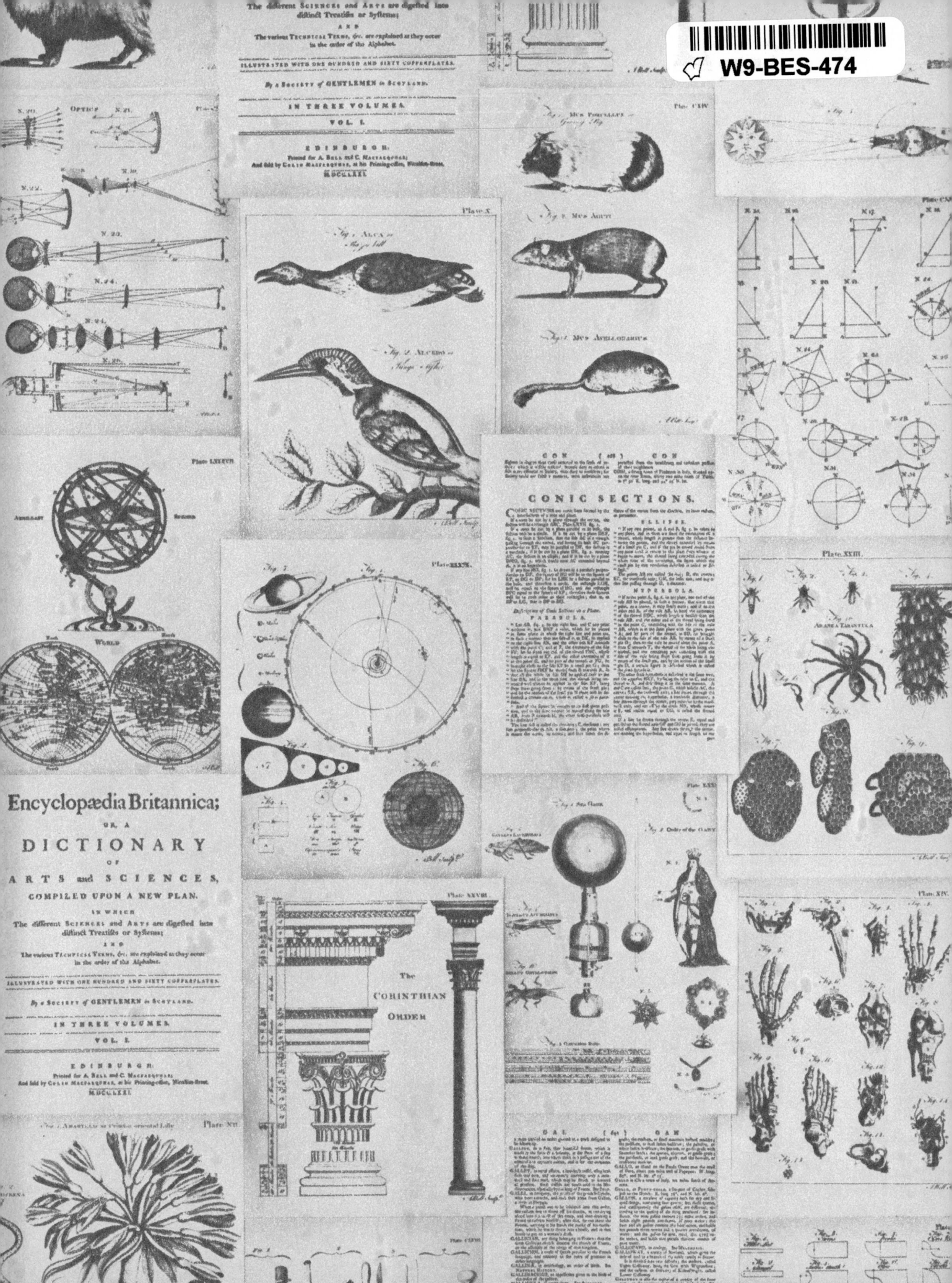

ENCYCLOPÆDIA
BRITANNICA

THE UNIVERSITY OF CHICAGO

*The Encyclopædia Britannica
is published with the editorial advice of the faculties
of The University of Chicago and of a
committee of members of the faculties of Oxford, Cambridge
and London universities and of a committee
at The University of Toronto*

*

"LET KNOWLEDGE GROW FROM MORE TO MORE
AND THUS BE HUMAN LIFE ENRICHED."

ENCYCLOPÆDIA
BRITANNICA

VOLUME

1

First Published in 1768
by A Society of Gentlemen in Scotland

ENCYCLOPÆDIA BRITANNICA, INC.

William Benton, Publisher

CHICAGO · LONDON · TORONTO · GENEVA · SYDNEY · TOKYO · MANILA

1968
1768

Editor's Preface

IF THE LIFE OF AN ENCYCLOPAEDIA is measured by editions and printings, then this printing of the *Encyclopædia Britannica* marks the completion of 200 years of its continuous publication. If the life of an encyclopaedia is measured by the passage of time, then December 1968 will mark the beginning of this encyclopaedia's third century of continuous existence as a survey of universal knowledge.

The historical fact that the Society of Gentlemen in Scotland, who were the putative authors of the first edition of the *Britannica,* released the first two serial sections of that edition in December of 1768 provides a fortuitous reminder that major anniversaries are most properly composed of a thoughtful look backward as prelude to a responsible look forward.

If it is a remarkable event for a set of volumes to be 200 years old, it is an awesome one for it to enter into its third century of service to man. Particularly is this true of the *Britannica,* whose successive editors have traditionally accepted a mission set for them by the first of their line.

The history of the *Encyclopædia Britannica* is set forth in the article ENCYCLOPAEDIA in the pages of the volumes that follow and need not be recounted here. It is interesting to note, however, that although the editor of the first edition of the *Britannica* was conscious of the importance of the new system of organizing knowledge on which his work was to be based, he elected to begin his preface to that edition not with grandiloquent praise of the system, nor yet with inflated intellectual pride in its invention. He began, instead, with a warning: "Utility ought to be the principal intention of every publication. Wherever this intention does not plainly appear, neither the books nor their authors have the smallest claim to the approbation of mankind."

To be useful is to be serviceable, and it seems not unreasonable to note with some pride that during its 200 years of growth, the *Britannica*'s durability has been a measure of its success in its mission to be useful.

By translation from the Greek, *encyclopaedia* means "instruction in the full circle of knowledge," and by intent each of the editions of the *Britannica* taken separately has been a summary presentation of the state of knowledge as it existed at the time of publication. Taken collectively, then, its successive editions and printings constitute a history of world knowledge during the 200 years of history through which man has just passed.

Save in history books, the historical ages of man have been but indistinctly marked. And yet it seems abundantly clear that in the years surrounding 1768 the world was taking its first major steps into a new age. The stirrings of that nascent era had already made themselves felt. New values, new theories, new ways of looking at things, new methods of doing what had to be done or what could be done, new beliefs, new creeds, new social, political, and economic ideas and ideologies were forcing themselves into existence. There was a common belief in the possibility, if not the inevitability, of progress as a goal and a general acceptance of science as the road that must lead to it.

From such stirrings there exploded a series of developments that left no part of man's life—from the most inward and private to the most outward and public—untouched. From them, there evolved a series of changes that in their intensity and importance can only be described as revolutionary. Man's knowledge of his past, of his world, and of himself increased exponentially; his political theory reshaped itself and covered great segments of the world with forms of government almost unrecognizable; his technological capabilities changed the very environment in which he lives, from layers below the surface of the earth to layers of the atmosphere above; his wealth aggregated; his powers for good and evil alike became manifest and his problems multiplied.

In its work of recording the evolving intellectual history of the last 200 years, the *Britannica* has established itself as something more than a passive mirror against which the images of time might be reflected. It has had a role to play in the shaping of the history of which it was a part. In its pages Malthus' theory that the world's population might someday exceed the world's capacity to sustain it found its first widespread audience well before actual fact seemed likely to overtake theoretical possibility; in its pages great men—like Thomas Thomson in chemistry and Stanley Morison in typography—first published germinal versions of later texts that were to influence whole generations of practitioners in those fields, and other great men published definitive papers; from its pages generations of readers were to gather inspiration that would shape their lives—as in the case of Michael Faraday—and the very structure of knowledge itself; while writing for its pages men like James Frazer were to be set off into research channels that would culminate in works like *The Golden Bough.*

Preeminently, however, the *Britannica* has played its own part in shaping the history of its own time by making available to millions of users—in schools and colleges, laboratories, research centres, public libraries, and in their own homes—the periodic distillations of man's knowledge that comprise its contents. One of the indisputable characteristics of the last two centuries has been a widespread awareness of the need for knowledge and an intense pursuit of it.

It is within this context that today's editors feel themselves under the greatest constraints as they look, not to the 200 years of history immediately passed, but to the third century immediately ahead.

There is an emerging consensus that the world of 1968 is—as it was in 1768—once more on the edge of a new historical era. Whether the 200 years just ended will go down in history books of the future as the age of the Industrial Revolution, or the age of the scientific-technological revolution, or something else, may be open to debate. That it has been a period of intense change is indisputable.

By the same token no one can now say for certain what the emerging age is to be, what its dominant characteristics will be. But it seems certain that it will be a new world. Commenting on the rapidity of change that seems to many to be the dominant characteristic of today's world, Margaret Mead once said that no one now alive will die in the same world into which he was born.

It is appropriate therefore that on the occasion of its 200th anniversary the *Britannica* should introduce the three volumes of *Britannica Perspectives* that are this year a part of its summary statement of man's knowledge. Developed as a special editorial project of the Board of Editors of *Encyclopædia Britannica* under the guiding direction of Robert M. Hutchins, its chairman, the articles constitute, as it were, thirteen separate analyses of the world, each seen through the prism of a different ordering of the elements of that world. The *Perspective* articles are not primarily for reference—it is unlikely that readers will "look up" anything in them—and they are divorced insofar as is possible from the academic disciplines into which knowledge is typically separated. They deal, therefore, not with economics as a subject or science, but with the aspects of world life that are economic; not with political science, but with the part of life that is political, and so on. They attempt, wherever possible, to demonstrate the interrelationships that exist within the orderings as set forth, and they strive to highlight the problems and the issues created in each of the orders, and between the orders. One function of an encyclopaedia might well be to make men think. The *Perspectives* were designed to suggest many of the problems man may be called upon to think about.

One thing that is quite clear about the world in which we live—and will live—is that it is no longer possible for man to live and function effectively within it if his learning is to be limited to the relatively short span of years traditionally set aside for formal education. His own successes in discovering knowledge, spurring scientific and nonscientific research, and accelerating the applications of both have created a world in which learning must become a lifelong activity. There is too much to be learned, and too much to be relearned in the face of new knowledge, for anything less to suffice.

The utility of the *Britannica* in its impending third century will be in direct proportion to its ability to meet, and indeed to stimulate, man's need for knowledge. In meeting its responsibilities, the editors of the *Britannica* are aware that for knowledge to be useful it must first be made meaningful, in its exposition and, equally important, in its organization. They are aware that whether or not knowledge was ever—as once conceived—a seamless fabric, it is not such today. They are aware that systems of organizing knowledge are not given by nature but must be created, and that none is necessarily perfect. And they are aware that one of the lessons derived from 200 years

of encyclopaedia publishing is that arrogance ill becomes those who deal with knowledge. Within its history, the *Britannica* has reported as scientific "fact" that the atom is the part of matter subject to no further division, that uranium is of value only as an additive in the manufacture of ceramics. Knowledge and the "facts" based upon it are never static, and it is not the function of an encyclopaedia to be a volume of permanent "truths."

Most of all, however, the editors of the *Britannica* are aware that their ability to carry out their function in the future is dependent upon the maintenance of the partnership that has existed between themselves and the authorities who are their contributors, the academic specialists who are their advisers, and their readers. We acknowledge our obligation to our partners of the past and affirm it for the future.

There is, of course, another way in which contemporary encyclopaedias are active partnerships. It goes without saying that no one man can master all of learning in today's world, and so, at the start, there must be a partnership between the editor and his staff and their advisers and contributors. There must, in addition, be a partnership between the editorial department and the many business specialists required to keep a modern business healthy and vital, and between the editorial department and the salesmen who, with dedication, follow in the footsteps of a long line of similar specialists whose job it has been to take information to the people who need it, where they needed it.

If these partnerships are to be kept healthfully operative, they must be organized, supported, and directed. That function, of course, belongs to the publisher. In 1968, therefore, the *Britannica,* in addition to its own 200th anniversary, takes note of the 25th anniversary of William Benton as its Publisher and Chairman of the Board. The history of the growth of this company and of its many interests under his leadership is a part of the history of the *Britannica,* and may be found in the article ENCYCLOPAEDIA as well as in his own biographical entry. Not the least of the *Britannica*'s assets, as it prepares for the challenging and difficult responsibilities of reporting knowledge in a changed and changing world, is his presence at the head of this company.

WARREN E. PREECE
Editor in Chief

This preface, the title pages, and several of the preliminary pages for this anniversary printing have been set in Times New Roman type, designed by the distinguished typographer and scholar of the press, Mr. Stanley Morison (1889–1967), who served on the Board of Editors of Encyclopædia Britannica. *The special anniversary thistle device was designed and executed by Mr. Reynolds Stone, English engraver and woodcutter, and the preliminary pages were designed by Mr. Walter Howe, American book designer, all in consultation with, and with the advice of, Mr. Morison before his death in London on October 11, 1967, while this edition was still in press.*

WARREN E. PREECE, *Editor in Chief*
PHILIP W. GOETZ, *Executive Editor*
DONALD E. STEWART, *Managing Editor*
CHRISTOPHER H. W. KENT, *Deputy Editor for London*

DEPARTMENTAL EDITORS AND ADVISERS

GERALD (ERNEST HEAL) ABRAHAM, *Assistant Controller of Music, British Broadcasting Corporation, London, England, 1962–67.* (MUSIC)

ROBERT McC. ADAMS, *Director, The Oriental Institute, The University of Chicago, Chicago, Illinois.* (ARCHAEOLOGY)

JACOB B. AGUS, *Rabbi, Beth El Congregation, Baltimore, Maryland.* (JUDAISM)

ROBERT E. ALBRIGHT, *Emeritus Professor of Social Studies, State University of New York College at Buffalo, New York.* (GEOGRAPHY: EAST CENTRAL U.S.)

FRANCIS A. ALLEN, *Dean of the Law School, University of Michigan, Ann Arbor, Michigan.* (LAW)

SIR R. G. D. ALLEN, *Professor of Statistics, London University, London, England.* (ECONOMICS)

SIR JOHN F. BAKER, *Professor of Mechanical Sciences and Head, Department of Engineering, Cambridge University, Cambridge, England.* (ENGINEERING)

C. N. BARCLAY, *Brigadier, Cameronians (Scottish Rifles) (retired). Editor, The Army Quarterly and Defence Journal, London, England, 1950–66.* (MILITARY AFFAIRS)

WILLIAM CARROLL BARK, *Professor of Medieval History, Stanford University, Stanford, California.*
(CLASSICAL AND MEDIEVAL HISTORY)

E. C. BARKSDALE, *Professor and Head, Department of History, Philosophy and Sociology, University of Texas at Arlington, Arlington, Texas.*
(GEOGRAPHY: WEST SOUTH CENTRAL U.S.)

EMMET BLACKBURN BAY, M.D., *Emeritus Professor of Medicine, The University of Chicago, Chicago, Illinois; Member, University of Chicago Advisory Committee on Encyclopædia Britannica.* (MEDICINE)

WALTER BLAIR, *Professor of English, The University of Chicago, Chicago, Illinois; Member, University of Chicago Advisory Committee on Encyclopædia Britannica.*
(AMERICAN LITERATURE)

ROBERT J. BRAIDWOOD, *Oriental Institute Professor of Old World Prehistory and Professor of Anthropology, The University of Chicago, Chicago, Illinois.* (ARCHAEOLOGY)

CARL FREMONT BRAND, *Emeritus Professor of History, Stanford University, Stanford, California.* (HISTORY)

CONRAD BRANDT, *Senior Research Fellow, St. Antony's College, Oxford University, Oxford, England.*
(FAR EASTERN HISTORY)

E. L. BREDSDORFF, *Reader in Scandinavian Studies, Cambridge University, Cambridge, England.*
(DANISH LITERATURE)

J HARLEN BRETZ, *Emeritus Professor of Geology, The University of Chicago, Chicago, Illinois; Member, University of Chicago Advisory Committee on Encyclopædia Britannica.* (GEOLOGY)

EDWARD ETTINGDENE BRIDGES, BARON BRIDGES, *Former Permanent Secretary to H.M. Treasury.*
(POLITICAL SCIENCE)

C. O. BRINK, *Kennedy Professor of Latin, Cambridge University, Cambridge, England.* (LATIN LITERATURE)

JOHN BROUGH, *Professor of Sanskrit, Cambridge University, Cambridge, England.* (PHILOLOGY).

D. A. BROWN, *Agriculture Librarian and Professor of Library Science, University of Illinois, Urbana, Illinois.*
(AGRICULTURE)

JOHN ELY BURCHARD, *Dean of the College of Environmental Design, University of California, Berkeley, California.* (ARCHITECTURE)

SIR CYRIL BURT, *Emeritus Professor of Psychology, London University, London, England.* (PSYCHOLOGY)

ALBERT BUSH-BROWN, *President, Rhode Island School of Design, Providence, Rhode Island.* (ARCHITECTURE)

CLAUDE A. BUSS, *Professor of History, Stanford University, Stanford, California.* (FAR EASTERN HISTORY)

JAMES HARMON BUTLER, *De Mille Professor and Chairman, Department of Drama, University of Southern California, Los Angeles, California.*
(THEATRE AND MOTION PICTURES)

THEODORE VERN BUTTREY, JR., *Associate Professor of Classics, University of Michigan, Ann Arbor, Michigan.*
(CLASSICAL STUDIES)

HORACE ROBERT BYERS, *Dean of Geosciences and Distinguished Professor of Meteorology, Texas A & M University, College Station, Texas.* (METEOROLOGY)

J. M. S. CARELESS, *Professor of History, University of Toronto, Toronto, Ontario, Canada.*
(CANADIAN GEOGRAPHY AND HISTORY)

ALONZO CHURCH, *Professor of Mathematics and Philosophy, University of California, Los Angeles, California.*
(PHILOSOPHY)

GERHARD LUDWIG CLOSS, *Professor of Chemistry, The University of Chicago, Chicago, Illinois.* (CHEMISTRY)

LOWELL T. COGGESHALL, M.D., *Trustee and Frederick H. Rawson Professor of Medicine, The University of Chicago, Chicago, Illinois; Member, University of Chicago Advisory Committee on Encyclopædia Britannica.*

RAYMOND COHEN, *Professor of Mechanical Engineering, Purdue University, West Lafayette, Indiana.*
(MECHANICAL ENGINEERING)

GRACE ROGERS COOPER, *Curator of Textiles, Smithsonian Institution, Washington, D.C.* (TEXTILES)

EDWIN ALFRED COURSE, *Resident Tutor, Department of Extra-Mural Studies, Southampton University, Southampton, England.* (TRANSPORT)

ENCYCLOPÆDIA BRITANNICA, INC.

HOWARD L. GOODKIND, *Executive Vice-President, Editorial*

HOWARD E. KASCH, *Managing Editor*

KENNETH KEITH COWART, *Vice-Admiral, United States Coast Guard, Retired.* (SHIPPING)

JOHN W. COWEE, *Professor and Dean, School of Business Administration, University of California, Berkeley, California.* (ECONOMICS)

PETER P. H. DE BRUYN, M.D., *Professor of Anatomy, The University of Chicago, Chicago, Illinois.* (MEDICINE)

HUBERT DESCHAMPS, *Professor of African History, the Sorbonne, Paris, France.* (GEOGRAPHY)

ALLISON DUNHAM, *Professor of Law, The University of Chicago, Chicago, Illinois; Member, University of Chicago Advisory Committee on* Encyclopædia Britannica. (LAW)

L(ESLIE) C. DUNN, *Emeritus Professor of Zoology, Nevis Biological Station, Columbia University, Irvington-on-Hudson, New York.* (ZOOLOGY)

ELDON DYER, *Professor of Mathematics, Graduate Studies Division, City University of New York, New York, New York.* (MATHEMATICS)

FRED R. EGGAN, *Harold H. Swift Distinguished Service Professor of Anthropology, The University of Chicago, Chicago, Illinois; Member, University of Chicago Advisory Committee on* Encyclopædia Britannica. (ANTHROPOLOGY)

RAYMOND WILLIAM FIRTH, *Professor of Anthropology, London University, London, England.* (ANTHROPOLOGY)

DARYLL FORDE, *Professor of Anthropology, London University, London, England.* (ANTHROPOLOGY)

PETER W. FRANK, *Professor of Biology, University of Oregon, Eugene, Oregon.* (ZOOLOGY)

HELLMUT FRITZSCHE, *Professor of Physics, The University of Chicago, Chicago, Illinois; Member, University of Chicago Advisory Committee on* Encyclopædia Britannica.

C. H. GIBBS-SMITH, *Keeper of the Public Relations and Education Department, Victoria and Albert Museum; Committee Member, Historical Group, Royal Aeronautical Society, London, England.* (AERONAUTICAL HISTORY)

JULIAN ROYCE GOLDSMITH, *Professor of Geochemistry and Chairman, Department of Geophysical Sciences, and Associate Dean, Division of the Physical Sciences, The University of Chicago, Chicago, Illinois.* (MINERALOGY)

ROBERT M. GRANT, *Professor of New Testament and Early Christianity, The University of Chicago, Chicago, Illinois.* (RELIGION)

FLETCHER MELVIN GREEN, *Kenan Professor of History, University of North Carolina, Chapel Hill, North Carolina.* (GEOGRAPHY: SOUTHEASTERN U.S.)

ALLAN GRIERSON, *Senior Lecturer in Mining, Royal School of Mines, Imperial College of Science and Technology, University of London, London, England.* (MINING)

CHARLES MEYER HARDIN, *Professor of Political Science, University of California, Davis.* (POLITICAL SCIENCE)

CHRISTINA PHELPS HARRIS, *Professor of Political Science, Stanford University, Stanford, California, 1959–67.* (NEAR EASTERN HISTORY)

DAVID HARRIS, *Emeritus Professor of History, Stanford University, Stanford, California.* (HISTORY)

ARNOLD HASKELL, *Director, Royal Ballet School, London England, 1947–65.* (DANCE)

PHILIP M. HAUSER, *Professor of Sociology, The University of Chicago, Chicago, Illinois; Member, University of Chicago Advisory Committee on* Encyclopædia Britannica. (SOCIOLOGY)

JOHN BAPTIST HEFFERNAN, *Rear Admiral, United States Navy, Retired. Secretary, Naval Historical Foundation, Washington, D.C.* (NAVAL AFFAIRS)

F. CLARK HOWELL, *Professor of Anthropology, The University of Chicago, Chicago, Illinois.* (ANTHROPOLOGY)

WARREN EVERY HOWLAND, *Professor of Sanitary Engineering, Purdue University, West Lafayette, Indiana.* (ENGINEERING)

CHARLES OSCAR HUCKER, *Professor of Chinese and Chairman, Department of Far Eastern Languages and Literatures, University of Michigan, Ann Arbor, Michigan.* (ORIENTAL LITERATURE)

G. DONALD HUDSON, *Professor of Geography, University of Washington, Seattle, Washington.* (GEOGRAPHY)

JOHN HUGHES-HALLETT, *Vice-Admiral, Royal Navy, Retired; Member of Parliament, 1954–64; Joint Parliamentary Secretary, Ministry of Transport, United Kingdom, 1961–64.* (NAVAL AFFAIRS)

HOWARD F. HUNT, *Chief of Psychiatric Research (Psychology), New York State Psychiatric Institute; Professor of Medical Psychology, College of Physicians and Surgeons, Columbia University, New York, New York.* (PSYCHOLOGY)

HANS HUTH, *Emeritus Curator of Decorative Arts, The Art Institute of Chicago, Chicago, Illinois; Lecturer, University of California, Los Angeles, California.* (ART)

FAHIR IZ, *Professor of Medieval Turkish Literature, Istanbul University, Istanbul, Turkey.* (LITERATURE)

ADRIAN WILLIAM JANES, *Editor of Publications, College of Agriculture, University of Illinois, Urbana, Illinois.* (AGRICULTURE)

MARSH JEANNERET, *Director, University of Toronto Press, Toronto, Ontario, Canada.*

JOHN J. JOHNSON, *Professor of History, Stanford University, Stanford, California.* (LATIN-AMERICAN HISTORY, GEOGRAPHY)

S. PAUL JOHNSTON, *Director, National Air and Space Museum, Smithsonian Institution.* (AERONAUTICS)

A. H. M. JONES, *Professor of Ancient History, Cambridge University, Cambridge, England.* (ANCIENT HISTORY)

FRANK LEROY KIDNER, *Professor of Economics and University Dean of Educational Relations, University of California, Berkeley, California.* (ECONOMICS)

JOSEPH B. KIRSNER, M.D., *Professor of Medicine, The University of Chicago, Chicago, Illinois; Member, University of Chicago Advisory Committee on* Encyclopædia Britannica.

JOSEPH M. KITAGAWA, *Professor of History of Religions, The University of Chicago, Chicago, Illinois.* (RELIGION)

MARTIN JESSE KLEIN, *Professor of History of Physics, Yale University, New Haven, Connecticut.* (PHYSICS)

W. C. KNEALE, *White's Professor of Moral Philosophy, Oxford University, Oxford, England; Fellow of Corpus Christi College, Oxford.* (PHILOSOPHY)

MICHAEL DAVID KNOWLES, O.S.B., *Regius Professor Emeritus of Modern History, Cambridge University, Cambridge, England.* (CHURCH HISTORY AND THEOLOGY)

HANS KOHN, *Emeritus Professor of History, City College of New York, New York; Fellow, Center for Advanced Studies, Wesleyan University, Middletown, Connecticut.* (HISTORY)

WILLIAM H. KRUSKAL, *Professor and Chairman, Department of Statistics, The University of Chicago, Chicago, Illinois; Member, University of Chicago Advisory Committee on* Encyclopædia Britannica.

PHILIP B. KURLAND, *Professor of Law, The University of Chicago, Chicago, Illinois.* (LAW)

DOROTHY MARGARET LEAHY, *Emeritus Professor of Home Economics Education, University of California, Los Angeles, California.* (HOME ECONOMICS)

DONALD WILLIAM LUCAS, *Perceval Maitland Laurence Reader in Classics, Cambridge University, Cambridge, England.* (CLASSICAL GREEK LITERATURE)

JO DESHA LUCAS, *Professor of Law, The University of Chicago, Chicago, Illinois.* (LAW)

O. R. McGREGOR, *Professor of Sociology, Bedford College, London University, London, England.* (SOCIOLOGY)

KENNETH CUNNINGHAM McGUFFIE, *The Admiralty Registrar, Royal Courts of Justice, London, England.* (MARINE LAW)

W. D. McHARDY, *Regius Professor of Hebrew, Oxford University, Oxford, England.* (OLD TESTAMENT)

D. McKIE, *Head, Department of History and Philosophy of Science, University College, and Professor of History and Philosophy of Science, London University, London, England.* (HISTORY OF SCIENCE)

D. G. MacRAE, *Professor of Sociology, London School of Economics, London University, London, England.* (SOCIOLOGY)

NORRIS McWHIRTER, *Television Commentator, British Broadcasting Corporation, London, England.* (SPORTS)

ANATOLE G. MAZOUR, *Professor of History, Stanford University, Stanford, California.* (RUSSIAN HISTORY)

GEORGE J. METCALF, *Emeritus Professor of Germanic Philology and Chairman, Department of Germanic Languages and Literatures, The University of Chicago, Chicago, Illinois; Member, University of Chicago Advisory Committee on Encyclopædia Britannica.*

REID T. MILNER, *Head of the Department of Food Science, University of Illinois, Urbana, Illinois.* (FOODS)

SIR ALAN MONCRIEF, *Nuffield Professor of Child Health, London University, London, England, 1946–64.* (MEDICINE)

WILLIAM WILSON MORGAN, *Professor of Astronomy, Yerkes Observatory, The University of Chicago, Williams Bay, Wisconsin.* (ASTRONOMY)

LON W. MORREY, *Editor in Chief, American Dental Association, Chicago, Illinois.* (DENTISTRY)

TERENCE PATRICK MORRIS, *Reader in Sociology (Criminology), London School of Economics and Political Science, London University, London, England.* (CRIMINOLOGY)

RHOADS MURPHEY, *Professor of Geography, Center for Chinese Studies, University of Michigan, Ann Arbor, Michigan.* (FAR EASTERN GEOGRAPHY)

JOHN COURTNEY MURRAY (1904–67), S.J., *Professor of Theology, Editor, Theological Studies, Woodstock College, Woodstock, Maryland.* (CATHOLICISM)

PETER MURRAY, *Lecturer, Courtauld Institute of Art, London University, London, England.* (ART)

RAYMOND MUSE, *Professor and Chairman, Department of History, Washington State University, Pullman, Washington.* (GEOGRAPHY: WESTERN U.S.)

NORMAN H(ARRY) NACHTRIEB, *Professor and Chairman, Department of Chemistry, and Professor, Institute for the Study of Metals, The University of Chicago, Chicago, Illinois.* (CHEMISTRY)

G. NANDRIS, *Emeritus Professor of Comparative Philology of the Slavonic Languages, London University, London, England.* (SLAVONIC STUDIES)

H. G. NICHOLAS, *Nuffield Reader in the Comparative Study of Institutions, Oxford University, Oxford, England.* (POLITICAL SCIENCE)

W. D. OLLIS, *Professor of Organic Chemistry, University of Sheffield, Sheffield, England.* (CHEMISTRY)

BERNARD PAGEL, *Senior Principal Scientific Officer, Royal Greenwich Observatory, Herstmonceux, England.* (ASTRONOMY)

THOMAS PARK, *Professor of Zoology, The University of Chicago, Chicago, Illinois; President, American Association for the Advancement of Science, 1961; Chairman, University of Chicago Advisory Committee on Encyclopædia Britannica.* (BIOLOGY, ZOOLOGY)

JAMES B. PARSONS, *Emeritus Professor of Chemistry, The University of Chicago, Chicago, Illinois.* (CHEMISTRY)

JAROSLAV JAN PELIKAN, *Titus Street Professor of Ecclesiastical History, Yale University Divinity School, New Haven, Connecticut.* (RELIGION)

STUART PIGGOTT, *Abercromby Professor of Prehistoric Archaeology, Edinburgh University, Edinburgh, Scotland.* (ARCHAEOLOGY)

JOHN LOWELL PRATT, *Sports Publisher, New York, New York.* (SPORTS)

DOROTHY PRICE, *Professor of Zoology, The University of Chicago, Chicago, Illinois.* (ZOOLOGY)

C(HARLES) HERMAN PRITCHETT, *Professor of Political Science, The University of Chicago, Chicago, Illinois.* (POLITICAL SCIENCE)

ROY PRYCE, *Senior Lecturer in Contemporary European Studies, University of Sussex, Brighton, England.* (POLITICAL SCIENCE)

SARVEPALLI RADHAKRISHNAN, *President of the Republic of India, 1962–67; Spalding Professor of Eastern Religions and Ethics, Oxford University, Oxford, England, 1936–52.* (EASTERN PHILOSOPHY)

J. R. RAEBURN, *Professor of Agriculture, Aberdeen University, Aberdeen, Scotland.* (AGRICULTURE)

KENNETH J. REHAGE, *Professor and Secretary, Department of Education; Dean of Students, Graduate School of Education, The University of Chicago, Chicago, Illinois.* (EDUCATION)

JOHN RICHARD REITZ, *Manager, Physics and Electronics Department, Scientific Laboratory, Ford Motor Company, Dearborn, Michigan.* (PHYSICS)

HERMAN G. RICHEY, *Emeritus Professor of Education, The University of Chicago, Chicago, Illinois.* (EDUCATION)

BENJAMIN CHARLES ROBERTS, *Professor of Industrial Relations, London School of Economics and Political Science, London University, London, England.* (INDUSTRIAL RELATIONS)

EDGAR EUGENE ROBINSON, *Margaret Byrne Professor Emeritus of American History, Stanford University, Stanford, California.* (AMERICAN HISTORY)

CARL A. ROEBUCK, *Professor and Chairman, Department of Classical Languages, Northwestern University, Evanston, Illinois.* (ARCHAEOLOGY)

BENJAMIN ROWLAND, JR., *Gleason Professor of Fine Arts, Ryerson Lecturer, Harvard University, Cambridge, Massachusetts.* (SCULPTURE)

E. G. RUPP, *Professor of Ecclesiastical History, Manchester University, Manchester, England.* (CHURCH HISTORY AND THEOLOGY)

SIR JOHN RUSSELL, *Director of Rothamsted (Eng.) Experimental Station, 1912–43, and of the Imperial Bureau of Soil Science, 1928–43; President of the British Association, 1949.* (AGRICULTURE)

J. COERT RYLAARSDAM, *Professor of Old Testament Theology, The University of Chicago, Chicago, Illinois.* (RELIGION)

SIR EDWARD SALISBURY, *Director, Royal Botanic Gardens, Kew, London, England, 1943–56.*
(BIOCHEMISTRY AND BOTANY)

PAUL ARTHUR SCHILPP, *Emeritus Professor of Philosophy, Northwestern University, Evanston, Illinois; Visiting Distinguished Professor of Philosophy, Southern Illinois University, Carbondale, Illinois; Editor,* The Library of Living Philosophers. (PHILOSOPHY)

ALBERT WILBUR SCHLECHTEN, *Professor and Head, Department of Metallurgical Engineering; Director, Institute for Extractive Metallurgy, Colorado School of Mines, Golden, Colorado.* (MINING AND METALLURGICAL ENGINEERING)

VICTORIA SCHUCK, *Professor of Political Science, Mount Holyoke College, South Hadley, Massachusetts.*
(GEOGRAPHY: NORTHEASTERN U.S.)

P. A. SHEPPARD, *Professor of Meteorology, Imperial College of Science and Technology, London University, London, England.* (METEOROLOGY)

NICHOLAS SLONIMSKY, *Writer, Musician and Teacher.*
(AMERICAN MUSIC)

GABRIEL SMITH, *Lecturer in Industry and Finance, City of London College, London, England.* (COMMERCE)

W. O. LESTER SMITH, *Professor of Sociology of Education, London University, London, England, 1949–53.*
(EDUCATION)

RIXFORD KINNEY SNYDER, *Professor of History and Director of Admissions, Stanford University, Stanford, California.* (HISTORY)

WILLIAM REED STECKEL, *Professor of History, University of Wyoming, Laramie, Wyoming.*
(GEOGRAPHY: WESTERN U.S.)

R. W. STEEL, *John Rankin Professor of Geography, Liverpool University, Liverpool, England.* (GEOGRAPHY)

WILSON STEPHENS, *Editor,* The Field, *London, England.*
(FIELD SPORTS)

HEINRICH STRAUMANN, *Professor of English Philology, University of Zürich, Zürich, Switzerland.* (LITERATURE)

DON R. SWANSON, *Professor and Dean, Graduate Library School, The University of Chicago, Chicago, Illinois; Member, University of Chicago Advisory Committee on* Encyclopædia Britannica.

WILLIAM H(AY) TALIAFERRO, *E. H. Moore Distinguished Service Professor Emeritus of Microbiology, The University of Chicago, Chicago, Illinois; Senior Immunologist, Division of Biological and Medical Research, Argonne National Laboratory, Argonne, Illinois.* (MEDICINE)

JOSHUA C. TAYLOR, *William Rainey Harper Professor of Humanities and Professor of Art, The University of Chicago, Chicago, Illinois; Member, University of Chicago Advisory Committee on* Encyclopædia Britannica.

JOHN W. THIERET, *Professor of Biology, University of Southwestern Louisiana, Lafayette, Louisiana.* (BOTANY)

D. LLOYD THOMAS, *Lecturer, Metallurgy Department, Imperial College of Science and Technology, London University, London, England.* (METALLURGY)

L. M. THOMPSON, *Professor of History, University of California, Los Angeles, California.*
(SOUTH AFRICAN HISTORY)

DAVID THOMSON, *Master of Sidney Sussex College, Cambridge, England.*
(HISTORY)

C. E. TILLEY, *Emeritus Professor of Mineralogy and Petrology, Cambridge University, Cambridge, England.*
(MINERALOGY)

ILZA VEITH, *Professor and Vice Chairman, History of Health Sciences, San Francisco Medical Center, University of California, San Francisco, California.* (MEDICAL BIOGRAPHY)

BIRGIT VENNESLAND, *Professor of Biochemistry, The University of Chicago, Chicago, Illinois.* (BIOCHEMISTRY)

W. H. WALSH, *Professor of Logic and Metaphysics, Edinburgh University, Edinburgh, Scotland.* (PHILOSOPHY)

J. W. C. WAND, *Canon and Treasurer, St. Paul's Cathedral; Editor,* Church Quarterly Review, *London, England.*
(RELIGION)

F. J. B. WATSON, *Director, Wallace Collection, London, England.* (APPLIED ARTS)

W. T. WELLS, *Queen's Counsel, Member of Parliament.*
(LAW)

RUPERT L. WENZEL, *Curator of Insects, Field Museum of Natural History, Chicago, Illinois.* (ENTOMOLOGY)

R. B. WERNHAM, *Professor of Modern History, Oxford University, Oxford, England.* (MODERN HISTORY)

RALPH HARTLEY WETMORE, *Emeritus Professor of Botany, Harvard University, Cambridge, Massachusetts.*
(BOTANY)

DOROTHY WHITELOCK, *Elrington and Bosworth Professor of Anglo-Saxon, Cambridge University, Cambridge, England.*
(ANGLO-SAXON LITERATURE)

ALLEN PAUL WIKGREN, *Associate Professor of New Testament Language and Literature and Chairman, Department of New Testament and Early Christian Literature, The University of Chicago, Chicago, Illinois; Member, University of Chicago Advisory Committee on* Encyclopædia Britannica.

BASIL WILLEY, *King Edward VII Professor Emeritus of English Literature, Cambridge University, Cambridge, England; Honorary Fellow of Pembroke College, Cambridge. Literary Adviser to Committee of the Translators of the* New English Bible. (LITERATURE)

OSCAR OSBURN WINTHER, *University Professor of History, Indiana University, Bloomington, Indiana.*
(GEOGRAPHY: NORTHWEST CENTRAL U.S.)

ROBERT WOERNER, *Business Manager, Midwest Program on Airborne Television Instruction.*
(ELECTRICAL ENGINEERING)

ROBERT SMITH WOODBURY, *Professor of History of Technology, Massachusetts Institute of Technology, Cambridge, Massachusetts.* (TECHNOLOGY)

QUINCY WRIGHT, *Emeritus Professor of International Law, The University of Chicago, Chicago, Illinois.*
(INTERNATIONAL RELATIONS)

DOROTHEA WYATT, *Professor of History, Flint College, University of Michigan, Flint, Michigan.*
(GEOGRAPHY: EAST NORTH CENTRAL U.S.)

THOMAS FRASER YOUNG, *Emeritus Professor of Chemistry, The University of Chicago, Chicago, Illinois.*
(CHEMISTRY)

A full list, in alphabetical order by initials, of all the writers for the *Encyclopædia Britannica* is to be found at the back of the Index volume. Following it is an alphabetical list by name.

HOW TO USE BRITANNICA

IN ORDER to make each of the thousands of articles in this Encyclopaedia easily accessible to the reader, the articles have all been placed in strictly alphabetical order throughout the set, regardless of the specialized fields to which they apply. An alphabetical listing on so large a scale requires clear and consistent methods for dealing with various details. The rules adopted by the editors of the *Encyclopædia Britannica* were designed on the basis of long experience for maximum usefulness to the reader, and a few minutes spent in becoming acquainted with them will amply repay every user of the set.

First, it is important to note that *titles of articles* are in strict alphabetical order *regardless of whether the title contains one, two, or more words.* Thus MOUNTAINEERING precedes MOUNTAIN GOAT. Headings containing more than one word are alphabetized as if they were one word and this system continues up to the punctuation mark. Words in parentheses are not generally considered as part of the heading for purposes of alphabetization. Names beginning with Mc or M', St., or SS. are alphabetized as though they were spelled out; *i.e.,* Mac, Saint, or Saints.

The position of articles that have the same name is determined by the order: (1) persons; (2) places; and (3) things. When there are a number of biographical entries for *persons bearing the same name,* they are arranged in the order: saints, popes, emperors, kings, nobility in order of precedence, persons other than the above bearing the one name only, and persons bearing the name as a surname. Thus JOHN, SAINT, THE APOSTLE, precedes JOHN I, Byzantine emperor; JOHN, duke of Burgundy, precedes JOHN OF ASIA, who in turn precedes JOHN, AUGUSTUS EDWIN.

Popes of the same name are included in one article. Within the article, the popes are listed in order by number. Kings of the same name are alphabetized by the name of their realms, and numbered kings of the same name and realm are arranged by number. Thus CHARLES III, king of France, precedes CHARLES I, king of Great Britain and Ireland. Others whose names include numbers, such as emperors, are also arranged by number.

Territorial designations and sobriquets (ROBERT OF GLOUCESTER; HOLBEIN, HANS, THE YOUNGER) are not considered in alphabetizing unless there are two or more entries with titles which are otherwise the same. These entries are then alphabetized by the first principal word of the subsidiary designation, the "of" or "the" being disregarded. Thus JOHN, SAINT, THE APOSTLE, precedes JOHN, SAINT, OF THE CROSS; JOHN OF ASIA precedes JOHN OF SALISBURY.

Persons with the same family name are arranged in relation to each other by alphabetizing the given name. Persons with the same family and given name are arranged by date of birth, the earliest coming first. Titles such as "Sir" or "Dame" are not considered in alphabetizing. Unused portions of given names, when they precede the name that is used, are enclosed in parentheses and are also disregarded in alphabetizing. CHAMBERLAIN, SIR (JOSEPH) AUSTEN thus precedes CHAMBERLAIN, (ARTHUR) NEVILLE.

Names with connectives such as "de," "von," etc., are generally alphabetized under the main part of the name—GOGH, VINCENT WILLEM VAN—except where the European form has been anglicized, as in DE QUINCEY and DU PONT.

Places of the same name are arranged in the order: (1) countries; (2) subordinate divisions, such as *département,* province, or state; (3) cities; and (4) geographic features, such as islands, mountains, lakes, and rivers. Cities of the same name are alphabetized, in relation to each other, by the names of their countries: ALBANY in Australia precedes ALBANY in New York, U.S. Cities of the same name and country are arranged by alphabetizing the territorial unit next below the country: ALBANY, Georgia, U.S., precedes ALBANY, New York, U.S.

In addition to the main articles, there are thousands of cross references throughout the *Britannica.* These appear as boldface entries in alphabetical position in the text (*e.g.,* DISRAELI, BENIAMIN: see BEACONSFIELD, BENJAMIN DISRAELI, EARL OF); the "*see*" and "*see also*" references to other titles in the body or at the end of articles; and the parenthetical *q.v.* (*quod vide,* "which see") references, which indicate that separate articles under the titles cited will be found in the *Britannica.*

Many of the boldface cross references in alphabetical position in the text are expanded to several lines to give minimal information about the subject; *see,* for example, AENEAS SILVIUS.

Other aids to the reader include the "Articles on Articles," which, for many major fields of study, outline *Britannica*'s basic coverage systematically. For an example of such articles, *see* BIOLOGY (ARTICLES ON). For the reader's convenience, these articles precede the main entry (ignoring the usual alphabetizing rules), as will be seen in the case of BIOLOGY.

Again for the convenience of the reader, tables of contents are given at the beginning of very long articles; for an example, *see* WORLD WAR II or BIBLE.

Authors of *Britannica* articles are identified in the text by initials only. Contributors' names are found in the list "Initials and Names of Contributors," the last section of the Index volume.

It is important to read, also, the introductory sections of the Index volume,
which explain how the articles are indexed alphabetically by subject matter.

FOUNDED A.D. 1768

ENCYCLOPÆDIA BRITANNICA

Volume
1

A TO ANSTEY

THIS letter has stood at the head of the alphabet (*q.v.*) during the whole of the period through which it can be traced historically. The name of the letter in the Phoenician period resembled the Hebrew name *aleph* meaning "ox"; the form is thought to derive from an early symbol resembling the head of an ox. The letter was taken over by the Greeks in the form of *alpha*. In the Phoenician alphabet the letter stood for a species of breathing, since vowels were not represented in the Semitic alphabets.

Throughout its history variations have occurred in the form of the letter. The Phoenician form was ⊀. In the Lydian alphabet of the 5th century B.C. it appeared as Λ, in the Carian alphabet A or Λ. In the early Greek alphabet from the island of Thera, which may possibly be dated as far back as the 8th century B.C., its form was A or A. In the Greek alphabet of classical times its form was usually Λ. Early Italic and Latin forms were Λ and A. As early as the middle of the 2nd century A.D. λ is found as a form of A, and this is the ancestor of the present minuscule printed a by way of uncial λ (4th century) and λ (8th century), uncial writing being the name given to the round hand which in late Roman times superseded the square capitals that had been suitable for inscription in stone. Under the influence of the uncial hand this form was adopted into Carolingian minuscules. The rounded minuscule a derives from Latin cursive, in which in the

5th century A.D. appeared the astonishing form ⟙. This was a hastily written majuscule A distorted by its apex having fallen to the left. In the 6th century the cursive form was ⟙, and from this in the 7th century developed the form ᘃ, from which the rounded form of the Irish and early English hands grew. The rounded capital α that sometimes appeared in handwriting was the minuscule letter written large.

The sound for which the letter consistently stood in Greek and Latin was the open low back vowel, sometimes known in modern English as continental a. There are of course countless slight variations in the method of pronouncing this sound. In English the sound has undergone far-reaching changes during and since the Middle English period. These are due to *fronting*, that is to say, pronouncing the sound more toward the front of the mouth, or to *rounding*, slightly rounding the lips, which has the effect of causing the sound to be pronounced higher in the mouth. At the present time the letter represents six principal vowel sounds: (1) its original value, the low back vowel, as in *father;* (2) an intermediate vowel, as in *man;* (3) a closer vowel, further fronted, as in *hare*, occurring only before the liquid *r;* (4) a diphthong (*ei*) as in *take, spade.* This is the sound that the letter now normally represents when the vowel is long.

(3) Represents a stage in the development of the sound on its way from (1) to (4) which was arrested at this point when the

word was followed by *r*. A similar fronting of this sound took place in the Ionic-Attic dialects of Greek, where sounds derived from the *a*-sound and represented in other dialects by *a* are represented by *η*.

The two remaining developments of the sound are due to rounding: (5) the vowel of *water* and (6) the vowel of *was*. This development is due to the influence of the preceding bilabial spirant *w*. (B. F. C. A.; J. W. P.)

In music, A is the name of the first note of the musical alphabet and constitutes the 6th degree of the scale of C. In respect of pitch A is equal to 440 vibrations per second, this being the standard pitch.

A is the note always given to orchestral players, usually by the oboe, for tuning purposes.

See PITCH, MUSICAL.

AA, the name of many small European rivers. The word is derived from the Old High German *aha*, cognate to the Latin *aqua*, "water" (*cf.* Ger. *-ach;* Scand. *å, aa,* pronounced *ō*). Among the streams of this name are: two rivers in western U.S.S.R., entering the Gulf of Riga with Riga lying between their mouths; a river in northern France flowing through St. Omer and Gravelines; and a river of Switzerland, in the cantons of Lucerne and Aargau, which carries the waters of the "finger" lakes of Baldegger and Hallwiler into the Aar (Aare). In Germany there are the Westphalian Aa, joining the Werre at Herford, the Münster Aa, a tributary of the Ems, and others. (A. F. A. M.)

AABENRAA-SONDERBORG (officially ÅBENRÅ-SØNDERBORG) is a county district of Denmark comprising the separate county council districts (*amtsraadskredse*) of Aabenraa and Sonderborg.

Aabenraa has an area of 305 sq.mi. and a population (1960) of 49,769 and its boundaries extend in an arc from Genner fiord to Flensborg fiord. It is centred on the town of Aabenraa (pop. [1960] 14,219), a port at the head of Aabenraa fiord (an arm of the Little Belt) which has a good harbour and a large import trade. Graasten (pop. [1960] 3,341) is another centre.

The county of Sonderborg embraces the island of Als and the adjacent Sundeved peninsula of southeast Jutland; area 170 sq.mi.; pop. (1960) 56,267. Hummocky moraine prevails in the east, and the fertile clay loams support wheat, barley, oats, roots, dairy cattle and pigs. In the west, poorer soils cover the outwash sands and gravels. The principal town is Sonderborg (pop. [1960] 20,-653), a port and seaside resort on the southwest coast of Als Island, connected with the mainland by a double-bascule bridge (built 1925–30). Sonderborg castle, dating from medieval times, houses a museum. Textiles, machinery, margarine and beer are manufactured. The town has existed since the mid-13th century and was burned down in 1864 during the assault by the Prussians on the Düppler trenches. With the whole district it then passed to Germany, but was restored to Denmark by the plebiscite of 1920. Dybbol Mill, the scene of the heroic Danish resistance in 1864, is now a symbol of national unity. (HA. T.)

AACHEN (Fr. AIX-LA-CHAPELLE; Dutch AKEN), an ancient city and spa of Germany, *Land* of North Rhine-Westphalia, Federal Republic of Germany, is situated under the northern slopes of the Ardennes, 70 km. (43.5 mi.) S.W. of Cologne by road. Pop. (1961) 169,769. Its municipal boundaries coincide on the west with the frontiers of Belgium and the Netherlands. The hot sulfur springs have been celebrated for centuries. In appearance it is a prosperous, modern commercial town but it is full of medieval associations. The outer town is mainly new, while the ramparts of the old inner town are now streets, with two ancient gates, Ponttor and Marschiertor, remaining. The conspicuous cluster of buildings in the centre of the city includes the cathedral and the Rathaus (town hall), a Gothic structure (1353–70) built on the ruins of Charlemagne's palace, which contains the magnificent hall of the emperors (143 ft. by 61 ft.). The two original towers, Granusturm and Glockenturm, were all but destroyed by fire in 1883; their restoration was completed in 1902. Near the Rathaus is the Grashaus, restored in 1889 to contain the municipal archives. The cathedral, where the German kings from the 10th to the 16th centuries were usually crowned, has two distinct styles:

the Octagon is Carolingian Romanesque and the choir is Gothic. The Octagon, begun about 796, was modeled on San Vitale at Ravenna and consecrated by Pope Leo III in 805. It is the finest extant building in that style. It suffered damage at the hands of the Normans in 881 and was later restored on the original lines. It is surrounded on the first story by a gallery (the Hochmünster) with antique marble and granite columns, of various sizes, brought from Rome, Ravenna and Trier. The columns were removed by Napoleon to Paris, but were in part returned after 1815. The mosaic representing Christ surrounded by "the four-and-twenty elders," which originally lined the cupola, was executed in 1881 from a 17th-century copy of the ancient originals. The bronze west doors date from 804. Underneath the dome, tradition places the tomb of Charlemagne, said to have been opened by Otto III in 1000 and to have shown the emperor's body on a marble chair which was removed and long used for coronations. It is now in the gallery. The site of the tomb is marked by a stone slab, with the inscription *Carlo Magno*, and above it hangs the famous bronze chandelier presented by the emperor Frederick I (Barbarossa) in 1168. In a chapel off the Octagon is kept the rich cathedral treasure, including the sacred relics and fine medieval work such as the 13th-century gold casket containing the remains of Charlemagne. The more sacred of the cathedral's relics are exhibited on occasion to large crowds of pilgrims. The Gothic choir was added during the 14th and 15th centuries and contains the tomb of the emperor Otto III. The pulpit, a gift of emperor Henry II, dates from *c.* 1020.

The churches of St. Foillan (founded in the 12th century, but twice rebuilt, in the 15th and 17th centuries, and restored 1883–88) and St. Paul, with its beautiful stained-glass windows, are interesting. The Suermondt museum contains good pictures by early German, Dutch and Flemish masters. There are many fine streets, squares and public monuments. The fountain in the market square is surmounted by a statue of Charlemagne. In the principal square, Friedrich-Wilhelmplatz, is the Elisenbrunnen, with its colonnade and garden, the chief resort of visitors taking the baths and waters. Educational institutions include the Rheinisch-Westfälische Technische Hochschule, a polytechnic founded in 1870.

BY COURTESY OF GERMAN TOURIST INFORMATION OFFICE

FOUNTAIN IN THE AACHEN MARKETPLACE, SURMOUNTED BY A STATUE OF CHARLEMAGNE. IN THE RIGHT BACKGROUND MAY BE SEEN A PORTION OF THE 14TH-CENTURY RATHAUS (TOWN HALL)

Aachen is on the main line from Cologne to Brussels. Since the working of extensive coal fields in the district almost every branch of iron industry has been carried on. Cloth, glass, needles and pins are important products. The suburb of Burtscheid, incorporated with Aachen in 1897, has old established manufactures of cloth and needles and contains, among frequented thermal springs, the Schwertbad-Quelle (171° F.), the warmest spring in Germany.

History.—The ancient city and watering place of Aachen represents the Aquisgranum of the Romans, named after Apollo Granus, who was worshiped in connection with hot springs. As early as A.D. 765 King Pepin III had a palace there, in which it is probable that Charlemagne was born. The greatness of Aachen was attributable to the latter, who between 777 and 786 built a magnificent palace, raised the place to the rank of the second city of the empire, and made it for a while the centre of western culture and learning. From the coronation of Otto I in 936 until that of Ferdinand I in 1531 the sacring of the German kings with few exceptions took place at Aachen. Late in the 12th century the city was surrounded with walls by order of the emperor Frederick I, to whom (1166) and to whose grandson Frederick II (1215) it owed its first important civic rights. In the 16th century Aachen began to decline. It lay too near the French frontier to be safe, and too remote from the centre of Germany to be convenient as a capital; and in 1562 the election and coronation of Maximilian II took place at Frankfurt am Main, a precedent followed till the extinction of the empire. Aachen was the scene of several important peace conferences, notably the treaty of 1668 that ended the War of Devolution, and the peace of 1748 ending the War of Austrian Succession. The city was occupied by French troops in 1794 and was annexed in 1801 by France, who held it until the congress of Vienna (1814–15), after which it was given to Prussia. The Aachen congress, sealed in 1818, regulated the affairs of Europe after the Napoleonic wars. In Nov. 1918, at the conclusion of World War I, Aachen was occupied for a period by Belgian troops. During World War II it was bombed many times and was captured on Oct. 20, 1944, the first large city on German soil to fall to the Allies.

AAHMES: *see* Ahmose.

AAL (A'l, Ach or Aich), the Hindustani names for the *Morinda tinctoria* and *M. citrifolia*, plants extensively cultivated in India because of the reddish dyestuff which their roots contain. The name is also applied to the dye, but the common trade name is *suranji*. Its properties are a result of the presence of a glucoside known as morindin.

AALBORG (officially Ålborg), a seaport in northern Jutland, Den., and capital of the *amt* (county) of Aalborg, lies on the south side of Limfjord, with its suburbs of Hasseris, Norresundby and Sundby-Hvorup extending on both sides of the fjord. Pop. (1960) 85,800.

Founded in 1342, and one of the oldest towns in Denmark, Aalborg has many buildings of interest including the Holy Ghost monastery (1431), the cathedral of St. Botolph, Aalborghus castle (1539) and several old merchant houses. There is a modern town hall and a theatre, as well as several schools and colleges, and six parks, fine zoological gardens and a racecourse. In the museum and art gallery some of the relics from the Viking village of Lindholm Hoje are preserved. Aalborg has an international airport with flights direct to Norway and Copenhagen. The port has considerable overseas trade and the town manufactures cement, tobacco, chemicals and spirits. It is also an important shipbuilding centre.

The *amt* (county) of Aalborg, bounded in the south by the Mariager fjord and in the north by the Geraa river, has an area of 1,125 sq.mi. (2,914 sq.km.). Pop. (1960) 239,041. It has poor quality soil and two large areas of moorland. (P. E. Je.)

AALSMEER, a village in the province of North Holland, Neth., lies about 10 mi. S.W. of Amsterdam. Pop. (1960) 14,973 (mun.). It is an important flower-growing centre with nearly 1,000 nurseries. The older part is on peaty soil at about sea level surrounded by polders with loamy soil, 9–15 ft. below sea level.

The principal products are carnations (approximately 119,000,000 a year), cut roses (88,000,000), lilacs (9,000,000), freesias (45,000,000), chrysanthemums and potted plants such as cyclamens and begonias. About half the flowers are exported and there is a big trade in seeds and nursery plants. There are two flower auctions and an experimental station for floriculture. The Westeinder lake is popular for sailing. (Ja. W.)

AALST (Fr. Alost), an industrial town of Belgium in the province of East Flanders, lies on the Dender river where the undulating countryside of mid-Belgium levels out to the coastal plain, 26 km. (16 mi.) by road west-northwest of Brussels. Pop. (1961) 45,092. The town hall, begun between 1200 and 1225, is the oldest in Belgium and contains a 43-bell carillon. The town archives include 12th-century manuscripts. The large, but unfinished, church of St. Martin has a transept containing remarkable furnishings, sculptures and a Rubens painting. Aalst is on the railway from Brussels to Ghent, and the E5 motorway from Brussels to Ostend skirts the town. The manufacture of textiles, from the linen thread to the finished cloth, and the making of clothing and textile machinery are the chief industries. Hops provide malt for flourishing breweries. The first printing shop in the Low Countries was established at Aalst by Thierry Martens (later a professor at the University of Louvain) in 1473. Marshal Turenne took the town after a four-day siege in 1667 during the War of Devolution that gave southern Flanders to France. During World War I the town was in German hands from Sept. 1914 until Nov. 1918. In World War II the Germans occupied Aalst from May 1940 until Sept. 1944. (R. M. An.)

AALTO, ALVAR (1898–   ), Finnish architect, designer and planner, whose works have influenced modern design throughout the world, especially for their sensitive treatment of natural materials, was born in Kuortane, on Feb. 3, 1898, and studied at the Helsinki Institute of Technology. His sanatorium at Paimio (1923–33), the library at Viipuri (1927–34, destroyed) and other buildings helped introduce modern architecture into Finland and Scandinavia. Featuring native materials, brick and timber, as well as concrete, his works range from private dwellings, like the Gullichsen house (1938–39), to the Sunila Cellulose Products factory (1937–39) and community buildings at Sänynätsala (1951–52). He built the Finnish pavilion at the New York World's fair (1939) and the Massachusetts Institute of Technology senior dormitory (1947–49). Aalto also designed influential standardized plywood furniture. He was ably assisted by his architect-wife Aino (1894–1949).

See Sigfried Giedion, *Space, Time and Architecture,* 3rd ed. (1954); Eduard and Claudia Neuenschwander, *Finnish Architecture and Alvar Aalto* (1954). (A. K. P.)

AARDVARK, "earth-pig," the Afrikaans name for an exclusively African termite-eating mammal of the genus *Orycteropus,* comprising the order Tubulidentata (*q.v.*). It is a curious looking

BY COURTESY OF NEW YORK ZOOLOGICAL SOCIETY

AARDVARK (ORYCTEROPUS AFER), NATIVE OF AFRICA

animal, of unknown relationships, having a stout piglike body, long snout, donkeylike ears and powerful short, thick legs armed with strong, blunt claws. The body averages four feet in length, with the tail an additional two feet. In colour the Cape aardvark is pale sandy to yellow, the hair being scanty and allowing the skin to show; the northern form has a still thinner coat, a shorter tail and longer head and ears; the western has the fullest coat, a glossy black fur.

The aardvark lives in both forest and plains country, wherever their insect food is plentiful. This highly specialized digger excavates large burrows in which it rests by day, venturing out at night to forage. After digging into and demolishing a large termite hill, the aardvark rapidly laps up the routed insects with its sticky, foot-long tongue.

Aardvarks are not aggressive, but when attacked, usually by larger carnivores such as lions and leopards, they roll over and use their powerful claws to good effect. A single young is born in summer. Besides keeping termites in check, the aardvark is also important in the native economy for its edible flesh and its teeth, prized as amulets to ward off evil.

AARDWOLF (*Proteles cristatus*), a mammal superficially resembling a small striped hyena and about 30 in. long, of which the tail accounts for 8 in. It has front legs longer than the hind, large ears and a pointed muzzle. The colour is buffish-gray with dark vertical stripes, dark muzzle and forefeet. A long, coarse-haired erectile mane runs the length of the back. Aardwolves live in the drier parts, but not the forests, of eastern and southern Africa and are usually nocturnal. They inhabit burrows, feed largely on termites, are usually solitary but sometimes forage in small packs. The litter averages three. They are mild, harmless animals whose only defense is to emit a musky smelling fluid and run away. *See* also Carnivore. (L. H. M.)

AARE or Aar, the longest river entirely within Switzerland, is 295.2 km. (183 mi.) long and the area of its basin is 17,779 sq.km. (6,864 sq.mi.). It rises in the Aare glacier in the canton of Bern, below the Finsteraarhorn and west of the Grimsel pass.

Near there an artificial lake, 7 mi. long, was created behind two dams which control the flow of water to the Grimsel underground power station. Below the Handegg falls, the Aare drains the Oberhaslital and there a power station was built in the Aare gorge at Innertkirchen above Meiringen. The Aare expands into the glacial lake of Brienz, on the southern shore of which the spectacular Giessbach falls occur. The river then crosses the lake delta of the Bödeli at Interlaken as a canalized river, before expanding into the similarly formed lake of Thun, at the lower end of which is the medieval castle town of Thun. Flowing northwest in a deeply entrenched valley, the Aare almost encircles the peninsula on which the medieval core of the city of Bern (q.v.) lies, then turns west and finally north to Aarberg, where it is diverted west by the Hagneck canal into the lake of Biel (Bienne). It subsequently flows northeastward parallel to the foot of the Jura, past the castle towns of Solothurn, Olten and Aarau. The chief right bank tributaries in this section are the Grosse Emme, Wigger, Suhr and Aa. Below Brugg, first the Reuss and then the Limmat converge on the Aare. The combined rivers turn north to join the Rhine at Coblenz.   (A. F. A. M.)

AARGAU (Fr. Argovie), a canton of northern Switzerland, takes in the lower course of the Aare river (q.v.), whence its name. The capital is Aarau and the total area of the canton is 1,403.5 sq.km. (542 sq.mi.). It forms the northeastern section of the great Swiss plateau between the Alps and the Jura. Its fertile valleys alternate with pleasantly wooded hills.

In 1415 the Aargau region, previously the centre of the Habsburgs, was taken from them by the Swiss Confederates. Bern kept the southwestern portion. In 1798 the Bernese part became the canton of Aargau of the Helvetic republic and the remainder of the Aargau region formed the canton of Baden. In 1803 the two halves (plus the Frick glen, ceded in 1802 by Austria to the Helvetic republic) were united under the name of Canton Aargau and admitted to membership of the Swiss confederation.

The population in 1950 was 300,782 and in 1960 was 360,940, almost exclusively German-speaking with Protestants predominating. The canton is governed by an executive council of five members who are elected by direct vote, and it sends 13 members (on the basis of the 1960 census) to the federal *Nationalrat*. The principal industries are agriculture, dairying and fruit growing, straw-plaiting, electrical engineering, the making of precision instruments, cement and cigars, and the mining and refining of salt. The canton has much to offer the tourist in its beautiful landscape, its ancient castles and its museums with their artistic treasures. Baden (q.v.), an important city in the canton, has a tourist industry based on hot sulfur springs.

Aarau, capital of the canton, had a population (1960) of 17,-045. At the southern foot of the Jura, it is built in terraces on the right bank of the Aare and is 50 mi. by rail N.E. of Bern and 31 mi. W. of Zürich. In the newer parts industries have grown up, the most important of which produce footwear and precision instruments.

Once an ancient fortress, it was taken by the Bernese in 1415, and in 1798 became for a time the capital of the Helvetic republic. The cantonal library has a fine collection of books and manuscripts, and the art gallery an important collection of pictures. Eight miles by rail northeast of Aarau is Schinznach Bad whose famous sulfur waters have been used for medicinal purposes since the end of the 17th century. Near Schinznach Bad is the ruined castle of Habsburg, or Habichtsburg (hawk's castle), the original home of the Habsburg family.

BIBLIOGRAPHY.—*Biographisches Lexikon des Kantons Aargau* (1957); Nold Halder, *Geschichte des Kantons Aargau 1803–1953*; Charles Tschopp, *Heimatkunde des Kantons Aargau* (1960).

AARHUS (officially Århus), a seaport, the capital of Aarhus *amt* (county), and the second town in Denmark, lies on the east coast of Jutland on Aarhus bay. Area 20.5 sq.km. (7.9 sq.mi.) (including suburbs, 114.2 sq.km. [44.1 sq.mi.]). Pop. (1960) 119,568.

The oldest buildings in the town are the 11th-century crypt of St. Nicholas under the Church of Our Lady and the 13th-century cathedral. The town hall built in 1941 by A. Jacobsen and E. Möller and the university (1932) by C. F. Möller are fine examples of modern Danish architecture. There is an art gallery, a prehistoric museum and Den Gamle By, a unique open-air museum of an early Danish town. Aarhus has a botanical garden and several other parks. In addition to the university (opened 1928) there are training establishments for dentists, journalists and technicians; a merchant high school; and four teachers' training colleges.

Aarhus is the centre of both transport and commerce in Jutland. The harbour, with a maximum depth of 33 ft., has eight docks. Daily services are maintained from Aarhus to Kalundborg; Copenhagen; Halmstad, Swed.; and Oslo, Nor. From the Tirstrup airfield, 37 km. (23 mi.) N.E., there are daily flights to Copenhagen. The major industries of Aarhus are metals and chemicals.

Though the origin of the town is unknown, it became an episcopal residence as early as 948. The oldest existing charter dates from 1441 and refers to a still earlier one. Since the beginning of the 19th century Aarhus has expanded rapidly.

Aarhus county (area 311 sq.mi. [804 sq.km.], pop. [1960] 221,895) is low-lying, fertile farming country with a large amount of woodland.   (J. Je.)

AARON, the traditional founder and head of the Jewish priesthood, who, in company with Moses, led the Israelites out of Egypt (see Exodus; Moses). He is described as a son of Amram and Jochebed of the tribe of Levi, and as three years older than his brother Moses (Ex. 6:20; 7:7). He acted together with his brother in the desperate situation of the Israelites in Egypt (Ex. 4 ff.) and took an active part in the exodus. While Moses was the actual leader, Aaron acted as his "mouth." The two brothers went to Pharaoh together, and it was Aaron who told the king to let the people of Israel go, using his magic rod in order to show the might of Yahweh. When Pharaoh finally decided to let the people go, Yahweh gave the important ordinance of the Passover to Aaron and Moses (Ex. 12:43 ff.). But Moses alone went up on Mt. Sinai, and he alone was allowed to come near to Yahweh (Ex. 24:2). Moses later was ordered to "bring near" Aaron and his sons (Ex. 28:1), and they were anointed and consecrated to be priests "by a perpetual statute" (Ex. 29; cf. Num. 3). Aaron's sons were to take over the priestly garments after him. Aaron is not represented as wholly blameless. It was he who, when Moses was delayed on Mt. Sinai, made the golden calf (q.v.).

Once a year, on the Day of Atonement, Aaron was allowed to come into the holy of holies (see Tabernacle), bringing his offering (Lev. 16). Together with his sister Miriam, Aaron spoke against Moses because he had married a foreigner (a Cushite woman), but as in the episode of the golden calf the narrative in Num. 12 tells how Aaron was merely reproved, though Miriam was punished, for the offense. In the rebellion of Korah the Levite, however, Aaron stood firmly at the side of Moses (Num. 16). Aaron died on the top of Mt. Hor at the age of 123 (Num. 33:39). In Deut. 10:6 which represents another tradition, he is said to have died in Moserah and was buried there, while Deut. 32:50 has the same tradition as Num. 20.

Aaron is a central figure in the traditions about the exodus, though his role varies in importance. At the beginning he seems to be co-equal with Moses (cf. also Mic. 6:4), but after the march out of Egypt he is only a shadow at Moses' side. Moses is obviously the leading person in the tradition, but it is also clear that he is pictured as delegating his authority in all priestly and cult matters to Aaron and "his sons."

Aaron and the Biblical Critics.—Scholars have long been aware that the figure of Aaron as it is now found in the Pentateuch (q.v.) is built up from several sources or layers of traditions. According to J. Wellhausen and his followers the Jahwist source (J) was the oldest one, followed in order by the Elohist (E), Deuteronomist (D), and Priestly code (P). Scholars have distributed the passages about Aaron to one or the other of these sources. Although their results differ, they do agree in ascribing about 90% of the material about Aaron to the Priestly source, which was written after the exile and is also the source that can be most easily traced. According to Wellhausen, Aaron was not mentioned at all in the early (Jahwist) narrative, but he may have been inserted by later redactors. It was Moses who was the hero of the priests before the exile (Ex. 4:17; 24), and it was Joshua, not Aaron, who officiated in the tabernacle (Ex. 33:7–11).

Other scholars, such as S. Mowinckel, are of the opinion that the narrative about the golden calf, which presents Aaron in an unfavourable light, was part of the ancient traditions in the Jahwist work, being the only passage in the latter that mentions him. This narrative, according to these scholars, originally came from the northern kingdom of Israel and described Aaron as the ancestor of the priests in northern Israel; later it was rewritten in a way defamatory to Aaron. But there are also features in the narrative which may indicate that a later source (or traditionist), the Elohist, tried to excuse Aaron and to put the main responsibility on the people. The Elohist narrator was credited with making Aaron the brother and helper of Moses (Ex. 4:14–17, 27–30), who stood at the side of Moses under the conflict with Pharaoh (Ex. 5, 7–10) and assisted Moses as a leader in battles (Ex. 17: 7–13) and in the cult (Ex. 18:12). It may also be the Elohist who provides the unfavourable story about Aaron's objection to Moses' wife (Num. 12). On the other hand it seems to be the same narrator who mentions Aaron at the side of Moses in the revolt at Meribah (Num. 20), but here also Aaron, together with Moses, is actually reproached. There is reason to believe that Aaron was not mentioned in the Deuteronomist work by the original author but that his name has been added by a redactor, for instance in Deut. 9:20, 10:6, and 32:50. The main bulk of the traditions about Aaron, and the frequent addition of "and Aaron" after the mention of Moses, are found in the Priestly source, which was written at a time when the priests had a more dominating position in Judah than they had before the exile. By then Moses had ceased to be the hero of the priests, and Aaron had taken over that role.

Many modern scholars prefer to speak of traditions and layers of traditions where their predecessors spoke of sources, but apart from this terminology the view concerning Aaron has not greatly changed. There have been new attempts, however, to see the contrasting figures of Moses and Aaron in new light. It has been suggested that the traditions about Moses represent a southern, Judaean tradition, while the old traditions about Aaron originated in the northern kingdom. It has also been indicated that the traditions about Moses are primarily concerned with a prophet, while those about Aaron are connected with priesthood. There may be a kernel of truth in all these suggestions, as also in the theory of I. Engnell that Moses represents the royal ideology while Aaron stands for priesthood and priesthood alone. The standing struggle between the king and the leading priests is reflected both in the laws and in the narratives of the historical books. The descriptions of the relationship between Aaron and Moses—priest and king—are coloured by this struggle, for instance in Lev. 16, Ezek. 45, II Chron. 26:16 ff. In the long run the priests were victorious, but Moses at the same time won an authority that could not be shaken.

Aaron in Later Jewish Thought.—Aaron continued to live as a symbol in Jewish religion and traditions. The position of the priests was strengthened after the exile, a fact which can be seen in Ezek. 40 ff., Chronicles, and Ezra. Also in the Qumran sect Aaron was a symbol for a strong priesthood, as can be seen from the Dead Sea Scrolls. At the end of time men of the community should be set apart, as a house of holiness for Aaron. Only the sons of Aaron should "administer judgment and wealth," and according to the *Manual of Discipline* two Messiahs were expected, one of Aaron, the priestly one, and one of Israel. According to a fragment found near Qumran the priest would have the first seat in the banquets in the last days and bless the bread before the Messiah of Israel. Here "the sons of Aaron" have the highest position.

In Midrash and Talmud, Aaron is seen not so much as a symbol as the leading personality at the side of Moses. The relationship between the two brothers is painted as prototypical in the *haggada*. Rabbi Hillel praised Aaron as peace-loving, a man of goodwill, who wanted to teach his fellow men the Law (Talmud, *Aboth* 1, 13). In the *haggada* his rod also played a role (*cf.* Num. 17:

1–10 [16–26 in the Hebrew Bible]). In Jewish exegesis little is said about him, though he is mentioned as a man who created peace among men. Many attempts have been made to explain the episode of the golden calf. According to some exegetes Aaron had to make the calf in order to avoid being killed. Gersonides (1288–c. 1344) explained that this would have been fatal not only for Aaron but even more for the people. Ibn Ezra (c. 1090–1164) underlined that here was no apostasy, and Rashi (1040–1105) contended that the calf was a symbol of the leader, Moses, who was at that time on the mountain. The relationship between Moses and Aaron also is discussed in the Talmud. Some traditionists have wondered why Aaron and not Moses was appointed high priest. The answer has been found in an indication that Moses was rejected because of his original unwillingness when he was called by Yahweh (Talmud, *Zebahim* 102a). It also seems to have been hard for some traditionists to accept that Aaron was described as older than Moses (*Sota* 12b). The death of Aaron is related in the Midrash *Petirat Aharon.*

Aaron in Christian Symbolism.—The first Christian communities admitted that Aaron, "the sons of Aaron," or "the order of Aaron" were symbols of the highest priesthood. But from the Epistle to the Hebrews (4 ff.), where Christ is described as a High Priest according to the order of Melchizedek, which was set over against "the order of Aaron" (Heb. 7), it can be seen that this caused problems. Of the church fathers, Cyril of Alexandria in his *De adoratione* i, 11 says that Aaron was divinely called to a priesthood in spirit and in truth, and that he was a type of Christ. Cyril also goes into the symbolism of Aaron's garments and their ornaments. Gregory the Great in his 33rd homily translates the name Aaron as "mountain of strength" and sees in him a redeemer who mediated between God and man. Isidore of Seville in his 60th scriptural allegory takes Aaron as a sacrificer, representing Christ who effaced the sin of the world through his blood. Alcuin in his commentary on Ps. 133 saw in Aaron the type of Christ, who penetrated into the holy of holies not with the blood of others but with his own blood, to intercede for the world with the Father. *See* also PRIESTHOOD: *Semitic and Israelite Priesthood.*

BIBLIOGRAPHY.—H. Gressmann, *Mose und seine Zeit* (1913); M. Noth, *Überlieferungsgeschichte des Pentateuch* (1948); I. Engnell, *Svenskt Bibliskt Uppslagsverk,* vol. i, col. 117–119 (1948); F. S. North, "Aaron's Rise in Prestige," in *Zeitschrift für die alttestamentliche Wissenschaft,* vol. lxvi, pp. 191–199 (1954); G. Widengren, *Sakrales Königtum im Alten Testament* (1955). (A. S. K.)

AARON'S-ROD, the popular name given to various tall flowering plants, such as garden orpine (*Sedum telephium*) or live-forever, great mullein (*Verbascum thapsus*), and goldenrod (*Solidago*).

AASEN, IVAR ANDREAS (1813–1896), Norwegian philologist, who constructed one of the two official languages of Norway, was born at Aasen i Ørsten, in Sunnmøre, Aug. 5, 1813. His first publication was a small collection of folk songs in the Sondmore dialect (1843). The *Grammar of the Norwegian Dialects* (1848) and the *Dictionary of the Norwegian Dialects* (1850) prepared the way for the wide cultivation of the popular language in Norwegian. With certain modifications, the language Aasen constructed, which is now called *nynorsk,* rapidly assumed an importance comparable to that of Dano-Norwegian. Aasen composed poems and plays in the composite dialect and continued to enlarge and improve his grammars and his dictionary. Quite early in his career (1842) he had begun to receive a stipend to enable him to give his entire attention to his philological investigations. Aasen died in Christiania (now Oslo), Sept. 23, 1896.

ABA, a town of Eastern region of Nigeria, Africa, lies on the west bank of the Aba river, about 40 mi. (64 km.) N of Port Harcourt, in the heart of the tropical rain forest but high enough above sea level to be clear of mangrove and fresh-water swamps. Pop. (1963) 131,003.

The town came into existence with the gradual pacification of the village communities of the area in the early years of the 20th century. Its development was hastened by the arrival in 1915 of the railway from Port Harcourt, extended to Enugu in 1916, and the subsequent construction of roads. By 1933 Aba was a settled urban area and a principal centre of trade. The town was laid out on modern lines around the main street, Asa road. There is a government school, a technical engineering school, Roman Catholic and Qua Iboe missions, a golf course and a prison.

Aba is the centre of a palm oil and palm kernel producing district and contains large and well-equipped soap factories. Other industries established or projected include furniture, textiles, concrete, aluminum ware and a brewery. The town is linked by road as well as by rail to Port Harcourt and Enugu (150 mi.), capital of Eastern region, and by road to the federal capital, Lagos (510 mi.). It is within reach of the airport at Port Harcourt.

(W. H. I.)

ABACÁ FIBRE (Manila Hemp), one of the most valuable of all fibres for cordage, is the product of *Musa textilis*, a plant of the banana family (Musaceae). This fibre is also known in the trade as manila and manila hemp, but abacá is a hard fibre and is entirely different from true hemp, which is a soft fibre and is the product of *Cannabis sativa*.

SHELL

STRIPPING, OR "TUXYING," STALK OF ABACÁ (MUSA TEXTILIS). STRIPS ARE CLEANED AND DRIED. AFTER WHICH THEY ARE GRADED AND BALED FOR USE IN MAKING CORDAGE

The abacá plant, which resembles in appearance the banana and plantain, to which it is closely related, is a perennial. Numerous suckers grow from the rootstocks, forming a cluster of stalks 10 to 25 ft. in height. These stalks, formed by the broad, overlapping leaf stems, bear at the top a crown of large, undivided leaves. The point of growth is at the base. The flower stalk is pushed up through the centre of the plant, bearing at the top flowers that are followed by fruits similar to small bananas but filled with black seeds. Abacá plants grown from seeds do not come true to type, so the plant is propagated from suckers or from rootstocks.

The abacá plant flowers when about two years old, at which stage it is in the most favourable condition for the production of fibre. The stalk is cut down, and the outer fibre-bearing layer of each successive leaf stem is stripped off in the form of ribbons known as "tuxies." The tuxies are scraped to remove the pulp and other waste material, leaving the cleaned fibre, which is then hung up to dry in the open air. Formerly, most of the processing was done by hand; more recently various machines, called decorticators, have been used. Without further treatment the fibre is graded and baled for shipment.

The outer sheaths of the abacá stalk contain a rather short, strong but discoloured fibre; the middle sheaths produce a fibre of medium colour and good strength; the sheaths near the centre of the stalk have a very white, fine fibre of medium strength. Delay and carelessness in drying affect both the colour and the strength of the fibre.

The exceptional strength of abacá fibre and its quality of resistance to the action of salt water make it particularly suitable for marine cordage. It is also largely used for well-drilling cables, hoisting ropes and various other types of rope where strength and durability are required. Henequen and sisal have largely replaced abacá as a binder twine fibre. In the Philippines the superior grades of abacá are used for textile fabrics, hats, slippers, rugs and various other articles. In Japan large quantities of abacá fibre, particularly the waste products, are used for the manufacture of paper. From the old and disintegrated ropes is made the well-known manila paper.

The abacá plant has been introduced into many different tropical regions, including Indonesia, India, the Andaman Islands, the West Indies and Central America; formerly the commercial production of this fibre was confined to the Philippine Islands. About 1921 shipments of abacá rootstocks were made from the Philippine Islands to Sumatra, where fairly large plantings were made. Despite some expansion of the industry there, it remained relatively unimportant. Small abacá plantings were also made in North Borneo.

In 1925 a shipment of propagating material of the superior varieties of abacá was brought from the Philippine Islands to the republic of Panamá by the United States department of agriculture. It was determined by experimental plantings that the climatic and soil conditions of this region are suitable for the abacá plant; that this plant is resistant to the more serious diseases of the banana plant, and that abacá fibre of excellent quality can be produced in tropical America. Little attention was given the Central American plantings until 1942 when the war cut off abacá supplies from the Philippines. At that time production of the fibre started in earnest in Costa Rica, Guatemala, Panamá and other countries of Central America.

In the early 1960s world production of abacá fibre exceeded 100,000 long tons, of which total the Philippines contributed over 90%.

(H. T. Es.; X.)

ABACUS, a calculating device of ancient origin still used in parts of the orient and middle east. The first abacus probably was a slab or board on which a Babylonian spread sand so he could trace letters. The word "abacus" is believed to be derived from the Phoenician *abak*, describing sand strewn on a surface for writing. As the abacus came to be used solely for counting and computing, its form was changed and improved. Wax-covered boards were introduced, and later a counter abacus was devised in which loose counters of bone, glass or metallic disks or rods were placed on a ruled table drawn on the board. In a still later form, the one used in some parts of the world today, the counters slide in grooves or on wires or strings.

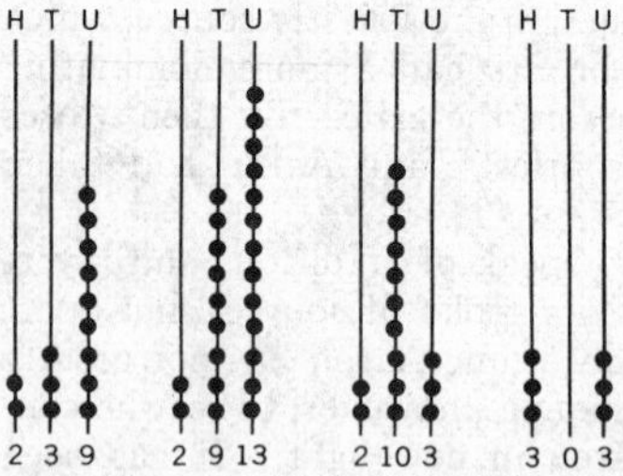

The table of the early counter abacus was composed of lines representing units, tens, hundreds, etc., or units of value, such as shillings, pence, pounds. Addition on an abacus of this type probably was performed as represented in fig. 1, which shows the steps in adding 64 and 239. Subtraction was simply the process of taking away counters; multiplication was considered as repeated addition, and division as repeated subtraction. This type of abacus was known in the Mediterranean countries, and Herodotus (*c.* 450 B.C.) is authority for the statement that the Egyptians wrote their figures and reckoned with pebbles "bringing the hand from right to left," while the Greeks proceeded in the opposite direction.

H T U	H T U	H T U	H T U

2 3 9   2 9 13   2 10 3   3 0 3

FROM D. E. SMITH, "HISTORY OF MATHEMATICS"

FIG. 1.—ADDITION ON ABACUS AS PRACTISED IN ANCIENT MEDITERRANEAN COUNTRIES

Lines represent hundreds, tens and units. The computation represented is: **239 + 64 = 29[13] = 2[10]3 = 303**

There are several references to the abacus in Roman literature, and what is apparently a Greek computing table was found in the 19th century on the island of Salamis.

Latin writers tell of three types of abacus in use in Rome, namely: (1) the sand board or wax tablet; (2) a marked table for counters; and (3) a table with grooves in which the counters were free to slide. Fig. 2 shows a late Roman abacus now in the British museum, each upper button representing five units of the order in which the column stands and each lower button representing one unit of the same order. Cicero speaks of the counters as *aera* ("bronzes") but the common name was *calculi* ("pebbles") or *abaculi*. The pieces were stone, ivory, metal or coloured glass.

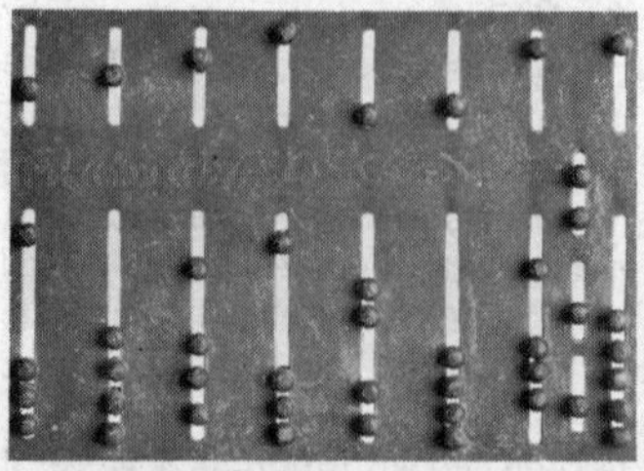

The earliest type of abacus in China seems to have been the bamboo rods that served instead of counters. These were known as early as the 6th century B.C. and they survived in Korea until the close of the 19th century. They found their way into Japan

BY COURTESY OF THE TRUSTEES OF THE BRITISH MUSEUM

FIG. 2.—LATE ROMAN ABACUS

Bronze table with each upper button representing five units and each lower button representing one unit of the order in which the column stands

about the year 600 and were known as *sangi* or *sanchu*. Until recent times they were used to represent algebraic coefficients, being placed on a ruled board. Since the 12th century the *suan-pan* ("computing tray"; *see* fig. 3) has been generally used throughout China. The chief difference between this and the Roman abacus lies in the fact that the latter has one less bead in each section. In the 16th century this type, slightly changed and bearing the kindred name of *soroban*, found its way into Japan, where it is still in use. An abacus differing considerably from the Roman or oriental types is found in the middle eastern countries. The Turks call it the *coulba*; the Armenians, the *choreb*; and the Russians, the *s'choty*. As in the case of the *suan-pan* and the *soroban*, this permits rapid computation and serves a purpose similar to that of the modern calculating machine.

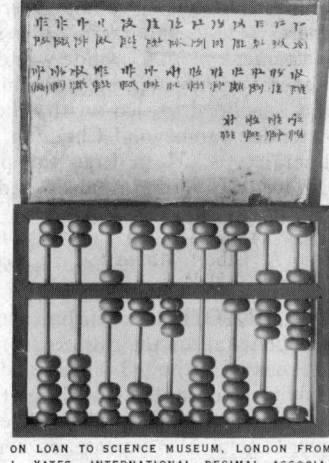

ON LOAN TO SCIENCE MUSEUM, LONDON FROM J. YATES, INTERNATIONAL DECIMAL ASSOCIATION

FIG. 3.—CHINESE SUAN-PAN
Each upper bead represents five units and each lower bead represents one unit of the order in which the column stands. The number represented is 7230189

A type of abacus called the line abacus appeared in Europe in the middle ages. It consisted of a table ruled with horizontal lines representing the successive powers of ten, each space between lines representing half the value of the line immediately above it. This type was used well into the 18th century.

Abacus disks used in computing were known in Great Britain as counters; in the Latin books as projectiles (*pro,* "forward," + *jacere,* "to throw"), being thrown or cast upon the counting board, or as *denarii supputarii* ("computing pennies"); and in France as *jetons* (from *jacere,* "to throw"). In Germany a counter was called a *Rechenpfennig* or *Zahlpfennig* ("number penny"). Such later expressions as "cast an account," "borrow one," "carry two" and possibly "lay a wager" have their origin in this kind of computation. The countinghouse, billiard counters, poker chips and various games trace their origin to the counting board.

By medieval times the counter abacus was being used in most regions of the known world, but it gradually was abandoned as the Arabic notation of nine figures and zero replaced the Roman numeral system in calculating. The abacus was last generally used in Spain and Italy in the 15th century, in France in the 16th century and in England and Germany in the 17th century.

(D. E. S.; X.)

BIBLIOGRAPHY.—F. C. Scesney, *The Chinese Abacus* (1944); D. E. Smith, *History of Mathematics* (1958); T. Kojima, *Japanese Abacus* (1954); C. C. Liu, *Principles and Practice of the Chinese Abacus* (1958).

ABACUS, in architecture, the upper member of a capital (*q.v.*) whose function is to provide a supporting surface for the structure above. In Egyptian capitals it is smaller than the parts below and in the late work it has great height. In the Greek Doric order it is a plain square slab, but in the Roman Doric it is usually crowned by a molding. In the Greek Ionic order it is at first rectangular, to cap the projection of the volutes, but later becomes square, except at corner capitals where it is curved out over the angle volutes. In both Greek and Roman Corinthian orders and in the composite and four-sided or Scamozzi Ionic order it is molded with concave sides and usually the corners are cut off slightly. In Romanesque architecture the abacus usually is square, with sides splayed or molded, and in the Gothic, outside of England, it is square or octagonal and richly molded. In English Gothic, however, circular forms are frequent, especially in 13th-century work. The diminutive, *abaculus,* is applied to the squares of tile, or tessera. *See also* ORDER.

ABADAN, a city of Khuzistan *ostan* (province) of Iran, lies on an island of the same name off the eastern bank of the Shatt al Arab, 33 mi. from its mouth on the Persian gulf. The island, 42 mi. long and from 2 to 12 mi. wide and known to the Arabs as Jazirat al-Khidr (from the tomb of a saint of that name), is bounded on the east by the Khowr-e Bahmanshir, a branch of the Karun river. The population of Abadan city in 1932 was about 40,000 and by 1956 had reached 226,083, with a further 57,522 in the area, mostly date-palm growers. The climate is extremely hot and often very humid for seven months of the year.

Abadan Island was referred to in the 13th century by the historian Nasir Khosrow as the southernmost settlement of Iraq. Its possession was long in dispute between Persia and Turkey but was awarded to Persia by the treaty of Erzurum (1847); the Turks retained control of the Shatt al Arab, while ensuring freedom of navigation to the Persians.

In 1909 the Anglo-Persian Oil company, by agreement with the sheik of Mohammerah, established its pipeline terminus and refinery there. Once the largest in the world, with a daily capacity of 500,000 bbl., it is served by 1,880 mi. of pipelines from the oilfields in the foothills of the Zagros range. The port has deepwater jetties for the loading of tankers and the discharge of other goods. A 590-mi. pipeline to Teheran was completed in 1959. Asphalted roads connect Abadan with the port of Khorramshahr (formerly Mohammerah) and with the oilfields. There is a separate crude oil port at Bandar-e Ma'shur, 55 mi. to the east.

The city is among the best equipped in Iran and consists mainly of a series of compounds for the company's staff and its labour force, which is recruited from all over the gulf and from the Bakhtiari tribes. There is a lively bazaar and poor housing quarters for unemployed immigrants.

The nationalization of the oil industry by the Iranian government in 1951 led to a virtual cessation of operations. Three years later an agreement to resume production was made between the government and a consortium of eight foreign oil companies, but it was not until 1959 that full production was restored.

(H. Bo.)

ABAE, an ancient town in Greece, in the northeastern corner of Phocis, north of Lake Copais and west of modern Topolia, famous for its oracle of Apollo, one of those consulted by Croesus. Its rich treasures were sacked in 480 B.C. by the Persians, who burned the temple. The oracle was, however, still consulted; *e.g.,* by the Thebans before the battle of Leuctra in 371 B.C. The temple, burned again during the Sacred War of 355–347 B.C., was very dilapidated when seen by Pausanias in the middle of the 2nd century A.D., although some restoration had been undertaken by Hadrian. Privileges due to the sanctity of the shrine were confirmed to the people of Abae by the Romans. The polygonal walls of the acropolis may still be seen, with one gateway and traces of town walls below.

ABAILARD: *see* ABÉLARD, PETER.

ABAKAN, the capital of the Khakass autonomous *oblast,* Russian Soviet Federated Socialist Republic, U.S.S.R., was created a town in 1931 and stands on the left bank of the Abakan river at its confluence with the Yenisei. Pop. (1959) 56,146. It is the terminus of the branch railway from Achinsk on the Trans-Siberian; a line from Abakan to Novokuznetsk in the Kuzbas was under construction in the 1960s. A branch links Abakan with the coal-mining town of Chernogorsk, 10 mi. N. A motor road from Abakan crosses the Yenisei to Minusinsk and runs on over the western Sayan mountains to Kyzyl, capital of the Tuva autonomous *oblast.* The town is a centre of metal-working and sawmilling, and of food-processing based on agricultural products of the fertile Minusinsk basin. It has a pedagogical institute.

(R. A. F.)

ABALONE, a common name of Spanish derivation, applied in California to various species of marine snails of the genus *Haliotis.* They are widely distributed and are called perlemeon in South Africa, ormer or ormier in the Channel Islands and France, paua in New Zealand and ear shells in Australia. The single flattened shell is earlike with the large body whorl perforated on the left side by a single row of small openings that become filled progressively during growth; the last five to nine remain open to serve as outlets for waste products. Depending on the species, abalones range from a few inches to ten inches across and up to three inches in depth. The lustrous, pearly interior of the shell is commonly iridescent and is utilized in the manufacture of attractive ornaments such as buttons and inlaying.

The large muscular foot of these snails was a popular food of primitive man and is still regarded as a delicacy in many countries. Commercial fisheries exist in California, Mexico, Japan, South Africa and the Channel Islands off England.

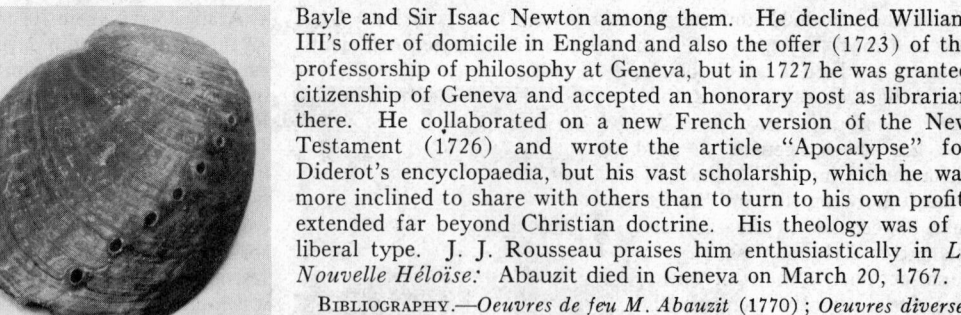

BY COURTESY OF AMERICAN MUSEUM OF NATURAL HISTORY

SHELL OF BLACK ABALONE (HALIOTIS CRACHERODII), SHOWING BREATHING HOLES

The west American species inhabit algal covered rocky bottoms from the tidal zone to depths of more than 100 ft. and are sought by skin divers and commercial fishermen using diving equipment. Of the eight Californian abalones, the red (*Haliotis rufescens*), pink (*H. corrugata*) and green (*H. fulgens*) are the important ones. *See also* SNAIL.

See "Review of the Abalone in California," *Calif. Fish Game*, 46:381–406 (1960).   (W. K. E.)

ABANDONMENT, a legal term denoting the relinquishment of an interest, claim or privilege by the owner. The conduct sufficient to manifest an intention to abandon and the consequences of such conduct vary according to the branch of law under which the issue arises. Thus, while the benefit of an easement may be abandoned by the owner of the dominant estate, mere nonuser for a period of time is usually not sufficient to manifest an intention to abandon (*see* EASEMENT). On the other hand, no matter how clear the intention to abandon an estate in land is expressed, such abandonment is not possible since this would leave the ownership vacant (*see* REAL PROPERTY AND CONVEYANCING, LAWS OF).

For abandonment of children, *see* CHILDREN, LAWS CONCERNING; for abandonment of domicile, *see* DOMICILE AND RESIDENCE.
(A. DM.)

ABARBANEL: *see* ABRABANEL, ISAAC.

ABAS, the name of several characters in classical literature and mythology.

1. Abas, son of Lynceus and Hypermestra (daughter of Danaus), was the 12th king of Argos and founder of Abae in Phocis. He was noted for his shield, which had been consecrated by Danaus to Hera but was given to Abas by his father on his report of Danaus' death. The gift was apparently the explanation of the prize given at an Argive festival, a shield rather than a crown.

2. Three persons by this name appear in Ovid's *Metamorphoses*: a centaur, a friend of Perseus, and a companion of Diomedes who was turned into a swanlike bird by Aphrodite.   (T. V. B.)

ABATEMENT, in law, the interruption of a legal proceeding upon the pleading by a defendant of matter which prevents the plaintiff from going forward with the action at that time or in that form. Pleas in abatement raise such matters as objections to the place, mode or time of the plaintiff's action, lack of proper parties to the action or lack of jurisdiction in the court to entertain it, without questioning the justice of the plaintiff's claim. In earlier procedures, abatement of proceedings in equity differed from abatement at law in that the former merely suspended the action, subject to revival when the defect was cured, while the latter entirely terminated it, although the plaintiff could start anew. The latter is now the more usual usage. *See also* PRACTICE AND PROCEDURE: *England: Civil Procedure.*   (C. E. CL.)

ABATTOIR: *see* SLAUGHTERHOUSE.

ABAUZIT, FIRMIN (1679–1767), French theologian, remembered both for the extent of his learning and for his great kindliness and modesty, was born of Huguenot parents at Uzès in Languedoc in Nov. 1679. His mother contrived his escape to Geneva in 1689 from enforced Catholicism in France. In 1698 he began to travel, visiting Germany, the Netherlands and England and making the acquaintance of learned and literary men, Pierre

Bayle and Sir Isaac Newton among them. He declined William III's offer of domicile in England and also the offer (1723) of the professorship of philosophy at Geneva, but in 1727 he was granted citizenship of Geneva and accepted an honorary post as librarian there. He collaborated on a new French version of the New Testament (1726) and wrote the article "Apocalypse" for Diderot's encyclopaedia, but his vast scholarship, which he was more inclined to share with others than to turn to his own profit, extended far beyond Christian doctrine. His theology was of a liberal type. J. J. Rousseau praises him enthusiastically in *La Nouvelle Héloïse:* Abauzit died in Geneva on March 20, 1767.

BIBLIOGRAPHY.—*Oeuvres de feu M. Abauzit* (1770); *Oeuvres diverses de M. Abauzit*, 2 vol. (1770–73; Eng. trans., *Miscellanies*, 1774). *See also* A. Gibert, *Abauzit et sa théologie* (1865); E. Stroehlin, *Firmin Abauzit* (1894).

ABBADIDS, a Muslim dynasty which arose in Andalusia on the downfall of the caliphate of Córdoba (*q.v.*).

ABBAD I (Abu'l-Qasim Mohammed) (d. 1042) was the qadi of Seville who, in 1023, with aristocratic support, declared his city independent from Córdoba. Before his death he had enlarged his territory at the expense of neighbouring kinglets by a mixture of political chicanery and indiscriminate border warfare.

ABBAD II, known as al-Mu'tadid (d. 1069), continued this policy of aggrandizement far more successfully by leading Muslims of Arab and native Spanish descent against the Berbers of eastern Andalusia and even aimed at taking Córdoba and restoring the caliphate. He failed in this mainly because of family defections and the opposition of the Castilian king Ferdinand I, whom he later appeased by becoming his tributary. A "vengeful, suspicious and bloody" character, poet and patron of poets, wine drinker and skeptic, he is said to have killed a rebellious son with his own hand and disposed of certain Berber chiefs of Ronda by smothering them in a steam bath in the Alcázar of Seville. Even more sadistically picturesque was his flower garden, planted over the skulls of his enemies, which he "contemplated with ecstasy."

ABBAD III (1040–1095), his son, generally known as al-Mu'tamid, the last ruling member of the dynasty, epitomizes the chivalrous, extravagant and tragic virtuosity of medieval Andalusia. Remembered as the poet-king of Seville, whose example and patronage made the city a brilliant centre of Spanish Muslim culture, he appointed as his vizier his fellow poet Ibn Ammar, and took as his queen a Sevillian slave girl, I'timad al-Rumaykiyah, who had capped one of his improvised couplets. Though he was a less ruthless character than his father, his political life was equally turbulent and scarred by repeated tragedies and failures. His son and namesake was killed in early youth during a struggle with the ruler of Toledo for possession of Córdoba. His alliance with the Catalans for the conquest of Murcia was destroyed by an unforeseeable mishap, and the conquest of that city by his troops led to a breach with Ibn Ammar, who lampooned his master so stubbornly that he had him strangled in jail. Al-Mu'tamid's downfall was precipitated by the outbreak of hostilities against the Castilian king Alfonso VI, whose Jewish envoy had accused al-Mu'tamid of debasing the tribute money. Al-Mu'tamid had him crucified, and in revenge Alfonso made a fruitless incursion into Andalusia. Christian progress in Aragon and Valencia and the fall of Toledo in 1085, together with pressure from religious enthusiasts at home, forced al-Mu'tamid to seek alliance with the Almoravid amir Yusuf ibn Tashfin (*see* ALMORAVIDS). Although the Sevillian had distinguished himself for generalship and personal valour in their joint victory in 1086 over the Castilians in the battle of Zallaka or Zalaca (Sacralias, north of Badajoz), the Almoravid later turned against his ally and besieged Seville. The city was betrayed by Muslim zealots after a heroic defense by al-Mu'tamid, who was taken prisoner (1091). Some of the elegies he wrote in his five-year captivity in north Africa won him popular sympathy, and for more than two centuries his tomb was a centre of pilgrimage.

BIBLIOGRAPHY.—R. P. A. Dozy, *Histoire des Musulmans d'Espagne*, 2nd ed. (1932), and *Historia Abbadidarum*, 2 vol. (1846–52). *See also* A. F. von Schack, *Poesie und Kunst der Araber . . .* (1877).
(K. GA.)

ABBADIE, ANTOINE THOMSON D' (1810–1897), and
ARNAUD MICHEL D' (1815–1893), geographers and travelers in north Africa who were born in Dublin, Ire., of a French
father and an Irish mother. Their parents moved to France in
1818. In 1835 the French Academy sent Antoine on a scientific
mission to Brazil, the results being published in 1873 under the
title of *Observations Relatives à la physique du globe faites au
Brésil et en Éthiopie*. Arnaud spent some time in Algeria before
the two brothers started for Abyssinia in 1837, landing at Massawa
in Feb. 1838. After collecting much information on the geography, geology, archaeology and natural history of Abyssinia, the
brothers returned to France in 1848. Arnaud then paid another
visit to Abyssinia in 1853.

Meanwhile Antoine had become involved in various controversies relating to both his geographical results and his political
activities in Abyssinia. Time and the investigations of subsequent explorers have shown that he was quite trustworthy as to
his facts, though wrong in his contention that the Blue Nile was
the main stream. The topographical results of his explorations
were published in Paris in 1860–73 in *Géodésie de l'Éthiopie*. Of
the *Géographie de l'Éthiopie* (1890) only one volume has been
published. *Un Catalogue raisonné de manuscrits éthiopiens* (1859)
contains a description of 234 Ethiopian manuscripts collected by
Antoine. He published numerous papers dealing with the geography
of Abyssinia, Ethiopian coins and ancient inscriptions. His *Recon-
naissances magnétiques* (1890) is an account of the magnetic observations made by him in journeys to the Red sea and the Levant.

The general account of the travels of the two brothers was
published by Arnaud in 1868 under the title of *Douze ans dans la
Haute-Éthiopie*. Antoine died in 1897 and bequeathed an estate
in the Pyrenees, yielding 40,000 francs a year, to the Academy
of Sciences, on the condition that it produce a catalogue of 50,000
stars within 50 years. His brother Arnaud died in 1893.

ABBA MARI (Abba Mari ben Moses ben Joseph), French
rabbi, was born at Lunel, near Montpellier, toward the end of the
13th century. He is also known as Yarhi from his birthplace
(Heb. *Yerah; i.e.,* "moon," *lune*), and he further took the name
Astruc, Don Astruc or En Astruc of Lunel. In Montpellier, where
he lived from 1303 to 1306, he was much distressed by the
prevalence of Aristotelian rationalism, which, through the medium of the works of Maimonides, threatened the authority of the
Old Testament, obedience to the law, and the belief in miracles and
revelation. He, therefore, in a series of letters (afterward collected under the title *Minhat Kenaot;* "Jealousy Offering") called
upon the famous rabbi Solomon ben Adret of Barcelona to come
to the aid of orthodoxy. Ben Adret, with the approval of other
prominent Spanish rabbis, sent a letter to the community at Montpellier proposing to forbid the study of philosophy to those who
were less than 30 years of age, and, in spite of keen opposition
from the liberal section, a decree in this sense was issued by Ben
Adret in 1305. The result was a great schism among the Jews of
Spain and southern France, and a new impulse was given to the
study of philosophy by the unauthorized interference of the Spanish rabbis. On the expulsion of the Jews from France by Philip IV
in 1306, Abba Mari settled at Perpignan, where he published the
letters connected with the controversy.

Bibliography.—Edition of the *Minhat Kenaot* by M. L. Bislichis
(1838) ; E. Renan, *Les rabbins français,* p. 647 ff.; Perles, *Salomo ben
Abraham ben Adereth,* p. 15–54; "Abba Mari," *Jewish Encyclopedia.*

ABBAS I (1571–1629), shah of Persia from 1587 to 1629,
is known as Abbas the Great. His brutal uncle Isma'il II ordered
his execution when he was a child, but he was saved by Isma'il's
death in 1577. Four years later he was proclaimed ruler of the
great province of Khurasan. He became shah of Persia on the
abdication of his father, Mohammed Khudabanda, in 1587. His
prospects seemed gloomy, as he was confronted with anarchy in
Persia due to the insubordination of the Turkmen tribal leaders,
and with invasion by the Ottoman Turks on the west and by the
Uzbeks on the northeast.

Faced with such odds, Abbas was forced to make peace with the
Turks on unfavourable terms in 1590, but he was then able to
subdue the rebels in his own country and to crush the Uzbeks and

drive them out of Persia. He reopened hostilities with Turkey in
1603 and in a series of campaigns regained the territory that had
been surrendered in 1590; the war against the Turks continued
with intervals, until the end of his reign. In 1621 his forces regained Kandahar, which the Mogul emperor Akbar had seized 30
years earlier. In the following year, with naval aid furnished by
the English East India company, Abbas expelled the Portuguese
from the island of Hormuz; much of the trade from there was diverted to Gombrun on the mainland, which was renamed Bandar
'Abbas after the shah. In gratitude for the East India company's
assistance against the Portuguese, the shah gave the company
valuable privileges at Bandar 'Abbas.

Abbas' military successes were largely the result of his thorough
reorganization of the army. In place of the tribal levies, whose
loyalties were primarily to their own chiefs, he created a regular
force, which gained both in reliability and in efficiency. In this
he owed much to the help of an English adventurer, Sir Robert
Shirley (Sherley), who also assisted him in the creation of an
artillery corps. Abbas' reign was distinguished by military successes and administrative efficiency, also by the magnificence of
his court and by his zeal as a builder. He largely replanned and rebuilt Isfahan, which he had made his capital in 1598; many of the
architectural glories of that city date from his reign. He fostered
trade and industry by constructing highways, bridges and cara-
vanseries and also by granting privileges to his Armenian subjects
(many of whom he had forcibly moved from their homes in the
north and settled in a suburb of Isfahan). He also encouraged the
English and Dutch East India companies to trade in Persia. He
was tolerant in religious matters and allowed foreign monastic
orders to establish missions in Persia.

Abbas' fame, however, was tarnished by some terrible deeds of
cruelty. At his orders Queen Ketevan of Kakhetia was tortured
and put to death. He blinded and imprisoned his father and two
brothers and had his own son Mohammed Baqir Mirza executed
and another son, Imam Quli, blinded. Although he had made
Persia a great power once again, he was nevertheless partially responsible for its subsequent decline by reason of his inauguration,
for reasons of security, of the practice of immuring the heir apparent (as well as the other royal princes) in the harem until the
moment came for his accession to the throne.

Bibliography.—Munshi Iskandar Beg, *Ta'rikh-i-Alam-Ara-yi-'Ab-
basi* (1896) ; J. Chardin, *Voyages du Chevalier Chardin,* ed. by L.
Langlès (1811) ; L. L. Bellan, *Chah 'Abbas I: sa vie, son histoire*
(1932) ; E. D. Ross (ed.), *Sir Anthony Sherley and His Persian Adventure* (1933) ; N. Falsafi, *Zindigani-yi-Shah 'Abbas-i-Avval* (1955).
(L. Lo.)

ABBAS I (1813–1854), pasha and viceroy of Egypt, a grandson of Mohammed Ali (*q.v.*), came to power in 1848, nine months
after the death of his uncle Ibrahim Pasha. Abbas was by nature
cautious and secretive. His years of office were marked by reaction against the westernizing tendencies of Mohammed Ali; he
curtailed the scope of government activity, reduced the fighting
services, closed factories and abolished, though only partially in
the Sudan, the state trading monopoly imposed by his grandfather
in defiance of Ottoman treaties with the Powers. He distrusted
western, especially French, thought and ways and dismissed many
European experts, while Egyptian intellectuals influenced by European culture, such as Rifa'a Bey al-Raf'i, were banished to the
Sudan. Nevertheless his retrenchment in government spending
lightened taxation and restored the Egyptian finances, strained by
Mohammed Ali's wars and economic experiments. Abbas permitted the construction of the Alexandria-Cairo railway by Robert
Stephenson (1852–56). His loyalty to the Ottoman empire was
expressed by the dispatch of an Egyptian contingent in 1853 to
support the Turks against the Russians (*see* Crimean War). On
July 13, 1854, he was murdered at Benha. (R. L. Hl.)

ABBAS II (Abbas Hilmi Pasha) (1874–1944), last khedive
of Egypt, was born in Cairo on July 14, 1874, the eldest son of
Mohammed Tewfik (Tawfiq) Pasha, whom he succeeded in the
khediviate in 1892. His relations with the British occupying power
were invidious. With studied indiscretion at a parade of troops
at Wadi Halfa during a tour of the frontier garrisons in 1894, he
publicly criticized the military efficiency of the British officers

serving in the Egyptian army, an incident which caused the fall of the Riyad ministry and brought no gain to his prestige in any quarter. His dealings with the Egyptian nationalists were equally unfortunate. So long as nationalist criticism was confined to agitation against the British occupation, he discreetly supported the nationalist cause and in 1904 procured from the sultan the grade of pasha for the nationalist leader Mustafa Kamil, who for a time pursued a pan-Islamic and pro-Ottoman policy. When, however, partly as a result of the Anglo-French settlement of 1904, the nationalists began to advocate a more liberal regime for Egypt, their relations with the khedive became estranged.

Abbas showed a lively interest in the social and economic welfare of Egypt and the Sudan. He visited Berber and Khartoum in 1901–02 and opened the new harbour at Port Sudan in 1909. While on a visit to Constantinople he was shot and wounded by an Egyptian student in July 1914. He was still in Turkey when the Ottoman empire entered World War I; his return to Egypt was forbidden by the British, who declared a protectorate over Egypt and, on Dec. 19, 1914, deposed him in favour of his uncle, Husain Kamil Pasha, who assumed the title of sultan. Abbas passed the rest of his life in exile, chiefly in Switzerland, and died at Geneva on Dec. 21, 1944. He wrote *A Few Words on the Anglo-Egyptian Settlement* (1930).

See Evelyn Baring, earl of Cromer, *Abbas II* (1915); A. A. H. Beaman, *The Dethronement of the Khedive,* ed., with introduction, by J. M. Robinson (1929).   (R. L. Hʟ.)

ABBAS, FERHAT (1899–   ), Algerian political leader of the Front of National Liberation (F.L.N.) in the Algerian rebellion against French rule, was born at a village near Djidjelli in the Constantine department. Son of a caid, he was educated at Philippeville and later at Algiers university. Entirely French-educated, he never spoke Arabic well. After two years' service with the French army, he became a pharmacist at Sétif and later a member of the *conseil général* of Constantine. In his first period of political activity Abbas stood for the emancipation of the Algerian Muslims as French citizens. "Algeria is French soil," he wrote in 1931, "and we are French Moslems." Bitterly disillusioned by the subsequent French rejection of the proposals in the Blum-Violette plan, he yet served as a volunteer with the French forces in World War II. Later he promoted the "Algerian manifesto" which was presented to the French and Allied authorities in North Africa Feb. 10, 1943. In its final form this envisaged an Algerian state at the end of the war, with a constitution to be worked out by a constituent assembly elected by universal suffrage; meanwhile a government should be formed with Muslim and European members in equal numbers and parity be established in all assemblies.

As leader of the Union Démocratique du Manifeste Algérien and member of the French constituent assembly, Abbas submitted in Aug. 1946 a project for the recognition of Algeria as a state federated with France. This, however, was not considered by the assembly. On the outbreak of the rising in 1954, he appeared at first taken aback and issued an appeal for calm. Later, however, with other former moderates of various tendencies, he escaped to Cairo and joined the F.L.N. (April 1956). On Sept. 19, 1958, the formation of a provisional government of the Algerian republic was announced in Cairo, with Ferhat Abbas as prime minister. He resigned in 1961 but was elected president of the Algerian parliament in Sept. 1962. A year later he resigned. As a leading critic of Ahmed ben Bella's government he was placed under house arrest in 1964 but was released in 1965.   (N. Ba.; X.)

ABBASIDS, the second of the two great dynasties of the Muslim Arab empire (*see* Caliphate). The name is derived from Mohammed's uncle, al-Abbas (566–652), of the Hashemite clan of the tribe of Quraysh in Mecca. From *c.* 718 some of the family of al-Abbas were planning to gain supreme power. By skilful propaganda their agents won much support, especially from Arabs and Persians in Khurasan. Open revolt in 747 under Abu Muslim led in 750 to the defeat of the Omayyad dynasty and the proclamation of the first Abbasid caliph, Abu'l-Abbas.

Iraq became the centre of the caliphate instead of Syria, Baghdad being founded as capital *c.* 762. Much of the support of the Abbasids came from Persian converts, and it was therefore natural for them to take over much of the Persian (Sassanian) tradition of government. Support by pious Muslims likewise led them to acknowledge publicly the embryonic Islamic law and to profess to base their rule on the religion of Islam. Under them commerce and the liberal arts expanded. The reigns of Harun al-Rashid (786–809) and al-Ma'mun (813–833) were periods of splendour.

Gradually Abbasid power decayed. First in the east, then elsewhere, provincial governors made themselves independent though still nominally receiving appointment from the caliph. In the 10th century, real power even at the centre passed into the hands of dynasties of military leaders, such as the Buyids and the Seljuks (*qq.v.*). The caliph retained the nominal power of making appointments while these rulers had titles such as sultan. This nominal power was ended in 1258. A branch of the family held formal, religious powers in Cairo until the death in 1538 of al-Mutawakkil III who had been moved to Istanbul in 1517. *See* also references under "Abbasids" in the Index.   (W. M. Wt.)

ABBE, ERNST (1840–1905), German physicist, is best known for his invention of the Abbe refractometer and his many improvements in microscopic and photographic lenses. He was born in Eisenach, Thuringia, Jan. 23, 1840. He was educated at Göttingen and Jena. In 1863 he became an instructor, and in 1870 was made a professor, in the University of Jena, at which in 1878 he was appointed director of the astronomical and meteorological observatories. In 1866 he became connected with the optical works of Carl Zeiss, was made a partner in 1875, and contributed in a very large degree through his experiments to the excellence of the instruments and lenses made by the firm.

In 1884, with Zeiss and Otto Schott, he established important works for the production of technical glass. Upon the death of Zeiss in 1888 he became the sole owner of the Zeiss optical works, which he reorganized as a co-operative establishment; the officials, the workmen and the university participated in its profits. His collected works were published in 1903–06. He died in Jena, Jan. 14, 1905.

ABBESS: *see* Abbot.

ABBEVILLIAN (formerly known as Chellean [*q.v.*]), the oldest Stone Age industry with hand axes, named after Abbeville in the Somme valley, France, where artifacts occur in terrace gravels believed to date from the first warm interval in the Pleistocene Ice Age, *i.e.*, more than 300,000 years old. These simple tools, also called *bifaces* or *coups de poing,* consist of a lump of flint or other suitable stone flaked to a tongue-shaped form with a margin for cutting, and may be pointed or oval. Abbevillian hand axes are coarsely flaked (probably with hammerstone) and have a thick, largely unworked butt. Lower Paleolithic hand-ax culture spread throughout Africa, western Europe and southwestern Asia. The development of hand axes from roughly chipped pebbles has been traced in Oldoway (Olduvai) gorge in Tanganyika. The Abbevillian type was superseded by the more regularly flaked Acheulian hand axes, associated with Ternifine and Swanscombe man. *See* also Archaeology.   (K. P. O.)

ABBEY, EDWIN AUSTIN (1852–1911), U.S. painter, one of the foremost illustrators of his day, was born in Philadelphia, Pa., April 1, 1852. After studying at the Pennsylvania Academy of Fine Arts, he became in 1871 an illustrator for the publishing house of Harper and Brothers in New York. Harper's, because of his success, was persuaded to send him to England in 1878 to gather material for illustrations of the poems of Robert Herrick. These drawings, published in 1882, and followed by illustrations for Oliver Goldsmith's *She Stoops to Conquer* (1887), *Old Songs* (1889), and the comedies of Shakespeare, among others, established his reputation in England and America. His water colours and pastels were no less successful, and he was elected a member of the Royal Institute of Painters in Water-Colours in 1883. He first exhibited an oil painting at the Royal Academy in London in 1890; he was elected an associate (A.R.A.) in 1896, academician (R.A.) in 1898, and to the National academy in 1902.

In his later years he created several large decorative schemes, including murals in the Boston public library and in the state capitol at Harrisburg, Pa. He painted the official picture of the coronation of Edward VII in 1902 and supervised the decoration of the peers' corridor of the houses of parliament just before his death, Aug. 1, 1911. His work, especially his perceptive drawings, water colours and sketches, was of consistently high academic quality. At his finest he achieved a degree of spontaneity and life seldom attained by artists of this persuasion. He is represented by works at the Metropolitan Museum of Art, New York; the Boston • Museum of Fine Arts; Carnegie institute, Pittsburgh; and the Tate gallery, London. The Yale University Art gallery, New Haven, Conn., possesses a large collection of his work.

BIBLIOGRAPHY.—Edwin A. Abbey and Alfred Parsons, *The Quiet Life* (1890); *A Catalogue of a Memorial Exhibition of the Work of Edwin Austin Abbey, R.A., N.A.* (1912); E. V. Lucas, *Edwin Austin Abbey*, 2 vol. (1921); *A Catalogue of an Exhibition of Paintings, Drawings and Pastels From the Edwin Austin Abbey Collection* (1939); George Heard Hamilton, "The Edwin Austin Abbey Show," *The Carnegie Magazine*, vol. xv, no. 3, pp. 83–86 (June 1941). (G. H. HN.)

ABBEY THEATRE, the national theatre of Ireland, began in 1902 when the Irish Literary theatre's work in Dublin was taken over by W. G. Fay's Irish National dramatic company, which presented Irish plays with Irish actors. In 1903 it became the Irish National Theatre society. This brought W. B. Yeats, J. M. Synge, Lady Gregory, George William Russell (Æ) and others into contact with the group of amateur actors which the brothers Frank and William Fay had been building up since 1891.

In 1904 an Englishwoman, Miss A. E. F. Horniman (*q.v.*), paid for the conversion of an old theatre and adjoining buildings into the Abbey theatre. Its early years were tempestuous. Synge's *The Playboy of the Western World* (1907) was greeted with almost riotous disorder. Tension and quarrels with the directors caused the resignation of the Fays later the same year—the chief but not the only schism of the early period. Two years later Miss Horniman withdrew her subsidy, by which time the company was strong enough to carry on. Lennox Robinson joined the management in 1910. He was active as dramatist, manager and director for more than 40 years and next to Lady Gregory (*q.v.*) did most to keep the Abbey going from 1916 to 1924, when the government subsidy was first given. Sean O'Casey brought a change in luck, and his plays, produced between 1923 and 1926, gave a splendid opportunity to a new generation of actors. George Shiels wrote plays from 1921 until his death in 1949, and Brinsley MacNamara, Paul Vincent Carroll and Denis Johnston made important contributions in the 1930s.

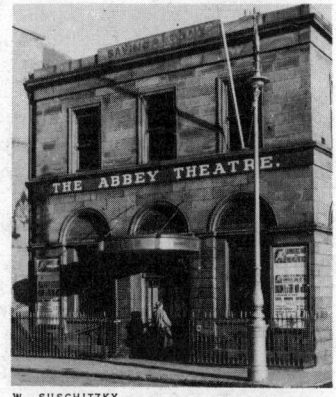

W. SUSCHITZKY

THE ABBEY THEATRE, DUBLIN, IRE., DESTROYED BY FIRE JULY 18, 1951

The Abbey's contribution to the world theatre is divided between a school of playwrights and a style of acting which abolished the "stage Irishman." Its plays are presented mainly in English but a few are in Irish. After a fire in 1951 the company moved to the Queen's theatre nearby. Plans were published (1958) for a larger theatre on the original site.

BIBLIOGRAPHY.—W. G. Fay and Catherine Carswell, *The Fays of the Abbey Theatre* (1935); U. Ellis-Fermor, *The Irish Dramatic Movement* (1939); Lennox Robinson, *Ireland's Abbey Theatre: a History (1899–1951)* (1951); Gerard Fay, *The Abbey Theatre: Cradle of Genius* (1958). (G. F. A. F.)

ABBON, SAINT, OF FLEURY (ABBO) (*c.* 940–1004), French Benedictine monk and scholar, who led a vigorous movement for monastic reform, was born near Orléans. In 985 he was invited to England to establish the monastery school at Ramsey. After his return to France, Abbon was elected abbot of Fleury on the Loire (988). He played a leading role at the synod of St. Basle where Archbishop Arnolf was tried for treason and deposed. At the monastery of La Réole in Gascony, he tried to re-establish strict Benedictinism by bringing in a group of his own reform monks. The original group at the monastery revolted against the reformers, and Abbon was killed during the ensuing fracas. His feast day is Nov. 13.

Abbon's life, written by his friend and disciple, Aimoin of Fleury (and reprinted in J. P. Migne, *Patrologia Latina;* vol. cxxxix, pp. 375–414), is an important source for the reign of Robert II of France.

See Dom Patrice Cousin, *Abbon de Fleury-sur-Loire* (1954). (E. G. RN.)

ABBOT, EZRA (1819–1884), U.S. biblical scholar, whose studies were chiefly in oriental languages and the textual criticism of the New Testament, though he was a remarkable bibliographer, was born at Jackson, Me., April 28, 1819. He graduated at Bowdoin college in 1840, and, after being principal of a public school in Cambridge, became assistant librarian of Harvard university. From 1872 until his death, on March 21, 1884, he was Bussey professor of New Testament criticism and interpretation in the Harvard divinity school.

Abbot's publications were largely dispersed in the pages of reviews and other publications, but to the enlarged American edition of Smith's *Dictionary of the Bible* (1867–70) he contributed more than 400 articles, besides greatly improving the bibliographical completeness of the work. His principal single production, representing his scholarly method and conservative conclusions, was *The Authorship of the Fourth Gospel* (1880; second edition, by J. H. Thayer, with other essays, 1889), up to that time probably the ablest defense, based on external evidence, of the Johannine authorship, and certainly the most complete treatment of the relation of Justin Martyr to this gospel. Abbot also was one of the original members of the American New Testament Revision company in charge of the Revised Version of the Bible.

See S. J. Barrows, *Ezra Abbot* (1884).

ABBOT, GEORGE (1562–1633), archbishop of Canterbury and the recognized leader of the Calvinists during the early years of the 17th century, was born on Oct. 19, 1562, at Guildford, Surrey, the son of a clothworker. Educated at Balliol college, Oxford, he became master of University college (1597) and dean of Winchester (1600). He was vice-chancellor of the university of Oxford at different times between 1600 and 1605, when his theological views brought him into conflict with Laud. He wrote *A Briefe Description of the Whole Worlde* (1599), *An Exposition upon the Prophet Jonah* (1600), and helped to prepare the Authorized Version of the New Testament (1611). James I sent him to Scotland in 1608 to arrange for the establishment of episcopacy there. In 1609 he became bishop of Lichfield and Coventry, in 1610 of London and in 1611 archbishop of Canterbury. He promoted the marriage between the elector palatine and Princess Elizabeth and resisted the proposal for the marriage of the prince of Wales to the Spanish infanta. In 1621 he accidentally shot a keeper while hunting. The question whether the homicide, though accidental, disqualified him from office was referred to a commission, on which King James exercised the casting vote in his favour. Under Charles I he was suspended from his functions as primate for refusing to license the assize sermon of Robert Sibthorp at Northampton (Feb. 22, 1627) advocating nonresistance to the royal demands, however arbitrary. He died at Croydon, Aug. 4, 1633. (G. HU.)

ABBOT, WILLIAM (1789–1843), English actor, of whom William Hazlitt said, "he never acts ill," was born in Chelsea, London, and made his first appearance on the stage at Bath in 1806, and his first London appearance in 1808. He created the parts of Appius Claudius in Sheridan Knowles's *Virginius* (1820) and of Modus in his *Hunchback* (1832). In 1827 he organized the company, including William Charles Macready and Harriet Constance Smithson, which played Shakespeare in Paris. Abbot's two melodramas, *The Youthful Days of Frederick the Great* (1817) and *Swedish Patriotism* (1819), were produced at Covent Garden. He died in poverty in Baltimore, Md., on June 6, 1843.

(W. J. M.-P.)

ABBOT is the official title of the superior of a monastic community that follows the Rule of St. Benedict (Benedictines [*q.v.*], Cistercians, Camaldolese, Trappists) and of certain orders of canons regular (Premonstratensians, Canons Regular of the

Lateran). The word derives from the Aramaic *ab, aba* ("father," "my father"), which in the Septuagint and New Testament Greek was written *abbas*. In early Egyptian monastic history, monks renowned for age and sanctity were called *abbas* by their disciples. The word signified the spiritual fatherhood which, according to the Scriptures of both Testaments, he exercises who teaches divine wisdom (*e.g.,* I Cor. iv, 15). This father-son relationship between Christian teacher and disciple was also recognized in nonmonastic circles—*e.g.,* by Irenaeus, Clement of Alexandria, Origen, etc.—and led to the term "Father" being applied subsequently to important early Christian writers. Originally, therefore, the title did not have the connotation of authoritative ruling. When monasticism in the east became more organized, under Pachomius and Basil, and more stress was correspondingly laid on the power of jurisdiction, the superiors of such monasteries were called not *abbas* but *proestos; i.e.,* "he who rules." Its Latin equivalent, *praepositus,* was adopted in western monasticism by Cassian.

It was Benedict, in his "Rule for Monks," who restored the word *abbas,* the abbot being regarded as the representative of Christ in the monastery, who teaches and instructs in Christ's name. To this earliest concept of spiritual fatherhood through teaching, connoted by the word abbot, Benedict added the concept of *patria potestas,* the authority wielded by a father according to Roman law. The abbot has the fullness of authority to rule the monastery in temporal as well as spiritual matters; and the monks, his sons, owe him the typically Roman virtues of reverence, obedience and filial piety. The abbot's rule may therefore rightly be called monarchic. Yet it is also clearly constitutional, for the abbot himself is bound by the Rule, details of which, however, he may adapt according to changing needs. In the course of the centuries the Rule was supplemented by decrees of popes and councils, and more recently by the Code of Canon Law. Yet the supremacy of the abbot and his government of the monastery has never been seriously weakened.

Abbots at first were laymen, but beginning about the 5th century in the east, and, under the influence of that example, in the 7th century in the west, only an ordained priest was normally elected abbot. This became mandatory through a council of Rome in 826.

The Rule of St. Benedict stipulates that the abbot be elected by the monks of the monastery. As the monasteries became more and more influential, however, bishops and secular rulers often interfered and claimed the right to name abbots, or appointed abbots *in commendam; i.e.,* persons who were granted the temporal revenues of the monastery. This latter abuse continued in some countries into the 18th century. It was so entrenched that every ecclesiastic of any standing possessed an abbey or two *in commendam,* and was therefore a commendatory "abbot." Hence it became customary to presume this honour in all ecclesiastics, and, in France, to address every priest as *Monsieur l'Abbé.*

As a protection against such encroachment, abbeys secured from Rome exemption from the jurisdiction of the local bishops, and also united in so-called "congregations." Such congregations become the norm in the 14th century, but the autonomy of the individual abbey, and correspondingly the authority of the abbot, were nonetheless jealously guarded, especially among the "black monks," the Benedictines. In 1893 Pope Leo XIII united all the Benedictine congregations into a federation presided over by an abbot primate who resides in Rome and has certain supervisional rights over the discipline of the abbeys. By the *Lex Propria* of 1947, the abbot primate's privileges and obligations were more closely defined. The Reformed Cistercians, or Trappists, were similarly federated under an abbot general in 1892.

According to law, an abbot is elected by the chapter of the monastery in secret ballot. He must be at least 30 years old, of legitimate birth, professed at least ten years and an ordained priest. An abbot is elected for life except in the English congregation, where by special dispensation he is elected for a term of 8–12 years. The election must be confirmed by the Holy See or by some other designated authority. The bishop of the diocese in which the monastery is situated confers the abbatial blessing, assisted by two abbots. This solemn rite, found in the Roman

Pontifical and dating back in part to the 8th century, strikingly resembles the consecration (*q.v.*) of a bishop, including a laying on of hands. Though not a sacrament, it is regarded as one of the most important sacramentals of the Roman Catholic Church because of the privileges and powers it confers. Chief among these are the power to administer tonsure and the four minor orders on his own subjects, and the right to celebrate Mass according to pontifical rite, to give many of the blessings normally reserved to a bishop, and to use the pontifical insignia of mitre, crosier, pectoral cross and ring.

Some abbots have ordinary jurisdiction over a given territory and govern it as a bishop does his diocese. They may administer confirmation, but, unless in episcopal orders, may not confer the major orders. Such an abbot is called *abbas nullius (dioecesis); i.e.,* abbot belonging to no diocese. Archabbot is a title borne by abbots of certain distinguished monasteries.

In eastern monasticism, the superior of a community of cenobite monks is called archimandrite (*q.v.*) or hegumen. Idiorrhythmic (*i.e.,* "self-governing") monasteries, which made their appearance in the 14th century, are ruled by several elder monks whose leader is given the name of abbot. The election of a monastic superior is confirmed by the diocesan bishop, who also officiates at the blessing. Abbatial insignia include the *mandyas* (similar to the western *cappa magna*) and the *pateritsa,* the pastoral staff.

Abbess is the title given to the superior of certain communities of nuns following the Benedictine Rule, of convents of the Second Franciscan order (Poor Clares) and of certain communities of canonesses The name is met with for the first time on a Roman inscription of 514. To be elected, an abbess must be at least 40 years old and a professed nun at least ten years. She is solemnly blessed by the diocesan bishop in a rite resembling that of the blessing of abbots. Her blessing gives her the right to specified pontifical insignia: the ring and, sometimes, the crosier. In medieval times, abbesses occasionally ruled double monasteries, of monks and nuns, and enjoyed various privileges and honours.

BIBLIOGRAPHY.—P. de Langogne, "Abbés," "Abbesses," in *Dictionnaire de Théologie Catholique,* vol. i, col. 10–20 (1903) ; F. A. Gasquet, *English Monastic Life* (1904) ; J. Chapman, "Abbot," in *Encyclopaedia of Religion and Ethics,* vol. i, pp. 8 ff. (1910) ; J. Baucher, "Abbés," "Abbesses," in *Dictionnaire de Droit Canonique,* vol. i, col. 29–71 (1935) ; *The Rule of St. Benedict,* trans. with notes by Justin McCann, 2nd rev. ed. (1952) ; D. Knowles, *The Monastic Order in England* (1940) ; P. de Meester, *De Monachico Statu iuxta disciplinam Byzantinam,* pp. 202–348 (1942) ; P. Delatte, *The Rule of St. Benedict: a Commentary* (1950) ; H. Emonds, "Abt," in *Reallexikon für Antike und Christentum,* vol. i, col. 45–55 (1950) ; P. Salmon, *Étude sur les insignes du pontife dans le rit romain,* pp. 49–90 (1955).   (G. L. D.)

ABBOTSFORD, the country seat of Sir Walter Scott (*q.v.*) from 1812 till his death in 1832, lies 3 mi. W. of Melrose, Roxburghshire, Scot. Scott bought, in 1811, from the Rev. Robert Douglas of Galashiels, a farm of 110 ac. on the right bank of the river Tweed opposite Galashiels. He renamed the land Abbotsford. By successive purchases he enlarged it to 1,200 ac., much of which he planted with trees. To the original farmhouse he built (1817–19) a Gothic addition which he extended (1822–25) over the site of the old house, which was pulled down. Although he consulted Edward Blore, Daniel Terry and others, he himself superintended the planning and building of the house, employing as architect William Atkinson. In 1823 Scott installed a gas plant to light the house with oil gas. James Hope-Scott added a south wing in 1855. The house, still owned and occupied by Scott's direct descendants, is furnished substantially as it was in Scott's day and contains a valuable collection of books and historic relics. It is open to the public from March to October.   (J. C. Co.)

ABBOTT, GRACE (1878–1939), U.S. social worker and reformer, influenced public opinion in favour of the child-labour amendment and related social legislation. She was born in Grand Island, Neb., Nov. 17, 1878, and educated at Grand Island college and The University of Chicago. In 1908 she went to Hull House, Chicago, as director of the newly formed Immigrants' Protective league. She exposed the exploitation of immigrants in a series of weekly articles ("Within the City's Gates") in the Chicago *Evening Post* (1909–10), in articles in the *Journal of Criminal Law and Criminology* (1911 and 1915) and in her book

The Immigrant and the Community (1917). As director of the child-labour division, U.S. Children's bureau (1917–19), she administered the first federal child-labour law. As chief of the bureau (1921–34) she administered the Maternity and Infancy act (1922–29). She was U.S. delegate to the International Labour organization in 1935 and 1937. While serving as professor of public welfare at The University of Chicago (1934–39) she edited the *Social Service Review* and published *The Child and the State*, 2 vol. (1938). Some of her papers were published posthumously under the title *From Relief to Social Security* (1940). She died in Chicago on June 19, 1939.

Her sister, Edith Abbott (1876–1957), was dean of The University of Chicago school of social service administration from 1924 to 1942. She died in Grand Island, July 28, 1957. (A. W. M.)

ABBOTT, JACOB (1803–1879), U.S. teacher and writer, was best known for his many books for young readers, including the "Rollo" series. Born at Hallowell, Me., on Nov. 14, 1803, he and his four brothers all attended Hallowell academy and Bowdoin college (Brunswick, Me.), studied at Andover Theological seminary (Andover, Mass.), and became teachers and ministers. After teaching at Amherst college (Amherst, Mass.), Abbott, in 1829, moved to Boston where he founded and was the first principal of the Mount Vernon school, a secondary school for girls. *The Teacher* (1833), which pioneered in advocating an appeal to students' honour and conscience in place of traditional disciplinary methods, was widely used as a textbook in early teacher-training institutions. In 1833 Abbott left Boston for suburban Roxbury, where his third son, Lyman Abbott (*q.v.*), was born. He devoted his time chiefly to writing. Later he established a home at Farmington, Me., where he died on Oct. 31, 1879.

He was sole author of 180 books, and co-author or editor of 31 others, notably the "Rollo" series (28 vol.). To accompany the earlier books (*Rollo at Work, Rollo at Play*), Abbott wrote a volume for teachers, *The Rollo Code of Morals, or the Rules of Duty for Children, Arranged With Questions for the Use of Schools* (1841). In following Rollo's travels about the world, with his all-knowing Uncle George, the young reader could improve himself with information on ethics, geography, science and history. Abbott also wrote 22 volumes of biographical histories and the *Franconia Stories* (10 vol.).

BIBLIOGRAPHY.—The memorial edition of *The Young Christian* (1882) contains a biographical sketch by his son Edward Abbott; Lyman Abbott, *Silhouettes of My Contemporaries* (1921); Carl J. Weber, *Bibliography of Jacob Abbott* (1948).

ABBOTT, LYMAN (1835–1922), U.S. Congregationalist minister, was editor for almost half a century of the *Outlook*, and influential as a leading exponent of the Social Gospel. He was born at Roxbury, Mass., on Dec. 18, 1835, the son of Jacob Abbott (*q.v.*). He graduated from New York university in 1853, studied law and was admitted to the bar in 1856, left the practice of law to study theology and was ordained a minister in 1860. After serving in two pastorates he became associate editor of *Harper's Magazine* and in 1870 editor of the *Illustrated Christian Weekly*. In 1876 he joined Henry Ward Beecher as associate editor of the *Christian Union*, an undenominational religious weekly founded by Beecher, and in 1881 became editor in chief. After Beecher's death, he succeeded in 1888 to his pulpit in the Plymouth Congregational church, Brooklyn, where he served until resigning in 1899.

Abbott early became interested in industrial problems. Under his editorship the *Outlook* (as the *Christian Union* was renamed in 1893) became the first leading religious journal to enter into a discussion of labour problems, both editorially and through the contributions of such economists as Ely and such ministers as Washington Gladden (*q.v.*). With Gladden and Walter Rauschenbusch (*q.v.*), Abbott was a leader in presenting the Social Gospel, which sought to interpret Christianity in terms of practical applications to industrial and social problems. His *Christianity and Social Problems* (1897), *The Rights of Man* (1901), *Industrial Problems* (1905), *The Spirit of Democracy* (1910) and *America in the Making* (1911) present his sociological views, which were middle-of-the-road, opposed both to socialism and to *laissez-faire* economics (*see* CHRISTIAN SOCIALISM).

On other problems Abbott led in presenting the viewpoint of liberal evangelical Protestantism. He sought to interpret rather than condemn the impact of the theory of evolution on religion. Abbott also popularized the point of view of "higher criticism." Among several popular devotional books, *The Other Room* (1903) and *The Great Companion* (1904) are notable. He published *Reminiscences* (1915; new ed. 1923). As editor he supported Theodore Roosevelt's presidential campaign of 1912, and early recognized as inevitable the entrance of the U.S. into World War I.

Abbott died in New York city, Oct. 22, 1922.

BIBLIOGRAPHY.—Character sketches and tributes in the *Outlook* (Nov. 8, 1922); Ira V. Brown, *Lyman Abbott, Christian Evolutionist: A Study in Religious Liberalism* (1953), containing extensive bibliography; C. H. Hopkins, *The Rise of the Social Gospel in American Protestantism 1865–1915* (1940).

ABBOTTABAD, headquarters of Hazara district and a military cantonment, lies 38 mi. N.N.E. of Rawalpindi. Pop. (1961) 31,036, including 15,081 in cantonment. Total area 7 sq.mi. Abbottabad lies 4,120 ft. above sea level on a saucer-shaped plateau at the southern corner of the Rash or Orash plain with the snow-covered Kagan and Bhogarmang to the north and the wooded hills of Thandiani and the Galis to the east. It contains a men's and a women's college affiliated with Peshawar university and two public parks. It is the chief market town for the surrounding countryside and lies on the main road running from the Indus plainlands of Campbellpur district northeastward to the Kagan valley and Srinagar (Kashmir). The railhead is Havelian (10 mi. S.), the end of a branch line from Taxila on the Lahore-Rawalpindi-Peshawar main line. At Kakul (5 mi. N.E.) is the Pakistan military academy. Abbottabad was founded in 1853 and named after Maj. James Abbott, the first British deputy commissioner of Hazara. (K. S. Ad.)

ABBREVIATION. Strictly a shortening, the word abbreviation commonly refers to a letter or group of letters taken from a word or words and employed to represent it or them for the sake of brevity. Abbreviations, both of single words and of phrases, having a meaning more or less fixed and recognized, were common in ancient writings and inscriptions (*see* PALEOGRAPHY). A common form of abbreviation is the substitution for a word of its initial letter, but one or more of the other letters are frequently added. Letters are often doubled to indicate a plural or a superlative. The list below gives a selection of common abbreviations with their meanings. Geographical names (for which *see* the list of abbreviations in the Index) are omitted; so are abbreviations for Christian names, weeks and months, points of the compass, and those which have passed into common usage as ordinary words, like Benelux, Cominform and gestapo. For symbols of the chemical elements, *see* ELEMENTS, CHEMICAL; for colloquial expressions (for example, O.K.) *see* AMERICAN ENGLISH and SLANG.

No universally accepted rule as to the use of periods in abbreviations has been followed. The method used in this article is to place periods after the initials of all organizations except U.S. government and United Nations agencies, and some, but not all, organizations whose letters form pronounceable words (called acronyms) such as WAVES. In cases where the abbreviation has multiple meanings, only the most common are given.

COMMON ABBREVIATIONS

	A				
a.	alto; adjective; answer; *ante*; at	A.A.	Automobile association (Brit.); Alcoholics Anonymous; associate in arts; anti-aircraft	A.A.A.L.	American Academy of Arts and Letters
A.	absolute (temperature)	A.A.A.	American Automobile association; Amateur Athletic association (Brit.)	A.A.A.S.	American Association for the Advancement of Science
Å	angstrom, angstrom unit, the international wave-length unit			A.A.U.	Amateur Athletic union
				A.A.U.P.	American Association of University Professors

A.A.U.W. American Association of University Women

A.B. able-bodied seaman; bachelor of arts

A.B.A. American Bar association

abbr., abbrev. abbreviated; abbreviation

ABC American Broadcasting company

ab init. (*ab initio*) from the beginning

abl. ablative

Abp. archbishop

A.B.S. American Bible society

ac. acre(s)

a/c account; aircraft

A.C. (*ante Christum*) before Christ; alternating current

acc. accusative

accel. (accelerando) with increasing speed

A.C.E. American Council on Education

ac.ft. acre foot (feet)

A.C.L.S. American Council of Learned Societies

A.C.L.U. American Civil Liberties union

A.C.S. American College of Surgeons; American Chemical society; American Cancer society

ACTH adrenocorticotropic hormone

A.D. (anno Domini) in the year of our Lord

A.D.A. Americans for Democratic Action; American Dental association

adag. (adagio) slow

ADC air defense command

A.D.C. aide-de-camp; Aid to Dependent Children

A.D. and C. advise duration and charge (telephone, Brit.)

ad fin. (*ad finem*) at or to the end

ad inf. (ad infinitum) to infinity

ad init. (*ad initium*) at the beginning

ad int. (ad interim) in the meantime

adj. adjective

Adj., Adjt. Adjutant

ad lib. (ad libitum) at one's pleasure

ad loc. (*ad locum*) at the place

Adm. admiral(ty)

adv. adverb

ad val. (ad valorem) according to value

A.E. and P. ambassador extraordinary and plenipotentiary

AEC Atomic Energy commission (U.S.)

A.E.F. American or Allied expeditionary force or forces

aet., *aetat.* (aetatis) aged

A.F.A.M. Ancient Free and Accepted Masons

A.F.C. air force cross (Brit.)

A.F.L.-C.I.O. American Federation of Labor-Congress of Industrial Organizations

A.F.M. air force medal (Brit.)

A.F.S. Auxiliary Fire service

a.h. ampere-hour(s)

A.H. (*anno Hegirae*) in the year of the hegira (Moslem era); (*anno Hebraico*) in the Hebrew year

A.I.A. American Institute of Architects

A.I.C. American Institute of Chemists; associate of the Institute of Chemistry (Brit.)

A.I.C.E. American Institute of Chemical Engineers; associate of the Institution of Civil Engineers (Brit.)

A.I.D. artificial insemination donor; American Institute of Decorators

A.I.E.E. American Institute of Electrical Engineers; associate of the Institution of Electrical Engineers (Brit.)

A.I.M. & M.E. American Institute of Mining and Metallurgical Engineers

A.I.M.E. associate of the Institution of Mechanical Engineers (Brit.); associate of the Institution of Mining Engineers (Brit.)

A.L. American Legion

A.L.A. American Library association

Ald. alderman

A.L.I. American Library institute

alt. altitude; alternate; alto

Am. American

AM amplitude modulation

A.M., a.m. (ante meridiem) before noon; (*anno mundi*) in the year of the world; master of arts

A. & M. ancient and modern (hymns)

A.M.A. American Medical association

A.M.D.G. (*Ad majorem Dei gloriam*) to the greater glory of God

A.M.E. African Methodist Episcopal

Amer. American

amp. ampere(s)

amp.hr. ampere-hour(s)

AMVETS American Veterans of World War II and Korea

A.N.A. associate of the National Academy of Design

and. (andante) moderately slow

Angl. Anglican

anon. anonymous

ANPA American Newspaper Publishers association

ant. antonym

ant., antiq. antiquities; antiquarian

ANTA American National theatre and academy

A.O.H. Ancient Order of Hibernians

A.O.L. absent over leave

a.p. aboveproof (spirits)

A.P. Associated Press; American Pharmacopeia

A.P.I. American Petroleum institute

A.P.O. army post office

A.P.S. American Philatelic society; American Philosophical society; American Physical society

A.R.A. associate of the Royal Academy (Brit.); American Railway association

A.R.A.M. associate of the Royal Academy of Music (Brit.)

A.R.C. American (National) Red Cross

Archd. archdeacon; archduke

A.R.P. air raid precautions (Brit.)

art. article

ARTC air route traffic control

A.R.V. American (Standard) Revised version (Bible)

A.S.A. American Statistical association; Acoustical Society of America

ASCAP American Society of Composers, Authors and Publishers

A.S.C.E. American Society of Civil Engineers

A.S.M.E. American Society of Mechanical Engineers

ASW antisubmarine warfare

ATC air traffic control

atm. atmosphere(s); atmospheric

Atty. Gen. attorney general

at. wt. atomic weight

A.U.C. (*anno urbis conditae* or *ab urbe condita*) from the founding of the city (Rome)

av. average; avenue

A.V. Authorized version (Bible)

A.V.C. American Veterans committee

avdp. avoirdupois

ave. avenue

avoir. avoirdupois

A.W.O.L. absent without leave

AWVS American women's voluntary services

B

b. born

B.A. bachelor of arts

B.A.A.S. British Association for the Advancement of Science

B.A.C. British Association of Chemists

Bank International Bank for Reconstruction and Development

Bapt. Baptist

BAR Browning automatic rifle

B.Ar., B.Arch. bachelor of architecture

bart. baronet

B.B.A. bachelor of business administration

B.B.B. Better Business bureau(s)

BBC British Broadcasting corporation

bbl. barrel(s)

B.C. before Christ

B.C.E. bachelor of civil engineering; bachelor of chemical engineering

BCG bacillus-Calmette Guérin

B.Ch., B.Chir. bachelor of surgery

B.C.L. bachelor of civil law

B.C.P. Book of Common Prayer

b.d. brought down (accounting)

B.D. bachelor of divinity

B.D.A. British Dental association

bd.ft. board foot (feet)

b.d.s. (*bis in die sumendus*) to be taken twice a day

Bé. Baumé (degrees)

B.E. bachelor of education; Buddhist era

B.E.A. British Engineers association; British European Airways

B.E.E. bachelor of electrical engineering

B.E.F. British expeditionary force

B.E.M. British empire medal

B. Eng. bachelor of engineering

BES bureau of employment security

Bev billion electron volts

bf, b.f. boldface (typography); brought forward

b.h.p. brake horsepower

Bib., bibl. Bible, biblical

bibliog. bibliography; bibliographer

B.I.S. Bank for International Settlements

Bl. (the) Blessed (title)

B.L. British Legion

B.Lit(t). bachelor of literature (or of letters)

B.LL. bachelor of laws

BLS bureau of labour statistics

blvd. boulevard

b.m. board measure; bench mark

B.M. bachelor of medicine; beachmaster; British Museum

B.M.A. British Medical association

B.M.E. bachelor of mechanical engineering; bachelor of mining engineering

B.M.I. Broadcast Music, Inc.

B. Mus. bachelor of music

B.O.A.C. British Overseas Airways corporation

B.O.Q. bachelor officers' quarters

bor. borough

B.O.T. board of trade

boul. boulevard

b.p. boiling point; below proof (spirits)

Bp. bishop

B.P. British Pharmacopoeia

B.Phil. bachelor of philosophy

B.P.O.E. Benevolent and Protective Order of Elks

B.R.C.S. British Red Cross society

Brig. brigadier; brigade

Brig. Gen. brigadier general

Brit. British; Britannica

bros. brothers

B.S., B.Sc. bachelor of science or sciences

B.S.A. Boy Scouts of America

B.S.T.	British summer time
bt.	baronet
B.T.	board of trade
B.Th.	bachelor of theology
B.Th.U.	British thermal unit(s)
B.T.U.	board of trade unit(s) (Brit.); British thermal unit(s)
bu.	bushel(s)
B.V.M.	the Blessed Virgin Mary
bx.	box(es)

C

c.	(circa) about
c., ¢	cents
c.	(caput) chapter
C.	centigrade; celsius
C.A.	chartered accountant; Catholic Action
CAB	Civil Aeronautics board
cal.	calorie(s); calibre
Cantab.	(Cantabrigiensis) of Cambridge (university)
cap.	(caput) chapter
cap., caps.	capital(s)
CAP	civil air patrol
Capt.	captain
car.	carat(s)
Card.	cardinal
CARE	Cooperative for American Remittances to Everywhere
Cath.	Catholic
C.B.	companion of the order of the Bath (Brit.)
CBC	Canadian Broadcasting corporation
C.B.E.	commander order of the British empire
C.B.I.	Cumulative Book Index
CBR	chemical, biological, radiological (warfare)
CBS	Columbia Broadcasting system
c.c.	cubic centimetre(s)
CCC	Commodity Credit corporation
C.D.	Corps diplomatique
Cdr.	commander
C.E.	civil engineer; Christian Endeavor; chemical engineer
C.E.F.	Canadian expeditionary force
cent.	(centum) a hundred; centigrade
cet. par.	(ceteris paribus) other things being equal
c. ft.	cubic foot (feet)
cf.	(confer) compare
cg.	centigram(s)
c.g.	centre of gravity; consul general
C.G.	coast guard; commanding general
C.G.I.A.	City and Guilds of London Institute insignia award
C.G.M.	conspicuous gallantry medal (Brit.)
C.G.S., c.g.s.	centimetre-gram-second(s)
C.G.T.	(Confédération Générale du Travail) General Confederation of Labour (Fr.)
ch.	chapter
c.h.	central heating
C.H.	companion of honour (Brit.)
chap.	chapter
Chem.E.	chemical engineer
CIA	central intelligence agency
CIC	combat information centre
C.I.D.	criminal investigation department (Brit.)
C.I.E.	companion of the order of the Indian empire (Brit.)
cie.	(compagnie) company (Fr.)
C.I.F.	cost, insurance, freight
C.I.G.S.	chief of the imperial general staff (Brit.)
CINC, C. in C.	commander in chief
cl.	centilitre(s)
cm.	centimetre(s)
C.M.G.	companion of the order of St. Michael and St. George (Brit.)
C.M.H.	(congressional) medal of honor

co.	company; county
c.o., c/o	care of; carried over
C.O.	commanding officer; conscientious objector
C.O.D.	collect or cash on delivery
co-ed.	co-educational
C. of E.	Church of England
col.	column
Col.	colonel
Comdr.	commander
Comdt.	commandant
Comm.	commander
comp.	compiled; compiler
con.	consolidated; consul; concerto; (contra) against
Conelrad	control of electromagnetic radiation
Cong.	congregation; Congregational; congress
cont.	contents; continue(d); continent; (contra) against
conv.	convent; convention; conversation; converter
co-op.	co-operative
corp.	corporation; corporal
cos	cosine
cot	cotangent
c.p.	candle power; chemically pure; common pleas; court of probate; centre of pressure
C.P.	Communist party
C.P.A.	certified public accountant; chartered public accountant
Cpl.	corporal
C.P.O.	chief petty officer
c.p.s., cps	cycles per second
C.R.	(Custos Rotulorum) keeper of the rolls
cres., cresc.	(crescendo) with gradually increasing volume
C.S.A.	Confederate States of America
csc	cosecant
CSC	Civil Service commission
C.S.I.	companion of the order of the Star of India; Church of South India
C.S.O.	chief signal officer; chief staff officer
C.S.P.	Congregation of Saint Paul
C.S.T.	central standard time
ct.	cents; count
ctn	cotangent
cu.	cubic; cumulus
cu.cm.	cubic centimetre(s)
cu.ft.	cubic foot (feet)
cu.in.	cubic inch(es)
C.V.O.	commander of the Royal Victorian order
CW	continuous wave (radio)
C.W.S.	Co-operative Wholesale society (Brit.)
cwt.	hundredweight(s)
C.Y.O.	Catholic Youth organization

D

d.	deceased; died; daughter
d.	(denarius) penny
da.	daughter
D.A.	district attorney
D.A.B.	Dictionary of American Biography
D.A.E.	Dictionary of American English
D.A.R.	Daughters of the American Revolution
dat.	dative
D.A.V.	Disabled American Veterans
db	decibel
D.B.E.	dame commander of the order of the British empire
D.C.	(da capo) from the beginning; direct current
dcg.	decagram(s)
dcl.	decalitre(s)
D.C.L.	doctor of civil law
dcm.	decametre(s)
D.C.M.	distinguished conduct medal (Brit.)

D.C.V.O.	dame commander of the Royal Victorian order
D.D.	doctor of divinity
D.D.M.	doctor of dental medicine
D.D.S.	doctor of dental surgery
DDT	dichloro-diphenyl-trichloroethane
dec.	deceased
decim.	decimetre(s)
decresc.	(decrescendo) with gradually decreasing volume
del.	(delineavit) he (or she) drew (it)
dele.	(deleatur) delete
Dem.	Democrat; Democratic
D.Eng.	doctor of engineering
dept.	department
DEW	Distant Early Warning radar line
DF, D/F	direction finding or finder
D.F.C.	distinguished flying cross (Brit.)
dg.	decigram(s)
D.G.	(Dei gratia) by the grace of God
diam.	diameter
dim.	(diminuendo) with gradually diminishing volume
D.J.S.	doctor of juridical science
dl.	decilitre(s)
D.Lit(t).	doctor of literature (or of letters)
dm.	decimetre(s)
D.M.D.	doctor of dental medicine
DME	distance measuring equipment
D.M.S.	doctor of medical sciences
D.Mus.	doctor of music
D.N.B.	Dictionary of National Biography (Brit.)
do.	(ditto) the same
doz.	dozen
DP	displaced person
D.Phil.	doctor of philosophy
dr.	drachma(s) or dram(s); debtor
d.r.	dead reckoning
Dr.	doctor
D.Sc.	doctor of science
D.S.C.	distinguished service cross
D.S.M.	distinguished service medal
D.S.O.	companion of the distinguished service order
D.S.T.	daylight saving time; doctor of sacred theology
d.t.	delirium tremens
D.T.	doctor of theology
duo.	duodecimo
D.V.	(Deo volente) God willing; Douay version (Bible)
D.V.M.	doctor of veterinary medicine
D.V.S.	doctor of veterinary surgery
dwt.	pennyweight(s)

E

e.	eldest
ea.	each
ed.	editor; edited; edition; educated
eds.	editors
e.e.	errors excepted
E.E.	Early English; electrical engineer
E.E. & M.P.	envoy extraordinary and minister plenipotentiary
e.g.	(exempli gratia) for example
e.h.p.	effective horsepower
E.M.	earl marshal; enlisted man
emf	electromotive force
E.M.U.	electromagnetic unit
ency., encyc.	encyclopaedia
Eng.	English
Ens.	ensign (flag); ensign (title)
Epis., Episc.	Episcopal
ESC	Economic and Social council
esp., espec.	especially
ESP	extrasensory perception

Esq. esquire
est. established; estimated; estuary
E.S.T. eastern standard time
E.S.U. electrostatic unit(s)
e.t.a. estimated time of arrival
et al. (*et alii* or *aliae*) and others; (*et alibi*) and elsewhere
etc. (et cetera) and so forth
et seq. (*et sequens, sequentes* or *sequentia*) and the following
etym. etymological; etymology
Euratom European Atomic Energy community
ev electron volt(s)
ex lib. (*ex libris*) from the books of
ext. extension; external(ly); extinct; extant

F

f. farad(s); father; folio; following; feminine
f. (*forte*) loud, powerful
F. Fahrenheit
FAA Federal Aviation agency
FAO Food and Agriculture organization
F.B.A. fellow of the British academy
FBI Federal Bureau of Investigation
FCA Farm Credit administration
FCC Federal Communications commission
FCIC Federal Crop Insurance corporation
F.C.S. fellow of the Chemical society (Brit.)
F.D. (*Fidei Defensor*) Defender of the Faith (Brit.); fire department
FDA Food and Drug administration
FDIC Federal Deposit Insurance corporation
fec. (*fecit*) he (or she) made (or did) (it)
fem. feminine
FEPC Committee on Fair Employment Practice
ff. following (pages); folios
ff. (fortissimo) very loud
F.F.P.S. fellow of the Royal Faculty of Physicians and Surgeons (Glasgow)
F.G.S. fellow of the Geological society (Brit.)
FHA Federal Housing administration
fig. figure(s)
fl. flourished
fl.oz. fluid ounce(s)
F.L.S. fellow of the Linnean society
fm. fathom(s)
FM frequency modulation
F.M. field marshal
F.O. foreign office (Brit.); flying officer
f.o.b. free on board
F.O.E. Fraternal Order of Eagles
fol. folio; following
f.p. foot-pound(s); freezing point
FPC Federal Power commission
F.Phys.S. fellow of the Physical society (Brit.)
f.p.s. foot-pound-second; feet per second
F.P.S. fellow of the Philological society (Brit.); fellow of the Philosophical society (Brit.)
fr. franc(s); from; father
Fr. Father (title); friar; French
F.R.A.I. fellow of the Royal Anthropological institute (of Great Britain and Ireland)
F.R.A.S. fellow of the Royal Astronomical society (Brit.)
F.R.C.M. fellow of the Royal College of Music
F.R.C.P. fellow of the Royal College of Physicians, London
F.R.C.P.E. fellow of the Royal College of Physicians of Edinburgh
F.R.C.S. fellow of the Royal College of

Surgeons, London
F.R.C.V.S. fellow of the Royal College of Veterinary Surgeons (Brit.)
F.R.G.S. fellow of the Royal Geographical society, London
F.R.Hist.S. fellow of the Royal Historical society, London
F.R.H.S. fellow of the Royal Horticultural society, London
F.R.I.B.A. fellow of the Royal Institute of British Architects
F.R.Met.S. fellow of the Royal Meteorological society
F.R.S. fellow of the Royal society (of London)
F.R.S.E. fellow of the Royal Society of Edinburgh
F.R.S.L. fellow of the Royal Society of Literature (of the United Kingdom)
F.S.A. fellow of the Society of Antiquaries (of London)
F.S.C. (*Fratrem Scholarum Christianorum*) Brothers of the Christian Schools (Christian Brothers)
F.S.S. fellow of the Royal Statistical society (of London)
ft. foot; feet
Ft. fort
FTC Federal Trade commission
Fund International Monetary fund
fur. furlong(s)
f.v. (*folio verso*) on the back of the page
fwd. forward
F.Z.S. fellow of the Zoological society, London

G

g. gram(s); acceleration of gravity; good; guinea(s)
gal. gallon(s)
G.A.O. general accounting office
G.A.R. Grand Army of the Republic
G.A.T.T. General Agreement on Tariffs and Trade
gaz. gazette; gazetteer
G.B.E. knight or dame grand cross of the order of the British empire
G.C. George cross
GCA ground-controlled approach
g.cal. gram calorie(s)
G.C.B. knight grand cross of the order of the Bath
G.C.E. General Certificate of Education (Brit.)
GCI ground-controlled interception
G.C.I.E. knight grand commander of the order of the Indian empire
G.C.M.G. knight grand cross of the order of St. Michael and St. George
G.C.S.I. knight grand commander of the order of the Star of India
G.C.T. Greenwich civil time
G.C.V.O. knight grand cross of the Royal Victorian order
g.d. granddaughter
gen. genitive; general; genus
Gen. general (title)
GG gamma globulin
G.H.Q. general headquarters
gi. gill(s)
G.M. general manager; George medal
gm. gram(s)
G.M.T. Greenwich mean time
G.O.E. General Ordination Examination
G.O.P. grand old party (Republican)
Gov. governor
g.p. general practitioner
g.p.m. gallons per minute
GPO government printing office
G.P.O. general post office
gr. grain(s); gross
g.s. grandson

GSA General Services administration
G.S.A. Girl Scouts of America

H

h. husband
H henry (elect.)
ha. hectare(s)
h. & c. hot and cold
h.c.f. highest common factor
H.E. his, or her, excellency; high explosive
Heb.,
  Hebr. Hebrew(s)
her. heraldic; heraldry
HF high frequency
H.G. his, or her, grace
hg. hectogram(s)
H.H. his, or her, highness; his holiness (the pope)
hhd. hogshead(s)
hi-fi high fidelity
H.I.H. his, or her, imperial highness
H.I.M. his, or her, imperial majesty
H.J.S. (*hic jacet sepultus*) here lies buried
hl. hectolitre(s)
hm. hectometre(s)
H.M. his, or her, majesty('s)
H.M.S. his, or her, majesty's ship, or service
H.M.S.O. his, or her, majesty's stationery office
Hon. honourable; honorary
h.p. horsepower; high pressure; hire purchase
H.Q., hq. headquarters
hr. hour(s)
H.R. house of representatives; house of representatives bill
H.R.H. his, or her, royal highness
H.S.H. his, or her, serene highness

I

I. island
ib., ibid. (*ibidem*) in the same place
I.C.A.A.A.A. Intercollegiate Association of Amateur Athletics in America
ICAO International Civil Aviation organization
ICBM intercontinental ballistic missile
ICC Interstate Commerce commission
I.C. 4-A Intercollegiate Association of Amateur Athletics in America
id. (*idem*) the same
i.e. (*id est*) that is
IFC International Finance corporation
IFR instrument flight rules
I.G. inspector general
IGY International Geophysical year
i.h.p. indicated horsepower
IHS a symbol representing IHΣ, the first three letters of the Greek name of Jesus; also *Iesus Hominum Salvator* (Jesus the Saviour of Men)
I.L.G.W.U. International Ladies' Garment Workers' union
ILO International Labour organization
ILS instrument landing system
IMCO Inter-Governmental Maritime Consultative organization
imp. imperative; imperfect (tense); imperial; (*imprimatur*) let it be printed
in. inch(es)
Inc. incorporated
incl. inclosure; inclusive; including
incog. (incognito) unknown
inf. (infra) below
infra dig (infra dignitatem) undignified
in loc. cit. (*in loco citato*) in the place cited
I.N.R.I. (*Iesus Nazarenus Rex Iudaeorum*) Jesus of Nazareth, King of the Jews

inst.	instant, the present month
int.	interest
int. al.	(*inter alia*) among other things
I.O.F.	Independent Order of Foresters
I.O.O.F.	Independent Order of Odd Fellows
I.O.U.	I owe you
I.P.A.	International Phonetic association or alphabet
i.q.	(*idem quod*) the same as
I.Q.	intelligence quotient
I.R.A.	Irish Republican army
IRBM	intermediate-range ballistic missile
IRO	International Refugee organization
IRS	internal revenue service
Is.	island(s)
I.S.O.	imperial service order
ital.	italics
I.T.A.	Independent Television authority (Brit.)
ITO	International Trade organization
ITU	International Telecommunication union
I.V.	initial velocity
I.W.W.	Industrial Workers of the World

J

J.A.	Junior Achievement (U.S.)
J.A.G.	judge advocate general
jato	jet-assisted take-off
J.C.D.	(*juris civilis doctor*) doctor of civil law
J.D.	(*jurum doctor*) doctor of laws
j.g.	junior grade (U.S. navy)
J.M.J.	Jesus, Mary and Joseph
jnr.	junior
jp	jet propulsion
J.P.	justice of the peace
Jr.	junior

K

k.	carat(s); knot(s)
K.	Kelvin
K.B.E.	knight commander of the order of the British empire
kc.	kilocycle(s)
K.C.	king's counsel; Knights of Columbus
K.C.B.	knight commander of the order of the Bath
K.C.I.E.	knight commander of the order of the Indian empire
K.C.M.G.	knight commander of the order of St. Michael and St. George
K.C.S.I.	knight commander of the order of the Star of India
K.C.V.O.	knight commander of the Royal Victorian order
kg.	kilogram(s)
K.G.	knight of the order of the Garter
kg.cal.	kilogram calorie(s); kilocalorie(s)
K.K.K.	Ku Klux Klan
kilo(s)	kilogram(s)
kl.	kilolitre(s)
K.L.M.	Koninklijke Luchtvaart Maatschappij voor Nederland en Kolonien N.V. (Royal Dutch Airlines)
km.	kilometre(s)
k.o.	knockout (pugilism)
K.P.	knights of Pythias; knight of the order of St. Patrick (Brit.); kitchen police (military)
kt.	carat(s); kiloton; knot(s)
Kt.	knight
K.T.	Knight(s) Templar; knight of the order of the Thistle (Scot.)
kv.	kilovolt(s)
kva.	kilovolt ampere(s)
kw.	kilowatt(s)
kw.hr.	kilowatt hour(s)

L

l.	litre(s); length; line(s)
L., £	(*libra*) pound(s) (money)
L.	(*liber*) book
lat.	latitude
lb.	(*libra*) pound(s) (weight)
l.b.w.	leg before wicket (cricket)
l.c.	lower case (typography); letter of credit; level crossing
L.C.	Library of Congress; lord chamberlain; lord chancellor
L.C.C.	London County council
l.c.d.	lowest common denominator
L.C.J.	lord chief justice
L.C.M.	least common multiple
LF	low frequency
L.H.D.	doctor of humanities
lib.	library; librarian
lib.	(*liber*) book
Lieut.	lieutenant
Linn.	Linnaeus; Linnaean
Lit(t).D.	doctor of literature (or of letters)
ll.	lines
L.L., L.Lat.	Law Latin
LL.B.	(*legum baccalaureus*) bachelor of laws
LL.D.	(*legum doctor*) doctor of laws
LL.M.	(*legum magister*) master of laws
loc.cit.	(*loco citato*) in the place cited
log	logarithm
long.	longitude
L.O.O.M.	Loyal Order of Moose
loq.	(*loquitur*) he (or she) speaks
LOX	liquid oxygen
LP	long playing (phonograph records); liquefied petroleum
L.R.A.M.	licentiate of the Royal Academy of Music (Brit.)
L.R.C.P.	licentiate of the Royal College of Physicians (Brit.)
L.R.C.P.E.	licentiate of the Royal College of Physicians, Edinburgh
L.R.C.S.	licentiate of the Royal College of Surgeons (Brit.)
l.s.	(*locus sigilli*) place of the seal
Lt.	lieutenant
l.t.	long ton(s)
Ltd.	limited
Luth.	Lutheran

M

m.	married; metre(s); minim; masculine
M.	(*meridies*) meridian, noon; mark(s); (*mille*) thousand(s); monsieur
M.A.	(*magister artium*) master of arts
Maj.	major
M. & B.	May and Baker 693 (drug)
Marq.	marquis
masc.	masculine
MATS	military air transport service
max.	maximum
M.B.	(*medicinae baccalaureus*) bachelor of medicine
M.B.A.	master of business administration
M.B.E.	member of the order of the British empire
MBS	Mutual Broadcasting system
mc.	megacycle(s)
MC	millicurie; medical corps
M.C.	master of ceremonies; member of congress; military cross (Brit.)
M.D.	(*medicinae doctor*) doctor of medicine
M.E.	Middle English; Methodist Episcopal; mechanical engineer; mining engineer
mem.	(*memento*) memorandum
m.e.p.	mean effective pressure
Messrs.	messieurs; sirs
Meth.	Methodist; methylated spirits
Mev	million electron volts
mf.	(*mezzo forte*) moderately loud

M.F.H.	master of foxhounds
mg.	milligram(s)
Mgr.	monsignor; monseigneur; manager
m.g.s.	metre-gram-second(s)
mh	millihenry
mi.	mile(s)
M.I.E.E.	member of the Institution of Electrical Engineers (Brit.)
M.I.Mech.E.	member of the Institution of Mechanical Engineers (Brit.)
M.I.Min.E.	member of the Institution of Mining Engineers (Brit.)
min.	minute(s)
misc.	miscellaneous; miscellany
M.Lit(t).	master of literature (or of letters)
ml.	millilitre(s)
Mlle.	mademoiselle
MM.	messieurs; sirs
mm.	millimetre(s)
mμ	millimicron(s)
Mme(s).	madame; mesdames
M.M.F.	magnetomotive force
mo.	month(s)
M.O.	medical officer; money order
mod.	(*moderato*) moderately fast; modern
mol.	molecule(s); molecular
mol.wt.	molecular weight
mp.	(*mezzo piano*) moderately soft
m.p.	melting point
M.P.	member of parliament; military police; Methodist Protestant
m.p.g.	miles per gallon
m.p.h.	miles per hour
Mr.	mister
M.R.C.P.	member of the Royal College of Physicians (London)
M.R.C.S.	member of the Royal College of Surgeons (Brit.)
M.R.C.V.S.	member of the Royal College of Veterinary Surgeons (Brit.)
M.R.P.	(*Mouvement Républicain Populaire*) Republican Popular movement (France)
Mrs.	mistress
ms.	manuscript
M.S., M.Sc.	master of science
Msgr.	monsignor
m.s.l.	mean sea level
mss	manuscripts
M.S.T.	mountain standard time
m.t.	metric ton
Mt., mt., mts.	mount, mountain; mountains
mth.	month
μ	micron(s); micro-
μv	microvolt(s)
μsec.	microsecond(s)
mun.	municipal
Mus.B., D., M.	(*musicae baccalaureus, doctor, magister*) bachelor, doctor, master of music
mv	millivolt(s)
MVD	(*Ministerstvo Vnutrennikh Del*) ministry of internal affairs, including secret police (U.S.S.R.)
M.V.O.	member of the Royal Victorian order
myth.	mythology; mythological

N

n.	noun; name; normal; neuter; note
N.A.	National Academician or Academy
N.A.A.C.P.	National Association for the Advancement of Colored People
N.A.D.	National Academy of Design
N.A.M.	National Association of Manufacturers
N.A.S.	National Academy of Sciences
NASA	National Aeronautics and Space administration
NATO	North Atlantic Treaty organization

n.b. (*nota bene*) note well
NBC National Broadcasting company
N.C.A.A. National Collegiate Athletic association
N.C.O. noncommissioned officer
N.C.W.C. National Catholic Welfare conference
N.C.Y.C. National Catholic Youth council
n.d. no date
n.e. new edition
N.E.A. Newspaper Enterprise association; National Education association
nem.con. (*nemine contradicente*) no one contradicting; unanimous
neut. neuter; neutral
New Test. New Testament
N.F.S. National Fire service (Brit.)
N.G. national guard; no good
NLRB National Labor Relations board
nn. notes
no. (*numero*) number(s)
nol. pros. (*nolle prosequi*) unwilling to prosecute
nom. nominative; nominated; nominal; nomenclature
non.seq. (*non sequitur*) it does not follow
Nor., Norm. Norman
NORAD North American Air Defense Command
N.P. notary public
n.p.t. normal (blood) pressure and temperature
nr. near
NRC National Research council
NS nuclear (powered) ship
N.S. new style (calendar); new series
N.S.P.C.C. National Society for the Prevention of Cruelty to Children
N.T. New Testament

O

o ohm
OASI old-age and survivors insurance (social security, U.S.)
ob. (*obiit*) he (or she) died
obdt. obedient
O.B.E. order of the British empire
OCD Office of Civilian Defense
OCDM Office of Civil and Defense Mobilization
O.C.S. officer candidate school
o.d. overdraft
O.D. officer of the day; olive drab; ordinary seaman
O.E. Old English
O.E.D. *Oxford English Dictionary*
O.E.E.C. Organization for European Economic Co-operation
O.E.S. Order of the Eastern Star (U.S.)
O.F. Old French
off. official; office; officer; offered
O.F.M. (*Ordo Fratrum Minorum*) Order of Friars Minor (Franciscans)
O.H.M.S. on his, or her, majesty's service
O.M. order of merit (Brit.)
O.O.D. officer of the deck
op. opus; opera; opposite
O.P. Order of Preachers (Dominicans); observation post
op.cit. (*opere citato*) in the work cited
ord. ordained; ordinance; ordnance
O.S. old style (calendar); outsize
O.S.A. Order of St. Augustine
O.S.B. Order of St. Benedict
O.S.F. Order of St. Francis
OSRD Office of Scientific Research and Development
O.T. Old Testament
Oxf. Oxford
Oxon. (*Oxonia, Oxoniensis*) Oxford; of Oxford (university)
oz. (*onza*) ounce(s)

P

P. parking

p. page
p. (*piano*) soft
par. parallel; parenthesis; parish; parochial; paragraph
para. paragraph
parl. parliament; parliamentary
P.A.S.I. professional associate of the Chartered Surveyors' institution (Brit.)
pat., patd. patent; patented
Pat. Off. patent office
P.A.U. Pan American union
P.C. privy council(or); police constable
pd. paid
P.D. police department
P.E. Protestant Episcopal
P.E.N. International Association of Poets, Playwrights, Editors, Essayists and Novelists
pert. pertaining
p.f. (*più forte*) a little louder
Pfc. private first class
P.G.A. Professional Golfers association
pH logarithm of the reciprocal of hydrogen-ion concentration
PHA Public Housing administration
phar. pharmacy; pharmaceutical
Ph.B. bachelor of philosophy
Ph.C. pharmaceutical chemist
Ph.D. doctor of philosophy
PHS public health service
pinx. (*pinxit*) he (or she) painted (it)
pizz. (*pizzicato*) plucked (music)
pl. plural; place; plate
P.M., p.m. past master; postmaster; (*post meridiem*) afternoon; provost marshal; prime minister; post mortem
p.o. post office; postal order; petty officer (naval)
POD post office department
P.O.E. port of embarkation
pop. population
POW prisoner of war
pp. pages
pp. (*pianissimo*) very soft
P.P., p.p. parcel post; parish priest; present participle; past participle; postpaid; *per pro.*
P.P.S. (*post postscriptum*) an additional postscript
P.R. proportional representation; public relations
prep. preposition; preparatory; preparation
Pres. president; present; presumptive
Presb. Presbyterian
P.R.O. public record office; public relations officer
proc. proceedings
Prof. professor
pron. pronoun; pronunciation
prop. proprietor; proposition; property
propr. proprietor
pro tem (*pro tempore*) for the time being
prov. provisional; provost; province
prox. (*proximo* [*mense*]) next month
P.S. (*postscriptum*) postscript
pseud. pseudonym
P.S.T. Pacific standard time
PT physical training
pt. part; pint(s); point; port
p.t. (*pro tempore*) for the time being
P.T.A. Parent-Teacher association
PTM phase time modulation
P.T.O. please turn over
pub., publ. publication; published; public
Pvt. private
PWA Public Works administration
pwt. pennyweight
PX post exchange
pxt. (*pinxit*) he (or she) painted (it)

Q

q. quintal; query; question

Q.C. queen's counsel
Q.E.D. (*quod erat demonstrandum*) which was to be demonstrated
Q.E.F. (*quod erat faciendum*) which was to be done
q.l. (*quantum libet*) as much as you please
Q.M. quartermaster
qq.v. (*quae vide*) which see (plural)
qr. quarter; quarterly; quire
q.s. (*quantum sufficit*) as much as is sufficient
qt. quart(s)
qu. query; question
quant. suff. (*quantum sufficit*) as much as is sufficient
q.v. (*quod vide*) which see; (*quantum vis*) as much as you will
qy. query

R

R. (*rex, regina*) king, queen; river
R., ℞ (*recipe*) take
R.A. Royal Academy (of Arts, London)
R.A.A.F. Royal Australian air force
rabb. rabbinical
R.A.C. Royal Automobile club
rad. (*radix*) root; radical
R.A.D.A. Royal Academy of Dramatic Art (Brit.)
RADM rear admiral (U.S. navy)
R.A.F. Royal Air Force
rall. (*rallentando*) gradually slower
R.A.M. Royal Academy of Music (Brit.)
R.A.N. Royal Australian navy
R. & I. (*rex et imperator*) king and emperor
R.B.A. Royal Society of British Artists
R.C. Roman Catholic; Red Cross
R.C.A.F. Royal Canadian air force
R.C.M.P. Royal Canadian mounted police
R.C.N. Royal Canadian navy
R.C.P. Royal College of Physicians or Preceptors
R.C.S. Royal College of Surgeons
rd. road
Réaum. Réaumur's thermometrical scale
REA Rural Electrification administration
Rear Adm. rear admiral
Reg. Prof. regius professor
rel. religion; relative
R.E.M.E. royal electrical and mechanical engineers
Rep. Republican; representative
ret. retired; returned
Rev. reverend
RFC Reconstruction Finance corporation
R.F.D. rural free delivery
Rh Rhesus factor
R.H.S. Royal Historical society
R.I.B.A. Royal Institute of British Architects
R.I.P. (*requiescat in pace*) may he (or she) rest in peace
rit. (*ritardando*) gradually slower
riv. river
rm. room(s)
R.M. royal marines; resident magistrate; royal mail
R.M.A. Royal Military academy (Sandhurst)
R.M.O. resident medical officer(s)
R.M.S. royal mail steamer (Brit.)
R.N. Royal Navy; registered nurse
R.N.V.R. royal naval volunteer reserve
R.N.Z.N. Royal New Zealand navy
Rom. Roman; romance
R.O.T.C. reserve officers' training corps
r.p.m. revolutions per minute
r.p.s. revolutions per second
rpt. repeat; report
R.R. railroad
R.S.M. regimental sergeant major, Royal Society of Medicine

R.S.P.C.A.	Royal Society for the Prevention of Cruelty to Animals
R.S.V.	Revised Standard version (Bible)
R.S.V.P.	(*répondez s'il vous plaît*) please reply
Rt. Hon.	right honourable
Rt. Rev.	right reverend
R.V.	Revised version (Bible)
Ry.	railway
R.Y.S.	royal yacht squadron

S

s.	son; second(s); series
s.	(*solidus*) shilling
S.	*san* (saint); senate bill
S.A.	Salvation Army
SAC	strategic air command
S.A.E.	Society of Automotive Engineers
Sans., Sansk.	Sanskrit
S.A.R.	Sons of the American Revolution
sb.	substantive
sc.	scruple; science
sc.	(*scilicet*) namely; (*sculpsit*) he (or she) carved or engraved (it)
s.c.	small capital letters
SC	Security council (of United Nations)
Sc.D.	(*scientiae doctor*) doctor of science
scr.	scruple
SCUBA	self-contained underwater breathing apparatus
sculp., sculpt.	(*sculpsit*) he (or she) carved or engraved (it)
sd.	said; signed
s.d.	(*sine die*) without (appointing) a day (on which to assemble again)
SEATO	Southeast Asia Treaty organization
sec	secant
sec.	section; second(s); secretary
SEC	Securities and Exchange commission
Sen.	senator; senate; senior
seq., seqq.	(*sequens, sequentia*) the following
sergt.	sergeant
sf.	(*sforzando*) with emphasis
Sgt.	sergeant
SHAPE	supreme headquarters Allied powers Europe
sin	sine
sing.	singular
S.J.	Society of Jesus (Jesuits)
SOP	standing operating procedure
sost.	(*sostenuto*) sustained
sp.	spelling; species; specific; spirit
s.p.	(*sine prole*) without offspring
S.P.	shore patrol
SPAR	women's reserve of the United States coast guard (contraction of coast guard motto, *semper paratus* [always prepared])
S.P.C.A.	Society for Prevention of Cruelty to Animals
S.P.C.C.	Society for Prevention of Cruelty to Children
S.P.C.K.	Society for Promoting Christian Knowledge (Brit.)
S.P.G.	Society for the Propagation of the Gospel (Brit.)
sp. gr.	specific gravity
sp. ht.	specific heat
S.P.Q.R.	(*senatus populusque Romanus*) senate and people of Rome
sq.	squadron; square
sq.	(*sequens, sequentia*) the following
sq.ft.	square foot (feet)
Sr.	senior; señor
Sra.	señora
S.R.N.	state registered nurse (Brit.)

S.R.O.	standing room only
Srta.	señorita
ss.	(*scilicet*) namely
SS.	saints
S.S.	steamship
S.S.R.C.	Social Science Research council
st.	stanza; stone (weight)
s.t.	short ton(s)
St.	saint; strait; statute(s); street
Sta.	(*santa*) saint; station
stacc.	(*staccato*) distinct; separated
stat.	statics; (*statim*) immediately; statistics
Ste.	(*sainte*) saint
S.T.P.	professor of sacred theology
sub.	subaltern; substitute(s); subeditor; submarine; subscription; subject; subjunctive
subj.	subject; subjunctive
sup.	(*supra*) above
supp., suppl.	supplement
s.v.	(*sub verbo, sub voce*) under the word (or heading)
syn.	synonym; synonymous

T

t.	ton(s); town; transitive
T.A.	territorial army (Brit.)
TAC	tactical air command
tan	tangent
TASS	(*Telegraphnoye Agenstvo Sovyetskovo Soyuza*) Soviet news agency
t.b.	tuberculosis, tubercle bacillus
TBS	talk between ships (radio)
tbs., tbsp.	tablespoon(s)
t.d.s.	(*ter in die sumendus*) to be taken three times a day
T.E.	topographical engineer
terr.	territory; terrace
t.i.d.	(*ter in die*) three times daily (pharm.)
t.k.o.	technical knockout (pugilism)
t.l.	trade last
TNT	trinitrotoluene (explosive)
tr.	translated; translator; transpose; transitive
trans.	transferred; translation
trem.	(*tremolo*) trembling; fluttering
tsp.	teaspoon
TT.	teetotaler; tourist trophy
T.U.C.	Trades Union congress (Brit.)
TV	television; test vehicle (guided missiles)
TVA	Tennessee Valley authority
twp.	township

U

UCMJ	Uniform Code of Military Justice (U.S.)
U.C.V.	United Confederate Veterans
U.D.C.	United Daughters of the Confederacy; urban district council (Brit.)
UES	electrostatic unit(s)
UFO	unidentified flying object
UHF	ultrahigh frequency
ult.	(*ultimo*) last (month)
UN	United Nations
UNAC	United Nations Appeal for Children
UNEF	United Nations Emergency force
UNESCO	United Nations Educational, Scientific and Cultural organization
UNICEF	United Nations Children's fund
univ.	university; universal
U.P.I.	United Press International
UPU	Universal Postal union
U.S.	unserviceable
u.s.	(*ubi supra*) in the place above mentioned
USA	United States army
USAF	United States air force
USCG	United States coast guard
USES	United States employment service

USGS	United States geological survey
USIA	U.S. Information agency
U.S.M.	United States mail
U.S.M.A.	United States Military academy
USMC	United States marine corps
USN	United States navy
U.S.N.A.	United States Naval academy
USNR	United States naval reserve
U.S.O.	United Service organizations
U.S.P.	United States Pharmacopoeia
USPHS	U.S. public health service
U.S.S.	United States ship; United States senate
U.S.S.S.	United States secret service

V

v.	volt(s); verb; very; verse; village
v.	(*vide*) see
v.	(*versus*) against; verse
VA	Veterans administration
V.A.D.	voluntary aid detachment
V.C.	vice-chancellor; Victoria cross
V.D.	venereal disease
Ven.	venerable
vet.	veterinary; veteran
VFR	visual flight rules
V.F.W.	Veterans of Foreign Wars
VHF	very high frequency
vic.	vicar; vicarage
vid.	(*vide*) see
Vis., Visc., Visct.	viscount
viz.	(*videlicet*) namely
v.l.	(*varia lectio*) varient reading(s)
voc.	vocative
vol.	volume(s); volunteers; volcano
vox pop.	(*vox populi*) voice of the people
V.P.	vice-president
vs.	verse
v.s.	(*vide supra*) see above
VTO	vertical take-off
Vul., Vulg.	Vulgate (Bible)

W

w.	watt(s); wife
WAC	women's army corps; World Aeronautic chart
WAF	women's air force
WAVES	women accepted for volunteer emergency service (United States naval reserve)
W.C.C.	World Council of Churches
W.C.T.U.	Woman's Christian Temperance union
WHO	World Health organization
W.I.	Women's institute
w.l.	wave length
WMO	World Meteorological organization
WPA	Works Projects administration
W.R.A.C.	women's royal army corps
W.R.A.F.	women's royal air force
WRENS, W.R.N.S.	women's royal naval service
W.S.	women's size
WSB	Wage Stabilization board
wt.	weight; without
W.V.S.	women's voluntary services
W.X.	women's extra (outsize)

X

X	Christ; Christian
XQ	cross question

Y

y.	youngest
yd.	yard(s)
Y.M.C.A.	Young Men's Christian association
Y.M.-Cath.A.	Young Men's Catholic association
Y.M.H.A.	Young Men's Hebrew association
yr.	year(s); younger; your
Y.W.C.A.	Young Women's Christian association
Y.W.H.A.	Young Women's Hebrew association

A.B.C. POWERS, a term used to denote the three leading nations of southern South America, Argentina, Brazil and Chile. The term refers particularly to their informal association, including the exchange of friendly speeches and official visits, which began about 1905 and was formalized in a five-year treaty in 1915. The treaty pledged the A.B.C. states not to war on each other without first attempting a neutral investigation of the causes of the conflict, but it was never implemented and had no lasting effect.

The most significant accomplishment of the A.B.C. countries was their joint mediation between the United States and Mexico in 1914. The mediation effort followed the U.S. bombardment of the port of Veracruz, Mex. (April 21–22, 1914). The mediation conference was held from May to August of that year at Niagara Falls, Ont. The good offices of the A.B.C. mediators contributed to a solution of the immediate dispute between Mexico and the United States if only by providing time for further diplomatic negotiations and, as it happened, for a change of presidents in revolutionary Mexico which worked to the advantage of the policy being pursued by Pres. Woodrow Wilson.

The importance of this South American "triple entente" lies in the indication it provided of the sensitivity of even remote Latin American nations to United States intervention south of the Rio Grande, and in the wider reputation it gave those nations as active partners in hemispheric affairs. (T. F. McG.)

ABD-AL-MALIK ('ABD-AL-MALIK IBN MARWAN) (c. 647–705), Omayyad caliph from 685 to 705 and reorganizer of the Arab Muslim empire after the civil war of 680–692, was born at Medina in Arabia and lived there until 683. His father, Marwan I, was proclaimed caliph in Damascus in June 684 but was assassinated in April 685. Abd-al-Malik succeeded him, but was at first recognized only in Syria and Egypt. Several years were spent in recovering the empire. The rival claimant, Abdullah ibn al-Zubayr, of Mecca, who was at first acknowledged in Iraq also, was defeated in 692 by Abd-al-Malik's able general al-Hajjaj. There were also bands of Kharijite and other rebels to be subdued and the Byzantines to be held in check. Eventually control was reasserted, and the closing years of the reign were prosperous. Frontier campaigns recovered lost territories (as in central Asia) or prepared for further advances (as by establishing a firm base at Kairouan in Tunisia). Important internal changes were also made. Arabic became the official language in the financial offices instead of Greek or Persian. The first Islamic gold dinars were minted. To al-Hajjaj were due both the founding of a new garrison city for Iraq at Wasit, and the edition of the text of the Koran with vowels. Abd-al-Malik died in Damascus in Oct. 705. *See* CALIPHATE. (W. M. Wt.)

ABD-AL-RAHMAN, the name of five Omayyad rulers, amirs and caliphs of Córdoba in Muslim Spain. (*See* CÓRDOBA, CALIPHATE OF.)

ABD-AL-RAHMAN I (Abd-al-Rahman ibn Mu'awiya ibn Hisham) (reigned 756–788) escaped the massacre when the Abbasids overthrew the Omayyad caliphate in Syria in 750 (*see* CALIPHATE). Abd-al-Rahman after adventurous wanderings accepted an invitation to intervene between two warring Muslim factions in Spain. His energy, generalship and political vision enabled him to master a bewildering situation and to found, in 756, an independent amirate centred on Córdoba. With a standing army of mercenaries he temporarily repressed the rivalries of the Arab aristocracy and the anarchic tribalism of the Berbers in Spain, while defending his territories against invasions organized by the Abbasid caliph of Baghdad and the ruler of Meknès. His internal reforms, which included the formation of a council of state, the reorganization of the judiciary under a senior qadi and the division of Spain into six military provinces, together with his embellishment of Córdoba (where he constructed the famous mosque with its schools and hospitals) and his clemency to the Christians, have led historians to treat him as the equal of Charlemagne, the defeat of whose army in 778 at Roncesvalles (*q.v.*) by the Navarrese marked the end of a Frankish invasion of Abd-al-Rahman's domains.

ABD-AL-RAHMAN II (reigned 822–852), son of the amir al-Hakam I, was the fourth Omayyad amir of Córdoba. In spite of internal troubles, increasing seditiousness on the part of his Chris-tian subjects and wars with the Franks, his reign was noted for the cultivation of the arts and sciences and for the enlightened encouragement of commerce and public works.

ABD-AL-RAHMAN III (Abd-al-Rahman ibn Mohammed ibn Abdullah) (reigned 912–961), the eighth and perhaps the greatest Omayyad ruler of Córdoba, was the first to use the title of caliph in Spain (Jan. 16, 929). He succeeded to the throne at the age of 22, when Omayyad rule was crippled by tribal warfare among the Arabs and by strife between them and Muslims of Spanish descent, while the greater part of Andalusia had seceded under the leadership of Ibn Hafsun. The first ten years of his reign were spent in restoring central authority, the rest in defending his northern borders against the inroads of the Leonese and in stemming the westward advance in north Africa of the Fatimids, who also claimed the caliphate. For a time his navy mastered the western Mediterranean, and he maintained diplomatic relations with the Byzantine emperor and with the princes of southern Europe. Under his rule Córdoba, with 500,000 inhabitants, was the largest and most civilized city of Europe. The seat of Europe's first academy of medicine, a centre for geographers, architects, craftsmen, artists and scholars of every kind, it rivaled for a brief period the splendour of Alexandria in the 4th century B.C.

ABD-AL-RAHMAN IV, styled al-Murtada (reigned 1018–1023), and ABD-AL-RAHMAN V, styled al-Mustazhir (reigned 1023–1024), succeeded to the caliphate in the death agony of the Omayyad dynasty. Both were puppets of factions which soon deserted them. The first was killed while fleeing from a battle in which his troops were victorious, while the second was dismembered, two months after his proclamation, by a revolutionary mob headed by his cousin.

See R. Altamira, "The Western Caliphate," *Cambridge Mediaeval History,* vol. iii (1922); P. K. Hitti, *History of the Arabs,* 5th ed. (1951). (K. Ga.)

ABD-AL-WADID DYNASTY (ZEIYANIDS or BENI ZEIYAN), a dynasty which ruled at Tlemçen (*q.v.*) in northwestern Africa from 1239 to 1554. In 1239, when the empire of the Almohads (*q.v.*) was breaking up, the amir Yaghmorasen, of the Abd-al-Wadid section of the Berber Zenata tribe, set up a new kingdom at Tlemçen, with the support of other Berber tribes and of immigrant Arab groups. This kingdom, however, had neither geographical unity nor fixed frontiers, being peopled mainly by Zenata tribesmen and equally nomad Arabs, and its internal life was much disturbed. The amirs, being unable to find enough Berbers for their armies, were forced to recruit from the unreliable Arab tribes, and their best troops were used for the suppression of internal rebellions. Attempts at expansion eastward and westward failed, and twice during the 14th century the kingdom was annexed by the Marinids of Fez. More than once also the Abd-al-Wadids acknowledged the Hafsids of Tunis as suzerains.

Tlemcen, on the trade route between the Mediterranean ports and Saharan oases, was long prosperous, and the Abd-al-Wadid amirs encouraged the growth there of Andalusian civilization. Several masterpieces of Spanish-Moorish art still bear witness to the city's past splendour. The Abd-al-Wadid kingdom, which had been declining since the 15th century, was overwhelmed by Ottoman Turkish troops from Algiers in 1554.

BIBLIOGRAPHY.—Various authors, *Initiation à l'Algérie* (1957); C. A. Julien, *Histoire de l'Afrique du Nord,* vol. ii, rev. ed. by R. le Tourneau (1952); E. F. Albertini, G. Marçais and G. Yver, *L'Afrique du Nord française dans l'histoire* (1937); G. Marçais, *L'Architecture musulmane de l'Occident* (1955); W. Marçais and G. Marçais, *Les Monuments arabes de Tlemçen* (1903). (H. L. E. T.)

ABD-EL-AZIZ IV (ABD-AL-AZIZ IBN AL-HASAN) (1878–1943), sultan of Morocco from 1894 to 1908, whose reign was marked by the failure of the sherifian empire to modernize itself by its own efforts. When Abd-el-Aziz succeeded his father Mulay el-Hasan at the age of 16, the government was carried on for six years, on traditional lines, by his late father's chamberlain, Si Ahmed ben Musa, who acted as regent. On the latter's death in 1900 the young ruler, whose mother was a Circassian and who was glad to seek European advice, attempted to modernize the country and in particular to reform the methods of taxation. These well-meant endeavours, defeated because of the complete lack of administrators trained on modern lines, caused great resentment among influential notables of the old school. This was further accentuated by the sultan's indulgence in childish and often fantastically expensive hobbies. The Anglo-French agreement of 1904, which deprived him of the hope of British aid to resist French encroachments, was a further blow. Nor did the German-sponsored conference of Algeciras (1906) help him in view of the increasing internal anarchy. A pretender, known as Bu Hamara, who claimed to be the sultan's elder brother, headed a rising and all but captured Fez. Though driven back he maintained himself in the eastern provinces. In 1907, the sultan's brother Mulay Abd-el-Hafidh raised the standard of revolt in the southern capital, Marrakesh. After seeking a loan in France, Abd-el-Aziz marched on Marrakesh in July 1908. His forces were however routed (Aug. 19, 1908) and he himself took refuge with the French troops established near Casablanca. Later pensioned by his brother, he spent the rest of his life at Tangier. *See* Morocco: *History.*

(N. Ba.)

ABD-EL-KADER (Abd-al-Kadir) (1808–1883), Algerian national leader, was born near Mascara in northwestern Algeria on Sept. 6, 1808, the third son of Mahi-ed-Din, head of the Kadria Muslim sect. Inured to hardship from early childhood, he became a fine horseman. He also received a sound education and grew up to be very devout. He made the pilgrimage to Mecca in 1827. In 1832, before the death of Mahi-ed-Din, who in 1832 had declared a holy war against the French in Algeria, Abd-el-Kader was proclaimed amir of Mascara. He built up his power astutely, taking advantage of the mistakes of the French and, when the French negotiated with him in 1834, making it clear to the Muslims that the French regarded him as the Muslims' leader.

Success, however, eluded him, and although he won a victory at La Macta (June 28, 1835) he could not prevent Gen. Bertrand Clauzel from sacking Mascara in December and was defeated by Gen. T. R. Bugeaud at Sikkah (July 6, 1836). Resourceful in adversity, he entered into negotiations, and the treaty of Tafna (May 30, 1837) saved his prestige just when the tribes were going to desert him. He still had difficulty, however, in establishing his authority over the tribesmen because of the rivalries of the different Muslim brotherhoods.

In 1839 Abd-el-Kader declared that the French by uniting Constantine and Algiers had broken the Tafna treaty, and holy war was again proclaimed. He laid waste the Mitidja and harried the French troops. In 1840, however, the French decided to compensate themselves in Algeria for the loss of prestige they had suffered over the Eastern Question and Bugeaud was given command of a reinforced army of 106,000 men. Abd-el-Kader lost Tlemcen in 1842, his Moroccan ally was defeated at Isly in Aug. 1844, and his success at Sidi Brahim (Sept. 1845) served only to postpone the French victory. He finally surrendered on Dec. 23, 1847, his only condition being a safe-conduct to the east for himself and his family. Although this was agreed, he was arrested and imprisoned in France first at Toulon, then at Pau and at Amboise (1848–52). He wrote at this time a philosophical treatise which was translated as *Rappel à l'intelligent, avis à l'indifférent.* Finally, on Oct. 16, 1852, he was released and, after a stay of nearly three years in Bursa in Turkey, he settled in Damascus (1855). There in 1860 he saved 12,000 Christians from a crowd of fanatical Muslims (for this he was awarded the *grand cordon* of the *Légion d'Honneur*). On a last visit to Paris (1863–65) he tried in vain to influence Napoleon III's Algerian policy. He died in Damascus during the night of May 25–26, 1883. *See* Algeria: *History.*

See Gen. Paul Azan, *L'Émir Abd-el-Kader, 1808–1883* (1925); P. d'Estailleur-Chantereine, *Abd-el-Kader: l'Europe et l'Islam au XIXème siècle* (1947). (L. G.)

ABD-EL-KRIM (Mohammed Abd-al-Karim al-Khattabi) (1881–1963) achieved fame as leader of the resistance in the Moroccan Rif mountains to the implantation of the Spanish protectorate. His father, a caid of the Berber tribe of Ait Wariyagher, or Beni Uriaghel, gave him a Spanish education and he became *qadi al-qudat* ("chief Muslim judge") at Melilla and

editor of the *Telegrama del Rif.* First known as friendly to the Spaniards, he took offense at a slight offered him by a Spanish officer, was imprisoned, then fled to Ajdir near Alhucemas and organized armed resistance among the Beni Uriaghel. In 1921 he achieved a tremendous success by completely routing a Spanish force of 20,000 men under Gen. M. F. Silvestre and pursuing them into the suburbs of Melilla. He then organized the whole of the Rif and much of the country to the east into a rudimentary state under his own leadership. The Spanish withdrew from the interior and maintained themselves only in Tetuan. In 1925, however, the French advanced from the south into the valley of the Wargla, from which Abd-el-Krim had drawn supplies. He thereupon attacked them also and in the first onslaught almost reached Fez. This produced a combined Franco-Spanish reaction. The Spanish dictator, Primo de Rivera, organized a successful landing at Alhucemas, in the immediate neighbourhood of Abd-el-Krim's capital, Ajdir; while Marshal Pétain took charge of a French army of 160,000 men and attacked from the south. Soon the end was no longer in doubt; in May 1926 Abd-el-Krim surrendered to the French forces and was sent into exile on the island of Réunion. In his heroic struggle he had displayed great qualities, both military and administrative. If the technical disparity between Morocco and Europe had been no greater than it was in earlier ages he might well have succeeded in driving out the foreigners. But times had changed, and there was no possibility of restoring Moroccan independence until a new generation had grown up, educated in modern schools and methods. While himself a Berber, Abd-el-Krim was a good Arabic scholar and the administration which he introduced was essentially Arab.

After he had spent 21 years in exile on Réunion, the French government in 1947 authorized his residence in France. While passing through the Suez canal he was persuaded by north African emissaries to accept an offer of refuge in Egypt. In Cairo, he presided over the organization known as the Maghrib office. He was, however, out of sympathy with nationalist leaders of the new school and, while disapproving of terrorism, was in other respects intransigent. After the restoration of Moroccan independence, Sultan Mohammed V invited him to return to Morocco. This he refused to do as long as foreign troops remained on north African soil. Abd-el-Krim died in Cairo on Feb. 6, 1963.

See W. B. Harris, *France, Spain and the Rif* (1927). (N. Ba.)

ABDERA (modern Avdira in the *nomos* of Xanthi in Greece), an ancient town on the coast of Thrace, near the mouth of the Nestos river, almost opposite the island of Thasos. An attempt in the 7th century B.C. by Greek colonists from Clazomenae to occupy the site failed; but the people of Teos, evacuating their homes when the Persians under Cyrus overran Ionia (c. 540 B.C.), succeeded in establishing a colony there, which developed a brisk trade with the Thracian interior. Abdera was a prosperous member of the Delian league in the 5th century but was crippled early in the 4th century B.C. by the incursions of Thracian marauders and declined sharply in importance. The air of Abdera was proverbial in causing stupidity, but among its citizens were the philosophers Protagoras and Democritus. The ruins both of the ancient town and of a medieval settlement survive in the neighbourhood of Avdira.

ABDIAS, PROPHECY OF: *see* Obadiah, Book of.

ABDICATION, the renouncing of office and of power before the end of the term for which it was assumed. In ancient Roman law *abdicare* meant primarily "to disown," as when a father disowned a son, who was thereby disinherited; but the word was also used in Latin as meaning "to renounce." In modern usage the word "abdication" is generally confined to signifying the renunciation of supreme power in a state. When it is said that a potentate abdicated, it may be implied that he did so voluntarily. But in many cases where abdication is alleged there is an obvious element of constraint, a show of willingness being put forward in order to avoid the consequences of what would otherwise have to be called deposition. Even so, in arguing that James II of Great Britain "abdicated" by his desertion of the kingdom, the Whigs of 1689 seemed to be straining the sense of the word.

Celebrated voluntary abdications include those of Sulla, of

Diocletian and of the emperor Charles V. The abdication of Edward VIII (*q.v.*) of Great Britain was the result of conflict between personal and political interests. Abdications in the face of military disaster, revolution or the threat of revolution include those of Napoleon I in 1814 and in 1815; of the French, Bavarian and Austrian sovereigns in 1848; of Tsar Nicholas II of Russia in 1917; of the German emperor William II and of the rulers of Bavaria, of Saxony, of Baden and of Württemberg, as also of the tsar of Bulgaria, after World War I; of Kings Victor Emmanuel III of Italy, Leopold III of Belgium and Michael of Rumania after World War II and during the Communist subjugation of eastern Europe; and of King Faruk of Egypt in 1952.

ABDOMEN, the belly, the body cavity lying between the chest or thorax above and the pelvis below. The diaphragm is its upper boundary. There is no wall or clear-cut boundary between it and the pelvis. It contains organs of digestion and the spleen, which are surrounded by a serous membrane, the peritoneum. *See* Anatomy, Gross; Gastrointestinal Tract.

ABDOMEN, SURGERY OF. The diseases of this region are dealt with generally in the article Gastrointestinal Tract, Diseases of, and under their own names (*e.g.*, Appendicitis).

The main barriers to be overcome in the advancement of abdominal surgery were pain and infections. The first was overcome by the introduction of ether in 1846 and chloroform in 1847. Prevention or reduction of infection became possible after the introduction of antiseptic drugs in surgery in 1867, and was further advanced in the latter half of the 19th century through the development of aseptic techniques. With further improvement in the selection of anesthetic and analgesic drugs and in methods of administration, the length of surgical operations could be increased without danger to the life of the patient. Proper preparation of the patient before the operation and adequate care afterward still further increased the safety of surgery, even when it involved extensive surgical procedures. (*See also* Anesthesia and Anesthetics; Gall Bladder, Biliary Tract and Liver, Surgery of.) Discovery of the therapeutic value of sulfa drugs and antibiotics greatly diminished the incidence of postoperative infection and further decreased the danger of abdominal surgery. (*See also* Antibiotics; Sulfonamides.)

Types of Operations.—Operations on the abdomen may be elective or emergency. The former are those planned beforehand and executed at a deliberately chosen time. Emergency surgery is that which has to be performed at once or within a very short time. In some cases the nature of a contemplated operation is envisioned beforehand; in others it is determined only after the abdomen is opened, that is, after exploratory laparotomy.

Gastrointestinal Surgery.—The stomach and the small and large bowel are the major organs in this category.

The commonest stomach operations are those performed for cancer or ulcer. The stomach may be removed *in toto* (total gastrectomy) or a portion may be removed (partial gastrectomy). In the operation called gastrojejunostomy an artificial communication is made between the stomach and a loop of small bowel (jejunum) in order to bypass a duodenal ulcer or a benign pyloric stricture. Gastrostomy is an operation employed on the stomach of patients suffering from constriction of the esophagus. It consists of making an opening in the stomach with an outlet on the anterior abdominal wall. Food is introduced into the stomach through this opening.

Operations on parts of the small bowel such as the duodenum, jejunum or ileum are employed when parts become gangrenous, as in intestinal obstruction or mesenteric thrombosis, or when they are invaded by malignant tumours. These conditions necessitate resection (removal) of the affected portion of the bowel. Among affections of the large bowel are appendicitis and cancer. Cancer may affect any part, but the rectum and the sigmoid are most often attacked. If cancer is detected early—that is, before there is involvement of other structures—it is possible to remove the diseased portion with the hope of a cure or of five-year survival. (*See* Intestine, Surgery of.)

Strangulation of loops of the bowel by a muscular ring of the abdominal wall (external hernia) or by peritoneal bands within the abdominal cavity (internal hernia) requires immediate surgical intervention, ranging from mere cutting of the ring or band to resection of a loop of bowel if gangrene has developed. (*See also* Stomach, Surgery of.)

Glands of the Digestive System.—Glands include the liver (with the gall bladder and extrahepatic biliary passages) and the pancreas. Resection of a portion of the liver was done occasionally in the second half of the 19th century for wounds or for removal of echinococcus cyst or carcinomatous growth. With the development of the control of hemorrhage by electrosurgery and particularly by suture methods, operations upon the liver ceased to be a rarity. Partial liver resection now is performed not only for the conditions mentioned above but also, for example, to expose branches of the biliary ducts and utilize them for establishment of anastomosis with a loop of jejunum. Operations upon the gall bladder include several procedures—cholecystostomy, cholecystectomy, cholecystogastrostomy and cholecystenterostomy.

Cholecystostomy implies the formation of a fistula between the gall bladder and the exterior surface of the abdomen. It is done occasionally after the removal of gallstones by inserting one end of a rubber tube into the gall-bladder cavity and bringing the other end outside, thus allowing bile to flow outside the body.

Cholecystectomy denotes removal of the gall bladder. It is usually performed for chronic diseases of the gall bladder or after gallstones have been cleared. Cholecystogastrostomy consists of making an artificial communication between the gall bladder and the stomach. In cholecystenterostomy such a communication is made between the gall bladder and a loop of small bowel, usually the jejunum. These operations are performed to sidetrack the common bile duct when the latter is obstructed and there is no possibility of removing the obstruction, as for instance when the duct is compressed by a malignant tumour from the outside.

Cholecystojejunostomy or choledochojejunostomy is one of the surgical steps in removal of the pancreas with a portion of the duodenum, an operation known as pancreatoduodenectomy.

Although some comparatively simple operations on the pancreas were performed in the last quarter of the 19th century, it was not until the 20th century that the more complicated operative procedures, such as removal of stones and resection of part of or even the entire pancreas, were attempted.

An operation is employed in which an artificial communication is established between the vena cava inferior and the vena porta (Eck's fistula), for relief of ascites or of hemorrhages from the veins of the lower esophagus, caused by cirrhosis of the liver.

Other Procedures.—These include sympathectomy, removal of the sympathetic nerves for spasm of the blood vessels in the legs; vagotomy, or division of the vagus nerves to the stomach to decrease the secretion of acid gastric juice; removal of the spleen for a variety of hematologic conditions; and replacement of the aorta with grafts for aneurysm or arteriosclerotic obstruction.

(J. L. Sk.; P. V. H.)

'ABDUH, MOHAMMED (1849?–1905), a pioneer of modern Islamic thought in Egypt, whose legacy of personal character and educational leadership has become formative in Arab history. After a traditional mosque-school education, he became a devotee of Sufi discipline according to the Shadhili order, until he encountered Jamal al-Din al-Afghani (*q.v.*), tireless advocate of Pan-Islamic revival, under whose powerful influence he was stimulated into fervent political and journalistic activity. Exiled to Syria in 1882, he traveled in France, Tunis and Lebanon. Returning to Egypt in 1888, he became convinced that the future called for a more Fabian approach. Thus he set himself to instigate wide legal and legislative reforms, to improve student conditions in al-Azhar university and to develop worthier standards among the sheikhs. But inertia and obscurantist hostility finally robbed him of any substantial fulfillment of his aspirations. He died on July 11, 1905.

It was this apathetic spirit of *taqlid,* or blind appeal to book-authorities, that 'Abduh sought by his writings to banish. His most significant works were an unfinished Koranic commentary and a treatise on divine unity (*Risalat al-Tawhid*) in which he set out his conviction of the essential rationality of Islam. He presupposed the corpus of orthodox theology, aiming only to rid it of this incubus of traditionalism—a negative but urgent task in his day. On the positive side, he tended to a placid concept of faith, "in the knowledge that every sound speculation leads to a belief in God as he is described in the Koran" (*Risalat*, p.10). Holding this harmony between sound natural reason and revealed theology, he did not examine further his assumption that Islam was the religion of reason and the finally perfect faith, or delve into attendant problems. In these terms of attained ultimacy, he interpreted the familiar phrase describing Mohammed as "the seal of the prophets."

'Abduh's greatest achievement lay in the reforming range and vigour of his official *fatwas* as grand mufti of Egypt and in the devotion his personality evoked among his disciples, notably Rashid Rida, Taha Husayn and Mustafa Abd al-Raziq.

See C. C. Adams, *Islam and Modernism in Egypt* (1933).

(A. K. Cr.)

ABDUL-AZIZ (1830–1876), Ottoman sultan of Turkey, second son of the sultan Mahmud II, was born in Istanbul on Feb. 9, 1830, and succeeded his brother Abdul-Mejid I as sultan on June 25, 1861. He belonged to the Mevlevi sect (dancing dervishes) and loved music, painting and wrestling. Between 1861 and 1871 Abdul-Aziz cultivated good relations with Great Britain and France, with whose collaboration the troubles in Syria, the Balkans and Crete were settled. He was the first Ottoman sultan to visit Egypt (1863) and western Europe (1867). At the same time he continued his predecessors' policy of westernizing Ottoman institutions. On the suggestion of the French government, a council of state was established; an imperial college was opened for both Muslims and non-Muslims; and the first Ottoman civil code was promulgated. Abdul-Aziz enriched himself through the constant issue of state loans but squandered money extravagantly. He also received valuable gifts from Ismail Pasha, the khedive of Egypt, for making the succession to the khediviate hereditary from father to son in direct line and for extending the khedive's prerogatives.

After the French defeat in the Franco-German War, Abdul-Aziz deprived the grand vizier of his prerogatives and made himself an absolute monarch. Abandoning western ideas, he turned to Russia for friendship. In 1870 he signed the firman creating an exarchate in Bulgaria. Finally, however, insurrections in Bosnia and Hercegovina (1875) and in Bulgaria (1876) caused an outbreak of Muslim discontent in Turkey itself and of fanaticism against Russia and the sultan. Abdul-Aziz was deposed on May 29, 1876, and his death in Istanbul four days later is attributed to suicide.

(E. Z. K.)

ABDÜLHAK HAMID (1852–1937), Turkish poet and playwright, who introduced western influences into Turkish poetry, was born in Istanbul, Jan. 2, 1852, and educated in Paris and Teheran where his father, Hayrullah Efendi, a famous historian, was ambassador. He held diplomatic posts in Paris and Bombay, where his wife became mortally ill. Deeply affected, he wrote his poetic masterpiece *Makber* (1885). Later, when counselor in London (1885–1908), he remarried, and subsequently became ambassador in Brussels, senator (1914) and, finally, member of parliament in Ankara. He died in Istanbul, April 12, 1937.

A follower of the Tanzimat school of literature which developed from the movement for political reform, he was strongly influenced by Shinasi, Ziya Pasha and especially Namik Kemal. He soon broke with classical tradition, introducing western genres, techniques and ideas into poetry. Shakespeare and Victor Hugo greatly influenced him. His poems, mainly romantic and contemplative, are obsessed by ideas of death and human destiny. His best dramas (*Tarik, Tezer, Eshber, Ibn-i Musa, Abdullahüssagir*, etc.), written between 1876 and 1885, are inspired by Muslim history, though *Finten* (1887), his own favourite, portrays London society.

His powerful influence completely changed literary taste in Turkey, and paved the way for the more radical reforms of Tevfik Fikret and his successors.

See E. Rossi, "In morte del poeta turco Abd ul-haqq Hamid," in *Oriente Moderno 17* (1937); A. Fischer, *Abdülhaqq Hamids dramatische Ruhlar,* text with German trans. (1941). (F. I.)

ABDUL-HAMID I (1725–1789), Ottoman sultan of Turkey, succeeded his brother Mustafa III on Jan. 21, 1774. He was a practical man, but at the same time superstitious, believing in his own sanctity. During his reign, the decline of Turkey became more pronounced: the disastrous treaty of Kuchuk Kainarji (1774) was concluded with Russia; Bukovina was ceded to Austria (1775); and the Russian annexation of the Crimea was recognized (1784). In order to prevent Russian schemes for the partition of his territories, the sultan in Aug. 1787 declared war on Russia and Austria, in accord with the Russian plans, joined in the war against Turkey the next year. Abdul-Hamid tried to reorganize his army with the help of French experts, but his efforts were frustrated by fanatics. He died on April 7, 1789, before the end of the war.

(E. Z. K.)

ABDUL-HAMID II (1842–1918), Ottoman sultan of Turkey from 1876 to 1909, was born in Istanbul on Sept. 21, 1842. A son of the sultan Abdul-Mejid I, he succeeded to the throne, at the deposition of his brother Murad V, on Aug. 31, 1876. Brought to power by a group of liberals led by Midhat Pasha (*q.v.*), he proclaimed the first Ottoman constitution on Dec. 23, 1876.

Circumstances, however, were ill-suited for liberal developments. Indignation had been aroused throughout Europe by the savage repression of the Bulgarian rising of May 1876; peace had not yet been ratified with Serbia; and the treasury was empty. Then, early in 1877, the disastrous war with Russia began (*see* RUSSO-TURKISH WARS). Though the hard terms of the treaty of San Stefano (*see* EASTERN QUESTION) were mitigated mainly through British efforts at the congress of Berlin (*q.v.*), it became clear to the sultan that he could expect little more help from the western powers whose demands for further reforms he was obstinately resisting. The first Turkish parliament, which had met in March 1877, was dismissed and the constitution suspended in Feb. 1878. Midhat Pasha was exiled in 1881 and died by violence in 1883. Thenceforward until 1908 the sultan's rule was absolute.

After the French had occupied Tunisia (1881) and the British had consolidated their hold over Egypt by overthrowing Arabi Pasha (1882), the sultan turned more and more to Germany for support. Germans were employed to re-organize his finances (by a decree of Dec. 1881 many of the imperial revenues had been handed over to the public debt administration for the satisfaction of bondholders) and to train the Turkish army. In return for this help, concessions had from time to time to be made to Germany, culminating in 1899 in permission to construct the Baghdad railway (*q.v.*).

Though he resented the Bulgarian occupation of eastern Rumelia in 1885, Abdul-Hamid was able to maintain toward Bulgaria an attitude astutely calculated to suit both German and Russian wishes. In Armenia, however, there was agitation from 1890 onward for the reforms promised at the congress of Berlin, and in 1894 a serious rebellion broke out. When this was ruthlessly suppressed, the European powers demanded reforms. The granting of these (autumn 1895) was followed by massacres of Armenians both in Armenia itself and also in Constantinople (mod. Istanbul), and the reforms came to nothing.

Meanwhile Crete had been constantly in turmoil, and Greek support for the Cretans led in 1897 to war. In this the Turks were easily successful (*see* GRECO-TURKISH WAR, 1897) and gained a small rectification of the frontier from Greece, but a few months later Crete was taken in trust by Great Britain, Russia, France and Italy who appointed Prince George of Greece as their mandatory. Germany and Austria did not participate in this, and in 1898 the sultan received the visit of the German emperor William II.

In his opposition to European pressure, Abdul-Hamid had always insisted on his role as the champion of Islam against Christian aggression. Pan-Islamic propaganda was encouraged; the privileges of foreigners in the Ottoman empire were curtailed; the Hejaz railway was pushed on toward the Muslim holy places in Arabia; and emissaries were sent far afield to preach Islam and the caliph's supremacy. This appeal to Muslim sentiment, however, failed to prevail over the disaffection caused by Turkish misgovernment. In Mesopotamia and Yemen disturbances were endemic, and in the nearer parts of the empire the loyalty of the army and the people could only be maintained by a police system of espionage and delation. Obsessed by the fear of assassination, Abdul-Hamid kept himself in fortified seclusion in the palace of Yildiz.

These conditions, together with fresh resentment at Turkish humiliations in the Balkans, led at last to the military revolution of the Young Turks (see TURKEY: History) in 1908. Abdul-Hamid capitulated, and on July 24, 1908, the restoration of the suspended constitution of 1876 was announced. The sultan, however, despite his correct behaviour, was suspected of intriguing with the reactionary elements in the empire, and this suspicion was confirmed by his acquiescence to the counterrevolution of April 13, 1909, when the new regime was temporarily overthrown. When the Young Turks' army from Salonika restored the new regime, Abdul-Hamid was deposed and his brother was proclaimed sultan as Mohammed V (April 27). Confined at first in Salonika, Abdul-Hamid was in 1912 brought back to Constantinople. He died in the palace of Beylerbeyi on the Bosporus on Feb. 10, 1918.

Abdul-Hamid had a great capacity for work: before his accession, unlike any other Ottoman prince, he had managed a farm. His system of personal rule, however, though apparently successful for many years, was an anachronism. An opportunist, he was not vindictive, but he had no friends and was so mistrustful of other people that he used to extract his own teeth and prepare his own medicines.

See Sir E. Pears, *Life of Abdul-Hamid* (1917); Joan Haslip, *The Sultan: the Life of Abdul Hamid* (1958).   (E. Z. K.)

ABD-UL-ILAH (1913–1958), regent of Iraq from 1939 to 1953 and crown prince thereafter, was born at Taif, the son of Ali ibn Husain who for a few months was king of the Hejaz. He accompanied his father thence to Baghdad in 1926 after the loss of the Hashemite family's throne and position in peninsular Arabia. Educated at Victoria college, Alexandria, interested in racing and polo, society and travel and possessing an attractive, intelligent personality, the amir Abd-ul-Ilah was called unexpectedly to act as regent for his cousin and nephew Faisal II when the latter, a child of four, succeeded to the throne of Iraq as a result of the death by accident of the boy's father, King Ghazi (April 4, 1939).

Abd-ul-Ilah showed throughout his regency an admirable loyalty and affection to the boy-king and resolutely upheld, with gifts and powers which steadily developed, the position of the throne. Compelled to leave Iraq for some weeks in 1941 on the seizure of power by Rashid Ali, he returned with British assistance; and thereafter, in close collaboration with Nuri as-Sa'id and other moderate statesmen, he opposed the more violent forms and personalities of local nationalism and saw Iraq's advantage in a policy of collaboration with the west. He paid numerous state visits to foreign capitals between 1945 and 1953 and, without unconstitutional action, played a considerable, indeed a central, part in Iraqi politics. Relinquishing his functions to Faisal II in 1953, Abd-ul-Ilah remained the king's constant adviser and supporter. He was assassinated with the king in the uprising in Baghdad on July 14, 1958. See HASHEMITES; IRAQ: History.   (S. H. Lo.)

ABDULLAH IBN HUSAIN (1882–1951), amir of Transjordan from 1921 to 1946 and king of Jordan from 1946 to 1951, may be said to have created that country. Born in Mecca, the second son of the sharif Husain (q.v.; later king of the Hejaz), he was educated in Turkey and became a member for Mecca in the Ottoman parliament. He played an outstanding role in preparing the Arab revolt against Turkey in World War I and in 1920 boldly occupied Transjordan, where he was recognized as amir by Great Britain, the mandatory power, in March 1921. He ruled as a benevolent autocrat, guided by British advisers, adroitly establishing Transjordan as an entity separate from Palestine by exacting a pledge from the British that Jews should not settle there. His Hashemite blood and typically Arab attributes—piety, courage, prowess as a marksman and love of poetry and laughter—endeared him to his people. But his unconcealed ambition to extend his rule to Syria and to form with Syria and Iraq a dominant Hashemite bloc embittered the long-standing feud between the Hashemites (q.v.) and the Wahhabi dynasty of Saudi Arabia. In World War II he sent his army, the Arab legion, to assist British

troops in Iraq and Syria. Rewarded in 1946 by the grant of full independence, he retained a treaty with Great Britain, renamed his country Jordan and became king.

When in 1947 the United Nations resolved to partition Palestine, Abdullah was the only Arab head of state to accept the plan. But, on failing to win his Arab neighbours to his view, he joined them in fighting the Jews in Palestine, where his army captured Old Jerusalem and played a decisive part in holding central Palestine for the Arabs. In 1950 he annexed these Arab-held territories to Jordan, thereby incurring the anger of the Egyptian, Saudi Arabian and Syrian governments, which considered that Arab Palestine should constitute a separate state under the control of Haj Amin al-Husaini, former mufti of Jerusalem. Thereafter Abdullah's problems increased. While his country was desperately impoverished by the arrival of thousands of refugees from Palestine, his new Palestinian subjects clamoured for a more democratic constitution. His enemies multiplied, and a plot to murder him was brought to fruition on July 20, 1951, when he was shot in the Aqsa mosque in Jerusalem by a young Palestinian Arab, a supporter of Haj Amin al-Husaini.

BIBLIOGRAPHY.—George Antonius, *The Arab Awakening* (1938); Abdullah I, King of Jordan, *Memoirs,* ed. by P. Graves, Eng. trans. by G. Khuri (1950); "King Abdullah's Assassins," *The World Today* (Oct. 1951); Sir John Glubb, *Soldier With the Arabs* (1957); Ann Dearden, *Jordan* (1958).   (A. DE.)

ABDUL-MEJID I (1823–1861), Ottoman sultan of Turkey, was born in Istanbul on April 23, 1823, and succeeded his father Mahmud II, on July 2, 1839, at the age of 16. Well-educated and able to speak French, Abdul Mejid was also liberal-minded and receptive of western ideas. He came to terms with Mohammed Ali (q.v.), the rebel Egyptian viceroy, and then attempted to carry through the program of reforms which he had inherited from his father. On Nov. 3, 1839, he issued an edict, known as the *Hatti-sherif* ("handwriting") of Gulhane, which contained some provisions regarding human rights. The lives and property of all Ottoman subjects, irrespective of race or creed, were safeguarded, and their right to justice guaranteed; and the incidence of taxation was determined and its collection regulated. A regular system of recruiting was introduced. These regulations heralded a new era known as the *tanzimat,* which was applauded by the liberals of Europe. Abdul-Mejid refused to surrender the Hungarians who had fled to Turkey after the rising in 1849. His liberal dispositions helped to secure for him the support of Great Britain, France and Sardinia in the Crimean War (q.v.) against Russia. In 1856, Abdul-Mejid issued a new regulation by which he accorded civil and political rights to his Christian subjects and opened the door to foreign capital. The later years of his life, however, were troubled by a financial crisis and by a conspiracy against him. He died in Istanbul on June 25, 1861.   (E. Z. K.)

ABDUL-MEJID II (1868–1944), the last caliph and crown prince of the Ottoman dynasty of Turkey, was born on May 30, 1868, in Istanbul, the son of the sultan Abdul-Aziz and Hayranidil Kadin. Although confined to the palace until he was 40, Abdul-Mejid was considered to be better-informed than other Ottoman princes of the time, but his inconsistencies and his behaviour created a general impression that he was psychologically affected like his father and his elder brother. In 1918, when Mohammed V died and Vahid-ed-Din ascended the throne as Mohammed VI, Abdul-Mejid became crown prince, but he lost this title when Mohammed VI fled the country (1922) and the sultanate came to an end. He was then chosen caliph, but, four months after the proclamation of the republic, the caliphate was abolished (March 3, 1924) and members of the Ottoman dynasty were expelled. Abdul-Mejid died in Paris on Aug. 23, 1944.   (M. P. P.)

ABDULRAHMAN (TUANKU ABDULRAHMAN) (1895–1960), the first king (*Yang di-pertuan Agong*) of the Federation of Malaya, was born at Sri Menanti, on Aug. 24, 1895, the son of Tuanku Mohammed, the ruler (*Yang di-pertuan Besar*) of Negri Sembilan. He accompanied his father to England in 1925 and remained to study law, being called to the bar from the Inner Temple in Nov. 1928. Returning to Malaya he held a variety of posts in the civil service. After his father's death he was, on Aug. 3, 1933, elected ruler of Negri Sembilan. A retiring but kindly man who had learned from his father a deep respect for constitutional law and a profound sympathy for his people, he was admirably fitted to be Malaya's first king when it became independent. He died on April 1, 1960. (R. O. Wt.)

ABDUL RAHMAN, TUNKU (1903–   ), first prime minister of Malaysia, was born at Alor Star, Kedah, on Feb. 8, 1903, the seventh child of Sultan Abdul Hamid Halim Shah and a Thai (Shan) mother. After early education in Malaya he went to school in England (1920), graduated at Cambridge, and then studied law. He returned to Malaya in 1931 to enter the Kedah civil service. Tunku ("Prince") Abdul Rahman remained in Kedah throughout the Japanese occupation (1941–45) and in 1947 went to England again to study law. Called to the bar in 1949, he was appointed a deputy public prosecutor in the Malayan Federal Legal Department. Two years later he resigned to begin a political career. Succeeding Dato' Onn bin Ja'afar (q.v.) as president of the United Malays' National Organization (UMNO) in 1951, he effected the alliance of UMNO with the Malayan Chinese Association (1951) and with the Malayan Indian Congress (1955). The Alliance Party swept the poll in 1955, and Tunku Abdul Rahman became chief minister and home minister. In January 1956 he led a mission to London to negotiate for independence. The mission secured immediate internal self-government and the pledge of independence by August 1957. He then became independent Malaya's first prime minister and foreign minister. It was acknowledged that multiracial agreement on the new constitution and the success of independence were due largely to his unselfish leadership and winning personality. When the federation of Malaysia was formed in September 1963, he became prime minister of Malaysia. In 1966 he played an important part in the negotiations that led to the end of the "confrontation" between Indonesia and Malaysia.

He is keenly interested in sports and is president of the Asian Football Federation. (A. Ke.)

ABDURRAHMAN KHAN (1844–1901), amir of Afghanistan from 1880 to 1901, was born in Kabul, the son of Afzal Khan and the grandson of Dost Mohammed Khan, the founder of the Mohammedzai (or Barakzai) dynasty. When his father was appointed governor of the northern province of Mazar, Abdurrahman, then about ten years old, went with him. Dost Mohammed died in 1863 and was succeeded by his third son, Sher Ali Khan, whose elder brothers Afzal Khan and Azam Khan, with Abdurrahman's support, then rose in revolt. For several years civil war was waged. When Sher Ali was finally victorious Abdurrahman Khan took refuge in Russian Turkistan. Warmly received by the governor, he lived at Samarkand from 1870 to 1880, profiting by his study of the Russian administrative system.

After the outbreak of war between the British and the Afghans (1878), which was followed by the death of Sher Ali and the deportation of his son Yakub Khan to India, Abdurrahman in 1880 returned to Afghanistan where he was heartily welcomed by the people. At a conference held at Kabul on July 22, 1880, the British, then in possession of Kabul and Kandahar, formally proclaimed him amir. All British troops were withdrawn from Afghanistan after Lieut. Gen. Frederick Roberts (later Earl Roberts) had relieved the siege of Kandahar, which Ayub Khan, Yakub's brother, had been besieging. Abdurrahman then set to work with great energy and determination to pacify the country and to consolidate his authority. His methods may have been grim and cruel but, as he himself confessed, he had to rule an iron people with a rod of iron. Ayub, who for a time was able to maintain himself in Herat, gave trouble intermittently till his final defeat in 1887.

After establishing law and order Abdurrahman turned his attention to the settlement of border disputes with his powerful neighbours. In 1887 agreement was reached on the demarcation of Afghanistan's northwestern border with Russia. At the end of a series of talks held near Kabul in Oct.–Nov. 1893 with a British delegation led by Sir Mortimer Durand, Abdurrahman was constrained to accept the Durand line as his frontier, relinquishing some of his hereditary rights over the tribes on the eastern border of the country.

In spite of these preoccupations Abdurrahman found time to reorganize the administrative system of the country and to initiate internal reforms. He brought foreign specialists and experts in and imported machinery for making munitions; factories were established for the manufacture of boots, soap and candles; distilling apparatus and new agricultural tools were successfully introduced; the first modern hospital was established; and mines were successfully opened. Abdurrahman Khan died in Kabul on Oct. 1, 1901.

BIBLIOGRAPHY.—S. Wheeler, *The Ameer Abdur Rahman* (1895); J. A. Gray, *At the Court of the Amir*, 2nd ed. (1901); C. C. Davies, "Abd al-Rahman Khan" in *Encyclopaedia of Islam*, 2nd ed. (1954); Mohammed Ali, *Afghanistan: The Mohammedzai Period* (1959). (Md. A.)

ABEL, the second son of Adam and Eve (q.v.), portrayed in the fourth chapter of Genesis. He was a shepherd and offered the first born of his flock to the Lord, comparable to a faithful Israelite in the nomadic tradition. In a jealous rage, Cain, his brother, slew him, thus committing the "first murder." Cain was a farmer, and many interpreters feel that the story constitutes a polemic against agriculture. Its major concern, however, is the guilt incurred by shedding innocent blood. Cain must become a fugitive because his brother's blood, spilled on the soil and unavenged, puts a curse on him. Matt. xxiii, 35 and Luke xi, 51 cite the blood of Abel as an example of the vengeance of violated innocence. In Heb. xi, 4 and xii, 24 the blood of Abel becomes a type of the blood of Jesus. *See* also CAIN. (J. C. Ry.)

ABEL, JOHN JACOB (1857–1938), U.S. pharmacologist and physiological chemist, was a specialist in the chemistry of the ductless glands. He was born on May 19, 1857, in Cleveland, O. After attending the University of Michigan, Ann Arbor (1876–79), he was principal of the high school and superintendent of the public schools of La Porte, Ind. (1879–80; 1880–82), receiving his Ph.B. in 1883. After a year of study at Johns Hopkins, Baltimore, Md., he studied chemistry and medicine at several European universities, receiving his M.D. from the University of Strasbourg in 1888. He was lecturer and professor of materia medica at the University of Michigan (1890–93); in 1893 he became professor of pharmacology at Johns Hopkins, and, in 1932, director of the Laboratory for Endocrine Research. From 1909 to 1932 he edited the *Journal of Pharmacology and Experimental Therapeutics*.

Abel isolated adrenaline (epinephrine), the blood-pressure raising constituent of the adrenal glands, in the form of a benzoyl derivative. He also isolated insulin in crystal form. He became internationally known through these discoveries and through his many studies on the chemical composition of animal tissue and fluids, albumoses in the tissues, the action of pthaleins, the poisons of mushrooms, hydrolytic products of proteids, carbamic acid and histamin. He died on May 26, 1938, in Baltimore, Md.

ABEL, KARL FRIEDRICH (1723–1787), German musician, one of the last great players of the viola da gamba, and a notable symphonist of the preclassical school, was born at Cöthen, Dec. 22, 1723. He played from 1748 to 1758 under J. A. Hasse in the famous Dresden court orchestra, and, going to England in 1759, became chamber musician to Queen Charlotte.

When J. C. Bach arrived in London in 1762 they became friends and later established a famous series of concerts, known as the Bach and Abel concerts, one of which, in 1775, inaugurated the celebrated Hanover Square rooms. At these concerts, Haydn's symphonies were first publicly performed in England. Abel himself was a fine performer and a gifted instrumental composer; his first set of symphonies was published c. 1761 and achieved great success. He wrote about 40 symphonies, most of which were published: one was long attributed wrongly to the youthful Mozart (the so-called K. 18). Abel also published several sets of quartets and trio-sonatas, and a set of harpsichord concertos.

After the death of J. C. Bach (1782), he allowed his weakness for alcohol to gain hold upon him, and the last part of his life was clouded by this failing. He died in London, June 20, 1787. Some of his music has been reprinted; it has formal neatness and balance, and considerable melodic facility. His technical knowledge was highly regarded, and he was esteemed as a teacher, one of his most famous pupils being J. B. Cramer, who published some of his adagios (1820).

See S. M. Helm, *Carl Friedrich Abel, Symphonist* (1953).
(Cs. Ch.)

ABEL, NIELS HENRIK (1802–1829), Norwegian mathematician, a pioneer in the development of modern mathematics, was born on Aug. 5, 1802, on the island of Finnøy, near Stavanger, Nor., where his father was a minister. Shortly after Abel's birth, his father was transferred to the parish of Gjerstad, near the town of Risör (southeast Norway), and there the boy grew up, the second of six children. His mathematical talent was recognized, while he was a student at the Cathedral school in Oslo, by a young teacher, B. M. Holmboe (who edited the first edition of Abel's work, in 1839). While still in school he believed he had found a solution of the general quintic equation, but he discovered an error before publication.

In 1820 Abel's father died, mainly from drink, and left the family in poverty. The boy was able to enter the University of Oslo in 1821, sponsored by personal contributions of several of the professors. His first papers were published in 1823 in the new periodical *Magazin for Naturvidenskabene*. The topics were functional equations, integrals and the first instance of the solution of an integral equation. At this time Abel received a small stipend from the mathematics professor Rasmussen, which enabled him to take a trip to Copenhagen to make the acquaintance of the Danish mathematicians. Upon his return Abel found the proof for the result that the general quintic equation or higher had no solution in radical expressions; it was published in a small pamphlet at his own expense. In 1824 he received a government fellowship for mathematical studies in Oslo and abroad. The winter of 1825–26 he spent in Berlin with Norwegian friends, mainly geologists. He had the good fortune of making the acquaintance of A. L. Crelle, who became his close friend and protector. Inspired by Abel, Crelle founded the important *Journal für die reine und angewandte Mathematik*, the first volume of which is filled with papers by Abel. They concern such topics as equation theory, functional equations, integration in finite form, problems from theoretical mechanics and others.

Abel's early mathematical training had been in the formal calculating school typified by Euler. In Berlin he came into contact with the new direction represented by C. F. Gauss and A. L. Cauchy, requiring a much stronger degree of logical stringency. Under this influence he wrote a study of the binomial series, considered to be one of the classics in function theory. It contains the principles of convergent series with special applications to power series (Ostwald's *Klassiker der exakten Wissenschaften*, no. 71).

During the spring of 1826 Abel undertook a journey with his Norwegian friends through Prague, Vienna, northern Italy and Switzerland to Paris. Upon his arrival there he completed his *Mémoire sur une propriété générale d'une classe très-étendue de fonctions transcendantes*, which he himself considered his masterpiece. In this he gives a theory of integrals of algebraic functions —in particular, the result known as Abel's theorem, that there is a finite number, the genus, of independent integrals of this nature. This forms the basis for the later theory of Abelian integrals and Abelian functions. The paper was submitted to the French institute Oct. 30, 1826. Abel had hoped that it would open the door to the French mathematicians, but he waited in vain until his money gave out and he had to return to Berlin. There he completed his first long article on elliptic functions, a topic he had worked on in his student days. Abel returned to Norway heavily in debt. He subsisted by tutoring and a small grant from the university; beginning tuberculosis of the lungs aggravated his situation. In 1828 he received a substitute teaching position. His poverty and ill-health had little influence, however, on Abel's scientific production. He poured forth a great number of papers, principally on equation theory and elliptic functions. Among them are found the theory of the Abelian equations with Abelian groups. The theory of elliptic functions was developed with great rapidity in competition with K. G. J. Jacobi.

By this time Abel's fame had spread to all mathematical centres, and strong efforts were made to secure a suitable position for him. Bernadotte, the king of Norway-Sweden, was addressed directly by a group of members of the French Academy; Abel's friend Crelle worked feverishly to secure a professorship for him in Berlin. But in the fall of 1828 Abel became seriously ill, and his condition deteriorated on a several-day sled trip at Christmas time to visit his fiancée at Froland. He died there on April 6, 1829, at the age of 26. The appointment to Berlin had just been made; posthumously he was awarded, together with Jacobi, the Grand Prix of the French academy for 1830.

Crelle stated in his obituary: "One may say that he was able to penetrate all obstacles down to the very foundation of the problems, with a force which appeared irresistible. . . . He distinguished himself equally by the purity and nobility of his character and by a rare modesty which made his person cherished to the same unusual degree as was his genius."

BIBLIOGRAPHY.—N. H. Abel, *Oeuvres complètes* (1839; new ed., 2 vol., 1881); *Abel (N. H.) Mémorial publié à l'occasion du centenaire de sa naissance* (1902); O. Ore, *Niels Henrik Abel; Mathematician Extraordinary* (1957), with a bibliography; E. T. Bell, *Men of Mathematics* (1937). (O. Oe.)

ABELARD, PETER (Lat. PETRUS ABAELARDUS; Fr. PIERRE ABAILARD or ABÉLARD) (1079–1142), theologian and philosopher, was the son of the lord of Le Pallet in Brittany south of the Loire. Between *c.* 1094 and *c.* 1106 he studied logic at Loches and in Paris under Roscelin and Guillaume de Champeaux (*q.v.*) and taught it at Melun and Corbeil. After one or two years in Brittany he returned to Guillaume's school; but the violent polemics with his master, whom he forced to change views on the nature of universals, made his stay in Paris difficult. He went again to Melun but was soon back in Paris as a teacher on the Mont Ste. Geneviève. After another interval in Brittany he attended Anselm of Laon's theological school (*c.* 1114) but alienated his masters by sharp criticism of their scholarship and went back to Paris as a teacher of logic and theology at Notre Dame. Fulbert, a canon there, entrusted him with the education of his brilliant niece Heloïse. Abelard's love for her led to the birth of a child and to a secret marriage; Fulbert took his revenge by having Abelard emasculated; whereupon Heloïse became a nun and Abelard a monk (*c.* 1118). In the monastery of St. Denis, he made himself unpopular by denouncing the worldliness prevailing there; and his success as a theologian prompted other theologians to probe his views on the Trinity. The council of Soissons (1121) ordered his first theological book to be burned and its author to retire to St. Médard. After returning to St. Denis, he fled to Provins because of the storm which he aroused by claiming that the traditional identification of St. Denis with Dionysius Areopagiticus was wrong. Soon he was allowed to found the community of the Paraclete (Le Paraclet, in the vicinity of Nogent-sur-Seine), which was later given to Heloïse and her nuns. As abbot of St. Gildas de Ruys in Brittany (1125–*c.* 1132), he struggled to rule over corrupted monks, who even tried to murder him. In 1136 John of Salisbury was his pupil on the Mont Ste. Geneviève. In 1140 or 1141 he was faced with a new and stronger attack, led by St. Bernard of Clairvaux (*q.v.*), against his theological doctrines. The council of Sens and the pope condemned him. He decided to appeal to Rome, but on his way there was persuaded by Peter of Cluny to submit to the verdict of the council and make peace with Bernard. From Cluny he passed to the priory of St. Marcel near Chalon-sur-Saône, where he died on April 21, 1142.

The mainspring of Abelard's thought and teaching was his optimism concerning the power of human reason to achieve true knowledge in the natural and supernatural spheres; unaided reason would not lead to "comprehension" of all truth accessible to man, but would "understand" much which is more directly and more completely available through faith. Thus pagan philosophers knew something about God's Trinity; and ancient philosophy (which Abelard knew almost exclusively through the evidence of the Fathers and from Cicero, Aristotle's *Categories* and *De Interpretatione*, a section of Plato's *Timaeus*, Porphyry's *Isagoge* and Boethius) provided sufficient evidence that God had also revealed himself, to some extent, outside Scripture, the incarnation and the church. Reason, philosophy and logic can still walk side by side with faith in the province of theology. The written words of Scripture and of the Fathers must be subjected to the scrutiny of reason; Scripture is God's work, produced through fallible men, transmitted by fallible scribes, interpreted by fallible apologists; language is liable to innumerable ambiguities and changeable. A healthy skepticism is a steppingstone to knowledge. Should the mind, however, find itself on the verge of an insoluble conflict, Abelard would rather reject Aristotle than St. Paul. The aim of his teaching and writing was to give a more logically argued foundation to Christian doctrine and thus to defeat the contemporary heresies or dangerous views of such thinkers as Roscelin and Gilbert de la Porrée, but St. Bernard, among others, saw in those methods the very source of heresy.

As a philosopher Abelard excelled in his study of the nature of abstraction and in his search for the source of responsibility in human actions. His inquiries into the problem of universals, far from crystallizing in a moderate nominalism or intellectualism, ranged from a critical survey of the opinions of other philosophers to an analysis of the functions—logical and grammatical—of universal words, to a research into the various levels of knowledge and to a metaphysical discussion on the similarities of things and on the relationship between God and universality in created things. His inquest into the components and aspects of human action made him conclude that intention is what makes an action good or bad, independently of its being performed or not.

A man enthusiastically devoted to the search for truth, intellectually self-centred, impetuous and uncompromising, Abelard stimulated and inspired large numbers of pupils, angered—and was feared by—many of his elders and provoked equally stubborn opponents, foremost of all St. Bernard, to fight him. The direct influence of his writings was limited; the indirect influence of his teaching has yet to be assessed. No other works of the early 12th century give as clear a picture as do Abelard's of that deep concern with a vast range of problems or of that critical attitude toward past and contemporary solutions which characterized the period. In his poetical compositions, particularly in his *Planctus,* Abelard also left a mark in the history of Latin metric.

Abelard's extant works may be divided among five groups: (1) theological writings; (2) philosophico-theological writings; (3) logical treatises; (4) letters; and (5) poetical compositions. To the first group belong the successive elaborations of his *Theologia,* namely, the *Theologia "Summi Boni"* (of which the so-called *De Unitate et Trinitate* is an incomplete text), the *Theologia Christiana* and the *Theologia "Scholarium"* (of which the so-called *Introductio ad Theologiam* is one of the five known recensions); the incomplete *Apologia; Sic et non* (a collection of apparently contrasting passages from the Fathers on various theological topics); the *Expositio in Hexaemeron* and the *Expositio in Epistolam ad Romanos;* the *Sermons;* and some shorter treatises. The second group comprises the *Scito te ipsum* (the *Ethica*) and the incomplete *Dialogus inter Philosophum, Judaeum et Christianum.* The logical treatises include short commentaries on some works by Aristotle, Porphyry and Boethius; longer commentaries (*Logica "Ingredientibus"* and *Logica "Nostrorum petitioni"*); the *Dialectica;* and possibly the *De intellectibus* and the *Sententiae.* The letters comprise his autobiography down to 1132 (*Historia Calamitatum*), five letters to Heloïse, a letter to St. Bernard and six other letters. The poetical compositions comprise hymns, sequences, the *Planctus* and the *Ad Astralabium filium.*

No complete edition of Abelard's works exists, and a few texts are unpublished. Collected works were edited by F. d'Amboise and A. Duchesne (1616); by Victor Cousin, *Ouvrages inédits* (1836), and, with Charles Jourdain, *Opera hactenus seorsim edita* (1849–59); and by J. P. Migne, in *Patrologia Latina,* clxxviii (1855). Editions of separate works include those of the *De Unitate et Trinitate* by R. Stölzle (1891); of the *Theologia "Summi Boni"* by H. Ostlender (1939); of the *Apologia* by P. Ruf and M. Grabmann, in *Sitzungsberichte der Bayerischen Akademie der Wissenschaften: Philos.-hist. Abt.* (1930); of *Sic et non* by E. L. T. Henke and G. S. Linderkohl (1851); of the *Logica "Ingredientibus"* (incompletely) and of the *Logica "Nostrorum petitioni,"* under the title *Peter Abelards philosophische Schriften,* by B. Geyer (1919–33); of the short commentaries and of the commentary on Boethius' *De Differentiis Topicis,* under the title *Scritti filosofici,* by M. Dal Pra (1954); of the *Dialectica* by

L. M. de Rijk (1956); of the *Historia Calamitatum* and other letters by J. T. Muckle, in *Mediaeval Studies,* xii, xv and xvii (1950–55); of the *Hymnarius* by G. M. Dreves (1891; also in *Analecta Liturgica Medii Aevi,* xlviii, 1905); of the *Planctus* by G. Vecchi (1951); and of the poem *Ad Astralabium* by B. Hauréau in *Notices et extraits,* xxxiv, 2, pp. 153–154 (1895).

There are English translations of the *Ethics* by J. R. McCallum (1935); of the *Letters to Heloïse* by C. K. Scott Moncrieff (1925; 1926); and of the *Historia Calamitatum* by J. T. Muckle (1954).

See also references under "Abelard, Peter" in the Index.

BIBLIOGRAPHY.—C. de Remusat, *Abélard* (1845); S. M. Deutsch, *Peter Abälard, ein kritischer Theologe* (1883); J. G. Sikes, *Peter Abailard* (1932); M. Grabmann, *Geschichte der scholastischen Methode,* ii (1911); P. Lasserre, *Un conflit religieux au XIIe siècle* (1930); J. Cottiaux, "La Conception de la théologie chez Abailard," *Revue d'histoire ecclésiastique,* xxviii (1932); J. R. McCallum, *Abelard's Christian Theology* (1949); E. Gilson, *Héloïse et Abélard,* 2nd ed. (1953). *See* also the introductions and studies appended to the editions by Cousin, Geyer, Ostlender and De Rijk. For additional literature *see* F. Überweg and B. Geyer, *Die patristische und scholastische Philosophie,* 11th ed. (1928); M. de Wulf, *History of Medieval Philosophy,* Eng. trans., vol. i (1954). (L. M.-Po.)

ABELL, SIR WESTCOTT STILE (1877–1961), British naval architect and engineer who did much to maintain the standards of British mercantile shipbuilding during and after World War I, was born on Jan. 16, 1877. After professional training at the Royal Naval colleges of Keyham and Greenwich and service in the admiralty as naval constructor, he was in 1910 appointed the first professor of naval architecture at Liverpool university, where he inaugurated a new course in that subject. From 1914 to 1928 he was chief ship surveyor, Lloyd's Register of Shipping, and greatly assisted the government's merchant shipbuilding program during World War I. Sir Westcott was created knight of the British Empire in 1920. Between 1928 and 1941, while professor of naval architecture at Armstrong college, Newcastle upon Tyne, he designed the Dover-Dunkirk ferry steamers. He was the author of several works on shipbuilding. He died on July 29, 1961.

ABENCERRAGES, a family or faction said to have been prominent in palace intrigues in the Moorish kingdom of Granada in the 15th century. The name seems to be derived from that of Yusuf ibn Sarraj, head of the tribe under Mohammed VIII of Granada. Ginés Pérez de Hita's romance, *Guerras civiles de Granada,* originally entitled *Historia de los bandos de los zegríes y Abencerrajes* (1595), celebrates the family's feud with the Zegris. A hall in the Alhambra (*q.v.*) is the reputed scene of the massacre of the family (*c.* 1485?). Chateaubriand's *Aventures du dernier Abencérage* (1826; new ed. with historical notes by P. Hazard and M. J. Durry, 1926) also has done much to preserve the name.

ABEOKUTA, town and capital of the province of that name of Western Region, Nigeria, Africa, lies on the east bank of the Ogun river, about 65 mi. N. of Lagos and 48 mi. W. of Ibadan, around a group of rocky outcrops about 600 ft. above sea level. The surrounding country is savanna.

The population at the 1963 census was 187,292. The inhabitants are of the Egba branch of the Yoruba (*q.v.*) and have four chiefs of whom the *alake* (king) of Abeokuta is *primus inter pares* ("first among equals").

In spite of the abundance of local stone from the the Aro quarries south of the town, which have supplied granite for much of the new building in Nigeria, the majority of the houses of Abeokuta are of pounded laterite mud with pan (metal) roofs. The more notable buildings include the Ake (residence of the *alake*), the Anglican church, the Centenary hall (1930) and Abeokuta grammar school.

There are six secondary schools, among them the Blaize memorial institute for handicraft training, founded in the early part of the 20th century.

Farming is the main occupation of the inhabitants and the town is a centre for palm kernels and cocoa. A traditional craft is the dyeing of cloth in Yoruba patterns and colours (especially blue). The women of the town have a strong organization for retail trade, of which they have a virtual monopoly.

Abeokuta is on the main railway from Lagos to the north and on the older trunk road from Lagos to Ibadan, now replaced for through traffic by the shorter road through Shagamu.

According to local tradition Abeokuta ("under stone") was first settled about 1830 by people from townships in Egba forest in the Ibadan area who fled when their homes were destroyed by slave raiders. Their association with the British crown developed after the arrival of Christian missionaries in 1842 (Abeokuta was for a long time the headquarters of the Yoruba mission), through one of whom in 1850 Queen Victoria presented them with two Bibles, in English and Arabic (since twice replaced by British sovereigns). They gave their co-operation in suppressing the slave trade which still persisted along the coast; and in 1893, through the intervention of the governor of the colony of Lagos, a united Egba government was formed to end local rivalries, and a treaty of friendship and commerce was concluded between the *alake* and the British sovereign. In 1914 the Egba kingdom came formally under British protection on the amalgamation of Northern and Southern Nigeria. *See also* NIGERIA. (W. H. I.)

ABERCORN, EARLS AND DUKES OF. The 1st earl of Abercorn, JAMES HAMILTON (*c.* 1575–1618), the eldest son of Claud Hamilton, Lord Paisley, and grandson of James, 2nd earl of Arran (*q.v.*), was probably born on Aug. 12, 1575. He gained favour with James VI of Scotland, who appointed him privy councilor (1598) and hereditary sheriff of Linlithgow (1600). He was created Lord Abercorn (1603), and in recognition of his support of a proposed union between Scotland and England was created earl of Abercorn, lord of Paisley, Hamilton, Mountcastle and Kilpatrick (1606). Later King James made him a privy councilor for Ireland (1615) and granted him estates in the barony of Strabane. He died at Monkton on March 23, 1618, and was succeeded by his eldest son JAMES (*c.* 1604–*c.* 1670), the 2nd earl.

The title of Abercorn, held by the head of the Hamilton family, became a marquisate in 1790 and a dukedom in 1868. JAMES (1811–1885), the 1st duke, was born in London on Jan. 21, 1811, and succeeded his grandfather JOHN JAMES (1756–1818), the 1st marquess. In the house of lords he consistently supported Tory policies and was by Conservative prime ministers appointed lord lieutenant of Ireland (1866–68 and 1874–76). He held strong views on Irish land problems and forced upon the Liberal government several amendments to the Irish land act of 1880. He also laboured to end religious discrimination in education and became in 1879 the first chancellor of the Royal University of Ireland. He died at Baronscourt, County Tyrone, on Oct. 31, 1885.

His son JAMES (1838–1913), the 2nd duke, was born at Brighton on Aug. 24, 1838. He became a member of the household of the prince of Wales (afterward Edward VII) and accompanied him on a visit to Russia in 1866. He was president of the Irish landlords' convention (1888) and opposed land purchase, although this was a Conservative policy; nevertheless after George Wyndham's act (1903) he was among the first to sell land to his tenants. He was a stalwart Unionist and opposed the Home Rule bill of 1912. He died in London on Jan. 3, 1913.

JAMES ALBERT EDWARD (1869–1953), the 3rd duke, was born on Nov. 30, 1869. Like his father and grandfather he supported the Unionist interest. After the passage of the Government of Ireland act (1921) he became a senator of Northern Ireland and served as governor from 1922 to 1945. He died in London on Sept. 12, 1953, and was succeeded by JAMES EDWARD (1904–), the 4th duke.

ABERCROMBIE, LASCELLES (1881–1938), English poet and critic whose work is distinguished by clarity, intellectual power and keen interest in structure and form. Born at Ashton-upon-Mersey, Cheshire, Jan. 9, 1881, he was educated at Malvern college and studied science at Manchester, 1900–02. He then became a journalist and began to write poetry. His first book, *Interludes and Poems* (1908), was followed by *Mary and the Bramble* (1910), a dramatic poem—*Deborah*—and *Emblems of Love* (1912) and prose *Speculative Dialogues* (1913). A leading member of the Georgian group of poets, he collaborated with John Drinkwater, Rupert Brooke and Wilfrid Gibson in the periodical *New Numbers* (1914). His chosen metres, the irregular choric ode

and blank verse, reflected his feeling for classical poetry, especially Greek, as did his increasing concern to establish a philosophy of poetry and his interest in prosody.

After World War I, Abercrombie began an academic career with his appointment to the first lectureship in poetry at Liverpool university. There, as professor of English literature at Leeds (1922–29) and London (1929–35), and as reader in English literature at Oxford (1935–38), he showed keen critical and philosophical powers. His critical works include *Thomas Hardy* (1912), *An Essay Towards a Theory of Art* (1922), *The Theory of Poetry* (1924) and *Poetry, Its Music and Meaning* (1932). His most mature poetic work, *The Sale of St. Thomas*, a poetic drama the first act of which appeared in 1911, was published in 1931. He died in London, Oct. 27, 1938.

Abercrombie's *Collected Poems* were published in 1930. A collection of lectures, *The Idea of Great Poetry* appeared in 1925. *See* also O. Elton, *Lascelles Abercrombie* (1939).

ABERCROMBY, SIR RALPH (1734–1801), British soldier, whose command restored discipline and prestige to the British army after the disastrous campaigns in the Low Countries between 1793 and 1799, and who prepared the way for the successful campaign against Napoleon in Egypt, was born on Oct. 7, 1734, at Tullibody, Clackmannanshire, Scot. He was educated at Rugby school and at Edinburgh and Leipzig universities, where he studied law. Preferring a military career, he entered the army as cornet in the 3rd dragoon guards in 1756, served in the Seven Years' War and was schooled in the methods of Frederick the Great. In 1774 he was elected member of parliament for Clackmannanshire in the Whig interest. His opposition to the American war impeded his professional advancement and, disgusted with politics, he went out of parliament in 1780. On the outbreak of war with France in 1793 he returned to the army and was appointed to the command of a brigade under the duke of York, for service in Flanders. Commanding the rear column, he had to protect the army in its retreat from Holland in the winter of 1794–95. Returning home, he was made a knight of the Bath and appointed to the command of the British forces in the West Indies, in which capacity he seized the French sugar islands. During his absence there he was re-elected to parliament for Clackmannanshire without a contest (1796), but resigned his seat in 1798. He commanded the troops in Ireland in 1797–98 but, finding all his efforts to tighten military discipline and to end the excesses of the militia were thwarted by the Irish government, he resigned the command and was at once appointed commander in chief in Scotland. He served under the duke of York in the second expedition to the Netherlands in 1799. In 1800 he was given the command of the troops in the Mediterranean. After the failure of a descent on Cadiz, he was ordered to Egypt to expel or destroy the army which Napoleon had left there in 1799. Landing at Abukir bay on March 8, 1801, he advanced toward Alexandria. A French attack before daybreak on March 21 was beaten back with heavy loss, but Abercromby was mortally wounded in the hour of victory. He died on board the flagship "Foudroyant" on March 28 and was buried at Malta. His widow was created Baroness Abercromby of Tullibody and Abukir Bay. Major General Hutchinson, who succeeded him in the command and quickly completed the reconquest of Egypt, wrote of him and his troops: "It was my fate to succeed such a man, who created such a spirit and established such discipline among them that little has been left for me to perform, except to follow his maxims and to endeavour to imitate his conduct."

See Lord Dunfermline, *Sir Ralph Abercromby K. B. 1793–1801*, a memoir published by Abercromby's third son (1861); Sir John Fortescue, *A History of the British Army*, vol. iv. part ii (1906). (A. AL.)

ABERDARE, HENRY AUSTIN BRUCE, 1ST BARON (1815–1895), British statesman, who was home secretary from 1868 to 1873 and lord president of the council from 1873 to 1874, was born at Duffryn, Aberdare, Glamorganshire, Wales, on April 16, 1815. Coal discovered on the Duffryn and Aberdare estates of the family made him a rich man, always prominent in Welsh affairs. Entering politics as a Liberal, Bruce represented Merthyr Tydfil from 1852 to 1868, and Renfrewshire from 1869 to 1873, when he became a peer. Efficient and conciliatory, he served under

Lord Palmerston and Lord John Russell, gaining a high reputation as undersecretary at the home office (1862–64) and vice-president of the council for education (1864–66). Until his death Aberdare took an active interest in social and economic questions. He presided over several royal commissions and was first chancellor of the University of Wales. From 1882, when he became chairman of the National African company (later the Royal Niger company), he was associated with developments in west Africa.

He was a lifelong ardent admirer of W. E. Gladstone who described him as "a heaven-born Home Secretary"; yet Gladstone's first administration was much damaged by Bruce's policies. The trade union legislation of 1871 was contradictory and generally unpopular. Bruce, a sincere churchman, came to be regarded by both Anglicans and Dissenters as evasive in ecclesiastical matters. Above all, his regulation of liquor licensing in 1872, an attempted compromise on a controversial topic, contributed significantly to the defeat of the Liberals, "borne down in a torrent of gin and beer," at the general election of 1874. Now a liability to his party, Aberdare retired from politics. He died in London on Feb. 25, 1895. (A. F. T.)

ABERDARE (ABERDÂR), an urban district in the Aberdare parliamentary division of Glamorgan, Wales, at the confluence of the Dar and Cynon (the latter being a tributary of the Taff), 23 mi. N.N.W. of Cardiff by road. Pop. (1961) 39,044. Area 23.7 sq.mi. The neighbouring moorlands show evidence of occupation in pre-Roman times. The parish church of St. John the Baptist dates from the 12th century. Aberdare has a fine public park.

The town remained but a small nucleus among the scattered farms of the moorlands until the beginning of the 19th century when it grew rapidly because of the abundance of its coal and iron ore, and the population of the whole parish (which was 1,486 in 1801) increased tenfold during the first half of the century. Ironworks were established at Llwydcoed and Abernant in 1799 and 1800 respectively, followed by others at Gadlys and Aberaman in 1827 and 1847. The building of the Glamorgan canal in 1811 connected these ironworks with the coast, but the railways superseded the canals and at the same time gave an impetus to the iron trade between 1820 and 1870. Previous to 1836, most of the coal mined in the parish was consumed locally, chiefly in the ironworks, but in that year the mining of steam coal for export was begun, pits were sunk in rapid succession and the coal trade, which at least since 1875 had been the chief support of the town, soon replaced the ironworks. Aberdare was severely affected by the depression of the 1930s. Some mines were abandoned, but others were modernized, while new fields and opencast sites were developed after 1945. There are several brickworks and breweries. After World War II many light industries were established in the vicinity, especially at Hirwaun. Cables, metal tubes and washing machines are made and a patent smokeless fuel is produced. A college of further education was opened at Cwmdare in 1955.

ABERDEEN, GEORGE HAMILTON-GORDON, 4TH EARL OF (1784–1860), British statesman, who was prime minister of the coalition government in office at the outbreak of the Crimean War, was born at Edinburgh, Scot., on Jan. 28, 1784. His parents both died before he was 12; his grandfather, the 3rd earl, who died in 1801, cared little for him, and he was brought up by his guardians William Pitt and Henry Dundas (later Viscount Melville). He was educated at Harrow and St. John's college, Cambridge. He traveled in southern Europe and the Levant during 1802–04, and made useful excavations at Ephesus and Athens (hence Byron's reference to "The travell'd Thane! Athenian Aberdeen"). In 1805 he married Catherine, daughter of the 1st marquess of Abercorn; they were ideally happy together, but she died of consumption in 1812, and none of her children lived to come of age. He wore mourning for her for the rest of his life.

In 1813 Viscount Castlereagh, then foreign secretary, appointed him special ambassador to Austria. For nine months Aberdeen was one of the central figures in European diplomacy, helping to form and to hold together the coalition that crushed Napoleon's power. He signed the treaty of Töplitz (Sept. 1813), was present at the battle of Leipzig (October) and at the congress of Châtillon, and signed the treaty of Paris on May 30, 1814. Castlereagh, who

thought him too lenient to the French, then took over all the principal negotiations himself, and Aberdeen retired. One of his brothers, Sir Alexander Gordon, aide-de-camp to the duke of Wellington, was killed at Waterloo. In July 1815 Aberdeen was remarried, to his first wife's sister-in-law Harriet, dowager viscountess Hamilton, who bore him five children and died in 1833.

Aberdeen devoted much time, thought and money to his large estates round Haddo house, Aberdeenshire; he planted numerous trees there, and greatly improved his tenants' conditions. In 1825 he persuaded parliament to pass the liberalizing Entail (Scotland) act. At Wellington's request, he became chancellor of the duchy of Lancaster in Jan. 1828, and in June took over the foreign secretaryship. He helped to settle the question of Greek independence, maintained neutrality in Portuguese affairs, and opposed France's designs on Algeria. Resigning in Nov. 1830, he did not again hold office for over a decade, except as secretary for war and the colonies in Sir Robert Peel's brief administration in 1834–35. Scottish church affairs much occupied him, and he strove without success to avert the disruption of 1843 (see SCOTLAND, CHURCH OF).

From Sept. 1841 to July 1846 he was again foreign secretary under Peel. The queen had confidence in him; his friendships with Metternich and Guizot, who became French foreign minister in Oct. 1840, and his pacific inclinations, helped him to do well. He established an effective entente with France, which survived a sharp quarrel over Tahiti in 1844, but not his own retirement. More importantly, he composed two long-standing boundary disputes with the United States, by the Webster-Ashburton treaty of 1842 and the Oregon treaty of 1846. He supported Peel in his corn law policy and resigned with him. On Peel's accidental death in 1850 he was acclaimed the leader of the Peelites.

They agreed with him in deploring Lord John Russell's Ecclesiastical Titles bill, introduced early in 1851, which forbade Roman Catholic bishops to use their territorial titles; but the measure was momentarily so popular that it prevented Aberdeen from accepting the queen's invitation to form a government on Russell's resignation that spring. In April he received Gladstone's ardent protests at the iniquities of the Bourbon regime in Naples, and took the matter up privately with Vienna; but the answer took so long to come that Gladstone published his *Letters* to him before it arrived, in July.

In Dec. 1852 Aberdeen succeeded in forming a coalition cabinet, composed of six Whigs, six Peelites and one Radical. The cabinet's harmony was almost entire, except for occasional notes of discord from Russell, who wanted to head it himself; and with Gladstone's celebrated first budget it had a successful year at home. Yet, during 1853, difficulties over the eastern question became so acute that war with Russia was unavoidable by the end of it. Public opinion in London forced war on a largely reluctant government. The prime minister, usually firm, upset Lord Clarendon, his foreign secretary, by vacillating. The two of them took a fatal step on Sept. 23; without consulting their colleagues, they ordered the fleet to Constantinople. The cabinet agreed, three months later, to send it into the Black sea; and the declaration of war that necessarily followed came in March 1854. At the time, Aberdeen could see no other step he could have taken; but in retrospect he felt himself responsible for the war. He never repaired a tumbledown church near Haddo; *I Chronicles* xxii, 7–8, David's account of his unwillingness to build the Temple, provided his reason. Aberdeen was ill-informed by the soldiers on the spot in the Crimea, but he was constitutionally responsible for their mistakes, and was driven from office by a strongly adverse vote of the commons in Jan. 1855. The queen created him a knight of the Garter on retirement. He lived on, an elder statesman and a Scottish patriarch, till his death in London on Dec. 14, 1860.

Though dour and stiff at first meeting, Aberdeen was a quick-witted man of great gentleness and sweetness of temper. Of singular uprightness and probity, he was almost too straightforward and naïve to tackle the diplomats and politicians of his day. He was a sincere lover of peace; the cries of the wounded at Leipzig never ceased to ring in his ears.

Of his sons, the eldest, George John James (1816–64), became the 5th earl, and the youngest, Arthur (1829–1912), a successful colonial governor, was created Lord Stanmore in 1893. His grandson, the 7th earl, was created marquess of Aberdeen and Temair in 1915.

BIBLIOGRAPHY.—Lord Stanmore, *The Earl of Aberdeen* (1893); Lady Frances Balfour, *Life,* 2 vol. (1923); H. W. V. Temperley, *England and the Near East: the Crimea* (1936). Aberdeen's papers (320 vol.) are in the British Museum. (M. R. D. F.)

ABERDEEN, a royal burgh, city and county of a city and the capital of Aberdeenshire (*q.v.*), Scot., is situated on a bay of the North sea between the rivers Dee and Don, 130½ mi. N.E. of Edinburgh by rail and 118 mi. by road and ferry. Pop. (1961) 185,379. It is the third city in Scotland and the chief seaport of the north of Scotland.

The City.—Aberdeen (Gaelic *Aber,* "mouth"; *deen,* "of the Dee") is called "the Granite city" from the gray granite of which it is largely built and which, gleaming in the sunshine, justifies the other popular name of "the Silver City by the Sea." The old market place (Castlegate), lying at the base of the Castle hill (this recalls the castle, which was demolished in the 14th century), has been a focal point of the burgh's activities since earliest times. Nearby are the oldest streets, dating from the 13th and 14th centuries. Union street, the principal thoroughfare (nearly a mile long) and King street, which were constructed early in the 19th century, form with Holburn street a main artery, 5 mi. in length, linking the Dee with the Don.

In the Castlegate stands the market cross (1686), an open-arched hexagonal structure, considered to be the most handsome of old crosses in Scotland. In the neighbourhood are three 17th-century houses, Wallace tower, Provost Skene's house (now a museum of local history) and Provost Ross's house. Behind a dignified granite façade in Union street stand the twin churches of St. Nicholas (the West, and the North and East), which occupy a building that until 1596, when it was divided, was the old parish church dedicated to the burgh's patron saint. The oldest parts of the structure are the transepts, which separate the two churches, and a small vaulted chapel (St. Mary's) built about 1430. The steeple above the transepts houses a carillon of 48 bells, the largest in Great Britain. The existing West church dates from 1755 (a famous Aberdeen architect, James Gibbs, was the designer) and its neighbour from 1838 (the work of another eminent Aberdonian, Archibald Simpson). In Old Aberdeen stand two pre-Reformation structures. One is the cathedral of St. Machar, built, partly of granite, between *c.* 1366 and 1530. Its heraldic ceiling is an interesting feature. The other, is the chapel of King's college with its stately Crown tower (1505). Within the chapel are exquisite examples of oak carving on stalls and choir screen, and there (as also in the cathedral) are to be seen beautiful stained-glass windows by Douglas Strachan, a native of the city. Two old bridges survive in Aberdeen: the Brig o' Balgownie, spanning the Don and built, it is said, by order of King Robert I about 1320; and the old Bridge of Dee, completed in 1527.

There are many handsome new granite buildings in the city, in both traditional and modern design. At the east end of Union street stand the imposing municipal buildings (with a main tower 200 ft. in height), which assumed their present form in 1868-74. In the charter room is a valuable collection of documents and relics. No other burgh in Scotland possesses so complete a record of its past. The council's records cover the burgh's activities from 1398 to date, with one break: vol. iii (1414-33) is missing. In Union street also are Trinity hall, the home since 1847 of the incorporated trades, the Music hall with a well-proportioned Grecian portico and, dominating the west end, Christ church (Divinity hall). In Broad street, on a site once occupied by Grey Friars, stands Marischal college, the largest granite building in Great Britain. Part of the existing structure was erected in 1844 (to the design of Archibald Simpson), and in 1893-1906 considerable alterations and additions were made, including a magnificent granite frontage (400 ft. in length) and the Mitchell hall with a lofty tower (235 ft.) named after the donor, an alumnus of the university. The Roman Catholic cathedral of St. Mary is in Huntly street. In an attractive setting in a residential district called Foresterhill are Aberdeen's main infirmary buildings, completed in 1936. The parks, recreational grounds and open spaces in the city total 2,185 ac.

History.—Aberdeen's recorded history goes back to the 12th century. The oldest extant charter is one granted by William the Lion (*c.* 1179) conferring trade privileges on the burgesses. The burgh supported Robert Bruce during his struggle for Scotland's freedom. By a charter dated 1319 he handed over to the burgesses (for a small yearly feu duty) the royal burgh itself and extensive lands adjoining it, but a large part of this valuable gift was alienated in the 16th century. The burgh was burned by the English in 1336. In 1638 Charles I acknowledged the support given to his religious policy in Aberdeen by granting a "Great Charter" amply confirming the burgh's ancient rights. In the wars of the 17th century between royalists and parliamentarians Aberdeen suffered severely, particularly in an attack on the city in Sept. 1644 by the marquis of Montrose, fighting then on the king's side. In 1715 and again in 1745 the Jacobite pretender to the throne was proclaimed king by his adherents at the market cross, but while in 1715 there was displayed in the city a measure of enthusiasm for the Stewart cause this had waned 30 years later. From the early 19th century Aberdeen grew in size and importance, and in 1891 large adjoining areas, including the two burghs of Woodside and Old Aberdeen, were incorporated in it.

The history of Old Aberdeen is bound up with that of the cathedral. Legend tells that St. Machar, a disciple of St. Columba, was instructed to build a church in the northeast of Scotland at a spot where a river took the form of a shepherd's crook. Not far from the sea the Don river assumed such a form and, in a tiny hamlet nearby, the church of St. Machar was built. In the 12th century the status of this Christian settlement was radically altered when it became the seat of the bishopric of Aberdeen founded by David I. Thereafter the cathedral of St. Machar dominated the life of what in old documents was called Aberdon, but later became known as Old Aberdeen (or Aulton). Charters granted by James IV in 1489 and 1498 created it "a free Burgh of Barony for ever," with the church as its superior. The administrative control of the church continued till some time after the Reformation. Till 1891 Old Aberdeen had its own council, provost, trade guilds, etc. Recalling its former independence there remain the old town house and, nearby, a fragment of the market cross.

From early times Aberdeen was prominent in cultural and other achievements. It claims as its son Scotland's first poet, John Barbour (*q.v.*), author of *The Brus.* The earliest mention of a "play" in Scotland is to be found in Aberdeen's records—a performance of *Halybluid* in 1440. George Jamesone (*c.* 1587–1644), the first Scottish painter of whom there is any record, was a native of the city. Among a large number of others whose fame spread far beyond their birthplace were Alexander Cruden (*q.v.*), author of the *Concordance of the Holy Scriptures* (1737), John Hill Burton (*q.v.*), the historian, William Dyce (*q.v.*), the painter, Mary Slessor (1848–1915), missionary in Africa, Sir George Reid (1841–1913), president of the Royal Scottish academy, and Sir Arthur Keith (*q.v.*), the anthropologist.

Education.—For more than 260 years there were two separate, autonomous universities in the northeast of Scotland within a mile of each other. Through the efforts of Bishop William Elphinstone (*q.v.*), Pope Alexander VI authorized, by a bull dated Feb. 10, 1494, the foundation of a university in Old Aberdeen, and King's college was built. From the beginning King's offered a course in medicine—the first recognition of this subject by a university in what was later to become Great Britain. The second university was Marischal college in the main burgh, founded in 1593 by George Keith, 5th earl marischal, as an essentially Protestant institution to offset the Catholicism that persisted at King's, which was under the influence of the stanch Roman Catholic, George, 6th earl of Huntly. From 1641 to 1661 King's and Marischal were united under the name of King Charles's university, but the union was merely formal (virtually no change took place in administration or policy) and it was not until 1860 that a complete union was effected. Other institutions of higher education are the Robert Gordon's technical college, the training college for teachers and (just outside the city) the North of Scotland College of Agriculture. Research work is carried out by the Marine laboratory and Torry station (fisheries), the Macaulay institute (soil) and (near the city) the Rowett institute (animal nutrition).

Of secondary schools the oldest is the grammar school, founded as the medieval burgh school. It occupies a handsome building in Scottish baronial style, opened in 1863. In the front quadrangle stands a statue of Lord Byron, who was a pupil there for a time. The only other old school is Robert Gordon's college, opened in 1750 as a "hospital" for the maintenance and education of "sons or grandsons of decayed Burgesses of Guild" of Aberdeen. The founder was an Aberdeen trader, Robert Gordon, who left his fortune of £10,000 to endow the institution. In 1881 the old "hospital" came to an end, its place being taken by the college, primarily a day school.

Communications, Commerce and Industries.—Not only has Aberdeen a good harbour and, at Dyce, 6 mi. N.N.W., its own airport, but it is also an important junction for rail and road communications between north and south. It is in fact the commercial capital of a large part of northern Scotland and, with its rich agricultural hinterland, is one of Scotland's largest livestock-selling centres.

The estuary of the Dee formed Aberdeen's first natural harbour, which was gradually improved in the course of the years. The construction of the North pier (1,200 ft.) in 1780 (on the advice of John Smeaton), the extending of this in the following century (after consultation with Thomas Telford), the completion of the South breakwater in 1878, etc., lessened the hazards of the navigation channel, while the building of quays, docks and warehouses and the diversion of the Dee into a new bed vastly improved the harbour facilities. The harbour can accommodate vessels drawing up to 27 ft. of water and is well provided with modern equipment. A dock bridge, opened in 1953, is of interest since it was the first aluminum-alloy bascule bridge to be constructed in Scotland. The harbour estate, administered by a board of commissioners, extends to 370 ac., of which 199 ac. comprise the water area. One valuable asset is the fish market (nearly half a mile in length with an average width of 52 ft.), which was opened in 1889 and considerably enlarged and modernized in the late 1920s. The trade of the port is extensive and links Aberdeen not only with other ports in Great Britain but also with the mainland of Europe (particularly Scandinavian, Baltic and Mediterranean countries), North and South America, Australia, etc.

Aberdeen owes its importance as the premier fishing port of Scotland and the third in Great Britain to the development of the steam-trawling industry. This was started in 1882 but is now being superseded by diesel-trawling. Linked with the fishing industry are ancillary trades, such as curing and ice manufacture. In the 19th century Aberdeen became famous for the construction of fast tea clippers (the best-known was probably the "Thermopylae") and, since iron replaced wood, its shipyards have launched trawlers, cargo vessels and tugs.

Since the middle of the 18th century granite has been quarried in Aberdeen (Rubislaw quarry is the main source) and, with other quarries in Aberdeenshire furnishing a plentiful supply of the stone, the city has become the largest centre of granite working in the United Kingdom, providing not only building material but also monumental work, sets for road paving, etc. Other industries include textile manufacturing (wool and linen), papermaking, engineering, the making of agricultural implements, plastics, paint, chemicals and fertilizers. Aberdeen has also become a popular holiday resort and it is the depot of the Highland brigade.

Administration.—The city returns two members to parliament. For local government it is divided into 12 wards, each returning 3 members to the council, on which also sits the dean of guild. The chairman of the council (and civic head) is designated lord provost.

BIBLIOGRAPHY.—J. Gordon, *A Description of Both Towns of Aberdeen* (with plan, written in 1661; pub. 1842); W. Orem, *A Description of the Chanonry in Old Aberdeen ... 1724 and 1725 etc.*, 3rd ed. (1830); W. Kennedy, *Annals of Aberdeen ...*, 2 vol. (1818); J. Robertson, *Book of Bon-Accord* (1839); J. Bruce, *Lives of Eminent Men of Aberdeen* (1841); E. Bain, *Merchant and Craft Guilds: a History of the Aberdeen Incorporated Trades* (1887); W. Robbie, *Aberdeen: Its Traditions and History* (1893); J. M. Bulloch, *A History of the University of Aberdeen 1495–1895* (1895); A. M. Munro, *Memorials of the Aldermen, Provosts and Lord Provosts of Aberdeen* (1897); E. H. B. Rodger, *Old Aberdeen* (1902); J. Milne, *Aberdeen* (1911); V. E. Clark, *Port of Aberdeen* (1921); H. C. Mackenzie, *The City of Aberdeen* (1953); Spalding Club (Aberdeen) publications and books, especially P. J. Anderson (*Charters and University*), H. F. M. Simpson (*Grammar School*), R. Anderson (*Gordon's College*), K. E. Trail (*Old Aberdeen*) and L. B. Taylor (*Council Letters*). (J. MH.)

ABERDEEN, a city of South Dakota, U.S., seat of Brown county, is located in the northeastern part of the state about 270 mi. W. by N. of Minneapolis, Minn. With more than 50 wholesale concerns in the city it is the financial and trading centre for a large wheat, corn, cattle and hog producing area extending into North Dakota.

Aberdeen's first settlers arrived in 1880 and the city, which was incorporated in 1882, has grown steadily since that time, exceeding 20,000 after mid-20th century. (For comparative population figures, *see* table in SOUTH DAKOTA: *Population*.) The state's early settlers were, for the most part, young men from the wooded areas of the east and, in smaller numbers, Scandinavians, Germans and Russians.

Northern State Teachers college, a four-year liberal arts and teacher-training college, was founded in Aberdeen in 1901. The largest teacher-training college in the state, it had an enrollment of more than 1,000 after mid-20th century. Presentation junior college, a Catholic school for girls, was founded there in 1951.

(M. G. Co.)

ABERDEEN, the largest city in Grays Harbor county, Wash., U.S., is located about 48 mi. W. of Olympia and Puget sound on the estuaries of the Chehalis, Wishkah and Hoquiam rivers which together make Grays harbour. It combines with its neighbouring communities of Hoquiam and Cosmopolis to form a single area of settlement.

Aberdeen is located just south of the wild areas of the Olympic peninsula and Olympic National park. The recreation facilities in the Olympic mountains, the Quinault Indian reservation and the nearby ocean beaches bring visitors from every state in the union. The foggy climate and heavy rainfall on the western slopes of the Olympics to the north promote the growth of vast stands of cedar, hemlock and Douglas fir. Although fishing is an important resource, Aberdeen's basic industry has always been lumbering. Many of its inhabitants are descendants of Finnish and Swedish immigrants who came to the region to work in the lumber camps and mills.

The site of Aberdeen was first visited by Capt. Robert Gray who came on the "Columbia" May 7, 1792. Gray named the bay Bulfinch harbour. Samuel Benn, a Scottish immigrant, established a cannery there in 1878 and platted the townsite in 1883. The population reached a peak of about 20,000 in 1930 and remained constant for the next three decades while that of the rest of the state increased about 81%. (For comparative population figures *see* table in WASHINGTON: *Population*.) Aberdeen is the home of Grays Harbor college, founded in 1930. (K. A. M.)

ABERDEENSHIRE, the sixth largest county in Scotland with a land area of 1971.4 sq.mi., projects shoulderlike into the North sea, bounded on the west by Banffshire and Inverness-shire, on the south by Perthshire, Angus and Kincardineshire. Pop. (1961) 298,503.

Physical Features.—Although the county lies north of the Highland boundary fault, it consists essentially of an agricultural lowland drained by rivers which flow generally in an easterly direction. This low coastal plateau rarely rises more than 400–600 ft. above sea level except where it is surmounted by resistant rock formations such as the quartzites of the Hill of Mormond in the northeast of Buchan or the outliers of the Highlands. Elsewhere it is a rolling countryside, wind-swept and almost devoid of trees except in sheltered situations. The gentle slopes are mantled with glacial debris and dissected by the melt-water channels of the ice sheets which converged from the Grampians, the Moray firth and Strathmore. Marshy wastes, peat bogs, lochans and infertile, often stony moorlands, penetrated by haughs or riverine lands along the Dee, Don, Deveron, Ugie and Ythan which were, and still are, liable to flooding, have been transformed by the plow and drainage to make the essentially agricultural landscape of today. Fertile raised beaches fringed with expanses of sand dunes alternate with magnificent cliffs cut in metamorphic and igneous rocks or Old Red Sandstone along the North sea and Moray firth to give an exposed coast broken only by small estuaries of which two, the Dee and Ythan, are navigable for a short distance inland.

The lowland of Buchan, and its southerly continuation in Formartine and Mar, terminates abruptly against the steep slopes of the Grampians (q.v.), which form a mountainous or upland rim to the west and south. From these heather-covered or cold stony wind-swept plateaus dissected by corries, which culminate in Ben Macdhui (4,296 ft.) and other peaks such as Braeriach, fingers of the Highlands spread north and east back into the lowlands while the valleys of Dee and Don and their tributaries bring lowland conditions far into the highland zone. These cultivated glens, straths or wider basins, such as the Howe of Cromar, Strathbogie, the Howe of Alford and the Garioch, offer a sharp contrast with the uninhabited peaty flat upland surfaces of the Hill of Fare, or the steep rocky slopes of Bennachie. Only at the southeastern and northwestern extremities is there easy connection with adjacent regions, although in the historical period the southern upland rim or Mounth was frequently crossed by glen and moorland routes which penetrate it from Strathmore in the south and from the Dee valley in the north.

The Old Red Sandstone rocks which probably once covered the whole area have been almost completely stripped away, except where preserved by down faulting, as in Strathbogie and in a belt between Turriff and the north coast, to reveal the underlying complex of igneous and metamorphic rocks. Although mainly composed of closely folded and faulted metamorphic rocks of the Dalradian series, with a Caledonian or north-northeast to south-southwest trend, the continuity is broken by masses of plutonic and hypabyssal intrusions, so that wide areas of gabbro and granite rocks occupy large parts of Aberdeenshire. These granites were formed both prior and subsequent to the folding of the main metamorphic rocks, and the Newer Granites such as the salmon pink variety from Peterhead, the gray of Aberdeen and the light-coloured rock from Kemnay have given rise to the important quarrying and polishing industries of the country. Over most of the lowlands and in the highland valleys, the solid geology is effectively masked by the deposits of the ice streams which invaded the district from the Cairngorms, the Moray firth and Strathmore, the latter leaving a characteristic belt of red clays and moraines with marginal channels along the coast as far north as Peterhead, covered in places by deposits of the valley glacier of the Dee. The salmon- and trout-bearing Dee, Don and other rivers have been diverted in many places, while lochs have been impounded by moraines as at Loch Kinord and Loch Davan on the Muir of Dinnet on Deeside.

Situated on the east of Scotland in the rain shadow of the Grampians, the climate of Aberdeenshire is generally dry with parts of the coastal strip receiving less than 25 in. of rain annually, but cold sea mists occasionally cover a narrow belt along the littoral and penetrate farther inland along the river valleys. Temperatures are warm for the latitude but exposure to cold winds from the north and east gives a somewhat harsh winter climate. High-level hill roads have been blocked with snow in June.

The subalpine vegetation on the highest summits and plateaus gives way at lower levels to heather moors, which are found also on the unreclaimed sections of the lowlands and on the older dunes along the coast. Elsewhere the natural vegetation of the lowlands has been modified by cultivation, except, for instance, on the sandy outwash deposits of the Dee valley which are still under forest. The fauna ranges from the eider ducks and waders of the nature reserve of Forvie, at the mouth of the muddy Ythan estuary, to the deer, mountain hares, golden eagles, grouse and snow buntings of the high Cairngorms. On the lowlands the development of agriculture has encouraged the growth of a vegetarian population, including hares and rabbits.   (K. W.)

History.—Some of the coastal stretches of the county and parts of lower Deeside have been occupied since Mesolithic times. One or two long cairns of the Neolithic period survive; but the effective colonization of the area dates from the settlement of the Beaker folk, coming direct from Holland at the commencement of the Bronze Age, about 2000–1800 B.C. To the latter part of this period belong the stone circles and round cairns in which the shire is so rich. A special type of stone circle, marked by a recumbent stone in the southwestern sector, is almost restricted to the area between Dee and Spey. The Iron Age is represented by numerous earth houses and a group of massive stone hill-forts—two of which, on Dunnideer and Tap o' Noth, are vitrified. At the dawn of history the county was occupied by Celtic tribes whom Ptolemy called Taixali. Later, Aberdeenshire formed part of the territories of the Northern Picts. Roman marching camps exist at Culter, Kintore and Ythan Wells. Christianity was introduced at an early period, and there were Celtic monasteries at various places, notably Old Deer and Monymusk. Early Christian sculptured stones of high artistic merit, many showing the mysterious Pictish symbolism, abound. Though the coast was exposed to Viking raids, definite traces of Scandinavian colonization are lacking; but with the advent of Anglo-Norman feudalism, sponsored by the Canmore dynasty, colonies of Flemings were introduced, by whom the wool trade was developed. Royal burghs were built at Aberdeen, Kintore and Inverurie, and were peopled mainly by English settlers. The great Celtic mormaorships of Mar and Buchan were in due course transformed into feudal earldoms (*see* MAR, EARLS OF; BUCHAN, EARLS OF). Gradually the old Celtic tongue became restricted to the upper parts of Deeside and Donside, and in the 20th century it became extinct in the county.

Aberdeenshire played its part in the long struggle between the rival houses of Canmore and Macbeth. It was at Lumphanan on Deeside that Macbeth (q.v.) fell in 1057, and his stepson Lulach, who continued the struggle, was killed next year at Essie in Strathbogie. During the Anglo-Norman penetration great families such as the Balliols, the Bruces and the Comyns obtained a footing in the shire. When the contested succession between these three houses resulted in the Scottish War of Independence, Edward I twice traversed the county, in 1296 and 1303; and a famous event was the heroic defence of Kildrummy castle in 1306. Robert Bruce's victory next year near Inverurie may be regarded as a turning point in the struggle, and was followed by the savage hership or wasting of the Comyn earldom of Buchan (*see* ROBERT I the Bruce). Another turning point was the victory of the nationalists at Culblean on Deeside in 1335. The triumph of Bruce resulted in the settlement of new families, among whom the Forbeses and the Gordons emerged as the principal rivals in the period of feudal strife during the 14th and 15th centuries. A deep mark was left upon the memory of after generations by the bloody battle of Harlaw (1411), in which Donald, lord of the Isles, seeking to enforce his claim to the earldom of Ross against the earl of Buchan, was defeated by Alexander Stewart, earl of Mar. Sir Alexander Forbes and Sir Alexander Seton of Gordon were created Baron Forbes and earl of Huntly respectively in 1445; and the struggle for power between these two families fills up the history of the next two centuries. Its bitterness was intensified by the fact that, in the main, the Forbeses accepted the Reformation, while the Gordons adhered to the ancient faith. Huntly castle, the chief seat of the Gordons, became in effect the Scottish headquarters of the counter-Reformation. A notable event in the struggle was the victory of the royal forces over the earl of Huntly at Corrichie on the Hill of Fare (1562) (*see* GORDON; HUNTLY [EARLS AND MARQUESSES OF]). During the Civil War of the 17th century Aberdeenshire emerged as a stronghold of royalism and episcopacy. The very first action of that war was known as the Trot of Turriff (1639). Inevitably the county was the scene of much fighting, notably the marquess of Montrose's victories in the royal cause at Aberdeen and Fyvie (1644) and Alford (1645). Aberdeenshire also witnessed some of the most agile marches and countermarches of John Graham of Claverhouse and Hugh Mackay during the Jacobite rising of 1689.

Meanwhile, trade with the low countries, the Hanseatic league, Prussia and Poland had flourished, and in the 17th century this laid the foundations of a new wealth among some of the ancient county families. The progress of learning is marked by the founding of three universities—King's college in Old Aberdeen (1494), Marischal college in the new town (1593) and the short-lived University of Fraserburgh (1597). The episcopacy of the northeast, more favourable to culture than was Calvinism, reached its fine flowering in the celebrated school of scholars known as the "Aberdeen Doctors"—scattered by the "club law" of the Covenant.

From 1690, after the Revolution settlement, more tranquil conditions prevailed. Yet local devotion to Jacobitism and episcopacy persisted and found vent in the risings of 1715 and 1745. It was at Braemar (q.v.) that the Stewart standard was raised in 1715, and later in that year James, the Old Pretender, landed at Peterhead. A brisk event in the 1745 rebellion was the Jacobite victory at Inverurie. Upon the collapse of this rebellion the penal laws destroyed the ascendancy of episcopalianism and the feudal power of the landowners, and paved the way for the ensuing era of agricultural and industrial progress.

The castles of Aberdeenshire range from Norman earthworks, like the Bass of Inverurie, the Peel of Lumphanan and the Doune of Invernochty, through the splendid royal stronghold of Kildrummy, to such fine Renaissance buildings as Huntly, Craigievar, Castle Fraser and Fyvie. Ecclesiastical architecture includes the Norman church of Monymusk and the remains of the Cistercian abbey of Deer. There are fine 16th-century sacrament houses, of a type peculiar to the northeast, at Kintore, Kinkell and Auchindoir. (W. D. S.)

Population and Administration.—The population in 1961 was 298,503, of whom 161,125 were in the Aberdeenshire portion of the city of Aberdeen (the small portion of the city south of the Dee is, for census purposes only, in Kincardineshire). The figures for the county were the lowest at any census since 1851 because of continued rural depopulation. The bulk of the rural population is found on the lowlands, where the larger towns such as Peterhead (12,497), Fraserburgh (10,462), Inverurie (5,152), Huntly (3,952) and Turriff (2,686) (qq.v.) are also situated. The supreme court of justiciary sits in Aberdeen to try cases from the counties of Aberdeen, Banff and Kincardine, while Aberdeenshire and Kincardineshire together return three members to parliament.

Agriculture, Industries and Communications.—The favourable environment of the lowlands has been intensively exploited since the re-organization of the economy and agricultural techniques which was completed by about 1850. Emphasis was laid on the rearing of beef cattle, especially the famous Aberdeen Angus (see CATTLE), in association with arable farming to provide fodder, with sheep also important in both highland and lowland areas. The cattle industry gathered momentum as communications with London and the industrial markets improved. Oats are the predominant crop, with turnips, swedes, potatoes, barley and sown grasses on the remaining cultivated acreage, which extends to an altitude of about 800 ft., varying locally with the degree of exposure. Dairying and pig and poultry keeping are increasing in importance with the establishment of a surplus milk conversion unit, a bacon factory and egg-grading stations. About two-thirds of the population depend on farming, practised principally on small farms and crofts, while the fishing industry is the second most important occupation.

The steam trawler, which caused the eclipse of numerous small fishing ports and gave the county town of Aberdeen pre-eminence as the Scottish centre for trawling and great-line fishing, making it the chief port for white fish, is itself on the decline. Its place is being taken by diesel trawlers which, although fewer in number, are much more efficient. Fresh fish is taken increasingly to the southern markets by road rather than by rail, while new techniques, such as fish freezing at the port, are being intensively employed. Fraserburgh and Peterhead, formerly most important as seasonal herring ports, now give increasing attention to white fishing using dual-purpose seine-net vessels. Stake nets for salmon fishing are found along many sections of the coast.

Auxiliary industries such as boxmaking, curing and kippering are important in each of the fishing ports and the food- and fish-canning factory at Peterhead is of especial interest. Shipbuilding is prominent in Aberdeen, where large coastal, ocean-going and fishing vessels are built, while smaller, principally wooden, fishing vessels are produced at Peterhead and Fraserburgh.

Although there are precision industries at Peterhead and Fraserburgh, where twist drills and pneumatic tools, respectively, are manufactured and give much-needed diversification of employment, industry is concentrated principally in Aberdeen and its vicinity and steps are being taken to increase industrial employment there. Papermaking is important along the lower reaches of the Don, newsprint and high-quality papers being produced from imported pulp, esparto grass and rags. Granite working, using local and imported stone, is concentrated in many small yards where monumental polished masonry, granite facings and blocks for constructional work are prepared. Engineering workshops, linen- and canvas-weaving factories, and paint, chemical and fertilizer industries are also found in Aberdeen, which acts as a market and distributing centre for most of the north of Scotland. Elsewhere in the county industries include distilling and forestry and a railway repair workshop at Inverurie.

J. ALLAN CASH

PASTURE LAND OF UPPER DEESIDE, ABERDEENSHIRE, WITH BALMORAL CASTLE IN THE BACKGROUND

The attractions of the coastal and mountain scenery bring increasing numbers of tourists while the association of the royal family with Balmoral castle (q.v.) and upper Deeside is well known. Winter sports in the Cairngorms are being encouraged by the construction of ski tows and huts, and hotels which formerly closed in the winter now remain open all the year round.

Guided by the relief features, the main road and rail communications enter the county at the southeastern and northwestern corners, and although there are roads through and over the mountain rim these are liable to be blocked by snow in the winter. Some local railway lines have been closed, but a system of bus routes connects rural districts with their market centres and with Aberdeen. Air services from Dyce airport near Aberdeen connect with all parts of the United Kingdom, including the Shetland and Orkney islands, while regular steamer services for passengers, freight and livestock operate from Aberdeen to the northern isles and the southern ports.

BIBLIOGRAPHY.—*A Scientific Survey of Aberdeen and District,* Report of the British Association for the Advancement of Science (1934); W. G. Ogg and A. Muir, *Land Utilisation Survey Report, Part 29, Aberdeenshire* (1946); H. H. Read, *The Grampian Highlands,* British Regional Geology (1948); W. D. Simpson, *The Province of Mar* (1943), *The Earldom of Mar* (1949); A. C. O'Dell and K. Walton, *The Highlands and Islands of Scotland* (1960). (K. W.)

ABERDOVEY (ABERDYFI, "mouth of the Dovey"), a small seaside town on the north side of the Dovey estuary, Merionethshire, Wales, lies 28 mi. N. of Aberystwyth. Pop. (1951) 1,262.

Its site has associations in Welsh folklore with coastal submergence (*see* CARDIGANSHIRE), and the song and legend of "The Bells of Aberdovey" are supposed to commemorate the inundation of the Lowland Hundred or Cantre'r Gwaelod (*c.* 520). During the 17th, 18th and 19th centuries Aberdovey had a considerable coasting and fishing trade and subsequently became a popular resort, because of its mild climate and pleasant scenery. It has a beach of firm sand which affords safe bathing, and there are excellent facilities for boating, fishing, golfing and rough shooting. The first Outward Bound Sea school for boys was established there in 1941.

ABERGAVENNY, a municipal borough and market town of Monmouthshire (*q.v.*), lies at the confluence of the Gavenny with the Usk, 15 mi. W. of Monmouth and 19 mi. W.N.W. of Merthyr Tydfil by road. Pop. (1961) 9,624. Area 3.7 sq.mi. Situated at the entrance of the pass between the Black mountains and the Brecon beacons, it is a popular tourist centre and a nodal point for roads joining England and Wales. It also lies on the main Newport-Hereford railway line.

Abergavenny (*Aber*, "mouth of river") was the Roman Gobannium, a legionary fortress guarding the road up the Usk. It grew under the Norman lords of Abergavenny and there are remains of its medieval walls and of the 11th-century castle built by Hamelin de Ballon or Baludin. He also founded the Benedictine mitred priory of St. Mary, the chapel of which later became the parish church. The town was frequently embroiled in the border warfare of the 12th and 13th centuries and was burned by Owen Glendower in 1404. At the dissolution of the priory part of its endowment went toward a free grammar school, founded in 1542, when the town received its first royal charter. Abergavenny showed strong royalist tendencies during the Civil War, when it suffered badly at the hands of Thomas Fairfax (1646), and in 1689 it lost its charter because of its Jacobite sympathies. The market was of consequence as early as 1200, but with the better roads and greater movement of the 18th and 19th centuries cattle and horse fairs became more important. Today trade is still largely agricultural, the cattle market being one of the largest in the south Wales area. In the 18th century Abergavenny was famous for its wigs and Welsh flannel; its present industries include iron founding, printing and the manufacture of machines and sweets (candies). Abergavenny was reincorporated in 1899 and its boundaries were extended in 1935.

ABERRATION (OF LIGHT). This is an astronomical phenomenon depending on the fact that light is not propagated instantaneously. Observations of the heavenly bodies are made from the earth, a planet whose speed of motion is not incomparably smaller than that of light; the result is that the apparent position of a star in the sky does not correspond to its true direction from the earth. It is customary to assume intuitively that a body is "where it is seen to be"; or, since the distance cannot always be judged, that at any rate it is in the direction in which it is seen. But actually vision gives only an indirect acquaintance with its position. That which affects the observer's eyes is the light which has traveled to him from the object; the circumstances of propagation of the light must therefore be taken into consideration. It is well known that a light ray changes direction in passing from one transparent medium to another, *e.g.*, water to air, and that its course is curved in a medium of varying density such as the earth's atmosphere; an object seen by these dislocated or curved rays is displaced from its correct position, and the corresponding correction for refraction by the earth's atmosphere is highly important in determining the positions of stars. The correction for aberration is also concerned with the propagation of light; it arises from the fact that an observer's actual judgment of the direction of a ray involves a combination of the earth's motion and the motion of the light.

The most elementary explanation can be given in terms of the old corpuscular theory of light—which was the theory accepted at the time aberration was discovered. If the ray of light be thought of as a stream of missiles proceeding from the star with a speed of 186,000 mi. per second, it is clear that the apparent direction from which the missiles come will be affected by the earth's

own velocity if that is not too insignificant in comparison. A common illustration is that of a man walking through a rainstorm with the drops falling vertically; the faster he walks, the more inclined is the position in which he must hold his umbrella to shield off the "missiles." The argument can be restated in terms of the wave theory of light without essential alteration; but reference should be made to an account of that theory for an explanation of the signification of "rays of light."

A rough way of aligning the direction of a star is to point a long, narrow tube so that the star can be seen through it. The alignment is given by the two apertures at the ends of the tube, which must be such that the small pencil of rays admitted through the one can make an exit through the other and thus reach the observer's eye (*see* diagram). The upper part of the diagram shows the rays of light coming from a star; the upper aperture E admits a narrow beam which continues in the original direction, so that F is the position in which the exit aperture has to be placed. Suppose that while the light travels the distance EF the earth moves through a distance GF; then the required direction of the tube is GE. It will then admit the light at E, and, by the time the light has traveled down the tube, the lower aperture will have reached the position F and the light will pass out. It will be seen that the tube GE does not point in the true direction of the star FE. The same principle applies when the tube is furnished with lenses, as in a telescope.

The alignment is the same whether the tube is long or short, and the relative proportions can be appreciated conveniently if EF is taken to be 186,000 mi. The light then takes 1 second to pass from E to F; and in 1 second the earth travels in its orbit $18\frac{1}{2}$ mi., represented by GF. Thus GF is $\frac{1}{10,000}$ of EF. The greatest possible angle between the observed direction and the true direction is $\frac{1}{10,000}$ of a radian, or more accurately 20.49″; this is called the constant of aberration. (For comparison the apparent radius of Jupiter is about 20″; so that [when the aberration is at maximum] the observer sees the centre of Jupiter when actually looking toward the edge of its disk.) As the direction of the earth's motion changes throughout the year so the direction of the aberration displacement of a star changes; the star is always displaced toward the "apex of the earth's way," *i.e.*, the point of the sky toward which the earth's motion is directed, which is a point on the ecliptic 90° behind the sun in longitude. The star apparently moves in an ellipse around its true position as centre, making a circuit once a year. For a star at the pole of the ecliptic this ellipse is a circle of radius 20.49″; for other parts of the sky the path may be regarded as a parallel circle which is projected into an ellipse by foreshortening. The major axis of the ellipse is always 40.94″, but the minor axis depends on the latitude (*i.e.*, distance from ecliptic) of the star.

Discovery of Aberration.—The discovery of the aberration of light in 1725 by James Bradley (1693–1762) is one of the most important in the whole domain of astronomy; and in pure physics it has provoked a succession of investigations culminating in the theory of relativity. It was entirely unexpected, and it was only by extraordinary perseverance and perspicuity that Bradley was able to explain the phenomenon in 1729. The discovery arose in the course of an attempt to discover whether the stars had appreciable parallaxes. The first authentic parallax was not measured until a century later, and it is now known that stellar parallaxes are less than a second of arc. Many observers had, however, claimed to have discovered such parallaxes. In 1680 Jean Picard in his *Voyage d'Uraniborg* stated, as the result of ten years' observations, that the pole star exhibited variations of position amounting to 40″ annually; some astronomers endeavoured to explain this by parallax, but the motion was at variance with that which parallax would occasion. John Flamsteed, from measurements in 1689 and succeeding years with his mural quadrant, concluded that the declination of the pole star was 40″ less in March than in September. Robert Hooke in 1674 concluded from his observations that γ Draconis was 23″ more northerly in July than in October.

When James Bradley and Samuel Molyneux entered this area of astronomical research in 1725 there was much uncertainty as to whether genuine stellar parallaxes had been detected or not; and it was with the intention of answering this question definitely that they erected a large telescope in Molyneux's house at Kew. They determined to reinvestigate γ Draconis, a star selected because it passed almost through the zenith in the latitude of London; its position would not therefore be affected by troublesome and uncertain corrections for refraction. The telescope constructed by George Graham (1673–1751), a celebrated instrument maker, was affixed to a vertical chimney stack; the eyepiece could be moved a little laterally by means of a screw so as to measure deviation from the vertical, which was fixed by a plumb line. The first observations were made on Dec. 3, 5, 11, and 12, 1725. On Dec. 17 Bradley found the star to be moving southward and confirmed this on Dec. 20. (The change of position in the north-south direction through aberration at this time of the year is rapid, and amounts to about 3.2″ in ten days.) γ Draconis was found to continue its southerly course until March when it was about 20″ south of the December position. By the middle of April it was apparent that it was returning north again. In September it reached its northerly limit, the extreme range between March and September being 40″.

Although the observers were seeking an apparent shift of the star, they immediately realized that what they had found could not be attributed to parallax. The maximum range of parallactic shift for γ Draconis should be between June and December. Aberration and parallax are easily distinguished by this three months' difference of phase; the displacement of a star due to aberration is always at right angles to that due to parallax. Bradley and Molyneux discussed several hypotheses in the hope of arriv-

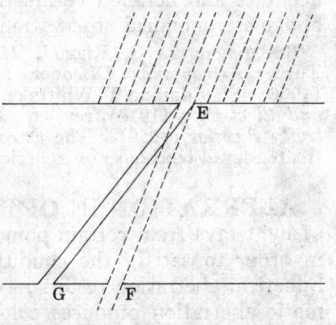

DETERMINING THE DIRECTION OF LIGHT FROM A STAR (*see* TEXT)

ing at an explanation. One hypothesis was that the direction of the earth's axis and therefore of the plumb line varied, causing an apparent displacement of the star when its position was measured with respect to the plumb line. Observations were therefore made of another star on the opposite side of the pole; from a comparison of its displacements with those of γ Draconis it was found that they could not be explained by a shift of the earth's axis. (The precaution, however, was fruitful, for by long-continued observation Bradley ultimately established that shifts due to a change of the earth's axis actually occurred; and he was led to his second famous discovery—nutation.) Bradley realized that observations of many more stars were required in order to determine the laws governing this mysterious effect of aberration. He therefore set up a more convenient telescope at the rectory at Wanstead, the residence of the widow of his uncle, James Pound, who had guided him in his early astronomical work. This telescope, erected in Aug. 1727, had a range of $6\frac{1}{4}°$ on each side of the zenith and thus covered a much larger area of the sky than the Kew instrument. Fifty stars were kept under close observation. Bradley disentangled from these observations the conclusion that a star had its extreme declinations at the times of the year when it passed through the zenith at 6 A.M. or 6 P.M.

The true theory of aberration was discovered by an accident reminiscent of the more apocryphal story of Newton and the apple tree. Sailing on the Thames, Bradley noticed the shifting of the vane on the mast as the boat altered its course; the shift was not due to unsteadiness of the wind but to the combining of the changing motion of the boat with the steady velocity of the wind. This suggested that the changing direction of the light ray from the star was the result of the combination of the changing motion of the earth with the steady velocity of the starlight. The finite velocity of light had been discovered by the Danish astronomer Ole Roemer 50 years earlier; Bradley's discovery enabled him to give a greatly improved value for this velocity.

Astronomical Effects.—In modern astronomy the aberration due to the earth's orbital motion is included along with precession and nutation as part of the "star correction" applied to reduce from apparent to mean place. A small correction is also applied for diurnal aberration arising from the motion of the observer caused by the diurnal rotation of the earth. For planets and comets a different procedure is adopted. It must be remembered that, even after allowing for the aberration, the body is seen not where it is now but where it was when the light left it (*see* fig.). Thus the corrected direction FE joins the position of the earth at the instant of observation of a planet to the position of the planet some minutes or hours before. Using the figure with a new connotation, let E be the planet when the light left it, and let F be the position of the earth when the light arrives. While the light travels from E to F the earth travels from G to F, so that the apparent direction of the planet GE is the actual direction joining the positions of the earth and planet at the time when the light left the planet. Accordingly there is no need to trouble about the hybrid direction FE. GE is accepted uncorrected, but a correction is applied to the time of observation, antedating it by the light time. This simple procedure is inapplicable to the stars whose light time is many years, because it assumes that the earth's velocity has been constant throughout the interval. But it answers a question often raised—whether a correction ought not to be applied on account of the aberration due to the motion of the whole solar system through space toward a point in the constellation Hercules. This motion, being uniform, admits of the above treatment; and the answer is that no correction is required provided it is understood that the observation relates to the state of things when the light left the star; the aberration rather helpfully "puts back the sun" to the earlier date which must in any case pertain to the star.

Since the velocity of light is known with great accuracy the observed value of the constant of aberration determines the earth's orbital velocity. This can also be calculated, when the radius of the earth's orbit is known, from observations of the solar parallax. There has long been a rivalry between the constant of aberration and the solar parallax as to which shall provide the more accurate determination; at present the degrees of accuracy seem to be about equal, and the two methods are in satisfactory accord.

Aberration, Ether and Relativity.—In the explanation of aberration, light was pictured as traveling in a straight line from the star uninfluenced by the motion of the earth carrying the observer. In the 19th-century picture of light as a wave train through a rarefied medium called the "ether," this would not be true if the ether in the earth's neighbourhood were carried along with it; for when the light reaches this moving region of the ether its course will be disturbed, the motion of the ether (if the phrase has any literal meaning) being superposed on the ordinary velocity of the light traversing it. According to the modern idea of the atom introduced by Ernest Rutherford (later Lord Rutherford) in 1911, the electrons and atomic nuclei are so minute that the ether can slip through the void interior of the atom as easily as through the solar system, and there is no longer any reason to anticipate a convection; but in the 19th century it seemed almost contrary to reason to imagine solid matter pushing its way through the etherial medium without serious disturbance. Apart from this prejudice, experimental evidence in the 19th century suggested that the ether in the lower part of the atmosphere was traveling with the earth, and, further, that moving matter such as a stream of water partially dragged the ether with it. Thus in 1818 the French scientist François Arago pointed out that the refraction by a prism (depending on the ratio of the velocities of light in air and glass) ought to be altered by the motion of the prism through the ether; since no such alteration was observed he concluded that the surrounding ether shared the motion of the prism. His co-worker A. J. Fresnel explained this effect by a "dragging coefficient," his hypothesis being that the "condensed" ether carrying the light inside the prism did not have the full motion of the prism but was only partially dragged in the same direction. This was apparently verified by A. H. L. Fizeau in 1851; he sent light in opposite directions around a circulating stream of water and thus studied its velocity with and against the current. In 1871 Sir George Airy performed his water-telescope experiment (originally suggested by the Italian Jesuit physicist Ruggiero Giuseppe Boscovich), in which he measured the constant of aberration with a telescope that had its tube filled with water. According to crude reasoning, the aberration should have been increased, since the velocity of light is less in water than in air; but the normal value was obtained. Fresnel had already predicted that there would be a compensation when account was taken of the alteration of refraction at the surface of the moving liquid.

When Fresnel's theory was taken into account, the conclusion seemed to emerge that the ether-drag was limited to the interior of the moving bodies, and that its effects were compensated by changes of refraction at the surface of the bodies, except when (as in Fizeau's experiment) differential motions were concerned. Thus the ether just outside the solid earth would be stagnant as the theory of aberration requires. But in 1887 the American physicists A. A. Michelson and E. W. Morley made a much more delicate attempt to detect the difference of velocity of the earth and surrounding ether (*see* Relativity: *Special Theory of Relativity*); this seemed to decide that the ether was carried with the earth. Thus the conflict between stagnant and convected ether was brought to a head, the former being demanded by astronomical aberration and the latter by the Michelson-Morley experiment and certain later experiments involving similar principles. A reconciliation was ultimately effected by the theoretical investigations of the Dutch physicist H. A. Lorentz and Sir Joseph Larmor. Their work showed that the electrical structure of matter involves an alteration of length of all material objects in the direction of their velocity through the ether, which would compensate the effect looked for in the Michelson-Morley experiment—confirming a suggestion originally made by George FitzGerald. When allowance is made for this contraction, none of the numerous experiments are capable of testing the relative motion of the earth and ether. The position just prior to 1905 could be summed up as follows: The earth moves through the stagnant ether without disturbing it, as the original explanation of astronomical aberration demands. The objection that bodies carried on the earth show no effects of this relative motion is of no value because in all experiments the effects are precisely compensated.

A more radical view of aberration—eliminating the ether from physical theory altogether—was put forward by Albert Einstein in 1905 in the special theory of relativity (*see* Relativity: *Special Theory of Relativity*), which asserts that the laws of nature, and the value of the speed of light in a vacuum, are the same for all observers in uniform relative motion. Einstein deduced from this that two such observers would measure slightly different time intervals and spatial distances along the direction of their relative motion, and that these time intervals and distances would be related by the Lorentz transformation. In the same paper, Einstein gave the relativistic theory of aberration, which leads to the same formula as the older theory provided that the velocities involved are much smaller than that of light; but with the essential difference from the older theory that only relative motions between observers are involved. The two observers in this case are terrestrial astronomers measuring the angular position of a particular star from the earth at two different points of the latter's annual orbit around the sun; the measured position of the star undergoes a shift in the direction of the relative motion between the terrestrial observers at different times of year. The resulting annual change in the star's apparent position in the sky is of exactly the same character, and for practical purposes of the same amount, as is given by the classical explanation discovered by Bradley. However, the change in direction is due to fundamental relationships between distances and times measured by observers in mutual relative motion, and is thus virtually unaffected by the presence of small local amounts of refracting material; *e.g.*, in Airy's water-filled telescope.

The constant relative motion between the solar system and individual stars naturally leads to no observable change in any angular position in relativity theory. However, an important effect still does arise when very high velocities are involved (as in the case of remote galaxies). Aberration necessitates a correction to the apparent brightnesses of the galaxies, because the angle subtended at the source of light by the light-receiving surface (such as the observer's eye or a telescope) appears smaller to an observer moving with the source than to one stationed on the earth; without this correction, the intrinsic brightness of a rapidly receding light source would be underestimated.

At the present time, the special theory of relativity has received such abundant confirmation from laboratory experiments that there is no longer any doubt that aberration is due to relative velocity, or rather to the differences in the earth's velocity at different times of year. According to current ideas, there is no all-pervading physical medium, such as the ether, which would transmit light rays at a certain velocity and thus make uniform motion through the medium detectable. In this connection it is of some interest to note that astronomical observations have shown that aberration is equal for observatories at sea level and at the tops of mountains, contrary to what could be expected if there were an ether which was, in addition, dragged along at the earth's surface, but was stagnant at greater heights. However, laboratory experiments showing the validity of the Lorentz transformation for the masses and lifetimes of atomic particles now provide much more accurate and detailed verifications of special relativity than the above astronomical observations.

Bibliography.—S. Rigaud, *Memoirs of Bradley* (1832); H. H. Turner, *Astronomical Discovery* (1904); J. Larmor, *Aether and Matter* (1900); Sir Edmond T. Whittaker, *A History of the Theories of Aether and Electricity* (1910), rev. ed., 3 vol. (1953); W. H. McCrea, *Relativity Physics* (1950). The astronomical application of aberration is treated in all textbooks on spherical astronomy.

(A. S. E.; B. E. J. P.)

ABERRATION IN OPTICAL SYSTEMS, the deviation of light rays from certain points through which they should pass in order to satisfy the conditions necessary for distinct focus. Spherical aberration results in distortion of the image, and chromatic aberration produces coloured fringes around an otherwise white image. *See* Optics; Microscope: *Simple Light Microscope*.

ABERTILLERY, an urban district in the Abertillery parliamentary division of Monmouthshire (*q.v.*), lies 22 mi. N.N.E. of Cardiff by road. Pop. (1961) 25,146. Area 10.1 sq.mi. It is a coal-mining town, with five collieries in the area, lying in the Ebbw Fach valley that runs south to Newport between two spurs of mountains. Formerly known for its stone quarries, it developed rapidly after the middle of the 19th century, the first coal mine being sunk at Cwmtillery about 1850, at which time the tin-plate works were already established.

Following the depression of the 1930s, a joint industrial development committee with the neighbouring towns of Brynmawr (Brecon), Nantyglo and Blaina (Monmouthshire) was formed and many factories were built in the valley.

ABERT RIM, a striking rock formation in south central Oregon, U.S., is one of the largest fault scarps in the world. (*See* also Fault.) The rim runs along the eastern edge of Abert lake for 19 mi., rising about 2,000 ft. above the lake, and has an 800-ft. lava cap ending in a sheer precipice.

Lieut. John Charles Frémont and his men discovered Abert rim and lake in Dec. 1843. Legend says that a party of Indians chased a wagon train of white people across the level plateau which slopes gradually from the east up to the summit of the rim, and drove them over the cliff. In the vicinity of Abert lake are found crude pictographs on rocks, rock foundations of dwellings of prehistoric people, arrowheads and skeletons.

Rhinoceros and camel fossil remains and those of many other animals have been found nearby.

ABERYSTWYTH, a municipal borough, seaside resort, university town and the county town of Cardiganshire, Wales, in the Cardigan parliamentary division. It stands on the shores of Cardigan bay, backed by hills, at the mouth of the artificially united Rheidol and Ystwyth rivers, 111 mi. N.N.W. of Cardiff by road. Pop. (1961) 10,427. Area 1.8 sq.mi. On Pen Dinas hill, south of the town, is one of the largest hilltop earthworks in central Wales. With the clearing of the lowland, Pen Dinas was superseded by Llanbadarn Fawr. Castell Aberystwyth—the most interesting of three Norman motte and bailey castles in the neighbourhood—stands above the bend of the Ystwyth and gave its name (*Aber*, "mouth of river") to the stone castle built about 1277–89 near the fishing village that grew up at the river mouths. The history of the castle was a troublesome one. It was finally captured by the English in 1407–08 and during the Civil War a mint was established there which was moved to Shrewsbury in 1642. In 1646 the castle surrendered to the parliamentarians and was destroyed. Restoration work was done on it in the 20th century. After about 1555 the fishing village of Llanbader was called Aberystwyth. Traces of the medieval town walls are still to be seen.

Aberystwyth shared in the mining (lead), agricultural and sea trade movements of the early 19th century and seems to have become at this time the social centre for the surrounding area. It has since gained favour as a summer holiday resort with its wide beaches of sand and shingle. The coming of the railways killed the coastal trade and the harbour is now little used. There are boatbuilding, brewing and mineral water works and the town is the centre for a large agricultural district. There is a plant-breeding station there. Aberystwyth became the site of the founder college of the University of Wales, founded in 1872 and incorporated by charter in 1889, and of the National Library of Wales, begun in 1911 and completed in 1955. The library, standing on a hill, has more than 1,000,000 books and thousands of manuscripts. In 1906 the Theological College of the Presbyterian Church of Wales was moved there from Trefecca.

Aberystwyth, whose first charter was granted in 1277, was incorporated in 1877. The Michaelmas fair (now called the November fair) and the Monday market (now for cattle), granted by the first charter, are still held.

ABETTOR, a law term implying one who is present, actually or constructively, and aids and abets another to commit an offense. An abettor differs from an accessory (*q.v.*) in that he must be present at the commission of the crime; all abettors (with certain exceptions) are principals in the second degree, and, in the absence of specific statutory provisions to the contrary, are punishable to the same extent as the actual perpetrator of the offense. *See* CRIMINAL LAW.

ABEYANCE, in law, is a state of expectancy with respect to property or title when ascertainment of the owner of a right must await the happening of some future event such as marriage or birth. If the next taker of an interest was unascertained at the time of the creation of the interest, strict common law rules required ascertainment prior to termination of a prior estate (*see* ESTATES, ADMINISTRATION OF); otherwise the title or seisin was in abeyance and the conveyance void (*see* REAL PROPERTY AND CONVEYANCING, LAWS OF). The term was also used in connection with offices and titles (*see* PEERAGE). (A. DM.)

ABGAR, the name of several kings of a dynasty that reigned in Osroene (*q.v.*) in Mesopotamia, with their capital at Edessa. According to legend, Abgar V, Ukkama ("the Black"), (4 B.C.– A.D. 50), afflicted with leprosy, had heard of Jesus' miracles, and wrote to Jesus acknowledging his divine mission, asking to be cured and inviting him to Edessa. Jesus wrote to him in reply that after the completion of his earthly mission he would send one of his disciples to heal the king. In its oldest form this legend emerges in Eusebius (*Ecclesiastical History*, i, 13), who claims that it had come into his possession from the archives of Edessa. A developed form of it exists in the *Doctrine of Addai*, a Syriac document that seems to contain some reflections of the primitive Christianity in Edessa. Jesus' reply to Abgar has long been used in the Syrian and Egyptian orient as a magic amulet.

It has been thought that the legend is an echo of the beginnings of Edessene Christianity, under Abgar IX (179–214). The view, however, that Abgar IX received the Christian faith, though popular, is doubtful. *The Book of the Laws of the Nations,* the earliest monument of Syriac literature, emanating from the traditions of Bardesanes (*q.v.*), says that when this Abgar became a believer he forbade castration. However, the words "became a believer" appear to be an interpolation caused by the Abgar legend. Eusebius quotes the same source *in extenso*, but these words do not appear in the text he used. *See also* EDESSA: *Edessene Christianity.*

BIBLIOGRAPHY.—G. Phillips (ed.), *The Doctrine of Addai* (1876); A. von Gutschmid, *Untersuchungen über die Geschichte des Königs- reiches Osroëne* (1887); L. J. Tixeront, *Les origines de l'église d'Édesse et la légende d'Abgar* (1888); W. Bauer, *Rechtgläubigkeit und Ketzerei im ältesten Christentum* (1934); A. Vööbus, *History of Asceticism in the Syrian Orient,* vol. i (1958). (AR. Vö.)

ABHDISHO BAR BERIKHA (EBEDJESUS; OF NISIBIS; d. 1318), was the last important writer among the Nestorians (*q.v.*). Abhdisho ("servant of Jesus") became bishop of Shiggar and Beth-Arbaye about 1285, and by 1291 was metropolitan of Nisibis and Armenia. Though few details of his life are known, a complete list of his writings prepared by Abhdisho himself is preserved. This includes some works no longer extant, such as his biblical commentary; 12 treatises on science, ecclesiastical decisions and canons, and another against heresies; and a commentary on a letter dealing with alchemy addressed to Alexander the Great allegedly from Aristotle. Among those extant are his *Marganitha* ("Pearl"), a theological treatise written in 1298 in five sections on God, the creation, the Christian life, the sacraments and the signs of the world to come, a work which may be regarded as a statement of Nestorian doctrine toward the end of its development. Parts of an Arabic translation of it made by Abhdisho in 1312 are cited by the historian 'Amr ibn Matta. The *Collection of Synodical Canons* or *Nomocanon* dealing with civil and ecclesiastical law depicts the organization of the Nestorian church in his day. His *Paradise of Eden,* 50 homilies published in 1291, is a metrical tour de force. The most cited of his works is his *Catalogue,* written in 1316, a list of titles covering the books of the Bible, Syriac translations of Greek fathers and works of Syrian fathers, chiefly Nestorian. It gives no information about dates or contents, but it does mention works otherwise unknown.

See A. Baumstark, *Geschichte der Syrischen Literatur,* pp. 323–325 (1922); J. B. Chabot, *Littérature syriaque,* pp. 139–141 (1934). (W. D. McH.)

ABHINAVAGUPTA (fl. A.D. 1014), an outstanding Indian philosopher, ascetic and writer on aesthetic theory, was a Kashmiri Brahman and a spiritual descendant of the 9th-century Kashmiri Somananda, founder of the "recognition" (pratyabhijna) school of Kashmiri Sivaist monism. Together with Somananda's disciple, Utpaladeva, he is the most important representative of this school. He conceived Siva, the I or consciousness, and the All as synonymous; and multiplicity or objectivity as an expression of the freedom and strength of the I which through it affirms and realizes itself precisely as I, consciousness or freedom. This concept of freedom (*svatantrya*) is one of the principal achievements of Kashmiri Sivaist thought. Abhinavagupta's chief philosophical works are the *Isvara-pratyabhijna-vimarsini* and the fuller *Isvara-pratyabhijna-vivriti-vimarsini.* The extensive *Tantra-aloka,* summarized by him in the *Tantra-sara,* is one of the most important works on Tantrism (*q.v.*). A beautiful and profound philosophico-religious work is his commentary on *Para-trimsika.* His most notable works upon aesthetics are his commentaries on the *Natyasastra* of Bharata, and on the *Dhvani-aloka* of Anandavardhana.

BIBLIOGRAPHY.—L. Silburn, introduction and French trans. of *Paramarthasara* (1957); R. Gnoli, *The Aesthetic Experience According to Abhinavagupta* (1956), introduction and Italian trans., *Tantrasara* (1961); K. C. Pandey, *Abhinavagupta* (1935), *Indian Aesthetics,* 2nd ed. (1959), Eng. trans. of *Isvara-pratyabhijna-vimarsini* in *Bhaskari,* vol. iii (1954); J. C. Chatterji, *Kasmir Saivism* (1914); L. D. Barnett, Eng. trans. of *Paramarthasara* in *J. R. Asiat. Soc.,* pp. 718–747 (1910). (R. GN.)

ABIATHAR, in the Old Testament, son of Ahimelech, priest of Nob. He alone escaped from the massacre carried out by Doeg. Fleeing to David, he remained with him throughout his wanderings and his reign. He was loyal through the rebellion of Absalom, but supported Adonijah against Solomon and was banished to Anathoth. He probably represents an early rival house to that of Zadok, the official priestly family of Jerusalem down to the exile. (*See* especially I Sam. xxii *et seq.*; II Sam. xv, xx; I Kings i, ii, iv.)

ABIDJAN, capital of the Ivory Coast, west Africa, stands on a promontory of the mainland shore, overlooking Ebrié lagoon and linked by bridge to its southern quarter on the island of Little Bassam. Pop. (1963 est.) 247,000. A village in 1898, it became capital of the colony in 1934. Its wide, shady avenues and gardened squares are flanked by modern buildings for the town hall, government offices, law courts, consulates and other public and private purposes. There are a *lycée*, a technical college, a theatre, and also a library and museum of ancient art under the direction of the Institut Français d'Afrique Noire. The town has an average temperature of 79.7° F. The beach, the forest of Banco, and the botanical gardens at the old capital of Bingerville to the east are popular resorts; there are three stadiums and two swimming pools.

Abidjan has been a rail terminus since 1904 but lacked port facilities, depending on the inadequate Port Bouet on the ocean shore of the sand bar south of the lagoon. But a long-cherished project of cutting the sand bar and linking the capital itself to the sea was consummated when the seaport of Abidjan was opened in 1951. The Houphouet-Boigny road-rail bridge, joining the mainland to Little Bassam, was opened to traffic in May 1958 and is a notable engineering achievement. The airport near Port Bouet, $10\frac{1}{2}$ mi. from the capital, is served by French and other airlines. Motorable roads run to Upper Volta, Guinea and Ghana.

Abidjan is a trading and commercial centre; its local industries include soap manufacture, canning, sawmills and breweries. Exports are coffee, cocoa, timber and bananas; imports include textiles, machinery, petroleum and food products.   (P. DU P.)

ABIETIC ACID is a constituent of the exudate (oleoresin) flowing from the incised trunks of conifers. Various species of pine may serve as a source, among them *Pinus abies* and *Pinus palustris*. Distillation of the exudate gives the volatile oil of turpentine, consisting largely of the monoterpenoid α-pinene and a residual resin known as rosin or colophony. This is rich in abietic acid, partly because of the oleoresin's original content and partly because other resin acids change to abietic acid during heat treatment. Abietic acid, a diterpenoid, is purified through the diamylamine salt and has the following formula:

If fresh oleoresin is allowed to stand at low temperatures, a crystalline mass of mixed acids known as galipot is formed. From this mixture some of the less stable resin acids can be obtained. Rosin is one of the cheapest large sources of organic acids. The sodium salt, a low-grade soap, is used as an emulsifying agent and as a size in paper-making. Since the rosin acids are highly susceptible to air oxidation, some of their heavy metal salts are used as driers for paints and varnishes. Rosin esters also are used in the paint industry. *See also* RESINS: *Oil-Soluble Resins;* ROSIN.
    (P. DE M.)

ABIGAIL (ABIGAL), in the Old Testament, the wife of Nabal the Carmelite of southern Judah, on whose death she became one of the earlier wives of David (I Sam. xxv). By her David had a son, whose name appears in the Hebrew of II Sam. iii, 3 as Chileab, in the Septuagint as Daluyah and in I Chron. iii, 1 as Daniel. The name Abigail also was borne by a sister of David's (I Chron. ii, 16 ff.). From the former (self-styled "handmaid"; I Sam. xxv, 25 ff.) is derived the 16th- and 17th-century colloquial use of the term for a waiting woman.

ABIJAH (Heb. ABIYYAH and ABIYYAHU, "Yah is father"), a name borne by nine different persons mentioned in the Old Testament, of whom the most noteworthy are the following. (1) The son and successor of Rehoboam, king of Judah (II Chron. xii, 16; xiii), reigned about two years (913–911 B.C.). The accounts of him in the books of Kings and Chronicles are very conflicting. The Chronicler says that he has drawn his facts from the Midrash (commentary) of the prophet Iddo. This is perhaps sufficient to explain the character of the narrative. (2) The second son of Samuel (I Sam. viii, 2; I Chron. vi, 28). He and his brother Joel judged at Beersheba. Their misconduct was made by the elders of Israel a pretext for demanding a king (I Sam. viii, 4). (3) A son of Jeroboam I, king of Israel; he died young (I Kings xiv,

1 ff., 17). (4) Head of the eighth order of priests (I Chron. xxiv, 10), the order to which Zacharias, the father of John the Baptist, belonged (Luke i, 5).

ABILDGAARD, NIKOLAJ ABRAHAM (1743–1809), Danish painter, was born in Copenhagen, Sept. 11, 1743, and studied in Rome during 1772–77. His style was classical, though with a romantic trend, and he had a remarkable sense of colour. He enjoyed great fame in his lifetime and taught at the Danish Royal Academy of Fine Arts, of which he became director in 1789. He died at Frederiksdal, Den., on June 4, 1809. Bertel Thorvaldsen was his pupil.   (S. Sz.)

ABILENE, a city of Kansas, U.S., located about 95 mi. W. of Topeka, was settled on the Smoky Hill river in 1858, and became the seat of Dickinson county in 1861.

In 1939 Abilene adopted a commission-manager form of city government. (For comparative population figures *see* table in KANSAS: *Population.*) Joseph McCoy (1837–1915), a cattle entrepreneur and later mayor of Abilene, selected Abilene for the northern terminus of the Texas cattle drives in 1867, the year the Kansas-Pacific railroad reached this point. The biggest year of cattle drives to Abilene over the Chisholm trail was 1870 when more than 5,000 cowboys driving 700,000 cows arrived at the yards. The appearance of homesteaders and fenced ranges discouraged the Texas cattle trade, much of which was diverted to Wichita. There is still a considerable trade in cattle, however, and grain and poultry markets are centred in the city. Flour and milk products are also important to the city's economy. The Eisenhower museum was opened in 1954 in Abilene, the boyhood home of the 34th president of the United States.   (D. P. G.)

ABILENE, a city of Texas, U.S., about 150 mi. W. of Fort Worth almost at the geographical centre of the state, is the seat of Taylor county. Named after Abilene, Kan., its site was determined by the route of the Texas and Pacific railway. On March 16, 1881, the first sale of building lots was held for the city of Abilene. The city adopted a council-manager form of government in 1947. Pop. (1960) 90,368; standard metropolitan statistical area (Jones and Taylor counties), 120,377. (For comparative population figures *see* table in TEXAS: *Population.*)

Abilene is the distributing centre for a farming and stock-raising region. Outside the city are many producing petroleum pools; natural gas is abundant. Abilene has more than 100 wholesale concerns and is headquarters for many oil companies and oil-well supply firms. Cottonseed and peanut products, feeds, pressed brick, dairy products, clothing, oil-field equipment, soap and watches are manufactured. The West Texas fair is held there. There are three denominational institutions of higher learning: Hardin-Simmons university (Baptist; 1891), Abilene Christian college (Church of Christ; 1906) and McMurry college (Methodist; 1922). The Abilene state school cares for and trains retarded pupils. Dyess air force base is located there.   (R. N. R.)

ABIMELECH (Hebrew for "the [divine] Father is King"), the name of two well-known Old Testament personalities, and a common west Semitic name known in various forms from extra-biblical documents.

1. ABIMELECH was a king of Gerar in south Palestine with whom Isaac had relations (Gen. xxvi). Isaac's dealings with Abimelech were a part of the common struggle over grazing and water rights during the period. The story of Isaac's representing his wife Rebekah to be his sister in order to facilitate his relations with Abimelech has its parallel in the story of Abraham's having declared Sarah to be his sister (Gen. xx); another close parallel appears in Gen. xii, telling of the pharaoh's having taken Sarah as his wife, believing her to be Abraham's sister. These stories are chiefly designed to show how God protected the people of the promise even when they lacked courage and faith. In the first two of these accounts, the foreigner Abimelech is represented to be more upright and ethically sensitive than are Isaac and Abraham.

2. ABIMELECH, a son of Jerubbaal or Gideon (*q.v.*) by his Shechemite concubine (Judg. viii, 31; ix). On the death of Gideon, Abimelech set himself to assert the authority which his father had earned, and through the influence of his mother's family won over the citizens of Shechem. Furnished with money from the treasury

of the temple of Baal-berith, he hired a band of followers and slew 70 (*cf.* II Kings x, 7) of his brethren at Ophrah, his father's home. Abimelech thus became king, and extended his authority over central Palestine. But his success was short-lived, and the subsequent discord between Abimelech and the Shechemites was regarded as a just reward for his atrocious massacre. Jotham, the only surviving son of Gideon, is reported to have denounced Abimelech to the Shechemites in a fable of the trees who desired a king to rule over them. Not one of the trees was willing to rule, but the bramble gladly accepted.

It has been supposed that this sharply negative attitude toward kingship belongs to a later period of Israelite life, after the prophetic denunciations of the kings of Israel and Judah. More probably, it represents a basic distrust of kingship characteristic of the 12-tribe system of Israel which, for a time, had its centre at or near the old Canaanite city of Shechem. The story of Abimelech's disastrous attempt to establish a kingship over Israel, culminating in his death at Thebez, reveals the importance of Shechem for the life of early Israel; it also indicates that the tribal confederation, despite its political weaknesses and disadvantages, would not yield easily to the monarchical system characteristic of Israel's neighbours. (W. HA.)

ABINGDON, a municipal borough of Berkshire, Eng., lies 7 mi. S. of Oxford and 20 mi. N. of Newbury, in the flat Thames valley where the small river Ock, draining the Vale of the White Horse, joins the Thames. Pop. (1961) 14,287. Area 2.7 sq.mi. The town grew up round a Benedictine abbey founded in 675 which, after being twice destroyed by the Danes, acquired great wealth and importance. The abbot controlled the town and despite serious riots in 1327 the townspeople did not gain local government until 1556 when, the abbey having been dissolved by Henry VIII, Mary I granted Abingdon its first charter, establishing it as a free borough corporate. Holders of the office of high steward have included Queen Elizabeth I's favourite, the earl of Leicester, and Edward Hyde, 1st earl of Clarendon, but after 1709 it became customary to appoint the successive earls of Lindsey and Abingdon. Abingdon was the county town from Tudor times until 1870.

Remains of the abbey comprise a beautiful Perpendicular gateway (the gatehouse now forms part of the guildhall); the Checker (*i.e.*, exchequer) with a vaulted undercroft and a rare chimney; the Long gallery, believed to have been a guesthouse; and the restored Checker hall, now used as an Elizabethan-style theatre. The arched bridge over the Thames (1416, widened 1929) gives fine views toward the old part of the town and the Early English tower and Perpendicular spire of St. Helen's church. This, having five aisles, is wider than it is long. In the churchyard are three sets of almshouses, the oldest erected in 1446. The guildhall (1440, with later additions), which has some fine portraits and plate, includes the Roysse schoolroom built in 1563. The county hall (1677) was for 200 years the assize hall of Berkshire and now houses a museum collection. Opposite is St. Nicholas' church, whose west front was built in 1180. Schools include Abingdon (Roysse's) school, which is one of the oldest public schools in England, and Radley college (1847).

A Thames-side resort, Abingdon is also a residential area for nearby establishments for research into atomic energy (Harwell) and petroleum. Its manufactures include automobiles, prestressed concrete, scientific instruments and leather products. There are also a large brewery and a substantial agricultural trade, a cattle market being held every Monday. The corporation owns, uniquely, fisheries in the Thames. Ancient customs still maintained are the Michaelmas fair in the main streets (on the Monday and Tuesday before Oct. 11), the Morris dance (*q.v.*) along Ock street (on the Saturday nearest June 19) and, on royal occasions, the throwing of 2,500 buns into the market place by the mayor and council from the roof of the county hall. (E. W. J. N.)

ABINGTON, FRANCES (FANNY) (née BARTON) (1737–1815), English actress, daughter of a private soldier named Barton, was first a flower girl (hence her later nickname, Nosegay Fan) and street singer. Employment by a French milliner gave her taste in dress and a knowledge of French that later stood her in good

stead. She first appeared on the stage at the Haymarket in 1755 as Miranda in *The Busybody*. In 1756 she joined the Drury Lane company but was overshadowed by Hannah Pritchard and Kitty Clive. After an unlucky marriage with her music master in 1759, she was known as Mrs. Abington. She spent five successful years in Ireland and was then invited by David Garrick to rejoin Drury Lane. There she remained for 18 years, creating many important roles, among which was Lady Teazle in *The School for Scandal* (1777). She was equally successful in drama, tragedy and comedy. In 1782 Mrs. Abington left Drury Lane and went to Covent Garden. She left the stage in 1790, returning for two years in 1797. Despite her humble origin, her wit, cleverness and ambition won her a place in society. She was a leader of fashion, and a headdress of hers called the "Abington cap" was very widely worn. She died on March 4, 1815. (W. J. M.-P.)

ABIOGENESIS: see BIOLOGY: *History: Biogenesis Versus Abiogenesis.*

ABIPÓN, a South American tribe of the Guaycuruan (*q.v.*) language family, which lived on the lower Bermejo river, in the Argentine Chaco. The Abipones acquired fame in anthropological literature because of the much-quoted description of their culture by a Jesuit missionary, Father Martin Dobrizhoffer (pub. in 1784; Eng. trans., *An Account of the Abipones, an Equestrian People of Paraguay*, 1822). These Indians—whose seminomadic bands lived on hunting, fishing, food-gathering and limited agriculture—obtained the horse in the 17th century and became the scourge of the Spanish settlements that they raided from the foothills of the Andes to the Paraná river. Their social structure combined the democratic features of primitive bands with incipient forms of a military aristocracy. Conjuration of spirits and spectacular recapture of lost souls by influential medicine men were the salient features of their simple ritualism. The Abipones were settled on various missions by the Jesuits in 1748 (the modern cities of Reconquista and Resistencia in the Argentine were former Abipón missions). Originally perhaps 5,000 strong, they vanished altogether as distinct people in the 19th century. (A. Mx.)

See A. Métraux, "Ethnography of the Chaca," in J. H. Steward (ed.), *Handbook of South American Indians,* vol. 1 (1963).

ABISHAG, in the Old Testament, the Shunammite nurse of David (*q.v.*) and last addition to David's harem. References to her occur in narratives relative to the close of David's reign, the coronation of Solomon and Solomon's establishment of his position as king (I Kings i, 3, 15–31; ii, 17, 21–22). Found as the result of a search for a beautiful young virgin, Abishag was brought to David's court to serve as nurse and bed mate for the aged king. In the latter role her function was to impart heat to the king's body and to restore his sexual potency. In the counterplot to have Solomon displace Adonijah, Abishag witnessed David's promise to Bathsheba that Solomon would succeed him. Abishag appears lastly as the favourite member of the harem that Solomon inherited from David. Abishag was requested as wife by Adonijah, who engaged Bathsheba to present his request to Solomon, whereupon Solomon had Adonijah murdered.

See Edith Deen, *All of the Women of the Bible* (1955). (C. B. Co.)

ABITIBI, a lake and river in Ontario, Canada. The name is an Algonkian Indian word descriptive of the lake's central location on an old canoe route halfway between Ottawa valley and Hudson bay. The lake, on the Ontario-Quebec boundary, is 55 mi. long and has an area of 350 sq.mi. It is shallow, island studded and a popular tourist area. The river, which flows northward 200 mi. to Moose river, is roughly paralleled by the Ontario Northland railway (Canadian National railways). It has a total length of 340 mi. The forested Abitibi valley is the location of an important pulp and paper industry. Power plants at Abitibi canyon, Island falls, Iroquois falls, and Twin falls provide 376,000 h.p. for northern mining developments. (F. A. CK.)

ABKHAZ AUTONOMOUS SOVIET SOCIALIST REPUBLIC (ABKHAZSKAYA AVTONOMNAYA SOVETSKAYA SOTSIALISTICHESKAYA RESPUBLIKA or ABKHASIA) is in northwestern Georgian S.S.R., U.S.S.R., between the Black sea and the crest of the greater Caucasus range (Bolshoi Kavkaz). Along the coast is a narrow lowland, broken by mountain spurs reaching almost to the sea, and widening to the southeast. Behind this lowland is a hilly foreland zone of eroded sea and river terraces, backed in turn by the steep slopes of the Caucasus, which rise to 13,254 ft. in Mt. Dombai-Ulgen. The sharp relief in close proximity to the sea gives Abkhazia a distinctive climate, the wettest in the U.S.S.R., with annual rainfalls of from 48 to 55 in. on the lowland to 80 in. on the slopes, where up to 120 in. have been recorded. Conditions on the lowland are subtropical and this is one of the few areas of the U.S.S.R. where January average temperatures remain above freezing point. The heavy rainfall gives rise to a large number of rivers, flowing usually in a southwesterly direction and subject to frequent floods during thawing and heavy downpours, while the subtropical climate leads to the formation of subtropical soils, yellow earths and terra rossa, bearing a luxuriant vegetation of more than 1,500 species. The forests of oak, beech and hornbeam which once covered all Abkhazia have been cleared from wide areas of the lowland and foreland zones. Higher up, the trees are mainly coniferous, giving way to meadow. At about 9,000 ft. the snow line occurs. Abkhazia, once the home of the Abkhaz tribe (in Abkhaz Apsua; in Greek Abasgoi) and part of the Roman empire, became Christian under Justinian (c. 550). In the 8th century, Leo, duke of the Abasgoi, formed the kingdom of Abasgia, independent of Byzantium and later part of Georgia. In 1463 the duchy became independent of Georgia only to come under the Ottoman empire in the 16th century when Islam replaced Christianity. In 1810 George I Sharvashidze, prince of Abkhazia, signed a treaty with Russia acknowledging a protectorate and in 1864 Abkhazia was annexed by Russia. The country proclaimed its autonomy in 1919 and was formed into an A.S.S.R. in 1921. The population of Abkhazia in 1959 was 400,000, of which approximately 37% (or 147,000) were urban dwellers. Most of the people are concentrated in the coastal lowland where the larger settlements are located—Sukhumi (q.v.), the capital, Ochamchire and a chain of resorts such as Gagra and Novy Afon (New Athos). The one large exception to a coastal location is the coal-mining town of Tkvarcheli in the Galidzga valley, which in 30 years has grown from a village of about 500 to a town of more than 28,000 inhabitants.

The agricultural economy of the country, thanks to the subtropical conditions, has an importance in the U.S.S.R. out of all proportion to its area. There is grown the best tobacco of the Soviet Union, particularly in the foreland zone, while the coastal zone is a major tea-producing region. There are 11 tea-processing plants. Other crops of importance are citrus fruits, although, since these have suffered greatly from the abnormal frosts of 1950 and the following years, special precautions are now taken, such as the use of gauze covers in winter. The tung tree, the nut of which is used for oil, is widely grown, while plantations of eucalyptus and bamboo add a characteristic element to the Abkhazian landscape. Orchards are numerous, not only of apples, pears, plums and cherries, but also of figs, medlars, quince and olives. The vine has been cultivated since ancient times, although the quality of the wine is not high. Silk is obtained in the lowland. Inland, on the higher areas, timber production is the major occupation, especially in the Bzyb and Kodori valleys. Beech and pine are the most common timbers. Coal was discovered at the end of the 19th century, but only since 1935 has it been mined, centred on Tkvarcheli. In the late 1950s nearly 1,500,000 tons were being produced annually, partly by the opencast process. The rivers are well suited to the production of hydroelectric power and several plants were built, the largest being at Sukhumi. The coastal resorts and the lovely Lake Ritsa are popular holiday and convalescent centres for people from all over the Soviet Union. The main line of communication is the railway along the coast, linking the major towns, with an electrified branch line to Tkvarcheli. Roads lead inland to Lake Ritsa and along the Kodori valley.

(R. A. F.)

ABLUTION, a religiously prescribed washing of part or all of the human body, or of possessions such as clothing or ceremonial objects, with the intent of purification or dedication (Lat. *ablutio,* from *abluere,* "to wash off"). Water, or water with salt or some other traditional ingredient, is most commonly used, but washing with blood is not uncommon in the history of religions, and urine of the sacred cow has been used in India. The devout Shintoist rinses his hands and mouth with water before he approaches a shrine (*haiden*) and prepares to clap his hands to draw the attention of the divine (*kami*) to his devotions. The monk of the southern Buddhist (Theravada) tradition washes himself in the monastery pool as he prepares to honour in his meditations an enshrined relic or image of the Buddha. The upper-caste Hindu bathes ceremonially in water before performing his daily morning worship (*puja*) in his home. The Jewish family that does not have a separate set of ritual dishes and glassware for the Passover meal (Seder) may take the traditional course of preparing such dishes by dipping in boiling water; at the same meal the family uses pitcher and towel for hand ablutions. The Roman Catholic priest (and priests of some Orthodox churches) celebrating the Mass prepares himself by ritual washing of his hands in the lavabo (a ceremonial basin); after the offertory of the sacred elements there is a ritual washing of the fingers. Seven days after baptism those newly baptized in Eastern Orthodox churches often go through a ceremony in which holy oil is washed from the forehead. In some of the Brethren sects in rural United States ceremonial foot washing is performed on stated occasions, continuing in Protestant life what was centuries ago common in Christian piety as a response to the gospel story of Jesus' washing his disciples' feet (John xiii, 1–15) and to the Pastoral epistle's description of upright widows as having "washed the feet of the saints" (I Tim. v, 10). In Muslim piety it is required that the devout wash their hands, feet and face before each of the five daily prayers; however, in keeping with the koranic claim that God does not desire needless suffering for believers, the use of sand is permitted in place of water where desert conditions make water difficult or impossible of access.

The Jewish Torah (Mosaic law, embodied in the Pentateuch) contains numerous examples of ablution. At this period of history ablution is only one of many methods for catharsis (*see* PURIFICATION) of the dangerous "charge" that was felt by Semitic peoples—as by the Greeks, Romans, Babylonians, Egyptians, Chinese and many primitive peoples—to be associated with death and corpses, women in childbirth, menstruating women, male nocturnal emissions, violent acts and booty of battle, certain diseases, initiation to high office, performance of priestly rites, etc.

Like most ritual acts, ablution may carry a wide range of meanings to those who perform it. The stain of ritual uncleanness may be felt to be as real as contamination with unseen germs is for the medically minded, and as productive of suffering and misfortune; or the act of cleansing may be only a gesture, symbolic of desired purity of soul, as Thomas Aquinas thought of ablution in the Mass. Probably both objective and subjective referents are often fused in the act, as C. G. Jung and others have suggested in studies of unconscious elements in religious symbolism. The cleansing often is sought in a perfunctory way. But it may also be sought as a matter of gripping holy (numinous) concern, as Rudolf Otto suggested in his analysis of such ritual elements as chants, art and sacrifices. Such concern, compounded of inarticulate awe and adoration, may have no ethical or rational content, as any review of the varieties of ablution will confirm. Yet, as Otto and others have shown, the irrational sense of the holy in such acts as ablution often serves as a vital background upon which worship may develop its profoundest rational and ethical content.

BIBLIOGRAPHY.—Geradus van der Leeuw, *Religion in Essence and Manifestation* (1938); Rudolf Otto, *The Idea of the Holy* (1925); *The Encyclopedia of Religion and Ethics* (1908); *The Jewish Encyclopedia* (1930); and statements about their worship by representatives of several religions in Kenneth Morgan (ed.), *The Religion of the Hindus* (1953), *The Path of the Buddha* (1956), *Islam, The Straight Path* (1958), with bibliographies in each volume; C. G. Jung, *Collected Works,* "Bollingen Series 20" (1953–).   (HA. H. B.)

ABNAKI (ABENAKI) designates a confederacy of Algonkian-speaking Indian tribes in northeast North America, which was organized to furnish resistance and protection against the warring encroachments of members of the Iroquois league of northern New York state, especially the Mohawk. In its earliest organization it consisted of tribes east and northeast of New York: Maliseet (Malecite) in New Brunswick; Passamaquoddy, a segment from the Maliseet; Penobscot in Maine; and tribes in Vermont and New Hampshire. Later it included some eastern tribes as far south as the Delaware tribe. Some agriculture was practised throughout the coastal region, more intensively from north to south. In the northern portion the typical dwelling was the birch-bark covered wigwam. The birch-bark canoe was in general use. Game was taken in snares and traps and by bow and arrow. Each tribe consisted of small bands under a head man or chief who had little compulsory authority. There was institutionalized comradeship with mutual responsibility, which united two men for life. Belief in a culture hero who will return to help the people in time of great need persists to the present. The population in the 1960s, including so-called Abenaki groups in Canada, was about 5,000.

See F. W. Hodge (ed.), *Handbook of American Indians North of Mexico* (1959); K. Hill, *Glooscap and His Magic* (1963).
(W. D. Wa.)

ABNER, in the Old Testament, Saul's cousin and commander in chief, comes into prominence only after the crushing defeat of Israel at Mt. Gilboa. This battle placed the Philistines in control of the whole of central Palestine, and the weakness of Israel was enhanced by the division into two parties, that of the south, which followed David, and that of Trans-Jordan, which remained faithful to Ishbosheth, the son who succeeded Saul. Ishbosheth himself, however, was a weak character, and the whole strength of the party was concentrated in Abner. The struggle between the two parties was continuous, and in the battle of Gibeon Abner killed Asahel, brother of Joab, thus exposing himself to the blood-vengeance of the dead man's whole family. It seems that Abner aspired to become the sole leader of his party and, as a step in the achievement of his aim, married Rizpah, one of the concubines of Saul. For this he was reproved by Ishbosheth and thereupon deserted to the opposite party. An agreement was made between David and Abner, by which David had restored to him Michal, daughter of Saul, thus establishing a claim on Saul's throne, and Abner was received into favour. Joab, however, in obedience to the binding law of blood-revenge, took an opportunity of putting Abner to death, and his disappearance practically brought to an end the resistance of the eastern party. David, of course, was not implicated in Abner's death, and his short dirge over the body, like that over Saul and Jonathan, is an exquisite specimen of the early poetry of Israel. See chiefly II Sam. ii. iii. iv.

ABNEY, SIR WILLIAM DE WIVELESLIE (1843–1920), English chemist, is best known for research on colour measurement and mixture and on photographic processes. He was born in Derby, July 24, 1843. He was educated at Rossall school and in 1861 obtained a commission in the royal engineers through the Royal Military academy. He was appointed instructor in chemistry and photography at the school of military engineering at Chatham and in 1874 was placed in charge when the department was made a separate school. In 1877 he entered the science and art department at South Kensington where he was appointed director in 1893. In 1899 he was made principal assistant secretary to the board of education. After his retirement from this position in 1903, he served as scientific adviser to the board.

Abney invented gelatino-chloride, or printing-out paper, and discovered the developing power of hydroquinone and the "failure of the reciprocity law." He made the earliest measurements of the relation of the transparency of a photographic image to the exposure and prepared red-sensitive plates, with which he made many observations in the red and infrared regions of the spectrum.

In 1900 he was made knight commander of the Bath. He was elected fellow of the Royal society in 1876. In 1882 the Royal society awarded him the Rumford medal for his work on spectrum analysis. He was president of the Royal Astronomical society from 1893 to 1895, of the Physical society from 1895 to 1897, of the Royal Photographic society from 1892 to 1894, in 1896, and for 1903 to 1905. He received the Royal Photographic society's progress medal in 1878 and 1890. Abney died in Folkestone, Kent, Dec. 3, 1920. (C. E. K. M.)

ABO: see TURKU.

ABODE: see DOMICILE AND RESIDENCE.

ABOLITIONIST, an advocate of the abolition of slavery. The term as used in the United States referred specifically to those persons who, during the years 1830–61, made it their mission to advocate the immediate abolition of Negro slavery. In spite of riots, assaults and persecutions of every kind, they carried on their task by means of the press, tracts, lectures and petitions to congress. Among the outstanding leaders of the abolitionist movement were William Lloyd Garrison, Wendell Phillips, Lucretia Mott and John Brown. See SLAVERY.

ABOLITION MOVEMENT, a movement primarily in Britain, the United States and western Europe, between about 1783 and 1888, to abolish the international slave trade and the institution of chattel slavery.

After Roman slavery was gradually converted into serfdom, slavery was virtually unknown in western Europe until 1442, when the Portuguese began to bring back Negro slaves from their explorations along the west coast of Africa. Soon after, the need for labour in the colonies of North and South America created an immense market for slaves. Consequently, a vast trade sprang up and flourished for more than three centuries, being dominated in turn by Portugal, Spain, Holland, France and England. Altogether probably more than 15,000,000 slaves were transported, and prior to 1800 far more African slaves than English or European colonists crossed the Atlantic—mostly to the West Indies and South America.

Despite its severity and inhumanity, the slave system aroused little protest until the 18th century. Rational thinkers of the Enlightenment then began to criticize it for its violation of the rights of man, and pietistic or evangelical religious groups condemned it for its unchristian and brutal qualities. In Britain and America, the Quakers, who began their criticism in 1671, were the first significant opponents of slavery, and the dynamics of the antislavery movement were largely religious throughout. Consequently the leaders were always more concerned with ending the sin of slavery than with finding a constructive social policy for the slaves. In France, where the Société des Amis des Noirs was founded in 1788, the rational factor was stronger than the evangelical.

By the late 18th century moral disapproval of slavery was widespread and antislavery reformers gained a number of deceptively easy victories. In Britain, Granville Sharp, working almost alone, secured a decision in the Somersett case (1772) that West Indian planters could not hold slaves in England, since slavery was contrary to English law. In America leading figures of the revolutionary period, such as Washington, Jefferson and Franklin, condemned slavery unequivocally. Between 1777 and 1804 all of the states north of Maryland abolished it—some by gradual, others by immediate action. Meanwhile, in the south, numerous and vigorous antislavery societies enjoyed considerable success in persuading owners to manumit their slaves voluntarily.

These victories, however, had little effect upon the centres of slavery, the great plantations of the deep south, the West Indies and South America. The antislavery movement, therefore, slowly turned to the problem of slavery in these areas, and as it did so, it passed through three major phases.

The first phase involved British and American efforts to prohibit the importation of African slaves into the British colonies and the United States. English Quakers began actively to campaign for such a prohibition in 1783. In 1787 the Abolition society, consisting mostly of Quakers, was formed. Under William Wilberforce (*q.v.*), who led the movement in parliament, and Thomas Clarkson (*q.v.*), who devoted many years to the tireless collection of evidence concerning the evils of the trade, the antislavery forces waged an unremitting contest against extremely powerful opposition. After two decades the trade to the British colonies was abolished in 1807.

Meanwhile in the United States, the Constitutional Convention in 1787 had considered placing in the constitution a prohibition of the trade, but in order to conciliate southern interests which opposed immediate action the convention agreed to a provision that congress might prohibit the trade after 20 years. Accordingly, in 1807 the United States also prohibited it.

Antislavery men had hoped that when the supply of new slaves was stopped, slavery itself would gradually wither away. But this did not follow, and in its second phase abolitionism concentrated upon the emancipation of populations already in slavery. In Britain antislavery leaders organized the Anti-Slavery society in 1823, made Thomas Fowell Buxton (q.v.) their parliamentary leader in place of the aging Wilberforce and, after another prolonged and dramatic contest, finally succeeded in 1833 in passing a law to free all slaves in the British colonies after a six-year period of apprenticeship, with compensation to their owners. In 1848 France also abolished slavery in its West Indian colonies. This was France's second attempt, for the French revolutionists in 1794 had proclaimed emancipation but the internal struggle over this question in Haiti had led to bloody and violent uprisings. During a vain attempt to restore French control of the island, Napoleon re-established slavery (1802), and it continued in other French colonies until 1848.

The British abolition movement had a deep influence in the United States. As the cotton economy developed, slavery gained new vigour and the south began to defend slavery in positive terms. Discouraged by these developments and disappointed by the limited results of their appeals to gradualism and persuasion and their attempts to colonize free Negroes in Liberia, U.S. antislavery men turned, about 1830, to a more militant policy. Denouncing all slaveholders, they demanded immediate abolition by law. In this aggressive program the most conspicuous and most extreme leader was William Lloyd Garrison (q.v.), editor of the Liberator (1831) and founder of the American Anti-Slavery society (1833). But Garrison's actual following was small, and it is quite possible that a greater influence was exercised by the burning evangelist Theodore Dwight Weld, who with his "Seventy apostles" carried the gospel of antislavery to pulpits throughout the north. Also, the activity of free Negroes, of whom Frederick Douglass (q.v.) was the most important, is not to be underestimated.

U.S. abolitionism laboured under the handicap that it threatened the harmony of north and south in the union, and it ran counter to the constitution, which left the question of slavery to the individual states. Therefore the northern public remained unwilling to adopt abolitionist policy and distrustful of abolitionist extremism, as illustrated by John Brown's raid at Harpers Ferry (1859). Even when convinced of the evil of slavery as they were by Harriet Beecher Stowe's Uncle Tom's Cabin (1852), most northerners rejected abolitionism. But they were prepared to resist the spread of slavery into new territories. The election of Abraham Lincoln as president on this issue in 1860 led to the secession of the southern states and to the Civil War (1861–65). The war, in turn, led Lincoln, who had never been an abolitionist, to emancipate the slaves in areas in rebellion (1863), and led further to the freeing of all other slaves by the 13th amendment to the constitution in 1865.

Meanwhile, the third phase of the abolition movement had already begun as Britain took the lead in efforts to break up the remaining slave trade. All leading countries, by this time, had enacted laws against the trade, but smuggling was extensive and open. In fact, the closing of U.S. and British markets had merely deflected the trade to Cuba, Brazil and elsewhere, and as late as 1850 more than 50,000 slaves a year were being transported. A new organization, the British and Foreign Anti-Slavery society, was therefore formed in 1839 under the leadership of Joseph Sturge. While this society kept up a public agitation, the British government sought to obtain international agreements to stop the trade by means of an effective naval patrol, but the profitability of the trade and jealousy of British naval power both stood in the way. In 1862, however, the United States signed a treaty conceding the right of search, which was necessary for effective enforcement. After this treaty, the slave trade was quickly reduced to a trickle. Later, the world-wide reaction against slavery led to abolition in Cuba, between 1880 and 1886, and in Brazil, between 1883 and 1888. Some slavery, of a rather different kind, still prevailed in parts of Africa and Asia and was still the target of reformers' activities. But the system of African slavery as a western phenomenon, after shaping the destiny of three continents and dominating the history of three centuries, had ceased to exist. See also SLAVERY.   (D. Pr.)

ABOMINABLE SNOWMAN, a mythical monster supposed to inhabit the Himalayas at about the level of the snow line. No one has ever seen an Abominable Snowman, or Yeti, alive or dead, but certain marks found in the snow have been attributed to it. Where these have not been caused by lumps of snow or stones falling from higher regions and bouncing across the lower slopes, they have probably been produced by bears: at certain gaits bears place the hind foot partly over the imprint of the forefoot, thus making a very large imprint that looks deceitfully like an enormous human footprint traveling in the opposite direction. Credulity is strengthened by the legends current among the Sherpa natives of the neighbouring regions about the Yeti, the local bogyman. Specimens of hair alleged to have come from the Abominable Snowman have proved on scientific examination to be hairs of bears, yaks or other well-known animals. One such specimen, a dried scalp, preserved in a monastery of Tibetan lamas, is the skin from the back of a serow, a mountain antelope. (L. H. M.)

ABOMINATION, anything regarded with aversion as things contrary to omen (Lat. ab, "from," omino, "I forebode"); in the Old Testament, evil doctrines, impure ceremonial practices and heathen idols. The Hebrew words thoava and shikkuz became bdelygma in the Septuagint (Greek version of the Bible) and abominatio in the Vulgate (Latin version), the latter term passing into modern European languages. The gospel expression translated in the Authorized Version as "abomination of desolation" (Matt. xxiv, 15; Mark xiii, 14; "desolating sacrilege" in the Revised Standard Version) derives from Dan. xi, 31 and xii, 11 ("the abomination that makes desolate"), where it refers to a statue of Zeus Hypsistos (Semitic Baal Shamaim, "Lord of Heaven") erected in 167 B.C. by the Seleucid king Antiochus IV Epiphanes in the temple at Jerusalem.   (J. T. M.)

ABOR (ADI), a hill tribe of 4,000 (1960s) north of the Brahmaputra river in northeastern India, subdivided into Minyong, Galong, Padam and other groups. They fall into patrilineal exogamous septs or clans with traces of dual organization. A cross division exists into Mishing and Mipak—pure and impure, the latter condition being hereditary and contagious as a result of sexual intercourse, though exogamy is not affected by it. The dead are buried; monogamy prevails, but the Galongs practise the levirate (q.v.) and polyandry within the family circle; slavery, tattooing and segregation of the unmarried obtain. Public affairs are managed by elders and offenders are fined by the random confiscation of property. Weapons used include long swords, crossbows, bows, poisoned arrows and spears. See also NORTH EAST FRONTIER AGENCY.

See L. Gogoi, "The Adis . . . ," Folk-lore, vol. 4 (Jan. 1963); S. Roy, Aspects of Padam-Minyong Culture (1960).

ABORIGINES, the inhabitants found in a country at its first discovery. The Aborigines were a mythical people of central Italy, supposed to have descended from near Reate (an ancient Sabine town) upon Latium, whence they expelled the Siceli and settled down as Latini under a King Latinus. The etymology of the name (ab origine) makes them the original inhabitants (Gr. autochthones) of the country, but is inconsistent with the fact that the oldest authorities (e.g., Cato in his Origines) regarded them as Hellenic immigrants, not as a native Italian people. Other explanations suggested are arborigines, "tree-born," and aberrigines, "nomads." See RACES OF MANKIND.

ABORTION may be defined as the termination of pregnancy before independent viability of the fetus has been attained. It is one form of human reproductive wastage, the general descriptive term for loss of embryonal and fetal lives in reproduction. Wastage may occur throughout pregnancy, during the birth process and in the first days following delivery. Very few fetuses weighing less than 1,000 g. (2 lb. 3⅓ oz.) and born earlier than 24 weeks after conception survive, and pregnancies terminated prior to this period are generally considered abortions. Expulsion of a dead fetus later in pregnancy is called stillbirth, and birth of a living infant before term is called premature birth. Miscarriage is a folk term for spontaneous abortion.

The distinction between abortion and stillbirth is not agreed upon by all persons and all governments, and the World Health organization in 1950 recommended that neither term be used, suggesting instead that when a fetus is born dead it be classified in one of four groups: group I, early fetal death—pregnancy of less than 20 weeks; group II, intermediate fetal death—pregnancy from 20 to 28 weeks; group III, late fetal death—pregnancy of more than 28 weeks; group IV, fetal death with length of pregnancy unknown.

It has been estimated that 10% to 12% of all pregnancies terminate as abortions. Early abortion may occur before the young pregnancy has obtained a secure attachment to the uterine lining. Many such early abortions are not recognized by the patient or her physician because they induce no recognizable symptoms.

The failure of a baby to survive pregnancy may be the result of a number of factors, among them physical impairment of the mother; a complication of pregnancy; or abnormal condition of the baby or its environment. Abnormalities of the developing embryo and chorionic sac which contains it are the result of intrinsic defects in the germ cells (that is, of defects existing in the egg or sperm before conception took place); uterine lining poorly prepared because of insufficient hormones; or gross alteration of the environment by tumours of the uterus, infections, or congenital or acquired defects. The ovarian hormones estrogens and progesterone are necessary for the establishment and normal progress of early pregnancy, and inadequate secretion of them may result in abortion. Psychogenic factors also are probably responsible in some cases. A mother who has acquired diabetes during childhood or adolescence may experience a fetal death or give birth to an excessively large child who may fail to overcome the results of the abnormal environment provided by its diabetic mother. The mother who has Rh-negative blood married to a husband who is Rh-positive may become immunized in her first or subsequent pregnancies and the baby may develop a serious anemia and succumb in the uterus or (rarely these days) after birth. A mother may have high blood pressure or kidney disease which become aggravated during pregnancy. The inadequate circulation to the uterus under such circumstances may interfere with the development of a normal placenta, or this important structure may undergo early senile changes, so that the baby is deprived of an adequate blood supply and it dies in the uterus or its growth and development are retarded.

A fetal death may result when a baby who moves freely in the uterus becomes entangled in its umbilical cord, cutting off its oxygen supply. The placenta may become partially separated from its uterine attachment, likewise interfering with oxygenation and occasionally initiating early labour. A baby may develop major malformations, resulting in its death during pregnancy or immediately after its birth. Infections of the baby can occur in late pregnancy, particularly if the fetal sac ruptures some time prior to the onset of labour, or in the early days following birth. Some of these infections are due to staphylococcus organisms which may be resistant to antibiotic therapy.

A few women, designated as habitual aborters, have repeated abortions. In these women some recurrent factor or factors predispose to the early termination of pregnancy. Complete and careful diagnostic study and proper therapy will prevent the recurrence of abortion in most of these women.

The course of an abortion varies. The embryo may die and its expulsion from the uterus may be delayed for several weeks or even several months. The abortion process may begin with lower abdominal pains, resembling menstrual cramps, and slight bleeding. At this stage damage to the gestation may be slight, and proper treatment may result in continuation of the pregnancy and a healthy child. In other cases the abortion process starts with profuse bleeding and severe cramps, indicating a rapid separation of the gestational sac from its uterine attachment and its expulsion from the cavity of the uterus. The physician will usually complete such an abortion surgically and make certain that no remnants of the pregnancy remain in the uterus.

In most countries medical ethics and the law permit the deliberate termination of pregnancy (therapeutic abortion) when the mother's health, life or reason are seriously jeopardized by the continuation of the pregnancy and when grossly defective offspring may surely be expected. The frequency of therapeutic terminations of pregnancy is decreasing rapidly with the advances of medical knowledge. In many parts of the world a person who willfully causes an abortion, as well as anyone who contributes to the act in the absence of medical indications, is liable to conviction of crime. The frequency of such criminal abortions is unknown, but they contribute to much invalidism and death. Infection is a common complication and may result in the inability to have children.

See EMBRYOLOGY AND DEVELOPMENT, ANIMAL; FETAL DISORDERS; OBSTETRICS; PLACENTA AND FETAL MEMBRANES, DISEASES OF; PREGNANCY; PREMATURE BIRTH; *see* also references under "Abortion" in the Index.

See P. H. Gebhard *et al., Pregnancy, Birth and Abortion* (1958); C. T. Javert, *Spontaneous and Habitual Abortion* (1957).
(M. E. Ds.)

ABORTION, CONTAGIOUS: *see* BRUCELLOSIS.

ABOUT, EDMOND FRANÇOIS VALENTIN (1828–1885), French novelist and journalist, a vigorous polemist who effectively introduced a mordant humour into the most serious subjects, was born on Feb. 14, 1828, at Dieuze, in Lorraine. After a period at the École Normale he went to Greece with a grant from the French school at Athens. On his return he published *La Grèce contemporaine* (1854), a bitingly satirical and occasionally unfair account of his personal impressions. Turning to novel writing, he published the whimsical *Le Roi des montagnes* (1856), showing an individual humour later echoed by Daudet, and attempted realism in *Tolla* (1855), *Germaine* (1857) and *Madelon* (1863). About resumed his humorous style with *Le Cas de Monsieur Guérin, L'Homme à l'oreille cassée* and *Le Nez d'un notaire* (all 1862), his best works.

Under Napoleon III, About proclaimed his liberal views in *La Question romaine* (1861) and *Le Progrès* (1864). Following the establishment of the Third Republic he founded in 1871 a periodical, the *XIXe Siècle,* in which he showed himself a brilliant journalist and controversialist, with a formidable wit. A convinced anticlerical, he campaigned for the secularization of French education. Elected to the Académie Française in 1884, About died in Paris on Jan. 16, 1885.

See M. Thiébaut, *Edmond About* (1936). (R. Dl.)

ABOYNE, a village of Aberdeenshire, Scot., lies on the river Dee, 31 mi. W. of Aberdeen by road. Pop. (1961) 1,555. It is a picturesque village with a large green where the Aboyne Highland games are held every September. To the north is Aboyne castle, for centuries the seat of the marquises of Huntly. At Aboyne the Dee is crossed by a fine bridge (leading to Glen Tanar), and nearby is the Queen's loch. Local industries are farming and sawmilling, and there is a fortnightly market for cattle and sheep. Michael fair is a well-known sheep sale held every autumn.
(Jo. F.)

ABRA, interior province in northwestern Luzon, Republic of the Philippines. Area 1,471 sq.mi. Pop. (1960) 115,193. Hilly and mountainous, it is drained by the Abra river, whose flood plain is the principal level terrain. The main crop is rice, with tobacco and corn of secondary and lumbering of minor importance. Bangued, the capital, is the chief settlement and commercial centre. The inhabitants are principally Ilocanos, and secondly Igorots (mountain people). (An. C.)

ABRABANEL (ABRAVANEL or ABARBANEL), **ISAAC** (1437–1508), Jewish statesman, philosopher, theologian and commentator, was born at Lisbon, Port., of an ancient family which claimed descent from the royal house of David. Like many of the Spanish Jews he united scholarly tastes with political ability. He was a favourite of King Alfonso V, who entrusted him with important state business, but after the king's death in 1481 Abrabanel was compelled to flee to Spain, where for eight years (1484–92) he held the post of a minister of state under Ferdinand and Isabella. After the expulsion of the Jews from Spain in 1492 Abrabanel resided at Naples, Corfu and Monopoli, and in 1503 moved to

Venice, where he was a minister of state until his death in 1508.

Abrabanel was one of the first to see that for biblical exegesis it was necessary to reconstruct the social environment of olden times, and he applied his practical knowledge of statecraft to the elucidation of the books of Samuel and Kings.

BIBLIOGRAPHY.—J. S. Minkin, *Abarbanel, and the Expulsion of the Jews From Spain* (1938); J. Sarachek, *Don Isaac Abravanel* (1938); B. Netanyahu, *Don Isaac Abrabanel, Statesman and Philosopher* (1953).

ABRACADABRA, a word analogous to abraxas (*q.v.*), used as a magical formula by the Gnostics of the sect of Basilides (*q.v.*) in invoking the aid of beneficent spirits against disease and misfortune. It is found on abraxas stones, which were worn as amulets. The Gnostic physician Serenus Sammonicus gave precise instructions as to its mystical use in averting or curing agues and fevers generally. Subsequently its use spread beyond the Gnostics, and in modern times it is applied contemptuously to complicated, unscientific hypotheses.

ABRAHAM, the first of the Hebrew patriarchs, stands at the fountainhead of the history of redemption in the Bible.

Traditions About Abraham in Genesis.—In the prologue to the tradition about Abraham in Gen. xi the origin of Abraham, at first called Abram, is traced to Harran in northern Syria and to Ur of the Chaldees in the lower Mesopotamia valley. The prologue connects the history of Abraham (Gen. xi, 26–xxv, 10) with the primeval history of Gen. i, 1–xi, 9. Therein Abraham is a symbol of God's plan of redemption for the world.

In Gen. xii Abraham's story proper begins. His call is described briefly (xii, 1 ff., part of the "J" tradition; *see* PENTATEUCH): God commands him to break away from his environment and to go out to a new land. The promise of progeny and of material felicity is given to him. Furthermore, he is to act as intermediary for this blessing to "all the families of the earth" (xii, 3).

The theological importance of these opening verses cannot be overemphasized. Abraham is from now on to live on God's word (God's providence) alone, but in a hostile world (xii, 6). Abraham's unhesitating acceptance of his call is described in a single word in the Hebrew ("so [he] went"; xii, 4). The meaning of the story lies in Abraham's obedience to God, his severing of his ties with his former life and his achieving of a new existence based on one single thing: God's promise.

The journeyings of Abraham are related in the subsequent material. He comes to Shechem, builds an altar there and receives the divine promise that his descendants will inherit the land (xii, 7). On his way south through the central mountain ridge of Canaan, he pauses at Bethel, where he builds another altar and worships, and then comes to the Negev, where he settles close to Hebron (xii, 9; xiii, 18). It is in this southern area that the traditions about Abraham most probably belong, and the body of the tradition actually begins to develop at this point (xii, 10). When Abraham journeys from Hebron down to Egypt for better grazing grounds, which is normal nomadic practice, the story for the first time takes on flesh and colour, reporting incidents and describing people. Because of the beauty of his wife Sarah, he meets trouble in the land of Egypt, but he is saved by his presence of mind and the power of Yahweh (xii, 11 ff.; *cf.* xx, 12, where Sarah is reported to be Abraham's half sister).

The narrative moves from the story of Lot in ch. xiii (continued in ch. xix) and the puzzling ch. xiv on toward the important event of God's covenant with Abraham in ch. xv. Ch. xiv is somehow intrusive in the story, and it is strangely foreign to the traditions about Abraham. In it Abraham appears as a warrior who, in order to help Lot, his captured kinsman, campaigns against four foreign kings who had made war on Bera, king of Sodom, and his four allies. (The names of these Canaanite allies do not occur in other sources, and scholars have not identified any of them with certainty.)

The campaign incident in ch. xiv connects Melchizedek, king of Salem (Jerusalem), with Abraham. He blesses Abraham who, in his turn, swears to Melchizedek's God, El Elyon ("God most high"). Here, then, the continuity between Abraham's God and native Canaanite worship is expressed. Thus too, Abraham is linked with Jerusalem, the later throne of David, and Melchizedek becomes a symbol of the promises to David (Ps. cx, 4).

Ch. xv contains the account of God's covenant with Abraham—material of unmistakable historical value for the understanding of Abraham and his religion. In several ways the chapter is comparable with the narrative of his call in ch. xii, and it has been suggested that in the oral stage of the tradition this account stood originally at the beginning of the story of Abraham in Canaan.

The chapter falls into two sections, xv, 1–6 and xv, 7–21, relating first the promise to Abraham and second the covenant with him. These two are inseparable and belong almost entirely to "J," the oldest literary tradition of the Pentateuch. In the first section Abraham receives God's promise of progeny in a vision. He was concerned about his childlessness and the possibility that his slave Eliezer would succeed him. (This point is clarified by comparison with the customary law of the 2nd millennium B.C. regarding adoption, as exemplified in tablets found at Nuzi, southeast of Nineveh. A childless man would adopt a son who would serve him in his old age. Should a son be born to the man, the adopted son's status as an heir would be changed.)

This section is highly theological; it brings together the themes of God's promise and man's doubt (xv, 2–4). The tension between the two is resolved only by Abraham's quiet and submissive acceptance and trust (*i.e.*, his faith), which is the occasion for the famous statement "And he believed the Lord; and he reckoned it to him as righteousness" (xv, 6).

The second section, xv, 7–21, is an account of the covenant (xv, 13–16, 19–21 are a later interpolation). During a sacrificial rite, in a "deep sleep" and in "dread and great darkness," Abraham perceives God as a flaming torch passing between the portions of the offering. Here, a covenant rite is easily recognizable (the "passing between" was a part of the ritual). The psychological mystery is expressed through the "deep sleep" during which Abraham's perceptive powers are heightened. Once more the promise given to Abraham concerns the land which his seed is to inherit (xv, 18). Through this account of the covenant, we are given an authentic glimpse into Abraham's cultic experience of the transcendent God who speaks into a human situation.

Abraham's concubine Hagar and her son Ishmael are introduced in the following chapter. In accordance with a type of marriage contract known from the 2nd millennium, Sarah, being childless, had provided her husband with a concubine, who bore him a son. The story of Hagar is resumed in ch. xxii, where Abraham is reluctant to "cast out this slave woman with her son" (xxii, 10 ff.) because of Sarah's jealousy. (Nuzi law forbade the expulsion of the slave wife in such cases.)

A second account, ch. xvii, of the covenant with Abraham (from the so-called Priestly tradition), although differing considerably in detail and in theological concern from its parallel in ch. xv, 7–18, is in essentials the same: God establishes a covenant with Abraham and gives him a promise of land and offspring. God reveals himself here as El Shaddai ("God Almighty"; xvii, 1), another form of revelation for Yahweh, as explained in Ex. vi, 3 (also from the Priestly source, "P"). Here, God announces that Abraham is to change his name from Abram to Abraham, showing that he is to become the father (Heb. *ab*) of a multitude of nations. This is probably a popular etymology. The name Abraham is a longer form of the shorter Abram with the same meaning: "The father [the deity] is exalted." In xvii, 9–14 the rite of circumcision is introduced as the sign by which Abraham's descendants shall be distinguished.

In the following section, also from "P," Abraham is promised a son (xvii, 15–27). The promise is repeated in xviii, 10 (from "J") when God appears in the form of three men whom Abraham entertains to a meal. Later, "at the appointed time," the child, Isaac, is born (xxi, 2; xviii, 14).

At this point a climax has been reached in the narrative. The promise of descendants has materialized at the birth of Isaac. This climax, however, is soon to be countered by the command to sacrifice the boy in ch. xxii.

In the meantime, other material is brought in before and after the birth of Isaac, some of which had belonged originally to independent cycles of traditions, such as the story of Lot's escape from Sodom in xix, continuing xiii, 5–13. Abraham journeys in Gerar (ch. xx), is in danger on account of Sarah (xx, 1 ff., a doublet to xii, 10 ff.), makes a treaty with Abimelech of Gerar (xxi, 22–32) and founds the cult of El Olam in Beersheba (xxi, 33).

The great testing point in Abraham's life is then described (ch. xx). God tests his obedience (it is stated explicitly in xxii, 1) by ordering him to offer up his only son, Isaac, as a burnt offering. Abraham leaves Beersheba in obedience and journeys to the land of Moriah (unknown; traditionally Jerusalem). The great scene, holding all the tension of tragedy, is, in true Hebrew narrative style, painted with few but bold strokes. There had been built up in the preceding chapters (xii; xvi; xviii) a climactic account of God's promises and their fulfillment in the birth of Isaac. All this is now to be nullified at one stroke. "The story tells of something far more terrible than human sacrifice: namely of being forsaken by God" (G. von Rad).

At the last moment, God releases Abraham from the terrible injunction. The story, then, finds its denouement in the redemptive word, the command not to harm the boy (xxii, 12), and the accompanying event, the finding of a ram which Abraham offers up in Isaac's place.

The tradition about Abraham in its present form ends with the death of Sarah and the purchase of the patriarchal burial chamber in Hebron (ch. xxiii), the death of Abraham himself and the burial of them both (xxv, 7–10).

Figure of Abraham Elsewhere in the Old Testament.— There is little doubt that David took up the tradition about Abraham to consolidate the religious authority of Jerusalem (Gen. xiv, 19 ff.; Ps. cx, 4). Abraham is the active symbol of the blessing and the promises of the covenant (Ex. vi, 8; Deut. i, 8; II Kings xiii, 23), and as such he is the symbol of the meaning of the nation's history. In Isa. li, 2 he is called the father of Israel, and in Isa. xli, 8 Israel is called "the offspring of Abraham" and Abraham the friend of God.

Abraham in Judaism and in the New Testament.—In rabbinic tradition Abraham occupies a position of eminence. His faith atones for the sins of Israel, and he was even the rock upon which God built and established the world. In the New Testament, allusions are made to this role of Abraham; e.g., in Matt. viii, 11 and Luke xiii, 28–29, where Abraham is an eschatological figure, represented as the host at the heavenly banquet (cf. Luke xvi, 22). The promises to Abraham are recognized as giving the Jews a special prerogative (Rom. ix, 8; xi, 1 ff.). Yet, being children of Abraham has a spiritual, rather than a national, meaning (Rom. ix, 7 ff.; cf. Gal. iii, 9). The true children of Abraham are "children of the promise" (Rom. ix, 8), and that promise is fulfilled in Christ (Gal. iii, 14). Thus Abraham becomes a precursor of Christ. In Him the promises to Abraham are fulfilled (Gal. iii, 25–29; cf. Heb. vii), and Christians, even the gentile ones, partake in the blessing in Abraham (Gal. iii, 8 ff.; cf. Gen. xii, 3). Paul seizes upon Abraham's righteousness by faith (Gen. xv, 6) in order to expound his central thesis that righteousness is granted through faith rather than through works (Rom. iv, 1 ff.; Gal. iii, 6 ff.). In the epistle to the Hebrews, Abraham is an example of the faith that receives God's promise and responds to it in obedience (Heb. xi, 8 ff.).

Abraham as a Historical Figure.—The traditions about Abraham in the Bible are derived from oral traditions in epic form. Successive generations retold the stories and applied them to the needs and concerns of their own particular cultic and social institutions. Some of the narratives were probably told in order to substantiate ancient blood ties between clans. Furthermore, the tradition about Abraham is involved with those of Isaac and Jacob in a simple manner, making of the whole a well-rounded story. Behind this simplicity, there undoubtedly lies a vastly complex picture of Hebrew origins in the pre-Mosaic era.

How much can be stated about Abraham as a historical person? Abraham and the other patriarchs have sometimes been considered to be personifications of clans or even figures of myth. This opinion has been proved erroneous. To be sure, the story of Abraham in the Bible is not a biography in the modern sense of the word. The ancients told stories of persons in order to illuminate the meaning of the clan's or the nation's life. Yet, there can be no doubt that Abraham existed. On the other hand, it is not possible to be specific either about when he lived or about the details of his life.

Excavations at Mari on the Euphrates, at Nuzi and elsewhere have yielded texts which illuminate customs, names and tribal history in the first half of the 2nd millennium B.C.; it has become evident that the narratives about Abraham in the Bible authentically reflect that age (or perhaps the middle of the millennium). Abraham was a seminomad who belonged perhaps to a social stratum called Habiru (cf. the word "Hebrew," possibly from the same root, in Gen. xiv, 13).

The religion of Abraham has now been shown, by Old Assyrian inscriptions from the 20th century B.C. and by material of a later period, to belong to a type of high-god religion, which fits the picture given in Genesis. The "God of the Fathers" was a type of deity intimately connected with the clan, whose "patriarch" consciously chose the God and became the founder of the clan's cult. Abraham was such a cult founder (cf. "the God of Abraham," Gen. xxvi, 24).

The literary history of the traditions about Abraham is uncertain in many points because an extremely complex tradition-history has been compressed into a relatively short cycle. As in other histories of the same type, groups of stories have been connected with a particular locality such as Beersheba and Mamre-Hebron. In some cases, the name of the locality has not been preserved, such as the scene of the covenant in Gen. xv. The stories of Lot in xix and of the courtship on Isaac's behalf in xxiv are but loosely tied to the traditions about Abraham. The stories connected with the terebinth grove in Mamre (xviii, 1 ff.) and the cave of Machpelah (xxiii, 19; xxv, 9) locate Abraham in Hebron, where his home probably was. The chronological framework and the ties between independent cycles come from the "P" tradition (xi, 10–27, 31, 32; xvi, 3, 15, 16; xvii; xxi, 3–5, 23; xxv, 7–10). Some of the material assigned to this source, such as the Machpelah story (xxiii), is among the oldest of the traditions about Abraham.

Abraham's Religious Significance.—The story of Abraham centres in three themes: God's call; Abraham's response, in obedience and faith, to God's call; and God's promise to Abraham and its fulfillment. These themes constitute the significance which Abraham had for religious thought in the Bible. The implications of faith for social responsibility were not spelled out until later, in the covenant theology of Moses and his followers (see COVENANT and MOSES), but Abraham, as a figure in history, furnished the directive principles for the life of God's people: faith in God's promise and obedience to God's call.

See APOCALYPTIC LITERATURE for the Apocalypse of Abraham and the Testament of Abraham.

BIBLIOGRAPHY.—G. von Rad, *Genesis: A Commentary* (1960); J. Bright, *A History of Israel* (1959); M. Noth, *Überlieferungsgeschichte des Pentateuch* (1948); C. H. Gordon, "Biblical Customs and the Nuzi Tablets," *The Biblical Archeologist*, 3:1–12 (1940); A. Alt, *Der Gott der Väter* (1929); J. Lewy, "Les Textes paléo-assyriens et l'ancien testament," *Revue de l'histoire des religions*, 110:29–65 (1934); G. E. Wright, *Biblical Archaeology* (1957); H. S. Nyberg, "Abraham," in I. Engnell and A. Fridrichsen, *Svenskt Bibliskt Uppslagsverk*, vol. 1, col. 8–11 (1948); R. de Vaux, "Les Patriarches hébreux et les découvertes modernes," *Revue biblique*, 53:321–348 (1946), 55:321–347 (1948), 56:5–36 (1949). (T. K. T.)

ABRAHAM, THE PLAINS OF, a plateau to the southwest of the city of Quebec, the scene of the historic battle between the French under Louis Joseph Montcalm (q.v.) and the English under James Wolfe on Sept. 13, 1759.

ABRAHAM ECCHELLENSIS: see ECCHELLENSIS, ABRAHAM.

ABRAHAM IBN DAUD (c. 1110–c. 1180), Jewish historiographer and philosopher of Toledo, Spain. His historical work was the *Book of Tradition* (*Sepher ha-Qabbalah*), a chronicle to the year 1161 (Latin trans. by Gilbert Génébrard in *Hebraeorum breve chronicon*, 1572). His philosophy was expounded in an Arabic work better known under its Hebrew title *'Emunah Ramah* ("Sublime Faith," Ger. trans. by S. Weil, 1852). Ibn Daud was one of the first Jewish scholastics to adopt the Aristotelian system. His work was, however, soon eclipsed by that of Maimonides and failed to exercise much influence.

ABRAHAM-MAN, the nickname for a vagrant who wandered in England in Tudor times. The phrase is as old as 1561, and was due to these beggars' pretending that they were patients discharged from the Abraham ward at Bedlam insane asylum in London; on his discharge the genuine Bedlamite, provided he wore a badge, was allowed to roam the country, soliciting alms. This privilege was grossly abused, and thus gave rise to the slang phrase "to sham Abraham"—meaning to feign illness.

ABRAHAMS, ISRAEL (1858–1925), the first native-born Anglo-Jewish Hebraist to enjoy a European reputation, was born on Nov. 26, 1858, into a rabbinical family in London. In 1902, after teaching for several years at Jews' college, London, he was appointed reader in Talmudic at Cambridge, where he remained until his death on Oct. 6, 1925. He was distinguished both for the range of his interests and for the lightness of his touch. His *Jewish Life in the Middle Ages* (1896; rev. ed. by C. Roth, 1932), a highly readable social history, was his first major book. His other works include several monographs on medieval Jewish literature and *Studies in Pharisaism and the Gospels* (1917; 2nd series, 1924). From 1889 to 1908 he was co-editor of the *Jewish Quarterly Review,* and he was a leading member of the Jewish Historical Society of England. Orthodox by upbringing, he was later among the founders of the Liberal Jewish movement in England.

(C. R.)

ABRASIVE, relatively hard material used to grind or polish materials softer than itself. Grinding wheels, oil stones and sandpaper are common examples of abrasives. The high precision and fine surface finish of many modern machine tools are obtainable only with the use of abrasive grinding operations. Most household cleansers use a mild abrasive to help the soap or detergent do its work.

Primitive man used abrasives to help shape his stone tools by rubbing them against harder stones. Drawings in ancient Egyptian tombs show the polishing of jewelry and vases with abrasives. In later historical times, craftsmen used natural abrasive stones shaped into wheels, such as grindstones and mill wheels, and into blocks for use by hand for sharpening scythes, knives, axes and woodworking tools. Powdered abrasives were used for polishing in much the same manner as they were used by the Egyptians.

It was not until late in the 19th century, when it became necessary to work with harder metals and to closer tolerances, that abrasives assumed a major role in the manufacturing industry. Synthetic abrasives were developed with improved and more uniform characteristics, and new machines were designed to use these abrasives to best advantage. Natural abrasives are still widely used in some applications, but in industrial grinding they have been largely replaced by synthetics.

Natural Abrasives.—Diamonds are the hardest of all abrasives. The small and imperfect diamonds are crushed and the abrasive powder obtained is graded and used in many grinding and polishing operations, especially on carbide tools, which are difficult to form by any other method. (*See* DIAMOND.)

Corundum (*q.v.*) is a crystalline form of aluminum oxide (Al_2O_3) mined principally in South Africa. It is quite high in cost but among natural abrasives is second only to diamond in hardness.

Emery (*q.v.*) is a mixture of corundum and magnetite (black iron oxide, $FeO \cdot Fe_2O_3$), which has been mined for several centuries on Cape Emeri on the island of Naxos in the Greek archipelago. For many years it was the standard industrial abrasive, being formed into emery wheels and emery stones and used to coat cloth. It has now been largely supplanted by synthetic abrasives such as silicon carbide and synthetic aluminum oxide.

Garnet is a silicate of iron and aluminum mined in the eastern United States and in Spain. It is used for making coated abrasive paper and cloth.

Quartz is among the commonest of all minerals and occurs in many forms. Quartz sand is used for making sandpaper and for sandblasting. Sandstone, of which quartz is the main constituent, is used for making grindstones and for sharpening stones. Some compact forms of quartz, such as Arkansas and Washita stone, make the finest oil stones for sharpening knives and other edge tools.

Pumice is the frothy part of lava. It is a relatively soft abrasive used in cleaning and scouring compounds. Other soft abrasives such as diatomite, tripoli, rouge and crocus are used primarily for buffing and polishing operations.

Synthetic Abrasives.—Carborundum, or silicon carbide (SiC), initially prepared in 1891, was the first important synthetic abrasive. It is made by fusing coke and sand at high temperature in an electric furnace. Silicon carbide is harder and stronger than corundum, but inferior to synthetic diamonds and boron carbide in hardness. It is second only to aluminum oxide in its importance as an industrial abrasive and is used for grinding cast iron, tungsten carbide and other hard materials. (*See* SILICON CARBIDE.) Other important synthetic abrasives, in order of hardness, are discussed in the following paragraphs.

Synthetic diamonds are produced commercially and are competing with the natural product. Their greater uniformity justifies their higher cost in some applications.

Boron carbide (B_4C) is, next to diamond, the hardest of all abrasives. It is used for grinding very hard materials such as tungsten carbide, which is widely used in dies and cutting tools.

Artificial aluminum oxide (Al_2O_3), or artificial corundum, is not so hard as silicon carbide but is stronger and is preferred for grinding the common grades of carbon and alloy steel. (*See* CORUNDUM, ARTIFICIAL.)

Iron and steel are sometimes used as abrasives in the form of shot and grit for air blasting and in the form of steel wool for rubbing and polishing.

Industrial Techniques.—Abrasives for industrial use are crushed into a powder which is graded according to size from the coarsest, #6, to the finest, #600. In some polishing and cutting operations these powders are mixed with a liquid or paste and rubbed against the work. Abrasive grains are also cemented or applied as a paste to soft polishing wheels of cloth, felt or leather which are used for buffing or polishing metal or plastic parts to impart a fine finish or as a preparation for electroplating. Most of this buffing is done by hand; however, some operations, such as the polishing of stainless steel sheets, are done in large automatic machines.

In most applications the abrasive grains are pressed into wheels or blocks, using various binders, or are glued to the surface of paper or cloth to form coated abrasives. The wheels may be used in simple hand grinders or in high precision machines for grinding of flat surfaces, for internal and external cylindrical grinding or for the grinding of screw threads or cutting tools. The abrasive blocks may be used as oil stones for the hand sharpening of knives and other edge tools or in honing machines for imparting a fine finish to such parts as automobile cylinders and crankshafts. Coated abrasives include sheets of sandpaper and emery cloth, which have been used for many years for hand finishing of woodwork and metal parts, and synthetic abrasive belts, which are used in belt grinding machines for finishing many metal surfaces.

In sandblasting, the abrasive grains are blown by air pressure or impelled by centrifugal force against the surface of metal castings or other materials for removing rust or scale or smoothing irregularities, or for imparting a slightly rough or matte finish, such as in ground glass. (*See* BLAST CLEANING AND SHOT PEENING.) Ultrasonic machining uses a liquid abrasive mixture flowing under a shaped tool of brass or soft steel which is caused to vibrate at a high frequency. The tool, working in combination with the abrasive, penetrates rapidly even the hardest materials such as ceramics, glass and carbides, leaving a smooth and accurate hole. *See* HARDNESS TESTING; *see* also Index references under "Abrasive" in the Index volume.

BIBLIOGRAPHY.—Johnson Heywood, *Abrasive Grains and Their Uses* (1943), *Grinding Wheels and Their Uses* (1942); Frank W. Wilson (ed.), *Tool Engineers Handbook,* 2nd ed. (1959).   (A. C. AN.)

ABRAUM SALTS (Ger. *Abraum-salze,* "salts to be removed"), a mixed deposit of salts originally regarded as rubble or waste material, including chlorides and sulfates of sodium, potas-

sium and magnesium, found in association with rock salt at Stass-
furt, Ger. They are a principal source of potassium (*q.v.*).

ABRAXAS (Abrasax), a word probably first used by the
Basilidians (*see* Basilides) and engraved on certain stones, called
on that account abraxas stones.
The Greek letters *abraxas* make
up the number 365, and the Basilidians gave the name to the 365
orders of spirits which emanated
in succession from the supreme
being. These orders were supposed to occupy 365 heavens,
each fashioned like but inferior
to that above it, the lowest being
the abode of the spirits who
formed the earth and its inhabitants, to whom was committed the
administration of its affairs. In
addition to the word abraxas the
stones often have cabalistic figures engraved on them.

BY COURTESY OF THE BRITISH MUSEUM
ABRAXAS STONE

ABREU, JOÃO CAPISTRANO DE (1853–1927), Brazilian historian, was born near Maranguape, Ceará, Oct. 23, 1853. In
Rio de Janeiro after 1875, he was a journalist, teacher and member
of the National Library staff. From 1883 to 1899 he was professor of Brazilian history at the Colégio Dom Pedro II. Distinguished as an editor and essayist, he was initially influenced by
Auguste Comte (*q.v.*) but soon embraced the German school of
historical realism. His critical editing of chronicles and of the
historian Francisco Adolfo de Varnhagen assured him of high rank
among Brazil's historians but his *Caminhos antigos e o povoamento*
(1899; 1924) and *Capítulos de História Colonial* (1907) give him
first place. The former work, often compared to Frederick Jackson Turner's frontier thesis, stressed the importance of the previously neglected backlands. The *Capítulos* reinterpreted and enlarged the scope of Brazilian historiography and became the guide
for subsequent historical research and writing. He died in Rio,
Aug. 13, 1927.   (G. C. A. B.)

ABRON (Brong), an Akan (*q.v.*) Twi-speaking Negro people
of more than 75,000 (1960s) in the vicinity of Bondoukou (*see*
Ivory Coast, Republic of). In the 20th century, the several
hundred villages in the Abron kingdom were about 70% populated
by Kulango, Diula, Agni (*q.v.*), and other peoples. Political and
judicial representation are made through the family head (the
eldest male) to the village chief, the chief of the province and the
king. Descent is patrilineal but inheritance passes normally to the
eldest younger brother, or if there are no brothers, to the eldest
sister's eldest son. The son of the deceased inherits only if there
are no brothers and no sisters' sons. These sedentary farmers
grow bananas, manioc, and taro. They identify their sky god with
Allah, have an earth god, river deities, and sacrifice to their
ancestors.

See A. Alland, Jr., "Residence, Domicile and Descent Groups Among
the Abron of the Ivory Coast," *Ethnology*, vol. 2 (July 1963).
                                                            (Wi. B.; X.)

ABRUZZI, Duke of the (Luigi Amedeo) (1873–1933),
Italian vice-admiral, mountaineer and explorer, born at Madrid on Jan. 29, 1873 (the son of the duke of Aosta, who was
then king of Spain as Amadeo), was the first to ascend Mt. St.
Elias in Alaska (1897). In 1899 he organized an Arctic expedition part of which reached latitude 86°34′ N, at that time the
record of northern exploration. In 1906 he was the first to
ascend the Ruwenzori in east Africa, reaching the twin summits
which he named Margherita and Alexandra. He also made the
first detailed map of the Ruwenzori. In 1909 he ascended K2
in the Himalayas to an altitude of over 20,000 ft. and on July 17
Bride Peak to 24,600 ft. During World War I he commanded
the naval forces in the Adriatic, but he resigned in 1917 owing
to disagreements with Adm. Thaon di Revel, his chief of staff,
and retired. Afterward he undertook colonization on the lower
Webi Shebeli in Italian Somaliland, and explored and mapped the
river. He died in Somaliland on March 18, 1933.

English translations of his works are *The Ascent of Mount St. Elias*
(1900); *Ruwenzori* (1909).

ABRUZZI E MOLISE, a region of south central Italy, comprises the provinces of L'Aquila, Campobasso, Chieti, Pescara and
Teramo, with a total area of 5,881 sq.mi. and a population of 1;-
457,764 in 1961. Most of the region is mountainous or hilly,
except for intermontane basins such as those of L'Aquila, Sulmona
and the Fucino. The Apennines cover the greater part of the
region, consisting of three chains with a northwest-southeast trend.
The easternmost of these is the highest, including such peaks as
the Gran Sasso d'Italia (9,592 ft.) and the Maiella (9,170 ft.);
the central group is lower, with Mt. Velino (8,159 ft.); while the
western group, comprising the Sabini and Simbruini mountains,
does not exceed 7,000 ft. The Apennines are chiefly of limestone,
and karstic phenomena (dolinas, caves, underground drainage)
are common. In the east, toward the Adriatic, the hills descend
gradually to the sea and are of sand or clay. The southernmost
part of the region is the rolling plateau of Molise. The coast
lacks good harbours for its entire length and fishing does not
play an appreciable part in the economy. The principal rivers
draining toward the Adriatic (Tronto, Pescara, Sangro, Trigno,
Biferno) provide water for irrigation in their fertile lower valleys.
The water level in these streams varies greatly according to seasons; and floods, due in large part to indiscriminate felling of
timber on the higher slopes, are frequent. Cutting of the forests
also contributes to the ever-present danger of landslides endangering roads and railroads. Agriculture does not thrive on the shallow
soils of most of the region and crop averages are low. Wheat is
the main cereal crop; grapes and, toward the Adriatic, olives and
fruit are grown, while among industrial crops tobacco, sugar beet
and saffron are of importance. Animal husbandry has long been
the mainstay of a large part of the population, and migratory
herding (transhumance) of sheep, from mountain pastures in the
Abruzzi to the lowland winter pastures of the Foggia plain and of
the Roman region, is still a feature of the economy. Pigs are
raised in large numbers, and hams and sausages of the Abruzzi are
well known. Industrial development has been negligible except
for food industries and artisan work on a small scale. The main
rail artery is the Rome-Pescara line, crossing the central part of
the region, connecting Rome with the Abruzzi and with the Adriatic. Lines of local importance include those connecting Sulmona
with L'Aquila and Terni to the north, with Venafro and Campobasso to the south, as well as the lines from Campobasso to
Benevento and to Termoli on the Adriatic. Important cities are
the provincial capitals L'Aquila, Campobasso, Chieti, Pescara and
Teramo.

The region had long resisted conquest and retained its own character even after Roman rule was imposed on it. During the early
middle ages all of it came under the Lombards, the Abruzzi being
controlled by the duchy of Spoleto, and Molise by the duchy of
Benevento. The Normans established themselves in the Abruzzi
during the 12th century, and the region sided with the Hohenstaufens during their long struggle with the papacy. After the fall
of the Hohenstaufens, the region came under the Angevin, Spanish
and Bourbon rulers of the kingdom of Naples (divided as Abruzzo
Ulteriore I, Abruzzo Ulteriore II, Abruzzo Citeriore and Molise)
and became part of the united Italian kingdom in 1860. Among
the natives of the region are two of the great writers of modern
Italy, Gabriele D'Annunzio and Ignazio Silone. In the field of the
fine arts, while the Abruzzi retain a few Roman monuments, their
period of greatest development was the 12th–14th centuries, and
cathedrals, churches and abbeys bear witness to the flowering of
Romanesque and Gothic architecture and sculpture. (G. Kh.)

ABSALOM, the third son of David (*q.v.*) and his father's favourite. The picture presented in II Sam. xiii–xix (which deals
mainly with his life) suggests that he was the Alcibiades of the
Old Testament, alike in his personal attractiveness, his lawless insolence and his tragic fate. He is first mentioned as murdering his
half brother Amnon, David's eldest son, in revenge for the
rape of his full sister Tamar. For this deed he was driven into
banishment, but he was eventually restored to favour through the
good offices of Joab. Later, when some uncertainty seems to have

arisen as to the succession, Absalom organized a revolt. For a time he seemed to be completely successful; David with a few followers and his personal guard fled across the Jordan, leaving to Absalom Jerusalem and the main portion of the kingdom. The usurper pursued the fugitives with his forces but was completely defeated in "the forest of Ephraim" (apparently west of Jordan) and killed by Joab, who found him caught by the hair in an oak tree. To the affectionate chivalrous heart of David, the loss of his son, worthless and treacherous as he was, brought grief which more than outweighed his own safety and restoration.

ABSALON (c. 1128–1201), Danish archbishop and statesman prominent in public affairs under Kings Valdemar I and Canute VI (qq.v.), was a younger son of Valdemar's foster-father Asser Rig and belonged to the powerful Hvide family of Zealand. After studying in Paris, he returned to Denmark in 1156 and sided with Valdemar in his struggle for the kingdom. After Valdemar's victory at Grathehede (1157), Absalon in 1158 was made bishop of Roskilde. Thereafter he was the king's closest adviser. In opposition to Archbishop Eskil (q.v.), he approved the king's support of the emperor Frederick I Barbarossa in his dispute with Pope Alexander III and also Valdemar's oath of fealty to the emperor. By 1167, however, Absalon and the king were reconciled to the pope and were aiming at independence from the emperor.

Absalon directed the building of the fortress of Havn (Copenhagen) and compaigned vigorously against the pagan Wends of the north German coast, whose base on Rügen was captured in 1169. Its incorporation, with papal permission, into Absalon's diocese marked the beginning of Danish supremacy in northern Germany.

Valdemar's claim to rule by divine right received papal sanction in 1170 when his father, Canute Lavard, was canonized and his son Canute VI was crowned as joint king, and Absalon was undoubtedly the author of this policy. Elected archbishop of Lund in succession to Eskil in 1177, Absalon combined Lund with Roskilde till 1192. His zeal for discipline, however, provoked a rising in Skaane when he became archbishop. As guardian of Canute VI, he prevented the renewal of the oath of fealty to the emperor after Valdemar's death (1182) and in 1184 won a decisive victory over a German fleet. He founded many churches in Skaane and Zealand, generously endowed his family's abbey at Sorö and, during his last years, tried to unify Danish ecclesiastical procedure. He died at Sorö in 1201. Saxo Grammaticus (q.v.), whose patron Absalon was, glorifies him as a hero, but modern historians tend to estimate Absalon's achievement less highly.

BIBLIOGRAPHY.—H. Olrik, *Absalon* (1908–09); E. Arup, *Danmarks Historie*, vol. i (1925); L. Weibull, *Skånes kyrka* (1946); H. Koch, *Den danske Kirkes Historie*, vol. i (1950).   (A. E. Cn.)

ABSAROKA, a range of mountains immediately to the east of Yellowstone National park in northwestern Wyoming. The range extends about 170 mi. in a northwest-southeast direction and has a width of 84 mi. Mid-Tertiary volcanic action built up a great plateau in the area. This volcanic accumulation was then uplifted and streams cut deep canyons into the plateau surface. Mountain glaciers have scoured the eroded surface and the resulting features are most spectacular. The upland surfaces (10,-000–12,000 ft. above sea level) rise from 2,000 to 4,000 ft. above Yellowstone park and 5,000–6,000 ft. above the Bighorn basin to the east.   (H. B. Ha.)

ABSCESS, a localized collection of pus in tissue spaces, hollow organs or body cavities. It is formed as the result of infection with pus-forming (pyogenic) organisms; there is local heat, redness, swelling and pain. The cells die and the centre of the inflammatory mass liquefies to form pus, which may break through the wall of the abscess or be emptied by incision. Various names are applied according to the location and the causative organism. The term "cold abscess" designates a localized collection of pus caused by the bacillus of tuberculosis. *See* BACTERIA; INFLAMMATION.   (F. L. A.)

ABSCISSA. In Cartesian co-ordinates (*see* ANALYTIC GEOMETRY) the abscissa of a point (P) is the part (OP') of the X axis lying between the origin (O) and the point (P') where a line (PP') parallel to the Y axis cuts the X axis. In each of the two figures, the line segment P"P is also called the abscissa of P. The axis of

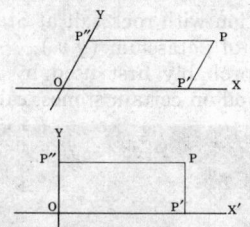

X (OX) is called the axis of abscissas.

ABSENTEE OWNERSHIP, a term originally used to describe the ownership of land by proprietors who did not reside on the land or cultivate it personally but enjoyed income from it. The term "absentee ownership" has come to have a social connotation not inherent in its literal meaning, based on the assumption that absentee owners lack the personal interest in and knowledge of their lands and tenants.

The fact of absentee ownership has been a social and political issue for centuries in many parts of the world. It was an important criticism directed at the absentee owners among the court nobility in prerevolutionary France, and it was a prominent issue in the debates concerning the alleged exploitation of Irish tenants by English absentee owners in the 19th century. It remains an issue in the numerous programs for land reform in many countries.

Early in the 20th century, Thorstein Veblen, the U.S. economist, also applied the term to owners of huge industrial combinations. He argued that, through their control of vast enterprises, they exercised control over industrial prices and output while not themselves engaging in industrial pursuits.

See T. Veblen, *Absentee Ownership and Business Enterprise in Recent Times* (1923); E. Roll, *A History of Economic Thought*, rev. ed. (1942).   (Fk. L. K.)

ABSENTEE VOTING. A system designed to permit the use of their vote to persons unable to appear at the polling place where they are registered by reason of their state of health, occupation, etc. Special administrative safeguards are necessary to assure the secrecy and legitimacy of absentee ballots; in practice, these keep some eligible persons from voting and have, in certain instances, involved some discrimination along party lines. The basic provisions are few, although arrangements vary in detail from country to country.   (X.)

United States.—Absentee voting in the United States was first provided for by state legislation during the Civil War, when 11 Union states permitted men serving in the Union army to vote in the federal election by absentee ballot or by proxy. There were then about 2,000,000 men under arms, of whom about 150,000 voted. But although more than three-fourths of the soldiers voted for the re-election of their commander in chief, Pres. Abraham Lincoln, their total vote scarcely affected the general outcome. There was relatively little interest in the soldier vote during the Spanish-American War or World War I. During the latter, some legislation was discussed, but no action was taken and the war department announced that there would be no voting overseas. It did, however, co-operate with those states which provided machinery for absentee voting within the U.S.

The first use of the absentee ballot by civilians was authorized by a Vermont law passed in 1896, and five years later a similar measure was adopted in Kansas.

Between 1917 and 1942 the number of states which extended this privilege to their citizens increased from 28 to 45. By the 1960s all states had established a system of absentee voting. Military personnel were permitted to vote by absentee ballot by all states, but, except for this common characteristic, great diversity existed in state absentee voting laws. Some states permitted any absent qualified voter to cast an absentee ballot. Others restricted the privilege to those engaged in certain duties, businesses or occupations. Some variation existed, too, in the types of elections in which absentee voting was authorized. The most restrictive laws limited the exercise of the privilege to elections for national office. At the other extreme, some states allowed it in all elections.

The trend has been toward extension and liberalization of the privilege of absentee voting. Many states have authorized the use of an absentee ballot by the physically incapacitated, whether they are located within or outside the state.

World War II experience showed the inadequacy of arrangements for absentee voting in time of war. Late in 1942 a Soldiers

Vote law was passed by congress to facilitate voting, but under its provisions only 28,051 votes were cast for members of congress in that off-year election. For the presidential election of 1944 the law was revised to provide a federal ballot for citizens of such states as approved its use, and then only if the serviceman had applied for a regular state absentee ballot by Sept. 1 and had not received it by Oct. 1. Twenty states approved the use of this ballot. About 2,800,000 servicemen, an estimated 30% of the total number of voting age, cast absentee ballots, state or federal, in this election.

The federal legislation and many of the state laws facilitating absentee voting by service personnel were temporary measures, which expired when peace was restored after World War II. As the presidential election of 1952 approached, with millions of Americans again in uniform, Pres. Harry S. Truman recommended that state laws be revised to remove obstacles to voting by absent military personnel. The president further recommended that a federal ballot be made available to servicemen from states which failed to make adequate provision for absentee voting, but congress failed to act on these recommendations. The defense department estimated that only 15% of the servicemen of voting age voted by absentee ballot in that election.

In the national election of 1956, by contrast, 35% of servicemen of voting age voted, although among the civilian population a smaller percentage of potential voters cast ballots in 1956 than in 1952. Instrumental in bringing about this change were the enactment of the Federal Voting Assistance act of 1955 by the congress and a general revision of state laws on the subject to enlarge the opportunities for absentee voting by removing such obstacles as tardy mailing of ballots to voters, the requirements of personal registration and payment of poll tax. (W. B. Pt.)

Great Britain, the Commonwealth and Europe.—The British Labour government's Representation of the People act of 1948 made eligible for a postal vote: (1) persons certified by a doctor as too ill to appear at a polling booth; (2) persons who would otherwise have to make a journey by sea or by air to reach a polling station; (3) persons who have moved from one electoral registration district to another since the register was compiled; (4) persons away from their place of voting on polling day by reason of their occupation. A proxy vote was allowed to servicemen, government employees and their dependents if they were outside Britain on election day. Few persons have claimed proxy votes, except at the 1918 and 1945 general elections. British law does not make provision for persons who are absent from their electoral district on vacation. It also discriminates against persons who have moved distances of up to 15 mi. within large cities; although they may have changed their constituency, they cannot have a postal vote since large cities are technically single registration districts.

Applicants for the postal vote in Great Britain must file their claim with the election officials for their place of registration at least nine working days before the election; often they do so at the behest of party canvassers. A postal ballot is then issued to them, along with a ballot-paper envelope (bearing on the outside the number of the ballot paper) and an identity form which must be countersigned by someone personally acquainted with the voter. Ballots must be returned by polling day; the election officials verify that the identity forms and the ballot-paper envelopes bear the same numbers and are properly filled out. The two are separated, the ballot envelopes opened and the postal votes then counted. Proxy voting requires an intending voter to nominate a proxy on an official form; the nominee then appears at the polling station with a certificate issued by the registration officer to substantiate his claim to cast a proxy vote.

The largest postal vote in Britain up to mid-20th century was in 1951 when 2.6% (742,000) of the total vote was so cast. In the 1959 election 692,000 postal ballots were issued of which 612,-000 were returned; of these, 13,000 were invalidated, usually for lack of a witness's signature. The number of such votes varied from a minimum of 113 to a maximum of 4,069 in individual constituencies; it was usually higher in sprawling rural seats, and lower in compact urban ones.

In close elections the postal vote has been of considerable political importance, because in almost every constituency the Conservatives have obtained well over half of it. Since postal voting figures are not officially announced, one must rely upon the estimates of people present at the count. The authors of *The British General Election of 1959* (*see* Bibliography) calculate that at that election, if the postal vote be reckoned at three to one in favour of the Conservatives it may be deemed to have won them 11 seats. At a minimum, with the vote divided only six to four in the Conservatives' favour, it accounted for five of their victories. The Labour party's special effort to increase its postal vote at this election apparently had little success. Observers attribute the Conservatives' advantage partly to their superior political organization and partly to the fact that the postal vote seems to be more readily claimed by educated persons and that such are more likely to vote Conservative. Similarly, in the general election of 1957 in the German Federal Republic the party of the better educated, the Christian Democratic Union, secured 60.3% of the 1,537,000 postal votes, although it obtained only 49.6% of the votes cast in person.

Because the proper use of absentee voting facilities is related to education, in parts of the commonwealth where illiteracy is fairly widespread absentee voting is either not allowed, as in Nigeria and Uganda, or allowed only on a severely restricted basis, as in India, Malaya and Jamaica. But in highly literate Australia, where voting is compulsory, generous provisions are made for the casting of absentee votes; there is also an election officer in London to aid Australians in the United Kingdom to vote in Australian federal elections. Where qualifications for electors are not primarily geographical, the postal vote may be the normal form of voting. Such is the case in the voting for the university representatives in the house of commons of Northern Ireland and for the university seats in the senate of the Republic of Ireland. In some European countries where elections are held on Sundays, persons traveling for pleasure are permitted to cast their votes at polling places other than those where they are registered, provided that they have first obtained a certificate from the election officials. Normally the voter, even though voting away from home, must cast his ballot for candidates in his constituency of registration.

BIBLIOGRAPHY.—F. A. Ogg and P. O. Ray, *Introduction to American Government*, 11th ed. (1956); W. J. M. Mackenzie, *Free Elections . . .* (1958); A. N. Schofield, *Parliamentary Elections*, 3rd ed. (1959); D. E. Butler, *The Electoral System in Britain, 1918–1951* (1953); D. E. Butler and R. Rose, *The British General Election of 1959* (1960); *Recueil des Textes relatifs à l'Élection des Députés à l'Assemblée Nationale* (Paris; Nov. 3, 1958); T. E. Smith, *Elections in Developing Countries* (1960). (R. Ro.)

ABSINTHE is a flavoured spirit and not, strictly speaking, a liqueur. It is yellowish-green in colour, dry and bitter, and of very high alcoholic strength, being 68% alcohol by volume. Its predominating ingredient is wormwood (*Artemisia absinthium*), but hyssop, fennel, aniseed, liquorice, angelica root, sweet flag, dittany leaves and star-anise fruit are also used. These herbs are found in the Val de Travers in the Swiss Jura.

Henri Louis Pernod first made absinthe commercially in 1797, after he had bought the recipe from Dr. Ordinaire of Couvet, Switz., but because of the danger to public health its manufacture was prohibited in Switzerland in 1908, in France in 1915 and, later, in other countries including the United States. Wormwood is habit-forming and can cause delirium, hallucinations and even permanent mental deterioration In 1918 Pernod Fils (Sons) built a factory at Tarragona, Spain, where they imported the necessary herbs, but this was closed down at the time of the Spanish Civil War (1936–39). Since then only imitation absinthe has been obtainable; it is usually made out of aniseed and contains no wormwood. (C. C. H. F.)

ABSOLUTE. The term has two chief uses: as an adjective it is used in contrast with relative, comparative or conditioned; as a noun it is used by philosophers to denote the universe conceived as a single whole or system.

Absolute v. Relative, etc.—1. Sometimes the contrast is between what stands in a certain relation and what does not. Thus the term teacher is described by traditional logic as relative because its meaning involves relation to a pupil; similarly, pupil is relative because it involves the relation to a teacher. But table and boulder are absolute terms because they do not refer to their objects as standing in any special relation. It has proved difficult at times to be sure whether a term is absolute in this sense or not. For example, are space, time and motion absolute or relative? Newton maintained that they were both. The space, time and motion of ordinary perception were relative, since the position of everything for it was determined by relations to other things; but there were also an absolute space, time and motion in which, for example, a thing would have a position even if there were no other thing in the universe. This absolute view was rejected by Albert Einstein, who held that when we speak of a position, a moment or a motion, relations to other things enter into the very meaning of the term; and this view has come to prevail.

2. Sometimes the term absolute refers to what has reached the extreme limit within its own kind, so that no further improvement or advance is possible. Thus the propositions of mathematics are said to be absolutely true, while most other propositions are conceded only varying degrees of truth or probability; and absolute zero is the temperature at which the motion of particles which constitutes heat (according to the kinetic theory) would cease; a more intense physical cold is inconceivable.

3. Closely connected with this usage is a third, in which absolute means that which is without conditions or reservations. Thus absolute monarchy is a government in which the power of the monarch is subject to no conditions or limitations. In ethics an action such as truth-telling is called absolutely right, or an attitude such as love absolutely good, to indicate that the rightness or goodness does not depend on the conditions of any particular society, but holds independently and universally.

The Absolute.—Among philosophers the notion of an Absolute has been common since the time of Plato, but the term is chiefly associated with the German school of Absolute Idealism, whose leading members were Johann Fichte, Friedrich Schelling and Hegel. The simplest way of arriving at the notion of the Absolute is as follows: start with any object or event and ask what are its causes. Repeat the question about the causes themselves and again about their causes. One finds that one is carried in thought along a set of radiating paths, all of which lead out into infinity. Philosophers have been led through such reflections to the notion of a being with the following characteristics: (1) It is all-comprehensive; there could not, even in theory, be anything outside it; to suppose there could only shows that we have not been thinking of the whole. This ultimate whole is the Absolute. (2) Furthermore, it is conceived as an intelligible whole, which implies that if enough is known about it, it is not a mere aggregate of parts, but it is seen that every part is necessarily connected with every other. (3) From this it is held to follow that ordinary beliefs are not wholly true, nor the things of common experience wholly real. Just as one cannot understand what a stomach or a heart is until seen in its place in the organism as a whole, so one cannot see what anything finally is until seen in its place in the Absolute whole. Only the Absolute is fully real. (4) It is timeless or eternal. All time is included within it, but it is not itself subject to change. (5) It is *causa sui*, self-caused; for there can be no cause or ground outside itself. (6) By its leading exponent, Hegel, it was conceived as a conscious whole or mind, consisting throughout of experience, though whether it was to be regarded also as personal and to be identified with God was a matter of dispute. Some philosophers, for example, Josiah Royce, have maintained the Absolute to be morally good; others have followed Spinoza in holding it to be above all distinctions of value. Again, for some who have accepted the notion, such as Plotinus and F. H. Bradley, the Absolute was a seamless whole, above relations and distinctions of any kind, and hence could be grasped only by a superrational or mystical insight, while for others, of whom Plato was apparently one, its parts were related very much as are the propositions in a system of geometry.

Critics of the notion of an Absolute have taken various lines. Many have pointed out that history could hardly be, as Hegel held,

a progressive realization of the Absolute if there were no real time or change and if the goal of the process were realized already. Others, such as Bertrand Russell, have insisted that not all present knowledge can be regarded as illusory appearance; if it is, this insight itself would have to be regarded as illusion. Others again have argued, with William James, that the world is a perfect whole and that belief in the Absolute is neither logically nor morally and that belief in the Absolute is merely a "tender-minded" faith that the world is more rational than in fact it is.

See histories of philosophy by Wilhelm Windelband, Harald Höffding, etc. Spinoza's *Ethics*, Hegel's *Phenomenology of Mind* and Bradley's *Appearance and Reality* develop the idea of an absolute in different ways; G. W. Cunningham, *The Idealistic Argument in Recent British and American Philosophy* (1933), considers the evidence pro and con.

(B. Bd.)

ABSOLUTE DIFFERENTIAL CALCULUS: *see* VECTOR ANALYSIS.

ABSOLUTE PITCH: *see* PITCH, MUSICAL.

ABSOLUTE TEMPERATURE SCALE, the scale of temperature based on thermodynamics, also called the Kelvin scale after Lord Kelvin (*q.v.*). The temperature scale derived from the law of expansion of a perfect gas is identical with this thermodynamical scale.

The usual abbreviations for absolute scale are abs., A. or K. Comparing it (approximately) with the centigrade scale, 0° C. = 273° A., 100° C. = 373° A., thus absolute zero is equivalent to −273° C.

See HEAT: *Thermal Properties of Gases*; THERMOMETRY.

ABSOLUTE UNITS, units of measurement of a physical quantity in terms of fundamental (arbitrary) units of length, mass and time. The implication of the word "absolute" is taken to mean that none of these units depends on variable factors that cannot be ruled out by the terms of their definition. The three absolute systems most commonly used are set forth in Table I for purposes of comparison.

TABLE I.—*Absolute Systems of Units, in Terms of Fundamental Units*

System	Abbre-viation	Fundamental Units			Force	Conversion factor
		Length	Mass	Time		
Metric	c.g.s.	Centimetre	Gram	Second	Dyne	
Metric	m.k.s.*	Metre	Kilogram	Second	Newton	10⁵ dynes
British	f.p.s.	Foot	Pound	Second	Poundal	1.38x10⁴ dynes

*This system of units, because of its advantages in electrical measurements, came into increasing scientific use in the U.S.

Engineers frequently use systems of units in which weight replaces mass; *i.e.*, the force of the earth's gravitational attraction for an object instead of the object's inherent inertia. Since the weight of an object depends on its position because of the variation of gravitational attraction over the surface of the earth as well as everywhere in space, these engineering systems, according to the above criteria of invariance of the fundamental units, are not entitled to the name of absolute systems. For comparison with the above, however, these units and conversion factors are shown in Table II.

TABLE II.—*Engineering Systems**

System	Length	Force	Time	Mass	Conversion factor
English Engineering	1 foot	1 pound-weight	1 second	Slug	32.174 poundals
metric	1 centimetre	1 gram-weight	1 second	Metric slug	980.665 dynes

*If, and only if, by agreement, weight is defined as being measured where the acceleration of gravity is 980.665 cm./sec.² can the above engineering systems be arbitrarily regarded as absolute, as indeed they often are.

See also MECHANICS: *Newton's Laws;* PHYSICAL UNITS; WEIGHTS AND MEASURES. (H. B. Lm.)

ABSOLUTION, in religion, is the pronouncement of remission to the penitent. Interpretations of absolution in the several Christian traditions vary in relation to two issues, the designation of penance as a sacrament and the designation of the ministry as a priesthood (*see* MINISTRY, CHRISTIAN). In Roman

Catholicism, where penance is a sacrament and the minister is a priest, absolution grants release from the guilt of sin to the sinner who is truly contrite over his sin, confesses his sin to a priest and promises to perform satisfaction to God for the offense. The doctrine of absolution is similar in Eastern Orthodox teaching; but in place of the Western formula, "I absolve thee from thy sins in the name of the Father and of the Son and of the Holy Ghost," Eastern churches generally employ some such formula as "May God, through me, a sinner, forgive thee. . . ." In Anglican and in Lutheran usage, formulas of absolution have ranged from the declaratory "I forgive you all your sins" or "I forgive thee" in the Visitation of the Sick, to the precatory "Almighty God, have mercy upon you, and forgive you all your sins." Some Anglican writers distinguish three forms of absolution in the usage of that communion: declaratory, intercessory and judicial. In keeping with their doctrines of the ministry and of the sacraments, other Christian traditions have confined absolution to prayers for forgiveness and the announcement of God's willingness to forgive all those who truly repent of their sins; hence absolution is neither a judicial act nor a means by which the forgiveness of sins is conferred, but a statement of divine judgment and divine forgiveness. Nevertheless, some formula for the public confession of sins and the public pronouncement of forgiveness is included somewhere in the liturgies of most Christian groups, even of those that avoid the term absolution altogether. *See also* CONFESSION.

(J. J. PN.)

ABSOLUTISM, POLITICAL. In its general sense, absolutism means a governmental system in which power is wholly concentrated in a single ruling agency, typically a single individual. The essence of such a system is that the ruling power is not subject to regularized challenge or check by any other agency, be it judicial, legislative, religious, economic or electoral. Louis XIV, who ruled France during the late 17th and early 18th centuries, furnished the most familiar assertion of absolutism when he said, "L'état, c'est moi" ("I am the state"). Fascist, nazi and communist dictatorships provide more recent examples. In fact, all governmental systems described as dictatorial, despotic, autocratic, authoritarian or totalitarian are absolutist in their concentration of political power. By the middle of the 20th century, absolutism came to mean the opposite of western democracy, in which government is limited by free elections and often by other means of distributing power.

Varying in form, political absolutism has prevailed in much of the world over long periods of time. However, the form originating early in modern European history became the prototype. Its character was definitely monarchical, based on the strong individual leaders of new nation-states created at the breakup of the medieval order. The power of these states was closely associated with the power of their kings, and to strengthen both it was necessary to curtail the restraints on centralized government which had been exercised by the church, feudal lords and medieval customs generally. By claiming the absolute authority of the state against such former restraints, the monarch as head of state claimed his own absolute authority as well.

By the 16th century monarchical absolutism was coming to prevail in much of western Europe, and it was widespread in the 17th and 18th centuries. Besides France, whose absolutism was epitomized by Louis XIV, well-known illustrations may be drawn from Spain, Prussia and Tudor England.

Ideological Basis.—In defense of monarchical absolutism, the simplest argument was that kings derived their authority from God. This view could justify even tyrannical rule as divinely ordained punishment, administered by rulers, for man's sinfulness. In its origins, the divine right theory may be traced to the medieval conception of God's award of temporal power to the political ruler while spiritual power was given to the head of the church. However, the new national monarchs asserted their authority in all matters, and tended to become heads of church as well as state. Their power was absolute in a way that was impossible for medieval monarchs confronted by a church that was essentially a rival centre of authority.

More pragmatic arguments than that of divine right were also advanced in behalf of absolute monarchy. Complete obedience to a single will was said to be essential to order and security. The alternative was the chaos believed to flow from challenging or dividing political power. Efficiency in protecting life and property required absolutism. In so justifying submission by subjects on the ground of self-interest, the most elaborate statement was made in the 17th-century work the *Leviathan* by Thomas Hobbes. Technically Hobbes's theory allowed the absolute sovereign to be a representative assembly instead of a monarch, but he regarded an individual ruler as more convenient. In this respect, Hobbes resembles other defenders of absolutism. The single will to which they assign all authority ordinarily turns out to be that of a single man or of a very small group. The same has often tended to be the case even with those theorists who have started with the premiss that there is a "general will" of the whole community whose authority is absolute when expressed by a majority. Although Jean Jacques Rousseau, the 18th-century French writer who developed the conception of the general will, apparently meant its absolute authority to be exercised by the people themselves, it has readily been converted into a justification for strong leadership ruling absolutely in the name of the people.

20th-Century Forms.—The 20th-century forms of absolutism appear no different in this important respect. Although nonmonarchical in leadership, fascist, nazi and communist systems strongly personalized the absolute power claimed for the state or for the sociopolitical movement dominating the state. Concentration of power thus approximated that of the older absolutist forms, but the 20th-century dictatorships were innovative in that they made absolute political authority virtually synonymous with society and accordingly more pervasive, or totalitarian, in its impact on the lives of individuals. Along with this went a much broader effort to manufacture popular support for absolute rulers than had been characteristic of the earlier monarchies.

Absolutism, especially in its later forms, is most clearly distinguished from democracy by contrasting the unlimited power claimed for dictators with the constitutional practices of democratic systems. The difference rests on more than the degree of popular support for governmental decisions. What is always absent in absolutism is restraint on the exercise of political power. No constitutional machinery exists to impose limits on what rulers may do. Not only are they unchecked by an electorate free to choose an alternative set of rulers, but they are conceived to be under no law or custom higher than their own will. Although absolutists are, in practice, likely to take some of their subjects' desires into account, if only as a means to maintain power, it is still true that law is a product of the will of the rulers alone. Furthermore this law of the rulers exhausts the meaning of justice in the absolutist state. No higher standard of right and wrong can be applied.

Nevertheless it is possible, and indeed frequent, for absolute rulers to claim that law as they make it is really based on some higher standard than that of their own will. From kings asserting that they represented God's will on earth to 20th-century leaders speaking in the name of a national, racial or class destiny, political absolutism cloaks itself in the language of philosophical absolutism.

The monopoly of political power is justified by a knowledge of absolute truth. Neither the sharing of power nor limits on its exercise appear valid to those who believe that they know, and know absolutely, what is right. *See* MONARCHY; *see also* Index references under "Absolutism, Political" in the Index volume.

(L. D. E.)

ABSORPTION OF LIGHT IN SPACE: *see* INTERSTELLAR MATTER.

ABSORPTION SPECTRUM: *see* SPECTROSCOPY: *Measurements;* LIGHT; MOLECULAR SPECTRA; SPECTROSCOPY, ASTRONOMICAL.

ABSTRACT AND ABSTRACTION. A number of things may be found to have some property or relation in common, to which an appropriate designation is then given. This procedure is commonly known as a process of abstraction. Thus, when it was discovered that certain bodies allow electricity to flow through them, they came to be known as conductors, and the common property was called conductivity. The word "conductivity" is said to be an abstract term; and conductivity itself is said to be an abstraction. Some writers also call the concept of conductivity an abstract idea. Abstraction may also occur when observation of a single thing leads to detection of some property or relation which can be shared with other things. In this way, the discovery that a man's blood fails to clot might lead to the introduction of the abstract term "hemophilia."

"Abstract" is contrasted with "concrete" (though there is no corresponding opposite for the word "abstraction"). A word or expression is said to be concrete if it refers to a particular thing. Thus the expression "World War I" is concrete, while the word "war" is abstract.

It is hard to give a satisfactory definition of "abstraction," since its use generally presupposes an oversimple conception of how thinking proceeds. It might be said that abstraction is a process in which consideration is given to some aspect or feature of a complex whole to the neglect of the remainder; but this statement is both too vague and too restrictive to cover all the cases in which abstraction is commonly said to occur.

In modern logic, the word "abstraction" has several more exact senses. For example, suppose a given relation R is transitive, symmetric and reflexive. And consider a class of objects, every two of which are connected by the relation R. Then to each such class there may be made to correspond a symbol, S_i. Each S_i can then be said to have been given a "definition by abstraction." This sense was introduced by Giuseppe Peano, who used it in defining cardinal numbers.

"Functional abstraction" is used for the process of obtaining a function from a given formula containing a free variable. If A is a formula, the notation "$\lambda x\,[A]$" is employed for the function obtained from A by abstraction relative to A; "λx" is called an *abstraction operator*. (The foregoing is Alonzo Church's notation, for which *see* bibliography; other logicians use different but equivalent notations.)

Other abstraction operators have been found useful. By prefixing the symbol "$\hat{x}$" to a propositional form containing a free variable "x," we can refer to the class of things satisfying that propositional form. The symbol "$\hat{x}$" is called the *class abstraction operator*. Again, by prefixing the symbol "$\hat{x}\hat{y}$" to a propositional form with the two variables, "x" and "y," we can refer to the relation in extension corresponding to the propositional form in question; "$\hat{x}\hat{y}$" is the *relational abstraction operator*. The above technical devices can be regarded as instruments for sharpening the vague notions discussed at the beginning of this article.

BIBLIOGRAPHY.—H. W. B. Joseph, *Introduction to Logic*, 2nd rev. ed. (1916); Heinrich Scholz and Hermann Schweitzer, *Die sogenannten Definitionen durch Abstraktion* (1935); Alonzo Church, *The Calculi of Lambda-Conversion* (1941).   (M. BK.)

ABSTRACT ART, or nonobjective, concrete, nonfigurative, or nonrepresentational art, is art in which the portrayal of things seen plays no part. All art consists largely of elements that can be called abstract—elements of form, colour, and texture, of size and inner scale and space—and it is they that principally determine style. In the past these abstract elements served descriptive and illustrative purposes to celebrate, comment upon, and portray divine and human personages and institutions—and exposition dominated over expressive function.

Historically, abstract art is the child of the 19th century. The period that saw so vast a body of elaborately representational art produced for the sake of anecdote saw also generations of painters engaged in extending what Delacroix called "the music of a painting" and in questioning inherited conventions of naturalism by attending closely to the visual facts of both subject and picture. The period of Romanticism (*q.v.*) had put forward ideas about art that denied classicism's emphasis on imitation and idealization and stressed the role of imagination, the unconscious, and even of chance as the essential creative factors. Gradually painters seized on the freedom, and recognized some of the duties, implied in this. Maurice Denis' statement of 1890, "It should be remembered that a picture—before being a war-horse, a nude, or an anecdote of

some sort—is essentially a flat surface covered with colours assembled in a certain order," summarizes the feeling among progressive artists of his time, and it is possible to see the bold experimental designing of the *art nouveau* (*q.v.*) phase, with its reliance on the expressive (as opposed to descriptive) properties of line, colour, surface, etc., as the first widespread exploration of abstraction in an area closely allied to painting.

All the major movements of the first decades of the 20th century in some way stressed the gap between art and natural appearances (while the cinema began to offer a form of visual narrative greatly superior, as such, to narrative painting): various forms of Expressionism (*q.v.*), encouraged by the art of primitive peoples, attempted to communicate strong feeling through distortion of the visible world; Fauvism (*q.v.*) exploited emancipation of colour, as already advocated by Gauguin; Cubism (*q.v.*), with Cézanne as its great forerunner, fragmented and reconstructed natural objects for the sake of an essentially pictorial structure; and Futurism (*q.v.*) attempted to find a visual idiom in which to express a sensation of speed in keeping with 20th-century dynamism. One of the Futurists, Giacomo Balla, ventured outside the usual range of Futurism to paint geometrical patterns, but generally the hold on artists of some part of the visible world, at least as pretext for a composition, remained strong.

There is, however, a deep distinction between abstracting from appearances, even if to the point of unrecognizability, and making works of art out of forms not drawn from the visible world. During the four or five years preceding World War I several artists in France, Germany, and the U.S.S.R. (Robert Delaunay, Wassily Kandinsky, Kazimir Malevich, Vladimir Tatlin) turned to fundamentally abstract art, but to the majority of even the progressive artists the abandoning of every degree of representation seemed perverse. During the war, the emergence of the de Stijl group in the Netherlands (Piet Mondrian, Theo van Doesburg, Georges Vantongerloo, and others) and of the Dada group in Zürich (notably Jean [Hans] Arp) further widened the spectrum of abstract art.

It is possible to divide abstract art into two sections: elementarism and free abstraction. Preeminently among the elementarists Malevich, who initiated Suprematism in the U.S.S.R., and Mondrian, the exponent of Neoplasticism, limited themselves to a few basic forms and colours. Other artists used geometry and mathematical calculations to direct their compositions. Generally the elementarists stressed the rational origin of their work and opposed it to nature. (*See* PAINTING: *Nonobjective Painting.*) Elementarist art exercised a lasting influence outside the fine arts, especially on typography and architecture; indeed the elementarists sought to refashion the whole human environment. The German Bauhaus, active from 1919 until 1933, sought to unify art and design education on elementarist principles. On the other hand, free abstraction, whether expressionist (Kandinsky, between 1910 and 1920) or lyrical (Arp), was founded on emotion and instinct and therefore had to be subjective in origin and effect. Kandinsky's book *Über das Geistige in der Kunst* ("Concerning the Spiritual in Art," 1912) and the *De Stijl* magazine (1917 to 1930) provided the basic philosophies on both sides.

Abstract art did not flourish between World Wars I and II. Beset by totalitarian politics and by art movements placing renewed emphasis on imagery, such as Surrealism, it received little notice. Groups in Paris exhibiting and publishing under the names of the *Cercle et Carré* and *Abstraction-Création* offered rallying points for abstract artists from several countries, and the 1930s saw some development of the abstract movement in sculpture. It was then that Alexander Calder produced his first mobiles, Henry Moore and Barbara Hepworth, at first influenced by Constantin Brancusi and later by the Constructivist, Naum Gabo, began to create abstract works that have played a pioneer role in the development of British sculpture.

After World War II an energetic American school of abstract art emerged and has had wide influence. In painting, products ranged from the warmest expressionism (Jackson Pollock, Willem de Kooning), to a more impersonal manner (Mark Rothko, Barnett Newman), and then to a variety of coolly controlled idioms. In

Great Britain, Ben Nicholson, continuing his role from the 1930s, Victor Pasmore, William Scott, Roger Hilton, Alan Davie, and others established the viability of abstract painting in Britain, and many younger artists have built on that foundation. In continental Europe such men as Max Bill and Victor Vasarely have pursued elementarist principles, while others, such as Lucio Fontana and Georges Mathieu have taken free abstraction or "Informal Art," as it may be called in Europe, to new extremes.

Abstract art has puzzled and indeed confused many people, but for those who have accepted its nonreferential language there is no doubt as to its value and achievements. It has been claimed that it appeals too exclusively to the sense of sight but, as in the case of music, this sensory appeal results from intelligible and analyzable means. Certainly sensibility to the abstract values of art in general has been greatly refined by it, and it has contributed to a growing understanding of nondiscursive communication.

BIBLIOGRAPHY.—A. H. Barr, Jr., *Cubism and Abstract Art* (1936); M. Brion (ed.), *Art Since 1945* (1958); W. Haftmann, *Painting in the Twentieth Century* (1960); M. Seuphor, *Abstract Painting* (1962).

(N. L.)

ABSTRACT OF TITLE: *see* TITLE TO LAND.

ABU, MOUNT, a mountain near a town of the same name, is just within the southern border of Rajasthan, India, 110 mi. N. of Ahmedabad. It is an isolated feature of the Aravalli range, detached from the chain by a valley seven miles across, in which flows the Western Banas. It rises from the surrounding plains like a precipitous granite island, its several peaks ranging in height from 4,000 to 5,650 ft. The hill has been a place of pilgrimage for at least 2,000 years, and is mentioned as such in the *Mahabharata* where it appears as Arbuda. The elevations and platforms of the mountain are covered with elaborately sculptured Jain shrines, temples and tombs. On the top is a small round platform containing a cavern, with a block of granite bearing the footprints of Data-Bhrigu, an incarnation of Vishnu. The two principal temples, at Dilwara, about the middle of the mountain, are built of white marble and are pre-eminent both for their beauty and as examples of the culminating baroque phase of Gujarat architecture.

The more modern of the two, the Tejpal temple, was built by two brothers, rich merchants, between 1197 and 1247, and for delicacy and richness of carving and minute beauty of detail, especially of the elaborately worked underside of its famous dome, it stands almost unrivaled. The other was built by Vimala, a local governor of the Solanki monarch, apparently about A.D. 1032; simpler and bolder in style, it is one of the oldest, as well as one of the most complete, examples of Jain architecture known. The principal object within the temple is a cell lighted only from the door, containing a seated figure of Parswanath, the 23rd *tirthankara*, or sage, of the Jain faith. The portico is composed of 48 pillars, the whole enclosed in an oblong courtyard about 140 ft. by 90 ft., surrounded by a double colonnade of smaller pillars, forming porticos to a range of 52 cells, each of which is occupied by an image of Parswanath. According to legend the Agni Kula (Firegroup) Rajputs originated in a fire pit around Mount Abu. This seems to represent a purgation rite by which the taint of foreign extraction of these Rajput clans was removed.

The town of MOUNT ABU (pop. 1961, 8,076), a much frequented hill resort, was the headquarters of the Rajputana states agency under British rule.

See C. E. Luard, *Notes on the Dilwara Temples and Other Antiquities of the Sacred Mount of Arbuda (Abu)* (1913).

ABU-AL-ALA AL-MAARRI (Arab. ABU-AL-'ALA' AL-MA-'ARRI) (973–1057), Arab poet and man of letters whose two famous collections of poems, *Saqt al-Zand* ("The Tinder Spark") and the *Luzumiyyat*, place him in the first rank of Arab poets. He belonged to the south Arabian tribe Tanukh, a section of which had migrated to Syria before the time of Islam. Born at Ma-'arrat al-Nu'man in north Syria, he was blind from early infancy as a result of smallpox. In 1007 he visited Baghdad and made the acquaintance of literary circles, but returned in 1009 to Ma-'arra, where he spent the rest of his days, until his death in 1057, in teaching and writing.

Apart from poetry, he wrote a volume of epistles on various literary and social subjects (*Mukatabat*), another of literary homilies, *al-Fusul wal-Ghayat* ("Chapters and Aims"), and a work on literary criticism in the unusual form of a description of a celestial journey, entitled *Risalat al-Ghufran* ("Epistle of Pardon"). The second collection of his poems, known as *Luzum ma lam yalzam* or the *Luzumiyyat* (a word meaning literally "necessities," descriptive of their complicated rhyming system), contains the more original, mature and pessimistic thoughts of the author in contemplating human life and death. Much interest has been shown in the author and his works by 20th-century scholars.

BIBLIOGRAPHY.—R. A. Nicholson, *Studies in Islamic Poetry*, with Eng. trans. of more than 300 poems from the *Luzumiyyat* (1921), his summary, with a partial Eng. trans., of the *Risalat-al-Ghufran* is in the *Journal of the Royal Asiatic Society* (1900 and 1902); A. Rihani, *The Luzumiyyat of Abu'l 'Ala*, Eng. trans. (1920); D. S. Margoliouth, *The Letters of Abu'l 'Ala' of Ma'arrat Al 'Nu 'man*, with Eng. trans. and biography (1898), and "Abu-al- 'Ala' al-Ma'arri's Correspondence on Vegetarianism" in *Journal of the Royal Asiatic Society* (1902); Ibrahim al-Arabi, Arabic ed. of the *Luzumiyyat* (1952); Taha Hussein and Ibrahim al-Abyari, *Sharh Luzum ma lam Galzam*, a commentary (1954). The *Saqt al-Zand* and *Risalat al-Ghufran* were published in Arabic in 1924 and 1950 respectively.

See also C. Brockelmann, *Geschichte der arabischen Literatur*, suppl. vol. i (1937).

ABU-AL-ATAHIYAH (ABU'L-ATAHIYA; Arab. ABU ISHAQ ISMA'IL IBN QASIM AL-'ANAZI) (748–828) was the first Arab poet of note to break with the conventions of the older poetry of the desert, and to adopt the simpler and freer language of the towns. Born at 'Ain al-Tamr on the Euphrates in 748, he was descended from clients (*i.e.*, loosely attached members) of the tribe of Anaza. His life was spent in Kufa and Baghdad, where he died in 828, during the reign of al-Ma'mun. In earlier life he wrote love lyrics, but his fame rests on the ascetic poems of his later years, the *Zuhdiyyat* (German translation by O. Rescher, *Der Diwan des Abu'l Atahija: Teil 1. Die Zuhdiyyat*, 1928), most of which are concerned with the observation of common life and mortality and are generally pessimistic in tone. In spite of this, and of suggestions of heresy in his verse, he was a favourite at the court of Harun al-Rashid. His poems were collected in part and published in Arabic (1887; reissued 1909).

On his position in Arabic literature *see* W. Ahlwardt, *Diwan des Abu Nowas* (1861); R. A. Nicholson, *Literary History of the Arabs* (1907; reissued 1953).

ABU-AL-FARAJ AL-ISFAHANI (ABU'L FARAJ; Arab. ABU-AL-FARAJ 'ALI IBN AL-HUSAIN AL-ISFAHANI) (897–967), Arab scholar, was the author of *Kitab al-Aghani* ("Book of Songs"), which gives an account of the chief Arabic songs known in his day, with the stories of the composers and singers. Born in Isfahan in 897, he was a member of the tribe of the Quraish (Koreish) and a direct descendant of Marwan, the last of the Omayyad caliphs who ruled at Damascus and were deposed and succeeded by the Abbasid caliphs in 750. He was thus connected with the Omayyad rulers in Spain, and seems to have kept up a correspondence with them and to have sent them some of his works. He spent his youth and made his early studies in Baghdad (the capital of the Abbasids), becoming famous for his knowledge of early Arabian antiquities. His later life was spent in Aleppo with Saif-al-Dawla (to whom he dedicated the *Kitab al-Aghani*), in Rai with the Buyid vizier Ibn Abbad, and in other cities in Moslem Arabia. In religion he was a Shiite and wrote a book on the martyrdom of the house of 'Ali, *Maqatil al-Talibiyyin*, but his fame rests on the *Kitab al-Aghani* which contains a mass of information as to the life and customs of the early Arabs, and is the most valuable authority for their pre-Islamic and early Moslem days. In the last years of his life he lost his reason. He died at Baghdad in 967.

The text of the *Kitab al-Aghani* was published in 21 vol. (1905–06). *See also Tables alphabétiques du Kitab-al-Agani*, a volume of elaborate indexes edited by I. Guidi (1900).

For his life *see* M'G. de Slane's French trans. of Ibn Khallikan's biographical dictionary (1843–71).

ABU BAKR (*c.* 573–634), later known as al-Siddik (the truthful, the upright, or the one who counts true), was the first Muslim caliph, reigning from 632 to 634. Of the Taim clan of the tribe of Quraish at Mecca, he was a merchant, probably in a small way, when he became a friend of Mohammed before the latter's call to preach. He is usually said to have been the first male convert to Islam; but this may only reflect his later position. Before the Hegira (Mohammed's migration from Mecca to Medina, A.D. 622), he was clearly marked out as second to Mohammed by the latter's betrothal to his young daughter 'A'isha and by Abu Bakr's being Mohammed's companion on the journey to Medina. He had spent most of his wealth to promote Islam by ransoming believing slaves and in other ways. From 622 to 632 he was Mohammed's chief adviser, but had no prominent public functions except that he conducted the pilgrimage to Mecca in 631 and led the public prayers in Medina during Mohammed's last illness.

On Mohammed's death (June 8, 632), Abu Bakr succeeded to his political functions by the choice of the Muslims of Medina, with the title of *khalifat rasul-Allah* ("deputy or successor of the Messenger of God," or caliph). His caliphate was occupied with suppressing the risings in various parts of Arabia known as the *ridda* ("apostasy"), in which, despite the religious description, politics were probably uppermost. His chief opponent, Musailima, was killed at a battle in eastern Nejd in May 633. While clearing operations went on, Abu Bakr began to direct expansionist moves from Arabia into Iraq and Syria. The Muslim conquests had thus begun before his death (Aug. 23, 634). The ascription to him of the first "collecting" or writing down of the Koran is probably mistaken. *See* CALIPHATE.   (W. M. WT.)

ABUKIR: *see* ABU QIR.

ABU 'L-FARAJ (13th century): *see* BAR-HEBRAEUS.

ABU'L-FAZL 'ALLAMI (1551–1602), secretary, historiographer, general and, in religion, tutelary genius of the great Mogul emperor Akbar. Born at Agra on Jan. 14, 1551, the second son of Shaykh Mubarak Nagauri and younger brother of the poet Fayzi, Abu'l-Fazl was presented to Akbar in 1574. A mystic and scholar, critical of the orthodox Moslem religious teachers, he assisted in the development of Akbar's eclectic *Din-i-Ilahi* ("The Divine Faith"). Appointed a military commander in the Deccan in 1599, Abu'l-Fazl distinguished himself there as a soldier and an administrator. He was assassinated at the jealous instigation of Akbar's eldest son, Salim (afterward the emperor Jahangir), on Aug. 22, 1602.

In Mogul Persian literature Abu'l-Fazl is famed for his *Akbarnama* ("Book of Akbar"), a history of Akbar's reign to 1601 supplemented by the *A'in-i-Akbari* ("Akbar's Institutes"), a "gazetteer" of the administrative and military organization and the social and religious life of Akbar's empire. Two collections of Abu'l-Fazl's letters are also extant.

See C. A. Storey, *Persian Literature: a Bio-bibliographical Survey,* vol. i, pt. ii (1954).   (P. H.)

ABULFEDA (ABULFIDA; Arab. ABU-AL-FIDA' ISMA 'IL IBN 'ALI 'IMAD-AL-DIN) (1273–1331), Arab prince, historian and geographer, best known for his *Mukhtasar Tarikh al-Bashar* ("Abridgement of the History of the Human Race"), extending from the Creation to 1329. He was born in 1273 at Damascus, whither his father, Malik al-Afdal, brother of the prince of Hamah, had fled from the Mongols. He was a descendant of Ayyub, the father of Saladin. In 1285 he was present at the assault of a stronghold of the Knights of St. John, and he took part in the sieges of Tripoli, Acre and Qal'at al-Rum. In 1310 he was appointed governor of Hamah by the Mameluke sultan Malik al-Nasir. In 1312 he became prince with the title Malik al-Salih, and in 1320 received the hereditary rank of sultan with the title Malik al-Mu'ayyad. For more than 20 years he reigned in tranquillity and splendour, devoting himself to the duties of government and to the completion of the works to which he is chiefly indebted for his fame. *Taqwim al-Buldan* ("Geography of Countries") was founded on the works of his predecessors, and so ultimately on the work of Ptolemy. Parts of the work were published and translated as early as 1650. He was a munificent patron of men of letters, who came in large numbers to his court. He died at Hamah in 1331.

The text of *Mukhtasar Tarikh al-Bashar* was published in 1869. There are translations of parts into Latin, French and English.

The *Taqwim al-Buldan* was edited by M'G. de Slane and M. Reinaud (1840), and translated into French, with introduction by M. Reinaud and S. Guyard (1848–83).

See C. Brockelmann, *Geschichte der arabischen Literatur,* vol. ii, (1902).

ABUL KASIM (Arab. ABU-AL-QASIM KHALAF IBN-ABBAS AL-ZAHRAWI; Lat. ALBUCASIS) (c. 936–c. 1013), a distinguished Arabo-Spanish physician, was born of Spanish parents about 936 at El-Zahra near Córdoba. His medical reputation was brought to the attention of Caliph Abd-ar-Rahman III (912–961), who named him as his court physician. He died about 1013.

Abul Kasim's magnum opus was his *Altasrif,* a comprehensive work devoted to medicine and surgery and divided into 30 parts. His surgical tract, which was translated into Latin by Gerard of Cremona, was the leading textbook on surgery in Europe for about 500 years. The material of the *Altasrif* was borrowed from the *Epitome* of Paul of Aegina (q.v.), but it eclipsed the *Epitome* and also the *Kitab al-Mansuri* of Rhazes because of its lucid descriptions and its remarkable illustrations of surgical instruments. Abul Kasim was not followed to any great extent by the Arab physicians, who favoured Rhazes and Avicenna (qq.v.) as medical teachers. His chief influence was in Latin Europe, where his lucidity and method of presentation were preferred even over Galen. More than anyone else, Abul Kasim helped raise the status of surgery in Christian Europe.

BIBLIOGRAPHY.—B. L. Gordon, *Medieval and Renaissance Medicine* (1960); D. Campbell, *Arabian Medicine* (1926); C. Brockelmann, *Geschichte der arabischen Literatur,* vol. i (1898); H. Handerson, *Baas' History of Medicine* (1910).   (B. L. G.)

ABU'L QASIM MANSUR: *see* FIRDAUSI.

ABUL WEFA (ABUL WAFA) (940–997/998), Persian astronomer and one of the greatest Moslem mathematicians, was born in Buzjan (now Buzdschan), Quhistan (now Khurasan), in 940, and flourished in Baghdad where he died in 997 or 998. He translated and commented on the works of the Greek mathematicians and made an exhaustive commentary on Diophantus, but these writings are lost; a book of applied geometry is probably the work of a pupil. He did not, as is sometimes claimed, discover the inequality in the moon's motion later called variation. He contributed much to the development of trigonometry, being probably the first to prove the generality of the sine theorem for spherical triangles; devised a new method for calculating sine tables; studied the tangent, drew up a table of tangents, and introduced the secant and cosecant.

See F. Woepcke in *Journal Asiatique* (1855); G. Sarton, *Introduction to the History of Science,* vol. i (1945).   (D. McK.)

ABUNÁ, a river in Bolivia, rising east of the Cordillera Vilcabamba and flowing northeast for about 200 mi. to join the Madeira. Rubber, Brazil nuts, quinine and other forest products are the principal items of commerce in the densely forested and sparsely inhabited Abuná region. The Abuná constitutes the northern boundary between Bolivia and Brazil.   (J. L. TR.)

ABUNDANTIA, Roman goddess, the personification of prosperity and good fortune. She appears holding a horn of plenty and distributing grain and money, or, in the aspect of Annona or Felicitas, almost exclusively on the coins, as representative of the personal power of the Roman emperor to induce prosperity. The numismatic representation occurs as early as Nerva and was especially popular under Antoninus Pius, Marcus Aurelius and Commodus. Because of the peculiarly single significance of the goddess she seems to have had no cult, unlike some other deified abstractions (*e.g.,* Clementia). Abundantia may be compared with Domina Abundia (O. Fr., Dame Habonde, Notre Dame d'Abondance), a beneficent fairy who brought plenty to those whom she visited (Grimm, *Teutonic Mythology*).   (T. V. B.)

ABU NUWAS (ABU-AL-HASAN IBN HANI' AL-HAKAMI) (c. 756–810), who is recognized as the greatest Arab poet of his time, was born about 756 in al-Ahwaz, Persia, of a Persian mother. His father was a native of Damascus and a soldier. He is said to have spent a year with the Arabs in the desert to gain purity of language. He settled in Baghdad, where he enjoyed the favour of the caliphs Harun al-Rashid and al-Amin, and died there in 810. Genial, cynical, immoral, Abu Nuwas drew on all the varied life of his time for the material of his poems. In his formal odes he followed on the whole the old Arab tradition, though with greater freedom than his predecessors, but his native genius probably found its best expression in the *Khamriyyat*, a famous collection of wine songs.

Abu Nuwas' collected poems were edited by M. K. Farid, *Diwan Abu Nuwas* (1932). The *Khamriyyat* was edited by W. Ahlwardt, *Diwan des Abu Nowas*, i. *Die Weinlieder* (1861).

See R. A. Nicholson, *Literary History of the Arabs,* pp. 292–296 (1907; reissued 1953).

ABU QIR (ABUKIR; ABOUKIR), a fishing village and summer resort on the Mediterranean coast of Egypt, 14½ mi. N.E. of Alexandria by rail. Pop. (1957) 10,224. The name means "Father Cyrus," who was a Coptic saint. From the protected anchorage the bay of Abu Qir sweeps eastward about 30 mi. to the Rosetta mouth of the Nile. Behind this coast line lies the lagoon of Lake Idku, a former embayment of the sea. A fish-smoking plant operates there and a paper mill, making wrapping paper from rice straw. In the bay on Aug. 1, 1798, Horatio Nelson defeated the French fleet in the battle of the Nile, and near Abu Qir on March 8, 1801, a British army commanded by Sir R. Abercromby landed in the face of strenuous opposition from a French force entrenched on the beach. The site of the ancient city of Canopus (*q.v.*) is about 2 mi. from the village.   (A. B. M.)

ABU SIMBEL (IPSAMBUL), three temples of Ramses II built (*c.* 1250 B.C.) in Aswan governorate of Egypt (ancient Nubia) on the west bank of the Nile 56 mi. S of Korosko by river. The temples were hewn in the sandstone cliffs at the riverside. The principal one, judged by some to be the greatest and most imposing of all rock-hewn monuments, was discovered by J. Burckhardt in 1812 and opened by G. B. Belzoni in 1817; the front was cleared several times, but sand pressed forward from the north end. The hillside was recessed to form the facade, backed against which four immense seated colossi of the king, in pairs on either side of the entrance, rose from a platform or forecourt reached from the river by a flight of steps. Of nobly placid design, the colossi were 65 ft. high and were accompanied by smaller figures of Ramses' queen and their sons and daughters; behind and over them was a cornice surmounted by a long row of apes standing as if in adoration of the rising sun. Large hieroglyphs just below the cornice gave the titulary of Ramses II, who built the temple primarily for the solar gods Amon-Re of Thebes and Re-Horakhte of Heliopolis, called the true sun-god; it was oriented to the east so that the rays of the sun in the early morning penetrated the whole length of two great halls to the innermost sanctuary and fell upon the central figures of Amon-Re and Ramses, enthroned there with Ptah of Memphis and Re-Horakhte on either side. The interior of the temple, a series of halls, penetrating for 185 ft. into the solid rock and decorated with coloured sculpture of fine workmanship was in a good state of preservation in the 1960s; some of the scenes had religious import (among them Ramses as king making offerings to himself as god), others illustrated war in Syria, Libya, and Nubia; another series depicted the events of the famous battle with the Hittites and their allies at Kadesh, in which Ramses saved the Egyptian camp and army by his personal valour.

Not the least important feature of the temple belongs to a later age when some Greek, Carian, and Phoenician soldiers of one of the kings named Psamtik (apparently I, 663–609 B.C.) inscribed their names upon the two southern colossi, doubtless the only ones then clear of sand. These graffiti are of the highest value for the early history of the alphabet, and as evidence of the presence of Greek mercenaries in the Egyptian armies of the period. The upper part of the second colossus (from the south) had fallen; the third had been repaired by Seti II not many years after the completion of the temple. A small temple, immediately to the south of the first, consisted of a single rock-cut chamber originally preceded by an exterior antechamber. The scenes on the inner walls indicated that the temple served as a repository for divine barks that were carried in procession. The third and northernmost temple, separated from the others by a ravine, was imposing; the six colossi of the facade were 33 ft. high, representing Ramses and his queen Nefertari, to whom he dedicated the temple for the worship of the goddess Hathor.

Years before the high dam at Aswan (*q.v.*) was completed, it was realized that Abu Simbel would be completely submerged as the Nile rose behind the dam to create a gigantic reservoir. In 1955 an international team of archaeological workers began to record the scenes and inscriptions at the site. By 1966 such features as the seated colossi had been cut out of the rock in huge blocks and raised for reconstruction to a cliff about 200 ft. above the old river bed. This salvage effort was supported by funds, equipment, and personnel from more than 50 nations in response to a drive conducted by UNESCO.

See NUBIA: *Excavation and Preservation of Nubia's Sites and Monuments.*   (E. F. W.; X.)

ABU TAMMAM (Arab. ABU TAMMAM HABIB IBN AWS) (*c.* 800–*c.* 845), Arab poet, best known as the compiler of the anthology of early Arabic poems known as the *Hamasah* (*q.v.*). He was born about 800 either in Jasim (Josem) or near Manbij (Hierapolis), and he died in Mosul about 845. Two other similar collections are ascribed to him. His own poetry has been variously judged by Arab critics, some of whom regard him as the greatest poet of the Abbasid era. For his collected poems *see* the critical edition by Muhammad 'Abduh 'Azzam (1951–   ).

For his life *see* Ibn Khallikan's biographical dictionary, in Eng. trans. by M'G. de Slane, vol. i, pp. 348 ff. (1842); and *Kitab al-Aghani* ("Book of Songs") of Abulfaraj, vol. xv, pp. 100–108 (1905–06).

ABUTILON, a genus of more than 100 species of tropical shrubs or herbs (rarely trees) of the mallow family (Malvaceae), including such greenhouse favourites as the flowering maple (*Abutilon hybridum*), which is often used as a summer bedding plant. Abutilons have alternate leaves, often showy bell-shaped flowers and dry, beaked fruits. Some have beautifully variegated leaves and there are many horticultural forms. All should be grown in a cool greenhouse, in reasonably rich potting soil. They are easily propagated by cuttings of young twigs inserted in moist sand. Abutilon is found throughout the world, except on the European continent, and one weedy species (*Abutilon theophrasti*), the velvetleaf, yields China jute, a bast fibre used for cordage. Besides the flowering maple, more than 15 ornamental species are cultivated in England, usually in the greenhouse; among them is *Abutilon esculentum,* the cooked flowers of which are eaten by Brazilians, under the name Bencao de Dios.

(N. TR.)

ABUTMENT: *see* BUTTRESS.

ABYDOS, an ancient town of Mysia, the site of which lies just northeast of the modern Turkish town of Canakkale on the east side of the Dardanelles (Hellespont) at the narrowest point of the straits. Probably originally a Thracian town, it was colonized about 670 B.C. by the Milesians. There Xerxes crossed the strait on his bridge of boats when he invaded Greece in 480 B.C. Abydos is celebrated for its vigorous resistance to Philip V of Macedon (200 B.C.) and for the legend of Hero and Leander. It survived until late Byzantine times as the toll station of the Hellespont.

ABYDOS (Egyptian ABDU, Coptic EBOT), one of the most sacred cities of ancient Egypt. The site, now called al-'Arabat al-Madfuna, is in the low desert west of the Nile, near al-Balyana, about 100 mi. N. of Luxor. Abydos was the necropolis city for nearby Thinis, capital city of the eighth nome of upper Egypt.

The history of Abydos is intimately associated with the political and religious development of Egypt itself and goes back to the beginnings of Egyptian history (*see* EGYPT). There, in two low mounds composed of votive potsherds of all ages, close to the foot of the cliffs, E. Amélineau late in the 19th century discovered a series of pit tombs, proclaimed by their contents and by the steles with royal names found above them to have been those of kings of the first two dynasties of Egypt. The full excavation and description of these tombs by Sir Flinders Petrie gave much information about the earliest dynastic culture of Egypt, although they had been extensively plundered. Doubt has subsequently been raised as to whether these tombs were the actual burial places of the pharaohs whose names they bore: in Saqqarah (*q.v.*), a series of mastaba tombs found by W. B. Emery contained objects bearing the same royal names, and the far greater size of these mastabas and the richness of their contents and decoration have led many scholars to suppose that these are the real resting places of the early kings and that the custom of constructing a sham burial, or cenotaph, at Abydos was practised as early as the Archaic period. Some of the 2nd-dynasty pharaohs, however, may in fact have been buried at Abydos, and they built imposing brick fortresses at the northwestern end of the necropolis area; one, Shunet ez Zebib, covers nearly two acres.

The tutelary deity of the necropolis city was the jackal-god, in the Old Kingdom called Khenti-amentiu. By the 5th dynasty a new deity, the god Osiris, whose cult spread from Busiris (Djedu) in the delta, had become associated with Abydos. The city soon became the focal point of the cult of Osiris, which gradually absorbed that of Khenti-amentiu. Various places mentioned in the Osiris legend were located in and around Abydos, and one of the early tombs most revered by later generations, that of King Djer, was eventually selected as the authentic tomb in which the dismembered god's head was thought to be buried. The city became known as Abdu ("hill of the reliquary"); Abydos is the Greek form. At least as early as the 12th dynasty a sacred drama or mystery play dealing with the death and resurrection of Osiris came to be enacted at Abydos.

Abydos became a place of pilgrimage for pious Egyptians, who desired above all else to be buried as close as possible to the tomb of Osiris. If burial in the sacred precinct was not attainable—and few could afford the expense involved—it was possible to set up a stone in the necropolis inscribed with the dead man's name and titles and a prayer to the god. Thousands of these steles have been found in the cemeteries. Over the mound where the early tombs were known to be, the mound of votive pots grew, and the site is now known to the Arabs as Umm el-Ga'ab ("mother of pots").

The pharaohs, though they were now buried near their residence city, encouraged the cult of the deified king at Abydos and took especial care to embellish and enlarge the temple of Osiris, erected on the site of an older temple of Khenti-amentiu. It was entirely rebuilt by Pepi I, of the 6th dynasty, and much enlarged by the pharaohs of the 12th. In the 18th dynasty Ahmose I built a chapel and Thutmose III a far larger temple (about 130 by 200 ft.). Thutmose also made a processional way from the temple to the cemetery, with a granite gateway. Ramses III added a large building and Ahmose II (Amasis) in the Saite period rebuilt the temple once more and placed in it a large monolithic shrine.

Some pharaohs had a cenotaph or a mortuary temple at Abydos. The temple of Seti (Sethos) I, first excavated by A. Mariette in 1859, is one of the most beautiful of all the temples of antiquity. Its plan is unique, for it has no fewer than seven sanctuaries, approached through two broad hypostyle halls. The sanctuaries are dedicated to the king and the principal gods of Egypt. Behind lie halls devoted to Osiris, Isis and Horus, and to the south, at right angles to the axis, are other halls dedicated to the god of the underworld, Sokaris, and to Nefertum. In a long gallery leading to these halls is a relief showing Seti and his son Ramses making offerings to the cartouches of 76 of their dead predecessors beginning with Menes. This is the so-called Abydos list of kings (*see* CHRONOLOGY: *Egyptian*). The reliefs decorating the walls of this temple are of particular delicacy and beauty. Nearby is a smaller temple, built by Ramses II.

Only 26 ft. behind the temple of Seti I is a remarkable structure known as the Osireion, but probably in reality Seti's cenotaph. This curious monument, completed by the pharaoh Merenptah, is an underground vaulted hall containing a central platform with ten monolithic pillars surrounded by a channel of water. Perhaps the whole was an allegory in stone, a cosmological symbol of the primeval hill amid the waters of the deep.

Around and between the temples is a vast complex of cemeteries of every period of ancient Egyptian history, from the prehistoric age to Ptolemaic and Roman times. Abydos is one of the most important archaeological sites in Egypt.

BIBLIOGRAPHY.—A. Mariette, *Abydos, description des fouilles* (1869–80); E. Amélineau, *Les Fouilles d'Abydos en 1897–8* (1898), *Les Nouvelles Fouilles d'Abydos,* 4 vol. (1899–1905), *Le Tombeau d'Osiris* (1899); M. A. Murray, *The Osireion at Abydos* (1904); J. Capart, *Abydos: le temple de Seti Ier* (1912); W. M. F. Petrie, *Abydos I–III* (1902–04), *The Royal Tombs at Abydos, I and II* (1900–02), *Tombs of the Courtiers* (1925); T. E. Peet, *The Cemeteries of Abydos, I–III* (1913–18); H. Frankfort, *The Cenotaph of Seti I at Abydos* (1933); A. M. Calverley and M. F. Broome, *The Temple of King Sethos I at Abydos,* 4 vol. (1933–59). Plan of the site in B. Porter and R. Moss, *Topographical Bibliography,* vol. v, p. 38 (1937). (M. S. DR.)

ABYSS, any deep place (Gr. *a*, "not"; *byssos*, "bottom"), a bottomless depth. In general, the abyss is regarded vaguely as a place of indefinite extent, the abode of mystery and sorrow.

In the Greek version of the Old Testament the word represents the original chaos (Gen. i, 2) or the Hebrew *tehom*, which is used also in apocalyptic literature and in the New Testament for hell. In the Septuagint cosmography the word is applied to the waters under the earth, from which the springs and rivers are supplied, and to the waters of the firmament, which were regarded as closely connected with those below. Derivatively it acquired the meaning of the place of the dead. In Revelation it is the prison of evil spirits, from which they may occasionally be let loose, and where Satan is doomed to spend 1,000 years.

In rabbinical cosmography the abyss is a region of Gehenna situated below the ocean bed and divided into three or seven parts imposed one above the other. In the cabala the abyss as the opening into the lower world is the abode of evil spirits, and corresponds to the opening of the abyss to the world above.

The adjective abyssal is used to describe deep regions of the sea. In heraldry the abyss is the middle of an escutcheon.

ABYSSINIA: *see* ETHIOPIA.

ACACIA, a large genus of trees and shrubs belonging to the pea family (Leguminosae); the genus comprises a group of several hundred species widely distributed over the warmer regions of the world, but particularly abundant in Australia and Africa. The leaves are usually twice compounded (bipinnate); in some instances, notably with Australian species native to arid localities, the leaflets are suppressed, their stalks (petioles) then becoming flattened and acquiring the physiological functions of leaves. These stalks are commonly vertically arranged, an orientation which precludes the inception of intense sunlight, thus apparently preventing injury through the retardation of excessive surface evaporation.

The small, frequently fragrant flowers are arranged in rounded or elongated clusters. The several seeded podlike fruits are either flattened or cylindrical, often with constrictions between the seeds. Sharp spines arm the branchlets of many forms.

True gum arabic is the product of *Acacia senegal,* a native of both east and west tropical Africa (*see* GUMS, PLANT). The Indian *A. arabica* yields a similar gum, but of inferior quality. Catechu (*q.v.*) or cutch is procured from *A. catechu* and several other species. Extractions from finely divided wood of this tree are employed in dyeing khaki cloth. The barks of most acacias are rich in tannin. Babul or babool, derived from *A. arabica,* is used in India for tanning. The Australian acacias, often called wattle barks, are important sources of tannin; especially valuable are golden wattle (*A. pycnantha*), green wattle (*A. decurrens*) and silver wattle (*A. d. dealbata*). The golden wattle is the Australian national tree and flower.

A few acacias are productive of valuable timber. Australian blackwood (*A. melanoxylon*) is a highly figured wood used in cabinetry. *A. homalophylla,* also Australian, yields a fragrant, decorative wood. Koa (*A. koa*), a native of the Hawaiian Islands, produces a handsomely figured wood used in the manufacture of

A. W. KERR

FLOWERING BRANCH OF SILVER WATTLE (ACACIA DECURRENS DEALBATA)

ukeleles. *A. heterophylla* from Mauritius and Bourbon is another excellent timber tree. The biblical shittah tree (*A. seyal*) is also a member of this group. Species noted for their heavily developed spines include the Australian kangaroo thorn (*A. armata*), the giraffe acacia or African camel's-thorn (*A. giraffae*) and the Central American *A. sphaerocephala* and *A. spadicigera*. The large thorn-like stipules of the two last-mentioned acacias are hollow and provide shelter for ants that feed on leafstalk secretions and curious food bodies at the tips of leaflets.

Sweet acacia (*A. farnesiana*) of the southwestern United States has been introduced into India and southern Europe. Its fragrant, yellow flowers are used in making perfume. The term acacia has been erroneously applied to species of the genus *Robinia,* also a member of the Leguminosae. The American black locust (*Robinia pseudoacacia*) is the false acacia so widely cultivated in milder parts of Great Britain. (E. S. HR.; X.)

ACADEMIC FREEDOM embraces freedom in teaching and freedom in learning, or *lehrfreiheit* and *lernfreiheit* in the language of Germany where the modern conception of academic freedom took form in the 19th century. It is that freedom of members of the academic community, assembled in universities and colleges, which underlies the effective performance of their functions. In modern understanding it embraces intellectual freedom, which is necessary to the acquisition and exchange of knowledge and to inquiry into the unknown, and freedom of creative activity in those arts which are practised in colleges and universities or in which training is offered: it includes also certain personal freedoms in relation to conduct outside of their institutions, which are deemed essential to faculty members and students as such. All of these freedoms exist elsewhere in society as well; but in higher education they occur in a specific institutional context which renders academic freedom distinctive.

Because of the social role of ideas, struggles over academic freedom between the academic community and other interests in society have taken place in all ages and in many circumstances. The nature and outcome of those struggles have been influenced by the forms of organization of academic institutions and the varieties of external authority over them. European universities began as self-constituted communities of scholars; but since these scholars were mainly ecclesiastics, the institutions they founded came under the sponsorship of the medieval church. Before the 18th century the Roman Catholic Church and in some areas its Protestant successors at times exerted a censorship with which the universities or members of their faculties found it necessary to contend. In the 18th and 19th centuries the political state became in many instances the supervising power. Aided by a tradition of faculty government within the institutions, relationships developed in most of the countries of western Europe which (with occasional lapses, notably in the Nazi period in Germany and in other dictatorships) eliminated external control over thought and teaching as an incident to the support and sponsorship of higher education. Faculty members were also left free of institutional control in their teaching and research. Students, similarly left largely free, were subject to the completion of examination and thesis requirements. In England, however, the relation of the established church to Oxford and Cambridge resulted in the maintenance of religious tests for university personnel of these institutions into the 19th century.

In the United States, in the absence of self-constituted communities of scholars, colleges and universities were established by religious or private nonsectarian groups and by states and, occasionally, cities for instruction and, later, for research and development of the arts and professions. Faculty members were hired. Representatives of the founders and their successors, established as boards of control, have remained vested with full legal authority over the institutions they head and have delegated much of it to academic administrators. The faculties usually lack legally secure authority to share in institutional government. Academic tradition and the professional status of faculty members have, nevertheless, served to establish a high degree of independence of the individual in teaching and research, and there has developed considerable faculty participation in college and university government. Students in the United States have been subjected to a rather paternalistic relationship which imposes significant curricular requirements and controls over conduct. Developments in the overseas countries of the British Commonwealth have been similar in various respects to those in both England and the United States.

The academic profession in the United States has formulated principles relating to academic freedom and to a correlative, academic tenure, which has grown up, for the purpose of clarifying academic freedom and of safeguarding it by protecting the faculty member against unwarranted loss of his position or dismissal without a hearing. Originally set forth by the American Association of University Professors in 1915, these principles were supported by other organizations as well and became incorporated into the bylaws of many universities and colleges. Because they are of varying legal effect, their observance rests largely on academic and public opinion, sometimes called into play by investigations of alleged violations and publication of reports upon them. Clearly stated religious limits to academic freedom when the aims of an institution require them are recognized as permissible, but are generally regarded as qualifications to freedom rather than as consistent with it.

Academic freedom in the United States has been strongly influenced by court interpretations of the constitutional freedoms of speech, press and assembly and is itself included to some extent in the protection these freedoms receive against governmental impairment. State requirement of military training of students in state institutions, exclusion of students and faculty from public institutions on account of race, the power of legislative investigators to inquire into educational affairs, and the validity of requiring political oaths of academic personnel have come under judicial scrutiny. The constitutional freedoms of faculty members outside their institutions, which may be vindicated in court, have also been brought within the protections accorded to academic freedom by professional action; for in a democratic society, in which scholarship often is directed consciously to the service of specific social interests, the scholar demands liberty of action in public affairs as a professional as well as a personal right.

Academic freedom on the part of faculty members is accompanied by recognized obligations: the obligation to preserve scholarly objectivity; to refrain from using the classroom for extraneous purposes; and to distinguish the individual's personal role from his institutional or academic capacity. Observance of these obligations is enjoined upon members of the academic profession in the United States by the nationally recognized principles of freedom and tenure.

See also CIVIL LIBERTIES; EDUCATION, HISTORY OF; EDUCATION, PHILOSOPHY OF; UNIVERSITY.

BIBLIOGRAPHY.—F. Paulsen, *Die deutschen Universitäten und das Universitätsstudium,* Bücher iii and iv (1902), Eng. trans. by F. Thilly and W. W. Elwang (1906); R. Hofstadter and W. P. Metzger, *The Development of Academic Freedom in the United States* (1955); R. M. MacIver, *Academic Freedom in Our Time* (1955); R. A. Kirk, *Academic Freedom* (1955); American Association of University Professors, "Declaration of Principles on Academic Freedom and Tenure," *Bulletin,* pp. 15 ff. (Dec. 1915), reprinted, vol. xxxiv, pp. 141 ff. (1948), "1940 Statement of Principles on Academic Freedom and Tenure," *Bulletin,* vol. xlv, pp. 107 ff. (1959); S. P. Capen, *The Management of Universities,* pp. 272–287 (1953); American Civil Liberties Union, *Academic Freedom and Civil Liberties of Students* (1956); J. L. Montrose, "The Legal Relation Between a University and Its Professors," *Universities Review,* vol. xxix, pp. 44–47 (1956); G. F. Kneller, *Higher Learning in Britain,* ch. iii, v (1955); C. Byse and G. L. Joughin, *Tenure in American Higher Education* (1959); *Adler* v. *Board of Education,* 342 United States Supreme Court Reports, 485 ff. (1952); *Sweezey* v. *New Hampshire,* 354 United States Supreme Court Reports, 234 ff. (1957). (R. F. Fu.)

ACADEMIES. The term "academy" is derived from the Greek *Academia,* originally an olive grove of a local hero, situated two miles from Athens. There Plato started his school, which became known by the same name (*see* ACADEMY, GREEK). Gradually the term acquired a general meaning of a higher school and in that sense it was used by Ptolemy I in Alexandria, by Spanish Muslim caliphs, by Charlemagne, by Alfred the Great and others. It is still used for some secondary schools and higher teaching institutions in many countries. The Calvinists in France, Switzerland and the Netherlands called their higher institutions "academies" until the 18th century, when the term "university" was generally adopted. In England both the dissenting and private institutions imparting secondary or higher learning were also called "academies," especially in the 18th century. In modern times many institutions for higher learning in special subjects such as naval, military, agricultural, fine arts, music or commerce have been called "academies." From the Renaissance the term was associated with learned societies which were not schools in the ordinary sense, and in this use "academy" may be defined as a society or institution for the cultivation and promotion of literature, of arts and sciences or of some particular art or science.

The beginning of such societies can be traced to the 13th and 14th centuries. Thus Brunetto Latini started a speculative society (*Accademia*) in Florence in 1270. The French troubadours started gatherings in Toulouse in 1323 for the promotion of poetry. In 1694 Louis XIV incorporated these gatherings as the Académie des Jeux Floraux. Most numerous and flourishing were these societies in Italy, where the movement started in 1439 in Florence subsequent to a Greco-Roman church congress. Two eminent Greek scholars, Gemistus Pletho and Johannes Bessarion, were present, and, influenced by the former, Cosimo de' Medici founded in 1442 the Accademia Platonica in Florence for the study of Plato's philosophy and Greek literature. Bessarion went to Rome where he became a cardinal and the promoter of the Accademia Romana di Storia e di Archeologia, incorporated in 1498. Another early academy, the Accademia Pontaniana, was founded in Naples in 1442 under the patronage of Alfonso V of Aragon.

The first scientific academies belong to the 16th century. In 1560 Giambattista della Porta founded the Academia Secretorum Naturae. In 1575 Philip II of Spain founded in Madrid the Academia de Ciencias Matemáticas. The famous Accademia dei Lincei in Rome, to which Galileo belonged, was founded in 1603 by Federigo Cesi, but closed on his death. In 1870 it was resuscitated as the Reale Accademia Nazionale dei Lincei. In 1657 Leopold de' Medici founded in Florence the Accademia del Cimento; the physicist Torricelli was a member.

In Germany the first academy was Die Fruchtbringende Gesellschaft, founded at Weimar in 1617 for the purification of the language and the promotion of literature. The first German scientific academy was the Societas Ereunitica, founded at Rostock in 1622. In 1652 the physician J. L. Bausch founded at Schweinfurt an academy for research in medicine and connected sciences, called the Academia Naturae Curiosorum. It published in 1670 the first German scientific periodical, *Miscellanea Curiosa*. In 1687, in honour of the emperor Leopold I, it was renamed Academia Caesarea Leopoldina; later it became known as the Leopoldinisch-Karolinische Deutsche Akademie der Naturforscher, with its seat in Halle.

It was also in the 17th century that the two pre-eminent scientific academies were founded. Both the English Royal society (*q.v.*) and the French Académie des Sciences began as informal gatherings of famous men. The "invisible college" of London and Oxford had its first meetings in 1645. It was incorporated as the Royal society in 1662. In Paris a group of men including Descartes, Pascal, P. Gassendi and M. Mersenne started private meetings almost at the same time. In 1666 they were invited by Colbert to meet in the royal library. In 1699 the society was transferred to the Louvre under the name of Académie des Sciences. The Académie Française also started as a private society of men of letters some five years before its incorporation in 1635 under the patronage of Richelieu. Another famous French academy, known as the Petite Académie, began as a committee of the Académie Française in 1663 for the study of ancient monuments, inscriptions and medals. In 1716 it became the Académie Royale des Inscriptions et Belles-Lettres.

In the 18th century the fame and achievements of the Royal society and of the Académie des Sciences were internationally recognized and many European countries started to found their own national academies of sciences. The chief promoter of this European movement was Leibniz. As early as 1676 he urged the establishment of an imperial academy of sciences at Vienna. He prompted Frederick III of Brandenburg to found the Berlin academy, at first as the Societät der Scienzien, in 1700. As Frederick was king in Prussia from 1701, this became known as the Königlich Preussische Societät der Wissenschaften. It was formally opened in 1711. In 1703 he presented a memorandum for the foundation of the academy of sciences at Dresden. During 1708–11 he wrote plans for a similar academy at St. Petersburg for Peter the Great. These and other plans were all realized and at the end of the period of enlightenment most European countries had their academies of sciences.

The academies of the 16th and 17th centuries were either scientific or literary. During the 18th century the rise of academies of the fine arts took place. As a rule they were societies closely connected with a higher teaching institution and thus differed from the earlier societies. The foundation of academies continued throughout the 19th century and in the 20th century national centres of sciences, literature and the fine arts were established in most of the new European and non-European countries.

Academies often have included by invitation distinguished foreigners among their members and so have helped to foster the international character of science and scholarship.

SCIENTIFIC ACADEMIES

Austria.—In 1786 I. von Born founded an international Society of Mining, but the Österreichische Akademie der Wissenschaften in Vienna originally planned by Leibniz was founded only in 1847 by the emperor Ferdinand I.

Belgium.—The Académie Royale des Sciences, des Lettres et des Beaux-Arts de Belgique acquired its present title in 1845. It originated in 1769 as a literary society of which one of the founders was the English naturalist J. T. Needham.

Czechoslovakia.—The Prager Gelehrte Privatgesellschaft was founded by I. von Born in 1771. In 1784 it became Societas Regia Scientiarum Bohemica and in 1952 was refounded as the Czechoslovak Academy of Sciences (Ceskoslovenska Akademie Ved).

Denmark.—The Royal Danish Academy of Sciences and Letters (Det kongelige danske videnskabernes selskab) was founded at Copenhagen in 1742 by Christian VI.

France.—The old Académie des Sciences, with all French academies, was suppressed in 1793 by the Convention. In 1795 its functions were assumed by a branch of the newly formed Institut National. In 1816 the former name was restored and this branch became one of the academies of the Institut de France.

Germany.—The Leibnizian society in Berlin was reconstituted by Frederick II as the Königliche, or Königlich Preussische, Akademie der Wissenschaften in 1744. In 1946 it was renamed Deutsche Akademie der Wissenschaften zu Berlin. The Bayerische Akademie der Wissenschaften in Munich was founded in 1759. Maximilian I entrusted it with the organization and supervision of public education. The Akademie der Wissenschaften at Göttingen was founded in 1751 by Albrecht von Haller. It was reorganized in 1897. The Akademie der Wissenschaften at Mannheim was founded in 1755 by the elector palatine. Scientific academies were founded at Leipzig in 1846 and at Mainz in 1949.

Hungary.—The Hungarian Academy of Sciences (Magyar Tudományos Akadémia) was founded in 1825 by Count István Széchényi.

Italy.—Scientific societies existed in many towns, but the beginnings of a well-established and permanent academy of sciences belong to Turin. In 1757 G. B. Beccaria, J. L. Lagrange and others founded a private scientific society called Philosophico-Matematica Società Privata Taurinensis. In 1761 it became Società Reale and in 1783 Regia Accademia delle Scienze. The second in importance of Italian academies of the 18th century was the Accademia delle Scienze e Belle Lettere at Naples (1779), promoted by Tanucci. One member was Gaetano Filangieri. The Accademia dei Ricovrati of Venice was also founded in 1779.

Netherlands.—The first scientific society, the Hollandsche Maatschappij der Wetenschappen, was founded in 1752. In 1774 a special section was added devoted to agriculture, industry and commerce. The Royal Institute of the Low Countries was founded by King Louis Bonaparte at Amsterdam in 1808. It was reorganized in 1851 and in 1855 became the Koninklijke Nederlandse Akademie van Wetenschappen.

Norway.—J. E. Gunnerus, the botanist, founded a scientific society at Trondheim in 1760. The Norske Videnskaps Akedemi at Oslo was founded in 1857.

Poland.—The first scientific society was founded in Warsaw in 1800 under the name of Towarzystwo Przyjaciol Nauk (Society of Friends of Science). The Cracow branch, opened in 1816, was reconstituted by the Austrian government in 1872 as an academy and in 1919 it was renamed Polska Akademja Umiejetnosci. In 1951 it was transferred to Warsaw as Polska Akademia Nauk.

Portugal.—The Academia Real das Ciências was founded in 1779 by the duke of Lafões and Correa da Serra, both members of the Royal society. In 1851 it was reorganized into two sections of sciences and literature and social sciences.

Spain.—Although scientific societies were founded in 1575 and 1657, the academy of sciences dates back only to 1774. In 1847 it became the Real Academia de Ciencias Exactas, Físicas y Naturales.

Sweden.—Archbishop Erik Benzelius, Emanuel Swedenborg and C. Polhem founded a private scientific society at Uppsala in 1710. In 1728 it received the title Kungliga Vetenskaps Societeten. Linnaeus was one of the founders, in 1739, of a society in Stockholm incorporated in 1741 as Kungliga Svenska Vetenskapsakademien.

Switzerland.—Several cantons have their own scientific societies. The oldest is the Société pour l'Avancement des Arts in Geneva, started as a private society by H. B. de Saussure. It was approved by the Geneva government in 1776. The Schweizerische Naturforschende Gesellschaft in Zürich, founded in 1815 on a national basis, has enjoyed the rank of an academy of sciences since 1931.

U.S.S.R.—The academy of sciences was founded by Peter the Great in St. Petersburg in 1724 and was opened by his widow, Catherine I, in 1725 as Rossiyskaya Akademia Nauk. The first Russian member was the scientist and poet M. V. Lomonosov. In 1934 the academy was transferred to Moscow. At Kiev the Academy of Sciences of the Ukranian S.S.R. was founded in 1918 and reorganized in 1919. The academies of other republics of the Soviet Union are of recent origin.

Yugoslavia.—Under Italian influence academies were flourishing in Dalmatia and Istria as early as the 16th century, for instance the Accademia dei Concordi at Dubrovnik. In Slovenia the Societas Unitorum at Ljubljana dates back to 1688. A society founded at Zagreb in 1848 by Bishop Strossmayer became in 1861 the Jugoslavenska Akademija Znanosti i Umjetnosti (Yugoslav Academy of Sciences and Arts). In Serbia the first society was founded in 1841. In 1864 it was named Srbsko Uceno Druzstvo (Serbian Learned society) and in 1886 it became the Srbska Akademija Nauka (Serbian Academy of Sciences) in Belgrade. The Slovenska Akademija Znanosti in Umetnosti (Slovene Academy of Sciences and Arts) was formed in 1937 from a society founded at Ljubljana in 1921.

English-speaking Countries.—The relations between state and society in the English-speaking countries differed from those in continental Europe. Culture, including religion, science, literature and the fine arts, was considered a prerogative of society and private initiative. Reflecting this attitude Great Britain, the commonwealth countries, Ireland and the United States have no state-established academies of sciences. They have, however, scientific societies which rival European academies in fame and importance.

Great Britain.—The oldest and best-known English scientific societies are the Royal society, the Gentlemen's Society of Spalding (1710), the Royal Society of Arts (1754), the Lunar society (1768) and the Royal Institution of Great Britain (1799). In Scotland the Royal Society of Edinburgh originated in 1739 as a philosophical society. In Ireland the Royal Dublin society was founded in 1731.

United States.—The most influential scientific society was founded by Benjamin Franklin in 1743. It was incorporated in 1780 under the name of American Philosophical Society Held at Philadelphia for Promoting Useful Knowledge and became recognized abroad as the national centre of scientific activities. In 1779 a group of Harvard graduates established a rival society in Boston, incorporated in 1780 as the American Academy of Arts and Sciences. The aims and organization were similar to those of Franklin's society and claims to represent the United States nationally were put forward. The New York lyceum, founded in 1817, was renamed the New York Academy of Science in 1876. The St. Louis Academy of Sciences was founded in 1856. The National Academy of Sciences was founded in 1863 in Washington, D.C. The Academy of Natural Sciences of Philadelphia was established in 1812. (*See also* ASTRONOMY, SOCIETIES OF; CHEMISTRY, SOCIETIES OF; HORTICULTURE AND BOTANY, SOCIETIES OF; ZOOLOGY, SOCIETIES OF.)

LITERARY ACADEMIES

The Renaissance was not only the rebirth of classical literature and science, it also promoted national languages and literatures. Literary societies or academies were founded everywhere, but Italy was the source and model of this movement. In the 16th century the number of Italian academies approached 700. The most famous of Italian literary academies was the Accademia della Crusca, founded in Florence by A. F. Grazzini in 1582. Its *Vocabolario della Crusca*, published in Venice in 1612, stabilized the Italian literary language on the basis of Tuscan speech. In France the institution of this group is the Académie Française. The old academy of Richelieu was dissolved in 1793 and reconstituted as the third class of the Institut National in 1795. Napoleon, by abolishing the class of moral and political sciences, promoted it to the second class. In 1816 it was reconstituted under its old name. In Spain a similar role was played by the Real Academia Española, founded in Madrid by the duke of Escalona in 1713. The Russian Academy founded in 1783 became the eighth department of the Academy of Sciences of the U.S.S.R. The British Academy in London was founded in 1901. Its aim is defined in its charter as "the promotion of historical, philosophical and philological studies," or more precisely "the promotion of the study of the moral and political sciences, including history, philosophy, law, politics and economics, archaeology and philology." It will thus be seen that the British Academy combines literary and social studies.

In Latin America academies belonging to this group include the Academia Hispano-Colombiana de la Lengua founded in Bogotá, Colombia, in 1871, the Academia Chilena de la Lengua in Santiago, Chile, founded in 1885, and the Academia Venezolana de la Lengua, founded in Caracas, Venez., in 1882. (*See also* LITERATURE, SOCIETIES OF.)

ACADEMIES OF SOCIAL SCIENCES

The two oldest academies of this group were founded in Portugal and Spain in the 18th century. They are the Academia Portuguesa da História (1720) and the Real Academia de la Historia (1738). The French Académie des Sciences Morales et Politiques can trace its origins to the Club de l'Entresol, known as the Académie Politique, which was influential until its closure by Cardinal Fleury in 1731. As the second division of the Institut National created in 1795 it was suppressed by Napoleon in 1803 as potentially subversive. In 1832 it was restored as one of the five academies of the Institut de France. The Academy of Social Sciences in Moscow (1946) is a training department of the central committee of the Communist party. In the U.S., the American Academy of Political and Social Science was founded in Philadelphia in 1889.

ACADEMIES OF FINE ARTS

The first academies of fine arts were in Italy. The Accademia di Disegno was founded at Florence in 1563. It was followed by the Accademia di Belle Arti at Perugia (1573), the Accademia di San Luca at Rome (1577) and the Accademia Albertina di Belle Arti at Turin (1652). The Akademie der Bildenden Künste in Vienna was started as a school in 1692 but was not incorporated as an academy until 1770. The French Académie Royale de Peinture et de Sculpture had its beginnings in 1648. It was reconstituted as the Académie des Beaux-Arts in 1795. In Denmark, Det Kongelige Akademi for de skønne Kunster (the Royal Academy of Fine Arts) was founded in Copenhagen in 1754. In the U.S.S.R., the academy founded in St. Petersburg in 1757 by Count Shuvalov was re-established as the Academy of Fine Arts of the U.S.S.R. in Moscow in 1947. The Royal Academy of Arts in London, founded in 1768, is described in a separate article. (*See* ACADEMY, ROYAL.)

In the Americas, the first academies of fine arts were the Academia das Belas Artes, founded in Rio de Janeiro, Braz., in 1816, and the National Academy of Design founded in New York in 1825, whose first president was S. F. B. Morse, later the inventor of the electric telegraph. (*See* also ART, SOCIETIES OF.)

MUSICAL ACADEMIES

Musical academies were started in Italy and grew from societies of musicians and poets in the 16th century. The Accademia della Fama in Venice was founded in 1558 by the musicians G. Zarlino, A. Gabrieli and others. The Accademia degli Arcadi in Rome, of which the composers A. Corelli, A. Scarlatti and B. Marcello were members, was founded in 1690. The Accademia Filarmonica of Bologna, founded in 1666, numbered Mozart among its members in the 18th century. In France, the Académie Royale de Musique, also known as the Théâtre National de l'Opéra, originated in 1669. The Austrian Akademie für Musik und darstellende Kunst was founded in Vienna in 1817. The first musical academy in England was the Academy of Ancient Music, founded in London in 1710. A Royal Academy of Music, under the direction of Handel, existed in London from 1720 until 1728, but the present institution was founded in 1822 and incorporated in 1830. (*See* also MUSICAL SOCIETIES AND INSTITUTIONS.)

MEDICAL AND OTHER ACADEMIES

The Académie Royale de Chirurgie founded in Paris in 1731 was suppressed in 1793 and reopened in 1820 as the Académie de Médecine. Since 1871 it has been called the Académie Nationale de Médecine. The Russian Military-Medical Academy was founded in 1799. Other medical academies are of the 20th century.

The first mining academy, the Bergakademie at Freiberg in Saxony, eastern Germany, was founded in 1765. In 1914 a mining academy was founded in Cracow, Pol. The first agricultural academy was founded in Venice in 1790. The Royal Swedish Academy of Agriculture and Forestry (Kungliga Skogs- och Lantbruksakademien) was founded in Stockholm in 1811. The Timiryazev Academy of Agriculture and the V. I. Lenin All-Union Academy of Agricultural Sciences in Moscow, founded in 1865 and 1929 respectively, and the Bulgarian agricultural academy founded in Sofia in 1948, are higher educational institutions with the title of "academy." Commercial academies, all 20th-century foundations, exist in the U.S.S.R., Poland, Rumania and other countries. *See* also MEDICINE, SOCIETIES OF; MILITARY, NAVAL AND AIR ACADEMIES.   (N. H.)

ACADEMY, GREEK. The Greek school of philosophy known as the Academy took its name from Academia (Akademeia), a locality in the northwestern outskirts of Athens, where Plato acquired property *c.* 387 B.C. and used to teach; the designation, however, is most usually applied not to Plato's immediate circle but to his successors down to Cicero's time. Legally, the school was a corporate body organized for the worship of the muses, the scholarch (or head of it) being elected for life by a majority vote of the members. Most scholars infer, mainly from Plato's writings, that instruction in the Academy originally included mathematics, dialectics, natural science and preparation for statesmanship. The Academy continued in existence until A.D. 529, when the emperor Justinian closed it, together with the other pagan schools. The problem of its intellectual unity has always been controversial, particularly if its post-Ciceronian phase is included. Major differences concern its dogmatism and antidogmatism; its exclusiveness (syncretism); the primacy of speculation or of ethics; its religious ("mystical") or its secular ("rational") character. If these points are borne in mind, it seems reasonable to consider the Academy in five phases as follows:

1. The Old Academy (4th century B.C.), with Speusippus, Xenocrates, Polemo and Crates as successive scholarchs and with Philippus of Opus, Heracleides Ponticus (who had strong supranaturalist leanings), Eudoxus of Cnidus (outstanding as an astronomer) and Crantor as outstanding members, seems to have devoted itself mainly to the dissection of reality into spheres such as numbers, geometricals, soul, down to sensibles; or into spheres of knowledge, of opinion, of sensation. These appear to have been derived from one another or from a set or sets of ultimate principles, called "the one" and "the indeterminate dyad" or by analogous expressions. Discussion of the nature of "the one" and its relation to the good on the one hand and of the nature of the other principle and its relation to matter and evil on the other was combined with number-speculations in Pythagorean style, sometimes also with theology and demonology. In many respects the Old Academy was closer to what Aristotle presented as Plato's "system" than to Plato's works. Especially characteristic is the displacing of ideas in favour of numbers.

In what sense we should consider Aristotle a member of the Academy is a moot point.

2. The Middle (or New) Academy (3rd–2nd centuries B.C.) was the result of developments under Arcesilaus, when the school, with an obvious preference for Plato's early dialogues and in accordance with his criticism of sensation, turned antidogmatic—this tendency reaching its climax under Carneades about a century later (on the meantime we know almost nothing). Whereas Arcesilaus had mainly refuted all claims to infallibility put forward by the Stoics for certain sense-presentations, Carneades extended this refutation to all types of knowledge and criticized specific Stoic doctrines; *e.g.*, their teleology, theodicy, astrology and theology. The key word of this antidogmatism is *epoche*, the withholding of assent. On the other hand, Carneades developed a doctrine of degrees of probability (of particular importance in matters of conduct). In ethics he professed or at least defended the doctrine that the goal of life and happiness consists in the fruition of "natural" things such as the integrity of one's own body and mind, to secure which man is instinctively driven. The text and the canon of Plato's work were probably established by the Academy early in this period.

3. In the 1st century B.C. a neodogmatic turn started with Philo of Larissa and reached its climax with Antiochus of Ascalon. The latter asserted that Academics and Peripatetics originally were simply two branches of Platonism; and he traced Stoic doctrines (particularly their derivation of the standard of conduct from nature and their concept of *oikeiosis*, that is, the "propriety" of certain things to our nature and their "appropriation" as a foundation of morality) back to the Academy, with Polemo as key figure. This historical interpretation (the correctness of which is controversial) provided the justification for his syncretism. He accepted the division of philosophy into ethics, physics and logic (in order of decreasing importance) and distinguished goods of the mind and of the body and external goods, the last-named being essential for a life if it was to be not only happy, but consummately so (*vita beata, beatissima*). The reconstruction of additional doctrines of Antiochus (he has, for example, been credited with being the first to identify Plato's ideas with thoughts of God) and the tracing of their influence has been the object of much controversy.

Plato and Aristotle being excepted, not a single writing of any Academic mentioned hitherto has been preserved in its integrity. Some writings ascribed to Plato might, however, be Academic (on the *Epinomis, see* PLATO).

Cicero (*q.v.*), strongly influenced by Philo and Antiochus, combined a noncommittal attitude in matters of speculation with the conviction that, as the result of experiences (he says: innate ideas) common to all men, there is universal consensus in all matters relevant to conduct and religion.

4. Of the Academy after the time of Cicero we know little. In the 2nd century A.D., Calvisius Taurus was one of its scholarchs, and Atticus, a violent critic of Aristotle, perhaps another. With Eudorus, Albinus, Apuleius, Maximus of Tyre, Plutarch of Chaeronea, etc., they represent the so-called Middle Platonism, out of

which Neoplatonism developed.

5. In the 5th century A.D., when Platonism had already turned into Neoplatonism (since the 3rd century A.D.), the Academy becomes visible again. Within the Neoplatonic movement it constitutes the so-called Athenian school, distinct, for instance, from the Alexandrian in that it remained closer to the spirit of Plotinus (who had literary contacts with Eubulus, scholarch of the Academy), of Porphyry and of Iamblichus and was devoted to polytheism. Other scholarchs were Plutarch of Athens, Syrianus, Proclus and Damascius, the last of them; and Simplicius was a famous member. Neoplatonism professed to be genuine Platonism but assimilated many doctrines belonging to other schools and to Greek and oriental religions. It teaches an ineffable deity, absolutely transcendent and yet the source out of which, in a nontemporal process, everything "flows," "dispersing" and thus decreasing in reality but longing to return to its origin; this return in man taking place in "ecstasy," an act of nondiscursive knowledge.

See also PLATO; NEOPLATONISM; and articles on various Academic philosophers.

BIBLIOGRAPHY.—General works dealing with the Academy are: F. Ueberweg–K. Praechter, *Die Philosophie des Altertums*, 12th ed. (1926; reprinted 1956); A. H. Armstrong, *Introduction to Ancient Philosophy*, 3rd ed. (1957). For the Old Academy *see* U. von Wilamowitz-Moellendorff, *Antigonos von Karystos* (1881); P. Boyancé, *Le Culte des Muses chez les philosophes grecs* (1937); H. Herter, *Platons Akademie*, 2nd ed. (1952); C. B. Armstrong, "Plato's Academy," *Leeds Philosophical and Literary Society Proceedings* vii, 2 (1953); L. Robin, *La Théorie platonicienne des idées et des nombres d'après Aristote* (1908); E. Frank, *Plato und die sogenannten Pythagoreer* (1923); H. F. Cherniss, *The Riddle of the Early Academy* (1945); P. Merlan, *From Platonism to Neoplatonism*, 2nd ed. (1960); R. Heinze, *Xenokrates* (1892); H. Karpp, *Untersuchungen zur Philosophie des Eudoxos von Knidos* (1933); F. Wehrli, *Herakleides Pontikos* (1953). For the Middle Academy and for the third period *see* R. Hirzel, *Untersuchungen zu Ciceros philosophischen Schriften*, 3 vol. (1877–83); E. R. Bevan, *Stoics and Sceptics* (1913, reprinted 1959); A. Goedeckemeyer, *Geschichte des griechischen Skeptizismus* (1950); H. Hartmann, *Gewissheit und Wahrheit* (1927); O. Gigon, "Zur Geschichte der sogenannten Neuen Akademie," *Museum Helveticum*, i (1944); G. Luck, *Der Akademiker Antiochos* (1953). For the fourth period *see* J. Baudry, *Atticos* (1931); R. E. Witt, *Albinus and the History of Middle Platonism* (1937); J. H. Loenen, "Albinus' Metaphysics," *Mnemosyne*, series iv, vol. 9–10 (1956–57). For the fifth period *see* K. Praechter, "Richtungen und Schulen im Neuplatonismus," *Genethliakon . . . C. Robert* (1910); T. Whittaker, *The Neo-Platonists*, 2nd ed. (1928); E. Bréhier, *The Philosophy of Plotinus* (1958). (PP. M.)

ACADEMY, ROYAL. The foundation of the Royal Academy of Arts in London in 1768 was the outcome of a memorial to George III presented by a group of the leading painters, sculptors and architects then in Great Britain, seeking his interest in setting up "a Society for promoting the Arts of Design" of which the two principal objects were to be the establishment of "a well regulated School . . . and an Annual Exhibition." The king signed the instrument of foundation on Dec. 10 of that year and graciously declared himself therein to be the Academy's "patron, protector and supporter." It decreed that there should be 40 academicians and it named the first 34; it defined the society's activities, the functions of the council and general assembly, the offices to be filled and the manner of electing new members.

The main terms of the instrument have always been observed and form the basis of the laws in force today, the sovereign's approval being necessary for any amendment and for the appointment of the president and other officers. There are still 40 royal academicians who serve in rotation on the council and on the selection and hanging committees of the annual exhibitions. Two major changes have been made, in 1769 and in 1918. The former instituted a class of associates (not less than 30 and not more than 35 in number) who are represented on various committees and from whom the academicians are elected. The latter change inaugurated the terms "senior academicians" and "senior associates" for members reaching the age of 75. They are then no longer eligible to serve in any office or committee although they retain their vote in general assembly and other rights. The vacancies thus created in the active lists, together with those caused by death or other reasons, are filled by election among all members. New royal academicians are each required to present to the Academy a specimen of their art before receiving their diplomas signed by the sovereign.

From small temporary quarters in Pall Mall and old Somerset house, the Royal Academy moved in 1780 into the Strand block of the present Somerset house where it remained for 57 years. From 1837 to 1868 it was housed in the eastern half of the building on the north side of Trafalgar square (subsequently entirely occupied by the National gallery) and finally, on attaining its centenary, took possession of Burlington house in Piccadilly and built the main galleries and schools at its own expense on part of the gardens. The house itself was adapted for the library, offices and meeting rooms, and a third story was added to accommodate the diploma works.

The annual exhibition, by which the academy is perhaps best known to the public, has been held every summer without a break since 1769. Each member is allowed to send in not more than six paintings, drawings, engravings, pieces of sculpture or architectural designs, and any other person, of whatever nationality or domicile, may submit three. Over 10,000 items are received every year and an exhibition of some 1,500 is formed. No commission is deducted from the prices of the many works which are sold.

The winter exhibitions in the main galleries, usually of the works of old masters, were started in 1870 and have included large-scale displays of the highest international importance. Since 1952 the diploma galleries also have been used for special loan exhibitions from time to time throughout the year.

Entrance to the Royal Academy schools has always been "free to all students who shall be qualified to receive advantage from such studies." Successful candidates for the schools of painting and sculpture are admitted for a period of three months and thereafter, if approved, for a studentship of four years. The school of architecture was run on similar lines till 1947 when it was reconstituted as a postgraduate course of one year.

The Royal Academy has never received any subsidy from the state and except for the first 11 years of its existence, when the deficits were reimbursed from the king's privy purse, it has been financially self-supporting. The maintenance of its premises and the general administrative costs, together with the provision of free training in the schools, have all been paid for from the public's support of the exhibitions. In addition the Academy has been enabled, through the receipt of certain trust funds, to give scholarships and prizes to its students, to award annuities and grants to artists in distress, and to purchase works of art under terms designed to encourage artists living in Great Britain.

BIBLIOGRAPHY.—W. Sandby, *The History of the Royal Academy of Arts* (1862); J. E. Hodgson and F. A. Eaton, *The Royal Academy and Its Members, 1768–1830* (1905); G. D. Leslie, *The Inner Life of the Royal Academy* (1914); Sir Walter R. M. Lamb, *The Royal Academy*, new ed. (1951); S. C. Hutchison, *The Homes of the Royal Academy* (1956). (S. C. HN.)

ACADIAN, a descendant of the French settlers in Acadie or Acadia, the French colony on the Atlantic coast of North America in what is now eastern Canada. The area, visited by Champlain (1603) and by De Monts (1604) and colonized by the French, was long a bone of contention in the wars between France and England. By the treaty of Utrecht (1713) Acadia became English. In 1755 the imminence of war with France, the vexed question of the neutrality of the Acadians and the possibility of revolt led to their forcible deportation—the theme of Longfellow's *Evangeline*. They were distributed among the English colonies, and one group made its way to Bayou Teche, La., where George Washington Cable (*q.v.*) described their subsequent life. After the treaty of Paris (1763) left the British in undisputed possession of Canada, and Acadia had ceased to exist as a political unit, a number of Acadians found their way back to Nova Scotia and New Brunswick. In many cases their descendants continued to form a distinctive part of the population. *See* NOVA SCOTIA: *History*.

See G. P. Bible, *An Historical Sketch of the Acadians* (1892); A. Doughty, *The Canadian Exiles* (1914); Grace Dean McLeod, *Stories of the Land of Evangeline* (1891).

ACANTHACEAE, containing about 240 genera and more than 2,200 described species, is a largely tropical family of plants allied to the Gesneriaceae and Bignoniaceae. They are perennial herbs, armed or unarmed shrubs, or rarely trees or vines. A few genera are cultivated as ornamentals. Chief among these, and probably the best known because of the use of the leaf pattern in the design on the Corinthian columns, is *Acanthus* (*q.v.*). Other genera grown in greenhouses or out of doors in warm climates are *Ruellia*, *Pseuderanthemum*, *Aphelandra*, *Thunbergia*, *Fittonia*, *Jacobinia* and *Justicia*. The family can be recognized botanically by the following combination of characters: the opposite, usually large and thin leaves, commonly provided on the surfaces with minute whitish lines (cystoliths); the absence of stipules; the usually compound inflorescences; the presence of persistent, often conspicuous, floral bracts; the irregular, tubular, two-lipped, often highly coloured (red, purple or yellow) corollas; the four (or sometimes two) stamens inserted on the corolla tube; the free two-celled ovary; and the often club-shaped capsule, opening elastically from the apex downward. (Ey. C. L.)

ACANTHOCEPHALA, the spiny-headed worms, a phylum of parasites characterized by an anterior attachment organ (the proboscis) covered with rows of recurved hooks. These elongate worms as adults are found only in the intestine of vertebrates, and no free-living stage is present in any phase of their life histories. They vary in length from about $\frac{1}{16}$ in. to over 1 ft.

The Acanthocephala exhibit many of the aspects of "degeneracy" usually associated with parasitism. There is not the slightest trace of a digestive system in any stage of their development, and the relatively few sense organs, when they are present, are small and inconspicuous. The "brain" consists of a small cluster of cells located in an anterior muscular sac, the proboscis receptacle, into which the proboscis is retractable. Only a few species have any excretory system.

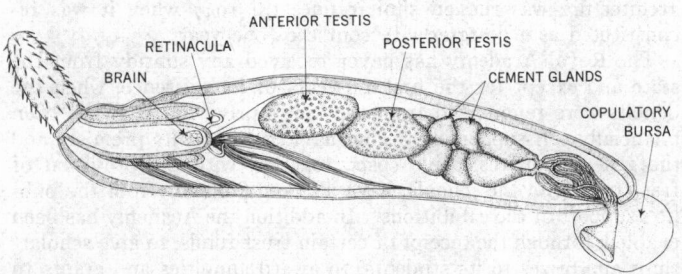

MALE ACANTHOCEPHALUS RANAE, A PARASITIC WORM THAT LIVES IN THE INTESTINES OF FROGS AND NEWTS

Natural History.—The spiny-headed worms undergo a two-host life history: the definitive host for the adult parasite is always a vertebrate, most commonly a fish or bird, and the intermediate host is always an arthropod such as an insect or crustacean. (Sometimes a "transport host" is interpolated between the intermediate and definitive hosts. It is not clear how necessary such transport hosts are for the completion of the life history.)

The arthropod host ingests the infective embryo which then hatches into the first larval stage, the acanthor. After penetrating the gut, the acanthor enters the body cavity of the host, where it successively develops into an acanthella and finally into a later larval stage, the cystacanth. Vertebrates are infected by feeding on arthropods containing infective cystacanths. Upon ingestion the cystacanth begins development to the adult stage. After anchoring itself, by means of its burrlike proboscis, to the intestinal lining of the host, the worm absorbs nourishment directly through its thin body covering.

Because of their method of attachment, the spiny-headed worms are relatively destructive parasites. Heavy infections, frequently fatal, have been reported among fish, birds and monkeys. Lighter infections produce significant damage to the intestinal wall.

Structure and Function.—The acanthocephalan body is divided into two structural units: The presoma and the trunk. The presoma consists of the proboscis, neck, proboscis receptacle, brain and two internal fingerlike projections (lemnisci) in the neck region. The proboscis varies from globular to elongate-cylindrical in shape and is armed with a varying number of hooks, usually arranged in a definite pattern and relatively constant in size and num-

ber for each species. Inside the proboscis a pair of muscles, the invertors, connect the tip of the proboscis to the posterior portion of the receptacle. Contraction of these muscles causes the introversion of the proboscis into the receptacle. The neck region extends from the basal row of hooks to the beginning of the trunk and is devoid of hooks and spines. It is usually quite short but in some forms, for example *Pomphorhynchus*, is remarkably elongated and specialized. The lemnisci are structurally and functionally connected to the subcuticula layer (*see* below) of the proboscis. Lemnisci are found in no other group of the animal kingdom and their function is unknown. Both the lemnisci and the proboscis receptacle project posteriorly into the trunk.

The trunk, the main part of the body, has a covering composed of a thin cuticula under which lies a thick, complex subcuticula. In many forms the cuticula is covered with spines which are primarily, if not entirely, limited to the anterior region of the trunk. The subcuticula is syncytial (lacking cell boundaries) and contains a rudimentary circulatory system, the lacunar system. The organs of the reproductive system are located in the trunk. In the male they consist of two testes, a variable number of cement glands and a muscular, copulatory bursa, within which is the penis. In the female, the ovary breaks up into "germ balls," where the eggs are produced, fertilized by the male's sperm and started on their development. After a period of maturation in the body cavity the embryonated eggs are passed into the anterior end of the female reproductive system, the uterine bell. From there a selective apparatus either passes the embryos on through the female ducts and out the genital pore or returns them to the body cavity for further development.

Classification.—There are approximately 400 species in about 85 genera. These are divided among at least three major groups.

1. The Archiacanthocephala are primarily parasites of terrestrial hosts. Examples include: *Macracanthorhynchus*, infecting beetle grubs and hogs; *Moniliformis* of roaches and rats; and *Mediorhynchus* of grasshoppers and birds.

2. The Palaeacanthocephala are parasites of aquatic and marine hosts. Examples include: *Polymorphus* of amphipods and ducks; *Echinorhynchus* of amphipods and fish; and *Corynosoma* of amphipods and ducks or seals, with fish serving to transport the parasite from amphipod to seal.

3. The Eoacanthocephala are primitive forms found almost entirely in fishes. Examples are: *Neoechinorhynchus* and *Octospinifer* of ostracods and marine or fresh-water fish.

Superficially, the Acanthocephala bear certain resemblances to the nematodes, and more basic characters suggest similarities with the flatworms. However, nearly all authorities agree in recognizing Acanthocephala as a separate phylum.

See also PARASITOLOGY.

See L. H. Hyman, *The Invertebrates*, vol. 3, *Acanthocephala, Aschelminthes, and Entoprocta* (1951). (W. L. Bu.)

ACANTHODIAN, a small armour-plated fish, among the oldest jawed vertebrates, of the extinct group Acanthodii, often misleadingly called "spiny sharks." *See* PLACODERM.

ACANTHUS, a genus of plants of the acanthus family (Acanthaceae [*q.v.*]), embracing about 20 species, mainly perennial herbs and small shrubs, native to the Mediterranean region and the warmer parts of Asia and Africa. They are bold, vigorous, handsome plants, with mostly broad, much divided, often spiny-toothed leaves. The erect stems bear stately spikes of showy white, purple or red flowers, surrounded by sharp-pointed, sometimes highly coloured bracts.

Several species are grown as ornamentals. These are mostly thistlelike plants, with stems three feet to four feet high. The best known is the bears' breech or brankursine (*A. mollis*), common in Mediterranean countries, with deeply cut, hairy, shining leaves, which are without spines, and whitish or rose-coloured flowers in spikes $1\frac{1}{2}$ ft. long.

The spiny acanthus (*A. spinosus*), native to southern Europe, is so named because of its very spiny leaves. *A. perringi*, a native of Asiatic Turkey, with red flowers, is suitable for rock gardens. *A. montanus*, native to Greece, with roseate flowers, is grown in greenhouses.

TYPICAL
GREEK ACANTHUS

CAPITAL
TEMPLE OF MARS

TYPICAL
ROMAN ACANTHUS

BY COURTESY OF BUHLMANN, "CLASSIC AND RENAISSANCE ARCHITECTURE" (NEFF AND HELBURN);
H. D'ESPOUY, "FRAGMENTS D'ARCHITECTURE ANTIQUE" (CH. MASSIN ET CIE)

ARCHITECTURAL USES OF THE ACANTHUS DESIGN

In architectural decoration the acanthus was first reproduced in metal and subsequently carved in stone by the Greeks. It was afterward, with various changes, adopted in all succeeding styles of architecture as a basis for ornamental decoration.

There are two types: that found in the *Acanthus spinosus*, which seems to have been followed by the Greeks; and that in the *Acanthus mollis*, which seems to have been preferred by the Romans.

ACAPULCO, a resort city and port of Mexico, at sea level on the Pacific coast in the state of Guerrero, 288 mi. by road S.S.W. of Mexico City. Pop. (1950) 28,512; (1960) 49,149, plus many transients. Acapulco has the best harbour on the Pacific coast of Mexico and one of the finest natural anchorages in the world; it is situated on a deep, semicircular bay, nearly landlocked and accessible by land. Acapulco was a main depot for Spanish colonial fleets plying between Mexico, the Philippines and the orient, and continued to be a port of call for steamship lines between Panama and San Francisco as well as coastwise trading vessels. The town lies on a narrow strip of land between the bay and steeply rising mountains which encircle it. From May to November the climate is hot and humid, but from December through April it is warm and pleasant; February, March and April are almost rainless. Long a regional economic centre, Acapulco exports hides, cedar and fruit, as well as cotton, tobacco, cacao, sugar cane, Indian corn and coffee grown in the adjacent district of Tabares. No railways connect to Acapulco but a spreading network of highways and frequent air service make it accessible to visitors. Acapulco became "The Riviera of Mexico."

Many luxurious hotels attract tourists, and its principal beaches, Caleta and Los Hornos, offer excellent bathing facilities. Its deepsea fishing is famous. A traditional tourist attraction is a spectacular dive into the sea from a high cliff by young men for whose benefit a collection is taken up by the spectators.

A main highway, passing through Taxco and Cuernavaca, runs to Mexico City. (R. B. McCk.)

ACARAÍ, SERRA (AKARAI MOUNTAINS), a range of low mountains on the border between Brazil and British Guiana, forming the watershed between the Rio Trombetas, which joins the Amazon just upstream from Óbidos, and the Oronoque river, which joins the Courantyne river on the border between British Guiana and Surinam. The underlying rocks are crystalline. On either side of the Serra Acaraí there is a gently rolling crystalline hilly upland. At the headwaters, however, there is an erosion remnant, preserving a surface, developed during an earlier erosion cycle, that stands at an elevation of about 1,600 ft. above sea level with steep sides and a flattish top. The whole area is covered with a dense tropical rain forest and is little explored. The range extends for about 80 mi. east and west on the southeasternmost part of the British Guiana border. To the east, the same surface feature runs along the border between Brazil and Surinam, where it is called the Tumuc-Humac mountains. The Serra Acaraí was formerly spelled Acarahy; in British Guiana the range is known as the Akarai mountains. (P. E. J.)

ACARINA (ACARI), the scientific name for the order of small arthropods comprising the mites and ticks. Many are parasites and become important for health and economic reasons when they attack man and animals and cause dermatitis or transmit diseases. *See* MITE; TICK.

ACARNANIA (AKARNANIA), a district of ancient Greece, bounded by the Ionian sea, the Ambracian gulf, Mt. Thyamus (Petalas) and the Achelous river; its most populous region was the fertile plain of the lower Achelous. The inhabitants emerged late from barbarism (Thucydides noted that in the 5th century B.C. they still carried arms in everyday life), but in the 7th century Corinthian colonists had already settled the coastal areas. The Athenians later helped the Acarnanians to repel attacks by these colonists (perhaps in 437 B.C.) and by the Spartans (429–426); but in 390 they were overcome by Agesilaus and fell successively under the sway of Sparta, Athens and Thebes. They joined the resistance against Philip II of Macedonia but after the battle of Chaeronea (338 B.C.) submitted to Macedonian control. In 314 they established a confederation of newly founded cities; but frontier disputes with Aetolia culminated in the partition of their country between Aetolia and Epirus (c. 243). The Epirote part of Acarnania recovered its independence after 230 and was closely allied with Philip V of Macedonia in his Roman wars. In 167 it lost its new federal capital of Leucas and was forced to send hostages to Rome; but the confederacy with its capital at Thyrrheum survived until the time of the Roman principate, when Augustus incorporated many Acarnanians into his new city Nicopolis Actia, and the rest were included in the province of Achaea. Acarnania took a prominent part in the Greek national uprising of 1821. In modern Greece it is linked with Aetolia in the prefecture (*nomos*) Aitolia kai Akarnania, with its administrative centre at Missolonghi.

BIBLIOGRAPHY.—L. Heuzey, *Le Mont Olympe et l'Acarnanie* (1860); E. Oberhummer, *Akarnanien im Altertum* (1887); article "Akarnania," Pauly-Wissowa, *Real-Encyclopädie der classischen Altertumswissenschaft,* vol. i (1894). See also S. I. Oost, *Roman Policy in Epirus and Acarnania in the Age of the Roman Conquest of Greece* (1954).
(F. W. WA.)

ACASTUS, in Greek mythology, son of Pelias and brother of Alcestis, but the friend of Jason; he took part in the Calydonian boar hunt and the Argonautic expedition. After his father had been murdered by Medea (who persuaded his daughters that if he were cut up and boiled he could be revived with renewed youth) he instituted splendid funeral games in honour of Pelias, having succeeded to the throne of Iolcus. His wife Astydameia (so named according to Apollodorus, but called Hippolyte in Horace's *Odes* and in Pindar) fell in love with Peleus (*q.v.*), who had taken refuge at Iolcus, and accused him falsely to her husband (*see* BELLEROPHON; HIPPOLYTUS). Acastus thereupon left Peleus asleep on Mt. Pelion, having first hidden his famous sword. On awaking, Peleus was attacked by the Centaurs but saved by Cheiron. Having recovered his sword he returned to Iolcus and slew Acastus and Astydameia. (T. V. B.)

ACCADIAN LANGUAGE: *see* AKKADIAN LANGUAGE.

ACCA LARENTIA (LARENTINA), a Roman goddess whose festival, the Larentalia, fell on Dec. 23. Her original functions and the nature of her cult remain obscure because her legend was humanized and rationalized by writers such as Livy, Ovid and Plutarch, the main literary sources. One tradition described her as a prostitute who, in the early regal period, was won by Hercules at dice, married a wealthy Etruscan, Tarutius, and bequeathed her husband's property to the Roman people. In another account she was the wife of Faustulus, the herdsman who rescued Romulus and Remus (*see* ROMULUS AND REMUS), and the original *fratres Arvales* were her sons (*see* ARVAL BROTHERS). Sometimes, as Romulus' foster mother, she was equated with the she-wolf (*lupa* can mean "prostitute"). Modern scholars suggest that she was mother of the Lares (*q.v.*) and symbolized the earth's fertility, but the evidence is inconclusive.

See T. Mommsen, "Die echte und die falsche Acca Larentia" in *Römische Forschungen,* vol. ii (1879). (D. E. W. W.)

ACCELERATION, as used in mechanics, denotes the rate of change, with time, in the velocity of a moving object or of some purely geometrical concept; *i.e.*, a point. Since velocity itself is by definition the time (t) rate of change of the distance (s) traversed by a moving object ($v = s/t$), this quotient is constant for uniform motion, or represents the average velocity during the interval t for nonuniform motion; measured in centimetres per second (cm. sec.$^{-1}$). Likewise acceleration ($a = v/t$) is constant for uniform acceleration, or represents the average during the interval t for variable acceleration. This is measured as a rate of change of velocity (cm. sec.$^{-1}$) per second; i.e., cm. sec.$^{-2}$ The term velocity is of a vector character, involving both magnitude (speed) and direction. A velocity may change in either or in both characteristics. Therefore, the idea of acceleration possesses vector characteristics. Near the surface of the earth and in vacuo, falling objects show slightly variable accelerations, depending on their location. The direction is approximately toward the centre of the earth and their rate of increase of speed is approximately 980.5 cm., or 32.2 ft. per second every second. See also MECHANICS.

See Index references under "Acceleration" in the Index volume. (H. B. LM.)

ACCELERATORS, PARTICLE.

In 1919 Sir Ernest Rutherford observed the disintegration of atomic nuclei under the impact of alpha particles emitted from a naturally occurring radioactive substance; this may be considered the beginning of nuclear physics as an experimental (rather than an observational) science. It was immediately apparent that a wider range of experiments could be performed if stronger and more flexible sources of fast nuclear particles could be made, and a great deal of effort during the next few years led to the development of several ways for producing such sources. In 1932 J. D. Cockcroft and E. T. S. Walton first observed the disintegration of a nucleus by artificially accelerated particles. Thereafter, the importance of particle accelerators in nuclear research became comparable to that of telescopes in astronomy or microscopes in bacteriology. The particles accelerated are usually the nuclei of light atoms, such as the proton or deuteron from light or heavy hydrogen, respectively, or the alpha particle from helium; heavier nuclei may also be used, or electrons, which are lighter than any nucleus. Since each kind of particle produces its own characteristic effects on nuclei, research with all kinds is desirable. In the simplest general type of accelerator the particle, which bears an electric charge, is pulled along by a steady electric field, just as a falling rock is accelerated by the force of gravity. The particle acquires a kinetic energy equal to its charge multiplied by the difference in electric potential through which it falls. This concept leads to a unit of energy, the electron volt (ev), based on the electronic charge and the volt as a unit of potential; the abbreviation Mev (million electron volts) represents 1,000,000 of these units. An accelerator of this type would comprise an ion source, in which the charged particles are produced (for example, protons from hydrogen gas by the action of an electric arc); an evacuated tube, in which they can travel freely while acted on by the electric field; and some means for providing the required electrical potential. Of greatest importance are machines using potential sources of the kinds first used in this connection by Cockcroft and Walton and by R. J. Van de Graaff; these are suitable for energies up to about 1 Mev and 8 Mev, respectively.

Resonance Accelerators.—The practical limitation on particle energies obtainable in the above way is imposed by the difficulty of preventing electrical breakdown at high voltages. This difficulty can be avoided if the particle is accelerated in steps by the repeated application of a relatively small voltage, as in the general category of machines that can be called resonance accelerators. (The induction accelerator, representing another way around the difficulty, is discussed below under Betatrons.) The first resonance accelerator, built by R. Wideröe in 1927, is illustrated in fig. 1. This device served to introduce the idea to a scientific world that was eagerly searching for ways of producing high-energy particles. It led in two directions. One was the simple

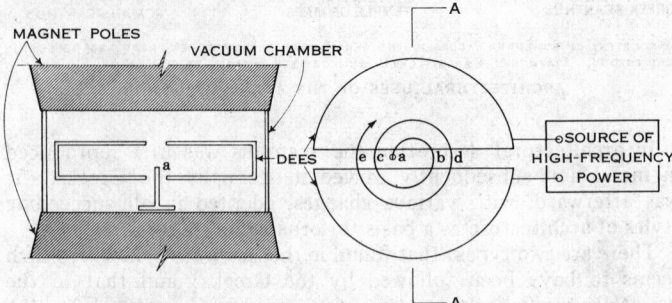

FIG. 2.—ELEMENTS OF A CYCLOTRON SHOWING (RIGHT) PLAN VIEW AND (LEFT) SECTIONAL VIEW AA

Ions from the source a are attracted by one of the hollow electrodes, called "dees" because of their shape. The magnetic field forces them to follow a circular path. When they reach the point b, the polarity of the electric field between the dees has reversed, and they are now repelled by the same dee that formerly attracted them. If the frequency of alternation is properly chosen, acceleration occurs also at points c, d, e, etc. The increasing energy causes the circular orbit to expand, resulting in a spiral path. When the ions reach the outer edge of the dees, they emerge through a channel not shown

extension to more and successive stages of acceleration, giving rise to the family of linear accelerators. The other was a basic modification, the cyclotron, proposed by E. O. Lawrence of the University of California, Berkeley.

In the cyclotron the particles are forced to move in a circular path by the action of a magnetic field. A particle of charge e (in absolute electromagnetic units) moving with velocity v (in centimetres per second) in a magnetic field of strength B (in gauss) is known to suffer a transverse force equal to Bev (in dynes). If the radius of the circular orbit is r, the centripetal acceleration is v^2/r and the radial force needed to keep the particle in the orbit is mv^2/r, where m is the mass in grams. Setting this equal to the magnetic force Bev and solving for r, we get

$$r = \frac{mv}{eB} \qquad (1)$$

The important thing to notice about (1) is that, since the size of the orbit is proportional to the velocity, the time per rotation is a constant. The frequency f (number of times per second around the orbit) is simply the velocity divided by the circumference, or

$$2\pi f = \frac{eB}{m} \qquad (2)$$

For a deuteron in a field of 13,000 gauss, f turns out to be 10,000,000 cycles per second; these values of field and frequency are easily attainable. Fig. 2 shows how the periodic electric impulses are applied to the particles as they travel around their orbit between the poles of a magnet. In the hands of Lawrence and others, the cyclotron quickly developed into a very powerful tool for nuclear research. For example, the 60-in. cyclotron completed at Berkeley in 1939 can deliver a current of more than 50 microamperes (μ amp.) of 20-Mev deuterons.

There is, however, a practical limit to the energy obtainable from a cyclotron, first pointed out by H. A. Bethe and M. E. Rose in 1937. According to the principle of relativity, the mass of a particle increases as its energy increases; in equation (2) the mass m varies as:

$$m = m_0 + \frac{W}{c^2} \qquad (3)$$

where W is the kinetic energy in ergs, c is the velocity of light in centimetres per second and m_0 is the rest mass of the particle.

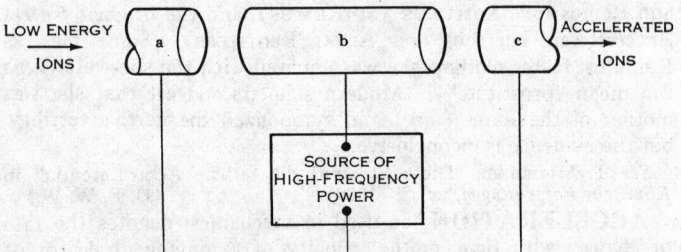

FIG. 1.—SCHEMATIC DIAGRAM OF SIMPLEST RESONANCE ACCELERATOR

Hollow cylinder b has an alternating potential with respect to a and c. If a positive ion enters the gap ab at a time when b is negative, it is attracted to b and thereby accelerated. The frequency of alternation is chosen so that when the particle reaches the gap bc the polarity has reversed and the particle, now being repelled by b, is accelerated again

To illustrate the magnitudes involved, the mass of a proton is doubled when its kinetic energy is 938 Mev; for an electron the corresponding figure is 0.51 Mev. Thus relativistic effects become important for electrons at much lower energies than for protons and other heavier ions. The effect on cyclotron operation is obvious: as the energy increases, the frequency of rotation decreases and the particle falls out of step with the applied high-frequency accelerating potential. Another fact to be noted is that, in a practical cyclotron, the magnetic field B must be weaker at the edge of the pole than in the centre, since this sort of field distribution serves to keep the orbits in their proper position, as explained in the section headed *Cyclotrons and Synchrocyclotrons*. Therefore one cannot compensate for the mass increase by using a field in which B increases with the radius.

Synchrotron and Related Machines.—A practical way for removing the relativistic limit from machines operating on the cyclotron principle was pointed out by V. I. Veksler in the U.S.S.R. and, independently, by E. M. McMillan in the United States in 1945. This is based primarily on the recognition of a property inherent in cyclotron operation, which has been called phase stability. Fig. 3 illustrates how this property comes about. The curve shows how the potential difference across an accelerating gap varies with time; and t_1 and t_3 are two successive times at which a particle is supposed to cross the gap, the energy gain at these times being such as to keep the particle at the required rate of acceleration. If the particle has less energy than it should have, according to equations (2) and (3), it will complete the orbit sooner than it should, and the second crossing of the gap will occur at a time such as t_2. The particle will therefore gain energy at an increased rate, tending to restore the initial deficit in energy. Similarly, an excess in rate is corrected by a motion of the time toward t_4. A more detailed analysis shows that the energy tends to oscillate about the correct value; the stability breaks down if a rate of energy gain greater than the peak of the curve is required. The stability in phase causes the motion of the ions to "lock in" to the applied radio frequency; or, in other words, the particles tend to seek out a state of motion in which equation (2) is satisfied, with f equal to the applied frequency. Thus a given set of

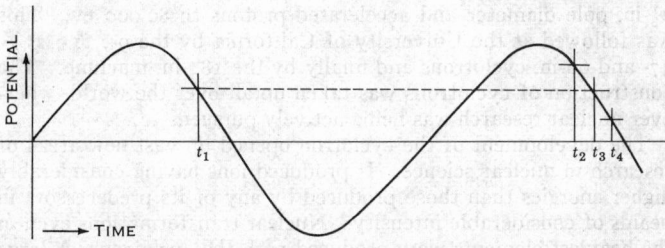

FIG. 3.—THE PRINCIPLE OF PHASE STABILITY

values of f and B determine a value of m and therefore, by (3), of the energy W.

Acceleration is achieved if f or B (or both) is made to vary slowly in time during the flight of the particle. At the start, f and B have values corresponding to the initial energy of the particles; a decrease in f or an increase in B will lead to an increase in particle energy. Machines in which B is constant in time belong to the general category of cyclotrons; if the frequency is modulated they are called synchrocyclotrons or simply FM cyclotrons. The general term synchrotron is now applied to machines in which B varies with time. This is technically more difficult than variation of f, and is done only when the mass varies by a large factor, as in the acceleration of electrons, or of protons to extremely high energies. Some practical realizations of these possibilities are described in later sections. *See also* ATOM; ELECTRICITY; ELECTRON; MAGNETISM; NUCLEUS; PARTICLES, ELEMENTARY; RADIOACTIVITY.   (E. M. MC.)

VAN DE GRAAFF ACCELERATORS AND COCKCROFT-WALTON GENERATORS

Van de Graaff Accelerator.—This is an accelerator in which power at high voltage is supplied by means of an insulating belt which carries charge from ground to the high-voltage terminal.

As pointed out by Van de Graaff in an early publication, a high-voltage machine utilizing a charge-carrying belt was first proposed by Lord Kelvin. Van de Graaff, while a Rhodes scholar at Oxford university, recognized the need for a steady, high voltage for particle acceleration and saw the possibilities of this device. After his return to Princeton university, Princeton, N.J., he built the first successful model in 1929.

In this device an electrical charge is deposited on a belt of insulating fabric. The charge is carried into a smooth, well-rounded

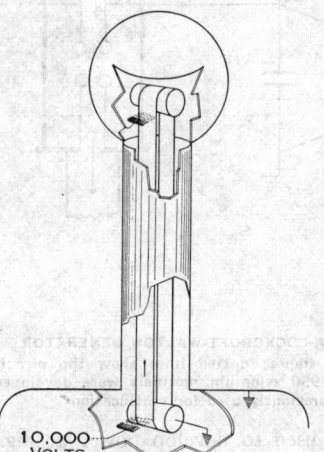

10,000 VOLTS

FIG. 4.—SCHEMATIC DRAWING OF A VAN DE GRAAFF ACCELERATOR

metal shell. Here it is removed from the belt; it passes to the metal shell, and the shell will increase in potential until electrical breakdown occurs or until the charging current is balanced by load current.

To charge the belt a corona discharge is maintained between a series of points or a fine wire on one side of the belt and a well-rounded electrode or inductor plate on the other side. Ionization takes place only near the sharp ends of the charging needles. If the needles are at a positive potential with respect to the inductor plate, positive ions move toward the inductor plate, which in many cases is a grounded metal pulley carrying the belt. The belt intercepts many of the ions and carries them into the metal shell, which serves as a high-voltage electrode. Here the charge is removed by an array of needle points electrically connected to the high-voltage electrode. The machine can be made to provide negative current to the high-voltage electrode by operating the charging needles at a negative voltage with respect to the inductor plate. Belt-charging electrodes must be electrically shielded from the field of the high-voltage terminal, and charge must be carried well within the high-voltage terminal before removal is attempted. Charging current is then independent of the potential of the high-voltage terminal. Terminal voltage will rise until it is limited by corona discharge, by leakage current along insulators, by spark-over or by some load such as ion current through an accelerating tube.

A working model which Van de Graaff built at Princeton consisted of a metal sphere 2 ft. in diameter supported by two Pyrex rods and charged by a silk belt 2.2 in. wide. Early machines followed closely the pattern of Van de Graaff's first model. Charging currents of several milliamperes were achieved, and voltages were commonly limited by spark-over through air from the high-voltage terminal. A smooth terminal approximately spherical in shape, with a radius of 1 m., was found to hold 1,000,000 v. satisfactorily; and from tests with a number of machines the maximum voltage appears to be approximately a linear function of the radius of the terminal.

Work at Princeton and at the University of Wisconsin, Madison, showed that the machine could be made much more compact by enclosing it in a pressure tank and utilizing the high dielectric strength of high-pressure gases. A series of developments at Wisconsin resulted in 1940 in a compact machine operating up to 4,500,000 v. From later development work at the Massachusetts Institute of Technology, Cambridge, a machine was completed in 1950 operating up to nearly 8,000,000 v. Nearly all machines of this type use high-pressure gases for insulation.

These machines came into wide use in nuclear physics laboratories throughout the world. They are specially suited for experiments requiring moderate currents of ions with accurately defined energies. Van de Graaff machines operating up to 6,000,000 v. became commercially available in the 1950s.

Cockcroft-Walton Generator.—This is a particle accelerator

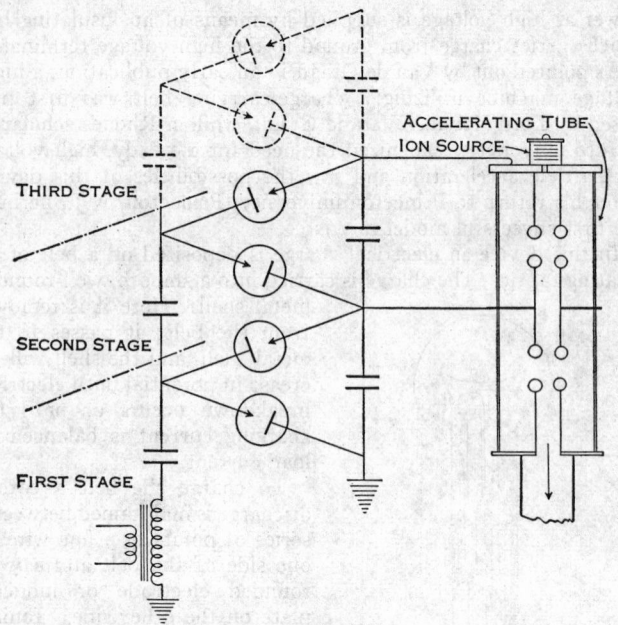

FIG. 5.—SCHEMATIC DRAWING OF A COCKCROFT-WALTON GENERATOR
The original machine consisted of two stages; dotted lines show the circuit arrangement for a third stage. After 1950 selenium rectifiers were developed for use in place of the electronic diodes previously used for rectification

in which a voltage multiplier is used to develop power at high voltage. The accelerator developed by Cockcroft and Walton for their transmutation experiments filled a need so successfully and proved so versatile that it was very widely copied.

In describing their early work, preceding completion of their successful machine, Cockcroft and Walton pointed out the advantages of a steady voltage for acceleration of charged particles. The stream of particles is then uninterrupted; and if fluctuation in voltage is held to a low value the variation of particle energy is small, and accurate measurement of transmutation phenomena is facilitated. Million-volt machines had been developed for the study of high-voltage insulators and for X-ray work, but they did not give the steady voltage desired.

For their high-voltage supply Cockcroft and Walton chose a circuit, commonly called a voltage multiplier, originated by H. Greinacher in 1920. This circuit consists of two stacks of series-connected condensers. One stack is fixed in voltage, except for ripple, with one terminal connected to ground and its other terminal connected to the load. One terminal of the second condenser stack is connected to a transformer; and if the peak voltage of this transformer is V, the voltages at all points along this condenser stack rise and fall within an amplitude of approximately $2V$. Series-connected rectifiers link the two stacks as shown in fig. 5. As the voltage on the oscillating stack rises and falls, charge is transferred stepwise from ground to the high-voltage terminal. Here the voltage is steady except for ripple caused by power drain and stray capacitance, and for no load it has a value of $2VN$ where N is the number of multiplier stages used.

Although extremely high voltages would appear to be attainable by use of many stages, certain practical difficulties set an upper limit to the voltage. One of the most severe limitations is imposed by electrical breakdown through air between neighbouring parts. A 1,000,000-v. machine must be housed in a large room. Exposed terminals must be well grounded, and components must be grouped to minimize electrical gradients. The practical upper voltage limit for these machines when operating in air at atmospheric pressure appears to be about 1,500,000 v.

The high-voltage supply serves to furnish power to an accelerating tube which is equipped with an ion source at its upper terminal. Many of the early machines were limited in voltage by electrical breakdown in the accelerating tube. Multisection tubes of large physical extent have been required to avoid this difficulty. Condensers and rectifiers were a major problem in early machines, and Cockcroft and Walton had to build these components for their

first machine. Later they became commercially available.

These machines are capable of relatively intense ion beams. The high-voltage supplies are usually capable of delivering many milliamperes of current, and ion sources yielding several milliamperes of ion current have been developed. Cockcroft-Walton machines are more numerous than any other type of particle accelerator. Many are designed for operation at only 100 or 200 kv. These are relatively compact and inexpensive and are used to provide neutron sources. Usually to provide neutrons, deuterons accelerated by the machine are directed onto a target containing deuterium or tritium. These reactions give prolific yields of high-energy neutrons at accelerating voltages even below 100 kv.

Low-voltage Cockcroft-Walton machines designed to serve as neutron sources are also commercially available. The N. V. Philips Gloeilampenfabrieken, Eindhoven, Neth., built a number of machines for 1,000,000 v. or more for general research work in nuclear physics. The company also produced machines of this type housed in pressure tanks. By taking advantage of the good insulating properties of high-pressure gases it developed a compact model operating up to 2,000,000 v.   (R. G. Hb.)

CYCLOTRONS AND SYNCHROCYCLOTRONS

The cyclotron is a major instrument for nuclear research. It is a device for accelerating protons and deuterons, as well as other heavier ions, to energies high enough to produce nuclear transformations in even the heaviest nuclei. The first machine to accelerate particles to high energies without the use of high voltages, it was for many years the only accelerator able to produce heavy particles with energies above 5 Mev. Among the various accelerators which were developed to produce high-energy particles, the cyclotron proved to be the most useful and the most popular.

The synchrocyclotron is a modification of the cyclotron that makes practical the acceleration of ions to energies about 20 times greater than otherwise: energies great enough to make possible the production of new particles of intermediate mass, called mesons. The creation of mesons by the synchrocyclotron is a striking example of the conversion of energy into matter.

Cyclotron.—The first cyclotron, constructed by E. O. Lawrence and M. S. Livingston in the early 1930s, had a magnet of only $2\frac{1}{2}$-in. pole diameter and accelerated protons to 80,000 ev. This was followed at the University of California by the 9-, 11-, $27\frac{1}{2}$-, 37- and 60-in. cyclotrons and finally by the 184-in. machine. The construction of cyclotrons was taken up all over the world, wherever nuclear research was being actively pursued.

The development of the cyclotron opened up vast new areas of research in nuclear science. It produced ions having considerably higher energies than those produced by any of its predecessors in beams of considerable intensity. Nuclear transformations even in the heaviest elements were produced with the cyclotron. A large variety of new radioactive substances was produced and isolated. It is fair to say that the whole important field of radioactive tracer

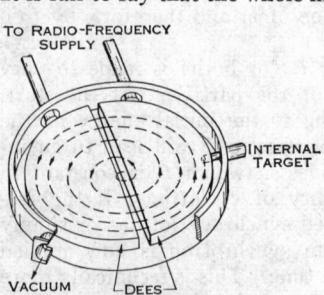

FIG. 6.—ARRANGEMENT FOR ACCELERATING IONS IN THE CYCLOTRON

technique in medical, biological and chemical research received a tremendous impetus as a result of the development of the cyclotron. The first tracer amounts of plutonium produced with the Berkeley cyclotron played an important role in the development of the plutonium bomb. By using the accelerated deuterons to bombard internal beryllium targets, neutron sources 50,000 times as intense as those obtainable previously from radon-beryllium mixtures were made

available. Moreover, studies of the scattering of protons by protons and of neutrons by protons, carried out in an energy range otherwise inaccessible, advanced the knowledge of the interaction of the fundamental particles.

In the cyclotron (*see* fig. 6) two semicircular (D-shaped) hollow electrodes, called dees, are arranged within a vacuum chamber between the poles of a magnet. The ions starting near the centre circulate inside the electrodes, crossing the gap between them twice in each revolution. A high-frequency potential difference impressed across the dees will produce a repeated acceleration at each crossing, provided its frequency is very close to the circulation frequency of the ions.

It is necessary to keep the ions from striking the dees. By arranging for a small radial decrease in the magnetic field, a slight outward curvature to the magnetic field is obtained (*see* fig. 7). The magnetic force on the particle then always has a small component toward the median plane. This keeps the particle within an inch or two of the plane median to the two magnet poles. This is important because the total length of the spiral path which the ions traverse may be several hundred feet.

The necessity of this focusing, together with the effect of relativity in increasing the mass of the particle as its energy increases, makes inevitable a difference between the circulation of frequency of the particle and the oscillation frequency of the accelerating potential over a considerable portion of the path. Under these circumstances the particle will get out of step with the dee voltage. The effect accumulates with each revolution; and if very many revolutions are made the particle will ultimately arrive at a phase in which the voltage is of the opposite sign, which means that the particle will be decelerated. Thus, a large number of revolutions has to be avoided and a very high voltage must be put on

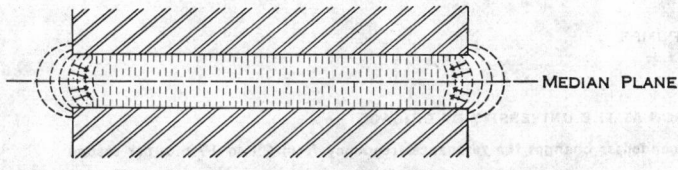

FIG. 7.—MAGNETIC FOCUSING IN THE CYCLOTRON

Arrows indicate direction of force on a particle moving in a radially decreasing magnetic field. The force is inward and toward the median plane

the dees. An extreme example is the 86-in. cyclotron at the Oak Ridge National laboratory, Oak Ridge, Tenn., where a dee voltage of 500 kv. is used to accelerate protons to 22 Mev. This requires a 400-kw. oscillator and represents a practical limit to what can be obtained from a conventional cyclotron.

At the University of Washington, Seattle, a 60-in. cyclotron modeled after the one at the University of California was completed in 1952. It has a 200-ton magnet operating at a field strength of 15,000 gauss with a power input of about 60 kw. The radio-frequency oscillator operates with a power input of 125 kw. and develops a peak dee-to-dee voltage of 250 kv. In discussing the performance of cyclotrons it is important to distinguish between the internal circulating beam and that fraction of it which is extracted by means of a deflector. In the University of Washington cyclotron the internal beam has about 800 μ amp. of 21-Mev deuterons. Thus, more than 12% of the oscillator power is converted to useful kinetic energy. About 25% of this beam can be extracted.

Some 50 cyclotrons are in use in research laboratories throughout the world. One-half of these are in the United States, and roughly an equal number are distributed throughout the world. These are of various sizes and some have special features. Thus, some of the more recent designs are arranged for easy changing of the energy. An example is the 90-in. cyclotron installed at Livermore, Calif., which can accelerate protons from 2.6 Mev to 14.0 Mev; deuterons from 5.2 Mev to 12.5 Mev; and tritons from 7.7 Mev to 8.3 Mev. Others are used largely for accelerating heavy ions. An example is the 1.2-m. pole diameter machine in Leningrad, U.S.S.R., which can accelerate nitrogen ions to 25 Mev.

The Oak Ridge National laboratory cyclotron produces what may be the world's record output of high-energy particles, 60 kw. of 22-Mev protons on an internal target.

Azimuthal Focusing.—In 1938, quite early in the period of cyclotron development, L. H. Thomas of Ohio State university described a means of obtaining additional focusing of the ions in the cyclotron by providing azimuthal variations in the magnetic field.

This feature promised more stable and efficient operation of the machine in general, and a considerable improvement in the maximum energy attainable.

The idea was not taken seriously until 15 years later when an extensive study, both theoretical and experimental, was undertaken at the Radiation laboratory at Berkeley, Calif. Models were built, and these verified the soundness of the ideas. At Los Alamos, N.M., the performance of the 42-in. cyclotron was greatly improved by the incorporation of Thomas focusing. This was accomplished rather simply by the insertion of three iron sector plates on the magnet poles. This kind of focusing can be augmented by spiraling the sectors. Such spiraled "hill and valley" magnetic fields appear to have useful applications in a variety of accelerator types for producing particles in the relativistic range of energy while using a fixed magnetic field and constant radio frequency. These designs were originated and have been developed extensively by the Midwestern Universities Research association (M.U.R.A.), Madison, Wis., under the name FFAG (fixed-field alternating-gradient accelerators).

Synchrocyclotron.—A more obvious way to overcome the energy limitation of the cyclotron is to provide a means of varying the frequency applied to the dees in accordance with the needs of magnetic focusing and the relativistic increase in the mass of the particle. The scheme is made practical by the existence of phase-stable orbits. Such an orbit is one in which the circulation frequency of the ion is the same as the oscillation frequency of the dee voltage. The circulation frequency of the ion decreases with increasing radius because of the decreased value of the magnetic field and the relativistic increase in the mass of the particle. When the frequency of the oscillator approaches the circulation frequency of the ion in the centre of the machine, some of these ions are caught into phase-stable orbits. As the frequency of the oscillator is decreased, the ions tend to stay in these orbits by absorbing energy from the electric field of the dees. By keeping in synchronism with the radio frequency, the particles gain energy and move in orbits of increasing radius up to the maximum allowed by the magnet design.

An important advantage of the synchrocyclotron is that, provided the vacuum is good enough, there is no limit to the number of revolutions the particle may make to obtain the desired energy. The desired acceleration may take place in quite small steps, 10 kv. per turn being the usual amount. This allows a more modest radio-frequency supply. Moreover, the shape of the magnetic field is much less critical. Another feature of the synchrocyclotron is the use of a single dee. This gives half the acceleration per turn of the two-dee system but has many mechanical and electrical advantages for synchrocyclotron use.

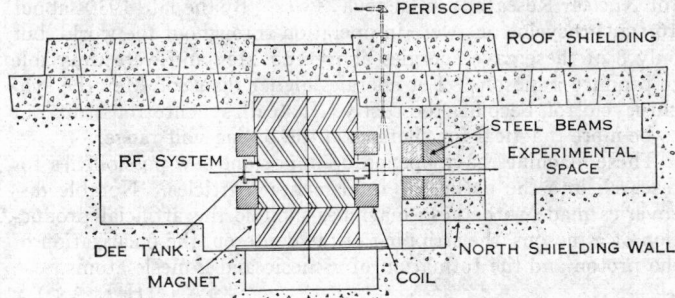

FIG. 8.—INSTALLATION OF THE 170-IN. SYNCHROCYCLOTRON AT THE UNIVERSITY OF CHICAGO

Heavy concrete and steel walls shield the working areas from the penetrating radiations emitted by the machine

On the other hand, the output intensity is much lower since the frequency is modulated. The ions are captured into stable orbits only during a small fraction of the modulation cycle. In the 170-in. synchrocyclotron at The University of Chicago, the beam appears as a pulse about 100 μ sec. long at a repetition rate of 60 cycles per second. The mean circulation current is about 2 μ amp. However, the energy is 450 Mev so the total beam power is almost 1 kw.

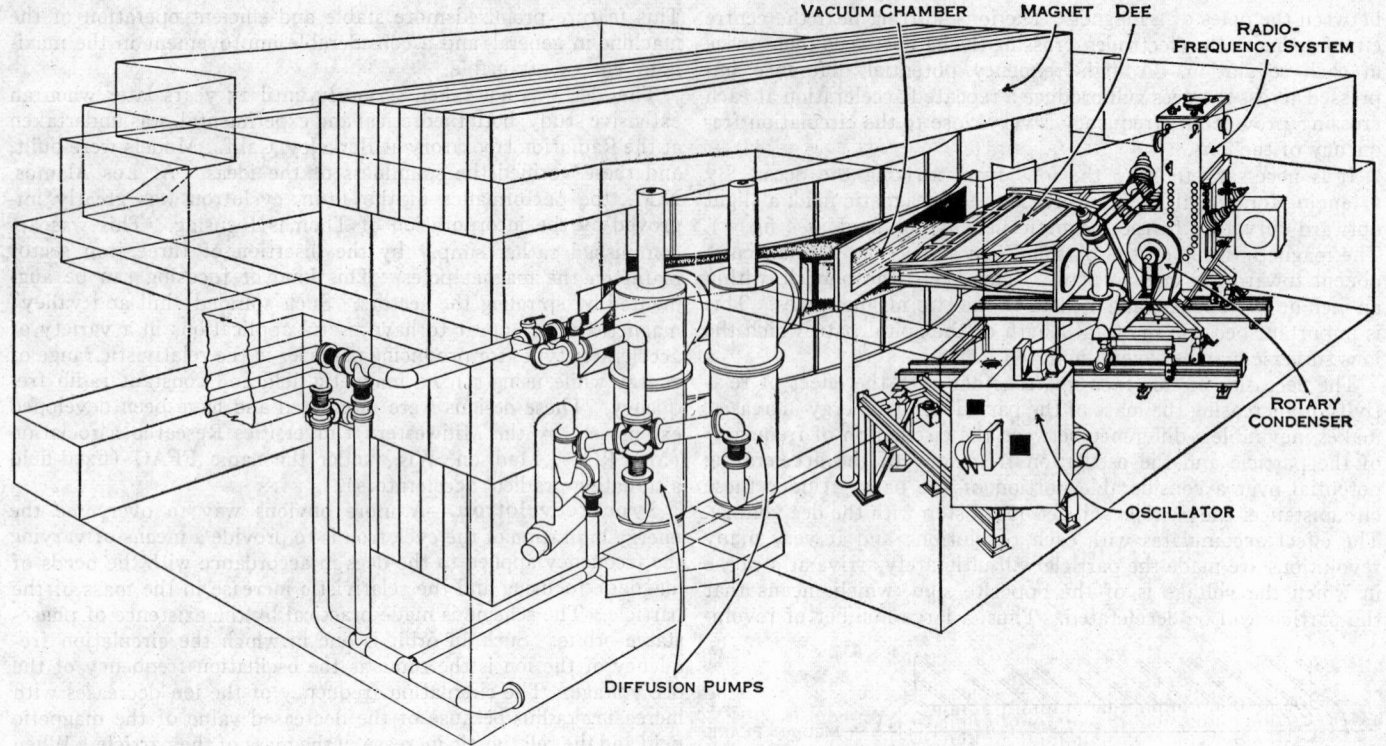

VACUUM CHAMBER   MAGNET DEE   RADIO-FREQUENCY SYSTEM

ROTARY CONDENSER

OSCILLATOR

DIFFUSION PUMPS

FIG. 9.—THE 170-IN. SYNCHROCYCLOTRON AT THE UNIVERSITY OF CHICAGO
The MacKenzie system of frequency modulation is used in which a rotating condenser changes the resonance frequency from 29 to 17 mc. per second

Following E. M. McMillan's suggestion, the first test of a frequency-modulated cyclotron was made by converting the 27-in. machine at Berkeley. The test was so successful that immediately afterward the 184-in. cyclotron, which was originally designed for conventional operation with about 1,000,000 v. on the dees, was operated as a synchrocyclotron and gave beams of about 200-Mev deuterons and 400-Mev alpha particles. In 1948 its radio-frequency system was changed to the MacKenzie circuit for operation with protons, and it then gave a beam of protons of an energy of 350 Mev. In 1957 an extensive conversion of both the magnet and the radio frequency brought the operating energy up to 750 Mev. This placed the Berkeley machine higher in energy than the 680-Mev machine in Dubna, U.S.S.R. (near Moscow), in operation since 1953; and the 600-Mev synchrocyclotron completed in 1958 in the laboratory of CERN (European Organization for Nuclear Research) in Geneva, Switz. By the late 1950s about 16 synchrocyclotrons were in operation throughout the world, but only 8 of these gave energies above 200 Mev and were thus able to produce π mesons. For energies higher than 800 Mev the synchrocyclotron becomes too costly. Instead, synchrotrons turn out to be more practical for energies in the billion-volt range.

These machines have opened up important new possibilities for research into the nature of fundamental particles. Notable discoveries made with these machines include the artificial production of π mesons, the stripping of the deuteron, the polarization of the proton and the formation of π-mesic and μ-mesic atoms.

(H. L. An.)

SYNCHROTRONS

Synchrotrons for Electrons.—The electron synchrotron utilizes the principle of phase stability to maintain synchronism between the circulating particles and an applied high-frequency electric field. A magnetic field deflects particles in a circular orbit, and the intensity of the field is modulated cyclically from low to high field strength as the particles gain energy, to maintain orbits of nearly constant radius. Since the magnetic field is required to maintain the orbit, but is not used for acceleration, magnetic field lines are needed only in the annular region defined by the orbit. This field may be produced by a ring magnet. The relatively low weight and cost of such a ring magnet compared with

the solid-core magnets required for cyclotrons or betatrons gives the synchrotron a significant economic advantage for high particle energies.

Electrons are well adapted to acceleration in a ring-shaped magnetic field, since they acquire a velocity essentially equal to the velocity of light at relatively low energies ($v = 0.98c$ at 2 Mev); for higher energies they circulate about an orbit of fixed radius at constant frequency. An electric field to provide acceleration is developed (by a resonant electrical cavity) across a gap in the vacuum chamber enclosing the orbit. The potential across the gap alternates at a frequency tuned to be identical with the orbital frequency of the electrons. This applied frequency is determined by the orbit radius r and is

$$f = \frac{c}{2\pi r} = \frac{\text{velocity of light}}{\text{orbit circumference}}$$

During the half cycle when the electric field is positive, the electrons acquire energy; they are reduced in energy during the other half cycle. So they become bunched into a phase where the voltage maintains a rate of increase in energy which matches the rising magnetic field. Under these conditions, an electron which crosses the gap at the wrong time, and which has the wrong energy, traverses an orbit of slightly smaller (or larger) radius. The resulting change in orbital frequency causes the electron to migrate toward the correct phase. This migration represents an oscillation in phase about the mean or equilibrium phase, at which the energy acquired per traversal is exactly that required to match the rate of rise of magnetic field. This type of stable-phase oscillation is inherent in the synchrotron. Electrons will follow any reasonable rate of rise of magnetic field; i.e., 60 cycles per second. If sufficient accelerating potential is available across the gap, the electrons will maintain synchronism and be accelerated to maximum energy.

Electrons must be brought up to constant velocity (taken as 1 to 2 Mev energy) by some auxiliary means. In early synchrotrons this was accomplished by magnetic induction, as in the betatron, by providing some linkage flux threading the orbit. Other installations use a low-voltage accelerator external to the magnet to preaccelerate the electrons, after which they are inflected into the orbit by a suitably shaped electric field. The vacuum chamber has the general form of a toroid, or "doughnut," and must be maintained at high vacuum (0.000001 mm. Hg) to avoid loss of electrons by scattering from the gas during the early stages of acceleration. When the electrons approach maximum energy, the oscillator providing the high-frequency accelerating field is turned off; the electrons spiral in to strike a target on the inside of the chamber and generate a narrow beam of energetic X-rays which emerge tangentially from the chamber and which can be used for experimentation.

The first electron synchrotron, for 8 Mev, was built in England in 1946 to test the principle of phase-stable acceleration. The first high-energy synchrotron developed 330 Mev in 1947, at the University of California. By 1956 more than 20 synchrotrons between 50 and 500 Mev were in use as research instruments in many countries. Two synchrotrons for 1,200 Mev were completed in 1957, one at the California Institute of Technology, Pasadena, and one at Cornell university, Ithaca, N.Y. The Cornell machine was the first of a new type of synchrotron using alternating-gradient magnets (see below, Synchrotrons for Protons). Electron synchrotrons have found their greatest use as X-ray sources for producing photonuclear reactions, especially the photoproduction of mesons, which occurs above a threshold of about 250 Mev. Synchrotrons of 100 Mev or less have also found useful applications in hospitals for treatment of cancer and in nuclear research laboratories.

The electron synchrotron has a unique property which leads to a practical upper limit of energy. When deflected in a magnetic field the electrons radiate electromagnetic energy in a continuous spectrum extending into the soft X-ray region, with an intensity which increases with the third power of electron energy. This radiated energy must be supplied by the high-frequency accelerating system, in addition to that required for synchronous acceleration. At very high energies the radiation disturbs particle orbits and produces transverse oscillations which throw the electrons out of the chamber. The Cambridge electron accelerator, a joint project of the Massachusetts Institute of Technology and Harvard university, is designed to produce electrons at an energy of 6,000 Mev (6 Bev), which approaches the practical energy limit. It uses alternating-gradient magnets in an orbit 236 ft. in diameter, op-

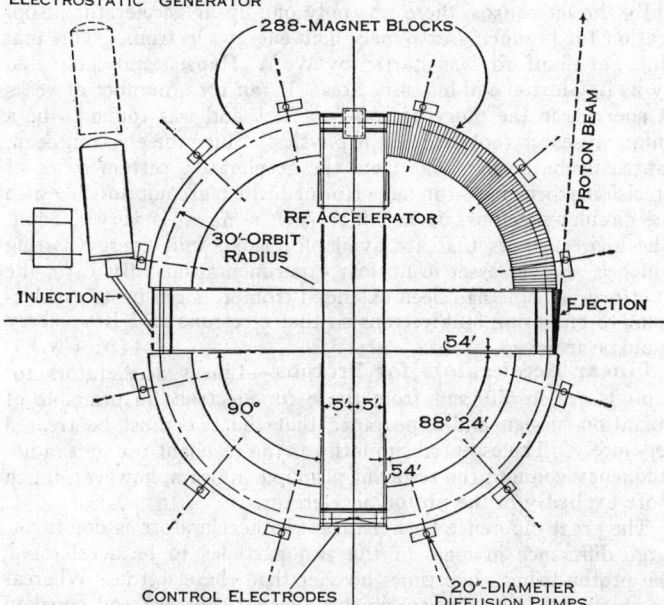

ELECTROSTATIC GENERATOR

288-MAGNET BLOCKS

RF ACCELERATOR

30'-ORBIT RADIUS

PROTON BEAM

INJECTION

EJECTION

54'

90°

5'-5'

88° 24'

54'

CONTROL ELECTRODES

20'-DIAMETER DIFFUSION PUMPS

FIG. 10.—PLAN VIEW OF THE COMPONENTS OF THE COSMOTRON, A 3-BEV PROTON SYNCHROTRON AT THE BROOKHAVEN NATIONAL LABORATORY, UPTON, L.I., N.Y.

erating at 60 cycles per second, and has many high-frequency accelerating cavities to provide the energy lost by radiation. A similar electron accelerator was under construction (1960) in the DESY project at the University of Hamburg in west Germany.

Synchrotrons for Protons.—The proton synchrotron also uses

a ring magnet and utilizes the principle of phase stability to maintain synchronism with the high-frequency accelerating electric field. A ring magnet is much lighter and less costly than the solid-core magnet of a synchrocyclotron, which also accelerates protons, but requires acceleration at essentially constant orbit radius. The magnetic field must be varied cyclically from low to high field strengths during the acceleration interval, matching proton energy. High-energy protons are produced in short bursts at the peak of each cycle, which results in a low average beam intensity. However, the advantage of higher energies for scientific research justifies reduced beam intensity, and proton synchrotrons have displaced synchrocyclotrons for energies above 1 Bev (= 10^9 electron volts).

Proton velocity increases continuously with increasing energy; so, unlike the situation with electrons, orbital frequency increases during acceleration, by more than 1:10. The applied electric field must be varied in frequency to match exactly the orbital frequency of the protons, which requires a precisely determined schedule of frequency modulation. To vary the frequency, the resonant cavities which provide accelerating electric fields are equipped either with rotating capacitors or with ferrite cores which are magnetically biased, or with both. In high-energy accelerators many such cavities are spaced around the orbit and operated in phase.

Protons are preaccelerated in an external accelerator to relatively low energy, and are inflected into the orbit when the orbit magnetic field reaches the proper value for deflection at the designed radius. At maximum energy the protons are directed against targets at the edge of the chamber by changing the applied frequency, or they can be deflected tangentially outward in an emergent beam for experimental studies.

The cosmotron at Brookhaven National laboratory, Upton, L.I., N.Y. (see fig. 10), completed in 1952, operates at 3 Bev and produces bursts of 5×10^{10} protons at 5-sec. intervals. The magnet is formed of four quadrants spaced by 10-ft. straight sections, forming a distorted circle of 75-ft. diameter. An electrostatic generator produces 4-Mev protons, which are inflected into the orbit at one straight section. A ferrite-loaded high-frequency resonant cavity in another straight section supplies about 3,000 v. per turn for acceleration and is modulated between 0.37 and 4.20 mc. per second. At high energy the protons are deflected outward in an emergent beam used for experiments. Significant research has been performed on the production of "strange" particles and the properties of high-energy mesons.

The bevatron at the Berkeley Radiation laboratory was completed in 1954. It produces 2×10^{10} protons per pulse of 6.2-Bev energy, at 10-sec. intervals. The magnet consists of four quadrants with 20-ft. separation, forming a circle of 160-ft. diameter. Protons are preaccelerated to 0.5 Mev in a Cockcroft-Walton generator and to 10 Mev by a linear accelerator, before being inflected into the orbit. Although structurally larger and heavier than the cosmotron, the bevatron is similar in basic principles of design and of operation. Research operations have been highly successful, the most dramatic results being the discovery of the negative proton (antiproton) and the antineutron.

The principle of alternating-gradient magnetic focusing, developed at Brookhaven starting in 1952, has been applied to several types of accelerators. It utilizes alternately positive and negative gradients in the magnetic field used to deflect particles around an orbit. A gradient field is one in which the field is stronger on one side of the orbit than on the other, so magnetic field lines are curved, and particles are deflected toward or away from the median plane and the central orbit. In effect, the successive sectors of alternating gradient are magnetic "lenses" which focus moving particles strongly about the chosen equilibrium orbit location. The use of such strong focusing fields reduces particle oscillation amplitudes, allowing much smaller magnets to be used and so reducing cost. Synchrotrons can be designed for larger orbit radii and higher energy.

An alternating-gradient proton synchrotron at the CERN laboratory in Geneva was brought into operation in 1959 at 28 Bev, and a similar machine at Brookhaven was completed in 1960. These super-energy accelerators are located in underground circular tunnels for radiation shielding; that at Brookhaven is 750 ft. in diameter. Scientists anticipate an exciting wealth of new experimental information on the properties of high-energy particles when these machines come into full operation. (M. S. Ln.)

LINEAR ACCELERATORS

Linear Accelerators for Electrons.—The term linear accelerator might be applied to any machine which accelerates particles in a straight line, but through common usage it has been restricted to the particular class of these machines which employs repeated use of a rapidly alternating potential in a resonant condition. It is a development and extension of the machine proposed by R. Wideröe, mentioned above under *Resonance Accelerators*. Because of the considerable difference in the design and operation of these machines for electrons and for heavy particles, they will be treated separately.

Linear accelerators were developed through the application of techniques developed by the radar programs of World War II. With few exceptions, they use an electromagnetic (or radio) wave with a frequency of the order of 3,000 mc. per second traveling down an evacuated wave guide as the medium of acceleration. A wave guide is a cylindrical pipe with conducting walls in which a radio wave may be propagated under suitable circumstances. Electrons are injected into the wave guide so that they travel in the same direction as the wave; and the wave guide is so constructed that the principal wave and the particle have the same velocity at all points along the guide. The wave guide is also arranged so that the electric field component of the wave is directed along the axis. Electrons entering the guide at the proper time (or phase) experience a force resulting from the interaction of their charge and the electric field; and since wave and particle travel at the same speed, this force continues throughout the length of the wave guide, accelerating the electrons to ever-increasing energies. The effect is similar to that of a surfboard rider on an ocean wave.

There are several possible conditions of phase for acceleration. The particle can be ahead of the point of maximum electric field in the wave. In this case it is phase stable, for if the acceleration is not sufficiently large to keep the electron in step with the wave, the electron moves back to a position of greater field and greater acceleration. It can be shown, however, that the electron is then radially unstable; *i.e.,* if the electron is deflected from its path, the deflection becomes progressively worse. The particle can also be behind the position of maximum electric field. It is then phase unstable and radially stable. As a third condition, the particle may be at the position of maximum electric field (which incidentally has a sine wave variation). In this case, it is in unstable equilibrium in regard both to phase and radial deflections.

Since it is not possible to fabricate the wave guide so that the wave will have exactly the right velocity, it is generally advantageous to operate the machine so that the electrons have phase stability and to overcome the radial instability with an axial magnetic field along the guide. In one notable case, however, the position of unstable equilibrium is used (the accelerator developed at Stanford university, Stanford, Calif.). The rate of acceleration is very high; the wave velocity is made equal to the velocity of light; and, because of the relativistic velocity of the particles, the accelerator appears so short that neither phase nor radial instability has a chance to operate.

In an ordinary wave guide with smooth conducting walls, the phase velocity of the electromagnetic wave is always greater than the velocity of light. Since particle velocities cannot exceed the velocity of light, it is necessary to slow the wave down. This is accomplished by placing iris diaphragms in the guide. Thus a practical accelerator wave guide consists of a metal tube of high conductivity and circular cross section with metal diaphragms placed at intervals of one-fourth wave length throughout the length of the tube. Each of these diaphragms has a circular opening at its centre through which the electrons pass. The phase velocity of the wave is determined by the difference between the diameter of the hole in the diaphragm and the inside diameter of the tube.

The final energy of electrons from a linear accelerator of optimum design is proportional to the square root of the product of wave-guide length and radio-frequency power input. Since the cost of long accelerator wave guides is very large, the power input must be as high as possible. Magnetrons operating at power levels of 500,000 to several million watts, and klystrons operating in the range of 10,000,000–30,000,000 w. have been used as power sources. These tubes are unable to handle such power continuously and therefore are turned on for periods of one or two millionths of a second, repeated 50 to 1,000 times per second.

Since magnetrons are free-running oscillators, it is very difficult to control the phase so as to operate several together. On the other hand, klystrons are power amplifiers, and it is easy to drive any number from a single source with complete control of the phases of the output. This fact makes possible the cascading of a number of separate sections of accelerator with each feeding into the next section with the proper phase. This scheme was adopted at Stanford university for acceleration to the 1,000-Mev (1-Bev) range. (L. S. Ss.)

The first linear accelerator was built by D. W. Fry and his associates at Malvern, Eng., in 1946. Further work continued in England and to some extent in the United States on obtaining large output currents and high efficiencies. A single magnetron feeding several feet of wave guide with magnetic focusing was used in this first accelerator. Subsequent accelerators were built in England, France and the United States that employed several klystrons feeding separate sections to obtain higher energies. In some of these machines, peak currents as high as 0.75 amp. have been obtained, with as much as 50% of the radio-frequency power being transferred to the electron beam. Some of these high-current accelerators are intended to generate pulsed neutrons for time-of-flight measurements. Others are intended for use in food and drug sterilization and for activation of chemical reactions. A number of lower-current accelerators are also in use as X-ray sources in the range of 4–6 Mev for the treatment of cancer. There are several machines in the range of 50 Mev being used for biological research and experimentation in the direct use of electrons for cancer treatment.

By the late 1950s, there was only one linear accelerator in operation for producing extremely high-energy electrons. This machine, at Stanford, was started by W. W. Hansen and completed by E. L. Ginzton and his associates. It ran for a number of years at energies in the range of 700–800 Mev and was found to be a unique research tool for nuclear physics. Since the electron beam can easily be brought out from the accelerator, certain types of precision experiments can be performed which are not possible with the circular machines from which such removal is very difficult. The high currents that are available also permit energy sorting which is another asset in nuclear experimentation. By 1959, the Stanford machine had been extended from a length using 21 klystrons to one using 30 klystrons so that electrons of 1-Bev energy could be achieved. (M. Cw.)

Linear Accelerators for Protons.—Linear accelerators for protons are so different from those for electrons in principle of operation, design and appearance that the two must be treated separately. The essential similarity is the resonant use of a radio-frequency voltage; the resonant principle appears, however, much more explicitly in the proton accelerator.

The great difference between the two accelerators is due to the large difference in mass of the two particles to be accelerated, the proton being 2,000 times heavier than the electron. Whereas an electron has a velocity which is nearly constant and equal to that of light at energies higher than 1 Mev, a proton is much slower and essentially obeys the classical laws of mechanics up to 100 Mev; that is, its velocity increases as the square root of its energy. This low velocity of the proton makes it impractical to reduce the velocity of an electromagnetic wave in a wave guide to the extent needed to use the principle of the electron linear accelerator. It is necessary to develop a new technique for protons.

Consider a large cavity in the form of a long, cylindrical tank with electrically conducting walls. When this cavity is fed with radio-frequency power of the proper frequency, a resonant condition is set up. The cavity is equivalent to a wave guide with closed reflecting ends, so that the wave is reflected from side to side, resulting in a standing wave at the resonant frequency much the same as a sound wave in an organ pipe. The cavity and the way in which power is fed are so designed that the electric field of the electromagnetic wave is in the direction of the long dimension of the cavity. Therefore, if protons are injected with the right phase in the direction of the long axis of the cavity, they will be accelerated at first; but when the phase of the oscillation changes, they will be decelerated. The result is no net gain in energy. To avoid this difficulty, a number of hollow drift tubes are placed nearly end to end along the axis of the cavity. These shield the protons while they are within the tubes from the effects of the decelerating field. The lengths of the drift tubes are so adjusted and the gaps so placed that the protons cross the gaps at the time the field is near a maximum in the accelerating direction. This requires the spacing between drift-tube centres to increase as the proton is accelerated; the distance being v/f, where v is the velocity of the proton and f is the frequency of the electromagnetic wave.

In proton linear accelerators, the particles must have the proper velocity at each gap. The machine will not operate unless the radio-frequency power level is above a minimum value. This disadvantage is not shared by the electron accelerator; but, on the other hand, the energy spectrum of the proton accelerator is much better (i.e., the spread of energies of the emergent particles is much less).

The drift tubes must have sufficient diameter to pass a reasonable beam of protons, but at the same time they must not be so large that there is appreciable penetration of the electromagnetic field into their interior. This leads to the use of relatively low frequencies—in the region of 200,000,000 cycles per second. The large size of the cavity leads to a long time for the build-up of resonant oscillations, requiring a long pulse of power. This is an advantage in nuclear disintegration work.

There are positions of phase stability and radial instability, or phase instability and radial stability, as in the linear accelerator for electrons. The radial instability can be eliminated by placing metallic grids across the drift tubes, changing the shape of the electric field in the gap region to one that has a focusing action.

Wideröe's two-stage linear accelerator was developed by E. O. Lawrence and D. H. Sloan, who built several multistage accelerators in 1930–32. The logical extension of their ideas to the acceleration of protons was accomplished by L. W. Alvarez and his associates at the University of California in 1947. As in the electron accelerator, this accomplishment was materially aided by the very extensive technical advancements in radar during World War II. The California accelerator operates at a wave length of 150 cm. The cavity has a diameter of 3.5 ft. and a length of 40 ft. Protons are injected from a Van de Graaff generator at 4 Mev and accelerated to 32 Mev. The 2.5 megawatts of radio-frequency power comes from six triode oscillators which are pulsed on for 500 μ sec., 15 times per second. The average beam current is $\frac{1}{3}$ μ amp. (L. W. A.; L. S. Ss.)

A second proton machine, operating at 60 Mev, was built at the University of Minnesota, Minneapolis, by J. H. Williams. In addition to these two machines intended for nuclear research, a number of proton accelerators were built as injectors for circular accelerators. Examples are at Berkeley and Brookhaven in the United States, at several Russian laboratories and at CERN in Geneva, Switz.

Another interesting application of linear accelerators is exemplified by two heavy ion accelerators at the University of California and at Yale university. These will accelerate a variety of ions, with energies of the order of 10 Mev per nucleon. These are also intended for bombardment experiments using such heavy nuclei as carbon, nitrogen, oxygen, etc. See also NUCLEAR ENGINEERING. (M. Cw.)

BETATRONS

The betatron is a circular accelerator for electrons, operating on the same principle of electromagnetic induction as the transformer. It produces electrons or X-rays of millions of electron volts of energy without the use of excessively high voltages. The need for such a machine is threefold: (1) in nuclear physics a source of high-energy electrons or X-rays is used to study fundamental properties of matter and radiation; (2) in industry the X-rays are used in radiography, where they are able to penetrate 12 in. of steel and still produce a good radiograph; and (3) in medicine X-rays of high penetrating power, producing a low skin dose and a high depth dose of radiation, are valuable for the treatment of cancer.

Description.—In a transformer the electrons in the secondary winding are guided by the insulated copper wire wound around the core, while the changing magnetic flux in this laminated iron core induces a voltage in the secondary winding that makes the electrons move. Similarly in the betatron there is a means of guiding the electrons along their circular path; at the same time they are accelerated by the electric field induced by changing magnetic flux within the orbit. However, the guiding process in the betatron is quite different: in the first place, the circular orbit is inside a high-vacuum tube in the form of a hollow glass or ceramic "doughnut"; in the second, the electrons are kept in the circular orbit or focused toward it by a specially shaped magnetic guide field. The magnitude of this field must be in a definite proportion to the magnetic flux through the orbit so that the circular path does not become either a decreasing or an increasing spiral. By travelling around the tube thousands of times the electrons build up a

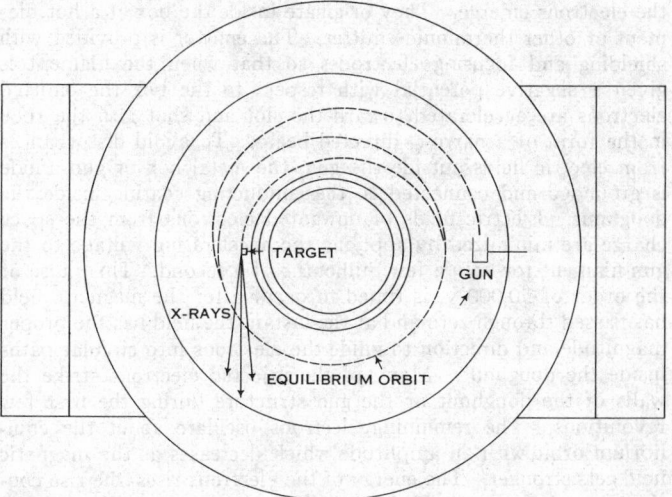

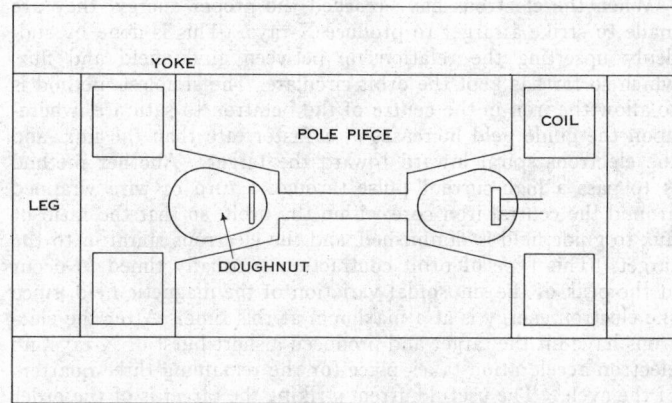

FIG. 11.—HORIZONTAL CROSS SECTION (TOP) AND VERTICAL CROSS SECTION (BOTTOM) THROUGH BETATRON

high energy measured in millions of electron volts, without the insulation problems associated with the actual production of a high potential.

The upper part of fig. 11 is a horizontal cross section through the centre of the betatron. The dotted line gives a rough indication of the path of an electron in the vacuum tube: starting from the electron gun, the electron goes thousands of times around at the equilibrium orbit and finally stops at the target where X-rays are produced, these being principally in the direction of the motion. The lower part of fig. 11 is a vertical section showing the magnetic circuit with the coils forming the primary winding and the doughnut representing the secondary. As can be seen, the magnetic guide field at the orbit and the magnetic flux passing through the orbit belong to a magnetic circuit. This consists of two specially profiled round pole pieces, two horizontal yokes and two vertical legs. All these parts are made of laminated silicon steel to keep eddy-current losses low. The frequency of operation ranges from the power-line frequency of 50 or 60 cycles per second to as high as 2000 cycles (in which case a motor generator is required). The magnetic circuit is energized by means of two primary windings which are connected to the power source in shunt with a capacitor bank. The capacitor bank is used to increase the power factor. The vacuum tube (or doughnut) is located between the profiled part of the pole pieces; its inside wall has a thin, high-resistance coating to keep static charges from disturbing the electron beam.

Electrons are introduced into the vacuum tube by an electron gun placed in the plane of the stable orbit and usually outside it. It is placed as far from the equilibrium orbit as possible in order to leave a maximum of unobstructed space, yet within the region where the magnetic field has the proper focusing effect. The electron gun is a small metal box with a slot through which the electrons emerge. They originate inside the box at a hot filament or other thermionic emitter. The emitter is provided with shielding and focusing electrodes so that when the filament is given a negative potential with respect to the box the emitted electrons are accelerated toward the slot and shot into the tube in the form of a narrow, directed beam. To avoid disturbances from electric fields outside the gun, the metal box or gun anode is grounded and connected to the conducting coating inside the doughnut. Electric fields of unwanted electrons from the space charge are minimized by applying the accelerating voltage to the gun filament for only a few millionths of a second. This pulse of the order of 50,000 v. is timed to occur after the magnetic field has passed through zero and at the instant the field has the proper magnitude and direction to guide the electrons into circular paths inside the doughnut. Many of the injected electrons strike the walls of the doughnut or the gun structure during the first few revolutions. The remaining electrons oscillate about the equilibrium orbit with an amplitude which decreases as the magnetic field gets stronger. The energy of the electrons rises, the rise continuing as long as the field increases.

When the electrons have reached the proper energy, they are made to strike a target to produce X-rays. This is done by suddenly upsetting the relationship between guide field and flux, which so far has kept the orbit circular. The simplest method is to allow the iron in the centre of the betatron to saturate, whereupon the guide field increases at a faster rate than the flux, and the electrons spiral inward toward the target. Another method is to pass a high-current pulse through a turn of wire wrapped around the central iron core within the orbit, so that the ratio of flux to guide field is diminished, and the electrons spiral in to the target. This type of orbit contraction is usually timed to occur at the peak of the sinusoidal variation of the magnetic field, since the electron energy is at a maximum at this time. After the electrons have hit the target and produced a short burst of X-rays, no electron acceleration takes place for the remaining three-quarters of the cycle. The useful current striking the target is of the order of a few microamperes.

Some betatrons are equipped to produce an external beam of electrons instead of X-rays. In this case the electron gun may be placed inside the equilibrium orbit. Near the outside of the doughnut is located an electrostatic or electromagnetic deflection system which, upon orbit expansion, directs the electrons toward and through a thin metal-foil exit window. The external electron beam has some use in physics research and cancer therapy.

Particle Dynamics.—The equations of motion of the electron in the radial direction and the tangential direction may be integrated, subject to the constraint of constant radius. Elimination of charge and momentum yields the required relationship between magnetic flux through the orbit and the guide field at the orbit. This condition is

$$\phi - \phi_0 = 2\pi r^2 B$$

Expressed in words, the equation states that the change of the magnetic flux $(\phi - \phi_0)$ from the time that the guide is zero is equal to twice the product of the area (πr^2) of the circular orbit and the flux density (B) in the guide field. In most betatrons, $\phi_0 = 0$, and the equation then shows that the flux density averaged over the orbit is twice the guide-field flux density. Therefore the guide field is relatively weak even when the iron in the centre of the machine tends to saturate. A great weight and size reduction is obtained in the so-called biased betatron by making ϕ_0 negative; this is done by means of a bias winding and appropriate currents. One of the remarkable things about the equilibrium orbit is that it does not change form as the velocity of the particle changes from the nonrelativistic to the extreme relativistic region. It is this fact which makes the betatron so simple a machine for electron acceleration, since injection occurs at low velocities, and acceleration is carried to velocities very close to that of light. It is only when the betatron principle is applied beyond 100 Mev that the above relation is insufficient to maintain a circular orbit. With this high energy an electron in circular motion radiates so much electromagnetic energy, including visible light, that the loss of energy (unless compensated for by additional magnetic flux) causes an appreciable contraction of the orbit.

For energies larger than a few million electron volts the kinetic energy of the electrons in a betatron can be given by a simple expression:

$$E = 3 \times 10^{-4} Br - 0.51$$

where E is the kinetic energy in millions of electron volts (Mev); B is the flux density at the orbit in gauss; and r is the orbit radius in centimetres. Practical values of B range from 2,000 to 8,000 gauss, depending on the size and on the use of bias.

History and Present Status.—The successful operation of a betatron was first demonstrated by D. W. Kerst at the University of Illinois, Urbana, in 1940. The concept of the equilibrium orbit was known many years before that time, but the careful theoretical study by Kerst and R. Serber of the conditions for injection and Kerst's use of the pulsed electron gun placed near the equilibrium orbit made the betatron practical.

Betatrons are now in commercial production in the U.S. and Europe in the energy range from 10 to 30 Mev. Most betatrons are in industrial radiographic use; a few are being used in cancer therapy; and some, including the largest, rated 300 Mev, in high-energy physics research. Above 50 Mev the betatron was superseded by the development of the synchrotron in 1946.

(W. F. Wp.)

BIBLIOGRAPHY.—A. K. Solomon, *Why Smash Atoms?*, rev. ed. (1946); W. B. Mann, *The Cyclotron* (1940); M. S. Livingston, *High-Energy Accelerators* (1954); R. R. Wilson, "Particle Accelerators," *Sci. Amer.*, 198:64 (March 1958); E. M. McMillan, "Particle Accelerators," in E. Segrè (ed.), *Experimental Nuclear Physics*, vol. iii (1959); R. J. Van de Graaff, K. T. Compton and L. C. Van Atta, "The Electrostatic Production of High Voltage for Nuclear Investigations," *Phys. Rev.*, 43:149 (1933); D. B. Parkinson, R. G. Herb, E. J. Bernet and J. L. McKibben, "Electrostatic Generator Operating Under High Air Pressure: Operational Experience and Accessory Apparatus," *Phys. Rev.*, 53:642 (1938); R. G. Herb, C. M. Turner, C. M. Hudson and R. E. Warren, "Electrostatic Generator With Concentric Electrodes," *Phys. Rev.*, 58:579 (1940); W. W. Buechner, R. J. Van de Graaff, A. Sperduto, L. R. McIntosh and E. A. Burrill, "Electrostatic Accelerator for Electrons," *Rev. Sci. Instrum.*, 18:754 (1947); J. D. Cockcroft and E. T. S. Walton, "Experiments With High Velocity Positive Ions; (I) Further Developments in the Method of Obtaining High Velocity Positive Ions," *Proc. Roy. Soc.*, A136:619 (1932); W. R. Arnold, "A 500-Kilovolt Linear Accelerator Using Selenium Rectifiers," *Rev. Sci. Instrum.*, 21:796 (1950); E. O. Lawrence and N. E. Edlefsen, "On the Production of High Speed Protons," *Science*, 72:376 (1930); E. O. Lawrence and M. S. Livingston, "A Method for Producing High Speed

Hydrogen Ions Without the Use of High Voltages," *Phys. Rev.*, 37:1707 (1931); R. R. Wilson, "Theory of the Cyclotron," *J. Appl. Phys.*, 11:781 (1940); W. M. Brobeck, E. O. Lawrence, K. R. MacKenzie, E. M. McMillan, R. Serber, D. C. Sewell, K. M. Simpson and R. L. Thornton, "Initial Performance of the 184-In. Cyclotron of the University of California," *Phys. Rev.*, 71:449 (1947); D. Bohm and L. Foldy, "Theory of the Synchrocyclotron," *Phys. Rev.*, 72:649 (1947); J. R. Richardson, B. T. Wright, E. J. Lofgren and B. Peters, "Development of the Frequency Modulated Cyclotron," *Phys. Rev.*, 73:424 (1948); H. L. Anderson, J. Marshall, L. Kornblith, Jr., L. Schwarcz and R. Miller, "Synchrocyclotron for 450-Mev Protons," *Rev. Sci. Instrum.*, 23:707 (1952); F. H. Schmidt, G. W. Farwell, J. F. Henderson, T. J. Morgan and J. F. Streib, "The University of Washington Sixty-Inch Cyclotron," *Rev. Sci. Instrum.*, 25:499 (1954); M. S. Livingston, "The Cyclotron," *J. Appl. Phys.*, 15:2,128 (1944); T. G. Pickavance, in O. R. Frisch (ed.), *Progress in Nuclear Physics* (1950); J. Rotblat, in H. R. Lang (ed.), *The Acceleration of Particles to High Energies* (1950); M. S. Livingston, in J. G. Beckerley (ed.), *Annual Review of Nuclear Science*, vol. i (1952); Wolfgang Panofsky, "The Linear Accelerator," *Sci. Amer.*, 191:40 (Oct. 1954); P. Howard-Flanders and A. W. Haslett, "Linear Accelerators in Use," *Science News*, 32:33–42 (May 1954); J. C. Slater, "Linear Accelerators," in J. G. Beckerley (ed.), *Annual Review of Nuclear Science*, vol. i (1952); D. W. Kerst, "Development of the Betatron and Application of High Energy Betatron Radiations," *Amer. Scient.*, 35:56 (Jan. 1947); E. L. Chu and L. I. Schiff, "Recent Progress in Accelerators," in J. G. Beckerley (ed.), *Annual Review of Nuclear Science*, vol. ii (1953); K. R. Symon, D. W. Kerst, L. W. Jones, L. J. Laskett and K. M. Terwilliger, "Fixed Field Alternating Gradient Particle Accelerators," *Phys. Rev.*, 103:1837 (1956); M. H. Blewett, "The Cosmotron: a Review," *Rev. Sci. Instrum.*, 24:725 (1953); E. D. Courant, M. S. Livingston, H. S. Snyder, "The Strong-Focusing Synchrotron," *Phys. Rev.*, 88:1190 (1952); E. D. Courant and H. S. Snyder, "Theory of the Alternating-Gradient Synchrotron," *Ann. Phys.*, 3:1 (1958); W. W. Hansen, R. L. Kyhl, R. B. Neal, W. K. H. Panofsky, M. Chodorow, E. L. Ginzton and the staff of the W. W. Hansen Laboratories of Physics, "Stanford High-Energy Linear Electron Accelerator (Mark III)," *Rev. Sci. Instrum.*, 26:134 (1955); L. W. Alvarez, H. Bradner, J. V. Franck, H. Gordon, J. D. Gow, L. C. Marshall, F. Oppenheimer, W. K. H. Panofsky, C. Richmond, J. R. Woodyard, "Berkeley Proton Linear Accelerator," *Rev. Sci. Instrum.*, 26:111 (1955); R. B. Neal and W. K. H. Panofsky, "The Stanford Mark III Linear Accelerator and Speculations Concerning the Multi-BEV Applications of Electron Linear Accelerators," *Proceedings of the CERN Symposium on High Energy Accelerators and Ion Physics*, 1:529 (1956); H. Leboutet, "Contributions to the Theory of the Linear Electron Accelerator," *Ann. Radioelect.*, 13:107 (1958); G. K. O'Niell, "Storage Rings," *Science*, 141:3582 (1963).

ACCENT, in speech, is understood colloquially in at least three senses: (1) the presence in an individual's speech of articulations not typical of the community (*e.g.*, a foreign accent); (2) a sustained quality of vocalization, outside the linguistic system, used to discriminate shades of meaning or personal characteristic (*e.g.*, to speak in tender accents); (3) a prominence given to a short span of speech and manifested as stress or pitch or some extralinguistic component.

In linguistics, accentual (also called prosodic or suprasegmental) features are sound units which may be manifested as pitch or tone (*i.e.*, acoustic fundamental frequency), stress (intensity), length or quantity (duration), and occasionally as glottalization, devoicing or nasalization.

In English, the most widely used notations for stress are: ´ for primary stress; ˆ for secondary stress; ` for tertiary stress; and ˘ for weak stress. Different stresses applied to the same words convey different meanings. For example, the same four words, "a-black-bird's-nest," according to their stress sequence may convey the following: ˘ ˆ ` ´ a *nest* (not a house) of a blackbird; ˘ ` ´ ˆ a nest of a *blackbird* (not a jay); ˘ ˆ ` ´ a nest of a black bird; or ˘ ` ´ ˆ a bird's nest that is *black* (not green). The difference between the tertiary and weak stresses is further exemplified by comparison of the final syllables in "Ándès" and "cándiĕs" or "pick-ùp" and "hiccŏugh." Pitch notation consists of numbers from 4 (for the highest) to 1 (for the lowest). Differences in pitch sequence in the word "yes" may convey the following: 4–1, impatient agreement, as after persistent urging; 2–3, abruptness, as in answer to an interruption; 3–2, apprehensive admission or concession; 4–4, high-pitched frightened acquiescence; 2–4–1, leering, lascivious approval or conniving agreement. Cut-offs are indicated as follows: ↓ sharp; ↑ up-glide; and → trail-off. The word "well," depending upon the cut-off, may indicate the following: 2–2 ↓, "let's get on with it"; 2–2 ↑, "and then—?" or "please explain yourself"; and 2–2 →, preoccupied indecision. (These examples are characteristic of a great many residents of the U.S., particularly in the north and east, but are not, of course, valid for all English-speaking persons.)

Accents form perhaps the most common basis in languages for the organization of syllables, most commonly by stress and pitch. While English seems to have four degrees of stress, one of which occurs with every vowel, Chinese has four tones, one of which occurs with most syllabics. Occasionally (*e.g.*, in Swedish) the pitch organizes a sequence of more than one syllable. The best-known language lacking an accentual organization of syllables is French.

Accent sequences frequently serve to integrate words; a word that lacks an independent accent pattern is either proclitic (if it depends upon the following word) or enclitic (if it depends upon the preceding word). Similar features, especially pitch (usually called intonation) and the distinctive manner of cutting off the voice (usually called terminal contour), are used to organize longer sequences—phrases and sentences. Spanish has an array somewhat similar to the four distinctive pitch levels and three types of cut-off of English. Japanese seems to have intonation patterns, but no terminal contours; Ojibwa has contours, but no intonations of the sort English has. No known language may be said to lack intonations and contours entirely. French employs stress, in addition to pitch, in contour patterns (as in *áttention!*).

Languages show great variety in their exploitation and distribution of accents. Thus, while English has only one major stress in a polysyllabic word, many languages permit more than one. In English, stresses occur only with vowels; in Czech, they occur also with the semiconsonants *r* and *l*; in South African Bushman, tones occur with vowels and often with nasals; in the Wahgi language of New Guinea, the stress-pitch accent occurs with all vowels and most consonants. Within the syllable there is also endless variety; though one may hear the accent as acoustically overlying the whole syllable, in some languages it has a structural position within the syllable. Stress in English and Spanish and tone in Japanese, Navaho and Cuicateco (Oaxaca, Mex.) cannot be assigned a sequential position. But the tones of Chinese and Lushai (India) seem to belong to the end of the syllable; those of Trique (Oaxaca) to the middle; those of South African Hottentot to the beginning; while the mobile stress of Lithuanian and Karok (California) and the pitch of Lettish may occur at distinctively different points along the syllable. The greatest number of level tones (five) yet described is found in Trique. On the other hand, Mazateco (Oaxaca) has four, but permits combinations of up to three within a single syllable; as a result, the sequence of tones carries so much of the distinctive features of words that Mazatecs can whistle complicated messages over distance. In many languages the simple accents are not level, but have a broken or gliding contour; in Burmese tones, pitch is associated with glottalization.

Accents are usually more difficult to reconstruct than other phonemes of dead or prehistoric languages. They are rarely recorded in writing systems, and they usually change in the course of time, making recovery difficult. Weakly stressed syllables are frequently lost in time, as from Latin to French (*frigidum* to *froid*). Other sounds may also change quite differently depending on their accentual environment.

The ancient Greek grammarians devised marks to indicate the accents of their language, the primary feature being pitch. The Greek term for accent was *prosodia* (literally translated by the Romans as *accentus*), which later came to be used to refer to metrical quantity (whence the English "prosody"). The ancient Hindus marked the accents in their Vedic hymns, and this system became known to Western scholars when they first learned Sanskrit. The modern scientific tradition represents a confluence of these two ancient traditions.

The diacritical marks, misleadingly called acute (´), grave (`) and circumflex (ˆ, ˆ and ˜) accents, used to distinguish different vowels in written European languages are not subsumed under any of the above senses.

BIBLIOGRAPHY.—K. L. Pike, *Tone Languages* (1948); G. L. Trager,

The Theory of Accentual Systems (1941); R.-M. S. Heffner, *General Phonetics* (1950); C. F. Hockett, *A Manual of Phonology* (1955); A. A. Hill, *Introduction to Linguistic Structures* (1958). (E. P. H.)

ACCEPTANCE, in law, an act of consent or approval, having special significance in different situations. Thus, the term may be applied to the act of a person in signing his name (or his name with the word "accepted") across the face of a bill of exchange or draft addressed to him. He thereby obligates himself, as acceptor, to pay the bill according to its tenor or, if the acceptance is qualified, according to the terms of the acceptance. A bill accepted by a bank, typically in a letter-of-credit transaction, is called a "banker's acceptance" and has the highest credit standing. (*See* COMMERCIAL PAPER.) Again, acceptance may refer to the act of a person in agreeing to the terms of an offer, thereby completing a contract with the offeror, as to perform services or to sell goods. The offeree, in so doing, makes himself liable to an action for damages in case of default, or, where the contract is for unique goods, to an action for specific performance. (*See* CONTRACT.) Acceptance may refer also to the act of a buyer in receiving goods delivered to him by the seller. Acceptance of the goods, although there is no written contract, will satisfy the Statute of Frauds. Acceptance of nonconforming goods, after inspection or a reasonable opportunity to inspect, will bar a subsequent return or rejection of the goods; but, to encourage acceptance in such cases and thus promote the flow of goods in commerce, an action against the seller for damages will survive. *See* SALE OF GOODS. (R. T. S.)

ACCESSORY, a person who incurs criminal liability for participating in the commission of an offense by another. An accessory before the fact is a person who urges or advises the principal offender to commit the crime; he is classed as principal in the second degree if he is present when the offense is committed and aids or abets its commission. At common law the distinction between principals and accessories applied only to felonies. In cases of misdemeanour or treason all participants were punishable as principals. The accessory after the fact falls in an entirely separate category and refers to a person who harbours or conceals a felon with intent to prevent apprehension of the felon. *See* ABETTOR; CRIMINAL LAW. (F. A. A.)

ACCIDENCE: *see* GRAMMAR.

ACCIDENT (Latin *accidens,* "happening" or "occurring"), a term used in philosophy with various meanings according to the term with which it is specifically or by implication contrasted. The principal philosophical meanings, summarized in this article, are historically connected with one another; and one of them (see *Accident, Necessity and Design,* below) is in turn connected with the ordinary use of the term to designate an unforeseen and often disastrous event.

Accident and Substance.—Perhaps the oldest use of the term "accident" was by way of contrast with the term "substance" or "thing." "Substance" means the basic reality which has various qualities, stands in various relations, etc. These qualities, relations, etc., on the other hand, need a basis or support to qualify—they are "accidents," accessions to something that is there to bear them (substance). Among the schoolmen, accordingly, almost any quality was commonly called an accident; and this usage was fairly common even in the 17th century—"accident" and "substance" corresponding roughly to "quality" and "thing" respectively, as these terms are commonly used.

Accident and the Self-Existing.—In the strict sense of the term, as distinguished from its more usual meaning even among philosophers, the term "substance" means that which exists in itself and through itself; and when so interpreted its familiar contrast with "accident" naturally prompts the application of the term "accident" to anything that is dependent on some other thing. In this case, even what are commonly called "things" or "substances" will be classed among "accidents." Thus for Spinozism there is only one Substance, namely God, who alone is self-existing, while all finite things and even the so-called "infinite modes" (such as motion) are really "accidents," or dependent existents. Cartesianism, too, made this admission, or one very like it to all intents and purposes, but allowed the name "substance," in a qualified sense (that is, in the popular sense) to finite bodies and to souls.

Real Accidents.—The antithesis between "accident" and self-existing "substance" clearly cuts across the distinction between "accident" in the sense of "quality," and "substance" in the sense of "thing." In considering the latter distinction, however, some of the schoolmen maintained that there are certain sense-qualities of things which are not dependent on the substances with which they are sometimes combined, but can exist by themselves, apart from such substances. These alleged independent or self-existing qualities they called "real accidents."

Accident and Essence.—The distinction between "substance" and "accident" naturally led people to regard an "accident" as something less important than substance, as something not essential to substance; and so the term "accident" was contrasted with whatever is not really essential to anything. Thus in logic, for instance, the so-called fallacy of accident is the erroneous assumption that a claim to know anything or anybody implies a knowledge even of all that is nonessential in relation to it or him. Similarly, in the doctrine of the predicables (*q.v.*), as commonly expounded in books on logic, the predicable "accident" is contrasted with the other four predicables in the sense that any predicate asserted of a subject but not essential to it is called an "accident" of it, whereas any predicate essential to the subject of which it is affirmed belongs to one or other of the remaining predicables.

Accident, Necessity and Design.—The kinship between what is "essential" and what is "necessary" has prompted the common use of "accident" for what is otherwise called a chance occurrence. Likewise, the term "accident" has come to be applied in law to any occurrence or result that could not have been foreseen by the agent (because not necessarily involved in his action), or to a result not designed (and, therefore, presumably not foreseen) or, lastly, to anything unexpected.

"Essential" and "Accidental" Accidents.—One curious consequence of the multiplicity of meanings of "accident" is that by using the noun in the sense of "quality" and the adjective in the sense of "not essential," the schoolmen came to distinguish between "essential" accidents and "accidental" accidents.

ACCIDENTALS, in music, are signs signifying that the notes to which they are attached have to be raised, lowered or restored to their original pitch, as the case may be. Thus a sharp (♯) raises a note a semitone; a flat (♭) lowers it a semitone; while a natural (♮) restores it to its former status. Each sign may also be doubled, though in the case of the double sharp, signifying the raising of the note by two semitones, the sign ✕ is used instead of ♯♯; ♭♭ indicates a double flat, signifying the lowering of the note by two semitones. A single natural is sufficient to cancel a preceding double sharp or double flat. Accidentals placed before a note normally affect that note only during the bar in which they occur. In some modern compositions, however, where the harmony is complex, accidentals refer only to the immediate notes with which they are associated. In such cases the composer gives a direction to this effect. Sharps and flats placed at the beginning of a staff denote the tonality of the music and are not classed as accidentals.

See also MUSICAL NOTATION.

ACCIDENT INSURANCE: *see* CASUALTY INSURANCE.

ACCIDENTS: *see* DANGEROUS OCCUPATIONS; INDUSTRIAL MEDICINE; DROWNING AND LIFESAVING; and INDUSTRIAL ACCIDENTS; SAFETY.

ACCIUS (ATTIUS), **LUCIUS** (170–*c.* 85 B.C.), greatest and most popular of the Roman tragic poets, came of freedman stock in Umbria. His plays, of which more than 40 titles and about 700 lines have survived, were mostly free translations from the Greek, ranging over the whole field of Greek tragedy from Aeschylus (*Myrmidones, Prometheus*) to Hellenistic drama (*Hellenes, Stasiastae*); some plays were taken from Sophocles (*Antigone?, Athamas, Tereus*), a great many from Euripides (*Alcestis, Bacchae, Phoenissae, Telephus*); others again apparently combined two originals (*Armorum iudicium,* from Aeschylus' *Hoplon krisis* and Sophocles' *Ajax*). But he also composed two plays, *Decius* and *Brutus,* on Roman subjects. Accius' passion, loftiness of diction and splendid use of rhetoric were admired by Roman critics and are discernible in the fragments. His plays were performed until the end of the republic. He also wrote love poetry and verse treatises in various metres on the history of Greek and Latin poetry and on agriculture.

BIBLIOGRAPHY.—Fragments in the "Teubner Series": *Scenicae Romanorum poesis fragmenta*, ed. by O. Ribbeck, vol. 1 (1897) and *Fragmenta poetarum Latinorum*, ed. by W. Morel (1927); also with Eng. trans. in the "Loeb Series," *Remains of Old Latin*, ed. by E. H. Warmington, vol. 2 (1936). *See also* Schanz-Hosius, *Geschichte der römischen Literatur*, vol. 1, pp. 131 ff. (1927).   (OT. S.)

ACCLIMATIZATION, in biology, originally was taken to mean only the ability of human beings or animals or plants to accustom themselves within the span of a lifetime to new and strange climatic conditions. (Adjustments due to genetic changes are called adaptations, as also are the rapid adjustments constantly being made by the sense organs; *see* below.)

A man moves to a hot climate and is uncomfortable there; but after a time he is better able to withstand the heat. Aside from temperature, however, there are other aspects of climate. A man or an animal may become adjusted to living at altitudes higher than those to which he was originally accustomed. At ordinary mountain altitudes this does not involve much of an adjustment to change in atmospheric pressure, for mountain climbers suffer more from lack of oxygen than from change in pressure (*see* HYPOXIA). However, at really high altitudes, such as airplane pilots may be exposed to, the low atmospheric pressure becomes a factor of primary importance. In changing to a new environment a man may meet new conditions of temperature or pressure, and in addition he may have to contend with different chemical surroundings. On high mountains he encounters relatively low concentrations of oxygen; in crowded cities he may become exposed to relatively high concentrations of carbon dioxide or even carbon monoxide; and in various areas he may be exposed to conditions in which the water content of the atmosphere is extremely high or extremely low. Thus, in the case of man and higher animals, the concept of acclimatization includes the phenomena of increased toleration of high or low temperature, of altered pressure and of changes in the chemical environment.

Lower animals and plants are exposed to an environment very different from the environment of a terrestrial mammal. Fishes may live at or near the surface of the ocean or at great depths; in fresh water or in salt water. The ability of an aquatic animal to change from one type of environment to another is the same sort of a phenomenon as the ability of a terrestrial animal to change from one climate to another. Numerous investigators have tried to transfer fish, clams, crabs, etc., from salt water to fresh, or from fresh water to salt, and they have examined the conditions which favour the success of such transfers. In order to include, therefore, all types of organisms and all types of environments a broader definition of acclimatization is required: the process in which an organism or a part of an organism becomes accustomed or hardened to an environment which is normally unsuitable for it or deadly for it. By and large, acclimatization is a relatively slow process. The term, therefore, should not be taken to include relatively rapid adjustments such as our sense organs are constantly making—the type of adjustment commonly referred to by the physiologist as adaptation. Thus after a time we fail to hear the ticking of a clock; to detect an obnoxious odour; to squint in bright light; etc.

On the other hand, when an adjustment to an unfavourable environment requires several generations, this is scarcely acclimatization in the strict sense (although often in the past it has been so considered). If a species of animal or plant is moved to an unfavourable environment, the individuals of the species may, after a number of generations, be better able to withstand the unfavourable conditions than were the animals and plants that first moved into the new environment. This may be due not so much to any change or acclimatization during the lifetime of the original animals or plants, or their descendants, but rather to changes or mutations from generation to generation. Such mutations are now known to be of relatively frequent occurrence (*see* HEREDITY; GENE). The mutations that are more apt to prosper in a given environment tend to survive (as a result of natural selection); the unfavourable

mutations tend to die off. Thus, wheat plants that are moved to an excessively cold climate may, during successive generations, produce mutations that are better able to withstand the cold; these mutants, then, would tend to survive and would pass on to their progeny the same hardiness. This type of natural selection is well known, and it can be hastened by artificial selection on the part of the agriculturist. The end result is to produce new strains or races which are better able to withstand a particular environment than did the original species. (*See* ADAPTATION, BIOLOGICAL.)

The change in a species is a very different process from the acclimatization change which occurs during the life of an individual. If one considers the behaviour of a species for a number of generations, it is hard to distinguish between the changes produced as a result of mutation followed by natural selection and the changes produced as a result of true acclimatization.

The fundamental fact about acclimatization is that all animals and plants have some capacity to adjust themselves to changes in their environment. This is one of the most remarkable characteristics of living organisms, a characteristic for which it is extremely difficult to find explanations. Before entering into a more detailed treatment of the various facts and theories concerning the different types of acclimatization, a brief discussion of the ability of various animals and plants to change their habitat from one region of the earth's surface to another is presented. This subject has been studied primarily from the viewpoint of human welfare and human economy.

Acclimatization of Various Species, Including Man.— Early writers on biology and natural history, as well as early travelers and explorers, were interested in the possibility of importing animals and plants from one country to another. Tobacco, originally found in America, was introduced into Turkey and other countries. Cotton likewise was transplanted. Rubber and quinine, originally produced in South America, became staple crops of the East Indies. Flowers and shade trees found their way from one country to another. So, too, horses were imported into the Americas, and various other domestic animals were introduced into different parts of the world. Sometimes noxious insects or other types of pests find their way into countries originally free of them. The entrance of such undesirable organisms is often a matter of great economic importance.

An animal or a plant from a strange country may be successfully introduced into the homeland, or it may not be able to live there. Usually the important variable is temperature. Some animals seem to be able to exist anywhere. As Charles Darwin pointed out in his *Origin of Species,* rats and mice can live in very cold climates as well as in the tropics. Some other animals are very sensitive to changes of temperature. Possibly, in part at least, the ability of rats and mice to live in different climates is due to their nocturnal habits. Both rats and mice are sensitive to high temperatures and are much more readily killed by heat than are cats and cows, for example. It is doubtful whether rats or mice could withstand any lengthy exposure to the rays of the tropical sun.

Years ago, as new countries were discovered and developed, societies were founded to promote the exchange of species of animals and plants from one part of the world to another. The most famous of these societies was the Société Nationale d'Acclimatation in Paris.

The introduction of a species is not always accompanied with difficulty. Some species thrive away from their natural habitat, often better than in their homeland. In such instances there is no need for the species to become accustomed to the new habitat, and in reality acclimatization does not occur. The organism becomes naturalized, but not acclimatized (*see* NATURALIZATION, PLANT AND ANIMAL).

The question of human acclimatization has interested historians, geographers, sociologists and medical men. The early Greek writers wondered why white men did not successfully colonize tropical countries. The difficulties of white settlers in the tropics are manifold, and the problems are extremely complex. It is hard to distinguish between the direct adverse effects of climate and the deterioration and death caused by the many types of tropical disease. In addition, the white man in the tropics often has had to face the competition of coloured races perhaps more capable of withstanding the heat. Then too the conditions of life often are strange and difficult and this may be a factor in the causation of what has been called "tropical neurasthenia," a neuropsychological affliction.

In the 20th century, when sanitary and health conditions have been improved, as in Panamá and in northeastern Australia (eastern Queensland), acclimatization of white settlers is favoured. Some medical authorities have urged that if tropical disease could be prevented, white men in the tropics would prosper. Others have insisted that, quite apart from disease, the climate itself is harmful. Women are said to be paler in the tropics. In very hot regions, according to some observers, the effects of old age appear earlier. Some physicians claim that old-age vision (presbyopia), which in temperate climates usually is not noticeable until a man reaches the age of about 45, may become evident in Europeans in the tropics about 10 years earlier. Hot climates have been blamed also for premature loss of memory.

Surprisingly enough, little attempt has been made to study conditions that favour successful existence in hot countries. Of course, air conditioning can change the climate within the home, which, along with the introduction of modern methods of transportation, eventually may effect a partial solution of the practical problem of life in the tropics; however, knowledge of the physiological aspects, is meagre. Authorities agree that excessive use of alcohol is fatal to anyone who attempts to live under tropic conditions. Some Australian experts believe that manual labour is helpful to the health of dwellers in the tropics.

Because salt is lost through the sweat, men in the tropics, as well as workers in industries in which exposure to high temperatures is common, are urged to eat salt occasionally. Presumably there are benefits from this practice, but they are not great.

Diet may be an important factor in determining human resistance to heat. It is generally agreed that in warm climates there is an unconscious tendency for people to choose diets lower in protein and fat and higher in carbohydrates. Such a practice is perhaps beneficial and there may be a theoretical reason why it should be (see below).

As is well known, men can to some extent become acclimatized to life at high mountain altitudes. This acclimatization is primarily an adjustment to the low oxygen concentration of the air over the mountains. When a man first ascends a high mountain, his heart beats faster and he becomes breathless; he may also be nauseated and vomit, his head may ache and his nose may bleed. After a short time these symptoms of mountain sickness tend to disappear. The physiological adjustment is somewhat complex, but for one thing there is an increase in the ventilation of the lungs so that more air passes through them in any given interval of time. Also the hemoglobin of the blood acquires a greater affinity for oxygen than it normally possesses. In addition the actual concentration of hemoglobin in the blood increases.

Heat.—In general, animals show a very definite ability to become acclimatized to temperatures somewhat above those they can normally withstand. For example, the common American black bass (*Micropterus salmoides*) if kept in warm water at a temperature of 86° F. for four days becomes more resistant to heat. Normally 50% of these fish die when exposed for an hour to a temperature of 93° F., whereas those conditioned in the warm water for four days reached their death point at a temperature of 100° F. Thus their tolerance to heat had been raised approximately 7°. On the other hand, when the fish were kept for 16 days at a temperature of 50° F., half of them died when exposed to a temperature of 86° F. for an hour. Other fishes show a similar behaviour. Toad tadpoles raised in the warmth were found to be able to stand temperatures about 6° higher than those raised in colder water.

Lower animals show a somewhat similar behaviour. For example, protozoa can be acclimatized so that they will withstand temperatures 4°–5° higher than those temperatures which normally kill them.

In the summer, as might be expected, animals are commonly better able to resist heat than in winter. In the case of the common sand or mole crab (*Emerita talpoida*) of the Massachusetts coast the lethal heat temperature is 18° higher in summer than it is in the winter.

The mechanism of heat acclimatization is uncertain. In man changes in the sweating mechanism or in the blood circulation may play a part. Only a few mammals sweat, however, and yet acclimatization to heat is very generally exhibited by all sorts of organisms, even by those which completely lack blood. As a matter of fact, essentially all living cells are heat sensitive, and the temperatures which kill them often are only a few degrees above those at which they are accustomed to living. In lower animals heat death is simply due to the death of the constituent cells. In higher animals some cells appear to be more sensitive than others, and the death or injury of these cells apparently produces toxic substances which injure and eventually kill the animal as a whole.

In general those organisms which are killed at the higher temperatures have more solid fats; that is fats with higher melting points. This is a broad truth which holds both for animals and plants: fishes, which die at relatively low temperatures, have fats fluid at ordinary temperatures; whereas the warm-blooded mammals and birds have solid fats. Similarly plants which grow in the tropics seem generally to have more solid fats than those which grow in temperate climates. Various experimenters have shown that when animals are reared at higher temperatures, their fats tend to become more solid. Such a change in the melting point of the fats may be a factor in the acclimatization of animals and plants to heat.

Further, recent nutritional studies have shown that if animals eat sugar, the fat produced within the body from this sugar has a high melting point. The fact that other animals (namely, rats) with fats of higher melting point are better able to survive higher temperatures perhaps indicates why men in hot countries seem unconsciously to prefer a diet relatively rich in carbohydrates.

Cold.—There have been relatively few studies on the ability of animals to become acclimatized to cold. Fishes accustomed to warm water are unable to withstand sudden transfer to cold water. At Naples, the eggs of the sea urchin (*Paracentrotus lividus*) cannot develop at temperatures below 61° F. in summer, but in the wintertime they can develop at temperatures as low as 47° F.

The ability of plants to become acclimatized to the cold is a matter of great practical importance. Tropical plants are killed at temperatures above freezing. In cold countries plants frequently suffer injury from frost. As a result of breeding experiments and as a result also of chance mutations, cold-resistant varieties of wheat and other crop plants have been obtained. These varieties have made farming possible in regions where it might otherwise have been impractical. But even for any given variety of a plant, some increase in so-called cold hardiness is possible. For when plants are grown at lower temperatures they are better able to withstand frost.

When plants are exposed to the cold, there may be an increase in the amount of sugar or salt contained in the plant cells, and such increases would tend to prevent freezing. Possibly also, in hardy plants, water is prevented from freezing by being bound chemically in such a way that it does not act as ordinary water. Some workers believe that cold hardiness primarily is caused by an increase in the amount of this "bound water." This explanation, however, does not seem to fit all cases. A protein jelly, such as a gelatin gel, does not freeze so readily as a fluid protein solution. It is possible, therefore, that the state of fluidity of the vital protoplasm may be a factor in determining cold hardiness.

Marine and Fresh-Water Acclimatization.—Ordinarily animals which live in the ocean die rather rapidly if they are placed in fresh water; also fresh-water animals die in sea water. This is not always true, however, for the eel and the salmon can pass from sea water to fresh water and back again without injury.

Fresh-water animals placed in water containing a large amount of salt tend to lose water from their cells (and in the case of simpler animals, there is a considerable loss of water); on the other hand, marine animals placed in fresh water tend to absorb water into their cells. The process producing this inflow and outflow of water is called osmosis, a general phenomenon operating throughout the animal and plant kingdoms.

The cells of all animals are in equilibrium with the solutions in which they are bathed. If these solutions become more dilute, the cells increase in volume; if on the other hand, the concentration of the solutions is increased, the cells lose water and shrink. Many higher animals are enclosed in stiff integuments which prevent the free passage of water to the constituent cells, and such animals are less sensitive to changes in the salt content of the outer medium; although, of course, within the bodies of the animals the cells are in equilibrium with the blood or other fluids of the animal.

Sea water contains many types of salts, but by far the most abundant of these is ordinary table salt (sodium chloride). The concentration of salt in sea water is approximately the same as that of a 3% solution of table salt. If fresh-water animals, normally incapable of living in sea water, are placed in a very dilute salt solution to which salt is gradually added over a period of weeks or even months, it is in some instances possible to acclimatize the animals so that they can live in solutions as salty as or even saltier than sea water. Also, with the gradual addition of fresh water to the sea water in which marine forms are living, marine animals can be made to live in solutions whose lack of salt ordinarily would kill them rapidly.

Different types of animals vary widely in their capacity to become acclimatized; all sorts of adjustments are involved. Presumably with an increase in salt content of the surrounding medium, both the cells and the body fluids of the animals become richer in salt. An important factor is the ability of an animal to excrete salt. Ordinary fishes are able to excrete salt through their gills; this aids them in their adjustment to the salt water of their surroundings. Marine birds are able to excrete salt through an enlarged nasal gland.

On the other hand, the excretion of water by animals enables them to get rid of excess water taken in through the skin. Thus a frog immersed in water is continually taking up water through the skin and excreting it by way of the kidneys. Obviously, excretory processes may play an important part in the ability of animals to accustom themselves to changes in the salt content of their watery environment.

Chemical Acclimatization.—All sorts of organisms show some power of accustoming themselves to a wide variety of poisons. Bacteria and protozoa may acquire an increased resistance to such substances as mercuric chloride, quinine, etc. Such acclimatization becomes a factor in the treatment of disease, for protozoan and bacterial parasites that are normally killed by a certain concentration of a drug may after a time become resistant.

Bacteria and protozoa reproduce very rapidly—on the order of once every 20 or 30 minutes—and accordingly, in studies of acclimatization in these lower organisms, the acclimatized organisms are descendants of the original organisms. Consequently, new types of organisms may arise in successive generations as a result of mutation. Some of these newly mutated types may be more resistant than the original forms and would tend to be selected out, that is, they would show a greater tendency for survival.

In higher animals true acclimatization to chemicals undoubtedly occurs. Mice and rabbits can become somewhat acclimatized to the presence of carbon monoxide in the atmosphere. Man can train himself to eat increasing amounts of certain poisons and thereby acquire a tolerance for these poisons. Various types of explanation are possible. One theory is that when a tolerance to arsenic is acquired, there is less absorption of the poison from the intestine. Earlier, tolerance to alcohol was thought to involve a decreased absorption, an increased or more rapid excretion, a decrease in the amount of alcohol which reaches the brain or an increase in the rate at which alcohol is chemically transformed within the body. Modern studies, however, tend to disprove all these possibilities; it seems that human tolerance for alcohol is primarily due to an acclimatization of the cells of the central nervous system.

Many living organisms produce poisonous substances. Thus toadstools are notoriously poisonous and so too are many higher plants, as well as scorpions, spiders, snakes, etc. In general the organism producing the poison is immune to its effects. A man can be made tolerant, that is, made immune, to a certain type of snake poison, and similar immunity may be acquired for various bacterial poisons. The attempt to understand this type of immunity is of such importance to bacteriology and medicine that an entire science, immunology, has been built around it.

One of the most interesting types of chemical acclimatization is that shown by bacteria and yeasts toward food substances in their environment. Yeasts, which commonly live by fermenting sugars, normally utilize certain types and not others. If, however, a yeast colony is grown in a medium containing an unusual type of sugar, one which it does not have the power to attack, it may after a time acquire this power.

In animals generally, cells and tissues may acquire an increasing ability to cope with substances originally more or less alien to them.

BIBLIOGRAPHY.—Charles Benedict Davenport, *Experimental Morphology,* vol. i (1897); Lewis Victor Heilbrunn, *An Outline of General Physiology,* 3rd ed. (1952); Archibald Grenfell Price, *White Settlers in the Tropics* (1939). (L. V. H.)

ACCOMPANIMENT, a musical term signifying an auxiliary part or parts of a composition designed to support the principal part or to throw it into relief. In secular medieval music and early folk music, instrumental accompaniments for singers consisted of unison or octave reduplications, novel rhythmic features or a primitive type of harmony in the form of a drone or sustained notes on wind or string instruments. In the 16th century, solo songs were sung with simple harmonic or contrapuntal lute accompaniments, notably those of John Dowland and the French *airs de cour*. With the introduction of the thorough bass at the beginning of the 17th century the art was gradually developed of harmonic accompaniments, improvised at the harpsichord or organ and based on chords which the composer indicated by figures. By the 18th century these improvised accompaniments, designed to support either a soloist as in the sonatas and solo cantatas of J. S. Bach, or an instrumental ensemble as in the operas of Alessandro Scarlatti, demanded from the performer a high degree of ornamental and contrapuntal invention. The accompaniment thus assumed a role as important as that of the soloist. (*See* also THOROUGH BASS.)

The term obbligato accompaniment was applied to this form, as opposed to ad libitum accompaniment, a term used for the optional reduplication of a part or unessential ornamentation performed on another instrument. Obbligato accompaniments were sometimes written out, among them one originally improvised by Bach for a movement of his Sonata in B minor for flute and harpsichord. In the second half of the 18th century the obbligato accompaniment assumed a primary role, the part of the solo instrument being reduced to an ad libitum accompaniment. Sonatas for harpsichord or piano with violin or flute accompaniment were written by Joseph Mondonville, and Mozart followed the example of Johann Schobert in writing four sonatas for harpsichord accompanied by the violin.

The influence of the obbligato style in the 19th century is suggested in Beethoven's statement, "I came into the world with obbligato accompaniment." It persisted in both the solo and the concerted works of the romantic composers where accompaniments became even more elaborate and expressive. The greater expressive resources of the piano, as opposed to the harpsichord, allowed the accompaniments of Schubert to illustrate pictorial or psychological aspects of the texts of his *Lieder*. His example was followed in the *Lieder* of Schumann, Brahms and Hugo Wolf. Piano accompaniments in works for string or wind instruments acquired the status of a concerted part. Orchestral accompaniment, which in the 18th century had hardly exceeded chamber-music proportions, was greatly developed in the romantic concerto and in songs or song cycles with orchestra by numerous composers from Berlioz to Alban Berg and Benjamin Britten.

The art of the piano accompanist flourished chiefly in response to the demands in the 19th century of the German *Lied* and the

French *mélodie*. Qualities of poetic and musical insight, and also of ensemble playing, distinguish the piano accompanist's art which resembles the art of performance in chamber music. Accompanists such as Gerald Moore and Conraed van Bos developed the art by their sensitive attitude to the soloist and by their power to interpret the composer's intention. Both Moore and van Bos have written valuable books on the art of the accompanist.   (E. Lr.)

ACCOMPLICE, a person who is associated with another in criminal activity. The category includes, but is not limited to, the accessory (*q.v.*). Some U.S. states provide by statute that testimony of accomplices is competent only when corroborated by other evidence. Elsewhere the jury is ordinarily cautioned as to the possible unreliability of testimony by accomplices. *See* CRIMINAL LAW.   (F. A. A.)

ACCORAMBONI, VITTORIA (1557–1585), the Italian lady whose story forms the basis of John Webster's tragedy *The White Devil*, was born in Gubbio, near Perugia, on Feb. 15, 1557. In 1573 she was married to Francesco Peretti, whose uncle Cardinal Montalto (Felice Peretti) was regarded as likely to become pope. In Rome she found many admirers, among them Paolo Giordano Orsini, duca di Bracciano. Her brother Marcello, wishing to see her married to Bracciano, had Peretti murdered (1581). Bracciano, who was already believed to have murdered his first wife, Isabella de' Medici, was suspected of complicity in this murder also, but proceeded to marry Vittoria. Early attempts by the Peretti family to have the marriage annulled had no result except that Vittoria was imprisoned for a short time. In 1585, however, Montalto was elected pope as Sixtus V, and the couple, fearing that he would avenge his nephew's death, fled to Salò in Venetian territory, where Bracciano died (Nov. 1585). Vittoria then retired to Padua. There she was followed by Lodovico Orsini—a remote cousin of Bracciano's—who hated her personally and resented her marriage as degrading to the Orsini family. On Dec. 22, 1585, he had her murdered. He and his accomplices were executed by order of the Venetian republic. Besides Webster's play, Vittoria was the subject of Ludwig Tieck's novel, *Vittoria Accorambona* (1840).

BIBLIOGRAPHY.—G. Marchetti Ferrante, *Rose del Mondo* (1932); B. Colonna, *La Nepote di Sisto V* (1936); C. Bax, *The Life of the White Devil* (1940).

ACCORDION, a musical instrument of the free reed class. The name first appears in the 1829 patent of C. Demian, Vienna, though an earlier model was patented by Friedrich Buschmann in Berlin in 1822. A free reed is a metal tongue screwed or riveted over a slot accurately cut in a metal frame. The pitch of a reed depends upon the length and thickness of the tongue, which can be tuned by filing near the free end to raise the pitch or near the fixed end to lower it. Each tongue is "sprung up" above its frame and vibrates when air is made to flow around the reed from this upper side; an air flow in the opposite direction does not cause the tongue to vibrate.

An accordion consists of a bellows fastened between two oblong wooden structures that carry the reeds, to which wind is admitted selectively through pallet valves controlled from a keyboard or set of finger buttons, each key or button bringing into action a pair of reeds, one of which is mounted to sound on the "press" of the bellows, the other to sound on the "draw." In some forms of accordion, including the early designs, the two reeds of a pair sound two adjacent notes of the scale, so that a button will give, for instance, G on the press and A on the draw ("single action"). By this arrangement ten buttons suffice for a diatonic compass of over two octaves, though at the cost of rendering each note available with a bellows movement in one direction only. For the left hand there are, typically, two keys or "basses" to provide bass notes and major chords respectively, sounding the tonic on the press and the dominant on the draw, in one tonality only. This single-action accordion has been developed, chiefly in Austria and Switzerland, by adding a second row of buttons giving a scale of F (the first-row scale being C), so arranged that almost every note of the diatonic series becomes available with a C-row button on the press and an F-row button on the draw, or vice versa. Semitones are provided by additional rows and the number of basses is increased.

In the piano accordion, with piano-style keyboard for the right hand, introduced in the 1850s and later perfected in Italy by Dallapè, the two reeds of each pair are tuned to the same note, thus making every note (also every bass) available from one key with both directions of movement of the bellows ("double action"). Among other improvements, steel reeds, instead of brass, give a steadier pitch to the notes. Couplers or "registers," developed in the 1930s, bring into action extra sets of reeds, one set pitched an octave below the main set and another off-tuned from the main set to give a tremulant through "beating." Other registers may include a high-octave set and a second tremulant. Each set may be used alone or in combination with others, by means of switches placed above the keyboard and identified by symbols or descriptive terms. The left-hand provision is also greatly extended, with up to 120 basses actuated by six rows of buttons. Two rows give bass notes arranged in cyclic order of tonalities (D, G, C, F, etc.), one row being offset against the other at the interval of a major third, to facilitate melodic passages for the left hand. The other rows give three-note chords, respectively major and minor triads and dominant and diminished sevenths. There are up to five registers for the basses, causing each bass note to sound over as many as five octaves if desired and each chord to sound in three.

A variant of the accordion is the bandoneon, a double-action instrument with square shape and finger buttons, invented by Band of Crefeld, Ger., and the leading solo instrument in modern Argentine tango orchestras. For precursors of the free-reed instruments, *see* the article HARMONIUM, and for other types *see* CONCERTINA; HARMONICA.   (A. C. Ba.)

BY COURTESY OF THE PHILIP LESLY CO.
ITALIAN ACCORDION, 19TH CENTURY

ACCORSO (ACCURSIUS), **MARIANGELO** (*c.* 1480–1546), Italian poet and critic, known for his satirical dialogues and his edition of the letters of the Roman statesman Cassiodorus, was born at Aquila, *c.* 1480. He became a favourite at the court of Charles V, by whom he was sent on numerous foreign missions. He is considered the first scholar to have investigated Roman epigraphs.

Though an accomplished linguist and, in his day, an acknowledged judge of Greek and Latin poetry, Accorso was himself not more than an academic poet.

He died at Aquila in 1546.

ACCOUNTING, a broad term that denotes certain theories, behavioural assumptions, measurement rules and procedures for collecting and reporting useful information concerning the activities and objectives of an organization. In less general terms, accounting consists of procedures for recording, classifying and interpreting selected experiences of an enterprise to promote effective administration.

It is now generally agreed that accounting and similar information-control systems must serve the needs of those who direct the organization. This approach requires that accountants know who is to use the information and must understand the objectives involved and the nature of the decisions to be made. It also requires that accountants select a consistent set of rules and conventions to accumulate and report information in a manner designed to encourage desirable performance. Accounting is used to denote the occupation of those who devote themselves to these activities. The term bookkeeping (*q.v.*) is used to indicate the gathering and classifying of data according to established rules regardless of whether the work is done by individuals, machines or electronic devices.

Accounting Functions.—The primary function of accounting is to help society administer its financial affairs. Specialized combinations from the field of accounting often are found in such related fields as engineering and operations research, but the following functions are performed primarily by accountants: (1) Determining acceptable cost and revenue standards by detecting variations between actual and desirable performance and by determining the causes of the variations. Flexible budgets and other forms of performance budgeting are expressions of this function. (2) Measuring the progress of an enterprise in terms of income or profit. Such measurements help channel future investment and act as yardsticks for evaluating the enterprise's management. (3) Helping to safeguard the properties of the organization by employing suitable devices for discovering shortages and misuse of funds. Much of the network of red tape associated with accounting systems is devoted to this end. (4) Providing information to help solve problems of short-run liquidity and financial stability. (5) Determining the rights and relative positions of owners, creditors, income beneficiaries, remaindermen and other equity holders, including the interests of governmental taxing and regulating agencies.

Reporting Viewpoint.—The impossibility of collecting all information about an enterprise that conceivably might be useful to someone means that accountants must limit their reporting to data that are important and are clearly needed. Many events in the history of an organization may be neglected, and data on other aspects may be required only intermittently for specialized nonrecurring decisions. Accountants must possess the ability to furnish such information through supplementary reports that do not interfere with the routine periodic reports.

One of the first requirements of an information-reporting system is the definition of an entity—an area of interest. Selecting an entity requires the identification of the purposes of collecting and reporting information. A large organization may be divided into many responsibility centres for certain reports; for other needs, the relevant entity may include many corporations, a sector of national activity or the entire world economy. Double-entry bookkeeping is sometimes based on the assumption that the entity and the proprietor are identical. Assets, liabilities, revenues, expenses and the interpretative viewpoint are defined and related to the position of the proprietor. The growth of large-scale enterprise has increased the number of identifiable interests (equities) in an organization, and reporting to the public now tends to take the form of stewardship reports that are focused on the entire organization as the basic entity and are geared to the needs of equity holders and other outside interests.

Internal reports to the various levels of management may be made frequently and may cover a wide range of topics. Reporting to outside interests is likely to include some combination of a financial status report in which assets are listed and classified in a meaningful fashion and are related periodically to equities, a profit-and-loss statement or a fund-flow report that summarizes changes in liquid resources.

System Requirements.—The design of an accounting system begins with a clear statement of the objectives of the enterprise, a description of the types of decisions required for guiding operations toward these objectives and an appraisal of the ability of individuals to adapt to new modes of reporting. An understanding of these features permits the designer to decide what information is necessary and to determine the form and content of the reports expected of the system. The data classification is set up to facilitate the preparation of the reports, and in turn the data-gathering system is designed to accumulate the required information with the least expenditure of enterprise resources. Inasmuch as accuracy and restraint of dishonesty are objectives, accountants have devoted considerable attention to devices of internal control so that the accuracy of the work of one employee will be checked by the work of another and so that misappropriation of assets will require collusion among two or more employees.

An important task for an accounting system often is to trace the cost of an operation, job, process or some other unit of activity with emphasis on accounting as an aid to internal managers. Special investigations and prospective cost studies improve decision-making in the fields of abandonment, expansion, shutdown, resource shifting, modernization and product planning. The field of cost accounting (*q.v.*) is concerned with performance levels and

acceptable costs of attaining these levels. Variations between actual and programed costs are shown in the accounts or on supplementary records with the hope that administrative action will be improved. Costs and variations are isolated and correlated insofar as feasible with individual responsibility so that remedial action can be made effective.

Budgeting is now acknowledged to be a major part of accounting and to be a legitimate accounting activity. The chief accounting officer—the controller—has responsibility for co-ordinating estimates, accumulating and reporting actual performance, issuing reports of variations from budget and in rare cases for enforcing the budget by encouraging laggards to better performance. Systems that combine budgetary and historical data for ready comparison are widely used.

Income Measurement Rules.—The usual concept of income is related to values that may be withdrawn without changing the prospects of an organization. Attempts have been made to make this concept operational by specifying rules for comparing discounted expectations at the beginning and end of each period, but accountants have been disturbed by the amplified effect of changes in optimism or pessimism in such a subjective measurement system.

Professional measurement conventions for income determination are more modest and consist of rules for recognizing and measuring new asset values (revenues), corresponding rules for recognizing and measuring declines in value (sacrifice) and further rules for matching (correlating) the results in periodic reports.

Asset value increases must meet certain standards of evidence. In rare cases (*e.g.*, installment method) only cash receipts are considered to be sufficient, but in most cases bona fide sale is acceptable evidence. In construction work the progress of physical construction may be used to support partial recognition. Many accountants build into their definition of income a further requirement that the net value increase be available in the form of additional working capital. Tax assessments on income and the historical association of income with dividends or other withdrawals have tended to focus attention on the liquidity aspects of enterprise operation. Even though value may be added when a favourable contract is procured, accountants will not report income at this stage. They may, however, insist on some form of disclosure.

The second aspect of the income measuring process concerns the measurement of effort exerted (capital consumed) in terms of costs expired. The profession has favoured the recording of explicit historical costs and a definition of income that calls for deducting from revenues sacrifice in terms of historical costs. Normally at the time of asset acquisition discounted service expectations are at least as great as the acquisition price of the productive agent. Actual services may yield discounted values far above or below cost. Depreciation and similar amortization problems are reduced to rules for spreading cost in proportion to services given. Inventory valuation becomes a process for assigning cost of goods available for resale to current and to future periods in proportion to similar estimates of benefit.

In times of changing price levels, revenues tend to adjust faster than costs with the result that costs of different vintages are matched with revenues. The unit for measuring cost has also changed and service estimates may thus be affected. Some accountants feel that current replacement costs best measure the sacrifice in getting revenue. Last in, first out (lifo) advocates are willing to match latest actual costs with revenue but as a group they prefer to measure capital consumption in terms of replacement cost at the time of sale. The implied definition of income is that the deductions from revenue should be sufficient to keep the physical assets intact. Other accountants feel that historical cost should be preserved by applying a general price index and converting the original costs and equities into current monetary units. The usual benefit (service) rule is applied to the restated and modified historical costs. Depreciation on replacement cost implies that income emerges only after provision for keeping physical assets intact and is therefore related to last in, first out.

Measuring income for short intervals is clearly subject to grave hazards. Cost expiration is difficult because many capital assets yield benefits over many accounting periods, and the critical tests for revenue recognition often are met in an irregular fashion. Accounting and some taxing authorities have recognized the difficulties of short-period profit measurement and permitted limited application of annual operating losses to past and future gains—a type of averaging. Obviously measuring and reporting rules for a concern that is presumed to be continuing are widely different from those appropriate for a liquidating enterprise. The going-concern convention hardly qualifies as a fundamental principle of accounting, but one of the first tasks of an accountant is to determine whether the measuring conventions for a going concern are or are not appropriate in the particular case.

A common misconception is that the grand total of all assets at current values should equal the value of the entire concern. Many specific assets may yield economic rents, and accountants traditionally do not consider all items of value (worker morale, for example) to be assets. The difference between the total of all recognized specific assets at current value and the value of the entire concern as a going business is normally taken to be goodwill (*q.v.*). Many have felt that accountants should value the entire business periodically and adjust the income and goodwill account to reflect this valuation, but accountants have preferred to let prospective investors make their own enterprise valuations.

The Field of Public Accounting.—Public accountants carry on many activities, but their chief function is to render independent, unbiased, professional opinions regarding the accuracy of representations made by a firm's management. The primary responsibility of auditors is not to management officials but to outside groups who are interested in the affairs of the concern and need dependable information. The primary problem of auditing is to establish standards of evidence to support professional opinion. Sampling procedures are clearly necessary, and in recent years auditors have supplemented their intuitive feeling of adequacy with statistical help. Management self-interest may sometimes lead to pressures that influence reporting, and the rules of evidence for accounting and auditing work are developed with regard to the direction of such pressures.

Many accountants devote a greater proportion of their time to management services, and many firms employ specialists in operations research, information theory, engineering, labour relations and the behavioural sciences. Public accounting firms are developing in the direction of industrial accounting, and a hoped for by-product may be an increased acceptance of more responsibility to the public by controllers and other private accountants. They engage in many activities of a nonauditing nature. They may, for example, design and install accounting and related information systems; develop cost and efficiency programs and standards; advise on income and other tax matters; serve as trustees in liquidation or bankruptcy; prepare schedules for property and business appraisals for loan and insurance purposes; testify in disputes involving financial liability and relative status of equity holders; consult on matters of wage and management compensation and incentives; install budgetary controls over expenditures; advise on such management problems as capital budgeting, expansion, shutdown, abandonment and modernization.

A code of ethics and highly formalized rules of professional conduct have developed over the years. A distinctive characteristic is the concept of independence which arises primarily because of the auditing function and the necessity for expressing an opinion that managements' representations fairly present the financial position and the results of operations. Independence is, of course, a frame of mind, but it is presumed that independence does not exist if the auditor has a financial interest in the business or is a director, officer, underwriter or promoter of the business. Following are some of the important rules of professional conduct recommended by the American Institute of Certified Public Accountants: Opinions or representations in financial statements must contain no false or misleading statements and must be prepared in accordance with accepted accounting and auditing principles. Professional fees for service must not be contingent upon the accountant's findings. There shall be no division of fees with nonprofessional persons. An accountant shall not violate any

confidence between himself and his client. Only partners or employees may use the accountant's name in professional practice. Accountants shall express professional opinions only with respect to work performed by themselves, their employees or other professionally qualified accountants with whom they have co-operated. Practice of accounting in the corporate form of organization is prohibited. An accountant may not advertise his professional attainments or services, or solicit clients or encroach upon the practice of another accountant, but he may give service and advice to any client upon request.

Status and Organization of Public Accounting.—Public accounting in Great Britain is regulated by professional institutes, societies and associations. The Institute of Chartered Accountants of Scotland is the outgrowth of local units, the first of which was established by royal charter at Edinburgh in 1854. The Institute of Chartered Accountants in England and Wales was chartered in 1880, as a merger of several associations, the first of which was established in 1870. The Irish institute was chartered in 1888.

The Society of Incorporated Accountants in England was registered in 1885, under the Companies act of that year. The Association of Certified and Corporate Accountants was established in 1904 and later absorbed the membership of several organizations. By 1960 total membership of these British accounting organizations was more than 50,000.

Each group imposed an experience requirement, and membership in an institute required a period of articled clerkship under the direction of a chartered accountant. Admission requires written tests in accounting theory and practice, as well as in the related fields of law, economics and business administration. The practice of public accounting is not legally restricted in the British Isles, but certain responsibilities may be discharged only by members of an institute authorized by royal charter or of the societies and associations established in accordance with statutory regulations. *The Accountant,* weekly publication of the Institute of Chartered Accountants in England and Wales, was established in 1874.

The title of certified public accountant (C.P.A.) and requirements for the certificate were first created in the United States by the state legislature of New York in 1896. Pennsylvania followed in 1899, and by 1923 each state and the District of Columbia had enacted legislation by which a commission or an educational institution authorized use of the title C.P.A. on the basis of written examinations and acceptable education and work experience. College instruction may be substituted in some states for all or part of the practical experience requirements. In New York state a bachelor's degree became a requirement for eligibility to take the examination in 1938, and other states are rapidly increasing their requirements to that level.

Written examinations prepared by the American Institute of Certified Public Accountants are uniform in all states and consist of questions from the fields of accounting theory and practice, auditing and commercial law. All states have a C.P.A. society or its equivalent to co-ordinate activities and work with the national organization. Most states grant certificates on a reciprocal basis to residents who have met similar educational and experience requirements. Some states also license public accountants who are not certified and permit them to carry on limited accounting and even auditing work.

The number of certified public accountants in the United States in 1960 was approximately 60,000 as compared with 250 in 1900; 5,000 in 1920; 13,500 in 1930; 20,000 in 1940; and 38,000 in 1950.

The American Institute of Certified Public Accountants, whose name was changed from American Institute of Accountants in 1957, developed from the American Association of Public Accountants, organized in 1887, and several national groups, including the important American Society of Accountants, have been merged with the institute. The institute conducts a program of education, professional improvement and research on such subjects as accounting procedure, auditing methods, federal taxation, education, ethics and history. The institute publishes monographs, bulletins and books related to accounting, and in 1912 the *Journal of Accountancy,* a monthly publication established in 1905, became the official periodical.

An institute of chartered accountants in Montreal received a royal charter in 1879, and later became a province-wide organization. Each Canadian province has an institute of chartered accountants with membership requirements patterned after those in Great Britain. Each provincial institute conducts an educational program as preparation for uniform examinations and membership. Their activities are co-ordinated through the Canadian Institute of Chartered Accountants, which publishes an official journal, *The Canadian Chartered Accountant.*

Societies of accountants in continental Europe have been established with much the same functions as those in Great Britain; *i.e.,* to examine and approve qualified persons for the duties of public accounting. There are records of an accounting association (*Collegio dei Raxonati*) in Venice in 1581, and another was known to exist in Milan in 1739. Whether these groups were composed of independent accountants or accounting employees is not authoritatively established. The organization dates for associations of accountants in other countries are: France, 1881; Australia, 1885; Netherlands, 1895; Germany, 1896; Sweden, 1899; Belgium, 1903; Austria, 1904; Denmark, 1909; Finland, 1911; Switzerland, 1916; Japan, 1917. Auditing the accounts of private and communal enterprises in the Union of Soviet Socialist Republics became a governmental function in 1917, and accounting has received serious intellectual attention there and in other socialist states. Organizations of independent public accountants exist in some form in almost all countries that are beyond the embryonic stage of industrial development.

Government Control Through Accounting.—The possibilities for using accounting as an instrument of control increased with the rise of corporations and the separation of ownership and control. The English Companies act of 1844 permitted stock companies with limited liability of stockholders and provided that railroads should engage auditors to examine and certify to the accuracy and completeness of their financial reports. The Act of 1862 recommended that all corporations be audited by independent accountants. This feature became a legal requirement in England in 1900 with the auditors to be elected by the stockholders.

U.S. legislation affecting accounting practices began with the need for regulation of public utilities to determine fair and equitable rates. The fair-return-on-a-fair investment and similar guides lean heavily on accounting conventions for measurement of both return and investment. The Interstate Commerce commission, organized in 1887, supplemented its rules in 1906 by a uniform accounting system of reports. The Federal Power commission and many state commissions have stressed uniform accounting methods.

The income tax laws of 1909 and 1913, the formation of the federal reserve system in 1913, and the rapid growth of stock market transactions increased the need for uniform accounting reports and independent verification. Such requirements were established by the New York Stock exchange in 1932, and in 1934, by the newly formed Securities and Exchange commission. In the latter year, the national bankruptcy act prescribed uniform procedures for corporate reorganizations.

The Robinson-Patman act of 1936 defined price discrimination for purposes of the Sherman and Clayton acts in terms of price differentials not justified by differentials in cost. Numerous states developed legislation that prohibited sales at prices below cost to the seller. During and after World War II many contracts for government work and renegotiation procedures were framed in terms of allowable costs and made wide use of other accounting conventions. Needless to say, accounting devices for control are a necessity in socialist states and in the publicly controlled sectors of any economy.

Accounting Origins.—Records and reports have characterized the exchange of goods or services from earliest times. The levy and collection of taxes in the Babylonian empire required proof of individual obligations and payments. Clay tablets as well as stone and wood devices were used to record payments for services in temples. Tally systems that used notched and marked branches as evidence of indebtedness and repayment were used in the British Isles. The development of papyrus (paper) and the calamus (pen) in Egypt, about 400 B.C., facilitated the recording of information. Government records of the Roman republic in 200 B.C. classified cash receipts in such items as rent and interest, and expenses included wages, entertainment and sacrifices. Officials known as quaestors were designated to examine the accounts of provincial governors. The emperor Augustus is said to have established the first government budget in the year A.D. 5.

During medieval times, advances in accounting were made by government and church officials. Charlemagne in 800 ordered in the *Capitulare de Villis* that an annual inventory of property be taken with separate books for income and expense. Audits were made in England during the reign of Henry I (1100–35). The English pipe roll, 1131, was a record of taxes, debts and other liabilities due the crown.

Accounting for private business in terms of ventures was an outgrowth of Italian commerce during the 13th century. Loans to trading firms and the investment of money by partners led to the development of double-entry records and reports (*see* BOOKKEEP-ING) which reflected the interests of both creditors and investors and helped the merchants control their relations with customers and employees. The auditing function was originally performed during the industrial revolution by certain accountants who placed their knowledge and competence at the disposal of other organizations, through part-time or intermittent employment. They were known as public accountants and also were employed to install bookkeeping systems for new enterprises. Many public accountants also engaged in the practice of law or the teaching of commercial subjects, foreign languages or arithmetic. These combinations were especially common in Holland, France and Great Britain during the 15th and 16th centuries. A Scotsman, Alexander Herreot, served annual engagements for a Haddington cloth manufacturer from 1681 to 1703 and was well established by 1697 as a teacher of bookkeeping in Edinburgh.

The first person definitely presumed to have practiced public accounting on a full-time basis in western Europe was George A. Watson, who was born in 1645 in Edinburgh. An Edinburgh directory listed seven accountants in 1773, and there were six names in a Glasgow record of 1783. The 1809–11 edition of *Holden's Triennial Directory* indicated that 24 public accountants were practising in London in 1800. The government of Milan, in 1742, announced a scale of charges to be made by accountants for services to clients, which suggests the existence of a profession of public accounting at that time.

Charles Emmanuel III, of Italy, in 1790, recognized chartered accountants as the only persons qualified to discharge the duties of public accountants. Napoleon decreed in 1805 that an accountant wishing to practice independently in Italy must pass a required examination after serving with an approved accountant. Uruguay, in 1825, became the first country in the western hemisphere to regulate the practice of public accounting.

The importance of independent examination of business records was increased by international trade and by wars such as the American and French Revolutions, which caused many bankruptcies for British businessmen and increased the need to determine the losses and equities of the owners and creditors of the various firms. Early public accounting methods in the United States were greatly influenced by practices in England and Scotland, and British accountants were frequently engaged for services in the U.S. during the latter half of the 19th century by British investors in American land and industry.

Education and Training.—The complexity of modern business, government and other organizations has increased the demands made on accountants and thus has emphasized the need for extensive education and training. While it is still true that many accountants begin as bookkeepers or as apprentices, have little formal education and develop on the job, a college education is generally recognized as a highly desirable if not necessary requirement. Early education for accounting careers was confined largely to the functional branches of business, narrowly conceived, with a heavy load of how-to-do-it courses in accounting practice as it then existed. Many of the quantitative requirements of the profession are now furnished by courses in statistics, mathematics, econometrics, engineering and related subjects, so that accounting courses are tending to become integrating courses with stress on professional and managerial adaptation to a changing environment.

Formal instruction in accounting was limited to public and private secondary schools until the late 19th century. In 1883, the Wharton school of finance and commerce of the University of Pennsylvania included an accounting course as part of the regular curriculum, and by 1900 accounting courses were offered at The University of Chicago and New York university.

Growth of the field and increased demands on practising accountants have led to the recommendation for a 5-year program of professional education for accounting. The American Institute has been active in education, and the American Accounting Association was organized in 1917 primarily for collegiate instructors and students of accounting. Many of the articles in *The Accounting Review* (1926) relate educational material to the teaching of accounting theory and practice.

Accounting courses for collegiate academic credit are less generally offered in universities in Europe than in the United States. Much basic instruction for public accounting in Great Britain is carried on by correspondence schools or through noncredit courses in the colleges and universities, but departments of accounting have been created in a number of universities. Emphasis is placed upon the economic and administrative aspects of the subject rather than training for careers in public accounting.

German universities regard accounting as an integral part of business administration (*Betriebswirtschaft*). Instruction places primary emphasis upon accounting as a tool of control, with special attention to such aspects as cost analysis and budgetary control. The public accountant (*Wirtschaftsprüfer*) offers opinions on the efficiency of management as well as on the accuracy and completeness of financial statements.

Educational training for public accounting in Canada is accomplished mainly through correspondence and special courses conducted by the provincial institutes of chartered accountants, but some instruction is offered at universities and colleges. *See* also Audit; Bookkeeping; Cost Accounting; Office Machines and Appliances; Operations Research; Value.

Bibliography.—William A. Paton and Robert L. Dixon, *Essentials of Accounting* (1958); Thomas M. Hill and Myron J. Gordon, *Accounting*, rev. ed. (1959); J. P. Powelson, *Economic Accounting* (1955); N. A. H. Stacey, *English Accountancy: a Study in Social and Economic History, 1800–1954* (1954); A. C. Littleton and B. S. Yamey (eds.), *Studies in the History of Accounting* (1956); A. C. Littleton, *Structure of Accounting Theory* (1953); W. T. Baxter (ed.), *Studies in Accounting* (1950); Perry Mason, Sidney Davidson and James S. Schindler, *Fundamentals of Accounting* (1959).   (C. T. D.)

ACCRA, capital, seaport and largest city of Ghana, formerly the Gold Coast. Pop. (1960) 337,828. The climate is warm and moist (temperatures, 73° to 86° F.; relative humidity, 81%; average rainfall, 32 in. falling during two rainy seasons on 79 days in the year). The town lies in an earthquake zone and has suffered from shocks, one of the most serious of which occurred in 1939. The name Accra seems to be a Europeanization of *nkran* (literally, "black ant"), applied by the Akan peoples of the Gold Coast to the Ga groups who, in the 16th century, arrived from Nigeria to settle on the Accra plain and to mingle with its inhabitants. The town lies partly on a cliff, 25 to 40 ft. high, and spreads northward over the undulating plains. The cliff projects at three points to form coves that afford partial shelter for the landing of boats through the surf. During the latter part of the 16th century the Portuguese possessed a fortified trading post on one of these points. In the 17th century the English built Ft. James on the westernmost promontory, the Dutch built Ft. Crèvecoeur on the point ½ mi. to the east, and the Danes built Christiansborg castle on the promontory at Osu, 1½ mi. along the coast. The attractions of trade with these European nations caused the Ga to move their towns from inland to sites under the walls of the forts.

Accra developed from the settlements by the Dutch and English forts. The people of Osu were a politically distinct community,

CENTRAL LIBRARY IN ACCRA, GHANA

though today the built-up area of Accra includes Osu and extends even farther east. Christiansborg and Ft. Crèvecoeur (renamed Ft. Ussher) were transferred to the British in 1850 and 1872 respectively, and in 1876 Accra replaced Cape Coast as the administrative capital of the British colony. The principal public buildings of the capital, including government departments and the supreme court, were built between Christiansborg castle (formerly the governor's residence, now the official residence of the president) and the old mercantile town. Higher ground to the north was laid out as a residential area for senior government officers. Still farther inland are large military cantonments and the airport, extensively developed during World War II and since used by international services of British, U.S., French, Portuguese and other airlines as well as by local services. A new international terminal building and another for internal services, as well as other improvements, were completed in 1957.

After 1961, Accra was largely superseded by an artificial harbour at Tema, 17 mi. E., to which it is linked by rail and road. Accra remains a busy port with about 1,000 tons a day being handled by surfboats. A 450-yd. breakwater running eastward from the Ft. James promontory affords increased shelter to the landing beach. The main export from Tema is cocoa, brought from points on the railway via Accra which extends 189 mi. inland to Kumasi, and on the numerous roads serving the hinterland.

From Accra tarred arterial roads lead westward along the coast to Cape Coast and Takoradi, eastward to Togoland and north to Kumasi and beyond.

Accra has electricity and piped water supplies, and an extensive municipal bus service. Besides the three forts, notable buildings include the State house, Parliament house, Korle Bu hospital, the Anglican and Roman Catholic cathedrals and many other churches, the Independence arch, the law courts, the law school, the National museum, the Central Ghana library, Broadcasting house, the Ambassador hotel, the offices of the Bank of Ghana, the Cocoa Marketing board and other public corporations, and the stores and offices of the major European trading concerns. On the northern outskirts are Achimota school, the leading secondary school in the country, opened in 1927; and, at Legon, the extensive new buildings of the University College of Ghana, founded in 1948 at Achimota.   (J. D. F.)

ACCRINGTON, a municipal and parliamentary borough in Lancashire, Eng., 5 mi. E. of Blackburn. Pop. (1961) 42,991. Area 6.9 sq.mi. It lies in the valley of the Hyndburn, a feeder of the Calder, on the western flank of the Pennines. The name of Accrington is said to derive from O.E. *Aecerntūn*, "village where acorns grow." The De Lacys were lords of the manor of Accrington (Akarinton from 1194) in Norman times, and about 1200 it was given by Robert de Lacy to the Cistercian monks of Kirkstall.

Returned for a time to the De Lacys in 1287, it had so developed by 1507 that a "New Accrington" was created. Old and New Accrington, straggling villages with about 5,000 inhabitants in 1836, were united in 1853 by which time textile print works and cotton mills were employing many people. The population, 17,688 in 1861, increased with the development of the Lancashire coal fields; the town was incorporated in 1878. Cotton and artificial-silk weaving, printing and dyeing and textile machinery manufacture, together with brick- and tilemaking and engineering, form, with the collieries, the industry of the area. The church of St. James, rebuilt in 1763, dates from 1546; the original chapel was probably an oratory which was an offshoot of Kirkstall abbey. Ecclesiastically Accrington was dependent on Altham till after the mid-19th century. The Haworth art gallery contains mostly British paintings. Five miles north-northeast, at Whalley, are the remains of a 13th-century abbey, belonging partly to the Church of England and partly to the Roman Catholics.

ACCULTURATION, the processes of change in artifacts, customs and beliefs resulting from the contact of peoples of different cultural backgrounds. The term is also used to refer to the effects of those processes, as in "an acculturated Navaho Indian," meaning a Navaho who has adopted Anglo-American behaviour while retaining some traditional Navaho ways. The word "acculturation" was first given currency in the late 19th century by U.S. anthropologists interested in the changing cultures of North American Indians. German anthropologists later also employed the term. Not until the 1930s, however, did it assume the status of a technical term in anthropology.

Anthropologists speak of the whole way of life of a people—the body of techniques, behaviours and ideas transmitted from one generation to another—as a culture. Cultures constantly change. A culture may change, on the one hand, as a result of innovations from within, that is, through discoveries and inventions. On the other hand, a culture may change as a result of influences from without, that is, through contact of its bearers with persons of a different culture. Acculturation includes those processes of change which result from contact conditions.

While it is recognized that acculturation has been instrumental in the building of every civilization, the processes have been studied thus far chiefly as they have operated in the spread of western civilization. It has been possible, especially during the 20th century, to make direct observations on the response of native peoples to different varieties of contact with European and European-derived peoples.

Incorporation.—Two major types of acculturation may be distinguished. One takes place when people of different cultures maintain an interchange without the exercise of military or political domination by one group over another. Such conditions were the rule during the long period of human development prior to the appearance of conquest states, but they have also existed more recently. An example of this type of free "borrowing" of cultural elements was that which took place during the 18th century between Spanish colonists and Navaho Indians in the area now called New Mexico. Unconquered by the Spaniards, the Navahos remained a free tribe at the Spanish colonial frontier. Frequent contacts occurred, ranging from trade in seasonally established markets to raids in which Navahos appropriated sheep and horses from Spanish settlements and Spaniards carried off Navaho captives as slaves. Under these conditions Navahos selected livestock, clothing, metalworking techniques and other elements of Spanish culture, integrating these into their own culture in their own way. The result was a culture new in content but with an organization that remained basically the same from the 18th into the 20th centuries. This kind of free borrowing with modification of customs to fit the borrowers' culture has been called incorporation.

Directed Change.—The second general type of acculturation takes place when one people establishes dominance over another through military conquest, political domination or other means of control. This has been called directed culture change in reference to the fact that whenever one people establishes control over another it seeks to change in some degree the way of life of the dominated group. It has been an important form of change ever since conquest states came into existence and it continues to be of great importance in the modern world. Extensive programs of directed change characterized the Roman conquest of the Mediterranean region and western Europe, the Spanish conquest of South and Central America, the British and American conquest of the Indians of Canada and the United States, the European domination of Africa, the Russian conquest of central Asia and Siberia and many other political expansions in the ancient and modern worlds.

Although they also involve selection and modification, the processes of directed culture change are more varied and their results more complex than those that take place under conditions of free contact. This is true because the changes are the result of interference in one cultural system by the agents of another. The determinants of change derive not from a single culture but from two or more in complex interaction. Three important processes which come into operation under various conditions of directed change may be discussed under the heads of assimilation, fusion and reaction.

Assimilation.—A term frequently used by anthropologists and sociologists to refer to the process by which one culture is replaced by another is "assimilation." It may also be used to refer to the replacement of single traits or trait-complexes. It is commonly believed by members of dominant societies that the cultural assimilation of subordinated ones is inevitable, as illustrated in American views concerning the future of North American Indians. Actually complete assimilation rarely takes place, unless the subordinated people are relocated and their family units broken up. The great diversity of local and regional cultures in Europe, despite centuries of conquest and recurrent attempts to force assimilation, testify to the rarity of the process continuing to completion. Some of the most notable instances of assimilation have taken place in the United States. A well-known one is that of the Negro slaves brought from Africa. The tribal cultures of the Negroes were almost completely replaced—languages, social organization, religions, as well as economic life. This came about under conditions of complete uprooting and breakup of family organization. However, even under such conditions some features of the older cultures survived. Another notable instance of assimilation is that of the millions of European immigrants to the United States, who through relocation, the influences of the public-school system and other forces in American life became almost completely assimilated within two or three generations.

Blending.—A commoner result of directed change is a blending of the cultures brought into contact, a process called fusion, accommodation or syncretism. Most of the North American Indian cultures in the area of the United States have undergone fusion, although this has been accompanied by varying degrees of replacement. The reservation system in the United States has operated strongly to set up conditions favouring fusion rather than assimilation. The results of fusion, embodying intricate combinations of Spanish, Anglo-American and various Indian elements, are to be seen in the cultures of the Pueblo Indians of New Mexico. The cultures of the Iroquois in the state of New York, the so-called "full-blood" Cherokees in Oklahoma, the Crow and other Plains Indians, as well as many others exhibit combination of elements from different cultures. In a more pervasive fashion among a far larger native population the results of similar fusional processes are to be seen in many parts of rural Mexico, Guatemala and South America. New syntheses of cultural elements, combining European and African or European and Asiatic cultures, seem to be a characteristic product of European expansion in the 20th century, as exemplified in India, Indonesia and west Africa. In such areas the processes of acculturation have resulted not in complete assimilation but rather in the formation of new cultures, which, with political autonomy, have begun their own independent courses of development, very much as new cultural syntheses arose after the termination of the Roman conquest.

Reaction.—A third common form of response to directed contact has been called reaction. It involves reaction against aspects of the culture of a dominant group by members of the subordinated society. Such reactions frequently take the form of nativistic movements. One of the most famous was the Ghost Dance among Paiute, Plains and other Indians of North America. This was a new religious cult led by a Paiute Indian named Wovoka in the 1880s. Wovoka, inspired by supernatural visions, preached a future in which white men would be eliminated and the old way of life restored. To bring this about it was necessary to dance the Ghost Dance, in the course of which dancers communicated with the dead ancestors. The cult spread rapidly among Indians in western United States and culminated in the tragic massacre at Wounded Knee creek, South Dakota. Similar forms of reaction against European domination have occurred repeatedly, such as the Vailala Madness among New Guinea natives and the Mau Mau rebellion among the Kikuyu of Kenya, Africa.

BIBLIOGRAPHY.—R. Linton, *Acculturation in Seven American Indian Tribes* (1940); B. Malinowski, *The Dynamics of Culture Change* (1945); R. Redfield, *A Village That Chose Progress* (1950); S. Tax (ed.), *Acculturation in the Americas* (1952); R. L. Beals, "Acculturation," in A. L. Kroeber (ed.), *Anthropology Today* (1953); E. Colson, *The Makah Indians* (1953); B. J. Siegel (ed.), *Acculturation* (1955); W. W. Newcomb, *The Culture and Acculturation of the Delaware Indians* (1956); W. R. Bascom and M. J. Herskovits (eds.), *Continuity and Change in African Cultures* (1959); E. H. Spicer (ed.), *Perspectives in American Indian Culture Change* (1961); M. H. Wilson, *Reaction to Conquest*, 2nd ed. (1961); M. Huxley, *Farewell to Eden* (1964); M. Mead, *New Lives for Old* (1956, 1966).   (E. H. Sp.)

ACERACEAE, the maple family of plants, comprising about 200 species of trees and shrubs in two genera, *Dipteronia* (two species) of central and southern China, and *Acer*, the maples, widely distributed in the northern hemisphere, crossing the equator only in Malaysia. In *Dipteronia* the seed is surrounded by a wing; in *Acer* it is winged only on the back. About 15 species of *Acer* are native to the U.S. Leaves of Aceraceae are opposite, simple or compound, and usually toothed or lobed. The small, clustered flowers are mostly unisexual and are sometimes without petals. The fruit, a samara, splits into two (rarely three) winged, one-seeded parts. Many maples are cultivated for ornament and shade (*see* MAPLE). Maple have a watery, sweet sap that in some species, especially sugar maple, is used to make sirup and sugar. Certain species of *Acer* are also important timber trees.

    (J. W. Tt.)

ACESTES (Gr. AEGESTES) was a mythological king of Segesta (Gr. Egesta) in Sicily. His mother, Egesta, had been sent from Troy by her parents to avoid feeding her to a voracious sea serpent that was ravaging the city because of Poseidon's anger against Laomedon (*q.v.*). Going to Sicily she met the river-god Crimisus, who appeared as a bear or a dog and by whom she became the mother of Acestes.

Acestes appears notably in the *Aeneid*, offering hospitality to Aeneas when he lands in Sicily (book 5). His function is to emphasize the mythological connection of that island with Troy: in Greek legend Aeneas traveled no farther than Sicily. Acestes brings the funeral games of Anchises to a climax by shooting into the air an arrow that becomes a comet, a sign of Anchises' eternal life (and a deliberate suggestion of the comet that appeared at Caesar's funeral games in 44 B.C. and that was hailed as proof of his divinity).   (T. V. B.)

ACETALDEHYDE, an aldehyde important as an intermediate product in the synthesis of acetic acid, *n*-butyl alcohol, ethyl acetate and other chemical compounds. It occurs in crude ethyl alcohol (*q.v.*) obtained by the fermentation of sugars and in crude methyl alcohol obtained by the destructive distillation of wood. Manufacture is by the oxidation of ethyl alcohol and the hydration of acetylene (*q.v.*). Acetaldehyde is transformed into ethyl alcohol by reduction and by oxidation into acetic acid (*q.v.*). The molecular formula is C_2H_4O and its structure is CH_3CHO. *See* also ALDEHYDES AND KETONES: *Aldehydes*.

ACETANILIDE (ANTIFEBRIN) is a drug made by interaction of glacial acetic acid with aniline (*q.v.*) and used in medicine to reduce fever. It does nothing to remove the cause of the fever and may result in aniline poisoning, a depressant action on the heart muscle resulting in collapse, nausea, vomiting and blueness of lips and nails. The last is caused by chemical changes in the blood, whereby red corpuscles lose their power to carry oxygen.

Acetanilide is a white, crystalline substance melting at $115°$ C., boiling at $305°$ C. and soluble in water, alcohol or ether. Its chemical formula is $C_6H_5.NH.CO.CH_3$.

ACETIC ACID is the most important member of the carboxylic acid group (*see* CARBOXYLIC ACIDS). It is produced on a vast scale technically, and the two principal methods which are now used for its preparation involve either biological oxidation (vinegar manufacture) or its synthesis from acetylene. Acetic acid is an important intermediate in many biosynthetic reactions, and it occurs naturally as a constituent of biological fluids and plant juices.

Pure acetic acid ($CH_3.CO_2H$) is often called glacial acetic acid. It is a colourless liquid (boiling point, $118°$ C.; melting point, $16.7°$ C.) which is completely miscible with water. The liquid has a corrosive action.

Manufacture.—Many processes have been devised for the synthesis of acetic acid on a technical scale. The steps which form the basis of most of these methods are (1) the preparation of acetylene from calcium carbide, $CaC_2 + 2H_2O \rightarrow Ca(OH)_2 + C_2H_2$; (2) the catalyzed hydration of acetylene to acetaldehyde, $C_2H_2 + H_2O \rightarrow CH_3.CHO$, which takes place in dilute sulfuric acid with mercuric sulfate as the catalyst; (3) the vapour-phase oxidation of acetaldehyde to acetic acid (*see* below). This process constitutes a very simple method for the synthesis of acetic acid, and the starting material, calcium carbide, is easily prepared by an electric arc process from limestone and coal.

The manufacture of vinegar consists of a fermentation process whereby carbohydrates such as starch, sugar or malt are fermented to yield ethyl alcohol, and this ethyl alcohol is then oxidized to acetic acid (*see* below). There are numerous species of aerobic bacteria (*e.g.*, *Acetobacter aceti* and *A. pasteurianum*) which may be used to effect the oxidation. Various names are used to describe vinegar, including malt vinegar and cider vinegar, and these indicate the origins of the carbohydrates used in the fermentation process. Vinegars usually contain about 5%–10% of acetic acid.

The oxidation of ethyl alcohol to acetic acid proceeds through acetaldehyde as an intermediate.

$$CH_3.CH_2OH \rightarrow CH_3.CHO \rightarrow CH_3.CO_2H$$

This reaction may be achieved either by using oxidizing agents, such as potassium dichromate and dilute sulfuric acid; or by vapour-phase oxidation in which a mixture of air and ethanol is passed over a heated vanadate catalyst. The biochemical oxidation of ethyl alcohol involves enzymes of the dehydrogenase type. (The souring of wines is due to the oxidation of the contained ethyl alcohol to acetic acid.)

Industrial Uses.—Acetic acid is used in the preparation of (1) metal acetates which are used in some printing processes; (2) the plastic polyvinyl acetate; (3) the further plastic cellulose acetate, which also finds extensive use in photographic films and in textile fibres (rayon); and (4) volatile esters such as ethyl acetate and amyl acetate, which are used extensively as solvents for resins, paints and lacquers. Amyl acetate is used as a flavouring agent in confectionery. *See* also references under "Acetic Acid" in the Index.   (W. D. Os.)

ACETOACETIC ESTER, or ethyl acetoacetate, an organic compound used industrially in the manufacture of synthetic drugs and dyes, is an outstanding example of a chemical substance having a dual character arising from the possession of two different molecular structures. Such substances are called tautomeric compounds. The substance is an ester, and has the molecular formula $C_6H_{10}O_3$. The two tautomeric forms are represented by

$$CH_3COCH_2COOC_2H_5 \quad \text{(ketonic form) and}$$
$$CH_3C(OH):CHCO_2C_2H_5 \quad \text{(enolic form)}$$

ordinary specimens of the ester as handled in commerce may be regarded as consisting of 93% of the first in equilibrium with 7% of the second. When treated by reagents which combine with ketones, such as sodium bisulfite hydroxylamine, phenylhydrazine and hydrocyanic acid, the ketonic character of the ester is manifested, and when acted upon by reagents such as phosphorus pentachloride, diazomethane, ammonia and amines, which detect alcoholic (enolic) groups, then its enolic nature is revealed.

In 1911 L. Knorr separated the two forms of the ester in a state of purity. The ketonic modification was frozen out of the equilibrium mixture at −78° C. and the enolic modification was isolated in the liquid condition by decomposing the sodium derivative with hydrogen chloride at the same low temperature. In these experiments it was found to be essential to use silica vessels. The ester was first discovered by A. Geuther in 1863. The original method of production is still employed on a manufacturing scale. Sodium, either molten or in wire form, is added to dry ethyl acetate containing a little ethyl alcohol. When all the metal has dissolved, the mixture is acidified with dilute acetic or sulfuric acid and the crude acetoacetic ester, which is partially miscible with water, separates as an oil on addition of common salt and is purified by distillation under diminished pressure. The ester is a colourless, fragrant liquid and boiling, with slight decomposition, at 181° C. under a pressure of 760 mm.

In the chemical laboratory acetoacetic ester is a valuable synthetic reagent, for its sodium derivative when acted on by an alkyl iodide yields an alkylacetoacetic ester, and the sodium derivative of the latter ester by similar means furnishes a dialkylacetoacetic ester. These alkyl- and dialkyl-acetoacetic esters may be employed in producing either higher ketones or higher fatty acids.

The ester has also been employed in the synthesis of pyridines, quinolines, furans, pyrazoles, pyrroles and compounds of the purine group.

ACETONE is an organic solvent of industrial and chemical importance, and is the simplest representative of the aliphatic ketones (*see* ALDEHYDES AND KETONES). It has very useful solvent properties, dissolving many fats and resins as well as cellulose nitrate and acetate. Because of the latter properties, it finds extensive use in the manufacture of explosives and artificial fibres. The numerous important chemical reactions of acetone make possible many organic syntheses in the laboratory and in industry.

Physiologically, acetone is present in the urine and in the blood; larger quantities are detected in diabetic patients. The ketones in general give rise to narcosis and lowering of blood pressure. Acetone itself produces intoxication and sleep but is less powerful than ether or chloroform, although less toxic than ethyl alcohol. When treated with chlorine, bromine or iodine in the presence of alkali, acetone is converted respectively into chloroform, bromoform or iodoform. It is the starting point in the production of the narcotic drug sulfonal.

Because of its valuable properties as a solvent and as an organic reagent, acetone is prepared commercially on a large scale, the processes available being as follows:

1. The dry distillation of calcium acetate leading to the formation of acetone and calcium carbonate.

2. The catalytic decomposition of glacial acetic acid into acetone, carbon dioxide and water when it is passed over heated metallic oxides such as alumina and thoria.

3. The fermentation of corn (maize), rice, horse chestnut meal or other starchy materials with a bacterium discovered by A. Fernbach, the starch present being converted into a mixture of normal butyl alcohol (6 parts), acetone (3 parts) and ethyl alcohol (1 part).

4. The dehydrogenation or oxidation by air of isopropyl alcohol in the presence of heated metallic or metal oxide catalysts.

Acetone has the molecular formula CH_3COCH_3 and is thus dimethyl ketone. It is a colourless, fragrant, inflammable, mobile liquid, boiling at 56.3° C. and miscible in all proportions with water, alcohol and ether.

See J. F. Thorpe and M. A. Whiteley, *Thorpe's Dictionary of Applied Chemistry* (1937).

ACETOPHENONE or phenyl methyl ketone, is an organic compound with anesthetic and soporific properties; under the name hypnone it has been used as a drug to induce sleep. It is the simplest representative of the mixed aliphatic-aromatic ketones. Acetophenone melts at 20° C. and boils at 202° C., is volatile in steam and has the composition, $C_6H_5COCH_3$. It occurs to a small extent in coal tar and, having feebly basic properties, is

extracted from the heavy oil fractions (boiling point 160°–190°) with sulfuric acid.

ACETYLENE is a colourless, gaseous hydrocarbon, widely used as a fuel in oxyacetylene welding and cutting of metals, and as a chemical intermediate in the synthesis of many organic chemicals and plastics. It was discovered and identified in 1836 by Edmond Davey. The properties of acetylene were first determined in 1862 by P. E. M. Berthelot who also showed that acetylene is formed in many high-temperature pyrogenic reactions; for example, acetylene is usually present in small amounts in coal gas. However, it was not until the discovery in 1892 by Willson and Moorehead of the electric-furnace method of producing calcium carbide from the combination of coal with lime that acetylene became of any commercial significance. Acetylene, generated when calcium carbide is brought in contact with water, was used for illumination because the acetylene flame, when supplied with the correct amount of air, gives a pure white light which is the nearest known artificial approach to sunlight. The widespread use of acetylene for illumination during the early part of the century has been supplanted by electric lighting, except for locations where electric power is not available; *e.g.*, in navigation buoys and miners' lamps.

The next stage in the growing importance of acetylene as an industrial commodity was the development of autogenous welding using an oxygen-acetylene flame in the so-called oxyacetylene torch. This oxyacetylene flame produces the highest flame temperature (about 6,000° F.) of any known mixture of combustible gases and, although originally limited to welding and joining of certain ferrous metals, can now be used to weld or cut practically all industrial metals.

Acetylene is an unsaturated organic compound, highly reactive toward many chemical reactants, so it soon became the basis for a rapidly growing chemical industry. Acetaldehyde, acetic acid, acetone and a wide range of chlorinated solvents were so derived. During the early 1930s, E. I. du Pont de Nemours and Co. developed in the United States the first synthetic rubber, Neoprene (Duprene) from acetylene. Subsequently the use of acetylene in chemicals continued to widen until more than 75% of the acetylene used was employed in synthetic chemicals, many of which appeared as such familiar household articles as water-base paints, vinyl fabric and floor coverings, dry cleaning solvents and aerosol insecticide sprays.

Properties of Acetylene.—Acetylene or ethyne, $HC \equiv CH$, is the simplest and best-known member of the acetylenic hydrocarbon series. As the formula shows, acetylene contains two carbon atoms, each joined to one hydrogen atom, and linked by a socalled triple bond. It is this triple bond which distinguishes acetylene from ethylene ($CH_2 = CH_2$) and which is responsible for many of its unusual properties and reactions.

Acetylene is an inflammable, gaseous compound having a molecular weight of 26.02 and containing 7.75% hydrogen and 92.25% carbon. When pure, it is a colourless gas with a pleasant ethereal odour. However, as prepared from calcium carbide, it usually contains traces of phosphine which cause an unpleasant, garliclike odour. The accompanying table lists many of the common physical properties of acetylene.

Physical Properties of Acetylene

Molecular weight	26.02
Melting point	−81.8° C. (−115.2° F.)
Boiling point	−88.5° C.; −83.6° C. sublimes
Critical temperature	36° C. (96.8° F.)
Critical pressure (atmospheres)	62
Density (g/l, 0° C., 760 mm.)	1.173
Density (lb./ft.³, 32° F., 1 atm.)	0.07323
Specific gravity (air=1)	0.9073
Inflammable limits in air (vol. %)	2.5 to 80
Auto-ignition temperature	635° F.
Heat of combustion/gram m.w.	1,238 BTU

Acetylene is a highly endothermic compound. It has a heat of formation in the gaseous state, from the elements carbon (graphite) and hydrogen at the absolute zero of temperature, of 54.33 kcal. per gram mole (about 3,800 BTU per pound weight); and, contrary to other hydrocarbons, it has a free energy of formation that decreases with an increase in temperature. Therefore, since the equilibrium constant at any particular temperature is a function of the free energy at that temperature according to the expression

$$\Delta F^\circ = -RT \ln K$$

(where ΔF° is the free energy, K is the equilibrium constant, R is the gas constant and T is the absolute temperature) it can be calculated that the equilibrium concentration of acetylene increases with temperature. The stability of acetylene in association with its elements thus increases with temperature and allows for improved yields of acetylene as the temperature is increased.

Acetylene can be decomposed into its elements with the liberation of heat. This decomposition may or may not give rise to explosions, depending on conditions. If acetylene gas is ignited at atmospheric pressure, decomposition occurs, but usually is not propagated beyond the ignition source. On the other hand, pure acetylene under pressure in excess of about 15 lb. per square inch, or in liquid or solid form, explodes with extreme violence.

The hydrogen atoms in acetylene are somewhat acidic in character and can react with metallic salts to form metallic derivatives of acetylene, the so-called acetylides. Either one or both of the hydrogens may be replaced. Metals of group I and group II of the periodic table and a few other metals form acetylides by direct reaction or by action of acetylene on a compound of the metal:

$$HC\equiv CH + Na \longrightarrow NaC\equiv CH + \tfrac{1}{2}H_2$$

$$HC\equiv CH + 2AgNO_3 \longrightarrow AgC\equiv CAg + 2HNO_3$$

As may be seen by the above equations, silver (and also copper, mercury and gold) displaces both hydrogens of acetylene, while the alkali and alkaline earth metals generally displace only one hydrogen atom, requiring elevated temperatures to replace both hydrogens. A further distinction of these acetylides is that the acetylides of silver, copper, mercury and gold are precipitated from aqueous or alcoholic solution while those of the alkali and alkaline-earth metals are not. Because of the insolubility of the copper and silver acetylides, these are used to detect small amounts of acetylene in other gases. The acetylides of silver, copper, mercury and gold darken on exposure to light and when dry are extremely sensitive to heat, friction or shock. Because of the explosive danger, these metals should be kept from acetylene.

In addition to its reactive hydrogen atoms, acetylene also contains a carbon-to-carbon triple bond. Physical evidence indicates that the $C\equiv C$ bond of acetylene (1.06Å) is shorter than the $C=C$ bond of ethylene (1.09Å) and that the electrons are more tightly packed in acetylene than in ethylene. This accounts for the fact that halogens and other electrophiles add to acetylene at a much slower rate than they do to ethylene. Acetylene, notwithstanding, is readily susceptible to both electrophilic and nucleophilic attack. It will add halogens, halogen acids, hydrogen cyanide, alcohols, acids, amines and amides; for example:

$$HC\equiv CH + Cl^+ \longrightarrow HClC=\overset{+}{C}H \xrightarrow{Cl^-} HClC=CHCl$$

$$HC\equiv CH + H^+ \longrightarrow H_2C=\overset{+}{C}H \xrightarrow{Cl^-} H_2C=CHCl$$

$$HC\equiv CH + CN^- \longrightarrow H\overset{-}{C}=CHCN \xrightarrow{H^+} H_2C=CHCN$$

$$HC\equiv CH + C_2H_5O^- \longrightarrow H\overset{-}{C}=CHOC_2H_5 \xrightarrow{H^+} H_2C=CHOC_2H_5$$

Acetylene can also provide the nucleophile for attack on polarized atoms. Thus, it can add to itself or to aldehydes and ketones:

$$HC\equiv CH + \overset{-}{C}\equiv CH \longrightarrow H\overset{-}{C}=CHC\equiv CH \xrightarrow{H^+}$$
$$H_2C=CHC\equiv CH$$

$$H_2C=O + \overset{-}{C}\equiv CH \longrightarrow H_2C\overset{O^-}{\underset{C\equiv CH}{<}} \xrightarrow{H^+}$$

$$HOCH_2C\equiv CH \xrightarrow{H_2C=O} HOCH_2C\equiv CCH_2OH$$

Manufacture of Acetylene.—Until about 1940, acetylene was usually derived from calcium carbide, the product of the reaction of coal and lime in an electric furnace at about 2,000° C.

$$\underset{coal}{3C} + \underset{lime}{CaO} \xrightarrow{heat} \underset{calcium\ carbide}{CaC_2} + \underset{carbon\ monoxide}{CO}$$

Reaction of water with calcium carbide in specially designed generators produces gaseous acetylene and solid hydrated lime.

$$\underset{calcium\ carbide}{CaC_2} + \underset{water}{H_2O} \longrightarrow \underset{acetylene}{HC\equiv CH} + \underset{hydrated\ lime}{Ca(OH)_2}$$

During World War II Germany installed in the synthetic rubber plant at Huls the first successful commercial installation for the cracking of hydrocarbons to acetylene by means of a high temperature electric arc. During the same period, Germany also operated a plant at Oppau for the production of acetylene by partial combustion of methane with air or oxygen. The combustion of part of the methane provided the heat required to raise the temperature of the injected hydrocarbon up to the cracking temperature. This latter process, sometimes referred to as the Sachsse process, later was further developed, particularly in the southwest United States where ample supplies of natural gas are available cheaply. Unlike the calcium carbide or arc processes, the Sachsse process does not require electrical power as a primary source of energy. Still a fourth method, a purely thermal hydrocarbon cracking process known as the Wulff process, is carried out in a regenerative type furnace consisting of carborundum refractory tiles in the heated section. The heat required to raise the temperature of the tiles to the cracking temperature of 1,250–1,450° C. is supplied by burning the waste gases, consisting of carbon monoxide and hydrogen, from the purification section.

One fundamental requirement in all high temperature cracking operations for producing acetylene is that the hydrocarbon feed be heated to the highest possible temperature in the shortest possible time and that the temperature of the cracked gases be lowered rapidly to minimize decomposition of the acetylene produced.

Acetylene generated from carbide is generally rather pure, containing less than 0.4% impurities, and is suitable for most uses except chemical synthesis, for which traces of phosphine, arsine and hydrogen sulfide must be removed to prevent poisoning sensitive catalysts. On the other hand, acetylene generated from cracking of hydrocarbons is in very dilute form, comprising only about 8% to 16% of the total gas. Purification may be carried out by several methods but, in principle, all depend on the selective absorption of acetylene in a solvent, generally under pressure, in which the acetylene is many times more soluble than the attendant impurities. This solvent stream, containing principally acetylene, when warmed up at lower pressures, releases the acetylene in fairly pure state. A major by-product in all cracking operations is a considerable amount of finely divided carbon, separation and disposal of which is often troublesome.

A substantial factor in the cost of pure acetylene from cracking operations is the expense of purification. In some cases this can be offset partially by processing the waste "tail gas," consisting essentially of carbon monoxide and hydrogen in roughly the correct percentages for synthesis of methyl alcohol (methanol), a useful industrial chemical. In other instances the carbon monoxide may be removed, leaving essentially pure hydrogen, also useful for chemical synthesis, for example, by reaction with nitrogen from the atmosphere to form ammonia, the basis of several forms of nitrogenous fertilizers.

Despite the wide differences in manufacturing technology, no one of these methods is universally used. Where electrical power is cheap and hydrocarbons scarce, the carbide method probably is prevalent, but where hydrocarbons are plentiful, as in the southwest United States, some form of hydrocarbon cracking is the method of choice.

Shipping of Acetylene.—Because of its inflammability and explosive nature under pressure, acetylene must be shipped in special containers, so constructed as to minimize danger. One basic feature of safe construction lies in packing the cylinders with a highly porous monolithic filler so that no pockets of significant size remain where free acetylene in gaseous form can collect. A second factor is the use of a solvent, acetone, which dissolves many times its own volume of acetylene. By this technique, acetylene can be shipped safely at pressures of 250 lb. per square inch (p.s.i.). Even so, in the United States the construction and shipping of acetylene cylinders must follow the specifications and regulations of the Interstate Commerce commission.

From the above, it is obvious that the weight of acetylene available in each cylinder is very small, usually less than 10% of the total shipping weight. If one takes into account the return of the empty shipping container, the net efficiency of shipping is less than 5%. On the other hand, calcium carbide gives off 31% of its weight of acetylene and is thus the cheapest form in which to transport acetylene by common carrier.

Fuel Uses.—Mixtures of air and acetylene are explosive over a wide range: from about 2.5% air in acetylene to about 12.5% acetylene in air. Acetylene requires 2.5 times its volume of oxygen or 11.95 times its volume of air to effect its complete combustion. It is used for lights in portable lamps, buoys, road signals, isolated premises, etc., but the consumption of acetylene for lighting is small compared with its use in the industrial welding and cutting of metals, for which purposes it is consumed in a blowpipe to which a supply of undiluted oxygen is fed from a steel cylinder containing that gas under pressure. In welding, a reducing flame is maintained by using less than the proportion of oxygen required for complete combustion, whereas in cutting metals an excess of oxygen is admitted to oxidize the metal. Since acetylene is an endothermic compound its heat of combustion is greater than that of the constituent carbon and hydrogen. For this reason acetylene affords a higher flame temperature than other fuel gases, about 6,000° F. in a correctly designed and operated torch.

Chemical Uses.—Ready availability, high reactivity and reasonable cost make acetylene a suitable starting material for the industrial synthesis of many organic chemicals. Together with ethylene, it forms the basis of much of the synthetic aliphatic chemical industry. In countries having abundant electrical power but limited oil reserves, acetylene is usually favoured as a raw material. However, in the United States acetylene and ethylene are often competitive; acetylene is generally more expensive than ethylene but processing costs may be lower because, in many cases, acetylene may offer a more direct route to the desired chemical. The use of acetylene as a raw material for chemical synthesis increased so rapidly that total usage in the United States was expected to reach 3,000,000,000 lb. per year by 1975.

The first major use of acetylene as a chemical raw material involved the addition of water to acetylene in the presence of sulfuric acid and mercuric sulfate to produce acetaldehyde. Oxidation of acetaldehyde gives acetic acid, a necessary component in the acetylation of cellulose to cellulose acetate, and in the synthesis of solvents for automobile lacquers.

Chlorination of acetylene to produce a series of chlorocarbons is a major consumer of acetylene. The chlorocarbons, which include trichloroethylene and tetrachloroethylene, are solvents for fats, oils and waxes and are widely used in metal degreasing, in dry cleaning, in scouring wools and in extracting oils. They are non-inflammable and, under most conditions, stable to oxidation and hydrolysis.

During the early 1930s, the du Pont company developed the first synthetic rubber, based on the original discovery of J. A. Nieuwland of the University of Notre Dame (Ind.) that acetylene could be converted to vinyl acetylene. Addition of hydrogen chloride to vinyl acetylene gives chloroprene which rapidly polymerizes to a rubberlike material, polychloroprene, known as Neoprene or Duprene. Actually, Neoprene is superior to natural rubber in resistance to heat and oxidation and to fuels such as gasoline and oils.

Much of the rapid increase in the use of acetylene as a chemical intermediate paralleled the amazing development and growth of plastics. Addition of acetic acid to acetylene produces vinyl acetate. Polymerized vinyl acetate is a component of water-base paints and textile finishes. Hydrolysis of polyvinyl acetate gives polyvinyl alcohol, a unique polymer which, after chemical modification, is widely used in safety glass lamination and in synthetic sponges. Addition of hydrogen chloride to acetylene yields vinyl chloride, the polymer of which is familiar commercially in the form of vinyl upholstery, vinyl floor tile and inflatable toys. Combination of acetylene with hydrogen cyanide gives acrylonitrile, the

major component of the acrylic fibres such as Orlon. Acrylate monomers are produced from the reaction of acetylene with carbon monoxide and an alcohol. Acrylate polymers such as Lucite and Plexiglas are familiar as transparent, optically clear plastic sheets and as the basic material in artificial dentures.

Acetylene is also a key raw material in the synthesis of vitamin A, an important food supplement. One of the chemicals based on acetylene reactions under pressure is polyvinyl pyrrolidone, a water-soluble polymer having many properties resembling natural proteins. Polyvinyl pyrrolidone was used in Germany as a blood plasma extender, but this use in the U.S. did not materialize.

Many potentialities of acetylene as a raw material for synthetic products have been realized, primarily by J. W. Reppe in Germany; knowledge of Reppe's work became generally available only after World War II. Reppe recognized that inability to handle acetylene safely under pressure was a very serious limitation to the discovery of new reactions of acetylene. He initiated an exhaustive study of the explosive characteristics of acetylene, as a result of which new techniques were devised which permitted acetylene to be used in chemical reactions under pressures of up to 250–300 lb. p.s.i. In brief, these techniques involved: (1) dilution of the acetylene with an inert gas such as nitrogen; (2) use of small-bore transmission lines; and (3) subdivision of all large areas of the container by packing with ceramic or metal rings or gauzes so that no acetylene molecule was more than one-half inch from a wall surface.

With these new techniques allowing the use of acetylene under pressure, Reppe was able to develop four new areas of acetylene chemistry: (1) vinylation, in which an alcohol, mercaptan, acid, amine or amide is added across the triple bond to produce vinyl ethers, vinyl thioethers, vinyl esters, vinyl amines and vinyl amides; (2) ethynylation, in which the acid hydrogens are added to aldehydes, ketones and amines to produce new acetylenic chemicals, still containing a triple bond; (3) carbonylation, in which carbon monoxide may be added in the presence of water or alcohol to give acrylate derivatives; and (4) cyclopolymerization, in which acetylene reacts with itself to produce cyclic hydrocarbons such as benzene, styrene and cyclooctatetraene.

This new chemistry of acetylene under pressure, sometimes referred to as Reppe chemistry, has made available many new acetylene chemicals but few have obtained large-scale usage as yet.

See also references under "Acetylene" in the Index.

BIBLIOGRAPHY.—R. E. Kirk and D. F. Othmer (eds.), *Encyclopaedia of Chemical Technology*, vol. i (1949–52); J. W. Copenhaver and M. H. Bigelow, *Acetylene and Carbon Monoxide Chemistry* (1949); S. A. Miller, *Acetylene*, 2 vol. (1964–66).   (Jn. W. C.)

ACHAEA (AKHAIA, ACHAIA), the name of a region of Greece, on the north coast of the Peloponnesus, bounded in ancient times to the south by Elis and the Erymanthus mountains and to the east by Sicyon and approximately corresponding to the modern Greek *nomos* or department of Achaea (area 1,239 sq.mi., pop. [1961] 239,206, administrative capital Patras [*q.v.*]). The 12 cities of ancient Achaea formed a religious confederacy, meeting in Poseidon's sanctuary at Helice: from this developed the Achaean league (*q.v.*) of Hellenistic times. After the war between Rome and the Achaeans in 146 B.C. Achaea was administered by Rome as part of the province of Macedonia and not organized separately as a senatorial province until 27 B.C., when the name was extended to comprise all of Greece south of Thessaly, with Corinth as capital. On the Latin conquest of the Byzantine empire in A.D. 1204, a Frankish principality of Achaea was established in the Morea or Peloponnesus. After various dismemberments, this was conquered by the Turks in 1460 (*see* GREECE: *History*). The name Achaea was applied in ancient Greece to a region west of the Gulf of Pagasae (mod. Gulf of Volos) in southern Thessaly, this being usually referred to as Achaea Phthiotis. *See* also ACHAEANS.

ACHAEAN LEAGUE, a confederation of the towns of Achaea (*q.v.*) in ancient Greece. Isolated on their narrow strips of plain, these towns were exposed to piratical raids from across the Corinthian gulf. As a protection against such dangers the earliest league of 12 Achaean cities arose. In the 4th century B.C. it was fighting with Sparta against Thebes both before and after the battle of Leuctra (371), and it shared in the resistance to Philip II of Macedonia (338) and Antipater (330) (*see* GREECE: *History*). In the period following the death of Alexander the Great this league fell apart. By 280, however, four towns had combined again, and soon the ten surviving cities of Achaea renewed their federation around the shrine of Zeus Homarios near Aegium. Much was due to Aratus (*q.v.*) of Sicyon, who in 251 brought his newly liberated city, and later other non-Achaean cities, into the confederation on equal terms. He thus initiated an expansive policy, and by 228 the confederation included Arcadia, Argolis, Corinth and Aegina.

Aratus probably also organized the federal constitution. The league embraced city-states which maintained their internal independence. Only in foreign politics and war was their competence restricted. The central government claimed to be democratic, but its democracy was modified by a high minimum age (30 years) for membership of the assembly and by the absence of payment for attendance, with the result that the expense of officeholding in practice left power in the hands of the well to do. The chief magistracy was the *strategia*, which combined unrestricted command in the field with considerable civil authority and had practically the sole power of introducing measures before the assembly. There were two annual generals (*strategoi*) down to 255, but subsequently only one; re-election was allowed only after a year's interval. Beside the general stood a board of ten *demiourgoi*, who shared in the administration and under his chairmanship presided over the assembly. There was a representative council (boule). Though the relations of this body with the assembly are a matter of controversy, the probability is that down to *c.* 200 B.C. there were regular meetings (*synodoi*) of both council and assembly throughout the year to transact normal business, but that after 200 the assembly was not ordinarily convened; thus from then onward Achaea was governed by a representative council, perhaps elected on a proportional system. At all times irregular meetings (*synkletoi*) of council and assembly could be summoned to debate such questions as war or alliance; and after 200 the primary assembly was convened only for this purpose or on the instructions of the Roman senate.

The confederacy prescribed uniform standards and coinage. There were federal law courts, and the assembly could transform itself into a court of justice. The federal authority summoned contingents, imposed taxes and fined or coerced refractory members.

The first federal wars were against Macedonia, against Antigonus Gonatas and Aetolia and, in alliance with Aetolia, against Demetrius II. But the admission of Megalopolis and other Arcadian cities to the league led to friction with Sparta. Shorn of much of its territory and in danger of complete disintegration before the assaults of the Spartan king Cleomenes III (*q.v.*), the confederacy was persuaded by Aratus to call in the Macedonians. Victorious at Sellasia, Antigonus Doson restored the lost districts, but retained Acrocorinth for himself (224–221). The Achaeans then joined his new Greek league and fought beside his successor, Philip V, first against Aetolia (220–217), then against Rome allied to Aetolia (211–205). Under Philopoemen (*q.v.*) a reorganized federal army defeated Nabis, the tyrant of Sparta (207). In the Second Macedonian War Achaea joined Rome (198), and this new policy led to the incorporation of nearly the whole Peloponnese; it also brought increased friction with Sparta and clashes with Roman officials, and after the Roman victory at Pydna (168) control by subservient representatives of the pro-Roman party. In 150, in defiance of Rome, the confederacy attacked Sparta. The federal army was routed near Corinth by Lucius Mummius (146), and the Romans dissolved the confederacy. However a smaller league was soon afterward set up, and this continued into the Roman imperial age; it was at one time a member of a larger Panachaean confederacy within the Roman province of Achaea.

The chief defect of the Achaean league lay in its lack of provision for securing efficient armies and regular payment of imposts and for dealing with disaffected members. Its achievement was to have combined city autonomy with an organized central administration, to have made noteworthy progress in the institution of representative government and to have served the interests of Greek liberty for more than a century.

BIBLIOGRAPHY.—Polybius, *History,* especially books 2, 4, 5, 22, 23 and 28, with the *Commentary* of F. W. Walbank on books 1–6 (1957); Livy, books 31–45; *Cambridge Ancient History,* vol. vii and viii (1928–30); G. Niccolini, *La confederazione achea* (1914); F. W. Walbank, *Aratos of Sicyon* (1933); A. Aymard, *Les Assemblées de la confédération achaienne* (1938) and *Les Premiers Rapports de Rome et de la confédération achaienne* (1938); J. A. O. Larsen, *Representative Government in Greek and Roman History* (1955). (F. W. WA.)

ACHAEANS, an ancient Greek people, whose eras of greatest importance belong to preclassical and postclassical times. In Homer, Akhaioi is the name chiefly used, along with Danaoi and Argeioi, of the Greeks besieging Troy, whereas the name Hellenes occurs only once ("Myrmidones and Hellenes and Achaeans"; *Iliad* ii, 684) and is used, as Thucydides noted, only of followers of the northern chief Achilles. Homer's Achaeans dominate the mainland and western isles of Greece (with "rich Mycenae" as capital of their strongest kingdom); Crete (where they are distinguished from "True-Cretans" and other peoples), Rhodes and adjacent isles, but not the Cyclades (where indeed Mycenaean imports recorded by archaeology are relatively scanty). Farther afield they are said to have contacts with Cyprus (where, according to Strabo, writing in the 1st century B.C., the place name "Achaean Shore" commemorated the first landing of Achaean settlers) and with Phoenicia and Egypt, a piratical raid on which is described by Odysseus in one of his "yarns." Their area as described by Homer is thus precisely that covered by the activities of the "Mycenaeans" in the 14th–13th centuries B.C., as revealed by archaeology. Moreover, the references in 13th-century Hittite documents to a powerful western kingdom of Ahhiawa, whose king is on occasion addressed as "brother" by Hittite monarchs, have been plausibly interpreted as referring to the Mycenaean world under Achaean domination. Modern scholars have also, more dubiously, identified as Achaeans the people denoted as "K-w-sh" in Egyptian hieroglyphics and recorded as invading Egypt from the west in alliance with Libyans in 1221 B.C.—the name being vocalized as "Akhaiwasha" (for Greek "Akhaiwoi").

It might be concluded from the above evidence that the Achaeans are coeval with the Mycenaeans and therefore the first Greeks in the Aegean, were it not that the linguistic affinities of the Achaeans present a more difficult problem. The language of the Mycenaean "Linear B" writing is generally believed to be an early form of Greek, having affinities with the Arcadian and Cypriot of classical times; and the written language of Mycenae was quite certainly also that of Crete, well before 1200 B.C. No break in the cultural development such as might be expected to accompany the coming of Greek, an Indo-European language, to the Aegean can be detected by archaeology later than the beginning of the Middle Bronze Age (*c.* 1900–1600 B.C.; *see* GREECE: *History*); however, the Achaeans of the northern Peloponnese in historic times, who were reckoned by Herodotus to be descendants of the earlier Achaeans, spoke a dialect of Greek akin to Doric (if we may judge by the inscriptions of their colonists in Italy), which suggests that they did not enter Greece until the Dorian invasions at the end of the Bronze Age (12th century B.C.). Since the genealogies of Homer's Achaean chiefs are very short (two or three generations) and since Homer's only reference to writing is in a story referring to a time two generations before the Trojan War, it seems at least possible that these chiefs, whose infiltration into Mycenaean kingships by way of military service and dynastic marriages is a frequent motif of Greek saga, were not the first Greeks in the south, but that they held power in the Mycenaean world only for a few generations in its last, warlike and semibarbarous phase and were relatively close kindred of the Dorians (*q.v.*) who were to replace them.

In the classical period, Achaea (*q.v.*) was the name of two districts in Greece, neither of them important. Twelve small Achaean cities held the coastal strip of the northern Peloponnese and were never brought by Sparta into the Peloponnesian league, Sparta being only at pains to keep the area out of hostile hands. The most important achievement of these little cities was their contribution to Greek colonization, with the foundation (by the "overspill" of population from their rocky and narrow land) of cities in southern Italy, c. 700 B.C.: Sybaris (q.v.), which colonized Poseidonia (Paestum, q.v.); Crotona (q.v.); Metapontum; and Caulonia. In their more spacious land, these Achaean colonists flourished so greatly that the region came to be known as Great Greece (Magna Graecia, *Megale Hellas*). Here, as in the line of Homer quoted above, Achaeans seem to have been early users of the Hellenic name. For Achaea's importance from the 4th century onward, *see* ACHAEAN LEAGUE.

The other Achaea of historic times, Achaea Phthiotis, was a district of southeastern Thessaly. Preserving, in the hill country of Othrys, a distinct dialect akin to Thessalian (Aeolic mingled with northwestern elements) and their own tribal organization, but politically dominated by the Thessalian league, these Achaeans played no independent part in Greek history.

BIBLIOGRAPHY.—M. Ventris and J. Chadwick, *Documents in Mycenaean Greek* (1956); M. I. Finley, "Homer and Mycenae," *Historia*, vol. vi (1957); D. L. Page, *History and the Homeric Epics* (1960).
(A. R. BU.)

ACHAEMENIDAE, Latin form of the Greek name of an ancient dynasty of Persian kings (*see* PERSIAN HISTORY). Achaemenes (Persian, Hakhamanish), their eponymous ancestor, is presumed to have lived early in the 7th century B.C., but nothing is known of his history. From his son Teispes two lines of kings descended. The kings of the older line were Cyrus I, Cambyses I, Cyrus II the Great and Cambyses II. After the death of Cambyses II the junior line came to the throne with Darius I, who in the Bisitun inscription traces his descent from Teispes through Ariaramnes, Arsames and Hystaspes, his father. Cyrus II, Darius I and all the later kings of Persia called themselves Hakhamanishiya (Achaemenidae). The dynasty became extinct with the death of Darius III, following his defeat (330 B.C.) by Alexander the Great.

The name Achaemenes was borne by a son of Darius I. After the first rebellion of Egypt, in 484 B.C., he was appointed satrap of Egypt by his brother Xerxes and commanded the Persian fleet at Salamis (480). In 460 B.C. he was defeated and slain by Inaros, the leader of the second rebellion of Egypt.

See also Index references under "Achaemenidae" in the Index volume.
(J. M. M.-R.)

ACHATES, the companion of Aeneas in Virgil's *Aeneid*. The expression "fidus Achates" became proverbial for a loyal and devoted companion.

ACHELOUS (mod. ASPROPOTAMOS or AKHELOOS "white river"), the largest river in Greece, is 137 mi. long. It rises in the Pindus mountains, and, dividing Aetolia from Acarnania, falls into the Ionian sea. Its water is charged with fine mud, which is deposited along its banks in fertile, marshy plains. At its mouth a number of small islands (Echinades) were enveloped in this deposit. In winter the river, which has a rapid pace, overflows the whole of its lower plain, and Hercules is said to have attempted to drain the region by confining the stream within its banks. At its mouth it has a depth of less than two feet and so is not navigable from the sea.

The river was formerly called Thoas, from its impetuosity, and its upper portion Inachus, the name Achelous being restricted to the shorter eastern branch. The name is given to several other rivers in Greece and appears in cult and in Greek mythology as that of the typical river-god. (WM. C. B.)

ACHENBACH, ANDREAS (1815–1910), German landscape painter, a pioneer of the German realistic school, was born at Cassel on Sept. 29, 1815. He studied at the Düsseldorf academy under Johann Wilhelm Schirmer, but emancipated himself from the contemporary school of landscapists which delighted in the representation of romantic scenery. He was the first artist of the Düsseldorf school who painted nature for its own sake. As a young man he sought inspiration in the Netherlands and Norway. His pictures of the stormy North sea, of Dutch canal scenes and of Rhineland villages contrasted favourably with the sentimental landscapes of his contemporaries. He died on March 31, 1910.

His brother, OSWALD ACHENBACH (1827–1905), is distinguished for his colourful renderings of the Bay of Naples, of Rome and

of Venice. He broke away from the traditional classicist interpretation of these scenes and reveled in strong and glowing colour effects.

ACHENE, a small, dry, one-seeded, indehiscent (closed at maturity) fruit with a thin pericarp, as the individual fruits of buttercups and sunflowers. *See* FRUIT.

ACHERNAR, α Eridani, the brightest star in the constellation Eridanus (q.v.), is located only 32.5° from the south celestial pole. The apparent magnitude of Achernar is 0.6 visual and it is one of the ten brightest stars in the sky.

The star is a blue subgiant about 120 light-years from the earth. Its true luminosity is more than 600 times that of our sun.
(D. L. H.)

ACHERON (Gr. etymology doubtful, traditionally river of woe), name of several rivers of Greece. In Greek mythology the name is specially given to a river of Hades, hence, particularly in Latin (Acceruns in Plautus), used to designate the lower world generally.

ACHESON, EDWARD GOODRICH (1856–1931), U.S. inventor who discovered silicon carbide (q.v.) and perfected a method for making graphite (q.v.), was born at Washington, Pa., on March 9, 1856. After completing elementary school he became interested in electricity, joining the staff of Thomas A. Edison in 1880. Acheson helped develop the incandescent lamp at Edison's laboratories at Menlo Park, N.J., and then in 1881 installed the first electric lights for Edison in Italy, Belgium and France. Upon returning to the U.S., Acheson began his own experiments on methods for producing artificial diamonds in an electric furnace. During these experiments he accidentally discovered silicon carbide (SiC), an abrasive of great cutting power, which he named carborundum. Later while studying the effects of high temperature on carborundum he found that silicon vaporizes from the compound at about 7,500° F., leaving behind graphitic carbon of superior quality. Acheson received patents for the graphite process and also for carborundum, and numerous others for methods for producing metallic silicon and graphite lubricants. He died in New York city July 6, 1931.

ACHILL, the largest island off Ireland, is separated from the Curraun peninsula of County Mayo on the west coast by the narrow Achill sound. It covers an area of 56.2 sq.mi. and is roughly triangular in shape. Pop. (1961) 4,069. Achill (meaning "eagle") is mountainous, the highest points being Slieve Croaghaun, which rises abruptly to 2,192 ft. from the magnificent cliffs of Achill head at the western tip of the island, and Slieve More (2,204 ft.), a regular cone of quartzite, on the northern side. The pre-Cambrian quartzites, which make up most of the island, weather into infertile soils, and peat fills many depressions on wild moorlands. Cultivable areas are few and small and farming has to be supplemented by fishing to provide even a scanty livelihood. Population is highest on the more sheltered eastern coast where a bridge joins the mainland. Railway connection to this point was replaced by motor bus in 1940. Domestic knitting and a small knitting factory provide employment for women. The main source of income is derived from migratory labour. Many men are away from the island for three months or more each year, working as agricultural labourers in England or the Scottish lowlands. (T. HER.)

ACHILLES, in Greek mythology, son of Peleus (q.v.) and Thetis; bravest, handsomest and swiftest of the army of Agamemnon. According to Homer, he was brought up by his mother at Phthia with his cousin and intimate friend Patroclus; his teachers were Phoenix and Cheiron. The non-Homeric tales of his childhood contain obvious folk-tale themes. Thetis had seven children, all of whom she put into the fire or a cauldron to make them immortal. All died save Achilles; because Peleus interfered at this point, Thetis left him (fairy bride theme).

Another version is that Thetis dipped the child in the waters of the river Styx, by which (like Sigurd Fafnirs-bane) he became invulnerable, except for the part of his heel by which she held him: the proverbial "heel of Achilles."

The later mythographers relate that Peleus, having received an oracle that his son would die fighting at Troy, sent him to the court of Lycomedes on Scyrus, where he was dressed as a girl and kept among the king's daughters. (From a liaison with one of these, Deidamia, Neoptolemus was born.) On the warning of Calchas, that Troy could not be taken without Achilles, Odysseus with Phoenix and Nestor searched for him. Coming to Lycomedes' court they presented to the king's daughters arms and stuff for weaving; the girls chose the latter, but Achilles revealed himself by seizing the arms.

During the first nine years of the war as described in the *Iliad*, Achilles ravaged the country around Troy and took 12 cities. In the tenth year the quarrel with Agamemnon occurred. In order to appease the wrath of Apollo, who had visited the camp with a pestilence, Agamemnon had restored Chryseis, his prize of war, to her father, a priest of the god. As compensation Agamemnon deprived Achilles, who had openly demanded this restoration, of his favourite slave, Briseis.

Achilles refused further service and rejected offers of gifts as compensation for the insult. During Achilles' absence the Greeks were hard pressed, and at last he allowed Patroclus to impersonate him, lending him his chariot and armour. Hector slew Patroclus, and Achilles, having reconciled with Agamemnon, obtained new armour from Hephaestus and slew Hector. After dragging the body about at the wheels of his chariot, he gave it to Priam at his earnest entreaty.

The *Iliad* concludes with the funeral rites of Hector. It makes no mention of the death of Achilles, but hints at its taking place "before the Scaean gates." The *Odyssey* mentions his funeral. The *Aethiopis* took up the story of the *Iliad*. It told how Achilles, having slain Memnon (*q.v.*) and the Amazon Penthesilea, was himself slain by Paris, whose arrow was guided by Apollo.

Achilles was worshiped in many places: at Leuke, where he was honoured with offerings and games; in Sparta, Elis and especially Sigeum on the Hellespont, where his famous tumulus was erected. Behind these legends there probably lies a real man, certainly not a sun-, river- or other god. No certain statue of him but numerous other representations in art survive.

BIBLIOGRAPHY.—L. Preller and C. Robert, *Griechische Mythologie*, vol. ii; A. Pauly and G. Wissowa, *Real-Encyclopädie der classischen Altertumswissenschaft*; Daremberg and Saglio, *Dictionnaire des antiquités*; W. Roscher, *Ausführliches Lexikon der griechischen und römischen Mythologie*; L. R. Farnell, *Greek Hero Cults and Ideas of Immortality* (1921).   (T. V. B.)

ACHILLES, TENDON OF, the large tendon at the back of the ankle. It is the tendon of the calf muscles that extend and invert the foot, and is inserted into the heel bone (calcaneus). According to Greek legend, when Achilles was born his mother plunged him into the Styx river. This made his whole body invulnerable except for the part of the heel by which she held him, and in this area he later received a mortal wound.

ACHILLES TATIUS (fl. 2nd century A.D., as recent papyrus discoveries demonstrate, and not 4th–6th, as previously believed), of Alexandria, wrote the Greek prose romance of Leucippe and Cleitophon. Nothing certain is known of his life. The romance, a typical adventure story of love triumphant over innumerable obstacles—shipwrecks, tortures, abductions and attacks by pirates—is related in the first person (an unusual feature in this genre) by Cleitophon himself, whom Achilles claims to have met in Sidon. The style is typical of Atticism, with its extreme purity of diction, short unconnected sentences, parallel clauses, detailed descriptions and frequent declamations and disquisitions, often in antithetical form (*e.g.*, on love for women and pederasty). Achilles shows uncommon ingenuity in inventing *coups de théâtre* (Leucippe apparently dies three times, but always reappears), but his characterization is poor, and plot is relegated to the background by numerous and irrelevant interruptions. His work was admired by the Byzantines, and translations of it influenced the development of the novel.

BIBLIOGRAPHY.—*Leucippe and Clitophon*, in Greek, ed. by E. Vilborg (1955); *Achilles Tatius*, Eng. trans. by S. Gaselee, in the "Loeb Series" (1917). *See also* E. Rohde, *Der griechische Roman und seine Vorläufer*, 3rd ed. (1914); F. A. Todd, *Some Ancient Novels* (1940).   (GI. G.)

ACHILLINI, ALESSANDRO (1463–1512), Italian philosopher and physician, was born on Oct. 29, 1463, at Bologna. Educated in the University of Bologna, he taught philosophy and medicine there from 1484 to 1512, except for a period between 1506 and 1508 during which he lectured at Padua and also disputed with Pietro Pomponazzi. An outstanding Aristotelian, he cites the commentaries of Averroës with respect. The human intellect he held to be a separate substance, one throughout the human species, yet at the same time the substantial form of the individual to whom it is united. He died on Aug. 2, 1512. Achillini's chief works, printed at Bologna, are: *Quodlibeta de intelligentiis* (1494); *De orbibus* (1498); *De universalibus* (1501); *De elementis* (1505); *De distinctionibus* (1510); and *Annotationes anatomiae*, ed. by his brother G. F. Achillini (1520).

BIBLIOGRAPHY.—*Alexandri Achillini opera omnia* (1508; augmented ed., 1545, 1551 and 1568); L. Münster, "A. Achillini, anatomico e filosofo," *Rivista di storia delle scienze mediche e naturali*, vol. xv, pp. 7–22, 54–77 (1933); C. F. Mayer, *Bio-bibliography of XVI Century Medical Authors* (1941); B. Nardi, *Sigieri di Brabante nel pensiero del Rinascimento italiano*, ch. ii (1945); and, for two manuscripts attributed to Achillini, "Appunti sull' averroista A. Achillini," *Giornale critico della filosofia italiana*, ser. 3, vol. viii, pp. 67–108 (1954); L. Thorndike, *History of Magic and Experimental Science*, vol. v, pp. 37–49 (1941).
                                                        (H. S. M.)

ACHIMENES, a genus of plants (family Gesneriaceae, to which belong also Gloxinia, Streptocarpus and the African violet), natives of tropical America, well known in cultivation as stove or warm greenhouse plants. There are over 30 species and many horticultural varieties, among the finest of which are Little Beauty, Dainty Queen, Margarita, Carmine Queen and Crimson Glory. They are herbaceous perennials, generally with hairy serrated leaves and handsome flowers. The corolla is tubular with a spreading limb and varies widely in colour, being white, yellow, orange, crimson, scarlet, blue or purple. The plants need a rich soil of compost, peat and manure, with enough sand to lighten the mixture.   (N. TR.)

ACHIN: *see* ATJEH.

ACHINESE (ATJEHNESE), a Sumatran tribe originally of Proto-Malayan stock, but much mixed because of contacts with foreign traders, slave raids and willingness to incorporate any person or group. Achinese numbered roughly 2,000,000 in the 1960s (*see* ATJEH; SUMATRA).

The Achinese of northwestern Sumatra probably were the first people of that island to feel Indian influence. Prior to 500 A.D. they had accepted the rule of Indian princes and had embraced Indian religion. This led to ideas of state and of a graded society—nobles, middle class and serfs or slaves—which have persisted to the present. Later they were converted to Islamism and about 1520 founded an independent sultanate. For a time they maintained trade with the Portuguese, but the demands of the latter led to war and their expulsion from Sumatra in 1641. For the next 100 years the Achinese were dominant in northern Sumatra, but the expanding power of the Dutch ultimately reduced their influence. The attempt of Holland to gain full control led in 1873 to the Achinese War which lasted about 40 years.

Today western influence is evident in public buildings and in the homes of the well to do. Otherwise the native type of dwelling is the rule. This consists of a three-room structure of wood or bamboo raised high above the ground on piles. The front gallery serves as a gathering place for the family and guests. Behind this is the sleeping room, and in the rear, a kitchen. Furnishings are scanty but elaborate hangings are common.

Marriage is matrilocal. The bride's family adds a room or provides a new house and perhaps some land. These remain the property of the girl. Despite Islamic influence the position of the woman is high. Her dress consists of a skirt over trousers, a jacket and scarf and many ornaments. She does not wear a veil. The man wears a jacket or shoulder cloth and trousers of great width, over which a loincloth is draped.

Each town is supposed to have a mosque and a man's house. The latter is the night dwelling for boys and male guests. It also serves as a house of prayer and as a Muslim school.

See C. S. Hurgronje, *The Achinese* (1906); R. T. McVey (ed.), *Indonesia* (1963).   (F.-C. CE.)

ACHROMATIC LENS, a combination of two or more lenses corrected for chromatic aberration. *See* OPTICS: *Chromatic Aberrations*; PHOTOGRAPHY: *Photographic Lenses*; TELE-

SCOPE: *Achromatic Telescopes*; MICROSCOPE: *Compound Light Microscope*; DOLLOND, JOHN.

ACIDS AND BASES. Acid is the name loosely applied to any substance that, in water solution, tastes sour, changes the colour of indicators (*e.g.*, reddens blue litmus), reacts with some metals (*e.g.*, iron) to liberate hydrogen and "neutralizes" bases. Base is the name loosely applied to any substance that, in water solution, is slippery to the touch, tastes bitter, reverses the colour changes produced by acids on indicators (*e.g.*, turns red litmus blue) and neutralizes acids. Neutralization is the process whereby an acid and a base enter into a chemical reaction which destroys the characteristic properties of both and produces a compound known as a salt.

There are several different scientific definitions of acids and bases in current use; these will be explained below.

Among the industrially important acids are sulfuric, nitric, hydrochloric, phosphoric and acetic; among the industrially important bases are sodium and potassium hydroxides, sodium and potassium carbonates, calcium oxide (lime) and ammonia. Sulfuric acid is one of the most important of chemical products in the United States; the tonnage produced annually greatly exceeds that of any metal except iron. Sulfuric acid is used in the refining of petroleum, in storage batteries, in "pickling" steel, in the manufacture of fertilizer, etc. Nitric acid and acetic acid are widely used in the chemical industry. Among the uses for the former are the manufacture of explosives and of dyestuff intermediates; among the uses for the latter are the manufacture of plastics and of solvents. Among bases sodium and potassium hydroxide (*see* ALKALI) are used in soap manufacture; sodium carbonate is one of the important ingredients for the manufacture of glass and is used in the household as washing soda. Ammonia is widely used, in the form of ammonium sulfate, as a fertilizer; it is also the raw material for the production of much nitric acid. The details of manufacture are described under individual articles on acids; and, for bases under ALKALI MANUFACTURE. Here only the theory of acids and bases is considered. For the principles used in naming acids and bases *see* CHEMISTRY: *Inorganic Chemical Reactions*.

History.—In ancient Mesopotamia and Egypt, vinegar was produced by the action of air on wine (fermentation). Vinegar is a dilute and impure solution of acetic acid in water; impure acetic acid (vinegar) was utilized industrially by the ancients. Theophrastus of Eresus, in the 4th century B.C., gave directions quite similar to comparatively modern ones for the preparation of white lead pigment from vinegar and metallic lead. Sodium carbonate (obtained by the evaporation of alkaline water from arid regions) and potassium carbonate (from wood ashes) were known in ancient times; lime was obtained, as it is today, by roasting calcium carbonate. The manufacture of sodium and potassium hydroxides by the action of lime on sodium and potassium carbonates was also practised. The exact dates at which these substances were first prepared is unknown, but the manufacture of glass (which required sodium carbonate) was practised in Egypt at least as early as 1400 B.C.

During the middle ages, the alchemists slowly increased the knowledge of acids and bases. The preparation of nitric acid (aqua fortis) by the destructive distillation of a mixture of alum, iron sulfate and potassium nitrate was described in a work by Geber translated about A.D. 1310, and the preparation of sulfuric acid by the destructive distillation of iron sulfate was known before 1600. Still later, an explanation was sought for the behaviour of acids and bases. One of the early theories was that of Bertrand (1683), who suggested that ". . . an acid is a liquid body composed of small, firm and pointed particles, slightly resembling fine and delicate needles." He supposed that alkalis consist of "particles which have between their junctions pores of different structures" and that neutralization results when the needles of the acid enter the pores of the alkali. According to the phlogiston theory current early in the 18th century, such acids as sulfurous, phosphoric, etc., which are produced by combustion, were regarded as elementary substances. This misapprehension was abandoned along with the phlogiston theory and temporarily replaced by Antoine Laurent Lavoisier's doctrine (1777) that oxygen is the acid-producing element. About 1808–10, the researches of Sir Humphry Davy and of J. L. Gay-Lussac and L. J. Thénard on hydrochloric acid established beyond doubt that hydrogen and not oxygen is the element essential (although not sufficient) for acidic properties. The hydrogen theory of acids was extended by S. A. Arrhenius, who showed (1887) that, in aqueous solution, acids are partly ionized—separated into electrically charged particles called ions. He further suggested that an acid should be defined as a substance that ionizes in water to yield hydrogen ions; a base should be defined as a substance that ionizes in water to yield hydroxide ions. The definitions of acids and bases given above will hereafter be called the "classical" ones. For example, nitric acid was assumed to ionize according to equation (1a); sodium hydroxide according to equation (1b):

$$HNO_3 \rightleftarrows H^+ + NO_3^- \qquad (1a)$$
$$NaOH \rightleftarrows Na^+ + OH^- \qquad (1b)$$

The characteristic properties of acids and bases were ascribed respectively to the hydrogen ion, H^+, and the hydroxide ion, OH^-. A substance containing hydrogen that does not ionize in aqueous solution to produce hydrogen ions (*e.g.*, methane, CH_4) is then not an acid. In qualitative terms, a strong acid, when dissolved in water, largely or completely ionizes and thus produces a high concentration of hydrogen ions, whereas a weak acid when dissolved in water is only slightly ionized, and thus produces only a low concentration of hydrogen ions. Modern concepts of both acids and bases have been developed from Arrhenius' theory.

The "Hydrogen-Ion" Theory of Acids.—An enormous amount of evidence supporting Arrhenius' theory of acids and bases has been accumulated since the 1880s. (*See* SOLUTIONS: *Solutions of Electrolytes*.) It is a pertinent fact, for example, that a solution of hydrochloric acid in water conducts electricity and that, when the current passes, hydrogen gas is liberated at the negative electrode or cathode. In dilute solutions of the acid, oxygen is liberated at the positive electrode or anode. These facts (and many others) can be explained by assuming that hydrochloric acid in aqueous solution is an assembly of chloride ions, Cl^-, and of hydrogen ions. The hydrogen ion, H^+, exists in water only as the hydrate, H_3O^+ (H^+ plus H_2O), called the hydronium ion; the evidence for this statement will be presented later.

Many of the reactions of aqueous solutions of acids and bases can be explained on the basis of the ionic theory. For example, the existence of charged particles in the solution accounts for the fact that the solution conducts electricity. The existence of H_3O^+ ions (hydrated hydrogen ions) is consistent with the fact that hydrogen gas is liberated at the cathode, for these positively charged hydronium ions are repelled by the positive electrode and attracted to the negative one, where they are discharged; hydrogen and water are thus liberated.[1] Similarly, a solution of sodium hydroxide in water is assumed to consist of an assembly of sodium ions, Na^+, and hydroxide ions, OH^-. During electrolysis, the negatively charged hydroxide ions migrate toward the anode and are there discharged to form oxygen and water. The interpretation here advanced is made much more plausible by quantitative experiments on the changes in composition which, during electrolysis, take place in those portions of the solution near the electrodes (transference experiments; *see* ELECTROCHEMISTRY).

The ionic theory helps to account for differences in the strengths of acids and bases. Any acid, HA, when introduced into water, rapidly comes to chemical equilibrium with its ions (see *Quantitative Studies of Acids and Bases*, below):

$$HA + H_2O \rightleftarrows H_3O^+ + A^- \qquad (2)$$

Bases ionize similarly to give (OH^-) hydroxide ions. Such an ionization reaction may be essentially complete, as it is in an

---

[1] Although all acids when electrolyzed liberate hydrogen at the cathode, it is not true that all compounds that liberate hydrogen at the cathode are acids. During the electrolysis of the aqueous solutions of some salts, the weak acid water, rather than the salt itself, is decomposed. Such salts, however, have no acidic properties; for example, they do not redden blue litmus.

aqueous solution of the strong base sodium hydroxide, which is largely ionized even in the solid state; or it may be far from complete, as it is in an 0.1 molar aqueous solution of acetic acid, where less than 1.5% of the acid is dissociated into ions, and the rest remains as un-ionized molecules.

Neutralization.—The ionic theory is also useful in explaining the process of neutralization, in which an acid and a base react to form water and a salt. When an acid and a base neutralize one another, the hydronium ion (hydrated hydrogen ion) and hydroxide ion combine to form water; if equivalent quantities of the two materials are present, the reaction proceeds essentially to completion because water is only slightly dissociated into ions. The chemical equation for the reaction between potassium hydroxide and hydrochloric acid is written

$$K^+ + OH^- + H_3O^+ + Cl^- \rightleftarrows K^+ + Cl^- + 2H_2O \qquad (3)$$

which may be simplified to

$$OH^- + H_3O^+ \rightleftarrows 2H_2O \qquad (3a)$$

where the potassium and chloride ions, which do not really enter into the chemical reaction, are omitted. However, these ions are present after the neutralization; with the water produced by the neutralization and the excess water present as a solvent, the ions form a solution of potassium chloride (a salt).

Many acids ionize in water to give more than one hydronium ion; these are called polybasic acids because each molecule of acid can neutralize more than one molecule of base. For example, sulfuric acid is dibasic; it ionizes in two steps:

$$H_2SO_4 + H_2O \rightleftarrows H_3O^+ + HSO_4^- \qquad (4)$$
$$HSO_4^- + H_2O \rightleftarrows H_3O^+ + SO_4^{2-}$$

and forms two series of salts, corresponding to $NaHSO_4$ and Na_2SO_4; phosphoric acid (H_3PO_4) is tribasic and forms three series of salts. Bases (e.g., $Ba[OH]_2$) that can ionize to give more than one hydroxide ion per molecule are called polyacid bases. The characteristic reactions of acids other than neutralization and salt formation (e.g., the colour changes of indicators, the formation of hydrogen with metals and of carbon dioxide with carbonates) can also be explained in terms of the ionic theory. Furthermore, this theory has led to an understanding of the mechanism by which acids catalyze some reactions. For example, the role of strong acids in the bromination of acetone is explained in terms of ionization equilibriums. The explanations for the characteristic reactions of bases parallel those for the reactions of acids.

Groupings of Acids and Bases.—Some acids are inorganic compounds and some are organic compounds. Among the former are sulfuric, nitric, hydrochloric, perchloric, hydrofluoric, hydrobromic, phosphoric, sulfurous, hypochlorous and arsenic acids. The organic acids are further subdivided according to the structural feature in the molecule which is responsible for the acid properties. For example, there are carboxylic acids (acetic, butyric, benzoic, phthalic, stearic, oleic, etc.), sulfonic acids (benzene sulfonic acid, naphthalene disulfonic acid, etc.), phenols (phenol or carbolic acid, cresol, etc.), enols (ascorbic acid or vitamin C, etc.) and other types too numerous to mention.

Bases include the hydroxides of sodium, potassium, calcium, barium, copper, iron and other metals, as well as the hydroxides related to ammonia and to numerous organic compounds, most of which are amines (compounds closely related to ammonia) such as methylamine and aniline. There are a few compounds, such as aluminum and zinc hydroxides and water, which have both slightly acidic and slightly basic properties; these substances are called amphoteric.

The Hydronium Ion.—The hydrogen ion in aqueous solution was for a long time written simply as H^+. This notation implied that the proton (the nucleus of a hydrogen atom) could exist free in solution. The proton has no electrons around its nucleus and is therefore a small particle. Hence, the electrostatic field in its neighbourhood should be great. On these theoretical grounds, the existence of protons in aqueous solution appears doubtful. All the ions known to exist under such conditions have two or more electrons around their nuclei. A number of experiments have lent

support to the notion that the hydrogen ion exists in aqueous solution only as the hydronium ion, H_3O^+. Among these can be cited the fact that liquid hydrogen chloride is a nonconductor of electricity. This compound, however, when dissolved in water, conducts current well.

These phenomena are just what would be expected if pure hydrogen chloride did not ionize (i.e., if H^+ alone could not exist under the conditions cited). When gaseous hydrogen chloride dissolves in water, the following strongly exothermic reaction presumably takes place:

$$HCl + H_2O \rightleftarrows H_3O^+ + Cl^- \qquad (5)$$

X-ray analysis shows definitely that the hydronium ion does exist at least under certain circumstances. For example, the lattice of crystalline perchloric acid monohydrate consists of hydronium and perchlorate (ClO_4^-) ions. It is true that ions other than the hydrogen ion interact with water; moreover, hydronium ions in aqueous solution tend to combine with additional water to form heavily hydrated ions. But whereas, in crystalline and molten salts, ions other than the hydrogen ion can exist, there is no evidence for the existence of uncombined protons in either solid or liquid phases. (Free protons can exist under special circumstances in the gas phase; e.g., in a cyclotron.) In view of these facts, the hydronium ion, H_3O^+, will here be written for the hydrogen ion in aqueous solution.

Brönsted-Lowry Definition.—A broader definition of acids and bases was introduced by J. N. Brönsted and T. M. Lowry simultaneously and independently in 1923. According to this definition, any compound that can transfer a proton to any other compound is an acid; the compound that accepts the proton is a base. Two considerable advantages of the Brönsted-Lowry definition are that it can be applied to nonaqueous solutions and that it codifies and simplifies acid-base reactions. It is not inconsistent with the classical definition of acids in terms of hydrogen ions, but is rather an extension of the older concept. According to the Brönsted-Lowry scheme, all acid-base equilibriums are then represented by the equation:

$$Acid_1 + Base_2 \rightleftarrows Base_1 + Acid_2$$
$$or \quad HA + B \rightleftarrows A^- + BH^+ \qquad (6)$$

Here A^- and B are described as the conjugate bases of the acids HA and BH^+, respectively; similarly, HA and BH^+ are the conjugate acids of the bases A^- and B.

In such generalized equations the presence or absence of an electric charge on any particle does not necessarily indicate the net charge on the particle in question. It merely shows that an acid has one more positive or one less negative charge than its conjugate base, and conversely that a base has one less positive charge or one more negative charge than its conjugate acid. Examples of acid base equilibriums are shown in equations (7a) and (7b):

$$H_3O^+ + NH_3 \rightleftarrows H_2O + NH_4^+ \qquad (7a)$$
$$H_2O + CH_3CO_2^- \rightleftarrows OH^- + CH_3CO_2H \qquad (7b)$$

In these equations, ammonium ion is the acid conjugate to the base ammonia, acetic acid is the acid conjugate to the base acetate ion, hydronium ion is the acid conjugate to the base water, and water is the acid conjugate to the base hydroxide ion. (Water is thus seen to be amphoteric.)

According to the Brönsted-Lowry scheme, the existence of acids implies the existence of bases (and vice versa), just as the existence of oxidizing agents implies the existence of reducing agents (and vice versa).

It has long been known that an aqueous solution of pure sodium acetate gives a basic reaction toward litmus. This fact may be explained by equation (7b), which shows that the reaction between water and acetate ion produces some hydroxide ions, which are responsible for the colour changes of the indicator. In classical language, reaction (7b) is described as the hydrolysis of the acetate ion; in Brönsted-Lowry's terminology, it is called the ionization of the base, acetate ion.

The hydrolysis (equation [7a]) of ammonium chloride (classical) is similarly replaced by the ionization of the acid, ammonium ion (Brönsted-Lowry). A solution of aniline hydrochloride has about the same acidity as one of acetic acid; it is, therefore, both convenient and informative to state that the anilinium ion, $C_6H_5NH_3^+$, is an acid of about the same strength as acetic acid.

The Brönsted-Lowry definition considerably enlarges the number of compounds considered (on the basis of the classical definition) as acids and bases. The class of bases is expanded to include not only the hydroxide ion and amines but also the acetate ion, phosphate ion, carbonate ion, sulfide ion, etc., since each of these negative ions can acquire a proton from an appropriate acid. Similarly, the class of acids is expanded to include the ammonium ion, anilinium ion, the oxonium ion of alcohol, etc., since each of these positive ions can transfer a proton to an appropriate base.

Furthermore, the hydrogen (or hydronium) and hydroxide ions are no longer considered the exclusive bearers of acidic and basic properties; an example in which un-ionized molecules function as acids is provided by the phenomenon of general acid catalysis.

One of the characteristic properties of acids and of bases is that they catalyze or increase the rate of certain chemical reactions. There are a number of reactions, such as the hydrolysis (inversion) of cane sugar, that are catalyzed exclusively by hydronium ions; similarly, there are reactions catalyzed exclusively by hydroxide ions. But there are reactions (e.g., the decomposition of tetryl) that are catalyzed by all bases, reactions (e.g., the hydrolysis of ethyl orthoacetate) that are catalyzed by all acids and reactions (e.g., the bromination of acetone) that are catalyzed by all acids and all bases, the terms acid and base being used here in the Brönsted-Lowry sense.

The rate constant for a reaction of the third type can be represented as a sum

$$k = k_o + \sum_A k_A c_A + \sum_B k_B c_B \qquad (8)$$

where k_A is the rate constant associated with each acid present at a concentration c_A, k_B is the rate constant associated with each base present at a concentration c_B, k_o is the rate constant for catalysis by water and the symbol $\sum$ indicates a summation over all acids (or bases) present in the solution. In those general acid or general base reactions, the mechanism of which is understood, the rate-controlling step is actually the acid-base reaction; e.g., the reaction whereby a base removes a proton from a weak acid. Here the usefulness of the Brönsted-Lowry definition is obvious.

Lewis Definition.—G. N. Lewis has suggested (1923) a definition for the word acid which extends this class of compounds even beyond the limits set by Brönsted and Lowry. According to the electronic concept of valence (q.v.), a proton from an acid, during neutralization, becomes attached to an unshared pair of electrons in the molecule of a base. Lewis used the word acid to include all substances which, during a chemical reaction, become attached to an unshared pair of electrons in some other molecule. This definition includes, besides the conventional acids, such substances as aluminum chloride, boron trifluoride and zinc chloride.

For example, boron trifluoride (see equation [9a]) reacts with ammonia much as does hydrogen chloride (equation [9b]). The electronic structures of the reactants and reaction products are shown in equations (9a) and (9b):

$$\begin{array}{ccc}
\text{H} & \;\; :\ddot{\text{F}}: & \text{H} \quad :\ddot{\text{F}}: \\
\text{H}:\ddot{\text{N}}: + \text{B}:\text{F}: & \longrightarrow & \text{H}:\overset{+}{\text{N}}:\text{B}:\ddot{\text{F}}: \\
\text{H} & \;\; :\ddot{\text{F}}: & \text{H} \quad :\ddot{\text{F}}: \\
\end{array} \qquad (9a)$$

$$\begin{array}{ccc}
\text{H} & & \text{H} \\
\text{H}:\ddot{\text{N}}: + \text{H}:\ddot{\text{Cl}}: & \longrightarrow & \text{H}:\ddot{\text{N}}:\text{H}^+ + :\ddot{\text{Cl}}:^- \\
\text{H} & & \text{H} \\
\end{array} \qquad (9b)$$

Furthermore, in certain nonaqueous solvents, boron trifluoride and aluminum chloride react with indicators to produce the same colour changes produced by conventional acids; these same reagents catalyze many reactions (e.g., the Friedel-Crafts reaction) which are known to be acid catalyzed. It should be noted that the Lewis definition of acid departs from both the classical and Brönsted-Lowry use of the word in that hydrogen is no longer considered essential to acidity.

The analogy which Lewis has pointed out between conventional acids such as sulfuric and materials such as boron fluoride is an important one. Whether these materials should be called acids is a matter of nomenclature depending on personal preference and usage. Most chemists, however, refer specifically to the substances in question as "Lewis acids" or as "electrophilic reagents" or as "cationoid reagents."

Quantitative Studies of Acids and Bases.—It has previously been pointed out that those acids which in aqueous solution are largely dissociated into ions are called strong acids; those which under similar conditions are only slightly dissociated are called weak acids. There have been many quantitative investigations of the strengths of acids in various solvents; here only aqueous solutions will be discussed.

In water, any acid HA is ionized according to equation (2),

$$\text{HA} + \text{H}_2\text{O} \rightleftharpoons \text{H}_3\text{O}^+ + \text{A}^- \qquad (2)$$

The equilibrium constant for the reaction is represented by equation (10):

$$\frac{[\text{H}_3\text{O}^+][\text{A}^-]}{[\text{HA}]} = \text{K}_A \qquad (10)$$

where the expressions in brackets represent the activities of the acid and its ions. (The activity of each ion or molecule is approximated in dilute solution by its concentration; see THERMODYNAMICS: *The Equilibrium Constant.*) The activity of water is omitted from equation (10) because it is for all practical purposes constant and can therefore be included in the equilibrium constant K_A. A strong acid then is one with a large value for its ionization constant K_A; indeed, the value of this constant is a quantitative measure of the strength of the acid in question. In accordance with the equation (10), the more dilute the solution, the more extensively is the acid ionized. If it is possible by some analytical technique to determine the concentration of hydronium ions in solution, where the gross concentration of ionized and unionized acid is known, K_A may be computed.

No purely chemical method of analysis for H_3O^+ can succeed because, when hydronium ions are removed by any reaction whatsoever, the equilibrium (2) is rapidly re-established and more acid is ionized. Chemical methods, therefore, determine only the gross amount of acid present, not the amount ionized at any given moment; these methods are then useful for quantitative analysis of solutions of acids and bases.

There are, however, many physical methods for determining the momentary concentration (or activity) of the hydronium ions. (See HYDROGEN IONS: *Indicators of pH; Glass Electrode.*) They include colorimetric, conductometric, electrometric, catalytic and other methods. Here only the colorimetric method will be outlined, as an example of the type of procedure that can be employed.

If the ion A^- or the acid HA is coloured, or if both are coloured and the colours differ, then the ionization constant can be determined colorimetrically. The colour intensity per mole of the ion A^- is determined from a solution of its sodium or potassium salt; the colour intensity per mole of the acid HA is determined from an aqueous solution of a mixture of the acid in question and some strong acid (such as hydrochloric) which represses the ionization of the weaker acid. The concentrations of the ion A^- and of the acid HA are then determined colorimetrically, or spectrophotometrically, for any solution in which both are present. From considerations of electrical neutrality, the concentration of hydronium ion can then be computed. The method described can be extended to include ultraviolet and Raman as well as visible spectra.

The ion product of water, K_w, has been accurately determined (see equation [3a]) and from this constant and the ionization constant of any acid, the ionization constant of the conjugate base may be computed as follows:

$$[H_3O^+][OH^-] = K_W = 1 \times 10^{-14} \text{ at } 25° C.$$

$$\frac{[H_3O^+][A^-]}{[HA]} = K_A \qquad (11)$$

$$\frac{[HA][OH^-]}{[A^-]} = K_W/K_A = K_B$$

Here as before the symbols HA and A⁻ do not necessarily represent uncharged and charged particles, respectively; they are intended only to show that any acid has one more positive charge (or one less negative charge) than its conjugate base. For example, it is convenient sometimes to speak of the acid strength of the ammonium ion and sometimes of the base strength of ammonia; the two ionization constants are related by equations (11).

It is to be noted that, with an amphoteric substance, HA, the equations (11) relate the acid ionization constant of HA with the basic ionization constant of the conjugate base A⁻ and also relate the basic ionization constant of HA with the acid ionization constant of the conjugate acid H_2A^+. There is on the other hand no general quantitative relationship between the acid and basic ionization constants of the amphoteric substance HA itself.

In aqueous solution, sulfuric acid, nitric acid and hydrochloric acid are all strong acids; that is to say, they are all largely ionized. The ionization constant of hydrochloric acid and the first ionization constant of sulfuric acid are in fact so large that they have not yet been properly measured in water; the ionization constant of nitric acid, although large, is measurable. Most organic acids, on the other hand, are weak acids, and some of them are very weak.

Table I contains the ionization constants of some representative acids.

TABLE I.—*The Ionization Constants of Selected Acids in Water (25° C.)*

Acid	K_A
Perchloric acid (HClO₄)	Too great to measure
Benzene sulfonic acid (C₆H₅SO₃H)	Too great to measure
Sulfuric acid (H₂SO₄)	Too great to measure
Hydrochloric acid (HCl)	Too great to measure
Nitric acid (HNO₃)	*c.* 24
Bisulfate ion (HSO₄⁻)	1.01×10^{-2}
Sulfurous acid (H₂SO₃)	1.7×10^{-2}
Phosphoric acid (H₃PO₄)	7.5×10^{-3}
Chloroacetic acid (CH₂ClCO₂H)	1.4×10^{-3}
Formic acid (HCO₂H)	1.8×10^{-4}
Acetic acid (CH₃CO₂H)	1.8×10^{-5}
Carbonic acid (H₂CO₃)	4.5×10^{-7}
Dihydrogenphosphate ion (H₂PO₄⁻)	6.3×10^{-8}
Phenol (C₆H₅OH)	1.3×10^{-10}
Bicarbonate ion (HCO₃⁻)	4.7×10^{-11}
Water (H₂O)	1.8×10^{-16}
Acetophenone (C₆H₅COCH₃)	Too small to measure
Triphenylmethane (C₆H₅)₃CH	Too small to measure

It should be pointed out that most of the ionization constants that cannot be measured for aqueous solution can be measured or at least estimated for solutions in other solvents. The strengths of some representative bases are shown in Table II.

It should be noted that with the aid of equations (11) all the data in Tables I and II could have been presented respectively in terms of the ionization constants of the conjugate bases and acids.

The differences in acid and base strength among compounds of the types listed have to a considerable extent been accounted for. The fact that ammonia is a much stronger base than water is related to the atomic structures of nitrogen and oxygen. Oxygen, with a higher nuclear charge, does not attract the positively charged protons as strongly as does nitrogen. The fact that aniline is a weak base compared with ammonia has been ascribed to quantum-mechanical resonance (*see* RESONANCE, THEORY OF), and the fact that chloroacetic acid is stronger than acetic acid has been ascribed to the electrostatic effect of the carbon-chlorine dipole.

For some purposes, it is convenient to speak not of the activity of the hydronium ion but of the logarithm of that quantity. For a discussion of this matter *see* HYDROGEN IONS.

TABLE II.—*The Ionization Constants of Selected Bases in Water (25° C.)*

Base	K_B
Sodium hydroxide (NaOH)	Too great to measure
Guanidine (NH₂C[NH]NH₂)	Too great to measure
Diethylamine ([C₂H₅]₂NH)	9.6×10^{-4}
Ammonia (NH₃)	1.8×10^{-5}
Diethanolamine ([C₂H₄OH]₂NH)	7.6×10^{-7}
Diethylaniline (C₆H₅N[C₂H₅]₂)	3.7×10^{-8}
Aniline (C₆H₅NH₂)	4.6×10^{-10}
Water	1.8×10^{-16}
Urea ([NH₂]₂CO)	1.5×10^{-14}
Acetanilide (C₆H₅NHOCCH₃)	Too small to measure

Nonaqueous Solvents.—Water solutions have been more thoroughly investigated than any other solutions, but the phenomena of acidity and basicity are by no means limited to solutions in water; in fact, nonaqueous solutions exhibit a broader range of acidity and basicity than do aqueous solutions. In water solution, no acid much stronger than H_3O^+ can exist, for otherwise it would transfer a proton to the solvent; similarly, in water solution no base much stronger than hydroxide ion can exist since otherwise this base would react with water and accept a proton from it.

For nonaqueous solvents, the classical definitions of acids and bases must be abandoned; the simplest adequate definition is that of Brönsted and Lowry.

Two solvents of particular interest, which illustrate the principles involved, are liquid ammonia (boiling point, −33.42° C.) and pure acetic acid (b.p. 118° C.). An acid dissolving in liquid ammonia reacts with the solvent according to equation (12):

$$HA + NH_3 \rightleftarrows A^- + NH_4^+ \qquad (12)$$

This equation is analogous to equation (2) for water. In liquid ammonia, the ammonium ion is the solvated proton; it functions as an acid.

Similarly, the amide ion, NH_2^-, functions as a base. Solutions of the ammonium ion in liquid ammonia liberate hydrogen from active metals (*e.g.*, sodium), change the colour of indicators, conduct electricity and neutralize solutions of amide ions. Both the acid in the ammonia system, NH_4^+, and the base, NH_2^-, exert strong catalytic effects on reactions carried out in ammonia.

Acids and bases function in analogous fashion in glacial acetic acid. Here the strongest possible base is the acetate ion; any stronger base reacts with the solvent

$$B + CH_3CO_2H \rightleftarrows BH^+ + CH_3CO_2^- \qquad (13)$$

Strong acids such as sulfuric ionize according to the equation

$$H_2SO_4 + CH_3CO_2H \rightleftarrows HSO_4^- + CH_3CO_2H_2^+ \qquad (14)$$

Solutions of both acids and bases in acetic acid neutralize one another, conduct electricity and strongly catalyze chemical reactions.

"Hard-Soft" Rule.—A rule for acid-base reactions, formulated in 1963 by R. G. Pearson of Northwestern University, takes into account the "hard" or "soft" nature of the electron clouds of the atoms involved. According to Pearson, hard-with-hard and soft-with-soft acid-base combinations occur more rapidly and are more stable than hard-with-soft combinations.

See also references under "Acids and Bases" in the Index.

BIBLIOGRAPHY.—J. M. Stillman, *The Story of Early Chemistry* (1924); T. M. Lowry, *Historical Introduction to Chemistry,* rev. ed. (1936); F. H. MacDougall, *Physical Chemistry,* 3rd ed. (1952); L. P. Hammett, *Physical Organic Chemistry* (1940); H. S. Harned and B. B. Owen, *Physical Chemistry of Electrolytic Solutions,* 3rd ed. (1958); Hans Landolt-Richard Börnstein, *Physikalisch-Chemisch. Tabellen* (1950); Victor Gold, *pH Measurements: Their Theory and Practice* (1956); *Handbook,* American Institute of Physics (1957); R. A. Robinson and R. H. Stokes, *Electrolyte Solutions* (1955); R. G. Bates, *Electrometric pH Determinations: Theory and Practice* (1955). (F. H. WR.)

ACIREALE, a town on the east coast of Sicily in Catania province, is built on terraces above the Ionian sea at the foot of Mt. Etna, 10 mi. N. of Catania by road. Pop. (1961) 44,166 (commune). The cathedral (1597–1618) has a modern façade.

Other features include the baroque church of S. Sebastiano; the church of SS. Pietro e Paolo; the town hall containing a library, museum and picture gallery; an observatory; a fruit experimental station; and the sulfur springs called Terme di Santa Venera. Acireale is on the railway from Messina to Catania. Mineral water, leatherwork, wine, rice and herbs are produced and exported. Known as Aquilia by the Romans, Acireale was called Reale by Filippo IV in 1642.

The first part of the name is derived from the river Aci, which according to mythology welled forth at the death of Acis, the shepherd beloved by Galatea and slain by the giant Polyphemus. After the earthquake of 1693 much of the present town was built. During World War II Acireale fell to the British 8th army in Aug. 1943. (SA. G.; F. V.)

ACIS, in Greek mythology, the son of Pan and the nymph Symaethis. He was a beautiful shepherd of Sicily, the lover of the Nereid Galatea. His rival, the Cyclops Polyphemus, surprised them together and crushed him to pieces with a rock. His blood, gushing forth from beneath, was metamorphosed by Galatea into the river bearing his name (modern Fiume di Jaci).

ACKERMANN, KONRAD ERNST (1712 [1710?]–1771), German actor-manager, was born at Schwerin on Feb. 1, 1712 (1710?). In 1740 he joined the company of Johann Friedrich Schönemann in Lüneburg. Schönemann specialized in German adaptations of French plays (Corneille, Racine. Molière, Voltaire), and Ackermann's initial training as an actor consequently was along formal French lines. In 1749 he married the actress Sophie Charlotte Schröder, and with her and a good company toured in Russia, the Baltic states and East Prussia until the Seven Years' War forced him to move to the south and into Switzerland.

Gradually Ackermann developed a taste for domestic drama and a technique for parts in which he could mingle the comic and the sentimental. In 1765 he built a modest playhouse in Hamburg, but by opening night he was heavily in debt; dissension fell over his company, and the next year he had to lease his theatre, not regaining control over it until two years later. Shortly before his death. on Nov. 13. 1771, he turned the management over to his stepson, Friedrich Ludwig Schröder, who was to begin the "naturalization" of Shakespeare in Hamburg.

See J. G. Robertson, *Lessing's Dramatic Theory* (1939); H. Kindermann, *Theatergeschichte der Goethezeit* (1948). (A. M. N.)

ACKERMANN, LOUISE VICTORINE (née CHOQUET) (1813–1890), French poet, whose best work is imbued with a deep pessimism. was born in Paris on Nov. 30, 1813. Educated by her father in the philosophy of the Encyclopédists, she went to Berlin in 1838 to study German, and there married in 1843 Paul Ackermann, an Alsatian philologist. Two years later her husband died, and she went to live at Nice, France. In 1855 she published *Contes en vers* and in 1862 *Contes et poésies,* but her real reputation rests on the *Poésies, premières poésies, poésies philosophiques* (1874). a volume of sombre and powerful verse, expressing her revolt against human suffering. She died at Nice on Aug. 2, 1890.

ACKERMANN, RUDOLPH (1764–1834), Anglo-German inventor who promoted the fashion for coloured prints. He was born on April 20, 1764, at Stolberg in Saxony. In his youth he visited various German towns and Paris; later he settled in London where he made designs for coach-builders. In 1795 he married an Englishwoman and established a print shop and drawing school in the Strand, London. In 1801 he patented a method for rendering paper and cloth waterproof. He was also responsible for the invention of movable carriage axles.

In the artistic sphere Ackermann perfected the aquatint and was among the first in England to establish lithography as a fine art for which, in 1817, he set up a press. His new lithographic process was used in his monthly publication, *The Repository of Arts,* to which Thomas Rowlandson and other artists were contributors. In 1822 he introduced the illustrated annual from Germany, and in 1825 edited the English annual *Forget-me-not.* He published illustrated volumes of topography and travel including histories of the colleges at Oxford and Cambridge. He did much to help foreign exiles in London.

Ackermann died at Finchley, Middlesex, on March 30, 1834.

See W. J. Burke, *Rudolph Ackermann, Promoter of the Arts and Sciences* (1935).

ACKNOWLEDGMENT, a term used in law in various connections, is a written admission that something has been given or done. In the United States it usually refers to a certificate of a public officer, the notary public, that a grantor of a deed has come to him and declared that he executed the instrument. *See* COMMERCIAL PAPER; REAL PROPERTY AND CONVEYANCING, LAWS OF; NOTARY. (A. DM.)

ACMITE (AEGIRITE): *see* PYROXENE.

ACNE: *see* SKIN, DISEASES OF.

ACOELOMATA, a term used in zoology to denote those animals in which no second body cavity (coelom) is present between the digestive tube and the body wall. Although the name has no special taxonomic rank, it serves as a convenient category for the flatworms (Platyhelminthes) and ribbon worms (Nemertinea). *See* FLATWORM; RIBBON WORM.

ACOEMETI, Latinized form of a Greek word (*akoimetai*) meaning "sleepless ones," which was applied to the monks of the Byzantine monastery at Irenaion (Tchiboukli), on the Asiatic shore of the Bosporus, because the divine office never ceased to be sung there, day or night. The monastery was first founded in Constantinople, *c.* 400, by St. Alexander, who after long study of the Bible put into practice his conviction that God should be perpetually praised by arranging for relays of monks to relieve one another without pause in the choir offices. They also practised absolute poverty and were vigorous missionaries. The idea, new to Eastern monasticism, attracted so many monks from other convents that hostility toward Alexander developed. Driven from Constantinople, he founded another monastery in Bithynia. After his death, in about 430, his successor, Abbot John, transferred the foundation to Irenaion, where the local people gave the monks the name of Acoemeti. In their enthusiastic attacks on the Monophysites, the Acoemeti fell into Nestorian error, and little is heard of them after the 6th century, when they were excommunicated by Pope John II. Later (the date is unknown) they moved their monastery to Constantinople, and they are known to have been in existence as late as the 12th century. They had a famous monastic library.

BIBLIOGRAPHY.—E. Marin in *Dictionnaire de théologie catholique,* vol. i, col. 304–308 (1903); J. Pargoire in *Dictionnaire d'archéologie chrétienne et de liturgie,* vol. i, col. 307–321 (1907); A. Vailhé in A. Baudrillart (ed.), *Dictionnaire d'histoire et de géographie ecclésiastiques,* vol. i, col. 274–282 (1912).

ACOLYTE, the highest of the four minor orders in the Latin Church. As its name suggests (Gr. *akolouthos,* "server," "companion," "follower"), the office, like that of the subdiaconate with which it is most often associated in ecclesiastical documents, was created in order to assist the deacons, who in a rapidly expanding church were no longer able to cope with all the duties traditionally assigned them (*see* DEACON).

The first probable reference to the office dates from the time of Pope Victor I (189–199). Pope Cornelius in 251, in enumerating the clergy of Rome, speaks of 42 acolytes active in the city's seven regions (Eusebius, *Historia Ecclesiae*). After the 4th century, Roman documents mention them frequently. Cyprian (d. 258) witnesses to their existence in north Africa. where their role however seems to have been limited to "carrying candles when the Gospel is read and the Sacrifice offered" and to the personal service of the bishop. Elsewhere in the west, until the fusion of the Gallican and Roman rites after the 9th century, the office was virtually unknown.

From the 10th century the order was gradually introduced everywhere as one of the four minor orders leading to the priesthood (the other three being porters, lectors and exorcists). It was so defined by the council of Trent (1545–63) in reply to the Protestant rejection of the sacrament of holy orders. At the present time, as a result of the liturgical movement in certain sectors especially of the Anglican and Lutheran churches, interest is occasionally expressed in the restoration of the pre-Reformation offices of minor orders. In the east, though mention is made of acolytes in the Apostolic Constitutions (Syrian, 4th century), the order did not find permanent acceptance, and it is not used by any of the churches except that in Armenia.

The duties of acolytes varied, historically, according to the extent to which they were permitted to assist the deacons and bishop. At first their tasks were chiefly charitable. In time they acquired a more prominent part in the divine worship: to the acolytes was entrusted the *fermentum* (part of the Host consecrated by the bishop) to be carried to the titular churches of the city as a sign of unity; acolytes accompanying the pope carried the chrism to be used for confirmation, and sometimes, when the number of catechumens was large, they were even permitted to administer the sacrament of baptism together with priests and deacons.

Originally the acolyte was simply named to the office; the present rite of ordination (in the Roman Pontifical) derives largely from an early 6th-century Gallican rite. It consists in the ordaining prelate's exhortation and prayers, and the candidate's touching a candlestick with unlit candle and an empty wine cruet, symbols of his office: for according to this rite the acolyte's duties are to light and carry candles for worship and to prepare the water and wine for the sacrifice. These tasks are now generally performed by laymen. The order of acolyte in modern times is no longer functional, except as a preparatory rite to major orders. The council of Trent had expressed hope for its reactivation on the pastoral level, and the modern liturgical movement has stirred up some concrete suggestions about its functional adaptation to present pastoral needs.

BIBLIOGRAPHY.—J. Morin, *Commentarius de sacris Ecclesiae ordinationibus,* vol. ii, p. 209 ff. (1685); H. Leclercq, O.S.B., in *Dictionnaire d'archéologie chrétienne et de liturgie,* vol. i, pt. 1, col. 348–356 (1907); M. Andrieu, "Les Ordres mineurs dans l'ancien rit romain," in *Revue des sciences religieuses,* vol. v, pp. 232–274 (1925); W. Croce, "Geschichte der niederen Weihen," in *Zeitschrift für katholische Theologie,* vol. lxx, pp. 257–314 (1948); M. Righetti, *Manuale di Storia Liturgica,* vol. iv, pp. 276–283 (1953).   (G. L. D.)

ACOMA, the westernmost Keresan-speaking Indian pueblo, located in Valencia county, N.M., U.S., 54 mi. W.S.W. of Albuquerque on an isolated 357-ft.-high sandstone mesa rising from the piñon and juniper-dotted Cebolleta mesa country in which lie the village sheep-grazing lands and irrigated fields along the San José river. The total acreage of land is about 256,000 of which 94,159 was the Spanish grant of 1689. The Acoma reservation was created in 1928 and has been supplemented by purchased and rented land. In the 1960s the bulk of Acoma population lived in the daughter villages of Acomita (Tichuna) and McCartys (Santa María), returning to the old town for ceremonies, the most important of which are the winter solstice, summer rain dance, and harvest dance and St. Stephen's day fiesta on Sept. 2. Outsiders are unwelcome at all but the September fiesta.

BY COURTESY OF NEW MEXICO STATE DEPARTMENT OF DEVELOPMENT

SAN ESTEBAN REY MISSION, ACOMA, NEW MEXICO

Acoma was established no later than A.D. 1250 according to archaeological evidence and has been occupied continuously. The name is from the native term *Akóme,* "people of the white rock," who call their stone masonry, terraced-house town, *A'ko.*

Marcos de Niza, Spanish Franciscan explorer, mentioned the town in 1539; in 1540 it was visited by Coronado's army, then in 1583 by Antonio de Espejo, and again in 1598 by Juan de Oñate. A Spanish force was ambushed at the pueblo in 1598, leading to Spanish reprisals in 1599 that killed half the population and partly burned the town.

The first church was established in 1629 by Padre Juan Ramírez; in 1699 it was either extensively remodeled or replaced by the present adobe structure. Acoma participated successfully in the Pueblo revolt of 1680 against the Spanish, but in 1699 again submitted to Spanish rule. From a population of 1,500 at the time of the revolt the town dwindled to around 500 in the first quarter of the 20th century.

Acoma is an independent social, political and ceremonial unit, traditionally headed by a cacique, always a member of the Antelope clan. The war chief is the next most important official. The population is divided into 14 matrilineal, exogamous, totemically named clans, but the economic unit is the household. Religious organization centres in the medicine societies and kachina (masked god) cult into which both boys and girls are initiated. There are seven ceremonial rooms (kivas) in the pueblo. The secular government, post-Spanish in origin, comprises a governor and appointed and elected subofficials. Federal administration is by the united Pueblos agency of the bureau of Indian affairs in Albuquerque. Acoma population during the 1960s was reported to be approximately 1,400 people. *See also* PUEBLO INDIANS.

BIBLIOGRAPHY.—L. A. White, "The Acoma Indians," in *47th Annual Report of the Bureau of American Ethnology* (1932); E. C. Parsons, *Pueblo Indian Religion,* 2 vol. (1939); F. W. Hodge (ed.), *Handbook of American Indians North of Mexico* (1959); F. R. Eggan, *Social Organization of the Western Pueblos* (1950); M. K. R. Sedgwick, *Acoma: the Sky City* (1963); W. R. Hunt, *The Dancing Horses of Acoma* (1963); W. R. Miller, *Acoma Grammar and Texts* (1965).
                                                                    (N. F. S. W.)

ACOMINATUS: *see* CHONIATES, MICHAEL; CHONIATES, NICETAS.

ACONCAGUA, a province in the northern part of central Chile, bounded on the north by Coquimbo, east by Argentina, south by Santiago and Valparaíso, and west by the Pacific. It has an area of 3,812 sq.mi. and a population (1960) of 140,528. It is divided into the departments of Petorca, San Felipe and Los Andes. The surface of the land is mostly mountainous, interrupted by broad valleys, including the northern reaches of the famous Central valley of Chile, which lies between the coastal ranges and the piedmont alluvial slopes of the Andes. The major valleys, however, are transverse and include those of the Aconcagua and Ligua rivers, together with those of their tributaries. Climatically the province lies in a transitional zone between the arid northern part of Chile and the subhumid central part. The annual rainfall, which amounts to but a few inches, coincides with the winter season; summers are rainless, but the drought is mitigated somewhat along the coast by the presence of persistent fogs. Inland the skies are clear in summer and the temperatures are high. The natural vegetation (cacti, scrub and grasses) resembles closely the *chaparral* of the southwestern Pacific area of the United States, or the *maqui* of Mediterranean Europe. The valleys are highly fertile, and where irrigation is employed crops of alfalfa, wine grapes, fruits and vegetables are produced in abundance. San Felipe, capital of the province, is on the Río Aconcagua in a rich agricultural area, connected by rail (Transandine railway) with Valparaíso (80 mi.), and by rail and car with Mendoza, Argentina.

ACONCAGUA, a mountain in the southern Andes, commonly regarded as the highest summit in the western world (22,-831 ft. above sea level). It is on the boundary of Chile and Argentina in 32° 39' S. and 70° 1'. W. The peak of Aconcagua is in Mendoza province in northwest Argentina, but its western flanks build up from the coastal lowlands of Chile. While Aconcagua is of volcanic origin it is not itself a volcano. The first attempted ascent, made by Paul Güssfeldt in 1883, failed. Aconcagua's summit was first reached by Stuart Vines and Mattias Zurbriggen of the Edward Fitzgerald expedition in 1897.
                                                                    (J. L. TR.)

ACONITE (*Aconitum*), a genus of flowering herbs belonging to the Ranunculaceae (*q.v.;* buttercup, crowfoot) family, includes many species which grow in cool, damp, mountainous areas of the northern hemisphere. The common names monkshood and friar's-cap are descriptive of the helmet- or hood-shaped blue or yellow flowers of the plant. The synonym wolfsbane indicates its poisonous nature. The aconites are ornamental, hardy perennials which are propagated by divisions of the roots or by seed. Prolonged storage and drying of the seeds results in a decreased ability to germinate.

Medicinally, aconite refers to the dried root of *Aconitum napellus,* which is extracted to provide useful tinctures and fluid extracts. Aconitine, an alkaloid present in the roots, is responsible for the pharmacological actions of the plant. The roots of *Aconitum ferox* are the source of the famous Indian (Nepalese) poison known as bikh, bish or *nabee. Aconitum ferox* owes its toxicity to the presence of pseudaconitine, one of the deadliest poisons known. Other allied species include *Aconitum lycoctonum, A. heterophyllum, A. paniculatum* and *A. spicatum,* all of which contain alkaloids with varying degrees of pharmacological potency.

J. HORACE MCFARLAND CO.

COMMON MONKSHOOD (ACONITUM NAPELLUS)

Medicinal Uses and Pharmacological Actions.—Since ancient times it has been known that aconite exerts a profound effect upon the physiological functions of the body. The ancient Chinese, Gauls and hill tribes of India used various species of aconite for preparing arrow poisons. The rational use of aconite in medicine began with the observations of Anton Stoerck in 1763. Stoerck described the tingling sensation, salivation and sweating caused by ingestion of the plant, and proposed its use for relieving rheumatic and neuralgic pain, for reducing swellings and healing ulcers. Alexander Fleming (1824–75) accurately described the actions of aconite in a report of a comprehensive experimental and clinical study of *Aconitum napellus* in 1845.

When applied locally, preparations of aconite produce a tingling sensation with warmth followed by numbness and anesthesia. These actions are not accompanied by redness, pain, swelling or other signs of inflammation, and the apparent irritation is therefore sensory. Aconite in the form of oil base liniments or ointments is absorbed through the skin. Preparations of aconite were formerly applied locally for the relief of toothache, neuralgia, migraine, rheumatic and similar pains.

Systemically, aconite in therapeutic doses causes a slowing of the heart rate with a slight fall in blood pressure and weakening of the pulse. If taken orally a numbness and tingling of the fingertips and arms occurs. Respiration is moderately slowed and laboured. Because of its action on the heart and circulation, aconite has been used systemically in the treatment of heart disease, hypertension and severe fevers. Aconite is seldom used in modern medicine, however, because of the toxic nature of the drug and its general inefficiency at therapeutic dosage levels. The local application of preparations of aconite to open wounds and abraded areas of the skin may also lead to systemic poisoning. The potency of aconite and its preparations is determined and standardized by biological assay. The assay consists of comparing the toxicity to guinea pigs of a tincture of aconite with the toxicity of a known quantity of the purified active ingredient aconitine.

Toxicology.—Poisoning by aconite may occur in connection with its medicinal use or by the accidental ingestion of the plants, which are grown in gardens as ornamentals. Aconite is rarely used deliberately as a poison because the tingling sensation in the mouth, stomach and skin warns the victim and is diagnostic for the drug. Full therapeutic dosage as formerly used may cause toxic symptoms consisting of giddiness, confusion, lethargy and a feeling of cold. Moderately toxic doses cause nausea, vomiting, diarrhea, difficult respiration, muscular weakness, cold skin, impairment of the special senses and speech, convulsions and death from respiratory or heart failure. Very large doses may produce rapidly fatal ventricular fibrillation. No specific antidote for aconite poisoning is available. The drug should be removed from the stomach and the patient kept warm. Atropine may be useful, and artificial respiration can be lifesaving. Intravenous epinephrine may be of value in extreme emergencies.

Chemistry.—The pharmacologically active ingredients of the aconites are alkaloids (*q.v.*). Aconitine ($C_{34}H_{47}O_{11}N$), obtained from *Aconitum napellus* and also found in the Soviet aconite *A. karakolicum,* is the acetyl-benzoyl-ester of aconine, a base derived from quinoline. It decomposes readily upon heating in solution to form benzoyl aconine (picroaconitine, isaconitine) and aconine which are only $\frac{1}{50}$ and $\frac{1}{2,000}$ as active as aconitine respectively. Small quantities of aconitine may be identified by mixing with a few drops of sulfuric acid containing ammonium vanadate; an orange colour is produced.

Other species of aconite contain alkaloids with similar chemistry and pharmacological actions. Pseudaconitine is obtained from Indian species of aconite: *A. deinorrhizum, A. balfouri, A. laciniatum* and *A. ferox.* Jesaconitine and japaconitine are found in the roots of the Japanese aconites. Bikhaconitine is present in *Aconitum spicatum,* and *A. chasmanthum* contains indaconitine. The base aconine is believed to be common to all aconitines.

(K. P. Du.)

ACONITINE, a poisonous alkaloid, the active principle of aconite, found particularly in plants of the monkshood or larkspur family. *See* ACONITE; ALKALOIDS.

ACONTIUS, in Greek legend, a beautiful youth of the island of Ceos. During the festival of Artemis, at Delos, Acontius saw and loved Cydippe, a girl of rich and noble family. He wrote on an apple the words "I swear to wed Acontius" and threw it at her feet. She picked it up and mechanically read the words aloud, thus binding herself by an oath. Therefore, although she was betrothed more than once, she always fell ill before the wedding took place. The Delphic oracle at last explained the matter, and she married Acontius.

ACONZIO (ACONCIO), **JACOPO** (JACOBUS ACONTIUS) (1492–1566?), pioneer of religious toleration, was one of the Italians who, like Peter Martyr (Pietro Martire Vermigli, *q.v.*) and Bernardino Ochino (*q.v.*), repudiated Roman Catholic doctrine and ultimately found refuge in England. His revolt against Roman Catholic doctrine, like theirs, took a more extreme form than Lutheranism. After a temporary residence in Switzerland and at Strasbourg he arrived in England soon after the accession of Elizabeth I. Aconzio had studied law and theology, but his profession was that of engineer, in which capacity he found employment with the English government. For some time he was occupied with draining Plumstead marshes, and in 1564 he was sent to report on the fortifications of Berwick. His importance, however, depends upon his contributions to the history of religious toleration.

Before reaching England he had published a treatise on the methods of investigation, *De Methodo, hóc est, de recta investigandarum tradendarumque scientiarum ratione* (1558), and his critical spirit placed him outside all the recognized religious societies of his time. On his arrival in London he joined the Dutch Reformed Church, but he was "infected with Anabaptistical and Arian opinions" and was excluded from the sacrament by Grindal, bishop of London. The real nature of his heterodoxy is revealed in his *Stratagemata Satanae* (1565). The "stratagems of Satan" are the dogmatic creeds which rent the Christian church. Aconzio sought to reduce dogma to a minimum in the hope of finding a common denominator for the various creeds.

ACORN SHELL, or acorn barnacle, popular name given to

sessile forms of barnacles common on rocks, piers, etc., on sea coasts. In the United States they are often called rock barnacles. See BARNACLE.

ACORUS CALAMUS, sweet sedge or sweet flag, a marsh plant of the family Araceae (q.v.), found throughout the north temperate zone. The name is derived from the Greek *acoros*, the classical name for the plant. It was the *Calamus aromaticus* of the medieval druggists and perhaps of the ancients, though the latter has been referred by some to citronella grass, *Cymbopogon nardus*.

The plant is a herbaceous perennial with a long, branched rootstock creeping through the mud, about three-fourths inch thick, with short joints and large brownish leaf-scars.

The leaves are tufted, flat, swordlike, sweet scented, three or four feet long and about an inch wide, closely arranged in two rows as in the true flag (*Iris*); the tall flowering stems (scapes), which very much resemble the leaves, bear an apparently lateral, blunt, tapering, spikelike cluster (spadix) of densely packed, very small flowers.

A long leaf (spathe) borne immediately below the cluster forms an apparent continuation of the scape, though really a lateral outgrowth from it, the spadix being terminal. The rootstock yields the drug calamus, and a variegated form is cultivated for ornament.

ACOSMISM. This term was coined by Fichte and Hegel on the model of the term atheism (q.v.). According to the ordinary view, reality consists of God and a world (cosmos) of finite objects usually conceived as having been created by Him and made to conform to certain laws. Now atheism is the theory which denies the existence of God, and so identifies reality with a godless world of objects and events which exist of themselves and have an inherent order of their own. Acosmism is the contrary view that denies the independent reality of a world of finite objects and events, and regards God as the sole ultimate reality. In accordance with the common practice of denouncing anybody as an atheist whose conception of God was different from theirs, Spinoza was generally described as an atheist by his contemporaries and others. Hegel protested against the injustice of this. Spinoza, he said, was so far from denying the existence of God that he acknowledged no other ultimate reality—so far from being an atheist he was an acosmist. Fichte similarly applied the term to himself in reply to similar accusations. The term acosmism has since been applied also to philosophies like those of the Vedanta, of Buddhism, and of Schopenhauer. Apart from its polemical uses the term acosmism, with its suggestion of an illusory world, is not a happy equivalent of the term pantheism. Strictly speaking, a pantheism like that of Spinoza no more denies the reality of the world than it denies the reality of God. It simply identifies the universe with God, and for that very reason regards the universe all the more as a world of order, a real cosmos. Moreover, there is an important sense in which pantheism is essentially cosmic, namely, in the sense that it regards man from the standpoint of the universe, instead of regarding the universe from the point of view of man. Acosmism is therefore not only an inadequate but also a misleading description of pantheism (q.v.).

ACOSTA, JOAQUÍN (1800–1852), Colombian scientist, historian and statesman, an officer in the patriot army under Simón Bolívar, who set himself the task of reviving Colombia's colourful past for his young fellow countrymen, was born in Guaduas, on Dec. 29, 1800. He first intended to reprint some of the chronicles originating during the period of discovery and colonization, but abandoned his plan on realizing that the accounts were incomplete, factually inaccurate and archaic in language. To fill what he considered a civic need, he composed his *Compendio histórico del descubrimiento y colonización de la Nueva Granada en el siglo décimosexto* ("A Historical Compendium of the Discovery and Colonization of New Granada in the 16th Century"), which was published in Paris in 1848. This work covers in 20 chapters the eventful years from Columbus' earliest landings and explorations on the mainland, in 1498, to the death in 1579 of the conqueror of New Granada, Gonzalo Jiménez de Quesada. The carefully documented account is based partly on Acosta's

findings in Colombian archives, partly on his research in the Archives of the Indies in Spain and partly on his travels throughout Colombia during military operations. Thus following the trail of the early conquerors, he was able to corroborate, or correct, the chronicles that served as his sources. Patriotism, humility and a succinct, unadorned, soldierly style mark the *Compendio*, as well as his many shorter historical and scientific works.

Acosta died in Guaduas on Feb. 21, 1852.

See Soledad Acosta de Samper, *Biografía del General Joaquín Acosta* (1883). (K. L. L.)

ACOSTA, JOSÉ DE (1540–1600), Spanish Jesuit missionary, who was the author of several works on the natural history of Spanish America, was born at Medina del Campo in Sept. or Oct. 1540. He joined the Jesuits in 1551, became a novice the following year and in 1571 was sent as a missionary to Peru. He acted as provincial of his order from 1576 to 1581, was appointed theological adviser to the council of Lima in 1582, and in 1583 published a catechism in Quichua and Aymará—the first book printed in Peru. After traveling to Mexico he returned, in 1587, to Spain where he remained thereafter, except for a visit to Rome in 1588. In 1597 he became rector of the Jesuit college at Salamanca, where he died on Feb. 15, 1600. His treatise *De natura novi orbis libri duo* (1588–89) may be regarded as the preliminary draft of his celebrated *Historia natural y moral de las Indias* (1590), which was speedily translated into Italian (1596), French (1597), Dutch (1598), German (1601), Latin (1602) and English (1604). Apart from his sophistical defense of Spanish colonial policy, Acosta deserves praise as an acute and diligent observer. Among his other publications is *De procuranda salute Indorum libri sex* (1588).

See Edward Grimston's translation of the *Historia* reprinted (1880) for the Hakluyt society, with introduction and notes by Sir Clements R. Markham; León Lopetegui, *El Padre José de Acosta y las misiones* (1942).

ACOSTA, URIEL (c. 1585–1640), Portuguese-Jewish philosopher and a significant forerunner of Spinoza and the Enlightenment, rejected revealed religions as false, and advocated a religion based on natural law and reason which would cherish life, property and human dignity. Born in Oporto to a noble Catholic family of Jewish descent, Acosta studied canon law and became the treasurer of a cathedral chapter. Disturbed by the conviction that there was no salvation through the church, he turned to the Judaism of the Old Testament. After converting his mother and brothers to his beliefs, he and the family fled to Amsterdam and embraced Judaism. Acosta soon discovered, however, that the prevailing form of Judaism was not biblical but an elaborate structure based on rabbinic legislation. Stunned, he formulated 11 theses (1616) attacking rabbinic Judaism as nonbiblical, for which he was excommunicated. Acosta then prepared a larger work condemning rabbinic Judaism and denying the immortality of the soul (1623–24). For this denial, the Amsterdam magistracy arrested, fined and deprived him of his books. A sensitive soul, Acosta was unable to bear the isolation of excommunication, and he recanted. Excommunicated again, he made a public recantation. This humiliation shattered his self-esteem, and, after penning a short autobiography, *Exemplar Humanae Vitae*, he shot himself, April 1640. Acosta's *Exemplar* attacks revealed religion as disruptive of natural law and a source of hatred and superstition. In contrast, the religion of nature and reason bids us love our fellowman.

BIBLIOGRAPHY.—J. Whiston, *The Remarkable Life of Uriel Acosta, an Eminent Freethinker; With His Reasons for Rejecting All Revealed Religion* (1740); Carl Gebhardt, *Die Schriften des Uriel da Costa* (1922); Carolina Michaelis de Vasconcellos, *Uriel da Costa* (1922); N. Porges, "Gebhardt's Book on Uriel da Costa," *Jewish Quarterly Review* (N.S.), xix, pp. 37–74 (1928–29). See also Karl Gutzkow's play *Uriel Acosta* (1847) and the novel by Israel Zangwill, *Dreamers of the Ghetto*, pp. 68–114 (1898). (Es. R.)

ACOUSTICS OF BUILDINGS. Acoustics of buildings, or architectural acoustics, is a field of engineering concerned with providing a satisfactory acoustic environment and good hearing conditions in every building. Acoustics is as important in the development of any building project as any other technical aspect of modern construction. Available information about architectural acoustics usually permits the design and construction of acoustically satisfactory buildings without need for later corrective measures. If the acoustics of a finished building is found unsatisfactory, it is often too late to do anything without great difficulty. Good acoustics must be planned in advance.

Everyone knows that an auditorium or a church needs special attention to acoustics, but few realize that the apartment house and the office building pose equally important and difficult problems, many of which can be handled with little or no additional expense. In a sense every element of design and construction of a building has some influence on its acoustical characteristics. The selection and utilization of the site, the horizontal and vertical interrelation of the spaces within the building, the general choice of materials and construction, and the shapes of rooms all determine the result. These matters of functional analysis, together with specific methods, will be discussed in the following sections.

ACOUSTIC ENVIRONMENT

Range of Sounds.—The table shows that the range of sounds that must be tolerated by the ear is enormous, extending from a threshold value of 1 arbitrary unit for a faint sound that can just be detected to 1,000,000,000,000 units for a very loud sound.

Intensity of Sound

Units	Decibels	Type of noise
1,000,000,000,000 . .	120	
100,000,000,000 . .	110	Airplane engine nearby
10,000,000,000 . .	100	Airplane cabin (normal flight)
1,000,000,000 . .	90	Heavy traffic, pneumatic drill
100,000,000 . .	80	
10,000,000 . .	70	Noisy office, telephone conversation, ordinary traffic
1,000,000 . .	60	Average office
100,000 . .	50	Ordinary conversation
10,000 . .	40	Quiet home, quiet conversation
1,000 . .	30	
100 . .	20	
10 . .	10	Rustle of leaves, whisper
1	0	

Smaller numbers to express this vast range have been developed by using the decibel unit, the number of decibels between two intensity levels being obtained by taking ten times the logarithm of the ratio of the intensities. Although the tolerable range is very great, the absolute energy of sound is very small, an average voice having only about one-millionth of the energy needed to operate an ordinary electric lamp. (For the general principles of acoustics and hearing *see* SOUND and HEARING.)

Noise.—A satisfactory acoustic environment is one in which the character and magnitude of all noises are compatible with the satisfactory use of the space for its intended purpose. Distracting noises can make it quite difficult to study in a library reading room, while the same noises might be acceptable in a large business office. But even in the business office there are limits of noise intrusion beyond which the workers find it difficult to maintain efficiency and composure. There is a wide range of acceptable background noise levels in rooms, depending on the occupancy, the time of day, the noise conditioning that the occupants have undergone, and other factors. A dripping faucet in the middle of the night can keep a person awake, while a gentle rain which actually makes more noise can put him to sleep. Noise, or unwanted sound in a building, comes from many sources: automobiles and airplanes, industry, adjoining apartments or offices, ventilating and air-conditioning equipment, typewriters, telephones, household appliances, children playing, and many others. A certain amount of noise from activity inside and outside gives the building life, but too much noise from any source can reach levels that actually impair health. (*See* also NOISE AND ITS CONTROL.)

"Acoustic Perfume."—We can understand the usefulness of a moderate amount of background noise in a case like a library located on a city street. Little attention is paid to continuous and expected traffic sounds unless something like a fire engine goes by. This background noise does, however, mask many sounds within the reading room, such as the conversations at the lending desk, the occasional telephone calls, the typewriting, the coming and going of other people. Privacy and lack of distraction

from the other activities in the room are made possible. This type of background noise is referred to as "acoustic perfume." The technique of hiding disturbing sounds with pleasant ones is sometimes the only solution to a problem of annoyance.

When a superhighway was constructed near a large country estate the owner was greatly annoyed. In his garden he felt the constant intrusion of automobile traffic. The solution he adopted was to install fountains. The splashing water hid the noise of the traffic, and gave the owner a sense of remoteness from the highway. There is a limit, however, to the use of noise as a "perfume."

GOOD HEARING CONDITIONS

In order to have good hearing conditions in any space, whether it be a courtroom, a church, a lecture room, an outdoor theatre or even a living room, it is essential that four basic requirements be met: (1) adequate loudness of the sounds to be heard; (2) good distribution of the sounds to be heard; (3) proper blending of the sounds with adequate separation for good articulation of music or speech; and (4) quiet.

Loudness and Distribution.—When sound is radiated from a source in free field, the spherical sound wave moves at about 1,100 ft. per second. The energy is spread over a sphere of increasing area, and the intensity decreases inversely to the square of the distance. When an audience is placed in front of a source (*e.g.,* a person speaking), the conditions found in free field do not exist. If the person talking is at almost the same level as the audience, there is an additional loss of intensity as the sound grazes over the people seated in the audience. This is especially important when the audience is on level ground (*see* fig. 1). The

FIG. 1.—DISTRIBUTION OF SOUND WHEN AUDIENCE IS SEATED ON LEVEL GROUND OUTDOORS

ancient Greeks and Romans understood this very well; they built their theatres on steep hillsides in quiet locations (fig. 2) and found that, with the audience placed at a very steep angle, conditions were almost as good as in free field. An alternative is to raise the source of sound high above the audience, but this is not usually convenient. A more satisfactory arrangement is to let the ceiling of the room act as a sound mirror, bringing reflected sound down on top of the audience to reinforce the direct sound. In most auditoriums more sound energy is actually received from the ceiling than directly from the source of sound. The ceiling is the most important surface in the room in assuring adequate loudness and good distribution. A ceiling in any room where hearing conditions for an audience are to be good must always be hard and sound reflecting, never sound absorbing. There is much misunderstanding of this point.

It is obvious that a listener must be seated so that he can "see" the ceiling if he is to receive useful reflections from it. If he is seated under a deep balcony, he often will not receive these reflections and will get only the direct sound which has grazed over the sound-absorbing audience ahead of him. The undersurface of a balcony should always slope, giving the people seated on the main floor a view of a large area of the main sound-reflecting ceiling. Many auditoriums

FIG. 2.—DISTRIBUTION OF SOUND IN AN OUTDOOR THEATRE OF THE CLASSICAL GREEK DESIGN

and churches have been built with sound-absorbing ceilings, and therefore require sound-amplifying systems for the spoken voice since ceiling reflections are lost. Without these reflections the members of a congregation do not hear each other very well, and each person feels as if he were singing or praying alone—there is little sense of congregational worship. This same principle of reflection applies to a chorus or orchestra. In order for the members to hear each other, and play together, it is essential to have a sound-reflecting ceiling not more than 25 or 30 ft. overhead. An orchestra finds it difficult to give a good performance in an auditorium filled with sound-absorbing scenery and draperies. Some surfaces in an auditorium can give reflections so long after the original sound that there are annoying echoes. Rear walls, excessively high ceilings and other distant surfaces can cause trouble of this sort. It is common practice to place sound-absorbing materials on these surfaces.

Sound Amplification.—If the background sound level is very high or if the volume of the room is too great, adequate loudness can sometimes only be achieved by using a sound-amplifying system. In general, the most realistic amplification is obtained when

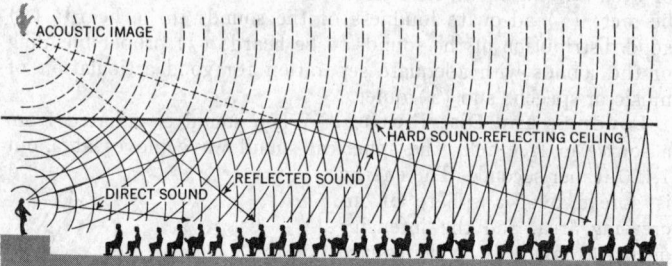

FIG. 3.—DISTRIBUTION OF SOUND IN WELL-CONSTRUCTED AUDITORIUM

the loud-speaker is placed directly over the source being amplified. The direction from which a sound has come is very readily located, so the amplified sound should come from the same direction as the original source. It is confusing to see a person speaking from the middle of a platform and hear loud-speakers at each side of the platform. Even worse is to hear a loud-speaker from behind when the original source is in front.

If it is not necessary to associate the amplified sound with the original source, as in an airport terminal, a distributed system of loud-speakers can be used. These must all be operated at a low level so that a listener hears only a loud-speaker that is near him. A distributed system of loud-speakers may be considered as analogous to a lighting scheme, in which each light covers a localized area.

Loud-speaker systems are often used when they are unnecessary. In a hall smaller than 50,000 cu.ft. a loud-speaker system is almost never necessary, and until the volume is greater than 200,000 cu.ft. it is seldom needed. In larger auditoriums many voices will need amplification, especially if the room is bigger than 500,000 cu.ft. In very large sports buildings, where the wall and ceiling surfaces are usually treated with sound-absorbing materials for the control of echoes and audience noise, a good public-address system is essential. Its design must be carefully integrated with the disposition of the audience and the shape and acoustical treatment of the building.

Blending and Separation.—The sound that is radiated by a source will fall not only on the audience directly and by reflection from the ceiling but will be reflected many times from all surfaces until all of the energy has been absorbed. This actually results in a persistence of the sound after it has left the source and is called reverberation. Reverberation time in a room is defined as the time required for the intensity of a sound to decrease to one-millionth of its original value. A longer reverberation time is desirable in a church, where music is important, than in a conference room. A concert hall should have a reverberation time somewhat greater than 1.8 sec., while for a multipurpose auditorium it should probably not be more than 1.5 sec. If it is too high, there may be too much blurring of successive sounds or syllables. If it is too low, there will be too much articulation or separation, and there will be no sense of fullness, especially for musical performances. While optimum reverberation is an essential attribute of a good auditorium, it is important to realize that it is only one of the four essential requirements.

Reverberation time is determined by the volume of the room

and by the sound-absorbing properties of the finishes, furnishings, and people in it. Sound absorption is specified in terms of sound-absorbing units. In most auditoriums the audience is the principal absorber of sound. Fabric upholstered seats, which have about the same sound-absorbing characteristics empty or filled, will minimize the variation in the reverberation characteristics of an auditorium with large or small audiences. If hard seats are used, the auditorium will sound more reverberant when it is empty.

Sound-absorbing treatment for the control of echoes usually produces the desired reverberation characteristic. The treatment of the entire ceiling of a room with acoustical materials not only deprives the listeners of needed reflections for adequate loudness but also results in extremely low reverberation time.

Quiet.—Unless there is quiet, really good hearing conditions cannot exist. Good hearing cannot be expected in an outdoor theatre in a city park with cars going by on all sides. An air-conditioning system for a church should not be so loud that it must be shut off during the service. Too much noise is very often the cause of poor hearing conditions.

Noise Control.—Noise control in buildings is achieved by means of: (1) proper planning to separate noise from quiet spaces; (2) proper design in detailing of structures to block effectively the transmission of sound; and (3) proper utilization of finishes and furnishings to absorb sound (drain off sound energy).

These three techniques are based on distinctly different physical principles. The first and simplest way to control noise is to separate the source as far as possible from the listener. In a school, the band room should be placed far away from the library and other classrooms. If it must be placed next to the library, the surrounding construction will be expensive, and the result will probably not be as satisfactory as if it had been placed far away. A television studio should not be located under a printing plant, nor should air-conditioning compressors be placed on the floor above an executive office. This relation between noisy and quiet spaces occurs often, and the solutions are almost always expensive and seldom completely satisfactory.

There are problems of noise isolation that cannot be solved by separation, such as neighbouring apartments, hotel rooms, offices, the psychiatrist's office next to his waiting room, and the Sunday school in the church basement during the regular morning church service.

Sound is a wave motion in which individual molecules of the air move back and forth at a rate determined by the frequency of the source of sound. This motion results in alternate compressions and rarefactions which act on the eardrums or other receiver. When these oscillating molecules of air encounter a barrier, such as a wall, they try to set it in motion. An effective sound-isolating wall or floor is one that is heavy, solid, impervious, with no leaks or cracks in or around it. The heavier the wall, the less it will move under the action of the sound waves. If it is lightweight, or porous, or has holes or cracks in it, the sound will be transmitted.

The amount that a construction reduces the transmission of sound, usually given in decibels, is called the transmission loss. In fig. 4 the average transmission losses for some common constructions are shown. Relatively high noise isolation can be achieved by using two separated heavy elements rather than a single extremely heavy unit. The transmission loss of a four-inch brick or concrete wall can be attained with a double plaster wall, using separated studs so that the two faces are not in contact with each other or resilient clips connecting the two plaster skins to a single set of studs. The equivalent of 12 in. of brick can be achieved with two $\frac{1}{4}$-in. sheets of glass, separated by 6 in. If the two elements of the wall are each reasonably heavy and airtight, and are not in direct contact with each other, they afford a much more efficient sound-isolating construction than a single massive unit. However, the control of the transmission of sound is governed almost entirely by the weight of the components.

Airtight construction can be very important in achieving good isolation between spaces. A solid flush wood door with a threshold crack has negligible transmission loss (perhaps ten decibels). With tight gaskets all around, it can have a transmission loss of 25 or

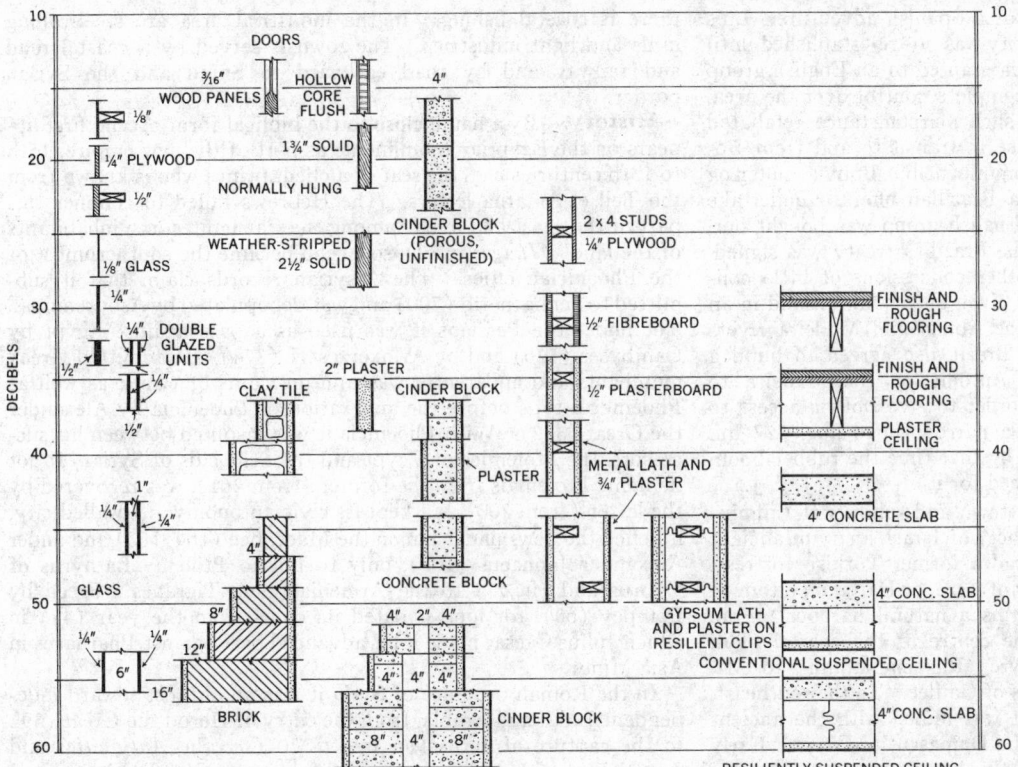

FIG. 4.—AVERAGE TRANSMISSION LOSS FOR TYPICAL KINDS OF CONSTRUCTION

must be understood. Sound absorption demands porosity which permits the molecules of air to move in and out freely. A sound-absorbing material, used alone as a barrier, permits a great deal of sound energy to go through it, and thus is a very poor sound isolator. A curtain hung over a wall, for example, will do almost nothing to increase its sound-isolation value. Sound isolation requires heavy, impervious elements. There is wide misunderstanding of this problem, and much time and money is wasted in attempting to improve sound isolation by the use of sound-absorbing materials. A common example is the home owner who nails standard acoustical tiles to the underside of the floor joist to improve the sound isolation between a noisy playroom and a living room. While the acoustical tile will absorb some sound energy in the noisy space below, it will add almost nothing to the sound-isolation properties of the floor construction. A plaster ceiling on the underside of the joists is needed, with the acoustical tile applied to it for reverberation control in the playroom.

Sound-absorbing treatment in a room, by controlling reverberation and spread of sound, gives a sense of comfort. Sounds stay where they belong and do not seem to jangle from everywhere. Everyone knows the difference between the sound of an empty house and of a furnished one. Sensible use of sound-absorbing materials can improve the acoustic environment in almost any space.

BIBLIOGRAPHY.—*Jour. Acoust. Soc. Amer.* (1929 et seq.); *Noise Control* (1955 et seq.); V. O. Knudsen, *Architectural Acoustics* (1932); R. H. Bolt and R. B. Newman, "Architectural Acoustics," *Archit. Rec.* (April, June, September, November 1950); L. L. Beranek, *Acoustics* (1954); C. M. Harris (ed.), *Handbook of Noise Control* (1957).
(R. B. Nn.)

30 decibels, which is enough to give adequate privacy in many cases. The back-to-back convenience outlet, the space around steam pipes and many other small leaks and cracks of this sort can ruin otherwise good construction. The design of a sound-isolating enclosure involves more than the choice of an adequate wall structure. Careful attention must be given to the proper detailing of all joints, inserted elements, and connections with the basic structure of the building.

Another difficult problem in noise isolation is that of impact sounds from spaces overhead. Pianos, footfall noises and the noises of machinery are transmitted directly through the floor construction. Carpets and resilient pads can help in reducing this problem. A piece of machinery should be mounted on resilient supports (specially designed rubber and steel spring mounts) so that there is no direct driving of the floor as a sounding board. Cork is seldom adequate for this although it is often used.

If extremely high sound isolation is required, as in a broadcast studio or a room for specialized audiometry research, it may be necessary to provide a completely floated interior construction, with the room itself forming an inner shell within the building structure. This involves many problems of resilient connection, of ventilation through lined sound-reducing ducts, etc., and is only necessary in extreme situations.

Sound Absorption.—In addition to planning for segregation of sound and designing and detailing structures to block effectively the transmission of sounds, one more control mechanism is available: sound absorption within a space. Every material in a room absorbs some sound, but those used for noise or reverberation control are usually soft, porous materials, like hair felt, carpeting, heavy fabrics and acoustical tiles. These materials almost always have fibrous structures which permit air to flow in and out. The air molecules in the sound wave encounter the fibres in the sound-absorbing material and experience a frictional drag. The spaces between the fibres must be very small if a significant amount of energy is going to be given up by the sound wave. This energy goes into heat, although the amount of heat produced is actually very small. A sound wave striking a one-inch blanket of hair felt can lose as much as 70% or 80% of its incident energy in heat and only 20% or 30% will be reflected back to the room.

The difference between sound absorption and sound isolation

ACRANIA, an obsolescent term for Cephalochorda, a subphylum of small marine animals, members of the phylum Chordata (*see* CHORDATE). The group is typified by the well-known lower chordate *Amphioxus* (*q.v.*).

ACRE, a state of Brazil named for the Acre river which rises on the Peruvian border and flows in a northeasterly direction through the territory to join the Purús river. The territory of Acre has a common border with Peru on the west and with Bolivia on the south. It lies entirely within the Amazon drainage system. The territory is in a region of heavy rainfall and dozens of rivers traverse its low, level lands. River boats provide the principal means of bulk transportation. Acre has an area of 58,915 sq.mi. and in 1960 had a population of 160,208. Its capital, Rio Branco, in the eastern portion of the territory, had a population of 17,245 in 1960. From the mid-1890s until about 1910, Acre was economically important as a rubber-producing area. Agricultural crops produced for local consumption include rice, sugar, manioc, coffee and corn. Cattle and hogs are raised on a small scale. The rivers contain many edible fish.

Until the 1890s when rubber gatherers from Brazil flocked into the region, Acre was considered to belong to Bolivia, although distances and jungles made tenuous that nation's hold on the area. In 1898, when it undertook to enforce its revenue laws by establishing a customhouse at Puerto Alonso (Pôrto Acre) on the Acre river, Bolivian authority was openly challenged by the rubber gatherers, armed by Brazilian entrepreneurs. Unrest and official indecision led to the proclamation of an independent state of Acre in July 1899 under the leadership of a Spanish adventurer, Luis Gálvez Rodríguez. Bolivian authority was not re-established until April 1901. About that time Bolivia granted to an English group a concession which gave it nearly complete control over the area. The Brazilian foreign office, fearing such a circumstance, retaliated by closing the Amazon to commerce in transit to and from Bolivia. Early in 1903 war appeared imminent but Bolivia, suffering from internal disorders, accepted a Brazilian offer to undertake the pacification of the area. The English group was bought out, and on Nov. 17, 1903, at Petrópolis, Brazil, a treaty was signed. Brazil received Acre and certain other concessions of little consequence. In exchange Bolivia was given 890 sq.mi. of land in an angle south of the confluence of the Abuna and Madeira rivers and an indemnity of £2,000,000. Brazil also agreed to build a railroad from the port of Santo Antônio on the Madeira to Guajará-Mirim on the Mamoré in order to give Bolivia access to the Amazon river. This railroad, a narrow-gauge line, 227 mi. long, was opened in July 1912, but by that time the rubber boom had collapsed and there was little need for it. (J. J. J.)

ACRE (Akko), a small seaport town and subdistrict (administratively within the Northern district) of Israel, a city of ancient Phoenicia and later of Palestine, and a former Turkish fortress, lies at the northern point of the Bay of Acre, or Haifa, on a tongue of land ending in a reef which forms a natural harbour. Pop. (1964 est.) 31,700. Acre is at the centre of the coastal plain stretching from the Ladder of Tyre (Ras en-Naqura) to Mt. Carmel and eastward to the foothills of Galilee. To the southeast, via the plain north of Nazareth, it was linked with the ancient caravan route from Mesopotamia and Damascus to Egypt. Early names for it were Egyptian 'Ak (a); Assyrian 'Akku; Hebrew 'Akko; Greek Ake, or in Josephus Arke; Latin Ac(c)e; Arabic 'Akka; under the crusaders, Ac(c)on, Ac(c)hon, or after the Arabic, Acre, Acri, whence St. Jean d'Acre, from the once prominent ruin of the hospital and church of the knights of St. John. The name Ptolemais, which was in use from the 3rd century B.C. until the 7th century A.D., is still the title of the Orthodox episcopal see.

The present town lies mainly within its Turkish ramparts of *c.* 1800. Its buildings date mostly from the 18th and 19th centuries but incorporate some remains of crusader times. There are four large caravansaries, one of which, Khan al Faranj, was originally that of the French merchants. The great mosque of Jazzar Pasha with its college, the citadel (Burj al Khazna), the Pasha's Baths (Hammam al Basha) and the covered "white" market (Suk al Abyad) are all of *c.* 1800. The Greek Orthodox cathedral (St. George) dates from early 17th century, the Franciscan convent from 1729 and their church (St. John) from 1737, the Maronite church from 1750; there is a rebuilt Greek Catholic cathedral (St. Andrew) on the site of the Templars' church. A modern residential and industrial quarter has been developed north and northeast of the old town. About 15 mi. N. is the Pilgrims' house of the Bahais, with the tomb of Baha'ullah (d. 1892), the chief prophet of the sect. Nearby is a government experimental farm.

In the old city Jews, Muslims, Christians, Druses and Bahais live and work side by side. Crafts are still carried on, such as the making of straw brooms and brushes, silver and bronzeware, earthenware and sponges, and

there is coastal fishing. In the industrial area are steel-rolling mills and light industries. The town is served by a coastal road and railway and by road eastward to Safad and the Syrian border.

History.—By a name close to the biblical form, Accho first appears on the Egyptian monuments as part of the new empire, 15th to 13th centuries B.C., the seat of a client prince who is known from the Tell el Amarna letters. The Hebrews failed to conquer this part of the coast and lived "among the Canaanites, the inhabitants of the land" (*Judges,* i, 32), so Accho became the southernmost of the Phoenician cities. The Assyrian records claim that it submitted to Sennacherib (700) and was depopulated by Ashurbanipal. Yet under the Persians it was used as a base against Egypt by Cambyses (526) and by Artaxerxes II (374). It admitted Greek merchants and apparently was minting coins of Greek as well as Phoenician type before the annexation of Phoenicia by Alexander the Great (332). With Phoenicia it was disputed between his successors, the Ptolemies of Egypt and the Seleucids of Syria. It got its name Ptolemais from the former (from 261), was recovered by the latter (from 200), but kept its civic autonomy. A walled city, it defied the Jews under Simon the Maccabee (164–163) and under Alexander Jannaeus (103), only to fall to Ptolemy Lathyrus of Cyprus and (in 71) to the Armenian king Tigranes. Freed by Pompey (63), for long it dated its coins from the year (47) in which Julius Caesar made it his advanced base against Pharnaces in Asia Minor.

In the Roman province of Syria it was an outpost toward independent Judea and Arabia, from the entry of Herod the Great (39) to the capture of Jerusalem in A.D. 70 (*see* the *Antiquities* and *Jewish War* of Josephus). From the emperor Claudius it received the Roman status of *colonia* (52–54). St. Paul landed there "and saluted the brethren" in *c.* 57 (*Acts* xxi, 7); and bishops of Ptolemais are known to have attended local and general councils of the church from *c.* 190. There is archaeological evidence that the inhabited area then reached its greatest extent.

Resuming its older name under the Arabs (from 638), it was developed as a naval base by several caliphs. It submitted to the invasions of the Fatimid caliphs of Egypt (from 969), the Seljuk Turks (from 1079) and the first crusade (1099). Then the best harbour on the Palestine coast, its seizure by King Baldwin I (1104) helped to establish the Latin kingdom of Jerusalem.

THE GREAT MOSQUE AT ACRE, BUILT IN THE 18TH CENTURY BY JAZZAR PASHA

For nearly two centuries Acre was a gateway for pilgrims and for trade between Asia and Europe. When Saladin took it (1187), King Guy and the third crusade made its recovery their first objective. The long siege of 1189–91 is an epic of medieval warfare, narrated in the Anglo-Norman poem *Carmen Ambrosii* ("Song of Ambrose") (*see* CRUSADES). Pending the recovery of Jerusalem, Acre became the capital and remained as such for another century. The walled town then stretched about twice as far from west to east as the present ramparts. It was refortified with a double wall (1202–12) which was extended (1250–54) to the north of the present line. It contained a patchwork of quarters or wards representing the religious and military orders of the Holy Land and European cities and nations. Not only for their merchants was it a base but also for St. Francis (1219) and his friars, *e.g.,* William of Rubruquis whose journal of his visit to the Great Khan was written there (1255), and for the journeys of the Venetian Polo brothers to China (1269, 1271). Twice threatened by the most powerful Mameluke ruler of Egypt, Baibars (1265, 1269), it was overwhelmed by one of his successors (1291). With its fall the remaining crusader strongholds on the coast were abandoned.

Out of its vast ruins the older part of the modern town has been built. There was little more than the Khan al Faranj (early 16th century) and some of the churches, when a semi-independent Arab chieftain Dahr al-'Omar began to rebuild about the middle of the 18th century. Ahmad al-Jazzar, the Turkish governor who replaced him, made the new town his capital and gave it much of its character, partly before and partly after the damage done by Napoleon's siege (1799). It was then fortified only with a new wall of medieval pattern, still to be seen in part behind the present ramparts, and the French attacks were foiled less by that wall than by the steadiness of the Turks and the ready aid of the small supporting British squadron. Afterward the present ramparts were constructed and the sea wall strengthened. Within these a Turkish garrison resisted an Egyptian army and fleet for six months (1831–32) before surrendering to Ibrahim Pasha. His subsequent victories over the Turks led to the bombardment of Acre by a combined British, Austrian and Turkish fleet (Nov. 3, 1840), and the fortress was restored to Turkey.

After the Allied conquest of Palestine and Syria in the war of 1914–18 the League of Nations included the town and district in the British mandate for Palestine (1920–48). In plans to partition Palestine into Arab and Jewish states, the town was allotted to the Jewish state by Britain but to a detached Arab district of western Galilee by the United Nations commission, whose report was accepted by the general assembly (Nov. 29, 1947). It was occupied by Israeli forces on the expiry of the British mandate (May 1948).

BIBLIOGRAPHY.—N. Makhouly and C. N. Johns, *Guide to Acre,* 2nd ed. rev. (1946). For ancient times: *Encyclopaedia Biblica,* s.v. "Ptolemais"; G. F. Hill, *Catalogue of the Greek Coins of Phoenicia* (1910), with E. T. Newell, *The Dated Alexander Coinage of Sidon and Ake* (1916); A. H. M. Jones, *The Cities of the Eastern Roman Provinces* (1937). For medieval times: *Encyclopaedia of Islam,* s.v. "'Akka"; G. Le Strange, *Palestine under the Moslems* (1890); Ambroise, *L'Estoire de la Guerre Sainte,* ed. by G. Paris (1897); W. B. Stevenson, *The Crusaders in the East* (1907); Beha ed-Din, *Life of Saladin,* ed. by C. W. Wilson (Library of Palestine Pilgrims' Text Soc., vol. xiii). On the ruins of Crusader Acre: C. Enlart, *Les Monuments des Croisés dans le royaume de Jérusalem,* vol. 2 and album (1925–28). On the sieges of 1799, 1831–32, 1840, Lt. Col. R. C. Alderson, R.E., *Notes on Acre and Some of the Coast Defences of Syria, 1843* (Works ed. by the Royal Engineers, *Papers,* vol. 6, 1844). (C. N. J.)

ACRIDINE, an organic compound, is the parent substance of several dyes and pharmaceuticals. The antimalarial quinacrine (Atabrine), for example, is an acridine derivative.

Acridine is a solid found in coal-tar anthracene. It is characterized by its irritating action on the skin and by the blue fluorescence shown by solutions of its salts.

Acridine and its homologues are stable compounds of feebly basic character, belonging to the general class of heterocyclic ring compounds (*see* CHEMISTRY: *Organic Chemistry*). They combine readily with the alkyl iodides to form alkylacridinium iodides, which are readily transformed by the action of alkaline potassium ferricyanide to N-alkylacridones.

Acridine has the molecular formula $C_{13}H_9N$.

ACRIFLAVINE, an acridine derivative obtained from coal tar, is a reddish-brown powder with antiseptic properties. Introduced as an antiseptic in 1912 by Paul Ehrlich as trypaflavine, it was used extensively in World War I but later was largely replaced by such chemotherapeutic agents as the sulfonamides and antibiotics. In solution it is used as the hydrochloride or as the less irritating base, neutral acriflavine, for irrigating wounds and for the treatment of gonorrhea. As a urinary antiseptic, it may be taken by mouth. (F. L. A.)

ACROMEGALY, a chronic disease characterized by overgrowth of the tissues, is caused by excessive production of growth hormone by the pituitary body. (*See* DWARFISM AND GIGANTISM; PITUITARY GLAND.) The disease is a form of gigantism occurring in persons who develop hyperpituitarism only after full growth has been achieved. It is usually first brought to notice by the necessity of increasing the size of the hat, gloves and shoes. The teeth of the lower jaw separate due to growth of the mandible, which results in a characteristic prognathism. The nose, lips, tongue, hands and feet broaden and enlarge, as do also the visceral organs. Treatment consists of X-ray irradiation of the pituitary. If loss of vision is threatened or if there is no response to irradiation, surgical removal of the gland may be necessary.

(A. GR.)

ACROPOLIS, in Greek literally "city at the top," is the general name in ancient Greek history for citadels built on elevated and easily defensible sites and usually forming the nuclei of large cities. By extension it can be applied to any such citadels, even outside Greek history. In several ancient Greek cities the acropolis survives, the most famous being that of Athens. *See* ATHENS; ARGOS; CORINTH; THEBES (Greece).

ACROPOLITES, GEORGE (1217–1282), Byzantine scholar and statesman, whose history provides a reliable and objective account of the Byzantine empire of Nicaea, was born in Constantinople and brought up at the imperial court which was then at Nicaea. He served John III Ducas Vatatzes, and his successors, Theodore II Lascaris and Michael VIII Palaeologus, and in 1246 held the office of logothete of the treasury and subsequently grand logothete. Under Theodore II he was active on campaigns against the Bulgarians and the Epirotes. He returned to Constantinople when it was recaptured from the crusaders in 1261, and his scholarly activities were interspersed with diplomatic missions. He represented Michael VIII in the negotiations for the reunion of the western and Byzantine churches which culminated in the second council of Lyons in 1274, where he acknowledged the papal primacy. In 1282 he was ambassador to John II Comnenus, ruler of Trebizond.

His *Chronike Syngraphe* continues the history of Nicetas Choniates and covers the years 1203–61. He also wrote theological and rhetorical works and poems; of these his funeral oration on John III is of special historical value.

BIBLIOGRAPHY.—Works ed. by A. Heisenberg in the Teubner series (1903). The *Chronike Syngraphe* is also ed. by I. Bekker in the Bonn corpus (1836) and in J.-P. Migne, *Patrologia Graeca,* vol. 140, col. 957–1220 (1887). For further bibliography *see* G. Moravcsik, *Byzantinoturcica,* vol. i, pp. 266–268, 2nd ed. (1958), and G. Ostrogorsky, *History of the Byzantine State,* pp. 371–372 and p. 409 (1956).

(J. M. HY.)

ACROSTIC, a short verse composition, so constructed that the initial letters of the lines, taken consecutively, form words (Gr. *akros,* "at the end," and *stichos,* "line" or "verse"). The fancy for writing acrostics is of great antiquity, having been common among the Greeks of the Alexandrine period, as well as with the Latin writers since Ennius and Plautus, many of the arguments of whose plays were written with acrostics on their respective titles. One of the most remarkable acrostics was contained in the Greek verses cited by Lactantius and Eusebius in the 4th century, the initial letters of which form the words *Iesous Christos Theou Uios Soter,* "Jesus Christ, the son of God, the Saviour." The first letters of each word make up the word *Ichthys* (fish), to which a mystical meaning has been attached, the fish being a symbol for Christ in early Christian literature and art, thus constituting another kind of acrostic.

The monks of the middle ages were fond of acrostics, as well as the poets of the Middle High German period, notably Gottfried von Strassburg and Rudolph von Ems. The great poets of the Italian renaissance, among them Boccaccio, indulged in them, and in 1599 the English poet Sir John Davies wrote 26 elegant *Hymns to Astraea,* each an acrostic on "Elisabetha Regina."

Acrostic verses, however, have been held in slight estimation from a literary standpoint. Samuel Butler says, in his "Character of a Small Poet," "He uses to lay the outside of his verses even, like a bricklayer, by a line of rhyme and acrostic, and fill the middle with rubbish." Addison (*Spectator,* No. 60) found it impossible to decide whether the inventor of the anagram or of the acrostic was the greater blockhead; and in describing the latter, says, "I have seen some of them where the verses have not only been edged by a name at each extremity, but have the same name running down like a seam through the middle of the poem." And Dryden, in *Mac Flecknoe,* scornfully assigned Shadwell the rule of "Some peaceful province in acrostic land."

The name acrostic is also applied to alphabetical or abecedarian verses. Of these we have instances in the Hebrew psalms (*e.g.,* Ps. xxv and xxxiv), where successive verses begin with the letters of the alphabet in their order. The structure of Ps. cxix is still more elaborate in the Hebrew, and in the King James version this is indicated in the translation by the successive letters of the alphabet standing before each of the 22 parts of the psalm.

At one period much religious verse was written in a form imitative of this alphabetical method, possibly as an aid to the memory. The term acrostic is also applied to the formation of words, from the initial letters of other words. *Ichthys,* referred to above, is an illustration of this. So also is the word "Cabal," which, though it was in use before, with a similar meaning, has, from the time of Charles II, been associated with a particular ministry, from the accident of its being composed of Clifford, Ashley, Buckingham, Arlington, and Lauderdale. In the 20th century a great many organizations were being named with this acrostic principle in mind, *e.g.,* CARE, the initials of Cooperative for American Remittances to Everywhere.

Double acrostics are such as are so constructed that not only initial letters of the lines, but also the middle or last letters, form words. For example: (1) By Apollo was my first made; (2) A shoemaker's tool; (3) An Italian patriot; (4) A tropical fruit. The initials and finals, read downward, give the name of a writer and his nom de plume. Answer: Lamb, Elia.

1. L yr E
2. A w L
3. M azzin I
4. B anan A

A curious and clever 20th-century development of the acrostic was the quadruple acrostic. The following, taken from R. A. Knox's *Book of Acrostics,* is a good example.

Uprights: Since there's no A, B, let us C and D.
Lights: 1. Reverse the name a schoolboy might apply, for briefness, to his weekly subsidy.
2. A lady thus (but with an S)
   In Southern lands you might address.
3. Initials seen on many a truck.
4. To cattle breeders brings bad luck.

SOLUTION

Uprights: "Since there's no help, come, let us kiss and part."
Lights: 1.   Hsa Cte Kco P (Reverse of pocket cash)
2.   (s) E n Or It A
3.   L. M. S. R. (London, Midland & Scottish Railway)
4.   P E S T

In the United States the Double-Crostic devised by Elizabeth Kingsley for the *Saturday Review,* beginning in 1934, had an acrostic in the answers to the clues giving the author and title of a literary work; the letters, keyed by number to blanks like those of a crossword puzzle, spelled out a quotation.

BIBLIOGRAPHY.—P. M. Pearson, *Acrostic Dictionary* (1901); R. A. Knox, *Book of Acrostics* (1924); L. C. Scott, *Acrostic Poems* (1924); Elizabeth Kingsley, *Double-Crostic,* 26 series (1934–52). (G. W. A.)

ACT, a statute or law adopted (enacted) by a national or state legislature or other governing body. Acts are distinguished from resolutions, which are usually used to express legislative opinion or to regulate affairs of the governing body itself, and from ordinances or bylaws of municipal corporations and rules and regulations of administrative agencies. *See* LEGISLATION; STATUTE LAW. (J. D. Ls.)

ACTA, the minutes of public business and gazette of political and social events in ancient Rome, began official publication in the first consulship of Julius Caesar (59 B.C.), in two forms: *acta senatus* and *acta diurna.*

The *acta senatus* or *commentarii senatus,* minutes of the proceedings of the senate, were published only occasionally and unofficially before 59 B.C. when Caesar ordered them to be issued regularly and with official authority. Augustus continued to keep them, but forbade their publication. From the reign of Tiberius a young senator was chosen by the emperor to draw up these *acta,* which were kept in the imperial archives and public libraries. Special permission from the *praefectus urbi* (city prefect) was necessary in order to examine them.

The *acta diurna,* which were called also *acta populi, acta publica* and simply *acta* or *diurna,* grew out of Caesar's arrangements for the recording and publishing of official business and matters of political interest. They were set up daily in a public place on a whitened board (*album*). After a reasonable time they were taken down and preserved with other public documents, so that they might be available for reference. Under the empire the *acta diurna* constituted a sort of daily gazette, providing an official account of noteworthy events at Rome. Its contents were partly official (court news, decrees, etc.), partly private (notices of births, marriages, deaths). Thus to some extent it filled the place of the modern newspaper. The publication of these *acta* continued until the transference of the capital to Constantinople in A.D. 330.

(A. H. McD.)

ACTAEON, in Greek mythology, son of Aristaeus and Autonoë, Boeotian hero and hunter. According to Ovid's *Metamorphoses,* having accidentally seen Artemis on Mt. Cithaeron while she was bathing, he was changed by her into a stag, and pursued and killed by his 50 hounds. The story was well known in antiquity; Pausanias says that he saw on the road from Megara to Plataea the very stone on which Actaeon sat as he gazed at Artemis. Several of the tragic poets presented it on the stage (*e.g.,* Aeschylus' lost *Toxotides,* "The Archeresses"), and many sculptured representations of Actaeon's death are known. Actaeon was worshiped in Plataea and Orchomenus. (T. V. B.)

ACTA SANCTORUM, a collection of the lives of the saints, compiled by the Bollandists. The work, first conceived at the beginning of the 17th century, was carried on thereafter, except during the period of the suppression of the Society of Jesus in Belgium. *See* BOLLANDISTS.

ACTING, DIRECTION AND PRODUCTION. The summits of world theatre are the Everests of dramatic literature and, as G. H. Lewes said, "the greatest artist is he who is greatest in the highest reaches of his art." But the sublimest theatrical mountaineering always begins before an audience, on one small, particular stage. Such masters of the drama as Shakespeare and Molière wrote for specific actors working within a specific kind of aesthetic and economic organization. Their work may be read with admiration in the study, but it is only in performance that it comes to life completely. Below those heights it is even more apparent that the play text is only one factor in the arts of the theatre and that its form, content and communication are intimately affected by the state of the stage. As critics in the 20th century came increasingly to emphasize, the history of acting, direction and production is integrally linked to the history of the drama. Upon the status and style of the actors, the ownership of the stage, the finance of "show business" and the control of its constituent arts depend, to a large extent, the dramatist's communication with his public and the condition of the theatre in general.

ACTING

Classical.—The essential words with which the nature of theatre is defined are of Greek origin: theatre, drama, chorus, tragedy, comedy, scene. The Greek theatre was a development from the primitive. But the theatre became a conscious creative art.

The actor occupied an honourable and special place. Contests were held not only for the best play but for the best actor. Acting began to be appreciated as a separate art and the discussions of acting sound oddly contemporary. Actors accused each other of over-acting and Aristotle censured the performers of his own day for representing degraded women. The speeches of the Greek plays created special problems, calling for strength, flexibility and emphasis in expression, but the drive toward naturalness and truthfulness gained as the art developed. The tragedian Theodoros was commended for his natural delivery, and his voice was described as sounding like a real person's whereas the others sounded artificial and "actory." The striving for reality or conviction in acting is illustrated by the story of the actor Polus, who is said to have taught Demosthenes elocution. In the scene where Sophocles' Electra brings on stage the remains of Orestes, Polus carried on the ashes of his own recently deceased son, and thereby expressed his own sorrow and pain.

Roman acting, like the Roman theatre, is shrouded in uncertainties. But the struggle between Christianity and paganism found the actor a victim, and at this time the conventional image of the actor was created, that of a vagabond, lascivious and vulgar, a mountebank, a comedian, whose sole purpose was to entertain. The rise of medieval Christian drama changed nothing in this respect.

The Beginnings of Modern Acting.—Modern acting began with the *commedia dell'arte*. The sudden efflorescence of these acting companies, the earliest mention of which is in 1545, is still unexplained. Until then, acting was an amateur occupation. The actor remained confined to simply illustrating the text by means of a narrow scheme of gesture and rhetorical speech. But in the *commedia dell'arte* the actor used only an outline, a plot; he improvised the play, giving free rein to the actor's art, developing his own characters or masks repeated in each play. Since this demanded high skill, the actors joined into companies. The actor became professional. By doing so he stimulated the development of modern drama. The essential requisite for the drama is its performance. The dramatist's creation finds its fulfillment not in the writer's study but on the stage. This fulfillment can best be achieved through the contribution of the professional actor. The amateur only repeats the words of the writer; the actor fuses with them and creates the real image of word and deed. "The professional actor is the prerequisite of great drama." (Max J. Wolff in Robert F. Arnold [ed.], *Das deutsche Drama*, C. H. Beck'sche Verlagsbuchhandlung, Munich, 1925.)

With Shakespeare the modern theatre created its major classic, and modern acting was fully born. It is unthinkable that Shakespeare would have created his major roles for actors who were unable to perform them. Shakespeare's "capital discovery is that physical action in itself and by itself is the least effective thing upon that stage . . . the why and the wherefore, what went before and what is to come after . . . they are the fruitful stuff of drama. From which it soon follows that not rhetoric merely or mainly, nor what may be openly said, but the thing only thought or felt will need to be expressed." (H. Granville-Barker and G. B. Harrison, *Companion to Shakespeare Studies*, Cambridge University Press, 1934.) It is not enough for the actor to pose and move and speak his lines magnificently. He must be able to create a character immersed in a situation, behaving in it and thinking and feeling beyond it. Shakespeare was aware that while the intention in acting is to "suit the action to the word, the word to the action," the real problem and mystery in acting is that the actor must be able "but in a fiction, in a dream of passion, [to] force his soul so to his own conceit." The exploration of this became the problem of the post-Shakespearean actor.

18th Century.—While the 17th century was taken up with the struggle for the acceptance of these principles, the 18th century dedicated itself to a deeper exploration of character and the actor's ability to fuse with his role. David Garrick (1717–79) "raised the character of his profession to the rank of a liberal art," according to Edmund Burke, who considered him "the first of ac-

tors, because he was the most acute observer of nature." His influence reached into the other arts and "his easy and familiar yet forcible style in speaking and acting, and the expression of the features from the genuine workings of nature" became the exemplar of 18th-century acting.

James Quin (1693–1766), who was more declaimer than actor, remarked that "if the young fellow is right, I and the rest of the players have been all wrong." Garrick's triumph was aided by the achievements of actors such as Lekain (Henri Louis Cain; 1729–78), described as "small, ugly and possessing a harsh voice," and François Joseph Talma (1763–1826) in France, and of Konrad Ekhof (1720–78), August Wilhelm Iffland (1759–1814), Johann Fleck (1757–1801) and Friedrich Schröder (1744–1816) in Germany. Discussion about acting and its problems flourished within the profession. Contrary to the philosophic ideas of Denis Diderot (1713–84) that "the possibilities of a good actor lie in the complete absence of sensibility," Luigi Riccoboni (c. 1675–1753), Remond de Ste. Albine, Talma and others concluded that acting demands a combination of "sensibility" (or "enthusiasm," "fire") and "intelligence."

19th Century.—The art of acting is kept alive by the performances of great actors: Sarah Siddons (1755–1831), the greatest tragic actress of the English stage, of whom Hazlitt wrote "Passion emanated from her as from a shrine. She was tragedy personified"; Edmund Kean (1787–1833), whose performances, "too often in the highest key of passion," were described by Coleridge as "reading Shakespeare by flashes of lightning"; Marie Dorval (1798–1849); Frédérick Lemaître (1800–76), whom Victor Hugo called "the greatest actor of his day, and perhaps the greatest of all time," who would have failed his examination at the Conservatoire except for Talma's voice saying "He has that which cannot be taught: the holy fire [spirit]"; Rachel (1820–58), who died early leaving a tradition of tragic acting which has hardly been surpassed; Gabrielle Réjane (1857–1920), who stated "I understand only what I feel, and I feel only what I also understand"; Ludwig Devrient (1784–1832), who after one of his death scenes, when he regained his senses, said, "I thought I had really died."

But by the last quarter of the 19th century the emphasis had shifted from the individual to the ensemble. The Meiningen players, though containing few outstanding actors, set a standard for ensemble acting and attention to the details of staging which proved what the actor of lesser talent could accomplish with proper direction. At the same time a number of Italian actors again electrified Europe with their terrific temperament and almost brutal theatrical realism. Ernesto Rossi (1827–96), Adelaide Ristori (1822–1906), Tommaso Salvini (1829–1915), Ermete Novelli (1851–1919), Ermete Zacconi (1867–1948) and Giovanni Grasso (1875–1930) were able to play both classics and contemporary plays. The appearance of Eleonora Duse (1859–1924) was a fitting climax. With a sensitivity so extreme that she could blush on the stage, yet simple and unmelodramatic, with gestures of great beauty and expressiveness, she set a standard for future generations.

Stanislavski.—Stimulated by this activity and supported by the traditions of the best of Russian acting, Konstantin Stanislavski (1863–1938) set himself to fuse all the random thought and experiences into a form that could help the beginner and be of service to the experienced actor. His aim was to find a "grammar of acting," to achieve that level of inspiration, or of living on stage, which great actors had found accidentally and sporadically. Without minimizing the value of voice, speech and body training, which are the actor's tools, Stanislavski tried to find means to stimulate and develop the actor's essential requirements: concentration, belief and imagination. He did not seek to fabricate inspiration, but to create the proper foundation for its appearance.

The actor, according to Stanislavski, should come on the stage not to play-act but to perform the activities required of the character, to act. His appearance on the stage is not the beginning but a continuation of the given circumstances that have previously taken place. The actor trains his concentration so that he is able to create the impression of being private in public. He trains his senses so that he is able to see, hear, touch, taste, smell and relate to the many objects which compose his imaginary situation. He learns to use not only intellectual knowledge but emotional experience by means of affective memory. Wordsworth defined poetry as originating in "emotion recollected in tranquillity." Shaw emphasized that "vital art work comes from a cross between art and life." Thomas Wolfe in one of his short stories and Proust in a passage in *Swann's Way* brilliantly described the workings of affective memory. It is not limited to the ability to recreate one's previously experienced real emotions, but also to learn to repeat previously experienced stage emotions. The actor's training of himself goes hand in hand with the actor's work on a role. The actor learns to delve beneath the lines to find the meaning or subtext of a play. He learns to find the "kernel" or core of a part, to find the actions of the character that define the important sections, to set smaller tasks or problems for his concentration throughout each section. In later years Stanislavski tried to correct the overly intellectual approach of this part of the work by simplifying the action work in terms of physical or psychophysical actions. Some have interpreted this as a reversal of his previous methods. Actually, it was intended not to rule out or contrast with but to serve as a life belt by means of which the previous preparation and work on a role could be securely held.

After Stanislavski.—Stanislavski's work with the actor was not limited to the realistic form. His own realistic productions tended to create that impression. But the pupils of Stanislavski, especially E. V. Vakhtangov (1883–1922), succeeded in combining the truthfulness and conviction of the actor that Stanislavski sought with the theatrical methods of V. E. Meyerhold (1874–1942), whose brilliant work represented a more formalized or stylized approach, without, however, following Meyerhold's "biomechanics" system of acting. In France Jacques Copeau (1879–1949) combined methods of inner truth with a search for theatrical form and this also characterized the work of H. Granville-Barker (1877–1946). While he never developed any complete system of aesthetics, the work of Max Reinhardt (1873–1943) combined an amazing variety of production methods with a use of ensemble, and he developed a group of actors of unusual talent and variety. Albert Bassermann (1867–1952), Emil Jannings (1886–1950), Werner Krauss (1884–   ), Alexander Moissi (1879–1935), Paul Wegener (1874–1948) and Rudolph Schildkraut (1862–1930) combined an extraordinary ability in the realistic drama with the temperament demanded by the classics.

In England, as elsewhere, acting was ruled by adherence to traditional patterns, strengthened by the principle that an actor played the same line of parts and usually the same way. But the profession boasted of this as the result of art and study. Sir Henry Irving (1838–1905) and others broke the spell. Irving's Iachimo was a new and independent creation—no bagful of tricks but a true impersonation, unbroken in its life current. Mrs. Patrick Campbell (1865–1940) as Ophelia, instead of being a strenuously earnest young lady giving a recitation, was mad—inspiredly mad. Sir Johnston Forbes-Robertson (1853–1937) created a Hamlet of "light, freedom, naturalness, credibility." Sir Gerald Du Maurier (1873–1934) established the acting thought of as typically English. He walked, talked and behaved as he believed the character would behave in natural circumstances ("Can't you just say, 'I love you,' and yawn, and light a cigarette and walk away?"). (Daphne Du Maurier, *Gerald: A Portrait*, Victor Gollancz, London, 1934.) What he achieved others only imitated. William Poel (1852–1934), most of whose work was done with largely amateur casts, revolutionized Shakespearean productions by preaching a return to the principle of Elizabethan staging. This placed the actor in a dilemma. He could not continue the development toward a realistic character approach and remain true to Elizabethan convention. Performers such as Sir Laurence Olivier (1907–   ), Sir John Gielgud (1904–   ) and Sir Ralph Richardson (1902–   ) reached great heights without, however, creating a style or basic approach. Michel Saint-Denis (1897–   ), a pupil of Copeau, tried to remedy this but left England without accomplishing his purpose.

It was at this point that United States acting began to influence the world arena. The U.S. theatre was conditioned in its beginnings by the tradition of English acting. Among the first actors

to develop typical American characters were "Yankee" Hill and "Jim Crow" Rice of U.S. minstrel shows and vaudeville, though Edwin Forrest (1806–72) and especially Edwin Booth (1833–93) became known in Europe. Toward the end of the 19th century, actors such as William Gillette (1853–1937) and Minnie Maddern Fiske (1865–1932) began to develop a more distinctively American type of acting, colloquial but forceful. After World War I American actors created outstanding performances that could be called great: Jeanne Eagels in *Rain*, Pauline Lord in *Anna Christie* and *They Knew What They Wanted*, Alfred Lunt in *The Guardsman*, Jacob Ben-Ami in *Samson and Delilah*, Laurette Taylor in *The Glass Menagerie*, the performances of John Barrymore and others. But these remained without influence in the rest of the world. The visits of Eleonora Duse and the company from the Moscow Art theatre created an additional stimulus which bore fruit in the ensemble acting created by the Group Theatre. For the first time the ideas of Stanislavski were tested and achieved unusual results outside of Russia.

The growth of motion pictures, especially the rise of the "talkies" beginning in 1927, greatly affected American acting. Two generations of theatre talent were diverted from the stage.

The requirements of acting in motion pictures, television, the theatre and opera are basically the same, although some of the techniques are different. It is possible to put strips of film together and create a performance that was never actually given. The performance is created by the director rather than by the actor. There were many performers in the silent pictures who were thus completely products of the camera and contributed little from an acting point of view, depending on their physical charms and personality (Rudolph Valentino, Theda Bara and others). However, individuals such as Charlie Chaplin and Lillian Gish were authentic actors, Chaplin being one of the greatest of all time in any medium. Werner Krauss in *The Cabinet of Dr. Caligari* created a masterpiece of the fantastic; the actors in Erich von Stroheim's *Greed* (Zasu Pitts, Jean Hersholt) attained a terrifying verisimilitude hardly matched on the screen since then, or, for that matter, on the stage. In the pictures directed by the Russians S. M. Eisenstein and V. I. Pudovkin, despite their use of the new principles of montage developed from D. W. Griffith, the acting reached a conviction and believability that revolutionized the medium, though it was difficult to tell whether it was achieved by the actor or the director. With the rise of sound movies, the role of the individual actor increased. Greta Garbo, Emil Jannings, Harry Baur, Bette Davis, Paul Muni, Luise Rainer, Spencer Tracy, Sylvia Sidney, Humphrey Bogart, Katharine Hepburn, Sir Laurence Olivier, Marlon Brando and others created authentic acting performances which could have held their own on the stage. In the U.S. motion-picture stars have come from the theatre to a greater extent than that permitted by the classical training of the English or French actor. Actors from the Actors Studio, especially under the direction of Elia Kazan (1909–   ), made a powerful impression, and showed a remarkable ability to bridge the gap between stage, screen and television to an extent that aroused excitement and interest in the rest of the world. So strong was the fusion of performer and role that many of the traits of the character were confused with those of the actor and led to serious misunderstanding. But at mid-20th century, for the first time, an American style of acting was being born.

The Nature of Acting.—Acting is the most appreciated and least understood of the arts. Taste is too often confused with judgment. But acting has a history of struggle, progress and development. Acting is not mimicry, exhibitionism or imitation. It is the ability to react to imaginary stimuli; and its essential elements remain the twin requisites enunciated by Talma, "unusual sensitivity and extraordinary intelligence," this latter not in the form of book learning but in the ability to comprehend the workings of the human soul. The essential problems in acting—does the actor "feel" or does he merely imitate? should he speak naturally or rhetorically? what is natural? etc.—are as old as acting itself. They derive not from the realistic movement but from the nature of the acting process. The commercial conditions of the theatre, screen and television make necessary a greater degree of training for the actor than ever before if the enormous talent that exists is not to be swamped by time and technical requirements. The training of the actor today is not a luxury but a necessity. (L. Sg.)

Schools of Acting.—During the greater part of the theatre's history actors have learned by doing. Their schools have been professional companies; their classroom, the stage; their curriculum, the drama in performance; their teachers, the audience and their fellow players. Academies of dramatic art, isolated from theatres or companies, are a relative innovation and are unknown in several European countries. Perhaps the most celebrated of all schools of acting, the Conservatoire in Paris—whose pupils have included Rachel, Sarah Bernhardt and Constant-Benoît Coquelin—has been intimately linked for nearly 200 years with one playhouse, the Comédie Française; and in the U.S.S.R. most of the major theatres include schools of acting as part of their basic organization. To such schooling there is no counterpart in the Anglo-American theatre.

In the pre-1640 English theatre training was organized inside the companies. Individual actors bought boy apprentices, coached them for a certain number of years (while renting their services to the company) and later sold them as trained actors. After the Restoration, "nurseries" were briefly in existence under the sponsorship of the rival "patent theatres," but this short-lived experiment was not repeated. At Drury Lane theatre, London, Garrick ran for some months in the mid-1750s a class of children who included Jane Pope, later celebrated on the stage. Some actors—notably, Charles Macklin—gave individual tuition to stagestruck aspirants: Sir Henry Irving, as a young clerk in London, went without food to pay for private lessons from a small-part player. And one couple, Samuel and Julia Glover, managed to establish a school in 1848 which kept alive for several years. Yet it was not until the beginning of the 20th century that a would-be actor could hope to learn his craft in an academy: if not "nursed on rose-pink and cradled in properties" (like Kean, Ellen Terry, Eleonora Duse or Lemaître), he joined a company and picked it up as he went along. In the stock-company system, before the advent of the metropolitan long run and the provincial touring company, there was ample opportunity for histrionic education. During three years of his provincial apprenticeship Irving played over 400 roles: in contrast, Gielgud played 80 roles in his first nine years on the stage and Sir Alec Guinness 54 roles in 21 years.

With the dissolution of the stock companies and the new respectability and popularity of acting among the Victorian middle class, the need for theatrical training on a less empirical basis became apparent in the 1880s, although the project of a dramatic academy—so often discussed in the past 200 years—was still hotly opposed by many actors. It was an actor-producer, Sir Herbert Beerbohm Tree, who took the lead by establishing a school of acting in 1904 in the dome of his London theatre, His Majesty's. In 1905 he moved it to a house in Gower street under the name of the Academy of Dramatic Art and set up a presiding council of other leading actors. A royal charter was granted in 1920 and from 1924 onward the Royal Academy of Dramatic Art—generally known by its initials as R.A.D.A.—received a small annual grant from the state. Other schools of acting such as the London Academy of Music and Dramatic Art and the Central School of Speech Training and Dramatic Art were instituted and were run on roughly similar lines, preparing pupils, in two-year courses, for the kind of work they might hope to find on the commercial stage in the open market.

The first school in the United States for the professional study of acting was the Lyceum Theatre school founded in 1884 by Franklin H. Sargent, Steele MacKaye and others. In 1888 it was renamed the American Academy of Dramatic Arts.

More radically comprehensive in their approach to acting, as an integral function of theatrical art rather than as an occupation for young ladies and gentlemen or as a form of casual labour marketable in the entertainment industry of the day, were several influential schools established in England and the U.S. in the 1930s and 1940s. Michel Saint-Denis, nephew of Jacques Copeau and former director of the Compagnie des Quinze, founded the London

Theatre Studio in 1936 but had to close it down on the outbreak of war in 1939. After the war he created the Old Vic school, linked with the Old Vic theatre, which offered instruction not only in acting but also in direction, design and other stagecrafts; and although the school was shut down in 1951 on grounds of economy, many of its pupils made their mark in the following decade. Saint-Denis' master, Copeau, was deeply influenced by Stanislavski and it was to Stanislavski that the leading U.S. schools of acting were principally indebted. Among them was the school established in New York in 1938 by Michael Chekhov, who had first opened it in England in 1936. Chekhov, nephew of the dramatist, had worked at the Moscow Art theatre with Stanislavski for many years. More than ten years earlier, when the Moscow Art theatre had visited the U.S., two members of the company—Richard Boleslavsky and Maria Uspenskaya—remained there and founded schools of acting. Among their pupils were three Americans who, in turn, became leader-teachers: Stella Adler, Harold Clurman and Lee Strasberg. Strasberg's Actors' Studio, which was attended in the 1950s by many professional actors in search of re-education, prompted the institution on both sides of the Atlantic of other postgraduate schools under the Stanislavski banner.

See also DRAMA. (Ri. F.)

BIBLIOGRAPHY.—Ivor Brown, *First Player* (1927); H. Granville-Barker, *The Exemplary Theatre* (1922), *Prefaces to Shakespeare* (1927–48); Toby Cole and H. K. Chinoy, *Actors on Acting*, especially the bibliography (1949); Lee Strasberg, "Acting and the Training of the Actor," in John Gassner, *Producing the Play*, pp. 128–162 (1941); William Archer, *Masks or Faces?* and D. Diderot, *The Paradox of Acting*, 2 vol. in 1 (1956); G. Henry Lewes, *On Actors and the Art of Acting* (1957); C. Stanislavsky, *My Life in Art*, trans. by J. J. Robbins (1924); G. Bernard Shaw, *Dramatic Opinions and Essays* (1907); J. Isaacs, *Shakespeare as Man of the Theatre* (1927); K. M. Lea, *Italian Popular Comedy* (1934); A. Vardac, *Stage to Screen* (1949).

DIRECTION

Among the principal changes in the balance of theatrical power during the 20th century was the actor's loss of control over the economic and aesthetic organization of the drama. New processes of specialization in function gave rise to the professional producer (the economic organizer of the play) and the professional director (the aesthetic organizer). Outside Anglo-American show business the director frequently exercised both economic and aesthetic control; in Britain he was generally known as the producer and elsewhere in Europe as the *régisseur* or *metteur en scène;* but to avoid confusion one may agree to call this specialist the director (a distinction officially made in Britain in the 1950s by the Society of West End Theatre Managers). He is responsible for the casting of a play (wholly or in part) and the conduct of rehearsals. He supervises the tempo, tone and traffic of the stage. As the interpreter of the text to the players and the audience, he is charged with the integration of performance, script, lighting and décor into a harmony of style and unity of theatrical effect. He is chairman, coach, umpire, conductor, choreographer and ideal spectator.

The Actors as Directors.—For more than 2,000 years the professional theatre existed without such an independent organizer of the show. During the middle ages something of the modern director's power was enjoyed by the pageant master or *maître du jeu* appointed by civic authorities to direct miracle and morality plays (with amateur actors), and throughout the history of the modern stage a small, subordinate role in the preparation and regulation of entertainment was played by the stage manager, the director's immediate ancestor. Playwrights were sometimes in control: from Sophocles to G. Bernard Shaw authors have directed their own plays. Yet aesthetic organization—as far as it went—was mainly the responsibility of the actor, who worked inside conventions of staging and performance. Instead of looking for realism and unity of effect in a coherent stage picture where every detail is planned and controlled, the audience up to the mid-19th century was content with scenic and histrionic clichés as the framework to displays of acting for "points." Painted scenery and standard properties out of stock were changed in full view of the public; plays of the past were costumed in a mixture of traditional, modern and haphazardly fancy dress from the theatre wardrobe; movement, grouping and even gestures were regulated by custom rather than dramatic truth; rehearsals were called mainly to demonstrate their exits, entrances and positions to subordinate actors; the stars —like operatic singers—played most of their big scenes by the footlights while the rest of the cast waited disinterestedly for their cues.

In the new art and industry of the theatre which began to emerge in the 1880s the need for an independent organizer of the play became apparent on several counts: the sheer physical expansion in the volume and range of theatrical production; the growing complexity of stage machinery, lighting and organization; the requirements of a new drama for a new mode of acting and for fidelity not only to the text but (as in the plays of Ibsen and Chekhov) to the stage directions; the public's mounting expectation of realism (both external and psychological) and unity (both visual and emotional); the influx of middle-class actors, outside the old craft system, who had to be coached and welded together from play to play; the eclecticism of taste, especially in revivals of past drama in appropriate styles; the breakup of the old conventions of performance and production; and (in the Anglo-American theatre, especially) the transference of productive power from the actor to the entrepreneur, who employed the director as his artistic agent.

First Directors in the 19th Century.—The era of the modern director was inaugurated in 1874, when a minor German aristocrat, George, duke of Saxe-Meiningen, startled Berlin playgoers with a revolutionary company from his court theatre. The duke was his own producer with his own stage, and a working guarantee of financial security (from his private fortune) freed him from the restrictions of immediate box-office budgeting. He designed all the sets and costumes; he supervised every detail in lighting and make-up, introducing a more realistic use of light and shade; he broke up the surface of the stage floor, establishing new levels of acting area; and he insisted on "the continuous and direct relation between the design of a setting and the actor's movements within it" (Lee Simonson, *The Stage is Set*). In training actors he attacked the baroque tradition of strut-and-bluster playing and with iron discipline he fused his players into an ensemble of which Europe had never seen the like. Especially impressive were the Meiningen crowd scenes, for every individual in the crowd was a trained actor (not, as was usual, an amateur "supernumerary"). Months of rehearsal went into every production and between 1874 and 1890 the Meiningen company visited 36 cities.

Other, more fundamental pressures were at work in the theatre —notably, the pressure toward naturalism, in the attempt to make the stage a more candid and "scientific" reflection of the contemporary world outside it. It was under the banner of Emile Zola that in 1887 the Théâtre Libre was founded in Paris by André Antoine. Photographic verisimilitude, in recreating the physical environment of the drama, was Antoine's aim as a director. He established "fourth wall" scenic realism (already heralded by Madame Vestris), developed a new ensemble pattern of naturalist playing among his troupe of amateurs and not only introduced outstanding foreign dramatists to the Paris stage—Ibsen and Tolstoi among them—but also brought new French writers (such as Eugène Brieux) into the theatre. Later in his career, during his ten-year directorship of the officially subsidized Odéon, he extended his methods from the contemporary drama to the classics. In Germany, within two years, the Théâtre Libre was followed by the Freie Bühne, which opened in Berlin with *Ghosts*. This company was founded and directed by Otto Brahm, a literary critic who did for the German stage what Antoine did for the French. Unlike Antoine he began with a company of professional actors, and his productions were sporadic and limited to matinee performances. The Freie Bühne collapsed after two seasons, but Brahm later worked at the Deutsches theatre in Berlin. In Russia in 1898 Konstantin Stanislavski—a wealthy dilettante who had worked for years with amateurs—founded the Moscow Art theatre, in collaboration with the playwright Vladimir Nemirovich-Danchenko. As in France and Germany, this enterprise was a platform for naturalist drama and new writers, notably Chekhov and Gorki, were introduced to the stage. Stanislavski's first productions, like those of Antoine and Brahm, were obsessively concerned with the

exact reproduction of reality (he insisted upon buying properties and clothes in the actual places where plays were set), although in the course of his long and influential career he moved away from external to inner realism, from scenery to psychology and from drilling his actors to collaborating with them, which illustrates the general trend of naturalistic direction.

After the foundation of the Théâtre Libre, stage realism and naturalism (the terms were never satisfactorily distinguished) survived as dominant influences in theatrical direction, especially in the Anglo-American theatre. Yet the early champions of the director's art advocated its use in the service of very different theatrical ideals: to express men's inner, emotional truths and to reflect not particular fact but universal reality. Richard Wagner developed the conception of the *Gesamtkunstwerk*, in which all components of the theatre arts were to be synthesized under the single authority of the director. In studying the problems of staging Wagnerian opera Adolph Appia demonstrated in two seminal books of the 1890s that the director had a new weapon at his command in electric light, used with deliberate unrealism to suggest (not to reproduce) in the illumination of three-dimensional settings without painted scenery or realistic properties. And Gordon Craig eloquently argued the need for the stage manager's dominion over the art of the theatre. Three years after the Théâtre Libre was established, the Théâtre d'Art was opened in opposition by a poet-director, Paul Fort. Believing in a theatre of fantasy not of fact, in evocation and not imitation, Fort introduced a simplified décor of draped curtains and formalized backcloths, instead of the "naturalistic lies" of the scene painter. Heralding later directors' attempts to subjugate the intransigent actor, Fort also ventured upon some stylization of performance by immobilizing his players in statuesque poses. The Théâtre d'Art lasted for only two years, yet Fort stands for all those directors who followed him in opposition to the naturalistic theatre, under the banners of symbolism, theatricalism, expressionism and other causes.

The 20th Century.—Selective realism and theatrical eclecticism characterized the leading directors of the 20th century. In Germany Max Reinhardt experimented in many kinds of theatres on many kinds of stages. Borrowing from Japanese, Greek and Elizabethan styles, from the circus and the passion play, Reinhardt directed plays old and new in places as different as Salzburg cathedral and the square outside it, a Venetian piazza and a Viennese ballroom, the Boboli gardens, Florence, and the vast arena of London's Olympia. He was as much at home as a director in the intimate Kammerspielhaus with Molière as in the Grosses Schauspielhaus in Berlin, a converted circus ring where he hoped to revive the mass theatre of antiquity. Reinhardt tried to change the theatre's relationship with its audience and with its past, especially in his insistence on the play script as being one element only in production. Whereas the realistic theatre of Antoine, Brahm and their successors depended upon the complete separation of the actor from the audience behind the proscenium arch and orchestra pit, Reinhardt brought the actor out of the picture frame into the middle of his public. He transformed German acting style in the classics, had a special gift for the orchestration of crowds which helped to make his international reputation as a master showman and founded the first school for directors.

Among other notable German directors were Leopold Jessner, whose productions at the Berlin State theatre between 1919 and 1925 were celebrated for his use of broad symbolic and expressionist effects on massive stairways connecting different levels of acting area, and Erwin Piscator, the pioneer of "epic theatre" who, after a stormy career in Berlin in the 1920s, spent the years 1934–51 in the U.S. Piscator was a ruthless opponent of theatrical illusion, atmospheric production and identification of the actors with their roles. He made no attempt to mesmerize the audience into oblivion: stridently and aggressively they were reminded that they were watching actors at work who were trying to prove a case, not to create a world of make-believe. Slogans blazed in electric lights above the proscenium; searchlights roved across the stage and the auditorium; loud-speakers blared and mobile scenic units were trundled on and off; while Piscator's actors were employed to present types, rather than to imitate people. Piscator made extensive use of stage machinery, which had been widely developed in the German theatre, and he believed in combining live and filmed action by the frequent interpolation of cinematic sequences. His theories of "epic theatre" were developed and enlarged by one of his early collaborators and authors, Bertolt Brecht, who later in the 1950s created and directed his own company, the Berliner Ensemble, with state aid from the German Democratic Republic.

In the U.S.S.R. Vsevolod Meyerhold experimented for 30 years in antirealistic theatre until his arrest in 1939. Like Reinhardt, Meyerhold pushed the actors into the audience and attempted a new social integration in his Theatre of the Revolution but, whereas Stanislavski ignored the audience, he attacked it. In place of Reinhardt's eclectic theatricalism, Meyerhold—"the Picasso of theatre," as he has been called—worked restlessly and adventurously toward a narrower aesthetic of abstraction. Often he filled the stage with constructivist settings—scaffoldings, ladders and ramps—and coached his actors as gymnasts and acrobats in a system of "biomechanics." Exhorting them to practise "the vigorous elimination of all humane feeling" and to suppress their "little, rickety egos," Meyerhold did his best to stylize them into puppets and machines. At Moscow's Kamerny theatre, from 1914 to 1934, Alexander Tairov worked along similar lines, putting his actors in exaggerated make-ups and masks and drilling them in formalized speech and gesture. For a few years in the 1920s E. V. Vakhtangov, a pupil of Stanislavski, tried to reconcile the methods of his master and Meyerhold against the background of a new socialist society at the Moscow Art Theatre Third Studio; and in the 1930s Nikolai Okhlopkov made significant experiments in central staging at the Realistic theatre in Moscow. After the disappearance of Meyerhold, experimental direction in the U.S.S.R. came to a virtual standstill; but the director—under political guidance—remained in supreme authority.

In France the outstanding director of the 20th century was Jacques Copeau, a literary critic who in 1913 founded the Théâtre du Vieux-Colombier in Paris. Copeau's explicit aim was to serve the author and to show the actor how to do it. Every play, Copeau insisted, has a rhythm of its own which determines its use of stage space and every literary style engenders its own appropriate style of performance: this rhythm and this style must be discovered by the director as the interpreter of the text and the actors' leader. He encouraged his actors to make their voices and bodies more flexible and to share his own dedicated sense of duty toward theatrical reform. Believing that the physical structure of the playhouse could enhance the intellectual structure of the drama, he presented his productions at the Vieux-Colombier on a small platform stage in front of a permanent architectural background, without footlights or proscenium. Copeau's first company included Charles Dullin and Louis Jouvet, who later emerged as two of Europe's leading directors. Other eminent French directors between World Wars I and II were Georges Pitoëff, Gaston Baty and Michel Saint-Denis, the nephew and disciple of Copeau, while in the 1940s Jean-Louis Barrault and Jean Vilar appeared as actor-director-producers at the summit of European theatre.

Thus throughout Europe after 1887 directors led the theatre in the service of a new drama, coaching new breeds of actors, introducing new methods of staging, reaching out for a new kind of audience. From the start, many of them controlled playhouses and companies of their own which played a significant and continuing part in the theatrical life of their nation. Many were supported by state or civic subsidy. In Britain and the U.S., however, the situation was very different. The outstanding director in the U.S., then and for years to come, was David Belasco, who was also his own producer at his own theatres, but this showman did nothing to promote new drama or acting. Although acclaimed for the meticulous efficiency of his stage management and lighting, Belasco's realism was an end in itself. The exact reproduction of life, in Zola's terms, shrunk to the careful copying of clothes and furniture. In the 1920s notable individual directors emerged inside the commercial theatre, such as Arthur Hopkins and Guthrie McClintic, with occasional productions of individual plays; Ken-

neth Macgowan worked with the play-producing societies of the Provincetown players and the Greenwich Village theatre; but it was not until 1931—when the Group Theatre was launched—that a U.S. director could enjoy any continuity of creative purpose among the anarchy and waste of the long-run system. In that year Harold Clurman, Lee Strasberg and Cheryl Crawford developed a more or less permanent ensemble of actors dedicated to and coached in the principles of naturalistic acting formulated by Stanislavski, employed in the production of new, naturalistic dramatists, of whom Clifford Odets was the most important. The Group Theatre exerted a far-reaching influence in the U.S. during the next 20 years and among its eminent graduates was Elia Kazan, who became one of the leading directors on the Broadway commercial stage.

In Britain, unlike the U.S., two significant attempts were made to establish a national equivalent of the Théâtre Libre before World War I. The first of these ventures, the Independent theatre, was founded in 1891 by an Anglo-Dutch dramatic critic, J. T. Grein, as a society of enthusiasts who financed special performances of plays, with scratch casts, on any stage that could be rented for a matinee or Sunday night. The direction was done by anyone available. Through this group and the Stage society many outstanding plays were shown to members and both helped to extend the horizons of the British drama. Yet, lacking an organizing director and a permanent home, their impact on acting and production was negligible compared with their European contemporaries. Their work, however, helped to prepare the way for a far more influential enterprise—the three-year management of the Court theatre from 1904 to 1907, backed by a commercial producer, John Vedrenne, and directed by Harley Granville-Barker. Avoiding conventional "slice of life" realism, Granville-Barker—perhaps the outstanding British director of the century—insisted on truth as opposed to effect. In an era of star-acting and spectacular scenery, he carefully schooled his company in "natural" ensemble playing, where even the smallest part was rehearsed and studied in detail and every actor was encouraged to develop for himself the truth of his role. Like Copeau, Granville-Barker put the author first and, as part of his ambition to reform the stage, he sought to raise the art of acting to new heights, not in histrionic display but in serving the drama. Later at the Savoy theatre from 1912 to 1914 he set new standards of production and performance in Shakespearean staging. But thereafter Granville-Barker—self-exiled from the commercial stage—made no further sustained contribution as a director to the British theatre.

Few other English directors enjoyed a similar opportunity in the next 50 years and for two generations the London stage seemed curiously insulated from cross-channel developments in dramaturgy, lighting, design and acting. Among the rare artists who achieved some continuity of theatrical control was Sir Nigel Playfair, who from 1918 to 1932 was director-producer of the Lyric theatre, Hammersmith. In 1926 a wealthy dilettante, Terence Gray, established Britain's only venture in antirealist staging at the Cambridge Festival theatre: under his control, until 1933, a wide range of plays was produced without props, scenery or proscenium arch on a multi-level stage jutting out into the auditorium, but these isolated experiments had little effect on the British theatre at large. It was in Shakespearean staging that the individual director had most power and prestige. At the turn of the century William Poel—Granville-Barker's master—had organized his Elizabethan Stage society which, from 1894 to 1905, demonstrated the importance of the theatrical conditions under which Shakespeare wrote. Attacking the "vice of scenery," the cluttering traditions of stage "business," the star-actors' mutilation of the text and the limitations of the picture-frame stage, Poel emphasized swift and musical speech, continuity of action in nonlocalized scenes, fidelity to the script and greater intimacy between the players and the public. Outside the commercial stage, at the Old Vic theatre, London, and the Shakespeare Memorial theatre, Stratford-upon-Avon, other directors made their name in Shakespearean revival. Among the most eminent were Tyrone Guthrie, Peter Brook, Peter Hall, Michael Benthall and Glen Byam Shaw, while Theodore Komisarjevsky and Michel Saint-Denis had a strong influence in the 1930s.

By 1960 stage direction in general was characterized by empiricism and eclecticism. In Britain and the U.S. most directors were still—compared with their European contemporaries—displaced persons without a theatre or company of their own. Hired by commercial producers as artistic free lances to organize scratch casts in a few weeks of rehearsal, they were committed to the diluted realism of the picture-frame stage, the dominant aestheticism of the entertainment industry on both sides of the Atlantic. Yet in the 1950s the London theatre was infiltrated by two highly successful and influential ventures under the control of individual directors (subsidized by state and civic enterprise) with permanent bases in the capital: Joan Littlewood's Theatre Workshop, which presented a bold range of classics and new drama under Brechtian influence with Britain's only permanent acting ensemble, and George Devine's English Stage company, which introduced many new writers, actors, designers and directors at the Royal Court theatre.

BIBLIOGRAPHY.—Gordon Craig, *The Art of the Theatre* (1905); Lee Simonson, *The Stage is Set* (1932); Harold Clurman, *The Fervent Years* (1945); Constantin Stanislavski, *My Life in Art* (1948); Toby Cole and Helen Krich Chinoy (eds.), *Directing the Play* (1953); Mordecai Gorelik, *New Theatres for Old* (1940); Norman Marshall, *The Producer and the Play* (1957); Lynton Hudson, *The English Stage, 1850–1950* (1951); Richard Findlater, *The Unholy Trade* (1952); Robert Speaight, *William Poel and the Elizabethan Revival* (1954); Phyllis Hartnoll (ed.), *The Oxford Companion to the Theatre,* 2nd ed., with illustrated supplement (1957).

PRODUCTION

In the course of its history the theatre has been variously sustained by the love of God, art, gold and glory—as a royal diversion, a religious ritual, a social service or a commercial speculation—but throughout its changing styles and forces of production it always depends upon one prime mover, the man who puts on the plays. In the London theatre he is the manager; in Germany, the *intendant;* in the English provincial repertories and other European playhouses, the director or administrator; in the U.S. theatre, the producer. To simplify the confusing nomenclature of the stage he will be called the producer in this article: the central organizer of the play's economics and administration as distinct from the aesthetic organizer, who will be called the director. It is the producer (in this sense of the term) who selects the plays; who engages the cast, designer, director, composer, orchestra and technical staff; who controls or (in the commercial theatre) rents the playhouse; who finds and spends the money required to finance the show. As the main middleman between the artists of the theatre and the audience, it is on his initiative, taste and industry—in using artistic supply to create and/or satisfy public demand—that the welfare of the theatre largely depends.

Subsidiary Role of Early Producers.—Sometimes theatrical production was organized by an outside financier, showman or theatre owner. In Shakespeare's day Philip Henslowe, a wealthy property dealer, owned three London playhouses and controlled several companies in turn. David Garrick's first producer at Drury Lane theatre in 1742 was a rich dilettante, Charles Fleetwood. Outside the Anglo-American theatre, production was often subsidized by the state and supervised by an official administrator (as in the Comédie Française). Yet, generally speaking, it was for nearly 2,000 years the main responsibility of the theatre's authors and actors. The artists of the theatre were usually their own producers.

At times the playwrights were in control of production. At the tragic festivals of Athens, Aeschylus was actor, director and producer. Shakespeare not only played in some of his own works but he was also co-producer, as a leading member of his fellowship with a share in both the company and the playhouse: it was his producer's profits, and not the relatively meagre rewards of his writing, that set him up as a country gentleman in Stratford. Molière, too, combined the roles of actor, author and producer. Ludwig Tieck in Dresden, Ferdinand Raimund in Vienna, August Iffland in Mannheim, Goethe in Weimar, Ludwig Holberg in Copenhagen, Henrik Ibsen in Bergen, Alexandre Dumas *père* in Paris, Henry Fielding and Samuel Foote in London—all for a time commanded theatres of their own.

But it was the actors who usually ruled the roost, especially in the Anglo-American theatre. Production was sometimes shared by the leading members of a troupe, as in the Elizabethan fellowships or Italian *commedia* companies, but more often it was organized by the star player who was, until the beginning of the 20th century, his own director, producer and even landlord. It is not only as actors but as producers that such names as Garrick, Samuel Phelps, William Macready, Charles Fechter, Richard Mansfield, William Evans Burton and the Wallacks are remembered; and all of them worked without official subsidy in the open market, usually with a permanent company of their own and sometimes with a playhouse on a long lease, often helped by a business manager. The heyday of the actor-managers (as they were known in England) came toward the end of the 19th century, with the recruitment of a vast new middle-class audience as the customers of a rapidly expanding entertainment industry. In England knighthoods signalized the unprecedented success and respectability of Sir Squire Bancroft, Sir Herbert Beerbohm Tree, Sir Charles Wyndham, Sir George Alexander, Sir John Martin-Harvey, Sir Johnston Forbes-Robertson and Sir Henry Irving. Commissioning plays, remodeling theatres, organizing tours, setting styles and standards, these actors ensured a continuity of production unknown to the modern commercial stage. But with their reign ended the traditional supremacy of the actor in theatrical production. Accelerated by World War I, the social forces that had helped them to make their fortunes also destroyed their kind of theatre. The actor's authority over both playhouse and production was dissolved and new powers took control.

Development of the Professional Producer.—The enormous increase in the potential profitability of theatrical enterprise, with the development of the long run and its provincial touring companies, attracted outside speculators and financiers who supplied the capital needed to build new playhouses and exploit new fields of production. Theatre owners in the 20th century sometimes engaged in production themselves, or let their stages to the highest bidder for the run of one show, and this bidder was, after World War I, no longer an actor but an entrepreneur, the old-style business manager transformed from the actor's servant into his master. Productive power was dominated increasingly by a few syndicates—notably, at first, in the U.S., where the Theatrical syndicate (formed in 1896) controlled for approximately 16 years most of the New York theatre and many playhouses outside it. Later the Shubert brothers—Lee, Sam S. and J. J.—dominated the U.S. stage for over 40 years: in 1950 the U.S. government filed a civil antitrust suit (later dropped) charging them with monopolistic practices. The Shubert Theatre corporation was then said to control 37 playhouses (including 17 in New York) and a large part of the nation's theatre bookings. In Britain it was not until 1942 (when Sir Oswald Stoll's death threw the control of his Theatres corporation on the market) that a concentration of power comparable to the Shuberts' empire was initiated. Under the leadership of Prince Littler, a small group of men extended control over nearly half of London's theatres and the chief "number one" stages in the provinces. By 1960 this group had a large stake in theatrical insurance, advertising, catering, entertainment agencies, the recording industry and independent television; it was linked with the country's most powerful producer of "straight" drama; and its members included Britain's biggest producers of light entertainment outside the legitimate theatre.

The golden age of theatrical expansion lasted, at most, about 30 years between the 1890s and the 1920s. When business declined, in an era of steadily rising costs and fierce competition first from the cinema and then from television, theatre owners on both sides of the Atlantic found compensation in the inflation of urban land values. Playhouses were destroyed in increasing numbers as expendable units in property deals: in Britain the number of professional stages, which had risen from about 100 in 1800 to about 700 in 1900, dropped by 1960 to less than 200. This liquidation of the theatre's physical assets, the concentration of economic power and the steep rise in costs had obvious repercussions on the forces of production in both Britain and the U.S., where there was no tradition—as in France and Germany—of state or civic subsidy and protection.

In London and New York commercial producers had to compete from play to play for the hire of a restricted number of theatres in private ownership. They were often obliged to present plays in buildings of the wrong size, or to jettison productions because no stage was available. Continuity in casting or policy was virtually impossible in the uncertain conditions of the entertainment industry. A show was rehearsed for a few weeks by a company of actors starting from scratch and was allowed to run just as long as it paid the lessee of the theatre and the producer, which might be for three years or three days. The producer had to mobilize his audience at once: a very high level of takings was necessary from the first week of the show's run if he was to keep a stage for it. For as soon as box-office receipts fell below a certain figure, the theatre lessee usually had the right to give the producer notice to quit. It was the man with the theatre who had the power in the long-run system. His rent was among the biggest items in the inflationary production budget, together with star salaries and (in the U.S.) the excessive backstage payroll caused by trade union "featherbedding" and restrictive practices. While prices of admission, on average, doubled between 1940 and 1960 in London, costs more than trebled. Yet a straight play costing £5,000 to stage in London would cost three times as much on Broadway, and a U.S. musical would probably have to run the best part of a year before it paid back its production costs (which might be in the region of $200,000) and the producer began to make a profit. In New York prices might soar to as much as $40 a ticket, but only a few shows every season inspired such speculation and only a small fraction of such inflated prices was taken by the producer. Generally speaking, his actual costs increased at a far higher rate than his potential revenue; he had to count in New York (and increasingly in London) upon an immediate smash-hit success, knowing the alternative to be an instant flop; and the virtual liquidation of the commercial stage outside these theatrical capitals radically reduced the possible compensations of a post-metropolitan tour.

In both Britain and the U.S. the primary factor in the future of the commercial theatre was that, in an era of continuing real-estate development, a playhouse was an uneconomic user of urban land. Moreover, the making of profits became—in New York especially—an increasing gamble every year. Between the 1920s and 1950s about 75% of New York's stages were lost to the living theatre and, although in the 1950s new outlets developed for productive forces in the "off-Broadway" theatre, the costs rose so rapidly that the producer of a success was lucky to break even. Whereas in the 1920s the U.S. producer was generally self-financing, in the 1950s he had to enlist the support of professional backers or "angels" to raise the necessary capital. This trend, still less significant in London during the 1950s, represented a further specialization in the forces of theatrical production and a decline in the authority of the individual producer.

Yet producers in the 1950s experienced little difficulty in recruiting the necessary cash for individual shows with a possible commercial future. For although the odds against survival were increasingly heavy, the rewards of success were increasingly high, not only from the local box office but from foreign rights, film rights, television rights and so on. Moreover, the system brought not only financial but artistic results. In spite of the wastage of talent involved in the hit-or-flop system, its successes were often widely staged throughout the western world. The Anglo-American commercial stage compared favourably in dramaturgical fertility and histrionic variety with the noncommercial theatre in Germany and the U.S.S.R.

For this, one reason was the developing importance of the noncommercial theatre as a training ground and shopwindow for actors, authors, directors and audiences. A vital role in British production was occupied by the leading repertory theatres in such cities as Birmingham and Bristol, which took the place of the stock companies in the 19th century. The pioneering producer of the repertory movement was Miss A. E. F. Horniman, who established the Repertory Theatre of Ireland at Dublin's Abbey theatre in 1904 and founded the first "rep" in Britain in 1908 at the Gaiety theatre in Manchester.

The principal British repertories are supported by state aid, distributed through the Arts Council of Great Britain, an independent body outside direct ministerial control and established in 1946, which played an important indirect role in production after World War II. After the Local Government act of 1948 civic authorities were also empowered to subsidize theatres from the rates and, by 1960, about a dozen municipalities gave direct aid to their local repertory companies. Production in the leading "reps" was organized on a short-run basis of two or at most three weeks, financed by a nonprofit-distributing trust which generally appointed a director-producer to control the theatre, assisted by a business manager. Although most of these repertories were afflicted by lack of capital, inadequate housing and the widening gap between costs and prices, there were signs by 1960 that their future role would be more secure. State aid was, in the late 1950s, increasingly supplemented by subsidies from television and other industries; and more civic authorities seemed ready to follow the lead of Coventry and build new playhouses for their local companies.

Of especial importance in noncommercial production of the classics was the Old Vic theatre in London, since 1914 the home of Shakespeare and the workshop of most of the stage's leading talents. Production was controlled, under a board of governors, by a director and an administrator in partnership and subsidized by the state and (in the 1950s) by various donations from industry. At Stratford-upon-Avon the Shakespeare Memorial theatre, after many years of relative obscurity, achieved in the 1950s an unprecedented commercial and artistic success—without any external subsidy—under the control of a director-producer, assisted by a business manager. In London the West End stage was transformed in the 1950s by the impact of two noncommercial organizations, both with a permanent stage of their own outside central London and both controlled by a producer-director: Joan Littlewood's Theatre Workshop and George Devine's English Stage company, based at the Theatre Royal, Stratford, and the Royal Court theatre, Chelsea, respectively.

In the U.S. theatre, unlike the British, noncommercial production in the first half of the 20th century was largely controlled by amateurs, often with stages of their own which put to shame the theatrical housing of London and New York. Ever since George Pierce Baker established his "47 Workshop" at Harvard in 1912 the arts of the stage occupied a place of increasing importance in the curricula of U.S. universities. By 1960 there were over 400 university stages, which represented almost the only U.S. theatre subsidized by public funds. Community theatres, usually financed by seasonal subscription, began to sprout in the 1920s as the old-style professional stage declined. By 1960 there were about 2,300 of them, including a few (as at Kalamazoo and Indianapolis) supported by civic funds, and an increasing number were partly or completely professional. The outstanding community theatres were—like Gilmore Brown's Pasadena playhouse and Frederic McConnell's Cleveland playhouse—created and run by director-producers. In the U.S. the state's only venture into theatrical production was the epoch-making Federal Theatre project, administered under the relief program of the Works Progress administration from 1935 to 1939. Under the leadership of Hallie Flanagan, Federal theatre sponsored nationwide production on an astonishing scale and with an immensely creative effect upon artists and audiences. In New York several attempts were made to establish a producing organization with a consistent policy and a continuous existence outside the cash nexus of Broadway show business. Eva Le Gallienne ran her Civic Repertory theatre from 1926 to 1933 and the Group Theatre (see *Direction*) survived from 1931 to 1941. Yet few of these enterprises did more than to introduce individual talents into the commercial stage and most were quickly swallowed up by the entertainment industry. *See* also MOTION PICTURES; STAGE DESIGN; THEATRE; MAKE-UP (STAGE, MOTION PICTURE AND TELEVISION). (RI. F.)

ACTINIUM. The metallic element actinium (after the Greek *aktis* or *aktinos*, "ray," in recognition of its radioactivity), with symbol Ac and atomic number 89, was discovered by A. Debierne in 1899 and independently by F. O. Giesel in 1902. The radio-active isotope discovered is known to have the mass number 227 and half-life 22 years and is a member of the natural, $4n + 3$ radioactive family. A number of other isotopes, natural and artificial, are known and are too short-lived to isolate in macroscopic quantity. Before 1950 the chemical properties were investigated by the tracer method.

The isotope Ac^{227} can be isolated in pure form from uranium ores, containing its precursor U^{235}, only with difficulty. A better source is the transmutation of radium through intense pile neutron bombardment according to the reactions Ra^{226} (n, γ) $Ra^{227\beta\rightarrow}$ Ac^{227}. This latter source was used by F. Hagemann in 1950 for his first isolation of actinium in the form of pure compounds and was used for subsequent investigation of the chemical properties of pure actinium compounds.

Actinium is colourless and exclusively tripositive in solution, closely resembles the tripositive rare-earth (lanthanide) elements in its chemical properties, and may be regarded as the prototype for the 14 following rare-earthlike (actinide) elements of atomic numbers 90–103 inclusive. It forms insoluble compounds of the same type as the rare-earth elements such as fluoride, oxalate, hydroxide and a number of crystallized double salts. However, actinium is more basic than even lanthanum, contributing to differences from rare-earth elements in the extent to which certain complex ions are formed. It may be separated from the rare-earth elements and the heavier tripositive actinide elements by use of ion exchange resins or distribution between aqueous and organic solvents. Known solid compounds are all tripositive, colourless (except the sulfide), isostructural with the analogous lanthanide and actinide compounds, and include the halides, oxyhalides, sesquioxide, sulfide, hydroxide, phosphate, oxalate and some double salts. *See* also RADIOACTIVITY. (G. T. Sg.)

ACTINOLITE: *see* ASBESTOS.

ACTINOMETER, an instrument or process for measuring the chemical effect of radiation, taking its name from the so-called "actinic" or chemically active rays. Intensity of fluorescence of various salts, rate of darkening of bromide paper, rate of decomposition of potassium permanganate or of hydrogen iodide, rate of formation of ozone and other chemical effects have been used to standardize the intensity of radiation in different frequency bands. Comparative measurements are relatively simple; absolute measurements of efficiency of quantum yield are difficult. Most actinometers are of an integrating type.

For more rapid measurements of radiation intensity, without respect to specific actinic or chemical action produced thereby, numerous electrical instruments are also available in recent forms of light meters, exposure meters and photoelectric cells (*see* PHOTO-ELECTRICITY).

The thermojunction, thermopile and bolometer were earlier instruments in this category. (R. M. Sn.)

ACTINOMYCOSIS (STREPTOTRICHOSIS or LUMPY JAW), a chronic infectious disease, occurring in cattle and in man and caused by the fungus *Actinomyces*. *See* FUNGUS INFECTIONS.

ACTION, in law, a proceeding in a court for enforcing legal rights. It may be civil or criminal, personal, real or mixed, local or transitory. Its objective is a judgment settling the rights asserted. *See* JUDGMENTS AND DECREES; PRACTICE AND PROCEDURE. (C. E. Cl.)

ACTIUM (modern AKRA NIKOLAOS), the ancient name of a promontory in the north of Acarnania in Greece, on the southern side of the strait leading from the Ionian sea into the Ambracian gulf. Actium belonged originally to the Corinthian colonists of Anactorium, who probably founded the worship of Apollo Actius and the festival of games called Actia, which was later amplified by Augustus. In the 3rd century B.C. it fell to the Acarnanians, who subsequently held their synods there.

Actium is famous chiefly as the site of Octavian's decisive victory over Mark Antony (Sept. 2, 31 B.C.), which made him in fact the undisputed master of the Roman world (*see* AUGUSTUS; also ANTONIUS). Both men had large naval and land forces: Antony commanded about 500 ships and 70,000 infantry; Octavian had

400 ships and 80,000 infantry. Octavian's forces arrived from the north and, by occupying Patrae and Corinth, cut Antony's communications with the Peloponnese. Deserted by some of his allies, Antony twice failed in attacks on Octavian's camp, and lack of provisions soon forced him to take action. He rejected a plan to retire to Macedonia and fight by land and followed Cleopatra's advice to use his fleet. His ultimate purpose is obscure. He probably hoped for a decisive battle, with the expectation that, if he failed, he might break off and escape to Egypt; alternatively, he may have been attempting merely to escape from the blockade. He drew up his fleet offshore, facing west, with Cleopatra's squadron behind. The course of the action is not certain; perhaps while he, on the right, was trying to turn the northern left wing of Octavian's fleet, which was commanded by M. Vipsanius Agrippa, part of the centre and left of his line retreated to harbour. He signaled to Cleopatra, who had the treasure chest aboard, to escape, broke off the engagement and with a few ships managed to follow her. Octavian received the surrender of the fleet and, a week later, of the land forces. He founded the city of Nicopolis Actia (*q.v.*) on the other side of the strait, in commemoration of his victory.

See W. W. Tarn, *J. Roman Studies,* vol. 21; pp. 173 ff. (1931) and *Cambridge Ancient History,* vol. x (1934); G. W. Richardson, *J. Roman Studies,* vol. 27, pp. 153 ff. (1937). (H. H. Sd.)

ACTON, JOHN EMERICH EDWARD DALBERG ACTON, 1ST BARON (1834–1902), English historian and philosopher of freedom, was one of the first to lay bare the tyrannical tendencies of the modern state. The grandson of the Neapolitan admiral, Sir J. F. E. Acton, 6th baronet (*q.v.*), he was born at Naples on Jan. 10, 1834. His father came from the English Roman Catholic squirearchy and his mother from an old south German aristocratic family.

In 1840 his widowed mother married Lord Leveson, the future Lord Granville and Liberal foreign secretary, an alliance which brought Acton early into the intimate circle of the great Whigs. Educated at Oscott college, Warwickshire, he went to Munich to study under Döllinger (*q.v.*), who grounded him in the new German methods of historical research.

Civilized and cosmopolitan, rich, learned and widely traveled, he spent much time in Europe and the United States, and then in 1859 was returned to the house of commons for Carlow. In the same year he became editor, following John Henry Newman, of the Roman Catholic monthly, the *Rambler,* but this experience was unfortunate. He himself believed that a rigorously scientific history would ultimately strengthen the church and that Christian doctrine would be harmonized with the findings of history. But when Pius IX indicated that it was wrong, though not heretical, to reject the opinion of the Roman congregations, Acton did not dispute the pope's authority, but held that it condemned the intellectual independence of his journal (by then called the *Home and Foreign Review*) and so laid down the editorship. In the crisis in the Roman Catholic Church in 1870 over the dogma of papal infallibility, Acton was in complete sympathy with Döllinger. "We have to meet," he wrote to Gladstone, "an organized conspiracy to establish a power which would be the most formidable enemy of liberty as well as of science throughout the world." He had a hatred of the papal temporal power and an outraged sense of the many instances of its misuse in history. But he was deeply rooted in Catholicism and, unlike Döllinger, did not secede. He regarded "communion with Rome as dearer than life." His parliamentary career had ended in 1865—he was an almost silent member—but his friendship with Gladstone, a fruit of the Whig connection, was of great consequence for the minds of both men. Matthew Arnold used to say that "Gladstone influences all around him but Acton; it is Acton who influences Gladstone." He claimed, in fact, to be the author of the home rule policy for Ireland. He was raised to the peerage by Gladstone in 1869, and in 1892 Gladstone repaid his services as adviser by making him a lord-in-waiting. Queen Victoria uttered the wish that Prince Albert could have known him. In 1865 he married Marie von Arco-Vallery, daughter of a Bavarian count, by whom he had one son and three daughters.

After 1870, Acton wrote little, his only notable publications being a masterly essay in the *Quarterly Review* (January 1878) on "Democracy in Europe"; two lectures delivered at Bridgnorth in 1877 on "The History of Freedom in Antiquity" and "The History of Freedom in Christianity" (both published in 1907)—these last the only tangible portions put together by him of his long-projected "History of Liberty" —and an essay on modern German historians in the first number of the *English Historical Review*, which he helped to found (1886). In 1895, on the death of Sir John Seeley, Lord Rosebery appointed him to the regius professorship of modern history at Cambridge. His inaugural lecture on "The Study of History" (published in 1895) made a great impression in the university, and his influence on historical study was felt in many important directions. He delivered two valuable courses of lectures, on the French Revolution and on modern history, but it was in private that the effects of his teaching were most marked. He died at Tegernsee, Bavaria, on June 19, 1902.

THE BETTMANN ARCHIVE
LORD ACTON

Although Acton sometimes fell into credulous error, no earlier English historian had inculcated such rigorous standards of accuracy. The ethical principles that he expected to see maintained in politics he applied to history; in his famous memorandum for contributors to the *Cambridge Modern History*, of which he was the planning editor, he declared: "Contributors will understand that our Waterloo must satisfy French and English, German and Dutch alike; that nobody can tell without examining the list of authors where the Bishop of Oxford laid down his pen and whether Fairbairn or Gasquet, Liebermann or Harrison took it up."

His fame rests less on his few historical writings than upon his prescient concern with problems of political morality. Deeply influenced by Plato, a disciple of Edmund Burke, and sympathetic to De Tocqueville, he saw the threats to liberty contained in democracy and socialism, and the evils of power when concentrated in the modern state. A stern critic of racialism and nationalism, his Liberalism was rooted in Christianity. "I fully admit that political Rights proceed directly from religious duties, and hold this to be the true basis of Liberalism." For him, conscience was the fount of freedom and its claims superior to those of the state. "The nation is responsible to Heaven for the acts of the State." If democracy could not restrain itself, liberty would be lost. The test of a country's freedom was the amount of security enjoyed by minorities. For Acton, in his judgment of politics as of history, morality was a matter of life and death. He was the great modern philosopher of resistance to the evil state.

Acton's *Lectures in Modern History* (1906), *History of Freedom and Other Essays* (1907), and *Historical Essays and Studies* (1907) were edited by J. N. Figgis and R. V. Laurence and his *Essays on Church and State* were edited with an introduction by Douglas Woodruff (1952). *Letters of Lord Acton to Mary . . . Gladstone* were edited with an introductory memoir and valuable references to authorities by H. Paul (1904); a selection from Acton's correspondence was edited with an introduction by J. N. Figgis and R. V. Laurence (1917–).

BIBLIOGRAPHY.—W. A. Shaw, *A Bibliography of the Works of . . . Lord Acton*, Royal Historical Society (1903); G. P. Gooch, "Acton: Apostle of Liberty," in *Foreign Affairs* (July 1947); D. Mathews, *Acton: the Formative Years* (1946); G. Himmelfarb, *Lord Acton* (1952); G. E. Fasnacht, *Acton's Political Philosophy* (1952).

(A. W. J.)

ACTON, SIR JOHN FRANCIS EDWARD (1736–1811), English baronet who was prime minister of Naples under Ferdinand IV, was the son of Edward Acton, a physician at Besançon, France, and was born there in 1736. He succeeded to a distant cousin's baronetcy and estates in 1791. Acton served in the navy of Tuscany and in 1775 commanded a frigate in the joint expedition of Spain and Tuscany against Algiers and distinguished himself in action. In 1779 Queen Maria Carolina of Naples, acting on the advice of Prince Caramanico, persuaded her brother the grand duke Leopold of Tuscany to allow Acton to reorganize the Neapolitan navy. He became commander in chief of both services, minister of finance, and finally prime minister. Acton's rise to power was rapid. The rivalry of Caramanico prompted Acton to send him as ambassador to England and then to France. Caramanico's sudden death while on a diplomatic mission to Sicily in 1794 cast suspicion on Acton, but no evidence of foul play has ever been discovered. Acton's policy aimed at substituting Austrian and British influence for Spanish in Naples, and consequently involved open opposition to the French in Italy during the French Revolutionary and Napoleonic Wars. In December 1798 he shared the flight of the king and queen. For the reign of terror which followed the downfall of the Parthenopean republic, five months later, Acton has been held responsible. In 1804 he was for a short time deprived of the reins of government at the demand of France; but he was soon restored to his former position which he held until, in February 1806, on the entry of the French into Naples, he had to flee with the royal family into Sicily. He died at Palermo on Aug. 12, 1811. (*See also* FERDINAND I [king of the Two Sicilies].)

Acton's elder son, Richard, was the father of Lord Acton, the historian. His second son, Charles Januarius Edward (1803–47), became a member of the Curia Romana, helped to secure the increase, in 1840, of the English Roman Catholic vicariates-general to eight (which paved the way for the restoration of the English Roman Catholic hierarchy in 1850) and was created cardinal in 1842.

See Harold Acton, *The Bourbons of Naples* (1956).

ACTS OF THE APOSTLES, the fifth book of the New Testament. This book was written in Greek by Luke as the sequel to his gospel, though it may have been penned after a first draft and before the final one of the gospel. Acts is historically of unique interest and value, being the one church history that is primitive both in spirit and in substance; apart from it a real picture of the apostolic age would be impossible. With it, the Pauline epistles are of priceless historical value; without it, they would remain bafflingly fragmentary, often even misleading, owing to their "occasional" nature and emphasis.

Contents.—After the first five introductory verses, addressed to Theophilus (an unknown person to whom the gospel of Luke also is addressed), Acts may be divided into six sections:

1. i, 6–v, 42. The origins of the church at Jerusalem (the Ascension; the choice of Matthias to take Judas' place as an apostle; the coming of the Holy Ghost at Pentecost; Peter's first speech, which won 3,000 converts; the healing of a lame man at the gate of the Temple by Peter and John, which led to their imprisonment by the Jewish authorities because they were preaching the resurrection of the dead; their release the next day after a severe caution to which they replied that they must obey God rather than man; the attempt among the Christians to have all things in common; further imprisonment of the apostles and their release on the Jewish rabbi Gamaliel's advice).

2. vi, 1–ix, 31. The death of Stephen and the spread of the church in Palestine, leading to Paul's conversion (the appointment of seven men to relieve the administrative burden of the apostles; the arrest of one of them, Stephen, by the Jews on charges of blasphemy; his defense and execution; the Jewish persecution of the church in Jerusalem which caused dispersal of Christians through Judaea and Samaria; the conversion of an Ethiopian eunuch by Philip, another of the seven; the conversion to Christ of Saul [Paul] the Pharisee on his way to Damascus to persecute the Christians).

3. ix, 32–xii, 24. The missionary work of Peter (Peter's curing of diseases at Lydda and Joppa; his dream at Joppa that he must not call things common which God had purified, followed by his visit to a gentile named Cornelius to whom the Holy Spirit was given in his presence; his baptizing of Cornelius and his household; his justification of disregarding the Jewish Law which convinced

the Jewish Christians in Jerusalem; the visit of Barnabas and Saul to Antioch and to Judaea with aid for famine relief; the martyrdom of James the son of Zebedee; the imprisonment and miraculous escape of Peter).

4. xii, 25–xvi, 5. The beginning of Paul's missionary travels and the apostolic council (Barnabas and Saul's journey from Antioch to Cyprus, Antioch in Pisidia, Iconium, Lystra and Derbe and their return; the apostolic council at Jerusalem which decided on what terms gentiles should be admitted to the church; the sending of Paul and Barnabas to Antioch with this message; Paul's second missionary journey with Silas to Syria and Cilicia).

5. xvi, 6–xix, 20. Paul's travels from Philippi to Ephesus (Paul and Silas' journey through Phrygia and Galatia to Philippi, Thessalonica, Beroea, Athens and Corinth; their return via Ephesus to Antioch; the third missionary journey through Galatia and Phrygia to Ephesus).

6. xix, 21–xxviii, 31. Paul's return to Jerusalem, his arrest and voyage to Rome (his address to the Ephesians after an uproar in favour of the goddess Diana; his visit to Macedonia; his return via Ephesus to Jerusalem, where he was arrested by the Jews for defiling the Temple; his appearance before the Sanhedrin; his removal to Caesarea and defense before Felix; his subsequent defense before Festus and appeal to Caesar; his voyage to Rome, including shipwreck on Malta; his meeting with the Jews in Rome, where he remained two years).

Authorship.—The name of the author of Acts appears in neither the title nor the book itself, but both external and internal evidence point to Luke, who is almost universally accepted as the writer. It is here assumed that Luke wrote the gospel that goes under his name (*see* LUKE, GOSPEL ACCORDING TO SAINT).

The earliest external evidence for Lucan authorship is found toward the end of the 2nd century. The so-called anti-Marcionite prologue to Luke's gospel (usually dated *c.* 180, though it may be later) states that Luke wrote Acts after his gospel. The Muratorian canon (*c.* 180–200; the oldest extant list of New Testament writings) also affirms Lucan authorship, and Irenaeus (*c.* 180) implies it. Clement of Alexandria (*c.* 200) and later church fathers accept it as Luke's work.

Internal evidence is found in the opening verse of Acts ("In the first book, O Theophilus, I have dealt with all that Jesus began to do and teach . . ."), which is addressed, like the dedication of Luke's gospel (Luke i, 1–4), to Theophilus, a Christian convert. It is natural to suppose that these two books, one of them apparently referring back to the other ("the first book") and both addressed to the same person, are the work of one author. Luke's gospel and Acts have strong affinities in both style and approach, which minute linguistic analysis has not been able to minimize.

Further, Luke is mentioned by Paul as a close friend and fellow worker (Col. iv, 14; Philem. 24). Now there are passages in Acts which appear to be written by a companion of Paul; in xvi, 10, without any previous warning, the narrative passes from the third person to the first: "And when he had seen the vision, immediately *we* sought to go on into Macedonia." Thenceforth "we" re-emerges at certain points in the story until Rome is reached. These parts at least are generally held to have been written by an eye-witness. If so, this eyewitness was almost certainly the author of the whole work, for the style of the "we" passages cannot be distinguished from that of the rest of the book. Thus Luke as a known companion of Paul is a possible author.

That Luke was a medical man is shown by Paul's reference to him as "the beloved physician" (Col. iv, 14), and some scholars have seen the medical cast of the language in certain passages of Acts as confirmation of Lucan authorship, though others have pointed out that no more medical knowledge is betrayed in Acts than would be possessed by any educated writer. The early tradition that Luke was born in Antioch suits the way in which the origin of the Antiochene church and its place in the extension of the gospel are described.

Although no one of the points here enumerated is alone conclusive, taken together they make a strong case for Lucan authorship, especially when it is remembered that this tradition is uncontradicted by any early Christian source. If Luke were not the

author there would have been no reason why his comparatively obscure name should ever have been associated with Acts at all.

Plan and Aim.—Acts is the work of an author of high literary skill, who exercised careful selection in the use of his materials, in keeping with a definite purpose and plan. It is therefore important to discover what these were. Luke himself gives hints about his aim at the beginning of the book (i, 1–11):

1. He implies that this second book is the logical sequence to his first. As his gospel set forth in orderly sequence the providential stages whereby Jesus was led, "in the power of the Spirit," to begin the establishment of the Kingdom of God, so Acts sets forth its extension by means of His chosen representatives or apostles.

2. This involves emphasis on the identity of the power, divine and not merely human, visible in the great series of facts from first to last; God's Spirit appears as active throughout.

3. But further, the divine energy in the disciples is conditioned by the continued influence and volition of their Lord at His Father's right hand in heaven: "Holy Spirit," the holy power of His personality (*cf.* xvi, 7 "the Spirit of Jesus"), is the living link between His actions and theirs (i, 2, 4 ff., 8; ii, 1–5; *cf.* Luke xxiv, 49).

4. And the scope of this action is nothing less than all mankind (i, 8; ii, 5 ff.), especially within the Roman empire.

5. Finally, as the parallel in Luke xxiv, 46–48 shows, the divinely appointed method of victory is through suffering (Acts xiv, 22), as it was for Jesus himself. This explains the space devoted to the tribulations of his witnesses, and their constancy amid them. It forms part of the virtual *apologia* for the absence of that earthly prosperity in which the ancient mind was apt to look for divine approval. Moreover, the church's enemies were chiefly Jews, whose opposition Luke regards as due to blindness to the wider reading of their own religion—to which the Holy Spirit had from of old been pointing (*cf.* Stephen's speech)—and to jealousy of those who, by preaching the wider messianic good news, were winning the gentiles, and particularly proselytes, in such numbers.

These, then, seem to be Luke's main motifs: the universality of the gospel, the jealousy of national Judaism, and the divine initiative, shown particularly in the gradual stages by which men of Jewish birth were led, in spite of their own prejudices, to recognize the divine will in the setting aside of national restrictions as alien to the universal destiny of Christ's church. The practical moral of the book is the divine character of the Christian religion, as evinced by the manner of its extension in the empire no less than by its original expression in its founder's life and death. Thus both of Luke's books tend to produce assured conviction of Christianity as of divine origin.

This view gives Acts a practical religious aim, for all early Christian writings were propaganda. In spite of the difficulties, Luke implies, this religion is worthy of belief, even though it means opposition and suffering. To meet this source of doubt Luke holds up the picture of early days, when Paul, the great apostle of the gentiles, enjoyed protection at the hands of Roman justice. It is implied that present distress is but a passing phase, resting on misunderstanding; for Christianity, as the true fulfillment of Israel's religion, had once been (and might again be) treated as a recognized (*licita*) religion, the more so in that it had deep kinship with non-Jewish philosophic monotheism. Meantime the example of apostolic constancy should inspire like fidelity. Acts is in fact an *apologia* for the church as distinct from Judaism, the breach with which is accordingly traced with fullness and care.

From this standpoint Acts does not, as some have thought, seem to end abruptly. Whether as exhibiting the divine leading and aid, or as recording the normal attitude of the Roman state, Luke at his conclusion reaches the climax of the gospel's progress: the arrival of Paul in Rome. In keeping with this, the solemn close of the book is xxviii, 26–28, the last two verses (30, 31) describing Paul's two-year stay in Rome being an appended observation. Yet even here, by the final word of all ("unhindered") Luke ends most fittingly on one of his keynotes.

The Question of Sources.—It is known that Luke used Mark's gospel and probably other sources when composing his own gospel. The question therefore naturally arises as to whether he also depended on earlier documents when writing Acts. He would perhaps have had more need to do so in the first 15 chapters, which describe events in which he had not taken part, but he might also have used sources for some of the rest of the book.

Attempts have been made to postulate sources deriving from the place that forms the setting of certain sections of the narrative. For instance, in the first part of the book some scholars have distinguished a Jerusalem source, a Jerusalem-Caesarean source and a Jerusalem-Antiochian source. Others have made supposed differences in theology, outlook and style the basis for the postulation of sources. The "we" passages can be pressed into service in this connection. If their author is not the same as the author of Acts, then they would be an earlier source used by the latter but so insufficiently edited as to stand out as unassimilated fragments of a diary. There is no trace in Acts of dependence on the Pauline epistles, the only relevant documents still extant which Luke might have read.

But the search for passages in Acts that are based on earlier documents is bound to be guesswork, for no such sources have actually survived, so suppositions about them cannot be checked. In any case it is perhaps more probable that Luke elicited the material for his book by questioning the persons directly concerned with the events.

Historical Accuracy of Acts.—Acts shows accurate knowledge of both geographical and political conditions in the Roman empire of Luke's day, insofar as it can be checked by secular sources and by archaeology. The different titles of the Roman imperial officials mentioned are correctly given; for instance: *anthypatos* ("proconsul") in Cyprus (xiii, 7), Asiarchs at Ephesus in the province of Asia (xix, 31). The historicity of the famine in xi, 28 is supported by contemporary information. The trustworthiness of Acts on such matters is an indication that it is also to be generally relied upon in giving an accurate account of events in the early church.

Problems of Correlation With Paul's Epistles.—It is not possible to check the accuracy of the narrative in the first 12 chapters of Acts—which deal with the church in Jerusalem and Judaea and with Peter as the central figure—with any other contemporary document, as there is none that touches on the same events. But the last part of the book pursues the history of the apostle Paul, and here it can be compared with the latter's epistles. The result of such correlation reveals a general harmony, without any trace of direct use by Luke of the epistles, and there are many minute coincidences. But there are also two remarkable discrepancies: the account given in Paul's epistle to the Galatians of his visits to Jerusalem as compared with the narrative of Acts, and the nature of his mission as it appears in his letters generally and in Acts.

Briefly, the first problem here is the difficulty of correlating the three visits of Paul to Jerusalem described in Acts with the two only that are mentioned by Paul himself in Galatians (*q.v.*). If the council visit in Acts xv is to be identified with the second visit in Galatians (Gal. ii, 1–10), for the subject of circumcising gentile converts to the faith came up on both occasions, it is surprising that Paul in Gal. ii, 1–5 never even mentions the actual council decision, which would have been relevant to the point he was trying to make in Galatians, namely that in Christ the gentile Christian is freed from the Law, including the necessity of circumcision. If, on the contrary, it is the visit of Acts xi, 27–30 (when Paul and Barnabas brought famine relief to the Jerusalem Christians) that is to be identified with the second visit in Galatians, then naturally the council decision is not mentioned in Galatians, as the council had not yet taken place. Too much however can be made of the difficulties of reconciling Acts and Galatians on this point. Both Luke and Paul had their own special aims in writing, and either may have omitted material that to the modern reader might seem essential but that to him was irrelevant. It must for instance be remembered that Paul's purpose in Galatians was to give an account not of his movements but of his authority as a preacher of the gospel.

The other discrepancy concerns the nature of Paul's mission. In his epistles Paul insists that he was the apostle to the gentiles, as Peter was to the circumcised, and that circumcision and the observance of the Jewish Law were of no importance to Christians as such. But in Acts it is Peter who first opens up the way to the gentiles (x, xi), and who uses the strongest language in regard to the intolerable burden of the Law as a means of salvation (xv, 10 ff.). Acts says nothing of the occasion in Gal. ii, 11 ff. when Paul rebuked Peter for inconsistency in his behaviour to gentile converts for fear of the Jewish Christians. In Acts, Paul is not shown as the unbending champion of the gentiles; he seems anxious to reconcile the Jewish Christians by personally obeying the Law, he circumcises his disciple Timothy, who had a Jewish mother, he performs his vows in the temple, he is particularly careful in his speeches to show how deep is his respect for the Law. On the other hand, however, Acts implies something other than what it sets in relief, for why should the Jews hate Paul so much if he was not in some sense disloyal to their Law?

There is, nevertheless, no essential contradiction here, only such a difference of emphasis as belongs to the standpoints and aims of the two writers and to different historical conditions. Peter's function in relation to the gentiles belongs to early Palestinian conditions, before Paul's distinctive mission had taken place. Once Paul's apostolate had proved itself by tokens of divine approval, Peter and his colleagues frankly recognized the distinction of the two missions, and were anxious only that the two should not fall apart through religiously and morally incompatible usages (Gal. ii, 10; *cf.* Acts xv). Paul on his side clearly implies that Peter felt that "a man is not justified by works of the law" (Gal. ii, 15 ff.), and argues that the Law could not now be made obligatory in principle, though for Jews it might continue for the time (pending Christ's second coming) to be seemly and expedient. To this he conformed his own conduct as a Jew, so far as his gentile apostolate was not involved (I Cor. ix, 9 ff.). Peter must have largely agreed with him, since he acted in this spirit himself until coerced by Jerusalem sentiment to draw back for expediency's sake (Gal. ii, 11 ff.). It did not fall within the scope of Acts to narrate this incident, since it had no lasting effect on the church's extension.

Speeches.—Ancient Greek historians used the liberty of working up in their own language the speeches they inserted into their narrative; they molded a speaker's thoughts to their own methods of presentation. Some went so far for the sake of vividness as to give to their characters speeches never really uttered. The author of Acts, heir to the Jewish as well as to the Greek methods of writing history, cannot be assumed to have used speeches as freely as Herodotus had done; some of the speeches in Acts are bare summaries. Others claim to be reports of speeches actually delivered. Many are based on the *kerygma* or pattern of apostolic preaching (*see* PREACHING). Though all have passed through one mind, and some mutual assimilation in phraseology and idea may have resulted, yet these circumstances, while inconsistent with complete verbal accuracy, do not destroy authenticity; in most cases there is varied appropriateness (*e.g.*, xiv, 15–17), as well as allusiveness, pointing to good information. There is no evidence that any speech in Acts is a free composition by Luke without either written or oral basis; and in general he seems nearer than most ancient historians, even Thucydides, to the essentials of historical accuracy.

Date.—External evidence points to the existence of Acts at least as early as the opening years of the 2nd century. Both Ignatius and Polycarp appear to quote from it, and if the author of the Second Epistle to Timothy drew his knowledge of Paul's career from Acts (II Tim. iii, 11) then Acts must have been written well before the year 100. It is further just possible that the unusual form of a quotation from Ps. lxxxix (lxxxviii), 20 in the first epistle of Clement may have been borrowed from Acts xiii, 22, in which case Acts was written before *c.* 96. It has been suggested that Acts used the later works of the Jewish historian Josephus, which would place it after 94, but the only passage which might show contact between them (the reference to Theudas and Judas in Acts v, 36 ff., compared with the account of Theudas and the sons of Judas in Josephus' *Antiquitates*) is more probably due to dependence on a common source.

The *terminus ad quem* of Acts is probably *c.* 90. The *terminus a quo* cannot be settled without consideration of the date of Luke's gospel, the relation of Acts to it, the ending of Acts and its lack of reference to Paul's death, to the fall of Jerusalem in 70 or to any Pauline epistle. A date prior to 70 can be maintained, for this would leave time for Luke to use Mark's gospel, written *c.* 64–67, as he clearly did (*e.g.*, Acts i, 7 picks up Mark xiii, 32; Acts vi, 11–12 alludes to Mark xiv, 58, 64; Acts xii, 4 picks up Mark xiv, 12; Acts ix, 40 echoes Mark v, 40). Acts may even have been written by Luke after an early draft of his gospel and before the final text of it (which omits Marcan parallels already used in Acts). However, many scholars, assuming that Luke wrote Acts after his gospel, prefer a date from 75–80. This later date is favoured by form critics and typologists, as it allows more time for the growth and formulation of oral traditions. Those who hold the unlikely theory that "Q" (the postulated common source other than Mark for the gospels of Matthew and Luke; *see* GOSPELS) did not exist, but that Luke's gospel used Matthew's, also welcome the extra time allowed by the date 75–80.

Text.—Acts offers complicated problems to the textual critic. There are two groups of manuscripts, the "Alexandrian" and the "Western" (*see* BIBLE: *New Testament; Text*). The misleading term "western" really stands for a glossing or paraphrastic text, comparable to a Targum (*q.v.*) on an Old Testament book; it became widespread in the east as well as the west from the 2nd century. The Western text of Acts seems to be a 2nd-century recension of a popular nature, to which other Western additions were made later; the Alexandrian revision was slighter and nearer the archetype. It is not possible that Luke himself was the author of both texts, the Western being, for Acts, the original. The Western text is of value not only because it preserves some variants lost in the Alexandrian stream of transmission but also because it sheds light on ecclesiastical thought as early as the 2nd century. Acts, from its very scope, was the book least likely to be viewed as sacrosanct in its text; indeed there are signs that its undogmatic nature caused it to be comparatively neglected at certain times and places.

BIBLIOGRAPHY.—Text with Eng. trans., introduction and commentary in F. J. F. Jackson and K. Lake (eds.), *The Beginnings of Christianity*, vol. i–v (1920–33); text with introduction and commentary by F. F. Bruce (1951); text with introduction and notes on selected passages by A. C. Clark (1933); Eng. trans. with introduction and commentary by F. F. Bruce (1954) and by C. S. C. Williams (1957); German trans. with introduction and commentary by E. Haenchen, 3rd ed. (1959). *See also* A. von Harnack, *The Acts of the Apostles* (1909); H. J. Cadbury, *The Making of Luke-Acts* (1927) and *The Book of Acts in History* (1955); W. L. Knox, *The Acts of the Apostles* (1948); A. H. McNeile, *Introduction to the Study of the New Testament*, 2nd ed., pp. 92–123 (1953); W. M. Ramsay, *St. Paul the Traveller and the Roman Citizen* (1903); E. Trocmé, *Le Livre des Actes et l'histoire* (1957); M. Dibelius, *Studies in the Acts of the Apostles*, ed. by H. Greeven (1956). (J. V. B.; C. S. C. W.)

ACTUARY, an expert who calculates insurance risks and premiums. He computes the probability of the occurrence of various contingencies of human life such as birth, marriage, sickness, unemployment, accident, retirement and death. The actuary also deals with the contingencies concerned with the hazards of property damage or loss and the legal liability for the safety and well-being of others. On the basis of these evaluations, risks affecting lives or property can be insured. This embraces the areas of life insurance, accident and health insurance, annuities, pensions and social insurance as well as fire, casualty and marine insurance.

The name is derived from the Latin *actuarius,* denoting the clerk who recorded the *acta* or proceedings of the senate, a court or a similar body. In its English form the word has undergone a gradual limitation of meaning. At first it seems to have been applied to any clerk or registrar in the sense that a clerk represented a person of book learning, and was especially applicable to a notary, secretary or accountant; then, before acquiring its present specialized meaning, it denoted the secretary and adviser of an insurance company.

Actuarial science developed from the concept that the experience of the past may be utilized to measure the chances of the future. It deals with monetary questions involving separately or in combination the mathematical doctrine of probabilities and the principles of compound interest.

Ever since an actuary was designated the founding chief executive officer of the first modern life insurance company in 1762 (the Equitable Society of England), most actuaries have been employed by insurance companies. The actuary is, in a way, the engineer of the insurance company; he makes statistical studies to establish basic mortality and morbidity tables, develops corresponding premium rates, establishes underwriting practices and procedures, determines the amounts of money (reserves) required to assure payment of benefits, analyzes company earnings and counsels with the accounting staff in establishing adequate records and preparing financial statements; he plays a major role in the development of new forms of coverage and the establishment of investment policy. He is also concerned with the application of electronic data processing machines to these operations. In many insurance companies he is a senior officer and in some the chief executive officer.

Some actuaries serve as consultants and some are employed by large industrial corporations to advise on insurance and pension matters. The government employs actuaries in its work of regulating the insurance business and in connection with social security programs, retirement plans, census taking and operations research for the military services.

There are two professional societies of actuaries in Great Britain and two in the United States to which membership admission is by formal examinations. These societies include members from Canada. The British societies are incorporated by royal charters—the Institute of Actuaries, London, founded in 1848, the oldest professional actuarial body in the world; and the Faculty of Actuaries, Edinburgh, founded in 1856. The United States societies are the Society of Actuaries, Chicago, formed in 1949 through merger of the Actuarial Society of America (founded in 1889) with the American Institute of Actuaries (founded in 1909); and the Casualty Actuarial society, New York, organized in 1914. The examinations for membership deal with fundamental mathematics; actuarial theory (including life and other contingencies, probability theory, statistics, demography and mathematics of finance); and elements of social security and insurance law, investments and accounting.

The Conference of Actuaries in Public Practice, Chicago, was organized in 1950. There are also many local actuarial clubs.

Besides Great Britain and the United States, many other nations have actuarial associations. The International Congress of Actuaries, with headquarters in Brussels, Belg., held its first meeting in 1895. Its affairs are directed by a permanent committee, membership of which is on an international basis. It customarily meets in a different country every third year if world conditions permit. The first International Conference of Social Security Actuaries and Statisticians was held in Brussels in 1956. (A. C. O.)

ACUÑA, CRISTÓBAL DE (1597–*c.* 1676), Spanish Jesuit missionary and explorer in the Amazon, was born at Burgos in 1597. He was sent on mission work to Chile and Peru and became rector of Cuenca college. In 1639 he accompanied Pedro Teixeira in his second exploration of the Amazon to take scientific observations and draw up a report for the Spanish government. The journey lasted ten months; on the explorer's arrival in Peru, Acuña prepared his narrative, while awaiting a ship for Europe. The king of Spain, Philip IV, received the author coldly and it is said even tried to suppress his book, fearing that the Portuguese, who had just revolted from Spain (1640), would profit by its information. Eventually Acuña returned to South America where he died, probably soon after 1675. His *Nuevo Descubrimento del Gran Río de las Amazonas* was published at Madrid in 1641; French and English translations (the latter from the French) appeared in 1682 and 1698.

ACUPUNCTURE, also known as needling, is a form of surgical procedure devised in China many centuries B.C. Its practice consists of the insertion of needles of various metals, shapes and sizes into one or several of 365 spots which are specified for this purpose on the human trunk, the extremities and the head. Acupuncture has been in continuous use in China and in Japan where it was introduced together with Chinese medicine. Since it is supposed to relieve internal congestion and to restore the equilibrium of the bodily functions, acupuncture has been used for a vast variety of diseases and especially for the treatment of arthritis, headache, convulsions, lethargy, colic, etc. In the 1930s the practice became popular and years later was still in use in several European countries, especially France and Germany.

A practice similar to acupuncture and of equal antiquity is that of moxibustion or moxa treatment, which also originated in China and thence spread to Japan. It is practised by placing little combustible cones of the dried leaves of *Artemisia moxa*, or wormwood, on certain designated spots, which generally coincide with those used for acupuncture. The cones are then ignited and burned down to the skin where a small blister arises. While moxa treatment has not been adopted by western medicine, it is practised in the United States by Japanese physicians, and occasionally Japanese patients with recent scars of moxa burns are seen in U.S. hospitals. There is no known physiological basis to either acupuncture or moxibustion.

See Ilza Veith, *The Yellow Emperor's Classic of Internal Medicine* (1949); Ming Wong, "Acupuncture ancienne et acupuncture moderne," *Bulletin de la Société de l'Acupuncture*, no. 54 (1964).　　(I. V.)

ADAB (mod. BISMAYA), an ancient city of the Sumerians situated in southern Iraq, about 25 mi. S. of Nippur. Small excavations made there by E. J. Banks in 1903–04 revealed buildings dating back from the reign of Ur-Nammu (at the end of the 22nd century B.C.) to prehistoric periods, as well as an inscribed statuette of a king Lugal-dalu, dressed in the characteristic Sumerian fleece garment. Adab was important only up to *c.* 2000 B.C. The Sumerian king list ascribed to it one of the early dynasties, comprising only one king, Lugal-anne-mundu, said to have reigned for 90 years; according to his position in the list, this would have been about 2400 B.C. An inscription of later date claims for him sovereignty over many lands east and west of Babylonia and the suppression of revolts. Otherwise, fragments discovered at the site show that Adab was held by successive rulers over the whole country such as Me-silim, Naram-Sin, Shulgi and Hammurabi. Its principal deity was the goddess Ninkhursag, whose temple was called *e-sar* or *e-makh* ("the exalted house"). During the 3rd dynasty of Ur in the 22nd and 21st centuries B.C. Adab was under governors appointed by the kings of Ur.

See E. J. Banks, *Bismya or the Lost City of Adab* (1912); S. A. Pallis, *The Antiquity of Iraq*, p. 367 (1956).　　(C. J. G.)

ADAD, the great weather god of the Babylonian and Assyrian pantheon, was known to the Sumerians as Ishkur and to the Canaanites and Arameans as Addu or Hadad (both variants of Adad) and as Ramman (Old Testament Rimmon, "the thunderer"). The name Adad would appear to have been brought into Mesopotamia during the later years of the 3rd millennium B.C. by western (Amorite) Semites. Related to this is the fact that one of the god's Babylonian names is Amurru.

Adad has a twofold aspect, being both the giver and the destroyer of life. His rains cause the land to bear grain, wine and food for his friends; hence his title "lord of abundance." His storms and hurricanes, evidences of his anger against his foes, bring darkness, want and death upon the earth. His destructive energy is represented on some seal cylinders which show him erect on a bull and holding a thunderbolt. The bull and the lion are sacred to him.

Adad's father was the heaven god Anu, but he is also designated as the son of Bel, "lord of all lands." His consort was Shalash, whose name may be Hurrian, and who is represented sometimes naked, at other times clothed. The symbol of Adad was the cypress, six was his sacred number and Shabat his month. In Babylonia and Assyria he was god of oracles and divination, being accompanied in the former country by the sun-god Shamash and in the latter by the heaven god Anu.

At Aleppo in Syria, too, Adad was an oracle-deity, and he sometimes figures alongside Sin (the moon-god) and Shamash in the secondary cosmic triad. Adad also figures in local myths. In the epic of the divine punishment of men, plants and grain fail because he withholds rain. In the deluge story he thunders in a black cloud which rises up from the horizon. In the ensuing darkness men are unrecognizable even by the gods, who, in terror, ascend to the heaven of Anu. In the myth of the Zu-bird, who had stolen the tablets of destiny, Adad is asked to slay the thief, but his father forbids it.

Unlike the greater gods, Adad quite possibly had no cult centre peculiar to himself. Early in the 2nd millennium B.C. his cult is evidenced chiefly by theophoric names which are almost all Semitic in form. In succeeding millennia he was worshiped in Babylon, where his temple bore the name "house of abundance," and in many of the important cities and towns of Mesopotamia. A great temple to him and to Anu has been found at Ashur, the capital of Assyria. *See* also BABYLONIA AND ASSYRIA: *Religion: Sumerian Pantheon;* HADAD.

BIBLIOGRAPHY.—G. Contenau, *La Vie quotidienne à Babylone et en Assyrie* (Eng. trans. by K. R. and A. R. Maxwell-Hyslop, *Everyday Life in Babylon and Assyria*, 1954); A. Deimel, *Pantheon Babylonicum* (1914); E. (Paul) Dhorme, *Les Religions de Babylonie d'Assyrie* (1945); S. N. Kramer, *From the Tablets of Sumer* (1956); J. B. Pritchard (ed.), *Ancient Near Eastern Texts Relating to the Old Testament*, 2nd ed. (1955); H. and H. A. Frankfort, J. A. Wilson and T. Jacobsen, *Before Philosophy* (1949).　　(T. FH.)

ADAIR, JOHN (*c.* 1654–56 to 1720–22), Scottish surveyor and map maker who completed maps of the counties along the Forth and charts of the Forth, Clyde and west of Scotland, of a high standard for their period (*c.* 1680–86). Manuscripts of these are in the Scottish National and other libraries. Other maps and charts prepared by Adair—those of the west coast at considerable risk and peril—were not printed. In 1688 he was elected a fellow of the Royal society. At about this time Capt. John Slezer claimed, and was granted, a share in the tax allotted by the government to Adair for surveying Scotland and navigating its coasts. In 1693 Slezer produced his *Theatrum Scotiae* (reprinted 1814), and in 1703 Adair published the first part of his *Description of the Sea Coasts and Islands of Scotland,* for the use of seamen. The second part never appeared. Judging from his delicate delineations, Adair's search for perfection may have delayed completion of his work. In 1723 a payment was made to Adair's widow for unpublished manuscripts which were deposited in the Bodleian library and British museum　　(AR. G.)

ADALBERON (ASCELIN) (d. *c.* 1030), Frankish bishop of Laon remembered for his role in the accession of the Capetian dynasty to the crown of France and as a poet. Bishop of Laon from 977, he was imprisoned for a time when Charles, duke of Lower Lorraine, the Carolingian claimant to the crown, took the city in 988. Subsequently, however, he won the duke's confidence and so was able, in 991, to betray Laon, together with Charles and Arnulf his relative, archbishop of Reims, into the hand of Hugh (*q.v.*) Capet. In 1017 Adalberon wrote a satirical poem, dedicated to Robert II of France, in which he criticized the elevation of men of humble origin to bishoprics and claimed that bishops had the right to guide the local princes. The text is printed by J. P. Migne in *Patrologia Latina*, cxli (1853).

BIBLIOGRAPHY.—The contemporary history of the period by Richer is ed. with Fr. trans. by R. Latouche as *Histoire de France (888–995)*, 2 vol. (1931–37). *See* further A. Olleris, *Vie de Gerbert, premier pape français sous le nom de Sylvestre II* (1867); the Benedictine *Histoire littéraire de la France,* vii, new ed. (1867); A. Luchaire, *Les Premiers Capétiens* (1901).　　(J. DE.)

ADALBERT (ADELBERT), **SAINT** (*c.* 700), English deacon, accompanied Willibrord in 690 in the evangelization of Friesland and is said to have been appointed archdeacon of Utrecht. He established a church at Egmont and apparently died there. His cult there is ancient; many miracles have been reported. In the 10th century he became the patron saint of a Benedictine abbey constructed by Theodoric, duke of Holland. At about the same time his life's story, attributed to Rupert of Mettlach, appeared which remains the chief source. St. Adalbert's feast is on June 25.

See H. Thurston and D. Attwater (eds.), *Butler's Lives of the Saints*, vol. ii, pp. 641–642 (1956).　　(Fs. P. C.)

ADALBERT (VOYTECH), **SAINT** (956–997), the first bishop (982) of Prague of Czech origin, was descended from the Slavnikovs, Bohemian princes. He was trained in theology at Magdeburg, which conformed to the strict principles of the Cluny reform; there he received the name Adalbert at his confirmation. As bishop he promoted the political aims of Boleslav II, the ruler of

Bohemia, by extending the influence of the church beyond the borders of the Czech kingdom. Critical of the superficial attitude to Christianity prevalent in the country, he departed in 988 with the intention of leading the ascetic life of a monk. On papal orders he returned in 992 to find but little change. He came into sharp conflict with some of the nobility, being probably drawn into the growing feuds between the Czech kings and the Slavnikov princes, and in 994 left the country again to become a missionary to Prussia, where he was martyred. He was canonized in 999, and his feast day is April 23.

ADALBERT (ADELBERT) (c. 1000–1072), German archbishop, the most brilliant of the medieval prince bishops of Bremen, and a leading member of the royal administration, was the youngest son of Frederick, count of Goseck (on the Saale river). Destined by his father for an ecclesiastical career, Adalbert attended the cathedral school at Halberstadt, becoming subsequently subdeacon and, in 1032, canon. In May 1043 he was appointed archbishop of Hamburg-Bremen by the emperor Henry III. High in the emperor's favour, Adalbert had ambitious plans for his see, dreaming of a "patriarchate of the North" which, by forestalling the creation of Scandinavian archbishoprics, would confirm the ecclesiastical supremacy that German missionaries had won for Bremen over all northern countries from Lapland to Iceland and Greenland. Pope Leo IX, however, though he made Adalbert his vicar for the northern countries in 1053, never allowed him to exercise the greater authority that he desired. In imperial politics, on the other hand, during the minority of Henry IV, Adalbert gained considerable influence as guardian and tutor to the young king. His secular ambitions involved him in conflict with the Saxon nobles and especially with the house of Billung (q.v.). In 1056 the lands of his bishopric were ravaged by Bernard II Billung, and he was humiliated in his own residence and had to flee to Goslar. Henry IV, however, granted Adalbert extensive powers in Saxony in 1063, but was obliged to dismiss him as royal adviser at the diet of Tribur in 1066, in view of the protests of the nobility. Although he was frequently at court after 1069, Adalbert never regained his political ascendancy. He died of dysentery at Goslar on March 16, 1072, and was buried in the cathedral at Bremen, the building of which he had done much to advance.

Adalbert's death was a serious blow to Bremen's commerce which under him had developed so rapidly that the town could be described as rivaling Rome in celebrity and as "the market of the northern peoples." Adam (q.v.) of Bremen has left a vivid description of his haughty, ambitious, pompous and yet personally irreproachable contemporary.

BIBLIOGRAPHY.—G. G. Dehio, *Geschichte des Erzbistums Hamburg-Bremen bis zum Ausgang der Mission* (1877).; B. Schmeidler, *Hamburg-Bremen und Nordost-Europa vom 9.–11. Jahrhundert* (1918); G. Misch, "Das Bild des Erzbischofs Adalbert in der Hamburgischen Kirchengeschichte des Domscholasters Adam von Bremen," *Nachr. Akad. Wiss. Göttingen,* no. 7 (1956).   (F. J. D. P.)

ADAM, the name of a family of French sculptors. LAMBERT SIGISBERT (1700–1759) executed many pieces for the French royal residences and for Frederick the Great of Prussia. NICOLAS SÉBASTIEN, his brother (1705–1778), was responsible for the tomb of Catherine Opalinska at Nancy. Another brother, FRANÇOIS GASPARD BALTHASAR, executed many of the monuments at Sans Souci and Potsdam.

ADAM OF BREMEN (11th century A.D.), German historian whose work on the archbishops of Hamburg-Bremen not only provides valuable information on German politics under the Salian emperors but also is one of the great books of early medieval geography. Of Franconian origin, he was probably educated at the cathedral school in Bamberg, but was introduced in 1066 or 1067 into the cathedral chapter at Bremen by Archbishop Adalbert (q.v.). In 1069 he was head of the cathedral school at Bremen. After Adalbert's death (1072), Adam began his *Gesta Hammaburgensis Ecclesiae Pontificum,* which he continually revised. He died on Oct. 12, in a year not long after 1081.

In four books, written with great care on the basis of old chronicles and documents, the *Gesta* constitutes a major source both for the diocese of Hamburg-Bremen in general and for the

life of Adalbert in particular, book iii containing a candid and vivid description of his personality and activities, which in turn leads inevitably to an account of the political affairs of the time. Book iv of the *Gesta,* moreover, gives a "description of the islands of the north" based on some trustworthy reports though also containing much hearsay. Besides dealing with Russia, the countries of the Balts, Scandinavia, Iceland and Greenland, Adam makes the earliest known reference to Vinland, that part of America reached by Leif Ericsson. The original Latin text is printed in *Monumenta Germaniae Historica,* vol. vii (1846). Translations include a German one edited by B. Schmeidler and S. H. Steinberg, *Hamburgische Kirchengeschichte* (1926); and an English one by F. J. Tschan, *History of the Archbishops of Hamburg-Bremen* (1959).

See B. Schmeidler, *Hamburg-Bremen und Nordost-Europa vom 9.–11. Jahrhundert* (1918); M. Dreijer, *Strövtåg kring mäster Adams av Bremen Nordenframställning,* with Eng. summary (1952).
                                                            (F. J. D. P.)

ADAM, ADOLPHE CHARLES (1803–1856), French composer, is remembered chiefly for his music for the ballet *Giselle,* which, although not distinguished in its own right, is notable for its power to enhance the dramatic situations which make the ballet one of the most popular with dancers and audiences. He was born in Paris, July 24, 1803, and became a pupil of Adrien Boieldieu. A prolific composer and a victim of his own facility, he wrote over 60 operas, of which the best are *Le Postillon de Longjumeau* (1836) and *Giralda* (1850). His ballets, subordinating music to choreographic demands, were written for production in London, Berlin and St. Petersburg as well as Paris, where the success of *Giselle* (1841) led to its inclusion in the repertory of most 20th-century ballet companies. He died in Paris, May 3, 1856.

ADAM, PAUL (1862–1920), French author whose early works exemplify the naturalist and symbolist schools and who later won considerable reputation for his historical and sociological novels. He was born in Paris, Dec. 7, 1862. Publication of his first naturalist novel, *Chair molle* (1885), led to his being prosecuted; his second, *Le Thé chez Miranda* (1886), written with Jean Moréas, is an early example of symbolism. In 1899, with *La Force,* he began a series of novels depicting French life during the period 1800–30; the last, *Au soleil de juillet,* appeared in 1903. He traveled widely and wrote two books on his American journeys, *Vues d'Amérique* (1906) and *Le Trust* (1910). His autobiography, in the form of a novel, *Jeunesse et amours de Manuel Héricourt,* appeared in 1913. He died in Paris, Jan. 1, 1920.

Adam's style is sometimes turgid, and he is better at conveying the force of ideas than of personalities, but his power of descriptive and poetic writing, nurtured by naturalism and symbolism, gives his work lasting literary value.

See F. Jean-Desthieux, *Paul Adam* (1928); T. Fogelberg, *La Langue et le style de Paul Adam* (1939).

ADAM, ROBERT (1728–1792), foremost British neoclassic architect and creator of the style named after him, was the second son of William Adam (1689–1748) and the most celebrated of four brothers, John, Robert, James and William. He was born at Kirkcaldy in Fife, Scot., on July 3, 1728. His father was the leading Scottish architect of his day and designed many country houses in a crude but vigorous Palladian style. Robert Adam was educated at Edinburgh high school and university. His architectural training was begun under his father and completed at Rome between 1755 and 1757 when he made an intensive study of imperial Roman architecture under the guidance of C. L. Clérisseau, the French architect and antiquary. With Clérisseau he also visited Naples, Florence, Vicenza and Venice, from where he made a voyage to Split in Dalmatia. The results of this archaeological expedition were published as *The Ruins of the Palace of the Emperor Diocletian at Spalatro* (1764).

After his return to England in 1758 Robert Adam rapidly achieved fame as an architect, being appointed architect of the king's works in 1761, together with Sir William Chambers. His younger brother James (1730–94), who made the grand tour with Clérisseau between 1760 and 1763, joined him in London.

In 1773 appeared the first volume of *The Works . . . of Robert and James Adam* in which the authors claimed "to have brought about . . . a kind of revolution in the whole system" of English architecture. By that date the Adam style (*see* the relevant sections of INTERIOR DECORATION, HISTORY OF: *Renaissance to the End of the 18th Century: England;* FURNITURE DESIGN), an elegant and sophisticated interpretation of neoclassicism, had completely superseded Palladianism in England and within a few years its influence had spread abroad as far as Russia in the east and America in the west. As designers of furniture the Adam brothers can claim to have been the precursors of the Louis XVI style in France. Their designs for ceilings and chimney pieces were widely copied by London and provincial builders and their influence was also felt in silver, metalwork and the applied arts generally.

Except at the Adelphi in London and, toward the end of his life, in Scotland, Robert Adam never obtained an opportunity to build on the scale his genius demanded. His English country houses were mostly adaptations of existing buildings and in some cases, for example at Syon house, his work was restricted to the interior. His best country houses—Harewood house, Kedleston, Newby hall, Kenwood, Luton Hoo, Nostell priory and Saltram— date from the 1760s and early 1770s. During the next decade he designed several important town houses, notably Home house, Portman square, London, which are masterpieces of ingenious planning and sophisticated decoration. He also prepared grandiose plans for Cambridge and Edinburgh universities, but neither was carried out. His only surviving monumental building is the Register house at Edinburgh. Although the Adam style is strictly

A. F. KERSTING

ENTRANCE HALL OF THE SYON HOUSE (C. 1761), ISLEWORTH, ENG., BY ROBERT ADAM

neoclassical, Robert Adam occasionally worked in a romantic neo-Gothic manner, notably in the now-destroyed interiors at Alnwick castle. He died on March 3, 1792. *See* also references under "Adam, Robert" in the Index.

BIBLIOGRAPHY.—John Swarbrick, *Robert Adam and His Brothers* (1916); A. T. Bolton, *The Architecture of Robert and James Adam* (1922); J. Lees-Milne, *The Age of Adam* (1948).   (J. FG.)

ADAM AND EVE. *Adam* (*'adham*) is one of several Hebrew words meaning "man," and usually designates man as a species. With the definite article or in the phrase "son of *'adham*" the word indicates an individual man. In Gen. i, 26–27 the word is used to designate the human species, created male and female, with no implication that a single couple or a group is meant. The word is used with the article through Gen. ii, 4—iii, 24 to designate the first man, the ancestor of the species. It does not appear as a proper personal name "Adam" before Gen. iv, 25 and v, 1. It is read as a proper name in the present Hebrew text of Gen. ii, 20 and iii, 17, but this is due to the vocalization of the Hebrew text, not to the consonantal text, which permits the word to be read as a proper name only in these verses. The use of the word as a personal name in later writings and in modern speech is not based upon the original text but upon a Jewish interpretation of the last few centuries B.C. The word has an assonance with the Hebrew word for soil (*'adhama*), and the two words may come from a root signifying "reddish," "ruddy."

The name Eve (Hebrew *hawwah*) is given to the first woman in Gen. iii, 20. The name is explained in this verse by a popular etymology as connected with the Hebrew word for "life." Modern scholars doubt the genuineness of this etymology, but of the several etymologies proposed none has been generally accepted.

The controversy between theologians and natural scientists concerning the story of Adam and Eve (Gen. ii, 4—iii, 24) was the result of a tacit understanding that the story was intended to convey historical and scientific information concerning human origins. Exegetes no longer understand the story in these terms. They take the chapters as an expression, in the form of a story, of certain Hebrew beliefs concerning the mutual relations of God, man and the universe. That the first man is called simply "the man" (or "Man") is not insignificant; he is intended to be typical. Hebrew folklore often represents the ancestor as a prototype, prefiguring not only in his character but also in his life the character and the experiences of his descendants. The early Hebrews had no historical or scientific information concerning human origins and constructed their story by the skilful combination of details drawn from popular traditions. The symbolism of most of these details can be understood by comparisons with the traditions of the ancient near east.

The story is attributed to the Jahwist source of the Pentateuch. It is often called "the second creation account" (after Gen. i, 1—ii, 4) but this designation is misleading. It contains nothing corresponding to the creation of the visible universe in Gen. i. It is an account of the origin of man, more precisely of man and of woman as sexually differentiated. In the religions of the ancient near east sexual differentiation was found in the gods and was thought to be as much a primary datum as the gods themselves. The Hebrews, rejecting any sexual character in the deity, insisted that sex is instituted in lower forms of being by a deity who is himself above sex.

Man is compounded of clay and of the animating breath of God (Gen. ii, 7). That man is clay is a literary commonplace not only in the Bible, but also in Mesopotamian and Egyptian literature. Man's origin from the soil is deduced from his return to the soil. Even the "molding" of the clay has an explicit parallel in Egyptian art, where the potter god Khnum is represented molding the human figure on the potter's wheel. The divine component in Mesopotamia was the blood of a slain god; Hebrew belief could not tolerate this grossness and replaced it with the more subtle element of breath. The man is placed in a garden in Eden (Gen. ii, 8–14); the geography of the passage is unreal and the garden has no location. The contrast between man's primitive bliss in the garden and the conditions of historical experience is explicit. No restraint is placed upon the man except the prohibition of eating the fruit of the tree of knowledge of good and evil (Gen. ii, 16–17). This tree has no parallel in ancient near eastern traditions; its symbolism is most probably to be understood in the context of the fall narrated in Gen. iii (*cf.* below). The tree of life, on the other hand, has numerous parallels in Mesopotamian literature and art. The tree stood next to the temple and was protected by guardian genii. In Mesopotamia life was communicated by touching a branch of the tree to the nostrils. The symbol in Genesis is obscurely drawn; the story is not interested in whether the fruit was to be eaten once or at regular intervals. The point of the symbolism is that primeval man had life without death within his grasp.

The story of the creation of the animals shows the difference between man and the animals and his superiority over them (Gen. ii, 19–20). The man gives them names; in the ancient world to confer a name was a sign of authority, and here also of superior intelligence. None of the animals is fit to live with man in society, and so the scene is set for the creation of woman. The creation of woman comes as the climax of the chapter, and this solemnity is not merely accidental. Her creation from the body of the man shows her community and equality with the man and her capacity to share his life. The protest against the depressed condition of woman in ancient society is as clear as it is surprising. The story places the institution of monogamous marriage, which is presented as the ideal relation of the sexes, at the beginning of the race; this ideal was not highly esteemed in the ancient east or even in Israel, but it was recalled by Jesus when he quoted the passage (Matt. xix, 3–8; Mark x, 2–9). The reflection upon the relation of the sexes in Gen. ii, 24 (union in one flesh) makes it highly improbable that the story intends to present the man and the woman as sexually immature, as many scholars have maintained. Rather their common life "without shame" seems to indicate an ideal of sexual morality in which the appetite is controlled. Gen. ii, 25, however, is somewhat obscure. It is possible that the original story contained at this point an account of the consummation of sexual union, which has been displaced by Gen. iii.

The situation of this couple suggests in its external features some details of Semitic mythology which it may echo. In the Mesopotamian deluge myth Ut-napishtim and his wife, the survivors of the deluge, live in isolated bliss in "a paradise of delight at the mouth of the two rivers" (the Tigris and Euphrates). The epic of Gilgamesh describes Enkidu, the companion of Gilgamesh, as created of clay, half man and half beast, living with the beasts in the open field. Gilgamesh instigated a harlot to seduce him; after his experience with the harlot Enkidu abandoned his wild manner of life and became a city dweller. The similarity must be pointed out, although the differences must not be ignored; Hebrew literature elsewhere has certainly borrowed colourful descriptive details from Semitic mythology.

The connection between Gen. ii and iii is obscure. Scholars have suggested various isolated stories from which the present narrative was composed; that these stories preceded the literary form is evident, but there is no agreement on their form. One may suggest three: the creation of man and the woman (perhaps originally two independent stories); the sin of the man; and the sin of the woman. The story of the sin of a man unaccompanied by a woman appears in Ezek. xxviii, 12–15. On the other hand, the man is strangely silent and inactive in Gen. iii, and it may be suspected that he has been inserted where he did not originally appear.

The symbolism of the serpent in ancient near eastern literature and art is multiple, but in general the serpent is a symbol of life (cf. the caduceus). In art the serpent is often represented with the nude goddess of fertility in such a way that it can be nothing but a sexual symbol. This suggests that the fall of man is represented as in some way a deviation from sexual morality. There is no probability in the opinion that the fall was the simple discovery and use of sex. This view is so foreign to the Hebrew attitude that it demands much more solid evidence than can be given. The presence of the serpent suggests the fertility cults of the ancient Semitic world, so often reprobated in the Old Testament.

The fertility cults, which attributed sex to the gods, expressed the belief that the renewal of life on earth is an earthly counterpart of the sexual union of the god and the goddess of fertility. This myth was re-enacted in the cult, and the worshipers shared in the divine life force by sexual intercourse with the sacred prostitutes, the representatives of the goddess. The story seems to present the radical deviation of man from God in terms of these cults, the worship of the mystery of sex made personal in divine

beings. The chapter so interpreted is a symbolic description of human corruption, not an essay in the history of human corruption; in the context of the Israelite monarchy, when these cults were so popular that they threatened the integrity of the Hebrew religion, such a description easily finds its place. Man's helper has become the goddess of fertility, inviting him to share in the life of the gods ("knowing good and evil," Gen. iii, 5 and 22) by participating in the mysteries of her cult.

This view also suits the curses uttered upon the man and the woman. The curse of the woman reduces her to the degraded position which she occupied in ancient society; once she becomes a goddess of pleasure, she loses the dignity and the security which are hers as the monogamous wife. The man is cursed in the cultivation of the soil; he has sought fertility from the cultic myth and ritual and not from Yahweh, and therefore the soil refuses its bounty. The serpent is not a symbol of the life force but a beast crawling on the ground. And man is cursed with death (i.e., is denied immortality) because he has sought life where it cannot be found.

The story and the beliefs which it expresses are distinctively Israelite, unparalleled in the ancient world, resting upon Israel's unique conception of God and of his relations to the universe and man. Mesopotamia and Egypt could accept the historical condition of man because the will of their gods, more powerful than the human will, did not surpass the human will in morality. The Israelites believed in the divine moral imperative and did not conceive that God could create a disorderly world. Therefore the evident disorder in the existing world cannot be due to the inability of God to create a world worthy of himself; it must be attributed to the rebellion of man—in the story, to man's refusal to recognize the true character of the deity. This rebellion of man is primeval and universal. Because of it man suffers in his family life, in his struggle with nature, in strife with his fellow man (cf. Gen. iv) and finally in death. None of these is his intended portion from his creator; they are the fruits of his efforts to rise to the divine level through superstitious cults.

One's wonder that Adam and Eve do not appear elsewhere in the Hebrew Old Testament (except I Chron. i, 1) is less if one remembers that the Old Testament rarely cross-references itself. They appear as the ideal of marriage in Tob. viii, 6. Adam is the first man (Wisd. Sol. x, 1). The tendency to exaggerate Adam's endowments is suggested in allusions to his wisdom (Wisd. Sol. x, 1) and to his excellence over every living being in his creation (Sirach [Ecclus.] xlix, 16). Sirach xxxiii, 10 alludes to his creation from the ground. The heavy yoke which rests on the sons of Adam (Sirach xl, 1) is the only possible allusion in the Hebrew or Greek Old Testament to the fall.

In contrast, the story of Adam and Eve was popular with the writers of the pseudepigrapha, who retold it with many embellishments. The Life of Adam and Eve contains a much fuller account of the fall and what followed. The fall of man is rationalized in a modern manner by the author of II Baruch, who states that each man is his own Adam.

Adam is mentioned in the Lucan genealogy of Jesus (Luke iii, 38). Paul illustrates human frailty by the serpent's seduction of Eve (II Cor. xi, 3). In I Tim. ii, 13 the authority of man over woman is argued from the chronological priority of the creation of the man; this is a rabbinical type of argument. Elsewhere in the New Testament Adam appears only in the Pauline writings, where he is given some theological importance. The conviction that all men die in Adam was already fixed in Paul's mind when he wrote I Cor. xv, 22. Here Adam, who brought death to all men, is the type of Christ, who brings the life of the resurrection to all men. In answer to the question of what kind of body the risen shall have, Paul appeals to the typology of Adam and Christ. Here he plays on the omission of the Hebrew word for spirit in Gen. ii, 7; the omission is probably coincidental, since the word is used elsewhere in the Old Testament for the animating principle, but Paul finds in it an occasion to explain what he understands by resurrection (I Cor. xv, 44–53). Adam had a "body" of earth and a "soul"; he did not receive the "spirit," and so he was mortal. His descendants like him have only a "psychic" body, a body with a "soul," and they too must die. Paul is certain that flesh and blood cannot possess the kingdom of God (I Cor. xv, 50); therefore the body must be changed. It will be changed by the reception of the life-giving spirit which is conferred by Jesus Christ. Adam is from the earth; Christ, the second Adam, who lives forever, is from heaven. The Christian becomes "heavenly" through his union with the heavenly man, Christ; his body is changed into a "spiritual" body, and he is free from death.

Paul again introduces Adam as "a type of the one who was to come"; *i.e.*, Christ (Rom. v, 14). As Adam initiated the life of man upon earth, so Christ initiates the new life of man. Because of the sin of Adam, death came upon all men; because of the righteousness of Christ, life is given to all men (Rom. v, 12–21). This had important consequences for Paul's theology. It was Adam's sin and not failure to observe the Law of Moses which made the gentiles sinners; therefore Jews also stood in need of the grace of Jesus Christ. Just as failure to observe the Law was not the formality under which man is sinful, so observance of the Law is not sufficient to reconcile man with God. It is likely also that this Pauline rereading of Genesis is responsible for his emphasis upon the universality and the gratuity of the redemption wrought by the Father in Jesus Christ. For if men, as attested by their universal mortality, are subject to the wrath of God for reasons which are antecedent to their personal conduct, so it is fitting that deliverance from wrath should come by the act of another antecedent to their personal conduct. This other is Christ, the new Adam, head of a new race. The Pauline theology of Adam as the type of Christ is the basis of the Christian belief in original sin, on which the reality of the redemption and the efficacy of baptism depend. *See also* EDEN; CREATION, MYTHS OF; GENESIS.

BIBLIOGRAPHY.—B. W. Anderson, *Understanding the Old Testament*, pp. 167–169 (1957); N. K. Gottwald, *A Light to the Nations*, pp. 224–227 (1959); J. L. McKenzie, *The Two-Edged Sword*, pp. 90–108 (1956); B. M. Vawter, *A Path Through Genesis*, pp. 50–71 (1956); T. C. Vriezen, *An Outline of Old Testament Theology*, trans. by S. Neuijen pp. 204–212 (1958). (J. L. McK.)

ADAMAWA, a region of tropical Africa, lies roughly between 6° and 11° N. and between 11° and 15° E. Formerly an independent native kingdom, it is now partitioned between the Northern Region of Nigeria and Cameroun. In these territories administrative units with the name Adamawa survive.

Adamawa owes its origin and name to Adama, a Fulani emir, who established the emirate during the first half of the 19th century. In 1809 the Muslim Fulani of the western Sudan, under the leadership of Othman dan Fodio of Sokoto, began a holy war (*jihad*) against the non-Muslim Negroes. Adama and his followers conquered the area now known as Adamawa and established a ruling aristocracy over the Negro tribes. Adama, who died in 1848, made Yola his capital and founded such cities as Garoua and Ngaoundéré.

Adama was succeeded by four of his sons. Lowal (1848–72) was ruling when H. Barth visited Adamawa (1851); Saanda (1872–90) consolidated the empire; Zubeiru (1890–1901) attempted to defend it against Great Britain and Germany but in 1903 he was killed by rebels when fleeing from his pursuers. After Adamawa had been partitioned in 1901, Bobo Amadu, Adama's fourth son, became emir of Yola in the British section of the state. His titular suzerainty as *lamido* of Adamawa continued to be recognized by Fulani (*q.v.*) across the frontier.

Western Adamawa includes the broad plains of the middle Benue valley, between 500 and 1,200 ft., which extend eastward to the foot of the highland masses which compose the rest of the area. The larger highland area runs from west to east along the southern boundary, with summits above 6,000 ft. A second highland area follows the present Nigerian frontier, though trenched through by the Benue valley east of Yola, also with summits above 6,000 ft. in the Vogel massif and the Mambila plateau, with slightly lower summits in the Mandara mountains north of the Benue.

The chief crops grown are millets, maize, rice, peanuts and cotton. Agriculture is the occupation of the Negro groups whereas the Fulani are primarily cattle breeders. Cattle are found on the mountain grasslands farther south than in other parts of West Africa. *See also* CAMEROONS; NIGERIA.

BIBLIOGRAPHY.—S. Passarge, *Adamaua* (1895); K. Strümpell, *Die Geschichte Adamauas* (1912); H. Barth, *Travels and Discoveries in North and Central Africa* (1857–58); A. H. M. Kirk-Greene, *Adamawa Past and Present* (1958). (J. C. PH.)

ADAM DE LA HALLE (ADAM LE BOSSU; *c.* 1250–*c.* 1306), a distinguished late-13th-century poet, musician, and dramatist from Arras (*q.v.;* then capital of the old French province of Artois). His lyric works set to music form a vital link between two ages: his 36 *chansons* and 18 *jeux-partis* are in the monodic tradition of the *trouvères* (*q.v.*), but his 16 rondeaux and 5 motets are polyphonic and point forward to "Ars Nova" (*q.v.*) and Guillaume de Machaut (*c.* 1300–77; *q.v.*). Adam's position as a dramatist is no less important, for three of the earliest secular plays in French are by him. (*See also* FRENCH LITERATURE: *Early Lyrics* and *The Beginnings of Drama*; RONDEAU.)

Adam studied *c.* 1275 in the University of Paris. His facetious poem of leave-taking, *Li Congé*, and his high-spirited *Jeu de la Feuillée* ("play of the greensward"), which satirizes himself, and his family and friends in Arras, were probably written then; it was certainly in Paris that he acquired the techniques of polyphony. While a minstrel in the service of Robert II, count of Artois, Adam visited Italy in support of a campaign by Charles I, count of Anjou, who had beeen crowned king of Naples and Sicily in 1266. It was, no doubt, for the court at Naples that Adam composed the elegant dramatization of the traditional *pastourelle* theme of the errant knight wooing a pretty shepherdess, his *Jeu de Robin et Marion*. This delightful entertainment of song and verse, sometimes called the first comic opera, shows the shepherdess Marion, with her rustic lover and village friends, getting the better of her overamorous suitor. A fragment remains of an epic poem, *Le Roi de Sezile*, which Adam composed on the death of Charles of Anjou in 1285. Sometime after 1288, when his friends in Arras had supposed him dead, Adam returned home and mocked their forgetfulness with his short *Jeu du Pelerin*, a play in which a pilgrim praises the poet and says he has seen Adam's tomb in Naples. Most modern critics have been misled by this into supposing that Adam had died in Naples *c.* 1288, and that the pilgrim play was an anonymous composition by a follower, but "*Adam le boçus*" is listed among entertainers at a royal function at Westminster in 1306, and it therefore seems likely that Adam was still alive later than has usually been supposed.

BIBLIOGRAPHY.—*Oeuvres complètes*, ed. by E. Coussemaker (1872; reprinted 1965); *The Lyric Works of Adam de la Hale*, ed. by N. Wilkins (1967); *Canchons und Partures*, ed. by R. Berger (1900); *Les Partures Adan*, ed. by L. Nicod (1917); *Le Jeu de Robin et Marion*, ed. by F. Gennrich (1962), and by K. Varty (1960) and E. Langlois (1958) with *Le Jeu du Pelerin*; *Le Jeu de la Feuillée*, ed. by E. Langlois (1911; reprinted 1951); H. Guy, *Essai sur la vie et les oeuvres littéraires d'Adan de la Hale* (1898); F. Gégou, "Adam le Bossu était-il mort en 1288?" in *Romania*, vol. lxxxvi (1965). (N. E. W.)

ADAMNAN (ADOMNAN or EUNAN), **SAINT** (*c.* 628–704), the biographer of St. Columba, was born in County Donegal, Ire. In 679 he was elected abbot of Iona, the ninth in succession from St. Columba, the founder. While on a visit to Northumbria he adopted the Roman rules on the date of Easter and on the tonsure, but failed to enforce the change at Iona. He then traveled much in Ireland to promote the same observances and, at the council of Birr (County Offaly), succeeded in ameliorating the condition of women, particularly by their exemption from military service, and in making regulations protecting children and clerics (Law of Adamnan). Adamnan wrote two valuable works, the *Vita S. Columbae*, in three sections, describing the saint's prophecies, miracles and visions, and the *De locis sanctis*, an account of the travels of Arculf (*q.v.*) to the Holy Land. Adamnan is sometimes credited with *Adamnan's Vision*, an Irish composition of the 10th or 11th century, on the other world. His feast day is Sept. 23.

BIBLIOGRAPHY.—The *Vita S. Columbae* was edited with introduction, Eng. trans. and notes by W. Reeves (1857 and 1874); ed., with Eng. trans., by A. O. and M. O. Anderson (1961). The *De locis sanctis* was edited and translated by D. Meehan (1958); Eng. trans., *The Pilgrimage of Arculphus* by J. R. Macpherson in *Palestine Pilgrims' Text Society*, vol. 3 (1897). For the Law of Adamnan *see* K. Meyer, *Cáin Adamnáin, an Old Irish Treatise on the Law of Adamnan* (1905). See further F. J. Kenney, *The Sources for the Early History of Ireland*, vol. 1 (1929). (PL. GN.)

ADAMS, ABIGAIL (née SMITH) (1744–1818), wife of John Adams, second U.S. president, and mother of John Quincy Adams, sixth U.S. president, was born in Weymouth, Mass., on Nov. 22 (new style; Nov. 11, old style), 1744. Scantily educated but intelligent and broad-minded, she became a terse and vigorous letter writer. In 1764 she was married to John Adams, then practising law in Boston. She resolutely supported him in his insistence upon the Declaration of Independence and aided him and his cause with loyal zeal. In 1784 she joined her husband in France and in 1785 accompanied him to England, where, as the wife of the first minister of the United States to the court of George III, she met with social discourtesies which she long resented. From 1789 to 1801, when her husband was successively vice-president and president, she lived in a simple manner. The publication by C. F. Adams in 1875 of *The Familiar Letters of John Adams and His Wife* increased interest in her career. She died at Quincy, Mass., on Oct. 28, 1818. (J. R. AL.)

ADAMS, BROOKS (1848–1927), U.S. historian, son of Charles Francis Adams and grandson of John Quincy Adams, was born in Quincy, Mass., June 24, 1848. He graduated from Harvard College in 1870 and practised law in Boston until 1881. A large inheritance enabled him to travel extensively in Europe, the Middle East, and India. Very close to his elder brother Henry, also a historian, Brooks carried on with him an active correspondence in which they both developed the idea, revolutionary at the time, that by its nature and substance U.S. democracy was foreordained to degradation and decay. In 1895 he published his *Law of Civilization and Decay* in which he developed his theory of history, the conviction that the centre of trade had consistently followed a westward movement from the ancient crossroads in the East to Constantinople, Venice, Amsterdam, and finally London, in accord with a law relating to the density of populations and the development of new and centralizing techniques of trade and industry.

His *America's Economic Supremacy* (1900) accurately foresaw within 50 years a world in which there would be only two powers, Russia and the United States, with the latter possessing economic supremacy. In 1913 he published *The Theory of Social Revolutions,* a study of defects in the American form of government, developing the idea of the imminent danger in the existence of great wealth exerting private power but declining to accept responsibility. After Henry Adams' death, Brooks Adams prepared for publication his brother's book *The Degradation of the Democratic Dogma* (1920), to which he wrote the introduction, a kind of family chronicle that began with John Quincy Adams' troubles and ended with the renunciation by the two grandsons of the democratic dogma. The roots of his Puritan ancestry were deep. An agnostic, a profound skeptic, he returned in the last years of his life to the church at Quincy where, overcoming his lifelong shyness, he stood up and made a public profession of his faith. He died in Boston, Feb. 13, 1927.

Adams other writings include *The Emancipation of Massachusetts: the Dream and the Reality* (rev. ed., 1919); *The New Empire* (1902); *America's Economic Supremacy* (rev. ed., 1947).

See A. F. Beringause, *Brooks Adams* (1955). (M. W. CH.)

ADAMS, CHARLES FOLLEN (1842–1918), U.S. regional humorous poet, is best known for his Pennsylvania German dialect poems. He was born on April 21, 1842, in Dorchester, Mass., and was educated in the public schools. During the American Civil War he was wounded and taken prisoner. In 1872 he began writing humorous verses for periodicals and newspapers in a Pennsylvania German dialect similar to that used by Charles Godfrey Leland in his "Hans Breitmann" ballads. Collections of his verse are *Leedle Yawcob Strauss, and Other Poems* (1877) and *Dialect Ballads* (1888). His complete poetical writings, *Yawcob Strauss, and Other Poems,* with illustrations by "Boz," were published in 1910. He died in Boston, Mass., March 8, 1918.

ADAMS, CHARLES FRANCIS (1807–1886), U.S. diplomatist, son of Pres. John Quincy Adams and grandson of Pres. John Adams, was born in Boston, Mass., Aug. 18, 1807. His father, having been appointed minister to Russia, took him in 1809 to St. Petersburg, where he learned French as his native tongue. After eight years in Russia and England, he attended the Boston

Latin school, and in 1825 graduated from Harvard. He lived for two years in the executive mansion, Washington, during his father's presidential term, studying law and moving in a society where he met statesmen such as Webster, Clay, Jackson and Randolph. At the age of 22 he married Abigail Brooks, daughter of Peter Chardon Brooks, wealthy Boston insurance broker.

Having returned to Boston, he devoted ten years to business and study and wrote for the *North American Review.* He also undertook the management of his father's financial affairs, and actively supported him in his contest in the house of representatives for the right of petition and the antislavery cause. In 1835 he wrote an effective and widely read political pamphlet, entitled, after Edmund Burke's more famous work, *An Appeal from the New to the Old Whigs.* He was a member of the Massachusetts general court from 1840 to 1845, and from 1846 to 1848 he edited a party journal, the *Boston Whig.*

In 1848 he was a prominent "Conscience Whig," presiding over the Buffalo convention which formed the Free-Soil party and nominated Martin Van Buren for president and himself for vice-president. He was a Republican member of the 36th congress, and during its second session (Dec. 3, 1860–March 4, 1861) he represented Massachusetts in the congressional committee of 33 at the time of the secession of seven of the southern states. Together with William H. Seward, he stood for the Republican policy of concession. For this he was criticized severely and charged with inconsistency in view of his record as a "Conscience Whig." He, with Lincoln, was willing to concede nonessentials but holding that there must be no extension of slavery. He believed that as the Republicans were the victors they ought to show a spirit of conciliation, and that the policy of righteousness was likewise one of expediency, since it would result in the holding of the border slave states with the north until March 4, when the Republicans could take possession of the government at Washington.

After inauguration of the new administration, Secretary Seward secured for Adams the appointment as minister to Great Britain. So much sympathy was shown in England for the south that his path was beset with difficulties. His mission was to prevent the interference of Great Britain in the struggle; as American minister, Adams was insistent and unyielding, and knew how to present his case forcibly and with dignity. He laboured with energy and discretion to prevent the sailing of the Confederate cruiser "Alabama," built in a British shipyard; and, when unsuccessful in this, he persistently urged upon the British government its responsibility for the destruction of American merchant vessels by the cruiser (*see* "ALABAMA" ARBITRATION). His diary shows that underneath his calm exterior was keen anxiety. Adams remained in England until May 1868. His last important work was as a member, in 1871–72, of the tribunal at Geneva which settled the "Alabama" claims. He died at Boston, Nov. 21, 1886.

He edited the *Works of John Adams* (1850–56) and the *Memoirs of John Quincy Adams* (1874–77).

See the biography (1900) by his son, Charles Francis Adams, Jr.; and E. D. Adams, *Great Britain and the American Civil War* (1925). An authoritative biography is by Martin B. Duberman, *Charles Francis Adams, 1807–1866* (1961). (S. F. B.)

ADAMS, CHARLES FRANCIS (1835–1915), U.S. railroad specialist, civic leader and historian, was born in Boston, Mass., May 27, 1835. He was one of the four sons of Charles Francis Adams (*q.v.*; 1807–86) and was the grandson of Pres. John Quincy Adams and the great-grandson of Pres. John Adams. He received his education at the Boston Latin school and Harvard college. He fought through the American Civil War, rising from the rank of lieutenant to colonel of the 5th cavalry (Negro). After the war his journalistic articles on railroad scandals led to the creation of the Massachusetts board of railroad commissioners (1869) with himself as chairman (1872–79). He was president of the Union Pacific railroad from 1884 to 1890.

The most important part of Adams' career was that of historian. He published several major works in history, politics and biography and served as president of the Massachusetts Historical society from 1895 until his death on March 20, 1915.

See Charles Francis Adams, 1835–1915: an Autobiography, with a

"Memorial Address" by Henry Cabot Lodge (1916).   (S. F. B.)

ADAMS, CHARLES FRANCIS (1866–1954), U.S. secretary of the navy, philanthropist and yachtsman, was born in Quincy, Mass., Aug. 2, 1866. He was a great-grandson of John Quincy Adams, sixth president of the United States, and great-great-grandson of John Adams, second president. He graduated from Harvard in 1888, took his law degree four years later and was admitted to the bar in 1893. He had a long career as a public-minded Boston lawyer, capitalist, and sportsman. He was amateur skipper of the yacht "Resolute," which won the international yacht races, 1920. From 1929 to 1933 he served as President Hoover's secretary of the navy. He was a trustee of the Adams Manuscript Trust, a great collection of Adams family papers turned over in 1956 to the Massachusetts Historical Society. Adams died in Boston on June 10, 1954.   (S. F. B.)

ADAMS, CHARLES KENDALL (1835–1902), U.S. teacher and historian, introduced the European seminar method in the U.S. He was born in Derby, Vt., on Jan. 24, 1835. Graduating from the University of Michigan (Ann Arbor) in 1861, he taught history there until 1885. Study in Germany and France in 1867–68 led to his introduction of the seminar method, which spread to other U.S. universities. Among his historical works were *Democracy and Monarchy in France* (1874), *A Manual of Historical Literature* (1882), and *Christopher Columbus* (1892). He edited *Representative British Orations* (1884). In 1885 he became president of Cornell University (Ithaca, N.Y.) and was president of the University of Wisconsin (Madison) from 1892 until his death in Redlands, Calif., on July 26, 1902.

ADAMS, HENRY BROOKS (1838–1918), U.S. historian, son of Charles Francis Adams and grandson of John Quincy Adams, was born in Boston, Mass., on Feb. 16, 1838. He graduated at Harvard in 1858, traveled abroad, and was private secretary to his father when the latter was a congressman and later minister to Great Britain. For a brief time he did political writing in Washington, D.C., and then in 1870 became assistant professor of history at Harvard. He taught at Harvard from 1870 to 1877 and became the first U.S. college professor to use the seminar method of teaching history. For most of the period he also served as editor of the *North American Review,* to which he had earlier contributed. At about this time he dropped the use of his middle name.

Adams wrote two novels: *Democracy* (published anonymously, 1880), and *Esther—A Novel* (under the pseudonym of Frances Snow Compton, 1884). His nine-volume *History of the United States from 1801 to 1817,* (1889–91 with new editions in 1909 and 1930), is considered to be the best work on the administrations of President Jefferson and President Madison. It is particularly notable for its account of the diplomatic relations of the United States during the early 1800s, and for its essential impartiality. Two books that represent editings of portions of this history are *War of 1812,* edited by Maj. H. A. DeWeerd, 1944, and *The Formative Years,* edited by Herbert Agar, 1947. The *History,* like his other historical and biographical works, such as *Chapters of Erie and Other Essays* (1871, with Charles Francis Adams, Jr.), *Life of Albert Gallatin* (1879), *John Randolph* (1882) and *Historical Essays* (1891), won for Adams a reputation among scholars. A prolonged visit to the South seas led him to edit and publish *Memoirs of Marau Taaroa, Last Queen of Tahiti* (1893, revised and enlarged 1901). His *Mont-Saint-Michel and Chartres* (1913, privately printed 1904) and *The Education of Henry Adams* (1918, privately printed 1906) revealed him to a much wider audience. *Mont-Saint-Michel and Chartres* is one of the most valuable studies of medievalism produced in America, not only for the aid it affords in the appreciation of the literary and architectural monuments of the past, but also for the conception it gives of the social and religious forces that produced these monuments. The *Education,* which attempted to show how ill-adapted 19th-century man and education were for the needs of the 20th century, was one of the most widely discussed books of its decade in the United States and is one of the world's great autobiographies. Other notable works by Adams are: "King" in *Clarence King Memoirs* (1904); *A Letter to American Teachers of History* (privately printed 1910); *Life of George Cabot Lodge* (1911); and *Degra-*

dation of the Democratic Dogma (posthumously, 1920, with introduction by Brooks Adams). In the years after his death in Washington on March 27, 1918, many of his letters began to appear in magazines, biographies and other books. They gave him the distinction of being one of America's great letter writers. The principal collections of these letters are: *Cycle of Adams Letters, 1861–1865,* in two volumes (1920); *Letters to a Niece and Prayer to the Virgin of Chartres, by Henry Adams, with a Niece's Memories,* by Mabel La Farge (1920); *Letters of Henry Adams, 1858–1891* and *Letters of Henry Adams, 1892–1918,* both edited by W. C. Ford (1930 and 1938 respectively); *Henry Adams and His Friends, A Collection of His Unpublished Letters, Compiled, with a Biographical Introduction,* by Harold Dean Cater (1947). Three volumes of an extended biography by E. Samuels are *The Young Henry Adams* (1948), *Henry Adams: the Middle Years* (1958), and *Henry Adams: the Major Phase* (1964).   (H. D. C.)

ADAMS, HENRY CARTER (1851–1921), U.S. economist, was born at Davenport, Ia., Dec. 31, 1851. He was educated at Iowa college (Grinnell, Ia.), Johns Hopkins university, and French and German universities, afterward teaching at Cornell university. In 1887 he became professor of political economy and finance in the University of Michigan. Adams served as statistician to the Interstate Commerce commission and was in charge of the transportation department in the 1890 census. His principal works include *The State in Relation to Industrial Action* (1887); *Public Debts* (1887); *The Science of Finance* (1898); *Economics and Jurisprudence* (1897); *Description of Industry* (1918); and *American Railway Accounting* (1918). He died Aug. 11, 1921.

ADAMS, HERBERT BAXTER (1850–1901), U.S. historian and educator was born at Shutesbury, Mass., on April 16, 1850. After graduating from Amherst college, Amherst, Mass., at the head of his class in 1872, he studied in Germany at Göttingen and Berlin before receiving the degree of Ph.D. from the University of Heidelberg in 1876. That same year he was appointed a fellow in the new Johns Hopkins university, Baltimore, Md. There he remained, becoming professor of American and institutional history in 1891, until his death on July 30, 1901. It was a crucial period for historical scholarship in America and he played an important part in it. The common belief that he introduced German methods is exaggerated as he had almost no contact with German scholars after his return to America while his correspondence and contacts with British scholars were numerous. He was an organizer and promoter of scholarship rather than a producer. He was one of the founders of the American Historical association and served as its secretary until 1900. He initiated in 1882 the "Johns Hopkins University Studies in Historical and Political Science," the first such series in the United States. To his seminar came the best graduate students of the period. They included Woodrow Wilson, J. Franklin Jameson, Frederick Jackson Turner, Charles H. Haskins, Charles M. Andrews and many others who achieved distinction and who testified to the personal and generous interest Adams took in his students. None of his own scholarly work was distinguished. Among his writings are: *Maryland's Influence in Founding a National Commonwealth* (1877); *Methods of Historical Study* (1884); *Maryland's Influence upon Land Cessions to the United States* (1885); and the *Life and Writings of Jared Sparks* (1893).

See *Herbert B. Adams: Tributes of Friends* (1902); *Historical Scholarship in the United States, 1876–1901: As Revealed in the Correspondence of Herbert B. Adams* (1938).   (W. S. Ht.)

ADAMS, JOHN (1735–1826), the first vice-president and the second president of the United States of America was born Oct. 30 (new style; Oct. 19, old style), 1735, in what is now the town of Quincy, Mass. His father, a farmer, also named John, was of the fourth generation in descent from Henry Adams, who emigrated from Devonshire, Eng., to Massachusetts about 1636; his mother was Susanna Boylston Adams. Young Adams graduated from Harvard college in 1755, and for a time taught school at Worcester and studied law in the office of James Putnam.

In 1758 he was admitted to the Boston bar. From an early age he developed the habit of writing descriptions of events and impressions of men. The earliest of these is his report of the argument of James Otis in the superior court of Massachusetts as to the constitutionality of writs of assistance. This was in 1761, and the argument inspired him with zeal for the cause of the American colonies. Years afterward, when an old man, Adams undertook to write out at length his recollections of this scene; it is instructive to compare the two accounts. John Adams had none of the qualities of popular leadership which were so marked a characteristic of his second cousin, Samuel Adams; it was rather as a constitutional lawyer that he influenced the course of events. He was impetuous, intense and often vehement, unflinchingly courageous, devoted with his whole soul to the cause he had espoused; but his vanity, his pride of opinion and his inborn contentiousness were serious handicaps to him in his political career. These qualities were particularly manifested at a later period—as, for example, during his term as president. He first made his influence widely felt and became conspicuous as a leader of the Massachusetts Whigs during the discussions with regard to the Stamp act of 1765. In that year he drafted the instructions which were sent by the town of Braintree to its representatives in the Massachusetts legislature, and which served as a model for other towns in drawing up instructions to their representatives; in Aug. 1765 he contributed anonymously four notable articles to the *Boston Gazette* (republished separately in London in 1768 as *A Dissertation on the Canon and Feudal Law*), in which he argued that the opposition of the colonies to the Stamp act was a part of the never-ending struggle between individualism and corporate authority; and in Dec. 1765 he delivered a speech before the governor and council in which he pronounced the Stamp act invalid on the ground that Massachusetts, being without representation in parliament, had not assented to it. In 1768 he removed to Boston. Two years later, with that degree of moral courage which was one of his distinguishing characteristics, as it has been of his descendants, he served as a lawyer for the defense in the trial of the British soldiers charged with murder as the result of the so-called "Boston massacre." Public sentiment was strongly against the accused. The trial resulted in an acquittal of the officer who commanded the detachment, and most of the soldiers; but two soldiers were found guilty of manslaughter. These claimed benefit of clergy and were branded in the hand and released. Adams' upright and patriotic conduct in taking the unpopular side in this case met with its just reward in the following year, in the shape of his election to the Massachusetts house of representatives by a vote of 418 to 118.

John Adams was a member of the continental congress from 1774 to 1778. In June 1775, with a view to promoting the union of the colonies, he supported the nomination of Washington as commander in chief of the army. His influence in congress was great, and almost from the beginning he was impatient for a separation of the colonies from Great Britain. On June 7, 1776, he seconded the famous resolution introduced by Richard Henry Lee (*q.v.*) that "these colonies are, and of a right ought to be, free and independent states," and no man championed these resolutions (adopted on July 2) so eloquently and effectively before the congress. On June 11 he was appointed on a committee with Jefferson, Franklin, Livingstone and Sherman to draft a declaration of independence; and although that document was by the request of the committee written by Thomas Jefferson, it was John Adams who occupied the foremost place in the debate on its adoption. Before this question had been disposed of, Adams was placed at the head of the board of war and ordnance, and he also served on many other important committees.

BY COURTESY OF THE INDEPENDENCE NATIONAL HISTORICAL PARK COLLECTION

JOHN ADAMS, PORTRAIT BY CHARLES WILLSON PEALE, PAINTED BETWEEN 1791 AND 1794

In 1778 John Adams sailed for France to supersede Silas Deane in the American commission there. But just as he embarked that commission concluded the desired treaty of alliance, and soon after his arrival he advised that the number of commissioners be reduced to one. His advice was followed and he returned home in time to be elected a member of the convention which framed the Massachusetts constitution of 1780, still the organic law of that commonwealth. With James Bowdoin and Samuel Adams, he formed a subcommittee which drew up the first draft of that instrument, and most of it probably came from John Adams' pen.

Before this work had been completed he was again sent to Europe, having been chosen, Sept. 27, 1779, as minister plenipotentiary for negotiating a treaty of peace and a treaty of commerce with Great Britain. Conditions were not then favourable for peace, however; the French government, moreover, did not approve of the choice, inasmuch as Adams was not sufficiently pliant and tractable and was from the first suspicious of Vergennes; and subsequently Benjamin Franklin, Thomas Jefferson, John Jay and Henry Laurens were appointed to co-operate with Adams. Jefferson, however, did not cross the Atlantic, and Laurens took little part in the negotiations. This left the management of the business to the other three. Jay and Adams distrusted the good faith of the French government. They persuaded Franklin to break the instructions to the commissioners from congress, which required them to "make the most candid confidential communications on all subjects to the ministers of our generous ally, the king of France; to undertake nothing in the negotiations for peace or truce without their knowledge or concurrence; and ultimately to govern yourself by their advice and opinion"; and, instead, they dealt directly with the British commissioners, without consulting the French ministers. Throughout the negotiations Adams was especially determined that the right of the United States to the fisheries along the British-American coast should be recognized. Political conditions in Great Britain, at the moment made the conclusion of peace almost a necessity with the British ministry, and eventually the American negotiators were able to secure a peculiarly favourable treaty. This preliminary treaty was signed Nov. 30, 1782. Before these negotiations began, Adams had spent some time in the Netherlands. In July 1780 he had been authorized to execute the duties previously assigned to Henry Laurens, and at The Hague was eminently successful, securing there recognition of the United States as an independent government (April 19, 1782), and negotiating both a loan and, in Oct. 1782, a treaty of amity and commerce, the first of such treaties between the United States and foreign powers after that of Feb. 1778 with France.

In 1785 John Adams was appointed the first of a long line of able and distinguished American ministers to the court of St. James's. When he was presented to his former sovereign, George III intimated that he was aware of Adams' lack of confidence in the French government. Replying, Adams admitted it, closing with the outspoken sentiment: "I must avow to your Majesty that I have no attachment but to my own country"—a phrase which must have jarred upon the monarch's sensibilities. While in London Adams published a work entitled *A Defence of the Constitutions of Government of the United States* (1787). In this work he ably combated the views of Turgot and other European writers who had criticized the framework of the state governments. Unfortunately, in so doing, he used phrases savouring of aristocracy which offended many of his countrymen—as in the sentence in which he suggested that "the rich, the well-born and the able" should be set apart from other men in a senate. Partly for this reason, while Washington had the vote of every elector in the first presidential election of 1789, Adams received only 34 out of 69. As this was the second largest number he was declared vice-president, but he began his eight years in that office (1789–97) with a sense of grievance and of suspicion of many of the leading men. Differences of opinion with regard to the policies to be pursued by the new government gradually led to the formation of two well-defined political groups—the Federalists and the Democratic-Republicans—and Adams became recognized as one of the leaders of the Federalists. He was less conservative than many other Federalists.

In 1796, on the refusal of Washington to accept another election, Adams was chosen president, defeating Thomas Jefferson; though Alexander Hamilton and other Federalists had asked that an equal vote should be cast for Adams and Thomas Pinckney, the other Federalist in the contest, partly in order that Jefferson, who was elected vice-president, might be excluded altogether, and partly, it seems, in the hope that Pinckney should in fact receive more votes than Adams, and thus, in accordance with the system then obtaining, be elected president, though he was intended for the second place on the Federalist ticket. The electoral college cast 71 votes for Adams, 68 for Jefferson, 59 for Pinckney and 78 scattered among other candidates. Adams' four years as chief magistrate (1797–1801) were marked by a succession of intrigues which embittered all his later life; they were marked, also, by events such as the passage of the Alien and Sedition acts (*see* UNITED STATES [OF AMERICA]: *History*), which brought discredit on the Federalist party. Moreover, factional strife broke out within the party itself; Adams and Hamilton became alienated, and some members of Adams' own cabinet looked to Hamilton rather than to the president as their political chief. The United States was, at this time, drawn into the vortex of European complications, and Adams, instead of taking advantage of the militant spirit which was aroused, patriotically devoted himself to securing peace with France, much against the wishes of Hamilton and of Hamilton's adherents in the cabinet. In 1800, Adams was again the Federalist candidate for the presidency, but the distrust of him in his own party, the popular disapproval of the Alien and Sedition acts and the popularity of his opponent, Thomas Jefferson, combined to cause his defeat. He then retired into private life. On July 4, 1826, on the 50th anniversary of the adoption of the Declaration of Independence, he died at Quincy. Jefferson died on the same day.

In 1764 Adams had married Abigail Smith (1744–1818), the daughter of a Congregational minister at Weymouth, Mass. She was a woman of much ability, and her letters, written in an excellent English style, are of great value to students of the period in which she lived. (*See* ADAMS, ABIGAIL.) President John Quincy Adams (*q.v.*) was their eldest son.

BIBLIOGRAPHY.—C. F. Adams, *The Works of John Adams, with Life* (1850–56); John and Abigail Adams, *Familiar Letters of John Adams and His Wife Abigail During the Revolution* (1875); Catherine D. Bowen, *John Adams and the American Revolution* (1950); Gilbert Chinard, *Honest John Adams* (1933); L. H. Butterfield, L. C. Faber and W. D. Garrett (eds.), *The Adams Papers*, vol. 1–4, *Diary and Autobiography of John Adams* (1961); Page Smith, *John Adams*, 2 vol. (1962). (E. C.; J. R. AL.)

ADAMS, JOHN COUCH (1819–1892), British mathematical astronomer who discovered the planet Neptune, independently of V. Leverrier, was born at Laneast, Cornwall, on June 5, 1819. Educated at St. John's college, Cambridge, he was senior wrangler and first Smith's prizeman in 1843 and was elected fellow of his college in the same year. On July 3, 1841, he had entered in his journal, "Formed a design in the beginning of this week of investigating, as soon as possible after taking my degree, the irregularities in the motion of Uranus, which are yet unaccounted for; in order to find whether they may be attributed to the action of an undiscovered planet beyond it; and if possible thence to determine the elements of its orbit, etc., approximately, which would probably lead to its discovery." By Sept. 1845 he obtained his first solution and handed to J. Challis, the director of the Cambridge observatory, the elements of what he described as "the new planet" and its position for Oct. 1, 1845. This position was actually within two degrees of the position of Neptune at that time but unfortunately the planet was not searched for at Cambridge until much later. Meanwhile, the French astronomer Leverrier, working successfully along similar lines, had sent a request for observations to the Berlin observatory where, as a result, Neptune was discovered on Sept. 23, 1846. A heated controversy arose, motivated largely by nationalistic feelings, but reason soon prevailed and the credit for this unsurpassed intellectual feat was equally divided between the two astronomers and the planet given the neutral name of Neptune.

In 1851 Adams became president of the Royal Astronomical society and in 1853 Pembroke college elected him to a fellowship which he held for the rest of his life. He became professor of mathematics at St. Andrews in 1858 and Lowndean professor of astronomy and geometry at Cambridge in 1859. Two years later he succeeded Challis as director of the Cambridge observatory where he resided until his death on Jan. 21, 1892.

Although Adams' researches on Neptune are his best-known work, subsequent memoirs on the moon's motion, terrestrial magnetism and the November meteors—or Leonids—were no less remarkable and won him the gold medal of the Royal Astronomical society in 1866. He presented his celebrated paper on the secular acceleration of the mean motion of the moon to the Royal society in 1853, revolutionizing that branch of physical astronomy. Some of his work in terrestrial magnetism, such as the determination of the constants in Karl Gauss's theory of magnetism, was published posthumously. The anticipated meteor shower of 1866 turned his attention to the Leonids, which, as he showed, traveled in an elongated ellipse with a period of 33 years and 3 months and were subject to planetary perturbations.

Adams wrote an account in 1888 of Newton's unpublished mathematical material in the Portsmouth collection. *The Scientific Papers of John Couch Adams* were edited by W. G. Adams, 2 vol. (1896–1900).

See Sir H. S. Jones, *John Couch Adams and the Discovery of Neptune* (1947). (O. J. E.)

ADAMS, JOHN QUINCY (1767–1848), eldest son of Pres. John Adams, and sixth president of the United States, was born on July 11, 1767, in that part of Braintree that is now Quincy, Mass. He had two notable careers: first as one of America's greatest diplomatists, and second as outstanding champion of the antislavery cause in the house of representatives during the last 16 years of his long life; between these two careers was the period of his presidency of the United States, from 1825 to 1829.

The infant entered the world at the same time his maternal great grandfather John Quincy (1689–1767), for many years a prominent member of the Massachusetts legislature, was leaving

BY COURTESY OF THE METROPOLITAN MUSEUM OF ART, NEW YORK (GIFT OF I. N. P. STOKES AND THE HAWES FAMILY)

JOHN QUINCY ADAMS (1848), DAGUERREOTYPE BY A. S. SOUTHWORTH AND J. J. HAWES

it; hence his name. He grew up as a child of the American Revolution. Tugging at his mother's apron strings he watched the battle of Bunker hill from Braintree on Penn's hill and heard the cannons roar across the Back bay. His patriot father, at that time a delegate to the continental congress, and his patriot mother, one of the intellectual mistresses of those stirring times, had a strong molding influence on his education after the war had deprived Braintree of its only schoolmaster. In 1778 and again in 1780, the boy accompanied his father to Europe. He studied at a private school in Paris in 1778–1779 and at the University of Leiden in 1780. Thus at an early age he acquired an excellent knowledge of the French language and a smattering of Dutch. In 1780, also, he began to keep regularly the diary that forms so conspicuous a record of the doings of himself and his contemporaries through the next 60 years of American history.

In 1781, at the age of 14, he accompanied Francis Dana (1743–1811), American envoy to Russia, as his private secretary and interpreter of French. Dana, after lingering over a year in St. Petersburg, was not received by the Russian government, and in 1782 Adams, returning by way of Scandinavia, Hanover and the Netherlands, joined his father in Paris. There he acted in an informal way as additional secretary to the American commissioners in the negotiation of the treaty of peace that concluded the American Revolution. Instead of remaining in London with his father, who had been appointed U.S. minister to the court of St. James's, he chose to return to Massachusetts where he graduated at Harvard college in 1787. He then read law at Newburyport under the tutelage of Theophilus Parsons, and was admitted to the bar in Boston in 1790. While struggling for a practice he wrote a series of articles for the newspapers in which he controverted some of Thomas Paine's doctrines in the *Rights of Man.* In another later series he ably supported the neutrality policy of Washington's administration as it faced the war that broke out between France and England in 1793. These articles were brought to President Washington's attention and resulted in Adams' appointment as United States minister to the Netherlands in May 1794.

The Hague was then the best diplomatic listening post in Europe for the war of the first coalition against revolutionary France. Young Adams' official dispatches to the secretary of state and his informal letters to his father, the vice-president, (read also by President Washington) kept the government well informed of the diplomatic activities and wars of the distressed continent and the danger of becoming involved in the European vortex. Some of his phrases appeared in Washington's Farewell Address of 1796. During the absence of the regular minister at London, Thomas Pinckney, on his famous mission to Spain (Pinckney's treaty, 1795), Adams transacted public business with the British foreign office relating to exchange of ratifications of Jay's treaty of 1794 between the United States and Great Britain. In 1796 Washington appointed him minister to Portugal, but before his departure his father John Adams became president and changed the young diplomat's destination to Berlin. While there John Quincy Adams negotiated (1799) a treaty of amity and commerce with Prussia. President Washington had come to regard Adams as the ablest officer in the foreign service. President Adams, after the election of Thomas Jefferson to the presidency in 1800, recalled the younger Adams from his post at Berlin. He reached Boston in 1801 and the next year was elected to the Massachusetts senate; in 1803 the Massachusetts legislature elected him as a member of the senate of the United States.

Up to this time John Quincy Adams was regarded as belonging to the Federalist party, but he found its general policy displeasing to him. He was frowned upon as the son of his father by the followers of Alexander Hamilton and the Essex junto, and soon found himself practically powerless as an unpopular member of an unpopular minority. Actually he was not then, and indeed never was, a strict party man: all through his life, ever aspiring to higher public service, he considered himself a "man of my whole country." Adams arrived in Washington too late to vote for ratification of the treaty for the purchase of Louisiana, opposed by the other Federalist senators, but he voted for the appropriations to carry it into effect, and announced that he would have voted for the purchase treaty itself. Nevertheless, he joined his Federalist colleagues in voting against a bill to enable the president to take possession of the newly acquired territory under officials of his own appointment: such a bill, he vainly protested, violated the principles of the constitution, the right of self-government, and imposed taxation without representation. In Dec. 1807 he supported President Jefferson's suggestion of an embargo and vigorously urged instant action, saying: "The president has recommended the measure on his high responsibility. I would not consider, I would not deliberate; I would act!" Within five hours the senate had passed the Embargo bill and sent it to the house of representatives. Support of a measure so unpopular in New England and so hated by the Federalists cost Adams his seat in the senate; his successor was chosen on June 3, 1808, several months before the usual time of electing a senator for the next term, and five days later Adams resigned. In the same year he attended the Republican congressional caucus which nominated Madison for the presidency, and thus allied himself with that party. From 1806 to 1809 Adams was Boylston professor of rhetoric and oratory at Harvard college.

In 1809 President Madison sent Adams to Russia to represent the United States at the court of the tsars. He arrived at St. Petersburg (Leningrad) at the psychological moment when the tsar had made up his mind to break with Napoleon. Minister Adams therefore met with a favourable reception and a disposition to further the interests of American commerce in every possible way. From this post of vantage he watched and reported Napoleon's invasion of Russia and the final disastrous retreat and dissolution of the *grande armée.* On the outbreak of the war between the United States and England in 1812 he was still at St. Petersburg. In September of that year the Russian government suggested that the tsar was willing to act as mediator between the two belligerents. Madison precipitately accepted this proposition and sent Albert Gallatin and James Bayard to act as commissioners with Adams; but England would have nothing to do with it. In Aug. 1814, however, these gentlemen, with Henry Clay and Jonathan Russell, began negotiations with English commissioners which resulted in the signing of the treaty of Ghent on Dec. 24 of that year. After this Adams visited Paris, where he witnessed the return of Napoleon from Elba, and then went to London, where, with Henry Clay and Albert Gallatin, he negotiated (1815) a "Convention to Regulate Commerce and Navigation." Soon afterward he became U.S. minister to Great Britain, as his father had been before him, and as his son, Charles Francis Adams, was after him. After accomplishing little in London, he returned to the United States in the summer of 1817 to become secretary of state in the cabinet of President Monroe. This appointment was due primarily to his diplomatic experience but also to the president's desire to have a sectionally well-balanced cabinet in what came to be known as the Era of Good Feeling.

As secretary of state, Adams played the leading part in the acquisition of Florida. Ever since the acquisition of Louisiana successive administrations had sought to include at least a part of Florida in that purchase. In 1819, after long negotiations, Adams succeeded in bringing the Spanish minister to the point of signing a treaty in which the Spaniards abandoned all claims to territory east of the Mississippi, and the United States relinquished all claim to what is now known as Texas. This Transcontinental treaty was the first treaty to draw a boundary of the United States from the Atlantic to the Pacific ocean. It was the greatest victory ever won by a single man in the diplomatic history of the United States. Adams himself was responsible for the idea of running the line from the Rocky mountains to the Pacific—a stroke of real diplomatic genius. In his own word it marked a triumphant "epocha" in our continental expansion. As secretary of state, Adams was also responsible for conclusion of the treaty of 1818 with Great Britain laying down the northern boundary of the United States from the Lake of the Woods to the Rocky mountains along the line of 49° N. lat. Years later, as a member of the house of representatives he supported 49° N. lat. as the boundary of Oregon from the Rocky mountains to the Pacific ocean: "I want that country for our Western pioneers." Polk's Oregon treaty of 1846 drew that boundary along the line of forty-nine. Before the Spanish government ratified the Transcontinental treaty in 1820, Mexico, including Texas, had thrown off allegiance to the mother country, and the United States had occupied Florida by force of arms. The Monroe Doctrine (*q.v.*) rightly bears the name of the president who in 1823 assumed the responsibility for its promulgation; but it was the work of John Quincy Adams more than any other single man.

As President Monroe's second term drew to a close, there was a great lack of good feeling among his official advisers, three of whom—John Quincy Adams, secretary of state, John C. Calhoun, secretary of war and William H. Crawford, secretary of the treasury—aspired to succeed him in his high office. Henry Clay, speaker of the house, and Gen. Andrew Jackson were also candidates. Calhoun was nominated for the vice-presidency. Of the other four, Jackson received 99 electoral votes for the presidency, Adams 84, Crawford 41 and Clay 37; as no one had a majority, the decision was made by the house of representatives, which was confined in its choice to the three candidates who had received the largest number of votes. Clay, who had for years assumed a censorious attitude toward Jackson, cast his influence for Adams and thereby secured his election on the first ballot. A few days later Adams offered Clay the secretaryship of state, which was accepted. The wholly unjust and baseless charge of "bargain and corruption" followed, and the feud thus created between Adams and Jackson greatly influenced the history of the United States.

Up to this point Adams' career had been almost uniformly successful, but his presidency (1825–29), in which the country's affairs were so prosperous, was in most respects a political failure because of the virulent opposition of the Jacksonians; in 1828 Jackson was elected president over Adams. (*See* UNITED STATES [OF AMERICA]: *History*.) It was during his administration that irreconcilable differences developed between the followers of Adams and the followers of Jackson, the former becoming known as the National Republicans, who with the Antimasons were the precursors of the Whigs. In 1829 Adams retired to private life in the town of Quincy; but only for a brief period, for in 1830, largely by Antimasonic votes, he was elected a member of the national house of representatives. When it was suggested to him that his acceptance of this position would degrade an ex-president, Adams replied that no person could be degraded by serving the people as a representative in congress, or, he added, as a select-man of his town. He served in the house of representatives from 1831 until his death in 1848. But he had not abandoned his hopes for a re-election to the presidency, whether as nominee of the Antimasonic party, in which he was very active as long as that party had political possibilities, or of the National Republican party, or of a union of both, or even of the later Whig party—always in his own mind as a "man of the whole nation." Gradually he had to abandon these hopes.

His long second career in congress was at least as important as his first career as a diplomatist. Throughout he was conspicuous as an opponent of the expansion of slavery, and was at heart an abolitionist, though he never became one in the political sense of that word. In 1839 he presented to the house of representatives a resolution for a constitutional amendment providing that every child born in the United States after July 4, 1842, should be born free; that with the exception of Florida no new state should be admitted into the Union with slavery; that neither slavery nor the slave trade should exist in the District of Columbia after July 4, 1845. The famous "gag rule," imposed by southern members of congress against all discussion of slavery in the house of representatives, effectively blocked any discussion of Adams' proposed amendment. His prolonged fight for the repeal of the so-called gag laws and for the right of petition to congress for the mitigation or abolition of slavery was one of the most dramatic contests in the history of congress. These petitions, from individuals and groups of individuals from all over the northern states, were increasingly sent to Adams and he dutifully presented them. Adams contended that these gag rules were a direct violation of the first amendment to the federal constitution, and refused to be silenced on the question, fighting for repeal with indomitable courage, in spite of the bitter denunciation of his opponents. Each year the number of antislavery petitions received and presented by him grew in great numbers; perhaps the climax was in 1837, when Adams presented a petition from 22 slaves, and, when threatened by his opponents with censure, defended himself with remarkable keenness and ability. At each session, also, the majority against him decreased until in 1844 his motion to repeal the 21st (gag) rule of the house was carried by a vote of 108 to 80 and his long battle was over.

Another spectacular contribution of Adams to the antislavery cause was his championing of the cause of the Africans of the *Amistad*, slaves who had mutinied, escaped from their Spanish owners off the coast of Cuba and brought the slaveship into United States waters in Long Island. He defended these Negroes as freemen before the supreme court in 1841 against efforts of the Van Buren administration to return them to their masters, and inevitable death, and won their freedom.

As a member of congress—in fact, through all his life—he was a constant supporter of improvement of the arts and sciences and the diffusion of knowledge, and did much to conserve the Smithson bequest, of an eccentric Englishman to the United States, and to create and endow the Smithsonian institution (*q.v.*) with the money.

The most dramatic event in Adams' life was its end. On Feb. 21, 1848, in the act of protesting an honorary grant of swords by congress to the generals who had won what Adams considered a "most unrighteous war" with Mexico, he suffered a cerebral stroke, fell unconscious to the floor of the house and died two days later in the capitol building. His obsequies in Washington and in his native Massachusetts assumed the character of a countrywide pageant of mourning, as if it were an emotional release at the end of a war which had troubled the conscience of millions of his fellow Americans.

Few men in American public life have possessed more intrinsic worth, more independence, more public spirit and more ability than Adams, but throughout his political career he was handicapped by a certain personal reserve and austerity and coolness of manner which prevented him from appealing to the imaginations and affections of the people. He had few intimate friends, and not many men in American history have been regarded, during the period of their lifetime, with so much hostility and attacked with so much rancour by their political opponents.

Adams was married in London in 1797, on the eve of his departure for the post as minister to Prussia, to Louisa Catherine Johnson (1775–1852), daughter of the United States consul Joshua Johnson, a Marylander by birth, and his wife, Catherine Nuth, an Englishwoman.

BIBLIOGRAPHY.—C. F. Adams (ed.), *Memoirs of John Quincy Adams, Comprising Portions of His Diary from 1795 to 1848* (1874–77); J. T. Morse, *John Quincy Adams* (1883, new ed., 1899); Dexter Perkins, "John Quincy Adams" in *American Secretaries of State and Their Diplomacy*, vol. iv (1928); Bennett Champ Clark, *John Quincy Adams, The Old Man Eloquent* (1933). Two basic volumes by Samuel Flagg Bemis, *John Quincy Adams and the Foundations of American Foreign Policy* (1949) and *John Quincy Adams and the Union* (1956), utilized the fabulous archives of the Adams family, now in the possession of the Massachusetts Historical society and in the process of voluminous publication, and a wealth of other official and private collections.

(E. C.; S. F. B.)

ADAMS, MAUDE (1872–1953), U.S. actress, best known for her charming portrayals of J. M. Barrie's heroines, was born in Salt Lake City, Utah, Nov. 11, 1872, daughter of James and Annie (Adams) Kiskadden. Her mother, whose maiden name she adopted, was leading lady of the Salt Lake theatre. Miss Adams was carried on stage as an infant and as soon as she could walk and talk played child parts, enjoying her first triumph at the age of five as Little Schneider in *Fritz* at the San Francisco theatre. She played all the usual child roles, and after an interval for education in 1888 joined E. H. Sothern as ingénue. From her appearance in C. H. Hoyt's *A Midnight Bell* (1889) her popularity grew rapidly. The next year Charles Frohman cast her in William Gillette's *All the Comforts of Home*, and when John Drew left Daly for the Frohmans in 1892 she became leading lady for five years to the "first gentleman of the stage." From 1897 she was for many years a Frohman star, especially successful in *The Little Minister, Peter Pan, What Every Woman Knows, Quality Street* and *A Kiss for Cinderella*. But she also played Juliet, Viola, Rosalind, and Joan of Arc in Schiller's play. She left the stage in 1918, experimented for a time with stage lighting, returned in 1931 as Portia to Otis Skinner's Shylock, and made her last appearance as Maria in *Twelfth Night* in 1934. She became professor of dramatic art at Stephens college, Columbia, Mo., in 1937. Miss Adams died at Tannersville, N.Y., on July 17, 1953. (B. HT.)

ADAMS, ROBERT (*c.* 1791–1875), Irish clinician noted for his contributions to the knowledge of various forms of heart disease and of rheumatic gout, was born in Ireland *c.* 1791 and educated at Trinity college, Dublin. After spending some time in medical study in Europe, he settled in practice in Dublin. He was surgeon successively to the Jervis Street and Richmond hospitals and was three times elected president of the Royal College of Surgeons in Ireland. In 1827 he described a condition of the heart characterized by a very slow pulse and by transient giddiness. Twenty years later attention was again drawn to this curious combination of symptoms by his colleague William Stokes, and it became known as the Adams-Stokes's syndrome (or disease). In 1861 he was appointed surgeon to the queen in Ireland and regius professor of surgery in the University of Dublin. He died in Dublin on Jan. 13, 1875.   (W. J. Bp.)

ADAMS, ROGER (1889–   ), U.S. chemist, best known for his studies of organic compounds, was born in Boston, Mass., on Jan. 2, 1889. Educated at Harvard university, he received the degree of Ph.D. in 1912. Following study in Germany and a period of teaching at Harvard, he went in 1916 to the University of Illinois, where he became professor of organic chemistry in 1919 and head of the chemistry department in 1926. In 1954 he accepted a research professorship and in 1957 he retired.

Adams' most important researches determined the chemical constitution of such natural products as chaulmoogra oil, gossypol, marijuana and numerous alkaloids. His other fields of research were stereochemistry, synthesis of medicinal compounds, and platinum catalysts. In recognition of his career as research chemist, teacher, consultant to the chemical industry and scientific adviser to the government in World War II, Adams was awarded many honours, including the Priestley medal (1946).   (D. C. Bm.)

ADAMS, SAMUEL (1722–1803), political leader of the period of the American Revolution and signer of the Declaration of Independence. He was born in Boston, Mass., on Sept. 27, 1722, a second cousin to John Adams, second president of the United States. He graduated from Harvard college in 1740, briefly studied law, and failed in several business ventures. As a tax collector in Boston, he neglected to collect the public levies and to keep proper accounts, so exposing himself to suit.

With the passage by parliament of the Sugar act in 1764 (*see* UNITED STATES [OF AMERICA]: *History*) Adams began a swift rise to power in Massachusetts. He denounced the measure, being one of the first of the colonials to cry out against taxation without representation. He played an important part in instigating the Stamp act riots in Boston, and he soon acquired influence

BY COURTESY OF THE CITY OF BOSTON, ON DEPOSIT AT MUSEUM OF FINE ARTS, BOSTON

SAMUEL ADAMS, PORTRAIT BY JOHN SINGLETON COPLEY

second only to that of James Otis among those who struggled against British authority in the colony. Elected to the lower house of the Massachusetts general court from Boston, he served in that body until 1774, after 1766 as its clerk. In 1769 Adams assumed the leadership of the Massachusetts "radicals." According to his cousin John, Samuel had committed himself to American independence a year earlier. John Adams may have erred in ascribing this extreme stand to his cousin at so early a time, but certainly Samuel Adams was one of the first American leaders to deny any authority over the colonies to parliament; and he was also one of the first to establish independence as the proper goal, this surely before 1774.

John Adams described his cousin as a plain, modest and virtuous man. But Samuel Adams was in addition a propagandist who was not overscrupulous in his attacks upon British officials and policies, and a passionate politician as well. In innumerable newspaper letters and essays over various signatures he described British measures and the behaviour of royal governors, judges and customs men in the darkest colours. He was a master of organization, arranging for the election of men who agreed with him, procuring committees that would act as he wished and securing the passage of resolutions that he desired.

During the crisis over the Townshend duties (1767–70) Adams was unable to persuade the Massachusetts colonists to take extreme steps, partly because of the moderating influence of Otis.

However, the British troops who were sent to Boston in 1768 offered a fine target for his propaganda; and he saw to it that they were portrayed in the colonial newspapers as brutal soldiery oppressing inoffensive citizens and assailing their wives and daughters. He was one of the leaders in the town meeting which demanded and secured the removal of the troops after the Boston massacre. When news came that the Townshend duties, except for that on tea, had been repealed, his following dwindled. Nevertheless, during the years 1770–73, when other colonial leaders were inactive, Adams persistently revived old issues and found new ones; he was responsible for the foundation (1772) of the committee of correspondence of Boston and of similar bodies in other towns, these later becoming effective engines against British tyranny.

The passage by parliament of the Tea act of 1773 gave Adams ample opportunity to exercise his remarkable talents. Although he did not participate in the Boston Tea Party, he was undoubtedly one of its planners. He was again a leading figure in the opposition of Massachusetts to the execution of the Coercion acts; and as a member of the first continental congress, he insisted that the delegates take a vigorous stand against Britain. As a member of the provincial congress of Massachusetts in 1774–75 he participated in making preparations for warfare, should Britain resort to arms. When the British troops marched out of Boston to Concord, Adams, with Hancock, was staying in a farmhouse near the redcoat line of march; and it is often said that the arrest of the two men was one of the purposes of the expedition. However, the troops made no effort to find them; and British orders called only for destruction of military supplies gathered at Concord. When Gen. Thomas Gage issued an offer of pardon to the rebels some weeks later, he excepted Adams and Hancock.

As a member of the continental congress, in which he served as a delegate until 1781, Adams was less conspicuous than he was in town meetings and the Massachusetts legislature. He and John Adams were among the first to call for a final separation from Britain. Both men signed the Declaration of Independence. They formed a political alliance with the Lees of Virginia and exerted considerable influence by means of it. With the departure of John Adams for Europe, Samuel became of less consequence in congress. In that body there were many men as able as he.

Adams was a member of the convention which framed the Massachusetts constitution of 1780, and also sat in the convention of his state which ratified the federal constitution. He was at first an anti-Federalist, but finally abandoned his opposition when the Federalists promised to support a number of future amendments, these including a bill of rights. He was defeated in the first congressional election by Fisher Ames. Returning to political power as a follower of Hancock, he was lieutenant governor of Massachusetts from 1789 to 1794 and governor from 1794 to 1797. When parties developed on a national scale, he affiliated himself with the Democratic-Republicans. He was defeated as a presidential elector favouring Jefferson in the election of 1796, and soon thereafter retired to private life. He died on Oct. 2, 1803.

BIBLIOGRAPHY.—R. V. Harlow, *Samuel Adams, Promoter of the American Revolution* (1923); John C. Miller, *Sam Adams: Pioneer in Propaganda* (1936); H. A. Cushing (ed.), *The Writings of Samuel Adams*, 4 vol. (1904–08); and *Warren-Adams Letters*, 2 vol., Mass. Hist. Soc. Collections (1917–25).   (J. R. Al.)

ADAMS, SAMUEL HOPKINS (1871–1958), U.S. journalist and author of more than 50 books, was born in Dunkirk, N.Y., on Jan. 26, 1871. He graduated from Hamilton college (Clinton, N.Y.) in 1891 and was a reporter and later a special writer for the *New York Sun* until 1900; from 1901 to 1905 he was associated in various editorial and advertising capacities with McClure's syndicate and *McClure's Magazine*.

One of the muckrakers (*q.v.*) of the period, he contributed to *Collier's Weekly* in 1905 a series of articles exposing quack patent medicines, followed by *The Great American Fraud* (1906), which furthered the passage of the Pure Food and Drug act in 1906. In 1915–16 in the *New York Tribune*, he exposed dishonourable practices in advertising. The novel *Revelry* (1926), and in 1939 a biography of Warren G. Harding, *The Incredible Era*, set forth the scandals of the Harding administration. Adams also wrote biographies of Daniel Webster (*The Godlike Daniel*, 1930) and of Alexander Woollcott (1945). *Average Jones* (1911) was one of many detective stories. Several novels became movie scenarios, notably *It Happened One Night* (1934). *Grandfather Stories* (1955) was based on reminiscences of his grandfather in upper New York state. Some of his books were published under the name Warner Fabian. He died Nov. 15, 1958, in Beaufort, S.C.

ADAMS, SARAH (*née* FLOWER) (1805–1848), English poet, best known for the hymn, "Nearer, My God, to Thee" (1840), was born at Great Harlow, Essex, on Feb. 22, 1805, the daughter of the republican author Benjamin Flower. In 1834 she married William Bridges Adams, a railway inventor and political pamphleteer. She contributed to the *Monthly Repository* and wrote many unpublished poems, chiefly for the Anti-Corn-Law league. A Unitarian, her writings were chiefly religious and her longest work, *Vivia Perpetua* (1841), a dramatic poem about the conversion to Christianity of a Roman girl, shows genuine feeling. Her hymns remain popular for their strong rhythms, simple imagery and their expression of devout self-dedication.

ADAMS, WALTER SYDNEY (1876–1956), U.S. astronomer, was for many years director of the Mount Wilson observatory near Pasadena, Calif. He was born in Syria on Dec. 20, 1876, of missionary parents who returned to the U.S. when he was 8 years old. He studied astronomy at Dartmouth college, The University of Chicago and the University of Munich, Ger.

From 1901 to 1904 he worked on stellar spectra at Yerkes observatory, Williams Bay, Wis. In 1904 he was invited to become a charter member of the staff of a new observatory being established by the Carnegie Institution of Washington on Mount Wilson in southern California. For many years he shared with George E. Hale responsibility for the administration of the growing observatory with its powerful solar apparatus and 60-in. and 100-in. stellar telescopes. He served as director from 1923 to 1946.

As an observer of the spectra of the sun and stars Adams was skillful and indefatigable. His most important investigations included: (1) a close study of the spectra of sun spots; (2) spectroscopic measurements of the rotation of the sun at various solar latitudes; (3) spectroscopic determinations of the velocities and distances of thousands of stars; (4) detailed observations of the spectra of peculiar stars; (5) studies of gases in interstellar space.

Adams was an important member of committees set up by the California Institute of Technology to plan and construct the 200-in. telescope on Palomar mountain. For outstanding contributions to solar and stellar astronomy he received many high honours. He died in Pasadena on May 11, 1956. *See* also OBSERVATORY (AsTRONOMICAL). (P. W. M.)

ADAMS, WILLIAM (1564–1620), English navigator and merchant adventurer, the first Englishman in Japan, was born at Gillingham, Kent, in 1564. When 12 years old he was apprenticed in the mercantile marine, afterward entering the British navy and later serving the company of Barbary merchants as master and pilot. Attracted by the Dutch trade with India, in 1598 he shipped as pilot major with a fleet of five ships which were to sail westward from the Texel via the Straits of Magellan to the East Indies. After storms and hostile attacks by Indians off the coast of Chile, the fleet was scattered, but in April 1600 the "Charity," with a crew of sick and dying men and with Adams on board, anchored off the island of Kyushu, Japan.

Summoned to Osaka, he was examined by Iyéyasu the guardian of the young son of Taiko Sama, the ruler who had just died. His knowledge of ships and shipbuilding and his nautical smattering of mathematics raised him in the estimation of the shogun who presented him with an estate at Hémi near Yokosuka, but refused him permission to return to England. In 1613, however, Adams decided to postpone his return home (permission for which had now been given him) in order to help with the establishment of an English trading factory for the East India company. He spent the rest of his life in Japan and married a Japanese woman. He was given the title Anjin Sama, and a street in Tokyo, Anjin-cho, was named in his memory. Adams died on May 16, 1620.

See N. Murakami (ed.), *Letters Written by the English Residents in Japan, 1611–23* (1900); C. J. Purnell (ed.), *The Log-Book of William Adams, 1614–19* (1916). (A. M. F.)

ADAMS, WILLIAM TAYLOR (1822–1897), U.S. juvenile writer, popularly known under the pseudonym of Oliver Optic, was born in Bellingham, Mass., on July 30, 1822. For 20 years he was a teacher in the public schools of Boston, and he served for a term in the state legislature. He wrote more than 100 books, chiefly juvenile stories of adventure and patriotism, which appeared in several series. In large part these were contributed to *Oliver Optic's Magazine,* of which he was founder and editor. Among the best known are the "Boat Club Series" (1854), the "Army and Navy Series" (1865–94) and the "Great Western Series" (1875–82). He died in Boston on March 27, 1897.

ADAM'S APPLE, a prominence in the middle of the front of the neck, which moves up and down with swallowing. It is more noticeable in men than in women. It is formed by the thyroid cartilage of the larynx, commonly known as the voice box. It is sensitive to pressure and blows.

ADAM'S BRIDGE (RAMA'S BRIDGE), a chain of sandbanks between the island of Mannar, near the northwestern coast of Ceylon, and the island of Rameswaram, off the Indian coast, and lying between the Gulf of Mannar on the southwest and Palk strait on the northeast. More than 30 mi. long, it seriously hinders navigation. Some of the sandbanks are dry and no part of the shoal has a greater depth than 3 or 4 ft. Dredging operations were begun as early as 1838 but were never successful in maintaining a channel for any except vessels of light draft; they have been abandoned. Geological evidence suggests that Adam's Bridge is all that is left of a former land connection between India and Ceylon. The banks and shoals of the "Bridge" are traditionally supposed to be the remains of a huge causeway constructed by Rama, the hero of the *Ramayana,* to facilitate passage of his army from India to Ceylon for the rescue of his abducted wife Sita. (B. H. F.)

ADAMSON, PATRICK (1537–1592), archbishop of St. Andrews, Scot., from 1576 and opponent of the Presbyterian party in the Scottish Kirk. He was born at Perth, probably in March 1537, educated at St. Andrews, was a tutor in Paris, Padua and Geneva, where he studied Calvinist theology, and returned to Scotland *c.* 1572. As archbishop he won the king's support but opposed the Presbyterianism of the general assembly and was excommunicated by the synod (1586). He lost the king's favour and spent his last years in poverty, although recantations of his earlier views, apparently signed but not necessarily written by him and not printed until 1598, gained him remission of the sentence. He died on Feb. 19, 1592. His collected works were published in 1619. His ability as scholar and preacher and his determination as theologian and controversialist were admired even by his enemies.

ADAM'S PEAK, a mountain in Ceylon, about 45 mi. E. by S. of Colombo. It rises steeply to a height of 7,360 ft. and commands a magnificent view. Its conical summit terminates in an oblong platform, 74 by 24 ft., on which there is a hollow, resembling the form of a human foot, 5 ft. 4 in. by 2 ft. 6 in. The footprint is held in veneration by Buddhists, by Muslims and by Hindus alike, and by them it is ascribed respectively to Gautama, to Adam and to Siva. It is in charge of Buddhist monks, and is a famous place of pilgrimage. Heavy chains on the southwestern face, said to have been left there by Alexander the Great, and mentioned by Marco Polo, mark the original route. The ascent is usually made from Maskeliya. At dawn the peak frequently casts a very well-defined shadow upon

CAMERA PRESS, PIX FROM PUBLIX
ADAM'S PEAK, CEYLON

the clouds.

ADANA (SEYHAN), the capital of Seyhan *il* (province) in southern Turkey, on the banks of the Seyhan river, of which it stands about 32 mi. from the sea; it is the fourth largest city in the country and one of the most prosperous. Pop. (1960) 231,548. The climate is cold in winter but hot and humid in summer with frequent thunderstorms. Most of the buildings are of mud brick but the streets are wide. There are several banks, a hospital, a museum, modern hotels, a meteorological centre, a government-sponsored agricultural research station and a malarial-investigation-commission centre. Industries include cotton, flour and saw mills; factories for soap, tobacco and explosives; olive oil refineries; and a government weaving plant. Adana lies on the Istanbul-Baghdad railway, with a branch line to the port of Mersin from which its produce is shipped. It is connected by tarmac roads via Tarsus to the west and eastward to Iskenderun (Alexandretta).

The modern town overlies the ancient one, which dates back at least to the period of the Hittite empire, when it was known as Ataniya, and probably earlier. It has been suggested that Velican Huyuk, lying nearer the sea, was the site of the early settlement. Excavations at Adana Tepe Bag, a mound in the centre of the town, have yielded material from the Islamic to the Hellenistic periods. One of the earlier standing monuments is the 220-yd.-long stone bridge across the Seyhan (ancient Sarus), dating from the time of Justinian and restored in the time of the Arab rulers al-Walid (743) and al-Mu'tasim (840) when they controlled this area. On the right bank of the river is the ruined fortress built by Harun al-Rashid in 782. The principal mosque, the Ulu Cami, dates from 1542. Situated close to the narrow pass known at the Cilician Gate, Adana was often taken by conquering armies, from those of Alexander to those of Ibrahim Pasha. After the Turkish defeat at Konya it was held by the Egyptians from 1832 to 1840. After World War I it was occupied for a short time by French forces in 1920–21, until the treaty of Lausanne returned the *il* to Turkey.

The *il* of Seyhan (*q.v.*) was known in classical times as Cilicia, and under the Hittites as Kizzuwatna. Adana is the centre of the cotton trade and the surrounding plain grows cereals, tobacco, sugar cane, sesame and citrus fruits.   (M. V. S.-W.)

ADAPA was a legendary sage, a citizen of Eridu, a city of Babylonia. Endowed with vast intelligence by Ea, the god of wisdom, he became the hero of the Eridu myth of the Fall of Man. Adapa, in spite of his possession of all wisdom, was denied immortality. One day, while he was fishing, the south wind blew so violently that he was thrown into the sea. In his rage he broke the wings of the south wind, which then ceased to blow. Anu, the god of heaven, summoned him before his gates to receive punishment, but jealous Ea cautioned him not to touch the bread and water that would be offered him. When Adapa came before Anu, Tammuz and Gizzida interceded for him and explained to Anu that as Adapa had been endowed with omniscience he needed only immortality to become a god. Anu then offered Adapa the bread and water of eternal life, which he refused to take. Thus mankind became mortal. The legend is preserved among the cuneiform tablets discovered during the 19th century in Ashurbanipal's library at Nineveh.   (T. V. B.)

ADAPAZARI (ADAPAZAR), the chief town of the *il* of Sakarya, Turkey, lies about 75 mi. E. of the Bosporus, on the old military road from Istanbul to the east. Pop. (1960) 79,420. It is an important commercial and industrial centre, and is connected by a branch line to the Anatolian railway. Its industries include sugar refining, silk, linen and the manufacture of pipes; its exports are tobacco, walnut wood, cocoons and vegetables for the Istanbul market. The country around is fertile and extensively cultivated, its chief crops being sugar beet, tobacco, potatoes and cereals.   (N. TU.; S. ER.; E. TU.)

ADAPTATION, BIOLOGICAL. The adaptations which, in the widest sense, fit an animal or plant to its environment are the result of natural selection acting upon heritable variation. Even the simpler organisms must be adapted in a great variety of ways: in their structure, physiology (the working and chemistry of their bodies) and genetics, in their locomotion or dispersal, in their

means of defense and attack, in their reproduction and development and in other respects. It should initially be noticed that there are two distinct means of achieving these results, though all intermediates between them may be encountered. Either the body may be adjusted accurately to particular types of environment or it may develop a tolerance to a wide range of them.

Accurate adaptations may involve migration to, or survival in favourable conditions such as temperature. Alternatively, organisms may manufacture their own environment as do the mammals that are precisely adjusted to their optimum temperature. This they create for themselves in whatever situation (consistent with survival) they may be. On the other hand, forms with a wide tolerance are fitted to the environmental range, great or small, to which they are normally exposed; they cannot evolve appropriate reactions to conditions they seldom or never experience.

It will be evident that, to be useful, adaptations must often occur simultaneously in a number of different parts of the body. A change from a more carnivorous to a more vegetarian diet necessitates alterations in the teeth, digestive juices and length of the digestive tract; it necessitates also modifications in habit and imposes a need for new types of defense. Such profound effects demonstrate that individuals best adapted to their environment tend to survive. (*See* SELECTION.)

Some of the most fundamental of biological adaptations are of a chemical and genetic kind. The conditions in which the cells of the body can live are really very restricted. They have, indeed, changed but little since life first arose. It did so in the sea, and it was not until long afterward that it became practicable to colonize fresh water and land. That achievement was possible only through the evolution of adaptive mechanisms capable of maintaining something like the original constitution of the body-fluids. Thus even in man and other mammals today, the blood is chemically quite closely related to sea water.

For general information on the genetic adaptations of organisms *see* GENETICS: *Population Genetics: The Role of Natural Selection*. It is useful, however, to draw attention to one or two aspects of them here. The gene-complex of an organism is controlled by selection to give rise to the most favourable effects from the genes and, as far as possible, to minimize the unfavourable ones. Furthermore, it might even have been deduced on logical grounds, in advance of the discovery, that some mechanism exists for holding together, generally but not irrevocably, those genes that interact in a favourable way. Not only, then, is the chromosome mechanism a predictable necessity, but it follows that the genes which each chromosome carries are not, as might appear from the linkage maps, a purely random assortment. That is to say, the chromosomes must be highly adapted systems.

C. D. Darlington has pointed out that the stability of the chromosome numbers in plants is associated with the length of the reproductive cycle. The values frequently vary within species, and usually within genera, in annuals; they do so within tribes in perennials, but hardly within families in trees. For chromosome changes at their onset interfere with fertility, and an error in the sexual mechanism does not become effective until maturity. This will be in a few weeks in an annual, but only after many years and great biological expenditure in a tree. Here we have one aspect of the way in which adaptation controls the chromosome system.

The means by which organisms are adjusted to their ecology may be either environmental or genetic. Thus we find that many plants are, for obvious reasons, of more prostrate growth in exposed positions, high up on mountains or by the seashore, than in sheltered habitats. In some species the forms maintain their characteristics when grown together in the same environment. Of this the bittersweet, *Solanum dulcamara,* and its dwarf phase *maritimum*, from shingle beaches, provides an instance; in others, the sea plantain, *Plantago maritima*, for example, they do not. The adaptations for pollination (*q.v.*) and seed dispersal (*see* ANGIOSPERMS: *Reproductive Characters;* FRUIT; WEED) possessed by plants are diverse and related to their ecology (*see* ECOLOGY: *Special Aspects of Plants*). Among animals, habits, in addition to structure, must be adapted correctly. Thus the swallowtail butterfly, *Papilio machaon,* is wide-ranging and scatters far over the countryside in continental Europe. In England, it is adapted strictly to life in the fens of East Anglia and from these it seldom strays, though powerful on the wing; for in these circumstances the wandering habits of the continental race would prove fatal.

Of all the adaptations, those involving colour-pattern are probably the best known. One of the most general of these is the evolution of paler colouring on the underside of animals to counterbalance their own shadow, as an aid to concealment. However, the heavy caterpillars of some moths habitually hang upside down from the branch upon which they feed. Consequently, their counter-shading is reversed, the back being paler than their true underside, as in the privet hawkmoth, *Sphinx ligustri;* this is an example that demonstrates clearly the force of selection and that the darker colour in the dorsal position is not merely an anatomical necessity.

In general, animal colour-patterns can be classified according to their adaptive functions. The cryptic or concealing type may enable a predator to approach its prey unobserved, as in the tiger, or to escape predation. Beautiful instances of the latter type are, of course, extremely numerous and familiar. They may involve a general resemblance to the background, like the woodcock when sitting in undergrowth or a leaf butterfly. They may, on the other hand, give security by matching some particular inanimate object likely to be avoided, such as a bird-dropping. Alternatively, the pattern may be so arranged as to alter the apparent shape of some well-known type of prey for which a predator is searching. (*See* COLORATION, BIOLOGICAL; BIRD: *Coloration.*)

Cryptically coloured forms sometimes, in addition, possess "flash coloration." Here some conspicuous mark, easily visible, is apparent when the animal moves, but is hidden when it comes to rest protected by its background. For instance, the gray and mottled forewings of the red underwing moth, *Catocala nupta,* match tree trunks and dark stones to perfection. In these circumstances, the scarlet hindwings are, of course, hidden, and the sudden disappearance of this colour when the flying insect settles is extremely confusing to a potential enemy. On the other hand, species that possess means of defense, such as certain wasps, or are inedible, like many butterflies and moths, advertise the fact by conspicuous warning colours, and these, unlike flash colours, are usually exhibited even at rest. Such species frequently move or fly slowly; it is to their advantage to be recognized and therefore avoided by their predators. Warning devices other than colour-patterns are sometimes employed, such as the rattle of the rattlesnake. Some of the most remarkable adaptations are those that involve deception, in which edible species without means of defense copy those that are genuinely protected and display warning colours (*see* MIMICRY).

A striking demonstration of natural selection is provided by those instances in which organisms have had to fit themselves to new environments. Since the mid-19th century more than 80 species of moths have lost their original pale cryptic colouring and have become black in the industrial areas of Britain, the United States, and elsewhere (*see* MELANISM). These species rest fully exposed on tree trunks or walls, deriving protection by their resemblance to bark and lichen; but the black forms are better concealed in the blackened countryside of manufacturing districts. A selective interpretation of this phenomenon implies that such species are preyed upon by birds or other predators hunting by sight. The proof of this contention, long denied by ornithologists, was supplied in Britain by H. B. D. Kettlewell, who showed that insect-eating birds selectively eliminate the inappropriately coloured specimens in great numbers, in this case the black ones in the normal countryside and the pale ones in regions polluted by soot. Here we can see biological adaptations evolving at the present time.

See PALEONTOLOGY: *Evolutionary Evidence: Adaptation;* EVOLUTION, ORGANIC: *The Species Concept;* MORPHOLOGY: *Form and Function;* ACCLIMATIZATION; GENE. *See* also references under "Adaptation, Biological" in the Index.

BIBLIOGRAPHY.—E. H. F. Baldwin, *An Introduction to Comparative Biochemistry,* 3rd ed. (1948); C. D. Darlington, *Chromosome Botany* (1956); E. B. Ford, *Moths* (1955); J. S. Huxley, *Evolution, The Modern Synthesis* (1942); H. B. D. Kettlewell, *Heredity, 10:* 287 (1957); W. B. Turrill, *British Plant Life* (1948). (E. B. F.)

ADDA (anc. ADDUA), a river of north Italy, rises in small lakes in the Rhaetian Alps at 7,660 ft. In its upper course, from Bormio to Tirano, it flows southward, turning west at Tirano and entering Lake Como near its northern end. The upper course of the Adda is sometimes known as the Valtellina (*q.v.*). Leaving Lake Como (*q.v.*) at Lecco, the Adda crosses the Lombardy plain, flowing past Lodi, and reaches the Po, after a course of 194 mi., just upstream from Cremona. The drainage basin of the Adda covers 3,081 sq.mi., its average flow in the lower course is about 8,800 cu.ft. per second, varying between 600 and 28,000. There are numerous hydroelectric plants on the upper Adda, and there is extensive irrigation on its lower course. (G. KH.)

ADDAMS, JANE (1860–1935), U.S. social reformer, founder of Hull House in Chicago, Ill., and co-winner of the Nobel peace prize in 1931, was born at Cedarville, Ill., Sept. 6, 1860. After graduating from Rockford college, Rockford, Ill. in 1881, she entered the Woman's Medical college of Philadelphia, Pa., but her health failed, and after two years of invalidism she traveled extensively in Europe. In London she visited the Toynbee Hall "settlement" in the Whitechapel industrial district. After her return she founded Hull House (1889), a pioneer U.S. social settlement (*q.v.*) in the old Hull mansion on Chicago's west side, where well-known social reformers lived as residents. In this large settlement she worked with labour and other reform groups for many pioneer welfare laws such as the first juvenile court law and the first "mother's pension" law, tenement house regulation, an eight-hour working day law for women, factory inspection and workmen's compensation. She was also an able supporter of woman suffrage. A well-known pacifist, she was chairman of the International Congress of Women at The Hague, Neth., in 1915, following which the Women's International League for Peace and Freedom, of which she became president, was established. She was the first woman president of the National Conference of Social Work (1910) and took an active part in the Progressive presidential campaign with Theodore Roosevelt in 1912. Author of many books and articles, Jane Addams used her influence for social justice for the immigrant, for the Negro, for labour and for the rights of women and children. She died in Chicago on May 21, 1935. (E. AT.; X.)

ADDAX (*Addax nasomaculatus*), a large antelope once distributed throughout the Sahara desert, but now much reduced in number and distribution. The summer coat shades from white underparts to sandy above; in winter, long brown hair develops on the neck, shoulders and forehead. Below the dark-brown forehead a white streak crosses the face. A heavy, short-legged, oryx-like antelope, the addax stands about 40 in. high. The closely ringed horns, up to 43 in. long, have a slight spiral twist. Desert adaptations include broad hoofs for travel in loose sand, moisture-conserving specializations and an ability to follow rains to vegetation-covered dunes. (H. K. B.)

ADDER, originally meaning "any snake," is now usually applied to the viper *Vipera berus,* a poisonous snake of Europe and northern Asia. In Norway it occurs slightly above the Arctic circle, farther north than any other known snake. Its colour is variable, with usually a zigzag black band running along the back; its length, 18 to 30 in. Six to 20 young are born during August or early September. Food consists of lizards and small mammals. The adder's bite is rarely fatal to man.

The puff adder (*Bitis arietans*), large and dangerous, and the night adders (*Causus* species), small and not so dangerous, are African vipers. The death adder (*Acanthophis antarcticus*), of another family, the Elapidae, is a dangerous Australian snake remarkably similar to a viper in appearance. (S. A. M.)

ADDER'S-TONGUE: *see* DOG'S-TOOTH VIOLET.

ADDICT, DRUG: *see* DRUG ADDICTION and articles on the various addicting drugs, as HEROIN; MORPHINE; etc.

ADDING MACHINES: *see* OFFICE MACHINES AND APPLIANCES.

ADDIS ABABA ("New Flower"), the capital of Ethiopia, Africa, lies in the Shoa province about 8,000 ft. above sea level and in the centre of a well-watered plateau surrounded by hills and mountains. In place of the original forest is a profuse growth of eucalyptus trees. The climate is healthful with warm, sunny days and cool nights. The rainy season extends from July to late September and the average rainfall is about 50 in. Addis Ababa is the administrative and business centre of the Ethiopian empire and the seat of government. Pop. (1961) 449,021, including about 10,000 foreign nationals.

The present site of Addis Ababa, then known as Finfinnie, was chosen in 1886 by Menelik II, then king of Shoa, as his capital. Building began in 1887, when the foundation stone of the palace (the "Old Ghibbi") was laid, and the town became the official capital of Ethiopia in 1889. It grew in a desultory fashion until, in 1936, the Italians occupied it and made it the capital of Italian East Africa. They carried out many constructive improvements during their occupation. The city was captured by the Allies in 1941 and Ethiopian rule was restored. Its growth accelerated after World War II, with considerable building and road construction, but although developing rapidly on modern lines it retained much of its character as an African town. The main thoroughfare, Churchill road, is long and rather steep and the city is laid out on different levels, owing to the hilly terrain. A town-planning scheme of Sir Patrick Abercrombie's was being gradually made effective, with striking results.

The University College of Addis Ababa was founded in 1950 and there are also two teacher-training colleges; a college of engineering; technical, commercial and handicraft schools; secondary schools; and a large number of primary schools. Certain of the foreign communities maintain schools which are open to all races.

There are two imperial palaces of modern design with large gardens; a national library and museum; and public buildings in various styles, notably a striking new parliament house. Among the numerous churches, some of which are picturesque, are a Coptic and a Roman Catholic cathedral. Addis Ababa has several large hospitals, an impressive opera house and several cinemas. Electricity and water supplies are adequate and keep pace with the city's growth. There are a large diplomatic colony and some imposing embassies. The United Nations Economic Commission for Africa has its headquarters in Africa House.

Addis Ababa is the centre of the growing coffee trade of the empire. There is no heavy industry, but light industries such as textile mills, shoe factories, a brewery, distilleries and flour mills are established on the outskirts of the city. In its large and colourful markets is distributed much of the produce grown throughout the empire.

Interest is being shown in developing Addis Ababa as a tourist centre and there are several first-class hotels. An automatic telephone system and modern telegraphic facilities are available and there is a radio station. From the airport, 2½ mi. from the city, there are services to Frankfurt, Ger.; Athens, Greece; the port of Aden; and to Nairobi, Kenya; Cairo, Egy.; Khartoum, Sudan; and other African towns. There is also a network of internal services. Addis Ababa is the terminus of the Franco-Ethiopian railway, which runs to Djibouti. A highway system, which is constantly being extended, fans out from the city to the provinces.

The city, which is divided into ten municipal districts, is governed by a nominated kantiba (mayor) with the aid of a council which comprises both elected and nominated representatives.

(F. E. Sd.)

ADDISON, JOSEPH (1672–1719), English essayist and critic who, with Sir Richard Steele (*q.v.*), wrote most numbers of *The Tatler* (1709–11) and *The Spectator* (1711–12 and 1714), was born at Milston, Wiltshire, on May 1, 1672, the eldest son of Lancelot Addison. His father, who had at one time been chaplain to the British garrison at Tangier, was rector of Milston: he later became the dean of Lichfield. Joseph Addison was educated at Lichfield grammar school and at the Charterhouse, where he made friends with Richard Steele, who often spent his holidays at the deanery. At the age of 15 Addison went up to Queen's college, Oxford, later being elected to a demyship and subsequently (in 1698) to a fellowship at Magdalen college which he retained until 1711. He first distinguished himself by his skill at Latin verse. His first biographer, Thomas Tickell, tells us that he "was admired as one of the best authors since the *Augustan* age, in the two Universities, and the greater part of Europe, before he was talked of as a Poet in Town." At this time he met John Dryden and the publisher Jacob Tonson, for whom he soon undertook some literary commissions. "To Mr. Dryden," his first English poem, was published in Dryden's third miscellany of poems, *Examen Poeticum* (1693), and an ode, two translations and a poem entitled "An Account of the Greatest English Poets" in the fourth, the *Annual Miscellany* (1694). He was soon introduced to William Congreve and other men of letters and through them he was presented to the lord chancellor, Sir John (later Baron) Somers, and to Charles Montagu (later earl of Halifax), then chancellor of the exchequer and leader of the Whigs, who persuaded him to write his *Poem to His Majesty* in 1695. He had to choose between taking holy orders, thus confirming his fellowship, and taking up a life of affairs in London. Montagu and Somers secured him a pension of £300 from the crown to enable him to travel and prepare for further literary undertakings. His Latin poem *Pax Gulielmi*, on the peace of Ryswick, and his essay on the *Georgics*, in Dryden's translation of Virgil, had appeared in 1697. Shortly afterward Addison left England for four years (1699–1703). During his travels, for much of the time as tutor to young Edward Wortley Montagu, he wrote his *Letter from Italy* (1704), one of the most agreeable of his poems, *Remarks on Several Parts of Italy* (1705) and *Dialogues upon the Usefulness of Ancient Medals*, posthumously published in Tickell's edition of the *Works* (1721) and separately in 1735.

The months immediately following his return to England in 1703 were among the least propitious of his career (though he became acquainted with many notable Whigs at this time, having been introduced into the Kit-Cat club), the Whigs being out of office and his principal patron in particular discredit at court; but his fortunes were quickly restored when the earl of Godolphin asked Halifax to find him a poet to celebrate Marlborough's glori-

ST. GEORGE CATHEDRAL IN ADDIS ABABA, CENTRE OF THE COPTIC FAITH IN ETHIOPIA ous victory at Blenheim. Halifax recommended Addison, who was immediately offered a commissionership of appeal in the excise (virtually a sinecure) and began work on his heroic poem *The Campaign* (1705). About this time he helped Steele to complete the comedy *The Tender Husband* (1705). Soon after (in 1706) he was promoted undersecretary of state to Sir Charles Hedges and some months after to his successor, the duke of Sunderland. It was at this time that his opera, *Rosamond* (1707) was produced. It failed. Later in his political career he was made chief secretary to the earl of Wharton, who became Lord Lieutenant of Ireland (1708–10): this gave Addison an opportunity of renewing his friendship with Jonathan Swift when he accompanied the lord lieutenant to Ireland, where he was also appointed keeper of the records, in 1709. Addison had been elected in 1708 as member of parliament in the Whig interest for Lostwithiel, Cornwall, and after 1710 represented Malmesbury, a seat he retained until his death, though he never spoke in the house of commons. In Dublin parliament he was one of the members for Cavan (1709–10).

JOSEPH ADDISON. PORTRAIT PAINTED BY MICHAEL DAHL (1656–1743)

One of his clerks in Ireland was his relative Eustace Budgell (*q.v.*), who later became his private secretary and contributed to *The Tatler* and *The Spectator*.

Addison's fame rests above all on these two periodicals, *The Tatler* and *The Spectator*. The honour of founding *The Tatler* (April 12, 1709) must go to Steele, but Addison quickly became involved and played a considerable part in determining the nature of the new periodical. In a sense *The Tatler* was an example of the increase in journalism which followed the refusal of the house of commons to renew the licensing act in 1695; but Addison, who was less passionate and less interested in politics than Steele, realized that it would be prudent to exclude politics altogether from their new publication. Within six months, accordingly, *The Tatler,* to which Addison contributed 46 numbers, collaborating with Steele in the writing of 36 other numbers, was almost wholly devoid of political news or comment. "Is it not much better," as he once asked, "to be let into the knowledge of one's self, than to hear what passes in Muscovy or Poland?" The concern of the essayists was not politics but life. "The general purpose of this paper," Steele wrote in the dedication of the first collected volume (1712–15), "is to expose the false arts of life, to pull off the disguises of cunning, vanity, and affectation, and to recommend a general simplicity in our dress, our discourse, and our behaviour." The last number of *The Tatler* appeared on Jan. 2, 1711, and the first number of its successor, *The Spectator* (in which Addison was from the first the leading spirit, contributing in all 274 numbers), came out on March 1, 1711. The object of the new work, which lasted until Dec. 6, 1712, and was revived by Addison for 24 numbers from June 18 to Sept. 29, 1714, was similar to that of its predecessor. "It was said of Socrates," as Addison wrote, "that he brought philosophy down from heaven to inhabit among men; and I shall be ambitious to have it said of me that I have brought philosophy out of closets and libraries, schools and colleges, to dwell in clubs and assemblies, at tea-tables and in coffeehouses." The club that centres in the Spectator himself is a brilliant device: Sir Roger de Coverley, Captain Sentry, Sir Andrew Freeport and the others represent important sections of the society of the day. Addison's instinct was to bring people together for reasonable discussion. Hence his hatred of rancorous party politics. "There cannot a greater judgment befall a country," as he wrote in No. 125, "than such a dreadful spirit of division as rends a government into two distinct peoples and makes them greater strangers and more averse to one another than if they were actually two different nations." Although he was equally opposed to violent religious controversy, he did not exclude religion from his pages. At one time he had intended to take holy orders and his resemblance to a parson was noted not only by Bernard de Mandeville (*q.v.*)—with his sneer about "a parson in a tye-wig"—but also by Tonson, who told someone that he "ever thought him a priest in his heart." The Saturday essays have usually a serious tendency. But although Addison wished to "recommend Christianity," he had no intention of encouraging passionate religious feeling, "enthusiasm" of the sort that had caused so much trouble in the previous century. His attitude is summed up in the motto of the *Spectator,* No. 112: "Honour the gods according to the established modes."

Two features of *The Spectator* deserve particular mention: the critical essays which it contained and the attention which it paid to the tastes of women readers. From the first Addison made a point of devoting a considerable proportion of the essays to literary criticism. He was a good critic, but to understand his historical importance in this respect it is as well to remember Dr. Samuel Johnson's observation that most earlier criticism had been intended "rather for those that were learning to write, than for those that read only to talk." Accordingly "an instructor like Addison was now wanting, whose remarks being superficial might be easily understood, and being just might prepare the mind for more attainments." Here, as in so many other respects, Addison felt the pulse of his time and dispensed precisely what was required. His criticism proved more influential than that of many profounder critics, helping (above all) to bring it about that writers and writing were considered proper subjects for conversation throughout the century. One reason for the essential simplicity of his critical essays was that they were intended for women as well as men. The accession of a woman to the throne had made the time propitious for the advocacy of a change of attitude to women. "There are none to whom this paper will be more useful than to the female world," Addison wrote in the tenth number. "I have often thought there has not been sufficient pains taken in finding out proper employments and diversions for the fair ones." Most people now agree with Swift, who found the tone in which Addison "fair-sexed it" intolerably condescending; but there is no doubt that the essayists of the period did a great deal to improve the status of women in English society.

In 1713 (to conclude the account of his life) Addison contributed 51 numbers, few of which were memorable, to Steele's periodical *The Guardian* (March 12—Oct. 1) and completed his tragedy, *Cato,* which was produced and received with the greatest approbation. Dr. Johnson considered it "unquestionably the noblest production of Addison's genius," yet described it as "rather a poem in dialogue than a drama, rather a succession of just sentiments in elegant language than a representation of natural affections." It may still be read with admiration but it will never again excite an audience. Its success may be regarded as the climax of Addison's good fortune. In 1714 he was secretary to the lords justices who formed the council of regency, from 1714 to 1715 chief secretary to the earl of Sunderland, who was then Lord Lieutenant of Ireland, and in 1715 became one of the commissioners for trade and the colonies. *The Freeholder, or Political Essays,* of which there were 55 numbers (Dec. 23, 1715–June 29, 1716) was entirely Addison's work. Though well-written, it is unremarkable. It seems unlikely that his marriage to the dowager countess of Warwick (in 1716) was a particularly happy one: his health was beginning to decline and he had a quarrel with the most gifted satirist of the age which made him the subject of what is perhaps the most celebrated satiric "character" in the language. In the summer of 1715, angered by Addison's support of a rival translation of the *Iliad,* Pope sketched the lines on "Atticus," the narcissistic and envious man of letters, "Willing to wound, and yet afraid to strike." A year later he sent Addison a copy of the lines. The details of the quarrel are obscure and it can merely be said that Addison seems to have behaved correctly to Pope for the remainder of his life and that Pope did not publish the "character" until 1735, when it appeared in *An Epistle to Dr. Arbuthnot.* Addison's prose comedy *The Drummer,* which was produced anonymously in 1716, was unsuccessful. In 1717 Addison became secretary of state, an arduous position from which he resigned in the following year. He was involved in a quarrel with Steele in the spring of 1719, defending, in two numbers of *The Old Whig,* the Peerage bill which Sunderland had introduced and Steele had attacked in the *Plebeian.* References became personal and the argument ended bitterly. Two months later, Addison died, on June 17, 1719, at Holland house, London, at the age of 47. He remains an outstanding example of a writer of the highest talents (rather than genius) who achieved celebrity in his own age and significantly influenced the course of English literary history by his application to the problems of his art and a careful study of the taste and the needs of his time.

See also Index references under "Addison, Joseph" in the Index volume.

BIBLIOGRAPHY.—There are collected editions of the *Works* by Thomas Tickell, 4 vol. (1721) and Richard Hurd, 6 vol. (1811, reprinted 1898). *The Miscellaneous Works,* ed. by A. C. Guthkelch, 2 vol. (1914), gives the best text of poems, plays and prose works (English and Latin) other than the periodical essays. The *Letters* were ed. by Walter Graham (1941). Of many reprints of *The Tatler* the best is that of G. A. Aitken, 4 vol. (1898–99): of the numerous editions of *The Spectator,* that by G. Gregory Smith, 4 vol., "Everyman's Library," nos. 164–167 (1907, 1950) may be recommended. The definitive edition is that by D. F. Bond (1962). A good brief biography is that by W. J. Courthope in the "English Men of Letters Series" (1884): there is a much fuller one by Peter Smithers (1954).

For criticism and comment, *see* Johnson's *Lives of the Poets,* ed. by Birkbeck Hill, vol. ii, pp. 79–158 (1905); T. B. Macaulay, *Critical and Historical Essays,* vol. ii, pp. 453–522, in "Everyman's Library," no. 266 (1907); A. Beljame, *Le Public et les hommes de lettres . . . 1660–1744* (1881; Eng. trans. *Men of Letters and the English Public in the Eighteenth Century, 1660–1744,* 1948); B. Dobrée, *Essays in Biography, 1680–1726,* pp. 201–345 (1925), *English Literature in the Early Eighteenth Century, 1700–1740* (1959), pp. 102–120 and 612–614, including a bibliography; C. S. Lewis, "Addison," *Essays on the Eighteenth Century presented to David Nichol Smith,* pp. 1–15 (1945).

(J. H. JA.)

ADDISON, THOMAS (1793–1860), English physician famous for his descriptions of Addison's disease of the suprarenal capsules and of pernicious anemia, was born at Long Benton, Northumberland, in April 1793. In 1837 he became full physician and joint lecturer on medicine to Guy's hospital, London, with Richard Bright. He died at Brighton, Sussex, on June 29, 1860.

Addison gave a preliminary account in 1849 of the two diseases named after him and described them fully in *On the Constitutional and Local Effects of Disease of the Supra-Renal Capsules* (1855). He was the first to correlate a set of disease symptoms with pathological changes in one of the endocrine glands, and it has been well said that "the whole of endocrinology dates from March 15, 1849." He was author with John Morgan of *An Essay on the Operation of Poisonous Agents Upon the Living Body* (1829), the first English book on the subject. Of Bright and Addison's *Elements of the Practice of Medicine,* only the first volume appeared (1839). Addison's original and important writings on pneumonia, tuberculosis and skin diseases mostly appeared in the *Guy's Hospital Reports* and were republished with a prefatory memoir as *A Collection of the Published Writings of . . . T. Addison* (1868).

(W. J. BP.)

ADDISON'S DISEASE (ADRENAL CORTICAL HYPOFUNCTION), a morbid state first described by Thomas Addison in 1855 as being characterized by "anemia, general languor and debility, remarkable feebleness of the heart's action, irritability of the stomach, and a peculiar change of the color of the skin." The cause of the symptoms (to which may be added also signs of emotional instability) is deficiency of adrenal cortical function, this deficiency resulting from fibrocaseous tuberculosis of the adrenal gland or from atrophy of the adrenal cortex of unknown cause (surgical removal of the gland of course also produces the same symptoms). The symptoms are related to the functions of the adrenal cortex, chief among which are regulation of the body's mineral metabolism (sodium, potassium and chloride), regulation of water balance and regulation of organic metabolism (carbohydrate, protein and fat).

Diagnosis of Addison's disease in its severe form is not difficult,

but demonstration of limitation of adrenal cortical function requires objective laboratory tests.

Before the development of crystalline cortical steroids for use in replacement therapy, life in the presence of Addison's disease was difficult and precarious. Any condition that resulted in loss of sodium and chloride, as excessive perspiration or a diet with high content of potassium and low sodium, could cause prostration or death. Physical exertion, strain from a surgical operation or administration of an anesthetic alone often was sufficient to precipitate a critical condition.

Moderately effective treatment of Addison's disease began to be possible in 1930, when an extract of the adrenal cortex was made available for patients in a critical condition; this material, however, remained scarce, not always reliable and very expensive. In 1932 Robert Loeb discovered that if the loss of sodium chloride was stopped by daily administration of large amounts of this salt, clinical improvement was often marked and sustained, and in 1937 the unfavourable effect of excess potassium was shown. The availability of desoxycorticosterone after 1937 made it possible to control mineral metabolism, but since desoxycorticosterone tended to increase the concentration of sodium and decrease that of potassium in the blood when large amounts were used, it was necessary to limit the intake of sodium and increase potassium in the diet. Many patients were greatly benefited by this treatment, but few were restored to a state of well-being and some patients died even though the electrolytes in the blood were within normal limits. It became evident that something more than control of mineral metabolism was essential.

Cortisone (*q.v.*) was prepared on a commercial scale in 1948, and in 1949 it was shown that a daily dosage of cortisone and desoxycorticosterone restored strength and a sense of well-being to patients who had Addison's disease. Treatment with cortisone alone is not satisfactory because sodium and chloride are rapidly lost from the body; but when mineral metabolism is controlled with desoxycorticosterone at the same time cortisone is administered, patients are able to resist fatigue and to enjoy an almost normal state of health.

See also Index references under "Addison's Disease" in the Index volume.

See George W. Thorn, *Diagnosis and Treatment of Adrenal Insufficiency* (1948). (E. C. KL.; X.)

ADDRESS, FORMS OF. Forms of address are the modes in which one person may speak or write to another. They vary from country to country, and in the great majority of cases are the result of custom and courtesy. Occasionally a form of address is prescribed by official ruling.

This article is divided into the following sections:

I. United States
    1. Spoken Forms of Address
        Presentations and Introductions
        Self-Introduction
        Presentation of a Speaker
    2. Written Forms of Address
        Business Forms of Address
        Social Forms of Address
II. Great Britain
    1. The Royal Family
    2. The Nobility
    3. Other Ranks
III. Europe
    1. France
    2. Spain
    3. Italy
    4. Germany
IV. Asia
    1. The Arab World
    2. India and Pakistan

I. UNITED STATES

1. Spoken Forms of Address.—In the United States the forms of address emphasize the position occupied by the person addressed. They are concerned with the correct use of the name or the label designating the position. Thus the president of the United States is addressed as "Mr. President" in speaking to him and as "Sir" when in conversation with him. In speaking of or quoting him he is referred to as "The President." In presenting him for an address he is announced as "The President of the United States of America." When the wife of the president is included in the address the speaker says "The President and Mrs. Surname." The vice-president is addressed and referred to in the same manner as the president.

An ambassador is addressed as "Mr. Ambassador" or "Your Excellency," his wife as "Mrs. Surname." The governors of the states are addressed as "Governor." The mayor of a city is addressed as "Your Honor."

In unofficial or private life the trend is away from the use of titles in verbal forms of address. It is not correct, according to distinguished social usage, to make the professional title of major importance in speaking to a person. This is especially true in academic and business circles. Such titles as "Dean," "Doctor" and "Professor" are gradually being dropped from social usage.

When in a strictly business or professional relationship, the title should be used. A student would address a dean as "Dean Surname"; he would probably address a professor with a doctor's degree as "Dr. Surname." It is generally considered antiquated to say "Professor Surname"; the term "Mr." is preferable if he is without a doctor's degree or administrative position. However, some persons, according to local customs, cling to the recognition by title.

In the medical profession "Doctor Surname" is always used. The title "Reverend" is seldom used verbally in addressing a clergyman; if he holds a doctor of divinity degree frequently he is addressed as "Dr. Surname." If he holds a position of rank in denominational organizations, such as bishop, he is addressed with a title according to the dictates of the church.

In business it is generally considered poor taste to refer to anyone as "the boss," or by his given name, although there is an increasing habit of using given names in informal fellowship. Deference to a superior should be shown in manner of approach; he is politely addressed as "Sir" or "Mr. Surname." In all of these and similar situations care must be taken not to offend the sense of dignity a person may feel about his position or rank. The speaker must be guided by his own wishes and local custom in choosing the form to use. When in doubt as to the proper title, or as to the use of a title as the proper courtesy, it is always acceptable to address the person as "Mr.," "Mrs." or "Miss."

Presentations and Introductions.—One of the most important forms of address is that used in introductions. An introduction is the form for making easier the beginning of an acquaintanceship between strangers. It must provide a means of identification for the persons being introduced. The form used may also indicate the degree of sponsorship the person making the introduction is assuming for the new relationship.

The simple form of "Miss Smith, Miss Jones" or "Mr. Blank, Mr. Doe," spoken with a genial smile or simple gesture, a glance (never point) or voice inflection, is the easiest form and most generally accepted for all chance meetings, whether in public places, among work associates or on informal occasions.

When respect or additional identification is to be shown, as when the sex, age or position is different, the introduction would be more formal, as "Mrs. Blank, may I present (or may I introduce) (or I would like you to meet my friend Miss Smith) (or Mary Smith) my escort Mr. Doe"; the names would then be repeated: "Miss Smith, Mrs. Blank." The name of the person to whom the greater respect is to be shown is spoken first—in this case Mrs. Blank.

In business introductions, the official title of the person of superior rank is used, as "President Brown, may I present (or introduce) Mr. Newcomer? Mr. Newcomer, Mr. Brown." Then give some identification as the reason for Mr. Newcomer's presence, as "Mr. Newcomer is a new employee in my department; we would like to discuss with you . . ."

Self-Introduction.—Frequently a person must introduce himself. In a business interview he should announce himself by giving his name or presenting a business card, give some identification such as place of residence or business connection, and then state the purpose of his visit, as "I am John Stranger, a senior at New York university. I would like to talk with you about . . ." In answering a telephone a person should always identify the telephone by number and himself by position, as "extension 262, secretary to the president speaking."

Presentation of a Speaker.—In presenting a speaker to an audience the person making the introduction should select carefully only such biographical facts about the speaker as have a direct relation to his qualifications to address the audience on the particular subject, or to the occasion for which they are assembled. These remarks should include the name of the person and his present position, and conclude with: "It is my pleasure to present you Mr. Surname (title if preferred)." The person making the introduction should then turn toward the speaker and say "Mr. Surname."

When the speaker is a person of great distinction, such as the president of the United States, no introductory remarks are made about him; the presiding officer simply announces "The President of the United States."

2. Written Forms of Address.—In all written forms of address the proper use of labels, identity and recognition of position are of paramount importance.

Business Forms of Address.—Great care should be taken in giving correct identification by title, name and position in the address at the head of a business letter. The salutation should be carefully worded so as to indicate a recognition of the respect due the person because of his position.

The title "The Honorable" should be used in writing to: governors, cabinet officers, United States ambassadors and ministers, judges, senators, members of the house of representatives, the secretary to the president, assistant secretaries of executive departments and the heads of independent boards and commissions.

The title "Esquire" should be used after the names of: chief clerks and chiefs of bureaus of the executive departments, mayors of towns and cities (when the name is used before the title, as "James Burrows, Esquire, Mayor of . . ."); although considered antiquated by some, "Esquire" may be added after the name of any individual gentleman.

Beginnings of formal letters should be as follows: to the president, "The or Mr. President"; to an ambassador, "Sir"; to a minister, "Sir." To the cabinet officers and the justices of the U.S. supreme court, "Sir" is used for formal salutations. To a senator, informally, the salutation would be "My dear Senator Smith"; to a member of the house of representatives, "My dear Mr. Jones." For the U.S. supreme court the informal form is "My dear Mr. Chief Justice" and "My dear Mr. Justice." For the supreme court of a state it is also "My dear Mr. Justice"; for the court of appeals of the state, it is "Chief Judge" and "Judge."

Social Forms of Address.—The president of the United States, according to social form, should never receive an engraved invitation to dinner from an individual. When his presence is desired the person inviting him should either call at the White House and ask him to select a date or write to him to that effect.

The most formal invitation should read:

Mr. and Mrs. John Doe
request the honor of
the company of
The American Ambassador to Great Britain and Mrs. Surname
(occasion, time and place)

The envelope addressed to officials should read:

The Title of the Position
and Mrs. Surname

The same form is used for invitations and envelope addresses for all dignitaries. The word "honor" instead of "pleasure" is suggested because of the position of the recipient of the invitation. Between host and guest who are officially equal in rank the word "pleasure" is preferable, but either is correct in all forms of invitations where the name of the guest is to be included.

Acknowledgment of the invitation, either accepting or declining, should be written in the same form as the invitation:

The Governor of the State of Virginia
and Mrs. Surname
regret that they cannot

accept the invitation of
Mr. and Mrs. John Doe
(occasion, time and place)

The place card would read "The President"; his wife's card would read "Mrs. Surname." Similar form for place cards should be used for ambassadors and governors and other ranking dignitaries who are addressed by title of office and not by name. In the case of the American ambassador to Great Britain and his wife, his place card would read "The American Ambassador to Great Britain," his wife's "Mrs. Surname."

The titles "Reverend" and "Honorable" should not precede a surname. The Christian name or title as "Dr." or "Mr." should be used:

The Reverend John Pastor, or the Reverend Dr. Pastor.

Academic degrees and title of position should follow the name: Mr. John Collegian, M.A., or Dr. John Collegian, Director of Admissions.   (E. W. Ch.; E. Pt.; M. L. Mt.)

II. GREAT BRITAIN

Forms of address have evolved over many centuries. They are almost all customary and are therefore variable by changes in the same usage which brought them into being.

1. The Royal Family.—A person speaking to the queen should begin "Your Majesty" and continue "Ma'am." Letters, headed "To the Queen's Most Excellent Majesty," should begin "Madam" and end "I remain, with the profoundest veneration, Your Majesty's most faithful subject."

The spoken form of address for the queen mother is the same as for the queen. Letters, headed "To her Gracious Majesty Queen Elizabeth the Queen Mother," should begin "Madam" and end "I remain Your Majesty's most faithful servant."

A person speaking to a prince of the royal family should begin "Your Royal Highness" and continue "Sir." Letters, headed "To H.R.H. the Duke of—" (or, if not a duke, "To H.R.H. Prince—"), should begin "Sir" and end "I remain, with the greatest respect, your Royal Highness's most obedient servant." Princesses of the royal family should be addressed *mutatis mutandis* as for princes, "Ma'am" taking the place of "Sir."

Those wishing to address royalty in writing should approach them through the lady or gentleman in waiting.

2. The Nobility.—The peerage in Great Britain has five degrees of rank, namely duke, marquess, earl, viscount and baron. Each of these, their wives and children require a different form of address.

Dukes and duchesses are always dukes and duchesses when addressed either in speech or in writing; the prefixes are "His Grace" for dukes, "Her Grace" for duchesses; e.g., His Grace The Duke of Norfolk. The spoken form of address is "Your Grace." Letters should begin "My Lord Duke" and end "I have the honour to be, my Lord Duke, Your Grace's obedient servant."

The full formal title is not used in addressing any member of the four succeeding grades of peers either in conversation or in the intimacy of a private letter. On envelopes, on invitations, in and on legal documents or tradesmen's communications and bills, they are addressed as marquesses and marchionesses, earls and countesses, viscounts and viscountesses. In conversation, and in letters beginning "Dear . . . ," they must be addressed as "Lord So-and-So" or "Lady So-and-So." In formal correspondence "The Most Honourable" for marquesses and marchionesses and "The Right Honourable" for earls, countesses, viscounts, viscountesses, barons and baronesses may be used.

For a baron, the use of the title is more restricted; it is used only in or on legal documents. On envelopes in nonlegal correspondence, on all invitations or in letters written in the third person, he is styled "Lord." However, a baroness in her own right is always called "Baroness" (e.g., Baroness Ravensdale, Baroness Wentworth) except in speech and in letters beginning "Dear." In invitations, the full title, except in the case of barons, is always used. In letters written in the third person, the full title is used in the first place, but afterward reference is made by means of the colloquial designation; e.g., "The editor presents his compliments to the Marquess of Piccadilly and will be much pleased if Lord Piccadilly . . . ," etc.

In the case of the three higher grades of peers, the eldest son bears a courtesy title; i.e., he is known by one of his father's subsidiary peerages (this, however, does not provide him with a seat in the house of lords).

The eldest son of the eldest son of a duke or of a marquess is also customarily known by one of his grandfather's subsidiary peerages. Never is the bearer of a courtesy title addressed as "The Right Honourable." The younger sons of dukes and marquesses have the prefix "Lord" placed before their Christian names and surnames; the younger sons of earls and all the sons of viscounts and barons have that of "Honourable," generally shortened to "Honble." or "Hon."

The daughters of dukes, marquesses and earls bear the title of "Lady" prefixed to the Christian name and surname. Thus Lady Mary will remain Lady Mary all her life, unless she marries a peer or a younger son whose father has a higher rank than her own father. If she marries a commoner, a knight, a baronet or an Honble., she remains Lady Mary and should always be addressed as such. It is wrong to use only her surname, as "Lady Debrett."

The prefix "Honble." is applied to the unmarried daughters of viscounts and of barons. When a daughter marries, the Christian name is dropped and she becomes The Honble. Mrs. Blank, unless she marries a peer or a man with a courtesy title in the peerage higher than her own. If, for example, she marries a younger son of a duke or a marquess, she becomes Lady (husband's full name), as Lady Edward Jones; she can never become Lady Mary Jones unless her father becomes a marquess or a duke. One great difference between these courtesy titles of Lord and Honourable is that the latter title is not used in conversation, and is never printed on visiting cards.

3. Other Ranks.—The wives of baronets and knights are known as "Lady X," but there is nothing in the wife's title to show to which order her husband belongs. The baronet's name is differentiated in writing because the abbreviation "Bt." or "Bart." (preferably the former) follows it on envelopes; the nine different orders of knighthood have their initial letters placed after the name (K.G., knight of the order of the Garter, etc.), but their "ladies" have no right to use these letters. To specify which lady of the same surname is meant, it has become the practice to use the husband's Christian name between parentheses, as Lady (James) Debrett, although this is contrary to tradition and heraldry.

Knights bachelor are knights who do not belong to any of the nine specified orders. They are correctly given the abbreviation, "Kt.," or "Kt. Bach." after their names. They may lay claim, if they possess the necessary qualifications, to such letters as M.D., R.N. or M.P.; the M.P. is always added to the name of any member of the house of commons, no matter what his titles may be.

The title of "Right Honourable" (Rt. Hon.; Rt. Honble.) is the prerogative of H.M.'s privy councilors and, as such, is borne by those of them who are not peers. It is used, in the same way as "Honble.," directly in front of the Christian name (e.g., Rt. Hon. R. A. Butler).

Professional designations, such as "Dr." or "Rev.," or naval or military rank precede the prefix of "Honourable," whereas titles of baronetcy and knighthood follow the prefix; e.g., The Rev. The Honble. Jonathan Kenworthy; Colonel The Honble. Edward Wyndham; The Honble. Sir Trevor Bigham, K.B.E., C.B.

Sailors, soldiers and airmen are always addressed by their professional titles—admiral, general, air marshal, captain, colonel, commander, squadron leader and so on, except sublieutenants in the navy, lieutenants and second lieutenants in the army and flying officers in the air force, who in private life remain Thomas Smith, Esq. Captains in the royal navy add R.N. after their names to show that they belong to the senior service.

Judges and doctors may choose titles as a matter of personal preference from equally correct forms of title. This can generally be discovered by noticing how they style themselves on their visiting cards; e.g., "Sir Henry Barnard" or "Mr. Justice Barnard"; or "Dr. Drennan."

Clergymen are spoken to and of as "Mr.," and on invitations and envelopes they are addressed as "The Revd. (or Rev.) George Burke." In conversation a canon is addressed as "Canon X," but on envelopes it must be as "The Revd. Canon X." Archdeacons when written to are "The Venerable," and deans are "The Very Reverend," but they are addressed orally as "Mr. Archdeacon" and "Mr. Dean." Bishops and archbishops on envelopes are respectively "The Rt. Revd." and "His Grace." The archbishop of Armagh, retired archbishops, the bishop of Meath and the primus of Scotland are "Most Revd." In the Roman Catholic Church archbishops are "Most Revd." and "His Grace," while a cardinal is "His Eminence." In formal speech and in formal writing the form of address for bishops is "My Lord." (Archbishops and bishops are never referred to by their surnames until they have retired; *e.g.*, Archbishop Lang or Bishop Gore, but during tenure of office, His Grace the Archbishop of Canterbury, etc.)

Although men in holy orders may be created knights of various orders (*e.g.*, the Royal Victorian Order and the Order of St. Michael and St. George) they do not receive the accolade and consequently must never be addressed as "Sir"; neither are their wives addressed as "Ladies." Peers and baronets in holy orders are, of course, given their titles, as the Revd. the Viscount Hurlingham.

Ambassadors, ministers (in diplomacy), governors-general and governors have the words "His Excellency"—often abbreviated to H.E.—prefixed to their official titles. It has also become a matter of courtesy to give the wives of ambassadors, of ministers accredited to foreign courts, and of governors-general the same titles and precedence accorded to their husbands. Neither the precedence nor the title applies outside the limits of the country in which the official holds office.

Special sections for women and the title "Dame" exist in the Order of the British Empire and the Royal Victorian Order. "Dame" is followed immediately by the Christian name (*e.g.*, Dame Edith Evans); and the title is not used by peeresses or by ladies whose rank is higher than that of "Dame."

Men who have no titles are termed "Esquire" (commonly shortened to "Esqre." or "Esq.") on their envelopes, and this mode of address is almost universal. This usage has completely swamped the small class of persons who are entitled to be called "Esquire," *e.g.*, landed gentlemen and bearers of coats of arms. Any qualifying letters, such as M.P., C.B., follow after the Esqre. A medical specialist may be addressed "C. Medico, Esqre." or as "Mr. Medico," but a general practitioner should be addressed as "Dr. J. Smith."

In the City of London and in large provincial towns, aldermen and mayors bear their titles in daily life, in speech and writing; in such cases, they should always be addressed on their envelopes according to their style: "Mr. Sheriff Jones"; "Alderman Brown"; "the Worshipful the Mayor of—." In speaking it is usual to say "Mr. Mayor," except in the case of lords mayor, where "my Lord" takes the place of "Mr."

In no case should "Esqre." end an address beginning "Alderman" or "Councilor." There is no definite rule for the use of civic titles, but when a letter is written to the holder of a municipal office at his official address, the envelope must be addressed to him showing his official capacity. In the case of a letter sent to him as a private citizen, at his home address, the civic title may be dropped.

Ministers and certain other holders of official positions in some of the dominions and crown colonies enjoy the prefix "Honble." during their term of office, and often on their retirement it is bestowed on them for life. Care should be taken, therefore, not to omit the prefix where it has been earned.

The word dowager is a source of perplexity to many people. The real meaning of the word (a woman who receives a dowry) has been lost. In medieval times, such recipients were almost always the widows of men belonging to the baronage or landed gentry, who lived in the "dower house" and remained under the protection of the head of the family. In those days, the widow was designated as dowager to differentiate her from the wife of the head. In modern times, its use is entirely a question of personal choice but the widow should show through her name that she no longer holds the position of wife of the leading member of her husband's family.

If the term dowager is disliked, the widow can use her Christian name instead. In that case the Christian name must precede the title; *e.g.*, May Lady Hemphill. The term dowager can either precede the title or be interpolated between the title and the surname; *e.g.*, the Countess Dowager of Plymouth, or the Dowager Viscountess Hailsham.

BIBLIOGRAPHY.—For social forms of address *see* Ellen Countess of Desart and Constance Hoster, *Style and Title: a Complete Guide to the Forms of Social Address* (1924). For official forms of address see *Debrett's Peerage, Baronetage, Knightage and Companionage;* and *Burke's Peerage, Baronetage and Knightage* (many editions).

(E. C. OF D.; C. HOS.; C. F. J. H.)

III. EUROPE

The varied and elaborate forms of address in Europe are the result of monarchical systems of government, with their hereditary and privileged social groups. They are numerous and their usage is sometimes complicated. Examples of them and the general principles from which they derive are given below for four major European countries.

1. France.—The republican constitution of 1792 abolished nobility as a social institution, but the first empire, the two monarchies (the absolute monarchy of 1815 and the liberal one of 1830), as well as the second empire continued to create titles of nobility. Beginning with the third republic new titles ceased to be bestowed, and officially titles are ignored. If, for instance, a Comte de X is appointed ambassador he is officially addressed as Monsieur de X. It is in fact an offense to give oneself a title.

In private intercourse traditional forms of address continue to be observed. Members of former reigning families are addressed as *Altesse Royale;* other princes as *Altesse Sérénissime.* A letter to one of them should begin with *Monseigneur* and end with *Je prie votre Altesse (R. or S.) d'agréer les assurances de ma trés respectueuse considération* ("I beg your highness to receive the assurance of my very respectful consideration").

A letter to a *duc* (and similarly to a *marquis*, a *comte*, a *vicomte* or a *baron*) is addressed to *Monsieur le Duc* and ends with a formula, *Veuillez agréer, Monsieur le Duc, les assurances de ma trés haute considération* ("please accept . . . the assurance of my very high consideration").

In conversation a prince is addressed as *Monseigneur* and other nobles as *Monsieur;* in the latter case, the title should be used once but not repeated.

The president of the republic is addressed as *Monsieur le Président de la République,* and a letter to him should end thus: *Veuillez agréer, Monsieur le Président de la République, l'hommage de mon profond respect* ("the homage of my deep respect"). When speaking to him the shorter form of *Monsieur le Président* is sufficient.

A cardinal is addressed as *Eminence Révérendissime* and a letter to him begins with *Éminentissime Seigneur.* An archbishop or a bishop is addressed as *Excellence* and, at the beginning of a letter or in speech, as *Monseigneur.*

A minister or an ambassador is addressed as *Excellence.* When writing or speaking to an army officer his rank is mentioned. In speech he is addressed as *Mon Colonel* or *Mon Général* (but *Monsieur le Maréchal*).

A barrister is addressed as *Mon cher Maître.* There are, of course, many variations in forms of address depending on the degree of personal relations between two people. A friend writing to a friend starts his letter with *Mon cher Ami* or *Cher Paul* and ends with *affectueusement votre* or *bien à toi.* A letter addressed to an untitled lady starts with *Madame* or *Chère Madame* and ends generally with a formula *Je vous prie, Madame, d'agréer les assurances de mon profond respect.*

2. Spain.—Officially a monarchy with a regent, Spain preserves its traditional and rather elaborate forms of address. The pretender is addressed as *Su Majestad* and his son as *Su Alteza Real.* A *grande de España* is addressed as *Excelentísimo Señor.* Nobles who are not grandees are addressed as *Ilustrísimo Señor el Conde* (or *Vizconde* or *Barón*).

In writing both forms are abbreviated (*Excmo.* or *Ilmo.*). Every man who had been awarded the grand cross of a Spanish order is also addressed as *Excmo.*, and every knight commander as *Ilmo.* Cardinals are addressed *Vuestra Eminencia* (*V.E.* in the text of a letter), ministers, ambassadors and bishops *Vuestra Excelencia* (*V.E.*).

An untitled gentleman (*caballero*) writing to another one addresses his letter to *Señor Don*—and starts with *Muy Señor Mío*. In the text he addresses him as *V.S.* (*Vuestra Señoría*) and ends his letter thus: *De Vd. atto. y s.s., q.e.s.m.* (*De usted atento y seguro servidor, que estrecha su mano,* "your attentive and constant servant, who shakes your hand"). Writing to a lady the last four initials would be *q.b.s.p.* (*que besa sus pies,* "who kisses your feet").

3. Italy.—There is less formality in Italy than in Spain in modes of address, but because of different historical traditions the Italian modes vary between the south and the north. The old titles were not abolished by the republican constitution of 1948. The pretender is styled by his supporters as *Sua Maestà* and members of the former reigning family are addressed with the qualification of *Altezza Reale*.

A letter to a nobleman should be simply addressed to *Il Principe* (or *Marchese, Çonte* or *Barone*), followed by his full name. A letter to him should begin with *Gentilissimo Marchese* (never *Signor Marchese,* a form used by servants). The president of the republic, a minister, an ambassador or a bishop is addressed as *Eccellenza* (a cardinal as *Eminenza*). Writing to a prominent professor a usual form is *Chiarissimo Professore;* to a famous writer in Naples the form *Illustre* would be used, while in Piedmont *Egregio* would be courteous enough. A letter never begins with the surname of the addressee, but always with his position or degree if he has any, the last-named being always abbreviated on the envelope (*Chiar^mo Sr. Prof., Gent^mo Sig. Dott.,* etc.). At the end of a letter the commonest forms are: *Con i piu vivi saluti ed ossequi* ("with the most sincere wishes and respect"; formal, to a superior) or *Con i migliori saluti ed ossequi* ("with the best ..."; formal, to an equal); or simply *Distinti saluti* ("respectfully yours," a business letter). To a lady, the form *Gentile Signora* is always correct, the ending being as to a gentleman but a degree more formal.

4. Germany.—The German republican constitution of 1920 did not abolish titles of nobility but stipulated that they were to be an integral part of the surname. The constitution of the German Federal Republic of 1949 confirmed that. In private intercourse the head of the Hohenzollern house would expect to be addressed as *Kaiserliche Hoheit* ("Imperial Highness"), while the head of a former reigning house in Bavaria, Saxony or Württemberg claims the qualification of *Königliche Hoheit* ("Royal Highness"). The latter form is used when addressing a former reigning grand duke. The heads of houses which were formerly principalities of the Holy Roman empire but which were later mediatized (*see* MEDIATIZATION) are entitled to the style *Durchlaucht* ("Serene Highness") and the heads of mediatized countships to that of *Erlaucht* ("Illustrious Highness"). A count (*Graf*) or a baron (*Freiherr*) is addressed simply by his name (*i.e.,* Karl Gf. von— or Georg Frh. von—).

A letter to a *Fürst* (prince) begins *Euer Durchlaucht* ("Your Serene Highness") and ends *Mit vorzüglicher Hochachtung, bin ich Euer Durchlaucht sehr ergebener* ("Yours respectfully, I am very devoted to your serene highness").

A letter to a member of the lesser nobility begins *Hochverehrter* (or *Sehr verehrter,* or *Sehr geehrter*) (all meaning "Honourable") *Graf Arnim* (von is dropped in this case), and ends as in the previous case, but without such qualification as *Euer Durchlaucht.* In a letter to a member of a liberal profession the beginning would be the same but the title would be replaced by the position or degree (examples: *Hochverehrter Herr Professor* or *Sehr geehrter Herr Doktor*).

The letter would end differently, according to the position of the addressee in relation to that of the writer, but *Mit vorzüglicher*

Hochachtung ("Yours respectfully") is always correct. A slightly less formal ending would be *Ihr ganz* (or *sehr,* or *stets*) *ergebener* ("Yours completely, or very, or always devoted").

A letter to a lady generally begins *Sehr verehrte Frau* (adding the title, position or degree) or *Gnädige Frau* ("Dear Madam"; followed by surname). In both cases it would end *Mit vorzüglicher Hochachtung, Ihr sehr ergebener.*

IV. ASIA

1. The Arab World.—In the Arab countries which until World War I had been part of the Ottoman empire, the old Turkish titles of pasha, bey and effendi were abolished at different dates after World War II. (In Turkey they were suppressed in 1934.) An Arab king (malik) is addressed as *Sahib el-Jalalat* ("Majesty"), a royal prince as *Sahib el-Semon el-Malaki* ("Royal Highness"), a prince (emir) not of royal blood as *Sahib el-Semon* ("Highness"). A prime minister (*rais el-wuzara*) is addressed as *Siadat el-Rais* ("His Excellency the Premier").

2. India and Pakistan.—The Indian and Pakistani princes continue to enjoy their titles in courtesy. They are usually known as His Highness (H.H.). The great division is between Hindus and Moslems. The Hindus had the following: maharaja bahadur (bahadur means "warrior"), maharaja, raja bahadur, raja, raj bahadur, rai sahib and rai. The Moslems had the following: nizam, nawab bahadur, nawab, khan bahadur, khan sahib and khan. Maharani is the female equivalent of maharaja and begum the female equivalent of nawab. The usage in address in writing and speech follows that used in addressing European royalty.

ADE, GEORGE (1866–1944), U.S. author, playwright and humorist, whose *Fables in Slang* summarized the kind of wisdom accumulated by the country boy in the city, was born in Kentland, Ind., Feb. 9, 1866, and graduated from Purdue university, Lafayette, Ind. For ten years (1890–1900), he was on the staff of the *Chicago Record,* and his editorial page column, "Stories of the Streets and of the Town," illustrated by his friend John T. McCutcheon won wide acclaim. Characters introduced in his column became the subjects of his earlier books, *Artie* (1896), *Pink Marsh* (1897), and *Doc Horne* (1899). His greatest recognition came with the publication of *Fables in Slang* (1899), which became a national best seller, and was followed by a weekly fable, syndicated to newspapers, and by 11 other books of fables. The fables actually contained only a little slang being, rather, examples of the vernacular. The fables had such flippant morals attached as, "Early to bed and early to rise, and you'll meet very few prominent people," and gave readers a chance to laugh at themselves.

In 1902 Ade's light opera, *The Sultan of Sulu,* was produced, and had a long run in New York. Then he did successful comedies, among them *The County Chairman* (produced 1903) and *The College Widow* (1904). Even before three of Ade's plays ran simultaneously in New York, he was recognized as one of the most successful playwrights of his time. His books and plays brought him wealth, and he established an estate of 2,000 ac. near Brook, Ind., which was his home for the rest of his life. He wrote many motion-picture scripts, and late in life during the prohibition era wrote what many called one of his most amusing books, *The Old Time Saloon* (1931). He died at Brook, May 16, 1944.

BIBLIOGRAPHY.—Fred C. Kelly, *George Ade: Warmhearted Satirist* (1947); Dorothy Russo, *Bibliography of George Ade* (1947); *The Permanent Ade,* ed. by Fred C. Kelly (1947) is an anthology of Ade's writings.   (F. C. K.)

ADELA (1062?–1137), daughter of William I (*q.v.*) of England and mother of King Stephen (*q.v.*), whose claim to the English throne was inherited through her, was born about 1062. In 1080 she married Stephen count of Meaux and Brie, son and heir of Theobald count of Blois and Chartres, who died in 1090. Adela shared actively in the government of her husband Count Stephen, ruling on his behalf during his absence on crusade from 1095 to 1099, and again in 1101 when he went back to the Holy Land. After his death at the siege of Rames (mod. Ramle), her regency continued, since her sons were minors, until 1109 when she had her second son Theobald made count of Blois, setting aside his elder brother as unfit to rule. After handing over the government to Theobald, Adela retired to the Cluniac priory of Marcigny-sur-Loire, in Burgundy, but this scarcely lessened her participation in public life, especially ecclesiastical politics. Before her retirement she had formed close friendships with St. Yves de Chartres and St. Anselm of Canterbury and given hospitality to Pope Paschal II. In disputes between lay rulers and reforming church leaders, Adela sometimes acted as mediator, but it is clear that the ruling passion of this forceful woman was the preservation and the strengthening of the great fief of Blois and Chartres: to this end she called in French aid in 1108, while in 1117 she brought about an alliance between Blois and Henry I of England against France. She died in 1137. (G. W. S. B.)

ADELAER (ADELER [Norwegian, "eagle"]; properly CORT SIVERTSEN) (1622–1675), Norwegian sailor, distinguished in Venetian and in Danish naval history, was born on Dec. 16, 1622, at Brevik. He entered the Dutch navy in 1639 and served under Martin van Tromp but moved into Venetian service in 1642 where he was known as Curzio Suffrido Adelborst (the last name being Dutch for "naval cadet"). He soon distinguished himself and in 1650 was sent to patrol the Dardanelles. On May 16, 1654, his Venetian squadron took part in the battle of the Dardanelles, when his ship alone sank 15 Turkish galleys, and on the following day he compelled the surrender of the Turks at Tenedos. In 1659 he was made a knight of St. Mark and given a pension for life (heritable to the first three generations of his descendants) and in 1660 he became lieutenant-admiral of the Venetian fleet. Two years later, however, he returned to Denmark as admiral of the Danish fleet, receiving at the same time various honours and revenues from Frederick III. His most important work was the refitting and reorganization of the fleet. In 1665 he received an invitation to command the Dutch fleet against England, but this he refused. He was ennobled by Frederick III in 1666 and was sent to India to negotiate with the court of Coromandel three years later (1669–70). Under Christian V he was appointed to command the Danish fleet against Sweden but died before the expedition, at Copenhagen on Nov. 5, 1675.

See P. Holck, *Cort Adeler* (1934).

ADELAIDE (ADELHEID) (931–999), queen of Italy and empress, was the daughter of Rudolf II, king of Burgundy, and Bertha, daughter of Burchard, duke of Swabia (d. 926).

Rudolf II had for a short time been king of Italy, and when he died, in 937, Hugh of Arles, who replaced him there, came north and married Bertha while betrothing Adelaide to his young son and heir Lothair. They married in 947, but Lothair died three years later, whereupon Berengar, margrave of Ivrea, took the Italian crown. Adelaide fell into Berengar's hands at Como in April 951 and was maltreated, stripped of her treasure and imprisoned at Garda. Then the German king Otto I came to the aid of Berengar's opponents. With a large German host, Otto marched into Lombardy in Sept. 951, seized Pavia, declared himself king and married Adelaide—who shortly before his arrival had escaped from custody.

Adelaide's entry into the Ottonian family circle led to a crisis, the rising of Otto's son by his first marriage, Liudolf, and his son-in-law Conrad the Red. It was suppressed with great difficulty, but from then onward Adelaide could enjoy her husband's almost unbroken success and in 962 she was crowned empress with him in Rome by Pope John XII. Of their children only Mathilda (d. 999), who became abbess of Quedlinburg, and Otto, who succeeded his father, lived. After Otto I's death (973) Adelaide's position at court deteriorated and her influence was challenged during the reigns of both her son Otto II (973–983) and her grandson Otto III (983–1002). During the latter's minority she shared responsibility and power with Theophano, her Byzantine daughter-in-law, and together they defended Otto III's rights and the integrity of his inheritance against the claims of his kinsmen Henry duke of Bavaria and the Carolingian king of France, Lothair. In 985, however, Adelaide had to give way to Theophano in Germany and went to Lombardy, where her authority always counted for something. After Theophano's death in 991 the old empress ruled—none too successfully—in Otto III's name until 994, when the young king assumed his majority. A small group of prelates

headed by archbishop Williges of Mainz were her most influential advisers. After 995 she devoted herself mainly to enlarging and embellishing the monastery that she had founded at Selz in Alsace, where she chose to be buried. The monks fostered her memory, miracles were reported at her tomb and a cult developed. She was canonized by Pope Urban II, probably in 1097.

Adelaide brought to the Ottonian dynasty a rich inheritance, connections in Burgundy and Italy and cultural traditions which were new to it and helped to change its character. It became less Saxon and through her also its religious interests were drawn toward the leaders of Cluniac monasticism, St. Majolus and St. Odilo.

BIBLIOGRAPHY.—Odilo of Cluny's biography of Adelaide, *Epitaphium Adalheidae imperatricis*, is ed., with the book of her miracles added to it at Selz in the middle of the 11th century, by G. H. Pertz in *Monumenta Germaniae historica: Scriptorum tomus iv* (1841). *See* further M. Kirchner, *Die deutschen Kaiserinnen . . .* (1910), with bibliography; R. Holtzmann, *Geschichte der sächsischen Kaiserzeit, 900–1024* (1943); G. Fasoli, *I Re d'Italia, 888–962* (1949). (K. J. L.)

ADELAIDE, the capital city and chief port of South Australia, named after Queen Adelaide, consort of King William IV, is in the county to which it gives its name. It is situated near the middle of the curving, eastern side of Gulf St. Vincent. Pop. of the city proper (1961) 23,051; including suburbs 587,957, (1963 est.) 600,200 (on this basis Adelaide is the fourth largest city in Australia). Total area 161 sq.mi. A fairly regular annual rainfall of about 21 in. falls largely between April and November. Temperatures are high in summer (January mean 73.4° F. with fairly frequent hot spells; highest recorded temperature in the shade 117.7° F.); but it is cool and bracing in winter (June mean 53.6° F. with occasional frosts). Land and sea breezes along the coast complete a typical Mediterranean climate.

As a result of the genius of Charles Sturt and, later, of William Light, the first surveyor general of the colony, a site was selected in 1836 upon fertile plains which swept up gently from the coast to a curving line of hills about 9 mi. inland. Light chose, not without opposition, a spot on rising ground, close to the Torrens river, the chief early source of water supply. Within eight miles lay the only considerable sheltered waterway along the coast, known as the Port Adelaide river, in reality a tidal inlet. This water—shallow and muddy but improved by dredging—became the site of Adelaide's port until the construction of the outer harbour provided a more accessible anchorage for larger vessels near the mouth of the inlet and facing the open gulf. Easy movement was possible also through mountain gaps to the Murray lowlands to the east and southeast and Adelaide thus soon became an important centre for lines of movement by land and sea. The fertility of the plains (deep alluvium washed down from the torrent-scarred hills), the presence of minerals in the hills (though in relatively small quantities) and the climate formed the bases of the city's prosperity.

After a somewhat checkered early history, Adelaide, by virtue

STATUE OF WILLIAM LIGHT OVERLOOKING ADELAIDE FROM MONTEFIORE HILL

of its commanding situation in relation to all parts of the state, steadily grew until by 1959 it had more than 61% of the total population of the state. Its commercially central position, good communications and ready supplies of raw materials, including brown and imported coal, aided the growth of a number of flourishing industries—the manufacture of motor bodies, farm implements and machinery, woolens, cottons, furniture, etc. Adelaide receives the bulk of the products of the lower Murray valley, which has no river-mouth port. The city's main airport, West Beach, 4½ mi. S.W., provides services to the other chief Australian cities.

Surrounding the city of Adelaide and completely separating it from the suburbs are the park lands of 1,710 ac. which have been reserved for recreation. The best use was made of the geographical advantages of the site selected. The city is laid out in two distinct sections, one to the south being square in form and the other, to the north, divided into rectangular blocks. The southern section, which has developed into the principal business area, is completely separated from the northern residential section by the Torrens river and extensive reserves and gardens. The city claims to have no slums. The climate and the presence of the Torrens, now artificially dammed to form a lake, lend Adelaide the peculiar charm and beauty of diversified vegetation.

Adelaide has many fine buildings, including Parliament house, Government house, the public library, and an art gallery and a university. The Adelaide Festival of Arts, held in 1960, was the first international festival of its kind in the commonwealth of Australia. Adelaide was the birthplace of municipal government in Australasia and gained a lord mayoralty in 1919. In 1956 construction work began on a new town, Elizabeth (*q.v.*), as a satellite of Adelaide, 16 mi. to the north of the city.   (W. C. D. V.)

ADELARD OF BATH (fl. early 12th century), English scholastic philosopher who was one of the first interpreters to western Europe of Arabic scientific knowledge. Adelard studied and taught in France and traveled in Italy, in Cilicia, in Syria, in Palestine, and perhaps also in Spain (*c.* 1110–25) before returning to Bath and becoming a teacher of the future king Henry II. In his platonizing dialogue *De eodem et diverso,* philosophy and the liberal arts, embodying permanent values (*idem,* "the constant"), are made to hold their ground against love of the diverse (*philocosmia*), but his atomism and his attempt to reconcile the reality of universals with that of the individual distinguish him from other Platonists. His *Quaestiones naturales* (76 discussions covering human nature, meteorology, astronomy, botany and zoology) are based on Arabic science, and his translation of an Arabic version of Euclid's *Elements* was to be for centuries the west's chief textbook for geometry. His other writings include works on the abacus, on the astrolabe and on hawking and a translation of Maslama's edition of al-Khwarizmi's astronomical tables.   (L. M.-Po.)

ADEN, a British colony and port on the southern coast of the Arabian Peninsula, and a member state of the Federation of South Arabia. The port lies about 100 mi. (160 km.) E of Bab el Mandeb, the entrance to the Red Sea. The high commissioner for Aden has direct legislative powers over the island of Perim (*q.v.*) in the Bab el Mandeb, and over the island of Kamaran (*q.v.*) off Yemen, about 200 mi. (320 km.) N of Perim, which are together administered by a commissioner. The high commissioner also has legislative powers over the five Kuria Muria Islands (*q.v.*) off the Dhofar (Zufar) coast of Oman which are administered by the British political resident in the Persian Gulf.

The area of Aden is 75 sq.mi. (194 sq.km.). In 1955 the population, which is about 90% Muslim, was 138,441, of which 103,879 were Arabs (including 48,088 Yemenis), 15,817 Indians, 10,611 Somalis, 4,484 Europeans, 831 Jews, and 2,819 others. In 1963 the estimated population was 225,000. The climate is hot and humid from April to October and cooler during the northeast monsoon. Rainfall is low and in some years there is none.

Aden consists of two peninsulas of volcanic rock rising to more than 1,000 ft. (300 m.). The eastern peninsula, on which is situated the town and port of Aden, is joined to the western peninsula, known as Little Aden, by a flat, sandy foreshore. The old town of Aden (formerly Aden Camp), known as Crater, is built in the crater of an extinct volcano in the northeast of the eastern

peninsula, surrounded on three sides by precipitous crags. The old harbour lay off the town, but the new port is on the northwestern side of the peninsula. In a rocky gorge above the town are the ancient Taweela rainwater storage tanks. To the northwest is the district of Ma'alah, where there is a dhow anchorage and construction yard; the Somali inhabitants are concentrated there. Wharves, warehouses, etc., have been built at Ma'alah on land reclaimed from the sea. West of Ma'alah are Steamer Point and the harbour suburb of Tawahi, with the consulates and the principal banks and shipping offices. To the north is the isthmus of Khormaksar, where Aden civil airport is located, about seven miles from the port. Farther north is the town of Shaykh 'Uthman (Sheikh 'Othman; *q.v.*), known for its cotton-dyeing industry and for its gardens. Nearby a new township, Al Mansurah, is being developed. Artesian wells at Shaykh 'Uthman and at Bir Nasr supply drinking water to Aden.

Aden possesses a technical institute, a teachers' training centre, secondary and intermediate schools for boys, and primary schools for boys and girls. There is a general government hospital. Aden has good bus communications. Internal airlines are operated as well as international services. There is a broadcasting station and a television station, the latter completed in 1964.

Aden is a free port and an important oil-bunkering point. Approximately 30 berths (including oil berths) accommodate vessels of various sizes, and there are also 3 floating docks. The colony is the centre of a large transshipment and distributive centre for the surrounding areas of Yemen and Saudi Arabia and for the Somali Republic, Ethiopia, and other parts of the African coast. There is considerable trade between Aden and the hinterland. Main occupations are those related to ship bunkering and cargo handling; others include the crushing of oilseeds; the reexport of hides, skins, coffee, gum, incense, and oyster shells; the making of soap, aluminum utensils, printed cotton cloth, and mineral waters; and inshore fishing. Services provided for the military base are also an important source of employment.

At Little Aden, on the western peninsula, a large oil refinery, with a refining capacity of 5,000,000 tons of crude oil a year, started operating in 1954, as did an oil harbour specially constructed to accommodate four 32,000-ton tankers at a time. A 20-mi. (32-km.) road was made across the foreshore between Little Aden and Aden, and a new town was built to accommodate workers at the refinery.

History and Administration.—Aden early became an important entrepôt of trade between Europe and the East. Spices, incense, etc., were brought to Aden and other South Arabian ports through the hinterland kingdoms of Saba (Sheba), Ma'in, Qataban, and Himyar until their high tolls made sea traffic cheaper and led to a decline.

Produce from India, China, Indonesia, and Africa was transshipped for carriage by camel caravans up to Egypt, Syria, and be-

STEAMER POINT, ADEN

yond until about the time of the Roman occupation of Egypt, when adventurous traders developed more direct and less taxed routes via the Nile Valley, Red Sea, and Indian Ocean, water transport replacing caravans where possible. Ancient ruined cities, with elaborate dams and irrigation works, and fortifications along these routes, both in South Arabia and in Yemen, indicate the importance and wealth of the traffic during the 1st millennium B.C. The *Periplus of the Erythraean Sea*, a Greek geographical work written about A.D. 50, describes the sea traffic which had by then replaced the caravans. Aden is called Eudaemon Arabia. Throughout the Middle Ages Aden was an important entrepôt for the Far Eastern trade, especially in textiles and commodities such as pepper.

In 1513 Aden was unsuccessfully attacked by the Portuguese. In 1538 it fell into the hands of the Turks under whom it declined while Mocha (Al Mukha) rose in importance. A century later the Turks were forced to relinquish it when the peninsula was captured by the Yemeni Arabs from the north. In 1728 the sultan of Lahej (Lahij) revolted against the imam of Yemen and in 1735 seized Aden, which he 'despoiled.

After the plunder of an Indian ship, the British East India Company captured Aden in 1839 and annexed it to India. The Island of Perim was occupied in 1857, and certain mainland areas were purchased between 1868 and 1888. These acquisitions completed the "Aden Settlement" administered first by the Bombay government and, from 1932 to 1937, by the (British) government of India. In 1937 these territories, together with the Kuria Muria Islands, became a British crown colony. An elected element was introduced into the Legislative Council established in 1947. In 1959 the council was given an elected majority, and in 1961 ministerial government was introduced.

Despite the fissile character of Arab society, Western-type nation-building efforts were made and led in 1953 to ideas of unifying Aden and the tribal states of the Aden Protectorate surrounding Aden. As a first step a federation of the protectorate states (known as the Federation of South Arabia) was launched in 1959. At the same time Perim and Kuria Muria were given separate constitutions. The mainland part of the colony, then called Aden State, was given a more advanced constitution in October 1962, with a Council of Ministers and an increase of elected members in the legislature. In January 1963 Aden State was included in the Federation of South Arabia. The governor of Aden then became high commissioner for Aden and the Protectorate of South Arabia. After this date efforts to create a unitary state continued without marked success. In 1964 it was agreed that the Federation of South Arabia should become independent no later than 1968. This was several times repeated, and in February 1966 it was added that British forces would be withdrawn at that time. Nevertheless, an Egyptian-inspired terrorist movement aimed at a forced evacuation by the British was in full force in Aden from 1963. In September 1965 the Aden state constitution was suspended and the high commissioner became the sole authority.

(W. C. Bu.; W. H. Is.)

There was a marked increase in the number of violent incidents, particularly against British troops, early in 1967 and the situation was complicated by a struggle for power between two rival nationalist organizations, the National Liberation Front (NLF) and

THE "CRESCENT" AREA OF STEAMER POINT IN THE SUBURB OF TAWAHI, WEST OF ADEN TOWN. A TANK FARM OF A BUNKERING STATION IS PARTLY SHOWN AT LEFT

the Front for the Liberation of Occupied South Yemen (FLOSY), led by Abdul Qawi Mackawi and Abdullah al-Asnag. A third organization, the South Arabian League (SAL), less violent and less powerful than the NLF and FLOSY, had links with Saudi Arabia.

A UN mission which visited Aden in April 1967 charged with the preparation of a report on the future government of the territory arrived during a general strike and scenes of violence. After a short stay the mission left stating it had not received the co-operation it expected from the British authorities.

See also ARABIA; SOUTH ARABIA.   (X.)

ADENA MOUND, a large, conical-shaped earthen burial mound just northwest of the city of Chillicothe, O., the type site of the North American Adena culture and period. It was probably built in late Adena times, about A.D. 400, and was excavated in 1901 by William C. Mills. The mound, as well as the cultural remains and the culture to which they belong, takes its name from the estate on which it stood.

The mound at the time of exploration was 26 ft. in height, with a basal circumference of 445 ft. It had been constructed in two different stages. The first stage represents the original or primary structure, which was 20 ft. high and 90 ft. in diameter and composed of a dark sandy loam soil. The second stage shows construction over and slightly to the north of the primary mound with a light-coloured soil secured from the surrounding surface.

The disposition of the dead in the first stage was different from that of the second. The remains, wrapped in coarsely woven textile or bark, were placed in rectangular log tombs, roofed with logs and poles. Burials made in the secondary stage were simple extended inhumations placed on bark and covered with bark.

One of the finest and most unusual objects discovered during the exploration of the mound is the Adena pipe, a stone pipe carved in the form of a human figure, found near the left hand of one of 23 burials. Standing eight inches in height, it is basically tubular in type with the figure of a dwarf carved in relief about the tube. The smoking chamber, drilled in the tube, extends nearly the entire length of the body, tapering from an opening between the feet to a small drilled perforation in the block-end mouthpiece at the top of the head. *See* also NORTH AMERICA: *Prehistory and Archaeology.*   (R. S. Ba.)

ADENAUER, KONRAD (1876–1967), German statesman, chancellor of the Federal Republic for its first 14 years, during which his country was restored to sovereignty, rearmed, and given

ADENAUER

a leading place in the movement for a voluntarily united Europe. He was born on Jan. 5, 1876, of a Catholic family, in Cologne. He studied law and economics at Freiburg im Breisgau, at Munich, and at Bonn, graduated as doctor of law, and, in 1906, was elected to the Cologne city council.

In 1917, during World War I, Adenauer was elected *Oberbürgermeister,* or chief mayor, of Cologne. In this post, which he retained till 1933, he created new port facilities, a green belt, sportsgrounds, and exhibition sites, and, in 1919, sponsored the refounding of the university.

In 1918 Adenauer had hoped at first that the Rhineland might become one of the member-states of the new republican Germany, but when the British had finally evacuated Cologne (1926), the city, with its district, remained part of the Prussian Rhine Province. Adenauer, who had been a member of the Prussian *Herrenhaus* (Upper Chamber of Parliament) before its abolition in 1918, was a member of the *Staatsrat* (the central organ representing the diets of the Prussian provinces) from 1920 and became speaker of it in 1928. Politically he belonged to the Centre Party, which reflected Catholic principles.

With the advent of the Nazis to power (1933), Adenauer lost all his offices and posts. After intermittent persecutions, he was finally sent to a concentration camp in 1944. At the end of World War II the U.S. military authorities restored him as chief mayor of Cologne, but the British, who assumed control of the city in June 1945, removed him from office in October.

By September 1945 Adenauer had already taken part in the foundation of the Christian Democratic Union (CDU), a new political party. He was elected chairman of the CDU for the British zone in 1946 and led its group in the *Landtag* of North Rhine-Westphalia from 1947. In 1948–49 he was speaker of the Parliamentary Council, which produced the constitution of the German Federal Republic.

In 1949 Adenauer became chairman of the CDU for the whole of Western Germany; and in the first elections under the new regime his party and its regular ally, the Christian Social Union (CSU), together won 139 of the 402 seats in the *Bundestag* (Federal Parliament). He managed to form a coalition government; but it was only by a majority of one vote that the *Bundestag,* on Sept. 15, 1949, confirmed his appointment as chancellor.

Adenauer soon made it clear that his predominant concern was with external affairs. His first aim was to keep the Federal Republic in the Western camp and to consolidate that camp in Europe against the Communist threat from the East. For this purpose he was determined to maintain the closest links with the United States and also to work for a lasting reconciliation with France. Pursuit of this policy was far more important to Adenauer than attempts to hasten the reunification of Germany: reunification was an ultimate aim, but its achievement was the duty rather of the powers which had partitioned Germany than of the Federal government. With regard to the internal affairs his main concern was to ensure victory for his party at successive elections, so that he could remain in office for his foreign policy's sake. He meant to govern firmly, however, and was ready to assume sole responsibility for decisions. While his methods were not always overscrupulous, he had a persuasive manner and a gift for political tactics, together with a directness and simplicity of expression.

The Federal Republic's history in the international field under Adenauer's guidance is described in the article GERMANY: *History.* Important events were: in 1950, the Federal Republic's associate membership of the Council of Europe; in 1951, the establishment of a German Foreign Office (with Adenauer himself as minister of foreign affairs till 1955), full membership of the Council of Europe, and founder membership of the European Coal and Steel Community; in 1952, the project for the European Defense Community (EDC); in 1954–55, after the collapse of EDC, recognition of the Republic as a sovereign state and its admission to the North Atlantic Treaty Organization (NATO), with the Western powers' approval of German rearmament; and in 1957–58, founder membership of the European Economic Community (EEC).

Meanwhile, Adenauer's rising prestige had been reflected in two successive elections (1953 and 1957; *see* again GERMANY: *History*) in both of which the CDU-CSU won a strikingly increased majority in the *Bundestag,* so that Adenauer's retention of the chancellorship had been unchallenged. Within the CDU, however, the terms on which he secured the Federal Republic's membership of EEC were criticized by Ludwig Erhard, who as minister of economic affairs from 1949 enjoyed the main credit for the "miracle" of West German economic recovery. Erhard became vice-chancellor also in 1957, but antagonism between him and Adenauer grew more pronounced, and in 1959 Adenauer tried to exclude him from eventual succession to the chancellorship.

In the elections of 1961 the CDU-CSU lost a number of seats in the *Bundestag.* If he was to form the next government, Adenauer had to bring the Free Democrats back into coalition with his own party (as in 1949 and in 1953, but not in 1957). The Free Democrats, however, made him promise to relinquish the chancellorship before the end of the parliamentary term. In 1963, after achieving his long sought treaty of cooperation with General de Gaulle's France (in Paris on Jan. 22), Adenauer accordingly resigned his government office as from Oct. 15. He was succeeded by Erhard.

Adenauer remained chairman of the CDU till March 1966. In February 1967, two months after Erhard had been replaced as chancellor by Kurt Georg Kiesinger, Adenauer visited General Franco in Madrid and De Gaulle in Paris. He also forcefully expressed German resentment at the U.S.-Soviet plan for a Nuclear Non-Proliferation Treaty, which he saw as a threat to subject German use of atomic energy to Soviet control and so to reduce the Republic to industrial backwardness.

On April 19, 1967, Adenauer died in his villa at Rhöndorf, near Bonn.

ADENET LE ROI (*c.* 1240–*c.* 1300; called by himself ROI ADAM, LI ROIS ADENÉS and officially styled ADAN LE MENESTREL, ADAM REX MENESTRALLUS), French poet and musician. The interest of Adenet for the literary historian lies not in his poetry, which is pallid and unoriginal, but in the detailed documentary evidence for his career as a household minstrel. He received his training in the court of Henry III, duke of Brabant; after his patron's death in 1261, his fortunes wavered, owing to dynastic rivalries and the growth of Flemish literature at the court of Louvain, until in 1268 or 1269 he entered the service of Guy of Dampierre, heir to the county of Flanders, as principal minstrel (whence his title of *roi, i.e.,* king of minstrels). Adenet accompanied Guy in 1270–71 on the Tunisian crusade led by St. Louis IX and Charles of Anjou; Guy returned by way of Sicily and Italy and Adenet's poems contain many precise references to parts of this itinerary. Of Adenet's written work there are preserved three *chansons de geste: Buevon de Conmarchis, Les Enfances Ogier* and *Berte aus grans piés;* and a romance in octosyllabic couplets, *Cléomadès;* this last work was written at the suggestion of Marie de Brabant, daughter of his old patron and queen to Philip the Bold.

BIBLIOGRAPHY.—A. Henry (ed.), *Les Oeuvres d'Adenet le Roi* contains background information and critical edition of the works: vol. i, *Biographie d'Adenet, La tradition manuscrite* (1951), vol. ii, *Buevon de Conmarchis* (1953), vol. iii, *Les Enfances Ogier* (1956). *Berte* is in editions by A. Scheler (1874) and U. T. Holmes, Jr. (1946) and *Cléomadès* in an edition by A. van Hasselt (1865–66).   (C. A. RN.)

ADENOIDS or ADENOID is an enlarged pharyngeal tonsil, which is a pad of lymphoid tissue attached to the upper and posterior walls of the upper or nasopharynx (the part of the throat that lies above the soft palate). The nasal passages open into the front of the nasopharynx, and on the sides are the openings of the Eustachian tubes leading to the middle ear, the air space behind the eardrum. The pharyngeal tonsil is a part of a ring of lymphoid tissue known as Waldeyer's ring that encircles the throat or pharynx.

The adenoid is made up of rounded, pale-staining germinal centres surrounded by mature lymphocytes. The surface is formed into ridges or clefts but no branching crypts. The surface layer consists of ciliated epithelium similar to that in the nose and lower respiratory passages and is covered by a thin film of mucus. The cilia, which are microscopic hairlike projections from the surface cells, move constantly in a wavelike manner and propel the blanket of mucus from the nasal passages down to the pharynx proper. From that point the mucus is caught up by the swallowing action of the pharyngeal muscles and sent down to the stomach. The adenoid also contains glands that secrete mucus to replenish the surface film. The fibrous tissue that surrounds and forms the framework of the adenoid does not form a distinct capsule.

The function of the adenoid as well as that of the other lymphoid tissue of Waldeyer's ring is protective. The moving film of mucus tends to carry infecting agents and dust particles from the nose to the pharynx, where the epithelium is more resistant. Immune substances or antibodies are thought to be formed within the lymphoid tissue, which, combined with phagocytic action, tends to arrest and absorb infecting agents. The lymphoid tissue usually enlarges in early childhood, the degree being influenced by infection and probably also by hormonal influence.

Infections in childhood cause acute swelling and inflammation of the adenoids and appear to be the main cause of a permanent enlargement. Large adenoids tend to obstruct breathing through the nose and interfere with drainage, thus predisposing to infection of the sinuses during an acute infection. Chronic obstruction and mouth breathing produce vacant facial expression. Enlargement and infection of adenoids predisposes to Eustachian tube blockage and middle ear disease. The detection of chronic tubal obstruction in the child is usually an indication for removal of adenoids as the first step toward preventing hearing impairment. Adenoids normally decrease in size after childhood. *See* also TONSILLITIS. (J. R. L.)

ADEODATUS, SAINT (d. 676), pope from April 672 to June 676, sometimes styled Adeodatus II or Deusdedit II, was a Roman. He played no known role in the political events of the day or in the liquidation of Monothelitism. Easy of access, he devoted his attention chiefly to restoring dilapidated churches. Himself a Benedictine monk, he took the abbey of SS. Peter and Paul, Canterbury, under his protection and seems to have recognized the exemption of the abbey of St. Martin of Tours from episcopal authority. He was the first pope to date his correspondence by the year of his pontificate. Some hagiographers give him June 26 as a feast day, although there is some doubt that this was ever done officially. (A. G. BI.)

ADHÉMAR DE CHABANNES (c. 988–1034), Frankish chronicler chiefly important for the history of Aquitaine, was born of a noble family at Chabannes in Limousin, France. At the monastery of St. Cybard in Angoulême, where he rose to high office, he made a large collection of manuscripts, most of which passed after his death to the abbey of St. Martial of Limoges. He died as a pilgrim in Jerusalem. Adhémar's *Chronicon Aquitanicum et Francicum* (critical ed. by J. Chavanon, 1897) traces the history of Aquitaine and of the Franks from the times of the legendary king Pharamond. Books i and ii are of little value but book iii is of great interest, particularly for the history of western France between 814 and 1028. His minor works, printed by J. P. Migne in *Patrologia Latina,* vol. cxli (1853), are an *Epistola de apostolatu S. Martialis* (representing St. Martial of Limoges as one of the apostles of Gaul), hymns in praise of St. Cybard and a work on the Limousin abbots.

BIBLIOGRAPHY.—L. V. Delisle, *Notice sur les manuscrits originaux d'Adhémar de Chabannes* (1886) ; J. A. Lair, *Études critiques sur divers textes des Xième et XIième siècles,* vol. ii, and *Historia d'Adhémar de Chabannes* (1899) ; L. Halphen, *À travers l'histoire du moyen âge* (1950). (J. DE.)

ADHÉMAR (AIMAR) DE MONTEIL (d. 1098), French bishop who, as papal legate, was one of the leaders of the first crusade. He became bishop of Le Puy when Pope Gregory VII deposed the former bishop in 1077 and is known to have made a pilgrimage in 1086–87, perhaps to Jerusalem. In Nov. 1095, when Pope Urban II began preaching the crusade at Clermont, Adhémar was the first of his hearers to take the cross and was appointed by Urban to lead the crusade as legate. He traveled to Constantinople with Raymond IV of Toulouse and the Provençal contingent. During the crossing of Asia Minor (May–Oct. 1097) and during the siege of Antioch (Oct. 1097–June 1098), when there was no supreme commander of the crusaders, Adhémar took a leading part in military counsels and operations. He also organized mass religious devotions at times of crisis, but hesitated to accept Peter Bartholomew's claim to have discovered the holy lance when the crusaders in turn were besieged in Antioch by Kerbogha. As well as beginning to establish friendly relations with the eastern Christians, Adhémar used his prestige to restrain the guards that arose from the conflicting ambitions of the lay crusaders. This was his greatest service to the expedition, as he commanded universal respect and affection. After his death of the plague in Antioch (Aug. 1, 1098), disputes within the army became so acute that the crusade almost foundered.

See S. Runciman, *History of the Crusades,* vol. i (1951).
(R. C. SMA.)

ADHESIVES, natural and synthetic substances used for joining or bonding other materials together by surface attachment. Examples are glue, paste, mucilage and rubber cement.

Adhesives have been used since prehistoric times, the first ones used probably being natural gums and waxes such as rosin, rubber, shellac and beeswax. All of these are exuded by certain trees and insects and still find limited use. One of the earliest uses of adhesives was the employment of animal and casein glues by the early Egyptians in making wood furniture and attaching ornamental veneers to wood surfaces. Both these glues are still commercially important in the woodworking industry.

Until the late 1930s, the only adhesives in common use were animal, casein and vegetable glues and natural resins. The principal commercial use was in the woodworking and paper industries. After synthetic plastic resins became available in almost limitless variety about 1935, new uses for adhesives were found in almost all industries, including the manufacture of automobiles, aircraft, electrical and electronic equipment and many other products. Many of the new adhesives give excellent bond strength in joining metals, glass, plastics and other nonporous materials as well as the more conventional porous ones such as paper and wood.

Uses.—Examples of uses of adhesives by industry in the early 1960s included the following:

In the automotive industry, adhesives are used for attaching sound-absorbing materials to metal surfaces, linings and floor covering to bodies, and rubber stripping to doors and trunk covers. Safety glass is made of two layers of glass with an adhesive film between. In some cases the entire automobile body is made of glass fibres bound together with an adhesive.

In the manufacture of aircraft, boats and house trailers, honeycomb cores of paper, fibre, wood veneer or metal are bonded by adhesives to surface layers of similar materials to form structural panels possessing very high strength-to-weight ratios. Many boats are made of glass fibres bound together by a synthetic resin adhesive. In some aircraft, the outer covering, or "skin," is bonded to the structural members by an adhesive instead of by rivets, resulting in a reduction of cost and air resistance. In electronics, copper foil is bonded to insulating panels to form the "printed circuits" that replace hand wiring in most radio and television sets, computers, and military and industrial electronic equipment. In electronic equipment for missiles and other applications requiring resistance to high shock and vibration, the resistors, capacitors, transistors, diodes and other components may be firmly cemented to the printed circuit board.

Theory of Adhesion.—The chemical or physical processes of adhesion are not completely understood, and so the technology tends to be experimental rather than theoretical.

The strength of a joint bonded by an adhesive depends on (1) adhesion of the adhesive to the surfaces joined and (2) cohesion within the adhesive itself. The adhesive must cover the surfaces thoroughly and form a continuous glue line. It is very desirable to have the glue line as thin as possible since the strength of a properly bonded joint, either in tension or in shear, is much greater than that of the adhesive in bulk. Surfaces to be joined must be clean and properly prepared. In the case of metals it is usually best to roughen the surface slightly, although this requirement differs according to the adhesive used.

To obtain good strength in adhesive bonds, it is important that the joints be properly designed. Adhesives are stronger in shear or tension than they are against a peeling stress. Some adhesives remain slightly flexible, which is desirable when materials with differing expansion and contraction characteristics are to be joined, but flexible adhesives are likely to be weak and to creep under continuous load. The area of the surfaces to be joined should be as large as possible in order to provide maximum strength. In the case of lap joints in thin sheets of metal or plastics, the joints should be supported or reinforced to make sure they are subjected only to a straight shearing stress rather than to bending and peeling. Joints that are designed and made properly with the most suitable adhesive can be strong and reliable.

NATURAL ADHESIVES

The principal types of natural adhesives, their general characteristics and chief uses are as follows:

Animal Glues.—These are made from hides and bones of various animals and are an impure form of gelatin. They are usually sold in the form of granules or flakes, which are heated in water before being used. They are applied hot and harden both by cooling and the absorption or evaporation of water. Animal glues, including fish glue, are also made in a liquid form that is used cold. The principal uses of animal glue are in woodworking and the manufacture of coated abrasives such as sandpaper. Even in these applications the newer synthetic resin adhesives are often preferred because of their shorter curing time and better resistance to moisture. All of the animal and vegetable glues may be attacked by fungus under tropical conditions of high temperature and humidity.

Casein Glue.—This type of glue, made from milk, is better suited than animal glue for some uses in woodworking and in the paper industry. Its adhesion to porous materials is good and its moisture resistance is somewhat superior to animal glue. It is usually sold as a powder that is mixed with water just before being used.

Vegetable Glues.—These are made from starches or dextrins and find their principal uses in the paper products industry and in woodworking in that order. They are low in cost but possess limited strength and moisture resistance. Gum arabic is a water soluble vegetable adhesive often used on gummed paper and stamps.

Natural Gums and Resins.—These usually possess low melting points and may be used hot or mixed with solvents. Natural rubber compounds are used in the building industry for bonding linoleum or tiles to floors and acoustical material to ceilings. The rubber cements used for bonding paper, rubber or leather are often made of natural rubber in a solvent, although synthetic rubber is also used for this purpose. Natural asphalt, which probably is of plant origin at least in part, serves as an adhesive in paving by bonding together the crushed rock or sand used as a filler.

"Marine glues" are often natural resins dissolved in a solvent that evaporates during hardening. Sealing wax is an example of a hot melt adhesive made of natural resins. Natural gums and resins usually have excellent moisture resistance and fair adhesion but soften and lose strength rapidly at even moderately elevated temperatures.

Sodium Silicate.—Water glass, or sodium silicate, is the only inorganic adhesive in general use. It is also the only adhesive that will stand temperatures in excess of about 500° F., although it has a tendency to deteriorate and crumble on aging, especially on nonporous materials. It is low in cost and used widely in the manufacture of corrugated boxes, for attaching labels to glass containers and as a binder for asbestos fibres in wallboard. Mixed with inorganic fillers it forms high-temperature cements used for electric lamp bases, heating elements and other high-temperature applications.

SYNTHETIC RESIN ADHESIVES

Synthetic resin adhesives may be divided into (1) the thermosetting types that undergo a chemical change on hardening and (2) the thermoplastics that can be softened repeatedly by the application of heat. The thermosetting types retain their strength much better at elevated temperatures.

Synthetic resins can be modified in many ways and are often combined to obtain the best characteristics for a particular application. For these reasons the following listings are quite general in nature.

THERMOSETTING SYNTHETIC ADHESIVES

Epoxies.—These are the most versatile of all the adhesives, providing excellent adhesion to both porous and nonporous materials, including metals. They harden by chemical action and so can be made without solvents. When used without solvents they shrink only slightly on hardening; this quality adapts them for use on poorly fitted joints or where a considerable build-up is required.

Epoxies are usually furnished in two parts, the resin and a catalyst, which are mixed together just prior to use. After mixing, the hardening proceeds quite rapidly. Formulations designed to harden at room temperature must be used within a short time after mixing, often within a half hour or less. This is known as the "pot life." Formulations that require heat to complete their cure may be kept at room temperature for several days or even months before hardening but will harden very rapidly if heated. The resin can be modified to cure quite hard or with slight flexibility. For joining metal to metal, epoxy gives very strong bonds with an average shear strength of 3,000 pounds per square inch (p.s.i.) and up to 7,000 p.s.i. under closely controlled conditions.

The epoxies are rather high in price but are widely used in the aircraft industry and in electronics, where their excellent electrical properties are valuable. Their moisture resistance is excellent and their bond strength is good up to about 350° F.

Phenolics.—Phenolics, also widely used in industry, are available as liquids that cure by evaporation of the solvents. For greatest bonding strength, the solvents are allowed to evaporate before the parts are joined under heat and pressure. Phenolic adhesive also is made available in thin sheets that are applied to the surfaces to be bonded; bonding with sheets also is done under heat and pressure. Sheets of adhesive are often used in the manufacture of plywood and of the lightweight honeycomb panels mentioned earlier. The commonly used phenol-formaldehyde adhesive provides good adhesion to wood and other porous materials but is not suitable for use with metals or glass. Other phenolic compounds and blends such as phenolic-epoxy, phenolic-polyamide, phenolic-vinyl acetals and phenolic-elastomers are excellent for this purpose.

Ureas.—Another important group of synthetic adhesives are the ureas. Like the phenolics, they work best on porous materials and are often used in the manufacture of plywood and in other woodworking applications. Urea-formaldehyde is the most commonly used adhesive of this group, but blends of urea and other resins, especially melamine, are better for certain applications. A related group of resins, the polyurethanes, are among the best of all adhesives for metal and glass as well as the porous materials.

Polyester Resins.—These adhesives are used in large volume as a binder for glass fibres to form structural panels, boats, luggage, electrical insulation, specialized automobile bodies, caskets and machine tool housings. Like the epoxies, they are usually made to harden by chemical action rather than by the evaporation of solvents; for this reason they cure with almost no shrinkage. Parts of complex shape can be built up over simple forms or in more elaborate molds by applying successive layers of glass fibre cloth or matting and polyester adhesive or binder. The curing of the resin is accelerated by heat.

Silicones.—Silicones withstand the highest temperatures of all the synthetic adhesives and retain good strength to about 500° F. While the bond strength of the harder resins is not as good as some of the other types of adhesive, some silicone rubber compounds are excellent in this respect. The silicones also have very high moisture resistance. They are used as binders for glass fibres to form electrical insulating sheets with characteristics that make them especially valuable in the electronics industry.

Resorcinol Resins.—These are excellent adhesives for wood and other porous materials although not generally satisfactory for metal and glass. Their water resistance is very good and they are often used in manufacturing plywood for exterior use.

Alkyd Resins.—Adhesives of this type are formulated with solvents to make adhesive varnish that is widely used in electrical and electronic manufacturing. The adhesion to metals is fair but not as good as that of the epoxies sometimes used for the same purposes.

Synthetic Rubbers.—In addition to the natural rubber mentioned above, synthetic rubbers are important bases for adhesives. They are flexible and well-adapted to such applications as the attachment of felt or similar materials to automobile body panels, fabric coating to metal and the joining of leather and rubber. The moisture resistance is excellent and the bond strength is adequate for many purposes, although flexibility and the tendency to creep under stress make most rubber adhesives unsuitable for highly stressed joints.

THERMOPLASTIC SYNTHETIC ADHESIVES

The following synthetic resin adhesives are of the thermoplastic type and do not retain their bond strength under elevated temperatures, although some of them display characteristics that make them useful below 180° F.

Vinyl Resins.—The most commonly used of the thermoplastic adhesives are the vinyl resins. Many modifications are available with the bonds formed either by fusing with heat or by solvent release. Some of the vinyl acetate, vinyl chloride and vinyl butyral formulations provide good adhesion to metal and glass. Vinyl resins are used in large volume in the manufacture of safety glass for the automobile industry. Polyvinyl emulsions have largely replaced the older types of animal and fish liquid glues for woodworking applications, since they harden more quickly and are more resistant to moisture.

Cellulose Derivatives.—Derivatives of cellulose, especially cellulose acetate and cellulose nitrate, are dissolved in solvents to form quick-drying, general purpose adhesives for household use. They are excellent for wood and paper and are moisture resistant, but their adhesion to metal and glass is rather poor.

Acrylics.—These are the most transparent of all the synthetic resins. Their transparency makes them useful for some applications even though their adhesion in general is not as good as that of some other resins. A notable exception is a cyano-acrylate formulation that hardens by chemical action, often in a few seconds or minutes, when it is pressed into a thin film between close-fitting surfaces. This form of acrylic displays excellent adhesion to metal and glass.

BIBLIOGRAPHY.—N. A. De Bruyne and R. Houwink (eds.), *Adhesion and Adhesives* (1951); Society of Chemical Industry, *Adhesion and Adhesives, Fundamentals and Practice* (1954); various articles in current issues of *Mod. Plast. Encycl.* (A. C. An.)

ADIABATIC CHANGE,

a change in the physical state of a body, whether this change be one of volume, strain, electric charge, etc., which occurs without loss or gain of heat in the body.

See THERMODYNAMICS: *Applications to Ideal Gases; see* also references under "Adiabatic Change" in the Index.

ADIABATIC PROCESSES IN ATMOSPHERE.

Because of the large volumes of air involved and the relatively small temperature differences between adjacent air parcels, it is common to assume that no heat is added to or withdrawn from the air (adiabatic process) during atmospheric processes.

This assumption appears to be justified for air which is not in contact with the ground and for processes which are completed in from a few hours to a day. When air ascends or descends it expands and contracts as a result of the change in pressure. If no condensation or evaporation of water occurs the air will cool about 1° C. per 100 metres rise (5.4° F. per 1,000 feet), which is called the dry adiabatic lapse rate.

When moist air is lifted it will cool at the dry adiabatic rate (the presence of moisture has a negligible effect until saturation is reached) until it becomes saturated. Further lifting will result in the condensation of water vapour or cloud formation. The latent heat of condensation is added to the air and as a result it cools less rapidly, at the so-called moist or saturated adiabatic lapse rate.

See LAPSE RATE OF TEMPERATURE; METEOROLOGY; THERMODYNAMICS; UPPER AIR SOUNDINGS. (H. G. HN.)

ADIAPHORISM

is the theory that certain doctrines or practices in morals or religion are "indifferent matters" (Gr. *adiaphora*). There were two adiaphorist controversies in Germany after the Reformation.

The first controversy arose over the religious compromise which certain post-Lutheran theologians, chiefly Philipp Melanchthon, were willing to make with Catholicism. It was an issue of the provisional scheme of compromise drawn up by Charles V in May 1548 and known as the Augsburg Interim, whose essentially Catholic theology made little concession to Protestant views. The elector Maurice of Saxony succeeded in making the Wittenberg theologians, for political reasons, accept the Leipzig Interim (Dec. 1548), which sanctioned the jurisdiction of Roman Catholic bishops and observance of certain rites (*e.g.*, extreme unction and confirmation), while all were to accept justification by faith, the added word "alone" being treated as one of the *adiaphora*. Matthias Flacius passionately opposed this policy on the grounds that under compulsion there could be no *adiaphora*, that the intention was to bring back popery and that no concessions would in fact be allowed. In practice the controversy was ended in Sept. 1555 by the religious peace of Augsburg, when Lutheranism was acknowledged as legitimate, but much bitter and dangerous internal strife was kept up by Protestants on the theoretical question of *adiaphora*. The tenth article of the Formula of Concord (1577) was an attempt to settle the matter on the lines laid down by Flacius.

Another adiaphorist controversy arose in the field of morals in 1681, when the building of a theatre in Hamburg was opposed by the Pietists (*see* PIETISM). They denounced worldly amusements as anti-Christian, whereas Lutherans normally defended the Christian freedom to use them.

BIBLIOGRAPHY.—A. Hauck (ed.), *Realencyklopädie*, vol. i, pp. 168–179 (1896); F. Hastings (ed.), *Encyclopaedia of Religion and Ethics*, vol. i, pp. 91–93 (1908); A. Ritschl, *Geschichte des Pietismus*, vol. ii (1884). (E. BI.)

ADIGE

(anc. ATHESIS; Ger. ETSCH), an important river of north Italy, 255 mi. long, with a drainage basin of 4,710 sq.mi. It rises as a small stream from two lakes below the Resia pass, at a height of 4,947 ft. During the first part of its course it flows as a rapid mountain stream through the Val Venosta, from Glorenza east to Merano and Bolzano. Having received the waters of the Isarco river at Bolzano, the Adige turns south and after a long and narrow middle course enters the Po lowland at Verona. Turning southeast at Verona, after several long meanders it enters the Adriatic sea at Porto Fossone, a short distance north of the Po delta. In the lower course, near the sea, the average volume of the Adige is about 9,000 cu.ft. per second, varying, however, from a maximum of 70,500 to a minimum of 2,000. In the early centuries of the Christian era, the river's course was probably several miles farther north, until, about A.D. 589, the river broke through its banks and built its present course. The dikes built during the past several centuries had to be raised several times, and the last 50 mi. or so of the river's course are entirely man-made. Besides hydroelectric plants utilizing the waters of the Adige and of its tributaries in its upper Alpine section, the river provides irrigation for the Veneto in its lower course. Sudden floods, as in 1951 and 1966, can do great damage and require constant control of the river bank. (G. KH.)

ADILABAD,

a town in Andhra Pradesh, India, the head quarters of Adilabad district and an agricultural trade centre, is 114 mi. S.S.W. of Nagpur. Pop. (1961) 20,970. It is on the Nagpur-Hyderabad section of the Benares-Cape Comorin national highway, and at the end of a branch from Mudkhed on the Central railway.

ADILABAD DISTRICT lies on a 2,000-ft. plateau between the Godavari (*q.v.*) and Penganga rivers. Pop. (1951) 831,600. Area 6,501 sq.mi. The eastern part of the district is served by the Wardha-Secunderabad broad-gauge section of the Central railway. Asifabad is a commercial centre on this line. Annual rainfall is about 40 in. and the district is well forested; teak and ebony are extracted. There is plentiful game in the wilder parts of the district. The main crops are jowar, rice, wheat, oilseeds, fibres and cotton. Coal is mined in the Pranhita valley and other minerals extracted are talc, limestone, iron ore (hematite) and sulfur. Local manufactures include paper, silk, chemicals and wooden toys. The fort near Mahur, 37 mi. N.W. of Adilabad, is a relic of the Muslim Bahmani and Imad Shahi dynasties (14th–16th centuries). (S. Ah.)

ADIPOSE TISSUE is a body tissue composed of specialized connective tissue cells that contain large globules of fat. The chief chemical constituents of this fat are the neutral glycerol esters of stearic, oleic and palmitic acids. The fat stored in these cells comes in part directly from the fats eaten, and in part is manufactured within the body from fats and carbohydrates in the food and sometimes from protein. The main reservoir of fat in the body is the adipose tissue beneath the skin, called the *panniculus adiposus*. There are also deposits of fat between the muscles, among the intestines and in their mesentery, around the heart and elsewhere.

Besides acting as a fuel reserve against times of starvation or great exertion, adipose tissue helps conserve the heat of the body and forms soft and elastic pads between the various organs.

ADIRONDACKS, a mountainous region in northeastern New York state, U.S., discovered by Samuel de Champlain in 1609. Adirondack means "tree eater," a name bestowed on a local tribe of Indians who sometimes were reduced by food shortages to making soup from the bark of trees. Covering 5,000 sq.mi., the region is bounded on the east by Lake Champlain, on the north by the St. Lawrence river and on the south by the Mohawk river valley. Although often included in the Appalachian system, the mountains are related geologically to the Laurentian highlands of Canada. The Adirondacks were formed partly by fracturing of the earth's crust, a process known as faulting, but mainly by long years of erosion. While they are primarily rounded in outline, several of the higher peaks reveal bare rock walls in vertical escarpments. Unlike the Appalachians, the Adirondacks do not form a connected range, but consist of many summits in isolation or in groups. There are about 100 peaks, ranging from 1,200 ft. to more than 5,000 ft. in height; the highest, Mt. Marcy, attains an elevation of 5,344 ft., and Whiteface mountain reaches a height of 4,867 ft. Motorists may approach the summit of Whiteface on the Whiteface Memorial highway.

As the Adirondacks were completely covered by an ice sheet during the last glacial period, glacial till (clay, sand, gravel and boulders intermingled) covers all but the highest surface areas of the region. The retreating glaciers contributed much to the beauty of the landscape by creating many spectacular gorges and waterfalls, and hundreds of lakes, ponds and swamps. More than 200 lakes, each more than a square mile in area, lie in a general northeast and southwest direction. The lake shore lines are usually rocky and irregular. The mountain region is circular in outline, with radial drainage from the centre forming many miles of streams that flow into the Hudson, Mohawk and St. Lawrence rivers and into Lake Champlain and the lakes of Ontario. The important rivers, famous for game fish, include the Black, Oswegatchie, Grasse, Raquette, Saranac and Ausable.

A large part of the Adirondack region is still in a primitive, natural state, protected by state law. The state of New York set aside a conservation and recreation area in 1892 and has continued to acquire land and control forest utilization in the Adirondacks since that time. The Adirondack forest preserve and state park consists of over 5,000,000 ac., and is one of America's outstanding attractions for tourists. Numerous state parks and private resort communities provide excellent facilities for camping, bathing, hiking and canoeing. Additional attractions include famous historical landmarks located at Ft. Ticonderoga, Saratoga, Lake George and Plattsburg. Good highways afford access to nearly all parts of the Adirondacks and to the many resort villages located along the shores of such lakes as Placid, Saranac, Tupper, Schroon, Long, Raquette, Cranberry, and Blue Mountain. There are no large cities in the Adirondacks; population density is very low compared to other regions of the state. The summer climate is moderated by cool mountain breezes. Although the winters are cold, the sub-zero temperatures are moderated by a normally dry atmosphere. As the climate has been considered beneficial to those suffering from pulmonary ailments, many sanitariums have been established in the Adirondacks, especially in the vicinity of Saranac Lake and Lake Placid.

Lumbering, although once a major industry in the Adirondacks, has been considerably restricted by the creation of the state forest preserve. The mountains, largely covered with spruce, hemlock, and pine forests with some hardwood trees growing on the lower slopes, appeal to the outdoorsman. Mineral deposits that have been mined profitably include iron and graphite. State counties in the region include Clinton, Essex, Franklin, Hamilton and Lewis, and parts of Ful-

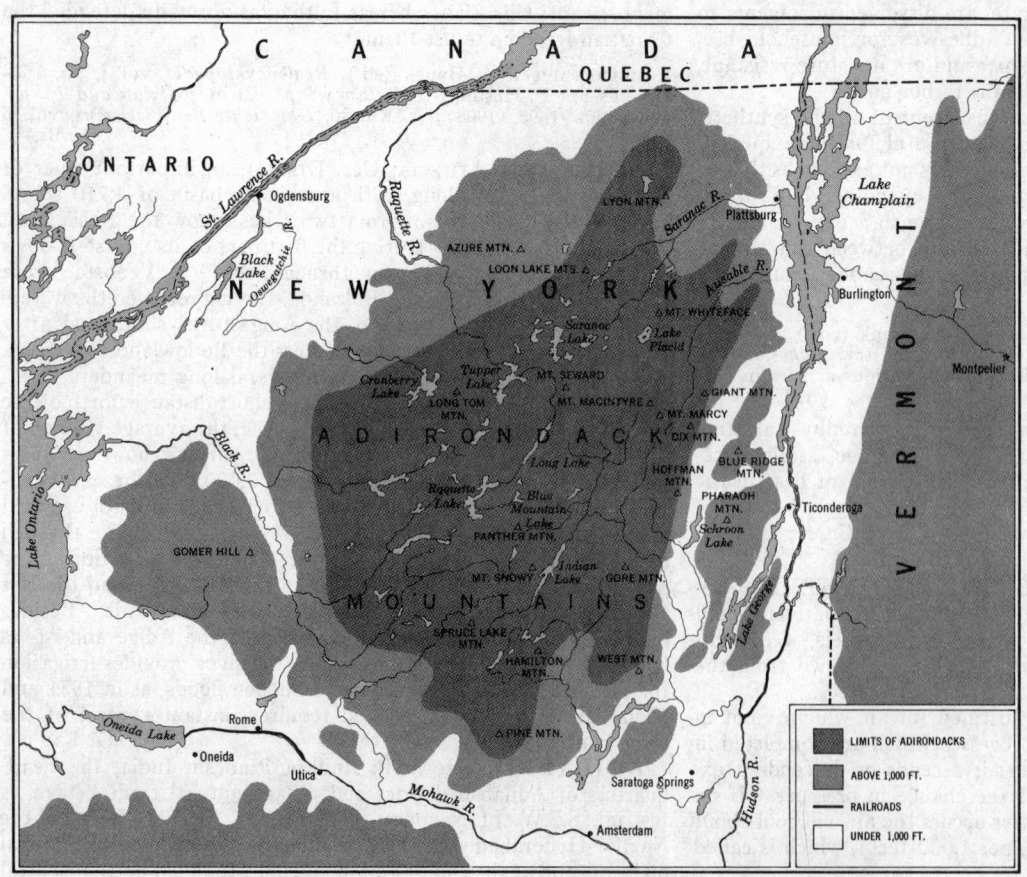

MAP SHOWING REGION OF THE ADIRONDACK MOUNTAINS, NEW YORK

ton, Oneida, St. Lawrence, Warren and Herkimer.   (D. E. A.)

ADIT, a horizontal opening, or entrance, made from the earth's surface to intersect a seam of coal or a mineral vein. The accompanying figure shows a seam of coal outcropping on the side of a hill with ventilating shaft, incline and adit. An adit is frequently called a tunnel, although the latter term is more properly reserved for a working open at both ends, such as through a mountain or a ridge, and inclines are sometimes erroneously called adits. Among U.S. miners adits also have been known in the past

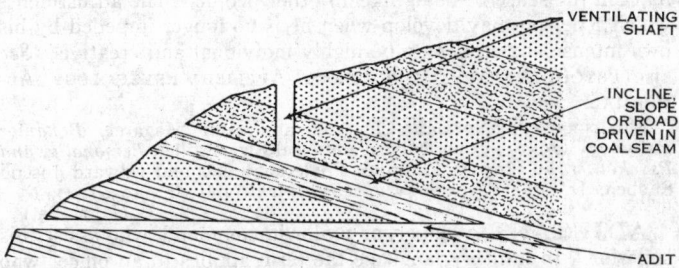

VENTILATING SHAFT

INCLINE, SLOPE OR ROAD DRIVEN IN COAL SEAM

ADIT

AN ADIT CUT ACROSS THE STRATA, TO WIN AND DRAIN A COAL SEAM

as adit levels and drifts, and among British miners as day drifts, day holes, surfs, soughs, watergates and audits.

The use of adits was perhaps the earliest method of gaining access to mines. Adits were driven at such a level as to drain off the water from the workings. In modern times and where topography permits, adits are driven below earlier mine workings for the purpose of draining water from old abandoned mines and also to enable mining on deeper levels.

The choice as to whether an underground objective is to be reached by shaft, slope or incline or by adit is dependent upon topography and economic considerations. Adits can be driven only in hilly country where the portal will be at such an elevation as to provide an adequate slope for water to flow out and to favour removal of coal or ore. Where either shaft or adit can be used, the saving in the generally lower cost of driving an adit over the cost of sinking a shaft, plus the saving in the cost of pumping water and hoisting the coal or ore in the shaft, will dictate that the adit is more economical. Consequently, adits of greater length than shafts, sometimes reaching one or two miles, are economically feasible.

The cross section of adits is square, round, elliptical or, more commonly, horseshoe shaped. The size range is from that which will allow a man to stand erect to that which will allow passage of haulage equipment. The walls may be of the natural rough rock, or may be lined with concrete, masonry, wood or steel.

(W. A. V.)

ADJUSTMENT (IN PSYCHOLOGY) is the process of behaviour by which men, and other animals as well, maintain an equilibrium among their various needs, or between their needs and the obstacles of their environments. A sequence of adjustment begins when a need is felt and ends when it is satisfied. For example, a hungry man is stimulated by his physiological state to seek, obtain and prepare food. He eats and thereby reduces the stimulating condition that impelled him to activity. He is then adjusted to this particular need.

Social adjustments are similar. Most people in many cultures want to be recognized and approved by their fellows. When a man is criticized, that need is thwarted. In response he may try various ways to regain approval; or he may belittle the critic or argue that someone else is to blame. The latter behaviours do not really bring approval, but they are adjustments of a sort because they tend to reduce the man's feeling of distress.

In general, the adjustment process involves four parts: (1) a need or motive in the form of a strong persistent stimulus; (2) the thwarting or nonfulfillment of this need; (3) varied activity, or exploratory behaviour; leading to (4) some response that removes or at least reduces the initiating stimulus and completes the adjustment.

Motives.—Some of the motives that stimulate adjustive behaviour are primary physiological needs such as hunger and thirst.

Certain other strong motives, such as the sex drives, combine physiological elements and cultural or learned factors. Of greatest importance in complex human adjustments are the social motives involved in interactions with other persons, including needs for security, approval, recognition, affection, conformity, prestige, mastery, self-realization and the like.

Social motives are not inborn, but are learned by each person during the course of his early development and socialization. Innate emotional responses provide the base from which many important social motives develop. A child fears pain instinctively. If scolding accompanies painful punishment, he may learn to fear all social criticism. The scolding thereby becomes an acquired drive which will evoke fear and arouse a need for adjustment. Similarly, motives to compete, strive and succeed may be learned as elaborations of the primitive response of anger which is caused by restraint.

Social motivation also may originate from the learning of secondary rewards. Feeding and comforting are intrinsically satisfying to a little child. If these are accompanied by attention and kind words, then recognition and approval from other people will become gratifying in themselves. Their absence will become an annoyance and will arouse adjustive behaviour. Repeated experiences during a lifetime of development typically cause certain social motives to be learned so thoroughly that they become stronger than some primary physiological drives. A hungry man often will not steal food because his socialization provides a stronger motive than his hunger.

Since social motives are learned, they tend to differ from one culture to another. Each society provides different learning experiences for its children. Thus, typical persons in the middleclass European-American culture have strong urges to succeed and excel, which are markedly lacking in members of some so-called primitive cultures.

One type of emotional motivation, anxiety, has an especially important role in the process of adjustment. The feeling-tone of anxiety is much like that of fear, but there are differences. Fear is evoked by a present external stimulus, anxiety by an apprehension of threat and a feeling of helplessness. A boy fears a larger bully, but he may have anxiety about his own strength or his acceptance in his group. There is no specific effective adjustment to anxiety. Anger may lead to aggression and fear to flight, but the anxious person is stirred up futilely. Anxiety is therefore at the root of many of the less effective adjustments. (*See* also MOTIVATION.)

Frustration and Conflict.—Two kinds of thwarting may prevent the fulfillment of motives—frustration and conflict.

A frustration is an external circumstance or an act of another person which prevents the satisfaction of an aroused motive. An adolescent may want to drive the family automobile to a dance, but be frustrated because the automobile is out of order or because his father forbids him to use it. Frustrations usually lead to increased effort, to anger and aggressive impulses or to immature and ineffective behaviour, but they do not often result in serious psychological difficulties. Some frustrations are even socially constructive, for they may cause the person to discover new solutions to problems.

A conflict is the arousal of two or more strong motives that cannot be solved together. A youngster wants to go to a dance to feel that he belongs to a group and does what his friends do. For an adolescent in western culture, that is a strong motive. But the youth may be a clumsy dancer, and sensitive to the real or imagined ridicule of his fellows. Therefore, he also has a motive to avoid the dance to escape humiliation. He is in a dilemma; whether he goes or stays he will experience distress. Psychologically, a conflict exists when the reduction of one motivating stimulus involves an increase in another, so that a new adjustment is demanded.

Conflicts are not all equally severe. A conflict between two desired gratifications, as when a youth has to choose between two attractive and practicable careers, may lead to some vacillation but rarely to great distress. A conflict between two dangers or threats is usually more disturbing. A man may dislike his job intensely but fear the threat of unemployment if he quits. A conflict between a need and a fear may also be intense. A child may be dependent on his mother but fear her because she is rejecting and punitive. The conflicts which involve intense threat or fear are not solved readily but make the person feel helpless and anxious. His subsequent adjustments may then be directed more to the relief of his anxiety than to the solution of his real problems.

Conflicts are often unconscious, in the sense that the person cannot clearly identify the source of his distress. Many strong impulses—such as fear and hostility—are so much disapproved by the culture that a child soon learns not to acknowledge them, even to himself. When such impulses are involved in a conflict, the person is anxious but does not know why. He is then less able to bring his rational thinking to bear on the problem.

Varieties of Adjustment.—Every person experiences some frustrations and conflicts, but is able to solve most of them normally with his own resources. A person engages in exploratory behaviour, trying one act and then another until he discovers one that overcomes the frustration, resolves the conflict or at least reduces its intensity.

Adjustments vary in quality. Suppose, for example, that a university student fails his examinations. This situation demands adjustment, for it not only thwarts his educational and vocational plans but also evokes conflicts about his personal adequacy. The student may adjust by finding and remedying the cause of his difficulties, by increasing effort or by making a rational change in his goals, all of which are direct and constructive solutions. Or he may adjust by blaming others for his failure, by emphasizing his attainments in other areas (as in athletics), by daydreaming of imaginary successes or by developing an apparent illness that excuses his failure. These acts do not solve his problem, but they are adjustments because they help him relieve his tension and reduce his anxiety. The indirect, substitutive methods of adjustment are often called adjustment mechanisms. (*See* DEFENSE MECHANISMS.)

The problem of defining what is a "good" adjustment is clarified by the concepts of integrative and nonintegrative behaviour. An integrative adjustment is one that not only satisfies the present motive but also facilitates the solution of subsequent problems. A nonintegrative adjustment, in contrast, reduces the anxiety of the moment but leads to more trouble in the future. A person who is one-sided in his satisfactions, who reduces one intense need at the expense of thwarting the rest, is nonintegratively adjusted. Such a person is usually so preoccupied with the overpowering need to reduce his immediate anxiety that he is blinded to other considerations more relevant to his ultimate welfare.

Counseling and Psychotherapy.—A person whose adjustments are not optimal often can be helped by the professional services of a counselor, a psychologist or a psychiatrist.

The term counseling is often used to designate the process of helping a person to make adjustments that deal with realities, such as educational or vocational plans, or the success of a marriage. A part of such counseling may be the giving of information that enables the person to increase the scope of his exploratory behaviour. The counselor, for example, may give him information about his own abilities and interests as determined by psychological tests, or about educational opportunities and the requirements of various occupations. The competent counselor does not attempt, however, to solve the person's problems for him. Adjustment is an individual matter which each person must discover for himself, and the counselor tries mainly to clarify the person's own thinking. The process has to be inductive and may require considerable time.

Psychotherapy is the process of helping a person, by psychological means, to resolve adjustive difficulties that are more personal and more pervasive in his whole life. The patient in psychotherapy may be an essentially normal person who is anxious and ineffective. Psychotherapy is also widely used to help neurotic persons and sometimes is an aid to the psychotic.

Psychotherapy establishes a special kind of interpersonal relationship. The therapist's task is to show a warm, calm, understanding and permissive interest. He is never shocked and never scolds. The patient's task is to keep talking about his anxieties.

In this trusting relationship a kind of learning takes place. The patient finds that he can remember, feel and express aspects of his life that he was unable to face earlier because of his emotional distress. He learns, at his own pace and through his own thinking, to respond with constructive exploration instead of with helpless anxiety. Improvement in his everyday adjustments is likely to follow.

Integrative adjustment does not imply conformity. The aim of the therapist, therefore, is not merely to make the patient "normal" in the sense of being like all other people. The adjustments which a person may develop when he is no longer impeded by his own intense anxieties may be highly individual and creative. *See* also PSYCHOTHERAPY; PSYCHOLOGY, APPLIED; PSYCHOLOGY, ABNORMAL.

BIBLIOGRAPHY.—Norman Cameron and Ann Magaret, *Behavior Pathology* (1951); John Dollard and Neal Elgar Miller, *Personality and Psychotherapy* (1950); Laurance Frederic Shaffer and Edward Joseph Shoben, Jr., *The Psychology of Adjustment*, 2nd ed. (1956).

(L. F. SR.)

ADJUTANT, a helper, or junior in command, who assists his superior. In military language the term applies to an officer who assists the commander of a military unit. In the British and U.S. services the adjutant is the principal administrative staff officer of the commander of a battalion, battle group, regiment, squadron or military post. An officer holding an appointment as adjutant in such units usually has the rank of captain. The adjutant publishes official orders of the unit, is responsible for superintending clerks and other administrative personnel, submits reports to higher headquarters, handles official correspondence and maintains records. "Adjutant's call" is a special bugle call sounded before certain ceremonies. An officer performing the adjutant function in a larger formation of the U.S. army, such as a division or corps, is entitled adjutant general (*q.v.*). In the French army, an officer performing the adjutant function is entitled *adjoint*, the word *adjutant* being the rank of senior noncommissioned officers, comparable to warrant officers in the U.S. services. *See* AIDE-DE-CAMP.

(T. N. D.)

ADJUTANT GENERAL, an army or air force official, originally the chief assistant or staff officer to a general in command but more recently a senior staff officer with solely administrative responsibilities. In Britain the second military member of the army council is styled adjutant general to the forces. His department is charged with all duties pertaining to personnel. The adjutant general of the U.S. army serves as a principal assistant to the chief of staff. He heads the adjutant general's corps, an administrative service that publishes all army orders, is responsible for army correspondence and takes charge of personnel actions, records, decorations and awards, publications, postal service, recreational activities and career guidance. The adjutant general of the U.S. air force has comparable functions. The principal administrative staff officers of large subdivisions of the U.S. army, such as divisions, corps and armies, are entitled adjutants general, though they usually hold the rank of lieutenant colonel or colonel. Each U.S. state has its own adjutant general, with administrative duties regarding the state national guard or militia. (T. N. D.)

ADLER, ALFRED (1870–1937), Austrian psychiatrist and founder of individual psychology, was born Feb. 7, 1870, in a Vienna suburb. Invited by Sigmund Freud (*q.v.*) in 1902 to join his circle, Adler became a prominent associate. Gradually, however, theoretical differences between the two became irreconcilable; he separated from Freud in 1911 and founded his own school and journal. In 1919 Adler founded the first child guidance clinics in the Vienna school system. After 1925 he regularly visited the United States and settled there in 1935. He died in Aberdeen, Scot., on May 28, 1937, while on a lecture tour.

Adler's main concepts are: (1) The dominant motive is the striving toward a goal of superiority or perfection, in compensation for the inferiority feeling postulated for everyone. (2) The individual cannot be considered apart from society; all important problems, including certain drive satisfactions, are social. (3) The socialization of the individual is afforded through social interest, an innate ability that must, however, be developed; socialization is not achieved at the cost of repression. (4) The individual is unique. His personality structure, which includes his unique goal and ways of striving for it, is his style of life. (5) The goal and the life style are more or less unconscious. (6) The individual is a self-consistent unity; psychological categories such as specific drives or the consciousness-unconsciousness contrast are only aspects of a field of processes subordinated to the life style. (7) The individual's opinion of himself and the world influences all psychological processes. (8) All objective biological and social conditions are mere raw material used by the self according to his life style. (9) Birth order or the sibling situation influences the individual at an early, formative stage. (10) The life style is ultimately the product of the individual's creativity.

While the normal person with a well-developed social interest will, according to Adler, compensate by striving on the useful side of life, the neurotically disposed person is characterized by increased inferiority feelings, underdeveloped social interest and an exaggerated, unco-operative goal of superiority, manifesting themselves as anxiety and more or less open aggression. Organ inferiorities and neglect or overprotection as a child make unfavourable development more likely, yet may lead to successful overcompensations.

Therapy consists in providing the patient with insight into his mistaken life style through material furnished by him in the psychiatric interview. The life style can be diagnosed from all verbal and bodily expressions, the individual speaking with his entire body ("organ dialect") as well as his tongue. Particularly useful are dreams, and early recollections as thumbnail sketches of the patient's opinion of himself and the world. Social interest is strengthened and inferiority feelings are reduced by encouragement and by an atmosphere of relaxed equality between patient and therapist.

Adler accepted from Freud the theorem that no psychological expressions are accidental (*i.e.*, psychological determinism). But whereas for Freud the determiners were in the last analysis objective biological factors such as instincts, especially sex, and past events, for Adler they were subjective psychological factors such as opinions and values, unified under the life goal.

Representative books by Adler include *The Practice and Theory of Individual Psychology* (1920; English trans., 1927); *Problems of Neurosis* (1929); *Social Interest* (1933; English trans., 1938).

BIBLIOGRAPHY.—P. Bottome, *Alfred Adler, a Biography* (1939); L. Way, *Adler's Place in Psychology* (1950; 1951); H. L. and R. R. Ansbacher, *The Individual Psychology of Alfred Adler* (1956).

(H. L. A.; X.)

ADLER, CYRUS (1863–1940), U.S. scholar and educator, a leader of Conservative Judaism in the United States, was born in Van Buren, Ark., on Sept. 13, 1863. He was graduated from the University of Pennsylvania, Philadelphia, in 1883 and received the Ph.D degree in 1887 from Johns Hopkins university, Baltimore, Md., where from 1884 to 1893 he was an instructor and associate professor of Semitic languages.

He was librarian, 1892–1905, and assistant secretary, 1905–08, of the Smithsonian institution, Washington, D.C. From 1889 to 1908 he was curator of historic archaeology and historic religions at the U.S. National museum, Washington. Adler became president of Dropsie College for Hebrew and Cognate Learning, Philadelphia, in 1908; he was acting president of the Jewish Theological Seminary of America, New York city, from 1916 and president from 1924. In 1892 he founded the Jewish Historical Society of America. He was an editor of the *Jewish Encyclopedia* and in 1899 was made editor of the *American Jewish Year Book*. He died on April 7, 1940.

Among his published works are *The Shofar, Its Use and Origin* (1893); *Told in the Coffee House*, with Allan Ramsay (1898); *International Catalogue of Scientific Literature* (1905); *Jews in the Diplomatic Correspondence of the United States* (1906); and *Jacob H. Schiff: His Life and Letters*, two volumes (1928).

ADLER, DANKMAR (1844–1900), U.S. architect and engineer, whose partnership with Louis Henri Sullivan (*q.v.*) was perhaps the most famous and influential in U.S. architecture, was born at Stadtlengsfeld, Ger., on July 3, 1844. He and his father

emigrated to the United States in 1854 and settled in Detroit, Mich., where he began his study of architecture in 1857. Later father and son moved to Chicago, where Adler became a draftsman in the office of Augustus Bauer. The American Civil War interrupted his career until 1865. On his return to Chicago he held a succession of positions in the offices of Bauer, A. J. Kinney and Edward Burling. The first of his important buildings was the Central Music hall in Chicago, in which he made the initial use of his unique knowledge of acoustics.

In 1881 the partnership of Adler and Sullivan was founded. The commercial buildings which they designed—particularly the Auditorium (Chicago), Wainwright (St. Louis), Guaranty (Buffalo)—constituted a new architectural style with the essential features of modern building art. Adler acted as engineering designer and administrator, while Sullivan worked as planner and artist. This fruitful association was terminated in July 1895. Adler did no distinguished work in the few years remaining before his death on April 16, 1900.

He wrote extensively on the technical and legal aspects of architecture and building construction. His most important paper is "The Influence of Steel Construction and Plate Glass Upon the Development of Modern Style" (1896).

BIBLIOGRAPHY.—Carl W. Condit, *The Rise of the Skyscraper* (1952); Hugh Morrison, *Louis Sullivan: Prophet of Modern Architecture* (1935); Arthur Woltersdorf, "Dankmar Adler," *West. Archit.*, 33:7 (July 1924). (C. W. Co.)

ADLER, FELIX (1851–1933), U.S. educationalist and founder of the Ethical Movement, was born at Alzey, Ger., Aug. 13, 1851. His father, a Jewish rabbi, emigrated to the United States in 1857, and the son graduated at Columbia college in 1870. After studying at Berlin and Heidelberg, he became professor of Hebrew and oriental literature at Cornell university, Ithaca, N.Y. (1874–76). He was appointed professor of political and social ethics at Columbia university in 1902.

In 1876 Adler established in New York city the Society for Ethical Culture. The history of the Ethical Movement and Adler's relation to it are described in the article ETHICAL MOVEMENT.

Adler took a prominent part in philanthropic and social reform movements, such as the erection of model tenement houses and the abolition of child labour. He published *Creed and Deed* (1877), *The Moral Instruction of Children* (1892), *Marriage and Divorce* (1905), *The Religion of Duty* (1905), *The World Crisis and Its Meaning* (1915), *An Ethical Philosophy of Life* (1918) and *The Reconstruction of the Spiritual Ideal* (Hibbert lectures at Oxford, 1923).

Adler died April 24, 1933.

ADLER, HERMANN (1839–1911), British chief rabbi, who was for many years a prominent figure in English public life, was born at Hanover, Ger., on May 30, 1839, the son of N. M. Adler (*q.v.*). He was educated at University College school and University college, London, and then at Prague, where he received the rabbinical diploma. Returning to England, he became temporary principal of the Jewish Theological college in London for two years. With this college he was associated in one capacity or another all his life.

He began his ministry at the Bayswater synagogue in 1864 and continued to preach there until 1891, when he became chief rabbi on the death of his father. Adler served on many Mansion House committees and on various bodies concerned with the improvement of social conditions in London. He died on July 18, 1911. A collection of his sermons, entitled *Anglo-Jewish Memories and Other Sermons*, was published in 1909.

ADLER, MORTIMER JEROME (1902–   ), U.S. philosopher and editor, advocated adult and general education by study of the great books of the Western world. He was born in New York City on Dec. 28, 1902. After teaching at Columbia University, where he received a Ph.D. (1928), he became professor of the philosophy of law at the University of Chicago. There, with Robert M. Hutchins, he led in the pursuit of liberal education through regular discussions based on reading great books. He had studied under John Erskine in a special honours course at Columbia, in which the "best sellers of ancient times" were read as a "cultural basis for human understanding and communication."

Adler was associated with Hutchins in editing the 54-volume *Great Books of the Western World* (1952), and conceived and directed the preparation of its 2-volume *Syntopicon*.

In 1952 Adler became director of the Institute for Philosophical Research, which prepared *The Idea of Freedom* (vol. 1, 1958; vol. 2, 1961). His books include *How to Read a Book* (1940); *A Dialectic of Morals* (1941); *The Capitalist Manifesto* (with Louis O. Kelso, 1958); and *The Revolution in Education* (with Milton Mayer, 1958).

With Hutchins, Adler edited the ten-volume *Gateway to the Great Books* (1963) and from 1961 an annual, *The Great Ideas Today*. Under the sponsorship of Encyclopædia Britannica, he delivered six lectures on philosophy at the University of Chicago in 1964, published as *The Conditions of Philosophy* (1965).

ADLER, NATHAN MARCUS (1803–1890), British chief rabbi, a moving spirit behind the establishment of the United Synagogue, was born at Hanover, Ger., Jan. 15, 1803. He took his Ph.D. degree at Erlangen in 1828 and was ordained the same year. He became chief rabbi of Oldenburg in 1829 and of Hanover in 1830, and on Oct. 13, 1844, was elected chief rabbi in London. There he originated and carried out his scheme for a Jewish college for teachers, which was founded in London, Nov. 11, 1855, with himself as first president. In 1860 he suggested the establishment of a United Synagogue which should bring all the British congregations under one central administration; this idea was realized in 1870, when the United Synagogue bill was passed in parliament. Adler died Jan. 21, 1890, at Brighton. He was succeeded as chief rabbi by his son, Hermann Adler (*q.v.*).

His writings include sermons and commentaries on Hebrew texts, the best known of which is *Nethinah la-ger,* a commentary on the Aramaic paraphrase of Onkelos on the Pentateuch (1874).

ADLER, VIKTOR (1852–1918), Austrian Social Democrat, mainly responsible for the continuing unity of the Austrian Social Democratic party, was born, the son of a wealthy merchant, at Prague in Bohemia on June 24, 1852. As a medical student at Vienna university he belonged to a German nationalist association in which he met E. Pernerstorfer, later his associate, and also H. Friedjung and G. von Schönerer. In 1881 Adler, a qualified doctor, joined the Social Democrats and worked on problems of industrial insurance. During a tour of Germany, Switzerland and England in 1883 he met Friedrich Engels and August Bebel. In 1886 he founded the Vienna weekly *Gleichheit.* When this was proscribed in 1889, he founded the *Arbeiterzeitung,* which became the main organ of the Austrian Social Democratic party.

Adler's greatest achievement was when, during the party convention at Hainfeld (Dec. 1888–Jan. 1889), he reconciled diverging factions among the Austrian Social Democrats. In 1899, moreover, he published a program for the Socialist parties of the various nationalities of the Austrian lands designed to maintain the unity of the empire. Between 1887 and 1899 he was imprisoned for 18 months for his political activities. He was elected, however, to the *Landtag* of Lower Austria in 1905 and had much to do with the introduction of general suffrage into the Austrian lands in 1907. In 1911, the breakaway of the Czech Social Democrats frustrated his hopes of complete party unity. Before and during World War I Adler used the Second International in repeated efforts for peace; *e.g.,* at Basel in 1912 and at Stockholm in 1917. After World War I he joined the provisional administration of "German Austria," advocating union with Germany. He died in Vienna on Nov. 11, 1918.

His speeches and letters are collected as *Aufsätze, Reden und Briefe,* 11 vol. (1922–29); there are also selections by A. Tesarek, *Aus Viktor Adlers Reden und Briefen* (1957).

See K. Renner, *An der Wende zweier Zeiten* (1946); L. A. Windisch-Grätz, *Ein Kaiser kämpft für die Freiheit* (1957).   (L. JE.)

ADMETUS, in Greek legend, son of Pheres, king of Pherae, in Thessaly. Having sued for the hand of Alcestis, the most beautiful of the daughters of Pelias, king of Iolcus, he was first required to harness a lion and a boar to a chariot. Apollo, who served him—either as a punishment for having slain the Cyclopes or out of affection for his mortal master—yoked the pair himself and gave them to Admetus, who thus obtained Alcestis.

Finding that Admetus was soon to die, Apollo persuaded the Fates to prolong his life, provided anyone could be found to die in his place. His parents refused, but Alcestis consented. She was rescued by Hercules, who wrestled with Death at the grave and made him give her back. The death and resurrection of Alcestis form the subject of many ancient reliefs and vase paintings, as well as the *Alcestis* of Euripides, which is extant.

See A. Lesky, *Alkestis: der Mythus und das Drama* (1925); W. Roscher, *Ausführliches Lexikon der griechischen und römischen Mythologie* (1884–1937).   (T. V. B.)

ADMINISTRATION, in law, is the management of an estate by a person, other than the legal owner, appointed or supervised by a court; especially the management of a decedent's estate by an administrator or executor, a ward's estate by a guardian, an insane person's estate by a conservator or committee, a bankrupt estate by a trustee in bankruptcy and, generally, of a trust fund by a trustee. Every such fiduciary is held to a high standard of care and is strictly accountable for his management. Ordinarily he is entitled to a fee. Fiduciary management is to a large extent carried on by professional trustees, especially trust companies. The total amount of personal funds administered by banks and trust companies in 1959 has been estimated to amount to approximately $50,000,000,000 in the United States. For the principles applicable to specific kinds of administration, *see* BANKRUPTCY; ESTATES, ADMINISTRATION OF; CHILDREN, LAWS CONCERNING; INSANITY; TRUST.   (M. RN.)

ADMINISTRATION, MILITARY: *see* LOGISTICS.

ADMINISTRATIVE AREAS. An administrative area is a portion of the earth's surface that has been officially delimited for the administration of one or more governmental functions. Administrative areas come into being in three ways. First, the total area of each government, whether national, state or local, is automatically an administrative area. Second, any such government may subdivide its area into smaller areas for administrative purposes. Thus, a city government may have police precincts, a state government have highway districts, a national government have administrative regions or districts. Third, an administrative area may be intergovernmentally created to combine all or parts of the areas of two or more governments for defined administrative purposes. Thus, the New York Port authority, established jointly by interstate compact between the states of New York and New Jersey, has jurisdiction in both states; similarly, three counties may agree to set up a joint health department with tri-county jurisdiction.

Number and Types of Areas.—An administrative area may be used for many functions or for only a single function. Of the 91,000 governmental units in the United States in the 1960s, about one-third were multifunctional and two-thirds unifunctional. The multifunctional units included the national government, the 50 states, and about 3,000 counties, 18,000 municipalities, and 17,000 towns and townships. In England and Wales the major multifunctional governmental areas numbered 145, including 62 administrative counties and 83 county boroughs (larger urban areas whose governments have both county and urban powers); in addition, the two-tier administrative counties included more than 1,000 urban and rural county districts, and more than 300 noncounty boroughs; still lower were 14,000 parishes. France's 38,-000 communes were multifunctional local governments.

The United States has, and England earlier had, a perplexing number of substantially autonomous single-function governmental units, each with its own area. The unifunctional areas in the United States in the 1960s included about 35,000 school districts and over 18,000 other special districts for such functions as fire protection, soil conservation, drainage, cemeteries, housing, water supply, and highways. The trends were downward for school districts, which were half as numerous as in the early 1940s, but upward for other special districts, as they increased 75% between the 1940s and the 1960s.

When a national or state government subdivides its territory it may establish a single master set of administrative areas and channel the field work for all its functions through a chief administrator of each area. Napoleon I established this system for France. It persists into the second half of the 20th century, with 90 administrative *départements* (*i.e.*, areas), each headed by a prefect. The major alternative is to allow each national agency to design its own scheme of administrative areas to fit its own function without any necessary regard to the areas used by other national agencies or to other governmental areas, such as states and counties; each agency, of course, directs its own field work. This pattern is followed by the national governments in the United States and England, neither of which has any official comparable to the French prefect.

Suggested Reforms.—Areal reform is widely advocated. It is not difficult to demonstrate that areas could be redesigned to satisfy criteria of symmetry, simplicity, uniformity and geographical correctness. But these are not the substantial questions. A more meaningful approach takes account of the degree to which existing administrative areas contribute to or obstruct effective governmental services to the people, democratic control of officials and maintenance of local government.

English, French and American all-purpose administrative areas were inherited from the 19th century—an age of less population, less urbanization, fewer governmental services, less need for staffs of professional, full-time officials and less technological mastery of transportation and communication. The artificiality of existing multifunctional administrative areas becomes more pronounced as the premises on which they were built increasingly lose validity.

A substantial official and professional literature in the United States urges increase in the average size of counties, expansion of city and town boundaries to include the suburbs and fringe areas, amalgamation or federation of immediately adjacent cities and towns to provide a single government for each large urban and metropolitan community and drastic reduction of special districts. Action along these lines has been slight.

The proposals rest on such premises as these: that the natural areas, self-defined by the problems with which a government is to deal, should be embraced by the official area of that government; that modern financing and staffing requirements for each of a number of functions dictate in each case a larger supporting and service area than was true earlier; that well-to-do sections of a community should not escape a share of responsibility for depressed sections or for leadership of the whole community, nor should residents of "dormitory suburbs" escape responsibility for supporting central city services they enjoy daily; that fragmentation of government among a variety of autonomous agencies, such as special districts and *ad hoc* joint authorities, precludes a unified approach to a community's interlocking problems and impairs popular control; that intergovernmental co-operation is an inadequate mode of action for an important continuing problem, as the least co-operative autonomous governmental unit in a community may exercise an absolute veto and so set the pace of joint action; and that local democracy is best served by areas that permit effective performance by government, control by a majority of the whole community and retention of responsibilities that might otherwise go by default to higher levels of government.

In Great Britain there have been proposals for devolution to English, Welsh and Scottish parliaments and for regional divisions of England itself. But the principal proposals have been for reform of local government areas. From 1945 to 1949 a Local Government Boundary commission studied the problem but hesitated to act, partly because of the county councils' unqualified resistance to important recommendations for urban areas. When the commission did announce its intention to act, parliament abolished it. In the 1950s the government negotiated with local officials to identify types of areal changes they would not oppose.

In France there is considerable regionalist literature, critical of the small size of the 90 administrative *départements*. This bore practical fruit under the Vichy government, which established 18 regions, and under the fourth republic, which grouped *départements* into 9 regions largely for internal security reasons. French national ministries tended increasingly to establish their own administrative area schemes, instead of channeling their functional

field work through the prefect and his *département*.

Metropolitan Areas.—Major urban communities—the 174 metropolitan areas in the United States and the "conurbations" in Great Britain—present the most pressing areal problem. Greater London contains more than 8,000,000 persons, but the London county council serves only between 3,000,000 and 4,000,000 of them. The 3,000 sq.mi. metropolitan area of New York and northeastern New Jersey in the 1950s included over 1,000 governmental units; New York city served only 8,000,000 of the 13,000,000 inhabitants in the area.

In the United States, efforts to provide suitable administrative areas for the metropolitan community and to rationalize the hodgepodge of governmental layering have been piecemeal and not widely successful. Among the methods advocated and attempted were annexation, unifunctional and multifunctional special districts, city-county consolidation, city-county separation, designation of the county as the metropolitan government, granting to the core city of extraterritorial jurisdiction over its fringe and voluntary co-operation among governmental units operating in the metropolitan community.

The most probable solution appeared to lie in metropolitan federation, whereby existing general-purpose local governments would continue to perform certain functions and a government with metropolis-wide jurisdiction would perform certain other functions. The first tests of this pattern in North America occurred in Toronto, Ont., and Dade county (Miami) Fla.

Area and Function as Conflicting Factors.—The common element in experiences with the administrative area problem is the conflicting and complementary claims of area and function. Function may dictate area. Thus, a school administrative area, it is said, should have at least 1,500 pupils (though 90% of school districts have less), and a local tax assessment district should have at least 10,000 inhabitants; health, welfare, police, fire and other functional requirements can be stated, each statement leading to a different area. So, too, each national agency can argue persuasively for a strictly functional administrative geography; customs collection and apprehension of counterfeiters have differing geographical requirements, though both are in the treasury department.

But over against the claim of function is the claim of each natural area, such as an urban community or an economic region, to be looked at as a whole for which the total range of administrative functions should make sense and so be co-ordinated. Reconciliation of these claims is thwarted both by the failure of existing local all-purpose administrative areas to expand to a size that would accommodate 20th-century functional requirements, and by the reluctance of functional specialists to accept direction by administrative generalists and political officials.

BIBLIOGRAPHY.—*General:* G. Montagu Harris, *Comparative Local Government* (1949); W. A. Robson (ed.), *Great Cities of the World,* new ed. (1957). *United States:* U.S. National Resources Committee, *Regional Factors in National Planning and Development* (1935); William Anderson, *The Units of Government in the United States,* rev. ed. (1945); Victor Jones, *Metropolitan Government* (1942); James W. Fesler, *Area and Administration* (1949); Lane W. Lancaster, *Government in Rural America,* 2nd ed. (1952); Charles McKinley, *Uncle Sam in the Pacific Northwest* (1952); U.S. Commission on Intergovernmental Relations, *Report* (1955); The American Assembly (Columbia University), *The Forty-eight States* (1956); Council of State Governments, *The States and the Metropolitan Problem* (1956); John C. Bollens, *Special District Governments in the United States* (1957); Roscoe C. Martin, *Grass Roots* (1957); Henry C. Hart, *The Dark Missouri* (1957); U.S. Bureau of the Census, *1957 Census of Governments,* vol. i, no. 1, "Governments in the United States" (1957), vol. i, no. 2, "Local Government in Standard Metropolitan Areas" (1957), and vol. i, no. 3, "Local Government Structure" (1957). *Great Britain:* G. D. H. Cole, *Local and Regional Government* (1947); Local Government Boundary Commission, *Report for the Year 1947* (1948); V. D. Lipman, *Local Government Areas, 1834-1945* (1949); J. W. Grove, *Regional Administration,* Fabian Research Series No. 147 (1951); W. A. Robson, *The Development of Local Government,* 3rd ed. (1954); W. J. M. Mackenzie and J. W. Grove, *Central Administration in Britain,* pp. 260-280 (1957). *France:* Brian Chapman, *Introduction to French Local Government* (1953), and *The Prefects and Provincial France* (1955). *Germany:* Arnold Brecht, *Federalism and Regionalism in Germany* (1945).

(J. W. Fr.)

ADMINISTRATIVE LAW is the law concerning the powers and procedures of administrative agencies, including the law governing judicial review of administrative action. An administrative agency is a governmental authority, other than a court or legislative body, which affects the rights of private parties through either adjudication or rule making, *i.e.*, through deciding cases or through subordinate legislation. An administrative agency may be called a commission, board, authority, bureau, office, officer, administrator, department, corporation, administration, division or agency. Nothing of substance hinges on the choice of name, and usually the choices have been haphazard.

Administrative law, as the term is generally but not always used, is limited to law concerning powers, procedures and judicial review. In England and the U.S. the term is used to some extent to include the mass of substantive law produced by the agencies; it is probably better to designate this substantive law by such names as tax law, labour law, transportation law, communications law, and zoning law. Some political scientists regard administrative law as all the law that relates to public administration, but this usage is uncommon among lawyers.

Administrative law consists of constitutional law, statutory law, common law, and agency-made law. The great bulk of administrative law is judge-made law. Some of the judge-made law either is or purports to be constitutional or statutory interpretation; some of it is common law in the sense that it is produced by courts without reliance on either constitutional or statutory provisions; and some of it is judge-made law that may or may not be directly or remotely anchored to constitutional or statutory provisions.

The three large segments of administrative law relate to transfer of power from legislatures to agencies, exercise of power by the agencies, and review of administrative action by courts. The important segment has become the exercise of power by the agencies, *i.e.*, rule making and adjudication, and such incidental powers as investigating, supervising, prosecuting, advising and declaring.

The Place of Administrative Action in Governmental and Legal Systems.—Justice Robert Jackson of the U.S. supreme court once asserted in a formal opinion: "The rise of administrative bodies probably has been the most significant legal trend of the last century and perhaps more values today are affected by their decisions than by those of all the courts, review of administrative decisions apart." The statement relates to U.S. law, but can perhaps be applied almost equally well to the law of western European nations, the major difference being that industries which are regulated in the United States are often directly operated by the governments of western Europe.

Another associate justice of the supreme court has pointed out: "Review of administrative action, mainly reflecting enforcement of federal regulatory statutes, constitutes the largest category of the (Supreme) Court's work, comprising one-third of the total cases decided on the merits." Constitutional law, including "cases with constitutional undertones," was in second place, with less than one-fourth of the cases.

The average person is much more directly and much more frequently affected by the administrative process than by the judicial process. The pervasiveness of the administrative process may be illustrated by samples of what it typically protects against in the U.S.: excessive prices of electricity, gas, telephone and other utility services; unreasonableness in rates, schedules and services of airlines, railroads, streetcars, and busses; disregard for the public interest in radio and television broadcasting; unwholesome meat and poultry; adulteration in food; fraud or inadequate disclosure in sale of securities; physically unsafe locomotives, ships, airplanes, bridges, and elevators; unfair labour practices by either employers or unions; false advertising and other unfair or deceptive practices; inadequate safety appliances; uncompensated injuries related to employment; cessation of income during temporary unemployment; subminimum wages; poverty in old age; industrial plants in residential areas; loss of bank deposits; and perhaps undue inflation or deflation. Probably the list could be expanded to a thousand or more items the public is accustomed to taking for granted.

Political Groups Affected.—The administrative process is a governmental tool, and as a tool it can be neither conservative nor liberal. It is used to promote probusiness policies, antibusiness policies, and policies having little or nothing to do with business. It has often been used as an instrument of law reform, but it is also used as a means of protecting vested interests. Yet the administrative process is always a tool for positive government, never a tool for *laissez faire*.

The all-too-prevalent assumption that positive government is contrary to the interests either of business or of big business is false about as often as it is true. Many measures are designed to protect the public against abuses by business, but many major regulatory programs are sponsored by business. In the U.S., radio broadcasters brought about the regulation of radio broadcasting because they wanted a system of assignment of frequencies. Airlines in need of subsidies helped promote the establishment of an administrative authority to dispense subsidies and to supervise the development of an orderly system of routes. Railways and large motor freight carriers joined in sponsoring regulation of the motor carriers. When corporations gained the political power to enact antiunion legislation in 1947, they did not destroy the National Labor Relations board but added to its powers; they authorized the board to administer a system of preventing labour unions from engaging in unfair labour practices. The major petroleum companies initiated the most drastic system of regulation administered by any state agency—oil proration in Texas. Nearly all occupational licensing agencies set up by state legislation, averaging perhaps thirty or forty in each state, have come into being at the instance of regulated groups.

Sometimes agencies established to protect the public are in some measure taken over by the regulated industry. Although much is spoken and written in criticism of the zeal of some agencies, deficiency of administrative zeal may be as grievous a fault as excessive zeal. One of the greatest dangers of the administrative process is that an agency, through lethargy or through immoderate yielding to the influence of the regulated groups, may thwart the democratic will by acting only when prodded by private interest. "Administrative arteriosclerosis" is a common disease among the older agencies. Excessive zeal, much feared, may be less dangerous than administrative apathy, much ignored.

Historical Development.—Administrative law existed long before the term for it came into use. In 1893 Frank J. Goodnow wrote: "The general failure in England and the United States to recognize an administrative law is really due, not to the nonexistence in these countries of this branch of the law but rather to the well-known failure of English law writers to classify the law. For . . . there (has) always existed in England, as well as in this country, an administrative law."

In the U.S. about one-third of federal peacetime agencies were created before 1900, and another third before 1930. The first federal agency was established in 1789 to "estimate the duties payable" on imports.

In 1916 Elihu Root said: "There is one special field of law development which has manifestly become inevitable. We are entering upon the creation of a body of administrative law . . . There will be no withdrawal from these experiments. We shall go on; we shall expand them, whether we approve theoretically or not, because such agencies furnish protection to rights and obstacles to wrong doing which under our new social and industrial conditions cannot be practically accomplished by the old and simple procedure of legislatures and courts as in the last generation." But leaders of the bar for the most part rejected this wise counsel. Emotional resentment against the rise of administrative power gradually welled up.

In 1929 Lord Hewart's book, *The New Despotism*, gave emphatic and emotional expression to the concern shared by most lawyers both in England and the U.S. But the British committee on ministers' powers investigated and reported "no ground for public fear, if the right precautions are taken." In the U.S. in the 1930s, with the coming of the New Deal, the agencies were not cut back but were multiplied. A host of new agencies were thorns in the sides of businessmen. If before the New Deal the antagonism toward administrative agencies was fast reaching the breaking point, the reasons for alarm were now explosive.

In 1937 came the report of the president's committee on administrative management, approved by Pres. Franklin Roosevelt: "Commissions . . . constitute a headless 'fourth branch' of the Government, a haphazard deposit of irresponsible agencies and uncoordinated powers." But congress rejected the recommendations of that committee, and in 1939 the attorney general's committee on administrative procedure was created. The elaborate report of this committee, together with the descriptive monographs on which it was based, has been a primary source of information about the federal administrative process. Out of the report grew the Administrative Procedure act, 1946, which regularized, improved and strengthened administrative procedure, and which preserved the basic limits upon judicial review of administrative action. The American Bar association seemed satisfied even though it had lost its battle for such propositions as "the decisions of controversies must be brought back into the judicial system." But in the late 1950s the American Bar association, following the lead of the second Hoover commission, was again sponsoring legislation designed to cut back administrative power. Attorney General Herbert Brownell, however, said of the Hoover commission's proposals: "These changes would substantially 'judicialize' the administrative process, with disastrous results to efficient and effective government. . . . Far from achieving the Commission's objectives of attaining economy, efficiency, and improved service in the transaction of public business, these proposals would do exactly the contrary."

In 1957 came the report of the British committee on administrative tribunals and enquiries, known as the Franks committee: "In recent years most other western Governments have been called upon to govern more extensively and more intensively. . . . Reflection on the general social and economic changes of recent decades convinces us that tribunals as a system for adjudication have come to stay. . . . Our general conclusion regarding tribunals is that, despite the haphazard way in which they have developed, this method of decision works reasonably well. . . . We regard both tribunals and administrative procedures as essential to our society."

Reasons for Growth of the Administrative Process.—The fundamental reason for resort to administrative agencies is the undertaking by government of tasks which from a strictly practical standpoint can best be performed through them. When U.S. collectors of customs were authorized in 1789 to decide the amounts of duties payable on imported goods, no one was thinking in terms of judiciary v. bureaucracy, capitalism v. socialism, or laissez faire v. governmental interference. The same is true of the creation of most other agencies. Practical men were seeking practical answers to immediate problems.

In the 1870s, railroad abuses were insufficiently checked by shippers' common-law actions for refund of unreasonable charges. Farmers in the midwest saw that what was needed was a governmental authority having power not merely to adjudicate but to initiate proceedings, to investigate, to prosecute, to issue regulations, to supervise. State legislatures responded, and then in 1887 the federal congress took action. The Interstate Commerce commission thus came into being and later congresses enlarged its powers as needs were felt. The impetus came not from philosophers or theorists but from down-to-earth men who sought workable machinery for stamping out particular evils.

Gradually the legislative bodies throughout the world developed the system of legislating only the main outlines of comprehensive programs requiring constant attention, and leaving to administrators the tasks of working out subsidiary policies.

The reasons for using agencies rather than courts for adjudication of controversies are numerous and variable. A major reason is that adjudication of issues often grows directly out of administrative handling; for instance, if 99 veterans are admitted to a hospital and only in the 100th case does a controversy arise, the hospital officials or members of their organization may most conveniently conduct whatever proceeding is needed. Much adjudication is outside the competence of courts, which are not qualified to fix rates or to determine what practices related to rates are to be preferred. Similarly, judges cannot supply the skills of an agency like the Interstate Commerce commission, which requires the assistance of experts on rates, locomotive inspectors, railroad reorganization specialists, explosives experts, valuation engineers, tariff interpreters, accountants, specialists in long- and short-haul problems, and experts on rail traffic congestion. Neither can judges handle 2,000,000 social security claims per year. Even for adjudication of workmen's compensation cases, widespread experience has shown that the courts are not the appropriate tribunals.

Another major reason for the legislative preference for the administrative process has been the belief that the judicial process is unduly awkward, slow and expensive. The public has demanded a speedy, cheap and simple procedure. The fact is that the administrative process is by no means always fast and inexpensive, but the prevailing belief has been that it is.

Some programs have been committed to the administrative process because of a widespread belief, whether or not justifiable, that the biases of judges disqualify them. Sponsors of reform legislation have often thought, rightly or wrongly, that judges, by reason of experience as advocates in favouring the interests of property, tend unduly to construe away sound and necessary reform legislation. In 1914 a senate committee in recommending creation of the Federal Trade commission said: "The people of this country will not permit the courts to declare a policy for them with respect to this subject."

The political outlook both in England and the U.S. is for a long-term continued growth of the administrative process. The Franks committee in England has found administrative tribunals "essential." The attorney general for a conservative administration in the U.S. said in 1955: "Administrative agencies must be enabled and permitted to function efficiently and effectively if the public interest, which is their primary concern, is to be preserved."

Supremacy of Law or Rule of Law.—Although the terms "rule of law" and "supremacy of law" are probably interchangeable, their meaning is far from clear. The terms are often emotional: appraisals of the importance of the rule of law usually vary in direct proportion to the vagueness of the meaning the writer or speaker assigns to it.

Seven separate meanings are common:

1. Most people agree with the rule of law in the sense of law and order as distinguished from resort to force. But resistance to the rule of law in this sense crops out from time to time; Sen. James O. Eastland said in 1955: "You are not required to obey any court which passes out such a ruling. In fact, you are obligated to defy it."

2. Exponents of the rule of law often mean merely that they prefer fixed rules to discretion; i.e., what the Massachusetts constitution calls "a government of laws and not of men." The problem of the proper proportion of rule and discretion is of course a central problem in our governmental system. Solutions we work out in practice vary from one context to the other; we inevitably allow wide play for discretion in many areas. The administrative process, as distinguished from the executive process, confines discretion through procedural safeguards and through judicial check; in this respect, as the attorney general's committee on administrative procedure asserted, "the administrative process, far from being an encroachment upon the rule of law, is an extension of it."

3. The rule of law sometimes means elimination of all discretion from governmental processes, and in this sense the rule of law seems impossible of accomplishment. For example, how can a congress be bound by fixed rules on such a question as whether or not to enact social security legislation? Even the U.S. supreme court is not bound by fixed rules in deciding whether or not to overrule a batch of precedents, as it has often done.

4. Sometimes the rule of law means democracy and fairness. Thus, the British committee on administrative tribunals and enquiries, reporting in 1957, referred to "the notion of what is according to the rule of law, its antithesis being what is arbitrary."

But the antithesis of principles or laws is not necessarily arbitrariness; it may be reasonable exercise of discretionary power. When the U.S. supreme court overrules a precedent, it may be creating a new principle, but it is not necessarily acting arbitrarily. Nor is an agency necessarily acting arbitrarily when it makes a change in announced policy.

5. The rule of law sometimes means due process, natural law or higher law. The concept of "a law which governs the governors" is a useful one. But the concepts of due process and of natural justice may often be more satisfactory.

6. The rule of law sometimes means a preference for decisions by judges rather than by administrators. John Dickinson, in his book *Administrative Justice and the Supremacy of Law in the United States,* says that "every citizen is entitled . . . to have his rights adjudicated in a regular common-law court." The existence of unreviewable administrative action contradicts Dickinson. His position borders on absurdity when he says that "the law ought to be applied by an agency whose main business is to know the law, rather than to enforce some part of it." This would mean that a judge, not an inspector of hulls and boilers, should decide whether a ship is seaworthy.

7. The rule of law sometimes means that administrative action should be reviewable. But the law, as stated by the U.S. supreme court, is that "courts are not charged with general guardianship against all potential mischief in the complicated tasks of government." Holdings preventing the courts from reviewing even questions of law are not at all uncommon. U.S. courts do not review (*a*) the budget bureau's recommendation that an appropriation be reduced; (*b*) the government's purchase of X's land but not Y's; (*c*) the president's recognition or refusal to recognize a foreign government; or (*d*) a refusal of executive clemency to a convicted criminal.

Separation of Powers.—Blackstone, drawing from doctrine stemming from Plato, Aristotle, Polybius, Cicero, Machiavelli, Harrington, Locke, and Montesquieu, wrote: "In all tyrannical governments, the supreme magistracy, or the right both of making and enforcing the laws is vested in one and the same man, or one and the same body of men; and wherever these two powers are united together, there can be no public liberty." But Joseph Story, in his *Commentaries on the Constitution,* wrote in 1833: "The slightest examination of the British constitution will at once convince us, that the legislative, executive, and judiciary departments are by no means totally distinct, and separate from each other." The British government of the 20th century continues to mix the three kinds of powers, and yet no government has been more completely free from tyranny.

The U.S. constitution contains no specific provision that the three kinds of powers shall be kept distinct, and the typical administrative agency exercises all three. The supreme court said in 1881 that "it is essential to the successful working of this system that the persons intrusted with power in any one of these branches shall not be permitted to encroach upon the powers confided to the others." But the court has never held that the blending of the various kinds of power in an agency is unconstitutional.

The realities of the law about separation of powers, along with innuendoes about its unrealities, have been stated by Justice Jackson in formal opinion: "They (administrative bodies) have become a veritable fourth branch of the Government, which has deranged our three-branch legal theories much as the concept of a fourth dimension unsettles our three-dimensional thinking. Courts have differed in assigning a place to these seemingly necessary bodies in our constitutional system. Administrative agencies have been called quasi-legislative, quasi-executive or quasi-judicial, as the occasion required, in order to validate their functions within the separation-of-powers scheme of the Constitution. The mere retreat to the qualifying 'quasi' is implicit with confession that all recognized classifications have broken down, and 'quasi' is a smooth cover which we draw over our confusion as we might use a counterpane to conceal a disordered bed."

In framing a constitution for a new government, the idea of separating the three kinds of powers from each other has much to commend it; modern totalitarian regimes show the advantages of avoiding concentration of power in the hands of any officer or group of officers. But in making relatively small arrangements within a framework already established, the idea that the three kinds of power should not at any level be blended in any one set of hands becomes so impracticable that legislative bodies all over the world reject it. And in the U.S. the supreme court has approved the rejection.

The U.S. constitution itself provides that the president shall participate in the legislative process by approving or vetoing bills and in the judicial process by exercising the power of pardon, that the house of representatives shall act executively in impeaching officers, that the senate shall act judicially in trying impeachments, and that the senate shall participate in an executive function in advising on and consenting to appointments to public office.

The blending of power in a modern U.S. agency can hardly lead to tyranny, for administrative power is typically hemmed in on all sides. Administrators are appointed and reappointed by the president with the advice and consent of the senate. They get their power from congress, which can always withdraw or modify the granted power, and frequently does so. Congressional committees, including appropriations committees, investigate and recommend, threaten and cajole. Within the limits that congress has thought appropriate, administrative action is subject to the check of judicial review. Both congress and the courts have imposed the further checks of procedural safeguards.

The principle whose soundness has been confirmed by both early and recent experience is not the principle of separation of powers but the principle of check. We have gone far beyond Montesquieu. We have learned that danger of tyranny or injustice lurks in unchecked power, not in blended power.

Delegation of Power.—Not only does the British parliament delegate power to whatever extent it chooses but it commonly authorizes ministers to redelegate power to other authorities; the courts do not interfere.

Although the U.S. constitution says nothing about delegation of congressional power except that "all legislative Powers herein granted shall be vested in a Congress" and that congress may "make all Laws which shall be necessary and proper for carrying into Execution the foregoing Powers," the supreme court created a nondelegation doctrine which was especially troublesome during the 1930s and 1940s. In 1932 the supreme court asserted: "That the legislative power of Congress cannot be delegated is, of course, clear." In two cases in 1935 congressional delegations to governmental authorities were held invalid, the only such holdings in U.S. history. But throughout American history congress has delegated legislative power to administrative agencies. Except for unrealistic verbiage that tends to persist, the effective law is in accord with a 1940 statement of the supreme court: "Delegation by Congress has long been recognized as necessary in order that the exertion of legislative power does not become a futility." Much of the judicial talk about requiring a statement of legislative standards in order that a delegation may be valid is contrary to the action the supreme court takes when delegations without standards are upheld.

The problem of delegation is not merely one of determining what organ of government is best qualified to determine particular policies, for whether powers are delegated or not they are often exercised through co-operative arrangements in which many organs of government participate; sometimes the most effective method for expressing legislative will may be delegation, with virtually no standards, but with strong legislative influence upon policy creation after the delegation has been made.

The nondelegation doctrine has been to a considerable extent a judge-made corollary of *laissez faire,* inconsistent with positive government. The ultimate determination of desirable boundaries for delegation must therefore depend in part upon a determination of the proper role of government in society—a determination that the supreme court probably should allow congress to make.

The Power of Investigation.—In England a ministry or tribunal may compel production of evidence pursuant to an authorizing statute and no constitutional principles stand in the way.

Witnesses have a privilege against self-incrimination, but since 1898 they can be compelled to give incriminating testimony or to produce incriminating documents if they are given a corresponding immunity from prosecution.

In the U.S., constitutional principles before the 1940s often stood in the way of effective administrative investigation. When in 1924 the Federal Trade commission sought records of a tobacco company, Justice Oliver Wendell Holmes said for a unanimous supreme court: "It is contrary to the first principles of justice to allow a search through all the respondents' records, relevant or irrelevant, in the hope that something will turn up." But during the 1940s the effective constitution with respect to the administrative power of investigation was largely turned right around backward by judicial decisions. In 1946 the supreme court made clear that a subpoena for records will be enforced if "the investigation be for a lawfully authorized purpose, within the power of Congress to command," including "general or statistical investigations authorized by Congress." In 1948 the court held that the privilege against self-incrimination does not apply to records required by law to be kept. In 1950 it declared: "Even if one were to regard the (Federal Trade commission's) request for information in this case as caused by nothing more than official curiosity, nevertheless law-enforcing agencies have a legitimate right to satisfy themselves that corporate behavior is consistent with the law and the public interest." Petty officials may now, when authorized by statute, enter a business establishment, demand that records and documents be made available for their inspection and enforce the demand by securing a court order requiring disclosure, even in absence of probable cause to believe that the law has been violated.

On the vital question of whether administrative agencies may have access to business records, three principal ways have been developed for getting around the 5th amendment's provision that "No person . . . shall be compelled . . . to be a witness against himself": (1) statutes provide for compulsory testimony or production of records and confer immunity from prosecution; (2) the courts have created law that records required to be kept are outside the scope of the privilege against self-incrimination; and (3) courts have created law that records of corporations and of some other organizations are not subject to the privilege.

Each step has followed inexorably: Industrialization brings regulation. Regulation necessitates administrative processes. Agencies cannot operate without access to facts. Ideas about privacy, standing in the way of agencies which seek information indispensable to intelligent regulation, have to give way. In the same way that the gasoline engine made inevitable the development of the airplane, mass production methods and all they symbolize produce complex business arrangements which bring forth equally intricate governmental mechanisms requiring effective exercise of the administrative power of investigation. And the courts as a result have felt called upon to write out of the constitution the protections that earlier courts felt called upon to write into it.

Rule Making.—A "rule" or a "regulation" is the product of administrative legislation. Interpretative rules have all degrees of authoritative effect, varying from about zero to full force of law, but legislative rules, if valid, have force of law; the authoritative effect in each instance goes back to statutory intent. Retroactive rule making is often permitted.

Rule-making procedures cover the spectrum from no party participation to full-fledged trials, but the mainstay is submission of tentative drafts to affected parties for written comments. The simple system of deferred effectiveness of published rules in order to allow criticisms has been quite successful. Other methods include consultations and conferences, advisory committees and speech-making hearings. The central problem about rule-making procedure usually is not whether a hearing ought to be held but whether parties should be allowed to participate by some other means.

The English parliament has a committee which systematically reviews rules issued by ministries, but the review concerns only such questions as improper use of power, not the wisdom of the policy expressed in the rules. The U.S. government has never had a systematic arrangement for legislative review of administrative rules, but congress unsystematically supervises administration as the occasion arises.

Requirement of Opportunity To Be Heard.—A "hearing" is any oral proceeding before a tribunal. Hearings are of two principal kinds—trials and arguments. A trial is a process by which parties present evidence, subject to cross-examination and rebuttal, and the tribunal makes a determination on the record. The key to a trial is the opportunity of each party to know and to meet the evidence and the argument on the other side; this is what is meant by the determination "on the record." The opportunity to meet the opposing evidence and argument includes opportunity to present evidence, to present written or oral argument or both, and to cross-examine opposing witnesses. A typical hearing before an appellate court is an argument, not a trial. A trial is designed for resolving issues of fact, and an argument, not a trial, is normally the appropriate oral process for resolving nonfactual issues of law and policy and discretion. These simple propositions are sometimes misunderstood; agencies sometimes develop nonfactual issues of policy by having "witnesses" express argumentative opinions, and by having opposing counsel present argument in the form of cross-examination.

Facts pertaining to the parties and their businesses and activities, *i.e.*, adjudicative facts, are intrinsically the kind of facts that ordinarily ought not to be determined without giving the parties a chance to know and to meet any evidence that may be unfavourable to them, *i.e.*, without providing the parties an opportunity for trial. But facts which are used only for their bearing upon issues of law and policy, *i.e.*, legislative facts, may often be properly developed without trial, either through presentation to the tribunal in briefs or arguments or through the tribunal's own research.

The key principle is that a party who has a sufficient interest or right at stake in a determination of governmental action should be entitled to an opportunity to know and to meet, with the weapons of rebuttal evidence, cross-examination and argument, any unfavourable evidence of adjudicative facts, except in the rare circumstance when some other interest, such as national security, justifies overriding the interest in fair hearing. Some major exceptions to the principle involve emergency or temporary action, inspection or testing (of an airplane, meat, an obscene book) as a substitute for hearing, and cases involving *de novo* judicial review.

Whether (or when) a party is entitled to a hearing if only a privilege, gratuity or act of grace is at stake has been a troublesome problem. A donee ought not to be allowed to compel the government to make a gift. Nor should a supplicant for an act of grace be permitted to coerce officers to make a favourable determination in the exercise of discretionary power. But the government cannot give to Baptists and withhold from Methodists; it cannot give to whites and withhold from Negroes. Can it, then, grant or deny privileges through flagrantly unfair procedure? The answer is sometimes yes and sometimes no.

Because of the concept of privilege, the U.S. supreme court in alien cases, even when human values of the highest order have been at stake, has interpreted vague statutory provisions against the alien and has observed: "Whatever the procedure authorized by Congress is, it is due process as far as an alien denied entry is concerned." Problems of privilege arise concerning government employment, passports, exemption from the draft because of conscientious objection, revocation of probation or parole, and revocation of certain occupational licences.

Institutional Decisions.—An institutional decision of an administrative agency is a decision made by an organization and not by an individual or solely by agency heads. The decision of a trial judge of an ordinary court is personal; the judge hears evidence and argument and decides the case. In the administrative process, evidence may be taken before an examiner (a subordinate officer who presides at a hearing), the examiner or other subordinates may sift the evidence, various kinds of specialists of the agency's staff may contribute to the writing of reports, and the agency heads may in fact lean so heavily on the work of the staff that they know little or nothing about the problems involved in many of the cases decided in the agency's name. In the institutional decision lie elements of special strength and weakness of the administrative process. The strength springs from the superiority of group work—from internal checks and balances, from co-operation among specialists in various disciplines, from assignment of relatively menial tasks to low-paid personnel so as to utilize most economically the energies of high-paid personnel, and from capacity of the system to handle huge volumes of business and at the same time maintain a reasonable degree of uniformity in policy determinations. The weaknesses of the institutional decision lie in its anonymity, in its reliance on extrarecord advice, in frustration of the parties' desire to reach the men who influence the decision behind the scenes, and in the separation of the deciding function from the writing of the opinion or report.

Problems about the institutional decision are little developed in case law or legal literature outside the U.S. The law in the U.S. is that deciding officers need not personally hear the witnesses testify, that they need not read transcripts of testimony fully, that they may base their decisions upon reports of subordinates analyzing the evidence and making recommendations, and that they must develop their own understanding of the issues and of the relevant evidence.

The volume of business of some regulatory agencies in the U.S. is such that agency heads are forced to rely heavily upon subordinates. Any proposal that the extent of such reliance should be reduced is unrealistic unless it is coupled with some practical suggestion for disposing of the case loads.

Deciding officers are allowed to consult agency specialists freely, so long as extrarecord facts are not improperly used.

Bias.—Courts uniformly hold that bias in the sense of preconceived views about issues of law or policy is not a disqualification, thereby rejecting the surprising position taken by the British committee on ministers' powers that "bias from strong and sincere conviction as to public policy may operate as a more serious disqualification than pecuniary interest." Legislative bodies have often created agencies in order to escape supposed biases of the judiciary or in order to obtain administration of a program in accordance with a desired point of view or bias. Prejudgment of facts bearing upon law or policy is no more a disqualification than prejudgment of philosophy about law or policy; all educated people inevitably have such prejudgments.

Even prejudgment of facts about particular parties is not necessarily a ground for disqualification; this is seen most clearly in cases in which a trial judge who has announced findings of fact is held not disqualified to hear the case a second time after an appellate court has reversed and remanded, and these holdings are generally applied equally to the administrative adjudicator.

Personal prejudice—an attitude of favouritism or animosity toward a particular party—is a disqualification when it is substantial. Of course, a judge or officer who stands to gain or lose by a decision may be disqualified by interest; a disqualifying interest may be pecuniary or professional, it may be based upon a relation to a party, or it may involve a predetermination to achieve a particular objective.

Rules about disqualification of officers are often defeated by "the rule of necessity," under which a disqualified officer may serve when no provision has been made for a substitute tribunal. Resort to the rule of necessity may well induce a court to intensify judicial review.

Combining Prosecuting With Judging.—Judging should not be contaminated by allowing officers who judge to perform inconsistent functions such as prosecuting. Yet the modern administrative agency, as is often pointed out, is sometimes the investigator, accuser, prosecutor, judge, jury and executioner. How can this be justified?

The answer is that incompatible functions ought not to be combined in individuals, but no principle is opposed to a combination of functions in large and complex organizations. After all, in a typical criminal case the governmental unit both prosecutes and judges—through the prosecuting attorney and the judge—and no harm results. When an agency keeps separate the staffs engaged in prosecuting and those engaged in judging, the cry of improper combination of functions may have emotional appeal but it is unsound.

Yet, on a subtler basis, the ways in which incompatible functions may be fused are numerous and intricate. Insulation of individuals from personal contact with those who perform incompatible functions may not be enough separation; access to files containing the products of investigation or advocacy might disqualify. Agency heads often read investigators' reports in approving prosecutions and later serve as judges in the same cases. Sometimes the same individual serves as prosecutor in one case and as deciding officer in the next. Advocates and deciding officers may both serve on the staff of the same immediate superior—or of the same remote superior. A supervisor of a staff of advocates may give advice to the agency on questions of law or policy. Research staffs may prepare studies to assist prosecutors and then advise agency heads on the same subject. Staff members may testify as experts at hearings and later give informal advice on the same questions to the deciding officers. These samples of the problem's many facets show that a broadside condemnation or approval of combination of functions is likely to be the product of ignorance. The problem calls for many highly particularized solutions.

By and large, the courts have failed to provide leadership in working out solutions. The controlling cases in the U.S. have held, with few exceptions, that the combination of judging and prosecuting does not deny due process. The U.S. congress has taken several inconsistent positions for different agencies, the most important position being that functions may be combined in agencies but must be separated among individuals within agencies.

Evidence.—The Anglo-American system of law is unique in the world in the extent to which relevant evidence is excluded from consideration. The most important rule in numbers of exclusions is the rule requiring, with exceptions, that hearsay be excluded. Hearsay is any written or oral statement made outside the tribunal and offered for the truth of what is asserted. The hearsay rule is based upon the needs, real or supposed, of protecting untrained jurors from relevant but possibly misleading evidence.

Because the hearsay rule and some other exclusionary rules are based upon the jury system, they are and should be usually inapplicable to administrative proceedings. But they persist to a considerable extent in judge-tried cases, both in England and the U.S., and they still have a good deal of effect in administrative proceedings. Yet the hearsay rule is unknown to the law of the rest of the world except the nations whose legal systems are based upon the English system.

Throughout the Anglo-American system of law, the direction of movement with respect to problems of evidence in all types of tribunals is toward (1) replacing rules with discretion, (2) admitting all evidence that seems to the presiding officer relevant and useful and (3) relying upon "the kind of evidence on which responsible persons are accustomed to rely in serious affairs." The movement has generally gone farther in administrative proceedings than in court proceedings. No good reason can be given for a holding that a rule designed to govern admissibility of evidence before a jury should govern evaluation of evidence before an agency. The alternative to such a holding is not to compel an agency to rely upon hearsay; it is to allow the agency to use its judgment as to whether or not particular hearsay is sufficiently reliable in the circumstances.

Official Notice.—Anyone who uses judgment either about fact-finding or about lawmaking must draw upon previous experience; the determination cannot be limited to the facts in the particular record. When a court properly takes facts from outside the record, it "takes judicial notice" of the facts; similarly, an agency "takes official notice" of extrarecord facts. No other major problem of administrative law surpasses in practical importance the problem of use of extrarecord information in an adjudication.

The cardinal principle of fair hearing that comes into play is not that all facts used should be in the record unless they are indisputable, nor that, as the U.S. supreme court several times has asserted, "nothing can be treated as evidence which is not introduced as such," but it is that parties should have opportunity to meet in the appropriate fashion all facts that influence the disposition of the case. What the appropriate fashion is depends upon three main variables—how far the facts are from the center of the controversy between the parties, the extent to which the facts are adjudicative facts about the parties or legislative facts of a general character, and the degree of certainty or doubt about the facts. Nothing short of bringing the facts into the record, so that an unabridged opportunity is allowed for cross-examination and for presentation of rebuttal evidence, will suffice for disputed adjudicative facts at the center of the controversy. Debatable and critical legislative facts probably need not always be brought into the record, but such facts should be subject to challenge through briefs and arguments, and the tribunal should have a discretionary power to determine whether cross-examination is appropriate in the circumstances. The most obvious facts often may be used without even stating that they are being noticed; 99% of the facts a tribunal uses come from outside the record without mention—that trains run on rails, that coal is not a food, that France is not a part of China, that a man is never 60 ft. tall.

When an officer who is studying a record finds that additional information is both needed and readily available, either from agency files or from agency specialists, a rule forbidding him to go beyond the record will almost surely defeat either the objective of assuring informed decisions or the equally meritorious objective of assuring parties a fair hearing; for if he obeys the rule available information will be kept out of the case, and if he violates the rule he will almost surely act surreptitiously and thereby deprive parties of a chance to meet the extrarecord information. To encourage the officer to use the information and to summarize it in his report will produce a superior substantive result and will also provide a better protection for the parties' procedural rights, for the parties then have opportunity to present argument about the new information or to move to reopen the hearing for cross-examination and rebuttal evidence.

Tort Liability of Governmental Units.—The governments of continental Europe have long made themselves liable for torts their agents commit against private parties. But in both England and the U.S., the prevailing doctrine has been that "the king can do no wrong." For instance, a pedestrian injured by the negligence of a driver may collect damages if the vehicle is owned by a private corporation but not if it is owned by the government. The doctrine of sovereign immunity came into U.S. law through judicial decisions but without a deliberate choice; the supreme court acknowledged in 1882 that "while the exemption of the United States and of the several states from being subjected as defendants to ordinary actions in the courts has since that time been repeatedly asserted here, the principle has never been discussed or the reasons for it given, but it has always been treated as an established doctrine."

Tort liability of the U.S. and British governments was at last established, with some exceptions, by the Federal Tort Claims act of 1946 and the Crown Proceedings act of 1947. But most U.S. state and local governments retain a large degree of sovereign immunity; a good deal remains to be done to make governmental units liable in tort whenever a private party would be liable in the same circumstances.

The problem that is in need of further study is the planning of a system of liability and immunity with respect to functions that have no private counterpart.

Officers' Tort Liability.—The central principle that takes care of the great bulk of practical problems concerning tort liability of public officers and public employees is that officers are generally immune from liability for their unintentional fault in the exercise of discretionary functions. By and large, the law both in England and the U.S. is the antithesis of A. V. Dicey's proposition that "every official, from the Prime Minister down to a constable or a collector of taxes, is under the same responsi-

bility for every act done without legal justification as any other citizen." It is doubtful that English courts at any time would have held the prime minister liable personally on account of an exercise of discretionary power.

Some cases hold that an officer exercising discretionary power may be liable for malicious action; the U.S. supreme court has held, five to four, that such an officer is not liable even for malicious action. Some cases hold that such an officer may be liable for tortious action in excess of his jurisdiction.

An employee performing ministerial acts has long been liable for his own torts even when he works for a governmental authority. But the supreme court has held that the government, after it had been held liable under the Tort Claims act for an employee's negligence in driving a government automobile, cannot recover indemnity from the employee.

Judicial Review.—When private rights are at stake, administrative action is usually subject to a limited judicial review, although some administrative action is unreviewable and some is subject to *de novo* review. A limited judicial review does not weaken the administrative process but strengthens it. Cutting off what the courts have to offer to a governmental program may violate the cardinal principle that functions should be allocated between courts and agencies on the basis of comparative qualifications of each tribunal. And a check upon administrative authority is usually desirable for the same reasons that an appellate court's check upon a trial court is desirable.

Subject to exceptions and qualifications, a party who seeks judicial review of administrative action (1) must exhaust his administrative remedies; (2) must satisfy the requirements of ripeness for review (so that the issues will be real and present, not hypothetical or remote); (3) must have standing to obtain review (*i.e.*, be properly qualified as a moving party); (4) must choose an appropriate form of proceeding; and (5) must satisfy the requirements of reviewability. The law of each of these four categories is highly technical and complex.

Although the scope of review of administrative action ranges from complete unreviewability to complete substitution of judicial judgment on all questions, the dominant tendency is toward a middle position under which the court decides issues of law but upholds discretionary determinations and findings of fact if they are reasonable.

Broadly, questions of law include not only common law, statutory interpretation and constitutional law but also questions of administrative jurisdiction, of fair administrative procedure and of protection against arbitrary or capricious action or abuse of discretion.

In general, the scope of review of administrative findings of fact is about the same as the scope of review of jury verdicts, but it is slightly narrower than the scope of review of findings made by a judge without a jury.

Unlike England, the U.S. has constitutional limits, both minimum and maximum, on judicial review. Two doctrines that have been important but are in process of dying are that a public utility which claims confiscation from a rate order is entitled to an independent judicial determination of both law and fact, and that a party to a workmen's compensation case is entitled to a judicial determination of facts on which constitutionality or the agency's jurisdiction depends. The maximum constitutional limit prevents a court from doing all over again what an agency has done in the exercise of nonjudicial functions.

Because review of law is broader than review of facts, the law-fact distinction becomes vital. But what is law and what is fact does not always reflect a literal meaning of those terms. Courts often decide on functional grounds whether or not substitution of judicial judgment is desirable; if it is, the question is called a question of law, and if it is not, the question is called a question of fact. The tendency to allocate powers between agencies and courts on the basis of policy considerations and then to attach labels accordingly resembles what common-law courts did centuries ago when they used policy reasons in dividing functions between judges and juries and then called jury questions "fact" and judge questions "law." Thus, what is fact and what is law is not a question of fact but a highly artificial question of law.

The principal consideration that determines the extent to which a court substitutes judgment for an agency's judgment is the comparative qualification of the court and of the agency on the particular question. When a problem of radio engineering has been decided by radio engineers who are members of the Federal Communications commission's staff, legally trained judges can hardly be expected to try to substitute their judgment, even though the specialists' determination may well be checked by the judges. However, substitution of judicial judgment is desirable in many categories of cases, including those involving problems which (1) transcend the single field of the particular agency, (2) call for interpretation of the common law, (3) are primarily problems of ethics or fairness of a common-law type, (4) are affected substantially by constitutional considerations, whether or not a constitutional issue is directly presented, (5) require analysis of legislative history, especially when political conflict is the essence and not legislative inquiry into technical understanding within the agency's field of specialization, (6) bring into question judge-made law previously developed in the course of statutory interpretation and (7) impel the reviewing court to make a discretionary choice for any reason, explained or unexplained, to create or mold law as a guide for the agency and for affected parties. *See also* REGULATORY AGENCIES COMMISSION. For administrative law on the Continent, *see* FRANCE: *History: Administration and Social Conditions: Government;* GERMAN LAW; ITALIAN LAW; etc.

BIBLIOGRAPHY.—Kenneth Culp Davis, *Administrative Law Treatise,* 4 vol. (1958); William A. Robson, *Justice and Administrative Law,* 3rd ed. (1951); James M. Landis, *The Administrative Process* (1938); Walter Gellhorn, *Federal Administrative Proceedings* (1941), *Individual Freedom and Governmental Restraints* (1956); J. A. G. Griffith and H. Street, *Principles of Administrative Law,* 2nd ed. (1957); Robert M. Benjamin, *Administrative Adjudication in the State of New York* (1942); Sir Cecil Thomas Carr, *Concerning English Administrative Law* (1941); Robert E. Cushman, *The Independent Regulatory Commissions* (1941); John Dickinson, *Administrative Justice and the Supremacy of Law in the United States* (1927); Ernst Freund, *Administrative Powers Over Persons and Property* (1928); Charles A. Horsky, *The Washington Lawyer* (1952); Emmette S. Redford (ed.), *Public Administration and Policy Formation* (1956); Attorney General's Committee on Administrative Procedure, *Report* (1941; with 27 monographs on particular agencies); British Committee on Ministers' Powers, *Report* (1932); British Committee on Administrative Tribunals and Enquiries, *Report* (1957); Commission on Organization of the Executive Branch of the Government (first Hoover commission), *Report* and *Task Force Report on Regulatory Commissions* (1949); President's Conference on Administrative Procedure, *Report* (1953); Commission on Organization of the Executive Branch of the Government (second Hoover commission), *Report on Legal Services and Procedure* (1955), and accompanying *Task Force Report*; Louis L. Jaffe, "The Effective Limits of the Administrative Process," *Harvard Law Review,* 67:1105 (1954); Ralph F. Fuchs, "Concepts and Policies in Anglo-American Administrative Law Theory," *Yale Law Journal,* 47:538 (1938); Felix Frankfurter, "The Task of Administrative Law," *University of Pennsylvania Law Review,* 75:614 (1927); Nathaniel L. Nathanson, "Central Issues of American Administrative Law," *American Political Science Review,* 45:348 (1951).　　(K. C. DA.)

ADMIRAL, the title and rank of a senior naval officer, often referred to as a flag officer, who commands a fleet or group of ships of a navy, or who holds an important naval post on shore. The term is sometimes also applied to the commander of a fleet of merchant vessels or fishing ships.

The title has an ancient lineage. It apparently originated with Muslim Arabs who combined *amir* ("commander"), the article *al,* and *bahr* ("sea"), to make *amir-al-bahr,* before the 12th century. Shortened to *amiral* it was adopted for naval use by the Sicilians. The French copied the word from the Genoese during the crusade of 1249. The Latin word *admirabilis* helped to produce the title admiral for the commander of the Cinque Ports (*q.v.*) in England before the end of the 13th century.

In Europe it became the title of a great officer of the crown: in France as *grand amiral,* in Spain as *almirante mayor,* and in England as lord high admiral. The noblemen who held these posts were not seamen and did not command at sea except on rare occasions; they were heads of departments that administered naval

affairs. They were responsible for providing ships for war and their duties usually brought them large fees. They also had jurisdiction in legal cases of the types afterward handled by admiralty courts. (*See* ADMIRALTY; ADMIRALTY, HIGH COURT OF.)

By 1620 the word admiral was used in England to denote a commander at sea. In that year the fleet was formed into three squadrons with the admiral commanding the centre squadron, his ships flying red ensigns. The vice-admiral in the van squadron flew white ensigns and the rear admiral flew blue ensigns in his squadron. By 1660 the fleet had grown so large that three divisions were created in each squadron and at the same time the white squadron was placed in the van and the blue squadron in the rear. There were then nine flag officers of the Royal Navy: an admiral of the fleet; admirals of the white and blue; vice-admirals of the red, white and blue; and rear admirals of the red, white and blue.

In 1718 the title admiral of the fleet ceased to be an office and became a rank. In later times it corresponded to the rank of field marshal in the army or marshal of the Royal Air Force. The rank of admiral corresponded to general or air chief marshal; vice-admiral corresponded to lieutenant general or air marshal; and rear admiral corresponded to major general or air vice-marshal. After 1864, ships of the Royal Navy flew the white ensign and the designation of admirals of the red, white and blue ended.

The U.S. navy had no admirals before the Civil War, the highest rank in those years being commodore. On July 16, 1862, congress authorized appointment of four rear admirals on the active list and eight on the retired list. David G. Farragut became the first officer of the U.S. navy to be promoted to the rank of vice-admiral, on Dec. 21, 1864. He attained the rank of admiral on July 25, 1866. David D. Porter succeeded him in these ranks, and Stephen C. Rowan succeeded as vice-admiral.

On March 3, 1899, following his notable service during the Spanish-American War, George Dewey was promoted to a new rank, admiral of the navy. Laws enacted in 1915 provided that the chief of naval operations and three commanders in chief of fleets were to hold the rank of admiral while serving in these positions. The laws also provided for three vice-admirals in the three fleets. In Dec. 1944 congress created a new rank, fleet admiral, and bestowed it upon three officers, William D. Leahy, Ernest J. King and Chester W. Nimitz. William F. Halsey was promoted to this rank a year later. Without additional legislation no other officer could be promoted to this rank. A fleet admiral ranks with a general of the army or general of the air force. Admiral ranks with general, vice-admiral with lieutenant general and rear admiral with major general. A fleet admiral's flag is blue with five white stars. An admiral's flag has four stars, a vice-admiral's three and a rear admiral's two. A rear admiral of the medical corps commanding a naval hospital flies a white flag with two blue stars; a rear admiral of the supply corps flies the same flag over a naval supply depot. Rank insignia for U.S. or British admirals consist of a broad gold stripe encircling the lower sleeve with one or more (depending on rank) narrower stripes above it (*see* INSIGNIA, MILITARY).

The Royal Navy appointed a second admiral of the fleet in 1862, a third in 1863. The number rose to four in 1898 and after World War II it increased until there were 16 in 1958. Admirals in the Royal Navy are not flag officers unless appointed as such; but they are officers of flag rank. The union flag is flown at the mainmast head by an admiral of the fleet. The flag of an admiral is the St. George's cross, that of a vice-admiral the cross with one red ball and that of a rear admiral the cross with two red balls.

(J. B. HN.)

ADMIRALTY. In Great Britain the board of admiralty, usually referred to simply as "the admiralty," is the government department that manages naval affairs. It corresponds in a general way to the navy department in the United States and to the ministry of marine in France. It is served by the admiralty divisions of the naval staff and by admiralty departments that deal with such matters as the provision of warships, aircraft, munitions, manning of ships, and the general organization and administration of the fleets and shore establishments.

The admiralty is unlike the ordinary British government departments, which are under a secretary of state or minister with powers defined by act of parliament. In ancient times the navy was governed by a "great officer of state" called the lord high admiral of England. Early in the 18th century the office was placed in the hands of commissioners known as the board of admiralty, and with rare exceptions has so remained ever since. Thus the board of admiralty derives its powers from the royal prerogative; no act of parliament defines or circumscribes them, except inasmuch as the discipline of the navy is regulated by a Naval Discipline act. In pure law, the commissioners share a joint and equal responsibility, but an order in council of 1869 conferred upon the first lord of the admiralty overriding powers and responsibilities.

In the late 1950s the "commissioners for executing the office of lord high admiral of the United Kingdom" were ten in number. Three of them were members of parliament; six were naval officers; and one was the permanent secretary. Each of the lords commissioners has special duties and responsibilities. The first lord of the admiralty must by law be a member of parliament, sitting in either the upper or lower house, and a privy councillor. He is the minister responsible to parliament for the navy. The first sea lord is chief of the naval staff and is the principal adviser to the government on professional naval matters. The second sea lord is chief of naval personnel and the third sea lord is the controller, responsible for engineering, equipment, ordnance and research. The fourth sea lord deals with supplies and transport and the fifth sea lord has responsibility for naval aviation.

The other commissioners are the vice chief of the naval staff, the parliamentary and financial secretary (a member of parliament), the civil lord (also a member of parliament), and the permanent secretary. The latter is the senior civil servant in the admiralty with responsibility for the general conduct of admiralty business. The titles indicate the nature of the duties and responsibilities of the members. The first lord, the civil lord and the parliamentary and financial secretary resign automatically whenever the prime minister resigns, and the resignations of the sea lords may also occur at the same time. The composition of the board of admiralty can be changed by order in council, and has in practice varied widely in modern times depending on the needs of the moment. In general, the board has been enlarged in time of war by the addition of a deputy first sea lord, by separating the offices of parliamentary and financial secretary, and by other devices to secure the presence on the board of men with specialized knowledge.

Another way in which the admiralty differs from the other British service ministries is that it functions as an operational authority, sometimes actually issuing direct orders to ships at sea. This has been so for three centuries, and before the close of the 18th century a chain of mechanical telegraphs linked the admiralty in Whitehall to the principal naval ports. Another relic of earlier times is the wind direction indicator in the board room, operated from a weather cock on the roof of the old building. The advent of wireless telegraphy greatly increased the practice of direct control from the admiralty. During World War I, an order in council gave power to the first sea lord, acting in conjunction with one other sea lord, to issue operational orders to fleets and ships. During World War II, an operational plot of all shipping in the Atlantic and home waters was kept at the admiralty, and frequent interventions were made from Whitehall in the hour-to-hour conduct of operations at sea. Although this practice has been criticized by postwar historians, the fact remains that the admiralty's advice and warning to ships operating in enemy waters concerning the movements of hostile ships and aircraft was usually prompt and accurate to an extraordinary degree.

The admiralty is responsible for the government's economic policy in the shipbuilding and ship repair industries, and in certain minor allied industries. It undertakes research to meet naval requirements and administers both the Royal observatory and the National Institute of Oceanography.

The military and civilian staff of the admiralty was much increased in numbers during World War II and in successive years,

and was not afterward cut back to its prewar level. The admiralty building in Whitehall, London, adjoining the Horse Guards, dates from 1722–26, while the quadrangle in the rear along the north side of the Horse Guards parade was added after 1887. The admiralty arch at the end of the mall was completed in 1910. Bombproof additions to the quadrangle were made in the years 1930–42 to house the operational plotting activities.

BIBLIOGRAPHY.—The work and organization of the admiralty are described in a series of articles by Sir Oswyn Murray in *Mariner's Mirror,* the journal of the Society for Nautical Research (1937–39). *See* also S. W. Roskill, *The War at Sea 1939–45,* vol. i (1954); T. K. Derry, *The Campaign in Norway* (1952); *Britain, an Official Handbook* (1958). (J. B. Hn.)

ADMIRALTY, HIGH COURT OF.

The high court of admiralty of England was the court of the deputy or lieutenant of the admiral. It is supposed in the *Black Book of the Admiralty* to have been founded in the reign of Edward I; but it appears that it was established as a civil court by Edward III in the year 1360, the power of the admiral to determine matters of discipline in the fleet, and possibly questions of piracy and prize, being somewhat earlier. At first there were separate admirals or rear admirals of the north, south and west, each with deputies and courts. These were merged in or absorbed by one high court early in the 15th century. Sir Thomas Beaufort, appointed admiral of the fleet 1407, and admiral of England, Ireland and Aquitaine 1412, certainly had a court, with a marshal and other officers, and forms of legal process—mandates, warrants, citations, compulsories, proxies, etc.

Jurisdiction.—The original object of the institution of the courts or court seems to have been to prevent or punish piracy and other crimes upon the narrow seas and to deal with questions of prize; but civil jurisdiction soon followed. The jurisdiction in criminal matters was transferred by the Offences at Sea act, 1536, to the admiral or his deputy and three or four other substantial persons appointed by the lord chancellor, who were to proceed according to the course of the common law. By the Central Criminal Court act, 1834, cognizance of crimes committed within the jurisdiction of the admiralty was given to the central criminal court. By an act of 1844 it was also given to the justices of assize; and crimes done within the jurisdiction of the admiralty are now tried as crimes committed within the body of a county.

The early jurisdiction of the court appears to have been exercised very much under the same procedure as that used by the courts of common law. Juries are mentioned, sometimes of the county and sometimes of the county and merchants. But the connection with foreign parts led to the gradual introduction of a procedure resembling that coming into use on the Continent and based on the Roman civil law.

Restraining Acts.—The material enactments of the restraining statutes were as follows: An act of 1389 (13 Ric. II c. 5) provided that "the admirals and their deputies shall not meddle from henceforth of anything done within the realm, but only of a thing done upon the sea, as it hath been used in the time of the noble prince king Edward, grandfather of our lord the king that now is." The act of 1391 (15 Ric. II c. 3) provided that "of all manner of contracts, pleas and quarrels, and other things rising within the bodies of the counties as well by land as by water, and also of wreck of the sea, the admiral's court shall have no manner of cognizance, power, nor jurisdiction; but all such manner of contracts, pleas and quarrels, and other things rising within the bodies of counties, as well by land as by water, as afore, and also wreck of the sea, shall be tried, determined, discussed and remedied by the laws of the land, and not before nor by the admiral, nor his lieutenant in any wise." The statutes of Richard, except the enabling part of the second, were repealed by the Civil Procedure Acts Repeal act, 1879. The formation of a high court of justice rendered them obsolete.

In the reign of James I the chronic controversies between the courts of common law and the admiralty court as to the limits of their respective jurisdictions reached an acute stage. It is recorded that, notwithstanding an agreement asserted to have been made in 1575 between the justices of the king's bench and the judge of the admiralty, the judges of the common law courts successfully maintained their right to prohibit suits in admiralty upon contracts made on shore, or within havens, or creeks, or tidal rivers, if the waters were within the body of any county, wheresoever such contracts were broken, as well as for torts committed within the body of a county, whether on land or water, and for contracts made in parts beyond the seas.

Judge's Patent.—All the while, however, the patents of the admiralty judge purported to confer on him a far ampler jurisdiction than the jealousy of the other courts would concede to him. The patent of the last judge of the court, Sir Robert Joseph Phillimore, dated Aug. 23, 1867, gave to him power to take cognizance of "all causes, civil and maritime, also all contracts, complaints, offences or suspected offences, crimes, pleas, debts, exchanges, accounts, policies of assurance, loading of ships, and all other matters and contracts which relate to freight due for the use of ships, transportation, money or bottomry; also all suits civil and maritime between merchants or between proprietors of ships and other vessels for matters in, upon, or by the sea, or public streams, or fresh-water ports, rivers, nooks and places overflown whatsoever within the ebbing and flowing of the sea, and high-water mark, or upon any of the shores or banks adjacent from any of the first bridges towards the sea through England and Ireland and the dominions thereof, or elsewhere beyond the seas." Power is also given to hear appeals from vice-admirals; also "to arrest . . . according to the civil laws and ancient customs of our high court . . . all ships, persons, things, goods, wares and merchandise"; also "to enquire by the oaths of honest and lawful men . . . of all . . . things which . . . ought to be enquired after, and to mulct, arrest, punish, chastise, and reform"; also "to preserve the public streams of our admiralty as well for the preservation of our royal navy, and of the fleets and vessels of our kingdom . . . as of whatsoever fishes increasing in the rivers"; also "to reform nets too straight and other unlawful engines and instruments whatsoever for the catching of fishes"; also to take cognizance "of the wreck of the sea . . . and of the death, drowning and view of dead bodies," and the conservation of the statutes concerning wreck of the sea and the office of coroner (1276), and concerning pillages (1353), and "the cognizance of mayhem" within the ebb and flow of the tide.

Later Developments.—The contention of the common law judges prevailed, and the admiralty court (except for a temporary revival under Cromwell) sank into comparative insignificance during the 17th century. The great maritime wars of the 18th century gave scope to the exercise of its prize jurisdiction; and its international importance as a prize court in the latter half of the 18th and the first part of the 19th centuries is a matter of common historical knowledge. There were upwards of 1,000 to 2,000 prize causes each year between 1803 and 1811.

In the reign of Queen Victoria, two enabling statutes, 1840 and 1861, were passed and greatly enlarged the jurisdiction of the court. The manner in which these statutes were administered by Dr. Stephen Lushington and Sir R. J. Phillimore, whose tenure of office covered the whole period of the queen's reign till the creation of the high court of justice, the valuable assistance rendered by the nautical assessors from the Trinity House, the great increase of shipping, especially of steam shipping, and the number and gravity of cases of collision, salvage and damage to cargo, restored the activity of the court and made it one of the most important tribunals of the country. In 1875, by the operation of the Judicature acts of 1873 and 1875, the high court of admiralty was with the other great courts of England formed into the high court of justice. The principal officers of the court in subordination to the judge were the registrar (an office which always points to a connection with canon or civil law), and the marshal, who acted as the maritime sheriff, having for his baton of office a silver oar. The assistance of the Trinity masters was provided for in the charter of incorporation of the Trinity House. These officers and their assistance have been preserved in the high court of justice.

Practitioners in the Court.—Till the year 1859 the practitioners in the high court of admiralty were the same as those in the ecclesiastical courts and distinct from those who practised in the ordinary courts. Advocates took the place of barristers, and proctors of solicitors. The place of the attorney general was taken by the king's or queen's advocate general, and that of the treasury solicitor by the king's or queen's procurator or proctor. There were also an admiralty advocate and an admiralty proctor.

In an act of 1859 the practice was thrown open to barristers and to attorneys and solicitors.

Upon the next vacancy after the courts were thrown open, the crown altered the precedence and placed the queen's advocate after the attorney general and solicitor general. There were two holders of the office under these conditions, Sir R. J. Phillimore and Sir Travers Twiss. The office was not filled up after the resignation of the latter, nor was the office of admiralty advocate filled up when next it became vacant.

Ireland.—The high court of admiralty of Ireland, being formed on the same pattern as the high court in England, sat in the Four courts, Dublin, having a judge, a registrar, a marshal and a king's or queen's advocate. In peace time and war time alike it exercised only an instance jurisdiction, though in 1793 it claimed to exercise prize jurisdiction. No prize commission ever issued to it. By the Irish Judicature act of 1877 it was directed that it should be amalgamated with the Irish high court of justice upon the next vacancy in the office of judge, and this subsequently took place. There was no separate lord high admiral for Ireland.

Scotland.—At the union, while the national functions of the lord high admiral were merged in the English office it was provided by the Act of Union that the court of admiralty in Scotland should be continued "for determination of all maritime cases relating to private rights in Scotland competent to the jurisdiction of the Admiralty Court." This court continued until 1831, when its civil jurisdiction was given to the court of session and the sheriffs' courts. *See also* MARITIME LAW. (P.; X.)

ADMIRALTY ISLANDS, a group of about 40 islands in the southwest Pacific about 380 mi. N.W. of Rabaul, New Britain. The group forms a northwest extension of the Bismarck archipelago and has an area of 800 sq.mi. With other small island groups to the west and southwest it constitutes the Manus administrative district of the trust territory of New Guinea (*q.v.*), administered by the commonwealth of Australia.

The only large island is Manus, or Great Admiralty Island, which is about 50 mi. long and 17 mi. wide. The highest point is Mt. Dremsel (2,356 ft.) in the southcentral part of the island; many ridges reach heights above 1,000 ft. Lowlands are restricted to the narrow east coast plain and the lower river valleys. Most of the island is densely forested, with mangroves along the coasts. The coasts are fringed with coral, which also composes most of the other islands.

Seeadler harbour on the northeast coast is a good natural harbour, and near it is Lorengau, the administrative centre. The indigenous population of the islands, of Melanesian affinities, numbered 20,202 in 1966; three major groups of people can be distinguished. After World War II Manus became a centre of the so-called "cargo-cults" (*see* NEW GUINEA: *Anthropology*). The nonindigenous population numbered 840, of whom fewer than 50 were Europeans. The only important product is copra. The coconut plantations are all long-established, but were considerably reduced in area after World War II. Fishing and local trading are carried on by the natives in outrigger canoes.

The islands were first sighted by Willem Cornelis Schouten in 1616 and were named by Capt. Philip Carteret in 1767. They became part of the German protectorate in 1884, were occupied by the Australians in 1914 and were included in the territory mandated to Australia in 1921. Taken by the Japanese in 1942, they were liberated in March 1944. *See also* PACIFIC ISLANDS.
(D. W. F.)

ADMIRALTY JURISDICTION. The judicial power vested in the U.S. federal courts by the constitution extends "to all Cases of admiralty and maritime Jurisdiction," and by act of congress this jurisdiction is explicitly withheld from the courts of the states. The exclusiveness of the federal jurisdiction is, however, greatly modified by an exception, "saving to suitors in all cases all other remedies to which they are otherwise entitled."

In practical effect, while any admiralty or maritime case may be maintained in a federal court, any civil maritime case except a libel *in rem* may be maintained in a state court. *See* MARITIME LAW. (B. CE.)

ADOBE is a Spanish word for sun-dried clay bricks (*q.v.*); it also applies to a structure built from such bricks and to the clay soil from which the brick or structure is made. It comes from the Arabic word *atob* meaning "sun-dried brick." Adobe is basically a calcareous, sandy clay, having good plastic qualities and drying to a hard uniform mass. Its use (or that of clays with similar properties) dates back many thousands of years in several parts of the world, particularly those areas with an arid or semi-arid climate. Techniques varied, but all took advantage of the special properties of adobe.

This use of earth for building construction resulted partly from the scarcity of wood as a building medium, partly from the ease of such construction and its insulation value against both heat and cold. Adobe or sun-dried bricks are found in the old world in the dry areas east of the Mediterranean sea, in north Africa and in southern Spain. In the western hemisphere adobe appears in many of the pre-Columbian sites from the U.S. southwest to Peru, always, again, in those regions with a dry climate. The American aborigines built walls by hand manipulation of the plastic clay into courses, allowing each course to dry before adding the next. Forms such as are necessary for rammed earth or concrete construction were not used.

Sometimes the bricks were hand shaped and more or less loaf-like. Molds for shaping the bricks, probably introduced into Spain from Africa, came to the new world at the time of the Spanish conquest.

The usual modern method of making adobe is very simple. It consists of wetting a quantity of suitable soil and allowing it to stand for a day or more to soften and break up clods. A small quantity of straw or other fibrous material is added and the materials are mixed with a hoe or similar implement. The mass is then trampled with the bare feet.

When it is brought to the proper consistency, the adobe is shaped into bricks in simple molds. The molds, made of smooth lumber or sheet metal, are four-sided and open at the top and bottom. Although they vary widely in size, depending on the intended use of the finished brick, they are usually from 3 to 5 in. thick, 10 or 12 in. wide and 14 to 20 in. long. The plastic adobe must be moist enough to fill the mold completely but not too wet to prevent its easy removal. The bricks are allowed to dry partially while flat on the ground; then they are stacked on edge to permit more thorough and uniform drying. The bricks are not used until thoroughly dry. This usually takes at least two weeks under average dry climate conditions. The addition of straw or similar material helps to prevent shrinkage cracks during the curing process but does not add any structural advantage to the finished product.

Adobe walls should be built on a solid, waterproof foundation of stone or concrete because otherwise the capillary action of ground water will cause the lower courses to disintegrate. The bricks are laid in a mortar of the same material, then finished with a coat of adobe, or sometimes with lime or cement plaster. With care in construction and protection against moisture by proper attention to repair, an adobe wall is very enduring. Some such walls, centuries old, are still in use.

The chief advantages of adobe as a building material lie in its availability in dry regions; its relative cheapness, particularly when labour costs are low; and its remarkable insulation properties.

The physical properties of adobe when tested as a building material indicate an optimum value for one-story structures with a possible limitation to three or four stories.

BIBLIOGRAPHY.—R. H. Clough, *Qualitative Comparison of Rammed Earth and Sun-Dried Adobe Brick,* University of New Mexico Publications in Engineering no. 4 (with bibliography, 1950); T. T. Eyre, "Physical Properties of Adobe Used as a Building Material," *University of New Mexico Bulletin,* Engineering Series, vol. 1, no. 3 (1935); S. A. Stubbs, *Bird's-Eye View of the Pueblos* (1950); E. Huntington, *Principles of Human Geography* (1940). (S. A. Ss.)

ADOBE SOIL, a term used in the western United States, particularly in California, to designate the structural quality of various clay soils, referring usually to the characteristic breakage of such soil material into small angular blocks when it dries. These soils are very heavy in texture, being composed of extremely fine-grained material, a large part of which is colloidal. Sands and loose sandy loams, for example, never display an adobe soil structure. Under proper conditions of moisture, soils of adobe structure are readily worked, but when too dry their hardness and coherence make tillage extremely difficult. When placed under irrigation, soils of this type usually display great fertility. For adobe building materials, *see* ADOBE.

ADOLESCENCE is usually defined as the period of transition between childhood and adulthood. Although some writers equate adolescence with puberty and the cycle of physical changes culminating in reproductive maturity, a more common view is to define adolescence in psychological and social terms as beginning with pubescence and terminating vaguely with "adulthood." Perhaps a better usage of the term is as a convenient label referring to a period of years (approximately ages 12 to 20) in the life of an individual, since such usage makes no a priori commitments regarding the character of adolescent development or the specific nature of the causal variables (*e.g.,* pubescence).

Any period of life tends to be characterized by a group of developmental problems which are biological, psychological and social in origin and timing. Among those which typically but not necessarily occur during the second decade of life are adjustments in the areas of heterosexual relations, occupational orientation, the development of a mature set of values and the development of responsible self-direction and the breaking of close emotional ties to parents. In a sense, such developmental tasks define adolescence and represent areas in which satisfactory adjustments must be made if future psychological development is to be possible.

Interpretations of Adolescence.—Authorities are not in agreement as to the nature of adolescence. To the popular mind and to many specialists, adolescence is presumed to be a psychologically stressful and critical period, characterized by a variety of special types of behaviour.

According to one viewpoint, essentially biological and stemming mainly from psychoanalytic literature, adolescence is initiated at pubescence by the sudden upsurge of sex feelings following the sexually tranquil period of latency. Adolescence is the period when the individual is learning to control and properly direct his sex urges and is terminated when such control and direction are established. The whole process is presumed to be highly stressful emotionally and to give rise to a variety of behaviours, ranging from avoidance of the opposite sex to the writing of diaries, which are thought to be characteristic of adolescence and which serve to reduce the sex-generated anxiety. A biological view of adolescence implies a certain universality of occurrence.

Cultural views, while typically assuming adolescence to be stressful, nonetheless specify that "adolescence" will occur only under certain circumstances. It is asserted that quite generally children are not given gradually graded opportunities for maturing experiences compatible with their physical and intellectual development, and thus they experience a sudden widening of their world during their teens. This relatively sudden encountering of new ideas, new concepts, new values, new types of people, as well as the relatively sudden responsibility for self-determination and self-sufficiency, force a whole array of adjustments upon the comparatively inexperienced young person and generate much apprehensiveness and anxiety. Furthermore, the teen-ager has no defined role of his own in society but is caught in the ambiguous overlap between the reasonably clearly defined roles of childhood and adulthood. Sometimes treated as a child, sometimes expected to be adult, he is uncertain how to behave. It is also pointed out that society serves to frustrate important psychological needs of the young person (*e.g.,* sex and desire for independence), thus generating aggression or other reactions, many of a socially disapproved type. Whatever the specific formulation, cultural views recognize that adolescence, as typically defined, will exist in the degree that conditions such as the foregoing prevail in a particular culture or a particular home.

The "Storm and Stress" Hypothesis and Adolescent Behaviour.—Theories of adolescence such as the preceding may be summarized as involving (1) causal conditions either biological or cultural (sudden emergence of the sex drive, sudden widening of life space, moving into an unstructured period of life where a well-defined role does not exist) which (2) generate anxiety or emotional stress to an unusual degree compared with other age periods, which, in turn, (3) provoke a variety of defensive behaviours or symptoms which constitute "typical" adolescent characteristics. Since in one way or another, explicitly or not, many professional and most popular views of adolescence assume some such sequence as the foregoing, the conception requires careful consideration and evaluation.

As will be noted later with respect to the first of these three phases, there is serious question as to whether the biological and cultural conditions assumed by various interpretations are in fact present. With respect to the second phase, actual data suggest that emotional stress is much less than ordinarily assumed; in fact, most studies involving sufficiently large samples of subjects and a wide enough age perspective show no increased incidence of anxiety symptoms associated either with pubescence or with the teens. Surveys of frequency of worries, observations of emotional episodes in classrooms, actual counts and questionnaire surveys of specific nervous symptoms, as well as data derived from specialized psychological tests (*e.g.*, the Rorschach ink-blot test), reveal no increased emotional disturbance. One extensive study (based on 3,300 subjects) led to the conclusion that while age gains were evident over the range 9 to 17 years, in measures reflecting competence (skill, problem solving, work habits) there were no increases correlating with age in measures relating to feelings and emotions.

The picture is not entirely one-sided, however. In one study 9th and 12th graders had more unpleasant and fewer pleasant experiences than did 6th graders. In another investigation, reaction time to stimulus words such as "worry," "afraid" and "unhappy" showed a sharp increase at age 13 for girls and 14 for boys and stayed high until 17 but declined in adult years. Such inconsistent findings are difficult to interpret, but if adolescence is a period of emotional upheaval, indications should appear in most rather than in only a few studies.

With respect to the third phase of the sequence, that relating to the types of behaviours presumed to be characteristic of adolescence and generated by the presumed emotional turmoil, the evidence is no more consistent. Marked vacillation in interpersonal attachments is often assumed, yet research indicates that teen-agers are more stable in their friendships and in other respects than are younger children. It is assumed that the frustrations posed by society will lead to aggressive behaviour which may find expression in delinquency (a striking out against society) or more commonly in conflict or belligerence toward adult authority figures such as parents or teachers. In general, available evidence shows that aggressive tendencies decline with age, with no peak at adolescence. Delinquency data pose special problems of interpretation since the term has a legal rather than a psychological definition. Crime rates (as reflected in admission to penal institutions) do increase during the teens but reach a peak in the young adult years. No special relationships to pubescence or adolescence are evident in the over-all picture. Evidence bearing on parent-child relationships fails to provide convincing proof of increased belligerency (*see* below). Daydreaming, which may be construed as a means through which gratification of frustrated needs is achieved, does seem to increase during the teens and to decline in frequency in the adult years.

The psychopathology of adolescence is of interest to many, and data showing the incidence of suicide and mental illness are often cited as indicative of one outcome of adolescent turmoil. While suicide and mental illness increase markedly from the early to the late teens, there is no adolescent peak; the rate curve continues to climb in adulthood. (*See* PSYCHOLOGY, ABNORMAL.)

Physical Growth.—On the average a child enters a period of accelerated growth just prior to pubescence. The greatest increase in height is at about 11.5 years of age for girls and about 13.8 years for boys according to one study, and at 12.6 and 14.8 according to another. There is no strong evidence that the general prepubertal growth spurt or the differential timing of growth in various dimensions causes a decline in motor co-ordination. Since larger children tend to enter the period of rapid growth early, the range of differences among individuals at any given age increases until the average ages noted above for the two sexes and then decreases as the slower developers catch up. Thus children of junior high school age are more heterogeneous in size and general maturity than young people of any other age. Because of their earlier development, girls are notably taller and more mature than boys at about this age.

The mean age of first menstruation, usually taken as the age of pubescence in girls, is approximately 13. About one-sixth reach the menarche before 12 and about the same proportion after 14, and about 95% between 11 and 15 years of age. However, the first externally discernible signs of sexual development occur at about $10\frac{1}{2}$ in girls (beginning of breast development) and at just under 12 in boys (increase in size of genitalia), but adult status as judged by external developments is not reached until the average ages of just under 14 in girls and just after 15 in boys. Reproductive capacity is not achieved in girls until some time after the menarche.

It is clear from this that the cycle of sexual maturation covers a substantial period of time and, since cultural adjustments are made to the first signs, it seems unlikely that the major psychological impact of sexual maturation can be specifically located in time. This, plus evidence suggesting the probability that sex interests increase steadily during childhood (*i.e.*, that a latency period does not exist), calls into question biological interpretations of adolescence that assume a sudden upsurge of sexuality.

Sexual maturation may not be a general cause of psychological stress, but its pervasive effect upon developing behaviour is evident in changing interests and social behaviour. Boys who mature early, for example, are on the average better poised and more adult in their social interactions than are those who mature late, a difference which persists, though to a lesser degree, beyond adolescence. Where ignorance regarding the nature of the physical changes he is experiencing characterizes the individual adolescent, where there exist marked deviations (as in time) from the generality or from the cultural ideal for the particular sex group, or where rearing has generated marked guilt feelings about sex, there may well be some anxiety or maladjustment. Thus early-maturing girls (who are likely to be oversized) and late-maturing boys (who are likely to be undersized) are most apt to exhibit anxiety about their growth. Many children pass through a temporary phase of moderate obesity during the prepubertal growth spurt; this circumstance often causes emotional disturbance which presumably could be alleviated if they were made aware that the condition is probably temporary.

Culture and Adolescence.—Studies of primitive societies reveal marked differences in the ages at which various ceremonies, or rites of passage, give recognition to the individual as an adult. Variations among technological societies are also great. At about mid-20th century, to take one illustration, the proportion of males in their late teens (15–19) who were economically active was 45% in the United States, 59% in Japan, 83% in the United Kingdom, 87% in Italy and 90% in Yugoslavia. The proportions of girls in these countries who were economically active were 26%, 54%, 78%, 47% and 87%, respectively. These employment figures suggest substantial differences from culture to culture in the degree to which teen-agers occupy significant responsible roles, but equally striking contrasts are to be found within any one country between social class groups, between urban and rural areas and between races.

Cultural heterogeneity poses special problems for the modern adolescent. Reared with one set of values, he is exposed to a broad and inconsistent array of other values in the larger society as he ranges farther from home. The degree of his bewilderment will reflect the suddenness of his introduction to this larger scene.

Rapid cultural change introduces further complications. Such change may not only pave the way for intergeneration misunderstanding and conflict, but may also pose problems for the parent who is uncertain as to the ends toward which training should be directed. In certain respects—as delay of admission to full-time employment—modern societies, as typified by the United States, seem to be prolonging adolescence, but in other respects—age of marriage—young people appear to be assuming adult roles at a younger age.

Although the broad cultural setting is important in determining the ease of transitions to adult roles, parents typically have sufficient control over the course of the child's development in the restricted "culture" of the home to effect important differences in the degree to which the child is gradually provided with opportunities for maturing experiences, self-direction and responsibility, and is afforded opportunity gradually to learn the values and ways of the larger society. Since adolescence does not, in fact, seem as stressful as ordinarily assumed, it may be inferred that parents and society are actually effecting a gradual introduction of the child to his larger world. With the passage of time, at least in the United States, this seems to be increasingly true. According to one investigation, 9th graders in 1959 were as mature as were 12th graders in 1938.

Areas of Adolescent Growth and Adjustment.—If adolescence is defined essentially as an age range during which certain patterns of development and adjustment typically occur, some description of these growth trends and adjustments is necessary to complete the definition. Although, as earlier noted, existing data do not unequivocally support the concept of generalized emotional disturbance in adolescence, there does seem to be increased tension (which later subsides) associated with particular adjustment areas, a finding consistent with a developmental task conception of adolescence.

Social Development.—One of the most striking developmental changes is the increasing cleavage between the sexes up to around 12 or 13 years of age with a subsequent reversal of the trend as interest in the opposite sex emerges. Although sexual maturation probably gives impetus to this reorientation, interactions between the sexes occur in a social context and subject to social controls to such a degree that wide variations in the timing and nature of the interaction exist from culture to culture and the influence of biology may be obscured. For example, despite the early maturity of girls, in the United States dating begins on the average at 14 years of age for both sexes.

Contrary to the popular view that adolescents are notably unstable in their friendship relations, evidence indicates that each year of age brings increasing stability in social relations, reflecting a gradual and steady trend toward maturity. However, shifts during childhood and adolescence in the social desirability of certain personal characteristics may cause gradual individual shifts in degree of social acceptance and create a degree of ambiguity, making perception of one's own status difficult. On the average, girls have stronger affiliation needs than do boys; this is reflected in closer friendships and greater cliquishness. During the course of development, the peer group becomes an increasing influence in the life of the young person, in some instances in opposition to parental influences but often reinforcing parental views and values.

Changing Values and Interests.—The basic values of a culture seem to be inculcated in the child well before adolescence. Nonetheless, significant changes occur as the child develops greater abstract ability, moves about more freely in his culture, reads more widely and comes more and more under influence of the peer group. Significant changes occur in religious values, social responsibility and attitudes toward truth. Generally there is a greater liberality of attitude toward borderline moral wrongs and a more tolerant attitude toward many matters, at least on a verbal-intellectualistic level. Compared with their parents and especially their grandparents, members of the younger generation seem more inclined to make moral and ethical judgments on the basis of intelligent judgment and aesthetic standards rather than on a strict rightwrong moral basis. These trends would seem to be in a desirable direction and reflect greater maturity.

Interests, hobbies and the like represent means of achieving satisfaction of various motives and needs. The relationship between breadth of interests, a positive orientation toward experience, and quality of adjustment has been well demonstrated. In view of the trend toward increased leisure and fewer opportunities for finding need satisfaction in work, this assumes special importance. During childhood and adolescence there is a decrease in number of activities but a greater involvement in those remaining. Better adjusted children appear to achieve deeper interests earlier. In view of such relationships and trends, it is notable that gaps in one's repertoire of interests and related skills that are not corrected in adolescence are likely to continue throughout life and thus restrict the range of satisfactions open to a person, especially when the significant and time-demanding roles of family rearing or career are terminated.

Vocational Orientations.—Occupational and career orientations develop slowly and reflect the personality and need structure of the individual. Consciously or unconsciously, the adolescent will tend to select that occupation which he perceives as potentially satisfying to his needs while at the same time being compatible with his personality characteristics. Compromises must be made, of course, if reality, in the form of limited ability, limited finances or strong opposing motives, stands in the way. Sound choices are more apt to emerge to the degree that there is opportunity during the course of development for adequate reality and role testing; *i.e.*, genuine opportunities to test one's own interests and abilities and to find if the work is really satisfying. Problems related to vocational choice in adolescence are relatively urgent because of the impending termination of school and are often critical because of the irreversibility of certain decisions. However, final decisions often are not made in adolescence; the typical person works on several jobs before settling down to one.

The importance of work and career and their meaning for the individual vary greatly with social class level. Middle-class individuals appear more concerned with career, are more future oriented and are more likely to be stimulated to career planning by parents and teachers. Lower-class individuals seem to be relatively apathetic regarding career, to view work mainly as a means of livelihood and to live in an environment relatively lacking in stimulation with respect to career planning.

Changing Relations With Parents.—It is not unlikely that the persistence in popular and professional opinion of the conception of adolescence as a period of stress and emotional upheaval is a product of the anxiety generated in the parents of adolescents. Such anxiety is likely to be perceived by the parent not as characterizing himself but as existing within the adolescent. Adolescence may be threatening to parents for a number of reasons. There are threats to parental authority and to parental codes of conduct. Parents become anxious because of the physical risk involved when inexperienced young people drive cars and are likely to experience a sense of personal failure if the teen-ager fails to conform to the hopes and ideals the parent held for him. Instead of accepting the youngster for what he is (there are many differing patterns of good adjustment and maturity), the parent may well experience ambivalent feelings and as a result increase the degree of pressure toward his goals and become even more restrictive.

Under these circumstances it would be expected that adolescence would be characterized by increasing conflict with parents, and this is probably true in individual homes or in cultures where parental domination is marked. The bulk of evidence on the teen-ager in the United States suggests that girls but not boys tend to experience increased conflict with parents, possibly because of the greater supervision and control exercised over daughters and hence the greater frustration experienced by them. Boys, in contrast, are likely to be given greater freedom and training for independence—marked differences, of course, exist among cultures and subcultures. It seems reasonable to expect that the path of development may be smoothed for both adolescents and their parents if unnecessary frustrations are reduced; if the child and adolescent are given increasing opportunities for freedom and self-direction and if restrictions, when necessary, are imposed only with due consideration of the adolescent's commitments and desires and after objective discussion of the situation; *i.e.*, reasonably rather than autocratically and arbitrarily.

It should be emphasized that the evidence dealing with age trends in parent-child relations is not consistent nor conclusive. One extensive study concluded that there is no strong evidence that adolescence is commonly a time of rebellion against parents.

Long-Term Outcome.—If adolescence is a critical period during which important personality reorganizations occur, significant shifts in developmental patterns of the types just described should result in the case of individual adolescents. However, the available information points toward continuity rather than marked reorganization in the sense that patterns of personality and adjustment once established tend to persist over long periods of time and to be modified only gradually. In laboratories where long-term studies have been conducted and individual growth curves plotted into the adult years, evidence points to long-term stability of traits. Changes do occur, and individual cases are occasionally noted in which the shifts are marked, but such shifts presumably could result from marked environmental changes (as moving to a new town, resulting in escape from reputation and social expectations that may have existed in the previous environment) or from changing physical status (as in the instance of an undersized late-maturing boy who finally catches up with his agemates and is no longer at a physical disadvantage). These exceptions must be noted as a qualification of the generality relating to continuity of psychological development.

The whole question of adolescence obviously needs further study. While the character of adolescence will vary in important respects from society to society and from one point in time to another, there is evidence indicating clearly that many existing views of adolescence do not gain unequivocal support. It may well be that in many settings adolescence is a calmer period than ordinarily assumed, and where this is not true, that appropriate changes in the environment may have the effect of reducing its stress and even of basically altering its nature.

See CHILD PSYCHOLOGY; CIVILIZATION AND CULTURE: *Role of Childhood;* FAMILY.

BIBLIOGRAPHY.—J. E. Anderson *et al., A Survey of Children's Adjustment Over Time* (1959); Mary Cover Jones, "A Comparison of the Attitudes and Interests of Ninth Graders Over Two Decades," *J. Educ. Psychol.,* vol. li, pp. 175–186 (1960); R. G. Kuhlen, *The Psychology of Adolescent Development* (1952); Arline B. Nicolson and Charles Hanley, "Indices of Physiological Maturity: Derivation and Interrelationships," *Child Development,* vol. xxiv (1953); J. M. Seidman (ed.), *The Adolescent: A Book of Readings,* rev. ed. (1960); J. M. Tanner, *Growth at Adolescence* (1955).   (R. G. KN.)

ADOLF OF NASSAU (*c.* 1250–1298), German king from 1292 to 1298, was the son of Walram II, count of Nassau, whom he succeeded as count in 1277. His inherited territories around Wiesbaden and Idstein were small in extent but he gained a military reputation as a mercenary captain over the next 14 years. On May 5, 1292, Adolf was elected German king at Frankfurt in succession to Rudolf I (the first Habsburg king), who had vainly attempted to engineer the election of his son Albert, duke of Austria. Adolf was crowned at Aachen on June 24, 1292, but his position was weakened by his inability to meet the exorbitant demands of his electors and by the hostility of Albert of Austria, whose territorial and financial resources were far superior.

Adolf sought to broaden the territorial basis of his power by seizing Meissen as a vacant fief and by purchasing the right of succession in Thuringia from the landgrave Albert. His alliance with Edward I of England against France, signed on Aug. 24, 1294, brought him an initial subsidy of £20,000, which he expended in crushing the resistance of the landgrave's disinherited sons, Frederick the Dauntless and Dietzmann (Dietrich).

The growing power of Adolf alarmed his electors who, after reaching an understanding with Albert of Austria, decided in Feb. 1298 to depose the king. The sentence of deposition was pronounced by six of the seven electors at Mainz on June 23, 1298. Albert, whose forces were present in strength, was elected king, as Albert I (*q.v.*), on the same day. Adolf attempted to reverse this decision on the field of battle but was defeated and slain by the superior forces of his rival at Göllheim, near Worms, on July 2, 1298.

See V. Samanek, *Studien zur Geschichte König Adolfs* (1930).
(C. C. BA.)

ADOLPHUS FREDERICK (1710–1771), king of Sweden from 1751 to 1771, was born at Gottorp on May 14, 1710. His father was Christian Augustus (1673–1726), duke of Schleswig-Holstein-Gottorp, bishop of Lübeck and administrator of the duchies of Holstein-Gottorp from 1702 to 1718 during the minority of his nephew Charles Frederick; his mother was Albertina Frederica of Baden-Durlach. Adolphus Frederick was bishop of Lübeck from 1727 to 1750 and administrator of Holstein-Kiel from 1739 to 1745 during the minority of Duke Charles Peter Ulrich (afterward Peter III of Russia). In 1743 he was elected heir to the throne of Sweden by the "Hat" faction in order that they might obtain better conditions of peace from the Russian empress Elizabeth, whose fondness for the house of Holstein was notorious. He succeeded to the throne in 1751 on the death of Frederick I.

During his whole reign Adolphus Frederick was little more than a state decoration, the real power being lodged in the hands of an omnipotent *riksdag* (parliament), distracted by fierce party strife. Twice he tried to free himself from its intolerable tutelage. The first occasion was in 1756 when, stimulated by his imperious consort Louisa Ulrica, sister of the Prussian king Frederick the Great, he tried to regain a portion of the attenuated royal prerogative and nearly lost his throne in consequence. On the second occasion (1768–69), under the guidance of his eldest son the crown prince Gustavus, he succeeded in overthrowing the tyrannous "Cap" party in the *riksdag* but was unable to make any use of his victory.

He died in Stockholm on Feb. 12, 1771.

See C. G. Malmström, *Sveriges politiska historia,* vol. iii–vi (1897–1907); Ingvar Andersson, *A History of Sweden,* trans. by Carolyn Hannay (1956).   (E. O. H. J.)

ADONAI, the name traditionally used in the synagogue liturgy as a surrogate for the ineffable name of the God of Israel (probably Yahweh [*q.v.*]). In form it is a plural of dignity of the noun *adon* ("lord") with a first person singular suffix: literally "my Lord." Long before the Christian era it had become customary to substitute this expression for the sacred tetragrammaton (YHWH) wherever the latter appeared in the consonantal Hebrew text. After the invention of vowel points, the tetragrammaton was provided with the vowels of Adonai, thus unintentionally giving rise to the bastard and impossible form "Jehovah" (YeHoWaH).   (R. C. DE.)

ADONI, a town in Kurnool district, Andhra Pradesh, India, 142 mi. S.W. of Hyderabad. Pop. (1961) 69,951. It is an important cotton cloth and carpet manufacturing centre on the Madras-Bombay railway route, 307 mi. from the former.

Adoni was a stronghold of the Hindu kings of Vijayanagar (*q.v.*). After their downfall it changed hands between local and imperial Muslim regimes until 1792 when, following the East India company's first war with Tipu Sultan (*q.v.*), it was allotted to the Nizam of Hyderabad. The Nizam ceded it to the British in 1800, however, in payment for military aid. Among Adoni's monuments are Jain figures carved in the rocks of the ruined fort and the beautiful Jami Masjid (great mosque) built in 1680 by Sidi Masud Khan.   (G. KN.)

ADONIJAH (in the Douai version of the Bible, ADONIAS), a name borne by several persons in the Old Testament, of whom the most noteworthy was the fourth son of David (*q.v.*). Adonijah was the natural heir to the throne. On the death of Absalom, and shortly before the death of David, he made preparations to seize his birthright, receiving the support of Joab and Abiathar the priest. However, Bathsheba, David's favourite wife, organized a counterintrigue in favour of her son Solomon (*q.v.*). Shortly after his accession Solomon had Adonijah put to death on the ground that by seeking to marry David's concubine Abishag he was aiming at the crown (I Kings i ff.).

ADONIS, in classical mythology, a youth of remarkable beauty, the favourite of Aphrodite. According to Apollodorus he was the son of the Syrian king Theias by his daughter Smyrna (Myrrha), who had been inspired by Aphrodite with unnatural love for her father and, by deceiving him as to her identity, conceived Adonis by him. When Theias discovered the truth he would have slain his daughter, but the gods in pity changed her into a tree of the same name. After ten months the tree burst asunder and from it came forth Adonis. Aphrodite charmed by his beauty, put the infant in a box and handed him over to the care of Persephone, who afterward refused to give him up. Zeus, on appeal being made to him, decided that Adonis should spend a third of the year with Persephone and a third with Aphrodite, the remaining

BY COURTESY OF NATIONAL GALLERY OF ART, WASHINGTON, D.C., WIDENER COLLECTION

"VENUS AND ADONIS" BY TITIAN (TIZIANO VECELLIO)

third being at his own disposal. In another version, given by Ovid, Adonis was killed by a boar, and this version was followed by Shakespeare. Apollodorus clumsily combines the two. Numerous other variants exist.

The name is generally supposed to be of Phoenician origin (from *adon*, "lord"), Adonis himself being identified with Tammuz (*q.v.*). (*See* also ATTIS.) Annual festivals called Adonia were held in his honour at Byblus, and also, from the 5th century B.C. onward, at different places in Greece. The central idea was the death and resurrection of Adonis and the mourning for Adonis, generally represented by an effigy which was afterward flung into the water. The very elaborate Alexandrian festival is described by Theocritus.

Most authorities agree that Adonis is a vegetation spirit, whose death and later return to life represent the decay of nature in winter and its revival in spring. He is born from the myrrh tree, the oil of which is used at his festival, and is connected with Aphrodite in her character of vegetation goddess. A special feature of the Athenian festival was the "Adonis gardens," small pots of seeds forced to grow artificially which rapidly faded (the custom is still practised by Christians in Cyprus). The dispute between Aphrodite and Persephone for the possession of Adonis finds a parallel in the story of Tammuz and Ishtar (*see* ISHTAR). In other words, Aphrodite is the oriental mother-goddess, Adonis her lover; the details have been influenced by the legend of Demeter (*q.v.*). The ceremony of the Adonia was intended as a charm to promote the growth of vegetation, the throwing of the gardens and images into the water being supposed to procure rain.

J. G. Frazer suggested that Adonis is not a god of vegetation generally, but specially a grain spirit, and that the lamentation is not for the decay of vegetation in winter but for the cruel treatment of the grain by the reaper and miller (*cf.* Robert Burns's *John Barleycorn*).

An important element in the story is the connection of Adonis with the boar; possibly Adonis himself was looked upon as incarnate in the swine. For a god sacrificed to himself as his own enemy, *cf.* the sacrifice of the goat and bull to Dionysus. It has been ob-

served that whenever sacrifices of swine occur in the ritual of Aphrodite there is reference to Adonis. In any case, the conception of Adonis as a swine-god does not contradict the idea of him as a vegetation or grain spirit, which in many parts of Europe appears in the form of a boar or sow.

BIBLIOGRAPHY.—W. Mannhardt, *Wald- und Feld-Kulte*, ii (1905); M. P. Nilsson, *Griechische Feste* (1906), *A History of Greek Religion* (1925); W. Roscher, *Ausführliches Lexikon der griechischen und römischen Mythologie*; A. von Pauly and G. Wissowa, *Realenzklopädie der klassischen Altertumswissenschaft*; J. G. Frazer, *The Golden Bough*, vol. v (1955); L. R. Farnell, *The Cults of the Greek States*, vol. ii (1896–1909); P. Lambrechts, "La Résurrection d'Adonis," *Annuaire de l'Institut de Philologie*, vol. xiii, pp. 207–40 (1953).   (T. V. B.; X.)

ADONIS, a genus of showy garden plants of the crowfoot family (Ranunculaceae) including the pheasant's-eye and several other cultivated species. They comprise about 20 Eurasian species, all with solitary flowers and dry fruits crowded into a head. They are erect herbs with much-divided leaves and yellow or red flowers.

Adonis vernalis is the perennial pheasant's-eye, with yellow flowers, but *A. aestivalis* and *A. annua* are annuals with red flowers, and are sparingly naturalized in eastern North America. The perennial species are easily cultivated in ordinary garden soil. Annuals should be sown one-fourth inch deep in sandy loam. The name is also given to the Adonis Blue butterfly (*Lysandra bellargus*), occurring in the chalk downs of southern England.   (N. TR.)

ADOPTION has been described as a way of conferring "the privileges of parents upon the childless and the advantages of having parents upon the parentless" (*Clarke Hall and Morrison's Law Relating to Children and Young Persons*, 5th ed., p. 502, Butterworth & Co. [Publishers] Ltd., London, 1956). More precisely, the act of adoption establishes a person as parent to one who is not in fact or in law his child. Adoption is so widely recognized that it can be characterized as an almost world-wide institution with historical roots traceable into antiquity. Greek and Roman practices form the earliest examples of persistent use of adoptions, notwithstanding the recording of adoptions in previous civilizations.

In ancient Greece and Rome, however, and in certain later cultures as well, the purposes served by adoption differed substantially from those emphasized in modern times. Continuity of the male line in a particular family was the main goal of these ancient adoptions. The importance of the male heir stemmed from political, religious or economic considerations, depending on the nation. The person adopted invariably was male and often adult, whereas contemporary adoptions commonly involve infants of either sex. In addition, the welfare of the adopter in this world and the next was the primary concern; little attention was paid to the welfare of the one adopted. As a result of the impact of Roman civil law upon the legal systems of Europe, the ancient traditions have left their mark on the adoption laws of a number of European and Latin-American nations and, in the United States, on the laws of Louisiana and Texas, which were colonized by French and Spanish settlers.

Nevertheless, it seems fair to state that in English-speaking and European countries, on the whole, contemporary laws and practices aim to promote child welfare and are regarded as but one facet of the state's program to protect its young. While the desire to continue a family line or to secure rights to inheritance are still among the motives for adoption, interest now centres more on the creation of a parent-child relationship between a married couple and a young child. This attitude developed primarily in the period following World War I, when vast numbers of children were left homeless by virtue of orphanage and an increase in illegitimate births. Adoption had popular appeal as a way to provide homes for these children. Its popularity was reinforced not only by the havoc of later wars but by the influence of psychiatry and allied fields, which have stressed the importance of stable family life from an early age in furthering the desired development of children.

Among English-speaking countries the United States is noteworthy for its relatively high rate of adoption and substantial experience in the administration of child welfare laws. Adoptions in the United States have grown in number and national interest. As elsewhere, the effects of war, as seen in increased illegitimacy, orphanage, divorce and separation, have accounted for much of the numerical growth. The adoption movement, however, began as early as the mid-19th century, when the first adoption statute, providing for judicial approval of such alliances, was passed in Massachusetts in 1851. The need for a judicial proceeding is universally recognized in the United States, save for a few exceptions related to a father's adoption of his illegitimate child. Adoption of adults is permitted in most jurisdictions; the legal provisions are generally formulated, however, in terms of child adoption, and the adopter must usually be an adult. It is not customary to require an age difference between adopter and the person sought to be adopted. The laws typically provide for the consent of the child's natural parents or guardian to the adoption, the consent of any older child (commonly one over 12 or 14 years), an investigation of the suitability of the prospective home according to criteria stated in the governing statute and a probationary period of residence in the adoptive home. During the probationary period, entry of a final decree of adoption is withheld pending evidence of the satisfactory adjustment of parent and child to one another. Provisions exist to secure the secrecy of the legal proceeding and to effect the necessary alterations on the child's birth certificate. In short, the laws endeavour to erase the natural parent-child relationship and create a wholesome replacement which intimately resembles it.

In the matter of inheritance, however, laws in the United States differ considerably. As a general rule, the child may inherit from the adopting parents and they from him. Inheritance by the child from his natural parents, once commonplace, is increasingly prohibited, with the exception of cases of adoption by stepparents. In addition, there has been a tendency to broaden the child's right to inherit from relatives of the adopting parents, although great variation appears among state laws on this subject.

In England adoption was first permitted only as recently as 1926. It was unknown to the common law, and the delay in passage of legislation can be attributed in part to the availability of devices which served to protect the continuity of family titles and estates, and in part to other legal means for protecting and caring for the dependent or homeless child. Under English adoption law the applicant must be 25 years old, he must generally be 21 years older than the person adopted, and the relationship is created through a judicial proceeding. In every case a guardian *ad litem* (for the purpose of the suit) is appointed for the child. The guardian's duties are not limited to the fulfillment of formal statutory requirements, as is often the case in the commonwealth countries and the United States; he also is required to investigate all aspects of the proposed adoption with a view to safeguarding the child's interests. The Adoption act, 1958, is a consolidating measure embodying the changes made in the Adoption act, 1950, and the Children act, 1958. The latter was of particular importance in giving effect to the recommendations of the Curtis committee in regard to the responsibilities of local authorities in relation to adoption.

The effects of an adoption order are to establish the usual parental rights and duties relating to support, education and custody. Inheritance follows the lines established for natural children, their parents and relatives, and inheritance by the child from his natural parents is prohibited. The adoption once made—if properly made —is final; the law does not permit annulment. English policy in this respect differs from that followed in several of the commonwealth and European nations, as well as a few U.S. jurisdictions. English law, in brief, though it was late in dealing with adoption, is advanced in its insistence on the similarity between natural and adoptive families.

Several of the commonwealth nations passed adoption laws well in advance of the English statute of 1926. In New Zealand, for example, the first law was enacted in 1895, and in Canada adoptions have been permitted in Nova Scotia since 1896. The statutes vary widely throughout the commonwealth. Some have been modeled on the English acts, while some reflect the influence of other nations.

Adoption of minors in the sense of creating permanent, comprehensive bonds between adopter and adoptee is a relatively recent phenomenon in France, dating from 1923. The law specifies the minimum age of the adopter and requires a 15-year difference in the ages of the parties. Two types of adoption are recognized. Simple adoption is available to single persons and is designed to restrict the effects of adoption to the relationship of adopter and adoptee. Adoptive legitimation, on the other hand, can be undertaken only by married people who propose to adopt a child under five years; this process has the consequence of creating ties between the child and the greater family of the adopter. The process is always a matter of public record.

In Germany and the Scandinavian countries adoption is part of comprehensive child welfare legislation. German provisions require that all adoptions involve the services of trained welfare workers. The validity of adoptions depends on confirmation by competent tribunals. Similarly, in Norway and Sweden adoption work is supported by sound social services for children and unmarried mothers. The extent to which adoption is regarded as an integral part of the Swedish child welfare program can be seen in the fact that adoptions do not become irrevocable, as they do in so many other places, but can be set aside when such action is in the best interest of the child. *See* also CHILDREN, LAWS CONCERNING.

BIBLIOGRAPHY.—Margaret Kornitzer, *Child Adoption in the Modern World* (1952); Chester G. Vernier, *American Family Laws*, vol. iv (1936); Michael Schapiro, *A Study of Adoption Practice*, 2 vol. (1956). (M. K. R.)

ADOPTIONISM, the title given to two Christian heresies, one originating in the 3rd and the other in the 8th century.

Adoptionism in the first sense is the belief that Christ was not the pre-existent Son of God but a mere man (Gr. *psilos anthropos*, hence psilanthropism), "adopted" by God at his baptism when he received the divine power (Gr. *dynamis*, hence dynamic monarchianism) to enable him to fulfill his mission of redemption. Propounded first by Theodotus of Byzantium *c.* 190, it was continued by Paul of Samosata (*q.v.*), who was condemned by a council at Antioch in 268. Nestorius was charged, probably incorrectly, with holding such a view, and hotly repudiated it. It was revived at the Reformation by certain Anabaptists and is the belief, at the present day, of many Unitarians. (*See* MONARCHIANISM.)

Adoptionism is also the name given to a controversy that broke out in Spain at the end of the 8th century. Under Islamic rule the Spanish church had tended to become isolated, and in an effort both to bind it closer to the apostolic see and to reform it a delegate was sent, named Egila, who took as his companion Migetius. Elipandus, archbishop of Toledo, resented this intrusion and found opposition easier because Migetius' teaching was suspect, the latter asserting that Jesus was one of the three persons of the Trinity and so confusing the two natures and the one person of the incarnate Son of God. Migetius was condemned by a council at Seville and Elipandus himself published a declaration of faith containing Christological statements that were soon to be challenged. Concerned to distinguish in Christ, who is both human and divine, the operations of each nature, Elipandus referred to Christ in his humanity as "adopted son" in contradistinction to Christ in his divinity who is the Son of God by nature.

He who is man among us was united in a single person with the Word. But it was not by him who was born of the Virgin that the world was created, but by him who is Son, not by adoption but by status, not by grace but by nature. It was by him who is both son of man and Son of God, adopted son according to his humanity, not-adopted Son according to his divinity, that the world has been redeemed. And if all the saints are imitators of the Son of God according to grace, they are also adopted sons like he.

The son of Mary, assumed by the Word, thus was not the Son of God by nature but only by adoption. Although this was not entirely unlike Nestorianism, no connection can be supposed; it was a somewhat archaic way of asserting that the divine Word had taken to himself a concrete human nature, whose properties were not impaired by the union.

Opposition to these views was first voiced by the priest Beatus and Etherius (later bishop of Osma), who, resident in Asturia, were motivated in part by a desire to be free from the jurisdiction of Toledo. At their instigation Pope Adrian I intervened and condemned Elipandus' teaching. The latter would have been wise to have let matters rest but instead he sought the support of Felix, bishop of Urgel, who expressed agreement. Urgel however had been occupied by the Franks between 785 and 790, and Charlemagne, who was not prepared to allow this questioning of the pope's decision, summoned Felix to Regensburg in 792, induced him to recant and sent him to Rome to be enlightened and disciplined by Adrian. Whereupon the Spanish church sent an open letter to the bishops of Gaul and a second to Charlemagne supporting the essential orthodoxy of both Felix and Elipandus. A council was summoned to Frankfurt in 794 which renewed the condemnation but an incursion of Arabs into Gothia prevented Charles from taking action and Felix returned to Urgel. A literary duel then ensued between him and Alcuin of York. In 798 Pope Leo III held in Rome a council of some 60 bishops which condemned the "adoptionism" of Felix and anathematized him. A commission was dispatched, under archbishop Leidrad of Lyons, which brought Felix to Aix-la-Chapelle (Aachen) in 799; after six days' dispute with Alcuin, Felix recanted again, was placed under the surveillance of Leidrad and died in 818. Elipandus remained unrepentant and despite further treatises by Alcuin continued undisturbed in his see; the adoptionist view, however, was almost universally abandoned after his death, apart from a temporary recrudescence in the 12th century in the teaching of Abelard and his followers.

See J. N. D. Kelly, *Early Christian Doctrines* (1958); E. Amann, *L'Époque carolingienne* (1937), vol. vi of A. Fliche and V. Martin (eds.), *Histoire de l'église.*   (J. G. DA.)

ADORATION, ultimately from the phrase *ad ora,* "to the mouth," designating the Roman's act of kissing the hand to the statue of the god he wished to honour, came to denote acts whereby man acknowledges God's supreme perfection and dominion. The chief of such actions in Christian worship is sacrifice, which can be made to God alone, accompanied normally by prayers of praise, etc. The Greek Christians used two words to distinguish carefully between the worship of God (*latreia*) and the veneration given to other sacred persons or objects (*proskynesis*). Both Greek words were translated into Latin by the one word *adoratio* and as a result the distinction of concepts was at times obscured. In English this confusion has been avoided by the use of "veneration" to designate the reverence paid to saints and images or relics of saints. Roman Catholics add a further distinction between such veneration as paid to the Blessed Virgin because of her singular pre-eminence (hyperdulia) and as paid to saints and sacred objects (dulia). By a natural transition "adoration" was also applied to the homage rendered to monarchs by the ceremony of striking the earth with the forehead. *See also* WORSHIP.

ADOUR, a river of southwest France, rises in the *département* of Hautes-Pyrénées, south of the Pic du Midi de Bigorre, and flows in a wide curve to the Bay of Biscay. It traverses the beautiful valley of Campan and, after passing Bagnères de Bigorre, enters the plain of Tarbes (*q.v.*). Beyond Tarbes numerous canals are drawn from the river for irrigation purposes; the most important is the Canal d'Alaric which follows the right bank for 36 mi. Within the *département* of Landes it flows west and later southwest becoming navigable at St. Sever, beyond which it is joined on the left by the Larcis, Gabas, Louts and Luy, and on the right by the Midouze. After Bayonne the river enters the sea through a dangerous estuary, after a total course of 208 mi. The mouth of the Adour has repeatedly shifted, its old bed being represented by *étangs* and lagoons extending northward as far as the village of Vieux Boucau (22½ mi.), where it debouched in the 14th century. The present channel was constructed in 1579.

ADRANO (ADERNO), a town of Sicily in the province of Catania, is near the Simeto river on a lava plateau on the western slopes of Mt. Etna, 36 km. (22 mi.) N.W. of Catania by road. Pop. (1961) 30,973. The ancient walls with ruined towers remain and there are traces of baths and burial grounds. The Ponte dei Saraceni, with bold 13th-century architecture, the 18th-century Ponte dei Biscari, an aqueduct with 40 arches, the 13th-century Norman castle and the 15th-century monastery of Sta. Lucia are

worthy of note. Oranges are the most important product of the district, but other fruits and vegetables are cultivated and honey is made. The old town, Hadranum, was founded by Dionysius the Elder, tyrant of Syracuse, in 400 B.C. near a sanctuary dedicated to the god Adranus, from which it took its name. It was conquered by the Romans in 263 B.C. In the middle ages it belonged to Roger I, count of Sicily. Emperor Frederick II made it a countship and in 1549 it passed to the Moncada, princes of Paterno, who held it until 1812. In 1928 it reassumed the classical name of Adrano, which had been corrupted into Adernò. In World War II Adrano was captured in Aug. 1943.   (M. T. A. N.)

ADRENAL GLANDS. These are two virtually identical glands, one situated above each kidney. Each gland consists of two parts. The inner portion, the medulla, produces epinephrine, also designated adrenaline, and norepinephrine or noradrenaline. The outer portion, the cortex, elaborates a group of hormones that are steroids closely related to progesterone.

The physiologic activity of the cortical hormones can be summarized under three aspects. First, mineral metabolism: the maintenance within narrow limits of the concentration in the blood of sodium, potassium and chloride is essential for life. The adrenal cortex exerts an important influence on this phenomenon by the secretion of the hormone aldosterone. Second, organic metabolism: the utilization and distribution of carbohydrates, proteins and fats are modified by cortisone and hydrocortisone. Third, tissue reactions such as hypersensitivity, allergic states and collagen diseases: the beneficial results produced by cortisone and hydrocortisone are manifested in the relief of rheumatoid arthritis and about 50 other diseases. The adrenal cortex did not appear to be directly involved in the etiology of any of these diseases and the manner in which cortisone and hydrocortisone produce their effect was not known as of the early 1960s. The activity of the adrenal cortex is controlled by the pituitary gland through an agent designated as adrenocorticotrophic hormone or ACTH. (*See* PITUITARY GLAND: *Hormones of the Pituitary Gland.*)

Until 1930 the mortality of patients who lacked adrenal secretion, a condition called Addison's disease (*q.v.*), was close to 100%. Administration of cortisone or hydrocortisone and small amounts of desoxycorticosterone or aldosterone permits these patients to lead a normal life and to undergo unusual stress, such as surgical operations.

Preparation of Extract.—To prepare an extract that contains these hormones, frozen adrenal glands from animals are passed through a meat grinder and extracted with cold alcohol. Water from the glands mixes with the alcohol and compounds soluble in water dissolve in the aqueous alcohol. The meaty portion of the gland, fat and other products remain insoluble. The aqueous alcohol is separated from the insoluble material, which is discarded. The alcohol and a large part of the water are removed by distillation under reduced pressure. The water solution that remains contains the hormones of the adrenal cortex. It also contains epinephrine that was originally present in the middle portion of the gland. For clarity this is designated solution A.

The concentrated solution A is thoroughly extracted with chloroform. Since hormones of the adrenal cortex are much more soluble in chloroform than in water this treatment provides a way to separate them from epinephrine and other compounds that remain in solution A. The chloroform is completely separated from solution A and is evaporated to dryness leaving a residue that contains the cortical hormones. In the commercial preparation of the extract the residue is dissolved in a volume of water such that one millilitre contains the extract of a constant amount of adrenal glands. Some pharmaceutical manufacturing companies have used 40 g. of adrenal glands for each millilitre of the water solution; other companies have used 75 g. of glands.

Solution A after extraction of the cortical hormones with chloroform still contains epinephrine. To obtain this valuable product solution A is concentrated to a small volume and ammonia is added. Epinephrine separates as a white crystalline precipitate that is filtered off and subsequently purified.

An extract of the adrenal gland was first prepared by methods similar to this by two groups of investigators working independently in 1929. Such extracts have served to provide substitution therapy for patients who were deficient in adrenal cortical function; to allow physiologists and clinicians to determine the physiologic activity of these essential compounds; and to permit chemists to isolate, identify and finally synthesize all of the cortical and medullary hormones.

Nature and Effects.—Epinephrine is a methylamine ethanol derivative of catechol. Norepinephrine has the same structure except the amino group is not substituted with a methyl group. Epinephrine when administered mimics the action produced by stimulation of the sympathetic nervous system and fortifies the body in an emergency—W. B. Cannon's theory. Among these effects are a rapid rise in blood pressure, an increase in the concentration of blood sugar and the flow of blood to the muscles and inhibition of digestion. However, the adrenal medulla is not essential for life. Activity of the medulla is controlled largely by stimulation of sympathetic nerves and by such agents as acetylcholine and insulin. Norepinephrine shares the stimulatory rather than the inhibitory properties of epinephrine.

Between 1930 and 1938 almost 30 different crystalline compounds were separated from the cortical adrenal extract and their chemical structures were determined. In 1937 the member with the simplest chemical structure, desoxycorticosterone, was made commercially available by alteration of the structure of another abundant steroid. Cortisone and hydrocortisone were made in small quantities in 1948 and in 1951 respectively. The last important member of the hormones, aldosterone, was separated in 1953, identified in 1954 and made synthetically in 1955. *See* ENDOCRINOLOGY: *Adrenal Glands;* ANIMAL EXTRACTS: *Adrenal Extracts;* ADRENAL GLANDS, DISEASES OF. *See* also Index references under "Adrenal Glands" in the Index volume.

BIBLIOGRAPHY.—C. H. Best and N. B. Taylor, *Physiological Basis of Medical Practice,* 6th ed. (1955); P. B. Hawk, B. L. Oser and W. H. Summerson, *Practical Physiological Chemistry,* 13th ed. (1954); R. S. Harris and K. V. Thimann (eds.), *Vitamins and Hormones,* vol. 10–17 (1952–59); F. D. W. Lukens (ed.), *Medical Uses of Cortisone* (1954).
(E. C. KL.)

ADRENAL GLANDS, DISEASES OF,

may be divided into diseases of the cortex and diseases of the medulla (*see* ADRENAL GLANDS). The only known disease of the medulla is a tumour (pheochromocytoma) which results in secretion of excessive quantities of epinephrine and norepinephrine. Symptoms are periodic episodes of high blood pressure, palpitation of the heart, sweats, pounding headaches, anxiety, nausea and vomiting. The only treatment is surgical removal of the tumour.

Adrenal cortical disease may be manifested as hyperfunction (overactivity) or hypofunction (insufficiency). The latter, known as Addison's disease, is discussed in a separate article (*see* ADDISON'S DISEASE).

Adrenocortical hyperactivity may be congenital or acquired; the former always is due to bilateral adrenal hypertrophy (enlargement), the latter to either tumour or hypertrophy. Congenital adrenal hypertrophy in the female infant results in masculinization with pseudohermaphroditism; in the male, sexual precocity occurs. In both, the virilism may be associated with a salt-losing syndrome. Acquired adrenocortical hyperfunction may be due to an adrenal tumour, benign or malignant, or to adrenal hypertrophy. Not infrequently, nontumorous adrenal hyperfunction is associated with no demonstrable enlargement of the adrenals. In nontumorous adrenal hyperfunction, a basophilic adenoma or basophilic hyperplasia is often present in the pituitary body.

Acquired adrenocortical hyperfunction is manifested by Cushing's syndrome, the adrenogenital syndrome, or both. Cushing's syndrome is characterized by obesity, rounding of the face, amenorrhea, high blood pressure, diabetes, osteoporosis, thinning and easy bruisability of the skin with appearance of violaceous striae, weakness and, often, mental disturbances. The adrenogenital syndrome consists of virilizing manifestations in the female, sexual precocity in the preadolescent male, and varying degrees of demasculinization in the adult male.

Treatment for adrenal tumour is surgical removal. For congenital hypertrophy, treatment consists of administration, for an indefinite length of time, of an adrenal hormone such as cortisone

or one of its synthetic analogues. In the presence of the salt-losing syndrome, a salt-retaining hormone, desoxycorticosterone or 9-alphafluorocortisol, may be added to the regimen. The forms of therapy available for acquired nontumorous adrenal hyperfunction with Cushing's syndrome are: (1) pituitary irradiation; (2) pituitary irradiation and removal of one adrenal gland; (3) removal of most of the adrenals; (4) total removal of the adrenals; (5) removal of the pituitary. Where both adrenals are removed or almost entirely removed or the pituitary body destroyed, replacement therapy with adrenal hormones must be instituted. *See* also ENDOCRINOLOGY.

Primary aldosteronism represents a selective form of adrenocortical hyperfunction, usually due to tumour, occasionally to nontumorous adrenal hyperfunction with respect to secretion of aldosterone. The syndrome is characterized by (1) hypertension, (2) reduction in the serum potassium level, (3) an increase in the blood CO_2 content, (4) evidence of renal damage, (5) an increase in the urinary excretion of potassium and (6) a considerable increase in the urinary excretion of aldosterone. The clinical manifestations often include tetany, muscle weakness and passage of large amounts of urine. Successful removal of the adrenal tumour generally results in a reversal of the laboratory and clinical manifestations.

See Louis J. Soffer, *Diseases of the Endocrine Glands* (1956); Louis J. Soffer, R. Dorfman and J. L. Gabrilove, *The Human Adrenal Gland* (1961). (L. J. So.)

ADRENALINE AND NORADRENALINE

(epinephrine and norepinephrine or levarterenol) are separate, active principles secreted by the medulla of the adrenal glands. They are also liberated at the ends of sympathetic nerve fibres where they serve as chemical mediators for conveying the nerve impulses to effector organs. Chemically, the two compounds differ only slightly, and they exert similar pharmacological actions that resemble the effects of stimulation of the sympathetic nervous system. They are therefore classified as sympathomimetic agents. The active secretion of the adrenal medulla contains approximately 80% adrenaline and 20% noradrenaline, but this situation is reversed in the sympathetic nerves, which contain predominantly noradrenaline.

The purified, active compounds are used clinically and are obtained from the adrenal glands of domesticated animals or prepared synthetically. The administration of adrenaline results in an increase in blood pressure by increasing the rate and force of contraction of the heart and by constricting the peripheral blood vessels. It also dilates the bronchioles and in this way is an aid to respiration. Adrenaline exerts a metabolic effect manifested by a rise in blood glucose. Noradrenaline elicits similar responses, but its metabolic effects and actions on the heart are much less than those of adrenaline. The rise in blood pressure after the administration of noradrenaline is due to its powerful vasoconstrictor action.

Adrenaline is used in combination with local anesthetics, since its vasoconstricting properties delay the absorption of the local anesthetics and in this way it prolongs their activity and reduces their toxicity. It is useful in acute allergic disorders such as drug reactions, hives and hay fever. Occasionally it is applied as a local vasoconstrictor in the control of superficial hemorrhage from the skin and mucous membranes and to relieve the nasal congestion of certain allergic conditions. Noradrenaline is administered by intravenous infusion to combat the acute fall in blood pressure associated with certain types of shock. Large doses of these compounds may result in such serious consequences as cerebral hemorrhage and cardiac abnormalities. *See* ADRENAL GLANDS; ANIMAL EXTRACTS; ENDOCRINOLOGY; HORMONES. *See* also references under "Adrenaline and Noradrenaline" in the Index.
(K. P. Du.)

ADRIA, a town of Rovigo province, Veneto region, Italy, is situated in the flat Po valley, 13 ft. above sea level, between the lower reaches of the Po and the Adige rivers, 16 mi. E. of Rovigo and 14 mi. W. of the Adriatic sea to which it gave its name. Pop. (1961) 25,669 (commune). It is an agricultural centre on the railway from Rovigo to Chioggia with another line to Mestre and Venice. Known to the Greeks and Romans, it was an important Etruscan harbour (Hatria or Atria) and was famous in Aristotle's day for a special breed of fowls. Even then river silt rendered access difficult and the historian Philistus excavated a canal to the sea which had gradually receded from the town. The canal was still open in the imperial period and the town possessed its own guild of sailors, but its importance gradually decreased in the middle ages because of continued silting by the Po and Adige. The Bocchi Municipal museum contains a fine collection of Etruscan remains and Roman glass from the old town, 10–20 ft. below the modern level. In World War II Adria was freed on April 27, 1945. (GI. S.)

ADRIAN (HADRIAN), **SAINT,** OF NICOMEDIA (3rd/4th century A.D.). Two saints of this name, both martyred at Nicomedia and buried at Argyropolis, one under Diocletian and one under Licinius, are commemorated on Aug. 26 in the Orthodox Church. Only the former, whose wife Natalia was a Christian, appears in the Roman martyrology, on March 4 and Sept. 8. Attempts to identify the two are probably mistaken, as their legends are quite distinct.

See A. Butler, *Lives of the Saints,* ed. by H. Thurston and D. Attwater, vol. 3, pp. 507–508 (1956).

ADRIAN (HADRIAN), the name of six popes.

ADRIAN I (d. 795), pope from 772 to 795, was a Roman aristocrat by birth and education. He was elected Feb. 1, 772. As pope he invoked Frankish aid against the Lombard king Desiderius and his Roman partisans. By Easter 774 Charlemagne was in Rome, having destroyed the Lombard kingdom. Thenceforth the Frankish alliance, and not that with Constantinople, determined Adrian's policies. Amicable rivalry marked the relations between Charlemagne and the pope. The former made use of the church to hold his empire together and enforced overlordship on the papal states while Adrian fought firmly but adroitly for ecclesiastical autonomy and painstakingly pieced together a papal domain that was lost only in the 19th century. Constantinople was conciliated by Adrian's co-operation in the anti-Iconoclast Council of Nicaea (787), which Charlemagne attacked. Adrian died on Dec. 25, 795. Charlemagne commemorated him in an epitaph, composed by Alcuin and preserved at St. Peter's.

ADRIAN II (792–872), pope from 867 to 872, was a Roman by birth and a relative of two previous popes, Stephen V (816–817) and Sergius II (844–847). He was elected on Dec. 14, 867. The papacy had reached a high point under his vigorous predecessor, Nicholas I, and Adrian struggled to maintain the advantageous position, not without some success. He readmitted Lothair II of Lorraine to communion but Lothair's early death created a difficult problem of succession in which Adrian ineffectually intervened. Adrian also had difficulties with Hincmar of Reims who developed a doctrine not unlike that of the later Gallicans.

Adrian approved the use of the Slavic language in liturgy by Cyril and Methodius and, by making Methodius archbishop of Sirmium, won the adhesion of the Moravians to the church. His legates took part in the eighth ecumenical council, the fourth of Constantinople (869–870), which deposed the patriarch Photius. For the sake of peace, Adrian accepted the 21st canon of this council which gave the patriarch of Constantinople rank second only to that of the pope. He refused, however, to sanction the transfer of the Bulgarians to the patriarchate of Constantinople, which was decided at the same time. He died on Dec. 14, 872.

ADRIAN III, SAINT (d. 885), pope from 884 to 885, was a Roman. He died, probably in Sept. 885, near Modena on his way to the diet of Worms, summoned by Charles the Fat to settle the succession to the empire. His feast day is July 8.

ADRIAN IV (Nicholas Breakspear) (d. 1159), pope from 1154 to 1159, the only Englishman to occupy the papal throne, was born at Abbot's Langley near St. Alban's in Hertfordshire. He was elected on Dec. 4, 1154. He became a canon regular of St. Rufus near Avignon and in 1150 cardinal bishop of Albano. Eugenius III sent him as legate to Scandinavia in 1152 to reorganize the hierarchy. His mission was a success and on his return he was chosen pope. Adrian crowned Frederick Barbarossa emperor in 1155 after Frederick had captured and handed over Arnold of Brescia

to him. The papal policy in regard to the Normans of southern Italy, however, aroused the emperor's anger and thereafter the relations between Adrian and Frederick form a preamble to the struggle between Alexander III and Barbarossa. Henry II of England in 1156 asked Adrian for permission to conquer Ireland. Even if the bull *Laudabiliter* were authentic, which is doubtful, it does not grant hereditary possession of Ireland to the English king. Adrian died on Sept. 1, 1159.

ADRIAN V (Ottobono Fieschi) (d. 1276), pope for about five weeks in 1276, was a native of Genoa and a nephew of Innocent IV who created him cardinal. He was legate to England (1265–68), charged with establishing peace between Henry III and the rebellious barons. Elected as successor of Innocent V on July 11, 1276, he died on Aug. 18, having, however, revoked the stern conclave regulations of Gregory X.

ADRIAN VI (Adrian Florisze Boeyens) (1459–1523), pope from 1522 to 1523, was born March 2, 1459, in Utrecht. He was elected on Jan. 9, 1522. The last non-Italian and the only Dutch pope, he studied at Louvain where he became priest, professor of theology, chancellor and rector of the university. Erasmus was one of his pupils. In 1507 Adrian was appointed tutor of Charles V, who afterward entrusted him with the highest offices. Bishop of Tortosa in 1516, he was created cardinal in 1517. He was crowned pope at Rome in Aug. 1522. Despite opposition and ridicule, Adrian took up the task of reform with great earnestness, beginning with the curia. An excellent but misunderstood pontiff, he reigned such a brief time that his accomplishments are disappointing. He did, however, point out the way to reform. He died on Sept. 14, 1523. (E. A. R.)

ADRIAN, EDGAR DOUGLAS ADRIAN, 1ST BARON, OF CAMBRIDGE (1889–   ), English physiologist and winner, with Sir Charles Sherrington (*q.v.*), of the 1932 Nobel prize in physiology and medicine for discoveries regarding the neuron, the ultimate anatomical unit of the nervous system. He was born in London on Nov. 30, 1889, and educated at Westminster school and Trinity college, Cambridge, qualifying in medicine in 1915. Apart from medical service during World War I his career was spent at Cambridge, as fellow of Trinity (from 1913), Foulerton professor of the Royal society (1929–37), professor of physiology (1937–51) and master of Trinity (from 1951). He was awarded the Order of Merit in 1942; elected president of the Royal society in 1950; and raised to the peerage in 1955.

Adrian became known for brilliant experimental researches in electrophysiology. His early work was concerned with nerve impulses from sense organs. The variations in electrical potential associated with such impulses amplified many thousands of times by means of thermionic valves, and it was found possible to record them. He later made recordings of nerve impulses from single sensory endings and from single motor nerve fibres. This made possible a better understanding of the physical basis of sensation and the mechanism of muscular control. After 1934 Adrian studied the electrical activity of the brain itself. His work on the variations and abnormalities of the changes known as the Berger rhythm opened up new fields of investigation in epilepsy and in the location of cerebral lesions. (W. J. BP.)

ADRIANOPLE: *see* EDIRNE.

ADRIATIC (anc. MARE ADRIATICUM), an arm of the Mediterranean sea between Italy and the Balkan peninsula, extends northwest to southeast from latitude 40° N. to latitude 45° 45′ N., a distance of nearly 500 mi. Its average width is about 110 mi., but at the Strait of Otranto only 45 mi. It shallows rapidly in its northern half, its depth north of Dubrovnik (Ragusa) being nowhere more than 130 fathoms, beyond Ravenna less than 50 fathoms. A narrow minor depression with depths of more than 100 fathoms crosses the sea between the Abruzzi and Sibenik (Sebenico). From Mt. Gargano southward to opposite Bari there is a much more extensive and deeper basin (more than 500 fathoms) where soundings of more than 765 fathoms have been recorded. Structurally the Adriatic sea and its western extension in the basin of the Po river occupy a downfold between the Tertiary fold ranges of the Apennines on the west and those of the Alps to the north, and the Dinaric system to the east. In the Po basin the depression has been infilled with detritus brought down from both the Alps and the Apennines, but more especially the former, partly by glacial action during the Ice Age but mainly by the violent flood streams characteristic of the tributaries of that river. The combined delta of the Po, Adige, Brenta and Piave rivers shows that this process is still continuing, for its front is advancing seaward, in places by as much as 30 ft. a year. It is only with great difficulty that the channels necessary to the continued existence of Venice as a port are kept open. To protect the Venetian lagoon, sea walls extend the Lido sand bar; in Nov. 1966 the sea, driven by high gales, breached them and Venice was flooded, while farther south incursions of the sea augmented river flood in the Po delta.

Adria (q.v.), which was a flourishing port in Roman times and up till the late 12th century, and which gave its name to the sea, is now 14 mi. inland. Beside being the shallowest of all the sections of the Mediterranean, the Adriatic is also distinguished in parts by the relative freshness of its waters. Its mean salinity is approximately $35^0/_{00}$ near the Strait of Otranto but falls to $18^0/_{00}$ near the head of the sea where it receives the surface flow of Alpine and Apennine streams and also submarine flows from the limestone plateaus of Istria and Dalmatia.

Though in general the Adriatic may be said to experience a Mediterranean climate, the more continental conditions prevalent over the north Italian lowland and the Danube basin are not without their effect on its northern sections. Their low winter temperatures, for example, cause the waters of the Gulf of Venice to show uniformly low temperatures at all depths during that season while off the Dalmatian coasts the surface waters are more than 3° F. colder than the underlying layers. When the cyclonic depressions that develop over the Po basin and Gulf of Genoa during the same season move southeastward, the whole coastal area is swept by the cold wind from the northeast (the bora) which brings some danger to small craft as well as general discomfort to the population. In southern areas, a warm damp sirocco (not to be confused with the dry dusty Saharan wind of the same name experienced on the north African coast) blows from the southeast. Surface currents move anticlockwise, entering the Adriatic on the east side of the Strait of Otranto, passing northward along the Dalmatian coast, southward along the Italian shores and leaving on the westward side of the strait. The southward movement, by carrying silt from the Po delta, has extended the lowland toward Ravenna and beyond.

There is a marked contrast between the Balkan and the Italian coasts. The former is rugged everywhere north of Albania, its main features evidently formed by submergence; the latter shows mainly emergent features, though the coastal belt shrinks to a narrow ledge in the Abruzzi. Marshes, lagoons and sandspits border the shores of the Gulf of Venice and extend for some distance south of the Po delta, low marshy ground reaching as far south as Rimini though narrowing to less than a mile beyond Ravenna. In northeastern Emilia-Romagna, side tracts were reclaimed by poldering. Foothills of the Apennines lie close behind the coast through the Marche and Abruzzi e Molise but from Mt. Gargano southward these are replaced by bare limestone plateaus and hills.

There is a marked absence of natural harbours all along the Italian coast. Ancona, on a bay sheltered by a limestone promontory, is the only port for many miles along the middle section. The marsh and lagoon type of coast stretches around the Gulf of Venice almost to Trieste where begins the low limestone plateau of the Istrian peninsula. Southward from the Gulf of Kvarner the coastlands rise very steeply inland, the 1,500-ft. contour being close to the sea everywhere. As far as Dubrovnik the land is fringed with islands (e.g., Krk, Cres, Brac and Curzola) and its coastal margin interrupted by frequent inlets (T- and L-shaped gulfs), all obviously produced by the submergence of valleys between the fold ranges which are there parallel to the shore line. In Albania the coastal plain is wider and more continuous but imperfectly drained.

Penetrating northward so close to the heart of central Europe, the Adriatic has always been of importance as a trade highway. From very early times traffic has passed across it between Italy and the Balkan lands in spite of the obvious difficulties presented by the lack of shelter on the Italian side and the absence of good natural routes leading inland from either shore. Durrës (Durazzo) was the western terminus of the great Roman and Byzantine highway from Constantinople and Salonika. Dubrovnik and Split were Roman ports on the Balkan side linking with Ancona, Ravenna and Adria on the Italian. Through routes across the Apennines were difficult but, in spite of this, the latter ports also handled trade between Rome and the eastern Mediterranean because of the difficult navigation involved in the voyage by way of the Straits of Messina.

The rise of Venice gave special importance to Adriatic routes because of its easy communication with southern Germany and northwestern Europe by the Brenner pass, as well as to Vienna and the Danube highway by the Semmering pass. Long before the opening of the Suez canal (1869) the main currents of Mediterranean trade had been diverted away from the Adriatic ports. Neither that event nor the frequent boundary changes around its northern land termini have completely robbed it of its former importance. The trade of Venice and Trieste indeed increased as a result of the opening of the Suez canal. Rijeka, Dubrovnik and Split still carry on more than purely local trade; Trieste handles a large traffic and Venice manages to maintain its position as an outlet for the Lombardy plain. Bari and Brindisi are large ports, while Ancona's trade is mainly coastal.

(T. Her.; C. G. Sm.)

ADSORPTION. All solid substances are known to be capable of attracting to their surfaces molecules of gases or solutions with which they are in contact. This phenomenon is known as adsorption. The solids that are used to adsorb gases or dissolved substances are called adsorbents; the adsorbed molecules are usually referred to collectively as the adsorbate. A well-known example of an excellent adsorbent is the charcoal used in gas masks. With its area of about 125 ac. per pound, it is capable of adsorbing and holding large quantities of poisons or impurities that one wishes to remove from a stream of air.

Adsorption refers to the taking up of molecules by the external surface or internal surface (walls of capillaries or crevices) of solids or by the surface of liquids. Absorption, with which it is often confused, refers, on the other hand, to processes in which a substance penetrates into the actual interior of crystals, of blocks of amorphous solids or of liquids. Sometimes the word "sorption" is used to indicate the process of the taking up of a gas or liquid by a solid without any specification as to whether the process is one of adsorption or of absorption.

It is now generally recognized that adsorption can be either physical or chemical in nature. For convenience, these two types of adsorption will be discussed separately. Adsorption from solution is also treated separately.

Applications of Adsorption.—Traditional applications of physical adsorption include the use of charcoal for removing poison gases from the air; hydrocarbons from natural gas; and oxygen, nitrogen or other gaseous impurities from helium during the separation and purification of the latter. Later applications were concerned with the measurement of the surface area of finely divided or porous solids and with the measurement of the pore size and pore distribution of porous solids. Also, in the analytical process known as gas chromatography (see CHROMATOGRAPHY) physical adsorption is responsible for the separation of the various components of a gaseous mixture to produce separate and characteristic peaks on the chromatograms.

Chemical adsorption or chemisorption, as pointed out below, is of general interest mostly because of its being one of the steps in catalytic processes (see CATALYSIS). Typical examples of important catalytic processes include, among others, the synthesis of ammonia, the cracking of hydrocarbons to form gasoline, the synthesis of methanol, the cyclization of heptane to form toluene, the oxidation of sulfur dioxide to sulfur trioxide and the hydrogenation of oils to edible fats. Chemisorption is, however, not an unmixed blessing in catalytic reactions, since it can also slow them down by holding poisons on the catalyst surface.

Adsorption from solution has even more applications than adsorption from the gas phase. Its importance in dyeing, photography, brewing, the purification of water, the clarification of oil and in making lubricants more effective is well known. Soils and soil colloids with their large surface areas (30 to 50 ac. per pound) are able by adsorption to remove from solution and retain fertilizer components essential to plant growth. Finally, the separation of components of a solution by liquid chromatography became important not only as an analytical tool for chemists but for separating out specific compounds from liquid solutions. For example, the aromatic, olefinic and paraffinic portions of liquid hydrocarbons can be separated by chromatography on a scale that promises to prove important in petroleum technology.

Physical Adsorption of Gases and Vapours on Solids.— Physical adsorption resembles the condensation of gases to liquids. It depends upon the physical or van der Waals forces of attraction between the solid adsorbent and the adsorbate molecules. As one might expect for a given solid, the adsorption of a gas will become larger as the temperature at which the gas and solid are in contact decreases toward the boiling point of the gas or as the pressure of the gas at a given temperature is increased toward the pressure that would be necessary to actually condense it to a liquid. There is no chemical specificity in physical adsorption, any gas tending to be adsorbed on any solid if the temperature is sufficiently low or the pressure of the gas sufficiently high.

The five fundamental types of isotherms (plots of volume of gas adsorbed against pressure), which separately or in combination can describe the behaviour of all known examples of physical adsorption, are shown in fig. 1.

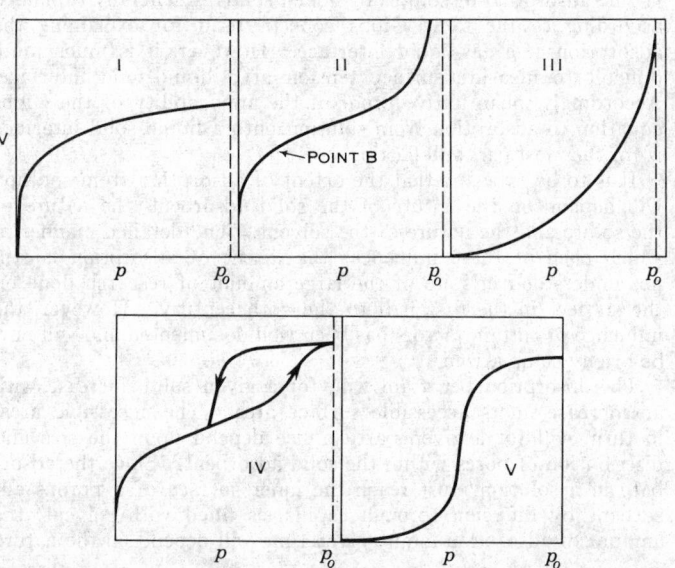

FROM S. BRUNAUER, "THE ADSORPTION OF GASES AND VAPORS," PRINCETON UNIVERSITY PRESS (1934)

FIG. 1.—TYPES I, II, III, IV AND V ADSORPTION ISOTHERMS. IN EACH PLOT THE VOLUME OF GAS ADSORBED (AS MEASURED AT A STANDARD TEMPERATURE AND PRESSURE) IS PLOTTED AGAINST GAS PRESSURE, P. THE LIQUEFACTION PRESSURE IS P_0

Type I isotherms are representative of solids such as activated charcoals, or natural or synthetic chabazites (q.v.) having very small pores (one to ten times the size of ordinary gas molecules). Type II isotherms are obtained on finely divided nonporous solids or on solids having fairly large pores, using as adsorbates inert gases such as nitrogen at temperatures close to their boiling points. Water vapour adsorbed on graphite yields a type III curve. It is generally believed that the heat of adsorption of the adsorbate molecules for type III isotherms is equal to or a little smaller than the heat of liquefaction of the gas being studied. On solid adsorbents having all of their areas located on the walls of cracks or crevices smaller than about $\frac{1}{1,000,000}$ in. in size, isotherms of type IV will normally be obtained. Finally, if the heat of adsorption is small but the pore size is also small, type V curves will be obtained as adsorption isotherms. Water vapour on charcoal gives such a curve provided the amount of surface oxide on the charcoal is relatively small.

Even though the chemical relationship of the gas and solid that is being studied is usually not important in determining the extent or nature of physical adsorption, a certain differentiation among the adsorbents can be made on a basis of the polarity of the solid or the adsorbate. For example, water vapour on graphite gives isotherms of type III, whereas nitrogen, argon, krypton and similar gases give type II isotherms. Apparently the exceptional behaviour of water vapour is to be attributed to the polar character of the —OH group and the nonpolar character of the carbon surface. On the other hand, polar solids such as silica gel adsorb water vapour even more strongly than adsorbates such as nitrogen.

Physical adsorption is characterized by low heats of adsorption and by rapid adsorption and desorption. The only systems in which physical adsorption is slow are those in which the pores are so small that an appreciable time is required for the adsorbate molecules to diffuse down the pores or capillaries to the inner surface on which they are finally to be adsorbed.

Numerous equations have been developed for representing the volume, v, of gas adsorbed as a function of pressure, p. One of these, the Langmuir equation, is of the form

$$v = \frac{abp}{1 + ap}$$

Another, called the Freundlich equation, is

$$v = kp^{1/n}$$

In these equations, a, b, k and n are constants. The Freundlich equation usually represents isotherms over certain restricted pressure ranges. At very low pressures or high temperatures the value of n approaches 1; at intermediate pressures, the constant $1/n$ assumes fractional values characteristic of the particular solid-gas system that is involved.

One of the more useful relationships for estimating the extent of adsorption at one temperature from that at another was due to M. Polanyi and his co-workers. In it the volume of gas adsorbed is plotted against the adsorption potential defined by the equation

$$\text{adsorption potential} = RT\ln p_0/p$$

where p_0 is the liquefaction pressure of the gas being studied, T is the temperature, R is the gas constant and p is the pressure at which the volume adsorbed (at a standard temperature and pressure) is being measured. Plots of such data show that except for a slight correction for the two-dimensional expansion of the adsorbed gas, the adsorption volumes taken at a series of temperatures and pressures will fall on a smooth curve.

In 1935 it was postulated that point B on type II isotherms for iron catalysts corresponded to a statistical monolayer of adsorbed gas and that the linear part of these isotherms and the portion convex to the pressure axis (to the right of point B in the type II curve of fig. 1) represents the building up of multimolecular adsorption layers. A theory designed to explain the shape of these isotherms in terms of multimolecular layers may in its simplest form be written

$$\frac{x}{v(1-x)} = \frac{1}{v_m C} + \frac{(C-1)x}{v_m C}$$

where v is the volume of gas adsorbed at the relative pressure, x, of the adsorbate gas and C is a constant. A plot of the left side of the equation against the relative pressure, x, yields a straight line from which v_m, the volume of gas in a monolayer, can be evaluated.

This equation has become known as the Brunauer-Emmett-Teller or BET equation. A simple multiplication of v_m by the cross-sectional area of each adsorbed molecule (as estimated from the density of the liquefied or solidified adsorbate) yields directly a value for the surface area of the solid in any convenient unit such as square metres per gram or acres per pound.

One theory of physical adsorption assumes that in porous solids a considerable portion of the adsorbate is held by what is known as capillary condensation. To express the vapour pressure, p, of a liquid in a capillary, Lord Kelvin derived the equation

$$\ln p_0/p = \frac{2\sigma V \cos \theta}{rRT}$$

where σ is the surface tension of the liquefied adsorbate gas, θ

is the contact angle between the liquid and the wall of the capillary, r is the radius of the capillary, V is the molal volume of the adsorbate and R, T and p_o are as defined above. The existence of capillary condensation is usually assumed to account for the hysteresis that is frequently found in adsorption isotherms representing physical adsorption of gases or vapours on porous solids (*see* type IV curve in fig. 1). By making proper allowance for the amount of monomolecular or multimolecular adsorption that occurs at a given relative pressure for a particular gas-solid system, it is possible to use the desorption isotherm of the type shown in fig. 1 for the type IV isotherm to calculate with the help of the Kelvin equation the pore size and the pore size distribution of capillaries.

This application of physical adsorption is one that is very valuable in studying the size of pores in catalysts and in other porous solids.

Chemical Adsorption of Gases on Solids.—When certain specially prepared samples of porous iron are placed in contact with a mixture of the two simple gases hydrogen and nitrogen at a dull red heat and at high pressure, a chemical reaction takes place between the hydrogen and nitrogen to form ammonia. In this typical catalytic reaction it can be shown that both the hydrogen and nitrogen are capable of being adsorbed on the surface of the catalyst.

The temperatures involved (450° to 550° C.) are too high to permit physical adsorption to take place. It is concluded that the gases in this high-temperature range are held by chemical forces and hence by what has been called chemical adsorption or chemisorption.

Chemical adsorption occurs usually at higher temperatures than those at which physical adsorption occurs; furthermore, chemical adsorption is ordinarily a slower process than physical adsorption and like most chemical reactions frequently involves an energy of activation.

The heat of chemical adsorption is much higher than that of physical adsorption and corresponds to heats that are involved in chemical reaction.

Thus, for example, the heat of physical adsorption of nitrogen on an active iron synthetic ammonia catalyst at −195° C. is in the range 1,360 to 3,000 cal. per mole of nitrogen compared with a liquefaction heat of 1,360 cal. per mole; in contrast with this the heat of adsorption of nitrogen at 450° C. on the same iron catalyst is about 35,000 cal. per mole of nitrogen. Chemical adsorption is perhaps most easily visualized as a surface compound between the atoms of the catalyst surface and the gaseous adsorbate formed under conditions which preclude the possibility of the adsorbate reacting with the main bulk of the catalyst to form a regular chemical compound.

As might be expected, chemisorption is chiefly of interest in connection with the occurrence of catalytic reactions. Apparently at least one of the reacting gases in a catalytic reaction has to be chemically adsorbed on the surface of the catalyst prior to reaction (*see* CATALYSIS).

One other application of chemisorption should be mentioned. It can be used to measure the surface concentration of components called promoters which are added to catalysts to the extent of a few per cent by weight to improve their activity. For example, the chemisorption of carbon monoxide by the iron atoms and of carbon dioxide by the alkali promoter has made it possible to ascertain that a few per cent of added promoter may cover as much as 50% to 75% of the surface of a doubly promoted iron synthetic ammonia catalyst.

Until relatively recently, little information was available as to the state of chemisorbed molecules on the surface of adsorbents. Only general inferences could be drawn based on the expected nature of interaction of the adsorbate and the adsorbent as judged by their respective chemical properties. In 1953 successful measurements were finally made of the infrared absorption bands of ammonia adsorbed on silica-alumina cracking catalysts and of carbon monoxide chemisorbed on such metals as iron, nickel, cobalt, platinum and palladium. The information obtained from such spectra relative to the nature and the strength of the bonds holding the adsorbed molecules onto the surface without doubt opened an entirely new approach to a better understanding of chemisorption.

Adsorption in Solution.—When a substance (solute) is dissolved in a liquid (solvent) to form a solution, the solute usually tends to concentrate either in the surface or in the bulk of the solvent. For example, soap tends to concentrate preferentially in the surface of an aqueous soap solution (positive adsorption). On the other hand, inorganic salts, such as ordinary table salt, tend to concentrate in the bulk of an aqueous solution rather than in its surface (negative adsorption).

These qualitative observations have been expressed in a formal manner by the Gibbs adsorption equation

$$\Gamma = \frac{-c\delta\sigma}{RT\delta c}$$

where Γ is the excess surface concentration of the solute in grammoles per square centimetre; c is the mean concentration of the solute; $\delta\sigma/\delta c$ is the change of surface tension of the solution with the concentration of solute; and R and T are as defined above.

Adsorption From Solution by Solids.—The adsorption of a solute on the surface of a solid in contact with a solution is of fairly common occurrence. For example, activated carbon is used for removing coloured impurities from solution; clay can remove coloured components from oil; and bone char is used to remove impurities from sugar solutions in sugar refining.

The adsorption of solutes by added solids is generally explained according to the same Gibbs concept used for explaining the adsorption at a gas-liquid interface. However, it is much more difficult to measure surface tension at a liquid-solid interface. Accordingly, quantitative proof of the applicability of the Gibbs equation to adsorption from solution onto a liquid-solid interface is for the most part still lacking.

It is to be expected that the extent of adsorption from solution will depend on the nature of the solid adsorbent, the nature of the solute and the nature of the solvent. The detailed manner in which each of these influences the extent of adsorption is still not understood in spite of the large amount of research done on the subject in the first half of the 20th century. However, the influence of certain factors has been well documented and will now be briefly summarized.

The adsorption per gram will, for a given solid, increase with an increase in its accessible surface area. The accessible area, in turn, will for a given particle size depend upon the size and distribution of pores within the solid adsorbent. Since the adsorbate in a solution must reach the inner surface of a porous adsorbent by diffusion through capillaries filled with solvent, the amount of adsorption in any given time will depend on the nature

TABLE I.—*Adsorption of Various Fatty Acids on Charcoals of Different Porosities*

Weight ratio*		Propionic acid		Valeric acid		Enanthic acid	
		Per cent ads.†	Time for 75% equil.	Per cent ads.	Time for 75% equil.	Per cent ads.	Time for 75% equil.
1.00	. .	15	96 hr.	5	150 hr.	3	380 hr.
.86	. .	47	3 hr.	58	3 hr.	45	60 hr.
.83	. .	30	< 1 hr.	68	< 1 hr.	95	< 1 hr.
.55	. .	55	< 1 hr.	88	< 1 hr.	98	< 1 hr.

*100 (1-weight ratio) is the percentage weight loss in the charcoal during activation.
†25 c.c. of .01N acid and 0.1 g. of charcoal were used in each case; "Per cent adsorption" is the per cent of the added acid that is adsorbed.

of the pores and capillaries as illustrated by the data in Table I (*see* M. Dubinin, Z. physik. Chem., 1931).

In the original unactivated material the pores were so small as to tend to screen out the larger molecules. With increased activation the charcoals increased their total adsorptive capacity and the pores became sufficiently enlarged to permit all of the solutes to be adsorbed regardless of molecular size.

It goes almost without saying that the time required to reach a given percentage of the final equilibrium values decreases as the pores become enlarged by activation. The rate of adsorption can be judged on these four charcoals by the time required to reach

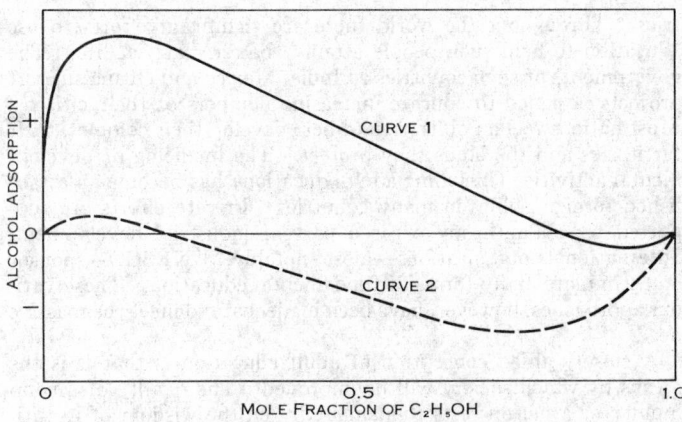

FROM F. E. BARTELL, G. H. SCHEFFLER, AND C. K. SLOAN; "J. AM. CHEM. SOC." 53, 2501 (1931)

FIG. 2.—THE ADSORPTION OF ETHYL ALCOHOL FROM A BENZENE SOLUTION ON SILICA GEL (CURVE 1) AND ON CHARCOAL (CURVE 2). THE POSITIVE ADSORPTION REGION CORRESPONDS TO A HIGHER RATIO OF ALCOHOL TO BENZENE ON THE SURFACE THAN IN THE BULK LIQUID; THE NEGATIVE REGION, TO A LOWER RATIO

75% of the final equilibrium adsorption (see Table I).

An excellent illustration of the influence of both solvent and solute is given by the data in Table II (see M. Dubinin and E. D. Zaverina, J. Phys. Chem. [U.S.S.R.], 1933).

TABLE II.—Adsorption* of Fatty Acids From Water and From CCl₄ on Birch Charcoal

Acid	From water		From CCl₄	
	k	$1/n$	k	$1/n$
Formic . . .	0.316	0.340	2.239	0.115
Propionic . .	.646	.238	.851	.131
Heptylic . .	1.203	.180	.158	.433

*The adsorption is given in terms of the constants k and $1/n$ of the Freundlich equation.

As is evident, the adsorption from water increases with the molecular weight of the acid, whereas from CCl₄ the extent of adsorption decreases with an increase in molecular weight. In both solvents the adsorption increases as the solubility of the solute decreases.

Not only the nature of the solute and solvent but the actual composition of a solution has a strong influence on the extent and nature of the adsorption on an added solid. This is illustrated by the curves in fig. 2, taken from the work of F. E. Bartell, G. H. Scheffler and C. K. Sloan, J. Am. Chem. Soc. (1931).

The solid curve shows that on silica gel small amounts of ethanol are strongly adsorbed from a benzene solution. At high concentrations of ethanol, on the other hand, benzene is preferentially adsorbed. The dotted curve shows the corresponding adsorption isotherm for a sample of activated carbon. Clearly, the polar ethanol is relatively much more strongly adsorbed by silica gel than by activated carbon.

Attempts are sometimes made to list adsorbents in order of their efficiencies. However, the nature of the adsorbate, the presence or absence of a solvent, the concentration of adsorbate, the temperature and the surface area and pore size of a particular sample of adsorbent are all factors that can influence the efficiency of a given chemical species of adsorbent. Reference should therefore be made to some of the comprehensive treatises for detailed information that would enable one to select the proper adsorbent for a given adsorption problem.

One special type of adsorption from solution merits special mention. It can be illustrated by zeolitic materials commonly used in water softening. Certain ions such as Ca^{++}, Mg^{++}, etc., are taken up by the zeolites. In the process, an equivalent amount of Na^+, H^+ or other ion is released to the solution. The resulting "adsorption" of the Ca^{++} is really an exchange reaction of the type

$$2NaX + Ca^{++} = CaX_2 + 2Na^+$$

where NaX represents the original zeolite or synthetic ion ex-

changer. Exchange adsorption does not represent a true adsorption in the strictest sense of the word. Nevertheless, it is extremely important in modern living and is fairly closely related to adsorption.

BIBLIOGRAPHY.—S. Brunauer, The Adsorption of Gases and Vapors (1943); B. Trapnell, Chemisorption (1955); H. Freundlich, Colloid and Capillary Chemistry, trans. by H. S. Hatfield (1926); J. J. Bikerman, Surface Chemistry for Industrial Research (1947); A. E. Alexander and P. Johnson, Colloid Science, 2 vol. (1949); P. H. Emmett (ed.), Catalysis, vol. i (1954), vol. ii (1955); Chemical Society, Chemisorption (1957).   (P. H. ET.)

ADULLAM, a Canaanite city with a king (Josh. xii, 15) in the Shephelah (Josh. xv, 35), fortified by Rehoboam (II Chron. xi, 7) and still a place of importance at the time of the Maccabees (II Macc. xii, 38). Its chief interest lies in its connection with David, who took refuge in its stronghold ("cave" is now generally admitted to be a scribal error; I Sam. xxii, 1); hence the allusion in the name Adullamites (q.v.) to seceders from a political party on some special issue. A site on the eastern edge of the Shephelah (Shefela) depression in southern Israel, in the neighbourhood of Socoh (Shuweikeh), seems to be indicated. Conjectural identifications have been (1) Khareitun in Jordan, southeast of Bethlehem, which has a large cave; (2) Deir ed-Dibban, about 6 mi. E. of Shuweikeh, where there are caves; and (3) 'Aid el-Ma' (an Arabic popular version of the name), south of Shuweikeh. The last identification is the one most favoured and the particular site is now held to be Tell esh-Sheikh Madhkur to the south of it.

See G. A. Smith, Historical Geography of the Holy Land, 25th ed. (1931).

ADULLAMITES is the name given to the English politicians who rebelled against their Liberal leaders and defeated the Reform bill of 1866, designed by Lord John Russell and W. E. Gladstone to enlarge the electorate by about 40%. These dissidents were aptly described by John Bright as a "political Cave of Adullam," attracting "every one that was in distress, and every one that was discontented." They eventually became about 40 strong; Russell's majority disappeared and his ministry resigned in June. Throughout a session remarkable for brilliance of debate and skill in parliamentary maneuver, the main attack upon the bill came from the Adullamites, a heterogeneous association with varying motives; and especially from Robert Lowe (later Viscount Sherbrooke, q.v.), who, according to Gladstone, "really supplied the whole brains of the opposition" and "had such a command of the House as has never in my recollection been surpassed."

Lowe's speeches form a classic statement of the view that democracy is inimical to good government. Such "distress" was genuine; but "discontent" was also important. Lowe and his lieutenants, E. Horsman and Bernal Osborne, were unrepentant Palmerstonians with frustrated ambitions, who resented the mounting influence of Gladstone and the radicalism of Bright in the Liberal party. Powerfully supported by John Thadeus Delane (q.v.) in the Times, they could rely upon "a last rally of aristocrats of the Whig decadence," in which heirs to peerages, notably Lord Elcho and Lord Grosvenor, played a prominent part; and they were followed by certain members for small constituencies who feared the loss of their seats.

The Adullamite revolt was symptomatic of the divisions within Liberalism after Lord Palmerston's death, and foreshadowed later secessions to Conservatism. However, its success was short-lived and the group soon dissolved. Popular demand for reform, previously limited, had been sharply stimulated by the bill's defeat; and in 1867 their recent ally, Benjamin Disraeli, passed a much more drastic measure, the second Reform act.   (A. F. T.)

ADULT EDUCATION, in its broadest sense, signifies any form of learning undertaken by or provided for mature men and women. Because of the scope of this meaning, the term has had many special interpretations, each built on a conception of the learning process, a historical movement or an institutional pattern.

Adult education deals with that whole span of life which begins when childhood is left behind and continues until death. The mature person passes through several stages that are perhaps as clearly differentiated as are the various periods of childhood. He lives in a social climate that influences his values and shapes the methods by which he achieves his goals. He is also an individual with his own abilities and interests. It is not surprising, therefore, that education carried out in such diverse circumstances presents a vast and varied panorama and one that obstinately defies exact analysis.

The very breadth of the picture, however, provides at least one safeguard: the student of adult education is less likely than the student of earlier education to believe that learning is purely an institutionalized process. Thus the education of the child from 6 to 12 years of age is often thought to be synonymous with the work of the elementary school in the U.S. and the primary school in England despite the obvious fact that the child learns many things not taught him in school. In adult education it is self-evident that no single institution or program can be dominant; central attention must always be given to the learning processes of individuals and groups and not to particular organizational forms.

Many who discuss adult education start from the premise that "education" and "life" are synonymous terms. Since the early Greeks, philosophers have argued that the duty of the statesman is to build a society which will instruct its citizens in the virtues. John Stuart Mill believed that "in its largest acceptation" education (either good or bad) is the result of all experience, a point also central to John Dewey's philosophy. Those who hold this view emphasize the educative impact of motion pictures, television and other mass media; they urge programs of housing, slum clearance or prison reform because of their positive influence; they contend that each person is a product of his relationships with other individuals and groups; and they argue that democratic government, voluntary association and other arenas of practical decision are the proper centres of adult education.

Despite the truth of this viewpoint, most people use the term "adult education" to mean only those experiences that are undertaken with the intent to learn or to teach others some skill, knowledge, understanding, attitude or appreciation. This limitation of the term is supported theoretically on the ground that purposeful learning is more effective than indirect learning, and practically by the fact that purposeful learning tends to be systematic and therefore can be analyzed and appraised without broadening the frame of reference to include all human existence. Those who hold that adult education is activity consciously directed toward learning tend to be interested in the self-education of individuals or to concentrate upon the work of such institutions as the school, the university, the library and the museum, or such educational programs as those carried on by churches, corporations, unions, government departments and co-operatives.

Some form of organized adult education may be discerned in virtually every human society. Anthropologists have noted that some tribes have mysteries to which the individual is not inducted before the years of maturity; one might say, therefore, that organized adult education appears even in primitive communities. Certainly it is present in every civilized society and, in general, the more complex that society, the more ample are its provisions for the education of mature people. The programs of all countries have surface similarities since many of the needs of adults for learning are universal, but essentially each country's work is unique, reflecting the distinctive culture of the nation.

AIMS

The conception underlying much adult education throughout the world is that of helping men and women acquire the knowledge they missed in childhood. Those who pioneer in developing schools for children quickly become aware of how many adults also are ignorant. In country after country the realization of this fact has led to the provision of night schools, evening colleges and other programs because adults demanded learning for themselves, because educators felt a mission to take knowledge to everyone regardless of his age, and because schools for children would not long survive if they had to depend for support on an ignorant citizenry. The major world-wide task of adult education is suggested by the often-quoted observation of James Yen that "three-fourths of the world's population are under-housed, under-clothed, under-fed, and illiterate." These people are to be found in even the most advanced nations, but they are concentrated in under-developed coun-

tries. Throughout the world there are significant efforts to use education to help such people attain a better material life. The governments of such countries as India, Mexico and Ghana support projects designed to educate increasing numbers of their citizens. Most nations feel an obligation to help develop their colonies, their territories and the lands they protect. The financing of developmental activities (including adult education) has become an established foreign policy in many countries. Private efforts are supported by philanthropy or as a part of industrial development. International organizations—most notably, UNESCO—sponsor and stimulate many forms of fundamental education. These various approaches, however, have been inadequate to meet the massive need.

A closely allied conception of adult education is that it is the means by which society will be improved. The quality of a community or a nation rests fundamentally on the wisdom of its citizens. The central task of adult education, therefore, should be to help mature members of society make wise choices on social matters and carry out needed changes. Such education may focus on the individual with the expectation that he will use his knowledge to improve society or it may operate more directly to analyze social ills and remedy them. The Danish folk high school, a secondary school for adult education, for example, became effective as an instrument of national regeneration after defeat by Germany in 1864. The program of St. Francis Xavier university in improving the conditions of fishermen, farmers and miners in the maritime provinces of Canada through the Antigonish movement combining adult education, credit unions and co-operatives is another outstanding example. Efforts to improve society by adult education are going forward throughout the world in countries at all levels of civilization.

The third and most profound conception is that education should be a continuous process throughout maturity, so that the individual may develop, as far as his span of years permits, the vast potentialities of his nature and so that society may benefit as he does so. Those who operate in terms of the first conception sometimes assume that when the existing group of underprivileged adults is cared for and a sound system of schooling for children is established, the need for adult education will disappear. What actually happens is that the need and desire for adult education increase and the ends sought become more varied and intricate. The same development often occurs in efforts to use education to advance society. As specific social needs are met, the surviving institutions broaden their programs to provide for lifelong learning. The folk movements of Sweden, for example, which were originally dedicated to such social goals as temperance, the organization of co-operatives and the advancement of labour unions, came to provide for a wide range of interests and needs.

The various institutions and movements of adult education can find their unifying aim only in such general conceptions as the three expressed above. This point is often obscured because the term "adult education" acquires certain values as it is used within a particular setting. It is sometimes assumed, for example, that adult education is inherently democratic or that it necessarily is concerned with the self-development of the individual. In fact, the massive efforts of Russia, China and other communist countries to use education to build a totalitarian society may closely resemble comparable programs in the free world. *See* also HIGHER EDUCATION: *Points of View.*

MEANS

Each major institution of adult education has its own method of work and its unique terminology. A librarian, a museum curator, a head resident of a settlement house, a dean of university extension and a director of an evening school each will have strong traditions that guide his efforts. Even though all may serve the same city, they may find it hard to communicate with one another or to discern the common unity of their work. The increasing alliance of such people with one another in various associations and councils indicates, however, that they have not only common aims but also fundamental methodological principles.

Since most studies of the learning process have used children as subjects, the psychology of adult education has not been very fully explored. Observation, however, makes clear some outstanding differences between learning in adulthood and in childhood. The adult, for example, has had more experience than the child, as well as kinds of experience that are denied to children, such as courtship, marriage and parenthood, which enrich and give perspective to his learning processes. Also, the child goes to school to fulfill an expected obligation, to prepare for later life and to receive the training which his society believes he needs, whereas adults undertake learning experiences chiefly in terms of immediate necessities or absorbing interests. The adult can learn most things more rapidly than can the child, although many adults encounter initial difficulties because of lack of practice and because their habit patterns are more fixed than are those of children, a fact which is often a deterrent, although not necessarily a block, to education. Another difference is that the teacher of adults has no generalized authority over his students such as that growing out of the adult-child relationship in earlier schooling. He has only the authority he can win by his demonstrated competence.

More exact investigation may lead to the conclusion that the successive stages of adulthood are as worthy of separate methodological consideration as are the various periods of childhood.

INSTITUTIONAL FORMS

As the foregoing suggests, organized adult education exists in all countries, although its institutional patterns vary markedly. In addition to the many illustrations already mentioned and the fuller treatment of activities in the United States and Great Britain, the following other significant programs might well be noted.

As a part of the process of helping its colonies toward full nationhood, Great Britain has established or assisted a number of institutions of higher learning in Africa, Asia and the Caribbean. These fledgling universities usually contain extramural departments, whose work is concerned chiefly with the further education of those who are capable of undertaking advanced studies.

The community development movement, by which local problems (chiefly in emerging nations) are attacked directly by the people themselves operating with skilled advice and assistance, has spread throughout the world. Such activities are supported by private ventures, by national governments, by colonial powers and by the United Nations and its affiliates. This movement has several emphases which are clearly educative in intent and execution. Among them are literacy campaigns and efforts to bring enlightenment to women, helping them to emerge from their subordinate positions and giving them a greater knowledge of sanitation, diet, child-rearing and other aspects of home and family living. The development and execution of local improvement projects (such as the building of roads, schoolhouses and latrines) is also treated in such a way as to create a greater awareness of the spirit and processes of democracy and is therefore fundamentally educational in purpose.

In many countries government departments often have an important role to play. The diffusion of agricultural knowledge, for example, which is essentially a university function in the United States, is a responsibility of the ministry of agriculture in almost all other countries. Many kinds of specialized assistance are also given by health, social welfare, correctional and other departments.

Public libraries are unevenly developed throughout the world. Where they do exist, they often provide important centres for individual study, supplementing the work of other institutions and helping to remedy deficiencies caused by the lack of formal and informal instructional programs.

Finally, it should be noted that throughout the world local initiative, individual leadership, and voluntary effort have produced many different kinds of institutions—missions, instructional centres, museums, mutual improvement circles, residential units and voluntary associations. Some are independent; others are affiliated with organizations which have more general purposes, such as churches, labour unions or political organizations. Each of these institutions approaches the task of education in its own distinctive fashion, and some of them mix education with fraternal, recreational or propagandistic purposes. While each of them is small and may even appear insignificant (particularly in terms of the overwhelming needs of underdeveloped countries), their total impact throughout the world may eventually prove to be very great. Some of them are the sources for later movements of more significant size. Others will achieve their impact by influencing individuals who are destined for leadership.

UNITED STATES

Early Organizations.—In the United States, organized adult education has existed from colonial days. The need to create the basic conditions of a satisfactory life on a new and unsettled continent led the early migrants from Europe to organize various forms of activity, of which the most important was the private school, which usually met in the evening and taught vocational subjects and the rudiments of language and arithmetic.

When the new nation was created, its founders realized that while they had gained political independence there remained the necessity of creating culture in a relatively primitive land. The first half of the 19th century was a period of rich development of institutions, each one unique and often unrelated to the others but all providing new channels of learning. Most important were the lyceums, local associations of men and women who had had some formal education and were concerned both with their own further learning and with the creation of a public school system. Paralleling the growth of the lyceums and to some extent developing out of them were libraries, museums, mechanics' institutes, lecture series, endowed institutions, publicly supported evening schools, and a host of other institutions, many of which achieved permanent status. (*See* also LYCEUMS and CHAUTAUQUAS.)

The 25-year period after the close of the American Civil War was another time of national appraisal and readjustment and therefore another era of growth for organized adult education. Old institutions gained strength. Sporadic university lecture series for the general public flowered into systematic programs of university extension. The Chautauqua institution had great influence and inspired other activities, such as reading circles, traveling chautauquas, summer schools and encampments, and correspondence instruction. Then and later the process of invention continued, often occurring by the creation of voluntary associations which in time were to achieve massive memberships. The National Congress of Parents and Teachers is the best known and largest organization of this type but it is paralleled by countless other groups which vary greatly in size and objectives.

20th Century Developments.—The drive toward the wider diffusion of scientific agriculture which had led earlier to the founding of land-grant colleges and experiment stations finally culminated in 1914 in the establishment by the federal government of the extension service in the department of agriculture. This service became the most highly organized and pervasive instrument of adult education in the United States (*see* AGRICULTURAL EDUCATION AND RESEARCH). When the country entered World War I in 1917, public attention turned to the need for vocational training and congress passed the Smith-Hughes act establishing widespread activities in this field for both young people and adults. The nation also became aware of the many illiterates and unassimilated foreigners in the population (*see* AMERICANIZATION). Programs designed for these two groups were greatly expanded, thereby creating a corps of teachers which later provided one nucleus for the development of a broad adult educational movement. The department of immigration education of the National Education association became the department of adult education in 1924.

In that same year the Carnegie corporation, under the leadership of Frederick Keppel, became interested in adult education and subsidized a number of exploratory inquiries. Observing European programs, Keppel believed that similar activities should be initiated in the United States, but eventually came to the conclusion that the chief need was not the creation of a new program but the extension and co-ordination of existing efforts. Accordingly the American Association for Adult Education (A.A.A.E.) was founded in 1926. This organization, largely financed by the Carnegie corporation until 1941, undertook a broad program studying adult education, bringing together those engaged in the field and, in other ways, stressing the importance of lifelong learning. The A.A.A.E. was particularly successful in enlisting the support of leading figures in political, literary and academic life. Its executive director, Morse A. Cartwright, was for many years the dominant figure in U.S. adult education.

Two enormous programs, one in the 1930s and the other in the 1940s, brought adult education to the attention of the general public and provided initial experience for many of those who were later to be the leaders of the field. The work-relief programs of the depression years used professional and other skilled workers as teachers for adult classes, enrolling at one time more than 2,000,000 students. An even larger program began when the United States entered World War II. In addition to the task of training about 16,000,000 civilians to undertake highly specialized technological warfare, the armed services provided a broad program of off-duty education through classes, discussion groups and correspondence instruction.

By the close of the war, it was apparent that adult education had become a mass movement of great size. The same expansion was taking place at the adult level as had occurred during the 19th century in elementary education and in the first quarter of the 20th century in secondary education. However, while there was great extension of opportunities, programs of service were often poor in quality, brief in duration and guided by either improvisation or the borrowing of procedures originally used in the education of young people but extremely inappropriate for more mature students. A number of attempts to develop a more vital approach were initiated, the most sustained being the group dynamics movement, in which a key figure was Leland Bradford. This was the first major development of educational psychology which worked out its principles with mature students, although it was later seen to have great implications for the education of children as well. A number of university departments of education also began to develop research and training programs, the latter intended primarily for administrators in the field.

In 1951 both the department of adult education and the A.A.A.E. disbanded and the Adult Education Association of the U.S.A. was founded to provide a unified focus for all workers in the field. That same year the Ford foundation created an independent organization, the Fund for Adult Education, to study the whole field and provide financial resources to those efforts which offered the best hope for the development of broad liberal study by adults.

Categories of Institutions.—Education in the United States is generally characterized by its decentralization of control, but nowhere more conspicuously than in adult education. The institutions operating in the field are myriad but they may be grouped together into certain large categories distinguished in terms of basic purpose.

The first category includes those institutions which are primarily concerned with the education of adults. Grouped here are the extension services, the private schools (including those which teach by correspondence), the vocational rehabilitation agencies, and specially endowed institutions (such as Cooper Union).

The second category includes those institutions which educate both adults and young people. The chief examples are the public schools and the institutions of higher learning. Since the control of these institutions in the United States is highly autonomous, the extent and quality of adult education they offer vary markedly.

The third category includes those institutions in which adult education is a co-ordinate function paralleling such other purposes as recreation, community service or fraternity. In this category are libraries, museums, group work agencies, voluntary associations, settlement houses, community centres and co-operatives.

The fourth category includes those institutions in which education is a subordinate function used to accomplish a primary end. In this category are churches; labour unions; industrial and commercial companies; governmental departments interested in defense, health, welfare, safety, conservation, correction and other purposes; hospitals; commercial mass media of communication; and associations whose aim is to improve or reform society.

Many of those professionally engaged in adult education are primarily identified not with any one institution but with a field of specialization which cuts across the work of many institutions. Health education, safety education, education for effective home living, vocational education and many other areas of work provide a focus for those with special training or interests.

A brief listing such as the foregoing can include only the major enterprises. It leaves out of account what may well be the largest and most important form of American adult education: the effort of the individual or of the small special group to achieve, with any resources at hand, a better understanding of the world and a greater capacity to deal with it.

BIBLIOGRAPHY.—UNESCO, *International Directory of Adult Education* (1953); British Ministry of Reconstruction, Adult Education Committee, *Design for Democracy* (1956); Robert Peers, *Adult Education* (1958); National Society for the Study of Education, *Community Education, Principles and Practices from World-Wide Experience,* 58th yearbook, part 1 (1959); Paul H. Sheats, Clarence D. Jayne and Ralph B. Spence, *Adult Education* (1953); C. Hartley Grattan, *In Quest of Knowledge* (1955); John Walker Powell, *Learning Comes of Age* (1956). (C. O. H.)

GREAT BRITAIN

Early Organizations.—The rise of organizations to promote adult education in Great Britain is generally dated from the end of the 18th century. An adult school was founded in Nottingham in 1798, and lectures given to artisans by George Birkbeck in Glasgow in 1799 led to the establishment of the first mechanics' institute. In the first half of the 19th century adult schools and mechanics' institutes were established in many parts of England. The inspiration and purposes of the two kinds of institutions were different. The institutes arose out of the desire of artisans to understand the sciences and applications of science which were transforming industrial processes and social conditions. The adult schools were formed largely by religious people who wished to reduce adult illiteracy, often with the hope of encouraging the reading of the Bible. Both the schools and the institutes were supported entirely by voluntary effort and financial contributions. After the middle of the 19th century both tended to decline. Some of the institutes became technical colleges, others middle-class reading and lecture societies. The adult school movement revived in the latter part of the century and was still active in the second half of the 20th century.

Apart from organizations concerned with adult education in its less formal modes, the 19th century saw the appearance of educational work promoted by co-operative societies, the establishment of people's or workingmen's colleges and the rise of the university extension movement.

The workingmen's colleges were in part the result of dissatisfaction with mechanics' institutes, in part the product of Chartism and of Christian Socialist ideas. The first was started in Sheffield in 1842 but the best known was established in London in 1854 under the leadership of F. D. Maurice. Others were founded in a number of towns but disappeared or changed their character. All were nonresidential, unlike Ruskin college, Oxford, which was founded in 1899 to provide workingmen with education designed to equip them for their responsibilities as citizens and trade unionists. A "strike" in Ruskin college against the "orthodox" teaching of economics led in 1909 to the establishment of a labour college in London and later to the foundation of the National Council of Labour Colleges, which rejects the idea of "objective" adult education.

The university extension movement, in its narrower sense of a movement for part-time adult education, owed its inception to James Stuart, a Cambridge university lecturer who in a private capacity delivered courses of lectures to audiences in the north and midlands in the late 1860s. As a result of his work, Cambridge university in 1873 set up a Local Lectures syndicate to provide lecture courses in many parts of the country and the universities of London and Oxford took similar steps in 1876 and 1878 respectively, the London work being confined to the metropolitan area. The provision of lecture courses increased rapidly in the 1880s and 1890s, in spite of the fact that all the costs of lecturers' fees had to be borne by the students. This was a principal reason for the comparative failure of the movement to attract large numbers of working-class students, but it met a strong middle-class and feminine demand for facilities for higher education, and in several towns extension societies were among the institutions out of which new university colleges, later to become universities, grew.

20th-Century Developments.—In the 20th century the term adult education has been used to denote the "liberal education of adults," in distinction from the term "further education," which has been used with reference to technological and other vocational education for adolescents and adults. Adult education thus interpreted has been the concern largely of voluntary organizations, especially the Workers' Educational association (W.E.A.), and the extramural departments of universities, with financial assistance from the board and ministry of education and from local education authorities.

The W.E.A. was founded by Albert Mansbridge in 1903. Mansbridge's original intention was to create an organization which would bring together the university extension movement and working-class people and organizations. In 1907, however, a conference held at Oxford considered afresh the best way in which universities might contribute to working-class education and in 1908 the University of Oxford sponsored two university tutorial classes. The purpose of the classes was to provide opportunities for working-class students to pursue long and thorough courses of study under university teachers, and though lectures formed part of the class proceedings, much importance was attached to discussion of the lecture and to regular reading and writing at home by the students. In the interests of tutorial work the size of classes was limited. With R. H. Tawney as tutor, the first classes were very successful and the quality of the work done impressed observers in the universities and the board of education. More classes were promoted by Oxford and by other universities, and in 1909 Oxford instituted a joint committee of members of the university and working-class representatives nominated by the W.E.A. to be responsible for the organization of this kind of work.

Similar joint committees were shortly afterward set up by most of the other universities in England and Wales, and by 1914 the tutorial-class movement was well established, with every university and university college participating.

The establishment of university extramural departments followed the publication in 1919 of the final report of an adult education committee of the ministry of reconstruction. In addition to suggesting that universities should institute departments of adult education with full-time academic heads and full-time as well as part-time staffs, the committee strongly urged that grants should be made directly to voluntary organizations by the board of education to enable them to provide facilities of a less advanced kind. In 1924 the board issued grant regulations giving effect to this proposal and before the outbreak of World War II was making contributions to the teaching costs of courses attended by some 66,000 students, of whom over 12,000 were in university tutorial classes.

After the passing of the Education act of 1944 the provision of publicly assisted adult education in Great Britain increased considerably. The number of students attending classes provided by universities and the W.E.A. with financial assistance from the ministry of education was in the second half of the 20th century more than 150,000, of whom more than half were women, though the number in university tutorial classes was little more than before 1939. Four universities which had not previously done so set up extramural departments. Approximately 30 new residential colleges for adult education were established. Some were provided by universities, a small number by voluntary effort, but the majority by local education authorities. They all differed from Ruskin college and several others established earlier in the 20th century in that they provided only short courses, lasting anything from a weekend to a few weeks, or occasionally two or three months. Wartime arrangements for providing civilian aid to adult education in the armed forces were replaced in 1949 by a permanent scheme comprising a central committee for adult education in her majesty's forces and committees for services' education at most of the universities, all providing for representation of the universities, local education authorities, the W.E.A. and the

education branches of the services. A number of full-time tutors were engaged for this work by universities and the W.E.A. and a considerably increased number for work with civilian students. A Universities' Council for Adult Education and a National Institute of Adult Education were founded, while a Central Joint Advisory Committee for Tutorial Classes, which was established in 1909, continued to be active.

Organizations providing less formal kinds of adult education (notably women's institutes) expanded rapidly, and local education authorities concerned themselves more with "liberal" adult education than in the past.

The distinctive features of British adult education remained: the large part played by the universities; the recognition of the importance of voluntary organizations; the substantial state assistance given both to universities and to voluntary organizations; and the concern with liberal and social studies.

See AGRICULTURAL EDUCATION AND RESEARCH; AUDIO-VISUAL EDUCATION; CORRESPONDENCE EDUCATION; ILLITERACY; UNIVERSITY EXTENSION; *see* also references under "Adult Education" in the Index.

BIBLIOGRAPHY.—M. E. Sadler, *Continuation Schools in England and Elsewhere* (1907); *Final Report of the Adult Education Committee of the Ministry of Reconstruction* (H.M.S.O., 1919); S. G. Raybould, *The English Universities and Adult Education* (1951); M. D. Stocks, *The Workers' Educational Association: the First Fifty Years* (1953).
(S. G. R.)

ADULTERATION, the act of debasing a commercial commodity or substituting an inferior article for a superior one in order to gain an illegitimate profit. The term is usually applied to the debasement of foods, drugs or cosmetics. *See* HEALTH AND SAFETY LAWS.

ADULTERY, sexual intercourse by a married person with someone other than the spouse. In some U.S. penal legislation the term includes also an unmarried person's sexual relations with one who is married. Adultery is almost universally regarded as the gravest infraction of marital vows and is, therefore, the commonest ground for divorce specified in the statutes. Except for an interlude in Cromwell's 17th-century theocracy, adultery has always been regarded in England as a matter exclusively within the cognizance of spiritual authorities. A number of other countries, *e.g.*, Japan, Uruguay and the U.S.S.R., have no penal provisions on the subject. Some codes, *e.g.*, those of France, Italy and Argentina, distinguish between adultery by a husband and adultery by a wife, punishing the latter more severely or in circumstances where the husband would not be guilty of an offense.

In the United States, as a result of Puritan influence and absence of any official church with acknowledged jurisdiction, criminal legislation against adultery (and even fornication between unmarried persons) is quite common. The maximum sentence authorized for adultery ranges up to 21 years, but 5 years is the typical maximum. It is remarkable that actual prosecutions have been extremely rare, even in a state such as New York where thousands of cases of adultery have been made a matter of judicial record every year in divorce proceedings. The practical nullification of the penal provisions against adultery probably reflects general recognition that adultery, although immoral, is not subject to effective restraint by the penal law and occurs so frequently as to make it unfair to select a few scapegoats for punishment. The American Law institute voted in 1955 not to include adultery in its Model Penal code. *See* also DIVORCE; MARRIAGE.

See A. C. Kinsey, W. B. Pomeroy and C. E. Martin, *Sexual Behavior in the Human Male* (1948); A. C. Kinsey *et al.*, *Sexual Behavior in the Human Female* (1953).
(L. B. S.)

ADUWA, a town in the province of Tigre, Ethiopia. It lies 6,500 ft. above sea level 17 mi. E. of Aksum, the ancient capital of Ethiopia, and 50 mi. W. of Adigrat, which is on the main Dessye-Asmara highway. It is a market centre of an agricultural district. Pop. (1965 est.) 12,450. About 2½ mi. to the northwest, on a volcanic outcrop, are the ruins of Fremona, the headquarters in Ethiopia of the Portuguese Jesuits during the 16th and 17th centuries. The site of the crushing defeat of an Italian force under Gen. Oreste Baratieri by Emperor Menelik II on March 1, 1896, is about 10 mi. E. of Aduwa, in a fantastic region of volcanic formations. His victory firmly established Menelik's authority in Ethiopia. The town was bombed and captured by the Italians in Oct. 1935 and incorporated into Eritrea. It was recaptured by British and Ethiopian troops in April 1941. *See* also ETHIOPIA: *History;* ITALY: *History.* (G. C. L.)

AD VALOREM, the term applied to tax rates which are imposed on the basis of value of the taxed items. Literally the term means "according to value." Traditionally in Great Britain, the U.S. and other countries most customs and excises had "specific" rates; that is, the tax base was defined in terms of physical units such as gallons, pounds or individual items. While many excises, such as those on gasoline, liquor and tobacco, and many customs duties still have specific rates, there has been a definite trend toward increased use of ad valorem rates.

The ad valorem basis has the important advantage of adjusting the tax burden in terms of consumer expenditures on the taxed items and avoids the serious discrimination of specific rates against the low priced varieties of the commodities. Cigarette producers have long argued that the specific rate on cigarettes has drastically checked the growth of economy brands. If customs duties are designed primarily for protection, the ad valorem basis provides more adequate protection for the more expensive articles in the class, and avoids the extremely detailed classifications of goods and rate structures often established in specific rate tariffs in an effort to adjust the duty in a rough fashion according to value.

The primary difficulty with the ad valorem basis, one of particular concern with tariffs, is that of establishing a satisfactory value figure. The usual practice is to define the dutiable value as the foreign export value (converted, when necessary, at the current exchange rate), that is, the actual cost to the importer or the domestic sale value in the exporting country, whichever is greater. An invoice must be submitted at the port of entry giving details of cost and final decision is made by the customs appraisers. Firms engaged in foreign trade occasionally complain of unreasonable valuations. With excise taxes the task is simpler since the rates can usually be applied to the actual selling price of the vendor liable for payment of tax, a figure readily available. However, a few difficulties are encountered, particularly when an ad valorem excise is applied at the manufacturing level. If the tax is applied to the actual price in all cases, those manufacturers who perform wholesaling functions and sell to retailers or consumers will be discriminated against compared to firms selling competing goods in large volumes at low prices to wholesale distributors.

Sales taxes of broad scope of necessity must have ad valorem rates. Property taxes are sometimes referred to as ad valorem levies since the rates are applied to the value of the property, as distinguished from special assessments, which are frequently imposed on a specific unit (*e.g.,* front footage) basis. (J. F. D.)

ADVANCED GUARD, the protective detachment pushed forward in advance of an army or smaller force, moving towards the enemy. Although protective in purpose, its action is largely offensive in order to fulfill its duties. These are to gain information of the position and strength of the enemy's main forces, to deny similar information to the enemy's reconnoitring troops, to brush aside his advanced detachments and so prevent delay to the march of the main body. When the advanced guard eventually comes to grips with the real strength of the enemy, it should fix him securely in order to allow its own main force to deploy and maneuver. Gaining time is then as vital as saving time in the earlier phase and for this purpose the advanced guard may have to resort to attack, defense, or an alternation of both.

The role of an advanced guard may be likened to that of an outstretched arm of a man moving in the dark. Flank guards and rear guards are variations of an advanced guard, whose names explain their roles. Outposts are a protective detachment to a force halted.

ADVANCEMENT, in law, a sum of money or other benefit conferred by a parent or a person *in loco parentis* (acting in place of a parent) upon a child, later to be deducted upon the parent's death from the child's share in the estate. The rule that an advancement must be brought into hotchpot (*q.v.*) has its basis in the presumption that generally a parent does not wish to treat his children unequally. The presumption is rebuttable, however, and the determination of whether or not a benefit conferred upon a child by his parent was meant as a gift, an advancement, or perhaps only as a loan may be difficult. In England a benefit conferred upon a child for the purpose of establishing him in life or upon the occasion of his marriage is rebuttably presumed to be an advancement. Some U.S. state statutes provide that no benefit conferred upon a child is to be treated as an advancement unless it has been clearly stated to be so at the time it was conferred. The rules on advancement apply only where the parent dies intestate. Where the parent has made a will containing a provision for the benefit of a child and afterward actually confers to that child a benefit of property of a description similar to that given by the will, under the rule against double portions the benefit is presumed to have been given in full or partial satisfaction of the legacy. *See* also INTESTATE SUCCESSION; INHERITANCE.

See D. H. Parry, *Law of Succession* (1953); T. A. Atkinson, *Law of Wills* (1937). (M. RN.)

ADVENT, a holy season of the Christian church, the period of preparation for the celebration of the Nativity or Christmas (Lat. *Adventus,* "coming"; *i.e.,* of Christ), and also as preparation for the second coming of Christ. In the Western Church Advent begins on the Sunday nearest to Nov. 30 (St. Andrew's day); in the Eastern churches it begins about the middle of November. It is uncertain at what date the season began to be observed. A council at Saragossa in 380 forbade the faithful to be absent from church from Dec. 17 to Epiphany, but the first unquestionable mention of Advent is at the Council of Tours (567). It had long been recognized in the west as the beginning of the ecclesiastical year. The season is a solemn one, though not now kept as Lent as it once was. The Roman Catholic Church forbids the solemnization of marriage during Advent. In many countries it was marked by a variety of popular observances, some of which still survive. *See* also CHRISTMAS; CHURCH YEAR.

ADVENTISM, a general term referring to a number of religious bodies a dominant element of whose doctrine is the imminent second coming of Christ. In the early decades of the 19th century there developed spontaneously, in various countries, an interest in the prophetic portions of the Bible. The result was a conviction that the end of the age was near at hand, an event to be marked by the literal, personal coming of Christ in glory.

Millerism.—In the United States this became a rather well-defined interchurch movement led by William Miller (*q.v.*), a Baptist and a former officer during the War of 1812. Prominently associated with him was Joshua V. Himes, a Boston minister of the Christian Church, who had been a leader in the abolitionist movement. Miller began to preach in 1831 but aroused no great interest until 1839. From then onward he rapidly gained adherents, both ministerial and lay, from the various Protestant churches. The press labeled such adherents Millerites. In the spring of 1843 the Millerites seem first to have used the name Adventists to describe themselves (from Lat. *adventus,* "coming").

At that time there was a rather widely held view among writers on biblical prophecy that the end of the present age of sin was near at hand. What would follow this soon expected end? The Millerites answered, fiery conflagration, then the new heaven and new earth, the eternal home of the redeemed in the immortal state. Other Protestant theologians declared, spiritual regeneration, this regeneration to be gradual till the whole world was converted. As the Millerite leaders sought repeatedly to emphasize, the heart of their preaching was not so much the time of Christ's coming as the nature of it. They affirmed that they were but restating the teaching of the apostles and 16th-century reformers. Some of their opponents declared that the coming of Christ would be spiritual, invisible, his spiritual coming into the hearts of men and converting them; others asserted that it would be literal, introducing a real kingdom on the earth during the millennium, before the end; others expected the advent after the millennium.

Miller set a tentative date of the coming of Christ between March 21, 1843, and March 21, 1844. The movement seems not to have been greatly shaken by what came to be called the First Disappointment, and in the summer of 1844 a second date was set by some (Oct. 22, 1844), though Miller, Himes, and certain other prominent leaders hesitated almost to the last to advocate so specific a time. Oct. 23 brought the Great Disappointment. The Millerite movement was stunned, though not quite shattered. Its peak number of believers, in 1844, may be conservatively estimated as totaling not fewer than 50,000, and possibly as many as 100,000 persons.

Sharpening the distress of the Millerites were the fanciful, even lurid tales that had been circulated for years in the public press, picturing them as a wildly fanatical group. One of the chief of these stories was that they had prepared ascension robes in which to go to glory, but search of the original sources leads to the conclusion that the ascension robe story is wholly groundless. Those stories of fanaticism that can be proved establish only that Millerism was troubled at times by the same kind of emotionally unstable enthusiasts that disturbed earlier religious awakenings, such as the Protestant Reformation and the Wesley movement.

Aftermath of Millerism.—On April 29, 1845, a representative company of Millerites met in Albany, N.Y., in what was announced as a Mutual Conference of Adventists. They had earlier been held together by the crusading momentum of the movement; now, in order to maintain cohesion, they needed a statement of doctrine and some kind of organization. But many of the Millerite leaders were suspicious of formal creeds and close-knit church organization, considering them to be repressive of the truth and fettering to the spirit. Though the meeting produced some results, it was evident that the Millerite movement as such had ended.

Certain modern church bodies, however, holding to a belief in the personal and imminent return of Christ, find their roots in Millerism. With variations, they believe that a man's failure to accept salvation through Christ will mean his final and complete extinction, not his conscious suffering in hell throughout eternity. With one exception (see below) they all observe Sunday as their weekly holy day. There is some question as to which of the presently existing Adventist-oriented churches are truly direct outgrowths of the Millerite movement rather than simply offshoots of one or another of such churches. There seems good evidence for accepting the following:

1. Advent Christian Church, organized in 1861, with a membership in the later 1960s of about 31,000. In 1964 the former Life and Advent Union merged with this body.

2. Church of God of the Abrahamic Faith, incorporated in Oregon, Ill., in 1921; membership about 5,800. Though this church is generally found in the list of those considered Millerite in origin, some of its spokesmen believe that it should not be considered an outgrowth of Millerism.

3. Seventh-day Adventists, organized in 1863, membership in the later 1960s about 1,660,000, including about 390,000 in the United States and Canada.

Except in the last-mentioned church, the membership of these bodies is confined almost wholly to the United States and Canada.

Seventh-day Adventists.—When no visible event occurred on Oct. 22, 1844, most Millerites took one of two positions: (1) that the date had been wrongly computed, thus stimulating believers to further time-setting, or (2) that the whole prophetic exegesis on which the date rested was invalid, thus prompting them to abandon the movement. Seventh-day Adventism began with the belief that the prophetic date was correct but that the event foretold was not the Second Advent but the opening of an investigative judgment in heaven, which would terminate in the coming of Christ to execute judgment on all. This group, which soon adopted the seventh-day sabbath from the Seventh Day Baptists, early established as one of its prime tenets that man cannot know the time of Christ's coming, though, in harmony with Christ's own words, he can know when "he is near, at the very gates" (Matt. 24:33).

History.—In their earliest years these Sabbath-keeping Adventists—the name Seventh-day Adventists was not officially adopted until 1860—were found largely in the New England states. In 1849 they started a paper called *Present Truth*, superseded in November 1850 by the *Advent Review and Sabbath Herald* (later renamed *Review and Herald*), one of the oldest continuously published religious journals in America. In 1855 a headquarters was established in Battle Creek, Mich., which marked the beginning of expansion westward. In May 1863 a general denominational organization was created and in 1874 the first missionary, J. N. Andrews, was sent abroad. In 1903 the headquarters was moved to Washington, D.C.

Organization and Government.—Direction of the denomination's world activities is by the General Conference of Seventh-day Adventists, headquarters at Washington, D.C. Sessions of this General Conference, constituted of delegates chosen on a membership basis from the various subdivisions of the organization over the world, are held quadrennially. Interim business is conducted by the executive committee. Under the General Conference are 13 world divisions, made up of union and local conferences. Each administrative unit has a president and an executive committee. The local congregations elect lay elders, deacons, and other officers to carry on the local church work. Pastoral supervision of churches is provided from the local conference office, which pays these pastors from a central fund.

Doctrine.—Seventh-day Adventists believe, among other things, in one God, revealed as Father, Son, and Holy Spirit; in the Bible as the inspired Word of God; in creation by divine fiat; in the fall of man and his redemption only through the substitutionary death of Christ; in the Ten Commandments as man's eternal moral standard, understanding that the command to keep holy "the seventh day" requires observing the seventh day of the week as the Sabbath; in the gift of prophecy in the church; in the mortality of man and his unconsciousness in death; in the resurrection at the last day, with immortality meted out to the righteous and annihilation by fire to the wicked; in the proper care of the body as the "temple of the Holy Ghost"; in the premillennial, personal, visible return of Christ at a time unknown but close at hand; in a new earth, created from the ruins of the old after the millennium, as the final abode of the immortal saints.

Activities.—The major activities of the church may be comprehended under four heads: (1) Evangelistic preaching is conducted in more than 800 languages and dialects. (2) Publishing plants are found in most of the principal countries; literature is sold from house to house by trained colporteurs. (3) A separate school system—primary, secondary, and college—is maintained in the U.S. and many other countries; there are also graduate schools and a medical college. (4) A chain of medical institutions, often called sanitariums, is operated; the first was the Battle Creek (Mich.) Sanitarium, founded in 1866.

BIBLIOGRAPHY.—William Miller, *Evidence from Scripture and History of the Second Coming of Christ, About the Year 1843* (1836); Sylvester Bliss, *Memoirs of William Miller* (1853); Isaac C. Wellcome, *History of the Second Advent Message and Mission, Doctrine and People* (1874); United States Department of Commerce, Bureau of the Census, *Religious Bodies: 1936* (1941); Francis D. Nichol, *The Midnight Cry* (1944), *Ellen G. White and Her Critics*, ch. xiii (1951); Le Roy E. Froom, *The Prophetic Faith of Our Fathers*, vol. iii and iv (1946, 1954); Arthur Whitefield Spalding, *Origin and History of Seventh-day Adventists*, 4 vol. (1961–62); Don F. Neufeld (ed.), *Seventh-day Adventist Encyclopedia* (1966); National Council of the Churches of Christ in the U.S.A., *Yearbook of American Churches* (annual); *Seventh-day Adventist Yearbook* (annual).

(F. D. N.; K. H. W.)

ADVERTISING, a form of paid public announcement intended to promote the sale of a commodity or service, to advance an idea or to bring about some other effect desired by the advertiser. It is essentially a form of communication through such diverse media as handbills, newspapers, magazines, billboards, letters, radio and television broadcasts and motion pictures. The term is broad enough to include a wide range of types, from a small two-line entry in a newspaper or magazine to a "spread" of several full pages, or from a small sign in a shop window to a huge billboard with changing designs in coloured lights. During the 20th century, particularly in the United States, advertising became a basic factor in merchandising. It was estimated that by the mid-1960s more than $15,000,000,000 was spent each year on advertising in the United States and nearly £570,000,000 (or $1,600,000,000) in Great Britain. (*See* also PROPAGANDA; PUBLIC RELATIONS.)

To a manufacturer, advertising is usually considered part of the firm's marketing program, along with personal selling, packaging, display, pricing and product design. To the retailer, it is also a part of his so-called "marketing mix," along with display, store promotions, etc. To the various media of communication it is both a major source of revenue and a means of providing information on products and services to their audiences. To the consumer it is a major source of information regarding products and services.

Purposes and Types.—Purposes of advertising may be divided, first of all, into two types, product and institutional. Product advertising emphasizes the type of product or the brand to be sold; institutional advertising concerns the firm that makes or sells the product. Automobile advertisements that emphasize the virtues of a particular car are examples of product advertising. Advertisements that strive to improve the public's impression of a firm by describing its research facilities are examples of institutional advertising. Retailers use product advertising to describe the products they have for sale, institutional advertising to build a favourable store image. Among both manufacturers and retailers, product advertising is the more common of the two types.

Advertisements may also be distinguished on the basis of whether they are designed for direct or indirect action. The direct-action advertisement aims at achieving some immediate action by the reader or viewer, such as buying a product or sending in a coupon. The indirect action advertisement is more concerned with building a favourable mental picture of the brand that will pay off later in sales. The manufacturer is more likely to use image-building advertisements, while the retailer is more concerned with gaining immediate action. The manufacturer thus builds acceptance for the brand and the retailer capitalizes on that acceptance at the local level and translates it into action.

A distinction may also be made between primary and selective purposes. When a dairy or group of dairies attempts to convince people they should drink milk rather than other beverages, it is engaging in primary advertising. When one dairy tries to build demand for its particular brand as compared with competitors, it is using selective advertising.

Historical Background.—The first advertising was by public criers in ancient times who circulated through the streets calling attention to the sale of such items as slaves, cattle and imports. An ancient written advertisement, perhaps 3,000 years old, was discovered by an archeologist delving in the ruins of Thebes. It offered a "whole gold coin" as reward for the return of a runaway man-slave named Shem. During the middle ages the spoken word was the principal means of communication and there was little of the activity that we now call advertising. The invention of movable type (c. 1450) by Johann Gutenberg made it possible to produce many copies of books and periodicals cheaply and quickly and ushered in the modern era of advertising.

Printing made possible the transition from simple announcement to the system of argument and suggestion which constitutes modern advertising, and the medium of this development was the newspaper. The weekly papers sometimes carried a few advertisements, including the first offerings of coffee (1652), chocolate (1657) and tea (1658). In June 1666 the *London Gazette*, no. 62, announced the first advertisement supplement as follows: "An Advertisement—Being daily prest to the publication of Books, Medicines, and other things not properly the business of a Paper of Intelligence. This is to notifie once for all, that we will not charge the *Gazette* with Advertisements, unless they be matter of state; but that a Paper of Advertisements will be forthwith printed apart, and recommended to the Publick by another hand."

The restriction of the word "advertisement," which for Shakespeare and the translators of the Authorized Version had meant information of any kind, to a business announcement was made in *The Tatler* of Sept. 14, 1710:

"It is my custom, in a dearth of News, to entertain myself with those Collections of Advertisements that appear at the end of all our Publick Prints. . . . Advertisements are of great use to the vulgar. First of all, as they are instruments of ambition. A man that is by no means big enough for the *Gazette* may easily creep into the advertisements. . . . A second use which this sort of writings have been turned to of late Years, has been the management of Controversy. . . . The inventors of *Strops for Razors* have written against one another in this way for several years. The third and last of these writings is to inform the World where they may be furnished with almost everything that is necessary for Life. If a Man has Pains in His head, Cholic in his Bowels, or spots in his Cloathes, he may here meet with proper Cures and Remedies. If a Man would recover a Wife or a Horse that is stolen or strayed; if he wants new Sermons, Electuaries, Asses' milk, or anything else, either for his Body or his Mind, this is the place to look for them in."

In 1712 all advertising was dealt a blow when the British government imposed a tax of one halfpenny on every newspaper or magazine sold and an additional tax of one shilling on every advertisement. This move was aimed at silencing press criticism, not raising money. In spite of this tax, however, advertising prospered during the 18th century. In 1758 Samuel Johnson wrote in *The Idler*:

Advertisements are now so numerous that they are very negligently perused, and it is therefore become necessary to gain attention by magnificence of promise and by eloquence sometimes sublime and sometimes pathetick.

Benjamin Franklin is regarded by many as the father of advertising in the United States. He put advertising before editorial in the masthead of the first issue of the *Pennsylvania Gazette* in 1729. But the *Boston News-Letter* had contained advertisements for the sale or rent of houses, farms, shops, vessels and other items in its first issue published in April 1704. Much of the early newspaper advertising in the colonies was for patent medicines and gave advertising a bad name that persisted for many years.

The 19th century was a period of expansion in advertising as well as in business generally. The Industrial Revolution expanded the output of factories and advertising helped market this output. The growth of the penny press and of magazines, combined with an increase in the educational level, brought forth an increase in audiences. Improvements in transportation made it possible to distribute magazines on a national basis. In 1830 there were an estimated 800 magazines and newspapers in the U.S.; by 1861 the number had risen to more than 5,000. By 1870 the use of magazines for general advertising was established. This permitted vast increase in circulation and a reduction in price. By the turn of the century *Cosmopolitan* and *McClure's* carried about 100 pages of advertising in a single issue. Slogans and jingles became favourite advertising techniques. Total advertising expenditures rose from $60,000,000 in 1867 to $360,000,000 in 1890. Some of the trade-marks famous today were popularized during this period.

During the first two decades of the 20th century, advertising was re-examined. Certain excesses in its claims had developed and caused widespread resentment. Regulation came both from within the industry and from the government.

In 1914 the Audit Bureau of Circulations (A.B.C.) was organized. It quickly became the main source of reliable information about the circulation of periodicals in the United States and Canada. Such information was obviously of great value to advertisers as a means of determining the size of the audience reached by each publication.

After World War I came the era of salesmanship. Advertising was accepted as an essential tool in selling the booming output of the nation's factories. "It pays to advertise" became a standard slogan. Soap companies and automobile companies were among the most important advertisers. It was discovered that testimonials by movie stars were very effective in selling such items as soap and cigarettes. Good advertising copywriters were much sought after.

A major new advertising medium, radio, was added during the 1920s. At first most radio commercials were indirect and there was doubt as to whether advertising would be allowed on the air. However, commercial radio thrived and by 1928 it accounted for $10,500,000 in advertising. Total advertising expenditures in the United States reached a peak of $3,400,000,000 in 1929.

The depression of the 1930s brought on a searching re-examination of the entire economic system, including advertising. Advertising was blamed for some of the nation's economic problems and total expenditures for advertising dropped to $1,300,000,000 in 1933, less than half the 1929 total. Much restrictive legislation was proposed and some of it passed. The sales resistance of consumers forced businessmen to turn to advertising research. Researchers like A. C. Nielsen, George Gallup and Daniel Starch were among the pioneers in trying to determine what kind of advertising was most effective.

During the years following World War II, U.S. advertising expenditures soared. From $3,400,000,000 in 1946 they rose to $5,700,000,000 in 1950 and exceeded $11,000,000,000 by 1960. Meanwhile the industry experienced further criticism. Two books, *The Hucksters* (1946) and *The Hidden Persuaders* (1957), became best sellers. Each painted a picture of the advertising world which disturbed both the friends and the critics of advertising.

A new medium, television, was added to the U.S. advertising scene immediately after the war. It had a spectacular growth. By the 1960s there were more than 46,000,000 homes with television sets and approximately 600 broadcasting stations in the U.S. Within less than ten years television had grown to be the third largest advertising medium in the U.S. (after newspapers and direct mail) in terms of total dollars spent and the largest in the top national advertisers' budgets.

Two new research tools—motivation research, which emphasized man's subconscious motives (*see* PSYCHOLOGY, APPLIED: *Other Areas of Applied Psychology: Motivational Research*) and operations research, which emphasized mathematical approaches to advertising—were used by advertising and marketing specialists. Although advertising had long been considered a tool of marketing, new emphasis was placed on co-ordinating advertising with other tools of the marketing program.

In Great Britain the government became one of the nation's largest advertisers. Among its most striking successes was the campaign for diphtheria immunization. Between 1941 and 1954 it virtually banished diphtheria as an epidemic disease. Other campaigns were launched on behalf of the fighting services, civil defense, blood donation, safety, and national health and nursing services.

Total advertising expenditures in Great Britain rose from approximately £68,200,000 ($273,000,000 before devaluation of the pound) in 1938 to over £400,000,000 ($1,128,000,000 after devaluation of the pound) in 1960. The estimated British ratio of advertising to national income was 1.5% in 1953 and 2.1% in 1959. Comparable figures for the United States were 2.6% for 1953 and 2.9% for 1959. The U.S. figure slightly exceeded the prewar figure while the British figure was slightly below the prewar figure. On the other hand, if 1948 is used as a base year, the advertising ratio increased more in Britain than in the United States.

The proportion of the British advertising handled by agencies grew from 42% in 1938 to 49% in 1956. This rise was probably due in large part to the growth of national brand advertising, which is almost always handled through agencies.

By mid-20th century the press accounted for about half the total normally spent for advertising in Great Britain. Restrictions on newsprint introduced during World War II and continued for many postwar years brought about a change in the relative proportions of advertising within the press section. Before the war the national newspapers carried about 17% of all advertising and the provincial press 15%. In 1952 the proportions were almost reversed, with 16.1% carried by provincial newspapers and 12.2% by the nationals. Trade and technical journals, magazines and periodicals increased their share of advertising revenue as compared with prewar. A study of the press by the royal commission on the press (1947–1949) indicated that attempts by advertisers to sway newspaper policy or obtain omission or insertion of specific items of news were generally unsuccessful.

The printed media's share of total advertising expenditures dropped from 58% to 49% between 1954 and 1958. There was, however, an even more dramatic shift in the expenditures of the top 20 advertisers in newspapers, magazines and television. In 1957 the top 20 spent 57% in newspapers and magazines and 43%

in television. In 1958 they spent 46% in newspapers and magazines, 54% in television.

The Television act of 1954 made one television channel an advertising medium in Great Britain. Advertisers were not given control of the program and thus were not sponsors, but they were permitted to buy spot announcements. Control of the service was placed with the Independent Television authority (I.T.A.) which was made responsible for seeing that the Television act was carried out. According to Mark Abrams of the London Press Exchange, Ltd., there were over 10,000,000 British homes equipped to receive television at the end of 1960. This provided advertisers with a potential coverage of about 50% of all consumers in the country.

Film became an important advertising medium in Great Britain. Apart from special showings of films or documentaries, motion-picture advertising was usually in the form of short films lasting only for 15 seconds, one minute or two minutes. Most of the theatres accepted advertising films or slides. (*See* also BROADCASTING.)

Social and Economic Aspects.—In his exhaustive report on *The Economic Aspects of Advertising*, published in 1942, Neil H. Borden, professor of advertising at the Harvard Graduate School of Business Administration, concluded that advertising's chief economic contribution was its ability to promote a dynamic, expanding economy. He found that one of its principal means of accomplishing this was through its encouragement of the development of new products. He emphasized the role of advertising in capitalizing on differences in brands and thus making it possible for an entrepreneur to regain fairly quickly a substantial part of his growth costs. Advertising thus encourages pioneering in new products and services.

Many people believe that advertising makes the goods and services they buy more expensive. The evidence accumulated by Borden and other investigators indicates it is even more likely to make them cheaper. A change in price of a product may result from changes in (1) cost of producing or marketing it and (2) changes in the demand for it.

In the case of such products as automatic washers and power mowers, advertising made possible a substantial reduction in costs by helping stimulate demand. This increase in demand increased the output of each factory and brought about a lower cost per unit. Where there are large overhead costs involved in producing a product, it is often possible to decrease the costs per unit significantly as the volume is increased. Marketing costs may be reduced by substituting advertising for some other marketing elements (*e.g.*, personal selling), thus making the marketing operation more efficient. But we must conclude, as Borden did, that the evidence is sketchy and the role of advertising too complicated to make any generalizations regarding the ultimate effect of advertising on price.

Another economic problem is the relationship between advertising and the level of national income. Both Borden and E. A. Lever, an English economist, have examined in some detail the nature of this relationship. Both concluded that advertising alone was incapable of causing either depressions or booms. However, wisely used it can act as a stimulant when sales are difficult to get. During the depression of the 1930s, for instance, several companies made substantial profits by making important product improvements and using advertising to tell people about them. In general, advertising expenditures as a percentage of U.S. national income have been tapering off since the 1921 peak of 4.5% and by 1960 were about two thirds of the 1920s level.

Advertising is sometimes accused of causing monopoly and a decrease in the number of choices open to the consumer. The evidence indicates that the opposite is somewhat more likely to take place. In those fields where advertising plays an important part in the marketing mix, the number of brands has been increasing rather than decreasing. There are some who accuse advertising of influencing the news and editorial columns of the various media. This criticism is based on the fact that the average U.S. newspaper received about 70% of its income from advertising and most radio and television stations are financed entirely by

advertising. Although there have been various attempts to influence the press—some much publicized—there is little evidence
that the attempts have succeeded. In its volume *A Free and Responsible Press,* the Commission on the Freedom of the Press
(copyright 1947 by The University of Chicago) concluded that
"the evidence of dictation of policy by advertisers is not impressive.
Such dictation seems to occur among the weaker units. As a
newspaper becomes financially stable, it becomes more independent
and tends to resist pressure from advertisers."

Advertising Agencies.—The advertising industry is divided
into three principal types of organizations—advertisers, advertising agencies and the media of communication. The advertiser is
the one whose brand or corporate name appears on the advertisement. The advertising agency handles the advertising for its client.
The media carry the advertising to the various audiences. These
three main types of organizations are aided by many specialists
such as typographers, engravers, artists, film companies and research agencies.

An advertising agency, Reynell and Son, was founded in London as early as 1812 but advertising agencies have achieved their
greatest development in the United States. In 1841 Volney
Palmer, who had been an editorial writer and later a member of
the advertising staff of the *Pottsville* (Pa.) *Miner's Journal,*
opened in Philadelphia what is generally considered the first advertising agency in the U.S. Unlike modern agents, he was primarily an agent for the publishers. They paid him a commission
of 25% for selling space, although he did not assume liability for
the credit extended to advertisers. Shortly after he began operations he had several competitors, including his former clerk S. M.
Pettengill.

George P. Rowell, who opened an agency in 1865, added two
features—wholesaling and the "list system"—to agency operation.
He contracted with a large number of weekly newspapers to sell
him a column of space for a certain period of time. He then
offered this space to advertisers in smaller units at retail rates
which were below rates charged by competitors. He advertised
his offering of "an-inch-of-space-a-month-in-one-hundred-papers-
for-one-hundred-dollars." He was, like Palmer, primarily a seller
of space but he offered exclusive lists of newspapers and magazines, and any advertiser who bought space in these had to buy
through the exclusive agent.

In 1875 N. W. Ayer & Son of Philadelphia developed the "open
contract" which gave advertisers access to the true rates charged
by the publishers. Ayer thus put the emphasis on the agency's
service to the advertiser rather than on selling space for the media.

The next major step was the development of a full line of services for the advertiser. In the late 19th and early 20th century
emphasis was on writing the advertising copy. After copy came
art services, advertising production and the selection of media.
By 1920 most agencies could plan complete campaigns for their
clients, including research and budgeting, and could also execute
these campaigns by preparing the advertisements and arranging
for their insertion in the various media, which now included outdoor advertising and direct-mail soliciting. The American Association of Advertising Agencies (A.A.A.A.) was founded in 1917
and the Association of British Advertising Agents (now the Institute of Practitioners in Advertising) that same year.

By 1960 there were slightly more than 3,000 bona fide advertising agencies in the United States, approximately 120 in Canada
and 500 in Great Britain. According to *Advertising Age,* a leading
trade publication, four U.S. agencies handled over $200,000,000
worth of advertising in 1960 and nine handled over $100,000,000.
The only agency outside the United States to have billings of over
$100,000,000 was in Japan. The largest British agency had bill-
ings estimated at £17,000,000 ($47,600,000).

Most of the general advertising (that done by firms not selling
directly to consumers) and some of the retail (that done by firms
selling directly to consumers) is handled by agencies. The former
classification accounts for roughly 60% of the total advertising
volume in the U.S. Most large agencies handle all types of accounts, but some of the smaller agencies specialize in a certain
type, such as drugs, financial services or agricultural products.

Many of the larger advertisers have several agencies serving them,
often one for each of their major brands, but as a rule agencies
do not serve competing firms or products.

The typical advertising agency is staffed to perform the following services for its clients: (1) supervision and servicing of all
advertising activities; (2) writing copy; (3) conducting market,
media and copy research; (4) working out a complete marketing
plan, budget and supporting activities; (5) selecting media; (6)
arranging for mechanical reproduction of the advertisement and
its insertion in the medium; (7) laying out the advertisement; (8)
buying any artwork or film needed for the advertisement; (9)
helping supervise the sales force; (10) arranging for appropriate
merchandising and public relations activities to help make the advertising more productive. It has thus tended to become a marketing agency, supplying a full range of marketing services, rather
than simply an advertising agency.

U.S. agencies tend to be organized on either a departmental or
a group basis. Under the former, specialists (artists or writers)
work in the same department and may service any of the accounts
in the agency. Under the group system the various specialists
are assigned to a group of accounts and work exclusively on these.

The bulk of the standard U.S. agency's income is derived from
the 15% commission which the media grant to recognized agencies
on the space or time bought in those media. Most U.S. agencies
also charge a commission on artwork for clients or television programs which they buy for their clients. In addition, they may
charge fees for special services such as research or public relations. British agencies that are recognized by the media receive
between 10% and 15% commission. In France agency commissions range from 10% to 20%, with commissions generally higher
in the provinces than in Paris. Only agencies recognized by the
media are granted commissions. Among the usual requirements
for recognition are the following: freedom from control by advertisers, financial resources sufficient to meet obligations incurred
on behalf of clients, and personnel of sufficient experience and
ability to serve general advertisers.

In 1955 the U.S. department of justice attacked this system of
compensation. It filed suit against the American Association of
Advertising Agencies and five media associations, charging them
with conspiracy in restraint of trade. It questioned the uniform
standards for recognizing agencies, the refusal to grant commissions to nonrecognized agencies and uniformity of the 15% commission. In 1956 the A.A.A.A. and the media associations entered
into a consent decree with the department of justice and the case
was dropped. They agreed to refrain from "fixing, establishing,
or stabilizing agency commission."

ADVERTISING PRODUCTION

The starting point for the planning and production of an advertising campaign is usually the over-all marketing program. Although the advertisements may be brilliantly conceived they are
not likely to be successful unless they are used in conjunction with
personal selling, display, packaging, pricing, product design and
other elements of the marketing program. Consequently agencies
and advertisers frequently talk of their marketing plan rather than
their advertising plan. The marketing plan consists of at least
three major elements: marketing objectives, the "marketing mix"
that is most likely to attain this objective, and the integration of
the various elements used.

Once the marketing plan is decided on, the advertiser and the
agency are ready to fit advertising into that plan. If they know,
for example, that the manufacturer's objective is to increase the
acceptance of his brand name within a certain segment of the
market, they can decide what part advertising can play in carrying
out that objective. In general, the steps an advertiser or agency
will follow in producing an advertising campaign are the following:
(1) finding all pertinent facts; (2) establishing objectives; (3)
setting the budget; (4) creating the advertisements; (5) inserting
them in the media.

Facts.—The most fruitful facts for planners of an advertising
campaign are likely to fall into these categories: characteristics of
the consumers, location of the markets to be covered, product or

service to be advertised, media to be used and past experience with different types of advertisements.

Among the facts which help the advertiser understand the consumer are the answers to questions such as these: What attitudes do people have toward this type of product? What psychological needs or desires does this product satisfy? What are the buying habits of people who buy this type of product? Research indicates that people often rationalize certain of their purchases. They will tell other people (and often themselves) that they bought a certain brand of automobile because it provides good gas mileage or has a high trade-in value. The real motivation is often more subtle and not so socially acceptable—for instance, the desire to keep up with one's neighbors. Among the most commonly used psychological wants featured in advertisements are: sex, food and drink, comfort, freedom from fear and danger, desire to be superior, social approval, long life and love of family.

Facts about the location of the market help the advertising people to select the correct media to reach the potential consumers and to design advertisements which will have maximum appeal. Some products are dramatic and easy to advertise. For instance, it is fairly simple to find some dramatic, want-satisfying feature of a new house or a new automobile. On the other hand, more prosaic products like tea or cleaning powder may require considerable analysis. There has been a decided effort since World War II to emphasize the building of a "product image." In a speech before the American Association of Advertising Agencies, David Ogilvy, a prominent agency president said, "Every advertisement must be considered as a contribution to the complex symbol which is the brand image . . . The manufacturers who dedicate their advertising to building the most favorable image, the most sharply defined personality for their brands are the ones who will get the largest share of these markets at the highest profits—in the long run."

Some of the media facts which are important in producing an advertising campaign are those dealing with where the medium is circulated, how thoroughly people read or listen to it, and whether they pay for it or receive it free of charge.

Facts on the message itself might cover the relative effectiveness of illustrations v. words for conveying various types of messages, long copy v. short copy, full-page advertisements v. fractional-page advertisements.

Objectives.—The ultimate objective of most advertising is to sell goods or services. Even public service campaigns are usually expected to produce some sort of long-range profit. However, individual campaigns may have various objectives. In the United States, where tea had been widely considered an effeminate drink, a successful campaign was designed for the Tea council to convince people that tea was a drink for the hale and hearty. Illustrations of vigorous men such as truck drivers and bold, masculine typography were used to suggest that the very virile enjoy tea just as much as do elderly women.

Setting the Budget.—Sometimes the advertising budget is determined in advance of the plan; sometimes the plan is the basis for it. In general, the budget is likely to be constructed by using either the task approach or the percentage-of-sales approach. The task method defines the job to be accomplished and a sufficient advertising fund to accomplish this job is appropriated. It is, therefore, necessary that the objective be defined as carefully as possible. For instance, a company may be considering the marketing of a new food product. It will decide how many advertisements are needed and what media should be used to accomplish the acceptance of this product. If the firm decides it cannot afford the amount involved, it has simply to trim its sights to coincide with what it can afford. This method is becoming increasingly popular —particularly for new products and for products sold to industrial users.

There are many variations of the percentage-of-sales method. In its simplest form it involves multiplying a fixed percentage (e.g. 3%) by the sales of the previous year. This is a simple method and will work out fairly well if the fluctuations from one year to the next are not too great. Small retail stores which have a stable business sometimes use this method. A variation that is somewhat more desirable is to predict next year's sales and then assign a certain percentage of that amount to advertising. For instance, a manufacturer may predict that his sales next year will be $1,000,000. If he customarily spends 5% for advertising his advertising appropriation will be $50,000. He can then divide this into the various media or functions as he sees fit. This method has the virtue of emphasizing the future instead of the past, but it is somewhat illogical to forecast what the results of advertising will be and then base one of the causes of those results on that figure.

Another variation of this method which is common in some industries is the unit-of-sale method. Instead of basing the appropriation on dollar sales it is based on the number of units sold or expected to be sold. For example, if a company produced 100,000 automobiles in a year it might appropriate $20 per unit or $2,000,-000. If it increased production to 200,000 units, it would keep the same amount per car on the basis that this is the amount of money needed to sell a unit of this car. Similarly, makers of package goods may budget a fixed amount of money per case.

The Message.—The first purpose of the advertising message is to get the reader's or listener's attention and hold it. The message should then arouse his desire for the product or service, and finally get him to buy it, desire it, prefer it or perhaps just recognize it.

There are two important steps in the creation of every advertisement, deciding what is to be said and deciding how to say it. The first of these should grow out of the objective of the campaign. In other words, many successive advertisements in a campaign might say much the same thing—an idea decided on by a group of planners or perhaps the copywriter or artist. One successful series for a soft drink emphasized year after year the same general idea—that is, "a light refreshing drink"—in a variety of ways.

In deciding how the message should be constructed, the creative person has certain elements with which he can work: in a print advertisement the headlines, illustrations, captions, trademarks, body text, white space, colour and type faces; in radio the spoken word; and in television all the above plus motion. In the case of print advertising the arrangement itself may help to communicate the idea. For example, a crowded layout suggests to most people that the product or store whose name appears is a bargain-type product. Conversely, a lot of white space suggests style and sophistication.

Some advertisements are mainly visual and thus start with the visual elements. A typical case is the fashion advertisement one finds in most newspapers and many women's magazines. In these advertisements the illustration itself suggests to the reader what the product looks like, what sort of people may be seen wearing it, in what kind of surroundings it may be worn, and it may attempt to suggest certain aesthetic associations. The visual elements of an advertisement usually have three functions: (1) attract the attention of the desired audience; (2) tell the reader something about the product; and (3) arouse sufficient interest so that the reader will want to read the body text, if there is any.

Colour is another commonly used visual element. It is used mainly for portraying goods in their natural colour, dramatizing the rewards from a product, providing a refined or symbolic atmosphere for a product or aiding the identification of a trademark or package by showing it in natural colour.

Agency art personnel will usually make "layouts" or "visuals" to show how the finished advertisement will look. Sometimes they make a drawing or painting that is reproduced, although most finished art work is done by free lance artists or those in studios. Much of the television art work is done by specialists.

The headlines of a print or television advertisement may account for as much as 25% of the effectiveness, according to one authority, John Caples. The headline, like the illustration, is designed to attract attention and to arouse interest in the body of the text. If the product is a very dramatic one, a headline talking directly about the product is customarily used. On the other hand, in such products or services as life insurance, a curiosity approach is often used in an attempt to intrigue the reader.

In most advertisements the heart of the advertising message is in the text. Some full-page newspaper advertisements have as much as several thousand words of copy. Some have practically none. The exact proportions of visual and verbal elements will be decided on by the advertising man. He will use either words or pictures according to how well he thinks each will tell the desired story.

ADVERTISING ORGANIZATIONS

United States.—Much of the improvement in advertising standards in the 20th century resulted from the efforts of various professional groups representing segments of the industry. In 1911 the Associated Advertising Clubs of America at their annual convention adopted the motto "Truth in advertising" and established a National Vigilance committee in the United States, later renamed the National Better Business bureau, to police advertising. The national committee worked with the local advertising clubs to organize local Better Business bureaus (*q.v.*) to eliminate objectionable or untruthful advertising. These bureaus are supported financially by local businessmen in an effort to curb unethical advertising and selling practices. Complaints concerning such practices are made to the local bureau, which then investigates the charge. If it finds the charge is true, it tries to persuade the offender to stop his methods of operation; if that approach fails, it may take legal action. Among the most common complaints are false and misleading comparisons of price and quality, exaggerated claims as to quality, and "bait" advertising (quoting a ridiculously low price for a product which is not really for sale in order to attract customers to a store).

The National Better Business bureau publishes a loose-leaf reference manual entitled *Do's and Don'ts in Advertising,* to keep advertising people up-to-date on current legislation, administrative orders, industry standards and court decisions. It covers a wide variety of product categories and is designed to assist advertisers and agencies in deciding what they may say and what should be avoided.

The Advertising Federation of America is the successor to the Associated Advertising Clubs of America. It was the parent of some of today's independent advertising associations, such as the Newspaper Advertising Executives association and the Direct Mail Advertising association. Like its predecessor organization it emphasizes the importance of truth in advertising. It often acts as the spokesman for the industry as a whole. For instance, during 1958 and 1959 much of its effort was directed toward opposing proposals made in various cities and states to levy a tax on advertising. It is also active in advertising club work and advertising education.

The Advertising Association of the West, a Pacific coast counterpart of the Advertising Federation of America, operates in 11 western states, British Columbia and Hawaii.

The Audit Bureau of Circulations is another organization supported by the entire advertising industry. It audits and verifies circulations of paid-circulation newspapers, magazines, business publications and farm publications in the United States and Canada. Another auditing organization, Business Publications Audit of Circulations, audits both paid and free-distribution publications.

The Advertising Research foundation is devoted to investigating problems of research interest to the entire advertising industry. For several years it sponsored readership studies of various media. The Advertising council is devoted to the planning, preparation and production of public service advertising campaigns. The defense bond campaign, safety, fire prevention and many others were Advertising council campaigns.

The Association of National Advertisers is an organization of about 500 companies which manufacture and advertise consumer goods. It was organized in 1913 for the purpose of exchanging information and conducting various activities of mutual benefit.

The National Industrial Advertisers association is an organization of firms engaged in marketing industrial, rather than consumer, goods.

The sales promotion division, National Retail Merchants association, studies methods of improving retail advertising. It is perhaps best known for its annual sales promotion budgeting planning calendar.

The American Association of Advertising Agencies is the leading organization of advertising agencies; 335 of the largest national agencies belong to it. It works with advertisers and media associations.

The American Newspaper Publishers association is the leading organization of daily newspaper publishers in the United States. It serves the advertising field primarily through its bureau of advertising, which acts as both a promotional and a research organization. Other newspaper organizations concerned with advertising are Newspaper Advertising Executives association, National Newspaper Promotion association, American Association of Newspaper Representatives and Association of Newspaper Classified Advertising Managers.

In the magazine field, the Periodical Publishers association, the Magazine Publishers' association, the Magazine Advertising bureau of the Magazine Publishers association, Associated Business Publications, National Business Publications, and Agricultural Publishers association represent the various segments of the industry.

The National Association of Broadcasters is the principal organization in the field of television and radio. Promotion and research for the radio industry are conducted by the Radio Advertising bureau and for television by the Television Bureau of Advertising.

Other important media groups are: Outdoor Advertising Association of America, Outdoor Advertising, Inc., the Direct Mail Advertising association, and National Association of Transportation Advertising.

All of these organizations exercise some control over the advertising excesses of their members, either directly or indirectly. The A.A.A.A. through its Committee on the Improvement of Advertising Content and the Advertising Federation of America have been among the most active in this respect.

The Federal Trade commission (*q.v.*), established in 1914 by the Federal Trade Commission act and strengthened by the Wheeler-Lea amendment in 1938, is the main U.S. government agency for policing advertising. Its power to regulate advertising is derived from its authority to regulate "unfair methods of competition." It issues cease and desist orders for any advertising which it believes is deceptive and which is in interstate commerce. It cooperates with the Federal Communications commission in policing false and misleading advertising on television and radio. The FTC also administers certain wool and fur labeling acts and the Food and Drug administration checks the labeling of foods, drugs and cosmetics. Misleading labels or those lacking essential information are prohibited by law.

The Federal Communications commission controls advertising through its power to grant (or refuse to grant) licences and renewals for television and radio stations. The post office department is most active in checking for obscenity, lottery and fraud in advertising which goes through the mails.

Other federal regulatory agencies of importance in advertising are: the seed act division of the department of agriculture (seed advertising), the alcohol tax unit (alcoholic beverages), the Securities and Exchange commission (stocks and bonds advertising), the U.S. patent office (trade-marks), and the Library of Congress (copyrighted material).

Great Britain.—The Advertising association is the central organization of the advertising industry in Great Britain. It combines the various groups—advertisers, agencies, media and ancillary services—and is thus similar to the Advertising Federation of America. Among its objectives are the promotion of public confidence in advertising and advertised goods through the correction or suppression of abuses which undermine that confidence; encouragement of the study of the theory and practice of advertising and the improvement of its technique by the institution of courses of study, holding of examinations and awarding of diplomas; the adoption of standard practices in relations between publishers, agencies and advertisers.

The British equivalent of the American Association of Advertising Agencies is the Institute of Practitioners in Advertising. Its main purpose is, according to its own statement: "establishing, once and for all, the position of the service advertising agency through the introduction and observance of professional standards of practice; thereby, helping to make possible as it has, both the quality and scope of the advertising and marketing services rendered to advertisers."

The Incorporated Advertising Managers includes many of the leading advertising people who work for manufacturers.

Self-regulation comes from the British Code of Standards in Relation to the Advertising of Medicine and Treatments. This code states that no advertisement should contain a claim to cure any ailment or symptoms of ill-health and that no advertisement should contain a word or expression used in such form or context as to mean, in a positive sense, the extirpation of any ailment, illness or disease.

Government regulation is carried out mainly through the various sections of the Food and Drug acts, together with the Merchandise Mark acts. Other government regulations deal with trade-marks, defamation, copyright and hire purchase. The last, which came into force in 1957, stipulates that in almost all advertisements for hire purchase (*i.e.*, credit sales) exact details of terms must be given.

Other Countries.—The parent advertising organization in France is Federation Française de la Publicité. There are approximately 1,300 "qualified intermediaries" (agents) in France. The Technical Advertising school gives a course in advertising, following which a student may take an examination which when passed entitles him to an advertising degree recognized by the state. Since 1956 three new organizations have been created in France: Center of Study of Advertising Media, Institute of Research and Advertising Studies (similar to the Advertising Research foundation in the U.S.) and the Great National Causes, an organization for promoting public interest campaigns. In most other western European countries there is an organization of the leading advertising agencies and in many a parent organization for all advertising. In west Germany most agencies that follow the American system of giving clients complete service are members of Werbeagentur-Gesellschaften.

See also references under "Advertising" in the Index.

(S. W. D.)

BIBLIOGRAPHY.—Roger Barton, *Advertising Agency Operations and Management* (1955), (ed.), *Advertising Handbook* (1950); Neil H. Borden, *The Economic Effects of Advertising* (1942); Darrell Blaine Lucas and Steuart Henderson Britt, *Advertising Psychology and Research* (1950); W. J. Leaper, *Law of Advertising* (1950); F. B. Lane, *Advertising Administration*, 2nd ed. by N. T. Sandbrook (1951); Ian Harvey, *The Technique of Persuasion* (1951); Rodney Silverman, *Advertising Expenditure 1952* (1954); F. P. Bishop, *The Ethics of Advertising* (1949); J. W. Hobson, *The Selection of Advertising Media* (1955); Mills and Rockleys, *The Size and Nature of the Poster Audience* (1955); Lyndon O. Brown, Richard S. Lessler and William Weilbacher, *Advertising Media* (1957); John Caples, *Tested Advertising Methods* (1961); Richard Crisp, *Marketing Research* (1957); S. Watson Dunn, *Advertising: Its Role in Modern Marketing* (1961); British Market Research Bureau, *Readings in Market Research* (quarterly); Ralph Harris and Arthur Seldon, *Advertising in a Free Society* (1959); Walter Taplin, *Advertising: a New Approach* (1960).

ADVOCATE, in law, a person who is professionally qualified to plead the cause of another in a court of law. As a technical term "advocate" is used mainly in legal systems derived from the civil law.

Thus in Scotland the word refers especially to a member of the bar of Scotland (*see* ADVOCATES, FACULTY OF), but is also used to denote a member of a society of solicitors in the city of Aberdeen. The chief law officer of the crown in Scotland is the lord advocate, the head of the public prosecution system.

In France *avocats* are an organized body of pleaders, but in Germany, until the distinction between counselor and pleader was abolished in 1879, the *Advokat* was the adviser rather than the pleader.

The term has traditionally been used of pleaders in courts of canon law, and thus in England, those lawyers who practised before the courts of civil and canon law were styled advocates (*see* LEGAL PROFESSION).

In the United States the term advocate has no special significance, being used interchangeably with such terms as attorney, counsel or lawyer.

(M. C. ME.)

ADVOCATES, FACULTY OF, the collective term employed to designate the members of the bar of Scotland. The faculty has grown out of the Scots act of 1532, which established the college of justice, or court of session, in Scotland. The advocates had, and still have, the sole right of audience in the court of session and high court of justiciary. By immemorial custom, they have formed themselves into a self-governing faculty under annually elected officers consisting of the dean of faculty and his council, the vice-dean, the treasurer and the clerk. When properly instructed by an agency of the law an advocate is, under pain of deprivation of office, bound and entitled to plead in any court in Scotland, civil or criminal, superior or inferior. He is also entitled to plead before the house of lords, the judicial committee of the privy council and parliamentary committees. The magnificent library collected by the faculty has now been formed into the National Library of Scotland.

ADY, ENDRE (1877–1919), probably the greatest Hungarian lyric poet, was born at Erdmindszent on Nov. 22, 1877, of an impoverished but noble family. On leaving school, he studied law for a time. In 1899 he published a somewhat insignificant volume of verse, *Versek,* and from 1900 until his death he worked as a journalist. In 1903 he published another volume of poetry, *Még egyszer,* in which signs of his exceptional talent could already be seen. With his next book, *Uj versek* ("New Poems"; 1906), he burst like a bombshell into Hungarian literary life. Poetry in Hungary had been dormant at the end of the 19th and at the beginning of the 20th century, and people had become accustomed to diluted and insipid imitations of Sándor Petofi and János Arany. None of the few original poets was powerful enough to make an impression on the public which was thus faced without transition with the "new verses of a new era," as Ady himself described his work. These poems were, indeed, revolutionary in form, language and content. Though Ady's strict use of rhyme could not shock even the most conservative reader, his frequent repetition of whole lines (sometimes two out of four in each stanza) was found greatly irritating, while his unconventional, though splendid, language, with its unusual choice of adjectives, shocked a public not accustomed to the unexpected. The outrage was completed by the general tone of his poems. At that time, Ady was an "angry young man" in whom a visit to Paris had unleashed a storm of violent and insulting attacks against his country. Though the artistic value of these "new poems" is beyond question, it is understandable that their provocative tone did not remain unanswered. Ady became the target of violent attacks which persisted well beyond his death, and which soon degenerated into a political struggle. Ady, backed by the left-wing radicals who hailed him as a prophet, was abused by right-wing nationalists. He emerged from these battles purified, and, abandoning gratuitous insult, he attained a higher level of social and political censure in his later work. His understanding of his country and of the social and political evils by which it was beset inspired him to find new accents of pain, anger and castigation, which reached apocalyptic vigour at the sufferings inflicted by World War I. By that time, Ady's failing health, undermined by a profligate life, was unable to stand up to the pressure of constant hard work. (He had published ten volumes of poetry in 12 years, as well as short stories and countless articles.) He reached the haven of a happy marriage too late (1914), and died, a victim of alcoholism, on Jan. 27, 1919, in Budapest.

Ady's love of the Hungarian people and the political preoccupations which developed from it was only one of his themes. His love poems, most of which had been inspired by a remarkable woman whom he called Leda, are striking in their originality and their mystical approach to physical love. His religious poems, which seemed blasphemous to many, reveal his search for God "who is at the bottom of all things, to whom all the bells toll and on whose left I, alas, sit."

Ady's poems are concerned with eternal problems. And if in many respects his own life was a failure, he at least attained one of his aims: "To write splendid things."

BIBLIOGRAPHY.—Béla Révész, *Ady trilogiája* (1935); Gyula Földessy,

Ady minden titkai (1949); László Bóka, *Ady Endre élete és müvei,* vol. i (1955).

(Ds. Sr.)

ADYGEI AUTONOMOUS OBLAST, established in 1922, is located in Krasnodar *krai* of the Russian Soviet Federated Socialist Republic, U.S.S.R. Its area of 2,934 sq.mi. extends from the left bank of the Kuban river opposite Krasnodar in a strip along the Kuban and its tributary the Laba and thence southward to the lower foothills of the Caucasus around Maikop (*q.v.*). Apart from the flood plain meadow soils along the rivers, the lower parts of the *oblast* are covered by black earth with steppe vegetation, giving way to deciduous forests on brown soil higher up.

The total population in 1959 was 284,690, of whom 95,462 were urban and about a quarter were Adygei, a branch of the Cherkess or Circassian people. It is one of the more densely settled parts of the territory. The administrative centre is Maikop with 82,135 persons. Nearly three-quarters of the *oblast* is agricultural land, with arable dominating on the black earth and a preponderance of hayland and pasture higher up. The marshy lands, subject to serious flooding, which lie along the Kuban are suitable for reclamation and approximately 20,000 ac. were reclaimed in 1955 by the Chibisky drainage scheme with 36 mi. of canals and two reservoirs. These fertile lands provide market gardens to supply Krasnodar. Agriculture is, in general, intensive, with maize the chief crop, together with wheat, sunflowers, hemp, tobacco, melons, potatoes and other vegetables. Flowers, especially Crimean roses and lavender, are grown for scent, and there is beekeeping. In the higher areas, dairy cattle and sheep are important. Food processing forms two-thirds of industrial production. The Adygei canning factory is located in Yablonovski. Timber processing is also important and oil is drilled in the neighbourhood of Maikop. The chief industrial centre is Maikop with a wide range of food-processing and canning industries, sawmills, factories for tannin extraction, furniture making, wood chemicals and machine building. In 1950 a hydroelectric power station was built there on the Belaya river. The town lies on a branch of the Armavir-Tuapse railway which crosses the southern part of the *oblast.*

(R. A. F.)

ADZHAR AUTONOMOUS SOVIET SOCIALIST REPUBLIC (ADZHARIA) lies in the southwestern corner of the Georgian S.S.R., U.S.S.R., on the Turkish frontier. Its area of 1,158 sq.mi. is largely mountainous. Only along the coast is a lowland strip, which widens somewhat south of Batumi and again in the north around Kobuleti, where it is swampy. The mountains consist of two main east-west ranges, the Adzharo-Imeretinski range, rising to 9,350 ft. (Mt. Mepistskaro), and the Shabshetski range, the crest of which, rising to 9,219 ft. in Mt. Kheva, forms the Turkish frontier. Between the ranges lies the deep valley of the Adzharis-Tskali, which is closed at the eastern end by a third range, the Arsianski mountains, where the Goderdzi pass leads into Georgia. The coastal lowland has a humid, subtropical climate with the smallest temperature range in the U.S.S.R., 27° F. Rainfall is high; the Batumi average is 93.3 in. Inland the climate becomes increasingly severe with height, and snow lies for six months on the summits. Rainfall there is still high, up to 60 in. or more. Vegetation ranges from the subtropical up through deciduous forest with rhododendrons and azaleas, to coniferous forest and alpine meadows.

From the 17th century to the end of the 19th century Adzharia was part of Turkey and suffered greatly in the troubled history of this area. It became Russian in 1878 and was made an A.S.S.R. in 1921. Its 1959 population of 245,286 includes, as well as Adzhars and Georgians, Russians, Armenians and others, most of whom live in Batumi (*q.v.*), the capital, which has 82,328 inhabitants.

The economy of Adzharia is based on the subtropical crops of the lowland, especially tea (11 tea-packing plants), citrus fruits (tangerines, oranges, lemons and grapefruits), other fruits, particularly avocados, tung trees (for oil) and, in higher areas, tobacco. The main field crops are maize in the lowland and potatoes in the mountains. There are sizable plantations of eucalyptus and bamboo. Stock-rearing is important in the mountains, while the lowland dairy cattle are noted for high yields. Most industries are concerned with processing agricultural products and are concentrated in Batumi. This town, at the terminus of two pipelines from Baku, is a large oil-refining centre and port. Adzharia is linked with the rest of Georgia by a road over the Goderdzi pass and by the Transcaucasian railway which runs north along the coast from Batumi, then eastward to Tbilisi and on to Baku. (R. A. F.)

AE.: *see* RUSSELL, GEORGE WILLIAM.

AEACUS, in Greek legend, was the son of Zeus and of Aegina, daughter of the river-god Asopus. His mother was carried off by Zeus to the island of Oenone, afterward called by her name. The island having been depopulated by a pestilence, Zeus changed the ants upon it into human beings, who were called Myrmidons (*murmekes,* "ants").

Aeacus was celebrated for justice and in Attic tradition became a judge of the dead, together with Minos and Rhadamanthus. His successful prayer to Zeus for rain at a time of drought was commemorated by a temple at Aegina, where a festival, the Aiakeia, was held in his honour.

AEDESIUS (d. *c.* A.D. 355), Neoplatonist philosopher, from Cappadocia, was a pupil of Iamblichus in Syria and afterward taught at Pergamum, where his principal disciples were Maximus, Chrysanthius and Eusebius Myndius. No writings of his remain; there is a biography of him by Eunapius.

See T. Whittaker, *The Neoplatonists,* 2nd ed. (1918); F. Copleston, *History of Philosophy,* vol. i (1946).

AEDILE, a title, probably derived from Lat. *aedes,* "temple," of magistrates in ancient Rome, who at first had charge of the temple and cult of Ceres. Originally they were two officials of the plebs, created at the same time as the tribunes (494 B.C.), whose sanctity they shared. These magistrates were elected in the assembly of the plebs. In 366 two curule aediles (*see* CURULE) were created. These were at first patricians, but those of the next year were plebeians and so on year by year alternately until in the 2nd century B.C. the system of alternation between classes ceased. They were elected in the assembly of the tribes, with the consul presiding. The privileges of the curule aediles included a fringed toga, a curule chair and the right to ancestral masks, privileges perhaps extended to the plebeian aediles after 100 B.C. Aediles ranked between tribunes and praetors, a greater proportion of the curule ones attaining the consulship, but the office was not necessary for advancement in a senatorial career. Their functions were threefold: first, the care of the city (repair of temples, public buildings, streets, sewers, aqueducts, traffic, supervision of public decency and precaution against fires); second, the charge of the provision markets, weights and measures and the distribution of grain, a function for which Julius Caesar added two plebeian aediles called Ceriales; third, organization of certain public games, the Megalesian and the Roman games being under the curule aediles and the Plebeian games as well as those of Ceres and Flora being under the plebeian. They had judicial powers and could impose fines.

Augustus transferred the care of the games and the judicial functions to the praetors and the care of the city to appointed boards and to the prefects of the watch and of the city. Under the imperial regime the office became a step in the senatorial career for plebeians until it disappeared after the reign of Alexander Severus in the 3rd century A.D.

In Roman municipalities aediles were regular magistrates and are recorded as officials in associations and clubs.

BIBLIOGRAPHY.—T. Mommsen, *Römisches Staatsrecht,* vol. ii, 3rd ed. (1887); T. R. S. Broughton and M. L. Patterson, *Magistrates of the Roman Republic,* vol. 1 and 2 (1951–52); D. Sabbatucci, *Memorie dell'Accademia nazionale dei Lincei,* series viii, vol. vi (1955).

(T. R. S. B.)

AEDON, daughter of Pandareus and wife of Zethus of Thebes, was the mother of a single son, Itylus. Envious of her sister-in-law Niobe for her many children, she undertook to kill the eldest while he slept, but in the dark she mistakenly killed her own son. She was transformed by the gods into a nightingale, whose song is a lament for Itylus.

(T. V. B.)

AEDUI, an ancient Celtic tribe of central Gaul (occupying most of what was later Burgundy), which was chiefly responsible for the diplomatic situation exploited by Julius Caesar when he began his conquests in 58 B.C. The Aedui had been supported by

Rome since 121, when they were recognized as "brothers and blood relations," but were heavily defeated c. 61 by their neighbours the Sequani, aided by the German Ariovistus. They then lost their revenue from the tolls on the Arar (Saône). Appealing to Rome, they were rescued by Caesar, who made them his principal allies; yet they joined the coalition against him in 52, though they quickly returned to their allegiance after the Gaulish leader Vercingetorix surrendered at Alesia. Under Augustus they became a *civitas foederata* (allied state) governed by magistrates with Roman titles; and their hill fort Bibracte, on Mt. Beuvray, was demolished, a new capital being built at Augustodunum (Autun). Another tribal centre of importance was Cabillonum (Châlon-sur-Saône). In A.D. 21 under Julius Sacrovir they joined the Treveri in a revolt against Roman exactions and were quickly crushed by the Rhine army. But it is unlikely that they still seriously wanted independence, for although they supported the revolt of Julius Vindex in 68 they resolutely opposed next year the attempt under Julius Classicus to establish an *Imperium Galliarum* ("Empire of the Gauls"). Moreover in A.D. 48 they had become the first tribe of Gallia Comata to send senators to Rome.

See T. R. Holmes, *Caesar's Conquest of Gaul,* 2nd ed. (1911).

(G. E. F. C.)

AEGADIAN ISLANDS (anc. *Aegates Insulae;* Ital. ISOLE EGADI), a group of mountainous small islands, lie off the western tip of Sicily in Trapani province and had a total population of 6,714 in 1951. Favignana, the largest (7 sq.mi., highest point 991 ft.), lies 11 mi. from Trapani, the nearest point on Sicily. Levanzo, 2½ mi. N. of Favignana (4 sq.mi., highest point 912 ft.), is known for the "Genovese" cave with prehistoric paintings. Marettimo, farthest west of the group, has an area of 5 sq.mi., highest point 2,251 ft.; formerly a political prison, it is known as the largest tuna fishing centre of Sicily. In 241 B.C. the Carthaginian fleet was defeated there by Gaius Lutatius Catulus, signaling the end of the First Punic War. (G. KH.)

AEGEAN CIVILIZATION is a general term for the prehistoric Bronze Age cultures of the area around the Aegean sea covering the period from c. 2500 B.C. or earlier until c. 1100 B.C., when iron begins to come into general use throughout the area. From the earliest times these cultures fall into four main geographical groups: (1) Crete, (2) the Cycladic islands, (3) the mainland of Greece, including Thessaly, and (4) the Troad (the land of Troy) in northwestern Asia Minor, together with the coasts of western Asia Minor, the great coastal islands (Lemnos, Lesbos, Chios, Samos) and Macedonia. The cultures of this fourth group have many affinities with the early cultures of central and southern Asia Minor and are really more allied to them than to the other cultures of the Aegean area.

The Bronze Age cultures of these four groups are known as (1) Minoan, (2) Cycladic, (3) Helladic and (4) Troadic. The Minoan, Cycladic and Helladic cultures are divided for convenience into three phases, Early, Middle and Late Bronze Age, with three further subdivisions (1, 2, 3) of each age. The Late Bronze Age phase of the mainland and of the islands (except Crete) is usually called Mycenaean after Mycenae, the chief Late Bronze Age site in mainland Greece. The Troadic culture is subdivided according to the "cities" (or superimposed levels of settlement found by H. Schliemann and his successors) at Troy, ranging from the earliest, Troy I, to Troy VII, the last Bronze Age settlement. Each of these "cities" is subdivided further according to occupation levels labeled *a, b, c,* etc. Various phases of Neolithic culture have been identified on the mainland of Greece (especially in Thessaly) and in Crete; but not yet for certain in the Aegean islands or in the Troadic area. Traces of Late Paleolithic occupation were found by R. Stampfuss during World War II at Haliartus on Lake Copais, and later by V. Milojcic along the Peneus river in Thessaly.

The first centre of high civilization in the Aegean area, with great cities and palaces, a highly developed art, extended trade, writing and use of seal stones, was Crete. Here from the end of the 3rd millennium B.C. onward a very distinctive civilization, owing much to the older civilizations of Egypt and the near east but original in its character, came into being. This rise of the first high civilization on European territory may have been stimu-lated by an actual immigration of new peoples into the island in the early part of the Bronze Age, c. 2500–2300 B.C.

The Cretan (Minoan) civilization had begun to spread before the middle of the 2nd millennium across the Aegean to the islands and to the mainland of Greece. During the Late Bronze (Mycenaean) Age (c. 1600–c. 1100), from the middle of the 16th century onward, a civilization more or less uniform superficially but showing local divergencies—with cities, palaces, writing and use of seal stones—is found throughout the Aegean area including Thessaly, the coasts of Macedonia, the rest of central and southern Greece, and the Aegean islands with Crete and Rhodes. Eventually people bearing this civilization spread colonies eastward to Cyprus and elsewhere on the southern and western coasts of Asia Minor as far as Syria; also westward to Tarentum in southern Italy and even perhaps to Sicily. In the latter part of this period, after about 1400 B.C., the centre of political and economic power, if not of artistic achievement, appears to have shifted from Knossos in Crete to Mycenae on the mainland of Greece.

HISTORY OF DISCOVERY AND DISTRIBUTION OF REMAINS

The first great landmark in the development of modern knowledge of the Aegean Bronze Age civilization was undoubtedly the excavation of the 16th century B.C. royal shaft graves at Mycenae by Schliemann in 1876. The second was the uncovering of the Bronze Age Palace of Minos at Knossos in Crete by A. J. Evans from 1900 onward. Mycenae and Tiryns near Argos in the Peloponnesus are the two principal sites at which evidence of a prehistoric civilization was remarked. But the Cyclopean walls of the citadel of Mycenae, its gate with heraldic lions, the royal tholos (or beehive) tombs, the so-called Treasury of Atreus and the galleries of Tiryns were supposed by scholars only to point to the civilization represented in Homer (*q.v.*) or, at farthest, the primitive stages of a Hellenic civilization. Not until Schliemann exposed the contents of the shaft graves that lay just inside the gate (*see* MYCENAE) did scholars recognize the advanced stage of art which prehistoric dwellers in the Mycenaean citadel had attained.

A good deal of other evidence was available before 1876, but it had not been collated and seriously studied. Although it was recognized that certain tributaries—represented, *e.g.*, in the 18th-dynasty tomb of Rekhmire at Egyptian Thebes—as bearing vases of peculiar forms—were of some Mediterranean race, neither their precise habitat nor the character of their civilization could be determined. Nor did the Aegean objects that were lying obscurely in museums before 1870 provide a sufficient test of what real basis there might be underlying the Hellenic myths of the Argolid, the Troad and Crete. Both at Sèvres and Neuchâtel Aegean vases had been exhibited since about 1840, one found at Philacopi in Melos, the other in Cephalonia. L. Ross, by his explorations in the Greek islands from 1835 onward, called attention to certain seal stones, since known as "island gems," but it was not till 1878 that C. T. Newton demonstrated that these were not Phoenician products. In 1866 primitive structures were discovered in the island of Therasia by quarrymen extracting *pozzolana* for the Suez canal works. When this discovery was followed up on the neighbouring island of Thera, by excavations of the French School at Athens, much pottery of a class now known to belong to the transition from the Middle to the Late Bronze Age (16th century B.C.), and many stone and metal objects, were found and dated by the geologist M. Fouqué, somewhat arbitrarily, to 2000 B.C. In 1868 tombs at Ialysus in Rhodes had yielded to M. A. Biliotti many fine Late Bronze Age painted vases, but these, bought by John Ruskin and presented to the British museum, were supposed to be of some local Asiatic manufacture of uncertain date. *See also* PRE-HELLENIC ARCHITECTURE.

Schliemann's Excavations.—Even Schliemann's first excavations at Troy (Hisarlik in Turkey) did not excite astonishment. But the "Burnt City" of his second stratum, revealed in 1873, with its fortifications, vases and a hoard of gold, silver and bronze objects, began to arouse curiosity. As soon as Schliemann came on the royal shaft graves at Mycenae three years later, the importance of his findings in relation to prehistoric Greece was widely recog-

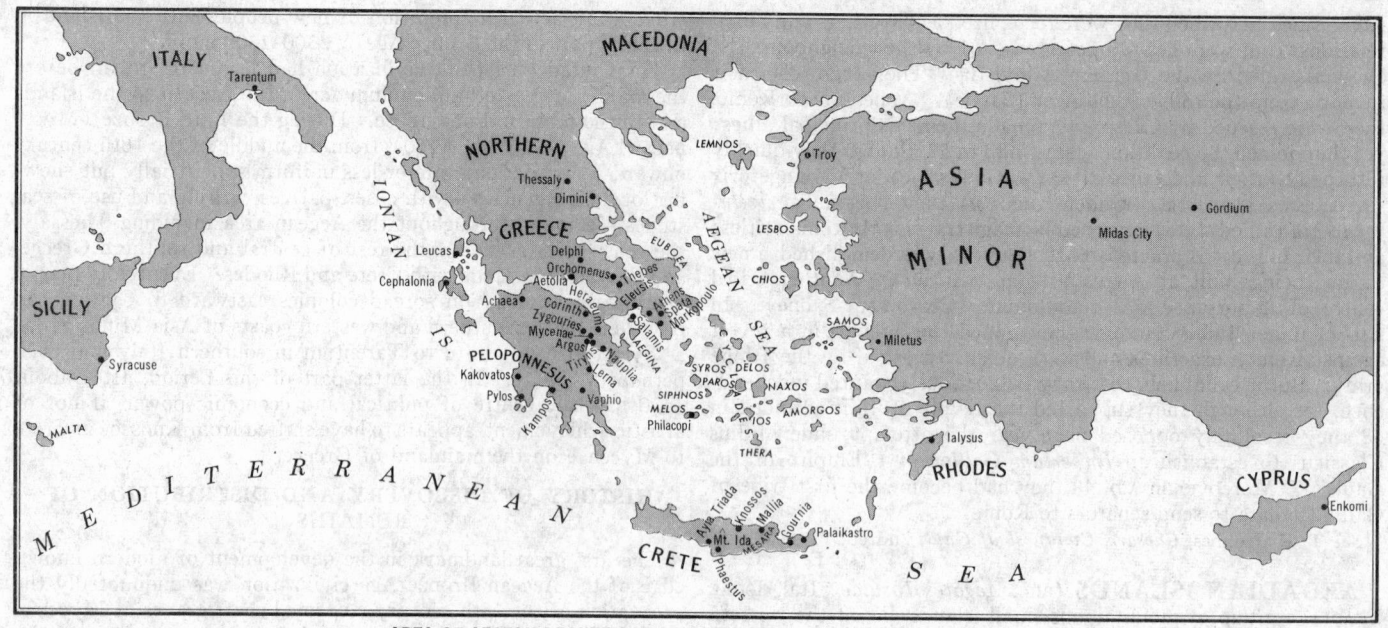

AREA OF AEGEAN BRONZE AGE CIVILIZATION, c. 2500 B.C.—c. 1100 B.C.

nized. Both the fabric and the decoration of the Mycenaean objects differed from any well-known art. The wide extent in space of this culture was proved by the identification of the "island gems" and the Ialysus vases with the newly discovered style; its wide extent in time was proved by collation of the earlier discoveries at Thera and Troy. A relation between objects of art described by Homer and the Mycenaean treasures was generally allowed, and a correct opinion prevailed that, while Homer was certainly later, the civilization described by him was in many respects reminiscent of the Mycenaean civilization. Schliemann resumed work at Troy in 1878, and greatly increased our knowledge of the lower strata. He did not recognize the Mycenaean remains in his "Lydian" city of the sixth stratum, which were not to be fully revealed till W. Dörpfeld resumed the work at Troy in 1892 after Schliemann's death. But by laying bare in 1884 the remains of a Mycenaean palace on the rock of Tiryns (q.v.), Schliemann made a contribution to knowledge of prehistoric domestic life that was amplified two years later by C. Tsountas' discovery of a similar palace at Mycenae. Work at Tiryns was not resumed till 1905, when it was proved that earlier strata dating back to the beginning of the Bronze Age lie below the palace cleared by Schliemann. In 1877 Late Bronze Age sepulchres were found outside the Argolid.

Between this date and the end of the 19th century many isolated tombs of the beehive type and cemeteries of rock-cut chamber tombs were explored in different districts of Greece. Chamber tombs were found in Attica (e.g., at Spata and Markopoulo) and in the Argolid (at Nauplia, and near the Argive Heraeum) and some late graves in Salamis. Beehive tombs, already rifled but retaining some of their furniture, were excavated at Dimini in Thessaly, Thoricus (Thorikon) in Attica, Orchomenus (Petromagoula) in Boeotia and Kampos in Laconia. The richest tomb of all was cleared at Vaphio in Laconia in 1889, and this produced, in addition to a fine series of engraved gems and miscellaneous goldsmith's work, two splendid golden cups chased with scenes of bull hunting, the famous Vaphio cups. The exploration of classical sites showed that many of these, too, had been important centres of culture in Bronze Age times. Thus the sanctuary at Delphi, the Argive Heraeum and the acropolis of Athens all yielded their quota of Mycenaean remains. A Cyclopean acropolis and palace were explored on the island of Goulas (Gla) in Lake Copais in Boeotia, the apparently prehistoric dikes of which were surveyed.

Mycenaean remains came to light in most parts of Greece, but except for Eleusis, the island of Aegina and Thoricus (all in the *nomos* of Attica) few settlements (as opposed to tombs) were excavated. At these last three sites pottery of new types was found dating from the Middle Bronze (Middle Helladic) Age; but

this and the discovery in 1894 in a barrow at Aphidna (Aphidnai) in Attica of burials accompanied by similar early wares remained almost unnoticed. Similarly some rock-cut tombs with Early Bronze Age (Early Helladic) handmade pottery found in the American excavations at Corinth in 1896 did not fall into their right context till the discoveries at Korakou, near Corinth, almost 20 years later.

Excavations Outside the Greek Mainland.—Meanwhile certain of the Aegean islands, Antiparos, Ios, Amorgos, Syros and Siphnos, were found to be singularly rich in remains of the local Early Bronze Age (Early Cycladic). The series of graves on Syros, containing crouching corpses, is most representative. Rich cemeteries in Naxos and Paros contained in addition to early graves some remains of the Middle Bronze Age (Middle Cycladic). Delos too proved an unexpected source of Bronze Age culture, with a settlement on Mt. Cynthus and tombs in the area of the later sanctuary of classical times at its foot. Melos, long marked as a source of early objects but not systematically excavated till 1896 by the British School at Athens, yielded at Philacopi remains of all periods except the Neolithic. Numerous cemeteries with Late Bronze Age pottery were found in Rhodes both in the 19th century and later by Italian excavators.

In Cyprus, where colonists from the Aegean area seem to have arrived during the Late Bronze Age, vast numbers of clay vases of Mycenaean type (mostly of local manufacture, but some imported) have been recovered. Even earlier in the Bronze Age vases and bronze weapons were apparently being imported into the island from Crete. A prolonged campaign of excavations was undertaken in Cyprus by the Swedish Cyprus expedition between World Wars I and II. After World War II the French under C. Schaeffer and the Cypriot Antiquities service under P. Dikaios made fruitful excavations at the chief Late Bronze Age site in the island, Enkomi.

The Troadic Early Bronze Age culture has been found throughout the whole region of the coast of western Asia Minor including the great islands of Lemnos, Lesbos, Chios and Samos. Excavations at sites in Macedonia by W. A. Heurtley and others in the 1920s and 1930s indicated the existence of an allied culture there. At Miletus, on the southwestern coast of Asia Minor, German excavations before and after World War II revealed Late Bronze Age pottery of Minoan and Mycenaean types, evidence of an actual colony of peoples from Crete or mainland Greece or both. In Egypt in 1887 W. M. Flinders Petrie found imported Cretan sherds of about 1750 B.C. at Birkat Qaroun in the Fayum, and in 1889 fragments of hundreds of Late Bronze Age (c. 1375–1350 B.C.) vases from the Aegean (thought to be of mainland rather than of Cretan

AEGEAN CIVILIZATION

PLATE I

Palace of Minos at Knossos; dating from before 1800 to c. 1400 B.C., Middle Minoan I—Late Minoan II

Linear B inscribed tablet from the Palace of Minos, Knossos; dating from c. 1400 B.C., Late Minoan II

Vase with octopus design found at Palaiokastron; dating from c. 1500 to 1450 B.C., Late Minoan I B

Faïence snake goddess from the Palace of Minos at Knossos; dating from c. 1600 B.C., Middle Minoan III B

Pitcher from Phaistos; dating from c. 1750 B.C., Middle Minoan II

Bronze helmet from warrior's tomb at Knossos; dating from c. 1400 B.C., Late Minoan II

MIDDLE AND LATE MINOAN BRONZE AGE CULTURE

Plate II

AEGEAN CIVILIZATION

Marble idol from Amorgos in the Cyclades

Early Cycladic "sauceboat" from Syros

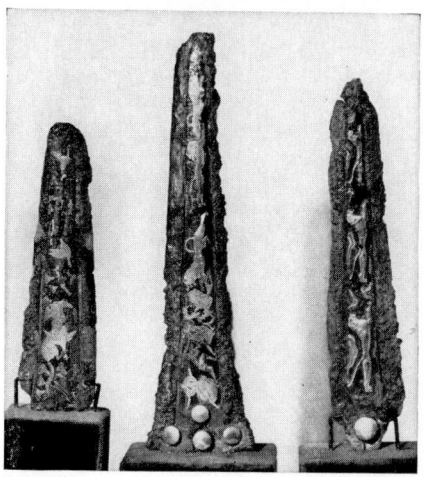

Dagger blades inlaid with gold and silver from royal tombs of Mycenae; 16th century B.C.

Gold cup with repoussé decoration, from a beehive tomb at Vaphio, in Laconia; 16th century B.C.

The Lion Gate leading into the citadel at Mycenae; c. 14th century B.C.

Two impressions of seal stones from Vaphio; dating from c. 1500 B.C.

The so-called Treasury of Atreus at Mycenae, the largest of the beehive tombs; dating from c. 1350 B.C.

CYCLADIC AND HELLADIC BRONZE AGE CULTURES

PHOTOGRAPHS, (TOP LEFT, CENTRE TOP) FROM "L'ART DES CYCLADES," CHRISTIAN ZERVOS, (OTHERS) FROM "CRETE AND MYCENAE" PUBLISHED BY THAMES & HUDSON, LONDON AND HARRY N. ABRAMS, NEW YORK

manufacture) from the rubbish dumps of the palace of the pharaoh Ikhnaton at Tell el-Amarna on the Nile. Vases of the Late Bronze Age imported from the Aegean also were found in tombs near Syracuse in Sicily. Aegean objects were reported from Sardinia and the Balearic Islands.

Crete.—The greatest Bronze Age city of the Aegean and the chief site of the Minoan Bronze Age civilization was Knossos in Crete, which has yielded the most various and the most continuous evidence from the Neolithic Age onward. It was in fact the fountainhead of Aegean Bronze Age civilization and probably for long its political and social centre. The remarkable archaic Greek bronzes found in a cave on Mt. Ida in 1885, and epigraphic monuments of the classical period such as the famous law of Gortyna (*q.v.*), first attracted the notice of archaeologists, but the first undoubted Bronze Age remains reported from it were a few objects extracted from the palace at Knossos by M. Kalokairinos in 1878. These were followed by important discoveries made in the southern plain (Mesara) by F. Halbherr and other Italian explorers. The American W. J. Stillmann and Schliemann both made unsuccessful attempts at Knossos, and Evans, going to Crete in 1893, traveled in succeeding years about the island exploring sites and collecting evidence which convinced him that greater things would eventually be found. He was able to forecast the discovery of written characters, till then not suspected in Aegean civilization. For the subsequent history of Evans' excavations at Knossos *see* CRETE.

Further Investigations on the Mainland After 1900.—The success of the excavations in Crete naturally caused fresh attention to be paid to Mycenaean remains on the mainland. At Thebes in Boeotia the ruins of the Late Bronze Age palace (the House of Cadmus) were found by A. D. Keramopoullos and yielded many fragments of brilliant frescoes and a store of inscribed vases; close to the city chamber tombs, stored with vases and other funeral furniture, were excavated. At Orchomenus the Mycenaean stratum was explored by A. Furtwängler and the underlying strata, earlier Bronze Age and Neolithic, began to reveal for the first time the pre-Mycenaean history of the mainland. Wares of the Early and Middle Bronze Age were unearthed at Aegina, and imported Cretan ware of the Middle Bronze Age also came to light there and, after World War II, at Lerna. At Tiryns many fragments of frescoes from the palace were found, and in the strata beneath the palace floor, reaching down to bedrock, remains of the Middle and Early Bronze Ages appeared. Further beehive tombs were excavated in Messenia at Kakovatos and Pylos (Pilos) and in the Argolid at Tiryns and at many other sites. More evidence for the Late Bronze Age came from Argos, Achaea, Aetolia, Locris and Cephalonia, showing that culture all over Greece at that time had been more or less uniform.

In Thessaly rich deposits of painted Neolithic pottery were found before World War I at Dimini and Sesklo by Tsountas. Further systematic excavation of other sites in Thessaly, notably by A. J. B. Wace and M. S. Thompson before World War I and after World War II by V. Milojcic and H. Biesantz, and researches by G. Soteriades and later by H. Goldman and S. Weinberg in Boeotia and Phocis, showed that the Neolithic pottery of the Greek mainland was different from that of Crete, having painted designs instead of plain burnished surfaces. Dörpfeld in Leucas (an island off the coast of Acarnania) found wares of all Bronze Age periods (Early, Middle and Late) and Neolithic pottery with painted decoration closely akin to the Thessalian. Euboea produced tombs of the Early Bronze Age, with pottery showing a striking likeness both to the wares of the Cyclades and to those of the mainland, and more Late Bronze Age tombs.

After 1915, American excavations there under C. W. Blegen and others threw light on the early history of the mainland. In the Peloponnesus, Neolithic wares similar to those of Thessaly have been found at Corinth, Nemea, the Argive Heraeum and Lerna. Excavations at Korakou and at Zygouries (southwest of Corinth), at the Argive Heraeum and, near Athens, at Ayios Kosmas have revealed further evidence of the three stages of Bronze Age culture on the mainland. In the Argolid, at Asine near Nauplia and at Berbati near Mycenae, Swedish expeditions under A. W. Persson recovered remains of all periods, and at Midea (Dendra) exca-

vated an unplundered beehive tomb that revealed evidence of the burial ritual and treasures richer than those of Vaphio. There was a splendid gold cup chased with a design of octopuses and dolphins, a gold and silver cup adorned with bulls' heads, silver cups, weapons of bronze, engraved seal stones and pottery dating the tomb to about 1350 B.C. Nearby a chamber tomb, with a hoard of 33 bronze vessels, empty of human remains, seemed to have been a cenotaph. Another tomb produced a bronze helmet, and one found in 1960 contained a bronze corselet.

But the most spectacular discoveries from the mainland of Greece in the 20th century have been at Mycenae itself and at Pylos in Messenia in the southwestern Peloponnesus. At Pylos in 1939 Blegen began to excavate a great Mycenaean palace (the Palace of Nestor) containing archives of clay tablets inscribed with a linear script (Linear B) like those found for the first time by Evans at Knossos about 40 years earlier. No such tablets had been found before this on the Greek mainland, although a few clay jars with painted inscriptions had come to light, for instance, at Thebes and Eleusis. After World War II many more tablets were found at Pylos, and similar tablets were recovered at Mycenae. In 1952 the language of these tablets (both those from Knossos and those from the mainland sites) was deciphered by M. Ventris and J. Chadwick as Greek. Their decipherment has been accepted by many authorities, but is challenged or doubted by others. At the same time more tholos tombs and rock-cut chambers with very rich finds rivaling those from Mycenae itself have been excavated by Blegen at Pylos near the palace and by S. Marinatos elsewhere in the Pylos area. Many other unexcavated tholos tombs and Bronze Age sites are known to exist in this region.

From 1920 to 1923 the British under Wace re-explored the Late Bronze Age palace and the great royal tholos tombs around the city at Mycenae, and cleared new cemeteries of rock-cut chamber tombs there. In 1939 Wace resumed excavations, and continued them again after World War II, excavating important Bronze Age houses outside the walls with a rich harvest of clay and stone vases, ivory inlays and inscribed clay tablets. In 1951 a new circle of royal shaft graves like those explored by Schliemann but in general somewhat earlier in date (they contained imported Cretan pottery of about 1550 B.C.) came to light in the same area outside the Late Bronze Age citadel walls and was explored by the Greek archaeologists J. Papademetriou and G. E. Mylonas. The wealth of gold cups, bronze weapons, vases and objects of rock crystal and jewelry from these graves rivals the treasures from the graves examined by Schliemann.

GENERAL NATURE OF THE EVIDENCE

The internal evidence comprises:

1. Structures: ruins of palaces, palatial villas, houses, built tholos (domed or beehive) tombs, rectangular built tombs (in Crete), cist graves and fortifications (Aegean islands, Greek mainland and northwestern Asia Minor). Large temples like those of Egypt and the near east do not seem to have existed. Small shrine buildings, however, have been noted at many sites in Crete, for instance at Gournia, in the centre of the town, and associated with the palaces at Mallia and Ayia Triada, and on a large number of mountain tops. On the mainland what appears to be a Late Bronze Age shrine has been recognized deep under the floor of the later Hellenic *telesterion* (hall of the mysteries) at Eleusis. Many pictures of shrines appear in fresco paintings, on stone relief vases and on gold plaques, and clay models of them exist. These, mostly of the Late Bronze Age, have been recovered from both Crete and the mainland. From like sources and from faïence and ivory inlays representations of palaces and houses also have been recovered.

2. Structural decoration (*i.e.*, architectural features), such as stone columns, friezes and various moldings; mural decoration, including fresco paintings, coloured plaster reliefs and perhaps mosaic inlay.

3. Furniture including: (*a*) Domestic, such as vessels of clay, stone, bronze, etc., from huge store jars down to tiny unguent pots; culinary and other implements; thrones, seats, tables, etc., of stone or plastered terra cotta. (*b*) Sacred, such as models or actual examples of ritual objects; of these there are also numerous pic-

torial representations. (*c*) Funerary; *e.g.*, coffins in painted terra cotta and occasionally stone.

4. Works of art; *e.g.*, objects carved in stone or ivory, cast or beaten in metals (gold, silver, copper and bronze) or modeled in clay, faïence, paste, etc. Little or no trace has been found of large sculpture in stone or any other material, but many examples exist of small sculpture in stone, bronze and ivory. There is some evidence from Crete, however, that there were larger statues in wood. There are vases of all kinds, carved in marble or other stones, cast or beaten in metals or fashioned in clay, the latter in enormous number and variety, richly ornamented with painted designs and sometimes bearing molded decoration; examples of painting on stone, opaque and transparent; engraved objects in great number, *e.g.*, ring-bezels and gems (seal stones); and an immense quantity of clay impressions, taken from these.

5. Weapons, tools and implements in stone, clay and bronze and, from *c.* 1100 B.C., iron, sometimes richly ornamented or inlaid. Numerous representations of these also have been found. Evidence for the use of body armour (bronze helmets, greaves, cuirasses) has been found, the rare surviving examples of these all being of the Late Bronze Age.

6. Articles of personal use; *e.g.*, brooches (only at the end of the Late Bronze Age), pins, razors, tweezers, etc., occasionally found as dedications to a deity.

7. Written documents; *e.g.*, clay tablets, engraved gems and gem impressions, legends written with ink or paint on pottery or painted on frescoes (rare) and characters incised on stone or pottery.

8. Excavated tombs, of either the pit or the chamber kind, in which the dead were laid together with various objects of use and luxury. The burials are almost invariably inhumations, but rare examples of cremations, mostly Late Bronze Age, have been found both in Crete and on the mainland. The bodies were placed in either coffins of clay or wood (in Crete) or simple wrappings.

9. Public works, such as paved and stepped roadways, bridges, systems of drainage, etc.

A certain amount of external evidence also may be gathered from:

1. Monuments and records of other contemporary civilizations. Among these are representations of alien peoples in Egyptian frescoes; imitation of Aegean fabrics and style in non-Aegean lands; allusions to Mediterranean peoples in Egyptian, Hittite, Semitic or Babylonian records.

2. Literary traditions of subsequent civilizations, especially the Hellenic, such as those embodied in the Homeric poems, the legends concerning Crete, Mycenae, etc.; and statements as to the origin of gods and cults transmitted by Hellenic antiquarians such as Strabo, Pausanias and Diodorus Siculus.

3. Anomalies in customs, creeds, rituals, etc., in the Aegean area in the periods after the Bronze Age, indicating survivals from earlier systems.

4. Philological evidence: survivals in Greek (an Indo-European language) of words of non-Indo-European origin.

GENERAL FEATURES OF AEGEAN CIVILIZATION

From the evidence classified above it is possible to deduce some leading features of Aegean civilization.

Political Organization.—The Cretan palaces, and the fortified citadels of Mycenae, Tiryns and Troy, containing little more than one great residence and dominating lower towns of meaner houses, point to monarchy at all periods. Local variations in the development of Aegean art before the middle of the 2nd millennium B.C. suggest the early existence of independent political units in various parts of the Aegean world, of which the strongest was that at Knossos.

Religion.—The kings were evidently priest-kings, if not themselves regarded as divine, as in Egypt and the near east. Religion in the area may have been essentially the same everywhere from the earliest period, though until the spread of Minoan civilization in the Late Bronze Age the evidence for it is virtually confined to Crete, viz., the cult of divine principles, resident in nature and controlling fertility. This cult in Crete passed through an aniconic

stage, from which fetishes survived to the last, these being rocks or pillars, trees and weapons (*e.g.*, the double war ax, the shield). When the iconic stage was reached, in Crete from early in the 2nd millennium B.C. or before, we find a goddess with a subordinate young god, as in many other eastern Mediterranean lands. The god was probably son and mate of the goddess, and the divine pair represented the genius of reproductive fertility in its relations with humanity. The goddess at times appears with doves, as uranic, at others with snakes, as chthonic. In the ritual, fetishes, often miniature, played a great part. Many plants and animals were sacred; animal sacrifice (but not normally burnt, in Crete at least), invocation and dedication of all sorts of offerings and effigies were practised. The dead may have been objects of a sort of hero worship both in Crete and on the mainland. This early nature cult explains many anomalous features of Hellenic religion, especially in the cults of Artemis and Aphrodite.

Social Organization.—Of the organization of the people under the monarch little is known. There are so few representations of armed men that it seems doubtful if there can have been any professional military class, at any rate until the Late Bronze Age. Theatral structures, found at Knossos and Phaestus within the precincts of the palaces, perhaps were used for shows of a religious character or for sittings of a royal assize, rather than for popular assemblies. The remains at Knossos contain evidence of an elaborate system of registration, account-keeping and other secretarial work, which perhaps indicates a considerable body of law.

The life of the ruling class in Crete at least was comfortable and even luxurious from early times. In Crete fine stone palaces, richly decorated, with separate sleeping apartments, large halls, ingenious devices for admitting light and air, sanitation and highly developed arrangements for supply of water and for drainage, attest this fact. There, even the smaller houses, after the Neolithic period, seem also to have been of stone, plastered within. After 1600 B.C. the palaces in Crete had more than one story, fine stairways, bath chambers, windows and folding and sliding doors. In the Late Bronze Age palaces of the mainland, the distinction of blocks of apartments has been held to indicate the seclusion of women at least among the ruling class; moreover, frescoes at Knossos show women grouped apart, and they appear alone on gems.

Meat, fish and many kinds of vegetables were evidently eaten, and wine and beer were drunk. There was evidently olive and vine culture on a large scale. Vessels for culinary and table use show an infinite variety of form and purpose. Artificers' implements of many kinds were in use, bronze succeeding obsidian and other hard stones as the material. Stone seats are found carefully shaped to the human body. Chariots were in use in the Late Bronze Age, as is proved by the pictures of them on the shaft grave steles (tombstones) at Mycenae, on Cretan tablets, and on gems and frescoes. The horse was also ridden, but chariots were no doubt used more than cavalry in war, as in Egypt and elsewhere at the time. Main roads were paved. Sports, probably more or less religious or magical in their object, are often represented; *e.g.*, bull-fighting, dancing, boxing and armed combat.

Commerce.—Trade was practised to some extent from the earliest times, as is proved by the distribution of obsidian from Melos over most of the Aegean area and by the Nilotic influence on early Minoan art. Early in the 2nd millennium Cretan vases were exported to Melos, Egypt, Cyprus and the Greek mainland; Melian vases came in their turn to Crete. After 1600 B.C. there is very close intercourse with Egypt, and Aegean things find their way to all coasts of the Mediterranean. No traces of currency have come to light, unless certain axheads, too slight for practical use, were used as such; but standard weights and ingots have been found. No Aegean written documents have been found outside the area and there is therefore no evidence of epistolary correspondence with other lands. Representations of ships are not uncommon on Aegean gems, gem-sealings and vases. There are also leaden and clay models of boats, of low freeboard, with masts. Familiarity with the sea is evinced in the free use of marine motives in decoration.

Disposal of the Dead.—Little is known about the burial customs of the Neolithic peoples whether in Crete or on the mainland.

In Crete at the beginning of the Bronze Age natural caves were being used as communal tombs by whole families or tribal groups. Somewhat later artificial caves—irregular chamber tombs with one or more compartments—began to be cut in the soft rock at sites such as Knossos. In other parts of the island tombs built of stone above ground, either rectangular with several chambers, or circular, domed in stone, mud or mud brick (remote ancestors of the great tholos tombs of the Late Bronze Age), were also in use. All these were communal tombs used for repeated burials over long periods of years, and they often contain the remains of hundreds of bodies. In the other Aegean islands cist graves (also found in Crete from an early period) and little stone-built tombs containing only one or two bodies were more often the rule. On the Greek mainland in the Early Bronze Age both stone-built communal tombs (at coastal sites such as Ayios Kosmas near Athens) and rock-cut chamber tombs with only one or two bodies are known.

About the beginning of the Middle Bronze Age (Middle Helladic), however, an intrusive culture brought by invaders apparently from somewhere in Asia Minor introduced new burial customs to the mainland. The dead were now buried individually in graves, often lined with slabs (cist graves), either under the floors of the houses or in the streets inside the settlements. Throughout the Aegean area, before this time, burial was always (except in the case of infants) outside the settlement area. In Crete from about 1600 B.C. the custom of communal burial began to give way, at the great centres like Knossos at least, to a practice of burying in small tombs or graves with only one or two bodies in each. But by a curious inversion, with the spread of the Minoan civilization to the mainland of Greece, large chamber tombs used by whole families for repeated burials largely replaced the Middle Bronze Age (Middle Helladic) custom of burial in single graves there.

On the mainland royal burials were at first in shaft graves, and later in tholos tombs apparently descended from the earlier Cretan circular tombs. In Crete the only "royal" tombs that have been identified are at Knossos; and they are either circular beehives or rectangular stone rooms with keel vaults, or (in the case of the Temple Tomb at Knossos) in the form of a regular funerary temple with a rock-cut burial chamber behind it.

In Crete during the early part of the Bronze Age burials were normally contracted (the body being often squeezed head or feet first into a clay store jar), but in the later Bronze Age loosely flexed and extended burials became common. At this time in Crete the bodies often were placed in wooden coffins or in clay imitations of them, or in clay bathtubs (the latter also used, but more rarely, on the mainland). Rare examples of cremation have been found dating from the Late Neolithic period in Thessaly, and from about the 17th century B.C. and later in Crete and on the mainland; but cremation was never a regular form of burial around the Aegean area (except perhaps in the Troad) until the beginning of the Iron Age after 1100 B.C.

In Crete there is evidence of an elaborate cult or tendance of the dead in the shape of vast numbers of vases, evidently once containing food and drink, placed outside the great communal tombs. In the later Bronze Age it became the custom throughout the Aegean area to put such grave goods together with the bodies inside the tombs. The arrangements in the royal Temple Tomb at Knossos, and the funerary scenes depicted on the painted stone sarcophagus found at Ayia Triada dating from about 1350 B.C., suggest an elaborate cult of the dead continuing into the Late Bronze Age in Crete. Above the shaft graves excavated by Schliemann at Mycenae was what appears to have been a circular altar. This and offerings in the form of terra-cotta figurines, bronzes, etc., placed, as well as vases of food and drink, outside the great royal tholos tombs at Mycenae, indicate a similar kind of cult on the mainland as well.

Artistic Production.—Ceramic art reached an especially high standard in its fabric, form and decoration by about 1750 B.C. in Crete. But the high-water mark of the Bronze Age civilization of Crete is in the 17th and 16th centuries B.C. It was during this period that the Cretan civilization spread its influence over the Aegean islands and the Greek mainland. The products of the Aegean gem (seal stone) engravers then probably excelled in fine-

ness anything of the kind made elsewhere at the time. The same may be said of fresco painting, and probably of metalwork. By the end of the 15th century B.C., however, the beginning of a decline in workmanship and style in all branches of the arts is visible. This decline was accelerated during the centuries that followed.

ORIGIN AND HISTORY OF AEGEAN CIVILIZATION

Distinctive Features.—The distinctive character of Aegean civilization is now clear enough. The truth was obscured for a time, however, by prejudices in favour of certain alien Mediterranean races long known to have been in relation with the Aegean area in prehistoric times; e.g., the Egyptians and especially the Phoenicians. Others put forward the Achaeans (q.v.) from the north as the people to whom this civilization belongs. But such claims to the authorship of the Aegean remains grew fainter with every fresh Aegean discovery; with the Cretan revelations they largely ceased to be considered.

The Aegean civilization developed these distinctive features:

1. Indigenous scripts expressed in characters of which only a small percentage are identical, or even obviously connected, with those of any other scripts (see CRETE).

2. Art quite distinct in character from any other known art. Its obligations to other contemporary arts (of Egypt and Babylonia, for instance) are many and obvious, especially in its later stages; but every borrowed form and motive is modified in the works of Aegean craftsmen and assumes a new character. In it may be detected the beginning of that naturalism, combined with a striving for the ideal, that afterward animated Hellenic art. The fresco paintings, ceramic motifs, reliefs, free sculpture and metalwork of Crete confirm the impression long ago created by the earlier discoveries on the Greek mainland (Mycenae, Vaphio, Tiryns).

3. Tomb construction of the tholos or beehive type, of which the grandest examples known are at Mycenae. The Cretan type of coffin, also, has no parallel outside the Aegean.

Chronology and History.—The Cretan Bronze Age was divided by Evans, on a basis of changes observable in the style of the pottery, seal stones and other objects, into three main periods, called by him the Early, Middle and Late Minoan after the legendary King Minos of Knossos. Some years later a similar scheme was proposed by Wace and Blegen for the Bronze Age sequences of the mainland (Early, Middle and Late Helladic) and the Aegean islands (Cycladic). These three systems do not by any means necessarily run parallel to each other except during the last (Late Bronze Age) phase from about 1600 B.C. onward, when Cretan civilization had spread its influence throughout the Aegean and over the Greek mainland.

The earlier Bronze Age (Early Minoan period) in Crete had many affinities with the end of the Old Kingdom (6th dynasty) and the First Intermediate period succeeding it in Egypt. There may even have been an influx of settlers from Egypt, and from the coasts of Syria and Palestine, into Crete during this disturbed time between about 2400 and 2200 B.C. But many of the basic elements of the Cretan (Minoan) Bronze Age civilization can be traced back into the local Neolithic civilization. At the same time, the earliest Bronze Age civilization of Crete had much in common with the earliest Bronze Age cultures of the islands and the Greek mainland, although the civilization of Crete from the start appears to have been much more advanced, with a knowledge of writing and extensive use of seal stones in commerce.

The distribution of place names of a peculiar non-Indo-European (see INDO-EUROPEAN) type, notably names with roots ending in -ss like Knossos or -nt(d) like Korinthos (Corinth) or Tiryns with genitive Tirynthos, together with words of the same type surviving in later Greek, suggest that at some point in time a people speaking the same or related non-Indo-European languages occupied the whole Aegean and the western part of Asia Minor. The spread of this language or languages may have been due to immigrations into the Aegean from the direction of Asia Minor at the beginning of the Bronze Age, or may reflect the position in still earlier Neolithic times.

In Crete a high civilization, with great cities and palaces, the arts of writing, fresco painting, stone vase making, gem engraving, ivory carving, and faïence molding, developed without any apparent break throughout the 2nd millennium B.C. On the mainland of Greece, however, the promise of the Early Bronze Age (Early Helladic) culture, apparently connected in many ways with the civilization of Crete, was cut short by an irruption of more barbarous people coming perhaps from the hinterland of central or eastern Asia Minor. These people lived in long houses of a primitive aspect with a main room and a porch in front, and often with a semicircular compartment at the back—a type of dwelling already found in Thessaly during Neolithic times and widespread throughout central Europe and Asia Minor—and they introduced the practice of burying their dead inside their settlements. But the influence of the rich and powerful Cretan civilization, now at its apogee, increasingly made itself felt and spread over the islands and the Greek mainland.

In some of the Aegean islands this spread of Cretan civilization was certainly accompanied by actual colonies of Cretans. Such a colony dating from the 17th or 16th century B.C. has been recognized at Trianda (near Ialysus) in Rhodes, and many others no doubt existed. On the mainland the position is less clear, and it is by no means certain that any part of the mainland was ever politically subject to Cretan rule. The kings of the shaft graves at Mycenae were clearly natives, although many of the fine things placed in their tombs (the gold cups, swords, gems, etc.) were of Cretan origin, either gifts from Cretan kings, or plunder taken by mainland kings in war, or manufactured by Cretan craftsmen, whether prisoners or volunteers, working at mainland courts. Moreover the Cretan civilization, which is best represented at the great centres like Mycenae or Pylos, does not appear really to have saturated the mainland. The use of seal stones, for instance, general in Crete, was evidently confined to a comparatively small class—kings, nobles and officials—on the mainland; for on the mainland seal stones are much rarer than they are in Crete, and the cheap crude seal stones used by ordinary people are almost entirely absent. Above all, the Late Bronze Age palaces of the mainland are of quite a different type from the earlier Cretan palaces. The latter were built around a large open court, while the former were dominated by a great hall or *megaron,* as it has come to be called from its resemblance to the *megara* (halls) that Homer describes, with a huge central hearth and a porch in front, a glorified version, in fact, of the long house of the Middle Bronze Age and earlier times on the mainland. It seems therefore that the kings of the mainland, even if at some point they were tributary to Cretan overlords, were not themselves Cretans.

About 1400 B.C. what Evans called the "Last Palace" at Knossos was destroyed. It may be that both at Knossos and other Cretan sites palaces existed after this time. But if they did they were almost certainly poor and mean compared with the great palaces that had preceded them. The archaeological evidence suggests that in the period immediately before 1400 B.C. Knossos was the centre of a great political power with a highly developed military system, ruling the whole of Crete and many of the islands if not parts of the mainland as well; but that after 1400 B.C. the centre of political power had shifted to Mycenae, which during the following century attained the height of its glory and prosperity. In this period the greatest of the beehive tombs like the Treasury of Atreus and the Cyclopean walls round the citadel were built.

The decline in the civilized arts that had already begun to be visible during the period of the so-called Last Palace at Knossos before 1400 B.C. continued throughout the 14th and 13th centuries. Internal wars or the threat of invasions from outside are reflected in the construction of great fortifications on the mainland of Greece, at Mycenae, Tiryns, Dendra, Athens and Gla in Lake Copais, for instance. There appears also to be a Mycenaean fortification wall crossing the Isthmus of Corinth to defend the Peloponnesus from the north. In the course of the 13th century the great palaces of the mainland were destroyed one after another, never to be rebuilt. But at Mycenae itself, and perhaps at Pylos, the final destruction of the city and palace apparently were delayed until 1200 B.C. or later.

About 1100 B.C., according to tradition, the last wave of Greek invaders, the Dorians, entered southern Greece. This period coincides with the ultimate degeneration of the Old Bronze Age civilization. It also coincides with the beginning of the extensive use of iron replacing bronze for tools and weapons in the Aegean area, and the spread of the practice of cremation burial.

When the earliest wave of Greeks had begun to enter the Aegean area is a more open question. If the language of the Late Bronze Age (Linear B) script of Knossos, Pylos and Mycenae is correctly interpreted as Greek, they clearly entered the Aegean before the time that such a script was evolved, in the 15th century B.C. or earlier. Many authorities would place the entry of the first Greeks into Greece at the turn of the Early and Middle Bronze Ages of the mainland, the beginning, that is, of the 2nd millennium B.C. There are many arguments in support of this view; and even if the language of the Linear B script is finally proved not to be Greek, the first Greeks may still have come into Greece then. But if the language of the script is *not* Greek, they may also have come later in the Bronze Age, during the 13th century B.C., only 100 years or so before the Dorians.

See also MINOAN LINEAR SCRIPTS; and references under "Aegean Civilization" in the Index.

BIBLIOGRAPHY.—*General works:* C. Tsountas and J. Manatt, *The Mycenaean Age* (1903); H. R. Hall, *Aegean Archaeology* (1915); D. Fimmen, *Die Kretisch-Mykenische Kultur* (1921); G. Glotz, *La Civilisation Egéenne* (1925); J. L. Myres, *Who Were the Greeks?* (1930); H. J. Kantor, *The Aegean and the Orient in the 2nd Millennium B.C.* (1947); F. Matz, "Die Agäis" in *Handbuch der Archäologie,* ii (1950); H. L. Lorimer, *Homer and the Monuments* (1951); F. Schachermeyr, *Die ältesten Kulturen Griechenlands* (1955). *Crete:* A. J. Evans, *The Palace of Minos,* vol. i–iv and index (1921–36); J. D. S. Pendlebury, *The Archaeology of Crete* (1939), *A Handbook to the Palace of Minos* (1954); *Etudes Crétoises* (1928 et seq.); L. Pernier, *Il Palazzo Minoico di Festos,* i (1935), ii (1951); F. Matz, *Forschungen auf Kreta, 1942* (1951). *Aegean islands:* British School at Athens, *Excavations at Phylakopi in Melos* (1904). *Mainland:* G. Karo, *Die Schachtgräber von Mykenai* (1930); A. J. B. Wace, *Mycenae, an Archaeological History and Guide* (1949); G. E. Mylonas, *Ancient Mycenae* (1957); H. Bulle, *Orchomenos,* i (1907); E. Kunze, *Orchomenos,* ii–iii (1931–34); A. J. B. Wace and M. S. Thompson, *Prehistoric Thessaly* (1912); A. Frickenhaus, G. Rodenwaldt and K. Müller, *Tiryns,* i–iv (1912–38); C. W. Blegen, *Korakou* (1921), *Zygouries* (1928), *Prosymna* (1937); H. Goldman, *Excavations at Eutresis in Boeotia* (1931); A. W. Persson *The Royal Tombs at Dendra Near Midea* (1931), *New Tombs at Dendra* (1942); W. A. Heurtley, *Prehistoric Macedonia* (1939); Lord William Taylour, *The Mycenaeans* (1964). *Religion:* A. W. Persson, *The Religion of Greece in Prehistoric Times* (1942); C. Picard, *Les Religions Préhelleniques* (1948); M. L. Nilsson, *The Minoan-Mycenaean Religion,* 2nd ed. (1950). *Pottery:* Catalogue of *Vases in the British Museum,* vol. i, pt. 1 (1925); A. Furumark, *The Mycenaean Pottery* (1941), *Chronology of Mycenaean Pottery* (1941); F. H. Stubbings, *Mycenaean Pottery from the Levant* (1951); W. Taylour, *Mycenean Pottery in Italy* (1958). *Seal stones:* F. Matz, *Die Frühkretischen Siegel* (1928); H. Biesantz, *Kretische-Mykenische Siegelbilder* (1954); V. E. G. Kenna, *Cretan Seals* (1960). *Picture books* (illustrating sites, works of art etc.): H. T. Bossert, *The Art of Ancient Crete* (1937); C. Zervos, *L'Art de la Crète* (1956), *L'Art des Cyclades* (1957); S. Marinatos and M. Hirmer, *Krete kai Mykenaike Hellas* (1959), Eng. ed. *Crete and Mycenae* (1960). *Writing and Language:* A. J. Evans, *Scripta Minoa,* vol. i (1909), vol. ii (1952); M. Ventris and J. Chadwick, *Documents in Mycenaean Greek* (1956); J. Chadwick, *The Decipherment of Linear B* (1958); A. J. Beattie, "Mr. Ventris' Decipherment of the Minoan Linear B Script," *Journal of Hellenic Studies,* 76 (1956). For an account of the controversy beginning in 1958 about the date of the Linear B tablets *see* articles by M. S. F. Hood, L. R. Palmer and J. R. Boardman in *Antiquity,* xxxv, no. 137–140 (1961).

(D. G. H.; A. J. B. W.; M. S. F. H.)

AEGEAN SEA (Gr. AIGAION PELAGOS; Turk. EGE DENIZI), an arm of the Mediterranean sea between Greece on the west and Asia Minor on the east, is connected by the Dardanelles with the sea of Marmara and closed by Crete to the south. The name "archipelago" was formerly applied specifically to the sea. Various derivations suggest the origin of "Aegean" from the town of Aegae (modern Limni), or from Aegea, queen of the Amazons, who perished in this sea, or from Aegeus, father of Theseus, who drowned himself there. Structurally the sea is a much-shattered old land block almost entirely submerged, outlined by younger fold mountains (being continuations of ranges of Asia Minor), also partly submerged. Both features have accounted for this island-studded sea with its alternating deeps and shallows. Island chains may be traced through Chios, Psara and Skyros to the northern Sporades; through Samos, Ikaria, Mykonos, Tenos and Andros to the southeast promontory of Euboea; and through Rhodes,

Karpathos, Crete and Cerigo to the southeastern promontory of the Peloponnesus. Between the two last chains is the great group of the Cyclades including Naxos, Paros and Melos. Islands in the northern section of the sea include Thasos, off the Macedonian coast, Samothrace, fronting the Gulf of Saros, and Imbros and Lemnos, in prolongation of the Gallipoli peninsula, while Mitylene lies off the coast of Asia Minor. Important sea basins are those of the Cretan sea with depths of over 1,000 fathoms, and the trough between Thessaly and the Gulf of Saros (over 600 fathoms). Many islands are of volcanic formation; and a well-defined volcanic group includes Melos, Cimolus, Thera and Therasia. The larger islands have some fertile and well-watered valleys and plains. The chief productions are wheat, wine, oil, mastic, figs, raisins, honey, wax, cotton and silk. The people fish for coral and sponges, as well as for bream and mullet. Greece owns most of the islands, since a number collectively known as the Dodecanese were transferred to Greece by Italy after World War II. Imbros (Imroz) and Tenedos (Bozcaada) remain Turkish. The storms which cross the sea in the winter months inhibit navigation, but in summer the gentle and regular Etesian winds, setting from the north, make movement by sea safe and easy. In the latter half of the 2nd millennium B.C., the Mycenaean thalassocracy, or maritime supremacy, was centred on the Aegean and controlled its shores. In later antiquity, the Aegean was the heart of the Greek world, and the Greek people lived along its shores, as Plato said, like frogs around a pond; indeed, the island of Delos was traditionally the centre or hub of the world, set between the foreshores of the three continents.

The ethnic unity of the islands and shores of the Aegean was only broken after World War I, with the exodus of a large Greek population from the western coasts of Asia Minor. Now that the frontier cuts the Turkish coast from all but a few minor inshore islands, coastal trade on this side of the sea has declined sharply. Geological changes, too, have affected shipping, for on all the Aegean coasts the accumulation of silt has swamped numerous small harbours since classical times, and traffic has concentrated increasingly in a few large silt-free ports, like Izmir (Smyrna) and Piraeus. There are separate articles on most of the islands; for historic aspects see AEGEAN CIVILIZATION; GREECE.

(WM. C. B.)

AEGEUS, son of Pandion and grandson of Cecrops, was king of Athens and the father of Theseus (q.v.).

AEGINA (mod. Gr. AIΓINA or AIΓINA), a Greek island in the Saronic gulf, lies 20 mi. from the Piraeus. In shape almost an equilateral triangle (each side about 8 mi. long), it has an area of about 33 sq.mi. and a population of (1951) 8,859. In the northwest is a stony but fertile plain which produces olives, figs, vines and almonds; along the east coast stretches a ridge of volcanic trachyte, its highest point the conical Mt. Oros in the south (1,745 ft.). The chief town, Aegina (pop. [1951] 6,217), whose sheltered harbour is now little used, lies at the northern end of the west coast. The island forms an eparchy of the modern *nomos* of Attica (q.v.).

Antiquities.—The site of the modern town has been occupied continuously since about 3000 B.C. Excavations on the promontory which shields the double harbour on the north have yielded abundant evidence of Neolithic and Bronze Age occupation. With the extension of the city southward in historical times this acropolis became more exclusively a religious centre and remains have been found of several small sanctuaries (notably that of Aeacus (q.v.), the hero whose mother gave her name to the island) and of a central temple (c. 500 B.C.), now known to be that of Apollo, of which the foundations and one interior column are preserved. Neolithic to late Mycenaean tombs have been discovered near the town, from one of which came the famous Aegina treasure in the British museum (now known to be of Cretan origin). At the northern end of the eastern ridge stands the sanctuary of Aphaea, a primitive local goddess of uncertain origin, associated by the systematic mythographers with Britomartis (Pausanias, II, xxx, 3). The sanctuary was already established in late Mycenaean times and traces of walls, an early temple and an even earlier altar testify to successive improvements before it reached its final form

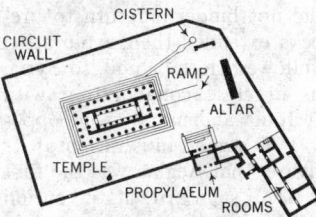

PLAN OF THE SANCTUARY OF APHAEA, 5TH CENTURY B.C., AEGINA

c. 490 B.C. (see plan). The temple, which is perhaps the finest example of late archaic architecture in European Greece, was a Doric peripteral structure of local limestone, coated with stucco and richly decorated. In the pediments were set two superb groups of marble sculpture, substantial fragments of which are now in Munich, Ger. The theme of each is similar, an Athena flanked by groups of combatants before Troy, but stylistically the eastern pediment is markedly more developed than the western, a discrepancy explained by the discovery near the east front of fragments of a third group on the same theme in the earlier style. This, the original east pediment, was probably damaged in the wars of 490–480 B.C. and then replaced by a more modern version (see GREEK ART).

The Munich sculptures were discovered by Charles Robert Cockerell (q.v.) and others in 1811 and sold to Louis of Bavaria who had them restored, disastrously, by Bertel Thorvaldsen (q.v.). Further fragments came to light and the whole plan of the sanctuary was established in the systematic excavations of Adolf Furtwängler (q.v.) in 1901. By 1960 the Greek Archaeological service had carried out extensive restoration.

The sanctuary was thought by early writers to belong to Zeus Hellanios; its real identity was proved by Furtwängler while substantial traces of the sanctuary of Zeus have now been discovered toward the summit of Mt. Oros.

History.—The dominating factor in Aegina's early history was trade. Commanding, as it does, the Saronic gulf, it was the natural clearinghouse in any dealings between central Greece and the east. The evidence of literature and archaeology bears witness to the devotion with which it exploited its natural advantages and to the profits which this devotion brought.

Already in the Early Bronze Age (2500–2000 B.C.) Aegina was importing from the Cyclades, Crete and Asia Minor while in the Middle Bronze Age (2000–1600) its own pottery was distributed throughout the neighbouring mainland states. To this period, perhaps, we should ascribe its membership in the shadowy association of Saronic states later remembered as the Calaurian league (Strabo, VIII, vi, 14). During the Mycenaean period (1600–1200) its individual style of pottery disappeared and this may be symptomatic of some more general decline; Homer makes it a dependency of Argos at the time of the Trojan War. As elsewhere the Dorian invasion (c. 1200; see DORIANS) brought an end to commerce, culture and history for several hundred years, although the island was not occupied by the invaders until 1000 B.C. or even later. They came in the end, traditionally, from Argos via Epidaurus (q.v.) on which Aegina long remained, in some sense,

EAST END OF THE TEMPLE OF APHAEA, AEGINA

dependent. But this dependence did not hinder a return to pre-Dorian habits of trade; as the Greeks extended their exploration of eastern waters, Aeginetan ships followed close behind, to Syria, Egypt and the Black sea; all this in close collaboration with Miletus and other friendly cities of Ionia and not without opposition from Miletus' enemy Samos. It is a good illustration of its interests and success, public and private, that Aegina was the first Greek state to introduce coinage (c. 620), soon after its invention by the Lydians, and that an Aeginetan citizen, Sostratus, was said by Herodotus (IV, 152) to have made more profit on a single voyage than any other merchant. Little is known of the nature of Aegina's commerce; but without many native resources it must have been chiefly as a carrier and distributor of corn (Herodotus VII, 147), oil, wine and slaves that it earned its profits. By 505 the aristocratic government was faced with a politically unsympathetic and economically formidable neighbour and rival, Athens (q.v.), whose new democracy had just survived a combined attack by Thebes, Chalcis and the Peloponnesian league (see SPARTA). Thebes appealed to Aegina, invoking a mythological connection, and Aegina replied, appropriately, with mythological aid. But the loan of statues of the Aeacidae did not help materially and a second appeal followed. This time the Aeginetans began a damaging series of raids on the Attic coast line, the resumption of an old quarrel, says Herodotus, referring to an early war, perhaps of the 7th century; but Aegina had more immediate reasons for wishing harm to Athens. Athens was diverted from prompt reprisals by other preoccupations which culminated, after 494, in the threat of an attack by Persia. Faced with the same threat Aegina decided to submit; with all its former partners and most of its markets in Persian hands, Aegina could hardly reconcile patriotism with profit. The crisis gave Athens a chance of revenge; an appeal to Cleomenes I (q.v.) brought the Spartan king to Aegina and, ultimately, ten Aeginetan hostages to Athens. This seems to imply that Aegina was at the time a member of Sparta's Peloponnesian league and we might, perhaps, suggest that Cleomenes' decisive defeat of Aegina's old friend Argos about 494, at a time when relations were strained between Sparta and Aegina's natural rival Corinth (q.v.), had brought it under Spartan influence. After Cleomenes' death the Aeginetans, through the Spartans, asked for the return of their hostages and, when Athens refused, reacted by seizing an Athenian ship. So war began—Herodotus implies in 490, the year of Marathon, but many modern scholars prefer a later date (c. 487) when, they argue, Athens would be free to think of revenge. Whatever the date, an Aeginetan nobleman, Nicodromus, was prepared to lead a democratic uprising against his fellow aristocrats and arranged for Athenian help. But by the time the fleet arrived Nicodromus had fled and, in spite of some initial successes, it was defeated and driven off. The war continued, for Nicodromus raided the Aeginetan coast from his base at Sunium, near Athens, and it was against Aegina that Themistocles (q.v.) persuaded the Athenians to build their new fleet in 483; but of the course of the war nothing is known. At least Aegina suffered no serious defeat for it was to the decade 490–480 that the ancient chronographers dated its thalassocracy, or rule of the sea.

By the time of the second Persian invasion (480 B.C.) Aegina had realized that collaboration with Persia was no longer practicable; in the crisis the quarrel with Athens was patched up and together they shared the responsibility for the naval defense of Greece. Eighteen Aeginetan ships served at Artemisium and perhaps 40 at Salamis—small numbers compared with the massive Athenian squadrons, but the skill and bravery of their crews earned the first prize for valour after Salamis. This was Aegina's finest period; the wealth of its ruling aristocracy bought luxury and culture (from abroad, for, apart from one or two sculptors in the late 6th and early 5th century, there were few native artists of distinction); their political security won the admiration of less happy aristocrats elsewhere. On both counts Pindar (q.v.) found Aeginetan society congenial and some of his finest odes were composed for the well-born athletes of the island. This same aristocratic sympathy brought 20 years of peace with Athens after Salamis. While Themistocles remained popular Athens had other

preoccupations; from about 474 until 462 the pro-Spartan Cimon (q.v.) could see no reason to resume the quarrel with his fellow aristocrats in Aegina, themselves Sparta's allies. The end came, however, in 457, three years after the outbreak of the first Peloponnesian War, when the city was besieged and captured by an Athenian fleet. By the terms of the peace treaty (446 B.C.) Aegina was abandoned by the Spartans to be "autonomous" but tributary to Athens. The former was an empty word, the latter meant the vast annual contribution of 30 talents (sufficient evidence of continued wealth). When war between Athens and Sparta was imminent again in 432 B.C., the Spartans chose to make much of Aeginetan complaints about this "autonomy"; the drastic Athenian reply was to expel the whole population and settle their own citizens in its place (winter 431). The exiles were given land by the Spartans in Thyreatis but even there the Athenians pursued them; most were killed in a naval raid in 424 and only a remnant could be restored to their home by the victorious Spartans in 404. Thereafter the impoverished island served only the strategic ends of others; it was used, for example, by the Spartans against Athens in 390 and 378, by Demetrius Poliorcetes against the Piraeus in 307 and by the kings of Pergamum as a base in European Greece from 210 until it passed into the hands of Rome in 133 B.C.

The *pax romana* brought no great benefits, the collapse of the Roman empire even greater trials. A renewed prosperity under Venetian control (from 1451) was broken by the terrible raid of the pirate Khair ed-Din, another Barbarossa, in 1537. From then, except for a brief Venetian interlude, it remained in Turkish hands until 1826, by which time it was again a modestly successful commercial centre and was chosen by Capodistria to be the temporary capital of independent Greece (1826–28). Since then the increasing concentration of business in Athens had led to a gradual decay until today it is little more than a holiday resort, an Athenian colony again.

See also Index references under "Aegina" in the Index volume.

BIBLIOGRAPHY.—*Authorities:* Pausanias, II, xxix, 2–xxx, 5; Herodotus, II, 178; III, 59, 131; V, 80–89; VI, 35, 49, 61, 64, 73, 85, 87–94; VII, 144–147, 203; VIII, *passim;* IX, 28, 31, 75, 76, 78–80, 85; Thucydides, I, cv, cviii; II, xxvii; IV, lvi–lvii. *See* also A. Furtwängler and others, *Aegina, Heiligtum der Aphaia* (1906); G. Welter, *Aigina,* with full bibliography (1938); A. Andrewes, *Annual of the British School at Athens,* xxxvii, pp. 1 ff.; T. J. Dunbabin, *Annual of the British School of Athens,* xxxvii, pp. 83 ff.   (W. G. F.)

AEGIRITE or ACMITE: *see* PYROXENE.

AEGIS (Gr. *aigis,* "goatskin"), a garment, obviously very ancient, worn especially by Zeus and therefore imbued with something of his supernatural power. On occasions he allows his favoured daughter Athena to have it, hence in time it becomes her ordinary dress, as in Aeschylus' *Eumenides,* where she uses it as a kind of sail. Less commonly, some other god has the use of it, as Apollo in *Iliad* xv, where he employs it to rouse panic in the Achaean host. This terror-producing property recurs in *Odyssey* xxii, when Athena shakes it against the suitors, and is part of the divine power resident in the garment. As early as Homer, it is something more than the ordinary goatskin cloak of a countryman in appearance, for it is decorated with golden tassels. A stout hide of this sort could turn a blow, like a buffcoat, and thus it often appears as a piece of armour. This no doubt is why Athena casts it about the unarmed Achilles' shoulders (*Iliad* xviii) and why it protects Hector's corpse (*Iliad* xxiv). Lastly, as improvised armour of this sort had long gone out of use and

ALINARI

DETAIL OF ATHENA PARTHENOS, 1ST CENTURY A.D., WEARING THE AEGIS

been forgotten, it is occasionally thought of as a metal corselet; so Horace (in the *Odes* iii, 4) describes it as "ringing" (*sonantem*) under the blows of the attacking giants. (H. J. R.)

AEGISTHUS, in Greek legend, the surviving son of Thyestes, who was driven out with his father after the Thyestean banquet (Aeschylus, *Agamemnon*). He plotted with Clytemnestra to kill Agamemnon. A story first alluded to by Plato (*Laws*), and told with fantastic details departing from all received versions of the legend by Apollodorus and Hyginus, makes him the son of Thyestes by his own daughter Pelopia, exposed in infancy and suckled by a goat (*aix*), hence his name, derived from *aigos*, its Greek genitive form.

See AGAMEMNON; ATREUS. (H. J. R.)

AEHRENTHAL, ALOYS, GRAF **LEXA** VON (1854–1912), Austro-Hungarian statesman who as foreign minister pursued a policy of short-term success that increased the international feeling of insecurity in the years preceding World War I. The son of an Hungarian landowner, he was born at Gross Skal in Bohemia, on Sept. 27, 1854. He began his career in 1877 as an attaché in Paris, but in 1878 was transferred to Russia, where he was attaché at St. Petersburg until 1883. Sent back to Russia in 1888, he remained there till he was appointed ambassador to Rumania in 1895. In 1899, however, he became ambassador at St. Petersburg.

Aehrenthal's experience of Russian affairs was expected to be of great value when he was appointed foreign minister of Austria-Hungary on Oct. 22, 1906. From the first his policy was more active than his predecessor, Agenor Goluchowski's. His first attempt to extend Austrian influence in the Balkans, by linking the Bosnian railway system with Salonika, miscarried. Then, in Oct. 1908, his diplomatically ill-prepared annexation of Bosnia-Hercegovina (*q.v.*), which had been under Austrian occupation since 1878, provoked an international crisis. Complete understanding had not been reached between Austria and Turkey, and Russia's consent, supposedly obtained in September at a meeting between Aehrenthal and the Russian foreign minister, Count A. P. Izvolski (*q.v.*), at Graf L. Berchtold's house at Buchlau (Buchlovice) in Moravia, was denied by Izvolski when the annexation had been announced. Izvolski's statement contributed greatly to European feeling against Austria. Turkey's consent was withheld until Feb. 1909, Russia's till March (when it was obtained through German mediation). Aehrenthal's policies also damaged the Austrian government's relations with its allies. Italy cooled noticeably toward Austria after the Bosnian crisis and was further alienated by Aehrenthal's conduct on the outbreak of the Italo-Turkish War in 1911, when Austria, despite German advice, maintained a reserved attitude toward Italian claims. The archduke Francis Ferdinand's circle, in particular the chief of staff F. Conrad von Hötzendorf, heightened the tension by demanding a preventive war against Italy, but Aehrenthal then had enough sense of responsibility to secure Conrad's dismissal. Finally, Aehrenthal's critical attitude toward Germany during the Moroccan crisis of 1911 impaired Austro-German relations without achieving any real *rapprochement* between Austria and France.

Recognizing the mistakes of German foreign policy, Aehrenthal tried to dissociate himself from them but could never in fact do so because his own policies depended on German support. He weakened the German and Austro-Hungarian position in Europe, as his rebuffs to Italy prepared the dissolution of the Triple alliance. His apparent foreign successes, however, set the Austro-Hungarian monarchy on a dangerous road. Aehrenthal died in Vienna on Feb. 17, 1912.

BIBLIOGRAPHY.—B. Molden, *Aloys Graf Aehrenthal* (1917); O. Hoijer, *Vers la grande guerre: le comte d'Aehrenthal et la politique de la violence,* 2nd ed. (1922); W. M. Carlgren, *Iswolsky und Aehrenthal vor der bosnischen Annexionskrise* (1955); and general histories of Austro-Hungarian foreign policy from 1908. (K. O. v. A.)

AELFRIC, called GRAMMATICUS, "the Grammarian" (fl. *c.* 955–*c.* 1010), English abbot and author, the greatest prose-writer of Anglo-Saxon times, was educated in the Benedictine monastery, the Old Minster at Winchester, under Aethelwold, one of the chief leaders of the 10th-century monastic reform, who was bishop of Winchester from 963 to 984. When the abbey of Cernel (Cerne Abbas, Dorset) was founded about 987, Aelfric was sent there by Aethelwold's successor, Bishop Aelfheah, at the request of the founder, Aethelmaer, to teach the monks. He was by that time in priest's orders. Aethelmaer and his father, the ealdorman Aethelweard, were enlightened patrons of learning and Aelfric's work owed much to their encouragement. Aethelmaer founded the abbey of Eynsham in 1005, and placed Aelfric as abbot over it. There he remained until his death. The date of this is uncertain, and the assertion sometimes made that he witnessed a document of 1020 rests on shaky evidence. His last datable work is the homily *In natale unius confessoris,* 1006–12.

His major works belong to his Cerne period. In 990–991 he issued the first volume of his *Catholic Homilies,* and the second volume followed a year later. Each volume contained 40 homilies for the chief festivals and saints' days celebrated by the English people, except that the copy of volume one for the ealdorman Aethelweard was to contain an extra four homilies. Only one manuscript contains the prefaces and has the two series arranged in the way Aelfric issued them, for the work proved popular, and the homilies were copied in many different arrangements. Aelfric's aims, to provide the clergy with orthodox sermons, is set out in his English preface to volume one, where he regrets that, except for Alfred's translations, Englishmen had no access to sound doctrine in their own language. His homilies are largely based on Latin writers, especially St. Augustine, St. Jerome, St. Gregory and Bede.

A translation of Bede's *De temporibus* was probably his next work, to be followed by his Latin *Grammar, Glossary* and *Colloquy* and then by the *Saints' Lives,* planned to include lives of the saints honoured by the monks, rather than by the people in general. He had doubts, however, regarding the wisdom of placing such translations in the hands of the unlearned, and resolved to translate no more, but pressure from others, especially from Aethelweard and Aethelmaer, caused him to continue. Thus, under protest, he translated at Aethelweard's wish parts of the Old Testament. His chief works written at Eynsham are a Latin *Life of St. Aethelwold,* an abridgement of the *Regularis Concordia* (the general rule of monastic observance in England, drawn up by the synod of Winchester) for the use of his monks, a *Treatise on the Old and New Testament* addressed to an Oxfordshire thegn, Siweard of Asthall, a treatise on chastity and one on the Trinity and the Atonement for a Warwickshire thegn, Wulfgeat of Ilmington. Some minor works survive from both the Cerne and the Eynsham periods, as well as some of uncertain date, including a translation of the *Hexameron* of St. Basil.

Aelfric's works reveal great learning in both the Fathers and later theological and canonical writings, and he was largely instrumental in spreading the teaching of the monastic revival of the 10th century. He was recognized as an authority in his own day, and was commissioned to write pastoral letters for Wulfsige, bishop of Sherborne (992–1001), and Wulfstan, archbishop of York (1002–23). Most of his works continued to be copied and studied throughout the middle ages, and he was the first Anglo-Saxon writer whose work was printed. Reformation ecclesiastics interpreted his teaching on the Eucharist as proof that the Anglo-Saxon church did not believe in transubstantiation, and so *A Testimonie of Antiquitie,* a work of religious polemic issued in 1567 under the auspices of Archbishop Matthew Parker, includes Aelfric's Easter homily from the second series of *Catholic Homilies.*

Though much of Aelfric's work is translated and compiled from Latin sources, it includes additions of his own which shed light on contemporary conditions and ways of thought. It is written in a style of singular clarity, variety and grace.

Current editions of his major works are: *Homilies of the Anglo-Saxon Church,* part i, *The Sermones Catholici,* ed. by B. Thorpe (1844–46); *Aelfric's Metrical Lives of Saints,* ed. by W. W. Skeat for the Early English Text Society (1881–1900) with a good study of the author; *The Old English Heptateuch, Aelfric's Treatise on the Old and New Testament and his Preface to Genesis,* ed. by S. J. Crawford for the Early English Text Society (1921); *Aelfric's Grammatik und Glossar,* ed. by J. Zupitza (1880); *Aelfric's Colloquy,* rev. ed. by G. N. Garmonsway (1947) and Eng. trans. by

A. S. Cook and C. B. Tinker, *Select Translations from Old English Prose* (1908) and by S. H. Gem, *An Anglo-Saxon Abbot* (1912); *De temporibus anni,* ed. by H. Henel for the Early English Text Society (1942); *Vita S. Aethelwoldi,* ed. by J. Stevenson, *Chronicon Monasterii de Abingdon,* "Rolls Series," ii, 253–266 (1858), Eng. trans. by D. Whitelock, *English Historical Documents c. 500–1042,* pp. 831–839 (1955); *Aelfric's Hirtenbriefe in altenglischer und lateinischer Fassung,* ed. by B. Fehr, Bibliothek der angelsachsischen Prosa, ix (1914).

BIBLIOGRAPHY.—Older incorrect identifications of the author with prelates of the same name were disproved by E. Dietrich, "Abt Aelfrik," *Zeitschrift für historische Theologie,* xxv, xxvi (1855–56). For general accounts *see* C. L. White, *Aelfric: A New Study of His Life and Writings* (1898); M.-M. Dubois, *Aelfric, sermonnaire, docteur et grammairien* (1943); K. Sisam, *Studies in the History of Old English Literature* (1953). For work on sources, and other detailed study, *see The Cambridge Bibliography of English Literature,* vol. i, pp. 89–92 (1940).
(D. Wk.)

AELIAN (AELIANUS TACTICUS), Greek military writer of the 2nd century A.D., resident at Rome. He is sometimes confused with his namesake Claudius Aelianus. Aelian's military treatise, *Taktike Theoria,* is dedicated to Hadrian, though this is probably a mistake for Trajan, and the date A.D. 106 has been assigned to it. It is a handbook of Greek (*i.e.,* Macedonian) drill and tactics as practised by the Hellenistic successors of Alexander the Great. The author claims to have consulted all the best authorities, the chief of which was a lost treatise on the subject of Polybius. Perhaps the chief value of Aelian's work lies in his critical account of preceding works on the art of war and in the fullness of his technical details in matters of drill. Critics of the 18th century thought Aelian greatly inferior to Arrian, but on the Byzantines and on the Arabs, who translated the text for their own use, Aelian exercised a great influence. The emperor Leo VI incorporated much of Aelian's text in his own work on the military art. The Arabic version of Aelian was made about 1350. The copious details in the treatise made it valuable to the army organizers of the 16th century, when translations of it formed the groundwork of many books on drill and tactics. The theory that Aelian wrote most of Arrian's *Tactica* and that the *Taktike Theoria* is a later revision of this original is not generally accepted. The *Poliorcetica* of Aeneas Tacticus is wrongly ascribed to Aelian in its manuscript suprascription.

A few editions by German editors were published after the *editio princeps* (Italian) in 1552, and an English translation was printed by Viscount Dillon in London in 1814. For a scholarly account with a bibliography *see* K. K. Müller, "Aelianus," in A. von Pauly and G. Wissowa, *Real-Encyclopädie der classischen Altertumswissenschaft.*

AELIAN (CLAUDIUS AELIANUS) (*c.* 170–235), Roman author and teacher of rhetoric, is best known for his stories in *De natura animalium* and *Varia historia.* He was born at Praeneste and flourished under Septimius Severus. His extant writings are in Greek, which he spoke so well that he was called "honey-tongued" (*meli-glossos*) and "honey-voiced" (*meli-phthongos*). The chief of them, both valuable for their many excerpts from earlier writers, are the *De natura animalium,* curious stories of animal life, frequently with moral lessons; and *Varia historia,* mainly anecdotes of men and customs.

His style is simple, and he was, like Lucian, an Atticist; in his views he was a Stoic. Twenty *Farmers' Letters,* after the manner of Alciphron but inferior, are attributed to Aelian; if this attribution is correct, they were probably composed in his youth.

BIBLIOGRAPHY.—Complete works ed. by R. Hercher (1864–66); for the *Farmers' Letters* with Eng. trans., *see* A. R. Benner and F. H. Fobes (eds.), *Letters of Alciphron, Aelian and Philostratus,* in the "Loeb Series" (1950).

AELLA (d. 867), king of Northumbria (*q.v.*), succeeded to the throne in 862 or 863 on the deposition of Osbert, although he was not of royal birth. In 867 he and the deposed Osbert joined forces against the invading Danes, whom they attacked in York on March 21 or 23. They were both killed in this attack. Later Scandinavian legend regarded Aella as the king responsible for the death of Ragnar Lodbrok by having him thrown into a snake-infested pit.

BIBLIOGRAPHY.—*Anglo-Saxon Chronicle; Symeonis Monachi Opera* *omnia,* ed. by T. Arnold, vol. i and ii (1882–85); *Rogeri de Wendover Chronica,* ed. by H. O. Coxe, vol. i (1841). (D. Wk.)

AELLI (d. 588 or 590), first king of Deira (*q.v.*), succeeded in 560. Tradition says that on his death, Aethelric of Bernicia seized his kingdom. Deira was certainly ruled by Aethelric's son Aethelfrith, king of Bernicia from 593 to 616, in the latter part of this period. Aelli was the father of Edwin, later king of the Northumbrians, and of Acha, wife of Aethelfrith. His name gave rise to Pope Gregory the Great's pun on the word "Alleluia," when he saw youths from Deira in Rome.

BIBLIOGRAPHY.—Bede, *Historia Ecclesiastica,* bk. ii; *Anglo-Saxon Chronicle; Life of Pope Gregory the Great,* ed. by F. A. Gasquet (1904); F. M. Stenton, *Anglo-Saxon England,* 2nd ed. (1947).
(D. Wk.)

AELLI (late 5th century A.D.), king of the South Saxons, founder of the kingdom of West Sussex, is said to have landed near Selsey Bill in 477, with his three sons. In 491 he and his son Cissa captured the Roman city of Anderida (Pevensey). His subsequent history is unknown, but Bede reckons him as the first king to be recognized as overlord of all the English peoples south of the Humber, which shows that he must have led the invaders against the Britons in the south. The *Anglo-Saxon Chronicle,* using Bede, puts him as the first *bretwalda* (ruler of Britain).

BIBLIOGRAPHY.—*Anglo-Saxon Chronicle;* Bede, *Historia Ecclesiastica,* bk. ii, ch. 5; F. M. Stenton, *Anglo-Saxon England,* 2nd ed. (1947).
(D. Wk.)

AELRED (AILRED, ETHELRED), **SAINT,** OF RIEVAULX (*c.* 1110–1167), Cistercian abbot, spiritual writer and historian, who exerted a powerful influence on the ecclesiastical affairs of northern England, was born at Hexham. Brought up at the Scottish court with the sons of King David I, he was the royal steward when he entered the monastery of Rievaulx in Yorkshire, probably in 1134. He was abbot of Revesby in Lincolnshire from 1143 to 1147 and then abbot of Rievaulx until his death there on Jan. 12, 1167.

Aelred's works include: *Speculum caritatis,* on the monastic life, written when he was novice master at Rievaulx; *Relatio de standardo,* an account of the battle of the Standard against David I in 1138; *De spirituali amicitia,* a Christian counterpart of Cicero's *De amicitia;* a treatise on the questioning of the 12-year old Jesus in the Temple; *Vita S. Edwardi,* written in honour of the translation of Edward the Confessor's body in 1163; *De anima,* Aelred's last work, on the nature of the soul; and various sermons.

BIBLIOGRAPHY.—Most works in J. P. Migne, *Patrologia Latina,* vol. 195, col. 197–796 (1855). Critical editions: *Relatio de standardo* by R. Howlett in the "Rolls Series" (*Chronicles of the Reigns of Stephen,* etc., 3: 181–199; 1886); *Sermones inediti* and *De anima* by C. H. Talbot (1952); *De spirituali amicitia* with French trans. by J. Dubois (1948), Eng. trans. by C. H. Talbot (1942); *De Jesu puero duodenni,* by A. Hoste, with French trans. by J. Dubois (1958).
See F. M. Powicke, *The Life of Ailred of Rievaulx by Walter Daniel,* with full introduction and Eng. trans. (1950); D. Knowles, *The Monastic Order in England* (1940); P. Grosjean, "La prétendue canonisation d'Aelred de Rievaux par Célestin III," in *Analecta Bollandiana,* vol. 78 (1960). (Pl. Gn.)

AEMILIAN (MARCUS AEMILIUS AEMILIANUS) (d. A.D. 253), Roman emperor in 253. A native of Mauretania, a senator and consul, he commanded the army of Moesia under the emperor Gallus (251–253). In the late summer of 253 he rebelled, invaded Italy, killed Gallus near Interamna (Narni) and was recognized by the senate and both armies. About 12 weeks later he was attacked by Valerian and killed by his own troops, near Spoleto. His wife was named Cornelia Supera. (Jn. R. M.)

AENEAS, mythical hero of Troy and Rome, son of the goddess Aphrodite and Anchises. Aeneas was a member of the royal line at Troy and cousin of Hector. He played a prominent part in the war to defend his city against the Greeks, being second only to Hector in ability. Homer implies that Aeneas did not like his subordinate position, and from that suggestion arose a later tradition that Aeneas helped to betray Troy to the Greeks. However, the commoner version made Aeneas the leader of the Trojan survivors. In any case, he came through the war, available to compilers of Roman myth.

The association of Homeric heroes with Italy and Sicily goes back to the 8th century B.C., and the Greek colonies founded there in that and the next century frequently claimed descent from leaders in the Trojan War. Legend connected Aeneas, too, with certain places and families, especially in Latium. As Rome expanded over Italy and the Mediterranean, its patriotic writers began to construct a mythical tradition that would at once dignify their land with antiquity and satisfy a latent dislike of Greek superiority. The fact that Aeneas, as a Trojan, represented an enemy of the Greeks and that tradition left him free after the war made him peculiarly fit for the part assigned him; that is, founding Roman greatness.

It was Virgil (q.v.) who gave the various strands of legend related to Aeneas the form they have possessed ever since. The family of Julius Caesar, and consequently of Virgil's patron Augustus, claimed descent from Aeneas, whose son Ascanius was also called Iulus. Incorporating these different traditions, Virgil created his masterpiece, the *Aeneid,* the Latin epic whose hero symbolized not only the course and aim of Roman history but also the career and policy of Augustus himself. In the journeying of Aeneas from Troy westward to Sicily, Carthage and finally to the mouth of the Tiber in Italy, Virgil portrayed the qualities of persistence, self-denial and obedience to the gods that, to the poet, built Rome.

When Troy fell to the Greeks, Virgil recounts, Aeneas, who had fought bravely to the last, was commanded by Hector in a vision to flee and found a great city overseas. He gathered his family and followers and took the household gods (small images) of Troy, but in the confusion of leaving the burning city his wife disappeared. Her ghost informed him that he was to go to a western land where the Tiber river flowed. He then started on his long voyage, touching at Thrace, Crete and Sicily and meeting with many adventures which culminated in shipwreck on the coast of Africa near Carthage. There he was received by Dido, the widowed queen, to whom he told his story. They fell in love and he lingered there, forgetful of his destiny, until sharply reminded by Mercury, at Jupiter's command, that Rome, not Carthage, was his goal. Guilty and wretched, he immediately abandoned Dido, who committed suicide, and sailed on in obedience to his fate.

When, after being shown the future greatness of Rome by the Cumean sybil, he finally arrived at the mouth of the Tiber, he was well received by Latinus, the king of the region, but other Italians, notably Latinus' wife and Turnus, leader of the Rutuli, resented the Trojan arrival and especially the plan for a marriage alliance between Aeneas and Lavinia, Latinus' daughter. When war broke out Aeneas found some support from Evander (significantly ruler on the site of later Rome), and succeeded in checking Turnus' attacks on the Trojan camp. After Turnus had broken truce negotiations, Aeneas engaged him in combat and killed him, thus ending the war. Aeneas then married Lavinia and founded Lavinium, the parent city of Rome.

Aeneas' character as portrayed by Virgil is not only that of a heroic warrior. In addition he guides his life by obedience to divine command, to which he sacrifices his own natural inclinations. It is in this sense that the epithet *pius,* so frequently applied to him in the *Aeneid,* is to be understood.

Aeneas' death is described by Dionysius of Halicarnassus. After he had fallen in battle against the Rutuli his body could not be found, and he was thereafter worshiped as a local god, *Juppiter indiges* as Livy reports.

See L. Matten, "Aineas," *Archiv für Religionswissenschaft,* 29: 33–59 (1931); J. Perret, *Les Origines de la légend troyenne de Rome (281–31)* (1942). (WM. S. A.)

AENEAS SILVIUS, the popular name of the voluminous author Enea Silvio de' Piccolomini (1405–64), who became pope as Pius II in 1458. *See* PIUS.

AENEAS TACTICUS (4th century B.C.), Greek writer. According to Aelian (Aelianus Tacticus) and Polybius, he wrote a number of treatises on the art of war; the only one extant deals with the defense of fortified cities and is chiefly valuable as containing a large number of historical illustrations.

Aeneas was considered by Casaubon to have been a contemporary of Xenophon and identical with the Arcadian general, Aeneas of Stymphalus, whom Xenophon mentions as fighting at the battle of Mantinea (362 B.C.).

Two English translations exist, accompanied by introductory and bibliographical material. They are *Aeneas Tacticus,* by the Illinois Greek Club, in the "Loeb Classical Library" (1923), and L. W. Hunter, *Aeneas on Siegecraft,* rev. by S. A. Handford (1927).

AENEID, THE, Latin epic poem by Virgil (q.v.), relating the adventures of the Trojan hero Aeneas (q.v.) who after the fall of Troy voyaged to Latium in Italy as the destined founder of Lavinium, the parent city of Rome.

The *Aeneid* was the model for the *Roman d'Énéas* (c. 1160), a French poem of uncertain Norman authorship, which in its turn provided the basis for the Flemish *Eneide* by Heinrich von Veldeke (c. 1190), now extant only in a Thuringian version. Another medieval French version was translated into English by Caxton (1490).

See also Index references under "Aeneid, The" in the Index volume.

BIBLIOGRAPHY.—For the Latin poem, *see* bibliography to VIRGIL. Critical edition of the French romance by J. S. de Grave (1891), of Veldeke's version by O. Behagel (1882) and of Caxton's by W. T. Culley and F. J. Furnival (1890).

AENESIDEMUS (fl. *c.* 80–60 B.C.), Greek philosopher and leader of what is sometimes known as the Third Skeptical school, was born at Cnossus in Crete and taught at Alexandria. He revived to a great extent the doctrine of Pyrrho and Timon. His chief work was the *Pyrrhonian Discourses,* addressed to Lucius Tubero. Although his work has been lost, its argument can be reconstructed from an analysis by Photius (9th century) and evidence furnished by Diogenes Laërtius and Sextus Empiricus.

First, as regards the meaning and criterion of truth, Aenesidemus distinguished himself from other *soi-disant* skeptics of his day, regarding them as tainted with dogmatism. A skeptic is inconsistent if he affirms that he knows that there is no criterion of truth—he believes this, indeed, but his skepticism is a manner of behaviour rather than a sect existing in rivalry to others. The dogmatic philosophers (*i.e.,* principally Epicurus and the Stoics) had found the criterion either in sense perception or in intellectual judgment or in some alliance between these. Aenesidemus showed that no variety of these views is tenable and further drew up the famous "ten tropes," a general statement of reasons why perception must not be trusted, as follows.

Things present a diverse appearance (1) to different species of animals, (2) to different men, (3) to the different senses of one and the same man, (4) to the same sense according to the man's circumstances and physical condition and (5) to the same sense according to distance and perspective. Moreover, perceptions vary (6) on account of mixture with one another in various degrees and (7) on account of their extent. In general, (8) perceptions depend upon the relation of the perceiver to his object, or of things or notions to one another, (9) their strength varies with habituation and (10) the beliefs, laws and customs of men are indefinitely variable.

Next, Aenesidemus proceeded to the criticism of signs and causality. Under the heading "signs" it was not the causal relation itself that was criticized, but the rules laid down by some philosophers for an inference from an observed fact to its concealed cause. But by a parallel line of reasoning he rejected as unintelligible the cause-effect relationship. To name a thing a cause implies that it has some intrinsic productive power, but of this power no intelligible account has been or can be given. In the last part of his *Discourses* he carried his criticism into the region of moral ideas and argued that neither pleasure nor happiness nor knowledge is the *summum bonum;* there is no such highest good. *See* also SKEPTICISM.

BIBLIOGRAPHY.—V. Brochard, *Les Sceptiques grecs* (1887; reprinted 1923); E. Bréhier, "Les Tropes d'Enésidème contre la logique inductive," *Revue des études anciennes,* vol. xx (1918); L. Robin, *Pyrrhon et le scepticisme grec* (1944). (D. J. A.)

AEOLIAN HARP, a stringed musical instrument, played by

the wind, and so-called from Aeolus, god of the winds. It consists of a wooden sound box, usually about three feet long, five inches broad and three inches deep, with raised ends into which are fixed tuning- and hitch-pins, and between which are loosely stretched 10 or 12 catgut strings, usually tuned in unison; these vary in thickness and therefore in elasticity and the play of the wind causes them to vibrate in aliquot parts; *i.e.* (the fundamental note not being heard), the half or octave, the third or interval of the 12th, the second octave and the third above it: in fact, the upper partials of the strings in regular succession. The Aeolian harp is generally placed by an open window or hung out of doors to catch the wind.

The principle of the natural vibration of strings by the pressure of the wind has long been recognized. According to legend King David used to hang his *kinnor* (a kind of lyre) above his bed at night to catch the wind, and Dunstan of Canterbury was charged with sorcery for producing sounds from a harp by allowing the wind to blow through its strings. Athanasius Kircher constructed such an instrument and described it in his *Musurgia universalis* (1650). It became popular in Germany and England during the Romantic movement; and models were made by the poet Robert Blomfield, author of a pamphlet about them (*Nature's Music*, 1808). There have been two attempts to construct keyboard instruments on this principle, using bellows-fed wind: J. J. Schnell's Anémocorde (Paris, 1789) and Isouard's Piano éolien (Paris, 1837).   (E. HA.)

BY COURTESY OF THE MANSELL COLLECTION, LONDON

AEOLIAN HARP

AEOLIAN ISLANDS, known in ancient times as the Aeoliae Insulae, a group of volcanic islands north of eastern Sicily; also called the Lipari Islands (*q.v.*).

AEOLIS (AEOLIA), the name applied collectively to a group of ancient cities on the west coast of Asia Minor founded toward the end of the 2nd millennium B.C. by Greeks from Thessaly, Phocis, Locris and Boeotia, speaking a dialect known as Aeolic. The earliest settlements on the islands of Lesbos and Tenedos and on the mainland opposite, between the Troad and Ionia, including Pitane, Gryneum, Myrina, Cyme, Temnos, Notium and Smyrna (which in the 7th century was taken by the Ionians), were the result of a wave of migration *c.* 1130–*c.* 1000 B.C. A wave of secondary colonization, perhaps in the 7th century B.C., gave rise to further Aeolian settlements in the Troad and in the region of the Hellespont. At the end of the 6th century Aeolis was merged in one of the 20 satrapies organized by Darius I. Aeolic was the dialect of the poets Alcaeus and Sappho.

AEOLUS, the name of two figures in Greek mythology.

1. AEOLUS, a mythical king of Magnesia in Thessaly, was the son of Hellen and father of Sisyphus. His daughter Canace and son Macareus committed incest and suicide, providing the subject of Euripides' lost *Aeolus*. Aeolus gave his name to Aeolis, a territory on the western coast of Asia Minor.

2. In Homer, AEOLUS was the son of Hippotes. He was controller of the winds and ruler of the floating island of Aeolia. In the *Odyssey* he entertained Odysseus, gave him a favourable wind and a bag in which the unfavourable winds were confined. Odysseus' companions opened the bag; the winds escaped and drove them back to the island, whence Aeolus dismissed them with bitter reproaches. Human in Homer, he later became a minor god. This was his status in Latin poetry especially. According to Virgil, in the *Aeneid,* Aeolus dwelt on one of the Aeolian islands to the north of Sicily, Lipara or Strongyle (Stromboli), where he kept the winds imprisoned in a vast cavern.   (T. V. B.)

AEPINUS (originally HOCH), **FRANZ (MARIA) ULRICH THEODOR** (1724–1802), German physicist, best known for his researches, theoretical and experimental, in electricity and magnetism, was born in Rostock, on Dec. 13, 1724, and died in Tartu (Dorpat), Estonia, on Aug. 10, 1802. He first studied medicine and then physics and mathematics, his original work in these new fields leading to his election to the Berlin Academy of Sciences and, in 1757 to professor of physics in St. Petersburg, where he remained until he retired in 1798. His principal work, *Tentamen theoriae electricitatis et magnetismi* (1759), was the first systematic attempt to apply mathematical reasoning to these subjects. He designed a type of parallel-plate electrical condenser. He improved the microscope and extended Franklin's one-fluid theory of electricity, which postulated an all-pervading electric fluid of particles which were mutually repellent but which attracted particles of ordinary matter. He studied the relation between electrical conductors and nonconductors and carefully investigated the phenomena of pyroelectricity. His discussion of the effects of parallax in the transit of a planet over the sun's disk excited great interest, having appeared in 1764 between the dates of the two 18th-century transits of Venus.

(D. McK.)

AEPYORNIS, the genus name for "elephant birds," large flightless forms extinct for several centuries. They comprised the family Aepyornithidae and the order Aepyornithiformes. *Aepyornis* species resembled the moas (*q.v.*) in many particulars, and inhabited the southern half of Madagascar. They are said to have been the origin of the legend of the roc (*q.v.*). Many species were the size of ostriches, but one, *A. titan,* apparently reached a height of 12 ft. Its egg was larger than that of any other bird, measuring more than 13 by 9½ in. and having a capacity of more than two gallons.

AEQUI, an ancient people of Italy originally inhabiting the region watered by the tributaries of the Avens (the modern Velino river in the province of Rieti). Hostile to Rome for centuries (according to Livy), they became a menace in the 5th century B.C., advancing to the Alban hills. The Romans attacked and ejected them from Tusculum *c.* 484 B.C. and drove them from the Alban hills and the Algidus gap in 431. The Aequi were not finally subdued, however, until the end of the second Samnite War (304 B.C.), when they received *civitas sine suffragio* (a limited form of Roman franchise). Rome established the Latin colony of Carsioli (302 B.C.) in the territory of the Aequi, through which, at about the same date, the Via Valeria was extended. Thenceforward the Aequi rapidly became romanized; before Latin, they had probably spoken Oscan, one of the chief non-Latin Italic dialects.

All that is known of their subsequent political condition is that after the Social War (90–89 B.C.) the people of Cliternia and Nersae appear united in a *municipium Aequiculorum* or *Aequiculanorum.* This name, which appears as Cicoli and Ecuiuli in medieval documents, survives in modern times as Cicolano, denoting the district north of the Lago Fucino.

See R. S. Conway, *Italic Dialects,* vol. i (1897); J. Whatmough, *The Foundations of Roman Italy* (1937).

AERARII, in ancient Rome, were citizens subjected to special tax by the censors as a mark of disgrace (from Latin *aes,* money). Theodor Mommsen (*Römisches Staatsrecht,* vol. ii, 3rd ed., pp. 399 ff., [1887]) thought (1) that they were the citizens without the vote and citizens subjected to civil degradation for following professions such as acting, for dishonourable acts or for certain crimes and excluded from the tribes and the centuries, from voting, from holding magistracies and from serving in the army; (2) that the original *aerarii* had been landless citizens excluded from registration in the tribes who were distributed among the tribes by the censor Appius Claudius in 312 B.C. but limited to the four city tribes by the censors of 304; and (3) that the term was later also applied to citizens demoted from a higher (rustic) to a lower (urban) tribe though not deprived of the right to vote or to serve in the army. It has been shown, however, (1) that *aerarii* did hold magistracies and serve in the army; (2) that landless citizens must have been registered in the tribes from the beginning of the Servian constitution, traditionally in the 6th century B.C.; (3) that the term *aerarii* is not used in connection with landholding, on which the evidence for the censorship of 312 has nothing to say; and (4) that to be moved to a lower tribe and to be made an *aerarius* were distinct penalties, though often imposed together. The term therefore must refer solely to payment of *aes,* and the penalty involved may have been payment of tax at a higher rate.

BIBLIOGRAPHY.—G. W. Botsford, *Roman Assemblies* (1909); H. M. Last, in *Journal of Roman Studies,* 35:30–48 (1945); P. Fraccaro, *Opuscula,* vol. ii, pp. 149–170 (1957). (T. R. S. B.)

AERARIUM, the treasury of the Roman people, was housed in the temple of Saturn at the west end of the Forum and in the adjacent *tabularium* (record office), built in 78 B.C. In it were stored coin and bullion, certain public records (including laws) and the public accounts. Under the republic it was managed by the two urban quaestors with a staff of permanent salaried clerks and controlled by the senate, without whose authorization no payment could be made except to the consuls. In theory all revenues were paid into the *aerarium* by the *publicani* who farmed the taxes or by the magistrates who collected them, and all public payments were made from it. In practice provincial governors were normally authorized to draw their allowances from the local offices of the *publicani* or from the provincial depots (*fisci*) into which local revenues were paid, and money was moved from the provinces to the *aerarium* only if a province produced a surplus, while conversely money was paid out of the *aerarium* only if the provincial revenue did not cover expenses. All magistrates and *publicani* had, however, to balance their accounts with the *aerarium,* which was thus a central clearinghouse.

Augustus in 27 B.C. transferred the control of the *aerarium* to two prefects of praetorian rank, elected by the senate, and in 23 B.C. to two of the praetors. Claudius restored the *aerarium* to the quaestors, who were nominated by himself and served three years. Nero went back to praetorian prefects, who were henceforth nominated by the emperor. Under the principate the *aerarium* gradually waned in importance as the emperors, who were responsible for the bulk of the public expenditure, drew the money from provincial *fisci* and, as they never laid down their office, did not account to the *aerarium.* They built up their own treasury and audit, the *fiscus.*

In A.D. 6 Augustus founded a second treasury, the *aerarium militare* (the old treasury was henceforth distinguished as *aerarium Saturni*). Its function was to pay bounties to discharged veterans or purchase land for them, and it was managed by prefects of praetorian rank, at first chosen by lot, later nominated by the emperor. The *aerarium militare* was initially endowed by Augustus out of his own pocket and fed by two new taxes payable by all Roman citizens, the 5% tax on inheritance and the 1% tax on sales.

See A. H. M. Jones, *Studies in Roman Government and Law* (1960). (A. H. M. J.)

AERIAL, an elevated wire or group of wires or rods forming the principal part of a radio antenna of the open or "condenser" type. *See* ANTENNA (AERIAL).

AERIAL MAPPING: *see* PHOTOGRAMMETRY.

AERODROME: *see* AIRPORT.

AERODYNAMICS, a branch of physics concerned with the study of the motion of air or other gases, and of the forces acting upon bodies passing through the air. In particular, it seeks to understand the principles governing the flight of aircraft through the earth's atmosphere and the flight of rockets and missiles. Aerodynamics has made important contributions to the design and development of modern aircraft and has promoted understanding of the special problems of supersonic flight. Aerodynamics has also been concerned in the design of ships, land vehicles such as streamlined trains and automobiles, and in the construction of tall buildings, towers and bridges to determine their resistance to high winds.

HISTORICAL DEVELOPMENT

Observation of the flight of birds and of projectiles stirred speculation among the ancients as to the forces involved and the manner of their interaction. These speculations were in general carried on without benefit of what has become known as the "experimental method." The ancients had no real knowledge of the physical properties of air nor did they attempt to study these properties, in the modern sense.

The ideas of the ancients usually involved the concept that the air provided a sustaining or impelling force. These ideas were based to a considerable degree on the principles of hydrostatics (the study of the pressures of liquids) as they were then known or understood. Thus, in ancient times, the view was held that the impelling force of a projectile was associated with forces exerted on the base by the closure of the flow of air around the body. This view of air as an assisting rather than a resisting medium persisted for centuries, even though in the 6th century men recognized that the energy of motion of a projectile was imparted to it by the catapulting device.

Near the end of the 15th century Leonardo da Vinci recognized that air offered resistance to the movement of a solid object and he attributed this resistance to compressibility effects. His theories of bird flight were also related to the compressibility properties of air. In his view, the rapid flapping of a bird's wings created a region of compressed air beneath the wings and thus provided the desired lift.

Using an experimental approach, Galileo later established the fact of air resistance and arrived at the conclusion that the resistance was proportional to the velocity of the object passing through it. The Dutch physicist Christiaan Huygens (*q.v.*), near the end of the 17th century, may have been the first to appreciate that the resistance of air to the motion of a body was proportional to the square of the velocity. Huygens used an experimental approach; at about the same time, Newton reached the same conclusion by deduction.

The work of Newton in setting forth the laws of mechanics marked the beginning of the classical theories of aerodynamics. Newton considered the pressure acting on an inclined plate as arising from the impingement of particles on the side of the plate facing the air stream. His formulation produced the result that the pressure acting on the plates was proportional to the product of the density of the air, the area of the plate, the square of the velocity and the square of the sine of the angle of inclination. Later, by a somewhat different argument, Leonhard Euler produced the same result with the exception that the effect of inclination was proportional to the sine rather than to the square of the sine, a result more in accord with experimental evidence. The arguments, of course, failed to show the important result, to come much later, of the effects of the flow on the upper surface of the plate where low pressures exist and from which a major portion of the lift of a wing is produced. The concept of air as a continuum with a pressure field extending over great distances from the plate was to come much later.

Daniel Bernoulli, a Swiss physicist, made a most important discovery in the middle of the 18th century. Proceeding, perhaps, from the then well-known principle of hydrostatics that the level of a liquid flowing from one tank to another would in the end achieve the same height in both tanks, Bernoulli arrived at the formulation of his well-known theorem

$$p + \tfrac{1}{2}\rho V^2 = \text{constant}$$

where p is the pressure in the stream, ρ is the density of the fluid and V the velocity of the fluid. This result evolved from the study of the flow of a fluid from a tank through a nozzle. The constant is the height of the fluid above the nozzle. This formulation expresses the interrelation of the pressure and velocity along any fluid streamline for incompressible flow, the constant being the pressure corresponding to that for zero velocity. The simple formulation is, of course, not correct for high velocities because air is compressible.

A somewhat more complicated form proceeding from the same basic considerations but including the compressibility effect is found for high speeds. The effect of the compressibility correction in the Bernoulli equation becomes about 1% of the value of the term $\frac{1}{2}\rho V^2$ when the Mach number is equal to 0.2 and increases rapidly with the speed.

Also in the 18th century, Jean Le Rond d'Alembert, apparently dissatisfied with the theories for resistance, tackled the problem. Considering air as an incompressible elastic fluid composed of small particles and, carrying over from the principles of solid body mechanics the view that resistance is related to loss of momentum on impact of moving bodies, he produced the surprising result that the resistance was zero. D'Alembert was himself dissatisfied with the result and, largely because of his own comments, the conclusion is known as "D'Alembert's paradox."

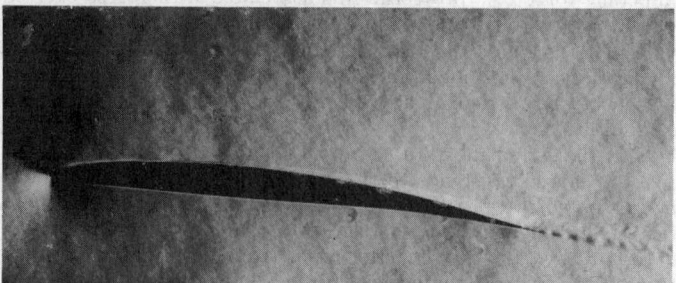

FIG. 1.—SCHLIEREN PHOTOGRAPH OF SUBSONIC FLOW FOR A WING SECTION
Bright area at the leading edge shows region where the impinging streamline is decelerated. Dark regions aft of the leading edge are areas of rapidly increasing speed as the streamline accelerates. The boundary layer is the thin bright region in contact with the wing. (The Schlieren method, widely used for the observation of flow phenomena, makes flow visible because regions of changing density bend light rays. The optical phenomena are similar to the "heat waves" frequently observed above hot surfaces)

The common physical characteristic of both Bernoulli's and D'Alembert's results follows from the law of the conservation of energy: in the absence of a dissipating agent such as friction the potential and kinetic energies of the flow are freely interchangeable. Actually, the body of the classical hydrodynamics that was so highly developed through the 19th century is based on these same assumptions. For many applications, the friction effect is small so that the pressures acting on bodies and the flow fields surrounding them may be calculated with surprising accuracy.

The relationship of resistance to the viscous properties of a fluid was appreciated to some degree by the beginning of the 19th century. Numerous investigators, including C. A. de Coulomb, J. M. H. Navier, A. J. C. Barré de St. Venant, J. L. M. Poiseuille, George G. Stokes and others made important contributions. In the 1880s Osborne Reynolds, experimenting with flows in pipes, demonstrated laminar flows (of a smooth, shear layer nature) and an abrupt transition region to turbulent flows. Only then did modern understanding of viscous effects begin. Reynolds observed that flow which may have started as laminar became abruptly turbulent when a particular value of the product of the distance along the tube and the velocity divided by the viscosity was attained. From this work the "Reynolds number" evolved. Dimensional analysis shows that the Reynolds number expresses the ratio of the mass forces to the viscous forces in a fluid; hence, flows at equal Reynolds numbers (other factors such as surface roughness and Mach number being the same) are similar.

Beginning with Newton and continuing until the end of the 19th century, the foundations of classical hydrodynamics had been developed. The period of modern aerodynamics then began at about the same time that the Wright brothers made their first powered flights. Frederick W. Lanchester in England at the beginning of the 20th century may have been the first to set forth the idea of the circulation theory of lift of an airfoil of infinite span and the idea of the vortex theory of the lift of a wing of finite span. His ideas did not receive wide circulation at the time. At about the same time or shortly thereafter (1901–10) M. Wilhelm Kutta in Germany and Nikolai E. Zhukovski in Russia came independently to the idea of the circulation hypothesis and produced the mathematical theory.

Ludwig Prandtl at Göttingen, who has been recognized as the "father of modern aerodynamics," arrived independently at the same hypotheses as Lanchester and developed the mathematical treatment. Many feel that Prandtl's mathematical formulation of the results is one of the most useful contributions ever made in the field of aeronautics. The lifting theory is based largely upon Prandtl's work as is the modern recognition that the total resistance of an aircraft is composed of three parts: skin friction (viscosity), form or pressure drag and the production of lift (induced drag).

Following Prandtl, the theoretical basis of modern aerodynamics was developed and expanded by a host of contributors in the first half of the 20th century. Among the most notable were contributions of Max M. Munk in the subsonic area and Theodore von Karman in the area of subsonic, supersonic and viscous flows. Like Prandtl, Karman's contributions embraced the original and applied fields, and as teacher Karman became the founder-leader of modern aerodynamics in the mid-20th century.

SUBSONIC AERODYNAMICS

General.—The forces and moments (tendencies to produce motion) acting on an aircraft are the sum of the forces and moments of its components. Lift, most of which is provided by the wing, balances the weight of the aircraft. It overcomes the force of gravity that tends to pull the aircraft back to the ground. At the same time, the wing and the body usually exhibit unstable moments tending to cause roll, pitch or yaw. The wings themselves are designed to prevent rolling of the plane about its longitudinal axis. The horizontal stabilizer at the tail of the plane, acting at a considerable distance from the centre of gravity, gives a counteracting moment that prevents pitching (rise or fall of the plane's nose or tail). The vertical stabilizer or fin, also at the tail, helps to keep the plane from yawing, or turning about its vertical axis. The drag of the aircraft (the force that resists its motion through the air) is balanced by the thrust from the engine.

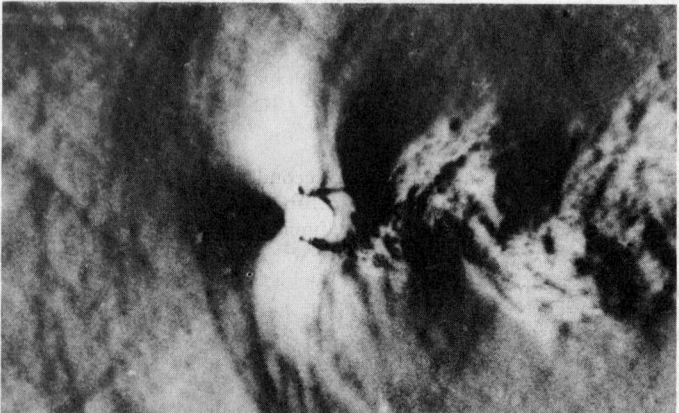

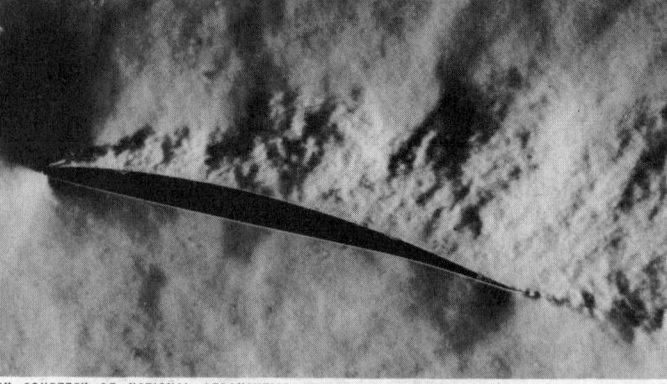

FIG. 2.—SEPARATED FLOWS SHOWN BY THE SCHLIEREN METHOD

(Top) The flow separates from the cylinder at approximately the maximum diameter as shown by the dark lines. (Bottom) The flow separates from the airfoil immediately behind the darkest region at the leading edge. The high shear stress in the high-velocity (dark) region and consequent loss of kinetic energy due to friction in the boundary layer leaves the boundary-layer air with insufficient kinetic energy to flow into the rising-pressure area and separation results

FIG. 3.—VORTEX FLOW AT TIPS OF A WING

A wire grid to which wool tufts are attached is placed in the wake of a delta wing. Examination shows that the vortex extends its effects a considerable distance from the tips. The induced drag is associated with the energy in the vortex shed at the tips

As noted above, the drag of the aircraft is composed of three factors: skin friction, drag due to lift (induced drag) and pressure drag. Skin-friction drag is due to the viscosity of air. Its effects are exhibited in the boundary layer (after Prandtl), the thin layer of air that is in contact with the surface. The boundary layer begins at the surface of the aircraft where the air in immediate contact with the surface is at zero velocity relative to the surface; the outer edge of the boundary layer is at air-stream velocity. There is, thus, a velocity gradient in this layer and a stress is produced in the layer. The skin-friction drag is the result of the stresses produced in this layer. The boundary layer starts as a laminar layer which terminates abruptly in a transition region after which the boundary layer becomes turbulent and increases in thickness. The boundary layer is illustrated in fig. 1.

The drag of the laminar boundary layer is very much lower than the drag of the turbulent layer, hence it is important to design for laminar layers. The transition from the laminar to the turbulent layer occurs at a critical value of the Reynolds number mentioned above. This critical value of the Reynolds number is lowered by the effects of surface imperfections and regions of increasing pressure. The boundary layer in subsonic flow is the only region in the whole flow where kinetic energy of the flow is lost from the main stream. In some circumstances, the kinetic energy lost from the flow in the boundary layer is so great that the flow separates from the body and produces large pressure or form drag. Examples of such separation are the flows for a cylinder and for a wing at high angles of attack, illustrated in fig. 2. In the design of aircraft, care is taken to produce the maximum extent of laminar boundary layer and no separation. Modern subsonic aircraft have insignificant form or pressure drag caused by separation effects.

The drag due to lift is associated with the shedding of vortexes from each wing tip. The flow from the lower surface, which is at higher pressure than the upper surface, rolls up over the tip and a vortex trails from the tip (fig. 3.). The drag due to lift, called induced drag, becomes smaller as the span of the wing is increased in relation to the chord (dimension of the wing in the stream direction). This point is important to aircraft designers. Airplanes that travel long dis-

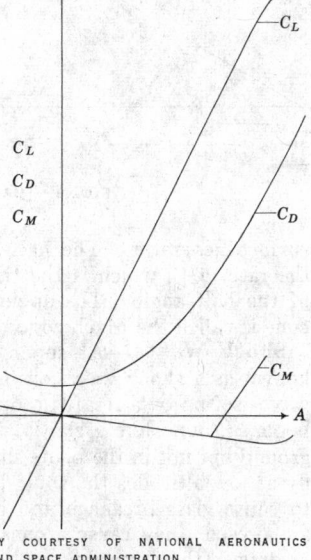

FIG. 4.—DRAWING OF WING CHARACTERISTICS

The lift increases along a straight line as the angle of attack is increased until separation of the flow when "stall" occurs. Further increase of the angle of attack results in decrease of lift, rapid increase of drag and reversal of the moment curve slope

tances at moderate cruising speeds minimize the induced drag by using long wing spans.

Aircraft Aerodynamics.—The characteristics of airplanes and airplane components may be represented by a system of nondimensional coefficients. Lift, drag and moment may be expressed as follows:

$$\text{Lift,} \qquad L = C_L \tfrac{1}{2}\rho V^2 A$$
$$\text{Drag,} \qquad D = C_D \tfrac{1}{2}\rho V^2 A$$
$$\text{Moment,} \; M = C_M \tfrac{1}{2}\rho V^2 Ac$$

A is the area of the wing, ρ is the mass density of the air, c is the chord of the wing and V is the velocity. The term $\tfrac{1}{2}\rho V^2$ is known as the dynamic pressure, one of the terms of the Bernoulli equation. The usual representation of wing characteristics is illustrated in fig. 4.

The lift increases as the angle of attack (the angle included between the direction of the air flow and the chord line of the wing) is increased up to the "stalling angle," after which the lift falls abruptly. At this angle, the flow fails to follow the contour of the wing; it separates from the upper surface (fig. 2), leaving a turbulent wake which is very unsteady. Many examples of loss of aircraft control have occurred at the stall. Because the lift must balance the weight of the aircraft, one can readily see that at high speed the wing or airplane is at a small angle of attack relative to the flight path. The minimum speed at which flight can be sustained is determined by the value of the maximum lift coefficient.

The drag coefficient curve shows a minimum at small values of the angle of attack increasing rapidly as the stall angle is approached. High-speed flight occurs near this minimum value. For good subsonic aircraft, this drag is essentially that due to skin friction.

The principal aerodynamic property determining the range of an aircraft is the maximum lift-to-drag ratio. It has been shown that this occurs for the attitude of the airplane at which the sum of the profile drag (essentially skin friction) and the induced drag is a minimum. The induced-drag coefficient is

$$C_{Di} = \frac{C_L^2}{\pi R},$$

where R, the aspect ratio, is the span squared divided by the area. To minimize this factor, the wings are of large span and small chord.

If the lift coefficient is plotted with the drag coefficient as a parameter, as in fig. 5, the line drawn from the origin tangent to this

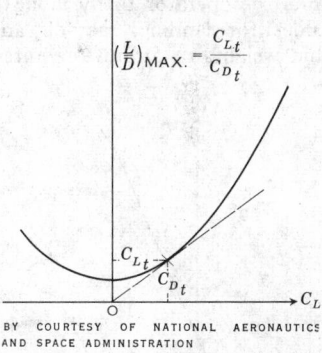

FIG. 5.—DRAG POLAR ILLUSTRATING DETERMINATION OF MAXIMUM LIFT-TO-DRAG RATIO

curve gives the point for which the lift-to-drag ratio is maximum.

The distribution of lift along the chord of the wing is illustrated by the pressure-distribution diagrams, fig. 6.

High-performance aircraft make use of auxiliary devices called flaps to increase the maximum lift so that the landing speed may be kept low. There is a wide range of flap types and the choice depends on the particular application. Frequently, such auxiliary devices are used to improve the climbing properties of an airplane. A simple type is illustrated in fig. 7. The action of such a flap is shown by the lift curves in the figure. At high-speed flight (low angles of attack), the flap is retracted and the low drag of the plain wing is achieved. The flap is extended or deflected for low-speed flight as at landing and the increased lift produced as shown by the upper curve permits the achievement of greatly reduced speeds.

Stability and Controllability.—Stability is that characteristic of a moving body which will cause it to return to its original path or attitude, without the application of control forces, following a disturbance of the original path or attitude. The stability

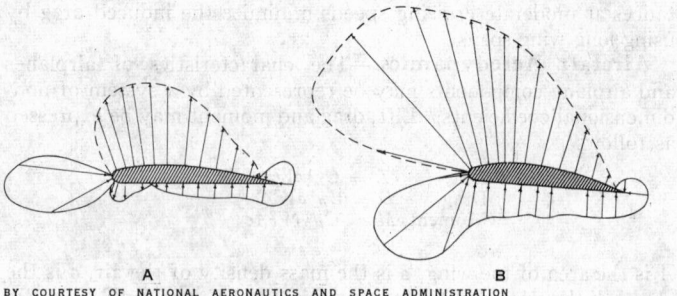

FIG. 6.—DISTRIBUTION OF LIFT ALONG THE CHORD OF A WING
The arrows show direction of pressures acting on wing surfaces; arrow lengths indicate magnitude of pressures for (A) high-speed (low angle of attack) condition; (B) low-speed (high angle of attack) condition; (C) "stall" (angle of attack higher than that for the maximum lift coefficient) condition

of aircraft is usually treated in terms of static stability and dynamic stability. Static stability is provided when the summation of the aerodynamic forces and moments is such as to cause a return to the original path or attitude. Dynamic stability treats of the interaction of the aerodynamic and inertial forces.

Aircraft may exhibit static stability, yet be unstable in maneuvers. This occurs when the inertial effects of the mass of the aircraft in the disturbed or maneuvering motions are too great in relation to the aerodynamic restoring forces. Thus, it is not sufficient that the aerodynamic forces and moments have stable rather than unstable characteristics; there must also be a static stability margin. If, on the other hand, this margin is too great, difficulties with control arise. The general stability equations have been well developed and have been used in various simplified forms. Increased speeds which bring about compressibility effects and the flexibility of the structures have required increasingly detailed analysis as well as more accurate knowledge of the aerodynamic, inertial and structural flexibilities of aircraft.

Controllability is that characteristic of an aircraft which permits the operator to fly along desired paths and at desired attitudes for landing, take-off and maneuvers. Increased speeds and weights of aircraft require increasing precision in the flight paths flown and accurate response to a control movement. Small aircraft usually have more or less direct connection of the control column and rudder pedals to the control surfaces of the aircraft. Large aircraft and high-speed aircraft usually require power-actuated surfaces because the control surfaces, even when aerodynamically balanced, require large forces. Mechanisms for actuating control surface sometimes become very complicated and their characteristics have to be taken into account in the stability and control analyses. On the basis of flight research, the flying and handling qualities of aircraft types (that is, transport, bomber, etc.) can be established for safety and ease of control.

Stability of an aircraft is usually fixed by the action of fixed surfaces—wings, horizontal stabilizer, vertical fin. Controllability is provided by control surfaces —elevator, hinged to the horizontal stabilizer; rudder, hinged to the vertical fin; and the ailerons, small, hinged outboard rear sections of the wings. Usually, of course, there is interaction of the controls and the motion of the airplane; seldom, if ever, is a maneuver made without simultaneous use of all control surfaces.

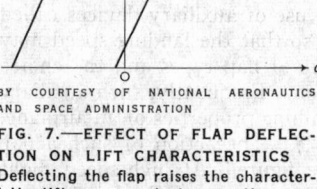

FIG. 7.—EFFECT OF FLAP DEFLECTION ON LIFT CHARACTERISTICS
Deflecting the flap raises the characteristic lift curve and changes the pressure distribution over the whole wing. The increase in the maximum lift coefficient enables an airplane to land at a slower speed

SUPERSONIC AERODYNAMICS

Pressure Fields.—The speed of sound (Mach 1.0) is important in aerodynamics because it is the speed at which small pressure disturbances, such as those caused by the shape or lift of a moving body, are transmitted through the surrounding atmosphere. When a body moves at subsonic speed, its pressure field extends far in front of the body. At supersonic speeds, the pressure field is confined to a region extending mostly to the rear and outward.

The first clear presentation of these phenomena was made by the Austrian physicist Ernst Mach, about 1881. Fig. 8 illustrates the Mach construction. The projectile at point A is assumed to move at twice the speed of sound (Mach 2.0). In a given time, it will have moved the distance AD. In the same time interval, the pressure disturbance at the nose will have traveled one-half of the distance AD, that is, to points on the circle with centre at A and radius a, the speed of sound.

Similarly, at all points along the path AD, the pressure disturbances will travel at the speed of sound and will have reached points on corresponding circles. The line DW is the tangent or envelope of these circles. The total pressure field caused by the projectile passage is, thus, contained within a cone having its vertex at the nose of the projectile with the line DW as its

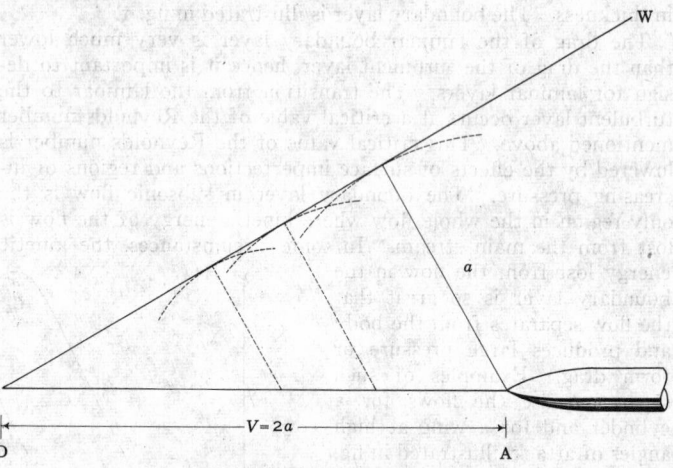

FIG. 8.—MACH CONSTRUCTION

surface generator. The half angle of this cone is measured by the ratio a/V, which is the trigonometric expression for the sine of the half angle. The angle is called the Mach angle and the cone is called the Mach cone.

Shock Waves.—At supersonic speeds a sharp pressure rise, known as a shock wave, occurs along the line DW. Such shock waves set up by aircraft produce the phenomenon known as sonic boom, a sound like a clap of thunder which can be heard on the ground but not in the plane that produces it. When such aircraft fly at low altitudes the sonic boom may be of sufficient intensity to cause glass breakage and other damage. When shock waves are present they cause a considerable energy loss which appears as drag in the forces on the body.

Referring to fig. 8, it can be seen that when a body travels at subsonic speeds the pressure disturbances set up along the path precede the body. Because this disturbance is transmitted to every point along the path, the pressure field ahead of the body is continuous, with no sharp disturbances or jumps, and shock-free passage of the body occurs.

Lift and Drag.—The next significant step following Mach's analysis was development of the theory of the supersonic flow into and around corners. This work, known as the Prandtl-Meyer turn, was first presented in 1908. It demonstrated that the streamlines of the flow turned along a line that began in the corner and had a slope related to the Mach angle of the flow. From this work the calculation of the pressures and forces on the cross section of a wing of large (infinite) span followed directly. This flow is illustrated in fig. 9.

The lift on the airfoil is the net difference between the upper and the lower surface pressures acting on the surfaces. With positive pressures acting on the forward surfaces and negative pressures acting on the rearward surfaces, there is a pressure drag acting on the airfoil section associated with the wave system. When the angle of attack (α) of the airfoil section is zero with respect to the air-stream direction, the pressure diagrams for the upper and lower surfaces become coincident. In this case lift becomes zero, but because of the positive pressure on the forward surfaces and the negative pressure on the rear surfaces, a pressure drag acts on the airfoil. This pressure drag is not experienced at subsonic speeds.

At a given Mach number, the pressure drag due to the shape of the airfoil increases approximately as the square of the thickness; the drag due to lift increases approximately as the square of the angle of attack.

From the method of characteristics and the conical flow theory developed by Adolf Busemann from 1930 to 1935, accurate representation of the flows for curved surfaces and bodies and their shock-wave systems can be made. Numerous investigations have refined and extended the Busemann theory so that general flows are well understood for most examples so long as aerodynamic frictional heating and large boundary-layer effects are not con-

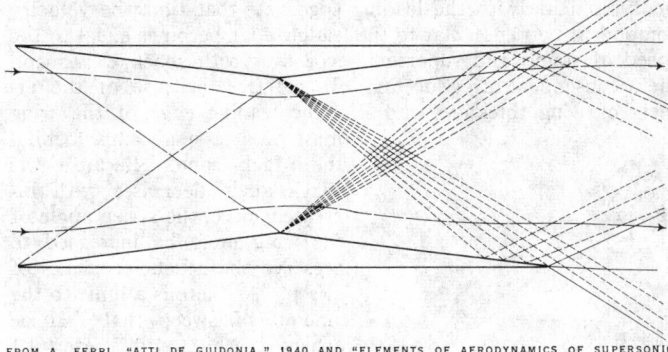

FROM A. FERRI, "ATTI DE GUIDONIA," 1940 AND "ELEMENTS OF AERODYNAMICS OF SUPERSONIC FLOWS"

FIG. 10.—DRAWING OF THE BUSEMANN SUPERSONIC BIPLANE

trolling factors.

Interaction of Waves.—The interaction of the shock and expansion waves from bodies in combination, such as wings and fuselages, is of foremost importance in practical applications. By the correct shaping and positioning of adjacent surfaces, shock and expansion waves can be made to interact to reduce drag. This was first illustrated by Busemann's concept of the supersonic biplane about 1935 (see fig. 10).

The Mach waves from the leading edges, when passing into the region between the wings, interact with the expansion waves and theoretically reduce to zero the pressure drag due to the thickness of the airfoil sections, known as shape drag. The outside surfaces, being parallel to the flow, produce no change of direction of the streamlines. Thus no pressure jumps and corresponding drag losses occur. The whole body acts as though it were a plate of zero thickness in the flow.

By increasing the angle of attack, lift and drag due to lift would be produced, but shape drag would still be nullified. Practical difficulties in the application of the biplane occur because the added surface area would increase skin friction as would any internal structure required to support the surfaces. A further restriction occurs in that precise contours could be made for only one value of the Mach number and one angle of attack. Nevertheless, the concept is of the first order of importance in the design of aircraft where the combinations of wings, bodies and air inlets for engines can be and usually must be carefully calculated to obtain favourable interactions.

Sweeping.—A most important contribution to the achievement of supersonic flight in the late 1940s was the recognition of the effect of sweeping the wings back or forward with respect to the line of flight. This work is attributed to Busemann, A. Betz and R. T. Jones, all of whom seem to have arrived at the result independently during World War II. The physical concept may be grasped by considering a wing in an air stream with its span perpendicular to the direction of flow.

If this wing is now moved continuously in the spanwise direction, no increase in the flow velocity occurs, yet the true velocity of a point on the wing is greater than the flow velocity. The resultant velocity of a point on the wing is in a direction different from the flow velocity by an amount determined by the sidewise velocity. This leads to the conclusion that it is the component of velocity perpendicular to the leading edge of the wing that determines whether the flow over the wing has subsonic shock-free flow or supersonic flow with shocks and consequent drag. Fig. 11 illustrates this effect.

The flight velocity is resolved into the components parallel and perpendicular to the leading edge. The Mach angle for the assumed Mach number is shown. The velocity V_{le} being less than the speed of sound a, the flow over the wing is of the shock-free subsonic type.

If the velocity of the wing is increased, the component perpendicular to the leading edge is increased and finally equals or exceeds the speed of sound. Similarly, if the velocity is increased while the speed of sound remains constant, the Mach angle is de-

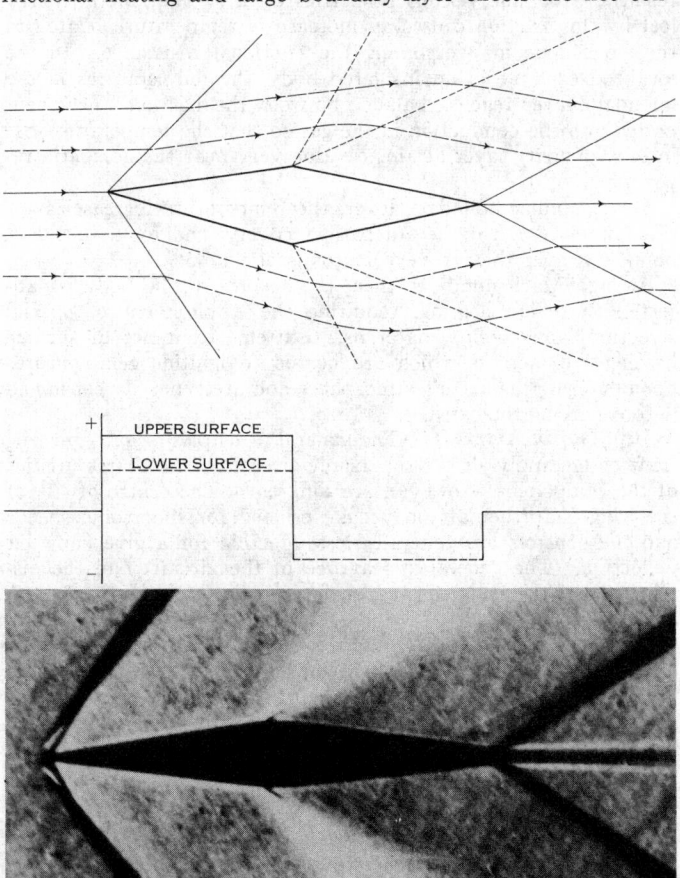

UPPER SURFACE

LOWER SURFACE

PHOTOGRAPH BY COURTESY OF ADVISORY GROUP FOR AERONAUTICAL RESEARCH AND DEVELOPMENT, NATO (AGARDOGRAPH 23, D. S. HOLDER AND R. J. NORTH)

FIG. 9.—SUPERSONIC FLOW AROUND A SIMPLE WING SECTION
(Top) Drawing of the waves originating at the leading edge. (Centre) Drawing of the pressure changes over the wing. (Bottom) Schlieren photograph of supersonic flow around a simple wing section. Dark regions are regions of sharp pressure jump. The bright fan-shaped area is the expansion zone

creased and the Mach line originating at the vertex will eventually coincide with the leading edge. At that time the velocity component perpendicular to the leading edge becomes equal to the speed of sound and supersonic-type flow with shock waves and their consequent drag occurs. In practice, because of the effects of wing thickness and lift, the leading edge of the wing must be at a small angle behind the Mach cone. Because the Mach angle decreases with increased speed, the sweep angle of the wing must be increased to preserve the beneficial effects of sweep. As there is a limit to the amount of sweep that can be achieved while still preserving some lifting area of the wing, there is a maximum Mach number, in the range of 2.5 to 3.0, for which the beneficial effects of sweep can be maintained. Photographs of the flow for a swept wing are shown in fig. 12.

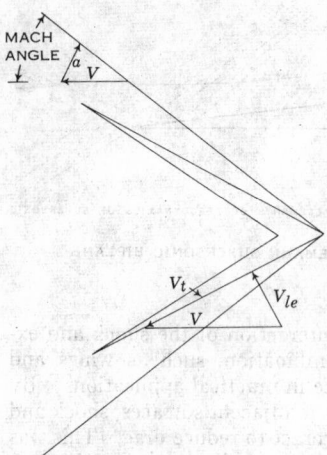

FIG. 11.—DRAWING OF VELOCITY AND MACH CONE FOR SWEPT WING WITH SUBSONIC LEADING EDGE

Boundary-Layer Effects.— The boundary layer introduces special problems at supersonic speeds. Under certain conditions, shock waves from one component surface impinging on another component surface may, because of the sharp pressure rise in the shock, cause the boundary layer to thicken and even separate from the surface upon which the shock wave impinges (fig. 13). Such types of flow interactions are very complicated and generally produce serious unfavourable effects on the stability and controllability of an aircraft. Knowledge in this field, however, is sufficiently advanced so that such adverse effects can be reasonably minimized by proper shaping and location of the aircraft components with respect to each other.

Surface Heating.—An even more serious problem is surface heating caused by the boundary layer. The simple form of Bernoulli's equation shows the relation between velocity and pressure at points in the flow about a body. At the nose of a body, the velocity of the body in the direction of the stream becomes zero and the pressure at this point, called the stagnation point, is consequently at its highest value. The temperatures at points in the flow are related to the density and the pressure of the gas by the general gas laws. At the nose of the body, the temperature, as well as the pressure, is at its highest value. Physically, what has occurred at this point is that the kinetic energy represented by the velocity of the impinging streamline has been converted to potential energy which is measured by the pressure and tempera-

BY COURTESY OF NATIONAL AERONAUTICS AND SPACE ADMINISTRATION

FIG. 12.—SCHLIEREN PHOTOGRAPHS OF FLOW FOR TRIANGULAR (DELTA) WINGS FOR MACH NUMBER 1.62

(Left) The Mach cone lies well ahead of the wing's leading edge, and the flow partakes of subsonic properties with little shock-wave drag. (Right) The Mach cone has become coincident with the leading edge. The Mach line has become a shock wave

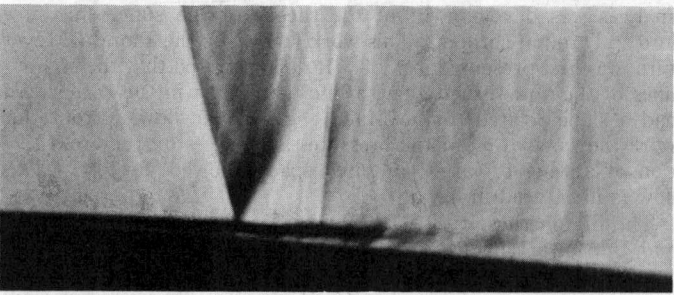

BY COURTESY OF NATIONAL AERONAUTICS AND SPACE ADMINISTRATION

FIG. 13.—SCHLIEREN PHOTOGRAPH OF SEPARATION OF BOUNDARY LAYER BY SHOCK WAVE
The line along which separation occurs is illustrated by the dark line in the photograph. The sharp line fades as mixing of the boundary layer occurs downstream of the separation region

ture for the zero velocity case.

When air is brought to rest, as at the stagnation point, the stagnation temperature is given by the formula

$$T_s = T\left(1 + \frac{M^2}{5}\right)$$

where T is the temperature of the surrounding atmosphere as measured from absolute zero (Fahrenheit temperature plus approximately 460) and M is the velocity of the flow expressed as a Mach number. Thus, very large local temperatures exist at the stagnation point when the Mach number is increased. The temperature difference $(T_s - T)$ is called the adiabatic recovery.

In the boundary layer the velocity is reduced by the friction resulting from the viscous properties of air. The kinetic energy lost by this friction causes an increase in temperature related to the work done in overcoming the frictional resistance. In the idealized example of an insulated body, the temperatures in the boundary layer reach a balance between the frictional heat generated and the conduction in the gas so that the temperature rise in the boundary layer attains a value very near the adiabatic recovery.

For a laminar boundary layer, the temperature increase is approximately 85% of the adiabatic recovery, and for a turbulent boundary layer the recovery factor is about 90%.

At high Mach numbers, then, the surface of the body is subjected to severe heating, requiring the employment of special structural and cooling materials. Extreme examples of surface heating are meteors which are heated to ignition temperatures upon entering the earth's atmosphere and are generally consumed before striking the earth.

Supersonic Aircraft.—The general principles of subsonic aircraft design apply also to supersonic aircraft. The characteristics of the components, however, are different. The centre of lift of the wing is further aft on wings designed for supersonic speeds and the controls are generally less effective for a given angular deflection. The general appearance of the aircraft and the distribution of the main masses, such as engine, fuel and pay load, are also different.

The aerodynamic heating due to the boundary-layer frictional effects probably accounts for the most serious difference. When the Mach number exceeds 2.0, the structure and the materials of the aircraft are markedly different. Aluminum, so widely used in subsonic aircraft fabrication, cannot be used and must be replaced by such materials as titanium and special steel alloys. When the Mach number exceeds 3.0, major changes in engine configuration become necessary.

TRANSONIC FLOWS

A special case of subsonic and supersonic flows occurs when the Mach number is near 1.0 and is termed transonic flow. As wings or other bodies approach the speed of sound, the velocities at local points on the bodies are increased in correspondence to the pressures acting at these points so that locally the velocity of sound may be exceeded. Strong shocks then form on the wing or body, usually causing separation of the boundary layer. These

and cargo transport, and describes the major world airlines.

The theoretical structure on which aeronautical science is built and the technical history of its development are outlined in AERODYNAMICS; AERONAUTICS; and FLIGHT (NATURAL). Some important experimental aspects of aeronautics are covered in WIND TUNNEL. Applications of aerodynamic theory in aircraft design are explained in AIRPLANE; SEAPLANE; HELICOPTER; and GROUND-EFFECT MACHINE. The evolution of aircraft power plants and the techniques on which modern types are based are treated in AIRCRAFT PROPULSION. Both the function and operation of basic flight instruments, engine instruments and auxiliary instruments are covered in AIRCRAFT INSTRUMENTS. Landing fields and service facilities for aircraft are discussed in AIRPORT.

AIR POWER discusses the military doctrine of air power and also traces the military use of aircraft, from the balloons used by the French during the siege of Paris in 1870 to the development of the intercontinental ballistic missile, which is treated in detail in ROCKETS AND GUIDED MISSILES. AIR POWER also discusses the organization of air forces, the development of air defense systems, and the military use of paratroopers. AIRCRAFT CARRIER surveys the emergence of the floating airfield in World War I, its formidable role in World War II and the Korean War, and its subsequent development.

Medical and legal aspects of aeronautics are discussed in AVIATION MEDICINE and AIR LAW.

The reader who wishes a broader theoretical perspective of the science of which aerodynamics represents a subdivision will find this in MECHANICS, FLUID. Similarly, AIRCRAFT PROPULSION is supplemented by the general article INTERNAL-COMBUSTION ENGINE, and AVIATION, CIVIL by TRANSPORTATION. Aerial navigation is included in the article NAVIGATION. The reader interested in specialized areas should consult the Index, which refers not only to major articles but to individual topics within them.

The theories on which the possibilities of flight into outer space are based are explained in SPACE EXPLORATION; the methods used in attempting to apply these theories are described there and also in ROCKETS AND GUIDED MISSLES. The phenomenon of "flying saucers" is discussed in UNIDENTIFIED FLYING OBJECTS.

Many of the key figures of aeronautical history whose work is described in the articles mentioned above are represented by biographical articles—for example, WRIGHT, ORVILLE AND WILBUR; LANGLEY, SAMUEL PIERPONT; BLÉRIOT, LOUIS; MITCHELL, WILLIAM, etc.

AERONAUTICS.

This term has been used for many years to describe generally the art and science of aerial flight. It included flight in lighter-than-air craft (balloons and airships) as well as in all forms of heavier-than-air machines. With the advent of vehicles capable of flight outside the earth's atmosphere, however, its implications were too limited, and a revision in terminology became necessary. Various combinations have been suggested (e.g., "aero-astronautics"), but most have proved to be too awkward for common use. A combination of "aeronautics" and "space" has resulted in the coinage of the word "aerospace" to describe the regions in which man may now navigate, and the science of aeronautics has become integrated into the aerospace sciences.

Because the aerospace sciences cover a wide range of diversified activities and applications, it is not feasible to treat them all under one entry. A series of articles on various aspects of the aerospace sciences is included in this edition, the major entries being listed in AERONAUTICS (ARTICLES ON); see also Index references under "Aeronautics" in the Index volume. The remainder of the present article deals with those facets of the aerospace sciences that are concerned with aircraft design, and presupposes an elementary knowledge of aerodynamics (q.v.). It consists of the following material:

    I. Introduction
   II. Forces Acting Upon Aircraft
  III. Aircraft Lift Systems
       1. Airfoils
            Boundary-Layer Phenomena
            Shock-Wave Phenomena
       2. Three-Dimensional Wings

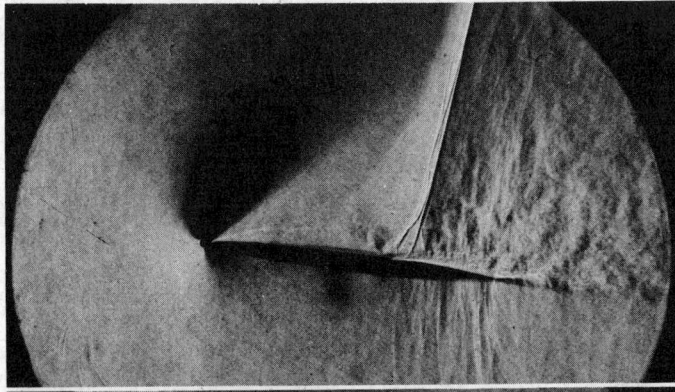
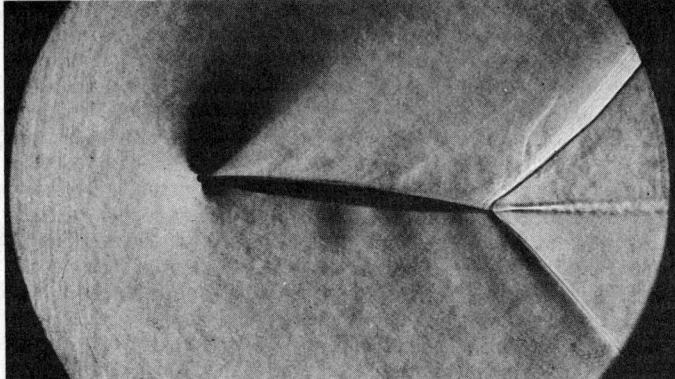

FIG. 14.—SCHLIEREN PHOTOGRAPHS OF TRANSONIC FLOWS FOR A WING SECTION

(Top) At Mach 0.92, a strong shock wave separates the flow. At the point where separation first occurs, a rearward sloping shock starts and terminates on intersection with the single strong shock. (Bottom) When the speed is increased the shock is swept to the trailing edge, becoming a sharply inclined shock. The separated flow disappears and supersonic flow occurs (Mach 1.2)

flows are very unsteady and give rise to severe buffeting and changes in the characteristics of the wings or bodies that may cause serious stability difficulties and losses in control effectiveness. An example of a transonic flow for a conventional wing section is illustrated in fig. 14. These effects are minimized by reducing the thickness of wings, by sweeping and by the proper combination of wings and bodies following a principle called the area rule.

In principle, the area rule combined with reduced thickness of components reduces to a minimum the differences between the flight velocity and the velocities of local points on the surface of the vehicle. Generally, vehicles properly designed for supersonic flight will not have great difficulty in passing through the transonic speed region, the so-called sound barrier. On the other hand, aircraft efficiently designed for subsonic speeds, with comparatively thick, unswept wings, may become extremely dangerous if through a dive maneuver they should enter the transonic speed range.

See also references under "Aerodynamics" in the Index.

BIBLIOGRAPHY.—William F. Durand (ed.), *Aerodynamic Theory*, 6 vol. (1934–35; reprinted 1943); N. A. V. Piercy, *Aerodynamics*, 2nd ed. (1947); Theodore von Kármán, *Aerodynamics* (1954); L. L. Beckford, *An A.B.C. of Aeronautics* (1957). (J. SK.)

AERONAUTICS (ARTICLES ON).

The history of the intellectual and physical pioneering by which the basic principles of flight were established is summarized in AVIATION, HISTORY OF, and the major applications of these principles are described.

The earliest type of exploration of the air and its modern applications are discussed in BALLOON FLIGHT, which deals with the history and methods of construction of balloons, from 18th-century France to the Skyhook balloons used for the study of cosmic rays. The evolution of modern techniques is described also in AIRSHIP, dealing with self-propelled dirigibles, and in GLIDING and PARACHUTE.

AVIATION, CIVIL surveys the general history of aerial passenger

3. Bodies of Revolution
    Design Considerations
    Interference Drag
4. Minimum Flight Speeds; High-Lift Devices
    Trailing-Edge Flaps
    Leading-Edge Slats and Flaps
5. Effect of Sweepback on Lift
IV. Aircraft Performance Estimation
    1. Propeller Design Considerations
    2. Thrust Considerations
    3. Range of Flight
V. Aircraft Stability and Control
    1. Longitudinal Control Systems
    2. Lateral and Directional Control Systems
VI. Aircraft Structures
    1. Wing Design
    2. Temperature Considerations

I. INTRODUCTION

To produce a successful aircraft, the airplane designer must blend the sciences of fluid mechanics and aerodynamics with the most advanced engineering techniques available. He must foresee any number of unexpected situations and applications for his machine. He must anticipate emergency situations of wide variety and provide the pilot and crew with systems and techniques for dealing with them. There is no single design that can optimize all factors. The design process is a process of compromise—the exercise of the designer's judgment about the interrelation and relative importance of the various functions that his product will have to perform.

Aircraft of today have become so complex that their design demands a detailed knowledge of physics, chemistry, electronics, fluid mechanics and the various branches of engineering. Frequently basic design decisions are based upon economic or political considerations. The job has become too large for one man and in most companies is handled by design teams ranging in size from a few men to thousands of highly trained specialists. Because each design is different, it is impossible to outline all of the factors that control the final appearance of the aircraft, but the following paragraphs discuss in a general way the major factors that lead to a particular configuration.

II. FORCES ACTING UPON AIRCRAFT

Vehicles moving through the air that are not directly supported from the earth's surface may, in general, be considered as being subjected to a system of body forces consisting of the weight and various inertia forces such as centrifugal forces, etc.; a system of aerodynamic forces arising from the relative motion of the vehicle with respect to the surrounding air; and lastly, the forces generated by whatever method of propulsion is employed. Efficiency of design requires that, for a given amount of power to be used, the maximum load must be carried at a given design speed. Furthermore, the machine must be stable; i.e., must return to its given flight condition when displaced by either mechanical or atmospheric disturbances. It must also be satisfactorily controllable throughout its entire range of possible flight conditions.

The aerodynamic forces acting upon a vehicle moving through the air arise from physical properties of the air such as density, viscosity and specific heat, and from the fact that the pressure throughout the flow is a function of the velocity, decreasing as the velocity increases. By proper design of the shape of the machine, these characteristics of the air can be made to produce sustaining or lift forces many times greater than the retarding or drag forces. In the case of an airplane (q.v.) or glider this involves shaping the craft, within the limits set by structural weight and strength, to produce the greatest possible ratio of lift to drag at the design speed. In the case of a lighter-than-air ship, or a missile, efficiency of design involves surrounding the required space within the machine with a structure of adequate strength offering the least possible resistance for the lowest possible weight.

III. AIRCRAFT LIFT SYSTEMS

When considering an airplane or glider it is natural to regard the wings as the major element of the lifting system, even though appreciable lifting forces may arise from the pressure distributions over the fuselage and control surfaces, as well as from components of the forces produced by the propulsive system. The lift of lighter-than-air craft is generally computed on the basis of the volume of lifting gas contained within the gas bags, even though a large contribution to the craft's over-all lift may result from the pressure distribution about the hull. The sustaining forces acting on a missile may come from many sources, such as the pressure distributions over the body and control surfaces, but the major contribution in the case of wingless designs arises from those components of the propulsive and body forces that act in a direction opposite that of the force of gravity.

To maintain steady level flight, forces must be created that are equal and opposite to the gravitational pull. In addition, the propulsive or thrust forces must exactly balance the aerodynamic resistance tending to retard the machine. The components of the aerodynamic forces created by the relative motion of the air flowing past the machine are related to the direction of the flow. The components perpendicular to the flow direction add to produce the force known as lift. The summation of the components of the retarding forces parallel to the direction of the flow is termed the drag.

Because the lift of a dirigible or blimp arises from the displacement of air by an equal volume of lighter gas, and that of a missile is frequently largely the result of a component of the propulsive force, the discussion of lifting systems will be narrowed to an investigation of the lift of wings. These wings may be either fixed, as is the case with airplanes and gliders, or rotating, as in helicopters or gyroplanes. In either case the fundamental flow mechanisms are much the same.

1. Airfoils.—A cross section of a wing, such as either of those shown in fig. 1, is termed an airfoil section. The operation of such an airfoil is best understood by considering a section such as that shown in fig. 1(A), in which the thickness is distributed symmetrically (a-a) about the line joining the leading and trailing edges, the so-called chord line. When the angle of attack a is zero, i.e., when the chord line is parallel to the direction of flow, the particles of air flowing over the upper surface travel the same distance from the point of flow impingement, the stagnation point located on the leading edge, as do the particles of air flowing

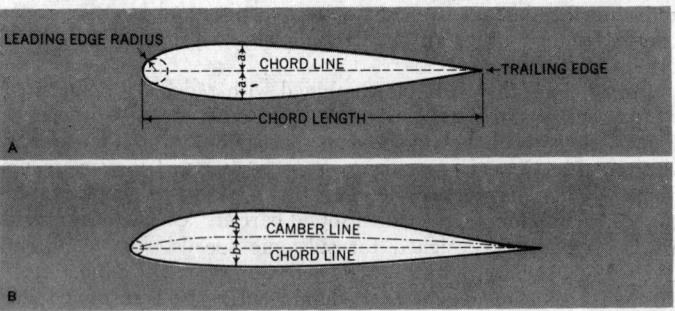

FIG. 1.—AIRFOIL SECTIONS: (A) SYMMETRICAL AIRFOIL WITH THICKNESS DISTRIBUTION (a-a) SYMMETRICAL ABOUT CHORD LINE; (B) CAMBERED AIRFOIL WITH THICKNESS DISTRIBUTION (b-b) SYMMETRICAL ABOUT CAMBER LINE

under the wing. Thus, two particles of air starting on either side of the stagnation point and flowing over the upper and lower surfaces, respectively, will arrive at the trailing edge simultaneously. Under these conditions the flow will leave the trailing edge smoothly, as illustrated by fig. 2(A).

If the angle of attack, the angle between the chord line and the undisturbed direction of the flow, is increased, as shown in fig. 2(B), the stagnation point moves under the leading edge so that the air flowing over the upper surface suddenly has a greater distance to travel to reach the trailing edge than does the air passing under the wing. As a consequence, the lower surface flow arrives at the trailing edge before the flow that started at the stagnation point at the same time but followed the upper surface.

There being no forces to prevent it, the lower surface flow attempts to expand around the trailing edge, as illustrated in fig. 2(C). As it flows about the sharp trailing edge, the magnitudes of the centrifugal and viscous forces are such that the flow separates, forming a vortex flow of the type illustrated. Because of the sense of rotation of this vortex, it serves to accelerate the upper surface flow so that the length of time required for a particle of air to move from the stagnation point at the leading edge to the trailing edge becomes the same for either the upper or lower surface routes.

The increased velocity of the upper-surface air produces two significant effects; it eliminates the tendency of the lower-surface air to expand about the trailing edge, and it produces lower pressures at each point on the upper surface than exist at the corresponding points on the lower surface. Each time the angle of attack is changed, an imbalance of velocities and pressure occurs at the trailing edge, producing another vortex which serves to establish the new upper-surface steady-state flow. Thus, as the angle of attack is increased, the upper-surface velocities increase, producing lower and lower pressures.

The summation of the pressures acting over the infinitesimal elements of area that make up the airfoil surface represents the resultant force on the section. The component of this force in the direction perpendicular to the flow is the lift; the component parallel to the flow is the drag. These forces can readily be measured in wind tunnels on models especially designed and constructed for the purpose (see WIND TUNNEL). In order to make the data so obtained applicable to wings of other sizes moving through the air at speeds other than those employed during the test program, these data are presented in a nondimensional form. Extensive investigations have shown these nondimensional coefficients to be functions of the airfoil shape, the angle of attack; the Mach number (ratio of the speed of the body to the speed of sound); and the Reynolds number.

Boundary-Layer Phenomena.—The influence of Reynolds number, which is merely the ratio of the inertial forces to the viscous forces within the fluid, becomes important only when the viscous forces become large. Even though air is a fluid of low viscosity, in certain regions within the flow field the magnitude of the viscous forces may become large enough to be the controlling factor determining the nature of the flow. One such region is the boundary layer, the layer of air adjacent to a solid surface over which air is flowing.

To examine the nature of this layer, consider a flow of the type pictured in fig. 3. In this case a thin, flat plate is placed parallel

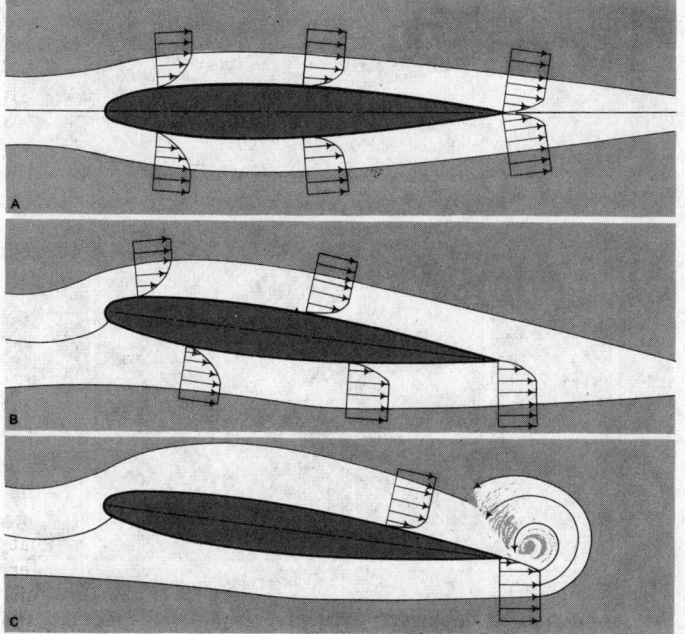

FIG. 2.—CHANGE OF AIR FLOW WITH CHANGE IN ANGLE OF ATTACK

to the oncoming flow, which has a velocity U. At the extreme leading edge of the plate, the particle of air immediately next to the surface is brought to rest. At each successive point along the plate, the molecules of air immediately adjacent to the surface are bound to the surface by the powerful attractive forces of

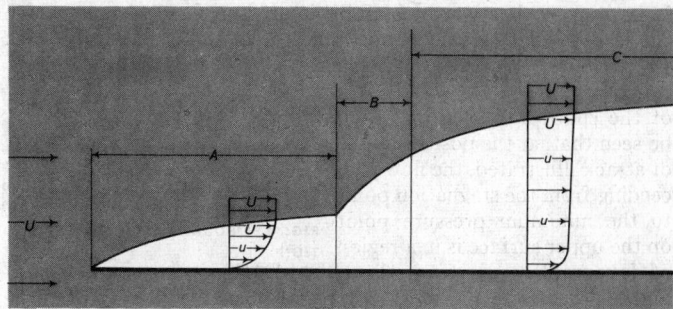

FIG. 3.—BOUNDARY-LAYER DEVELOPMENT OVER A FLAT PLATE: *A*, REGION OF LAMINAR FLOW; *B*, TRANSITION REGION; *C*, REGION OF TURBULENT FLOW; *U*, VELOCITY VECTORS OF UNDISTURBED AIR STREAM; *u*, VELOCITY VECTORS IN SAME DIRECTION BUT OF SMALLER MAGNITUDE

the molecules making up the solid boundary. This is the so-called no-slip condition, and has been found to exist in air flows up to very high Mach numbers when the energies involved in the flow are so great that the chemistry of the air undergoes a change, with ionization and dissociation taking place.

The molecules of air immediately above those bound to the surface are slowed to a velocity *u* by their contact with these stationary particles. As they move away from the surface under the influence of their random molecular motions, they collide with other molecules and are slowed, while the latter in turn are speeded up. Thus, a molecular mixing region exists which thickens as the flow proceeds downstream. The existence of this region is indicated by the loss in velocity shown by the typical velocity profiles sketched in fig. 3. Because the decrease in velocity in this region of the boundary layer is produced primarily by molecular action, the flow itself is relatively smooth and tends to move in layers parallel to the surface. This portion of the boundary layer is thus referred to as laminar.

As the flow proceeds along the solid boundary, it loses energy through the molecular action at a rate which depends upon its viscosity. Because of this loss of energy, the stability of the flow (its ability to damp out disturbances) is affected. As a result, slight velocity components normal to the surface, produced perhaps by freestream disturbances or by irregularities in the surface itself, tend to grow instead of diminish. If they grow sufficiently large, the fairly regular motion of the laminar boundary layer is destroyed, and the boundary layer is said to undergo transition; it thickens rapidly, and becomes characterized by large random motions or turbulence.

The sensitivity of the boundary layer to transition has been found to be a function of the amplitude and frequency of the disturbance, the Reynolds number, the freestream turbulence, the surface smoothness and temperature and most important, the pressure gradient along the surface.

If the flow is proceeding from a region of high pressure to one of low pressure (*i.e.*, in a favourable pressure gradient), it can be likened to a stone rolling downhill, and small disturbances are readily damped out; however, if it is proceeding in the other direction (*i.e.*, in an adverse pressure gradient), it is extremely sensitive, and will almost immediately undergo transition to the turbulent state.

One other boundary-layer phenomenon must be understood to appreciate the behaviour of airfoils. This is the tendency of the boundary layer to become thicker and thicker as the flow proceeds against an adverse pressure gradient. The layers of air next to the surface become more and more retarded until, as shown in fig. 4, the velocity above the surface, instead of increasing, remains equal to zero for a short distance. Under these conditions, the air will react to the higher pressure downstream, and will actually begin to flow upstream along the surface, forcing the freestream flow away. Such a flow is said to be separated, and the point at which it first occurs is termed the separation point.

These characteristics of the flow, arising from the viscosity of the air, have a profound effect upon the behaviour of the air as it passes over the airfoil. If, for the moment, consideration is limited to the type of airfoil pictured in fig. 5(A), in which the leading edge is well rounded and the airfoil is relatively thick (maximum thickness being roughly between 10% and 20% of the chord line length), it will be seen that, at the positive angle of attack illustrated, the flow proceeding from the stagnation point to the minimum pressure point on the upper surface is in a region of favourable pressure gradient,

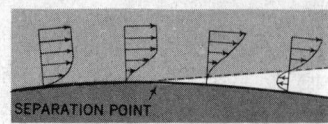

FIG. 4.—BOUNDARY-LAYER SEPARATION

and is, therefore, probably laminar. Once the flow is past the minimum pressure point, the gradient reverses and transition occurs. The boundary layer may thus be considered as turbulent from this point aft to the trailing edge. The flow under the airfoil could remain laminar all the way or might, under the action of large disturbances, undergo transition, but is certainly in a much less critical position than the layer above the airfoil.

As the angle of attack is increased, the depth of the turbulent boundary layer at the trailing edge increases until separation occurs. Further increases of angle of attack cause the separation point to move upstream, as shown in fig. 5(B). Because more and more of the profile is covered by the separated region, the increase of lift for each incremental change in angle of attack after separation has begun is less than for the case of completely attached flow. As the angle of attack is further increased, a point is reached where no further increase in lift results. This is the point of maximum lift, and further increases in angle of attack cause the lift to diminish, in some cases very rapidly. An airfoil in this flow situation, in which most of the upper-surface flow is separated, is said to be stalled.

The characteristics of the boundary layer also have a controlling influence upon the drag of the airfoil profile. The action of the surface molecules in decreasing the velocity of the air flowing past is manifested as an equal and opposite force termed the skin friction. This skin friction is a function of the viscosity of the fluid and the rate at which the velocity increases above the surface. In the laminar portions of the boundary layer in which the change of velocity is accomplished solely by molecular diffusion resulting from the random motion of the air molecules, this rate of change of velocity normal to the surface is relatively small.

Once transition has taken place, and the boundary-layer flow has become turbulent, the molecular mixing throughout the layer is much more rapid, molecular diffusion giving way to conduction by means of large turbulent eddies as the primary mixing process. As a result, the rate at which the velocity above the surface increases to nearly the freestream value is much more rapid than in the laminar case.

The difference in shape between typical laminar and turbulent velocity profiles is shown in fig. 3.

The rapidity of the velocity rise normal to the surface results in a much higher skin friction being associated with a turbulent boundary layer than with a laminar one.

It would thus be expected that as the region of turbulent flow

FIG. 5.—GROWTH OF TRAILING-EDGE SEPARATION ON THICK AIRFOIL: (A) AIR FLOW AT SMALL POSITIVE ANGLE OF ATTACK; (B) AIR FLOW AT INCREASED ANGLE OF ATTACK WHICH LEADS TO TRAILING-EDGE SEPARATION

over the surface of the airfoil profile increases with angle of attack, the drag of the profile will also increase. In addition, as separation occurs, the change in pressure distribution results in a large increase in the component of force in the direction parallel to the freestream; i.e., a large increase in the pressure drag.

In an attempt that was initially intended to produce a reduction in drag by increasing the extent of the laminar flow areas over the surface of the profile, the so-called high-speed profiles were developed. As shown by fig. 6(A), the geometry of these profiles from their relatively small-radius leading edges to their point of maximum thickness well aft on their chord line is arranged to maintain favourable (or at least zero) pressure gradients over the greater part of the chord for the given range of design lift coefficients.

Figure 6(B) shows typical lift and drag characteristics of such a profile. In this figure C_L, called the lift coefficient, and C_D, the drag coefficient, are nondimensional quantities proportional to the lift and drag, respectively. The most notable feature is the abrupt reduction in drag in the range of low lift coefficients, the so-called drag bucket. This reduction represents the increased region of laminar flow that results when the surface of such a profile is polished and maintained to a high degree of smoothness. Unfortunately, disturbances such as mud, or even scratches, are sometimes sufficient to disrupt the flow, causing premature transition and loss of the entire drag advantage.

The second feature of the curves shown in fig. 6(B) that requires comment is the abrupt nature of the stall. Typically, this type of profile displays a flattening of the lift-coefficient v. angle-of-attack curve near the stall, and when stall occurs, the loss of lift is apt to be sudden and severe. Unlike the stall of conventional airfoils, which originates as a trailing-edge separation of the turbulent boundary layer, the stall of a sharp-leading-edge profile originates as a separation of the laminar boundary layer at the leading edge. The exact nature of this separation depends upon the Reynolds number, the curvature of the leading edge and the thickness distribution of the profile.

The mechanism of this leading-edge separation arises from the fact that as the angle of attack increases, the forward stagnation point moves below the leading edge. The air must thus accelerate

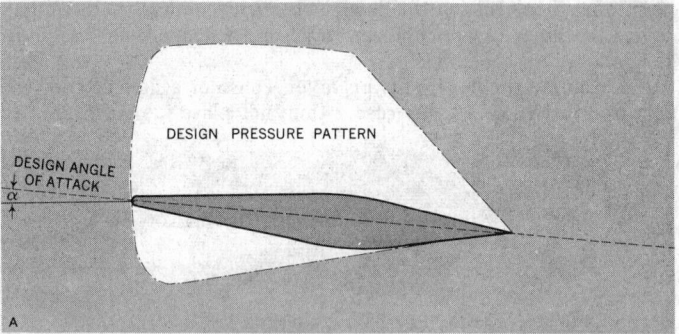

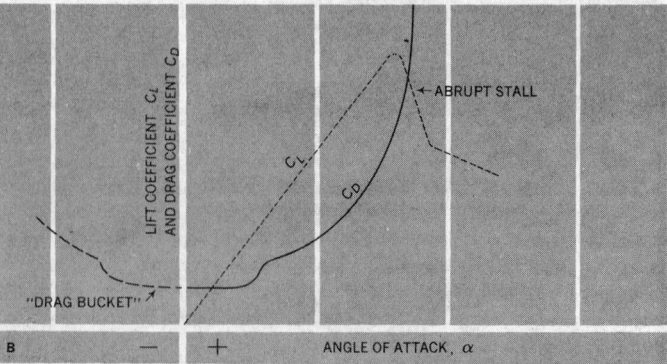

FIG. 6.—DESIGN OF HIGH-SPEED AIRFOILS: (A) AIRFOIL PROFILE AND PRESSURE GRADIENTS AT ANGLE OF ATTACK a; (B) VARIATION IN LIFT AND DRAG COEFFICIENTS AT VARYING ANGLES OF ATTACK

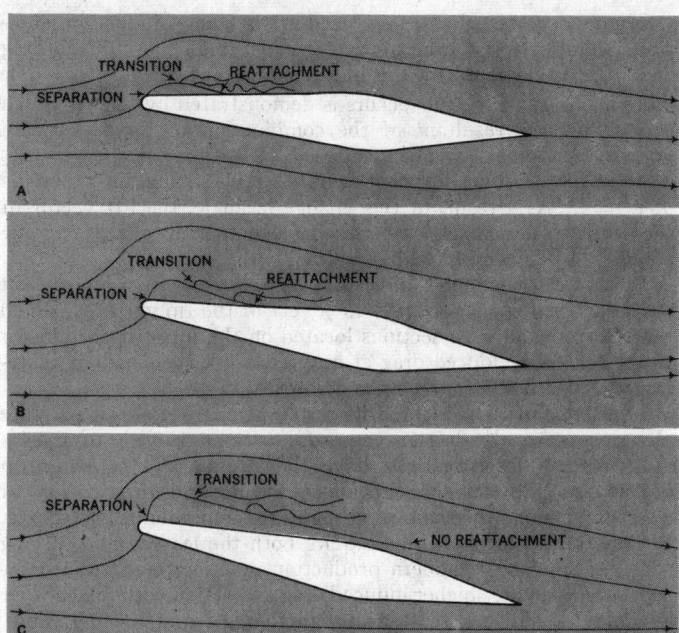

FIG. 7.—LEADING-EDGE SEPARATION ON HIGH-SPEED AIRFOIL OF THICK PROFILE: (A) LEADING-EDGE BUBBLE FORMS; (B) BUBBLE MOVES FORWARD WITH INCREASED ANGLE OF ATTACK; (C) SHORT-BUBBLE STALL OCCURS WITH FURTHER INCREASE IN ANGLE OF ATTACK

past a region of very abrupt curvature to reach the upper surface. The velocities at such a point can be very high, and although the pressure gradient may be strongly favourable, the centrifugal forces acting on the air as the air attempts to turn around the leading edge become so large that the air is pulled from the surface. The laminar flow leaving the surface moves into a region of adverse gradient as it proceeds downstream. Under the action of this gradient it undergoes transition, and as a result of the growth of turbulence it reattaches to the upper surface, forming a leading-edge bubble, as shown in fig. 7(B).

If the profile is relatively thick and the leading-edge radius large, the separation point and the reattachment point will move forward as the angle of attack increases; therefore, the bubble does not grow appreciably but remains small while moving forward on the profile. Quite abruptly, a point will be reached where the growth of turbulence causes the flow to expand along a line that, instead of intersecting the surface and producing reattachment, becomes merely tangent, thereby producing the abrupt and violent stall associated with the small or so-called short bubble. This sequence of events is shown in fig. 7(C).

In the case of a very sharp leading edge, separation occurs either right at the leading edge or possibly slightly below it. Under these circumstances the separation bubble is large and becomes larger with increasing angle of attack. Final stall occurs when the reattachment point on the downstream end of the bubble reaches the trailing edge. Fig. 8 demonstrates this set of circumstances. Because of the growth of separation over the upper surface, the lift curve of such a profile demonstrates a much more gradual stall than the small-bubble case. The maximum lift coefficient obtainable, however, may be only about one-half that which can be obtained from a thicker wing having a trailing-edge stall.

Shock-Wave Phenomena.—The major reason for employing high-speed profiles, rather than the trailing-edge stalling type of profiles, is to reduce the high-speed drag. Curiously enough, this is not so much to reduce the skin-friction drag which they were originally designed to overcome, but rather the drag associated with the change of flow that takes place when the velocity at some point on the profile approaches the velocity of sound.

Pressure waves move through the air with the speed of sound; thus, as a wing moves along at some velocity well below that of sound, the pressure disturbance it causes is transmitted to the

air ahead, enabling the air to flow smoothly over the surfaces. If at some point the local velocity, *i.e.*, the flow velocity at that point, becomes equal to the speed of sound, the pressure disturbances cannot propagate forward; instead, they build up to form a surface of discontinuity of pressure and density known as a shock wave.

When a shock wave first forms on the wing, it is limited to a relatively small region, as shown by fig. 9(A). Tending to be somewhat unstable, it dances back and forth over the boundary layer, producing large disturbances and leading to premature separation aft of the shock. As previously pointed out in the discussion of trailing-edge stalls, such a separation reduces the lift and increases the drag. Because of the similarity of the effects produced by the shock-induced separation and the trailing-edge stall, this condition is sometimes referred to as a shock stall. The speed at which the shock wave is first encountered is called the drag divergence Mach number, or the critical Mach number, of the section. Because it is a function of the local pressure distribution, the speed at which the condition is first encountered will vary with the angle of attack, and hence with the lift coefficient of the section.

An airfoil designed to avoid high-velocity peaks, *i.e.*, low local pressures, in the range of low angles of attack will have good high-speed characteristics in that the formation of the disruptive shock waves will be delayed. The high-speed profiles have just such peakless pressure distributions at these angles of attack, being so designed in the attempt to avoid boundary-layer transition. These profiles thus delay shock-wave formation until high speeds are attained, and as a consequence have found extensive use on high-speed airplanes. Reducing the thickness of the airfoil also reduces the magnitude of the difference between the local velocities on the surface and the freestream. For this reason the wings of high-speed aircraft are as thin as the demands of structure and fuel storage space will allow.

If the velocity is increased beyond that at which shock waves first appear, the region of supersonic velocities (velocities greater than the speed of sound) increases, the shock wave splitting as shown in fig. 9(B). When the freestream velocity becomes supersonic, the shock waves are located at the leading and trailing edges. Further increases of speed merely reduce the angle between the shock wave and the profile surface, but do not appreciably change the location of the waves.

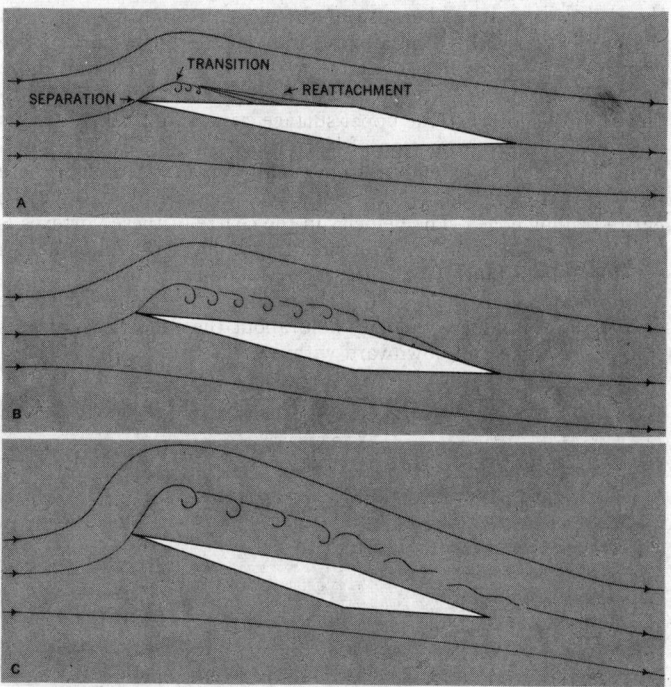

FIG. 8.—SEPARATION ON HIGH-SPEED AIRFOIL WITH SHARP LEADING EDGE: (A) LEADING-EDGE BUBBLE FORMS; (B) BUBBLE ENLARGES WITH INCREASED ANGLE OF ATTACK; (C) LONG-BUBBLE STALL OCCURS WITH FURTHER INCREASE IN ANGLE OF ATTACK

With the first appearance of a shock wave, the lift of the profile tends to drop while the drag starts to rise rapidly. This increase in drag arises partly from the induced separation produced by the shocks, but as the flight speed increases, the major contribution arises from the energy necessary to maintain the shock pattern, the so-called wave drag. As shown by fig. 10, which is a plot of the typical variation of drag coefficient with Mach number for constant values of lift coefficient, the drag coefficient ceases to increase once completely supersonic flow has been achieved. This reflects the steadier nature of the purely supersonic shock patterns.

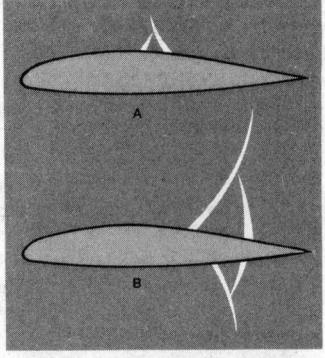

FIG. 9.—SHOCK-WAVE PATTERNS: (A) SHOCK WAVE AS INITIALLY FORMED; (B) SPLIT SHOCK WAVE FORMED AT INCREASED SPEEDS

2. Three-Dimensional Wings.—The preceding discussion has dealt solely with airfoil sections. If the entire wing is considered, still another method of delaying the advent of the drag rise associated with local velocities equal to the speed of sound can be added to the use of thin high-speed sections. This is the utilization of wing sweep as explained in AERODYNAMICS. The importance of sweep decreases as the speed of flight increases to the point at which the component normal to the wing becomes supersonic. Fig. 11 shows the drag coefficient variation of straight, swept and delta wings at various speeds. It will be seen that although there are large differences between the wing types in the region of Mach number one, they become of relatively little significance as the velocity increases beyond Mach two.

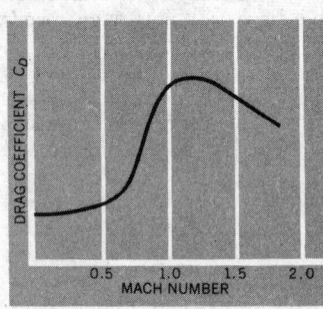

FIG. 10.—VARIATION OF DRAG CO-EFFICIENT WITH MACH NUMBER

One other important difference between the wing section and the entire wing arises because of the existence of wing tips. In the production of lift, the air pressures on the upper surface are negative, i.e., below the freestream static pressure, and those on the lower surface are positive. As a result, the air tends to flow from the lower to the upper surface, as shown in fig. 12. This flow results in the formation of large wing-tip vortexes, horizontal tornado-type flows extending from each wing tip. Although these flows are strongest at the tip, similar vortexes are shed along the entire trailing edge. The velocity in the centre of these vortexes is very high, resulting in low pressures that influence the flow field a considerable distance from the wing. As indicated by fig. 12, one of the major consequences of this trailing vortex pattern is the creation of an induced velocity field about the wing, upward outside of the wake and downward within it.

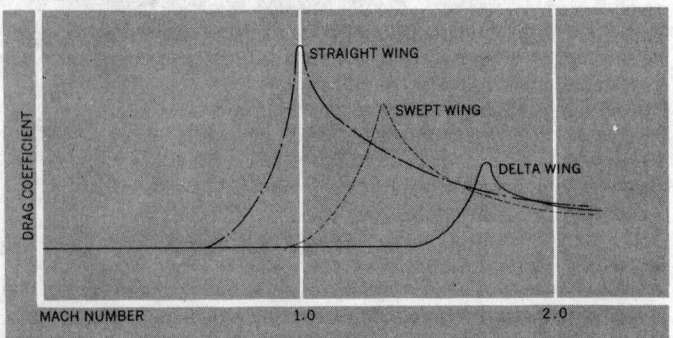

FIG. 11.—VARIATION OF DRAG COEFFICIENT WITH MACH NUMBER FOR THREE WING FORMS

The downward velocities induced at the wing produce an additional component of drag appropriately termed the induced drag and usually indicated by the induced drag coefficient, C_{Di}. The mechanism by which this occurs is demonstrated by fig. 13, which shows how the resultant of the combination of the freestream velocity vector V_1 and the induced velocity or down-wash V_2 at the wing combine to produce an effective change in the angle of attack. As a result of this change in angle, the lift vector of the wing is rotated backward, creating a component of force arising from the lift but oriented like a drag.

By constructing long slender wings, i.e., wings with a high aspect ratio (ratio of span to chord) the effect of the tip vortexes is held remote from the wing sections located on the inboard portions of the span. The induced drag at any given lift coefficient is therefore reduced if the aspect ratio is large.

The shape of the wing and its resultant distribution of pressure along the span also has an effect upon the magnitude of the induced drag. Investigations have shown that a wing planform having an elliptical shape produces a uniform distribution of down-wash along the span, resulting in the minimum induced drag. Because elliptical planforms require both the leading and trailing edges to be curved, modern production practice tends toward accepting the slightly higher induced drag associated with the cheaper and more easily constructed straight leading and trailing edges.

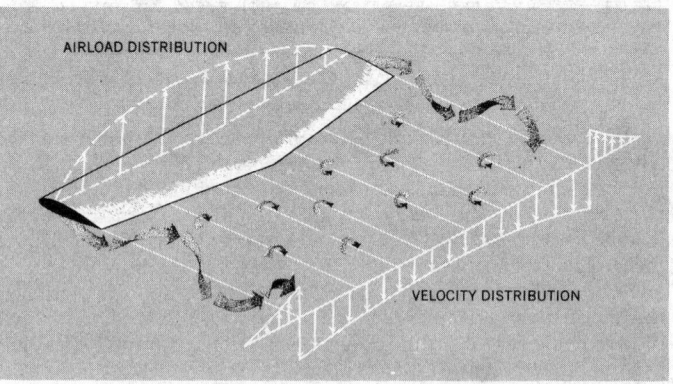

FIG. 12.—VORTEX TURBULENCE PATTERN BEHIND WING

However, use is made of wing taper, i.e., utilizing a tip section that is smaller than the root, so that an elliptical planform is roughly approximated.

3. Bodies of Revolution.—Three-dimensional bodies approximating bodies of revolution in appearance, such as the fuselage and nacelles of an airplane or the body of a missile, are also subject to the four types of drag arising from the skin friction, the pressure distribution, the formation of shock waves and the induced effects resulting from the creation of lift. Because the lift created by the fuselage is small compared to that of the wings, it is generally assumed that the drag contribution arising from the induced drag of the fuselage and nacelles is negligible, and that the total lift of an aircraft arises from the wings.

The design considerations applied to airfoil sections to reduce the skin friction and pressure drags are also applicable to three-dimensional bodies. In order to minimize pressure drag, the body should be designed in a so-called streamline shape to avoid regions of appreciable separation. To reduce skin friction, every precaution must be taken to maintain laminar flow in the boundary layer over as great a portion of the forebody as possible. This includes shaping the body to maintain favourable pressure gradients as far aft as practicable, as well as maintaining at least the forward portions of the body as smooth as possible, using flush rivets, faired windows, etc.

Design Considerations.—To reduce wave drag, it is necessary to produce as little initial disturbance to the flow as possible. This is generally accomplished by the use of a spike- or needle-nose design. In such a design the initial wave created by the spike slightly reduces the velocity downstream of the shock front. The next increase in body diameter downstream of the spike creates another shock wave, but because the velocity is less than freestream, the strength of this second wave is not as great as would be the case if the spike had not previously formed its shock. This procedure persists until the full diameter of the fuselage is achieved.

Studies have shown the drag created by this successive weak-wave generation to be much less than that associated with a single strong shock wave from the bow.

Interference Drag.—The total drag of the complete aircraft is greater than the sum of the drags of its individual components. This is because of the change in the velocity and pressure fields about one element created by the pressure of another. As an example, consider a low wing attached to a fuselage. The high-velocity air passing over the wing will increase the skin friction of the adjacent portions of the fuselage above that which would be created by only the freestream velocity.

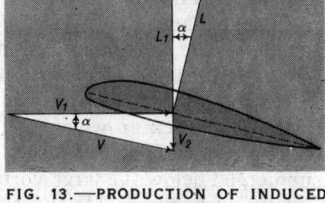

FIG. 13.—PRODUCTION OF INDUCED DRAG C_{D_i} BY ROTATION OF LIFT VECTOR L; V_1, FREESTREAM VELOCITY; V_2, INDUCED VELOCITY; V, RESULTANT VELOCITY; L_1, LIFT PERPENDICULAR TO FREESTREAM; L, LIFT RESULTING FROM PRESENCE OF INDUCED VELOCITY

In addition, the presence of the adverse pressure gradient over the aft portion of the wing may produce local separation in the junction between the wing and fuselage, with a resultant increase in pressure drag. The creation of these interference drags in the subsonic regime has driven designers to develop fairings and fillets to avoid separation areas at the intersection of a lifting surface and a body.

In addition, attempts have been made to reduce the number of such intersections. These attempts have concentrated on tail design, and have given rise to such arrangements as the butterfly tail, in which the conventional horizontal and vertical surfaces are replaced by diagonal surfaces, and the T-tail, in which the horizontal surfaces are removed from the fuselage altogether and placed at the top of the vertical fin.

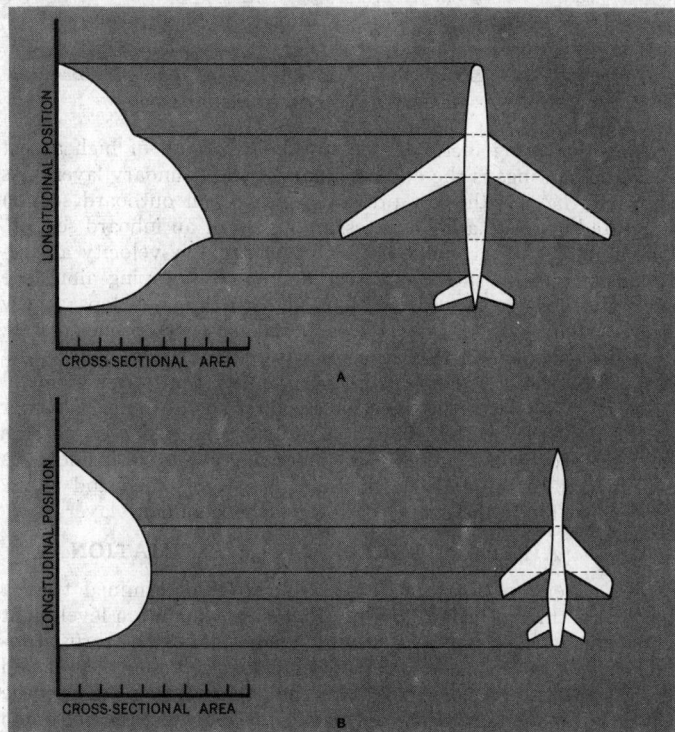

FIG. 14.—REDUCTION OF DRAG BY VARIATION OF TOTAL CROSS-SECTIONAL AREA: (A) CONVENTIONAL SWEPT-WING DESIGN SHOWING ABRUPT CHANGES IN CROSS-SECTIONAL AREA AT POINTS OF ATTACHMENT OF WINGS; (B) AREA CURVE SMOOTHED BY ALTERING FUSELAGE TO "COKE BOTTLE" SHAPE

In the transonic regime, that range of flight speeds in which the velocity field about the aircraft is mixed (in some portions being supersonic and in others subsonic), the interference drags can have a profound influence on the design. It has been found theoretically, and confirmed experimentally, that in this velocity range the aircraft can be considered as an equivalent body of revolution having at each section a cross-sectional area equal to that of the actual aircraft. The drag of such a body of revolution is a function of the rate at which the cross-sectional area varies along the longitudinal axis. If the variation is smooth and steady, the drag is low; if it is abrupt and sudden, the drag is high.

When moving aft on a conventional subsonic airplane, it is found that the variation of cross-sectional area is likely to be smooth until the location at which the wings are attached is reached (fig. 14[A]). At this point an abrupt change is experienced, due to the fact that the cross-sectional area added by the wing is appreciable. The area of outboard nacelles must also be included, and this tends to make the variation even more abrupt. Highly swept wings somewhat alleviate the situation, but to achieve a truly smooth variation of cross-sectional area it is necessary to reduce the fuselage area to compensate for the increase produced by the wing. This gives rise to designs displaying the distinctive "coke bottle" shape shown in fig. 14(B).

Similar considerations also determine the optimum shape for supersonic aircraft, although additional factors must be considered. Under proper conditions, it is possible to utilize shock-wave interactions to reduce interference drags, the higher pressure behind the shock being employed to increase pressures on bodies in favourable locations. In certain supersonic ranges, it is desirable to keep the leading edges of the wings within the shock cone emanating from the nose spike. For this reason many such designs have a canard or tailfirst configuration, the smaller control surface fitting within the narrow confines of the forward part of the cone, the larger wing filling the more ample space further downstream.

4. Minimum Flight Speeds; High-Lift Devices.—For an aircraft to fly in steady level flight, the lift must equal the weight, and the thrust must equal the drag. If the lift is set equal to the weight for a given weight and altitude, the velocity is controlled by the value of C_L. The pilot controls the value of C_L through his longitudinal control system, the elevators. By deflecting these he is able to pitch the aircraft about its centre of gravity, thereby increasing or decreasing the angle of attack, and hence the lift coefficient, at will. It is thus, with the elevators rather than with the throttle, that the pilot controls the speed of his aircraft.

The minimum speed at which flight is possible is determined by the maximum lift coefficient that can be achieved. This, of course, occurs just before the stall. The equation for the minimum speed obtainable in level flight is

$$V_{\min.} = \sqrt{\frac{2\,W/S}{\rho C_{L_{\max.}}}}$$

where W = aircraft weight, S = wing area, ρ = air density and $C_{L\,\max.}$ the greatest value of the lift coefficient obtainable. When applying this expression, it must be remembered that $C_{L\,\max.}$ occurs at a high angle of attack, implying a rather large angle of pitch. If the power plant is producing high thrust under these conditions, an appreciable component of the thrust vector may add to the total lift force. In addition, if the propellers are employed, the slip stream passing over the wings will also result in values of $C_{L\,\max.}$ considerably higher than those obtained in free air, a characteristic that has been extensively employed in the development of short take-off and vertical take-off aircraft.

As the speeds of aircraft have increased, it has become more and more desirable to reduce wing drag by reducing wing area. This means that the wing loading W/S has been increased. Since $C_{L\,\max.}$ is limited by stall, this trend has resulted in the minimum speeds of aircraft, the speeds used for landing and take-off becoming higher. These higher speeds have, in turn, necessitated longer runways. Because the space available for such runways is limited, this trend has also produced a search for methods of increasing $C_{L\max}$.

Trailing-Edge Flaps.—The most common method of increasing $C_{L\max}$ is the deflection of a trailing-edge flap. Although, as shown by fig. 15, there are many varieties of such devices, they all work on the same principle. Deflection of the trailing edge increases the camber or mean line curvature of the profile and thus causes the upper-surface flow velocities to increase. These increased velocities, in turn, produce lower pressures, thereby increasing the lift of the profile.

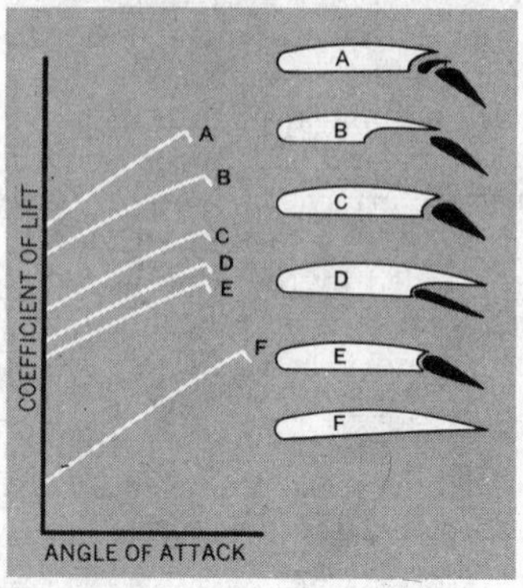

It has been shown that there is an adverse pressure gradient over the after portion of a wing profile. This gradient becomes more severe when the flap is deflected, thereby producing a premature separation before the flow reaches the trailing edge and thus limiting the effectiveness of the flap. To overcome this, the slotted flap was developed. In this design, higher-energy air is led through a slot from the lower surface to the upper surface and blown into the low-energy boundary layer. This arrangement, particularly when a multiple-slot design is employed, has proved very effective.

Because of the success achieved with the slotted flaps, systems have been developed in which the blowing air is supplied at even higher energy levels by using compressed air from a separate blower located within the wing or fuselage (frequently the compressor of a jet engine) which is piped along the wing, ejected through small slots and blown over the flaps. Other systems have been developed which accomplish the same end of energizing the boundary layer by removing the lower-energy air next to the surface by sucking it through slots or holes. This latter arrangement of powered suction has also been used to reduce the skin-friction drag by maintaining the boundary-layer laminar over the entire wing surface. Such arrangements, in which power is supplied to alter the aerodynamics of the boundary layer, are termed boundary-layer control systems.

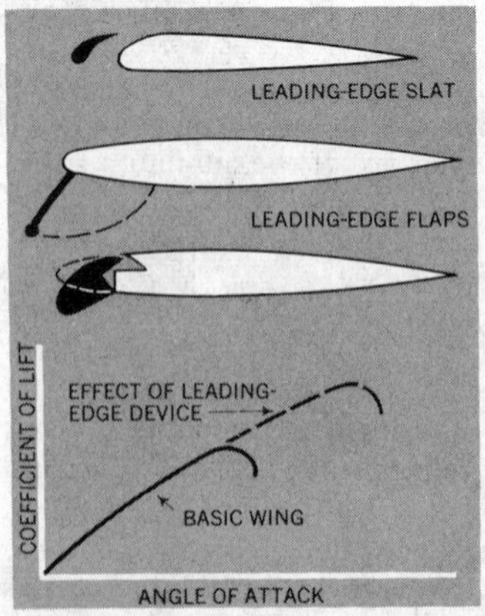

Leading-Edge Slats and Flaps.—Fig. 15 shows that the effect of the flap is to increase the lift coefficient at a given angle of attack. Occasionally it is desirable to extend the lift curve to higher angles of attack. This can be done by means of a slat, as shown in fig. 16. A slat is a small surface, sometimes retractable into the wing, sometimes fixed in place, which serves much the same purpose as the slot of the slotted flap, postponing the stall by energizing the boundary layer with higher-energy air from the lower surface.

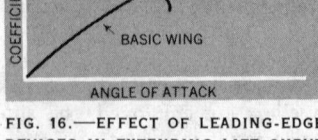

FIG. 15.—EFFECT OF VARIOUS TRAILING-EDGE FLAPS IN INCREASING COEFFICIENT OF LIFT AT GIVEN ANGLES OF ATTACK: (A) DOUBLE-SLOTTED FLAP; (B) FOWLER FLAP; (C) SLOTTED FLAP; (D) SPLIT FLAP; (E) PLAIN FLAP; (F) PLAIN WING

FIG. 16.—EFFECT OF LEADING-EDGE DEVICES IN EXTENDING LIFT CURVE TO HIGHER ANGLES OF ATTACK

The slat is particularly effective for profiles that display leading-edge stalling characteristics, and is frequently used on such profiles in addition to flaps because the flap alone tends to induce premature leading-edge stall. Other devices which are used for this same purpose are termed leading-edge flaps, two examples of which are shown in fig. 16. The primary purpose of these devices is to increase the effective radius of curvature at the leading edge, thereby reducing both the centrifugal forces and the severe pres-sure gradients associated with small leading-edge radii.

5. Effect of Sweepback on Lift.—The use of sweepback has a significant effect on the maximum lift coefficient that can be achieved. Experiments have shown that when a transverse velocity is imposed upon a separation bubble such as that at the leading edge, a vortex results. The spanwise component of the freestream velocity along the swept wing provides the required transverse velocity, and a conical vortex is formed. As the angle of attack increases, the magnitude of the vortex also grows.

If the wing under consideration is of relatively low aspect ratio, it is practically buried under these vortexes. Although the lift coefficient under these circumstances is not great, it is nearly constant; the maximum lift in some cases is not reached until the angle of attack is nearly 40°, and even then the decrease of lift as the angle is increased is slight. On wings of larger aspect ratio, the vortex grows along the leading edge. When the angle of attack is sufficiently large, the wing tips become completely submerged below the large vortexes.

This is an undesirable effect for two reasons. First, it produces thick turbulent flow (in a sense a separated flow) in the region where the lateral control ailerons are customarily located, thereby severely limiting lateral control; for this reason, many swept-wing aircraft have ailerons located well inboard on the span. Second, as the lift on the tips is decreased, the centre of action of the resultant lift vector on each wing panel moves forward, producing a "nose-up moment" or "pitch-up" that is difficult for the pilot to control.

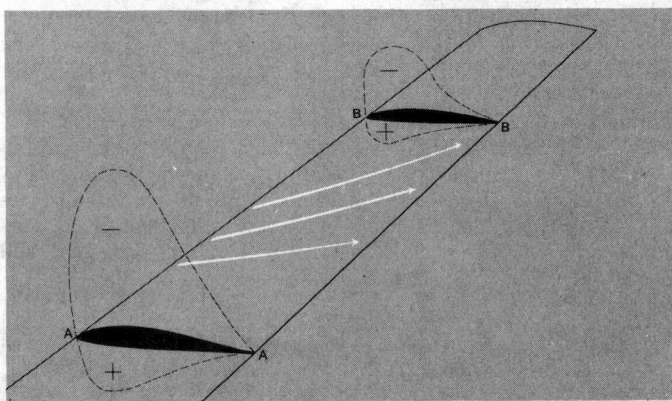

FIG. 17.—SPANWISE FLOW OF BOUNDARY LAYER

An aggravating factor in the so-called tip stall of high aspect ratio swept wings is the outboard flow of the boundary layer. As shown in fig. 17, the low pressure point of an outboard section is located opposite a higher pressure region of an inboard section. The boundary layer, made up of low-energy, low-velocity air, responds readily to such a pressure difference, sweeping along the span and flowing toward the tip. The tip thus develops a very deep low-energy boundary layer and becomes very prone to stall.

It has been found that in some cases this type of flow is decreased by the use of boundary-layer fences, thin strips of metal fastened to the wing in the flowwise direction forming a barrier to the drift of the boundary layer. In other cases, the pressure field created by the presence of underwing-mounted engine pods is sufficient to cause the leading-edge vortex to shed and in the process to block the spanwise flow of the boundary layer.

IV. AIRCRAFT PERFORMANCE ESTIMATION

The general performance of an aircraft is determined from a plot of its thrust (or horsepower) required to maintain level flight versus flight velocity, superimposed upon a plot of the thrust supplied by its power plant. The power plants commonly employed for aircraft propulsion (*q.v.*) are the reciprocating engine; the turbine propeller, or turboprop engine; the turbojet; the pulse jet; the ram jet; and the rocket. The first two, the reciprocating and turboprop engines, are designed primarily for the production of shaft horsepower which is converted into thrust by means of a propeller or rotor. The remainder produce thrust directly by using chemical energy to exhaust a stream of high-velocity gases. It is the momentum of these gases that creates the thrust force. All but the rocket use atmospheric air as their working fluid. The rocket's fuel and oxidizer are both carried within the rocket, thus permitting the production of thrust in the rarefied atmospheres encountered at great altitudes and in space.

The location of the power plants is an important decision for the designer. If propellers are used, there must be sufficient ground clearance, but the landing gear weight should not be excessive. Low- or mid-wing-mounted engines are generally decided upon for multiengine machines, fuselage mounting being usual for single-engine aircraft. To reduce the high drag associated with the slip stream passing over the nacelle or fuselage, rearward-mounted or pusher propellers have been used on some designs. Usually the slight gain in drag reduction is more than offset by the loss in propeller efficiency arising from its operating in the wake of upstream bodies, as well as by the more severe mechanical problems such as engine cooling, etc.

The large air-breathing engines, such as turbojets, must be so located that their performance is not adversely affected by inlet restrictions and obstructions, because much of their ability to produce thrust depends upon achieving appreciable amounts of ram pressure recovery by well-designed inlets and diffusers which slow the flow ahead of the first engine compressor stage. To ensure optimum conditions when the inlet is located next to the fuselage, a diverter plate is used to prevent the fuselage boundary layer from entering the inlet duct. At supersonic speeds, centre bodies, not unlike the spiked-nose body of revolution already discussed as a drag-reduction device, are used to slow the flow with the smallest loss of pressure recovery possible. To maintain optimum conditions at all speeds, the position of these bodies is frequently adjustable.

Mounting such engines within the fuselage can, of course, be accomplished only on relatively special design types such as fighters. The space requirements on other types dictate other mounting locations. Mounting the engines in the wing roots relieves their drag but compromises their performance because of the variable up-wash field which is created as the angle of attack is changed. A location within the fuselage results in high noise levels, and high-temperature jet impingement on other parts of the aircraft downstream of the engine is also a factor that must be considered. Pod mounting below the wing eliminates the flow difficulty and is possibly somewhat safer in the event of violent engine failure, but produces higher drag and creates a control problem should one engine fail. If noise is a problem, as it is for commercial passenger aircraft, a rearward location on the fuselage may be desirable, although the thick fuselage boundary layer may cause a loss in efficiency.

1. Propeller Design Considerations.—A propeller or rotor produces thrust in the same manner as a wing creates lift. A velocity-vector diagram of a typical blade section is shown in fig. 18. The resultant velocity is the summation of the freestream and rotational velocities. The thrust is the summation of the force components parallel to the propeller shaft; the torque is the product of the force components perpendicular to the shaft times the distance from the axis of rotation to the blade element under consideration. Summation of the contributions of each element over the entire disk area gives the total thrust and torque of the propeller.

Because the velocity at each blade section is a function of the radius, the blades are twisted to maintain a reasonable distribution of angle of attack along the span of the blade. Adjustable-pitch propellers are designed to maintain propeller efficiency as the forward velocity changes by giving the pilot control over the pitch angle β (*see* fig. 18). As the forward velocity increases, this angle is increased in such a manner as to keep each section operating close to its maximum value of L/D, the ratio of lift to drag, or, alternatively, to keep the engine rotating at a constant speed.

An additional complication is introduced when there is a velocity component parallel to the plane of rotation, as in the case of a helicopter rotor. The velocity of the forward-moving blade is

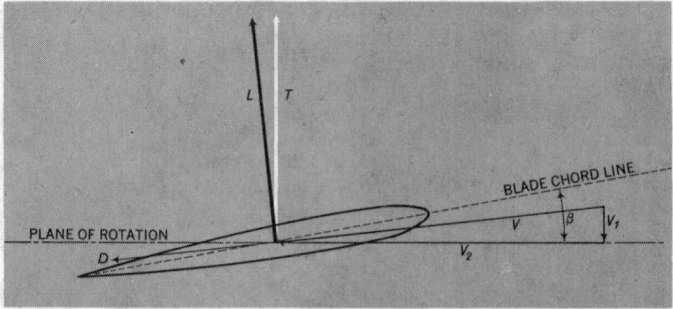

FIG. 18.—VELOCITY-VECTOR DIAGRAM OF SECTION THROUGH A PROPELLER OR ROTOR BLADE: V_1, FREESTREAM VELOCITY; V_2, TANGENTIAL VELOCITY DUE TO ROTATION; V, RESULTANT VELOCITY; β, BLADE PITCH ANGLE; D, DRAG COMPONENT; L, LIFT COMPONENT; T, RESULTANT THRUST

greater than that of the retreating blade, and if the blade is rigid and the angle of attack is not changed mechanically, an imbalance of lift results, the lift on the forward-going blade being considerably greater than that on the retreating blade. The result is a large rolling moment tending to bank the machine. It has been found that the most convenient way to overcome this rolling moment is to hinge the blade at the shaft, thereby moving the point at which the load is transmitted to the aircraft from well out on the blade inboard to the shaft axis.

This, of course, eliminates the rolling moment, but allows the blade to tilt or flap about this hinge under the action of this unbalanced load. The exact arrangement used for tilting the axes depends upon the rotor configuration. It may vary from a seesaw scheme used on two-bladed rotors to individual hinges on multibladed designs, but in all cases the blade is prevented from merely being deflected to an upright position by the magnitude of the centrifugal forces.

The forces required to move the helicopter in any direction are produced by tilting the rotor in that direction. This is achieved by cyclic pitch control, an arrangement whereby the pilot can increase the pitch of the blades over a portion of the rotor disk, causing the blades in that region to flap upward, while decreasing the pitch over that portion of the rotor disk 180° away, causing these blades to flap downward.

2. Thrust Considerations.—Fig. 19 shows the variation of thrust, T, with velocity for various types of power plants. Fig. 20 shows the variation of thrust required to maintain level flight of a typical aircraft, indicating the relative importance of each of the varieties of drag as the flight speed changes. Fig. 21 gives graphs depicting the thrust available from a typical turbojet engine, with a superposed curve of required thrust. The two points of intersection of each set of these curves represent the minimum and maximum velocities at which level flight can be maintained

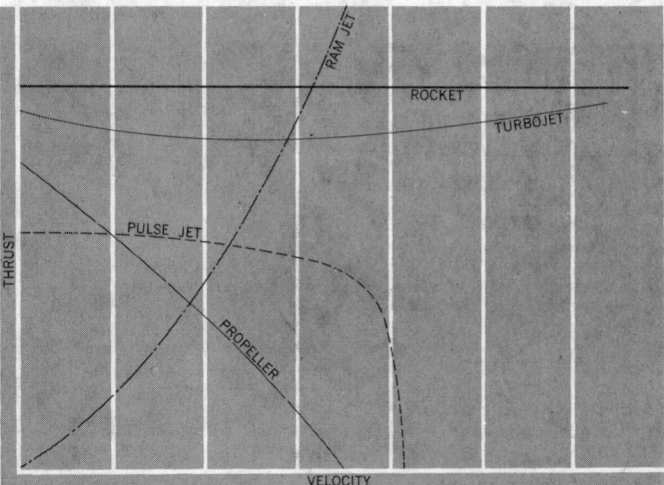

FIG. 19.—EFFECT OF VELOCITY ON AVAILABLE THRUST FOR VARIOUS TYPES OF POWER PLANTS

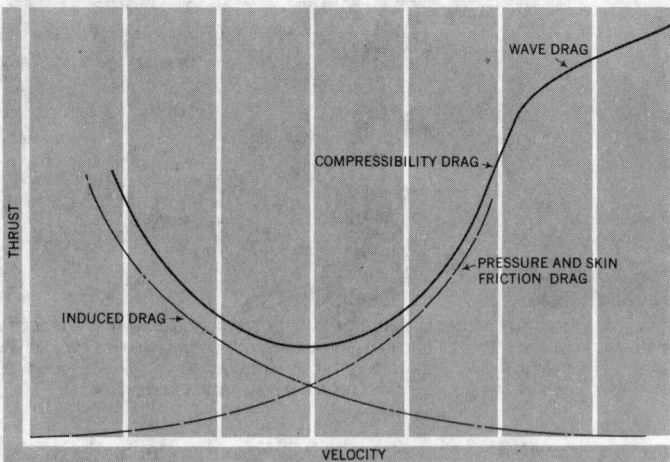

FIG. 20.—EFFECT OF VARIOUS DRAG FACTORS ON THRUST REQUIRED TO MAINTAIN LEVEL FLIGHT AT DIFFERENT VELOCITIES

under the conditions of engine thrust depicted.

Velocities lying to the left of the intersection of the thrust-available and thrust-required curves represent conditions under which level flight is impossible, the power required being greater than the power available. In most cases, it is likely that a factor contributing to the rapid drag rise in this region is the proximity of the stall, a fact which, coupled with the difficulty of control encountered at these low speeds, makes even nonlevel flight in this region dangerous and undesirable. Velocities lying to the right of the intersections at the right side of the graph also lie in a region in which level flight is impossible because the thrust required is greater than the thrust available; in this case, however, higher velocities can be achieved by placing the aircraft in a dive, thereby adding a component of the weight to the thrust available.

Velocities between the intersections of the curves lie in a region in which the thrust available is greater than the thrust required. If a constant lift coefficient is maintained, the excess thrust available causes the aircraft to climb. If the throttle setting is such that there is less thrust available at any given speed than the thrust required for level flight, the rate of sink of the machine can be computed from the deficiency of thrust.

Both the thrust available at a constant throttle setting and the thrust required are affected by a change in altitude, the curve representing the thrust available lowering with increasing altitude and the thrust-required curve moving upward and to the right. As a result, the excess thrust available for producing climb falls off with altitude, lowering the rate of climb. The altitude at which the rate of climb falls to 100 ft. per second is termed the service ceiling, and the altitude at which it falls to zero is called the absolute ceiling.

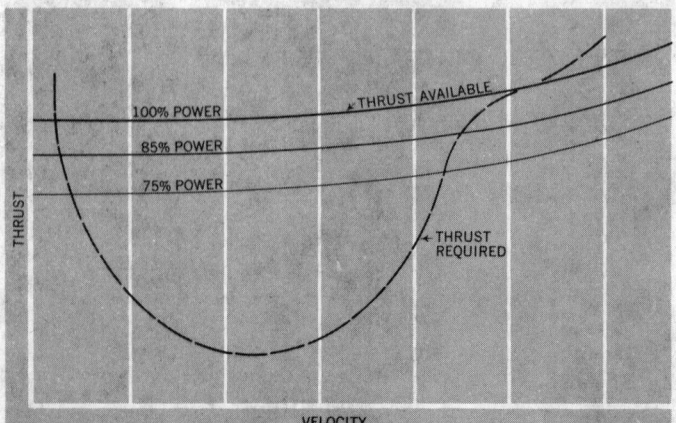

FIG. 21.—THRUST AVAILABLE FROM A TURBOJET ENGINE AT THREE POWER SETTINGS AND THRUST REQUIRED TO MAINTAIN LEVEL FLIGHT AT VARIOUS SPEEDS

3. Range of Flight.—A major performance item that exerts an influence on the design of an aircraft is the range over which it is desired to fly. The factors that contribute to the range are the airframe efficiency, as reflected by its lift-to-drag ratio; the engine efficiency, expressed by the specific fuel consumption, which relates the pounds of thrust produced per unit time to the pounds of fuel consumed; the weight of fuel carried; and the speed at which the flight is conducted.

It was formerly believed that the influence of the lift-to-drag ratio, L/D, which is high at low speeds and falls off with velocity together with the specific fuel consumption, would limit truly long-range aircraft to relatively low speeds. These low speeds correspond to relatively large values of C_L and hence to a large induced drag. To overcome this, high aspect ratios are used and have become a characteristic of long-range transports and bombers. Developments have shown, however, that it is possible to obtain acceptable lift-to-drag ratios at supersonic speeds by making full use of the possibilities of favourable supersonic interference drags. Much the same has proved true of the specific fuel consumption. As a result, it appears that it will be possible to achieve long ranges at supersonic speeds because the increase of speed more than compensates for the loss of airframe and engine efficiency. This is the major reason why the development of supersonic transports is considered both feasible and desirable.

V. AIRCRAFT STABILITY AND CONTROL

Stability may be defined as the ability of a system, when disturbed from its equilibrium position, to create forces and moments that tend to restore equilibrium. The control characteristics include both the aircraft's response to a given control movement and the force required of the pilot to produce such a desired response.

As applied to aircraft, stability can be defined as the machine's tendency to return to a trim speed if it is disturbed. If, for example, the airplane encounters an upward gust of air, its angle of attack will be increased. Because the speed of flight does not change instantaneously, this increment in angle of attack will result in an unbalanced lift force which will start to curve the flight path upward. Both this upward motion and the increase in induced drag will tend to slow the machine below its trim speed. If the airplane is neutrally stable, it will reach a new equilibrium point, but will generate no forces or moments tending either to slow it further or speed it up. If it is unstable, slowing the machine will produce the tendency to slow it more. If it is stable, slowing it will create the forces and moments necessary to speed it up. In a like manner, if the aircraft were inadvertently to increase its speed without a corresponding change in angle of attack, a stable machine would tend to slow down.

If the pitching moment about the centre of gravity is considered, nose-up moments are, by convention, referred to as positive and nose-down moments as negative. To provide stability, a sudden increase in coefficient of lift should produce a nose-down pitching moment, tending to reduce the angle of attack; or it should produce a nose-up pitching moment, should the initial disturbance be a decrease in angle of attack. This means that the change in pitching moment, or of pitching moment coefficient C_m as defined in fig. 22, should be of a sense opposite to the lift coefficient; a decrease in lift, or negative lift increment, should produce a positive or nose-up moment, and a positive lift increment, a nose-down moment.

The major components contributing to the pitching moment of an airplane are the propellers, the fuselage, the wing and the tail. A propeller ahead of the centre of gravity produces a nose-up moment; one behind, a nose-down moment. The contribution of the fuselage is always nose up. The major contribution of the wing arises from the lift vector acting on a lever arm about the centre of gravity; it may be either nose up or down depending upon whether the point of action of the lift force, termed the aerodynamic centre, is ahead or behind the centre of gravity. The magnitude of the wing's contribution varies directly as the distance between these two points.

The greatest nose-down effect comes from the horizontal tail.

Tailless airplanes can, of course, be stable, but this can be achieved only by a careful balance between the location of the aerodynamic centre and the centre of gravity. Not only does this serve to limit severely the amount of travel permitted the centre of gravity, but, in general, these machines are unable to trim out the large moments associated with high-lift devices, such as flaps, etc. If care is taken to avoid the stall, a tailforward, or canard, configuration can also be made stable. A stall of the forward trimmer, however, can produce dangerously severe nose-down pitching moments and must be avoided. A stall of the main lifting surface prior to the stall of the trimmer produces an unstable nose-up moment, and stalling both simultaneously produces a dangerous controlless situation. The canard and tailless configurations are thus used only if the performance gains to be achieved by employing them outweigh their stability disadvantages.

The horizontal tail is so designed that its position and size serve to produce a change in stabilizing moment greater than the destabilizing contribution arising from the change in lift coefficient. Thus stability can be assured about a given equilibrium position. A change in the position of the centre of gravity, by changing the arm between it and the aerodynamic centre, changes the magnitude of the stability contribution of the wing. If the centre of gravity is too far behind the aerodynamic centre, this destabilizing contribution becomes equal to the stabilizing contribution of the horizontal tail, canceling it out and producing neutral stability. The centre-of-gravity position at which this occurs is termed the neutral point and forms the aftmost limit of centre-of-gravity travel, for to go aft of this point will cause the machine to become unstable.

1. Longitudinal Control Systems.—Although, as can be seen from fig. 22, a change in the centre of gravity changes the equilibrium trim point, it does so by changing the slope of the C_m v. C_L curve, the so-called stability level of the aircraft. This is an unsatisfactory system of achieving control, because it produces a change of stability at each speed. For this reason, elevators that are merely controllable trailing-edge flaps located on the horizontal tail are employed. These elevators change the tail lift coefficient, and hence its pitching moment contribution, forcing the machine to pitch about the centre of gravity. This produces a change in angle of attack and lift, resulting in a new equilibrium speed.

The application of such a control deflection, unless the system is completely powered, will require the pilot to exert a control force on the stick. Because this force is required continuously to maintain trimmed equilibrium, it can become most fatiguing. To avoid this, the control surfaces are equipped with small trailing-edge flaps, termed tabs, which the pilot can deflect (in a manner exactly analogous to a wing flap) to produce a small force opposite in direction to that produced by the main control deflection. These forces are small enough so they do not appreciably affect the overall control effectiveness, but being remote from the hinge line they allow the total hinge moment to be reduced to zero, thereby relieving the pilot of the necessity of applying a constant correcting force.

Just as the neutral point forms the after limit on the permissible centre-of-gravity travel, the forward limit is set by the elevator's ability to produce a large enough control force to maintain flight at a speed corresponding to $C_{L\max}$. If the centre of gravity is too far forward, the rate of change of pitching moment with lift coefficient becomes so large that at high values of C_L the elevator cannot create a sufficiently large counteracting moment. The forward limit on the centre-of-gravity travel is set so that the elevator not only can trim out $C_{L\max}$ in flight, but has some reserve power to provide proper control during landing.

Other limits, possibly more severe than the ones described above, restrict the centre-of-gravity travel. These arise from the character of the air loads on the control surfaces and from the necessity of keeping the control forces within certain predetermined bounds, and will not be discussed here. The examples just given serve to demonstrate the extreme importance of designing the machine in such a way that all permissible loading arrangements keep the centre of gravity within well-defined limits.

2. Lateral and Directional Control Systems.—No less important than the longitudinal stability and control of the aircraft are its lateral and directional stability and control characteristics. In this case, there being no large side loads corresponding to the wing lift, the exact location of the centre of gravity is of minor importance. The vertical tail and rudder operate in a manner completely analogous to the horizontal tail and elevator, producing yawing moments tending to force the airplane back to a condition in which the freestream approaches from directly ahead (zero sideslip). The size of the rudder is generally determined by the most severe conditions anticipated for the given design; for example, the need to hold zero sideslip at low speeds on a multiengined aircraft when one engine is inoperable.

Lateral control, *i.e.*, control over the angle of bank or the rate of roll, is achieved by means of ailerons, which are differentially acting flaps located on the trailing edges of the wings. Whereas the rudder is employed to maintain zero sideslip angle, the ailerons are used to bank the airplane, thereby tilting the lift vector and producing a component of lift at right angles to the flight path. It is this component of lift that turns the airplane; the steeper the angle of bank, the steeper the turn.

In the lateral-directional modes of motion, the directional stability, *i.e.*, the ability of the aircraft to return to a condition of zero yaw when disturbed, corresponds to the longitudinal stability level, dC_m/dC_L. This stability is produced by the vertical tail in a manner exactly analogous to the horizontal tail's role in the longitudinal case. There is no equivalent stability laterally, but there is a coupling between sideslip and roll known as the dihedral effect. As a sideslip is produced, the geometry of the aircraft is such that a rolling moment is also produced. If this rolling moment is in such a sense that the forward-going wing is raised, it is said to be a positive dihedral effect.

VI. AIRCRAFT STRUCTURES

Aircraft structural technique differs from structural practices in other fields primarily in the emphasis placed upon weight. In order to minimize weight, extensive testing of sample elements of the aircraft, in many cases to failure, is resorted to in an effort to eliminate all unnecessary structural weight. Because of this extensive testing it is possible to design to much smaller margins of safety than in most other fields. Unlike other structures, for which the maximum anticipated loads are multiplied by a safety factor and the resulting product required to be less than the proportional limit of the material, aircraft design practice merely requires that the maximum anticipated loads shall be less than the proportional limit of the material, and that these loads when multiplied by a safety factor of the order of 1.5 shall be less than

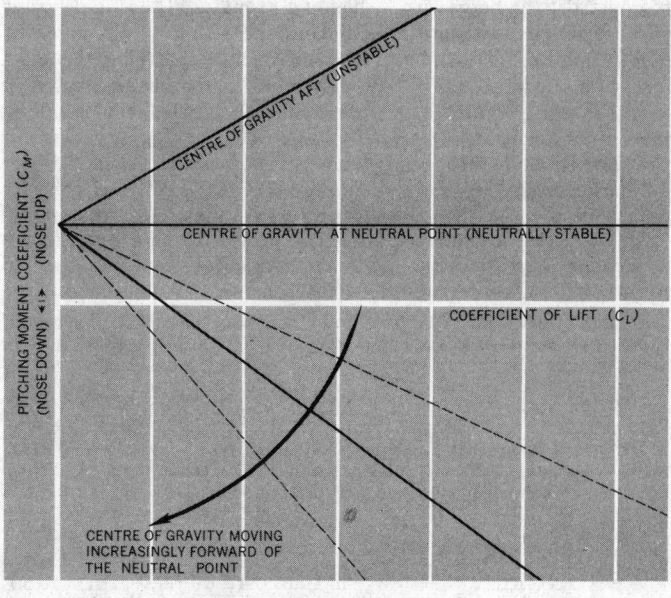

FIG. 22.—STABILITY CRITERIA

the ultimate strength of the material.

1. Wing Design.—The aircraft wing is probably the most difficult structure to design, because of the fact that air loads produce large bending moments while aerodynamic considerations require that the beam carrying these loads be thin, the maximum depth being limited by the maximum thickness of the airfoil section employed. In addition to the lift loads it carries, the wing is also subjected to drag loads in the chordwise direction, and to a torsional load arising from moments created by the basic section and by any high-lift devices that might be employed.

In order for the wing to carry these loads, design techniques have been developed which concentrate the main structural load-carrying members as far from the neutral axis as possible. This means that the skin giving the wing its aerodynamic shape must be highly stressed. To keep it from deforming under load, particularly under compressive loads, use is frequently made of stiffeners or stringers running in the spanwise direction.

Another method which has found considerable application is the use of sandwich construction, in which the material actually withstanding the applied loads is stiffened by a low-density core which might be constructed of balsa wood, plastic or thin aluminum sheets formed into a honeycomb-type structure placed edgewise between the two cover plates. The bond between the core and cover plates may consist of any one of a number of high-strength resins.

Irrespective of the type of construction employed, the designer has to exercise great caution to ensure that the mass distribution of the structure and its elastic constants are adjusted in such a way as to damp any vibrations that might arise from unsteady or vibratory aerodynamic loading. The study of the deformation of the aircraft structure under load comes under the heading of aeroelasticity, and its response to vibration comes under the heading of flutter.

Although the wing is probably the most critical element of an aircraft structure, the same general structural techniques are employed for all other elements, and the search continues both for better materials and for better ways of operating higher-strength structures.

2. Temperature Considerations.—Another problem which has become of increasing importance as the speeds of aircraft have become higher is that of temperature. The temperatures associated with the very high energies dissipated during re-entry of a missile are frequently above the melting point of most materials. Even the temperatures associated with the leading edge of airplanes in supersonic flight are high enough to reduce severely the strength characteristics of the structural materials.

Three methods have been used to overcome the temperature problem. For certain missile re-entry applications, it is possible to construct the body with a shielding of material that is designed to absorb the heat generated during the re-entry maneuver by merely melting or burning away the shielding, leaving the main structure undamaged. In cases where such an approach would be unsatisfactory, efforts have been made to combat the temperature by utilizing cooling systems such as bleeding water under pressure through the leading edge and absorbing the excess heat by converting it to steam. At lower speeds, merely switching to temperature-resistant materials, such as stainless steel or titanium or even certain aluminum alloys, has proved to be a satisfactory approach. *See* AIRCRAFT INSTRUMENTS; ROCKETS AND GUIDED MISSILES; and references under "Aeronautics" in the Index.

BIBLIOGRAPHY.—I. H. Abbott and A. E. von Doenhoff, *Theory of Wing Sections: Including a Summary of Airfoil Data* (1949); A. F. Donovan and H. R. Lawrence (eds.), *Aerodynamic Components of Aircraft at High Speeds* (1957); A. F. Donovan *et al.* (eds.), *High Speed Problems of Aircraft and Experimental Methods* (1960); H. W. Liepmann and A. Roshko, *Elements of Gasdynamics* (1957); R. von Mises *et al.*, *Theory of Flight* (1945); L. E. Neville, *Aircraft Designers' Data Book* (1950); A. S. Niles and J. S. Newell, *Airplane Structures,* vol. 1, 4th ed. (1954), vol. 2, 3rd ed. (1943); D. J. Peery, *Aircraft Structures* (1950); C. D. Perkins and R. H. Hage, *Airplane Performance Stability and Control* (1949); H. Schlichting, *Boundary Layer Theory* (1955).   (D. C. HA.)

AERONOMY, the study of that part of the earth's atmosphere in which ionization and dissociation are important phenom-

ena; *i.e.*, the part above about 20 mi. The word gained in usage after 1954 when it was incorporated in the name of the International Association of Geomagnetism and Aeronomy. It has been justified as a science distinct from conventional meteorology because it involves techniques of astrophysics, physics, chemistry, radio propagation and rocket and missile technology as well as meteorology.

See also ATMOSPHERE; IONOSPHERE.   (H. R. B.)

AEROPLANE: *see* AIRPLANE.

AEROSOL, a system of very finely subdivided liquid or solid particles dispersed in and surrounded by a gas. The earth's atmosphere, in which minute particles of many kinds are suspended, is an aerosol. In common parlance, however, an aerosol denotes a product dispensed from a pressurized container. Food products are pressurized with a compressed gas such as nitrous oxide or carbon dioxide. Nonfood products are generally packed with a propellant gas, usually a fluoro-hydrocarbon, in two-phase or three-phase systems.

In a two-phase system, the propellant gas in liquid form is mixed with a product, such as an insecticide or room deodorant. Released to the atmosphere, the liquid propellant vaporizes, causing the product to disperse in minute particles. Such dispersions in space are true aerosols. However, increasing the quantity of the product to between 20% and 75% of the total content produces a spray of material on a surface.

In a three-phase system, the product is contained between a layer of vaporized propellant occupying the top, or head space, of the dispenser, and a layer of liquid gas propellant at the bottom. When the actuating button is pressed, vapour pressure in the head space forces the product up the dip-tube and out the valve. The increase in head space resulting from the loss of product is filled by vaporization of the liquid gas. Powders and foams are pressurized in three-phase systems. In foam packs, however, the liquid propellant and the product, such as a shaving cream, are present as an emulsion. Upon reaching the atmosphere, the liquid gas immediately vaporizes, whipping the whole into a foam.

See AGRICULTURE: *United States;* BACTERIA; MOSQUITO: *Control Measures.*   (E. L. Y.)

AERSENS (AERSSEN), **FRANÇOIS VAN** (1572–1641), Dutch statesman influential in his country's foreign affairs in the later phases of the war of independence against Spain, was born in Brussels, in the Spanish Netherlands, but went with his parents to the United Provinces. Educated at Leiden university, he was sent in 1598 to be the agent of the states-general at the court of France, where he was subsequently accredited ambassador. He favoured Johan van Oldenbarnevelt's policies until 1607, but supported Prince Maurice of Nassau in his fruitless opposition to the signing of the Twelve Years' truce in 1609. His position in France became so difficult after the death of Henry IV (1610) that he was recalled in 1613. He sided with Prince Maurice against Oldenbarnevelt in the bitter struggle which led to the latter's execution in 1619. Thereafter as a member of the states of Holland and of their delegation to the states-general he exercised a decisive influence on foreign policy, and was instrumental in concluding the Franco-Dutch treaty of 1635. He also took part in the negotiations for the marriage of William II of Orange and Mary Stuart (1641).

He died at The Hague on Dec. 27, 1641.   (E. H. K.)

AERTSEN (AERTSZEN, AARTSEN), **PIETER** (1508?–1575), Dutch painter, known for his meticulous renderings of still life and genre, was called "long Peter" because of his height. He was born and died at Amsterdam. When a youth he distinguished himself by painting homely scenes, in which he reproduced articles of furniture, cooking utensils, etc., with marvelous fidelity. An excellent specimen of his style on a small scale, a picture of the Crucifixion, is in the Antwerp museum. Aertsen was a member of the Academy of St. Luke, in the books of which he is entered as *Langhe Peter, schilder.* Three of his sons attained to some note as painters.

AESACUS, a Trojan seer, son of Priam. He learned the interpretation of dreams from his grandfather Merops, by which he foretold that Paris would cause the destruction of Troy and argued that the infant be exposed (which was unsuccessful). He committed suicide by jumping into the sea, grieving for the death of his wife, but Thetis changed him into a diving bird.

(T. V. B.)

AESCHINES (5th–4th century B.C.), Athenian writer of Socratic dialogues which were praised for their authentic portrait of Socrates, came from the Athenian deme of Sphettus and was still a boy or young man at the time of Socrates' death, at which he was present (Plato, *Apology,* 33 e; *Phaedo,* 59 b). After an interval into which presumably the composition of his dialogues falls, he was attracted to Syracuse (c. 368–356 B.C.) by the temporary enthusiasm of Dionysius II for philosophy. He gained his livelihood by teaching rhetoric and writing speeches.

Of the dialogues passing under his name, seven were singled out by ancient critics as genuine; these were entitled *Miltiades, Callias, Axiochus, Aspasia, Alcibiades, Telauges* and *Rhinon.* At least four of them were in the form of a reported dialogue, with Socrates himself as the narrator (a form perhaps imitated from Plato). The titles confirm the impression given by Plato that Socrates consorted on terms of familiarity with Athenians of high rank and members of the Periclean circle. Aeschines seems to have agreed with Plato rather than with Xenophon in his presentation of Socrates' tenets and manner of life. But the extant fragments are so scanty that any attempt to reconstruct the dramatic situation or argument of his dialogues is conjectural.

See Diogenes Laertius, ii, 60–64; editions of the fragments of the dialogues by H. Krauss (1911) and by H. Dittmar (1912); and A. E. Taylor, *Philosophical Studies,* ch. i (1934). (D. J. A.)

AESCHINES (389–c. 314 B.C.), Athenian orator who advocated peace with Philip II of Macedonia and was a bitter political opponent of Demosthenes (q.v.). His father Atrometus lost his property during the Peloponnesian War, and Aeschines was brought up in humble circumstances. During his early career he held minor posts in the state service and was a professional tragic actor. He is first heard of as prominent in public life in 348 B.C., when he served on a mission sent by the Athenians to Arcadia. Two years later he, like Demosthenes, was a member of the embassies to Philip II of Macedonia which resulted in the peace of Philocrates (see GREECE: *History*). During the negotiations he changed his policy in favour of Macedonia, and after the peace had been concluded Demosthenes together with a certain Timarchus prepared to prosecute him for treason. He retaliated by successfully indicting Timarchus for gross immorality. Aeschines' trial took place in 343 B.C., when he was acquitted by a narrow majority.

In 339 B.C., by provoking the Amphictyonic council to declare a sacred war against the Locrians of Amphissa, Aeschines enabled Philip to enter central Greece as champion of the Amphictyonic forces. The bitter hostility between Aeschines and Demosthenes culminated in the years following the defeat of Athens and Boeotia at Chaeronea. In 336 B.C. Aeschines brought an action against a certain Ctesiphon for illegally proposing the award of a crown to Demosthenes in recognition of his services to Athens. The case was not heard until 330 B.C., when Aeschines was overwhelmingly defeated, largely, no doubt, because of Demosthenes' brilliant speech for Ctesiphon ("On the Crown"). He left Athens for Rhodes, where he is said to have taught rhetoric.

Aeschines was a political opportunist rather than a statesman. His own speeches suggest that he had little understanding of Philip's intentions or the wider implications of the struggle with Macedonia. There is, however, no evidence to support Demosthenes' accusation that he was a paid agent of Philip.

Three speeches by Aeschines are extant: (1) in accusation of Timarchus; (2) in defense of his own conduct on the embassies to Philip; and (3) in accusation of Ctesiphon. These appear to have been the only speeches which he wrote, as opposed to those which he delivered extempore. They show a tendency to superlative expression and exaggeration, free use of rhetorical figures, variety of sentence construction, fondness for poetical quotations and ready wit. As a literary stylist he has imperfections, although there are fine passages. The effectiveness of his oratory was enhanced by his impressive voice and dignified bearing.

There are editions of the speeches by F. Blass, 2nd ed. in the "Teubner Series" (1908); by C. D. Adams with Eng. trans. in the "Loeb Series" (1919); and by V. Martin and G. de Budé with French trans., 2 vol. in the "Budé Series" (1927–28). (H. L. H.-W.)

AESCHYLUS (?525–456 B.C.), the earliest and perhaps the greatest Greek tragic poet of whom completed plays have survived. Without abandoning the lyrical and ritual character which can be assumed for early tragedy, he added the second actor (according to Aristotle), developed the possibilities of dialogue and pioneered the characteristic forms of the 5th century. The first-known writer to express in dramatic form that vision of life which is recognized as "tragic," he may well merit Gilbert Murray's description of him as "the creator of tragedy."

Life.—Son of Euphorion, a landowner of aristocratic family, Aeschylus was born at Eleusis in Attica. The known facts of his life are few. He fought at Marathon, where his brother Cynegirus fell; and in his own epitaph, which he probably wrote himself, Marathon is mentioned to the exclusion of his poetic achievements. He doubtless fought at Salamis, a battle brilliantly described in his *Persae,* and perhaps also at Plataea. In his poetry the miseries of war are more prominent than its glories, though both were known to the full by his generation. Between 472 and 468 he visited the court of Hiero I at Syracuse, where he is said to have revived the *Persae* and to have produced in honour of the newly founded city of Aetna a play (*Aetnae* or *Aetnaeae*), part of the argument of which may be preserved on a papyrus. He revisited Sicily in 458 or later, and died there at Gela in 456. It is possible that among the western Greeks he became acquainted with the philosophy of Pythagoras. But this influence has not been demonstrated, nor has that of the famous mysteries at Eleusis, his birthplace. It is related on fair authority that, when he was accused of having violated their secrecy, he pleaded successfully that he had done so without knowledge. If in fact he was initiated, it seems unlikely that his thought was greatly affected by ceremonies mainly concerned with the life after death, a theme not prominent in his plays.

Plays.—Aeschylus won his first victory in 484, and was victorious not less than 13 times. The figure of 28, also given, may include victories won after his death, when he was granted the unique honour that his plays might be revived in subsequent competitions. One authority puts the number of his plays at 90, including satyr plays as well as tragedies; about 80 titles are known. Seven tragedies only have survived entire.

The *Persae* was produced in 472; the *Septem contra Thebas* (Gr. *Hepta epi Thebas,* "Seven Against Thebes") in 467; the *Agamemnon,* the *Choephori* ("Libation bearers") and the *Eumenides,* which together constitute the trilogy of the *Oresteia,* in 458. The dates of the other surviving plays are unknown. Most scholars are now inclined to place the *Prometheus Vinctus* (Gr. *Prometheus desmotes,* "Prometheus Bound") late. The *Supplices* (Gr. *Hiketides,* "Suppliant Women"), because of archaic features in its technique, was generally regarded as the earliest extant play, until the publication in 1952 of a fragmentary argument on papyrus which implies that the trilogy of which the *Supplices* formed part was produced in competition with Sophocles, who first competed in 468; there is an indication that 463 may be the date. Though doubts still remain, it can no longer be assumed that this is an early play. There is thus no certain knowledge of the early work of Aeschylus.

Persae.—This play is unique in two important respects. (1) Each competing poet was required to produce three tragedies and a satyr play. It was evidently the practice of Aeschylus, at least in his later period, to link his three tragedies closely in subject matter and treatment—to write, that is to say, trilogies or (including the satyr play, which took its subject from a related myth) tetralogies. The trilogy, which may have been his own invention, enabled him to transcend the temporal limits imposed on each single play by the chorus, to achieve a grand architecture and to explore the problems of human destiny upon an extended scale. How he handled this form at the height of his powers can be seen in the *Oresteia.* The *Septem,* the *Supplices* and the *Prometheus* all formed part of trilogies; and various lost tragedies can be grouped together in this way. But between the tragedies of 472—(asterisk indicates a lost play) *Phineus**, *Persae*, *Glaucus Potnieus**—there is no obvious link of any kind. (2) The *Persae* is the only extant Greek tragedy on a theme taken from contemporary history. Phrynichus had produced his *Miletou halosis** ("Capture of Miletus") about 493; his *Phoenissae** of 476 (?) had dealt with the defeat of Xerxes at Salamis, and it was to this theme that Aeschylus returned in 472.

Aeschylus treats his historical subject with some freedom; and patriotic exultation takes second place to a broad religious view. The action is of archaic simplicity. The play opens with the chorus of Persian councilors. Concerned that no news has come from the great expedition, they declaim and sing for 150 lines before the entry of the first character—the mother of Xerxes. She tells them of an ominous dream. A messenger brings news of the disaster of Salamis. The return of the humiliated Xerxes and the lamentations between king and chorus with which the play ends are delayed, while the spirit of the dead Darius is evoked from his tomb. The use by Aeschylus of overwhelming spectacular effects was noted by ancient critics. Such an effect is the evocation of Darius, but it is not used for mere sensation: Darius is central to the play, for it is his function to expound the moral order of Zeus and so give meaning to the events.

Septem contra Thebas.—This play was the third of a trilogy dealing with the well-known legend of Laius, Oedipus and his sons. It is uncertain how the earlier events were distributed between the first two plays, *Laius** and *Oedipus**, but, clearly, after Laius had disobeyed the oracle and begotten a son, the family had been doomed and the city endangered. When the *Septem* opens, Oedipus is dead; Thebes is besieged by an army of Argives come to place Polyneices on the throne; his brother Eteocles leads the defenders. The action is again extremely simple, but, unlike the *Persae* (and the *Supplices*), the play opens with a prologue scene. This difference in technique may be connected with the fact that, whereas in the *Persae* there is little interest in individual personages as such, the dramatic issues are here focused upon Eteocles, both "captain of the ship of state" and son of Oedipus, whose decision to fight his brother is the climax of the play. It is to this decision that the earlier scenes lead up. When the chorus of frightened women break in tumultuously, Eteocles, to calm their fears, promises to fight as one of the seven champions at the gates; and at the seventh gate he is to meet his brother in fratricidal combat. Toward this combat dramatic tension is built up in the most striking—and archaic—scene of the play. In seven pairs of speeches, a scout describes the enemy champions and Eteocles posts a defender against each. But at the seventh gate the foe will be no Argive, but the Theban Polyneices. Eteocles recognizes the fulfillment of the curse of Oedipus, that his sons should divide their inheritance with the sword. Soon the messenger reports that the brothers have killed one another, but the city has been saved. (There is grave doubt whether the end of the play in the extant text is genuine; most scholars think that the decree forbidding the burial of Polyneices has been imported for a revival subsequent to the *Antigone* of Sophocles.)

Supplices.—Of the Danaid trilogy the first play alone is extant. The archaic features which led to belief in its early date are evident. The play opens, like the *Persae*, with the chorus, to which well over half the lines belong. The dramatic interest is in their fate, and the dramatic tension is largely generated through their songs. They are the 50 daughters of Danaüs, who have fled with their father from Egypt to Argos, home of their ancestors, to escape a hated marriage with their cousins, the sons of Aegyptus. They appeal for protection to the king of Argos, who is confronted with a dilemma: war, if he protects them, or the wrath of Zeus, if he rejects the suppliants. He decides to commend their case to the people of Argos, who have the final word. This word is favourable, but a herald lands from the Egyptian fleet and with barbarous violence seeks to drag the suppliants from the altars at which they have taken refuge. They are saved by the king; and the play ends with the Danaids and their handmaidens on the way to safe quarters in Argos, the Danaids singing to Artemis, their handmaidens (surprisingly) to Aphrodite. The *Supplices* was followed by the

Aegyptii* and *Danaides**. It is probable that after a battle in which the king was killed the city was besieged. It is certain that the Danaids were given as brides to their cousins, but on the counsel of Danaüs slew their husbands on the wedding night, with the exception of Hypermestra, who spared Lynceus and by him became the ancestress of the Argive kings. In the *Danaides**, Aphrodite appeared, proclaimed her universal power, justified Hypermestra and (it may be) reconciled her sisters to the state of marriage.

Prometheus Vinctus.—Prometheus, who in defiance of Zeus has saved mankind by the gift of fire, is riveted to a Caucasian rock. There he is visited by the chorus of ocean nymphs, by their father Oceanus, by the "cow-headed" Io (another victim of Zeus) and finally by Hermes, who vainly demands from him his knowledge of a secret threatening the power of Zeus. At the end of the play Prometheus sinks into Tartarus for further torture. A motionless hero, and a minimum of action; much of the play is taken up with long expository speeches, as he recounts to the chorus his services to mankind or prophesies to Io her future wanderings (there is a strong geographical interest in Aeschylus) and her glorious destiny. The drama resides in the clash between the irresistible power of Zeus and the immovable will of Prometheus, rendered more stubborn still by Io's story. It has been doubted whether this is the first or second play of a trilogy, though the former is more likely, and whether the trilogy was ever completed, though this play was certainly followed by the *Prometheus lyomenos* ("The Loosing of Prometheus") and perhaps by the *Prometheus pyrphoros* ("Prometheus the firebearer"). (Few have accepted the view, advanced on stylistic and other grounds, that Aeschylus was not the author of the play.) It appears that in the sequel Heracles, descended from Io, shot the eagle that feasted on the liver of Prometheus and loosed him from his bonds. Zeus and Prometheus must have been reconciled, but it is not known how this was achieved, nor how Aeschylus developed the most controversial feature of the *Prometheus Vinctus*—that Zeus is there presented as a tyrant.

Oresteia.—This trilogy deals with the criminal history of the house of Atreus. In the *Agamemnon* the conqueror of Troy returns to Argos to be killed by his wife Clytemnestra in vengeance for the sacrifice of their daughter Iphigenia before the Trojan war. In the *Choephori* his son Orestes avenges his father by an act of matricide. In the *Eumenides* Orestes is pursued by the furies (Erinyes) of his mother, first to Delphi, where he is purified by Apollo, then to Athens, where he is acquitted before the court of the Areopagus. (Such a change of scene is uncommon in Greek tragedy.) The trilogy forms a single artistic whole unified by the themes which run throughout its length, but each play has its own dramatic action, its own tone and character.

The *Agamemnon* is the most complex, as it is the longest, of the plays of Aeschylus. It is complex in exposition; and, as facts and implications are gradually revealed through the speeches of the watchman, of Clytemnestra, of the herald and above all through the songs of the chorus of elders, so foreboding accumulates, up to and beyond the entry of Agamemnon. Though Aeschylus now has three actors at his disposal, he is still using in the main an old technique. The choral odes bulk large; scenes are often between one actor and the chorus; genuine dialogue is rare—the greater, therefore, the effect when Clytemnestra persuades her husband to enter the palace treading on scarlet draperies. In no scene are there three speaking parts; Cassandra the prophetess is silent while Clytemnestra and Agamemnon are on the stage. Alone with the chorus, she weaves past, present and future into a single fabric, as the poet weaves them in his trilogy: it is the masterstroke of Aeschylus. But the play is dominated by Clytemnestra. Characterization in Aeschylus is and remains austerely limited, but he can now place a person vividly in the centre of the stage with a power that foreshadows Sophocles. Minor characters are now naturally portrayed: the watchman, the herald—and the nurse in the *Choephori*.

The *Choephori* contains a recognition and an intrigue: Electra recognizes her brother Orestes on his return from exile, and with him plots the deaths of Aegisthus and Clytemnestra. The action moves more rapidly, and the old nurse of Orestes is used to make it go forward. But, compared with the wide horizons of the *Agamemnon* (which embrace the sack of Troy), the interest is sombrely concentrated upon the theme of vengeance through matricide. The most elaborate and impressive feature in the play is lyrical, when son and daughter join with the chorus of palace slaves in invoking the aid of the dead Agamemnon from the earth.

The *Eumenides* is a play of gods; even the chorus is divine. It is a play of brilliant variety and scenic effect: at Delphi, where Orestes is disclosed in the shrine of Apollo surrounded by sleeping furies; at Athens, when the furies dance round Orestes and sing their binding song, when Athena empanels the Areopagus and Apollo enters to conduct his defense. After Orestes has gone free, Athena persuades the furies to accept worship at Athens, and the play ends with a procession, as, scarlet-robed and singing good songs, they are escorted by torchlight to their new home in the rock.

Staging.—Apart from the *Oresteia*, no play certainly demands a substantial edifice in the background. Visual attention was then concentrated upon costume and grouping, upon the chorus in the orchestra, for whom Aeschylus devised new dance movements. There were often large numbers to be deployed in and behind the dance floor, when supplementary choruses, as in the *Supplices* and the *Eumenides*, and other supernumeraries, were employed. The *Oresteia*, however, not only requires a solid structure in the background to represent palace and temple fronts, but Aeschylus there seems to have used the *eccyclema* or wheeled platform to expose an indoor scene. His use of other stage devices, *e.g.*, the crane, particularly concerns the staging of the *Prometheus*, on which there is little agreement.

Style and Structure.—Aeschylus can write with great simplicity, and to humbler characters he sometimes gives colloquial turns of speech. But in general his style, both in lyric and dialogue, is grand. His vocabulary owes much to his epic and lyric predecessors, though he was doubtless a bold innovator in his own right, particularly in the coinage of those compound epithets which are characteristic of his diction. But the richness of his style is seldom, if ever, used for mere decoration, the firm dramatic control being most evident in his later work. In the bold use of metaphor Aeschylus has no peer but Pindar. While he can elaborate a single figure, he does not hesitate to combine different metaphors and may sometimes be felt to have strained figurative language almost to its breaking point.

It is characteristic of Aeschylus to sustain an image or images throughout a play: the ship of state in the *Septem*, the birds of prey in the *Supplices*, the snare in the *Agamemnon*. Such sustained images perform a structural function, but are only a special case of a more general aspect of his art, which is the deployment throughout a play or trilogy of leading themes, often associated with a particular word or group of words. In the *Oresteia*, for instance, such themes as wrath, mastery, persuasion and the contrasts of light and darkness, dirge and triumph song, run throughout the trilogy. Another point of style and structure is the use of symmetry and correspondences. A minor aspect of this artistic method shows itself in the way that speeches, odes and scenes constantly recur at the end to a word or theme from the beginning (sometimes called ring composition). But major symmetries are visible in the shaping of whole plays. In the *Persae*, themes from the earlier part of the play recur toward the close with the effect of isolating the Darius scene (from which they have been absent) and establishing its dominance in the thought structure of the play. The same pattern of action and emotion is repeated from the *Agamemnon* to the *Choephori;* and there is reason to suppose that a similar correspondence existed between the *Prometheus* and its sequel. Such principles of construction have been traced in Homer and, thanks to Pindar, can be inferred for the earlier lyric poetry: they are wholly consonant with the sense of form which the Greeks displayed in their visual art. The appreciation of them is a valuable aid in the interpretation of the dramatic thought of Aeschylus.

Dramatic Conceptions.—Aeschylean tragedy deals with the plight, decisions and fate of individuals, but the destiny of the community is also at stake; both individual and community stand in close relation to the gods. Personal, social and religious issues are integrated, as they still were in the Greek civilization of the poet's day.

The concern of Aeschylus with the events of his own time is most obvious in the *Persae*, where he interprets a contemporary event as though it were myth. In dealing with the mythical subject matter of the *Oresteia*, he is not without thought for the political circumstances of his own day. That he hints in passing at a recent alliance between Athens and Argos is a minor matter: more important is the establishment of the Areopagus as a court to try cases of homicide. To this function the ancient council had been all but confined by the democratic reforms of 462; in dignifying it Aeschylus may well be accepting and commending the new order in the state. But if so it was not mere propaganda; murder and feud might be incidents in political strife, and it was essential that the state should control the punishment of homicide—a primary issue of the trilogy. Again, it was in the lifetime of Aeschylus that the reforms of Cleisthenes had sought to reduce the political power of the clans; and it has been plausibly suggested that the Theban trilogy dramatizes the disentanglement of the fortunes of clan and state, the guilty family being annihilated without bringing ruin on the city.

A different social question occupies the mind of Aeschylus both in the Danaid trilogy and in the *Oresteia:* marriage, and the right relationship of man and woman in society. This issue arises naturally out of the myth in the former trilogy; it is given stress in the *Oresteia* by the portrayal of Clytemnestra as a woman of manly and dominating character. It is hard to believe that Aeschylus treated this theme without thought of the social conditions of his time. To later generations he has often seemed to deal in a remote and awful way with the problems of theodicy in terms of strange and even barbaric myths. But, though the myths provided him with symbols, his thought was firmly rooted in his own experience of life, which for him as a Greek was political and social life. The gods were still at work in the world he knew; and to him a contemporary reference would in no way detract from the solemnity of his tragedy.

Theodicy, the justifying of God's ways to men, which was the concern of Milton, was in some sense also the concern of Aeschylus, though it might be truer to say that he aimed through dramatic conflict to throw light on the nature of divine justice. The Greeks had pondered much upon the operations of the gods. Though Homer had established the Olympian family with clear anthropomorphism, popular belief tended to think of divinity in vaguer terms; but in either case it was power rather than goodness that characterized the divine. It was commonly believed that the gods grudged human greatness, sent infatuation upon a man at the height of his success and so brought him to disaster. But his infatuated act was one of impiety or pride (Gr. *hubris*), for which his downfall could be seen as a just punishment. Thus the jealousy and the justice of heaven fought a battle in the Greek mind. The more articulate thinkers wrestled with this problem. Hesiod saw in Zeus, supreme among the gods, the guardian of a just moral order. But the unjust are not always punished in their lifetime: it is upon their descendants, according to Solon, that the punishment may fall. Aeschylus received a tradition of thought from Hesiod and Solon—belief in a just Zeus and in hereditary guilt. The simplest case is that of Xerxes and his Persians, who, as Darius says, were punished for their own offences. (*Persae*, 827 ff.) But in the *Agamemnon*, where the chorus explicitly rejects the doctrine of divine jealousy (750 ff.), Agamemnon is punished not only, through Clytemnestra, for his own slaying of Iphigenia, but also, through Aegisthus, for the sin of his father Atreus at the Thyestean banquet. Guilt haunts the house; and in the next phase Orestes, who kills his mother to avenge his father, is the sinner-victim, saved only at the last by divine interposition.

That divine justice punishes pride and impiety is certain for Aeschylus, but is not the end of the matter. Troy was punished for the sin of Paris, but the innocent suffered with the guilty; Iphigenia died as the inescapable preliminary to an act of justice. As for such a sinner as Eteocles or Agamemnon, how can he be responsible, if he is not free? How can he be free, if he is bound by evil heredity and divine compulsions? How can he be justly punished, if he is not responsible? Early Greek thought had hardly clarified these issues; and the opinions of interpreters differ as to the insight with which they are handled by Aeschylus. To some it seems that he has envisaged with clarity and presented with power contradictions which still baffle the human intellect. The nearest perhaps that he comes to a formulation is when the chorus of the *Agamemnon* (1505 ff.) refuse to allow that Clytemnestra is without responsibility, while admitting that the avenging spirit of the crime of Atreus may be lending her his aid. Human action is both responsible and determined; and the same action can, as in Homer, be seen on two planes, divine and human. The divine justice uses human motives to carry out its decrees: among these motives is the desire for vengeance, basic to the ancient Greek scheme of values.

In the one complete extant trilogy the notion of retaliation is dominant. Retaliation is a motive of Agamemnon, Clytemnestra, Aegisthus and Orestes. Upon Orestes there is no human being to take vengeance, and it is the Erinyes—divine avengers—who seek to enforce upon him the *lex talionis*. But even before these grim earth bogeys take up their role, *talio* has been seen as a principle of divine justice and human avengers as incarnations of an Erinyes. It was Zeus who sent Agamemnon as an Erinyes against Troy to do indiscriminate justice, and Apollo who commanded Orestes to kill his mother under threat of persecution by Erinyes. Justice is done, but crime is punished by crime, until at last we see the hideous aspect and hear the odious words of the divine avengers themselves. Here we touch the essence of the tragic thought of Aeschylus, but do not exhaust it. For the poet must not only end his trilogy, but solve his problem, must show that divine justice is more than the perpetuation of evil and that the Zeus to whom the chorus of the *Agamemnon* prayed does really teach by suffering (176 ff.). To this end the acquittal of Orestes upon an equal vote may be less significant than the institution of the Areopagus; more important still may be the reconciliation of the Erinyes by the persuasions of Athena and their transformation into Eumenides ("spirits of good will"). It will be more important, if those scholars are right who see in the contrast of force and persuasion a significant category of Aeschylean thought and find the most original product of his religious genius in the demonstration that the divine power operates through persuasion no less than through force. It may be that the solution of the problem of the Promethean trilogy was upon the same lines, that the Zeus first presented as the master of might and force was reconciled to his intransigent opponent by persuasion. It seems certain that in the Danaid trilogy sexual passion, which under the mode of violent pursuit gives rise to deeds of violence, was presented by Aphrodite toward the end of the trilogy as a persuasive influence. But it is in the *Oresteia* alone that the full facts can be studied. The trilogy ends with reconciliation and with joy in the triumph of good. That good could triumph was not the conclusion of a mystic or a metaphysician, but something based upon the poet's experience of life, in which perhaps the defeat of Xerxes counted for less than the fact that society showed some sign that its problems could be solved without violence. By setting up the Areopagus, Athena had shown a better way. She persuaded the Erinyes, and persuasion is the cardinal democratic virtue.

In writing tragedy which, for all its power in depicting evil and the fear of evil, ends with joy and reconciliation, Aeschylus has found few, if any, imitators. But this is only one of several conjunctions which make him unique. Master of an intricate verbal technique and an elaborate architectural structure, he is no less the master of spectacular effect and emotional crisis. Heir to the archaic poetry of Greece with its direct physical apprehension of emotion, living at a time when men could still feel themselves surrounded by gods, he had a capacity for general thought which was typically Greek and, in the judgment of many, treated the problem of evil with singular honesty and success.

Finally, this tragedian of superhuman stature was known as the best writer of satyr plays. It is astonishing that the sublime close of an Aeschylean trilogy could be followed by a grotesque treatment of myth, with a chorus of satyrs, as the *Oresteia* by the

Proteus*, the Theban trilogy by the *Sphinx**. These plays are now lost, but papyrus finds of the *Diktyoulkoi* ("Net-fishers") and the *Isthmiastae* show what lightness of touch Aeschylus could use in this genre, with what charm he could invest the traditional obscenity.

See also Index references under "Aeschylus" in the Index volume.

BIBLIOGRAPHY.—*Editions of the complete text:* U. von Wilamowitz-Moellendorff, (1914); Gilbert Murray, Oxford Classical Texts, 2nd ed. (1955); P. Mazon in the "Budé Series," with French trans., 6th ed. (1953); H. W. Smyth in the "Loeb Series," with Eng. trans., 2 vol. (1923–26; vol. ii reprinted in 1957, with appendix by H. Lloyd-Jones containing the principal papyrus fragments); M. Untersteiner with Italian trans. (1946–47).
Fragments: ed. by H. J. Mette (1959).
Texts with commentary: F. A. Paley, 4th ed. (1879); *Persae*, ed. by H. D. Broadhead (1960); *Oresteia*, ed. by G. Thomson, with Eng. trans., incorporating the important work of W. Headlam (1938); *Agamemnon*, ed. by E. Fraenkel with Eng. trans., 3 vol., of major importance (1950) and by J. D. Denniston and D. Page, giving a different view of the theology of Aeschylus (1957). *Choephori:* U. von Wilamowitz-Moellendorff with German trans., *Aischylos Orestie*, vol. 2 (1896). *Prometheus Bound*, ed. by G. Thomson with Eng. trans. (1932); all plays except *Supplices* ed. with Dutch commentaries by P. Groeneboom (1928–52).
Manuscript Studies: A. Turyn, *The Manuscript Tradition of the Tragedies of Aeschylus* (1943), and the editions of Wilamowitz-Moellendorff and Fraenkel.
Lexicon: G. Italie, *Index Aeschyleus* (1954–55).
Translations: (into English prose), W. and C. E. S. Headlam (1909); (into English verse), Gilbert Murray, collected ed. (1952); *The Complete Greek Tragedies*, ed. by D. Grene, R. Lattimore and S. G. Benardete, *Aeschylus*, 2 vol. (1953–56); P. Vellacott, *The Oresteian Trilogy* (1956); *Prometheus and Other Plays* (1961).
Criticism: U. von Wilamowitz-Moellendorff, *Aischylos Interpretationen* (1914); H. W. Smyth, *Aeschylean Tragedy* (1924); G. Méautis, *Eschyle et la trilogie* (1936); Gilbert Murray, *Aeschylus, the Creator of Tragedy* (1940); W. B. Stanford, *Aeschylus in His Style* (1942); G. Thomson, *Aeschylus and Athens*, 2nd ed. (1946); F. R. Earp, *The Style of Aeschylus* (1948); F. Solmsen, *Hesiod and Aeschylus* (1949); K. Reinhardt, *Aischylos als Regisseur und Theologe* (1949); E. T. Owen, *The Harmony of Aeschylus* (1952); J. de Romilly, *La Crainte et l'angoisse dans le théâtre d'Eschyle* (1958). *See* also M. Untersteiner, *Guida bibliographica ad Eschilo* (1947).   (R. P. W.-I.)

AESCULAPIUS: *see* ASCLEPIUS.

AESOP (d. ? 564 B.C.), famed as the composer of short animal fables, was regarded throughout classical antiquity as the exponent of fables par excellence. He used them to carry his point in debating or pleading with others in the conflicts of real life, but it is improbable that he wrote anything for publication. Similar fables had been employed in the wisdom literature of the Sumerians, Babylonians and Assyrians throughout the second millennium B.C., as well as by other Greek authors before him.

A slave most of his life, Aesop lived on the island of Samos in the early part of the 6th century B.C., being a contemporary of Solon and the so-called Seven Wise Men of Greece, with whom he is closely associated by writers from the 4th century B.C. onward. An inscription of 16 A.D. and the chronicle of Eusebius (fl. 4th century A.D.) fix his death at Delphi in 564 B.C. Since this was four years before Croesus became king of Lydia, it is probable that the tradition, known chiefly from Plutarch, which represents Aesop as adviser and diplomatic courier to Croesus originated in Alexandrian times by assimilation with stories about the Seven Wise Men at Croesus' court. The oldest information about Aesop comes from Eugeon (5th century B.C.) who according to the Suda lexicon said that he was a Thracian. It is probably Eugeon also, in his lost chronicle of Samos, who was the source for Herodotus' statement (2:134) that Aesop was put to death unjustly by the Delphians, whom he had offended or insulted, and for the tradition that he became the slave of Xanthus in Samos and later of Iadmon, who freed him. Aristophanes (*Wasps* 1446–48) relates that Aesop was accused by the Delphians of stealing a goblet from Apollo's temple, and told the fable of the eagle and beetle to the Delphians in pleading for his life, and Aristotle (*Rhetoric* 2:20) that he used the fable about the fox's ticks in defending a politician on trial for embezzlement at Samos.

A romantic biography of Aesop, written in Egypt in the first century A.D., has many stories about him: describing his outwitting of his master, Xanthus the philosopher, his sojourn with

Croesus, his career as minister and riddle-solver for King Lycurgus of Babylon (taken from the Assyrian story of Ahikar, *q.v.*), and his death at Delphi. This biography, of which the Byzantine scholar Maximus Planudes (*c.* 1300 A.D.) made a truncated edition, was first printed entire in 1952 from the only manuscript (10th century). Herein originated the idea of Aesop as physically ugly and deformed, on the analogy of Socrates. Demetrius Phalereus (fl. *c.* 320 B.C.) is probably the source of the statement widely made by later rhetoricians, and in the biography, that Aesop was a Phrygian by birth. There is no evidence for the improbable theory that a folk book about Aesop was written in the 6th or 5th centuries B.C.

The first-known collection of fables ascribed to Aesop, published in one short book by Demetrius Phalereus, has not survived, but it was extant in the 9th century, was apparently well known to the Greek rhetoricians as the official Aesop, and was probably the chief source used by Phaedrus for his Latin versification. The next oldest collection of Greek fables in prose, ascribed by an anonymous collector to Aesop and written probably in the 2nd or 1st century A.D., consists of about 230 fables and is known as the *Augustana* (first printed entire in 1812). This is independent of Babrius, who versified a number of Aesopic fables in the 2nd century A.D. and probably antedates him. In Byzantine times the prose fables of the *Augustana* passed into various shorter and slightly reworded recensions, which, together with a prose paraphrase and a few metrical adaptations of Babrius, constitute the entire corpus of Greek fables fancifully ascribed to Aesop in more than a hundred manuscripts. This corpus has not been influenced in any way by the *Fables of Bidpai* (*q.v.*) or any other Indian sources. The contents of modern editions have varied widely according to the manuscripts on which they were based. Planudes' selection, first printed in 1479, was long the standard one.

In antiquity the Aesopic fable was never popular literature. Normally it was told very briefly in a learned context for the sake of its metaphorical meaning. Fable collections in prose were made originally as repertories for the use of writers and speakers. Phaedrus (fl. 1st century A.D.) was the first to publish fables in verse meant to be read consecutively as literature; and this classical precedent, together with that of Avianus (late 4th century A.D.), both very popular authors in medieval and early modern times and much used in the schools, sanctioned and made fashionable the publication of fable books as belles-lettres in the hands of such able stylists as Jean de La Fontaine, and as moral instruction addressed by writers of lesser artistic claims to both children and elders in innumerable translations, adaptations and imitations of "Aesop" throughout Europe. Like fairy tales told purely for entertainment, amusing stories about the clever or stupid actions of animals have always been popular in oral folklore, and never more so, perhaps, than in early modern times; but the recognition in intellectual circles of the Aesopic fable as wisdom literature—Luther reckoned it next to the Bible— gave it a far greater proliferation in literature than was possible for the fairy tale, which had no such sanction. *See also* FABLE.

BIBLIOGRAPHY.—All the Greek proverbs and fables ascribed to Aesop together with Latin translations as well as the lives and the references to him in classical literature are ed. by B. E. Perry, *Aesopica*, vol. 1 (1952). The Eng. trans. by S. A. Handford (1954) is closest to the Greek text of the *Augustana*. *See* also B. E. Perry, "Fable," *Studium generale*, 12:17–37 (1959). (B. E. PE.)

AESOPUS, CLAUDIUS, Roman tragedian, flourished in the 1st century B.C.

Cicero was on friendly terms with him. Aesopus made a last appearance in 55 B.C.—when Cicero tells us that he was advanced in years—on the occasion of the splendid games given by Pompey at the dedication of his theatre.

Horace (*Sat.* iii, 3, 239) mentions his taking a pearl from the eardrop of Caecilia Metella and dissolving it in vinegar, that he might have the satisfaction of swallowing £8,000 worth at a draught.

AESTHETICS (Gr. *aisthesis*, "sense perception") is the theoretical study of the arts and related types of behaviour and experience. Traditionally regarded as a branch of philosophy, con-

cerned with the understanding of beauty and its manifestations in art and nature (*see* AESTHETICS, HISTORY OF), it is still so classed by some writers. In the 20th century, however, there developed a tendency to treat it as an independent science, concerned with investigating the phenomena of art and their place in human life. The data for such study consist of (1) works of art in all media, to be analyzed, described and compared; (2) human behaviour and experience directed toward works of art.

Aesthetics studies all the arts, including music and literature, theatre, dance and film, as well as painting, sculpture, architecture, landscape design and town planning. It deals with the "useful" as well as the "fine" arts insofar as they appeal to aesthetic taste. When covering so broad a field, it is sometimes called general or comparative aesthetics. Some writers specialize on theoretical problems within a single art.

Modern aesthetics collects information from the older sciences and from every other source which may contribute to a fuller understanding of the arts and their changing roles in civilization. It makes especial use of psychology (including psychoanalysis and depth psychology) for the light it throws on the processes of artistic creation and appreciation, including the symbolic meaning and emotional effects of various images. It looks to the social sciences, such as anthropology, for information on the ways in which the arts have fitted into the cultural patterns of different peoples and periods. It draws upon the histories of the various arts and on cultural history in general, but differs from them in organizing its materials and conclusions in theoretical rather than chronological order. General theories of art history are on the borderline between aesthetics and history. Aesthetics is also closely related to art criticism, but differs in emphasizing general principles and problems in that field, rather than the merits of particular artists or works of art. It examines the standards used in evaluation and criticism. As an empirical subject, it is regarded as primarily descriptive; *i.e.*, concerned with discovering and generalizing on the facts of art and related human activities. It does not abandon the problem of value, but approaches it more indirectly through a search for fuller understanding of the actual nature, functions and effects of art, which need to be considered if evaluation is to be more than a mere dogmatic assertion or expression of personal taste. Modern aesthetics makes no claim to proving universal laws of value, but seeks to provide relevant knowledge and methods which may help to make evaluation more informed and intelligent. It does not ignore the subject of beauty, but is less narrowly devoted to the task of defining "the beautiful," "the sublime," "the ugly," etc., than traditional aesthetics. Instead, it tries to describe the many specific processes and configurations involved in aesthetic experience, both in the observer and in the work or other object which stimulates it. Defining such terms as "beautiful" is seen as partly a semantic problem for which there is no one right answer; the main task is to analyze the various phenomena to which such terms are applied and then to seek more adequate ways of describing them verbally. The concept of beauty holds a less pre-eminent place in modern than in traditional aesthetics, being only one of many aspects of art and aesthetic experience which calls for investigation. This reflects the tendency of contemporary artists to aim at other qualities and of critics to put less emphasis on beauty in judging the value of art.

Origins and Development.—Some disagreement about the proper definition of aesthetics survives from the conflict of rival schools of thought in philosophy and art criticism during the 18th and 19th centuries, when it first achieved recognition as a distinct field of knowledge and inquiry. In France and England during the Enlightenment (*q.v.*), theories of art and beauty followed a naturalistic, empirical approach, but toward the end of the 18th century, beginning with Immanuel Kant's *Critique of Aesthetic Judgment* (1790), this empirical approach was temporarily overwhelmed by the powerful influence of German idealism, and the approach to beauty and art became more metaphysical and transcendental, more devoted to the search for a priori, universal principles of beauty and aesthetic value.

The empirical study of works of art continued along other lines, however, and that of aesthetic psychology revived soon afterward. The former continued in the researches of 19th-century anthropologists and archaeologists on primitive and prehistoric art and in those of art historians on historic styles, especially in architecture, painting and sculpture. A leader in this renewed attempt at a science of art was Hippolyte Taine, who in 1864 proposed that styles of art should be studied in the same way as the kinds of plants are studied by the botanist and as subject to evolutionary development. In Germany the name *Kunstwissenschaft* was applied to the historical writings of Gottfried Semper, Konrad Fiedler, Jacob Burckhardt, Alois Riegl and Heinrich Wölfflin on the history of styles in the visual arts. These writers strove for objectivity in comparative analysis, through the avoidance of personal value judgments, and sought to understand each style as the expression of a certain way of seeing, thinking and feeling. They also sought to explain, in various ways, the causation of stylistic change: some attributing it to economic or technological factors; some (especially Riegl) to a collective will or striving toward some type of form; some to factors inherent in art. Such *Kunstwissenschaft*, restricted to a certain art or group of arts, was both historical and theoretical; it aimed at a grasp of underlying trends and principles rather than a superficial account of individual artists and their works.

In the meantime aesthetics in the narrow sense, as the study of aesthetic experience rather than of art, was also being recalled to scientific aims and methods. It gradually became not only the "philosophy of beauty" but also the empirical psychology and sociology of artistic creation and appreciation. Chief leader in this revival was G. T. Fechner (1801–87), whose *Vorschule der Ästhetik* (1876) proposed an approach to aesthetics "from below" —that is, by observation of particular phenomena—rather than "from above,"—by deduction from metaphysical assumptions. His so-called "experimental aesthetics" (also called "laboratory" or "biometric" aesthetics) emphasized the statistical study of individual aesthetic preferences for standardized types of object, such as rectangles of certain sizes. Because of its reliance on exact measurement it has sometimes been regarded as equivalent to scientific aesthetics in general; but it is only one of many approaches in that general direction. It was actively developed early in the 20th century by such psychologists as C. W. Valentine and Edward Bullough in England, Lightner Witmer in the United States and Charles Lalo in France, but declined in activity after World War II. An initiator of another main line of psychological investigation was F. T. Vischer (1807–87), who formulated the theory of empathy (*Einfühlung*) in his *Ästhetik oder Wissenschaft des Schönen,* first published in 1846. It describes how the observer of a work of art or other aesthetic object tends to project his own feelings into it, exploring its form imaginatively and deriving therefrom an enjoyment similar to that of play. (Schiller, Herbert Spencer and others also noted the analogy between art and play.) Theodor Lipps developed this hypothesis in detail (*Ästhetik,* 1903–06), showing how the process of empathy is not purely subjective but dependent for its satisfaction on the nature of the work of art. Hence both subjective and objective phases in aesthetic experience must be studied in their interrelation. Other important contributions to aesthetics were made from the standpoint of psychoanalysis (notably by Sigmund Freud and C. G. Jung) and from that of Gestalt psychology (for example, in K. Koffka's *Problems in the Psychology of Art,* 1940).

Most important of all is the general, naturalistic account which modern psychology has provided of human nature in all its integrated functions, including those which operate in art. This includes the evolutionary account of the human species with its innate perceptual, mental and affective functions, predispositions and aptitudes, especially man's power to learn and to accumulate culture. It includes the unconscious and preconscious realms of human experience as revealed by depth psychology, with the light it throws on dreams and creative imagination. General psychology provides a framework within which aesthetics can focus its special studies on the creation and appreciation of art and related varieties of experience.

The social sciences, especially anthropology, sociology and cultural history, have provided another framework for aesthetic theory in their accounts of the various culture patterns which man has developed in successive periods in different parts of the earth. In these, the arts are more fully understood as interacting with economic, technological, social, political, religious and intellectual factors, as well as with natural conditions and resources. Art is shown as profoundly influenced by these and as expressing aspects of them in its varied forms, but also as affecting them in return, especially in advanced civilizations.

Early in the 20th century Max Dessoir, professor at the University of Berlin, sought to enlist the co-operation of many different approaches under the double name "aesthetics and general science of art." This implied that aesthetics was still to be understood in the early, narrow sense as philosophy of beauty, but that a new, empirical science of art was to be recognized as allied and parallel with it. A more synthetic and general (*allgemeine*) kind of *Kunstwissenschaft* was to be formed through integrating the specialized historical and critical studies. The "double-barreled" name was used as the title of a society and a quarterly review, the *Zeitschrift für Ästhetik und allgemeine Kunstwissenschaft,* which Dessoir edited from 1906 until the time of Hitler. However, it did not find favour outside of Germany, and since World War II the single term aesthetics has been more commonly used instead, in a sense broad enough to include all the various lines of research and schools of thought.

The work of synthesizing the prerequisites for a broadly scientific study of art, that had been accumulated since the latter years of the 19th century, was undertaken by scholars in the field with the aid of universities, museums, libraries, research foundations, professional societies and periodicals. One of the most important comparatively new resources was the greatly increased supply of works of art for observation and comparative analysis. Until the late 19th century, there was little opportunity in Europe or in the United States for intensive study of oriental, archaic and primitive types of art. European aesthetics was accordingly restricted to generalizing mainly on the styles and guiding principles of European art from the classical Greek and Roman through the Renaissance and baroque styles which had been deeply influenced by the classical. In the 20th century, however, a flood of art works in all media from China, Japan, India, Indonesia, Iran, Arabia, Egypt, Negro Africa, the Pacific islands and the western hemisphere became available to scholars. This vastly greater sampling of the world's art profoundly affected the theories of aesthetics. Confronted with such diversity, western scholars became more modest and more relativistic in their standards of value. They saw that modern western art, though possessed of many important values, is not the only good or important kind; that the rules and standards developed by western philosophy and criticism cannot be assumed as valid for art in general; and that each style of art had to be understood and appreciated in terms of the aims and value system of the group wherein it was made. It was learned, moreover, that nonwestern as well as western civilizations had much to say on the philosophy of art: for example, the theory of rasa (aesthetic flavour) in Indian aesthetics.

The Scope of Modern Aesthetics.—As a result of the convergence of these many approaches, each providing new materials and concepts, aesthetics gradually developed new divisions and subdivisions as a large, diversified science. Among theoretical studies focused on the arts, there are (1) systematic classifications of the arts (the arts and their interrelations); (2) aesthetic morphology (the descriptive study of form and style in the various arts); (3) theories of art history (evolutionary and other hypotheses about the main trends, patterns and causal influences in the sequence of styles with the study of the relations between art and other cultural factors). Among studies focused on human behaviour and experience in relation to the arts are: (1) aesthetic psychology, the subjects of which include the nature of the artist and the processes involved in artistic production, the relations between art and personality and children's art expressions; (2) the sociology of art, including the economics, anthropology and cultural history of art; (3) the logic, semantics and semeiology of art, dealing especially with language, signs and symbols, concepts, propositions and inferences used in discussing art; and (4) the epistemology and ontology of art, which examine the nature of the work of art or other aesthetic object in relation to existence and to human knowledge. A third main division must be recognized for the subject of aesthetic value theory or axiology, since it requires attention to both the work of art and the observer or user in almost equal degree and involves (1) a knowledge of the various types and styles of art and of their relations to human nature, individual and social; (2) of the kinds of effect that they tend to have on various types of person under various conditions; and (3) of the relation of such effects to various ideal goals and standards of value, including moral and practical as well as aesthetic.

Principal Exponents.—The theories of past and present philosophers still provide enlightening hypotheses. Idealism as developed from Plato through Hegel and Emerson and dualism as set forth by St. Thomas Aquinas, Descartes, Jacques Maritain and others still hold many followers especially in Germany, France and Italy. These traditional philosophies maintain that art is essentially spiritual and supernatural; that the work of true art is a sensuous manifestation of eternal ideas; and that it can reveal divine truths and point the way to higher values in the next life. Naturalistic and empiricist philosophers stress rather the natural basis of art in man's animal origin and evolution, its sensuous forms and the impossibility of separating it from man's practical, social activity. At the same time, they recognize its value in serving ideal goals through the improvement of experience in this life on earth. The empiricist trend toward science in aesthetics, strong in the United States, France and England, is derived from the humanism of Aristotle's *Poetics,* Lucretius, the naturalism of the French Enlightenment, Hume, Edmund Burke, Auguste Comte, Herbert Spencer, Taine, George Santayana and Lalo. The pragmatism of John Dewey has also helped to shape it. Long overshadowed by the prestige of German transcendentalism, this tradition revived in Europe toward the end of the 19th century and now dominates American thinking in the field.

In England, Herbert Read, a leading writer on aesthetics, approached the subject mainly as a poet and critic of the visual arts. In British philosophy and in American philosophy under its influence, the school of thought known as logical positivism (*q.v.*) achieved wide influence after World War II. Its occasional discussions of aesthetics were highly specialized on semantic, logical and epistemological problems—not so much on the phenomena of art or aesthetic experience as on the language used for discussing them and the logic of inferences made about them. In Europe and South America, the phenomenology of Edmund Husserl and the existentialism of Sören Kierkegaard, Martin Heidegger, Karl Jaspers and Jean-Paul Sartre were applied to aesthetics, most explicitly by Sartre in his philosophic and literary writings. Aesthetics and criticism in the U.S.S.R. and other Communist countries were dominated by the theories of art developed by Marx, Engels, Georgy Plekhanov, Lenin and others. They emphasized the economic determination of styles in art as a phase in the dialectical process of cultural evolution and the role of art in strengthening (or sometimes undermining) the current socioeconomic order at various periods of history. Selected aspects of the Marxist or sociological approach are accepted in modified form by many noncommunist writers, in stressing the influence of socioeconomic factors in art history.

General Characteristics.—Modern aesthetics does not expect to discover exact, permanent laws like those of physics, but only approximate accounts of recurrent types and tendencies, correlations and causal connections. The phenomena of art and taste are obviously among the most variable, complex and often intangible of those presented to scientific inquiry. They vary somewhat from person to person, from culture to culture, from period to period; their changing and unique aspects are often among their most important. They cannot be reduced to fixed, numerical formulas, but they are not completely unique or chaotic, and it is the business of aesthetics to describe both their constant and their variable aspects. Where direct sensory observation is im-

possible, as in the case of past events and inner experiences, all available clues to their nature can be examined, including those of introspection. Along these lines, aesthetics is trying to achieve the status of an empirical science in spite of the serious difficulties involved in interpreting the data.

Opinions differ as to whether aesthetics is now a science or can ever become one, in the strict sense of that word. If the concept of science is limited to subjects in which exact measurement and logical proof are highly developed, as in mathematics and physics, then aesthetics cannot be a science. Attempts at the measurement of aesthetic phenomena by laboratory and statistical devices have achieved comparatively little of importance. Much of the central subject matter of aesthetics remains inaccessible to exact measurement. But there is a broader sense of science which includes the rational pursuit of knowledge by other means where measurement is impossible: that is, by controlled, systematic observation and logical inference, eliminating guesswork, personal bias and subjectivism as far as possible; by testing hypotheses and comparing results to achieve the utmost objectivity and a gradual increase in the reliability of generalizations. As an attempt to set up absolute laws of value and beauty, traditional aesthetics could not achieve even this modicum of scientific status; but as an attempt to discover the facts about art, modern aesthetics has made considerable progress.

Two other criteria of scientific status are also, in some degree, within the reach of empirical aesthetics: namely, prediction and control. Through systematic observation and experiment, we can gradually learn the effects of certain types of art on certain types of persons under certain conditions. Understanding these general tendencies, even in a rough, approximate way, enables one to predict with some reliability what the effect will be in a particular case. Such knowledge has been applied for centuries in the use of art for political, military and religious propaganda and, in modern times, for commercial advertising. Only a slight beginning has been made toward the scientific investigation of the psychological and social effects of art. Education, both general and artistic, is one potential laboratory for testing the effects of different kinds of art and activity on different kinds of persons.

Obviously the power to control the human mind by art may be used for bad ends as well as good: for destructive or mercenary ends or far-reaching benefit. It is part of the task of contemporary aesthetics to consider how the power of art and of knowledge about art can be devoted to the best possible ends, such as the enrichment of experience, the development of mental powers and better social and material conditions. It is not assumed that art should be actively used or regulated by governments or other social agencies as a means of social improvement, but as pressures grow to use its resources for commercial, political and other interests not always consistent with public welfare, society is forced to take more careful note of them and to decide the extent to which it wishes to adopt collective policies in the realm of art—perhaps only to protect individual freedom and initiative, as through laws of copyright and free press.

Organization.—The international leadership in aesthetics which had long been exercised by German scholars ceased with World War II. The *Zeitschrift für Ästhetik und allgemeine Kunstwissenschaft,* edited first by Max Dessoir and later by Richard Müller-Freienfels with the co-operation of a distinguished list of writers, ceased publication in 1943, though steps toward revival in Germany were taken in the series of yearbooks on aesthetics, edited by Heinrich Lützeler from 1951. Meanwhile, other countries carried on more actively. French aestheticians, led first by Victor Basch, then by Charles Lalo and then by Étienne Souriau at the Sorbonne, organized before the war an Association pour l'Étude des Arts et les Recherches Relatives à la Science de l'Art. Revived in 1945 under the simpler name Société Française d'Esthétique, it began publishing a quarterly *Revue d'Esthétique* in 1948. In the United States, the quarterly *Journal of Aesthetics and Art Criticism* first appeared in 1941, being edited from 1945 by Thomas Munro. The American Society for Aesthetics, founded in 1942, publishes it under the auspices of the Cleveland Museum of Art and Western Reserve university in

Cleveland, O. The British Society of Aesthetics was founded in 1960, with Sir Herbert Read as president. It publishes the *British Journal of Aesthetics*, with Harold Osborne as editor. In Tokyo there is a Japanese Society for Aesthetics and a quarterly, *Bigaku* ("Aesthetics"), sponsored by the faculty of letters of Tokyo university. In Spain the Instituto Diego Velázquez (Madrid) publishes its *Revista de Ideas Estéticas*. In Italy, at the University of Turin, the Instituto di Estetica publishes a quarterly *Rivista de Estetica* (1956 ff.) under the editorship of Luigi Pareyson. A congress on aesthetics was held in Berlin in 1913 by Dessoir and his group; a second, more international in scope, in Paris in 1937 under the leadership of Paul Valéry, Paul Claudel, Victor Basch and Charles Lalo; a third in Venice in 1956, with Luigi Pareyson as chairman of the executive committee; and a fourth in Athens in 1960, with P. A. Michelis as chairman. A standing executive committee was appointed to further international co-operation, with Étienne Souriau as chairman.

See also Index references under "Aesthetics" in the Index volume.

BIBLIOGRAPHY.—Edward Bullough, *Aesthetics* (1957); Max Dessoir, *Ästhetik und allgemeine Kunstwissenschaft* (1906); John Dewey, *Art as Experience* (1934); Friedrich Kainz, *Vorlesungen über Ästhetik* (1948); Charles Lalo, *L'Expression de la vie dans l'art* (1933); Earl of Listowel, *A Critical History of Modern Aesthetics* (1933); Thomas Munro, *Toward Science in Aesthetics* (1956); K. C. Pandey, *Indian Aesthetics* (1959); Herbert Read, *The Anatomy of Art* (1932); George Santayana, *Reason in Art* (1906); Étienne Souriau, *La Correspondance des arts* (1947). (T. M.)

AESTHETICS, HISTORY OF.

AESTHETICS, HISTORY OF. The history of aesthetics (*q.v.*) puzzles the student by its paradoxes. Aesthetics as a branch of philosophical inquiry was constituted under its now familiar name as late as 1750 by Alexander Baumgarten (1714–62), author of *Aesthetica,* a book in Latin which was never reprinted or translated into a modern language. If aesthetics is regarded as beginning with the publication of this highly successful but little-read treatise, it will seem to be a modern invention and its history a relatively short one. But the long preparatory stage before Baumgarten's book is at least as important to the study of aesthetics as its historical life under its own name. For most of the ideas developed by the modern science of aesthetics were conceived before by earlier thinkers ignorant of the name and possessing no terminological equivalent to it. Even after the unpresumptuous start of 1750 the unity of aesthetics as a philosophical discipline was by no means taken for granted. The first important journal in the field, *Zeitschrift für Ästhetik und allgemeine Kunstwissenschaft,* founded in 1906 by Max Dessoir, suggested by its dual title that the theory of our perception of beauty and the theory of the principles of art were kindred but independent studies. Yet Baumgarten was apt with his name-giving precisely because for him aesthetics embraced both the study of beauty and the theory of art. The unsolved problem underlying the dynamic pattern of the history of aesthetics throughout the ages was this duality, which there were many attempts to resolve, as unity could only be effected if art could be interpreted as that type of human creativity whose purpose is to embody beauty.

CLASSICAL ANTIQUITY

Plato.—The great author whose work was to become the fountainhead of aesthetic thought down to modern times spoke disparagingly of works of art—including the Homeric poems—which we are accustomed to exalt. Plato (*q.v.*) was of course not blind to the grandeur and loveliness of Greek poetry or sculpture. But his own writing extolled a beauty unknown to previous poets, painters and sculptors. Their failure, in Plato's judgment, was to have missed the true object of poetic praise. The essential nature of beauty, in Plato's *Symposium,* reveals itself to the enraptured beholder who, guided by love (*eros*), has ascended from the admiration of physical perfection to the discovery of inward beauty and thence to an ultimate vision. The beautiful as such, hardly distinguishable from the good as such, a nonsensuous transcendent splendour, was characterized by Plato with a series of negations: not subject to growth and decay, not like a bodily frame, not mutable or enmeshed in relativities, but "being itself by itself

with itself sempiternally uniform." This negative science of beauty was counterbalanced by a theory of participation: everything is beautiful through participating in the "beautiful as such," and love, though a yearning after transcendent beauty, is kindled by visible loveliness. So the attempts made in Plato's dialogue *Hippias Major* at defining sensuous beauty were not unrelated to the subject matter of the *Symposium.* There was at least no contradiction between Diotima's lofty teaching and the more empirical definition of the beautiful in *Hippias Major* as that which is "pleasing to the eye and ear." Both the straining of later occidental art after "the light that never was, on sea or land" and the ever-repeated attempts to interpret this urge in terms of aesthetic theory were to testify to the fruitfulness of Plato's discovery.

For Plato love, inspired by beauty, especially by the beauty of a human being, and yearning after immortalization, was in its turn creative of beauty: the lover desires to "engender in the beautiful." But among the fair works and deeds which, according to the *Symposium,* bear testimony to love's creative power, "works of art" (in the modern sense of this term) were not explicitly included. And this is all the more noteworthy as the theory of art, in the sense of man's rational productivity, played an important part in Plato's thought. At the same time, Plato did view poetry as closely linked to the erotic vision of beauty. The poet, Plato made Socrates say in the *Phaedrus* and the *Ion,* chants his praises in a sacred madness, and no sober speech can compete with the words inspired by enthusiasm. But the "fine frenzy" which Plato attributed to the poet—another concept which was to echo through centuries of occidental civilization—did not belong to him as to a representative of art in general. On the contrary, in Plato's mind this distinction of poetry, which disabled the poet from giving a rational account of his own works, set it apart from the rest of those arts or crafts which through their purposive structure furnished to both Plato and Aristotle a model of rationality. The good poets, Plato affirmed in the *Ion,* do not compose their poems "by art" but under divine inspiration. Just as the Greek language knew of no word which corresponded to our "art" with its aesthetic overtones, so we shall look in vain for an aesthetic theory of art in Plato. Yet an approach to this modern concept was effected through an association of art with imitation (mimesis)—a word which in Greek is closer to "re-enactment" than to "copying." The idea of an "imitative art" might seem peculiarly apt to suggest a generic likeness between poetry on the one hand and sculpture and painting on the other, while at the same time hinting at an analogy between the human artificer and the divine demiurge who, in the *Timaeus,* fashioned the world by copying an ideal pattern. For Plato, the opponent of naturalistic tendencies in contemporary sculpture and painting and the critic of traditional poetry, this concept generally served to disparage all copy-making on account of the distance separating the copy from the ultimate original, the "form" or *eidos.* But again mimesis meant also a kind of participation, and Socrates, drawing the picture of a blessed city, was cast by Plato in the role of a painter. In addition, Plato was heir to the Pythagorean theory of music, based as it was on the conviction that the same numeric harmony which becomes audible through music determines the order of the universe as well as that of the soul. So the constructive power of mimesis was evident especially in the eminence assigned to music in the educational process: "rhythm and harmony sink into the innermost recesses of the mind."

Aristotle.—Plato objected to tragedy on the ground that tales of weepings and wailings weaken rational self-control through their appeal to passion. Aristotle (*q.v.*), while following to some extent the argument of Plato's *Republic,* book iii, in writing his *Poetics,* turned his teacher's verdict into a defense. The high hopes which Plato, a believer in divine justice, cherished for the just man's destiny after death were not entertained by his pupil, and therefore tragedy, which in Aristotle's opinion was largely concerned with the incongruity between the relative slightness of the hero's guilt and the awful magnitude of the disaster visited upon him, had to be recognized as true to life. Thus the two passions of fear and pity, arising out of sympathy, were according to Aristotle not only stimulated but also cleansed by tragedy. At the same time, the divine madness as a source of poetic inspiration was replaced by a natural talent, the ability of the poet's sensitive mind to adopt the gesture and attitude of his fictitious characters. So, together with a rationally justifiable purpose, the title of art could be restored to poetry. In spite of being anti-Platonic in some respects, Aristotle's *Poetics* served as a vehicle for other Platonic concepts and so helped to pass on Plato's notion of the poem, or more generally of speech, as an integrated whole like a living creature to later books of poetics, of which Horace's *Ars Poetica* (*Epistula Ad Pisones*) was the most celebrated example.

The Later Classical Writers.—Thought on aesthetics in late antiquity was rich and varied. Fresh insights were gained less through clarifying the theoretical principles than through direct knowledge of a variety of creative processes. A unity existed in aesthetic thought, but it was concealed by a multiplicity of *artes* with their sets of rules, which were continually revised and enriched by new observations. A number of classic works emerged as a result, and the authority of some of them survived antiquity. Horace (*q.v.*) wrote his epistle to the Pisos (an "Art of Poetry"), Vitruvius his *De Architectura,* Aristoxenus his *Harmonics.* Rhetoric, the most productive member in this family of aesthetic technologies, found its lawgivers in Quintilian and Cicero (*qq.v.*). While the authors of these writings generally made no claim to speak as philosophers, the pervasive influence of the Platonic theory of beauty remained noticeable in most of them. The observation that the sculptor Phidias wrought his statue of Zeus on a model visible only to the eyes of the mind rather than after a man of flesh and blood was a commonplace with Hellenistic writers on the arts. When at last Plotinus, in the 3rd century A.D., repeated this well-worn affirmation it once more regained some of its authentically Platonic ring. With him the repudiation of a bare reproduction of things visible was a move involved in the mind's ascent toward a vision of "the beautiful." But this Platonic vision as renewed by Plotinus had no longer the dignity of an ultimate consummation: it was the prelude to a mystic union in which the seer and the seen became indistinguishably one (*see* NEOPLATONISM). The fine essay *On the Sublime,* wrongly attributed to Longinus, which established the idea of sublimity as an aesthetic counterpart to the ethical notion of magnanimity or greatness, was a product of the combined influences of the art of oratory and Neoplatonism.

THE MIDDLE AGES AND THE RENAISSANCE

Augustinian Platonism.—The beginning of the Christian era was less of a break in the development of aesthetic ideas than in some other fields of philosophical thought. To be sure, Christian asceticism deepened the distrust of the arts and their effects on the human mind, and there were frequent complaints about those who pleased congregations by their music while displeasing God by their lives. But the Christian criticism of aesthetic pleasures merely continued a line of thought traced before by Plato. At the same time the fight against Gnostic and Manichaean heresies helped to make it clear that hostility directed against sensuous delight as such was alien both from the Christian idea of the world as bearing imprinted upon it the vestiges of its creator and from the spirit of the divine Master who put man's idle worries to shame by letting him "consider the lilies." The Platonic idea of poetry as praise gained a wider bearing and a fresh radiance in minds familiar with the Psalms. *"Ore canunt alii Christum, canit arte fabrili Hugo"* ("Others sing of Christ with their mouths, I with my craftsmanship") read the inscription by a medieval sculptor, Hugo d'Oignies. Thanks to educated and sensitive leaders of the early church such as the Cappadocian fathers in the east and, above all, St. Augustine in the Latin world, the aesthetic culture of ancient Greece was, after severe scrutiny and not without grievous omissions, preserved for Christendom. Accordingly the approach to the aesthetic problem continued to follow a path mapped out by classical philosophy. On the one hand, beauty was made the object of analysis and of a speculation which, while taking its departure from its sensuous appearance, tended to veer toward the beautiful as a purely spiritual brilliance. This was the

Platonic or Augustinian strain. On the other hand, the theory of the arts, an Aristotelian heirloom, was appropriated and, especially during the 12th and 13th centuries, developed, systematized and refined far beyond what could be found in Aristotle. Art (*ars*) for these thinkers, and here again they followed an ancient tradition, signified invariably a knowledge of how to make something, in other words, a "poietic" knowledge as distinguished from both theoretical knowledge (*i.e.,* knowledge for knowledge's sake) and practical knowledge. The medieval thinkers eagerly studied Plato's *Timaeus,* substituting for the mythical figure of the demiurge the God who spoke through the prophets. So man the maker was viewed in the light of the humbling idea of God the Creator. This analogical view was instrumental in conferring a higher degree of systematic consistency upon the theory of the arts, especially in the school of Chartres in the 12th century, but otherwise the principles laid down by Greek philosophy were maintained. The more science there was in an art, and the less its work required the services of the body for its execution, the higher it ranked and the better founded was its claim to be classed as "liberal." It is quite true that medieval painters, sculptors, architects, illustrators and goldsmiths attained to high personal fame and developed a great professional pride; it is also true that a lofty idea of the perfect craftsman-artist was held out for admiration and emulation. Furthermore, the medieval theorists were not unaware of the difference that existed between useful arts and those which simply aimed to give pleasure or to satisfy a desire for purposeless play. Yet for all that they remained, like their ancient predecessors, ignorant of the idea which in modern times was expressed by the term "fine arts." To them it seemed evident that all arts, weaving or agriculture no less than painting or sculpture, strove after beauty as one form of perfection. So the idea of singling out certain arts as "fine" (*i.e.,* as specifically designed for materializing beauty) did not enter their scheme of thought.

Plato was the mastermind that dominated aesthetic theory throughout the history of occidental civilization. But in the Christian era this influence was exercised largely through the medium of later authors, especially through the Pseudo-Dionysian writings and through St. Augustine (354–430). In the chapters of *De Trinitate* that dealt with the Word, Augustine defined the transcendent basis of all beauty. He sought the principle of beauty in unity, from which its further characteristics, order, harmony and proportion, were to flow, and found the paragon of this unity in the Word as the perfectly adequate expression of the Father. At the height of scholastic philosophy in the 13th century St. Bonaventura and St. Thomas Aquinas reaffirmed this aesthetic doctrine, and the latter developed it into the well-known triad of marks of things beautiful: integrity or perfection, due portion or consonance and finally clarity (understood as the radiation of the form). On the one hand beauty was held to subsist in God, on the other it was discovered through the ear and the eye, as sound and colour. But whether transcendent or sensuous, it was covered by the general formula: beauty is that which pleases the beholder. This definition set a clear distinction between the beautiful and the good, relating the beautiful to cognition and the good to appetition; and, again, this dual conception of beauty as of a perfection both sensuous and supersensuous derived from Augustinian Platonism.

Of the six books of St. Augustine's *De Musica,* five were devoted to questions such as metre, rhythm, scale and the like, all treated with an eye to discovering numerical relationships as the basis of musical delight. But the sixth book of the fragmentary treatise purported to show the fruits of the preceding argument by lifting the reader "on the wings of charity" from the visible and audible and mutable numbers to the immutable numbers through which the invisible things of God became clearly seen, "being understood by the things that are made, even His eternal power and Godhead." What began as a dialogue on one of the liberal arts ended as a Pythagorean-Christian version of the Platonic ascent of the love of beauty toward a beatific vision.

This Augustinian appraisal of beauty was to predominate throughout the middle ages, and it by no means vanished with the beginning of the modern era. The mind of St. Augustine—and that is generally true of those who followed him—was open to the glory of the created world, to the loveliness and grandeur of nature as well as to the majestic and awe-inspiring spectacle of human history, the *ordo saeculorum*, which he likened to a most beautiful poem composed of antitheses. Man's predilection for fair things offered him through eye and ear appeared to him not only legitimate but good: it could provide steppingstones for the spiritual ascent of the mind. Yet it held also a temptation. For because of the depravity of man the love of sensuous beauty might exceed the place assigned to it within the order of things, with the result that the inferior love would turn against the love of divine beauty. Accordingly the praise of beauty had to be kept in balance by words cautioning the lover of beauty against the perils of disorderly affection. This was the twofold lesson taught by Augustine, Christ's follower and a pupil of the Greeks, to the theologians and philosophers of subsequent centuries: while knowing that only an obtuse and ungrateful mind will blind itself to beauty, we must also bear in mind that even after his rebellion Lucifer retained the fair aspect of his celestial origin. How else could he tempt the proud and the high-minded?

The Renaissance.—When Petrarch (*q.v.*), who is usually considered one of the early embodiments of post-medieval man, had ascended Mont Ventoux, he stood long transfixed by the grandeur of the panorama. Then it occurred to him to open the copy of St. Augustine's *Confessions* which he used to carry with him, and the first lines to catch his eye were those which exhorted the reader not to forget the beauty of the soul in seeking external beauty: "*Et eunt homines admirari alta montium . . . , et relinquunt se ipsos*" ("And men go to wonder at mountain heights . . . and leave themselves behind"). On reading these words aloud the poet, abashed and silent, began to descend with his companions: "*Tunc vero . . . in me ipsum interiores oculos reflexi*" ("Then indeed . . . I turned my inward eyes on to myself"). The story has a symbolic significance. Great though the artistic achievements of the Renaissance were, the pattern of ideas by means of which this burst of aesthetic creativity was interpreted showed no great departure from classical tradition. A period of relative philosophical sterility had intervened between the breakdown of medieval philosophy and the Cartesian renewal. Consequently the idea of beauty at the same time sensuous and supersensuous lingered on in the minds, though the framework of medieval metaphysics to which it belonged had less importance. Humanist philosophers like Marsilio Ficino (1433–99) became Platonists by reading all or most of Plato's dialogues instead of reading St. Augustine and Pseudo-Dionysius. But what they found in Plato's dialogues differed surprisingly little from what others had found in St. Augustine and in *De Divinis Nominibus*. Platonism, in the minds of the educated, eclipsed Aristotelianism. But while astronomy and physics were to reap marvelous benefits from this turning of the philosophical tide and while the influence of Platonism as a spiritual atmosphere was all pervasive, the philosophical insight into the nature of beauty was not much advanced.

The general theory of the arts, so important a part of ancient and medieval philosophy, had likewise come to a standstill. All the greater was the theoretical vitality exhibited by the special theories devoted to poetry, the pictorial arts, architecture and music. Boccaccio, Lodovico Castelvetro and J. C. Scaliger wrote on the art of poetry, Leon Battista Alberti on architecture and painting, Cennino Cennini on painting, and then came the long procession of authors of "defenses of poetry," headed by Sir Philip Sidney. The title suggested a program: the Platonic theory of inspiration was invoked for a refutation of the verdict passed on poetry by Plato. The evaluation of this vast literature is the business of historians of the various arts concerned rather than that of the historian of aesthetics, yet certain ideas and tendencies of general import stood out. There was a novel insistence on the value of artistic mastery measured by the magnitude of the difficulties overcome; and the pride of human achievement expressed itself in other ways also. To relate man the maker to God the Creator was a commonplace with medieval theologians and philosophers. When, however, Scaliger dared to describe the

poet as "another god" he seemed to view this analogy in a light more flattering to human self-esteem than might have seemed permissible in the middle ages. The new consciousness of man's power and dignity involved liberation from the shackles of tradition. The artist was bidden to seek his models in nature rather than in art: "He who can go to the fountain does not go to the water vessel," wrote Leonardo da Vinci. But nature, the artist's fountain, was for Leonardo something recondite rather than the surface aspect of things met with in everyday life. The limited antitraditionalism of the Renaissance is not to be confused with 19th-century naturalism. Michelangelo, for instance, frowned upon Flemish painting, with its records of the contemporary scene, as a sort of pictorial heresy. As a rule the exaltation of nature went hand in hand with an equally enthusiastic admiration of antiquity. A recognition of the authoritative greatness of Greek and Roman art, feeding as it did on archaeological discoveries and on the translations of the ancient classics multiplying in the 16th century, did not seem to contradict the idea of nature as the fountain of art. The ancient masters, closer to nature than the artists of the middle ages, were believed to be nature's true interpreters. Yet this duality of authorities—nature and classical antiquity—was to become the source of the "quarrel of the Ancients and Moderns," the great theme not only of French criticism in the 17th century but also of classicist and romantic aesthetics at the turn of the 18th and 19th centuries. "We are greater than the ancients," asserted Giovanni Pico della Mirandola, writing to Pietro Bembo, a man of letters and a Platonist, on Sept. 19, 1512. At the end of the 17th century this battle cry was raised again by Charles Perrault and by Fontenelle in their onslaught against classical orthodoxy as represented by Racine and Boileau.

A historian writing about a Renaissance theory of art (taking this word in its modern sense) would still be guilty of an anachronism. There were arts and theories relating to these various arts, and there were, of course, mutual influences and interdependencies combining these theories into a vaguely circumscribed whole. But the idea of art as such, the indispensable counterpart to aesthetics as a unified field of study, was as yet unknown. An important step, however, was taken toward forming this decisive concept. The idea of the artist began to take shape. This was not a discovery of philosophers but rather the fruit of a theoretical self-consciousness developing in some of the great painters and sculptors of the time. Certain sociological elements were involved in this process. The Greek civilization, with the contempt for manual labour characteristic of a slaveholding society, celebrated the works of Phidias and Zeuxis but paid very little attention to Phidias and Zeuxis as persons. Again, in the feudal society of the middle ages, the *artifex*, or artisan, was by and large kept in a lowly though respected position roughly corresponding to that of the artisans in Plato's ideal state. With the disintegration of feudalism and the growth of a new urban society, at first in the Italian city-states, the artist was given a chance to throw off the social limitations placed upon him by his membership in a guild and to demand for himself the dignified place which antiquity had freely granted to the poet and which Dante had regained for him. However, the social change favoured but did not produce the decisive event—the discovery, or rediscovery, of the fundamental truth that there is a poetry not only of words but also of colours and lines, of sculptural and architectural forms. If the poet is moved by "love" to feel a sensual-spiritual aspiration in which his mind has to be fructified by an immediate contact with transcendent reality, so also is the pictorial artist. This idea, though never developed by Plato, was yet touched upon by him in a sentence which, in his suggestive brevity, taxes the understanding of the modern interpreter. Love, so Diotima taught Socrates, is a desire "to engender in the beautiful." While some are creative in their bodies, others are pregnant in their souls and give life to what is proper for the soul to beget and bring forth: wisdom and virtue in general. "And such creators are all poets and those of the artificers who are called inventors." It took two great inventor artificers, Leonardo da Vinci and Albrecht Dürer (*qq.v.*) to revive this insight, the idea of a poetical power shared by the poet with his brother-artists—a revival due primarily not to a study of Plato's words but to encountering, through personal experience, the very reality with which Plato had been confronted. This was the deeper significance of Leonardo's struggle after winning for painting a rank equal to or even above poetry. Beauty, Dürer affirmed, "stands firmly fixed in nature," and nature in God. Therefore a painter must study God through science and observation, for only by such submission—which entails imitation—shall a man ever be able to make a beautiful figure. Here, at long last, the point was discovered at which the essential kinship not only of poet and painter but of all "artists" in our sense of the word became clear—a discovery that made it possible to advance from the ancient theory of art as "knowledge of how to make things" toward aesthetics as a philosophy of art. This point, moreover, was found to lie not in the sphere of art itself but in that of religion.

THE CARTESIAN ERA AND THE 18TH CENTURY

Classicism.—The enthusiastic appraisal of man's eminence as expressed in the *Oration on the Dignity of Man* by Giovanni Pico della Mirandola (1463–94)—"to him is granted to have whatever he chooses, to be whatever he wills"—seemed to be borne out in the following centuries by an achievement of staggering greatness: the modern technological civilization began to take shape. The philosophical guidance needed for the development of a science which made man the master of nature was provided by Descartes (1596–1650), and the new science itself reached a first apogee in Newton's *Philosophiae Naturalis Principia Mathematica* (1686–87). Philosophers, bent on co-operating in this enormous enterprise, were, on the whole, not too much concerned about art and its problems. Leibniz (1646–1716), critical though he was of some aspects of Cartesianism, could quote with approval the tsar Peter the Great confessing that "he admired more certain pretty machines than all the beautiful paintings in the king's palace." Enthusiasm was frowned upon in the Age of Reason, and John Locke (1632–1704) in the role of an educator offered advice for combating it in young people. In this dry intellectual atmosphere the French developed their classic literature, which succeeded in attaining to poetic greatness by pleasing in accordance with rules. Paradoxically, these rules, thought through and applied in a Cartesian spirit, were borrowed from Aristotle. But whereas Aristotle had been looking back upon a period of poetical creativity which in his time had already spent its force, Corneille (1606–84) rewrote Aristotle's *Poetics* in three prefaces ("On the Function and Parts of the Dramatic Poem," "On Tragedy" and "On the Three Unities") as a set of interconnected precepts at a time of vigorous poetic creation in France. So Corneille's code of rules was more nearly an "art" in the traditional sense (*i.e.*, knowledge of how to write a dramatic poem) than his ancient model. The premise of this normative theory was belief in the ultimate identity of nature and reason. The rationality exhibited in coherent rules was conceived as an expression of the very nature of things themselves and especially of man, and a poem obeying these rules could not fail to give pleasure to the audience while benefiting it morally. For Descartes the clarity and distinctness of our ideas produced the conviction of truth. Not only that, said Boileau (1636–1711) in *L'Art poétique,* but they are likewise productive of poetic beauty.

The forceful elegance of versification attained by the French classics and successfully emulated in England by Dryden and Pope was a short-lived triumph. When G. E. Lessing (1729–81) in his *Hamburgische Dramaturgie* (1767–68) attacked the artificiality of the French rules in the name of "untrammeled" nature (which supposedly spoke through Greek tragedy and had been listened to by Aristotle), the classical code had already lost its sway. The postclassic generation, encouraged by critics and theorists like Jean Baptiste Dubos, Charles Batteux and Diderot, looked for the unaccountable charm, the *je ne sais quoi*, the surprising departure from the expected norm, the emotional impact which can do without mediating concepts. French classicism had shown how far it was possible to go in contravening Plato's statement that the good poets do not write their poems "by art." The limit was

reached and a small host of avenging Platonists stood in readiness biding their time. But first we must look at the contribution made by the Cartesians toward forming a body of aesthetic thought.

The Subjective Approach.—The Cartesians' contribution to aesthetics was an important one. But its significance consisted less in throwing a fresh light on the twin problems of beauty and art than in providing a psychology of aesthetic experience. Descartes himself, in his *Compendium of Music* (1618) and in his correspondence with Marin Mersenne, found the basis of beauty in agreeableness, which in its turn he explained as resulting from the adaptation of stimulus to response. The human voice impressed him as more agreeable than other sounds, "because it holds the greatest conformity to our spirits." The aptness of sensation to the recipient he conceived furthermore as a mean between extremes: that is pleasing which neither bores nor fatigues. There was nothing really new in all this. The idea that the pleasure which we take in beautiful objects involves a harmonious relationship between man who perceives and the object perceived was part of the Platonic teaching and was reaffirmed by Thomas Aquinas. Again, the idea of a mean between extremes was clearly derived from Aristotle's functional theory of pleasure and pain. The novelty, however, was in the emphasis placed upon the emotional response. "Beauty pleases"—this was a truism conceded by everyone, and attempts had been made to show why its pleasingness is an essential rather than an accidental attribute of beauty. But Descartes and his followers turned the self-evident assertion around so as to read: "Whatever pleases in a certain way is beautiful." Pleasure, hitherto understood as the mark by which beauty can be known, was now considered the fundamental fact, mental or physiological, from which beauty derives. For the new kind of investigation the centre of theoretical interest had shifted from the beautiful object as perceived and enjoyed by the mind to the subject; *i.e.*, to the perceiving and enjoying mind.

The subjective approach won, and along with it there developed a new vocabulary. Imagination, fancy, taste, sense of beauty, sentiment and the like became the cardinal words of an emerging science. The influence of Locke, in England and also in France, combined with and generally outweighed that of Descartes. Psychological hypotheses abounded. The *abbé* Jean Baptiste Dubos (1670–1742) regarded our instinct to be always in motion and to avoid ennui as the source of our love of the beautiful. For the *abbé* Charles Batteux (1713–80) "imitation of nature" was the key to artistic perfection, and that might suggest a concentration of analysis on the object. Yet Batteux believed the artist's concern with nature to be through sentiment rather than through the intellect, and this view leads back to that of Dubos with his fear of boredom. Lord Kames (1696–1782) moved in the same direction when he connected aesthetic pleasure with readiness of apprehension, liking for novelty and social sympathy. Similarly Edmund Burke (1729–97), not quite able to disentangle his sentimental and amorous experiences from among his aesthetic ones, asserted: "I call beauty a social quality" (*A Philosophical Inquiry Into the Origin of Our Ideas of the Sublime and Beautiful*, 1756). David Hume (1711–76) finally brought to a logical conclusion the process by which beauty self-subsistent and real was dissolved into the mental life with its throng of ideas and impressions: pleasure and pain, he maintained, "are not only necessary attendants of beauty and deformity, but constitute their very essence" (*A Treatise of Human Nature*, 1739–40). One may well sympathize with the "common-sense" philosopher, Thomas Reid (1710–96), who was dismayed at seeing his contemporaries "resolve all our perceptions into mere feelings or sensations"; or with the obstinacy of William Hogarth (1697–1764) who, in the face of psychologically inclined critics, clung to his "precise serpentine line" as the standard of beauty.

The psychological analysis was in danger of explaining away its object: the sense of beauty, under the scrutiny of the psychologist, turned out to be something else in disguise—human sympathy or desire for change or self-assertiveness or a longing for emotion. Against these aberrations the great influence exercised by the 3rd earl of Shaftesbury (1671–1713) and his disciple Francis Hutcheson (1694–1746) served as a counterweight, not only in England but also on the continent of Europe and especially in Germany. It was largely through Shaftesbury that sense, inner sense and sense of beauty became key words in the language of literary and artistic criticism. But though the method that he promoted had been initiated by Locke, Shaftesbury was also a Platonist and, as such, was bitterly critical of the "physiologist" Locke. By Shaftesbury the way into the inward life was once again understood as part of a movement ultimately raising the mind to the vision of spiritual beauty.

Vico, Herder and Winckelmann.—The analysts of the mind had generally adopted the point of view of the receptive rather than of the creative mind—another weakness of their theories. Thomas Hobbes (1588–1679), who spoke of the architectural and philosophical nature of poetical fancy, was one of the exceptions to this rule. Then Giambattista Vico (1668–1744) sought to remind his contemporaries—who were tastefully dallying with things that flattered a refined sense of beauty—of a forgotten truth. He stepped forth as a witness to the power of imagination, whose heroic strength was manifest in ancient poetry, especially in Homer. The dormant potentialities of St. Augustine's idea of the Word, perfect expression of the Godhead and thereby source of all beauty, came to life in Vico's concept of a poetical wisdom which, in the early phase of human civilization, acquainted man with truth through language and myth. So he anticipated J. G. Hamann (1730–88), for whom poetry was "the mother-tongue of the human race" and who exalted the archaic simplicity of the language of the Pentateuch and the New Testament above Greek tragic poetry. At the same time, the life of poetry was viewed by Vico in a historical context, as exercising an important function in the growth of human civilization. A deep affinity rather than effective influence connected Vico with J. G. Herder (1744–1803), the rediscoverer of folk poetry of many languages and the visionary who surveyed the history of mankind as the epic of humanity triumphant. With all his fondness for national and historical colour and character, Herder aspired with the ardour of a Platonist toward the idea of beauty which is one and the same for all men and for all times. Also a Platonist, or rather a Plotinist with Stoic leanings, was J. J. Winckelmann (1717–68), who with his *Geschichte der Kunst des Altertums* (1764) laid the foundations of the modern study of the history of art. At the same time, Winckelmann's book became the bible of the classicist dogma which was to dominate aesthetic thought for more than a century. In the majesty and repose of Greek sculpture he saw the unique revelation of beauty pure and unalloyed, the incarnation, as it were, of a Platonic form.

The New Notion of Art.—The subjective approach, first conceived in the spirit of Cartesian and Lockian psychology, broadened into a genetic or historical study of man's artistic creativity. The new emphasis placed on man the spectator or the creator or, finally, the genius (the Platonic inspiration transfigured into a talent) helped to decrease the distance which to earlier thinkers separated activities such as the writing of verses, painting, play-acting, building, dancing and others. "Art" was now more and more frequently coupled with the predicate "fine," but the prevailing use of the plural showed that the minds did not yet have a firm hold on the essential unity of "art as such." The current expression read: *les beaux-arts,* the fine arts, *die schönen Künste,* sometimes with the addition *et sciences* (*und Wissenschaften*), which provoked Herder's vigorous protest. In fact it showed that the ancient idea of art as "poietic knowledge" was still abroad. The work of two great poets and critics, Goethe and Schiller, finally succeeded in firmly establishing the modern usage, now accepted by all European languages, which leaves no doubt about the primary meaning of "art." Only by keeping in mind this development can one understand the limited but real importance of Alexander Baumgarten's idea of beauty as a "phenomenal perfection," corresponding to the lower form of apprehension. Though by no means original or profound, it was instrumental in furthering the growth of the concept of art with its new unified meaning. Baumgarten's two books, a thesis *Meditationes philosophicae de nonnullis ad poema pertinentibus* (1735) and the first volume of *Aesthetica* (1750), foreshadowed the beginning of a new epoch. Posterity paid Baumgarten the not undeserved compliment of accepting the name he had chosen for a philosophical science both old and new.

KANT AND LATER AESTHETICS

Kant.—Immanuel Kant (*q.v.*) in his *Critique of Judgment* (1790), the third of his three fundamental works, applied the transcendental method of philosophical analysis to the problem of aesthetics. What are the conditions, he asked, implied by the existence of the phenomenon of beauty? What are the presuppositions which give validity to our aesthetic judgments? The *Critique of Pure Reason* had outlined the realm of phenomenal necessity, determined by the a priori laws of creative understanding (*Verstand*). Then the *Critique of Practical Reason* had granted a glimpse into the realm of freedom where reason (*Vernunft*) holds sway in the role of moral legislator. The dualism of the phenomenal world on the one hand and the noumenal world on the other (or of the corresponding faculties of the mind) required a mediation, and beauty as analyzed in the first part of the *Critique of Judgment* furnished the connecting link. Through the harmonious design of a shell or a melodious sequence of sounds the effectiveness of reason in the phenomenal world is borne in upon the mind which intuitively recognizes in these forms a "purposiveness without purpose"; *i.e.,* they appear to be designed to fit our needs and desires although there is no rational ground for supposing this. This recognition gives a peculiar pleasure at the harmonious interplay of our cognitive faculties, and it expresses itself in a judgment which, though incapable of demonstration, can claim universal validity.

As against the confusion of aesthetic pleasures with other pleasurable feelings which had marred the theories of the 18th-century psychologists, Kant sharply distinguished the disinterested pleasure, fruit of the contemplation of the beautiful, from "agreeableness." At the same time, he restored to beauty the dignity of a power mediating between two worlds. But the mediating function assigned to beauty by Kant characteristically differed from the classical or Platonic mediation. Instead of inflaming the passionate yearning of love and thus initiating an ascent toward beauty as a transcendent form, beauty was now conceived as healing an otherwise incurable wound by reconciling the intelligible to the sensuous, freedom to necessity. Beauty, in this view, became an essentially and exclusively sensuous phenomenon, though one of great spiritual significance. Kant's followers, however much they modified the master's theory, generally maintained this his fundamental thesis, thereby justifying the title of "aesthetics," derived as it is from *aisthesis* or sense perception. Beauty is "the ideal informing the real," as Schelling (1775–1854) asserted; or "the sensuous appearance of the idea," in the formula of Hegel (1770–1831). The conception of an "aesthetic at-one-ment" as envisaged by Kant became the germinating idea which, at the turn of the 18th and 19th centuries, gave rise to a breath-taking wealth of intellectual creations. System after system was forged, and almost all of those philosophical constructs included aesthetics as an essential part of the systematic whole—a novelty in the history of philosophy. Moreover, though most of these systematic treatises on aesthetics dealt separately with beauty in nature and with artistic beauty, they were all animated by the conviction that man holds commerce with beauty chiefly through art.

Goethe.—Kant himself, by taste and culture a man of the Enlightenment, was out of touch with the new creative movement heralded by the early phase of romanticism. Yet his *Critique of Judgment* ushered in a new epoch of aesthetic thought because those who felt the impact of his teaching were influenced by another master as well—one who taught them less through his arguments than through his presence and his poetical work. Goethe (1749–1832) seemed to his contemporaries the incarnation of poetical power and wisdom. The lesson that he taught was all the more impressive as neither as an artist nor as a thinker did he start from the Kantian experience of an ultimate duality: the harmony symbolized, according to Kant, by the beautiful form seemed to be the principle animating both his life and his thought. He, too, used Platonic language, knowing that he received "the veil of poetry out of the hands of Truth." But the spiritual significance of beauty appeared to him in the light of a formative ascent rather than as the healing of a fatal breach—the roots of his thinking reached more deeply into the past than those of his philosophizing contemporaries. Their idealist aesthetics was, to a large extent, an attempt to understand art and the artist, typified by Goethe and his work, with the help of concepts derived from Kant.

Schiller and the Notion of Play.—Friedrich Schiller (1759–1805) took up and transformed Kant's idea of an interplay of faculties in his *Letters on the Aesthetical Education of Man* (1793–94). Man's inner life, composed, as he thought, of the two basic drives *Stofftrieb* ("sensuous instinct") and *Formtrieb* ("formal instinct"), can attain to balanced unity only through a third force, the play-impulse which constitutes beauty and art. Hence art appeared to him an indispensable instrument for fashioning man into the kind of harmonious personality which he admired in Goethe. A little less than a century later, Herbert Spencer (1820–1903) read Schiller's essay, forgot the name of the author and made the idea of play the cornerstone of his sociological aesthetics. The theory was then adopted and variously modified by psychologists such as Karl Groos (1861–1946) and Konrad Lange (1855–1921), until a growing realization of the importance of the festival as a matrix out of which the arts developed reminded scholars of the religious and metaphysical significance of play.

Later Romantic Aesthetics.—Friedrich Schlegel (1772–1829), the master theorist of the romantic movement in Germany and one of the representatives of Christian idealism, combined the idea of play with another element of Kant's aesthetics, the notion of freedom, interpreting the latter as the freedom of the creative mind to rise by means of play above the limitations imposed by fixed form. Thus he arrived at his concept of irony, which then furnished to S. A. Kierkegaard (1813–55) the dominant trait for characterizing the aesthetic type of life and served K. W. F. Solger (1780–1819) as an axis around which he constructed his system of aesthetics. The climax of romantic thought was finally reached by Novalis (Friedrich von Hardenberg, 1772–1801), with whom poetry, philosophy and life came to be fused in the ecstatic vision of a "magic universe." A curious reversal of the preceding development took place. Through the constitution of aesthetics, an area of its own had been set aside for man's artistic creativity. Now autonomy turned into hegemony, and the tendency toward differentiation gave way to desire for total inclusiveness. Art, after liberating itself from service under alien powers, aspired in its turn to embrace life in its entirety. In German romantic thought, especially in Novalis and E. T. W. Hoffmann, we find the seeds of 19th century aestheticism—the movement which tried to raise beauty to the rank of the sovereign good. Edgar Allan Poe, Gustave Flaubert, Théophile Gautier, Charles Baudelaire, Walter Pater and Oscar Wilde—all had undergone, directly or indirectly, the influence of German romantic aesthetics.

The Creative Imagination.—The harmonious attunement of the cognitive faculties as a natural gift was for Kant the mark of genius. Schelling, carrying the idealist principle beyond the limits of Kantian phenomenalism, took a further step by developing the idea of a creative imagination as a faculty analogous to the power of intellectual intuition. Both imagination and philosophical vision, he asserted, achieve a reconciliation of the finite and the infinite—imagination in the sphere of the real, philosophical vision in the sphere of the ideal. Art, like philosophy, discloses metaphysical truth, not under the form of concepts but by the imaginative creation of symbols. The spread of the concept of the symbolizing imagination, however, owes much to Samuel Taylor Coleridge. It is reflected in his distinction between fancy on the one hand, which plays only with fixities and definites, and imagination on the other, a "living Power and prime Agent . . . a repetition in the finite of the eternal act of creation in the infinite I AM." Largely through Coleridge, the same idea was carried to America, where it inspired Emerson and the New England transcendentalists.

The "Naïve" and the "Sentimental."—One may wonder how an aesthetics spellbound by Winckelmann's classicist dogma and looking backward to ancient Greece as to the unique revelation of absolute beauty could give guidance to the forward-going creative movement of German classical and romantic poetry. An answer to this question was first suggested by Schiller. Through him the problem that had agitated the combatants in the quarrel of the Ancients and Moderns gave rise to a scheme boldly conceived as the outline of a philosophy of history. This scheme achieved the seemingly impossible: a justification of modern art which left to the ancients the prize of unmatched perfection. All poets, he held, are nature or seek nature: in the "naïve" poet, the perfect accord between imagination and understanding is the source from which his creation springs; the "sentimental" poet strives after this accord which to him is a remote ideal. Naïve poetry and art in general were typified for Schiller by the Greeks and among his contemporaries by Goethe; sentimental poetry by the moderns in general and especially by his own works. Of the Greeks he wrote: "They are . . . what we must be again some day . . . We perceive eternally in them that which we have not, but which we are continually forced to strive after; that which we can never reach, but which we can hope to approach by an infinite progress." Friedrich Schlegel appropriated and reinterpreted this scheme in broadening its historical basis and in replacing Schiller's "sentimental poetry" with his idea of a "progressive universal poetry" and of the "characteristic" as a hallmark of the modern artistic achievement.

Hegelian Aesthetics.—The scheme of a universal history of artistic creation yielded a program for the romantic school of poetry. In a revised form it was adopted by G. W. F. Hegel (q.v.; 1770–1831), the beneficiary and at the same time the adversary of romanticism. In his famous *Lectures on Aesthetics* he distinguished three phases: (1) in the "symbolic art" as produced by the nations of the ancient orient, the idea is still recalcitrant in its relation to form; (2) Greek art alone attains a perfect equilibrium of the ideal and the sensuous form ("Nothing more beautiful can ever be"); and (3) in the Christian era, the aesthetic achievement of antiquity is surpassed by a spiritual comprehension of the idea as such, which gives rise to a new form of art, called "romantic" by Hegel. This art may still rise to its peculiar kind of greatness, though art has outlived its former vitality: "For us art is no longer the highest form under which truth can become real." Nevertheless, Hegel firmly established the place of art in the highest sphere of the creations of the mind. In the sphere of the "absolute spirit," "the identity eternally subsisting in itself and returning to itself," art comes first, and it is surpassed only by revealed religion and philosophy. Long after the decline of idealism, Hegelian aesthetics, in one form or another, continued to survive, in Germany chiefly through the magisterial work of F. T. Vischer (1807–87), whose *Ästhetik oder Wissenschaft des Schönen* first appeared in 1846, and in England through Bernard Bosanquet (1848–1923), who published a *History of Aesthetic* in 1892.

Schleiermacher.—Through art a fundamental duality is resolved into a happy consonance—this was the conviction shared by all the representatives of German idealist aesthetics. F. D. E. Schleiermacher (1768–1834) developed this idea of reconciliation through art with an unparalleled analytic subtlety. He showed that expression and imaginative play are two aspects of the same peculiar semblance which characterizes the work of art—a semblance which lifts the artistic image out of the context of reality and confers upon it a symbolic significance. So the aesthetic *via media* between construction and experience leads the mind to a vision of the absolute.

Schopenhauer and Nietzsche.—Art became an instrument of liberation rather than of reconciliation in the system of Arthur Schopenhauer (1788–1860), who inherited the riches of the Platonic-Kantian tradition and out of them erected a towering metaphysical structure. At the same time he vitiated the meaning of it all by putting a blind will as the ultimate reality in the place of the absolute as understood by his brother-idealists. Art, within this strangely inverted idealist scheme, was viewed as a substitute for religion. In the creations of art, Schopenhauer taught, the mind intuits Platonic forms, thus freeing itself for a while from the curse of existence and "keeping the Sabbath of the penal servitude of willing."

Friedrich Nietzsche (1844–1900) recognized Schopenhauer as his true master: the idea of a liberation through art was at the core of his famous essay on *The Birth of Tragedy From the Spirit of Music*. In a luminous symbolic dream-picture an Apollonian vision of life redeems the primordial pain of Dionysian ecstasy—such was for Nietzsche the essence of Greek tragedy. Again art was conceived as a road toward salvation, but this saving power was not only distinguished from but opposed to reason.

Conclusions.—In Plato's dialogues Socrates is depicted as the true lover, the only one worthy to receive out of the seer's mouth the disclosure of the mystery of the love which, through beauty, creates wisdom. In Nietzsche's view the same Socrates appears as a fiendish character who destroys the heroic wisdom of the early Greeks by propagating a reason hostile to art. Thus the path which has been traced here through the centuries come full circle. First, the two lines of thought—the one which pursues the idea of beauty and the other trying to determine the nature of art as a form of human productivity—will not fit into a harmonious pattern: the essence of beauty appears to be a transcendent entity, and art seems much more, and again much less, than "fine art." Then a *rapprochement* takes place, and finally, in the heat engendered by an overwhelming experience, a fusion is effected: a unified idea of art emerges, modeled, roughly speaking, on a Platonic concept of poetry. But the solution, hardly achieved, creates fresh difficulties. Art, placed in the neighbourhood of religion and metaphysics, reveals its innate dignity but also a tendency toward beguiling the mind into an idolatry of beauty, whereupon, defeated in its attempt to dominate life, it becomes divorced from life, and writers on aesthetics spread the false gospel of "art for art's sake." So the history of aesthetics is in fact a guide to aesthetic truth. But the art of interpreting the guide's language must be acquired through a renewed study of the phenomena. One lesson, however, stands out and, as formulated by Franz Baader (1765–1841), has a direct bearing on the difficulty under which 19th-century aesthetics laboured: "The deeper the mind of an artist and the more intensely he lives in ideas and ideals, the more certain it is that, even in the moments of supreme enthusiasm, the idea will flash through his inward life: alas, I have only painted pictures, and yet I feel I am created for realities."

For later developments see AESTHETICS.

BIBLIOGRAPHY.—Hermann Lotze, *Geschichte der Ästhetik in Deutschland* (1868); B. Bosanquet, *A History of Aesthetic* (1892); W. A. Knight, *The Philosophy of the Beautiful, Being Outlines of the History of Aesthetics* (1891); H. Kuhn and K. E. Gilbert, *A History of Esthetics*, rev. ed. (1953); B. Croce, *Estetica* (1902); E. von Hartmann, *Die deutsche Ästhetik seit Kant* (1886); M. Menéndez Pelayo, *Historia de las ideas estéticas en España* (1883–91; new ed., 1940).　　(Ht. K.)

AETA, a collective name by which the Negrito (*q.v.*) groups in the Philippines are known. They are short (pygmoid) with woolly hair and dark skin, believed to be an early land-migrating people related physically to the Semang of the Malay peninsula and to the Andaman Islanders. Comparisons of blood types contradicted an earlier assumption that they have a common origin with the African Pygmies. The Aeta are semisedentary and continue to derive a major part of their subsistence from hunting, fishing and food gathering. They inhabit the remote upland regions of the larger islands. The basic social unit is the extended patricentric family. The bow and arrow are used by all groups. Personal ornamentation includes scarification, teeth chipped to a sharp point and unusual bamboo combs. Though technologically primitive, they possess a phenomenal knowledge of plant and animal life. Religious beliefs and practices centre on a complex of potentially helpful or harmful spirits, *anitu,* whom they believe inhabit the proximate environment. Aeta numbered about 30,000 in the 1960s.

BIBLIOGRAPHY.—M. Vanoverbergh, *Negritos of Northern Luzon* (1925); H. W. Krieger, *Peoples of the Philippines* (1942); R. B. Fox, "The Pinatubo Negritos: Their Useful Plants and Material Culture," *Phil. J. Sci.* (1952–57); P. Schebesta, *Die Negrito Asiens* (1952); J. M. Garvan, *The Negritos of the Philippines* (1963).　　(R. B. Fx.)

AETHELBALD (ETHELBALD) (d. 757), king of the Mercians from 716 to 757, succeeded Ceolred after some years in exile, during which he visited St. Guthlac, the hermit of Crowland. By 731 all the provinces south of the Humber were subject to his overlordship. He occupied Somerton in Wessex in 733 and controlled Berkshire some time between 740 and 757. He held London by 733. He made war on Northumbria in 737 or 740 and on the Welsh in 743. Though defeated by the West Saxons in 752, one of his charters shows that he could dispose of land in Wiltshire in 757. He made many gifts to the church, and Boniface and other Anglo-

Saxon missionary bishops in Germany praised his generosity in almsgiving and his strong, just rule in a joint letter written primarily to dissuade him from loose living and from violating ecclesiastical privileges. His charter of 749, freeing the church from public burdens except bridge repair and fortress building, may be a response to this letter. His charters use the regnal style "king of Britain." He was murdered in 757 by his followers.

BIBLIOGRAPHY.—*Felix's Life of Saint Guthlac,* ed. by B. Colgrave (1956); *English Historical Documents,* vol. i, ed. by D. Whitelock, pp. 21 ff., 158–163, 259, 449–454, 682, 751–758 (1955); F. M. Stenton, *Anglo-Saxon England,* 2nd ed. (1947).　　(D. Wk.)

AETHELBERHT (ETHELBERT) I (d. 616), king of Kent from 560 to 616, was son of a certain Eormenric. Bede attributes to him an imperium over all England south of the Humber, a position which he probably obtained only late in his reign, for he was defeated by the West Saxons in 568 at a place called Wibbandun. He married Berhta, daughter of Charibert, king of Paris, and she brought with her Bishop Liudhard, but they seem to have made little attempt to convert the people of Kent to Christianity. This marriage may, however, account for the tolerant reception that Aethelberht gave to the missionaries sent by Pope Gregory the Great. These landed in Thanet in 597. The king gave them a dwelling in Canterbury and later accepted Christianity himself, though he did not attempt to force it on his subjects. A second see for Kent was established at Rochester in 604; and one also at London, where the king, Saeberht of Essex, was Aethelberht's nephew. Aethelberht's conversion of Raedwald of East Anglia had only a temporary effect. Aethelberht issued the first code of Anglo-Saxon laws, which established the legal position of the clergy and put into writing many secular regulations.

BIBLIOGRAPHY.—Bede, *Historia Ecclesiastica,* bk. i, ch. 25–33, bk. ii, ch. 3, 5; *Anglo-Saxon Chronicle;* F. M. Stenton, *Anglo-Saxon England,* 2nd ed. (1947). For the laws, *see* F. L. Attenborough (ed.), *The Laws of the Earliest English Kings,* with Eng. trans. (1922).　　(D. Wk.)

AETHELBERHT (ETHELBERT) (d. 865), king of the West Saxons, an elder brother of King Alfred, succeeded to the underkingdom of Kent, Essex, Surrey and Sussex on the death of his father Aethelwulf in 858 and to the whole kingdom of Wessex (*q.v.*) after his brother Aethelbald's death in 860. A great force of Vikings stormed Winchester in that year, but were later defeated. In 865, the year of his death, a Viking force raided Kent.

See *Anglo-Saxon Chronicle;* also King Alfred's will, in *English Historical Documents,* vol. i, ed. by D. Whitelock (1955).　　(D. Wk.)

AETHELFLAED (ETHELFLEDA) (d. 918), "lady of the Mercians," played an important part in the struggle against the Scandinavians during the reign (899–924) of her brother Edward the Elder (*q.v.*). Daughter of Alfred the Great and wife of Ealderman Aethelred of the Mercians, she became effective ruler of Mercia (*q.v.*) some years before Aethelred died in 911.

Her fame rests chiefly on her close and successful co-operation with Edward against the Danish armies of eastern England. To supplement Edward's fortified enclosures (boroughs) in the southeast midlands, she built fortresses at "Bremesburh" (910), "Scergeat" and Bridgnorth (912), Tamworth and Stafford (913), Eddisbury and Warwick (914), and Chirbury, "Weardburh" and Runcorn (915). She also restored the defenses of Chester (907). The joint attack on Danish positions was launched in 917. Aethelflaed captured Derby and in 918 occupied Leicester. Edward had advanced to Stamford but before the campaign could be successfully completed Aethelflaed died at Tamworth on June 12, 918, and he at once rode there to claim Mercian allegiance. Within a few months he was formally accepted as lord by all Danes and Englishmen south of the Humber.

Aethelflaed ordered at least one expedition into Wales, against Brecknock (916), and she probably compelled the princes of Wales to recognize her overlordship. She also intervened in Northumbria, and Irish annals suggest that she led a temporary alliance of Picts, Scots, Britons and Anglo-Danish Northumbrians against raids by Irish-Norse adventurers. She made possible Edward's reconquest of the Danish midlands, she facilitated his integration of Mercia and Wessex and, by extending her influence into Wales and Northumbria, she ensured that he was accepted as the most powerful ruler in Britain.

See F. T. Wainwright, "Aethelflaed Lady of the Mercians," in *The Anglo-Saxons,* ed. by P. Clemoes (1960). (F. T. W.)

AETHELFRITH (ETHELFRITH) (d. 616), king of Northumbria (q.v.), succeeded his father Aethelric as king of Bernicia (q.v.) in 593 and later ruled Deira (q.v.) also. He married Acha, daughter of Aelli of Deira. His advances against the northern Britons brought him also into conflict with Aidan (Aedan), king of the Dalriad Scots, whom he defeated at a place called Degsastan in 603. Between 613 and 616 he routed the Britons at Chester, killing a host of monks from Bangor Iscoed who had come to pray for the British army. He extended his authority so far southwest that by the end of his reign the Britons of Wales had become separated from those of Strathclyde. He tried to persuade Raedwald (q.v.) of East Anglia to surrender or kill Edwin, the refugee heir to the Deiran throne, but Raedwald refused and restored Edwin, after killing Aethelfrith at the battle of the Idle in 616.

BIBLIOGRAPHY.—Bede, *Historia Ecclesiastica,* bk. i, ch. 34, bk. ii, ch. 2, 12; *Anglo-Saxon Chronicle;* F. M. Stenton, *Anglo-Saxon England,* 2nd ed. (1947). (D. WK.)

AETHELNOTH (ETHELNOTH, EGELNODUS; called THE GOOD) (d. 1038), archbishop of Canterbury from 1020 to 1038, son of the ealderman Aethelmaer (a descendant of King Alfred's brother Aethelred), was a monk at Glastonbury and then dean of Canterbury before being consecrated archbishop on Nov. 13, 1020, by Archbishop Wulfstan of York. He translated the relics of St. Alphege (Aelfheah) from London to Canterbury. The *Encomium Emmae* has a story that he refused to crown Canute's son, Harold Harefoot. He died on Oct. 29, 1038.

BIBLIOGRAPHY.—*Anglo-Saxon Chronicle;* William of Malmesbury, *Gesta Regum,* ed. by W. Stubbs (1887–89); F. E. Harmer (ed.), *Anglo-Saxon Writs* (1952). (D. WK.)

AETHELRED (ETHELRED) (d. 716), king of Mercia (q.v.) from 674 to 704, succeeded his brother Wulfhere (q.v.) as ruler not only of Mercia but also of Middlesex and the once West Saxon area north of the Thames, where he placed a Mercian see at Dorchester-on-Thames in Oxfordshire. He also had influence in Wiltshire and Berkshire. He married Osthryth, daughter of King Oswiu of Northumbria, but this did not prevent warfare against her brother King Egfrith, over whom he won a great victory at the Trent in 678, by which he obtained Lindsey. Peace was made by Theodore, archbishop of Canterbury, and Aethelred paid a wergild for Egfrith's brother Aelfwine who was killed in the battle. Meanwhile, in 676 Aethelred had raided Kent, and he had some power there about ten years later. But he lost to Ceadwalla of Wessex the control in Surrey and Sussex which Wulfhere had held. He was a protector of Bishop Wilfrid (q.v.) in his exile and was a benefactor of churches. In 704 he retired to the monastery of Bardney, where he died in 716.

BIBLIOGRAPHY.—Eddius, *Life of Bishop Wilfrid,* ed. by B. Colgrave (1927); F. M. Stenton, *Anglo-Saxon England,* 2nd ed. (1947); *English Historical Documents,* vol. i, ed. by D. Whitelock, pp. 20, 154–157, 629, 653, 659 ff. (1955). (D. WK.)

AETHELRED (ETHELRED) **I** (d. 871), king of Wessex from 865 to 871, was the fourth son of Aethelwulf (q.v.) and succeeded his brother Aethelberht (q.v.) in the year when the great Danish army began its attempt to conquer England. Aethelred went with his brother Alfred (q.v.) to help Burgred of Mercia against the Danes, who were in Nottingham in 868, but the Danes refused battle and the Mercians made peace. Late in 870, the Danes invaded Wessex, and Aethelred and Alfred unsuccessfully attacked them at Reading. The brothers won a victory on the Berkshire downs, then called Ashdown, where Aethelred refused to begin battle until divine service was over. Defeats followed at Basing and a place called Merton (Meretun). Aethelred died in 871 and was succeeded by Alfred.

BIBLIOGRAPHY.—*Anglo-Saxon Chronicle;* Asser, *Life of Alfred,* ed. by W. H. Stevenson (1904); King Alfred's Will, in *English Historical Documents,* vol. i, ed. by D. Whitelock (1955). (D. WK.)

AETHELRED (ETHELRED) **II** (968?–1016), king of the English from 978 to 1016, surnamed "the Unready" (originally *unraed,* "evil counsel"), was the son of King Edgar and his second wife Aelfthryth. His accession after the murder of his half brother Edward (q.v.) the Martyr in 978 was an inauspicious beginning responsible for much of the distrust and disloyalty prevalent during his reign. Danish raids recommenced in 980. In spite of some heroic defense, especially of London, bad leadership and mismanagement made the history of his reign a sad tale of defeat. The attackers were bought off in 991 and at ever-increasing price on many later occasions. Almost the whole country was ravaged. The massacre of the Danes on St. Brice's day, Nov. 13, 1002, provoked a great invasion by Sweyn of Denmark in 1003, and another great army arrived in 1009. St. Alphege (Aelfheah), archbishop of Canterbury, was captured by the Danes in 1011 and martyred in 1012. By the end of 1013 Sweyn was accepted as king and Aethelred fled to Richard of Normandy, whose sister he had married. When Sweyn died early in 1014, Aethelred was invited back on condition that he would rule better, but Sweyn's son Canute returned with an army and war was raging when Aethelred died at London on April 23, 1016.

The reign is disfigured by the treachery of English leaders and by murders instigated by the king, such as that of Aelfhelm, a Northumbrian ealderman, in 1006 and of the northern thegns Sigeferth and Morcar in 1015. Aethelred was unhappy in his dealings with the north. Yet the picture in the *Anglo-Saxon Chronicle* may be one-sided. Archbishop Wulfstan of York strove for reform and composed several law codes for the king, and numismatic evidence suggests a high degree of administrative efficiency. The reign saw a great production of literary and artistic works.

See *English Historical Documents,* vol. i, ed. by D. Whitelock, pp. 210–226, 293–297, 318–321, 401–414, 525–547, 823 ff., 854–859 (1955); F. M. Stenton, *Anglo-Saxon England,* 2nd ed. (1947). (D. WK.)

AETHELSTAN (ETHELSTAN or ATHELSTAN) (d. 939), king of the English from 924 to 939, son of Edward the Elder, was the first Saxon king to have effective rule over the whole of England. He called himself *rex totius Britanniae* ("king of all Britain"), on his coins, attested charters with the same title, and used flamboyant styles such as "*basileus* of the English and in like manner ruler of the whole orb of Britain." He was brought up at the court of his aunt, Aethelflaed, lady of the Mercians. On his father's death (924), he was elected king by the Mercians and then crowned king of the whole country at Kingston on Sept. 4, 925. He gave his sister in marriage to Sihtric, Scandinavian king of York, on Jan. 30, 926, but when Sihtric died in 927 he seized control in Northumbria and on July 12 received at Eamont near Penrith the homage of Constantine of the Scots, Owain of Strathclyde, Howel of Dyfed, Owain of Gwent and Ealdred, the English high reeve of Bamburgh. Welsh princes and Northumbrian magnates attended the great courts which he held between 931 and 935. At a meeting at Hereford he forced Welsh rulers to promise tribute and fixed the river Wye as a boundary. He made the river Tamar the boundary for the Britons of Cornwall, refortifying Exeter after evicting the British population. He established the see of St. Germans for the region beyond the Tamar. In the north, he bought the district of Amounderness (north Lancashire) from the Scandinavians, no doubt in order to prevent attack from the northwest. He attacked Scotland in 934, when he reached Fordoun (in Kincardineshire) by land, and Caithness by sea. Constantine of the Scots, Owain of Strathclyde and Olaf Guthfrithson, claimant of the kingdom of York, combined against him in 937 and invaded England with a large force, but were utterly routed by the West Saxons and Mercians at a place called Brunanburh. The Anglo-Saxon Chronicle enters a poem on this battle and later Anglo-Saxon writers regarded it as the main event of Aethelstan's reign. He died on Oct. 27, 939.

Aethelstan played a part in continental politics. His father had given one of his daughters in marriage to Charles III the Simple, king of the West Franks, and their son Louis was brought up at Aethelstan's court until recalled to his father's throne in 936. Aethelstan married his sisters to continental rulers including the emperor Otto I and Hugh the Great, duke of the Franks. He had stood godfather for Alan of Brittany, who was brought up at his court and won back Brittany by his support. A third foreign prince reared at his court was Haakon, son of Harald Haarfager, who sailed with English men and ships to win Norway and to attempt its conversion to Christianity.

Aethelstan was a generous donor to churches, both in England and on the continent. His gifts included relics, of which he was a famous collector, and books, some imported from abroad. Six of his law codes are extant and show him active in suppressing theft, in removing to other districts men too overbearing in their own and in punishing corruption. An unusual note of leniency is found in his concern to mitigate the punishment of young offenders. His reign is important in numismatic history, for he pronounced that one coinage should be current throughout the realm, and that money should not be minted outside a town.

BIBLIOGRAPHY.—F. M. Stenton, *Anglo-Saxon England,* 2nd ed. (1947); *English Historical Documents,* vol. i, ed. by D. Whitelock, pp. 38–43, 95 ff., 199–202, 277–283, 316 ff., 381–391, 503–508 (1955); J. Armitage Robinson, *The Times of Saint Dunstan* (1923).   (D. Wk.)

AETHELWEARD (ETHELWERD) (d. 998?), English chronicler and ealderman of the western provinces (probably the whole of Wessex; *q.v.*), was a descendant of King Alfred's brother Aethelred. He wrote, in elaborate and peculiar Latin, a chronicle for his continental kinswoman, Matilda, abbess of Essen. In the printed version of the text, the chronicle stops in 975, but fragments of the burned manuscript show that it continued in this into the reign of Aethelred (978–1016). Up to 894 it is based on a version of the *Anglo-Saxon Chronicle* (*q.v.*) more ancient than any now surviving; thereafter it is an independent authority. Aethelweard was the patron of Aelfric the homilist. The last certain mention of him is in 998.

BIBLIOGRAPHY.—H. Petrie, *Monumenta Historica Britannica* (1848) gives a text of the chronicle. *See* also E. E. Barker, "Cottonian Fragments of Aethelweard's Chronicle," in *Bulletin of the Institute of Historical Research,* vol. xxiv (1951); F. M. Stenton, "The South-Western Element in the Old English Chronicle," in *Essays in Medieval History Presented to T. F. Tout* (1925), "Aethelwerd's Account of the Last Years of Alfred's Reign," in *English Historical Review,* vol. xxiv (1909) and "The Danes at Thorney Island in 893," in vol. xxvii (1912); K. Sisam, "Anglo-Saxon Royal Genealogies," in *Proceedings of the British Academy,* vol. xxxix (1953).   (D. Wk.)

AETHELWULF (ETHELWULF) (d. 858), king of the West Saxons from 839 to 858, was the son of Egbert and father of Alfred the Great. On his accession he relinquished to his son Aethelstan the subkingdom of Kent, Essex, Sussex and Surrey which he himself had ruled since 825. He was constantly at war with the Danes and his great victory in 851 at a place called Aclea in Surrey against a large force, which had stormed Canterbury and London and put Beorhtwulf of Mercia to flight, was widely acclaimed. But it did not prevent further raids and the Danes wintered in Sheppey in 855. Aethelwulf showed wisdom in his dealings with Mercia. He helped King Burgred (Beorhtwulf's successor) against the Welsh in 853 and gave him his daughter in marriage. During Aethelwulf's reign the long struggle for the possession of the lands on both sides of the Thames was amicably settled, Aethelwulf receiving Berkshire, and presumably renouncing all claim on the lands north of the upper Thames. He was a religious man, who freed one-tenth of his demesne from secular dues and services for the benefit of churches, and in 855 he took his son Alfred to Rome. On his way back he delayed at the Frankish court to marry Judith, the daughter of Charles II the Bald. Under pressure from a faction in Wessex he agreed to relinquish that kingdom to his son Aethelbald, retaining only his previous subkingdom in the east.

BIBLIOGRAPHY.—*Anglo-Saxon Chronicle; Asser, Life of Alfred,* ed. by W. H. Stevenson (1904); F. M. Stenton, *Anglo-Saxon England,* 2nd ed. (1947).   (D. Wk.)

AETHRA, in Greek legend, was the daughter of King Pittheus of Troezen, who married her to Aegeus, king of Athens, who had previously been childless. She became mother of Theseus by Aegeus or by Poseidon, who had attacked her in Troezen. (The two versions may reflect the antique confusion of Aegeus with the sea-god; *e.g.,* the Aegean sea.)

Many years later she guarded Helen when she had been stolen from Sparta by Theseus; in retribution Aethra was carried to Sparta by the Dioscuri to be Helen's slave, thereafter following her to Troy. Freed after the ten years' war, Aethra later killed herself in grief for her son.   (T. V. B.)

AETIUS (FLAVIUS AETIUS) (d. 454), Roman general and statesman, the commander of the imperial army at the battle of the Catalaunian plains, was born at Durostorum (Silistra in Bulgaria), probably toward the close of the 4th century. He was the son of Gaudentius, the *magister equitum* ("master of the cavalry"), and of his Italian wife. As a youth Aetius spent some time as a hostage with Alaric, leader of the Visigoths, and later with the Huns, thus acquiring valuable knowledge of the leading barbarian peoples of his day. He supported the usurper John in Italy in 423–425 and brought to Italy a force of Huns, alleged to number 60,000 to help him. Although John died three days before his arrival, Aetius forced the government to grant him an amnesty. After successful battles in Gaul against the Visigoths and the Franks, he was appointed in 430 as *magister utriusque militiae* ("master of both services"). His rival Bonifacius having died in 432, he soon gained almost complete control over the young emperor Valentinian III, and from this time until the end of his life he was the dominating personality in the western empire. He became consul three times (432, 437 and 446), a unique distinction for a commoner; and it was said that envoys from the provinces were no longer sent to the emperor, but to Aetius. He was given the title of patrician in 433 and for several years thereafter fought continuously and successfully in Gaul against rebels and barbarians. In 435–437 his general Litorius crushed the Armoricans, who had revolted. In the same years, aided by Hunnish troops, Aetius mercilessly destroyed the Burgundian kingdom at Worms, an event which made a deep impression in the barbarian world and is remembered in the *Nibelungenlied* (*q.v.*). In 437–439, despite the defeat and death of Litorius, he checked the Visigoths of Toulouse. He returned to Italy in 440. In 443 he transferred the remnants of the Burgundians from Worms to Savoy, where their kingdom survived until 534. In 446, during his third consulate, the Britons appealed to him for help against the barbarian invaders of their island, but there is no evidence that he was able to do anything to aid them. In 451 he joined with the Visigoths in defeating Attila and the Huns at the battle of the Catalaunian plains (*q.v.*), but when Attila invaded Italy in the following year, Aetius could do little to oppose him. He next secured the engagement of his son to Placidia, the emperor's daughter; but on Sept. 21, 454, at the height of his power, he was assassinated at the instigation of Petronius Maximus, the future emperor. Valentinian III struck him down at an audience.

See J. B. Bury, *History of the Later Roman Empire,* vol. i (1923).   (E. A. T.)

AETOLIA (AITOLIA), a district of ancient Greece, directly north of the Corinthian gulf, bounded on the west by the Achelous river, on the north and east by the western spurs of Mt. Parnassus and Mt. Oeta. The land falls into two divisions. The basins of the lower Achelous and Euenus (Evinos) form a series of alluvial valleys intersected by detached ridges which mostly run parallel to the coast, the hinterland being the rich agricultural country of the central Aetolian plain north of Lakes Hyria (Lisimakhia) and Trichonis. Northern and eastern Aetolia is a complex of chains and peaks, whose rugged limestone flanks bear only stunted shrubs and leave scarcely room for a few precarious mule tracks. These heights often rise in the frontier ranges of Tymphrestus, Oxía and Corax (Vardhoúsia) to more than 7,000 ft.; snow-capped Kiona attains to 8,235 ft.

In early legend Old Aetolia, with its cities of Pleuron and Calydon, figures prominently. During the great migrations (*see* GREECE: *History*), the earlier inhabitants were largely displaced. Those who were left long remained backward; in the 5th century some tribes still lived in open villages under petty kings, addicted to piracy and hardly recognized as Hellenes. But the successful repulse by their archers and slingers of the Athenian invasion of 426 indicates a fairly advanced organization, and by 367 the Aetolian league (*q.v.*) was in existence. The subsequent history of Aetolia is the history of this body. In 27 B.C. Augustus included Aetolia in the province of Achaea. In the 15th century it passed first under the rule of Skanderbeg and the Venetians and later under Turkish rule, in the reign of Mohammed II. In the War of Greek Independence it saw much severe fighting, including the sieges of Missolonghi. In modern Greece it is linked with the ancient Acarnania in the department (*nomos*) Aetolia-Acarnania with its administrative centre at Missolonghi.

See W. J. Woodhouse, *Aetolia* (1897). (F. W. WA.)

AETOLIAN LEAGUE. The tribes of ancient Aetolia (*q.v.*) possessed some degree of central organization by 426 B.C., when they repelled an Athenian invasion; by 367 they had united in a federal state or "sympolity," perhaps under Theban influence (*see* GREECE: *History*). In return for helping Epaminondas (367) and Philip II of Macedonia (338) they recovered their seaboard, including Naupactus, later adding Oeniadae (*c.* 330). Aetolia thus became one of the four leading military powers in Greece. Its subsequent prosperity depended partly on the wealth and influence acquired by Aetolian mercenaries in Hellenistic courts, but chiefly on the strength of the confederacy which, after successfully resisting the punitive invasions of Antipater and Craterus (322) and of Cassander (314–311), grew rapidly during the ensuing period of Macedonian weakness. By *c.* 300 (the exact date is uncertain) Aetolia, expanding eastward, had gained possession of Delphi and formed an alliance with Boeotia. This led to war with Demetrius Poliorcetes, but in 280 the Aetolians fought beside Antigonus Gonatas against the Peloponnesians led by Areus of Sparta and successfully extended their influence in central Greece, where Heraclea furnished a strong point against northern invaders and their control of the Amphictyonic council provided a useful political instrument. Aetolian valour was conspicuously displayed in 279, when it broke the strength of the irruption of the Celts and played a leading part in preserving Delphi. The commemorative festival of the Soteria ("Salvation"), which the league established at Delphi (246), obtained recognition from many leading Greek states. In 245 the Aetolians brought the Boeotians into subjection after defeating them at Chaeronea, thus gaining control of all central Greece. They then joined Antigonus Gonatas against the Achaean league (*q.v.*) and Sparta and made acquisitions in the Peloponnesus for their allies in Elis, Megalopolis and Messene.

Later in the century their power was attenuated by Macedonia. From 239 to 229 they combined with Achaea against Demetrius II of Macedonia and in 230–229 against the Illyrian pirates, who outdid them in unscrupulousness and violence. Although by this time their power extended to Cephalonia and several Aegean islands, the provinces of Thessaly which they seized on Demetrius' death were promptly recovered by his successor, Antigonus Doson, and eastern Phocis and Boeotia detached themselves from the confederacy. Moreover in 229 Cleomenes of Sparta annexed several Arcadian towns which the Aetolians had recently acquired from Achaea. Aetolian raids on Achaean territory (220) led to a war with Philip V of Macedonia and many members of Antigonus Doson's Greek league. Philip displayed great energy, expelling the invaders from the Peloponnesus and even marching into Aetolia, where he sacked the federal capital, Thermum (now Thermon); but when he was lured by the war between Hannibal and Rome he made peace with Aetolia on the basis of the *status quo* (217). The Romans solicited Aetolian help against Philip in 211; the subsequent war against the Greek league ended with a separate peace in 206. In the second Macedonian war (200–197) the Aetolians again fought with Rome against Philip, and their cavalry largely secured the victory at Cynoscephalae (197). The Romans handed over Dolopia, Phocis and eastern Locris to the Aetolians in return but excited deep resentment by withholding Aetolia's former Thessalian possessions. The Aetolians then (192) invited Antiochus III of Syria to European Greece, thus precipitating a conflict with Rome. In this they wasted their chances. Sparta refused support, and the Aetolians' failure to hold Thermopylae (191) rendered Antiochus' position untenable. His defeat at Magnesia left the Aetolians in isolation, and despite their fierce resistance the Romans refused all compromises and after their surrender in 189 B.C. restricted the league to Aetolia proper and assumed control of its foreign relations. The importance of the league as an independent state was at an end, and by the time of Sulla its functions were purely nominal.

The federal constitution closely resembled that of the Achaean league, for which it doubtless served as a model. The primary assembly was normally convoked twice a year, at Thermum each autumn to elect officials, and at various cities to transact other business in early spring. Apparently all adult males voted, though in practice the richer citizens controlled affairs. A council ("boule," "synedrion") of about 1,000 members, in which cities were represented in proportion to their population, met more frequently to supervise administration. But, especially in wartime, many essential duties fell to a smaller body of at least 30 *apokletoi*, who were perhaps a committee of the council. An annually elected general ("strategos"), assisted by the *apokletoi*, had complete control in the field and presided over the assembly. Leadership within the league was always kept in Aetolian hands, since the more distant states were linked to the confederacy by "isopolity," a "potential" citizenship which gave full civil but no political rights unless one migrated to a community enjoying full Aetolian citizenship. The Aetolians deservedly enjoyed an evil reputation for lawless violence; hence their grants of *asylia*, a guarantee against seizure of property, were highly valued. But as champions of republican Greece against foreign enemies no other Hellenistic power rendered greater service.

BIBLIOGRAPHY.—E. A. Freeman, *History of Federal Government in Greece and Italy,* 2nd ed. (1893); M. Holleaux, *Études d'épigraphie et d'histoire grecques,* vol. i (1938); G. Klaffenbach, introduction to *Inscriptiones Graecae* (editio minor), vol. ix, fasc.i, (1932); R. Flacelière, *Les Aitoliens à Delphes* (1937); J. A. O. Larsen, in *Transactions of the American Philological Association,* vol. 83 (1952) and *Representative Government in Greek and Roman History* (1955); F. W. Walbank, *Historical Commentary on Polybius* (1957). (F. W. WA.)

AETOLUS, in Greek mythology, was the son of Endymion (*q.v.*), king of Elis in northwestern Peloponnesus. To determine the succession to the throne of Elis, Endymion ordered a foot race at Olympia between his sons Aetolus, Paeon and Epeius, of whom Epeius won the race and crown. Paeon left Elis in a rage, moving "as far away as possible" (Pausanias), to that part of northern Greece to which he gave his name, Paeonia. Aetolus remained in Elis but later fled the Peloponnesus after accidentally running over and killing a spectator during a chariot race. He took refuge in Aetolia, so called after him. The whole myth represents the historical fact that in Greek prehistory dissensions in the Peloponnesus forced some of its people to migrate northward. (T. V. B.)

AFAR: *see* SAHO-AFAR; AFRICA: *Ethnography (Anthropology): Northeast Africa.*

AFER, DOMITIUS (d. A.D. 59), a Roman orator and advocate, was born at Nemausus (Nîmes) in Gallia Narbonensis and was among the first men of provincial birth to enter the Roman senate. A prominent delator (*q.v.*) under Tiberius, he was consul under Caligula (39) and superintendent of the water supply from 49 to 59, when he died. Quintilian calls him the greatest orator of his age, but only a few mots are preserved. (P. A. BR.)

AFFIDAVIT, a written statement of fact signed before an officer empowered to administer oaths. It recites the place of execution, that the person making the affidavit (affiant or deponent) states certain facts, that he appeared before the officer on a certain date and "subscribed and swore" the statement, and a jurat (*q.v.*). *See* OATH AND AFFIDAVIT. (R. E. DE.)

AFFILIATION, in law, the procedure by which paternity of an illegitimate child is determined and responsibility for its support is fixed. In England and the United States affiliation statutes provide the chief means of securing support for the illegitimate child from its putative father. *See* BASTARD; CHILDREN, LAWS CONCERNING. (M. K. R.)

AFFINE GEOMETRY: *see* PROJECTIVE GEOMETRY.

AFFINITY, in law, denotes relationship by marriage as distinguished from blood relationship (consanguinity; *q.v.*). The subject is important chiefly because of legal prohibitions against marriages between certain persons closely related by affinity, such as marriage between a widower and the mother of his deceased wife. *See* MARRIAGE, LAW OF. (B. CE.)

AFFIRMATION, in law, is the form of safeguard against false testimony allowed to those who cannot because of conscience swear an oath and to those who have no religious faith. Affirmation is appeal to the penalties of perjury rather than to eternal damnation. *See* OATH AND AFFIDAVIT. (R. E. DE.)

AFFRAY is the misdemeanour of breaking the peace in public to the terror of the public. Fighting in public is an affray, but no actual violence is necessary, and the offense is committed even where a man arms himself with weapons so as to cause terror to the public. However, abusive and threatening words alone will not amount to an affray. In the United States the English common law concerning affray applies, subject to certain modifications by the statutes of particular states. *See* CRIMINAL LAW.

AFFRE, DENIS AUGUSTE (1793–1848), French prelate, the first of the three archbishops of Paris to die by violence between 1848 and 1871, was born at St. Rome-de-Tarn (Aveyron) on Sept. 28, 1793, and was educated at the seminary of St. Sulpice in Paris, where he was for a time professor of theology. He became archbishop of Paris in 1840. Opposed to the July monarchy of Louis Philippe, he welcomed the establishment of the second republic in 1848. When, on June 23, 1848, the Parisian workers rose in revolt, Affre was led to believe that by intervening in person he might be able to restore order. Accordingly, on June 25, he mounted a barricade at the entrance to the Faubourg St. Antoine, but had only spoken a few words when, in a moment of confusion, firing broke out and he was struck by a stray bullet. He died on June 27. On June 28 the national assembly issued a decree expressing their sorrow at his death. His immediate successor, M. D. A. Sibour, was killed by a mad priest in 1857, and Georges Darboy (*q.v.*) was shot during the commune.

See L. Alazard, *Denis-Auguste Affre, archevêque de Paris* (1905).

AFFREIGHTMENT. The contract of affreightment is a contract for the carriage of goods by water, "freight" being the price paid for the service of carriage. Such contracts are of immense importance in the world's economy; they make up the legal structure governing the arterial traffic of the oceans. Contracts of affreightment are highly standardized, both by the requirements of law and by custom. Their terms are considerably complex, but the basic arrangement is very simple. There are two parties: (1) the carrier (or, by familiar personification of maritime law, the ship); and (2) the shipper and his successors in interest, the persons (if any) to whom he transfers his title to the goods in transit and his rights in the contract of carriage. The fundamental undertakings are that the carrier will carry the goods to a specified destination and that the shipper (or his successors) will pay the freight. The entire contract of affreightment consists in such qualifications and additions as the parties may expressly make to this simple arrangement or as the law may read into it irrespective of the expressed intention of the parties.

The formation of the contract is usually evidenced, and its terms stated, by one or both of two documents: the charter party (often shortened to charter) and the bill of lading. The charter party engages the whole capacity of the ship for a single voyage or for a period of time. The bill of lading is a receipt for goods taken on board for carriage and (if it is an "order" bill) functions also as a negotiable document of title, *i.e.*, its endorsement and transfer puts title to the goods in the transferee, the ship being obliged to deliver the goods at destination to the person presenting a duly endorsed bill. In the text of the charter or of the bill of lading (usually a printed form) are embodied any special terms on which the parties may have agreed. For reasons which will be made clear, many shipments are documented both by charter party and by bill of lading, but in numerous other cases (principally the less-than-shipload shipment) the bill of lading alone covers the shipment, and in some cases the charter party alone expresses the contract of carriage. It is evident from what has been said that consideration of the contract of affreightment amounts in effect to considering the content and import of these two documents.

The Bill of Lading.—As stated above, this document is first of all a receipt for goods taken aboard for carriage. As such, it names the vessel and the ports of loading and destination, describes the cargo, with needful particulars as to measure, weight and apparent condition, and states the freight payable on delivery (if freight has not been prepaid). Though no modern bill of lading stops with this, the legal position can best be clarified by reference to the rights that would arise if no further contractual

terms were added and if no statutes modified the old law of public carriage.

There are no problems, of course, if all goes well, *i.e.*, if the goods are delivered to the right person in the right place at the right time and in good condition, and if freight and other charges are duly paid. The most important part of the law pertaining to the carriage of goods concerns the allocation of responsibility when the goods are lost or damaged. In the absence of a special contract or statute (and it must be emphasized that in modern times this is a hypothetical situation) the public carrier is said to be responsible as an "insurer" for the safety and due delivery of the goods, by which is meant that, entirely without reference to any fault of his, he must pay the shipper or consignee for any loss unless it occurs through a catastrophic happening without human agency ("act of God"), through an act of the public enemy, through some defect in the goods themselves or through some negligence or misconduct of the shipper. (There is also a special arrangment, known as "general average," for dealing with the deliberate sacrifice of goods to save other goods and the ship; this will be touched on later.)

It could hardly be expected that shipowners would be satisfied to rest under this drastic liability if means were available for avoiding it. Accordingly, they sought to contract out of it by the insertion of exculpatory language in their bills of lading. (It is normally the carrier and not the shipper who prepares the printed bill.) During the 19th century, with the advent of steam, the shipping lines (dominantly British) attained a degree of economic power that enabled them to go very far in inserting clauses that exempted them from liability for loss or damage to cargo; shippers, relatively weak and unorganized, had to accept the terms offered on the carriers' printed forms or let their goods rot on the dock. The result was that, by "contract," the legal position was virtually reversed; instead of being responsible for almost all cargo loss and damage, the carrier came to be responsible for almost none, insofar as his exculpatory clauses, shortly referred to as "exceptions," were effective.

Shippers were dissatisfied with this situation, and their dissatisfaction was focused on bill-of-lading clauses that exempted the carrier from liability for the negligence of his employees. As a concrete example of the operation of such a clause, a shipper might ship farm machinery, and the carrier's sea personnel might through sheer negligence fail to close ports near this machinery, with the result that it was ruined by rust; but, with an appropriate negligence clause in the bill of lading (and a willingness by the courts to enforce the clause), the shipper or consignee could not recover damages. The U.S. federal courts refused to honour these negligence clauses, on the ground of inequality in the bargaining position of the parties, and of the clauses' repugnance to public policy. But the British courts and some U.S. state courts gave them full effect as valid terms of a contract. The position was therefore confused as well as oppressive to the cargo interests, and since the United States was then dominantly a cargo-shipping rather than a cargo-carrying nation, while British ships did most of the carrying, some international feeling was aroused.

In 1893, in the United States, the Harter act tried a compromise. The act followed the federal decisions by outlawing the negligence clause, insofar as that clause related to the carrier's duty to furnish a seaworthy and properly outfitted ship and to his duty to care properly for the goods. But it made a concession to the carrier interests by giving them (if due diligence had been used to furnish a seaworthy vessel) a positive immunity from liability for the negligence of master and crew in the navigation and management of the ship. For example, if a ship carrying goods that required refrigeration were to sail with its refrigerating gear in a defective state, proper inspection having been neglected by the carrier, or if the carrier's employees (ship's crew) negligently failed, during the voyage, to keep the refrigerating equipment turned on when needed, then the carrier would be liable for any cargo damage resulting from either of these causes. But if, due diligence having been used to make the vessel seaworthy, she struck a reef through negligent navigation and was stranded, with consequent spoilage of the goods, the carrier would not be liable. Doubtless the thought behind this compromise was that, where navigation or management of the whole ship was concerned, the carrier was sufficiently motivated by his interest in his own property, while the spur of liability was necessary to make him see that the ship was fit to receive cargo and that the cargo was properly handled.

This compromise seemed to work well and commended itself to the leading maritime nations of the world. In 1912 the Hague rules, adopting the substance of the Harter act compromise (as well as other provisions), were proposed for general voluntary inclusion in bills of lading, and in 1924 these rules were embodied in a proposed international convention. Ratification has been widespread though not universal. The United States and Britain have adhered; the U.S. version is the Carriage of Goods by Sea act of 1936, which may be taken as typical of the law of bills of lading throughout most of the world.

It is this act that governs and prescribes the terms of the bill of lading in the U.S. with respect to the vital matter of responsibility for cargo loss or damage; the contract of affreightment, in this regard, is no longer a bargained-out contract but one read into the bill of lading by law. Every bill of lading in foreign trade is required to embody a "clause paramount" subjecting it to the act, but the act would govern even if this requirement were not obeyed. (In domestic water carriage—from one U.S. port to another—the Harter act still governs unless the Carriage of Goods by Sea act is expressly stipulated for, as by its own terms it may be.)

Essentially, the act does two things: (1) it imposes on the carrier (and forbids him to avoid by contract) the obligations of using due diligence to furnish a proper ship, properly equipped and manned, and of carefully caring for the cargo while it is aboard; (2) it immunizes the carrier entirely from liability for all losses which do not result from his negligence and that of his employees, and even exonerates him in some cases of negligence (*e.g.*, in the navigation and management of the ship—the Harter act formula). Besides this basic distribution of responsibilities, the act regulates various other matters; it forbids, *e.g.*, the insertion of clauses placing a valuation on the goods lower than $500 per package or customary freight unit, and on the other hand limits the carrier's liability to that amount unless a greater value is agreed on.

Thus, there is little left for the bill of lading to do, as pure contract, with respect to this vital matter of cargo damage; its terms are laid down by law. Outside the ambit of the act, however, the parties may still contract with some freedom, though the freedom, it must be emphasized, is largely a freedom of the carriers to insert terms they feel to be advantageous to them. The act generally forbids any stipulations lessening the carrier's obligations under the act.

Implied in the contract of carriage is a "warranty not to deviate," *i.e.*, the carrier undertakes to proceed on his voyage by a customarily direct route; the deviating carrier becomes liable for subsequent cargo damage. The Carriage of Goods by Sea act allows "reasonable" deviation but no more. Modern bills of lading have sought to avoid the deviation rule altogether by defining the "voyage" in extremely broad terms. The courts have in turn indicated that they will not give effect to these clauses where the result would be to defeat altogether the obligation not to deviate.

Reference has been made above to the functioning of the bill of lading as a document of title, the ownership of the carried goods following ownership of the bill of lading. Doubtless the most important use resulting from this characteristic of the bill is its employment as security in the financing of the sale of goods. In the most common transaction, the buyer of the goods opens a letter of credit, directing a bank to pay the seller's draft for the purchase price "against documents," *i.e.*, on presentation, along with the draft, of a bill of lading, an insurance policy and perhaps other less important documents. The seller thus gets paid at the time of shipment, and if the bank has extended credit to the buyer it is secured by the fact that it holds the bill of lading, which carries title to the goods. The use of the bill of lading in this and similar transactions principally motivated the passage of

the Harter act and the Carriage of Goods by Sea act; under the older bills of lading, with their broad negligence clauses, neither bank nor buyer could have much idea of the value of the bill of lading as security, though their positions were softened by the partial protection of insurance. (*See* also COMMERCIAL PAPER.)

The Charter Party.—Basic commodities (corn, oil, coal, iron ore, as well as many others) move in shipload lots, and the charter arrangement is the typical one. Leaving out of account the demise or "bareboat" charter, which amounts to the lease of a ship and is not a contract of affreightment at all, there are two types: the voyage charter and the time charter. In both, the shipowner continues to control the navigation and management of the vessel, but its carrying capacity is engaged by the charterer.

The voyage charter is a simple engagement for the carriage of a whole cargo from one port to another. Such charters are fixed by the activity of brokers, and their terms are highly standardized for each trade. For example, there is a form known as the Chamber of Shipping Australian Grain Charter 1928 (code name "Austral" for use in cable negotiations); most grain shipments from Australia will move under such a form, in which the principal matters shown by experience to give rise to dispute will be dealt with. Freight under a voyage charter may be a lump sum or may be calculated on intaken or delivered quantity.

The time charter places the capacity of the ship at the charterer's disposal for a definite period. He may order the ship to go anywhere not forbidden in the charter and to carry any cargoes that are not excluded by the charter's terms. Payment under such a charter is by the month or other unit of time.

By operation of law (absent special agreement) the shipowner is absolutely bound to furnish a seaworthy ship, properly equipped and manned and fit for carriage of the particular goods, and is also under an obligation to use care in the stowing and custody of the cargo; he must pay for damage ensuing from breach of either of these obligations. His obligation not to deviate is similar to that resting on the carrier under a bill of lading. But the disparity of bargaining position that led to judicial and legislative protection of the bill-of-lading recipient against too drastic contractual modification of these obligations has not been thought to exist in the charter relation; charters may therefore freely alter the shipowner's liabilities, though in fact, precisely because the shipper of large bulk cargoes is likely to have a good bargaining position, typical charters are by no means the one-sided documents that bills of lading were in the pre-Harter act days.

The Carriage of Goods by Sea act has no application to charter parties as such but does apply to bills of lading issued for goods carried under charter. This leads to the consideration of the problem of the simultaneous coverage of a shipment by charter and by bills of lading. This is the typical situation when goods move under charter, for the charter is not a document of title and cannot be used in the financing transaction discussed above. The shipper of coal, *e.g.*, who has a voyage charter wants bills of lading for the coal so that he can get his money at once by using the bills as security. Most charters expressly provide that bills of lading shall be issued by the master of the vessel on loading. In most charter shipments, therefore, two documents are extant expressing the contract of affreightment, and since the Carriage of Goods by Sea act fixes the terms of one but not of the other they are likely to differ in the legal obligations they embody, the bill of lading (under the act) being usually somewhat more favourable to the cargo interest than the charter. While the decisions are confusing, some points seem fairly well settled: (1) as long as the bill of lading remains in the hands of the charterer, the charter is the governing contract and the bill of lading is a mere receipt; (2) if the bill of lading is transferred without notice to the transferee of the existence or terms of the charter, then the bill of lading alone governs; (3) subject to the reservation in the next sentence, effective notice to the bill-of-lading transferee of the terms of the charter (usually by some form of stamped or typewritten clause on the bill of lading) makes them effective against him; (4) in no case, regardless of notice, may a bill of lading, in the hands of a party to whom it has been transferred for value, import obligations less than those imposed by the Carriage of

Goods by Sea act; this point, though dealt with confusedly in the decisions, seems clear on the face of the act.

The interest of the shipowner, in the voyage-charter situation, lies in finishing the voyage as quickly as possible so that he can start another; thus he gets the most income from his ship. Hence such charters always put a penalty (demurrage) on the cargo owner for delay in loading or unloading. In the time charter it is the charterer who is interested in speed; hence such charters make detailed provision for the allocation of loss in the event of the disablement of the ship or of any of its essential gear.

General Average.—There is a distinctively maritime term in every contract of affreightment to the effect that, if either the ship or the cargo makes a sacrifice for the purpose of rescuing the entire venture from peril, the saved interests will contribute pro rata to equalize the loss; this system of loss distribution is known as general average (*see* AVERAGE for more detailed treatment). The most important contractual modification of general-average rights, now found in virtually all bills of lading and charter parties, is the Jason clause. Under maritime law, a ship could not recover general average from cargo when the peril that led to the ship's sacrifice arose through the ship's fault. The Jason clause changed this rule; under it, *e.g.*, a ship that has negligently run astrand and that deliberately damages her engines to get free can enforce a general-average contribution from cargo.

Obligations of the Shipper.—The obligation to pay freight, unless there is a contractual agreement to some other effect, does not become complete until the goods reach their destination. In modern practice, freight is often prepaid by small shippers. In voyage-charter carriage, the older rule is more usually adhered to.

The shipper may also make himself liable to the carrier by his own negligence or misconduct. If, therefore, he negligently ships dangerous goods, without notice to the carrier, he may be held to pay for consequent damage to the ship.

Remedies.—Generally speaking, the obligations arising under the contract of carriage may be enforced by suit either in admiralty or in the ordinary law courts. Besides this personal remedy applicable to all contracts, breach of the contract of carriage gives rise to a maritime lien, either on the cargo or the ship. Thus the carrier not only may sue the shipper (or, in some cases, the consignee) but may also hold the cargo until the amount due is paid or procure its sale for satisfaction of the claim. Similarly, the shipper or consignee to whom the carrier is liable for cargo damage not only may sue the carrier but may libel the ship (*i.e.*, procure her seizure) and enforce his claim against her directly, by sale under court order and by the satisfaction of his claim out of the proceeds. In practice, in most such suits against the ship, the owner posts a bond to cover the claim and so procures the release of his vessel. *See* also MARITIME LAW.

See T. G. Carver, *Carriage of Goods by Sea*, 10th ed. revised by R. P. Colinvaux (1957); G. Gilmore and C. L. Black, Jr., *The Law of Admiralty*, ch. iii and iv (1957). (C. L. B.)

AFGHANISTAN (DOULAT E PADSHAHI YE AFGHANISTAN), a kingdom of central Asia, is bounded on the north by the U.S.S.R. (the Turkmen, Uzbek and Tadzhik Soviet Socialist Republics), on the west by Iran (Persia) and on the east and south by West Pakistan; in the northeast it touches the Sinkiang Uigur Autonomous Region of China and Hunza in Kashmir. For information about border disputes and agreements see *History*, below. Area: 250,965 sq.mi. (650,000 sq.km.). Pop. (1965 est.) 15,500,000. The capital is Kabul (*q.v.*).

Afghanistan has been a crossroads for historical and religious forces between Europe and Asia since the days of Alexander the Great. Genghis Khan and Tamerlane crossed it. Buddhism flowed westward from India, Islam eastward from Africa. The many peoples in transit have made for internal dispute, and at the sign of any amalgamation of local forces, influence there has been assiduously contested by the British and imperial Russia in the 19th century, and after World War II by the Soviet Union, Communist China, and the United States. The outer aspects and many traditions of Afghanistan are among the most ancient in the world; Afghanistan, in contemporary perspective, can also be viewed as a relatively new, independent nation. (X.)

This article contains the following sections and subsections:

I. Physical Geography
   1. Physiography
   2. Climate
   3. Vegetation
   4. Animal Life
II. The People
   1. Anthropology
   2. Languages
   3. Culture and Beliefs
III. Archaeology
IV. History
   1. Early Period
   2. The First Muslim Dynasties
   3. The Mongol Invasion
   4. The Timurids of Herat
   5. The Mughals
   6. The National Awakening
   7. Nadir Shah
   8. Ahmad Shah and the Durrani Dynasty
   9. Dost Mohammed and the Rise of the Barakzai
  10. Sher Ali
  11. Yakub Khan
  12. Abdurrahman Khan
  13. Habibullah Khan
  14. Amanullah Khan
  15. Nadir Khan
  16. Zahir Shah
V. Administration and Social Conditions
VI. The Economy
   1. Agriculture and Animal Husbandry
   2. The Helmand River Project
   3. Minerals
   4. Industry
   5. Communications

I. PHYSICAL GEOGRAPHY

1. Physiography.—The dominant feature of Afghanistan is the great central range of mountains which divides the country approximately from east to west. This range, known in its eastern portion as the Hindu Kush (*q.v.*), takes off from the Little Pamir in the extreme northeast, and after forming the boundary between Chitral (in northwest Pakistan) and Afghanistan to a point south of the Dorah pass turns westward, and spreads across central Afghanistan in a series of deep ravines and broken ridges gradually diminishing in height from the eastern peaks of 25,000 ft. Opposite Kabul and about 100 mi. to the north of it, the main ridge rises to peaks of about 20,000 ft. Farther west it spreads out fanwise in a series of subsidiary ranges, such as the Paghman range (15,500 ft.), while the main ridge continues westward under the names of the Koh-i-Baba (16,900 ft.), the Band-i-Bayan (12,300 ft.), the Safed Koh (10,400 ft.) and the Paropamisus mountains (11,800 ft.), which continue as a series of low ridges in a northwesterly direction until they reach the valley of the Hari Rud.

Around the central structure the country is divided into four main divisions depending on the four principal river systems. In the north the gorges of Badakhshan and the high pastures of Mazar-i-Sharif and Kataghan descend to the valley of the Amu-Darya (*q.v.*) and the rich lands of Afghan Turkistan with its principal city, Mazar-i-Sharif. In the west the valley of the Hari Rud (*q.v.*) contains the city of Herat and the fertile surrounding country. In the southwest the Helmand and Arghandab with their tributaries water the provinces of Kandahar, Girishk and Farah. In the centre and east the Kabul river (*q.v.*) system, which includes among its tributaries the Logar, Panjshir and Kunar rivers, waters the Kabul plateau, the rich valleys of Chahardeh and Koh-i-Daman, and at a lower altitude the country of Nangrahar province around Jalalabad. Subsidiary to these main divisions are the valley of the Murghab river in the northwest, the plains of the Harut Rud (Adraskan), Farah Rud and Kash Rud in the southwest and the area around the headwaters of the Kurram, Tochi and Gumal rivers in the southeast.

2. Climate—Three main traits are characteristic, namely, extremes of temperature (both seasonal and diurnal), wind and dryness, in respect of which elevation rather than latitude is the chief deciding feature. In Seistan and in the north along the valley of the Amu-Darya temperatures may rise to more than 115° F. in the summer, while in the highlands of Kabul and Ghazni on the southern side of the main range the maximum shade temperature rarely rises above 100° F. The minimum temperature in these areas falls as low as −10° to −15° F. in February. Jalalabad (2,000 ft.) and Kandahar (3,500 ft.) have a subtropical climate; *i.e.*, the mean temperature of the coldest month keeps above 50° F.

The heat of summer is aggravated by hot winds, particularly on the western frontier from Herat to Seistan where a wind with a velocity which reaches 110 m.p.h. blows continuously from June to September. In winter periodic blizzards from the northwest bring heavy falls of snow at altitudes of more than 5,000 ft.

The average yearly rainfall varies. In Seistan and in Wakhan it is 2 in. along the lower Kabul river and along the lower Amu-Darya it is 5 in.; in Kabul it is 12 in., the greater part of which falls between December and April. An occasional shower

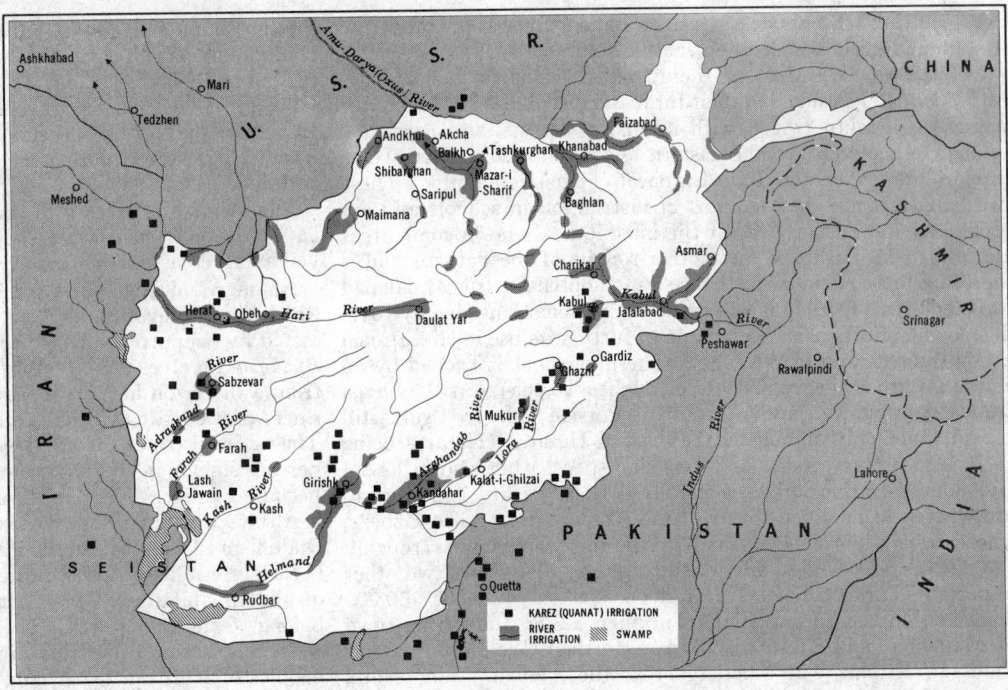

JOHANNES HUMLUM

RIVER SYSTEMS AND IRRIGATION OF AFGHANISTAN

falls in summer, but the influence of the southwest monsoon hardly extends beyond Jalalabad in eastern Afghanistan.

In the central highlands the climate is brisk. The spring and autumn are particularly fine, with clear, cool days and nights and a dry, invigorating atmosphere. At lower altitudes, below 3,000 to 4,000 ft., winters are pleasant but the heat in summer is intense.

3. Vegetation.—On the main ranges at 6,000 to 11,000 ft. grow large forest trees, among which the most prominent are conifers, such as deodar cedar, weeping spruce and pines. Yew, hazel, juniper, walnut, wild peach and almond are also found. Growing under the shade of these are several varieties of rose, honeysuckle, currant, gooseberry and hawthorn, and luxuriant herbage—the buttercup family being abundant and rich in genera. The lemon and wild vine are commonest on the northern mountains. The walnut and holly oak descend to the secondary heights, where they become mixed with alder, ash, arborvitae, juniper, *Indigofera* and dwarf laburnum, with species of *Astragalus*, etc. Lower again and down to 3,000 ft. grow wild olive, species of rockrose, wild privet, acacias and mimosas, barberry and *Zizyphus*, trumpet flower, sissoo, mustard tree, verbena, acanthus and species of *Gesneria*. The lowest terminal ridges, especially toward the west, are naked in aspect. Their scanty vegetation is almost wholly herbal, shrubs are only occasional and trees almost nonexistent. Labiate, composite and umbelliferous plants are most common. Ferns and mosses are almost confined to the higher ranges. On the dreary Kandahar tablelands grow many vigorous plants, such as the camel's-thorn; *Zygophyllum*; *Artemisia*; *Astragalus* in several species; spiny restharrow, the fibrous roots of which often serve as toothbrushes; mimosa; also certain orchids and several species of *Salsola*. Many plants are used domestically for medicinal purposes. The chief cultivated trees are mulberry, apricot, willow, poplar, ash and occasionally the plane.

Of some commercial value is the gum resin of *Ferula assafoetida* of the high and dry plains of western Afghanistan, especially between Kandahar and Herat. In the highlands of Kabul edible wild rhubarb is a local luxury. Walnut and edible pine kernels are both found wild and are exported. The *sinjid* or Russian olive common on the banks of watercourses, furnishes an edible fruit. A subspecies of *Pistacia terebinthus*, called *khinjuk*, affords a mastic. The pistachio is found along the northern slopes of the Hindu Kush and is an important article of export. Mushrooms and other fungi are also used as food.

4. Animal Life.—Wild animals include the wolf, fox, hyena, wild dog, wildcat, common leopard, mongoose, wild sheep, mole, shrew, hedgehog, bats, several species of jumping mouse, jerboa and pica hare. Bears are found in the forests and the Mongolian tiger is said to inhabit the thick reed country of the Amu-Darya.

Of the goat family the markhor, urial and ibex are found in the central ranges, while wild sheep inhabit the Afghan Pamirs.

The birds include several varieties of pheasant, goose, duck, teal, crane, pelican, snipe, woodcock, partridge and chukar. Smaller birds include the garden oriole, magpie, bulbul, swallow, quail and sparrow. Brown trout are plentiful in all streams north of the Hindu Kush; mahseer and snow trout, or *chush*, are found in the rivers of the Indus watershed. (J. P. C. N. H.)

II. THE PEOPLE

The origin of the name Afghan is obscure, but it has been in consistent use since its first known appearance in a Sanskrit text of the 6th century.

1. Anthropology.—The inhabitants of the modern state are divisible into four main ethnies, or cultural groups: the Pashtun (Pathan; *q.v.*), the Tadzhik, the Uzbek and the Hazara (*qq.v.*). The Pathans, *i.e.*, the Afghans proper, form about 60% of the population. The Tajiks or Tadzhiks represent the next largest ethny, 31%, followed by the Uzbeks or Usbegs, 5%, and the Hazaras, 3%. The remaining 1% comprises Hindus, Jews, Sikhs and a congeries of central Asian tribal elements. Members of the four principal groups are scattered throughout the country, but the bulk of the Pathans occupy its eastern and southeastern parts as well as Herat and Seistan. Most Tajiks live in the provinces of Herat and Kabul; the Uzbeks in northern and central Afghanistan; and the Hazaras in the mountainous district of Hazarajat, south of the main range of the Hindu Kush, and in the region west of Anardarra (Gandarra) bordering Iran. In physical type the Pathans belong to the Caspian branch of the Europiform Mediterranean race. They have sallow skins and dark hair and eyes, are of medium stature with very long, high heads, prominent occiputs, well-developed brow ridges, and large, moderately broad aquiline noses depressed at the root. The Tajiks are pale-skinned hirsute Europiform Pamirians with lighter hair (10% blonde) and eyes (15% blue) than the Pathans. Their stature is medium, their heads are short and high with flattened occiputs, receding frontal bones, and pronounced brow ridges, and their narrow noses straight in profile with curved wings. The Uzbeks, of recent mixed Europiform Mongoliform descent, are on balance Mongoliform. The Hazaras, also, are part of the far-flung Mongolian race. They are glabrous, short-headed, of medium stature, and have elongated oval faces, jutting cheekbones, straight salient noses of moderate breadth and eyelids with an epicanthic fold.

2. Languages.—Most of the 20 or so Afghanistan languages are inadequately studied in their form and distribution. The major languages—Pashto (*q.v.*), with its many dialects, and Persian—belong, respectively, to the eastern and western divisions of the Iranian branch of the Indo-European linguistic family. These two languages are the mediums of instruction in schools and are spoken by more than 75% of the inhabitants, who in some areas are bilingual. Pashto is the mother tongue of the Pathans and is therefore most common in the east and southeast, from Jalalabad to Kandahar. In 1936 it was made the national language by royal decree and efforts have been made to further its use in educational establishments and in the press. The movement is backed by an active Pashto academy (Pashto or Pakhtu Tolena). As the lingua franca, however, an archaic form of Persian akin to Tajiki still prevails, not only among the Tajiks and Hazaras (Hazaras being the last to preserve relics of Mongolian speech) but also in Kabul and administrative circles generally. Both Pashto and Persian are written in modified forms of the Arabic script. The Uzbeks, whose urban centre is Mazar-i-Sharif and who number roughly 1,000,000, speak Uzbek, a Turkish language. There are two other important Turkish dialects: Turkmen, spoken by about 200,000 Turkmen on the border of the Turkmen S.S.R. and in the town of Maimana; and Kirghiz, spoken in northern Wakhan by a few thousand Kirghiz who wander across the Afghan, Chinese and Soviet frontiers. Dardic languages (*q.v.*), the precise status of which is disputed, but which appear to belong to an undifferentiated stage of Indo-Iranian, are spoken by 50,000 or so Nuristanis who occupy the remote and inaccessible valleys draining into the northern affluents of the Kabul river. The Indians of eastern Afghanistan and Kabul, principally traders, speak Lahnda, a Panjabi dialect. The few immigrants from Baluchistan, living as nomads in the frontier regions southwest of Quetta, speak both the Balochi and Brahui languages (*see* BALOCHI; BRAHUI).

3. Culture and Beliefs.—Two million Afghans, mostly Pathans, are pastoral nomads and practise transhumance, changing the grazing grounds of their cattle and sheep with the seasons. The sedentary Tajiks are agricultural and irrigate their crops. They also engage in business and form the main urban communities north of the Hindu Kush. A group of Pamirian *Galchas* ("mountaineers"), speaking ancient Persian, live in the alpine regions of Badakhshan and Wakhan; these people rarely leave their villages. The Hazaras are both agriculturalists and pastoralists. In winter they are often snowbound and their cattle and sheep, which are pastured during the short summers, have to be stabled and fed. Different forms of the vendetta exist, and even the settled Afghan is often a warrior. Women still occupy a subordinate position in society but they are no longer required to wear the veil and increasing numbers are employed outside the home.

Among favourite sports is a kind of team wrestling (*ghosai*) in which the protagonist hops on one leg to reach a goal while protected by supporters against opponents, all similarly handicapped. *Buzkashi* involves the attempt to retrieve a decapitated calf's body from a ditch, on horseback, and carry it to the goal, hundreds of riders participating in the contest. Polo is also an Afghan game. The national dance, *Attan,* is performed in a circle by 50 or more persons singing in chorus accompanied by native instruments, steps becoming progressively faster as the tempo increases.

Although Afghanistan was once among the main centres of Buddhism, Islam has predominated since the 10th century and is the state religion, being professed by an overwhelming majority of the inhabitants. Most Afghans follow the Hanafi rite and belong to the Sunni sect. The Hazaras, apart from those of the west, and a few other minorities are Shi'as (*see* ISLAM). The peoples of Nuristan (*i.e.,* "land of light") were forcibly converted to Islam when the amir Abdurrahman Khan sent a military force to their mountain valleys in 1895. Before that they were known as Kafirs and their area as Kafiristan (*i.e.,* "land of the infidels"). Traditional proselytizers of peninsular India, the Afghans are intolerant of Christian evangelism, but freedom of belief is constitutionally accorded to its resident non-Muslims. (J. C. TR.)

III. ARCHAEOLOGY

Afghanistan forms the northeastern portion of the Iranian plateau. Its political frontiers include several natural regions. In the north is the narrow plain lying between the Amu-Darya (ancient Oxus) and the Hindu Kush, the ancient Bactria; in the centre is the mountain mass of the Hindu Kush and its subsidiary ranges, which may be further subdivided historically in terms of the watershed and drainage pattern; the southern extensions of the mountains are little explored and their archaeology is little known, but they extend to a line from Kandahar to Farah; in the south and west of the country are areas of desert and near-desert extending to the hills of Baluchistan, Seistan and the Iranian desert.

The earliest trace of human activity so far discovered is in Bactria (*q.v.*) where a Mousterian-type flake industry is suggested by finds near Balkh and at Haibak. At Kara-kamar cave near the latter a sequence of several industries was discovered, the earliest having blades and steep-ended scrapers of Upper Paleolithic type and the uppermost being described as Mesolithic. This suggests a sequence similar to that reported at Teshik Tash and other sites in Uzbek S.S.R. north of the Amu-Darya. In the south the earliest sites are Chalcolithic. At Mundigak, northwest of Kandahar, a prolonged occupation is attested. The earliest settlement produced painted pottery with affinities to Quetta ware,

MARC RIBOUD FROM MAGNUM

FUNERAL CUSTOMS: (LEFT) THE TRADITIONAL BANQUET IS SERVED AFTER AN AFGHAN RURAL FUNERAL; (RIGHT) FOLLOWING THE BANQUET, THOSE ATTENDING PRAY FOR THE DECEASED

while the pottery of the middle periods suggests relationship with the Harappa culture. At this time (middle of the 3rd millennium B.C.) a great mud brick platform was constructed about the central mound. Finally in the upper levels plain gray and buff pottery are found with the first iron. Slightly later in time may be the site at Nad-i-Ali in Seistan. In the north no Chalcolithic sites are yet known and the sequence begins again with evidence of an Iron Age settlement at Balkh with plain buffware akin to that of Anau IV and many other sites in Soviet territory. This culture was associated with an eastern Iranian-speaking people who settled widely in the area during the 1st millennium B.C. No Achaemenid sites have yet been identified in Afghanistan, but at least part of the "treasure of the Oxus" and the coin hoard of Chaman-i-Hazouri near Kabul are certainly pre-Alexandrine. Again, archaeologists cannot yet identify any traces of Alexander's invasions, although the edicts of the Mauryan emperor Asoka in Greek and Aramaic versions discovered near Kandahar (ancient Alexandria Arachosiorum) about 1956 and in Aramaic near Jalalabad at Pul-i-Darunta, discovered about 1936, testify to these territories having fallen into Indian hands soon after. It is certain that in Bactria the vast mounds at Balkh (q.v.), Kunduz and Khulm must contain monuments and relics of the Greek cities constructed at that time; while the ancient city of Kapisa at Bagram must indicate, with its hoards of Indo-Greek coins, the Greek campaigns south of the Hindu Kush and the centre from which the Greeks invaded north India.

The last two centuries B.C. witnessed an extension of the Parthian influence, at least in the north and west, while the barbarian Yue-chi (Yüeh-chih; q.v.) were establishing themselves in Bactria. At Balkh and other sites pottery and architectural fragments recall the Parthian influence. In the 1st century A.D. the Kushans (a branch of the Yue-chi) followed the Greeks through the mountains and into India, and under Kanishka established a vast power that straddled the mountains. The temple at Surkh-Kotal near Baghlan in the Hindu Kush, excavated between 1952 and 1957, with its Bactrian inscription of Kanishka, commemorates this power, as does the treasure of Indian and Mediterranean *objets d'art* discovered at Bagram. The succeeding centuries produced many monuments of a Buddhist character in which Indian influence is strongly felt. These are found mainly in the north and east, particularly around Hadda, near Jalalabad and around Kabul. The earliest show typical Gandharan influence, but by the 6th century a powerful new hybrid style developed which had its contacts with the caves of the Takla Makan and the frontiers of China. Foremost among these later sites are the caves at Bamian (q.v.) with their two colossal Buddha figures and rich frescoes. The main political forces at this time were the Hephthalite and Chionite princes and the western Turks, all apparently recent invaders from central Asia, but the main cultural influences were still from Iran. To this period must belong the great brick fortress of Zohak near Bamian, so evocative of Sassanian work, and the many other ruined forts of the valleys of the Hindu Kush and Bactria.

Few remains of the early Muslim invaders survive. Of the Ghaznevid period, however, the great palaces of Lashkari Bazar (Bust) southwest of Kandahar form a splendid monument, and many others must await discovery or description.

Again many monuments of the Ghorids survive, including a minaret near Djam, a village in the valley of the Hari Rud, 150 mi. E. of Herat, discovered in 1957, and the neighbouring city of Firoz Koh, the Ghorid capital whose site was identified in the same year. Many of these monuments bear traces of the Mongol inroads, but sufficient remains to indicate the wealth that yet awaits study. Of the Timurid period mention may be made of the fortifications and mosques at Balkh and Herat.

IV. HISTORY

1. Early Period.—The earliest recorded use of the name Afghan is by the Indian astronomer Varaha-mihira (of 6th century A.D.), in the form "Avagana." The Afghans proper form a group of tribes speaking an Iranian language, Pashto, and centred, since first they are recorded, in the Sulaiman mountains in the east of modern Afghanistan. Their legendary history survives in traditional forms of which none is more than 500 years old. There is no evidence that the Afghans anciently occupied any areas of modern Afghanistan other than those in which Pashto is spoken, and only in modern times have they settled in the parts occupied by peoples such as Tajiks and Hazaras over whom they hold feudal domination. The previously recorded distribution of Pashto as the predominating local language is from a little north of Jalalabad in the northeast, southward to Kandahar and thence westward to Farah and Sabzevar. Pashto extends also into the Northwest Frontier region of West Pakistan and thence southward throughout the Sulaiman ranges as far as Quetta.

Geographically and culturally Afghanistan forms the northeast portion of the Iranian plateau through which passed the routes which anciently linked India with the middle east, and both these regions with China and central Asia. It is thus to be expected that while the main cultural influences were those of Iran, others from India and central Asia have been constantly in evidence. The area enters history with the Achaemenid rulers of Iran, and although it is not easy to locate all the names derived from their inscriptions or from Herodotus (whom the inscriptions remarkably confirm) and other sources the principal regions are recognizable. Thus Bactria must have included the plain of the Amu-Darya, Arachosia (the neighbourhood of Kandahar) and Aria (the country of the Hari Rud valley around Herat), while the Drangiana of the inscriptions and later Greek sources must have been a region of southwestern Afghanistan including perhaps parts of Seistan. Sindhu and Gandhara may be taken as the Sind and Northwest Frontier regions of West Pakistan and probably did not include lands of Afghanistan. There are also problematic names: Herodotus mentions in the seventh satrapy of Darius, along with the Gandharians, the Sattagydae, Dadicae and the Aparytae (?Afridi, an Afghan tribe), and one of these may indicate tribes occupying the country around Kabul and the ancient Kapisa, which was included from the time of Alexander with the Hindu Kush mountains in Paropamisus, whence arose the satrapy of Paropamisadae. Mention must also be made of the Pactyes of Herodotus, for it has been sought to connect them with the Pathans, speakers of Pashto with the modern dialectic variant Pakhtun.

Achaemenid rule was first established in the regions of Afghanistan by Cyrus (559–530 B.C.) and consolidated by Darius I (522–486 B.C.). It survived until Alexander the Great (q.v.) overthrew the dynasty. After Alexander's death his empire broke up and the eastern satrapies passed to the Seleucid dynasty (q.v.). Already by 322 B.C. Chandragupta Maurya (q.v.) had gained control of northern India, and after his defeat of Seleucus (c. 305 B.C.) he gained also the eastern provinces of Afghanistan, Paropamisadae and Arachosia. Confirmation of the Indian hold over these two provinces half a century later is provided by the Asokan edicts discovered at Kandahar and Pul-i-Darunta. By c. 250 B.C. the local Greek ruler in Bactria, Diodotus, broke away from the Seleucids and established an independent kingdom. At the same time the Parthians also broke away. Probably Seistan and Aria were in dispute between Bactria and Parthia, finally falling to Parthia. The Bactrian Greek dynasty, famed for its coins, flourished for about a century (*see* BACTRIA). Soon after 175 B.C. its ruler Demetrius moved south through the mountains to capture the region of Kabul and thence to invade northwestern India and establish the Indo-Greek dynasty there. Parthian power, however, was increasing along the western frontiers of Bactria, and to the north beyond the Oxus, some time before 125 B.C., the barbarous Yue-chi appeared in Sogdiana. This tribal group was driven from the Chinese frontier region by a non-Iranian group, the Hsiung-nu. Before or with them came Iranian tribes of nomadic Saka (q.v.) who seem, before 130 B.C., to have made a pact with the Parthians and to have settled in Seistan (Sakastan). Thence they spread east through Arachosia and in the 1st century B.C. extended their power into India. Meanwhile the Yue-chi had wrested Bactria from the Greeks and settled there.

At the beginning of the Christian era one group, henceforward known as the Kushans, followed the Greeks into the mountains and shortly after emerged as conquerors of northern India. The

AFGHAN INFORMATION BUREAU, LONDON

ONE OF THE BUDDHAS CARVED IN THE CAVE-PIERCED ROCKS OF THE BAMIAN VALLEY; 6TH TO 7TH CENTURY A.D.

which included Balkh and Herat in its kingdom of Khurasan. They were succeeded there by a native Iranian dynasty, the Saffarids, of whom Yakub ibn Laith (867–870) made a series of whirlwind campaigns throughout Afghanistan. In the north, soon after, the local princes became feudatories of the powerful Samanids, also an Iranian house, under whose rule Bukhara, Samarkand and Balkh enjoyed a golden age. In the middle of the 10th century the former Turkish slave Alptigin seized Ghazni from its former ruler and built up for himself a principality. He was succeeded by another former slave, Subuktigin, who extended the conquests to Kabul and the Indus. His son was the great Mahmud (*q.v.*) of Ghazni who came to the throne in 997. Mahmud not only made extensive conquests in the north and west, thus bringing all Afghanistan under his sway, but also conquered the Punjab and Multan and carried his raids into the heart of India. The hitherto obscure town of Ghazni (*q.v.*) became a splendid city, as did the second capital at Bust (Qala Bist). Mahmud's descendants continued to rule from Ghazni over a gradually diminishing empire until 1152, when Ala-ud-Din of Ghor, a mountain-locked region in northwestern Afghanistan (*see* GHOR), descended upon the city, sacked it and drove the last Ghaznavid out to India, thereby earning the cognomen of Jahansuz ("World Burner"). The Ghorids appear to have been of Iranian origin. The nephew of Ala-ud-Din, Muizz-ad-Din Mohammed, commonly known as Mohammed of Ghor, drove out Ghuzz-Turkmen nomads from Ghazni and in 1175 invaded India. After his death in 1206 his general Qutb-ud-Din Aibak became the first sultan of Delhi.

(F. R. A.)

zenith of Kushan power was reached under Kanishka (*q.v.*), whose rule stretched from beyond Mathura (*q.v.*) to Kabul and thence from Bactria to the frontiers of China. During this time (2nd century A.D.) Afghanistan may have been momentarily united under one rule. The Kushans were patrons of the arts and of religion, and under Kanishka Buddhism flourished.

The empire did not long survive Kanishka, but for centuries Kushan princes continued to rule in the various provinces. During the 4th century the Sassanids offered a growing challenge from Iran, while in the latter half of the century fresh incursions of northern tribes, the Little Kushans under their leader Kidara, closely followed by or associated with the White Huns or Chionites, took place. These latter are generally associated with a branch of the Hsiung-nu, the Mongolian tribes who centuries before had driven forth the Yue-chi. Two branches were discerned. The northern settled in Bactria and the Hindu Kush and were known eponymously as the Hephthalites (*q.v.*) (after their hero Hephtha), while the second (*Zavula*) branch moved south through the mountains to Kabul and Arachosia. There they, too, came under Sassanid influence and formed the centre for their raids of India between 455 and 510 under their rulers Toramana and Mihiragula. In India they were long remembered for their barbarity and Hunas, as they were called, became a name to be regarded with horror. At about the same time, A.D. 484, their victory over the Sassanid king Firuz marks the beginning of a period in which they were more the masters than the vassals of Iran. The Hephthalite domination lasted for a century until in 565 the western Turks, another newly arrived tribal group from central Asia, made an alliance with the Sassanid Khosrau Anushirvan and destroyed their power. For the next century the Turks ruled Afghanistan until their defeat by the Chinese in 658, when already Arab armies had reached the area.

2. The First Muslim Dynasties.—The advance of Islam into Iran and central Asia was rapid, but in the mountain fastnesses of the Hindu Kush it was much slower, and it was not until the 9th and 10th centuries that the last non-Muslim dynasties disappeared from Kabul. The initial control of the caliphate soon declined in these remote areas and the 9th and 10th centuries also witnessed the rise of numerous local dynasties, both Turkish and Iranian. One of the earliest of these was the Arab Tahirid dynasty,

3. The Mongol Invasion.—Shortly after Mohammed of Ghor's death the Ghori empire fell apart and Afghanistan was occupied by Sultan Ala-ud-Din Mohammed, the Khwarizmshah or shah of Khwarizm (Khiva), an incapable ruler who was merely a tool in the hands of his mother, Turkan Khatun. The Khwarizmshahi dynasty was at this time at the zenith of its power, its territories extending from Chinese Turkistan in the east to the borders of Iraq in the west, but Ala-ud-Din Mohammed planned also to take the place of the Abbasid caliphs and early in 1219 (616 *anno Hegirae*), marched with a large army against Baghdad. Hardly had he reached his destination, however, when news was brought that Mongol hordes under Genghis Khan had invaded the eastern part of his empire, seizing some of the most important cities of Transoxiana and everywhere spreading death and destruction. Hurriedly he turned to repel them but, though he had 400,000 horsemen under his command, he was not equal to the occasion. Shirking a battle, he retreated hastily to a small, deserted island in the Caspian sea, where he died shortly afterward (1220).

Soon after Ala-ud-Din's death, his energetic son Jalal-ud-Din Munkabirni decided to wage a war of liberation against the Mongols. With Ghazni as his military headquarters, he allied the Afghan highlanders and at Parwandarah near Kabul inflicted a crushing defeat on the Mongols under Kutikonian. Genghis Khan, who was then at Herat, hastened to avenge the defeat and laid siege to Bamian, a place of great strategical importance in the Hindu Kush. Here Mutugen, his grandson, was killed and this so infuriated Genghis Khan that when he captured the citadel he ordered that no living being was to be spared. The beautiful city of Bamian was utterly destroyed.

Advancing on Ghazni, Genghis won a great victory over Jalal-ud-Din, who then fell back toward the Indus (1221). Here he made a final but unsuccessful stand. Seeing that all was lost, he threw his family into the river to save them from the wrath of the Mongols and then, with a few faithful adherents, jumped in the river on horseback, still exchanging arrows. Thereupon Genghis Khan gave up the pursuit, thus permitting Jalal-ud-Din to escape into India. Genghis Khan returned to Afghanistan through Peshawar and the Afghans' gallant resistance then brought a dreadful retribution. The whole country from Herat and Balkh to Kandahar and Ghazni was turned into a wilderness, and many thousands of people were butchered. After his death in 1227 Genghis Khan's vast empire fell to pieces. In Afghanistan some local chiefs succeeded in establishing independent principalities, while others acknowledged Mongol princes as suzerains. This state of affairs continued until the end of the 14th century, when Timur (q.v.) conquered a large part of the country. The horrors of the Mongol invasion were then repeated, though on a lesser scale.

4. The Timurids of Herat.—Timur's successors, the Timurids, were great patrons of learning and the arts and enriched their capital city Herat (q.v.) with fine buildings. Under their rule 1404–1507) Afghanistan enjoyed peace and prosperity. The first Timurid king, Shahrukh Mirza, Timur's fourth son, was an enlightened monarch of literary taste. He was greatly assisted in his work by his queen, Gohar Shad Agha. During his reign Herat became an important centre of Islamic civilization.

Sultan Husain Bayqara, another Timurid king (1468–1506), was also, with his minister Mir 'Ali Shir, a patron of scholars and artists. Jami (q.v.), the great Sufi poet, and Behzad, the painter, flourished at his court.

5. The Mughals.—Early in the 16th century the Uzbeks, under Mohammed Khan Shaibani, rose to power in central Asia and when Mohammed Khan Shaibani entered Herat triumphantly in 1507 the rule of the Timurids was practically at an end. Babur (q.v.), a direct descendant of Timur and the founder of the Mughal dynasty in India, was at this time in possession of Kabul. Driven from Fergana by the Uzbeks, he had crossed the Hindu Kush in 1504 and established an independent principality in central Afghanistan with Kabul as its capital. When he heard that the Uzbeks had captured Herat he joined forces with the Safavid shah Ismail against Mohammed Khan Shaibani. In 1510, when Mohammed Khan was killed in battle near Merv, Babur thought that the time was opportune to reestablish his authority in central Asia, but again he was defeated and forced to quit the country. Falling back on Kabul, he decided to make it a base for conquests in the east and south. He took Kandahar in 1522 and then turned his attention toward India. A series of expeditions enabled him to seize the Punjab and in 1526 he marched on Delhi. Ibrahim, the last of the Lodi Afghan kings of India, came out to meet him at Panipat, 80 mi. N. of Delhi. After a hotly contested battle in which Ibrahim was killed, Babur was victorious. He could then lay the foundations of the Mughal empire, which lasted until the middle of the 19th century. Babur made Agra his capital and the whole of eastern Afghanistan right up to the Hindu Kush became a part of the Mughal empire. When he died (1530), Babur's body, in obedience to his wishes, was taken from Agra to Kabul to be buried in his favourite garden.

For the next 200 years Afghanistan lost its political entity and was parceled between the Mughals of India and the Safavids of Persia, the former holding the regions south of the Hindu Kush, while the latter held Herat and Seistan. Kandahar was for many years in dispute between them.

6. The National Awakening.—Although it was not until later in the 18th century that Afghanistan emerged as a united nation under Afghan rule, the national awakening may be said to have started when, in 1709, Mir Vais Khan, an influential leader of the Hotaki Ghilzai tribe, led a rising against Gurgin Khan, the Persian governor of Kandahar. The Persians, caught unawares, could offer no effective resistance and were slaughtered. Mir Vais Khan governed Kandahar until his death in 1715. In 1716 the Abdalis of Herat, encouraged by this example, took up arms against the Persians and under their leader, Asadullah Khan, succeeded in liberating their province.

Mahmud, Mir Vais's young son and successor, was not content with possession of Kandahar. He resolved to invade Persia and, in 1722, at the head of about 20,000 men, marched on Isfahan. The degenerate Safavid government could offer no effective resistance and after a siege of six months, Shah Husain surrendered.

Mahmud was a man of talent and energy and immediately set himself to reorganize the Persian administration and economy. He was not destined to see the fruits of his labours, however, for he died in 1725 and was succeeded by his young cousin Ashraf. Ashraf, too, was energetic, but he came to power at a critical time. The Afghans in Persia were threatened on all sides. The Russians were advancing from the north, while the Ottoman Turks seized part of western Persia. Internal strife and jealousy among the Afghan chiefs made the situation worse. Shah Ashraf met the

dangers with courage and determination. He halted the Russian advance at Darband and in 1726 inflicted a crushing defeat on the Turks, who were marching on the capital. Meanwhile news was brought to him that a brigand chief, Nadr Quli Beg, had attacked Tus and was on his way to take Meshed and Herat. Collecting all available troops Ashraf hastened north to meet him, but after a fierce encounter was defeated at Damghan on Oct. 2, 1729. The Afghan position in Persia was thereafter untenable, and during the retreat Ashraf himself was murdered by a Baluchi chief in Seistan.

7. Nadir Shah.—After consolidating his position in Persia, Nadr Quli Beg turned his attention to the east, against Herat. The Abdali chief Zulfikar Khan appealed to Kandahar for help, and Saidal Khan, a Ghilzai chief of repute, was sent to his aid. In an engagement at Kafir Kila, near the Afghan border, the Afghans inflicted a crushing defeat on the Persians (1731). Nadr himself, with only 80 men, was cut off from the rest of the army, but made good his escape and, in 1732, on receiving reinforcements, marched again against Herat. The besieged fought desperately, but dissension in their ranks forced them to sue for peace. Impressed by their valour, Nadr treated them with courtesy and recruited many of them into his own army. He was elected shah of Persia, with the name Nadir Shah, in 1736.

In 1737 Nadir Shah advanced with an army of 80,000 men against Kandahar. The city fell after a year's siege and Nadir then came into conflict with the Mughal empire of India. He seized Ghazni and Kabul and, advancing into India, defeated the Mughal army at Karnal, north of Delhi, in 1739. Then having seized the jewels and treasure of the capital, including the famous peacock throne, he returned through Afghanistan to Persia. He was assassinated at Khabushan in 1747.

8. Ahmad Shah and the Durrani Dynasty.—After the death of Nadir Shah his empire disintegrated. In Afghanistan, Ahmad Khan Abdali, with a contingent of 4,000 Afghans, entered Kandahar and there, in 1747, was elected king of the Afghans by a tribal assembly. Ahmad Shah (q.v.) was a member of the noble Sadozai clan of the Abdali tribe of Afghans. He changed the tribal name from Abdali to Durrani. Though barely 25 years old, he soon proved himself a capable ruler. Securing the affection of his people and welding them into a strong nation, he was able in 25 years not only to liberate Afghanistan from foreign rule but also to lead conquering armies from Meshed to Kashmir and Delhi and from the Amu-Darya to the Arabian sea. He defeated the Marathas at the third battle of Panipat (Jan. 14, 1761). His popular manners, indomitable courage, and other martial virtues, won him the title of *Baba* ("Father of the Nation").

Ahmad Shah died about 1773 and was succeeded by his son Timur, who bore no comparison with him. He received but nominal homage from the feudal chieftains and much of his reign

AFGHAN TRAVELERS RESTING AT PUL-I-KHUMRI, A TOWN ON THE ROAD NORTH OF KABUL

was spent in quelling their rebellions. Seeing how the people of Kandahar hated him, Timur decided to shift his capital to Kabul.

After the death of Timur in 1793, his fifth son, Zaman, seized the throne with the help of Sardar Payenda Khan, the influential chief of the Barakzai. Zaman was from the beginning of his reign beset with difficulties, both external and internal. His elder brothers, Humayun and Mahmud, governors of Kandahar and Herat, respectively, took up arms against him. At first Zaman was successful, Humayun being defeated and blinded and Mahmud forced to take refuge in Persia. Zaman then turned to India with the object of repeating the exploits of Ahmad Shah. This alarmed the British, whose Indian possessions were now threatened both by the French and by the Afghans. After the way had been paved for him by the dispatch of a Persian agent in 1798, Capt. John Malcolm was sent in 1800 as envoy to Persia to induce Fath Ali Shah to bring pressure upon the Afghan king and to divert his attention from India. The shah went a step further, helping Mahmud, the ex-governor of Herat, with men and money and encouraging him to advance on Kandahar. Mahmud, assisted by Fath Ali and by his vizier Fath Khan, eldest son of the Barakzai chief Sardar Payenda Khan, took Kandahar after a 42-day siege and then pushed on toward Kabul. Zaman was at this time in India but learning of Mahmud's activities, he hurried back to Afghanistan. There, after various vicissitudes, he was betrayed by an old adherent, Ashiq Khan. He was handed over to Mahmud, blinded and imprisoned in the Bala Hissar fort at Kabul (1801).

Mahmud was an incapable, selfish and indolent ruler. He took no interest in the welfare of his people, squandered the nation's treasure on his personal pleasures and left all affairs of state in the hands of his vizier Fath Khan. Jealousies between Fath

Khan and his rival Akram Khan Alizai caused unrest throughout the country, and finally some of the chiefs, who had grievances against the king or one of his ministers, joined forces and invited Shah Shuja, a full brother of Zaman, to Kabul. The intrigue was successful. Shah Shuja occupied the capital, and Mahmud sued for peace. His life and eyes were spared, but he was imprisoned in the Bala Hissar.

The new king, Shah Shuja, who ascended the throne in 1803, was unable to restore peace. The chiefs had become too powerful and unruly, and the outlying provinces were trying to assert their independence. The Sikhs of the Punjab were encroaching upon Afghan territories from the east, while the Persians were threatening from the west, and the shah could not conciliate Fath Khan.

At this time Napoleon, the French emperor, was at the zenith of his power in Europe. After the signing of the treaty of Tilsit in 1807 he and Alexander I of Russia decided on a combined invasion of India. This once more aroused the British to action, and a mission, headed by Mountstuart Elphinstone (q.v.), was sent to meet Shah Shuja at Peshawar to discuss mutual defense against this threat. The mission was warmly received by Shah Shuja and a treaty of friendship was concluded (June 7, 1809), the shah promising to oppose the passage of foreign troops through his dominions. Hardly had the mission left Peshawar, however, when news was received that Kabul had been occupied by the forces of Mahmud and his vizier Fath Khan. Shah Shuja's troops were thereafter routed in a brief encounter near Gandamak and Shah Shuja himself withdrew from Afghanistan. In 1810, after making some ineffective efforts to recover his throne, he was captured and imprisoned in Kashmir. He escaped in 1812 and came to Lahore, hoping to receive help from Ranjit Singh, the ruler of the

(ABOVE LEFT AND LEFT) MARC RIBOUD FROM MAGNUM, (ABOVE) PIERRE STREIT

Aspects of Afghan life: (Above left) street scene in Kabul, capital of Afghanistan; (Left) Turkmen woman spinning wool outside her northern village hut; (Above) merchant at a bazaar in Kabul

Punjab, but instead the Sikh ruler robbed him of the famous Koh-i-Nor diamond. Finally Shah Shuja found asylum under the British at Ludhiana.

9. Dost Mohammed and the Rise of the Barakzai.—The Barakzai were now dominant throughout Afghanistan. This incited the jealousy of Kamran, Mahmud's eldest son, who had a grudge against Fath Khan and sought an opportunity to ruin him and his brothers. His chance came in 1816 when Fath Khan and his younger brother Dost Mohammed Khan, who had been sent to defend Herat against a Persian army, insulted Kamran's sister, who was the daughter-in-law of the governor of Herat. When she called on her brother to avenge the insult, Kamran seized and blinded Fath Khan. Retribution immediately followed this outrage. The vizier's brothers, 21 in all including Dost Mohammed who had escaped to Kashmir, took up arms. Shah Mahmud asked Fath Khan to write to his brothers and order them to submit. Fath Khan replied that he was blind and had no control over them. Enraged by this answer, the shah ordered the unfortunate minister to be cut to pieces. Fath Khan met his death calmly and died as he had lived—dauntless and resolute. The end of the vizier was the death knell of the Durrani dynasty.

The first of the Barakzai brothers to enter the field was Dost Mohammed. Advancing from Kashmir in 1818, he took Peshawar and Kabul and drove the shah and Kamran from all their possessions except Herat, where they maintained a precarious footing for a few years. The rest of Afghanistan was parceled out among the Barakzai brothers. In the confusion that followed, Afghanistan suffered heavily. Balkh was seized by the ruler of Bukhara; the trans-Indus Afghan districts were occupied by the Sikhs; the outlying provinces of Sind and Baluchistan assumed independence. In the partition which took place in 1826, Ghazni, Kabul and Jalalabad fell to the lot of Dost Mohammed, who thus became the most powerful of the Barakzai Sardars.

It was Dost Mohammed who established the Barakzai or Mohammedzai dynasty in power. As soon as his position was secure at Kabul, he decided to recover Peshawar by force from the Sikhs. Declaring a jihad or holy war in 1836 he collected an army of Muslims from far and wide and advanced on Peshawar confident of victory. But the shrewd Sikh leader, finding himself too weak to meet Dost Mohammed in the open field, sowed dissension in his camp, so that the invading army melted away and Peshawar was permanently lost to the Afghans.

In Nov. 1837 Mohammed Shah of Persia laid siege to Herat, which was looked upon by the British as the key to India. The Russians supported the Persians in their designs, and the British, fearful that Persia was falling completely under Russian influence, determined to stem the tide by entering into alliances with the rulers of Herat, Kabul and Kandahar. A British mission to Kabul under Capt. (later Sir) Alexander Burnes (q.v.) in 1837 was welcomed by Dost Mohammed, who hoped that the British would help him to recover Peshawar. Burnes, however, would not give him the required assurances, and when a Russian agent, Capt. P. Vitkevich, appeared in Kabul, the British broke off negotiations and were ordered to leave at once.

The failure of Burnes's mission gave the governor general of India, Lord Auckland, a pretext for the invasion of Afghanistan, with the object of restoring Shah Shuja to the throne. This was the origin of the first war between the British and the Afghans (1838–42). A British army assembled at Ferozepur in Dec. 1838, and Shah Shuja was supplied with funds to raise an army of his own. As the Sikhs did not allow the British to pass through their territories, the British army had to take a circuitous route to the Bolan pass in order to advance on Kandahar. In April 1839, after suffering great privations and guerrilla attacks on the way, the British army under Gen. Sir John Keane, entered Kandahar. Shah Shuja was then crowned in the mosque next to the mausoleum of Ahmad Shah. Ghazni and Kabul were captured in the following July and August, Shah Shuja being crowned again at Kabul. Dost Mohammed escaped first to Balkh, then to Bukhara, where he was treacherously arrested. The Afghans, however, could tolerate neither a foreign occupation nor a king imposed on them by a foreign power and insurrection broke out on all sides. Hearing of

the risings, Dost Mohammed escaped from prison and returned to Afghanistan to lead his partisans against the British. In a battle at Parwandarah on Nov. 2, 1840, Dost Mohammed had the upper hand but it was found the next day, to the astonishment of the Afghans, that he had surrendered to the British in Kabul. He was honourably treated by the British and deported to India with the greater part of his family.

After Dost Mohammed's departure the situation did not improve. Outbreaks continued all over the country and, when winter set in, the British garrison in Kabul found their position untenable. Terms for their withdrawal were discussed with Akbar Khan, Dost Mohammed's son, but the negotiations were delayed by the tactics of Sir William Hay Macnaghten, the British political agent, who was in no mood to quit Kabul. His attempts, however, to sow dissension among the Afghan chiefs were frustrated, and finally he was invited to a meeting by Akbar Khan, who killed him with his own hands.

On Macnaghten's death the British garrison decided to leave the city at once. On Jan. 6, 1842, in severe cold, approximately 4,500 British and Indian troops, with 12,000 camp followers, marched out of Kabul. Bands of Afghans swarmed around the line of their retreat, and the retreat ended in a massacre which few survived.

Though in the summer of the same year British forces under Gen. William Nott and Gen. George Pollock reoccupied Kabul, the new governor general, Lord Ellenborough, decided on the immediate evacuation of Afghanistan. In 1843 Dost Mohammed was released and allowed to return to his country, which was now without a ruler, as Shah Shuja had been killed by his own subjects after the British had left the capital. Thus ended the final phase of the war, which left bitter memories behind it.

Dost Mohammed reigned until 1863. During the last 20 years of his reign he occupied Kandahar, Mazar-i-Sharif, Kataghan and, at last, Herat, but died 13 days after capturing the last-named city.

10. Sher Ali.—Sher Ali Khan, Dost Mohammed's third son, then became amir, but his elder brothers Afzal and Azam rose against him. For five years fratricidal war went on until, in autumn 1868, Sher Ali was finally able to establish his authority. The British again became apprehensive of Russian designs on Afghanistan, and Sher Ali's reception of a Russian mission at Kabul and his refusal to receive a British one, intensified their suspicions and led directly to the war of 1878–81. On Nov. 21, 1878, the three great passes leading into Afghanistan were entered by British armies. They met stiff resistance, but by the end of the year Jalalabad and Kandahar had fallen. Sher Ali, leaving his son Yakub Khan as his regent in Kabul, went to Mazar-i-Sharif to seek help from the Russians, but the Russians advised him to make peace. Worn out by disease and worry, Sher Ali died at Mazar-i-Sharif on Feb. 21, 1879.

11. Yakub Khan.—By the treaty of Gandamak (May 26, 1879) Yakub Khan agreed to receive a permanent British embassy at Kabul; to conduct his foreign relations with other states in accordance "with the wishes and advice" of the British government; and to allow such rectification of the frontier as was demanded by the advocates of a "forward policy" for the British in India. In return he was promised help against foreign aggression. This British triumph, however, was short-lived. On Sept. 3, 1879, Maj. Sir Pierre Louis Cavagnari, the British envoy, and the whole of his escort were murdered in the Bala Hissar. British forces were again dispatched, and before the close of October Lieut. Gen. Frederick (later Field Marshal Earl) Roberts had occupied Kabul. Yakub abdicated and was sent to India (where he died in 1923).

12. Abdurrahman Khan.—The British remained in Kabul during the winter of 1879–80. In the meantime Lord Lytton, a supporter of the "forward" policy in Afghanistan, was succeeded by Lord Ripon who had instructions to bring about a speedy but peaceful settlement of the Afghan question. Accordingly, when Abdurrahman Khan (q.v.), a grandson of Dost Mohammed, appeared on the scene in July 1880, the British recognized him as amir of Kabul and undertook not to require the admission of a British resident anywhere in Afghanistan.

As the British were preparing to leave Kabul, news reached

them that at Maiwand, near Kandahar, a British force had been annihilated by Ayub Khan, Yakub Khan's brother. Roberts, with 10,000 picked men, at once started for Kandahar and on Aug. 31, 1880, attacked and defeated Ayub at Baba Wali, 3 mi. (4.8 km.) W. of the city. The British then handed over Kandahar to a governor deputed by Abdurrahman and evacuated Afghanistan. After the departure of the British, Ayub, from his base at Herat, once more seized Kandahar, but he was decisively defeated there by Abdurrahman, who thus won possession of both Kandahar and Herat. Ayub fled to Persia.

With great energy and determination Abdurrahman then set about establishing peace and a strong central government in Afghanistan. In this he was entirely successful. It was during his reign (1893) that the Durand line (named after Sir Mortimer Durand) was laid down to fix the boundary between Afghanistan and the North-West Frontier province of India. He died in Oct. 1901 and was succeeded by his eldest son Habibullah Khan.

13. Habibullah Khan.—Habibullah was an enlightened amir. In his reign the foundations of the Habibia school were laid, roads were constructed and steps were taken to introduce machinery and other modern appliances. A weekly Persian paper, *Siraj-ul-Akhbar*, was started and entrusted to the well-known Afghan writer, Mahmud-i-Tarzi. This paper infused new life into the country and played a great part in the national awakening. In Feb. 1919, having observed strict neutrality during World War I, Habibullah wrote to the viceroy of India demanding recognition by the Paris peace conference of Afghanistan's "absolute liberty, freedom of action and perpetual independence." But on the night of Feb. 20, 1919, he was assassinated.

14. Amanullah Khan.—After Habibullah's death his third son Amanullah Khan (*q.v.*), seized the throne and proclaimed himself king, displacing Habibullah's younger brother Nasrullah Khan. Amanullah's first act after his accession was to proclaim Afghanistan's complete independence in both internal and external affairs. He communicated his decision to the viceroy of India, and it was the reluctance of the government of India to recognize this independence that led to the third war between Great Britain and Afghanistan. Hostilities began on May 3, 1919, but the fighting was inconclusive and when peace was signed at Rawalpindi on Aug. 8 (supplemented by further agreements signed Nov. 22, 1921) the independence of Afghanistan was recognized. Amanullah then established diplomatic relations with the outside world.

Having achieved his first purpose, Amanullah started to introduce internal reforms on European lines with a view to preparing his people for the responsibilities of modern international life. This brought him into conflict with a group of reactionaries who rigidly opposed the modernization of Afghanistan. Civil war broke out and in Jan. 1929 a brigand chief Habibullah took advantage of the confusion to seize Kabul. Amanullah abdicated and left for Kandahar. In the spring of the same year, having made an unsuccessful attempt to recover the capital, he left the country and went into exile. Habibullah declared himself king, and ushered in a reign of terror which lasted for nine months.

15. Nadir Khan.—Sardar Mohammed Nadir Khan, Amanullah's cousin, was in Nice, France, and not in good health, but on hearing the news from Afghanistan decided to return home at once. There he and his brothers played a leading role in the struggle against Habibullah, who was finally driven from the capital in Oct. 1929. In a tribal assembly held shortly afterward in the Salaamkhana (audience hall) at Kabul, Mohammed Nadir Khan was unanimously elected king.

The first aim of the new king was to restore peace. Habibullah and his accomplices, who were still at large, were arrested, court-martialed and executed. Thereafter the king ruled without challenge and devoted his attention to internal reforms. New schools, a literary academy, a military college and a medical college were established; some Afghan graduates were sent abroad for higher education; and, as the crowning achievement of the reign, a constitution was introduced in 1930 providing for a bicameral legislature. Unfortunately, this steady progress was interrupted by the murder of the king during a prize distribution for schoolchildren on Nov. 8, 1933.

16. Zahir Shah.—Nadir Khan was succeeded by Mohammed Zahir, his only surviving son, then 19 years of age. On the day of his accession the king declared that he would scrupulously follow in his father's footsteps and fulfill his program. Internal peace was maintained and steady progress in all walks of life continued. Neutrality was observed in World War II as in World War I. In the years following Pakistan's achievement of independence (1947) there was friction between Afghanistan and Pakistan (*q.v.*) over the establishment of an independent Pathan state. The disputed area, based on the "Durand line," originally comprised the free tribal territory bordering the North-West Frontier province, afterward incorporated in the province of West Pakistan. In 1956 a five-year plan for the construction of better roads and better means of communication and for the development of mines, industry, education and agriculture was drawn up. The plan was successfully completed in 1961. To finance this vast development, the Afghan government signed agreements with certain foreign governments, notably the U.S.S.R. and the U.S., for loans and financial assistance. Afghanistan also brought in foreign experts and construction firms and welcomed specialists and educationists to help advance its modernization.

(MD. A.)

A second five-year plan was launched in 1961. In 1964 a motorway and tunnel, completed by Soviet engineers, through the Hindu Kush mountains, linking Kabul with the Oxus (Amu-Darya) valley was but one of several important roads constructed or under construction by Soviet and U.S. engineers.

Afghanistan acceded to the Colombo plan in March 1964.

MARC RIBOUD FROM MAGNUM

THE HISTORIC KHYBER PASS, THROUGH WHICH PASSES THE ROAD FROM AFGHANISTAN TO PAKISTAN

Diplomatic relations with Pakistan, which had been broken off in Sept. 1961 as a result of the quarrel over the establishment of an independent Pathan state were resumed in May 1963 through the good offices of the shah of Iran. A border agreement with Communist China was signed on Nov. 24, 1963.

In March 1963 the king accepted the resignation of his cousin, Sardar Mohammed Daud Khan, from the office of prime minister. The new government formed by his successor, Mohammed Yusuf, appointed a committee to draft a constitution which would be based on democratic principles. The new constitution, which excluded members of the royal family from key positions in the government, was approved by a specially convened *loe jirga* (grand council) on Sept. 19, 1964. After a general election in Sept. 1965 Mohammed Yusuf was reappointed prime minister. There was opposition to the appointment, however, in the newly elected people's assembly, and rioting by students broke out at the end of October. The prime minister resigned and the king called on Mohammed Hashim Maiwandwal to form a government. This was immediately approved by the assembly. (X.)

V. ADMINISTRATION AND SOCIAL CONDITIONS

Until 1919 the government of Afghanistan was an absolute monarchy. King Amanullah Khan, however, introduced a system of democratic government, though evolution was inevitably slow. The constitution adopted in 1931 provided the framework of a constitutional monarchy based on the *shari'a* (Islamic law, q.v.). Although after the accession of Mohammed Zahir Shah in 1933 the king no longer took any direct part in the administration, much power still rested in the hands of the royal family, who held the more important offices of the state. A new constitution promulgated in 1964 excluded the members of the royal family from the government and provided for freedom of speech and of the press, the right to form political parties and free trial in all criminal cases.

Legislation is effected by the people's council (national assembly), elected for four years by universal, secret and direct vote, and by the council of elders (senate), one-third of whose members are nominated by the king and the rest elected. The administration is carried on by a cabinet selected by the prime minister, who is appointed by the king and need not be a member of the legislature. The prime minister and the ministers are collectively and individually responsible to the people's council. In addition there is the *loe jirga*, consisting of members of parliament and chairmen of provincial councils, which is summoned in matters of great importance. The king has the power to dissolve parliament, but the members of the *loe jirga* retain their positions until a new parliament is convened.

Afghanistan was reorganized into the following 29 provinces in 1964–65: Farah, Herat, Seistan, Helmand, Kandahar, Zabul, Badghis, Ghor, Faryab, Jowzjan, Balkh, Uruzgan, Ghazni, Bamian, Samangan, Kunduz, Takhar, Badakshan, Katawaz and Urgoon, Paktia, Maidan and Wardak, Logar, Parwan, Kabul, Kapisa (Bagram), Pul-i-Khumri and Baghlan, Nangrahar, Kunar and Laghman. Each province is subdivided into districts and has an elected provincial council which advises the provincial government. The cities are controlled by municipal committees under a president.

Judiciary is an independent agency in the state; it consists of a supreme court and other courts and provides for military tribunals. In the absence of specific provision in the constitution or the laws, the courts are guided by the Hanifite version of the *Shari'a*. Punishments vary from the death sentence to fines.

Primary education is compulsory and primary schools exist throughout the country, but secondary schools only in the larger cities. Kabul university, known as the Pahantun, was founded in 1946 and incorporated a number of existing faculties, the oldest being the faculty of medicine, established in 1932. A university campus was under construction in the mid-1960s. The University of Nangrahar was founded at Jalalabad in 1963. There are teachers' training institutes and facilities for technical education.

Progress has been made in controlling malaria, smallpox and tuberculosis, and there are about 60 hospitals. The provincial capitals have social welfare centres.

Every Afghan has to serve two years in the army. The strength

ISTALIF, A TOWN NORTH OF KABUL IN THE FOOTHILLS OF THE PAGHMAN MOUNTAINS

of the army in the mid-1960s was about 90,000. There are army corps in Kabul and Paktia provinces, and infantry division headquarters at Ghazni, Kandahar, Herat, Mazar-i-Sharif and Jalalabad. In addition there is the royal bodyguard of brigade strength. Approximately 300,000 to 400,000 armed levies can also be called upon in emergency. The regular forces are armed with modern weapons. A military academy at Kabul trains cadets. A new training school for infantry and artillery was opened in 1957. Training for cadets is provided by an air academy, opened in 1958.

A small air force is equipped mostly with Russian aircraft. Two bases at Mazar-i-Sharif and at Bagram (completed in 1960) provide facilities for jet bombers. Another Russian-built air base at Shindand in the Helmand valley was completed in 1963.

VI. THE ECONOMY

Afghanistan is self-supporting in food (except for tea and sugar) and in cotton and wool, the two raw materials most important to its industries. The national income is obtained chiefly from land taxes and customs duties, and to a lesser extent from the profits of state trading and the Afghan National bank. This income pays for defense and for development. A plan for the economic development of the country was adopted by Nadir Shah and his advisers in 1932, and was steadily pursued. It was based on the partial industrialization of Afghanistan, and included the installation of hydroelectric works, the erection of textile factories, of machinery for the extraction of sugar from beets, of cotton gins and of other plants. The principal object of these schemes was to enable Afghanistan to be self-supporting so far as possible in certain essential commodities, and so to avoid the necessity for extensive importation of basic requirements. At the same time state-controlled companies were formed to regulate the purchase and sale of the principal imports and exports, the financial equilibrium of the state being maintained by the establishment of a national bank with branches at home and abroad. The first five-year development plan (1956) was completed in 1961. The second five-year plan provided for storage dams and irrigation channels and for the establishment of large mechanized farms.

The bulk of Afghanistan's export trade was with, or passed through, the undivided Indian subcontinent; in 1947 it was seriously disturbed after the independent countries of India and Pakistan were created. Lambskins continued, however, to go principally to the United States and a barter agreement with the U.S.S.R., first negotiated in 1943 for the exchange of Afghan wool for Soviet gasoline, piece goods, etc., was renewed in 1950 and afforded some relief to the country's economy. Under the Point Four program an agreement with the U.S. was signed in Kabul in Feb. 1951 to assist the Afghan government in the economic development of the country. A similar agreement was later signed with the Soviet Union and some of the east European states.

The principal export commodities are the Afghan lambskin

sists of desert land in the south and southwest and of highland country providing seasonal grazing. On the whole the soil is fertile, particularly in the wide loess plains north of the Hindu Kush and in the eastern and southern areas. In these places and along the valleys wherever irrigation is possible good crops are obtained. Irrigation is carried out by means of a network of channels, often many miles in length. The cultivators are skilled irrigators, utilizing every fragment of profitable land. Some of the Ghilzai are specially skilled in building underground water channels called *karez* (*see* KANDAHAR). Modern irrigation works have been constructed at Pul-i-Khumri, Baghlan, Sarobi and Kunduz in the north and at Girishk near Kandahar. Dry farming is also practised in certain areas. Under construction in the early 1960s were the 344 ft. (105 m.) high Naghlu dam and a dam at Darunta, both on the Kabul river, which were designed to enlarge the irrigated area and provide about 70,000 kw. of electric power for urban and industrial use in and around Jalalabad in Nangrahar province.

The principal crops are wheat, the staple food of a large portion of the inhabitants, rice (particularly in the valleys), barley and lucerne for fodder, cotton, sugar beets, sugar cane, Indian corn, millet, lentils and mustard seed. Vegetables are extensively cultivated and include potatoes, carrots, turnips, onions, chilies, tomatoes, beans, peas and cabbages.

Horticulture is largely practised, particularly around Kabul and Kandahar where the Sardas melon is famous. Grapes, of excellent quality, and dried apricots are exported in large quantities. Other fruits include all well-known European varieties. The mulberry is grown extensively and in some localities forms the staple food of the inhabitants. Dried and crushed with walnuts it is made into a cake (*talkhan*) and stored for winter use.

Domestic animals include sheep; horses, of which the northern variety (Turkmen) is the best-known; donkeys, extensively used for light transport; camels of two types for heavy transport (the dromedary south of the Hindu Kush); goats; and poultry.

The principal wealth of Afghanistan lies in the immense flocks and herds which roam the great pasture lands below the mountains. From the pastures around Andkhui, Akcha and Shibarghan come the highest-quality lambskin or astrakhan, while from the southern sheep come wool, mutton and butter (which is used in the clarified form of ghee). The cattle are kept chiefly for milk and also provide a considerable quantity of skins and hides.

2. The Helmand River Project.—After World War II the Afghan government invested a great part of the economic re-

OLIVER CLUB—PIX FROM PUBLIX

KARAKUL FLOCK FINDS POOR GRAZING IN A PARCHED VALLEY; IN THE BACKGROUND, THE HINDU KUSH

(karakul), of which 1,500,000 to 2,500,000 are exported in a normal year; wool; cotton; fruit, both fresh and dried; nuts; hides and skins; cattle felts; sheepskin coats (*poshtins*); carpets; asafetida; and timber. Imports consist principally of textiles, piece goods, sugar, tea, petroleum products, machinery, motor vehicles, hardware and rubber goods. The chief commercial centres are Kabul, Kandahar, Herat, Mazari-i-Sharif and Jalalabad.

The monetary unit is the afghani, with a par value of 45 afghanis to the U.S. dollar or 126 to pound sterling.

1. Agriculture and Animal Husbandry.—Afghanistan is mainly a pastoral country. Of the total area of 250,000 sq.mi. (647,500 sq.km.) probably not more than 32,000 sq.mi. (82,880 sq.km.), or about 13%, are under cultivation. The remainder con-

sources of the country in the construction of a multipurpose project in the regions of the Helmand and the Arghandab, its main tributary. In addition a large part of the necessary capital was obtained from the U.S. and the International Bank for Reconstruction and Development. The aim of the Helmand River project (carried out by an Afghan subsidiary company of an American firm) is to enlarge the irrigated area, increase and modernize agricultural production and at the same time to make the settlement of a great number of nomads possible. Further, the plan is to enlarge the road system in the Helmand region, produce hydroelectric power through two large dams on the Helmand and the Arghandab, and develop trade and industry.

The Kajakai dam on the Helmand is 360 ft. (110 m.) high and

forms an artificial lake 50 mi. (80 km.) long, with a capacity of 1,498,000 ac.ft. This reservoir ensures the irrigation of about 355,000 ac. (143,668 ha.) divided into eight districts along the Helmand. It has a power potential of 130,000 kw. About 1,000 nomad families and other landless Afghans have been settled; but beside difficulties of adaptation there have been problems with regard to the unfavourable soil (too salty or too alkaline), bad drainage, the tendency of the farmers to use too much water (when it is available), etc. In the Arghandab region difficulties have been considerably smaller, chiefly because there it is the water supply of already existing holdings that is being increased and regulated. The Arghandab dam is 230 ft. (70 m.) high with a reservoir of a capacity of 388,000 ac.ft. After the final extension it will provide water for 184,000 ac. (74,465 ha.), about half of which will be new land, while the rest formerly had an uncertain and strongly seasonal supply from primitive canals. The growing of grapes, peaches, apricots, almonds and other fruits is important for the Arghandab region, while the produce in the Helmand regions consists mainly of wheat, alfalfa, cotton, melons and vegetables.

3. Minerals.—Much work was done on the geological survey of the country by various agencies after 1930, but although Afghanistan is rich in minerals, its mountainous nature and its remoteness from the sea make the profitable exploitation of this source of wealth a matter of extreme difficulty.

Extensive coal-bearing strata were located in the Hindu Kush north of Bamian, but the only mines sufficiently accessible to work are at Ishpushta on the north road near Doab and at Karhar south of Khanabad, though the coal is not of the highest quality. A survey of the country in 1937–38 and later surveys in the 1950s located oil in the north and near Herat. In 1960 there was some production of oil for experimental purposes.

Large deposits of rock salt in Badakhshan, supplemented by brine deposits in Andhkui and Herat supply the greater part of the country's needs. There are alluvial gold deposits in the Amu-Darya and a disused gold mine in Kandahar. However, these are not rich enough for profitable exploitation, and neither is the silver that exists in the Hazarajat and the Panjshir valley. There is also a ruby mine in the Jagdalak pass, east of Kabul, and lapis lazuli of a high quality is found in Badakhshan and has been utilized for thousands of years.

Plentiful supplies of lead, zinc and iron ore of excellent quality have been proved near Kandahar and in the Ghorband valley, which also contains copper and manganese. Chrome ore has been found in the Logar valley about 35 mi. S. of Kabul, beryl in Nangrahar province and talc in Shinwari tribal territory adjoining Pakistan. Sulfur, gypsum, alabaster and saltpetre are also found.

4. Industry.—Except for cotton textiles and cement, Afghanistan's industries are on a small scale. The largest of the textile mills is at Gulbahar, 60 mi. (97 km.) from Kabul. There are cement factories at Jabal us-Seraj and Pul-i-Khumri, woolen mills at Kandahar and Kabul, a beet-sugar plant at Baghlan, and a fruit-processing and canning factory at Kandahar. Kabul and Kandahar have industrial districts which include a lumber mill, woodworking mills and metalworking shops.

5. Communications.—There are no railways and virtually no navigable rivers in Afghanistan. Main roads connect the principal centres of the country and link up with the road system of Pakistan: from Kabul via the historic Khyber pass (q.v.), and from Kandahar via Chaman and the Khojak pass. From Ghazni old trade routes lead through the Gumal pass and Kurram. A road links Herat with Iran via Islam Qala. Principal connections with the U.S.S.R. are by ferry across the Amu-Darya to Termez and from Herat to the Soviet railhead at Kushka. A road driven through the passes of the Hindu Kush to connect Kabul directly with the northern provinces was opened in 1933, and in the following 12 years fair-weather roads to all the larger towns were constructed. In 1964 a tunnel was completed below the Salang pass in the Hindu Kush to allow the main road from Kabul to Mazar-i-Sharif to be shortened by 120 mi. (193 km.). Several of the main roads are being asphalted, but many secondary roads are rough and liable to be blocked by snow or damaged by floods in the winter and spring. Bus services ply on the main roads with fair

regularity. Camel caravans and pack animals are still used.

Ariana Afghan Airlines was founded in 1955, and there is regular air service between major towns and between Kabul or Kandahar and airports in the U.S.S.R., Iran and India, and direct lines to the near east and Europe. An international airport was built at Kandahar, and the airport near Kabul was enlarged.

Afghanistan is a member of the International Postal and Telegraph union. Post offices have been established in the principal towns and regular motor mail services are in operation. A telegraph and telephone system links the provinces with the capital, while a world-wide radio installation connects Kabul with the outside world. There are subsidiary radio stations at Kandahar, Herat and Mazar-i-Sharif. *See* also references under "Afghanistan" in the Index.

(J. P. C. N. H.)

BIBLIOGRAPHY.—Mohammed Akram, *Bibliographie Analytique de l'Afghanistan* (1947); H. W. Bellew, *An Inquiry Into the Ethnography of Afghanistan* (1891), *Afghanistan and the Afghans* (1879); G. Morgenstierne, *Report on a Linguistic Mission to Afghanistan* (1926); *Encyclopaedia of Islam*, 2nd ed. (1954–); K. Ferdinand, "Preliminary Notes on Hazara Culture," *Hist. Filos. Medd. Dan. Vid. Selsk.* 37, no. 5 (1959); C. S. Coon, *Seven Caves* (1957); J.-M. Casal (preliminary account of Mundigak) in *Illustrated London News* (May 1955); *Mémoires de la Délégation Archéologique Française en Afghanistan*, i: xvi; for Lashkari Bazar (Bust) *see* D. Schlumberger in *Illustrated London News* (March 1950); for Surkh-Kotal see *J. Asiat.*, pp. 4, 5 and 9 (1952); F. R. Allchin, "The Culture Sequence of Bactria," *Antiquity*, xxxi (1957); A. Maricq, *Le Minaret de Djam* (1959); Sir Percy Sykes, *A History of Afghanistan* (1940); Sir Olaf Caroe, *The Pathans, 500 B.C.–A.D. 1957* (1958). For early history *see* works cited under BACTRIA; PARTHIA; and the articles on the various peoples, Iranian and non-Iranian, mentioned in the text above. For later history *see* also G. P. Tate, *The Kingdom of Afghanistan*, 2 vol. (1911); W. K. Fraser-Tytler, *Afghanistan: a Study of Political Developments in Central and Southern Asia*, 2nd ed. (1953); C. E. Yate, *Northern Afghanistan* (1888); Sir G. S. Robertson, *The Kafir of the Hindu Kush* (1896); Lord Roberts, *Forty-One Years in India* (1897); Sultan Mohammed Khan (Mir Munshi) (ed.), *Constitution and Laws of Afghanistan* (1910); T. L. Pennell, *Among the Wild Tribes of the Afghan Frontier* (1911); J. Hackin, *Guide de Bamiyan* (1924); R. Furon, *L'Afghanistan* (1926); R. Dollot, *L'Afghanistan* (1937); R. Byron, *The Road to Oxiana* (1937); L. Lockhart, *Nadir Shah* (1938); W. O. von Hentig, *Ins verschlossene Land* (1942); E. F. Fox, *Travels in Afghanistan* (1943); *Report on Development of Helmand Valley, Afghanistan* (1956); Donald N. Wilber (ed.), *Afghanistan*, rev. ed. (1962); A. A. Michel, *The Kabul, Kunduz and Helmand Valleys and the National Economy of Afghanistan* (1959); J. Humlum, *La Géographie de l'Afghanistan* (1959); Mahmoud Habibi, *Evolution économique et sociale des populations de l'Afghanistan à l'époque contemporaine* (1959); M. B. Watkins, *Afghanistan: Land in Transition* (1963); Mohammed Ali, *A Cultural History of Afghanistan* (1964); P. A. Macrory, *The Fierce Pawns* (1966). Current history and statistics are summarized annually in *Britannica Book of the Year*. (X.: F. R. A.; MD. A.)

AFONSO, the name of six kings of Portugal.

AFONSO I (Afonso Henriques) (1109?–1185), the first king of Portugal, was the son of Henry of Burgundy and Teresa, an illegitimate daughter of Alfonso VI of León and Castile. Henry, a grandson of Duke Robert I of Burgundy, had become count of Portugal in 1095, and on his death in 1112 Teresa took charge of affairs. On Afonso's coming of age, Teresa refused to surrender her powers, but Afonso defeated her forces on June 24, 1128, and took over the government. After a period of conflict with Alfonso VII of León, he obtained the latter's recognition of his title as king of Portugal at the conference of Zamora (Oct. 4–5, 1143). Subsequently he extended the Portuguese frontier southward by expeditions against the Muslims, capturing Santarém and Lisbon (1147), Beja (1162), Évora (1165) and Juromenha (1166). He had securely established Portuguese independence by the time of his death (Dec. 6, 1185).

AFONSO II (1185?–1223), king of Portugal from 1211 to 1223, was the son of Sancho I and Dulcia, daughter of Ramón Berenguer IV of Barcelona. His reign was distinguished by his army's share in the victory over the Muslims at Las Navas de Tolosa (1212) and by the conquest of Alcácer do Sal (1217) but was also marked by conflict with the clergy and the nobility, who resented Afonso's policy of strengthening the crown to their detriment. He was excommunicated in 1220 and died on March 25, 1223.

AFONSO III (1211?–1279), king of Portugal from 1248 to 1279, was the son of Afonso II and Urraca, daughter of Alfonso VIII of Castile. He became regent after the deposition of his brother,

Sancho II, in 1245, and king on his death in 1248. He conquered Faro in 1249 and established his dominion over Algarve, thus securing to Portugal the natural limits of its southern frontier. The first known meeting of the *curia regis,* in which the municipalities were represented, dates from his reign (1254). Afonso III died on Feb. 16, 1279.

AFONSO IV (1291–1357), king of Portugal from 1325 to 1357, was the son of King Diniz, whom he succeeded, and Isabella, daughter of Peter III of Aragon. He was at war (1336–40) against his son-in-law, Alfonso XI of Castile, but later allied himself with him against the Muslims to win the battle of the Salado river (1340). In 1355 Afonso ordered the assassination of Inês de Castro (*q.v.*) and so provoked his son and heir, Pedro, into rebellion. Afonso IV died on May 28, 1357.

AFONSO V (1432–1481), king of Portugal from 1438 to 1481, was born at Sintra in Jan. 1432, the son of King Duarte and Leonor, daughter of Ferdinand I of Aragon. He succeeded his father at the age of 6, under his mother's regency. This she was obliged to yield, in 1440, to Afonso's uncle, Pedro, duke of Coimbra. At the end of his minority, in 1448, Afonso embarked on a series of campaigns in north Africa. He conquered Alcácer Ceguer in 1458 and, after subduing Arzila in 1471, occupied Tangier. Ambitious of achieving the union of Castile with Portugal, he invaded Castile in support of the claims of his wife Joan, daughter of Henry IV of Castile, against those of Isabella I. In this same cause he went to France in 1476, hoping to enlist the support of Louis XI. When he failed to win this, he abdicated in favour of his son John, who, however, restored the crown to him on his return to Portugal in Nov. 1477. Afonso died on Aug. 28, 1481.   (V. R. R.)

AFONSO VI (1643–1683), king of Portugal from 1656, when he succeeded his father John IV, to 1683, was born in Lisbon on Aug. 21, 1643. In fact he ruled only from 1662, when he came of age, until 1667, when his brother Pedro (afterward king as Pedro II) seized power, keeping Afonso prisoner until his death at Sintra on Sept. 12, 1683. The reign was marked by internal disputes between partisans of the king and of his brother, and by a series of victories against Spain, including the battles of Ameixial (1663), Castelo Rodrigo (1664) and Montes Claros (1665) which led to the recognition of Portuguese independence by Spain in 1668.   (DA. A. P.)

A FORTIORI (Lat. "from a stronger [ground]"), a type of argument in which the conclusion is supported by a ground stronger than one that has already been accepted in a previous argument as sufficient justification for a similar conclusion about a subject of the same kind. For example, when it has been accepted that in a right-angled triangle the side opposite the right angle must be greater than either of the other two sides because the right angle is greater than either of the other two angles, then it can be argued that in an obtuse-angled triangle a fortiori the side opposite the obtuse angle must be greater than either of the other two (an obtuse angle being even greater than a right angle).

AFRANIUS, LUCIUS, Roman general, a devoted adherent of Pompey. In 60 B.C., chiefly by Pompey's support, he was raised to the consulship, in which office he proved himself utterly incompetent to manage civil affairs. In the following year, while governor of Cisalpine Gaul, he obtained a triumph, and on the allotment of Spain to Pompey (55 B.C.), Afranius and M. Petreius were sent to govern it as legates. On the rupture between Caesar and Pompey, Afranius and Petreius were compelled, after a short campaign in which they were at first successful, to surrender to Caesar at Ilerda (49 B.C.). Caesar dismissed them on their promise not to serve again in the war. Afranius, however, went to join Pompey, and at the Battle of Pharsalus (48 B.C.) he had charge of Pompey's camp. On Pompey's defeat, Afranius, despairing of pardon from Caesar, went to Africa, and was present at the disastrous Battle of Thapsus (46 B.C.), at which Caesar defeated the supporters of Pompey and gained control of Roman Africa. Though he escaped from the field with a strong body of cavalry, Afranius was afterward taken prisoner and handed over to Caesar, whose veterans rose against him in anger and put him to death. *See also* CAESAR, GAIUS JULIUS; POMPEIUS.

AFRICA, the second largest of the continents, has an area (including offshore islands) of approximately 11,690,000 sq.mi. (30,277,135 sq.km.) and a population estimated at more than 230,000,000. Though stretching for about the same distance north and south of the equator (from Ras ben Sekka near Cape Blanc, Tunisia, 37° 21′ N., to Cape Agulhas, South Africa, 34° 51′ S., about 5,000 mi. [8,000 km.]), two-thirds of the continent lies north of the equator, while nearly four-fifths is within the tropics. The west-east extent is 4,600 mi. (7,400 km.) from Pointe des Almadies, 17° 32′ W., on Cape Verde, Senegal, to Ras Hafun, 51° 25′ E., near Cape Guardafui, Somali Republic. It is joined to Asia in the northeast by the Sinai peninsula, cut by the Suez canal, and its nearest contact with Europe is across the Strait of Gibraltar. Some areas have long been known to Europeans, notably in North Africa, a part of the Mediterranean world, but western contact with much of Africa is relatively recent and accounts for the great international interest in territorial expansion during the 19th century as well as for the upsurge for political independence after World War II.   (L. C. KG.)

The article contains the following sections:

   I. Physical Geography
      A. Geology
      B. Physiography
      C. Climate
      D. Vegetation
      E. Animal Life
  II. Natural Resources
      A. Water
      B. Soils
      C. Minerals
      D. Land Use
 III. Ethnography (Anthropology)
      A. North Africa
      B. Northeast Africa
      C. West Africa
      D. East Africa
      E. West Central Africa
      F. Central Africa
      G. Southern Africa
  IV. Archaeology
      A. Fossil Hominid Remains
      B. Southern Africa
      C. Central and West Africa
      D. East Africa
      E. North Africa
      F. Carthaginian and Classical
   V. History
      A. North Africa
      B. Sahara and Sudan
      C. Guinea
      D. Central Africa
      E. Southern Africa
      F. East Africa
      G. Partition of Africa
      H. Africa After World War I
  VI. Population

I. PHYSICAL GEOGRAPHY

It is sometimes suggested that the physical characteristics of Africa—its climate, vegetation and soils as well as its relief and drainage—help to explain why Africa remained the "dark continent" for so long and until so recently. Certainly the physical environment has presented mankind in Africa with many obstacles and challenges. There are no deep bays or gulfs penetrating far inland and comparatively few rocky headlands to afford shelter to adjoining bays. Beaches are often surf bound, and sometimes backed by large though shallow lagoons, frequently with mangrove forests in them. Large rivers are relatively few and, apart from the Congo, end in deltas or are blocked by sand bars. Rapids and falls comparatively near the coast have discouraged penetration upstream, and navigation on most African waterways is inevitably restricted both by the grading of the river and by the often great seasonal fluctuations of volume. It is doubtful whether these difficulties would have proved insuperable had the resources of the continent been sufficiently attractive to encourage men to overcome them: but it is almost certainly true that they long discouraged, even where they did not actually prevent, European penetration. The realities of the limitations imposed on development by physical conditions must also be recognized, and several large-scale projects carried out after World War II have failed largely because adequate attention was not given to the facts of physiography, climate, water supply and soils.

(R. W. Sl.)

A. Geology

Africa is a plateau. Except in the north where the continent stands lower and was occasionally flooded by transgressive seas, it has remained stable and emergent practically since Precambrian time. Upon a basement of Archean (Early Precambrian) rocks, highly metamorphosed and much intruded by granites of various ages, rest numerous sedimentary rock sequences, mostly nonmarine in origin. The materials of sequences such as the Lubilash of the Congo and the Karroo of South Africa were derived in part from beyond the borders of the present continent. This fact, with the truncation of older structures at the coasts and the similarity with late Paleozoic and Mesozoic formations in South America, India, Australia and Antarctica led to the conception of a formerly vast southern land mass, Gondwanaland (q.v.), of which Africa formed a part. The existing outline of the continent, including Arabia, which is geologically a part of Africa, dates from the earliest Cretaceous as is shown by the occurrence of seaward dipping marine Cretaceous rocks in many maritime provinces.

Few severe orogenic movements have affected Africa. The Atlas mountains, which geologically and biologically resemble Europe more than they do the rest of Africa, are the only example of Tertiary mountain making, while the Cape ranges at the opposite end of the continent were crumpled during the Triassic. Paleozoic folds in the Sahara are apparently not as extensive as Eduard Suess formerly suspected; but Precambrian deformation is widespread, and dated radioactively to several phases. Not all instances of folding and metamorphism in the basement are orogenic. A. M. Macgregor defined in Southern Rhodesia a number of mantled gneiss domes closely crowded together. Between these domes the Archean rocks crop out as arcuate or triangular areas in which the foliation is parallel to the curving edges and gneissic structure of the intruding domes. Such assemblages are likely to prove widespread in the African basement.

Deformation has generally taken the form of broad basins separated by axial upwarps: Congo cuvette, Kalahari basin, Chad depression. Such features are of all ages from Precambrian to modern times. Most are occupied in part by sedimentary accumulations. Spectacular are the Rift valley troughs extending from Jordan to Mozambique. In their present form dominantly of mid-Pleistocene age, the Rift valleys are sited upon earlier rift structures of Tertiary, Cretaceous (Mesozoic), Paleozoic and possibly also Precambrian which were probably equally impressive in their time. Despite the general rise of adjacent country toward the rifts so that the sides frequently rise to (or near) 10,000 ft. (3,000 m.) and the floor of the rift stands even above the general elevation of the African plateau, the origin of the rifts is usually ascribed to tensional forces.

Volcanism has been endemic throughout geologic time. Most of the rock systems have associated intrusive or extrusive rocks; some phenomena are on a magnificent scale. The Lebombo basalts and rhyolites concluding the Karroo sequence are estimated at 29,000 ft. (8,800 m.) in thickness by A. L. du Toit, who also calculated the volume of magma in Karroo intrusions as between 50,000 and 100,000 cubic miles. At Calvinia and Hopetown in South Africa individual dolerite sheets are quoted as 3,500 and 5,000 sq.mi. (9,100 and 13,000 sq.km.) in area, respectively. Plateau-making floods of phonolite welled out in Kenya during the mid-Tertiary.

Recent and subrecent volcanism in Central Africa has been aligned closely along the Rift valleys. Mt. Kenya is a denuded cone, the summit of which projects as a neck; Kilimanjaro was similar, but a new cone with a semiactive crater, Kibo, now makes the highest eminence. Ruwenzori (the Mountains of the Moon) is nonvolcanic, consisting of a huge mass of Basement rocks warped and faulted differentially. Volcanic emissions along the eastern rift are strongly sodic in composition, those of the western rift through the Congo are strongly potassic. Mt. Lengai (Doinyo Lengai) of Tanzania and Mt. Nyamlagira and Mt. Niragongo of the Congo have been active in modern times, the 1939–40 outflows of basalt from Nyamlagira being among the largest witnessed by man. Recent volcanicity is also displayed in the Cameroons and at Emi Koussi and Tibesti in North Africa.

Stratigraphy.—Correlation among formations is usually based upon stratigraphic criteria. Fossils are scarce and of limited value for correlation before the late Paleozoic. The absence of fossils from formations such as the Transvaal and Waterberg systems does not prove them Precambrian as they accumulated within inferred continental basins of Gondwanaland.

In the Precambrian rocks radioactive age determinations are beginning to be useful. A. Holmes and L. Cahen indicate seven Precambrian geological cycles besides others extending into or belonging to the Paleozoic. In only a few localities are minerals older than 3,000,000,000 years; the Witwatersrand uraninite is 2,600,000,000 years, the Kibara-Karagwe-Ankole rock systems are indicated at about 1,400,000,000 years and there is abundance of ore deposits in the 630,000,000 years age group.

The solid foundation, exposed over about a third of the continent, is a mixed assemblage of Archean schists and paragneisses (of sedimentary origin) everywhere intruded by granites of various ages. Upon this lie thick Proterozoic sequences in which strikes are variable, while folding and metamorphism are in some places intense, in others relatively weak. The most complete subdivision of the Archean is established for Southern Rhodesia where three accumulative phases are followed, respectively, by three intrusive phases. The Sebakwian system comprising several thousand feet of rock, originally sediments and basic volcanics (now converted to hornblende schist), is intruded by serpentinites and Older Gneiss with an age of 2,900,000,000 years. The Bulawayan, which includes all the larger gold belts of the country, is a monotonous greenstone succession of 30,000 ft. (9,100 m.) of onetime basic lavas. It is intruded by the Younger Gneiss. The Shamvaian is mostly fine-grained arkoses (separated by unconformities into three series), and is intruded by younger (Matopo) granite dated as 1,900,000,000 to 2,150,000,000 years old. The threefold subdivision of the east African Archean into Basement, Nyanzian, and Kavirondian shows several lithological parallels with the Rhodesian classification. The Basement is heavily migmatized, the Nyanzian consists mainly of acid and basic volcanics and the Kavirondian resembles the Shamva grits.

Archean rocks in a series of major anticlinals make a chain of inliers along the Tropic of Cancer from former French West Africa to Egypt and Sudan and appear also about Ghana, Nigeria, and the Cameroons region, but detailed correlation with the Archean systems of Rhodesia is not yet possible. Mineralizations within the Archean systems are mainly hydrothermal, and associated with episodes of granitic intrusion. Gold, silver, copper, tin, chrome, beryl, asbestos, rare earths and mica are locally developed.

Proterozoic (Late Precambrian) rocks may be divided into older and younger groups, represented in South Africa by the Witwatersrand and allied systems, and the Transvaal and related systems respectively. The first group, richly gold-bearing, finds few extensive correlatives farther north, but the latter assemblage has representatives in almost every African territory. Arkoses, quartzites, shales, mica schists, limestones and dolomites are the typical rock types, and ore deposits due to abundant intrusions are often associated; e.g., Bushveld complex.

Early Paleozoic rocks are scarce in Africa. In the north, the Cambrian is identified only in Morocco, near Tetuán, and the Ordovician is restricted to a small area within the Sahara. Marine Silurian, with fossils including certain brachiopod species and crinoids, is, however, encountered at intervals right across North Africa. Post-Silurian folding was mild. In the south, the fossils *Rangea schneiderhöhni, Pteridinium simplex, Orthogonium parallelum* may indicate a Cambrian age for part of the Nama system, but no Ordovician formations have been identified. Reddish Silurian sandstones and conglomerates of continental rock formations are widespread (see *Geologic Formations,* below) from the Cape to the Democratic Republic of the Congo and Tanzania. Only in Congo are these fossiliferous (fish scales, Crustacea, hexactinellid sponge spicules and Radiolaria), and only in Congo and Cape Province have they undergone severe folding.

The Devonian is widely fossiliferous. It includes the Bokkeveld series of the southern Cape, and is extensive in the Sahara, Libya and the western Sudan. On the Ghanaian coast it reaches the Atlantic; marine representatives occur of the lower, middle and upper divisions. The Carboniferous of North Africa is widespread and generally continental. Between Ennedi in Chad and Uweinat (Libya-Egypt-Sudan border) the change of facies began in late Devonian time with the appearance of plant fossils—*Lepidodendron, Archaeosigillaria* and *Stigmaria;* but in Mauritania terrestrial conditions did not supervene until the mid-Carboniferous. In Egypt marine intercalations from the north appear in a predominantly continental sandstone series which continued to accumulate probably until the mid-Mesozoic. Central and southern Africa display the continental Karroo system over vast tracts of country. The lowest series is late Carboniferous in age and includes the glacial Dwyka tillite, 2,000 ft. (600 m.) thick in Cape Province but thinning northward to the Transvaal. Patches of it occur as far afield as Congo and the island of Madagascar.

The succeeding Ecca series (Permian) contains the rich coal deposits of South Africa, Southern Rhodesia and Tanganyika (Tanzania) with the fossil seed fern *Glossopteris;* while the Beaufort series (Triassic) of the Cape is famous for its fossil reptiles (*Pareiasaurus, Dicynodon, Cynognathus*). Equivalent formations in the Congo basin make the Lukuga series. The Stormberg series contains a Triassic flora (*Dicroidium, Baiera, Dadoxylon*) with the dinosaurs *Gryponyx, Plateosaurus* and the mammallike *Tritylodon*. Aeolian sandstones commonly conclude the Karroo sedimentary sequence before the extrusions of Drakensberg basaltic lavas (Lower Jurassic). Totaling 4,500 ft. (1,400 m.) thick in the Drakensberg, these eruptives extended from the east coast to the west, and from the Cape mountains to Victoria falls. Immediately following the extrusions the residual magma invaded the subjacent Karroo sediments as the largest network of associated dikes and sills extant. Except along the Atlas and in southern Tunisia no marine Triassic is established in Africa.

Outside Congo (Lualaba series), continental Jurassic sediments are scarcely known in Africa; instead, a phase of erosion was ubiquitous and virtually the whole continent was reduced to a plain. Remnants of this plain may still be identified in existing landscapes. The hypothesized breakup of Gondwanaland was begun by penetration of the Jurassic sea from Somalia to Tanzania, whence from Tendaguru come marine shells and fossil reptiles of which *Gigantosaurus* is the largest known animal. Madagascar was separated from the mainland. The isolation of Africa was completed during the early Cretaceous, when arms of the sea passing down the east and west coasts respectively met around the southern Cape. The faunas of these seas were Indo-Pacific and

TABLE I.—*Correlation of Sequences, South Africa*

Continental erosional stages	Succeeding continental deposition	Succeeding coastal deposition
Congo cycle . .	Pleistocene and Recent sands and terrace deposits with implements	Beaches and dunes
"Post-African" cycle (later Tertiary) .	Kalahari-type sand, chalcedonic, with abundant fauna including Australopithecines. Late Pliocene	Late Pliocene sands (Zanzibar)
African cycle (early Tertiary) . .	Plateau sands (chalcedonic)	Early Miocene (Uloa and Inharrime)
"Post-Gondwana" . (late Cretaceous)	*Grès polymorphes*, Botletle beds (late Cretaceous-Oligocene)	Senonian-Eocene
Gondwana landscape (Jurassic)	Série de Kwango	Neocomian-Cenomanian

Mediterranean respectively; *e.g.*, Cretaceous faunas of Zululand and Angola. All stages of marine Cretaceous (*q.v.*) are known along the east coast, the most widely distributed being the Neocomian and Senonian. Cretaceous epicontinental seas spread widely over North Africa reaching to latitude 24° N. up the Nile valley and in Libya. Cenomanian seas spanned West Africa, from

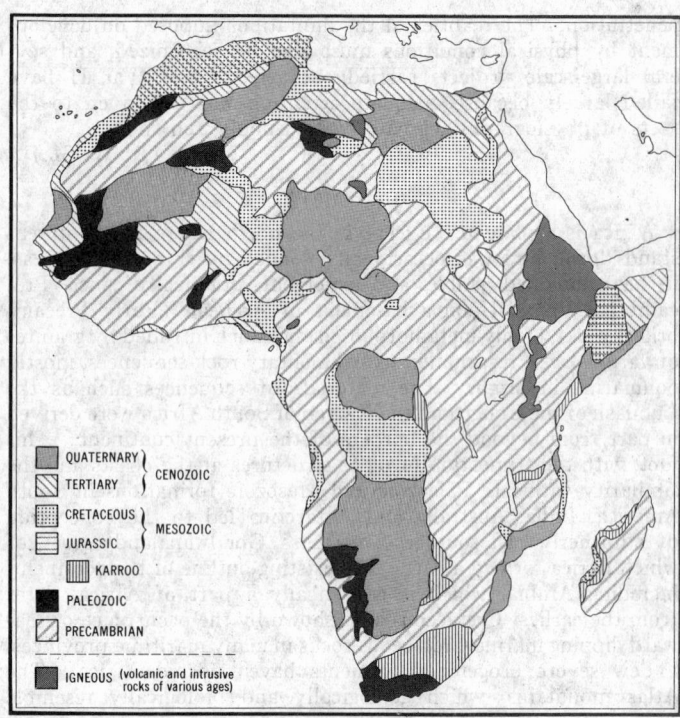

FIG. 1.—GEOLOGIC AGE OF SURFACE ROCK FORMATIONS OF AFRICA

QUATERNARY	CENOZOIC
TERTIARY	
CRETACEOUS	MESOZOIC
JURASSIC	
KARROO	
PALEOZOIC	
PRECAMBRIAN	
IGNEOUS (volcanic and intrusive rocks of various ages)	

Geologic Formations

CENOZOIC

Quaternary . . Alluvia, raised beaches, desert sands, etc., with neolithic and paleolithic implements. Lavas and tuffs of recent volcanoes.

Tertiary

  Pliocene . Marine beds in Algeria, Tunisia and Egypt. Limestones of Zanzibar and Angola. Bone beds of Omo valley and South African caves (with Australopithecines). Older lavas of Central African volcanoes.

  Miocene . Marine limestones of northern and eastern coasts. Rusinga Island beds of Lake Victoria; plateau sands of Congo and Kalahari desert. Kapitian phonolites of Kenya.

  Oligocene . Marine limestones in Algeria, Tunisia, Egypt, Somalia and Tanganyika. Lake beds of Fayyum.

  Eocene . . Nummulitic limestone of North Africa, Somalia and Mozambique. *Aturia* beds of South West Africa, Niger valley and Sokoto. *Grès polymorphe* of the Congo and Angola. Widespread eruptions in Kenya.

MESOZOIC

Cretaceous . . Almost complete marine sequences in former French West and North Africa, Mozambique and Zululand. Coastal Angola and Benue valley. Kwango series in Congo and Angola. Continental intercalary and Nubian sandstone of North Africa.

Jurassic . . . Late Jurassic marine and continental facies of Somalia and coastal Tanganyika. Lualaba series of Congo basin. Liassic effusion of Drakensberg lavas.

  Triassic . Upper Beaufort and Stormberg series of South Africa, terrestrial Trias of Tunisia and Atlas.

PALEOZOIC

  Permian . Ecca and Lower Beaufort series of South Africa, Tanga beds, Lualaba sandstones of Congo.

  Carboniferous . Dwyka series (with tillite), Witteberg series of Cape, terrestrial and marine sandstones of Egypt.

Devonian . . Bokkeveld series, marine and terrestrial beds of Sahara, Libya and Sudan.

Silurian . . . Table mountain, Umkondo, Upper Kundelungu series. Sandstones of central Sahara.

Ordovician . . Sahara.

Cambrian . . Northwest Morocco, Gulf of Aqaba. ?Nama system (in part).

?LATE PROTEROZOIC OR TRANSITIONAL

Transvaal system, Lomagundi, Katanga group (Roan and Kundelungu); Bakoban system arkoses, mica schists and limestones of Tibesti and Ahaggar.

?Early Proterozoic

?Early Proterozoic

Witwatersrand system, Frontier system, Kibara system; Lépi formation, Ankolean system; ?bankets of Ghana.

Archean

Onverwacht, Figtree and Moodies systems of South Africa; Sebakwian, Bulawayan and Shamvaian of Southern Rhodesia; Tugela-Mfongozi system of Zululand; Basement, Nyanzian and Kavirondian of East Africa; Benguela gneiss, Nigeria, Tibesti and Egypt.

Tunis and Morocco to the Gulf of Guinea. Limestones are typical in North Africa, for little terrigenous waste was supplied to the epicontinental sea from the low, smoothly planed Gondwana landscape. About emergent areas in the Saharan Ahaggar, Tibesti and the Sudan, accumulated continental and lagoonal sandstones with plants and crocodile remains.

After the Cretaceous the sea shrank, leaving a number of Eocene relicts of much smaller dimensions upon the rising land. Chief areas of sedimentation were the lower Nile valley, central Libya, the Niger valley from Tombouctou (Timbuktu) to the river mouth, Sokoto in northern Nigeria and the interior of Senegal. Across the northern Sahara retreat was rapid, leaving the Cretaceous hammadas (stony desert plateaus) to be covered by various continental Tertiary and Quaternary deposits, including the ergs (deserts of shifting sand dunes, or sand seas). Tertiary basins (e.g., Chad) received appropriate sedimentation. The Faiyum (Fayyum) sequence of Egypt contains the earliest fossil elephants and ancestral apes.

In the western Sahara there was no Eocene sea, only Algerian and Moroccan bays, for a convulsion of the Tethyan geosyncline created an early phase of the Atlas mountains. The Miocene sea covered only Cyrenaica and Degardaia in Algeria. The Pliocene sea was even more restricted. Elsewhere North Africa was land throughout the Neogene (Miocene and Pliocene). Erosion carved a set of cyclic erosional bevels that can be correlated with similar features in the south.

Marine Tertiary formations are strictly coastal about East, South and West Africa. Lower Miocene occurs at Mombasa (Kenya), Lindi (Tanzania), Inharrime (Mozambique) and St. Lucia (South Africa) along the east coast and in Angola in the west. Pliocene is best known in Zanzibar (Tanzania) and Angola. Marine faunas are again of contrasted Indo-Pacific and Mediterranean types on the east and west coasts respectively.

In southern Africa the correlation between (1) cyclic erosional landscapes, (2) sedimentary sequences of continental type and (3) coastal marine sequences which rest upon marginally downwarped land surfaces is tabulated in Table I. The same scheme may be extended, with slight modifications, to most of the continent.

South African Pliocene cave deposits have yielded Australopithecine man-apes and associated fauna (cf. alluvia at Olduvai gorge, Tanzania); and the Pleistocene throughout the continent is rich in stone tools and other evidences of early man.

(L. C. Kg.)

B. Physiography

Relief.—The physiography of Africa is largely a reflection of the geological history and geology described in the previous section. The continent, largely composed of a vast rigid block of ancient rocks, has geologically young mountains at its extremities in the highlands of the Atlas mountains in the north and the Cape ranges in the south. Between them are series of plateau surfaces, with huge areas that are level or slightly undulating, above which stand occasional harder and more resistant rock masses. Surrounding these plateaus is a zone of plateau slopes below which are narrow coastal belts widening along the Mediterranean coast, the coastlands of Tanganyika and Mozambique, a narrow belt between the Kunene and Niger rivers, and an area northward of the Gambia and Senegal rivers.

In proportion to its size Africa has less high mountain and less lowland plain than any other continent. The limited areas above 8,000 ft. (2,500 m. [1 ft. = 0.3048 m.]) are either volcanic peaks or resistant massifs. All the land below 500 ft. occurs within 500 mi. (800 km. [1 mi. = 1.6093 km.]) of the coast, except for two small basins in the Sahara.

The relief map (fig. 2) shows a contrast between the higher plateau areas of the south and east (to which the name "High Africa" is sometimes given) and the generally lesser elevation of "Low Africa" in the west and north. South of a line drawn from near the mouth of the Congo river to the Gulf of Aden most of the land lies 1,000 ft. or more above sea level, and much of it exceeds 3,000 and even 4,000 ft. North of the line there is relatively little land above 3,000 ft., most of the area being between 500 and 1,000 ft. above sea level; there are also broad coastal lowlands, except in the northwest and in the east beyond the Nile.

These contrasts between High and Low Africa are not only important physical differences, but are also full of consequences for economic development, for European settlement and for political status. An effect of elevation is to modify temperature conditions and, in a tropical area, generally to ameliorate the climatic environment so that the majority of the permanent white settlers in Africa, apart from those of the northwest, live either near or southward of the equator. The highest extensive areas are in Ethiopia, parts of which exceed 15,000 ft. Southward the East African plateau is highest in Kenya, where it is often 8,000 ft. or more above sea level; there are occasional volcanic peaks that are much higher, such as Kilimanjaro (19,340 ft.), Kenya (17,058 ft.), Meru (14,979 ft.) and Elgon (14,178 ft.). Ruwenzori or the Mountains of the Moon (16,763 ft.), on the borders of the Democratic Republic of the Congo (former Belgian Congo) and Uganda, is not volcanic in origin. From East Africa the plateau extends southward, often with a well-defined, though by no means continuous, escarpment which is particularly noticeable in the Drakensberg mountains of southern Africa (Thadentsonyane 11,425 ft. and Mont aux Sources 10,822 ft.). There the plateau edges are especially marked because the rock formations are hard and horizontal, whereas in Ethiopia they are conspicuous because of recent faulting. Where the rocks are softer and less resistant the escarpment is not so pronounced and so forms less of a barrier to climatic influences and to human movement.

Northward and westward of the plateau area of High Africa there is a decline in altitude to the lower areas of the basins of the Congo, Niger and Nile. The only large areas above 3,000 ft. are in the folded ranges of the Atlas mountains and in the central Sahara where resistant granites form the massifs of Ahaggar (Hoggar) and Tibesti. The interior uplands of West Africa and of Cameroon consist of ancient crystalline rocks, reaching considerable heights only in the Fouta Djallon plateau in Guinea and on the borders of Sierra Leone and Liberia, and in Nigeria in the Jos plateau, and Adamawa and Cameroon highlands. There are extensive low-lying areas near the coast and in the basin of rivers such as the Senegal, Gambia, Volta and Niger Benue. The high areas of Darfur in the Sudan (over 10,000 ft.) and of Mt. Cameroon (13,350 ft.) are volcanic in origin and are evidence of the same tensions that have resulted in rifting and vulcanism in East Africa.

The ancient crystalline Archean base, sometimes described as the Basement complex, is exposed at the surface over vast areas amounting in all to about one-third of the surface of the whole continent. Sometimes granites are predominant: elsewhere there has been much metamorphism, and schists and gneisses are common. Where erosion is vigorous, surfaces may be very uneven, since the granitic rocks erode rapidly while the metamorphosed rocks, which are often highly folded, form irregular and rugged ridges. In drier areas the more resistant rocks stand up sharply above their surroundings to give the inselberg (q.v.) or island-mountain topography so characteristic of much of Southern Rhodesia, Zambia and Tanganyika. Parts of the Basement complex are highly mineralized, as are some of the sedimentaries that rest on it, and there are important mineral-producing areas in southern Africa, on the Congo-Zambezi watershed and in western Africa (see Mining below).

Over very extensive periods of time, the African land mass has been subject to vertical movements of elevation and depression, but there has been relatively little folding. Exposure to atmos-

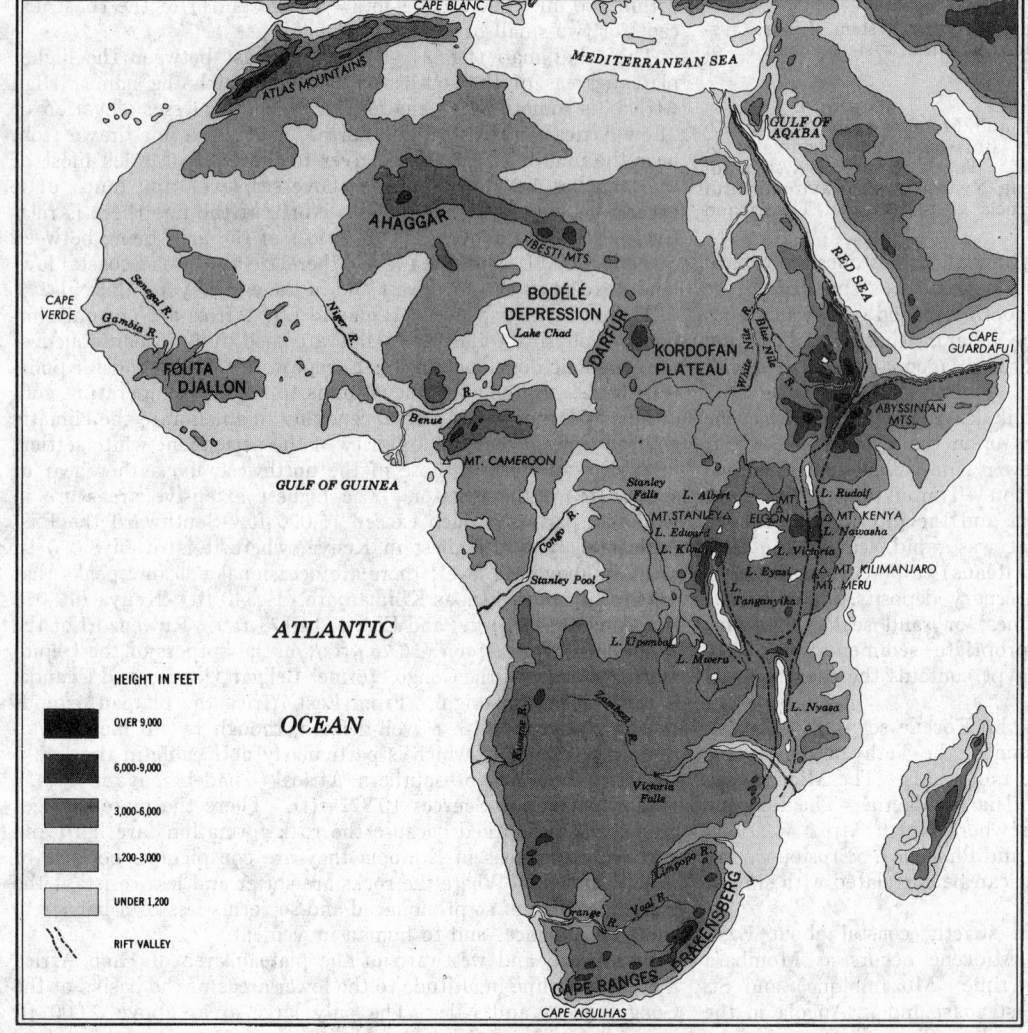

HEIGHT IN FEET

OVER 9,000

6,000-9,000

3,000-6,000

1,200-3,000

UNDER 1,200

RIFT VALLEY

R. W. STEEL

FIG. 2.—RELIEF OF AFRICA

with easily erodable Karroo sedimentary rocks. The third well-developed surface, occurring at between 2,500 and 4,000 ft., is Pliocene or late Tertiary and is most marked where the sedimentary rocks are weaker and in the Cretaceous beds of the Luangwa valley and of the Lake Nyasa trough. Detailed studies in other parts of the continent may help to elaborate and perhaps to modify this outline of the geomorphological history of Africa.

The Rift valleys of East Africa, though directly affecting only one part of the continent, are nevertheless most striking and distinctive features of the relief of Africa. Numerous theories have been advanced for their formation. They probably came into existence in Cretaceous or late Tertiary times and were contemporaneous with the separation of the island of Madagascar from the mainland of Africa. Associated with their formation was the volcanic activity responsible for most of the higher peaks of East Africa, including Kilimanjaro, Africa's greatest mountain, which is always snow-capped, near though it is to the equator. Seismic and volcanic disturbances are still recorded in the western portions of the Rift valley system. In the Virunga (Mfumbiro) mountains northeast of Lake Kivu there are periodic outbursts every 10 or 12 years which have created a series of lava flows of known dates. One of these volcanoes dammed the Rift valley and converted a large area, formerly drained by a tributary of the Nile, into Lake Kivu.

The Rift valley extends for about 4,000 mi., its course being clearly marked out by many of the lakes of East Africa as well as by the adjacent volcanic peaks. From the Gulf of Aqaba it can be traced southward along the Red sea and into the Ethiopian massif to the lakes Rudolf, Naivasha and Magadi in Kenya. Farther south the line is less obvious through Tanzania. The walls that constitute the eastern rim have been more easily eroded, while the lakes are generally smaller and not in line and some of them are only waterless salt beds: the largest lakes are Natron and Manyara, with Eyasi in a side branch of the main rift. The edges are obvious enough to the south in Malawi where a huge crusted block collapsed along the parallel faults that constitute the steeply rising slopes of Lake Nyasa. The lake is 360 mi. long but never more than 50 mi. wide, and has a maximum depth of 1,226 ft. The rift then follows the line of the Shiré valley to reach the coast of the Indian ocean near Beira, Mozambique.

The western branch or Western Rift valley extends from the northern end of Lake Nyasa in a great arc taking in the lakes Rukwa, Tanganyika (after Lake Baikal in Siberia the deepest lake in the world with a sounding of 5,715 ft.), Kivu, Edward and Albert. Subsidiary branches of this valley include the basins in which lie lakes Mweru and Upemba.

Most of the Rift valley lakes lie well below the general level of the plateau, ranging from 1,300 to 3,000 ft. above sea level. They are generally very deep and fjordlike, and some, though with surfaces many hundreds of feet above sea level, have their floors well below sea level.

pheric weathering resulted in the reduction of practically the whole land area to an almost level surface or peneplane in Miocene times. Subsequent elevation of this surface through thousands of feet led to the faulting and fracturing responsible for the formation of the Great Rift valley (q.v.) and to the associated volcanic activity. It also created huge inland seas and lakes in shallow basins on the uplifted surface, and in these areas were deposited large quantities of Quaternary and Recent alluvium. In some areas, however, the older rocks have remained hidden beneath a thick cover of aeolian or wind-borne deposits, as in parts of the Sahara and in the Kalahari.

Vast areas of Africa are characterized by uniformity and monotony of land form and natural vegetation. Level or slightly undulating surfaces occur widely and sometimes give the impression of being a lowland plain, even though lying at a considerable elevation above sea level. Much geomorphological investigation remains to be done, and more precise correlation is needed between the surfaces recognized in different parts of the continent. There is a fair measure of agreement for the view that at least three major cycles of erosion have been completed and are represented by well-marked surfaces, certainly in southern Africa where most field study has so far been done. The oldest of these is a high-level erosion surface of late Jurassic age at between 7,000 and 8,500 ft. above sea level. It has been recognized in the Cape ranges, the Basuto mountains and, farther north, in the Nyika plateau of Malawi. The second surface (of Miocene or mid-Tertiary age) stands at about 4,500 ft. and is best preserved where rivers like the Orange and Limpopo and, to the north, the Zambezi and Congo have carved out great valleys in troughs that were filled

In complete contrast is Lake Victoria, the greatest of all East Africa's lakes. This occupies a shallow depression on the plateau, 3,720 ft. above sea level, between the major branches of the Rift valley. Its greatest depth is only 270 ft. but its area (26,828 sq.mi. [69,485 sq.km.]) makes it the third largest of the world's great lakes after the Caspian sea and Lake Superior.

Drainage.—Both High and Low Africa are similar in that they consist of blocks elevated to form saucerlike depressions surrounded by land higher than their centres. On the seaward side the blocks generally slope steeply down and are deeply cut by relatively short but rapidly flowing streams. On the inland side the descent is usually gradual, except in the cases of the Atlas mountains, the Drakensberg and the Ethiopian highlands. The drainage pattern of the continent is determined by the nature and extent of these depressions and of their surrounding uplands. Formerly there were, as a result of uplift of the plateau surface, numerous vast inland lakes and seas. These have now either disappeared or been much reduced in size, through being drained by streams that have cut back through the plateau rim. Thus the Niger and Congo now drain the lake basins of the upper Niger and central Congo, the rivers meandering across the huge stretches of Quaternary and Recent alluvium before tumbling over the plateau edge to reach the sea. Yet despite the evolution of the drainage system, nearly one-third of the continent (3,750,000 sq.mi.) still consists of areas of inland drainage with no outlet to the sea.

Apart from the many short, and often seasonal, streams that are usually limited to the coastal zones, there are only nine major river systems, and one of these (the Lake Chad system) fails to reach the sea. Even these main rivers have not yet had time to grade their courses, and falls or cataracts occur where the rivers descend from the interior basins across the hard rocks of the plateau rim to the narrow coastal plain below. Energetic, short coastal streams are actively cutting back by headward erosion into the plateau, especially in the better watered areas, and in due course will drain to the sea areas that are at present inland drainage basins.

Part of the explanation of the apparent drying up of some inland lakes like Ngami, Makarikari, and Chad since Europeans first saw them may be at least as much concerned with changes in drainage as of climate.

The Congo.—This river has the largest drainage system (1,425,-000 sq.mi. drained, 2,716 mi. long). It lies entirely within the tropics, the main river running at times astride the equator. Thus most of its basin experiences the heavy and fairly evenly distributed rainfall of equatorial latitudes, so that all the main rivers are perennial, with many of them available for navigation during most of the year in those stretches between falls and rapids. Much of the basin of the central Congo is 1,000 ft. or more above sea level tilting gently from southeast to northwest. It is surrounded by uplands such as the Katanga–northern Angola plateau on the south, the Rift highlands of East Africa to the east, and the uplands of the watershed between the Congo and the Niger–Chari in the north. The alluvial plain is crossed by ill-defined channels with numerous lakes, marshes and swamps—parts of the basin that have never yet been fully drained.

All the tributaries join the main stream before breaching the Crystal mountains in a long series of 32 rapids and cataracts known as the Livingstone falls which take the river down 700 ft. in a stretch of 220 mi. immediately below Stanley pool. By contrast the difference in height between Stanley pool and the Stanley falls farther upstream (on the eastern edge of the former inland lake) is about 800 ft., spread over more than 1,000 mi. The Congo, unlike the other great African rivers, has an estuary and not a delta. (*See* CONGO RIVER.)

The Nile.—Though with a smaller drainage area than that of the Congo (1,110,000 sq.mi.), the Nile (*q.v.*) is one of the world's greatest rivers, comparable with the Mississippi and the Amazon, with a total length of 4,157 mi. It maintains its volume during a passage across a wide rainless desert area because much of its water comes from the equatorial regions of the East African plateau where it is stored in the huge natural reservoir of Lake Victoria (*q.v.*). Its tributary, the Blue Nile, brings the seasonal rainfall of the summer monsoon from Ethiopia and is thus mainly responsible for the great fluctuations in the amount of water in the lower parts of the valley. Navigation on the river is checked by six cataracts between Khartoum and Aswan (*q.v.*) as well as by the irrigation barrages and dams constructed since the mid-19th century.

The Niger.—This river drains 580,000 sq.mi. and, while rising only 200 mi. from the Atlantic ocean in the Fouta–Djallon plateau, has a total length of 2,600 mi. before reaching the sea in the Gulf of Guinea. The lower Niger, formerly a separate stream, has cut back into the plateau to drain the middle basin, a former inland lake, which still floods very easily during the rainy season in the area above Tombouctou (Timbuktu). The Niger's main tributary, the Benue (*q.v.*), is gradually working back, in the same manner, into the Lake Chad basin, by cutting its way through the upland area linking the plateaus of northern Nigeria to the mountains of Cameroon. (*See* NIGER RIVER.)

The Zambezi.—The Zambezi (*q.v.*) is 2,200 mi. long and its basin covers 513,500 sq.mi. Its upper course drains a huge shallow alluvial basin more than 4,000 ft. above sea level: many of its tributaries there are intermittent because of the highly seasonal nature of the rainfall and the intensity of evaporation. The falls and rapids are in its middle course, the most spectacular being the Victoria falls, 355 ft. high (*cf.* Niagara, 167 ft.). Below the falls the river follows a narrow zigzag course developed along successive fault lines. Farther downstream the Kariba dam has formed a huge lake in the section known by the Matabele (Ndebele) people as Gwembe. Nearer the Indian ocean the river becomes in places 5 mi. or more wide.

The Orange.—This river, with only one important tributary, the Vaal, is 1,300 mi. long but has a relatively restricted basin of 170,000 sq.mi. It drains some of the higher parts of the South African plateau westward to the Atlantic; but it loses so much of its water through evaporation and, in the 20th century, through withdrawal for irrigation, that in drought years it may even be dry. Much of the rainfall never reaches the main river but collects in shallow lakes (*vleis*) and is evaporated so that they become salt encrusted. (*See* ORANGE RIVER.)

Other Rivers.—Three other rivers deserving individual mention are the Limpopo (*q.v.*), draining an area between the Zambezi and the Orange, and the Volta and Senegal rivers (*qq.v.*) of West Africa, but none has a catchment area comparable with the five larger systems already described.

The great desert areas of northern Africa contain several basins with no outlets to the sea. Lake Chad (*q.v.*) is a shallow body of water whose volume and area fluctuate greatly from year to year largely because of the highly irregular seasonal discharge of the Shari (*q.v.*) river. Northeastward lies the lower-lying Bodélé depression, into which Chad water occasionally overflows. From the Gulf of Gabès in southern Tunisia there is a line of depressions extending southwestward across the desert from the *chotts* or salt lakes (some of which are below sea level) to the salt desert of El Djouf. The few streams that flow in the Sahara all lose themselves in the desert and fail to reach the sea. (R. W. SL.)

C. CLIMATE

Africa extends from 37° N. of the equator to almost 35° S. and hence the climates of the continent are largely tropical and subtropical in character. Temperate climates are found on the Mediterranean shores in the north, in the southern and southwestern Cape Province and on the higher parts of the great inland plateau. The cold ocean currents flowing equatorward on the western side of Africa cool the climates of the coastal zones for a few miles inland. In the east the climatic influence of the warm ocean currents is stronger and warm humid air penetrates far inland.

The amount of rainfall and its distribution throughout the year vary greatly. The outstanding feature of the rainfall is its seasonal distribution; almost everywhere, apart from the equatorial lowlands, there are marked wet and dry seasons, wet seasons as the sun passes overhead and dry seasons in the intervening periods. (*See* fig. 3.)

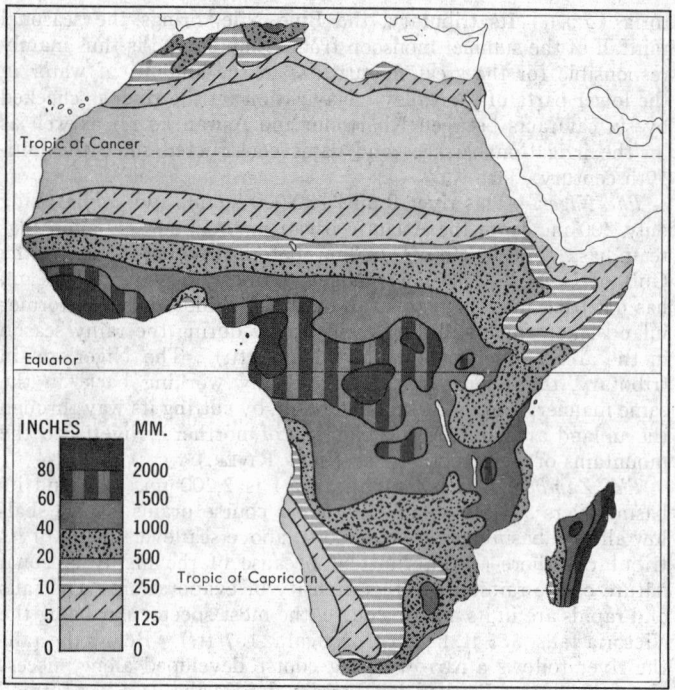

FIG. 3.—AVERAGE ANNUAL RAINFALL OF AFRICA

Air temperature is about as variable as rainfall. From the human point of view the climates of most of Africa are warm, though cold weather is common in the deserts, on the plateau and in the mountains. At times some regions are uncomfortably hot but only the deserts are too hot for active life. Statistics of average temperature for some representative stations are included, but the great differences of temperature between day and night make these figures difficult to interpret in the light of experience in temperate countries. (*See* fig. 4.)

There are seven major types of climate which occur in zones roughly symmetrical about the equator corresponding in a general way to the major zones of natural vegetation.

Equatorial Climate.—This is the climate of the basin of the Congo river west of Rwanda, Burundi, the Central African Republic, part of the Guinea coastlands extending to southern Nigeria, Ivory Coast and a small part of Ghana. The heavy convectional rainfall has no marked dry season but an interruption in the rains between two periods of maximum. Rains are heaviest when the sun is overhead; near the equator the equinoctial months are the wettest, but farther from the equator the two maxima merge into one, in midsummer—January in the southern hemisphere and July in the northern.

The change from a southern hemisphere regime of rainfall to a northern hemisphere one takes place about 3° N. of the equator. At Abidjan (77 in. [196 cm.; 1 in. = 2.54 cm.]), the first rains come from March to July; August and September are relatively dry and the second rains occur in October and November. At Léopoldville, June to August is a dry season and the rains occur from October to May with maxima in November and April. The average rainfall over most of the Congo basin is 60–70 in. a year, but some areas on the west coast receive 150–200 in. The hill slopes in the Cameroons are exceptionally wet. These heavy rains are influenced by the moist southwesterly monsoon wind that blows inland in the hot season, May to October. When this wind augments the ordinary convectional processes of the equatorial zone there is no interruption in the rainy season and no dry months. (Douala 156 in., Port Harcourt 98 in., Harbel 154 in.) On the other hand, where the influence of the monsoon predominates, as at Conakry (169 in.) in Guinea, there is a single, though long, rainy season followed by five months of drought when the dry northeasterly harmattan blows.

Temperatures in the equatorial region do not vary much throughout the year. The annual mean for the basin of the Congo

is about 27° C. (1° F. = 9/5° C. +32) with only a small difference between the means of the warmest and coolest months. The daily range (approximately 7°–11°) exceeds the annual range; in fact, cool though humid evenings are not uncommon on the banks of the Congo. Where there is a dry season the mean daily range may be as much as 17° even a short distance from the coast. Mean monthly temperatures: Coquilhatville, hottest month March 26°, coolest July 23°, greatest range January 11°, least July 9°; Stanleyville, hottest month March 26°, coolest August 24°, greatest range January 11°, least range July 8°; Douala, hottest month March 28°, coolest July 25°, greatest range April 9°, least July 5°.

Tropical Climates.—These are found in the savanna lands which enclose the equatorial regions. Precise definition of their extent is difficult but, taking the 30-in. rainfall line as a rough limit, the northern boundary would be somewhere between the parallels of 12° N. and 14° N. and the southern boundary near the parallel of 16° S. The rainfall varies from 30 to 60 in. except on the windward slopes of high mountains like Kenya and Kilimanjaro and in favoured situations like the northwestern shores of Lake Victoria (Entebbe 66 in.). Tropical climates are distinctly drier than the equatorial climates and are characterized by a rainy season in the summer of either hemisphere and a dry season in the winter. Rainfall decreases fairly rapidly in the direction of the tropics and the vegetation of tall trees and high savanna deteriorates into scrub.

The relatively cool highlands of East Africa which lie across the equator have a tropical rather than equatorial climate because of their altitude. Rainfall in the wetter parts of Kenya and Uganda is about 60 in., with local variations due to relief; the Rift valley, for example, is notably dry with only about 30 in. and densely populated Rwanda and Burundi have about 45 in. Temperatures in the warm months are higher than in the equatorial regions. But these climates are not always oppressive; relative humidity is usually low in the daytime when the temperature is high, and there is considerable range of temperature between day and night; in the warm weather before the rains day temperatures are above 27° C. but with a range of 11°–17° the nights are comfortable. Uganda, at a somewhat lower altitude than the highlands of Kenya and with a similar rainfall, has a warmer climate.

The region of tropical climate stretches westward from Uganda through Chad to West Africa. There the prevailing southwest

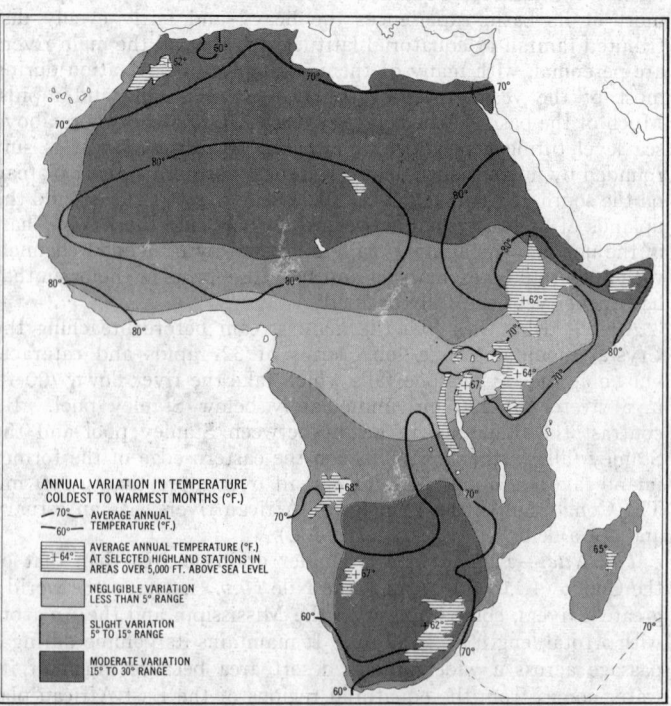

FIG. 4.—AVERAGE ANNUAL TEMPERATURE RANGE OF AFRICA

winds, from the Gulf of Guinea, carry moist air inland. The months April to October are rainy. The rest of the year, when the northeast winds blow, is dry and hot; temperatures are above 32° C., but the daily range is about 11° and on the hottest days the relative humidity is below 50%. The discomforts of the hot season are often exaggerated. Mean temperatures; Kano 31° in April and 22° in January, Jos 25° in April, Nairobi 18° in March and October and 15° in July, Kampala 23° in January.

The corresponding tropical climate of the southern hemisphere is in Southern Rhodesia, Zambia, Malawi, and Angola. With the exception of the deep Zambezi valley, the whole of this area lies above 3,000 ft. and in the east some of it is above 6,000 ft. Rainfall is moderate (30–50 in.) and the temperatures are lower than in the tropical region north of the equator. The daily maximum temperature in summer at about 5,000 ft. is approximately 27°–29° C. The hottest areas are in the deep valleys of the Zambezi (Luangwa and Kafue) where temperatures of more than 38° (100° F.) are common, and the coolest are near the eastern mountains.

On the desert side of the tropical climates is a dry region with the same essential characteristics forming a zone of transition from the savanna to the deserts. The northern Sudan, the northern frontier district of Kenya, the Karamoja district of Uganda, the Nyika zone in East Africa, southern Tanganyika, northern Kalahari and southern Angola all belong to this dry region. Rainfall is low (15–30 in.) and the rainy season lasts only three to five months (Kayes 30 in., Niamey 23 in., Dodoma 22 in., Maun 17 in.). Temperatures are high throughout the year (Kayes, mean maximum in May 42° C., daily range 15°; Niamey, mean maximum in May 41°, daily range 17°; Dodoma, mean maximum in November 31°, daily range 13°; Maun, mean maximum in October 35°, daily range 17°). The seasonal range of temperature is small (Niamey 5°, Dodoma 5°, Maun 10°) and there is no real winter. The hot weather at the end of the long drought is uncomfortable and despite the rise in humidity the arrival of the rains brings relief from the heat.

Desert Climates.—These are found in both hemispheres—the Sahara (q.v.) in North Africa and the smaller deserts of the Kalahari and South West Africa in the south. The former extends across the continent from the Atlantic to the Red sea and, for the most part, is a true desert. Except in the mountains' massifs years may pass without rain; vegetation is sparse and stunted and the surface consists largely of sand and broken rock. Apart from the lack of rain, one of the most interesting features of the climate is the great range of temperature: dry northerly currents of descending air prevail most of the time and the sky is hazy as even a light wind raises the dust. There is no cloud and the sun scorches the ground. Summer temperatures are among the highest in the world; day after day the thermometer rises above 43° C. (110° F.). But as the air is dry the ground cools rapidly when the sun begins to set and the night seems cold. Daily ranges of more than 10° are usual. In the winter, on the other hand, the days are pleasant; the temperature is about 16° but severe frosts follow at night. There are occasional violent dust storms known by local names like simoom, sirocco and the khamsin.

The Kalahari desert in the southern hemisphere extends from the Orange river to the Zambezi and has a summer rainfall varying from 10 in. in the south to more than 25 in. in the north. Practically the whole area supports a natural vegetation of some economic value. Normal summer maximum temperatures are close to 32° C. and days with temperatures as high as 41° can be expected only about once a month. The winter temperatures are over 21° in the daytime with light frosts at night and occasional severe frosts at altitudes above 3,500 ft. The Namib and the southern end of the plateau in South West Africa, Namaqualand, the drier parts of the South African Karroo and the lower reaches of the Orange river valley, where the rainfall is less than 5 in. (Goodhouse 2 in.), also belong to this region of desert climates. Though the rainfall (5–15 in.) is meagre, nearly half of it falls in winter and the vegetation of low scrub provides grazing for sheep and goats. Summer temperatures are similar to the Kalahari but winters are somewhat colder.

The coastal zone of the Namib is a narrow sandy desert, cool and almost rainless, stretching from Angola to Cape Province. True desert begins some distance south of Luanda where the mean annual rainfall is 13 in.; Moçâmedes (Mossâmedes) has only 3 in. of rain and the coast of South West Africa almost no rain at all. The upper air over the coast is warm but the surface air is cooled by the Benguela current and the coast is liable to frequent low cloud and fog. Called *cacimbo* in Angola, it occurs mainly in the cool season, spreading inland from the sea in the early morning and dispersing a few hours later. In South West Africa, however, it becomes a thick layer of stratus cloud about 1,000 ft. high extending from the seaward limit of the cold water to about 30 mi. inland. Almost every morning in summer and on many days in winter the sky is overcast and a fine drizzle falls and wets the ground. Toward afternoon the sky clears and a strong, almost violent, sea breeze comes up to raise the loose sand of the desert into clouds of dust. The hottest days are in the winter months when the cool weather is occasionally disturbed by the familiar berg winds of South Africa—hot dry winds from the direction of the interior of the plateau which make the temperatures on the cool coast rise to over 32° C.

Mediterranean Climate.—This occurs on the coast of the Mediterranean Sea, beginning in Morocco and extending eastward through northern Algeria and Tunisia, and in southwestern Cape Province. Both areas are mountainous and the rainfall, which is cyclonic, varies considerably with altitude and exposure. The characteristic feature of the Mediterranean climate is winter rainfall (15–30 in.) and a long dry summer.

In North Africa the Mediterranean region includes the coastal strip, a plateau 3,000–4,000 ft. high and the wooded ranges of the Atlas mountains in which there is abundant rain in both summer and winter. The climate of the Atlantic coast is moderated by the cool Canaries current. Summer is cool and the low cloud and fog are the cause of high humidity and a small range of temperature. Summer temperatures increase eastward along the North African coast (Mogado 20° C., Algiers 33°, Tunis 33°) and the contrast between summer and winter becomes much more pronounced. The extreme maximum temperatures in the hottest months may exceed 38° (Algiers, mean August maximum 32°). Winter depressions with their westerly winds and clouds, bring cool weather (Algiers, mean January temperature 13°); frost is rare on the coast but common on the drier steppe-covered plateau of the Shotts between the Atlas ranges. There the winter climate is severe and the summer is as hot as it is near the coast.

The Mediterranean region of Cape Province is small in comparison with the coast of North Africa but has large variations of rainfall and temperature. Winter is cool and wet and the summer dry and warm near the coast, though at times the weather may be uncomfortably warm only a short distance inland (Wellington, mean January maximum 31° C.). Both seasons suffer from strong winds—in winter the northwesterly gales and in summer the monotonous and regular "Cape southeaster" which, in the neighbourhood of Cape Town, may blow gale force for two or three days at a time. Rainfall varies greatly with exposure. The city of Cape Town has a rainfall of about 25 in. but the mountain slopes receive 60–70 in. The rainfall decreases rapidly northward and inland toward the Karroo where the Mediterranean climate merges into semidesert (Saldanha Bay 12 in., Garies 5 in., Worcester 9 in., Laingsberg 4 in.). In the warm summer (mean January temperature: Cape Town 22°, Stellenbosch 21°, Worcester 23°) weeks may pass without rain; the southeaster blows persistently, covering the mountains with whitish clouds like the "tablecloth" on Table Mountain.

Humid Subtropical.—The plain in the southeast of Mozambique and its continuation in the narrow coastal strip in South Africa have a warm and humid climate which is distinctly subtropical in the north but temperate in the south where it becomes cooler and merges into the region of year-round rainfall found on the south coast and on the forested southern slopes of the mountains of Cape Province (Harkerville near Knysna, mean annual rainfall 43 in., wettest month September 5 in., driest month April 3 in.). The extent of the region is restricted by altitude, losing its subtropical character above 2,000 ft. Rainfall occurs mainly in summer and varies from about 30–50 in. (Lourenço Marques 32 in., St. Lucia bay 51 in., Durban 45 in., Port St. Johns 48 in.). The warm Mozambique current exerts a strong influence on the temperature of the whole coastland of Mozambique and Natal and daily maxima in summer vary between 27° and 32° C. (Mean January maximum: Lourenço Marques 30°, St. Lucia Bay 28°, Durban 27°, Port St. Johns 26°.) These temperatures combined with a relative humidity of about 65% are uncomfortably warm, but in the winter the climate of this coast is the most genial in southern Africa. (Mean July maximum: Lourenço Marques 24° C., Durban, St. Lucia Bay, Port St. Johns 22°.)

The rainy season in Mozambique (November to April) corresponds to the season of the northern monsoon which is a southern extension of the Asian circulation into the Mozambique channel. The southern monsoon which blows in winter is part of the trade wind circulation of the southern hemisphere and does not usually bring rain. The coast of Natal, however, does not experience these winds and the most notable feature of the wind there is the fresh northeasterly sea breeze relieved occasionally by stray southwesters bringing clouds and rain. East London has a high frequency of southwest winds and there the average velocity for the year is 14 m.p.h.

Temperate Plateau.—This is the grassland plateau, 3,000–6,000 ft. high, and includes the high veld on which the Witwatersrand gold fields and the principal farming lands of South Africa are situated. The main features of the climate are low rainfall, cloudless skies and large diurnal changes in weather. Local differences of rainfall and temperature are due to relief and exposure, and a number of isolated areas of wet, cool and misty mountain climates are found on the prominent eastern escarpment. Seasons are sharply contrasted: summer is warm and the rains, mostly convectional, occur then; winter is cool and dry. Mean annual rainfall varies from about 20–40 in. decreasing from east to west (Standerton 28 in., Johannesburg 30 in., Bloemfontein 22 in., Kimberley 16 in.). Moisture for the summer rains appears to come from the Indian Ocean in a deep northerly to northeasterly current which becomes unstable and produces convectional showers with only a small ascent. Most of the plateau is cool in summer. (Mean January maximum: Ermelo 26° C., Johannesburg 26°, Bloemfontein 30°.)

The winter weather is fine and warm in the daytime followed by cold nights, and in the mornings the thick haze in the valleys and depressions reveals the inversions of temperature. In winter outbreaks of cold air from the south sweep across the plateau now and then bringing snow and rain to the mountains. Severe frosts are not unusual, as at Bloemfontein in July when this occurs on about one night in four.

Highland Climates.—These climates occur, in small areas, throughout eastern Africa where the altitude exceeds 6,000 ft., notably on the mountain slopes of Ruwenzori, Kilimanjaro, Kenya and Elgon. The Ethiopian plateau is an extensive area of highland climate—a rugged massif in which difference of altitude and exposure are responsible for important local differences of climate. But for the mountain peaks reaching 15,000 ft. the general level of the plateau is about 8,000 ft. The land between 6,000 and 8,000 ft. has a pleasant climate. The rain (Addis Ababa 49 in.) is monsoonal and falls mainly from June to September.

In the southern hemisphere the Basuto highlands with their natural vegetation of mountain grass should be included in the region of highland climates. The higher mountain slopes are cool, misty and often wet; in the winter they are snow-covered and intensely cold. The population is therefore concentrated in the valleys where conditions are less severe. (Mokhotlong 7,800 ft., rainfall 22 in., mean July maximum −4° C.).   (S. P. Jn.)

Effects of Climate.—Climatic conditions, particularly rainfall, have very important effects on other aspects of the physical environment and on economic and settlement possibilities. There is a direct correlation with vegetation types and with hydrographic conditions, especially in relation to the regime of rivers. Navigability, the possibilities of irrigation and the generation of hydro-

electricity are all affected by the markedly seasonal nature of most African rivers. The Congo benefits in that its catchment area extends both north and south of the equator so that the volume of water in all the main rivers fluctuates relatively little from season to season, while the Nile has the advantages of year-round rainfall over much of its upper basin and of the vast storage capacity of natural reservoirs like Lake Victoria.

The types of agriculture practised in different parts of Africa (fig. 8) are closely influenced by climatic conditions, and the predominance of crops or livestock in the rural economy is determined largely by rainfall. In areas with considerable altitudinal differences, with consequent variations in temperature, such as the uplands of Ethiopia, the East African plateau, and the Atlas mountains, there is usually a well-marked correlation with vegetational belts, and a wide range of products can be grown.

The links between climatic conditions and human activities are also revealed by a study of the distribution and incidence of disease. The effects of malaria, carried by the *Anopheles* mosquito, and of trypanosomiasis or sleeping sickness, which is spread by the tsetse fly (*Glossina*), are seen in the health of humans and of animals and in the nature of the farming systems practised (see *Natural Resources: Land Use,* below). Climate has also been a leading factor in determining those areas in tropical Africa that are suitable for permanent European settlement. Thus the hot, humid and relatively unhealthful conditions of the coastlands of the Gulf of Guinea for long gave West Africa its not wholly deserved reputation as "the white man's grave." In contrast Europeans were attracted to the healthful inland areas of East Africa, especially above 5,000 ft., and to the high veld areas of the Zambezi basin at a rather lower altitude. In subtropical Africa (*e.g.,* Algeria and South Africa) there are continuous areas of European settlement; but within the tropics the European-settled areas generally form relatively small islands in the midst of predominantly African areas. The extent and nature of white settlement have an obvious relevance to the problems of inter-racial co-operation and political progress.

Rainfall Probability Forecasting.—Since World War II the shortcomings of mean annual rainfall figures have been recognized by economists as well as by agriculturalists and climatologists, partly as a result of costly failures in agricultural planning, such as the East African Groundnut Scheme of 1946–51 for the raising of groundnuts (peanuts) in Tanganyika. What matters from an agricultural point of view is not average conditions but actual totals of rainfall during a particular year or growing season. In general, variability from year to year appears to be greatest in those districts where total rainfall is generally low, as for example in arid and semiarid areas. Under less dry conditions, the variations may be smaller, but they can still have vital consequences, especially in areas of intermediate average rainfall (20–40 in. per year).

Investigations carried out in East Africa showed that there was a very close relationship between rainfall reliability and the various ecological zones. Less than a quarter of the total area of East Africa was found to have reasonable prospects of receiving 30 in. of rainfall in a year (and much of this was already rather more densely peopled than most other areas). Although similar studies have not been available for most parts of the continent, it is widely accepted that accurate measurement of rainfall probability information is essential for sound and realistic planning of agricultural development.   (R. W. Sl.)

D. Vegetation

The greater part of Africa is covered by desert and by grasslands with or without trees; dense forest and thickets cover less than a tenth of the continent. The extratropical regions of North and South Africa both have a Mediterranean type of vegetation, but they are very different from each other floristically. The intertropical regions have belts of vegetation ranging from desert to luxuriant lowland rain forest, while the high mountains have their own special varied and exceptionally interesting vegetation. (*See* fig. 5.)

African vegetation is constantly being modified or destroyed

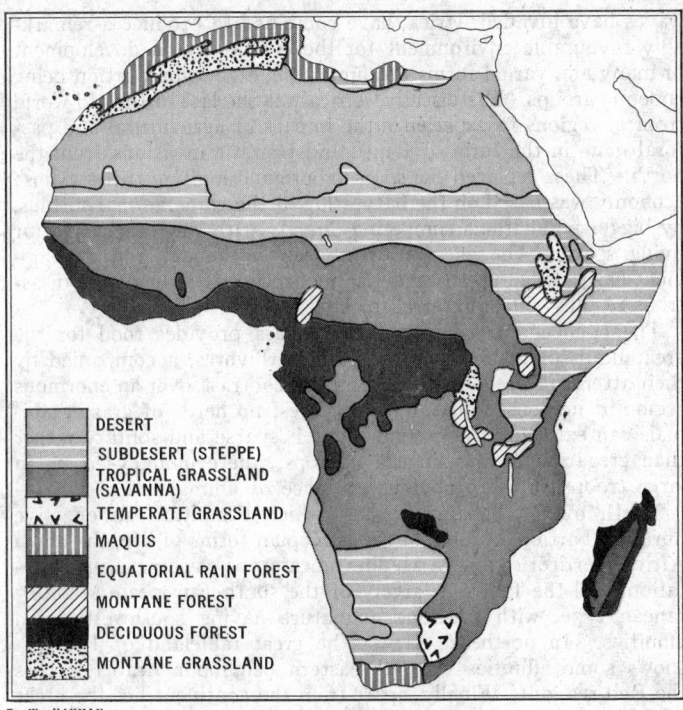

DESERT
SUBDESERT (STEPPE)
TROPICAL GRASSLAND (SAVANNA)
TEMPERATE GRASSLAND
MAQUIS
EQUATORIAL RAIN FOREST
MONTANE FOREST
DECIDUOUS FOREST
MONTANE GRASSLAND

R. W. HAYMAN

FIG. 5.—VEGETATION ZONES OF AFRICA

by man, his animals and the fires he starts. The most striking change is when humid forest is degraded to savanna, but a more widespread, though less dramatic, change has also occurred in the broad-leaved woodlands. In these a shrubby understory has been replaced by tall grass and the trees have become more widely spaced.

Many changes have undoubtedly taken place within living memory but certain features are probably the result of more ancient changes. In particular, the alternating humid and arid phases of the Quaternary seem to be responsible for the disjointed distribution of many genera and species. Fires have been prevalent in most areas at least since the last humid phase of the Quaternary, so that the climax vegetation may never have had a chance to become continuously established.

North African vegetation contains a considerable proportion of European genera and species, besides certain native species in and south of the Atlas mountains. Forests of cork oak and of Atlas cedar occur in Morocco, Algeria and Tunisia. Mediterranean maquis, composed of evergreen shrubs with hard leathery leaves, occurs in these countries and also in Libya. High plateau steppe is extensive in the Atlas mountains and subdesert steppe is found in the western desert. The Egyptian farmlands depend entirely on the Nile waters, while the rest of this country is arid desert. Plants of European affinity are found in scanty fragments of vegetation in the Saharan mountains and in oases with their characteristic date palms. The southern edge of the Sahara is wholly tropical in its flora.

Cape maquis occupies a narrow strip in the extreme south. The flora of the Cape is extraordinarily rich and resembles certain features of the Australian flora, the peculiar families Proteaceae and Restionaceae and certain groups of Leguminosae being common to the two areas but rare in other parts of the world. Many of the maquis shrubs contain oil or resin and have a brown or grayish appearance, such as many species of heather and composite plants. The few trees, such as the cypress pine (*Callitris juniperoides*) and the silver tree (*Leucadendron argenteum*), are thought to be remnants of more extensive forests. There are many beautiful herbs such as ground orchids, oxalis and members of the geranium and lily families.

Behind the maquis lies the vast Karroo, a subdesert plateau that extends to the northwest and merges with the coastal desert of South West Africa and Angola. The Karroo vegetation is extremely well adapted to the arid climate and is very rich in species.

Among the commonest shrubs and shrublets are *Pentzia, Chrysocoma* and *Euryops* and, on saline soils, *Salsola* and *Atriplex*. North of the Orange river the commonest shrub is *Rhigozum trichotomum*. In certain areas low succulent plants are abundant, especially the genus *Mesembryanthemum* and its segregates, which sometimes have strange leaves which can easily be mistaken for stones. Heathlike shrublets and taller succulents such as aloes and euphorbias also occur. Acacias and evergreen sumacs are often abundant along watercourses; trees also occur on mountain slopes.

On its eastern side the Karroo type of vegetation has invaded degraded areas of temperate and subtropical grassland. The latter, known as high veld, occupies vast areas above about 3,500 ft. (1,000 m.); *Themeda triandra* is a widespread and abundant grass there, as on certain tropical mountains.

Evergreen forest in Cape Province is confined to small areas of which the Knysna forest is the largest. Although growing in a temperate or subtropical climate, these forests have close floristic affinities with the montane evergreen forests of the intertropical regions. Trees include the conifers *Podocarpus* and *Widdringtonia* as well as wild olives (*Olea*) and stinkwood (*Ocotea*).

The eastern coast of South Africa is much wetter than the western, and the plains are occupied by savanna and patches of forest, both of distinctly tropical aspects. The savanna, composed of tall rank grasses, nutritious for game only in their early stages, is called "sour veld" in contrast with the "sweet veld" of higher altitudes, where the grass remains nutritious even when dry.

Mangroves grow in brackish swamps by river estuaries. Those of eastern Africa have a strong Asiatic affinity and are found in small patches from the Red sea to south of Durban. On the west coast they are found from the Senegal river to the Longa river in Angola; the dominants are three species of red mangrove which also occur on the Atlantic shores of America.

The coastal areas of West Africa are more or less humid from the Senegal to the Congo rivers; the coastal areas of Angola and South West Africa are, however, extremely dry. The position is reversed on the east coast where there is a relatively humid strip all the way from South Africa to the equator, but farther north in the Horn of Africa the coastal area, as well as the interior, is very dry.

The equatorial forests of the Congo basin do not extend east of the great lakes, except for outliers such as the Kakamega forest in Kenya. A broad tract of dry country separates these forests from the moister coastal areas. The latter have patches of dense forest rather different in floristic composition from that of the main equatorial block which extends as far west as western Nigeria. A relatively dry area of savanna vegetation in Dahomey and Togo separates the main forest block from the western block which extends from Ghana to Guinea.

The largest trees in the lowland rain forest are about 200 ft. high; many of them have buttresses and some yield valuable timber, such as African mahogany (*Khaya*), iroko or mvule (*Chlorophora*) and obeche (*Triplochiton*). In the moister areas the Leguminosae (*e.g., Brachystegia, Cynometra* and *Gilbertiodendron*) are the most important family of large trees. The Sterculiaceae, Ulmaceae, Moraceae and Meliaceae are more important in the peripheral areas.

Understory trees and shrubs include many Rubiaceae, Euphorbiaceae, and species of wild kola nut and ebony. Lianas and epiphytes, including many ferns, orchids and begonias, abound.

Farmed areas have many oil palms, kapok or silk-cotton trees and secondary growth trees, such as the umbrella tree (*Musanga*). Plantations of rubber, cocoa, kola and robusta coffee are found in the forest regions.

Although the belts of vegetation surrounding the humid forest are not arranged symmetrically, there is a fairly uniform sequence of types as one moves toward the desert. Immediately surrounding the forest regions are belts of tall grass savanna with relic patches of forest. This savanna has been formed by the destruction of forest for cultivation and the consequent incidence of fire. Elephant grass (*Pennisetum purpureum*) is characteristic of this type. In places where there is some protection from fire it is possible to observe the recolonization of the savanna by forest species.

In somewhat drier regions there is broad-leaved woodland, often known in East Africa as "myombo." The genera *Brachystegia, Isoberlinia, Julbernardia, Monotes, Combretum* and *Terminalia* have numerous tree species typical of this woodland. Much of it has been modified by fires to a savanna type with a continuous layer of tussocky grass 3–7 ft. high (especially *Andropogon* and *Hyparrhenia*), with rather widely spaced and often gnarled trees 20–60 ft. high. Farmed areas usually have native fruit trees, such as baobab, shea nut, locust bean and tamarind. The streams are fringed by evergreen forest in these moister savanna regions.

In the more arid regions there is an increasingly large proportion of fine-leaved and thorny trees, and the grass is shorter. A dry type of deciduous forest dominated by Rhodesian teak (*Baikiaea plurijuga*) is found in Barotseland (in Zambia) and neighbouring districts. The forest has a dense deciduous understory which is readily burned, and with increasing human activity big areas are being degraded by fire to an open savanna type. Woodland of mopane (*Colophospermum*) is extensive in the hot dry valleys of the Zambezi and Limpopo. Dense thickets are found in central Tanganyika and in Ethiopia; in the latter area, as in parts of western Uganda, candelabralike euphorbias are conspicuous. Vast tracts, including the Kalahari and a long belt extending from Senegal into most of East Africa, are covered with thorn woodland. The acacias, including gum arabic (*A. senegal*), and myrrh (*Commiphora*) are by far the commonest trees. The grass is short and feathery and is often regarded as steppe rather than savanna. This type gradually merges into subdesert steppe, which has widely spaced low perennial plants, as well as annual herbs which flourish for only a few weeks after rain. The extraordinary *Welwitschia*, unique in the plant kingdom, occurs in this type from Walvis Bay to Moçâmedes.

Mountain vegetation includes evergreen forest, woodland, grassland and bamboo (*Arundinaria alpina*) brakes. The forest at lower elevations is usually richly draped with mosses, ferns and other epiphytes (*e.g., Begonia, Impatiens, Peperomia*); tree ferns (especially *Cyathia*) are also characteristic. The trees in this type of forest include conifers such as junipers and podocarps, and dicotyledons such as *Olea, Ocotea, Schefflera* and *Pittosporum*. At higher altitudes the woodland of such trees as *Hagenia, Gnidia, Erica, Phillipia* and *Hypericum,* is festooned with lichens and is rather easily destroyed by fire. Grassland of species such as *Themeda triandra, Andropogon distachyus* and *Loudetia simplex* covers considerable areas at altitudes between about 5,000 and 7,000 ft. (1,500–2,100 m.). Higher up the grassland is often quite short and is composed of genera such as *Festuca, Agrostis* and *Pentaschistis*.

A characteristic and highly interesting feature of the mountain flora is the presence of numerous European genera and some species, which are absent from vast areas of intervening hot lowlands. Good examples of this flora are violet, dock, cranesbill, wood sanicle, buttercup and scabious. Above about 10,000 ft. (3,000 m.) on the mountains of East Africa are remarkable communities of tree lobelias and tree senecios, as well as shrubby *Alchemilla* and everlasting flowers (*Helichrysum*).

There is a strip of rain forest on the eastern side of the Malagasy Republic (Madagascar) and a strip of dry deciduous forest on the west. Forest has, however, been destroyed by fire in the centre of the island, and there is now a wide expanse of almost treeless grassland. There are extensive thickets containing many succulents in the southwest. The flora of Madagascar is very rich and is strikingly different from that of the mainland. (R. W. J. K.)

E. Animal Life

Several factors, geographical, climatological, evolutionary and historical, have contributed to the extraordinary richness of animal life on the African continent (including the island of Madagascar). The enormous area of the land mass, the fact that the greater part lies within the tropics and has benefited by a stable equatorial climate since the earliest times, and its long connections with the Eurasian land masses, from which successive faunal waves have invaded Africa, have combined to produce a remarkably favourable environment for the evolution and development of many and varied forms of animal life, a good proportion being endemic groups. Historically, Africa was the last of the old world tropical regions to experience the impact of agricultural and pastoral man, in the form of Bantu and Hamitic invasions from the north. These replaced the sparse aboriginal hunting tribes, whose economy was based on the harvesting of the game animal surplus, by bigger populations competing directly with the animal life for living space. The effect of European settlement and development has speeded up enormously the process of change: the disastrous results will be referred to later.

The open country south of the Sahara provides food for the great herds of grazing and browsing herbivores, accompanied by their attendant predators. In complete contrast, over an enormous region of immense equatorial rain forest no herds of grazing animals can exist and the ground fauna is sparse and solitary rather than gregarious. Only in the treetops, where monkeys roam in large troops, is there obvious evidence of animal life.

North of the Saharan wastes, which constitute an effective northern barrier for most of the Ethiopian forms of life, the north African territories have a Mediterranean type of climate and vegetation, and the fauna is largely of the south European–Mediterranean type, with a strong admixture having southwest Asian affinities. In northeast Africa, the great tableland of Ethiopia shows some affinities with its eastern neighbour Arabia, across the Red sea gulf. Finally, apart from the continent lies the great island of Madagascar, where a very high proportion of endemic groups and a lack of many of the continental types give evidence of a remote separation and subsequent isolation.

The once teeming African animal life has been disastrously affected by rapid economic and political changes so that possibly only precarious relics of its former glory may survive. (*See also* Wildlife Conservation: *International Co-operation.*)

Among the mammals, no fewer than 13 orders out of the 17 Recent orders listed for the whole world (excluding the purely marine Cetacea) are represented. Of the Insectivora, four of the six families are endemic: the tenrecs (Tenrecidae) of Madagascar, the golden moles (Chrysochloridae) of South Africa, the elephant shrews (Macroscelididae) from North Africa to the Cape, and the primitive otter shrews (Potamogalidae) of the equatorial forest streams. Many shrews and hedgehogs are also found.

Bats are richly represented, but not one of the ten families is peculiar to Africa, all having Asiatic affinities, although many of the genera are endemic. Among the abundant fruit bats is the largest in Africa, the grotesque hammerhead (*Hypsignathus*) of West Africa; it is noteworthy that the most important and wideranging genus in the Indo-Malayan region (*Pteropus*) has never reached the African continent although it has colonized Madagascar and the East African coastal islands. There are no vampire bats in Africa.

The order Primates is abundantly represented. In Madagascar alone all the Primates are lemurs in great variety. None of the continental groups is found on the island, but in Africa the pottos of the forests and the bush babies of the savannas are widespread, forming part of the oriental family Lorisidae. The true monkeys of the old world are represented by many species of guenons, mangabeys, baboons, colobi and, in northwest Africa only, one species of macaque, the Barbary ape. It is particularly in the forest regions that the monkeys have reached their peak in variety and numbers. Finally, Africa is noted for the two great anthropoid apes, the chimpanzee and gorilla. Both are confined to the forest regions. A very primitive order, Pholidota, contains only the toothless scaly anteaters or pangolins, an oriental group; and another small and primitive order, Sirenia, contains only the manatee and dugong of coastal waters and estuaries.

The Lagomorpha, containing rabbits and hares, has many representatives, but it is in the order Rodentia that Africa is particularly rich. The most notable of the native rodents are the scaly-tailed flying squirrels and the Cape jumping hares. Tree and ground squirrels, tree rats, grass rats, banana mice, mole rats, porcupines and scores of others make up a great variety in many different habitats. Jerboas, an Asiatic group, are found only in North Africa.

The predators and scavengers forming the order Carnivora are numerous. On the plains, lions and cheetahs, hyenas, jackals and hunting dogs follow the game herds, while in forest and bush, leopards, genets, civets, mongooses and others pursue the smaller prey animals. No wolves or bears are found in Africa. Madagascar has only one family of carnivores, the Viverridae.

A peculiar Ethiopian order, the Tubulidentata, contains a single genus and species, the termite-eating aardvark, a primitive type known also as a fossil from southeast Europe.

It is among the hoofed animals, now divided into Proboscidea (elephants), Hyracoidea (hyraxes), Perissodactyla (zebras, asses, rhinoceroses) and Artiodactyla (antelopes, pigs, hippopotamuses and giraffes), that Africa's greatest glory lies. More families, genera and species have evolved on the continent than in any other region of the earth. Its big-game fauna has never been excelled in variety and numbers, and includes the elephant of savanna and forest, the rock or tree hyraxes, the zebras, the fantastic variety of the antelopes, the unique giraffe and okapi of the thornbush plains and the equatorial forest respectively, wild pigs, the hippopotamus of the rivers and great lakes, and the black Cape buffalo. Formerly, immense numbers of antelopes such as wildbeest (gnu), hartebeest, waterbuck, gemsbok, gazelle and many others astonished the early travelers on the plains of South and East Africa. The inevitable encroachment of man has decimated these wild herds in most areas, so that it is only in the national parks and reserves that the visitor today can glimpse something of the real Africa of former days. Even in these reserves the need for constant struggle by the authorities against native poaching, competing cattle, threats of economic development and the general pressure of the rapidly increasing human population of the surrounding territories, allied to the political uncertainty for the future maintenance of the reserves, all give grounds for deep misgivings as to the eventual fate of the finest forms of animal life on the African continent.

Two further groups of hoofed animals, widespread elsewhere in the northern hemisphere, the deer and the wild sheep and goats, are barely represented in Africa, with one small population of north African red deer in Tunisia, one species of wild sheep and two forms of ibex also in North Africa. (For livestock see *Land Use: Agriculture—Tropical,* below.)

The bird life is no less rich and varied, in its way, for in addition to the great variety of groups native to the continent, a large part of the migrant species from the northern hemisphere spend half their lives in East or South Africa, traveling by several routes of which the Nile valley is one of the most important. Of the approximately 70 families recorded in the region, only about one-tenth are peculiar to Africa. These include the ostriches, the secretary birds, the whale-headed storks, the touracos or plantain eaters, the mouse birds or colies, the helmet shrikes and the sugar birds, while several subgroups such as guinea fowl, oxpeckers and honey guides are predominantly Ethiopian. An interesting recent discovery in the Congo forests is the African peacock (*Afropavo*), but such traditionally tropical birds as parrots are scarce. The Madagascan avifauna is much more restricted, and has greater affinity with the orient than with Africa, on the whole.

The reptiles and amphibians are largely representative of groups widespread in the old world tropics, with some South American affinities in some groups. Among the snakes, a python is the largest. The large family Colubridae contains a great many types, including the cobras and mambas, and the vipers include the puff adder and horned adder. The primitive Typhlopidae, or blind snakes, are well represented. No poisonous snakes are found in Madagascar. Lizards in many forms, from geckos, skinks, chameleons to the large Nile monitor, abound. Madagascar is particularly rich in chameleons. Frogs and toads swarm wherever there is sufficient moisture; they contribute a major share of the sounds that enliven the African night. Most belong to groups widespread outside Africa, but one of the most remarkable, the clawed frog (*Xenopus*), is confined to South and tropical Africa. Tortoises and turtles exist in suitable habitats. The best known

and most feared of all the reptiles is the Nile crocodile, growing up to 16 ft. long and living in most of the rivers and lakes. Smaller types inhabit the forest regions of West Africa and the Congo basin. (*See* also NATIONAL PARKS AND NATURE RESERVES.)

Fresh-water fishes are numerous. The extraordinary lungfish (*Protopterus*), which burrows into the mud as the pools dry up, to wait for the next rains, has South American affinities. Finally mention must be made of the enormous number of invertebrates including the vast insect life of tropical Africa, which, in the disease-carrying types (mosquitoes, tsetse fly, etc.) has in the past been a considerable drain on the human resource of the continent.

See also the *Physical Geography* sections of the articles on individual countries. (Ro. W. H.)

II. NATURAL RESOURCES

The preceding sections under *Physical Geography* suggest that much of Africa is a difficult and harsh environment for human occupation and development. Some areas have a variety and range of resources, but in only relatively few agricultural commodities and minerals is the continent in an outstandingly strong economic position; cocoa, gold and diamonds are examples of these, but there are also other cases. It is sometimes said, with truth, that Africa needs overseas capital and enterprise much more than overseas capital and enterprise need Africa. In the years between World Wars I and II, it was estimated that Africa's share of the world's trade was 4.5% of total exports and 4.8% of total imports, while in 1935 Africa was thought to be responsible for 2.8% of the world's primary production (rather more, 3.2%, in agricultural commodities but substantially less, only 1.3%, in nonagricultural production). African economic development is still in an early stage, with limits imposed on its future expansion by the type of its natural resources.

A. WATER

Perhaps more than any other single factor, water supply controls the habitability of an area, for plants and animals as well as for human beings. In many of the wetter parts of the African continent, water supply is not a matter of great concern (drainage, on the other hand, may well be). But it clearly is a vital problem in the many extensive arid and semiarid areas. Furthermore, availability of water may present real problems even where average rainfall totals might seem to be adequate for agricultural or pastoral needs; and in the section above on *Climate* reference has been made to the need for forecasting rainfall probability in such areas. Often there is a reasonably close connection between rainfall and availability of water. Areas receiving fair totals of rainfall not confined to one season in the year are generally well supplied with both surface and underground water. Where the rainfall is distinctly seasonal, however, as it frequently is, the availability of water may depend largely upon underlying geology. The nature and type of soil may also be significant: granitic soils, for example, hold water comparatively well and are often capable of supporting a considerable agricultural population.

Prospects for irrigation are fairly limited in Africa, outside the Nile valley in Egypt and some of the oases of North Africa. Egypt presents special conditions that are found nowhere else in Africa: it is the classic example of flood plain and delta irrigation, and the lower Nile valley is thus able to support the highest density of agricultural population in the continent. Of a total cultivable area of 9,000,000 ac., 6,000,000 ac. are in fact cultivated, and entirely dependent upon irrigation. About four-fifths is supplied with water controlled by barrages and the remainder depends upon the traditional basin system.

The French encouraged irrigation schemes in Algeria, Morocco and Tunisia, in the Saharan oases, and in the Niger project in Mali. In Sudan the Gezira scheme was successfully carried through as an enterprise of the state in partnership with private capital. Elsewhere irrigation possibilities are very limited, even in such countries as South Africa where capital for developing large schemes (such as the Vaal-Hartz undertaking) is available. Attention, therefore, is being increasingly directed to the small-

ELLIOTT ERWITT—MAGNUM

WORKER IN THE NILE VALLEY, EGYPT, USING AN ANCIENT IRRIGATION DEVICE, THE SHADOOF, CONSISTING OF A LEVER WITH A BUCKET AT ONE END COUNTERBALANCED BY A WEIGHT AT THE OTHER

scale water-storage project, created by digging wells rather than by building dams, to provide domestic supplies or to water stock. More care is also being taken to conserve water supplies and to prevent the excessive use of particular water points, especially in stock country during the dry season. This is singularly difficult in communities where overstocking is common and where congestion at a few points at certain times of the year may be very great.

The hydroelectric potential of Africa exceeds that of any other continent, even if estimates of future developments are accepted with considerable reserve. One such estimate puts the potential water power at 190,000,000 h.p.; *i.e.*, three times the estimated potential of Europe. Another estimate credits Africa with two-fifths of the world's potential, or four times that of North America; one-quarter of this is stated to be in the Congo basin alone. As yet, however, only 0.1% of the estimated potential is used. Major power schemes in operation include various installations in Katanga (Democratic Republic of the Congo), the Owen Falls dam at Jinja (in Uganda) where the Nile leaves Lake Victoria, and the Kariba dam on the Zambezi which supplies both the Copperbelt of Zambia and the rapidly growing manufacturing industries of Southern Rhodesia. The Volta dam project is basic to Ghana's seven-year development plan.

B. SOILS

In tropical Africa the exuberance of the natural vegetation has sometimes been taken as an indication that the soils are rich; in fact they are usually rapidly exhausted under cultivation, and latterly there has been a tendency to emphasize the poverty of African soils, especially those within the tropics. Reference is made, for example, to the leaching that takes place under heavy rainfall conditions, and to the absence of elements essential for plant growth, such as calcium and phosphorus. In arid and semiarid regions there is usually a shortage of humus and sometimes a tendency for sodium salts to form layers that are harmful to plant life. As the scientific knowledge of African soils increases, however, their potentialities as well as their shortcomings may be recognized. Some workers stress that many soils appear to be of at least average fertility, a fortunate state of affairs since they rarely receive additional fertilizers of any kind. They suggest that the abundance of energy from the sun, together with the range of root systems and water storage, permits plant growth of greater rapidity and bulk than in temperate areas.

Soil Groups.—Maps of the major soil groups of Africa closely resemble the main climatic belts. In a continent with the climate and geological history of Africa, soils are generally more closely related to the climates in which they have evolved than to the rocks from which they are derived because weathering is able to continue throughout the year, unchecked by frozen ground, and because so much of the surface has remained undisturbed for long geological periods. The wetter areas are characterized by red and red-brown tropical soils (the soil is leached of its plant food and underlain by a lateritic hardpan of fine particles). The desert soils of the arid and semiarid areas are brown, coarse and undifferentiated, with a variety of minerals including the salts needed for plant food. In the intermediate areas between the generally wet and the always dry regions there are intermediate types of soil,

including chestnut soils, chernozems and black soils.

Two exceptions to the general poverty of African soils should be noted, though they are limited in area. They are (1) those formed from recent alluviums (so that they are neither leached nor oxidized), as in the lower Nile valley and in the frequently flooded middle reaches of the Niger, Congo and Zambezi; and (2) the young soils derived from volcanic rocks, as on the slopes of the peaks of East Africa or of Mt. Cameroon. In both cases they are highly valued by farmers, as for example for cotton cultivation, with the aid of irrigation, in Egypt and for coffee growing by the Chaga (Chagga) people on the fertile, well-watered lower slopes of Mt. Kilimanjaro.

Soil Erosion.—The downward washing of soil is a normal geomorphological process in most parts of the world, but it can be greatly accelerated by the activities of man. Thus the excessive clearance of natural vegetation from the surface, the cultivation of very steep slopes or the overstocking of a grassland area can result in the complete removal of the soil cover over wide areas. The liability to erosion is especially great where torrential rains mark the beginning of the wet season following a period of drought lasting several months.

Three main types of erosion are commonly recognized: (1) sheet erosion, which causes the removal of a film of soil from the surface over a wide area especially during heavy rainfall; (2) gully erosion, where this destructive work is concentrated along stream beds, footpaths or shallow depressions in the surface to such an extent that the lines become deep, gorgelike gullies, making communications across the area difficult and plowing impossible; and (3) wind erosion, characteristic of most arid landscapes where exposed areas may be swept bare to bedrock as the finer particles are blown away.

During the 20th century, and particularly since the 1930s, soil erosion has been recognized as a major problem of several African territories, and remedial action has been taken wherever possible. The problem is especially serious in a continent where the areas of good soil are so restricted and where farming remains the chief occupation. It is particularly unfortunate where soil loss affects countries with rapidly increasing populations that are attempting to improve their standards of living.

Apart from desert areas, South Africa is as much affected by soil erosion as any part of the continent. It is estimated that 200,000,000 tons of soil are removed from the surface every year and deposited in the Indian ocean. Though European farmers

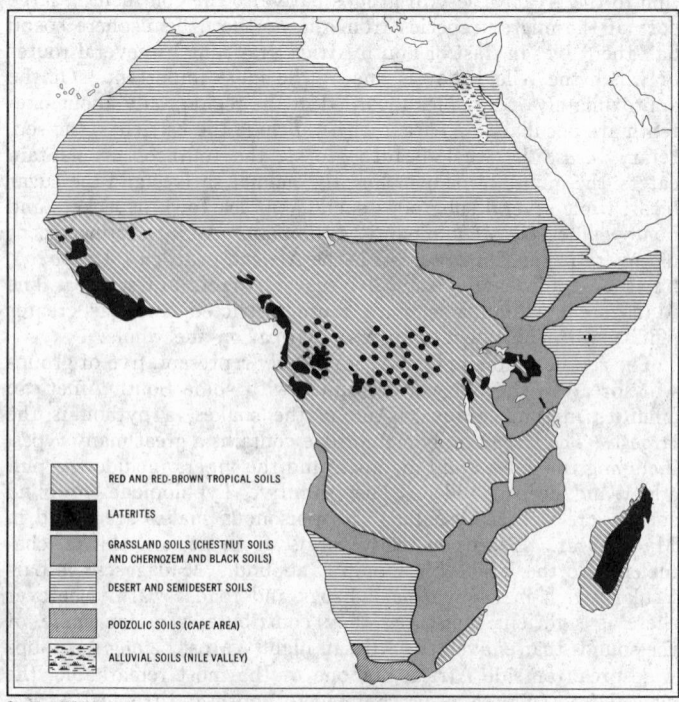

R. W. STEEL

FIG. 6.—SOILS OF AFRICA

RED AND RED-BROWN TROPICAL SOILS

LATERITES

GRASSLAND SOILS (CHESTNUT SOILS AND CHERNOZEM AND BLACK SOILS)

DESERT AND SEMIDESERT SOILS

PODZOLIC SOILS (CAPE AREA)

ALLUVIAL SOILS (NILE VALLEY)

Wind-blown dunes on the Sarir as Sab'ah, a part of the Sahara desert in the Fezzan, southwestern province of Libya. The largest desert in the world, the Sahara covers an area of about 3,500,000 sq.mi.

Arab woman selling bread at Tetuán, Morocco. Many people of the Mediterranean coast are of mixed Arab and Berber ancestry

Rugged peaks of the Ahaggar mountains in the central Sahara, southern Algeria

Berbers of Mauritania. Man at right, a marabout or a holy man, is holding a Koranic tablet

Oasis with some arable land near Djerba on the Mediterranean coast of Tunisia

Hamitic girl from the Hun oasis, Libya

THE LAND AND THE PEOPLE: NORTH AFRICA

PHOTOGRAPHS, (TOP LEFT, BOTTOM RIGHT) EMIL SCHULTHESS FROM BLACK STAR, (TOP RIGHT, CENTRE RIGHT) MARC AND EVELYNE BERNHEIM—RAPHO GUILLUMETTE, (CENTRE LEFT) CAMERA PRESS —PIX FROM PUBLIX, (BOTTOM LEFT) INGE MORATH—MAGNUM

PLATE II   AFRICA

Woman of the Goram tribe, Lake Chad area

Palm trees on the beach of the coastal plain near Lomé, Togo

Cliffs of the Bandiagara escarpment, a sandstone plateau near the valley of the Niger river, southern Mali republic

A chief of Nsukka, eastern Nigeria

Surfboats on the coast of Liberia

Fulani girls. Originally a non-Negroid race, the Fulani intermarried with the Negro Hausa of Nigeria

THE LAND AND THE PEOPLE: WEST AFRICA

PHOTOGRAPHS, (TOP LEFT) PAUL ALMASY, (TOP RIGHT) KAY LAWSON—RAPHO GUILLUMETTE, (CENTRE LEFT) AUTHENTICATED NEWS, (CENTRE RIGHT, BOTTOM RIGHT) ANTHONY HOWARTH—CAMERA PRESS, (BOTTOM LEFT) THECLA

Native dhow on the Blue Nile (Bahr el Azraq) which rises in northwestern Ethiopia

Woman of the southern Sudan region grinding cassava flour

Ethiopian man of the Amhara group, a Semitic-speaking people, who are mostly Christians

View of the White Nile (Bahr el Jebel) near Juba, Sudan. From Lake Albert, Uganda, the river flows across southern Sudan for more than 1,000 mi. before joining the Blue Nile at Khartoum

Rolling forested upland in the Shoa province, central Ethiopia

Hadendoa men, pastoral nomads of the Red sea coast of Ethiopia

THE LAND AND THE PEOPLE: SUDAN AND THE HORN

BY COURTESY OF (CENTRE RIGHT) SHELL PHOTOGRAPHIC UNIT, (BOTTOM LEFT) UNITED NATIONS; PHOTOGRAPHS, (TOP LEFT) C. TRIESCHMANN FROM BLACK STAR, (TOP CENTRE) "THE TIMES," LONDON FROM PICTORIAL PARADE, (TOP RIGHT) PAUL ALMASY, (BOTTOM RIGHT) CAMERA PRESS—PIX FROM PUBLIX

PLATE IV   AFRICA

Giraffes on the Amboseli plain, Kenya. In the background is Mt. Kilimanjaro, the highest peak in Africa

A Masai youth. Once famous warriors, the Masai, a Nilotic people of Kenya and Tanganyika, are now nomadic cattle herders

Kuja river, western Kenya, near the shore of Lake Victoria. The meandering watercourse is typical of many of the rivers of the African plateaus

Bantu tribesman of Kenya. The Bantu peoples are one of the largest native groups in East Africa

A view of Lake Victoria, largest lake in Africa, and the third largest in the world. It lies between Kenya, Uganda and Tanganyika

Elgeyo (Keyu) tribesmen of Kenya, dressed in traditional warrior costumes, standing at the edge of an escarpment on the western side of the Rift valley 700 ft. below

THE LAND AND THE PEOPLE: EAST AFRICA

PHOTOGRAPHS, (TOP LEFT) YLLA—RAPHO GUILLUMETTE, (TOP RIGHT) EMIL SCHULTHESS FROM BLACK STAR, (CENTRE LEFT) J. BRODIE—CAMERA PRESS, (CENTRE RIGHT, BOTTOM RIGHT) CAMERA PRESS—PIX FROM PUBLIX, (BOTTOM LEFT) HANS LEUENBERGER FROM BLACK STAR

Falls of the Kalule River, a tributary of the Lualaba or Upper Congo. Near Jadotville, Democratic Republic of the Congo

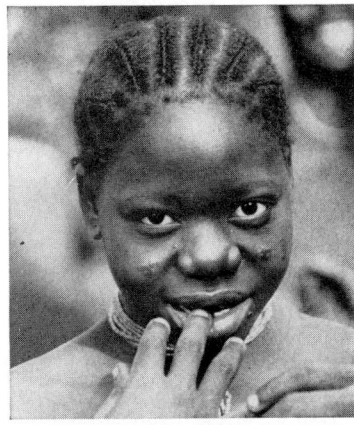

Girl of the western equatorial region, probably a Baya, one of the eastern Nigritic peoples

A woman of the Bushman group which were once widely distributed in southern Africa, but are now confined to small areas

Tutsi, or Watusi, of Burundi. Well known for their height—men often 7 ft. tall—the Tutsi are a Nilotic people

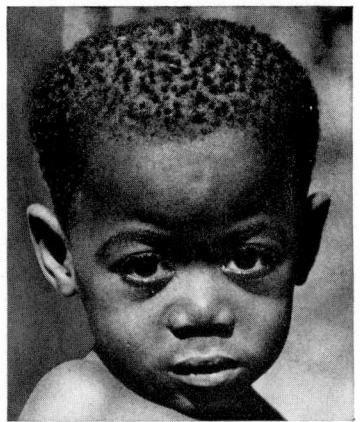

Pygmy child of the rain forests of the eastern Congo region. Adults rarely exceed a height of 5 ft.

Mangbetu woman of the Congo. A central Sudanic people, the Mangbetu often live in economic association with pygmies

One of a chain of volcanoes lying in Rwanda and Burundi, a former trust territory on the east shores of Lakes Kivu and Tanganyika between Uganda and Tanzania

THE LAND AND THE PEOPLE: EQUATORIAL AFRICA AND THE CONGO

BY COURTESY OF (TOP RIGHT) NORTHERN RHODESIA INFORMATION DEPARTMENT, (BOTTOM LEFT) BELGIAN GOVERNMENT INFORMATION CENTER; PHOTOGRAPHS, (TOP LEFT) ACTUALIT—PIX FROM PUBLIX, (TOP CENTRE, CENTRE RIGHT) ANTHONY HOWARTH—CAMERA PRESS, (CENTRE) AUTHENTICATED NEWS, (BOTTOM RIGHT) A. VAN SPRANG FROM BLACK STAR

PLATE VI AFRICA

Xhosa women dancing as they return to village from the fields. The Xhosa are one of several tribes living in the Transkeian Territories, eastern South Africa

Angling on the Vaal river near Vereeniging in the Transvaal. The Vaal and the Orange are the two principal rivers of South Africa, with a combined length of about 1,300 mi.

Warrior of Swaziland. The Swazi are a Bantu people, most of whom intermarried with the indigenous Bushmen during the period of Bantu expansion in the south

Table mountain, rising sharply to a height of more than 3,500 ft. behind the suburbs of Cape Town, South Africa

A Zulu chief of Natal, South Africa. Zulus, a Bantu people, represent an amalgamation of many original tribes in Natal

THE LAND AND THE PEOPLE: SOUTHERN AFRICA

BY COURTESY OF (CENTRE RIGHT) SATOUR; PHOTOGRAPHS, (TOP, CENTRE LEFT, BOTTOM RIGHT) AUTHENTICATED NEWS, (BOTTOM LEFT) CAMERA PRESS—PIX FROM PUBLIX

are by no means blameless, Africans by their careless agricultural methods and their tendency to overstock their farms are chiefly responsible for soil erosion, partly because they are rarely allowed sufficient land to support themselves by cultivation and stock raising. The contrast between well-tended European pastures and farms and overgrazed, exhausted and eroded African areas is often very striking in South Africa and in the highlands of Kenya and adjacent African areas of the Nairobi district. Other areas that are relatively overpopulated and where soil erosion can be seen include parts of Rwanda, Burundi, Uganda, southern Malawi and eastern Nigeria.

Remedies adopted, often with considerable success, include the reservation of forests to prevent further clearance by cultivation and the destruction of deep-rooted trees that help to bind the soil together; the training of farmers to cultivate along the contour rather than downslope; and the planting of trees, grasses and other crops on steep bare slopes to check further erosion. The whole appearance of the Kigezi district of southwestern Uganda has been altered by the measures introduced by the government to check soil erosion, to encourage contour farming, to consolidate scattered farm holdings and to resettle people on the land. Kigezi is now able to support a density of population that is, by common African standards, surprisingly high, and the exodus of its inhabitants to find work elsewhere in Uganda has been reduced.

C. Minerals

Precious metals gave rise to the first Arab contacts with Africa. The Portuguese were mining gold in Ghana before the end of the 15th century and numerous expeditions were sent to the kingdom of Monomotapa (q.v.) as a result of accounts of the gold available at Sofala. Mineral discoveries in the southern parts of the continent have transformed the modern economic and social history of Africa by bringing in both capital and European settlers. Exports of minerals play a very important part in Africa's external trade and dominate the economy of certain countries such as Zambia. Minerals have also been the reason for much of the initial railway construction in countries like Ghana, Nigeria, Zambia and Southern Rhodesia.

One-twentieth of the annual value of the world's mineral products comes from Africa. All but a very small proportion is exported, since minerals can generally bear the fairly high cost of transport to a consuming centre. The production of heavier minerals is only slight—coal, less than 2% of the world's tonnage; petroleum, by the mid-1960s, under 1%; salt 1.5%; bauxite 1.5%; and iron ore 2%. In contrast, Africa leads easily in the production of certain precious and rare minerals. About 98% of the world's diamonds come from various African territories, especially the Democratic Republic of the Congo (85% are used in industry and only 15% as gem stones). The Congo also had the world's first important uranium mine and was the only source of radium for several years.

More than half the world's gold comes from Africa, a high proportion still from South Africa. Africa produces substantial supplies of those minerals that are used to strengthen steel, including cobalt (70% of the world output, chiefly from the Katanga region of the Democratic Republic of the Congo, and from Zambia), chrome ore (40%, South Africa, Southern Rhodesia), manganese (30%, Ghana, Congo) and vanadium (20%, South West Africa, Zambia). Three nonferrous minerals are important —platinum (24%, South Africa), copper (about 24%, Zambia, Katanga) and tin (15%, Nigeria). One-fifth of the world's asbestos comes from South Africa, Southern Rhodesia and Swaziland, and more than one-third of the phosphate rock from Morocco, Algeria and Tunisia.

Important oil and gas strikes were made in the Sahara after World War II, and pipelines to the Mediterranean were constructed. Several new mines were developed elsewhere on the continent, some in old established mining districts and others in new areas to which railways were built. These include the Orange Free State gold fields in South Africa, the Kilembe copper deposits in Uganda (refined at Jinja, by the Owen Falls dam), the Mpanda lead mine in Tanzania and the Bomi Hills iron field in

Liberia. Bauxite production in Ghana was stimulated by the Volta project.

Mining creates many social and political problems, such as the migration of labour, detribalization, housing and food supply difficulties, and the question of whether labour should be encouraged

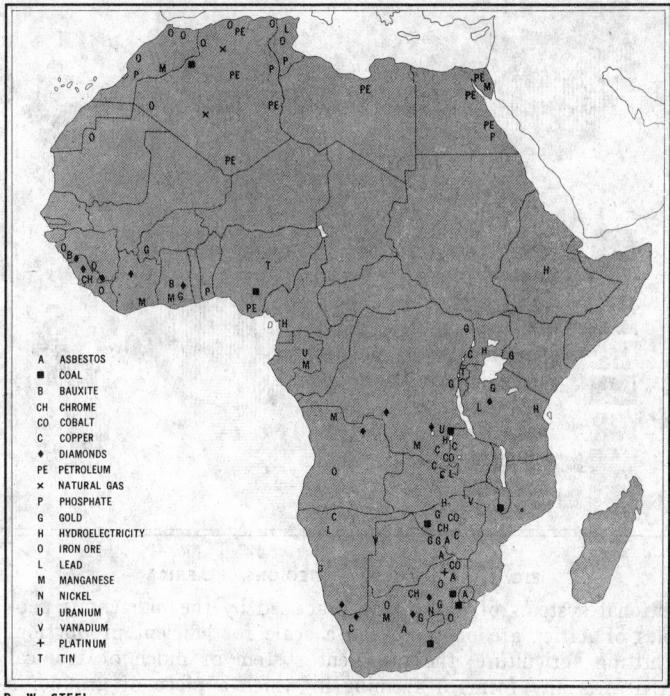

ASBESTOS
A ASBESTOS
■ COAL
B BAUXITE
CH CHROME
CO COBALT
C COPPER
♦ DIAMONDS
PE PETROLEUM
× NATURAL GAS
P PHOSPHATE
G GOLD
H HYDROELECTRICITY
O IRON ORE
L LEAD
M MANGANESE
N NICKEL
U URANIUM
V VANADIUM
+ PLATINUM
T TIN

R. W. STEEL

FIG. 7.—MINING AND HYDROELECTRIC SITES IN AFRICA

to settle permanently. Difficult though these problems are, the countries concerned value the revenue and the prosperity that comes from mining, and the contrast between mineralized and other territories in material terms is often very striking.

D. Land Use

A summary account of the agricultural activities of a vast continent can do little more than note certain major features. It is impossible to present the main facts about agriculture in Africa in a comprehensive statistical form because of the extreme paucity or inaccuracy of the figures available, especially for certain regions where nothing like an agricultural census has been taken and where often no real records are available even for individual farms or districts.

Agriculture: Tropical.—Large areas within the tropics are used for shifting agriculture, for subsistence cultivation and livestock, and for semidesert grazing and nomadic herding. By comparison the areas that are irrigated or farmed intensively or commercially are only small, and these are characteristic of European rather than African farming. Even though it is not easy to draw a clear line of distinction between crops grown by Europeans and those grown by Africans, since some are produced by both, there is nevertheless a great difference between the two types of farming. The African is nearly always a peasant cultivator, still interested mainly in subsistence cropping; even if he has extended his activities to produce certain cash crops, his methods are still largely determined by the needs of subsistence cultivation. The European, by contrast, is usually a farmer employing paid labour or the manager of a company with adequate capital both for cultivation and for marketing and processing the commodities grown: he must, therefore, depend greatly upon the availability of relatively cheap African labour or upon mechanization to replace such labour. Unfortunately, with the independence of many colonial units after 1960, there followed a considerable exodus of European farmers and settlers because of political uncertainty.

Shifting Agriculture and Bush Fallowing.—Nearly all the tra-

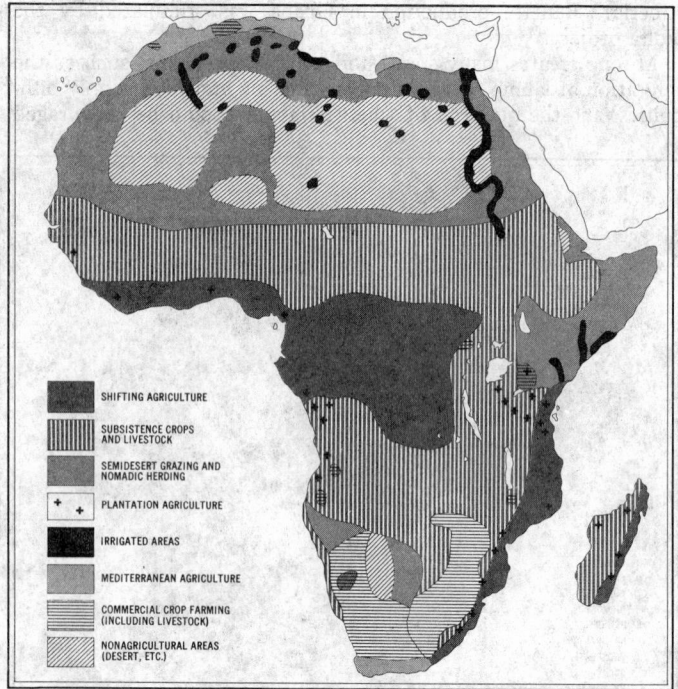

SHIFTING AGRICULTURE

SUBSISTENCE CROPS
AND LIVESTOCK

SEMIDESERT GRAZING AND
NOMADIC HERDING

+   + PLANTATION AGRICULTURE

IRRIGATED AREAS

MEDITERRANEAN AGRICULTURE

COMMERCIAL CROP FARMING
(INCLUDING LIVESTOCK)

NONAGRICULTURAL AREAS
(DESERT, ETC.)

R. W. STEEL

FIG. 8.—AGRICULTURAL REGIONS OF AFRICA

ditional systems of agriculture practised by the indigenous peoples of Africa are on too small a scale for efficient production. Shifting agriculture, the prevalent system of much of tropical Africa, is any form of farming in which a piece of ground is cultivated for a period of one, two, three or more years until the soil shows signs of exhaustion or the land is overrun by weeds, upon which the plot is abandoned to the regrowth of the natural vegetation while another patch is cleared and brought under cultivation. The original plot will be farmed again, after a period of years, when natural growth has restored fertility and checked the growth of weeds; the longer the fallow period, the better for subsequent cultivation.

At one time it was customary to regard shifting cultivation as a relic of barbarism and an indication of primitive social organization; but it is now generally recognized as basically a concession to the nature of tropical soils that require long periods for recovery and regeneration. Indeed in areas where the density of population is low, so that there is plenty of land available for farming and adequate fallow periods are possible, the system is in effect a rotational method of farming, a system of bush fallowing, and has much to be said in its favour. Details for individual tribes differ widely, as do conditions in forest and in savanna areas. Methods and crops vary according to the topography and the quality of the soil, to the availability or otherwise of livestock and to the community's dietetic habits. But everywhere it is a farming system in which groups co-operate to produce some of the necessities of life, recognizing empirically the value of crop rotation, the use of different soils and the importance of maintaining fertility and even of preventing soil erosion.

Circumstances have so changed, however, that shifting cultivation is no longer an adequate farming system for much of the tropics. No longer is there an abundance of land, for populations are increasing, often very rapidly. Many of the young men who used to clear the forest are away for long periods earning wages at the mines or in the towns. An increasing amount of land may be taken to grow crops for sale as well as for subsistence. It is vital, therefore, that farming methods be improved and crop yields increased. Scientific research has not been very successful in finding easily applied solutions to these problems of subsistence farming, apart from the greater use of livestock to graze and fertilize the crops, and this is not possible in many areas where the tsetse fly makes it impossible to keep most domestic animals.

Plows have been introduced in some districts, though as they go more deeply into the soil than the hoe does, they sometimes contribute to soil erosion. The crops grown vary widely with environmental conditions. In the wetter forest country root crops predominate—yams, sweet potatoes, cassava (manioc) and cocoyams—supplemented by plantains or bananas and by grain crops. In drier areas cereals are more common, notably maize (corn; introduced by the Portuguese from America) and the indigenous sorghum and bulrush millets.

Livestock.—In the 1960s Africa had about 26% of the world's goats, 15% of the sheep and 11% of the cattle. Animals, especially cattle, often have great social and religious significance, a man's status in society being judged by the size of his flocks and herds. Quantity, therefore, tends to be regarded as more important than quality and there is a strong preference for keeping animals alive rather than slaughtering them. (See *Ethnography*, below.)

In certain areas, particularly in eastern and southern Africa, pastoralism has often dominated the economy in the past. It is probably no longer so except among tribes such as the Masai who depend wholly upon their cattle for subsistence and who despise all cultivation. Nowadays even tribes with strong pastoral traditions often recognize the value of food crop cultivation.

Africa has more than its share of animal diseases, of which by far the most serious is trypanosomiasis, spread by the tsetse fly. The area affected, about 4,000,000 sq.mi., is bounded on the north by a line from the Senegal river through Lake Chad and Lake Rudolf to the Somali Republic coast and on the south by a line that passes through central Angola and roughly follows the course of the Zambezi to Mozambique. Between two-thirds and three-quarters of this broad area is infested by tsetse fly to a greater or lesser extent, making the successful rearing of domestic livestock almost impossible. This is particularly unfortunate with the growing recognition of the necessity for mixed farming to replace exclusive dependence upon either crops or animals. It also hinders the improvement of crop cultivation, as noted above. (*See* further TSETSE FLY.)

Other animal diseases include rinderpest, East Coast fever, contagious pleuropneumonia and tuberculosis. Veterinary work has been successful in certain directions, but constant vigilance is necessary, and epidemics often have serious and widespread consequences. The common breed of cattle in the tropics is the indigenous, often humped zebu (Brahman) type; European breeds have been introduced on some upland farms in areas such as the Kenya highlands.

Cash Crops.—In many parts of tropical Africa crops are increasingly produced for sale and export by African, as well as by European, farmers. The cessation of the slave trade and the abolition of slavery during the 19th century coincided with an increased demand in Europe for West African palm oil as an ingredient of soap. Later palm kernels became valuable as a constituent of margarine. Peanuts and other oilseeds were also in demand, and cotton and rubber plantations were established in some areas. Coffee, tea and sisal production was usually in European hands, at least in the early stages, but cocoa growing was from the first an essentially African enterprise which transformed the economy of southern Ghana and southwestern Nigeria. These developments have affected methods of land use, standards of living, provision of communications, population patterns and indeed every aspect of the lives of the peoples concerned.

Africa is the source of most of the world's supply of palm kernels and nearly two-thirds of its palm oil and cocoa, together with substantial quantities of cotton, sisal, tea, coffee and peanuts. More commercial use is also being made of tropical African livestock, and meat-packing stations have been established in several countries.

Much useful study has been given to the problems of commercial crops and considerable success achieved in plant breeding, in increasing yields, in minimizing the effects of disease and in the general improvement of farming methods. Even financially unsuccessful projects (like the East African Groundnut Scheme in Tanganyika shortly after World War II) have subsequently produced valuable information about mechanization under African farming conditions.

The principal plantations owned and managed by Europeans within the tropics have been in the highlands of Kenya, Tanzania, the high veld areas in Zambia, and Southern Rhodesia, the higher parts of the Democratic Republic of the Congo and in a few districts in West Africa (though not generally in the former British West African territories). The importance of these areas to the economy of the countries is far out of proportion to their size or to the scale of their contribution to world supplies. The resulting social and political problems have been sometimes very great, however.

Agriculture: Extratropical.—Relatively small areas occur outside the tropics, but some of them are very important farming lands. In the more favoured, better-watered and cooler parts of South Africa and of North Africa, particularly Algeria and, to a lesser extent, Morocco and Tunisia, European farming has been established on a large scale, though many settlers in the north returned to Europe in the 1960s.

The basis of the agricultural and pastoral economy of South Africa consists of livestock, especially sheep with cattle in the less dry areas, associated where possible with maize production; but there are also special features such as dairying in the Transvaal, sugar production in Natal and citrus and vine growing in the southwestern Cape. Southern Rhodesia, with many similarities to South Africa even though it lies within the tropics, has good cereal and pasture country and is a leading producer of tobacco. North Africa's principal crops, grown by non-Europeans as well as Europeans, include wheat, barley, olives and vines.

Scattered around the edge of the Sahara are numerous intensively cultivated oases, while the Nile valley in Egypt is able to support a very high density of population because of irrigation and successful commercial cotton growing.

Forestry.—The botanical aspects of the forests of Africa are described above, under *Vegetation*. Forests now occupy only about one-eighth of the total area of the continent. Even the tropical rain forest and the high forest of equatorial districts have been vastly reduced in area, largely because of the bush-fallowing agricultural system. There are extensive areas of the more open type of woodland known as savanna, while temperate forests occur at higher elevations in eastern and southern Africa, and there are limited forests in Mediterranean North Africa.

Reservation of forests by government legislation is now common (though not as widely practised as it should be) to promote soil and water conservation in watershed areas, African subsistence farming, and for local fuel and timber needs. Exploitation of timber resources for export proved difficult in the past, except in certain areas such as Gabon, because of the diversity of species, the problems of transport and the uncertainties of overseas demand. World War II greatly stimulated activity, and flourishing timber industries have been established in the Ivory Coast, Ghana, Nigeria and the Congo Republic. In addition to the export of sawn timber, integrated industries are being developed, and the manufacture of paper pulp has been successfully established in West Africa. Most of the trade is concerned with fewer than 40 of the 300 or more species of marketable size.

Outside tropical Africa certain forest products have long been of commercial value, particularly the cork-oak forests of North Africa and the hardwoods of Knysna in South Africa.

Fisheries.—Africa has little continental shelf. There is usually a sharp drop of 2,000 to 3,000 fathoms to the ocean depths, quite near to the mainland, so that there are no prospects of large-scale commercial fisheries such as have developed off northwest Europe or eastern Asia. But many forms of aquatic life abound along the African seaboard as well as in the large lakes and long rivers. So far, however, most attempts to develop the fishing industry have failed, though determined efforts are being made in some newly independent countries, and Ghana is planning extensive fisheries for the Volta lake. Fish farming, especially that based on a species of *Tilapia*, has proved successful, notably in the Congo basin. The South African marine fisheries are growing steadily, in trawling and in catches of pilchard. South Africa with an annual catch of about 655,000 tons of fish is one of the principal producers in the southern hemisphere.

Manufacturing.—Only in the extreme north and south of Africa had manufacturing industry made much progress before World War II, in both cases in close association with a fair-sized settled European population and with the exploitation of mineral resources (see *Minerals,* above). A few, relatively minor, secondary industries were established in the principal tropical African towns before 1939. World War II provided a tremendous stimulus by creating large overseas demands for certain African primary products and by cutting off the supply of many manufactured goods from Europe for several years. Industries started then have been maintained and some have expanded since, while new concerns have been established elsewhere, particularly in the newly independent countries. The problems of industrialization (including mining) are closely associated with those of the increasing movement of people into towns (see *Population,* below).

For more detailed information on land use, *see* articles on the individual countries.   (R. W. Sl.)

III. ETHNOGRAPHY (ANTHROPOLOGY)

Since the African continent is ethnographically most diverse in all respects the more detailed characteristics of its peoples can only be satisfactorily grasped by a consideration of its various regions. No such regions are, however, homogeneous or completely distinctive in character. It is therefore necessary to consider the nature and distribution of some prominent features that are significant over wide areas.

In physical or racial type most of the peoples of Africa south of the Sahara and the Ethiopian highlands are predominantly Negroid and there are Negroid enclaves in northern Africa as for example in the Tibesti highlands, the Nuba mountains and along the middle Nile. On the other hand, it would appear that the basic racial stocks of northern Africa, which are sometimes regarded as part of the "Mediterranean" or "brown" race, have been the source of many incursions into tropical Africa. These may have given rise to distinctive local types by Negroid admixture as among the pastoral Fulani (Fula) of the western Sudan, the Galla and some of the Nilo-Hamites of East Africa. Lighter skin colour, tall stature and absence of marked prognathism and platyrrhiny among other East and West African peoples have also been attributed to mixtures of northern and Negroid elements and subsequent southward migrations. But there is little documentary or biological evidence concerning these (*see* NEGRO).

Both the supposedly mixed stocks and the Negro peoples themselves have expanded over long periods in the past at the expense of other older stocks in central and southern Africa that once occupied extensive areas as hunting populations. In the tropical forest areas there are a number of enclaves of pygmoid groups while the ancient Bushman stock, now confined to a semidesert area in the southwest, appears to have been formerly more widespread in central and eastern Africa.

The languages of Africa also show a general cleavage between the various Hamito-Semitic languages on the one hand, which are spoken in North Africa, much of the Sahara and the eastern Horn, and the several major language groups associated with Negroid peoples to the south. The classification and the determination of the genetic relations of these African languages, many of which are still little known, is by no means definitive. In particular, the question of Hamitic elements in some East African languages is still being debated. But apart from the survival of the distinct Bushman and Hottentot (Khoisan) languages in the southwest and among one or two small East African peoples, the greater part of central and southern Africa is occupied by peoples speaking a large number of clearly related languages known collectively as Bantu. These in turn are held to be more remotely related to another large family of languages spoken in West Africa commonly labeled as Western Sudanic. But not all the Negro peoples of Africa speak Bantu or related languages. Those of the Negroid populations from the region of the upper Nile westward to Lake Chad belong to several distinct and apparently unrelated linguistic stocks such as Nilotic (to which the Nilo-Hamitic tongues of East

Africa are closely related), Eastern Sudanic and Central Saharan. Finally, Hamitic languages are found among them to the west of Lake Chad; *e.g.*, Hausa over much of northern Nigeria.

Modes of life over most of North Africa, the Sahara and much of the Ethiopian highlands are continuations of patterns characteristic of southwest Asia and range from fixed plow cultivation of temperate cereals and irrigated gardening in oases, to nomadic pastoralism often based mainly on camel herding but including the rearing of goats or sheep and in some regions cattle.

The economies of the tropical and southern African peoples have been less directly affected by northern techniques. Those of the Bushmen and pygmies retain archaic modes of hunting in a food-gathering economy. But most of the Negroid peoples, while they formerly engaged extensively in hunting, are predominantly agriculturists. Since primitive forms of iron smelting have been long established in many areas, nearly all have iron tools and in particular hoes for cultivation. But the rapid exhaustion of tropical soils with shallow cultivation and limited means for regularly restoring fertility has nearly everywhere imposed a pattern of shifting cultivation in which tracts of forest, bush or grassland are cleared afresh by felling and burning for each year's crops and are left to recover indefinitely or for a period of years, according to the conditions and the pressure of population, before being brought under cultivation again. But within these general limitations, to which there are also exceptions such as the permanent cultivation of banana groves in the East African highlands, there is considerable diversity of farming methods and efficiency.

Root crops predominate as food staples over most of the forest areas and their fringes in central and western Africa, while coarse grains are characteristic of the wide arc of tropical woodland and grassland with its long dry season that extends from Senegal in West Africa eastward to the southern Sudan and thence southward through East Africa to the southern plateaus of Southern Rhodesia, Zambia, Bechuanaland and Angola. Techniques range from the dibbling of a catch crop on patches of charred forest or burned grass to the systematic provision of fertilizer, *e.g.*, by pollarding trees for supplies of ash as in the *chitemene* system of Zambia, or the hoeing of high ridges for grain planting as among the Hausa of Nigeria and of large hills for yams as in southern Nigeria to secure an adequate depth of soil for large crops.

The grain and root staples include both African and introduced crops. *Eleusine* and *Pennisetum* (bulrush millet), which are widespread savanna grains, may have been first cultivated in the Ethiopian region; while *Sorghum* (Guinea corn) includes both Asian and perhaps indigenous West African varieties. Several of the varieties of the forest root staple, the yam, are Asian in origin but indigenous varieties are also cultivated in West Africa. The banana or plantain which is widespread and forms the staple in parts of eastern Africa was, like one species of cocoyam (*Colocasia*), also introduced from south Asia. The antiquity of agriculture in tropical Africa and the periods at which the various Asian cultivated plants were introduced have not yet been determined. But some plants which have become staples over wide areas are known to be recent since they are of new world origin and could not have been introduced before the end of the 15th century. These include the root crop cassava or manioc which has been adopted at the expense of yams in more densely populated areas of western and central Africa, a second species of cocoyam (*Xanthosoma*) and maize, a staple over the subtropical grasslands of the south and east.

Domestic goats and chickens, which are ubiquitous among the tropical cultivators, were an early introduction from Asia. Cattle were introduced many centuries ago from the north and have become an important element in the economy over wide areas. Small short-horned cattle resistant to fly-borne and other diseases are reared in small numbers by some forest cultivators, especially in West Africa, but the larger long-horned cattle are confined to the fly-free savanna in the north, east and south. Among some of the peoples of these regions cattle are the central element of the economy and hence of major social and religious importance. Pastoralism has been variously combined with agriculture according to circumstances. Although in West Africa many of the Fula-speaking peoples from Senegal to Lake Chad have specialized almost exclusively in cattle rearing, formerly depending on serfs and now on the trading of milk for supplies of grain, the agricultural populations rarely keep cattle for milking. Most of the eastern and southern African pastoral peoples combine grain farming with cattle rearing and prize milk highly as food.

The scale and complexity of political organization in Africa has depended only to a limited degree on the character of the econ-

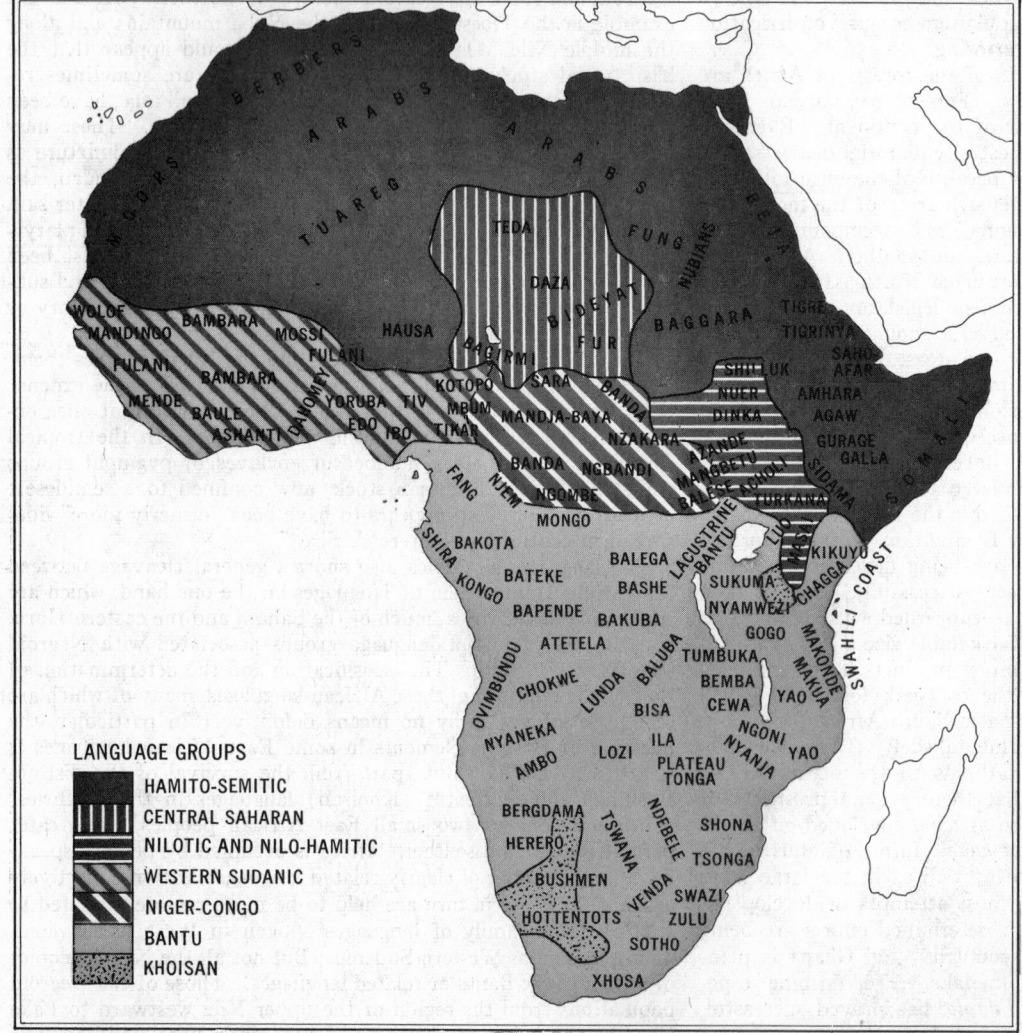

LLOYD A. FALLERS

FIG. 9.—MAJOR PEOPLES AND LANGUAGE FAMILIES OF AFRICA

omy. While pygmy and Bushman organization has been limited to small scattered and independent bands, among both the agricultural and the pastoral peoples the foundations of organization are usually enduring kin groups united according to a definite principle of descent, usually either patrilineal or matrilineal. Among many such peoples there were traditionally no formally political offices or central organization. Kin groups, fluctuating in scale according to the circumstances, co-operated and competed under their leaders, while religious sanctions reinforced by priesthoods and recurrent rituals supported a moral order among them. Such chiefless or segmentary societies are to be found in all regions among both agricultural and pastoral peoples. Well-known examples are the Tiv of northern Nigeria, the Nuer of the southern Sudan and the Cewa of Zambia. Some peoples, notably certain pastoral tribes of East Africa such as the Nandi and the Masai, have a territorial age-set organization through which limited political power is exercised in turn by the sets as they reach certain grades. But political centralization under a hierarchy of chiefs and their councils has long been developed among many peoples. Many of these in West Africa (*e.g.*, Yoruba and Akan) and in East Africa (*e.g.*, Nyoro and Ganda) have traditions of ancient foundation under sacred rulers who came with their followings from farther north. But strong chiefdoms were also early developed in the western and southern Congo basin and later among the Bantu of southeastern Africa. In many cases there is evidence of the peaceful incorporation or forceful domination of earlier peoples in the formation of these states.

While in Ethiopia early monophysite Christian kingdoms have persisted, political organization over most of North Africa, among both sedentary and pastoral peoples, has received the imprint of the Islamic Arab conquests which began in the 9th century A.D. Islamic principles of government and law as well as religious doctrine have also been superimposed in varying degrees on the political life of many of the chiefdoms of the savanna belt to the south of the Sahara from the Senegal to the middle Nile.

The foregoing and other aspects of the indigenous cultures and social life of African peoples, including religion and art, are considered in more detail below within the framework of a series of major regions. These regions, while severally manifesting considerable internal diversity, have each some degree of coherence with respect to certain predominant cultural patterns or the historic movements and interrelations of peoples within them.

See also AGRICULTURE; AFRICAN LANGUAGES; RACES OF MANKIND; KINSHIP TERMINOLOGY: *Africa;* DWELLINGS, PRIMITIVE: *Africa;* LAND TENURE, PRIMITIVE; MARRIAGE, PRIMITIVE; SECRET SOCIETIES, PRIMITIVE; PRIMITIVE ART: *Africa;* CURRENCY, PRIMITIVE; articles on the various African countries should also be consulted.   (D. F.)

A. NORTH AFRICA

North Africa extends from the Atlantic to the Red sea and from the Mediterranean to the northern bend of the Niger river and a line from the peak of this bend to the Red sea. This vast region is divided into numerous territories which do not correspond to the simple lines of relief or population. In the north the mountain folds from Morocco to Tunisia are continuations of the Mediterranean chains. In the south the Sahara extends the great artery of nomadism from the steppes of central Asia as far as Africa. Two isolated mountain massifs have particular populations: the Ahaggar (Hoggar) at the very heart of the Sahara, and Tibesti farther southeast. Neither relief nor natural resources have profoundly marked the life of the people. The great invasions of the past came from east to west, but constant exchanges have occurred from south to north and from north to south, with less obvious, but slower and deeper effects.

Physical Types.—The northern mountain chains are inhabited by the Berbers, a fair Mediterranean race of varied lineage. The Sahara artery is peopled by the same Semitic nomads as the near east, mixed in greater or lesser degree with Negroid elements. The oases of the south are inhabited by Negroids; the Tuaregs of the Ahaggar are so mixed with Negroids that their original type cannot be distinguished. Tibesti and Borku are also inhabited by Negroids

under various names: Tilda on the massif itself, Daza in the north and south of Borku; the Bideyat and Zaghawa from the south of Ennedi to the north of Wadai and Darfur extend eastward to the south of the Libyan desert. (*See* BERBER; TUAREG; ZAGHAWA.)

Languages.—The spoken Arabic is noticeably different from classical Arabic and the difference increases from east to west. Subject to modification by regional accents, it is the language of the majority. Berber is also a Semitic language, spoken especially in the massifs of the Moroccan Atlas, and in Algeria in the Zakkar, Kabylia and Aures. In Tunisia it is spoken in the 11 villages of the Matmata to the south of Gabès. In the Sahara Berber is spoken in most of the oases from Tabelbala to Agades, with a significant centre in Mzab. Farther south it is represented by the important group of the Mauritanian tribes: Tekura, Rigibat and Arusigin; and by the Tuaregs of the Ahaggar. To the east, in Egypt, it is practically confined to the oasis of Siwah.

In Tibesti the languages of Teda, Bideyat and Kanuri are the heart of the Sudanese languages. But Arabic has infiltrated across the whole of the Sahara, from Fezzan and northern Libya to Chad, through the migration of the Awlad Sliman about 1840 and, after 1850, by the religious brotherhood of the Senusi (Sanusi). (*See* ARABIC LANGUAGE; SEMITIC LANGUAGES; SUDANIC LANGUAGES.)

Population Movements.—In North Africa these are independent of the linguistic situation. There are arabicized Berbers where tribes of the latter have come under Arab cultural influence; on the other hand, there are berberized Arabs where the reverse has been the case. In the heart of Kabylia are found important Arab elements, the Beni Thour and the Beni Sliyam on the Kabylia coast and the Beni Husain in the Azazga region, who have become entirely Berber-speaking. The Arab tribes of Djedjelli region are partly berberized and speak, indifferently, a corrupt Arabic.

Living Conditions.—There is a clear distinction between the settled peoples and the tented nomads. Houses with double-sloped roofs cover a region stretching from the mountain chains of Morocco to the Krumirian mountains in Tunisia, and from the littoral to the high plains. The flat-roofed and terraced house covers all the rest of the northern area and the whole of the central area of North Africa. The domed house is often a stage toward permanent settlement of the nomads. Dugout dwellings or adapted caves are sometimes used by nomads in the process of settlement, as for example the Beni Bahdel near Tlemcen in Algeria, the inhabitants of the Jebel Ussalet settlement of Kairouan in Tunisia and those of the Jebel Nefusa in Libya. In Tunisia the Matmata have dwellings deeply dug into the ground.

The tents of North Africa are similar to those of the east, from where they were brought by the Bedouin tribes, made of bands woven from wool and goats' hair. Often the tent is surrounded by a dry stone wall, against which came to be erected domed storehouses; this is the beginning of the settled life. In eastern Morocco and western Algeria tents are often made of plaited matting. In Mauritania and the Ahaggar are found leather tents. Palm huts are used by the seminomad Teda in Tibesti and Borku and by the settled people of Kufra.

Mode of Life.—The settled peoples of the northern mountains are cultivators of trees and grain. The Ksuri of the south live essentially on their dates. The nomads throughout the Sahara raise sheep entirely for food; their main resources derive especially from their role as navigators of the Sahara, formerly by camel caravan, but now more and more by the organization of motor transport. The cycle of life depends on the production of resources. Among the settled peoples of the north, after the tillage, the men leave the mountain villages and go to work in the cities of the coast and more frequently in the industrial towns of France, Belgium and Germany. The high rewards of European industry cause this emigration to become intensified and prolonged. The money sent back to the villages provokes a veritable inflation because the necessities of life remain underdeveloped as the fields are increasingly deserted. The men return at the beginning of summer for the harvest, when a relative abundance reigns in the villages.

For the Ksuri of the Sahara dates provide a sufficient basic food so that the men do not seek to emigrate. The new oil and gas industry attracts labour (formerly restricted) from the north. Among the nomads of the Sahara movement begins in mid-November after sowing the barley at the foot of the palm trees. Their route covers more than 500 mi. and the journey takes two or three months with halts which combine pilgrimages to the tombs of saints. The duration of the nomadic movement never exceeds nine months.

In Tibesti and Borku the nomadic cycle covers about 300 mi. in the irrigated valleys during the wet season from August to January. The true nomads of Tibesti, Mauritania and the Sahara have no agriculture but live alongside the settled inhabitants of the oases.

PAUL CONKLIN—PIX FROM PUBLIX

A NOMADIC HERDSMAN WITH HIS FLOCK AT THE EDGE OF THE SAHARA IN SOUTHERN TUNISIA

Social Organization.—Among the settled and nomad peoples alike the family is patrilineal and patrilocal. It is basically a cult community. The father is head of the family. Polygamy is little practised and is found more in the cities than outside; but where it occurs the mistress of the house is always the first wife or the one whose first child is a boy. The husband's mother plays a pre-eminent part. Families sharing a communal life form a clan; thus communal life may derive from a common ancestor or from an alliance made by a sacrificial contract. The nomads throughout the high plains and the Sahara have the same social organization. The sons live a communal life with the father, and he has the sole right to allow them to pitch their tents near his, when they are married, to form a *duwar* or group of tents.

Families who share the same food cooked on the same fire may not intermarry. The *horma* ("sanctity of the house") forms an obstacle to the marriage of close cousins, but this obstacle disappears between families living under separate roofs. The bride preferred is usually a cousin on the mother's side.

Every human community, family, village or tribe, is basically a sacrificial community; it is also linked directly or by alliance with a common ancestry. Every year, generally in the autumn at the first plowing among the settled peoples and before the annual movements among the nomads, the members of a village or group repeat the ceremony that marked the arrival of their founder ancestor: a sacrifice of cattle in the north, of sheep and camels in the south.

The quarters of a village are grouped in *sof* ("halves"), opposed and complementary. These *sof* have a matrimonial significance: the men of the upper *sof* take their wives from the lower *sof;* the men of the lower *sof* seek wives among the lower *sof* of a neighbouring village. "A man does not climb the village hill to seek his wife" is the first and plainly expressed principle; "every village is also the upper *sof* of another village" is the second. Every family has its special tabus concerning food or clothing, as does every *sof*, and sometimes the villages and the tribes.

Among the nomads is found the same structure and the same idea of opposed and complementary clans. The founder ancestor is reputed to have come from Arabia and his descendants have formed numerous groups of tents arranged in *ferqa* of 15 to 20 tents which journey together. The different *ferqa* are divided into *sof*, distributed according to the direction of movement, *e.g.*, northern *sof* or southern *sof*, and they form matrimonial categories as with the settled peoples. The 40 clans of Tibesti have much the same organization.

Administration.—Among the settled peoples of the north authority is exercised by the assembly of heads of families, the *Jema'a.* Executive power is delegated for one year to an *amin* or sheikh, chosen alternatively from the two *sof*, who is assisted by *tamen*, the responsible heads of the quarters. The executive sees to the application of the customary law, the *kanun*, which is the expression of the will of the *Jema'a.*

Among the nomads power resides with the eldest male descendant of the family of the founder ancestor, assisted by the assembly of heads of groups. There are also more complex structures involving several villages or tent groups; the alliance of divers of these larger groupings constitute a tribe and several tribes may form a confederation.

Technical Trades.—Skilled workers in North Africa form castes: they include butchers, potters, stonemasons, hunters, blacksmiths and, in the Sahara, well cleaners. The blacksmith's skill includes magic as well as technique, as he is often the healer of heat disorders, fevers, etc. He also plays a social part: it is often his task to inaugurate the plowing, and among the northern settled peoples he was formerly war leader. In the Ahaggar, blacksmiths are frequently Hausa. In Tibesti they also form a separate nomad caste, and no observer has yet been able to say whether this caste is of different racial origin from the rest of the population. The existence of hunting clans appears to establish that a ritual chase once preceded the plowing. In Tibesti the blacksmith has the privilege of hunting the antelope with hounds.

Economic Activity.—The existence of groups with their particular tabus has entailed the existence also of complementary productive castes; exchange in its simplest form of barter has long been the only means of bringing these human groups together. The market, the place of exchange, is consecrated with magical rites; like the house, it has a sacred character which assures its protection, and men belonging to different clans can meet there unarmed to exchange their products. Barter has an important place in the economic life and makes it impossible to evaluate family budgets in terms of money. Earthenware vessels, for example, are exchanged for one or several times their content of grain; two or more goats are exchanged for one sheep and so on.

Towns.—The large towns have been founded on the sites of the Phoenician wharves and the Roman garrison quarters. Like all Mediterranean cities they have separate ethnical quarters. The gates which formerly pierced their walls were always placed under the protection of a saint whose sanctuary has often survived. Craftsmen occupy particular streets or quarters (*suqs*), which conform to the same tabus as in the rest of the country.

Arts and Handicrafts.—The arts and domestic crafts are part of the cycle of the life of the fields. Weaving is linked to plowing and to marriage. Women weave in winter, for then "the fields are covered with vegetation as the loom with wool." The two beams of the loom form a couple; the woven cloth is regarded like a living being and the ritual for separating it from the loom when it is finished is the same as that which attends the cutting of the umbilical cord of a newborn child. The striped blankets decorated with lozenges, common in the Berber regions, recall, according to tradition, the skin of serpents and the parallel bands of the fields.

In the high plain region the women weave pile carpets designed to cover the ground of the tent. Some, such as those of Kairouan in Tunisia, have achieved renown.

Domestic pottery is made by women, provided they have learned the art before puberty. Pottery is the object of many tabus and many groups may not make it. The patterns of Berber pottery symbolize the world and social organization: water, clouds, houses, the reed of a loom, or the fields are their principal elements. Pottery is made in springtime when the ears of corn are forming; it dries in the shade while the ears ripen and bakes under the open sky when the harvest is ended and there is no more fear that fires will parch the earth.

Remarkable pottery has long been made at Fès and Meknes in Morocco; at Nabeul and Djerba in Tunisia production has almost reached industrial scale. Leatherworking has given rise to corporations, especially in Morocco. The making of silver and gold jewelry has long been an activity of the blacksmith caste.

The music of North Africa can be clearly differentiated according to whether it is Berber music, which is related to the popular music of the northern Mediterranean, or Arab music, which is the mark of eastern influences. The latter may be divided into rural music, represented principally by the songs of the nomads to the accompaniment of the flute, of which the rhythms are the same from Syria across all the Sahara to the Atlantic, and urban music where the chief instrument is the lute, which is also the sign of eastern influences, doubtless from Iran. This music has undergone a considerable Spanish influence. There are groups of professional men singers whose social standing varies with their type of singing, sacred or secular. They move from village to village at the time of plowing, when obscene jokes are customary. The broadcasting of thoroughly arabicized songs over the extensive radio system is a great threat to rural music.

Religious Life.—The basis of the religious life of the people is the linking of society with the invisible world. The dead ancestor is at the root of a family cult. It is his duty to bring fertility to the earth, especially for his direct descendants, who in return must carry out funeral rites at fixed times. Among the people ancestral tombs take the place of martyrs' tombs among Christians and those of holy men among Muslims. At the mercy of desecrators, their name is often unknown or forgotten; they are simply *jedna* ("our ancestor") to the peasants. Religious life is thus composed of rites intended to propitiate and strengthen the spirit of the ancestor within the framework of the agricultural year.

Pilgrimages, the expression of popular piety, are seasonal rites. In spring they are accompanied by prayers for rain; in summer by offerings of first fruits after the harvest; at the beginning of autumn they are a consecration of the plowing and a reminder of the alliance between the descendants of the same ancestor and their relations by marriage. The family house is the principal temple, sanctified from the time of its construction by foundation sacrifices. Every domestic object is regarded as the abode of a guardian spirit and ritual offerings are placed by each at the time of every festival.

Passage Rites.—These rituals are parallel to the agricultural rites, and they also sanction entry into the family conceived of as a cult community. Birth is surrounded by ceremonies which aim at fixing the human spirit in a body and protecting the mother and the newborn baby from evil influences—evil spirits and the evil eye. Circumcision is practised throughout North Africa. The traumatic experience of the operation brings the child out of the world of women into the world of men. The age of circumcision varies from 1 year or less to 12 years; in the first case it is the survival of a very old Jewish custom. Female excision is practised in Egypt and Tibesti; it has not been noted in the rest of North Africa. Marriage is the keystone of all fertility rites; by virtue of this it assumes many of the aspects of the plowing rites. It is also the sign of alliance between two families, with the exchange of gifts of food and presents. The escorting of the bride to the conjugal home may be preceded by a pretense of abduction. Her departure from her paternal home is surrounded with ritual signalizing the abandonment of her father's authority and her passing under that of her husband. Her arrival at her conjugal home is marked by a series of fertility rites which are repeated seven days after consummation of the marriage.

The rites connected with death are governed by the rules of orthodox Islam. A very ancient past, however, controls the tabus and the mourning obligations, which are in fact relative tabus to those connected with germination in the plowing season—the forbiddance to cut the hair, beard or nails.

Agricultural Rites.—Plowing is accompanied by the same rites all over North Africa. After the sacrifice at the tomb of the founder ancestor, the eldest of his descendants or "a man with a lucky hand" cuts the first furrow, having placed an offering of multiple-seeded fruit on the soil, an offering often made in marriage rituals. Spring rites are especially for the protection of the green corn and of milk; by extension they have also become rites for the protection of the young and of the flocks. Harvest rites are essentially parallel to funeral rites. Special rituals surround the reaping of the first ears or the last sheaf.

The solar year was undoubtedly formerly divided into two seasons and began with the heliacal rising of Sirius at the beginning of August. The different phases of plant growth were calculated by the moon. Later the Arabs brought into use the Julian calendar borrowed from the Egyptian Copts, and their religious lunar calendar. The solar year has retained the names of the months of the Julian calendar and of festivals common to all Europe. The new year is marked by rites designed to avert famine and to foretell the fortune of the months to come. For the nomads this festival, called the festival of the tent pegs (*Bu inian*), marks their departure on their nomadic journey. June 24 (Julian) is celebrated throughout North Africa by the fires of 'ainsara which, according to tradition, perpetuate the memory of a sinful "pagan" woman who was burned alive. In reality these fires are an extension of the solstice fires which are found all over Europe.

Islam.—Officially Islam is practised in North Africa according to the Malikite rite, but there is a strong Ibadite community in Mzab and some Hanifites in the towns formerly occupied by the Turks. The Islamic religion of the people has had to take into account the essential facts of North African thought, the ancestor cult and the cycle of the fields. Islam penetrated North Africa in the Shi'ite (Shi'ah) form of the Omayyads in the 8th century, and later of the Fatimids. The memory of the Shi'ite faith is kept alive by the "hand of Fatima," an old symbol known to the Phoenicians but which Shi'ite Islam made the symbol of "the five most precious things in the world."

The principal Islamic festivals in North Africa are: 'Ashura, Mulud, Sha'aban, Ramadan (or the Little festival which marks the end of the fast of Ramadan) and the Great festival 40 days later. These festivals have borrowed numerous rituals from the ancient festivals of the solar year. 'Ashura, the first feast of the lunar year, has drawn on many new year rituals. Mulud, the birthday of the Prophet, has become a festival of lamps all over North Africa, the flame being the symbol of the return to earth of the spirits of the dead. The 15th night of Sha'aban is the anniversary of the ascension to heaven of the Prophet, on al-Mihraj. Peasants regard this night as one of destiny, in the course of which God allots the goods of this world for the year to come.

The Mrabtin, whose name comes from a root meaning "to bind," form a sacred caste of intermediaries and conciliators between this world and the next. They are forbidden to carry arms. Their villages are often situated on the plain, since they have no fear of any attack. Their weapon is the *da'a* or "power to curse." Among the Tuaregs of the Sahara they form special tribes. Mrabtin all over North Africa claim descent from the Prophet through Idris, and a common place of origin, Saguia el Hamra in Río de Oro.

Brotherhoods.—Dey Obayd Allah, who came from Iran to Little Kabylia about the 9th century, brought with him the idea of a secret mystical society. It is not surprising to see appearing much later, in the 17th century but in the same region, the first Muslim brotherhood, the Rahmaniya, founded by Si Abd-ar-Rahman, with seven degrees like the mystical Persian Order of the Deys. Other brotherhoods have followed, all borrowing their ritual from the first. The most popular is the Qadiriya, the most important politically the Senusi (*q.v.*), which for long held all the Sahara and converted Tibesti, Borku and the Ahaggar to Islam. The part played by these brotherhoods, important up to the beginning of the 20th century, has waned with the development of Muslim Reformism, and especially with the growing disaffection of the masses for the mystical aspects of Islamic thought.

Evolution.—At the beginning of the 20th century the social ideal was the western *petit bourgeois,* an official or member of a liberal profession. After World War I the Muslim Reformists of Cairo inspired a renewed idealism and the hope of a rebirth of Muslim civilization. In fact the achievement of independence by the states composing North Africa (Egypt before World War II and Libya, Tunisia, Morocco and Mauritania after) has seen the continuance of the European administrative structures and the domination by an intellectual minority of a peasant population still faithful to its traditional systems. Reformism has shaken the cult of the saints and with it Islam, which was scarcely known to the masses except through the tombs and holy places. In its turn Reformism has been abandoned by the young, leaving only a great vacuum in the minds of nearly 40,000,000 persons. *See* also BEDOUIN; KABYLE; MZAB; SAHARA.   (J. H. SE.)

B. NORTHEAST AFRICA

This region, usually taken to include the Republic of the Sudan and the Horn of Africa (in its widest use Ethiopia, including Eritrea, Somalia and French Somaliland), is one where political frontiers bear particularly little relationship to ethnic divisions. The Sudan embraces an area of 967,491 sq.mi. (2,505,782 sq.km.) and, like the Horn, has a long and varied history. The earliest name of the country is the vague Egyptian *Ta-Nehesu* which like the *Bilad as-Sudan* of the early Arab geographers means "land of the blacks." In fact, however, although Negroid features are widely diffused in the Sudan they are particularly pronounced only in the physical characteristics of the inhabitants of the south, and it is usual to recognize a general division between the predominantly Arabic-speaking and Muslim desert regions of the north and the Negroid and largely pagan areas of the less arid south. The Arab and Muslim influence which is dominant in the north has been superimposed upon earlier Hamitic cultures which survive little changed in the Red sea and Kassala provinces of the east. The earlier Hamitic populations were first influenced by Arab penetration in the middle of the 7th century when the Egyptian amir Abdullah ibn Sa'd led a well-equipped expedition into Nubia, reaching as far as Dongola, and concluded a treaty of peace with the Nubian king. But the first considerable Arab incursions came three centuries later when armies largely composed of Arab nomads were sent from upper Egypt and many Arabs settled among the Nubians and among the Beja. Christianity, which had been implanted about the 6th century, began to wane, especially after Arab immigration through Egypt reached a peak in the 13th century.

The Sudan.—The peoples of the Sudan whose culture and physical features represent the admixture in varying proportions of the three basic stocks, Negroid, Hamitic and Arab, can be classified as follows:

Nubian-Speaking Peoples.—The Nubians, who probably number more than 200,000, live along the Nile in U.A.R. (Egyptian) territory from Aswan to Halfa, and in the Sudan in Halfa district and Dongola as far south as Debba. The earliest inhabitants of this region were of the same stock as the predynastic Egyptians, but through assimilating successive waves of Negroid immigrants have come to speak a language (Nubian) which is regarded as belonging to the Sudanic (Negro) family. In physical type the population is a fairly homogeneous Negroid cross. The Barabra, who may be taken as representative, are fairly tall with a medium- to dark-bronze skin, thick lips and black hair which is curly rather than kinky. They are essentially an agricultural riverain people dependent upon the Nile for their livelihood and forced by the poverty of their habitat and pressure of population to travel widely as traders and seek work in the towns of the Sudan and the U.A.R. (Egypt). Occupational groups are organized into guilds under a sheikh. Descent is generally patrilineal and tribes have a segmentary lineage structure akin to that of the Arabs.

(*See* BARABRA; NUBIA.)

Beja Tribes.—Beja is the name given by Arabic writers to the large group of Hamitic-speaking, nomadic and seminomadic peoples who inhabit the eastern district between the Nile, the Atbara river and the Red sea, and who number about 300,000. Their largest group is the Haden Dowa (Hadendoa) who number about 70,000 and are known popularly as the "fuzzy wuzzies" from the wavy character of their hair. The Beja are essentially pastoralists wandering over wide distances with their flocks and herds of cattle and camels on whose produce (milk, butter and meat) they subsist almost entirely. There is a complex of attitudes surrounding milk which is regarded as in a sense sacred. Although there is evidence that in the past descent was matrilineal, it is now patrilineal and the tribes have a segmentary lineage organization similar to that of the Arabs. Authority is vested in the heads of kin groups, and in the case of larger groups which hold territorial rights in sheikhs. As Muslims, they practise polygyny but usually only the rich have several wives. Following the *shari'a,* father's-brother's-daughter marriage is preferred and bride wealth is paid generally in livestock. Boys are circumcised and girls subjected to clitoridectomy, but age sets are lacking. War and feud are common with such a virile and independent people and only recently has the Muslim Arab custom of paying blood compensation (*diya*) been introduced. Most of the Beja still speak To Bedawi, their Hamitic tongue, although some have adopted Arabic, and in the case of the Beni Amer the Semitic Tigre. (*See* BEJA.)

Arabic-Speaking Peoples.—The term Arab has in the modern Sudan the vaguest connotation, and many of the Hamitic Beja and the Nubian tribes as well as Negroid groups (such as the Fung) have Arab pedigrees and claim Arab ancestry. Nevertheless it is possible to distinguish a congeries of peoples who descend from the earlier Arab invasions and preserve their Arab characteristics in varying degrees. These have been divided by Sir H. A. Mac-Michael into two groups: the Ga'alin-Danagla (Ja'aliyyin-Danaqla) and the Guhayna (Juhaina). Together they are estimated to number about 5,000,000 and constitute the largest element in the population of northern Sudan.

The Ga'alin-Danagla, who include most of the riverain and Kordofan sedentaries, have less Arab heredity than the predominantly nomadic Guhayna. Some have been completely negriticized. They are distributed in cultivating villages under headmen (*'umdas*) who hear and try cases. Characteristic features are the numerous markets (*suqs*) which are held regularly and permit the grain, sugar, dates, etc., of the cultivators to be exchanged for the livestock and livestock produce of the pastoralists, for both groups are economically interdependent. The larger *suqs* have developed into market towns where trades are organized in guilds each under its own sheikh. Descent is patrilineal and the sedentaries, who are generally despised by the proud nomads, have a weaker tribal structure than the latter.

There is not, however, a complete division between the sedentaries and the Guhayna nomads, for some tribes have nomadic and sedentary sections, and true nomadism often gives place to transhumance; *e.g.,* a tribe cultivates in oases in the autumn and then moves out into the pastures with its livestock until the spring. But it is the Guhayna nomads who preserve the highest proportion of Arab heredity. They comprise the camel-owning nomads of Kordofan (the Kababish, Dar Hamid and Hamar), those of the Butana and Jezira (the Shukriya and Rufa'a) and the cattle-owning Baggara (Baqqara or Bakkara). The Baggara cattle people are less mobile than the camel pastoralists and are more mixed in ethnic composition. They have evolved a distinctive dialect and distinctive customs and are among the most warlike of the Arabs in the Sudan, being good horsemen. Their tribes, which like those of the other Arabs have a genealogical structure, are large and organized under *nazirs* whose lieutenants (*'umdas*) lead their segments. The less heterogeneous camel people (or Ahl Ibl as they are called) move over wider distances than the Baggara. Each tribe (*qabila*) has its own grazing area (*dira*) and wells. The tribal head (sheikh or, in administrative terminology, *nazir*) is a *primus inter pares* ("first among equals") whose office is not necessarily hereditary. The tribal war drum (*nahas*) is the traditional symbol of tribal unity and sheikhly authority. War and feud are common, friction over grazing and water rights being a frequent source of conflict, and blood compensation (*diya*) is regularly paid by all the nomads. Descent is patrilineal. (*See also* BAGGARA; GA'ALIN; KABABISH.)

Muslim Negroids.—Many Negroid groups chiefly in central and western Sudan have become Muslim, but most have retained their own languages and cultures. They may be divided into the following: (1) Fallata: colonies of West Africans settled in eastern Sudan, mainly immigrant Hausa, Fulbe, Kanuri and Borku. They probably number a few hundred thousand. (2) Fung (*q.v.*): groups of semi-arabicized Negroids of mixed ethnic composition known to the Arabs as Hameg living in Darfung. (3) Non-Arab peoples of Darfur, including seminomads such as the Tebu (Tibbu) and the sedentary agricultural Fur. (4) The Nuba (*q.v.*) of southern Kordofan, a heterogeneous group numbering several hundred thousand, mainly engaged in cultivation in terraced fields. They have many cattle and other livestock. They live in small sedentary hamlets united in larger hill communities. There are religious leaders (*kujurs*) and secular leaders (*mek*). All the Nuba have descent groups; the Tumtum of the south are exclusively matrilineal while the northern and central Koalib are patrilineal; others have dual descent. Age sets are common but not universal. (*See* DARFUR; HAMEG; TEBU.)

Pagan Tribes of Southern Sudan.—These have been classified by C. G. Seligman as follows: (1) Nilotes: those living in the Sudan have a total population of almost 1,000,000, the chief peoples being the Dinka, Nuer, Anuak and Shilluk. Although all engage in some cultivation and in fishing and other activities, they are predominantly pastoralists possessing large herds of cattle. All are patrilineal. There is considerable variation in political structure from the extremely egalitarian Nuer, who have a segmentary lineage structure, to the Shilluk who were united under a divine kingship. The Nuer and Dinka have strongly monotheistic religions centering in the cult of spirit and differ markedly in this respect from most Negroid peoples. (2) The Nilo-Hamites: the Bari, Mandari, Kuku, etc., and Lotuko and Luluba stocks (numbering scarcely more than 100,000) among whom pastoralism seems generally less important than agriculture. All are patrilineal and most are divided into small political units among whom ritual "earth chiefs" and rainmakers play an important role. An age-set organization is a general feature. (3) The Fung-Nuba peoples mentioned above. (4) The southwestern peoples: of whom the Azande of the Ironstone plateau, with their conquest-state political organization and numbering about 200,000 in the Sudan, are the best known. They are a conglomerate people welded together under the political ascendancy of the Ambomu whose ruling clan is the Avungara. They have a hierarchical system, are patrilineal in descent, and are known for their preoccupation with magic and witchcraft. They are agricultural and have no cattle. (*See also* AZANDE; BARI; DINKA; LOTUKO; NILOTES; NUER; SHILLUK.)

The Horn.—Most of the peoples of Sudan's eastern frontiers extend into the Horn giving this region considerable ethnic and cultural continuity with the Sudan. The pastoral Hamites of northeastern Sudan reach far into Eritrea; the Arabic-speaking Shukriya and other peoples to the southeast of Khartoum extend into central and western Ethiopia; and the pagan peoples (Beni Shangul, Nuer and Anuak) of southern Sudan spread into southwestern Ethiopia. As in the Sudan the physical characters and cultures of the present inhabitants are the result of the mixing of Negroid, Hamitic and Semitic stocks over a long period. This has led to a remarkable diversity of peoples and cultures, such indeed that Ethiopia has been described as a "museum of peoples" (Conti Rossini). The aboriginal population of at least part of Ethiopia was probably Negroid. But there is nevertheless a considerable uniformity of physical type due especially to the Hamitic strain which predominates and is assumed to date from several millennia B.C. This absorbed a later population introduced by Semitic migrations from southern Arabia probably in the 1st millennium B.C. The population may conveniently be divided into the following main groups:

Semitic-Speaking Peoples.—(1) Tigre-speaking communities:

the Beni Amer (60,000) of eastern Sudan extend into Eritrea along the Red sea coast. Contiguous Tigre-speaking peoples are the Bait Asgade (including the Habab) and the Marea (Marya) and Mensa, the total Eritrean Tigre-speaking population numbering about 260,000. Most of the Bait Asgade are pastoral nomads; the Marea combine pastoralism with cultivation; and the Mensa are sedentary cultivators. All are Muslims, patrilineal in descent, and constitute tribal federations with a ruling and a serf class. The serfs (Tigre) are in most cases the descendants of various earlier communities upon which the present aristocracies imposed their dominion. Among the Mensa, who still preserve traces of their former adherence to Christianity, each tribal section is under an elected chief (*kantebai*) whose position is symbolized in the possession of a tribal drum. (2) Tigrinya-speaking peoples: these are mainly Christian, although some are Muslim, and number about 1,150,000 of whom 430,000 (the Akkele-Guzai, Hamasien and Serae tribes) live in Eritrea. The majority, however, live on the northwest Ethiopian plateau. They are mainly cultivators, using the ox-drawn plow common in Ethiopia, and grow a wide range of crops. Livestock are also reared, milk being an important item of diet. Descent is patrilineal. Their social and political organization is similar to that of the neighbouring Amhara. (3) The Amharic-speaking community (the Amhara) is the ruling Christian aristocracy of Ethiopia and numbers at least 3,000,000. In contrast to the Tigrinya-speakers, to whom they are otherwise similar, descent is apparently bilateral. Both groups are settled in villages on the central Eritrean plateau and in the northern highlands of Ethiopia where the fundamental political unit is the large kinship group (*enda*) which is a territorial unit with hereditary land rights. Society is traditionally divided into landholders (*restenyatat*) and tenants (*sedbi*). In the Amhara feudal system of government the village headman has authority under the local chieftain and local representative (*ras*) of the emperor. The traditional hierarchy presided over by the emperor (*negus*), whose dynasty claims descent from the queen of Sheba, has only been slightly modified by recent reforms and, although parliamentary government has been introduced, the Amhara political system conserves much of its feudal character. (4) The Gurage are a patrilineal people numbering about 350,000 who live as sedentary cultivators with large herds of livestock in the fertile mountains south of the Awash river and west of Lake Zwai. They are partly pagan, partly Christian, partly Muslim and, although they speak a Semitic language, are closely related to the Cushitic-speaking Sidama. (*See also* AMHARA; MENSA; GURAGE.)

Cushitic-Speaking Peoples.—(1) The Bogos (Bilen), who number about 20,000, inhabit the northern part of the high plateau north of the Gash (Marab) river and are predominantly Muslim. They are mainly agriculturists, living in small hamlets, and have a hierarchical political structure in which the ruling class (*simager*) derive from Agau immigrants, the serfs (*mikeru*) descending from the earlier Tigre-speaking inhabitants. (2) The Agau (Agaw), who are a distinct strain of Cushitic stock, are scattered in several small pockets to the northwest of Addis Ababa in Ethiopia and probably number 100,000. Most are Muslim and sedentary cultivators with a social structure similar to that of the Amhara and Bogos. Of particular interest are a northern group, the Falasha (or "black" Jews), who number about 50,000 and live scattered in the northwestern provinces of Ethiopia practising primitive Judaism. They have no knowledge of Hebrew and their priests use the canonical and apocryphal books of the Old Testament in Ge'ez. (3) The Saho-Afar: two Muslim and predominantly pastoral peoples (Afar 100,000, Saho 50,000) who live south of the Bait Asgade along the Red sea coast of Eritrea extending for a considerable distance into northeastern Ethiopia and French Somaliland. Both are patrilineal and have a segmentary lineage structure with chiefs, the Afar having rigid class divisions. (4) The Somali, who number between 2,500,000 and 3,000,000, are a Muslim and essentially pastoral people closely related to the neighbouring Afar and Saho, although their social organization differs from that of the latter in several respects. There is some cultivation in northern Somalia, but agriculture is most developed in the region between the Juba and Webi Shibeli rivers in southern

Somalia. Descent is patrilineal and the Somali have a clearly defined lineage structure in which political contracts play an important role. Although many clans have sultans, the northern Somali particularly have an egalitarian and nonhierarchical political structure. (5) The Galla peoples who, with the exception of the Boran group of the northern province of Kenya, call themselves Oromo, dominate most of south and southeast Ethiopia and are the largest single ethnic group in the Ethiopian population. It is possible to make a rough division in economy and way of life between the eastern Galla or Baraytuma, who are mainly agricultural, and the western Galla or Boran, who are essentially pastoral. Some Galla have adopted Christianity but the majority are Muslim or pagan preserving much of their Cushitic monotheistic religion centring in the cult of the sky god (*Waq*). Descent is patrilineal and all the Galla have a highly developed cyclical system of age sets (*gada*) with important political functions and presided over by the Abba Boku or "father of the sceptre." This type of organization is entirely lacking among the Somali to whom the Galla are closely related. (6) The Sidama are a congeries of peoples representing an early Cushitic stock which, prior to the Galla incursions of the 16th century, occupied most of southern Ethiopia. They number about 1,500,000 and are concentrated in southwestern Ethiopia, bordered to the west by the Nilotes and to the north and east by the Galla. Agriculture is strongly developed, the ox-drawn plow being generally used, and in some places there is irrigated terrace cultivation. Descent is patrilineal and marriage mainly virilocal. Most of the Sidama have a monarchical type of political system which is most elaborate in the traditional structure of the Gibe, Janjero and Kafficho states which were ruled by divine kings. (*See* also Cushitic Peoples; Falashas; Saho-Afar; Galla; Janjero.)

Negroid Groups.—(1) The Baria (Barea) and Kuṇama: these groups situated in the Barentu region of southwest Eritrea number about 15,000 and are sedentary agriculturists who were formerly regularly raided by the Beja and other neighbouring peoples. The Baria are patrilineal and solidly Muslim, while the Kunama are matrilineal and mainly pagan. (2) Beni Shangul: this term is used by the Arabic-speaking tribes of the Sudan to refer to a group of agricultural tribes living in Ethiopia between the Blue Nile and the Sudan frontier. They are called by the Ethiopians *Shanqela* (a term applied to Negroes in general) and are an islamized segment of the Berta of the Sudan. (3) Bantu and Swahili-speaking communities of southern Somalia: these are predominantly Negroid but partly hamiticized tribes living among the Somali, especially in pockets along the Webi Shebeli and Juba rivers. They are Muslims like their stronger Somali neighbours, to whom they are allied, and are essentially cultivators. They number about 80,000 and represent the remains of the pre-Hamitic population which before the Galla and Somali invasions formerly occupied this region. *See* Saho-Afar.   (I. M. L.)

C. West Africa

South of the western Sahara desert from Dakar on Cape Verde (Senegal) to Lake Chad about 2,500 mi. to the east, West Africa extends southward for about 1,000 mi. to the Guinea coast of the Atlantic ocean. This extensive region, which is divided among many territories, is far from uniform in physical conditions or in the culture and social organization of its peoples. But, as will be seen, important and widespread internal developments, often under the impact of prolonged external influences, have given it a character of its own. The greater part of the interior (generally known as the Western Sudan) is tropical savanna or orchard bush, covered with waist-high grass during the summer rains and studded with low trees. To the north along the lower Senegal river, the bend of the middle Niger and in the region of Lake Chad, trees give place to thorn bush. The grass is thin and short-lived, and disappears in the sands and bare rock of the Sahara. But 700 mi. farther south the savanna merges insensibly into the rain forests of the coastal belt which, but for human intervention, would extend almost continuously for a depth of about 200 mi. behind the surf-beaten shores and mangrove swamps.

This north-south gradation of climate and vegetation gives a beltlike character to the West African environment. Between the open interior and the forested coastlands there have been marked contrasts in opportunities for human settlement, external contact and cultural development. To the north the Sahara has been no complete barrier. For at least 2,000 years there has been continuous, if restricted, communication between the Western Sudan and the ancient and later Muslim cultures of North Africa. On the south from the end of the 15th century, the hitherto empty beaches and mangrove swamps of the coast, which had so long been ultimate limits to movement and settlement in West Africa, became the sites of European trading posts, through which direct contact with western mercantile civilization has been established for over 400 years. Thus on both the northern and southern flanks the lure of gold, ivory, tropical products and slaves has long sustained external trade and political relations, stimulating complex but very different cultural and social developments in the two zones.

Peoples and Languages.—There are, however, common features which indicate long prehistoric periods of internal development, diversification and expansion. Thus, despite very considerable variation in physical types, the overwhelming predominance of Negroid characters ultimately links all the peoples of this area with the rest of tropical Africa. Moreover, the great majority of the hundred or more languages of West Africa appear to have been diversified from a common stock generally known as Western Sudanic. Only to the east in the country from the Niger bend to Lake Chad have languages like Hausa, which belongs to the Northern Hamito-Semitic group, and Kanuri, which is similar to the Saharan languages of the central oases, spread deeply into the Western Sudan. The internal groupings of the Western Sudanic languages suggest an early cultural separation of the populations which spread into and through the forest belt from those occupying the savannas to the north. Among the former, over a distance of 1,000 mi. from Liberia to beyond the lower Niger, although individual languages unintelligible to outsiders are sometimes confined to a few thousand people, linguistic studies have revealed underlying similarities of vocabulary and structure that justify their grouping into a single family known as Kwa languages. This in turn suggests the proliferation through the forest belt of early communities stemming for the most part from a single stock. It points also to the obstacles which the forests presented to large-scale penetration from the north. Although later intrusions of far-reaching cultural importance occurred in some areas, these appear to have been confined to small if dominant groups that were absorbed linguistically by the local populations. Only in the west did northerners penetrate in large numbers to establish petty chiefdoms like those of the Mende of Sierra Leone, which carried Mande languages from the Western Sudan right down to the coast.

Most of the Western Sudanic languages of the wider savanna zone also fall into a few major and divergent groups; broadly speaking each occupies a block of country extending across it from the desert to the forest margin. In the upper basins of the Senegal and Niger, the widespread group of Mande languages predominates. Linguistic and other cultural distributions show that the Mande-speaking peoples such as the Mandingo (*q.v.*) and Bambara of Senegal and Mali, most of whom share a tradition of military organization under strong chiefs, have in the course of time expanded at the expense of other stocks to the west and east. This expansion, which was still in process at the time of European pacification, corresponds to the main sphere of influence of a vigorous civilization that the medieval Arab chroniclers described as long established in the Western Sudan. (*See* also Sudanic Languages.)

Forest Belt, Mode of Life.—An early and important cultural differentiation between these zones is also reflected in modes of subsistence. The forest people were and have remained hoe cultivators depending basically on root crops, yams and cocoyams and fruits, especially varieties of the cultivated banana, supplemented by semicultivated tree crops, notably the oil and raffia palms and the cola tree. Hunting and trapping, although now much reduced, were prominent in the traditional economy but livestock was confined to small numbers of fowl, goats, pigs and in a few areas dwarf cattle attached to the household. There was no continuous loom weaving, fabrics being made of raffia and pandanus matting and beaten bark cloth. Iron tools were scarce but available to most peoples by traffic from scattered centres of ore smelting. On these depended not only more efficient forest clearing and cultivation, but also well-developed woodworking crafts, the products of which included massive assembly houses, stools, slit gongs, drums, statuary and masks for which distinctive aesthetic canons developed among different peoples. Pottery, which was also generally available, was often traded over considerable distances from specialized centres of production.

The development of this forest economy appears to have depended on early introductions from the east since the main crops, the domestic goat and fowl, and the crafts of bark cloth and raffia matting are also widespread among the forest people of central Africa and most are ultimately of south Asian origin. But some important local additions were made; notably the cultivation and improvement of two local species of yam. In the west, from Gambia to Liberia, rice was also established as both a rain and swamp crop, a development which is perhaps explained by the fact that rice had early been introduced, possibly across the Sahara, as a riverain crop along the upper Niger, where it could have been carried south into the wet forests.

Social and Political Organization.—Apart from a few more complex state organizations ascribed by their own traditions to incursions from the north and some later developments of trading oligarchies on the coast in response to commerce with Europeans, indigenous political organization in the forest belt has been small in scale, remaining rooted in ties of neighbourhood and kinship. Communities of only a few hundred strong were often virtually autonomous, each with its own organization of groups of kinsmen in an internal system of authority. Their relations with one another were not regulated from above but depended on mutual obligations and alliances maintained by traditions of common descent and intermarriage, ratified by collective ceremonies and feasts and economic exchange. Such ties were liable to disruption and realignment by rivalries and mutual suspicions that could lead to hostilities.

A system of lineages, whereby a body of kinsmen in one line of descent maintained collective claims to resources, co-operating and competing with similar groups for various ends, appears everywhere to have provided the first order of political organization within a locality. Among some peoples, like most of the Ibo and Ibibio of eastern Nigeria who were dispersed in small compounds or hamlets, this lineage grouping operated to unite smaller or larger bodies of kin according to the activity or issue involved. There were often fertility and other cults whose priests had ritual and moral authority to declare, and prescribe remedies for, breaches of custom in an area. But the larger groups which were united on occasion in defending their rights against more distant kin, themselves dissolved into ever smaller units on narrower issues; so that the authority of elders to mobilize and represent a following and to settle disputes among them by arbitration or threat of retaliation varied according to circumstances and size of groups which opposed or competed with one another.

Among peoples who congregated in compact villages separated geographically and socially from one another, there was usually a more definite local organization, including a village council variously composed of the priests of village cults, the leaders of local men's associations or of senior age groups, which directed village affairs and settled disputes between the kin groups holding rights in land and other resources. Political relations between such villages were often those of give and take between independent groups. But whether the social organization was one of proliferating lineages or of independent villages, communication through trade, intermarriage and ceremonial exchanges could maintain common speech, custom and pattern of organization over populations of several thousands. Despite the small size of the independent political units, technical skills, aesthetic styles, beliefs and rituals, as well as valued commodities, could be and were transmitted over wide areas.

FRANCIS THOMPSON LTD.

LOADING AVODIRE TIMBER AT FOSO IN SOUTHERN GHANA

Thus, while most of the forest peoples lived in small self-contained communities, persistent if slow diffusion of techniques and ideas, as well as territorial expansion under favourable conditions, can account for the fact that their cultures show many common elements in technology, art, beliefs and institutions.

But in some parts of the forest belt, notably among the Akan-speaking peoples of Ghana and the Ivory Coast and the Yoruba and Edo (Beni) of southwest Nigeria, both technical skills and the form and scale of political organization were far more elaborate. Thus the Akan, as the records of travelers from the 18th century show, had long been organized in states with a hierarchical organization and complex ritual focused on a sacred chief in whom political as well as religious authority was vested. Prompted by the opportunities for enrichment by control of trade to the north, and later with Europeans on the coast, some states secured dominance over others which they organized in military confederations. Of these, Ashanti, which united the greater part of the forest belt of Ghana, in the 18th and 19th centuries was the best known and most powerful. The Akan languages belong to the Kwa group of the forest belt and most of their crafts and religious beliefs are characteristic of that zone. But the older Akan states lay on the savanna borders, and all ascribe their origins to the successive hiving off of state after state from more northern centres.

Before the arrival of Europeans in West Africa, chiefdoms had also been established among the Yoruba in the forests right down to the Guinea coast, and among the Edo to the east in the kingdom of Benin. According to their own traditions these too had been formed by the repeated hiving off of members of the chiefly houses and their followers to found new chiefdoms on the model of the old. The old capital of Oyo, which was paramount in the 18th century, lay north of the forests and the founders of the first chiefdoms were believed to have come from the north.

Despite variations in detail, whether in craft or social organization, the techniques and skills characteristic of such chiefdoms present a remarkable contrast to those of the rest of the forest belt. Cotton was usually grown for weaving, the high status of the chief and other officeholders was marked by elaborate robes, ornaments and headgear. Bronze, brass, gold and precious stones were used to fabricate ceremonial objects; extensive buildings were erected for the court. Towns were protected by wide ditches and walls; armies were raised for conquest and defense. The subsistence economy and many elements of the ancestral and other spirit cults among their peoples were similar to those of other forest communities and there was some diffusion of particular crafts, customs and beliefs among other groups who were not fully incorporated into state organizations. Nevertheless, the association of these centralized political systems in the forest zone with sacred chiefship and new crafts justifies acceptance of their traditions of northern origins, even though archaeological and documentary evidence is so far lacking.

Western Sudan, Modes of Life and Political Organization.—The peoples of the savannas of the Western Sudan are predominantly grain cultivators as contrasted with the root- and fruit-growing peoples of the forests. Their essential agricultural tool (the broad-bladed, short-handled hoe) is the same, but their food staples and patterns of farming belong to a different tradition. Cereals, including *Sorghum, Pennisetum* and *Eleusine,* are their food staples, although a wide range of subsidiary field and tree crops is obtained. These two West African farming traditions were combined in some areas along the forest margins. This may well be the result of later interpenetrations such as the extensive but comparatively recent northward expansion of the Tiv into the orchard bush of the Benue valley in Nigeria. Originally, however, they appear to have been separate. Thus the early linguistic divergence of the language families of the forest belt and the savannas may well have been associated with these two distinct patterns of cultivation and the separate westward expansions of agricultural populations that they made possible.

Moreover, there appear to have been several phases of agricultural development within the savanna zone as additional crops and associated crafts were established in some areas. Thus there is great variation among its peoples in technical skills. Among some there persisted until recently a more primitive economy with a less productive agriculture, lacking textiles and dependent on sporadic trade for iron tools. Some of these people grew only inferior grains such as *Digitaria.* Others, although they cultivated several kinds of the better-yielding millets, merely dibbled in the seed and weeded with light hoes. Such peoples living dispersed in small hamlets or clustered in hill villages for protection, had no central organization of government. As in the forest belt the kin groups or the village communities of a locality allied themselves or disputed with each other on equal terms as occasion arose. Societies of this type are to be found in the more remote areas in many parts of the Western Sudan, as for example in the interior of Guinea and Liberia, the northern territories of Ghana, the north of Dahomey and the hill country of northern Nigeria and the Cameroons region.

Many other peoples, however, such as the Hausa and Kanuri of northern Nigeria or the Mandingo and Bambara of Mali (former French Sudan) and other territories, have practised a much more elaborate agriculture. With deep hoeing and ridge cultivation they raised a wide variety of grain and other crops, sometimes by irrigation. The level of agricultural production was correspondingly higher and could normally provide a surplus for trade and tribute. Cotton was generally grown to supply the weavers who were but one among a variety of specialist craftsmen. These populations have also long been organized in centralized chiefdoms which, while varying greatly in size from extensive empires to much smaller areas, shared many basic features of organization and ceremonial. Authority was concentrated in the ruler who, with his councilors and nobles, constituted a hereditary aristocracy often by tradition of conquest. The ranking and subordination both of offices and of classes was expressed in an elaborate etiquette. Slaves, whose numbers were continually augmented by periodic raiding of the more primitive peoples and by warfare between states, were important as a class not only for providing farm labour on the big estates, but as trusted and often powerful agents of their masters at all levels from the chief downward. The more primitive tribes of dispersed kin groups and isolated villages had for centuries been subject to conquest, slave raiding and incorporation by expanding chiefdoms. In many areas only small remnants had survived in independence at the time of European intervention at the end of the 19th century.

Impact of Islam.—The rulers and most of the populations of many chiefdoms have been at least nominally Muslim for many centuries. But both the chronicles of medieval North Africa and of the Western Sudan itself and modern ethnographic studies show that while the adoption and promotion of Islam have been potent factors in the growth of later chiefdoms, many of the basic ideas and customs associated with chiefship and other social relations are much older, and that in varying degrees, elements of pre-Islamic rituals and social codes have persisted. The earliest accounts of these ancient chiefdoms and empires are those of Muslim Arabs who crossed the western Sahara in the 10th and 11th centuries to report vivid if fragmentary impressions of the empire of Ghana which already extended from the Senegal to the upper Niger and to an unknown extent southward into the gold-bearing highland and forest. It claimed a history of many centuries at that time and its ruler was a sacred figure possessed of supernatural powers and the centre of elaborate ritual. The authority of the state was extended over a wide area by means of a standing army and control of vassal chiefs. Tribute was collected from its provinces, dues were levied on trade and there was a state monopoly of the traffic in gold from the south which appears to have been all important in sustaining the trans-Saharan caravan traffic. The early Muslims who came from North Africa were welcomed as merchants and advisers but were kept apart from the political and ceremonial life of this pagan kingdom. It was not until late in the 11th century that the Almoravid Berbers immediately to the north conquered part of Ghana and began the imposition of Islam. By the early 14th century, when this region was visited and described by Ibn Khaldun, Mali or Mande (Mandingo) had replaced Ghana as the centre of empire with an essentially similar but Muslim state organization. Many of the rulers of Mali made the pilgrimage to Mecca and it maintained diplomatic and scholarly as well as commercial relations with the Arab world until it in turn dwindled to a vassal chiefdom in the 17th century after the rise of the Songhai (Sonrhaï) empire based on the middle Niger.

Although contemporary records do not go back so far, pre-Islamic foundations for states that were early established on the Niger bend and in the region of Lake Chad are claimed in later chronicles. The traditions of Kanem-Bornu in the latter area ascribe its foundation to northern immigrants at least two centuries before the introduction of Islam in the 11th century. By the 13th century this empire controlled the chiefdoms that had been established among the Hausa to the west and extended northward into the Saharan oases of Fezzan (in Libya). An established route by way of the Bilma oases was regularly used by North African caravans and provided the main link with the outside world until the end of the 19th century. For, despite many vicissitudes, the kingdom of Bornu maintained itself until it became part of Nigeria (*see* Bornu; Kanem).

The widespread adoption of Islam in the many chiefdoms and successive empires that controlled different parts of the Western Sudan strengthened commercial and cultural links across the Sahara. But the first development of more productive agriculture and elaborate crafts, the specialization of occupations and the development of trade, are likely to have been associated with an earlier establishment of ruling aristocracies and administrative government before the Arab conquest of North Africa and the subsequent penetration of Islam into the Western Sudan. This is consistent too with the character and traditions of chiefdoms of the southern margins of the savanna and the forest belt. The Akan, the Yoruba and the chiefdoms of the southern Cameroons region knew of Islam only through traders and later military incursions from the north. But they ascribed their founders to earlier arrivals from older centres there.

Thus the emergence of the more complex cultures and political systems of the Western Sudan and of parts of the forest belt is linked with the early practice of superior crafts as well as elaborate doctrines whereby the authority of chiefs is derived from their supernatural powers as incarnations of gods or ancestors. Some of these traditions have individual parallels in the crafts and rituals of the ancient east whose beginnings go back before the 2nd millennium B.C. Although evidence of the processes of early cultural diffusion from the ancient east to western Africa is meagre in the extreme, such clues as are available point to intermittent incursions and traffic by way of North Africa and the oases of the central and western Sahara. And it is probable that early in the 1st millennium A.D., if not before, large chiefdoms had already been established in several parts of the Western Sudan. The domesticated camel, which was first introduced into North Africa at this time and provided the means of carrying men and goods in large numbers across desert country may have greatly reinforced this development. The introduction of the horse and donkey were also of key importance for political organization and long-distance trade within the Western Sudan. Horses provided the means for the concentration and rapid movement of military force, administrative control over provinces and vassals and raiding into distant areas for slaves. The modern ceremonial horse-riding displays in the northern chiefdoms and the elaborate Yoruba carvings of chiefs on horseback amid their wives and dependents are still symbols of chiefly power and recall the former importance of the horseman as the key to political control. The economical donkey afforded a great advance on human porterage for the transport of harvests and goods from farm to granary and from villages to central markets and storehouses.

The Hausa chiefdoms in northern Nigeria came under the control of local leaders of a remarkable and alien people at the beginning of the 19th century. Known there as the Fulani, they conquered and united in an empire based on their new capital Sokoto the Hausa states and several other peoples of this region in the course of a holy war (*jihad*) for the purification and re-establishment of Islam. These ancestors of the chiefs and nobles of the Nigerian emirates who are of Fulani descent came from tribes of a distinctive pastoral people who are found dispersed across the Western Sudan from Senegal to the Cameroons region where most of them have lived for centuries in small scattered groups. Their initial expansion was not by conquest but through a slow dispersion of migrant cattle-herding groups keeping to the outskirts of the chiefdoms to whose peoples they were often linked in the exchange of products. Lighter-skinned and non-Negroid in appearance, their common language (Fufulde) suggests that they began to spread less than 1,000 years ago from the region of the lower Senegal river. As pastoralists they long remained pagans, but some groups in the west embraced Islam with fanaticism in the 17th century. From among these, Muslim teachers and leaders gained influence in several areas to capture or found Fula-governed chiefdoms on the Senegal, the Niger and in the Futa highlands of Guinea, as well as in Nigeria. They were outstanding among the great chieftains whom the French and British encountered in the interior at the end of the 19th century. But their pastoral cousins have continued to herd their cattle from migrant camps in the remote bush.

European Influence on Coastal Chiefdoms.—Quite independently of the trans-Saharan stimulus, the European trading posts established on the Guinea coasts also from the 16th century onward offered new opportunities which profoundly affected cultural patterns and political organization along parts of the coastal belt. The traders provided muskets and gunpowder which, with the European demand for slaves, fostered the growth of larger and militarized chiefdoms there. Slave raiding and trading became the new means to power. Inland chiefdoms like Akwamu, Ashanti, Dahomey and Oyo fought for control of routes from the interior to the coast and sought to dominate its peoples. Benin temporarily achieved hegemony over most of the coast of western Nigeria. In the lagoons of the Niger delta, on the Calabar river and elsewhere small fishing communities were slowly transformed by leaders who built up bodies of kinsmen and slave dependents for their fleets of canoes to monopolize the creeks and organize the traffic in slaves and later in palm oil. Thus there grew up miniature trading empires composed of wealthy and competing houses as in Bonny and Old Calabar in Nigeria and Grand Bassam in Ivory Coast, which carried commerce and new forms of political organization into the forested hinterland.

Among such peoples as the Efik and Ibo of eastern Nigeria and also among some forest chiefdoms, such as the Yoruba and Mende in Sierra Leone, religious cult groups (into which some or all of the men were initiated) developed considerably under the stimulus of increasing wealth from raiding and trade as political forces that both supported and curbed the authority of elders or chiefs. At the same time these secret societies organized elaborate rituals that included dramatic public performances in which ancestral and other spirits were portrayed by elaborately masked dancers. Masks used in such rites are among the better-known examples of West African woodcarving. This art, which also includes statuary and other forms and played a great part in chiefly ceremonial, had, as is clear from Yoruba and Benin, a long history. Indeed it is part of an older and more widespread African tradition that existed to the east throughout the Congo basin and to the north in the savannas. Although some conventions, symbols and decorative elements are widespread, a multitude of highly distinctive local styles have developed among different peoples, giving a character of great richness and diversity to the West African art which has so greatly influenced styles and theory in European art of the 20th century.

Many features of the older cultures and forms of social organization in West Africa are now, at the insistence of native peoples, being superseded by new patterns that reflect an increasingly rapid incorporation into the economic and political life of the modern world. But some of the traditional elements are still vigorous in all spheres of village life, and are manifest in periodic rites and festivals which express underlying beliefs and values.

See also AKAN; ASHANTI; BENIN; EDO; EFIK; FULANI; HAUSA; KANURI; IBIBIO; IBO; MENDE; TIV; YORUBA.   (D. F.)

D. EAST AFRICA

East Africa has been the meeting place of many ethnically diverse groups, most of them immigrants from the west and north. The environment varies considerably, and high population densities are found in only a few favoured areas where intensive agriculture can be practised; these are especially the northern and western shores of Lake Victoria and the highland areas near Mounts Kenya, Kilimanjaro, Elgon and Ruwenzori. Over most of the remainder of the region only shifting agriculture or herding is possible with traditional techniques.

The remnants of aboriginal non-Negro peoples are found in a few scattered and unfavourable places, to which they have been driven by later immigrants. A few thousand people known as Dorobo or Okiek still live in the forests of the mountainous parts of Kenya and eastern Uganda, gathering forest products and speaking the language of their more powerful neighbours (usually Nandi and Kikuyu). In western Uganda there are a few hundred pygmies, and in the Lake Eyasi basin in northern Tanganyika there are about 600 hunters called Hadzapi or Tindiga. They speak a Bushmanlike language and have been thought to be a northern remnant of the Bushmen of whom only those that migrated to southern Africa survive in large numbers (see *Southern Africa,* below).

The aboriginal tribes were probably once dispersed over wide areas of East Africa, and were driven into their present habitats (and also absorbed by intermarriage) by immigrants. Most of the latter were Negroes from the west and north, although there have been non-Negro invasions from the northeast and Arab, Indian and European contact from the coast. The history of early immigration into the region is confused and uncertain, resulting from lack of adequate archaeological and documentary information. Most knowledge comes from linguistic studies and from traditional oral legends which provide little sound material for historical reconstruction.

The earlier immigrants were almost certainly Bantu-speaking Negroes from the west or northwest. They are primarily agriculturists, usually with grains as their staples (traditionally millets and sorghums, but later maize in most areas); they keep livestock where this is possible. They certainly brought a knowledge of ironworking with them. It seems likely that most of their differences, in both culture and social organization, are caused by differences of ecology and to the influences of later invaders, mainly from the north. The first of these later immigrants were probably Sudanic-speaking peoples from the region of Lake Chad, now represented only by the Lugbara (244,000) and Madi (67,000) of northwestern Uganda. They have had little influence on the rest of East Africa, although some observers have detected a substratum of Sudanic culture among many southern Uganda tribes. The Sudanic tribes are agriculturists, with little interest in cattle, and lack any developed form of political authority. Later came the Nilotic-speakers, known generally as Lwoo, who moved southward up the Nile valley from the Sudan. In the vanguard of the movement were the Luo (Lwo) of western Kenya (757,000), who were followed by the various Nilotic groups in Uganda (Lango [*q.v.*], Acholi, Alur, in all 654,000); and there are others still in southern Sudan. They are traditionally cattle keepers, with great cultural emphasis on the values associated with cattle, although the modern southern Nilotes of East Africa are all agriculturists. All those in East Africa, with the exception of the Alur, lack any formal political authority and are organized largely in strongly patrilineal descent groups (lineages and clans). Both Sudanic and Nilotic Negroes are tall and extremely dark people, renowned for their physical strength and generally regarded as "savages" by their Bantu neighbours to the south.

A further immigrant grouping consists of the many tribes speaking Nilo-Hamitic languages. These peoples are clearly physically of mixed Negro and non-Negro origin; they are often said originally to have been Hamites, although the precise ethnical connotation of "Hamite" (a linguistic rather than a racial term) is open to doubt. Traditionally all were transhumant pastoralists, despising agriculture. They occupy the floor of the Rift valley in Kenya and northern Tanzania (Masai, Nandi, Kapsigis, Turkana, etc.) and the drier regions to its west in northeast Uganda (Karamojong, Teso, etc.) and in southeast Sudan (Bari, Lotuko, etc.). In all they number almost 2,000,000. They all lack formal centralized political authority, but possess prophets such as the famous Masai *laibons;* all have an elaborate age-set system, based upon the initiation of boys by circumcision, the age sets providing the basis for an extremely efficient military organization. Some of them are settled agriculturists (especially the Teso, Nandi and Kipsigis) but most of them have turned their backs on European influence, preferring to retain their traditional dependence upon cattle herding. Many of them are dying out. (*See* Nilo-Hamites.)

In northern Kenya there are a few tribes of Hamitic speakers, especially Galla and Somali, numbering about 100,000; their influence has been negligible. And lastly, on a plateau in the Rift valley in northern Tanganyika is a cluster of tribes of which the largest is the Iraqw (103,000), whose language is said to show strong Semitic affinities and who seem ethnically to be quite unrelated to other peoples in the region.

The early history of East Africa is thus one of displacement of aboriginal tribes by Bantu peoples and then of the Bantu agriculturists by northerners, the Nilotes and Nilo-Hamites being the most important. The Bantu tribes near the invaders show differing degrees of influence. To the north and west of Lake Victoria is a cluster of kingdoms, the Lacustrine Bantu states, with a population of about 1,500,000 in Uganda. There something approaching a caste system is found, the state consisting of, originally, a non-Negro king and aristocrats exercising power over subordinate Bantu and pygmy servile classes. The aristocrats, known as Hima in the northern kingdoms (Nyoro, Toro, Nkole and Ganda, although they are no longer a distinct group in the last) and as Tutsi in the southern (Ruanda, Rundi and others) are tall fair-skinned people, keeping cattle of a type not found elsewhere in Africa and scorning the agriculture of their once servile peasants. The peasants are Bantu, known in the north as Iru and in the south as Hutu, who once provided tribute through a hierarchy of Hima–Tutsi chiefs set over them.

In some kingdoms pygmies known as Twa are found; they are hunters and gatherers and also provide bodyguards and soldiers for the aristocrats. The classes do not intermarry, although aristocrats take peasant concubines. All speak the Bantu languages of the peasants. It is generally accepted that the aristocrats came from the north, probably by the 12th century and before the Nilotic invasions mentioned above; they probably came from the region of the Ethiopian province of Kaffa. There is some evidence of Nilotic influence in the royal lines of the northern kingdoms, although the neighbouring Nilotic tribes do not possess kingship themselves. The influence of these invasions spread southward in an attenuated form to the peoples south of Lake Victoria (Ha, Nyamwezi, Fipa, numbering in all 750,000).

The Nilo-Hamitic invasions, down the line of the Rift valley, have affected the neighbouring Bantu peoples considerably. These are mainly tribes of agriculturists who have lived in uneasy relationship with their warlike pastoralist neighbours. Some, such as the Kikuyu (1,250,000) and Kamba (612,000) of Kenya, have adopted the age-set systems of the Masai. Clothing decorations and other features have also been affected, especially among the Gogo (271,000) who have intermarried with Masai and are in many ways similar to them (except in language).

All the Bantu peoples of East Africa are culturally fairly similar, although there are marked differences in some aspects of social organization and in size and density of population. Except for the Lacustrine kingdoms and the small tribe called Wanga in western Kenya, all lack traditional kingship, although the Chagga (237,000), the Sukuma (889,000) and several other tribes had a form of chieftainship. Almost all reckon descent patrilineally, but there are a few groups in southeast Tanganyika (Makonde 281,000, Makua 95,000, etc.) which trace descent matrilineally, through women only. These are part of a belt of matrilineal peoples stretching across Africa from Mozambique to Angola. There are a few matrilineal tribes on the coast (Digo, Bondei, etc.).

The influence of the outside world has always been felt at the coast. Arab city-states were founded at many places from Cape Guardafui to Kilwa in the early centuries of the Christian era, and persisted until weakened by the Portuguese in the 16th century. Later, Arab influence from Muscat became important as the power of the Portuguese waned, and in the 19th century Arab influence was considerable as far as the great lakes, as Zanzibar became the seat of the East African slave trade. The modern coastal population is distinct from that of the hinterland, and is known as Swahili, or in Zanzibar as Shirazi. It is ethnically and culturally mixed, with many Arab and Indonesian features, the latter from Madagascar; its language, Swahili, is basically Bantu but with much Arabic influence in its vocabulary. The coastal tribes are also mainly Muslim, which has further distinguished them from the peoples of the interior.

Indians have been settled in the coastal towns throughout their history and are found throughout East Africa, mainly as traders. Europeans are administrators, missionaries, settlers and traders, with an influence out of proportion to their relatively small numbers. The whole region was administered by European powers from the late 19th century. Intertribal warfare and raiding, such as that by the Masai of their neighbours, have been stopped. Non-traditional chiefly authorities have been created, with new roles and new sanctions for their position; where there were traditional rulers the basis of their authority has been changed and they have tended to become bureaucrats rather than primarily ritual leaders.

Much in traditional religion has been changed: either tribes have become Christian or indigenous religious beliefs and practices have died out without being replaced. The introduction of cash crops (especially of cotton and coffee), of cash markets for livestock and for labour in new enterprises, and the possibility of movement between tribal areas, have all affected the traditional economic and social systems. A formerly egalitarian standard of living, with few marked differences of status, is giving way to a situation in which there are considerable differences of wealth and of political power. An incipient class system is emerging, based mainly upon the larger towns.

The over-all picture is one of a few wealthy, densely populated and "progressive" areas, interspersed with areas of comparative poverty and social stagnation. The progressive and wealthy areas include southern and parts of eastern Uganda where wealth is based largely upon cotton and coffee; the Kavirondo area of Kenya; the Kikuyu highlands; the Chagga area of Kilimanjaro; and to a less extent parts of the coast. In all these what is usually called detribalization is taking place, with loss of narrow tribal loyalties and the appearance of new political and class movements. From the poorer and more rural areas there is often considerable emigration, especially of men who move away for a year or two as labourers in the industrial centres and then return to their homes; this has led to a degree of breakdown of traditional tribal life. These are all features characteristic of rapid social and economic change, part of the process of change from tribal subsistence small-scale societies to a wider-scale society based upon a cash economy. *See also* BANTU (INTERLACUSTRINE); CHAGGA; GANDA; HAMITE; KAMBA; KAVIRONDO; KIKUYU; LUGBARA; LUO; MADI; MAKONDE; MASAI; NANDI; NYAMWEZI; NYORO; PYGMY; RUNDI; SANDAWE; SUKUMA; SWAHILI LANGUAGE; TESO. (J. F. M. M.)

E. WEST CENTRAL AFRICA

The following areas may be included in this region: the Cameroons region, Chad, the Central African Republic (Ubangi-Shari), Gabon, Republic of Congo (former Middle Congo), Democratic Republic of the Congo (former Belgian Congo), Angola north of the Kalahari, Zambia and Malawi. The habitat ranges from semidesert in northern Chad and southern coastal areas in the west to open woodlands (savanna) and tropical rain forest. The northern limits of dense forest are situated toward the 5th parallel, but there are grasslands and savanna in the eastern and southern Congo, Angola and Zambia. The peoples of this diverse area are heterogeneous. They include pastoral or agricultural Arabs in the north; pastoral seminomad or sedentary Fulani living as minorities or as dominant groups in the Cameroons region; pygmies in Gabon and the Congo republics; Sudanic-speaking tribes, including some Nilotes, in the northeast of the Democratic Republic of the Congo; and to the south and west many subdivisions of Bantu are found. Moreover, there are numerous ethnic mixtures which often make strict classifications difficult, while linguistic groupings do not coincide with racial or cultural ones.

Agriculture is of primary importance throughout the area; but hunting, fishing, food gathering and herding are also widely practised. Pure hunters survive among the pygmies; elsewhere, though dependent on an agricultural economy, some tribes have strongly preserved the outlook of hunters. The staple crops cultivated in different habitats are: millets and maize, roots (yams, manioc or cassava, taro and sweet potatoes), bananas and peanuts. The oil and the raffia palm are important in the forest regions. Bows and arrows, spears, throwing knives, knives, clubs and shields are found as weapons of war and the chase. Dwellings range from tents in the north and rudimentary shelters in the forest to quadrangular or round huts and rectangular houses. Settlements may be small and dispersed or large and compact; royal capitals and other towns occur among some tribes.

Social groupings often depend on descent systems that range from patrilineal to matrilineal and double; but residence is generally patrilocal although the practice of bride service may result in the temporary residence of husbands with their wives' families. Marriage payments (in iron, cattle and sheep) are common. In some areas exchange marriages predominate. Some societies are organized into larger or smaller chiefdoms; while in others, small autonomous village groups with a segmentary structure form the ultimate political units. Associations may have great political significance. Tribal or village initiation is general and may be accompanied by widely different forms of body markings. Besides a general belief in a supreme being, ancestral, skull and spirit cults are much developed. Islam has spread among certain northern tribes. Many of the tribes are renowned carvers and craftsmen practising ironworking, plaiting, basketworking and weaving.

The Cameroons Region.—The people of the northern Cameroons are subdivided into numerous small groups: some are culturally similar to the plateau tribes of northern Nigeria, whereas others are linked with groups from Chad or the Central African Republic. The Kirdi (pagan sedentary tribes), Bata, Bura, Vere, Mumuye, Chamba, Namshi, Kotopo, Mbum and Wute are the better-known peoples. Most peoples speak languages of the Adamawa-Eastern branch of the Niger-Congo family. Fulani are also present everywhere and are politically dominant in Adamawa. Shifting hoe cultivation is practised; some groups also keep cattle

and milk them. Bride service and elopement are very common. Most tribes have patrilineal descent, but some also stress matrilineal ties. Some groups have been incorporated by the Fulani into their chiefdoms.

The central Cameroons highlands are inhabited by peoples of diverse origins, such as Tikar (*q.v.*) and Nsaw, Bamum, Bamileke, Banen, Bafia, Bali. Linguistically some of them are Bantu (*e.g.*, Bafia); others are Sudanic (Bali). Most of those that have been called semi-Bantu have been shown by modern research to belong to the Bantu group. Culturally many are complex groups in which different elements have been combined. Thus the Bamum invaded some of the Bamileke and their ruling clan is said to be of Tikar origin. Agriculture is important, millet, maize, cassava and cocoyams being the staples. A few groups have small cattle, but these are not milked. Nearly all tribes of this area are patrilineal and patrilocal. Marriage payments are common, but simple marriage gifts with bride service do occur. The social organization is based upon a lineage system. Most people live in small compact villages or dispersed in neighbourhoods, but there are some large settlements. They are organized in chiefdoms of varying size, with sacred chiefs and special status attributed to queen mothers. Men's associations, often important, exercise military or police functions or are mainly religious in character. Cults of ancestors, twins and skulls are widespread. Some of these peoples (Bamum, Bamileke) are well-known artists and craftsmen working in wood, bronze and terra cotta. King Njoya of the Bamum invented a system of pictographic signs for writing (*c.* 1895).

The coastal area of the Cameroons is peopled by various Bantu-speaking groups, such as Kpe-Mboko, Duala, Limba, Tanga-Yasa, which are linked by common myths of origin. They are fishermen, but cultivation and cattle keeping are not unknown. Settlements may be small and dispersed or concentrated. The Duala are famous traders. There is generally some stress both on patrilineal and matrilineal descent and some tribes have a clear-cut double descent system; virilocal residence is general. Marriage payments (goats) are common. The social organization is of the segmentary type and leaders are often merely village headmen. But some groups (Duala) have developed larger chieftaincies. Dance associations are prominent and there are cults of ancestors and water spirits.

The southern Cameroons are inhabited by Bakoko, Ngumba, Mabea, Bulu, Beti and the larger Fang (*q.v.*) group which also extends into Gabon. There are also some pygmies. The progressive expansion of the Fang has often disrupted earlier tribal organization and Fang influences have been profound. (*See also* BAMILEKE; BAMUM; DUALA; NSAW; KPE.)

Chad.—In the Republic of Chad a large number of groups which present varied aspects of language, origins and modes of life may be distinguished. A mosaic of small tribes of Negro origin was overrun and broken up by waves of invading peoples, including Arabs, Fulani and Kanuri-speakers. The northern parts are inhabited by people of Kanuri linguistic stock, such as Teda, Daza, Bideyat, who are seminomadic herders (camels and cattle). Agriculture (date palms, millet) is left to the descendants of ancient captives, and hunting to some specialized groups. Descent is either bilateral or double, but residence is virilocal. Political organization does not extend beyond autonomous local communities or small chiefdoms. They are partly pagans and partly Muslims.

More or less pure Arab groups (Ouled Sliman, Ouled Rashid) are dispersed throughout the Teda area. Farther south are the heterogeneous peoples of the old kingdoms (Kanem [*q.v.*], Bagirmi, Wadai, Bulala, Kotoko). Some speak independent languages, others belong to Chadic, Kanuri (*q.v.*) and Central Sudanic linguistic stocks. They practise hoe cultivation; most groups keep cattle and fishing is important along the rivers. Descent is patrilineal and residence patrilocal. Social stratification is complex and the political organization is strongly centralized. There are compact villages and towns. Arab groups (Ouled Rashid) are particularly numerous in Wadai and Bagirmi. On the Lake Chad islands, in the marshy regions and in the mountainous areas there are also isolated groups of heterogeneous origin which

PAUL ALMASY
CATTLE AT A MEAT-PACKING PLANT IN FORT-LAMY, REPUBLIC OF CHAD

have been forced back by conquest. The Yedina are fishermen and herders; the Kinga and Dadjo are agriculturists and herders. They are patrilineal and seem to be organized in small chieftaincies. The southern areas of Chad are inhabited in part by Logone populations (Mbum, Mundang, Masa) and by the more numerous Sara group. The term Sara refers to a mosaic of agricultural patrilineal tribes who also keep cattle and camels.

Central African Republic.—The Central African Republic (formerly Ubangi-Shari) is peopled by Sudanic-speaking groups that suffered heavily from slave raiding during earlier centuries. There are some Sara and Wadai groups to the north and some Azande, Nzakara and riverain groups (Banziri, Buraka, Ngbaka, Ngbandi) along the Ubangi to the south. But the bulk of the population is formed by Mandja-Baya groups to the west and Banda to the east. The former are related to the Mbum and Wute of the Cameroons; the Banda are composed of a large number of small tribes which settled in these areas during the 19th century. Hoe cultivation (millet, maize) is developed throughout the area, but hunting, fishing and gathering have considerable importance. Descent is patrilineal and residence is virilocal. There are dispersed exogamous totemic clans, but the patrilocal extended family is basic to the social organization. Living generally in small dispersed settlements, they are subdivided into autonomous village groups with headmen and elders. Among the Azande, however, there are strong chiefdoms. Circumcision is not widely diffused, but girls' initiations are common. Ancestral cults, beliefs in semihuman fabulous heroes and closed associations are very general. (*See* AZANDE.)

Gabon.—In northern Gabon live the Fang, who seem to constitute a special group within the Bantu linguistic family. They migrated from the northeast in mid-19th century and settled in forest areas which were occupied by pygmies (Babinga) and Bantu groups (Mekae, Ngumba, Njem). These and other surrounding tribes are strongly influenced by Fang culture. To the south of the Fang there are the Mpongwe who, with other smaller tribes, form the Omyene cluster. The other major groups are the Bakota to the northeast, the Shira to the southwest, the Okande to the centre and the Mbede-Nzabi to the east. The Fang and the other tribes which have been influenced by them are agriculturists (manioc, bananas, maize, palm trees) and gatherers, but hunting is important. Fang are renowned carvers in wood and steatite. They are patrilineal and patrilocal. Settlements are small; there is no central political organization. Fang are both egalitarian and competitive; rich people are looked upon with suspicion. Their associations have a marked religious or magical character.

Republic of Congo.—In this country, the former Middle Congo, the following clusters may be noted: the Sanga, the Njem (Bakwele) who are influenced by the Fang; the Bangi; the Bateke and Bakongo, including many subdivisions; there are also pygmies. Some links between Bakongo and Bateke exist; Shira have come under the influence of Bakongo. Some of these tribes

are also largely represented in adjoining parts of the Democratic Republic of the Congo (former Belgian Congo). They are agriculturists (manioc, bananas, palm trees, peanuts), but hunting and fishing are prominent among some of them. Most of them are very good carvers. Descent is patrilineal among the northern but matrilineal among the southern groups, and notably the Bakongo among whom residence was formerly avunculocal. The social organization is segmentary in type; there are no large chiefdoms, although the Bakongo once formed part of the powerful Kongo chiefdom (from the 1400s to the 1700s) and the Bateke have small chieftaincies.

All these tribes belong to different groups of the Bantu linguistic stock.

Democratic Republic of the Congo.—The savannas, grasslands and rain forests are peopled by substantially more than 200 tribes which claim widely different origins. Many of those on the margins are closely related to peoples of the former Middle Congo, the Central African Republic, and the Sudan, or of Angola, Zambia, Rwanda, Burundi and Uganda. The larger part of the tribes speak various Bantu languages, but there are also in the northern regions people of Sudanic linguistic stock and in the east and northeast a very few groups of Nilotic and Hamitic stock.

The tribes may conveniently be grouped into a number of cultural clusters the most important of which are: (1) Bakongo, Bateke and groups of Lake Leopold II, Bayaka-Basuku and Bapende clusters mainly in Kinshasa, Bandundu and Kongo-Central provinces; (2) Mongo, Ngombe, Ngbaka and Ngbandi clusters in Equateur province; (3) Azande, Meegye-Mangbetu, Mamvu-Balese, Bakumu-Babira, Babua, Balendu, Lugbara, Alur clusters in Uele, Kibali-Ituri and Haut-Congo provinces; (4) Banande, Bahunde-Banyanga, Bashi-Bahavu, Balgea-Babembe and lubaized clusters in Sud-Kivu province; (5) Baluba, Lunda-Chokwe, Babemba in Nord-Katanga and Sud-Katanga provinces; (6) Atetela, Bakuba-Bashilele, Baluba-Bambo, Bakete and Asalampasu clusters in Kasai-Occidental and Kasai-Oriental provinces.

It should be noted, however, that these clusters do not correspond exactly with the boundaries of the several provinces. The various pygmy groups, who may in all number up to 300,000 persons, are found in the rain forests and along the large belt of the Congo river.

Shifting hoe cultivation is practised everywhere by the other peoples, the staple crops according to the area being bananas, manioc (cassava), yams, millet and maize. But food gathering, hunting and fishing continue to play a very important role in the economic, social and religious life of many tribes. In the highlands of the eastern Congo there are some peoples with a mixed pastoral-agricultural economy. Most of the Congo peoples are organized by patrilineal descent and patrilocal residence. In the southwestern Congo, particularly in the Kinshasa and Kasai areas, several tribes have matrilineal descent groups with avunculocal or virilocal residence. A few tribes show features of double descent grouping. The Lunda have complex descent groups of bilateral composition. Ritually important clans which may be dispersed in varying degrees and corporate localized lineages are common. Minor lineages and extended families play a foremost part in the social organization. While all tribes accept polygyny, this may be very restricted or, as among Kuba, Luba or Azande chiefs, very elaborate. Widow inheritance is widely practised, as are the sororate and sororal polygyny. Cross-cousin marriage is less frequent. High marriage payments occur in most tribes, but exchanges of women, elopement and true purchase of women are also known.

Political organization ranges from small autonomous states with petty chiefs of a sacred nature and larger kingdoms with divine kings (Bakuba, Lunda) to states of the feudal type (Bashi) and military conquest states (Azande); from complex segmentary structures with or without special functions vested in lineages or closed associations (Atetela, Balega, Mayumbe) to small band organization (pygmies) and small autonomous villages or village groups (Bakumu, Mongo). Some tribes too, which are of the segmentary type were once organized in powerful states (Bakongo, Luba). Circumcision, tribal and youth initiations, closed associations and corporations are very widespread. Most tribes have a belief in a supreme being and in heroes; ancestral, twin and spirit cults are very general. Most Congo peoples are exceptional craftsmen. Ironwork (knives, spears, arrowheads, bracelets) attains an extraordinary variety. Masks are made in wood, ivory, bone, gourd and wicker; statues are made from the same materials, but some are also made in pottery or steatite. Outstanding carvings are known from the Luba, Bakuba, Bapende, Bayaka, Chokwe, Bakongo-Mayumbe, Balega, Benalulua and Asalampasu. (*See* also KONGO; KUBA; LUBA; LUNDA; MONGO; MAMVU.)

Angola.—In Angola the large Ovimbundu tribe occupies a central position on the Benguela highlands. North of them are the Ambundo and Kongo tribes which are related to groups of the southern Congo. To the east live the Imbangala, Songo, Chokwe, Lwimbe and Luchazi who are linked to tribes of the southern Congo and Zambia. To the south are localized cattle-owning tribes, like Nyaneka, Cipungu, Cilengi, Ambo. Many customs and institutions of the Angola peoples are comparable to those described for the Democratic Republic of the Congo. All groups speak various Bantu languages. They practise hoe cultivation, but hunting is important. Long-distance trading, especially between the coast and the interior, played a prominent role in the past centuries. Some tribes keep small herds of cattle.

Marriage payments are not usually high; polygyny is common and cross-cousin marriages are allowed. Descent is either matri-

CENTRAL PRESS LTD.

FISHERMEN PREPARING TO CAST THEIR NET ON LAKE KIVU IN THE DEMOCRATIC REPUBLIC OF THE CONGO

lineal or double; residence is patrilocal. Some groups, like Chokwe, are organized in autonomous villages; others like Ovimbundu, are divided into a number of independent or tributary chiefdoms under the control of paramount chiefs. Youths' initiations and circumcision masks are common among Chokwe, Luchazi and Ovimbundu. Earth and celestial gods are worshiped; cults of ancestors are much practised. *See* AMBO; CHOKWE; MBUNDU.

(D. P. Bi.)

F. CENTRAL AFRICA

Central Africa as here defined includes Zambia and Malawi. Most of the inhabitants of this region belong to the ethnic group known as the Central Bantu, although in Barotseland in northwestern Zambia or the Ngoni districts of Malawi there were intrusions of warrior bands from Basutoland and Natal respectively in the 19th century.

Zambia.—The inhabitants of the northeastern plateau of Zambia and the swamps of Lake Bangweulu include the dominant Bemba (*q.v.*; 150,000), widely dispersed over an area of around 20,000 sq.mi.; the Bisa, their neighbours on the west, south and east; the Unga and Twa, small tribes living in the swamps and

islands of Lake Bangweulu; and the Ushi on the plateau between Fort Rosebery and Kawambwa. The ruling group of the Lunda of the Luapula area south of Lake Mweru were also originally of the same stock as the Bemba. South of the Bemba country where the high plateau land begins to slope to the Zambezi plain are the Lala (50,000) and the Lamba (20,000). Similar in culture are the Kaonde (38,000) of northwestern Zambia and the Senga of the upper Luangwa valley. Groups of Lamba, Lala and Ushi are to be found over the border of the Democratic Republic of the Congo.

This group of tribes claim to be of Congo origin. They speak dialects so similar that they are all classed as Bemba at the Zambia copper mines where they go to work in large numbers. Like the peoples of the west central region they are predominantly agriculturists and, though livestock are occasionally kept in the regions free of tsetse fly, the ritual attitude to cattle found in parts of East and South Africa does not exist. Hunting was formerly an important activity but game is now nearly extinct. The soil of the northeastern plateau is poor and finger millet and cassava are the staple crops. The people are shifting cultivators, moving their villages every four to five years and sowing their millet in the ash beds formed by the burning of piled-up branches lopped from the savanna forest trees (*chitimene* system). No cash crop has been found for the area and the people now make money in the copper mines farther south. The emigration rate for adult males is 40%–60% in Bembaland.

The Central Bantu are predominantly matrilineal. Descent, clan affiliation and succession to office follow the matrilineal line. Marriage is matrilocal, at any rate initially, and the labour given by a bridegroom to his father-in-law is a more important element of the marriage contract than the passage of goods. The period of service varies from tribe to tribe and is now often replaced by money. The Bemba and kindred tribes are divided into matrilineal clans with totemic names. Girls' initiation ceremonies (*chisungu*) are characteristic of this group. All these people acknowledge the rule of hereditary chiefs, although only in the case of the Bemba (who dominated the region in the 19th century) and of the Luapula Lunda is there anything like a centralized state with a king or paramount chief ruling over lower chiefs. The *chitimukulu* ("paramount chief") of the Bemba had a court with titled councilors, army captains and executioners. Chiefs were believed to have supernatural powers by virtue of access to the ancestral spirits of the tribe and the *chitimukulu* must be classed as a "divine king" in Sir James Frazer's sense.

Other matrilineal tribes in Zambia are the plateau Tonga south of Mazabuka, a people without chiefs and organized on the basis of villages linked to rain shrines. They have girls' initiation ceremonies and also rites for boys. The Ila-speaking peoples on the Kafue river follow matrilineal clan descent but combine this with patrilocal marriage and patriarchal authority, a combination due, it is thought, to southern influences. Girls' initiation ceremonies are practised. The Ila are a cattle-keeping people formerly renowned as warriors. (*See* ILA-TONGA.)

In marked contrast to the organization of the Central Bantu was the kingdom of the Lozi (Barotseland) on the upper Zambezi plains, which had special treaty rights under Great Britain. The Lozi people (300,000) are formed of many ethnic groups. The original inhabitants, Aluyi, were conquered in 1810 by Kololo of Basutoland origin and, though the Aluyi ousted the Kololo chiefs in 1864, they continued to use their language. The kingdom was ruled by a paramount chief associated with a chief princess established in a secondary capital. The organization of titled ministers and councilors is elaborate. The country is divided into neighbourhoods centred around royal villages. There is no clan system but names are inherited by patrilineal descent. The Lozi follow a unique system of cultivation on mounds raised above the plains which are annually flooded by the Zambezi (*see* BAROTSE).

A group of Ngoni is settled in the Fort Jameson area of Zambia (*see* *Malawi*, below) and there are two patrilineal cattle-keeping peoples, the Mambwe and the Lungu, in the Abercorn area.

Malawi.—Inhabited by a complex mixture of tribes, the Arab influence was very marked in this region in the 19th century.

Some tribes such as the Nyanja and some of the Cewa were decimated by slave raids; others, such as the Yao, adopted Arab culture, became Muslim and engaged in slave raiding themselves. In 1835 the Ngoni, a group of Nguni (Zulu) scattered by Shaka's wars in Zululand, moved north and crossed the Zambezi. They raided the indigenous inhabitants and finally settled in what is now Malawi in a number of separate districts.

With the exception of these recent Ngoni immigrants, most of the Malawi peoples follow matrilineal succession and resemble the Bemba-Bisa-Lamba group in Zambia. They tend, however, to be organized in small independent village units under headmen rather than in chiefdoms. They can be roughly divided into the following groups: (1) The inhabitants of southwest Malawi, who have been called the Maravi group. These include the Nyanja (312,500), who are much interspersed with Ngoni and Yao; the Cewa (576,000), who constitute more than 60% of the population in five districts; the Nsenga (45,000), of whom the majority live in the Petauke district of Zambia; and the Cikunda (47,500), scattered among Nsenga and other peoples. This group is said to be of Congo origin and to have migrated earlier than the Bemba. Like them they are divided into matrilineal, totemic clans and practise matrilocal marriage. They hold elaborate girls' initiation schools (*vinyau*). (2) The peoples of northwest Malawi, such as the Tumbuka (110,000) and Tonga (50,500) who live on the western shores of Lake Nyasa; the Tonga are mainly fishing people. The history and ethnography of the area is confused and there has evidently been much movement of groups, mainly as the result of Ngoni raids. These are, however, all matrilineal peoples practising matrilocal marriage. They differ from the Maravi group in having no girls' initiation schools. (3) The peoples of eastern origin, such as the Yao (281,000), who are akin to the Makonde in Tanzania. The Yao had evidently achieved a dominant position in Malawi when missionaries arrived in 1876. They now live in the upper Shiré and south Nyasa districts, the Blantyre and Zomba districts, at Domira Bay on the west coast of the lake, and north of Dedza and in the east of the Ncheu district. The Yao were converted to Islam in the middle of the 19th century and took to trade and slave raiding. They are divided into matrilineal clans, practise matrilocal marriage and organize elaborate initiation ceremonies for girls, but they also circumcise boys. They grow maize and tobacco as cash crops. (4) The Ngoni (193,500) live in three chiefdoms in Malawi: Mombera in Tumbuka country, Ciwere in the Dowa district and Gomani in Dedza and Ncheu; but Mpeseni's Ngoni live around Fort Jameson in Zambia and there are further groups in Tanzania. The Ngoni language has now been adulterated or forgotten, but the Ngoni remember much of the historic tradition of their journey from the south and their military exploits. Their clan organization is patrilineal and they are strongly patriarchal. The political system is an adapted form of the old Zulu organization. All these areas of Malawi form labour reserves for Zambia, Southern Rhodesia and South Africa, but the rate of emigration among the Ngoni is particularly high. (5) The northern Nyasa group of people including the Ngonde and the Nyakyusa who live mainly over the Tanzania border. These people appear to be immigrants from the east. The Ngonde of Malawi number 62,000; they live in the mountainous country between Lake Nyasa and the Misuko hills. Their staple crop is the plantain but they now cultivate coffee. Cattle take a foremost place in the economy. The Nyakyusa peoples were divided into a number of independent chiefdoms. Among the Ngonde a paramount chief with divine powers was recognized. Characteristic of these cultures is the system of age-villages by which young boys build villages with their own age sets in adolescence and continue to live in them all their married lives. Descent and succession are patrilineal but there are no clans. *See* also Ngoni; Nyakyusa; Yao.

(A. I. R.)

G. Southern Africa

Grouping and Distribution.—The natives of southern Africa are conventionally classified into four major divisions: Bushmen, Hottentots, Bergdama and Bantu. The Bushmen, originally scattered throughout the region, are now found chiefly in the Kalahari desert and adjacent areas to the north and west. Numbering about 50,000, they are divided into many linguistic groups; the best known are the Auen, Naron, Kung and Heikum. The Hottentots are represented only by the Nama (30,000) in the southern half of South West Africa. Farther south and east there were formerly three other groups: Cape Hottentots, Eastern Hottentots and Korana. These have disappeared almost completely, partly because of the effects of war and disease but mainly as a result of absorption into the Cape Coloured and other mixed-blood communities of which they were a basic element. The Bergdama (40,000) live chiefly in the centre and north of South West Africa, to which in historical times they have always been confined. The Bantu, far more numerous and widespread, consist of the following four subdivisions:

Eastern.—Located in the coastal regions east of the Drakensberg mountains and south of the Sabi river, the Eastern division comprises two main clusters, Nguni and Tsonga. The Nguni (*q.v.*) includes the Cape Nguni (2,380,000) of the Ciskei and Transkei (Xhosa, Tembu or Thembu, Mpondo, etc., also the Fingo, fugitive remnants of tribes broken up in Natal during the great intertribal wars at the beginning of the 19th century); Natal Nguni or Zulu (*q.v.*; 2,048,000) of Natal and Zululand, with their offshoot the Ndebele (Tebele) of Southern Rhodesia; Swazi (410,000) of Swaziland and eastern Transvaal; and Ndebele (144,000) of central and northern Transvaal. The Tsonga (1,369,000), subdivided into Tsonga, Ronga and Tswa, are found chiefly in Mozambique, with offshoots in eastern and northern Transvaal.

Central.—This subdivision occupies most of the interior plateau north of the Orange river and west of the Drakensberg. It also comprises two main clusters: (1) Sotho, including the Southern Sotho of Lesotho (Basutoland) and adjoining districts (1,391,000), Tswana (Tlhaping, Rolong, Hurutshe, Kwena, Ngwaketse, Ngwato, Tawana, Kgatla, etc.) of Botswana (Bechuanaland) and western Transvaal (816,000) and Northern Sotho (Pedi and many others) of central and northern Transvaal (772,000). (2) Venda (133,000), a homogeneous cluster inhabiting the Soutpansberg district of northeastern Transvaal.

Shona Peoples.—These groups (over 1,000,000) of Southern Rhodesia and Mozambique are subdivided linguistically into Zezuru, Manyika, Karanga, Kalanga, Korekore and Ndau.

Western.—The fourth group comprises the Ambo (150,000) in northernmost South West Africa and the Herero (45,000) in central South West Africa and northwestern Botswana. The Ambo consist of several distinct tribes, notably Ndonga, Kwanyama, and Kwambi; the Herero are customarily divided into Herero, Mbanderu and Tjimba.

Physical Characteristics.—The classification given above is based partly on physical differences. As commonly visualized, the Bushmen are short and yellowish-brown, with wrinkled skin, "peppercorn" hair, low heads, broad flat faces, poorly developed bodies, slender limbs, small hands and feet. These features are especially typical of the southern groups (mostly extinct). The northern groups, mainly because of Bantu admixture, tend to be taller, darker, more muscular, longer and higher in head and face. The Hottentots closely resemble the southern Bushmen in colour and build, skin, hair and facial features, but are taller in stature, longer and narrower headed and somewhat more prognathous.

The Bergdama, in contrast, are of true Negro type; they are mostly very dark (often blue-black) and stocky, with woolly hair, long heads, broad flat noses, thick everted lips and strong prognathism. The Bantu are also basically of Negro stock, but because of early inbreeding with other African peoples vary greatly in appearance. They are, on the whole, taller and less sturdy than the Bergdama and often lighter in colour. Many Tswana, especially, are little darker than Bushmen. Sometimes too, notably among Zulu and Herero, they have narrower and higher noses, thinner lips and similar facial features.

Mode of Life.—Cultural distinctions do not coincide with either racial or linguistic divisions. (*See* Bantu Languages; Bushman Languages; etc.) Bushmen and most Bergdama live entirely upon the natural resources of their environment. The men hunt wild animals and birds, the women gather edible wild plants; other foods include many kinds of reptiles, rodents and insects (especially locusts and termites). Some Bergdama, however, also keep goats and grow tobacco and dagga (*Leonotis leonurus*), used mainly for barter. Hottentots and Bantu likewise eat many kinds of wild vegetables and fruits and depend largely upon hunting for meat. But they also keep cattle, sheep and goats, whose milk, either fresh or fermented, is part of their staple diet. The animals are seldom slaughtered except on ceremonial occasions, although all animals dying of disease or other causes are eaten. Everything connected with them is normally done by men and boys—Hottentots and Herero are exceptional in entrusting the milking to women. With the outstanding exception of the Herero, all Bantu (but not Hottentots) further cultivate sorghum, millet, maize and such minor crops as pumpkins, melons, peas and beans. From the cereals they make porridge (their usual daily food) and beer; the others are eaten either raw or cooked in various ways. Agriculture, done by means of hoes, is essentially women's work, though men clear new fields and occasionally help in other strenuous activities.

Because of the nature of their food supply, Bushmen and Bergdama are nomadic; whenever game and edible plants fail in their immediate vicinity, the group must move somewhere else. Their dwellings, often erected in a wide circle around a large tree, are usually flimsy bush screens or at best small hemispherical huts made of branches and grass. Hottentots and Herero are also nomadic, their arid environment forcing them to trek periodically in search of new grazing and water for their stock. Settlements among both peoples are circular in form, the huts surrounding a large open space in which the animals are kept at night. The Hottentots live in beehive huts made by covering a framework of slender poles with reed mats, and whenever camp is moved these are dismantled and transported on ox-back until needed again. Herero huts, abandoned when the owners move, are similar in shape but more solidly constructed. All other Bantu have relatively stable villages which, except sometimes among Tswana, are close to or even (as among Ambo) amid the fields cultivated by the inhabitants. The Nguni live in beehive huts, made typically of wattle and daub or wattle and thatch; elsewhere huts normally have a circular wall of wood or earth and a conical roof of thatched poles. The basic settlement pattern is generally similar to that of Hottentots and Herero. Kraals for livestock usually form part of the central enclosure, though in Bechuanaland and other arid regions the animals are kept mostly at grazing posts out in the veld.

Clothing varies considerably in detail, but is everywhere made chiefly of skins. All peoples also make household utensils of wood, skin and bone. Metalwork, in iron and copper, is confined to Bantu and Hottentots, though early writers say that some Bergdama also practised the art. Each household as a rule builds its own home and makes its own clothing and most of the other goods it uses. However, all metal objects are produced by specialist smiths, who barter them for cattle, grain, etc. Most ornaments and implements can also be exchanged for other commodities and are freely traded, both internally and between different communities. Among Bantu and Hottentots poor persons serve others as herdsmen, receiving milk and an occasional heifer in payment. Among Bantu beer and porridge are used widely as payment for labour and to satisfy social obligations toward kinsmen and neighbours. But nowhere do people depend solely on manufacture and trade for their livelihood; even smiths, magicians and other specialists carry on the same subsistence activities as the rest of the community, their special craft being an additional source of income.

Social and Political Organization.—Every major division consists of many independent political communities, each with its own territory and government. Bushman and Bergdama communities (bands) seldom contain more than 80 persons and often, especially among Bergdama, 30 or even fewer. Hottentot communities (tribes) generally have between 500 and 2,500 members each. Many Bantu tribes are no bigger, but in others, notably among Sotho, Nguni and Ambo, the population exceeds 50,000.

The members of a band are as a rule all related closely by kinship or affinity; those of a tribe are invariably of diverse origins and, as among Tswana, may even differ in culture, language and race.

The Bergdama band is a compact residential group. A Bushman band likewise camps together for at least part of each year. Hottentot tribesmen are, however, permanently dispersed over their territory, the men of each local group belonging typically to a single clan. The members of a Bantu tribe are also dispersed. Venda and most Sotho live in compact villages of from 10 to 50 different households; elsewhere each household normally occupies its own hamlet. The Tswana are unique in having relatively large settlements, some with more than 5,000 inhabitants; these are divided into wards under local headmen.

The basic social unit everywhere is the household, consisting typically of a man with his wife or wives and dependent children. Except among Bushmen, married children (especially sons) and their families are often also included. Polygyny is customary everywhere, though only Bantu practise it extensively. Few polygynists have more than two or three wives; among Bantu, however, four to six are not uncommon and some chiefs have many more. Marriages are usually arranged by parents in consultation with close relatives; several groups of Bantu formerly practised infant betrothal. Marriage among all Bantu except Ambo is legalized by a special "gift" of cattle to the bride's parents. There is no corresponding payment elsewhere. A wife normally settles in her husband's local group, though among Bushmen, Bergdama, Hottentots and some Tswana, he must live with her own people for a year or so immediately after marriage.

Hottentots and Bantu, but apparently not Bushmen and Bergdama, also have unilateral descent groups of various kinds. The most widespread is the lineage. The Ambo are matrilineal, all others patrilineal except the Herero, who have a double descent system. Bantu (but not Hottentot) lineages are often subdivided into localized sections, which rank according to seniority of descent. Among Hottentots, Nguni and Tsonga lineages are all component units of exogamous nontotemic clans, whose members (except among Hottentots) are usually widely dispersed. Sotho and Venda lineages belong to much larger totemic groups, which cut across tribal boundaries; among Venda, but not Sotho, people with the same totem were considered relatives and formerly could not intermarry. Shona and Ambo lineages are similarly grouped into clans that are exogamous, totemic and dispersed. Herero lineages are also subdivisions of totemic clans, and every person belongs to both his father's patriclan (*oruzo*) and his mother's matriclan (*eanda*). The former functions chiefly in religious and political life, the latter in inheritance of property. The patriclan is exogamous and so is the matrilineage (but not the matriclan).

The only other major kinds of social grouping are the age sets characteristic of all Central and Eastern Bantu except Cape Nguni. These are created periodically by the tribal chiefs, at intervals of say four to seven years, when all the adolescent boys are initiated simultaneously. Each set has its own name and leader (always of the chiefly family) and membership is for life. In most tribes there is a parallel grouping of women. The sets, ranked according to priority of creation, feature prominently in tribal affairs. They are often used by the chief for various kinds of public service, and those of able-bodied men fight as separate regiments in the army. Members usually live at home. But among the Zulu, in the heyday of their power, the younger regiments each had its own village, close to the chief's, where its members remained continuously for several years before being released and allowed to marry. The Swazi have a somewhat similar but less comprehensive residential system. The Bergdama are said to have age sets too, though little is known about them. They do not occur anywhere else in the region.

Systems of government differ widely. Each Bushman and Bergdama band has a hereditary headman, but public issues are decided by all the men in council. The headman has no judicial powers, the principal remedy for wrongs being self-help. His main task is to direct migrations and other collective activities, though among Bergdama and some Bushmen (Kung and Heikum) he is also the band's priest. Every Hottentot clan also has a headman, who with the help of its other men judges internal disputes, punishes criminals and decides on such matters as seeking new pastures. The clan heads together constitute the tribal council, the head of the senior clan presiding as chief. The council deals with intertribal relations and other matters of common concern, and also adjudicates upon disputes between people of different clans. The chief cannot act independently of its other members.

Every Bantu tribe also has a chief. He rules with the aid of several confidential advisers and a large formal council including all heads of major local segments; among Sotho, especially Tswana, he must also habitually consult a mass meeting of tribesmen. But his authority is supreme. He has both legislative and judicial powers, and although local subchiefs and headmen also try cases he only can impose the death penalty. He is the tribal priest and rainmaker and (like his Hottentot counterpart) often the leader in war. He regulates the distribution of residential and cultivable land, controls such other aspects of economy as the cycle of agricultural activities and receives tribute from his subjects in both kind and labour. In return he rewards his assistants with gifts of cattle and other commodities, supports the destitute and on great public occasions provides meat and beer for all who assemble at his village. One quality always required of him is generosity, failing which he soon becomes unpopular.

Religion and Magic.—The Bushmen pray to the moon and other celestial bodies, about which the southern groups especially have a rich and extensive mythology. They also recognize a supernatural being known variously as Cagn, Huwe, Hishe or Tora. He controls rain, thunder and lightning; he is invoked for abundance of plant foods, good luck in hunting, recovery from illness, protection, etc. The northern groups also speak of Gaua, a being associated primarily with the ghosts of the dead and, like them, considered a source of illness and death. He is apparently not worshiped nor are the spirits of deceased ancestors.

The Hottentots similarly connect the ghosts of dead persons with a being named Gaunab. Both are greatly feared as causing sickness or death. In mythology Gaunab features as an evil chief always in conflict with Tsui-Goab, the creator god who is invoked for health, prosperity, abundance and above all rain. Another leading figure in ritual and belief is Heitsi-Eibib, the central personage of a great mythical cycle in which he and members of his family have many wonderful adventures. His "graves," large heaps of stones, are found all over the country, and whoever passes by adds a stone or twig, usually with a prayer for good luck. Some early writers say the Cape Hottentots also prayed for food and rain to the moon, which among all Hottentots figures prominently in myths about the origin of death.

The supreme being of the Bergdama is Gamab, whose home in the sky is also the afterworld of the dead. His name, and the belief that he causes death, are reminiscent of Bushman "Gaua" and Hottentot "Gaunab," but unlike them he stands alone and is worshiped. His cult is connected with the sacred fire kept burning perpetually in every band. All game killed in the chase and all plant foods as they ripen are brought to it for the headman to bless before they are eaten. Whenever the band moves he also prays there to Gamab for abundance and good fortune. Scarcity of food, drought and other ills, are ascribed to the pollution of the fire, which the headman must then extinguish and renew with elaborate ceremonial. On certain occasions he also deposits offerings and prays at the grave of a deceased ancestor.

Among Bantu the dominant religious cult is ancestor worship. Every family and descent group worships its own ancestors, the head of the group conducting the rites. On important tribal occasions the chief also prays to his ancestors on behalf of all his subjects. The spirits of the ancestors are believed to guide the destinies of their living descendants, who propitiate them with prayers and offerings both whenever they reveal themselves through dreams or calamity, and on such occasions as birth, marriage or the start of some new enterprise. The Herero link ancestor worship with the cult of the sacred fire. Every household has its own fire, kindled originally from that of its *oruzo*

head. This fire, which should burn perpetually, is the domestic altar. At it the family priest prays to his ancestors and blesses the daily yield of milk before it can be consumed.

The Bantu also have some conception, often rather vague, of a universal power apart from the ancestors. It is variously known by such names as Tilo (Tsonga), Unkulunkulu (Zulu), Modimo (Sotho) and Raluvhimba (Venda). The beliefs and practices relating to it differ considerably. The Sotho, for example, regard Modimo as the creator of all things and the molder of destiny. He is associated with the phenomena of the weather, and punishes innovations or departures from custom by sending wind, hail or heat and withholding the rain. But he is considered too remote from the world of man to be directly approached in prayer, though at times the ancestral spirits may be implored to intercede with him. The Tsonga, in contrast, think of Tilo as an impersonal power presiding over all unaccountable and inevitable phenomena of the atmosphere, of the fields and of human existence, and try to propitiate it in times of drought or other extreme distress. There is little to suggest that these universal powers play as intimate a part in everyday religion as the spirits of the ancestors.

All South African peoples further make considerable and frequent use of magic. Certain individuals, women as well as men, are specialists in the art and are paid for their services. Their main activity everywhere is treatment of the sick; they also practise divination, charm people for success and protection from misfortune, officiate at puberty and similar ceremonies, and perform rainmaking rites in time of drought. Among Hottentots and Bantu they likewise "doctor" cattle (and among Bantu also fields) to insure fertility and other blessings. Any misfortune, especially sickness or death, may be attributed to the malevolent use of magic and the culprit if discovered is punished severely, sometimes by death. All peoples also have much faith in omens, of which there are many kinds. The wearing of amulets is likewise common everywhere; hunters, warriors, herdsmen and others tie around their necks small pieces of wood, bone and similar objects obtained from the magicians and believed to ward off danger, maintain health or deliver the possessor from evil.

Major Population Movements.—The Bushmen, because of their linguistic and other affinities with such peoples as the Hadza and Sandawe of Tanzania, have generally been held to have entered southern Africa from the northeast. By the 1960s, observers had come to maintain instead that they evolved locally from pre-existing and now extinct types of Stone Age man, subsequently spreading north of the Zambezi. It is, however, generally agreed that they have occupied southern Africa since the beginning of the Late Stone Age (about 8,000 years ago) and possibly earlier, and are the oldest of its modern inhabitants. Their relics (*e.g.*, skeletal remains, stone implement industries, pictorial art and place names) are found widely scattered throughout the region and furnish good evidence of their former presence in areas where they are no longer seen—notably Cape Province, Orange Free State, Basutoland and Natal.

The Hottentots have similarly been thought to have originated in East Africa from a mixture of Bushmen and early invading Hamites, to whom were attributed also their language, livestock and other cultural peculiarities. The modern view is that they developed in southern Africa by hybridization among "three basic strains—the small Bushman, the long-headed Bushmanoid (Boskop) type and a long-headed non-Bushmanoid form represented by the Kakamas type" (J. D. Clark). It is to the last-named, immigrants of Caucasoid stock who "probably originated somewhere in northeast Africa," that they are said to owe the distinctive features of their culture, brought into the country about 1,500–2,000 years ago.

The Bergdama are a mystery. Because they speak the same language as the Nama Hottentots, one view is that they were subjected by the Nama somewhere in central Africa and brought to the south as servants. It is generally and more plausibly assumed that in fact they represent an old Negro stock which, with the possible exception of the Bushmen, preceded all other inhabitants of South West Africa. It is established that by the end of the 18th century many had become serfs of Nama, Herero and

Ambo. But how and when they acquired their language is still a moot problem, since when first seen by Europeans (1792) they were living north of the Nama tribes, not in their midst.

The Bantu are universally held to have moved into South Africa from the north, the lake region of East Africa often being regarded as their centre of origin. They apparently came in many separate bodies and along diverse routes, each of their main groups representing a different series of migrations. Archaeological evidence, notably from Zimbabwe (*q.v.*) and similar ruins, suggests that the ancestors of the Shona were already in Southern Rhodesia by the 8th century A.D. Other evidence indicates that the Nguni and Sotho had reached their present habitats by the 14th century A.D., that the Venda migrated from Southern Rhodesia to the Soutpansberg about A.D. 1600, and that the Ambo and Herero entered South West Africa from the upper reaches of the Zambezi about the same time. More cannot be said with much plausibility, and even the dates mentioned are hypothetical.

The impacts upon one another of different native peoples and the later advance of European settlers inland from the Cape resulted in many local upheavals, during which various groups of Bushmen and Hottentots ceased to exist and the Bantu also were greatly affected. In particular, the wars of conquest initiated by the Zulu chief Shaka (Chaka; 1818–28) led to widespread devastation and enforced migration. One sequel was the creation of several other strong native states. Mzilikazi, after dominating central and western Transvaal (about 1821–37), went on to conquer the Shona in Southern Rhodesia, where he established the Matabele (Ndebele) kingdom. Soshangana subjugated most of the Tsonga in Mozambique and founded the Gasa (Shangana) kingdom, while Zwangendaba and others founded Ngoni kingdoms north of the Zambezi. Moshesh from the remnants of many scattered tribes similarly created the modern Basuto nation in Basutoland. Thulare and his son Sekwati brought many northern (Transvaal) Sotho tribes under the rule of the Pedi; Sebetwane, leading a horde of Sotho refugees from the south, established in far-off Barotseland the great Kololo kingdom. The wholesale destruction of life and dispersal of people resulting from these upheavals facilitated the subsequent extension of European settlement over the country. By the end of the 19th century, European armies had destroyed most of the new kingdoms, but such large tribal states as the southern Sotho (of Basutoland), Swazi and Ngwato still survive as examples of the political development to which the Bantu could sometimes attain.

See also BERGDAMA; BUSHMAN; HERERO; HOTTENTOT; NDEBELE; SHONA; SWAZI; TSWANA; XHOSA. (I. S.)

IV. ARCHAEOLOGY

The first factor which must be taken into consideration in discussing the archaeology of Africa is the vast size of the continent, which stretches from the equator to the edge of the temperate zone in both the northern and the southern hemisphere. This wide expanse is interrupted by few geographical barriers except those created by changing climate. Northward from the equator there is a steady transition from tropical rain forest to more open forests and rich grasslands, then to drier grasslands, woodlands and thorn scrub and so to semidesert and the extreme desert conditions of parts of the Sahara. Northward again the extreme aridity of the desert decreases and there is a fairly rapid transition to more hospitable conditions along much of the southern shore of the Mediterranean. From the equator southward this pattern is repeated, but in a somewhat modified form as a result of the eastern mountains and plateau, which extend from Ethiopia to the Cape of Good Hope and cause a considerable increase of rainfall down the entire southeastern part of the continent. Similarly, the Nile valley forms a bridge across the desert conditions of the northern half of the continent, locally upsetting the absolute regularity of the climatic pattern.

In general outline, this pattern has remained constant throughout the period of man's existence in Africa, but from time to time it has been considerably modified. Thus there have been periods when the desert was the habitat of grazing animals, which now live only on its fringes, and of the men who hunted them.

There have also been times when the tropical forests extended or receded beyond their present limits. Thus any particular area may form a barrier to human contact at one period and quite the reverse at another.

Sub-Saharan Africa has yielded a wide variety of early human and near-human skeletal remains, extending well back into geological time, and also what is probably the most complete series of Early Stone Age hand-ax industries known anywhere in the world. Taken together these strongly suggest that it was one of the centres of early human evolution, possibly even the region in which the all-important change from animal to man took place —a change signalized by the appearance of deliberately made tools which reflect developing manual and intellectual skills.

The fact that during much of this stage of human development the Sahara desert enjoyed a more humid climate than it does in modern times, and therefore was not such an obstacle to the movement of animals and man as it later became, may to some extent account for the remarkable uniformity of the hand-ax industries throughout Africa, southern Europe, western Asia and India. Later the climate of the desert belt became more intensely arid and human cultures in different regions, both in Africa and outside, began to develop along their own lines of local specialization. From then on, with certain notable exceptions, African culture tends to be more and more diversified. The climax comes with the final intensification of desert conditions in the Sahara and the early rise of civilization in the Nile valley. From that point onward Egypt and the north African littoral tend to form part of the Mediterranean world and Sub-Saharan Africa to go its own way.

Stone Age cultures succeeded one another in the various regions south of the Sahara. In the savanna regions of the south and east these were clearly based upon hunting the numerous species of larger game animals, and the diet was augmented by vegetable foods. In the forest regions vegetable foods must have played a more important part in the inhabitants' diet, but at what stage they began to encourage and then to cultivate the plants they found most palatable is not clear. Nor is it clear how far the change to food production was a spontaneous development or was due to direct or indirect influences from outside. Egyptian and Mediterranean influences are apparent around the fringes of the Sahara, but farther southward their traces tend to disappear.

During the Late Stone Age, Sub-Saharan Africa was a region of relative cultural and physical diversity; ideas spread from group to group and occasional movements of population no doubt took place, but the general trend was toward regional continuity. No Bronze Age revolution cut across this pattern as it did in Europe and northern Asia. The two factors which brought the whole region back into contact with the outside world might be summarized as iron and trade. In the last centuries before the beginning of the Christian era the knowledge of iron smelting and ironworking began to reach the Sudan, probably from Nubia, and then to spread southward, taking with it the possibility of numerous agricultural and technological advances and all that these implied. Following the Arab conquest of North Africa, Arab traders began to cross the Sahara and to sail down the east coast, chiefly in search of gold and other minerals, which they found in plenty. Partly no doubt as a result of these stimuli, large tribal groups, kingdoms and empires emerged in many parts of Africa, like those described by Arab geographers and Portuguese travelers in West Africa and the Sudan, and those which have left evidence of their presence in the extensive ruins of East and southern Africa. It is with the Iron Age also that the expansion of Bantu peoples in East and southern Africa may be associated. It is only in relatively recent years that the African Iron Age has begun to receive the attention it deserves.

The study of African archaeology has naturally tended to be approached from two directions. The archaeology of Egypt and North Africa has been studied in relation to that of the Mediterranean, Europe and western Asia, and is described in similar terms; that of Sub-Saharan Africa has developed its own terms, as an independent field. (B. AL.)

A. Fossil Hominid Remains

Africa is a part of that old world land mass which contains some of the earliest-known protohuman fossils as well as extremely ancient cultural traces of man. It was regarded by Charles Darwin as the continent which probably first witnessed the appearance of man, a view later revived by prehistorians of such distinction as P. Teilhard de Chardin. Moreover, Africa contains two of man's closest primate relatives, the gorilla and chimpanzee. The weight of conservative opinion, however, tended to view Asia as the more likely centre of human origins. Partly this was the result of earlier historic and philosophical ideas, partly the natural outcome of the discovery of Miocene and Pliocene apes in the Siwalik fossil beds of northern India. In addition, the late-19th-century discovery of a primitive type of man, *Pithecanthropus erectus*, in Java and, beginning in 1929, the uncovering in China (near Peking) of an almost equally primitive fossil form of man, *Sinanthropus pekinenis,* tended to strengthen the view that man had arisen in Asia.

This ancient controversy was revived by two dramatic events: first, the discovery in South Africa and later also in East Africa of a remarkable group of upright-walking man-apes classified taxonomically as the family Australopithecinae; second, the discovery in Kenya of an early Miocene ape, *Proconsul africanus,* and, in 1961, of a late Miocene ape, *Kenyapithecus,* which may be directly ancestral to man.

Proconsul africanus and Kenyapithecus wickeri.—In old lake deposits of Lower Miocene Age have been located the remains of primitive anthropoid apes known under the generic name of *Proconsul* (*q.v.*). These finds include the most complete skull so far recovered of any ape of this period, as well as other bones including femurs, a humerus, and numerous teeth and jaws. In *Proconsul* the upper canine tooth is large and the dentition not only is related to that of the later great apes but also shows certain more human features. The skull lacks the heavy brow ridges associated with many early human skulls and with the great apes. All in all, *Proconsul* suggests a fairly primitive ape, slender bodied, walking on four feet as well as swinging by the arms. *Kenyapithecus wickeri,* from Fort Ternan in western Kenya, dates from the end of the Miocene. It is represented by fragments of an upper jaw, including a canine tooth much smaller than those of apes and showing affinities with the hominids.

Australopithecinae.—In 1924 the first of a series of discoveries made in Bechuanaland and the Transvaal, in South Africa, revealed a creature intermediate in character between ape and man. From 1959 onward, similar discoveries were made at Olduvai gorge in Tanzania. The Australopithecinae, as these creatures have been named, come close to satisfying the idea of what the earliest "half men" looked like. They have been classified as members of the Hominidae, the family to which man belongs, and are described in separate articles. (*See* AUSTRALOPITHECINE; MAN, EVOLUTION OF: *Australopithecinae.*)

Fossil Men.—From 1954 onward, fossil human remains were discovered associated with Acheulean hand axes at Palikao near Ternifine in Algeria and at Sidi Abderrahman in Morocco. They consist of lower jaws and a piece of skull. The chin region is receding, and this feature, as well as the teeth, recalls *Homo erectus* (*Pithecanthropus*) of Java and Peking. These fossils all belong to one type, "*Atlanthropus mauritanicus,*" which apparently represents the African form of the Asian *Homo erectus* and could well be the next stage in hominid evolution after the australopithecines. In 1960 a skull of this type was found at Olduvai gorge, accompanied by hand axes of the Chellean stage. It has been dated by the potassium-argon method to 490,000 years.

Other early forms of man which are known to have inhabited Africa during the Pleistocene fall into two main categories. The first is a gerontomorphic group of hominids with heavy facial bones and large brow ridges, which belong to the widespread type known as Rhodesioids; the second is a remarkably pedomorphic *Homo sapiens* type apparently preceding and related to the existing Kalahari Bushmen. The Rhodesioids are known from three specimens: (1) the Broken Hill skull from a mine in northwestern Zambia; (2) certain fragmentary remains originally classified

under the title *Africanthropus* (*Homo njarensis*); and (3) a skull from Hopefield near Saldanha Bay, Cape Province.

Homo rhodesiensis.—Often termed Rhodesian man, he is represented by one of the most complete Pleistocene crania discovered by the mid-20th century. The skull was found, with a few other bones, in an old cave 60 ft. (about 18 m.) beneath the surface during the course of mining operations by the Broken Hill company in 1921. The skull itself, save for breakage in the region of the right parietal bone and the right side of the occiput, is complete, the face being in perfect condition. The mandible was never recovered. The salient feature of the cranium is its great size and massiveness. The supraorbital torus is exceptionally large, measuring 139 mm. across, a width greatly in excess of that of recent man. The skull is low and of great length (208.5 mm.), being rather similar to the European Neanderthaloids in this respect, and the occipital torus is heavy and pronounced. The cranial capacity is about 1,300 c.c., a lower figure than that observed for some European Neanderthals of similar size. The palate is much larger than in modern man and the face was undoubtedly huge and of a formidably primitive aspect. Morphologically the skull seems to belong to roughly the same level as European Neanderthal skulls, though its physical characters do not permit ranging it in an identical position with the Neanderthals, and it perhaps approximates a little more closely to the *Homo soloensis* form from Java. Its geological dating is early Upper Pleistocene. (*See also* MAN, EVOLUTION OF: *Neanderthal Man and Neanderthaloids.*)

"*Africanthropus.*"—The discovery of "*Africanthropus*" (this name has been abandoned) was made in the Eyasi Lake basin of northern Tanganyika, Tanzania, in 1934. Remains of three crania were recovered, but in an extremely fragmentary condition, from a lake deposit of early Upper Pleistocene Age. Fragments indicate a heavy supraorbital torus, said to be thinner and more delicate than in the Neanderthals or *Homo rhodesiensis*. This, however, might represent only a sex difference, as the small and delicate mastoid also suggests. Probably the form is of the same type as Rhodesian man, but the fragmentary character of the remains and the difficulties of restoration make a detailed study impossible.

Saldanha Man.—In 1951 pieces of a fossilized human skull were found on the farm of Elandsfontein near Hopefield, 9 mi. inland from Saldanha Bay, Cape Province. The skull, as well as fossil fauna and two different stone industries, came from lime-impregnated sand which probably represents the dried-up floor of an old pan. The skull is very similar to that of Rhodesian man, with heavy brow ridges, receding forehead and a low vault. The fauna includes some extinct forms, notably the giant buffalo *Homoioceras;* fluorine tests have shown that the human skull is contemporary with this Upper Pleistocene fauna and so presumably with the earlier Fauresmith industry rather than with the Stillbay industry found on the surface of the site.

Neanderthal Man.—In Africa, Neanderthal men seem to be confined to the North Atlantic coast and the Mediterranean shores, for instance at Jabal-Irhoud in Morocco and at Haua Fteah in Cyrenaica. The African equivalents of *Homo neanderthalensis* south of the Sahara appear to be the Rhodesioid types discussed above.

Early Forms of "Homo sapiens."—*Kanam Man.*—Very much earlier than the Rhodesioids and Neanderthaloids described above, according to its discoverer, L. S. B. Leakey, is a fragmentary human mandible from Kanam on the shores of Kavirondo gulf of Lake Victoria. Not only was it said to be associated with pebble tools and a Lower Pleistocene fauna but it was also claimed to be of *Homo sapiens* form, principally because it does not have a receding chin. The individual, however, had a tumour of the bone which may make the chin appear more prominent than it would otherwise be. If the fossil is really of Lower Pleistocene Age, the possibility of its being an australopithecine should not be ruled out; but possibly it may be a Rhodesioid of much later date.

Kanjera Man.—At Kanjera not far from Kanam, fragments of four human skulls were found; one of these includes the brow region, which is quite smooth as in modern man. The skull is ultradolichocephalic. The fossils were in the same state of mineralization as Middle Pleistocene fauna from the site and were associated with Acheulean hand axes. Recent tests have revealed a similar uranium content in the human skulls and the extinct fauna, which supports the view that they were contemporaneous.

Florisbad Cranium.—A remarkable specimen is the Florisbad cranium discovered by T. F. Dreyer and originally called *Homo helmei.* The bones were recovered in 1932 from an old spring deposit at Florisbad, 25 mi. (40 km.) N. of Bloemfontein. Several extinct animals were found in general association with the skull, including the giant African buffalo, *Homoioceras,* and two species of horse. The human skull fragments consist of part of the frontal, the right parietal, maxilla and molar. The skull has the immense minimum frontal width of 120 mm. as contrasted with an average Caucasian width of about 99 mm. The breadth across the supraorbital process approaches very close to *Homo rhodesiensis,* measuring as it does 136 mm. In spite of being pronounced, however, the brow ridge is divided in a manner resembling that of *Homo sapiens.* Unlike Neanderthal man, who had round and open orbits, the Florisbad orbital height is much less than the width. The skull must have been huge, perhaps as much as 210 mm. in length, but there are indications that it sloped rapidly away from a high point at the bregma toward the occiput. This feature suggests that the brain was rather low and flat in the occipital region. The face is extremely prognathous. The majority opinion regards the skull as a primitive form of *Homo sapiens,* probably an ancestral Bushman type. It is curious and unique, and can be better understood only as more complete specimens are obtained. Its date is probably early Upper Pleistocene. The age of the peat in which the skull was found has been dated by the radiocarbon method to about 37,000 years.

Boskop Cranium.—In 1913 a human calvarium of quite remarkable size was turned up in a drainage ditch near Boskop, in the Transvaal. It is 205 mm. in length with a basibregmatic height of 140 mm. The cranial capacity was probably about 1,700 c.c., which is markedly above the modern average. A single stone implement found with the skull shows Middle Stone Age affinities and may indicate the approximate age of the human remains. The most striking features of the skull, apart from its size, are the pentagoid shape when viewed from above, the bosses on the sides and the bulging forehead. Remains of Boskopoid individuals turn up with considerable frequency in the lower strata of cliff shelters and seashore middens in various parts of southern Africa. The term Boskopoid came to be applied to a pedomorphic type showing some trace of Bushman characters. The other finds are probably very late Pleistocene to early Recent. The cranium to face ratio in the Boskop skull is almost five to one, and the face is quite orthognathous. In other words, this is a human type in which the retention of infantile characters is more marked than in other varieties of *Homo sapiens.*

Singa Cranium.—A skull from Singa on the Blue Nile bears a marked resemblance to the Boskop cranium, but certain studies suggest that the resemblance may be fortuitous and that in fact this individual may be of Rhodesioid type, though abnormal. An accompanying industry is of Middle Stone Age type, described as Proto-Stillbay, and the skull is dated to the early part of the Upper Pleistocene.

Insofar as the skeletal material so far described has any cultural associations, they are with Early or Middle Stone Age industries. It is noteworthy that as in Europe the Mousterian industries are so often associated with the heavy-browed Neanderthal man, so in Africa the early Middle Stone Age industries are frequently associated with the large-faced Rhodesioids. With succeeding cultural developments of the Middle and Late Stone Age in southern Africa there is a tendency for more and more specialized Boskop and Bushmanoid types to be associated. This adds to the considerable ethnographic evidence that the immediate ancestors of the modern Bushmen of southern Africa were the makers of the final phases of the Late Stone Age industries in many parts of the region. (L. C. E.; S. M. C.)

B. SOUTHERN AFRICA

The study of archaeology in Southern Africa grew up in much the same way as it did in Europe—that is to say, through the collection of objects and their arrangement first in groups and then in a sequence of related groups. Later this sequence was altered or confirmed as similar objects were found stratified in river gravels or cave deposits which indicated their chronological relationship to one another in geological terms. Following the Pretoria conference of 1927, a systematic account of these findings was put forward by A. J. H. Goodwin and C. van Riet Lowe in "The Stone Age Cultures of South Africa" (*Ann. S. Afr. Mus.,* xxvii [1928]). Here they make it clear that in South Africa at any rate the stone industries fall into three major groups, which they called Early, Middle and Late Stone Age respectively. As the established European terminology, involving the use of Paleolithic and Neolithic cultural groupings with their subdivisions, is patently unsuitable, their terminology has now been generally accepted and their system of classification, with certain minor modifications, has been extended to much of Sub-Saharan Africa.

Early Stone Age.—This includes a series of hand-ax industries closely comparable to those found in Europe, western Asia and India. This is best represented in collections from the gravels of the Vaal river, where the evolution from simple pebble tools to finely worked hand axes and cleavers can be clearly seen. By general consent the term Chelles-Acheul is now used to describe these industries, as it is for their European counterparts. In the later stages the Levallois technique of making tools of flakes struck from prepared cores is seen to develop from the original core technique and to continue alongside it. Technically these industries are close to those of the Lower Paleolithic of Europe, but in Africa the proportion of cleavers to hand axes is much higher, as it is in India, and the core and flake aspects of the industries are more closely integrated than in Europe. The dating of these industries and the question of the existence of Pre-Chelles-Acheul pebble industries is discussed in the following section on the archaeology of Central and West Africa.

Middle Stone Age.—This follows after a transitional period, known as the first intermediate phase, which is represented in Southern Africa chiefly by the Fauresmith industry in which the hand axes of the Early Stone Age continue to be made but in much smaller sizes, and an increased range of small flake tools and points makes its appearance. The Fauresmith is widely distributed in Southern Africa, and is evidently associated with fairly open country; in places variants of the related Sangoan industries of the more thickly wooded country to the north also appear for the first time. In the industries of the Middle Stone Age proper, which correspond to a period of generally increased rainfall, the tendency to reduction in size and refinement of technique continues; they are characterized by the production of flakes from small carefully prepared cores, and of finely worked points of various kinds. These are accompanied by an increasing range of scrapers, blade flakes, large crescents and so on, like the tools of the Stillbay industries of Central and East Africa. There are a number of local variants which include the Rhodesian Stillbay, the Pietersburg and Hagenstad variants of the Transvaal and Orange Free State, the Mazelspoort and Alexandersfontein variants farther west, and the Mossel bay variant in the extreme south.

The meaning of the reduction in size which began in the preceding intermediate phase is clear: the tools of the Middle Stone Age industries were intended for hafting and not simply for use in the hand, as was the case with those of the Early Stone Age. At this period also man began to inhabit caves and rock shelters with increasing regularity. This may have been partly a result of climatic conditions, but it was undoubtedly due also to a knowledge of the use of fire, and an increasing ability to control it. During the greater part of the Early Stone Age fire was clearly unknown, and living sites were always in the open; but in the final stages of this period in South Africa there are indications both of its use and of the regular habitation of caves. Only when he had fire at his command was it possible for man to live in caves and defend himself from the attacks of large carnivores. Fire also made possible the hafting of stone tools in mastics such as resin and similar substances, a practice for which there is considerable evidence from Southern Africa and from many other parts of the world, and it also opened up many new possibilities in all directions.

As the Middle Stone Age drew to a close its final expression is to be found in the Magosian industries, which are also widely distributed in Southern Africa, and which are in many ways transitional between the Middle and Late Stone Age. For this reason they are regarded as occupying the second intermediate phase, which corresponds with an interpluvial or dry phase in the climatic sequence. This possibly accounts for the fact that the majority of Magosian assemblages have been found in the open, and not in caves or rock shelters like the industries which came before and after them. The assemblages include not only small, highly developed Middle Stone Age forms, but also small blades and geometric microliths, which distinctly foreshadow succeeding developments. Whether the bow and arrow also made their first appearance at this stage is uncertain, but a good case can be made for their having done so, as for the first time stone points appear which are light enough to be used as arrow heads.

Late Stone Age.—The age of the bow and arrow and of the final refinement of both hunting and stoneworking techniques, the Late Stone Age was the high period of the arts of rock painting and engraving. Both arts probably began in earlier periods but then reached their zenith in Southern Africa with a richness and variety, particularly in the case of the paintings, which has been attained by hunting people in few other parts of the world. The use of arrow poisons, which made fatal the smallest puncture of the skin, allowed bows and arrows to be extremely small and light; a great variety of small delicate tools of both stone and bone characterize this period.

The Late Stone Age industries of Southern Africa may be divided into two major groups, which are known as Smithfield and Wilton. The latter are similar to the Wilton industries of Central and East Africa in general respects, including a considerable range of geometric forms (among which lunates are the dominant type), thumbnail scrapers, hollow scrapers, awls, backed blades and other stone tools, often accompanied by bone tools, ostrich eggshell beads, large globular stones with hourglass-shaped perforations (used among other things as weights for digging sticks), grooved stones for straightening arrows and hollow stones for making arrow poison. Assemblages of the Smithfield group of industries are substantially similar, but lack the geometric forms. The Smithfield industries appear to be centred upon the interior plateau, but sometimes extend into the surrounding Wilton provinces. The line of demarcation between the two groups is nowhere clear-cut.

The immediate ancestors of the Bushmen were responsible for a great part of these Late Stone Age industries and there are abundant records of their making or using such tools after the middle of the 18th century. A number of stone tools of this period have also been found hafted with mastic in wood or bone handles, and the use of others is clearly shown in the rock paintings. Consequently it is possible to gain a much fuller insight into this period than into those which preceded it.

Iron Age.—The Iron Age is a somewhat elusive term in Southern Africa. When Jan van Riebeeck established a permanent foothold for the Dutch East India company at the Cape of Good Hope in 1652, it appears that both the hunting Bushmen and the cattle-keeping Hottentots were entirely ignorant of techniques of iron smelting. But they quickly made use of any scrap metal which came their way, hammering it into arrow- or spearheads as the Kalahari Bushmen do today. Iron-using agriculturists had arrived in the northern part of the region several hundred years earlier and built massive stone structures, which still can be seen in Rhodesia and the northern Transvaal. From these places they carried on trade with the inhabitants of the east coast and ultimately perhaps with Arabia and India. How soon the hunting people of surrounding regions obtained iron in a similar manner from them is impossible to know at present. At Zimbabwe (*q.v.*) and other sites a series of Iron Age cultural levels has been distinguished, but their relationship to similar cultures farther north, although generally established, has not yet been worked out in detail. Their relationship to existing ethnic groups in Southern Africa is only beginning to emerge. (B. Al.)

Rock Painting and Engraving.—Two broad periods are discernible in the prehistoric rock paintings. The earlier antedates the appearance of the Bantu-speaking invaders whose vanguard probably reached South Africa about 1,000 years ago; the later postdates this invasion.

In the earlier period the art is natural and restful, the work of men of leisure and peace. It develops from single animal studies in monochrome in the order yellow, red, maroon, black and white, through bichromes where perspective and composition first appear and finally to shaded polychromes often showing remarkable grouping and perspective. The paintings give an idea of the dress, arms, customs and beliefs of the artists. It was during the earlier monochrome phase of this development that Stone Age men in Southern Africa passed through a stage of artistic expression which shows striking affinities with the Paleolithic art of Europe, the Sahara and East Africa. So alike indeed are certain of the rock paintings of the Sahara, Tanzania, Zambia, Southern Rhodesia and South Africa that parallel evolution does not seem to afford a wholly satisfactory explanation. The bichrome and polychrome phase of the earlier period is notable for the emphasis first on a variety of gazelles and then on the eland, paintings of which are found superimposed on those of gazelles. Paintings of gazelles are usually small but always beautifully executed; those of eland are usually large individual pictures sometimes reaching several feet in length. These two phases represent the acme of prehistoric rock paintings in South Africa.

The later period is characterized by a restlessness which had a profound effect on the artist. He continued with the knowledge he had previously gained and certainly maintained the tradition of his ancestors, but he never seems to have had either the leisure or the inclination to paint as easily, skilfully and restfully as did his predecessors. This period is characterized by the first appearance in paintings of men with shields and spears, of cattle, sheep and other objects first brought to the south by Iron Age agriculturists, and the paintings occur as palimpsests over the works of the earlier period. Many of the lively scenes of this later period recall the paintings of eastern Spain, which are almost certainly post-Pleistocene in age. On the grounds of style and subject matter as well as technique there appears to be a general division into cave paintings and petroglyphs or rock engravings, which are generally found in the open. While many of the petroglyphs, whether pecked or engraved into the rock, reveal remarkable affinities with the rock paintings, many others do not. The oldest petroglyphs are finely incised line engravings in which single animal studies in profile appear over finely engraved but crudely drawn figures of triangles, zigzag lines, ladders, chevrons and so on. The animal figures include most of the still-living forms. Composition or grouping and perspective are very rare. Superimposed over these engravings is a vast array of figures, both animal and schematic, the profiles of which were pecked into the rock by a crumbling as opposed to a cutting process. Rarely are the two styles combined in a single figure. Although both rock painting and rock engraving were extensively practised by Bushmen during the Late Stone Age, the inception and earlier practice of these arts may have taken place toward the close of the Middle Stone Age. (S. M. C.)

C. Central and West Africa

It would be convenient to view the progress of African prehistory against a chronological backdrop of climatic change just as one does in northern latitudes, where a series of four major periods of ice-sheet formation can be recognized by the deposits they left behind, as well as by their effect on relative levels of land and sea and on river valley formation. Such a scheme has in fact been proposed for Africa in which four major pluvials (periods of increased rainfall) provide the counterpart of, and have been tentatively correlated with, the northern ice advances. The names proposed, Kageran, Kamasian, Kanjeran and Gamblian, were based on sites in East Africa where evidence was believed to exist for former relatively wet periods, and by tacit agreement these names had been extended throughout the continent wherever evidence of a wetter climate of the right order of age had been found. The validity of such long-distance correlation, based on climate rather than stratigraphy, has, however, been challenged by R. F. Flint and H. B. S. Cooke, as also has the climatic interpretation of the deposits themselves. At the fourth Pan-African Congress on Prehistory in 1959 it was agreed that the notion of a Kageran pluvial should be discarded, while Flint recognized evidence of only a Gamblian and a pre-Gamblian pluvial and two post-Gamblian minor wet phases (Makalian and Nakuran).

In Central and West Africa the evidence for past climatic change is meagre and not easily interpreted. The major river valleys such as those of the Zambezi and Congo and lesser rivers (Kalomo, Bembesi and Volta) display terrace formation which may, in part, be a result of climatic fluctuations. Evidence of former higher rainfall is to be found in the distribution of ferricretes (soil zones partially cemented by iron oxides) in areas where the rainfall required for their formation is now inadequate, while considerably drier conditions are suggested by the successive redistributions of wind-blown sands. At Kalambo Falls in Zambia, examination of fossil pollen grains has shown that part of the lake deposits containing Acheulean camping sites was formed when conditions were considerably cooler and wetter than they are to-day. This "cooling off," radiocarbon dated to 52,000 B.C., is taken to represent the early Gamblian pluvial and to be the equivalent of the onset of the Würm glaciation in Europe.

Pre-Chelles-Acheul Pebble Cultures.—A culture stage, preceding the great hand-ax complex, in which the surviving tools consist solely of simply split or flaked pebbles, was first recognized by E. J. Wayland in 1919. Its distribution is now known to be very wide in Africa, sites occurring sporadically from Ain Hanech in Algeria as far south as Durban in Natal and the Vaal river. Two forms of the culture have been identified: the Kafuan and the Oldowan. The first, which is generally considered to represent an earlier stage than the Oldowan, has been subdivided into four stages showing a development from the simplest form of split pebble to more complex forms in which several flakes are removed to provide a sinuous cutting edge; but it is doubtful if such a subdivision is really justified. Leakey showed that the Oldowan pebble culture at Olduvai gorge in Tanzania is truly ancestral to the Chelles-Acheul stages that follow. In the Zambezi valley near Livingstone, pebble tools of Oldowan type and large thick flakes occur heavily abraded in the older gravels alongside hand axes in a fresher state of preservation. This suggests that the former have been derived from still earlier deposits which have been completely eroded away and incorporated in the older gravels. Other sites exist in Zambia at Ngwezi and Kalomo, but generally speaking the evidence for this stage is not clear in that area.

Farther north in the Katanga province of the Democratic Republic of the Congo, G. Mortelmans recorded rich sites on the Kundelungu plateau, west of Lake Mweru and in the Kafila river basin. To the west, specimens are recorded by Leakey from the region of the diamond workings at Dundo in Angola. Northward one enters the region of tropical forest which seems to have been avoided by earliest man. If pebble tools exist along the northern fringe of the forest belt they have not yet been recorded, except for rather dubious reports from Ghana. Fossil remains of this period are known only from northern Malawi and southeast Angola, and no human remains are known. The evidence of the Transvaal caves and Olduvai gorge suggests that the makers of the pebble tools may have been of the *Homo habilis* type, recently described from Olduvai gorge.

Chelles-Acheul Culture.—The human workmanship of some of the earlier stages of the Kafuan has been questioned by certain authorities, but there is no doubt that the Oldowan-type tools are the work of man or that they are an early stage in the development of the hand-ax cultures. The transition is clearly seen at Olduvai and less clearly in the Vaal river; Kalomo in Zambia has also yielded what may well be transitional types, though good stratigraphical evidence is lacking at this site. From the fine stratigraphy of Olduvai and the Vaal it is known that a number of valid stages of the Chelles-Acheul culture exist, though in Central and West Africa no such long stratigraphic sequence is known and

the best that can be done is to assign individual sites to early, middle or late Chelles-Acheul on typological grounds.

The environment favoured by these early hunter-gatherers seems to have been that of the river valleys in reaches that cut across fairly open savanna country. Thus the equatorial forest belt is again lacking in finds of this period, and even the more densely wooded savanna of the plateau regions appears to have been generally avoided. The period is well represented in Southern Rhodesia and Zambia and in the eastern regions of the Congo. Northeastern Angola has yielded a few sites, and a few specimens are known from the lower Congo river. In Nigeria Acheulean sites are known only from the mines field area within 80 mi. of Jos. It is likely that the environment of the Guinea coast was unsuitable for occupation by hand-ax man, but little or no field work has been done in this area.

The most important site of Early Stone Age date from the area is undoubtedly that at Kalambo falls discovered by J. D. Clark in 1953. There an almost unbroken succession of camping sites is preserved in the accumulated lake deposits covering the period from an evolved stage of the Acheulean almost to the present. The Acheulean floors uncovered have yielded vast quantities of hand axes, cleavers, cores, hammerstones and flake tools in almost mint condition. But the greatest value of the site lies in the quantities of vegetable remains preserved in the waterlogged deposits. These include a number of wooden implements and sufficient plant remains to make it possible to reconstruct in remarkable detail the environment in which the hunters lived —an environment then apparently somewhat cooler and wetter. Careful plotting of the distribution of artifacts on one floor has revealed actual working spots and what may be sleeping places as well as a semicircle of large stones marking the edge of a windbreak—the oldest artificial dwelling known anywhere in the world. Carbon 14 dates from this site give an age earlier than 52,000 B.C. for the Acheulean living floors.

First Intermediate Period.—There is no reason to suppose that there is anywhere more than a purely local break in the sequence of African Stone Age cultures. In fact the evidence strongly supports the notion of a series of evolutionary developments in different regions out of the previously existing cultures. Such changes may be the response to new needs and new potentialities arising from changes imposed by nature on the environment, or the result of pure invention in a relatively static environment. Such a widespread and general change as marks the close of the Chelles-Acheul tradition in Africa, however, suggests strongly that the causes were largely environmental. In Southern and East Africa the first intermediate period is marked by the appearance of the Fauresmith culture, in which more refined and smaller versions of the Acheulean continue alongside an increased industry of flake tools and new techniques of stoneworking in which carefully prepared cores play an important role.

In Central Africa, however, in country that is believed to have been more heavily wooded, a culture appears to which the generic name Sangoan has been given. A few hand axes and cleavers continue the tradition of the Acheulean, but there is a tendency for workmanship to become somewhat coarser. Heavy triangular picks and flat-bottomed choppers, of rostrocarinate form (*i.e.,* resembling an eagle's beak in shape), in which the ventral edges and ends formed the working parts, become important and characteristic elements. Much of the tool kit of Sangoan man appears to be designed for woodworking. Various regional variants appear, due partly to the form in which raw material was available and partly to varying environment and traditions of toolmaking; culture contact no doubt played its part in marginal and outlying regions. In Southern Rhodesia the Bembesi variant has fewer typically Sangoan elements, while in Zambia the Zambezi and Luangwa variants appear to be due to differences in the form of the raw material. In Angola and the lower Congo river region the early manifestations of the Sangoan are remarkably similar to those of the type area in Uganda, but in successive stages these areas develop along very different lines from the Rhodesian Sangoan. Fine lance heads evolve (formerly East African Tumbian) as well as slipper-shaped chisels and woodworking tools. There is a marked encroachment toward the forest areas, until then unoccupied. Little is known of events in Nigeria and the Guinea coast, but B. Fagg makes no mention of Sangoan or Fauresmith tools from Nigeria, and it may well be that the sequence of events in these areas is considerably different. At Kalambo falls the Sangoan has been carbon dated to between 38,000 and 43,000 B.C.

Middle Stone Age.—Moving upward through the cultural succession in Africa, the number of regional variants increases until in the Middle Stone Age there are something like nine or ten throughout the continent. In the area of Central and West Africa there are two, and perhaps three, such variants which to some extent reflect the nature of the underlying Sangoan. In Zambia and Southern Rhodesia the form is known as Rhodesian Stillbay. In this the heavy elements of the Sangoan disappear except for a few pebble choppers, and there is a general tendency toward reduction in the size of artifacts. The prepared disk-shaped core is perfected and neat leaf-shaped points appear, both unifaced and bifaced, often very expertly flaked. These were almost certainly hafted as missile heads. Various scrapers and stone balls (possibly missile stones) of reduced size complete the assemblage. The culture has been found in good stratigraphical relationship to other cultures in Southern Rhodesia at Bambata cave and the Khami waterworks site, and in Zambia at the Mumbwa caves. The younger gravels in the vicinity of the Victoria falls have also yielded good assemblages. At Kalambo falls the industry shows an interesting blend of Rhodesian Stillbay elements and Lupemban forms more at home in the more northerly and western regions. This is presumably a reflection of the geographically intermediate position of the site. The Broken Hill skull (see above) was associated with an industry of the Rhodesian Stillbay referred to as Proto-Stillbay, tentatively dated by Clark to about 38,000 B.C.

To the northwest, in Angola and the lower Congo, as well as in the eastern Congo, the Middle Stone Age is represented by the Lupemban, a culture subdivided by Leakey and Mortelmans into several stages. The stratigraphical evidence for the stages is not good and the division is based mainly on typology. In the early stages a strong element of the Sangoan survives in the form of picks and a few hand axes. These gradually decline in importance and there is a development and refinement of new forms such as chisels, gouges and specialized adzes as well as tranchet axes, scrapers and narrow lanceolate points finely worked on both faces. The later stages of the Lupemban mostly represent a refinement of these various elements. Pressure flaking is used and true blades, sometimes backed, appear. Foliate points are deliberately serrated along to the edges, particularly toward one end, and true tanged points appear. Tranchets assume proportions which suggest their employment as transverse arrowheads. These special refinements appear in the final stage of the Lupemban which in Angola has been carbon dated to about 12,500 B.C.

To the north of the equatorial forest, in Nigeria and the Guinea coast region, information is again scanty. Fagg mentions an undifferentiated Middle Stone Age industry from the mines field area; O. Davies speaks of a "quasi-Magosian" but mentions no true Middle Stone Age from Ghana. He has also spoken of tanged points of Aterian appearance. In 1940, R. Delcroix and R. Vaufrey described an industry from Guinea which they compared with the "Tumbian" of Uganda and the Congo. This industry, however, contained a mixture of early and late forms, and cannot be taken as typical of the Middle Stone Age stage in that region.

Second Intermediate Period.—As the Gamblian wet phase comes to a close, and during the ensuing dry period about 10,000 B.C., a number of variants of a culture intermediate between the late Middle Stone Age and the true Late Stone Age appear. The tendency toward reduction in size noted in the Rhodesian Stillbay is carried still further in the succeeding Magosian culture to an extent where it clearly indicates that a number of tiny artifacts or microliths were being hafted together in groups to form barbs to spears (and possibly arrows) and to produce composite knives of the kind found at Mt. Carmel in the Natufian. True burins of the kind associated with the Upper Paleolithic and Mesolithic of

Europe occur in small numbers, and small punch-struck blades form another new element. These latter are frequently worked into various kinds of microlith such as crescents and backed blades. Two types of special woodworking tool are present: the thick crescent adz and the so-called *outil écaille* ("gouge" or "flake tool"). The unifaced and bifaced points, triangular and leaf-shaped, continue the tradition of the Stillbay but are generally smaller and often finely shaped with the aid of pressure flaking. Scrapers, drills, mullers and grindstones and the occasional bored stone complete the assemblage. It has been suggested that the culture is the result of a mixture of the indigenous Rhodesian Stillbay, and blade and burin and microlith makers infiltrating from East Africa. Whether this is true or not, the Magosian, with minor variations, is the ensuing culture in those parts of Central Africa formerly occupied by the Rhodesian Stillbay. The known distribution appears to be somewhat more restricted than the Stillbay, and this may indicate a greater degree of concentration of population because of deterioration in climate; this is suggested by the redistribution of aeolian sands in and below which the Magosian is frequently stratified.

In those areas in which the Middle Stone Age is represented by the Lupemban the second intermediate period is represented by the final expression of that culture, generally known as the Lupembo-Tshitolian. In a diminutive and refined state many of the ancestral forms of the Sangoan and Lupemban are present. The significant elements are the denticulated and tanged points, backed blades, crescents and trapezes and true punch-struck bladelets.

Late Stone Age.—In those areas occupied by the Lupembo-Tshitolian the final expression of the full Stone Age is the Tshitolian; a culture which, from its distribution and industrial content, was well adapted to life in the forest regions. The laurel leaf points of Lupemban type remain and leaf-shaped arrowheads, some denticulated, and tanged points are common. There are no true microliths, but tranchets of various sizes, probably transverse arrowheads designed to leave a good blood spoor, are abundant. Chisels and gouges reflect an interest in woodworking. In the later stages polished stone axes, adzes and grindstones occur. Occasional finds of pottery suggest contact with food-producing communities. The term Neolithic applied to assemblages with polished axes is inappropriate as this implies food production which is by no means certain. To the south, in Angola, there are differences in that microliths form part of the assemblage, and bored stones are present, probably as digging stick weights, whereas the polished ax is absent. In Katanga the culture shows a blending of Tshitolian and Nachikufan elements. A most important site at Ishango, on the shore of Lake Edward, has yielded a rather crude quartz industry associated with quantities of bone harpoons and barbed points, as well as simple bone points.

Southward over the plateau country of the major part of Zambia the culture is known as Nachikufan, the earliest stage of which has been carbon dated to about 4350 B.C. Three stages were established stratigraphically at the type site. In the earliest, very small nongeometric microliths are abundant, associated with trapezes, semicircles and double-backed microliths. Larger elements include grindstones and rubbers, numerous bored stones, bone points and ochre pencils. In the second stage the very small microliths are rare while to the other elements are added hollow and strangulated scrapers and numbers of polished stone adzes and axes. The number of bone points also shows a marked increase. In the final stage the microliths show a closer similarity to the Wilton forms, and the presence of pottery suggests the arrival of immigrant farmers into the area.

In the Zambezi valley the industry is known as Rhodesian Wilton and more closely resembles that of the type site in South Africa. The forms are mostly rather rough-backed blades, neat lunates and semicircles, some double-backed microliths and a few trapezes. *Outils écailles* and small scrapers are present and polished axes and bored stones are very rare. Two stages are recognized by Clark, the earlier with generally larger microliths and the later with a high percentage of crescent adzes, ostrich eggshell beads and occasional sherds of pottery. A date of about 240 B.C.

has been obtained for this later stage. In Southern Rhodesia, in areas close to the Zambesi, the industry is similar to that just described. But farther south an open grassland variant is recognized for Matabeleland and a woodland variant with axes and chopping tools for Mashonaland. The abundant naturalistic rock art of Southern Rhodesia is generally attributed to the Late Stone Age, while in Zambia there is some evidence for associating the geometric art of the northern and eastern parts of the territory with an early stage of the Nachikufan culture. In Ghana the Late Stone Age is best represented from the cave of Bosumpra at Abetifi, with a microlithic industry in quartz with lunates, backed blades, burins and simple points. Pottery and polished axes occur in the later stages. Biconically bored pebbles which are abundant in Ghana were also associated. Fagg described a similar industry from Rop rock shelter in Nigeria, including a polished ax with hourglass perforation.

Iron Age.—All the cultures thus far described were based on a hunting and food-gathering economy. There is some evidence that Late Stone Age man was taking a marked interest in vegetable foods, but none to suggest that agriculture had been independently discovered. This state of affairs was brought to an end by the movement into West and Central Africa of primitive farmers who brought with them the arts of metalworking and pottery manufacture. Evidence for the physical type of these people is not incontrovertible. There is no doubt that in a number of areas the Negro element was strong, and it is probably this which has contributed so much to the make-up of the present Bantu-speaking tribes. But at Bambandyanalo in the Transvaal an Early Iron Age culture is associated with a very definitely non-Negroid population. The claim that this culture is Proto-Hottentot is subject to serious doubt.

In Southern Rhodesia the earliest Iron Age tradition, which precedes the great ruins complexes, is marked by the fairly widespread occurrence of thick but well-made pottery decorated predominantly by comb impressions. Other elements in the culture are clay figurines, mainly human but with some animals, clay spoons and possibly some very rough terracing in the Inyanga area. Storage pits have been located and fragments of the walls of pole and daga huts, but the houses themselves have not been identified. From the exclusive occurrence of stamped ware in many of the ancient mines in Southern Rhodesia it would appear that these people were responsible for the mining of gold, and possibly copper and tin also. Work in Zambia suggests strongly that the Kalomo culture in the south may be related to the stamped ware tradition. Sites in the south of Barotseland have produced carbon 14 dates of around A.D. 90 for this stage. In the north of the territory, at Kalambo falls, the earliest pottery is more closely allied to the "dimple-based" tradition which is widespread throughout Rwanda and Burundi, in Kenya and as far west as the lower Congo basin. Dates for the Kalambo Iron Age range from the 6th to the 11th century A.D.

In the northern Transvaal and throughout Southern Rhodesia there exists a great complex of stone ruins. These mark the beginning of a new phase in the Iron Age. The earliest of these are probably Zimbabwe and Mapungubwe, whose origins have been carbon dated to approximately the 11th and 14th centuries A.D. respectively. Zimbabwe itself, despite the romantic tales that have grown up about it, is probably the kraal of a paramount chief, possibly connected with the Monomatapa empire. Buildings of different periods are distinguished, and the latest of these probably dates from the 17th century A.D., approximately contemporary with the ruins complexes of Inyanga, Khami, Dhlo-dhlo and Nalatali. Little is known of the origins of the ruins builders, but they possibly represent the first of a series of migrations whose epicentre may have been in the southern Congo basin.

In West Africa the earliest Iron Age culture, the Nok figurine culture, is best known from the tin mines of the plateau mines field area. The most striking features are the beautifully naturalistic clay animal figurines and the more stylized human figurines, mostly heads. These appear to have been made in clay molds possibly formed around a wax model as in the *cire perdue* method of bronze casting. With the figurines are found evidence of iron smelting, polished stone axes and one iron ax, pottery, stone ornaments including ground quartz beads, and bored stones (possibly digging stick weights). The current estimate of its chronology, based on radiocarbon measurement, is that it flourished from soon after 500 B.C. to around A.D. 200. Its origins and its influence on subsequent events are obscure.

To the west of Nok the finds of finely cast brass, and terracotta heads and figurines at Ife and Benin appear to belong to related kingdoms ancestral to the modern Yoruba. The differences in style between the Ife and Benin products are considerable and support other lines of evidence suggesting that Ife is the earlier and probably ancestral to Benin. The Ife bronzes are probably to be dated to between A.D. 1000 and 1500, and those of Benin to the 16th, 17th and 18th centuries. (R. R. In.)

D. East Africa

Much information about the Stone Age sequence of East Africa was derived from studies of the Rift valley. High terraces above the Rift valley lakes point to their extended area in Quaternary times. Partly from this evidence it was deduced that there was a series of pluvial periods during the Pleistocene, followed by two postpluvial wet phases, each separated by a period of drier conditions. Prehistoric industries and cultures have been correlated with these climatic phases, but attempts at wider correlations throughout Africa and with glacial and interglacial phases in Europe must still be regarded as tentative.

Pebble Culture.—The existence of the Kafuan pebble culture in East Africa, as well as in other parts of the continent, is very doubtful; it seems probable that these crude pebble tools were fashioned by natural agencies. The later Oldowan pebble tools, however, are undoubtedly of human workmanship. First recognized in the lowest bed of Olduvai gorge (Tanzania), they date from the Villafranchian period or Lower Pleistocene.

Chelles-Acheul Culture.—During the Middle Pleistocene, the Chelles-Acheul hand-ax culture was widespread in Kenya, Uganda and Tanzania. Its evolution, including its development from the Oldowan pebble culture, is clearly shown at Olduvai gorge, beginning in the upper part of Bed II. There thousands of implements as well as numerous fossil mammal remains are preserved in successive lake beds. In Bed I and the lower part of Bed II australopithecines and *Homo habilis* were found together with Oldowan tools. Associated with the following Chellean stage was a skull of *Homo erectus* type; also in Bed II was a butchering site where gigantic animals had been driven into a swamp and dismembered with hand axes and cleavers. Hand axes reached their peak during the Acheulean stage, represented at many sites in East Africa besides Olduvai. Among these are Paraa Lodge and Mweya Lodge in Uganda; Isimila in Tanzania; Kariandusi and Olorgesailie in Kenya. At all of these sites implements exist in great profusion; and at Olorgesailie they are accompanied by fossils of extinct mammals similar to the gigantic fauna of Olduvai.

The Chelles-Acheul was succeeded by the Fauresmith culture during the first intermediate period in Kenya as it was in Southern Africa. The Fauresmith appears to be confined to high altitudes; it is supposed that the camps belonging to this culture were situated beside streams that would continue to flow during the drier period which followed the Kanjeran pluvial. In other parts of the area, particularly in western Kenya and Uganda, the Chelles-Acheul was followed by the Sangoan, first discovered at Sango bay on Lake Victoria. At Nsongezi on the Kagera river it immediately succeeds the Chelles-Acheul culture and is characterized by rough hand axes and heavy picks.

Middle and Later Stone Age in Kenya.—During the time of the Gamblian pluvial, the regional specialization of Middle Stone Age times is as noticeable in East Africa as in other parts of the continent. In Kenya two main industries existed side by side. One is the Stillbay, which is found over most of the drier country of eastern Africa; the other is the Lupemban, which succeeded the Sangoan in wetter areas. During the Lupemban and the Tshitolian stages of the Later Stone Age, beautifully flaked lance heads and tranchets appear both in Uganda and in the

Kavirondo district of western Kenya.

The Magosian of the second intermediate period was first discovered at a water hole named Magosi in Karamoja, eastern Uganda. The industry includes points of the Stillbay type, little tortoise cores, and microlithic tools of various kinds as well as grindstones and a perforated stone. Probably also post-Pleistocene in age is a blade and burin industry named the Kenya Capsian, which is exclusive to the Rift valley but similar in certain respects to the Capsian industries of North Africa dating from about 6,000 B.C. At Gamble's cave near Elmenteita human burials associated with an Upper Kenya Capsian industry are of Caucasoid type. The implements include backed blades, lunates (crescent-shaped arrow or harpoon barbs), burins, scrapers and other tools all made of obsidian, as well as bone awls and harpoons. Two small fragments of pottery found in the excavation were associated with this industry. The whole assemblage would be regarded as typically Mesolithic in Europe; the bone harpoons are similar to those of the Ishangian culture of Lake Edward, which is dated on extrapolated radiocarbon evidence to about 6000 B.C., a date much later than that originally suggested for the Upper Kenya Capsian.

During Late Stone Age times tools tended to become increasingly smaller, notably in the Wilton industries which are widespread in East Africa, particularly in less heavily forested areas. Some Wilton sites are found in the open, others in rock shelters and others again accompanied by huge shell middens beside the shores of Lake Victoria, where they are associated with heavily built skeletons with skulls of Bushman type.

Rock Paintings.—Little in the way of rock art has been discovered in Kenya and Uganda other than very late paintings and engravings. In Tanzania, however, there are a large number of painted shelters, particularly in the neighbourhood of Kondoa. Many different styles have been distinguished and some are associated with an industry similar to the Nachikufan of Zambia. Some of the naturalistic animal paintings are comparable to those of Zambia and Southern Rhodesia and South Africa.

Neolithic.—The earliest "Neolithic" culture described in East Africa stems from the "Mesolithic" Elmenteitan, which includes long, two-edged blades and sophisticated pottery. It developed during the first postpluvial wet phase into the Hyrax hill variant of the stone bowl culture, of which three other later variants were distinguished: Gumban A, Gumban B (now considered to be Iron Age) and Njoro River cave. The last has been dated by radiocarbon to about 960 B.C. These variants are distinguished by different forms of stone bowl and by distinctive methods of burial. At the Njoro River cave cremation was practised. The skulls are all of Caucasoid type and show no trace of Negroid features. The assemblage includes many beads, a carved wooden vessel, pestles and grindstones, bone pendants and awls, basketwork and plaited cord.

Iron Age.—Few Iron Age sites in East Africa had been excavated before the late 1950s and it then became clear that the earliest evidence of ironworking was associated with "dimple-based" pottery, found in western Kenya, Uganda, Congo, Rwanda and Zambia (where it dates from the first few centuries A.D.). At Hyrax hill near Nakuru an Iron Age village which included large horseshoe-shaped enclosures and hut circles was excavated. In 1957 a similar industry was found nearby and called the Lanet culture; it was dated by radiocarbon to A.D. 1585 ± 175. In Uganda there are remarkable earthworks of which the most extensive is Bigo on the Katonga river. These constructions, which were presumable large cattle kraals, are attributed to the legendary Bacwezi, probably a ruling clan of the Hima, a pastoral aristocracy. At Ntusi are huge middens containing animal bones and potsherds—some of which are painted. Other large middens with innumerable potsherds occur at Kibiro on the eastern shore of Lake Albert. (C. V. R. L.; S. M. C.)

The Horn.—Since the earliest evidence of man's presence in the Horn (Ethiopia and the Somali Republic), the climate at its best seems never to have been more than semiarid. Doubtless the more even distribution and small increases of rainfall during the pluvial periods had an important effect on the vegetation pattern and the surface water supply, yet only the Ethiopian high plateau was ever especially inviting to permanent settlement and food production. This predominantly dry ecology, therefore, had an important effect on the human population, and before the end of the Middle Pleistocene the Horn appears to have been unoccupied by man and was probably heavily covered with thicket vegetation. About 100,000 years ago, however, groups practising a stone culture (Acheuleo-Levallois) intermediate in form between that of the Early and the Middle Stone Age are found in the northern parts, particularly in the northwestern part of the Somali Republic. Finely made hand axes, both pointed and pear shaped, cleavers and stone balls are found associated with numerous flake tools struck from large, circular, radially prepared Levallois-type cores. From then on there was continuous occupation and many stone implements have been collected from the widely eroded Pleistocene deposits. The material most commonly used was a fine chert, but sometimes quartzite was employed and, in the Danakil rift and on the Ethiopian high plateau, fine-grained lavas and obsidian from volcanic rocks.

By the falling out of the heavier hand-ax elements, human culture, during the more favourable conditions pertaining in the Horn during the last or Gamblian pluvial, passed through an unspecialized Middle Stone Age (Levalloisian) using flakes with little secondary trimming and comparable to the contemporary form in Egypt. There followed from this a fully bifacial phase (Somaliland Stillbay) where the flakes were worked by controlled percussion and pressure on one or both sides to form projectile points, knives and scrapers of various kinds. The points, scrapers and crudely backed flakes are similar in technique of manufacture and typology to those from East and southern Africa, as also is the prepared core technique employed for striking the primary flakes. It may be that the onset of drier conditions had severed the link with northeast Africa though still preserving that to the south.

By the end of Pleistocene times, about 10,000 years ago, there is evidence of a blade and burin (chisel) element in the north, particularly in the area of the former British protectorate and the Mijiurtein, which was probably derived from southwest Asia via the Red sea hills. Large as well as microlithic blades were struck from cores of black Eocene chert, and finished implements were angle and *bec-de-flûte* burins, single and double end scrapers and straight-backed microliths often with basal retouch. This industry was contemporary with a diminutive and evolved form of Middle Stone Age (Magosian) in the Danakil rift and the southern parts of the Horn. Perhaps this intrusive culture (Hargeisan) was brought by long-headed Afro-Mediterranean peoples, whose fossil remains have been found in Kenya in association with similar Stone Age cultures both contemporary with and earlier than this time. Unfortunately, in the Horn no human fossils except comparatively recent ones have been discovered, except for a jaw fragment said to show Neanderthal characteristics and to be associated with a final Middle Stone Age industry in the Porc Epic cave near Dire Dawa.

After the end of the Pleistocene, connections seem to lie essentially with northern Africa. The so-called Neolithic wet phase in the Sahara, probably lasting from the 6th to the 3rd millennium B.C., permitted Saharan forms of hollow-based and other types of pressure-flaked arrowheads to enter the Horn, probably brought by immigrants from the eastern desert who settled in central and southern Somalia. There is nothing as yet to show that these people were food producers and they must still have relied on hunting and collecting for their food supply. At a time not yet determined but perhaps in the 3rd or early 2nd millennium B.C., when the drying up of the pastures in the central Sahara drove cattle-owning peoples there to seek fresh country for their stock, pastoralists entered the eastern parts of the Horn. Rock paintings near Harar and Dire Dawa in Ethiopia and in northwestern Somali Republic depict herdsmen with long-horned, humpless cattle. A most important new area of rock paintings was discovered in 1961 in the Senafe and Adi Ugri regions of Ethiopia. The style of painting is similar to the later Saharan styles and the people seem to be of Afro-Mediterranean stock with weapons and clothing similar to those seen in the Sahara paintings.

No settlements of these people have yet been found, unless they can be associated with some of the microlithic industries in the rock shelters in the northern part of the Horn, and some of the "Galla graves" (stone cairns for burial and other purposes that are found throughout the dry areas of the Horn) may date back to these times, though the majority are undoubtedly much later. Some of these people may also have practised a simple form of millet agriculture but the majority are likely to have been purely nomadic as are most of the modern Somali Danakil-speaking peoples. The Egyptian expedition of Queen Hatshepsut (15th century B.C.) to the land of Punt, which most writers are agreed is the northern Somali or Ethiopian coast, shows that "Hamitic" and Negroid peoples, long- and short-horned cattle and evidence of cultivation were present there by that date.

Little is known of the prehistoric archaeology of the Ethiopian high plateau and Eritrea but it is likely that this was one of the first areas south of the Sahara to adopt the cultivation of cereal crops (wheat and barley). These must have both competed with and acted as a stimulus for the development of local indigenous food plants such as *teff*, *ensete* and the *Eleusine* millets. The date when cereal crop cultivation first began in the Horn is not known, but it is unlikely to have been prior to the middle of the 4th millennium (the Khartoum Neolithic dates to 3253 ± 415 B.C.) and it is possible that the crops and techniques traveled up the Nile and across the southwestern desert to Ethiopia.

Obsidian blade industries with pottery exist in the Tigre (at Quiha and elsewhere) but their date is unknown. Polished axes and adzes have been found in western Ethiopia. Similar forms associated with maceheads, stone palettes and pottery having affinities with the C group culture of Nubia have been described from Agordat in Eritrea and would seem to be the products of a sedentary and fully agricultural economy for which a date of the early to middle 2nd millennium B.C. is suggested.

By the early centuries of the Christian era, however, the camel and zebu or humped cattle (which have now quite superseded the long- and short-horned breeds in the Horn) are believed to have been introduced by Himyaritic peoples from southern Arabia. These Arabian peoples crossed the Red sea during the 1st millennium B.C. and gradually occupied the northern part of the highlands, intermarrying with the Hamitic-speaking peoples and forming the kingdom of Aksum (Axum) which apparently covered what is now the Tigre province. The earliest record of this kingdom is in the first century A.D. Ironworking probably spread to the Horn from the kingdom of Meroe on the upper Nile sometime after 500 B.C., but it is not known whether bronze or copper was smelted there prior to that time. Greek sailors from Egypt had reached the Eritrean coast in the 3rd century B.C., probably in search of elephants for the Ptolemaic army. By the 1st century A.D. the king of Aksum controlled the ivory, and probably the incense trade on that coast, and by the 3rd century most of the northern part of the Horn seems to have been conquered. It may have been this process of subjugation of the indigenous Ethiopian peoples to the kingdom of Aksum that set off movements of Hamitic-speaking and Negroid peoples into the southern parts of the continent. While during the later Pleistocene the cultural connections of the Stone Age peoples in the Horn were with East Africa, from the end of that time they have been linked more particularly with northeast Africa and southern Arabia.   (J. D. CL.)

E. NORTH AFRICA

In comparatively recent years the archaeology of North Africa has assumed a detailed aspect and general importance in human history unsuspected previously, as a result in part of its geographical position as a link between Asia, tropical Africa and southwestern Europe. Ecologically it subdivides into well-defined territories whose geographical pattern in turn has conditioned both its history and its prehistory.

Geography and Climate.—The most important territory for human occupation is the Maghreb (Maghrib), the Africa Minor of the ancients. This comprises the western half of the Mediterranean littoral and consists essentially of the Atlas massif and coastal plain from Morocco to Tunisia. The mountains cause the Atlantic westerlies to drop their moisture mainly on the northern slopes and narrow coastal plain, where under natural conditions the vegetation would be of Mediterranean evergreen and maquis type. Rainfall on the southern slopes of the massif is sufficient to maintain desert scrub fading into true desert in the Saharan plain to the south. A small appendage of the Maghreb area of fertility is formed by the high ground of northern Tripolitania, but eastward for about 600 mi. along the shores of the Gulf of Sidra (Sirte) the desert reaches practically to the sea. A second small coastal area comparable in fertility to the Maghreb is the Jebel Akhdar of northern Cyrenaica. Though much smaller in extent it is of importance ecologically as providing a natural staging post halfway between the Maghreb and the Nile.

A quite different ecological role is played by the Nile valley, which constitutes the only permanent corridor of access between Central Africa and the Mediterranean. A much more tenuous line, revived in classical times by the introduction of the camel, runs from northern Tripolitania to the Niger bend via the central Saharan highlands. The latter consist of a system of volcanic outcrops and tectonic ridges extending from the Ahaggar in the centre southeastward along the Tummo ridge to Tibesti and ultimately to Darfur. At the present time this feature has only minor climatic consequences, but its importance in the past during periods of over-all increased precipitation is proved by a remarkable relict fauna and flora including such species as crocodile, Asiatic cobra and a conifer that could not possibly spread to the area under conditions prevailing today. One such period of greater rainfall certainly occurred during the Middle Acheulean and enabled human settlements to extend far over regions now totally uninhabitable for lack of water; and a second of less pronounced character during the diffusion of pottery and other traits associated with the Neolithic of the 4th and 3rd millenniums B.C. Signs of other fluctuations of minor and perhaps regional importance have been reported, but the attempt made by some investigators to construct an ambitious scheme of pluvials and interpluvials and to correlate it with European glaciations must be regarded as quite hypothetical as yet.

Lower Paleolithic.—More direct evidence for correlation can be derived from the combined study of ancient marine shorelines and vertebrate paleontology along the northern littoral. The most ancient certain traces of man in northern Africa consist of cores (possibly tools) and flakes accompanied by a rich Lower Pleistocene (Villafranchian) fauna, discovered at Ain Hanech, Alg., in 1948. Their age is thus as great as that of the earliest certain human industries in any part of the world, and in particular may be compared with the oldest horizon (Bed I) at Olduvai gorge in East Africa of comparable typology and associated with the very primitive hominid *Zinjanthropus* or else the newly suggested *Homo habilis*. The second stage in the North African archaeological succession is represented by a somewhat archaic Middle Acheulean, in which the usual pointed types of hand axes are associated with true cleavers of central African type. The absence of any traces of the earlier precleaver stages in the hand-ax tradition such as those recorded at Olduvai (Bed II) and elsewhere south of the Sahara may well indicate a severance of the western trans-Saharan route at this time; such industries do occur in the Nile valley but are unknown farther west.

The most notable occurrence of the Middle Acheulean in question is at Ternifine in northern Algeria, where it is dated by an early Middle Pleistocene fauna with Villafranchian survivals including a sabre-toothed tiger, a giant wart hog and an extinct cynocephalous ape. Also associated are the only known human fossils definitely attributable to this culture stage. They comprise three admirably preserved mandibles and a parietal, and show anatomical affinities to *Pithecanthropus*, the earliest human strain of the far east. They also exhibit some novel features especially in the dentition, on the strength of which their discoverer C. Arambourg proposes separate generic status under the name *Atlanthropus*, though most authorities agree that no more than specific differentiation from *Pithecanthropus* is indicated.

Apart from the character of the associated fauna, the age of the Ternifine stage is supported by geological evidence from the

Sidi Abderrahman quarries near Casablanca, Morocco. There an identical industry is included in a beach deposit underlying an apparently unwarped strand line at +30 m. attributed by most authorities to the Tyrrhenian I or Great Interglacial stage. If this correlation is correct it would follow that Ternifine belongs at latest to the equivalent of a Mindel interstadial or more probably the preceding (antepenultimate) interglacial. This date, if transferred to East Africa on the basis suggested above, would suggest a Lower Pleistocene date for *Zinjanthropus*, or *Homo habilis*, not unreasonable if either is to be regarded as a true human ancestor. It would also be in accord with a recent reassessment of the Bed I fauna at Olduvai also as Lower Pleistocene (Villafranchian) rather than Middle Pleistocene, as previously supposed.

Middle Paleolithic.—The final stages of the Lower Paleolithic in the western Maghreb are represented at Sidi Abderrahman also by an evolved Acheulean associated with human fossils believed to indicate a later, more developed form of *Atlanthropus*. They are dated stratigraphically as post-Tyrrhenian I (most probably the equivalent of Riss) and paleontologically by the presence of some intrusive Eurasiatic species. The latter were absent from the Acheulean fauna, which had been of purely African character, but are a regular feature of the biotope associated with the subsequent Middle Paleolithic culture stage. In eastern Tunisia the great length of duration of the hand-ax tradition is shown by the inclusion of typical hand axes in deposits which were warped by tectonic movement on a large scale before the beginning of the Middle Paleolithic. While the fauna associated with the Middle Paleolithic of the Maghreb and Cyrenaica clearly indicates that the east-west corridor along the coast was still biologically viable, there are indications that movement of men and animal species across the Sahara from north to south was considerably less than in Lower Paleolithic times. It is interesting to note that detailed observations in the Nile valley give geological evidence also that desiccation of the later Pleistocene made itself first felt in the south. The apparent effects of this change can be seen in several ways.

In Kharga (Al Kharijah) oasis in the extreme southeast of the Sahara the passage from the final Acheulean hand-ax tradition to the most evolved Middle Paleolithic flake tradition, with a highly evolved technique of cores prepared in the Levalloisian style, is a gradual process with many terms of transition and spread over a long period of climatic change. The same type of gradual evolution is a regular feature of tropical Africa and the Nile valley. Farther north in the Jebel Akhdar the later terms only of this sequence are known, and have recently been shown to be superimposed, not on an Acheulean substratum as at Kharga, but on an early horizon otherwise unique in the African continent, consisting of flake blades and burins. This newly discovered tradition finds its nearest affinities with a flake-blade culture in the Levant known as the Pre-Aurignacian and geologically dated there to the last interglacial. Marine shells associated with the Cyrenaican variant suggest a similar date.

The overlying Middle Paleolithic in both Cyrenaica and Palestine is similar and known as Levalloiso-Mousterian from the combination in it of the two traits of a miniature type of Levalloisian core technique together with various tools finished by unifacial trimming like those of the Mousterian of Europe. This complex tradition is associated both in Cyrenaica (at the cave of Haua Fteah) and Palestine with fossil human remains of Neanderthaloid type sharing a number of peculiarities not known elsewhere, and incidentally contrasting in almost every detail with the corresponding features of *Atlanthropus*. It is dated by radiocarbon in both areas to between 35,000 and 50,000 B.C.

The situation in the Maghreb is different again. Earlier facies of the Middle Paleolithic have left few if any certain traces, and there is so far no clear indication of a parallel evolution of this stage out of the preceding final Acheulean. The overwhelming majority of Middle Paleolithic finds belong unquestionably to a single pattern termed the Aterian. This contains all the main features of the Levalloiso-Mousterian coupled with additional elements of a still more specialized kind, above all the device of a carefully contrived hafting projection or tang, clearly implying that many of the tools and weapons were mounted in handles and shafts. A significant feature is the sporadic use of bifacial trimming, sometimes for the manufacture of small hand axes, but sometimes so fine as to indicate a true pressure-flaking technique comparable with that of the Solutrians of Europe. Over a restricted area in the extreme west of the Maghreb the application of this method to the production of tanged points led in the very latest Aterian to a form virtually indistinguishable from Neolithic or Bronze Age arrowheads. Remarkably similar forms occur in the Solutrian of southeastern Spain and it seems not improbable that culture contact in some form was established across the Strait of Gibraltar at this time. If so we have an implied date of about 15,000 B.C. for the final Aterian in the Tangier-Morocco region. An earlier stage of this tradition in the same region (at the cave of al-'Aliya) is associated with fragmentary human fossils which appear still to show some of the peculiarities of *Atlanthropus* in attenuated form, and are almost certainly distinct from the Neanderthaloids of Cyrenaica.

A working theory might be postulated on the strength of these observations as follows: The final Lower Paleolithic in both Cyrenaica and the Levant during the last interglacial is characterized by the appearance in both areas (sporadically in the latter and in isolation in the former) of flake blades. This stage is overlaid in both areas by an identical variant of evolved Middle Paleolithic, the Levalloiso-Mousterian, most probably of ultimate Central African origin and spreading northward along the Nile valley to fan out east and west along the Mediterranean coast. During this time a residual Acheulean may well have survived in the Maghreb, cut off by growing desiccation from the south, and undisturbed until reached by the westward spread of the Levalloiso-Mousterians along the coast. Culture contact between these and the final Acheuleans to produce the Aterian would not contradict the typological evidence as it stands, and would accord well with such elements as the bifacial technique. Finally, it may be noted that both in Cyrenaica and in Kharga the final term of the Middle Paleolithic succession is in fact supplied by Aterian of a moderately evolved kind.

Upper Paleolithic.—In eastern North Africa the earliest true blade and burin assemblage of Upper Paleolithic type, the Dabban, takes the form of an industry with both primitive backed blades and steep scrapers comparable to the corresponding initial stage of the Upper Paleolithic in the Levant, the Emiran. It is found in the Haua Fteah where it abruptly succeeds the Levalloiso-Mousterian at or shortly before 38,000 B.C. according to the radiocarbon dates. In the Maghreb not only are all traces of this early tradition lacking but it has been seen that the final Aterian may well have survived as late as the 15th millennium. True blades and burin industries there fall into two classes known respectively as the Oranian (or Ibero-Maurusian) and the Capsian. Contrary to what was at first suggested on purely typological grounds, the Oranian now proves to be very much the older, as well as by far the most widely spread. It is found along the whole coastline and penetrates some distance inland in both Morocco and Tunisia, and has been identified in Cyrenaica where it replaces the earlier Emiranlike tradition about 14,000 B.C. Typologically it is distinguished above all by the immense preponderance of small backed blades over all other tool forms. The date of its substitution for the Aterian in the Maghreb is not yet precisely known but certainly antedates the 10th millennium, a date obtained for an evolved variant at the cave of Taforalt in Morocco.

Human remains are relatively common with the Oranian and extremely uniform in character; they belong to the Mechta al-Arbi type. The sudden appearance of the Oranian clearly indicates an incursion into northern Africa on a large scale, and the recent discovery in eastern Spain of a skull dated to the Solutrian showing all the peculiar features of the Mechta al-Arbi type provides a clue to the source of this immigration. In many traits the Oranian closely resembles an impoverished version of the Magdalenian IV of southeastern Spain, for which a date in the 15th millennium B.C. is probable.

Epi-Paleolithic.—The Capsian, once thought to typify the Upper Paleolithic of northern Africa, is now known to be wholly postglacial in date and is only certainly known from a very restricted area in southern Tunisia. It differs from the Oranian in displaying a far more varied tool kit distinguished by large, backed blades and burins in its earlier phase and a gradual development of geometric microliths later. These become its leading feature by the 6th millennium B.C. when they seem to have been transmitted to the final Oranian groups along the coast. Its origin has been sought in an Epi-Gravettian tradition which seems to have survived down to a late period in Sicily and the Sicilian islands. In Cyrenaica the final Oranian is replaced by 8,000 B.C. by a blade and burin tradition resembling an impoverished Capsian without the microlithic element.

Neolithic.—Shortly afterward, by 4,500 B.C., signs of contact with the early Neolithic (Fayyum A) cultures of Egypt are apparent in the form of pottery, pressure-flaked tools of distinctive types and domestic goats or sheep. The pottery is for the most part plain self-coloured and burnished, and doubtless ultimately of Levantine inspiration.

West of the Gulf of Sidra the earliest evidences of pottery and domestic animals, accompanied by certain changes in the flintwork, follow a different pattern. Widespread adoption of final Capsian microlithic forms, notably the trapeze and scalene triangle, are coupled with small pressure-flaked types such as stemmed arrowheads. This Neolithic of Capsian tradition has a wide extension in space and time; it occurs far south of the Maghreb into the western Sahara and down the Atlantic littoral to tropical West Africa. Its earliest dated occurrence in the Sahara goes back to the 4th millennium B.C. (Meniet) and echoes of its influence can still be detected at the time of the earliest introduction of iron into West Africa.

In the Maghreb itself two distinct provinces can probably be detected: (1) a northern coastal variant with undecorated pottery and virtually lacking in arrowheads and (2) a southern variant with impressed pottery of a type found virtually throughout the Sahara, abundant arrowheads and above all associated with a remarkable style of rock engraving. The latter generally takes the form of large-scale figures of animals or scenes with human figures grouped on slabs near water holes or shelters. Many of the human figures show details of dress, hairstyle, etc., reminiscent of those of the ancient Libyans in contact with Egypt during the 2nd millennium B.C. These occur in a well-studied cluster of sites in southern Algeria; sometimes in connection with curious figures of a ram wearing a round object on its head with snakelike projections recalling the well-known symbol of Amon. In a second large group of sites in the Fezzan district of southern Tripolitania further evidences of Egyptian influence include copies of the Bes design. Scattered finds of a seemingly degenerate version of this style occur as far south as the Ahaggar, but more characteristic of this southern area is a different style of remarkable rock paintings showing numerous human figures engaged in hunting, herding cattle, dancing, etc. The distribution of these overlaps with the engravings in the Fezzan and vicinity to the west. There a clue to the age of the former is afforded by representatives of chariots of almost certainly first millennium date, not improbably to be identified with the Garamantes of Herodotus.

Southeastward the distribution of these paintings can be traced along the high ground to Tibesti, and thence via Aweinat and the Gilf Kebir to the southern confines of Egypt and Nubia. Impressed pottery of Saharan type was in use there during the middle kingdom but an earlier centre of diffusion of pottery making of probable 4th millennium dates occurs in the Old Khartoum culture of the Sudan. The latter shows some possible signs of influence from the Neolithic of Capsian tradition in the flintwork but elsewhere, along the southern Sahara as far west as the Aïr, Egyptian influence is evident in the stonework generally.

Egypt.—The earliest phases of Egyptian prehistory are recorded in the system of ancient terraces of the Nile which reflect its geological history from late Tertiary times to the present. The earliest cultural remains belong to an early stage of the hand-ax tradition comparable to the remains from Olduvái (Bed II) in East Africa, before the first appearance of the cleaver. It is remarkable that this latter form so common in the later stages in East Africa and western North Africa should be virtually unknown in Egypt throughout the long development of the hand-ax tradition there. While an explanation may be sought in part in local peculiarities of raw material, almost exclusively flint, it seems also to be in part a reflection of the cultural autonomy which characterizes the Egyptian sequence in general.

Hand axes make their first appearance in the 100-ft. terrace of upper Egypt together with rarer pebble tools, and last through the period of the 50-ft. down to the 30-ft. stage when Middle Paleolithic flaking techniques begin to be associated with them. In lower Egypt a pure Acheulean occurs in a terrace at about 80 ft. above the Nile which can probably be equated with the Tyrrhenian I stage, but no earlier occurrence is known. The gradual emergence of Middle Paleolithic out of an Acheulean industrial matrix resembles the normal sequence south of the Sahara rather than that of farther west. The general pattern is that of a gradual reduction in size culminating in a Levalloiso-Mousterian contained in a terrace of fine silty sediments which appears to correlate with a low sea level in all probability of Würmian age.

Several workers have sought in the past to distinguish a final stage—the "Sebilian"—at the top of the silt terrace and subsequently, during which this refined Middle Paleolithic was supposed to have given rise directly to a microlithic blade industry by a process of independent evolution. The reality of this "Sebilian" industry may now be seriously doubted in view of the pattern of normal Upper Paleolithic spread and development known from the rest of North Africa. Thus it is practically certain that the bearers of the Emiran type of tradition of Palestine must have passed to Cyrenaica across the delta region shortly before 38,000 B.C. A number of undated surface sites of a blade industry, almost certainly a marginal variant of the Oranian, have been recorded from the Fayyum depression in lower Egypt; and there is evidence of acculturation between this indigenous hunting culture and the Fayyum B Neolithic sometime during the early 4th millennium B.C. or perhaps slightly earlier. The latter is clearly a final stage of the Neolithic A tradition established in the area by the 5th millennium and almost certainly ancestral to the initial Neolithic of middle Egypt represented by the Tasian culture. Both derive their principal culture traits in all probability from the somewhat earlier Levantine Neolithic tradition in existence by the 7th millennium B.C. and connected with still earlier food-producing societies in that area. *See* also EGYPT: *Archaeology* and *History*.

(C. B. M. McB.)

F. CARTHAGINIAN AND CLASSICAL

Carthaginians.—The central point of the North African coast, commanding the passage between the continent and Sicily, was bound to attract sea traders opening up the western Mediterranean, and the position of Carthage (*q.v.*), on a peninsula offering good opportunities for defense and with a fertile hinterland, had special advantages.

The development of Punic Carthage is indicated by the position of its successive cemeteries. Structural remains are rare, not only because of the destruction by Scipio in 146 B.C. but because of the Roman city that rose above the earlier debris and endured for 700 years. Two lagoons now represent the outer and inner harbours, and the foundations on the islet in the northern one may be those of the Carthaginian admiralty. The hill of St. Louis, farther northwest, is the ancient citadel Byrsa; on this Punic walls and houses have been found. Traces of the seaward fortifications and of the southern city wall have been located, and a part of the fortifications across the isthmus was excavated in 1949.

The earliest settlement is believed to have lain near the southern lagoon west of which an ancient sanctuary was discovered. Among the pottery in the latter were Greek vessels datable to *c.* 725 B.C. The site is a sacred enclosure of Canaanitish type in which young children were sacrificed (*see* CARTHAGE: *Religion*). The calcined bones of the victims were placed in urns which were buried in the holy place. At first small cairns and then simple memorial stones were set up over the urns, giving place in their turn to larger stelae carved to represent small shrines. As the temenos filled up, the earlier stelae were covered with soil so that fresh urns might be accommodated above them. More than 1,000 urns have been excavated, the uppermost (2nd century B.C.) at a point about four metres under the level of subsequent Roman buildings. Analogous shrines are known at several other places, including Sousse (Hadrumetum), where, however, the later urns contain animal bones. Inhumation was the commonest funerary rite, though cremation was also practised, especially from the 3rd century B.C. Many Punic tombs are chambers cut deep in the rock, reached by vertical shafts. Most knowledge of Punic culture is derived from tomb offerings of pottery, jewelry, etc. Punic pottery has been found at sites all along the coast from Tripolitania to Morocco and is in general inferior to Greek or Italian wares. Grotesque terra-cotta masks were made to be placed in graves as protective amulets. Knowledge of Punic architecture has to be deduced from the sculptures on votive stelae, from rare fragments of decorative elements such as cornices or capitals, and from a few Numidian tombs. In the early days the predominant influence was from the east, especially Egypt, and the shrines depicted on the stelae have the concave Egyptian cornice, decorated with rows of uraei and flanked by lotus capitals; from the 4th century B.C. contacts with Greek architecture appear. The final Carthaginian style (if such it can be called) was a florid mingling of elements culled from Egypt, the orient, the Greek and the Hellenistic worlds. In such sculpture as has survived there is similar development. At first sacred stones (baetuli) are shown within the shrines but certain images were adopted quite early, including an Egyptian-looking Baal at Sousse. Greek influence followed and finely sculptured effigies are found on sarcophagus lids of the 4th and 3rd centuries. These are regarded as the work of Greek sculptors settled in Carthage, though the subjects, especially a figure of the goddess Tanith encased in wings, are Punic. Many symbols are engraved on the votive stelae, including the triangle with circle and two arms at the top, the sign of Tanith.

Numidia.—Punic culture did not disappear with the fall of Carthage. Other Punic cities had come to terms with the conquerors, and survivors of the siege, scattered through Africa and especially in Numidia (*q.v.*), carried their customs with them. Sanctuaries of Punic type later than 146 B.C. have been found at Numidian cities such as Constantine (Cirta) and Dougga (Thugga). Their votive stelae exhibit a further proliferation of the old motifs, with the Neo-Punic alphabet gradually ousting the earlier Punic one. The Libyan alphabet appears on the mausoleum at Dougga, persisting on tombstones in outlying areas of Roman Africa, to survive as the *tifinagh* script of the Tuareg.

Four tombs afford evidence of the influence of mixed Punic-Hellenistic architecture, the large cylindrical mausoleums with conical tops of the Medracen, near Batna (3rd century), and the Kbor Roumia (late 1st century B.C.) near Tipasa, and the tower-like 2nd-century-B.C. tombs of Dougga and of Al Khroub near Constantine. The Medracen (18 m. high, 59 m. across) is encircled by engaged Doric columns with an Egyptian cornice above. The tomb at Dougga, three stories topped by a pyramid, is the ancestor of the tower tombs with slender pyramids which are characteristic of Roman Africa. Numidian territory has also long been noted for its many megalithic tombs. Their date can rarely be determined, but some as at Mactar overlap with the Roman period. It may also be appropriate to mention two groups of late Berber tombs: the Djedar of the *département* of Oran near Tiaret. These are large tumuli on square bases, 30–40 m. across, strongly reminiscent of the old royal tombs; they appear to be monuments to the Christian kings of the independent Moorish dynasties of the 5th and 6th centuries A.D.

Roman Africa.—The prosperity of Roman Africa is reflected in the quantity and splendour of its ruins. Their remarkable state of preservation is due in part to the climate, in part to the fact that so many of them were deserted after the Arab invasions. They have yielded many thousands of inscriptions which have furnished material of the highest importance for the history of the empire.

Under the republic a comprehensive land survey was undertaken. As a result huge areas of Tunisia are still marked with the boundary lines of the Roman centuriation, which show up clearly in aerial photographs. In the Augustan age the cities began to blossom with all the paraphernalia of municipal adornment, exhibiting an ever-increasing prosperity which reached its climax in the early 3rd century. The impressiveness of their ruins has been enhanced in many places by a partial restoration of fallen columns and other elements. The classic Roman colonial foundation is Timgad (A.D. 100) in Algeria, built by Roman legionaries from Lambaesis (Lambessa). Within its original square plan is a chessboard grid of 12 insulae each way, those south of the centre being occupied by the forum and civic buildings. The town outgrew its original plan and a large suburb arose to the west. The old Numidian town of Dougga retained its primitive appearance, with narrow streets winding up and down the hillside and with houses adapted to the terrain by having their stories stepped down the hill. Ports, generally very ancient, are again more individual in pattern. The oldest quarter of Sabratha, close to the shore, has the irregularity of the old Punic colony, whereas the later Roman quarters are regularly laid out.

Buildings throughout Roman Africa are frequently constructed of a framework of large dressed stones, with smaller masonry or rubble and concrete in between. This is found in many public buildings, in houses, and in farms and seems to be of Punic origin. Houses were built around patios of Hellenistic type, and nearly every house and public building had its cistern.

Standard Roman temples, generally pseudoperipteral and Corinthian, arose in honour of many gods, especially for the official cults of the Capitoline deities and the deified emperors. The capitolium usually stood in or near the forum, as at Sabratha, Dougga or Volubilis, though in Timgad it is on a low hill outside the original colony. The temple of the Severi at Djemila typifies the widespread building programs undertaken in Africa under the Severan dynasty. The temple of Caelestis (Tanith) at Dougga is peripteral, set within an unusual semicircular portico, and is a link with a group of temples which have preserved features derived from the old Punic sanctuary. This was essentially a court shielded from the outer world by a temenos wall, with perhaps a few small shrines in it. The court was maintained in the Roman period, generally with an internal portico, or there might be, as at Thinissut, a succession of courts, with several shrines in each, and an inner holy of holies. The temple of Saturn at Dougga, on the site of the sanctuary of Baal Hammon, his Punic equivalent, has a monumental propylaeum at the northeast end and a porticoed court, along the southwest side of which are three chapels in a row.

The forum of Carthage has disappeared, but many others can be studied, from the standard type at Timgad, with its curia, tribune for orators, porticoes, shops and basilica and its many statue bases, to the magnificent imperial forum built by Septimius Severus in his native city of Leptis (Lepcis) Magna (*see* LEPTIS) in Tripolitania. This forum is part of a monumental new quarter of the city, on a slightly irregular site, and is so ingeniously contrived that it appears to be perfectly symmetrical. Its architecture departs in certain ways from previously accepted practice, notably in the use of arcading for its porticoes instead of the classical architraves. Its basilica was of exceptional splendour, largely the work of Greek masons brought to Leptis for the purpose.

The public library at Timgad is the only one so far discovered in Africa, but other public monuments are repeated from town to town. The four-way triumphal arches at Tripoli (Marcus Aurelius), Leptis (Septimius Severus) and Tebessa (Caracalla) are particularly notable; immense public baths were built, innumerable fountains and many theatres and amphitheatres. The amphitheatre at Al Djem, one of the most complete surviving examples in the empire, dominates a wide expanse of country. Remains of circuses are rarer, but that at Leptis is still impressive.

Nowhere was the Roman concern for the water supply better displayed than in thirsty Africa. The greatest of the aqueducts is that of Carthage, 50 mi. long, of which the collecting basin survives in the hills of Zaghouan. There are long stretches of the arches bearing the channel across the plain, with massive cisterns at its point of arrival at the city. The aqueduct of Cherchel is carried across a valley by a bridge (128 ft. high) of tall arches with two lower tiers of supporting arches. In the country districts farms and grazing areas were provided with numerous large cisterns. Maximum use for agriculture was made of the spates which periodically flood the wadi beds, and numerous concrete dams were built to hold back the water and retain the silt. In the shallower, broader wadis dry stone walls were regarded as adequate for water spreading. Aerial photographs have revealed many networks of these wadi walls and of hillside terracing. A notable dam was built to divert the channel of the Wadi Labdah above Leptis to prevent silting up of the port.

The sites of olive farms can be recognized by the remains of presses, notably by the upright stones constructed to hold one end of the pressing beam. Large areas in Tripolitania, Tunisia and Algeria, where now there is little or no cultivation, have many presses, attesting their former prosperity. Morocco also has its Roman olive farms.

The garrison of Roman Africa had its headquarters in the fortress of Lambaesis. Large parts of the site have been excavated and the standard barracks and other buildings, including a hospital, identified. The chief structure still to be seen is the entrance hall of the headquarters building. Outside the fortress was a large town. A section of the *fossatum* mentioned in the Theodosian code survives in the Seguia Bint al Krass, a ditch 37 mi. long south of Biskra. It resembles other *limites* of the empire, with a line of fortified posts along it. Aerial photography in the 1940s revealed new lines of *fossata,* from the Al Kantara pass northwest to Tobna. In association with these works, which are dry stone walls or sometimes earthworks, is a series of forts. Gemellae and Ad Majores are of the standard mid-empire form with rounded corners; others with projecting towers (Aquae Herculis) are of a type built under Diocletian or later. An advance post, Castellum Dimmidi (198–238), has been found far to the southwest toward Laghouat. An interesting complementary system, without a *fossatum* as far as is known, has been observed in Tripolitania, where a deep frontier zone is guarded by fortified farms along the wadis and by advance oasis forts at Bu Ngem, Gheria al Gharbia and Ghadames on the routes to the Sahara. Trade with the south is attested by the large quantity of Roman pottery and glass found in the tombs of the Garamantes in Fezzan near Jerma, where there is also a well-preserved mausoleum of Roman type, and Roman objects have been found at the tomb of Tin Hinan in the Ahaggar. In the far west the Moroccan frontier still presents some problems, but there appear to have been posts south of Volubilis and a short stretch of frontier ditch south of Sala.

African museums have many art treasures, some acquired through strange chances. Thus, the philhellene king Juba II filled his capital at Caesarea with the finest copies of Greek masterpieces then to be had, and some of these are now in the Cherchel museum; and a wreck of the 1st century B.C. found off the coast at Mahdia has yielded a collection of Greek works for the Bardo museum. Of greater interest, however, are the works of art made for Africa itself. An altar from a temple of the Gens Augusta at Carthage has some of the quality of the work on the Ara Pacis in Rome. The finest work of the Severan period is to be found, not in Rome, but in Leptis Magna; much of this is the work of sculptors trained in the school of Aphrodisias in Asia Minor. From the 3rd century onward there is a resurgence of indigenous Berber influence, related to the earlier Punic carvings. This is found on pagan tombs, such as those of Ghirza in Tripolitania, and on the Christian churches which spread all over the country districts in the 4th and 5th centuries.

The mosaics are the special glory of Roman African art. Outstanding work is found throughout the Roman period and into the Byzantine age, and the museums at Tunis, Sousse, Tripoli, Bône, Cherchel and elsewhere are full of examples. In these are subjects common to the Roman world and others which reflect the African scenes which the artists saw about them, and their passion for hunting, the amphitheatre and chariot racing. Particularly remarkable are the mosaics of country life on the great demesnes of the rich landowners, with their fine towered houses.

The fame of the church of Africa in history and patristic literature is equaled by the abundance of its material remains. The Christian quarter of Hippo (Bône), the city of Augustine, is being rejuvenated; Carthage has several fine basilicas; Timgad has a Donatist cathedral. The favourite type of church is the three-aisled basilica, with deep chancel and altar well forward in the nave, and with a raised apse which, especially in Tripolitania, is frequently in the west end of the church. A church of this type is shown on a mosaic found at Tabarka. Djemila has an important 5th-century baptistery. One of the most imposing Christian buildings is the basilica of Tebessa and its dependencies. The main church is probably to be assigned to the 4th century; later a great square was built out in front, and around the edge of the church itself cells were constructed for members of the religious community established there. The monuments of the Byzantine period are mainly fortifications and churches. Cities, depopulated and impoverished, were given walls which enclosed only a fraction of their old areas. The centre of modern Tebessa is still enclosed by the Byzantine walls with large projecting towers. A fort with well-preserved barrack blocks stands outside Timgad. The Byzantine walls of Leptis enclose the Severan forum as a citadel. (*See also* AFRICA, ROMAN PROVINCE OF.)

Greek and Roman Cyrenaica.—The eastern end of the Greater Syrtis marks a natural boundary, the effects of which can be observed in the Neolithic period and earlier, as noted above. There also the Carthaginian territory matched with the lands of the Greek colonies of Cyrenaica, of which the earliest and most august was Cyrene founded by Battus about 631 B.C. Although most of the visible monuments date from the Roman period, much is nevertheless known of the Greek buildings which preceded them, and the Greek layout has left its character imprinted strongly on the remains of later ages. For the history and archaeology of the city, *see* CYRENE.

Cyrene is the most interesting of the sites, but its port, Apollonia (Susa), has fine churches, a Byzantine wall and the palace of the Byzantine governor. Its harbour, now mostly submerged, was surveyed by underwater explorers in 1958–59. Ptolemais, farther west, is a fine Hellenistic city with a Roman overlay. The site of Euhesperides, predecessor of Berenice (Benghazi), was revealed by aerial photography; both there and at Tocra important finds of early Greek pottery have been made. Outside the cities many sites are known, among them a temple of Asclepius near Beda and a church with rich mosaics at Gasr Lebia. The defensive system of Cyrenaica, comparable in many respects with that of Tripolitania, consisted of a network of fortified posts. (O. P. F. B.)

V. HISTORY

A. NORTH AFRICA

Evidence has been uncovered in East Africa suggesting the great antiquity of man in Africa (see *Archaeology,* above). However, the continent's history begins with the gradual development of Egyptian civilization in North Africa.

The western part of North Africa, comprising modern Morocco, Algeria and Tunisia, known as the Maghreb (Maghrib) or Barbary, forms a well-marked zone completely surrounded by sea or desert. To the east of this, from Tunisia to the Nile, the Sahara extends northward almost to the Mediterranean sea, and the Cyrenaican plateau is the only substantial area of non-desert character in this stretch. The history of North Africa as thus understood, together with the distinct history of Egypt, which is excluded from this survey, belongs rather to the Mediterranean world than to that of the rest of Africa.

Native history until the arrival of the Muslims late in the 7th century A.D. is practically nonexistent, so that information is chiefly derived from the accounts of the peoples who successively conquered or colonized the region. The oldest inhabitants, who have been there since the dawn of history, are the Berbers (*q.v.*), from whom the name Barbary is derived, a people of diverse physical and cultural types whose only clear unity is that of language. Their own traditions accord them an eastern Mediterranean origin, but it is difficult to detach the genuine Berber elements in the legend from additions resulting from the Berbers' desire to assimilate themselves to their Phoenician and Arab conquerors.

Phoenicians and Greeks.—The earliest settlements from outside were those of the Phoenicians in Tunisia (*see* PHOENICIA). Their most famous settlement was the city-state of Carthage (*q.v.*), founded on a site with many natural advantages at one of the few sheltered points of the Barbary coast. Carthage commanded the passage between the eastern and western Mediterranean and so controlled the western Mediterranean for more than 600 years. The Carthaginians were interested primarily in maritime trade and made little attempt to penetrate far from the coast. Their activities were concentrated in a series of trading posts along the coasts of the Mediterranean and the Atlantic to where the desert again comes down to the sea in southern Morocco. Isolated expeditions pushed on much farther than this; Hanno in the 5th century B.C. voyaged at least as far as Sierra Leone.

During the heyday of Carthage, Greek power began to grow. A Greek colony settled in Cyrenaica (*see* CYRENE) about 630 B.C. and the first dispute between Greeks and Carthaginians arose out of the settlement of the boundary between the Greek colonies in Cyrene and those of the Carthaginians to the west. Wars with the Greeks continued for centuries all over the Mediterranean, but especially in Sicily and southern Italy. About 300 B.C. the Carthaginians were supreme in the Tyrrhenian sea and Sicily, but by this time they were threatened by the growing power of Rome, and it was in defense of these interests that the Carthaginians found themselves at war with the Romans.

Romans.—The three Punic Wars (*q.v.*), from 264 to 146 B.C., destroyed the power of Carthage, and Barbary became absorbed into the Roman empire, under which it remained until the coming of the Vandals. At its best the Roman government ran the country well and endowed it with a good system of communications. The southern frontier of the territory which it controlled, the *limes,* roughly corresponding with the boundary between desert and cultivated land, was guarded by a series of forts which kept the inhabitants of the "granary of Rome" free to follow their occupations under the *pax Romana.* The numerous and magnificent Roman remains still visible, not to mention less conspicuous but ubiquitous traces in areas which are now often uncultivated steppe, bear witness to the prosperity under Roman rule. Apuleius, St. Augustine of Hippo and the emperor Septimius Severus were all born in North Africa. (*See* AFRICA, ROMAN PROVINCE OF; NUMIDIA; MAURETANIA.)

Vandals.—The Vandals (*q.v.*) invaded Barbary from Spain in A.D. 429. The decadent Roman regime gave way before them, and for a century they ruled the country. Hostility between them and the romanized natives led to the collapse of orderly government and they could not resist a renewed onslaught from the Byzantine empire.

Byzantines.—By the 6th century the centre of gravity of the Roman empire had shifted from Rome to Constantinople. The Byzantine general Belisarius, sent from Constantinople in 533, landed in Africa, routed the Vandals and re-established the Roman empire in eastern Barbary. Central and western Barbary passed into a period of obscurity of which little is known, though it is evident that Christianity and the Latin language continued vigorous in many places. Though the Byzantine government was oppressive, archaeology shows that it brought to the land an economic and artistic revival.

First Muslims.—The romanized order in Barbary was swept away by the Muslim invaders of the latter half of the 7th century. Their first expeditions were mere raids from bases in Egypt, and it is a moot point whether pillage or proselytization was the dominant motive. The definite establishment of the Muslims may be considered to date from the foundation of Kairouan (in modern Tunisia) by Uqba (Okba) ibn Nafiʻ about A.D. 670. Tradition credits Uqba with two extensive expeditions, one as far as Kawwar (about 300 mi. N. of Lake Chad) and the other to the Sous (southern Morocco), but these may be legendary. Tradition also describes the whole of Barbary as rapidly islamized, but in fact it seems to have taken nearly a century for all the Berber tribes to become even nominally Muslim, and the Berbers tended to express

their national feeling by the adoption of the Khawarij (Kharijite) heresy of Islam as in Roman times they had adopted Donatism.

The first wave of Arab invaders was numerically small and had little ethnic or linguistic effect. Barbary remained overwhelmingly a Berber country until the Bedouin invasion of the 11th century. The Muslim government was based on Kairouan and was at first under amirs subject to the caliph at Damascus or at Baghdad, but these were succeeded in 800 by the independent dynasty of the Aghlabids (*q.v.*). Aghlabid rule covered what is now Tunisia and eastern Algeria. In 788 a descendant of the Prophet Mohammed, Idris the Elder, fleeing from Abbasid persecution, set himself up in the far west and founded the Idrisid dynasty, whose capital his son established at Fès. In the central Maghreb the Rostemids formed a small but successful Kharijite state based at Tahert (modern Tiaret). Thus, by about 900, Barbary was more or less completely under the control of Muslim governments, and so it remained until the advent of the Europeans in the 19th century.

The Muslim states, however, did not live at peace with one another, and the history of Barbary is a depressing recital of wars, rebellions, misgovernment and anarchy only rarely relieved by short periods of peace and good management. It is remarkable that Barbary, so clearly a geographical unit, was only once unified politically under a single regime of native origin. Nevertheless, the deeply ingrained traditions left by centuries of Roman rule were not yet obliterated. The sedentary elements of the population still predominated and were capable of resisting the disruptive and anarchical tendencies of the nomads. The country, especially the eastern part, seems to have remained prosperous.

The Aghlabids were succeeded in 909 by the Fatimids (*q.v.*), the first of whom was an easterner of Shiʻite persuasion (*see* SHIʻISM). Despite their successful political and military career in the Maghreb, the Fatimids had no success in converting their subjects to their faith, and their ambitions from the beginning appear to have been directed toward the east. In 972 they moved their capital to Cairo, leaving the Zirids as their vassals in Tunisia. The Zirids soon declared their independence, and in revenge the Fatimids let loose upon them the nomad hordes of Beni Hilal, Beni Sulaim and Beni Maqil. This is the received account, but it is permissible to wonder whether the Fatimids did not so much plan and organize this emigration as take advantage of a movement over which they had no real control. At all events these Bedouin fell upon the Maghreb, as Ibn Khaldun says, "like a swarm of locusts."

This catastrophe had profound effects. It brought about a great contraction of the settled areas with a consequent sharp decline in cultural life and prosperity. The turbulent and destructive Bedouin made government extremely difficult and large areas were administered only sporadically when a government was able to mount an armed expedition to extort taxes. What is now Algeria remained virtually without central government until the French arrived in the 19th century. The Bedouin invaders were far more numerous than the few thousand of the first Arab invasions, and they greatly affected the demographic situation of the country. The Berbers, with their language, were driven into the more inaccessible regions while the open country became the domain of Arabs and Arabic. The arabization of Barbary, greatly helped by the prestige of Islam but also hindered by the fiercely independent spirit of the Berbers, remains incomplete even today. If language is taken as the criterion, arabization is virtually complete in Tunisia but not far beyond the half-way mark in Morocco.

Berber Dynasties.—In the 11th century, just before the advent of the Hilali at the eastern end of Barbary, a new and powerful dynasty was growing in the west. The veiled Almoravids (*q.v.*), emerging from the western Saharan deserts, quickly took control of Morocco and crossed the Strait of Gibraltar to breathe a new life into the flagging Islam of Spain. Meanwhile the Hammadids had split off from their cousins the Zirids and instituted in central Barbary a regime remarkable for its unusually tolerant attitude toward Christians and its diplomatic relations with the pope.

The Almoravids, crude Saharans debilitated perhaps by a too

sudden introduction to the degenerate ways of Spanish Islam, gave way in less than a century to the Almohads (*q.v.*), a Berber dynasty having its roots in the High Atlas mountains of southern Morocco. These remarkable people not only checked the slow but sure progress of the Christian reconquest of Spain but, for the first and only time, by clearing away the decrepit remnants of Hammadid and Zirid authority and carrying out a skilful policy of force and alliances against the Arabs, united all the Maghreb from the Sous to Tripoli under one effective administration (1159).

In the course of time the Almohad empire too began to break up. In Morocco their successors the Marinids pursued essentially the same policy with the same administrative machinery. In western Algeria the Abd-al-Wadids of Tlemçen (*see* ABD-AL-WADID DYNASTY) led a precarious and turbulent existence between their more powerful neighbours. In Tunisia the Hafsids (*q.v.*), legitimate heirs to the Almohad authority, succeeded on the whole in keeping the Arabs at bay and maintaining the country in a state of reasonable prosperity until the arrival of the Turks.

After the disappearance of the Almohads a gradual decline in the capacity of Barbary to remain impervious to the outside world was matched by the growth of interest from outside. The Spaniards and the Portuguese were eager to extend their conquests into Africa. The Portuguese founded fortresses along the Atlantic coast. The Spaniards did the same along the Mediterranean coast, but in the east they collided with the expanding power of the Turks.

Turks.—The first Turkish establishment in Barbary dates from 1514, when the corsair Aruj established himself at Djidjelli in Algeria. This originally private enterprise later received official recognition from the Ottoman government in Istanbul, and the regency of Algiers was born, to be followed 70 years later by that of Tunis. Two other corsairs, Dragut and Sinan, established themselves at Tripoli in 1551. The Turkish settlements in the Maghreb were only nominally dependent on the central Ottoman government.

The Turks were interested solely in piracy. Though they claimed authority over an area stretching well inland and had garrisons in some of the towns, most of the country in fact escaped their rule entirely and they made only half-hearted attempts to impose it. So long as they were accorded the minimum co-operation necessary for the pursuit of their "trade" they were ready to leave the indigenous inhabitants to their own devices. The activities of the corsairs brought retaliation from Europe, but the Europeans were too divided among themselves to act effectively. Piracy could thus be carried on successfully right up to the 19th century, although united action by the European powers could probably have easily suppressed it. (*See* BARBARY PIRATES).

Sharifian Morocco.—*Sa'adi Dynasty.*—The decline of the Marinids led to the establishment of the first of the sharifian dynasties of Morocco, that generally known as the Sa'adi or Hasani. Tradition has given to their reign an aura of splendour, as one in which Islam was revivified and the jihad (holy war) against the infidel renewed, but historical appraisal does not confirm this tradition. Their jihad was a defensive one: the great "battle of the three kings" at Kasr al Kebir (Alcázarquivir) in 1578, in which the sultan 'Abd ul-Malik, the sultan Mohammed XI (whom he had deposed) and King Sebastian of Portugal were all killed, though a victory for the Muslims, was fought on Moroccan soil; and in fact they even entered into an alliance with the infidel Spaniards against the Muslim Turks. Their splendour was that of courtly pomp supported at the people's expense by an alien apparatus of renegade officials and mercenary troops. The Sa'adi sultans managed skilfully on the limited resources at their disposal to maintain a precarious independence despite lack of moral support from within and pressure from Spaniards, Portuguese and Turks. The great expedition of the sultan Ahmad al-Mansur to the Niger in 1590–91 was a costly failure in spite of the prestige which it brought.

Filali Dynasty.—The second sharifian dynasty, that of the Filali or Alawi, dates from the middle of the 17th century. Their history up to the middle of the 20th century was also one of

gradual decline. Though occasionally checked by an energetic sultan such as Mulay Ismail (1672–1727), internal anarchy increased until much of Morocco (the *bled es-siba*), while nominally under the central government's control, was in practice governed by tribal or religious leaders (marabouts). The country began a life turned in on itself, hopelessly archaic, and by the middle of the 19th century was incapable of resisting the covetousness of Europe.

Return of Europe.—The intention behind the French occupation of Algiers in 1830 was ostensibly a desire to stamp out piracy, but it was complicated by Charles X's need to distract attention from events at home. The French exhibited much indecision as to their aims and were baffled by the nature of the resistance. Nurtured under European conditions, they imagined that the submission of the dey of Algiers entailed the submission of all Algeria. They did not appreciate that the country had not been united under an effective Turkish administration but owed such stability as it had to an intricate interlocking of numerous interests (Turkish, tribal, religious, etc.) which had to be brought one by one under a single control. Thus the conquest of Algeria was prolonged, though the issue was never in doubt. In spite of the valiant efforts of Abd-el-Kader (*q.v.*), who managed to organize opposition by a call to Islam, the conquest is generally reckoned to have been complete by 1847. Tunisia and Morocco were then threatened by the same fate. In Tunis, after years of increasing European intervention, the bey formally submitted to a French protectorate in 1881 (confirmed 1883). In 1912, likewise, the sultan of Morocco was obliged to accept a French protectorate over the southern part of his empire and a Spanish one over the northern zone. France exercised a form of indirect rule in the two protectorates, but Algeria was administered as far as possible as if it were part of metropolitan France.

The Italians entered late into the race for the partition of Africa, but in 1911 they took Tripoli from the Turks and proceeded to annex Fezzan and Cyrenaica (*see* ITALO-TURKISH WAR). The ancient name Libya was revived to designate the union of these three territories. In Cyrenaica the Italians met fanatical resistance from Bedouin, the Sanusiyah (*see* SENUSI).

World War II ushered in a period of ferment in North Africa. The problems facing France and Italy, coupled with the liberal professions of the victorious powers, encouraged independence movements which were difficult to resist. In 1951 Libya, ravaged by war, totally lacking in resources (oil was not discovered in Cyrenaica until 1959) and without a government, was given independence, with the leader of the Sanusiyah as king (*see* IDRIS I). Morocco attained independence with its sultan as constitutional monarch in 1956. Tunisia also attained independence in 1956 and, by the deposition of the bey the next year, became a republic. Both in Morocco and in Tunisia a lively national feeling and the survival of Muslim institutions allowed these transformations to take place fairly smoothly.

In Algeria, however, the long duration of direct French rule and the policy of integration with France had given rise to a substantial European population so that when the Muslim movement for independence developed into rebellion in 1954 it was long impossible to see how the conflict could be resolved. The Algerian war severely strained France's relations with Morocco and Tunisia, which supported the rebels though economically closely linked with France, but a new era in North African history opened with Algeria's attainment of independence in 1962.

See also *History* sections of ALGERIA; LIBYA; MOROCCO; TUNISIA. (J. F. P. H.)

B. SAHARA AND SUDAN

The name Sahara is derived from the Arabic *as-Sahra* ("the waste" or "wilderness") and the name Sudan from the Arabic *Bilad as-Sudan* ("land of the black men"). The Sudan, in fact, being the savanna country between the southern limits of the Sahara desert in about 17° N. and the northern limits of the tropical African forest in about 8° N., is the region in which North African peoples came most directly into contact with Negroes. The Sahara, moreover, has become desert only since Quaternary times, when it was well-watered grassland supporting a rich fauna preyed on by hunters of Negro and Mediterranean stock alike. Subsequent desiccation drove the population outward into the Sudan, into the Mediterranean coastlands and into the Nile valley. In this way the Negroes tended to become separated from the Mediterranean peoples. The desiccation of the Sahara was doubtless a factor in encouraging the Neolithic revolution, in which the growing populations of the better-watered peripheral regions learned first to domesticate animals and then to grow crops. In the Nile valley the Neolithic revolution proceeded rapidly, and led to the emergence by the end of the 4th millennium B.C. of Egyptian dynastic civilization, but in the Sudan south of the Sahara the development of the isolated Negroes was slower. However, through commerce and colonization, Egypt exercised a significant influence on the mixture of brown and black peoples higher up the Nile in Nubia (q.v.), which resulted in the development there of the independent Sudanese kingdom of Cush, centred first on the region of Napata (q.v.) and later, farther south, on Meroe (q.v.).

In the middle of the 8th century B.C., Cush was strong enough to conquer Egypt and to establish there the 25th dynasty, which ruled until expelled by the Assyrians in the 7th century B.C. Thereafter the Egyptian-inspired divine monarchy of Cush continued to rule the mixed population of the Nilotic Sudan. Meroe became one of the earliest centres of ironworking in Negro Africa, and the Negroes went straight from the use of stone tools to those of iron without passing through a copper or bronze stage. Meroitic civilization declined when the increase in population and in the number of cattle began to denude the land of vegetation, and the incorporation of Egypt in non-African empires caused north–south trade to be diverted from the Nile route to the Red sea. In the early centuries of the Christian era, Meroe was superseded as a centre for trade with interior Africa by the Semitic kingdom of Aksum (see ETHIOPIA: History: Kingdom of Aksum). About A.D. 350, Meroe was sacked and Cush finally destroyed by Aksum.

Farther west, the influence of Phoenician, Greek, Roman and Jewish civilizations emanating from their colonies in North Africa seems to have penetrated into the Sahara toward the Sudan only indirectly, through the activities of pastoral Libyan Berber tribes on the steppes fringing the settled coastal regions. Some of these tribes (e.g., the Garamantes described by Herodotus) early developed the habit of crossing the desert in horse-drawn chariots in search of such commodities as gold dust, ostrich feathers and slaves, for sale in the coastal towns. The evidence of prehistoric rock drawings in the desert suggests that two major trans-Saharan routes developed leading toward the headwaters of the Niger and Senegal rivers, a region rich in alluvial gold, later known by the Arabs as Wangara.

Kingdom of Ghana.—By about the 5th century A.D. there had emerged in the savanna bordering the desert just north of Wangara the kingdom of Ghana, founded apparently by Libyan Berber migrants, possibly possessing some Semitic strain, who had established an ascendancy over the Mandingo-speaking Negro clans of the area. Later rulers of Ghana were undoubtedly Negroes themselves, and it has been suggested that the alien element in early Ghana was expelled westward into Tekrur and Futa (Fouta Tovo) on the lower Senegal. There intermarriage with the local Tukulor eventually produced the Fulani, a pastoral people, who subsequently spread eastward throughout the Sudan to the Cameroons, infiltrating among, but keeping themselves separate from, the predominantly agricultural local Negroes.

By the time of the arrival of the Arabs in the Maghreb in the 7th century, Ghana was already renowned there as "the land of gold." Its wealth and greatness, however, seem to have stemmed less from actual possession of gold mines than from its role as a centre where the products of the western Sudan, of which gold was the most important, were collected to be exchanged for exports from North Africa and salt from the Sahara brought to Ghana's markets by the Berber tribes who controlled the desert trade roads. (See also GHANA [ANCIENT].)

Spread of Muslim Influence.—The pattern of trans-Saharan relations thus established was confirmed by the introduction of the camel and by the coming of the Arabs and Islam. The camel,

established in the Maghreb before the end of the Roman period, secured the Berber nomads in their mastery of the desert. It increased their mobility and made them less dependent on oases tilled by Negro agriculturalists, and the frontier of Negro agriculture in the Sudan itself was pushed southward, perhaps as much a result of the destructive propensities of the desert nomads' camels and goats as of deliberate aggression.

Arab penetration of the Maghreb (7th–11th centuries) drove southward some of the fringing Berber tribes most determined to maintain their independence and also, through their eventual islamization, perhaps gave them a new impulse toward southern conquests. Saharan and Sudanese history between the 5th and the 13th centuries was thus one of considerable movement of peoples, except in Nubia, where the adoption of Christianity in the 5th century by the rulers of the Nobatae, of Mukurra and of Alwa added new strength to the culture they had inherited from Cush (see DONGOLA). These kingdoms, however, were eventually undermined by the growing infiltration of Muslim traders and Bedouin tribesmen from Egypt and finally disappeared in the 14th century. The advent of the Bedouin meant the arabization of the peoples of the eastern Sudan and the replacement of centralized government by tribal rule, except in the south, where the "black sultans" of the Fung maintained their kingdom of Sennar (q.v.) from the 16th to the 19th century.

Elsewhere in the Sudan the effects of the coming of the camel and of Islam were rather different. Migrants from the desert infiltrated among the sedentary Negro agriculturalists and, possessing organized cavalry and a hierarchical social order, were often able to incorporate the native Negro kinship groups into tribute-paying territorial states. As information on these developments depends mainly on remote oral traditions often surviving only through their incorporation in later Arabic texts (which tend to put an Islamic or at least a Semitic gloss on them), it is not easy to be precise as to the origins of these state-founding immigrants. However, it can be said that, although they inspired Negro clans to imitate their methods and, once established as rulers, became themselves increasingly Negro through intermarriage, they were not Negroes in origin. It may also be affirmed that they were not Muslims: if their coming into the Sudan is to be associated with Islam, it seems rather to have been in reaction to its advent elsewhere. Probably they were connected with the Berber tribes and confederations who dominated the Sahara; e.g., the Sanhaja in the west, the Lemta and Ahaggar toward the centre and the Zaghawa farther east. About this time such tribes were developing into the people later known as Tuareg.

There seem to have been two main streams along which successive waves of alien influence reached the central and western Sudan during this formative period of its history: one from the Maghreb, the other from the Nile valley and the Red sea. These two streams met and intermingled, in overlays which are difficult to disentangle, in the region which is now Nigeria. The state of Kanem and its successor Bornu (qq.v.)—respectively to the north and to the west of Lake Chad—after their conversion to Islam claimed to have been founded by the Sefawa, thought to have arrived from the east before the 11th century. On the other hand, the traditions of the Songhai (Sonrhaï), who in the 14th century created the great empire of Gao (see TOMBOUCTOU), suggest that on an earlier influence from the east was imposed that of Lemta Berbers from the north, the latter having settled among the clans of the eastern Niger bend from about the 8th century. The intervening Hausa states seem certainly to have been the product of at least two major waves of immigration, from the north and the east, between about the 7th and the 11th centuries. The legends of peoples farther south (e.g., the Jukun of the Benue valley and the Yoruba in western Nigeria) suggest that they too felt at least a reflection of these great influences. Farther east, the origins of states like Darfur (q.v.) can perhaps be more confidently associated with the Zaghawa and with echoes of Meroitic culture.

Empires of Mali and of Gao.—In the west meanwhile, the kingdom of Ghana, by then essentially Negro, had come into conflict with the Sanhaja Berber tribes. The imposition on the latter of a puritanical Islamic code gave them a temporary unity, and the Almoravids used this unity to grasp at the wealth which lay at either end of the desert trade road which they controlled. The kingdom of Ghana was eventually conquered in 1076, but the Almoravids as a whole were more strongly attracted by the Maghreb. Ghana soon regained its freedom, but not its former greatness and prosperity. The incursion of the Almoravids had disrupted Ghana's trading system, and their flocks and herds brought about a disastrous deterioration of marginal agricultural land. Subject clans asserted their independence of the capital, which declined in commercial importance. The Muslim merchants retreated northward to Walata, while political power in the western Sudan eventually passed to another Mandingo group farther to the south, whose leader Sundiata had by 1240 destroyed Ghana and laid the foundations for a new and greater Mandingo empire, that of Mali. Mali reached its apogee in the time of Mansa Musa (1307–32), who received tribute from the borders of Tekrur eastward to the growing commercial emporia of Tombouctou and Gao, and from Wangara in the southwest far into the desert in the north.

The commercial and cultural influence of Mali reached even farther afield and was enhanced by its rulers' adoption of Islam, which secured recognition from the North African states at a time when the merchants of Mali were developing the trade of a wide area, reaching toward the gold- and kola-producing areas of the southern forest and eastward into Hausaland, whose conversion to Islam they initiated. On the basis of the exchange of North African exports and desert salt for gold, kola nuts and slaves, Mali, Tombouctou and Gao achieved great prosperity, and Tombouctou became recognized as a centre of Islamic learning and culture. Only the emergent Mossi–Dagomba states of the upper Volta, offshoots of the impulses which had produced the Hausa states and Bornu, stood out against the power of Mali.

In the 15th century, the empire of Mali began to decline. Its political power had been extended over many peoples, including the Songhai, who had no natural bonds of allegiance to the ruling Mandingo group and would remain subject only so long as Mali's supremacy went unchallenged. Succession disputes weakened the military supremacy of Mali at a time when its commerce was suffering from the decay of the western trans-Saharan trade roads caused by the political weakness of Morocco and by the rise of the more central route which led to Tunis. The Tuareg began to encroach from the north and the Mossi to raid from the south. In the east the Songhai regained their independence and, controlling the navigable middle Niger at its junction with the central caravan roads, began to build up the empire of Gao which, because of the military genius of Sonni Ali (c. 1464–92) and Askia Mohammed (c. 1493–c. 1528), reduced Mali to insignificance and more than took its place as the dominant power of the western Sudan.

The power of the new empire, however, was even shorter lived than that of Mali. Islam had been a source of strength for Mali, but among the Songhai it provoked pagan reactions which Askia Mohammed's heirs, unable to agree on an orderly succession of power, either failed to control or used for their own selfish ends. This proved fatal, since the Songhai's control of the Saharan salt mines provoked a series of interventions from Morocco, now united and strong under the Sa'adi sultans, who were anxious to exploit the trans-Saharan trade. In 1590–91, in the time of the sultan Ahmad al-Mansur, a small Moroccan expedition crossed the desert, and its discipline and firearms secured the defeat of the massed cavalry and bowmen of the Songhai emperor. But the Moroccans were strong enough to occupy only the three principal centres of Gao, Tombouctou and Jenne, which they held with difficulty against the remains of the Songhai state in Dendi, against Tuareg raiders from the desert and against a renascent Mandingo power in the west in the form of the pagan Bambara (q.v.) kingdom of Segu and its offshoot Kaarta. The coveted gold-producing regions of the forest proved far beyond the Moroccans' reach and, in the absence of any strong central government for the Sudan, their victory brought no lasting economic gain.

Decline of Trans-Saharan Commerce.—The great days of the trans-Saharan trade and of the Sudanese empires that it fostered were passing. From the 15th century onward, the Portu-guese and their western European rivals had been developing the Atlantic approach to western Africa. The trade which had flowed northward from the Guinea forest lands began to find new outlets in European entrepôts on the coast. The Barbary states, which were the northern termini for the trans-Saharan trade, became involved in struggles for power between Portugal and Spain, Morocco and the Ottoman Turks. Access to Turkish firearms and military ideas proved an important element in the rise of Bornu under Idris Alooma (c. 1580–c. 1617). But Bornu had less commercial wealth than Ghana, Mali or Songhai had had and so was less significant internationally, though it remained a local centre for an Islam inspired from Egypt rather than from the Maghreb, as had been the case with Mali. Such trans-Saharan trade as remained flowed mainly to the city-states of the Hausa, small in size but growing in agricultural and industrial wealth. Freed from the pressures of the Mandingo and Songhai empires and with attacks from the pagan Jukun of Kwararafa checked by the advance of Bornu, the Hausa extended their economic and cultural influence to the south and west through their itinerant Muslim traders, who joined with those of the Mandingo as the principal purveyors of commerce and Islam to the peoples of the forest.

Extension of British and French Authority.—In the 19th century, the Sudan experienced a political resurgence which, despite its ostensibly religious colour, seems ultimately to have been a reaction against the pressures which foreigners were exerting on African trade and territory. The French were well established on the Senegal river, and the British, despite their abolition of the slave trade, were diverting coastward the trade of the Gold Coast-Nigeria region. Mohammed Ali's successors in Egypt had embarked on the conquest of the Nilotic Sudan and, through the slave and ivory trades, on its exploitation.

In Nigeria the Fulani rose in a jihad against the corrupt and weakening rule of the Hausa amirs and, between 1804 and 1810, incorporated their states in the twin empires of Sokoto and Gando. Checked in the east by the equally righteous Muslim rulers of Bornu, they then began to sweep southward into Yorubaland. Farther west, the Fulani in Massina also set up a new state. A Tukulor from Futa, Omar el-Hadj, launched another jihad, conquered the Bambara kingdoms, absorbed Massina and, by 1863, had created an empire reaching from the French outposts on the upper Senegal to Tombouctou. In 1881, Mohammed Ahmed (q.v.), the Mahdi, led a rising which cleared the Nilotic Sudan of its Egyptian oppressors.

These movements naturally came into collision with the advancing power of the British and French, whose explorers from about 1788 had been penetrating the Sudan and stimulating their countries' economic ambitions. The western empire of Omar el-Hadj, weakened by internal revolts, was systematically conquered from 1879 onward by the French, who advanced against it from the Senegal. By the 1890s the French were eroding the hinterland of British trade from the Gold Coast and lower Nigeria and threatening the upper Nile, vital to British interests in Egypt and Uganda. Conflict between the two European powers was narrowly avoided as the British conquered northern Nigeria as far as Sokoto and the southern approaches to Lake Chad (1894–1906) and, in association with Egypt, defeated the Mahdists on the Nile (1898). The French and the British, however, co-operated to defeat the Mandingo leader Samory and the slave-raiders Babatu (Upper Volta) and Rabah (Chad). During the first three decades of the 20th century, the French, overcoming bitter resistance from the Tuareg tribes, became masters of the greater part of the Sahara, and so linked their West African colonies with the Maghreb. In the east, the British had established their rule throughout the Anglo-Egyptian Sudan by 1917. See also History sections of CAMEROON, REPUBLIC OF; CHAD, REPUBLIC OF; FRENCH EQUATORIAL AFRICA; FRENCH WEST AFRICA; GHANA; MALI, REPUBLIC OF; NIGER, REPUBLIC OF THE; NIGERIA; SAHARA; SENEGAL, REPUBLIC OF; SUDAN, REPUBLIC OF THE.

C. GUINEA

Attempts have been made to derive the name Guinea from Ghana or from Jenne, but it would seem to be a version of the

Berber word *Aguinaw* or *Gnawa,* meaning "black man" or Negro. *Akal-n-Iguinawen,* equivalent to the Arabic *Bilad as-Sudan* ("land of the black men"), was the Berber name for Negro Africa. Western Europe's earliest knowledge of Negro Africa came through its relations with Barbary, and the name Guinea, in forms such as Guinuia, Ginya, Gheneoa and Ghinea, began to appear on maps drawn in the Mediterranean lands of western Europe in the 14th century. When the Portuguese explorers of the west coast of Africa first sailed beyond the region of Berber or Moorish dominance and came to the Senegal river and Cape Verde and so to country inhabited by Negroes, they applied to both people and land the name that they had learned in Morocco. Since the Portuguese, together with their European successors until the 19th century, were almost entirely concerned with trade at the coast, the name Guinea came to mean the West African coastlands and the forest adjacent to them.

The history of Guinea before about the 11th century is almost totally unknown. Archaeology has done little to compensate for the absence of written records among the Negroes of Guinea, and the value of oral traditions varies with the degree of political organization of their possessors. The traditions of the best-organized Guinea states may sometimes provide an acceptable historical record reaching back as many as 500 years, but beyond this they tend to require much interpretation before they can be made to yield useful information. Fortunately, some of these legends have affinities with similar legends of the Sudan which can be more readily placed in a historical setting, since, from the 8th century onward, the western Sudan became increasingly well known to Arab geographers, chroniclers and travelers. By reference to the Sudan it is thus possible to attempt a tentative historical framework for Guinea which may go as far back as the 11th century, about 600 years before European sources begin to afford an increasing amount of reasonably intelligible information about the peoples of the Guinea coast.

This is particularly true of the region lying between the Ivory Coast and the Niger, apparently because its inhabitants were more forward than others in setting up organized states. A state cannot exist without some conscious record of its origin and subsequent history, and the rulers of this part of Guinea took special care to preserve intact the formal traditions of their states. Examination of these suggests that the process of state formation in Guinea was generally begun by emigrants from the Sudan.

The influences from east and north which resulted in the emergence of the states of the central Sudan continued southwestward. Throughout middle Nigeria, from the upper Benue to Bussa on the Niger, there are legends of Kisra, usually represented as a Persian king who fled with his men from Egypt to Napata and then moved westward, followed by the Napatan king and his supporters. Beyond Lake Chad they are remembered as founding a series of states, including Nupe and Borgu, the Jukun state of Kwararafa, some of the states (notably Gobir) which became Hausa states and perhaps the earliest Yoruba states. The historical basis for this story is difficult to assess, but the name Kisra seems to be an echo of Khosrau II, the Sassanid king who conquered Egypt and ruled it during 616–628. Names remembered in connection with the Napatan king, notably Issa (Jesus) and Mesi (Messiah), together with some other evidence, suggest an emigration about the 7th century from the Christian kingdoms which succeeded Cush in the Nilotic Sudan.

Analysis of Yoruba legends suggests that the Yoruba states were formed by two main waves of settlement. The first was the Kisra migration, which gave rise to a number of small independent agricultural colonies. A later and better-remembered immigration, associated with the name of Oduduwa (Odudua), the Yoruba god of creation, caused the settlement at Ife to branch out and dominate the others. This migration may be linked with the second major movement into Hausaland about the 10th century. These events in Yorubaland had their repercussions in neighbouring territories. The tradition of Benin, immediately to the southeast, makes it clear that it experienced the same two formative influences. Farther along the coast, the traditions of the Adja, Fon, Ewe, Adangbe and Ga indicate a westward expansion from Yorubaland which reached its limit in the southeast of modern Ghana only about the 15th century.

The problem of Yoruba origins is complicated by theories concerning the exceptionally fine sculpture, particularly in brass, found chiefly at Ife (*q.v.*) and reflected in the art of Benin. The art of Benin (*q.v.*) is unquestionably an offshoot of the art of Ife, but the magnificent craftsmanship of the earliest-known Ife heads has given rise to the idea that the art must have originated in the work of some non-Negro artist. Since the evidence from Benin makes it plain that the origins of the art must precede the first arrival of Europeans in the area by sea in the 15th century, it was suggested that some Greco-Roman influence reached across the Sahara. However, finds associated with the Nok culture, on the Jos plateau, which may be dated between about 900 B.C. and A.D. 200, show that early inhabitants of the Nigerian region had already reached a very high standard in the making of figures in terra cotta, and the only innovation of Ife need have been the introduction of the lost-wax method of casting.

This tends to confirm evidence implicit in the early legends and traditions that the migrations which gave rise to the eastern Guinea states were not generally mass invasions of uninhabited land, but that comparatively small numbers of immigrants brought new ideas and techniques to already established Negro kinship groups, fused these groups into political units and in the course of time largely merged with them. There is indeed an underlying cultural continuity throughout the region. A similar picture emerges farther west, among the Akan-speaking peoples of modern Ghana and the eastern Ivory Coast. There the external influences were not from the northeast, from the direction of Lake Chad, but from the north or northwest, from the direction of Mandingoland. The earliest Akan states seem to have been set up on the northern edge of the forest by emigrants from the Sudan by about the 13th century. By the 14th century, states such as Bono and Banda were beginning to prosper on the proceeds of a trade in gold and kola nuts with the Mandingo emporia. Later waves of pioneers pushed south through the Volta gap to the coast and also to some extent infiltrated into and through the forest. At two points, in what is now northeastern Ghana (where the Akan touched the Mossi-Dagomba) and by the Volta mouth (where they came into contact with the Ga and Adangbe), this movement of state-formation stemming from the northwest met the similar movement from the northeast.

There is little positive evidence to indicate the motives for these migrations from the Sudan into Guinea. While the movement from the northwest may have been connected with the expansion of trade from the ancient kingdom of Ghana and from Mali, the survival of the horse as a symbol of chieftaincy even in such unsuitable regions as Benin suggests that the migrations from the northeast were the products of the political revolutions which created the states of the central Sudan. From the 15th century onward, however, the Sudanic influence on the Guinea peoples began to be eclipsed by the more readily discernible influence deriving from the establishment on the Guinea coast of European trading posts.

First European Trade and Its Effect.—By 1445 the Portuguese, aiming to outflank the trans-Saharan trade of the north Africans, reached the Senegal by sea. Forty years later they were establishing trading posts on the Gold Coast (later Ghana) and at Benin. Except in what ultimately became the colony of Portuguese Guinea, a region naturally exploited by the colonists of the Cape Verde Islands, the Portuguese largely neglected the coast between the Gambia and the Gold Coast, and the pattern thus established was also followed by other European countries trading with West Africa during the next 400 years. One reason for this seems to have been that the peoples of the region from the Gambia to the Gold Coast were still organized in simple kinship societies, which were economically self-sufficient and possessed none of the surplus of wealth required for international trade. Such surpluses, however, did exist in the Senegal region (on the edge of the Sudanese trading system) and in the more complex state systems of the region from the Gold Coast to the lower Niger. In particular the Gold Coast provided substantial quantities of gold dust, and the Portuguese built a number of strong stone forts on its shores in an attempt to exclude their rivals from this trade.

Portugal's near monopoly of maritime trade with West Africa was broken during the first half of the 17th century by the Dutch, who concentrated on providing slaves to meet the ever-growing demand for labour on the European plantations in tropical and subtropical America. In the latter part of the 17th century, however, the Dutch met with increasing competition from French and English slave-trading interests and by the beginning of the 19th century, when efforts were being made to stop the transatlantic slave trade, the British had become the most important agents in the West African trade except around the Senegal river, where French influence was dominant.

The European slave traders concentrated their activities on those parts of the Guinea coasts where earlier traders in gold, ivory, gum, pepper, etc., had already created a demand for European exports (cloth, hardware, raw metals, spirits, arms and ammunition) and where native trading systems were consequently well developed.

The bulk of the slaves taken to America were in fact purchased from African middlemen on the coasts east and south of the Gold Coast. Though politically the power of the Europeans hardly extended beyond their forts and factories on the coast, the trade that they brought engendered a political as well as an economic and social revolution. Whereas hitherto the main centres of wealth and power in West Africa had been in the Sudan, greater wealth was now coming in from the sea, and attempts to control and to exploit it led to the emergence of Guinea states similar in many respects to earlier Sudanese states and empires.

As the coastal entrepôt for Yorubaland in the 16th and 17th centuries, Benin experienced a period of great prosperity during which it expanded its territory by conquest and colonization. Then, while Benin decayed, one of the more northerly Yoruba states, Oyo, began to advance southward, establishing a political primacy over its fellows comparable with the spiritual primacy of Ife and so coming to control the foreign trade of the whole productive region. Oyo itself did not reach to the sea, but found outlets through small coastal states like Lagos and Badagry. Farther west, however, the Fon state of Dahomey, pursuing similar aims, succeeded in the early years of the 18th century in swallowing up its small kindred on the slave coast, and a similar policy was adopted by Akwamu, an Akan state which between 1670 and 1730 established a short-lived empire over the Ga, Adangbe and Ewe peoples of the coast from Accra to Ouidah. Akwamu's imperial experience was drawn on to aid in the organization of the Ashanti union, in which a group of small Akan forest states joined together to impose their will on their neighbours in the forest and north of it.

By the end of the 18th century the Ashantis were seeking direct access for their trade to the European forts on the coast (see also ASHANTI).

European Government Intervention.—During the early years of the 19th century, the various European nations concerned with trade to West Africa outlawed what had been its most valuable element, namely the slave trade. There followed a period of confusion which lasted until the end of the 1870s. Many European merchants withdrew from West Africa altogether, either because they could not find a successful staple to replace slaves or because, continuing to deal in slaves, they came into conflict with the antislavery trade patrols maintained by the British navy. The French and the British remained, however—the French mainly because they hoped that their foothold in Senegal could be expanded to give access to the wealth of the Sudan, the British partly because some of their merchants found the palm-oil trade of the coasts east of the Gold Coast an acceptable substitute for the slave trade, and partly because of their continuing interest in the fight against the slave trade, which still went on inland after export by sea had finally been suppressed (about 1880). Explorers and missionaries joined the traders, and the British government sent out consular agents briefed to try to induce local rulers to abjure the slave trade and to protect the interests of "legitimate" British traders. All these groups tended to conclude that West

Africa could not be peacefully opened to Christianity, commerce and civilization without direct intervention in Africa by the British government.

The troubles resulting from Ashanti invasions of the coastal states of the Gold Coast, Dahomey's continuing activity in the slave trade, and the anarchy and civil war in Yorubaland following the decline of Oyo power and the invasions of the Fulani, all lent force to the views of the traders and missionaries, but showed at the same time that government intervention was bound to involve Great Britain in responsibilities and expense which it would be very difficult to limit.

On the whole, therefore, the British government gave little consistent support to the interventionist cause until the 1880s, when German imperialism and the success of the French in conquering the western Sudan and linking up with hitherto weak and isolated French *comptoirs* in Guinea, the Ivory Coast and Dahomey made action essential if any hinterland was to be preserved for British trade.

Thus while the French were creating the eight colonies which became the federation of French West Africa and the Germans were establishing their colonies of Togo and the Cameroons, Great Britain acquired, besides Gambia and Sierra Leone, the two commercially most attractive territories in West Africa—the Gold Coast and Nigeria.

When after World War I the former German colonies were mandated to Great Britain and France, these two countries ruled all West Africa except for Portuguese Guinea and the republic of Liberia, which, like Sierra Leone, had its origin early in the 19th century in colonization by freed slaves. French policy was in essence to rule directly and to expect the Africans gradually to assimilate French ways. The British allowed somewhat more freedom to indigenous ways of life and hoped for an eventual synthesis which might lead to autonomy under local parliamentary governments.

However, the opening up of the colonies by railways and roads, the vast expansion under government auspices of the education systems initiated by the Christian missions and the great increase of wealth resulting from the production for the world market of crops such as cocoa, palm oil and kernels, coffee, peanuts, bananas and cotton led eventually to the growth of nationalist movements which found the programs mapped out by the British and French too limited.

After World War II these movements were able to make rapid headway and the colonies began to secure self-government. The Gold Coast led the way, achieving independence as Ghana in 1957; it was followed by former French Guinea (which became the Republic of Guinea), Nigeria, Sierra Leone, the French Cameroons (which became the Republic of Cameroun), Togoland and by the other former French West Africa territories.

See also *History* sections of DAHOMEY, REPUBLIC OF; FRENCH WEST AFRICA; GAMBIA; GHANA; GUINEA, REPUBLIC OF; IVORY COAST, REPUBLIC OF; LIBERIA; MAURITANIA, ISLAMIC REPUBLIC OF; PORTUGUESE GUINEA; SIERRA LEONE; TOGO, REPUBLIC OF; UPPER VOLTA, REPUBLIC OF.

D. CENTRAL AFRICA

Apart from a few insignificant groups, such as the pygmies of the Congo forests, the indigenous inhabitants of central Africa are Negroes speaking Bantu languages. Comparative study of these languages suggests that somewhere in central Africa close by the Zambezi valley was the centre from which the Bantu-speaking Negroes, themselves probably originally an offshoot of the west African Negroes whose languages are classified as Sudanic, spread out to occupy the greater part of central, eastern and southern Africa south of the Bantu line, absorbing or displacing earlier inhabitants akin to the modern Bushmen and Hottentots. This expansion of the Bantu cannot be accurately dated, but it seems likely that it began early in the first Christian millennium. It was certainly still in progress in southern Africa during the 18th century (see *Southern Africa,* below), and there is also evidence for the northward expansion of the Bantu during the last few centuries in the great lakes region of East Africa. This rapid settlement by the Bantu of so large an area was probably facilitated not only by their Iron Age technology but also by their acquisition and development of new food crops of East Indian origin, such as the banana, yam, cocoyam and sugar cane, which proved well suited for cultivation in equatorial Africa. The introduction of these crops to Africa was probably in some way associated with the East Indian settlement of Madagascar, which, on both linguistic and cultural grounds, seems likely to have taken place between the 5th and the 8th centuries.

Bantu States.—The earliest historical references to the central Bantu are in Arabic accounts of the east coast from about the 10th century A.D. onward. These accounts are scanty and not easy to interpret, but it is clear that from the hinterland of Sofala (Mozambique) Arab traders received gold for which they exchanged Asiatic products. When the Portuguese arrived in the Congo and Angola (from 1483) and in Mozambique (from 1505), in both regions they made contact with a number of well-organized Bantu kingdoms. Those on the west coast—Kongo, Kakongo, Loango, Ndongo, etc.—may have been relatively recent foundations, for the traditions of the not dissimilar Kuba kingdom farther in the interior (which was not known to the Portuguese) suggest that it was formed about 1570, after a period of migrations. Beyond Sofala, however, on the highlands between the Zambezi and Limpopo rivers, Portuguese explorers and missionaries discovered an impressive complex of states commonly referred to as the empire of Monomotapa (*q.v.*). The numerous dry stone ruins (*zimbabwe*) of this region, the best-known and most impressive of which is Great Zimbabwe, near Fort Victoria in Southern Rhodesia, have been investigated by archaeologists. (*See* ZIMBABWE.) For the most part the stone walls seem to have been fortifications for mud dwellings, and it has been shown that the practice of building in stone dates from at least as early as the 10th century and continued, gradually deteriorating, until at least the 18th century. The builders of the *zimbabwe* are generally considered to have been ironworking and gold-mining Bantu, the ancestors of the modern tribes of the region, but there is some evidence (*e.g.*, at Mapungubwe in the northern Transvaal) to suggest that the Monomotapa-Zimbabwe culture may have been originated by earlier inhabitants, probably the ancestors of the modern Hottentots, who were subsequently overrun and absorbed by the Bantu.

The Monomotapa culture was probably already in decline when the Portuguese encountered it. Its deterioration seems to have been connected partly with a decline in the gold yield and partly with the disturbances caused by successive waves of Bantu invasion and conquest. The earliest Bantu elements of the Zimbabwe culture may have been akin to the modern Sotho of southern Africa, and it seems likely that they were invaded first by the ancestors of the modern Karanga and Shona peoples of Southern Rhodesia, and then (about 1700) by the Rozwi, who created the Mambo empire which survived until its destruction by the Ngoni and Ndebele in the 1830s.

Northwest from the Zambezi toward the lower Congo there was a group of comparable states which, though sometimes more extensive, seem generally to have been less stable. This was possibly because, without the stimulus of foreign trade (as in the Monomotapa region from about the 10th century and on the lower Congo from the 16th century), the tendency of the population to increase following the establishment of organized governments was apt to overstrain the resources of wealth available from cultivation of the dry savanna soils. Among these northern states of the central Bantu was the empire of the Luba in the southeastern Congo, at its peak in the 15th and 16th centuries. This seems to have influenced the subsequent rise of the Lunda empire farther to the southwest (which flourished in the 16th and 17th centuries), the kingdom of Cazembe in northeastern Zambia (18th century) and the Lozi kingdom in the richer riverain lands of the upper Zambezi (Barotseland), which reached its apogee in the 19th century. Most of the central Bantu monarchies seem to have been influenced in their beliefs, ritual and methods of organization by the divine kingship of the states of the Lacustrine Bantu in East Africa. Lacustrine influences

doubtless entered the Congo through the Luba, but their mode of transmission to the Monomotapa region is uncertain.

Portuguese Exploitation.—Both on the lower Congo and in the hinterland of Mozambique, the Portuguese attempted to control the native states and their trade by converting their rulers into Christian vassals of the Portuguese kings, but they achieved little permanent gain. In the west, political and religious intervention by the Portuguese and their attempt to monopolize foreign trade occasioned stresses which gravely weakened organized government in the Bantu kingdoms. In the east, Portuguese hopes of engrossing the gold exports were frustrated by the difficulty of communication with inland Monomotapa and by the growing weakness of its governments. In the 17th and 18th centuries, therefore, the Portuguese fell back upon direct exploitation of the coastal regions of Angola and Mozambique, developing a meagre plantation economy in the latter and treating the former principally as a reservoir from which slave labour could be exported through their ports at Luanda and Benguela to their plantations in Brazil. Portuguese activities in the interior were increasingly left to half-caste *pombeiro* traders, though the Christian missionary work, which had begun so brilliantly in the 16th century, never entirely ceased.

European Exploration.—In the 19th century central Africa began to be influenced by the growth of European settlement farther south. First, the increasing shortage of land led some southern Bantu groups to raid and conquer to the north. The Rozwi state was destroyed by the Ngoni, who then pressed on to settle and raid in Nyasaland (later Malawi), leaving the Shona of Southern Rhodesia to be preyed on by another Zulu splinter-group, the Ndebele under Mzilikazi (Umsilikazi, Mosilikatze), who established themselves around Bulawayo. The Lozi kingdom was conquered by the Kololo, an offshoot of the southern Sotho. Secondly, European hunters, traders, missionaries and concession-seekers began to penetrate northward despite the hostility of Mzilikazi and his successor Lobengula. Southern Rhodesia and its gold resources were revealed to the outside world from 1860 onward through the journeys of men like Karl Mauch, Thomas Baines and F. C. Selous.

The great explorations (1852–73) of David Livingstone (*q.v.*) had much wider consequences: during 1852–56, desiring to widen the field of missionary activity, he traveled to the upper Zambezi from Bechuanaland and, having been favourably received by the Kololo rulers of Barotseland, went first westward to Luanda and then eastward to Quelimane, seeking an easier route of access to their country. In so doing he began to appreciate the extent to which central Africa was suffering from the slave trade that was being developed by the Zanzibar Arabs and countenanced by the Portuguese; he concluded that only through the example of pioneer settlements of European missionaries and farmers could central Africa be rescued from barbarism. Livingstone's accounts of his two subsequent journeys, which did much to awaken European hostility to the east coast slave trade, led to the first missionary settlements in Nyasaland and inspired H. M. Stanley's transcontinental expedition of 1874–77, with its revelation of the great Congo waterway to the heart of Africa. (*See* STANLEY, SIR HENRY MORTON.)

Colonization of Central Africa.—The exploitation of Stanley's work by Leopold II of Belgium, led to the establishment of the Congo Free State and to the Berlin conference on Africa (1884–85), and ushered in the colonial phase of central African history. During 1885–94 there was intense competition for the possession of central African territories. Portugal's ancient claim to suzerainty over all land between the coasts of Angola and Mozambique was ignored. Cecil Rhodes's British South Africa company sought, in competition with trekkers from the Transvaal, to expand the frontiers of European settlement from the south. The British Protestant missions in Nyasaland consolidated their position with the aid of Scottish merchants who waged war on the Arab slave traders. Agents of the Congo Free State, having limited French competitors to the regions north of the Congo (which became French Equatorial Africa), penetrated eastward to the great lakes and southward into Katanga.

Despite opposition from Portugal and from the Transvaal, pioneers from Rhodes's company occupied Mashonaland in 1890, and in 1893–94 conquered Lobengula and the Ndebele. The Ndebele and Shona risings of 1896–97 ended with the disruption of Bantu society, and although the gold resources proved disappointing, the British South Africa company had by 1914 established Southern Rhodesia as a colony of European settlement in which a growing voice in the government was entrusted to the settlers' representatives. Lack of resources and poor communications made the comparable development of the larger territory of Northern Rhodesia (later Zambia) much slower. Barotseland became a protectorate, and after about 1909 the British South Africa company's administration was thinly extended over the rest of the colony. Nyasaland became a British protectorate in 1891. Its dense African population and lack of minerals did not encourage European settlement, and it remained essentially an African territory, though linked to the Rhodesias through its transport system and its export of labour.

The Portuguese took measures for the proper administration and economic development of the lands remaining to them in Angola and Mozambique. On the economic side this was facilitated by encouraging the investment of foreign capital. Politically the Portuguese endeavoured gradually to assimilate their African subjects to Portuguese civilization.

During 1885–1908 the Congo was under the personal rule of Leopold II. His administration eradicated the slave trade, but, lacking the financial resources available to the colonial administrations of European governments, it embarked on desperate measures to make its vast undeveloped territory economically profitable, leasing out large concessions to companies and, in common with them, employing forced labour and other unsavoury means to bring in revenue. International public opinion was eventually aroused, with the result that in 1908 control of the Congo passed to the Belgian government.

French Equatorial Africa was organized as a federation of four colonies—Gabon, French Congo, Ubangi-Shari and Chad. Attempting to speed up the economic development of the two southern colonies, the French adopted a concessions policy similar to that of Leopold II, with comparable unhappy results. However, steps were taken after 1906 to end the abuses of company exploitation and to enforce proper administrative control.

See also *History* sections of ANGOLA; BELGIAN CONGO; CENTRAL AFRICAN REPUBLIC; CONGO, DEMOCRATIC REPUBLIC OF THE; CONGO [REPUBLIC]; FRENCH EQUATORIAL AFRICA; RHODESIA AND NYASALAND, FEDERATION OF; GABON REPUBLIC; MALAWI; RHODESIA; ZAMBIA.

E. SOUTHERN AFRICA

By about the 15th century A.D., Bantu-speaking Negroes, who, in the region from the Limpopo to the Zambezi valleys, had already developed advanced states where agriculture was practised and iron and gold were mined and worked, were expanding southward across the Limpopo into country inhabited by more primitive peoples—groups of Stone Age Bushmen hunters and tribes of pastoral Hottentots. The main route of the migration, which was probably caused by pressure of population on land, was down the better-watered eastern side of the subcontinent, and by the latter part of the 18th century the Bantu had occupied all the fertile eastern coastlands as far as the Great Fish river, and were also more thinly spread over the dryer high veld south to the Orange river and west to the upper Limpopo. The surviving Bushmen had been pushed westward toward the Kalahari desert. Many of the Hottentots had been absorbed in the society of the newcomers, and those of their tribes that had survived were confined mainly to what is now the western part of the Cape province.

The early history of the southern Bantu is not easily unraveled from the surviving traditions. The land they had entered was both extensive and relatively thinly populated, and they were apt to spread widely over it, with the result that tribal groupings were continually fragmenting. Later arrivals would often consolidate earlier settlements into new groupings which would in turn divide as elements moved farther afield. However, by the mid-18th century, the four major modern divisions of the southern Bantu were probably already discernible. In the northern Transvaal and southern Southern Rhodesia were the Lemba and Venda tribes, both probably southern survivors from the early Limpopo-Zambezi states. Farther east, in the lower Limpopo valley and southern Mozambique, were the agricultural Tonga, also relatively long established. South of these, on the rich coastal plain east of the Drakensberg, were the numerous Nguni tribes. The presence of clicks in many of their languages, and perhaps also the importance attached by them to cattle keeping, suggest that the Nguni had absorbed a considerable Hottentot element. Farther west, the Sotho tribes, probably the most recent arrivals, were dispersed over the high veld. The eastern Sotho had absorbed some Nguni elements while the western Sotho incorporated some Bushman stock.

European Settlement, 1650–1814.—Until the 17th century European expansion took little account of South Africa. Its coastal peoples could not offer much trade to offset the lack of safe anchorages, and on their way to the east the ships of the early explorers and traders (predominantly Portuguese) made no regular calls before Mozambique. In the first half of the 17th century, however, the Dutch East India company pioneered a quicker route to the East Indies, by-passing East Africa and sailing directly eastward in about latitude 40° S. after rounding the Cape of Good Hope. In 1652 the company sent out a small party of soldiers and officials under Jan van Riebeeck to establish a base on Table bay at the northern end of the Cape peninsula. The intention was to control this vital point which all ships sailing from the Atlantic into the Indian ocean had to pass, and to provide there a supply station for the company's ships. To this end Riebeeck's men were to grow foodstuffs and secure cattle by barter with the local Hottentots, but they were to avoid involvement with the country and its peoples. However, settlement solely by employees of the company proved an expensive and inefficient expedient for a commercial enterprise anxious to limit costs. To provide an adequate military force to defend the fort (begun in 1666 to meet possible English and French threats) and also to ensure an adequate and cheap supply of farm produce, the company encouraged independent farmers to settle at the Cape. The immigrants were mainly Dutch but also, after 1688, French Huguenots. Under the governorship of Simon van der Stel (1679–99) and of his son Willem (1699–1707), a successful agricultural community began to emerge. The land by the fort, however, was poor, and settlement quickly extended to the valleys fringing the interior plateau.

By the early 18th century the settlers had begun to feel discontent with the role assigned to them by the company, which controlled prices in the limited local market for their produce, forbade them to engage in more lucrative enterprises such as tobacco-growing and trading with the Hottentots, and allowed them no voice in the affairs of the colony. The company sought to lower the costs of farming by bringing in slaves from elsewhere in Africa and from the East Indies, but succeeded only in confirming a growing belief that the role of the white man was to direct coloured labour rather than to work with his own hands. Miscegenation between Europeans, Hottentots and slaves laid the foundations for a new intermediary class, the Cape Coloured. The younger sons of the prolific settler families, unhappy at the lack of opportunity under the company's regime, began increasingly to turn their backs on the Cape and to make their way into the interior. They began by hunting and trading (illegally) with the natives, and gradually established a new society of their own, that of the *trekboeren* (seminomadic farmers). The main features of this society were extensive, pastorally based farming (indifferent water supplies made 6,000 ac. the average size for a farm) which was nearly self-sufficing, and a sturdy belief that the *trekboeren* could rely on no one but themselves and God. The government at Cape Town was regarded as alien and hostile, neither able to afford them protection and civilized administration nor willing to allow them independence. In the circumstances, the Calvinist Boers began to see themselves as the children of God in the wilderness, a Christian elect to whom God had given the right freely to take the land and to whom he had also entrusted a natural and lasting dominion over its backward native inhabitants.

The general trend of Boer expansion was east and northeast toward the area of better rainfall, and at first there was no effective check to it. Proclamations from Cape Town attempting to establish boundaries for the colony and so avoid conflict with the Africans were ignored, and the scattered Hottentot tribes were easily driven away or absorbed by the Boers. By the 1770s, the Boer vanguard had reached the Great Fish river and had made contact with the foremost Bantu, advancing in the opposite direction. Their tribes were appreciably better organized and stronger than those of the Hottentots, and like the Boers they were constantly seeking more land for their growing populations and herds of cattle. Conflict between the two expanding pastoral peoples was inevitable, and in 1779 the first of the Kaffir wars broke out along what had become the eastern frontier of the Cape colony (*see* KAFFIR WARS).

The company was neither willing nor, by this time, able to afford to garrison and govern the frontier effectively. Its attempts at intervention eventually led the frontier Boers, already organizing commandos for their own defense and electing their own local military and civil officers, to proclaim the independent republics of Graaff Reinet and Swellendam (1795). In the same year, Great Britain, at war with a France whose army had occupied Holland, took possession of the Cape in the name of the prince of Orange in order to prevent its use by French warships preying on British communications with India. After the treaty of Amiens (1802), the Cape was returned to the government of the Batavian republic, but in 1806 the British re-occupied it. In 1814 the Cape was formally ceded to Great Britain.

Conflicts Between Bantu, Boers and British, 1814–1910.— Like the Dutch, the British were mainly concerned with the strategic importance of the Cape. In 1820 they attempted to seal off the eastern frontier by planting along it 5,000 British settlers—former soldiers and their families. On both sides of the frontier, however, there was pressure on land, so that the wars with the Bantu continued, involving the British in expensive and unwanted military commitments. The European frontier had checked the advance of the southern Nguni, with the result that the northern Nguni could expand only at their expense. Under two great kings, Dingiswayo (*c.* 1790–1818) and Chaka (1818–28), the Zulu clan of the northern Nguni developed a formidable fighting machine, grouping the young men in disciplined regiments which, fighting in close order with the stabbing assegai, carried all before them. Some Zulu elements struck out on their own: Mzilikazi's Ndebele onto the high veld, the Shangaans to conquer the Tonga and Zwangendaba to lead his Ngoni to raid as far north as Lake Nyasa. Southern Natal became depopulated, the pressure on the eastern frontier increased and the Basutoland and Swaziland mountains became areas of refuge where eventually able leaders like Moshesh, Sobhuza and Mswazi arose to form new nations to match the Zulu power.

Meanwhile British rule at the Cape meant for the scattered Boer communities more effective administration and, with the increase of missionary activity among the native Africans, new ideas. From 1828 onward legislation was introduced which gave non-Europeans equality before the law and brought Boer dealings with natives and their transactions over land under administrative control. In 1834 Sir Benjamin D'Urban (*q.v.*) arrived as governor with instructions both to liberalize the government and to reduce its cost. Seeking to cut down military expenditure, he brought the frontier Bantu under British rule, a measure which also promised more land for European settlement. However, this annexation and racially discriminatory legislation introduced into the new legislative council by settler representatives were both disallowed by the colonial office at a time when there was dissatisfaction with the compensation provided after the freeing of slaves under the emancipation act of 1833. Consequently in 1836 a growing stream of Boers began to move out of the eastern Cape colony intending, under the inspiration of men like Piet

Retief (*q.v.*), to establish new independent communities in the relatively empty spaces of the high veld and southern Natal in which they might lead their traditional life free from interference. The Ndebele were driven northward across the Limpopo and, after some bloody fighting with the Zulu, the republic of Natal was proclaimed in 1839.

The British, however, not wishing Port Natal (Durban) to be controlled by an independent government, and concerned also at the effect the expansion of Boer settlement might have on the frontier tribes, annexed Natal in 1843. Many of the Boers, led by Andries Pretorius, trekked back to the high veld. In 1852 the British government agreed to recognize the independence of the settlers in the Transvaal (later the South African Republic) and in 1854 of those in the Vaal-Orange area (later the Orange Free State). In 1852, on the understanding that it would henceforth pay for its own defense, Cape colony was granted representative government, with an electorate open to all men possessing certain property qualifications. Self-government followed in 1872 when first the export of wool and then the discovery of diamonds had laid the foundations for economic advancement. Natal (where the Europeans were very few in relation to the Bantu) became a separate crown colony in 1856.

The two Boer republics and the two British colonies expanded at the expense of the Bantu tribes. The Cape absorbed the old frontier districts, achieving a common boundary with Natal by 1894, and thus acquiring a considerable Bantu tribal population difficult to assimilate into its nonracial parliamentary democracy. Natal, granted responsible government in 1893, when sugar-planting with immigrant Indian labour had begun to afford some prosperity for its predominantly English settlers, finally absorbed Zululand in 1897. Continued trekking occasioned difficulties for the economically stagnant Boer republics. Incessant warfare between the Orange Free State and the Basuto ended only when Basutoland was annexed to Cape colony in 1871. The diamond-bearing region of Griqualand West, claimed by the Orange Free State, became a British possession in 1871 and was transferred to Cape colony in 1880. The bankrupt Transvaal was involved in border disputes with the Zulu and Swazi, which brought about the British annexation of the republic in 1877. This annexation was a stage in the plan of Lord Carnarvon (British colonial secretary, 1874–78) to federate the South African administrations so as to allow a unified approach to the many frontier and racial problems —an idea already put forward by Sir George Grey (governor at the Cape, 1854–59). However, when the Transvaal did not receive the self-government promised at the time of annexation, its burghers rose and in 1881, after defeating a British force at Majuba, regained their independence subject to British supervision of their frontiers, their foreign policy and their dealings with the Africans. (Pretoria convention, 1881, subsequently relaxed by the London convention, 1884). Meanwhile, encroachment by Transvaalers into Bechuanaland, across the route used by traders and missionaries from the Cape, together with the appearance of Germany in South West Africa, induced the British to occupy Bechuanaland in 1884–85.

South African affairs were revolutionized by the rapid exploitation of the gold of the Witwatersrand, discovered in 1886, which made the Transvaal potentially the richest state in South Africa. Under the presidency of Paul Kruger, its burghers were able to consolidate their republic and to aspire to extend its principles throughout South Africa.

Within the Transvaal opposition developed among the growing number of non-Boer settlers (*Uitlanders*), attracted by the development of the mining economy. Outside the Transvaal, Kruger was opposed by Cecil Rhodes who made a fortune through the amalgamation of the diamond mines, entered Cape politics and in 1890 became prime minister. Rhodes, generally supported in Great Britain by the Conservative party, aimed at unifying South Africa under the leadership of Cape colony in a self-governing British parliamentary democracy, which would serve as a base for the development of central and eastern Africa through European settlement. (*See* KRUGER, PAUL; RHODES, CECIL JOHN.)

The conflict between Rhodes and Kruger was first apparent in economic issues. Rhodes wanted the Boer republics to be linked with the Cape and Natal through common railways and customs tariffs, but the opening of its own railway to Delagoa bay in Portuguese East Africa in 1893 gave the Transvaal an independent outlet, and the occupation of the lands north of it by the pioneers of Rhodes's British South Africa company in 1890 served more to antagonize the Transvaal than to force it into closer relations with the south. The *Uitlanders,* restive under a government which taxed their wealth but which was increasingly reluctant to accord them citizenship lest they subvert the Boer state, plotted rebellion, to aid which Rhodes countenanced the invasion of the Transvaal by an armed force under Leander (later Sir Leander) Starr Jameson (*q.v.*) in 1895. However, the *Uitlanders* failed to rise as had been planned and Jameson's men were rounded up by Transvaal commandos. Rhodes subsequently resigned his premiership. The Transvaalers, convinced that the British wished to destroy their republic, prepared for war and the Orange Free State, hitherto not committed in the struggle, finally aligned itself with the Transvaal.

In the South African War (*q.v.*) the Boers gained initial successes (1899), but by 1900 a large British army had entered the capitals of the Boer republics. After two years of increasingly bitter guerrilla warfare, the Boers surrendered and agreed to the treaty of Vereeniging (1902). The republics became British colonies and their badly damaged economies were rapidly restored under Sir Alfred Milner (high commissioner, 1897–1905). However, little progress had been made with Milner's cautious policy of political rehabilitation when Britain's attitude toward South Africa was radically changed following the Liberal party's electoral victory in 1905–06. Full self-government was granted to the Transvaal in 1906 and to the Orange Free State in 1907. Under Lord Selborne (high commissioner, 1905–10), political leaders in the four colonies came together and worked out a scheme of union, implemented in the South Africa act (1910). The surviving Bantu territories—Basutoland, Bechuanaland and Swaziland—remained as separate British protectorates.

See also History sections of BOTSWANA; CAPE OF GOOD HOPE; LESOTHO; NATAL; ORANGE FREE STATE; SOUTH AFRICA, REPUBLIC OF; SOUTH WEST AFRICA; SWAZILAND; TRANSVAAL; ZULULAND.

(J. D. F.)

F. EAST AFRICA

The earliest written reference to the east coast of Africa is contained in the *Periplus of the Erythraean Sea,* a work of the 1st century A.D. This account suggests that there was regular trade from southern Arabia to the East African coast south of the Horn of Africa, but there is no indication as to how far south the traders sailed nor is it known with whom they carried on their trade. The geographer Ptolemy (2nd century A.D.) confirmed the account of the earlier writer but added no new information. Roman coins, however, have been found at Bircao (Port Durnford) in Somalia and coins of the Egyptian dynasty of the Ptolemies as far south as Msasani near Dar es Salaam. Ruined buildings on some of the islands off the coast of Tanzania may belong to the pre-Islamic period, but the next written records occur in the works of medieval Arab geographers who described Arab trading posts along the coast dating from the 10th century. None of these sites has been identified and the earliest archaeological evidence dated with certainty belongs to the 13th century, although the mihrab (prayer niche) in the mosque at Kizimkazi on Zanzibar Island bears the date 500 A.H. (A.D. 1107).

Supremacy of Kilwa.—For a long time it was believed that the town of Kilwa on the coast of Tanzania was founded in the 10th century by migrants from Shiraz in Persia. This legend stemmed from the *Chronicle of Kilwa,* a record of the ruling family of the town, which, although probably accurate from the late 14th century, is less reliable as regards the earlier period. Archaeological evidence in fact suggests that Kilwa belonged in its earliest days to an Islamic culture of Arabian origin which flourished in a number of coastal towns from the 13th century and reached its peak in the 15th. The traveler Ibn Batutah, who visited the East African coast in 1332, spoke with admiration of the fine mud and wattle buildings of Kilwa and of its inhabitants' devotion to Islam. It is probable, too, that the rulers of Kilwa exercised some form of authority over some of the other towns for limited periods.

In spite of Ibn Batutah's reference to warfare against the pagans of the hinterland, the relations between the Arab settlers and their African neighbours appear to have been generally friendly. There was some intermarriage and a mixed Arab and African (Swahili) culture sprang from the association between the two peoples.

The pre-eminence of Kilwa rested largely upon its control of the gold supplies from what is now Southern Rhodesia. The gold was brought to Sofala (on the Mozambique coast), which for a considerable period was controlled by Kilwa. The trade of East Africa, however, consisted of a variety of items, among which ivory and slaves were always important, while numerous other products such as tortoise shell and frankincense may well have been imported for re-export. The principal commercial contacts were with India and Arabia, and both these countries influenced the cultural development of the east coast. Chinese celadon of the Ming period was in regular use in a number of towns, but only two Chinese expeditions are known to have visited East Africa. The first, between 1417 and 1419, reached Malindi, while the second (1421–22) only traveled as far south as Brava and Mogadiscio on the Somali coast.

Portuguese Settlements.—The decline of Kilwa and of some of the other more southerly towns began with the arrival of the Portuguese at the end of the 15th century. During the course of his first voyage around the Cape of Good Hope in 1498 Vasco da Gama called at Mozambique, Mombasa and Malindi on his way to India, but was carried past Kilwa. At Malindi he met with a friendly reception which laid the foundations of an alliance between Malindi and Portugal. This alliance survived the conflicts between Portugal and the other coastal towns during the 16th century.

In 1502 Vasco da Gama forced the ruler of Kilwa to acknowledge the overlordship of the king of Portugal and to promise to pay an annual tribute. On the departure of the Portuguese fleet, however, the promise was forgotten until 1505 when another Portuguese force arrived under the leadership of Francisco de Almeida. Sofala had already fallen to these conquerors and Kilwa quickly followed. The ruler fled, a Portuguese nominee was appointed sultan and a fort erected. The Portuguese occupation, however, was short, the garrison being withdrawn in 1513 and the fort dismantled, as the capture of Sofala and the construction of a fort at Mozambique made Kilwa less important.

After his capture of Kilwa, Almeida sailed on to Mombasa, where the resistance of the defenders was overcome and the town looted. No fort was built, however, and the Portuguese force withdrew to continue its northward voyage of conquest as far as Socotra Island at the southern end of the Red sea. Left to its own devices, Mombasa became the centre of resistance to the Portuguese and succeeded to the pre-eminence of Kilwa among the coastal towns. So strong, however, were the jealousies existing among the ruling families along the coast that no united front was presented to the Portuguese, and when in 1529 a further attack was launched against Mombasa a number of towns supported the Portuguese in their operations.

The Portuguese made little attempt to exploit their conquest. Their objective was to capture the trade of the Indian ocean, and when it was seen that the limited produce of East Africa could be controlled from a handful of bases at Mozambique, Sofala, Zanzibar, Pemba and Malindi, no effort was wasted on administering the coast. Gradually, too, it was recognized that the best route to India lay directly across the Indian ocean, so that the towns on the East African coast north of Mozambique lost their earlier importance as stations along a vital line of communication. After the first years of conquest the East African settlements were administered from Goa, mainly with the assistance of friendly local rulers. Even the Portuguese flair for exploration found little outlet. Apart from a journey to Ethiopia in the 16th century the only exploration of the East African hinterland was undertaken by Gaspar Bocarro who, early in the 17th century, traveled up the Zambezi to take charge of some tin mines near Tete (Mozambique) and, after being attacked by the local population, made his way to the coast at Kilwa in 1616. His record of what he saw on the way is the only account of the interior before the coming of the Arabs in search of slaves. From Bocarro's writings it is clear that although neither Arabs nor Portuguese penetrated far into the continent, trade goods found their way a considerable distance into the hinterland. This was mainly the result of the movement of caravans between the interior (particularly Unyamwezi in western Tanzania) and the coast, a practice which became increasingly common in the later 17th and 18th centuries.

In 1585 the east coast was subjected to the attention of raiders. Mirale Bey, a Turkish corsair, sailed down the coast and, though he achieved no important conquests, was encouraged by the friendship of Mombasa to visit the coast again in order to challenge the power of the Portuguese. In 1589 he occupied Mombasa but was attacked by a Portuguese fleet from Goa. The Turkish squadron was defeated, Mirale Bey surrendered to the Portuguese and the town was destroyed by the warlike Zimba tribe.

The Zimba appeared on the scene with the destructive force of a swarm of locusts. Coming, in all probability, from the upper reaches of the Congo, they sacked Kilwa in 1587. Turning northward they arrived outside Mombasa just at the moment when the Portuguese were engaging Mirale Bey. After the destruction of the town the Zimba turned northward again and launched an assault on Malindi. The walls of the town were breached, but the attackers were almost completely wiped out by the defending force and by the Segeju, a local tribe which came to help the townsmen. The Zimba then disappeared from history, and the Segeju advanced against Mombasa, which they captured in 1592. They delivered the town to their ally, the sultan of Malindi, who transferred his headquarters there, and then in turn handed the town over to the Portuguese. In 1592 work began on the construction of Fort Jesus which became the most important Portuguese station north of the Rovuma river.

Predominance of Oman.—The resurgence of Portuguese interest in East Africa was brief. In 1631 the sultan of Mombasa, whose father had been killed at the instigation of the Portuguese, rebelled against his family's former allies and, though quickly driven from the town, maintained a sporadic resistance against the Portuguese for several years. The rising struck a serious blow at their precarrously balanced authority and a number of other towns followed the example of Mombasa. These individual uprisings were dealt with one by one, but a more serious threat occurred in 1696 when forces from Oman on the Arabian peninsula laid siege to Mombasa. An epic resistance lasting three years ended when the handful of survivors of the garrison were forced to surrender. After this victory the ruler of Oman received the submission of the other coastal towns and either appointed governors or else left the existing rulers in direct charge under his suzerainty.

In 1728 the Portuguese made their last bid for power. Taking advantage of the preoccupation of the sultan of Oman in his own country they once again seized Mombasa, but were able to hold it only until the following year. From this time they continued to maintain forts at Mozambique and Sofala but their authority north of the Rovuma river was at an end. The rivalries between the coastal towns soon threatened the temporary unity imposed by the Omani victories. In 1741 the Busaidi family overthrew the Ya'rubid dynasty in Oman, and this provided the opportunity for a number of the towns to renounce their allegiance. First among these was Mombasa, where the Mazrui family claimed authority over a considerable section of the coast north and south of the island and challenged the sultan of Oman to dispute their independence. Kilwa also rejected the Omani overlordship.

Slave Trade and Zanzibar.—The next outsiders to exert their influence on the coast were the French, who, in search of slaves, entered into negotiations with the sultan of Kilwa in 1776. There began the revival of the slave trade which was to reach vast proportions in the 19th century, and the renewed importance of Kilwa induced the sultan of Oman to make an effort to reassert his authority in the early 1780s. Henceforward, the French traded with the sultan's representatives. Zanzibar, meanwhile, had remained loyal to Oman, but the sultan's authority in East Africa extended no farther.

The next important developments along the coast took place as a result of British interest in the antislavery campaign that began in the early 19th century. During the Napoleonic Wars the British hesitated to take any steps that might offend their ally Sa'id ibn Sultan, the ruler of Oman, but the flourishing trade from Kilwa and Zanzibar induced the British authorities in India to take action as soon as peace was restored. In 1822 a treaty was signed between Sa'id and the British which restricted the East African slave trade to the sultan's possessions in East Africa and Arabia. Though the treaty's reference to his East African possessions gave an exaggerated impression of Omani authority along the coast, Sa'id felt encouraged by British friendship and decided to attack the Mazrui of Mombasa. The town fell, as a result rather of his guile than of his military prowess, and he then moved on to visit his loyal subjects in Zanzibar.

The attractive climate of Zanzibar Island and the obvious trading prospects appealed greatly to Sa'id, who, though he had to return to Oman, probably decided during his visit to transfer his headquarters to Zanzibar. Mombasa, however, continued to be a problem and it was not until 1837 that the pretensions of the Mazrui were finally destroyed. Sa'id spent increasingly lengthy periods in Zanzibar from this time and set himself the task of increasing the prosperity of the island by planting cloves and by financing trading caravans and encouraging them to venture into the interior of the continent. During the second quarter of the 19th century Arab and Swahili traders began for the first time to push beyond the immediate hinterland of the East African coast and to penetrate ever farther toward the great lakes of central Africa in search of slaves and ivory.

As the slave trade grew the British became more intent on restricting its effects. In 1841 a British consul was posted to Zanzibar in order to be in touch with the sultan, whom the British believed to be the one man with whom they could negotiate in the hope of controlling the trade still further. In 1845 Sa'id reluctantly agreed to another treaty which restricted the slave trade to the East African coast alone. While he did his utmost to fulfill his obligations he recognized that he did so against the wishes of almost all his Arab subjects, and the British naval patrol operating against the slave trade along the coast achieved only limited success in the face of almost universal opposition.

Whereas the only interest displayed by Great Britain in East Africa had been in the suppression of the slave trade, other countries now began to be attracted by the prospects of legitimate trade along the coast. Americans, Germans and Frenchmen all obtained trading rights from Sa'id ibn Sultan, although the trade was limited and could provide profit for only a few merchants. British influence, however, continued to be paramount in Zanzibar and increased after Sa'id's death in 1856, when his son Majid was established as successor with the support of the British consul and a body of British sailors who helped him to put down the revolt of his brother Barghash. In 1860 an appeal was made to Lord Canning, the governor general of India, who decided that the sultanates of Zanzibar and Oman should henceforward be separated, and in 1862 Great Britain and France agreed to recognize the independence of Majid as sultan of Zanzibar. This independence was of doubtful value. The French gave up their attempts to acquire slaves from the coast and ceased to interfere in the political affairs of Zanzibar, but the sultan's efforts to observe the terms of the antislavery treaties made him dependent upon British support against his own subjects. This dependence was still further increased in 1873 when Barghash, who had succeeded his brother in 1870, was forced by Great Britain to abolish the slave trade in Zanzibar and the coastal towns.

It was in the 1870s that the relationship between Zanzibar and the mainland was first questioned. The main interest of Sa'id and of his two sons in both the coast and the hinterland had been in their commercial possibilities. They had maintained a few small garrisons in some of the coastal towns and had representatives at some of the main trading centres in the interior. They had never sought to administer the mainland, however, and in spite of their political claims the suzerainty that they exercised was of a purely commercial character.

In the 1850s through the 1870s, a number of European explorers using Zanzibar as their base had penetrated to the region of the great lakes and several missionary societies had established themselves in Zanzibar and on the mainland. Moreover, after Stanley's great journey across Africa from east to west there had been a growing interest on the part of certain European powers in tropical African trade and colonization. Fearing an attempt to encroach upon Zanzibar's trading activities on the mainland, the British consul general, Sir John Kirk (q.v.), urged Barghash to seek British aid in establishing his claim to sovereignty in East Africa. Having lost the profits from the slave trade as a result of the most recent treaty with Great Britain, Barghash had already in 1878 offered a concession of all his mainland territories "between the coast and the great lakes" to Sir William Mackinnon, chairman of the British India Steamship company. Mackinnon, however, had been unable to obtain the British government's approval for his acceptance of the offer, and the British government was equally unwilling to become involved in Kirk's attempt to define the limits of the sultan's authority on the mainland. Barghash consequently was at the mercy of the rival contenders for supremacy in East Africa.

Chief among these contenders was Germany, which first took an interest in the mainland through the activities of Karl Peters, who, late in 1884 and in spite of the sultan's protests, made a number of treaties in the Usambara area which were subsequently ratified by the German government. Some British businessmen had also shown interest in the Kilimanjaro area with the sultan's approval, but they got little support from their own government. To avoid disputes the British agreed in 1886 to a German proposal that the limits of the sultan's authority on the mainland should be defined and that the rest of the territory should be divided into British and German spheres of influence. A boundary commission was appointed and as a result of its efforts the sultan's territories on the mainland were recognized as comprising a strip 10 mi. wide and stretching from the Rovuma river in the south to the Tana river in the north with, in addition, a few coastal towns extending as far northward as Mogadiscio.

Colonization of East Africa.—In 1888, Mackinnon's British East Africa association (incorporated by royal charter as the Imperial British East Africa company) was authorized to develop the British sphere of influence in East Africa on behalf of the British government. Next, by the Anglo-German agreement of 1890, the British and the German spheres of influence in East Africa were further defined, and Germany recognized a British protectorate over the dominions of the sultan of Zanzibar. Then, in 1891, the German government proclaimed a protectorate over its sphere of influence in East Africa. The British East Africa company in 1895 surrendered its charter to the British government, which then took direct responsibility for its territories as the British East African protectorate (later Kenya colony and protectorate).

During World War I, German East Africa was occupied by Allied troops. After the war the administration of the major part of it was assigned to Great Britain under a League of Nations mandate, its name being changed to Tanganyika. The Ruanda-Urundi area was assigned to Belgium. A British protectorate had been proclaimed over Buganda in 1894 and later extended to other parts of Uganda. To the south, moreover, the Anglo-Portuguese treaty of 1891 had confirmed the Portuguese in their possessions there.

See also *History* sections of KENYA; MALAGASY REPUBLIC; MOZAMBIQUE; PORTUGUESE EAST AFRICA; RUANDA-URUNDI; TANZANIA, UNITED REPUBLIC OF; UGANDA. (K. I.)

G. PARTITION OF AFRICA

Before the last two decades of the 19th century Europe showed little interest in colonizing tropical Africa. Where climate permitted Europeans to settle permanently, the French had established themselves in Algeria and the British in the Cape colony and in Natal. Elsewhere, European colonies were confined to coastal enclaves, often legacies of slave-trading days. Portugal had claims to the interior of Angola and Mozambique, but maintained only a sketchy administration over the coasts. Lack of interest in Africa was partly due to the fact that all the major western European powers, except Great Britain, had internal problems so acute as to preclude a sustained policy of colonial expansion. The British were mainly concerned with attempting to expand trade in Africa and to put down the traffic in slaves, without undertaking the costly and troublesome task of establishing colonies.

Tunis and Egypt.—By the end of the 1870s most of the internal problems of the major European states were resolved. Germany had emerged as the strongest military power in Europe, having in 1870 inflicted a crushing defeat on France. The German chancellor, Otto von Bismarck, hoped to lessen the hostility of France, embittered by the loss of Alsace and most of Lorraine, by diverting its energies into colonial activity. During the congress of Berlin (q.v.) in 1878 he urged France to take Tunis, which exposed the eastern frontiers of Algeria. The French feared Italian designs on Tunis, which had 20,000 Italian settlers, and in 1881 a French force occupied the country. The bey was made to sign a treaty accepting a French protectorate, Italy remaining powerless in the face of Bismarck's tacit support of the French.

Meanwhile in Egypt in April 1879, the khedive Ismail, nominally a vassal of Turkey, dismissed the British and French financial officials who had been imposed upon him in 1876. In reply Great Britain and France arranged for the sultan of Turkey to depose Ismail, and replace him with Ismail's son Tewfik Pasha. This action sparked off a nationalist revolt among army officers, led by Arabi Pasha (q.v.), who gained control of Egypt. Britain and France, in May 1882, agreed on a joint intervention, but as a result of maladroit diplomacy and political changes in France it was eventually the British alone who bombarded Alexandria and landed the force which defeated Arabi. The British had no plan for establishing a colony or even a protectorate in Egypt. The prime minister, W. E. Gladstone, thought that Great Britain could "restore the khedive's authority" and withdraw, but the restoration of the khedive's authority (*i.e.,* Egypt's ability to pay its debts) proved to be the work of more than a generation of financial, political and social reform.

The British occupation of Egypt was deeply resented by the French, who had long believed that their financial investment in Egypt and the fact that the Suez canal had been a French project entitled them to a predominant position there. It set the pattern for intense rivalry between Great Britain and France in Africa, which was to remain constant until 1898. French statesmen, such as Jules Ferry, convinced that France's trade and industry needed colonial markets that could be protected by tariffs, began to feel that the French must act quickly in other areas if they were not to be forestalled by the British.

Tropical West Africa and the Berlin Conference.—In 1884 the British position on the western side of tropical Africa suffered a severe setback. Through his supposedly philanthropic International Association for the Exploration and Civilization of Africa, King Leopold II of the Belgians had been laying plans for the creation of a personal domain in the Congo. The French countered by sending out the explorer Count Savorgnan de Brazza, who by 1882 had secured the north bank of the Congo mouth for France and laid the foundation for the colony of Gabon. At the same time the French government began actively to support its traders on the Niger, where British trade had been predominant. In the Anglo-Portuguese treaty of Feb. 1884, Great Britain, by recognizing Portuguese claims to the Congo mouth in return for the granting of easy access to this region to British missionaries and traders, tried to thwart both the French and King Leopold.

It was this situation which Bismarck decided to exploit in order to create a German empire in Africa. He himself did not favour the idea of founding colonies, but by launching Germany as a colonial power he was bidding for votes in the German elections and hoped to win over France and so to create some kind of Franco-German entente based on a common anti-British policy in Africa.

Throughout 1883 Germany had been sounding the British as to their claims around Angra Pequena in southwest Africa, where a German merchant, Franz Lüderitz, was asking for his government's protection. Germany was met first with evasion, but in

November was told that although Great Britain did not intend to establish any authority in the region, any German claim would infringe British "legitimate rights." This attitude infuriated Bismarck and in April 1884 he proclaimed a German protectorate over Angra Pequena. France and Germany then together denounced the new Anglo-Portuguese treaty and in June the British, seeing their isolation, recognized the German protectorate at Angra Pequena and abandoned the Portuguese treaty. In July the German consul in West Africa, G. Nachtigal, proceeded to annex Togoland and the Cameroons. In August, Bismarck extended the Angra Pequena protectorate to cover all the territory between Angola and Cape colony. Finally the fruits of Franco-German co-operation were revealed when the two powers invited Great Britain to a conference at Berlin to discuss ways of establishing international control over the Congo and Niger rivers and of defining future acquisitions on the coasts of Africa.

The Berlin conference, which began its work in Nov. 1884, finally rejected any Portuguese claims to the Congo region, which became the Congo Free State under the personal sovereignty of King Leopold. On the Niger the British managed to retrieve something of their predominant position, largely because George Goldie Taubman (later Sir George Dashwood Goldie [q.v.]) had succeeded in buying out the French traders on the eve of the conference, so that the British were alone on the lower Niger. Meanwhile the Franco-German entente was breaking down, as the French government feared that the electorate might turn violently against policies which appeared pro-German. As a result, Great Britain was made responsible for administering the Niger. Accordingly, in 1886 Goldie's company was granted a royal charter of administration and became the Royal Niger company. East of the Niger, where there were several British firms, the foreign office administered the Oil Rivers region.

British and German Rivalry in East Africa.—Throughout the 19th century British consuls, notably Kirk, had worked to make Zanzibar a progressive Arab state controlling the East African coastline. After the German annexations in West Africa some British cabinet ministers wanted to forestall any German moves in East Africa by establishing a British protectorate, but Gladstone vetoed the idea; in Nov.–Dec. 1884, Peters (working for the German Colonization society) succeeded in making treaties inland, in what is now Tanzania. In 1885, Peters' society was granted German protection and the right to administer its claims.

The international situation did not allow Britain to resist Germany in East Africa. The Germans were allowed to expand inland to establish themselves farther up the coast at Witu and to force the sultan of Zanzibar, under threat of naval bombardment, to accept what had been done. A joint British-French-German commission "delimited" the sultan's possessions exactly as the German representative wished.

The British attempt to salvage some position in East Africa was made expressly with German approval. The initiative came once more from private interests, prompted by the consular officials at Zanzibar. It was proposed to revive a scheme broached in 1879 and to rule what is now Kenya by a chartered company headed by Mackinnon under concessions from the sultan of Zanzibar. Though Mackinnon's associates began to make treaties in 1886 they could not at once obtain open official support. In Oct. 1886, an Anglo-German agreement was reached to divide the mainland between the Rovuma and Tana rivers along a line from the Umba river to Lake Victoria, retaining Witu as a German enclave inside the British sphere. Yet the German government still hesitated. The Conservative prime minister, Lord Salisbury, intended to restore control of Egypt to Turkey. Salisbury's negotiations failed, however, because of French and Russian opposition, and he then saw that if the British could not evacuate Egypt, Mackinnon's British East African association would have to protect the approaches to the sources of the Nile (on whose waters Egypt depended) and, if possible, occupy Uganda. In 1888 the association was incorporated by royal charter as the Imperial British East African company.

There followed a period of intense rivalry between the British and German companies for the control of the Nile sources. At first the rivalry concentrated on the Equatoria province of the Egyptian Sudan, where a German, Emin Pasha, still held out against the Mahdists. At the end of 1889 Emin was relieved by Stanley's expedition, and the Mahdists occupied Equatoria. Uganda then became the centre of competition. Both British and German companies sent expeditions to Buganda, but the Germans were first to make a treaty. By the Anglo-German agreement of 1890, Germany withdrew from Witu, recognized Uganda as within the British sphere and accepted that the island possessions of Zanzibar should become a British protectorate; Great Britain ceded to Germany the island of Heligoland in the North sea.

The sole remaining rival to Great Britain with regard to the eastern approaches of the Nile was Italy, already established in Eritrea and Somaliland. France, Great Britain and Italy were all established in Somaliland soon after the British occupation of Egypt. In 1888 France, and in 1889 Italy, made agreements with Great Britain which divided Somaliland into separate spheres. Also in 1889, the Italians concluded a treaty with the emperor Menelik of Ethiopia, which, they claimed, gave Italy a protectorate over his country. If substantiated, such a claim would have given Italy control of the Blue Nile. In 1891 Great Britain agreed to recognize Italy's claims, but the boundaries were drawn to preclude Italian access to the Nile, and Italy agreed not to alter the flow of water by building dams on the Nile tributaries. In return, Great Britain in 1892 persuaded the sultan of Zanzibar to lease the Benedir coast to Italy. In 1905 the lease was ceded outright and the territory incorporated into Italian Somaliland.

Anglo-French Rivalry in Guinea and the Sudan.—The Anglo-German treaty had recognized a British protectorate over Zanzibar despite an Anglo-French agreement of 1862 to maintain the sultan's independence. The French used this to extract a British recognition of a French protectorate over Madagascar and to try to limit British expansion in West Africa. The Anglo-German treaty had also settled the boundaries between British possessions and the German colonies of Togoland and the Cameroons, hinting moreover at a partition of the Lake Chad region. The French feared that the Royal Niger company might advance right across to the Nile and prevent France joining Algeria and Senegal with Gabon in one block. Thus they readily agreed (in the Anglo-French declaration of Aug. 1890) that the frontier between French and British spheres should be a line from Say on the Niger to Barruwa on Lake Chad, leaving the Sokoto empire in the Niger company's sphere. The company's eastern and western boundaries, however, remained exposed to future rivalry. Goldie in 1893 obtained an Anglo-German agreement extending German Cameroons so far northward that the company's eastern frontier was protected by German territory, but the western frontier of Nigeria remained open. The French, after conquering Dahomey, began pushing troops into areas claimed by the company, and by 1898 there was danger of war. The "Niger crisis," however, was settled by a frontier agreement in June 1898, which established the basis of Nigeria's frontiers and also settled the limits to the hinterlands of the other French and British West African colonies.

The Niger crisis was almost immediately followed by the Fashoda crisis. Whereas in 1893 the British had hoped that German expansion from the Cameroons might prevent the French approaching the Nile from Gabon, a Franco-German agreement of March 1894 drew a frontier to the Cameroons that left the Nile approaches open. The British thereupon agreed with King Leopold (May 1894), to seal off the Nile by leasing the Bahr al Ghazal to Leopold, who leased to the British a strip of territory linking Uganda with Rhodesia. France and Germany protested and in August the French persuaded Leopold to drop the agreement. The French then began to organize the expedition to cross Africa from Gabon to the upper Nile. Furthermore, when the Italians tried to control Ethiopia (they were to be disastrously defeated by the Ethiopians at Aduwa in March 1896), the French supported the Ethiopians and Great Britain feared that the Nile now lay open on both sides. Two weeks after the Italian defeat, the British decided to reconquer the Sudan. Sir Herbert (later Earl) Kitchener's army from the north and J. B. Marchand's French expedition from the west met shortly after Kitchener's defeat of the Mahdists at Omdurman in Sept. 1898. After a period of acute tension the French, failing to obtain diplomatic support, withdrew and, in March 1899, accepted exclusion from the Nile valley in an agreement with the British. The Anglo-French colonial conflict was virtually over and the basis laid for the realignment of European powers in the entente cordiale of 1904.

Southern Africa.—The partition of southern Africa was influenced much more by local factors, particularly the rivalries of British and Boer settlers. Great Britain had consistently refused to permit the Boer republics of the Orange Free State and the Transvaal to obtain access to the sea, so that no help could come to them from other European powers. When the Germans established themselves in East Africa and southwest Africa during 1884–85, there seemed a danger that the two German colonies might expand to join together, preventing British expansion northward and giving Germany a contiguous frontier with the Transvaal. German intervention also stimulated Portuguese efforts to realize claims to territories joining Angola and Mozambique. It therefore seemed essential that "the road to the north" should be secured and once more Great Britain was able to use private interests. Cecil Rhodes in 1889 obtained the incorporation by royal charter of the British South Africa company, and soon began the settlement of Mashonaland. The company also undertook to subsidize the administration of the Nyasaland protectorate. There was bitter rivalry with the Portuguese until the boundaries of Mozambique were settled in the Anglo-Portuguese convention of 1890–91. Rhodes then turned to the problem of unifying southern Africa. The Jameson raid of Dec. 1895, originally planned to assist a revolution in the Transvaal, ended disastrously.

Germany attempted to use the raid to build a league against Great Britain, but France and Russia remained aloof. The German navy was not strong enough to permit German assistance to the Boers, who in the succeeding years were isolated by British diplomacy. In Aug. 1898, the Germans renounced all interest in Delagoa bay, the Mozambique port which was the Transvaal's outlet to the sea. The South African War of 1899–1902 was the final act in the partition of southern Africa, ending in complete British control of the Transvaal and the Orange Free State.

Final Acquisitions.—Morocco and Tripoli remained the only considerable states in Africa still ruled independently, except Ethiopia and Liberia. France did not want a foreign protectorate in Morocco, lying next to Algeria, while Great Britain feared that any French control of northern Morocco would nullify the strategic importance of Gibraltar. After the settlement of the Fashoda incident, however, France and Great Britain drew together, and in 1904 France obtained British and Italian recognition of French preponderance in Morocco, recognizing in return British control of Egypt and giving Italy a free hand in Tripoli. In the same year a secret Franco-Spanish agreement delimited two zones in Morocco, the northern to be Spanish. Although Germany was not much interested in Morocco, the German foreign office used the Moroccan question to promote a series of incidents designed to test the strength of the Anglo-French entente. The effect was merely to cement Anglo-French co-operation. In Nov. 1911 Germany, in return for French territory transferred to the German Cameroons, accepted the French position in Morocco. In March 1912 Morocco was made a French protectorate, and later in the year the Spanish zone was finally delimited.

The Italians did not take up their option in Tripoli until 1911, when they invaded the country (see ITALO-TURKISH WAR). Local resistance during World War I delayed effective Italian occupation. After the war the Italians pursued the conquest ruthlessly, but the last resistance was not crushed until 1932.

The Versailles peace treaty of 1919 substantially altered the map of Africa by allocating the German colonies under mandates to the victorious allies. The French and British partitioned Togoland and the Cameroons; the British obtained most of German East Africa (renamed Tanganyika), the remainder going to Belgium; South Africa was given German South West Africa.

Ethiopia, which alone of all the African countries, except Liberia, was still independent after World War I, was invaded by the Italians in the autumn of 1935. Great Britain and France attempted a solution in the old style, which would have granted what Italy demanded, preserved British and French interests and left a truncated Ethiopian state, but opposition in Great Britain caused the plan to be dropped. The League of Nations tried unsuccessfully to check Italy with economic sanctions. In 1936 the Italian conquest of Ethiopia was completed. (J. E. FL.)

H. AFRICA AFTER WORLD WAR I

The most distinctive feature of African history during the four decades following World War I was the creation of African nations within the territorial limits laid down by the colonial powers. Territorial boundaries changed very little after 1918–19. The four German colonies were transferred to Allied powers under a mandate from the League of Nations. German South West Africa was entrusted to South Africa, and German East Africa was divided between Great Britain and Belgium, creating Tanganyika and Ruanda-Urundi. Both Cameroons and Togoland were divided between France and Great Britain, with France receiving the larger share in each case.

Most of the European conquest of Africa had been accomplished before World War I, and postwar military operations were mainly concerned with the suppression of African resistance on the fringes of the Sahara and in a few remote areas in other parts of the continent. In 1935, however, Italy began the invasion of Ethiopia. The Italian occupation of Ethiopia was cut short in 1941 during World War II by the intervention of British forces, and Ethiopia's independence was re-established.

Administration and Development in Colonial Territories.—The principal concern of the European powers in the interwar period was the extension of their administration and the economic development of their spheres of control. All the colonial powers (and the self-governing European minorities in South Africa and Southern Rhodesia) organized their respective territories on the initial assumption that their rule would last for an indefinitely long period. Ultimate responsibility for government was therefore retained in the hands of the Europeans. A full administrative bureaucracy on the European model staffed by Europeans, however, would have been prohibitively expensive. The colonial powers, therefore, tended to use the traditional African political authorities where possible as the basis of local government, while European officials occupied the higher posts in the administration. In British territories this system of mixed administration was called "indirect rule," and it was most fully developed in northern Nigeria.

Other powers, however, did much the same thing under different names, and even where "direct administration" was established in theory the need for cheap government forced a great deal of *de facto* delegation of power to African chiefs and village heads. African political traditions thus retained some of their vitality throughout the colonial period.

The new African nations which emerged at mid-20th century were not, however, to be based on the traditional political units of the pre-colonial era. They developed instead within the colonial framework, in which national life was gradually superimposed on the existing diversity of traditional cultures by unified economic development and a unified educational system.

Planning for economic development was of vital importance to the colonial territories from the beginning of European rule. There was a European demand for tropical products, and it was essential to have a taxable economic base in order to pay for the colonial administration. Economic development meant first of all the development of transport, and new transport networks, by river, rail and road, were constructed to serve each colony. The flow of trade and the movement of people followed the pattern of the transport routes, which led to the sea and contact with Europe rather than across colonial boundaries. Mining centres and the new distribution centres (such as Port Harcourt in Nigeria, Stanleyville in the former Belgian Congo and Bangui in former French Equatorial Africa) attracted people of many different cultures, speaking a variety of languages, and subjected them to the influences of urban life. The circle of vision of urban Africans gradually extended from the village and the traditional

society that they had left behind
to the new colonial territory.
Social and political organizations,
even in the urban areas, were
at first ethnic or local, but as
time passed more and more of
them became general and national in scope.

The process of nation building
was accelerated between the wars
by the development of education. Even primary education
brought young people into contact with a wider world, and the
secondary schools were the principal training ground for the new
African leadership. Teaching in
secondary schools—which were
often boarding schools serving a
wide area—was always conducted
in the language of the colonial
power. Achimota college in the
Gold Coast and Fourah Bay college in Sierra Leone drew students from all parts of British
West Africa, while the *lycées* at
St. Louis and at Dakar served not
only Senegal but the whole of
former French West Africa. Students established broad contacts
and came to see themselves as
members of a nation conterminous with the colonial boundaries
rather than as subjects of the
traditional African states. Ultimately they, and not the traditional rulers, formed the principal cadres for the nationalist
movements.

Rise of Nationalism.—The
processes of education, economic
growth and nation building were
not uniform throughout the continent. Nationalist movements
on the European pattern had de-
veloped on a small scale before World War I in some parts of
Africa—notably in Egypt, in the French North African territories,
in Senegal and in British West Africa. Elsewhere there were
movements of protest against colonial rule, but they were often
traditional in organization and aimed at creating something less
than a modern national state. Some were aimed to counteract the
European cultural influence by combining protest with a syncretic
mixture of Christianity and the traditional religion, as in the case
of Kibangism in the lower Congo during the 1920s. Others were
local protests against specific grievances, such as the "women's
riots" in Aba (Nigeria) in 1929. Still others combined both of
these elements with ethnic particularism, as in the Mau Mau revolt in Kenya during the early 1950s; and there were many other
variants. Some of these prenationalist protest movements were
important in preparing the way for later national independence,
but most were unsuccessful in achieving their own aims. In the
long run, the only successful movements opposing European rule
were those led by men with enough western education to take over
and operate the administrative organization created by the colonial
powers. This stage in the maturity and growth of nationalist
movements was not reached till after World War II.

Although military operations in Africa during World War II
were limited to the north and to Italian East Africa, the effect
of the war on Africa was far-reaching: Africans participated in
the war effort, and urbanization and economic development were
accelerated. Before the end of the war, it was clear to Great
Britain and to France alike that Africans would demand a greater

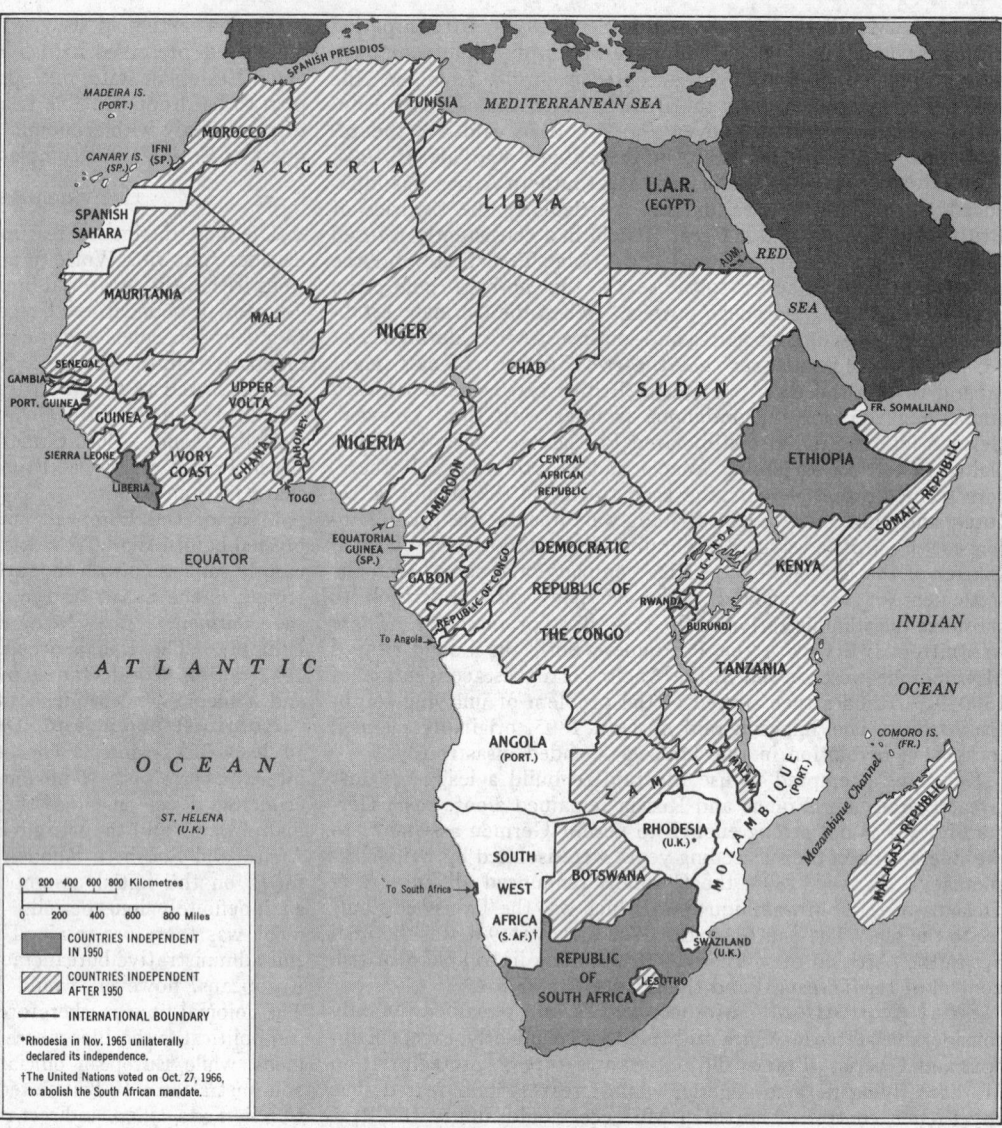

FIG. 10.—POLITICAL DEVELOPMENT OF AFRICA

share in the colonial governments, and both countries made plans
for new departures in their colonial administrations by introducing an element of African representation in government. Portugal
and Belgium, however, retained their nonrepresentative administrations, and in the 1950s and 1960s the government of South
Africa assumed even stricter control of the country's African majority.

Toward Independence.—The movement for national independence followed different courses in the various major divisions
of the continent. (*See* fig. 10.) In North Africa, where there
was a long history of contact with Europe, Great Britain ended
its military occupation of Egypt in 1947, withdrawing its troops
to the Suez Canal Zone. Libya became independent in 1951 and
the Anglo-Egyptian Sudan became a republic in 1956. In the
Maghreb, where there were large minorities of European settlers,
the independence movement was slower, but the two French
protectorates, Tunisia and Morocco, became independent by
agreement with France in 1956, and Spanish Morocco was reunited
with the rest of Morocco in the same year. After a rising in 1945,
the Algerian nationalists organized a rebellion in 1954, which continued until 1962 when France granted Algeria independence.

South of the Sahara two quite different situations confronted
the European powers. In those regions north and west of the
Congo and Ubangi rivers, there were only negligible numbers of
European settlers. South and east of the Congo-Ubangi line,
however, there were substantial minorities of Europeans and
Asians, and the European powers took the view that the rights of

the settlers should be safeguarded. They were therefore reluctant to allow democratic self-government, since this would mean government controlled by the African majority.

In the region where settlers were few, both France and Great Britain introduced a measure of local representation in the colonial governments in the years immediately following World War II. At that time, however, the West African nationalist movements were still small organizations of the educated elite, and the balance of political power rested firmly with the ruling countries. The movement toward independence depended on two developments still to come. One of these was the broadening of the nationalist movements into well-organized political parties with mass support throughout the various countries, a change that was accomplished in most of the West African territories before the end of the 1940s and spread gradually east and south during the course of the 1950s. The second necessary development was the recognition in Europe that token representation would have to give way to genuine self-government. This change was achieved in British policy toward West Africa in 1949, and it led to the independence of Ghana in 1957, Nigeria in 1960 and Sierra Leone in 1961.

The equivalent change in French policy came in 1956 with the passage of a new constitutional act (*loi cadre*), which granted substantial rights of internal self-government to elected assemblies in all French territories south of the Sahara. This was followed in 1958 by the formation of the French Community (*q.v.*), whose member countries possessed even greater powers of local self-government and the option of independence through referendum. Only Guinea seized the opportunity for immediate independence (1958), but in 1960 a new status of independence within the community was recognized and available to those territories that might choose it. Consequently, after 1962 the only area of continental Africa remaining under French control was French Somaliland.

In the early 1960s all African countries north and west of the Ubangi-Congo line were thus independent with the exception of Spanish and Portuguese possessions. At the same time the movement for national independence was spreading east and south into the regions of European settlement. The granting of independence to the Congo by Belgium in 1960 was followed by turmoil. Within the British sphere in central and East Africa there was also a major change in policy, which resulted in the independence of Uganda (1962), Kenya (1963) and Nyasaland (renamed Malawi) and Northern Rhodesia (renamed Zambia) in 1964.

In effect, a new line of demarcation equivalent to the older division along the Ubangi and Congo came into existence farther south. The white government of Southern Rhodesia declared the country to be independent of Great Britain in 1965 and set out, in the face of British and UN opposition, to create a police state under a minority government, following the model of South Africa. The Portuguese were also determined to fight rather than yield control of their overseas territories in Guinea, Mozambique and Angola. The southern boundaries of Congo (Kinshasa), Zambia and Tanzania thus became a frontier of hardening animosities between independent Africa and a southern region still dominated by Europeans. (P. D. Cu.)

VI. POPULATION

The racial composition, tribal groupings and characteristics, and social organization of the peoples of Africa have been described above (see *Ethnography*). This section is concerned with numbers and the distribution and density of population.

Knowledge of even the approximate size of the population of Africa in past centuries is very slight, for little contact was made between Europe and Africa. Information given to 18th- and 19th-century explorers was often incorrect, and their observations were not always objective. In East Africa, where the Arab-controlled slave trade continued until the last quarter of the 19th century, people tried to live well away from slave trade routes. Travelers did not hesitate to make estimates of population not only for the areas through which they passed but also for much larger regions and sometimes even for the whole continent. Thus there is a range of estimates early in the 19th century varying between 28,000,000 and 41,000,000—all figures considerably below

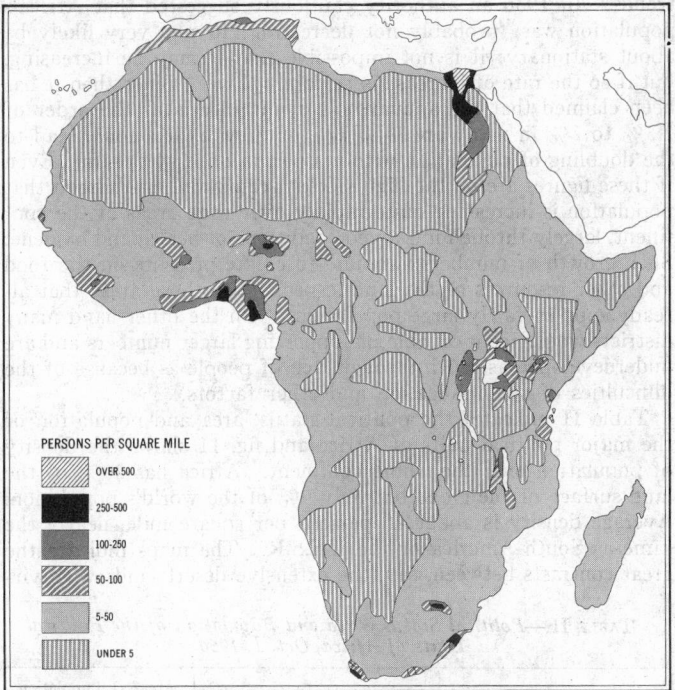

FIG. 11.—DENSITY OF POPULATION IN AFRICA

PERSONS PER SQUARE MILE

- OVER 500
- 250-500
- 100-250
- 50-100
- 5-50
- UNDER 5

that of 150,000,000 which was current during the previous century. Later, under the influence of the explorer Stanley in particular, the estimate moved up to 180,000,000.

The generally accepted figure early in the 20th century was of the order of 120,000,000 to 130,000,000. After World War I statistics were collected through the League of Nations secretariat and, subsequently, the United Nations. These figures are as reliable as any others available, especially with the proviso with which they are published that they may be out by up to ±10,-000,000. They suggest a fairly steady increase from 140,000,000 in 1920 to more than 230,000,000 in 1960. (*See* Table II.)

The problem of the over-all continental figure arises not particularly from the size of the area or of the population but from the multiplicity of political authorities and from the poverty and inaccuracy of the census data available. No territory has had accurate counting for long, except Algeria after the French occupation of 1830 (and the early non-European figures are suspect). Few detailed counts were taken before 1900, and these were for very restricted areas or groups of people; more elaborate, and thus more valuable, censuses are nearly everywhere features only of counts after World War II. Even in the 1960s there were political areas where no census had ever been taken or where it was admitted that the figures produced were valueless. Population study in Africa is full of pitfalls, and inexplicable anomalies are common. An oft-quoted example is that of the former Belgian Congo, which at one time was stated to have 40,000,000 inhabitants but whose official population in 1910 was given as 15,500,000 and in 1933 as only 9,250,000. It seems unlikely that population could have declined so strikingly simply as a result of mismanagement of the Free State before it came under direct Belgian control, and this would not explain the further marked decline between 1910 and 1930. The 1911–36 figures for former French Equatorial Africa are even more puzzling: the figure for 1911 was given as 20,000,000, but only 7,500,000 for 1921 and only one-third of this figure, a mere 2,500,000, for 1932. This was followed five years later by a French official figure of 3,400,000.

Census-taking operations in most parts of Africa are beset with difficulties: a predominantly illiterate population, a suspicion of the intentions of authority, a lack of precise information about age and a shortage of skilled personnel for use as enumerators. Undue reliance must not, therefore, be placed upon such figures as are available, and it must be recognized that there is rarely enough information on which to base any reliable forecast of trends. In 1936 an authority cautiously suggested that Africa's population was "probably not decreasing: it may very likely be about stationary: it is not impossible that it may be increasing, but if so the rate of increase is certainly slow." Since then it has been claimed that the annual rate of increase is of the order of 1.5% to 2% in many areas—a rate of growth that could lead to the doubling of population within a period of 35–40 years. Even if these figures are on the high side, it seems well established that population is increasing quite rapidly over wide areas of the continent, largely through improved conditions of health and hygiene. Such growth of numbers is bound to create pressure on the food and other resources of the land, especially in those areas that already support fairly large populations. On the other hand many districts would seem capable of supporting larger numbers and are underdeveloped as much through lack of people as because of the difficulties of communication and other factors.

Table II indicates the political status, area and population of the major political units of Africa and fig. 11 shows the density of population over the whole continent. Africa has 20% of the land surface of the globe but only 9% of the world's population. Average density is about 26 persons per square mile, nearly the same as South America or the U.S.S.R. The maps indicate the great contrasts between, say, the extensive desert lands with vir-

tually no inhabitants and the smaller, but very marked, areas of concentrated population in the Nile valley, in Rwanda and Burundi or in the Witwatersrand area of South Africa. Figures of density of population per square mile do not, however, tell the complete story and can in fact be misleading. Population needs to be seen in relation to the cultivable and other resources of the area in which it lives, especially in countries with large uninhabitable tracts. Thus Bechuanaland with only 2.5 persons to the square mile or Somali Republic, with 9.4, would be hard-pressed to support many more people in their semiarid environments. Ghana and Nigeria, on the other hand, with about 83 and 156 per square mile respectively, have shown an ability to maintain a greater population. Other territories—Rhodesia, for example—might be able to make better use of their resources if they had greater populations so that they were less dependent upon migrant labour.

There are, however, some countries or at least areas within certain countries where the density of population is high by African standards and where there is a state of overcrowding if not of overpopulation under present economic conditions and with existing agricultural methods. For example, many of the interior districts of the former French West Africa, some of the African tribal areas in Kenya, and parts of southern Malawi and of Rwanda and Burundi have to support more people, often at a very low standard of living, than their resources justify; and from them all there is considerable movement of people to areas such as Ghana, the Kenya highlands, Rhodesia and Uganda where there are much greater economic opportunities and a constant demand for labour. In these more densely peopled areas the signs of overpopulation include declining crop yields, soil exhaustion, the cultivation of excessively steep slopes, soil erosion, overstocking and the overuse of grazing grounds and falling water tables. Fortunately at this stage the problem is essentially not one of chronic overpopulation but rather occasional and local overcrowding; it can generally be met by redistribution of population, the opening of new areas to settlement, the improvement of farming methods and the development of other resources. Many governments are conscious of the need for a careful watching of the situation in the light of population trends, if more serious problems are to be avoided in future years. In Africa as a whole the more significant problem is lack of population, and the emphasis has been on the desirability of increased numbers in many areas for the sake of more complete and balanced economic development.

Migration.—Reference has already been made to movements of people from one area to another. Migration has always been a characteristic of the population of Africa, as suggested by the spread of Arabs (together with Islam) throughout North Africa and the gradual extension of Bantu-speaking tribes from Ethiopia across the equator and almost to the extreme south of the continent. In modern times these migrations have become permanent features between some of the poorer (but sometimes quite densely peopled) areas that have remained isolated from commercial development and those districts whose economic progress has demanded greater supplies of labour. In North Africa movements have been well established throughout the period of French occupation, and there are also regular seasonal migrations of tribes between the mountains and the lowlands and on the northern fringes of the Sahara. Mining areas have frequently become particular focal points of labour, often from remote places. In the gold mining and industrial districts of the Witwatersrand of South Africa, for example, there is a tremendous concentration of tribesmen from the Bantu areas of the republic itself; as well as from Basutoland, Mozambique and even Malawi. The European farmers, as well as the mines and industries of Rhodesia, are especially dependent upon Malawi labour. There is a steady flow of workers to the copper belt of Zambia and to the mining centres in Katanga. European estates are major users of African labour in East Africa, though the bulk of the large-scale labour migration from Rwanda and Burundi (with 250 persons per square mile, the most densely peopled agricultural area in Africa) is directed toward the African cotton-farming district of Buganda in Uganda. Similarly in West Africa there is (alongside the move-

TABLE II.—*Political Status, Area and Population of the Political Units of Africa, Oct. 1, 1966*

Unit	Political Status	Area* (sq.mi.)	Population 1963–65 (est.)
CONTINENTAL AFRICA			
Algeria	Republic	919,591	12,000,000
Angola	Overseas province (Portugal)	481,351	5,119,000
Basutoland (Lesotho)	Colony (U.K.)	11,716	733,000
Bechuanaland (Botswana)	Protectorate (U.K.)	220,000	543,000
Burundi	Monarchy	10,747	2,410,000
Cameroon	Federal republic	183,568	5,150,000
Central African Republic	Republic	241,313	1,306,000
Chad	Republic	490,733	2,800,000
Congo, Republic of	Republic	132,046	900,000
Congo, Democratic Republic of the	Republic	905,562	15,449,000
Dahomey	Republic	43,483	2,244,000
Equatorial Guinea			
Fernando Po	} Autonomous Region (Spain)	{ 785	70,000
Rio Muni		10,045	193,000
Ethiopia	Constitutional monarchy	457,142	22,200,000
French Somaliland	Overseas territory (France)	8,958	82,100
Gabon	Republic	102,317	463,000
Gambia	Parliamentary state	4,361	323,000
Ghana	Republic	92,100	7,637,000
Guinea	Republic	94,925	3,357,000
Ifni	African province (Spain)	579	50,000
Ivory Coast	Republic	124,503	3,665,000
Kenya	Republic	224,960	9,376,000
Liberia	Republic	43,000	1,041,000
Libya	Constitutional monarchy	679,536	1,559,000
Malawi	Republic	45,725	3,753,000
Mali	Republic	464,873	4,398,000
Mauritania	Republic	419,229	1,000,000
Morocco	Constitutional monarchy	171,834	12,959,000
Mozambique	Overseas province (Portugal)	303,073	6,914,000
Niger	Republic	489,206	3,193,000
Nigeria	Federal republic	356,669	55,620,000
Portuguese Guinea	Overseas province (Portugal)	13,948	550,900
Rhodesia (Southern Rhodesia)	Internally self-governing colony (U.K.)	150,333	4,210,000
Rwanda	Republic	10,169	2,971,000
Senegal	Republic	76,124	3,630,000
Sierra Leone	Parliamentary state	27,925	2,180,000
Somali Republic	Republic	246,155	2,300,000
South Africa†	Federal republic	471,819	17,488,000
South West Africa	Mandate (Rep. of S.Af.)	317,887	554,000
Spanish Presidios	Part of Spain *metropole*	12	158,000
Spanish Sahara	African province (Spain)	102,703	42,000
Sudan, The	Republic	967,491	13,372,000
Swaziland	Protectorate (U.K.)	6,705	292,000
Tanzania			
Tanganyika	} Republic	{ 361,800	9,990,000
Zanzibar		1,044	320,000
Togo	Republic	21,853	1,620,000
Tunisia	Republic	63,378	4,546,000
Uganda	Federal parliamentary state	91,134	7,367,000
United Arab Republic	Republic	386,872	29,200,000
Upper Volta	Republic	105,869	4,500,000
Zambia	Republic	290,587	3,610,000
OFFSHORE ISLANDS			
Canary Islands	Provinces (2) (Spain)	2,808	1,017,000
Cape Verde Islands	Overseas province (Portugal)	1,557	218,000
Comoro Islands	Overseas territory (France)	902	207,000
Madeira Islands	District (Portugal)	308	269,000
Malagasy Republic	Republic	230,035	6,016,000
Mauritius	Colony (U.K.)	805	734,500
Reunion	Overseas *Département* (France)	969	375,000
Saint Helena	Colony (U.K.)	156	6,000
Sao Tome and Principe	Overseas province (Portugal)	372	56,000
Seychelles	Colony (U.K.)	145	45,000

*Areas correspond to population figures as listed. †Includes Walvis Bay.

309

ment of labour to mining areas in Nigeria and Ghana and to the towns and ports of the Guinea coast) appreciable employment of Africans by Africans, particularly on the cocoa farms of southern Ghana and western Nigeria. Such economic development makes possible the support of larger populations and, ultimately, an improvement in the standard of living.

Migration may be regular, as with the seasonal movements of pastoral tribes, or spasmodic, as with mining labour. In South Africa a deliberate attempt has been made to prevent the permanent settlement of Africans in mining and industrial centres, and the policy of apartheid seeks ultimately to restore all those at present living in towns to permanent homes in the Bantu areas. Elsewhere many workers prefer to remain only temporary residents in the towns. By maintaining their mobility they are free to return to the rural districts whence they came after the accumulation of sufficient earnings or in the event of sickness or prolonged unemployment or when they are too old to work regularly. But in some countries governments and employers have come to recognize the desirability of a stable population and a regular labour force that can be well trained and acquire considerable skill. Stabilization of labour, as it is called, is increasingly common in Southern Rhodesia, Zambia and Katanga, and ever-growing numbers of Africans are settling, of their own volition, in towns in northwestern and eastern Africa.

Urbanization.—This tendency may be noted in all those parts of Africa where there is considerable economic development. Conditions along the North African seaboard are rather different from those elsewhere, the coastal town always having been characteristic of the pattern of population in the Mediterranean area. Cities like Marrakesh, Fès, Algiers, Tunis, Alexandria and Cairo are old established places with large populations. South of the Sahara the towns are usually predominantly non-African creations, though with notable exceptions, such as the Hausa town of Kano and the Yoruba towns in Nigeria, particularly Ibadan. They are, therefore, of recent growth, and the increase of population, especially after World War II, has sometimes been spectacular. Probably more than 10% of all the people in intertropical Africa now live in towns with 5,000 or more inhabitants. The towns are increasingly becoming centres of social and intellectual life as well as focal points of economic activity and political influence. They are not, however, without their problems. Apart from those of housing, food and water supply, and communications there are the social problems that arise from the admixture of different tribes and from the tendencies toward detribalization resulting from the relaxation of the accepted conventions and restraints of the tribal society to which most of the peoples were previously accustomed.

Non-African Population.—So far reference to the non-African population of Africa has been incidental. Though numerically insignificant (less than 2% of the total population), some elements, particularly the European, have played an overwhelmingly important part in the economic development and political life of many countries, particularly in Algeria, South Africa, Southern Rhodesia and Kenya. These are the countries where large settled European populations have been established and they contrast markedly with the West African territories where the European works for relatively short periods, as government official, teacher, trader, engineer or missionary. But even in these areas an important and indispensable contribution was made by the European to the organization of countries like Ghana, Guinea and Nigeria during the period leading to political independence.

Other nonindigenous communities include the Syrian and Lebanese traders of West Africa and the considerable Asian (predominantly Indian) populations of South Africa, Tanzania, Kenya and Uganda. In South Africa, Indians first came as indentured labourers for work on the sugar plantations of Natal in the 1860s, but they have remained in various occupations and now number nearly 500,000. The Asians of East Africa have for many years played a large part in the organization of the retail trade and, in Uganda, of the cotton export trade.

For further information *see* articles on the individual countries and regions. *See* also references under "Africa" in the Index.

(R. W. Sl.)

BIBLIOGRAPHY.—*Geology:* See publications of the various regional geological surveys and museums of Africa; the *Transactions* of the Geological Society of South Africa and publications of geological societies of France, Great Britain and Belgium. E. Krenkel, *Geologie Afrikas,* 4 vol. (1925–38); A. L. du Toit, *Geology of South Africa,* 3rd rev. ed. (1954); L. C. King, *South African Scenery,* 3rd rev. ed. (1963); L. Cahen, *Géologie du Congo Belge* (1954); S. H. Haughton, *Stratigraphic History of Africa South of the Sahara* (1963). For radioactive age determinations, *see* A. Holmes and L. Cahen, *African Geology and Mineral Resources* (1955). (L. C. Kg.)

Climate: Climatological Atlas of Africa, C.C.T.A., Lagos and Bukavu; W. G. Kendrew, *Climates of the Continents,* 4th ed. (1953); R. J. Harrison Church, *West Africa* (1957); *Atlas des Colonies Françaises* (1933); S. P. Jackson, "Climates of Southern Africa," *S. Afr. Geogr. J.* (1951); *Atlas of Kenya* (1959); *Atlas of Tanganyika* (1956); *Atlas of Uganda* (1962). (S. P. Jn.)

Vegetation: J. P. H. Acocks, "Veld Types of South Africa," *Mem. Bot. Surv. S. Afr.,* vol. xxvii (1953); A. Aubreville, *Climats, forêts et désertification de l'Afrique tropical* (1949); R. Capot-Rey, *Le Sahara français* (1953); M. Darrer, "Egypt, Eritrea, Libya and the Sudan," L. Emberger, "Afrique du Nord-Ouest" and R. Pichi-Sermolli, "Tropical East Africa," *UNESCO Arid Zone Research: VI-Plant Ecology* (1953); O. Hedberg, "Vegetation Belts of the East African Mountains," *Svensk Bot. Tidskr.,* vol. 45 (1951); H. Humbert, "La Destruction d'une flore insulaire par le feu. Principaux aspects de la végétation à Madagascar," *Mem. Acad. malgache,* vol. v (1927); R. W. J. Keay, *Vegetation Map of Africa South of the Tropic of Cancer* (1959); T. Monod, *Les Grandes divisions chorologiques de l'Afrique, C.S.A. Publ.* vol. 24 (1957); H. L. Shantz and C. F. Marbut, *Vegetation and Soils of Africa* (1923). (R. W. J. K.)

Anthropology: General: H. Baumann, D. Westermann and R. Thurnwald, *Völkerkunde von Afrika* (1940); M. Fortes and E. Evans-Pritchard (eds.), *African Political Systems* (1940); H. Wieschhoff, *Anthropological Bibliography of Negro Africa* (1948); Daryll Forde (ed.), *African Worlds* (1954); D. Forde and A. R. Radcliffe-Brown (eds.), *African Systems of Kinship and Marriage* (1950); P. S. Wingert, *Sculpture of Negro Africa* (1950); M. H. Hailey, *African Survey,* rev. ed. (1956); C. G. Seligman, *Races of Africa,* 3rd ed., ed. by I. Schapera *et al.* (1957); G. P. Murdock, *Africa, Its Peoples and Their Culture History* (1959). *See* the International African Institute's "Africa Bibliography Series" in regional parts (1958 ff.) and "Ethnographic Survey of Africa Series" (1950 ff.); *see* also the periodicals: *Africa* (1928 ff.), *African* (formerly *Bantu*) *Studies* (1921 ff.), *Zaire* (1947 ff.) and *J. Soc. Afric.* (1931 ff.). (D. F.)

Anthropology: North Africa: Neville Barbour, *Survey of North-West Africa* (1959); Jean Despois, *L'Afrique du nord* (1949) and *La Tunisie* (1930); C. A. Julien, *Histoire de l'Afrique du nord* (1949); A. Basset, *La Langue Berbère* (1952); J. M. Dallet, *Le Verbe Kabyle* (1953); M. W. Hilton-Simpson, *Among the Hill-Folk of Algeria* (1921); J. Matéa-Gaudry, *La Femme Chaouia de l'Aurès* (1929); E. Westermarck, *Ritual and Belief in Morocco* (1926); R. Montagne, *Les Berbères et le Makhzen* (1930); G. Boris, *Documents linguistiques et ethnographiques sur une région du Sud-Tunisien* (1951); E. Evans-Pritchard, *Sanusi of Cyrenaica* (1949); G. W. Murray, *Sons of Ishmael* (1935); W. Blackman, *Fellahin of Upper Egypt* (1927); W. Cline, "Notes on the People of Siwah and El Garah in the Libyan Desert," *Gen. Ser. in Anthrop.,* no. 4 (1950) and "Teda of Tibesti, Borku and Kawah in the Eastern Sahara," no. 12 (1950); F. R. Rodd, *People of the Veil* (1926); C. de Foucauld, *Dictionnaire Touareg-Français,* 4 vol. (1951); Institut Français d'Afrique Noire, *Contribution à l'étude de l'Aïr* (1950); R. Capot-Rey, *Le Sahara* (1953); A. M. Goichon, *La Vie féminine au Mzab* (1927); F. Nicolas, *La Langue Berbère de Mauritanie* (1953); "Mauritania" in *Études Mauritaniennes,* 5 vol. (1952); C. Le Coeur, *Dictionnaire Ethnographique Teda* (1950) and with M. Le Coeur, *Grammaire et textes Teda-Daza* (1955). (J. H. Se.)

Anthropology: Northeast Africa: N. A. MacMichael, *Tribes of Northern and Central Kordofan* (1912) and *History of the Arabs in the Sudan,* 2 vol. (1922); D. Westermann, *Shilluk People* (1912); C. G. and B. Z. Seligman, *Pagan Tribes of the Nilotic Sudan* (1932); E. Evans-Pritchard, *Witchcraft, Oracles and Magic Among the Azande* (1937), *Nuer* (1940), *Political System of the Anuak of the Anglo-Egyptian Sudan* (1940) and *Nuer Religion* (1956); S. F. Nadel, *Nuba* (1947); J. Trimingham, *Islam in the Sudan* (1949); G. Huntingford, *Northern Nilo-Hamites* (1953); A. Paul, *History of the Beja Tribe of the Sudan* (1953); *Sudan Notes and Records* (1918 ff.). For the "Horn" especially *see* International African Institute, "Ethnographic Survey of Africa Series," Daryll Forde (ed.), *North-Eastern Africa.* (1950 ff.); A. Cecchi, *Da Zeila alle frontiere del Caffa,* 3 vol. (1886–87); G. Montandon, *Au Pays Ghimirra* (1913); K. G. Roden, *Le Tribu dei Mensa* (1913); E. Cerulli, *Etiopia Occidentale,* 2 vol. (1933) and *Studi Etiopici,* i–iv (1936–51); A. Pollera, *Le popolazioni indigene dell'Eritrea* (1935); A. E. Jensen, *Im Lande des Gada* (1936); C. Conti Rossini, *Etiopia e genti di Etiopia* (1937); L. Cipriani, *Abitazioni indigene dell'Africa Orientale Italiana* (1940); V. L. Grottanelli, *Missione etnografica nell'Uollega Occidentale: I Mao* (1940); S. F. Nadel, *Races and Tribes of Eritrea* (1943); W. Leslau, *Ethiopic Documents: Gurage* (1950); J. Trimingham, *Islam in Ethiopia* (1952); *Rassegna di Studi Etiopici.* (I. M. L.)

Anthropology: West Africa: International African Institute (formerly the International Institute of African Languages and Cultures),

Ruth Jones (comp.), *West Africa,* "Africa Bibliography Series" (1958); International African Institute, Daryll Forde (ed.), *Western Africa,* in "Ethnographic Survey of Africa Series" (1950 *et seq.*); R. S. Rattray, *Ashanti* (1923); M. J. Herskovits, *Dahomey,* 2 vol. (1938); D. Forde, *Marriage and the Family Among the Yakö* (1941); D. Forde and R. Scott, *Native Economies of Nigeria* (1946); S. Nadel, *A Black Byzantium* (1942); M. Fortes, *Dynamics of Clanship Among the Tallensi* (1945); K. Little, *Mende of Sierra Leone* (1951); G. Dieterlen, *Essai sur la Religion Bambara* (1951); P. Bohannan, *Justice and Judgement Among the Tiv* (1957); D. J. Stenning, *Savannah Nomads* (1959); M. G. Smith, *Government in Zazzau* (1960). (D. F.)

Anthropology: East Africa: International African Institute, *East Africa,* "African Bibliography Series" (1960) and D. Forde (ed.), *East Central Africa,* in the "Ethnographic Survey of Africa Series" (1950 ff.); G. Huntingford and C. Bell, *East African Background* (1950); A. W. Southall, *Alur Society* (1956); J. E. Goldthorpe, *Outlines of East African Society* (1958); L. Fallers, *African Bureaucracy (Soga)* (1956); A. I. Richards (ed.), *East African Chiefs* (1960); J. Beattie, *Bunyoro* (1960). (J. F. M. M.)

Anthropology: West Central Africa: International African Institute, D. Forde (ed.) *West Central Africa,* in the "Ethnographic Survey of Africa Series" (1950 *et seq.*); F. Eboué, *Les Peuples de l'Oubangui Chari* (1933); H. Baumann, *Lunda* (1935); J. Van Wing, *Études Bakongo* (1938); H. A. Bernatzik, *Afrika: Handbuch der angewandten Völkerkunde,* 2 vol. (1947); I. Dugast, *Inventaire ethnique du Sud-Caméroun* (1949); P. Schebesta, *Les Pygmées du Congo Belge* (1952); A. Leroi-Gourhan and J. Poirier, *Ethnologie de l'Union Française:* vol. i *Afrique* (1953); J. Vansina, *Les Tribus Bakuba et les peuplades apparentées* (1954); H. Van Geluwe, *Les Bira et les peuplades limitrophes* (1956); *Mamvu-Mangutu et Balese-Mvuba* (1957); P. Alexandre and J. Binet, *Le Groupe dit Pahouin* (1958); H. Burssens, *Les Pleuplades de l'entre Congo-Ubangi* (1958); A. H. M. Kirk-Greene, *Adamawa Past and Present* (1958); A. M. D. Lebeuf, *Les Populations du Tchad* (1959); F. M. Olbrechts, *Les Arts plastiques du Congo* (1959); M. Soret, *Les Kongo nord-occidentaux* (1959). (D. P. Bi.)

Anthropology: Central Africa: J. A. Barnes, *Politics in a Changing Society* (1954); E. Colson, *Marriage and the Family Among the Plateau Tonga of Northern Rhodesia* (1958); E. Colson and M. Gluckman (eds.), *Seven Tribes of British Central Africa* (1951); I. Cunnison, *Luapula Peoples of Northern Rhodesia* (1959); M. Gluckman, *Economy of the Central Barotse Plain,* Rhodes-Livingstone Papers no. 7 (1941); J. C. Mitchell, *Yao Village* (1956); A. I. Richards, *Land, Labour and Diet in Northern Rhodesia* (1939); E. W. Smith and A. M. Dale, *Ila-Speaking Peoples of Northern Rhodesia,* 2 vol. (1920); W. Watson, *Tribal Cohesion in a Money Economy* (1958); International African Institute, Daryll Forde (ed.), *East Central Africa,* in the "Ethnographic Survey of Africa Series" (1950 *et seq.*). (A. I. R.)

Anthropology: Southern Africa: For a comprehensive annotated list of publications to 1939, *see* Isaac Schapera (ed.), *Selected Bibliography of South African Native Life and Problems* (1941); H. Ashton, *Basuto* (1953); A. T. Bryant, *Zulu People* (1949); J. D. Clark, *Prehistory of Southern Africa* (1959); C. H. L. Hahn *et al., Native Tribes of South West Africa* (1928); J. F. Holleman, "Some Shona Tribes of Southern Rhodesia" in E. Colson and M. Gluckman (eds.), *Seven Tribes of British Central Africa* (1951); M. Hunter, *Reaction to Conquest* (1936); I. Irle, *Die Herero* (1906); H. A. Junod, *Life of a South African Tribe,* 2nd ed., 2 vol. (1927); E. J. and J. D. Krige, *Realm of a Rain-Queen* (1943); H. Kuper, *An African Aristocracy* (1947) and *Swazi* (1952); I. Schapera, *Khoisan Peoples of South Africa: Bushmen and Hottentots* (1930), *Tswana* (1953), *Government and Politics in Tribal Societies* (1956) and (ed.) *Bantu-Speaking Tribes of South Africa* (1937); V. G. Sheddick, *Southern Sotho* (1953); H. A. Stayt, *BaVenda* (1931); H. Tönjes, *Ovamboland* (1911); N. J. van Warmelo and W. Phophi, *Venda Law,* 4 vol. (1948–49); H. Vedder, *Die Bergdama,* 2 vol. (1923), *Das Alte Südwestafrika* (1934), Eng. trans., C. G. Hall (ed.), *Southwest Africa in Early Times* (1938). *See* also *African* (formerly *Bantu*) *Studies* (1921 ff.). (I. S.)

Archaeology: H. Alimen, *Prehistory of Africa* (1957); Basil Davidson, *Old Africa Rediscovered* (1959) and *Lost Cities in Africa* (1959); L. S. B. Leakey, *Stone Age Africa* (1936); A. J. H. Goodwin, *Method in Prehistory* (1945) and *Loom of Prehistory* (1946); R. Broom, *Finding the Missing Link* (1950); Sir W. Le Gros Clark, *History of the Primates* (1949) and *Fossil Evidence for Human Evolution* (1955); Sir Arthur Keith, *Antiquity of Man* (1925) and *New Discoveries Relating to the Antiquity of Man* (1931); M. C. Burkitt, *South Africa's Past in Stone and Paint* (1928); 3rd Pan-African Congress on Prehistory, J. D. Clark and S. Cole (eds.), *Proceedings* (1959); J. D. Clark, *Prehistory of Southern Africa* (1959); A. R. Willcox, *Rock Paintings of the Drakensberg* (1956); G. Caton-Thompson, *Zimbabwe Culture* (1931); R. Summers, *Zimbabwe: a Rhodesian Mystery* (1964); R. Delcroix and R. Vaufrey, "Le Toumbien de Guinée Française," *L'Anth.,* vol. 49 (1939–40); R. Summers *et al.,* "Prehistoric Rock Art of the Federation of Rhodesia and Nyasaland," *Nat. Pub. Trust* (1960); R. R. Inskeep, "Some Iron Age Sites in Northern Rhodesia," *South African Archaeological Bulletin,* vol. 17 (1962); B. M. Fagan, "The Kalomo Choma Iron Age Project," *South African Archaeological Bulletin,* vol. 18 (1963); S. M. Cole, *Prehistory of East Africa,* rev. ed. (1964); L. S. B. Leakey, *Stone Age Cultures of Kenya Colony* (1931), *Stone Age Races of Kenya* (1935) and *Olduvai Gorge* (1965); C. van Riet Lowe, *Pleistocene Geology of Uganda,* pt. ii, *Prehistory* (1952); T. P. O'Brien, *Prehistory of Uganda Protectorate* (1939); J. D. Clark, *Prehistoric Cultures of the Horn of Africa* (1954); P. Graziosi, "New Discoveries of Rock Paintings in Ethiopia," *Antiquity,* vol. xxxviii, no. 150 and 151 (1964); A. J. Arkell, *Early Khartoum* (1949); O. Bates, *Eastern Libyans* (1914); L. Balout, *Préhistoire de L'Afrique du Nord* (1955); G. Caton-Thompson and E. W. Gardner, *Desert Fayum* (1934); C. B. M. McBurney, *Stone Age of Northern Africa* (1960) and *The Haua Fteah* (1965); K. S. Sandford and W. J. Arkell, *Palaeolithic Man and the Nile Valley in Lower Egypt* (1939); L. S. B. Leakey, "A New Species of the Genus Homo from Olduvai Gorge," *Nature* (1964); S. Gsell, *Les Monuments antiques de L'Algérie* (1901); C. Courtois, *Timgad* (1951); L. Leschi, *Djemila* (1953); D. Harden, *The Phoenicians* (1963); G. Charles Picard, *La Civilisation de l'Afrique romaine* (1959); D. E. L. Haynes, *An Archaeological and Historical Guide to the Pre-Islamic Antiquities of Tripolitania* (1956); R. G. Goodchild, *Cyrene and Apollonia* (1959); C. H. Kraeling, *Ptolemais* (1962); A. Driss and G. Caputo, *Tunisia: Ancient Mosaics* (1962); also the journals *Karthago* (1950–); *Libyca* (1953–); *Libya Antiqua* (1964–). (X.)

History: North Africa: C. A. Julien, *Histoire de l'Afrique du Nord: Tunisie, Algérie, Maroc, des origines à la conquête arabe,* rev. ed. by C. Courtois (1951), and *Histoire de l'Afrique du Nord de la conquête arabe à 1830,* rev. ed. by R. Le Tourneau (1952); B. L. Warmington, *Carthage* (1960). (J. F. P. H.)

History: Sahara, Sudan and Guinea: A. J. Arkell, *History of the Sudan . . . to 1821,* 2nd ed. (1961); M. Delafosse, *Haut-Sénégal-Niger,* 1st series, vol. ii, *L'Histoire* (1912), *Negroes of Africa* (1931); H. Lhote, *Les Touaregs du Hoggar,* 2nd ed. rev. (1955); E. W. Bovill, *Caravans of the Old Sahara* (1933), *Golden Trade of the Moors* (1958); Y. Urvoy, *Histoire des populations du Soudan central* (1936) and *Histoire de l'empire du Bornou* (1949); J. Rouch, *Contribution à l'histoire des Songhay* (1953); J. D. Fage, *An Introduction to the History of West Africa,* 3rd ed. (1962); W. E. F. Ward, *History of Ghana,* rev. ed. (1958); T. L. Hodgkin, *Nigerian Perspectives* (1960); Sir Alan Burns, *History of Nigeria,* 6th ed. (1963); E. L. R. Meyerowitz, *Akan Traditions of Origin* (1952); A. B. Mathews, "The Kisra Legend," *Afr. Stud.,* ix (1950).

History: Central and Southern Africa: D. L. Wiedner, *A History of Africa South of the Sahara* (1964); A. Keppel-Jones, *South Africa: a Short History,* 3rd rev. ed. (1961); J. Walton, *African Village* (1956); J. Duffy, *Portuguese Africa* (1959); A. J. Hanna, *Story of the Rhodesias and Nyasaland* (1960); J. Simmons, *Livingstone and Africa,* (1955); R. Slade, *Belgian Congo,* 2nd ed. (1961); I. Schapera (ed.), *Bantu-Speaking Tribes of South Africa* (1937); C. W. De Kiewiet, *History of South Africa, Social and Economic* (1941); E. A. Walker, *History of Southern Africa,* 3rd ed. rev. (1957), *The Greak Trek,* 4th ed. (1960); E. A. Ritter, *Shaka Zulu* (1955); W. M. MacMillan, *Bantu, Boer and Briton,* rev. ed. (1963); Basil Williams, *Cecil Rhodes,* rev. ed. (1938), *Botha, Smuts and South Africa* (1946); L. M. Thompson, *Unification of South Africa, 1902–1910* (1960). (J. D. F.)

History: East Africa: K. Ingham, *A History of East Africa,* 2nd ed. (1963); *History of East Africa* (in progress), vol. 1, ed. by R. Oliver and G. Mathew (1963), vol. 2, ed. by V. Harlow and E. M. Chilver (1965).

History: Partition of Africa: N. Barbour (ed.), *Survey of North West Africa* (1959); R. Coupland, *Exploitation of East Africa, 1856–1890* (1939); J. E. Flint, *Sir George Goldie and the Making of Nigeria* (1960); W. Langer, *Diplomacy of Imperialism 1890–1902,* 2nd ed. (1951); R. Oliver, *Sir Harry Johnston and the Scramble for Africa* (1957); M. Perham, *Lugard: The Years of Adventure, 1858–1898* (1956); S. H. Roberts, *History of French Colonial Policy,* 2 vol. (1929); A. J. P. Taylor, *Struggle for Mastery in Europe, 1848–1918* (1954).

Current history is summarized annually in *Britannica Book of the Year* under "Africa" and the individual countries. (J. E. Fl.)

Population and General: A. Bernard, *Afrique septentrionale et occidentale,* vol. xi, *Géographie universelle* (1937); W. Fitzgerald, *Africa* (1934); S. H. Frankel, *Capital Investment in Africa* (1938); E. F. Gautier, *Sahara* (1935); Lord Hailey, *An African Survey,* rev. ed. (1957); H. E. Hurst, *The Nile* (1952); F. Jaeger, *Afrika* (1928); G. H. T. Kimble, *Tropical Africa,* 2 vol. (1960); R. R. Kuczynski, *Demographic Survey of the British Colonial Empire,* vol. i and ii (1948–49); F. Maurette, *Afrique équatoriale, orientale et australe,* vol. xii, *Géographie universelle* (1938); S. Passarge, *Geographische Völkerkunde,* vol. ii, *Afrika* (1933); C. Stillman (ed.), *Africa in the Modern World* (1955); J. Weulersse, *L'Afrique noire* (1934); H. A. Wieschhoff (ed.), *African Handbooks,* 7 vol. (1943); E. B. Worthington, *Science in Africa* (1938) and *Science in the Development of Africa* (1958). *See* also for reading lists: J. Comhaire, *Urban Conditions in Africa* (1952); J. H. Wellington, *Southern Africa,* 2 vol. (1955); A. Hazlewood, *The Economics of Under-Developed Areas,* 2nd ed. (1959); K. M. Barbour and R. M. Prothero (eds.), *Essays on African Population* (1961); M. Cole, *South Africa* (1961); L. D. Stamp (ed.), *A History of Land Use in Arid Lands* (1961), *Africa: a Study in Tropical Development,* 2nd ed. (1964); R. J. H. Church *et al, Africa and the Islands* (1964); W. A. Hance, *The Geography of Modern Africa* (1964); R. W. Steel and R. M. Prothero (eds.), *Geographers and the Tropics: Liverpool Essays* (1964); *Bibliographie géographique internationale* (1923 *et seq.*); *Oxford Regional Economic Atlas* (1965).

(R. W. Sl.)

AFRICA, ROMAN PROVINCE OF. The Roman province of Africa consisted of a territory with varying boundaries which at times roughly corresponded with those of modern Tunisia. The name Africa was also used by the Romans to denote (1) the whole continent, and (2) Africa north of the Sahara, but was given specifically to the province proper, this being the first piece of African territory acquired by the Romans, into whose hands it came in 146 B.C. when Carthage (q.v.) was destroyed. It first comprised the territory which had been subject to Carthage in 149 B.C., when the 3rd Punic War broke out, and was divided from the kingdom of Numidia (q.v.) by a ditch and embankment running roughly southeastward from Thabraca (Tabarka) to Thaenae (southwest of Sfax), leaving Vaga (Béja) to the west. Its area amounted only to about 5,000 sq.mi., much of it belonging to seven former Carthaginian cities which were given local independence for having sided with Rome. The indigenous Libyans were mostly still backward in culture and living in small villages. The province was governed by a praetor stationed at Utica (near the mouth of the Medjerda river).

Roman interest in the territory was negligible till Gaius Sempronius Gracchus passed a law (123 or 122 B.C.) establishing a colony to be called Junonia on the site of Carthage. Although the project collapsed after the assassination of Gracchus, many of the proposed 6,000 colonists had already taken possession of their allotments and were left undisturbed. Interest among Roman farmers and investors was now stimulated, and in 111 B.C. a law was passed to regulate the different forms of tenure and exploitation in the province. Next, veterans of the army of Gaius Marius were given land in the Bagradas (Medjerda) valley shortly before 100 B.C., and the boundary of the province was extended westward almost as far as the present Algerian-Tunisian border. During the next 50 years there was some further immigration, but political uncertainties caused land to fall mainly into the hands of large landowners, often absentee.

The turning point in the province's history came in the 1st century B.C. when Julius Caesar and later the emperor Augustus founded between them some 19 colonies of Roman citizens both from army veterans and from civilian immigrants. The most notable foundation was Carthage itself which rapidly became the second city in the western part of the Roman empire. A number of native communities which were relatively advanced thanks to earlier contacts with Carthaginian civilization were given local independence. Augustus extended the province southward as far as the Sahara and, by controlling destructive nomadic movements, created conditions for four centuries of prosperity. To the east, the coastal area as far as Arae Philaenorum (at the southernmost point of the Gulf of Sidra), which marked the western boundary of Cyrenaica, was added to the province.

In the west, after the battle of Thapsus (46 B.C.), Caesar had formed a new province called Africa Nova out of the old Numidian kingdom of Juba I, and after the death of Bocchus (q.v.) in 33 B.C. the Romans took over his kingdom of Mauretania. Augustus, after restoring Juba II to the throne of Mauretania and part of Numidia (25 B.C.), eventually amalgamated the old province of Africa Vetus with Africa Nova. The western boundary now lay on the Ampsaga (Rummel) river in what is now northeastern Algeria and ran southwest toward the Chott el-Hodna lake. In the division of responsibility for imperial provincial government made by Augustus Africa was controlled by the senate; its governor was of proconsular rank, and it was unique among senatorial provinces in that it had a legion (*legio III Augusta*) stationed in it. The position was altered by Caligula, who placed the *legatus* (commander) of the legion directly under the emperor's orders and gave him jurisdiction over the area in which the army was most active. This military zone comprised most of the old Numidian kingdom with the exception of the area east of a line from Rusicade to Theveste (Philippeville and Tebessa in northeastern Algeria), together with that part of the hinterland of Tripolitania which is not desert. In effect a new province of Numidia was created, though it was not formally constituted till the reign of Septimius Severus (A.D. 193–211).

The first century A.D. was a time of rapid growth in African prosperity. Private estates of considerable size grew up which at-

ROMAN RUINS OF ANCIENT LAMBAESIS (LAMBESSA, ALGERIA)

tracted the greed of the emperor Nero, who executed a number of wealthy landowners and took their lands. This was the foundation of a vast imperial domain in North Africa. Cereals remained the chief crop, but late in the century olives became profitable, especially around Taparura (Sfax). Vast quantities of these and other products such as fruit and hides were exported. The period from the reign of Nerva (A.D. 96–98) to that of Alexander Severus (A.D. 222–235) was probably the most prosperous and peaceful that the area ever enjoyed. The amenities of urban life became available in many cities and over much of the country opulent villas were built. Many public buildings were erected, important remains of which may still be seen in Tunisia, at Carthage, Thysdrus (El Djem) and Utica (qq.v.) and at Thuburbo Maius (Henchir Kasbat), Thugga (Dougga), Mactaris (Mactar) and Sufetula (Sbeitla, q.v.). Substantial elements of the Libyan population were romanized and many communities received Roman citizenship, with the title of *municipium* or *colonia*, long before it was extended to the whole empire in A.D. 212. More and more men from Africa began to enter the imperial administration, and at the end of the 2nd century, an African, Septimius Severus, became emperor. In the rural areas, however, many of the Libyans were little affected by Roman civilization.

In the later 3rd century Africa, in common with the rest of the empire, suffered a decline in prosperity, though relatively free from invasion and war. When the empire was reorganized by Diocletian, two provinces, Byzacena and Tripolitania, were formed from the southern and eastern parts of the old province. The most important events in the 4th century were connected with the Christian Church. Christianity, established in Africa in the 1st century, had rapidly spread. There were more than 100 African bishops by A.D. 256, and Africa had produced such distinguished figures as Tertullian and Cyprian (qq.v.). The African Church had its share of martyrs up to the time of the final persecutions of A.D. 303–305 under Diocletian; its strength was subsequently reduced by the Donatist schism (*see* DONATISTS) from 312. In this, however, the majority of the African clergy and laity supported the Catholic cause, whose principal champion was Augustine, bishop of Hippo Regius. Imperial intervention in the dispute culminated in a council held at Carthage in 411 at which Donatism was condemned, and persecution of its adherents followed.

Africa fared better than most parts of the empire in the 4th century and even enjoyed a modest amount of prosperity, but there were symptoms of decline. City life decayed particularly toward the end of the century, and while wealth was concentrated in the hands of a few, the peasants tended to become poorer and more oppressed. In addition, the inhabitants had lost any military tradition that they may have had and were an easy prey to invaders. In A.D. 429 the Germanic tribe of the Vandals under Gaiseric (q.v.) crossed from Spain to Morocco, and in 430 they arrived in the province of Africa. After a short period of truce (A.D. 435–439) Carthage fell and became the capital of the Vandal kingdom. Roman civilization decayed more rapidly in spite of the numerical inferiority of the Vandals, and though the latter were destroyed by Belisarius, general of the Eastern emperor Justinian I, in 533 and imperial control was restored, the decline was irreversible. Africa offered little resistance to the Arab invaders who took Carthage in 697.

BIBLIOGRAPHY.—S. Gsell, *Histoire ancienne de l' Afrique du Nord* (1928); T. R. S. Broughton, *The Romanization of Africa Proconsularis* (1929); B. H. Warmington, *The North African Provinces from Diocletian to the Vandal Conquest* (1954).   (B. H. WA.) .

AFRICAN LANGUAGES.

The number of separate languages spoken by the inhabitants of the African continent is variously estimated as from 600 to 800. Until more data are available from some areas and until a more rigorously defined criterion as to what constitutes a separate language is agreed upon, no exact number can be given. The figures quoted are sufficient, however, to show the great linguistic diversity that is characteristic of Africa, particularly that portion which lies south of the Sahara. In certain parts of Africa, such as the Bauchi plateau of Nigeria and the Nuba hills of Kordofan, scores of distinct languages are spoken in a relatively small area. There are also languages with millions of speakers, answering to the needs of wider communication both before and after European contact. Examples of such languages are Swahili in east Africa, Lingala in the Congo basin, Sango in equatorial Africa, Hausa in west Africa and Arabic in north Africa and large areas of the Sudan. In spite of the fact that the languages of Africa cannot be shown to have a common origin, the cultural unity of Africa south of the Sahara is reflected in certain widespread common features which distinguish this region linguistically from the neighbouring area of the near east.

The prevailing classification of African languages which became established in the period 1910–20, chiefly as a result of the work of Carl Meinhof and the earlier work of Diedrich Westermann, divided African languages into five families, Semitic, Hamitic, Sudanic, Bantu and Bushman, forming, in general, successive east-west layers from Semitic and Hamitic in the north to Bushman in the extreme south. This scheme underwent considerable modification through the efforts of Marcel Cohen, Johannes Lukas, Joseph Greenberg and the later works of Diedrich Westermann. The chief points of criticism of this earlier classification, on the basis of which the present version is presented, are as follows:

1. It is evident that Semitic is not an independent family but is related to Hamitic.

2. Hamitic, as pointed out by Cohen, is not itself a unity as against Semitic. The situation is rather that Semitic is but one of a number of branches in a larger Hamito-Semitic family to which Greenberg has applied the name Afro-Asiatic.

3. Most of the various extensions of Hamitic proposed by Meinhof in *Die Sprachen der Hamiten* are invalid. There is general agreement that Hottentot, Fulani (Ful, Fulfulde) of west Africa and the so-called Nilo-Hamitic languages of east Africa (Masai, Nandi, Turkana, etc.) are not Hamitic.

4. The earlier all-embracing Sudanic unit, to which were assigned all the languages spoken by Negroes except the Bantu languages of the southern part of the continent, has been successively broken into smaller independent units in the later work of Westermann, who first proposed it. The same author showed the relation of the Bantu family, hitherto considered independent, to the western section of the former Sudanic family (*i.e.*, West Sudanic). Greenberg pointed out the special position of Bantu as a member of one of the subdivisions of the West Sudanic group spoken in Nigeria and the Cameroons, languages often called semi-Bantu because of their resemblances to the Bantu languages (*q.v.*).

5. Lukas has distinguished a separate Saharan family, formerly assigned to Sudanic and containing, as principal languages, Kanuri, Teda and Zaghawa.

The Hamito-Semitic (Afro-Asiatic) Languages.

This family of languages covers all of northern Africa while its Semitic branch extends into the adjoining areas of Asia. It consists of five branches: (1) Berber, formerly spoken in all of north Africa except Egypt, by the Tuareg of the Sahara and in the Canary Islands. It is now largely confined to Morocco, Algeria and parts of the Sahara. Ancient Berber inscriptions, known as Libyan, are found written in an alphabet probably derived from that of the Phoenicians of Carthage. This alphabet is still in use. (2) Ancient Egyptian, known from hieroglyphic inscriptions and in its later form, called Coptic, written in an alphabet derived from Greek. It is now extinct. (3) Semitic, including Arabic, which is dominant in north Africa, the Ethiopian Semitic languages, as well as languages in western Asia. Ethiopian Semitic is usually divided into a northern subdivision with Tigre and Tigrinya and a southern subdivision consisting of Amharic, the Gurage dialects, Gafat and Harari, the language of the Moslem centre of Harar in southern Ethiopia. (4) The Cushitic languages spoken in Ethiopia and neighbouring areas. Cushitic consists of five groups of languages: (*a*) Beja; (*b*) Agau group; (*c*) Eastern Cushitic (Galla, Somali, Afar, eastern Sidamo, Konso, Arbore, Geleba); (*d*) Western Cushitic (Kaffa group); and (*e*) Southern Cushitic (Mbugu and Mbulunge in Tanganyika). (5) The Chad languages of northern Nigeria and surrounding area. The most important of these languages is Hausa, a large group which can only tentatively be grouped. Among the better-known languages are Angas, the Kotoko group of dialects including Buduma and Logone, the Bata dialects, Mandara, Musgu, Somrai, Sokoro, Tuburi and Mubi.

The characteristics of Hamito-Semitic speech include: (1) absence of tone; some or all of the Chad languages, however, have acquired tonal systems under the influence of neighbouring languages; (2) grammatical gender—Shilh (Berber): masc. *idilli*, fem. *t-idilli-t* "black"; Hausa (Chad): *yazo* "he came," *tazo* "she came"; (3) a variety of plural formation in the noun including the use of suffixes, internal change, particularly to *a*, and partial reduplication, as Shilh (Berber): *iliwi*, pl. *ilawan* "thorn"; Logone (Chad): *ngun*, pl. *ngwaren* "belly." Hebrew (Semitic): 'ir, pl. *'arīm* "city"; (4) presence of internal change combined with both prefixes and suffixes to form verb conjugational systems; and (5) a complex system of forming derivative verbs, causative, reflexive, passive, etc., usually by prefixes. Bedauye (Cushitic): *kehan* "to love," *atkehan* "to be loved," *gumad* "to be long," *sugumād* "to lengthen," *dir* "to kill," *mdedar* "to kill each other."

The Niger-Congo Family.

This family has a vast and nearly continuous distribution, covering almost all of west Africa south of the Sahara, and most of the Congo basin and south Africa. The problem of subdivisions within this family had yet, at mid-20th century, to be solved in a definitive matter. Certain groupings, however, can be tentatively described.

1. In the far west are the West Atlantic languages subdivided into an eastern group comprising Temne, Bulom, Kissi, Limba and Gola and a western group containing Dyola, the Bissao-Bolama cluster (Bola, Sarar, Pepel, Kanyop), Bijogo, Bulanda, Cobiana-Cassanga, Banyun, Nalu, Serer-Sin, Serer-Nono, Konyagi, Wolof and Fulani. The position of Fulani, spoken by several million people scattered from Senegal to Wadai, east of Lake Chad, was long disputed, but it clearly belongs in the West Atlantic subgroup of this family. Within this subgroup, it is most closely related to Serer-Sin, and somewhat more remotely to Wolof, Serer-Nono and Konyagi.

2. A second subdivision is that of the important Mandingo languages, spoken in the central and lower Niger valley in former French West Africa, and in much of Liberia and Sierra Leone. The traditional division into Mande tan and Mande fu based on the numeral for ten is misleading. Mande tan is but one subgroup among several. Mandingo languages include Malinké, Bambara, Soninke, the Kpelle-Mende group in Sierra Leone and Liberia and a number of small languages as far east as Boko-Busa in the northwest corner of Nigeria.

3. The Gur subdivisions, including the following groups: (*a*) Mossi (Mossi, Dagomba, etc.); (*b*) Grussi; (*c*) Tem; (*d*) Bargu; (*e*) Gurma; (*f*) Kilina; and (*g*) Senufo. This latter group is somewhat remote from the remainder of the Gur languages but should probably be classed with them.

4. The Kwa subdivision contains the middle Togo group, hitherto classified separately, the Ewe-Akan languages (Ghana,

Dahomey) and Yoruba, Nupe, Ibo, Edo and probably the Yala (Idoma) group, all in Nigeria. The Ewe-Akan languages, including Ewe, the Fō of Dahomey, Twi, Ashanti, Fanti, Agni, Guang and Gã belong in the same subdivision with the Togo languages (Avatime, Adele and others) and the various languages of the Ivory Coast lagoon. The Kru languages of Liberia probably belong in the Kwa subdivision also.

5. The central group contains as a subdivision Bantu which covers the vast areas of the Congo basin, Angola, Mozambique and much of South Africa; the rest of the languages are in Nigeria and the western Cameroons. They include Bassa, Kamuku, Katab, Munshi (Tiv), Jukun, Ekoi and Efik. The Bute language of the Cameroons may belong to this group.

6. The Ijo (Ijaw) language of the Niger delta seems to form a separate group.

7. A large group of little-known languages mostly in the Cameroons constitute the Adamawa group. Examples of Adamawa languages are Chamba, Daka, Vere, Longuda, Yungur, Jen, Kam, the Mbum group, Masa and Bua-Nielim-Koke.

8. An eastern group extends as far as the Sudan and includes Banda, Zande, Sango, Bwaka, Mondunga, Sere-Ndogo, Barambo and possibly Gbaya. Gbaya shows some evidence of affiliation with the Adamawa group, and the Adamawa and eastern groups may turn out to form a single group.

The Niger-Congo languages are tonal with few exceptions. Nouns are generally divided into classes each marked by a pair of affixes, one for the singular and one for the plural. These changes are marked by either prefixes, suffixes or both in combination. Examples are: (1) prefixes, Yasgua (central group): u-tu, pl. a-tu "ear"; (2) suffixes, Guresha (Gur group): tu-i, pl. tu-e "ear"; (3) both in combination, Gurma (Gur group): o-yomb-o, pl. i-yomb-i "slave." Human beings, without regard to sex, usually belong to a single class, liquids to another. All names of trees are usually found in another class but along with nouns having other meanings. For other classes, no general principle of classification is discoverable. A minority of languages such as Ewe (Kwa group), Malinke and many other Mandingo languages, Jukun (central group), Kam (Adamawa group) and Bwaka (eastern group) have lost most or all of this system of classification. These languages generally resort to the addition of the pronoun "they" to form a plural and rely on word order in place of the agreement between noun and adjectives or noun and verbs characteristic of the class languages of the family, such as Bantu. This process of agreement may be illustrated from Swahili, a Bantu language. In the sentence ki-su ki-kali ki-moja ki-me-potea "knife sharp one has-been-lost," i.e., "one sharp knife has been lost," -su "knife" has ki- as its class prefix, and this is repeated before every word agreeing with -su. The plural prefix corresponding to ki- is vi-; thus the plural of the preceding is: vi-su vi-kali vi-nane vi-me-potea, "eight sharp knives have been lost."

The affixes, whether prefixed, suffixed or both, are in general agreement throughout the Niger-Congo family and must therefore belong to the original language from which the modern languages have evolved.

The Niger-Congo verb is usually unchanged except for tonal modifications. Tenses and moods are indicated by such changes and by the use of auxiliary verbs, for example, the verb "to come" to indicate the future. Some languages particularly in the West Atlantic, Gur and central groups including Bantu, have elaborate systems of verb derivation. To cite Swahili again, from pata "to obtain" the following derivatives may be formed; patana "make an agreement," patanisha "to unite," patia "to obtain for somebody," patika "to be vexed," patiliza "to vex someone," patilizana "to vex each other" and others.

The Macro-Sudanic Family.—This group of languages is widespread in east Africa and the upper Nile valley. It extends westward in the Congo-Nile divide area as far as the Sara languages near Lake Chad. The subdivisions of this family are (1) East Sudanic, containing: (a) the Nubian dialects of the Nile valley and of Kordofan and Darfur to the west; (b) Tabi; (c) Didinga-Murle; (d) Merarit; and (e) Dagu. The most important branch is a southern group (f), of which there are two subgroups, Nilotic

(Shilluk, Dinka, Nuer, Acholi, Anuak, Lango, Jur, etc.) and Great Lakes (so-called Nilo-Hamitic; Masai, Bari, Teso, Karamojo, Turkana, Lotuko, Nandi, Suk). (2) Central Sudanic with the following branches: (a) Bongo-Baka-Bagirmi-Sara; (b) Kredj (Kreish); (c) Moru-Madi; (d) Mangbetu; (e) Mamvu-Balese (including the language of the Efe pygmies of the Congo); and (f) Lendu. (3) Kunama, spoken in northwestern Ethiopia; and (4) Berta, spoken in the Ethiopia-Sudan border area. Berta is particularly close to Eastern Sudanic and probably forms a group with it.

These languages are likewise tonal as far as is known. Nouns have complex plurals but no division into noun classes. The Great Lakes division of the Eastern Sudanic family has grammatical gender and some other languages of the Eastern Sudanic family exhibit traces of it. Eastern Sudanic languages often have a complex system of verb derivatives; e.g., Nubian and Masai.

The Click Family.—This family contains three branches: (1) the Khoisan languages of the Bushman (q.v.) and Hottentot (q.v.) of south Africa; (2) Sandawe of east Africa; and (3) Hadzapi of East Africa. The Khoisan languages in turn fall into a northern, central and southern branch. The Hottentots form a subdivision of the central branch along with the closely related Naron and Auen Bushman languages.

As indicated by their name, these languages are characterized by the presence of click sounds, sounds not found anywhere in the world outside Africa. A few of the neighbouring Bantu languages have borrowed click sounds from their Khoisan neighbours. The click languages are probably all tonal. Hottentot, Naron, Auen and Sandawe have grammatical gender; e.g., Nama Hottentot khoi-b "man," khoi-s "woman." There are traces of a verbal derivative system particularly in Hottentot. Plural formation is usually simple, outside of some southern Bushman languages.

The Central Saharan Family.—This comprises: (1) Kanuri, the chief language of the aboriginal Bornu kingdom on the borders of Lake Chad in northern Nigeria; (2) Tebu of Tibesti, the large mountainous region of the central Sahara; and (3) Zaghawa and Berti, spoken farther to the east. These languages are probably all tonal, though there is no information in this regard except for Kanuri. They differ somewhat in type from the languages already described. They have neither noun classes nor gender divisions. On the other hand the noun has a case system, a feature also found in Nubian and Nuer in the Eastern Sudanic subdivisions of Macro-Sudanic. The verb has an elaborate conjugational set of inflections for person and number in various moods and tenses and a set of subordinating forms by means of which complicated periodic sentences can be constructed. There is also a fairly simple system of verb derivatives.

Minor Families.—In addition to these major families, there are a number of other families of minor size which on present evidence must be considered independent. However, some of the languages were not at all well known in the 1950s and might prove their membership in one of the larger families. The Kordofanian family consists of a large number of languages spoken in the Nuba hills of Kordofan in the Sudan. These languages have class prefixes whose function is very similar to that of affixes of the Niger-Congo family, although they show little evidence of etymological connection. These languages are insufficiently known but are probably tonal. There is some evidence for a verb derivational system. The Coman family consists of the various Coma dialects, Gule (Hameg) and Gumus all found in a relatively restricted area of the Ethiopian-Sudan border area. They are little known. Gule, at least, appears to have grammatical gender. In the western part of the Sudan is found Fur, the chief language of Darfur and still further west in Wadai a group consisting of Maba, Mimi and other related languages of the Maban stock. Both Maba and Fur are of the same general type as the Central Saharan languages. Maba is definitely known to be tonal. An important isolated language is Songhai, the speech of Tombouctou, of the city of Agades in the air oasis of the Sahara, and of the Niger valley farther south in the region of Djarma. This language has neither noun classes nor gender; in its general grammatical simplicity, it reminds one of English. The verb has a causative suffix. Minor, almost unknown languages, which must be considered independent are Nyangiya, surrounded by Lotuko (Eastern Sudanic) dialects in east Africa and two related languages of the Nuba hills, Temainian and Teis-um-Danab, both only known from a 20-word vocabulary. The languages of the island of Madagascar are Malayo-Polynesian being most closely related to those of Indonesia. Meroitic was spoken in the area of the junction of the Blue Nile and White Nile and written in a hieroglyphic alphabet for several centuries before and after the birth of Christ. In the absence of bilingual inscriptions it is only imperfectly known and thus cannot be related to any other language.

The outstanding problems of classification which remain are the precise subdivisions of the Niger-Congo family and of the Bantu subgroup within it and the status of the smaller families.

Common Features of African Languages.—From this review it can be seen that there are certain features common in African languages. Among those which have been mentioned are tone, the presence of noun-classes and of verb derivational systems. Other general characteristics of African languages are the following. Vowel systems most commonly contain five vowels as in classical Latin (a, e, i, o, u) or seven as in Italian (a, ε, e, i, ɔ, o, u). Umlauted vowels like those of German are quite rare. In addition to the clicks already mentioned there are labiovelar consonants (kp, gb) over a widespread and continuous area mostly occupied by Niger-Congo and Macro-Sudanic languages and there are implosive consonants. While neither labiovelars nor implosives are confined to Africa, they are rare elsewhere in the world. Outside of Hamito-Semitic, consonant systems tend to be simple. Tones are based on pitch levels usually two or three in number. They are thus unlike the contours of rises and falls characteristic of Chinese and other tonal languages of southeastern Asia.

There are many features of semantics and idiom which are widely distributed in Africa. For example, a verb meaning "to surpass" is used to express the comparative. Hausa yā fīni girmā, "he surpassed-me size"; i.e., "he is larger than I am." Parts of the body are often used as prepositions; "upon" is, literally, "head of," "in front" is "chest of," etc. Other examples of such semantic resemblance is the use of a single term meaning both "animal" and "meat" and the extended metaphoric use of the verb "eat" in the sense of "conquer, win, gain, etc."

Language and History.—The linguistic groupings enumerated above are, as might be expected, only in imperfect agreement with the distribution of physical types in Africa. The clearest correlation is that between the Hottentot-Bushman racial type and the click language. On the other hand, the Pygmies have not yet been demonstrated to have a language of their own, though such may exist. The Hamito-Semitic family is spoken both by Caucasian and Negro peoples. The speakers of Semitic, Berber, and the extinct Egyptian languages are white while those of the Cushite and Chad branches are predominantly Negro. The origin of this situation is unknown. It has been noted that the term Hamitic does not designate any linguistic entity. Whatever its racial value may be, it therefore has no linguistic support.

Distributions of language are valuable indicators of movements of people in the absence of direct historical records. The most important conclusions regarding the pre-history of Africa to be drawn from linguistic evidence are (1) the origin of the Bantu in the Nigeria-Cameroon area followed by a general southeastward movement beginning perhaps 2,000 years ago, and (2) the African, probably upper Nilotic or Abyssinian, origin of the Hamito-Semitic peoples, the Semitic branch resulting, no doubt, from a migration into Asia, probably Arabia. Many other details of movements can be reconstructed from linguistic evidence used in conjunction with written documents, recorded traditions and archaeology. Much work which will be of value for African history remains to be done with loan words which reflect cultural contacts. Words from Greek, Latin and Punic have penetrated into the Sudan, usually via Berber. Moslem influences are discernible in the spread of words from Arabic and more recent European influence, particularly Portuguese, is found in words for domestic plants and animals and technological terms.

BIBLIOGRAPHY.—M. Delafosse, A. Caquot and G. van Bulck in A. Meillet and M. Cohen (eds.), *Les Langues du Monde,* new ed. (1952), pp. 733–940, bibl. 844–45, 951–52, 904, 926, 1207, M. Cohen, pp. 86, 148–76, 179–81; L. Homburger, *Les Langues négro-africaines,* (1941; English trans., 1949); R. Lepsius, *Nubische Grammatik mit einer Einleitung über die Völker und Sprachen Afrikas* (1880); A. Werner, *The Language-Families of Africa* (1925); J. H. Greenberg, "The Tonal System of Proto-Bantu" in *Word* (1948), "Studies in African Linguistic Classification" in *Sthwest. J. Anthrop.,* vol. 5–6 (1949–50); D. H. Westermann and I. C. Ward, *Practical Phonetics for Students of African Languages* (1933); D. Westermann, *Die Sudansprachen* (1911); H. H. Johnston, *Bantu and Semi-Bantu Languages,* 2 vol. (1922); M. A. Bryan, *Notes on the Distribution of the Semitic and Cushitic Languages of Africa* (1947), *Distribution of the Nilotic and Nilo-Hamitic Languages of Africa* (1948); A. N. Tucker, *The Eastern Sudanic Languages* (1940); D. Westermann and M. A. Bryan, *Languages of West Africa* (1952); N. W. Thomas, *Specimens of Languages from Sierra Leone* (1916); M. Delafosse, *Vocabulaires comparatifs de plus de 60 langues parlés à la Côte d'Ivoire et dans les régions limitrophes* (1904); F. St. Strümpell, "Vergleichendes Wörterverzeichnis der Heidensprachen Adamauas," in *Z. Ethn.,* vol. 42 (1910); D. F. Bleek, *Comparative Vocabularies of Bushman Languages* (1929); C. Brockelmann, *Grundriss der vergleichenden Grammatik der semitischen Sprachen,* 2 vol. (1908–13); M. Cohen, *Essai comparatif sur le vocabulaire et la phonétique du chamito-sémitique* (1947); C. Meinhof, *Introduction to the Phonology of the Bantu Languages* (1932), *Grundzüge einer vergleichenden Grammatik der Bantu-sprachen,* 2nd ed. (1948); W. Bourquin, *Neue Ur-Bantu-Wortstämme* (1934); C. M. Doke, *Bantu; Modern Grammatical, Phonetical and Lexicographical Studies Since 1860* (1945); M. Guthrie, *The Classification of the Bantu Languages* (1948); W. E. Welmers, *A Descriptive Grammar of Fanti* (1946); D. W. Westermann, *A Study of the Ewe Language* (1930); I. C. Ward, *The Phonetic and Tonal Structure of Efik* (1933), *An Introduction to the Ibo Language* (1936); R. C. Abraham, *The Grammar of Tiv* (1933); D. M. Beach, *The Phonetics of the Hottentot Language* (1938); L. F. Maingard, "The Linguistic Approach to South African Prehistory and Ethnology" in *South African Association for Advancement of Science, Report of the Annual Meeting* (1934); U. Hintze, *Bibliographie der Kwa-Sprachen und der Togo Restvölker* (1960). (J. G.; J. WH.)

AFRICAN LILY (*Agapanthus africanus*), a member of the family Liliaceae, a native of the Cape of Good Hope, from whence it was introduced at the close of the 17th century. It is a handsome greenhouse plant, which is hardy in the south of England and the warmer parts of the United States. The basal, tufted leaves are long, narrow, arching, six inches to two feet long. A central flower stalk, two to three feet high, ends in an umbel of bright blue, funnel-shaped flowers. The plants are easy to cultivate and are generally grown in large pots or tubs which must be protected from frost in winter. During the summer they require plenty of water and are effective on the margins of lakes or running streams, where they thrive admirably. It may be propagated by dividing the rootstock in early spring or autumn. Dwarf and white-flowered forms are known in cultivation.

AFRICAN MUSIC. Africa falls, musically, into two main areas separated by an east-west line running south of the Sahara and Ethiopia. North of this line the music is predominantly Arabic; south of it is found what is called African music—the music of the Negroid peoples. In spite of the different language families represented by the large number of tribes (more than 2,000), the music of this huge area is fundamentally homogeneous and its chief characteristics are: (1) Spontaneous creation; while the tune and words of a song or the drumming for a dance will keep within the traditional pattern of melody or rhythm, they are not crystallized in a standard form, but are modified at each rendering by the creative genius of the performers. This modification is not an embellishment but a fundamental principle of the system, which may be defined as "free creation around a traditional framework." (2) A melody tied to the rise and fall of speech in the "tonal" languages, where the meaning of a word depends on the pitch at which each syllable is spoken—in such cases, the course of a melody cannot be dictated solely by musical principles, but must (to preserve the word sense) move generally up and down in conformity with the spoken word, a powerful inhibiting factor to the development of musical form. (3) A limited harmonic development. (4) An exceedingly complex rhythmic structure.

Rhythmic System.—The essence of the African rhythmic system is tension. Thus, while in western music the accents of a melody usually coincide with time beats (indicated by a baton or a handclap), in African music they normally must not do so. The melodic accents are in free rhythm (yet, in repetitions, always falling in the same places), and although the melody itself is tied to the claps, which may be either a regular beat or an irregular short pattern constantly repeated, the claps do not determine the rhythm.

The principle of rhythm in drumming is different. Here tension is attained by a deliberate staggering of the main accented beats of the several drums. To state the matter at its simplest, if two drums were to beat in triple time, the main beats of the second drum would fall on the second or third beat of the first drum's bar, never on its first beat. In addition, the various drums may be playing in different metres, thus further staggering the main beats (e.g., 3 against 2: 4 against 3); but this is not necessarily the case. In practice, where three drums are used, the small drum beats a simple duple or triple pattern while the master drummer, playing the big drum, has in each different kind of dance five or six fairly long standard patterns in free rhythm, the accents of which lie athwart those of the small drum. Using one of his patterns as a basis, the master drummer plays spontaneous variations on it with great virtuosity, modifying them to suit the style of individual dancers. Meanwhile, the middle drum gives standard "replies" to the master drum, the accents of which also cross those of the small drum. Thus a full dance, which is both the norm and the flower of African music, is a complex interweaving of melodic and rhythmic patterns the inherent accents of which are in a constant state of tension.

Use of Harmony.—Both vocal and instrumental forms of simple harmony or heterophony are found, though some tribes restrict themselves to unison. This heterophony is usually in the form of organum and is either in parallel thirds or in fourths or fifths. The groups favouring the one or the other are mutually exclusive, though there are a few borderline tribes which use both. There is reason to think that the thirds tradition is of Indonesian origin: it is met with in pockets in the Malay archipelago and notably on the Island of Madagascar, while in Africa it seems to have started on both the east coast and the west (Gulf of Guinea) and to have spread inland.

Instruments.—African musical instruments (a great variety of drums, xylophones, strings, horns, flutes and idiophones) even if of primitive appearance, often exhibit a considerable musical precision, although it is necessary to distinguish between an instrument as it leaves the craftsman and as it is later modified by indifferent performers. Functionally, instruments may be classified according to whether they are used for community occasions, for solo playing or solo accompaniment or for the performer's own pleasure. In areas where Islamic influence is felt, such as the lake regions of Uganda, in the northeast part of the Republic of the Congo and in Nigeria, stringed instruments are prominent.

Among the Chopi in Mozambique, where the xylophone is paramount, drums play a minor role. The Venda of South Africa use a flute ensemble for some dances. All these instruments are used for communal dances but usually the drums, with rattles and often iron clapperless bells, are the main communal instruments.

Of special interest are the *sansa* (known also as the *mbila* and as the Kaffir piano) and the xylophone. The former consists of a calabash resonator with a small soundboard on which is mounted a tuned series of metal or bamboo prongs which are played by the thumbs, the instrument itself being supported by the fingers of both hands. The *sansa* has not been found in any other part of the world, yet its distribution in Africa is similar to that of the xylophone, with which it sometimes shares the name *mbila* and to which it is similar in tuning. The African xylophone has two characteristic tunings: equitonal heptatonic and equitonal pentatonic.

Close parallels with the African xylophone in tuning and pitch are found in the xylophones of Thailand and Cambodia (for heptatonic) and in those of Java (for a modified heptatonic scale known as *Pelog,* and also for the pentatonic *Slendro* system). Recent research suggests that Africa may owe a large musical debt to Indonesian colonization. (*See also* MUSICAL INSTRUMENTS:

Chronological Evolution of Instruments; PERCUSSION INSTRUMENTS.)

Relation to Tribal Life.—Music is of the very fibre of African tribal life. It is an essential part (and not an adornment) of religious ceremonies. It is integrally associated with the events of the life cycle—birth, marriage and death—with initiation (for which special music is learned) and with serious sickness (when the patient must be induced to dance to the music). It is closely associated with royalty, the chiefs owning court orchestras and their movements being accompanied by music. It is the universal spur to protracted work, and here the rhythms of work are deftly exploited: pounding grain, paddling canoes, hoeing the fields, rock drilling in the copper mine, are all accompanied by singing, while even the operation of a European sewing machine is turned into a rhythmic pattern. Communal recreation must have music: folktales are interspersed with songs in which the chorus is sung by the audience; a "beer-drink" has singing and dancing; and the most common recreation for the whole village is to gather for drumming, singing and dancing. But besides this communal aspect, music (instrumental or vocal) is a form of individual delectation. One sings or plays to oneself just for pleasure. Music thus plays a part in African life which is vital both to society and to the individual. African music proliferates without any conscious theoretical system, depending entirely on creative musicianship within traditional practice.

Modern Developments.—After about 1920, there developed all over this area a new type of music, part western, part African, deriving from the spread of popular American dance music, heard on phonograph records, and from four-part western harmony learned in schools and churches. Basically this music is western in rhythm (usually in common time) and in harmony (the most usual chordal sequence being the triads on tonic-subdominant-dominant and tonic, constantly repeated) but the melody tends, as time passes, to become more and more African. It is played on western dance band instruments, particularly the guitar and the accordion, though occasionally (*e.g.,* in Ghana) indigenous instruments or their substitutes are used (for instance, a wine bottle struck with a spoon in place of an African iron bell and wooden striker). This hybrid music, which has tended to replace the traditional forms at least in urban areas, has a great urge; new musical forms in this idiom and new modifications of it appear every few years.

BIBLIOGRAPHY.—A. M. Jones, *Studies in African Music,* 2 vol. (1959) and "Indonesia and Africa: the Xylophone as a Culture Indicator" in *J. Roy. Anthr. Inst.,* vol. 89, pt. ii, (July–Dec. 1959); Jaap Kunst, "A Musicological Argument for Cultural Relationship Between Indonesia—Probably Java—and Central Africa," *Proc. Mus. Assn.,* lxii (1936).

(A. M. J.)

AFRICANUS, SEXTUS JULIUS, a Christian traveler and historian of the 3rd century, wrote a history of the world in five books, from the creation to A.D. 221, which introduced a system of chronology widely adopted in the eastern churches. He was probably born at Aelia Capitolina (Jerusalem) and lived at Emmaus, and may have served under Septimius Severus against the Osroenians in A.D. 195. In his history he calculates the period between the creation and the birth of Christ as 5,499 years, antedating the latter event by three years. This method of reckoning was known as the Alexandrian era. The history, which had an apologetic aim, is no longer extant, but copious extracts from it are to be found in the *Chronica* of Eusebius of Caesarea. There are also fragments in Syncellus, Cedrinus and the *Paschale Chronicon.*

Eusebius also gives a letter to Aristides, and one to Origen, impugning the authority of the book of Susanna. The ascription to Africanus of the *Kestoi,* a work on agriculture, natural history, military science, etc., has been disputed. Neander suggests that it was written by Africanus before he had devoted himself to religious subjects.

BIBLIOGRAPHY.—Edition in M. J. Routh, *Rel. Sac.,* ii, 221–509 (1846); trans. by S. D. F. Salmond in *Ante-Nicene Christian Library,* ed. by A. Roberts and J. Donaldson, vol. vi, 125–40 (1867–97). *See also* H. Gelzer, *Sex. Iul. Africanus und die byzant. Chronographie* (1880–98); G. Krueger, *History of Early Christian Literature,* pp. 248–53, trans. by C. R. Gillett (1897). For fragment of *Kestoi* see *Oxyrhyncus Papyri,* vol. iii, pp. 36 *et seq.,* ed. by B. P. Grenfell and A. S. Hunt (1898).

AFRICAN VIOLET, also known as Usambara violet, belongs to the genus *Saintpaulia* of the botanical family Gesneriaceae. Several species are known in tropical Africa; among the prominent ones, *S. ionantha,* the common African violet, and *S. kewensis,* the Kew African violet, appear to be in cultivation. The plants are small and often stemless, hairy, perennial herbs, with basal long-stalked leaves and two-lipped, almost white to violet or red flowers in few flowered cymes. Through breeding and careful selection after about 1925 a large number (perhaps as many as 200) of horticultural varieties were developed and named, although the plant had been discovered only late in the 19th century. It became a popular greenhouse plant and one of the favourite potted window plants for home growing.

Propagation is by seed and by leaf cuttings inserted in sand. The ripened leaves should be cut off with about an inch of the petiole attached, and inserted in sand with only a little of the leaf blade covered. The sand should be kept moist but not too wet while rooting is occurring to avoid rot.

The method of watering and the temperature of the water have a marked influence on vigour and flowering, although plants watered in different ways may do equally well.

One common method is to permit the plants to become fairly dry, then soak thoroughly by placing the pot in a shallow pan of

JOHN H. GERARD

AFRICAN VIOLET (SAINTPAULIA IONANTHA)

water overnight; allow to again dry fairly well before watering again, but take care to prevent water reaching the leaves or washing over the rim of the pot. Although the size and type of pot, the season of the year, the weather and temperature and the light condition are all important factors affecting the water requirement, no fast rule can be prescribed. Cleansing the foliage of dust at intervals by means of a syringe or a rubber sprayer is beneficial and recommended. The temperature of the water preferably should be warmer than that of the room in which the plants have been growing. Allow drying to occur away from direct sunlight and in warm circulating air. With experience and care African violets may be grown easily and successfully. It is easily possible to keep them flowering through the entire year, or the plants may be given periods of rest by reducing the supply of water.   (J. M. BL.)

AFRIDI, a powerful Pathan (*q.v.*) tribe, with a fighting strength estimated at about 50,000 men in the 1960s, inhabiting the hill country from the eastern spurs of the Safed Koh to the borders of the Peshawar district in West Pakistan. Important because they straddle the Khyber pass, they have a fertile but inaccessible base in the Tirah (*q.v.*) uplands (6,000–7,000 ft.).

Zahir-ud-din Babur, the Mogul invader of India, found them in the Khyber area in 1504, outside the control of any organized government. They remained so despite repeated Mogul efforts to control the road to Kabul. The emperor Akbar (*q.v.*) drove a cart road through the Khyber in 1581, but Afridi resistance, inspired by Jalal-ud-din, leader of the heretical Roshania movement, closed the pass to the emperor's first governor of Kabul, Man Singh, in 1585. Heavy fighting and the grant of allowances were needed to reopen it.

In 1622 a Mogul attack on Afridi and Orakzai Roshanias in Tirah ended in disaster on the Sampagga pass. Then, in 1630, after another Kabul governor, Muzaffar Khan, had suffered ignominious loss in the Khyber, a general tribal rising occurred, and Peshawar city was taken. The tribesmen were caught in the city and thoroughly beaten, and the Roshania leaders were exiled to India, but in 1672 another Mogul commander lost his entire army to the attacks of Afridis, who went on to capture Nowshera fort. The em-

peror Aurangzeb himself had to come north in 1674 to restore order by multiple campaigns and bribes.

The Afghan amir Ahmad Shah Durrani (*q.v.*) in the 18th century also paid allowances to the Afridis and employed them in his armies, and his grandson Shah Shuja received considerable support from the Afridis and asylum in defeat. They joined Dost Mohammed in attacking the Sikh, Hari Singh, at Jamrud in 1837.

British encounters with the Afridis began during the first Afghan War (1839–42), notably when Gen. George Pollock, marching his avenging column to Kabul, first used the flank picket technique against them with success. After the British annexation of the Punjab in 1849 all the old expedients were tried to keep the Khyber open: allowances, punitive expeditions such as those of 1878 and 1879 against the Kohat and Khyber Afridis, and the use of tribal militia (the Khyber Rifles, raised by Sir Robert Warburton). More novel and lastingly effective were the building of the Khyber railway and the foundation, by Sir George Roos-Keppel, chief commissioner of the North-West Frontier province, of Islamia college, now the University of Peshawar. Throughout the 1930s the British position was complicated by the Indian Congress party's success in enlisting tribal support for the Red Shirt political movement under Khan Sahib and his brother Abdul Ghaffar Khan. After 1947, moreover, Pakistan had to face an Afghan-supported movement for an independent Pakhtunistan or Pathan state and to protest against Afghan support for Afridi attacks.

The Afridis, wiry, shaven-headed, full-bearded, Pakhtu-speaking hillmen, are of uncertain origin. Their genealogies loosely connect them by the adoption of a foundling child with the other Pathan tribes, but they also link them with Urmaris, who speak an East Iranian language, so that it seems probable that the Afridis are older settlers who have adopted the Pathans' language and customs. Indeed, the Afridis have been identified with the Aparytae mentioned by Herodotus as living in the Peshawar area. While Henry Bellew, Sir George Grierson and Sir Aurel Stein supported this identification, G. Morgenstierne and H. W. Bailey rejected it, but a persuasive restatement of it was made by Sir Olaf Caroe (see *Bibliography,* below).

BIBLIOGRAPHY.—W. H. Paget and A. H. Mason, *A Record of the Expeditions Undertaken Against the North-West Frontier Tribes Since the Annexation of the Punjab* (1884); Sir Robert Warburton, *Eighteen Years in the Khyber* (1900), an excellent book by one who was himself of part Afghan descent; C. C. Davies, *The Problem of the North-West Frontier, 1890–1908* (1932); Sir Olaf Caroe, *The Pathans 550 B.C.–A.D. 1957* (1959).   (J. B. HA.)

AFTERBIRTH includes the placenta, amniotic fluid, fetal membranes and umbilical cord. They are usually expelled from the uterus in a single mass 15 to 30 minutes after the birth of the child. The placenta is a soft, beefy red disk, about 8 to 10 in. in diameter and 1 to $1\frac{1}{2}$ in. in thickness. It is the organ by which the mother nourishes the child and is composed largely of capillary loops from mother and child, in close contact. While the mother's blood does not pass into the blood vessels of the child, the constituents necessary for growth pass through the capillary walls into the child's circulation by a process called osmosis, and the waste products in the fetal blood pass in the other direction and are eliminated by the mother. One surface of the placenta is attached to the inside of the uterus, whence it draws its maternal blood. The other surface presents the branching blood vessels of the fetus, which unite into two arteries and one vein. These vessels form the umbilical cord, which usually starts from the middle of the placenta and enters the body of the fetus at the navel. It is about 22 in. long. Around the edge of the placenta is the thin torn membrane which envelops the fetus in the womb. It forms the water bag in which the fetus lies and usually breaks shortly before the birth of the child. If the child is born with the membranes intact, he is said to be born in a caul. See CHILD-BIRTH; EMBRYOLOGY AND DEVELOPMENT, ANIMAL; OBSTETRICS; PLACENTA.

AFTERDAMP: see COAL AND COAL MINING: *Hazards of Mining.*

AFTERGLOW: see TWILIGHT.

AFYONKARAHISAR, the popular name of Kara-hisar Sahip, the chief town of an *il* (province) of the same name in western Asiatic Turkey, nearly 200 mi. E. of Izmir and 50 mi. S.S.E. of Kutahya. Pop. (1960) 38,392. Called Nicopolis by Leo III after his victory over the Arabs in 740, the town's name was changed by the Seljuk Turks to Kara-hisar. It stands partly on level ground and partly on a declivity, and above it rises a precipitous trachytic rock (400 ft.) on the summit of which are the ruins of a Byzantine castle. It contains several mosques, one of them a very handsome building. It is an important railway junction, connected with Izmir, Konya, Ankara and Istanbul, and is on the Konya-Istanbul road. The town is a centre of trade, notably for opium, which is produced in large quantities in the vicinity. Wheat and barley are the other chief products of the district, and stock raising is an important occupation. Black felts and carpets are manufactured.

(N. Tu.; S. Er.; E. Tu.)

AFZELIUS, ADAM (1750–1837), Swedish botanist who founded the Linnaean institute at Uppsala, in 1802, was born at Larf, Västergötland on Oct. 8, 1750. From 1792 he spent several years on the west coast of Africa, and in 1797–98 he acted as secretary of the Swedish embassy in London. In 1812 he became professor of materia medica at the University of Uppsala. In addition to his various botanical writings he published the autobiography of Linnaeus in 1823. Afzelius died at Uppsala in 1837.

His brother JOHAN AFZELIUS (1753–1837), known as Arvidson, was professor of chemistry at Uppsala; another brother PER AF (1760–1843), who became professor of medicine at Uppsala in 1801, was distinguished as a medical teacher and practitioner.

AGA (AGHA), a Turkish word indicating, under the Ottoman empire, a person of high rank or social position. Combined with the names of military units or administrative departments it formed the official titles borne by the chief officers of the janizaries and of the cavalry, by the principal members of the imperial household and by the eunuchs controlling the sultan's harem. Later it was applied to officers of lower rank and, socially, as a term of respect to heads of families and villages and to landowners. In republican Turkey the official title disappeared, the social use of the word surviving only among the lower classes. (A. D. A.)

AGADE, a city founded as his capital in Babylonia by the Semitic conqueror Sargon I about 2300 B.C.; from it the northern part of the country was called Akkad (q.v.). The proposed location of it at Tall ad-Der, near Sippar, is questionable; as a chronicle records that Sargon took earth from Babylon to build his new city, it cannot have been far from the later capital. After its foundation Agade was the seat of a dynasty of 11 kings, but only the first four or five of these ruled over neighbouring lands. The city, as a principal sanctuary of the goddess Ishtar, remained of some religious importance until Babylonian rule ended in the 6th century B.C.

See S. Langdon, *Excavations at Kish*, 1,7 (1924). (C. J. G.)

AGADIR, a town on the Atlantic coast of southern Morocco, Africa, about 6 mi. N. of the Wadi Sous, and capital of the province of the same name, was entirely destroyed by a severe earthquake on Feb. 29, 1960. The site was flattened and plans were made for a new town about 3 mi. S., with buildings incorporating antiseismic features. The port, constructed in 1914, enlarged in 1930 and again greatly enlarged and refitted in 1953 was not entirely destroyed and was brought into use again. The population in 1960 was 16,695, of whom 15,828 were Moroccans. Its growth from 1,000 in 1913 was due to the development of agriculture in the Sous plain, to the exploitation of mineral resources in the interior and to the large fish-canning industry (mainly sardines).

Agadir was occupied by the Portuguese in 1505 and known as Santa Cruz del Cabo de Aguer. The Berber tribes of Sous carried on an intermittent holy war against the fortress and it was captured in 1541 by the Saadian king of Sous. The town came into prominence during the Moroccan crisis of 1911 when a German gunboat appeared off the town "to protect German interests" in spite of the international agreement of Algeciras in 1906 to which Germany was a party. This crisis was settled between France and Germany on Nov. 4, 1911, and Agadir was occupied by French troops in 1913.

The province of Agadir extends over the plain of Sous and over part of the western High Atlas mountains and of the Anti-Atlas, and has a population of (1960) 843,758. (A. Am.)

AGA KHAN, title of the imam or spiritual leader of the Nizari Isma'ili sect of the Shi'ite Muslims.

AGA KHAN I (Hasan 'Ali Shah) (1800–1881), the first holder of the title, claimed to be directly descended from 'Ali, the son-in-law of the prophet Mohammed, and his wife Fatima, Mohammed's daughter, and also from the Fatimid caliphs of Egypt. He was the governor of the Persian province of Kerman and was high in the favour of the shah, Fath 'Ali. It was from the Persian court that he acquired the title of Aga Khan. Under Mohammed Shah, however, he felt his family honour slighted and rose in revolt in 1838, but was defeated and fled to India. He helped the British in the first Afghan War (1839–42) and in the conquest of Sind (1842–43) and was granted a pension and also the style of "His Highness." After he had settled in Bombay, he encountered some opposition from a minority of his followers, who contested the extent of his spiritual authority and in a lawsuit challenged his control over the community's funds, but he won his case (1866). He died in April 1881.

AGA KHAN II ('Ali Shah) (d. 1885), the eldest son of the Aga Khan I, succeeded his father in 1881 and, in his short imamate, sought to improve the conditions of his community. He died at Poona in Aug. 1885.

AGA KHAN III (Sultan Sir Mohammed Shah) (1877–1957), only son of the Aga Khan II, succeeded his father in 1885. He was born at Karachi on Nov. 2, 1877. Under the care of his mother, a daughter of the ruling house of Persia, he was given not only a religious and oriental education but also a western one. Besides attending diligently to the affairs of his own community, he rapidly acquired a leading position among India's Muslims as a whole. In 1906, he headed the Muslim deputation to the viceroy, Lord Minto, which claimed that in any extension of representative institutions in India the Muslim minority should be granted a position that accorded not merely with their numerical strength but with their loyalty and political importance. The Morley-Minto reforms of 1909 consequently provided for separate Muslim electorates. He served as president of the All-India Muslim league during its early years and initiated the fund for raising the Muslim college at Aligarh to university status, which was effected in 1920.

When World War I broke out the Aga Khan cabled to the *jamats* or councils of the millions of Isma'ilis within British territories and on their borders, directing his followers to place themselves unreservedly at the disposal of the British authorities. When Turkey was drawn into the war, he issued a manifesto calling upon the Muslims of the British empire to remain loyal. However, at the peace conference and subsequently he urged that Turkey should be leniently treated. For his services during the war he was granted a salute of 11 guns. He played an important part in the Round Table conferences on Indian constitutional reform in London (1930–32): besides leading the Muslim delegation, he was made chairman of the entire British-Indian delegation. He also represented India at the World Disarmament conference in Geneva, Switz., in 1932, and at the League of Nations assembly in 1932 and from 1934 to 1937. He was appointed president of the league in 1937. During World War II he lived in Switzerland and withdrew from political activity.

In his leadership of the Isma'ilis the Aga Khan concerned himself with their temporal as well as spiritual welfare. Though they are distributed over a large area (including Syria, Iran, central Asia, India, Burma, Malaya and east Africa), he was able to make his views known to them as a result of their organization into local and regional councils. In general, he advised them to conform to the customs of whatever country they happened to be living in. He took particular care to encourage them to form co-operative enterprises such as banks, insurance companies, building societies and organizations for social welfare.

The Aga Khan was well known as a successful owner and breeder of thoroughbred horses and won the English Derby five times. He died at Versoix, Switz., on July 11, 1957.

AGA KHAN IV (Prince Karim) (1936–), nominated to the imamate by his grandfather, the Aga Khan III, was born at Geneva, Switz., on Dec. 13, 1936, the elder son of Prince Aly Khan by his first wife, the daughter of the 3rd Baron Churston. The new Aga

Khan, having completed his studies at Harvard university in June 1959, continued the visits to his Isma'ili peoples which he had started in the first year of his reign. *See also* Isma'ilism.

Bibliography.—Sultan Sir Mohammed Shah, *The Memoirs of Aga Khan* (1954); N. M. Dumasia, *The Aga Khan and His Ancestors* (1939); J. N. Hollister, *The Shi'a of India* (1953). (Ke. A. B.)

AGALMATOLITE, a compact variety of the soft mineral pyrophyllite (*q.v.*), hydrous aluminum silicate, also called pagodite, used by the Chinese for carving, especially into grotesque figures (hence called figure stone).

AGAMEDES, in Greek legend, king of Orchomenus in Boeotia. He and his stepbrother Trophonius were skilled architects and constructors of underground shrines and treasure houses. When building a treasure house for the Boeotian king, Hyrieus, the brothers fixed one of the stones in the wall in such a manner that they could remove it whenever they pleased and help themselves to the treasure. Hyrieus set a trap in which Agamedes was caught; Trophonius to prevent discovery cut off his brother's head and fled with it. He was pursued by Hyrieus, and swallowed up by the earth in the grove of Lebadeia. On this spot was the oracle of Trophonius in an underground cave; those who wished to consult it, first offered a ram and called upon the name of Agamedes. A similar story is told of the treasure of Rhampsinitus by Herodotus. The brothers built the temple of Apollo at Delphi. When they asked for a reward, the god promised them one in seven days; on the seventh day they died.

AGAMEMNON, a Homeric hero, king of Mycenae (according to Homer) or Argos (according to Aeschylus), son of Atreus and Aërope, grandson of Pelops, great-grandson of Tantalus and brother of Menelaus. After the death of Atreus (*q.v.*), Agamemnon and Menelaus took refuge with Tyndareus, king of Sparta, and his wife Leda, whose daughters, Clytemnestra and Helen, they respectively married. By Clytemnestra, Agamemnon had three daughters, Iphigenia (Iphianassa), Electra (Laodice) and Chrysothemis, and a son, Orestes. Menelaus succeeded Tyndareus, while Agamemnon, with his brother's assistance, drove out Aegisthus and Thyestes and recovered his father's kingdom. He extended his dominion by conquest and became the most powerful prince in Greece. In some ancient sources he is represented as ruler of a large part of Achaea.

When Paris (Alexandrus), son of Priam, had carried off Helen, Menelaus' wife, Agamemnon went to the princes of the country and called upon them to unite in a war of revenge against the Trojans. He himself furnished 100 ships, the largest contingent of the expedition, and was chosen commander in chief of the combined forces. The fleet, numbering 1,200 ships, assembled at the port of Aulis in Boeotia, but was prevented from sailing by calms or contrary winds. Agamemnon had in some way offended Artemis (perhaps by shooting a sacred stag, as related in Sophocles' *Electra*), who in revenge refused to permit the fleet to proceed. Calchas announced that the wrath of Artemis could be appeased only by the sacrifice of Agamemnon's own daughter, Iphigenia (*q.v.*), to which he consented. The fleet then set sail.

Little is heard of Agamemnon until his quarrel with Achilles (*see* Homer). After the capture of Troy, Cassandra, the daughter of Priam, fell to Agamemnon's lot in the distribution of the prizes of war. On his return, after a stormy voyage, he landed in Argolis. Aegisthus, who in the interval had seduced Agamemnon's wife, treacherously plotted the murder of Agamemnon. According to Homer, Aegisthus arranged a feast to welcome the returning king and slew him, his comrades and Cassandra as they dined. The version of Aeschylus' *Agamemnon* attributes the murder to Clytemnestra alone (out of mixed motives: in retribution for the sacrifice of Iphigenia, out of jealousy of Cassandra and in order to continue her life with Aegisthus). Helping her husband in the bath, she enveloped him in a great robe and stabbed him to death. The murder was avenged by Orestes, who returned to slay both his mother and her paramour (Aeschylus, *Choephoroi*; Sophocles, *Electra*; Euripides, *Electra*).

Agamemnon is quite possibly a more or less historical character, overlord of the Mycenaean or Achaean states of the Greek mainland. In Hellenistic times, at Sparta, he was worshiped under the title of Zeus Agamemnon.

Bibliography.—L. R. Farnell, *Greek Hero-Cults and Ideas of Immortality* (1921); W. H. Roscher, *Ausführliches Lexikon der griechischen und römischen Mythologie,* vol. 1, col. 90–97 (1884–86); A. Pauly and G. Wissowa, *Real-Encyclopädie,* vol. 1, col. 721–729 (1894).
(T. V. B.)

AGANA, the capital of Guam, an unincorporated Pacific island territory of the United States. It is situated at the centre of the west coast of the island on a sandy beach surrounding Agana bay and at the mouth of the small Agana river. A city of 10,000 inhabitants in 1940, it was destroyed in World War II. Its population increased slowly after the war, reaching 1,827 in 1964.

Reconstruction was retarded by the fact that it was very difficult to determine the ownership of many small, scattered pieces of land used for new, wide streets constructed by the U.S. navy after reoccupation of the island in 1944. As a result of the difficulty of obtaining clear title to real estate, few new buildings have been erected. The town of Tamuning, just north of Agana, and Piti to the south have grown to be important business centres at the expense of the capital. The mean annual temperature, about 81° F., is nearly constant. Tropical hurricanes which hit the town almost every year occasionally do considerable damage. Agana is the seat of the unicameral legislature of the territory. The non-American population is made up of Chamorros and Filipinos. Agana has been the seat of government for Guam under three nations—Spain, which ruled the island for 300 years; the United States, which acquired it on Feb. 1, 1899; and Japan, which occupied it from 1942 to 1944. (J. W. Cr.)

AGAPE, a Greek word understood in two senses in Christian religion.

1. The word appearing in translations of the New Testament as *caritas* (Vulgate), "charity" (Douai-Reims, Authorized Version), "love" (Revised Standard Version). The Greek term is normally retained in contemporary discussions to draw attention to the distinctive character of "love" in the New Testament. Both the category of virtue and that of feeling are inadequate as a point of departure. Man's "love" for God and for the "neighbour" (or "brother") is the activity of him who acknowledges the lordship of God. A more specific conception of this lordship is found where *agape* itself is regarded primarily as God's act of love in Jesus Christ (*e.g.,* I John 4:19).

2. The word used by the Church Fathers (as early as Ignatius) of the "love feast." The latter was both a meal (of fellowship to which the poor were invited or from which charity was dispensed) and a rite (with the use of bread and wine an important feature). The classical description of it is found in Hippolytus' *Apostolic Tradition.* Its practice was restricted especially by the councils of Laodicea (363) and Trullo (692). Its origin is a matter of dispute. Two main problems arise:

What was the relation between the *agape* and the Eucharist? Two typical solutions may be mentioned: (i) The *agape* was a later form of the "Lord's Supper" (I Cor. 11:20) and the Eucharist the isolation (by the time of Justin, *c.* 150) of the "sacramental" side of this celebration. (ii) The *agape* reflected a fellowship meal of Jesus and his disciples; the eucharistic element (emphasizing Christ's death) intruded itself by the time of Paul and later was separated from the meal. The *Didache* (9–10) has been thought to point to a stage before the complete separation of the two rites in which the *agape* served as a preliminary to the Eucharist. The *agape* preceded or followed the Eucharist, however, in some quarters, even after the time of Justin.

What influence did Jewish models (the Kiddush meals [*see* Kiddush and Habdalah] or the sacral meal of the Essenes) have on the *agape?* The detection of such models, according to some, strengthens the possibility that the early church at first celebrated only a fellowship meal (the "Last Supper" is regarded as distorted or unhistorical). Others believe that Jesus himself impressed a new character on the fellowship meal the night before his crucifixion. In that event it is simplest to regard the Passover setting of the Last Supper as unhistorical; but if arguments for retaining it seem convincing, a more complex relation between the fellowship meals, the Last Supper, and the *agape* must be reconstructed.

Bibliography.—For *agape* in the first sense, *see* G. Quell and E.

Stauffer, *Love* (1949); C. Spicq, *Agape in the New Testament* (1963). For the second sense, *see* G. Dix, *The Shape of the Liturgy* (1945); H. Lietzmann, *Mass and Lord's Supper* (1953); K. G. Kuhn, in K. Stendahl, *The Scrolls and the New Testament* (1957); O. Cullmann, *Early Christian Worship* (1953). (W. R. Sc.)

AGAPĒTUS (AGAPITUS), the name of two popes.

SAINT AGAPETUS I (d. 536), pope from 535 to 536, was a nobleman born at Rome, the son of Gordian, a priest. He was elected bishop of Rome on May 13, 535. At the time of his elevation he was an archdeacon. At the urging of the Ostrogoth king Theodahad, he headed an unsuccessful mission to Constantinople to deter the emperor Justinian I from his plans to reconquer Italy. While there he did succeed in choosing and consecrating Menas as successor to the patriarch Anthimus, whom he deposed as a Monophysite. Agapetus died in Constantinople April 22, 536, but his remains were buried in Rome. His feast is commemorated on April 22 and Sept. 20. (JN. F. B.)

AGAPETUS II (d. 955), pope from 946 to 955. He was elected on May 10, 946. A wise and pious administrator, he endeavoured to restore ecclesiastical discipline. The chief events of his pontificate are the spread of Christianity in Denmark, the settlement of the dispute over the see of Reims and the attempt of the German king Otto I to become emperor in 951, which failed because the real ruler of Rome, Alberic, son of Marozia, was too powerful. Agapetus died in Dec. 955. (C. P. L.)

AGAR, or AGAR-AGAR, is a gelatinlike product of red seaweeds, made from *Gelidium* and other agarophytes (agar-bearing plants) such as *Gracilaria, Ahnfeltia* and *Pterocladia*. It is best known as a bacteriological culture medium and is extensively used for food, as roughage, and in making jelly desserts, confectionery, icings, salad dressings and dairy products. It is employed in canning meat and poultry, in laxative preparations, as a constituent of medicinal pills and capsules, in numerous pharmaceutical and cosmetic creams and jellies, as a dental impression mold base and in wire-drawing lubricants. Agar is prepared by boiling the agarophytes in water and subsequently purifying and drying the product. It is produced chiefly in Japan and also in China, the U.S.S.R., the United States, Mexico, South Africa, New Zealand and Australia. It is amorphous and translucent and may be found on the market in the form of powder, flakes, shreds or bricks.

Agar is insoluble in cold water, but swells considerably, absorbing as much as 20 times its own weight of water. It readily dissolves in boiling water and is able to set to a firm gel at concentrations as low as 0.5%. Although a 1% agar sol solidifies at about 104° F., its gel does not melt until about 203° F., showing a striking case of hysteresis. Agar gels carry small negative electric charges. Like other gels, they exhibit syneresis. Chemically, agar is the sulfuric ester of a linear galactan, consisting of a long chain of *d*-galactose residues attached to each other by a 1, 3-glycosidic linkage. This chain is terminated by one *l*-galactose residue which is attached to the rest of the chain through carbon atom 4, and is esterified at carbon atom 6 with sulfuric acid. There are probably as many as 53 galactose units to each SO_4H group. In the natural state, agar occurs as a cell wall constituent of the agarophytes, probably existing in the form of its calcium salt or a mixture of calcium and magnesium salts.

BIBLIOGRAPHY.—W. G. M. Jones and S. Peat, "The Constitution of Agar," *Jour. Chem. Soc.*, 225–231 (1942); V. C. Barry and Thomas Dillon, "A Formula for Agar," *Chem. and Ind.*, 167 (1944); C. K. Tseng, "Agar: A Valuable Seaweed Product," *Scientific Monthly*, 58: 24–32 (1944); C. K. Tseng, "Phycocolloids: Useful Seaweed Polysaccharides," in Jerome Alexander, *Colloid Chemistry*, vol. vi, *Technology and Applications of Colloids*. (C. K. T.)

AGARDE, ARTHUR (1540–1615), English antiquary, a friend of Sir Robert Cotton and William Camden, and one of the group of early antiquaries and bibliophiles on whose industry later scholars depend for their materials. He was born at Foston, Derbyshire, in 1540. He was trained as a lawyer, although eventually he entered the exchequer as a clerk. Anthony à Wood stated in his *Athenae Oxonienses* that Agarde was appointed deputy chamberlain in 1570 by Sir Nicholas Throckmorton and that he held this post for 45 years, but his patent of appointment proves that he succeeded one Thomas Reve in the post on July 11, 1603.

Agarde was an early and keen member of the Society of Antiquaries founded by Archbishop Matthew Parker in 1572, and later joined by Camden, Cotton and Selden. He devoted much time to cataloguing the exchequer rolls and state papers, and made special studies of the Domesday Book, the origin and privileges of the inns of court, the antiquity of shires and the ancient character of parliament, earning John Selden's description of him as "a man known to be most painful, industrious, and sufficient." Six of his essays were published in the enlarged edition of Thomas Hearne's *Collection of Curious Discourses Written by Eminent Antiquaries* (1771).

Agarde died on Aug. 22, 1615. The manuscripts relating to the exchequer he bequeathed to it, the remainder to Cotton; these were later acquired by the British museum.

AGARIC, any fungus having the spores borne on gills (mushrooms), from the generic name *Agaricus*. Also, an obsolete medicinal preparation derived from the fungus *Fomes officinalis* (*Fomes laricis*) a polypore growing principally on larch and pine. (V. E.)

AGASIAS, the name of two Greek sculptors. Agasias, son of Dositheus, signed the "Borghese Warrior" in the Louvre. Agasias, son of Menophilus, was the sculptor of a number of portrait statues found at Delos. Both were Ephesians, and perhaps of the same family. They probably flourished in the late 2nd or early 1st century B.C. (C. M. RN.)

AGASSIZ, ALEXANDER (1835–1910), U.S. marine zoologist, also did valuable work on mine surveying. The son of J. L. R. Agassiz (*q.v.*), he was born in Neuchâtel, Switz., on Dec. 17, 1835. He went to the United States with his father in 1849; graduated from Harvard in 1855, subsequently studying engineering and chemistry, and taking the degree of bachelor of science at the Lawrence scientific school of the same institution in 1857; and in 1859 became an assistant in the U.S. coast and geodetic survey.

Although a specialist in marine ichthyology, Agassiz devoted much time to the investigation and superintendence of mines, being superintendent of the Calumet and Hecla copper mines, Lake Superior, from 1865 to 1869, and afterward, as a stockholder, he acquired a fortune, out of which he gave to Harvard, for the Museum of Comparative Zoology and for furthering the study of biology at Harvard and elsewhere, more than $1,000,000. In 1875 he surveyed Lake Titicaca, Peru, examined the copper mines of Peru and Chile, and made a collection of Peruvian antiquities for that museum, of which he was curator from 1874 to 1885. He assisted Sir Wyville Thomson in the examination and classification of the collections of the "Challenger" exploring expedition, and wrote the *Revision of the Echini* (1872–74) in the reports. Between 1877 and 1880 he took part in the three dredging expeditions of the steamer "Blake," of the U.S. coast and geodetic survey, and presented a full account of them in 1888.

Of his other writings on marine zoology, most are contained in the bulletins and memoirs of the Museum of Comparative Zoology; but he published in 1865 (with Elizabeth Cary Agassiz, his stepmother) *Seaside Studies in Natural History,* an exact and stimulating work, and in 1871 *Marine Animals of Massachusetts Bay.*

He died at sea on the "Adriatic" bound for the United States on March 27, 1910.

See G. R. Agassiz (ed.), *Letters and Recollections of Alexander Agassiz; With a Sketch of His Life and Work* (1913).

AGASSIZ, (JEAN) LOUIS (RODOLPHE) (1807–1873), Swiss-U.S. naturalist, geologist and teacher whose studies ranged from fish forms to glaciers, was born on May 28, 1807, the son of the Protestant pastor of Motier, on the shore of Lake Morat, Switzerland. His father was the last of a long line of clergymen, the first of the series having been driven from France by the revocation of the Edict of Nantes. His mother, Rose Mayor, was a gifted woman from whom especially he inherited his love of animals and plants. In boyhood he spent four years at the gymnasium in Bienne and later attended the academy at Lausanne. He then entered, successively, the universities of Zürich, Heidelberg and Munich. On completion of his academic courses, Agassiz took at Erlangen the degree of doctor of philosophy and at Munich that of doctor of medicine.

Although as a youth he gave some interested attention to the ways of the brook fish of western Switzerland, his permanent and lifelong interest in ichthyology arose from his being chosen to study the fishes of Brazil. In 1819 and 1820 two eminent naturalists of Munich, J. B. Spix and C. P. J. von Martius, had made an extensive tour in Brazil, bringing back a large collection of fishes, mostly from the Amazon river. The classification of these species was begun by Spix; he died in 1826, however, and the whole collection was then turned over by Martius to Agassiz. The work was completed and published in 1829, as *Selecta Genera et Species Piscium.* This was a splendid accomplishment, the author being at that time only 22 years old. The study of fish forms became henceforth the prominent feature of Agassiz's scientific research. In 1830 he issued a prospectus of a *History of the Fresh Water Fishes of Central Europe,* a valuable contribution printed in parts from 1839 to 1842.

The year 1832 proved the most significant in Agassiz's early career, because it took him first to Paris, then the centre of general scientific as well as medical research, and afterward to Neuchâtel where he spent many years of amazingly fruitful effort. While in Paris he lived the life of an impecunious student of the *quartier latin,* supporting himself, helped at times by the kindly interest of friends, such as Baron von Humboldt, who soon secured for him a professorship at Neuchâtel, and Baron Cuvier, the most eminent ichthyologist of his time. At Paris his scientific activities largely centred in the Natural History museum of the great park now known as the Jardin des Plantes.

Already Agassiz had become interested in the rich stores of the extinct fishes of Europe, especially those of Glarus in Switzerland and of Monte Bolca near Verona, of which only a few at that time had been critically studied. As early as 1829, Agassiz planned a comprehensive and critical study of these remains. To this end he gathered material wherever possible. His epoch-making work, *Recherches sur les Poissons Fossiles,* appeared in parts from 1833 to 1844. In it the number of named fossil fishes was raised to nearly 1,000, and the ancient seas were made to live again through disclosure of their inhabitants. The great importance of this foundation work rests on the impulse given to the study of extinct life itself. Turning his attention to other extinct animals found with the fishes, Agassiz published in 1839–40 two volumes on the fossil echinoderms of Switzerland, and later (1840–45) his *Études Critiques sur les Mollusques Fossiles.*

From 1832 to 1846 he served as professor of natural history in the University of Neuchâtel. In Neuchâtel he acted for a time as his own publisher, his private residence even becoming a hive of activities. Numerous young men were co-workers with him, dividing between themselves the scanty returns from his lectures and publications. He now began his *Nomenclator Zoologicus,* a catalogue, with references, of all the names applied to genera of animals from the beginning of scientific nomenclature, a date since fixed at Jan. 1, 1758.

In 1836 Agassiz began a new line of studies, that of the movements and effects of the glaciers of Switzerland. Several writers had expressed the opinion that these rivers of ice had once been much more extensive, and that the erratic boulders scattered over the region and up to the summit of the Jura mountains were carried by moving glaciers. On the ice of the Aar glacier he built a hut, the "Hôtel des Neuchâtelois," from which he and his associates traced the structure and movements of the ice. In 1840 he published his *Études sur les glaciers* in some regards the most important of all his works. In it Agassiz was able to show that at a period geologically recent Switzerland was covered by one vast ice sheet. His final conclusion was that "great sheets of ice, resembling those now existing in Greenland, once covered all the countries in which unstratified gravel (boulder drift) is found."

In 1846 Agassiz was led to visit the United States for the general purpose of studies in natural history and geology, but immediately to give a course of lectures in the Lowell institute in Boston. These were followed by another series in Charleston, and afterward by lectures both popular and technical in various cities. In 1848 he accepted a professorship of zoology at Harvard university.

In America his chief volumes of scientific research were the following: *Lake Superior* (1850); *Contributions to the Natural History of the United States* (1857–1863, in several quarto volumes, the most notable being on the embryology of turtles); and the *Essay on Classification,* a brilliant production, which, however, failed to grasp the trend of modern zoology. Besides these extensive contributions appeared a multitude of short papers on natural history and especially on the fishes of America. His two excursions of highest importance were, first, to Brazil in 1865, and second, to California in 1871, the latter trip involving both shores of South America. *A Journey in Brazil* (1868) by Mrs. Agassiz and himself, gives a very interesting account of their experiences on the earlier voyage. His most important paper on American fishes dealt with the remarkable group of viviparous surf fishes of California.

Agassiz was deeply absorbed in his cherished plan of developing at Harvard university a comprehensive museum of research in zoology. This institution, which was established in 1859 and ultimately grew into the present splendid museum of comparative zoology, enjoyed his fostering care during the rest of his lifetime. In America Agassiz's industry and devotion to scientific pursuits were as strongly marked as in Europe, but two other traits here assumed a much greater importance. As a teacher of science he was extraordinarily skilful, certainly the ablest America has ever known. In addition he was personally devoted to his students, who were in the highest sense co-workers with him.

Agassiz's method as teacher was to give contact rather than information. He discouraged the use of books except in detailed research. Among his favourite expressions were: "If you study nature in books, when you go out-of-doors you cannot find her." "It's not text-books we want, but students. The book of nature is always open." "Strive to interpret what really exists." The result of his instruction at Harvard was a complete revolution in natural history study in America. The purpose came to be not a category of facts taken from others, but the ability, through contact, to gather the needed facts. As a result of his activities every notable teacher of natural history in the United States for the second half of the 19th century was at some time a pupil of Agassiz or of one of his students.

In the interests of better teaching and of scientific enthusiasm, he organized in the summer of 1873 the Anderson school at Penikese, an island in Buzzard's bay. "The school of all schools which has had the greatest influence on science teaching in America was held in an old barn on an uninhabited island, 18 miles from the shore; it lasted but three months; it had virtually but one teacher. It existed in the personal presence of Agassiz. When he died, it vanished." (David Starr Jordan, *Agassiz at Penikese.*)

As Agassiz was beyond question one of the ablest, wisest and best informed of the biologists of his day, it is often asked why his attitude towards Darwinism was, throughout all his lifetime, cold and unsympathetic. It seems possible that his position was determined in part by a misunderstanding. He seemed to regard Darwinism as a theory of continued progress instead of one of divergence, tempered by the weeding out of unadapted individuals. He failed to recognize the importance of separation and segregation in the development of new specific forms. He once said that in his studies of fossils he "was on the verge of anticipating Darwinism," but was withheld by the discovery that "we had the higher fishes first." In a sense this was true, for the brain development of the sharks is higher, as a whole, than that of the bony fishes. But the latter are far more specialized in fitness for aquatic life. In his philosophy each species of animal or plant was in itself "a thought of God." Their homologies or fundamental unities were "associations of ideas in the Divine Mind."

He married twice. His first wife, Cecile Braun, was the sister of an eminent botanist. In 1850, after his first wife's death, Agassiz married Elizabeth Cabot Cary, of Boston, well known as a writer and as a promoter of the education of women.

Agassiz died on Dec. 12, 1873. He was buried in Mt. Auburn at Cambridge, and by his grave stands a boulder from the moraine of the Lauteraar.

BIBLIOGRAPHY.—J. Marcou, *Life, Letters and Works of Louis Agassiz* (1896); L. Cooper, *Louis Agassiz as a Teacher* (1917; rev. ed., 1945); James D. Teller, *Louis Agassiz, Scientist and Teacher* (1947).
(D. S. J.; X.)

AGATE, a variety of silica composed of alternating layers of variously coloured chert or granular cryptocrystalline (very fine grained) quartz. (*See* CHERT AND FLINT.) According to the Greek philosopher Theophrastus the agate was named from the Achates river (modern Acate), where the stone was originally found.

Agate is a widely scattered material and is found in many countries throughout the world. In the United States it is produced in several western states, with Oregon, Washington, Idaho and Montana the chief sources of gem stones. The most agates occur in eruptive rocks or ancient lavas, where they fill the cavities which were produced by the liberation of gas during the solidification of the molten rock. These agates have a banded structure, successive layers being approximately parallel to the sides of the cavity.

A number of varieties of agate are characterized by peculiarities in the shape and colour of the bands, which are seen in sections cut at right angles to the layers. In riband agate the bands are plane or nearly plane surfaces which in cross section appear as straight lines. Such agate with cloudy bands alternating with bands of another colour is known by the general term onyx. Many cross sections of agate give patterns that mimic familiar objects and are named accordingly. A ring or eye agate is one which, when sectioned, has the differently coloured bands disposed in concentric circles. A Mexican agate, showing only a single eye, has received the name of cyclops. When the banding forms a zig-zag pattern, suggesting the plan of a fortress, it is called fortification agate.

B. M. SHAUB

BANDED AGATE

Certain agates occur, to a limited extent, in veins, of which a notable example is the beautiful brecciated agate of Saxony—a stone mostly composed of angular fragments of agate cemented with amethystine quartz. A variety having included matter of a green colour, embedded in the agate and disposed in filaments and other forms suggestive of vegetable growth, is known as moss agate. Dendritic, or branchlike, markings of black or brown colour, due to infiltration of oxides of manganese and iron, produce the variety known as Mocha stone.

It is probable that agates occurring in cavities in lava flows have been formed in a number of ways, and various theories of their origin have been proposed. The theory which is now generally accepted is as follows. During cooling of the lava, but before solidification, gas and steam accumulate to form bubbles. These bubbles slowly rise; some escape at the top but others, overtaken by solidification, are frozen in, forming cavities. Long after, when the rock has solidified, water carrying silica in solution, probably as alkali silicate, penetrates into the region where the bubble is located. It then diffuses into the cavity and subsequently the solution coagulates to a silica gel. The alkali present with the silica attacks the iron-bearing rock surrounding the cavity, giving rise to iron salts. These diffuse into the silica gel and produce the regular layers of iron hydroxide after the manner of Liesegang rings (*see* COLLOID). Finally the whole mass gradually hardens with loss of water and crystallization of much of the silica as quartz or chert. During the process of crystallization the coloured bands are not disturbed and hence we have the final agate as it is now found.

Agate is essentially quartz and thus its physical properties are in general those of that mineral. It has a hardness of 7 on Mohs' scale (*q.v.*). Its specific gravity is 2.65, and it breaks with a conchoidal fracture.

The agate working industry grew up in the Idar-Oberstein district, Ger., many centuries ago by reason of an abundance of agates in the region. After 1900 the stones used were mostly imported from Brazil and Uruguay.

Most commercial agate is artificially stained so that stones naturally unattractive because of their dull gray tints come to be valuable for ornamental purposes. The colouring matter is absorbed by the porosity of the stone, but different stones and different layers of the same stone exhibit great variation in absorptive power. To produce a dark brown or black colour, the agate is soaked in a sugar or honey solution for several weeks, after which it is treated with sulfuric acid. The acid carbonizes the sugar, thus colouring the more porous layers brown or black but leaving the more impermeable layers white to obtain an alternation of light and dark bands. Agates are stained red by ferric oxide; green by chromium and nickel solutions; and yellow by hydrochloric acid.

Among the uses to which agate is applied may be mentioned the formation of knife-edges of delicate balances, small mortars and pestles for chemical work, burnishers and writing styles, umbrella handles, paper knives, seals, brooches and other ornaments. Real cameos are cut from banded onyx (*q.v.*), one layer forming the medallion, the other the design in relief.

BIBLIOGRAPHY.—H. C. Dake, F. L. Fleener, B. H. Wilson, *Quartz Family Minerals* (1938); E. H. Kraus and C. B. Slawson, *Gems and Gem Materials,* 5th ed. (1947); R. E. Liesegang, *Die Achate* (1927).
(W. A. W.; C. S. H.)

AGATHA, SAINT, a Sicilian martyr put to death at Palermo or, more probably, Catania, perhaps in the 3rd century. The traditional particulars of her martyrdom are of no historical value; according to them she resisted the advances of a Roman official who thereupon ordered her to be tortured, and she died in consequence. In the torture her breasts were cut off, a circumstance reflected in her iconography. She is named in the canon of the Roman mass, and her feast is kept on Feb. 5, on which day she figures in the calendar of the Book of Common Prayer.

See H. Thurston and D. Attwater (eds.), *Butler's Lives of the Saints,* vol. i, pp. 255–256 (1956). (D. AR.)

AGATHIAS (*c.* 536–before 582), Byzantine poet and author of a history covering part of Justinian I's reign, was born at Myrina in Aeolis in Asia Minor. After studying law at Alexandria, he completed his training at Constantinople and practised in the courts as an advocate (*scholasticus*). He wrote a number of short love poems in epic metre, called *Daphniaca.* He compiled an anthology of epigrams by earlier and contemporary poets, including his own. About 100 epigrams by Agathias have been preserved in the *Greek Anthology.* After the death of Justinian I (565), some of Agathias' friends persuaded him to write the history of his own times. This unfinished work in five books, which begins where Procopius ends, is the chief authority for the period 552–558.

BIBLIOGRAPHY.—Works ed. by L. Dindorf, *Historici Graeci minores,* vol. 2 (1871). History also ed. by B. G. Niebuhr in the Bonn Corpus (1828), and in J. P. Migne, *Patrologia Graeca,* vol. 88, col. 1249–1608 (1860). Poems also ed. with Eng. trans. by W. R. Paton, *Greek Anthology,* in the "Loeb Series," 5 vol. (1916–18). *See also* G. Moravcsik, *Byzantinoturcica,* vol. i, pp. 214–217, 2nd ed. (1958); P. N. Ure, *Justinian and His Age,* pp. 184–187, 190–193 (1951); F. A. Wright, *History of Later Greek Literature,* pp. 388–397 (1932). (J. M. HY.)

AGATHO, SAINT (*c.* 577–681), pope from 678 to 681 was of Sicilian origin but became a cleric at Rome. He was elected in June 678. He judged that Wilfrid, bishop of York, had been unjustly deprived and ordered his restoration, and he received the submission of Theodore of Ravenna, whose predecessors had aspired to autonomy. Through legates, he participated in the sixth ecumenical council (680–681), which accepted his definition of two wills in Christ. He prevailed upon the emperor Constantine IV to abolish the tax formerly exacted at the consecration of a newly elected pope. Agatho died in Jan. 681. His feast is celebrated on Jan. 10. (A. G. BI.)

AGATHOCLES (361–289 B.C.), tyrant of Syracuse from 317 to 304 and self-styled king of Sicily from *c.* 304 to 289, was born at Thermae Himerenses (mod. Termini Imerese) in Sicily. He moved to Syracuse (*q.v.*) in 343 and served with distinction in its army. In 333 he married the widow of his wealthy and influential patron Damas. He was twice banished from Syracuse for attempting to overthrow the oligarchical party there, but in 317 he returned with an army gathered from Sicel towns discontented at the growth of Syracusan influence. He then banished or murdered about 10,000 citizens (including the oligarchs) and, proclaiming himself champion of the people and exacting the support of the popular assembly, seized the tyranny.

Agathocles now embarked on a long series of wars. His first campaigns, against the other Sicilian Greeks (316–310), won him control of many of their cities, including Messana, but this made the Carthaginians fear for their own possessions in Sicily. They therefore sent a large force to the island, and the struggle that had gone on intermittently since the 6th century between the Sicilian Greeks and Carthage was renewed. In 310 Agathocles, defeated and besieged in Syracuse, resolved to break through the blockade and attack the enemy in Africa. He carried on the war in Africa with considerable success till 308. Then reverses in Sicily caused him to leave Africa when he was blockading Carthage, and on returning to Africa in 307 he was defeated. Nevertheless, the peace concluded in 306 with the Carthaginians restricted their power in Sicily to the area west of the Halycus (Platani) river, the frontier being the same as that previously agreed to between Carthage and the tyrant Dionysius (q.v.). Agathocles continued, moreover, to strengthen his rule over the Greek cities of Sicily and by c. 304 B.C. felt secure enough to assume the title of king of Sicily. He also extended his influence into southern Italy and the Adriatic.

The reign of Agathocles as king was orderly and peaceful, and he enriched Syracuse with many public buildings. Dissension among his family about the succession caused him in his will to restore liberty to the Syracusans. His death was followed by a recrudescence of Carthaginian power in Sicily.

AGATHON (b. c. 445 B.C.), Athenian tragic poet, whose innovations as a dramatist are mentioned by Aristotle, and whose first victory (416 B.C.) in the contest for tragic poets held at the Dionysiac festival became the imagined occasion of Plato's *Symposium*.

Like Euripides, he accepted the invitation of King Archelaus to the court of Macedon about 407. The length of his stay and the date of his death are uncertain. The 40 surviving lines of his plays make little impression save of a turn for paradox and antithesis, borne out by an anecdote in Aelian's *Varia Historia* and by Plato's characterization of his prose rhetoric in the speech given to him in the *Symposium*. In Plato's *Protagoras* he makes his appearance as a beautiful boy already at home in aristocratic and sophistic circles, and it is clear from his style that he learned much from the sophists, Gorgias especially; but he seems to have been a dramatist of some importance and originality.

In the prologue of the *Thesmophoriazusae* Aristophanes not only makes rude fun of him as an effeminate aesthete but parodies the style of his lyrics at some length, and in the *Frogs*, though Dionysus' approval should not be taken too seriously, he is not dismissed with contempt like most of the minor tragedians. From references in Aristotle's *Poetics* it seems that he was not afraid to go the whole way in "modernist" tendencies in drama: he sometimes overcrowded his plots; he was the first to write a play (*Antheus*) about imaginary characters instead of taking them from heroic mythology, and the first to compose lyrics as pure choral interludes instead of as a comment on the dramatic situation and an integral part of the play.

For the fragments of Agathon's plays, *see* A. Nauck (ed.), *Tragicorum Graecorum Fragmenta*, "Teubner Series" (1926).   (A. M. De.)

AGATHOS DAIMON, in ancient Greek religion, the "good spirit" protective of individuals and families. He received a libation of pure wine at the end of each meal. In Hellenistic and later times he was associated with Tyche, the goddess of luck, as a somewhat impersonal providence. He is portrayed as a serpent or as a young man with a horn of plenty and a bowl in one hand and a poppy and ears of corn in the other.

See M. Nilsson, *Geschichte der griechischen Religion*, vol. ii, pp. 202 ff. (1950).   (H. W. Pa.)

AGAVE, a genus of about 300 species of plants of the amaryllis family (Amaryllidaceae). Some agave species may require many years to bloom, especially in cultivation, hence the name century plant is applied to members of the genus, particularly the larger species such as *Agave americana*. Agaves may also be called American aloes because they resemble plants of the old world genus *Aloe*.

The genus was originally confined to the Americas but many species have been planted in warmer parts of the old world, where in certain areas (as in India) some are naturalized and appear native. The plants grow mainly in dry habitats and are typically stemless or shortstemmed, producing a rosette of large, elongate, fleshy and often spiny-margined and spine-tipped leaves that persist from year to year.

WILLIS PETERSON

CENTURY PLANT (AGAVE AMERICANA), WHOSE FLOWER STALK MAY REACH 40 FT.

A frequently massive and tall flower stalk bearing many greenish or yellowish flowers arises from the centre of the rosette. Some agaves flower annually, others occasionally, but many flower once and then die, often leaving basal suckers that develop into new plants.

Most agaves (99%) are North American, the greatest concentration of species being found in the highlands of central Mexico. About 150 native species occur in Mexico, 50 in the West Indies, and 20 in the United States, mainly in the southwest, 10 in Arizona alone. In South America, one species occurs in Venezuela, and two are reported from Colombia. Many species are known only in cultivation. Agaves range in size from dwarfs such as *A. parviflora*, with leaves 4 in. long and a thin flower stalk 5 ft. high, to enormous plants such as *A. atrovirens*, which may have leaves 8 ft. long and a flower stalk as thick as a man's body and 30 ft. high. The flower stalk of *A. neglecta* may reach 42 ft.

Several agaves are among the world's major cordage fibre plants, including henequen (*A. fourcroydes* and *A. zapupe*) cultivated extensively in Cuba and Yucatan, and sisal (*A. sisalana*), in East Africa and Indonesia. Other species are locally much used for fibre in Latin America. Agave fibres are obtained from the leaves. Pulque (q.v.), a Mexican beverage important both as food and drink, is fermented sap of several large species, especially *A. atrovirens*, great plantations of which are maintained for pulque production. Mescal is a liquor distilled from fermented mash made from stems and leaf bases of various *Agave* species. Tequila, made chiefly in Jalisco (Mex.), is one of many varieties of mescal. Some agaves contain in their leaves significant quantities of a compound (hecogenin) that is convertible into cortisone. Many species are cultivated as ornamentals outdoors in frost-free regions or as conservatory and house plants. Agaves are much used for hedgerows and for erosion control.

The genus is divided into 3 subgenera: (1) *Euagave*, plants with a flower cluster (panicle) having candelabralike branches; (2) *Littaea*, plants with a long cylindrical cluster of flowers that are in groups of from two to several; and (3) *Manfreda* (often given generic rank), plants that die down annually and have a slender spike of flowers that are borne singly. Flowers of *Agave* are more or less fleshy and cylindrical or funnel-shaped. The three sepals and three petals are similar and are usually exceeded in length by the six stamens, which bear large elongate anthers. The ovary is inferior, three-celled with axile placentae, and the style is long and slender with a usually capitate three-lobed stigma. Numerous flat, thin, black seeds are borne in two rows in each cell of the leathery or woody capsule.

See also SISAL FIBRE; AMARYLLIDACEAE. (J. W. TT.)

AGAZZARI, AGOSTINO (1578–1640), Italian musician less distinguished for his compositions than for his short treatise *Del sonare sopra il basso* (1607; facsimile ed. 1933), one of the earliest instruction books for performing from the thorough bass (*q.v.*). The treatise is particularly important because in it he distinguishes between "melody" and "fundamental" instruments and thus recognizes that, whereas usually in Renaissance music all voices of a composition had been equally important, in baroque music a new and significant concept was being developed—the polarity of the upper and lower parts, with neutral improvised inner parts. Agazzari was born in Siena, Dec. 2, 1578, and died there, April 10, 1640. He held various church appointments, and wrote music in both the old and the new styles.

See O. Strunk, ed., *Source Readings in Music History* (1952) for a complete Eng. trans. of *Del sonare sopra il basso.* (N. Fo.)

AGELADAS or (as the name is spelled in an inscription) HAGELAIDAS, a great Greek sculptor of Argos who flourished in the latter part of the 6th and the early part of the 5th century B.C. Ageladas was said to have been the teacher of Myron, Pheidias and Polycleitus; this tradition is a testimony of his wide fame, though historically doubtful.

AGEN, a town in southwest France, capital of Lot-et-Garonne *département*, 88 mi. S.E. of Bordeaux by road. Pop. (1962) 30,639. It lies at the foot of Ermitage hill, and is skirted on the west by the Garonne river, which is spanned by road and canal bridges. Two boulevards cross the town at right angles and others run round the edges, while in the centre are many narrow streets dating from the middle ages. The Promenade du Gravier, an open space alongside the Garonne is a well-known local beauty spot. The cathedral, dedicated to St. Caprais, was built between the 12th and 14th centuries; the church of the Jacobins has two naves, a relic of the days when it was used by the Dominicans. The museum, in two 16th-century mansions, contains valuable collections of ceramics, paintings and archaeological remains.

Agen is on the railway from Bordeaux to Sète, and another runs to Paris. There is a bus service to Toulouse. Its canals make it the outlet for the rich agricultural produce of the district, the chief being plums, which are dried and filled with almond or plum paste. It is a market for early vegetables, fruit, eggs, poultry, cattle and *foies gras* (fattened goose liver). Cold storage enables fruit and meat to be kept for long periods.

As the capital of the Nitiobriges, Agen (Aginnum) is mentioned by Caesar. The district was converted to Christianity by St. Foy about the 4th century. Later, Agen was the headquarters of the earldom of Agenais (*q.v.*), and played a part in the Albigensian War, the Hundred Years' War and, subsequently, the Wars of Religion. It is the seat of a bishop, a court of appeal and assizes, a chamber of commerce and the prefecture of Lot-et-Garonne.

(A.-M. L.)

AGENAIS or AGENOIS, a former province of France, of which Agen was the centre and to which the modern *département* of Lot-et-Garonne (*q.v.*) nearly corresponds. In ancient Gaul it was the country of the Nitiobriges, then a Gallo-Roman *civitas* (the 4th-century *Civitas Agennensium*), whose limits became those of the diocese of Agen. Having in general shared the fortunes of Aquitaine during the Merovingian and Carolingian periods, Aegnais eventually became an hereditary countship. From the middle of the 10th century it was part of the demesne of the counts of Bordeaux, dukes of Gascony, from whom it passed in 1036 to Eudes of Poitiers, later duke of Aquitaine. The marriage of Eleanor of Aquitaine with Henry Plantagenet in 1152 brought it under England; but when Richard I married his sister Joan to Raymond VI of Toulouse in 1196 Agenais formed part of her dowry, although remaining in the vassalage of Gascony. In 1249, with the other estates of Raymond VII, it lapsed to Alphonse of Poitiers, his son-in-law and the brother of Louis IX of France; but in 1259, by the treaty of Paris, Louis IX promised that if Alphonse and his wife Jeanne died childless their demesnes in Agenais would return

to the king of England. When Jeanne did die childless in 1271, Philip III of France had the country occupied; but Edward I recovered it for England by the treaty of Amiens in 1279. Yet the king of France claimed direct overlordship on a number of places, and the dispute over one of them, Saint-Sardos, brought a renewal of the war between England and France under Charles IV. During the Hundred Years' War Agenais was several times taken and retaken until the final retreat of the English.

In 1578 the countship was given to Margaret of France (Marguerite de Valois) in part settlement of the dowry due on her marriage to Henry of Navarre. On her death (1615), it was finally reunited to the French crown. In the last years of the *ancien régime* Agenais was a *sénéchaussée* within the *gouvernement* of Guienne and the *intendance* of Bordeaux. Since the late middle ages the country has been agriculturally rich, subject, however, to alternating phases of depopulation and immigration.

BIBLIOGRAPHY.—J. Andrieu, *Une province à travers les siècles: histoire de l'Agenais,* 2 vol. (1893), *Bibliographie générale de l'Agenais,* 3 vol. (1886–91); P. Deffontaines, *Les Hommes et leurs travaux dans les pays de la Moyenne Garonne* (1932); *Histoire de l'Agenais,* issued by the Société des Sciences, Lettres et Arts d'Agen (1943). (F. CT.)

AGENCY, broadly speaking, refers to the relationship that exists whenever one person engages another to act for him, *e.g.* to do his work, to sell his goods, to manage his business.

The essential quality of agency is that the agent, whether he be printer's devil or editor, office boy or chairman of the board, acts *for* another. He is to follow instructions, and may be discharged for cause if he fails to do so or if he is insubordinate. His is a personal-service relationship, terminable upon the death of either party. Equally significant, the gains or benefits of the agent's activities are to go to the proprietor; the agent is paid a wage or commission for his services. The agent, moreover, is placed by the courts under strict fiduciary duties to his principal; a legal sanction is thus added to the moral one, to make sure that gains reach the proprietor's pockets, not those of his agents.

In commercial matters it has long been the rule that the principal must indemnify his agent for pecuniary losses growing out of the work. This principle was even applied in so unusual a case as *D'Arcy* v. *Lyle* (1813) to give recovery for money the agent had been compelled to pay out (under threat of having to stand trial by battle before King Henry Christophe in Haiti) after his agency had ended. Some courts refuse to give indemnity to corporate officers or directors for their expenses incurred in successfully defending a shareholder's action for mismanagement. Many corporations, however, now expressly agree to indemnify officers and others for such losses.

No similar remedy was developed in the courts to put personal injury losses on the employer. These, it was assumed, were to be borne by agent or workman, much as any other member of society would bear his losses. In the famous case of *Priestly* v. *Fowler* (1837), the court refused to hold the employer liable for injuries caused by the negligence of a fellow servant. Thus was born the "fellow servant" rule (or, in England, the "common employment" rule) which was not to be set aside for the better part of a century. In fact, in the U.S. it remained for the legislature to abolish the rule, first by enacting the Federal Employers' Liability act (1908) in the case of carriers, and then by adoption of the various Workmen's Compensation statutes for other occupations.

Respondeat Superior.—Much of the early law of agency came to be classified under the heading master and servant. This topic covered not only the relationship between master and servant but also the very large area of litigation concerned with injuries to third persons, brought about by the servant's departure from instructions or by his negligence in carrying them out. The master, of course, could be held liable on ordinary tort principles when he was negligent or had directed the particular wrongful act. But by the end of the 17th century in England, the courts had announced the doctrine of *respondeat superior,* by which the injured person is given a direct recovery against the master, even though the injury was due to the fault of the servant.

Though *respondeat superior* is firmly established in the U.S., as in other common-law countries, there has been no agreement on the basis for the doctrine. The early rationalization that master and servant are one, and hence that the master should be liable for whatever his servant does, is both artificial and inaccurate; that the master selected the servant and could direct his actions, while true, would find fault in the employer, for which he might well be liable, but on quite different grounds. Actually, the doctrine may have been a pragmatic outgrowth from early custom; the feudal landholder enjoyed the fruits of his serfs' labour and, as matter of course, seems to have been responsible to third persons for their actions.

It is hard to gainsay that the doctrine has survived as a tacit recognition of the economic stratification existing between proprietor and employee. The injured third person must, as a matter of social policy, be given recourse to the "deep pocket"; it would be quite unrealistic to put him off with a judgment against the servant, while allowing the employer to take the gains from the business, which in ordinary course should be used to meet such losses. Or, as Lemuel Shaw put it in 1842, it is for the employer to so conduct his affairs, "whether by himself or by his agents or servants," as not to injure others.

Whether *respondeat superior* permits a master (who has had to pay a third person for injuries) to shift his losses to the negligent workman, was not litigated when the doctrine was announced. That may have been because the workman of that day did not have money, but in the U.S. the courts have come to give the master a recovery by holding, somewhat mechanically, that he is subrogated to the rights of the injured third person. In Britain, the same result was reached in the *Lister* case (1957), but there the house of lords improvised a contract on the part of the servant, by which he was said to have agreed to indemnify his employer against any losses caused by his negligence. In both countries, there is opinion that unintended risks of this sort should be borne by industry.

Principal and Agent.—The great increase in shipping, banking, insurance and mercantile transactions generally, which occurred in the late 18th and early 19th centuries, brought another kind of agent to the fore. The ship's captains, insurance brokers, bank managers, factors and salesmen of the time were concerned with commercial transactions. Moreover, they could not aptly be called "servants"; indeed, it is not appropriate, as a matter of common parlance, to speak of the modern industrial workman as a servant, even though he is still classified that way by the courts. At all events, the branch of agency dealing with salesmen and others having power to make contracts for their employers came to be separately treated under the topic principal and agent.

There have been many fruitless attempts to define "servant" and "agent" as mutually exclusive terms. Plainly, a useful distinction may not be drawn with respect to the employment relationship, for both "agent" and "servant" must follow orders and both are under strict fiduciary duties. Nor will it do to say that an employer is liable only for the torts of his "servant," not the servant's contracts; for it is only too plain that a chauffeur, for example, who as a "servant" may make his employer liable for injuries to others, may have some power to contract, as for fuel or repairs. And the bank manager, whose work as "agent" may be that of making contracts, also may subject his employer to liability for fraud or misrepresentation. Thus, if there are two concepts, the same man may wear both hats, that of "agent" and of "servant."

This concern with definition has not been just a battle of words. It marks a line behind which the employer has sought to limit his liability for injuries to third persons. For illustration, it is one thing for an employer to be liable when his messenger boy carelessly bumps into a woman on the street, injuring her; and perhaps an entirely different thing for an employer to be liable if a salesman, the manager of the business or its president, were to behave similarly while in course of his work. The difference lies in two things: the employer's assumed right to control physical conduct becomes increasingly tenuous in the latter cases; and, equally important, the ascending pay scale gives increasing assurance that the agent may be able to pay for his carelessness out of his own pocket. Hence, it is possible for the courts to say, consistently with *respondeat superior,* that at some point the employer is not to be held liable.

The courts speak of a salesman, for example, as an "independent contractor" when he is held solely responsible for physical injuries to others, or, speaking more strictly, he is a contractor as to so much of his work, for he may be both agent—in the commercial sense—and independent contractor at the same time. Thus, a bank in handling a customer's paper for collection, or a factor in selling a consignor's goods, acts both as agent and as independent contractor. The contractor, as an essential part of the bargain recognized by the courts, undertakes for a consideration to do the work in his own way without exposing the employer to liability for collateral negligence.

Agency in Commercial Matters.—In *Combes* case (1613), it was recognized that a principal may conduct most transactions by means of an agent quite as effectively as if he were present and acting for himself. There were relatively few cases concerning agents however, until late in the 18th century; by the end of the 19th century, the outlines of the subject were well defined.

An agent may ordinarily be appointed very informally—by word of mouth, by letter or by power of attorney. At common law, in the case of instruments under seal, however, it was required that the agent's authority must be executed with equal dignity. And while, in the U.S., many states have passed statutes abolishing the significance of seals, it is still not unusual to require that an agent's authority to make a conveyance of land must be under seal. Moreover, in those cases where the statute of frauds requires written record, the substance of the equal-dignity rule is usually retained by requiring that the agent's authority also must be in writing.

It was held quite early that a principal may ratify contracts made in his name by an unauthorized agent. The effect of this is to give the principal the same rights (and subject him to the same liabilities) as if he had originally authorized the transaction, for, as the courts put it, ratification relates back. But the doctrine requires that the entire contract be ratified; a principal may not take the good and reject the bad. In the case of promoter's contracts, it is said not to apply at all, for, literally speaking, the promoter cannot be an agent for a not-yet-in-existence principal. But, in the U.S., much the same result is obtained by permitting the newly-born corporation to "adopt" its promoter's contracts. Upon adoption, as in the case of ratification, the corporation is bound and the agent released.

The undisclosed-principal doctrine, also, has raised some theoretical problems. In *Watteau* v. *Fenwick* (1893) an undisclosed owner of a beerhouse was held liable for the price of supplies purchased by his agent (who appeared to be owner), even though the purchases were not authorized. Some writers have insisted that there could not be a contract in such case. But the doctrine is well established, for here, as in *respondeat superior,* a principal may not take the benefits of a venture and limit the third person to an action against the agent. The split today arises when, on discovering the principal, the third person seeks to hold both agent and principal until he gets satisfaction, as if he had bargained for two contracts. Most jurisdictions give him a choice of one or the other, but not both. Were it not for the undisclosed-principal doctrine, many realty transactions could not be conducted without greatly inflating prices.

Much litigation centres on questions concerning the agent's apparent authority. As early as 1812, it was recognized in England that a principal may be held liable despite the fact that the agent exceeded his express authority; in this instance the agent's sale of a quantity of hemp belonging to the principal was sustained, upon the theory that the principal, by permitting the hemp to be put in the agent's name on the wharfinger's books, had held him out as having an authority to sell. In a sense this is an estoppel, but in the U.S. the view prevails that a contract is made at the time of the negotiation, regardless of any change of position by the third person.

In broader context, it is evident that by use of apparent authority, the courts may increasingly give effect to business expectations. While in the older, landed society, they stressed the security of property, now, in a commercial world, they emphasize the security of transactions. In a way this compares with the development under *respondeat superior* through which the courts make use of another variable, scope of employment, to give sanction to social change; that is, many acts of a servant which, in an earlier and simpler economy, might well have been found to fall outside the scope of his employment, may now be held to come within the test, and thus subject the employer to liability. The employer, more often than not, is amply insured.

The Agent's Role.—The agent or broker, who may have exceeded his authority in dealings with third persons, was originally held liable in deceit. Some courts made him a party to the contract, although neither he nor the third person intended that. But in *Collen* v. *Wright* (1857) an English court gave recovery upon the theory that an agent impliedly warrants his authority to third persons. Thus, it became much simpler to achieve recovery, for the older action of deceit required a showing of intent to injure, which often was difficult to prove. While most courts in the U.S. recognize the warranty doctrine, many still award damages measured by the tort test; that is, they give judgment for those losses which naturally flow from the wrong, and deny a benefit-of-the-bargain recovery.

When an agent acts within his authority, however, as in selling goods for his principal, he is without liability to the third person. There are exceptions, of course, for the agent may so sign the contract as to bind himself, or he may have failed to disclose his principal and thus have made himself liable at the election of the other party. Similarly, the agent is not ordinarily liable to his principal, should the third person default. But there has long been a custom in some fields for the agent to act on a del credere basis; that is, for an additional commission the agent undertakes that should the buyer default, he will pay the amount due. For a form of agency known as factoring, *see* FACTOR.

During the 19th century, manufactured goods were generally marketed through a system of jobbers and dealers. Each transaction took the form of a sale and, in legal theory, the buyers were free to dispose of the goods as their own. Thus, they were not agents, and the customer had no direct recourse to the manufacturer. However, in the 20th century the independent jobber's lot has become a difficult one. Many manufacturers, because of a desire to control resale prices, to save costs of distribution, and so on, have set up their own sales organizations. While this has brought them nearer to the consumer, the courts have been reaching in that direction anyway. This they have done by stressing that even a jobber or dealer is in some sense an agent, as in advertising or warranting the product. In other instances, by treating the product as "inherently dangerous," they have disregarded the jobber or dealer and held the manufacturer directly liable for negligence. *See* also MASTER AND SERVANT. (R. T. S.)

AGENOR, the name of three figures in Greek legend and mythology.

1. Agenor, the son of Poseidon, grandson of Epaphos and great-grandson of Io, is usually agreed, although the genealogy is greatly confused, to have been father to Europa, Phoenix, Cadmus and Cilix. When Europa was stolen by Zeus, the brothers were ordered by their father to search for her and not to return without her. Consequently Cilix settled and gave his name to Cilicia, as Phoenix did to Phoenicia; Cadmus (*q.v.*) eventually reached Boeotia.

2. Agenor, one of the sons of the Arcadian king Phegeus, was the slayer of Alcmaeon (*q.v.*).

3. Agenor in the *Iliad* was a Trojan warrior who fought Achilles singlehanded. His form was taken by Apollo to confuse Achilles and to permit the Trojans to withdraw. (T. V. B.)

AGENT: *see* AGENCY.

AGESANDER, a Rhodian sculptor who is mentioned by Pliny in his *Natural History* as author (with Polydorus and Athenodorus) of the group of the Laocoön. Inscriptions found at Lindus in Rhodes date Agesander and Athenodorus to the period 42–21 B.C.

AGE SET is the name given to a system of compulsory grouping by age found among certain peoples of east and northeast Africa. In these societies every male of the tribe belongs either from birth or from a determined age to a named set which is connected with circumcision or initiation and which plays an important part in social and political organization. Women do not have age sets. The sets are not age grades (although they used so to be called in the older anthropological literature); for, once a man has entered a set, he remains a member of it for the rest of his life. Age grades, on the other hand, may be complementary to and coexistent with age sets, and men pass through them in succession, remaining in each grade for a fixed period; but they always belong to the same age set. The basic features of the age-set system are: (1) the number of sets is limited, and their names recur in a cycle, apparent exceptions being due to modification or breakdown; (2) at any given time one set is always that of the warriors or power group; (3) every male must belong to a set; (4) each set has a corporate unity. This pattern of age sets differs in a number of respects from age groups found elsewhere in Africa, and the east African age set, although it has military and governmental functions, is not primarily a regimental system like the age groupings of, *e.g.*, the Swazi of south Africa.

The age-set systems found in east and northeast Africa may be divided into categories according to the extent of their divergence from an assumed prototype. This prototype is believed to be the Galla system, and although this assumption is not accepted by all ethnographers it was not yet disproved in the early 1960s. The categories are: (A) Galla, with age sets working through a series of grades; (A1) Darasa; Konso (both southwest Ethiopia); (B) Nandi and other tribes of the Nandi (Kalenjin) group in Kenya; Masai (Kenya and Tanganyika); Dorobo (Kenya); (C) Central Nilo-Hamitic: Suk, Turkana, in Kenya; Teso (obsolete), Jie, Toposa, in Uganda; Donyiro (Sudan)—all accompanied by systems of age grades, some strongly, others weakly developed; (D) Northern Nilo-Hamitic: Bari, Lotuko, Lokoiya, Laŋo, all in the Sudan; (E) Nilotic: Nuer, Shilluk, Dinka, in the Sudan; Laŋo of Uganda (obsolete); (F) of uncertain pattern: Didiŋa, Gelaba, Murle, all on the Sudan-Uganda-Ethiopia border. The age-set system has been borrowed by various Bantu peoples, those possessing age sets or comparable institutions being the Luhya (Kavirondo) of western Kenya, who have borrowed them from the Nandi, some with Nandi names, others with topical names; the Chagga of northern Tanganyika and the Taveta of southern Kenya, both of which have borrowed from the Masai, those of the Taveta being a very close and old copy; the Ngurimi and Nata (Ikoma) with grades of Galla type and the Kurya (Tende) with linear sets, all in northern Tanganyika; the Giryama of the Nyika group and the Pokomo of the Tana valley, the latter having the Galla grade system without age sets; the Kikuyu of Kenya with topical names and institutionalized grades of elders.

Categories A, B and C, to which should be added the Nuer, are integral parts of the social system and their removal would have meant the collapse of the social and political order. Among many of the Bantu peoples, on the other hand, the age set is a borrowed feature fitted into tribal culture without real integration.

The principle of the Galla system was that all the males in a tribe were included in ten groups called *gada,* which were divided into two half-cycles of five, the sons of members of the first half-cycle being automatically members of the second half-cycle. A man belonged to the same *gada* all his life. Until its members reached the age of 40 each *gada* in turn passed through a series of five eight-year grades which were also called *gada,* although members belonged to each of these for eight years only, and on completion of the 40-year period ceased to belong to any grade, but were still members of their set. As an example, the ten age sets recorded by Antoine d'Abbadie were these:

First half-cycle: Birmaji Malba Mudana Robale Dulo; their sons
belonged to: ↓ ↓ ↓ ↓ ↓
Second half-cycle: Aldada Horata Bifole Sabaqa Kirole

Each of these sets passed in succession through these grades:

Age		status
1 to 8 years:	Daballe	status: boys, of little account
8 to 16 years:	Folle	status: boys, of little account
16 to 24 years:	Qondala	status: "learners," more important
24 to 28 years:	Dori ⎫	status: first half of governing period
	Luba	
28 to 32 years:	Luba ⎭	status: second half of governing period
32 to 40 years:	Yuba	status: advisory only

Circumcision took place in the Luba half-period. By the time that Birmaji, for example, had reached the end of the Yuba grade, their sons, Aldada, entered the Daballe grade, and so on. The names of the *gada* sets recurred after the completion of the 80-year cycle, and this type of age set may thus be called cyclic to distinguish it from the kind in which a new name is chosen for each set as it is formed, this latter type being called linear.

The Nandi system had no progressive grades, but every male in the tribe belonged from birth to a set which was normally that next below his father's. There were seven sets, *ipinda*, with recurring names, on the principle that at any given time there is one set of warriors, two of boys and four of elders. The names of the sets and their order at three different periods were as follows:

1908		1923		1938	
Maina:	boys	Juma:	boys	Sawe:	boys
Nyongi:	{circumcision 1911–15	Maina:	{circumcision 1926–30	Juma:	{circumcision 1940–44
Kimnyike:	warriors	Nyongi:	warriors	Maina:	warriors
Kaplelach		Kimnyike		Nyongi	
Kipkoimet	}elders	Kaplelach	}elders	Kimnyike	}elders
Sawe		Kipkoimet		Kaplelach	
Juma		Sawe		Kipkoimet	

Sons of Nyongi are normally Juma, sons of Kimnyike are Maina, etc. Every 15 years the warrior set handed over its functions to the set which had been circumcised during the previous 15 years and became the junior set of elders; *i.e.*, in 1923 Kimnyike gave place to Nyongi, the senior set of elders (all its members being dead by then) disappeared as such, and its name became that of the small boys' set. Since 15 years is too long a period for a man to be an active warrior, there was an institutionalized overlap by means of which men after they had been circumcised became junior warriors, relieving senior warriors of their active duties although their set did not become officially the warrior set till the full 15-year period was completed.

The Masai did this somewhat differently. They had a system which is now apparently linear but seems formerly to have been cyclic. The men of each tribe are divided into "generations," *ol-aji*, each of which is subdivided into two age sets, *ol-poror*, the senior being called *e-murata e-tatene*, "the right-hand circumcision," and the junior *e-murata e-kedyanye*, "the left-hand circumcision." Those of the right hand are circumcised first, during a period of four years; when this is finished, the new warriors are formed into companies, *i-sirit*. About seven or eight years from the beginning of the right-hand set, the members of the left-hand set are circumcised, becoming warriors three to four years later. Thus there are two warrior sets and the overlap practised by the Nandi is not necessary. The left-hand set, however, has a shorter warrior life than the right-hand set, because both right and left become elders simultaneously. The left hand is thus considered slightly inferior to the right hand.

An example of a Bantu age-set system is that of the Isukha (Kakumega) of North Nyanza (Luhya group, Kenya). They had a linear system in which age sets, *elikhula*, were formed as required when the circumcision periods were finished, at irregular intervals ranging from two to five years, each set taking its name from some current event, such as *Intsike*, "locusts," given to a set formed in 1928 when there was an infestation of locusts.

It may be said of age sets in general that, besides being corporate, they provide a means of tribal education and training in discipline when the boys are collected in groups for initiation; that hospitality and mutual assistance are practised within the group; and that they tend to affect rules of kinship and behaviour, since there is often a great gulf between senior and junior sets. However slight may be the degree of integration of age sets into the structure of a tribal society, membership produces a bond of comradeship between age mates; and in societies where the sets are deeply integrated they influence not only social behaviour but also the political system. Among the Galla, for example, within the framework of the *gada* sets the members of the fourth grade formed the tribal government, one of them being the tribal ruler, the *Abba Boku*, "father of the staff." In the Nandi and Masai systems three age groupings, of boys, warriors and elders, were clearly distinguished and separated; and this separation ensured

readily available manpower for fighting at all times. Where integration was less, the effect was mainly on the social side, and age sets played little or no part as military or governmental factors.

BIBLIOGRAPHY.—E. E. Evans-Pritchard, *The Nuer* (1940); G. W. B. Huntingford, *The Nandi of Kenya* (1953), *The Northern Nilo-Hamites* (1953), *The Southern Nilo-Hamites* (1953), *The Galla of Ethiopia* (1955); Pamela Gulliver and P. H. Gulliver, *The Central Nilo-Hamites* (1953); J. Middleton, *Central Tribes of the North-Eastern Bantu* (1953); N. Dyson-Hudson, "The Karimojong Age System," *Ethnology*, vol. 2 (July 1963).   (G. W. B. H.)

AGESILAUS II (*c.* 444–360 B.C.), king of Sparta from 400 or 398 to 360 B.C., of the Eurypontid house, was a son of Archidamus II and succeeded his half brother Agis II after he and Lysander (*q.v.*) had persuaded the city to set Agis' son Leotychidas aside as illegitimate. Sparta was at war with Persia in Asia Minor, an aftermath of the expedition of the younger Cyrus (*q.v.*), and news of naval preparations in Phoenicia caused the dispatch of Agesilaus to Asia in 396 with Lysander, who hoped to re-establish his influence there. Imitating the legendary Agamemnon, Agesilaus sailed from Aulis in Boeotia, but the Thebans, already on bad terms with Sparta, prevented him from sacrificing there. On arrival at Ephesus he made a three months' truce with the Persian satrap Tissaphernes, during which he succeeded in shaking off Lysander's control.

Agesilaus raided Phrygia later in 396, organized a cavalry force, made a successful incursion into Lydia in spring 395 and then ravaged Phrygia again. He was unable, however, to prevent the building up of a powerful Persian fleet under the Athenian Conon, or to co-operate effectively with the Spartan navy in the south. His plan for 394 was said to be a march deep into the interior of Asia Minor, and Xenophon and others believed that he was on the brink of important conquests when he was recalled by war in Greece, though it is hard to see what he could have achieved. The Spartan navy was completely defeated by Conon at Cnidus soon after his departure. Sparta had already in 394 defeated the coalition of Thebes, Athens, Argos and Corinth, near Corinth, before Agesilaus' rapid march home, and Agesilaus defeated them again in the same year in the battle of Coronea (*q.v.*) but not decisively, and Sparta's hold in central Greece was for the time lost. He fought round Corinth in 391 and 390 and conducted a subsidiary campaign in Acarnania in 389.

In spring 386 the war of the coalition was ended by the peace of Antalcidas. Agesilaus exploited this peace to the full, using the clause that guaranteed the independence of all Greek cities to enforce the dissolution of the Boeotian league and of the union between Argos and Corinth. When the Spartan Phoebidas seized the citadel of Thebes in 382, Agesilaus supported his action, and after the liberation of Thebes in the winter of 379–378 he brought the city near starvation in two campaigns in 378 and 377. At the conference in Sparta in 371 he refused to allow the Thebans to sign the peace on behalf of all Boeotia, and this precipitated the campaign against Thebes in which the other Spartan king, Cleombrotus, was heavily defeated in the battle of Leuctra (*q.v.*). This battle altered the whole balance of power and put Sparta on the defensive. In 370 Agesilaus invaded Mantinean territory in an attempt to restore Spartan prestige, but later in the year had to defend Sparta itself against Epaminondas. Some time afterward he went abroad to gain money for the war by assisting the rebellious Persian satrap Ariobarzanes. In 362 he again rescued Sparta from Epaminondas, but he took no part in the subsequent battle of Mantinea. In 361 he was abroad again, serving Zedhor (Tachos), king of Egypt, in his invasion of Phoenicia and Syria. During the campaign a revolt broke out in Egypt, and Agesilaus, who had already quarreled with Zedhor, eventually went over to his rival Nekhtharheb (Nectanebo II) whom he helped to defeat a further rival. On his way home from Egypt he died, at Cyrene, at the age of 84.

Agesilaus was an adroit politician and a brave commander with great tactical skill. He embodied the opportunist spirit shown by Sparta in the 4th century. The panegyric of him by Xenophon (*q.v.*) set the tone for later writers but other contemporaries were sometimes critical, arguing that it was his hatred of Thebes that led, through the battle of Leuctra, to the loss of Spartan supremacy in Greece.

See Xenophon, *Agesilaus;* Plutarch, *Life of Agesilaus.*   (A. As.)

AGGEUS, PROPHECY OF: *see* HAGGAI, BOOK OF.

AGGLOMERATE is a term generally applied to coarse fragmental rock produced by explosive volcanic action. Although similar in appearance to conglomerates, which are produced by sedimentary processes (*see* CONGLOMERATE), the agglomerates consist almost wholly of angular to subrounded fragments of lava in a poorly sorted tuffaceous matrix or rock composed of volcanic dust or ash. Agglomerates are closely associated with lava flows.

The term is restricted by some to rocks composed of volcanic bombs—gobs of lava at least partly plastic when erupted—and the term volcanic breccia is reserved for those fragmental accumulations which were erupted in a solid condition.

See also BRECCIA; VOLCANO.   (F. J. P.)

AGGLUTINATION, in philology, is the method by which two significant words or roots are joined together in a single word to express a combination of the two meanings each of which retains its force (Lat. *ad* and *glutinare,* literally "to fasten together with glue"). This juxtaposition or conjoining of roots is characteristic of languages such as the Turkish and Japanese, which are therefore known as agglutinative, as opposed to others, known generically as inflectional, or fusional, in which differences of termination or combinations in which all separate identity disappears are predominant. *See* LANGUAGE: *Language Typology.*

AGGLUTININ is a typical antibody that occurs in the serums of immunized and normal human beings and animals. When added to uniform suspensions of particles containing specific antigens on the surface, with which agglutinins react, such as bacteria, protozoa and red cells, the suspended objects adhere to each other, form clumps, fall to the bottom and leave the suspending diluent clear. This phenomenon of agglutination is a typical antigen-antibody reaction, is highly specific, is reversible and involves small reacting groups on the surface of each. An agglutinin may act as a precipitin or as other antibodies under appropriate conditions.

A particular antibody is usually in greatest amount (titer) in individuals who have been immunized with the specific antigen by infection or by other active immunizing procedures. For this reason, agglutination is used as a test for the presence of agglutinins in the serum and indirectly for past or present infection or immunization with the specific antigen. Conversely, serums containing agglutinins to known antigens can be used to identify various bacteria, red cells and other particulate materials containing the specific antigen.

Isohemagglutinins that clump red cells are found in man. The four main blood groups are separated with respect to two antigens, A and B, in the red blood cells and two isohemagglutinins, anti-A and anti-B, in the serum. Thus, in man, type O has neither antigen but both agglutinins, type A has A antigen and anti-B agglutinin, type B has B antigen and anti-A agglutinin and type AB has both antigens but neither agglutinin. These substances are unique markers because they are present at birth. There are also many additional red cell antigens in man, such as the MN and Rh_o or D ones. In fact, it has been estimated that several million different blood groups could arise from various combinations of the known antigens.

The blood groups are of great importance, especially from the standpoint of human genetics and medicolegal applications, blood transfusions, and hemolytic diseases of the newborn. Blood group factors are used medicolegally in such problems as questioned parenthood and the matching of blood stains with their suspected source. The determination of the blood group of a prospective donor and his recipient is a usual preliminary before transfusion because incompatible blood cells may result in intravascular agglutination. The anemia of the newborn, erythroblastosis fetalis, is most frequently associated with an antigen designated Rh_o or D. It is an extremely serious but, fortunately, rare disease caused by antibodies produced in the mother which react with antigens in the fetus that were derived from the father.

See BLOOD: *Plasma; Red Blood Cells* (*Erythrocytes*); *Individuality of Human Blood;* IMMUNITY AND IMMUNIZATION; PARASITOLOGY: *Host-Endoparasite Relationships;* PATHOLOGY: *Immunity;* VACCINE THERAPY; TOXIN; ANTITOXIN.

BIBLIOGRAPHY.—J. E. Cushing and D. H. Campbell, *Principles of Immunology* (1957); R. R. Race and R. Sanger, *Blood Groups in Man,* 3rd ed. (1958); A. S. Wiener, *Rh-Hr Blood Types; Applications in Clinical and Legal Medicine and Anthropology* (1954).   (W. H. T.)

AGGREGATE, a term used in building and construction to designate the material with which cement, bitumen, lime, gypsum or other adhesive material is mixed to form a concrete (*q.v.*) or mortar. The most common aggregates are sand, crushed or broken stone, gravel or pebbles, broken blast-furnace slag, boiler ashes or clinkers, burned shale and burned clay. The purpose of the aggregate is to provide the finished product with volume, freedom from change in volume, resistance to wear or erosion and other desired physical properties.

Aggregates are divided into two general classes, fine aggregate and coarse aggregate. The fine aggregate is generally sand, crushed stone or crushed slag screenings; the coarse aggregate is gravel (pebbles), fragments of broken stone, slag and the other substances mentioned above. The dividing line between fine and coarse aggregate is usually a $\frac{1}{4}$-in. screen opening, sometimes a $\frac{1}{8}$-in. opening. Aggregates are mixed with the cement or binding material in proportions varying from one part of cementing material to one part of fine aggregate for a "rich" grout to one part of cement to nine or ten parts of mixed fine and coarse aggregates for a "lean" concrete. The theory upon which such mixtures are proportioned is that there shall be sufficient cementing material to coat all of the particles in the fine aggregate, and that sufficient mortar will be produced to fill all the voids in the coarse aggregate. The ideal concrete would consist of closely packed fragments of crushed stone, slag or pebbles in which all the fragments are coated with mortar, and all the voids between the coarser fragments filled with mortar. Under actual conditions in construction work there is practically always an excess of mortar.

Preparation of aggregate depends upon the requirements of the job. Specifications usually include cleanliness (with a maximum set on extraneous impurities), allowable percentages of the various sizes of aggregate components, and soundness (*e.g.,* tests for freezing, thawing and mineralogical composition). After the raw materials are mined, they are processed into aggregate by washing, screening, crushing, grading and mixing. Fine aggregate often is graded and mixed hydraulically. For the strongest mortar or concrete, fine aggregate requires a gradual variation in material size from about 50 mesh (50 openings per linear inch) to $\frac{1}{4}$-in. mesh. For coarse aggregate, any hard, tough, durable material ranging in size from $\frac{1}{4}$ in. to $3\frac{1}{2}$ in. or more may be used.

It was long the custom to refer to mineral aggregates as "inert." It is now recognized that certain silica or silicate aggregates react chemically with the alkalies in portland cement and cause ultimate disintegration of concrete. Hence, chemical as well as physical tests are now considered essential for most aggregates that have not proved their stability by experience.

See American Society for Testing Materials, *Standards on Mineral Aggregates and Concrete* (1958).   (N. C. R.; X.)

AGGREGATES, THEORY OF: *see* SET THEORY (THEORY OF AGGREGATES).

AGGREGATION, in physics, a collective term for the forms or states in which matter exists. Three primary states of aggregation are recognized—gaseous, liquid and solid. Generally, if a solid is heated to a certain temperature, it melts or fuses, assuming the liquid condition (*see* HEAT: *Change of State*); if the heating is continued the liquid boils and becomes a vapour (*see* VAPORIZATION: *One-Component Systems*). On the other hand, if a gas is sufficiently cooled and compressed, it liquefies; this transition is treated theoretically in the article LOW-TEMPERATURE PHYSICS.

In a more technical sense the term molecular aggregation, a clustering together of molecules into groups, is used antithetically to the term molecular dissociation, the breaking up of molecular groups.   (H. B. LM.)

AGGRESSION refers in a psychological sense to any manifestation of a self-assertive disposition, in a political sense to any manifestation of an expansive policy, in a military sense to an unprovoked military attack and in a legal sense to the use of armed force by a government in violation of an obligation under international law or treaty. In the last sense, the term has appeared in numerous treaties and official declarations since World War I, including the League of Nations covenant (art. 10) and the United Nations charter (art. 39). The acceptance by most states of obligations not to "resort to war" (covenant, art. 12), not to use nonpacific means for the settlement of disputes (Kellogg-Briand pact, art. 2), and to "refrain in their international relations from the threat or use of force" (UN charter, art. 2, par. 4) has often made it necessary for international organs to consider the problem of aggression in the hostilities which have occurred after World War I. In such cases the League of Nations and the United Nations have usually followed the procedure of ordering a "cease fire" ("provisional measures") and have considered a government an aggressor only if it failed to observe that order.

Such cease-fire orders ended the hostilities between Turkey and Iraq in 1925, Greece and Bulgaria in 1925, Peru and Colombia in 1933 (Leticia Trapezium), Greece and its neighbours in 1947, the Netherlands and Indonesia in 1947, India and Pakistan in 1948 (Kashmir), Israel and its neighbours in 1949 and Israel, Great Britain and France against Egypt in 1956. None of these states was at the time declared an aggressor. On the other hand, Japan was found to be an aggressor in Manchuria in 1933, Paraguay in the Chaco area in 1935, North Korea and the People's Republic of China in Korea in 1950 and 1951, and the Soviet Union in Hungary in 1956 because they refused to observe cease-fire orders. The aggressions of Italy in Ethiopia in 1935 and of the Soviet Union in Finland in 1939 were so flagrant that aggression was found without cease-fire orders. In Italy's attack on Corfu (1923), the Italian and German interventions in the Spanish civil war (1936) and axis attacks after 1938, cease-fire orders were not given for political reasons, but a commission of jurists implied that Italy was an aggressor in Corfu and the axis aggressions were established by general recognition and the post-World War II war crimes trials.

International organs have usually been able to stop hostilities or to determine the aggressor but they have often failed to frustrate the success of the aggressor, at least for a considerable period. Economic sanctions have proved inadequate and military sanctions have not been undertaken for they might widen local hostilities into general war unless it appeared that overwhelming force could be collected as in the case of Korea. Eventually, however, Japanese aggressions in Manchuria, Italian in Corfu and Ethiopia, Russian in Finland, and axis aggressions in World War II failed.

For the purpose of reparation or punishment after hostilities, aggression has been defined as any use of armed force in international relations not justified by defensive necessity, international authority or consent of the state in whose territory force has been used. This conception was applied by the Nuremberg and other war crimes tribunals in dealing with the indictment of certain axis leaders for initiating aggressive war and was accepted by the United Nations International Law commission in its draft code of "Offenses against the peace and security of mankind." This code included among acts of aggression "the employment by the authorities of a state of armed forces against another state for any purpose other than national or collective self-defense or in pursuance of a decision or a recommendation of a competent organ of the United Nations."

The United Nations general assembly has recognized the need for a definition of aggression which would command universal acceptance, but continuous efforts have failed to produce such a definition largely because of the desire of some states to include "indirect aggression" such as subversion, infiltration, hostile propaganda and other acts of psychological or political aggression. The purpose of a definition of aggression is, however, to designate the circumstances which justify military action in self-defense or as an international sanction. That such action is permissible only in response to an illegal use of armed force has been affirmed by practice and by art. 42 and 51 of the charter. *See also* BELLIGERENCY; CONQUEST; LEAGUE OF NATIONS; PEACE, INTERNATIONAL; UNITED NATIONS; WAR; WAR CRIMES.

BIBLIOGRAPHY.—Q. Wright, "The Concept of Aggression in International Law," *Amer. J. Int. Law,* vol. xxix, p. 373 (1935), "The Prevention of Aggression," *Amer. J. Int. Law,* vol. l, p. 514 (1956); Harvard Research in International Law, "Draft Convention on Rights and Duties of States in Case of Aggression," Philip Jessup (ed.), *Amer. J. Int. Law,* supp., vol. xxxiii, p. 829 ff. (1939). (Q. W.)

AGHLABIDS (BANU 'L-AGHLAB), an Arab dynasty which ruled Ifriqiya (Tunisia and eastern Algeria) from A.D. 800 to 909, nominally subject to the Abbasid caliphs of Baghdad but in fact independent. Their capital city was Kairouan. The most interesting of the 11 Aghlabid amirs were the energetic and cultured Ibrahim ibn al-Aghlab (ruled 800–812), founder of al-Abbasiyya (2 mi. S. of Kairouan), who received an embassy from Charlemagne; Ziyadatallah I (817–838), who broke the rebellion of the Arab soldiery and sent it to conquer Sicily; Abu Ibrahim Ahmad (856–863), who commissioned many public works; the neurotic Ibrahim II (875–902), founder of Raqqada; and the depraved Ziyadatallah III (903–909), whose inability to defend his territory against the Kutama Berber tribe of Kabylia led to the accession of the Fatimids (*see* FATIMIDS).

During the 9th century the brilliant Kairouan civilization was evolved. Thanks to Sahnun and his disciples Malikism became the religion of the people, while Mu'tazilism and Hanafism were predominant at court and Kharijism in the south; philosophy and the exact sciences were studied in a sort of university, the Bayt al-Hikma ("House of Wisdom"). The Aghlabid amirs maintained a splendid court and are frequently reproached by historians for their oppressive taxes. Their magnificent buildings in addition to al-Abbasiyya and Raqqada, include the mosques of Kairouan, Tunis and Sfax and the *ribats* (hermitages) of Sousse and Monastir; their public works for the conservation and distribution of water contributed to the prosperity of a country which was on the whole peaceful. Their fleet was supreme in the central Mediterranean.

See M. Vonderheyden, *La Berberie orientale . . .* (1927); G. Marçais, "Aghlabids," *Encyclopaedia of Islam,* vol. i, 2nd ed. (1954–60). (H. R. I.)

AGIN-BURYAT NATIONAL OKRUG (AGINSKIY BURYAT NATSIONALNYY OKRUG) lies in Chita *oblast* of the Russian Soviet Federated Socialist Republic, U.S.S.R., on the left bank of the lower Onon, a headwater of the Amur, with the tributary valley of the Aga as its main axis. The western part of the okrug (district) consists of hilly country of the Onon and Daurski ranges. The area has a relatively mild climate for central Siberia, with a low rainfall (Chita has 12.3 in. a year). As a result the vegetation is mostly of a steppe type in the lower east, with forests on the higher hill slopes of the west. The population of 49,109 (1959) consists largely of Buryats, who form an exclave of the larger Buryat group living east and south of Lake Baikal. There are no towns in the district, the administrative centre being the village of Aginskoye. The economy is essentially pastoral and large herds of cattle and sheep are kept. The okrug and neighbouring parts of Chita *oblast* form the major stock-rearing region of the eastern U.S.S.R. The thin snow cover on the steppe pastures allows grazing all year. Spring wheat and oats are the main crops. Tin and gold are found in the area but the chief mining centres lie just outside the okrug borders. The former Chinese Eastern railway from Chita to Harbin crosses the eastern part of the district, while the west is traversed by the highway from Chita to Choybalsan in Mongolia. (R. A. F.)

AGINCOURT, BATTLE OF (Oct. 25, 1415), the victory of a small English army led by King Henry V over a French force commanded by Charles d'Albret, constable of France, during the Hundred Years' War. It was fought near the village of Agincourt (Azincourt in the modern French *département* of Pas-de-Calais). After capturing Harfleur in Normandy (Sept. 1415), Henry had decided to return to England via Calais but on Oct. 24 he found the French blocking his line of advance. Although his men had marched for 18 days and were tired and hungry, Henry saw that he had to fight. At dawn on St. Crispin's day (Friday, Oct. 25) the armies prepared for battle. The French had unwisely chosen a site with a narrow frontage, being enclosed on two sides by the woods of Agincourt and Tramecourt and only about 1,000 yd. wide. Thus it became impossible to make effective use of an army which outnumbered the English by at least three to one. Three French divisions, the first two dismounted, were drawn up one behind another. Henry had only 800–900 men-at-arms and 3,000–5,000 archers whom he arrayed in dismounted line between the southern ends of the woods. On each flank was a mass of archers set forward in wings and projecting wedges of archers also linked three groups of men-at-arms. After waiting for a French attack, Henry led his men forward and archery shots from long range at last provoked the French to action. Small cavalry charges upon the English wings ended in confusion and the re-treating horsemen broke through the French van as it moved for-ward. Sodden plowed land and heavy armour also hampered the French, who were bunched so tightly that some could barely raise their lances. Despite heavy archery shooting the French advanced bravely and at the first clash the English line yielded, only to recover quickly. Then Henry signaled his archers to attack with ax and sword. This was the decisive moment of the battle, for the lightly armed bowmen wrought havoc upon the French. Within three hours the van and second line had been routed, and most of the rear had fled. The dead lay in heaps and there were many prisoners, some of whom were later killed when a fresh attack appeared imminent. The French losses were commonly believed to amount to about 10,000 dead. Contemporary estimates of Eng-lish losses range from 14 to 1,600, but clearly they were relatively light. At Agincourt the English, brilliantly led by their king, snatched victory from what had appeared a desperate situation, but the incoherent tactics of the French greatly influenced the re-sult. Although the battle brought Henry no immediate territorial gains, this display of his military ability and the resultant de-moralization of the French, who were already politically divided, contributed to his later successes.

See Sir Nicholas Harris Nicolas, *Battle of Agincourt*, 2nd ed. (1832); J. H. Wylie, *The Reign of Henry the Fifth*, vol. ii (1919).

(J. W. Se.)

AGING, a part of living, involves growth and development as well as senescence or deterioration. As a complex biological process, which begins with conception, accompanies growth and often accelerates as growth ceases, its most obvious signs are a continuing reduction of the capacity of self-maintenance and repair of cells to the point at which death occurs. See GERONTOLOGY AND GERIATRICS; GROWTH; DEATH (BIOLOGICAL).

AGIO, a term used in commerce in three connections.

1. The variations from fixed pars or rates of exchange in the currencies of different countries. For example, in most gold-standard countries, the standard coin is kept up to a uniform point of fineness and so bears a constant relation to coins of other coun-tries in a similar condition. This is what is known as the mint par of exchange. The balance of trade between the various coun-tries is the factor determining the rate of exchange. Should the balance of trade be against one country, that country must remit money as payment for the indebtedness. Because of the expense of shipping gold there will be a demand for paper money for which it will be necessary to pay a premium, called the agio.

2. The term is also used to denote the difference in exchange between two currencies in the same country. Where silver coinage is the legal tender, agio is sometimes allowed for payment in the more convenient form of gold. Where the paper currency of a country is reduced below the bullion which it professes to repre-sent, an agio is payable on the appreciated currency.

3. Lastly, in some states the coinage is so debased because of the wear of circulation that the real value is greatly reduced below the nominal value. Suppose this reduction amounts to 5%. If 100 units of money are offered as payment of a debt in the coun-try where the units are current at their nominal value, they will be received as just payment. If they are offered as payment of the same amount of debt in a foreign country, they will be received only at their intrinsic value of 95 units, the additional 5 units con-stituting the agio. When a country keeps its coinage up to a standard value no agio is required. (F. Gr.)

AGIS, the name of four Spartan kings, the first of the Agiad family, the rest of the Eurypontid house.

AGIS I was traditionally the son of Eurysthenes (one of the legendary twin founders of Sparta). The Agiad line of kings was named after him, which may indicate that unlike Eurysthenes, he was an historical figure. Ephorus, writing in the 4th century B.C. attributes to him the capture of the city of Helos in Laconia and the reduction of the inhabitants to helots (*q.v.*).

AGIS II (d. 400 or 398 B.C.), son of Archidamus II, succeeded his father probably in 427 B.C. From 426 to his death he com-manded all operations of the regular army. In 418, when the peace of Nicias (see PELOPONNESIAN WAR) had produced much disaffection in the Peloponnese, he invaded the Argolid and cut the Argive army off from their city while his allies threatened their rear, but then made a truce and withdrew. His reason is not clear—the timing of the operation perhaps went wrong—but each side believed that it had the other at its mercy and was indignant with its leaders, and Agis only escaped heavy penalties by promis-ing better performance. A few weeks later he defeated the Argive alliance at Mantinea and restored Spartan prestige.

In 413, when war with Athens was formally resumed, Agis led the force which thereafter occupied Decelea in Attica, and Thu-cydides stresses the influence that he exerted from there. Though the occupation caused great hardship to Athens, it was Lysander's naval victory that ended the war in 404. Agis took no part in the subsequent settlement at Athens. In 402 (or 400) war broke out with Elis, and by ravaging the countryside Agis brought Elis to surrender in spring 400 (or 398). He fell ill on the way home from dedicating spoils at Delphi and died soon after.

AGIS III (d. 331 B.C.), succeeded his father Archidamus III in 338. After Alexander the Great (*q.v.*) had embarked on his cam-paigns in Asia Minor, Agis prepared to profit by his absence from Greece by raising the Greek cities against the Macedonians. With Persian money and 8,000 Greek mercenaries who had escaped from the battle of Issus (333) he tried to hold Crete against Alexander. In 331 he raised a coalition in the Peloponnese and laid siege to Megalopolis. Alexander's regent Antipater patched up peace with the Thracians with whom he was engaged, marched south and won a hard-fought battle near Megalopolis (331). Agis was killed and Spartan resistance was broken.

AGIS IV (d. 241 B.C.), succeeded his father Eudamidas II in 244 when he was 19 years old. Land and wealth were then very unequally distributed in Sparta, many estates were mortgaged and the poor heavily burdened with debt. The system of common meals and military training had lapsed, and there were only 700 full citizens. Tradition about the Lycurgan system (see LYCUR-GUS) helped to shape Agis' scheme of reform, which included can-cellation of debts; the division of the Spartan homeland into 4,500 lots for citizens, their number to be made up with perioeci (*q.v.*) and foreigners; the distribution of 15,000 lots to the remaining perioeci; and the restoration of the Lycurgan discipline.

Agis was supported by his wealthy mother and grandmother, who surrendered their property; by his uncle Agesilaus, whose estates were much encumbered; and by Lysander, ephor in 243, who put his proposals before the council. The wealthy, led by the other king, Leonidas II, defeated them by a bare majority, whereupon Leonidas was deposed in favour of his son-in-law Cleombrotus. When the ephors of 242 tried to reverse this, they were replaced by a board headed by Agesilaus.

Agesilaus now persuaded Agis to carry out the cancella-tion of debts first and then delayed the redistribution of land. Aratus (*q.v.*) of Sicyon, temporarily Sparta's ally, asked (241) for help against the Aetolians, and Agis went to the Isthmus of Cor-inth with an army, but Aratus declined battle. Agis returned to find that his supporters were disillusioned by the delay of his reforms and discontented under Agesilaus' rule, and that Leonidas had returned to power, supported by mercenaries. Agis took sanctuary rather than engage in war with Leonidas, but was en-ticed out, given a form of trial and executed with his mother and grandmother.

Such radical reform was almost equally unwelcome to the Macedonians and to the Achaean league, the two major powers struggling for domination in Greece; it was therefore unlikely to succeed by peaceful means. Agis' opponents were less scrupulous than he (who twice spared Leonidas' life), and even his supporter

Agesilaus was merely exploiting him. (A. As.)

AGLAUROS (AGRAULOS), in Greek mythology a daughter of Cecrops, was killed with her sisters by the infant Erichthonius (*see* ERECHTHEUS). But Ovid relates that Aglauros was turned to stone by Mercury in retribution for her attempt to frustrate his abduction of Herse.

Aglauros and her sisters were originally, apparently, fertility deities. She had a sanctuary on the Acropolis in which young men of military age swore an oath to her as well as to Zeus, Ares and minor deities. The honour may stem from yet another legend, that Aglauros had sacrificed herself for the city during a protracted war. (T. V. B.)

AGNANO (LAGO DI AGNANO), a lake that formerly occupied an extinct volcanic crater and was drained in 1870. The lake bed, in the volcanic region 6 mi. W. of Naples, Italy, was known to the Greeks and Romans for its thermal baths, but its present name is assumed to be of Norman origin. There are 75 springs and an active *solfatara*. The large thermal establishment utilizes mineral waters, gushing forth at various temperatures. (G. KH.)

AGNELLI, GIOVANNI (1866–1945), founder with others, in 1899, of the Fiat (Fabbrica Italiana Automobili Torino) company of Italy and the chairman and managing director almost from its inception, was born in Villar Perosa, Piedmont, on Aug. 13, 1866. He entered the military academy in 1884 and became a cavalry officer in 1886. Agnelli was largely responsible for establishing the ball- and roller-bearing industry in Italy. In 1906 he founded the Officine di Villar Perosa company (RIV bearings) and in 1907 he was made a Knight of Labour. He was a senator from 1923. Before and during World War II, Agnelli was one of the chief mobilizers of Italian industry for war. He personally survived the fall of the Mussolini government although he lost his factories. He was responsible for many philanthropic works. Agnelli died at Turin on Dec. 16. 1945. (St. J. C. N.)

AGNES, SAINT, one of the most celebrated Roman martyrs, who suffered possibly at the beginning of the 4th century; her epitaph, written by Pope Damasus I (d. 384), is extant. According to the tradition, of uncertain value, Agnes was a girl of about 13 years old who refused a good marriage for the sake of religious virginity and in punishment was exposed in a brothel. There she suffered no harm and so was put to death by being either beheaded or stabbed in the throat. She is mentioned in the canon of the Roman mass and her name figures in the calendar of the Book of Common Prayer. Her feast is kept on Jan. 21; on that day two lambs (Lat. *agnus*) are blessed in the church of Sta. Agnese in Rome and from their wool are made the pallia sent by the pope to archbishops as tokens of jurisdiction. Agnes is a patron saint of girls, and Keats's poem "Eve of St. Agnes" refers to a superstition connected with this aspect of her cult.

See H. Thurston and D. Attwater (eds.), *Butler's Lives of the Saints,* vol. i, pp. 133–137 (1956). (D. AR.)

AGNES OF MERAN (d. 1201), queen of France, was the daughter of Bertold IV, duke of Meran in Tirol. In June 1196, despite Pope Celestine III's protest, she was married to Philip II, king of France, who had repudiated Ingeborg of Denmark in 1193. Pope Innocent III, however, protested more forcefully in 1198 and in 1200 put France under an interdict, whereupon Philip pretended to agree to a separation from Agnes. In fact he did not turn her away and Ingeborg was imprisoned. Agnes died at Poissy in Aug. 1201. Innocent legitimized her children by Philip; viz., Marie (*c.* 1198–1238), later countess of Namur; and Philippe Hurepel (1200–34).

See Duc de Lévis-Mirepoix, *Les Trois Femmes de Philippe-Auguste* (1947); E. Rossier, *Sur les degrés du trône* (1940).

AGNESI, MARIA GAETANA (1718–1799), Italian mathematician and philosopher, was born on May 16, 1718, in Milan, where her father was professor of mathematics. She was an extremely precocious child. At an early age she mastered Latin, Greek, Hebrew and several modern languages; when she was only nine years old her Latin discourse in defense of higher education for women was printed. In 1738 appeared her *Propositiones philosophicae,* a series of essays on philosophy and natural science, based upon discussions before a scientific group meeting in her father's house. Her best-known work, *Instituzioni analitiche ad uso*

della gioventù italiana, dedicated to the empress Maria Theresa, was published in 1748. It enjoyed great popularity and was translated into several languages (Eng. trans. by John Colson, 1801). In this text is found a discussion of the Agnesi curve, a cubic, the *versiera* or versed sine curve, which, through a misunderstanding, became known as the Witch of Agnesi in English (*see* CURVES, SPECIAL).

In 1749 Agnesi was appointed honorary lecturer at the University of Bologna by Pope Benedict XIV. She was always deeply religious, and after the death of her father in 1752 devoted herself almost exclusively to charitable work and religious studies. In 1771 she was appointed director of the Pio Albergo Trivulzio, a charitable institution; there she died on Jan. 9, 1799.

Her sister, known as MARIA TERESA D'AGNESI-PINOTTINI (1720–1795), was an amateur composer of operas and instrumental works.

See A. F. Frisi, *Elogio storico di Domina Maria Gaetana Agnesi milanese* (1799); L. Anzoletti, *Maria Gaetana Agnesi* (1900). (O. OE.)

AGNI, the fire god of the Hindus, second only to Indra in the Vedic mythology of India. He is invoked as "priest of sacrifice" in the first verse of the Rigveda and, since he acts as messenger between gods and men, sacrifices to him are upborne to the deities. On earth his parents are the two sticks of the fire drill and every day he is reborn an immortal, living among men and supreme director of religious rites and duties. His form is, however, threefold—fire on earth, lightning and the sun—and in art he is depicted as ruddy, with two faces, one beneficent and one malignant, and three-legged (as in the swastika, with seven arms). Later he was identified with Rudra (*q.v.*). In modern India he has no professed sect but is invoked in many ceremonies, especially by Agnihotri Brahmans. *See* also HINDUISM.

AGNI. The Agni (Anyi) belong linguistically and culturally to the Akan (*q.v.*) peoples of the Kwa subfamily of the Nigritic (Western Sudan) stock. They live in southwestern Ghana and the Ivory Coast, between the Ashanti and the Baule. The Agni embrace the Arichin, Asaye, Bettie, Bini, Bonai, Brisa, Dadia, Kumwe, Moro, Ndeye, Safudi, Sanwi and Sika tribes. They number about 100,000. They live largely in dispersed homesteads, practising shifting hoe cultivation and fallowing. Yams, bananas and taro are among the staple crops. Inheritance, succession and political allegiance are determined by matrilineal descent though, like other Akan peoples, they recognize partially exogamous patrilineages.

See also AFRICA: *Ethnography* (*Anthropology*): *West Africa.* (K. A. BU.)

AGNOETAE (THEMISTIANS) (Gr. *agnoeō,* "be ignorant of"), a small monophysite group of eastern Christians of the 6th century who, contrary to the prevailing view, maintained that Christ as man was ignorant of many things (Mark xiii, 32; Luke ii, 52); founded by Themistius, a deacon of Alexandria. The doctrine was condemned by Pope Gregory the Great. *See* MONOPHYSITES.

(V. C. S.)

AGNOLO, BACCIO D' (BARTOLOMEO D'AGNOLO BAGLIONI) (1462–1543), Florentine wood carver, sculptor and architect, exerted an important influence on the Renaissance architecture of Florence. Born on May 15, 1462, he started as a wood carver, and between 1491 and 1502 did much of the decorative carving in the church of Sta. Maria Novella and the Palazzo Vecchio in Florence. At the beginning of the 16th century he was engaged with Il Cronaca in restoring the Palazzo Vecchio, and in 1506 he was commissioned to complete the drum of the cupola of the metropolitan church of Sta. Maria del Fiore. The latter work, however, was interrupted on account of adverse criticisms from Michelangelo, and it remained unexecuted. Baccio d'Agnolo also planned the Villa Borghese and the Bartolini palace, with other fine palaces and villas. The Bartolini palace was among the first houses to be given frontispieces of columns to the door and windows, previously confined to churches, and he was ridiculed by the Florentines for this novelty. He designed the campanile of the church of S. Spirito. His studio was the resort of the most celebrated artists of the day, Michelangelo, Sansovino, the brothers Sangallo and the young Raphael. He died March 6, 1543, in Florence, leaving three sons, all architects, the best known being Giuliano.

AGNON, SAMUEL JOSEPH (formerly SHMUEL YOSEPH CZACZKES) (1888–), foremost 20th-century Hebrew novelist and short-story writer, who shared in 1966 the Nobel Prize for Literature with Nelly Sachs, was born on July 17, 1888, in Buczacz, eastern Galicia, the setting of many of his stories. These form a saga of the decline of Galician Jewry from the golden age of Hasidism (1750–1850)—theme of *Hakhnasat kallah* (1922; Eng. trans. *The Bridal Canopy*, 1937)—to the apocalyptic ruin after World War I depicted in *Oreah natah lalun* (1945; Eng. trans. *A Wayfarer in the Night*, 1966). Almost all Agnon's other stories are set in Palestine, where he lived from 1908 to 1913 and to which, after some years in Germany, he returned in 1924. They deal with the replacement of the religious world of the "Old Settlement" by the secular and scientific society of European Zionist settlers, which Agnon faced at first with deep misgivings (expressed in situations of Kafkaesque failure) but later with greater sympathy. The treatment varies from the straight narrative of his greatest novel, *Temol shilshom* ("Yesterday and the Day Before Yesterday," 1945), the epic of early pioneer immigrants, to the nightmares of *Sefer ha-maasim* ("The Book of Deeds") and the satire of *Sefer ha-medinah* ("The Book of the State"). An anthologist of hasidic and other religious thought (as in the collection *Yamim Noraim*, 1938; *Days of Awe*, 1948), Agnon nearly always uses the simple yet allusive 18th-century hasidic style. This, different from contemporary Hebrew, and difficult to translate, has been adopted by several younger Israeli-born novelists.

BIBLIOGRAPHY.—Collected writings (in Hebrew), 12 vol. (1956–); Eng. trans.: *In the Heart of the Seas* (1948), *Tehilla and Other Israeli Tales* (1956), *Two Tales* (1966). See also D. Sadan, *Al S. J. Agnon* (1959); article by Misha Loubish, in the *Jewish Quarterly*, winter number (1966). (C. RN.)

AGNOSTICISM is, strictly speaking, the doctrine that man cannot know the existence of anything beyond the phenomena of his experience. The doctrine has been applied especially to the three unresolved antinomies defined by Kant's *Critique of Pure Reason*—God, freedom and immortality (*see* KANT, IMMANUEL). From this application the term has come to be equated in popular parlance with skepticism (*q.v.*) about religious questions in general, and in particular with the rejection of traditional Christian beliefs under the impact of modern scientific thought. Disregarding the nice distinctions developed by philosophers and theologians, many persons use such terms as agnostic, atheist, infidel, deist and skeptic quite indiscriminately. Agnosticism both as a term and as a philosophical position gained currency through its espousal by Thomas Huxley, who seems to have coined the word agnostic in 1869 to designate one who repudiated traditional Judaeo-Christian theism and yet disclaimed doctrinaire atheism, transcending both in order to leave such questions as the existence of God in abeyance. Huxley himself defined agnosticism as the principle

... that it is wrong for a man to say that he is certain of the objective truth of any proposition unless he can produce evidence which logically justifies that certainty. This is what Agnosticism asserts; and, in my opinion, it is all that is essential to Agnosticism. That which Agnostics deny and repudiate, as immoral, is the contrary doctrine, that there are propositions which men ought to believe, without logically satisfactory evidence; and that reprobation ought to attach to the profession of disbelief in such inadequately supported propositions (*Science and Christian Tradition*, p. 310, 1900).

From this definition and from the way the word has been used in ordinary speech it is evident that there are two related but nevertheless distinct viewpoints suggested by the term agnosticism. It may mean no more than the suspension of judgment on ultimate questions because not all the evidence has come in or because not all the evidence can ever come in. In this sense even the New Testament's definition of faith as "the assurance of things hoped for, the conviction of things not seen" might conceivably be called agnostic in its tenor, for it asserts that the final grounds of man's belief lie beyond the realm of evidence and experience. As doubt has been a path to faith in the thought of men such as St. Augustine, Pascal and Kierkegaard, so agnosticism in this sense belongs to the biblical interpretation of man's relation to God.

But the setting of Huxley's words quoted above makes clear that this very biblical interpretation of man's relation to God was the intended polemic target of agnosticism. The suspension of judg-

ment on ultimate questions for which it called was thought to invalidate Christian beliefs about "things hoped for" and "things not seen." Indeed, Huxley's essay on "Agnosticism and Christianity" was actually a discussion of such questions as the Mosaic authorship of the Pentateuch, the credibility of biblical miracle stories and the superiority of the ethic of Jesus. The inventor of the word agnosticism was himself responsible for its nontechnical use as a designation for one of the combatants in the 19th-century "warfare of science with theology."

Huxley's role in the struggle over the teachings of Charles Darwin helped to establish this connotation as the primary one in the definition of agnosticism. When such prominent defenders of the Darwinian hypothesis as Clarence Darrow likewise labeled themselves as agnostics, the writers of popular apologetic pamphlets found it easy to equate agnosticism with hostility to conventional Christian tenets. Because of the opprobrium attaching to it, the term agnosticism had lost favour by the second half of the 20th century. Its place was taken by the older term skepticism, but the field of the battle had likewise been shifted. Not the question of Christian evidences but the problem of evidence and verification as such had become the central issue among philosophers. Thus logical positivism (*q.v.*), which bore certain resemblances to agnosticism in its refusal to speculate about ultimate and unknowable questions, also went beyond the agnosticism of Huxley.

See T. H. Huxley, *Science and Christian Tradition* (1900); J. Ward, *Naturalism and Agnosticism,* Gifford Lectures for 1896–98 (1899). (J. J. PN.)

AGNUS DEI, "Lamb of God," a designation of Jesus Christ in Christian liturgical usage. It is based upon the saying of John the Baptist quoted in John i, 29: "Behold, the Lamb of God, who takes away the sin of the world!" In the Roman Catholic liturgy of the Mass (*q.v.*) the Agnus Dei is employed in the following text: "Lamb of God, who takest away the sin of the world, have mercy upon us! Lamb of God, who takest away the sin of the world, have mercy upon us! Lamb of God, who takest away the sin of the world, grant us peace!" Coming as it does between the Lord's Prayer and the communion, the Agnus Dei sounds the themes of sacrifice and of adoration. Thus it unites the sacrifice of the Mass to the sacrifice of Christ on the cross as the Lamb of God, and calls to mind the sacrifice of the lamb in the cultus of the Old Testament. Both Anglican and Lutheran liturgies have retained the Agnus Dei in their eucharistic rites. It appears also as a part of many of the litanies. The name Agnus Dei is applied as well to figures of Christ as the Lamb of God, especially to waxen disks impressed with this figure and blessed by the pope. (J. J. PN.)

AGOBARD, SAINT (*c.* 769–840), Frankish prelate active in ecclesiastical and political affairs under the emperor Louis I the Pious, became archbishop of Lyons in 816, in succession to Leidrad, having been a suffragan bishop in the archdiocese since 804. While he wrote against the adoptionist heresy of Felix of Urgel (who was confined at Lyons from 800 to 818), Agobard's zeal for reform led him to attack trial by ordeal and image worship, and his critical spirit went so far as to deny the verbal inspiration of the Bible and to object to the invocation of the saints.

Agobard was in frequent conflict with the secular power from 821, when he and Nibridius, bishop of Narbonne, ignoring the lay overlord, supervised the election of an abbot of Aniane in Languedoc. His struggle to reclaim ecclesiastical lands in accordance with the diet of Attigny (822) was ineffective, as were his protests against imperial protection of the Jewish communities (827). Having written a public justification of the deposition of Louis the Pious in 833, Agobard lost his see when Louis was restored (835). He retired to Italy until 838, when he was reinstated. He died in Saintonge on June 6, 840. Agobard is revered as a saint in Lyons, although his canonization is not recorded. His works are printed by J. P. Migne in *Patrologia latina*, vol. 104 (1851).

See A. Bressolles, *Saint Agobard évêque de Lyon* (1949); Allen Cabaniss, *Agobard of Lyons, Churchman and Critic* (1953).

AGONOTHETES, in ancient Greece, the president or superintendent of the sacred games. At first the person who instituted the games and defrayed the expenses was the Agonothetes. In the public games, however, such as the Olympic and Pythian, these superintendents represented different states, or were chosen from the people in whose country the games were celebrated; thus at the Panathenaea at Athens ten *athlothetai* were elected for four years to superintend the various contests. They were variously called "regulators," "arbitrators," "judges of contests," "stewards of the games" (at Athens), "rod-bearers" (from the rod or sceptre emblematic of their authority), but their functions were generally the same.

AGORA, a word found in Homer's works meaning both assembly of the people and meeting place and in later writings meaning also market place, was the name given by the classical Greeks to what they themselves regarded as a typical feature of Greek life: the daily scene of their religious, political, judicial, social and commercial activity. The agora was an open space, either in the middle of the city or near the harbour, which was surrounded by public buildings (such as the council house or *bouleuterion*) and by temples. Colonnades, or stoas, often served to enclose the space, and statues, altars, trees and fountains adorned it. There might be shops inside the colonnades. Earlier stages in the evolution of the agora have been sought in the east and, with better results, in Minoan Crete (for instance at Ayia Triada) and in Mycenaean Greece (for instance at Tiryns).

In the 5th and 4th centuries B.C. two types of agora competed with each other. Pausanias, writing in the 2nd century A.D., calls one archaic and the other Ionic. He mentions the agora of Elis (built after 470 B.C.) as an example of the archaic type in which colonnades and other buildings were not co-ordinated. The general impression was one of disorder. The agora of Athens (*q.v.*) was one of this type even when it was rebuilt after the Persian wars. The Ionic type was more symmetrical, often combining colonnades to form either three sides of a rectangle or a regular square; Miletus, Priene and Magnesia ad Maeandrum, cities in Asia Minor, provide early examples. This type prevailed and was further developed in Hellenistic and Roman times. The general trend was to isolate the agora from the rest of the town. In this later period the agora influenced the development of the Roman forum and was in turn influenced by it.

Even in classical times the agora did not always remain the place for popular assemblies. In Athens the ecclesia, or assembly, was moved to the Pnyx (a hill to the west of the acropolis) though the meetings devoted to ostracism were still held in the agora; the main tribunal remained in the agora. A distinction was maintained between commercial and ceremonial agoras in Thessaly and elsewhere (Aristotle, *Politics*, vii, II, 2). In the highly developed agora like that of Athens each trade or profession had its own quarter. Many cities had officials called *agoranomoi* to control the place.

The agora also served for theatrical and gymnastic performances until special buildings and spaces were reserved for these purposes. In Athens respectable women were seldom seen in the agora, and men accused of murder and other crimes were forbidden to enter it before their trials. But free men went there not only to transact business and to act as jurors, but to talk and idle—a habit often mentioned by comic poets. A tomb in the agora was granted in exceptional circumstances as the highest honour for a citizen.

BIBLIOGRAPHY.—W. A. McDonald, *The Political Meeting Places of the Greeks* (1943); R. E. Wycherley, *How the Greeks Built Cities* (1949); R. Martin, *Recherches sur l'agora grecque* (1951). On agora and forum *see* E. Gjerstad, *Opuscula archaeologica*, vol. 3 (1944).
(A. D. Mo.)

AGORACRITUS, a Parian and Athenian sculptor, said to have been the favourite pupil of Pheidias. His most noted work was the statue at Rhamnus of Nemesis, by some ancient authorities attributed to Pheidias himself. Part of the head is in the British museum; fragments of the pedestal reliefs are in Athens.

See Gisela M. A. Richter, *Sculpture and Sculptors of the Greeks*, rev. ed., pp. 240–242 (1950).

AGOSTINO DI DUCCIO (1418–1481?), one of the celebrated Florentine marble sculptors of the 15th century. His style, with its linear emphasis, cursive drapery and flat, schematic forms, lacks the fundamentally naturalistic intention of most Florentine sculpture of his time, and owes its mannerisms largely to the humanist environment of Rimini, where his best work was pro-

duced. In 1433 he left his native Florence, and in 1442 carved an altar at Modena (later on an outer wall of the cathedral). Subsequently he returned to Florence; from there he fled in 1446 (apparently accused of larceny) to Venice. In 1454 he was employed at Rimini, and between 1457 and 1462 was at work on the façade of S. Bernardino at Perugia. In 1463–73 he was active in Florence and in the latter year returned to Perugia, where he undertook an altar in S. Domenico, the altar of the Sacrament in the cathedral, the so-called "Maestà delle Volta" (figures from which survive in the Pinacoteca Nazionale) and the Porta di S. Pietro. Agostino's name is associated mainly with the wealth of sculptured decoration in the Tempio Malatestiano at Rimini. The only work in the Tempio with which he can certainly be associated is the Arca degli Antenati, and it is likely that his share in the sculptures was limited to those in the chapels of S. Sigismund, the "Sibyls" and the "Infant Games," and to some decorative carvings. Whether or not he also carved the much superior reliefs in the Chapels of the "Planets" and the "Liberal Arts," he was profoundly influenced by the Neo-Attic reliefs on which these were based. Of his smaller sculptures the most notable are reliefs of the Virgin and Child in the Victoria and Albert museum, London, the National Gallery of Art, Washington, D.C., the Museo Nazionale, Florence, and the Louvre, Paris.

See A. Pointner, *Die Werke des florentinischen Bildhauers Agostino d'Antonio di Duccio* (1909); C. Ricci, *Il Tempio Malatestiano* (1925).
(J. W. P.-H.)

AGOSTINO DI GIOVANNI, Italian sculptor, is first heard of in Siena in 1310 and was again resident in Siena in 1340–43. After 1320 he seems to have been active, with Agnolo di Ventura (documented 1312–49), at Volterra, where the two sculptors executed a number of scenes from the lives of SS. Regulus and Octavian. Between 1329 and 1332 they were jointly employed at Arezzo on the monument of Guido Tarlati in the cathedral.

In 1337 Agostino di Giovanni was at Orvieto, and later he seems to have been responsible for the monument of Cino da Pistoia (d. 1336) in the cathedral at Pistoia. The work of the two sculptors cannot be clearly differentiated and stems mainly from that of Tino di Camaino.

Agostino di Giovanni and Agnolo di Ventura were also active as architects, and a number of buildings in Siena, among them the Porta Romana and the church of S. Francesco, are conjecturally ascribed to them.
(J. W. P.-H.)

AGOULT, MARIE CATHERINE SOPHIE DE FLAVIGNY, COMTESSE D' (pseudonym, DANIEL STERN) (1805–1876), French writer, famous for her position in Parisian society in the 1840s and for her liaison with the composer Franz Liszt, was born Dec. 31, 1805, at Frankfurt am Main, Ger., the daughter of the *émigré* comte de Flavigny. In 1827 she married Col. Charles d'Agoult, 20 years her senior. She had early shown strength of will and enthusiasm for justice and freedom, and her marriage disappointed her expectations. Meeting Franz Liszt, she decided in 1834 to run away with him. Their relationship lasted till 1839 when Liszt, who had no private income and a strength of will to equal hers, felt that his musical career prevented a settled life. Their separation became permanent in 1844. Of their three children, Blandine married Émile Ollivier, Napoleon III's future minister, and Cosima married the pianist and conductor Hans von Bülow but divorced him to become Wagner's second wife.

Returning to Paris in 1839, Mme d'Agoult began her career as a writer and in 1846 published a largely autobiographical novel, *Nélida*. A close friend of George Sand, whose views on morals, politics and society she shared, and in whose house she had lived for a time with Liszt, she also became the leader of a *salon* where the ideas which culminated in the revolution of 1848 were discussed by the outstanding writers, thinkers and musicians of the day. Her own writings included *Lettres républicaines* (1848), *Histoire de la révolution de 1848* (1851–53), a play, *Jeanne d'Arc* (1857), a dialogue, *Dante et Goethe* (1866) and *Mes Souvenirs 1806–1833* (1877), supplemented by *Mémoires, 1833–1854* (1927), as well as articles for liberal and republican journals. She died in

Paris, March 5, 1876.

BIBLIOGRAPHY.—The *Correspondance entre Liszt et la comtesse d'Agoult* was published by their grandson, Daniel Ollivier (1933). *See* also M. O. Monod, *Daniel Stern, comtesse d'Agoult* (1937); C. Aragonnes, *Marie d'Agoult* (1938); S. Gugenheim, *Madame d'Agoult et la pensée européene de son époque* (1937); Jacques Vier, *Marie d'Agoult, son mari, ses amis* (1949). (R. Dl.)

AGOUTI (AGOUTY), any rodent of the genus *Dasyprocta* of tropical America. They range from northern South America to southern Mexico, including the Lesser Antilles. Agoutis attain the size of a large rabbit; they have an elongate body, small ears, a vestigial tail and slender feet terminating in long, hooflike claws. The fur is reddish-brown and wiry, the individual hairs being multibanded (agouti pattern). Agoutis are terrestrial herbivores mostly active during the night; they eat roots, leaves and fruit. Two to four young are produced in burrows, situated among boulders or roots on the forest floor. Their flesh is a prized food of the Indians. (E. T. Ho.)

ARTHUR W. AMBLER FROM NATIONAL AUDUBON SOCIETY

CENTRAL AMERICAN AGOUTI (DASY-PROCTA PUNCTATA)

AGRA, a city in Uttar Pradesh, India, headquarters of Agra district and division, lies on the Jumna river, 117 mi. S.S.E. of Delhi. Pop. of city (1961) 503,360.

Monuments.—Agra is essentially the city of the Taj Mahal (*q.v.*), held by generations of travelers and art critics to be the world's most sublime building. The earliest surviving monument, however, is the fort, built in 1564–75 by the emperor Akbar. Its 70-ft. high red sandstone walls are 1½ mi. in circumference. Within are the famous Pearl mosque (Moti Masjid), built by Shah Jahan in 1648–55, and the Jahangiri Mahal or palace (*c.* 1570). The former, of simple white marble, is noted for the beauty of its proportions and design; the latter is a fine Mogul adaptation of the stately solidity and commanding symmetry of the Hindu style. Next to the fort is the Jami Masjid (great mosque) built in 1644–49 by Shah Jahan's daughter Jahan Ara. On the east bank of the Jumna is the elegant tomb (built *c.* 1628–30) of Itimad ud-Daula, father of Jahangir's empress. Architecturally, it is important as marking a transition from the *opus sectile* (pierced stonework) to the *pietra dura* (solid stonework) style; it represents the first triumph in Mogul India of marble inlaid work in imitation of Persian ceramic decoration.

Five miles northwest of Agra is Sikandra, Akbar's burial place (though the emperor's remains were later looted and scattered by Jat raiders). His tomb (completed 1613) is a noble building in a fine setting, with an imposing gateway surmounted by four minarets.

The Modern City is crowded and busy near the fort but extends out to spacious suburbs. It is a military and air force centre with a fine cantonment. In the suburbs are Dayalbagh, a colony of the Radhaswamy sect formed there in 1861, and the state mental hospital. Agra university (1927) conducts most of its teaching through more than 100 affiliated colleges and institutes in Uttar Pradesh. In the city itself are seven of its degree colleges, including a medical school, an engineering college, an educational institute and a women's college.

Agra is a communications centre, being on the air route linking Delhi and Bombay; on the Grand Trunk road from Delhi to Calcutta; and at the junction of the Central railway (Delhi-Bombay via central India), the Western railway (Agra-Bombay via Baroda and the west coast) and the Northern railway, a spur of which connects the city with the main Northern system, Delhi-Kanpur, etc. A metre-gauge line of the Western railway runs westward from Agra into Rajasthan.

The city is also a big commercial centre with several markets. Its main industries are cotton ginning and pressing, carpet weaving, tanning and shoemaking; shoes are exported.

History.—The city is relatively modern, having been founded by the Moguls. They made it their capital for more than 100 years in the 16th and 17th centuries, until Aurangzeb removed the seat of the monarchy to Delhi in 1658. It was in Agra that Akbar received a letter from Queen Elizabeth I of England and Jahangir issued a *firman* (charter) to Thomas Aldworthe, a merchant of the British East India company, granting freedom to trade in India (1612). In Agra too was founded and flourished the Mogul school of painting. In the latter half of the 18th century it was taken successively by Jat, Maratha and Mogul forces, by Scindhia of Gwalior and by the English. Under the East India company the city was the capital of Agra (later Northwest) province from 1833 to 1858. In 1863 it was made a municipality and from 1959 was administered by a city corporation.

AGRA DISTRICT is mainly level plain (650–700 ft. above sea level) intersected by several rivers, the principal being the Jumna (*q.v.*). Area 1,861 sq.mi. Pop. (1961) 1,862,142. To the southwest is a succession of parallel sandstone ridges, with watercourses running in ravines. On the western border is the Thar desert (*see* THAR DESERT) of Rajasthan. The district's main crops are millets, pulses, barley, wheat and cotton. Twenty-three miles by rail W.S.W. of Agra is the deserted, but intact, Mogul city of Fatehpur-Sikri (*q.v.*).

AGRA DIVISION comprises the districts of Aligarh, Etah, Mainpuri (*qq.v.*) Mathura (*q.v.*) and Agra. Area 8,662 sq.mi. Pop. (1961) 7,179,264.

See K. C. Majumdar, *Imperial Agra of the Moghuls* (1934). (B. Si.)

AGRA CANAL: *see* JUMNA.

AGRANULOCYTOSIS, is an acute disorder usually characterized by fever, prostration and overwhelming infection especially involving the mouth and throat. There is a striking diminution or complete absence from the blood of a particular type of white blood cell known as the granulocyte (polymorphonuclear leukocyte), the cell that normally functions in combating invading bacteria. The severe sepsis that develops in agranulocytosis is therefore attributed to absence of cellular defense mechanisms with subsequent bacterial invasion.

Agranulocytosis is a disorder of multiple causation. Many medicinal agents have been implicated, among them sulfonamides, certain analgesics and drugs used in treating rheumatism, hyperthyroidism, epilepsy, leukemia and malignancies. In persons with unusual sensitivity, agranulocytosis may result from a single dose of a drug. Decrease in granulocytes also may develop following exposure to excessive X-irradiation. Since granulocytes are formed in the bone marrow, direct damage to the marrow may result in complete absence of these cells or granulocytes may be released in the earliest stages of their development (maturation arrest). Other possible mechanisms include toxic effects on circulating granulocytes or formation of leukocyte antibodies.

Treatment consists of prompt removal of the offending agent and use of antibiotics to combat infection until recovery occurs and normal defense mechanisms are restored. (A. S. WE.)

AGRAPHA ("unwritten [sayings]"), the name given to certain utterances ascribed, with some degree of certainty, to Jesus and preserved in documents other than the Gospels; *e.g.*, Acts xx, 35, and the Logia discovered in 1897 and 1903 at Oxyrhynchus. *See* also APOCRYPHA, NEW TESTAMENT.

AGREDA, MARÍA DE (1602–1665), Spanish mystical writer, was born in Agreda, Spain. Her real name was María Fernández Coronel, her name in religion Sor María de Jesús. In 1620 she made profession of a Franciscan rule for nuns and in 1627 became abbess of a Franciscan monastery in Agreda, retaining this office, except for a brief period, until her death in 1665. Her virtues and holy life were universally acknowledged, but controversy arose over her mystical writings, her political influence and her missionary activities. Her best-known work is *The Mystical City of God* (1670; English trans., 4 vol., 1916), a life of the Blessed Virgin based on revelations granted to María. The Roman Index condemned it in 1681, but the ban was lifted in 1747, Spanish theologians having maintained from the start that most of the opposition arose from a misunderstanding of the Spanish text. Though the book contains evident historical, geographic and chronological errors, it is valuable as an ascetical and mystical treatise.

In 1643 Philip IV paid María a visit, originating an interchange which was maintained either through personal visits or letters until her death. The letters form an invaluable source for the later period of Philip's reign. María gave a marked impetus to mission activity, especially among the Franciscans. She frequently repeated that God had revealed to her his desire to convert the Indians and assured the missionaries the reward of an apostle, and though some thought her words fanciful, many others, fortified with this assurance of success, took up mission work, among them Junípero Serra and Antonio Margil. María de Agreda died on May 24, 1665.　　　　　　　　　　(A. S. Tr.)

AGRICOLA, ALEXANDER (1446?–1506), one of the leading composers of the late Burgundian polyphonic school. Born in the Netherlands, probably in 1446, he was educated there and later went to the court of Milan. In 1474 he was at the court of Lorenzo de' Medici and in the same year returned with his family to the Netherlands. In 1500 he was appointed chaplain and chanter to Philip the Fair, whom he accompanied to Spain. He died at Valladolid in 1506. Of his masses and motets the *Missa in die pasce* and the motet *Regina coeli* are highly esteemed for their musical quality.

AGRICOLA, GEORGIUS (Georg Bauer) (1494–1555), German scholar and man of science, known as "the father of mineralogy," was born at Glauchau in Saxony on March 24, 1494. After studying philology at the universities of Leipzig, Bologna and Padua, he earned a degree in medicine at the University of Ferrara. From 1527 to 1533 he was city physician in the flourishing mining town of Joachimsthal in Bohemia and from 1534 to the end of his life practised medicine in Chemnitz. He adopted the latinized form of his name and wrote in Latin.

Although he made contributions to medicine, chemistry, mathematics, theology and history, his most important writings were on mineralogy and mining. Living in what was then the greatest mining region in Europe, and in close touch with all phases of the industry, his intimate and practical knowledge enabled him to become the first writer on these subjects to rely on direct observation rather than on speculation. He exerted a direct influence on his contemporaries and successors and through them on the development of geological science. Best known of his six books on geological subjects is *De re metallica,* published posthumously in 1556, dealing chiefly with the arts of mining and smelting and containing many informative and attractive woodcuts. It was translated into English by Herbert Clark Hoover and Lou Henry Hoover, appearing in a limited edition in 1912 and in a trade edition in 1950.

In Agricola's *De natura fossilium* (1546), translated into German by Ernst Lehmann (1809–10) and into English by Mark C. Bandy and Jean A. Bandy (1955), and considered the first mineralogy textbook, he presented a new classification of minerals based on their physical properties; he described many new minerals, chiefly metallic ores, their occurrence and mutual relationships. His first mineralogical work, *Bermannus, sive de re metallica dialogus* (1530), was a treatise on the Erzgebirge mining district. In *De ortu et causis subterraneorum* (1546) he recognized clastic rocks and mineral-bearing solutions. His other geological works are *De natura eorum quae effluent ex terra* (1546) and *De veteribus et novis metallis* (1546).

Agricola died Nov. 21, 1555.

See Frank D. Adams, *The Birth and Development of the Geological Sciences* (1938); Bern Dibner, *Agricola on Metals* (1958).
　　　　　　　　　　(L. W. P.)

AGRICOLA, GNAEUS JULIUS (A.D. 40–93), Roman general celebrated for his conquests in Britain and as the subject of a biography by his son-in-law the historian Tacitus, was born on June 13, A.D. 40, at Forum Julii (modern Fréjus) in Gallia Narbonensis. His grandfathers were of equestrian rank; his father became a senator but was executed by Caligula, and Agricola was brought up by his mother at Massilia (Marseilles). He served as military tribune (59) on the staff of Suetonius Paulinus in Britain, returning to Rome in 61 and marrying Domitia Decidiana, of a dis-

tinguished Narbonese family. In 64 he was quaestor in Asia, in 66 people's tribune, in 68 praetor, and in the civil war took the side of Vespasian, who appointed him in 70 to command the 20th legion in Britain. On return to Rome in 73 he was created a patrician and appointed governor of Aquitania, where he spent three years (74–77). Appointed consul in 77, he was admitted to a priesthood and made governor of Britain. In the same year he betrothed his daughter to Tacitus.

Agricola spent seven years in Britain, from 77 (if we reckon his term of office as beginning in the late summer of that year and not in 78) to 84. After conquering in north Wales, the Ordovices and the island of Mona (Anglesey), he forwarded the construction of a new legionary fortress for the 2nd legion (*Legio II Adiutrix*) at Deva (Chester). During the next two years he completed the conquest of what is now northern England and advanced to the river Tay. Between campaigns he encouraged the romanization of the province. In his fourth year he established a line of posts between the firths of the Clota and Bodotria (Clyde and Forth) rivers as a temporary frontier behind which he was to achieve in the fifth year the occupation of Galloway and the Ayrshire coast. After Agricola's army had spent the two following years in reconnaissance by land and sea, the Caledonians north of the Forth, commanded by Galgacus, were provoked in Agricola's seventh year by naval forays and an advance through the territory of the Venicones and Taexali (Angus, Kincardineshire and Aberdeenshire) to a decisive battle at an unidentified site called Mons Graupius, which ended in their complete defeat. Agricola's permanent occupation of Scotland reached the fringe of the highlands (*see* Britain); he blocked the main passes with forts and placed a legionary fortress at Inchtuthil (near Dunkeld in Perthshire). He was recalled to Rome after his victory, where he lived in retirement, refusing the proconsulship of Asia.

See I. A. Richmond, "Gnaeus Iulius Agricola," *Journal of Roman Studies,* vol. xxxiv, pp. 34–45 (1944); R. Syme, *Tacitus* (1958).
　　　　　　　　　　(I. A. Rd.)

AGRICOLA, JOHANN (Johannes; originally Schneider, then Schnitter) (1494?–1566), German Lutheran reformer and advocate of antinomianism (*q.v.*), was probably born on April 20, 1494, in Eisleben. A student at Wittenberg in 1515, he was recording secretary at the Leipzig debate between Martin Luther (*q.v.*) and Johann Eck in 1519. He became an influential member of the theological circle around Luther and helped to introduce Lutheranism in Frankfurt in 1525. Having taken the position of preacher and schoolmaster in Eisleben, he began to teach that repentance comes only from the message of love in the Gospel, not from the Law, which he regarded as a Jewish code: "The Decalog belongs in the courthouse, not in the pulpit. . . . To the gallows with Moses!" Returning to Wittenberg in 1536, Agricola energetically espoused this antinomianism. Luther replied with five disputations and the treatise "Against the Antinomians." Agricola retracted and in 1540 was appointed court preacher in Berlin by Joachim II of Brandenburg, and later general superintendent. Welcoming Charles V's victory over the Protestants, he helped write and promote the provisional religious settlement, the Augsburg Interim (1548), which earned him the hatred of staunch Protestants.

Meanwhile, he defended strict Lutheranism in other theological controversies. He died Sept. 22, 1566. A gifted preacher, theologian and administrator, Agricola's character was marred by vanity, contentiousness and moral weakness. Lasting achievements were his collections of German proverbs published in 1528, 1529 and 1548.

Bibliography.—B. Kordes, *Joh. Agricolas Schriften möglichst vollständig verzeichnet* (1817); G. Kawerau, *Johann Agricola von Eisleben* (1881), and notice in *The New Schaff-Herzog Encyclopedia of Religious Knowledge.*　　　　　　　　　　(Ro. H. F.)

AGRICOLA, MARTIN (1486?–1556), German composer, teacher and writer on music, was one of the first musicians to concern himself with the needs of the Reformed churches and to publish musical treatises in the vernacular. Much of the German musical vocabulary which he invented is still in use and his books give a valuable picture of the musical life of his time, particularly in his descriptions of early 16th-century instruments. Born, according to his own doubtful testimony, on Jan. 6, 1486, at Schwiebus, he was self-taught, called to music "from the plough" as his chosen surname suggests (his real name was Sore or Sohr). He worked in Magdeburg from about 1520 and died there on June 10, 1556. Most of his unpublished compositions are lost but his printed volumes include a good deal of functional sacred music and many instrumental pieces which are transcriptions of vocal part-songs.

BIBLIOGRAPHY.—Agricola's German publications include *Ein kurtz deudsche Musica* (1528); *Musica instrumentalis deudsch* (1529, completely revised 1545; modern ed. of both versions by R. Eitner, in *Publikationen älterer praktischer und theoretischer Musikwerke*, vol. 20, 1896); "Instrumentische gesenge odder exercitia" (in *Duo libri musices*, 1561; mod. ed. by H. Funck, 1933); *Ein Sangbuchlein aller Sontags-Evangelien* (1541). See also H. Funck, *Martin Agricola, Ein frühprotestantischer Schulmusiker* (1933). (B. L. TR.)

AGRICOLA, RODOLPHUS (properly ROELOF HUYSMAN) (1443 or 1444–1485), Dutch humanist, important as an exponent of Renaissance ideas in northern Europe, was born at Baflo, north of Groningen, and educated at Groningen, Erfurt, Cologne and Louvain, where he graduated in 1465. After some months in Italy in 1469, he returned to the Netherlands for about three years and then returned to Italy. He seems to have been in Pavia from 1473 to 1475 and in Ferrara, studying Greek under the protection of the reigning duke, from 1475 to the end of 1478. For the next five years he traveled between centres of learning in northwestern Germany and the Netherlands; in 1481 he went as envoy from Groningen to the court of the emperor Maximilian I in Brussels. In 1484 he went to Heidelberg to lecture on classical literature at the invitation of the bishop of Worms, Johann von Dalberg, whom next year he accompanied to Rome. Agricola died, on his return to Heidelberg, on Oct. 27, 1485.

Agricola's writings include an oration in praise of philosophy (1476), a life of Petrarch (1477), *De inventione dialectica* (1479; a criticism of scholastic philosophy) and *De formando studio* (1484; on education). His emphasis on individual freedom and on the cultivation of a complete personality, with attention both to intellectual attainments and to physical development, had an important influence on Erasmus and other 16th-century thinkers.

His works were edited, in two volumes, by Alard of Amsterdam (1539).

See P. S. Allen, "The Letters of Rudolph Agricola," *Eng. Hist. Review,* vol. xxi (1906); H. E. J. van der Velden, *Rudolphus Agricola* (1911).

AGRICULTURAL ECONOMICS, primarily applies the principles of economics and other sciences to organizing resources in agriculture for their most economical or efficient use. Agricultural economics has been described as "the business side of farming," using the term business in the broadest sense and projecting the concept of farming to include production, marketing and questions of farm policy.

Agricultural economics is an applied field. It is related to sociology and political science on the one hand and to the various production sciences of agriculture on the other. These include fields in animal industry, agronomy, soils, etc.

Agriculture is the major source of food, fibre and raw materials essential to human life. Consequently agriculture has been one of the basic occupations of man throughout the world. Interest in the economic aspects of production, distribution and economic policy relating to agriculture and to the use of farm products is, therefore, world-wide.

This article is divided into ten main sections covering the principal aspects of agricultural economics. In addition to the cross references to related articles given under the various headings of this article, *see* the summary AGRICULTURE (ARTICLES ON). For general discussion *see* also AGRICULTURE; FARM MANAGEMENT.

Following are the main divisions of this article:

I. History
II. Agricultural Prices and Income
III. Farm Appraisal
IV. Agricultural Credit Systems
V. Agricultural Insurance
VI. Farm Taxation
VII. Marketing Agricultural Products
VIII. Agricultural Co-operation
IX. Agricultural Labour
X. Law in Agriculture

I. HISTORY

1. Early Developments.—Agricultural economics is relatively new in comparison with most disciplines and is still in a stage of rapid development. Economic problems of agriculture received the attention of many of the 18th- and early 19th-century economists such as Adam Smith and David Ricardo in England, and the German, Austrian and French economists in Europe. Evidences of this development appeared in the course offerings of leading German universities, often under the title of *Agrarpolitik* (agriculture in relation to the state and society). As early as 1851 the Institute of Agronomy at Versailles, France, offered a course named *économie rurale*. In 1875 a book by Alexei P. Ludogovsky was published in Russia on *Fundamental Outlines of Agricultural Economics and Farm Accounting*. In the United States, a few courses were offered in universities after the Civil War but major development of the field did not occur until the turn of the 20th century.

2. Growth in the United States.—In the United States the first public appropriation for work in fields relating to agricultural economics was a modest grant to the patent office in 1839. In this grant, congress provided for "the collection of agricultural statistics, investigations for promoting agriculture and rural economy and the procurement of cuttings and seeds for gratuitous distribution among farmers." This work laid the foundation for the United States department of agriculture. Work in the United States was largely statistical until about the 1890s when, as a result of an agricultural depression, agitation was carried on by farmers' organizations and other rural groups to try to improve the economic position of agriculture, and from then on development of the field was more rapid. During the "golden era of American agriculture," from 1895 to 1914 when farm prices reached their most favourable balance with other prices, attention rested primarily on questions of credit and agricultural co-operation. During the decade from 1910 to 1920, a small number of persons in U.S. universities became concerned primarily with problems of farm efficiency, farm ownership, credit and tenure. Toward the end of the 1920s, attention was on the immediate problems brought on by World War I and agricultural economists were strongly influenced by the depressed condition of agriculture as related to other parts of the economy. This gave considerable force to the discussion of agricultural prices, marketing, co-operatives and tariff policy.

In the 1930s farm economists gave greater emphasis to methods for lifting agriculture out of its depressed condition. Major interest centred on agricultural adjustment to reduce surpluses and raise farm income. This included national legislation to control agricultural output, programs of land-use planning and farm planning which involved adjustments in individual farm organization. During the 1940s agricultural economics was greatly influenced by World War II. Ways of increasing agricultural output received major attention. Finally more effort was put into the study of national policy. Adjustments in size and type of farm, and studies in marketing and land use also received considerable attention.

3. European Development.—In many European countries, agricultural economics centred largely on problems associated with management of the individual farm business. Particular attention has been given to farm accounts and farm costings (production costs). This has been particularly true in most of the countries of northern Europe. In Germany, two main lines have been followed: one, *Agrarpolitik,* centred on questions of policy at the national and international levels. The other concerned problems of the individual farm, including production costs and credit. Germany, in fact, pioneered in a system of co-operative agricultural credit and this system has been used as a model in other countries. Agricultural co-operation has played a leading role in marketing of farm products throughout the Scandinavian countries. Sweden has developed a unique system for pricing farm commodities which involves government pricing and the marketing of a large part of its agricultural produce through co-operatives. Problems of land use and land evaluation received considerable attention in Italy especially after World War II (see ITALY: *The Economy*).

In Great Britain work in agricultural economics developed in several universities and in the British government. Considerable attention has been given to farm accounts and production costs. During World War II considerable attention was given to national policy and to methods for increasing agricultural output. Britain pioneered in using local boards to set production goals and establish practices for increasing agricultural output.

4. Development in Other Countries.—In most other countries of the world agricultural economics developed more slowly. After World War II, as countries moved from a relatively underdeveloped situation to a more developed status, one of the major problems was the reorganization of agriculture to save labour and to make use of more modern equipment. Consequently, agricultural economics received increased emphasis in various countries.

5. Professional Development.—The most extensive work in agricultural economics developed in the United States, although agricultural economics gained prominence in Europe, Canada, Australia and New Zealand, and increasing interest was shown in Latin America and many of the countries in Asia. Students from India, China, Japan, the middle east and other areas came to universities in the United States and Europe in increasing numbers to secure training in agricultural economics. At mid-20th century several of the larger universities in the United States had large numbers of graduate students from other countries. Part of this development was the result of the awakening world-wide interest in improving diets and levels of living and in promoting economic development.

All of the land-grant colleges in the United States and many universities throughout the world provide courses in agricultural economics. These involve courses in farm management, agricultural marketing, agricultural policy, land economics, agricultural credit, production economics, agricultural prices, statistical methods and techniques.

In all of the large countries agricultural economic associations provide a basis for professional interchange of ideas and for growth and development. Most of these associations publish individual journals. The Agricultural Economics society (Great Britain) publishes the *Journal of Agricultural Economics;* the Indian Society of Agricultural Economics, one of the newer organizations, publishes the *Indian Journal of Agricultural Economics;* the Canadian Agricultural Economics society publishes the *Canadian Journal of Agricultural Economics;* the American Farm Economic association in the United States publishes the *Journal of Farm Economics.* Journals such as these carry reports of research and discussions about major problems of the day and suggested improvements and research methods. The journals also carry discussions pertaining to agricultural policy, agricultural marketing, land economics, etc. The International Conference of Agricultural Economists, which meets every three years in various countries, provides a basis for exchange of professional ideas on a world-wide scale. Agricultural economists meeting in their national and international associations discuss how technical changes can be brought about and how advancement can be made in development of the agricultural economy.

In summary, agricultural economics started in the early 19th century. It developed in the latter half of the century as the result of increasing interest in economic problems associated with agriculture. In the 20th century agricultural economics expanded and the work developed to embrace all the major countries. The work centred on analysis of the economic problems involved in obtaining more efficient use of agricultural resources both in production and marketing. Questions of national policy were involved in many countries. Much interest centred on the question of how low income in agriculture could be alleviated. The three central objectives, therefore, involved (1) more efficient use of

resources; (2) elimination of poverty; and (3) the promotion of economic development.

BIBLIOGRAPHY.—Murray R. Benedict, *Can We Solve the Farm Problem? an Analysis of Federal Aid to Agriculture* (1955); C. E. Bishop and W. D. Toussaint, *Introduction to Agricultural Economic Analysis* (1958); Harold G. Halcrow, *Agricultural Policy of the United States* (1953), (ed.), *Contemporary Readings in Agricultural Economics* (1955); Earl O. Heady, *Economics of Agricultural Production and Resource Use* (1952); International Conference of Agricultural Economists, *Proceedings* (1929–55); Robert C. Ross, *An Introduction to Agricultural Economics* (1951); H. W. Spiegel (ed.), *The Development of Economic Thought* (1952); Henry C. Taylor and Anne Dewees Taylor, *The Story of Agricultural Economics in the United States, 1840–1932* (1952); United Nations, *World Economic Survey* (annual).
(H. G. Hw.)

II. AGRICULTURAL PRICES AND INCOMES

1. Past Instabilities.—The prices of agricultural products vary relatively to prices of nonagricultural products and to each other. The incomes received by agricultural producers have been generally lower and more variable over periods of time than those of other entrepreneurs.

The economic forces determining price changes are numerous. The general level of prices, both for farm products and for other products and services, varies (1) with the general level of demand for goods and services; (2) inversely with the general level of their supply; (3) with the supply of money; and (4) inversely with demand for money. These forces tend to operate on a world-wide basis, but as a result of different monetary and fiscal policies, individual countries experience different general price movements. Inflation of prices can result from demand for goods increasing more rapidly than supply, or from demand for money falling relative to supply of money, as typically in times of war. Inflation can also come about through an increase in the supply of gold or other base of a currency, or from devaluation of a currency.

Michael Rostovtzeff (*Social and Economic History of the Roman Empire,* 1926) produced evidence that price increases in the 3rd and 4th centuries A.D. were related to the successive debasement of the currency—silver in the 3rd century and silver-washed bronze in the 3rd and 4th centuries. George F. Warren and Frank A. Pearson showed that in the 16th century prices in Spain rose with increasing supplies of gold and silver and that in the 18th and 19th centuries there was a close correlation between the general movement of agricultural prices and the ratio of the supply of gold to the demand for it in Europe and North America. But long-run changes in the supply of agricultural products and in population can themselves cause price changes. Michael Postan (in *The Cambridge Economic History of Europe,* vol. ii, 1952) showed that the threefold rise in agricultural prices in England between 1150 and 1225 and the 50% increase in southwestern Germany between 1250 and 1350 were not general in Europe, but related to the pressure of population on the land more than to the influx of silver.

In periods of comparatively rapid changes in the general price level, prices paid to farmers tend to be more flexible than prices paid by them for many of the goods and services used in production or consumed on farms. Agricultural production is slow to respond to a fall in demand, for example, and agricultural prices fall further than industrial prices. The terms of trade of agriculture with other industries, and of agricultural countries with nonagricultural, have therefore been unfavourable in depression periods; and these unfavourable terms have tended further to reduce agriculture's effective demands on other industries. John R. Bellerby concluded that before 1939 the general average reward for human effort in agriculture was only 55% of that outside. Of the countries studied, only in Australia, New Zealand, France and possibly China was the return to farmers approximately equal to that in the average of nonfarm occupations over any considerable period of time.

This relatively low level of incomes is related to the lower productivity of labour in agriculture. But where in industrial countries, as in North America, a big increase in national income is brought about, the low income elasticity of demand for foodstuffs still keeps agricultural incomes relatively low, even though agricultural productivity is increasing; as incomes rise the demand for foodstuffs rises but little, whereas that for manufactures and urban services expands greatly.

In the richer countries, likewise, price elasticities of demand for foodstuffs are comparatively low, so that large harvests may cause price reductions sufficient to depress incomes. However, prices fall less than outputs rise where domestic disposals, exports or stocks expand sufficiently. And in the poorer countries such as India consumption may increase markedly in response to a fall in price or an increase in real income. The more serious year-to-year fluctuations in incomes are attributed to highly variable harvests of particular products in individual countries. Because these countries export or import only small parts of the world's total supplies of these products, world prices are not substantially affected. Thus northern Nigeria may have a poor peanut harvest but world prices of oilseeds and edible oils are not raised much in consequence.

2. Past Attempts to Control Price Fluctuations.— Throughout history, up until the 1930s, governments were concerned more with maintaining supplies and stable prices of foodstuffs for their urban populations than with safeguarding the incomes of agricultural producers.

In the imperial age of Egypt supplies were stored against famine years and stability of prices was partially maintained through imposition of taxes on land which were collected in kind and stored in treasury granaries. Under the Roman empire, taxation in kind removed during several centuries large quantities of agricultural products from the market and reduced the scope of the money economy. The direction of imports and exports of food products was controlled. The large imports of grain from Egypt, Sicily and north Africa were imported and stored under government control. The emperor Diocletian went farther in the direction of a controlled economy and by the edict of A.D. 301 fixed maximum prices for many commodities, including foodstuffs, throughout the empire. The edict was a failure for, according to Lactantius Firmianus, black market operations ensued.

In England, also, the earliest government intervention was designed to protect the urban populace rather than to help the agricultural producer. In the 14th century the long series of statutory corn laws was begun that only ended in 1846. The policy followed by Edward III was to keep internal prices down by forbidding almost all exports of corn. His successor, Richard II, encouraged corn growing by permitting corn exports on payment of duties and subject to orders in council. No import restrictions were imposed until 1463, when imports of corn were forbidden so long as the home price was under 6s. 8d. a quarter. The landed interests became aware of the benefits to themselves of keeping up farmers' prices, and variations in the corn laws were employed to this end for nearly 400 years. (*See* CORN LAWS.)

In the 20th century many governments intervened in the marketing of agricultural products and attempted to control price movements directly or indirectly. The period between World Wars I and II was marked by attempts to raise the prices of agricultural products by restricting supplies. It has been estimated that the operation of the Agricultural Adjustment act of 1933 reduced the U.S. cotton crop of 1933 to 25% and the tobacco crops of 1933 and 1934 to 33% below the 1932 output. In Great Britain the hops and potato marketing boards, set up in 1932 and 1934 respectively, restricted production of those crops by a strict acreage quota system. Other countries tried to keep up world prices by restricting supplies to export markets. The Stevenson scheme of 1922 aimed to restrict production of rubber in British territories by production and export quotas. In 1931 the Chadbourne plan for sugar allotted an annual export quota to each participating country. In 1931–37 the government of Brazil took strong measures to reduce supplies of coffee on the export market by a ban on planting and by destroying a substantial part of the harvested crop. The chief result of these schemes was a fall in the share of the world output of these commodities produced by the participating countries. After 1945 international commodity schemes attempted to secure wider support among producing countries and a measure of agreement between the major exporting

and importing countries.

3. Modern Systems of Agricultural Income and Price Supports.—There are significant differences between the objectives pursued by different countries through their agricultural protection policies. Certain governments undertake to maintain the general level of farm incomes; some maintain price support or controls only for particular commodities; others only give encouragement to increasing production and efficiency.

At the beginning of the 1960s the position in individual countries was as follows. In the United Kingdom and Sweden there were statutory obligations to ensure an appropriate level of income for the greater part of the agricultural industry, but the incomes of individual farmers were not guaranteed. In the United States the policy was to support the prices of individual commodities. Since a large proportion of the output of smaller farms was in products whose prices were not supported, the effect on their incomes was mostly indirect through increases in the general agricultural price level. In Austria, Belgium, France and the Netherlands there were no provisions for total income maintenance but, in the formulation of general agricultural policy, attempts were made to secure a considerable degree of income control. In Germany, Iceland and Switzerland there were statutory provisions to improve agricultural incomes, and to secure equality with the wages of certain groups of industrial workers. In other European countries such as Spain, Greece, Portugal, Turkey and Yugoslavia the emphasis of policy was on increasing production and reducing price fluctuations. In Canada, too, the state had no clear income obligations but aimed to secure increased efficiency in production. In the countries of eastern Europe the official policy after 1956 was to increase the material incentives to agricultural producers by raising product prices, reducing prices of factors and services involved in agricultural production and relaxing the system of compulsory deliveries of produce.

Modern systems of price support in selected countries are reviewed below in more detail.

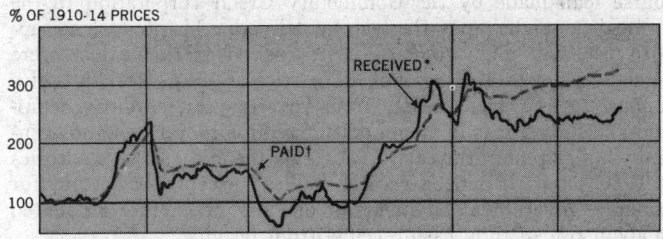

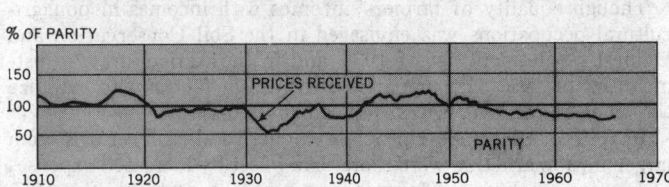

* Monthly data.
† Includes interest, taxes, and wage rates.
 Annual average data, 1910-1923; by quarters, 1924-1936;
 by months, 1937 to date.
BY COURTESY OF U.S. DEPARTMENT OF AGRICULTURE, ECONOMIC RESEARCH SERVICE

U.S. PARITY PRICES, 1910–66

United States.—The Agricultural Adjustment act of 1933 had as its goal the restoration of prices received by the farmers for their products to a level that would be equivalent in purchasing power to that of 1910–14, a period of comparative stability. The ratio between an index of prices received for the farmer's products and an index of prices paid by him for supplies during that period was taken as parity, or 100, as indicated in the accompanying chart, and this was made the chief basis for setting price-support levels. The index of prices received by the farmer for his products is indicated by the solid line in the upper part of the chart; the index of prices paid, by the broken line. The ratio between the two indexes, shown in the lower part of the chart, represents the purchasing power of farm products per unit (per bushel, bale, etc.): when the two indexes are equal, the ratio between them is 1,

TABLE I.—*Index Numbers of U.S. Farm Incomes*

Year	Income per head of farm population from all sources	Total farmers' net income from all sources*	Per capita disposable income of farmers as percent of other incomes
	1960=100		
1950 . . .	74	114	58
1955 . . .	77	95	48
1960 . . .	100	100	55
1961 . . .	108	107	58
1962 . . .	112	109	58
1963 . . .	118	109	59
1964 . . .	116	101	54
1965 . . .	140	126	63

*Conterminous U.S. only.
Source: U.S. Department of Agriculture, *Farm Income Situation* (July 1966), *Farm Income* (Aug. 1966).

or at parity. Subsequent legislation, while retaining 1910–14 as the base period for the ratio between the general level of prices received and prices paid, modified this strict concept of parity; and a more flexible system, basing parity for individual commodities on average prices over the most recent ten-year period to reflect the changing relationships among commodities, provided support for basic commodities—wheat, corn (maize), cotton, rice, tobacco and peanuts—within a range of 60%–90% of their purchasing power parities. The support prices were linked by a sliding scale to the relationship between their estimated and normal supplies. A system of loans near world prices, plus payments to increase the farmers' income on at least major parts of the crop consumed domestically, was adopted for some grains and for cotton in the 1960s. Certain nonbasic commodities were also included in the support formula but their relation to parity was determined by different criteria. Farmers' prices for meat, poultry, eggs, potatoes and fruit were not supported directly but were assisted on occasion of temporary surplus and severe price depression by special purchases of surplus for diversion to noncommercial outlets.

The method of price support most widely used was the nonrecourse loan made by the Commodity Credit corporation to the farmer; he might repay the loan by delivering his produce at support prices or might redeem it by cash if market prices were higher. Though the amount of particular crops seeking price support loans varied greatly from year to year, as did redemptions, surplus stocks in Commodity Credit corporation hands generally built-up until the early 1960s. By the mid-1960s inventories in CCC hands had been greatly reduced except for cotton, for example, government payments of one sort or another amounted to about 6% of total cash receipts from farming.

Though equality of farmers' incomes with incomes in nonagricultural occupations was envisaged in the Soil Conservation and Domestic Allotment act of 1936, and in the Agricultural Adjustment act of 1938, the support system did in fact aim to stabilize the level of the real prices of farm products.

In spite of the support program, higher total cash returns from larger farm marketing were more than offset by increased expenses of farming; realized net farm income generally declined after 1952 but recovered in the 1960s. A reduction by some 35% in the number of farms after 1952 left fewer units to share total income. Even so, in 1965 average income of persons on farms (with about two-thirds of the total derived from farming and one-third from non-farm sources), was less than two-thirds as high as the average for persons not on farms (*see* Table I).

United Kingdom.—The Agriculture act of 1947 aimed to secure continuously "a stable and efficient agricultural industry capable of producing such part of the nation's food and other agricultural produce as in the national interest it is desirable to produce in the United Kingdom, and of producing it at minimum prices consistent with proper remuneration and living conditions for farmers and workers in agriculture and an adequate return on capital invested in this industry." An elaborate system was therefore built up of guaranteed prices and assured markets for the main products, accounting for 80% of the total United Kingdom's agricultural output.

The guaranteed prices reviewed each year took into account the general level of costs and the income of the agricultural industry

as a whole. Under the *Long Term Assurance for Agriculture* (*Cmnd. 23,* published Nov. 1956), the government undertook not to reduce the total net income guaranteed (assuming normal weather conditions) by more than $2\frac{1}{2}$% in any one year, nor the prices guaranteed for individual products by more than 4% in any one year, nor those for livestock products by more than 9% over any period of three years. The Agriculture act of 1957, among other provisions, gave statutory form to these assurances.

The methods used to support prices and incomes after 1947 were various. Until 1953 many of the major products were purchased by government agencies at the guaranteed prices. After 1954 a system of "deficiency payments" was introduced by grains and fatstock, the state making good the difference between the open market price and a guaranteed minimum. This system left market prices free to fluctuate, but, without recourse to import controls, provided support levels for farmers' returns. Under the Agriculture act of 1957 the government had the right to limit the guarantee to specified quantities of any product. The Agricultural and Horticultural act of 1964 enabled minimum import prices to be established and levies to be imposed, if necessary, to support them.

In addition to these commodity subsidies, 60% of which it has been estimated went to one-third of the farmers, the government subsidized fertilizers and some other factors and farming operations and made various grants for improvements to the smaller and poorer farms and to amalgamate a substantial number of such units with viable farms.

France.—The price control policy pursued in France aimed at the modernization of agricultural structures and the improvement of agricultural incomes per holding, with special attention to small family farms. For the main products "target" prices were fixed either for unlimited quantities or for specified amounts, or alternatively (*e.g.,* for meat) as the base prices for fixing minimum and maximum limits. French farmers, as comparatively low-cost producers for some major agricultural products, were indicated as holding an advantageous position in the European Economic Community (EEC) (*see* ECONOMIC UNION).

German Federal Republic.—The Agricultural act of 1955 aimed to secure that efficient farmers obtained incomes equivalent to the earnings of workers in comparable industries. For major commodities, except meat, prices were fixed at the producer or consumer stage, and imports were adjusted to enable supplies to balance demand at that level. The changes necessitated by the EEC's Common Agricultural policy appeared likely to result in reduction in the overall level of German farm product prices.

U.S.S.R.—The freedom of peasant holdings, sanctioned by early Soviet agrarian legislation (1917–18), was limited during the period of War Communism (1918–21); crops were requisitioned and free markets in farm products were abolished. The New Economic Policy of 1921 restored free markets and substituted taxes for the requisitioning of crops, but under the first five-year plan of 1928–33 the agricultural industry was consolidated into two forms of organization, state farms and collective farms, and a regular form of crop requisitioning at fixed prices was established. Collective farms had to deliver fixed quotas of their produce to the state at prices considerably lower than free prices would have been and also make payments in kind to the machine-tractor stations in return for work done. Any surpluses could either be sold to the state for somewhat higher prices and some priority in the distribution of scarce manufactured goods, or could be sold in local free markets which were restored in 1933. This system favoured the geographically and climatically more fortunate areas and kept agricultural prices lower than they would have been in relation to those of manufactured goods.

From 1953 the Soviet government undertook to increase agricultural production and bring about a big investment in agriculture. Procurement obligations were lowered, higher purchase prices were established and incentives were offered to peasants to sell more from their individual holdings. But the price structure remained unbalanced; for instance, prices for cotton and cottonseed, flax and hemp were high relative to prices for grain and meat.

In 1958 a complete reappraisal of the pricing policy aimed to

TABLE II.—*Index Numbers of Monetary Prices and the Real Value of Prices Received by Farmers*

	Germany, West	Japan	France	Austria	United Kingdom	Netherlands	Australia	India	Canada	United States
	1961–63=100	1960–61=100	1955=100	1958=100	1954–57=100	1949–53=100	1945–50=100	1938–39=100	1935–39=100	1935–39=100
Monetary prices*										
1951–52	85	...	106	90	...	107	185	505	285	274
1954–55	90	...	100	94	101	104	177	445	235	222
1957–58	98	93	130	101	101	103	173	572	240	226
1960–61	97	105	141	107	96	101	178	561	256	223
1963–64	106	131	165	114	97	116	187	676	263	222
	1962–63=100	1960–61=100	1960=100	1958=100						
Real prices†										
1951–52	82	...	...	85	...	109	181	532	224	227
1954–55	85	...	...	92	...	117	196	470	224	220
1957–58	90	96	...	100	...	134	214	570	241	232
1960–61	96	103	101	108	...	149	229	612	257	241
1963–64	104	115	109	123	...	179	236	701	278	250

*Prices received in terms of local currency.   †Prices received in terms of goods and services bought by farmers.
Source: Food and Agriculture Organization, *Production Yearbook* (1965).

secure a more equitable distribution of income between collective farms and to increase their production of meat and dairy products. The obligatory deliveries to the state by collective farms and the payments in kind to the machine-tractor stations were formally abolished. The stations were disbanded and the machines distributed to the collectives. Farms were still under an obligation to sell substantial portions of their production to the state for cash but quotas were varied according to soil fertility. Multiple pricing was abolishèd. Regional prices were set to cover average production costs and a residual income to collective farmers in the area. They were, however, to be related to average costs for the whole of the U.S.S.R., although they might be altered in the republics according to yield fluctuations and production trends.

Eastern Europe.—In Poland agricultural incomes rose after 1956 following the increase in the fixed price level of state purchases, while costs were kept proportionally lower by reductions in land taxes and by state investment in agriculture.

In Rumania, Hungary and Bulgaria, compulsory deliveries to the state at fixed low prices were replaced by contractual delivery systems. The governments undertook to maintain the relation between prices paid to and by farmers. Compulsory deliveries of farm produce were also abolished in Yugoslavia in 1957 and were replaced by a system of guaranteed minimum prices for most cereals and meats. These were implemented by state-purchasing organizations which contracted with farms in advance.

4. Farm Price Levels and Income Trends.—World economic conditions during World War II and immediately afterward altered the relationship between the prices of agricultural and industrial products and raised agricultural incomes above the relatively low level of the 1930s.

After 1945 short-term fluctuations were reduced and prices received by farmers were kept more stable than in the years following World War I. Prices after 1946 rose more gradually than in 1919–20 and there was no sudden fall such as occurred in 1920–21. But price control did not eliminate longer-term price fluctuations resulting from the major economic forces. The experience of the 1950s and 1960s showed that it was not possible for countries with considerable trade to keep national prices above the international market level for an indefinite period. The support system practised in North America, involving government purchases and storing, led to serious surpluses. The experience of marketing boards in west Africa also illustrated the difficulty of attempting long-term stabilization of prices of export products.

Table II shows that between 1952 and 1964 monetary prices received by farmers fluctuated least in countries such as Canada and the Netherlands which were most dependent on export market prices and did not try to maintain a high internal price structure. The table also indicates that from 1952 to 1964 in most of the countries represented the indexes of real prices received by farmers rose. This was because prices paid by farmers continued to rise, however they did not rise as much as agricultural prices.

BIBLIOGRAPHY.—G. F. Warren and F. A. Pearson, *Gold and Prices* (1935); P. Lamartine Yates, *Commodity Control* (1943); T. W. Schultz, *Economic Crises in World Agriculture* (1965); D. G. Johnson, *Forward Prices for Agriculture* (1947); G. S. Shepherd, *Agricultural Price Analysis,* 5th ed. (1962); D. E. Hathaway, *Government and Agriculture* (1963); D. Paarlberg, *American Farm Policy* (1964); Organization for Economic Co-operation and Development, *Interrelationship Between Income and Supply Problems in Agriculture,* Agriculture Policy Reports (1965).   (JN. R. R.; W. MN.; J. K. R.)

III. FARM APPRAISAL

A farm appraisal is a valuation of farm real estate made by one skilled in this task. Farm appraisals are made for four major purposes: (1) for use in making farm mortgage loans; (2) for the use of buyers and sellers of farms; (3) for assessments used in levying property taxes; and (4) for condemnation where governments and other agencies with the power of eminent domain use appraisals in acquiring farm land.

Down through history there have been varying amounts of emphasis placed on farm appraisal. In China as early as the 23rd century B.C., the government had a system of rents based on soil properties. The Greeks and Romans of ancient times levied taxes in relation to estimated crop yields. During the middle ages in Europe, attention was given to land surveying which included not only measurement of land but rating of land productivity.

1. Modern Practice.—In modern times farm appraisal has taken on a stronger economic base, with specialists in Italy, Germany and Switzerland pioneering in the development. Italy, through a long tradition of appraisal writings by economists, has a highly developed farm appraisal profession which uses a combination of sales comparisons and income estimates. Germany, through the writings of Friedrich Aereboe, pioneered in the use of sale value comparisons and later, under Walter Rothkegel, developed a unique bench mark system of land assessment. Under this system a farm in Magdeburg was given a rating of 100 and other farms in Germany were rated up or down from this standard of 100. In Switzerland Ernst Laur used farm account records as the base for valuations. In Great Britain chartered surveyors, who represent the farm appraisal profession, not only value farm real estate but also handle many valuation questions connected with farm leasing. The Royal Institution of Chartered Surveyors had its beginning in Great Britain in 1868. In France the Ordre des Géomètres-Experts Français existed continuously under various names from 1838 and its journal, the *Revue des géomètres-experts et topographes français* (Paris), became the official organ for the International Federation of Surveyors or Fédération Internationale des Géomètres (F.I.G.).

In the United States extensive development of the farm appraisal and emergence of a farm appraisal profession was the result of faulty farm valuations made for the most part following World War I. Farm mortgage foreclosures in the 1930s indicated that appraisals had been too high on the poor land, too low on the best land. Reform by farm lenders was the logical result and formation of the American Society of Farm Managers and Rural Appraisers in 1929, with its provisions for certification of appraisers, gave the movement professional support.

2. Physical Inventory and Monetary Valuation.—The modern farm appraisal fundamentally is made up of two parts—the physical inventory and the monetary valuation. A brief description of a typical appraisal follows:

The physical inventory generally contains the location and legal description of the farm, an aerial map where one is available, and an appraisal map showing areas of uniform producing soil, slope, erosion, areas of nontillable land, drainage, orchards, timber, farmstead and other features. The map is made as the appraiser walks over and inspects the farm, using a soil auger or spade to evaluate the soil. Additional material is gathered on buildings and improvements, including measurements, descriptions and sometimes photographs. Information is also noted on climatic data, and typical crops grown and their yields. With this information the appraiser estimates the over-all productivity of the farm in the hands of a typical or average operator.

The second major aspect of appraisal—conversion of this physical classification into a monetary value—can be accomplished by estimating net income, by comparing sales of similar properties or by a combination of both procedures. The combination method has received wide acceptance.

Net income is estimated by putting an estimated price on the production of the farm, and subtracting expenses to get the net income likely in the years that lie ahead. Either net landlord income or net owner-operator income can be used as a base. Net income can be converted into value by the process of capitalization; that is, by dividing net income by a rate of capitalization (value = income/rate). This rate can be based on the farm mortgage interest rate since investment in a farm is an alternative to investment in a mortgage. For example, a farm yielding a net income of $1,000 annually with a 5% rate of capitalization would have an income value of $20,000.

Sale value comparisons require a search for farm sales within the neighbourhood or district of the farm being appraised. Each of the farms sold has to be compared in terms of productivity with the farm being appraised. Further, if there has been a change in the general market value of farms since one of the farms was sold, this has to be taken into consideration by an adjustment in the sale price. The sale value, determined by comparison, will in all probability be higher than the income value arrived at by capitalizing net income because the sale value includes nonincome features. For example, a sale value estimate of $25,000 might be indicated for the farm that had a capitalized net income value of $20,000.

Since both net income estimates and sale value comparisons involve estimating and judgment, farm appraisers generally have found it desirable to have as many checks on their work as possible. In consequence, the professional farm appraiser commonly uses both net income and sale value approaches in arriving at the final amount which in his best judgment represents the value of the farm.

BIBLIOGRAPHY.—Earl F. Crouse and Charles H. Everett, *Rural Appraisals* (1956); Giuseppe Medici, *Principii di Estimo* (1948; Eng. trans. by O. R. Agresti, *Principles of Appraisal*, 1954); W. G. Murray, *Farm Appraisal*, 3rd ed. (1954).   (W. G. My.)

IV. AGRICULTURAL CREDIT SYSTEMS

1. Nature and Role of Agricultural Credit.—In agriculture, as in commerce or industry, credit is needed to overcome a shortage of capital. Lack of capital and too little capital are major problems facing many farmers in various countries. These problems are more acute in underdeveloped countries where incomes are generally low and contribute relatively little to the building up of capital through savings.

Credit, in effect, is a tool to increase production, raise the quality of what is produced, or otherwise improve operations to make them more profitable. Its use must at least result in producing enough additional income to pay for the cost of the money borrowed and also assure repayment of these funds within the specified period of the loan.

A system of credit geared to the requirements of commerce and industry is not, without modifications, suited to the needs of financing in agriculture. The farm business and the home are closely associated. Many farm units are small and are operated by the persons who own them and production is normally on a seasonal basis. The primary fact that farming is based on plant and animal life results in a slow rate of turnover of invested capital and

an uneven flow of income. The nature of farming is such that risks in agricultural lending are usually greater than is generally true in the case of commercial or industrial borrowing, and cash incomes in relation to capital invested and to production are low compared with commerce and industry.

2. Kinds and Sources of Credit.—Agricultural credit must of necessity be adapted to the peculiarities of farming. Loans are made for longer periods than in commerce or industry. The term of agricultural loans must be flexible and all such loans should have a repayment plan consistent with income.

Credit in agriculture can be placed in three groups according to the terms of the loans: (1) short-term; (2) intermediate; and (3) long-term. Short-term loans are used for annually recurring production and other cash expenses. Intermediate-term loans are used to finance such items as machinery, equipment, tools, breeding animals, work stock, drainage and soil terracing. Long-term loans are used to purchase land, construct buildings and to make other lasting improvements so that the farm will become more productive.

There are various sources of agricultural credit, including merchants, moneylenders, banks, co-operative organizations and governmental agencies. In many countries co-operatives and governmental agencies have developed into major sources of agricultural financing. Credit from merchants and moneylenders is usually costly in one way or another, and the financing from these sources is mostly short-term. Banks in some countries are cautious in making agricultural loans because of the risks involved. The borrower has to compete with local businesses for the funds available for loans.

Co-operatives or credit unions (q.v.) or societies have been formed by farmers in many countries for the purpose of financing farmers. By pooling their resources and credit needs through such organizations, farmers are able to improve their bargaining power and fill their requirements at lower cost and at terms adapted to their needs.

Governmental agencies are providing agricultural credit in an increasing number of countries. The state may have many purposes for entering this field, but usually one is to provide more adequate credit to farmers at low cost in order to encourage increased production and offer an incentive to greater development.

3. Co-operative Credit Systems.—Although credit co-operatives are often supported one way or another by the government, they function in many countries with only limited state intervention and provide for their farmer-members a good measure of self-help in meeting credit needs.

In Europe, for example, the local co-operative society constitutes the base of these credit structures. These bodies are associated in regional or state institutions which, in turn, are usually joined together in a single national government organization. The credit and other financial activities of these societies are generally subject to government regulation, but responsibility for management and control rests in the hands of their members and administrative staffs.

Many of the local credit societies, as in Austria, west Germany and the Netherlands, have unlimited liability on the part of their members. Others, especially in Belgium, have restricted this feature. Usually the local societies are relatively small in size and serve a village or other limited area. Their credit operations are sometimes combined with other co-operative activities such as purchasing, marketing or providing other services. (*See* CO-OPERATIVES.)

There usually are other sources of agricultural credit in addition to co-operative lending organizations. Countries such as Austria, Belgium, Sweden, Denmark, west Germany, Italy, the Netherlands and Switzerland also have systems of savings banks. In some countries such as west Germany, Austria and to some extent Switzerland, these savings banks are chartered and their obligations are guaranteed by towns or other governmental units.

4. Credit Systems Associated With State Management.—In some countries the government has taken a direct hand in sponsoring, financing and even participating in the management of co-operative credit organizations. Under certain conditions, the co-operative status is maintained, but the organization has to depend more or less on the state for financing. In other cases, the co-operative is subject to some degree of administrative control by the government.

In France, farmers obtain about three-fifths of the money they borrow from a state-supported farm credit system. This credit system is administered by the Caisses de Crédit Agricole Mutuel which are co-operative societies. At the lowest level, there are the Caisses Locales which are private institutions covering a canton or commune. Next are the Caisses Regionales which are also private institutions organized in the same way as the Caisses Locales but covering the area of a *département*. The various Caisses Locales in their area are subordinate to them. The head organization is the Caisse National, a government body enjoying financial autonomy and administered by a plenary commission and a board on which the Caisses Regionales are abundantly represented. The supervisory powers of the Caisse National are such that it has an important say in the business and administrative activities of the Caisses Regionales.

Italy also has an agricultural credit system partly administered and financed by the government. Agricultural credit is supplied by several institutions which by law are required to hold authorization from the government. The Consorzio Nazionale per il Credito Agrario, which operates throughout Italy, and a number of other national and regional banks are authorized to make farm-improvement loans, the cost of which to the borrower is subsidized in part by the ministry of agriculture and forestry. Farm-operating loans are made by special farm credit banks and other authorized banks, including many which make farm-improvement loans. The small loans are usually made by rural co-operative banks (casse rurali).

In addition to its co-operative credit structure, Japan has the Agricultural, Forestry, and Fisheries Finance corporation, an independent government institution entirely capitalized by the government. Its purpose is to give long-term credit at low interest rates to farmers, forestry men, fishermen and their organizations where such credit is difficult to obtain from private institutions such as the Central Cooperative Bank for Agriculture and Forestry and other commercial banks. The corporation has no local branches of its own but, instead, its local business is entrusted to the Central Cooperative bank, the prefectural credit federations and local commercial banks.

In Turkey, the financing of about three-fourths of the loans to farmers is done by the Agricultural bank, a government-owned institution. This bank has branches and agencies serving nearly all of the rural areas. The second most important source of agricultural credit in Turkey is the more than 1,400 co-operatives. They serve about 10,000 villages. The remaining 25,000 villages depend on the Agricultural bank to provide credit to farmers directly. The co-operatives borrow from the bank to finance their lending operations.

5. Centralized Government-Controlled Credit Systems.—

In countries where capital is scarce and farmers cannot readily organize credit co-operatives to meet their needs for financing, the government may be called upon to establish lending facilities and provide funds. In other countries, particularly as new lands are opened or where private capital shuns investment in agriculture, the government may organize a credit structure to finance agriculture directly. In still other countries, where government desires to exert direct control over the development of agricultural resources by allocating the flow of investment capital into particular areas and specific farming activities, the state may establish and operate a strongly centralized farm credit system. Although in all such situations some credit may be available from various private sources, the biggest part of the lending to farmers is done by the government-controlled institutions.

The primary source of agricultural credit in Argentina, the Banco de la Nación, operates through its 278 main branches and 21 regional offices of loans and savings, and is a direct dependency of the ministry of finance.

In Chile, there are several government agencies supplying agricultural financing, but the most important credit source is the Banco del Estado de Chile. Various other government agencies such as the Colonization bank and the ministry of agriculture are active in providing agricultural credit, but the loans are mainly for special purposes.

In Colombia the Caja de Crédito Agrario, Industrial y Minero, a government credit institution for agricultural production and development, is practically the only source of credit for the small and middle-sized farmer, the share cropper and squatter.

In Guatemala autonomous government credit institutions furnish from one-half to two-thirds of all active bank credits for agriculture. The biggest agricultural lender is the Crédito Hipotecario Nacional de Guatemala. The most important source of financing for small farmers is the Banco Nacional Agrario which makes supervised loans primarily in connection with the establishment of family-type farms under the country's rural development program.

The Farm Credit corporation, established in 1959 as successor to the Canadian Farm Loan board (1929), is Canada's central agricultural credit institution. It provides loans under the Farm Credit act (1959) and the Farm Machinery Syndicates Credit act (1964).

Two government-controlled credit institutions which make agricultural loans were established in Egypt. One is the Agricultural and Cooperative Bank of Egypt, established primarily to make short-term loans. The Egyptian government owns only one-half of the capital stock, but controls the policies and credit operations of the bank including types of loans and repayments. The other is the Agricultural Mortgage Bank of Egypt which is entirely owned by the government and was established to handle long-term real estate loans.

6. Agricultural Credit Systems in the United States.—

Practically every system of agricultural credit is available in the United States. Government-sponsored credit systems frequently have paved the way for improved or increased agricultural lending activity by privately controlled institutions.

Commercial banks have long been an important source of credit for agriculture. Of some $4,500,000,000 in farm loans held by banks in the second half of the 20th century, non-real estate loans accounted for more than twice as much as real estate-secured loans.

Insurance companies, with outstanding agricultural loans approximating $2,500,000,000, also are important lending agencies in the farm mortgage field. Many banks enter into contracts with life insurance companies for sharing the farm mortgage business originated by the banks. Such arrangements often enable a bank to provide farm mortgage credit locally in greater volume and on longer terms than would otherwise be possible.

The Co-operative Farm Credit System.—U.S. farmers, soon after the turn of the 20th century, began to recognize that they should have mortgage credit better suited to their needs. Congress passed the Federal Farm Loan act in 1916. That act set up the co-operative land bank system.

Soon it became evident farmers also needed better short-term credit facilities. Congress created the federal intermediate credit banks in 1923 as wholesalers of such credit. These banks discount or purchase farmers' notes secured by chattel mortgages originally taken by local lending organizations and use these notes as collateral for short-term securities known as debentures. The credit banks also make loans to farmers' marketing co-operatives on the security of commodities in storage.

In 1933 congress provided for the establishment of a nationwide system of production credit associations as retailers of funds from the federal intermediate credit banks. In the same year congress also recognized that farmers needed permanent credit facilities to finance their marketing and purchasing activities. This need was met by the creation of 13 banks for co-operatives.

The co-operative farm credit system had grown until by the second half of the 20th century it consisted of over 1,000 local national farm loan associations, almost 500 local production credit associations, 12 federal land banks, 12 federal intermediate credit banks and 13 banks for co-operatives.

While the banks and the associations making up the system are chartered by the federal government, operate under laws passed by the U.S. congress, and are supervised by the Farm Credit administration, a government organization, they are so set up as to provide for complete ownership by farmers. Farmers elect the members of the board of directors of their local credit co-operatives and have a part in electing five of the seven members of the farm credit district board of directors. Farmers also have a voice in the selection of the 13-member part-time, policymaking federal farm credit board which was established to direct, supervise and control the Farm Credit administration.

Early in the second half of the 20th century, farmers and their co-operatives had about $3,316,000,000 outstanding in loans from the co-operative farm credit system. This consisted of some 367,-000 long-term land bank loans for about $1,900,000,000; some 260,000 loans for about $961,000,000 from production credit associations; some 2,300 loans amounting to about $384,000,000 from the banks for co-operatives; and about $71,000,000 of financing by the federal intermediate credit banks through other financing organizations.

U.S. farmers finance about 18% of their outstanding farm mortgage loans through national farm loan associations. About 8% of the non-real estate credit they use is production credit association loans. About one-half of farmers' co-operative credit is from the banks for co-operatives.

Farmers Home Administration.—The Farmers Home administration, an agency in the United States department of agriculture, was established in 1946 to meet certain credit needs of farmers not being met by other lenders. Congress since has extended to nonfarmer rural residents the use of this agency's credit for purposes including housing, central water distribution systems, and certain other co-operative or community enterprises. Most loans are made for the operation, purchase and improvement of family-type farms. All loans are made through the agency's 1,600 local offices serving all agricultural counties. Loans are subject to approval of applicants' eligibility by the Farmers Home administration committee for the particular county.

The Farmers Home administration supervisors in charge of the local offices, many serving more than one county, receive applications, make loans, assist borrowers with planning and carrying out farm and home plans, receive payments and handle other phases of program administration.

Rural Electrification Administration.—The Rural Electrification administration (REA), a lending agency in the United States department of agriculture, was established in 1935 by presidential executive order and given permanent status in 1936 under the Rural Electrification act. Until 1949 loans were made only for rural electrification; in that year congress granted authority also to finance rural telephone service.

In its first 25 years of operation, REA made, to more than 1,000 local co-operative organizations electrification loans amounting to $3,500,000,000 of which $2,900,000,000 had been invested by the borrowers in electrical facilities, including 1,390,000 mi. of line, to serve 4,350,000 farmers and other rural consumers. Loans for rural telephone service were made to commercial and nonprofit type telephone corporations. In the first 10 years of this program, REA had approved loans totaling more than $391,000,000 to about 350 commercial companies and 200 nonprofit borrowers to serve 863,000 rural families over 105,000 mi. of line.

Commodity Credit Corporation.—The Commodity Credit corporation (CCC), established in 1933, functions primarily in connection with commodity price support programs of the U.S. department of agriculture. The CCC is managed by a board of directors appointed by the president, subject to general supervision and direction of the secretary of agriculture, who is an ex officio director and chairman of the board. It also has a five-member advisory board.

One of the major activities of CCC is the making of nonrecourse price-support loans on agricultural commodities. Legislation in effect early in the second half of the 20th century provided mandatory price support for corn, wheat, rice, tobacco, cotton, peanuts, wool, mohair, tung nuts, honey and milk and butterfat. It provided permissive price support for other commodities.

Under the nonrecourse loan feature, the farmer has the right to redeem the price-support loan by paying off the principal plus interest, or to deliver the commodity given as security in full settlement of the loan. Commodities acquired by CCC are dispersed of through domestic and export sales, transfers to other governmental agencies and donations for welfare use.

The CCC also administers a storage facilities program under which it makes loans for the construction or expansion of farm storage facilities, and undertakes other operations necessary to provide storage adequate to meet its program needs.

BIBLIOGRAPHY.—W. G. Murray, *Agricultural Finance*, 3rd ed. (1953); S. G. Hooper, *Finance of Farming in Great Britain* (1955); D. C. Horton, *Patterns of Farm Financial Structure* (1957); A. S. Tostlebe, *Capital in Agriculture: Its Formation and Financing Since 1870* (1957).

(E. L. B.)

V. AGRICULTURAL INSURANCE

Various risk-meeting devices used by farmers, as well as by early shepherds and herdsmen, are as old as the arts of agriculture. These devices were the forerunners of insurance. The earliest forms of risk meeting involved mutual aid in the preservation of life and property, including the safeguarding of food supplies. Protection of this kind became a discipline of the family, the clan or the local group. If unfortunate events occurred to either property or person, the loss was alleviated by services or other aid that members of the group could contribute.

The developments of trade and a money economy brought new methods of risk bearing. Over a long period in history, the emphasis on risk sharing gradually shifted from "the recourse of neighbors" to greater dependence on money. During the change, there was a period in which reliance was placed on voluntary contributions to alleviate any loss sustained by a member of the group, but the dependability of this device for adequate relief broke down. From this experience, the idea of organized risk sharing against common perils, based on a businesslike method of collecting contributions, gradually evolved into the modern institutions of insurance.

1. Early Plans.—The earliest insurance plans were in effect before the Christian era, with the insurance of hazards peculiar to commerce and sailing. At first, thought was given only to protection against hazards to property. Life insurance, as well as social security programs, were later developments.

By comparison with commerce and industry, insurance programs for agriculture developed more slowly. In general, they followed the mutual principle of sharing unpreventable losses. The main reasons for this lag in the application of insurance to agriculture were that farmers, who were largely self-sufficient, were willing to accept the risks connected with small property valuations that were relatively easy to replace. They also felt that insurance was too expensive. As specialization developed under technological advances, the need for financing greater investments in properties grew and along with it the need for insurance. But into the second half of the 20th century, legislation authorizing farmers' mutual insurance companies remained limited. Also, a lack of knowledge of the effect of the various risks slowed down efforts to include many of them.

The more important hazards to agricultural production are fire and weather risks, such as cold, heat, hail, lightning, windstorm, drought or too much rainfall; diseases among both plants and animals; insect infestation, as well as animal damage to crops; risks of inefficient management; risks of sickness, injury or death to the breadwinner; and risks that arise from price fluctuations.

There is some evidence that the idea of nonprofit mutual insurance for farmers developed rather extensively first in Germany in about the 15th or 16th century. In Iceland, mutual insurance of livestock has been traced back to A.D. 1100. At first, small assessment companies or local co-operative societies were established by farmers themselves. They were designed to operate at low overhead costs. At the start, assessments were levied after each loss by a member. Later, as the societies began to gain experience, they tended to change over to a system of collecting in advance an amount based on average underwriting experience. Rate refinements by classes of property developed as loss experience was gained. As the business grew, the idea developed for the organization of reinsurance pools based on regional, as well as national, federations.

Because of the difficulty of insuring the varied risks of production, government aid has been enlisted in insuring against some types of risks. This has been particularly true with respect to crop and livestock insurance. In some countries, governments have promoted the organization of farm mutual insurance companies by direct grants and with liberal laws, sometimes exempting them from taxation. In other instances, subsidies have been granted, even subsidies for paying part of the premium tax when the risk was great. In some instances also, governments have entered directly into the agricultural insurance field, thus making it possible for farmers to obtain insurance that otherwise would not be available to them.

2. Property Insurance.—Starting with buildings and cattle, insurance programs gradually added other properties, including general lines of livestock, stored produce, farm implements and machinery, automobiles and motor trucks and growing crops.

3. Fire and Lightning Hazards.—From earliest times, insurance against damage caused by fire was provided widely. The earliest contracts did not cover damage from lightning in all instances. Later, lightning was covered if fire ensued, and the basic fire contract has been expanded to include windstorm and several minor risks, such as damage caused by falling aircraft and by motor vehicles, explosion, riot and smoke. Other coverages added include damage to an upset tractor, theft of property and loss of livestock if killed on the highway by passing traffic. A plan of forest fire insurance was developed early in the Scandinavian countries; it spread to countries with large timber reserves. Fire insurance on growing crops has been made available in countries where dry weather may increase the fire hazard at harvesttime.

4. Windstorm and Hail Hazards to Buildings.—Early windstorm insurance programs for agriculture were developed in Switzerland, Argentina, Denmark and the United States. Because of the catastrophic effects of windstorm and hail damage, these perils are more hazardous to insure than fire.

5. Livestock Insurance.—Crude forms of risk sharing against loss of livestock, particularly work cattle, are known to have antedated the modern forms of insurance. Some form of group risk sharing against loss of work stock was in operation in China many centuries ago. Although insurance against death from accident and disease has been made available in a number of countries, probably most livestock have been covered only against damage caused by fire, lightning and windstorm. All-risk coverage has been offered only on highly valued animals. The need for all-risk protection has been more acute for a farmer with only one or two head of livestock.

6. Multiple-Line Insurance.—For a long time, insurance companies were organized to undertake only one main line of underwriting, such as fire, windstorm or casualty insurance. The tendency, however, has been to combine these three lines into one basic contract.

7. Crop Insurance.—Earliest efforts toward insuring crops undertook to insure only against the single peril, hail, a practice that is still in force in many countries, particularly in Europe and North America. But the tendency has been to expand the list of perils until all-risk crop insurance has been offered in a number of countries, often with government aid. The catastrophic character of crop risks has brought support for subsidies, or government insurance as a monopoly or to compete with private companies.

In the U.S.S.R. crop insurance has been offered as a state monopoly. For the main crops and for certain minimum insurance requirements, the program has been on a compulsory basis. Supplementary insurance has been on a voluntary basis. In general, the hazards covered have been fire, wind, hail, frost and flood. However, industrial crops such as cotton, castor beans and tobacco, also have been covered against drought. Damage from hail causing deterioration in the quality of tobacco also has been covered.

A program for covering bananas against hurricane damage operates in Jamaica through a quasi-governmental agency. In Puerto Rico, a government agency has been established to insure coffee beans and coffee shade trees against windstorm damage. In Mauritius, a British colony in the Indian ocean, windstorm and drought insurance have been made available to cover damage to sugar cane plantations.

8. All-Risk Crop Insurance.—In a number of countries, all-risk crop insurance systems, either supported partly by governments or actually operated by them, or with private insurers subsidized, have been made available for some crops. In Brazil, a quasi-government corporation, the National Agricultural Insurance company, has a part of its capital stock subscribed by the government and the rest by private insurers and investors. It was established to insure crops and livestock.

Compulsory crop insurance covering damage to paddy and upland rice, grain and silkworms has been developed in Japan. This is a heavily subsidized semigovernment program and has had underwriting deficits. The farmer pays a part of the premium and the government the rest. Insurance covers if the yield of rice is below 70%, but is limited to 50% of normal yields. In 1954, the Mexican government sponsored a two-part subsidy program for all-risk crop insurance covering only investment and labour costs. The program utilizes the services of both stock and mutual companies. Insurance is voluntary, although the two national farm credit banks grant loans only to those who carry insurance.

In the United States, an all-risk form of crop insurance operated by the federal government was begun in certain counties in 1938 with the insurance of wheat. In 1942 cotton was added. Because of adverse experience, the program was abandoned in 1944 but was revived in 1945. Beginning in 1948, the program was placed on an experimental basis to obtain experience on additional crops as well as tree crops. Under the program as it started, farmers were offered all-risk insurance, which essentially covered production costs. The administrative expense was borne by the government. But beginning in 1955 some provisions were made to charge part of the operating costs against the premium income. By 1956 the accumulative experience showed that outgo exceeded income in the programs with cotton, beans, grain, multiple crops and corn, in that order. Over the total experience, premiums were adequate to cover losses to flax and tobacco.

9. Flood Insurance.—As early as 1846 flood insurance was undertaken in Austria. In 1865 it was undertaken in France but did not succeed. In the United States flood loss was included in the all-risk insurance program. In 1956 congress adopted a federal flood indemnity program which was abolished in 1957 because of lack of appropriations.

10. Liability Insurance.—With the development of financial responsibility laws, farmers were faced with increasing need for insurance to cover their liability for injury to others through use of their machinery and motor vehicles. Farmers also needed liability insurance to protect them against lawsuits if through their negligence a visitor should be injured on the farm premises, or if someone should be injured as a result of any activity in connection with their operations wherever the operations may occur.

11. Workmen's Compensation Insurance.—If power machinery is used or if a specified minimum number of employees are hired regularly, farmers are specifically required to comply with workmen's compensation laws, which provide relief for injured employees in at least 30 countries. Workmen's compensation laws also are of general application to all employers, including farmers, in 12 additional countries. In most states of the United States, farmers generally may elect to obtain this protection even if they are not required to do so.

12. Life Insurance.—For the most part, farmers obtain life insurance from private stock or general writing mutual companies. More and more, life insurance is used to strengthen the family financial position.

13. Social Security Insurance.—Laws in at least 16 countries specifically include small farmers or agricultural employees under old-age, disability and survivors insurance in which benefits are provided without an income test. In addition, laws of this kind are in effect and applicable to all citizens without regard to occupation in 10 countries.

BIBLIOGRAPHY.—*Crop and Livestock Insurance—a Selected List of References,* U.S. Department of Agriculture, Library List No. 47

(1949); Ralph R. Botts, "Fitting Insurance to Farmers' Needs and Circumstances," *Agric. Fin. Rev.,* vol. 16 (Nov. 1953); R. Botts and others, "Farmers' Mutual Fire and Windstorm Insurance in the United States," U.S. Department of Agriculture, *Agric. Inform. Bull.,* 165:1–87 (1956); "Farm Credit, Farm Insurance, Farm Taxation," *Agric. Fin. Rev.,* vol. 19, supp. vol. 18 (1956–57); "Expand Crop Insurance," *Wallace's Fmr.,* 82:69 (April 6, 1957); Carl H. Farman and Veronica Marren Hale, *Social Security Legislation Throughout the World,* Federal Security Agency Report No. 16 (1949).   (J. D. Rн.)

VI. FARM TAXATION

Agriculture, perhaps more than any other industry, has given shape to systems of taxation. At an early date, the organization of society under clans or tribes gave rise to crude forms of taxation as a recognized right of the leader or chief. In this primitive stage, cultivation of the soil remained the principal form of production, and land and livestock, the principal form of wealth, so that virtually all tax revenue came of necessity from agriculture. A certain proportion of the produce was commonly pre-empted for the chief or, later, the sovereign, and payment was often made in kind. This simple form of taxation endured in some parts of the world into the second half of the 20th century. Economic change has contributed to its rapid disappearance.

At a later stage in economic development, the rise of nonagricultural employments created new forms of wealth and new sources of income for the payment of taxes. In time, the revenue system of earlier periods was found to be ill suited to taxation of the developing manufacturing and commercial industries, and other taxes were devised for this purpose. These newer methods, which relied heavily on money payments, in turn were imperfectly adapted to obtaining revenue from agriculture. Thus it frequently came about that two separate tax systems existed side by side, one applicable to farming, the other to nonagricultural pursuits.

As subsistence farming has gradually given way to commercial agriculture, the distinctions between farming and other trades or businesses have diminished and the necessity for special tax treatment has become less urgent. This synthesis requires that agriculture be fairly well integrated into the money economy. Important also is the achievement of effective techniques of tax administration, especially in connection with taxation of agricultural income.

In most of the English-speaking nations, agriculture has come to be taxed under the same laws and rate schedules that apply to other industries.

For additional information on the history and development of taxes in various countries *see* TAXATION; LAND TAX.

1. Property Taxation.—Property taxation in one form or another is almost universal. Some countries tax only land. In others, structures are also included and in still others, the tax base includes many types of personal property. The tax may apply to the estimated value of the land, the annual rental or the yield or income (see *Farm Appraisal,* above). In the United States, taxes on the assessed value of real and personal property are the chief source of revenue for local governments. State governments collect but little revenue from property taxation, and the federal government none at all. In Great Britain, taxes on the rental value of real estate are important to local governments, but farm property has been exempt since 1929.

The farm business, with its heavy investment in land and buildings, is peculiarly vulnerable to property taxation. In the second half of the 20th century, taxes levied on U.S. farm real estate amounted to about 3% of gross farm income. These taxes averaged $0.91 per acre of farm land, and were equal to about ninetenths of 1% of the estimated market value of farm real estate. Levies on farm personal property, such as livestock, farm machinery, motor trucks and automobiles, involved substantial but smaller amounts.

The combined burden of real and personal property taxes on U.S. agriculture has occasionally given rise to serious economic problems. Property taxes are a relatively fixed charge on the farmer. The amount of the tax is affected very little by the value of current farm output, so that adjustment of the property tax load to changing economic circumstances is slow. During the depression of the 1930s, the burden of property taxes in relation to shrunken incomes and property values increased to a point at which many farmers were unable to carry it. Rural tax delinquency reached serious proportions in a number of farm states and remained troublesome for several years. Improved farm incomes and property values, as well as more favourable financial conditions for most farmers, caused the problem to diminish after a few years.

In its place came a new cause for concern. After World War II, property taxes turned sharply upward. By accentuating inequalities in valuations placed on property for tax purposes, higher tax rates focused attention on the need for improved methods of assessment. Various studies showed that farm land and buildings as a class were generally carried on the tax rolls at a higher fraction of true market value than were most other categories of property. Moreover, serious inequalities were found in the assessment of individual properties. Increasing awareness of these inequalities, coupled with a steady uptrend in revenue requirements of state and local governments, stimulated considerable interest in thoroughgoing reassessment programs. By the 1960s, several states had carried through complete revaluations of taxable property and others had plans to do so.

Efforts at property tax reform in the years following the close of World War II were not confined to the United States. Certain countries of Asia, Africa, the middle east and Latin America undertook basic revisions in their systems of land taxation as part of broad efforts to improve the productivity of agriculture. In many parts of the world, land tenure and taxation systems handed down from antiquity tended to keep much of the arable land out of cultivation and in the hands of large-scale landowners. Land tax reforms usually attempted to substitute an assessment based on potential yield for one based on actual yield or output, in order to encourage owners to place additional land under cultivation. For fuller discussion of the historic development of land taxes and tenure and their relation to modern programs and problems, especially in India, China and other countries of the far east, Italy and other countries of the Mediterranean, Mexico and Hispanic America, and of the trend toward compulsory collectivization in the countries of eastern Europe, *see* LAND REFORM.

2. Income Taxation.—Farm incomes have been taxable under the British income tax since its original enactment in 1799. For 150 years, however, they were subject to a special lower rate schedule and were eligible for optional treatment under a provision that allowed farm taxes to be based on a certain proportion of the annual rental value of the land rather than on actual income. The aim of these special provisions was twofold—to facilitate compliance for the many farmers who maintained no adequate records, and to soften the impact of the tax on agriculture. In 1948, both the special rate schedule and the presumptive basis for taxing farming profits were abandoned. Since then, agriculture has been taxed like any other trade or business.

Farmers in the United States were never singled out for special treatment under the federal income tax, as to either rates or method of reporting. Until the outbreak of World War II, however, a combination of low farm income and high personal exemptions kept all except a few farmers off the income tax rolls. After 1940, lower personal exemptions and improved farm incomes brought many more farmers under the tax. In the immediate postwar period, when agriculture was especially prosperous, income tax payments of farmers rose to an estimated $1,365,000,000, or more than double the tax bill on farm real estate at that time. In the decade following the close of the war, total income tax payments of farmers varied from 4% to 7% of their net income from all sources.

By the second half of the 20th century, however, federal income taxes were taking such a large share of income that few farmers could afford any longer to ignore the tax consequences of various management decisions. Strong interest developed in ways of minimizing taxes on farm income, for example, by timing of sales of crops or livestock to avoid undue concentration of income in any one tax year, and through devices whereby income could be realized in the form of capital gains, which are subject to preferential rates, rather than in the form of ordinary income. Several new provisions enacted in the early 1950s also had the effect of reducing farmers' taxes. Thus, income realized on sales of draft, breeding or dairy livestock held six months or more was made eligible for low-rate taxation as a capital gain. And outlays for soil and water conservation were declared to be deductible expenses, even though they ordinarily added value to the land.

In the 1960s, apart from the federal government, about 30 of the states were collecting some form of personal income tax. In general, the provisions of these laws, like the federal income tax laws, applied to income regardless of industrial origin. The rates, however, were much lower than those of the federal levy, so that farmers' payments in state income taxes totaled only a small fraction of that paid to the federal government.

3. Other Forms of Agricultural Taxation.—Taxes paid primarily by the consumer in the form of higher prices, including sales taxes of various kinds, are important components of the revenue systems of many countries. The Canadian excise tax on manufactured goods and the British system of consumption taxes doubtless account for a significant share of the tax load of agriculture in those countries, although the precise amount would be difficult to determine. Still other countries, especially those with low per capita incomes, depend greatly on consumption taxes that bear heavily on the poor, including those in rural areas. Communist countries in which the state has resold agricultural products commonly have added a so-called turnover tax which in the U.S.S.R. in the mid-1950s accounted for about one-half of the budget revenue. (*See* also EXCISE TAX.)

In the United States, two-thirds of the states collected taxes on retail sales in the 1960s. The rates were typically 2% or 3%. These taxes were not levied on farming as such, but they applied to a wide range of consumption items purchased by farmers, as well as to many types of material and equipment bought for use in the farm business. It was estimated that U.S. farmers paid about $300,000,000 annually in state sales taxes.

Federal and state taxes on motor fuel, together with charges for automotive licences and permits, cost farmers about $400,000,000 (net of refunds) a year. The state levies were viewed as highway use taxes, and taxes paid on fuel used off the highways were either wholly or partially refunded. Starting in 1956, the federal tax on motor fuel was also restricted to fuel consumed on the highways. In consequence, farmers were almost completely freed of taxes on fuel used in tractors or in other farm machinery. They continued, however, to pay taxes on motor fuel used on the public roads.

Finally, some countries tax agriculture indirectly through such devices as multiple exchange rates, export taxes, fiscal monopolies or government marketing boards. These methods are most effective and commonest where agriculture is dominated by one crop. Multiple exchange rates, as found in the exchange control policies of several Latin-American countries, may involve a relatively unfavourable exchange ratio for export crops. The usual result—a lower net return to the primary producer—is the same under an export tax.

Fiscal monopolies and government marketing boards are methods by which the government can exact a monopoly price for products obtained from the farmer at a lower, competitive price. The difference between buying and selling prices is a form of tax on agricultural production.

See Harvard University, *International Program in Taxation,* papers and proceedings of the conference on agricultural taxation and economic development, 1954 (1954); "Farm Credit, Farm Insurance, Farm Taxation," *Agric. Fin. Rev.,* vol. 21 (July 1959).

(F. D. Sr.)

VII. MARKETING AGRICULTURAL PRODUCTS

Marketing centres upon the exchange of goods and services, whether by barter or by purchase and sale for money, but agricultural marketing is usually defined to include much more than the act of exchange. It includes a great variety of acts to facilitate exchange—for example, processing, storing, transporting, grading, inspecting, pricing, advertising, wholesaling and retailing. In short, agricultural marketing refers to everything that is done to a commodity from the time it leaves the farm until it reaches the final consumer. Thus, hog marketing includes the processing of the hog and the distribution and selling of fresh and cured pork, sausage and numerous by-products.

1. Primitive Forms of Marketing.—In the simplest societies there is little marketing of any kind. Each family or local tribe is practically self-supporting, gathering or producing most of the foodstuffs it consumes. Even so, some form of trade is found in the most primitive societies and early in history men began to exchange foods (*see* TRADE, PRIMITIVE). Two reasons impelled them to do so: first, to obtain more varied diets; second, to receive the advantages of specialization.

To obtain varied diets, fruit or grain was exchanged with neighbouring hunters or nomadic herders for meat; expeditions were sent from interior points to the seacoast for salt and fish; islanders traded with mainlanders. As towns and cities grew, an increasing number of professional men, traders and soldiers produced no food at all. They could buy it to better advantage from farmers, and even farmers began to specialize; each producing only a few items which were suited to his land and his skills. Many of the most successful farmers have no garden, no poultry, no hogs. They, like the factory worker and the doctor, buy most of their own food. Marketing has made such specialization possible.

In the earliest forms of marketing, the farmer doubtless sold directly to the final consumer. There was no middleman between farmer and consumer. To make direct marketing more convenient to buyer and to seller alike, specific market places and definite times of business were designated. The farmers' market is an ancient institution throughout the world. The city authorities usually set aside a suitable space, provided simple facilities, established and enforced rules of trading and collected rents from the farmers who used the market (*see* MARKET).

Usually only farmers were allowed to sell in a farmers' market. If dealers were allowed, they might be required to use a special part of the market and often they were charged a higher rate than farmers. Moreover, some markets gave preferential treatment to local farmers, and even excluded distant producers.

Farmers' markets still exist in most countries. Also, other forms of direct marketing are fairly common. Farmers may peddle their eggs or milk from door to door; they may sell apples by parcel post; or they may sell fruit or vegetables at a roadside stand.

2. The Rise of the Middleman.—Although many kinds of direct marketing continue, the great bulk of agricultural products is marketed through a chain of processors, transporters, wholesalers, retailers—in short, middlemen. This is especially true in the most highly industrialized countries. Direct marketing of foods is an exception to the general rule in western Europe and in the United States, for example, and few farmers in these countries sell their products to the final consumer.

Traditionally, both the farmer and the consumer have been suspicious of the middleman. They have looked upon him as unproductive, parasitical and often dishonest. Several centuries ago, laws were passed in England and in other countries to forbid forestalling—that is, buying from a farmer before he reached the market in order to resell to the public. Similar laws tried to suppress engrossing—that is, selling goods at a higher price than was paid to the farmer.

Yet middlemen, like moneylenders, continued to do business because they performed useful services. Some philosophers, Plato and Thomas Aquinas, for example, and such early economists as Adam Smith, understood that the middleman was necessary in order to obtain the benefits of specialization. But only from about 1900 have students generally recognized that the services provided by middlemen in agricultural marketing are often truly productive. By transporting farm products, they produce space utility; by storing them, they produce time utility; by processing them, they produce form utility; and by buying and selling, they produce possession utility.

3. Transportation and Geography.—Marketing would be impossible without transportation. In early history, the lack of dependable and efficient transportation greatly limited the areas in which goods could be distributed. Even in the second half of the 20th century, producers and consumers in many parts of the world were unable to trade freely because of poor transportation.

From the time of the Phoenicians, the development of ocean and river transportation opened up large areas of the world to agricultural marketing. Later, highways, canals and railroads brought better transportation into the interior parts of most countries. The airplane and the development of air freight transport brought some transportation even to tropic jungles and to arctic outposts. (*See* Transportation.)

Johann Heinrich von Thünen (1783–1850) was the first major economist to analyze how transportation costs affect the geography of agricultural production. He pointed out that some foods, such as butter, can be shipped for long distances because their value is high in relation to their weight. At the other extreme are bulky foods, such as fluid milk, the value of which is low in relation to their weight. If such foods were shipped long distances, the freight bill would be more than they were worth. Partly for this reason (and also because of many local regulations) market areas for fluid milk (often called milksheds) usually are limited in size. Market areas for cream, condensed milk and butter are much larger, because of their higher value in relation to weight.

In a perfectly competitive situation, each producer would ship to whatever market offered the highest net price (*i.e.*, market price less freight). This would lead to definite, predictable, geographic patterns of prices, shipments and consumption. On the one hand, the wholesale price of U.S. number 1 Maine potatoes in any consuming market would be the f.o.b. Maine price plus freight, so market-price differentials would equal freight differentials throughout the area in which Maine potatoes were sold. On the other hand, if Maine and Idaho both ship potatoes to Chicago, Ill., the relation between the f.o.b. prices in Maine and in Idaho depends upon two factors: (1) differences in the quality of the potatoes, leading to premiums or discounts in the consuming market; and, (2) differences in freight rates.

Market news has been developed both by private industry and by governments in order to help shippers find their most profitable markets, and is a powerful aid to competition.

Although economists sometimes have assumed that the ideal market is purely competitive, it is clear that in many cases the purely competitive market is not the most profitable to the producer or the shipper. He can often gain from "dumping" part of his supplies in one area in order to maintain a higher price in other areas. Export dumping is a case in point. Here domestic producers export their surpluses at a low net price in order to maintain a higher price in the domestic market.

4. Storage and Timing.—In the case of extreme perishables, such as fresh fish and fresh strawberries, man in the past has had little choice as to the timing of marketing. Until he had some way to keep these foods without spoiling, he had to sell them when they were ready, or not at all. But many agricultural products could be readily stored for considerable periods of time, without serious deterioration of quality. Aging actually improves the quality of some meats, cheeses, tobacco, wine and other farm commodities.

Great advances have been made in methods of preserving and storing foods. Improvements in canning, dehydration and freezing have brought year-round markets for such perishables as peas and orange juice as well as fish and strawberries. Experiments with radiation offered promises of extending still further the markets for many perishable foods. Farmers and food processors can choose when, within a considerable period of time, they will sell their goods. If they expect higher prices next week, next month or next year, (or if it will improve their tax situation) they may decide to hold their goods off the market for a time. On the other hand, before the seller even owns any wheat or cotton, he may sell a futures contract, *i.e.*, a contract to sell a specified amount and grade at a specified time in the future.

In a purely competitive market, price differentials might be expected, over a period of time, to equal the costs of storage. For example, the November price of storage eggs might be expected to equal the April price, plus the cost of storing eggs from April to November. Actually, the price differentials through time often differ widely from this theoretical model. The departures are attributed in part to imperfect knowledge of future demand and supply conditions. And in part they are the result of institutional factors that cause such phenomena as "inverted markets," in which the futures price may be typically less than the current price (commonly called the spot price).

Many governments store agricultural products, or assist farmers to store them in order to help to stabilize prices. In the United States, for example, the Commodity Credit corporation (CCC) offers loans for cotton, wheat and several other farm products. The farmer can repay his loans and take back his commodity within a certain period of time, but he has the option of leaving it with the CCC to sell (see *Agricultural Credit Systems*, above). In periods of surplus production and low prices, the CCC obtains large stocks of farm products. In periods of high demand, such as occurred during World War II and again in 1950–51, the stocks are sold. Such a program to stabilize market supplies and prices has been called an ever-normal granary. Most storage programs operated by modern governments are intended not only to stabilize prices, but to raise them. To succeed, this usually requires measures to reduce production, to increase consumption or to divert the surpluses into noncompetitive markets where they may be sold at lower prices.

5. Different Forms of the Commodity.—Most agricultural commodities can be sold in several different forms. Milk may be sold as fresh whole milk, skim milk, cream, butter, cheese and other products. Tomatoes may be sold fresh, canned or made into juice, soup or catchup.

The economic principles here are the same as those applying to the geographical and time dimensions discussed above. Thus, assuming perfect competition each unit of the commodity would be sold in whatever form would return to the producer the largest net price.

The differentials between prices of the different forms of a commodity would tend to be equal to the differentials in cost. For example, the price of canned tomatoes would tend to equal the price of the tomatoes plus the costs of canning.

In actual practice, the differentials between market prices of different forms of a commodity may be substantially different from those that could be explained by differences in cost alone. In some cases, this difference is accidental, because of imperfect information. In other cases, it reflects business decisions. For example, surplus walnuts may be shelled, canned and sold at prices lower than those charged for walnuts in the shell. Again, surplus lemons may be converted into citric acid, even though the net price is far below that for fresh lemons.

E. H. Chamberlin made "product differentiation" a main factor in the theory of imperfect competition. There is very little product differentiation in the case of unprocessed agricultural products, although some of it is done through packaging and through brand names. But there is a growing proliferation of brands and packages of most processed foods.

Also, in times of agricultural surplus, there is great interest in the possible development of industrial uses of farm products, even though such uses might have to be subsidized. A case in point was the development from surplus corn of dialdehyde starch, a potentially cheap agent for tanning leather.

6. The Perfect Market Reconsidered.—Some economists have thought that perfect and pure competition would be the ideal, or the perfect market. In actual markets for farm products, the student can observe many departures from this norm. These departures are indicated by price differences in space, in time, by form of the commodity, or by groups of consumers. Such departures are profitable to farmers in some cases. Also, they may benefit certain groups of consumers. The pre-World War II food stamp plan in the United States was profitable to farmers and also helped low-income families. In some situations, at least, price differentiation—involving purposeful departures from the competitive norm—may benefit the general public.

7. Government Agricultural Marketing Services.—All governments assist marketing to some degree. Some governments go to the extremes of setting prices, rationing food or even establishing a governmental monopoly to distribute farm products. Except in time of war, the democracies generally avoid programs of these types. Instead, they generally rely mainly upon free, private enterprise and competition. This is not, however, a program of *laissez-faire,* it involves many governmental services and regulations. Among the oldest government services that assist marketing are police protection, the protection of public health and the enforcement of standard weights and measures. All governments have programs in these fields and most governments provide some agricultural statistics and some current market news. In the United States, the federal and state governments co-operate to supply detailed statistics on planted acreages, the condition of growing crops, production, storage stocks and similar factors of importance to marketers. They also supply day-to-day information on shipments, market receipts and market prices. In addition, they supply current outlook and situation reports, discussing current and foreseeable trends for the principal farm products.

Many governments have established official grades for farm products, and have set up inspection services to determine the actual grade of any specific lot of a commodity. Official grades have greatly facilitated marketing over long distances. For example, a carload of California lettuce may be sold in New York by wire on the basis of an inspection certificate. Or a shipload of North Dakota wheat may be sold in Liverpool. In general, grades are not based upon nutritive values, but upon market preferences. Foods that qualify for any of the official grades of the United States are good nutritionally.

In addition to such services as market news, grades and inspection, healthy competitive marketing requires some supervision of trade practices, especially some deterrants to antisocial forms of monopoly. The growth of large corporations in meat packing, cigarette manufacturing, milk distribution and food retailing has been in part a result of economies of scale. But they have also concentrated great power in the hands of a few large concerns. The aim of governmental programs in this field is to give the public the benefits of greater efficiency because of bigness, and also to protect the interests of both farmer and consumer.

While most democratic countries attempt to suppress monopoly, many of them also have programs to enable groups of farmers to work together in setting prices, or in regulating the flow of their products to market. Examples are the marketing schemes of several countries in the British commonwealth, and the marketing agreements and orders in the United States. Such programs are generally effective only when adopted by growers in a referendum and when approved by some responsible agency of the government. (*See also* MARKETING.)

BIBLIOGRAPHY.—E. H. Chamberlin, *Theory of Monopolistic Competition,* 6th ed. (1948); W. C. Waite and H. C. Trelogan, *Agricultural Market Prices,* 2nd ed. (1951); G. S. Shepherd, *Marketing Farm Products,* 3rd ed. (1955); F. L. Thomsen, *Agricultural Marketing* (1951); L. J. Norton, *Markets for and Marketing of Farm Products* (1954); F. V. Waugh (ed.), *Readings on Agricultural Marketing* (1954); U.S. Department of Agriculture, "Marketing," *1954 Yearbook of Agriculture* (1954); "Agricultural Markets in Change," *Agri. Econ. Report no. 95* (1966); National Commission on Food Marketing, *Report,* "Food From Farmer to Consumer" (1966), technical studies no. 1 through 10 (1966).   (F. V. WH.)

VIII. AGRICULTURAL CO-OPERATION

Farmers in most countries have developed business enterprises known as co-operative associations. These organizations differ from other forms of business in that the patrons or customers (those who use the services of the associations) own and operate them. For discussion of the history of co-operatives and their development and operation in various countries *see* CO-OPERATIVES.

1. Organization.—The members of co-operatives provide the capital required, elect directors to determine policies and programs to be followed, and delegate to them authority to employ an operating manager. Farmers use co-operative associations to market their products, to procure farm supplies and to obtain such services as insurance, irrigation, credit and electric power.

Co-operatives are usually incorporated. The incorporators may organize an association with capital stock, or a nonstock membership organization. In a capital stock co-operative, each member is required to purchase one or more shares of common stock. This stock carries voting rights and may be held only by members. In a nonstock co-operative, a membership fee is assessed. Additional financing may be derived from the sale of nonvoting, preferred stock, or from the purchase of certificates of interest by members of the association. The revolving capital plan is a method frequently adopted to maintain ownership of an association in the hands of active members. Under this plan members contribute capital in proportion to their individual use of the services of the association. The oldest outstanding contributions are repaid to members usually at the discretion of the board of directors.

Whatever form incorporation may take, the co-operative nature of the enterprise is safeguarded by the following provisions of its articles of incorporation or bylaws: (1) savings above operating costs are paid, or allocated, to each member in direct proportion to his patronage; (2) interest or dividends on invested capital, if paid, are limited to nominal rates of return; (3) voting by members usually is on a one-man, one-vote basis; occasionally it is based on patronage with a low limit on the number of votes one member may cast. In a capital stock association, the number of voting shares a member may own is limited, usually one qualifying share.

2. Development.—Farmer co-operatives developed over a wide front in Europe and North America in the last half of the 19th century. Their activities varied widely in different areas, but the common objectives were to provide at cost needed services that were not performed satisfactorily by existing agencies. Credit, insurance, marketing and the purchase of farm supplies were among the earliest services provided.

The first associations were small community organizations. As the needs of farmers became more complex, with the general economic expansion in many countries, co-operative progress and growth continued. Many local associations formed federations to extend their services and increase their bargaining power. During the first half of the 20th century, co-operatives developed broad marketing and purchasing programs and established substantial facilities to package and process farm products and manufacture farm supplies. They kept pace generally with the great technical and industrial expansion following World War II.

Throughout most of the world, agricultural co-operatives fall into three broad classes: (1) those selling members' products; (2) those furnishing farm supplies, such as fertilizer, feed and petroleum products; and (3) those providing essential business services. Many co-operatives fall in all classes.

3. Services.—A marketing co-operative may handle a farmer's product at one or more stages as it moves from the farm to the consumer. Some act only as bargaining associations to represent farmers in transactions with dealers and processors. Some associations process commodities, producing, for example, cottonseed oil, butter, canned fruits or dressed poultry. Others advertise and merchandise the members' products under the co-operative's own trade-mark, selling direct or through brokers to wholesalers and large retailers.

In the second half of the 20th century, supply associations increased rapidly in the more mechanized agricultural areas where farming required increased investments in feed, petroleum products, fertilizer and other supplies. More and more local supply associations affiliated with the larger regional co-operatives that owned and operated manufacturing facilities. The local association usually was a member of the regional association and as such was entitled to patronage refunds which then were allocated or paid to its farmer members. Some regional co-operatives, either individually or in co-operation with other regionals, acquired oil wells and refineries, and were engaged in mining chemicals required in the manufacture of fertilizer and insecticides.

Co-operative business services offered farmers in many countries included insurance, rural electric service, transportation, irrigation, cotton ginning and rural health and hospital care. Some predominantly rural countries established handicraft and similar co-operatives in agricultural communities.

Although the principles of co-operation remain reasonably constant throughout the world, the operations and the progress of farmer associations were affected by the economic development of agriculture in each country. In the more highly industrialized nations, such as Canada, Denmark, Sweden and the United States, local associations originally offered one type of service. They were formed to market one farm product, to buy a limited number of supplies or to perform one general service. Over the years, however, many of these single-purpose associations broadened the scope of their operations. In the second half of the 20th century, for example, 63% of the marketing co-operatives in the United States handled some supplies, while 27% of the farm supply associations also marketed certain farm products. Credit, insurance and electric power co-operatives, however, rarely engage in multiple activities. In other countries, less highly industrialized, a single community co-operative may provide insurance, credit and marketing services for farm products and purchase supplies, as well as perform other services. In parts of India and in Burma, for example, the policy has been to organize one multipurpose co-operative in each village.

The attitude of most governments toward farmer co-operatives ranges from neutrality to strong support. Generally, the nature of the support varies with the development and progress of the agriculture of the country. The governments of some highly agricultural countries often exercise extensive supervision over farmer associations, including audits of financial and operating records and reviews of performance programs. In other countries where agriculture is further developed, governments rarely exercise controls which are not applicable to all business. Technical help in organization and operation is extended to co-operatives by many governments whose policy is to render assistance to farmers in connection with their economic problems.

The need for farmers to be represented by organizations operating in their interests has sparked the development of agricultural co-operatives in all countries. The average farmer is a comparatively small producer. Membership in a co-operative increases his bargaining power when he sells his crops, when he purchases farm supplies or when he requires credit, insurance or other services that he can obtain by joint efforts through co-operatives.

Furthermore, supply co-operatives have pioneered in improving the quality of feed, fertilizer, seeds and other items farmers buy. Marketing co-operatives have been leaders in developing methods of operation that recognize superior product quality and tend to minimize speculative risks. One method employed to reduce speculative risks is the co-operative practice known as pooling. Returns from sales of members' products of like quality are pooled by many associations. This practice involves recording, according to quality and quantity, all products delivered by each member during the pooling period and making payment of sales returns to members based on the average price received per unit for all products of the same quality. In individual associations, the pooling period may extend from a few days to an entire marketing season.

Co-operatives, in addition, promote operating economy. If their capital permits, they invest in more efficient plants and laboursaving machinery and equipment whenever the directors are convinced that the investment will reduce handling margins or provide needed services. Such action by a co-operative is an application of the practice of improving service for members. As other efficient firms usually follow the lead of co-operatives in reducing handling margins, all farmers in the area benefit, whether they are members or not.

BIBLIOGRAPHY.—*American Cooperation,* proceedings of the American Institute of Cooperation (annual); *Year Book of Agricultural Co-operation,* recent developments by countries (annual); *Agricultural Cooperation—Selected Readings,* ed. by Martin A. Abrahamsen and Claud L. Scroggs (1957); *Farmer Cooperatives in the United States,* FCS Bulletin 1, Farmer Cooperative Service, U.S. Department of Agriculture (1955); *Bibliography on Cooperation in Agriculture, 1946–1953,* Library List No. 41, Supp. 1, U.S. Department of Agriculture Library (1954). Select bibliography on co-operation included in *Year Book of Agricultural Co-operation,* pp. 363–384 (1955).   (J. G. KP.)

IX. AGRICULTURAL LABOUR

Agricultural labour or work on farms in many respects is unique among the major occupations. In no other major industry does so large a proportion of the work force consist of self-employed operators, or so small a proportion of wage or salary workers. Because farms produce living things, the activities on them are affected by natural factors such as climate, weather, life cycles of animals and other physical and biological factors. This results in a larger month-to-month variation in the need for workers than in most

TABLE III.—*Agricultural Employment in Selected Countries*

Country	Year	Total population (in 000)	Total economically active population (in 000)	% (2) of (1)	Active population in agriculture (in 000)	% (4) of (2)
		(1)	(2)	(3)	(4)	(5)
United States (Continental excluding Alaska)	1940	131,669	44,888	34.1	8,372	18.7
	1950	150,697	60,037	39.8	7,331	12.2
	1960	178,464	73,126	41.0	5,723	7.8
	1965	193,608	78,357	40.5	4,585	5.9
Italy	1936	42,399	18,345	43.3	8,843	48.2
	1951	47,516	20,672	43.5	8,261	40.0
	1960	49,361	21,418	43.4	6,320	29.5
	1964	51,090	20,130	39.4	5,012	24.9
Venezuela	1940	3,851	1,241	32.2	636	51.2
	1950	5,035	1,706	33.9	705	41.3
	1961	7,622	2,407	31.6	774	32.2
Japan	1930	63,872	29,377	46.0	14,131	48.1
	1950	83,200	35,720	42.9	19,203	53.8
	1960	93,200	44,009	47.2	14,326	32.6
	1964	96,906	47,860	49.4	13,120	27.4
Canada*	1941	11,507	4,196	36.5	1,082	25.8
	1950	14,009	5,286	37.7	830	15.7
	1960	17,852	6,234	34.9	755	12.1
	1964	19,235	6,609	34.4	630	9.5
United Kingdom (excluding Northern Ireland)	1931	44,795	21,075	47.0	1,258	6.0
	1951	50,225	22,579	45.0	1,116	4.9
	1960	50,952	25,100	49.3	635	2.5
	1965	52,967	26,099	49.3	497	1.9
Germany, West (excluding West Berlin)	1939†	38,682	20,065	51.9	5,399	26.9
	1950	47,696	22,074	46.3	5,114	23.2
	1960	55,433	26,247	47.3	3,623	13.8
	1965	59,012	27,153	46.0	2,966	10.9
India	1931‡	352,838	148,817	42.2	109,731	73.7
	1951§	356,628	140,323	39.3	100,104	71.3
	1961§	441,631	188,676	42.7	137,546	72.9
New Zealand	1936	1,574	644	40.9	150	23.3
	1951	1,939	740	38.2	129	17.4
	1961	2,414	895	37.1	123	13.7
Chile	1930	4,287	1,460	34.1	506‖	34.7
	1940	5,024	1,812	36.1	616‖	34.0
	1952	5,933	2,155	36.3	648‖	30.1
	1960	7,290	2,389	32.8	662‖	27.7
Sweden	1930	6,142	2,872	46.8	943	32.8
	1945	6,674	2,988	44.8	615	20.6
	1950	7,042	3,105	44.1	540	17.4
	1960	7,497	3,244	43.3	447	13.8
Czechoslovakia	1930	13,998	6,719	48.0	2,484	37.0
	1950	12,338	5,577	45.2	1,626	29.2
	1960	13,654	6,063	44.4	1,468	24.2
	1965	14,159	6,477	45.7	1,262	19.5

*Excludes Yukon and Northwest Territories and Newfoundland.   †Official estimates covering present boundaries.   ‡Prepartition India.   §Excludes Jammu and Kashmir.   ‖Includes workers in forestry and fishing.

Source: From individual country official government publications and FAO, United Nations, *Yearbook of Production* (1965).

other industries. During periods of crop harvesting, for example, many more workers usually are required than during other seasons. Mechanized farming, however, tends to reduce the seasonal variations. Also, chiefly because of the natural factors, agricultural work consists of many separate tasks. And as most farm workers are not specialists, the work they do varies more from time to time than that of most nonfarm workers.

There are many kinds of agricultural workers. There is first the operator of the farm—whether owner or tenant, such as the European peasant or the United States family-type farmer—who himself works in the fields and cares for the farm animals. Next, there are the sharecroppers and similar types of labourer-tenants, who in many parts of the world work the land and share the proceeds with the owner. In some countries they are classified as farm operators, but in many instances they have more of the characteristics of workers than of operators. While they usually furnish the bulk of the labour, they own few tools and other farm resources and seldom make major management decisions. (See FARM TENANCY.)

Another group consists of members of the operators' family—chiefly wives and children—who work on the farm as unpaid workers. During slack seasons or school periods, they may help with only the usual farm chores or light routine work, but in the busy periods, they may work on a more nearly full-time basis. In some countries, school periods, at least for the older children, are adjusted to avoid conflict with peak periods of farm work. In many countries, however, there are regulations that govern the use of child labour and minimum school attendance.

Finally, there are the hired workers who may work on farms the year-round or only seasonally. The year-round or permanent workers derive their entire income from farm work. In many instances, they are farm boys who intend to make farming their lifelong occupation and are working as farm labourers to accumulate sufficient capital to begin farming for themselves. In many parts of the world—in Turkey, for instance, and several Asian countries—seasonal workers are generally operators of small holdings who supplement their income by working on other farms as wage labourers. Other hired workers have regular urban or rural employment, but work on farms during the busy seasons. Still others have no other employment, but come to the farms for harvest work. An important group of seasonal workers are those who migrate from area to area with the crop, as in the United States, and who rely on farm work for the major source of their income.

For many reasons, valid statistics that are comparable from country to country are difficult to obtain. Table III presents data for selected countries, for which statistics are available over a period of years. While total population has increased, as has the number of the economically active population in most countries, there has been a marked decline in the economically active population engaged in agriculture. The decline is less marked in the so-called underdeveloped countries. In many of the industrially advanced countries less than 20% of the active population is engaged in agriculture. The proportion is much higher in most of the less-developed countries.

Hired workers comprise a relatively small part of the farm work force in typical European peasant countries and in countries such as the United States and Canada, where family-type farming is the rule. Hired workers are even less important in Japan, with its large number of small farms. In countries such as Argentina and Chile, where large-scale farming is important and where mechanization has not advanced, the proportion of hired workers is high. It is highest of all in Great Britain chiefly because of high labour needs for intensive crops such as vegetables.

Historically, the level of farm wage rates has fluctuated in response to prevailing conditions of farm labour supply and demand including the lack or abundance of nonfarm employment opportunities, and to the general economic conditions as these affect the prices and income received by farmers. Additional factors affecting farm wages and income, especially after about 1950, included soil improvement, principally through use of fertilizers, and increased mechanization. Thus, with growing demands on the world's food supply, surplus producing countries like Australia

TABLE IV.—*Agricultural Wages in Selected Countries**

Country	Unit of currency	Period	1930†	1940†	1950†	1960‡
Denmark	krone	day	4.78	6.11	18.88	29.80
France	franc	day	20.85	28.79	421.00	196.80§
Germany, West	deutschemark	hour	0.33	0.29	0.76	1.73
Italy	lira	hour	1.52	1.64	60.16	...
Sweden	krona	day	4.19	5.75	15.16	4.18‖
United Kingdom¶	shilling	week	31.7	48.1	94.0	209.25
Australia	shilling	week	93.0	85.0	194.6	353.42
India	rupee	day	0.453	0.287	1.35	1.29
Japan	yen	day	1.14	2.07	201.0	372.0
New Zealand	shilling	week	71.6	76.6	148.7	210.75
Philippines	peso	day	...	0.56	1.70	1.94
Canada	dollar	month	47.42	38.70	110.68	163.0
Chile	peso	day	5.33	10.73	77.66	.62♀
Mexico	peso	day	1.09	1.30	2.66	9.38
United States	dollar	month	48.10	36.68	121.00	192.0

*Figures are for the year indicated or the nearest year for which data were available. †Exclusive of the value of such allowances as board and lodging except for France, Japan, New Zealand and Chile. ‡Inclusive of the value of such allowances as board and lodging for Australia, Chile, Mexico, Philippines and United States. §Monthly wage in New francs. ‖Hourly wage. ¶Minimum wage rates. ♀Daily wage in escudos.
Source: *Yearbook of Labour Statistics,* published by the International Labour Office (Geneva), and official statistics.

and Canada, by using fertilizers and adding agricultural land, were able to produce more with less labour; and this was reflected in their agricultural wages (see Table IV). In Mexico, the successful land reform of the early 1950s helped raise wages. But in India, planned soil improvement failed to reach goals, and the evergrowing supply of labour depressed already low wages.

The economic and social well being of farm labourers varies greatly among and within countries. An increasing number of countries have taken action to improve employment conditions in agriculture, giving attention to such problems as wages, hours, regularity of employment, housing and medical care. In some, such as several Latin-American countries, provisions of the general labour code apply to agricultural workers. In other countries, the regulation is entrusted to joint boards on which workers and employers are represented. Although trade unionism has lagged in agriculture, it is well established in a number of European countries, and regulation is effected by collective bargaining between workers' and employers' organizations. Various provisions of social security programs have applied to farm workers in an increasing number of countries. International labour conferences have adopted standards for improvement of living and working conditions in agriculture. The aim of these standards is to place farm labourers on an equal footing with industrial workers.

BIBLIOGRAPHY.—Organization for European Economic Cooperation, *Labour Management on the Farm* (1957); F. Wunderlich, *Farmer and Farm Labor in the Soviet Zone of Germany* (1958); T. K. Warley and K. A. Ingersent, *Use of Labour in Farm-Scale Vegetable Production* (1957); W. D. Weatherford, *Geographic Differentials of Agricultural Wages in the United States* (1957); F. Dovring, *Land and Labor in Europe, 1900–1950* (1956); *Agricultural Labor in the United States, 1943–52, A Selected List of Annotated References,* Library List No. 61, U.S. Department of Agriculture (mimeographed) (1954); W. S. Woytinsky *et al., Employment and Wages in the United States,* ch. 26, 30 and 42 (1953); International Labour Office, *Yearbook of Labour Statistics* (annual); *Productivity: A Bibliography,* Bulletin No. 1226, U.S. Department of Labour (1957). (M. O.; R. W. HT.)

X. LAW IN AGRICULTURE

Much of the law which affects the farmer is not agricultural in the sense that it is designed especially for agriculture. Laws on property, contracts, taxation, agency and the administration of estates, for example, affect the farmer vitally, but for the most part are of general application. Only occasionally are laws molded especially to fit agriculture. For general discussion of laws as they affect the farmer in various countries see LANDLORD AND TENANT and LAND TENURE: ECONOMIC AND AGRARIAN ASPECTS. *See* also LAW (ARTICLES ON) for references to articles in that field, and articles on separate countries.

A vast body of law, however, mainly administrative and regulatory in character, has been promulated for the benefit of agriculture. Hence, the farmer has become familiar with regulations and administrators, but he has not developed an easy familiarity with the principles of statutory and common law which are important to him. Nor have lawyers developed an easy familiarity with a myriad of principles regarding land tenure, the farm landlord-tenant relationship or the agricultural credit structure—to mention only a few areas of common interest.

Broadly viewed, farm law includes the legislation from which economic and social programs for agriculture have been constructed. It might even comprehend all policy-determining legislation having a direct bearing on agriculture. But for certain purposes there is something to be gained by excluding such legislation and considering farm law as those statutory and common-law principles which affect the personal and property rights of the farmer. In this light, farm law may be divided into several major areas—the legal incidents of property ownership and transfer; the use of farm property as security for credit; the landlord-tenant relationship; the employment of labour on the farm; drainage, irrigation and water rights; farm taxes; farm animals; fences; trespass; custom operators and other agents; liability and regulatory laws.

1. Farm Land Ownership.—Members of landowning farm families are vitally affected by law on property. Often the ability of a family to remain intact and continue a wise use and management of land after the termination of a present ownership depends upon the kind and quality of interest possessed by the member or members of the family holding the title. Present land use, future farm business plans and the ability to sell or mortgage depend to a large extent upon the kind of interest possessed by the present owner and upon the disposition which will be made of the property when that interest ends.

Members of landowning farm families are entitled to know the answers to such questions as these: Who holds the title to the farm? Is the owner a fee simple owner, life tenant, remainderman, corporation or individual? Is the title vested in more than one person? If so, are they joint tenants, tenants in common, or do they each own separate parts of the farm? What would happen to the farm if the owner were to die suddenly? Who would own it? Who would have the right to operate it? Would it have to be sold to pay debts? If it passed by descent, could those inheriting it co-operate in giving it proper management? Would they be apt to make a fair settlement within a reasonable period?

2. Farm Property as Security.—The use of land and personal property as security for an increased amount of rural credit focuses attention on laws relative to mortgages, trust deeds, chattel mortgages, land title transfer, interest rates, foreclosure and priority of creditors. To some extent laws on real estate and chattel mortgages have been modified to fit the farm enterprise. Likewise, bankruptcy laws have sometimes been altered to give preferred treatment to farm debtors.

3. Landlord-Tenant Relationship.—Most farm tenants and a great many farm landlords know little about the legal aspects of the landlord-tenant relationship. Yet where misunderstandings arise, as they often do, the parties must finally depend upon the various principles of tenancy recognized in law for a settlement of their differences. A better knowledge of the nature and effectiveness, under the law, of agreements made by landlord and tenant, and of the rights and duties of the two parties, would prevent many misunderstandings.

But much more than the avoiding of misunderstandings between landlord and tenant is involved in the matter of a legal basis for tenancy. Proper use of land and satisfactory economic, social and cultural levels of farm life are all bound up in the question of adequate functioning of the landlord-tenant relationship. If improvement is to be made in tenant farming, general knowledge of legal provisions is necessary on the part of both tenants and landlords. Dependence on oral leases and local custom tends to discourage change and to preserve the existing practices and systems of farming, whether good or bad.

4. Employment of Labour on the Farm.—The thoroughness with which farm employers and farm labourers discuss the terms of employment varies considerably. Many times such agreements are oral, and important items, such as the term of employment, Sunday work and perquisites of the labourer, are not discussed. Farm owners and operators, moreover, are faced with many problems about their liability for injuries to farm labourers or other labourers they employ, particularly as to liability under the provisions of workmen's compensation or employers' liability laws.

5. Drainage, Irrigation and Water Rights.—Common-law rules, statutory controls and laws enabling the organization of drainage, irrigation, water conservancy and other types of districts or public corporations all attest to the importance of law in the area of water rights.

6. Farm Taxes.—Tax laws generally give some special treatment to farmers. These are changed and modified frequently, yet up-to-date information on the various kinds of taxes that affect the farm business—property, income, gift, estate and other—is essential to the farm operator and owner. (See *Farm Taxation*, above.)

7. Farm Animals.—Many laws apply to the ownership of farm animals—relating to disease, animal trespass, cruelty to animals, liens for sire owners, injury by railroads, indemnity for loss from dogs, to mention only a few.

8. Fences.—Division fence laws requiring adjoining farm landowners to share in the construction and maintenance of such fences, laws defining a "legal" fence and laws requiring the trimming of hedge fences are common. However, the specific requirements of such laws vary a great deal.

9. Trespass.—One of the oldest and most venerated principles of property law is that which holds that an owner of land has the exclusive right of possession. This right is particularly important to farmers, whose crops, fences and livestock may be damaged by the entry of unauthorized persons. In many common-law jurisdictions the right as it pertains to farmers has been strengthened by statute.

10. Custom Operators and Other Agents.—Laws covering the independent contractor and agency generally are important because of the large amount of baling, threshing, grinding, construction, painting and other farm work done by contracting parties as distinguished from employees; and because of the use of farm managers to look after the owners' interests in rented land.

11. Liability.—Farmers annually pay out large sums to satisfy claims for damage. These payments are made to hired men, visitors, neighbouring farmers and many other classes of persons injured by the activities of the farm operator. To protect farmers against some of these risks, various types of liability insurance have been developed. The purpose of such insurance is to pay to injured persons the amount of damage the insured farmer would otherwise have to pay. Obviously the probability of some events happening is remote and need not be insured against—and insurance for certain other things would cost too much. Sound information on the principles of liability insurance, therefore, is important to farmers. (See *Agricultural Insurance*, above.)

12. Regulatory.—Seed, feed, fertilizers, stock remedies, community or auction sales, commission merchants and plant nurseries are a few of the many items or enterprises that are regulated and sometimes licensed by law. A knowledge of those regulations applying to a particular farm business is essential to the farmer. *See* REAL PROPERTY AND CONVEYANCING, LAWS OF; *see* also references under "Agricultural Economics" in the Index.

BIBLIOGRAPHY.—Jacob H. Beuscher, *Law and the Farmer*, 2nd ed. (1956); R. L. Adams and W. W. Bedford, *Everyday Farm Laws* (1949); A. E. Korpela, *Federal Farm Law Manual* (1956); Harold Winford Hannah, *Law on the Farm* (1948), "Law and Agriculture," *Virginia Law Review*, 32:781 (June 1946), and "An Educational Program in Agricultural Law," *J. Fm. Econ.*, 30:770 (Nov. 1948).

For law in agriculture in Great Britain *see* Laws, statutes, etc., *Agricultural Holdings*, 10th ed. (1949); *Agricultural Law and Tenant Right*, 4th ed. (1949); *Guide to the Agricultural Holdings Act, 1948* (1948).

For an introduction to problems of law in agriculture in underdeveloped countries *see* R. Barlowe, "Land Reform and Economic Development," *J. Fm. Econ.*, vol. 35, no. 2 (May 1953); Hassan A. Dawood, "Agrarian Reform in Egypt: A Case Study," *Current History*, vol. xxx, no. 178 (June 1956). (H. W. Hh.; N. G. P. K.)

AGRICULTURAL EDUCATION AND RESEARCH.

Almost every country has its agricultural research stations and teaching organizations. The research stations are of two types: those concerned with the development of a subject; *e.g.* soil science, plant nutrition or plant pathology; and those using the knowledge thus gained for obtaining higher yields and better quality of crops and animal products. The education offered is of three categories: university departments for training experts and teachers; farm schools for prospective farmers; and itinerant instructors and advisers who help those actually farming.

This article is divided into the following main sections: United States, Canada, Australia and New Zealand, Western Europe, Eastern Europe, the Soviet Union, Asia and the Middle East, North Africa, Central and Southern Africa, Latin America, Inter-American and UN Institutions.

UNITED STATES

EDUCATION

The impetus for agricultural education in the United States has been associated with demands for farm products by the increasing proportion of the total population engaged in nonfarming occupations. In 1820 only 13% of the population was engaged in nonagricultural occupations. A century later the proportion of rural farm population to the total population had decreased to 30%, and by the second half of the 20th century only 15% of the population lived on farms.

Until about 1900 new land was available as an additional source of food for the growing population. The U.S. farmer thereafter was confronted with the dual challenge of producing more total products and of obtaining increased yields per acre on the available land. The necessity of producing more products for each farm worker required increased mechanization and production efficiencies. Also the standard of living in the United States has improved from generation to generation, and no doubt agricultural education has had a significant role in this evolutionary process.

Early Agricultural Institutions.—Various agricultural institutions existed in the United States prior to the founding of the agricultural colleges and the development of public secondary schools in which formal education in agriculture is presented.

In 1743 Benjamin Franklin led in the organization of the American Philosophical Society, which gave much attention to agriculture. The members' interest in agriculture led to the organization in 1785 of the Philadelphia Society for the Promotion of Agriculture, of which George Washington was an honorary member. Other agricultural societies were organized in several states about the same time. In 1852 it was estimated that there were about 300 active organizations in the 31 states and 5 territories, and in 1860 there were 941 agricultural organizations recorded in the books of the United States Agricultural Society.

A second type of institution which preceded formal education in agriculture was the agricultural fair. What appears to have been the first fair of a modern kind was staged in 1810 in the District of Columbia with many notables in attendance, including Pres. James Madison and his wife. Elkanah Watson is credited with organizing the Berkshire Agricultural Society at Pittsfield, Mass., which presented its first fair in 1811. Thereafter agricultural fairs increased rapidly in New England, the Middle Atlantic states, and the new regions of the West.

The farm press was another forerunner of the agricultural colleges and of agricultural education. The *Agricultural Museum* (Georgetown, D.C.) was founded in 1810 as a full-fledged agricultural journal. The *American Farmer* (Baltimore, Md.) and the *Plough Boy* (Albany, N.Y.) appeared in 1819. The *Prairie Farmer* (Chicago, Ill.) began its long career in 1841. By 1850, 40 or more agricultural journals had been established. Some did not last long, many being absorbed by other journals; *e.g.*, the *American Agriculturist* (1842) took over the *Genesee Farmer, American Farmer, Plow, Loom and Anvil*, and more than two dozen others. Those journals that survived exerted great influence.

Agricultural Colleges.—Agricultural colleges came into existence about the middle of the 19th century. A state agricultural college was established in New York in 1853. The oldest surviving state agricultural college in the second half of the 20th century is that of Michigan (now Michigan State University), which began classes in 1857. Similar colleges were established in Pennsylvania and Maryland (1859), and the incorporation of agricultural colleges was authorized in Iowa and Minnesota (1858).

Major developments in U.S. agriculture have been associated with national emergencies. In the midst of the Civil War, Pres. Abraham Lincoln signed the Morrill Act of 1862, under which Congress granted to each state 30,000 ac. of land for each representative and senator for "the endowment, support and maintenance of at least one college where the leading object shall be—without excluding other scientific and classical studies and including military tactics—to teach branches of learning as are related to agriculture and mechanic arts." Sixty-nine state colleges were organized under provisions of the Morrill Act. The land-grant colleges and universities (*q.v.*) are intimately associated with the U.S. Department of Agriculture.

In 1887 Congress passed the Hatch Act, which made provisions for agricultural research to be conducted by the state colleges of agriculture in cooperation with the U.S. Department of Agriculture. State agricultural experiment stations had been established previously in Connecticut (1875), California and North Carolina (1877), New York (1879 and 1882), New Jersey (1880), Ohio, Tennessee, and Massachusetts (1882), Alabama and Wisconsin (1883), Nebraska (1884), and Michigan, Indiana, Kentucky, Maine, and Minnesota (1885). In 1914 Congress passed the Smith-Lever Act providing for agricultural extension teaching and the demonstration of improved agricultural and home economics practices. The creation of the extension service was related to World War I, as the land grants of the Morrill Act had been to the Civil War. The extension service is recognized as an outstanding example of adult education in the United States.

Agricultural Schools.—The demand for instruction in agriculture at the secondary level gained momentum with the growing popularity of high schools about the beginning of the 20th century. Previously some agricultural schools were founded through private initiative in certain states, including New York and Connecticut. A noncollegiate school of agriculture based on the folk school concept was started at the University of Minnesota in 1888.

In 1908 Rufus Stimson was appointed director of the Smith's Agricultural School at Northampton, Mass., where he is credited with having developed the "home project" plan of teaching agriculture. In 1911 a report on the program was presented to the Massachusetts Legislature with a request for state aid to subsidize the teaching of agriculture. In 1908 after Walter H. French became professor of agricultural education at Michigan State College, a new position created in the agricultural college, 67 agriculture departments in Michigan high schools were organized before federal aid was available for teaching vocational agriculture. The General Assembly of Indiana enacted a vocational education law on Feb. 22, 1913.

Among other states in which systems of vocational education in agriculture were established prior to World War I were New York, Pennsylvania, New Jersey, Minnesota, and Wisconsin. In 1916 the U.S. Bureau of Education reported that agriculture was being taught under state supervision in 421 high schools and without state aid in 2,760 public high schools.

Federally aided programs of vocational education in agriculture originated with the passage of the Smith-Hughes Vocational Education Act in 1917, providing assistance to states. The act specified that the instruction must be designed to meet the needs of persons over 14 years of age who were preparing for farming or were engaged in farming. After 1917 additional acts, including the George-Barden Act of 1946, were passed providing funds to supplement the Smith-Hughes Act. Instruction in vocational agriculture involves three major groups—high school students who are preparing for farming, out-of-school young men who are enrolled in young-farmer classes, and adults who are enrolled in adult-farmer classes. In the second half of the 20th century an average of about 750,000 students were enrolled annually in such classes in approximately 10,000 departments of vocational agriculture in the United States. (*See also* AGRICULTURAL ORGANIZATIONS; FOUR-H CLUBS; FUTURE FARMERS OF AMERICA.) (G. F. E.)

AGRICULTURAL RESEARCH

Agricultural research has helped to provide the people of the United States with ample food supplies, better nutrition, and a host of valuable new products, from life-giving drugs to frozen concentrated orange juice. It has meant greater efficiency in crop and livestock production, higher yields per acre, more eggs, milk, and meat from less feed, more effective control of diseases and pests, better use of land and water, and improved methods of harvesting, storing, processing, and marketing farm products.

Measured by the developments in the United States, agriculture had made more progress in the 75 years preceding the middle of the 20th century than in the previous 75 centuries. Agricultural research in America, of course, started very early. Christopher Columbus, on his second voyage in 1493, brought livestock, alfalfa, and other farm products to America to see if they would thrive. Later explorers and settlers also brought seeds and cuttings to plant in the new world. The culture of figs, olives, grapes, and many other crops dates to the early Spanish missions. Experimentation with such crops as rice and tobacco led to the successful colonization of the Carolinas.

For 300 years after the arrival of Columbus, agricultural research in North America was confined to the testing of crops and livestock introduced from Europe, Africa, and Asia. The selection of those plants and animals that produced most abundantly led to the development of new varieties and breeds better adapted to North American soils and climate.

Introduction and development of improved plants and animals were conducted in the early years entirely by private individuals and companies. Washington, Jefferson, and Franklin were among those who aided or encouraged the development of new plant varieties and new mechanical methods to handle crops. The growth of agricultural societies, beginning in colonial days, furthered agricultural research by coordinating the work of many agriculturists.

As the country expanded, the need for agricultural research increased. Soon private individuals could no longer afford to carry the full load. Although the idea of a department of agriculture in the federal government was voiced by Washington soon after he became president, it was not until 1862, during Lincoln's administration, that a federal agency devoted to the welfare of agriculture was created. The U.S. Department of Agriculture achieved cabinet rank in 1889. Federal-grant funds were made available to the states by the Hatch Act of 1887, the Adams Act of 1906, the Smith-Lever Act of 1914, the Purnell Act of 1925, the Bankhead-Jones Act of 1935, the Agricultural Adjustment Act of 1938, and the Research and Marketing Act of 1946. These federal laws established the cooperative extension service, set up regional laboratories to discover basic scientific laws and principles relating to agriculture, and later to find new uses for farm products, and authorized the U.S. Department of Agriculture to contract with other public and private agencies for the conduct of certain types of research, especially that aimed at improved utilization

and marketing of agricultural commodities.

Federal and state governments together contributed about equally with industry in the second half of the 20th century in the financial support of agricultural research. The total investment in this research effort amounted to about $470,000,000 annually. Funds spent by the public agencies, divided roughly half and half between USDA and the states, supported the work of some 13,000 scientists. About $32,000,000 of federally appropriated funds went to state agricultural experiment stations as federal grants and became part of the state research budgets. Contributions by private industry to agricultural research included work aimed at improvement of farm and forest production and farm machinery, research on farm chemicals, and development of new and improved agricultural products and methods of handling and marketing them. Industry also made sizable grants to public research agencies, plus land, facilities, materials, and services.

Although federal research in agriculture began modestly, with simple objectives, many early advances were impressive, such as the development by Marion Dorset of a serum to combat hog cholera (swine fever); the fundamental discovery by Theobald Smith that insects transmit tick fever of cattle—a discovery that paved the way for control of malaria, yellow fever, and other insect-borne diseases; valuable basic discoveries in human nutrition; and the breeding of many new varieties of plants with superior food qualities and resistance to disease and insects.

As more funds became available from both federal and state

GROWTH REGULATION

(Above) Studying the effect of artificial light on the growth and hardiness of young cedars; (below left) effect of the chemical growth regulator phosphon, added to soil to restrict stem growth of chrysanthemum at right; (below right) applying colchicine to bud of a grape cutting to induce genetic changes

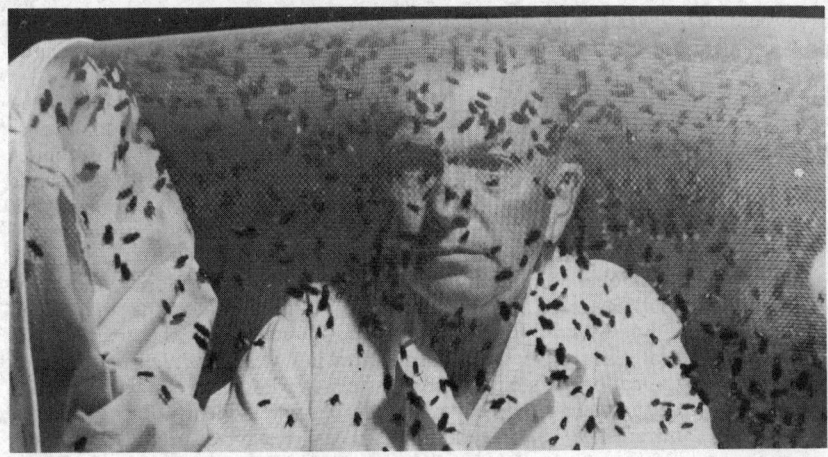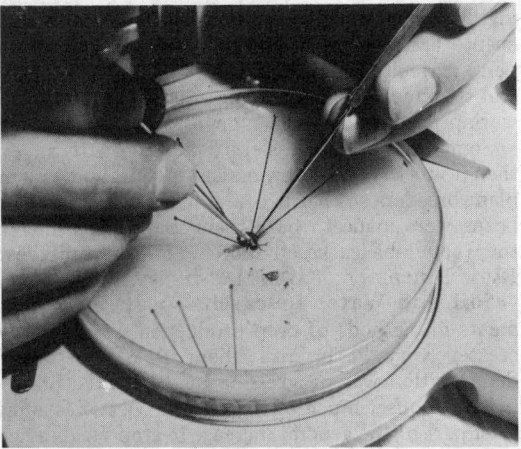

INSECT CONTROL

(Left) Screwworm flies, selected from strains most likely to survive and to compete with native flies; male flies are sterilized for use in control of the screwworm. (Right) Organs of an anesthetized fly are removed to study the effects of chemical insecticides

budgets, government research activities expanded until in the second half of the 20th century work was carried out at more than 500 stations located in every section of the country.

Broadly speaking, agricultural research in the various states is aimed at the solution of problems affecting farm production, marketing and distribution, and the welfare of the people within the states. Research agencies of the federal department of agriculture, on the other hand, concern themselves mainly with problems that are national or regional in scope. Many regional research projects are studied cooperatively by two or more states, USDA agencies, and privately supported organizations.

The state experiment stations provided a practical basis for cooperation with farmers and farm organizations, foundations interested in agricultural research, and private organizations. Although federal grant funds have constituted a nucleus of financial support, more than three-fourths of the funds spent for state experiment station research have come from state legislative action, plus gifts or grants from cooperative farm groups, industry, and other sources.

Crop Production Research.—Improved crop varieties that resist insects and diseases, better management of soils, more efficient methods of crop cultivation and harvesting, and better means of handling, packaging, and marketing farm products have all contributed to increased farming efficiency. Hybrid corn was undoubtedly the most significant single development in crop production in the first half of the 20th century. High-producing hybrids, developed through research, enabled farmers to harvest about a third more corn per acre than they could with open-pollinated varieties. (*See* also CORN; PLANT BREEDING.)

The scientists who opened the way were engaged in basic research. Their concern was to advance knowledge of plant genetics, with little thought of immediate application. But they soon saw the practical value of their work for corn farmers and turned their new basic knowledge over to other scientists for economic development.

Basic research does not always result in startling new discoveries of immediate practical value, but most of the really big developments can be traced back to this type of scientific study. With this fact in mind, the USDA established in 1957 a number of Pioneering Research laboratories, organized around outstanding scientists, to give added emphasis to work in basic research.

Hybrid corn is only one example of the revolutionary changes in farming made possible by research. In little more than 20 years, improved varieties of soybeans put this crop near the top of the list of major crops in the U.S. Yields per acre, oil content, and the area where this crop could be grown were all increased by soybean breeders.

Potato farmers before World War II often complained that their seed stock had "run out." They meant that yields were getting smaller each year. Tomato growers lost entire crops from wilt, and cabbage farmers were in trouble with a disease known as yellows. Nationwide breeding programs were organized with state and federal agencies cooperating. Most of the commercial varieties of these and other vegetables used since that time are an outgrowth of this teamwork.

In the second half of the 20th century, research aided the sugar beet and sugar cane growers economically, giving them varieties that resisted mosaic and curly-top disease, which once threatened to wipe out the U.S. sugar industry.

Other research developments were undertaken because of demands by housewives, who wanted better fruits, vegetables, and other products. As a result many new varieties were developed, ways were found to insure that fresh and processed foods would arrive at retail stores in prime condition, and retailers were taught to care for these foods so that the consumers would receive them in their most attractive, nutritious, and appetizing condition.

Stem rust and other diseases took an enormous toll of wheat and other cereals until resistant varieties were developed and came into general use. After a few years, however, some of these new varieties also succumbed to disease. E. C. Stakman, a research scientist in Minnesota, demonstrated that there were many races or forms of stem rust and that varieties of wheat and other grains could be resistant to one form but not to another. Later it was learned that the rust spores could hybridize in nature just as research men hybridize plants. This discovery indicated that the struggle by scientists to save cereal crops from the ravages of plant-disease organisms was likely to continue for many years to come. (*See* PLANT DISEASES.)

Insect Control.—Reducing agricultural losses from insects is a major function of research. Control of the housefly, mosquito, grasshopper, and many other disease-carrying and harmful insects has been instrumental in reducing damage to crops and livestock and various threats to human life. Many plant-breeding and management practices developed by research were primarily instituted to outwit insects. The use of one insect to control another and the discovery of many new insecticides helped to reduce the dangers from insect pests.

The control of malaria and other diseases carried by mosquitoes and the control of hookworm giving protection from trichinosis were brought about by the endeavours of agricultural scientists. For example, USDA entomologists had a leading part in testing and promoting the use of DDT following the discovery of its insecticidal properties in 1939. It has been applied in more ways to protect more crops and livestock from insects than any insecticide ever discovered. (*See* further PEST CONTROL and ENTOMOLOGY: *Applied Entomology*.)

Mechanization.—Grain combines, hay balers, corn and cotton pickers, and many other machines have been perfected by the farm-equipment industry, aided by research done by agricultural engineers in the public service. Mechanical devices for planting, weeding, thinning, fertilizing, spraying, and cultivating have helped ensure better farm products. Aircraft has been adapted to disperse agricultural chemicals and to do many other jobs for farmers and stockmen. Laboursaving equipment, improved buildings, and work procedures have been developed.

Sometimes it was easier to fit a crop to an existing machine than it was to build a new machine. Sorghum was made a dwarf by plant breeders so that it could be harvested with a combine. Soybeans were made to bear their seed pods higher on the stalk so they could be gathered more easily by a harvester. (*See also* FARM BUILDINGS; FARM MACHINERY.)

Soil and Water Research.—In spite of the many improvements in methods of crop production, average yields per acre increased very little until about 1935. Before that time, soil deterioration was progressing in the United States at a rate sufficient to offset much of the effect of better farming methods. At least part of the general increase in crop yields after the mid-1930s resulted from the slowing down of soil deterioration or, in many cases, to the actual improvement of the soil.

Research has made possible the use of all classes of land in more effective ways. The control of erosion and soil deterioration made other advances even more striking. The amount of water available for crop growth is one of the major limiting factors in crop production. Improved tillage and terracing practices were devised to conserve soil moisture; soil-management and land-use practices were developed to increase infiltration of snow, rain, and irrigation water, thereby reducing losses due to runoff (*see also* DRY FARMING; IRRIGATION; SOIL: *Soil Erosion and Conservation*).

Research in the use of fertilizers and in methods of soil management has revealed many facts useful to farmers in aiding nature to make specific soils more productive. Much has been learned about crop rotations, legumes, and green manure for replenishing soil humus and nitrogen; methods for determining and supplying the nutrient needs of crops; and soil management under irrigation, including salt control. Techniques based on these findings were put to use on farms to increase crop yields and improve soil fertility.

Fertilizers have been improved through both public and private research. The importance of the minor plant nutrients has become more generally understood. Between 1940 and 1965, farmers in the United States more than tripled their use of chemical fertilizers, applying them in granular, liquid, and gaseous forms (*see* FERTILIZERS AND MANURES; SPRAYS AND DUSTS IN AGRICULTURE).

Scientists discovered how to use radioactive isotopes to unlock a vast storehouse of knowledge regarding plants. Chemicals

BY COURTESY OF PENNSYLVANIA AGRICULTURAL EXPERIMENT STATION

AN EXPERIMENTAL MACHINE TRANSPLANTS SEEDLINGS AND LAYS A POLYETHYLENE PLASTIC MULCH TO PREVENT WEED GROWTH AND TO HOLD SOIL MOISTURE

"tagged" with these isotopes were employed, for example, to follow the processes by which plants take up soil nutrients to yield fruits, grains, and fibres.

Radioactive materials were used also to fight animal pests. One result was the complete eradication of screwworms from the island of Curaçao in the Netherlands Antilles in 1955. Entomologists saturated the wild population of screwworms with thousands of laboratory-reared male flies made sterile by exposure to gamma rays from radioactive cobalt. The sterile males mated with the wild females so that finally all eggs laid failed to hatch. Similar techniques were used against the screwworm in Florida and other southeastern states in larger eradication efforts that began in 1958.

Forest and Range Research.—Next to soil, the greatest natural resource in the United States is its forests. During most of the nation's history, these forests were destructively exploited, until the danger of their extinction became evident. Early research in forestry was concerned with measuring forest products and estimating volumes of standing timber on a given tract of land. Later research turned to finding the minimum requirements for keeping forest land productive. The practice of leaving seed trees to ensure reseeding of desired species became common. Experiments in many parts of the country proved that forests could be managed to produce annual crops through selective cutting. Many farmers gained worthwhile supplemental income from such practices.

In many places where millions of acres of forest land had become barren, research found ways of growing trees in nurseries, transplanting them, and making them live. Planting machines were developed to save as much as half the planting costs. Hybrid trees capable of growing larger and faster than native varieties were developed.

Much of the forest land is also range land. Almost half of the continental United States is in range, much of which has suffered from overuse. Research demonstrated that both forest and open ranges responded to good management, and helped cattlemen to produce twice the amount of beef they formerly could raise without the improved practices. Reseeding of western ranges increased the supply of forage in some localities by five to twenty times. This reseeding, along with better management practices, also contributed to soil and water conservation. (*See also* FORESTS AND FORESTRY; RANGE [IN AGRICULTURE].)

Livestock Research.—Successful efforts to safeguard and improve domestic animals give man better food, fur, fibre, and other useful animal products and often also protect human health. A contagious cattle disease, pleuropneumonia, was by 1884 so crippling exports of U.S. cattle that Congress for the first time authorized the Department of Agriculture to begin research on livestock problems. From such research has come a long series of victories against such livestock pests and diseases as new world hookworm, trichinosis, hog cholera, and cattle-tick fever. Veterinarians developed a vaccine against brucellosis in calves that also, indirectly, protects man from this disease, undulant fever, which is transmitted by drinking raw milk from an infected cow. As recently as 1910, many doctors and public health officials regarded pasteurized milk as unsafe for babies. Years of bacteriological research proved it safe even for babies and invalids, and brought about general pasteurization of milk.

Modifying livestock to meet present or anticipated demands of consumers requires more than health protection. Research on the pig (*q.v.*), for instance, has changed its basic characteristics. Consumers demanded more meat and less fat in pork. The meat-type hog was developed in 16 years of research by crossbreeding. It has more lean pork, less lard, and produces larger litters of bigger pigs that grow faster and require less feed to reach market weight than did the old-fashioned hog. Proper selection can produce such a hog in any breed. The Beltsville small white turkey was developed for smaller refrigerators, ovens, and families. The Columbia sheep was a breed made to order to yield more good wool and more meat in the intermountain area of the United States.

In attempts to breed dairy cows that can produce more milk during the long, hot summers of the region bordering the Gulf of Mexico, it has definitely been established that tolerance to heat can be bred into dairy cattle. Some of the most significant re-

CONTROLLING THE POLLINATION OF A WESTERN PINE BY ENCLOSING THE YOUNG CONE IN A CASING BAG, AND FERTILIZING IT WITH POLLEN THROUGH A HYPODERMIC SYRINGE

search on breeding of livestock has been done with dairy cattle, and has established the proved sire system of animal breeding (*q.v.*). Proved sires and artificial insemination enable the dairyman to constantly improve his herd. Advances in artificial insemination of swine point to more efficient pork production for the future. Along with increased emphasis on performance testing—proving a sire by testing performance of his offspring—efforts have been made to predict at a progressively earlier age whether a young animal will grow into an efficient milk or meat producer. Success in predicting the future of dairy heifer calves, beef cattle, and young chicks has made for early culling and better herds and flocks.

To understand how livestock converts plant food into milk, eggs, meat, bone, and fibre, scientists have undertaken broad investigations. Many discoveries—that feed flavours and odours are transmitted to milk directly through the body of the dairy cow, of ways to preserve the vitamin A and protein content of forage crops and to inject vitamin B_{12}, riboflavin, and other growth-promoting supplements into poultry feed, that antibiotics stimulate growth in poultry and swine—have brought about better feeds. Study of life processes in farm animals—in the rumen of a cow, for example—may help in developing the perfect nutriment for each animal (*see* also FEEDS, ANIMAL).

Utilization Research.—In the early days, the main problems of United States research in agriculture were in production, but as export markets decreased and production rose beyond current needs, research turned to finding new and wider outlets for farm products. This utilization research was aimed at improving and extending the markets for existing foods, fibres, and other farm products; at creating new products; and at finding new uses for farm output, including its wastes and residues.

The frozen juice industry was developed by utilization researchers, as were improvements in dried eggs that led to whole-egg cake mixes and similar convenience foods. Soybeans would not have become a major crop had not new food and industrial uses been found to stimulate a demand for greater production. Improvement of turpentine manufacture from pine-tree gum ushered in a

new era in pine farming in the South Atlantic and Gulf Coast states.

Large-scale methods for commercial production of penicillin were developed at one of the USDA utilization laboratories during World War II. This research aided in the discovery and production of many other antibiotics.

Finding uses for agricultural wastes, such as corn cobs, vegetable tops, inedible fats, and fruit pulp, has been an important job of utilization research resulting in new products and industries.

Spruce pulpwood once furnished most of the country's paper. But scientists concerned with forest utilization found ways to use some of the more plentiful tree species, such as southern pine, and at the same time to increase their yields. Fastening together of small pieces of wood to form beams, arches, and other structural members was brought to a high state of perfection as the large trees of the virgin forests disappeared. Plywood was transformed from a novelty product into a dependable material that could be used for a great variety of purposes. With research-developed glues the gluing of wood has progressed from a traditional and secretive process into a well-established commercial operation. Seasoning and preservation of wood have been vastly improved, swelling and shrinking of timber can be prevented, and softwoods can be treated to closely resemble hardwood in appearance and performance.

Much has been learned about wood chemistry. Cellulose can now be changed to sugar and it in turn to ethyl alcohol, feed yeast, molasses, or other products. Lignin, a substance in woody tissue that serves to bind together other constituents in the tissue, is a source of various chemicals (*see* WOOD: *Wood Chemistry*).

Home Economics Research.—The U.S. government's research in human nutrition began in 1894. To improve the nutrition of a nation, researchers must prove three unknowns—the exact nutrients the human body requires at different ages for growth and health; how much of each nutrient agriculture supplies in the various foods; and just what people are buying and eating. Changing people's food habits is difficult, but it can be done. A comparison of family diets in the U.S. in the second half of the 20th century and a century earlier shows the great strides made toward better health for all. (*See* also NUTRITION.)

Research at Work in Regulatory Programs.—The inadequacy of research organized along purely scientific disciplines became evident in the 1870s when the central United States was set upon by devastating hordes of grasshoppers. When Congress established an entomological commission to study the problem, it was the beginning of economic entomology in government, using science to solve practical problems and as a weapon against insect pests. An even stronger endorsement for the problem approach came in 1884 when Congress set up the Bureau of Animal Industry to deal with the cattle disease, pleuropneumonia. It not only authorized research, but it granted regulatory powers to bring the disease under control. Thus, research and regulation were combined, and the pattern for future development was established. Research is frequently directed toward specific regulatory problems —such as pest control, for example. In the same way, pest control operations in the field provide practical tests for research findings and suggest directions for new research to take.

As speedy transportation shrinks the world, the danger of foreign crop and livestock pests threatens the remotest corners of the earth. Between the U.S. farmer and foreign livestock and crop insects and diseases stands a thin line of federal plant- and animal-quarantine inspectors. Second line of defense is a system of surveys and alerts for new pests made by veterinarians, entomologists, and plant pathologists across the nation.

When foreign agricultural pests do invade, or when farmers or local agencies cannot control destructive native pests, large-scale federal-state control or eradication campaigns may be organized. Domestic quarantines are usually invoked to prevent spread. Latest research-proved weapons are used. Through such programs several livestock and crop diseases and pests have been eradicated from the U.S., and many another reduced to economic unimportance.

Since 1906, the meat marketed across state lines has been safeguarded by federal inspection, with close cooperation of industry.

This continuing inspection has been maintained at a cost annually of less than ten cents per person.

Economic and Marketing Research.—Research economists of the USDA and the land-grant colleges help to supply factual economic data to aid farmers. They have also helped to combine the separate contributions of research on plants, animals, and machines into efficient and profitable farm-management programs.

When farmers grew everything they needed and their wives made everything the family used, there were few marketing problems and little need for marketing research. As farming became a specialized business, the need increased for research in agricultural marketing relating to the entire range of activities that arose in moving products from farms to the consumer. Research assistance has been provided to farmers in organizing and operating co-operatives for marketing, purchasing, or other business service, and continuous research has been conducted to improve the marketing, handling, storage, processing, transportation, and distribution of agricultural products. (*See* also AGRICULTURAL ECONOMICS.)   (B. T. S.)

CANADA

Agricultural education in Canada is the responsibility of local or provincial authorities, while research is in charge of the central or federal authorities: this has the advantage that it can be based on broad ecological regions or on commodities of wide national importance.

The Ontario Agriculture College, Guelph, the oldest in the country, was established in 1874; later it was linked with the University of Toronto. In 1907 Sir William Macdonald founded the college in Quebec that bears his name and became the agricultural faculty of McGill University, Montreal, with the largest postgraduate school in Canada. The French agricultural college at Ste.-Anne de la Pocatière, Que., is linked with Laval University. The three prairie provinces have their universities, each with its agricultural faculty. These provide staff for the experimental farms and the extension services; candidates for the higher posts usually do postgraduate work of doctorate level at one of the U.S. universities where greater facilities are available.

The experimental farms were established in 1886 as a federal responsibility: the Central Experimental Farm is at Ottawa, and it had at the outset four branch farms in widely different parts of the country. The first director, William Saunders, recognizing that Canada's special climatic conditions would necessitate the breeding of crop varieties suited thereto, made crosses of wheat with the purpose of combining suitability, high quality, and early ripening. Among them was marquis; its virtues were not immediately recognized but later it dominated the prairies and became the most famous variety of its day. The experimental farms proved so useful that their numbers were increased and by the 1960s had risen to about 40 with more than 20 substations and a staff of about 1,000 graduates in addition to technical and other assistants. The Ottawa and Charlottetown, P.E.I., stations are the plant breeding centres for the eastern provinces, and those at Winnipeg, Man., and Lethbridge, Alta., for the western. The new varieties of wheat bred at Winnipeg have markedly benefited Canada's economy. Progressive shortening of the period of growth enabled the wheat belt to be pushed further north, and greater resistance to drought facilitated western extension. Increased resistance to rust reduced greatly a serious hazard in the eastern prairies, and resistance to sawfly did the same in the western area.

Problems of soil management are studied at Swift Current, Sask. For conserving soil moisture no improvement on the old practice of fallowing every second or third year had been found by the 1960s, but the action was much better understood and the procedure was more effective and safer. The older methods often led to soil erosion while modern ones evolved by research did not; they were based on strip farming, weed destruction, and trash or rough-surface fallowing. Extensive rehabilitation of eroded lands was carried out under the Soil Conservation Service.

The plant breeders of the eastern provinces have rendered great service to Canada's important and growing livestock industry by producing higher-yielding and disease-resistant grasses such as climax timothy, large-seeded hybrids of wheat and agropyron (wheat grass, or couch grass), and earlier maturing strains of soybean. Other research activities deal with pasture improvement.

Fruit problems are studied at Kentville, N.S., and in the western and northwestern stations; other investigations deal with the possibilities of growing vegetables in the far north thereby mitigating the harsh conditions for its inhabitants; the program includes hydroponic methods.

The experimental farms always have been active educational agencies. They are the basis of the extension service which, modified to suit Canadian conditions, is patterned after that of the U.S. Closely linked with the experimental farms are a series of illustration farms, ordinary commercial farms on which promising new results can be tested under practical conditions. The experimental farms staffs are associated with the provincial departments and the universities in carrying out the soil survey.

AUSTRALIA AND NEW ZEALAND

The first agricultural society in Australia was formed in 1822 at Parramatta, New South Wales, by a group of farmers with the purpose, among others, of "communicating their mutual experiences and benefiting by their reciprocal advice," and also of making experiments on the growth of products. Other societies followed, often short-lived; finally the Royal Agricultural Society of New South Wales was incorporated in 1869. Systematic agricultural education began in 1881 when the government of South Australia appointed a professor of agriculture who set up an experimental farm in 1882 which later became the Roseworthy Agricultural College. Victoria followed with the college at Dookie in 1885 and afterward another at Longerenong; New South Wales established Hawkesbury Agricultural College in 1891; Queensland set up the Gatton College (later called the Queensland Agricultural High School and College) in 1897; and last of all, in 1925, Western Australia established Muresk. There are also some agricultural high schools. Each of the universities has a faculty of agriculture; Sydney since 1910; Melbourne since 1911 (created 1905, but not staffed until 1911); the others later. These confer degrees in agriculture and prepare men for the higher teaching, advisory, and administrative posts, while the college training is more vocational in character and suited to farmers and managers of large sheep stations.

The earliest systematic agricultural research in Australia was done by William Farrer at his home at Lambrigg near Canberra, New South Wales, between 1886 when he settled there and 1906 when he died: for the first 12 years the research was conducted at his own expense; later he had a post in the Department of Agriculture. There he bred varieties of drought- and rust-resistant wheats suited to the Australian environment which made a great expansion of wheat growing possible. But for nearly 20 years he had no successors, and by 1920 unsolved difficult problems in soil management, animal health, and other subjects were causing loss to agriculturists and sheep farmers, or pastoralists.

As in Great Britain, New Zealand, and India, the first institute devoted entirely to research and free of departmental responsibilities resulted from the efforts of a private individual: in this case Peter Waite, a sheep farmer, whose benefactions to the University of Adelaide made possible the founding of the institute in 1924. It has since become Australia's greatest agricultural research station. Its investigations include the water requirements of the wheat crop, Australian meteorology and hydrology, soil surveys, and the trace elements in plant and animal nutrition. Another independent research institute is in Western Australia, also associated with the university; it deals largely with the problems of the sheep industry.

In 1926 the Commonwealth Scientific and Industrial Research Organization was established to ensure systematic investigation in all necessary directions. It set up a number of research institutes to study among other subjects the introduction and proper management of new fodder plants, the reclamation of soils hitherto infertile, problems of irrigation, and factors determining the quality of wool. Each state has its experiment stations for dealing with problems of more local interest.

New Zealand was fortunate in that its early settlers included a number of men and women who wanted to see education take an important place in the new country. The botanical flora was early studied by Sir Joseph Hooker; in 1864 a geological survey was organized; in 1867 the New Zealand Institute (now the Royal Society of New Zealand)was founded, and in 1872, 100,000 ac. of pastoral land in the South Island were set aside to endow a college of agriculture. This was opened in 1880 and called Lincoln Agricultural College, but was later (1896) reorganized as the Canterbury Agricultural College. In 1920 the first agricultural research institute was founded by Thomas Cawthron at Nelson, also in the South' Island. Educational and research activities expanded rapidly about this time as both soils and pastures began to show signs of deterioration, causing much anxiety about the future. In 1923 and 1924, two professorships of agriculture were established in the North Island, one each at the university colleges of Wellington and Auckland; they amalgamated in 1926 and transferred to Palmerston North where much more land was available; they were reorganized as the Massey Agricultural College. This and the Canterbury College became part of the University of New Zealand; both provide courses ranging from diplomas to doctorates.

Another reorganization took place in 1926: the various government research agencies were linked by the establishment of the Department of Scientific and Industrial Research on lines similar to those of the United Kingdom and Australia. This resulted in the setting up of research bureaus and institutes. Among them are: dairying (1927), grassland (1929, reorganized in 1936), and plant chemistry, all at the Massey College; cereals at Canterbury College where useful plant breeding has been conducted since 1910; soils at Rukuhia (North Island); horticulture at Te Kauwhata and Levin. Notable successes have been achieved: the dairy industry has become one of the most efficient in the world; new and highly productive strains of grasses and clovers have produced superb pastures; the cause of the sterility of large areas in the volcanic regions of the North Island (deficiencies of the trace elements boron, cobalt, copper, and molybdenum) has been discovered and rectified, dramatically transforming this once dreary waste into a prosperous countryside. The pasture improvement investigations at Marton begun in 1928 opened the way for aircraft dressings of superphosphate on hills too steep for farm implements thereby greatly enriching them. Meanwhile the Cawthron Institute has continued its studies of the intensive crops of the northern part of the South Island.

WESTERN EUROPE

United Kingdom.—There are three types of agricultural education. (1) County farm institutes for vocational training give one-year courses. Students number about 2,000 in England and Wales. In April 1959 the institutes were transferred from the Ministry of Agriculture to that of Education. (2) Agricultural colleges, founded by private benefactors but now state-aided, provide two-year diploma courses. The Royal Agricultural College at Cirencester, founded in 1845, and the Shuttleworth College, Biggleswade, Bedford, are for men; Studley College, Studley, Warwick, is for women; the others, the Harper Adams and Seale-Hayne Agricultural colleges at Newport, Shropshire, and Newton Abbot, Devon, respectively, are coeducational. (3) A National College of Agricultural Engineering was established in 1960 at Silsoe, Bedfordshire. Most of the universities have faculties of agriculture and award degrees; Wye College, Kent, is the agricultural department of London University.

Extension services for those already farming include demonstrations and lectures arranged by the county authorities and farmers' organizations. The chief agency, however, is the National Agricultural Advisory Service formerly under the county authorities but unified under the Ministry of Agriculture in 1946; its staff numbers about 1,300.

Central expert services are provided by the ministry at the National Institute of Agricultural Botany and Seed Testing Station at Cambridge, the Plant Pathology Laboratory at Harpenden, the Veterinary laboratories at Weybridge and at. Lasswade (Scot.), and the station at Tolworth, Surrey, for control of large pests (rodents, birds, etc.).

For many years agricultural research in the United Kingdom was carried out by individuals or societies at their own expense. Sir John Lawes (q.v.) personally financed the Rothamsted Experimental Station during its first 60 years. But in 1909 Lloyd George, then chancellor of the exchequer, set up a development fund of £3,000,000 to last five years, out of which research could be aided. A. D. Hall devised the plan. Autonomous agricultural research institutes were established on the basis of subjects, not commodities; they were associated with universities where practicable

AERIAL APPLICATION OF FERTILIZER IN REGION OF LOW FERTILITY AND RUGGED TERRAIN NEAR AUCKLAND, N.Z.

and linked at first through the Ministry of Agriculture, but later through a specialized autonomous body, the Agricultural Research Council.

The oldest station, the Rothamsted Experimental Station (*q.v.*) conducts unique field experiments in which the same crop has been grown on the same land with the same fertilizer for long periods. The investigations include the chemistry, physics, and biology of soils, and the growth of the plant in health and disease. Since 1921 much work has been done on applications of statistical science to agricultural problems. The next oldest station, Woburn, is part of the Rothamsted organization.

The Long Ashton Fruit Research Station (University of Bristol) was started in 1903 as the National Fruit and Cider Institute (in succession to Butleigh court, 1893) but now deals with all fruit in the wetter western region; much work has been done on plant nutrition, especially on the trace elements, and on protection against disease and pests. Fruit problems of the drier, eastern part of England are studied at East Malling, Kent (established 1913). For crops grown under glass a station was established at Cheshunt in 1914 and transferred to Rustington, near Worthing, in 1954. The plant physiology department of the Imperial College, South Kensington (London University), is associated with the crop investigations of these various stations. Problems of vegetable growing are dealt with at Wellesbourne (established 1949), Invergowrie (1950), and the John Innes Horticultural Institution (1910), Bayfordbury.

Three principal stations are devoted to plant breeding: (1) Cambridge (1912), which developed out of R. H. Biffen's work begun in 1899 and where success with wheat and barley has been outstanding and fundamental genetical studies have also been made; (2) Aberystwyth (1919) where Sir George Stapleton inaugurated the successful work on grasses and clovers; and (3) Pentlandfield (Scot.), in succession to Corstorphine, where potatoes and other crops are studied, especially in relation to disease resistance.

The nutritive value of pastures as affected by their botanical composition and management is investigated at the Grassland Research Station at Hurley, near Maidenhead (1948, in succession to Drayton, 1941); one of its practical achievements has been a marked extension of the grazing season. The National Institute for Research in Dairying at Shinfield (1912) took the lead in the clean milk movement and has done much work on the chemistry and physiology of milk production. Animal nutrition is studied at the Rowett Research Institute, Aberdeen (1914), special attention being given to its relation to animal health and to metabolism. Much work on the subject was previously done at the Cambridge school of agriculture by T. B. Wood and his colleagues.

The Agricultural Economics Research Institute, Oxford (1912), has developed methods of farm bookkeeping and cost accounting that form the basis of the economic surveys now made in different parts of the country. The Macaulay Institute at Aberdeen (1930) investigates soils, especially their mineral components including the trace elements. In addition to these major institutes there are several more specialized ones, and also some research units of the Agricultural Research Council placed in appropriate laboratories for particular studies.

In 1927 a research station of a new type was set up by Imperial Chemical Industries, Ltd., at Jealott's Hill, near Bracknell, where products of modern technological chemistry have been tested for possible agricultural uses and fundamental work has been done and published. Among other discoveries was the first of the selective herbicides. Since 1950 other industrial organizations associated with agriculture have established research stations.

The Agricultural Improvement Council was set up in 1941 to ensure that promising results obtained at the research stations should be applied in practice and also to report on agricultural problems needing further investigation. As agricultural research develops it becomes more abstruse and more in need of interpreters; and so massive, that no one person could hope to apprehend more than a fraction of it. The Commonwealth Agricultural Bureaux were accordingly set up in 1929 to collect the results and pass them on. The agricultural bureaus supply other information on request and

especially help those working in isolated conditions.

France.—The problems of agricultural education and research are associated in France with the peasant structure of much of the rural community, desired on social and political grounds; also with the need to attain greater self-sufficiency in food supplies (especially wheat) and to foster production of certain valuable export products (notably wine). There is a long tradition of agricultural education and research: the École Nationale d'Agriculture at Grignon was founded in 1826, that at Rennes in 1830, and the Institut National Agronomique in Paris, largest of all, in 1848, and reorganized in 1876. There are other colleges at Montpellier, Beauvais, and elsewhere and a horticultural college at Versailles.

Agricultural research is organized by the Institut National de la Recherche Agronomique in Paris in two main groups of institutes: those for soils and crops form the Centre National de Recherches Agronomiques at Versailles, and those concerned with animals and their products form the Centre National de Recherches Zootechniques at Jouy-en-Josas. The Institut National de la Recherche Agronomique also has an institute at Narbonne for research on wine (oenology), cider and fruit juices, and research laboratories attached to the colleges at Grignon (plant physiology), Rennes (crop improvement), and Montpellier (plant nutrition). Other institutes deal with machinery, farm buildings, and irrigation, and there are seven regional institutes for studying local problems.

Belgium.—Higher agricultural education is provided by the agricultural institutes of Gembloux (founded 1860), of Louvain (Catholic University, 1838), and of Ghent (Flemish University, 1920). Research is concentrated in these institutes and is closely linked with the corresponding teaching section; it comes, however, under the Ministry of Agriculture while the teaching activities are under the Ministry of Education. The Institut Agronomique de l'Etat at Gembloux is the chief centre covering almost all the agricultural subjects.

The Institute for Encouraging the Application of Science to Industry (set up in 1944) organizes joint research on specific subjects by members of the various research institutes, providing funds and necessary facilities. Among its activities are the soil and vegetation survey of the whole country, research on sugar beets (Tirlemont), fruit trees, wines, and other subjects.

Netherlands.—High quality in its agricultural exports is so vitally important to the Netherlands that it has developed very efficient systems of agricultural education and research. Farmers actively participate through their old-established societies for the improvement of agriculture, subsidized by the government. The centre for higher agricultural education and research is at Wageningen which began as an agricultural school in 1876, became an experiment station in 1877, when Dutch agriculture was behind that of neighbouring countries, and now comprises a group of important institutes dealing with all branches of agriculture. Other institutes in the appropriate districts deal with specific subjects: soils and plant production at Groningen, soil survey at Bennekom, soil testing at Oosterbeek, fruit and vegetables at Alkmaar, greenhouse crops at Naaldwijk, and bulbs at Lisse. Animal husbandry is studied at Hoorn; livestock investigations at several stations include pasture problems and associated animal disorders such as grass tetany (hypomagnesaemea). Problems of the Zuider Zee (IJsselmeer) reclamation are studied at Kampen and elsewhere. About 500 graduates assisted by 1,500 technicians are engaged in research. The coordinating body is the National Council for Agricultural Research, a branch of the Central Organization for Applied Scientific Research in the Netherlands. The corresponding centre for Veterinary Research is at Utrecht.

German Federal Republic.—Germany has long been distinguished for the number and efficiency of its institutes for agricultural education and research. The agricultural faculty of the Munich Technische Hochschule was founded in 1803; the much larger ones at Bonn (Friedrich-Wilhelms University) and Stuttgart-Landwirtschaftliche Hochschule Hohenheim, go back to 1818. There were in the early 1960s eight university schools, many farm schools, and about 250 research institutes. The latter are of four types: (1) federal, under the federal Ministry of Food, Agriculture and Forestry in Bonn, among which are institutes for investigating quality in crops (Giesenheim), dairying (Kiel), animal health (Dahlem), biology of crops and forests (Brunswick); (2) state, associated with agricultural colleges or faculties of universities and financed by the respective ministries of education—these include names well known in the history of agricultural science such as Giessen, Dahlem, Göttingen, and others: (3) state, under the respective ministries of agriculture and usually dealing with crops or problems of local importance—these are the most numerous; and (4) private institutions run by manufacturing or other groups dealing with specific subjects. The German Academy of Agriculture has its research institute in Berlin.

Switzerland.—Higher agricultural education is a federal responsibility and has been provided at the Eidgenössische Technische Hochschule, Zürich, since 1871, and under the federal Department of the Interior. Its associated institutes are the chief research agencies. There are ten federal institutes in different parts of the country for studying local problems, but they are also responsible for various control and advisory activities. The agricultural schools were provided by the cantons.

Austria.—The centre for higher agricultural education is the Hochschule für Bodenkultur (soil science) founded in 1872, and for livestock subjects at the Veterinary College, both in Vienna and under the Ministry of Education. There are a number of farm schools adapted to local requirements under the Ministry of Agriculture. Research is centred at the institutes of the Hochschule, of plant protection and of horticulture, all in Vienna. The Alpine Institute is at Gumpenstein, Styria.

Scandinavia.—*Denmark.*—Like that of the Netherlands, Denmark's economy depends on the export of high-quality agricultural products. Higher agricultural education was provided early in Denmark; the Technical University sent out its first agricultural graduate in 1849. The subject was transferred to the Royal Veterinary and Agricultural College when it was founded in 1858; this is now the centre for agricultural, dairying, and horticultural education. At least three years' work on a farm must be done by the student before entering; he must also have attended a nine-months course at an agricultural school. Vocational training begins on farms at about the age of 14, day or evening classes being attended. After about four years a full-time five- to eight-months course is taken at an agricultural school or a Folk high school, where, however, the emphasis is on general education. The working farmer is helped by two advisory services, one provided by the state, the other by the farmers' organizations.

Research is centred at the Royal Veterinary and Agricultural College. Closely associated with it is the National Research Institute on Animal Husbandry (1883). The animal problems studied at the various stations include pig progeny testing, immunogenetics, blood grouping, etc. The first blood-typing laboratory in Europe was set up in Copenhagen.

A number of state institutes under the Ministry of Agriculture in different parts of the country deal with particular crops and local problems. The important group at Lyngby includes plant diseases and pests (founded 1905), plant research (1909), and variety testing. Fertilizer investigations are done at Askov; they were started in 1893 to compare farmyard manure and artificial fertilizers as agents for conserving soil productiveness. An experimental dairy has been set up at Hillerød, and the Atomic research centre at Risø studies possible uses of radiation in plant breeding, meat conservation, etc.

Among the privately organized institutes are the Viborg station of the Danish Heathland Society founded by Enrico Dalgas in 1866; the Danish Farmers Cooperative Seed-Growing Association's station at Øtoftogaard, and the Meat Research Institute of the Federation of Cooperative Bacon Factories.

Sweden.—Agricultural education in Sweden began in 1862 at the Alnarp Institute. In 1932 the Royal Agricultural College was founded at Uppsala and took over most of the subjects, leaving Alnarp with dairying and horticulture. Six agricultural schools train youths of 18 and over in one- and two-year courses for posts as instructors and farm managers, while more than 50 farm schools give courses for prospective farmers.

The advisory and extension work includes a correspondence school founded in 1943 by the Federation of Agricultural Societies for the benefit of some of the 80% of the farmers who never attended farm schools. These societies have long played an important part in the improvement of Swedish agriculture: the first was founded in 1791. Agricultural research is organized under the Swedish Agricultural Research Council: since 1948 the chief institute has been attached to the Royal Agricultural College: its numerous departments cover most branches of crop and animal husbandry. Other institutes have been founded for dairying and horticulture (both at Alnarp), farm buildings (Lund), and economics (Stockholm). Two private plant breeding and seed stations operate at Svalöv and at Landskrona; both receive state subventions. The Dairies Association has also its well-equipped station.

Norway.—Norway's agricultural problems differ greatly from those of Sweden and Denmark; there are no agricultural exports, only about 2.5% of the land area is cultivated and the farms are very small. The Agricultural College at Vollebekk and the Veterinary College at Oslo provide higher education, and a number of schools for young farmers offer 6- to 18-months courses which, however, were not well attended. The advisory service is in three groups: state, county, and district. Research is centred at the two colleges and there are state institutes (12 in all) distributed over the country to deal with local problems. The Agricultural Research Council has general supervision: its distinguishing feature is that its activities are financed by the state football pools. Researches of special interest include those on fur-bearing animals (fox, mink, etc.), on the effects of sunlight on plant growth, and on regrouping and reallocating small holdings.

Finland.—Finnish agricultural problems derive from the fact that it is the only country lying wholly north of lat. 60° N. The agricultural faculty of the University of Helsinki (established 1902) provides higher education (though many entrants do not graduate) and formerly organized all the research, but in 1923 the Ministry of Agriculture took over the more practical and local sections leaving the university to develop the basic subjects, including soil science, plant pathology, and dairying.

The ministry's stations are supervised by the Central Board of Agricultural Research and are distributed over the country. The most important group is at Tikkurila and includes the stations for soil management, grassland problems, pest control, dairy and animal production (including mink). The plant breeding centre is at Jokioinen as is also the state institute for dairying; the Frost Research Institute is at Pelsonsuo. The Biochemical Institute, well known for Artturi Virtanen's work on silage, is at Helsinki, as are also the centres for soil science and seed testing, and the Plant Breeding Institute of the Cooperative Wholesale Society.

Portugal.—Higher agricultural education is given at the Instituto Superior de Agronomia at Lisbon (founded 1852). Research on soils and crops in all branches is centred at Sacavém, on animal husbandry at Santarem, and on veterinary subjects at Lisbon. There are stations for plant breeding at Elvas and Oeiras (industrial crops); for fruit at Setúbal and Alcobaça; oenology (wine) at Lisbon, Regua, and Dois Portos; and a port wine station run by the industry at Oporto.

Spain.—The highest centre for agricultural education is the Instituto Nacional Agronómico (founded 1855) in Madrid which offers a five-year course. Other centres were reorganized in 1957 in three groups: (1) higher level under the Ministry of Education—technical high schools with five-year courses, the last to be spent at a research institute; (2) medium level under the Ministry of Education for training experts (*peritos agrícolas*)—in 1958 there were five schools; (3) vocational schools under the Ministry of Agriculture (started 1949)—these are of several types selected respectively for prospective foremen on large estates, agricultural workers, administrators, etc.

Agricultural research is under a special council and is centralized at the Instituto Nacional de Investigaciones Agronómicas, Madrid, under the Ministry of Agriculture. A number of stations have been established in various parts of Spain for studying problems of the region or for special purposes: citrus fruits at Valencia, grapes at Barcelona, cereals at Cádiz. A parallel organization, the Consejo Superior de Investigaciones Científicas, associated with the Ministry of Education, is responsible for the more fundamental studies: one of its stations, the Aula Dei at Saragossa, deals with plant breeding, cytogenetics, plant physiology, and pathology; another deals with edaphology (the relation between the soil and the growing plant).

Italy.—Twelve of the Italian universities have faculties of agriculture but although the student entries are large only a small proportion graduates. Pisa is the oldest (founded 1840), Milan (1872) and Naples (1873) come next; the largest is Bologna (1900). Research is carried out at these centres and also at some 40 institutes of the Ministry of Agriculture dealing with local problems in different parts of the country. There are stations for wheat, especially macaroni sorts, at Rome, Pisa, Rieti, and Catania; for rice at Vercelli; flowers at San Remo; sericulture (silkworms) at Ascoli Piceno and Padua; wine at Conegliano; and for soils at Rome, Turin, Udine, Gorizia, and elsewhere.

Greece.—The physical conditions of Greece are ill-suited for many crops, but olives, vines, tobacco, and citrus fruits grow well in places. The research problems consist in seeking for higher output, better quality, and for new crops, including cotton, rice, and wheat, to broaden the basis of production. The agricultural faculty of the University of Salonika (founded 1927) provides for higher agricultural education and research. The Ministry of Agriculture has a number of stations dealing with soil management and crops: at Salonika for cereals and cotton, at Larissa for fodder and leguminous plants, in the province of Attica for vegetables, at Drama for tobacco, and at Pyrgos for raisins, the three last-named being helped by the industry. General supervision is exercised by the ministry's Bureau of Agricultural Research. An important private foundation, the Benakeion, deals with insect and fungus pests; it is now subsidized by the state. The Fertilizers and Chemical Company has its own station.

Yugoslavia.—Being a federation of six socialist republics, Yugoslavia has six universities each with faculties of agriculture: Zagreb (1919), Belgrade (1921), Ljubljana (1947), Sarajevo (1947), Skopje (1947), and Novi Sad (1954). Each faculty has specialized research institutes for different branches of agricultural science or technology. These are financed by the federal state. Another group of institutes carries out investigations for the regional and provincial authorities and is supported by them. The degree course at each university lasts four years for the *inžinjer agronomije* ("agricultural engineer") qualification.

EASTERN EUROPE

The organization of agricultural education and research in the Communist countries is generally similar to that of Western Europe. No fees are charged at the teaching institutions, and the number of students is very large; many are women and a large proportion of the students complete the full four- or five-year course and graduate. Research for the development of a subject is commonly in the charge of the Academy of Agriculture which, except in Poland, is entirely distinct from the Academy of Sciences. Research on particular crops or problems of local importance is under the ministry of agriculture of the country concerned.

Poland.—Agricultural education and research began in Poland in 1818 at Marymont, a suburb of Warsaw. In 1862 the Russians transferred this institute to Pulawy, the estate of Prince Adam Czartoryski, confiscated by them and renamed Novo-Aleksandria; the institute was reopened in 1869. In 1916 the old name was resumed, the teaching work was given up, and the institute was developed as Poland's chief centre of agricultural research. Higher agricultural education is given at the universities, which are under the Ministry of Higher Education and award the qualification of *inżynier magister* ("master engineer").

Below the colleges come the technical schools of agriculture. The technical schools are under the Ministry of Agriculture and most of them specialize in one main subject such as seed production, grassland, horticulture, economics, etc.; some of them conduct their five-year courses by correspondence. The diploma admits the student to the colleges. Other schools have two-year courses, both internal and correspondence, and confer the title

of practical technician; this, however, does not admit the student to college. At a still lower level are the residential schools offering one-year courses on agriculture and animal husbandry for men, and home economics for women; also one- or two-year courses for pupils of 13 or over, leading to admissions to the technical schools.

Section V of the Polish Academy of Sciences includes nine agricultural and forestry science research institutes. The Pulawy Institute, now called the Institute of Soil Science and Plant Cultivation, has a farm of 7,000 ac. where much variety testing is done; it has several associated institutes in other parts of Poland and a widespread extention service which annually makes some 2,000 field experiments adequately controlled by a special statistical section. The extension service also appoints an agricultural inspector or adviser to each of the provinces, together with a scientific and technical assistant. Various unions, *e.g.*, the Sugar Beet Union, also conduct experiments.

Other research institutes include those for plant breeding and acclimatization in Warsaw, for plant protection in Poznan, and for agricultural economics in Warsaw, the two latter subjects being studied at Pulawy, too. The Veterinary Research Institute is also at Pulawy.

Czechoslovakia.—There are four levels of agricultural education leading from one to another. (1) Apprentice schools for those leaving the elementary school at the age of 14 give two- or three-year courses, half the time being spent at the school and half on a training farm. Those wishing to specialize in practical branches can have two- or three-years' training on cooperative and state farms, tractor stations, or forestry establishments, according to their choice. Pupils can then pass to (2) schools for training group leaders on cooperative farms which give appropriate courses lasting two winters. (3) Agricultural technical schools give four-year courses for pupils from elementary schools. (4) The University of Agriculture at Prague and the University of Agriculture at Brno have large enrollments. These institutions also provide correspondence courses leading to the same qualification as for residential students.

Agricultural research is immediately under the Academy of Agricultural Sciences which consists of 15 members and was established in 1953 in succession to the older Academy of Agriculture. It controls the 30 research institutes and 22 research stations and appoints the staff and awards honours. Each institute, however, has its own council for detailed management; each also has substations. There are also 21 independent stations within the academy.

Rumania.—Five institutes of higher agricultural education exist in Rumania. The chief is the Niculae Bălcescu Agronomic Institute at Bucharest founded in 1885; it is one of the largest in the world. Other agricultural institutes are at Iaşi, Craiova, Cluj, and Timişoara; a high proportion of the students graduate.

The chief research institute is under the Rumanian Academy; set up in 1928 it covers the whole range of subjects dealing with crops and soils, including horticulture, forestry, agricultural economics, and meteorology. The Ministry of Agriculture has some more specialized institutes for animal husbandry, forestry, corn (maize) production, and horticulture and viticulture. Research is also carried out at the teaching institutions mentioned above.

THE SOVIET UNION

Prior to the 1917 Revolution the volume of work on agricultural science in Russia was small, but it included some brilliant investigations which after many years are still proving fruitful: among others those on soil formation and classification by V. V. Dokuchaiev (1846–1903), on soil bacteriology by S. N. Vinogradsky (*q.v.*) from 1890 onward (not all done in Russia), by M. F. Ivanov (1871–1935) in the early 1900s on artificial insemination, by K. K. Gedroits (1872–1932) on soil colloids in the years before World War I.

After the Revolution agricultural and other sciences came under the influence of political dogma, and scientific writings of the 1920s and 1930s had to conform to the tenets of dialetic materialism; they usually included quotations from the writings of Marx,

Engels, Lenin, or other political authorities. Geneticists suffered particularly; Western ideas were banned; N. I. Vavilov (q.v.), their most brilliant exponent, who had assembled at what is now the All-Union Institute of Plant Breeding, Leningrad, the finest collection in the world of the wild species of cultivated plants with the purpose of carrying out genetical investigations, was accused by T. D. Lysenko (1898–   ) of ideological impurity and banished to the Arctic regions where he died. Lysenko was elevated to the highest rank for a time and enjoyed great popularity as a man of peasant origin who rose to become an academician. Many scientific workers were required to devote much time to Stalin's grandiose plan for combating drought in the arid steppe region by planting protective forests and by other devices. After Stalin's death agricultural science appeared to be allowed more freedom; the political quotations were fewer; the Stalin plan seemed to have faded out and Western distrust diminished. Occasional short visits by Western scientists were arranged and in some instances a longer stay became possible.

As in certain other European countries, the applied sciences (including agricultural science) are studied principally at special institutes, although some universities have faculties of agriculture or of biology and soil science. The chief institutes, however, are of university rank. These are widely distributed over all the constituent republics, but the most important are in Moscow. Of the institutes for higher agricultural education the best known was the Timiryazev Academy of Agriculture, Moscow, founded in 1865: specialists are trained under seven faculties.

The separation of agricultural science from the pure sciences holds also for research: pure sciences come within the purview of the Academy of Sciences (founded in 1724) while those concerned with agriculture are within the province of the All-Union V. I. Lenin Academy of Agricultural Sciences (founded in 1929 and reorganized in 1956), which has 150 scientific institutions in six departments.

There are three main groups of agricultural stations. (1) The all-union institutes deal with fundamental studies and major problems of wide importance. Some are for subjects: e.g., the Dokuchaiev Soil Institute at Moscow, founded in Leningrad, where the museum of soil science is still located, in 1881 but greatly developed in 1926; the K. A. Timiryazev Institute of Plant Physiology, formerly in Leningrad but in 1934 transferred to Moscow in accordance with the centralizing tendency of the time; also the Institute for Fertilizers and Soil Science, Moscow, which has a large outside staff to organize fertilizer trials in many parts of the union. Others are for special crops; e.g., the sugar beet station at Kiev. These institutes serve the whole of the U.S.S.R.; they are affiliated to the Lenin All-Union Academy of Agricultural Sciences except for the Timiryazev and the Dokuchaiev institutes which retain their old affiliation with the Academy of Sciences. (2) The regional institutes, of which each republic has at least one, are for the study of local problems; they collaborate with the all-union institutes when necessary. Other subjects studied have been the possibility of growing vegetables in northern latitudes, agricultural developments in Siberia, and the acclimatization of livestock and its improvement by crossbreeding. (3) The state variety testing stations of which there are about 1,500 are under a special commission to deal with new varieties of crops.

The total output of work is enormous. Much of it, however, is little known outside the U.S.S.R.

ASIA AND THE MIDDLE EAST

China.—Each province of the Chinese People's Republic has its agricultural institute, some with about 5,000 students. There are two academies, the Academia Sinica (or Academy of Sciences) and the Academy of Agricultural Sciences. Each has its research institutes and journals (for agriculture, the *Journal of the Agricultural Association of China*). Plant improvement is studied in both groups of institutes; in the agricultural group the emphasis is on variety testing and regionalization; there are branch research institutes in each of the provinces. Research is also done at some of the institutes; e.g., Fukien, Szechwan, Chekiang. Soils are

studied at the Institute of Pedology, Peking, the Nanking Institute, and elsewhere. The volume of research is considerable but the work is little known in the West.

Japan.—Japan developed its agricultural education in the second half of the 19th century. The Hokkaido University began it in 1875; Tokyo followed in 1889 and two other agricultural institutes were founded in 1909 (Kagoshima and Chiba). Others were set up after World War I, and at the outbreak of World War II there were 15 in all. After the war ended there was great activity, fostered by the U.S. authorities. The agricultural institutes were reorganized (1949) and new ones set up: by the 1960s there were more than 50 institutes and university departments offering two- and three-year courses for masters' and doctors' degrees, while other junior colleges provided two-year courses but no title. Tokyo had three institutes: the largest, the Faculty of Agriculture of the University of Tokyo, had about 1,000 students, practically all males.

Fundamental research in the basic sciences is carried out at the universities. A research station for forestry was set up in 1878 and one for agriculture in 1893; later came stations for sericulture (1911), livestock (1916), and horticulture (1921). A comprehensive scheme was started in 1950. There are eight regional institutes where agricultural research is applied to the development of the local agriculture; eight fisheries research stations, and also one (1955) which is devoted to cultivated pearls. All these are under the Ministry of Agriculture; the staffs numbered nearly 6,000. A coordinating council was set up in 1956.

Indonesia.—Under its old name of Netherlands Indies, Indonesia had one of the best tropical agricultural research services in the world. The work had begun early: a botanical laboratory was set up in 1884 in the old Buitenzorg (renamed Bogor) Botanic Gardens (Java; 1817), the first to be established in the tropics, and was opened to visiting scientists. Later there followed a college of agriculture and an important group of agricultural research institutes dealing with soils, phytopathology, and crops, and the planters set up special institutes for tea, rubber, and cinchona. A sugar experiment station was established (1880) at Pasuruan (Java); Sumatra also had its Botanic garden and a tobacco experiment station. A steady stream of able young scientists came from the Netherlands to staff these stations and valuable work was accomplished. Much damage was done to these stations during the Japanese invasion. There are university faculties of agriculture at Bogor (University of Indonesia and the private Universitas Bogor); Jogjakarta, Bandung, and Semarang (Java); Padang (West Sumatra); Medan (North Sumatra); and Kalimantan (Borneo); and a faculty of veterinary science and cattle breeding at Denpasar (Bali).

Malaysia.—The University of Malaya, at Pantai Valley, Kuala Lumpur (1962; formerly the University of Malaya at Kula Lamphur, 1959), instituted a degree course in agriculture in 1960. The College of Agriculture, at Serdang, Selangor, offering a three-year course, was founded in 1931. The Division of Agriculture, Kuala Lumpur, undertakes agricultural research. Headquarters of the Rubber Research Institute of Malaya also are at Kuala Lumpur. In Sarawak are a school of agriculture, at Semongok, offering 12-month courses in basic agriculture and home economics, and an extension training centre, at Tarat.

India.—The teaching of better methods to the cultivator began in India as early as 1839 when the East India Company, anticipating a modern method, brought in a group of American cotton planters to show how cotton should be grown. This and some similar efforts proved unrewarding and it was gradually realized that success could be achieved only by making investigations in the country itself. The Famine Commission of 1880 discussed the problems and in 1889 J. A. Voelcker was called in to advise the commission. First a government agricultural chemist was appointed, then in 1892 a technical agricultural director for Bombay presidency. Six years later a sugar cane expert was brought from the West Indies to deal with the increasingly serious disease problems. Research on a broader basis free from routine duties became possible in 1903 when the Pusa Research Institute was founded by a generous donation by Henry Phipps, of the United States; it attracted a very able British staff, and much work was done on the breeding of improved wheats and potatoes, on the control of insect pests, on the increase of milk yield, and on other subjects. From 1905 departments of agriculture were established in the different provinces and states charged with the provision of agricultural education: they set up a number of colleges at some of which (*e.g.*, Nagpur, Poona, Lahore) useful research was also carried out. The Linlithgow Commission of 1926 recommended the appointment of the Indian Council of Agricultural Research with ample funds for the proper organization of research over the whole country. This was done in 1929. The Pusa Institute was destroyed by earthquake in 1934; it was replaced by a larger and better-equipped one at New Delhi which has an estate of 1,000 ac.; this was opened in 1936 and continues to deal with fundamental problems. A number of other institutes deal with specific crops or subjects, including sugar cane at Coimbatore, rice at Cuttack (this also has international responsibilities aided by the Food and Agriculture Organization of the United Nations), potatoes at Patna, dairying at Bangalore (the home of the Indian Institute of Science), and veterinary problems at Mukteswar-Kumaun.

The several state governments foster research on crops specially important to their regions. In addition, various crop and commodity committees provide for research on their particular subject, financed either by a special tax, or cess, or by a government grant; tea research, for instance, is thus carried out at Tocklai.

Education and extension services are the responsibility of the state governments and are under the directors of agriculture. Much ingenious thought has gone into the task of teaching the cultivator better methods. The problem is complicated by the widespread poverty of the peasants. Most of the larger states have agricultural colleges affiliated to the appropriate university and provided with an experimental farm for demonstration and research.

Israel.—The Central Institution for Agricultural Research and the College of Agriculture of the Hebrew University, formerly the Agricultural College, are at Rehovot, also the site of the Centre for Scientific Research and the Weizmann Institute of Science. An experimental farm deals with citrus and other irrigated horticultural and fodder crops. Another farm, near Haifa, is concerned with dry land crops—cereals, unirrigated pastures, and the breeding of hybrid corn (maize) and sorghum; and a farm in the northern Negev studies the adaptability of crops to semidesert conditions. The Negev Institute for Arid Zone Research was founded with help from United Nations Educational, Scientific and Cultural Organization in Nov. 1957; its program includes the utilization of solar energy and of dew, the desalting of saline waters, and the study of effects of desert conditions on human beings and animals and of the phenomena of acclimatization to them. Attempts are being made to reconstruct the conditions under which the region had supported a considerable Nabatean population for 1,000 years between the 2nd century B.C. and the 8th century A.D.

Agricultural engineering and food processing are both studied at Technion, Haifa, which offers courses in agricultural engineering to students from developing countries. There is also a two-year course for agricultural teachers and advisers for the advisory field service, offered by the College of Agriculture at Rehovot.

For children who have completed the elementary school course there are a number of agricultural boarding schools with more than 12,000 pupils at the beginning of the 1960s. The annual intake was planned to be at least 15% of all leaving the elementary school, this corresponding with the labour structure of the whole population. The ordinary course lasts for three years but a fourth-year course leads to the university.

There are also centres where unemployed young people are taught agricultural work. Evening classes are arranged for young people actually at work on farms. Transportation is organized to take them twice a week from their villages to study centres: the syllabus includes agriculture, arithmetic, Hebrew, and social activities. The studies last four to five hours at a time and the course extends over two years.

Instruction has long been available for farmers and is well developed in the older villages. Special arrangements are required for the new villages because of the diversity of the settlers, many of whom are in great need of both instruction and guidance. The necessary efforts are organized jointly by the Ministry of Agriculture and the Jewish Agency, the body that had enabled many of the settlers to reach the country.

Turkey.—The agricultural faculty of the University of Ankara (founded 1933) provides higher education, and its associated research institutes cover the whole range of soils, crops, and livestock problems. The Ministry of Agriculture has a number of stations distributed over the country dealing with agricultural and horticultural crops of local importance, with bees and silkworms, and also has five government studs. Research on wine and tobacco, however, is the responsibility of the Ministry of Monopolies. Veterinary research is similarly organized by the University of Ankara and the state stations, and that on forestry by Istanbul University. Atatürk University, at Erzurum (1957) and Aegean University, Bornova, Izmir (1955) have faculties of agriculture.

The Arab Countries.—With the exception of the agricultural department, now the School of Agricultural Sciences, of the American University of Beirut in Lebanon, very little agricultural education or research in the sense of scientific agriculture covered in this article existed in the Arab countries of the Middle East before the second half of the 20th century. Beginning in the 1950s the number of educational and research institutions of all types, including colleges, institutes, and faculties of agriculture, has been expanding. In Iraq, for example, a College of Agriculture, founded 1952, and a College of Agriculture and Forestry, founded 1964, are incorporated colleges of the University of Baghdad, and the Institute of Technical Agriculture, founded 1964, is affiliated with the university. In Syria, the University of Aleppo and Damascus University have faculties of agriculture; the Higher Agricultural Institute is at Damascus. All branches of agricultural research in Jordan are centred in the Department of Scientific Research (Agriculture), founded 1958, at Amman.

Iran.—Better provided than the Arab countries, Iran had a school of agriculture established in 1930 under the Ministry of Agriculture; it was transferred in 1944 to the University of Teheran and became a faculty in 1949. No fees are charged, and the course lasts three years. The universities of Shiraz and of Tabriz also have faculties of agriculture and Gondishapour University at Ahwaz includes an agricultural college, founded 1955.

NORTH AFRICA

United Arab Republic.—A college of agriculture was established in 1890 at Giza on what had been the home farm of Ismail Pasha's palace: in 1935 it became the faculty of agriculture of the Cairo University. Alexandria University also has a faculty of agriculture (1942) as has the Ain Shams University (1950) and Al-Azhar University, both in Cairo. In each case the course lasts for three years and leads to the B.Sc. degree.

Research began under the British with the formation of the Khedival Agricultural Society in 1898 which was given half the land at Giza. In 1903 its laboratories were built on the nearby Nile island of Gezira. After 1914 it became the Royal Agricultural Society and built new laboratories on Gezira. The Egyptian government took over the experimental farm at Giza for cotton research under the direction of the cotton board. More experimental farms and laboratories since have been set up there and at Bahtim and Heliopolis, and useful work on the development and productive powers of livestock under local conditions has been carried out. It is now the Egyptian Agricultural Organization. The Agricultural Research Executive Organization, Cairo, also undertakes research, and the National Research Centre has laboratories for biology and agricultural science.

Tunisia.—Tunisia started its independent career with an organization of agricultural education and research similar to that of France. The leading institute was the École National Supérieure d'Agriculture de Tunis (founded 1898 as the École Coloniale), for training the higher staffs; lower in the scale came the École Nationale d'Agriculture of Boghrana (1946) for training advisers, and at a still lower level the three agricultural schools. Research is done by the Institut National de la Recherche Agronomique de

Tunisie (founded 1914 as the Service Botanique et Agronomique de Tunisie).

Algeria.—Higher education is given in the Institut Agricole d'Algerie, founded 1905. The École Supérieure d'Agriculture Africaine, 1957, specializes in the problems of the Mediterranean and semiarid regions. At a lower level are the regional colleges and the agricultural schools.

Morocco.—There is a school of agriculture, the École Nationale d'Agriculture, founded 1951, at Meknès and a research organization at Rabat with stations for cotton at Tadla, and for hydraulics at Marrakesh, Tadla, and Berkane.

CENTRAL AND SOUTHERN AFRICA

Former French Territories.—Higher agricultural education is given at the École Supérieure d'Agriculture Tropicale in Paris and at agricultural schools in each of the former French territories. As production is entirely by small farmers a wide-ranging extension service has been developed including advisers, pilot schemes, and *paysannat* ("peasant cooperative areas"). Pilot schemes (*section d'aménagement rural*) are large comprehensive schemes which may involve a whole village or even a canton of 5 to 15 villages, while a *paysannat* is an area of small schemes, often 25 or 50 ac., entirely for African cultivators.

Research is centred in Paris in the Office de la Recherche Scientifique et Technique Outre-Mer and in several *instituts professionels,* each for a special commodity. The office (*Orstom*) has two teaching and research institutes, one at Bondy near Paris, the other near Abidjan (Ivory Coast) and a few centers of wide scope; Tananarive (Malagasy Republic), Bambey (Senegal), Bouaké (Ivory Coast), and others. The *instituts professionels* have stations for their special commodities: Pobé (Dahomey), and others for oil palm; Bouaké and others for cotton; Abidjan and others for fruits; Divo (Ivory Coast), and one in Cameroun for coffee and cocoa. Some large production organizations have their own stations: there is one on the island of Casamance (Senegal) for peanuts (ground nuts). In Tananarive, the university has a school of agriculture and there is also an agricultural college, both founded in 1966.

The commission set up in 1948 by the governments of the countries south of the Sahara to secure technical cooperation for dealing with problems of wide geographical range such as soil conservation and water resources, gives useful help in research. It organizes conferences, exchange of technicians and research workers, and seeks to secure uniformity of procedure and nomenclature in surveying and mapping.

Sudan.—Before World War II the Sudan Scientific Service was almost unequalled in the tropics. The irrigation station at Wad Medani in the Gezira and the cotton-breeding station at Shambat carried out superior research work and the Gordon Memorial College at Khartoum rose to become a university giving degrees in association with London University. An upheaval followed the establishment of the new republic in 1956; the connection with London University was broken and most of the British staff left. The University of Khartoum came into being in 1956 and included a faculty of agriculture.

Malawi, Rhodesia, and Zambia.—The chief experiment station of Rhodesia is at Salisbury (1914); it is now also the centre for hybrid corn (maize) seed production: a separate breeding station has been set up at Panmuri. The Grassland Research Station at Marandellas, about 50 mi. E of Salisbury, deals with the intensive production of milk and beef on the veld; there are also stations for tobacco at Kutsaga (financed by the industry), for cotton at Gatooma, and for pigs near Salisbury; one for irrigated crops in the Sabi valley about 100 mi. S of Umtali, another for low rainfall conditions at Matopos. Zambia has a research station at Mount Makulu near Lusaka, and Malawi has one at Lilongwe.

The multiracial University College in Salisbury, opened in 1957 and associated with London University, has a faculty of agriculture and a farm adjoining the Henderson Research Station where investigations are concentrated on the integration of crops, animals, and pastures. Gwebi Agricultural College at Salisbury offers a two-year course leading to the diploma in agriculture and Chibero

College of Agriculture at Norton offers a three-year diploma in agriculture for Africans. In Malawi, Chitedze Agricultural Research Station, at Lilongwe, founded 1948, in 1956 became a centre for agricultural and veterinary training and research.

The Agricultural Research Council of Central Africa, at Salisbury, was founded in 1964, succeeding the Agricultural Research Council of Rhodesia and Nyasaland. It operates research teams in Rhodesia, Malawi, and Zambia.

East Africa.—The East African Agriculture and Forestry Research Organization founded in 1948 with large and well-equipped laboratories and 1,600 ac. of land at Muguga, Kenya, deals with the fundamental problems of plant and animal growth in tropical conditions and is free of local and departmental responsibilities. The investigations include soil and water conservation, resistance of crops to disease and pests, the effects of changes in land use on the flow of rivers, water relationships of soils and plants, the plant nutrient status of African soils, and the nutritional value of African pasture plants. A parallel organization on an adjacent site deals with veterinary problems. The Veterinary Research Laboratory at Kabete was founded in 1911. The Tea Research Institute of East Africa, at Kericho, has substations in Tanzania and Uganda. There is a Cotton Research Station at Namulonge, Uganda, and research stations for coffee (Ruiru, Kenya, and Lyamungu, Tanzania), for sisal (Thika, Kenya, and Mlingano, Tanzania), and for cereals (Njoro, Kenya). The department of agriculture in each of the three countries carries out field experiments with crops of local importance.

Agricultural education in Kenya is complicated by the dual nature of the agricultural community, the European and the African differing so completely that no one system could serve both. The multiracial University of East Africa, at Kampala, Uganda, founded in 1963 and comprising Makerere University College (Kampala), University College (Nairobi), and the University College (Dar es Salaam), has faculties of agriculture and veterinary science. All three countries have farm schools for Africans which do not, however, lead up to the university.

West Africa.—In Nigeria, the University of Ibadan (1962; formerly University College, 1948), Ahmadu Bello University at Zaria (1962), the University of Ife, Ibadan Branch (1961), and the University of Nigeria at Nsukka (1960), have faculties of agriculture, and there are agricultural colleges at Akure (1957)

TECHNICIAN SHOWING YOUNG FARMERS AT THE WANBUGA FARMERS TRAINING CENTRE IN KENYA HOW TO CLIP A SHEEP'S HOOF TO PREVENT THE DEVELOPMENT OF FOOT ROT

TECHNICIAN EXAMINES WHEAT FOR DISEASES, INCLUDING SYMPTOMS OF STEM RUST, AT THE NJORO BREEDING STATION, KENYA

and Moor Plantation, Ibadan (1921). Agricultural Research Station is at Umudike, and the Agronomic Research Division is at Moor Plantation. Institute for Agricultural Research, Ahmadu Bello University, research staff covers agronomy, plant breeding, plant pathology, cotton, entomology, crop physiology, animal nutrition, pastures, soil science, soil survey, and agricultural engineering and economics. The headquarters of the West African Institute for Oil Palm Research is at Benin City and there is a substation in Annang province.

The University of Ghana, at Legon, near Accra, (1961; formerly a University College, 1948) has a faculty of agriculture; attached institutions include the Kade and Nungua Agricultural Research stations and an agricultural irrigation research station at Kpong. The University of Science and Technology at Kumasi (1961; formerly Kumasi College of Technology, 1951), also has a faculty of agriculture. The Ghana Academy of Sciences maintains the Animal Research Institute, at Achimota; the Cocoa Research Institute, at Tafo; the Crops Research Institute and the Soil Research Institute, at Kumasi; and the Forest Products Research Institute, at Takoradi.

Sierra Leone's Njala University College, at Njala, was established in 1963 as a major collegiate institution for agricultural education, research, and extension work. The internationally known West African Rice Research Station, at Rokupr, became a part of the college, which also includes the oil palm research station and the experimental station. The University of Illinois contracted with the United States Agency for International Development to assist in the development of Njala. S. B. Thomas Agricultural College, Mabang, was the first agricultural college in West Africa.

Republic of South Africa.—Agricultural education began in South Africa in 1898 with the founding of the Elsenburg School of Agriculture in Cape Province. Research began in 1902 at the end of the South African War when two experimental farms were established, one at Cedara in Natal, the other at Potchefstroom near Pretoria. Both agricultural education and research are organized regionally on an ecological basis. The Directorate of Agricultural Research, at Pretoria, manages, plans, and coordinates all agricultural research and controls the specialized and regional research institutes. Six regions are distinguished: (1) The winter rainfall region is served by the agricultural faculty of the University of Stellenbosch founded in 1926 by amalgamation with the Elsenburg

School of Agriculture. (2) The Karoo and eastern Cape region has the Grootfontein College of Agriculture, established in 1911, possessing a farm of 22,000 ac. and a flock of more than 6,000 sheep as well as Percherons and dairy cattle (Jersey and grade Frieslands). It deals with both crops and stock but it specializes in Merino sheep and wool. (3) The high-veld region has the Potchefstroom experiment farm to which in 1909 a college was added and later two outstations: it deals with all summer crops. (4) The South African plateau is served by the Glen College and experimental station near Bloemfontein. The rainfall averages only 20 in. a year and comes in summer when evaporation is high; the investigations include dryland production of maize and other crops, beef production with Afrikandar cattle on the veld, and the combining of improved systems and methods of veld management with soil and water conservation. (5) Natal has an Agricultural Research Institute at its university at Pietermaritzburg and also the Cedara College with a farm where winter crops, sown pasture, and dairy farming are among the chief studies. The South African Sugar Association has its wide-ranging experiment station at Mount Edgecombe (1924), with substations at Chaka's Kraal (1946) and Mtunzini, Zululand (1955). (6) The Transvaal region is served by the faculty of agriculture of the University of Pretoria associated with the government Soil Conservation and Extension services. Its outstations include one for grassland at Athlone, in the mistveld, cattle ranching stations at Mara and Messina where climatological reactions of cattle are studied; and one at Brits for the study of irrigation problems.

There is also a research station for wattle (acacia) in Pretoria. No systematic soil survey of the whole Union had been made but good work on soil conservation has been done; general soil problems are dealt with by the division of chemical services.

The most widely known of all South African institutions is the great Veterinary Research Institute at Onderstepoort.

LATIN AMERICA

Most of the universities of South America have faculties of agriculture offering five-year courses and giving the *ingeniero agrónomo* ("agricultural engineer") qualification; there are also a number of agricultural schools of college rank, 34 teaching institutions in all. The results, however, are not impressive. A large proportion (80% or more) of the students entering fail to complete the course; among the various reasons are the low educational standards in rural areas, the inadequacy of secondary education, the poor reward for those who finally graduate (the remuneration for agricultural technicians in government service being low), and the consequent attraction of other professions enjoying a higher social standing.

Argentina.—There are six agricultural teaching institutes: the oldest and largest is the La Plata National University (founded 1882); the University of Buenos Aires also has an agricultural and veterinary faculty (est. 1904). Others include the national universities of Cuyo, Tucumán, and the North-East (Corrientes).

Brazil.—Brazil has the greatest number of agricultural colleges, the largest being that of São Paulo (founded 1901) with more than 300 students; schools of agriculture are also found at the universities of Ceará and Rio Grande do Sul. The facilities for training have generally exceeded the demand.

Chile.—There are four university schools: the oldest in South America is the faculty of agriculture of the University of Chile (1876). Others are the Catholic University of Chile, the Southern University of Chile, and the University of Concepción.

Peru.—The university of agriculture at Lima has the largest school of agriculture in Latin America, with more than 800 students. The university at Cuzco and the new national universities at Lanbayeque, Huancayo, and Ica have faculties of agriculture.

Uruguay.—An agricultural faculty exists at the university at Montevideo.

Paraguay.—The school of agriculture of Paraguay, at Asunción, was founded in 1956.

Other Latin-American Institutions.—Some provision for agricultural education and research is made in the other Latin-American countries. The history of the stations has been checkered; some have been started and then closed before accomplishing anything. Useful work has been done in Venezuela at the Sosa Station, near Caracas; at Majaguez under Atherton Lee; at the Insular Station in Río Piedras, Puerto Rico, under J. A. B. Nolle; and at the Tropical Forest Station under Arthur Bevan. Mexico offers greater facilities for agricultural education, including more financial aid to the students, than any other of the Latin-American countries. It has four agricultural colleges, the oldest and best-known being at Chapingo (founded 1854), which has a seven-year course. The path from school to university is smooth, the school certificate being sufficient qualification for admission.

THE WEST INDIES

Introduction and acclimatization of plants was begun early in the West Indies. The Spaniards brought in cotton and sugar cane in the 16th century. The Botanic Garden of St. Vincent was set up in 1763, and was enriched in 1783 by the collection made by Capt. William Bligh (of the "Bounty") in the south seas. Jamaica had a considerable establishment in the 1870s. In the 1880s and 1890s subsidized beet sugar from Europe almost drove cane sugar out of the British market causing great distress to West Indian growers. A professor of chemistry, J. B. Harrison, was appointed in Barbados in 1882 but the economic situation grew so serious that a royal commission was appointed in 1896; on its recommendation a Department of Agriculture including a chemist, an economic botanist and entomologist was established in 1897. This organization grew and was able to effect considerable technical improvements; an unintended result was that some of the staff, having acquired experience with tropical crops, migrated to India where they rendered valuable service.

The West Indies were by the second half of the 20th century the chief training ground for tropical research workers. In 1921 the Imperial College of Tropical Agriculture was started, at first a centre for local advisory service and training, and later becoming a postgraduate institution for the whole British Commonwealth. From 1944 it became the centre of research on bananas, cocoa, soils, and sugar cane, chiefly for the West Indies, but in the case of cocoa for other countries also. It also provides a three-year diploma course for the West Indies. In 1960 it was incorporated into the University of the West Indies as the faculty of agriculture. There are farm schools in a number of the islands giving instruction at certificate level.

INTER-AMERICAN AND UN INSTITUTIONS

The Inter-American Institute of Agricultural Sciences, a specialized agency of the Organization of American States (OAS) mainly financed by the United States, maintains a research and training centre at Turrialba, Costa Rica, for studying major problems concerning livestock, pastures, coffee, forestry, and other subjects. Two important stations deal with veterinary problems: the Pan-American Zooanosis Centre at Azul, Arg., and the Pan-American Foot and Mouth Diseases Centre at Rio de Janeiro, Braz., run by the Pan-American Sanitary Bureau in association with the World Health Organization. An international forestry research station in Venezuela is sponsored by the Food and Agriculture Organization of the United Nations.

In addition the U.S. Overseas Aid Program, operated by the International Cooperation Administration, in most of the countries provided missions which deal comprehensively with important development problems, including education and research, while Rockefeller and Kellogg Trust funds are both available for research and training in selected fields. The UN Food and Agriculture Organization through its agricultural education and administrative branch advises on organization of educational, advisory, and research activities. *See also* FOOD AND AGRICULTURE ORGANIZATION.

For further discussion of agricultural education *see* ADULT EDUCATION; LAND-GRANT COLLEGES AND UNIVERSITIES; EDUCATION, HISTORY OF. For additional information on various aspects of agricultural research *see* ANIMAL BREEDING; PLANT BREEDING; PLANTS AND PLANT SCIENCE; VETERINARY SCIENCE; and articles on crops and products, as CORN; ENSILAGE; PIG; etc. *See also*

references under "Agricultural Education and Research" in the Index. (E. J. R.; X.)

BIBLIOGRAPHY.—*United States:* A. C. True, *A History of Agricultural Education in the United States, 1785–1925,* Miscellaneous publication no. 36 (1929); U.S. Department of Health, Education, and Welfare, *Statistics of Land-Grant Colleges and Universities* (annual); H. M. Hamlin, *Public School Education in Agriculture* (1962); U.S. Agricultural Research Service, *Questions and Answers on Agricultural Research in U.S. Department of Agriculture and State Agricultural Research Stations,* ARS-20-5 (1957), "The Agricultural Research Center of the United States Department of Agriculture," *Agric. Inform. Bull.* 189 (Oct. 1958), "New Uses for Farm Products," *Agric. Inform. Bull.* 209 (June 1959); U.S. Department of Agriculture, *Agricultural Research,* (monthly), *Yearbook of Agriculture,* agricultural problems, new developments and research findings (annual), *Agricultural Science Review* (quarterly), *Bibliography of Agriculture,* index of world literature in agriculture and the related sciences (monthly).
United Kingdom: Reports of the *Luxmore Committee,* Cmd. 6433 (1943); Ministry of Agriculture and Fisheries, *Report of the Loveday Committee* (1945, 1947, 1949), *Report of the Working Committee on Agricultural Education* (1953); *Report of the de la Warr Committee,* Cmd. 614 (1958); E. H. Dale, *Daniel Hall: Pioneer in Scientific Agriculture* (1956); Sir E. J. Russell, *A History of Agricultural Science in Great Britain* (1966).
Commonwealth of Nations: The results achieved at a number of the agricultural research stations in the Commonwealth during 1833–1958 are described in the *Empire Journal of Experimental Agriculture,* 26: 77–194 (April 1958) and some later issues. Each of the larger countries issues a *Yearbook* annually containing information about agriculture and research. For the colonial territories see *Colonial Research* (HMSO, annually).
Europe: Organization for European Economic Co-operation, *Agricultural Advisory Services in European Countries: Report of a Working Party of Experts* (1950); Food and Agriculture Organization, *Organization of Agricultural Research in Europe* (1953).
Other countries: The subject is by its nature very fluid: *see* the annual reports, published by most of the national research stations. *See* also UNESCO, *Educational and Agricultural Development* (1964).

AGRICULTURAL ENGINEERING has become an increasingly important part of the technical foundation for supporting agricultural productivity well above the subsistence level.

Agricultural production involves many engineering problems and opportunities. Agricultural operations to aid biological productivity—soil conservation and preparation, planting, cultivation, pest control, harvesting, hauling, processing, packaging and storage—are in many respects precision operations involving large tonnages, heavy power and critical factors of time and placement. Homes and work buildings functionally designed to aid farm operations help farm families to minimize the time and energy requirements of routine jobs.

Farmers use some of the same products engineered for urban use, but many conditions, operations and problems of agriculture are specialized. There is no urban use for a combine harvester thresher or a mechanical cotton picker. The primary use of much other equipment—plows, sprayers, dairy barns, electric brooders and terracing graders, to mention only a few items—is in agriculture. Agricultural engineering has developed to serve this need for engineering of and for agricultural activities, guided by a practical and scientific knowledge of agricultural considerations.

Early History.—In the United States, the field for agricultural engineering was recognized in part by such early leaders as George Washington and Thomas Jefferson, in improvements on the equipment and structures on their plantations. The term agricultural engineering came into occasional use before 1900 and became firmly established early in the 20th century with the organization of agricultural engineering departments and professional curriculums at Iowa State college and the University of Nebraska. This was followed by the organization of the American Society of Agricultural Engineers (ASAE), acceptance of the term agricultural engineering by a number of other colleges, universities and experiment stations, recognition by the federal civil service and some industrial employers, provision in the laws of certain states for the registration of agricultural engineers and accrediting of some curriculums by the Engineers Council for Professional Development.

Branches.—Four primary branches developed within agricultural engineering, based on natural groupings of the types of problems encountered. They deal with the following subjects:

Farm Power and Machinery.—This branch is concerned with advances in farm mechanization in terms of tractors, field machinery and other mechanical equipment.

Farm Structures.—This includes the engineering necessary to provide shelter in houses, barns, livestock buildings and crop storage and special purpose buildings, as well as fencing.

Soil and Water Control.—Agricultural engineering deals with the problems of water and soil as they influence farm operations, in drainage, irrigation, soil conservation, hydrology and to some extent, flood control.

Electric Power and Processing.—Distribution of electric power on the farm and its application to a wide variety of uses present primary problems. They include engineering electric power use to improve results in established stationary power and lighting jobs; and development of the full potential of electric power for new functions that could not otherwise be performed economically on farms, such as lighting to control plant growth and insect pests, electric fencing to control livestock and automatic control of various operations.

In these fields the general pattern of progress toward the solution of specific problems is (1) research to more accurately define functional requirements to be served; (2) design and development of machines, structures, electrical equipment and operations to better serve the functional requirements; and (3) adult education and related measures to introduce improved equipment or methods.

Professional Education.—It proved generally more practicable to develop agricultural engineers by providing a sound basic training in engineering supplemented by training in agriculture, rather than by making agriculture the prime requirement, to be supplemented by something less than the usual basic training for engineers.

Early in the second half of the 20th century, recognized professional curriculums in agricultural engineering were offered in 46 schools in 41 U.S. states and in 3 provinces of Canada. Provision for graduate study in agricultural engineering to the master of science degree had been made by 34 of these schools and 8 offered graduate study for the doctor of philosophy degree. Comparable engineering education with specialized attention to agricultural applications is available in a number of universities in other parts of the world where engineering education is well advanced and agriculture is an important factor in the national economy.

Applications.—In addition to training professional agricultural engineers, college agricultural engineering departments serve three other main functions. These include the education of students in related departments; adult education; and research projects.

The agricultural engineering departments provide service courses for students of agriculture who need to develop familiarity with farm mechanical, electrical and structural equipment, and soil and water control from a practical operating standpoint without becoming professional engineers. In many cases, the same department handles extension work or adult education in agricultural engineering in close co-operation with the federal agricultural extension service.

Independently and in co-operation with the agricultural experiment stations and in some cases the engineering experiment stations, the college agricultural engineering departments conduct research to develop new information in their field. This generally represents a more specific definition of physical conditions favourable to efficient production and handling of high-quality agricultural products.

Comparatively few agricultural engineers are directly engaged in farming. About 60% are employed in private enterprise and the other 40% in public service, including federal, state and local agencies. Private employers include farm-equipment manufacturers, component materials and parts manufacturers, trade associations, electric utilities, distributors and dealers and farm product processors.

In the U.S. department of agriculture, the soil conservation service and the agricultural research service are the primary employers of agricultural engineers, with smaller numbers in several other agencies. Land-grant universities and agricultural experiment stations are the largest employers of agricultural engineers on the state level.

American Society of Agricultural Engineers.—This is a national professional organization having membership or representation in other engineering, agricultural, educational, scientific, governmental and trade organizations. The society was organized in 1907 with 17 charter members. In 1935 it was chartered in Michigan as a nonprofit membership corporation for scientific and education purposes.

The objectives outlined in its constitution are to encourage, advance and improve (1) the science and art of engineering in agriculture; (2) agricultural engineering education; (3) the standards of agricultural engineering; (4) relations among agricultural engineers and with allied technologists; (5) the professional progress of its members; and (6) the usefulness of agricultural engineering. There are 27 regional branches in the United States and parts of Canada. The society publishes *Agricultural Engineering,* a monthly journal.

Agricultural Engineering Outside the United States.—A somewhat parallel development of agricultural engineering was taking place in other countries, modified by the composite influence of their agricultural problems, over-all economy, social customs, technical progress, educational and professional development and national outlook on material progress.

The extent of this development in the late 1950s was indicated briefly by the *International Directory of Agricultural Engineering Institutions* published in 1957 by the Food and Agriculture Organization of the United Nations. It listed 628 governmental services and institutes concerned with agricultural engineering in 75 countries. It also showed 41 national associations of manufacturers and distributors in related product fields, 33 related national meetings and shows, 54 technical and trade periodicals entirely or partly in this field and 129 reference books on various phases of the subject.

In its program of technical aid to other countries, the United States included teams of agricultural engineers to contribute to the development of agricultural resources. This usually involves considerably more than the transplanting of mechanization; it requires recognition of the existing agricultural, economic, scientific and social development of the country.

See also Farm Buildings; Farm Machinery; Fence; Fertilizers and Manures; Irrigation; Land Reclamation; Rural Electrification; Soil.   (R. A. Pr.)

AGRICULTURAL ORGANIZATIONS.

Agricultural associations range in scope from local clubs to national and international organizations that wield appreciable economic and political power and promote far-reaching technological programs. In the following discussion, the more important agricultural organizations are grouped geographically.

UNITED STATES

Farmer Movements.—Farmer movements in the United States can be grouped roughly into two types: (1) spontaneous mass efforts to change conditions regarded as intolerable by large numbers of farmers; and (2) the more closely knit continuing organizations designed for specific purposes. The first is well illustrated by the Greenback and Free Silver movements and the Populist Revolt of the late 19th century, the second by such general-purpose, continuing organizations as the Grange (Patrons of Husbandry), the Farmers Educational and Cooperative Union of America (Farmers Union), and the American Farm Bureau Federation.

Movements of the first type have sprung up from time to time, sometimes locally, sometimes on a regional basis, and at times on a scale that was almost nationwide. Among the early and local examples were Shays's Rebellion (1786–87) (*see* Massachusetts: *History*), the Whisky Insurrection (*q.v.;* 1794) and Fries's Rebellion (1799) in Pennsylvania, and the Antirent War (1839–46) against patroonship in New York. These were sharp, violent protests against taxes and inadequate amounts of money and credit. Much broader agrarian and semiagrarian movements developed later. The movement which led to the election of Thomas Jefferson in 1800 had its roots in the rural areas of the West and South, as did that which centred around Andrew Jackson and his opposition to the banking system in the period 1824–36.

From the 1830s until about 1870 there were no large-scale, general farmer campaigns of the protest type. In this period, farmers' clubs and rural fairs, organized mainly for social and educational purposes, sprang up in nearly all parts of the country, but they were almost exclusively independent and local. The most extensive and vigorous farmer movements were those of the late 19th century, from around 1870 to about 1896. The causes underlying them were, in the main, the poverty and hardships of pioneer life in the West and the flagrant abuses and corruption that characterized the railroad, marketing, and political organizations of that period.

Immediately after the Civil War (1861–65) the most significant struggle was over the issuance of United States notes, known as greenbacks (q.v.). It was essentially a protest against deflation and a return to the gold standard. The Greenbackers, mainly the farmers of the West, demanded that the amount of paper currency issued during the Civil War be maintained or expanded, as a means of keeping money in circulation and helping to keep prices up. The movement gained enough strength to halt the retirement of greenbacks but was not able to prevent the return to the gold standard in 1879. It eventually merged with the Free Silver movement of the 1880s and 1890s, which had similar objectives but advocated the use of silver instead of paper currency.

The so-called Granger movement of the 1870s and 1880s included many of the same persons and was part of the general protest against low prices, high and discriminatory freight charges, and corporate and political corruption. Largely as a result of it, railroad rates were brought under public control and a national regulatory body, the Interstate Commerce Commission, was established in 1887. A later outgrowth of the movement, though not specifically spearheaded by the Grangers, was the Sherman Anti-Trust Act of 1890.

The Farmers' Alliance movement, mainly in the 1880s and early 1890s, was a more general protest against the railroads, middlemen, banks, "trusts and monopolies" and the major political parties. It consisted of many organizations, some of which were absorbed into while others merely joined forces with the alliance in the pursuit of common ends. The shift to political party status in 1890 and 1892 resulted in defeat at the polls and the disintegration of the movement.

No new large-scale farmer movements developed thereafter until the 1920s, except for the Nonpartisan League, which gained considerable strength in the northern plains region between 1915 and 1924. The league had many of the characteristics of the Populist movement, though its program looked more specifically to state socialism than did that of the alliance or the Populist Party. It did not expand beyond a regional basis and its effective program was confined largely to one state, North Dakota.

A large-scale farmer movement of a different kind developed in the 1920s as a campaign for adoption of the McNary-Haugen two-price plan for farm products. It grew out of the severe decline in farm prices that followed World War I and was much more highly organized and ably led than the earlier protest movements. The plan itself lost out, but the strength developed by the farm groups in supporting it undoubtedly contributed to the actions later taken by the federal government in establishing the Federal Farm Board (1929–33) and the Agricultural Adjustment Administration of 1933 and after.

Smaller and less continuing farmer movements have sprung up from time to time, among them the Farmers' Holiday movement which swept over parts of the Middle West in 1932 as a protest against low prices and farm foreclosures.

The movements described above were of the mass-protest type. In addition, U.S. agriculture has developed a vast array of more formally organized, continuing organizations including marketing and service associations numbering in the tens of thousands. At times their rate of growth has been such as to constitute something approaching a "movement," though usually they are looked upon as being merely a special type of business organization.

General Organizations.—The general farm organizations constitute an intermediate group. The oldest of them, the Grange (Patrons of Husbandry), was started as a fraternal, educational, and social organization in 1867. It expanded rapidly, achieving a membership of nearly 1,000,000 by 1875. It soon launched into many types of activity not contemplated by its founders. The railroad laws and related legislation passed in the 1870s and 1880s are commonly referred to as the Granger laws, though the Grange itself was merely the largest and most prominent of the many farm organizations that took part in this movement. The Grange later declined to a membership of little more than 100,000, but it grew again after 1900 and became one of the largest and most stable of the farm organizations. When the Grange observed its centennial in 1967, its membership was well over 500,000.

The Farmers Educational and Cooperative Union of America was organized in Texas in 1902. Its early leadership consisted largely of former Farmers' Alliance men, and its strength in the early years was chiefly in the cotton states. Later its membership shifted to the northern plains states.

The other major farm organization, the American Farm Bureau Federation was organized in 1919. It consists of state farm bureau federations, which in turn are made up of county farm bureaus originally organized as educational groups for collaboration with the agricultural extension services. By 1922 the American Farm Bureau federation had a national paid-up membership of 450,000 families. Its membership declined sharply in the late 1920s and early 1930s but increased appreciably thereafter. The federation and the state and local farm bureaus continued to work in close collaboration with the agricultural extension services and the state colleges of agriculture.

Other farmer organizations of similar type gained temporary followings at various times but either did not survive or did not become important nationally.

Improvement Societies.—Agricultural improvement societies constituted another group of organizations, composed both of farmers and of others interested in farming. The first of these societies in the U.S. of which there is a definite record was the Philadelphia Society for the Promotion of Agriculture and the South Carolina Society for Improving Agriculture and Other Rural Concerns, both organized in 1785. The pioneer in establishing societies that would reach the working farmer was Elkanah Watson of Pittsfield, Mass., who organized the Berkshire Agricultural Society in 1811 to sponsor an annual cattle show or agricultural fair. County societies founded on the Berkshire plan multiplied rapidly until about 1825 when state aid was withdrawn and most of the societies disbanded.

About 1840 interest in improvement societies revived and both county and state societies were organized, many state governments appropriating funds for their support. From about 1840 to 1870 these societies bore virtually the entire burden of agricultural experimentation and instruction. After 1870 the number and influence of the societies declined as they were replaced by state and county boards of agriculture and later by state departments of agriculture, and their educational functions were taken over by other institutions (see AGRICULTURAL EDUCATION AND RESEARCH: *United States*).

See also AGRICULTURAL ECONOMICS: *Agricultural Co-operation;* AMERICAN FARM BUREAU FEDERATION; EXHIBITIONS AND FAIRS; FARMERS UNION; FOUR-H CLUBS; GRANGE, THE; EDUCATION, HISTORY OF. (M. R. BT.; W. W. WX.)

COMMONWEALTH OF NATIONS

Great Britain.—In the latter half of the 18th century numerous societies were formed in Great Britain whose objects were entirely or mainly to foster agricultural development.

In Scotland the Edinburgh Society of Improvers in the Knowledge of Agriculture, founded in 1723, dissolved for financial reasons in 1764, but out of it developed the Highland and Agricultural Society of Scotland, formed in 1784. In 1787 the latter society was granted a royal charter, and although its first aim was the development of the Highlands, its operations soon extended over the whole of Scotland. It offered premiums for plowing matches, land reclamation, plans for new villages and for the best-manured farms and encouraged research and education. It became known as the Royal Highland and Agricultural Society of Scotland.

In England, the Bath and West and Southern Counties Society, founded in 1777, started by collecting information about the best farming practices, arranged a plowing match said to be "the first of its kind in any country," and offered premiums for improved livestock. In 1799 it acquired an experimental plot of ten acres, the forerunner of the research stations of today.

Before the end of the century local associations had sprung up in numerous counties. Among them was the Herefordshire Agricultural Society, which was formed in 1797. In 1894 this society was enlarged to include Worcestershire, and 28 years later the Gloucestershire Agricultural Society, formed in 1829, joined with the other two counties to form the Three Counties Agricultural Society.

In 1798 the Smithfield Cattle and Sheep Society, which in 1802 became the Smithfield Club, was founded to improve farm live-stock and particularly to bring out the principle of early maturity by scientific farming and breeding. At its first show in 1799 prizes were offered in four classes, for the best beast and best sheep fed on grass, hay, turnips, or cabbages, and for the best beast and best sheep fed on corn or oil cake.

In 1838 a meeting of landowners and farmers formed the English Agricultural Society to encourage improvement in every branch of agriculture, by methods which ranged from the collection and distribution of available information to the award of grants and prizes for research, new equipment or better livestock. The society came to exert a great influence on the farming of England. During its first 50 years it undertook much of the work later done by government departments. In 1840 it was granted a royal charter as the Royal Agricultural Society of England (RASE). Its recommendations to government on many occasions laid the foundations for new agricultural legislation, for example, the organization of a conference in 1944, the recommendation of which formed a foundation for the Agriculture Act of 1947. In addition to its other activities one of the greatest tasks of the RASE is the organization of the annual Royal Show.

After World War II an important feature of its work was the organizing of conferences and of visits by its council members to overseas countries. Out of this developed the organization known as the Royal Agricultural Societies of the Commonwealth in which are represented the Royal Agricultural Societies of the United Kingdom and all the Commonwealth countries. The organization's object is to encourage and arrange the interchange of knowledge and experience in the practice and science of agriculture in order to improve methods of crop growing, the breeding of livestock, and the efficiency of agricultural machinery, and to encourage the exchange and settlement of young farmers within the Commonwealth.

Besides the large societies concerned with all sides of agriculture, there are many that deal with specific sections of the industry, such as the pedigree-breed societies for all the pure livestock breeds. The British Dairy Farmers' Association, founded in 1876, was established to improve dairy stock and produce and to support the interests of dairy farmers. In addition to organizing the London Dairy Show, it publishes a journal and, in conjunction with the RASE and the Royal Highland Society, forms the National Dairy Examination Board. It has given financial assistance toward research in dairying. Other such groups include the National Cattle Breeders' Association, formed in 1907, which works in conjunction with the cattle-breed societies; the National Sheep Breeders' Association, incorporated in 1892, which represents all the 35 sheep-breed societies in England; and the National Pig Breeders' Association, founded in 1884, which incorporates nine of the pig-breed societies.

Ministry of Agriculture.—In 1793 a board of agriculture was created by royal charter. The government financed and patronized it but had no direct control. It was dissolved in 1822 and in 1889 a new board of agriculture was established by act of Parliament and to the board were transferred the duties of the land commission and the responsibility for ordnance (government) survey, agricultural research, education, and statistics. In 1903 it took over the administration of the fishery laws. In 1919 it was reconstituted by act of Parliament as the Ministry of Agriculture and Fisheries, and its activities steadily increased. The minister of agriculture is assisted by two parliamentary secretaries, one in the House of Lords and one in the Commons. At the outbreak of World War II the ministry virtually assumed command of the country's farming resources, and war agricultural executive committees were formed in every county from representatives of farmers and farm workers. These committees acted as the ministry's agents in the county. Under the Agriculture Act of 1947 they were reconstituted as permanent county agricultural executive committees.

The Agricultural Research Council was established in 1931, and the Agricultural Improvement Council was set up in 1941 by the ministry to encourage the application of research to practical farming. In 1946 the national agricultural advisory service of the ministry came into being, took over the existing advisory services, and set up a chain of experimental husbandry farms.

The ministry's policy applies to Wales as well as England, but a Welsh department at Aberystwyth deals with problems specific to that country.

In 1911 the Department of Agriculture for Scotland was created and assumed all the ministry's functions in Scotland with the exception of animal health matters. Because animal disease does not stop at country boundaries, the authority of the ministry's animal health division extends over Scotland as well.

There is a separate Ministry of Agriculture for Northern Ireland.

Farmers' Clubs.—Another type of organization for farmers which grew up in Britain in the 19th century was the farmers' clubs—local groups that met to read papers and exchange information on agricultural subjects. The largest of these is the Farmers' Club of London, founded in 1842.

The organization of young farmers' clubs in England was begun largely through the influence of Lord Northcliffe, who had studied the work of the 4-H clubs (*q.v.*) of the United States. The first such club in England was organized in Devon in 1920. Later the movement was given financial assistance by the Ministry of Agriculture, and in 1932 the National Federation of Young Farmers' Clubs was inaugurated. By the 1960s it had about 1,500 local clubs in England and Wales and in the Channel Islands. Similar youth organizations for young farmers are to be found in many other countries, including Australia, Belgium, Canada, Denmark, France, Finland, the Netherlands, Ireland, Luxembourg, New Zealand, Northern Ireland, Scotland, Sweden, Switzerland, and the West Indies.

Farmers' Union.—The Chamber of Agriculture, founded in 1866 and intended to unite all organizations interested in agriculture, died out through lack of support. In 1904 nine farmers in Lincolnshire founded a local union of farmers, and the idea spread to adjoining counties. In 1908 these branches were incorporated in the National Farmers' Union, which by the second half of the 20th century had more than 200,000 members in more than 1,000 local branches in England and Wales. The union promoted most of the existing marketing schemes and maintained close contact with overseas agriculturists.

Similar organizations are the National Farmers' Union of Scotland, founded in 1913, and the Ulster Farmers' Union in Northern Ireland.

Agricultural Workers' Unions.—There are also unions which protect the interests of farm workers. In 1906 George Edwards, a Norfolk farm labourer, started in East Anglia a farm workers' union that, in 1919, became the National Union of Agricultural Workers. It has branches in England and Wales. In Scotland the farm workers are represented by the Scottish Farm Servants section of the Transport and General Workers' Union, and in Northern Ireland this same union also has an agricultural section.

Canada.—The Canadian Federation of Agriculture, which has a membership comprised of most of the farm operators in the country, was formed in 1935 when all organizations of farmers in the various provinces were invited to join in provincial federations and in one national body. The federation advises the government on agricultural matters and the government has followed the federation's policy of establishing marketing boards for various commodities.

Australia.—The National Farmers Union of Australia, a nationwide federation of associations of agriculture founded in 1943, includes the great majority of farm operators in the country. It is represented in government committees and statutory authorities dealing with matters of production and distribution of primary produce as well as such related matters as immigration and taxation. Among its accomplishments was the appointment of a minister for primary industry with full cabinet status in the federal government.

New Zealand.—The organization called the Federated Farmers of New Zealand was founded in 1945 and took over the functions of the New Zealand Farmers Union formed in 1900. About 80% of all farm operators in the country are members. It links all farming organizations in the country and has sections for every commodity of primary produce, each section having a large measure of autonomy.

India.—There are two main farmers' organizations in India: the Federation of Rural Peoples' Organizations and the Farmers' Forum of India. The Farmers' Forum, founded in 1954 had the union minister of agriculture as its first president. It is a federal organization that affiliates the farmers' forums established in various states as well as the agricultural commodity organizations which have been established at national level.

EUROPE

Belgium.—The chief organization looking after the interests of farming in Belgium is Boerenbond Belge, which has a large membership. Among its aims are the development and strengthening of the spirit of fellowship within the rural population; the maintenance of faith and morality in the country; the dissemination of agricultural skills; the improvement of conditions for farmers; and the economic and technical perfecting of agricultural and horticultural practices.

Denmark.—Nearly every farm operator in Denmark is a member of the Agricultural Council (Landbrugsraadet), founded in 1919 and composed of the Federation of Danish Co-operative Societies and the Federation of Danish Agricultural Societies. Negotiations are carried out by the council with the government on behalf of agriculture and the organization also takes part in trade negotiations with other countries and represents Danish agriculture abroad.

Finland.—There are two main agricultural organizations in Finland: Pellervo-Seura, founded in 1899, and Maataloustuottajain Keskusliitto (MTK), founded in 1917. One of the most important accomplishments of Pellervo-Seura was the new Cooperative Societies Act that came into force on Jan. 1, 1955. The MTK maintains close relations with members of Parliament and with cabinet members. It is represented on the most important committees dealing with agriculture and forestry.

France.—The Confédération Générale de l'Agriculture (CGA) was formed in 1945 as a free professional agricultural organization grouping the different branches of agriculture which were themselves formed into various federations.

German Federal Republic (West Germany).—The German Farmers' Association (Deutscher Bauernverband) is the central organization of 15 independent regional unions. Another 19 specialized professional associations extending their activities over the republic are affiliated with the union. The Association of German Farmers' Co-operative Unions (Deutscher Raiffeisen-Verband) is the central organization of the 12 independent regional associations with more than 23,000 single cooperative unions of all kinds.

Netherlands.—The Dutch National Farmers Union (KNIC) is a federation of ten provincial organizations. As with the other Dutch farm organizations (the National Catholic Farmers' Union and the National Protestant Farmers Union) most of its relations with the government are handled through the public body (Land-bouwschap) that deals mainly with negotiations on price policy, agricultural wages, and technical matters.

Norway.—The Norwegian Farmers' Union (Norges Bondelag) was founded in 1896. It negotiates with the government when a long-term agreement regarding agricultural prices is to be fixed. The Norwegian agricultural cooperative marketing, purchasing, and other organizations working on a nationwide scale are eligible for membership in Landbrukets Sentralforbund. This organization carries out certain statistical services and has a special division dealing with current marketing and price reports.

Sweden.—The Federation of Swedish Farmers' Associations (Sveriges Lantbruksförbund), founded in 1917, is the central body of the Swedish farmers' cooperatives. Affiliated to it are the 12 national organizations in various branches of production and most of their provincial societies. Practically all farmers are members of one or more regional farm cooperatives, and hence indirectly of SL. Riksförbundet Landsbygdens Folk (the Swedish National Farmers' Union), which was founded in 1929, has grown from a membership of 18,000 in 1930 to about 200,000 farmers.

The two organizations cooperate with agricultural organizations from Denmark, Finland, Norway, and Iceland in the NBC (the Joint Council of the Farmers' Organizations in the Nordic Countries), which handles issues of common interest and provides guidance on current problems affecting agriculture and farmers' organizations in the Nordic countries.

Switzerland.—The Swiss Farmers' Union (Union Suisse des Paysans) was founded in 1897 by grouping together all farm organizations then in existence. It consists of 65 regional groups with a total membership of 580,000 and its structure has remained basically unchanged since its establishment. The union is represented on about 30-odd official permanent government commissions and is frequently consulted by the government on matters of common interest.

JAPAN

The National Chamber of Agriculture was founded in 1954 and is made up of representatives of local chambers of agriculture, of national federations of agricultural cooperatives and other agricultural organizations. It works closely with the government on matters concerning agricultural policies. It also carries out research and extensive educational and publicity services for farmers and cooperates with the government in promoting measures concerning agriculture, forestry, and fisheries.

The Central Union of Agricultural Co-operatives was founded in 1955 for the purpose of encouraging the formation of cooperatives in the agricultural field on a nationwide basis.

INTERNATIONAL ORGANIZATIONS

The International Federation of Agricultural Producers was formed in 1946 at a conference called by the National Farmers' Union of England and Wales. Its headquarters in Washington, D.C., and Paris kept in close touch with the FAO and it became the spokesman for agricultural interests in international negotiations. By the 1960s it comprised about 50 member organizations from more than 30 countries. On IFAP's 20th anniversary in 1966, these included, in addition to the countries discussed above, Greece, Iceland, Ireland, Italy, Luxembourg, and Yugoslavia in Europe; Morocco, Niger, Rhodesia, South Africa, Tunisia, Uganda, and Zambia in Africa; Pakistan and the Philippines in Asia; Mexico in Latin America; and Israel in the Middle East.

The Food and Agriculture Organization of the United Nations (FAO), an international organization of governmental departments or ministries of agriculture, came into being in 1945 with Lord Boyd-Orr as its first director general. It succeeded the International Institute of Agriculture (*q.v.*). The governments of 71 nations (more than 100 nations in the late 1960s) combined in FAO to increase food production throughout the world. The work was organized under five technical divisions—agriculture, economics, fisheries, forestry, and nutrition. Technical advisors helped the member governments to improve their agriculture and social conditions by assisting such projects as land reclamation and drainage, the improvement of water supplies, the provision of improved varieties of seeds and plants, pest destruction, and the control of disease, fish culture, and forestry development.

See also Food and Agriculture Organization; International Trade Associations and Congresses: *Agriculture.*

(A. Hn.; X.)

BIBLIOGRAPHY.—Solon J. Buck, *The Granger Movement* (1913; reprint 1963); John D. Hicks, *The Populist Revolt* (1931; reprint 1961); Orville Merton Kile, *The Farm Bureau Through Three Decades* (1948); Charles M. Gardner, *The Grange, Friend of the Farmer* (1949); W. L. Robinson, *The Grange, 1867–1967* (1966); Murray R. Benedict, *Farm Policies of the United States, 1790–1950,* particularly ch. 6, 9, and 10 (1953; reprint 1966); Carl C. Taylor, *The Farmers' Movement, 1620–1920* (1953); Gilbert C. Fite, *George N. Peek and the Fight for Farm Parity* (1954); Fred A. Shannon, *American Farmers' Movements* (1957); J. A. S. Watson and M. E. Hobbs, *Great Farmers* (1937); J. A. S. Watson, *The History of the Royal Agricultural Society of England, 1839–1939* (1939); L. Bull, *History of the Smithfield Club from 1798–1925* (1926); Food and Agriculture Organization of the United Nations, *Growing Food for a Growing World: the Work of F.A.O., 1952–53* (1954); International Federation of Agricultural Producers, Handbook, *The First Ten Years* (1957).

AGRICULTURE (ARTICLES ON).

In spite of the industrialization of many parts of the world, agriculture still drafts into its service more of the world's aggregate manpower than all other occupations combined. The following article Agriculture deals with its changing methods of employing men and machines and gives a general view of its contemporary status. The history and current status of individual phases of the subject are treated in four additional survey articles: Agricultural Economics; Agricultural Education and Research; Agricultural Engineering; and Agricultural Organizations.

An additional background article, Agriculture, Primitive, discusses the link between the origins of agriculture and of civilization. Food Supply of the World describes regional production of various foodstuffs, outlines the nutritional patterns of various nations, and discusses the net food supply and the challenge of feeding the world's growing population. Significant basic material is contained also in the sections of Natural Resources captioned *Vegetation; Soils; Animal Life;* and *Water.*

Agronomy, the branch of agriculture concerned with field-crop culture and soil management, is represented by many articles. Soil deals with the natural processes by which soils are created, the methods by which they are classified and their physical and chemical properties, microbiology and productivity. Fertilizers and Manures identifies the elements necessary for normal plant growth, and discusses the major commercial fertilizers and manures and their production and use. Among other articles dealing with problems of agronomy are Seed; Crops; Rotation of Crops; Sprays and Dusts in Agriculture; Liming; Irrigation; Land Reclamation; Plant Breeding; Plant Diseases; Pest Control; Weed; and Grain Production and Trade.

Among the articles on individual grains are Wheat; Corn; Oats; Rye; Rice; Barley; etc. Information on pastures and hay crops is given in Grassland and in Range (in Agriculture). Articles dealing with forage and legumes are Ensilage; Leguminosae; and the specific crops Alfalfa; Lespedeza; Peanut; etc. Articles devoted to fibre crops are Fibre; Flax; Hemp; Jute; and Cotton.

Sugar crops are discussed in Sugar and Beet. Other important crops are discussed in such articles as Potato; Tobacco; Oil Plants; Tea; Coffee; and Rubber.

Horticulture surveys the principles and methods of the culture of fruits, vegetables and ornamental plants. This article is supplemented by Fruit Farming; Vegetable; and Flower, which has a section on *Commercial Flower Growing.* Individual articles are devoted to various fruits, berries, nuts, flowers and shrubs.

Soilless plant culture is discussed in Hydroponics; also in a section on hydroponics in Plants and Plant Science. Among the articles dealing with trees are Arboriculture; and Forests and Forestry.

Animal agriculture is treated in Animal Breeding; Dairy Industry; Feeds, Animal; Veterinary Science; Poultry and Poultry Farming; Turkey; and Fur, which contains a section

on *Fur Farming.* Individual articles are devoted to the various types of livestock—Horse; Cattle; Sheep; Goat; Pig; etc.; also, to such specialized farm interests as Rabbit; Game Birds; and Beekeeping.

Agricultural buildings, machinery and equipment are treated in Farm Buildings; Farmstead Arrangement, U.S.; Granary and Grain Elevator; Farm Machinery; Planting Machinery; Crop-Processing Machinery; Harvesting Machinery; Rural Electrification; Tillage Machinery; Sprays and Dusts in Agriculture; Tractor; etc.

Among the articles devoted to processed agricultural commodities are Milk; Cheese; Ice Cream; Dairy Industry; Food Preservation; Canning, Commercial; Oils, Fats and Waxes; Flour; Cider; Wine; and Honey.

Articles of specialized interest include Tropical Agriculture; Weather Forecasting; and Entomology.

Agricultural economics, treated in a survey article under that title, is discussed from various points of view in Farm Management; Marketing; and Farm Tenancy. Among the articles dealing with social, legal and political considerations are Farm Colony; Land Tenure: Economic and Agrarian Aspects; Small Holdings; and Land Reform. The historical uprooting of large populations because of land hunger is described in Migration.

Information on the agricultural methods and products characteristic of various regions will be found in articles on nations, states and other geographical units.

AGRICULTURE.

In the second half of the 20th century the people of the world were living very largely on the produce of an area of cropland equivalent to about one acre per person. This suggests the extent to which the land had been made productive by man's efforts, for they could not have lived as they did, and where they did, on the native vegetation and wildlife. Agriculture, the art of making land more productive, is practised throughout the world—in some areas by methods not far removed from the conditions of several thousands of years ago; in others, with the aid of science and mechanization, as a highly commercial type of endeavour.

In addition to the cross references to related articles given below, *see* Agriculture (Articles on). For agriculture in primitive societies *see* Agriculture, Primitive.

The main divisions of this article are as follows:

I. World Agriculture
  A. Origins of Agriculture
    1. Cultivation and Land Use
    2. Livestock
  B. Agricultural Expansion to the New World
  C. Land Use and Production
  D. Population and Food Supplies
  E. Soil Conservation
  F. Land Tenure and Agrarian Reform
  G. Productivity and Increased Output
  H. World Census of Agriculture
II. United States
  A. Agricultural Beginnings
    1. Indian Agriculture
    2. Colonial Land Policies
    3. Colonial Agriculture
  B. Developments up to the Civil War
    1. Federal Land Policies to 1862
    2. Southern Staple Crop Production
    3. Northern Mixed Farming
    4. Livestock
    5. Agricultural Journals
    6. Science in Agriculture
  C. From the Civil War to the 20th Century
    1. The Civil War and Agriculture
    2. Agriculture in the New West
    3. Agrarian Politics, 1870–96
    4. Government Collection of Agricultural Data
  D. Farming in the 20th Century

E. Type-of-Farming Regions
  1. Cotton Belt
  2. Wheat Areas
  3. Corn Belt
  4. Dairy Areas
  5. General and Self-Sufficing Areas
  6. Range-Livestock Areas
  7. Western Specialty-Crop Areas
  8. Other Areas

III. Commonwealth of Nations

  A. The United Kingdom
    1. Early and Medieval Times
    2. The Era of Improvement
    3. Victorian Prosperity
    4. Depression and Its Aftermath
    5. World War I
    6. Years Between the Wars
    7. World War II
    8. British Agriculture After World War II

  B. Canada
    1. General
    2. Quebec
    3. Ontario
    4. New Brunswick
    5. Nova Scotia
    6. Prince Edward Island
    7. Manitoba
    8. Saskatchewan
    9. Alberta
    10. British Columbia
    11. Canada's Agricultural Production

  C. Australia
    1. General Survey
    2. Queensland
    3. Northern Territory
    4. New South Wales
    5. Victoria
    6. South Australia
    7. Western Australia
    8. Tasmania
    9. Further Development

  D. New Zealand
    1. General
    2. North Island
    3. South Island

  E. India
    1. General
    2. Crops
    3. Livestock
    4. Food Production and Population: the Five-Year Plans

  F. Pakistan
    1. General
    2. West Pakistan
    3. East Pakistan
    4. Summary

  G. Rhodesia, Malawi and Zambia
    1. Rhodesia
    2. Malawi
    3. Zambia

  H. West Africa
    1. Introduction
    2. Nigeria
    3. Ghana
    4. Sierra Leone
    5. Gambia

  I. East Africa
    1. General
    2. Kenya
    3. Uganda
    4. Tanzania

  J. The Smaller Tropical Countries and Islands

I. WORLD AGRICULTURE

A. ORIGINS OF AGRICULTURE

The earliest human societies subsisted by hunting and gathering. About 10,000 years ago there arose in the old and new worlds a set of circumstances from which the discovery of plant and animal domestication became not merely a possibility but a likelihood. The glaciers were in full retreat. The next few millenniums were to see the continued extinctions of migratory Pleistocene fauna which had been the main food supply of Upper Paleolithic hunters. Humanity had begun a long period of settling down in various local environments, of learning to exploit particular plant and animal resources to the fullest. Above all, there was a new emphasis on the use of wild plants—roots and seeds. Speaking very generally of the origins of agriculture, archaeological evidence strongly indicates that the first use of cultivated plants was by societies which had achieved some degree of sedentary life through intensive collection of wild foods. Judging from observation of recent tribal peoples, it is also supposed that those early societies had a sustained practical interest in and a detailed knowledge of wild plants and their properties.

Knowledge of the specific times and places of the first plant domestications is derived from the study of present distributions of ancestral wild forms and from archaeological finds of preserved specimens of the plants and seeds themselves. The same methods are used to study the domestication of animals but less is known of the early stages of animal domestication than of plants because it is often difficult to distinguish the bones of the domesticated species from their wild counterparts.

In the second part of the 20th century information concerning the early development of agriculture was accumulating at an unprecedented rate as more archaeological explorations were being undertaken and in greater co-operation with botanists and zoologists. In consequence much that had been written only a few years earlier was becoming outdated. The evidence, however, suggests two major centres of plant domestication—southwestern Asia (the near east) in the old world and Mesoamerica (northern Mexico to northern South America) in the new. The old world centre from the beginning was also the scene of animal domestication. Plant and animal husbandry were early woven into the close relationship which characterizes western European farming. In the ancient Americas, however, animal domestication was less important, perhaps because of the absence of larger species which would be suitable as draft animals and which would submit to domestication.

The southwest Asia centre of plant and animal domestication has been described as a fertile crescent, extending from the alluvial plain of Mesopotamia through Syria and down the eastern coast of the Mediterranean to the Nile valley of Egypt. It is doubtful if all innovations in this region occurred at any single locale, and the most important evidence has come from two major sites: Jarmo (c. 6000 B.C.) in Iraqi Kurdistan, on the flanks of the Zagros mountains, and ancient Jericho (c. 7000 B.C.), by a gushing spring in the Jordan valley. Both localities indicate the goat as the first farm animal domesticated. Pigs, sheep and cattle—the major food animals of modern agriculture—were being hunted and eaten but were probably not domesticated at that time. Numbers of wild and cultivated grains were found in the excavations at Jarmo but by 1960 none had been discovered at Jericho. The suggestion that plants were grown there is based principally on the size and substantial character of the settlement, not a completely safe assumption.

At Jarmo occurred the large-grained wild wheat (*Triticum dicoccoides*), the small grained wild wheat (*T. aegilopoides*) and a two-row barley very like the wild species (*Hordeum spontaneum*). Cultivated grains included the large-grained emmer (*T. dicoccum*), which is ancestral to all other species of cultivated wheat except einkorn. The latter is the descendent of the small-grained wild wheat (*T. aegilopoides*). (*See* also WHEAT.)

Radiocarbon dating techniques suggested that plant and animal domestication probably were underway at Jarmo at 6000 B.C. and at Jericho perhaps 1,000 years earlier. Later between 6000 and 5000 B.C., farming villages spread over the Mesopotamian plain, Anatolia and Egypt. Emmer was adapted to the irrigated lands of Mesopotamia. Einkorn apparently was not, but continued with emmer in the agricultural settlements of the Danubian loessic lands of eastern Europe about 4500 B.C. Successive migrations of farmers and herders were responsible for the introduction of plant and animal husbandry to western Europe. In the 3rd millennium B.C. club wheat, which had had an earlier sporadic occurrence in Egypt, was the main wheat crop in Switzerland. In the meantime, other farming communities had appeared to the eastward in Iran; it was probably from these that Indus valley agriculture was derived early in the 3rd millennium B.C. The Yang-shao period of northern China apparently possessed cultivated millet (*Setaria* and *Panicum*), kaoliang (*Andropogon*) and rice (*Oryza*) and probably had domesticated cattle, pigs, sheep and goats; the relationship between this well-developed Neolithic agriculture and the southwestern centre is not at all clear.

The independent development of agriculture in Mesoamerica was also a complex affair. An excellent archaeological sequence from Tamaulipas in northeast Mexico shows supplementary cultivation emerging about 6000 B.C. among peoples who relied mainly on game and wild plant foods. The cultigens at this time were the pumpkin (*Cucurbita pepo*), pepper (*Capsicum frutescens*) and the runner bean (*Phaseolus coccineus*). Unlike the old world situation, where the important plants, wheat and barley, were present from the beginning, corn (Indian corn or maize), the most important plant of Mesoamerican agriculture, did not appear until later. An early race of maize appeared in Tamaulipas and at Bat Cave, New Mexico, about 3000 B.C. An earlier view held that maize was derived from teocentli, or teosinte; a more recent opinion is that a wild form was the ancestor of the cultivated species (*see* also CORN: *Origin and History*). In the meantime other varieties of beans (*Vulgaris*) were developed. Somewhat later the warty squash (*Cucurbita moschata*) appeared. Again, unlike the old world situation, several thousand years elapsed between the initial cultivation of plants (6000 B.C.) and the appearance of communities in which the main subsistence was derived from food production (1500 B.C.).

In the forests of the Amazon and Orinoco a tradition of cultivating tropical root crops—bitter manioc (*Manihot utilissima*), sweet manioc (*M. aipi*), and the yam (*Ipomoea batatas*)—arose sometime before 1000 B.C. On the Peruvian coast another series of cultivated plants had appeared by 2200 B.C.—squash, peppers, gourds, cotton, achira tubers and a local bean (*Canavalia*). These were in semisedentary shellfish and marine economies which utilized wild plants as well. In the northern Mississippi valley another group of plants which may have been cultivated as early as 1000 B.C. included gourds, pumpkin and squash, goosefoot (*Chenopodium*) and sunflower. The last two, at least, were local domesticates.

It is possible that the Mississippi valley and Peruvian centres somehow reflect an early diffusion of cultivated plants from the Mesoamerican region, but for the Amazonian root-crop tradition, there is, as in the case of the southeast Asia root-crop tradition, a greater likelihood of independent origin.

Whatever the case, the outward spread of Mesoamerican maize drew Peru, the North American southwest and the Mississippi valley into the orbit of Mesoamerican agriculture. In the southwest the eventual result was the establishment of village farming communities at about 300 A.D., or more than 3,000 years after the introduction of maize. During this long period of supplementary agriculture the bean, squash, pumpkin and improved races of maize were developed or introduced. In the northern Mississippi valley a certain amount of Mesoamerican maize was grown during the last centuries B.C. Again, not until 1,000 years later was heavy dependence placed upon cultivated plants. Indeed, nowhere in forested eastern North America did agriculture, which was essentially a part-time occupation of the women, play as decisive an economic role as in southwestern Asia and Mesoamerica.

The preceding discussion follows closely the views set forth in three distinguished papers in *Science*: H. Helbaek, "Domestication of Food Plants in the Old World," vol. 130, no. 3,372 (Aug. 1959); C. A. Reed, "Animal Domestication in the Prehistoric Near East," vol. 130, no. 3,389 (Dec. 1959); and G. R. Willey, "New World Prehistory," vol. 131, no. 3,393 (Jan. 1960). *See* also J. R. Caldwell (ed.), *New Roads to Yesterday* (1965).   (JH. R. C.)

1. Cultivation and Land Use.—Early methods of cultivation were limited to the digging stick and the hoe. The stick was

the ancestor of the mattock, pick, spade and fork. Since a few years of cultivation of upland soil led to depletion, hoe culture was associated, in most places, with a seminomadic way of life. In fertile river valleys where irrigation was possible and where fruit trees could be grown, populations tended to be more stable.

The plow is believed to have originated in the eastern Mediterranean region, some time before 3000 B.C. The use of plows, even those of the simplest type, marks the beginning of some system of land tenure and the development of a more complex form of agriculture.

Iron plowshares were used in Britain about 400 B.C. and colters (cutters on plows) made their appearance about the 1st century B.C. Early Roman agriculture in Britain is believed to have been based on the colter plow and strip cultivation in contrast to the pointed plows and square plots which characterized the native farming. The pointed plows, giving rise to cross cultivation, resulted in a system of small squarish fields averaging from one-half to two acres in area and found throughout Europe. The plots, separated by linchets or terraces, were clustered around villages. In Britain this form of agricultural economy is referred to as the Celtic field system. It appeared there during the late Bronze Age, about 1000 B.C., and lasted until the end of the Roman period, about A.D. 400. While it appeared to be the predominant system of community organization and land use then in effect there were exceptions, one of which, based on the Roman strip-shaped fields, has been noted.

With the coming of the Angles and Saxons, the Celtic field system was replaced by the open-field system of tenure which included the use of colter plows and strip cultivation. This was a co-operative system, the arable land being held in common but divided into strips which were apportioned among those entitled to them. The land was worked in common with plows and oxen owned by individuals. A man's holdings could be numerous and widely scattered. The plots were worked in rotation.

The Domesday survey, undertaken in Britain in 1086, revealed that the early Saxon form of tenure had been replaced by a manorial system. The land was owned by the king, by a lord or by the church, and the village community lived in serfdom upon it. Part of the land was operated as the home farm of the lord of the manor; the balance was operated by tenants who were required to perform military service and to work on the lord's demesne for a specified period each year. The land of the manor was divided into two or three large fields, each of which was subdivided into numerous strips. A serf or tenant had land in each field. The fields were tilled in rotation, one being in winter wheat, a second in barley, oats or beans and the third lying fallow. Livestock grazed on the fields after the harvest.

The Domesday survey recorded 9,000,000 ac. of arable land south of Yorkshire and Cheshire, 275,000 farm workers and 75,000 plow teams.

See FEUDALISM; MANOR; SERFDOM AND VILLEINAGE.

2. Livestock.—The domestication and raising of livestock in the eastern Mediterranean region was carried on by people who led a nomadic life. Bones found in early excavations indicate, however, that there was some association or trading of products between the herdsmen and those who raised crops.

By the time agriculture had spread over Europe the distinction between herdsmen and cultivators was disappearing and the two forms of agriculture were practised together. There were variations, however. The people of central Europe were nomadic cultivators who kept some cattle whereas the Breton was first and foremost a herdsman, for whom the cultivation of crops was a minor activity. The nomadic life of the herdsman was associated with tribal development and is not conducive to the creation of permanent habitations and institutions or to the leaving of records for archaeologists to discover.

The diffusion of knowledge of the plow and the discovery that manure would restore soil fertility gave a great stimulus to agriculture as contrasted with pastoralism. As the production of grain increased there was less need to raise cattle for food. There was also a change in the climate of Britain and northern Europe at the beginning of the Iron Age (500–400 B.C.). The much colder climate necessitated some form of housing and the growing of crops for winter feeding. The slasher or leaf knife used for stripping leaves from trees and the scythe used for cutting hay for winter feeding are products of this period.

A system of modified pastoral nomadism has survived in Europe down to the present. In Spain, Italy, Switzerland, the Balkans, Norway and Britain the presence of mountains and plains or valleys led to the cultivation of crops on the lowlands and the pasturing of cattle and sheep at the higher elevations. Transhumance —the migration of herds, herdsmen and even families from the lowlands to the uplands in the spring and back again in the fall— was and still is to some extent a custom. But the end of widespread herding in Europe began about 1750. When the common fields were enclosed and yields of grain and grasses increased, cattle and sheep could be enclosed in pastures in the summer and housed and fed in barns during the winter. With these changes the development of animal husbandry entered a new and interesting phase all over Europe, particularly in Britain.

The Romans had found large numbers of cattle in Britain and had also brought some of their own. Later, Anglo-Saxons brought cattle of the Devon type from western Germany. The Scandinavians contributed hornless or polled breeds. But it was in Britain that the characteristics of breed were established. The Shorthorn, Devon, Hereford, Aberdeen-Angus, Ayrshire and several other breeds of cattle are credited to contemporaries or followers of Robert Bakewell in 18th-century Britain (see *The United Kingdom*, below). As with cattle, so with sheep and pigs: selective breeding was applied in Britain during that same period and from it came the Leicester, Shropshire, Suffolk and Oxford breeds of sheep and Yorkshire, Berkshire and Tamworth pigs.

For details on the origins of various crops including those mentioned above *see* separate articles on those crops, as CORN; WHEAT; etc.

For the story of livestock development *see* ANIMAL BREEDING and CATTLE; PIG; etc. The history of the development of agriculture in early Britain and Europe is given in *United Kingdom: Early and Medieval Times*, below.

B. AGRICULTURAL EXPANSION TO THE NEW WORLD

The Industrial Revolution of the 18th and 19th centuries was accompanied by an agricultural revolution. With the growth of industry people gathered together in urban centres. The industrialist with his hired workers replaced the master and domestic craftsmen. The demand for food for this new urban population soon exceeded the capacity of the open-field tenure system, and husbandry and enclosure became necessary. Between 1750 and 1850 several thousand parishes were enclosed in Britain.

These changes were accompanied by great disturbances, aggravated by the Napoleonic Wars and the severe economic depression which followed. In some cases large farmers benefited but small holders, landless labourers, craftsmen and many others experienced difficulties. In the depression period, 1815-40, all of Europe suffered.

But this was also the period of spectacular development in the new world following two centuries of exploration and conquest. Britain, France, Germany, Spain, Holland, Portugal, Italy—the countries in which great progress had been made in agriculture— were also the countries that became associated in one way or another with the settlement and development of overseas territories. In some of these territories agriculture had to await the exploitation of other industries such as the fur trade, fisheries and forestry, but from 1750 onward agricultural growth was rapid.

The industrial and agricultural revolutions in Europe made not only the products of industry and agriculture available for export, but also millions of restless people who sought release from economic, religious and other restraints. They took with them the skills, the enterprise and the enthusiasm needed in the new world. They also took cattle, horses, sheep, pigs, fowl, seeds and plants which established these breeds and varieties in the new countries and led to a substantial export trade.

The agriculture that developed in the new world was a blend of the new and the old. Though influenced in all cases by the land-tenure practices and general farming experiences of the mother countries, it was also to a large extent the product of the local geography, climate and population. Plantation and estate farming became important in many tropical countries where a combination of native labour, climate and the adaptability of certain crops to that system existed. The production of coffee, tea, cocoa, rubber, coconut, cotton, pineapple, bananas, palm oil and similar products was the result. (*See* TROPICAL AGRICULTURE.) Side by side with the establishment of large estates and the employment of the native population, varying degrees of independent and small-holder operations came into being.

The seignioral system of tenure was introduced from France to the St. Lawrence river region of North America. The plantation system came into being in the deep south. But in other parts of what is now the United States and Canada, the pattern of tenure and operation that was emerging in 17th- and 18th-century Britain took root. In the people who came to settle in these areas there was a deep-seated desire for the possession of land. Accordingly, during the colonial period and later, the selling or granting of land for free title became the dominant policy. This culminated in the Homestead acts of the 1860s and 1870s. Based upon this policy the family farm became an institution in North America.

Land policies of somewhat the same general nature characterized New Zealand and Australia. There, shifts in emphasis between freehold and leasehold and variations in trend as regards small and large holdings occurred, but gradually the pattern shifted toward ownership and the family-farm type of operation. The family farm there, as in North America, may employ additional hired labour.

In Latin America the pattern of agriculture was predominantly monopolistic control and estate operation. In most if not all of these countries, however, some measure of small-holder operation also developed and in a few countries, such as Brazil, a family-farm type of tenure and operation prevailed.

C. LAND USE AND PRODUCTION

From the early beginnings of plant and animal domestication in southwest Asia and Europe, agriculture has spread to most parts of the globe. The Food and Agriculture Organization of the United Nations (FAO) estimated the total world area of "arable land and land under tree crops" at 1,457,000,000 ha. for the 1960s and permanent meadows and pastures at 2,633,000,000 ha. making a total of 4,090,000,000 ha. (Table I). The unused but poten-

TABLE I.—*Land Use*
(in 000,000 ha.)

| Continent | Total area | Agricultural area | | Other land unused but potentially productive, built-on area, wasteland and other |
		Arable land and land under tree crops	Permanent meadows and pastures	
Europe (excluding U.S.S.R.) . .	493	152	90	114
U.S.S.R. . . .	2,240	230	370	760
North and Central America . .	2,424	261	368	981
South America .	1,779	62	324	477
Asia	2,758	457	385	1,390
Africa . . .	3,021	260	636	1,374
Oceania (including Australia) . .	855	35	460	279
World total . .	13,570	1,457	2,633	5,375

Source: FAO, *1965 Production Yearbook*, vol. 19 (1966).

tially productive and built-on area, waste and other land was estimated at 5,375,000,000 ha. The area used for agricultural purposes was thus a little more than a quarter of the total land area of the world. The proportion of arable land to total area was highest (30.8%) in Europe and lowest (4.1%) in Oceania.

The arable land of the world is very unevenly distributed among countries and continents and in relation to population. Asia (excluding U.S.S.R.) has more than one-half of the world's population with less than one-third (about 31%) of the world's arable land. North and Central America, on the other hand, with less than 10% of the world's population, have almost 20% arable land. In Africa and the Soviet Union, in the 1960s the population per-

TABLE II.—*Area Under Major Crops in the World*
(in 000,000 ha.)

Crops	World* 1934–38	World* 1965	Europe 1934–38	Europe 1965	North and Central America 1934–38	North and Central America 1965	South America 1934–38	South America 1965	Asia† 1934–38	Asia† 1965	Africa 1934–38	Africa 1965	Oceania 1934–38	Oceania 1965
Wheat	127.9	216.9	29.8	29.1	33.1	32.8	8.6	8.7	45.5	105.8	5.6	7.7	5.3	7.3
Rye	37.6‡	28.3	13.5	8.9	1.6	1.0	0.5	0.8	22.0‡	17.5	—	—	—	—
Barley	35.7	72.3	9.4	13.3	5.7	6.7	0.9	1.2	15.3	32.7	4.2	4.4	0.2	0.9
Oats	37.9	30.8	14.6	8.2	19.6	11.7	1.0	0.8	1.6	6.3	0.4	0.4	0.7	1.4
Maize	85.9‡	113.3	11.7	11.1	41.9	33.5	10.0	14.5	15.6‡	14.5§	6.6	13.9	0.1	0.1
Millet and sorghum	69.2	103.0	0.3	0.1	1.7	5.6	...	0.9	48.2	43.1	19.0	25.8	...	0.2
Rice, paddy	85.8	123.9	0.2	0.3	0.5	1.3	1.2	4.9	82.0	84.6	1.8	3.2	...	0.3
Total grains	480.0	688.5	79.5	71.0	104.1	92.6	22.2	31.8	230.2	320.0	37.6	55.4	6.3	10.2
Potatoes	13.5	23.3	10.0	8.4	1.5	0.7	0.6	1.0	1.2	9.6	0.1	0.3	0.1	0.1
Sweet potatoes and yams	6.4	14.7	...	...	0.6	0.3	0.2	0.3	3.2	14.1	2.9		...	—
Total pulses‖	33.4	54.2	5.6	6.0	1.7	3.4	1.5	3.5	22.5¶	32.5¶	2.1	2.8	...	...
Total oilseeds9	68.6	109.4	1.2	2.5	14.2	22.8	5.8	9.0	41.6	40.0	5.8	10.5	...	0.1
Cotton, lint	31.2	34.6	0.1	0.4	11.8	6.9	2.7	4.8	14.0	14.2	2.5	3.9	...	...
Total	633.1	924.7	96.4	88.3	133.9	126.7	33.0	50.4	312.7	419.0	48.1	75.8	6.4	10.4

Note: Figures do not necessarily total because of rounding.
*Includes estimate on mainland China. †Includes European and Asiatic U.S.S.R.; excludes mainland China. ‡Includes U.S.S.R. 1938. §Excludes U.S.S.R. ‖Includes dry beans, dry peas, dry broad beans, chick peas, lentils. ¶Includes also vetch, lupins, and serradella for the U.S.S.R. 9Includes soybeans, peanuts, cottonseed, linseed, sesame, rapeseed, sunflower seed.
Source: FAO, *1965 Production Yearbook*, vol. 19 (1966), *Monthly Bulletin of Agricultural Economics and Statistics*, vol. 15, no. 6 (June 1966).

centages were 9.3% and 6.9% respectively; and the percentages of arable land were 17.8% and 15.8% respectively. In Europe (excluding the Soviet Union) and South America, the percentages of population were 13.5% and 5.1% respectively; and of arable land the percentages were 4.3% and 10.4% respectively. Oceania had the most balanced relationship between arable land and population but both were very small. Estimates of the world's potentially productive land vary from 400,000,000 to 3,500,-000,000 ha.

The area in the world under major crops was substantially greater after World War II than in the prewar years 1934–38 (Table II). The area in wheat increased substantially more than world population during the period 1937–60 (Table V). The area in oats and rye declined slightly despite the larger population. The decline occurred mainly in North and Central America and in Europe. In Asia, on the contrary, the acreage of grain crops including rice increased by nearly 40%. These crops also increased in Africa. Increases in all other major crops also occurred in these regions. The data indicate that the per capita consumption of the bread grains and potatoes declined in Europe and in North America.

Crop yields vary from country to country and from continent to continent. In 1965 for instance, European countries harvested about 19.8 metric quintals (1 q. = 220 lb.) of wheat per hectare

TABLE III.—*World Production of Selected Commodities*
(in 000,000 metric tons)

Commodity	Average 1935–39	Average 1956–58	1965
Wheat	166.0	209.6	273.5
Rye	44.0	36.2	32.8
Rice	162.3	203.5	255.8
Bread grains	372.3	449.3	562.1
Maize	121.3	172.9	225.9
Oats	67.3	64.1	45.2
Barley	51.7	71.3	110.5
Coarse grains	240.3	308.3	381.6
Total grains	612.6	757.6	943.7
Potatoes	158.9*†	188.3*‡	296.7
Meat§	30.9†	43.3	52.6
Milk (cowsmilk)	241.3†	297.4	327.5
Eggs (000,000,000)	131.5*†	200.1*	264.9‖
Wool (greasy)	1.8	2.3	2.5
Cotton, lint (000,000 bales)	31.7	42.9	54.7
Coffee	2.5	3.2	3.2
Tobacco	3.0	3.9	4.5

*Excluding U.S.S.R. †1934–38 average. ‡1955–57 average. §Production in 43 principal meat-producing countries. ‖1964.
Sources: U.S. Department of Agriculture, *The World Agricultural Situation* (1958, 1959), *Foreign Crops and Markets, World Summaries* (1959 issues); FAO, *1958 Production Yearbook* (1959), *Monthly Bulletin of Agricultural Economics and Statistics* (1966 issues).

(2.471 ac.) but the average yield in other continents was considerably lower. The yield per hectare of rice (paddy) in Asia, where rice is the staple food of the people, was 18.3 quintals. Yields were highest in Europe—46.5 quintals—and lowest in South America—15.3 quintals. The highest corn yields were obtained in North and Central America—30.7 quintals—and the lowest in Africa—10.8 quintals. Cotton yields at 6.0 quintals per hectare were also highest in North and Central America, but at

1.9 quintals per hectare were lowest in Asia. Yields of potatoes and root crops vary greatly although these crops are usually grown under better conditions.

The average level of crop yields was considerably higher in Europe, North America and Australia in 1945–65 than in pre-World War II years. Average cereal yields in western Europe, for instance, were 64% to 65% higher in 1965; potato yields increased still more. Wheat and corn yields in the United States in 1965 were, respectively, 90% and 137% higher than in the period 1925–39.

Potato yields in the same period were about 2½ times as great as before World War II. Wheat yields in Australia in 1965 were 85% above the 1925–39 average. In the case of the other continents there is no clear evidence of general or substantial increases in crop yields.

The average annual world production of the principal cereals in 1965 was about 943,700,000 metric tons (Table III). Production of bread grains—wheat, rye and rice—which are utilized mainly for human consumption was 562,100,000 metric tons or about 60% of the total grain output. Wheat represented 273,500,000 metric tons and was produced mainly in North America, western Europe, the Soviet Union, China, India, Argentina and Australia. Production of rice, about 255,800,000 metric tons, was concentrated mainly in the far east (India, China, Japan, Indonesia). Corn was third in importance with world production of about 225,900,000 metric tons. It is grown in North and Central America, South America, eastern Europe, India and China, and is used chiefly for feeding livestock. Barley and oats are also used for livestock feed; their annual production amounted to 110,500,000 metric tons and 45,200,000 metric tons, respectively.

The output of sugar was about 66,240,000 metric tons in 1965. Cane sugar is produced mainly in Latin America (Caribbean area and Brazil) and the far east (India, Pakistan and mainland China) and beet sugar in Europe, the Soviet Union and North America. Lentils, beans and other pulses, important as a source of vegetable protein, are raised mainly in Asia (China and India), South America and Europe. Vegetable oilseeds and nuts are produced in widely separated parts of the world: soybeans and cottonseed in North and Central America; sunflower seed in South America; peanuts, rapeseed and soybeans in Asia; and copra and palm oil in Africa (*see* OIL PLANTS). Cocoa is produced mostly in Africa and Brazil; tea in China, India and Ceylon; coffee in South America (particularly Brazil and Colombia); and tobacco in North America, Asia and Europe.

Production of fruits is concentrated in various parts of the world. Commercial output of apples and pears occurs in Europe and North America, grapes in Europe, figs in Europe and the near east and bananas in Latin America and the far east. (*See* FRUIT FARMING.)

Of the world's total milk production in the mid 1960s about 56%, about 200,000,000 metric tons, came from Europe and North America. Meat production (beef and veal, pork, mutton and lamb) in the major producing countries amounted to about 52,-

614,450 metric tons, most of it beef and pork. For all meats, as for milk, Europe and North America are the most important producing regions. Foremost producers of eggs and poultry are North America, Europe and Asia.

Production of fibre crops has been localized in various parts of the world. Cotton production is concentrated in North America, South America (Brazil), Asia (U.S.S.R. and China) and Africa (Egypt). Flax is grown mainly in Europe, including European U.S.S.R., and in the United States, Argentina and India. Two-thirds of the world's sisal is produced in Africa and South America (Brazil); two-thirds of the hemp in Europe (including the U.S.S.R.); and almost all the manila hemp in the Philippines and Malaysia. Asia produced almost the entire world supply of natural rubber.

World numbers of livestock units by continents in 1965 are shown in Table IV. (A livestock unit is a measurement designation which permits the grouping of livestock in terms of feed requirements. Thus, using the FAO scale, 5 pigs, 10 sheep or goats,

TABLE IV.—*Livestock Units in the World*

Area	Total* (000,000)		Per 100 ha. of arable land		Per 100 ha. of agricultural land	
	Prewar	1965	Prewar	1965	Prewar	1965
Europe . .	140.1	146.9	93.4	96.6	59.6	60.7
U.S.S.R. . .	79.5	101.3	36.2	44.0	16.3	16.9
North and Central America . .	122.1	168.0	47.9	64.4	20.0	26.7
South America .	128.0	193.7	185.5	312.4	33.5	50.2
Asia . . .	334.8	352.5†	81.9	77.1†	38.7	41.9†
Africa . . .	102.3	150.2	42.1	57.8	11.9	16.8
Oceania . .	30.4	44.1	126.7	126.0	75.8	89.1
World total .	937.2	1,157.0	68.4	79.4	24.4	28.3

*Includes: horses, mules, asses, cattle, pigs, sheep, goats, buffalos, camels.
†Excludes mainland China.
Source: Food and Agriculture Organization, Rome.

1 horse or buffalo or mule, 1.25 cows or asses, 0.91 camel, each represents 1 livestock unit and the 18.16 animals combined represent 5 livestock units.) The heaviest concentration of livestock units per 100 ha. of agricultural land was in Oceania and Europe, where the figures were 89.1 and 60.7 respectively. For other parts of the world the figures were as follows: Africa, 16.8; U.S.S.R., 16.9; North and Central America, 26.7; South America, 50.2; and Asia, 41.9. The total number of livestock units was greater in 1965 than before World War II although there had been a considerable drop in the horse and mule population. The num-

TABLE V.—*World and Agricultural Population**
(population figures in 000,000)

Continent	1937		1960		Percentage of agricultural population†	
	Population total	Population agricultural	Population total	Population agricultural	1937	1960
Europe (excluding U.S.S.R.) .	372	133	425	99	36	23
North and Central America .	179	56	266	54	31	20
North America (excluding Hawaii) . . .	(140)	(32)	(199)	(16)	(23)	(8)
Central America . . .	(38)	(24)	(67)	(38)	(63)	(56)
South America . . .	84	52	144	65	62	45
Asia (excluding mainland China) .	691	504	998	639	73	64
Africa	168	128	274	192	76	70
Oceania (including Hawaii) .	11	3	16	2	26	14
World (excluding mainland China and U.S.S.R.) . .	1,504	876	2,123	1,051	58	50
China, mainland . .	447	. . .	686	446	76	65
U.S.S.R.	190‡	109‡	214	75	57	35
World total	2,141	1,324	3,023	1,572	62	52

*Totals and derived figures were obtained before rounding. †Data must be regarded as only rough estimates. ‡Adjusted estimate for present territory. For the prewar territory, the 1939 census enumerated a total population of 170,000,000.
Source: FAO, *1965 Production Yearbook*, vol. 19 (1966).

ber of cattle, pigs and sheep increased considerably in the postwar period.

The world population in 1960 was 3,023,000,000 of which 1,572,-000,000 or 52% were engaged in agriculture. The lowest percentage of agricultural population in the total population was in North America 8%, followed by Oceania 14% and Europe 23%. In other continents the proportion of agricultural population ranged from 45% to 70%. In several of the leading industrialized countries that are also major food exporters, the percentages of the

population engaged in agriculture were low: in the United States, 7% (1964); the Netherlands, 11% (1960); Canada, 11% (1962); New Zealand, 14% (1961); and Denmark, 17% (1960).

D. POPULATION AND FOOD SUPPLIES

In 1798 the English economist Thomas R. Malthus published *An Essay on the Principle of Population*. His main thesis, that population would increase more rapidly than food supplies, had a profound effect on the thinking of the early 19th century and has been the subject of much discussion since that time. A hundred years after Malthus set down his views Sir William Crookes, in a presidential address to the British Association for the Advancement of Science, told his listeners that there seemed to be no possibility of increasing the wheat-producing area of the world sufficiently to provide for the wants of the rapidly increasing population of bread-grain eaters. This, too, had a pronounced effect—the more so because it came after a hundred years of advances in agriculture which seemed to have discredited the gloomy predictions of Malthus.

The experiences of the 1930s and of World War II and the subsequent widespread interest in the economic and social conditions of people throughout the world gave rise to the United Nations and its Food and Agriculture organization, World Health organization and other specialized agencies, all of which again stirred up interest in the matter of population and food supplies. The prediction of UN experts in 1958 that the world's population, then estimated at 2,737,000,000, would reach more than 6,000,000,000 by the beginning of the 21st century tended to extend the controversy.

According to the FAO, total world food production for the decade ended 1965 had risen to an index of 129 (1952–53 to 1956–57 = 100) whereas population had increased to an index of 122, thus allowing an overall per capita food increase of 7%. However, all the per capita increase had occurred in the first half of the decade. There had been a 14% increase in the developed areas, whereas within the developing regions, with about two-thirds of the world's total population, per capita food supplies in 1964–65 were lower than they were five years earlier.

There are three ways of increasing the world's supply of agriculturally produced food. One is to increase the output on existing land; another is to add to the cultivated area. The third might be to extend or make better use of the foods produced. Increased output offers much hope for the foreseeable future. In many areas revolutionary changes are occurring. In the decade following World War II total output in many countries was increased by 25% to 50% and the output per worker by even greater amounts. These increases were made possible by advances in scientific achievement and by the acceptance and application of the knowledge available. In the temperate zones better seed, improved cultural practices and greater use of fertilizers and pesticides resulted in larger yields. Irrigation of dry lands, the drainage of wet lands, the introduction of new grasses and plants brought increased output. The development of earlier maturing varieties extended the area of production northward. In the tropical forest areas, drainage, better management of soils, improvement of varieties and substitution of crops raised production. Better breeding, care and management of livestock greatly increased the output per animal unit and per acre. In general, less human labour but more capital and improved management practices brought results that had not been foreseen even a generation earlier. These developments indicate that with known methods the output of food in many countries and on the lands now cultivated can be considerably enlarged, probably doubled.

It is reassuring to know that increased output need not be hampered by any shortage of fertilizers or pesticides. Raw materials are abundant, and the chemical and engineering facilities and technology necessary to production are available.

As regards potential land area, the soil scientist Charles E. Kellogg in 1955 summarized certain conclusions that he and others had put forward in a UNESCO report issued several years earlier. He said that with the general adoption of practices already being used by good farmers occupying the various kinds of soil, the acreage of cropland in the world could be increased by more than 50% or from 1,000,000,000 ha. to 1,500,000,000 or 1,600,-000,000. The report indicated that while a part of this additional land lay in the temperate or cool temperate region, most of it lay in the tropics of South America, Africa and some of the larger islands.

Much of this land, while potentially suited to agricultural use, will not be farmed for many years. In Canada, for instance, there were about 73,000,000 ha. of unoccupied land with agricultural possibilities of some sort. Probably not over a quarter of that area will be brought into farms in the foreseeable future. If population pressure becomes acute enough, however, more of such land may be brought into food production.

Kellogg stated that "the estimates of the available soils for agricultural use and the production possible from those soils are considerably higher than the prospective population of this century." Sir E. John Russell, too, completed his study of 1954 on an optimistic note, saying ". . . world agriculture is developing and its possibilities are vividly emphasized by the circumstances that at present (1) less than 10 per cent of the earth's land surface is cultivated: the rest is largely waste; (2) only about one-tenth to one half of 1 per cent of the sun's radiation received at the earth's surface is fixed as organic material; the rest is lost; (3) only about half or less of the organic material ultimately reaches the table as human food; much of the rest is wasted. Taking the earth's surface as a whole, for each million calories of energy received from the sun only one calorie is converted into human food. And lastly, little attention has been paid to the conservation and most efficient use of water, the factor finally limiting food production. The problem of improving our utilization of these natural resources is being studied in many countries and it offers the best method of increasing the total supply of human food." (*World Population and World Food Supplies,* George Allen and Unwin Ltd., London, 1954.)

It is probable that most agricultural authorities support the views expressed by Russell and Kellogg but there are others who are not so optimistic.

The third method of increasing food supplies will not be dealt with here. It is not strictly a method of increasing but rather of preserving and extending the foods that are produced. That means reducing loss in storage, improving transportation, eliminating waste and deterioration, improving methods of processing and preservation, increasing extraction rates and the like (*see* Crop Drying and Processing). Attention to these matters could contribute substantially to the food supplies of the future; research into possible synthetic production of some essential items is also considered promising.

E. Soil Conservation

The problem of maintaining and restoring soil fertility is one that is common to farmers the world over. Through the centuries changing climates and the cropping practices of man have resulted in the permanent or temporary loss of large areas of land to agriculture. The full extent of the vegetative cover in the eastern Mediterranean region during the pre-Christian period and at the beginning of the Christian era is not known but the available evidence indicates substantial areas of tree and plant growth. Much of that growth later disappeared and millions of hectares of land became desert. After 1945 extensive land development and reclamation projects were initiated by India, Pakistan, Iran, Israel and other countries in the area extending from India to the Mediterranean. By the 1960s such development and reclamation projects, some completed, were making major contributions to increased agricultural production.

Old Chinese records tell of land destruction and abandonment centuries ago. In later periods many thousands of hectares of land were either completely eroded or buried and abandoned. In south China nearly all of the cleared hillsides were stripped of their soil cover. In some areas soil on the upper slopes of hillsides became so thin that crops such as sugar cane and corn had to be replaced with sweet potatoes and peanuts, or abandoned to brush and weeds, providing a poor harvest of fuel. Records indicate that the Yellow river in 1934 carried silt equivalent to 145,000 ha. of land with soil one metre deep.

Much of the land in the densely populated parts of Latin America is extremely susceptible to erosion. Removal of the original cover and cultivation of the slopes and valley lands of the Andean region has resulted in extensive soil loss. Wind erosion on the great plains of Argentina and Uruguay and in parts of Paraguay and southern Brazil has been the cause of much concern. Loss of soil from erosion is thought to have contributed to the low-calorie diet of the people in certain Central and South American countries, as revealed by the FAO world food survey of 1946.

In tropical countries where rainfall is heavy the removal of forest cover and the planting of land to coffee, bananas, pineapple and other crops results in heavy erosion, particularly where contour cultivation is not practised. In northern Thailand, Sumatra, Sarawak and elsewhere, large-scale soil erosion and floods result from the custom of felling virgin jungle, planting from two to four crops of upland rice and then abandoning the land to the elements. In Malaya upland tea production has developed on strip terrain where, on many estates and small holdings, good management and conservation practices are largely lacking. The sand and silt load of some rivers, the banks of which are being cultivated, has resulted in deposits that restrict navigation.

Wheat yields in medieval Britain are variously estimated at from six to nine bushels per acre. Some economic historians attribute these low yields to loss of soil fertility. With better husbandry and the use of manure and fertilizers, yields have been increased severalfold since then.

In the 18th century rapid settlement of the piedmont plateau of the southeastern United States led to the clearing of woods from land that went into cotton, corn and tobacco. With the land under clean cultivation and the rows running up- and downhill, the heavy rains of the region washed the soil away. This happened, too, on the heavy black soils of Alabama, Mississippi and Texas. Millions of acres were cleared and cultivated, a great proportion was seriously damaged and much of it was abandoned.

On the western Great Plains of the United States and Canada, farming practices involving large-scale mechanization led to severe loss of organic matter. In dry years, particularly during the 1930s, dust storms resulted in much drifting of soil and serious land and crop loss.

The conditions described have probably been experienced by new countries everywhere. Land is at first plentiful and cheap. Labour and capital are scarce and expensive. Economic conditions dictate that more of the cheaper factors of production be used than good husbandry would prescribe, so land is used extensively and production per acre is low. Production in terms of labour—a scarce factor—is high. Fertility is sacrificed to the building of capital goods.

In time the seminomadic and soil-depleting phase of farming passes. Population becomes more stable. Capital is acquired. Motor power and machinery supplement labour. Fertilizers, pesticides, weed killers and better seed can be purchased and used. Fence rows and stones can be removed, land can be leveled and tile-drained. In short, a better balance of production factors can be applied.

Along with these changes comes increased knowledge of how to prevent erosion. The scientist and experimenter have contributed new varieties of grass that provide better cover and sod, thus holding the soil in place. New techniques in cultivation—contour farming, the use of trash or mulch cover, the planting of windbreaks, alternate use of grain and row crops or summer fallow—help to control both wind and water erosion.

It would be a mistake to assume that these new techniques and aids to production are everywhere in use and that beneficial results are everywhere apparent, for they are not. But there are some very encouraging developments. Yields of grain in Britain and in the countries of western Europe have been increased very appreciably. There is evidence here and there of improvement in the newer countries where records are available for half a century or more. More and better animal husbandry is also contributing to soil conservation. With the knowledge of husbandry now available and with the power and materials of industry at hand it is actually possible not only to restore fertility but to build a more productive soil than nature provided originally.

One should not dismiss this topic without a reference to river basin or watershed development. Typically, the planning of a river-basin development includes measures to prevent too rapid runoff of water from rain or melting snow. Preservation and restoration of forest cover may be involved. Land on the hill slopes may be farmed on the contour or even terraced. A portion of the land devoted to annual crops is converted to pasture and to forage crops. Sheet and gully erosion is checked by various kinds of restraining works. Destruction of riverbanks is impeded by tree plantations and brushwork. The rapid flow and destructive effect of streams and rivers is reduced by the introduction of dams and other built-in impediments.

The water of many river basins is used to irrigate land. In temperate zones where variations in rainfall require the storage of water from rain and melting snow to ensure supplies for the dry season, dams are built to create storage reservoirs. From these, water is conveyed in ditches to land prepared for irrigation. In parts of the world where rainfall occurs frequently and with more or less uniformity throughout the year, thus ensuring a fairly constant river flow, water is diverted into irrigation ditches with the aid of gates and simple weirs or barrages, no reservoir being required.

In addition to these conservation and irrigation aspects, a river-basin program may afford the basis for a forest products industry; provide electrical power and water supplies for both urban and rural use; prevent flooding and destruction of farmlands and urban property; contribute to navigation; improve sanitary conditions where urban or industrial waste is discharged by ensuring year-round supply and flow of water; and improve the fishing and hunting opportunities and provide water-front building sites and camping grounds for recreational purposes.

F. LAND TENURE AND AGRARIAN REFORM

Outdated systems of tenure often prevent the adoption of new methods of farming. Insecurity of tenure may result in lack of incentive to improve a holding—to maintain or build soil fertility or to improve buildings and fences. Rigid laws and customs may perpetuate cropping systems and practices which deplete the soil and reduce yields. Excessively large holdings may impede progress if the owners lack the desire, the ability or the capital to develop their property. Excessively small, fragmented farms lead to much waste of effort and prevent the adoption of modern methods of husbandry.

Land-tenure reform attracted attention following World War I and played a still more important role in agricultural development after World War II. The measures adopted concerned redistribution of land, consolidation of holdings, land registration, improved leasehold arrangements, control of rents and changes in land taxation. For discussion of the history and development of programs in this area *see* LAND TENURE: ECONOMIC AND AGRARIAN ASPECTS; LAND REFORM.

G. PRODUCTIVITY AND INCREASED OUTPUT

World agricultural production in 1964–65 according to the FAO, was about 43% above the average of 1948–52. Output in developing areas was running behind annual increases in world population. The increase in productivity, particularly in countries of the western world, following the mid-1930s is one of the striking achievements in agriculture. What has occurred might well be referred to as a second agricultural revolution.

In the United Kingdom productivity in agriculture in 1952–53, expressed in terms of labour, was 58% above the 1937–39 average per man-hour, at 1951–52 prices. Between 1940 and the mid 1960s the total output of farm products in the United States increased about 45% while output per worker more than doubled. Based mostly on data from the 1950s, the FAO reported in 1963 that gross output per man in agriculture in 21 countries had grown at annual rates ranging from rather less than 2% in India to around 8% in Belgium and the Federal Republic of Germany.

Most of the economically advanced countries showed relatively high rates, generally exceeding 4% per year. Mexico and Venezuela showed increases comparable with those of the economically advanced countries. For most of the countries, output per man in agriculture had grown more than the per capita national income.

The major part of these increases probably resulted from the use of more machinery, power and materials of production. Much of it, too, was attributable to science, technology and education. For example, the increase already quoted for the United Kingdom was achieved with the aid of a 168% increase in farm machinery and very great additions in the amount of lime and fertilizer used. In Canada annual purchases of machinery by farmers from 1948 to 1954, with adjustments for changing prices, ran four to five times the purchases of the period 1935–39. World summaries exclusive of the U.S.S.R. provided by FAO indicate that in the mid-1960s about 3 times the amount of the major fertilizer ingredients were used than in 1938. There were 13,000,000 tractors in use in the mid-1960s compared with 5,700,000 in 1949–52.

But back of the machinery and materials of production, the better husbandry and the use of available equipment to best advantage was research and experimentation. From the tropics to the subarctic, in hundreds of centres throughout the world, research and experimental effort were contributing to increased productivity. Advances were made through the development of new varieties of plants to withstand drought or mature quickly enough to avoid freezing; the creation of new fertilizers, pesticides, fungicides and weed killers; the development of new production techniques and improved farm management; improvements in breeding, feeding, housing and management of livestock; and better understanding of nutrition and disease control. Extension services spread the techniques of good farming. This together with progress in transportation and marketing greatly expanded the frontiers of production.

See also AGRICULTURAL EDUCATION AND RESEARCH.

BIBLIOGRAPHY.—T. Bedford Franklin, *A History of Agriculture* (1948); G. E. Fussel, *Farming Techniques from Prehistoric to Modern Times* (1966); Food and Agriculture Organization, *Soil Conservation, an International Study* (1948), *The State of Food and Agriculture 1966* (1966); E. Cecil Curwen and Gudmund Hatt, *Plough and Pasture, the Early History of Farming* (1953); George B. Cressey, "Land for 2.4 Billion Neighbors," *Econ. Geogr.,* 29:1 (Jan. 1953); Sir E. John Russell, *World Population and World Food Supplies* (1954); L. Dudley Stamp, *Man and the Land* (1955); Charles E. Kellogg, "World Food and Agriculture Potentialities," *J. Fm. Econ.,* vol. 38 (May 1956); U.S. Department of Agriculture, Foreign Agricultural Economic Report No. 25, *Increasing World Food Output: problems and Prospects* (1965), Foreign Agricultural Economic Report No. 33, *The World Agricultural Situation 1967* (1967). (J. F. Bh.; J. K. R.)

H. WORLD CENSUS OF AGRICULTURE

Censuses of agriculture are held periodically in many countries. Originally, each of the various national censuses followed its own pattern in accordance with national needs and conditions. To promote the collection of comparable agricultural statistics, the former International Institute of Agriculture (*q.v.*) launched a program for a world census of agriculture in 1930. Forty-six of the 42 countries and 24 territories participating took a census by farm holdings for the enumeration of areas under crops and livestock in one operation in accordance with a standard form. The institute presented a program for a 1940 census of agriculture, but the outbreak of World War II prevented its completion.

A flexible plan for the 1950 world census of agriculture was presented by the FAO, which took over this responsibility from the International Institute of Agriculture. The minimum program covered principal characteristics of the holding such as size, form of tenure, land use and means of production available, including numbers of residents and livestock. An expanded list (for those countries able to undertake it) included such additional items as number and characteristics of the people employed in agriculture and the volume of crop production and of wood and fishery products in the agricultural holdings. Fifty-two countries and 54 territories participated in this world census.

For the 1960 census the FAO proposed a more flexible program with considerable expansion of some sections including those relating to land tenure. The scope of information on certain other items, especially in the expanded list, was broadened in view of the increased possibility of obtaining data through the use of sampling techniques. While in the past information on all census items was usually collected simultaneously from all holdings by interview and related to a predetermined point or period of time, by mid-20th century many countries had used a sampling approach. The 1960 census program recognized the value of this trend and of the study over a period of time of certain items such as employment in agriculture.

Ideally a census should include all agricultural holdings whatever their type (family or commercial), size and location. Practical considerations, however, have limited the enumeration to holdings that conform to certain criteria as to size of holding or operation or both. These criteria vary from country to country.

The 1960 world census of agriculture envisaged the collection of data for all individual holdings by direct enumeration wherever possible; but in countries lacking the necessary funds, personnel and physical facilities to prepare and carry out such operations, sampling methods were effectively substituted. In other countries where detailed information is needed for some census items and only national totals for the others, a combination of complete enumeration and sample survey was used.

Sampling helps ensure the quality of data. The measurement of sample areas for area statistics and the weighing of crops from small sample plots for yield statistics provide examples of such refinements. Such methods are particularly useful in countries where the majority of farmers are illiterate. Sampling methods are also used in assessing the accuracy of census data already collected, by making one or more follow-up surveys taken by specialists.

In addition to sampling, other methods and techniques are applied for improving the quality of national censuses. Special procedures often are needed in countries where agricultural practices are primitive. The use of independent sources of information to obtain or to check data is of great importance. To test the census questionnaire, definitions and enumeration procedures and to determine appropriate methods for the collection and processing of data, pilot censuses and pretesting surveys are useful, particularly in countries lacking previous experience in census work.

Participation in the world census project is promoted by the FAO through assistance to countries in planning, taking and tabulating the censuses in various ways. FAO has published reports on the experience gathered from past world censuses. FAO also advises countries on census questionnaires and instructions and has provided a number of studies of sampling procedures. Government officials are given training in special regional training centres on censuses set up for the purpose and experts in censuses and sampling are provided to countries requesting them. In view of the difficulties experienced by the countries in organizing and completing the tabulations of census data, FAO made a particular effort to assist various countries in data processing and tabulating by: (1) studying the existing facilities, methods and techniques for data processing, and the preparation and dissemination of informational and training materials on this subject; (2) developing plans to provide assistance, advice and special training on the organizing and operating of census tabulations through experts, and by organizing special training centres for census tabulations; and (3) exploring possibilities for central tabulation of agricultural census data by electronic equipment for those countries which may desire such a service. Several countries expressed interest in participating in such a scheme, provided the confidentiality of their census data is ensured by international supervision, and should there be savings in processing costs and time. (See also FOOD AND AGRICULTURE ORGANIZATION.)

See also Food and Agriculture Organization, *Monthly Bulletin of Agricultural and Economic Statistics,* C. P. G. J. Smit, "Plans for the 1970 World Census of Agriculture," vol. 13, no. 1 (Jan. 1964).

(A. H. BA.)

II. UNITED STATES

The first immigrants to America in the 17th century went not to set themselves up in farming but to trade with the natives, fish and search for gold. Trading and fishing from the outset absorbed the attention of some, but most immigrants were soon forced to turn to agriculture, which continued to be the mainstay of colonial life thereafter. The agriculture they practised was very different from that of the old world. English practices influenced colonial agriculture everywhere, particularly in New England, but in the middle colonies the Dutch, Germans, Welsh, Scotch-Irish and Swedes and in the southern colonies the French Huguenots contributed to the developing agricultural pattern. All these groups brought with them agricultural practices, seeds, farm tools, livestock, cuttings and plants that varied widely and ensured a cosmopolitan mixture of methods, techniques, plants and livestock.

More important in shaping the growth of agriculture in the new world was the great abundance of land, its cheapness and ease of acquisition, the dissimilarities of soil and climate, the freedom of enterprise, the initiative of the settlers and new commodities and practices acquired from the Indians.

A. AGRICULTURAL BEGINNINGS

1. Indian Agriculture.—The agriculture practised by the Indians varied widely from section to section. Corn or maize, the Indians' greatest gift to the white man, was commonly grown throughout the western hemisphere, but in what is now the United States it had perhaps attained its highest state of cultivation and was grown on the largest scale in the Iroquois country of the Mohawk valley. There were found substantial fields of corn and storehouses filled with grain. Farther south, tobacco was grown for smoking, but corn constituted the principal food of the Indians other than meat and fish. Sweet potatoes, squashes and beans were other important foods in the Indian diet, as was wild rice in the lower south and in the upper Mississippi valley. In the semiarid interior basin, a highly organized form of communal irrigation was practised which was to point the way centuries later for reclamation of dry lands.

Most Indian groups in the colonial period had a complex and fairly well-organized system of agriculture which was highly useful to the conquering Europeans. The Indians' clearings in areas of heavy forests were quickly seized for grain production, and their stores of grain were robbed or destroyed in the frequent wars. During some of the most trying times in the early days of Plymouth and Jamestown, these stores of grain were opened to the settlers for barter. The Indians' knowledge of the soil, their primitive methods of cultivation that required little labour, the vegetables and grains that they produced and their utilization of wildlife were all borrowed by the settlers struggling to adapt themselves to pioneer life.

In the first years of Jamestown and Plymouth the immigrants had considerable difficulty in adjusting themselves to the new country, ravaged as they were by disease and Indian conflicts. Though at first succoured by the Indians, the newcomers were actually close to starvation more than once. During this time they were dependent upon England for many of their foodstuffs, so slow were they to recognize and take advantage of the possibilities of the land surrounding them. At times malnutrition, dysentery, malaria and typhoid so weakened them as to make impossible the labour of clearing the land of its heavy forest cover for the planting of grain.

Gradually the first settlements became self-sustaining and even able to sell surplus foodstuffs to newer colonies. Better order was established through the use of more rigid political and social sanctions and the elimination of malcontents. Increased immigration of yeoman farmers and the coming of indentured servants and Negro slaves provided the labour essential to clearing land, preparing the soil and planting and harvesting the crops. Abandonment of communal and company ownership of the land and its fruits, the recognition of individual rights in land and the greater freedom allowed settlers further contributed to the progress of colonial agriculture.

2. Colonial Land Policies.—When the promoters of the trading companies were brought to realize that profits would not be forthcoming from company operation of the settlements, they turned to the land, from which they hoped, through sale, leasing or quitrents, to derive revenue. In Virginia and the Carolinas some early investors came to control large tracts. Elsewhere, in Pennsylvania and Maryland, income from rents and sales was relatively large. Efforts to establish aristocratic systems of land tenure with great estates held by the few, and with tenants, servants and slaves performing the labour, however, were not so successful as anticipated. The existence of 13 colonies, all having virutal control over their own internal problems and long neglected by the British privy council, each attempting to attract population, develop its resources and settle its abundant lands, made difficult the kind of tenure from which land promoters might benefit.

Early plans, consequently, for establishing the manorial system or, if not quite that, at least for keeping ownership of land in the hands of an aristocracy were discarded in practice if not in law. Instead, full ownership was made easy in most colonies. In a few, notably New York, where huge grants were made by the governor's council to favourites and men of influence, a concentration of ownership was established which was to retard development for nearly two centuries.

The founders of New England favoured an orderly, systematic growth with a fairly tight rein being held by the controlling Puritan group. The movement of individuals helter-skelter to the frontier was certain to irritate the Indians and endanger peace and security. Better, it was thought, to ensure a compact movement by requiring that groups interested in establishing new communities petition the legislature for a grant of a township of six or eight square miles, in the centre of which a town would be laid out. After survey, the petitioners or proprietors would be assigned residence lots in the village and meadow and forestland outside for farming operations. The original proprietors could divide the land among themselves, whether they settled in the town or not, or they might admit later applicants to share in the division. Newcomers not having proprietor's rights would have to buy from existing owners. The system was not intended to be revenue producing, and access to land by discreet persons in good standing was not difficult. Though there was some speculation in proprietors' rights, the township grant to groups and subsequent division among the members tended to produce a widespread diffusion of land ownership that was in sharp contrast with the situation developing in the Hudson-Mohawk valley or in the southern plantation country where great estates were being created.

In the middle colonies, notably in Pennsylvania and Maryland, land distribution was planned to produce revenue. Manors and other large holdings were established, but so were the more numerous small holdings. Rents constituted a major source of revenue to the proprietors and their families throughout the colonial period, but they were not oppressive nor did they retard immigration and development. On the contrary, an enlightened policy of easy land distribution, the degree of freedom guaranteed and vigorous efforts to solicit immigration combined to make Pennsylvania the fastest growing and most prosperous of the colonies.

South of the Potomac a more aristocratic system of land ownership emerged, not so much the result of policy as of economic conditions. There the headright of 50 ac. was assured to each person coming into the colonies. Indentured servants were entitled to the headright when they had served their period and were ready to start farming. Ship captains, slave importers and others bringing servants or slaves were entitled to a headright for every person they transported. With these rights it was possible to accumulate large ownerships. Although large and small owners existed together, there is little evidence that the small farmer played an important role in the economy or politics of the south.

3. Colonial Agriculture.—The pattern of land ownership in the American colonies was shaped as much by the nature of the land as it was by land-disposal policies. New England is a plateau

region extending from the mountains of the west and north to the narrow coastal plain, cut deeply by swift-flowing and unnavigable rivers with narrow valleys. Its soil is thin, rocky and infertile and could not produce the lush rural life of parts of the south. Unless he lived near the growing seacoast towns, where there was a market for cheese, butter and vegetables as well as for grain and meat, the Yankee farmer usually could not specialize. Remote from markets and lacking transportation facilities, he could expect to sell only what he could drive to market—livestock. He had little income and could buy little; hence he had to produce most of the items he needed. In his near-subsistence condition, he became ingenious in making his own tools, clothing and furniture, and at the same time he learned how to wrest from the land the most that it could produce.

Fuel came out of the Yankee farmer's wood lot, sugar and sirup were made from the sap of the maple tree, forage in the summer and hay for the winter feeding of sheep, cattle and horses was provided by the meadows and patches of cleared land too rocky for cultivation. Corn, wheat and rye were produced on the more level upland plots. Steeper-sloped land was used for pasture. Such a diversified economy did not call for extensive tracts, and the average farm was small. This made possible a relatively dense rural population having no wide disparity in wealth.

In New York and Pennsylvania with their wider valleys, more level land and better soil and with navigable rivers such as the Hudson, Delaware and Susquehanna, farms operating on a commercial scale with wheat as their major cash crop were common. The large Hudson river estates farmed by numerous tenants were unmatched elsewhere in the north. On the rich limestone soils of southeastern Pennsylvania the Germans followed the best farming practices in America, though even they concentrated primarily on one crop—wheat.

Tobacco was the staple crop of Maryland and Virginia. An increasing demand for it in England and Europe and the adaptability of American soil and climate to its culture encouraged its widespread planting. Tobacco raising requires intensive labour in the preparation of the seedbed, the transplanting of the seedlings, frequent cultivation, elimination of worms, picking, curing, packing and transporting to market. On the tobacco farms and plantations, indentured servants in the 17th century and Negro slaves in the 18th provided labour for the planters. Eventually, favourable prices led to overproduction with attendant price declines. Efforts to control production took various forms, including legislation requiring that only superior grades be exported.

Tobacco and Negro slavery made possible the successful development of the plantation economy in Virginia and supported the fine homes, lavishly furnished and bountifully supplied with the best of food and drink for owners and guests. They made possible the leisure time which the southern planter could devote to travel and education, political activity and leadership at all levels. Except on the remote frontier, small farmers also made tobacco their major crop.

In Georgia and South Carolina, rice and indigo were the major staples. Rice cultivation required a greater capital investment than tobacco or wheat. After the arduous task of clearing the low tidal lands along the streams was accomplished, canals, ditches and control valves had to be constructed to flood fields in the early season and to drain them later. Heavy investments, moreover, had to be made in machines for hulling and polishing the rice. These requirements plus the necessity for rotating fields made large-scale operations essential. Men of small means were able to engage in tobacco or cotton raising but not in rice cultivation.

The backwardness of agricultural practices in colonial America impressed English and European travelers, who could not understand the reasons for thin plowing, absence of rotation, neglect of livestock and manures. They did not realize that the abundance of land, the ease with which it could be acquired, its cheapness and the high cost of labour made land expendable. Also, colonial farmers and planters, in building a new country which lacked capital, were erecting farms and plantations with their own labour and that of their servants, and had to make their capital out of the land. Hence, they followed practices long since abandoned in the old world. They exploited the land without regard to its future use, mining the soil of its mineral and vegetable matter.

Agricultural tools in use in the colonial period were primitive. (The history of farm machinery is covered in FARM MACHINERY.) The sickle and cradle were both used in harvesting wheat. Threshing was still done by the flail or by treading out the grain. Hoes and mattocks were employed to prepare land for seeding, though crude plows replaced them on all but the most backward farms as draft animals were imported. Two-wheeled wooden carts hauled by oxen or horses carried produce to market in the summer; sleds were used in the northern colonies in winter. Great tobacco casks were rolled to the rivers for shipment. Hoes, axes, spades, simple harrows, pitchforks, scythes and wheelbarrows were improvised by the farmers themselves, with the ironwork being hammered out by nearby blacksmiths. Badly designed plows permitted only slight breaking of the soil. Not until Charles Newbold of New Jersey produced a cast-iron plow in 1797 and Jethro Wood of New York patented a plow with interchangeable parts in 1814 and 1819 was a practical, cheaply produced and light draft plow that worked well in most eastern U.S. soils available.

Livestock importations began almost with the arrival of the first settlers. Cattle, hogs, sheep and horses were brought from England, Sweden, Spain and the Netherlands and contributed their characteristics to American stock. Along with them were brought English grasses, for the native grasses, though rank, lacked nutriment. Fencing and stabling were not thought to be so essential as other factors in farm making and were among the last tasks to be undertaken. Beef became an item of export, though its quality was low, but for the most part cattle, sheep and swine were kept for domestic use.

British colonial policy, though based on the mercantilist idea that the colonies should supplement the economic life of the mother country, was doubtless more beneficial than it was harmful. Virginia and Maryland tobacco farmers found a ready market for their produce in England, where they had no competitors. Indigo and naval stores produced by Georgia farmers were subsidized. Rice was admitted free into the English market. The British-owned West Indian islands offered markets for wheat and flour, corn, beef and pork. Similarly, agricultural exports to the French and Dutch colonies flourished, in spite of the Navigation laws. After 1763, when enforcement of restrictive measures was tightened, farmers had more cause to complain of the imperial ties.

The loss of British and West Indian markets during and after the Revolution was a heavy blow to American farmers, particularly to producers of tobacco, rice and indigo. For a time the newly independent country was open to competition from imported goods, unable to shut them out or to bargain for concessions. Only with the adoption of the new constitution and the exercise by the national government of its treaty- and tariff-making powers did agriculture emerge from its post-Revolutionary disturbances and enter a new era of expansion with favourable prices. The long conflict between Great Britain and France in the Revolutionary and Napoleonic period assisted this development by creating a demand for American goods.

B. DEVELOPMENTS UP TO THE CIVIL WAR

1. Federal Land Policies to 1862.—With independence the 13 original states retained control over land within their immediate jurisdiction. Massachusetts kept its Maine lands, New York and Vermont fought over the New Hampshire grants, Virginia and North Carolina continued to grant lands in Kentucky and Tennessee, and Georgia, until 1802, sold, resold and forfeited the sales of its Yazoo lands in Mississippi. Ultimately, however, states with western land claims were induced to convey their rights in lands north of the Ohio and in Mississippi and Alabama to the federal government. With the adoption of the land ordinance of 1785, federal policy provided for the rectangular system of survey before sale, the offering of land at public auction and for private purchase after the auction.

The Federalists planned to make the public lands a major source of revenue by selling them at $1, later $2, an acre in large tracts which they expected would be bought for speculation. They also sought to control the westward movement of population by the high price and to make for orderly settlement by systematic and slow surveys and competitive bidding at auctions. There was logic in their plans, but they ran counter to long-established traditions and could not be maintained. Squatting, the practice of moving to new areas before the surveyor had run his lines or the land had been offered for sale, was opposed by federal troops but not for long. It was too unpopular for an administration to evict hardy pioneers struggling to make homes for themselves. Slowly the emphasis upon revenue gave way to a policy of facilitating the development of the west and aiding pioneer settlers to become farm owners.

Between 1800 and 1820 credit was extended to purchasers of government land, but it was halted because it had induced speculators and settlers to buy beyond their means. From 1820 until the end of government land sales, $1.25 an acre was the basic price. The minimum-sized tract subject to purchase was gradually reduced from 640 ac. in 1785 to 40 ac. in 1832. Pre-emption, the right to buy the land they settled on and improved, was extended to squatters in a series of special acts. In 1841 prospective pre-emption, or the right to settle upon surveyed public lands before they were offered at public sale, was conceded and in 1854 squatting was legalized on unsurveyed lands for which the Indian title had been surrendered. At the same time, lands which had been open to sale for 10 years or more were graduated in price in inverse proportion to the length of time they had been subject to purchase, the lowest price being 12½ cents per acre for tracts which had been on the market for 30 years.

In the meantime, congress granted land to subsidize state universities, agricultural colleges, roads, canals, railroads, swampland drainage and common schools. Beneficiary states, colleges and canal, railroad and construction companies all vied with each other for the sale of their lands. All were expected to get as much for their lands as the market would allow. Hence, while congress and the general land office were easing the path to ownership (the Homestead act of 1862 offered free land to actual settlers), the major grantees of the federal government were asking from $2.50 to $5 and more an acre.

Not until the Civil War did the federal government curb the speculative buying of public land and such restrictions were not to be altogether effective. Anticipating the settler, speculators invested heavily in the purchase of new land as it was placed on the market. Three great periods of speculation in which many millions of acres were thus acquired were 1816–19, 1835–37 and 1854–57. Speculators, whether small buyers who entered two or three quarter sections or individuals and companies that acquired from 10,000 to 100,000 ac., in no way contributed to the development of the west unless they also invested capital to improve their holdings. Instead, they slowed down progress by forcing settlers looking for cheap lands to go farther afield in their search, pushed the frontier deeper into the Indian country, aggravated the problem of transportation, delayed the extension of local government, the school and the church and made for greater isolation of the settlers. Most serious, the speculator, by intruding himself between the government and the settler, raised land costs substantially, aggravated an already serious credit problem in the west and contributed to the early development of tenancy.

2. Southern Staple Crop Production.—Staple crop production in the south was not the same after the Revolution. Indigo planting flourished for a time, but without subsidies it soon disappeared as a major crop. Two important new staples quickly pushed to the fore, attracting large capital investments and creating a constantly growing demand for slaves. Cotton had for its kingdom the region from North Carolina west through Tennessee to Arkansas and southwest to Louisiana and Texas. Sugar, like rice, was concentrated in a relatively small area, the lower Mississippi delta and lands adjacent to the bayous of Louisiana. Meanwhile, the other great staples, tobacco, flax and hemp, were moving westward, following the streams of population into Kentucky and Missouri.

Perfection of the cotton gin in 1793 capped a series of inventions for the utilization and manufacture of cotton that so lowered the cost of separating the seed from the short-staple lint, spinning the thread and weaving the cloth as to enable cotton to compete with wool in the world market. Demand and prices shot upward and farmers in Georgia, South Carolina and later elsewhere in the south soon began to raise cotton. From a crop of 10,000 bales in the year the gin was made workable, production increased 12-fold in the first decade and went on to make new records year after year. In 1835 the first 1,000,000-bale crop was raised. The record ante-bellum output was 4,508,000 bales in 1859. Cotton had become "king," having long since pushed tobacco aside as the principal staple crop.

Profits in cotton led to a scramble for land suitable to cotton culture. By the hundreds of thousands planters with numerous slaves and substantial bank credit and small farmers dissatisfied with their lot in older and perhaps declining areas sought out places in the piedmont of Georgia and the black prairie and alluvial lands of Mississippi, Alabama and Louisiana where they might plant cotton. These mushrooming cotton areas needed the surplus slaves who could no longer be profitably employed on the worn-out tobacco lands of Maryland and Virginia, and were responsible for the internal slave trade which so scandalized northern abolitionists and foreign travelers. The rapid engrossment of potential cotton land led southern leaders to feel the need for additional territory into which they could carry their slaves and their cotton economy. The annexation of Florida and Texas, the war with Mexico, the move to acquire Nicaragua and Cuba, the conflict over slavery in the territories and the Kansas imbroglio all resulted, at least in part, from the changed situation of cotton and the importance it had in the southern mind.

Cotton was raised by small farmers in 1- or 2-bale lots and by great planters with their many slaves in lots of 100 to 200 bales and more. It was an exacting crop which required much labour, from the planting early in spring throughout the long growing season to the picking, ginning, baling and shipping that extended into the next year. Because it provided work almost the year round, rough work such as chopping, picking, handling and baling, it was well suited to the use of slaves under the charge of overseers. The small farmer who worked in the field with his family and perhaps a slave or two did not count costs, including his own labour, as seriously as did the large planter. Yet he was eager to enlarge his operations, own more slaves and free himself from field work. The larger planter, trying to achieve efficient operation for his extensive capital investment, was even more anxious to expand. He could not capitalize his earnings and float securities to finance expansion as could the industrialist. Instead, he had to undertake expansion through the use of earnings of the land and slaves and such funds as he could borrow.

The ease with which farmers could shift to cotton and sell their crop and the adaptability of much of the southern land to its cultivation induced farmers and planters to lean ever more heavily upon it as their major crop. The high returns of the early period did not last long in the face of rapidly expanding production. From 33 cents per pound in 1818, cotton fell to 9 cents in 1827. In the middle 1830s the price recovered to 15 cents but continued expansion and declining economic activity forced it down to a low of 5 cents in the 1840s. In the late 1850s the price was again up to 11 and 12 cents. The economic pressure upon the planters for increased output was always strong. Capital costs of expansion, including the rising value of slaves, combined with the diminishing margin of profit to ensure the continued cropping that had so ravaged older portions of the south. Soil continued to be expendable.

Fearful of the results of constant cropping, planters tried to anticipate their future land needs by engrossing tracts far larger than they could expect to use for years. In the principal staple-producing areas all the better land not requiring expensive drainage and levees was in private ownership by the 1840s, but only a small part was in cultivation. Land engrossment by the planters dispersed the population, delayed the building of roads and railroads and prevented the compact and intensive development that

was proceeding north of the Ohio. This is not to say that small farmers were not found in the south, but they were fewer and their progress was retarded by the scattered character of population, the distance between farms and the slowness with which transportation facilities were introduced.

Low cotton prices in the 1840s and 1850s, while stimulating planters to enlarge their output, also led to more careful attention to costs. Experiments were made with improved seeds, new varieties were introduced and low-yielding lands were abandoned for freshly opened tracts. The saving feature in the southern cotton economy seemed to be that the value of land and slaves was rising rapidly. Upon this increased value planters could finance their deficits.

Emphasis upon cotton did not mean that the planters raised little else. They tried to make their plantations self-sufficient by producing corn, pork and beef—sometimes on land that was not well suited to such purposes—and emphasis was placed on making the plantations independent of foodstuffs, clothing and even ironware from the north. A few leaders who were well in advance of current agricultural practices preached in the farm journals the need for rotation and manuring but they did not win many converts. On the other hand, the regionalists who were arguing for self-sufficiency no matter what the cost had great influence.

In the tidewater counties of Virginia, however, tobacco cultivation, having seriously depleted the soil, was replaced by wheat farming. An agricultural revival of these depleted areas, stimulated by the example and admonitions of John Taylor and by Edmund Ruffin in his *Farmer's Register*, brought about a notable recovery. Crop rotation, the application of marl, gypsum and guano and local animal manures, deeper plowing and better cultivation made possible large yields. The new tobacco region was in the piedmont of Virginia and North Carolina and across the mountains in the bluegrass country of Kentucky.

Rice and sugar cultivation flourished in limited areas of Georgia, South Carolina and Louisiana, and it was there that the plantation aristocracy reached its highest development. In the sugar region of Louisiana, for example, 1,161 producers shared in the 1858 sugar crop that was worth $25,000,000, and only 208 of these were large producers of 500 hogsheads or more. One hundred and six planters received an average of $55,506 for their crops.

There has been much argument as to whether Negro slaves contributed to or detracted from the prosperity of the south. It is certain that the bulk of the immigrants, repelled by slavery, went elsewhere, and they constituted one of the greatest potential additions to the wealth of a community. It is also clear that the south was not able to hold its own population, for there was a substantial emigration from the slave states to free territory.

The south had been led by economic forces to invest its surplus capital in an institution which the rest of the civilized world was turning against. Not for long could the section stand against the tide of moral opinion that was demanding restriction and abolition of slavery. Yet the institution of slavery, or the presence of the Negro, so unified the south—the piney woods farmer, the southern mountaineer, the Cajun and the planter—as to enable it to fight four years of bloody civil war to protect itself against the northern interference it feared.

3. Northern Mixed Farming.—Farming in the north was more self-sufficient in character and less devoted to the production of staple crops than in the south. True, every farmer sought to produce marketable crops to finance capital improvements. Dairy farming near growing cities served this purpose. Wheat qualified as a staple cash crop for a few years until the accumulation of parasites, diseases and exhaustion of the soil necessitated rotation of crops. Livestock farming required capital investments that were beyond the reach of most farmers, who raised cattle, sheep and hogs as a side line.

In Virginia and Pennsylvania at the opening of the 19th century, wheat was the major crop. Its keeping qualities, value in relation to its bulk, the almost universal demand for it and the fact that it could be grown almost anywhere in the north with no great amount of labour led to its widespread distribution. Wheat was grown most extensively on the rich limestone lands of southeastern Pennsylvania by the descendants of the early Mennonite and Dunker immigrants. In the 1820s the Genesee valley of New York, which had a similar soil and climate, became a major wheat area. Later Ohio and, just before the Civil War, Illinois became centres of wheat production.

Purchasers of or tenants on the lands of the Holland Land company, the Pulteney associates, the Livingstons, Schuylers and Van Rensselaers of New York sought to meet their obligations by tendering wheat. Like the southern planters, they were driven to plant their staple year after year with similar results. Disease and insect infestation, soil depletion and declining production with rising costs made it difficult for them to compete with farmers on the cheap virgin soils farther west. Troubles over collections and antirent wars resulted. Discouraged farmers by the thousands gave up the struggle, abandoned their farms and joined the westward trek. The older parts of the north were having to adapt themselves to the new competition of the west as English farmers after the repeal of the corn laws (q.v.) had to adapt their scheme of farming to the flood of cheaply produced U.S. grain. Abandoned farms soon dotted the hillsides of New York and New England, but there was no great loss. Much of this abandoned land was probably marginal when it was first settled and had been made to support families only by the hardest labour. When wheat as a major cash crop was no longer economically feasible for the better valley lands of New York and Pennsylvania, the farmers turned to dairying, sheep raising, vegetable crops and truck gardening and other specialties.

The flow of population from the older states was joined by increasing numbers of immigrants from England, Germany, Norway and Sweden. Some new immigrants, notably the Irish, stayed in the east to take construction jobs, but others sought the cheap and fertile lands of the west which were being brought to their attention by emigrant agents and representatives of land companies.

Most people moving westward took no great amount of capital with them. Some grabbed more land than they could develop, a common failing so agricultural authorities said, but the expense of farm making and the meagreness of their resources soon turned their operations into small-farm development. Following the quarter-section lines of federal surveys, tier after tier of farms were established, fairly compactly arranged except where the speculators intruded. These farms were not separated by the hundreds of acres of unused land found in the south and as a result, schools, churches, roads and local government all came earlier. Ohio, Indiana, Michigan and Wisconsin were filled with small, single-family farms, mostly owned by the operators. Despite the existence of speculative holdings and a few large estates, Jefferson's ideal of an agrarian democracy came closest to realization there.

As settlers moved out of the previously wooded region of the older states into the prairies of Indiana, Illinois and Iowa they met with conditions which called for greater capital investment. Lumber for building and fencing had to be brought into the treeless prairies. Heavy breaking plows hauled by a number of pairs of oxen were needed to break up the thick prairie turf, and lighter steel plows, first perfected by John Deere in the 1840s, were thereafter required for the annual turning of the soil. To meet the cost of the land and the improvements it was necessary to raise grain on a substantial scale, and this required expensive machinery. Some men of capital came to the west to develop estates manned by hired hands and tenants. They appeared in almost every community, where they provided jobs for less-fortunate immigrants not able to begin farming on their own. Some of these workers by hard labour and careful saving were able to attain ownership, but others remained permanently as labourers or tenants. A few great estates were thus established at an early date.

Seventy years after the constitutional convention of 1787 agriculture had changed greatly. The population had spread over large areas in the Mississippi valley, creating more than 1,000,000 new farms. Cotton, tobacco and wheat pouring from these farms found markets abroad which provided exchange to balance U.S. trade. England's reliance upon U.S. cotton and wheat was to be of importance in the shaping of U.S.-British relations during the Civil War. The building of roads, canals and railroads had opened up new areas previously inaccessible to farmers and had made it possible for them to ship their surpluses to market. Commercial agriculture had made great strides. Farm machines such as the reaper, improved plows, drills and harrows and the substitution of the speedier horse for the cumbersome ox had contributed to this end. Farmers were getting to market more frequently; their families had easier access to the churches; schools were becoming available. The old type of near-subsistence farming and the old isolation were passing.

Increasing commercialization of agriculture made the farmer more subject to the fluctuations of the market and aggravated his distress in periods of low prices. This was the more true because the capital demands of agriculture made borrowing common, the mortgage a feature well known to most farmers. The depression years of 1858–61 brought hard times to many, particularly those who had bought land in the high-price period just preceding. Many failed in their efforts to become owners and were reduced to tenancy. Some moved elsewhere to try again, perhaps to Kansas, Nebraska or Minnesota where free homesteads were available.

4. Livestock.—From early times livestock constituted a minor yet significant feature of farm economy. Cattle, sheep, swine and horses—mostly grade (hybrid) stock in the colonial period—were given little attention as to breeding, feeding and housing. Cattle herding in North Carolina and Louisiana developed into a considerable business for a time. Hogs ran wild in the forests and swamps, living on mast (nuts), roots and seeds and providing, when dressed, pork of a distinctly inferior quality. Sheep likewise produced inferior wool which was used on the farms for homespun goods.

Before the end of the 18th century farmers and planters of wealth had imported purebred stock that contributed to raising the standards of cattle. First the Devons, then the Durhams were brought to Virginia; later Kentucky, New York and Ohio became centres for fine stock. Descendants of these early importations were popular for more than half a century until the better milk breeds and the Hereford and Angus replaced them. Early cattle fanciers prized heavy fat stock that took years to reach the desired weight, but pasture and corn were cheap.

The abundance and cheapness of grassland in Ohio, Indiana, Illinois and Missouri and the large surpluses of corn these states produced ensured that cattle and hog feeding would be centred there. Dealers bought the farmers' surplus stock, drove them to a central feeding ground where they were fattened and then drove them overland to market. Cattle droving thus flourished until the coming of the railroads to the middle west in the 1850s. The feeder-cattle industry was well under way before the Civil War, providing a pattern for corn-belt agriculture which, with the feeding of hogs, was to continue into the 20th century.

Everywhere the ox was an important beast of burden. In most of New England oxen were employed more commonly than horses, although the Morgan horse held sway in Vermont. Where time was of less importance and agriculture was more primitive the ox prevailed. Oxen could be raised and trained on the farm, while few small farmers could afford to enter horse breeding. Oxen, moreover when past their prime were useful for their meat. More progressive farmers in better areas, however, relied on the horse or mule.

The Morgan horse, a good all-purpose animal, and the Conestoga horse, a heavy draft animal developed by Pennsylvania Germans, were the best U.S. types at the opening of the 19th century. Later, Kentucky became famous for its fast driving horses and Missouri for its mules. The cost of rearing horses in the west was low because of the abundance of grassland.

The typical hog was a long-legged animal with a long snout, lean shanks and little meat. Much of the time hogs depended on their own ability to find food in the forests and to escape the

RICE PADDIES IN THE LAM TSUEN VALLEY, NEW TERRITORIES, HONG KONG

Known to have been under cultivation since 2800 B.C., rice continues
to be the staple food for about half of the world's population. It is second
only to wheat in planted acreage and annual crop production

PLATE II   AGRICULTURE

Harvest scene from ancient Egypt, a wall painting from a tomb of the Theban acropolis, 15th century B.C., probably during the reign of Thutmose IV. An inscription notes that the dead official was a scribe of the fields of the lord of Egypt

Plowing in medieval England with oxen. From a 14th-century manuscript

Aerial view of Fyfield Down, Wiltshire. Pattern of ridges lying beneath the present topsoil shows the division of lands of the Celtic (late Bronze Age) farmers

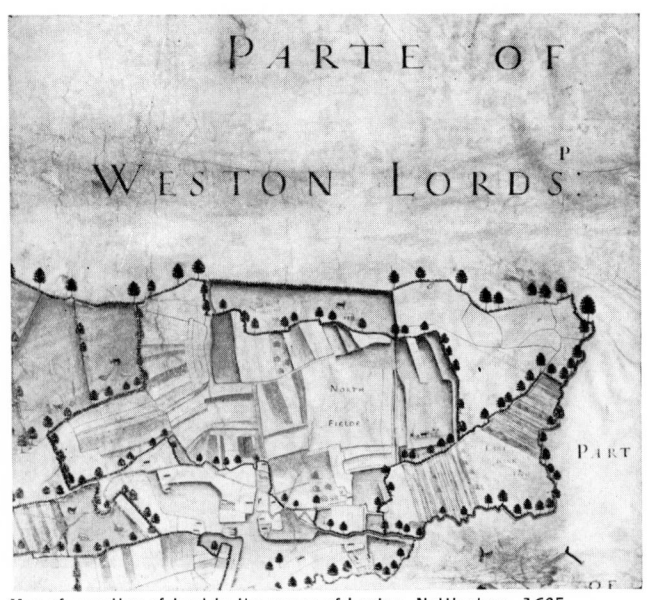

Map of a section of land in the manor of Laxton, Nottingham, 1635

Thomas William Coke, later earl of Leicester of Holkham, inspecting some of his Southdown sheep, 1808. Coke was an early developer of the crop rotation system

PRIMITIVE AGRICULTURE IN EGYPT AND EARLY PRACTICES IN ENGLAND

BY COURTESY OF (TOP) THE ORIENTAL INSTITUTE, CHICAGO, (CENTRE LEFT, BOTTOM RIGHT) ROTHAMSTED EXPERIMENTAL STATION, ENG., (CENTRE RIGHT) ASHMOLEAN MUSEUM, OXFORD, (BOTTOM LEFT) BODLEIAN LIBRARY, OXFORD

Colonist's engraving showing Indians at work in their fields. Woman in the background is using a planting stick to make holes for seeds. Men are breaking ground with a spadelike mattock

Threshing in the barn, a drawing of 1879 by W. M. Cary. A horse-driven endless belt was used to supply power to the thresher

Farm scene in Nebraska, c. 1900. Steam tractor was used to thresh grain in the fields

Homesteaders seeking land in Idaho in 1925, the final phase of agricultural expansion in the west

Abandoned farm in Oklahoma in the late 1930s. Poor farm practices turned promising crop areas into dust-blown wasteland

Artist's drawing of a Wisconsin farm, c. 1880. Ideally suited for livestock and pasture, Wisconsin rose quickly to its rank as the nation's leading dairying state

SCENES OF EARLY FARMS AND FARMING IN THE U.S.

BY COURTESY OF (CENTRE LEFT) NEBRASKA STATE HISTORICAL SOCIETY, (CENTRE RIGHT, BOTTOM LEFT) U.S. DEPT. OF AGRICULTURE, (BOTTOM RIGHT) NEW YORK STATE HISTORICAL ASSN., COOPERSTOWN; PHOTOGRAPHS, (TOP LEFT) BROWN BROTHERS, (TOP RIGHT) THE BETTMANN ARCHIVE

PLATE IV

AGRICULTURE

Turning the soil with mattocks on an experimental farm in the Najd desert area of Saudi Arabia

Sowing rice by hand in a paddy of Ceylon. This method is still predominant in Asia, where most of the world's rice is grown

Ethiopian tribesmen threshing millet by beating the harvested grain

Threshing wheat in central Spain. The grain is thrown into the air, and wind separates the chaff from the wheat

Cultivating on a co-operative farm in communist China. The labour gang is using a three-tined fork with a bamboo handle to loosen the soil

Harvesting potatoes on a mountain farm of the central Cordillera, at an altitude of about 9,000 ft., in Colombia

FARM PRACTICES: MANUAL LABOUR AND SIMPLE TOOLS

Oxen pulling a simple, single-blade hand plow on a farm in India. Cultivation depth is controlled by adjustment of the height of the hitch to the animals' yoke

Girl of western Sumatra guiding a water buffalo through a ditch in a rice paddy to prepare it for seedling transplants. The buffalo's hooves stir and mix the flooded topsoil

Threshing wheat on an Egyptian farm. The bullocks are pulling a wooden platform which crushes the stalks, thus releasing the grain

Mule-drawn cart being filled with hand-picked tobacco leaves on a farm near Danville, Virginia

A camel in Saudi Arabia being used to haul a load of freshly-cut alfalfa to market

Gaucho of the Argentine pampas using his horse to help him round up beef cattle

FARM PRACTICES: USE OF DRAFT ANIMALS

BY COURTESY OF (CENTRE RIGHT) VIRGINIA CHAMBER OF COMMERCE, PHOTO BY FLOURNOY, (BOTTOM LEFT) STANDARD OIL CO. (N.J.); PHOTOGRAPHS, (TOP LEFT) PIERRE STREIT, (TOP RIGHT) MARC RIBOUD—MAGNUM, (CENTRE LEFT) EWING GALLOWAY, (BOTTOM RIGHT) DAVIS PRATT—RAPHO GUILLUMETTE

PLATE VI

AGRICULTURE

Tractor pulling eight gangs of disk harrows over a wheat field in northeastern Bulgaria

Women loading potatoes into a sorting machine on a state co-operative farm in East Germany

Harvesting a crop of lucerne (alfalfa) on a farm in England with a tractor-mounted forager which cuts and chops for ensilage

Using a power sprayer to prevent fungus disease at a banana plantation in Guatemala

Two-man multi-bladed disk plow being operated at a co-operative farm in China

Diesel-powered tractor mounted with an eight-row cultivator being used in a U.S. cornfield

FARM PRACTICES: USE OF MACHINERY

BY COURTESY OF (TOP) BULGARSKA PHOTOGRAPHICA, SOFIA, (THIRD ROW LEFT) JOHN WILDER LTD., (CENTRE RIGHT) UNITED FRUIT COMPANY, (BOTTOM RIGHT) INTERNATIONAL HARVESTER CO.; PHOTOGRAPHS, (SECOND ROW LEFT) DALMAS—PIX FROM PUBLIX, (BOTTOM LEFT) EASTFOTO

Sheep grazing on the slopes of the Dartmoor plateau in Devon, a principally agricultural county in the southwest of England with raising of livestock its major activity

Spraying weed killer on emerging grain crop by helicopter in Cambridgeshire where the large size of fields makes this operation practical and efficient

Herd of purebred Sussex cattle, a strong beef animal originally bred to pull plows through the heavy soils of the area

Horses pulling a spike harrow in a field on the island of South Uist, one of the Outer Hebrides, off the northwest coast of Scotland. The soil in this area, called the *machair*, is sandy and calcareous. Oats and potatoes are the chief crops

Autumn plowing in East Anglia (comprised of the counties of Norfolk, Suffolk, parts of Essex, Cambridgeshire and Hertfordshire), one of the oldest agricultural areas of England and still its major granary

Hay raking on a farm near Brynmawr, Brecknockshire, Wales. Acreage in grass almost doubled in Wales after World War II and lent support to the country's rapidly growing dairying industry

Thinning turnip plants on a farm in County Down, Northern Ireland, where they are grown chiefly for local consumption. The soil in this area is well suited for turnips, giving a high yield per acre

FARMLANDS AND FARM PRODUCTS OF THE WORLD: THE BRITISH ISLES

PLATE VIII

AGRICULTURE

Girl of Lapland with her reindeer. With virtually no arable land, the Lapps depend upon reindeer for meat, skins and horns to trade, and for transportation

Terraced vineyards, rising up the steep slopes behind San Lourenço, Santa Maria Island, the Azores. Grapes are grown throughout Europe, and many countries, like Portugal, depend upon wine production as a significant factor in the agricultural economy

Loading cabbages for market on a scow in the Netherlands. The lowland countries are important vegetable producers in Europe

Sheep on a mountain farm of western Norway. The use of lowlands for crops and highlands for grazing is a survival of pastoral nomadism in Europe

Hay raking in the *département* of Basses-Pyrénées, France, in the mountains near the Spanish frontier. Europe is the leading continent in percentage of land under cultivation

Wheat harvesting with a combine in the Ukraine, U.S.S.R. Although in area the Ukraine is only 2.68% of the Soviet Union, it produces about a third of the nation's wheat

Dairy cows on gently rolling farmland of Belgium. Twelve of the world's sixteen leading milk producing countries are in Europe. Belgium is one of these despite its small size

FARMLANDS AND FARM PRODUCTS OF THE WORLD: EUROPE AND SCANDINAVIA

BY COURTESY OF (SECOND ROW RIGHT) CAS OORTHUYS; PHOTOGRAPHS, (TOP LEFT) AUTHENTICATED NEWS, (TOP RIGHT) J. ALLAN CASH—RAPHO GUILLUMETTE, (THIRD ROW LEFT, BOTTOM) © ENCYCLOPÆDIA BRITANNICA, (THIRD ROW CENTRE) YAN—RAPHO GUILLUMETTE, (THIRD ROW RIGHT) IRVING LEVINE—PIX FROM PUBLIX

Farmlands and irrigation canals of an Egyptian village in the Nile river delta. Irrigation of crop fields, in one form or another, has been practised in Egypt for 4,000 years

Workers setting out to tap latex at a rubber plantation in Liberia. West Africa is the only important producer of natural rubber outside of Asia. Exports of rubber account for about half of Liberia's annual total

Cutting sisal in East Africa. Kenya and Tanganyika are two of the world's leading producers of this fibre plant

Wind winnowing of grain in Ethiopia. The country is largely agricultural, producing a variety of cereal grains, coffee, livestock

Transplanting cuttings from cocoa trees at a plantation in Cameroun, one of the four African countries which together produce more than 60% of the world's cocoa

Bags of peanuts stacked as pyramids at Kano, Nigeria, largest producer of the continent and third in the world (after India and China)

Long-horned Ankole cattle of Uganda. Livestock represent the wealth of a number of pastoral tribes of East Africa

FARMLANDS AND FARM PRODUCTS OF THE WORLD: AFRICA

BY COURTESY OF (TOP RIGHT) THE FIRESTONE TIRE & RUBBER CO., (CENTRE LEFT) BRITISH INFORMATION SERVICES, (CENTRE) UNITED NATIONS, (CENTRE RIGHT) COMPAGNIE FRANCAISE DE L'AFRIQUE OCCIDENTALE; PHOTOGRAPHS, (TOP LEFT) J. ALLAN CASH, (BOTTOM LEFT) WIDE WORLD, (BOTTOM RIGHT) PHOTO YLLA—RAPHO GUILLUMETTE

PLATE X   AGRICULTURE

Part of a herd of 1,200 beef cattle being driven from their range lands to Lundbreck, Alta., for shipment to U.S. feeders. Alberta is the leading cattle-producing province of Canada

Two mechanical cotton pickers in a field near Belzoni, Miss. The U.S. produces more than twice as much cotton as any other nation in the world

Harvesting potatoes on a farm in Ohio. Potatoes are the leading fresh market vegetable grown in the U.S.

Harvesting wheat with a combine in Manitoba, one of the three prairie provinces of Canada which produce 90% of the nation's wheat

Typical dairy farm in Quebec. The province has the largest number of milk cows in Canada, with about one-third of the nation's total

Bringing in boxes of grapes at an Ontario vineyard in the Niagara peninsula, centre of Canada's wine-making industry. Ontario is the leading province in commercial fruit production

Potato farm on Prince Edward Island, often called the "garden" province of Canada with about three-fourths of its total land under cultivation. Seed potatoes are the chief commercial crop

Fruit orchard in the Hood river valley, Ore., (Mt. Hood in background). The states of the Pacific northwest are important producers of tree fruits, especially pears, apples and plums

FARMLANDS AND FARM PRODUCTS OF THE WORLD: NORTH AMERICA

BY COURTESY OF (SECOND ROW LEFT) STANDARD OIL CO. (N.J.), (SECOND ROW RIGHT) DEPARTMENT OF INDUSTRY AND COMMERCE. MANITOBA, (THIRD ROW LEFT) OFFICE PROVINCIAL DE PUB-LICITÉ QUÉBEC, (BOTTOM RIGHT) OREGON STATE HIGHWAY DEPARTMENT; PHOTOGRAPHS, (TOP) KLOPPENBORG—CANADIAN PRESS, (SECOND ROW CENTRE) NILS LINDQUIST, (THIRD ROW RIGHT) SENTINEL SERVICES, (BOTTOM LEFT) KARSH OF OTTAWA

Mixed farming in the Powells valley of the Appalachian mountains in Pennsylvania. In the foreground brown field (at left) is corn, green is winter wheat; golden-coloured field in background is oats

Rows of beans growing in Florida muckland

Rice fields of eastern Arkansas. Levees control the flow of water on the fields

TYPICAL FARMING LANDS OF EASTERN AND SOUTHERN U.S.

Montana wheat plains near Broadview. Each stripe is 10 rods wide, the golden ones planted in winter wheat, the brown ones fallow to conserve ground moisture

Wisconsin dairy farm. Land is sown for feed: corn, hay and pasturage

Corn and oats planted along the contours of rolling land in Nebraska

Irrigation in the west: ditch divides sagebrush wasteland (left) from alfalfa and wheat fields in the Kittitas valley, Washington

CROPLANDS OF THE MIDDLE AND FAR WEST

Horses grazing on pasture in the Cauca river valley near Cali, Colombia. A long-term development program, similar to that of the Tennessee Valley authority of the U.S., was begun in this area in the 1950s to provide balanced agricultural and industrial growth

Cutting sugar cane in the Dominican Republic, one of the Caribbean countries whose economies are based on sugar growing and refining

Carnauba trees, wax palms which are found in northern Brazil. The fronds yield a hard wax which is exported for use in polishes, explosives and phonograph records

Husking coconuts at a plantation in British Honduras. Once a major crop, coconut production declined until the late 1950s when a colonial board was established to redevelop cultivation and expand plantings

Sheep grazing lands in the Argentine pampas, a plain of about 293,000 sq.mi. which serves for high-grade cattle and sheep raising and, in its more fertile areas, for crop production. Argentina has a livestock population of about 100,000,000, most of it on the pampas

Workers picking okra (gumbo) at a state-owned collective farm in Cuba. Excellent soil and climate conditions are widespread on the island, permitting a diversification of farm products. The U.S. was the principal importer of Cuban fruit and vegetables until the advent of the Castro government

FARMLANDS AND FARM PRODUCTS OF THE WORLD: LATIN AMERICA

BY COURTESY OF (TOP) STANDARD OIL CO. (N.J.); PHOTOGRAPHS, (CENTRE LEFT) STOPPELMAN—PIX FROM PUBLIX, (CENTRE) EDGAR AUBERT DE LA RÜE, (CENTRE RIGHT) CAMERA PRESS—PIX FROM PUBLIX, (BOTTOM LEFT) DAVIS PRATT—RAPHO GUILLUMETTE, (BOTTOM RIGHT) BOB HENRIQUES—MAGNUM

PLATE XIV

AGRICULTURE

Israeli farmer picking cotton, a crop virtually unknown in the country until the early 1950s when cotton planting was started with the assistance of the UN Food and Agriculture organization

Bagging grain in a field near Politiko, Cyprus. Diversified agricultural production of the island permits it to be largely self-sufficient in food crops except for wheat and sugar

Olive trees growing on terraced strips on the lower slopes of the Mount of Olives, Jerusalem. Both Israel and Jordan raise substantial amounts of olives, and Jordan exports olive oil

Goatherd of Iran driving his flock of astrakhans along the shore of the Caspian sea. Goats and sheep are the principal livestock of the country, supplying skins, hides and wool for export

Jordan farmer inspecting figs being dried after picking. Vine- and tree-grown fruits and vegetables are the principal crops of Jordan's agricultural economy

Gathering dates at a large oasis near Jidda, Saudi Arabia, third greatest (after Egypt and Iraq) date-producing country in the world

FARMLANDS AND FARM PRODUCTS OF THE WORLD: ASIA MINOR AND THE NEAR EAST

Flooded fields in the Vale of Kashmir, India, a high-producing agricultural area with extensive irrigation facilities

Drying rice on a Japanese farm near Mt. Fujiyama. The harvested grain is spread out on mats and turned occasionally for even drying. Japan has a very high rice yield per acre

Tapping a rubber tree in Ceylon which, despite its small size, is the world's fourth largest producer of natural rubber

Clearing jungle for agricultural land in Thailand, part of a traditional system of shifting cultivation. Cleared land is planted in vegetables, rice and teak trees. As the teak trees grow, agriculture is abandoned, and the farmers move to a new area

Farmers in northern China covering young vegetable seedlings with clay pots to protect them against the frost. Wheat, rather than rice, is the principal grain of the region

Nomad encampment of Outer Mongolia. More than 80% of the population of Mongolia is engaged in pastoral agriculture, and the number of livestock per capita is the highest in the world

FARMLANDS AND FARM PRODUCTS OF THE WORLD: THE FAR EAST

BY COURTESY OF (CENTRE RIGHT) UNITED NATIONS; PHOTOGRAPHS, (TOP LEFT, CENTRE LEFT) J. ALLAN CASH—RAPHO GUILLUMETTE, (TOP RIGHT) WERNER BISCHOF—MAGNUM, (BOTTOM LEFT) MARC RIBOUD—MAGNUM, (BOTTOM RIGHT) ERGY LANDAU—RAPHO GUILLUMETTE

PLATE XVI # AGRICULTURE

Hop fields along the banks of the Derwent river, Tasmania, one of the few places outside of Europe and the U.S. where this crop is grown. It is a primary export item of Tasmania

Hereford beef cattle at a stream in Victoria. Australia has a cattle population of more than 15,000,000 head, and exports about 30% of its annual slaughter

A flock of sheep in north central Tasmania. New Zealand and Australia, including Tasmania, produce almost half of the world's wool and herd more sheep than any other continent

Cutting wheat in New South Wales. Wheat is the principal field crop of Australia, and New South Wales leads all states in production

Coconuts drying on the beach of Takoto atoll, Tuamotu archipelago, near Tahiti. Coconuts are the principal commercial crop of French Polynesia

Spraying pineapples on Molokai Island, Hawaii. The islands produce most of the world's supply of this fruit, which, after sugar, is the state's principal agricultural product

FARMLANDS AND FARM PRODUCTS OF THE WORLD: AUSTRALIA AND THE PACIFIC ISLANDS

BY COURTESY OF (TOP LEFT) AUSTRALIAN EMBASSY, WASHINGTON, D.C., PHOTO BY VICTORIAN DEPT. OF AGRICULTURE, (TOP RIGHT, CENTRE LEFT) AUSTRALIAN NEWS AND INFORMATION BUREAU, (CENTRE RIGHT) "THE MERCURY," HOBART, (BOTTOM RIGHT) U.S. INFORMATION AGENCY; PHOTOGRAPH, (BOTTOM LEFT) E. AUBERT DE LA RÜE

wolves. On the southern plantations where droves of them were kept in the woods, unattended and unfenced, slaughtering was done by rifle in annual hunts. The pork was heavily salted, the poorer grades being doled out to the slaves. Only in the upper Mississippi valley was hog raising becoming a major feature of the farm economy. There, with rich pasture and cheap corn, hogs could be fattened to considerable size, dressed and shipped by flatboat down the Ohio and Mississippi rivers to markets at Natchez, Memphis and New Orleans; or they could be driven overland to Cincinnati, St. Louis or Indianapolis for slaughtering. Hog drovers worked through Ohio, Indiana and Illinois, buying the surplus stock of individual farmers. Improvement in the quality of swine came through the use of better breeds, confinement and grain feeding, and by 1860 the modern corn and hog belt was becoming well defined, stretching from Ohio into Missouri and Iowa.

The modern sheep industry began with the importation of fine-wooled Spanish Merino sheep in 1800–12, followed by the Saxon breed from Germany and the Rambouillet from France. Sheep farming flourished on the hillsides of Vermont and New Hampshire where clearings were being abandoned by grain farmers who could not compete with the Genesee and Ohio regions. For a time Vermont led the union in numbers of sheep in proportion to its population. The high quality of its purebred animals with their large yields of fine wool assured a demand for all the state could produce and brought high returns to the breeders. But New England farmers could not compete for long with sheep raisers in Ohio and Michigan where land was cheaper and pastures were richer, and by the 1840s sheep farming was moving westward into the newer states of the upper Mississippi valley.

5. Agricultural Journals.—Before the day of agricultural colleges and experiment stations, leadership in agricultural improvement was in the hands of a notable group of writers, editors and farm journalists. Among these were John Taylor of Virginia, who preached deep plowing, rotation and manuring; Edmund Ruffin, also of Virginia, who advocated the use of marl; Jesse Buel and Luther Tucker, prominent agricultural editors; John Johnston, vigorous advocate of tile draining, with which he experimented on his New York farm; Solon Robinson, a shrewd, noncontroversial writer; and, finally, the ubiquitous and effervescent Horace Greeley. Important journals were the *American Farmer, Genesee Farmer, Country Gentleman, Cultivator, American Agriculturist, New England Farmer* and *Prairie Farmer*. See also AGRICULTURAL EDUCATION AND RESEARCH.

6. Science in Agriculture.—Technical knowledge of the chemical composition of soils and the essential elements that make for good crops was transplanted belatedly to America through the writings of German and English scientists, the visits of eminent European agricultural scientists such as James F. W. Johnston of the University of Durham and the pilgrimages of Americans to England and Germany for study with men like Johnston and Justus von Liebig. At Yale notable work in agricultural chemistry was being done in the middle of the century by Benjamin Silliman, John P. Norton and Samuel W. Johnson. The latter, having established the essential elements for plant growth, examined the brands of commercial fertilizer then widely advertised and determined the truth or falsity of their claims.

The next step in the application of science to agriculture was the appointment of state geologists who made analyses of rock and soil structures to determine the productive capabilities of various types of soil, the details of which were extensively copied in the agricultural periodicals. Then came the appointment of specialists in the taxonomy of insects who, though they made little progress in developing insecticides of value, did provide useful information concerning ways of combating pests. Agricultural surveys by reputable authorities and government action in importing seeds, cuttings, shrubs and trees from all over the world contributed to the broadening of knowledge of modern methods of farming and to diversification of crops. Most important of the imported crops was sorghum, a cornlike cereal grown for the sweetness of its stalk and for its grain.

C. FROM THE CIVIL WAR TO THE 20TH CENTURY

1. The Civil War and Agriculture.—The Civil War was accompanied by major political and economic developments that had marked effects on agriculture. Southern staple production was brought to a low point by the destruction left in the wake of the armies and by the drafting of field hands. Fields became neglected and weed infested and drainage ditches clogged and overgrown; livestock was destroyed; levees were breached and bridges and roads became impassable. The freedmen in many cases, refused to accept the work conditions their former owners offered. After a period of unrest they (and many poor whites) were compelled by circumstances to become sharecroppers instead of acquiring the elusive "forty acres and a mule" which radical Republicans had held out to them. Rice cultivation never recovered and sugar and tobacco came back only slowly.

By 1880 a new optimistic spirit pervaded the south. Cotton planting was pushed into central Texas and the northern delta of Mississippi and Arkansas. Diversification, better soil practices and increasing use of fertilizer along with expansion in beef and dairy cattle and the introduction of new crops all aided materially. But this improvement was followed by such problems as the boll weevil, overproduction and marketing problems that were to call for long-range planning and action by the federal government.

Northern agriculture prospered as that in the south suffered during the war. Army demands and renewed dependence of England upon U.S. wheat produced a scramble for the grain. Beef and pork also were in increased demand and prices rose to a level not witnessed since the Napoleonic Wars. Despite the drafting of younger men for the army, farmers met the demands upon them by substituting machines for the labour they were losing. Improvements were made in the reaper, mower, drills, plows, harrows and threshers, and the easing of credit and the rising price level enabled farmers to acquire such machines and actually to expand their operations.

War inflation brought high returns to farmers, but it also induced them to borrow heavily to acquire additional land, purchase needed machinery and build up their livestock. The roots of many of the western farmers' difficulties in the last third of the century lay in the fact that they had borrowed heavily in a period of marked inflation. In the meantime, the northern-controlled congress, freed of the strict constructionist views of the southerners, enacted a series of measures that profoundly influenced agriculture.

The Homestead act of 1862 offered free 160-ac. tracts to persons who would settle upon and improve them over a period of five years. It was this offer of free land that was to draw to the new west hundreds of thousands of peasant farmers from Europe and perhaps as many discouraged and debt-ridden farmers and tenants from older parts of the United States.

The Land-Grant College (Morrill) act of 1862 granted lands to each state to aid in establishing colleges of agricultural and mechanical arts and led to the beginning of scientific education for farmers and mechanics (engineers). The subsequent Hatch act of 1887 and the second Morrill act of 1890 went further by contributing to the establishment of experiment stations, extension work and agricultural research. By these three acts congress provided for the development of technical knowledge in the fields of farm management, agronomy and animal husbandry. In 1862 congress also recognized agriculture's importance by creating the department of agriculture. This was an outgrowth of work begun by Henry L. Ellsworth many years earlier when, as commissioner of patents, he had initiated the practice of collecting and publishing, in an annual volume, statistics of agriculture and reports on innovations in farm practice.

Finally, in 1862 congress promised as much as 100,000,000 ac. to assist the building of railroads connecting the Mississippi and the Gulf with the Pacific coast. A decade earlier congress had given land to numerous railroads in the Mississippi valley. The beneficiary railroads, anxious to develop their areas, undertook elaborate advertising schemes to bring them to the attention of prospective settlers and to stimulate and direct emigration thither.

Some of these land-grant railroads organized agricultural departments to aid the land buyers by disseminating information concerning modern farm practices, contributed to agricultural fairs, granted low rates for transportation of farmers' machines and exhibits and imported purebred bulls.

2. Agriculture in the New West.—The discharge of the veterans at the end of the Civil War, the rapid construction of western railroads (the Union Pacific was completed in 1869 and the other transcontinental lines were finished in 1883 and 1884), the extensive emigration-promotion work done by landholding companies in the eastern United States and in Great Britain, Germany and the Scandinavian countries, all contributed to a great migration to the west. Directed by the railroads, homesteaders swarmed over the undeveloped lands in Illinois and Iowa, took up the homestead and railroad lands of Kansas, Nebraska, North and South Dakota and the Pacific coast states and rushed into Oklahoma, where they crowded aside the Indians. By 1880 the modern corn belt was already sending out emigrants to seek land farther west. In the high plains the cattle kingdom had its brief but dramatic day, only to be pushed aside by the more prosaic wheat farmers. Before the end of the century this wheat belt was well on its way toward overflowing, and population was already crossing into the Canadian prairie provinces and into the interior basin of the United States, an area of limited rainfall where an agricultural pattern different from that farther east was developing.

The growth of the corn belt, which extended from Ohio through eastern Kansas and Nebraska, was accompanied by the emergence of tenancy and a small class of landlords owning from 2 to 60 and more farms. In Illinois, for example, only a generation out of the frontier stage, nearly one-third of the farms were operated by tenants; in the richer prairie counties tenants operated as many as one-half. Many of these tenant farmers were taking over the farms of their fathers, which they expected ultimately to inherit, but others were farming land they had no expectation of owning. This latter group of tenants might have considerable livestock and farm machinery and might, as on the hundreds of Scully farms in Illinois, Kansas and Nebraska, own the improvements. It was, however, the landlord who profited from the rise in real-estate values and who had the greater legal protection. As new immigrants pressed into the corn belt the demand for land further strengthened the position of the landlord, who felt justified in increasing cash rents or his share of the crops. Tension between landlords and tenants reached a high point in the late 1880s, with the latter seeking legislation to curb the growing concentration of ownership and to compel fairer treatment of tenants. (*See* FARM TENANCY: *United States.*)

Corn-belt farm practices continued much as before the Civil War. Increasing dependence was placed on farm machines. Corn was planted year after year on land the farmers thought was inexhaustible, and too many farmers neglected the need for manures, lime, phosphate and cover crops. Agricultural authorities continued to urge that farmers feed more livestock, particularly cattle, and thereby get the profits from feeding while providing the manure essential for the soil. Corn-belt farmers' prosperity, however, came more from the rise in land values and the swift utilization and exploitation of the soil than from intelligent long-range planning. A major development in the corn belt was the extension of tile draining, which made possible planting of corn on land previously too wet for anything but hay and pasture.

Removal of the Indians and the opening of the Kansas-Nebraska country by the railroads made possible the establishment of the cattle kingdom which flourished in the high plains area from the end of the Civil War to the droughts of the late 1880s. Texas longhorns, unmarketable during the war, were driven north in great herds to the railheads at Abilene, Newton, Dodge City or Ogalalla, feeding on the way on the unfenced public domain. When in good condition they were carried by rail to feed lots in the corn belt, where they were fattened for slaughter. The Texas cattle brought with them into the feed lots the tick *Boophilus annulatus,* which promptly infected the local cattle with the deadly cattle tick fever, also known as Texas cattle or Spanish

tick fever. The prairie states retaliated by barring further imports.

The Texas cattle reservoir was huge but it consisted of inferior stock that produced low-quality beef. Efforts to improve cattle by importing purebred stock from England promised steady stock upgrading in the long run, but through the 19th century the bulk of the plains cattle remained inferior to the purebred herds that were developing in smaller lots in the corn belt.

Development of the refrigerated car and artificial refrigeration made possible the shipment of beef to England, which, for a time, frightened the English into believing that such imports might have as serious effects on English agriculture as had the earlier flood of U.S. grain.

The Great Plains cattle kingdom lasted for a generation, but well before 1890 the region was being transformed into the wheat belt. Homesteaders advanced relentlessly into the short-grass country, taking up their quarter sections and pushing the open range farther west. Conflicts between the "nesters" and the cattlemen followed, but time was on the side of the former. What was once considered the American desert was proving to be productive wheat country. Displaced corn-belt tenants, Mennonite farmers from southern Russia, Germans, Swedes and Norwegians joined in this trek into the American frontier. They brought with them strains of hard winter wheat that were resistant to drought, disease and insects. Despite cold winters, grasshopper plagues, long droughts and low prices, the wheat farmers advanced to and beyond the 100th meridian, breaking into thin-grassed land as they proceeded—a development which subsequent events were to show was unwise. Unusually dry years and severe winters forced some of these hardy pioneers backward, but with more favourable weather and rainfall, western Kansas, Nebraska and North and South Dakota again proved attractive.

3. Agrarian Politics, 1870–96.—Post-Civil War agriculture, especially in the new areas of the west and southwest, was largely commercial with emphasis on one crop, such as cotton, corn or wheat. Heavy capital investments for land and its improvement, farm machinery and livestock, including horses and mules, and the high cost of farm credit, generally acquired when money was cheap and prices were high, made the position of the farmer particularly vulnerable when the downward movement of prices set in. With interest, taxes and the cost of the goods he bought made stable by the tariff and monopolistic practices, the farmer found his income shrinking badly while his necessary expenditures remained stationary. After 1873 distress was common among the farmers of the west and south. Since freight rates did not decline in proportion to the decline in agricultural prices, they absorbed an increasing amount of the Chicago price for wheat, hogs and cattle. This led the Iowa or Kansas farmer to blame the railroads for his plight.

There followed a series of agrarian movements that had as their object the ending of the monopolistic practices of the great trusts, the curbing of the railroads by rate-control legislation and inflationary legislation including the reissue of greenbacks and extensive silver purchase and coinage. The greenbackers, the Anti-Monopoly movement, the Farmers' Alliance and the Populists directed their demands to these ends. They also sought to encourage farmers' co-operatives and government farm credit institutions. The agrarian movements provided the only real opposition to the Democratic and Republican parties, which differed little on the fundamental issues of the time. Farmers learned to work together for common ends and won some important state victories; they also had a major share in the enactment of the federal Interstate Commerce act, but their successes were later weakened by the hostility of the supreme court to social control. (*See* also AGRICULTURAL ORGANIZATIONS.)

Great gold discoveries and the revival of foreign trade brought an improvement just before the turn of the century, and agriculture entered its halcyon days culminating in what have been called the "parity years," 1909–14, when farm commodity prices were most favourably related to other prices indexes.

4. Government Collection of Agricultural Data.—Collection of agricultural statistics by the U.S. government was first authorized in 1839 when an appropriation of $1,000 was made to the commissioner of patents for this and other purposes relating to agriculture. Until the creation of the department of agriculture in 1862 this office continued to publish agricultural statistics that it compiled or that were borrowed from the census reports.

In the sixth census in 1840 the first detailed statistics were compiled of the number of farms, their ownership, acreage, improvements, crop yields, livestock and value. Unfortunately, the collection of the data was in the hands of federal marshals and temporary appointees having political influence. The work was poorly done and the data were carelessly transcribed, unscientifically tabulated and inaccurately checked, if they were checked at all. The results were replete with errors, some obvious and easily corrected by anyone using them seriously, others impossible to check without going back to the original manuscript schedules, many of which were lost.

Criticism of the 1840 census figures and methods of compiling them by the American Statistical association led to improvement, but for years the political selection of census takers and clerks resulted in large numbers of errors. Also, the number of inquiries was increasing steadily, making the burden of the questioners difficult. In 1840 the number of agricultural inquiries was 27; in 1850, 45; and in 1860, 55. In that year a misunderstanding between the census takers, the marshals and the tabulators led to the omission of large numbers of livestock—as much as 18%—from the totals of horses, mules, cattle, sheep and hogs. To rectify the blunder a second tabulation of omitted data was included under a cryptic and unclear caption that was only made understandable by a footnote. Most users, having overlooked the footnote, used the inaccurate schedule.

While all early censuses have to be used with caution, later censuses presented their own difficulties by breaking up and changing earlier inquiries, thus making comparisons with previous data difficult or misleading.

The first census in which advance thought and planning were given in the preparation of schedules, by congress and by a board of the census set up by congress, was that of 1850, and the results proved to be a marked reform. In 1870 Francis A. Walker, an outstanding statistician, brought a touch of professionalism to the gathering of statistics. Thereafter, continued improvement was made in collecting, processing and publishing data. In 1902 congress provided for a permanent census bureau to replace the previous temporary bureaus. Statisticians and other experts in various government bureaus, the universities and professional organizations were utilized in planning for data gathering but politics continued to be influential in the appointment of the census takers.

Before 1860 there had been considerable criticism of the agricultural censuses by various states on the ground that their production of farm goods and numbers of livestock were not properly recorded and hence the census minimized their rank in U.S. agriculture. On the eve of the Civil War the census was collecting data which showed that the public land system was not working as its framers and defenders maintained it was. The census of that year revealed a relatively high ratio of agricultural labourers to farms in the frontier states of Kansas, Minnesota, Iowa and Wisconsin. In 1870 the statistics of the amount paid farm labourers further revealed that many thousands of western land seekers had had to settle for farm jobs, not farm ownership. In 1880 the census bureau for the first time collected statistics of farm tenancy which shocked the country, so high was the proportion of tenancy in the new west. Finally, in 1890 the census bureau, under pressure from the west which was greatly concerned about the farm mortgage problem, collected statistics of the number of mortgaged farms, their acreage and the dollar value of the mortgages. These data confirmed widely held views that the west was deeply in debt to eastern creditors, and they contributed to the growing agrarian unrest in the west and the demand for reform of land policies and the establishment of government farm credit.

In the 20th century the statistics of agriculture were found useful in so many ways by governmental and private groups that after 1920 the collection of such data was made every five years.

D. Farming in the 20th Century

U.S. agriculture has gone through a series of changes in the 20th century that have accentuated many of its problems. From "parity years" through the inflation of World War I to the distressing 1920s, the tragic 1930s and the recovery with World War II, farmers plunged from the heights to the depths and then cautiously watched the recovery of the 1940s and the rising production accompanied by rising costs of the 1950s. During this period scientific farming as taught in the colleges of agriculture and practised in the experiment stations and on the more progressive farms was having its effect everywhere. Improved farm machines, the combine harvester and thresher, corn and cotton pickers, mechanical planters and milkers and, more than anything else, the introduction of the rubber-tired tractor and the extension of electricity worked a revolution in farming.

Twentieth-century homesteaders continued to press into the new west, mostly the semiarid lands of the region extending from western Texas, the panhandle of Oklahoma, western Kansas, Nebraska and the Dakotas to the Pacific coast. Wheat was their principal crop. Dry farming (q.v.) techniques were developed which enabled farmers to conserve the meagre moisture in the soil by a process of dust mulching and by permitting the land to lie fallow to build up moisture for the following crop year. Thomas D. Campbell developed a huge wheat ranch in Montana on which dry-farming techniques were practised, and gave wide publicity to the methods he used. Because the homestead unit was too small for the extensive farming the semiarid lands required, congress in 1904 allowed full section homesteads in the sand-hills region of western Nebraska, which Mari Sandoz was later to picture in *Old Jules*. In 1909 and 1916, 320- and 640-ac. homesteads were authorized. Free land available in such quantities, whatever its character, proved a powerful attraction. World War I brought high prices and a demand for wheat that furthered the movement into the region beyond the 102nd meridian. In a half century an area equal to ten states the size of New York was brought under cultivation.

In the older states of the northeast farming continued to contract, so far as the number of farms and acreage in farms was concerned. Despite certain alarmists, however, the contraction was regarded by most agricultural economists as just and sound. Poor, unproductive land was reverting to forest. On better land farmers were doing well. The growing demand for dairy products and the extension of hard roads made possible the enlargement of urban milksheds so that few regions in the northeast were too distant to feel the pull of the city market. Fast milk trains and milk trucks brought the milk from pasteurizing plants in the dairy centres to New York, Boston, Philadelphia and other cities. Sanitary improvements were made in the housing facilities for cattle and the care of the milk on the farm. Emphasis was placed on quantity of milk and the amount of butterfat it contained. Farmers were urged to cull their poorer stock and substitute high-producing cows and progeny-tested bulls and to follow the techniques being developed at the agricultural colleges for wiping out Bang's disease and tuberculosis. The perfection of the milking machine was a boon to dairy farmers, for it freed them from some of their hardest labour, made them less dependent on hired help, which was increasingly difficult to retain, and made possible the management of larger herds. Another near-revolutionary improvement was artificial insemination, which shortly accomplished much in herd improvement (*see* Animal Breeding).

Until settlers reached areas where rainfall was insufficient to make fruit flourish they set out apple trees, grapevines and small fruits such as raspberries and strawberries. Regions of specialization developed where the tempering effects of lakes encouraged peaches and grapes, as in the Finger lakes country of New York and on the shores of the Great Lakes. Truck gardening flourished in the Connecticut valley along with tobacco cultivation, on Long Island and in the muckland area of upstate New York. By the 1860s southern Illinois had become an important fruit-producing area, and special fast fruit trains were run to Chicago to carry the region's produce. In the 20th century Florida and California oranges, Texas grapefruit and lettuce and other early vegetables grown in the deep south were shipped north in refrigerated cars to the rapidly expanding urban markets. A complex transportation network of truck and train was employed to bring to the great cities the seasonal products raised in every part of the country. Specialty crops, including vegetables, fruit and nuts, had become a big business.

Migratory labour was common in the wheat belt until the coming of the modern combine which both cut and threshed the wheat. Threshing crews started in midsummer in Texas and worked north through Kansas, Nebraska and the Dakotas. The migratory labourer was paid a higher wage than the ordinary farm hand and he had his living where he was employed, but he lacked security and decent housing conditions. During World War I wheat threshers, apple and strawberry pickers in Washington and Oregon and other migratory workers were drawn into the Industrial Workers of the World (q.v.) a radical labour union that sought by violent and revolutionary means to gain better wages and working conditions for its members. In the early 1930s residents of Oklahoma, Texas and other parts of the cotton south, driven to desperation by drought, dust storms, credit difficulties, diminishing soil fertility and the consolidation of small cotton and wheat farms into larger units suitable for modern machine farming, migrated to California, where they joined other migratory workers in search of fruit- and vegetable-picking jobs. John Steinbeck's *Grapes of Wrath* painted a classic picture of this displaced group as it slowly worked its way westward. The rapidly expanding airplane industry of World War II absorbed these workers, and the "stoop-crop" work in the lettuce and onion fields and fruit picking in the citrus belt began to be done by Mexicans, including "wetbacks" who crossed illegally into the U.S. Farther east, Puerto Rico provided migratory labourers for truck-gardening jobs. Bad conditions in housing camps for them attracted attention, and improvements required federal and state action. (*See* AGRICULTURAL ECONOMICS: *Agricultural Labour*.)

European dependence on U.S. grain, meat, fats and cotton in World War I and the accompanying high prices resulting from wartime demand made it possible to disregard costs and the economics of marginal land use and thereby to enlarge production strikingly. In accomplishing this, farmers bought, at war prices, expensive machines and land that had increased sharply in value, and borrowed heavily from banks and insurance companies. In 1920 the turn came. Prices dropped to prewar levels while the farmers' costs did not. The reasons for the collapse are diverse. European nations, in the throes of nationalism, sought to free themselves from dependence on U.S. foodstuffs, and the foreign market for wheat products and other exports dried up. The Fordney-McCumber and later the Smoot-Hawley tariff acts led to retaliation by Europe against U.S. imports that further cut demand.

At the same time U.S. farming was becoming more efficient as a result of the teaching of the agricultural economists and extension agents, the increased use of fertilizer, the development and wide introduction of machines, notably the combine, the tractor and the corn picker, the substitution of hybrid corn for the open-pollinated variety, all of which brought better yields in the face of lower demand. The tractor freed millions of acres previously used for raising oats or grass for horses and mules for commercial crops.

Farm surpluses became a major economic and political problem. Corn, wheat, tobacco and cotton farmers grimly watched their incomes shrink and their purchasing power decline in a period of general prosperity. Mortgage foreclosures, increase in tenancy, unemployment among farm workers and sharply contracted sales to farmers reflected this distress. Political efforts to deal with the farm crisis through the Nonpartisan league, the Farmer-Labor party, the McNary-Haugen movement and the farm bloc came to little for it was impossible, except in a few states, to get farmers and workers to agree on a common program.

Farm credit was extended in the 1920s, and in 1930, as a result of pressure by the American Farm Bureau federation, the Grange (Patrons of Husbandry) and the Farmers union, the Agricultural Marketing act was adopted. These organizations, in addition to being spokesmen for major groups of farmers, had set up co-operatively owned grain mills, processing plants and wholesale and retail stores to aid farmers in eliminating the middleman's profits. The marketing act provided for the establishment of a farm board which might lend funds to co-operatives to buy and hold nonperishable commodities the price of which had fallen below the cost of production. Lacking production controls, the measure slowed price declines only for a time.

After the election of Franklin D. Roosevelt as president in 1932, the Agricultural Adjustment administration was established to curtail production through the domestic allotment plan, whereby farmers were paid to withdraw from cultivation a portion of their land previously planted in major crops. A processing tax was levied at the point of ginning the cotton or milling the wheat and given to co-operating farmers in the form of benefit payments. Limitation of output and the tax and inflationary action, including the reduction of the gold content of the dollar, substantially raised the farmers' income. These steps were followed by the creation of the National Resources Board and Advisory committee to draw up long-range plans and make recommendations for the best use of various types of publicly and privately owned land. A major recommendation of the board that was soon acted upon was that several million acres of land classed as submarginal for farm purposes because of low yield, degree of erosion and soil depletion should be withdrawn from cultivation and placed in forests, parks, recreation areas or other controlled use. When the great drought of 1934 occurred and dust storms blackened the nation's skies, and land made productive by dry-farming techniques was stripped of every vestige of growth and left barren, the government took quick action to aid

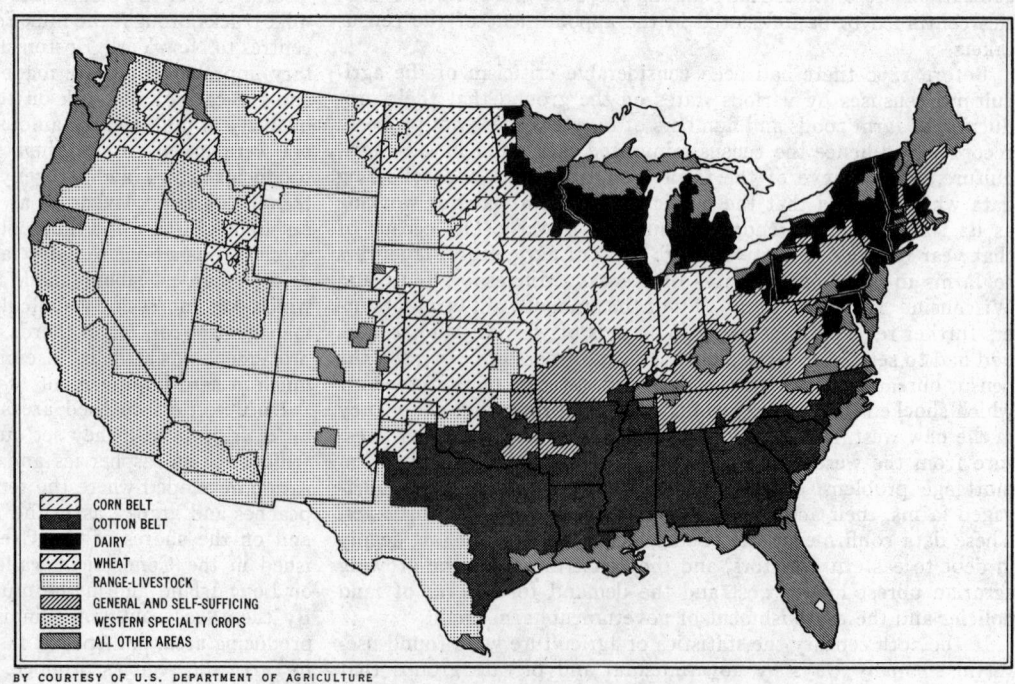

BY COURTESY OF U.S. DEPARTMENT OF AGRICULTURE

CORN BELT
COTTON BELT
DAIRY
WHEAT
RANGE-LIVESTOCK
GENERAL AND SELF-SUFFICING
WESTERN SPECIALTY CROPS
ALL OTHER AREAS

REGIONALIZED TYPES OF FARMING IN THE UNITED STATES

the ravaged area. Starving cattle were moved to better ranges or bought and slaughtered, and loans were extended to the distressed farmers. Mortgage foreclosures were stopped in 1933 by the swift extension of government credit. Soil erosion, long one of the gravest losses sustained by the country, was attacked by offering farmers payments to use cover crops, rotate their crops and institute grass waterways, terracing, strip cropping, contour farming and better drainage practices. Lime was widely distributed, and fertilizer prices were reduced through the threat of prosecution of the fertilizer "trust." (*See* also IRRIGATION; LAND RECLAMATION.)

Tenancy had been somewhat complacently regarded by agricultural economists of an earlier day, but its rapid growth in the depression (the agricultural censuses of 1930 and 1935 each showed more than 200,000 new tenant-operated farms, a total of more than 400,000 additional in a ten-year period) created alarm. A land-purchase program was initiated for tenants to aid them in becoming owners, though congress was reluctant to vote substantial funds for the plan. During World War II farmers' income improved, the cycle was reversed and the percentage of farms operated by tenants diminished from more than 40% in the 1930s to less than 20% in the 1960s.

Subsidies to maintain prices, once introduced, proved difficult to end. Representatives of farm states fought for their continuation, despite the high prices farm commodities were bringing after World War II and the growing surplus. Vast quantities of butter, wheat and cotton accumulated in government warehouses where the cost of maintaining them was high even while they depreciated in value. Neither major political party voiced opposition to subsidies and high parity prices, but by 1954, under pressure from some farm organizations, rigid price supports were breached. The administrative machinery for the soil conservation program was changed and the soil bank plan (not dissimilar from the old soil conservation procedure of the 1930s and 1940s) and government-subsidized sale of surpluses abroad at such prices as they might bring were pushed vigorously. The government attempts to have less-productive land withdrawn from cultivation, thereby reducing the yield of basic crops, and to unload unwanted surpluses abroad did not bring the hard-pressed farmer the relief he needed. Prices received in relation to prices paid by the farmer dropped below parity in the 1950s, while the federal government was spending substantial amounts in attempting, without notable success, to bolster farm income (*see* AGRICULTURAL ECONOMICS).

In the second half of the 20th century, high labour costs encouraged the use of corn pickers, wheat combines, cotton pickers, milking machines, bulk tanks and other large and expensive machines which, to be used efficiently, required larger farm units than had formerly been the norm. The average size of farms increased from about 150 ac. in the 1930s to over 300 ac. in the mid-1960s, mostly through the elimination of small farms. In 30 years more than 2,500,000 farms had been eliminated and an equal number of farmers displaced. The resulting emigration from the rural areas was even more rapid than immigration to those areas had been in the 19th century. These kaleidoscopic changes in agriculture seemed to threaten the old concept of agriculture as a "way of life" and to reduce further the influence of the once-powerful farmers in national politics. For production and acreage statistics *see* separate articles on various crops, as CORN; RYE; WHEAT; etc. *See* also FARM MANAGEMENT; FARMSTEAD ARRANGEMENT, U.S.

E. TYPE-OF-FARMING REGIONS

There are eight major classes of farming area in the United States, commonly referred to as type-of-farming regions. The proportion of farm income in an area which is derived from a given commodity or combination of commodities determines to a large extent the type into which the area is classed. The major types are (1) cotton belt; (2) wheat areas; (3) corn belt; (4) dairy areas; (5) general and self-sufficing areas; (6) range-live-stock areas; (7) western specialty-crop areas; and (8) all other areas, a residual category in which tobacco, sugar cane, fruits,

vegetables and potatoes predominate. These broad areas are shown in the accompanying map. Hawaii and Alaska, being unique agriculturally and falling outside the eight major type-of-farming regions, are dealt with in separate articles (*see* ALASKA; HAWAII).

Although major type-of-farming regions when described graphically seem to end abruptly at their borders, their outer fringes are transitional zones which shade into the contiguous regions. Each major type-of-farming region has a core or heart in which the physical features and location produce a technology, economy and social life different from those found in the cores of the others. The common activities engaged in by rural persons in making a living in each region produce broadly similar interests, attitudes, values and life patterns. Although there are occasional groups within a region which are different from the group prototype (such as the Amish, whose culture prohibits the use of many types of farm machinery, or the Mormons, the only large group with a high birth rate as well as a relatively high income), each major region is in general homogeneous with respect to technological, economic and social factors in the core area and less so near the boundaries of adjacent regions.

1. Cotton Belt.—The main factors determining the location of the cotton belt of the old south and the new cotton-producing areas of the southwest are climate and water for irrigation. The core areas of the cotton belt are the high plains and Corpus Christi areas of Texas and the delta counties of Arkansas, Louisiana and Mississippi. By the second half of the 20th century cotton production was firmly established in the San Joaquin valley of California and on irrigated land in Arizona, and these states ranked third and sixth, respectively, in the production of the staple. In some areas of the cotton belt small, family-owned farms are found. In others the sharecropper system, with small acreages per family, persists as a remnant of slaveholding days. The commonest pattern, especially in the core areas, is that of large farms situated on level ground and operated by up-to-date machinery. Other crops are grown in the cotton belt. Grain sorghums, corn, oats, soybeans, peanuts, tobacco, sugar cane and rice, separately or in various combinations, are produced on cotton farms in different parts of the cotton belt. Pasture, live-stock and dairy enterprises are also found. The cotton boll weevil, which spread over the cotton belt from 1892 to 1920, provided a strong incentive toward diversification.

In the older cotton areas where mechanization has proceeded slowly the cycle of growing and harvesting cotton determines school vacations, social events, business activities and church revivals. In contrast with the slack period in winter and early spring, the heavy work period during the picking season from September to November absorbs the efforts of almost everyone. The original plantation organization permitted only a relatively few to initiate action, make important decisions or engage in concerted community efforts. Influence and control by relatively few persisted into the 1960s, and segregation of Negro and white persons prevailed throughout the whole cotton belt. The Farm bureau became the strongest of the general farmers' organizations. The co-operative movement was particularly weak.

Use of the cotton picker and new systems of planting and cultivation made it possible to reduce greatly the amount of hand labour needed. This, together with the high birth rate of the people in the cotton belt, resulted in a steady exodus of white and Negro residents to the cities of the south and to the north. At the beginning of the second half of the 20th century approximately one-third of the farm population of the nation lived in the cotton belt, which matched its high birth rate with low standards of living, high proportions of native American stock, and, except in the western portion, high proportions of nonwhites and non-owners. It is the most rural of the regions. According to the 1960 federal census, of the 15 largest cities in the United States only one fell in the cotton belt, which contained only 4 of the 25 largest cities. True cotton-belt cities like New Orleans, Dallas, Fort Worth, Baton Rouge and San Antonio were growing phenomenally, however. Some of the most solid neighbourhoods in the entire country, often organized around a church, are found in the cotton belt. This is particularly true of Negro neighbourhoods. In general the interaction between groups is largely informal, with traditional and religious activities dominant. Rural religion is generally fundamentalist. Discussion meetings which permit participation of large segments of neighbourhoods or communities are extremely rare. (*See also* COTTON BELT.)

2. Wheat Areas.—Although wheat is grown in most parts of the United States, approximately three-fourths of the nation's wheat crop comes from the 250 counties delineated on the map as the wheat areas. In these areas there is insufficient moisture for heavy corn or row-crop yields, however sorghum grows well. In terms of acreage and production central and western Kansas, southwestern Nebraska, eastern Colorado and northwestern Texas and Oklahoma, known as the hard winter wheat region, excels the others. The spring wheat area in western Minnesota, North and South Dakota and Montana ranks second in production. In the eastern part of this spring wheat area farms are smaller than elsewhere in the wheat areas. Toward the west rainfall decreases, summer fallow becomes more important and acreages become larger. The wheat area of north central Montana is characterized by extensive farming operations and, as in most of the other wheat areas of the high plains, range livestock production is common. In the Pacific northwest region in the Columbia river basin both soft red and soft and hard white wheats are produced. There rainfall ranges from 20 in. annually in eastern Washington and northern Idaho to a low of 10 in. to the west in the Big Bend area.

The rural culture of the wheat areas stands in sharp contrast to that of the cotton belt. Levels of living and income are high, the birth rate is low, relatively little of the produce is consumed by the family. Like the cotton belt, the wheat areas are highly rural. Unlike the cotton belt, however, the neighbourhoods are weak with comparatively few open-country churches. The trade centres are relatively important gathering points for economic and social life. Farms are large, and people are settled sparsely. Towns are few and there are no large cities. The maintenance of adequate rural schools, libraries and similar agencies is a critical problem. Churches are usually in the towns, and the differences between rural and town people are inconspicuous.

In many of the wheat areas rainfall is uncertain and hailstorms and pests are common. The farmers are familiar with crop failure and have been characterized as willing risk takers. The Great Plains portion has been called the dust bowl. Farm tenancy is comparatively high even though farm enterprises are usually managed by families. Tenants have relatively high status. More than three-fourths of the work involved in wheat production is concentrated in the four months of planting and harvesting. In some instances "suitcase farmers" who live on the farms only during planting and harvesting are the operators, but townspeople and country people all sense their dependence on the wheat crop and the weather. The Farmers union became the strongest organization in these areas, particularly in the northern part, which was settled largely by northern Europeans.

3. Corn Belt.—Although corn (maize) is the dominant crop of the so-called corn belt, a more descriptive title and one frequently used is the feed-grains and livestock region. Soils there are deep, warm, fertile and rich in organic material and nitrogen and the land is relatively level. This is the area of warm nights, hot days and rainfall well distributed throughout the growing season—ideal conditions for corn. In practically all parts of the region the feed crops—corn, oats, grasses and legumes—plus large acreages of soybeans, some wheat and many hogs and cattle form the basis for the farming system. Corn is used chiefly for feeding hogs, and beef cattle.

The chief subdivisions of the region are determined by the basic relationship between the grains and the livestock fed from them. Thus much of the level, fertile land of central Iowa and east central Illinois is devoted to grains and farmed with relatively little livestock. Share renting is common. On the more rolling areas where there is considerable permanent pasture, livestock raising is combined with grain farming. Hogs, which convert concentrated feeds into meat efficiently, get most of the corn fed to livestock. On the boundaries of the area the chief products

of the adjoining type-of-farming regions are mingled with and influence the combination of feed grain and livestock.

Grain-livestock farms are usually family-operated commercial enterprises, averaging perhaps 300 ac. Little of the family's food supply is now produced on the farm. The value of land, buildings, implements, machinery and livestock is nearly double the national average. Tenant improvements are commonly inferior to those on owner-operated farms.

Approximately 14% of the nation's farmers lived in the corn belt at mid-20th century. High standards of living and large farm incomes coupled with low birth rates characterize the area. In no other major type-of-farming region is the proportion of extremely rich and poor lower. The one-room neighbourhood school is gone by now; in educational, social and economic activities the trade centre is very important and neighbourhoods located outside the centres are dying out. Rural churches are more frequently built near the trade centres than in the cotton belt. The Farm bureau became strongest in this area, but special-interest groups are usually organized around farm commodities. Producers' co-operatives also flourish. The farm work is distributed through the whole year, with the busiest seasons in the spring and fall, when the work days are long.

4. Dairy Areas.—Dairying is centred in the northeast, in the Great Lakes states, in small areas on the northern Pacific coast and in smaller areas adjoining large cities. There the soils and the terrain are not suitable to cereal farming, but the cool climate and plentiful, well-distributed rainfall are favourable to hay and pasture. Proximity to large cities provides markets for fluid milk in most of the areas.

The core dairy areas are the central northeast, eastern Wisconsin and northeastern Illinois. All these areas supply fluid milk to urban centres and to cheese factories and condenseries. A large proportion of the grain and other concentrates fed to the dairy herds are produced on the family farms. Other enterprises, most commonly poultry, fruit and truck farming, are usually combined with dairying.

The relationship between a common manner of earning a living and basic attitudes and habits is illustrated in the dairy areas. These areas are widely scattered and they vary considerably in climate, soil type and terrain. Settlement history, forms of local government, ethnic composition and other cultural factors also differ greatly, but the activities involved in producing dairy products stamp the farmers and their families with distinctive characteristics not found elsewhere. The general orientation of the farmers of the dairy and wheat areas may be compared. In the former, the income and work load are relatively constant and predictable throughout the year and from generation to generation; in the latter, principally because of the vicissitudes of the market and weather, great fluctuations occur within the year and through the years. In the dairy areas the work and marketing pattern lead to a high evaluation of thriftiness and hard work, the outward signs of which are solvency and attainment. There is little chance for making a "killing" in a short period of time. The gambling spirit is less apt to appear under these conditions. Soil building and conservation are common. In this respect, the dairy areas resemble the corn belt except for livestock feeding in the latter areas, which involves considerable risk.

The Grange, the Farm bureau and numerous co-operatives flourish in the dairy areas. Many special-interest groups, including various dairy herd and breed associations and artificial insemination co-operatives, exert considerable influence. There are some factory farms, but by and large dairy farming is a family enterprise. Small operations are also few, most of the herds carrying 40 or more cows.

This is the most urban major type-of-farming region. Within its boundaries as depicted on the map are many of the nation's largest cities. In the area as a whole, seven-tenths of the people live in cities and another two-tenths are rural but do not farm. The most rapidly growing segment of the population is the suburban nonfarm, most of which live in the fringe areas extending out from the metropolitan centres along the main highways.

5. General and Self-Sufficing Areas.—These are the areas which are left over after the major type-of-farming regions which are dominated by one or two agricultural enterprises are delineated. In the eastern areas as indicated on the map, corn, wheat, oats, hay and to a lesser extent soybeans, tobacco, fruit and truck crops are grown and much of the rougher land is kept in pasture and hay. Hogs, beef cattle and poultry are found on the majority of the farms, with some scattered dairy cattle and sheep. Livestock, truck crops and cotton are important in the southern Ozark and Ouachita mountain area. A detailed type-of-farming map with subregions would show numerous small general farming areas under irrigation in western Nevada, the lower Snake river basin in Idaho and Oregon, central Utah, southeastern Idaho, western Montana, the upper Arkansas valley, the San Luis valley and San Juan basin in Colorado and northwestern New Mexico and the Yakima valley in Washington. Other irrigated areas lie in Nebraska and central and northern New Mexico. There are small-scale and part-time general farming areas along the Atlantic and Gulf coasts where forest products, truck crops and cotton are common. Other small, nonirrigated general farming areas are in northeastern New Mexico and northwestern Texas.

The larger areas as shown on the map contain the most rugged terrain east of the Rockies. It is this terrain which makes isolation play such a dominant role in the lives of the people. Folk dances, music and crafts still live in the most remote sections. Traces of Elizabethan English are still evident. These areas are characterized by limited land resources, small, uneven fields and badly eroded, hilly land. Population pressure is great, and many marginal lands have been opened for cultivation, resulting in the depletion of game and forest resources. Outward migration is significant, as many as one-fourth of the people having left some mountain counties during World War II—many never to return except for an occasional visit. Others returned because of the strong family and locality ties characteristic of the region. Although the region is varied and the culture as a whole difficult to characterize, it may be said in general that a high premium is placed on independence among the people, an apparent heritage of the Anglo-Saxon rural culture which produced men like Daniel Boone, Davy Crockett and Andrew Jackson. Most of the farmers trace their ancestry to England, Scotland and Northern Ireland, although some are descended from Germans, Welsh or Dutch or the French Hugenots.

In general, relationships in business and politics are extremely personal. Special-interest or formal organizations are less widespread than in other regions. Tools are simple, life is unhurried and leisure is no luxury. The bulk of the farm work comes in the spring plowing and planting season and in the fall harvesting period. Emotional revival meetings are held frequently before the harvest begins. Most farmers supplement their incomes with off-farm work, and home production of food is relatively important.

6. Range-Livestock Areas.—This region comprises approximately 30% of the land area of the United States and carries 14% of the cattle and 45% of the sheep. Forming a band 500 to 1,000 mi. wide, it stretches from Mexico to Canada and has the roughest and most varied landscape of any region. It is made up mainly of areas which are too infertile, high or dry for other agricultural uses. About half the western range is federal- and state-owned land, a considerable portion of which is in federal grazing districts and national forests. In Nebraska, Kansas, Oklahoma and Texas private ownership is dominant. Elsewhere ranchers lease grazing rights on public lands, usually to supplement their private holdings. Throughout the ranch country there are mining enterprises, irrigated farming areas and recreation centres, including dude ranches. The most important subregions of the range-livestock region are the areas of (*a*) year-long grazing; (*b*) seasonal grazing for non-migratory use; (*c*) seasonal grazing for migratory use; and (*d*) upland summer grazing.

The cultural influence of the range-livestock areas upon American life is out of proportion to the number of persons and value of products within its boundaries. The only agricultural life of the United States generally known in many countries of the world is the life of the ranch country.

The range-livestock areas provide farmers and ranchers with more leisure time than any other farming region. Busy periods occur when animals are dipped to remove insect pests, calves castrated and branded, yearlings prepared for market and, in the migratory areas, when livestock is transferred from one area to another. The great climatic changes and the fluctuations of the market require adjustments which dominate the people everywhere. The old traditions of the "wild and woolly west" are kept alive through such events as rodeos, but ranchers who make their living from their agricultural operations have little use for dude or luxury ranches.

In social life the dominating factor is distance. The range or "spread" is usually measured in square miles called sections and towns are small and far apart. In no other agricultural region do schools, libraries, public health units, road maintenance divisions and other social and economic agencies suffer so much from lack of an adequate population base. (The population gains in these states shown in the 1960 census was accounted for by the spectacular growth of certain urban areas, and depended on industrial development rather than agriculture.) There are few open-country churches. All parts of the range-livestock areas have relatively high rates of operator ownership. Birth rates are high, but because of migration rural population was decreasing in the second half of the 20th century. Levels of living are relatively high, except in the Spanish American and Indian areas.

7. Western Specialty-Crop Areas.—The areas falling in this category are similar chiefly because they are devoted to specialty crops rather than diversified farming and because they are irrigated areas in arid territory. The 88 counties designated as belonging to this type-of-farming region are chiefly in California, Idaho, Utah and parts of Washington. They cover 8,000,000 ac. on which the major portion of the nation's almonds, apricots, alfalfa, asparagus, carrots, cantaloupes, cherries, lettuce, prunes, walnuts, lemons and grapes are grown. There are wide variations in climate and soil in the region.

Utah and the irrigated and specialty-crop areas of Idaho under the influence of the Mormon culture produced a distinct social and economic life. Relatively high birth rates are coupled with rural levels of living which are among the nation's highest, an exceptional relationship. The family-type farm prevails, and family and religious life are of great importance.

The irrigated specialty-crop section of California falls in a subarea sometimes called the factory-farm area. There a very high plane of living for operators is coupled with a very low birth rate. Approximately 40% of the population is foreign-born. As in the other non-Mormon parts of the western specialty-crop areas, farming is industrialized and commercialized. California farms averaged over 450 ac. in the 1960s; the average size for the 48 conterminous states was about 350 ac. About 7% of those in California and nearly 5% of those in the nation exceeded 1,000 ac. But all farm products sold averaged over $43,000 per farm in California (1964), nearly four times the national average of approximately $11,000.

Producers of citrus fruits, vegetables and nuts attempt through their specialized associations to control and regulate marketing. Even though irrigation reduces dependence on climate, the perishability of the crops places the producer at the mercy of the markets. The Farm bureau, Grange and Associated Farmers are strong organizations on the west coast.

Outside the Mormon areas, class distinctions are accentuated and dependence on transient labour is great. Tenants hold about the same social-economic position as owners. Transient labourers —largely Mexican—are the lowest in the social scale. Although the areas have excellent schools, the children of migrant workers are handicapped in obtaining a good education and in becoming integrated into the communities in which their families work.

8. Other Areas.—The cutover area of the Great Lakes states is often classified as part of the dairy areas, but it is more like the general and self-sufficing areas. New sources of income have been opened up by tourist and recreation industries, and a large proportion of the rural nonfarm inhabitants are dependent on off-farm work, especially in the mines and woods. There low farm incomes are associated with a high birth rate; a considerable proportion of the people are foreign-born.

The tobacco-growing counties of Kentucky, Tennessee, Virginia, North Carolina and Maryland stand out on the map as areas outside the seven major regions. In these areas people are dependent on the intensive cultivation of the cash tobacco crop mixed with the crop of the surrounding major type-of-farming region. Tobacco requires a great deal of carefully directed labour for preparing the soil, seeding, transplanting, cultivation, harvesting, curing and marketing. These operations set the rhythm of life for the areas. Otherwise, the life of the people resembles that of the general and self-sufficing areas.

The Gulf coast fringe and much of Florida is the largest subarea outside the seven major type-of-farming regions. There sugar cane, citrus fruits and vegetables are grown. The areas resemble the western specialty-crop areas, especially in the need for transient labour. Small family operations are common. The Atlantic seaboard portion is a small but important vegetable-producing section. Noted for its potato production, the northern portion of Maine also falls outside the seven major regions. Another such area, on the northern Pacific coast, includes commercial orchards, part-time farming operations for rural nonfarm dwellers and dairy enterprises. Potatoes, sugar beets, peanuts, rice and dry beans are grown under varying conditions in small enclaves scattered throughout the other regions.

BIBLIOGRAPHY.—Everett E. Edwards, *Bibliography of the History of Agriculture in the United States* (1930). For detailed description and analysis of agriculture before 1860, see Percy W. Bidwell and John I. Falconer, *History of Agriculture in the Northern United States, 1620–1860* (1925); Lewis C. Gray and E. K. Thompson, *History of Agriculture in the Southern United States to 1860*, 2 vol. (1933). For land policy see Roy M. Robbins, *Our Landed Heritage: the Public Domain, 1776–1936* (1950); E. Louise Peffer, *The Closing of the Public Domain: Disposal and Reservation Policies, 1900–50* (1951). For agriculture in the setting of economic history and regional history see Henry David et al., *Economic History of the United States*, particularly vol. v, Fred A. Shannon, *The Farmer's Last Frontier: Agriculture, 1860–1897* (1945); Ray A. Billington and J. B. Hedges, *Westward Expansion: a History of the American Frontier* (1949); A. M. Tang, *Economic Development in the Southern Piedmont, 1860–1950* (1958); Edward C. Higbee, *American Oasis: the Land and Its Uses* (1957); James H. Copp, *Our Changing Rural Society* (1964); U.S. Department of Agriculture, *Information Bulletin No. 3*, "Generalized Types of Farming in the United States—Including a List of Counties in Type-of-Farming Regions and Subregions," by Sherman E. Johnson et al. (1950), *Information Bulletin No. 30*, "Guide to Agriculture, U.S.A.," by Arthur F. and Martha J. Raper (1951), Yearbooks of Agriculture, *After A Hundred Years* (1962), *Farmers World* (1964); U.S.D.A.-E.R.S. *Agricultural Economic Report No. 101*, "Rural People in American Economy" (1966).

(C. P. Ls.; P. W. G.; J. K. R.)

III. COMMONWEALTH OF NATIONS

A. THE UNITED KINGDOM

1. Early and Medieval Times.—The first food producers in Britain were the peoples who arrived about the middle of the 3rd millennium B.C. bringing seeds of cereals—and their accompanying weeds. They probably cleared patches of ground by burning the vegetation and scattered their seeds among the ashes; there is no evidence of the use of hoes or other implements. They kept cattle, pigs and a smaller number of sheep and goats. Their Bronze Age successors (c. 1500 B.C. onward) were pastorally minded. Sheep predominated over pigs and were relatively abundant in the early Iron Age. The Bronze Age people in Europe used the ard or scratch plow. It is not known when this reached Britain but its presence is indicated by the spread of small, rectangular, "Celtic" fields in the last phase of the Bronze Age. No remains, however, have been found. Ards and Celtic fields were in full use during the pre-Roman Iron Age (450 B.C.–A.D. 54) and persisted throughout the Roman period (into the 5th century). Meanwhile plows with iron shares had been brought in, perhaps by the Belgae (50 B.C. onward); they are associated with long rectangular fields. Probably both systems were in operation in Roman times, the ard being used by the peasants and the plow by the villa farmers.

Sir Mortimer Wheeler's estimate of 1,000,000 inhabitants at the height of the Roman period implies a cultivated area of about 2,000,000 ac.—a considerable proportion of the more easily culti-

vable land then available. There followed a period of decay. Recovery began under the Anglo-Saxons who made many clearings in the forests for their village settlements. By the end of the 11th century agriculture had developed sufficiently to carry a population of about 4,000,000. Over much of the country—Wessex, the midlands, Lindsey and Deira—the arable land was in large unenclosed areas called open fields. These were divided into three or, on heavy soils, two sections, and each peasant's holding was in a number of strips scattered in such a way that he had approximately an equal area in each section. In the eastern districts of the country—Kent, much of Essex and probably East Anglia—each of the original settlers had his own compact area which, however, became much subdivided by inheritance. The chief crop was winter-sown bread grain (wheat where possible, but rye in wet districts with acid soils), or oats in the north. This was usually followed by a spring-sown crop of barley, peas or beans. A fallow period was then necessary. On heavy soils the fallow might be needed in alternate years. All strips in the same section carried the same crop, and the rotation went round the two or three sections.

The livestock grazed on the stubbles after harvest and on the untended common land, each eligible person having his allowance or "stint" of animals. There was, however, insufficient food to carry all the animals over the winter, and a number had to be slaughtered and salted down in the autumn when, as Thomas Tusser wrote in his *Five Hundreth Pointes of Good Husbandry* (1573), the husbandman's feasting began. The management was communal and it was almost impossible to effect changes, however desirable they might be.

The manorial system of the Normans after the Conquest gave farms to the lord of the manor and to the monasteries. On some of these farms, especially the monastic ones, improvements were made, but in general the system was static. Not infrequently a man's aggregate holding in the three fields would be about 30 ac., one-third being in wheat yielding approximately 10 bu. per acre; 2 bu. would be needed for seed leaving 8 bu. per acre, or, reckoning the weight of a bushel at 60 lb. (later it rose to 62-63 lb.), about 4,800 lb. for his disposal, reduced, however, by harvesting losses. But there were often local failures and records of hunger are not infrequent.

The peasants held their land from the lord of the manor and owed him certain obligations, though, as Walter of Henley (13th century) shows in *Le Dite de Hosebondrie*, they had their ways of evasion and deceit. Gradually changes set in, hastened by the Black Death of 1348–49. Villeins commuted their services for cash and so became free to leave the village. Enclosures began and by the time of Queen Elizabeth I were already causing concern as peasants suffered through the loss of grazing rights. However, the enclosed land was in individual farms managed by their owners (or by a tenant) and improvements could thus be introduced.

2. The Era of Improvement.—By the 17th century the south of France and Flanders each had well-developed and productive systems of agriculture. Sir Richard Weston, a royalist landowner in Surrey who fled to Flanders during the Great Rebellion, learned something of these methods and described them in a letter to his sons which Samuel Hartlib published under his own name in 1650 as *A Discours of Husbandrie*, though acknowledging Weston's authorship in the enlarged edition of 1651 (*His legacie*). The methods included a four-year rotation: first flax, next turnips, and then oats undersown with clover. This produced so much food for the animals that larger numbers could be kept in better condition providing more meat and more manure, thus greatly enriching the soil. Improvement became a mounting spiral: more crops gave more manure which in turn gave still more crops.

In the south of France Jethro Tull had seen cultivation implements which suggested to him the idea of the seed drill whereby the turnips could be sown in rows and kept free from weeds by hoeing, thus much increasing their yield. In 1730 Charles Townshend, 2nd Viscount Townshend (1674-1738), retired from political life to Raynham, Norfolk, and, adopting these improvements, worked out a new farming technique including the four-course rotation of crops. Thomas Coke, earl of Leicester, elaborated it from 1778 onward and made it into a highly productive system.

Meanwhile Robert Bakewell (*q.v.*; 1725–95) of Dishley near Loughborough had been carrying out his famous experiments on the improvement of livestock by selective breeding. He had the vision of the perfection he wished to attain and an artist's eye for recognizing the animals he should use. He developed the Leicester breed of sheep and stimulated Charles Colling of Ketton near Darlington to improve the Shorthorn breed of cattle (*see* CATTLE; SHEEP).

A flourishing period began about 1780. Agricultural improvements became the fashionable occupation of great landowners and King George III had his own model farm at Windsor. A board of agriculture was set up that organized the most complete set of agricultural surveys of Great Britain ever made. Its secretary was Arthur Young (*q.v.*), whose vivid accounts of his farming tours in England, Ireland and France are classics. Sir John Sinclair, the president of the board, arranged a detailed survey of Scotland. The surveys revealed considerable differences in farming efficiency in different parts of the country, but also showed where and how improvements had been made.

Then came the French Revolutionary and Napoleonic Wars (1793–1815) during which 14 bad harvests and only 2 really good ones forced wheat prices up to a height that stimulated further improvement. After the wars came a long period of severe depression when many farms were abandoned and their occupants ruined. These included a large number of freeholders of small farms, which in many instances had been in their families for generations. England became a land of large estates and tenant farmers.

3. Victorian Prosperity.—Recovery began in the late 1830s. The Royal Agricultural society, founded in 1838 and incorporated by royal charter in 1840, exerted a great influence by its shows, its premiums for high-quality animals and useful inventions, its journal and its advisory staff. In 1842 John Bennet Lawes of Rothamsted (*see* ROTHAMSTED EXPERIMENTAL STATION) set up the first fertilizer factory, greatly facilitating the enrichment of the soil. Methods of drainage were developed and agricultural implements and machines were improved. The new iron plows were lighter than the wooden ones and could be drawn by a pair of horses instead of the larger team, often of slow-moving oxen. They could, moreover, do the work more easily and at a greater speed. The yield of wheat, which had risen from about 10 bu. an acre to 20 bu. through the improvements of the late 18th century, rose still further to about 30 bu. an acre. By the 1860s British agriculture was so productive that visitors came from overseas to admire and to learn.

4. Depression and Its Aftermath.—In the late 1870s came a collapse. The North American prairies were opened up by the completion of the transcontinental railways and linked by steamer services to British ports. Wheat, the most easily managed crop for the pioneer farmers, began to pour into British markets. Its price fell from 58s. 8d. per imperial quarter (480 lb.) in 1873 to 31s. in 1886 and 22s. 10d. in 1894; 1879 was the wettest season and its harvest the most disastrous that farmers had ever known. Then came the shattering blow. Throughout the years prices of meat had generally been high when those of corn were low and vice versa: "Down horn, up corn" was an old adage. But in 1882 a refrigerator vessel brought the first frozen mutton and lamb from New Zealand to England, and in the following year frozen beef began to arrive from the Argentine. The quantities rapidly increased, and the selling prices were so low that British farmers could not compete. They asked for protection by tariff but this ran counter to the political theories of the time.

In this long run of bleak depression two periods were especially bad: 1875–84 and 1891–99. During each of these a commission of inquiry was held, each made very gloomy reports, especially the second, for in the interval the value of farm produce had fallen by nearly one-half while the cost of production had, if anything, risen. This second period was one of the saddest in the history of the countryside; it crushed out of existence those many conscientious farmers who regarded themselves as trustees of the land with the duty of leaving it in at least as good a condition as they had found it, and if possible, better. Their motto had been "Live as

if you are going to die tomorrow, but farm as if you are going to live for ever." They tried but went bankrupt.

Thousands of acres in Essex and other wheat-growing districts became derelict. Farm rents had to be reduced so much that landlords could no longer maintain buildings or drainage systems in proper order and were fain to make a little money by accepting shooting tenants. The board of agriculture was re-established in 1889 but achieved little. A high official was heard later to say that British agriculture was dead and the business of the board was to give it a decent burial. Certain advanced politicians thought that it was in any case superfluous: food could be imported more cheaply than it could be produced in Britain; it could be paid for by British manufactures and the land could be used for recreation by the people.

Salvation came from within the farming industry. It was the grain farmers who had suffered most; the grass farmers producing milk and meat were less affected. British meat was of higher quality than imported, and a sophisticated urban population then emerging was prepared to pay a higher price for it. A number of young farmers from the west of England and from Scotland, hear-

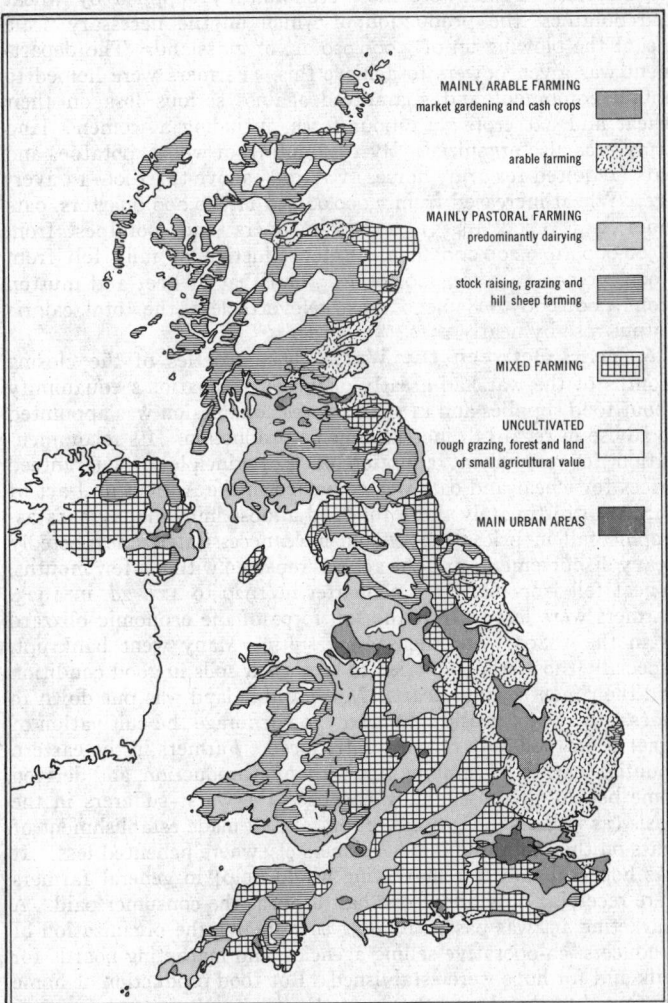

AGRICULTURAL AREAS OF THE UNITED KINGDOM

ing of derelict farms in Essex to be had for little or no rent, took them and started producing milk and potatoes for London and other towns. There was no overseas competition, and the rising standard of living was creating new and expanding markets. Arable farming gave place to low-level grass farming. There had been 14,900,000 ac. of arable land in England and Wales in 1871, but only 12,100,000 in 1901. The area of grassland, however, rose from 11,400,000 to 15,400,000 ac., an additional 1,200,000 ac. having been recorded. With the shrinkage of arable land came a fall in the number of workers required. The numbers of cattle rose from 4,270,000 to 5,530,000 while those of sheep fell from 20,230,000 to 19,000,000.

Agricultural education had greatly expanded. More and better machinery was becoming available and prices were improving. By about 1909 tenants were seeking farms and by 1912 rents were rising from their subeconomic level. When A. D. Hall made his well-known tours in 1910, 1911 and 1912 he found much good farming and quiet prosperity. The Agricultural Holdings acts gave farmers sufficient security to justify their spending money on improvements. Hall was, however, critical of the "low mental calibre" of some of the farmers and noted with regret the poverty of the workers: wages were low, hours long and holidays few. There was as yet no trade union to look after the interests of the farm labourers.

5. World War I.—For the first two years of the war there was little interference with food supplies, but by the end of 1916 the depredations of German submarines were creating a very serious situation. A food production department was therefore set up with T. H. Middleton as its technical director. The basic need was for calories. These were most economically supplied by wheat and potatoes, the production of which on the necessary scale meant the plowing up of 3,000,000 ac. of grassland. The department was given powers to achieve this. Farmers were helped to obtain equipment and guaranteed against serious loss on their wheat and oat crops; a labour force, including a women's land army, was also organized. By 1918 output of wheat, potatoes and oats (required for army horses) was 50% above the 1909–13 average. Wheat increased from 7,000,000 to 11,600,000 quarters, oats from 21,600,000 to 31,500,000 quarters and potatoes from 6,500,000 to 9,200,000 tons. But production of milk fell from 1,900,000,000 to 1,500,000,000 gal., and that of beef and mutton from 1,000,000 to 830,000 tons. Nevertheless, the total calorie output rose by nearly 25%.

6. Years Between the Wars.—The anxieties of the closing months of the war had greatly disturbed the nation's equanimity about food supplies and in 1919 a royal commission was appointed to advise in regard to increased home production. Its recommendation for permanent adoption of the principle of guaranteed prices for wheat and oats was embodied in the Agricultural act of 1920. Unfortunately there followed almost immediately a catastrophic fall in prices that would have necessitated unexpectedly heavy disbursements and the act was repealed within a few months. Wheat fell from 80s. 10d. a quarter in 1920 to 42s. 2d. in 1923. Farmers were left to bear the full force of the economic blizzard as in the 1880s, with the same results. Many went bankrupt, especially those who had tried to keep their soils in good condition and their men in good heart. Much arable land was put down to grass. In 1925 a subsidy was given to encourage the cultivation of sugar beet, then only recently introduced. Farmers in the eastern counties learned to combine this with milk production, and derived some benefit thereby. They had been the worst sufferers in the crisis (as in the 1880s) because low rainfall made establishment of grass on their land difficult. Farmers elsewhere benefited less. It was hoped that better marketing would help; in general farmers were receiving only about one-half of what the consumer paid. A marketing act was passed in 1931 encouraging the organization of producers' co-operative selling agencies, and marketing boards for milk and for hops were established. But food production at home continued to shrink and the international situation was deteriorating. The drastic step was therefore taken of abandoning the old policy of free trade in food adopted in 1846, and substituting instead some degree of control. Horticultural products were subjected to a tariff, bacon imports were restricted, wheat had a guaranteed price and sugar production a subsidy. Even these measures did not suffice, however, for prices continued to fall and land to go out of arable cultivation. By 1938 the arable area was down to 8,880,000 ac., the lowest on record. In May 1939, therefore, the further step was taken of giving a subsidy of £2 an acre for all grassland seven or more years old converted to arable. Subsidies were given also for various land improvements including the application of lime and fertilizers.

7. World War II.—By Sept. 1939 each county had an agricultural committee and one or more trained agricultural advisers, while nearly all farmers were enrolled in the National Farmers' union. Organization for production was therefore simpler than in 1914. No food production department was set up. Instead there were county agricultural war committees with the ministry of agriculture in general charge. Each county was given a target. Much rehabilitation of the farms was needed to repair the losses of the previous 15 years and much land had to be reclaimed. The committees were empowered to do this and any other necessary work that the farmers could not undertake. They could also impose cropping programs and remove unco-operative farmers. The expenditure was colossal but the food was produced.

8. British Agriculture After World War II.—The profound political, social and economic changes consequent to the war revolutionized British agriculture. The old sense of national security disappeared. It was felt that the country could no longer rely on importing so much of its food; much more must be produced at home, and agriculture must be maintained in such efficient condition that expansion could be rapidly achieved should the need arise.

Previous periods of depression had proved very costly. That of the 1880s had swallowed up the reserves accumulated in the 1860s and 1870s, and when World War I broke out heavy government grants for re-equipment became necessary to carry out the food-production program. But this and much privately owned capital was lost in the depression of the 1920s, and rehabilitation and re-equipment on a large scale at government expense were needed in World War II. Further, difficulties about balance of payments were compelling agriculture to become more self-supporting and to reduce imports of foods for livestock. The new policy necessitated the continued cultivation of marginal and hill land, and also keeping many marginal farmers in business with farm subsidies and control of food imports. No control was imposed on farmers, but agricultural production was steered by a system of support prices (subject to annual review) that applied to about 80% of the total produce. The change in utilization of land is shown in Table VI.

Another result of World Wars I and II was a radical change in the structure of village life. The landowning and county families were so impoverished that estates had to be broken up and many farmers were compelled to purchase their holdings, raising the money on long-term loans far more costly than rents and having imposed on them charges and obligations previously borne by the landlord. The growth of urbanism and industrialization continued to take land from agriculture, at first with but little control. In the 1930s the loss had been estimated at 60,000 ac. a year but this caused so much apprehension that a ministry of town and country

TABLE VI.—*United Kingdom: Utilization of Land**
(in 000,000 ac.)

Type of land	England and Wales		United Kingdom	
	1939	1965	1939	1965
Arable land	8.93	14.13	12.91	18.52
Permanent grass	15.71	10.22	18.77	12.14
Total cultivated	24.64	24.36	31.68	30.66
Rough grazing	5.54	4.83	16.54	17.83
Total agriculture	30.18	29.19	48.22	48.49
Nonagriculture	7.16	6.95	11.93	11.05
Total all land	37.34	37.13	60.15	59.54

*Due to rounding of figures the parts do not necessarily add up to the totals.
Source: Ministry of Agriculture, Fisheries and Food, Guildford, Eng.

planning was set up and given considerable power of action. The average net loss per year for 1939–57 was approximately 22,000 ac.; the overall net loss for the same period was approximately 360,000 ac.

This might be less serious than it appears since no account was taken of holdings of less than one acre, some of which were very productive. After 1957 the trend was reversed. In the 1960s the lands in agriculture exceeded slightly the total in 1939, but with arable land much increased and permanent grass sharply reduced (Table VI).

Motors and tractors replaced horses, farming became highly mechanized and the work was speeded up. A plowman with horses usually plowed less than an acre a day; with a tractor he could do from half an acre to two acres an hour. More timely sowing and planting thus became practicable, in many instances increasing the yields, especially of cereals, sugar beet and potatoes. Harvesting was similarly expedited, thereby saving much grain in bad weather. Mechanization was much more economical of man power: one man for 25 ac. was needed for a horse-drawn reaper; with a tractor and combine one man sufficed for 100 ac.

TABLE VII.—*United Kingdom: Area and Production of Chief Crops*

Crop	1939		1965	
	(in 000,000 ac.)	(in 000,000 tons)	(in 000,000 ac.)	(in 000,000 tons)
Wheat . . .	1.86	1.65	2.54	3.73
Barley . . .	0.93	0.76	5.39	7.40
Oats . . .	2.40	1.94	1.01	1.32
Sugar beets . .	0.33	2.74	0.45	6.22
Potatoes . .	0.72	4.87	0.74	6.95
Fodder roots* .	—	—	0.39	8.43
Meadow hay† .	4.92	5.00	3.08	4.22

*Includes: turnips, swedes, fodder beets, mangels. †Of permanent meadows only.
Source: Ministry of Agriculture, Fisheries and Food, Guildford, Eng.

and the grain was not only reaped but threshed. Wages rose accordingly; for the 1964–65 season, agricultural workers in the U.K. averaged £12 15s. 9d. weekly. The numbers of regular workers on the farms of Great Britain fell from 600,000 in 1939 to 527,800 after World War II, and 402,300 in June 1966, but the value of the output rose.

After World War II farming efficiency increased the output in spite of the loss of land and workers. Full advantage was being taken of educational and advisory services (*see* AGRICULTURAL EDUCATION AND RESEARCH). Crops and seeds were improved at plant-breeding stations at Cambridge (cereals and others), Aberystwyth (grasses and clovers), Pentlandfields (potatoes) and by some of the seed firms. Much help was provided by the National Institute of Agricultural Botany at Cambridge. Fertilizers were more extensively employed.

In terms of plant nutrients the quantities used (1964, prewar figures in parentheses) were: nitrogen 576,000 tons (60,000); phosphate 467,000 (170,000); and potash 420,000 tons (75,000). Weeds, pests and diseases were more effectively controlled by the new products of technological organic chemistry and yields continued to rise. The average yield in hundredweights per acre of wheat rose from 17.8 before World War II to 33.0 in 1964, that of barley from 16.5 to 29.4 and that of oats from 16.1 to 23.6. An efficient farmer obtained considerably higher yields (*see* Table VII). The output from grassland did not increase so much as from the arable, although investigations at Aberystwyth, Hurley, Jealott's Hill and elsewhere showed great possibilities.

The management of livestock improved. Artificial insemination was raising the quality of animals. Fuller knowledge of the nutri-

tional requirements in the various phases of the lives of animals led to improvements in their rations. Concentrated foods can be fortified with the necessary minerals and vitamins, and farmers can adequately control the supplies of carbohydrates and protein equivalent. Milking parlours facilitated the clean handling of milk and the adjustment of food to performance, besides saving labour. Inoculations, modern insecticides and vermicides and more efficient management improved the health of the animals and reduced wastage. Tuberculosis and mastitis were eliminated from many herds although foot-and-mouth disease continued to give trouble.

In consequence of these better conditions animal performance improved: the average gross yield per cow in milk-selling herds rose from 2,185 kg. in 1938–39 to 3,680 kg. in 1964, and the total production from 5,043,908 to 13,375,000 metric tons.

The numbers of livestock in the United Kingdom in the mid-1960s (1964), with totals for England and Wales only shown in parentheses, were: cattle 11,627,000 (8,475,000); sheep 29,657,-000 (over 14,000,000); pigs 7,379,000 (5,708,000); and poultry 118,377,000 (88,832,000).

The gross value of the annual agricultural output before 1939 was estimated at £290,000,000 and in 1965 at £1,796,900,000. The net output rose by about 60%. Whereas just before the war some two-thirds of the volume of United Kingdom's total food supplies were imported, by the mid-1960s, about half were produced domestically, and for a substantially larger population. Output approximately double the pre-war level had been stimulated by carefully planned Exchequer support in the form of price guarantees as well as direct grants and subsidies, amounting to an annual total in the mid-1960s of about £300,000,000. Schemes to reduce subsidy costs included a doubling by 1970 of the rate of small farm amalgamations.

BIBLIOGRAPHY.—J. G. D. Clark, *Prehistoric Europe: the Economic Basis* (1952); J. and C. Hawkes, *Prehistoric Britain* (1953); Lord Ernle, *English Farming, Past and Present,* 5th ed. (1936); C. S. and Christabel S. Orwin, *The Open Fields* (1938); A. D. Hall, *A Pilgrimage of British Farming* (1913); T. H. Middleton, *Food Production in War* (1923); *National Farm Survey of England and Wales* (1946); J. A. S. Watson *et al.*, *Agriculture,* 11th ed. (1962); Sir E. John Russell, *World Population and World Food Supplies* (1954); "Changes in Britain's Agriculture—Government Policy and Farm Output," *Midland Bank Review* (August 1964); county surveys by the Royal Agricultural society; *Agricultural Statistics* (annually, compiled from farmers' returns).

B. CANADA

1. General.—Most of Canada is physiographically unsuited to agriculture, and climatic factors restrict it chiefly to the southern regions. The Precambrian shield occupying more than half the country and the Cordilleran region occupying about 20% contain little land suitable for arable cultivation. The main agricultural areas of eastern Canada lie south of the shield, roughly south of latitude 45° N; and those of western Canada are the great plains between the shield and the Rockies, mainly south of

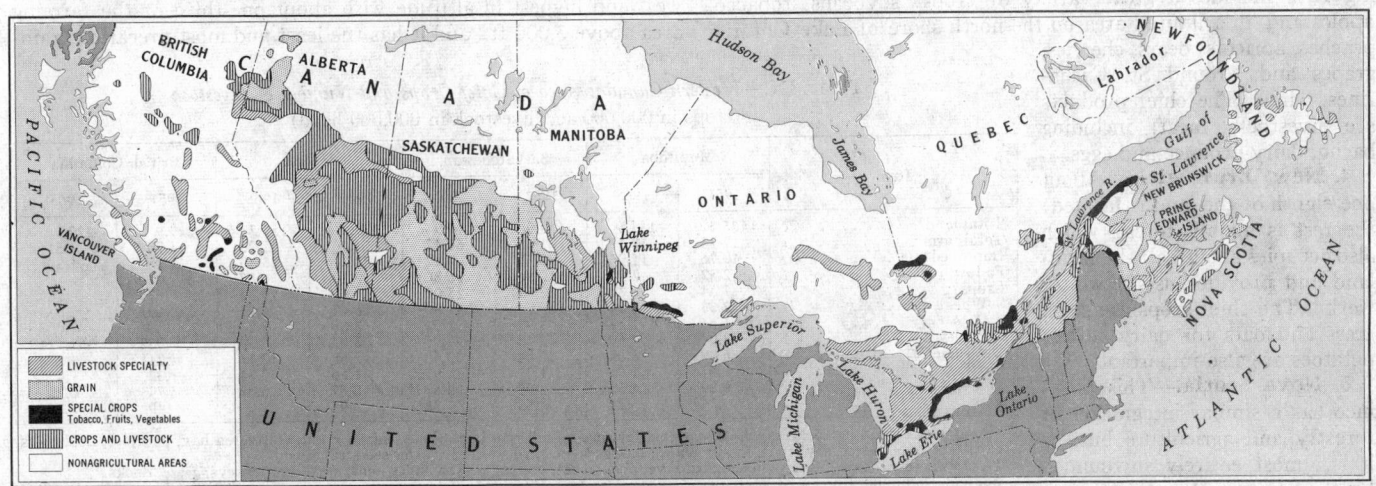

GENERALIZED AGRICULTURAL AREAS OF CANADA

TABLE VIII.—*Eastern Canada: Area of Chief Crops and Numbers of Livestock*
(crops in 000,000 ac.; livestock in 000,000 head)

Item	Ontario		Quebec		New Brunswick		Nova Scotia		Prince Edward Island	
	1951	1965	1951	1965	1951	1965	1951	1965	1951	1965
Total land*	213.7	220.22	335.3	335.27	17.58	17.81	13.28	13.06	1.40	1.40
Total farm*	20.88	18.57	16.79	14.20	3.47	2.20	3.17	2.23	1.10	.96
Improved*	12.69	12.03	8.83	7.86	1.01	.73	.662	.498	.646	.580
Crops†	8.65	7.55	5.79	4.89	.71	.441	.477	.281	.426	.378
Wheat	.75	.38	.012	.012	.003	.006	.0012	.0012	.0047	.0038
Oats	1.75	1.58	1.40	1.16	.175	.086	.062	.031	.100	.089
All cereals‡	3.84	3.64	1.69	1.30	.199	.107	.077	.043	.181	.152
Cultivated hay	3.41	3.10	3.65	3.41	.441	.275	.345	.229	.204	.181
Improved pasture*	3.24	3.30	2.69	2.31	.243	.200	.155	.127	.198	.168
Cattle	2.47	3.22	1.64	1.73	.162	.127	.166	.145	.098	.121
Poultry§	24.77	23.85	10.58	16.38	1.28	.989	1.67	2.180	1.03	.305
Pigs	1.76	1.96	1.11	.91	.0078	.039	.048	.062	.072	.072

*Figures of 1961. †Includes wheat, oats, barley, mixed grain, potatoes, cultivated hay, field roots, fall rye, buckwheat, peas, beans, fodder maize, maize, sugar beets, flaxseed, soybeans. ‡Includes wheat, barley, oats, mixed grain, maize, rye, buckwheat. §Includes hens, chickens, turkeys, geese, ducks.

Source: Dominion Bureau of Statistics, *Canada Yearbook 1965, Quarterly Bulletin of Agricultural Statistics (Jan.–March 1966), Livestock and Animal Products Statistics* (1965).

latitude 55° N, with some possibilities of extension as far north as latitude 62° N.

Eastern Canada was the first part of the British empire to be developed agriculturally. The first settlers were French *émigrés* of the 17th and 18th centuries. Starting from the rivers, the chief means of communication, they cut their farms out of the forest, so founding the linkage of agriculture and forestry still so important in the eastern provinces. The farming at first was necessarily for subsistence; as the population increased, more forest had to be cleared and more farm produce was sold.

2. Quebec.—Most of the farming is still in the hands of the French *habitants,* and much of its old pattern survives, but with great improvements. About 96% of the province is forest and waste for reasons stated above, and of the 4% in farms (most of which lie south of the St. Lawrence river) only about half is in crops or tended grassland. Forest and grass constitute the natural vegetation, and the farmland includes both. About 60% of the sown area is grass lea usually left down for four years, followed by two years of cereal crops, chiefly oats, leaving only about 8% for other crops including fodder crops, potatoes and, in favoured districts, apples.

Livestock thus became the chief interest, and butter, cheese, eggs and meat the chief products. This type of husbandry is well suited to the small farms that the social structure encourages; three-quarters of them are between 10 and 180 ac. The forest provides work during the winter.

3. Ontario.—This province was settled later, chiefly by the British. Its climate is milder than that of Quebec and productivity is greater. But the agricultural pattern is broadly similar in the two provinces, for both are naturally grass and forest regions. About 90% of Ontario is in forest and waste, and of the area farmed only about 60% is arable and tended grassland. Approximately half the arable area is in cereals—chiefly oats and mixed grain with a little winter wheat—and 40% is in leas. The remaining 10% includes a great variety of crops: soybeans, tobacco, apples and, in a limited area on the north shore of Lake Ontario, peaches, apricots, pears, cherries, grapes and, around St. Catharines, wine. The chief products are livestock, meat, including bacon, dairy produce and eggs.

4. New Brunswick.—About one-eighth of the land is farmed; the rest is mainly forest, which also occupies about half the farmland and provides useful winter work. The chief crops are sown grass and oats for dairy cattle; potatoes are also important.

5. Nova Scotia.—This province has a similar integration of forestry and agriculture but, as it is almost entirely surrounded by the sea, the climate is better and yields are higher. The richest section is the Annapolis valley, where good-quality apples can be grown.

6. Prince Edward Island.—This is the most fully farmed of all the provinces, about 70% of the total land being utilized. About half the improved land is in grass and half in tillage; the system is mainly dairying combined with pig production and potato growing. Yields are high, in some years the highest in Canada. Farms are small, the average being about 100 ac., and there is considerable prosperity.

Crops and livestock of eastern Canada are shown in Table VIII.

7. Manitoba.—The agricultural history of western Canada differs completely from that of the east. The first settlers, brought into the Winnipeg district by the earl of Selkirk in 1812, tried to grow English winter wheat but failed. After four years of heroic effort and pitiful suffering the settlement was abandoned. Subsequently the Hudson's Bay company, to which the prairies had been assigned, transferred vast areas to the Canadian government in 1869 for £300,000. Later it was discovered that Red Fife wheat, a hard spring variety which was popular with the bakers and had gotten into Canada in 1842 by an almost incredible chain of accidents, grew well on the prairies and was indeed the only known type that would.

The opening of the transcontinental railway in the 1870s and 1880s made wheat farming practicable and a wheat-fallow system of farming entirely for market, fundamentally different from the system of eastern Canada, was adopted. The farms also were larger, usually 160 ac., and as labour-saving machinery was invented they became larger still: 640 ac. is usual.

8. Saskatchewan.—This province lies farther west and at a higher level than Manitoba. It has a higher evaporation rate and lower rainfall: about 18 in. a year in the east and 12 to 14 in. in the west, fortunately coming in late spring or early summer when the crop most needs it.

Plant breeders, agronomists and engineers have enabled Saskatchewan to achieve by far the largest acreage of wheat and other cereals of all the provinces, although yields are lower than those of Manitoba. (*See* Table IX.)

The general system is that a one-year fallow is followed by two cereal crops, the first being wheat while the second may be either wheat, oats or barley. An area in the south is particularly liable to dry seasons. The farms are large, commonly a section (640 ac.; *i.e.,* 1 sq.mi.) in area.

9. Alberta.—Of the three prairie provinces this is the farthest west and highest in altitude with about one-third of the farming area above 3,000 ft., and it has the least and most precarious rain-

TABLE IX.—*Western Canada: Area of Chief Crops and Number of Livestock*
(crops in 000,000 ac.; livestock in 000,000 head)

Item	Manitoba		Saskatchewan		Alberta		British Columbia	
	1951	1965	1951	1965	1951	1965	1951	1965
Total land*	135.5	135.5	140.9	140.9	159.2	159.2	229.9	229.9
Total farm*	17.73	18.17	61.66	64.42	44.46	47.23	4.70	4.51
Improved*	10.76	11.96	38.81	43.12	22.27	25.30	1.15	1.30
Fallow	2.52	2.90	12.86	16.80	6.19	6.88	.07	—
Crops†	7.34	8.30	23.71	25.02	14.43	16.32	.67	.76
Wheat	2.33	3.24	15.63	18.50	6.42	6.05	.101	.053
Oats	1.64	1.52	3.82	1.92	2.86	2.20	.103	.093
Barley	2.04	.60	2.45	1.75	3.04	3.39	.032	.124
All cereals‡	6.09	5.69	22.64	22.63	12.68	12.17	.241	.283
Cattle	.67	1.01	1.27	1.97	1.56	2.84	.32	.47
Poultry§	6.89	4.59	9.07	2.53	8.87	5.32	3.74	6.22
Pigs	.34	.44	.53	.38	.93	.38	1.20	.38

*Figures of 1961. †Includes wheat, oats, barley, maize, fall rye, buckwheat, mixed grain, cultivated hay, potatoes, field roots, sugar beets, peas, beans, soybeans, fodder maize, flaxseed, mustard seed, sunflower seed, rape seed. ‡Includes wheat, oats, barley, mixed grain, rye, buckwheat, maize. §Includes hens, chickens, turkeys, geese, ducks.

Source: Dominion Bureau of Statistics, *Canada Yearbook 1965, Quarterly Bulletin of Agricultural Statistics (Jan.–March, 1966), Livestock and Animal Products Statistics* (1965).

fall. In its western part the uncertainty is so great that cattle ranching replaces arable cultivation. The cropping system is very similar to that of Saskatchewan but yields are lower. The cattle are largely beef animals and many are sold as stockers and feeders to the United States.

The movement of wheat growing has been westward. In 1891, out of a total wheat area of 2,700,000 ac., 53% was in Ontario, 33% in Manitoba, and only 4% in Saskatchewan and Alberta together. During 1962–65 when the total average wheat area was 28,000,000 ac., less than 2% were in Ontario and about 12% in Manitoba, while Saskatchewan had 65% and Alberta 22%.

Considerable soil erosion had resulted, however, especially in Saskatchewan and Alberta. The virgin prairie soil usually had a good crumb structure formed during the long years of undisturbed vegetation. The continuous arable cultivation breaks the crumbs down to dust, which is easily blown away by the hot dry wind. This can be considerably checked by strip farming and tillage practices that retain most of the stubble on the surface. Some of the land, however, has suffered serious losses. Rehabilitation is effected by sowing suitable grasses followed by proper management of the resulting pasture.

10. British Columbia.—This province is a region of lumbering and fishing rather than cultivation. In some of its delightful valleys apples are grown and in others dairying is practised.

11. Canada's Agricultural Production.—The total area of wheat increased up to about 1928 but then remained fairly stable at about 24,000,000 ac. until World War II. It was pushed up to 28,000,000 ac. in 1940 and remained about 26,000,000 ac. until 1952 after which it began to fall. By 1957 it was down to 21,000,-000 ac. In 1962 it was up again at about 26,000,000 and by 1965 was back above 28,000,000 ac. The yield fluctuates from year to year between extremes of 7 and 26 bu. per acre depending on the rainfall. Usually it is between 15 and 20 bu. (between 8.3 and 11 cwt.) and there is no clear indication of any increase in spite of the great amount of good scientific work. Production fluctuates between about 8,500,000 and 25,300,000 tons a year. There is little possibility of irrigation and the climate remains the unconquered element determining production. The occasional high yields put a great strain on transport, storage and marketing services. The acreage of oats fell as tractors largely displaced horses.

Livestock is next to cereals in importance for Canada's agriculture. In the five years after 1960 (June) cattle increased from 11,337,000 to 13,001,000, about a third being milch animals; pigs dropped from 5,483,000 to 5,136,000. Poultry however were unchanged at about 75,500,000. The production of milk decreased from 8,384,485 metric tons to 8,310,671 metric tons, but the quantity used in manufacturing dairy products rose from 4,966,265 metric tons to 5,280,064 metric tons. About 63% was used for manufacturing in each year, most of it (71% in 1961 and 1963, 73% in 1962) for creamery butter, the output of which rose from 3,204,030 to 3,371,210 cwt. The production of dairy butter remained stable. Production of cheese rose from 1,388,960 to 2,483,-980 cwt., cheddar cheese increasing from 1,103,720 to 1,446,440 cwt. and the amount of milk going into the various concentrated forms, particularly evaporated milk, increased from 249,098 to 260,131 metric tons.

Canada plays a vital part in the feeding of Great Britain and the question was arising as to whether its agriculture could expand sufficiently to continue supplies despite its own growing population. In the survey of 1961 the total land area of 2,278,-552,000 ac. was used as follows: total farm area 172,551,000 ac.; improved (i.e., tended land) 103,403,000 ac.; under crops and summer fallow 90,679,000 ac.; pasture (a) "improved" 10,247,900 ac., (b) unimproved 42,101,800 ac.; and woodland 17,247,400 ac. Less than 8% of the total area is in farms and it is not clear that this could be much increased. Perhaps another 200,000,000 ac. could be utilized if the causes of their infertility could be discovered and remedied. A more hopeful prospect would be to increase the area of improved land; i.e., arable and tended grassland on the farms. In 1941 this had been 91,600,000 ac. and within 20 years it had increased to 103,403,000 ac.: it remained,

however, only 58% of the total farm area. The demands of urban and industrial expansion in eastern Canada were absorbing more and more useful land from farms. From 1951 to 1961 there was a net loss in farm area of about 1,500,000 ac.

Progress with irrigation continued and in the 1960s projects in Alberta and Saskatchewan together would provide water for more than 1,000,000 ac. Community pasture development included some 2,500,000 ac. Optimistic estimates were that in addition to present arable lands as much as 40,000,000 ac. of virgin land could be developed for arable crops if needed. Consumption of fertilizer increased, and in 1965 in terms of plant food was: nitrogen 170,707 metric tons; phosphate 266,491 metric tons; and potash 122,838 metric tons. Herbicides were increasingly effective against weeds, which had often reduced cereal yields.

BIBLIOGRAPHY.—A. R. Ross, *The Red River Settlement* (1856); A. H. R. Buller, *Essays on Wheat* (1919); Montell Ogdon, "Canadian Agriculture; Its Competitive Position," U. S. Department of Agriculture-Foreign Agricultural Service, Report No. 110 (1958); *The Canada Year Book; Census Returns* (agricultural section).

C. Australia

1. General Survey.—The agriculture of Australia is both modern and exotic. Everything had to be introduced, much of it within living memory. The older agricultural exports were wheat and wool from the fine-wooled Merino sheep introduced by John Macarthur in the 1790s. Later, as refrigerator transport developed, dairy products, fruit and frozen meat were added. Later still the meat was chilled only, which improves its quality.

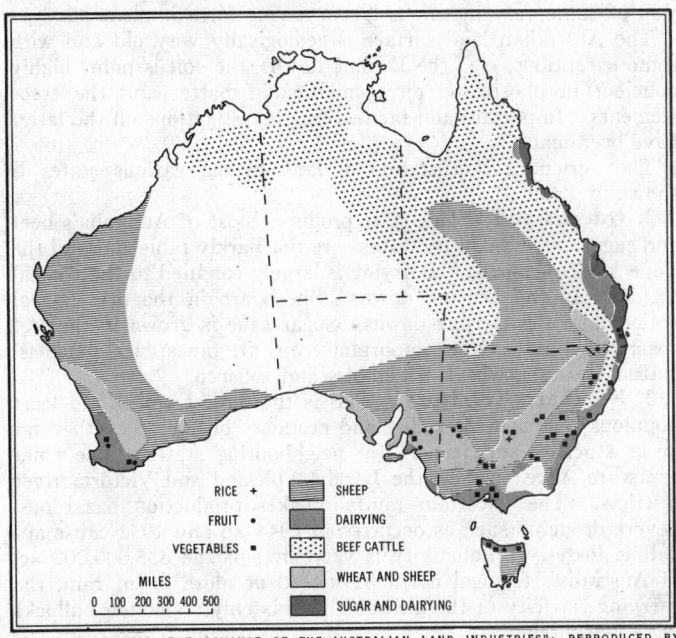

RICE +   SHEEP
FRUIT •   DAIRYING
VEGETABLES ▪   BEEF CATTLE
   WHEAT AND SHEEP
MILES   SUGAR AND DAIRYING
0 100 200 300 400 500

FROM R. D. WATT'S "THE ROMANCE OF THE AUSTRALIAN LAND INDUSTRIES"; REPRODUCED BY PERMISSION OF ANGUS & ROBERTSON LTD., SYDNEY

PRINCIPAL USES OF LAND IN AUSTRALIA

The northern part of Australia is tropical; the southern has a mediterranean climate. The rain in the southern part comes mostly during the winter months, from April to September, and is fairly reliable; in the northern part it comes chiefly in summer, from October to March, and is more erratic. It is highest—50 in. or more a year, 160 in. in the far north—on a narrow belt along the east coast. It decreases going inland; the inner core, two-thirds of the continent, has only 20 in. or less, and half of this area is desert or nearly so.

There is much intensive and varied farming in the well-watered coastal zone; fat-lamb production and dairying and, in places, fruit production are widely practised. In the adjacent inland zones (rainfall 15 to 25 in. yearly) farming is commonly restricted to wheat, barley and wool. The early settlers grew English varieties of wheat and suffered considerable losses until William Farrer in the 1880s and 1890s started breeding drought- and rust-

TABLE X.—*Australia: Area and Production of Chief Agricultural Products (1965)*

Area	Pop. (in 000,000)*	Area (in 000,000 ac.)	Area under crop (in 000,000 ac.)†	Area sown to pasture (in 000,000 ac.)‡	Wheat Area (in 000,000 ac.)	Wheat Production (in 000,000 U.S. bu.)	Sheep (in 000,000 head)	Cattle (in 000,000 head)
New South Wales§	4.23	199	10.01	11.17	5.76	156.4	72.40	4.60
Victoria	3.22	56	5.02	14.83	3.24	80.7	30.44	3.32
Queensland	1.66	427	3.87	3.44	1.03	23.6	24.02	7.39
South Australia	1.09	243	5.83	5.67	2.73	54.5	17.30	.70
Western Australia	.84	625	7.29	10.43	5.15	65.1	22.39	1.26
Tasmania	.37	17	.23	1.61	.02	.4	3.79	.45
Northern Territory	.04	333	.004	.01	—	—	.01	1.03
Total ‖	11.55	1,899	32.25	47.16	17.92	380.6¶	170.62	18.78

*1966 census.   †Excludes duplication on account of area double cropped for New South Wales and South Australia.   ‡Includes paspalum, clovers and grasses cut for hay and seed.   §Including Australian Capital Territory (Canberra, Jervis Bay).   ‖Because of rounding, parts do not necessarily add up to the totals.   ¶In 1964–65, about 206,645,000 U.S. bu. were exported.
Source: Department of Primary Industry, Canberra (1966); Commonwealth Bureau of Census and Statistics, *Pocket Compendium of Australia*, No. 51 (1966).

resistant varieties. This work has been continued with great success.

In the lower-rainfall regions Merino sheep are kept for wool production. The rate of stocking is low: from 5 to 30 ac. per head, and dams are constructed for storing water against the long dry periods. The farms or stations have to be very large, and while some of the older and more acessible ones are extremely pleasant habitations, many of the others suffer from being isolated. This is mitigated, however, by radio and by air transport.

Because of rainfall deficiencies only about 1.7% of the total area is sown, and another 2.5% is under improved pastures. The great areas involved and the low manpower have led to the invention of some very ingenious labour-saving farm implements.

The Australian land surface is geologically very old and with some exceptions, *e.g.*, the Darling downs, the soil is poor, highly deficient in phosphate, nitrogen, organic matter and the trace elements. Important and far-reaching investigations on the latter have been made.

The agricultural utilization of land in the various states is shown in Table X.

2. Queensland.—This state produces most of Australia's beef and sugar. The main beef areas are the Barkly tableland and the Cape York peninsula. Dairying is largely confined to the coastal regions and the Darling downs. Sheep are in the dry central regions and the Darling downs. Sugar cane is grown in the wet coastal sections. Other important crops are pineapples, bananas, cotton, peanuts, wheat, vegetables and tobacco.

3. Northern Territory.—This is the most tropical and least populous region in Australia and produces beef cattle either fat or as stockers and feeders for neighbouring states. The chief areas are Alice Springs, the Barkly tableland and Victoria river districts. The uncertain rainfall makes production hazardous. Severe droughts such as occurred in 1944–46 and 1952 cause appalling losses. Productivity is very low: of the 335,000,000 ac. of Australia's tropical north having 20 or more in. of rain, the carrying capacity of the utilizable land is only about ten bullocks per square mile.

4. New South Wales.—This is the most populous and productive of all the states, and produces half of Australia's wool, mainly in the central division and in the drier western districts of the Riverina. No food is grown for the sheep and the carrying capacity of the land is very low, being limited by the amount of native vegetation available during the hot dry summer. The stations have to be very large.

Much wheat is grown, chiefly in the 15- to 20-in. rainfall zones of the central region and in the Riverina. In the well-watered coastal belt there is considerable dairying, especially in the northern section of good summer rainfall. Bananas and citrus fruits are also grown. Of some 1,060,000 ac. irrigated in 1964, nearly one-half was in the Murray-Murrumbidgee basin, with sown pasture a major use.

5. Victoria.—Victoria is the chief dairying state. The dairying is carried on in the higher-rainfall areas of Gippsland and elsewhere, and on the irrigated pastures of the north. Much wool is produced on the western plains (rainfall 20 to 30 in.). After World War II Victoria had more land under irrigation than any other state (more than 1,100,000 ac. in the 1960s), partly because of its geographical position and partly because of the advocacy of Alfred Deakin, a former prime minister. Two-thirds of this area was under pasture, mainly for dairying, and the remainder under orchards, vines and market gardens. Important fruit-canning and grape-drying industries had been developed.

Victoria shares with New South Wales the Snowy mountains irrigation project, one of the most remarkable in the world since it involves decapitating the river which flows uselessly to the Tasman sea and diverting its headwaters into the Murray-Murrumbidgee irrigation system.

6. South Australia.—The chief products of this state are wool and cereals, especially barley, and in favoured districts dairy produce and fruit. The wine industry (about 20,000,000 gal. annually), established by British settlers from 1838 onward, was expanded in the Barossa valley in the 1850s by German immigrants.

Some 118,000 ac. were irrigated in 1964. Portions of the former Ninety Mile desert, barren in spite of suitable rainfall, were reclaimed in the second half of the 20th century, the sterility having been traced to deficiencies of phosphorus, copper, zinc and, in places, molybdenum. This was rectified and sheep grazing and dairying are successfully practised. The region has been renamed Coonalpyn downs. Once they were recognized, these deficiencies were found to be widespread in the southern coastal regions of Australia, and large areas have been reclaimed or improved.

7. Western Australia.—This is the newest state to be developed, chiefly in the southwest. The coastal region produces apples and other European fruits, in association with dairying and timber. The section of the tableland lying beyond and averaging about 1,000 ft. in altitude, with annual rainfall between 10 and 20 in., produces wheat and sheep in alternate husbandry.

8. Tasmania.—The island of Tasmania is Australia's chief exporter of apples and pears, produced with small fruit in the southern river basins. There is much mixed farming in the northern coastal area, including dairying and production of fat lambs, potatoes and vegetables; in the midlands and east coast region wool is the chief product. About half the island, however, is too mountainous or heavily timbered to be agriculturally or pastorally useful.

9. Further Development.—Australia's great difficulty is the widespread shortage of water. Only the Murray-Murrumbidgee basin is suited for large-scale irrigation. Queensland has a greater potential supply of water (runoff), but its rivers are very difficult to harness economically. By 1964 total capacity of large water storage was near 24,000,000 ac.-ft., triple that of a decade earlier. Lake Eucumbene in the Snowy mountains provided about one-sixth of the total. In all, more than 2,650,000 ac. were irrigated.

The 1949 marketing agreements and the fifteen year meat agreement of 1952 with the United Kingdom encouraged the export of meat. The 1964 United States-Australia meat agreement limits Australian meat exports to the United States; however, these limits are subject to modification in accordance with the increase of the United States meat market. The numbers of cattle rose from 14,500,000 during 1947 to 19,055,000 in 1964 and those of sheep from 111,000,000 to 164,981,000.

Except in the low-rainfall, unirrigated areas pasture improvement was progressing rapidly. By 1965, 47,160,000 ac. had been sown. Some useful grasses and other forage crops have been introduced, at first accidentally (*e.g.*, subterranean clover), but later on a planned scientific program. The rabbit population was for a time almost completely controlled by the myxomatosis virus liberated in 1950, but the older methods were having to be used again. The area under wheat fell from 13,000,000 ac. before

World War II to 7,900,000 in 1957, but as the yields had risen the total output did not correspondingly suffer. For a long period agricultural output appeared to stagnate but by 1965 Australia had brought a total of 32,250,000 ac. under crops and about tripled the wheat production of 1957.

BIBLIOGRAPHY.—A. R. Callaghan and A. J. Millington, *The Wheat Industry in Australia* (1956); M. H. Ellis, *John Macarthur* (1955); R. D. Watt, *Romance of the Australian Land Industries* (1955); D. B. Williams, *Economic and Technical Problems of Australia's Rural Industries* (1957); Sir S. M. Wadham and G. L. Wood, *Land Utilization in Australia*, 3rd ed. (1957); *Official Year Book of the Commonwealth of Australia;* Commonwealth Scientific and Industrial Research Organization, *The Australian Environment*, 2nd ed. (1949); Australian News and Information Bureau, Department of the Interior, *Official Handbook* (annual).

D. New Zealand

1. General.—The two main islands of New Zealand form a crescent about 1,100 mi. in length facing westward, but tilted somewhat to the northwest, and so narrow that no part is far from the sea. The north end is subtropical and produces citrus and other warm-climate products; the south end is cooler but still mild.

New Zealand has always been predominantly a pastoral country. In the mid-19th century the main product was wool for export to Great Britain. The invention of refrigerator transport in 1873 and its practical development in the 1890s permitted the much more lucrative export of lamb, dairy produce and fruit in addition to that of wool. Production difficulties during the 1920s led to the development of scientific services, and these, combined with labour-saving methods, greatly increased the value of the output from the land. The land is cultivated as shown in Table XI.

Production steadily increased. New Zealand became Britain's chief supplier of dairy produce, lamb and mutton, besides sending an important quantity of crossbred wool. Consumption of phosphatic and potassic fertilizers rose rapidly, and by 1965 was 298,400 tons of phosphate and 88,800 tons of potash, compared with

TABLE XI.—*New Zealand: Land Utilization* (1964)
(in 000,000 ac.)

Total occupied land area	Total area cultivated*	Area under field crops	Pasture land	Plantations	Fallow	Barren and unproductive land†
66.4	21.99	2.56	18.25	1.04	0.11	20.4

*Excludes areas in residences, private grounds, gardens, domestic orchards. †Includes land in cities, national parks, reserves, domains, state forest land, and wasteland such as mountains, bare rock, water surfaces, roads.
Source: New Zealand Department of Statistics, *New Zealand Official Yearbook 1965.*

pre-World War II averages of 102,000 and 6,000 tons, respectively. Consumption of nitrogenous fertilizers, 4,700 tons before World War II, was 7,300 tons in 1965. Over 1,000,000 ac. of exotic (planted) forests, mostly pines, are now capable of supplying merchantile produce. More than two-thirds of this crop is in the South Island. About 86% of the cattle and 56% of the sheep are in the North Island. Numbers of all livestock have continued to rise (*see* Table XII). On the other hand the acreage under wheat has fallen heavily but in the mid-1960s the total sown acreage again came close to the prewar figure and wheat production increased to 65% over the 1934–38 average (*see* Table XIII). Up to 1911 wheat was exported; after that imports increased to

TABLE XII.—*New Zealand: Livestock Production*

Item	1947–52 average	1964	Item	1947–52 average	1964
Total cattle (000,000 head) . .	4.96	6.70	Wool (000,000 lb.) . .	462	617
Milch cows (000,000 head) . .	1.85	2.01	Butter (000 tons)* .	200	231.5
Sheep (000,000 head) .	33.4	51.29	Cheese (000 tons) . .	96.3	95.1
Pigs (000,000 head) .	.564	.77	Lamb and mutton (000 tons) .	352	455.3
			Beef (000 tons) . .	225	266.2

*Creamery butter including 2,800 tons of whey-butter.
Source: New Zealand Department of Statistics, *New Zealand Official Yearbook 1965, Statistics of Farm Production 1965.*

about 8,000,000 bu. after World War II. Wheat imports in 1964 were down at 6,499,000 bu. Acreage and output of oats also fell; on the other hand production of barley increased to almost 700% of the prewar level.

New Zealand is famous for its highly productive small farms, but they occupy only a small proportion of the total area. In 1960, 55% of the farms were smaller than 200 ac. in size, whereas less than 9% of the units, holding 64% of the occupied land were 1,000 ac. and upwards in size.

2. North Island.—The North Island has the higher rainfall

TABLE XIII.—*New Zealand: Area and Production of Cereals**
(harvest of 1964)

Item	Wheat		Oats		Barley	
	1934–38	1964	1934–38	1964	1934–38	1964
Thousands of acres . .	215	203.96	65	26.57	22	93.98
Yield hundredweight per acre	16.9	26.44	15.8	20.80	16.6	27.43
Production (000 tons) . .	179	273.99	50	28.08	19	130.99

*Grain production only, not including pasture and fodder.
Source: New Zealand Department of Statistics, *Statistics of Farm Production 1965.*

(35 to 70 in.) and so little difference between summer and winter temperature that the cattle can be out all year. The soils are naturally poor, lacking phosphate, often lime, and some of the trace elements, cobalt, molybdenum and others; but they become extremely productive when the deficiencies are rectified. Some of the native tussock grasses, especially *Danthonia pilosa*, have a limited pastoral value, but perennial rye grass, cocksfoot and white clover introduced from Great Britain thrive amazingly, yielding 9,000 to 12,000 lb. or more dry matter per acre (even 16,000 lb. under spray irrigation) and making the grazing lands among the richest in the world.

The dairy farms are small: a usual range is from 50 to 200 ac. A hundred acres has been a common size but the tendency is toward the 150-ac. farm. Stocking is heavy—at least 60 or 70 and, on the best farms, 100 cows (mostly Jerseys) per 100 ac.—and so well mechanized and organized that where, as is usual, there is no hand stripping one man can look after 60 cows and two men after 100 to 120. The animals live almost entirely on grass—either green or as hay or silage. The yield of milk is usually about 350 to 400 gal. per acre, giving about 200 lb. of butterfat. Up to 400 lb. has, however, been obtained.

The cream may be separated on the farm and sent to the co-operative factory to be made into butter, the separated milk going to the pigs; or the whole milk may go to be made into cheese, milk powder, casein or other products.

New Zealand stands highest among the world's exporters of butter and cheese. These go chiefly to the United Kingdom. Fruit is grown in Hawke's Bay province.

Much of the North Island (about 20,000,000 out of 25,000,000 ac.) is hilly, even mountainous, and unsuited for dairy farming or, in its natural state, fat-lamb production. Spectacular improvements have, however, resulted from the application of superphosphate and trace elements by airplane, and where necessary also white clover seed. Farms at 1,000 ft. elevation can now produce fat lambs (Romney Marsh crossed with Southdown).

Several million acres of New Zealand's hill-country pastures are fertilized by aerial techniques; included are portions of the previously barren central volcanic plateau reclaimed by treatment with superphosphate and appropriate trace elements.

3. South Island.—The South Island is cooler and drier, the rainfall being about 25 to 45 in. in the settled areas. The northern part is very attractive with long hours of sunshine. It produces hops, tobacco, fruit and a variety of canning crops. The central part includes the 1,000,000-ac. Canterbury plains, where much of the land is arable, producing rape or leas for the fattening of lambs (Southdown crossed with Corriedale) and for maintaining the productivity of the land. High winds have caused erosion but this has been checked by erecting windbreaks.

In the far south (Otago district) grass farming using improved strains (*e.g.*, HI rye grass) has become more important. Fat lamb is the chief product; stone fruit is also grown. Much of the hill country is too dry for this system of husbandry, the rainfall being only 15 to 12 in. or less a year. It is in large holdings for Merino or crossbred sheep. The native vegetation is coarse and poor; production of wool is low but quality is high.

The Corriedale is an inbred half-breed, based on the Merino ewe and the English Long wool ram. It is a valuable dual-purpose animal (carcass and wool) whereas the Merino is kept only for its wool.

BIBLIOGRAPHY.—New Zealand .Department of Agriculture, *Farming in New Zealand* (1950), *Primary Production in New Zealand* (1957); F. R. Callaghan (ed.), *Science in New Zealand* (1957); Mary E. Long, "New Zealand's Agricultural Production, Marketing and Trade Policies and Their Bearing on U.S. Farm Exports," U.S. Department of Agriculture, *Foreign Agricultural Economics Report No. 9* (July 1963).

E. INDIA

1. General.—The agriculture of India is dominated by the amount and distribution of the rainfall. This comes mainly during the southwest monsoon, from June to September. It is highest (80 to 100 in. or more a year) in the region at the head of the Bay of Bengal and on a strip of the southwest coast. It is low and uncertain in the south central Deccan region and lowest in the northwest. The main crop in wet regions is rice; in the drier but irrigated regions of the north, wheat; and in the dry central region, the millets. The utilization of the land in the 1960s (in millions of acres) was as follows: geographical area 806; reporting area (Indian statistics have relation only to the "reporting area") 741, forest area 140; agricultural 330 (sown area including area sown more than once 386 and fallows 52); noncultivated areas 411; and area not available for cultivation 121. The area of irrigated land in the early 1960s was about 60,000,000 ac. net and 73,000,000 ac. gross (*i.e.*, total crops), whereas in 1950 it had been 49,000,000 ac. net.

Most of the former large estates have been broken up and the agricultural land is mainly in peasant cultivation. The holdings are small (averaging 7.5 ac.) and become smaller as the population increases. At the beginning of the second half of the 20th century, about 80% were under ten acres except in the Punjab and Gujarat state (northwest and west), where the percentages were respectively 50 and 70. This small size results in great poverty and makes improvements difficult. The soils are naturally poor, yields are low and the greater part of the land has to be in human food crops, chiefly cereals (*see* Table XIV). The increased output of the 1964–65 growing season reflects very well

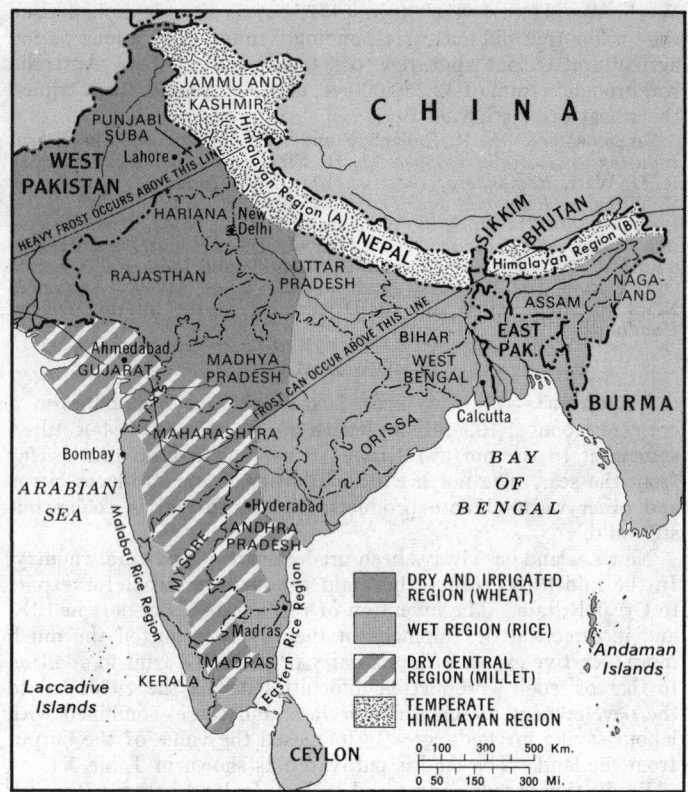

BY COURTESY OF INDIAN COUNCIL OF AGRICULTURAL RESEARCH

AGRICULTURAL REGIONS OF INDIA

TABLE XIV.—*India: Area, Production and Target Figures of the First and Third Five-Year Plans: Chief Crops*

Crops	Area (in 000,000 ac.)		Production (in 000,000 tons)		Production targets (in 000,000 tons)		
	1955–56	1964–65	1955–56	1964–65	First five-year plan, 1956	Third five-year plan, 1966	Fourth five-year plan, 1971
Food crops							
Cereals	214.1	231.5	54.5	76.6	52.5	84.3	120.0
Pulses	57.1	58.8	10.8	12.4	.9.1	17.3	...
Total	271.2	290.3	65.3	89.0	61.6	101.6	...
Oilseeds, edible	24.7	31.3	5.2	7.8	5.5*	9.9	10.0*
Sugar cane, as raw sugar and gur	4.6	6.4	6.0	12.0	6.3	10.2	13.5
Total food crops	300.5	328.0			...	...	...
Cash crops							
Oilseeds, nonedible	5.2	6.2	0.5	0.6	...	9.9	...
Cotton	20.0	20.5	4.0†	4.7†	4.2†	6.9†	...
Jute	1.7	2.0	4.2†	4.5†	5.4†	6.2†	...
Others	2.1	2.9	...	.8	...	...	...
Total area cropped‡	329.5	359.6	...	...	...	...	...

*Edible and nonedible combined. †Million bales (bale of cotton, 392 lb.; bale of jute, 400 lb.). ‡Taking into account the area sown more than once (1963).
Source: Ministry of Food, Agriculture, Community Development and Cooperation, New Delhi (1967).

the efforts of the first three five-year plans though production still depends very much on the amount of precipitation brought by the southwest monsoons.

2. Crops.—*Rice.*—This is the most important of the human foods. By long experience cultivators have picked out from the many Indian varieties those best suited to their local conditions and most acceptable to their tastes. Some varieties tolerate dryness, but most grow in well-watered or even swamp conditions. The best are grown in low-lying areas with standing water. The grain as reaped is called paddy and when dehusked it becomes rice. One hundred parts of paddy give 66.7 parts of rice. The average yield is about 9.5 cwt. of rice per acre but far higher yields are

obtained in good areas.

Millets.—The millets are all tolerant of drought and soil poverty and they replace rice in regions of low and uncertain rainfall. Jowar (*Sorghum vulgare*) is the most important, followed by bajra (*Pennisetum glaucum*) and ragi (*Eleusine coracana*). Lower-yielding smaller varieties with even higher tolerance of drought and poverty are grown in poor districts.

Wheat.—Wheat does not grow well in hot or very wet conditions. It is confined to a belt in the drier part of the north and is grown only as a winter crop; about a third is irrigated. Average yields range about eight hundredweight per acre. Severe losses are periodically caused by rust and smut, and much effort has been devoted to the breeding of resistant varieties. (*See* Table XV.)

Pulses.—Many kinds of pulse are grown. The chief are gram

TABLE XV.—*India: Area and Production of Cereals, End of Third Five-Year Plan (1964–65)*

Crops	Area (in 000,000 ac.) 1964–65	Production (in 000,000 tons) 1964–65	Production (in 000,000 tons) 1955–56
Kharif crops (May–mid-Oct.)			
Rice	89.9	38.7	26.8
Total millets	90.1	18.1	13.7
Jowar	44.2	9.7	6.6
Bajra	28.9	4.5	3.4
Raggee	5.9	1.9	1.8
Small millets	11.1	2.0	1.9
Maize	11.4	4.7	2.6
Rabi crops (mid-Oct–mid-April)			
Wheat	33.4	12.3	8.6
Barley	6.7	3.5	2.7

Source: Ministry of Food, Agriculture, Community Development and Cooperation, New Delhi (1967).

(*Cicer arietinum*), nearly half the total production, and pigeon pea (*Cajanus cajan*), about a fifth. The total area is about 60,-000,000 ac. and the product about 12,000,000 tons.

Vegetable Oils and Fats.—Peanuts, an early introduction (16th or 17th century from South America), are the chief crop. They also provide a good deal of protein. They are grown mainly in the states of Madras (in the south), Andhra Pradesh (central India) and Gujarat (west). The others, chiefly rape and mustard (treated as one crop) and sesamum, are much more widely distributed. (*See* Table XVI.)

Sugar Cane.—This is grown wherever sufficient water is available. The area in the mid-1960s was 6,286,500 ac. which produced the equivalent of 12,315,000 tons of gur (unrefined, non-centrifugal molasseslike concentrate from the juice crushed out of sugar cane), a very popular product. The average yield of 4,300 lb. of gur per acre gives the highest calorie return per acre of any

TABLE XVI.—*India: Area and Production of Oilseeds, End of the Third Five-Year Plan (1965–66)*

Crop	Area (in 000,000 ac.)	Production (in 000,000 tons)	Oil* (in 000 tons)
Edible:			
Peanuts (groundnuts) . .	17.8	4.0	900
Rape and mustard . . .	7.2	1.3	400
Sesamum	6.2	.4	100
Total	31.1	5.07	1,400
Nonedible:			
Linseed	4.4	.3	90
Castor beans	1.0	.1	20

*Estimates.
Source: Ministry of Food, Agriculture, Community Development and Cooperation, New Delhi (1967).

crop in India. In the mid-1960s, 3,512,000 tons of refined sugar were produced.

The 328,000,000 ac. of food crops recorded in Table XIV amount to about 85% of the total cropped area.

Cotton.—This is grown mainly in the drier districts and occupies about 80% of the total area of the cash crops. Short-staple

TABLE XVII.—*India: Area and Production of Cash Crops, End of Third Five-Year Plan (1965–66)*

Crops	Area (in 000 ac.)	Production
Cotton (bales of 392 lb.) . . .	19,300	4,700,000
Jute (bales of 400 lb.)	1,700	4,500,000
Tea (tons)	825	372,600
Coffee (tons)	320	60,600
Rubber (tons)	378	49,400
Tobacco (tons)	1,000	400,000

Source: Ministry of Food, Agriculture, Community Development and Cooperation, New Delhi (1967); The Times of India, *Directory and Year Book 1965–66*.

Asian varieties are grown in rain-fed districts and medium-staple American varieties in those irrigated. The surplus seed furnishes edible oil and a residual cake which can be fed to animals (usually milch buffaloes) or used as manure.

Jute.—This requires enormous quantities of water and is confined to the low-lying Gangetic delta in the northeast where floods and high rainfall furnish ideal conditions. It yields 600 to 1,000 lb. of yarn per acre and as textiles and yarn it heads India's list of export commodities.

Other Crops.—Tea comes second in importance as an export. It is grown in three regions where high rainfall has made the soil sufficiently acid: the hills of Assam, of the Darjeeling district and of Kerala and the Nilgiris in the south. The drier parts of the Nilgiris also produce coffee. Both crops are more suited to large plantation companies than to small farmers. The demand is not greatly expansible and neither area nor product has changed much since 1950.

Two other cash crops, however, have increased in area and output: tobacco and rubber. (*See* Table XVII.)

3. Livestock.—Cattle are the main source of power on the farm, but they provide little milk and meat. Slaughter is prohibited by the Hindu religion and castration is far from common. A vast cattle population, estimated at 176,670,000 in 1961, has, therefore, grown up and for most of it, apart from the working animals and the milch buffaloes, there is no food beyond the farm wastes and the quite inadequate grazing on wasteland or forest verges.

Meanwhile the grassland is overgrazed and eroded. The animals are half starved and very inefficient; the milk yield is a few pints daily and even the dung does not get to the farmed land but is dried into cakes for domestic fuel. The 22,000,000 milch buffaloes

provide most of the milk. Though they constitute only 30% of the number of total milch animals, they provide 56% of the total milk production. This is used for making the staple cooking fat, ghee, a kind of butter.

4. Food Production and Population: the Five-Year Plans.—At the beginning of the second half of the 20th century India's diet was definitely poorer than before World War II and the rising population threatened a further reduction. The five-year plans aimed at averting this calamity by increasing food output, lowering the birth rate and increasing industrial development. The agricultural methods included more irrigation, soil conservation and reclamation, greater use of fertilizers, better farming techniques and reduction of wastes and losses. By the end of the first five-year plan about 5,000,000 ac. were added to the total irrigated area, 34,000,000 ac. had been added to the food-crop area, and crop yields were higher. The food production part of the first five-year plan, as Table XIV shows, was accomplished. Import of cereals fell from 4,300,000 tons (1951–52 average) to 770,000 tons (1954–55 average) and the calorie consumption per head per day in 1955–56 rose from 1,700 (FAO estimate) to 2,200.

The second five-year plan aimed at still further progress. Its calorie target for 1960 was 2,400 per head per day, but severe drought in some areas threatened the food supply. Under the third five-year plan the irrigated area was increased by 29% to 90,000,000 ac. and 3,600,000 ac. of agricultural land was reclaimed; and the fourth plan included irrigation of an additional 13,000,000 ac. Food grain production by the end of the third plan had increased 82% since 1951 and 32% since 1960. Though the achievements were impressive, production could not keep up with rising consumption. The per capita calorie target was not reached (1960–62, 2,020 cal.; 1964–65, 1,880 cal.); and imports of food grain rose again, from 1960 to 1964 averaging 4,660,000 tons annually with a high in 1964 of 6,360,000 tons.

BIBLIOGRAPHY.—Ministry of Food and Agriculture, *Indian Agriculture in Brief*, 3rd ed. (1957); Narayan Aiyer and A. K. Yegna, *Principles of Crop Husbandry in India* (1948); S. Thirumalai, *Post-War Agricultural Problems and Policies in India* (1954); R. O. Whyte, *The Grassland and Fodder Resources of India* (1957); William F. Hall, *Agriculture in India*, U.S. Department of Agriculture, "Economic Research Service Series" (Jan. 1964); S. C. Jain, *Agricultural Planning in India* (1964).

F. PAKISTAN

1. General.—Pakistan, which lies in the north of the Indian subcontinent, comprises two provinces, West Pakistan and East Pakistan, widely different from each other and separated by 1,000 mi. Its total area is 365,529 sq.mi. (233,938,560 ac.) but only about 72,310,000 ac. are in agricultural use. About 53,970,000 ac. of this area is sown, but since some of it carries two or three crops a year the area of crops exceeds 63,940,000 ac. (47,000,000 ac. in 1949–50). About 9,680,000 ac. are fallow and 8,660,000 are forest.

2. West Pakistan.—West Pakistan is the larger but less populous of the two provinces (area 198,657,920 ac.; pop. [1961] 42,-978,261), much of it mountain and desert. The agricultural part is about 44,890,000 ac. mainly on the plain of the Indus system running north and south for approximately 800 mi., with a fall over the whole distance averaging only a foot a mile. The holdings average about five acres. There is, however, much division and fragmentation, especially on the unirrigated land. The rainfall is low—about 40 in. in the foothills and 4 in. at the sea—and comes mostly in July and August. The rivers are fed by the snows and glaciers of the Himalayas and are in spate during summer and early autumn, sometimes causing destructive floods when the embankments are breached. The land is admirably suited for irrigation and some impressive systems were set up under the British administration, notably the great Sukkur barrage designed to water 7,500,000 ac.

The canal system, the longest in the world, commands about 23,-000,000 ac., 35% to 55% of which can be cropped in winter and 30% to 40% in summer. Cultivated farmland was reported in the 1960s as 36,200,000 ac., of which 24,300,000 were irrigated.

Wheat (13,140,000 ac.) and cotton (3,624,000 ac.) were the

two chief crops. The production of wheat in 1965 was 4,518,000 tons and the yield was 7.6 cwt. per acre, back up from an average of only 6 cwt. per acre during the early years of the second half of the 20th century. Wheat, pulses, oilseeds and berseem, the fodder for the cattle, are winter crops. Those grown in summer include cotton, the millets, some oilseeds and rice. Most of the millets, about a third of the wheat and some of the cotton are grown on *barani*, or unirrigated land; the other crops are irrigated.

The output of cotton in the mid-1960s was about 2,000,000 bales (bale = 480 lb.) annually, of which about 1,700,000 are medium-staple, American upland type, and the rest (10% of the cotton area) are native short-staple varieties. The average yield is fairly steady at about 240 lb. of lint per acre. Weeds cause considerable loss; the native implements were designed for bullock power and are not very effective. Insect pests also cause serious trouble.

Since the partition of India, Pakistan has had to import both wheat and rice, with the aid of considerable overseas subventions. Sugar also is imported. Experimental yields are considerably higher than the average, showing that improvements are possible. Unfortunately many peasants have to burn their farmyard manure for fuel and cannot afford adequate fertilizers. Serious irrigation troubles cause increasing anxiety: waterlogging and accumulation of salt in the surface soil are making it sterile. About 2,000,000 to 3,000,000 ac. are affected. After partition in 1947 the waters of the Indus system were a matter of dispute. The Indus Water Treaty of 1960, mediated by the World Bank, provided for a ten-year Indus Basin development plan, with Pakistan farms to receive water from the Indus river and two western tributaries; and the flow of the three eastern tributaries (about 20% of the yearly flow of the system) to be released for use in India.

3. East Pakistan.—East Pakistan is much the smaller of the two provinces but by far the most populous (area 35,280,640 ac.; pop. [1961] 50,853,721). It lies on some of the mouths of the Ganges and Brahmaputra, and stretches up into the hill region of the east. The rainfall varies from about 50 to 135 in. a year, and as the riverbanks are not protected by levees, the floodwaters spread uncontrolled over the low-lying land.

These conditions suit rice and jute admirably, and in summer every available acre is cropped. In winter there is little rain and only about 20% of the land carries crops. The government was, however, promoting extensive schemes of pump irrigation. There is a little lift irrigation on some of the land bordering the rivers but none by canals. Some of the 20,940,000 ac. of crop land are sown twice and some even three times a year, making the total area of crops about 27,470,000 ac.

Rice occupies about 80% of the cropped area. About 75% of it is a *kharif* or summer crop (the *aman* varieties), sown in nurseries in March and June and transplanted to catch the monsoon rains (July to September). It is harvested about December. About 20% is broadcast during March–May (*aus* varieties) and, being harvested during July–August, can be followed by a winter crop. These varieties do best on good high land. The remaining 5% (*boro* varieties) is a winter crop started in nurseries, transplanted during October–January and harvested during March–May. Many types are grown including some adapted to flooded areas. The yields fluctuate about 11 cwt. of paddy, or unmilled rice, per acre (in Pakistan 100 lb. of paddy is estimated to give 70 lb. of rice). The total area of rice in the two provinces is about 22,500,000 ac.

The other food crops are other grains and the pulses, occupying about 350,000 ac. and oilseeds, chiefly rape and mustard, occupying a little over 500,000 ac.

Jute is the chief cash crop. It is confined entirely to the low-lying districts of East Pakistan because of its great need of water. The fibre is contained in the stems which may be ten or more feet high. The area, about 1,660,000 ac. is fixed annually to avoid overproduction and the yield per acre is about five bales of 400 lb. each.

There are also some minor crops: betel nuts (260,000 ac.) used for chewing, some being exported to India, tobacco and small areas of potatoes, tea and cotton. Because of the dense population the holdings are very small; the average size is about two

acres. In the two provinces numbers of livestock in the 1960s were about 33,531,000 cattle, 8,402,000 buffaloes, 12,921,000 goats and 10,263,000 sheep.

4. Summary.—Pakistan has had to face many difficulties. Nevertheless, food production per head of population was for many years higher in Pakistan than in India, giving (on the average of East and West Pakistan) more than 2,100 cal. a day. The protein supply also is better: beef (but not pork) is permitted to Moslems. In East Pakistan both inland and marine fish are available, and there is great scope for development. The Punjab is probably the best-fed region in the Indo-Pakistan subcontinent. The cattle, having between 2,000,000 and 3,000,000 ac. of fodder crops, are among the best producers.

G. RHODESIA, MALAWI AND ZAMBIA

1. Rhodesia.—Rhodesia was developed late. Much of it is high-lying savanna (the high veld and middle veld), which contains the farming area. Its rainfall is moderate but unreliable. It comes in the summer months from October or November to March or April, and is higher in the east and northeast and lower toward the south and west. Much of the soil is light and poor. The low veld, a region of wide river valleys with low rainfall and often high temperatures, occupies about 40% of the country. It is unsuitable for ordinary farming and is used for large-scale cattle ranching. Irrigation was, however, being introduced in the second half of the 20th century.

The European-farmed area is about 30,000,000 ac., of which about 1,000,000 are cropped. The acreages of the chief crops in the second half of the 20th century (1964, with 1950–51 figures shown in parentheses) were: maize 371,150 ac. (343,000 ac.); tobacco 260,140 ac. (169,000 ac.); green manure 31,580 ac. (110,-000 ac.).

The most distinctive feature of the farming is that green manuring, chiefly with leguminous crops, is more extensively used than in any other country. Three and four years' leas of selected and improved grasses are grown to restore soil structure destroyed by cultivation, especially on the light tobacco soils, and also to provide food for early maturing mutton sheep. Yields per acre were rising, indicating a steady improvement in the farming. These were in 1964 (harvest) with 1951–52 figures shown in parentheses: maize 23 cwt. (12); tobacco 1,115 wet pounds (523); and peanuts (unshelled) 9.2 (= 598 lb.) bags (5.9).

Tobacco, nearly all flue-cured Virginian, is commercially the most important crop and it is admirably suited to Rhodesia's great stretches of poor sandy soil. The other main crops are peanuts, potatoes (both summer and winter grown) and fodder. There is very little wheat. Sugar and citrus fruits are grown on the irrigated land in the low veld and tea along the high eastern border districts. Also grown in high districts is *Hibiscus cannabinus*, needed for local sack and bag manufacture, and in the lower rainfall areas, castor beans for export.

Cattle are the most important of the livestock. Their numbers increased from 2,960,000 in 1951 to 3,543,000 in 1964, more than half (1,916,000) being on the African farms. Beef production increased from 35,400 tons to 69,000 tons. An ample store of food must be provided for the long dry season and in years of drought losses may be heavy. Sheep are far fewer. They are liable to suffer in the high-lying districts because of the high rainfall and heavy mists, and everywhere they may pick up internal parasites. Properly managed, however, and given clean water and good pasture, they do well. Pig husbandry was expanding in the early part of the second half of the 20th century.

Soil erosion is an ever-present danger, but vigorous steps are taken against it. Practically all the arable land on European farms is protected, and the African farmers are becoming more cooperative. The area under irrigation was slowly increasing. In 1951 it was only 17,600 ac. but by 1955 it had risen to 31,200 ac. and some larger schemes were projected, including dams at the Kariba gorge and on the Sabi river.

2. Malawi.—This is the smallest but most populous member of this group. Maize and the sorghums are the chief food grains, and tobacco, tea, cotton, peanuts and tung oil the chief cash crops.

Of all these except tobacco Malawi produces more than Rhodesia.

3. Zambia.—Zambia is really a mining country but it was developing its agriculture in the 1960s, and a useful ecological survey had been made.

H. West Africa

1. Introduction.—Agricultural development in west Africa followed naturally from its opening up by the British in the latter part of the 19th century. There was already a primitive agriculture based on bush fallow (leaving exhausted land to cover itself with natural vegetation for several years and then cropping it again) or shifting cultivation (abandoning the exhausted land and moving on elsewhere). Africa is very poor in native food plants. Sorghum, various millets and roots, yams, etc., are indigenous. The Portuguese Jesuit fathers in the 16th and later centuries introduced some others from America, including maize, cassava and peanuts. The only implements were the hoe and a large knife. There were no plows, wheels or carts; transport was on human heads. The agricultural system was very inefficient and served only because famine, pestilence and tribal warfare kept the population low. The British policy was to improve the native crops and methods and to develop cash cropping so that Africans could purchase goods and services from outside countries.

2. Nigeria.—The coastal zone combines high rainfall (50 to 150 in. a year) with high temperature and is a region of tropical forest giving the impression of high production potential. Actually the soils are poor. The luxurious forest growth is due to the fact that the leaves falling to the ground decompose rapidly, liberating plant nutrients which are absorbed by the tree roots and so used over and over again. This region produces tree crops: oil palm (the most important), cocoa, rubber and, locally, kola, besides timber. The oil palm is a native tree and is usually wild, not cultivated. Both the pericarp oil and the kernels are valuable. Cocoa and rubber were both introduced and are grown from seed. The chief food crops are yams (*Dioscorea* species), coco yams (*Colocasia* species) and cassava, and all are interplanted with maize. Other crops include cowpeas, beans and bananas. Bush fallow is at present the best method of dealing with the soil poverty, and experiments are being made to improve it.

Farther inland is a belt of country with lower rainfall (60 to 80 in.), formerly mostly deciduous forest. As a result of much burning and clearing, it has become a man-made savanna where the crops are maize, sorghum, yams and cassava. Still farther north, beyond about latitude 11° N., is a drier and healthier zone where some of the best farming is found. This is the grain belt (millet and sorghum) and the chief source of cotton and peanuts. Fertilizers, particularly phosphates, markedly increase the yields. Their application is especially needed because the large export of peanuts permanently removes much phosphate from the soil.

Still farther inland the rainfall is too low and uncertain for much crop production except on some of the river flats. Most of Nigeria's cattle are there. The forest regions cannot carry them because of the prevalence of tsetse fly and other disease-bearing insects. Only the small imported Ndama breed appears to be resistant.

About two-thirds of Nigeria is forest, uncultivated bush or waste, and less than 10% is under farm crops. Farms are small and there is much interplanting of food crops.

3. Ghana.—Ghana is much smaller than Nigeria but its physiography is generally similar, except that it has a rather dry coastal belt and does not stretch inland beyond the savanna. It has no semiarid or desert region. In the wet forest zone cocoa is by far the most important product. It is not a native tree but was brought to the island of São Tomé about 1822, apparently from Brazil. Propagation did not begin, however, until about 50 years later and even then it was slow. Once expansion began it proceeded rapidly and by 1926 the export of cocoa beans amounted to 228,500 tons; and in 1965 it was 580,000 tons. Nigeria produces about 200,000 tons and the two together amount to 50% of the world total. When the contribution of the Ivory Coast (over 100,000 tons) is added the total comes to a substantial part of the total world output. However, diseases and pests gradually have

come in, and Swollen shoot, a serious virus disease, has caused great difficulties in cultivation. The Cocoa Research institute at Tafo, set up in 1944, investigates technical problems and the Cocoa Marketing board deals with business matters.

The savanna country beyond the forest produces, as in Nigeria, maize, peanuts, yams and, in places, rice.

The dry Northern Territories contain most of the livestock. As elsewhere in Africa burning and overgrazing have led to soil erosion and deterioration of the herbage; steps for control have, however, been taken.

The Volta River project, with the high dam completed in 1966 at a cost of about $400,000,000 though first of all a hydroelectric project, will impound water for irrigating as much as 6,000 sq.mi., thus permitting diversification of the agricultural economy by production of rice, cotton and sugar cane.

4. Sierra Leone.—This small but interesting country has the highest rainfall in west Africa, and grows the same crops as Ghana except that rice is far more important and cocoa less so. Bush fallowing is widely practised, but is being shortened because of the increasing population.

5. Gambia.—This is the smallest of the west African countries. It has a low rainfall and the tree crops cocoa and oil palm are of very little importance in its economy. Peanuts are the chief export crop, millets and rice the chief food crops. Depredations by baboons, other monkeys and wild pigs formerly caused considerable losses, but have been kept down by a well-organized shooting campaign.

I. East Africa

1. General.—East African territories lie mainly on the great African plateau. The rainfall is less than in the west and it is seasonal and irregular. There is a long dry season and the rivers offer little scope for irrigation. There is some forest on the higher ground and a good deal of scrub, but much of the land carries grass that varies in height from six feet or more to short tussocks, according to the rainfall. Some of the tribes are settled cultivators, others are cattlemen grazing over considerable areas. Hopes have sometimes been raised that a livestock industry might be developed, as in South America. But the conditions are completely different. Rinderpest is still prevalent and this excludes the possibility of an export trade. The carrying capacity of the pasture is low, and it is difficult to accumulate sufficient reserves of fodder to carry large numbers of animals over the dry season. The cattle tribes do not in general regard their animals as merchantable commodities but as marks of wealth and rank. They are also the price of a bride. For these purposes quantity rather than condition is important. Numbers were kept down so long as diseases remained uncontrolled, but with the introduction of veterinary services they increased, the land was overgrazed, bush encroachment and erosion were much intensified.

This same result followed the introduction of health services for the people. More land was needed for food crops; the period under bush fallow had to be reduced or eliminated and the land became impoverished and much of it eroded. Remedial measures were necessarily unpopular and for various reasons it has not always been possible to combat erosion effectively.

2. Kenya.—Kenya is agriculturally extremely important because the highland region, a relatively small block of country 6,000 to 10,000 or more feet in altitude, much of it in grass, has a cool climate suitable for European settlement. Being devoid of surface water it was almost uninhabited when the British went there toward the end of the 19th century. Comprising more than 11,000 sq.mi. in all, or about 5% of the total land area, the Highlands were largely reserved for non-Africans and for commercial crop production. In 1964 this commercial agriculture contributed more than 80% of the agricultural exports as well as large quantities of maize, meat, and dairy products for the domestic market. When the Highlands were opened in 1961 to African settlement, their 3,000 farms contrasted with perhaps 1,000,000 African holdings in the rest of Kenya.

The numerous African tribes long remained on the lower land. Of the cultivating tribes the Kikuyu are among the most numerous and efficient. They grow maize, potatoes, beans, bananas and yams for subsistence, and vegetables, pineapples, coffee, pyrethrum and wattle for cash. Much of their soil is a fertile red loam, sufficiently supplied with water and capable of giving good yields. Their land system, however, includes the fragmentation and scattering of the holdings and is wasteful both of land and of effort. The British agricultural staff worked out a much more effective system, including consolidation of the scattered holdings, the collection of the people into villages, antierosion measures, especially terracing, planned cropping, rotations and proper cultivating implements. Persuasion failed to secure its acceptance. The Mau Mau disturbances, however, compelled the government to remove the leaders and to build villages to which the people could be transferred. The advantages of village settlement and land consolidation were then so obvious that the cultivators themselves applied to the department of agriculture to have their scattered land consolidated, and this proceeded as rapidly as was practicable. The aim was to make compact holdings, providing food for the family and the livestock and a cash income of not less than £100 a year. It was necessary that industrial development proceed simultaneously to provide work for those not needed on the land.

To help the cattle tribes markets are being established and steps taken to ensure honest dealing. The meat can be sold for the mine workers in Malawi, Rhodesia, Zambia and South Africa and efforts are made to induce the owners to improve their stock.

The European farming is entirely for cash and the products include wheat (the chief arable crop), maize and other cereals, meat and dairy produce and, in regions suited to them, coffee (*Coffea arabica*), tea (best as plantation crops), pyrethrum and sisal. Coffee grows best on the deep red loam with moderate rainfall—about 35 in.—little mist and good sunshine. Tea grows well in regions of mist, high rainfall and acid soils. Pyrethrum must have a period of low temperature to stimulate the formation of flowers and sisal grows well in dry conditions. Much effort is devoted to the search for improved varieties of crops and of grasses, better management of pastures and better modes of cultivation of the arable land and avoidance of erosion, an ever-present danger in Africa. Dairying, bacon production and other livestock industries are being developed. The farms are large—500 ac. and more—and much labour and expense have been incurred in carving them out of the waste and in sinking bore holes for water, which may be 200 to 600 ft. deep. As methods are improved some of the larger arable farms are subdivided and the system intensified. A considerable amount of work is provided for Africans. These farms not only add greatly to the national income, but also furnish valuable information about possibilities of increasing output from the land, which will always be Kenya's crying need, there being no valuable minerals or fuels for mining.

The total land area of Kenya is 140,664,960 ac. Of this about 7,809,000 ac. are under crops, the chief of which, in the 1960s were (in thousands of acres): wheat 285; sisal 283; maize 2,965; wattle 160; coffee 126; and sugar 110. The numbers of livestock on farms by the mid-1960s were (in millions, with 1945 figures shown in parentheses): cattle 7.24 (5.28); sheep 6.57 (2.69); pigs 0.37 (0.35 [1947 figure]); and poultry 0.203 (.181). In 1964, 10,202,000 lb. of factory butter was produced compared with 5,000,000 in 1945.

3. Uganda.—The agriculture is almost entirely African. Over most of the country the rainfall is very reliable. The Baganda area is very fertile. The export products are cotton, coffee (mainly *C. robusta*), tobacco, peanuts and maize. The food crops include bananas, maize, sorghum and cassava, roughly in that order. The small area of non-African farming produces sugar, tea and coffee.

4. Tanzania.—The export products are plantation sisal, tea, sugar, maize, African coffee, cloves and cotton. By far the greater share of the export is produced by a small number of white cultivators.

BIBLIOGRAPHY.—R. J. M. Swynnerton, *A Plan to Intensify the Development of African Agriculture in Kenya* (1955); Carey B. Singleton, Jr., "The Agricultural Economy of Tanganyika," U.S. Department of Agriculture, Foreign Agriculture and Economic Research Service Report 92 (Sept. 1964); *Foreign Agriculture* "Special African Issue," U.S. Department of Agriculture (Nov. 1966).

J. THE SMALLER TROPICAL COUNTRIES AND ISLANDS

The agricultural problems are generally set by the circumstance that while an acre of land may grow enough food to provide an adequate, if uninteresting, diet for one or two persons it will, if growing a remunerative cash crop, provide for the purchase of a fuller and better diet as well as other requirements for a larger number. Search is therefore made for suitable cash crops and for means of securing higher yields of better quality. The West Indies produce sugar and its products rum and molasses, cotton, and, in Jamaica, bananas, citrus fruits, cocoa and coffee. Ceylon produces tea, coconuts, rubber and smaller quantities of cinnamon, citronella and cocoa. Malaya produces rubber, palm oil, coconut oil and copra. Mauritius produces sugar, tea and some tobacco. Fiji produces sugar and copra. All, however, import food. *See* TROPICAL AGRICULTURE; *see* also references under "Agriculture" in the Index.

(E. J. R.; J. K. R.)

AGRICULTURE, PRIMITIVE. Agriculture, the cultivation of fields (Lat. *ager*) for the production of a regular supply of crops for food and other needs, is the technical foundation on which the development of stable and sedentary human communities and the elaboration of most other arts and crafts has almost everywhere depended. Ethnographical records include a number of instances of primitive hunting and foraging peoples who sought to increase their supply of one or more of their collected vegetable foods by establishing proprietary rights over naturally productive tracts, by protecting seedlings, by burning the bush at certain seasons to inhibit the growth of unwanted plants and even by diversion of streams to promote the growth of seed-bearing grasses and wild roots by irrigation. But the crucial step toward cultivation consists in the deliberate and regular planting of stored seeds, tubers or cuttings in ground which has been sufficiently cleared and prepared to yield a crop.

Considerable empirical knowledge of the sprouting of seeds and tubers and of vegetative reproduction has been reported from collecting peoples. But for agriculture, however primitive, an element of foresight, planning and an established routine of cultivation is also necessary. The archaeological record shows that agriculture was a late development in the history of mankind. For by far the greater part of their existence, human communities were limited to small, widely dispersed and often migratory encampments of food gatherers.

Some natural environments have afforded an abundance of wild plant supplies that agriculture at a primitive level could not surpass. But under most conditions the successful cultivation of one or more staple crops, which can provide the greater part of the food supply, greatly reduces the extent of territory on which a given population needs to rely to secure its food. At the same time it can provide, according to the crop and climatic conditions, a harvest of storable supplies for the rest of the year or, as in the humid tropics, an almost continuous supply of maturing tubers and fruits. Both induce a greater fixity and concentration of settlement.

With the regular replanting of the more rewarding crops, incidental selection in favour of higher-yielding or otherwise desirable varieties takes place so that, over considerable periods of continuous cultivation, new mutant and hybrid plants may come to preponderate and thus effect a general improvement and an increase in the number of varieties adapted to different conditions. Already before the spectacular advances achieved by the genetically controlled methods of modern plant breeding, a wide range of improved and locally adapted varieties of cereals such as wheat, rice and corn or maize, of tropical root crops such as yams, taro and cassava and of many other cultivated plants had been developed in primitive agriculture.

EARLY AGRICULTURAL COMMUNITIES

Evidence for the antiquity of agriculture and the character of the earliest known farming communities has been derived from several sources. Archaeological discoveries of carbonized grains and other plant remains, or their impression, accidental or deliberate, on pottery before firing, together with other less-certain indications of cultivation, such as flint sickles, grindstones, mortars

PRIMITIVE METHOD OF PLOW CULTIVATION BEING PRACTISED ON AN ALGERIAN FARM

and hoelike tools, have been recovered from prehistoric settlements. Estimations of the absolute dates of some of these have been obtained by carbon-14 dating (*see* RADIOCARBON DATING). The geographical distributions and especially the clustering within limited regions of many varieties of some cultivated plants have been interpreted to indicate the probable areas of their first cultivation, while genetic studies have yielded valuable information on the course of the development of cultivated mutants and hybrids. (*See* AGRICULTURE: *Origins of Agriculture;* ARCHAEOLOGY.)

Old World.—Modern man (*Homo sapiens*) has existed from at least the period of the late Pleistocene glaciation and he survived as a food gatherer for more than 50,000 years before any human community began to rely on the effective and regular cultivation of plants for its food supply. In the old world the earliest known agricultural communities probably developed only about 7,000 or 8,000 years ago in the seasonally watered and lightly wooded grasslands to the east of the Mediterranean. The Natufians of Palestine with their harvesting sickles and mortars appear to exemplify an incipient agricultural community that heralded this development. The details of the process and the conditions in which these advances were achieved remain to be determined. But by at least 4000 B.C. the cultivation of wheat and barley, with which was combined the raising of goats, sheep and, later, cattle, was spreading widely over southwestern Asia, northeastern Africa and Europe to effect the Neolithic revolution—so called because these early agricultural communities, unlike their Paleolithic predecessors, generally employed ground stone "axes" as chopping and sometimes as digging tools.

While most early Neolithic settlements were still small communities of 20 or 30 households, they were more stable than those of Paleolithic hunters and the agricultural economy afforded time and energy for other activities including the new crafts of potmaking and weaving, as well as for the regular construction of durable dwellings. The potentiality for further development afforded by agriculture is shown by the comparatively rapid extension of such settlements over wide areas. This points in turn to a growth of population, made possible by a more assured food supply, and a recurrent hiving off of segments of expanding communities to establish new settlements.

Some similarities in the cultivated plants and farming methods of the Indus civilization in northeastern India and of Neolithic sites in Honan and Kansu in eastern Asia with those of the ancient near east suggest that the former may owe their beginnings to an early eastward diffusion of Neolithic farming. But at the beginning of the 1960s there was no archaeological or other evidence to indicate whether any links with southwestern Asia underlay the development of rice cultivation in southern and southeastern Asia which was well established before the Christian era. In the latter region, too, the cultivation of root and tree crops, notably yam and taro, the coconut palm and the breadfruit tree, which were subse-

quently introduced as food staples in Oceania, was also developed at an early but unknown date.

Little is known of the antiquity of agriculture in trans-Saharan Africa. Yam cultivation was established in the tropical forests of western Africa long before European penetration. Some of the African varieties of yams and other forest crops are common to southern Asia and were probably introduced. But others are unknown elsewhere and it is uncertain whether these result from an independent agricultural development in Africa or are secondary additions. Bananas and plantains, which are widely cultivated and afford the staple crop in some areas, are on botanical grounds to be regarded as introductions and may not have reached Africa before the development of the Arab trade down the east coast. From the 15th century European traders also introduced many plants from the far east and the new world which spread rapidly and widely through tropical Africa.

The cultural history of another group of food grains including sorghum (*q.v.*) and collectively known as millets (*see* MILLET), which have become staples over the dryer tropical and subtropical areas of Asia and Africa, remains largely unknown, but in the absence of archaeological evidence for their great antiquity it is assumed that their first cultivation was a secondary development in areas marginal to the ancient east; from there they spread through central Asia and over the tropical savannas of eastern and western Africa.

New World.—The archaeological record in the new world shows that agriculture was first established in the tropical and subtropical areas of central America where maize became the food grain. Detailed studies have shown that maize has a long and complex genetical history including the hybridization of distinct species. Although the basis for any absolute chronology is limited to carbon dating of only a few sites, settlements based on primitive maize cultivation may have existed 4,000 years ago. By 1000 B.C. farming communities that also cultivated beans, gourds and cotton as a textile material were established over a wide region extending from coastal Peru to Arizona, suggesting a rapid proliferation of the new and more productive economy analogous with but—as far as is known—independent of the Neolithic revolution in the old world. Maize growing was later introduced throughout the eastern woodlands of North America, and by the time of European discovery its cultivation had extended north and west to the climatic limits of cold and drought. In the west, on the other hand, although grown along the lower Colorado river, it had not been adopted by the Indians of the Californian woodlands who continued to rely on an abundance of wild acorns, nuts and seeds.

Although maize was known and cultivated under rather unfavourable conditions over much of the Amazonian tropical forest, an indigenous root, *Manihot* (cassava), had also been brought under cultivation at an unknown date to provide a continuously yielding food staple. On the high plateaus of the Andes beyond the climatic limits of maize cultivation, the potato became a cultivated food staple. (*See* INDIAN, NORTH AMERICAN; INDIAN, LATIN-AMERICAN.)

DIFFUSION OF PLANTS AND TECHNIQUES

In the course of the growth and movements of human populations and the secondary development of new food crops, a very wide range of combinations of cultivated plants had been established in the farming patterns of different regions. Crops that may have been originally secondary and minor sources of food have, like the sago palm in parts of Melanesia or the banana in parts of eastern Africa, become the food staple in new areas. World-wide voyaging and trading by Europeans added greatly to the range of crops available to primitive cultivation by introducing plants from other continents, some of which, like cassava in western Africa or maize in southern Africa, displaced the older staple foods.

But primitive forms of cultivation with simple hand tools were superseded well before the Christian era in the areas of early agricultural development in the old world. In southwestern Asia the harnessing of draft animals for plow cultivation and large-scale basin irrigation in the riverine lowlands had been developed by the 2nd millennium B.C. Plow cultivation and the rotation of fields extended through the Mediterranean, central and western Europe in the Iron Age to provide the economic foundation of the classical and medieval civilizations of Europe. Intensive agriculture with regular manuring and continuous cultivation was also developed in the higher civilization of southern and eastern Asia.

CONTEMPORARY AGRICULTURAL COMMUNITIES

It is only in remote hill areas of southern Asia, in some of the islands of Indonesia, in the Melanesian and Polynesian archipelagoes of Oceania, in trans-Saharan Africa and in the new world that hand cultivation has survived into modern times. Such areas do, however, include a wide range of physical environments and great diversity of crops. Techniques of cultivation and the organization of labour for the planting, tending and storage of crops are equally diverse in detail. It is therefore illusory to conceive of any single pattern of culture or form of social organization to which primitive cultivators will conform. The techniques involved range from the crudest dibble planting in sloughs or partially burned-over ground to the careful preparation of seedbeds, fertilizing with ash and sweepings, the terracing of hill slopes with stone revetments, ridge and mound cultivation and the irrigation of plots enclosed by bunds (embankments). Successful hand cultivation does not depend on any great elaboration of implements. Land can be sufficiently cleared by burning in the dry season, the scattered ash increasing the fertility of the soil. Simple digging sticks can, as in Oceania and the Americas, suffice for dibbling in seeds or tubers.

On their forested tropical islands the Melanesians practised a highly successful yam cultivation before iron tools were introduced and they continue to rely mainly on their digging sticks for planting. In the eastern Solomons they maintain coconut and breadfruit groves along the coast and make yam gardens on the rising ground inland. Groups of kinsmen co-operate to ring the trees and burn the undergrowth over acre-sized clearings which are fenced with the larger logs against the depredations of their domesticated pigs. Within the clearing the separate gardens of each household are marked out but all co-operate to rake over the ground and plant the yams of each garden in turn. The details of cultivation manifest an intimate empirical knowledge of the requirements of good farming and a strong spirit of emulation in the effort to obtain a good harvest of large yams. In the display of the harvests and the reciprocal gifts of food among kinsfolk great prestige is gained by the successful and social obligations are fulfilled. After one or two seasons a new clearing has to be made since fertility rapidly falls off and weeds choke the ground. But each co-operating kin group in a Melanesian village has claims to one or more extensive tracts of ground over which it shifts its clearings from year to year. After about a decade when saplings and dense bush have grown up on an old clearing it can be burned and cleared again in the dry season and replanted.

The vast river-threaded forests of the Amazon basin are still occupied by innumerable small communities of American Indians who successfully maintain themselves with even more meagre equipment. Stone axes are extremely scarce and many groups can obtain them only one at a time by infrequent barter. Nevertheless patches of forest extending over several hundred yards are periodically cleared of all but the largest trees by burning and prizing, using heavy stakes as levers. A whole season's work is often needed to clear this charred wilderness of trunks and creepers sufficiently to erect the single communal dwelling for the hundred or so villagers and to lay out plots in which crops can be planted. These include several root crops including yams and sweet potatoes but the food staple is cassava flour. A continuous supply of cassava roots can be obtained, for a plant will yield for several seasons and cuttings can be taken from the old growth for further plantings. But the tubers are poisonous in their raw state. They have to be soaked, fermented, grated and squeezed dry before the edible flour is obtained. Beans, pineapples and sometimes maize are planted in and around the cassava plots as well as tobacco and coca shrubs that yield narcotics. When, after four or five years, the yield of cassava tubers falls off markedly work on a new clearing must begin. An old site vacated a decade or so

before is usually chosen since although the undergrowth is denser this can be burned and there will be fewer large trees. Thus, as in Melanesia, a community migrates over a familiar tract of country occupying a series of clearings in succession.

This pattern of shifting cultivation by slash-and-burn methods is characteristic of primitive tropical-forest root-crop farming in all parts of the world, and is also used for dry rice cultivation in forested hill country in southeastern Asia. It allows for the development of settled village communities surrounded by their farming tracts within which plots are periodically cleared and planted. But the large total area per household that it entails limits their growth to a few hundred persons. Where, as in western and north central Africa, iron tools—especially machetes—are used for the effective clearing of the forest and hoes for the deep cultivation and mounding of the soil, considerably higher production can be obtained. Heavier dressings of fertilizing ash are obtained and fully cleared plots can be more closely cultivated, so that population densities of over 100 to the square mile and sometimes much higher can be maintained under shifting cultivation. Where the settlement pattern is compact, villages several thousand strong are established under favourable conditions.

In parts of the forest belt of west Africa, for instance, where the growth of trade, population and larger political organizations has also been stimulated for over four centuries by coastal commerce with Europe, intensive patterns of shifting cultivation have been established by large settled communities. Yams are usually the staple crop and extensive areas can be hoed into yam hills to provide the depth of soil required for these large tubers. A household plot will vary from one to several acres according to the size and other resources of the family. A wide range of secondary crops including coco yams, beans and gourds are grown on and between the yam mounds, while groves of bananas, peppers and fruit trees are established along the paths leading to the plots and round the large open barns in which the bulky yam harvests are stored on scaffolding to protect them from pests. Such intensive cultivation rapidly exhausts tropical soils and fresh plots are needed each year. But once a sufficient area of high forest around a settlement has been gradually cleared, the close secondary growth that develops on untilled ground can be cleared fairly rapidly in the dry season by teams of kinsmen with machetes and burning. Thus a system of rotating bush fallowing can be established whereby a given tract of land is farmed for one season and then allowed to revert to bush for four or five years before being cleared again by the household or kin group which retains continuous rights to its use for farming and as a collecting area for wild and semiwild produce. The latter includes the oil palms which colonize forest clearings and are of outstanding importance for both food and trade. On the better soils permanent crops such as cocoa and coffee are grown specifically for export overseas in plantations established by further clearing of the forest. Household surpluses of foodstuffs and produce for export are sold at recurrent village and district markets at which a wide range of imported manufactures are available for purchase. Both men and women engage in trade, some on a considerable scale in export produce, while local shortages of farm labour in productive areas are met by seasonal and periodic immigrations of farm workers from poorer regions. Dense sedentary populations are thus maintained, whether in large villages or spread over innumerable neighbouring hamlets that are connected by forest paths and focused on local markets. In southern Nigeria local population densities commonly exceed 200 per square mile and may rise much higher where substantial cash crops can be grown for export or where seasonal wage labour is available in accessible commercial centres. With such pressures of population, land rights for house sites as well as farms become increasingly important and the successive rights of the individual holder, his heirs, his wider group of kin and his local community become the subject of precise rules in customary law which are enforced according to the judgments of courts in the local community or chiefdom. Although the explicit sale of land is usually excluded by the collective rights of kin groups supported by religious sanctions, the needs and opportunities for land transactions between individuals in these more commercialized economies are met by forms of land pledging which result in permanent transfers. The division and organization of labour and the allocation of rights to the produce are similarly defined with increasing precision both within the household and within the groups of kinsfolk and villagers who co-operate in farming both for subsistence and for the market.

In the Mato Grosso and similar regions in South America the tropical wooded grasslands and scrublands proved very intractable to primitive agriculture before the advent of iron tools. Although the tall grasses could be burned after the long dry season, the hard ground was difficult to break and dibble with wooden sticks and the maize crops were often washed away by torrential rains. But in tropical Africa where the craft of ironworking was widely known and practised long before modern European penetration, millet cultivation was successfully established throughout such areas with the aid of the iron hoe. The problem of fertility on the characteristically poor and leached soils was met throughout much of central Africa by lopping trees over a wide area round the plot to provide the wood for heavy dressings of ash.

The steppes or temperate grasslands with their short growing season and root-matted soils appear never to have been conquered by the primitive hand cultivator. In the old world, prehistoric cultivators only penetrated the fringes of the Pontic and Siberian steppes which remained hunting and grazing territories well into historic times. The Great Plains and the pampas of North and South America were only opened up to agriculture by the steel plows of European pioneers in the 19th century. But primitive cultivators established themselves early in the semidesert areas of the new world and in a few of them the obstacles to European colonization have enabled them to survive. The Indian pueblos of New Mexico and Arizona preserved an essentially pre-Columbian pattern of primitive agriculture into the 20th century.

These small but compact Indian villages of the American southwest, to which the name pueblo, originally given by their Spanish discoverers, is generally applied, are dispersed over the semidesert intermontane plateaus from the Rio Grande to the Little Colorado. These are climatically marginal lands for agriculture, since the direct rainfall is inadequate for growing the staple crop, maize, and late winter frosts at these high altitudes of several thousand feet severely curtail the growing season. But, by taking advantage of the runoff and seepages from the higher plateaus which receive more rain and by deeply planting crop varieties that, as a result of centuries of practical selection, are resistant to drought and mature quickly, it is possible to secure good harvests on the wide alluvial basins lying below and between the mesas or plateaus.

Along the larger streams with permanent flow, such as the tributaries of the Rio Grande, irrigation channels can be taken off to lead water to the farmlands. Elsewhere, as in the Hopi pueblos of Arizona, fields can be made in the valleys at places where the floodwaters of intermittent streams from the mesas spread over the flats to produce natural and temporary inundations after rains in the higher ranges. Along the lower slopes at the foot of the mesas small but frequent natural springs afford opportunities to make irrigated gardens and seepages provide sufficient moisture for further cultivation. The scantiness of the vegetation of shrubs and cacti at lower altitudes and the friability of soils make it possible to clear and plant the ground with the simplest of wooden tools to uproot bushes and dibble in the seeds. Brushwood fences can be erected to afford some protection against the washing out of crops by heavy floods or their destruction by wind-blown sand. Plants are widely spaced and soil fertility is restored by the deposition of new soil so that a suitable area can often be used indefinitely for cultivation. The shortness of the season has induced careful attention to the timing of agricultural activities which is regulated by a calendar based on the daily shift in the position of sunrise along the southern sky line. By these means the Hopi, Zuñi and other Pueblo peoples have for centuries raised crops of maize, beans, squashes, melons, peppers, onions and formerly cotton between April and September in the various tracts of better-watered land which have been appropriated by the kin groups of which the villages are composed. But the hazards of farming are

such that a prudent household endeavours to keep most of a year's maize harvest in reserve, storing it on the ear in dry inner chambers of the house. The securing of the donkey and some new crops such as peaches from the Spaniards and of steel tools and wagons from Americans has not greatly altered the general pattern of Pueblo farming in which individual households still raise their crops by hand cultivation within the framework of village organization.

In addition to the references given above, see also articles on the various plants mentioned (such as CORN and POTATO) and on geographical regions (such as AFRICA; MELANESIA; NORTH AMERICA).

BIBLIOGRAPHY.—D. Forde, Habitat, Economy and Society, 7th ed. (1950), "The Human Record," Diogenes, 9, pp. 1–26 (1955), The Native Economies of Nigeria (1946); C. O. Sauer, Agricultural Origins and Dispersals (1952); V. G. Childe, New Light on the Most Ancient East, 4th ed. (1952); R. J. Braidwood, The Near East and the Foundations for Civilization (1952), "Jericho and Its Setting in Near Eastern History," Antiquity, vol. 31, pp. 73–81 (1957); K. M. Kenyon, "Jericho and Its Setting," Antiquity, vol. 30, pp. 184–195 (1956); F. E. Zeuner, "Cultivation of Plants" in C. Singer et al., A History of Technology, vol. i (1954). (D. F.)

AGRICULTURE, TROPICAL: see TROPICAL AGRICULTURE.

AGRI DECUMATES, a name given by Tacitus to the Black Forest and adjoining areas of southwestern Germany between the Rhine, Danube and Main, which Rome began to annex under the Flavian emperors, starting in A.D. 74. Tacitus, writing in A.D. 98, does not explain the name, but it probably derives from a pre-Roman term whose meaning had been forgotten; it may imply earlier occupation by a tribe with ten cantons. The area was once owned by the Helvetii (q.v.) but later was precariously inhabited, so Tacitus says, by vagabonds from Gaul. The Roman advance was doubtless due to the desire to secure better communications inside the imperial frontier by moving it farther east so as to include behind it the territory partly encircled by the loop of the Rhine as it changes its course from westward to northward. The Alamanni occupied the territory c. A.D. 260.

BIBLIOGRAPHY.—E. Norden, Altgermanien (1934); The Cambridge Ancient History, vol. xi (1936). (G. E. F. C.)

AGRIGENTO (formerly GIRGENTI; AKRAGAS of the Greeks, AGRIGENTUM of the Romans), an ancient and wealthy city near the south coast of Sicily. Founded c. 582 B.C. by Greek colonists from Gela on the site of an existing native settlement, it prospered rapidly, reaching its peak in 480, when Theron (488–472), in alliance with Syracuse, won the decisive battle of Himera over the Carthaginians. In 470 the tyranny that had existed until then was replaced by a democracy. It was the birthplace of the philosopher-politician Empedocles and under the tyranny it was a considerable centre of the arts. Pindar, who calls it the "fairest of mortal cities," and Simonides of Ceos were frequent visitors, and its wealth, founded on agriculture, stockbreeding and commerce, was a byword. Neutral in the struggle between Athens and Syracuse, it was sacked by the Carthaginians in 406 B.C., a disaster from which it never really recovered. It was refounded by Timoleon in 338 and achieved some local importance under the tyrant Phintias (289–279), but soon after fell victim to the rivalry of Rome and Carthage. It was sacked successively by the Romans (262) and the Carthaginians (255), and fell finally to the Romans in 210. Under Roman rule its agricultural wealth and the exploitation of the nearby sulfur mines ensured a modest prosperity, and it was not until late antiquity that the inhabitants withdrew to the relative security of the medieval hilltop town of Girgenti, the nucleus of the modern town of Agrigento. In 828 Girgenti was occupied by the Saracens and colonized. It was captured in 1086 by the Norman conqueror of Sicily, Roger Guiscard (Roger I), who established a Latin bishopric.

The site is beautiful and unusual, occupying a basinlike plateau, encircled on three sides by the low cliffs that overlook the junction of the ancient rivers Hypsas and Akragas (now called Drago and San Biagio respectively), and dominated from the north by a ridge with twin peaks, the so-called Rock of Athena and the eminence later occupied by Girgenti. Which of these peaks was the acropolis (q.v.) has been disputed, some scholars maintaining that the latter lay outside the town. However, reasons of defense seem to

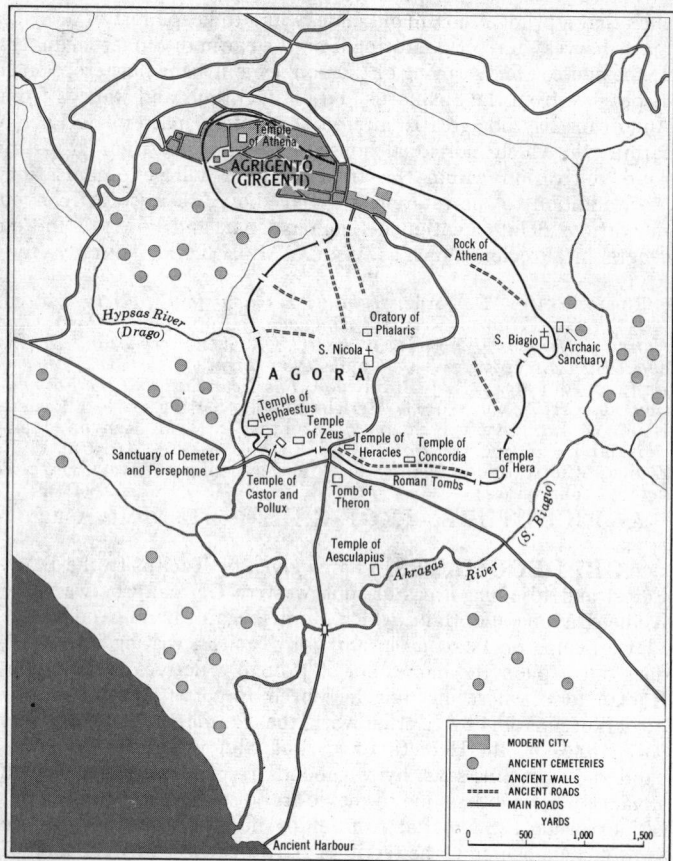

PLAN OF ANCIENT AGRIGENTUM (AKRAGAS) SHOWING SITE OF THE MODERN CITY OF AGRIGENTO

demand its inclusion, and the remains of an early 5th-century Doric temple under the church of Sta. Maria dei Greci may well be those of the temple of Athena, known to have been founded on the acropolis by Theron. That of Zeus Atabyrios perhaps underlies the cathedral. Except to the north and northeast the site is not one of great natural strength, but it was readily defensible by means of a wall which can be traced almost continuously from the Rock of Athena round to the head of the valley south of the hill of Girgenti, a distance of more than 4 mi.; in this stretch there are the remains of eight gates.

The principal excavated remains of the Greek city are its temples, of which no less than seven formed an almost continuous sacred area along the ridge that carries the south line of the city's defenses. All are Doric buildings. (For explanation of terms see GREEK ARCHITECTURE.) All except for the temple of Heracles (peripteral, hexastyle; late 6th cent.; eight standing columns) belong in their present form to the great burst of building activity that followed the victory at Himera in 480. The best preserved are the two very similar peripteral, hexastyle temples conventionally, though wrongly, attributed to Hera and to Concordia; the latter temple, which lacks little but the roof, owes its remarkable conservation to having been converted into a church in A.D. 597. In front of the temple of Hera stood a huge altar, as long as the façade of the temple itself, a feature which is repeated in the temples both of Heracles and of Zeus. This latter temple ($368\frac{1}{2}$ x $184\frac{1}{2}$ ft., a double square) was planned on a scale to which temple G at Selinus (q.v.) offers the only parallel in the field of Doric architecture, and it is one of the most original of all Greek buildings. The huge figures of Atlas, one of which has been recomposed on the site, supported the trabeation between the half-columns of the exterior order, which was unique in consisting not of columns but of half-columns linked by a continuous partition wall. The façade was heptastyle and the cella was open to the sky. Still unfinished in 406, its ruins were quarried in the 18th century to build the jetties of Porto Empedocle and very little is now standing. The sanctuary of Demeter and Persephone, founded on the site

of a pre-Hellenic shrine, is notable for the many remains of its archaic cult-buildings; the familiar standing structure (formerly known as the temple of Castor and Pollux) is largely a 19th-century pastiche. Of the temple of Hephaestus (hexastyle, peripteral; built c. 430) only the platform and two columns have survived. The little Doric temple of Aesculapius outside the walls, in antis (see ANTA), with a false rear porch indicated by half-columns, is notable for its architectural refinements, the lines being all slightly convex. Another simple Doric temple in antis is that of Demeter, underlying the church of S. Biagio; the cave sanctuary at the foot of the cliffs beneath goes back to pre-Hellenic times. The Agora, later the Roman forum, probably lay just north of the temple of Zeus, but apart from the extensive remains of aqueducts and cisterns little is known of the civil or domestic architecture of the Greek city. The "Tomb of Theron" just outside the south gate is a late Hellenistic funerary monument; and the "Oratory of Phalaris," adjoining the picturesque 13th-century Cistercian church of S. Nicola (the setting of Pirandello's *Il Signore della Nave*), is a *heroon,* or heroic shrine, of the 1st century A.D. A short distance to the east of it a considerable quarter of the Hellenistic and Roman town has been excavated. It is laid out on a strictly rectangular plan and includes houses of both Greek peristyle and Italic atrium type.

Although by late antiquity the cemeteries were invading the temple area (the many tombs around the temple of Concordia include a Christian catacomb) the earlier classical cemeteries lay on the slopes and in the valleys beyond the walls to the east and west. The earliest of these, on the low hill of Montelusa, west of the river mouth and the ancient harbour, offers clear evidence of a Greek trading settlement before the formal establishment of the colony.

The modern town, whose name was changed from Girgenti to Agrigento in 1927, is the capital of the province of Agrigento and an episcopal see, 58 mi. south by east of Palermo direct and $84\frac{1}{2}$ mi. by rail. Pop. (1957 est.) 44,338 (commune). The old quarter contains many historic buildings, notably the cathedral (14th century), the medieval churches of S. Giorgio and S. Spirito, and a number of baroque churches and palaces; there is a large modern quarter spreading over the Rock of Athena. The museum contains fine vases, sculptures, terra cottas, etc. Porto Empedocle (pop., [1957 est.] 17,513 commune), $5\frac{1}{2}$ mi. S.W. by rail, was founded in the 18th century by Bishop Gioeni of Agrigento. It is the best harbour on the southwest coast of Sicily, and serves the important sulfur mines in the hills just to the north of Agrigento. It was heavily bombed by the Allies during World War II.

See P. Griffo, *Guide to the Monuments of Agrigento* (1956).

(J. B. W.-P.)

AGRIMONY, a slender perennial herb (botanical name, *Agrimonia eupatoria,* family Rosaceae), $1\frac{1}{2}$ to 3 ft. high, growing in hedge banks, copses and borders of fields. The leafy stem ends in spikes of small yellow flowers. The flower stalk becomes recurved in the fruiting stage, and the fruit bears a number of hooks which enable it to cling to rough objects, such as the coat of an animal, thus ensuring distribution of the seed. The plant is widely spread through the north temperate region. The underground woody stem is astringent and yields a yellow dye.

The name has been unsystematically given to several other plants; for instance: bastard, Dutch, hemp or water agrimony (*Eupatorium cannabinum*); noble or three-leaved agrimony (*Anemone hepatica*); water agrimony (*Bidens*); and wild agrimony (*Potentilla anserina*).

AGRIONIA (the "gathering"), an ancient Greek festival celebrated annually at Orchomenus in Boeotia and elsewhere in honour of Dionysus by women and priests at night. The tradition is that the daughters of Minyas, king of Orchomenus, having despised the rites of the god, were driven mad by Dionysus and ate the flesh of one of their children; as punishment they were turned into bats, or birds. At this festival it was originally the custom for the priest of the god to pursue a woman of the Minyan family with a drawn sword and kill her.

AGRIPPA, a skeptical philosopher to whom are ascribed the "five tropes" (types of skeptical argument) which, according to

Sextus Empiricus, summarize the attitude of the later ancient skeptics. His date cannot be accurately determined but he must have lived later than Aenesidemus. He argued: (1) there is a clash of opinions, both in daily life and in the debates of philosophers; (2) nothing is self-evident—what is called a proof is a second proposition which itself needs demonstration, and so on ad infinitum; (3) perceptions and judgments are relative in a double sense—each is relative to a subject, and each is affected by concomitant perceptions; (4) dogmatic philosophers, to avoid the infinite regress, simply offer hypotheses which they are unable to prove; and (5) philosophers are involved in the vicious circle of proving the sensible by the intelligible and establishing the intelligible in its turn by the sensible.

The general result is that we have no starting point for knowledge. No perception or judgment guarantees its own truth, and the methods of proof which philosophers have attempted to use are all invalid. The ten tropes of Aenesidemus (*q.v.*) were concerned mainly with presentations of the senses and occupied a subordinate place in his defense of skepticism. Agrippa's tropes are integrated with one another and deal not merely with perceptions, but also with modes of proof. *See* also AENESIDEMUS.

For sources *see* Diogenes Laertius, ix, 88 *et seq.*, and Sextus Empiricus, *Hypotyposes*, i, 164–169. (D. J. A.)

AGRIPPA, HEINRICH CORNELIUS (AGRIPPA VON NETTESHEIM) (1486–1535), German writer, soldier and physician whose works on occult subjects gained him a reputation as a magician, was born at Cologne on Sept. 14, 1486, of the lesser nobility. From 1501 to 1507 he was a captain in the emperor Maximilian I's army. In 1509 his lectures at Dôle university, in the Franche-Comté, on the *De verbo mirifico,* Johann Reuchlin's liberal treatise on religion, roused ecclesiastical opposition. In 1510 he left Dôle for London, where he stayed with the humanist John Colet. He married his first wife in 1514, at Cologne. Eustache Chapuys, later imperial ambassador to England, stood godfather to their son. In 1515 Agrippa was lecturing at Pavia university and remained in Italy until 1518, when, recommended by William VI of Montferrat, he became public orator and advocate at Metz. His defense of an accused witch brought him ecclesiastical condemnation, and in 1520 he left Metz for Cologne, where his first wife died. In 1524 he went to Lyons as physician to Louise of Savoy, but in 1527, having received no salary, he again moved. He was appointed historiographer to the emperor Charles V at Antwerp in 1529. Imprisoned for debt in Brussels in 1531, he was rescued by Chapuys. He died at Grenoble in Dauphiné, on Feb. 18, 1535, having been three times married and leaving seven children.

Agrippa's principal works are *De occulta philosophia,* written about 1510 in Cologne and published in revised form in Antwerp in 1531; and *De incertitudine et vanitate scientiarum et artium atque excellentia Verbi Dei declamatio,* written between 1527 and 1528, and published at Antwerp in 1531. The latter work, influenced by Pico della Mirandola and Reuchlin, is a biting satire on the state of science, attacks the belief in witches, denounces the accretions which had grown up around the simple doctrines of Christianity and attacks the reactionary schoolmen of his time. The *De occulta philosophia,* a fascinating mixture of Neoplatonic and Christian beliefs, contains a system of cabalistic-mystical philosophy in which magic emerges as the most perfect science which can lead men to a knowledge of nature and God. It contains Agrippa's doctrine of the three worlds—those of the elements, of the stars and of the spirits, corresponding to the physical world, to the heavenly world and to the world of the mind—and postulates a fifth element (quintessence) that presides over the four elements. Agrippa displays many features later to be embodied in Goethe's *Faust.* An edition of his works was published at Leiden in 1550. Book i of *De occulta philosophia* was also reprinted in *Three Books of Occult Philosophy,* ed. by W. F. Whitehead (1898).

BIBLIOGRAPHY.—H. Morley, *Life of H. C. Agrippa* (1856); A. Prost, *Cornelius Agrippa, sa vie et ses oeuvres* (1881); J. Orsier, *Henri Cornélis Agrippa: sa vie et son oeuvre d'après sa correspondance* (1911); J. Meurer, *Zur Logik des C. Agrippa* (1920). (D. G. D.)

AGRIPPA, MARCUS VIPSANIUS (63–12 B.C.), Roman statesman and general, the chief agent of Octavian in his rise to power and chief support of the Augustan monarchy. Agrippa was with Octavian at Apollonia when the news arrived that Julius Caesar had been assassinated, and went with him to Rome to claim the inheritance (44 B.C.). Their path led through hazard and violence. Before long Agrippa helped Caesar's heir to recruit a private army. No action of his is recorded in the campaigns of Mutina and Philippi, but he played an important role in the War of Perusia (41–40).

Two years later, while governing Gaul for Octavian, he crushed a rebellion of the Aquitanian tribes and led an expedition across the Rhine. The consulate was his reward (37). Meanwhile Octavian had been calamitously defeated by Sextus Pompeius, who commanded the seas adjacent to Italy. Agrippa's help was needed. He trained fresh crews and constructed a great harbour on the Bay of Naples, using the Lucrinus (Lucrino) and Avernus (Averno) lakes. Then in the next year an attack was launched against Sicily, Pompeius being overcome by Agrippa at the battles of Mylae and Naulochus. When at last the uneasy alliance that apportioned the Roman world between Octavian and Mark Antony broke down, it was Agrippa's talent that won the decisive victory at Actium (31).

Agrippa proceeded to a second consulate as colleague of Octavian in 28 (when they held a census together and purged the Roman senate), likewise to a third in 27. In January of that year Octavian announced that normal government had been restored to Rome and took the cognomen Augustus. For the next 15 years Agrippa seems to have functioned as deputy to Augustus, alternating between Rome and the provinces; the two men were seldom in the same place. The year 23, in which occurred a conspiracy against the principate and the grave illness of Augustus, was critical for the new system of government, but it did not shake the power or diminish the utility of his ally. Agrippa went to the east (presumably on some important mission the nature of which is not recorded). In 23 the young Marcellus, nephew of Augustus and husband of his daughter Julia, died, and when Agrippa was recalled in 21 he received the widow as his bride. He then went to Gaul and Spain, where he completed the subjugation of the north and northwest.

In 18 Augustus admitted Agrippa to partnership in some of the special powers of the principate; and the sons whom Julia had borne him, Gaius (b. 20) and Lucius (b. 17), were promptly adopted by Augustus, who was anxious for the dynastic succession. In 17 Agrippa went away to supervise the provinces of the east, with extensive powers. He stayed there for four years during which he settled the affairs of the Bosporan kingdom, planted veteran colonies at Berytus (Beirut) and Heliopolis (Baalbek) and pursued a policy of friendship with Herod the Great. He came back in 13 to open operations against the Pannonians in Illyricum, but died early in the next year.

Agrippa was not merely a great general, but an organizer and an engineer. When aedile at Rome in 33 he had carried out many improvements, repairing sewers and aqueducts. He built a new aqueduct, the Aqua Julia. The Pantheon (built in 25) is also his. He prepared a map of the world and left behind notes on geography and a record of his own life.

Agrippa was a parvenu of obscure parentage. He is represented as self-effacing and tireless in his loyalty to Augustus. He was married three times, first to Caecilia Attica, the daughter of Cicero's friend T. Pomponius Atticus; a daughter of this marriage, Vipsania, married Tiberius Claudius Nero (later the emperor Tiberius). The death or divorce of Attica *c.* 29 qualified him for a dynastic match with Augustus' niece, the elder Marcella, whom he divorced in 21 in order to become the son-in-law of the *princeps.* Julia had three sons, Gaius, Lucius and Agrippa Postumus, and two daughters, Julia and the elder Agrippina (mother of Caligula and grandmother of Nero).

BIBLIOGRAPHY.—T. Rice Holmes, *The Architect of the Roman Empire,* 2 vol. (1928–31); M. Reinhold, *Marcus Agrippa, a Biography* (1933); F. A. Wright, *Marcus Agrippa, Organizer of Victory* (1937); R. Syme, *The Roman Revolution,* 2nd ed. (1951). (R. SE.)

AGRIPPINA THE ELDER (*c.* 14 B.C.–A.D. 33), daughter of Marcus Vipsanius Agrippa and of Augustus' daughter Julia, was born about 14 B.C. and married her second cousin Germanicus Caesar (*q.v.*) about A.D. 5. She accompanied her husband to Germany and to the east and after his death at Antioch in A.D. 19 promoted the trial of Gnaeus Piso for his murder. The death of Tiberius' son Drusus in 23 brought her sons into direct hope of the succession, and she became the object of attacks from Sejanus (*q.v.*), who had his own alternative designs. Finally in 29 she was exiled to Pandateria off the coast of Campania, where on Oct. 18, 33, she died, starved to death by herself or, according to some, by order of Tiberius. Her two elder sons, Nero and Drusus, had already died violent deaths. Of her nine children by Germanicus one son and three daughters survived her, the son being the emperor Gaius (Caligula) and the most famous of the daughters being Agrippina the mother of Nero. Her arrogance had moved Tiberius to protest that she must not take it as an insult that she was not actually queen of Rome, but her private life has escaped reproach.

There are several fine portraits of her, the most famous in the Capitoline museum at Rome, and a coin issue of which there are examples in the British museum commemorates the return of her ashes to Rome under Gaius' order.

BIBLIOGRAPHY.—Tacitus, *Annals* i–vi; Suetonius, *Tiberius; Cambridge Ancient History,* vol. x and volume of plates, iv (1934).   (G. E. F. C.)

AGRIPPINA THE YOUNGER (A.D. 16–59), daughter of the elder Agrippina, sister of the emperor Gaius (Caligula) and mother of Nero, was born at Oppidum Ubiorum on the Rhine, afterward named in her honour Colonia Agrippinensis (mod. Cologne). By her first husband, Gnaeus Domitius Ahenobarbus, she was the mother of the emperor Nero; her second husband was Passienus Crispus, whom she was accused of poisoning in 49. In 39 she was involved in a conspiracy against Gaius and exiled, but returned to Rome in 41.

In 49, after the death of Messallina, she married the emperor Claudius I (*q.v.*), her uncle, and induced him to adopt the future Nero as heir to the throne in place of his own son (Britannicus). She also protected Seneca and Burrus, who were to be Nero's tutors and advisers in the early part of his reign. In 54 she is said to have poisoned Claudius and secured the throne for her son. She exercised a considerable influence on political life during the first years of Nero's reign, but later her power declined. She quarrelled with Nero about his private life and opposed his liaison with Poppaea. Nero thereupon decided to get rid of his mother. Pretending a reconciliation, he invited her to Baiae, where an unsuccessful attempt was made to drown her on a vessel constructed to founder. Eventually he had her put to death at her country house. Agrippina wrote memoirs, referred to by Tacitus and Pliny the Elder.

BIBLIOGRAPHY.—Tacitus, *Annals* xii, xiii, xiv; Suetonius, *Nero;* B. W. Henderson, *The Life and Principate of the Emperor Nero* (1903).
							(A. D. Mo.)

AGRONOMY. In the middle 1890s the term agronomy, used to designate the branch of agriculture dealing with climate, soils, fertilizers and crops (plant production), was introduced into the agricultural colleges and experiment stations of the United States. The term later came to be used generally to indicate that branch of agriculture dealing with the science and the art of field crop culture and soil management. However, in some institutions the term agronomy is limited to the culture of field crops. *See* also Index references under "Agronomy" in the Index volume.						(A. D. T.)

AGUADILLA, a municipal district that forms the northwest corner of the island of Puerto Rico. Its population in 1960 was 47,864. The town of Aguadilla itself is located on the west coast of Puerto Rico, on the Mona passage that connects the Atlantic ocean with the Caribbean sea. The excellent port facilities provided by a deep bay, formed on the south by Point Jigüero and to the north by Point Boriquén, the northwest tip of Puerto Rico, are strategically located close to the shipping routes. The agricultural area around Aguadilla produces principally sugar, coconuts and tropical fruits such as avocados and grapefruit. Excellent roads lead to Mayagüez to the south, east to San Juan, the capital of Puerto Rico, and into the interior towns of San Sebastián and Lares. Slightly to the north of the town is Ramey air force base, one of the largest U.S. air bases in the Caribbean zone. Overlooking the town, the bay, and Mona passage is a well-serviced and popular tourist hotel.

Although the town was not founded until 1775, its historical tradition dates from 1493 when Columbus, on his second voyage, supposedly refilled the fleet's water casks from a spring which still flows in the centre of the town.				(T. G. Ms.)

AGUASCALIENTES, an inland state of Mexico, bounded north, east and west by the state of Zacatecas, and south by Jalisco. Pop. (1950) 188,075; (1960) 236,574. Area 2,499 sq.mi. The state occupies a part of the plateau of central Mexico about 6,000 ft. above sea level, extending from two spurs of the Sierra Madre, called the Sierra Pinal and Sierra de Laurel, eastward to the rolling fertile plains of its eastern and southeastern districts. It is well watered by numerous small streams and one large river, the Aguascalientes or Río Verde, and has a mild healthful climate with a light rainfall. The fertile valleys of the north and west are devoted to agriculture and the plains to stock raising. Indian corn, flour, cattle, horses, mules and hides are exported to the neighbouring states.

The area was explored by the Spaniards in the 16th century and was a mining centre of colonial days. Its name, Aguascalientes, meaning "hot waters," stems from the many thermal springs in the vicinity. The state is one of the smallest in Mexico; its present boundaries were delineated by the constitution of 1857. During the revolution of 1910–20 it was the centre of bitter fighting and was occupied by successive factions in the struggle. The capital city, also named Aguascalientes (*see* below), was a military prize because of its important rail terminals.

Aguascalientes is the centre of many beautiful orchards and vineyards, and produces excellent wines and fruits. Irrigation projects carried out in the 1950s greatly increased the productivity of the land. The state is also noted for its mining products: zinc, copper, gold, silver, lead and antimony. The ranches of Aguascalientes raise bulls for the *corridas* all over Mexico. The state and capital city have excellent rail, air and highway connections with all parts of Mexico.						(J. A. Cw.)

AGUASCALIENTES, a city of Mexico and capital of the state of the same name, 364 mi. N.W. of Mexico City. Pop. (1960) 122,809. Altitude 6,261 ft. Aguascalientes was founded Oct. 22, 1575, and became the state capital when the area was created a separate state during the 1850s. The city contains cotton and other textile factories, potteries, tobacco factories, distilleries and other industries. It is also the centre of a rich agricultural region producing many varieties of fruits and vegetables. The city contains many fine public buildings and churches. The most notable churches are San Juan de Dios, San Francisco and La Parroquia, each of which possesses outstanding examples of colonial religious art. The city is sometimes called La Ciudad Perforada (the perforated city) because of a labyrinth of tunnels beneath it excavated in pre-Columbian times by some unidentified tribe.
							(R. B. McCʏ.)

AGUE, the common name given to a form or stage of malarial disease; the ague fit is the cold, shivering stage, and hence the word is also loosely used for any such paroxysm.

See MALARIA.

AGUESSEAU, HENRI FRANÇOIS D' (1668–1751), French jurist and statesman who as chancellor of France made many important reforms in his country's legal system. He was born at Limoges, Nov. 27, 1668, the son of Henri d'Aguesseau, who held a number of high positions in the government. Educated for the law under Jean Domat, he distinguished himself as an advocate and in 1700 was appointed procurator general. As such, he defended the rights of the Gallican Church against Rome in the controversy over the promulgation in France of the papal bull *Unigenitus.* The regent Philippe d'Orléans made him chancellor and keeper of the seals in 1717 but withdrew the seals and exiled him to Fresnes in 1718 because of his opposition to John Law's projects. D'Aguesseau recovered the seals on his recall in 1720 and then, reversing his original attitude, helped Guillaume Dubois in his efforts to register the bull *Unigenitus.* However, he opposed other measures of Dubois and forfeited the seals again when Dubois became chief minister (1722). After five years spent in study at Fresnes, he was recalled by Cardinal Fleury in 1727 (though G. L. de Chauvelin was *garde des sceaux* till 1737). D'Aguesseau failed in his attempt to codify French law, but formulated several enactments concerning donations, testaments and successions and also introduced regulations for improving the forms of procedure and for effecting a greater uniformity in the execution of laws. He died in Paris on Feb. 9, 1751.

The chancellor's grandson, Henri Cardin Jean Baptiste, Marquis d'Aguesseau (1752–1826), who was born in Paris on Aug. 23, 1752, became advocate general in the *parlement* of Paris (1772), a member of the Académie Française (1787) and a deputy in the estates-general (1789). Under the consulate he was appointed president of the court of appeal of Paris and then minister to Denmark (1803). He was a member of the senate from 1805 to 1814, in which year Louis XVIII made him a peer of France. He died in Paris on Jan. 22, 1826.

Bibliography.—A selection of H. F. d'Aguesseau's own works ed. by E. Falconnet, 2 vol. (1865), includes a biographical notice. *See also* Charles Butler, *Memoir of the Life of Henry Francis d'Aguesseau* (1830) ; F. Monnier, *Le Chancelier d'Aguesseau,* 2nd ed. (1863).

AGUILAR, GRACE (1816–1847), English poet and novelist who wrote on Jewish history and religion, was born in London on June 2, 1816, of a family of Spanish-Jewish origin. An early book of poems, *The Magic Wreath,* appeared when she was 19. In *The Spirit of Judaism* (1842) she wrote in defense of her faith. She died, Sept. 16, 1847, at Frankfurt am Main, Ger. Many of her works were published posthumously. A branch of the New York public library is named after her.

AGUINALDO, EMILIO (1869–1964), Filipino leader who fought first against Spain and later against the United States for independence of the Philippines. He was born on March 23, 1869, near Cavite, Luzon, of Chinese and Tagalog parentage. He completed his education at the University of Santo Tomás, Manila. In Aug. 1896 he was mayor of Cavite Viejo and was the local leader of the Katipunan, a revolutionary society which fought bitterly and successfully against the Spanish. In Jan. 1898 he signed an agreement called the pact of Biac-na-Bató with the Spanish governor-general. He agreed to leave the Philippines and to remain permanently in exile on condition of a substantial financial reward from Spain coupled with the promise of liberal reforms. While in Hong Kong and Singapore he made arrangements with representatives of the American consulates and of Commodore George Dewey (*q.v.*) to return to the Philippines to assist the United States in the war against Spain. (*See* Philippines: *History;* Spanish-American War.)

After the power of Spain was destroyed in the Philippines, Aguinaldo broke with the U.S. authorities because he wanted complete independence for his country. His followers adopted their own flag, organized an army, assembled a congress and proclaimed the first Republic of the Philippines at Malolos, Bulacan, just a few miles away from the U.S. headquarters in Manila. After three years of costly fighting, General Aguinaldo was captured on March 23, 1901, and the insurrection came to an end. Aguinaldo took an oath of allegiance to the United States, was granted a pension from the U.S. government and retired to private life.

In 1935 when the commonwealth government of the Philippines was established in preparation for independence, Aguinaldo ran for president but was decisively beaten. He returned to private life until the Japanese invaded the Philippines in 1941. The Japanese used Aguinaldo as an anti-American tool. They caused him to make speeches, sign articles, and to address a radio appeal to Gen. Douglas MacArthur on Corregidor to surrender in order to spare the flower of Filipino youth. When the Americans returned, Aguinaldo was arrested and, together with others accused of collaboration with the Japanese, was held for some months in Bilibid prison until released by presidential amnesty. As a token vindication of his honour, he was appointed by Pres. Elpidio Quirino as a member of the council of state in 1950. In the later years of his life, he devoted his major attention to veterans' affairs, the promotion of nationalism and democracy in the Philippines, and the improvement of relations between the Philippines and the United States. He died in Manila on Feb. 6, 1964. (C. A. B.)

AGUIRRE, LOPE DE (1518–1561), a Spanish adventurer, born in Oñate, in the province of Biscay in 1518, and known as the "traitor." Arriving in Peru in 1544, he took part in the internal strife among the Spaniards that followed the defeat of the Incas. In 1560 he joined the expedition that Pedro de Ursúa organized to search for the legendary "El Dorado." After reaching the headwaters of the Amazon, Aguirre incited a rebellion which resulted in Ursúa's death. Fernando de Guzmán met the same fate at the hands of Aguirre after failing to co-operate in the latter's plans for renouncing allegiance to Spain. During the course of travel to Venezuela by way of the Amazon and a tributary of the Orinoco, Aguirre was responsible for the death of about 80 persons, including women, priests and his own daughter. Aguirre was captured and executed at Barquisimeto in 1561. (J. L. Tr.)

AGUSAN, a province in northeastern Mindanao, Republic of the Philippines, with a land area of 4,458 sq.mi. Its population in 1960 was 271,010. After 1950 there was rapid immigration from Cebu, Bohol and Leyte as new lands were opened and new roads constructed. The economy of the province is related to the forest and the farm. There are many lumber mills; the one at Nasipit is among the largest in the far east and operates a kiln dryer and a hardboard plant. Agricultural products are principally corn, coconuts and abaca. The area is drained by the Agusan river, which is navigable for river craft and log rafts throughout the length of the province. The river and a highway that parallels it are the routes to the interior settlements.

The capital, Butuan, lies on the west bank of the Agusan, near its mouth. It has several sawmills and is a regional depot for a few petroleum companies. Pop. (1960) 82,485. (An. C.)

AHAB (in the Douai version of the Bible, Achab), son of Omri, king of Israel from *c.* 874 to *c.* 853 b.c. (I Kings xvi, 29–xxii, 40). In some respects his reign represented the high-water mark of the success of the northern kingdom. In the reigns of Omri (*q.v.*) and Ahab the northern kingdom for the first time took an important part in international politics. Omri left to his son an empire which comprised not only territory to the east of Jordan, in Gilead and probably Bashan, but also the land of Moab, whose king was tributary. Judah (and probably Edom also), if not actually subject to Omri, was certainly a subordinate ally. Ahab's marriage with Jezebel (*q.v.*), daughter of Ethbaal of Sidon, revived an alliance which had been in abeyance since the time of Solomon.

Throughout the reign of Ahab, however, a fierce border war was waged with Damascus in which Israel, in spite of occasional victory, proved the weaker, while Mesha, king of Moab, successfully revolted and occupied the southern portions of the territory of Gad. The forces of Israel retained strength enough to contribute the second largest contingent of soldiers (the largest force of chariots) to the combined armies which, under the leadership of Bar-Hadad I of Damascus (Hebrew, Ben-Hadad; throne name, Hadadezer; Akkadian, Adad-idri), checked the westward movement of Shalmaneser III of Assyria at Karkar. After the Assyrian repulse, however, the alliance broke up, and Ahab met his death fighting the Syrians in a vain attempt to recover Ramoth Gilead.

Domestically, contact with a wider world and, especially, the alliance with Phoenicia had far-reaching results for the kingdom of Israel itself. Jezebel attempted to introduce into religion and government elements which were common enough elsewhere in the ancient world but strange in Israel. She endeavoured to set up the worship of the Tyrian Baal in Samaria and to maintain the familiar oriental principle of the absolute despotic power and authority of the sovereign. This roused the bitter hostility of that conservative party, which clung to the sole worship of the national god, Yahweh, and at the same time held to those democratic conceptions of society which the Hebrews had brought with them from the wilderness and had consistently maintained. The spirit of this party found expression in the prophet Elijah (*q.v.*), who protested alike against the establishment of the Baal priests and the judicial murder of Naboth. He and those who came after him seem to have been successful in eliminating the foreign worship, though in the end their purpose was achieved only by a bloody revolution, but they were powerless to stem the tide of social and moral deterioration. To the reign of Ahab may be traced the beginning of that sapping of the national life which led to the condemnations of the 8th-century prophets and to the downfall of

Samaria.   (T. H. R.)

AHAD HAAM (literally "One of the people"; real name ASHER GINZBERG) (1856–1927), Hebrew writer and leader of "spiritual Zionism." Born Aug. 18, 1856, in Skvira, Ukraine, and reared in a strictly orthodox family, he acquired a mastery of rabbinic literature but was early attracted to the rationalist school of medieval Jewish philosophy and soon turned to the writings of the modern Jewish "Enlightenment" (*Haskala*). At the age of 22 he went to Odessa, the centre of the Jewish nationalist movement, *Hoveve Zion* ("Lovers of Zion"). There he came under the influence of both Jewish nationalism and the teachings of the Russian thinker D. I. Pisarev and the English and French positivists. He joined the central comittee of *Hoveve Zion* and published his first essay "Lo ze ha-Derekh" ("This is not the Way," 1889), which opened a new epoch in Jewish nationalist ideology. It contained all the basic features of what was later called "spiritual Zionism" and, though praised and welcomed by many, was also severely criticized by the more practically minded. Ahad Haam thus became involved in controversy and was thereafter to remain so. In 1891 and 1893 he visited Palestine to study the movement's colonizing methods, and recorded his impressions and reflections in two critical essays, "Emeth me-Erez Yisrael" ("The Truth from Palestine"). In 1895 he published a collection of essays, *Al Parashat Derakhim* ("At the Crossroads"), followed by three further volumes (1903, 1904, 1913). In 1897 he founded the periodical *Ha-Shiloah* in which he severely criticized Theodor Herzl's political Zionism. He remained outside the Zionist organization, although in deep sympathy with the goal of a Jewish national centre in Palestine. In 1908 he moved to London and in 1912 visited Palestine a third time, later describing his observations in the essay "Sakh ha-Kol" ("Sum Total"). His last years he spent in Palestine editing his *Letters* (*Iggeroth Ahad Ha-Am*, 6 vol., 1923–25). He died on Jan. 2, 1927, in Tel Aviv. Further letters, notably from the last phase of his life, and his memoirs were published in *Ahad Ha-Am: Pirqe Zikhronoth we-Iggeroth* (1931).

Ahad Haam's doctrine blends an idealist conception of Judaism with a positivist and sociological approach. He interprets the Jewish religious and ethical teachings as expressions of Jewish culture and stresses the rational and moral character of Judaism. Unlike the Jewish reformers in western Europe and America, however, he also stresses that the national spirit is essential both for Jewish survival and as a means of expressing moral values in a distinctly Jewish way of life. He therefore calls for a renaissance of Hebrew culture and to this end urges the creation of a Jewish national home in Palestine as the centre and model for Jewish life in the Diaspora. He believes that this goal cannot be achieved by purely political means but primarily through spiritual rebirth. He rejects the solutions of thinkers who sought to recreate Jewish nationhood by a radical "transformation of values." Though himself deeply affected by secularizing tendencies, he retains a passionate love for what he regards as the essence of traditional Judaism. He is convinced that the Jewish people have not lost their creative capacity and proclaims his faith in the establishment of a Jewish culture in Palestine embodying the ideals of social justice and righteousness.

He expressed his lofty program in language of superb clarity and precision. His Hebrew style, though employing to some extent the allusive imagery (*meliza*) of an earlier period, paved the way for modern Hebrew prose and was a very important formative influence. Above all, his high moral pathos had a tremendous impact on his contemporaries. A more critical attitude to his ideology later began to assert itself, however, chiefly because of his excessive rationalism.

BIBLIOGRAPHY.—His collected writings appeared in 1947, 1 vol. (German trans., 4 vol., 1923). For a full bibliography in Hebrew *see* Arye (Sir Leon) Simon and Yosef Eliyahu Heller, *Ahad Ha-am, Ha-Ish, Poalo we-Thoratho* ("The Man, His Work and Doctrine," 1955). For English translations see *Selected Essays* (1912) and *Essays, Letters, Memoirs* (1948) translated by Arye (Sir Leon) Simon.   (A. AN.)

AHAGGAR MOUNTAINS, a large plateau region, also spelled HOGGAR, in the north centre of the Sahara (*q.v.*), lies on the Tropic of Cancer between longitude 5° and 7° E., about 900 mi. S. of Algiers. Its height is above 3,000 ft. culminating in Mt.

Tahat (9,842 ft.). The plateau is rocky desert composed of rocks with low dips. The main caravan route from Algiers to Kano in northern Nigeria passes along the western margin through the important oasis town of Tamanrasset. There has been exploration for oil northwest of the plateau.   (J. I. P.)

AHASUERUS (in the Douai version of the Bible, ASSUERUS; in the Septuagint, ARTAXERXES), a royal Persian name occurring in Ezra iv, 6, Dan. ix, 1 and throughout the book of Esther. Its occurrence in Tob. xiv, 15 in some Greek manuscripts is the result of a copyist's error. In Ezra iv, 6 Ahasuerus is mentioned as a king of Persia, to whom the enemies of the Jews sent representations opposing the rebuilding of the temple at Jerusalem. He thus occupies a place in a chronological series of those Persian rulers who were directly concerned with events of Jewish history. (*See* EZRA AND NEHEMIAH, BOOKS OF.) Immediately preceding Artaxerxes I Longimanus, he is evidently to be identified with Xerxes. In the book of Esther the king, at whose court the scene is laid, bears the same Hebrew name. Probably Xerxes is again the king intended. (*See* ESTHER, BOOK OF.)

In Dan. ix, 1 "Ahasuerus" is the father of "Darius the Mede," who is said to have become king over Babylonia upon the death of Belshazzar. The name seems impossible here, however, and may be the result of some accident in the literary transmission. No other name resembling Ahasuerus, nor any name like Darius, is to be found in the list of Median kings. It is known, moreover, that the immediate successor of Nabonidus and Belshazzar as ruler of Babylonia was Cyrus. Comparison with the list of Persian kings in the book of Ezra seems to show that in the Jewish tradition Darius I Hystaspis was placed before Cyrus as "Darius the Mede."   (C. C. T.; X.)

AHAZ (Assyrian JEHOAHAZ; in the Douai version of the Bible, ACHAZ), king of Judah. After the death of Menahem, Pekah, king of Israel, and Rezin (Rasun), king of Syria, allied against Assyria and invaded Judah. At the same time the Edomites recovered Elath on the Gulf of Akabah and Judah was isolated. Notwithstanding the counsel of Isaiah (*see* ISAIAH, BOOK OF), Ahaz called in the aid of Tiglath-Pileser I who, after attacking the Philistines, destroyed the power of Syria and exacted heavy tribute from Judah. It was as a vassal that Ahaz presented himself to the Assyrian king at Damascus, and he brought back religious innovations described in II Kings xvi, 10–18.

See W. R. Smith, *Religion of the Semites,* 2nd ed. (1894).

AHAZIAH (in the Douai version of the Bible, OCHOZIAS), the name of two biblical kings. (1) Ahaziah, eighth king of Israel, was the son and successor of Ahab and reigned for less than two years. On his accession the Moabites refused to pay any further tribute. Ahaziah lost his life through a fall from the lattice of an upper room in his palace (II Kings i, 2–17). (2) Ahaziah, sixth king of Judah, son of Jehoram and Ahab's daughter Athaliah, reigned one year. He, together with Jehoram, king of Israel, was slain by Jehu, son of Jehoshaphat (II Kings viii, 25–ix, 28). *See* also ELIJAH; ELISHA.

AHENOBARBUS, the name of a distinguished plebeian family of the Roman *gens Domitia*, members of which held consulships in 192 (from which time the family had the status of nobility), 162, 122, 96, 94, 54, 32, 16 B.C. and A.D. 32.

GNAEUS DOMITIUS AHENOBARBUS (consul 122 B.C.), helped to subdue southeastern Gaul and gave his name to the Via Domitia, the highway from Italy to Spain; his son of the same name (consul 96) opened the office of *pontifex maximus,* the head of the official religion, to popular election and was himself elected in 103.

LUCIUS DOMITIUS AHENOBARBUS (consul 54; d. 48 B.C.), was a die-hard member of the class of *optimates* (families whose power in the later republic was due to wealth and to distinction in public office throughout successive generations). A bitter enemy of Julius Caesar, he took Pompey's side in the civil war of 49 (when he was appointed to succeed Caesar in Gaul), although a kinsman had been put to death by Pompey as a supporter of Gaius Marius in 81. He tried to secure the loyalty of 10,000 or more troops under his command by promising each man 25 ac. out of his own estates, but his men went over to Caesar. Domitius was spared by Caesar, but resumed the struggle; he raised Massilia (Marseilles) against Caesar and fell fighting against him at Pharsalus.

GNAEUS DOMITIUS AHENOBARBUS (d. 31 B.C.), a son of Lucius, was, according to Suetonius, the best of a family notorious for its pride and cruelty. He had taken the same side as his father, and after Caesar's death he espoused the cause of Brutus and Cassius and commanded their fleet in 42. After their defeat by Mark Antony at Philippi he held out as a privateer, but was reconciled to Antony in 40 and became one of his chief partisans. A consul in 32, the year when the final breach occurred between Antony and Octavian, he fled from Italy to the east. But he could not brook Cleopatra's dominance over Antony and deserted him just before the battle of Actium (q.v.), only to die soon after, allegedly of remorse. The Enobarbus of Shakespeare's *Antony and Cleopatra* portrays him imaginatively but unhistorically.

LUCIUS DOMITIUS AHENOBARBUS (consul 16 B.C.), son of the last-mentioned Gnaeus, was promoted by Augustus to high commands, despite his family's past record. About A.D. 1 he carried Roman arms to the Elbe river. He was married to Antony's daughter by his wife Octavia, Augustus' sister, and their son Gnaeus was given in marriage to the younger Agrippina (q.v.). A son of this union, adopted by Agrippina's third husband, the emperor Claudius, became the emperor Nero (q.v.), the last Ahenobarbus.

See R. Syme, *The Roman Revolution*, reprint (1951).   (P. A. BR.)

AHIKAR, WISDOM OF,

the title of a story and collection of proverbs connected with the wise Ahikar, originating almost certainly in Babylonia, probably about 550 B.C. The oldest version of the text is in some 5th-century B.C. Aramaic papyrus fragments. In it the Assyrian kings Sennacherib and Esarhaddon are mentioned. Two other persons in the narrative bear Babylonian names: Ahikar's nephew Nadin (Nadan) and Nabusumiskun, who is known to have been one of Sennacherib's officers. Ahikar's own name appears as Ahiyaqar. The collection of proverbs is chronologically the fourth oldest extant, following the Egyptian, Mesopotamian (cuneiform) and Old Testament ones.

The Aramaic version relates how Ahikar was the counselor of the kings of Assyria. As he had no children of his own he brought up his sister's son, Nadin, as his heir. But he was ill rewarded, for Nadin aroused the suspicions of King Esarhaddon against Ahikar. He was sentenced to death, but managed to escape. At this point the story breaks off, but later versions tell how Ahikar regained his position, and Nadin was put in prison, where he had to listen to the proverbs and moral sayings of his uncle. It is not known if this is how the proverbs were originally attached to the story.

The story and sayings of Ahikar enjoyed great popularity. His name, in the form Achiacharus, is mentioned in the book of Tobit (i, 21, 22; xiv, 10), and some passages in both the Old and the New Testaments perhaps show acquaintance with episodes from the story. A life of Aesop takes material from it, and Theophrastus and Democritus were reputed to have known and used the sayings. Ahikar is also mentioned in the Koran. More or less complete versions, exhibiting minor and sometimes fantastic variations, are extant in Aramaic, Syriac, Arabic, Ethiopic, Armenian, Slavonic, Old Turkish and Rumanian.

BIBLIOGRAPHY.—Aramaic version with Eng. trans. in A. E. Cowley, *Aramaic Papyri of the 5th century B.C.*, pp. 204–248 (1923); versions (save for the Rumanian) translated with introduction in F. C. Conybeare, J. Rendel Harris and A. S. Lewis, *The Story of Ahikar*, 2nd ed. (1913); Syriac, Arabic and Armenian versions translated in R. H. Charles, *The Apocrypha and Pseudepigrapha of the Old Testament*, vol. ii, pp. 715–784 (1913), cf. vol. i, pp. 189–192 (1913). *See also* R. Smend, *Alter und Herkunft des Achikar-Romans und sein Verhältnis zu Aesop* (1908); T. Nöldeke, *Untersuchungen zum Achiqar-Roman* in *Abhandlungen der königlichen Gesellschaft der Wissenschaft zu Göttingen*, new series, vol. 14, no. 4 (1913).   (G. WI.)

AHITHOPHEL

(in the Douai version of the Bible, ACHITOPHEL), one of David's most trusted advisers, whose counsel was "as if one consulted the oracle of God." He took a leading part in Absalom's revolt, and his defection was a severe blow to the king, who prayed that God would bring his counsel to "foolishness." At Ahithophel's advice Absalom (q.v.) first took the precaution of asserting his claim to the throne by seizing his father's concubines. The immediate pursuit of David (q.v.) was then suggested, but Hushai recommended waiting till the levies of all Israel could be called up. This advice was adopted, and David had time to escape across the Jordan. Finding that his policy was neglected and foreseeing the disaster which actually occurred, Ahithophel went home and hanged himself. (II Sam. xv, 31–37; xvi, 20–xvii, 14, 23.)

AHLEN,

a town of Germany which after partition of the nation following World War II was located in the *Land* (state) of North Rhine-Westphalia, Federal Republic of Germany. It lies on the Werse river, 17 mi. S.E. of Münster, on the northeastern edge of the Ruhr district. Pop. (1961) 40,485. Ahlen is on the main Cologne-Hanover-Berlin railway and about 5 mi. from the Cologne-Hanover autobahn. A coal-mining town, its chief manufactures are enamelware (it once had the biggest enamel works in Germany), shoes, and industrial and agricultural machines. The town charter was granted in 1224 and industrial development began about 1900. St. Bartholomew is the patron saint of Ahlen.

AHMADOU

(d. 1898), the ruler of a Toucouleur empire in the western Sudan, celebrated for his resistance to the French occupation. Succeeding his father Omar el-Hadj in 1866, Ahmadou ruled over a great empire centred on the ancient Bambara kingdom of Ségou (his first capital) and including (1), in the west, the Kaarta country and the fortresses of Nioro, Koniakory, Diala, Koundian and Mourgoula; (2), farther to the south, the fortress of Dingguiraye; and (3), in the northeast, the Macina country around Bandiagara. Despite his great religious authority, Ahmadou could not count on the obedience of all his vassals or even on those of his own family. By the treaty of Nango signed with the French commander J. S. Gallieni in 1881 Ahmadou granted France most-favoured-nation status. Then, after the advance of the French to Kita and Bamako, he abandoned Ségou as his capital and accepted a French protectorate (treaty of Gouri, May 12, 1887). In 1888, however, Col. Louis Archinard, supported by the "colonial party" in Paris, took the offensive against Ahmadou. By 1891 Archinard had seized most of Ahmadou's strongholds in the south and west. When Ahmadou retreated into the Macina, Archinard pursued him and seized his remaining fortresses. Ahmadou sought refuge in the mountains to the east. He died in 1898 in the province of Sokoto (Nigeria).   (JE. B.)

AHMAD SHAH

(1725–1775), Mogul emperor in India from 1748 to 1754, son and successor of Mohammed Shah, was born in Delhi on Dec. 24, 1725. His father had kept him in penurious obscurity, so that on his accession he was wholly inexperienced in affairs and ready to fall victim to the opportunities for sensual gratification which was almost all that the throne then offered.

Twice during Ahmad Shah's reign, in 1748 or 1749 and in 1751-52, the Afghan Ahmad Shah Durrani (q.v.) invaded the Punjab, obtaining grants of revenue and territory from the Mogul. Further, in 1750, the Mogul wazir Safdar Jang was defeated by the Afghans of the Doab and, enlisting the aid of the Marathas, provided him with the spectacle of "his" servants struggling over the spoils of "his" empire.

In Delhi, Ahmad Shah fell first under the control of his mother Udham Bai and the eunuch Javid Khan. Safdar Jang had Javid murdered in 1752, only then to emphasize his own greed and incapacity. In 1753, Safdar Jang was ousted as wazir by Intizam ud-Daula and withdrew to Oudh. Then Imad ul-Mulk, grandson of Asaf Jah, first nizam of Hyderabad, won the alliance of the Marathas and, in 1754, expelled Intizam ud-Daula and deposed and blinded Ahmad Shah. Ahmad Shah lived in confinement until Jan. 1, 1775.

See Sir Jadunath Sarkar, *Fall of the Mughal Empire*, vol. i, 2nd ed. (1949).   (P. H.)

AHMAD SHAH

DURRANI (1722?–1772?), founder of the state of Afghanistan and ruler of an empire which stretched for a time from the Oxus (modern Amu-Darya) across Baluchistan to the Indian ocean and from Khurasan into Kashmir, the Punjab and Sind. He was born, probably at Multan late in 1722, in the noble and sacrosanct Sadozai clan, the second son of Mohammed Zaman Khan, a hereditary chief of the Abdali tribe of Afghans. When Nadir Shah of Persia conquered the Afghans in 1738, Ahmad entered his personal service and rose to command an Abdali contingent of cavalry. On the assassination of Nadir in 1747 his Afghan troops returned home; their chiefs declared themselves independent and elected Ahmad as shah. He took the title Durr-i-

Durran ("Pearl amongst Pearls"), changed the name of the Abdali tribe to Durrani, and from it chose most of his high officers. He was crowned that year near Kandahar, which became his capital. The spirit of his government was essentially Afghan and tribal but his administration and army were modeled largely on those of Nadir Shah. To gain prestige and wealth, to unify his people and to satisfy their marauding proclivities, he adopted a policy of raids and limited conquest toward his then chaotic neighbours. In 1747–48 he invaded India, capturing guns, horses and much wealth, but was finally repulsed near Sirhind, north of Patiala. He returned to Afghanistan; but in 1748, or 1749, he again invaded India and won from the Mogul emperor what had formerly been granted to Nadir Shah: India west of the Indus and the revenues of four districts of the Punjab. About 1750 he took Herat; in 1751 Nishapur and Meshed in Khurasan, as ruler of which he confirmed Shah Rukh, the blinded grandson of Nadir Shah. Balkh and Badakhshan were gained for him that year. The revenues from the Punjab were not paid, and in 1751–52 he returned and extorted the virtual grant of the Punjab from the Moguls. They attempted to reassert their supremacy and provoked a fourth invasion in 1756–57. He plundered Delhi; sacked with great slaughter the Hindu holy cities, Mathura and Vrindaban; confirmed the weak Alamgir II as emperor; and allied himself and his son Timur by marriage with the imperial family. Cholera among his troops forced him home that summer. Timur was driven out of the Punjab in 1758 by a force of Sikhs, Moguls and Marathas, the latter having intervened at the invitation of Imad ul-Mulk, wazir in Delhi. In 1759, however, Ahmad Shah swept the Marathas from the Punjab and joined forces with the Afghans settled in Rohilkhand; and on Jan. 14, 1761, at Panipat north of Delhi, they destroyed a large Maratha army sent from the Deccan (enabling the British in Bengal to strengthen their position decisively). In 1762, 1764–65, 1766–67 and 1769 Ahmad Shah marched to crush the Sikhs, but they were elusive and had local support, whereas his empire was restive: he lost control of the Punjab to them.

Ahmad Shah died at Maruf, or perhaps at Margha, east of Kandahar. He had been a bold yet careful general, a rapacious and cruel conqueror. The Sadozais ruled Afghanistan until 1818, when the Barakzai branch of the Durranis succeeded them. See also AFGHANISTAN: History.

BIBLIOGRAPHY.—Ganda Singh, Ahmad Shah Durrani (1959); J. Sarkar, Fall of the Mughal Empire, 2nd ed., vol. i and ii (1949–50); T. S. Shejwalkar, Panipat: 1761, in the "Deccan College Monograph Series" (1946).   (P. H.)

AHMAD SHAUQI (1868–1932), one of the outstanding Arab poets and dramatists of his time, was born in Cairo in 1868 of a family attached to the khedival court. A brilliant pupil, he was sent by the khedive to study at Montpellier and Paris universities and on his return the path of quick promotion lay open to him. By 1914 he was the leading literary figure in Egypt. He was exiled to Spain during World War I but on his return continued to dominate the Egyptian literary scene. In 1927 he was proclaimed amir al-shu'ara ("prince of poets"). He died in Cairo on Oct. 13, 1932.

He was a prolific writer with a fine command of Arabic rhyme and poetic diction, his themes varying from conventional encomia to poetical plays following western models (e.g., Shakespeare, Corneille, Racine). His efforts, however, to copy the ancient Arabic poets were not successful. He was, in fact, an innovator and his poem Muluk al-Arab shows him as a precursor of modern Arab nationalism. A pioneer, too, of the modern movement in Arabic poetry, he attempted to adapt traditional metres to dramatic dialogue in his remarkable poetical plays.

Ahmad Shauqi's collected poems were published in Cairo in four volumes (1948–51).   (A. EL-T.)

AHMED I (1590–1617), Ottoman sultan of Turkey, was born at Manisa (Magnesia) on April 18, 1590, and succeeded Mohammed III, his father, on Jan. 22, 1603, in his 13th year. When his first child was born, Ahmed wished to put his brother Mustafa to death, but was restrained by the ulema. His authority was weakened by wars, rebellions and misrule but, despite his youth, he took an active part in the government. The peace of Zsitvatörök (1606) which he signed with Austria was a blow to Turkey's pres-

tige, and he was compelled to renew the capitulations (q.v.) with France and Venice and to conclude a capitulation with the Dutch, by which the Dutch merchants were able to introduce the use of tobacco into Turkey. Ahmed tried to re-establish order in the country and administration: he put down the rebellion of the army deserters in Anatolia and the revolts of Fakhr al-din in the Lebanon and of the sipahis in Istanbul; he executed some of the viziers and exiled many palace dignitaries for bribery and intrigue; and he introduced a new regulation for the improvement of land administration.

Ahmed was strong willed and pious and he succeeded in rescuing his authority by skilful and drastic action. He made many donations, especially to the holy places of Mecca and Medina, and he built the great Blue mosque near the church of Hagia Sophia. He died on Dec. 22, 1617, leaving seven sons, of whom Osman II, Murad IV and Ibrahim I eventually succeeded to the throne.

(E. Z. K.)

AHMED II (1642–1695), Ottoman sultan of Turkey, son of Ibrahim I, was born on Aug. 1, 1642, and succeeded his brother Suleiman II in 1691. Continuing the war against the "Holy league" (Austria, Poland and Venice), the Turks sustained a crushing defeat in the battle of Slankamen (Szalankamen) at the hands of the Austrians under Louis, margrave of Baden (Aug. 19, 1691); the grand vizier Mustafa Koprulu was killed and the Turks were driven from Hungary. Crete also was attacked and Chios taken by the Venetians. Ahmed tried to retrieve these disasters, by changing grand viziers, but without success. He died on Feb. 6, 1695, in Edirne and was buried in the mausoleum of Suleiman I, in Istanbul.

(E. Z. K.)

AHMED III (1673–1736), Ottoman sultan of Turkey, son of Mohammed IV, succeeded to the throne in 1703 on the deposition of his brother Mustafa II. He cultivated good relations with England and France and afforded a refuge to Charles XII of Sweden after his defeat by Peter the Great at Poltava (1709). Forced into war with Russia (1711–13), he came nearer than any other Turkish sovereign to breaking that power. His grand vizier, Baltaji Mohammed Pasha, encircled the Russians near the Pruth (1711), and Russia had to agree to retrocede Azov, to destroy the Azovian forts and to abstain from interference in Polish or Cossack affairs (Turkish discontent at the leniency of these terms nearly brought on a renewal of the war). In 1715 the Morea (Peloponnesus) was taken from the Venetians, but when Austria intervened the Turks suffered reverses, losing Belgrade in 1717. Under the peace of Passarowitz (1718), concluded through Anglo-Dutch mediation, Turkey retained its conquests from the Venetians but ceded Hungary and part of Serbia.

Both Russia and Persia seized the opportunity to invade Turkey. Peace was made with Russia in 1724, but the struggle with Persia for Azerbaijan continued. Deposed during the uprising led by Patrona Khalil in 1730, Ahmed died in captivity in 1736. His reign was known as the Age of Tulips (see TURKEY: History: The Tulip Age; NEDIM, AHMED) and saw the first steps taken toward the westernization of Turkish institutions.   (E. Z. K.)

AHMEDABAD (AHMADABAD), a city in Gujarat state, India, and headquarters of Ahmedabad district, lies 275 mi. N. of Bombay on the Sabarmati river, crossed there by four bridges, including the 1,450-ft. Nehru bridge. Pop. (1961) 1,149,918. Urban area 20 sq.mi. The city presents a conflict between bustling mills and factories and ancient architectural glories. A local peculiarity is the planning of some sections in pols, self-contained blocks of houses sheltering several thousand people. Some are virtually small townships, crossed by a street with gates at either end. An attractive feature of the city is Lake Kankaria, with promenades, boating and a hill garden. The museum was designed by Le Corbusier. Ahmedabad is also the seat of Gujarat university (1950) and 20 of its 43 affiliated colleges. On the northern boundary is the military cantonment. Sabarmati, a suburb west of the river, became well known as the seat of Mahatma Gandhi's ashram or religious retreat.

Ahmedabad is at the junction of main roads giving access to Bombay and central India, the Kathiawar (Saurashtra) peninsula and the Rajasthan border. It is a major junction on the Western

W. SUSCHITZKY

HEADQUARTERS OF THE ASSOCIATION OF COTTON MILLOWNERS, AHMEDABAD; DESIGNED BY LE CORBUSIER (C. E. JEANNERET), 1955

railway: a double-track route (309 mi.) goes south to Bombay; other lines run to Delhi via the Rajasthan metre-gauge system and into Kathiawar.

About one-half of Ahmedabad's population depend on the cotton industry: there are about 70 cotton mills and 50 other major plants for oil, flour and silk milling, soap, match, glass, tobacco and hosiery manufacture, carpet weaving and tanning. The city's handicrafts include brocades, "atlas" and tinsel lace, copper and brassware, jewelry and wood carving.

History and Monuments.—Ahmedabad was founded in A.D. 1411 by the Moslem ruler of Gujarat, Sultan Ahmad Shah, next to the earlier Hindu town of Ashawal. It grew in size and wealth until the death in 1511 of Ahmad's grandson Mahmud Begara, the most (and last) eminent sovereign of the line. Then dynastic decay and anarchy brought decline until the city's capture by the Mogul emperor Akbar in 1572. Its renewed eminence under the Moguls ceased only with the death in 1707 of the last notable emperor, Aurangzeb, who had been viceroy at Ahmedabad in 1645-47. Further decline under the later Moguls and the Marathas was arrested by the British annexation of Gujarat in 1818. Ahmedabad's subsequent rise to the rank of India's sixth largest city and biggest inland industrial centre was promoted by the opening of the first cotton mills in 1859-61. In 1960 Ahmedabad became the temporary capital of Gujarat.

Dynastic changes made Ahmedabad the meeting place of Hindu, Muslim and Jain architectural traditions. Ahmad Shah and his successors ordered the dismantling and adaptation of Hindu temples in order to build mosques. This and the employment of Hindu artisans gave many of Ahmedabad's mosques and tombs a Hindu flavour in motifs and planning. The dense "forest" of 260 richly carved columns within the Jami Masjid or Great mosque (completed 1423) recalls the *mandapa* or hall of a Hindu temple (from which it was probably converted). At the mosque's entrance is the domed tomb of Ahmad Shah (completed 1441) and on the road leading to it the Tin Darwaza or triple arch (*c.* 1425), a triumphal gate through which the sultan was borne to worship. Among the city's many other fine Muslim buildings are the delicate mosque (*c.* 1505) at Rani Sipri's tomb; the Sidi Said mosque (1510-15), with minutely pierced arch-screens in the "palm and parasite" design; and the exuberantly rich Rani Rupmati mosque (1515). (For others *see* P. Brown, *Indian Architecture: Islamic Period,* pp. 48-58, 1942.) A notable later building is the Jain Hathi Singh temple (1848).

AHMEDABAD DISTRICT (3,461 sq.mi.; pop., 1961, 2,231,534) extends across the neck of the Kathiawar peninsula. The northeastern part is dotted with low hills, which gradually give way southwestward to a great plain subject to floods at its western end. Except in this latter area, the soil is fertile, the chief crops being millet, cotton, wheat and pulses. Some parts are wooded. The main rivers are the Sabarmati and its tributaries, flowing southward into the Gulf of Cambay. (D. G. K.)

AHMEDNAGAR (AHMADNAGAR), a city and district, in Maharashtra state, India; till April 30, 1960, in Bombay state. The city lies on the left bank of the Sina river, 130 mi. E. of Bombay. Pop. (1961) 118,266. It was founded in 1490 on the site of a more ancient city, Bhinar, by Ahmad Nizam Shah, who established a monarchy which lasted till its overthrow by Shah Jahan in 1636. Thereafter it passed into the hands of the Marathas, but during the war with them in 1803 it was captured by General Wellesley. Restored to the Marathas, it again became a British possession in 1817 under the treaty of Poona.

The city has a commonplace appearance and is surrounded by a dilapidated earthern wall with decayed bastions and gates. Monuments of interest are the fort about half a mile to the east, numerous specimens of Mohammedan architecture including the Damji Masjid, and several other mosques, a palace, the Paria Bagh (fairy garden), the tomb of Ahmad Nizam Shah, and Alamgir's Dargah (tomb). The city is a military station of the Poona district and an important mission station. It has a municipality established in 1854, and a college affiliated to the University of Poona. There is a large trade in cotton and silk goods. The chief industries are weaving of saris, cotton ginning and pressing, manufacture of copper and brass pots, indigo works and tanning. Ahmednagar is on the Dhond-Manmad loop line of the Central railway.

AHMEDNAGAR DISTRICT is a comparatively barren tract with a small rainfall. Area 6,591 sq.mi.; pop. (1961) 1,771,066. On the north the district is watered by the Godavari and its tributaries, the Pravara and the Mula; on the east by the Sephani which flows through the valley below the Balaghat range, and in the extreme south by the Bhima and its tributary the Dor. The Sina river, another tributary of the Bhima, flows through the Nagar and Karjat *talukas*. The Western Ghats, which cross the western end of the district from north to south, are its principal geographical feature. The staple food grains grown are the millets jowar (*Sorghum vulgare*) and *bajri* (*Pennisetum typhoideum*). Other crops include cotton, millet, pulses, wheat and ragi (*Eleusine coracana*). The forest cover consists of characteristic tropical dry deciduous and thorn trees. The chief industries are weaving, dyeing, and the manufacture of copper and brass pots. (M. R. P.)

AHMED VEFIK PASHA (1823-1891), Ottoman Turkish grand vizier and man of letters, was born in Istanbul on July 6, 1823, and educated in Paris. Appointed to a post in the translation office of the ministry for foreign affairs, he devoted his leisure to translating Molière's plays into Turkish and to compiling dictionaries, historical and geographical manuals, etc., for use in schools. In 1847 he brought out the first edition of the *Salnameh*, the official annual of the Ottoman empire.

Ahmed Vefik was appointed imperial commissioner in the Danubian principalities in 1849 and ambassador to Persia in 1851. After his return he was appointed a member of the grand council of justice and entrusted with the revision of the penal code and the code of procedure. In 1860 he was sent as ambassador to Paris, to avert the intervention of France in the affairs of Syria. Ahmed Vefik was president of the first Turkish parliament (1877) and twice prime minister (1878 and 1882), but the position in which he rendered his most distinguished service was as vali (governor) of Bursa (1879-82).

The drainage of the pestilent marshes, the water supply from the mountains, the numerous roads, the suppression of brigandage, the multiplication of schools, the vast development of the silk industry through the substitution of mulberry plantations for rice fields, the opening out of the mineral springs of Chitli, the introduction of rose trees, the production of attar of roses and the foundation of the first Turkish theatre—all these were Ahmed Vefik's work. A few days after his return he was again appointed grand vizier (Dec. 1, 1882), but he made conditions that were unacceptable to the sultan and Said Pasha was appointed in his place. For the rest of his life Ahmed Vefik, by the sultan's orders, was practically a prisoner in his own house at Rumili Hisar on the Bosporus, where he died on April 2, 1891. His library was sold for the payment of his debts.

AHMOSE (AAHMES; Gr. AMASIS or AMOSIS), from the Egyptian Iah-mose, "the moon has begotten him," the name of two Egyptian pharaohs, one in the 18th dynasty and one 1,000 years later, in the 26th.

AHMOSE I (reigned c. 1570–1546 B.C.), the first king of Manetho's 18th dynasty, bore the praenomen Neb-pehti-Rē, "the sungod Rē is lord of might." His predecessor Kamose, who may have been his brother, began the war of liberation against the Asiatic invaders known as the Hyksos, but died, perhaps in battle, before capturing their stronghold Avaris in the eastern delta. Ahmose took the city after a siege and pursued the fleeing Hyksos into Palestine; the occupation of Sharuhen after three years' siege laid the foundations of Egypt's future empire in Asia. Before proceeding to further conquests there Ahmose had to reorganize the newly reunited kingdom and to carry Egyptian arms into the long-abandoned province of Nubia, whose paramount chief had been an ally of the Hyksos. Nubia was subdued in three campaigns in which the Egyptian frontier was pushed at least as far south as Toshkeh. Later the king campaigned in Phoenicia. He appears to have done little large-scale building, but the dynasty that he established was one of the most glorious in Egyptian history.

AHMOSE II (reigned 569–526 B.C.) is generally known as Amasis Herodotus in his second book draws a vivid portrait of the shrewd, convivial soldier king. He was the general sent by Apries (q.v.) to quell a revolt among the Egyptian troops who had been sent on an abortive expedition to Cyrene in 570 B.C. The Egyptians proclaimed him king, and in a battle at Momemphis against the Greek mercenary army of Apries the latter was defeated and taken prisoner. In Amasis' third year, according to a stele in the Cairo museum, Apries again raised an army but was killed in battle. As champion of the native Egyptians Amasis at first played the role of xenophobe, but had the good sense to cultivate the friendship of the Greeks and other neighbouring powers. He married a Greek princess, Ladike of Cyrene, contributed 1,000 talents to the rebuilding of the Delphic shrine and made Polycrates of Samos and Croesus of Lydia his allies. Early in his reign he sustained an attack by Nebuchadrezzar of Babylon, but Egypt was apparently saved from invasion. Later he conquered Cyprus and was master of part of Phoenicia. Herodotus avers that under his wise administration Egypt was very prosperous. His last years, however, were disturbed by the threat of Persian invasion.

See A. Wiedemann, Herodots zweites Buch (1890); F. K. Kienitz, Politische Geschichte Ägyptens, vom 7 bis zum 4 Jahrhundert (1953). (M. S. Dr.)

AHO, JUHANI (real name JOHANNES BROFELDT) (1861–1921), a writer of central importance in the development of Finnish literature, was born in Lapinlahti, Sept. 11, 1861. A country clergyman's son, he studied at Helsinki university, worked as a journalist and was an active member of the liberal group Nuori Suomi ("Young Finland"). Aho's early realistic stories and novels describe with humour life in the Finnish backwoods he knew so well. His novel Rautatie ("The Railway," 1884; Swedish trans. 1920), the story of an elderly couple's first railway trip, is a Finnish classic. Influenced by contemporary Norwegian and French writers—Ibsen, Björnson, Maupassant and particularly Daudet—he described the life of the educated classes in Papin tytär ("The Clergyman's Daughter," 1885; German trans. 1899) and Papin rouva ("The Clergyman's Wife," 1893; German trans. 1896). In the 1890s he was drawn toward romantic nationalism: the long novel Panu (1897; German trans. 1899) dealt with the struggle between paganism and Christianity in 17th-century Finland and Kevät ja takatalvi ("Spring and the Untimely Return of Winter," 1906; Swedish trans., 2 vol.) with the national awakening of the 19th century. His soundest romantic work, Juha (1911), is the story of the unhappy marriage of a cripple in the Karelian forests. Aho's short stories, Lastuja ("Chips," 8 series, 1891–1921; partial Swedish trans. Spånor, 4 vol., 1891–99; selection in French trans. Copeaux, 1929), have lasted best: they are concerned with peasant life, fishing and the wild life of the lakelands. In these, as in his reminiscences of childhood, Muistatko-? ("Remember?" 1920), Aho's quiet lyricism is at its best. He died in Helsinki, Aug. 8, 1921.

See G. Castrén, Juhani Aho, 2 vol. (1922); A. J. Aho, Juhani Aho, 2 vol. (1951). (K. L. K. L.)

AHOM, an offshoot of the large family of Tai-speaking peoples whose migration from the Chinese province of Yunnan southward into Indochina and upper Burma began in the first centuries A.D. A tribal group called the Ahoms moved from the Irrawaddy region of Burma into the upper Brahmaputra valley of Assam early in the 13th century. Under the leadership of kings, whose names and deeds are recorded in chronicles originally written on strips of bark, the Ahoms began a long struggle with the indigenous Bodo peoples such as the Kacharis, and by the end of the 16th century controlled the whole of upper Assam. (This country's name is derived from the word Ahom.) Their system of government was based on a balance between the power of the king and that of an aristocracy, which elected the king from among the members of the royal lineage. This aristocracy also furnished three ministers of state, whose offices were the monopoly of five clans. By the end of the 18th century the Ahom kingdom, which had beaten back repeated attacks by Mogul armies, had extended its power also over lower Assam. Its end came in 1838 with the establishment of British rule.

Ever since the 15th century the Ahoms had been influenced by Hinduism, but they formally embraced the Hindu faith in 1714 and even then continued to practise the old tribal religion without hindrance. Yet traditional Ahom culture rapidly changed. While as late as the 16th century the Ahoms had lived in pile dwellings, they now built houses on solid foundations in Indian style. Similarly, cremation replaced burial and Hindu marriage rites the ancient ritual. The traditional division of Ahom society into a number of exogamous groups persists to the present day, however, and groups of different status do not intermarry. The original Ahom language and script (the latter akin to that used by the Siamese (Thais) and other Tai-speakers) have become extinct and the Ahom now speak Assamese, an Indo-Aryan language related to Bengali. No longer a nation of distinct identity, they are today a Hindu caste of good status. Their Mongoloid physical features, however, still distinguish them from the Assamese castes of Indian origin.

BIBLIOGRAPHY.—Sir E. A. Gait, A History of Assam, 2nd ed. rev. (1926); A. C. Banerjee, The Eastern Frontier of British India (1941); P. R. Gurdon, "Ahoms," Encyclopaedia of Religion and Ethics, ed. by J. Hastings et al., vol. 1 (1908); E. T. D. Lambert, "A Short Account of the Ahom people," J. Siam. Soc., 40:39–65 (1952); F. M. LeBar et al., Ethnic Groups of Mainland Southeast Asia (1964). (C. v. F.–H.)

AHRENS, FRANZ HEINRICH LUDOLF (1809–81), German philologist, was born at Helmstedt, June 6, 1809, and died Sept. 25, 1881. His most important work is De Graecae Linguae Dialectis (1839–43, new ed. by Meister, 1882–89), which, although unfortunately incomplete, dealing only with Aeolic and Doric, and in some respects superseded by modern research, remains a standard treatise. A volume of his minor works (ed. by Haeberlin, 1891) contains a complete list of his writings.

AHRIMAN (ANGRA MAINYU, the "Destructive One"), the principle of evil in the dualistic doctrine of Zoroaster. As the Evil Spirit, representing untruth, unrighteousness and disorder, he is contrasted with the Wise Lord, Ahura Mazda. He is the all-destroying, the source of all evil in the world; eventually, in the great world catastrophe, he will be defeated by Ahura Mazda and disappear. See AHURA MAZDA; DUALISM; ZOROASTRIANISM.

AHUACHAPÁN, department and city in northwestern El Salvador. Population of the department (1961) 130,710; area 472 sq.mi. Except for Pacific coastal plain about 8 mi. wide, the department consists of deep valleys and mountains, which include several volcanoes, the highest being Cerro Chichicastepeque, altitude 6,075 ft. The Río Paz to the west forms the natural boundary with Guatemala. Coffee is grown on volcano slopes 1,800 to 4,000 ft. altitude. Corn, beans, other food crops, livestock and blooms from the flower garden of El Salvador, Apaneca, are sent to all parts of the country.

Ahuachapán city (pop. [1961] 13.261), the departmental capital, is a manufacturing and distributing centre. Coffee is the most important product. It is noted for its hot mineral waters which are drawn from mountain springs, notably below Malacatiupan falls nearby. Ahuachapán is connected by rail and highway (64 mi.) with the national capital, San Salvador. (C. F. J.)

AHURA MAZDA, the supreme god, "Wise Lord," in the religious system of the Iranian sage Zoroaster (7th century–6th century B.C.), worshiped by the Persian king Darius (reign, 522 B.C.–486 B.C.) and his successors as Auramazda, greatest of all gods and protector of the just king.

According to Zoroaster, Ahura Mazda created the twin spirits Spenta Mainyu and Angra Mainyu, the former beneficent, choosing truth, light and life, the latter destructive, choosing lie, darkness and death. Their struggle against each other makes up the history of the world.

In the developed religion reflected in the Avesta, Ahura Mazda became identified with the beneficent spirit and directly opposed to the destructive one; the two being conceived as mutually limiting, coeternal beings, the one above and the other beneath, with the world in between as their battleground. There was thus lacking an infinite principle, and this sometimes was supplied by Zurvan, "Time." In late sources (3rd century A.D. onward) Zurvan is made father of the twins Ormazd (Ahura Mazda) and Ahriman (Angra Mainyu) who, in orthodox Mazdaism, reign alternately until Ormazd forever triumphs.

Something of this conception is reflected in Manichaeism, in which God is sometimes called Zurvan, while Ormazd is his first emanation, Primeval Man, who is vanquished by the destructive spirit of darkness and rescued by God's second emanation, the Living Spirit.

The modern Zoroastrians of India, the Parsees (q.v.), tend to diminish the importance of Ahriman by explaining him away as an allegory of man's evil tendencies, thus restoring omnipotence to Ormazd. *See also* DUALISM; ZOROASTRIANISM. (J. D.-G.)

AHVAZ (AHWAZ), a city of southwestern Iran and capital of Khuzistan *ostan* (province), is situated on both banks of the Karun river where it crosses a low range of sandstone hills. The climate is dry and very hot in summer. Pop. (1956) 120,098.

Ahvaz has been identified with the Aginis of Nearchus, and approximately occupies the site of a once extensive and important city of which very few traces remain. Its old Persian name was Hurmuz Shahr. Arab historians of the 12th century describe it as the centre of a large sugar-cane, rice and silk growing area irrigated by a system of great canals from a stone weir constructed across the river on solid rock. It exported its products all over Persia and to the west.

Since the opening of the Karun to foreign commerce in 1888 a new settlement, called Bandar Nasiri in compliment to Shah Nasr-ed-Din (d. 1896), has arisen on the left bank one mile below the rapids. Steamers anchor there. The town was well laid out in a grid pattern between 1903 and 1925. Extensive new quarters including the seat of government and the main railway station developed on the right bank after the construction of a concrete road bridge, whereas the workshops, stores and workers' quarters of the former Anglo-Iranian Oil company were built north of the old centre, near Karun station.

Ahvaz is the junction of the two branches to the termini of Khorramshahr and Bandar-e Shahpur of the Trans-Iranian railway. The Bandar-e Shahpur line crosses the river on a steel bridge more than 1,000 yd. long. Motor routes connect Ahvaz with Abadan (78 mi.), Khorramshahr (85 mi.), Shushtar (64 mi.), Dezful (94 mi.) and the oilfields. Air services to Teheran are frequent. The pipelines from the oilfields of Masjed Soleyman,

Naft-e Safid and Haft Gel meet there, and the pipeline (1959) from Abadan to Teheran passes by. The town was scheduled for industrialization under the Khuzistan development program. A faculty of agriculture was founded in 1959. (H. Bo.)

AHVENANMAA or **ÅLAND ISLANDS,** an archipelago at the entrance to the Gulf of Bothnia, separated from the Swedish coast by the 25 mi.-wide Åland sea and from the archipelago of Turku (Åbo) by the islanded strait of Skiftet. Area 581 sq.mi. Pop. (1960) 20,981. The islands (Finnish Ahvenanmaa, Swedish Åland) comprise the smallest of the ten *lääni* (counties) of Finland, but have unique autonomy in the republic. The county consists of about 80 inhabited islands, about 6,000 other identifiable islands and a large number of rocky reefs. The bedrock is primarily granite of varying age and character which supports depositional features of glacial and marine origin. The surface, depressed in the shallow central Bay of Lumparn, rises to upstanding heights toward the north coast, *e.g.*, Orrdalsklint (423 ft.). There is much evidence of land upheaval in both archaeological remains and place names. Soils are principally of clay or sand. Pine, spruce and birch are the chief trees, but there are also groves of oak, alder, maple and hazel. For the latitude, natural vegetation is remarkably varied and reflects the relatively mild climate. Mariehamn (Maarianhamina), the administrative centre and chief port, has average February temperatures of 25° F., July temperatures of 61° F. Rainfall is about 22 in. annually.

Population is concentrated in Åland "mainland," on which Mariehamn is located; founded in 1861, it has a population (1960) of 6,685. The Ålanders, who are Swedish-speaking, are mostly farmers, seamen and fishermen. Farms are small, intensively operated, well-mechanized and centred upon substantial buildings. The chief crops are spring and autumn wheat, oats, barley, sown grasses and clovers, potatoes, rape, beet, cucumbers and onions. There are nearly 700 ac. of apple orchards. Ayrshire cattle dominate the dairy farms. Sea-going enterprise is represented by a fleet of 100,000 gross registered tonnage and is reflected in an excellent maritime museum. The fisheries are a relatively declining source of income. Åland is linked by daily ferry and steamship services to the Finnish and Swedish mainlands, and by air services from Mariehamn airport. Icebreakers aid winter shipping. Workshop industry is mostly concerned with processing farm and forest products, and surplus grain and softwoods are exported. A shaft has been sunk to undersea iron workings at Nynäs, near Mariehamn. Depopulation and desertion of the outlying parts of the archipelago are social problems. There is also steady emigration to Sweden.

History.—The higher parts of Åland archipelago display ample evidence of Bronze and Iron Age settlement, while, as in adjacent

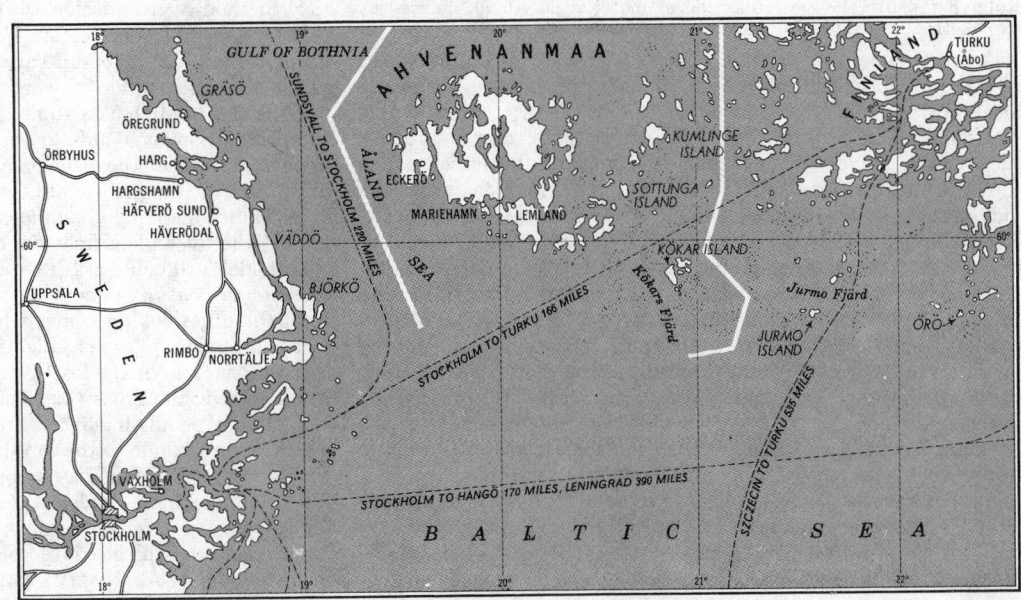

AHVENANMAA (ÅLAND ISLANDS) BETWEEN FINLAND AND SWEDEN IN THE BALTIC SEA

parts of Sweden, Viking age graveyards are common. Åland was a steppingstone on the way to Finland during the crusades of the middle ages and has impressive granite churches with a wealth of medieval wall paintings. Kastelholm has the remains of a major Swedish fortress restored as a museum. In early 18th-century campaigns, the islands were harried by Russians and, as church records attest, most people fled to Sweden. When the grand duchy of Finland was ceded to Russia in 1809, the islands were included; but Sweden was able to secure a provision that they should not be fortified. Nevertheless, fortification of the islands was initiated by Russia in the 1830s when the garrison of Bomarsund with its outworks was created. Bomarsund became the principal objective of the Anglo-French force during the first phase of the Crimean War. In Aug. 1854 the fortress was destroyed. A special Åland convention between Britain, France and Russia of March 30, 1856, stipulated that "The Åland Isles shall not be fortified and that no military or naval establishments shall be maintained or created on them." By article 33 of the treaty of Paris (1856) this convention was given "the same force and validity as if it formed part thereof." With the growth of German rearmament in the early 20th century, Russia again debated the status of the islands.

The Åland question assumed a new character when Finland declared its independence in 1917. The Ålanders claimed the right of self-determination and unofficial plebiscites showed an overwhelming vote in favour of union with Sweden. Finland granted the islands autonomy on May 7, 1920, but refused to contemplate their secession. In June leaders of the secession movement were arrested for high treason and Finnish troops were sent to the islands. On June 19, 1920, the attention of the council of the League of Nations was formally drawn to the serious tension prevailing between Finland and Sweden. With the consent of Finland and Sweden, the council asked a special commission of jurists whether the question was international or the exclusive concern of Finland. It was declared international and a commission of inquiry was dispatched to Åland. The commission reported against the claim to secede from Finland, but declared that the Ålanders formed a distinct group within the Finnish state. The commission also reported in favour of a new convention of neutralization and demilitarization to replace the international convention of 1856. This report was accepted by the council and the two nations. The new neutralization convention came into effect on April 6, 1922. The U.S.S.R. called for no concessions in Åland either in 1940 or 1944. Åland flies its own flag.

BIBLIOGRAPHY.—H. Smeds and S. Jaatinen (eds.), *Atlas of the Archipelago of S.W. Finland* (1961); *League of Nations Official Journal*, special supplements 1 and 3 (1920); the Swedish case was reported in *Ålands Frågan inför Nationernas Förbund* (1920–21); the Finnish case is found in *The Åland Question and the Rights of Finland* (1920); H. Tingsten, *The Debate on the Foreign Policy of Sweden*, trans. by J. Bulman (1950); the best collection of material on Åland, indexed by its collector R. T. Hausen, is in *Åbo Akademi* library. (W. R. Me.)

AI, the name of a Canaanite town destroyed by Joshua (Josh. vii–viii). Since biblical references agree without exception in locating this town (whose name in Hebrew, Ha-'ay, means simply "the ruin"), just east of Bethel (modern Beitin in western Jordan), there can be no doubt that it is to be sought in the unusually large Early Bronze Age site now called et-Tell. Excavations were conducted there by a French expedition led by Mme Judith Marquet-Krause in 1933–35, and very important remains of the 3rd millennium B.C. were recovered, including especially a large temple (believed at first to be a palace) with smaller adjacent shrines. This early occupation came to an end c. 2500 B.C., after a great conflagration, and there was no later reoccupation except briefly in the 12th–11th centuries B.C., whereas the events described in the book of Joshua are assigned by biblical scholars to a period between c. 1400 and c. 1200 B.C. A widely accepted solution of the dilemma is that early Israelite tradition identified the Canaanite town which was buried under the Israelite Bethel (and which is known to have been destroyed by fire about the time of Joshua) with the imposing ruins of the still earlier et-Tell, only 1½ mi. E.

See J. Marquet-Krause, *Les Fouilles de 'Ay (et-Tell) 1933–1935* (1949); G. E. Wright, *Biblical Archaeology*, pp. 80 ff. (1957).

(W. F. A.)

AICARD, (FRANÇOIS VICTOR) JEAN (1848–1921), French poet, novelist and dramatist known as a writer on Provence, was born at Toulon in 1848. In his youth he was influenced by Lamartine, and his *Poèmes de Provence* (1874) brought to French literature the most sensitive evocation of the Provençal scene since Mistral's *Mirèio*. The most successful of his 14 plays was *Le Père Lebonnard* (1889). Most of his novels, the best of which is *Maurin des Maures* (1908), are also based on Provençal life. Aicard became a member of the Académie Française in 1909. He died in Paris on May 13, 1921.

See C. Jullian, *Jean Aicard, la Provence et le félibrige* (1925).

AICHI, Japanese prefecture (area 1,953 sq.mi.; pop. [1960] 4,206,282) on the Pacific coast of central western Honshu. More than one half its area lies within the Nōbi plain and two smaller plains to the east. The irregular coast line is marked by the Chita and Atsumi peninsulas. In addition to growing food, Aichi is a leading industrial prefecture. Its capital, Nagoya (*q.v.*), and surrounding industrial satellite cities constitute Japan's third-ranking industrial concentration. Cotton textiles are the leading product, but ceramics, automobiles, wood products and many other items are made. Main port facilities are in Nagoya.

(J. D. Ee.)

AICHINGER, GREGOR (1564–1628), German composer of church music. Born at Regensburg in 1564, he may have been a pupil of Orlando di Lasso (Lassus) before taking holy orders and becoming organist to the family of Jakob Fugger at Augsburg from 1584. He visited Italy (1584–87) and Rome again in 1599–1600. He died at Augsburg, Feb. 21, 1628. His music is chiefly choral and ecclesiastical, to Latin words, and shows a conservative taste influenced by the Venetian school of composers, especially Giovanni Gabrieli. His motets were well-known, and frequently appeared in contemporary collections. (C. P. Co.)

AID, the name for a wide variety of taxes levied in the middle ages. The underlying idea was that they were granted (Lat. *dona*, "gifts"; Fr. *dons gratuits*) in aid (*auxilia*, "help"; *aides*) by persons or communities to someone in authority who asked for them or assessed them. Aids could be demanded (1) by the crown from its subjects; (2) by a feudal lord from his vassals; and (3) by a manorial lord from the inhabitants of his seigniory.

All over Europe princes had to resort to forms of direct taxation since the other revenues of the crown were insufficient, especially in emergencies. In Carolingian times "gifts" (*dona*) were regularly offered to the king. In the later middle ages the crown negotiated with various sections of the population for aids. Thus on pressing occasions (wars, etc.) towns (or communes) would be asked for certain lump sums by the crown. It was up to them to collect the money from their burgesses. This way of obtaining aids from separate communities was superseded by the more practical method of negotiation with the representatives of the whole country assembled in "estates." How much the sovereign could in fact obtain depended on various incidental considerations, such as the actual strength of the crown, the real urgency of its financial needs and its willingness to make concessions in exchange. Thus the negotiation over aids in the assemblies of estates played an important role in the development of representative institutions in Europe. Attempts to limit the amount that could be asked were occasionally made by communes, but were never really successful against the overriding financial needs of the crown.

A feudal lord could ask his vassals for an aid, as they owed him *auxilium et consilium* (help and counsel). In course of time, however, the occasions on which a lord could ask for a subsidy came to be limited (1) to the knighting of his eldest son; (2) to the first marriage of his eldest daughter; (3) to the payment of his ransom; and sometimes (4) to his going on crusade. These feudal aids should be distinguished from the feudal relief (*relevium*), which was a tax due to the lord by a new vassal upon entering into possession of a fief. They were also different, at least in origin, from scutage (*q.v.*), which was a payment in lieu of the military service due by a feudal tenant.

For the aids which a lord could demand from the inhabitants of his seigniory, *see* TAILLE; TALLAGE.

For England, aids were dealt with expressly in Magna Carta

(*q.v.*). Clause 12 established that the king should demand no aid or scutage without the common counsel of the realm, except for the payment of the king's ransom, for the knighting of his eldest son or for one marriage of his eldest daughter; and even in these cases the aid would have to be reasonable. Clause 15 extended this regulation between the king and his tenants in chief to all feudal lords and their respective vassals. Before, they had taken aids at their own pleasure. The last English king to levy these feudal aids was James I.

From early times the crown occasionally levied tallages or aids (also called *dona*) on the royal demesne lands including the towns of the realm. Exemptions were sometimes obtained by charter or custom. Lords could tallage their lands if they had in the past been royal demesne lands. From the reign of Henry II onward aids consisting of a certain proportion of movables (one-tenth, one-fifteenth, etc.) were levied at irregular intervals. Their frequency was reduced after the accession of Edward I, mainly because of the progress of taxes on movables and the effective liability of towns and rural demesne to them. The replacement of tallages by aids on movables and revenues occasionally had taken place earlier; thus in 1188 practically all the unpaid tallages of 1187 were pardoned and the aid on movables and revenues substituted. The yield of the latter was found more satisfactory. The fact that various sections of the country had to consent to the aids was an important factor in the history of parliament. By a statute of 1340 it was provided that the nation should not be called upon "to make any common aid or sustain charge" except by consent of parliament. The important but controversial document *De tallagio non concedendo* of 1297 said that no tallage or aid was to be imposed by the king without the common assent of the prelates, earls, barons, knights, burgesses and other freemen of the realm, thus turning the demesne tallage from a due into a gracious aid. Its text was more sweeping than the official confirmation of Magna Carta by Edward I, which merely stipulated that no aid levied for a special emergency should ever be regarded as establishing a precedent for a customary due. Whatever the nature of *De tallagio*, tallage on the demesne was only levied twice thereafter.

Finally there also existed in England the so-called sheriff's aid, which was a local payment of a fixed nature paid in early days to the sheriff by the county.

BIBLIOGRAPHY.—C. Stephenson, *Medieval Institutions: Selected Essays* (1954). For general English aspects *see* J. H. Round, *Feudal England* (1895) and *The Commune of London* (1899); S. K. Mitchell, *Taxation in Medieval England* (1951). For particular aspects *see* F. W. Maitland, *Domesday Book and Beyond* (1907); W. S. McKechnie, *Magna Carta*, 2nd ed. (1914).   (R. C. v. C.)

AIDAN, SAINT (d. 651), first bishop of Lindisfarne, was a monk at Iona when in 634 Oswald sent there to ask for a new bishop for his kingdom of Northumbria. Northumbria had only recently been converted to Christianity by Paulinus, a missionary from Rome. Aidan was appointed bishop, and settled on the island of Lindisfarne (Holy Island; *q.v.*). He founded churches and monasteries, and a school where 12 boys were trained for the ministry.

Aidan was successful in spreading Christianity throughout Northumbria, partly because he was building on foundations laid by Paulinus, partly because of Oswald's friendship, but chiefly because of his own character. Bede praises him for his learning, generosity, simplicity of life and the way he practised what he preached. After the defeat and death of Oswald at Maserfeld (641), the kingdom was divided, but Aidan retained his see. He always kept to the practice of the Celtic church on the date of celebrating Easter. He died at Bamburgh on Aug. 31, 651, and his feast day is Aug. 31.

See R. H. Hodgkin, *A History of the Anglo-Saxons*, 3rd ed., ch. 8 (1952); *Butler's Lives of the Saints*, ed. by H. Thurston and D. Attwater, vol. iii, pp. 451–452 (1956).   (PL. GN.)

AIDE-DE-CAMP (Fr. for camp assistant or perhaps field assistant), an officer on the personal staff of a general, admiral or other high-ranking commander who acts as his confidential secretary in routine matters. On Napoleon's staff such officers were frequently of high military qualifications and acted both as his "eyes" and as interpreters of his mind to subordinate com-

manders, even on occasions exercising delegated authority. In modern times they are usually of junior rank and their duties largely social. Traditionally, however, there are military, naval and air force officers, frequently of high rank, who act as aides to the president of the U.S.; governors of states also have aides-de-camp with the title of colonel. In Great Britain, the office of aide-de-camp to the king or queen is given to senior officers of the three services as a reward or honorary distinction. Civil governors serving the British crown, such as the governor of Northern Ireland, have also, as a rule, officers on their staffs with the title and functions of aide-de-camp.

In many countries, the word adjutant (*q.v.*) is used for aide-de-camp and adjutant general (*q.v.*) for a royal aide-de-camp. The common abbreviation for aide-de-camp in the U.S. is aide and in Britain A.D.C.

AIGUES-MORTES, a town of southeast France, *département* of Gard, 24 mi. S.W. of Nîmes. Pop. (1962) 3,776. It is a well-preserved medieval port now silted up. Situated at the western extremity of the Rhône delta, it was named for the *aquae mortuae* (dead waters) of the surrounding marshy plain. Aigues-Mortes is 3½ mi. from the Gulf of Lions, to which it is connected by a canal. The Rhône—Sète canal also serves the town.

Aigues-Mortes is almost entirely enclosed by medieval walls, forming an oblong roughly half a mile by a quarter. The crenelated walls are 25 to 30 ft. high, and are dominated by towers, the chief being the Constance tower once used as a prison for Protestants after the revocation of the Edict of Nantes. The main street leads from the central gate to St. Louis square and the other streets run parallel with or at right angles to it. Notre Dame du Sablon (1248) and the chapels of the Pénitents Gris and Blancs are interesting old churches.

Aigues-Mortes is on a branch railway line and has bus services to Nîmes and Montpellier. The salt marshes provide the main industry, the salt being extracted, processed and exported. The vineyards are preserved from disease by periodic submersion. Fishing and soda manufacture are other industries, and there is trade in coal, fruits and wine.

Louis IX (St. Louis) embarked from Aigues-Mortes in 1248 and 1270 for the 7th and 8th crusades. Only the Constance tower dates to his day and the fortifications were completed by Philip III. Although of declining importance, Aigues-Mortes remains as an example of medieval town planning.   (G. Bo.)

AIGUILLON, EMMANUEL ARMAND DE VIGNEROT DU PLESSIS DE RICHELIEU, DUC D' (1720–1788), French statesman, whose career illustrates the difficulties of the central government of the *ancien régime* in dealing with the provincial *parlements* and estates, the extent to which powerful ministers were at the mercy of court intrigue and how French diplomacy suffered under Louis XV as a result of secret diplomacy. Born on July 31, 1720, he succeeded in 1750 to the peerage duchy of Aiguillon (created for his great-great-grandfather's sister, a niece of the cardinal de Richelieu, in 1638). In 1753 he was appointed military commander for Brittany, where his wife, Louise-Félicité de Bréhan-Plélo, had numerous family connections. In the governor's absence he was the chief representative in the province of the central government and so incurred the hostility of the *parlement* of Rennes and of the provincial estates, which resisted the government's fiscal reforms of 1764–65. He also aroused the personal enmity of L. R. de Caradeuc de La Chalotais (*q.v.*) the powerful *procureur-général* of the *parlement*. These quarrels led to his recall in 1766. D'Aiguillon, however, was a man of great ambition and, after the fall of the duc de Choiseul, was appointed minister of foreign affairs (June 1771), though he had neither taste for nor experience of diplomacy. He was closely associated with the chancellor, René de Maupeou, and with the controller-general, the *abbé* J. M. Terray, in the so-called "triumvirate," which attempted to destroy the political powers of the *parlements*. As foreign minister he was unable to prevent the rapid decline of French influence in central and northern Europe. Though this was partly due to the rising power of Prussia and Russia, he gave no firm direction to French diplomacy and could not save Poland from being partitioned in 1772. His only—

dubious—success was the help that he gave to Gustavus III of Sweden in effecting his *coup d'état* of 1772. Dismissed from office on the accession of Louis XVI in 1774, he died in Paris on Sept. 1, 1788.

BIBLIOGRAPHY.—H. Carré, *La Chalotais et le duc d'Aiguillon* (1893); M. Marion, *La Brétagne et le duc d'Aiguillon* (1898); H. Fréville, *L'Intendance de Bretagne, 1689–1790*, vol. ii (1953); P. Rain, *La Diplomatie française d'Henri IV à Vergennes* (1945). (A. GN.)

AI-HUN (AIGUN), a Chinese city on the south bank of the Amur river in the province of Heilungkiang (49° 58′ N.; 127° 35′ E.). Opposite it is the Russian city of Blagoveshchensk (Hailanpao in Chinese). Ai-hun became an important entrepôt after the treaty of Aihun concluded in 1858 between China and Russia, dealing in the shipment of cattle, meat and food grains across the Amur to Blagoveshchensk. But after the building of the Chinese Eastern railway at the turn of the century its importance was reduced. Aihun is one of the major gold-producing districts of Manchuria, with important placer deposits. It is also a timber centre, getting supplies from the Little Khingan ranges.
(KN. C.)

AIKEN, CONRAD POTTER (1889–   ), U.S. poet and man of letters, explored the subconscious mind in symphonic poems and meditative prose. Born of New England stock in Savannah, Ga., on Aug. 5, 1889, he was the oldest son of a physician who killed his wife and himself when the boy was eleven. Sent to live with relatives in New Bedford, Mass., he was educated at private schools and at Harvard (class of 1911), where he was a friend and contemporary of T. S. Eliot. Most of his mature life was divided almost equally between England and the U.S., but after 1947 he was permanently established at Brewster, Mass.

Aiken was never anything but a writer. After three immature collections of verse, he entered an extremely fruitful period. 1915–20, during which he wrote five "symphonies" in an effort to create what he called "a sort of absolute poetry" that would resemble music. Then came a period of narrative poems, then several volumes of lyrics and meditations, and after World War II a return to the musical form, in poems that were simpler in conception than the symphonies but had richer overtones of philosophical and psychological meaning.

Besides his poems, Aiken produced distinguished work in many fields. He wrote five novels (beginning with *Blue Voyage*, 1927) and four books of short stories (notably *The Short Stories of Conrad Aiken*, 1950), many of them dealing with inhibited characters studied almost psychoanalytically. He also wrote many critical essays, a play (*Mr. Arcularis,* with Diana Hamilton, 1949) and an experimental essay in autobiography (*Ushant*, 1952). He worked in obscurity, sometimes in extreme poverty, during much of his career.

Although his *Selected Poems* received a Pulitzer prize in 1930, it was not until 1953, when his *Collected Poems* appeared in a volume of 900 pages, that he was widely recognized as a major writer.

Besides *Ushant, see* Houston Peterson, *The Melody of Chaos* (1931). *Wake 11: Conrad Aiken Number* (1952) contains an extensive bibliography. (M. CY.)

AILANTHUS (more correctly *ailantus,* from *ailanto,* an Amboyna word probably meaning "tree of the gods," or "tree of heaven"), a genus of trees belonging to the quassia family (Simaroubaceae). The best-known species, tree of heaven (*Ailanthus altissima*), is a handsome rapidly growing tree with spreading branches and large pinnately compound leaves bearing many lance-shaped leaflets with conspicuous glandular bases. The small greenish flowers are borne in branched panicles; the staminate (male), upon opening, exhale a most disagreeable odour. The fruit is a samara with a single centrally disposed seed in the elliptical, twisted, fibrous wing. This tree, which is a native of China and Japan, was introduced into England in 1751 and is a favourite in parks and gardens. It has been planted extensively in the eastern United States and is one of a few trees capable of thriving in smoky atmospheres adjoining industrial centres. Two other species, *A. imberbiflora* and *A. punctata,* are Australian trees of secondary importance; *A. excelsa* is a common tree in India. (E. S. HR.)

AILLY, PIERRE D' (1350–1420), French churchman, cardinal and scholar, the chief aim of whose life was to heal the great western schism of 1378–1417, was born at Compiègne and studied at the College of Navarre of the University of Paris, where he became doctor of theology (1380) and soon acquired a position of leadership. Although he recognized the Avignon pope as early as 1379, D'Ailly advocated the conciliar theory as early as 1380. According to this view, also adopted by the University of Paris, a general council is superior to the pope, whom it may, if necessary, depose. Acting as spokesman of the university before the royal council in 1381, D'Ailly advocated the convocation of a general council to end the schism. After temporary retirement, he became master of the College of Navarre in 1384, where he had as one of his pupils Jean de Gerson (q.v.). He became chancellor of the university as well as the king's confessor and almoner in 1389, but displeased the university by supporting Benedict XIII after the latter's election to succeed Clement VII (1394). Benedict appointed him bishop of Le Puy in 1395 and then bishop of Cambrai in 1397. Although D'Ailly opposed withdrawal of French allegiance from Benedict, he worked for the voluntary abdication of both pontiffs. He gradually broke with the intransigent Benedict XIII and returned to his old conciliar doctrine, which steadily became more extreme. He played a prominent part in the general council of Pisa (1409), which declared both popes deposed and elected a third, Alexander V. John XXIII, who succeeded Alexander the following year, made D'Ailly a cardinal (1411) and bishop of Orange, as well as his legate to Germany. But since the schism persisted, D'Ailly supported the convocation of a new general council at Constance (1414–18), where he was influential in its decisions to insist on the abdication of John XXIII, condemn the Hussites, vote by nations, support conciliarism and compromise concerning the parts of the council and the cardinals in the election of a new pope. He was also an advocate of church reform. (*See* CONSTANCE, COUNCIL OF.) The possibility that D'Ailly might be elected pope was ruled out by a hostile coalition of Italians, Germans and English. Since he was unacceptable to the English and Burgundians, who were now in control of most of France, he was forced to retire to Avignon, where he was legate for Martin V.

D'Ailly was the author of numerous works, several of which were very influential. Although many of his views on the constitution of the church, such as the independent superiority of the general council, the autonomous jurisdiction of bishops and the reservation of infallibility to the universal body of believers, were later rejected as heretical, they became temporarily ascendant as the only apparent way of ending the great western schism, and were later echoed by Protestant reformers. In philosophy, D'Ailly supported Ockhamistic nominalism (q.v.), which became ascendant at the University of Paris and later influenced Luther. Interested in science, he advocated calendar reform, later effected by Gregory XII; and his *Image of the World,* which supported the idea that India could be reached by sailing west, encouraged Columbus. Several of his works were printed in the 15th and 18th centuries; others remain in manuscript.

Biographies of D'Ailly have been published by P. Tschackert (1877), L. Salembier (1886) and John McGowan (1936). (D. D. McG.)

AILSA CRAIG, an island rock at the mouth of the Firth of Clyde, 10 mi. W. of Girvan, Ayrshire, Scot. Pop. (1951) 14. "Paddy's milestone," as it has been called because it is about halfway between Glasgow and Belfast, is cone-shaped and rises abruptly to a height of 1,114 ft.; it is 3,900 ft. long and 2,600 ft. wide. The only side from which the rock can be ascended is the east, the other sides generally presenting lofty columnar forms. The island is composed of microgranite with riebeckite—a rare type in Britain. Pebbles were carried far south (*e.g.,* to Wales and Ireland) by the retreating glaciers. The rock is a favourite material for curling (q.v.) stones, hence their popular name of "Ailsas" or "Ailsa Craigs." The rock is also used for paving stones. A columnar cave exists toward the north of the island, and on the east are remains of a tower. The Garry loch is 800 ft. above sea level. Two springs occur near the summit and some scanty grass affords subsistence to goats. After myxomatosis was introduced in 1956 the rabbit population almost died out, but it had risen again to about 10% of its former numbers by 1959 when the disease recurred. The precipices have large breeding colonies of gannets and other sea birds; the brown rat is firmly established. A lighthouse on the south flashes a light visible for 13 mi. and there are two alternating foghorns.

AIMAK, a Mongol term which Genghis Khan applied to a tribal group fighting as a military unit. In the 18th century the Chahar Mongols of Inner Mongolia comprised a single aimak, while in the 1960s 18 of the 19 administrative divisions of the Mongolian People's Republic (*q.v.*) were called *aymags*. Among the Kalmyks, who migrated to southern Russia in the 17th century, the aimak was a comparatively small subtribal group sharing a common territory. In western Afghanistan the term originally meant "nomadic tribe," but later was used only in the name Chahar Aimak ("Four Tribes"), which includes the Djamshidi, Firuzkuhi, Hazara and Taimani. Of these only the Hazaras (western Hazaras) are Mongol. The Firuzkuhi have a tradition of Persian origin. (EL. B.)

AIMARD, GUSTAVE (pseudonym of OLIVIER GLOUX) (1818–1883), French novelist who wrote adventure stories of the American frontier, was born in Paris in 1818. He went to sea at 12 and witnessed local wars and conspiracies in Turkey, the Caucasus and South America. He took part in the 1848 revolution in Paris, returned to America in an unsuccessful armed expedition to Sonora, Mex., under Count Raousset-Boulbon in 1854 and shortly afterward began a series of novels that extended to his death. Many of them, first published in serial form, were translated into English, including *The Border Rifles, The Trappers of Arkansas* and *The Missouri Outlaws.* Aimard fought in the siege of Paris in 1870 and died in Paris on June 20, 1883.

AIMOIN (*c.* 960–*c.* 1010), French Benedictine monk whose history of the Franks was highly esteemed in the middle ages. Having entered the abbey of Fleury-sur-Loire (between 979 and 985), he devoted much of his time to writing on St. Benedict; the second and third books of the *Miracula sancti Benedicti* were written by him in 1005. Encouraged, however, by the abbot Abbon (d. 1004), whose biography he also wrote, Aimoin began to compose his *Historia Francorum* or *Libri IV de gestis Francorum* from various texts on the Merovingian period (notably the works of Gregory of Tours), which he collected and rewrote in better Latin. Left incomplete, his history ends at the year 653. Later writers adapted, lengthened or expanded it, and its substance reappears in a number of 12th-century works.

BIBLIOGRAPHY.—For the *Miracula* see *Les Miracles de Saint Benoît,* ed. by E. de Certain (1858). For the life of Abbon, valuable for its use of authentic letters, *see* the *Annales ordinis Sancti Benedicti,* ed. by J. Mabillon, vol. vi, pt. 1 (1668). The *Historia* is printed by J. P. Migne, *Patrologia latina,* vol. cxxxix (1844). (JE. H.)

AIMORÉS, SERRA DOS, is a region of southeast Brazil divided between the states of Minas Gerais and Espírito Santo. Pop. (1960) 384,297; area 3,914 sq.mi. Until 1963 the area was claimed by Minas Gerais and Espírito Santo, but in that year the dispute was settled by dividing the territory between those two states. It is crossed by the São Mateus river and several smaller streams, and the Rio Doce follows closely its southwest border. In surface characteristics Serra dos Aimorés is mainly crystalline hilly upland, covered with semideciduous forest; elevations average close to 3,000 ft. Rainfall is in the range of 40 to 60 in. annually. It is a frontier region with fertile soils capable of producing coffee, beans, cereals, vegetables and livestock. The proximity of the Rio-Bahia highway and the Estrada de Ferro Vale do Rio Doce enhance the economic value of the region. Mantena is the principal town. (J. L. TR.)

AIN, a *département* of eastern France, formed from Bresse, the Pays de Dombes on the lowland and the Pays de Gex, Valromey and Bugey among the high parallel ridges of the Jura (*q.v.*) reaching south to the Rhône river between Geneva and Lyons. Pop. (1962) 327,146. Area 2,238 sq.mi. The Ain river roughly separates the lowland areas from the other districts, running north to south at first between outer hill ridges and then along the foot of the highland to join the Rhône. The western boundary is the Saône river, the southern the Rhône, the eastern Switzerland and the northern the *départements* of Saône-et-Loire and Jura, the boundary over against the latter being closely linked with that of old between Burgundy and Franche-Comté. The Pays de Gex includes some of the highest Jura scarps (Crêt de la Neige 5,653 ft.), the Pays de Valromey flanks on the west the deep Rhône gorge below Bellegarde, the Pays de Bugey is the south-pointing triangle of the Rhône focussing on Belley. West of the hills, Bresse occupies the fertile north part of the *département* and is effectively drained to the Saône, thus contrasting with the Pays de Dombes, mantled in boulder clay, with innumerable pools and marshes and, still, a good deal of consequent malarial trouble. The summers are warm in the lowland but the winters, generally, are cold; the precipitation rises above 40 in. per annum in the highland.

The farms of Bresse are famous for pigs and poultry and the latter (especially geese) are bred in Dombes, which also raises horses. In the Jura hills are extensive forests and pastures. Cheese is a noteworthy product. Bresse produces considerable cereal and other crops but the rest of the *département* is concerned mainly with stockraising, activities connected with its forests (of fir and oak) or with extensions of the silk industry from Lyons, made possible by the water power available from the rivers among the gorges of the limestone country.

Bourg (*q.v.*) is the capital of the *département;* the four *arrondissements* take their names from Bourg, Belley (the seat of a bishop in the archiepiscopal province of Besançon), Nantua and the Pays de Gex. The departmental appeals are heard at the court of Lyons and the *département* is also under Lyons educationally. Bourg is a market town specially known for the famous church of Brou. Among silk towns are Jujurieux, Tenay, St. Rambert and St. Bernard en Bugey; Bellegarde and St. Rambert make wood pulp; and Oyonnax, a rather larger town than several of the others, north of Nantua, makes articles in wood and horn and is specially well known for its combs. Seyssel, on the far east, yields asphalt, and many parts of the *département* produce building stones, cement or potter's clay. There is a thriving tourist industry for winter sports, angling, etc., and some of the gorges and ridges are very striking. Near Bellegarde, at the Perte du Rhône, the river formerly disappeared down a fissure. Though the main Sud-Est (formerly Paris-Lyon-Méditerranée) railway from Dijon to Lyons lies west of the Saône, and so outside the *département,* the main line from Paris to Geneva runs through Bourg and Ambérieu to Bellegarde; both the Saône and the Rhône are navigable for considerable lengths along the confines of the *département.* Historical aspects may be found in BRESSE; BURGUNDY; DOMBES; parts of which comprise Ain. (AR. E. S.)

AIN RIVER, of eastern France and a tributary of the Rhône (*q.v.*), flows through the *départements* of Jura and Ain. Rising in the Jura (*q.v.*) plateau above Champagnole, it flows southward for 124 mi. through the limestone plateau in a deep valley, receiving left-bank affluents from the Jura mountains. Approaching the Rhône, it emerges from its gorge to flow past Pont d'Ain across the hummocky moraine country of the Dombes. Several hydroelectric power stations are located along the courses of the Ain and its tributary the Bienne in the Jura mountains. (AR. E. S.)

AINSWORTH, HENRY (1571–*c.* 1622), English Nonconformist theologian and rabbinical scholar, a leader of the English Separatist colony in Amsterdam, was born at Swanton Morley, Norfolk, in 1571. He was a scholar of Caius college, Cambridge, and joined first the Puritan and eventually the Separatist party in the church. Driven abroad in the persecution of 1593, he found a home in "a blind lane at Amsterdam." He acted as "porter" to a scholarly bookseller in that city who, on discovering his skill in Hebrew, enabled him to continue his Hebrew studies. When part of the London church, of which Francis Johnson (then in prison) was pastor, reassembled in Amsterdam, Ainsworth was chosen as their doctor or teacher.

In 1596 he drew up a confession of their faith, which he reissued in Latin in 1598. Johnson joined his flock in 1597, and in 1604 he and Ainsworth composed *An Apology or Defence of Such True Christians as Are Commonly but Unjustly Called Brownists.* In 1610 he was forced reluctantly to withdraw, with a large part of the church, from Johnson and his adherents on a question of church government, Ainsworth taking the more congregational view. (*See* CONGREGATIONALISM; BROWNE, ROBERT.) He died in Amsterdam, probably in 1622.

The fruit of Ainsworth's rabbinical learning appeared in his *Annotations*—on *Genesis* (1616), *Exodus* (1617), *Leviticus* (1618), *Numbers* (1619), *Deuteronomy* (1619), *Psalms* (including a metrical version, 1612) and *Song of Solomon* (1623). These were collected in folio in 1627 and again in 1639. From the outset the *Annotations* took a commanding place, especially among continental scholars.

BIBLIOGRAPHY.—H. M. Dexter, *Congregationalism of the Last Three Hundred Years* (1880); W. E. A. Axon, *H. Ainsworth, the Puritan Commentator* (1889); F. J. Powicke, *Henry Barrow and the Exiled Church of Amsterdam* (1900); J. H. Shakespeare, *Baptist and Congregational Pioneers* (1906).

AINSWORTH, WILLIAM HARRISON (1805–1882), English writer of popular historical romances, was born in Manchester, Feb. 4, 1805. In 1824 he went to study at the Inner Temple, but abandoned law for literature and collaborated with J. P. Aston in writing *Sir John Chiverton* (1826). Success came in 1834, with *Rookwood*, which includes a vivid description of Dick Turpin's famous ride. It was followed by many other historical novels, of which *Jack Sheppard* (1839), *The Tower of London* (1840), *Old St. Paul's* (1841), *Windsor Castle* (1843) and *The Lancashire Witches* (1849) are the best known.

In 1839 Ainsworth became editor of *Bentley's Miscellany,* which he owned from 1854 to 1868, and in 1842 he founded *Ainsworth's Magazine.* He later edited the *New Monthly Magazine.* His fame as a writer, and his generous encouragement of other authors, gave him social standing. His books brought him wealth, but his ventures as editor and publisher were not financially successful. He died at Reigate, Jan. 3, 1882.

Ainsworth's novels, lacking coherence of plot or subtlety of characterization, excel in conveying a sense of the bustle and pageantry of history and in their historical accuracy and local colour.

BIBLIOGRAPHY.—S. M. Ellis, *W. H. Ainsworth and His Friends,* 2 vol. (1911); H. Locke, *A Bibliographical Catalogue of the Published Novels and Ballads of W. H. Ainsworth* (1925); M. Elwin, *Victorian Wallflowers* (1934).

AINU, a people living in Hokkaido, Sakhalin and the Kuril Islands, who are physically unlike their Mongoloid neighbours and may be descendants of early Caucasoid type peoples once widely spread over northern Asia. The Ainu of modern times are extremely reduced in numbers and appear to be dying out except as they are intermarried with Japanese and other settlers. Formerly they may have extended southward to the Ryukyu Islands. Some scholars see relationships between the Ainoid (Ainulike) type and the Australoid type aboriginal peoples of Australia and New Guinea. Short statured and brunette, they have the most profuse body hair of any known human group. Japanese migrations northward involved centuries of sporadic warfare with Ainu groups before final pacification of the remnants in the Hokkaido area. Ainu speech, with a number of dialects, has no known relation to any other language. The Ainu live in small villages near the sea, with hunting, fishing, gathering wild plants and, in modern times, minor gardening as an economic base. Houses are of reed thatch, and formerly included pit dwellings. Men usually have heavy beards, and women moustachelike tattooing around the mouth. Traditional clothing consists of bark cloth or skin

BY COURTESY OF CONSULATE GENERAL OF JAPAN, NEW YORK, N.Y
AINU COUPLE IN CEREMONIAL DRESS

drapes often decorated with geometric designs characteristic of their art. Village chiefs and kin elders provide leadership. Religion centres around local forces of nature and a cult of ancestors, with a bear sacrifice ritual as a high point. Many aspects of Ainu life show past Japanese influences, and the younger generations of Ainu in north Japan show extensive adaptation to modern Japanese culture. *See* JAPAN: *The People.*

BIBLIOGRAPHY.—J. Batchelor, *The Ainu of Japan* (1901), *Ainu Life and Lore* (1927); G. P. Murdock, *Our Primitive Contemporaries* (1934); C. Etter, *Ainu Folklore* (1949); S. Takakura, *Ainu of Northern Japan* (1960); J. A. Harrison, *Japan's Northern Frontier* (1953); N. G. Munro, *Ainu Creed and Cult* (1963); J. B. Cornell, "Ainu Assimilation . . . ," *Ethnology,* vol. 3 (July 1964).   (F. M. KG.)

AIR is the gaseous envelope that surrounds the earth. It is a mixture of gases, the most abundant of which are nitrogen and oxygen. Near the end of the 18th century the word air was applied to several common gases; *e.g.,* nitrogen was known as phlogisticated air, oxygen as dephlogisticated air, hydrogen as inflammable air and carbon dioxide as fixed air (*see* CHEMISTRY: *History of Chemistry: The Understanding of Combustion*). The name air now is used ordinarily only for the mixture of substances which constitute the gaseous components of our atmosphere.

The composition of the air is not constant. The principal variable components are water and carbon dioxide. If these substances are removed from samples of air collected in many places and at many times, the compositions of the remainders of the samples are virtually constant. Table I shows the concentrations of the nonvariable components of air.

TABLE I.—*Nonvariable Components of Air From Which Water and Carbon Dioxide Have Been Removed*

Constituent	Formula	Volume %*
Nitrogen	N_2	78.110
Oxygen	O_2	20.953
Argon	Ar	0.934
Neon	Ne	0.001818
Helium	He	0.000524
Krypton	Kr	0.000114
Xenon	Xe	0.0000087
Hydrogen	H_2	0.00005
Methane	CH_4	0.0002
Nitrous oxide	N_2O	0.00005

*Volume per cent of any gas is the volume of that gas isolated and purified in a total of 100 vol. of gas mixture.

Table II contains a list of other gases commonly found in air. The last four probably arise from industrial sources and perhaps should be regarded as contaminants rather than as constituents of natural air.

The amount of moisture in the air is very variable and has important effects on climate, radiation, weather and comfort (*see* HUMIDITY, ATMOSPHERIC). The absolute humidity may be as high as 7 volume per cent of water vapour if the temperature is 40° C. (104° F.) and if the relative humidity is 100%.

TABLE II.—*Variable Components of Air*

Constituent	Formula	Volume %
Water	H_2O	0 to 7*
Carbon dioxide	CO_2	0.01 to 0.1; average 0.033
Ozone	O_3	0 to 0.000007
Formaldehyde	CH_2O	?
Sulfur dioxide	SO_2	0 to 0.0001
Nitrogen dioxide	NO_2	0 to 0.000002
Ammonia	NH_3	0 to trace
Carbon monoxide	CO	0 to trace

*Approximate value for 40° C. (104° F.) and a relative humidity of 100%.

The ozone concentration is highly variable. Ozone is both produced and destroyed by absorption of ultraviolet radiation. Most of it is found at great altitudes. It is important in meteorology largely because it absorbs ultraviolet and infrared radiation.

Variations in the carbon dioxide content of the air are interesting and some of them are very important. Carbon dioxide concentration is relatively high over decaying leaves of forest floors and in enclosed spaces such as crowded rooms, city subways, caves and wells. It is relatively low over fields of growing vegetation, in polar regions not covered by ice and in regions where the air has recently passed over the ocean.

Carbon dioxide in the air reduces the loss of heat by infrared radiation from the earth. The widespread burning of fossil fuels (*e.g.*, coal and oil) increased the carbon dioxide content of the air by about 12% during the first half of the 20th century. This, in turn, caused an increase in the average temperature of the earth of 1.1° C. during the same period. It is estimated that all of the fossil fuels will be consumed in about 1,000 years, if the present rate of consumption is maintained. It has been further estimated that this will cause the temperature of the earth to rise 7° to 14° C. (13° to 25° F.), giving most of the earth a tropical and semitropical climate by the end of the period.

Density.—The density of the air can vary greatly. It is reduced by the lowering of barometric pressure, rise of temperature and increase of humidity. Since lowered density greatly reduces the lifting capacity of airplanes, density must be considered whenever heavily loaded planes are being prepared for flights.

Particulates.—Suspended in the air are liquid droplets and a wide variety of small solid particles called particulates. A very prominent class of particulate is salt raised by winds from ocean spray and carried to great altitudes and great distances over the earth. The salt particles are highly important in the condensation and precipitation of water. *See* ATMOSPHERE; *see* also references under "Air" in the Index.

BIBLIOGRAPHY.—G. P. Kuiper (ed.), *Atmospheres of the Earth and Planets* (1949); T. F. Malone (ed.), *Compendium of Meteorology*, esp. "The Composition of Atmospheric Air" by E. Glueckauf (1951); G. N. Plass, "Carbon Dioxide and the Climate," *American Scientist*, vol. 44, 302–316 (1956). (T. F. Y.)

AIR (AYRE). In general the musical term air (like its cognate forms in French, *air*, and Italian, *aria*) signifies a tune or song, and hence a type of music in which the upper (melody) line predominates. In the 16th century in particular these terms (*e.g.* as used in the compound *air de cour*, of a particular type of courtly song) indicated forms of art song, simpler in texture than the polyphonic madrigal (*q.v.*). The spelling "ayre" is used to refer to the rich and clearly defined repertory of late Elizabethan and Jacobean songs for solo voice, usually with lute accompaniment, inaugurated by John Dowland's *First Books of Songes or Ayres of Foure Partes, with Tableture for the Lute* (1597) and ending with John Attey's similarly named collection of 1622. This brief period saw the publication in London of more than two dozen collections of "ayres." The principal composers were Dowland (four books), Robert Jones (five books), Thomas Campion (four books), Philip Rosseter and Thomas Morley (one book each). Not only do their songs run the gamut of expression from gaiety to mourning, passion to frivolity; they also represent a relationship between music and poetry more intimate than any to be found in English song writing before the 20th century. Of the composers only Campion is known to have been a poet, but many of the texts of these collections were written by the finest poets of the day.

BIBLIOGRAPHY.—The complete repertory was edited by E. H. Fellowes, *The English School of Lutenist Song-Writers*, 32 vol. (1920–32). *See also* P. Warlock, *The English Ayre* (1926); B. Pattison, *Music and Poetry of the English Renaissance* (1948). (J. J. N.)

AIR-BORNE TROOPS: *see* AIR POWER.

AIR CONDITIONING,
the control of temperature, humidity, purity and motion of the air in an enclosure. Air conditioning is used for industrial processes as well as for human comfort. The production of uniformly good quality cotton yarn requires nearly constant temperature and high moisture content of the air in the cotton mill. During the manufacture of extremely delicate equipment, such as inertial guidance systems for rockets, airplanes or submarines, temperature and humidity must be closely controlled and air purity maintained at an extremely high level. Air conditioning for human comfort is employed in both large and small installations, such as theatres, office buildings, department stores, residences, airplanes, railway cars and submarines.

History.—The Romans used panel heating systems (*see* HOUSE DESIGN), and in India wetted grass mats were hung over the windward openings of houses to cool the incoming air.

The beginnings of modern air conditioning occurred in the textile industry, where the term "conditioning" was applied to the determination of the moisture content of textiles. In order to reduce breakage and the effects of static electricity, the air in the textile mills was humidified by evaporating water from steam pots.

In 1842 Dr. John Gorrie of Apalachicola, Fla., designed and built for the treatment of yellow-fever patients an apparatus that used air as a refrigerant. In the latter part of the 19th century, cotton mills used atomized sprays of water for simultaneous humidification and cooling. In the same period, methods of controlling the ambient air were used in many other industries also. In 1897 Joseph McCreary of Toledo, O., patented an air washer which cooled and humidified in addition to its primary function of cleaning the air.

In 1906 Stuart W. Cramer of Charlotte, N.C., and Willis H. Carrier of Buffalo, N.Y., working independently, made two important contributions. Cramer used individual spray heads in a room and controlled humidity by a system that depended upon the relation between the wet- and dry-bulb temperatures (*see* below). He first suggested the use of the term "air conditioning." Carrier devised the "dew point control," a central air-conditioning unit of the air-washer type which saturated the air and controlled automatically the saturation temperature. This system thus determined the moisture content of the air supplied. Carrier initiated the scientific approach to air conditioning in a paper presented to the American Society of Mechanical Engineers in 1911.

The form of air conditioning used first in textile mills was extended to other industries. In the early 1920s new refrigerants began to appear, enabling the manufacture of lighter, safer and more efficient refrigerating equipment. Air conditioning for human comfort was first used in 1922 in a motion-picture theatre. Its great success caused the widespread use of air conditioning in other public buildings, such as department stores, hotels and restaurants. The early 1930s saw the development of the first small unitary air conditioner for railway coaches and the beginning of the scientific study of human comfort requirements. The John B. Pierce Laboratory of Hygiene, the U.S. bureau of mines and the American Society of Heating and Ventilating Engineers, together with the United States department of public health, started studies of man's relationship to his thermal environment from both the physical and physiological standpoints.

After World War II the air-conditioning industry expanded at an extremely rapid rate. The use of air conditioning became universally accepted in various applications, particularly in the United States. New public buildings, office buildings and factories are almost always built with air conditioning included in the original design. Ships, particularly passenger vessels, use air conditioning. Medium-size unitary systems find widespread use in residential central units, offices, restaurants and in specialized applications such as buses, airplanes, submarines and space vehicles. Examples of the smallest units are air conditioners installed in the windows of homes and in automobiles.

Psychrometric Properties of Air.—Psychrometry is essentially the thermodynamics (*q.v.*) of air and water-vapour mixtures as applied to air conditioning. Atmospheric air is considered to be a perfect gas consisting of a mixture of dry air and water vapour. At the usual temperatures and pressures encountered, each of these components can also be considered as a perfect gas; *i.e.*, each component as well as the mixture follows the relation $pv = RT$, where p is absolute pressure in pounds per square foot, v is specific volume in cubic feet per pound, R is the gas constant of the particular gas in foot-pounds per pound-degree Fahrenheit (for air, $R_a = 53.35$; for water vapour $R_w = 85.71$) and T is the temperature in degrees Fahrenheit absolute. In addition, Dalton's law of partial pressures holds. Accordingly, atmospheric, barometric or total pressure is equal to the sum of the pressures exerted by dry air and water vapour independently of each other. The maximum partial pressure that water vapour can exert at any temperature is equal to its saturation pressure at that temperature (*see* VAPORIZATION). This saturated condition also determines the maximum quantity of water vapour that air can hold at any temperature.

Humidity per se denotes the water vapour mixed with dry air. Absolute humidity is the actual mass of water vapour in one cubic foot of space, and is equivalent to the density. It is usually expressed in pounds or grains per cubic foot (1 lb. = 7,000 gr.

avoirdupois). Specific humidity or humidity ratio is the mass of water vapour in pounds or grains that is mixed with one pound of dry air. Relative humidity is the ratio of the actual partial pressure of water vapour to the saturated vapour pressure at the same dry-bulb temperature. It is usually expressed as a percentage. (*See* HUMIDITY, ATMOSPHERIC.)

Percentage saturation is 100 times the ratio of the actual mass of water vapour mixed in one pound of dry air to that required to saturate one pound of dry air at the same dry-bulb temperature and absolute total pressure.

Dry-bulb temperature of the air is measured by a clean, dry thermometer properly shielded against radiation.

Wet-bulb temperature of the air is indicated by a wetted thermometer bulb when evaporation from its surface occurs in an air stream moving with a velocity of at least 1,000 ft. per minute. For dry-air and water-vapour mixtures this temperature is essentially equal to that of adiabatic saturation; *i.e.*, the temperature the same air would reach if brought in contact with a large surface of water inside a well-insulated chamber through which no heat flows and inside of which no work is done.

Sensible heat is the heat absorbed by a body when its temperature is changed. Latent heat (*q.v.*) is the heat absorbed by a body when it changes its physical state without change of temperature; *e.g.*, ice melting to form water.

Psychrometers are devices for measuring dry-bulb and wet-bulb temperatures.

Dew point is the temperature at which condensation of the water vapour in the air begins. Consequently, it is the saturation temperature corresponding to the partial pressure of the water vapour.

Enthalpy of a substance is its internal energy plus the product of its absolute pressure times its specific volume expressed in consistent units, usually B.T.U. per pound. In psychrometric calculations enthalpy is the measure of the energy that can be converted into heat. For dry-air and water-vapour mixtures the enthalpy per pound of dry air depends almost exclusively on the wet-bulb temperature.

Psychrometric charts present graphically the relations between the various properties of dry-air and water-vapour mixtures. They are of great help in air-conditioning calculations, providing not only a quick way of finding properties but also allowing convenient presentation and calculation of processes.

Air-Conditioning Equipment.—Air-conditioning systems may be classified in several ways. According to their purpose, they can be described as winter, summer or all-year systems. (For a discussion of winter systems, *see* HEATING AND VENTILATION.) Considering their basic design, they are called unit or central air conditioners.

Summer air-conditioning equipment can lower the dry-bulb temperature in several ways. In hot, dry climates, evaporative coolers are very effective and are also the most economical to install and to operate. These coolers use recirculated water to saturate adiabatically the air passing through. Such a process lowers the dry-bulb temperature and increases the humidity; it is of little effect when the outside humidity is above 40%.

In hot, humid climates air can be cooled and dehumidified by passing it through either a finned cooling coil or a spray of chilled water in an air washer. The air leaving either of these units is usually too cold and has to be passed through a reheat coil to bring it up to the desired dry-bulb temperature. The finned cooling coil can be of the direct expansion type when it serves as an evaporator of the refrigerant, or it can be cooled by chilled water that is refrigerated elsewhere. The latter arrangement has the advantage of permitting the use of the coil for heating applications if hot water is circulated through it. The self-contained cooling units are usually of the direct expansion type, which require only electrical connection to operate the compressor and fan motors if the condenser is air cooled but need both electrical and water connections if the condenser is water cooled. The air washer is essentially an all-year unit because it can provide heating, cooling, humidifying and dehumidifying by changing the temperature of the water spray. Dehumidification can also be achieved with absorption by a hygroscopic material, such as a lithium

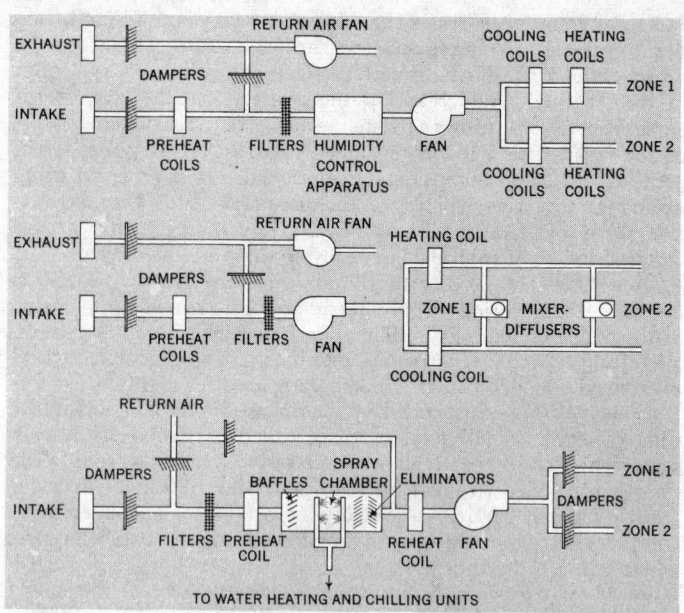

SCHEMATIC DIAGRAMS FOR REPRESENTATIVE ALL-YEAR AIR-CONDITIONING SYSTEMS

(Top) Zone control by individual cooling and heating coils; (centre) dual-duct system controlled by mixer-diffusers; (bottom) air-washer system with individually controlled zone dampers

chloride solution, or with adsorption by such substances as silica gel or activated alumina. With these types of systems, bypass arrangements and additional means for cooling and heating the air are usually required to obtain the desired final dry-bulb temperature.

All-year air-conditioning systems must provide means for performing all the processes required for winter and summer air conditioning. The basic pieces of equipment are the filters, preheat coils, humidifiers, dehumidifiers, reheat coils, additional cooling coils (if chemical dehumidification is used), fans and controls. The figure shows typical arrangements of all-year central systems.

Special Systems.—Special designs include the so-called high-velocity, the induction and the heat-pump systems. The high-velocity systems, with air moving up to 6,000 ft. per minute, require relatively small ducts, but their operating cost is high and the noise problem is severe. Special diffusers have to be used in the rooms to reduce air velocities and thus obtain a lower noise level.

The induction-type systems combine the principles of self-contained units and central systems. Primary conditioned air is supplied to a nozzle in the induction units in the rooms, where it is mixed with secondary air drawn from the room. The principal advantages of this system are individual controls for each room, reduced power cost due to the small amount of centrally supplied air and (usually) better circulation of the air in the rooms.

The major disadvantage of this system is the difficulty of providing enough fresh air to all rooms at all times.

The heat pump system is essentially a vapour compression refrigeration cycle system (*see* REFRIGERATION). For cooling, the air is passed over an evaporator coil. The heat from the condenser is rejected either to the outside atmosphere or to cooling water. For heating, the air is passed over a condenser coil, while heat can be absorbed in an evaporator from the outside atmosphere, from the ground or from some other available source. Such a system requires a rather complicated layout of ducts, pipes, dampers and valves.

Control Methods.—The control of unit or induction-type air conditioners is done directly from the room in which they are located. In central air-conditioning systems control can best be achieved by dividing the total space into zones and arranging the equipment so that the condition and quantity of air supplied to each zone can be controlled individually. The figure indicates types of zone controls.

The three basic functions of an automatic control system of air conditioning are performed by the following instruments: (1) controllers, such as thermostats, humidistats and pressure controllers, sense changes in temperature, humidity and pressure; (2) actuators operate dampers and valves to regulate the flow of air and the various fluids used in the system in response to signals received from the controllers; and (3) limit and safety controls operate the actuators when a potentially dangerous condition develops in the system; the controls can be operated either electrically or pneumatically.

Air Purification.—The control of air purity can be achieved in various degrees. As a minimum control, some sort of filtering must be done near the entrance of the air-conditioning system. There are four basic types of air filters.

1. The impingement filter stops dirt particles attempting to pass through by causing them to impinge on the surfaces of a closely packed filtering material, such as cellulose or glass fibres. This material may be dry or it may be coated with some suitable viscous liquid to improve filtering efficiency.

2. The directional-change or dynamic air-cleaning device separates the suspended particles from the air stream by producing rapid directional changes of the air flow which the particles cannot follow. A typical example is the so-called cyclone separator.

3. Possibly the most efficient (and most expensive) filtering device is the electrostatic precipitator. With this device, the particles in the air are charged by passing the flow through a strong electrostatic field, and are then precipitated on alternately placed, positively and negatively charged plates.

4. The air washer also acts as an air cleaner, but it can eliminate only contamination which can be wetted, such as ordinary dust.

Specialized air-purification problems include the removal of odours, most effectively done by activated charcoal filters, and air sterilization by ultraviolet rays or germicide sprays (*see* ANTISEPTICS).

Load Calculations.—In order to establish the size and operational requirements of an air-conditioning system, the maximum probable heating and cooling demands have to be calculated. These depend on the required conditions inside the enclosure, the expected outside design conditions and the various heat losses and heat gains occurring. The maximum probable heating demand is usually for winter air conditioning and it involves heating and humidifying. The maximum probable cooling demand is generally for summer applications and requires cooling and dehumidifying.

In calculating the various loads it is important to distinguish between sensible loads, which involve only a change in dry-bulb temperature, and latent loads, which involve only a change in humidity. The operating conditions of the air-conditioning system have to be so established that the air supplied to the enclosure will be able to satisfy the requirements of both sensible and latent loads. For example, if cooling and dehumidifying are required in the enclosure, the supply air has to be colder and drier than the inside air to such a degree that, as the supply air reaches the design conditions during its diffusion in the enclosure, it absorbs just the required amounts of sensible and latent heats.

Design Conditions.—The inside design conditions depend entirely upon the purpose for which air conditioning is used. Certain industrial process requirements and human comfort are the two major factors encountered. If the installation is for human comfort the usual inside design conditions for winter differ from those for summer. Summer air conditioning requires a closer control of humidity and higher dry-bulb temperatures (76°–80° F.) to reduce the cooling load on the equipment and lessen the temperature difference experienced by the people when they leave the air-conditioned space. The maximum outdoor-indoor temperature difference used is about 20° F.

The outside design conditions depend entirely upon the geographic location of the enclosure and should follow established local practices. If no local standards are available, the outside design dry-bulb temperature may be taken as 10 to 15 degrees above the minimum ever recorded in the winter and 5 to 15 degrees below the maximum ever known in the summer.

Heating Load.—The heating load is generated by the following phenomena:

1. Sensible heat is conducted through the walls, ceilings and floors in proportion to the dry-bulb temperature difference between inside and outside, and also in proportion to the over-all coefficients of heat transmission and the areas of these boundaries. If proper vapour barriers are installed, no latent heat will pass through these surfaces.

2. Outside air entering by ventilation and by infiltration through window and door cracks constitutes both sensible and latent loads since it has to be both heated and humidified.

3. Any process in the enclosure which absorbs heat and/or moisture contributes to the load.

Cooling Load.—The cooling load results from the following phenomena:

1. Sensible heat is conducted through the boundaries because of the dry-bulb temperature difference. This is the same effect described under item 1 of the heating load phenomena except that the heat flows in the opposite direction.

2. Sensible heat is conducted through exterior surfaces because of absorption of solar radiation. This effect depends upon the altitude of the sun, the clearness of the atmosphere, the position of the surface with respect to the direction of the sun's rays, the thermal absorptivity and construction of the surface, and the temperature of the surroundings with which radiant heat exchange may occur. Exact calculation of the resulting heat flow is difficult due to its periodic nature and the many variables involved. The usual design method is to determine the so-called sol-air temperature on the outside and the corresponding equivalent temperature differential, which gives the actual heat flow through the surface when multiplied by the over-all coefficient of heat transmission and the area. These equivalent temperatures depend upon all the factors enumerated above. Consequently, they have to be found specifically for each application.

3. Sensible and latent heats are given off by the occupants. Representative values are given in the accompanying table.

*Rates of Heat Emission from Occupants of Conditioned Spaces**

Degree of activity	Sensible heat, B.T.U./hr./person	Latent heat, B.T.U./hr./person
Seated at rest	195	155
Seated, very light work	195	205
Moderately active office work	200	250
Standing, light work; walking slowly	200	250
Sedentary work	220	330
Light bench work	220	530
Moderate dancing	245	605
Walking 3 m.p.h.; moderately heavy work	300	700
Heavy work	465	985

*Tabulated values are based upon 80° F. room dry-bulb temperature. For 78° F. room dry-bulb total heat remains same, but sensible heat values should be increased by approximately 10% and latent heat values decreased accordingly.

Source: American Society of Heating, Refrigerating, and Air-Conditioning Engineers, *Heating, Ventilating, and Air Conditioning Guide* (1960).

4. Sensible and/or latent heats are given off by lamps, motors, machinery, appliances, industrial processes, etc. To find the heat liberated in B.T.U. per hour, the electric power in watts which is converted into heat must be multiplied by 3.416. In the case of electric motors driving equipment within the air-conditioned space, the heat load can be calculated from the equation

$$\text{heat gain} = \frac{\text{horsepower rating} \times \text{load factor} \times 2,545}{\text{motor efficiency}} \quad \text{(B.T.U./hr.)}$$

The load factor is the fraction of rated load actually used under normal continuous operation. Allowances must be made if only the driving motor or only the driven machinery is within the air-conditioned space.

In calculating the latent heat load the number of B.T.U. required to either condense or evaporate one pound of moisture from or into the air is taken as 1,076.

BIBLIOGRAPHY.—W. H. Severns and J. R. Fellows, *Air Conditioning and Refrigeration* (1958); C. Strock (ed.), *Handbook of Air Conditioning, Heating and Ventilating* (1959); C. E. A. Winslow and L. P. Herrington, *Temperature and Human Life* (1949); W. R. Woolrich and W. R. Woolrich, Jr., *Air Conditioning* (1957).   (J. C. Ch.)

AIRCRAFT CARRIER, a naval vessel specially designed to serve as a floating base from which airplanes may take off and on which they may land.

The outstanding development in warfare during the first half of the 20th century was the rise of aviation. The airplane exercised perhaps an even more decisive effect on naval than on land warfare. At sea, air power reached its greatest effectiveness in the planes flown from aircraft carriers. In fact, by the end of World War II the carrier had succeeded the battleship as the dominant type of combatant vessel in the principal navies of the world. (*See* AIR POWER.)

Evolution of the Carrier.—As early as Nov. 1910 a U.S. civilian pilot, Eugene Ely, flew a plane off a specially built platform on the deck of the cruiser "Birmingham" at Hampton Roads, Va. On Jan. 18, 1911, in San Francisco bay, Ely landed on a platform built on the quarterdeck of the cruiser "Pennsylvania," using wires attached to sandbags on the platform as primitive arresting gear, and then took off from the same ship. Lieut. T. G. Ellyson of the U.S. navy experimented with a catapult launching device in 1912 at Annapolis, Md.

The British navy had meanwhile also been experimenting with the airplane, and during World War I developed the first aircraft carrier. The first true carrier, distinguished from other aircraft ships of the time by its unobstructed flight deck, joined the Royal Navy in 1918, but the war ended before it was used in major operations. This vessel, H.M.S. "Argus," displaced 14,000 tons and had a flight deck approximately 560 ft. long by 64 ft. wide.

Built on a merchant ship hull converted during construction, the "Argus" was one of three carriers begun in 1917. A second, the "Eagle," was built on a battleship hull originally intended for the Chilean navy, while the third, H.M.S. "Hermes," had been designed from the keel up as a carrier. With the signing of the Armistice on Nov. 11, 1918, construction of the "Eagle" and the "Hermes" was suspended until more could be learned about the requirements for carrier operations from trials with the "Argus."

Prior to the start of World War I in 1914, naval opinion had looked to seaplanes, *i.e.*, planes that could alight on and take off from the water, as the type of aircraft best suited to accompany the fleet to sea. As early as 1912 the Royal Navy converted an old cruiser, also named "Hermes," to accommodate three seaplanes. Although these planes were generally hoisted over the side for take-off from the water, there was a deck built forward from which the planes could be launched by means of dollies.

After the outbreak of hostilities, the Royal Navy converted more ships for use with seaplanes and employed them successfully in all theatres of war. The seaplane of that time, however, was no match for land planes, so it became increasingly evident that to achieve full effectiveness for aviation some means of taking land planes to sea would have to be devised. In 1916 the Royal Navy selected one of its larger vessels, the battle cruiser "Furious," on which to erect a flight deck both fore and aft with the conventional bridge structure between. Land planes flown off forward conducted successful raids against zeppelin sheds at Tönder, Den., on July 19, 1918. Landing on either deck, however, had proved impracticable as an operating procedure, although under favourable conditions it could be done. The result of these experiments was the carrier construction program of 1917 of which the "Argus" was the first product.

With the end of hostilities the United States and Japanese navies followed the British lead. The first United States carrier, a converted collier renamed the U.S.S. "Langley," joined the fleet in March 1922. The Japanese, on the other hand, chose to design a ship especially for the purpose of operating aircraft. This vessel, the "Hosyo," entered service in Dec. 1922, thus allowing the Japanese to claim that they had the first operational aircraft carrier designed as such from the keel up. The British completed the "Hermes" a few months later in 1923.

Like the "Argus," the "Langley" and the "Hosyo" were frankly experimental. Upon their decks the fundamental techniques of take-off and landing were worked out. Particularly important was the development of arresting gear that would bring an airplane to

a halt after a short run along the deck. The lack of any sort of bridge structure on these ships proved an impediment to running the ship or controlling air operations. The need was first recognized by the British who added a temporary bridge to the starboard side of the "Argus." This bridge, called the island, was soon made permanent and was adopted by all navies. Only the Japanese continued to operate a small number of flush-deck carriers and on two of their ships located the island to port rather than starboard.

Obviously, the lessons learned aboard the three experimental carriers influenced all carriers built in later years. An equally decisive influence came from the Washington naval treaty of 1922. Among the provisions of the treaty were a total carrier tonnage allowed each signatory and a limitation on the size of newly built carriers to 27,000 tons. An escape clause, however, allowed the conversion to a carrier of any ship up to 33,000 tons that might otherwise have to be scrapped under the terms of the treaty. All signatories, except Italy, took advantage of this clause to obtain large carriers quickly. The United States converted two battle cruisers, and Japan one battle cruiser and one battleship. Britain completed the "Eagle," reworked the "Furious" into a flush-deck carrier to which an island was later added, and converted two other battle cruisers, sister ships of the "Furious." France turned the battleship "Normandie" into the carrier "Béarn." British, French and some Japanese aircraft carriers differed from United States fleet carriers in having lightly armoured flight decks for added protection against aerial bombs.

Having used a large share of their total tonnage on conversions, the naval powers faced the problem of obtaining a maximum number of effective ships from the remainder. As a result, carriers built in the latter 1920s and early 1930s were under 20,000 tons and formed the basis for a class of light fleet carriers. The 27,000-ton limitation also had a lasting effect on carrier size. Except for the earlier conversions and the Japanese "Shinano," converted from a battleship hull during World War II, fleet carriers used in that conflict were all built in conformity with the 27,000-ton figure.

In addition to fleet carriers and light fleet carriers, a third class developed under the stress of conflict. No belligerent had sufficient fleet carriers to meet all its needs. The solution was found in the conversion of merchant hulls by the addition of flight decks, antiaircraft guns and basic equipment needed for air operations. The resulting ships, known as escort carriers, varied greatly in size and characteristics. Organized into task groups with screens of destroyers and destroyer escorts (mainly for antisubmarine protection), they supported troops in amphibious operations.

The development of flying techniques accompanied the development of the ships themselves. Fundamentally, the carrier was an airfield at sea with many special features imposed by size and by the medium on which it operated. To increase air speeds over the deck, the ship turned into the wind for take-off and landing. Catapults flush with the flight deck were also devised to assist in launching aircraft when wind was insufficient or the plane was overloaded. Since no more than half the deck was available for landing, the aircraft was fitted with a retractable hook which engaged one of a series of transverse wires, thus bringing it to a quick stop.

During intensive operations, planes could be rearmed and refueled on the flight deck. Rapid handling under combat conditions required large deck crews of specialists; each specialty had jerseys of a distinctive colour to indicate its function. Aircraft in need of more extensive attention could be lowered to the hangar deck. This large space contained equipment to replace engines, guns and all types of gear and do other maintenance work. Extensive repair and overhaul, however, were not usually done aboard carriers; badly damaged aircraft were returned to shore bases.

The vital nerve centres of a carrier were centred in the island, the only part of the superstructure extending above the flight deck. There the ship was controlled and operated, and there all flight operations were handled. Due to the din of dozens of motors connected with any flight operation, spoken conversation was practically impossible, and various hand signals were used by plane crews and plane handlers, although orders from the island could be given to the flight deck with a "bull horn," an electrical amplifier capable of magnifying the voice hundreds of times.

The actual landing of the planes aboard the carrier was under the control of one officer stationed at the after end of the flight deck. Highly experienced in the operation of carrier aircraft, he watched the approach of each plane, indicating to the pilot through a series of hand signals the proper moves to make in bringing the plane in to a landing. At any time that the landing officer judged the approach unsafe, he waved the plane off and the pilot withdrew into the landing circle of other planes to await his turn to come in for another landing.

History of Operations.—Before World War II, prevailing opinion held that the battleship would continue to dominate naval warfare. Although the increasing power of aircraft tended to enlarge the role of aviation, carriers were still believed to have a supporting rather than a principal function in naval tactics.

Doctrines for their employment stressed air defense of the battle fleet, control of the air over the enemy's fleet, and attacks on his surface units, not so much with the expectation of sinking his ships as of slowing them down so that they could be overtaken by other units and brought to a decisive engagement. Carriers were also to be used for scouting and to conduct surprise raids on enemy bases. The use of carriers in antisubmarine warfare seems not to have been extensively contemplated.

Carrier aircraft were developed with these roles and missions in mind. There were three principal types: fighters, torpedo planes and dive bombers. The dive bombers also had the additional role of scouting and reconnaissance. Because of the time required to design and produce new models of aircraft, World War II was fought with aircraft that had, at least, been on the drawing boards before hostilities began. In a word, although the concepts of carrier employment changed, both the ships and the airplanes continued to be those originally produced to meet the theories of the 1930s.

In the first phase of World War II, from the outbreak of hostilities in Europe, Sept. 1939, to the Japanese attack on Pearl Harbor, Dec. 1941, many of these theories seemed to be well-founded. At the battle of Matapan, in March 1941, the Royal Navy used its carrier aircraft to track the enemy, and hits on an Italian cruiser slowed down certain units until British surface vessels could engage them. This experience was repeated when the German battleship "Bismarck" sortied into the North Atlantic during May of the same year. Airplanes from the carriers "Victorious" and "Ark Royal" brought the "Bismarck" to a virtual standstill with aerial torpedoes and left it to be finished off by the big guns of the fleet. Raids on Italian naval bases were also effective, particularly a daring night attack against Taranto on Nov. 11, 1940, that resulted in so much damage that the Italians withdrew their heavy units to less exposed bases to the north.

Carriers played a minor role in the Norwegian campaign of early 1940, but their real test came in the Mediterranean after Italy entered the war in June of that year. Although they did useful work against the Italian fleet and in raiding bases, superior German and Italian land-based airpower forced the British to withdraw their carriers from the eastern Mediterranean. Operations, however, were continued from Gibraltar. There, the principal task was to provide air cover for Malta-bound convoys. This was dangerous and difficult work, but the carriers performed their duties well, aided by the British possession of radar and the adaptation to carrier defense of the fighter direction techniques first successfully employed in the battle of Britain.

During this period the British lost four carriers. Two were sunk by submarine torpedoes in the Mediterranean while engaged on convoy duty. A third likewise fell victim to submarine attack, this time in the Atlantic. The fourth was lost to the fire of German surface ships while ferrying a deck load of Royal Air Force fighters from Norway to Britain.

Because of the priority in aircraft production given to planes for the defense of Great Britain, the Royal Navy had on the whole inferior equipment with which to work. Its carriers, however, did remarkably well, and in the development of radar techniques it helped to prepare the way for United States success against the Japanese in the Pacific.

Japan opened the Pacific war on Dec. 7, 1941, with a devastating surprise attack on the United States base at Pearl Harbor, Hawaii. Its carrier force then turned westward to strike at Allied bases and concentrations of air power in the East Indies, Australia and Ceylon. The force was seldom sighted and never attacked.

Whatever may have been its prewar theories about the relative roles of battleships and carriers, the United States navy had no choice in the opening months of the war. Its carriers had escaped destruction by being absent from Pearl Harbor while the Japanese were rendering the battleline largely inoperative. To the three carriers already in the Pacific, two others were quickly added by transfer from the Atlantic. During the first seven months of the conflict these five ships steamed more than 180,000 mi. in their successful effort to check the Japanese offensive.

Their early operations, a series of raids against enemy positions in widely scattered areas of the central and South Pacific, while skilfully executed, failed of their principal purpose to divert the Japanese from their drive through the East Indies toward Australia. Two fleet engagements fought a month apart finally checked the Japanese offensive. In the first, the battle of the Coral sea, May 4–8, 1942, each side lost a carrier, and the Japanese turned back from an invasion of Port Moresby in New Guinea. The second occurred off Midway Island, located in the sea approaches to Hawaii, between June 6 and 8, 1942. The Japanese lost four carriers and the United States one. In neither engagement did the surface fleets sight one another; both were exclusively carrier actions.

After Midway, United States forces went over to the offensive on a limited scale, seeking to dislodge the Japanese from the southern Solomons. The Japanese reacted violently to the landing of Aug. 7, 1942, and in the confused naval fighting that followed the United States lost two additional carriers and the Japanese one. Total carrier losses for the first year in the Pacific were six of their original ten for the Japanese and four of the original eight for the United States.

With the end of the naval engagements in the Solomons both sides withdrew their remaining carriers. In the months that followed the belligerents hastened to outfit more ships, train additional aircrews and prepare to resume the conflict. In any production race the United States had great superiority, and in this instance it also excelled in applying the lessons of the conflict.

In laying its plans for the offensive, the United States navy acknowledged that the carrier would play the dominant role in future fleet engagements. It also recognized the lesson in the Japanese sweep of early 1942 from Hawaii to Ceylon. If sufficient carriers were concentrated their aircraft could overwhelm enemy air power at the point of contact and, by preventing the enemy from bringing up reinforcements, maintain control of the air in the objective area. For these purposes it organized fast carrier task forces. Each force was composed of one or more task groups made up of three or more fleet and light fleet carriers and an accompanying screen of battleships, cruisers and destroyers.

The task group had the added advantage of increasing defensive power by concentrating antiaircraft fire, providing better protection against submarines and permitting a smaller number of fighters to carry out an effective air defense than if the carriers were operated singly. The task group, however, would have been impossible without radar, which not only gave early warning of air attacks but also made possible accurate station keeping by the ships under all conditions of visibility. Finally, the technique of replenishment at sea, by which the force received fuel, munitions, supplies, replacement aircraft and fresh aircrews without return to port, allowed the carriers to remain in operation for periods up to 70 days.

With its forces organized, the United States began its great central Pacific offensive in Nov. 1943. Less than a year later, it had reached the Philippines and in two great battles had destroyed the Japanese navy as a cohesive fighting force. Beginning in early 1945, the offensive turned northward through Iwo Jima and Okinawa toward the Japanese home islands, which were first attacked in February. During the closing phases of the campaign, United States carriers were reinforced by a fast carrier task force of the British Pacific fleet.

Fast carrier task forces formed the principal striking element of the Allied navies, overwhelming the Japanese whenever they were encountered and seizing and maintaining control of the air over wide areas of naval operations. Some idea of their size may be had from the force that attacked Tokyo during Feb. 1945. It was composed of 11 fleet and 5 light fleet carriers with more than 1,200 aircraft on board and accompanied by 8 battleships, 17 cruisers and 81 destroyers. No such assemblage of naval power had ever been gathered together before.

The war in the Atlantic was quite different. The use of carriers in amphibious operations was the exception, although British and United States carriers were used to cover the North African landings of Nov. 1942 and those in southern France during Aug. 1944, and British carriers participated in the Salerno, Italy, landings of Sept. 1943. The British also achieved considerable success in laying aerial mines in Norwegian waters. Principally, however, the carriers were employed in antisubmarine operations. In this type of warfare hunter-killer groups composed of an escort carrier and a number of destroyers or destroyer escorts proved especially valuable in searching out and destroying packs of submarines that waylaid convoys in the mid-Atlantic beyond the range of land-based aircraft. Escort carriers also helped to run supplies through to the U.S.S.R. on the northern route around the North Cape to Murmansk.

The outstanding characteristic of carriers as employed in World War II was their ability to move quickly into an area, overwhelm opposing air power and maintain this control once gained. They also greatly extended the sphere of fleet action by attacking enemy naval units at great distances, sinking merchant shipping, raiding objectives for considerable distances inland and supporting troops in land operations.

They had many of the attributes of a tactical air force, which in part they were. This fact led to efforts to compare carrier-based and land-based aircraft. Exact measures of comparison, however, are difficult to establish because of the differences in manner and purpose of operation. Each has its distinctive sphere of activity, even though at times they complement one another.

Perhaps the clearest measure of the tactical effectiveness of carrier aviation is the record of the United States against the Japanese in the Pacific. From Pearl Harbor to V-J day, carrier aircraft destroyed 12,000 enemy aircraft, about 6,500 in air combat and the remainder on the ground. They accounted for 168 enemy warships, totaling more than 778,000 tons and including 11 carriers, 5 battleships, 19 cruisers and 31 destroyers. They also sank 359 merchant vessels of more than 1,390,000 tons, a total exceeded only by action of U.S. submarines.

Carrier losses to accomplish these results were not excessive. The United States had 10 carriers sunk in the Pacific and 1 in the Atlantic and lost only 451 planes in air combat. The accompanying table shows carrier losses of all belligerents.

Carrier Losses by Cause of Loss, World War II

Cause	United States	Britain	Japan	Total
Carrier air	6*	1	11†	18
Submarine	3	7	8	18
Carrier air and submarine	1	—	1	2
Naval gunfire	1	1	—	2
Carrier air and naval gunfire	—	—	1	1
Accidental	—	1	—	1
Total	11	10	21	42

*Includes one loss to Japanese carrier aircraft probably flown from a land base.
†Includes one case of U.S. carrier and U.S. army air forces planes combined.

It is noteworthy that after the task force system was introduced in 1943 neither the British nor U.S. navies lost a fleet carrier and only the U.S. lost a light fleet carrier.

Postwar Developments.—With the end of World War II in 1945, the Japanese navy ceased to exist and the United States and British navies sharply reduced their carrier fleets to a peacetime basis. Many vessels were disposed of and others laid up in reserve. Except for a few ships nearing completion, building programs were either canceled or suspended. Notable among the completions were three United States fleet carriers of the new

45,000-ton "Midway" class. The 930-ft. flight decks of these ships were armoured, an innovation in United States carriers introduced because of wartime experience with light bombs and Japanese suicide planes.

Size alone, however, would not solve the problems presented by post-World War II aircraft. The new jet-propelled airplanes were not only heavier than their predecessors but also were slower to accelerate, had higher landing speeds and consumed greater quantities of fuel. From the first trials by the Royal Navy with "Vampire" jets on Dec. 4, 1945, and by the United States with "Phantoms" on July 21, 1946, it was evident that World War II fleet carriers had marginal characteristics for jet operation. Programs were immediately inaugurated to extend the usefulness of existing carriers by strengthening the flight decks to carry heavier loads, increasing the aviation fuel capacity and making other improvements.

Due to their flight characteristics, jet aircraft had to be catapulted from the deck. Their relatively short time in the air and rapid fuel consumption also made traditional landing procedures obsolete. Three British developments, widely adopted by the United States, greatly increased the effectiveness of carriers in these respects. The first, a steam-powered catapult, made possible the successful launching of any plane in production or under design. The second was the angled or canted flight deck, permitting planes to land and take off simultaneously. The third, the mirror landing system, relieved the pilot of dependence upon an officer who formerly had directed approach and landing by means of hand signals.

These innovations were back-fitted into older carriers, including the "Midway" and its sister ships. They were likewise incorporated in new carriers that appeared during the 1950s. The British resumed work on two 37,000-ton fleet carriers, construction of which had been suspended in 1945. The first of these ships, a second "Eagle," joined the fleet in 1952, while the other, named "Ark Royal" after a carrier also lost during World War II, went into service during 1955. On Oct. 1 of the same year the United States commissioned the "Forrestal," first of a new class of aircraft carriers of postwar design. This ship displaced about 60,000 tons and had a flight deck in excess of 1,000 ft.

When the communists invaded the republic of Korea on June 25, 1950, the United States fleet carrier "Valley Forge" and the British light fleet carrier "Triumph" were in the far east. Both ships were immediately ordered to join the United Nations naval forces, and they commenced operations with simultaneous strikes at the communist capital of P'yŏngyang on July 3, the first occasion on which carrier-launched jets entered combat. From that date forward aircraft carriers played an important role in Korea. British and United States carriers covered the amphibious landing at Inchon in Sept. 1950 and United States carriers the withdrawal of United Nations forces from Hungnam in Dec. 1950. Their principal contribution, however, was in support of general land fighting and in the campaign to keep the enemy from bringing up supplies and reinforcements.

From Oct. 1950 a United States fast carrier force operated continuously off the east coast of Korea until the conclusion of hostilities on July 27, 1953. The force was replenished at sea, and individual ships were relieved on station. On the other side of the peninsula, a United States escort carrier with marine corps pilots on board alternated with a British light fleet carrier, including the Australian ship "Sydney," in supporting ground troops and maintaining the naval blockade.

Later Trends.—Except for the Soviet Union, the principal navies continued to operate aircraft carriers. By 1960 France had three carriers, Australia two, Canada and the Netherlands one each. Argentina and Brazil were also reported to be obtaining one carrier each, and training air groups. These vessels were primarily equipped for antisubmarine warfare. The British navy had on active service three fleet carriers and three light fleet carriers, all but one fleet carrier completed after 1950. An additional light fleet carrier was under construction.

In the United States, light fleet and escort carriers, with one exception, had by 1960 ceased to engage in air operations. Four

The U.S.S. "Card," an early escort carrier, relatively small in size, built on a merchant ship hull

French aircraft carrier "Béarn," an early carrier converted from the battleship "Normandie," showing a parasol-type airplane taking off from the flight deck

H.M.S. "Eagle," 37,000-ton British fleet carrier designed after World War II to accommodate jet fighter planes

The U.S.S. "Enterprise," the first nuclear-powered carrier, launched Sept. 24, 1960. The 83,350-ton ship had planes carrying guided missiles for defense

H.M.S. "Centaur," with sister ship, H.M.S. "Albion," in the background, British light fleet carriers with canted (oblique) decks

The U.S.S. "Essex," the principal type of fleet carrier used by the United States during World War II

The U.S.S. "Shangri-la," an attack aircraft carrier of the improved "Essex" class

BRITISH, FRENCH AND UNITED STATES AIRCRAFT CARRIERS

BY COURTESY OF (TOP LEFT, CENTRE RIGHT, BOTTOM LEFT AND RIGHT) U.S. NAVY, (TOP RIGHT, CENTRE LEFT BELOW) BRITISH INFORMATION SERVICES, (CENTRE LEFT ABOVE) MARIUS BAR

Plate II

AIRCRAFT CARRIER

Douglas A4D "Skyhawk" making preparations for take-off from a canted-deck carrier. Flight deck officer (right) guides the pilot with a series of hand signals

Launching "Fury" jets by steam catapult. Plane on right is taking off, one on left is being positioned for catapult shot, third plane is moving up to starboard catapult

U.S.S. "Forrestal" showing layout of flight deck with three launching areas. Designed after World War II to meet the demands of jet aircraft operations, the carrier can launch and retrieve planes simultaneously

U.S.S. "Saratoga" simultaneously catapulting two McDonnell F3H "Demons" during carrier qualification operations near Guantanamo bay, Cuba

McDonnell F2H-2P "Banshee" approaching carrier for landing. Hook lowered from tail of plane engages arresting cables stretched across deck. If landing gear fails, barricade in front of island will halt plane

Douglas F3D fighter touching down on deck of U.S.S. "Antietam" equipped with an automatic landing system which guides plane completely by radio and radar

LAUNCHING AND LANDING OPERATIONS

of the escort type were still in use as aircraft transports and a number of both types were held in reserve for similar duty in an emergency. Of 24 "Essex" class fleet carriers, the basis of World War II task forces, 20 were still active early in 1960, 8 of them as attack carriers, 10 as antisubmarine carriers and 2 as amphibious assault ships.

The last of these categories was a new one and involved the modification of the ship to handle helicopters and marine combat teams. The first experiments with this type of vessel were begun in 1956 on an escort carrier. In addition to the "Essex" class carriers, the United States navy had available the three "Midway" class ships completed shortly after the war. Four of the "Forrestal" class, the first truly postwar design, were also in service. A program of gradual replacement was keeping the fleet modernized.

At the same time, the aircraft carrier of the future was taking shape. On Sept. 24, 1960, the first nuclear-powered carrier, the "Enterprise," was launched. Displacing 83,350 tons, this ship had a flight deck 1,101 ft. by 252 ft., providing about 4,000 sq.ft. more operating space than aboard "Forrestal." Great size and almost unlimited cruising range without sacrifice of speed was only one of the advantages sought in the design. Ship's fuel ceased to be a problem, and the bunker space could be devoted to additional aviation fuel. Removal of the smokestacks and the elaborate system of ducts for elimination of gases increased safety, reduced chances of detection and eliminated the flying hazard of gas-induced turbulence across the deck.

Named after a famous World War II carrier, the "Enterprise" possessed improved radars and all the latest equipment, including planes carrying guided missiles for defense. The place of the carrier in the atomic age seemed assured.

See also references under "Aircraft Carrier" in the Index.

BIBLIOGRAPHY.—Lieut. Comdr. P. K. Kemp, *Fleet Air Arm* (1954); Capt. A. D. Turnbull and Lieut. Comdr. C. L. Lord, *History of United States Naval Aviation* (1949); Office of the Chief of Naval Operations, United States Navy, *U.S. Naval Aviation in the Pacific* (1947); Lieut. A. R. Buchanan (ed.), *The Navy's Air War* (1946); Lieut. Comdr. H. M. Dater, "Aviation and Sea Power," *U.S. Naval Institute Proceedings,* vol. 80, no. 4 (April 1954); William Jameson, *Ark Royal* (1957). (H. M. DR.)

AIRCRAFT INSTRUMENTS.

There are three main classes of aircraft instruments: flight instruments, navigational instruments and power plant instruments. Flight instruments assist the pilot in maintaining the desired attitude of the craft and include the air speed indicator, rate of climb indicator, turn and bank indicator and gyro horizon. The flight instruments make blind flying possible; that is, control of the aircraft when the pilot cannot see where he is going. Navigational instruments are analogous to those of a ship with the addition of altimeters (barometric, radio and sonic) that help the pilot to fly his vehicle at the proper

PILOT INSTRUMENT PANEL

Top row: (left to right) air speed indicator, gyrosyn compass indicator, horizon flight direction indicator, chronometer. Second row: (left to right) Mach meter, altimeter, deviation indicator, rate of climb indicator, radio magnetic indicator. Third row: turn and bank indicator. Bottom row: speed brake position indicator

height above the earth or at a suitable distance above or below other aircraft. Navigational instruments include compasses (magnetic, gyro and astro), the air speed indicator, which is also a flight instrument, and various radio direction and position finding systems. (*See* NAVIGATION.) Power plant instruments are comparable to those used on an automobile to show fuel supply, oil pressure and engine temperature. (*See* also AERONAUTICS.)

Flight Instruments.—The attitude of an airplane is determined by the positions of its fore-and-aft or longitudinal axis, its thwart-ship or lateral axis and its rudder axis, relative to a horizontal plane and to an axis perpendicular to the horizontal. Attitude in relation to all three axes is shown by the horizon flight direction indicator. An attitude indicator, which forms the background of this instrument, provides a pictorial horizon reference. Horizontal and vertical bars move in response to motion of the airplane about its lateral and rudder axes. By maintaining the two bars centred the pilot keeps the airplane on the desired flight path.

Another indication of attitude is provided by the turn and bank indicator. In this instrument a gyroscope rotates on an axis normally parallel to the lateral axis of the airplane within a frame pivoted on an axis parallel to the longitudinal axis, about which it is restrained by a spring. Turning of the airplane about its rudder axis causes the gyroscope to precess, moving the frame against the force of the spring and causing a pointer to indicate the rate of turn.

The bank indicator consists of a ball in a curved glass tube. When the airplane is not turning the ball remains in the centre of the tube so long as the wings are level. If one wing drops, the ball rolls to the side with the low wing. When the airplane is turning the ball remains in the centre of the tube when the angle of bank is correct: that is, when the resultant of the force of gravity (vertical) and of the centrifugal force (in a horizontal plane) is parallel to the rudder axis of the airplane. If, in a turn, one wing is lower than it should be for a correct bank, the ball rolls to that side.

The air speed indicator provides information both for maintenance of attitude and for navigation. It is a pressure gauge in which the position of the hand indicates the difference between the dynamic pressure generated by a pitot tube (a tube with its open end pointed into the air stream) and the static pressure corresponding to the altitude at which the airplane is flying. The instrument's dial is graduated in knots for standard sea-level air.

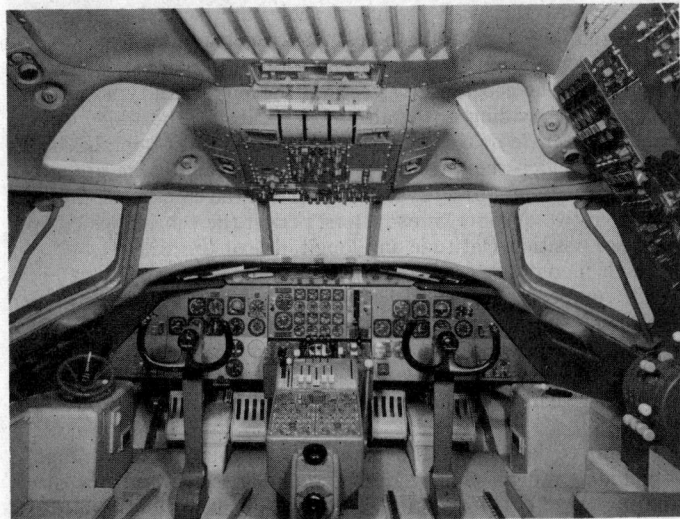

GENERAL VIEW OF THE COCKPIT INSTRUMENTS ON THE DC-8

The air speed indication is a measure of the support provided by the passage of the airplane's wings through the air. In taking off and landing, the pilot observes this instrument to maintain the air speed of the airplane above the stall speed where the flow of air over the wings is just sufficient to maintain support.

In navigation, the indicated air speed must be corrected for reduced air density to give true air speed. A true air speed indicator is a computer that correlates indicated air speed and air density to show true air speed. The true air speed must be corrected for the effect of the wind to give the airplane's speed relative to the ground.

Navigational Instruments.—The altimeter is an indicator of atmospheric pressure. Its dial is graduated in feet of height according to the following formula which relates altitude to pressure:

$$H = 221.152 \ (273 + T_{ms}) \ \log \frac{29.921}{P_h}$$

in which H is the altitude in feet, T_{ms} is the standard mean temperature in degrees Centigrade of the air from the ground to the altitude H, and P_h is the pressure at the altitude H in inches of mercury absolute. This formula assumes standard air, with a sea-level barometric pressure of 29.92 inches of mercury absolute. To determine the correct altitude when the barometric pressure is other than 29.92, the altimeter may be adjusted to indicate the actual elevation of the airport above sea level when the airplane is on the runway. At other altitudes the altimeter will show the actual height above sea level only when the temperature is standard, that is, the temperature assumed in the pressure-altitude formula. When the temperature drops below standard, the air contracts and the actual height is then less than that indicated by the altimeter.

The climb indicator (or rate of climb indicator or vertical speed indicator) is a pressure gauge with a dial graduated to show rate of climb or descent in thousands of feet per minute. It comprises a sensitive differential pressure element, one side of which is connected directly to the ambient static pressure, and the other side connected to static pressure through a constriction. Hence, the differential pressure across the element is a function of the amount the static pressure has changed in a unit of time, and the indication is in rate of change of altitude. Pilots use the climb indicator to keep on a level course and to maintain a constant rate of climb or descent.

The magnetic compass, when corrected for the effects of magnetic materials on the aircraft, gives the heading of the craft in relation to magnetic north. Mechanical compasses comprise magnets, supported on a pivot, which move to align themselves with the earth's magnetic field. Electrical compasses utilize the interaction of the earth's field with that of an electrically induced flux

BY COURTESY OF DOUGLAS AIRCRAFT CO.

FIRST OFFICER'S INSTRUMENT PANEL

Top row: (left to right) air speed indicator, gyrosyn compass indicator, horizon flight direction indicator, clock. Second row: (left to right) Mach meter, altimeter, deviation indicator, rate of climb indicator, radio magnetic indicator. Third row: (left to right) automatic pilot control, flap position indicator, turn and bank indicator. Bottom row: true air speed indicator

field pattern.

Except at the equator, the earth's magnetic field is not horizontal, but is inclined, becoming vertical at the poles. As the compass indications are used for navigation in a horizontal plane the instrument is useful only to the extent that its indications correspond to the horizontal component of the earth's field. The magnetic element is therefore stabilized, either by making it pendulous or by associating it with a gyroscope.

The gyrosyn compass comprises a remote compass transmitter (flux valve), a directional gyro, and a compass indicator, together with the necessary servo amplifiers. The magnetic heading is sensed by the flux valve, depending on the orientation of its sensitive element to the horizontal component of the earth's magnetic field. The directional gyro provides directional stability to the compass system, with the flux valve transmitting signals to correct for any wandering of the gyro. At high latitudes, where the earth's magnetic field is unsuitable for a directional reference, the flux valve is disconnected from the system. The compass indicator also incorporates radio-actuated direction pointers.

Two factors must be allowed for in using the gyrosyn compass. First, because the earth's magnetic poles are located at some distance from the geographic poles, compass readings must be corrected for variation: the angle by which the magnetic direction differs from the geographic direction. Second, both types of compass give the heading of the aircraft. To it must be added or subtracted the angle of the drift caused by the wind to obtain the direction in which the airplane is moving relative to the ground.

Radio position finding systems, based on the transmission of signals from two or more transmitters, permit the continuous computation of position (latitude and longitude) of the aircraft.

Mach meters are used on high-speed airplanes to indicate the Mach number: the ratio of the speed of the aircraft to the speed of sound. The Mach meter is a computer, the inputs of which are air speed pressure, static pressure and temperature of the air. The permissible top speed of the airplane is stated in Mach number rather than in terms of indicated air speed as on slower airplanes.

An aid to landing is the pictorial deviation indicator that is actuated by radio signals from the ground and from the gyro direction system. This instrument pictorially presents the position of the airplane relative to the radio guidance beams and its displacement from the glide path beam. A pointer moves with aircraft

BY COURTESY OF DOUGLAS AIRCRAFT CO.

CENTRAL INSTRUMENT PANEL

Top row: thrust (pressure ratio) indicators. Second row: ram air thermometer and four exhaust thermometers. Third row: static air thermometer and four turbine speed indicators. Bottom row: fuel flow meters

heading changes, or lateral departures from the correct path. A horizontal bar moves up or down as the airplane goes below or above the radio-beamed glide path.

The automatic pilot substitutes for the human pilot in flying the airplane. Horizontal and directional gyro sensers transmit signals to servomotors that operate the airplane's controls to maintain straight and level flight. Sophisticated versions of the automatic pilot provide controlled flight at a pre-set altitude or on a radio-monitored glide path.

Power Plant Instruments.—These instruments indicate engine speed (revolutions per minute) and, for reciprocating engines, manifold pressure, oil pressure, oil temperature, fuel pressure, cylinder-head temperature and propeller blade pitch. For jet engines, in addition to speed (usually shown as per cent of rated speed), indicators show thrust (pressure ratio) and exhaust temperature.

On large aircraft, indicators of fuel flow (in thousands of pounds per hour) to each engine, fuel quantity remaining in each tank, and of ram and static air temperatures are also provided. Other indicators show the positions of trim tabs, flaps, speed brakes and landing wheels.

See P. V. H. Weems, *Air Navigation*, 4th ed. (1955); Thoburn C. Lyon, *Practical Air Navigation*, 7th ed. (1955).   (C. H. C.)

AIRCRAFT PROPULSION. Although free balloons and gliders operate without means of propulsion, it was clear from the earliest experiments with flight that if air transportation was to be practical, some propulsive device was essential (*see* AVIATION, HISTORY OF). The content of this article is as follows:

    I. Introduction
   II. Air Resistance
  III. Propulsion Theory
   IV. Propellers
        1. Materials
        2. Pitch
             Continuously-Variable Pitch
             Feathering
             Reverse Pitch
             Pitch-Changing Mechanisms
        3. Counter-Rotating Propellers
        4. Supersonic Propellers
        5. Propeller Strip Theory
        6. Vertical Take-Off
    V. Piston Engines
        1. Advantages of Gasoline Engines
        2. Types of Gasoline Engines
        3. Superchargers
        4. Post-1927 Developments
   VI. Turbo-Superchargers
  VII. Jet Engines
        1. Turbojets
             Centrifugal Compressor Development
             Axial Compressor Development
             Combustion
             Turbines
             Bearings
             Afterburner
             Water Injection
             Thrust Reversal
        2. Turboprops
        3. Pulse Jets
        4. Ram Jets
        5. Turbofans
        6. Rockets
 VIII. Aircraft Fuels
        1. Fuel Composition
        2. Fuel Development
        3. Turbine Fuels

I. INTRODUCTION

Lighter-than-air craft (balloons, dirigibles) need expend no power to remain aloft, but unless one is content to drift with the wind, a propulsive device is necessary. To be an effective machine for transportation it is necessary that an aircraft be able to make headway against the winds ordinarily encountered. This requirement calls for a substantial amount of power. Even the most highly developed rigid airships sometimes found themselves being carried backward by the wind in spite of their propulsion engines. Early prints show balloons with sails blowing full. This, of course,

is an artist's misconception because a balloon drifts freely with the wind and in this situation sails can only hang slack and useless. Propulsion of a balloon by human effort is possible, but the speed that can be achieved in this manner is very low indeed and thus this method of propulsion is little if any better than drifting. Drifting can be controlled to a certain extent by controlling the altitude at which the balloon flies by valving gas or throwing out ballast, thus taking advantage of the fact that the direction and velocity of the wind vary with height. (*See* BALLOON FLIGHT.)

In 1851 a Frenchman, Henri Giffard, built the first engine to power a manned aircraft. It was a steam engine which, with its boiler, weighed 350 lb. and developed only 3 h.p. Nevertheless, it made possible the first controlled flight of the air on Sept. 24, 1852, when Giffard piloted his airship from Paris to Trappes at an average speed of 6 m.p.h. (*see* AIRSHIP). The first internal-combustion engine was flown in 1872 when a German, Paul Haenlein, piloted an airship powered by a four-cylinder engine using coal gas as a fuel. The first use of gasoline in aircraft was in a two-cylinder engine designed by David Schwarz to propel the first rigid airship in 1897. All of these engines turned screw propellers, which were well known as devices for marine propulsion.

All of the more modern dirigible airships have been powered by reciprocating internal-combustion engines burning gasoline, diesel oil, hydrogen, or a combination of these. Blaugas is a combustible oil gas with approximately the same density as air and having the advantage of leaving the lifting power of the machine unaltered as the fuel is consumed.

Heavier-than-air craft (airplanes, helicopters), unlike their lighter-than-air counterparts, require power to remain aloft. The power requirement of an airplane (*q.v.*) is considerable. Gliders without means of propulsion can remain aloft only if they are flown in a rising current of air (*see* GLIDING).

In the days of the Wright brothers, the screw propeller was universally recognized as being suitable for providing the necessary thrust for aircraft propulsion. The missing element needed to complete the propulsion system was a lightweight engine to turn the propeller. The Wright brothers' attempt to find a builder for such an engine took them to Europe, but they could find no one who would undertake to build an engine which they considered sufficiently light. An engine of their own design and construction powered the first controlled flight of an airplane on Dec. 17, 1903. It was a four-cylinder gasoline engine which developed 12 h.p. and weighed 179 lb.

In the same year Charles M. Manly designed and built a noteworthy engine for the ill-fated Langley "Aerodrome." Manly's engine developed 52 h.p. for 151 lb. weight. Its weight/power ratio of 2.90 lb./h.p. was remarkably low at that time and compares not unfavourably with the weight/power ratio of modern engines of similar power. Furthermore, this engine in later tests demonstrated durability and reliability far beyond that demonstrated by any comparable contemporary power plant. In Manly's engine there were five water-cooled cylinders arranged radially around a single crank. The radial form was an excellent design choice and contributed substantially to the light weight of the machine. All large air-cooled piston engines are now built in this form.

II. AIR RESISTANCE

A body moving in still air experiences a "drag"; *i.e.*, a force opposing and tending to reduce its velocity (*see* AERODYNAMICS; MECHANICS, FLUID). In the case of a body with wings, such as an airplane, a portion of the drag force is the result of the lifting force on the wings ("induced drag") while the remainder is the result of fluid friction and of pressure waves in the air caused by the body's motion. In the case of a lighter-than-air machine, such as a dirigible, virtually all the drag force results from friction. On the other hand, a large part of the drag force of a vehicle that travels near or above the speed of sound may be due to wave making. For modern aircraft at cruising conditions the drag force is somewhere between one-sixth to one-fortieth of the weight. The former figure applies to supersonic machines, the latter to highly developed gliders. The modern transport machine has a drag amounting to about one twenty-fifth of its weight.

A propulsive device is required to provide a "thrust"; *i.e.*, a force on the body opposing the drag force. In order for the aircraft to fly horizontally at constant speed, the thrust force must be equal and opposite to the drag force. Additional thrust must be supplied if it is desired to accelerate or climb.

III. PROPULSION THEORY

There are a number of possible methods of applying a propulsive force to an aeronautical vehicle. Perhaps the simplest method is to pull the vehicle with a tow rope from a ground vehicle or from another air-borne vehicle. A rope tow is a standard method of launching gliders. Gliders towed by airplanes were used during World War II for the purpose of delivering troops and supplies to places without landing fields adequate for powered airplanes. Another possible method of propulsion is to make use of a force acting at a distance, such as electrical attraction, magnetic attraction or gravitation. Electrical and magnetic attractive forces are much too weak when acting at the long distances required for aerial navigation. Gravitation can be used only if the destination is at an altitude considerably lower than the origin of the flight.

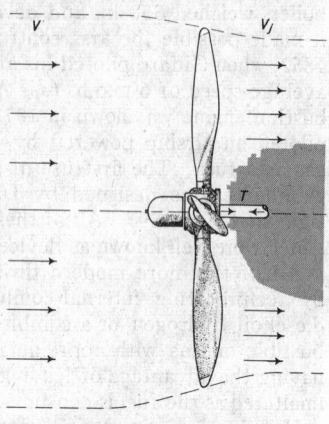

FIG. 1.—PROPULSION IN PROPELLER-DRIVEN AIRCRAFT

Rotation of the propeller results in the increase of air velocity (V) to the higher value (V_j) and produces thrust (T) in propeller shaft, which pulls the plane forward

The only practical means of propulsion so far devised is to take advantage of Newton's third law of motion. (Before Newton, Leonardo da Vinci enunciated a similar law specifically applied to flight: "An object offers as much resistance to the air as the air does to the object." His notes remained unpublished and unknown for nearly 300 years.) Usually this law is stated as "action and reaction are equal and opposite" (*see* MECHANICS). This somewhat cryptic statement may be explained as follows. It is observed in nature that forces ("pushes" or "pulls") never occur singly but always in equal and opposite pairs. Thus the existence of a force on a body requires the coexistence of an equal and opposite force. Two equal and opposite forces acting on the same body have no net effect upon its motion. The saying that a man cannot lift himself by his bootstraps is an expression of this observation.

If a pair of forces acts between two separate bodies (and if no other forces act) the bodies will be impelled to separate or come together depending upon whether the force pair is repulsive (a push) or attractive (a pull). Combining Newton's second and third laws shows that the resulting motion of the two bodies can be expressed by the statement that "the change in momentum of the two bodies is equal and opposite" and along the line of action of the force pair. Momentum is the product of mass and velocity, and because (at aeronautical velocities) the mass of any body remains constant, a force pair acting between two (otherwise free) bodies produces a change in the velocity of each. It is clear that in order to propel a body it is necessary to find something to push against. All aircraft propulsion devices except the rocket push against the air itself. If air is used as the propelling medium it must experience a change in momentum; that is, it must be accelerated toward the rear of the airplane and thus discharged rearward with increased velocity.

When an airplane is in flight, air appears to approach it at the flight speed, V. If a portion of this air is subjected to a steady rearward force it leaves the vehicle rearwardly with a velocity V_j which is greater than V. If all particles of air are assumed to be identical, it may be shown by using Newton's second law that the propulsive force or thrust T is

$$T = \frac{m}{g_0}(V_j - V)$$

where m is the mass of air flowing per unit time which is subjected to acceleration and g_0 is the proportionality constant (depending upon the units used) in Newton's second law:

$$g_0 \times \text{force} = \text{mass} \times \text{acceleration}$$

The agent that applies the force to the stream of air can be a propeller or a jet engine. If it is a propeller the situation can be pictured as shown in fig. 1. In this diagram the thrust, T, appears as tension in the propeller shaft.

A jet airplane produces thrust in the same way, except that in this case air is taken into an opening in the front of the engine and discharged to the rear (fig. 2).

The power, P_i, required to increase the velocity of the air from V to V_j is, if all losses incident to the process are neglected,

$$P_i = \frac{m}{2g_0}(V_j{}^2 - V^2)$$

while the power required to accomplish the propulsion by pulling with a rope would be

$$P_p = TV = \left[\frac{m}{g_0}(V_j - V)\right] \cdot V$$

The propulsive efficiency E_p is the ratio of these two powers, or

$$E_p = \frac{P_p}{P_i} = \frac{\frac{m}{g_0}(VV_j - V^2)}{\frac{m}{2g_0}(V_j{}^2 - V^2)} = \frac{2}{\frac{V_j}{V} + 1}$$

The quantity E_p is known as the Froude efficiency after R. E. Froude who, with W. J. M. Rankine, first advanced this theory. As stated, V_j must be larger than V for a propulsive force to exist; however, it may be seen that high efficiency can occur only if the ratio V_j/V is close to unity.

For propeller-driven airplanes that cruise at 200–400 m.p.h. V_j/V is nearly 1 and propulsive efficiency can be 80%–90%. Propellers maintain their efficiency reasonably well at the low speeds encountered during take-off. Turbojet-propelled aircraft in general have higher jet velocities and hence lower propulsive efficiency

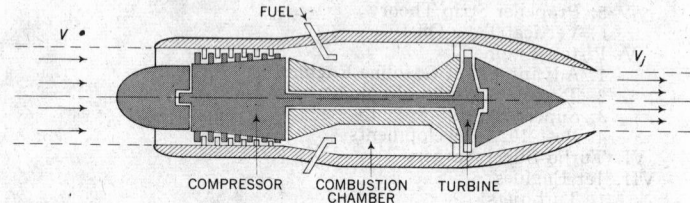

FIG. 2.—PROPULSION IN JET AIRCRAFT

Burning gases in the combustion chamber produce the increase in air velocity (from V to V_j), yielding the thrust to propel the plane

at cruising speed and particularly at take-off. This fact accounts, in part, for the long runways required for getting turbojet-propelled airplanes into the air (*see* AIRPORT).

IV. PROPELLERS

The principle of the aircraft propeller is essentially similar to that of the marine propeller, which was reasonably well understood at the time of the Wright brothers. There are, however, outstanding differences in the requirements of aircraft and marine propellers which made the problem of designing and constructing an air propeller quite different from that of a marine propeller. The most important difference is the relatively low density of air. Water is about 800 times as dense as air at standard sea level conditions. For a given thrust, an air propeller must therefore be much larger in diameter than a marine propeller. It can also run at a very much higher peripheral speed. The combined effects of these differences make stresses due to centrifugal force more important, and those due to fluid pressure less important, in air propellers than in marine propellers.

1. Materials.—For early airplanes, hardwood was a suitable propeller blade material, and up to the mid-1920s wooden blades were universally used. With the advancement of the aluminum industry came techniques for rolling and forging the relatively large sections of high-strength aluminum alloys which made it possible to construct propeller blades of this material (originally Duralumin). Aluminum-alloy blades are not affected by weather and are not eroded by water drops, as are wooden blades. Propeller blades have also been made of compressed wood, laminated plastic (Micarta) and hollow steel.

2. Pitch.—The first metal propellers were made of a single piece of rolled aluminum alloy twisted and machined to form a two-bladed propeller. Later, individual blades were forged separately and assembled into a steel hub. By loosening a clamp, the propeller blade could be turned about its own longitudinal axis and clamped again at any desired position, thus changing the angle of attack of the blade relative to the air. This adjustment of pitch (the distance advanced by the propeller in one revolution) made it possible to use one hub design and one blade design for several different airplanes or even for different engines. Furthermore, hubs could be constructed for any number of blades.

The advantages of adjustable pitch pointed the way to even larger advantages which could be obtained by a pitch-changing mechanism that could be controlled in flight. The increase in speed of airplanes made a controllable-pitch mechanism even more desirable.

A propeller of fixed pitch subjected to a constant turning force will turn faster as altitude increases and air density decreases. A fixed propeller designed for high-altitude operation will turn too slowly at sea level, and if designed for sea level it will turn too fast at high altitude. The advent of supercharged engines that could maintain sea-level power up to high altitude made the controllable-pitch propeller essential.

In the early 1930s a suitable controllable-pitch propeller was perfected and was (along with propeller reduction gearing, wing flaps and retractable landing gear) one of the important reasons for the superiority of the Douglas DC-2 and DC-3 transport airplanes. The mechanism was arranged so that the propeller could operate in either of two pitch positions under the control of the pilot—a low-pitch position primarily for take-off and climb and a high-pitch position for cruise and high flight speed. The angle through which the blade was turned was about 20°.

Continuously-Variable Pitch.—In the mid-1930s the mechanism was improved to make the pitch continuously variable. The pitch setting was controlled by an engine speed governor. The pilot had merely to set the desired engine r.p.m. and the governor then controlled the propeller pitch to maintain this r.p.m. This ar-

rangement made it possible to provide for greater range of control of propeller pitch without danger of overspeeding the engine. The range of pitch change for a constant-speed propeller is about 50°.

Feathering.—A further improvement was made when the "feathering" propeller was perfected in the late 1930s. This development made it possible to increase the pitch to a "feathered" position and thus stop the rotation of a damaged engine which would otherwise be rotated by the propeller acting as a windmill in flight. The drag of a windmilling engine is large. In addition, an important safety advantage was gained because damaged windmilling engines often catch fire. The total change of pitch necessary with the feathering feature is about 90°.

Reverse Pitch.—A still further increase in the amount of pitch change (to about 115°) was brought about by the incorporation of reverse pitch—an arrangement which made it possible to reverse the thrust of the propeller (without reversing the direction of rotation), which thus served as a brake. This feature, which first appeared in the late 1940s, has also contributed greatly to the safety of air transport by making it possible to stop an airplane quickly on the ground without relying on mechanical brakes, which, on an icy runway, can be nearly useless.

Pitch-Changing Mechanisms.—With all variable-pitch propellers there is a gear mechanism to ensure equality of pitch of all blades. Some mechanisms accomplish pitch change by means of one or more hydraulic pistons, others by electric motors. Modern pitch-control mechanisms often use a combination of electric and hydraulic elements. A typical hydraulic pitch-changing mechanism is shown in fig. 3.

3. Counter-Rotating Propellers.—Experiments have been conducted with counter-rotating propellers. The counter-rotating propeller consists of two coaxial propellers, one ahead of the other, rotating in opposite directions. In theory it can provide a slight improvement in efficiency over a conventional propeller. Several aircraft are equipped with counter-rotating propellers.

4. Supersonic Propellers.—Because of the rotation, the speed of a propeller blade relative to the air is higher than the forward speed of the airplane. This fact may be seen from the velocity diagram of fig. 4. Thus the propeller must contend with sonic velocity and the attendant wave-making losses before the airplane itself attains sonic velocity. This is one of the major reasons why propeller-driven airplanes do not ordinarily fly at speeds much greater than 400 m.p.h. Efforts have been made to improve the efficiency of propellers at high speed, but the jet engine appears to offer an easier solution to the problem of high speed and no supersonic propeller has come into use.

Some aircraft of the 1930s were not equipped with propeller reduction gearing and had propeller tip speeds approaching the velocity of sound at the takeoff condition when high revolutions per minute were used. These airplanes were very noisy and it seems probable that any supersonic propeller would constitute a severe noise problem.

5. Propeller Strip Theory.—The theory of Froude is unsuited to the calculation of the performance of propellers, and another theory, the strip theory, was developed for this purpose. In this theory, the propeller blade is divided into thin transverse slices and each slice is assumed to behave like a section of a wing. In the original strip theory each section was assumed to be uninfluenced by the remainder of the propeller. The velocities and forces on a strip are shown in fig. 4. The advantages of adjustable pitch may be seen by careful study of this figure.

The engine must supply turning effort (torque) to balance the

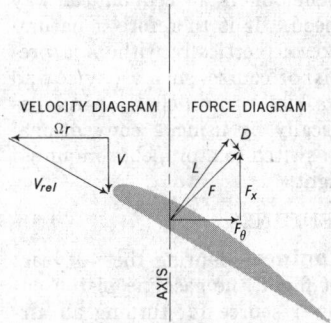

FIG. 4.—APPLICATION OF PROPELLER STRIP THEORY

Forces and velocities involved are (in velocity diagram) Ωr, rotational velocity; V, speed of air approaching propeller; V_{rel}, speed of air relative to the section; and (in force diagram) L, lift; D, drag; F, force resulting from lift and drag; F_x, forward thrust; F_θ, tangential force

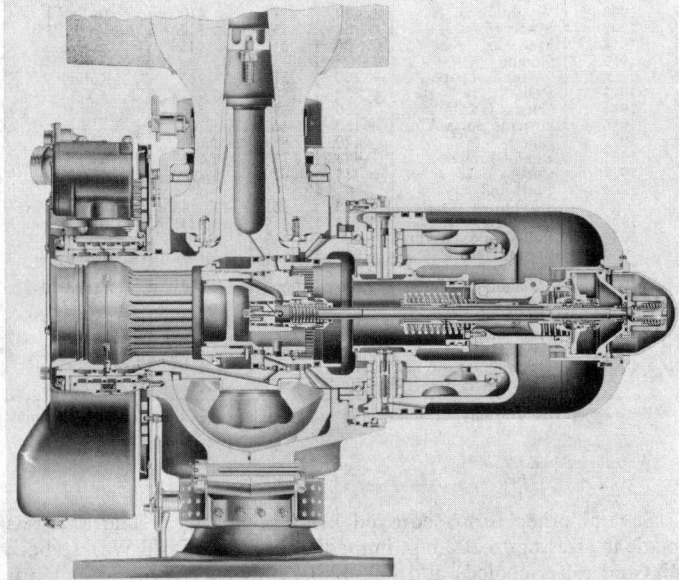

FIG. 3.—HYDRAULIC PITCH-CHANGING MECHANISM OF VARIABLE-PITCH PROPELLER

contributions of all sections to the torque sum of the quantities rF_θ. The resulting thrust is the sum of all the axial forces F_x.

With some modifications, the strip theory can predict the performance of propellers adequately and hence can be useful in design. A more rigorous theory, the vortex theory, is considerably more cumbersome and will not be treated here.

6. Vertical Take-Off.—A propeller offers an economical way of obtaining large thrust at low speed. It is therefore a natural choice for an airplane that can take off vertically without a preliminary run. A helicopter (q.v.) is, of course, such a device and the rotor of a helicopter is indeed a kind of propeller. Airplanes have been built that take off vertically by using a conventional propeller on a vertical axis and then switch to a propeller mounted on a horizontal axis for cruising flight.

V. PISTON ENGINES

1. Advantages of Gasoline Engines.—During the 40 years following the Wright brothers' first flight, the gasoline piston engine was highly developed as a power source for turning an aircraft propeller and thus completing the propulsive machinery. Although a few diesel engines were built for aircraft use (notably the Packard aircraft diesel, a nine-cylinder radial air-cooled engine, and the somewhat more successful Junkers six-cylinder opposed-piston two-stroke aircraft diesel engine), the gasoline piston engine was for 40 years virtually the only power plant used for aircraft. The success of the gasoline engine was due to a number of inherent advantages it had over other forms of power plants.

The steam engine has often been considered for aircraft. In fact, as has been noted, many of the early experiments were with steam power plants. The steam engine (see STEAM) is an external-combustion engine; that is, while it derives its energy from the combustion of fuel with the oxygen of the air, the energy thus made available must be transferred to the steam in the form of heat by means of a boiler. The surfaces of the boiler must be somewhat hotter than the water (or steam) inside in order for heat to flow. Thus, steam can be heated no hotter than the highest temperature that the material of the boiler can withstand. Although this temperature limit is slowly rising as better materials are developed, there seems little likelihood that it will ever approach the temperatures in common use in gasoline internal-combustion engines, these latter temperatures being limited only by the temperature attainable by the combustion of hydrocarbon and air (roughly 3,500° F.). In the case of the internal-combustion engine, there need be no heat-transfer device comparable to the boiler. The products of combustion are themselves used as the working fluid to push the piston and thus deliver power to the crankshaft. The walls of the cylinder and piston which contain the products of combustion are cooled by circulation of air or liquid on the outside of the cylinder so as to maintain these parts at a low temperature, and there is thus no need to limit the combustion temperature. (See INTERNAL-COMBUSTION ENGINE.)

The amount of power that may be obtained by burning fuel at a given rate (i.e., the thermal efficiency) depends upon the ratio of the highest to the lowest absolute temperature of the working substance; hence there is great advantage in the high temperatures that can be used in the internal-combustion engine. Furthermore, the elimination of the boiler results in an important saving of weight, but even more important for weight saving is the elimination of the need for a condenser. Early aircraft steam engines did not use a condenser but exhausted the used steam to the atmosphere. Since the airplane must carry its water as well as its fuel this is an intolerably wasteful process. The combustion of one pound of fuel (e.g., kerosene or gasoline) releases enough energy to evaporate about 18 lb. of water. A condenser to recover this water becomes essential in an aircraft steam engine—another heavy piece of equipment which is unnecessary with an internal-combustion engine. In view of these facts it is not surprising to find that even today all aircraft power plants (including jet engines and turbo-propeller engines) are of the internal-combustion type. In all these devices the products of combustion are the agents that push the piston or turn the turbine.

It does not seem possible to use the internal-combustion principle in conjunction with an engine powered by a nuclear reaction. The necessary limitation of maximum temperature and the weight of the necessary heat-transfer device are two of the many obstacles in the way of a practical nuclear-powered airplane.

Every engine that uses atmospheric air to burn fuel is limited in power essentially by the amount of air that can be passed through the machine. The spark-ignition (gasoline) engine is the only engine that can successfully use all of the oxygen in the air for combustion. The diesel engine can burn only about 60% of the oxygen in the air. Consequently, a diesel engine is, in general, larger and heavier than a gasoline engine of the same maximum power.

The gasoline engine, then, has great advantage for aircraft, and it is not surprising to find it used for 40 years to the virtual exclusion of all other types of prime mover. During this period great progress was accomplished in making airplane engines powerful, reliable, light in weight and economical of fuel.

2. Types of Gasoline Engines.—The first 20 years of this 40-year period were occupied mostly in perfecting details of design and manufacture and in experimenting with almost every conceivable arrangement of the cylinders around the crankshaft. One of the more interesting forms, which was extensively used during World War I and subsequently abandoned, was the rotary engine. This had a radial arrangement of cylinders around a single crank similar to Manly's engine, with the difference that the cylinders were attached solidly to the propeller and the crank was fixed to the airplane frame; because of this the cylinders revolved and the crank remained stationary. This arrangement was used to eliminate the necessity for a flywheel (which proved unnecessary in any case) and to improve the cooling of the engine by the motion of the cylinders, thereby making air cooling easier. One of the early rotary engines, the Gnome Monosoupape (see Table I), had an unusual valve arrangement which necessitated controlling the engine by means of the ignition switch. When the pilot required reduced power (e.g., for landing) he shut off the ignition, turning it on again at intervals in order to keep the engine running. It is not difficult to see the disadvantages of this technique, not the least of which was that it entailed releasing a quantity of unburned fuel from the exhaust. Later rotary engines did not have this objectionable feature, but as time went on it became clear that other engine forms were simpler and lighter, and the rotary form was abandoned shortly after World War I.

TABLE I.—*Some Important Aircraft Piston Engines*[*]

Approx. date first engine	Name	Horse-power	Weight, lb.	Displacement, cu. in.	Cylinder arrangement and number
1902	Wright Bros.	12	179	410	In-line 4
1902	Manly	52	151	540	Radial 5
1912	Mercedes	80	312	443	In-line 6
1913	Gnome Monosoupape	100	270	783	Rotary 9
1914	Rolls-Royce Eagle	350	880	1,241	V-12
1914	Curtiss OX5	90	390	568	V-8
1916	Hispano Suiza-A	150	467	718	V-8
1917	Liberty	420	857	1,650	V-12
1921	Bristol Jupiter	485	775	1,253	Radial 9
1922	Curtiss D-12	435	680	1,210	V-12
1926	Pratt and Whitney Wasp	600	865	1,344	Radial 9
1929	Wright Cyclone 9	1,525	1,469	1,823	Radial 9
1934	Rolls-Royce Merlin	1,730	1,450	1,649	V-12
1936	Bristol Hercules[†]	1,980	2,115	2,360	Radial 14
1937	Pratt and Whitney Double Wasp	2,050 2,500[‡]	2,390	2,800	Radial 18
1937	Junkers 211C	2,136			V-12
1944	BMW	1,700	1,940	2,550	Radial 14
1945	Pratt and Whitney Wasp Major	3,250 3,800[‡]	3,670	4,363	Radial 28
1948	Wright Turbo-compound	3,400 3,700[‡]	3,675	3,347	Radial 18

[*]With exception of Manly, all rotary and radial engines are air-cooled; others liquid-cooled.
[†]Sleeve valves.
[‡]Water injection.

Several other forms enjoyed brief popularity. The V-8 was made in sizes up to 300 h.p. immediately after World War I (both air- and water-cooled) and was moderately successful, although it vibrated badly, a fault corrected in later automobile V-8s by using a different arrangement of cranks together with counterweights on the crankshaft.

The three-cylinder radial type appeared and disappeared (it also had excessive vibration) as did the five-cylinder fan engine. Four- and six-cylinder in-line engines were used in both air- and liquid-cooled forms. Many small air-cooled, four-cylinder, in-line engines were made in the late 1920s and early 1930s for light planes. Some engines of these types are still being produced in Europe, but in the U.S. these forms have been superseded by horizontally opposed four- and six-cylinder air-cooled engines.

In later years the search for better forms (and the desire to increase power by putting more cylinders on a single crankshaft) led to the 12- and 18-cylinder and the 24-cylinder X forms. Single-row radial air-cooled engines appeared with 5, 7, 9 and 11 cylinders, two-row radials with 6, 10, 14, 18 and 22 cylinders, a four-row radial with 28 cylinders and finally a six-row radial with 42 cylinders, this latter design establishing the record for the highest number of cylinders on a single crankshaft. Horizontally opposed (flat) 12-cylinder engines were designed with the object of making an engine that could be placed within the wing, thereby eliminating unnecessary drag; however, wings became thinner faster than the engines could be developed and therefore these engines were abandoned. In addition there were engines having two crankshafts (24-cylinder H engines and a 24-cylinder double V engine).

By 1927 three very successful forms of aircraft engines had evolved: the air-cooled single-row radial engine of 7 or 9 cylinders, the double-row radial with 14 cylinders and the liquid-cooled 12-cylinder vee. All of these types were in production in Great Britain at this time, all but the two-row radials were being produced in the U.S. and some of the types were being produced in France. The gear-driven centrifugal supercharger was in production in the U.S. and the propeller reduction gear, by means of which the propeller was made to rotate at a speed lower than that of the engine crankshaft, had made its appearance in France and was spreading rapidly to England and the U.S. The original Wright brothers' airplane had a chain drive incorporating a speed reductor, but the speed of later airplanes was sufficiently great that this feature gave insufficient advantage to warrant its extra weight. Still later, with the advent of engines having a large number of cylinders and running at higher revolutions per minute, the reduction gear again became worthwhile.

The nonstop transatlantic flight of Charles A. Lindbergh in 1927 dramatized air transportation in a way not achieved by the previous nonstop flight of Sir John William Alcock and Sir Arthur Whitten Brown (1919). The U.S. navy had announced its decision to back the air-cooled radial engine and to abandon the development of liquid-cooled engines. In the United States fierce competition between the Pratt and Whitney company and the older Wright Aeronautical corporation led to a period of rapid development of the air-cooled radial engine, culminating in engines having more than 3,500 h.p.

3. Superchargers.—A supercharger is a blower that raises the pressure of the air entering the engine and thereby makes it possible to get more air into the engine in a given time and hence obtain more power. Because the density of air decreases rapidly with increasing altitude, an engine normally has less power available at higher altitudes. Also, a certain amount of power is required to overcome engine friction, primarily friction of the pistons. The net result is that for piston engines the power available goes to zero at about 53,000 ft. altitude. Below this altitude power increases approximately linearly with air density. The supercharger was originally conceived as a device to be used to increase the amount of air passing through the engine at altitude to make up for the loss in power. A small amount of power is sufficient to drive the supercharger.

A supercharger normally is geared to turn three to ten or more times crankshaft speed. The gear ratio is selected for operation at a certain altitude, but because the supercharger operates at all altitudes, it is necessary to operate the engine with the throttle partly closed below the design altitude in order to prevent damage to the engine. (The regulation of power of a gasoline engine is accomplished by a valve or "throttle." By closing this valve, the pressure in the inlet of the engine can be reduced. This in turn reduces the quantity of air [combustible mixture] entering the engine and thus the power. It would seem that the throttle could undo the effect of the supercharger in raising the inlet pressure. Except for the power required to drive the supercharger and the increase in temperature of the entering air resulting from this expenditure of power, this assumption is indeed true.) This fact required a complete change of attitude on the part of the engine operator (the pilot). The power that an engine could produce was no longer limited to what could be obtained with the throttle fully opened but was limited by what the structure of the engine could withstand without damage or too rapid deterioration. The pilot therefore had the added responsibility of seeing that this limit was properly observed. The limit was ordinarily set by the tendency of the fuel to "knock" or detonate. When the spark ignites the gasoline-air mixture in the cylinder, normal burning takes place progressively, the flame spreading from the source by a process of conduction of heat from the flame front to ignite the adjacent mixture. During this process the pressure rises and the unburned part of the mixture is progressively compressed. If compressed too much, it burns with explosive violence. The result is a pressure wave within the gas in the cylinder which causes the audible "ping" familiar to automobile drivers and known variously as knocking, fuel-knock, spark-knock or detonation. In an aircraft engine, detonation can be very destructive, resulting in erosion of pistons, piston rings, cylinder heads or valves which can lead to catastrophic mechanical failure. The tendency to detonate increases with increased inlet pressure and temperature and therefore with supercharging.

Another limiting factor (in air-cooled engines, at least) was the tendency of the cylinder temperature to rise above a safe value when extra power was called for. Knocking, but not overheating, can be controlled by altering the fuel composition, as measured by "octane number" (see *Aircraft Fuels*, below). The advent of the supercharged engine put additional importance on fuel composition and led to a revolution in methods of producing fuel.

Although some earlier engines had blowers running at crankshaft speed and a few experimental engines had been equipped with geared superchargers, the first production engines with geared superchargers appeared (in both England and the U.S.) in 1927. The amount of supercharging of these engines was trivial, still both the principle and the mechanism were present and in a very few years the gear ratio was increased to produce significant supercharging.

Even before the 1920s, Rateau in France and General Electric in the U.S. had demonstrated in-flight superchargers driven by turbines operating on the exhaust gases, but the development of these devices was slow because of various difficult problems connected primarily with control and with the very high temperatures of the exhaust gases.

The years from 1927 on were marked by great increases in power from an engine of given size. These increases were largely due to increases in supercharging, which was found to be effective at sea level as well as at altitude. The horsepower ratings of many engines more than doubled during this period. Increase in power made it necessary to strengthen and redesign practically every part of the engine. Redesigning for the most part was based upon endurance testing, which more often than not ended in failure of one or more engine parts. These failures were studied, corrective measures taken and the tests repeated. This technique still remains the cornerstone of the development of successful aircraft engines.

4. Post-1927 Developments.—Developments of the reciprocating engine after 1927 resulted in the 18-cylinder two-row radial engine—a logical step from the 14-cylinder design—and later the somewhat more daring 28-cylinder four-row, radial, air-cooled engine. In the early 1930s the principles of aerodynamic design of a cooling system became known, and the amount of drag caused by the cooling system of an air-cooled engine was greatly reduced by the Townend ring, NACA cowl and pressure baffles, all these devices being used for guiding air through the cooling fins of the engine and subsequently directing it rearward. These advances also pointed the way to reductions in the drag caused by cooling of liquid-cooled engines, but the problem here was not so severe and the improvement not so marked.

Other improvements during this period were fully lubricated valve mechanisms; greatly improved carburetors; two-speed superchargers, which allow supercharging to higher altitudes; fuel injection, which improves the metering of fuel to individual cylinders and eliminates the danger of fire in the inlet system; and water injection, used for take-off, which suppresses knocking and relieves the cooling problem, thus allowing the throttle to be opened further to obtain more power.

VI. TURBO-SUPERCHARGERS

The turbo-supercharger is of importance not only as a useful accessory to a piston engine but also because of the part it played in the development of the jet engine. In 1911 the Swiss firm of Brown-Boveri constructed and tested one of these devices, using the design of Alfred Büchi. The first aircraft turbo-supercharger was built five years later by Rateau in France. A Le Père biplane powered by a Liberty engine equipped with a turbo-supercharger of General Electric design broke the world's altitude record in 1920.

The turbo-supercharger consists of a turbine, operating on the exhaust gases from the engine (see Turbine), which directly drives a centrifugal compressor used as a supercharger. This device is attractive for several reasons. First, it provides an easy means of varying the revolutions per minute of the supercharger and thus the pressure supplied to the engine. This is accomplished by a "waste-gate," a valve in the exhaust pipe between the engine and the turbine which, when open, allows some of the exhaust to escape without passing through the turbine. Second, because the supercharger is not connected to the engine crankshaft, full engine power is available for driving the propeller.

Originally, the turbo-supercharger was conceived as a device for providing the engine with a sea level environment when operating at altitude and thus alleviating the reduction in power which otherwise accompanies increasing altitude. To accomplish this end it was necessary that the turbine and compressor be efficient enough to provide compressed air at sea level pressure at the engine inlet, with sea level pressure also maintained at the engine exhaust and turbine inlet. In addition, an intercooler cooled by atmospheric air was used to reduce the high temperature of the supercharger discharge before the discharge entered the engine. This objective could be accomplished with only modest efficiency of turbine and compressor. The temperature of the exhaust of a gasoline aircraft engine can easily exceed 2,000° F., and the development of the turbo-supercharger required the development of turbine nozzle and blade materials that were able to withstand high temperatures. Turbo-superchargers were successfully used on several bombers (Boeing Fortress and Superfortress and Consolidated Liberator) and on the Republic Thunderbolt fighter, all of World War II.

As the design of turbines and compressors improved, it became evident that an efficient turbo-supercharger could provide sea level pressure at the engine inlet and exhaust and have some power left over which could be used to help turn the propeller. This led to the development of the turbo-compound engine, which is essentially a reciprocating engine with an integral supercharger and one or more exhaust turbines geared to the crankshaft. Engines of this type have remarkably good efficiency and high power-to-weight ratio and consequently are useful for long-range aircraft.

Before the advent of the turbojet airplane, most of the improvement in speed of transport airplanes came from flying at higher and higher altitudes, where the air resistance was less because of lower density. High-altitude flight required the successful utilization of several devices—the high pressure-ratio supercharger, the controllable-pitch propeller and the cabin supercharger. These three devices are all essential to modern piston-engine transport planes.

VII. JET ENGINES

1. Turbojets.—From 1903 to 1939 the reciprocating internal-combustion engine with propeller was the sole means used to propel both heavier-than-air and lighter-than-air craft. On Aug. 27, 1939, the first jet-propelled airplane flew in Germany. The engine was designed by Hans von Ohain (patented by von Ohain and Max Hahn), who had conceived the idea when he was a student at the University of Göttingen. Unknown to von Ohain, Frank Whittle in England had arrived at the same concept some years earlier and was actively working on it when von Ohain's engine first flew. Whittle's engine had its first flight on May 15, 1941.

Whittle's and von Ohain's devices were both what have come to be called turbojet engines. The basic idea of this engine is simple. Air taken in from the atmosphere is compressed to 3 to 12 times its original pressure in a centrifugal or axial compressor. Sufficient fuel is added to the air and burned to raise the temperature of the fluid mixture to between 1,200° and 1,700° F. The resulting hot air is passed through a turbine whose sole function is to drive the compressor. If the turbine and compressor are highly efficient, the pressure at the turbine discharge will be nearly twice atmospheric, and this excess pressure is used in a propelling nozzle to produce a high-velocity stream of gas and hence a thrust.

The most important advantage of the jet engine is that it is extraordinarily light compared to an engine-propeller combination having similar thrust at cruising speed. This advantage makes it possible to use much more powerful engines in jet planes. In addition, the elimination of the propeller makes possible a simpler, lighter and aerodynamically cleaner (i.e., more streamlined) air frame. Furthermore, the propulsive efficiency of a propeller is low at high (above 500 m.p.h.) forward speed while the propulsive efficiency of a jet is particularly good at very high speed. All these advantages taken together have made it possible to build turbojet-powered aircraft having a speed advantage over their engine-propeller counterparts of more than three to one.

In order to produce a large thrust, a turbojet engine must be capable of handling a large flow. At the same time it must not be excessively heavy or bulky. Unless the compressor, combustion chamber and turbine of a jet engine are highly efficient, the machine will be heavy and will use an excessive amount of fuel. It is also necessary for the temperature of the products of combustion entering the turbine to be high, otherwise the ratio of thrust to weight will be low.

The requirements faced by the turbojet pioneers were clear:

1. A light machine with a high capacity for air flow.

2. Highly efficient compressor, combustion chamber and turbine.

3. A turbine which could withstand high temperatures.

Centrifugal Compressor Development.—Both Whittle and von Ohain used centrifugal compressors for their first machines (see Table II). The alternate choice was an axial compressor. During those years the performance of the axial compressor was less predictable, and in the interest of rapid development the choice was undoubtedly well made. Von Ohain's machine was abandoned for an entirely new design (which used an axial compressor), but Whittle's was developed and was the direct ancestor of the Rolls-Royce Welland, Derwent, Nene and Tay engines, the General Electric I-16 and I-40 engines, and the Russian engine used in the MiG-15 fighter in the Korean War. The first two Rolls-Royce types were built in quantity during World War II and were used in the Gloster Meteor fighter against German V-1 rockets.

TABLE II.—*Some Important Turbojet Engines*

Name	Thrust, lb.	Weight, lb.	Type
Whittle W-1	850	623	Centrifugal
Junkers 004	1,980	1,630	8-stage axial
Rolls-Royce Derwent	4,000	1,250	Centrifugal
Bristol Siddeley Sapphire ASSa.-7	11,000	3,050	13-stage axial
Pratt and Whitney J-57 (JT3C-6)	13,000*	4,234	2-spool 16-stage axial
Rolls-Royce Avon RA.28	10,000	2,890	15-stage axial
Pratt and Whitney J-75 (JT4A-3)	15,800	5,020	2-spool 16-stage axial
General Electric J-79	11,000	3,190	17-stage axial

*Water injection.

During the 1940s a significant improvement in the performance of centrifugal compressors was accomplished. Efficiency was increased from somewhat better than 70% to over 80%. The ratio of discharge pressure to inlet pressure was raised from less than 3 to 1 to more than 4 to 1 and the flow capacity of a given size machine was greatly increased. These improvements were made largely by empirical methods, with little guidance from theory. From the beginning it was clear that the pressure ratio of the centrifugal turbojet compressor was limited to about 5 to 1 without using two compressors in series (two "stages"), an arrangement that involved a heavy and awkward construction.

Axial Compressor Development.—In the axial compressor, air passes axially through alternate sets of rotating and stationary blades. The rotating blades are arranged to increase the tangential component of velocity of the air, while the stationary blades are arranged to remove this increase and thus prepare for similar action by the following row of rotating blades. One set of rotating blades and its accompanying set of stationary blades is called a "stage." If it has a large number of stages, the axial compressor can be made to produce a much higher pressure ratio than a centrifugal machine can produce. Furthermore, it can be made very much smaller in diameter (about one-half), a factor that is important in reducing the aerodynamic drag of externally mounted engines. Moreover, axial compressors can be made with extremely high efficiency. These obvious advantages led to the design of axial turbojet engines by Junkers and BMW in Germany and by the Royal Aeronautical establishment in England even before the first jet-powered flights. During the 1940s these engines and others, notably the General Electric TG-180, were developed. The Junkers 004 was produced in quantity late in World War II and used in the Messerschmitt 262 fighter against Allied bombers with considerable effect.

The empirical development process, with slight assistance from theory, did not succeed nearly so well in the case of the axial compressor as it had in the case of the centrifugal machine. The Junkers engine was a very effective machine for its time, but it had a very low pressure ratio (about 3 to 1). Its development was stopped with the end of World War II in Europe. It was necessary to build up theoretical and practical knowledge before it was possible to design efficient high pressure-ratio axial compressors with confidence that engines with these devices would operate satisfactorily, or indeed at all. By the early 1950s such a background of knowledge had been built up by several manufacturers. The design processes involved complex theories and the use of large electronic computers. By such processes a sufficiently good first approximation to the final design is possible, so that with a reasonable amount of experimental work and subsequent modification a satisfactory machine can be expected. The efficiency of the best axial machines was about 5% better than the best centrifugal machines throughout the period when both were under development. In the 1950s a large number of axial machines were developed in England, France, the U.S. and the U.S.S.R. It appears that the centrifugal turbojet has become obsolete for all but small engines.

The demand for increased pressure ratio led to trouble in the form of instability of flow in the machine, a phenomenon called surge. Surging can occur in centrifugal compressors but it is a much more serious problem in high pressure-ratio axial machines. This trouble ordinarily occurs at revolutions per minutes that are lower than those for which the machine is designed. Three methods of alleviating the difficulty have been devised:

1. Blow-off valves which allow some air to escape part way through the compressor.

2. Two-spool machines which consist of two separate compressors, each driven by its own turbine and thus capable of operating independently at different revolutions per minute.

3. Stator blades which can be controlled as to angle in a manner similar to the pitch-changing in a controllable-pitch propeller.

Combustion.—The combustion chamber of a turbojet engine is required to raise the entering air temperature uniformly to the desired turbine inlet temperature without imposing too great a restriction on the flow of air. This problem turned out to be considerably more difficult than at first anticipated. Theoretical analysis that could be used as a guide to its solution was practically nonexistent, and experimentation was almost the sole means of

progress. The problem was complicated by the fact that to attain the desired temperature less than one-third of the available oxygen in the air had to be burned. Further, the combustion chamber was expected to operate smoothly and efficiently over a wide range of pressures and fuel flow. Early troubles with hot spots in the combustion chamber itself causing distortion and cracking and hot spots in the turbine causing nozzle and blade failures were remedied, only to be followed by troubles with low efficiency and extinction of fire at high altitude. Although the theory of combustion is still too complex to be of much assistance, the early troubles of the combustion chamber have been satisfactorily solved for present purposes.

Two types of combustion chambers are used. In the spray type, fuel is introduced in the form of a fine spray, mixed with sufficient air for its combustion, evaporated and burned. The products of combustion are then diluted by mixing with excess air to produce the desired temperatures. The vaporizing type of combustion chamber is similar except that the fuel is introduced in a stream and evaporated by contact with a hot surface. Either type can be made to give good service and to burn efficiently up to very high altitudes. At normal operating conditions efficiency of combustion, as measured by the amount of unburned fuel discharged, can be expected to be very nearly 100%. Combustion chambers of reasonable size can be made with a pressure drop of less than 4% of the entering pressure.

Turbines.—The steam turbine industry provided much background experience which could be drawn upon by the designers of turbojets. The principal new problems were the necessity of operating at very high temperatures and of keeping the weight down. These problems were also present in the turbo-supercharger, and materials developed for this device were useful (particularly in the U.S.) for application to early turbojets. Later developments involving materials, notably vacuum melting, have helped to make modern turbine blades more reliable.

Centrifugal engines require only a single turbine stage, but the increase in pressure ratio made possible by the axial compressor requires two or more turbine stages. Some minor improvements in turbine efficiency have been made by the application of the methods of aerodynamics to turbines, but for the most part improvements have been metallurgical and mechanical rather than aerodynamic.

Bearings.—Another problem facing the designers of turbojets was that it was necessary to use large-diameter bearings running at very high revolutions per minute. These bearings were of the antifriction (ball or roller) type and in early engines gave considerable trouble. Close attention to quality control together with improved methods of feeding lubricant has successfully solved these problems.

Afterburner.—The afterburner is a device that capitalizes on the fact that less than one-third of the oxygen of the air is consumed in the turbojet engine. It is merely a second combustion chamber placed after the turbine and before the propelling nozzle. By means of this device the temperature of the gas ahead of the propelling nozzle can be increased to 3,000° F. or more. The velocity of the propelling jet is approximately proportional to the square root of the absolute temperature of the gas entering the propelling nozzle. The result of the increase in temperature is an increase of nearly 50% in thrust at take-off and much larger increases at high speed. This increase in thrust is gained at the expense of three to four times the fuel consumption without the afterburner, but it is useful for short duration requirements such as take-off and also for extreme speeds, where the increase in thrust nearly matches the increase in fuel consumption. The very loud noise accompanying afterburning has thus far restricted its use to military airplanes.

When the afterburner is ignited, the propelling nozzle must be made larger (in proportion to the square root of the gas temperature) in order to accommodate the increased volume of gas. Thus an adjustable propelling nozzle, automatically controlled, is part of every afterburning system.

Water Injection.—A somewhat more modest increase in thrust can be obtained by injecting water either before the combustion chamber or before the compressor. The cooling effect of the water can be counteracted by burning additional fuel to bring the temperature back to the limit, and the result is about a 20% increase in thrust without the large increase in noise of an afterburner. A very large flow of water is required, and this method of operation is useful for take-off only. Some modern jet transports use water injection for this purpose.

Thrust Reversal.—The reversible propeller is highly effective in reducing the length of landing run of propeller-driven airplanes. Jet-propelled aircraft normally land much faster and need a retarding device even more than do propeller-driven airplanes. Thrust-reversing devices, which reverse the direction of the jet after landing, have been developed and are used in commercial jet transports.

2. Turboprops.—The turbo-propeller engine, called a turboprop, was another important development of the 1940s. In a certain sense it was the result of the development of the jet engine, because the same problems (high-efficiency compressor and high-temperature turbine) had to be solved before the turboprop could be successful. Although the concept of the turboprop engine is much older than that of the turbojet, the basic problems were first solved for the turbojet engine. Like the turbojet, the turboprop engine comprises a compressor, combustion chamber and turbine, but in this case nearly the full pressure drop is used to run the turbine, which therefore develops more than enough power to drive the compressor. The excess power is used to drive a propeller through reduction gearing. The turboprop is very much lighter in weight than a reciprocating engine of comparable power and is easier to construct in very large sizes (over 4,000 h.p.). Compared with a turbojet engine, the turboprop has better propulsive efficiency at flight speeds below about 500 m.p.h. It seems particularly suited for a helicopter engine, where its very light weight is an especially great advantage and where fuel consumption is not so important because the duration of flight is usually short.

In the development of the turboprop engine, two severe problems arose which had not been encountered with the turbojet. Because a turbine turns about ten times as fast as a propeller, a reduction gear is essential. No previous experience was available with light reduction gears having such large power capacity coupled with high input revolutions per minute. While no new principles were needed to make a successful reduction gear, a considerable improvement in the art of gear making was required before such a gear was successfully made. The other problem was associated with the control of the machine. Overspeeding is particularly serious in the case of a turbine engine, and special attention to both the engine control and the propeller pitch-control system is necessary in order to provide safe operation at all times. This problem needed only the intelligent application of known principles for its solution, but it required considerable development time.

TABLE III.—*Some Important Turboprop Engines*

Name	Max. h.p.	h.p./lb.	Type	Application
Rolls-Royce Dart Mk 525	1,990	1.6	2-stage centrifugal	Vickers Viscount transport
Bristol Siddeley Proteus 765	4,445	1.5	12-stage axial and 1 centrifugal	Bristol Britannia transport
General Electric T-58-GE-8	1,350	4.5	10-stage axial	Helicopter engine
Pratt and Whitney T34-P-3	6,000	2.3	13-stage axial	Douglas military transport C-133
Allison 501-D13	3,750	2.1	14-stage axial	Lockheed Electra transport

Turboprop engines appeared in commercial airliners in the middle 1940s, several years before successful turbojet service was inaugurated. At least one of these transport airplanes, the Vickers Viscount (*see* Table III), was notable for its quiet and vibration-free operation. This was partly due to the absence of the low-frequency exhaust noise of the reciprocating engine and partly to the smooth operation of the turbine power plant. Intelligent placement of the propeller with respect to the airplane also considerably reduced the noise and vibration.

Both the power and the efficiency of turboprop engines would be greatly improved if the turbine inlet temperature could be raised, and improvement in this direction could well result in the efficiency of the turboprop engine exceeding that of the reciprocating engine. The efficiency and power of the turboprop is also sensitive to atmospheric temperature, the highest power and efficiency being available at low temperature. For this reason the efficiency of the turboprop is best at high altitudes.

3. Pulse Jets.—The German V-1 weapon used in World War II was a pilotless airplane provided with an intermittent jet propulsion device called a pulse jet. In this device air entered at the front through a nonreturn valve and passed into a combustion chamber, where it was mixed with a suitable quantity of gasoline and ignited. Because return of the air was prevented by the valve, the resulting combustion raised the pressure in the chamber and forced the products of combustion to flow out of a nozzle at the rear. Inertia of the flowing gas in the nozzle caused the gas to continue to flow until the pressure in the combustion chamber was reduced below atmospheric pressure, at which time the nonreturn valve opened and allowed a new charge to enter. It was found that residual fire from one explosion would ignite the next, hence an ignition device was necessary only for the first explosion. This device was simple, cheap and effective for its intended purpose. It has never become a propulsive device for manned aircraft because of its inherently high fuel consumption and because it produces an almost intolerable noise.

4. Ram Jets.—The simplest of all aircraft propulsive devices is perhaps the ram jet. It is essentially a turbojet in which the rotating machinery has been omitted. It functions only at high airplane speed. Air entering the front of the device at flight speed is slowed to a low velocity (relative to the airplane velocity) by providing a properly shaped inlet passage. If this process is done efficiently the pressure will be raised. Fuel is added and burning takes place at the higher pressure. The hot products of combustion are re-expanded to atmospheric pressure and flow out at high velocity through a rearward-facing nozzle. Because of the higher temperature of the gas after combustion the velocity at the nozzle exit is higher than the flight speed; therefore a thrust is produced. The ram jet can be an efficient device only at very high speeds. It can produce no thrust at standstill and very little at low forward speed. It therefore needs some form of assisted take-off. Rocket-assisted ram jets are used in guided missiles.

5. Turbofans.—Ducted fan, ducted propeller and turbofan are all names for a hybrid form intermediate between the turbojet and the turboprop engine. Turbofan engines can be looked upon as turbojet engines in which a portion of the energy normally used in the propelling nozzle is employed by a turbine which in turn drives an additional compressor. This additional compressor functions exactly like a propeller but only a fraction of the available power is used in the fan; a large part of the thrust is still supplied by the propelling nozzle in the jet engine. Troubles caused by the near sonic velocities are reduced by lowering the speed of the air in a diffuser ahead of the fan. The fan is very much smaller and lighter than a normal propeller and runs at turbine speed, thereby eliminating the need for reduction gears. The turbofan is somewhat more efficient than the turbojet at low speeds, and is also quieter. Compared with the turboprop it is lighter, less economical at low speed and more economical at high speed.

6. Rockets.—Rockets have been used in the propulsion of aircraft. One use of rockets is to provide additional thrust for the purpose of shortening take-off distances. Many such rockets were used in World War II. German rocket assist take-off devices of World War II used hydrogen peroxide as a fuel. Those of U.S. manufacture use solid propellants. Rockets have also been used as the primary power plant in interceptor aircraft, such as the Messerschmitt 163 used by the Germans in World War II. Experimental high-speed aircraft, such as the United States' X-1 and X-15, use rockets to achieve very high speeds and altitudes.

The advantage of a rocket is that it provides very high thrust for its weight. On the other hand, rockets use fuel at a very rapid rate (approximately 16 times as fast as a turbojet engine of the same thrust). For this reason rocket power can be used only for a very short duration. Rocket engines used for primary aircraft power plants differ from rocket engines used for other purposes in that in aircraft it is essential to be able to turn the thrust off and on again and also extremely desirable to be able to adjust the thrust. This feature makes it necessary to use liquid propellants. (*See* ROCKETS AND GUIDED MISSILES.) (E. S. T.)

VIII. AIRCRAFT FUELS

Until the advent of the gas turbine essentially all aircraft fuel was of the gasoline type (*see* GASOLINE). A few diesel engines were used but diesels never became important for aircraft propulsion. As a result of the gas turbine, development of high-power aircraft piston engines and of aviation gasoline largely ceased by about 1947.

Improvement of aviation gasoline was an essential factor in the development of the piston-engine aircraft, which reached their most advanced stages about 1950. At the end of World War II an engine of given size was producing at least four times as much power as at the end of World War I. Supercharging was a major factor in this power gain and was made possible by fuels having at least four times as much resistance to knocking as World War I fuels. Increased knock resistance permitted marked reduction in fuel consumption at the cruise condition, thereby increasing aircraft range. Increased knock resistance permits increased density of the fuel-air mixture in the cylinder at the time the spark passes. This increased density can be obtained by increase of cylinder compression ratio (as in automobiles) or by means of supercharging. The power output of a gasoline engine is closely proportional to the weight of air consumed per unit time, and supercharging may increase this by at least 200%.

1. Fuel Composition.—Data are lacking regarding the composition of aircraft fuels used prior to World War I, but they were probably straight-run motor gasolines; *i.e.*, hydrocarbons naturally occurring in crude oil and produced by simple distillation.

Gasolines, for both motor and aviation use, consist of mixtures of hydrocarbons of different types and boiling points. Motor fuels may contain thousands of different compounds with boiling points varying from about 30° to over 400° F. Aviation gasoline is much more restricted in both types of compounds and their boiling points. The types of chemical compounds in aviation gasoline are paraffins of straight and branched chain types, aromatics (the ring type compounds, of which benzene [benzol] is the simplest) and naphthenes. The compounds in aviation gasoline have boiling points ranging from about 85° to about 350° F., with the great majority boiling below 275° F. Both motor and aviation gasolines often contain antiknock agents (usually tetraethyl lead) in small concentration.

2. Fuel Development.—After World War I perhaps the most important development concerning aviation gasoline was standardization of quality so that an aircraft landing almost anywhere in the world could obtain suitable fuel. Standardization and improvement of distillation range (volatility) was also an important factor. The fuel must be sufficiently volatile so that it evaporates readily in the air taken in by the engine. The volatility, however, must not be too high, lest it cause the formation of ice in the carburetors (from atmospheric moisture) or boiling in the engine and aircraft fuel systems (vapour lock).

The increase in knock resistance has resulted from selection of gasolines, blending selected gasolines with benzol and other aromatics, and development of suitable methods for measuring and expressing knock resistance. The discoveries of tetraethyl lead and of the knock-resisting properties of the branched chain paraffins were the most important advances. The branched chain paraffins (octanes) were synthesized on a large scale during World War II.

Knock resistance is expressed in octane numbers (ON) for motor and aviation gasolines and in performance numbers (PN) for aviation gasolines of over 100 ON. In World War I U.S. aviation gasoline was often only of 50 ON (largely straight chain paraffins), and the best used by the Allies was only about 75 ON. By the end of World War II grade 115/145 fuel was in use. This fuel had 115 PN under cruising conditions and 145 PN at maximum power conditions. Grade 115/145 has about four times the knock resistance of 50 ON fuel at maximum power conditions and three times as much at the cruising condition. During World War II the Germans used highly leaded fuels of about grade 90/130.

During World War II and subsequently the maximum power available with grade 100/130 (which preceded grade 115/145) and with grade 115/145 was insufficient. Injection of a 50–50 mixture of water and methanol (wood alcohol) into the carburetor, in addition to the fuel, enabled power to be increased by about 20%.

Four grades of aviation gasoline of uniform volatility and varying knock resistance are in use. They are grades 80/87, 91/98, 100/130 and 115/145.

3. Turbine Fuels.—When the aircraft gas turbine first came into use it was believed that any liquid that would burn and that had a low enough freezing point would constitute a suitable fuel. Experience proved, however, that the combustion characteristics of aircraft turbine fuels were very important. The initial work with aircraft gas turbines was conducted mostly with kerosene (frequently known in Europe as lamp oil or paraffin oil). This is a straight-run product distilling between about 325° and about 525° F. Kerosene, as sold for use in lamps, proved to have too high a freezing point and sometimes possessed unsatisfactory combustion characteristics. Consequently, aircraft kerosene had to be modified somewhat from the lamp oil grade. Aromatics are undesirable in turbine fuels because they produce carbon deposits in the combustion system. The aromatic content of kerosene is frequently too high for satisfactory combustion. Modified kerosene has been used in the majority of the world's turbine civil transport aircraft.

The world supply of kerosene appears to be insufficient for it to be used in the pure form for military use; consequently, what is essentially a mixture of 65% gasoline and 35% kerosene, known as JP4, is widely used in military turbine-powered aircraft.

In turbine aircraft the fuel is often used to cool the engine lubricating oil. Fuel that is used for cooling purposes should not cause deposits in the cooling system. (S. D. H.)

BIBLIOGRAPHY.—M. J. B. Davy, *Interpretive History of Flight* (1937); R. O. Schlaifer and S. D. Heron, *Development of Aircraft Engines and Fuels* (1950); C. H. Chatfield and C. F. Taylor, *The Airplane and Its Engine* (1949); F. E. Weick, *Aircraft Propeller Design* (1930); T. Theodorsen, *Theory of Propellers* (1948); C. F. Taylor and E. S. Taylor, *The Internal Combustion Engine* (1948); P. H. Wilkinson, *Aircraft Engines of the World*, 4 vol. (1949–52); G. D. Angle, *Aerosphere* (1939); C. M. Harris (ed.), *Handbook of Noise Control* (1957); *Jane's All the World's Aircraft*, (annually, 1909–   ).

AIR DEFENSE: *see* AIR POWER.

AIRDRIE, a large burgh of Lanarkshire, Scot., 11½ mi. E of Glasgow. Pop. (1961) 33,620. The Monkland Canal (constructed 1761–90 and now derelict) connected Airdrie with Glasgow and the Forth and Clyde Canal near Maryhill.

Airdrie, originally a farming and weaving village, became a market town after 1695; its later prosperity was due to local coal and ironstone beds and its proximity to Glasgow. Its chief industries include the manufacture of tubes, boilers, paper, electrical equipment, foodstuffs, chemicals, clothing, drugs, and cigarettes.

AIREBOROUGH, an urban district (1937) in the Pudsey parliamentary division of the West Riding of Yorkshire, Eng., 8 mi. NW of Leeds and 7 mi. NE of Bradford. Pop. (1961) 27,508. Area 10.7 sq.mi., of which nearly one-third is moorland. The residential village of Rawdon contains large 16th- and 17th-century houses, a Baptist college (1859), and orchid nurseries. The textile-making town of Yeadon has an airfield, and two fine old mansions, Hawksworth Hall (Elizabethan) and Low Hall (1624). The district is connected with the Brontë family, Charlotte having taught for a time in Rawdon and her parents having been married in Guiseley Church. Many members of the Longfellow family, ancestors of the poet, are buried in the churchyard.

AIR FORCES: *see* AIR POWER.

AIRGLOW is the faint luminescence of the earth's upper atmosphere. Unlike the aurora, airglow does not exhibit structures such as arcs, and is emitted from the entire sky at all latitudes and at all times. The nocturnal phenomenon is called nightglow. Dayglow and twilightglow, or twilight airglow, are analogous terms. Little is known about dayglow, as it cannot be studied from the ground because of the solar radiation scattered by the lower atmosphere.

Nightglow is very feeble in the visible region of the spectrum, the illumination it gives to a horizontal surface at the ground being only about the same as that from a candle at a height of 300 ft. It is possibly about 1,000 times stronger in the infrared region. Considerable variations of intensity occur. The spectrum of nightglow contains the following features: the forbidden green line and the forbidden red lines of atomic oxygen at 5,577Å; 6,300Å and 6,364Å; the pair of yellow lines of atomic sodium at 5,890Å and 5,896Å; the Meinel band system of hydroxyl (OH) in the visible and infrared regions; the Herzberg band system of oxygen (O_2) in the ultraviolet region and a single member of the atmospheric band system of the same molecule in the infrared; and, finally, a continuum beginning just below 4,000Å and extending indefinitely toward longer wave lengths. From the rocket and other research completed up to the end of 1959 it appeared probable that the altitude of the source of the red oxygen lines was very great, perhaps about 150 mi., and that the altitudes of the sources of the other spectral features were within 10 mi. of 50 mi. Nightglow represents the release of solar energy which has been stored in the upper atmosphere. It is thought that the red oxygen lines are emitted as a result of recombination between oppositely charged particles in the F layer of the ionosphere, and that the other spectral features are emitted as a result of a variety of chemical reactions.

Twilightglow differs from nightglow mainly in that the red oxygen lines and the yellow sodium lines are much enhanced. In the case of the latter the mechanism responsible has been identified: it is simply resonance scattering of solar radiation by free sodium atoms. Each sodium atom in the illuminated portion of the atmosphere acts, in effect, as a tiny mirror reflecting the characteristic yellow light. *See also* ATMOSPHERE: *The Terrestrial Atmosphere.*

(D. R. B.)

AIR GUNS, weapons in which the force employed to propel the bullet, shot charge or dart is derived from compressed air, liquid carbon dioxide, or an ignitable fuel combined with compressed air. They are developments of the basic principle employed in the primitive blowgun (*q.v.*). Air guns are often called gas guns, spring-operated guns or BB guns. Most are relatively inexpensive and are usually thought of as children's toys, but many are used for target shooting or training in marksmanship. Although the term air rifle is loosely applied to all toy shoulder arms that use compressed air as a propellant, the term applies in strict accuracy only to weapons with rifled bores. Other varieties are air pistols, which are small enough to be held and fired with one hand, and air shotguns, which are shoulder weapons that shoot a quantity of small pellets at each firing. Total annual sales of air weapons throughout the world run into the millions.

The common forms of air gun are charged by compressing a spiral spring, one end of which actuates a piston working in a cylinder. When released by a pull on the trigger, the spring expands and compresses air which forces out the projectile. More complex air guns incorporate a reservoir of compressed air permitting one or several discharges. Gas guns utilize liquid carbon dioxide in a reservoir attached to or within the guns. A pull of the trigger opens a valve allowing a portion of the carbon dioxide to escape as a gas and propel the projectile from the barrel. Combination air and ignitable fuel guns utilize highly volatile gases pumped into the compression chamber where they form an ignitable mixture with air which is exploded by compression.

Elastic-operated guns utilizing the springiness of synthetic or natural rubber bands to propel a projectile may be considered in the spring-gun category. The projectile is ejected from a sliding carrier rather than through a barrel.

For historical background and detailed data on types and systems of operation *see* W. H. B. Smith, *Gas, Air and Spring Guns of the World* (1957). (M. D. W.; X.)

AIR LAW, the law governing use of the airspace and occurrences therein. Although radio waves, projectiles and other objects may traverse the airspace, air law has usually been related to aircraft, including operation thereof in the airspace or on the surface, rights therein, persons or property thereon, and events connected therewith. (For the meanings of airspace, aircraft and spacecraft, see *Space Law,* below.)

Sovereignty.—A fundamental principle of international law is that of national sovereignty over the airspace.

Early in the 20th century many jurists thought that airspace, like the high seas, should be free and outside national sovereignty; others regarded the airspace as part of the territory of the subjacent state; yet others attempted to reconcile "freedom of the air" with national rights in the airspace. Around 1910 it appeared that governments would regard control over the airspace as essential to national safety. Eventually the principle of state sovereignty became firmly established and was recognized in the Convention Relating to the Regulation of Aerial Navigation (Paris, 1919). That convention was replaced by the Convention on International Civil Aviation (Chicago, 1944) which also recognized that: "Every State has complete and exclusive sovereignty over the airspace above its territory."

Transit Rights.—Over the high seas there is freedom of air navigation, but aircraft cannot fly over any state without its permission. However, in the Chicago convention (following a similar principle of the Paris convention) each contracting state agreed that civil aircraft of the other contracting states would have the right, when not operating scheduled services, to fly across its territory or halt therein for nontraffic purposes, subject to the rules of the convention. As regards scheduled (regularly operated commercial) air services, privileges of transit and landing for nontraffic purposes were extended to one another's aircraft by the states that were parties to the International Air Services Transit agreement of 1944.

Traffic Rights.—Aircraft may not exercise traffic rights, that is, pick up or set down passengers or cargo, in any country without its authorization. Under the Chicago convention aircraft of a contracting state may exercise traffic rights in the territory of another contracting state on nonscheduled flights, but the privilege is subject to the latter's right "to impose such regulations, conditions or limitations as it might consider desirable." The International Air Transport agreement was formulated in 1944 to enable aircraft on scheduled services to exercise traffic rights in foreign territory, but it proved unacceptable to most states. Consequently, bilateral agreements were made by states to enable their airlines to pick up and set down traffic in each other's territory.

Territorial Law.—An aircraft must comply with the laws of the country where it flies, including the rules of the air and air traffic control, and regulations relating to entry, clearance, immigration, passports, customs, health and documents relating to the aircraft, crew, passengers and cargo. However, the states that were parties to the Chicago convention must apply their air regulations, including any which levy airport and similar charges, to the aircraft of all contracting states without distinction as to nationality.

National Legislation.—The common law was inadequate for regulation of aircraft operations and almost all nations enacted legislation for that purpose. These laws generally provided for carrying out international obligations, such as the Chicago convention, for ensuring safety of air navigation, registration of aircraft and verification of their airworthiness, licensing of crew, establishment of airports and acquisition of land or rights over land, provision of radio aids and other air navigation facilities, control of air traffic, investigation of accidents and for the administration of such regulations. Legislation also provided for economic regulation and licensing of commercial flying and for specifying conditions of commercial carriage of passengers or goods. In many states air transport was wholly or partly nationalized by legal enactments. National legislation in many instances included provisions governing the liability of the air carrier in respect of passengers or goods and third-party insurance.

Usually such legislation was supplemented by detailed regulations promulgated by the governments under delegated powers. For example, in the United Kingdom the Civil Aviation act of 1949 (consolidating and replacing earlier enactments) was a comprehensive statute but it authorized the government to promulgate orders in council to make provision for multifarious matters and "generally for regulating air navigation."

In the United States federal competence to enact air legislation was questioned as late as 1918 but eventually was justified on the basis of the interstate commerce clause of the constitution. Such legislation concerning rules of flight, navigation lights and licensing of aircraft personnel was held valid for purely intrastate operations also, on the ground that departure therefrom would present hazard to interstate air navigation.

The Air Commerce act of 1926 authorized the secretary of commerce to make safety regulations, grant licences and registrations and install and operate facilities necessary to safe navigation, such as airway lights and radio stations. Such rule-making powers were transferred by the Civil Aeronautics act of 1938 to a board with a view to promote development of safe, efficient air services at reasonable charges under regulated competition. The Federal Aviation act of 1958 continued the board and created a Federal Aviation agency to control use of the navigable airspace and develop and operate air navigation facilities and air traffic control. In 1966 the agency was included in the Department of Transportation.

Private Ownership in Airspace.—Here the trend was opposite to that in national sovereignty: it was toward freedom of flight. The right of the landowner to make unlimited use of the superjacent airspace was maintained, with only a few exceptions (see *The Law of Airports*, below), but judicial decisions and national legislation denied him any right to forbid, or to receive compensation for, the mere passage of aircraft, without producing material damage, through that part of the airspace of which he was making no effective use. In the United States the supreme court (*Causby* v. *United States*, 1946) observed: "It is ancient doctrine that at common law ownership of the land extended to the periphery of the universe . . . but that doctrine has no place in the modern world. The air is a public highway, as congress has declared. . . ." The court, however, upheld the landowner's claim for compensation since he suffered actual, material damage from frequent flights of aircraft over his land. In the United Kingdom a law of 1920, re-enacted in 1949, provided that no action would lie in respect of trespass or nuisance by reason only of the flight or the ordinary incidents of flight of an aircraft over any property at a reasonable height if the flight was conducted in accordance with regulations. However, if aircraft operations resulted in material loss or damage to any person or property on land or water, then (unless the complainant negligently caused or contributed to the damage) compensation would be recoverable without proof of negligence or intention.

The Law of Airports.—Actions for aerial annoyance usually come from people domiciled near airports where aircraft operate frequently and at low altitudes. Courts have prohibited the establishment or the continued operation of airports where a strong showing of injury to the neighbours was made. The British Civil Aviation act of 1949 met the resultant hazard to airport operation by providing that no action would lie in respect of nuisance by reason of the noise and vibration caused by aircraft on any airport where the terms of an order in council regulating such matters had been complied with.

The owner of property adjacent to an airport may be prevented by legislation from using his property in a manner which would create a hazard for air navigation. In the United States local regulations prohibited the erection of structures of more than a limited height in the neighbourhood of airports. Such zoning was not to entail serious hardship to landowners. If it did, as for example if safety of flight required that the structures on a given piece of land be only a few feet in height, compensation would have to be paid. The acquisition of the owner's rights in the airspace above his property, subject to compensation, is a possibility where such extreme restrictions are necessary; but airport zoning ordinarily imposes only moderate restrictions and entails no compensation.

In most countries airports are nationally licensed, and unlicensed places can be used for the landing and taking off of aircraft only under restrictive conditions, if at all. In the United States no such licensing exists, and any attempt to establish it might encounter constitutional difficulties on the ground that an airport is purely an intrastate activity. Federal control over airports is possible, however, through conditions attached to the grant of national aid to airports.

Codification of International Air Law.—The extreme mobility of aircraft and their frequent crossing of international boundaries make it particularly necessary that air law should be uniform. This can be achieved by international agreement. Certain rules of public air law are codified in the Chicago convention: for example, that aircraft have the nationality of the state where they are registered and that such state has to ensure that the aircraft is airworthy, that its crew is competent according to international standards, and that it complies with the laws in force wherever the aircraft may be. Considerable uniformity in the aeronautical regulations, standards and procedures of states that are parties to the Chicago convention results from their endeavour to follow the international technical standards and procedures formulated from time to time by the council of the International Civil Aviation organization (I.C.A.O.) established by the convention. That convention and the International Air Services Transit agreement mentioned above embody international agreements for aerial transit.

The function of developing studies with a view to unification of private air law was performed by C.I.T.E.J.A. (Comité International Technique d'Experts Juridiques Aériens) from 1926 until 1947 when that body was dissolved and its work taken over by the legal committee of I.C.A.O. Drafts prepared by those bodies resulted in the adoption of international air law conventions.

Warsaw Convention.—The convention for the Unification of Certain Rules Relating to International Carriage by Air, adopted at Warsaw in 1929, provided that the carrier would be liable for accident, in such carriage, to passengers or goods, unless he proved that all necessary and possible measures were taken to avoid the accident. However, his liability would be limited, except in cases of willful misconduct, to specified maxima.

The Hague Protocol.—In 1955 a protocol was formulated at The Hague, Neth., to effect amendments to the Warsaw convention, including one to double the limit of liability in respect of a passenger.

Rome Convention.—A convention on Damage Caused by Foreign Aircraft to Third Parties on the Surface was adopted at Rome in 1952 (replacing one of 1933 and a 1938 protocol). It made the operator absolutely liable for such damage subject to specified limits.

Geneva Convention.—In 1948, the convention on the International Recognition of Rights in Aircraft was formulated at Geneva, Switz. Its objective was that proprietary and other rights in aircraft would be protected in all countries participating in it.

Precautionary Attachment.—A convention was drawn up at Rome in 1933 to protect certain aircraft against attachment before judgment in pursuit of private interests.

Drafts and Projects.—In 1957 the I.C.A.O. legal committee prepared a draft convention on the unification of certain rules relating to international carriage by air performed by a person other than the contracting carrier. Projects on which the legal committee was engaged included study of the legal status of the aircraft, particularly with a view to formulating rules applicable to events happening on board aircraft, such as crimes, commercial transactions, torts, births, deaths and marriages. A closely related subject was that of the status of the aircraft commander. Another concerned the principles of liability and any limitation in cases of collision between aircraft.

Space Law.—The launching of the first artificial space satellites by the U.S.S.R. in Oct.–Nov. 1957 aroused popular interest in legal problems that for some years previously had been studied by jurists in many countries. The problems involved the legal status of spacecraft and of the outer space they would traverse. The primary question was whether national sovereignty extended to outer space. The declaration of state sovereignty over the airspace contained in the Paris convention of 1919 and the Chicago convention of 1944, as well as in the legislation of many countries, did not appear conclusive, since those instruments spoke of "airspace," but did not define or delimit it, or make any reference to outer space. Furthermore, those conventions and statutes were essentially linked with aircraft. The accepted technical definition of aircraft was "any machine that can derive support in the atmosphere from the reactions of the air." Thus it could be argued that the sovereignty of a state extended from the earth's surface as high as aircraft could fly, but no higher. Technical indications were that such height could not exceed 50 miles. On the other hand, there was no international agreement placing a maximum height for state sovereignty.

It was argued that the failure of any state to object to the actual launching of satellites by the U.S.S.R. and the United States evidenced consent. But "consent" obviously implied existence of a legal right on the part of the nations. In any case the military potential of spacecraft or of the establishment of a space-station by one state above another's territory was very grave, and nothing indicated that nations, mindful of considerations of national safety, would forgo, or refrain from claiming, sovereignty over several hundred miles of space above their territories.

Preoccupation over the military aspects was evident when, in Dec. 1957, the United Nations general assembly adopted a resolution on disarmament including a provision calling for a joint study of an inspection system designed to ensure that the sending of objects through outer space would be exclusively for peaceful and scientific purposes.

The legal status of satellites or spacecraft was clearer: they were not "aircraft" since they could operate without deriving "support in the atmosphere from the reactions of the air" and could ascend to infinite heights above the earth's surface where air is nonexistent. However, they would use the airspace while ascending or descending, possibly endangering the safety of navigation of aircraft, and would therefore become liable to be controlled at such time by air law.

General legal opinion tended to regard as insupportable the extension of state sovereignty literally to infinity or even thousands of miles above the earth. Various theories were advanced in regard to the height up to which state sovereignty extended: thus, one stipulated the height of 50 miles above the earth because of certain mathematical calculations concerning gravity and centrifugal force, and another a height of 300 miles. In Dec. 1959 the United Nations established a committee to co-ordinate and promote all activities for the peaceful uses of outer space and to study the nature of the legal problems arising from exploration of outer space.

BIBLIOGRAPHY.—C. N. Shawcross *et al., Air Law,* 2nd ed. (1951); Charles S. Rhyne, *Airports and the Courts* (1944); John C. Cooper, *The Right to Fly* (1947); *U.S. Aviation Reports* (1928 *et seq.*), reporting important judicial and administrative decisions and legislation; American Society of International Law, *Proceedings,* pp. 97–98 (1956).
　　　　　　　　　　　　　　　　　　　　　　　　(P. K. R.; Ed. W.)

AIR LOCK, a device to permit passage between regions of differing atmospheric pressures, most often used between the outside air and working places in compressed air, such as pneumatic caissons and subaqueous tunnels. A typical lock consists of a cylinder of steel plate with air-tight doors at both ends, one opening from the outside into the lock, the other from lock into compressed air, together with valves to admit or to exhaust compressed air into or from the lock. One of the doors must always be closed; before opening the other the pressure within the lock must be equalized with that on the opposite side. The employee who operates valves and doors is known as the lock tender.

Two types of lock are in general use, the horizontal, for tunnels, in which the doors are hinged on vertical axes, and the vertical, for caissons; in the latter the door arrangement must make provision for the cable which hoists material from working chamber to surface; several forms have been developed. On a large caisson the lock consists of a horizontal cylinder with a closed end, mounted on a caisson shaft. *See* CAISSON; TUNNEL.　(F. DN.)

AIR MASS. In synoptic meteorology, air mass is the designation for a vast body of air in which certain physical properties—mainly those of special value in analysis for weather forecasting purposes—vary but slightly in the horizontal.

The basic properties of air masses which determine characteristics of the weather are the vertical distribution of temperature and moisture content. These properties determine the actual or potential development of clouds and precipitation. Two air masses of similar horizontal homogeneity and similar average temperature and moisture at the ground may have very different vertical distribution of these properties. The practice of air mass analysis for weather forecasting therefore requires upper-air soundings to determine the vertical distributions, although it is possible to infer to some extent the latter from the conditions measured at or seen from the ground.

The origin and persistence of distinctive air masses are explained by the facts: (1) that there are certain large source regions of the earth's surface where conditions are sufficiently uniform so that the overlying air can acquire similar characteristics; *i.e.,* horizontal homogeneity, throughout the region; and (2) that the general circulation of the world's atmosphere has large-scale streams that are more or less steady and permit the travel of the air masses over long distances without being dispersed into small eddy branches.

The primary source regions are the polar areas and the subtropical belts (around 10°–30° latitude). The middle latitudes are the scene of interactions between the polar and tropical air masses, which intertwine and over- or underrun one another in great spiral trajectories that constitute the traveling cyclones and anticyclones (*q.v.*).

Such interactions produce the major weather variations in these latitudes (*see* METEOROLOGY). There is a subsidiary class of source regions in middle latitudes where the effects of the prevailing difference in temperature between ocean and continent surfaces tend to transform originally polar or tropical air masses passing over them into subtypes with distinctive and important characteristics.

Thus polar (or tropical) maritime and polar (or tropical) continental air masses are created, which also may interact in cyclones and anticyclones as a result of the large-scale air circulation bringing them together.

Near the coasts very rapid and striking transformations in air mass properties often take place when, for example, warm continental air moves onto cold ocean waters (in summer) or (in winter) cold continental air moves onto warm ocean waters; although such effects do not reach to very high levels in the atmosphere and are usually limited in area, locally they may play a dominant role in the weather.

Small-scale phenomena, such as sea and land breezes, mountain and valley breezes, may be considered as the result of contrasting local or pseudo air mass source regions. (*See* WIND.)

Although the air mass concept was recognized in a general way by H. W. Dove and others before the middle of the 19th century, its practical significance in weather forecasting was first realized in 1917 by Norwegian meteorologists hard pressed for a new technique to compensate for their lack of foreign weather reports withheld by the neighbouring warring nations. In less than two decades thereafter it had been adopted in most advanced countries. It greatly improved accuracy of forecasting, but only for periods up to 24 or 36 hr. in advance, and clarified the under-

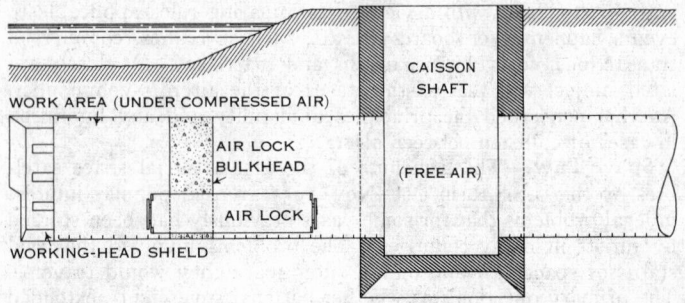

AIR LOCK IN VEHICULAR TUNNEL DRIVEN UNDER COMPRESSED AIR

standing of many familiar weather phenomena. (*See* WEATHER FORECASTING.)

In physical meteorology, air mass is the term for unit of mass of the atmosphere passed through by the sun's rays in reaching from outside the atmosphere to the earth's surface. Air mass of value 1 is defined as the amount of air passed through by the vertical rays when the sun is in the zenith. Then for lesser elevations of the sun above the horizon, the air mass m is nearly proportional to the secant of the sun's zenith distance, and may be described as the equivalent number of atmospheres of air mass 1 which the rays would pass through at any given solar elevation.

Tables of m values for various zenith distances are required for convenience in calculating the absorption of solar energy by the atmosphere.

In order to avoid confusion with the expression air mass as used in synoptic meteorology, E. W. Woolard and I. F. Hand suggested the word air path for m.   (R. G. SE.; X.)

AIR NAVIGATION: *see* NAVIGATION.

AIRPLANE. The concept of mechanical flight was almost a century old before modern aeronautical terminology began to take definite shape. During the early part of the 19th century, inventors referred to aerial vehicles variously as aerial ships, flying machines, aerial machines or aerial steam carriages. As late as 1903 the American inventor Samuel Pierpont Langley called his machine an aerodrome, from a combination of Greek words meaning aerial runner.

According to Svante Stubelius, the term aeroplane was first used by F. H. Wenham in England in 1866 to describe a wing, or "a plane in the air." From 1873 onward, the word was used to refer to the whole aircraft. In British usage this term is still employed. In the United States, however, the simplified form airplane was officially adopted by government agencies in 1916 and subsequently came into general use.

An airplane is a power-driven, heavier-than-air craft, usually manned, which derives its lift, *i.e.*, its support in the air, from the dynamic reaction of air flow over a system of fixed surfaces, or wings.

The essential components of an airplane are a wing system to sustain it in flight, tail surfaces to stabilize the wing, movable surfaces to control the attitude of the machine in flight and a power plant of some kind to provide the necessary thrust to push the machine through the air. Some sort of provision also must be made to support the machine when it is at rest on the ground or on water, or during take-off and landing operations. In addition, to make it a useful device, an enclosed body (fuselage) to house the crew, passengers and cargo must be provided, as well as controls and instruments for the pilots and navigators. These general characteristics distinguish the airplane from other common forms of aircraft, such as balloons and airships, which derive their support from the displacement of large volumes of air by large containers (bags) of lighter-than-air gas; gliders and sailplanes, which resemble airplanes in form but which do not carry power plants; helicopters and Autogiros, which derive their lift from systems of rotating wings; and rocket craft or spacecraft, which usually are wingless vehicles designed to operate outside the boundaries of the earth's atmosphere. (Discussions of these types of aircraft appear in AIRSHIP; BALLOON FLIGHT; GLIDING; HELICOPTER: ROCKETS AND GUIDED MISSILES; and SPACE EXPLORATION.)

Airplanes may be classified into two broad categories by: (1) their design configuration; or (2) the mission that they are intended to perform. The various types of airplanes are discussed in this article under the following headings:

I. Classification by Configuration
II. Classification by Mission
   A. Civil Airplanes
     1. Commercial Transport
     2. Industrial or Executive Transport
     3. General Utility Airplanes
     4. Private Airplanes
     5. Training Airplanes
   B. Military Airplanes
     1. Fighter Airplanes
     2. Attack Airplanes
     3. Bombing Airplanes
     4. Reconnaissance Airplanes
     5. Transport Airplanes
     6. Training Airplanes
     7. Research Airplanes and Special Types

An account of the development of the airplane may be found in the article AVIATION, HISTORY OF. For a discussion of the physical principles upon which mechanical flight is based, as well as the practical applications of these principles, *see* AERODYNAMICS and AERONAUTICS. The nonmechanical flight of the more talented animals is described in FLIGHT (NATURAL).

I. CLASSIFICATION BY CONFIGURATION

Most modern airplanes are monoplanes; *i.e.*, their lift is derived from one horizontal fixed-wing system. The biplane (using two horizontal wing systems, one above the other, connected by a series of struts and wires) was the almost universally accepted form up to the mid-1920s, but it later virtually disappeared from use. The few that remained were employed for primary pilot training, for sport flying or for agricultural crop dusting. During World War I, several multiplane designs appeared (triplanes, quadriplanes, etc.), but they subsequently disappeared entirely.

Modern monoplanes may be further catalogued by the plan form of their wings, which may be rectangular, tapered, swept-back or delta. The theoretical considerations on which the selection of various plan forms is based, and the resulting characteristics, are discussed in the article AERONAUTICS.

Another observable variation in modern airplane configuration lies in the number and location of the power plants. Airplanes are driven by means of the thrust developed by engine- or turbine-driven propellers, or from the reaction of streams of hot gases (jets) developed by gas turbines. For single-engine designs, the engines (or turbines) are usually located in the body, or fuselage. For multiple-engine designs, the power plants are usually distributed outboard along the wings, either in nacelles projecting from,

BY COURTESY OF (LEFT) THE AERONAUTICAL ARCHIVES OF THE INSTITUTE OF THE AEROSPACE SCIENCES, (RIGHT) U.S. DEPARTMENT OF DEFENSE, AIR FORCE PHOTO

(LEFT) MODIFIED NO. 3 GLIDER BY ORVILLE AND WILBUR WRIGHT AT KILL DEVIL HILL, N.C., 1902. (RIGHT) GLENN CURTISS' SEAPLANE OF 1911, THE FIRST U.S. AIRCRAFT SUCCESSFULLY TO TAKE OFF FROM, AND LAND ON, WATER

or in pods suspended below, the wing. Pods housing turbine power plants have also been attached to the rear of the fuselage.

Finally, as to over-all configuration, airplanes are either land based or water based. In the first case, they are equipped with wheels or skids; in the second, they are mounted on floats, or the main hull is so designed as to permit take-off or landing on water.

There is no one best solution to any given design problem. The general size, shape and configuration of an airplane are closely related to the mission for which it is intended. The final design is always a series of compromises among many interrelated elements. This is why airplanes designed for different purposes have varying external characteristics. For example, a long-range, high-altitude photographic mission calls for minimum total weight and large wing area (low wing loading); a high aspect ratio (ratio of wing span to wing width) for long-range cruising efficiency; a single engine, economical in fuel consumption; and a fuselage just sufficiently large to house the necessary equipment and a single pilot.

On the other hand, maximum speed calls for small, compact machines with very small, thin, swept-back or delta wings (i.e., high wing loadings), high landing and take-off speeds, large, uneconomical (in fuel) power plants and restricted crew accommodations.

If comfort, convenience and safety for a large number of passengers are paramount, lower wing loadings for slower landing and take-off speeds must be selected, and higher over-all drag (air resistance) must be accepted because of the necessity for larger fuselage (for passenger, crew and cargo accommodations), multiple power plants, large quantities of fuel, etc.

In making up specifications for an airplane of any category, the basic mission must be clearly defined and all design factors carefully studied to effect proper compromises to yield the desired result. It is impossible to attain the ideal in aircraft design. The "safest" airplane would be one that could not fly at all. The "fastest" airplane would have no practical utility except to establish speed records. The "highest flying" airplane would be merely a complicated and expensive research tool designed only to make a shallow penetration of outer space. And the "farthest flying" airplane would have very little practical utility except to establish endurance records.

Modern airplanes are so complicated, and such a large number of variables enter into their design, that many hundreds of thousands of engineering man-hours go into their specification, design, construction, testing and evaluation. After the mission has been defined and the basic configuration agreed upon, thousands of hours of detailed study must be spent upon the preliminary design before prototype construction can begin. Carefully built, geometrically and dynamically accurate scale models must be tested in wind tunnels to test the flying characteristics and to furnish information on the air load distribution in different flight conditions. Vibration and flutter induced by fluctuating air-flow patterns on wing, body and tail surfaces must be identified and evaluated.

Because designers are always pushing the state of the art to extreme limits and must work to the highest attainable strength-to-weight ratios in the use of materials, calculations must be exact. Margins for error are very small. Rule-of-thumb methods cannot be applied to airplane structural design. Simply to double the thickness (and therefore the weight) of any structural element to be certain of its strength or rigidity would be unthinkable. Each part must be examined in detail and then be designed for maximum efficiency. The problem is made doubly difficult because of uncertainty in determining the magnitude and exact location of points (or areas) of air loads on airplane structures. Often, actual full-scale structural components must be built and tested to destruction in laboratories to be certain that they will stand up under the dynamic and vibrational loads to be encountered in flight.

This detailed process may be repeated many times before the final design is accepted and the first prototype built. The assembled airframe is then subjected to many complicated load and vibrational tests to be certain that it will meet the intended strength specifications. After the power plants and all other auxiliary equipment are thoroughly tested for functional integrity on the ground, the complete machine is ready for flight testing.

This is always a critical operation. In spite of endless computations, the testing of components, and the experience and expectations of the designers, the actual performance of the airplane in flight cannot always be predicted with accuracy. In earlier days the question was whether or not the machine would fly at all; now it is whether or not the machine will fulfill all the expectations of the designer. A long series of well-engineered, well-instrumented test flights is usually required to guarantee that the original specifications for performance and safety have been met. For large aircraft this phase may last a year or more.

Even after such long and careful testing, it is not always possible to anticipate and to provide for all conditions that may be encountered in flight. On at least two occasions, large commercial airplanes that were exhaustively studied in design stages and subjected to rigorous testing on the ground and in the air subsequently experienced catastrophic failures in service. When working far out on the fringes of human knowledge, a totally unanticipated combination of events may lead to disaster. In such cases, the experience can only be recorded for future guidance.

II. CLASSIFICATION BY MISSION

Airplanes of any of the configurations discussed in the preceding section may be classified also by the use for which they are intended. The two broadest categories are civil and military. In some classes—for example, training and transport—the general appearance of civilian and military airplanes may be quite similar. In many details, however, they are different, and the specifications to which they are designed and manufactured differ materially.

A. Civil Airplanes

1. **Commercial Transport.**—This type of airplane is intended for carrying passengers or cargo, or both, for a profit. Commercial transports must be fast, efficient and reliable. (The jet transports of the 1960s cruised comfortably at 600–700 mph, depending on altitude.) For passenger service they must provide com-

BY COURTESY OF (ABOVE) RYAN AERONAUTICAL CO., (BELOW) VICKERS-ARMSTRONGS, LTD.

(ABOVE) "SPIRIT OF ST. LOUIS," RYAN MONOPLANE IN WHICH CHARLES A. LINDBERGH MADE THE FIRST SOLO NONSTOP FLIGHT BETWEEN NEW YORK AND PARIS, MAY 1927. (BELOW) SUPERMARINE S 6B, BRITISH SEAPLANE DESIGNED BY R. J. MITCHELL, SET THE WORLD'S SPEED RECORD AT 407.5 MPH IN 1931

(TOP LEFT) DE HAVILLAND ALBATROSS, BRITISH FOUR-ENGINED TRANSPORT OF 1937, A LOW-WING MONOPLANE WHICH SEATED 20-30 PASSENGERS. (TOP RIGHT) VICKERS VISCOUNT, 1948; THE FIRST TURBOPROP AIRLINER, THIS BRITISH MODEL WAS DESIGNED TO CARRY 48 PASSENGERS AT 315 MPH FOR 1,400 MI. (BOTTOM) DOUGLAS DC-8 SUPER 62, A U.S. JET, HAS A RANGE OF NEARLY 6,000 MI. AND CAN ACCOMMODATE UP TO 189 PASSENGERS

fortable seating, proper air conditioning (at all altitudes), and proper food services and toilet facilities consistent with the length of flights for which they are employed.

For short-haul service, where flights may be no more than one to two hours, personal conveniences can be minimized. For long runs, however (transcontinental or intercontinental), passengers will be aboard from 4 to 8 hours; thus more space per passenger and more service facilities are required. Such airplanes, moreover, must be provided with all available safety services and equipment. Extensive navigation and communication equipment must be supplemented by emergency gear for rapid and safe evacuation of the airplane on the ground or for emergency landings at sea.

Large airplanes for overseas or transcontinental use also require considerable crew space. In some cases as many as ten crew members are carried, including pilots, navigator, radio operator and cabin attendants. For the short-haul services two pilots and one cabin attendant make up the usual crew complement.

One of the most significant characteristics of commercial transport aircraft is the complete pressurization of the passenger and crew compartments. Modern airplanes, particularly if jet powered, operate most efficiently when flying at very high altitudes (25,000–40,000 ft.). At such heights the oxygen content of the atmosphere and the atmospheric pressure are both far below the limits of human tolerance, and it is necessary to supercharge all personnel spaces to somewhere near sea-level conditions. This means that the fuselage must be airtight, and air compressors must be provided to force sufficient extra air into the cabin to provide tolerable living conditions. Usually no attempt is made to reproduce actual sea-level conditions, but most airplanes maintain cabin temperatures and pressures equivalent to those prevailing at about 8,000 ft. above sea level, regardless of the actual flight altitude. Pilots and crews are readily conditioned to work at such equivalent altitudes, and the average passenger, if in normal health, can tolerate such conditions, particularly if seated and not doing any physical work.

All high-flying airplanes carry emergency oxygen supplies so that if the pressurizing system should fail, passengers can be supplied with oxygen until the airplane can descend to a lower altitude.

Most passenger airplanes, in addition to carrying the passengers' personal luggage, carry also a certain amount of cargo, usually mail or freight. Cargo and luggage commonly are carried in compartments at the bottom of the fuselage, easily accessible from the ground through doors and hatches.

Airplanes intended only for cargo carrying dispense with all the comforts and conveniences that are provided for passengers. The pilots' compartments are usually of the same design and arrangement as for passenger airplanes, but the interior equipment of the fuselage is reduced to a minimum. Sound insulation, an essential for passenger carriers, is usually nonexistent. Suitable anchor points are provided in the deck and interior walls so that cargo of a variety of shapes and sizes (barrels, boxes, crates, oil drums, etc.) may be safely secured. In addition, cabin doors are much larger than those required for passenger accommodation; in the case of very large airplanes designed to handle heavy equipment, built-in cargo hoists and rear-opening doors are provided.

During the period of transition from propeller-driven to jet-powered transports, many airlines used the older, internal-combustion-engine airplanes for cargo carrying. The passenger accommodations were removed, and the airplanes were modified with facilities for carrying cargo. Later, however, many of these older freight carriers were retired from service, and a number of jet transports were used as all-cargo carriers.

2. Industrial or Executive Transport.—With the world-wide spread of commerce and business enterprises and with the availability of good airports in many parts of the world and an extensive system of government-controlled airways, many commercial firms began to own and operate their own airplanes or fleets of airplanes. Such machines are used to transport personnel or goods from plant to plant or country to country. Many of the twin-engined airplanes that made up the fleets of air transport companies in the late 1940s or early 1950s were sold to nontransport business enterprises because they were largely replaced by four-engined or jet-powered airplanes on the airlines. A number of large companies (steel manufacturers, petroleum refiners, parts manufacturers, etc.) maintain their own fleets, their own pilot and flight personnel and even their own maintenance facilities.

Their airplanes operated under the same general conditions and operating requirements as airline airplanes. They carried suitable navigation and communication equipment to operate safely anywhere in the world. Many of them provided luxurious office and living accommodations for traveling executives. An increasing number are jet-powered and can equal commercial airliners in performance.

3. General Utility Airplanes.—Certain specialized forms of airplanes have been developed for commercial purposes apart from the transportation of passengers and goods.

One of the most common forms is the so-called crop duster,

designed to be flown at very low altitudes over growing crops to distribute insecticides or other forms of chemicals for the improvement or protection of crops. Such chemicals may be in the form of aerosols or finely divided powders. The airplanes must therefore be provided with proper containers and means of distribution and control, such as hopper valves, spray heads, etc.

These airplanes usually are single-engine craft of relatively small dimensions, flown by a single pilot. Primary requirements are good control at slow speeds and low altitudes, and safe maneuverability. Another desirable characteristic is the ability to land and take off from small, unprepared fields. This is one of the few categories of modern airplane in which the biplane type still persists.

Many farmers and cattle raisers in countries where large land holdings are commonplace use small airplanes for general survey and inspection purposes. These aircraft can also carry light equipment and supplies to outlying farm areas.

Oil companies, mining interests and professional aerial photographers use small airplanes in their businesses, but the airplanes generally are standard types in which specialized equipment has been installed. One such specialized use of aircraft in the more sparsely populated areas of the world is the Australian "Flying Doctor" service. Airplanes for such purposes must be sturdily built and dependable. In lake country they are often mounted on floats for off-water operations.

4. Private Airplanes.—The ownership of airplanes for pleasure or for personal convenience (entirely apart from business usage) is growing. Airplanes in this category range from small, single-seated, single-engined types, used purely for sport flying, to twin-engined airplanes capable of carrying eight to ten people in all types of weather along established airways.

At the lower end of the scale such private airplanes are rela-

BY COURTESY OF (BELOW) LOCKHEED AIRCRAFT CORP.; PHOTOGRAPH, (ABOVE) KEYSTONE

(ABOVE) CARRIER-BASED GRUMMAN WF-2; THE LARGE RADOME HOUSES LONG-RANGE DETECTION EQUIPMENT THAT PROVIDES EARLY WARNING TO FLEET UNITS. (BELOW) U-2 RECONNAISSANCE PLANE FURNISHES WEATHER, FALLOUT, RADIATION, AND PHOTOGRAPHIC DATA FROM FLIGHTS AT ALTITUDES UP TO 75,000 FT.

tively inexpensive and simple, designed to be flown only under fair conditions in the vicinity of suitable airports. At the other end of the scale, airplane ownership is expensive—comparable, indeed, to the ownership of seagoing yachts. Such airplanes are similar to small airliners and must be equipped with the same kinds of communication, navigation and survival gear. Between these two extremes is a wide range of aircraft for the private owner.

The majority of these airplanes are single-engined, cabin-type monoplanes, usually designed for two to four people, including the pilot. They are generally powered with air-cooled reciprocating engines, driving fixed-pitch propellers. Landing gear is simple, strong and, in some of the larger types, retractable in flight. Ease of control and ability to get in and out of small fields are highly desirable. A few private airplanes are mounted on floats for operation from water.

5. Training Airplanes.—In civil aviation the training airplane, as such, has practically disappeared. Pilots (or potential customers for private-aircraft purchases) are usually trained on the machines they intend to fly. These generally are in the small, private-owner class described above.

The essential element in a training type is the fitting of dual controls so that the instructor and pupil each can fly the airplane. Students usually begin by following through. The motions are made by the instructor, and the student gradually takes over control of the machine as he develops experience.

Good visibility for the pilot and pupil, ease of control, and sturdy landing gear are generally considered essential for training airplanes.

B. Military Airplanes

Until well into the middle of World War I the principal requirement of a military airplane was simply its ability to fly. If it proved successful in that particular, it often replaced cavalry or scouts as a means of collecting battlefield intelligence. Military leaders soon discovered, however, that the airplane had many more capabilities than simply to act as "flying eyes" for the army. Fighter aircraft evolved from the necessity of arming airplanes for their own protection. Specialized forms then began to be developed for many specific missions.

Generally speaking, whether for the army, navy or air force, all military aircraft fall into one or another of the following categories: (1) air-to-air combat (fighters); (2) ground support (attack); (3) air-to-ground bombardment (bombers); (4) surveillance (reconnaissance and command); (5) logistical support (transport and cargo carriers); (6) training (trainers); and (7) special missions (including research).

1. Fighter Airplanes.—The primary mission of fighter airplanes (for either air force or navy) is to secure the control of essential air spaces by attacking and destroying all types of enemy aircraft that may be operating in their area.

The opposition may consist of high-performance fighters of equal capability, or of high-altitude, high-speed bombers carrying armour or protective armament. For such purposes fighters must be capable of the highest possible performance in order to be able to outfly and outmaneuver opposing fighters; in addition, they must be armed with specialized weapons capable of hitting and destroying enemy aircraft.

At the speeds and altitudes at which such aircraft can operate, the problem of striking and destroying enemy aircraft becomes extremely complicated and requires an array of electronic, navigational and computing gear. A single-seated, high-performance fighter of the 1960s might weigh as much as, and be vastly more complicated than, many of the multiengined bombers of World War II. In many cases the search and attack functions are completely automatic, the pilot's role in combat being virtually reduced to monitoring the operation of the equipment. Indeed, with the most modern jet-powered fighter airplanes, a point has been reached where the performance capabilities of the machine far exceed the capabilities of a human pilot to control it.

In the so-called dogfighting aerial combat of World Wars I and II, pilots could recognize enemy aircraft and maneuver themselves into positions for combat by visual means. They controlled their

XB-70A SUPERSONIC TRANSPORT PATHFINDER AND BOMBER WITH TIPS OF DELTA WINGS FOLDED IN
HIGH-SPEED FLIGHT CONFIGURATION, AT AN ALTITUDE OF 15 MI.; RANGE APPROXIMATELY 7,600 MI.

machines manually and operated their guns by pressing triggers when they were in proper firing position. In supersonic aircraft at extremely high altitudes, such maneuvers were no longer possible. Human eyes and human reaction time are neither acute enough nor quick enough to bring two opposing aircraft within combat range or to aim and fire accurately and effectively. The modern fighter airplane must therefore be an almost completely automatic weapons system that will detect, identify, close with and open fire upon an enemy with very little help from the man in the cockpit. The pilot must rely upon electronic devices to find his enemy and upon electronic computers carried in his plane to lock onto his target and fire his guns at the proper moment. It is still his responsibility to take off and to fly his plane into combat areas, to decide when to engage in or to break off combat, and to return safely to base after combat; but during actual engagement (which may be a matter of only a few seconds) the pilot really is little more than a passenger.

In appearance a modern supersonic fighter bears a close relationship to a guided missile, with embryonic wing and tail surfaces. The fuselage is usually long, narrow and pointed, with the pilot's cockpit well forward in the nose. Wings are of short span, generally well swept back, frequently of delta configuration. Because of the somewhat peculiar weight distribution in the fuselage, with pilot and armament well forward and the heavy jet engine aft, the wing systems are generally located well to the rear of the fuselage, giving a characteristic long, needle-nosed look. The wings themselves are quite thin, and their surfaces are smooth and free from protuberances.

Very little space is available for the comfort of the pilot in a fighter airplane. Every available cubic inch in the airplane is utilized for the storage of fuel, ammunition, guns, computers, power plant and miscellaneous equipment.

The pilot's cockpit is heated and pressurized for high-altitude operation, but he must also wear protective pressurized clothing to enable him to withstand the high accelerations to which he is subject during high-speed maneuvers, together with a protective helmet for crash survival. Automatic ejection-type seats which incorporate parachutes are installed to provide emergency means of escape from fighter airplanes. When such equipment is operated, seat and pilot are literally blown out of the airplane, after which a parachute opens automatically.

Fighter airplanes for air force and naval use are basically similar in design and appearance. Fighters designed to operate from, and to land on, aircraft carrier decks, however, must be more stable, land at slower speeds and be fitted with proper catapult attachment gear and tail hooks to engage arresting gear for deck landings.

2. Attack Airplanes.—Attack airplanes closely resemble fighters but are designed to operate at lower altitudes and to carry rockets or other forms of missiles for use against ground targets. They may also be used as dive bombers. These planes are generally somewhat larger than the high-altitude fighters, with one or more engines mounted either in the fuselage or outboard on the wings. They are sometimes designed for extremely low-level attack, approaching their targets by profiling the ground at altitudes of 50 to 100 ft. They may thus effect surprise by their ability to approach their targets under defensive radar screens and get safely away before defensive armament can be brought to bear from the ground.

3. Bombing Airplanes.—Conventional bombers are designed to make high-altitude attacks against ground targets, using nuclear or conventional weapons. Prior to the era of nuclear warfare, bombers were usually relatively large and heavy, needing protection by high-speed fighter escorts against enemy attack.

With the advent of powerful jet engines, however, and the introduction of nuclear weapons of relatively small physical dimension and weight, it became possible to design long-range bombardment aircraft with performance capabilities approaching those of the best fighter types. Mach-2 and Mach-3 bombers (see MACH NUMBER) became theoretically possible, and with nuclear power plants, their range would be almost unlimited.

The long-range, high-altitude bomber is the basic offensive weapon of strategic air forces. By refueling in the air from flying tankers, such aircraft have flown around the world nonstop. However, it was claimed by some that intercontinental ballistic missiles rendered the long-range, high-altitude, manned bomber obsolete. Proponents of the bomber, on the other hand, argued that the presence of the crew on board the airplane provides an element of judgment lacking in the missile. Human navigators can make corrections in the flight plan which might be dictated by local conditions for which the unmanned missile could not possibly make allowance.

4. Reconnaissance Airplanes.—A knowledge of the enemy's whereabouts and intentions has always been of paramount importance in warfare. The airplane gave military commanders entirely new opportunities for reconnaissance, opportunities ranging from low-altitude observation of a battlefield from light, single-engined airplanes, to the continuous observation of an entire nation's industrial and military complex, using specially designed airplanes flying at very high altitudes and carrying highly refined photographic and other recording apparatus.

The classic method of aerial reconnaissance has been high-altitude photography, using techniques that were developed to a high degree during World War II. By taking photographs of a certain area at intervals and comparing them by very accurate photogrammetric techniques, it is possible to determine with a high degree of accuracy the kind and character of military installations or operations that may be in progress at the time (see PHOTOGRAMMETRY).

Later reconnaissance techniques, using radar, infrared or electronic radiations from ground targets, made it possible to identify certain military activities over very great distances. Such information is invaluable in determining the state of readiness or the intentions of a potential enemy. Modern high-speed airplanes of almost every type may be fitted out with photographic or other sensing apparatus for surveillance of enemy operations.

Except for certain specialized operations, the external configuration of the airplane is generally unaffected. Internally, cameras and associated equipment simply replace the guns and ammunition of the ordinary attack or fighter airplanes. An exception to this general rule is the antisubmarine warfare machine.

The detection of submerged submarines is a very difficult task, for which special airplanes were developed. A submarine traveling with only its snorkel above water is extremely difficult to detect on surface radars, and airplanes patrolling areas in which the presence of a submarine is suspected must be equipped with radar antennas of very large size if they are to be at all effective.

The housing of such radar antennas on a moving airplane presents a difficult aerodynamic problem and results in airplanes of unusual configuration. However, these ungainly looking machines play an essential part in antisubmarine warfare.

An example of a very specialized design for surveillance purposes was the American Lockheed U-2 airplane that was shot down over the territory of the U.S.S.R. early in 1960. This airplane represented an excellent design solution for the mission for which it was intended. Efficient cruising performance at very high altitudes was achieved by careful attention to aerodynamic and structural details. The machine had a very high aspect ratio, characteristic of high-performance sailplanes or gliders, for long-range cruising efficiency. Structural and equipment weights were kept to a minimum to yield a low wing loading (pounds per square foot of area) for the same reason. Its single turbine power plant was designed for long-range fuel economy at cruising speed at the design altitude. This is an example of a highly specialized design, of little practical value apart from the specific mission for which it was designed.

5. Transport Airplanes.—Although in general configuration military transport airplanes may resemble those used on civil airlines, the basic requirements differ greatly. Airline airplanes operate on regular schedules, along prescribed routes and between fixed terminals, where routine maintenance and servicing operations can be carried out regularly. Military transports, on the other hand, may be called upon to operate in any part of the world, in a wide range of climatic conditions, along unmarked routes and often from poorly prepared fields. The character of the cargo handled also is different from that carried in ordinary commercial services. Passenger accommodations need not be as spacious or luxurious and must be readily removable, in whole or in part, to accommodate cargo. In fact, for combat troop carrier operations personal comfort is a minor consideration.

BY COURTESY OF LOCKHEED AIRCRAFT CORP.

C-141 STARLIFTER FANJET CARGO-TROOP CARRIER CAPABLE OF TRANSPORTING 30 TONS OF CARGO OR 123 COMBAT TROOPS 6,000 MI. AT SPEEDS UP TO 500 MPH

For general cargo carrying, the facilities and equipment are similar to those described above for commercial cargo airplanes. Where air drop of military equipment (by parachute) is contemplated, airplanes are arranged so that large cargo packages or heavy equipment items (up to and including field artillery and light tanks) may be jettisoned from the rear of the airplane over the designated drop zone. For dropping paratroops extra doors are generally provided in the rear of transport airplanes so that the parachutists and their equipment can be evacuated from the airplane in the shortest possible time.

Very large military transport airplanes are capable of handling a number of trucks, tanks or other motor vehicles—or a complete intercontinental ballistic missile—in a single load. The cargo space of such airplanes may be of the order of 70 ft. in length and 15 to 20 ft. in diameter. Access to the cargo compartment is through large, double doors in the nose or near the tail of the airplane. Hoists and ramps are provided for easy loading of large and bulky pieces of equipment.

In the late 1950s the U.S. navy developed large cargo-carrying flying boats for operation at sea almost in the same way as light, cargo-carrying surface vessels. They were designed to load and discharge cargoes directly on beaches through doors and ramps at the bow. It was found, however, that loading, servicing and refueling were too time-consuming to be practical, and flying boats were abandoned in favour of large land-based airplanes.

A wide range of small civil-type airplanes are used in a number of ways by both the ground and air forces. Light, single-engined,

BY COURTESY OF LOCKHEED AIRCRAFT CORP.

YF-12A (A-11) INTERCEPTOR, DESIGNED TO FLY THREE AND ONE-HALF TIMES THE SPEED OF SOUND AT ALTITUDES IN EXCESS OF 90,000 FT. A SLIGHTLY DIFFERENT VERSION WITH AN OBSERVATION POD, DESIGNATED THE SR-71, IS A STRATEGIC RECONNAISSANCE PLANE

two-seated airplanes may be used in battle areas for rapid transport of staff officers or the evacuation of wounded. Four-, six- or eight-seated airplanes (single- or twin-engined) are also used for transporting military personnel or equipment. Built to more exacting specifications than the commercial versions, these light military transports are capable of operating successfully under difficult and hazardous conditions all over the world.

One highly specialized type of logistical support airplane is the flying tanker. The technique of refueling fighters and bombers in flight became commonplace after World War II. It is obvious that the tanker must be compatible with the airplane it is intended to serve; *i.e.*, it must be capable of flying at a range of speeds and altitudes at which the fighters and bombers fly.

Planes to be refueled approach the tanker from below and from the rear, where trailing tubes or a refueling hose can be picked up. With the planes flying in close formation, connections are established between the tanker's pumps and the aircraft to be refueled, and the required amount of fuel is transferred from one airplane to the other. One bomber or as many as three or four fighter airplanes may be refueled at the same time by a single tanker. Such operations came to be performed as a matter of routine by military aircraft. The record-breaking around-the-world flight of a U.S. bomber in 1958 was accomplished by refueling the airplane in this way.

6. Training Airplanes.—The complicated modern military airplane requires a high degree of skill on the part of pilots. Military training programs commonly make use of single-engined, piston-powered aircraft for primary training phases, with twin-jet trainers for transition stages. However, the British Royal Air Force in 1959 dispensed with piston-engined trainers and began initial pilot training on jet aircraft.

Primary training airplanes are generally of simplified construction, with a minimum of complicated equipment. The transition trainers are considerably more complicated. They are fast and highly maneuverable and can be fitted with a variety of complicated equipment found also in combat types.

Training in navigation is generally given on a class basis, in which groups of students are taken aloft in "flying classrooms," usually a twin-engined transport airplane containing a number of navigator's stations at which each student can make his own observations and computations while in the air.

Because the use of high-speed, high-performance military airplanes for training purposes is expensive, difficult and dangerous, a great deal of pilot and crew training came to be done on flight simulators. These consist of a completely instrumented airplane cockpit or flight deck installed in a classroom. By properly setting electronic controls, the instructor can present to the student, through the ordinary flight and navigation instruments, problems representing any conditions that may be encountered in actual flight. Some training machines are equipped to simulate visual and sound effects and even the motion of the aircraft. Flight simulators are expensive to build, but the saving of time and equipment is considerable, and invaluable hours of experience closely resembling that encountered in flight can be accumulated by the trainee on the ground. Not only military air services but the larger commercial airlines as well came to rely on flight simulators as an important training aid.

7. Research Airplanes and Special Types.—Apart from prototype and development models of airplanes designed for specific military uses, research projects involving special types of airplanes are sometimes sponsored by military departments. Such airplanes are not in themselves useful from the military standpoint, but they may lead to the discovery of new principles on which future military aircraft can be based. Such projects may range from a packaged single-engined, inflatable rubber airplane to the supersonic U.S. X-15, designed to explore the fringes of outer space. One strictly military application is the unmanned target drone. Any operational airplane, from a fighter to the largest bomber, may be fitted with radio-operated controls and used as a target by other airplanes using live ammunition. Sometimes drone airplanes have been flown through nuclear-bomb clouds, or in close proximity to nuclear explosions, to register the results of such

explosions on the aircraft and on equipment carried by it. More frequently, however, small, high-speed, relatively inexpensive unmanned airplanes are designed, built and flown as targets for air-to-air or ground-to-air gunnery or rocket practice. Many of these airplanes are powered by small turbojet engines.

Specialized research aircraft include ground-effect machines, heavily slotted and flapped airplanes designed for short landings and take-offs, and "convertiplane" configurations designed for vertical take-off and high-speed horizontal flight by the rotation of complete wing and propeller systems from vertical to horizontal positions.

Two of the more important of these nonconventional types are the STOL (Short Take-Off and Landing) and VTOL (Vertical Take-Off and Landing) aircraft. The exact definition of a short take-off and landing aircraft has not yet been standardized. Two definitions that have been employed are: (1) take-off and landing over a 50-ft. obstacle in less than 500 ft.; and (2) take-off and landing over a 50-ft. obstacle in less than 5 aircraft lengths. In either case such take-off and landing performance requirements confront the designer with a unique set of problems.

A conventional airplane derives the majority of its lift from its relative motion with respect to the air. In order to take off it must accelerate until its minimum speed is sufficient to keep it airborne. In its landing maneuver it decelerates from a similar speed. If conventional lifting systems were to be employed for STOL aircraft, the resulting accelerations and decelerations would in all probability be unacceptably great unless the minimum flight speeds were very low. As a consequence, STOL aircraft endeavor to utilize appreciable amounts of their thrust in a vertical direction to reduce the lift load that must be generated by their conventional lifting systems (wings, flaps, slats, etc.). For vertical flight the entire vertical force is achieved by some power-driven device that produces a vertical thrust equal to the weight.

Many arrangements for achieving successful vertical flight or short landings and take-offs have been designed or are under investigation. The first and so far the most successful is the helicopter. In this design the rotor produces the necessary lift, and translational motion is achieved by tilting the rotor plane in the desired direction. Greater thrust can be achieved by the addition of separate propulsive engines driving conventional propellers.

In some designs attempts have been made to reduce the high-speed vibration and drag of the rotor by the addition of stub wings that produce appreciable lift loads at high forward speeds, thereby unloading the rotor in this critical regime. The disadvantage of such arrangements is that, in hovering, the down-wash of the rotor produces large down loads on such wings, thereby compromising

WIDE WORLD

B-52 BOMBER AT 45,000 FT. DROPPING AN X-15 SPACE RESEARCH ROCKET PLANE. THE X-15 REACHED SPEEDS IN EXCESS OF 4,000 MPH AND ALTITUDES ABOVE 67 MI.

the hovering performance. In an attempt to avoid this difficulty, several alternate approaches have been attempted. These have ranged from tilting the entire aircraft through 90° after a vertical take-off from a tail sitting position, to tilting the power plants or the power plants and wings in combination. Propellers and rotors have been employed in many designs, and pure jet aircraft have also been used.

Irrespective of the technique employed to achieve the vertical thrusting force, all of these machines have certain problems in common. The first of these is the highly detrimental effect of the high-energy slip stream or jet striking the ground. Any loose material is thrown around with violence and forms a severe hazard both to the machine and to any personnel in the vicinity.

Because the entire lifting force arises from the engines in the hovering or low-speed regimes, power failure might prove to be catastrophic. The designer must therefore strive for the highest possible reliability and also provide adequate emergency systems to ensure the safety of the machine and its occupants.

The last major problem is that of low-speed stability and control. Because there is little or no flow over the normal control surfaces, entirely different types of controls must be utilized in the low-speed regime. Many different control systems, ranging from auxiliary jets and fans to differential control of the engines and propellers, are under study, but no single system has demonstrated clear superiority.

All of the aeronautical configurations described above are manufactured in small numbers and are then put through exhaustive test and evaluation programs at civil and military test centres.

See also references under "Airplane" in the Index.

BIBLIOGRAPHY.—Douglas Rolfe, *Airplanes of the World From Pusher to Jet, 1490–1954* (1955); M. J. B. Davy, *Interpretive History of Flight* (1937); Svante Stubelius, *Airship, Aeroplane, Aircraft: Studies in the History of Terms for Aircraft in English* (1958); Newton H. Anderson, *Aircraft Layout and Design* (1946); D. M. Desoutter, *All About Aircraft* (1954); Harold E. Baughman, *Aviation Dictionary and Reference Guide,* 3rd ed. rev. by E. J. Gentle and C. E. Chapel (1951); Gerald Pollinger and William Green, *Aircraft of the World,* rev. ed. (1956); Hugh Melvin Samuelson, *The Executive Aircraft* (1963); Frederick Gordon Swanborough, *Turbine-Engined Airliners of the World* (1963); John W. R. Taylor (ed.), *Jane's All the World's Aircraft* (annual).
(S. P. J.)

AIRPORT, a land or water area on which aircraft may land, and from which they may ascend. Airports are also called airdromes (aerodromes), air terminals, air parks and air fields. In addition to the basic provision of a runway for aircraft operations, an airport must provide additional facilities in varying degree according to the functions and volume of operations planned for it. Airport runways, locations, control towers, passenger and cargo terminals, lighting, and standards for construction and operation are the major topics discussed in this article.

Runways.—A conventional heavier-than-air craft requires forward speed through the air in order to sustain flight. Attainment of the required speed is accomplished by means of a runway on which the aircraft is accelerated forward from a standing position to the take-off speed. The runway is used in the opposite manner for a landing. The aircraft is brought down to the runway at a speed which will just barely sustain flight, and then after the airplane is on the ground it is braked to a stop.

The runways are strips of the over-all airport area and are usually hard-surfaced with concrete or asphalt. In the case of a water surface for seaplane operations, the principles involved are the same, and protected strips of water are utilized for transferring the seaplane from water to air and return. In the case of ground facilities for helicopters, advantage is taken of the fact that these aircraft can rise and descend vertically. Even so, a limited area of land must be made available for maneuvering and landing purposes in helicopter operations.

Configuration.—An aircraft's speed is relative to the speed of the air in which the aircraft flies. Thus if an airplane is coming in to make a landing at a speed of 100 mph and is flying directly into a wind of 20 mph, the airplane's speed over the ground is only 80 mph. When this airplane touches a runway, the heading of which coincides with the wind direction, the airplane must slow down to a stop from 80 mph; in this case, the wind helps it to

slow down. If the airplane had landed with the wind, it would have been going over the ground at 120 mph. It can be seen that a basic advantage is gained in bringing an airplane to a stop by heading it into the wind.

In the early days of aviation large open grass-covered fields were normally used for airports. Known as landing fields, these airports allowed a pilot to head directly into the wind to aid take-off and landing operations. The early aircraft were light in weight and could be supported by grass turf. Furthermore, the early aircraft were very sensitive to wind currents, and it was important for them to be headed directly into the wind for both take-off and landing. Under these circumstances an open field which could be utilized for take-off or landing in any direction became the most desirable type of airport.

In the 1920s, when aircraft became so heavy that hard surfaces were required to keep them from sinking into the turf or mud, efforts were still made to allow take-offs and landings in any desired direction. Several airports were constructed with large pads or hard surfaces in the middle of the landing fields, which allowed the aircraft to head in any direction for take-off or landing. Most airports, however, met the need for hard surfaces by the construction of concrete or asphalt runways. The aircraft of the 1920s —and to a lesser extent, of the 1930s—were still sensitive to cross winds, and most airports were provided with several runways in order that pilots could choose one having a minimum amount of cross wind at the time of take-off or landing. Furthermore, a study of wind directions and velocities for a particular airport location always preceded runway layout—as it still does today. These studies allow the runways to be so laid out as to minimize the amount of cross-wind operations required.

As aircraft have become heavier and faster, they have become less sensitive to cross winds. As a result, the number of runways required per airport has been reduced. A good example of this trend is shown by the experience at LaGuardia Airport, New York City. When this airport was designed and constructed in the late 1930s, it was equipped with four runways, enabling pilots to land or take off in eight different directions. In the mid-1940s one of the runways was closed because it was too short for the large four-engined planes then being introduced. This deserted runway was then converted to aircraft parking purposes. In the late 1950s a second runway at LaGuardia was closed, leaving just two runways, with four possible directions for take-off or landing.

In some localities it has been found practical to operate from a single runway. The runway at Hong Kong, commissioned in the late 1950s, is an example of single runway operation.

In addition to the numbers of runways necessary to provide orientation with respect to the wind, there must be enough runways to provide adequate capacity for heavy traffic areas. By the 1960s a number of airports had been equipped with dual runways which permit simultaneous handling of incoming and outgoing traffic or provide extra capacity for the handling of heavier traffic in one direction. Other configurations include tangential schemes, where the runways in effect radiate tangentially from a centre which serves as the terminal area. Simultaneous operations are carried on, with incoming aircraft landing toward the terminal area, and outgoing aircraft taking off in a direction away from the terminal area.

Lengths.—As aircraft have become faster, heavier and of longer-range operation, the requirement for runway length has grown. Table I shows how this growth has taken place for commercial passenger aircraft. The trend has been similar for military aircraft.

The runway lengths shown in this table are based upon standard sea level conditions; actually, the length of runway required for take-off depends somewhat upon the density of the air. When the temperature is high, the density of the air is relatively low and the aircraft requires a longer than usual run along the runway before it can take off. The altitude of the airport also affects the air density. The airport at La Paz, Bol., must have much longer runways at its altitude of approximately 12,000 ft. than would be required were La Paz at sea level.

The lower air densities at high altitudes require all aircraft to accelerate for a longer distance along the runway before attaining flight speed. The airplane must move along the runway at a sufficient speed to deflect downward a given mass of air. If the air is

TABLE I.—*Runway Lengths*

Aircraft description	Time of introduction	Runway length required
Twin-engined 20-passenger plane with 180 mph speed and 24,000 lb. weight . .	mid-1930s	3,000 ft.
4-engined 50-passenger plane with 240 mph speed and 65,000 lb. weight . .	mid-1940s	4,500 ft.
4-engined 60-passenger plane with 325 mph speed and 85,000 lb. weight . .	late 1940s	5,500 ft.
4-engined 80-passenger plane with 360 mph speed and 120,000 lb. weight .	early 1950s	6,500 ft.
4-engined 110-passenger jet plane with 550 mph speed and 300,000 lb. weight.	late 1950s	8,500 ft.
4-engined 250-passenger jet plane with 600 mph speed and 350,000 lb. weight. .	mid-1960s	10,000 ft.

of relatively low density (high temperature or high altitude), the airplane must move faster to deflect the same mass of air, and to move faster the airplane must run along the ground for a longer distance.

In addition to providing sufficient length for the ground run on take-off and landing, a runway must be sufficiently long to allow for emergency conditions, such as an engine failure. Under governmental regulations prevailing in most countries, all aircraft designed and constructed after 1940 must have the capability, should an engine fail during take-off, of being able either to continue its take-off successfully with the power remaining from those engines still operating or to come to a stop. These regulations thereby establish on the runway a point before which an aircraft taking off must be brought to a stop should an engine fail, and after which the aircraft must be capable of continuing and sustaining flight with its remaining power.

Some airports utilize arresting gear at the ends of runways for emergency purposes. This gear is designed to stop an airplane should it for any reason not be able to complete take-off or come to a stop on the runway. Military operations of the gear have been highly successful.

Surfaces.—Both asphalt and concrete have been used extensively for airport runway surfaces and for secondary surfaces, such as taxi ways and aircraft parking ramps. Each of these surfaces has its own advantages. For example, concrete is more visible under nighttime landing conditions, while the black surface of asphalt aids snow clearing during winter months by absorbing heat and thereby speeding the melting process.

The friction (resistance to motion) of runway surfaces began to assume increasing importance during the late 1950s and 1960s because of the long runway requirements of new aircraft being introduced at that time. In the Scandinavian areas an instrument which indicates values of the coefficient of friction of runway surfaces when the surfaces are covered by snow or rain water has been used. This instrument has been considered as a useful means for advising the pilot in the air as to what braking action he could expect at a runway. Such meters, if found fully practical, would be of use at airports all over the world.

Location of Airports.—The utility of an airport in serving a community is partially determined by its convenience of location to the businesses and residents served. Whereas the major trans-

portation terminals for railroads, steamship lines and bus companies have been located in central metropolitan locations, the comparatively large land area required for airports, together with the need for a minimum of surrounding obstructions, has required relatively remote locations.

Most airport locations for the major cities of the world were selected and activated in the 1920s and 1930s. At the time of selection they generally represented a compromise between convenience of location and requirement for space and minimum obstructions. As aircraft have become larger and faster, they have required larger airports, and in a number of instances new locations became necessary. In the 1940s London, New York, Los Angeles, Calif., Baltimore, Md., Paris, and other cities moved commercial air traffic to larger airports usually located more remotely than the previous airports. In the 1950s and 1960s a few new airports were opened, but by and large the expansion of aviation facilities took the form of runway lengthening and terminal building enlargement or replacement. The locations and distances of a number of the major commercial airports of the world are given in Table II.

The situation at Detroit represents an interesting example in the trends of location. In the 1930s the airlines used the City Airport, only $5\frac{1}{2}$ mi. from the downtown area. In the mid-1940s, however, it was necessary to move to a larger airport because of the requirement for longer runways by the new aircraft then being introduced. The only available airport with suitable runway lengths was Willow Run, which is 31 mi. from Detroit. The need for a more conveniently located airport was felt keenly throughout the late 1940s and early 1950s. In the late 1950s a number of airlines moved their operations to the "Metropolitan" airport.

In the case of London the movement was from Croydon before World War II to Heathrow in the late 1940s, with Gatwick coming into service in the late 1950s to share the commercial load with Heathrow. Croydon could not be enlarged; it accommodated private flying until it was closed as an airport and converted to other purposes in the late 1950s.

Airport Communities.—Large airports have proved to be centres of self-created business and commerce. In a number of instances where airports have been constructed in relatively remote areas, housing has been constructed to accommodate airport workers, motels and hotels have been erected to accommodate travelers, businesses have found that travel and shipping advantages are obtained by having airport locations for offices and manufacturing plants, and airport communities have therefore grown into being.

Drainage and Soil.—One of the most important considerations governing the location and selection of an airport site is the nature and composition of the soil and subsoil upon which the airport is to be built. For the economical development of the area for aviation purposes, and especially for the life and durability of paved runways, taxi strips and aprons, detailed knowledge of the soil at the site, and especially its behaviour in contact with water, is vitally important.

Adequate drainage is especially essential to the proper maintenance of paved runways, for experience shows that more runway paving failures occur because of unstable subsoil conditions caused by lack of proper drainage than for any other reason.

Airport Control Towers.—In order to keep the air traffic within the immediate vicinity of the airport on an organized basis and to provide maximum protection against collision, a control tower is located at any airport having an appreciable amount of air traffic. The control tower operators normally talk by radio with pilots of arriving and departing aircraft to give them traffic directions and to notify them of the exact positions of other aircraft in the area. They also assign landing positions to incoming aircraft when there is more than one aircraft in the so-called landing pattern. The landing pattern represents the traffic flow of aircraft existing at any one time under the existing wind conditions. Thus a typical landing instruction from a control tower operator might be: "Eastern 33, you are number one to land; American 42, you are number two to land, follow Eastern in . . ." Under these circumstances the pilot of the American Airlines plane makes sure

TABLE II.—*Major Commercial Airports*

City	Airport	Code	Miles from downtown
Buenos Aires, Arg. . .	Ezeiza	EZE	32
Chicago, Ill. . . .	O'Hare	ORD	16
Detroit, Mich. . .	Metropolitan	DTW	16
Geneva, Switz. . .	Cointrin	GVA	3
Hong Kong . .	Kai Tak	HKG	$4\frac{1}{2}$
London, Eng. . .	Heathrow	LHR	15
	Gatwick	LGW	27
Los Angeles, Calif. .	International	LAX	14
Moscow, U.S.S.R. . .	Sheremetyevo	SVO	15
	Vnukovo	VKO	18
New York, N.Y. . .	La Guardia	LGA	8
	J. F. Kennedy Int'l.	JFK	17
Paris, France. . .	Le Bourget	LBG	$9\frac{1}{2}$
	Orly	ORY	$9\frac{1}{2}$
Rome, Italy . .	Leonardo Da Vinci	FCO	22
Tokyo, Japan . .	International	TYO	11
Washington, D. C. . .	National	DCA	$4\frac{1}{2}$
	Dulles	DIA	27

he sees the position of the Eastern Air Lines plane, and pilots of any following planes conduct their operation likewise. At the major airports tower operators also watch the progress of aircraft in their control area on radar scanning screens.

In addition to directing the traffic flow in the air, the control tower operators must direct aircraft on the ground. When traffic becomes too heavy for one set of control tower operators to handle both air and ground traffic, the job is divided between two different groups of tower operators, one group directing traffic in the air, the other directing traffic on the ground.

Passenger Terminals.—Purchase or confirmation of tickets, checking of baggage, and boarding of aircraft are accomplished at the passenger terminal. In addition to these basic functions, the modern terminal building is being used more and more not only to accommodate waiting passengers but also to house shops, banks, restaurants, drug stores, hotels, etc.

Boarding Systems.—The systems for boarding passengers onto their aircraft have undergone extensive analysis and development, but as of the mid-1960s there was no standard system for getting passengers from the terminal to the aircraft. Two systems have been in prevalent use: the trickle system and the group movement system. In the trickle system the airplane is parked at the gate approximately 20–30 minutes before departure and the departure time is announced. The passengers then trickle onto the airplane with check-in procedures stretched out over the trickle period. In the group movement system the passengers are assembled in a group. All processing is then completed before they are moved in a group to the aircraft immediately before departure.

Ownership.—Passenger terminals and the airports on which they are located are normally owned and operated by some agency of the state or city government. In some instances they are operated by publicly owned authorities (such as the Port of New York authority, which operates the airports of metropolitan New York City) which function under the administration of the state or other governmental appointed administration.

Cargo Terminals.—During the period immediately after World War II there was serious discussion about the possible establishment of separate airports for use by cargo aircraft exclusively. Detailed consideration of the problems involved showed that such establishment would not relieve air traffic congestion or airport congestion because the heavy traffic periods for passenger traffic and cargo traffic do not coincide. Cargo nearly always moves at night. The shipper wants the cargo to be removed from his dock in the late afternoon and to be on the dock of the consignee early in the morning. Such a schedule calls for the cargo aircraft to be departing about midnight, when passenger traffic is at a low ebb. Also, much of the cargo moves on combination passenger-cargo aircraft, and it is therefore advantageous for both cargo and passenger terminals to be located at the same airport.

Cargo terminals are utilized largely for processing and sorting cargo as to destination. Through the mid-1960s, the majority of cargo moving by air did so in less than plane-load shipments. Therefore, the terminals were being used as marshaling points for full plane loads as well as distribution points for transfer to combination passenger-cargo aircraft. The growth of air cargo in the 1960s brought about corresponding increases in the number of all-cargo aircraft and necessitated construction of vast cargo terminals at the major airports. The means of transfer from terminal to aircraft were many and varied. They included forklift trucks with pallets, cargo cart trains, endless belt conveyors, and lift-bed trucks.

Delivery of cargo at the terminals was practically 100% by truck, and the usual air cargo terminal was equipped with a truck level floor, at least for its receiving dock. The eventual use of full plane load shipments would permit the development of cargo terminals having direct transfer design features.

Airport Lighting.—Of increasing interest to airport operators and those who use airports is the matter of lighting. The revolving searchlight with green on the reverse side of the white beacon has long been the mark of an active airport.

Of maximum interest to pilots are the high-intensity approach lights which were introduced in the late 1940s and have become a standard installation item for all busy airports. These lights are normally installed along a line leading up to the runway, thereby directing the pilot to the active runway. The line of lights is normally along the centre-line extension of the runway and may extend beyond the bounds of airport property.

Other lighting installations at airports include runway lights which can be turned on or off by individual controls for each runway. The control tower operator can therefore turn on a set of lights which outlines both sides of the runway in use at the time. Runway lights are white, slightly elevated from the ground and are spaced 200 ft. apart along each side of the runway. Green threshold lights are placed across the ends of runways. Lights are installed along taxi-ways (along which aircraft move between runways, terminal areas, and maintenance hangar areas) for guidance of pilots at night. By international agreement, these taxi-way lights are blue in colour. Recently developed airport visual landing aids which assist pilots include in-runway lighting (touch down zone, runway centre-line and taxi-way turn off lighting), visual approach slope indicators, and runway end identifier lights.

Red obstruction lights clearly mark all obstructions surrounding an airport. High obstructions such as radio towers, are identified by flashing red lights at the top and intermediate levels and by markings of alternate bands of orange and white paint.

Air markers, signs painted or constructed on roofs or on the ground or painted directly on highways, are especially valuable to private flyers. The marker letters should be 10–20 ft. high and legible under good visibility conditions from a height of at least 3,000 ft. Runway and taxi-way markings, which consist of numbers, letters, and lines painted directly on the airport pavements, also furnish valuable visual guidance to pilots. These markings identify the runways, taxi-ways, holding points, centre-lines, and edges of runways and restricted areas.

Standards for Construction and Operation.—In order that logical construction criteria may be applied generally to airports, the governments of individual countries normally establish airport construction standards. The International Civil Aviation Organization (ICAO) also adopted standards and recommended practices that prescribe the physical and associated characteristics to be possessed by and the equipment to be provided at airports used or intended to be used for the operations of airplanes engaged in international air navigation. The ICAO airport specifications prescribe the appropriate relationship between a number of different physical characteristics. Following are the major items covered by these standards:

Runways—number, orientation, basic length, width, separation of parallel runways, slopes, and surfaces.
Taxiways—width, minimum clearances, slopes, strength, and surface.
Aprons—size, strength, slopes, and surface.
Landing strips—width, length, and slopes.
Clearways and stopways—location and dimensions.
Visual ground aids—runway marking and lighting.
Obstruction removal and marking.

While the construction standards establish various categories of airports, the purpose to which each individual airport is to be put is determined by the airline operators. Although a given airport may have been classified for short domestic flights, traffic demand and airline planning may require the airport's use for long-range flights. Under these circumstances, the airport runway length or surrounding obstructions may be restrictive to the aircraft operation. Also, an aircraft with relatively limited airport performance may not be able to operate at full design weights out of existing airports.

Limitation of airport funds, as well as natural and physical obstacles to expansion programs, often curtail scheduled airline operations. In order for an airline to operate safely and efficiently under these conditions, it is necessary for it to establish and maintain specifications for take-off weights and landing weights at each airport on its system. These specifications establish weights based upon existing temperature and wind at time of take-off for each operating runway at each airport.

See AVIATION, CIVIL; *see* also references under "Airport" in the Index.   (R. D. SP.)

London airport (Heathrow), showing the runways and terminal buildings. One of two commercial airports serving London, it is equipped with two separate terminal areas, one for short-haul European flights, the other for long-distance intercontinental flights

John F. Kennedy International airport (Idlewild), Queens, New York city. Under construction since 1942, it has facilities for accommodating all types of aircraft traffic, ranging from local commuter helicopters to long-distance transcontinental jet planes

TWO OF THE WORLD'S BUSIEST AIRPORTS

Zürich airport at Kloten, Switz., 7½ mi. from Zürich, showing the terminal building, with built-in control tower, and the passenger loading area

Expressway leading to the main entrance of the terminal building (foreground) of Orly International airport, Paris. The major airport construction was completed in the early 1960s

Gatwick airport, London, showing the 7,000-ft. runway. Built alongside the London-to-Brighton railway (foreground), it was the first airport in the world to contain road, rail and air services in one unit

Runway at Kai Tak airport, Hong Kong. The airstrip, built on a man-made promontory in Kowloon bay, is 8,350 ft. long and equipped to handle the heaviest jet aircraft traffic

O'Hare International airport, Chicago, Ill., showing the passenger terminals and aircraft parked along the loading tunnels. Major construction was completed in 1963

OTHER MAJOR AIRPORTS OF THE WORLD

BY COURTESY OF (TOP LEFT) SWISSAIR, (CENTRE LEFT) B.E.A., (CENTRE RIGHT) HONG KONG GOVERNMENT PUBLIC RELATIONS OFFICE; PHOTOGRAPHS, (TOP RIGHT) AÉROPORT DE PARIS, (BOTTOM) METRO NEWS PHOTOS

Pinwheel passenger loading ramps at San Francisco airport. Telescopic corridors connect the terminal to entrances at front and back of DC-8 jet airliners

Central telephone office, Rome airport. Equipped to handle 2,000 simultaneous calls, it is able to service the requirements of flight assistance, internal airport traffic, administration and information

Customs office in the International Arrival building at John F. Kennedy (Idlewild) airport, showing the "supermarket" inspection system employed for examining the baggage of incoming passengers

Shopping area on the second floor of the terminal building, Orly International airport. The nine-story building is a miniature city. Its facilities include a postoffice, theatre, hotels, restaurants and chapel

Loading operations at the cargo terminal of Stapleton airfield, Denver, Colo. Freight is being loaded into a Douglas cargo aircraft by means of mobile, power-driven conveyer ramps

PASSENGER AND CARGO OPERATIONS

PHOTOGRAPHS, (TOP LEFT) AUTHENTICATED NEWS, (TOP RIGHT) HAMILTON WRIGHT ORGANIZATION INC., (CENTRE LEFT) D. JORDAN WILSON—PIX FROM PUBLIX, (CENTRE RIGHT) AÉROPORT DE PARIS, (BOTTOM) RALPH MORGAN AND ASSOCIATES

PLATE IV

AIRPORT

T-shaped landing apron of Westland heliport, on the Thames, London. Opened in 1959, it was designed to accommodate all types of British and U.S. helicopters currently in use

Electronic flash approach system at Cleveland-Hopkins airport, Cleveland, O. Moving bursts of light (top) supplement the regular approach lights to guide plane under poor visibility conditions

New York downtown heliport on the East river, showing the 80- by 85-ft. landing strip. Manhattan's second heliport, put into operation in 1960, it provided 22 daily flights to and from LaGuardia, John F. Kennedy (Idlewild) and Newark (N.J.) airports

View of the main terminal building and loading area at Orly International airport seen from inside the control tower. Originally located at the eastern end of the field, the tower eventually was to be rebuilt on top of the terminal building

Newark, N.J., airport control tower at night. The 150-ft. tower, located between the two active runways, is electronically equipped to guide air and ground aircraft traffic

SPECIALIZED AIRPORTS AND CONTROL OPERATIONS

BY COURTESY OF (CENTRE RIGHT) THE PORT OF NEW YORK AUTHORITY; PHOTOGRAPHS, (TOP LEFT) UNITED PRESS INTERNATIONAL, (TOP RIGHT) CENTRAL PRESS, (BOTTOM LEFT) DALMAS— PIX FROM PUBLIX, (BOTTOM RIGHT) AUTHENTICATED NEWS

AIR POWER. The U.S. naval historian Alfred Thayer Mahan defined sea power (*q.v.*) as the ability to use the element to go where desired when convenient and to prevent the enemy from doing likewise. Because, far more than the sea, the ocean of the air is three-dimensional and has neither shallows nor bottlenecks, complete command of the air has been almost impossible without the use of overwhelming force. In naval warfare narrow straits such as those at Gibraltar or Malacca could be controlled, and canals such as Suez and Panama could be closed. But there are no such natural passages in the air. Thus the doctrines of air power, which have tended to be dogmatic to the point of absolutism, have so far not worked out in practice during actual air warfare.

In the 20th century theory about air power blossomed rapidly as advocates fought the conservatism of the officers dominating the other, older branches of the armed forces. Especially during periods of peace, this need to make their way against the established branches caused airmen to make claims which, because of technological limitations, they were later unable to substantiate. Thus, air power has generally seemed less effective during wars than the public had been led to believe it would be in prewar years. That was particularly true of strategic bombing before the advent of the atomic bomb in 1945. However, tactical air power achieved some notable successes as in the German blitzkriegs of 1940 and in Allied operations in Europe in 1944–45 and the naval operations in the Pacific throughout World War II.

This article covers the doctrine and history of air power. It is divided into the following sections:

I. The Doctrine of Air Power
    1. Origins of Theory
    2. Influence of Douhet
    3. Basic Tenets of the Douhet Philosophy
    4. The Test in World War II
    5. Nuclear Weapons and Missiles
    6. The Philosophy of Limited War: Korea; Vietnam
II. History of Air Warfare
    A. Early Organizational and Technological Developments
    B. World War I
        1. Equipment and Organization
        2. Tactical Air Support
        3. Long-Range Bombing
        4. Naval Aviation
    C. Interwar Years
        1 Evolution of Separate Air Forces
        2. Technological Developments
        3. Interwar Air Defense Systems
        4. Use of Air Power
    D. World War II
        1. Strength of Air Forces
        2. Campaign in Europe, 1939–40
        3. Battle of Britain
        4. The Mediterranean
        5. War in the Soviet Union
        6. Strategic Air Offensive Against Germany
        7. Battle of the Atlantic
        8. Invasion of Fortress Europe
        9. Italian Campaign
       10. Pilotless Aircraft and Rocket Campaign
       11. Air War in the Pacific
    E. Air Power in the Cold War
        1. Post-World War II Air Forces
        2. Guided Missiles
        3. Postwar Air Defense Systems
    F. Air Power in Limited Wars
        1. Korean War
        2. Minor Conflicts
        3. War in Vietnam
        4. Summary

I. THE DOCTRINE OF AIR POWER

By the end of World War I the doctrines of air power had already been fairly well developed. The definition took a number of different forms. First, there was the popular conception of Brig. Gen. William "Billy" Mitchell, who said that air power is "anything that flies." Second was the development by Giulio Douhet in Italy, Sir Frederick Sykes, P. R. C. Groves, and Sir Hugh Trenchard in Britain, and by the U.S. Army school at San Antonio, Tex., of the concept that air power was strategic bombing. This latter term denotes aerial attack upon targets usually well beyond the zones of ground and naval fighting—targets which mainly contain the bases of enemy strength or of his potential military power. Third was the tactical concept of air power as used in direct conjunction with surface forces.

The strategic bombing view of air power emphasizes its independence from land and naval power in structure, operations, and mission. It is thus differentiated from other forms of military aviation, such as naval aviation operated from ships or naval shore stations and the so-called tactical aviation; *i.e.*, the operations of military aircraft in direct support of fighting ground forces. As one might expect, in practice these forms tend to merge. Naval aircraft operated from aircraft carriers may be used to attack enemy strategic targets ashore. Also, aircraft operating in direct support of armies will usually be operated and controlled by the same national air force which controls the strategic bombing force, and they may, in fact, comprise segments of that force. In addition, a type of attack known as interdiction bombing falls somewhere between strategic and close-support bombing; it is directed against targets, such as transportation bottlenecks, that are usually far behind enemy lines.

The implements of air power formerly comprised only military aircraft and supporting facilities, such as air bases. Now air power is considered to embrace also guided missiles wherever those missiles have taken over the functions of aircraft rather than merely of artillery. The difference is, of course, one of range. There is some tendency to use "space power" for long-range or intercontinental ballistic missiles, but space power has not yet and may never become operationally distinct from air power.

The concept of air power today may also include military air transport, which made a notable contribution in World War II, and also the aircraft industry. The comparable maritime elements were included by Mahan in his definition of sea power.

A final problem of identification concerns defense against strategic air attack, especially active defenses. These comprise instruments for shooting down attacking planes, as differentiated from passive defenses, which are concerned rather with the protection of targets through various forms of dispersion, concealment, and "hardening" (or armouring, as in shelters). One would logically suppose that active defenses against attacking air power would also be considered to be an essential part of air power, but in these matters logic rarely prevails. Traditionally, the part of the active defenses that comprises fighter aircraft, known at one time as interceptors, was identified with air power, whereas the operation of antiaircraft guns was entirely an army function. When ground-to-air missiles of various ranges began to take over the functions of both antiaircraft guns and interceptors, the allocation of duties, functions, or missions became blurred. In the United States the short-range defensive missiles, such as the Nike-Hercules, were operated by the Army; the long-range missiles, such as the Titan, were operated by the Air Force. In other countries the pressure of actual combat conditions forced closer cooperation as early as World War I. This developed in part because not until late in the war was any air force established as a separate military entity. In Britain in both world wars a tight working liaison was established between guns and aircraft and the same was true in Germany in World War II. Commonly guns were concentrated close to potential targets or along coasts and corridors, while defending aircraft roamed the air between.

1. Origins of Theory.—Practically all theorizing about air power, as distinct from operational doctrine, has been concerned with establishing and emphasizing the importance of strategic bombing as a method of warfare. Because of the opposition in the older branches of the military to this point of view, much of the literature on the subject has, in fact, been polemical. Outstanding among the air power polemicists have been the U.S. Brig. Gen. William Mitchell (*q.v.*), the Englishman P. R. C. Groves, and the Italian Brig. Gen. Giulio Douhet. But only the latter two were sufficiently gifted dialectically to be able to develop publicly a coherent philosophy of the use of air power as a distinctive and independent method of warfare.

The basic ideas that Douhet was later to elaborate were, however, advanced in British and U.S. official circles more than a

DRAWING OF A PROPOSED SCHEME OF NAPOLEON I TO INVADE ENGLAND.
FEATURING AIRBORNE TROOPS IN BALLOONS, RIGHT. ANTICIPATED BARRAGE
BALLOON DEFENSE, LEFT, HAD ITS MODERN COUNTERPART IN WORLD WAR II

The effect of this new thinking in the U.S. was also absorbed and exercised through the Bolling mission (headed by Col. R. C. Bolling) that left for Europe in the middle of 1917 to gather information about military aviation in Britain, France, and Italy. Its members were considerably influenced by an Italian plane designer, Giovanni Caproni, who was a close friend of Douhet and also of another Italian air theorist, Nino Salvaneschi. Salvaneschi, sponsored by Caproni, had already published, in 1917, in English, a book advocating strategic bombing as a means of ending the war. It was entitled *Let Us Kill the War; Let Us Aim at the Heart of the Enemy*.

2. Influence of Douhet.— All this, however, was merely a prelude to the work of Giulio Douhet. His rather stormy wartime career (he was jailed for a year for his published criticism of the Italian general staff, but officially vindicated when the Italian disaster at Caporetto in 1917 was held to have confirmed his criticisms) demonstrated his penchant for courageous and original thinking, which the new Air Ministry (1922) liked.

Douhet gained during World War II an inflated popularity as the supreme philosopher of air power, with a reputation something akin to that of Mahan in naval strategy. In fact, there is no evidence that he had any influence upon the British Royal Air Force, which, as indicated, had already developed its own strategic doctrine by 1918 and refined it in 1922. Writers saw in British practice the similarity to Douhet and assumed that he, rather than Lanchester, was responsible. Mitchell was, by contrast, not a strategic theorist at all, being simply concerned with asserting the importance of military aircraft in all military uses, tactical as well as strategic. He was, like Douhet, intensely in favour of an independent air force, but more because he distrusted the conservatism of the older services than because he thought in any profound sense of an independent mission. He produced many original and valuable tactical ideas, now of strictly historical interest; Douhet's and Lanchester's ideas are in their main outlines still alive.

Douhet's principal work was an essay published in Rome in 1921 entitled *Il dominio dell' aria: saggio sull' arte della guerra aerea (The Command of the Air: Essay on the Art of Aerial Warfare)*. The version published in 1927 was somewhat enlarged. This, plus several other essays published between 1927 and 1930, constitutes his major published work. In 1922 Douhet's ideas appeared in the U.S. in a short article by the Italian air attaché. However, they made little impact until in 1932 a French translation of a substantial part of the second edition of *The Command of the Air* was, in turn, translated into English in 1933 and reproduced for officers of the U.S. Army Air Corps. In that critical formative period of American air power development, it was bound to be well received. Since Douhet supported the British views, his work was given a limited welcome in England. In Germany, where Hermann Göring was reviving the *Luftwaffe*, his ideas were taken up by Gen. Walter Wever but lapsed on Wever's death in 1936. Both the British and German air forces were basically tactical organizations in 1939. In Japan, which started war with China in 1931, efforts were concentrated on tactical work because Japan's major opponents, both immediate and potential (China and the Soviet Union), had no suitable strategic targets.

year before the end of World War I. In Great Britain, the aeronautical engineer F. W. Lanchester had published in 1916 *Aircraft in Warfare: the Dawn of the Fourth Arm*, summarizing a series of articles he wrote during the previous two years. These were adopted by Maj. Gen. Sir David Henderson, whose memorandum was accepted by a committee under the nominal chairmanship of the prime minister, but actually headed by Lieut. Gen. Jan C. Smuts (*q.v.*). This committee presented to the War Cabinet on Aug. 17, 1917, a memorandum recommending that a separate air ministry be formed without waiting for the war's end. That recommendation was acted upon favourably, and the Air Ministry, together with the Royal Air Force (RAF) was formed within a year. The memorandum contained also the following observation: "As far as can at present be foreseen there is absolutely no limit to the scale of its [air power's] future independent war use. And the day may not be far off when aerial operations with their devastation of enemy lands and destruction of industrial and populous centres on a vast scale may become the principal operations of war, to which the older forms of military and naval operations may become secondary and subordinate." By June 1918 Sir Frederick Sykes as Chief of the Air Staff had submitted to the Cabinet a memorandum in which he predicted that any future war would start with a knockout blow at the enemy's capital city. This view was revived at an aeronautical conference in Paris in early 1922 and published in Britain by P. R. C. Groves, who had been chief of staff to Sykes in 1918. Air Chief Marshal Sir Hugh Trenchard, later Marshal of the Royal Air Force Lord Trenchard, has been credited erroneously with developing the idea of a counterstrike deterrent force to meet such a threat. In fact, Trenchard only became a convert to the idea about 1922 and never supplied the aircraft to make it a reality, despite an announced program for a 52-squadron Home Defense Air Force. Mitchell met Trenchard in May 1917 and was influenced by him in tactical matters. Later writers forgot that the term "strategic" as used by Trenchard at that date meant simply matters under Army headquarters concern as opposed to tactical actions by lesser units. They also failed to note that the so-called Independent Air Force of 1918 was to be independent only in the sense that it was not to be commanded by the Allied generalissimo.

In the Soviet Union the control of the armed services by the government was absolute and complete. The purge of leading military officers that took place in the late 1930s swept away Lieut. Gen. V. B. Khripin, deputy air force commander up to 1937 and chief Soviet air theoretician. He had written, in 1935, the introduction to the Russian translation of Douhet's major work, and shortly before the end of his career he had been named first commander of the short-lived "Army of Special Designation," a combined long-range bombing and air-borne forces organization. A purge environment is not generally conducive to new ideas, and the special identification of Khripin with Douhet did not help the spread of the latter's ideas in the U.S.S.R.

Although military establishments are reluctant to admit that ideas have come from other sources, there has been too strong a tendency to give Douhet credit for more than his actual influence. He apparently had more impact on the U.S. Army Air Force than on any other outside Italy. Even in the U.S. service, however, many of the ideas existed before the 1933 translation, having been picked up by Mitchell and others traveling abroad, especially in 1922. The U.S. Army Air Force entered World War II without a full appreciation of the value of long-range fighter escorts, though with an awareness of the need for defensive fighters. It also insisted on bombing in daylight and its B-17, or Flying Fortress, came closest to Douhet's concept of a battleplane.

3. Basic Tenets of the Douhet Philosophy.—To Douhet the old military maxim, derived from Jomini, that "methods change but principles are unchanging" made no sense. To him the advent of the airplane changed the basic character of war. For that reason he was totally uninterested in pre-World War I military history. He was even prepared to reject as irrelevant—presumably because it was too much concerned with the aerial duel—the experience in the military use of aircraft which World War I had provided and which was the only such experience available at the time of his writing. The lessons he did draw from World War I were of an entirely different order. He was convinced, first of all, that that war proved the ascendancy of the defensive in ground warfare. Because of the strength of ground defenses, inferior forces could easily hold the enemy on the frontiers or wherever else they pleased, and he felt they should not try to do more. In the air, however, the offensive was not only the stronger form of war, it was the only valid form. Thus Douhet's first and most basic tenet was: "Resist on the ground in order to mass in the air!" The nation's military resources, he held, ought to be mainly concentrated in air power, and all its air power ought to be concentrated in what he called the independent air force, rather than being dispersed in naval and army air arms.

The enemy air forces were to be destroyed where they could be most easily met and where they were most vulnerable, which was not in the air but on the ground. They should therefore be attacked immediately, in full force, at their bases. Douhet scorned air defenses and felt the attackers had nothing to fear from them. The side that moved first and most aggressively would, if it had the requisite strength, quickly win the air battle, after which everything else would fall into order. The morale of the enemy population was the next target, and because it involved civilians rather than professional military people, he assumed that it would be extremely vulnerable. He felt there would be no real occasion for air support of armies and navies, but insofar as it might prove useful he greatly preferred interdiction bombing to close support of ground troops.

Thus, the correctness of Douhet's position depended on: (1) the existence of static land fronts, relatively easily held by inferior forces; (2) a high incidence of physical damage and, hence, strategic and moral effects from each ton of bombs dropped; (3) the ineffectiveness of air defenses; and (4) the great vulnerability of civilian morale. The weakness of Douhet's theories in general application lay in the fact that they were promulgated in the Italian geographical setting with an easily defended mountain bastion protecting the northern end of the peninsula. Similar theories also suffered from the assumptions built upon a minute factual base that was statistically unreliable; the effectiveness of bombing was, despite battlefield experience with shelling, vastly overrated. More than this, little allowance had been made for improvements in antiaircraft defenses despite the lessons of the attacks on London, and no account was taken of the effect of air attack on a population that included many veterans of trench-warfare, who were not so likely to be demoralized by bombing.

4. The Test in World War II.—World War II did not test Douhet's theories but rather the idea of strategic bombing. Only when the atomic bomb became available in 1945 did air forces have the means to deliver a massive first blow by which an opponent might be paralyzed at the outset of a war. Far from proving Douhet right, it can be argued that World War II proved him wrong. Ground fronts were fluid, and armies roamed widely. No capital city was devastated to the extent he foresaw by air attack. Even industrial targets were only finally reduced to impotence after repeated raiding, and the economic collapse of no country was achieved by air power alone. In many cases strikes against enemy targets were used to create a battle of attrition between enemy fighter forces.

Even in Germany strategic bombing seemed to produce decisive results only in the very last stages of the war, when, first, the German oil and chemical industries and, later, the transportation system were effectively paralyzed. By that time the German armies had been defeated in the field. The part of the strategic bombing campaign that contributed most directly to the success of the Allied armies was the destruction of the German Air Force, due less to the bombing of aircraft production than to the aerial fighting which attended the bombing forays and to direct attacks on German airfields. Also, in the late stages of the war the Germans were putting about one-third of their total military resources into defense against Allied bomber attacks, and were short of fuel. Had it not been for the bombing raids these resources could have been added to Germany's formidable ground strength.

It is also clear that in the strategic bombing of Germany the Allies made many critical mistakes, largely because of lack of experience. Part of this can be blamed upon the same wishful thinking that characterized intelligence services in World War I, together with lack of sufficient information, gathered in peacetime, on the nature of the German economy. Thus the Allied air forces made many mistakes in their choices of industrial target systems and of actual aiming points, in the size of the bombs dropped (which were usually too small), and in the early rejection of fighter escorts for daylight bombing (later remedied for the U.S. forces with the introduction of the P-51 long-range fighter). If the Allies could have assured fewer critical mistakes because of more experience or better planning, there can be no doubt that the effects of the strategic bombing of Germany could have been felt decisively much sooner.

Some of the lessons of the German experience were absorbed early enough to be applied to the bombing of Japan. It is clear that far fewer tons of bombs did far more damage to the industry and population of that country than was true of Germany. But as in Europe it was the incendiary rather than the high-explosive bomb which proved the more effective, especially in the particularly flammable Japanese cities. As in Germany, gutting the homes of war workers did not so much undermine morale as it disrupted production systems. But the use of firebombs on factories was not so effective unless high explosives disrupted the foundations upon which machine tools stood. The combined air and submarine assault of 1944 had already convinced Japanese naval and military leaders that theirs was a defeated country before the major strategic bombing campaign began in 1945. The destruction wrought by the bombers did, however, put urgency into the work of the proponents for peace in Japan and forced the recalcitrants to recognize that further resistance would be hopeless and extremely costly.

The great and unequivocal successes for air power in World War II are to be found rather in tactical military aviation, both on land and at sea, than in strategic bombing. Many of the sea battles in the Pacific were mainly battles of carrier-borne aircraft against ships. In the Atlantic, aircraft played an important role in the fight against the German submarines. And in the European war their tactical role in support of ground troops was often the dominant feature in the battle. The most spectacular demonstration of direct air support to ground troops took place in air operations during the landing in Normandy on June 6, 1944. The Allied air forces based in the United Kingdom, including the strategic bombing forces, through their interdiction bombing successfully isolated the battlefield before the landing; they also prevented the German Air Force from offering any real opposition.

One could say that if airmen were inclined to repeat their successes and recoil from efforts which were less successful, the experience of World War II would have caused them to drop their preoccupation with strategic bombing in favour of tactical operations. Instead, they remained loyal to ideas which antedated that war. One reason for this was that leaders of strategic bomber commands remained dominant in certain air forces into the 1960s. The atomic bombs which appeared at the very end of the war actually vindicated them in their continued adherence to the Douhet philosophy. (For further analysis of World War II air operations, see *History of Air Warfare,* below.)

5. Nuclear Weapons and Missiles.—There can be no doubt that the coming of nuclear and especially of thermonuclear weapons established the dominance of strategic bombardment in any unrestricted war of the future. If Douhet exaggerated the effects of high-explosive bombs, then nuclear weapons far more than made up the difference. Nor can there be any doubt that the results of strategic bombing would now be achieved swiftly. Because each weapon can accomplish so much damage, one can now agree with Douhet that aerial defenses have an exceedingly difficult job to accomplish and very little time in which to do it. Moreover, because a small load of weapons can be so devastating, distance to the target no longer has the significance that it had in World War II, when every extra pound of fuel meant one less pound of bombs. Finally, with thermonuclear weapons, one of which can effectively destroy an entire city with all its industry, the problem of selection of target systems and of aiming points presents none of the special difficulties that it did in World War II.

In fact, it could be said that because of other technological trends affecting both the offense and the defense in strategic bombing, Douhet's philosophy and indeed the whole idea of strategic bombing would now be absolutely dead if it were not for nuclear weapons. Advances in jet propulsion and in the effectiveness of the defense have been such that bombers, in order to overcome that effectiveness, have had to attain a performance which has made them exceedingly costly to purchase and to operate. In repeated wartime sorties their attrition would undoubtedly be very high. Such sorties could hardly begin to be worthwhile if they could carry only chemical weapons. But so long as each aircraft can carry one or more nuclear weapons, the whole perspective of costs and attrition changes in favour of the offensive operation.

However, for a time another change apparently clinched the issue. The development of guided missiles, especially of the long-range ballistic variety (of which the German V-2 in World War II was the prototype), made the prospect for successful active defense appear hopeless. Yet, as in the past, every new weapons system has bred a counter system. The rapidity of this development has always depended upon the amount of effort and money put into constructing either a defense or a deterrent. For the interim between a new threat and its counter, passive defense in the form of shelters was proposed for limited protection (*see* CIVIL DEFENSE). The most effective counter to modern nuclear attack was considered by many analysts in the 1960s to be the counterstrike deterrent force; it had been advocated by Sykes, Groves, and Mitchell in the 1920s and even before them in the retaliatory force conceived by Henderson, Smuts, and Lloyd George in 1917. *See* further sections on the nuclear period in ATOMIC ENERGY; STRATEGY; and TACTICS. *See* also COLD WAR and INTERNATIONAL RELATIONS.

6. The Philosophy of Limited War: Korea; Vietnam.— It may be said that the nuclear bomb no sooner eliminated doubts about the effectiveness of strategic bombing than it began to stimulate questions about whether it had not become too effective.

Is not strategic bombing too dread a sanction to be invoked in any but the most desperate circumstances where sheer survival is threatened? Would it not be possible for each side to stand down the strategic bombardment forces of the other by its threat of retaliation, while forcing the more or less inevitable outbreaks of local violence to be settled by local limited means? It would hardly have been possible to ask such questions, in view of the previously prevalent dogma that all modern wars must be total wars, if it had not been for the Korean experience of 1950–53, when the United Nations unexpectedly found itself in what turned out to be a limited war. That it remained limited despite an enormous U.S. superiority in strategic bombing forces and nuclear weapons, which were not used, could have been predicted because there were no targets in China large enough to warrant the use of nuclear weapons.

Unanswered Questions.—The idea of limited war leaves many questions unanswered. It has been easily assumed in some quarters that total wars are now impossible and that all attention can henceforth be devoted to finding ways of conveniently winning limited wars. For that reason many have advocated even the fighting of limited wars with nuclear weapons. In fact, very little is known about how to keep wars between great powers limited. The special circumstances which limited the Korean War of the early 1950s and the war in Vietnam of the late 1960s may not be present on a similar occasion in the future. There are a number of reasons why the danger of total war is likely to remain real and substantial, and the dangers will definitely increase if they are ignored. On the other hand, probably never before in the history of mankind have so many nations been anxious to avoid total war, nor has so much scholarly, political, and public discussion taken place on the topic of preventing war.

In limited wars, which may have to be fought with nonnuclear weapons, there was by 1960 no important experience more recent than the Korean War. In that war, air power made an important contribution in a tactical role, especially that part of it devoted to close support. Naval and marine aviation operated from U.S. and British aircraft carriers had no doctrinal reluctance to engage in that kind of support, as well as in interdiction bombing and even some strategic bombing. The U.S. Air Force, however, found itself uncomfortable in a close-support role and insisted on putting its major effort into an interdiction operation informally known as Operation Strangle. This effort, carried on for some months with the cooperation of U.S. naval aviation, finally proved to be a failure, chiefly for three reasons: (1) the ground fighting during that period was relatively quiescent, and the Communist troops were, therefore, not forced to use up their ammunition and supplies as fast as they would have in more active fighting; (2) attacks on vehicles being necessarily halted at night, the Communist traffic limited itself to nighttime hours; and (3) the masses of cheap coolie labour available to the Chinese and North Korean Communists for hand transportation were extremely difficult to attack, and the patience and ingenuity of the whole organization was foreign to the non-Oriental Allied intelligence assessors.

The war in Vietnam provided further evidence, as of the latter 1960s, that a limited war could be contained. There, as in Korea, a combination of U.S. carrier- and land-based aviation provided battlefield support together with penetration strikes against limited targets in North Vietnam. On the whole, unlike the Korean War, there were few battles between fighters, most of the U.S. casualties being from ground fire and guided missiles. Even more interesting, and reminiscent of the use of heavy bombers to help smash German defenses around the Normandy beachhead in 1944, B-52 strategic bombers flew on tactical strike missions from their base in Guam.

Many have believed that in an unrestricted nuclear war the role of aircraft and ballistic missiles would be decisive. However, as counter weapons and even bases in space become more fully developed, the certainty of destroying an enemy before he could launch a counterstrike of similar annihilating destructiveness seemed to be receding. Even if all efforts were concentrated on eliminating his retaliatory ability, the chances of doing so were

BY COURTESY OF (LEFT) SPERRY GYROSCOPE DIVISION, SPERRY RAND CORP., (RIGHT) U.S. AIR FORCE

(LEFT) GYRO-STABILIZED BOMBSIGHT FIRST DEVELOPED DURING WORLD WAR I.   SHOWN IS A 1915 MODEL WITH SIGHTING TELESCOPE AND
RANGE ANGLE SCALE.   (RIGHT) TWIN-ENGINED HANDLEY PAGE, FIRST HEAVY BOMBER FOR BRITISH AND U.S. AIR FORCES IN WORLD WAR I

by no means certain. This in itself reintroduced a mode of caution about nuclear warfare.

So far as limited war is concerned, everything depends on the kind and degree of limitation. If the use of nuclear weapons can be avoided, then the manipulators of air power have to reconcile themselves to playing a role ancillary to ground forces. In that case the doctrinal preference for interdiction, which had Douhet's sanction and which allows the air force an independent role, deserves to be reexamined. A movement in this direction was made in 1961 in the U.S. when Strategic Army Corps and Tactical Air Command forces were combined under the command of an army general. However, the use of nuclear weapons is bound to increase the relative importance of air power, and the air forces may be expected to have a bias for their use. The chief danger in their employment is that they will make it more difficult to keep wars limited. Vietnam seemed to demonstrate that unless an enemy has targets worth both the use of nuclear weapons and the resultant risks of escalation of the war into a major conflict, nuclear weapons would remain an unused, if not an unusable, item in the armoury.

II. HISTORY OF AIR WARFARE

As understood during the first half of the 20th century, air warfare was based on the use of armed and armoured flying machines capable of carrying bombs. Strategic air warfare was concerned with bombing attacks against an enemy's industrial home front, although the strategic bombers themselves were also used for other purposes. Tactical air warfare was concerned with operations by fighter bombers, light bombers, and transports in the immediate vicinity of ground or naval battles.

The dawn of 20th-century military aviation occurred at the end of the 18th century when Montgolfier balloons first began to appear and when Sir George Cayley began to achieve some success with model gliders. A balloon school was organized in the first days of the wars of the French Revolution, and the French victory at Fleurus in 1794 has been attributed largely to the advantages they enjoyed from balloon reconnaissance. During the siege of 1849 the Austrians employed unmanned balloons to drop bombs on Venice. During the American Civil War, Thaddeus Lowe and others used balloons to provide observation and intelligence of Confederate movements. Their use was not followed up until in 1892 a balloon section was established in the U.S. Signal Corps and a rather feeble attempt was made to use a balloon at San Juan Hill during the Spanish-American War of 1898. In the meantime, however, the British under the leadership of Col. Robert Baden-Powell (q.v.) had employed balloons in colonial operations in Bechuanaland and Suakim in 1885 and again during the Boer War in 1899–1902. The French had also used balloons to take military leaders and messages out of Paris during the siege by the Germans of 1870. By the end of the 19th century two lines of development were about to bear fruit, thanks to the invention of the internal-combustion engine and of the radio. Ferdinand von Zeppelin, the German cavalryman who had observed the American

Civil War, was about to fly his rigid airships successfully, and the Wright brothers in the United States were almost ready to make their vital contribution by achieving successful powered flight. Military interest in aviation was stimulated both by the successful Zeppelin flights and those of the Wright brothers and by the aviation meeting at Reims, France, in August 1909. Thereafter, given the state of technology, developments were fairly rapid and by World War I, despite the doubts of many older officers, nascent air arms existed in the British, French, German, Russian, and Italian armed forces. The Italians had, in fact, already in operations in North Africa made use of airships in a tactical role.

World War I saw the rapid technological development of the airplane. But though there were a number of spectacular achievements, such as the German bombing of London, most of the war in the air was limited to tactical operations over the Western Front. And despite the emphasis placed on fighters and outstanding fighter pilots, much of the really important work was done by reconnaissance machines until late in the war.

By World War II technological developments, together with a greater appreciation of aircraft by military leaders, resulted in large-scale use of aircraft by the major belligerents. Air forces were used in tactical roles in support of the armies, including airborne assaults. Land-based aircraft were used to attack both convoys and submarines, while naval tactical aircraft engaged in both offensive and defensive work. In addition, the air arms undertook a primary role in the gathering of photographic intelligence and in testing the prewar concepts of strategic bombing.

In 1944 the arrival of combat jet aircraft and of ballistic missiles foreshadowed postwar developments which in the next decade of cold war led directly to the exploration of space as well as to the annihilation of distance as a sufficient form of security from attack. Jet aircraft were used extensively in a continuing series of limited wars from Korea in 1950–53 to Vietnam in the 1960s. Despite the rapid transition from piston engines, most air forces retained transport and even strike aircraft fitted with the piston-engine type of propulsion, while at the same time devoting considerable research and development funds to helicopters and to vertical (VTOL) or short (STOL) take-off-and-landing types. *See* also AIRCRAFT CARRIER; AIRPLANE; WORLD WAR I; WORLD WAR II; KOREAN WAR.

A. EARLY ORGANIZATIONAL AND TECHNOLOGICAL DEVELOPMENTS

From the beginning air forces emerged as special military organizations to maintain, control, and operate all types of aircraft. After World War I these organizations became branches of national armies and navies, and, in some cases, were organized as independent services.

Early balloon units were attached to armies, but after the success of Zeppelin and the Wright brothers, navies also became interested in flying. After the Reims meeting of 1909, it was obvious that war was likely, and this acted as a major stimulus to the development of military aviation in Europe. In the U.S.,

(Above) Gotha G.IV, twin-engine German bomber used during World War I. (Below) Gunner in open nose of a Gotha G.IV. He is dressed for high-altitude flight and holds an oxygen tube in his mouth. (Left) German bombs used during World War I, ranging in weight from 44 to 661 lb.

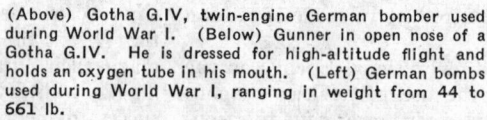

and European designers moved ahead of the Wrights. In 1910 the rigid airship Zeppelins began to serve passengers in Germany, and the Germany Army became interested. The success of the second de Havilland design led H. M. Balloon Factory at Farnborough to take up airplanes again, despite a British government ban of the year before, and to employ Geoffrey de Havilland (q.v.) as chief designer. In France a cavalry ground in the Paris suburbs was also the principal airfield. At last in 1911 the military and naval authorities, who had so much influence on financiers and politicians, began to see that aircraft were likely to become weapons that could not be ignored. Though the experimental British rigid airship No. 1 "Mayfly" broke in half before becoming airborne, money was voted for aviation and members of the British Cabinet witnessed the May aviation meeting at Hendon. In France the first *Concourse Militaire* took place in October, and in most countries military types of aircraft began to appear. And with the Italian use of an airplane against the Turks in 1911 in North Africa, military aviation had arrived. In April 1912 Britain founded the Royal Flying Corps with military and naval wings, encouragement was given to designers through competition, and machine guns and light bombs were tried out as well as radio and artillery spotting equipment. At sea aircraft took off both from a battleship at anchor and from cruisers underway.

despite an early beginning, progress was slow, though on Aug. 1, 1907, less than four years after the Wright brothers made their first successful flight, the U.S. Army organized an aeronautical division within the Signal Corps. Its original personnel consisted of one officer, Capt. Charles deF. Chandler, and two enlisted men. Two years later, on Aug. 2, 1909, the Army, urged on by Pres. Theodore Roosevelt, purchased its first heavier-than-air machine from the Wrights. In 1913 the aeronautical division had grown to a strength of 23 officers, 83 enlisted men, and 15 flying machines. In 1914 the U.S. Congress gave statutory recognition to the air arm as the aviation section of the Signal Corps, and later as the Air Service, independent of the Signal Corps. The first U.S. aero squadron was used in the pursuit of Pancho Villa in 1916, but its aircraft were by then obsolete and broke down in the early stages of the campaign. By that time the war in Europe was entering its third year.

Similar developments were taking place in Europe. France and Germany led in military aviation, while Britain followed close behind in both military and naval aviation. By the time war broke out in 1914 aircraft speed exceeded the Wrights' 30 mph of 1903 by as much as 70 mph and the range was nearly 100 mi. France was the centre of aeronautical development in Europe, and Louis Blériot's crossing of the English Channel on July 25, 1909, caused the French military to pay attention to the new developments. This was reinforced by the Reims meeting a few weeks later, which confirmed the importance of aviation. Also in 1909 airplanes were flown and under development in Germany, Austria, and Russia,

In Germany public action forced both naval interest in Zeppelins and military in airplanes, as well as the official establishment of a flying school. This alarmed the French, who redoubled their efforts not only to defend against what they saw as the potential Zeppelin hazard, but also to develop bombing aircraft. The following year, 1913, saw the development of deliberate aerobatics, a prelude to combat maneuvers, and of the inherently stable airplane, which allowed the pilot to concentrate on other things besides simply flying his machine. The Sopwith Tabloid could climb to 15,000 ft. in 10 minutes, while the new Deperdussin achieved 126 mph in level flight. In Russia Igor Sikorsky (q.v.) produced the first four-engined airplane.

The military organization in most air forces was the squadron, a term adopted by armies from cavalry units and by navies from cruiser organization. By 1914 the Royal Flying Corps (RFC) was a unit in the British Expeditionary Force, and it proceeded to France upon the outbreak of war. The Royal Naval Air Service had ceased to be even in name a part of the RFC with the promulgation of the royal warrant on July 1, 1914. In France the Army had its own aviation units, while in Germany both a military and a naval air service existed, the former under the influential patronage of Prince Henry of Prussia, Kaiser William's brother. In Italy and in Russia military air forces were in existence, and naval ones were emerging. All of these services grew, especially after 1916, though the Russian force was hampered by the revolution of 1917 and eventually went through a number of crises. Its principal designer, Sikorsky, emigrated to the U.S., as did one of its naval aviators, Alexandre de Seversky (later to write *Victory Through Airpower;* 1942). Indicative of the differences of scale is the fact that the Russian air forces totaled about 300 aircraft in 1917, whereas the British, the world's largest air force at the end of the war, numbered about 22,000.

B. WORLD WAR I

When World War I broke out, a small nucleus of persons in the armed forces of each of the major powers had faith in either or both lighter-than-air or heavier-than-air weapons. But military leaders as a whole were not convinced that aircraft had much more than a reconnaissance role. Progress in the development of such important elements as bombsights and aerial machine guns, for instance, was made by individual inventors on their own initiative, frequently in the face of lack of interest or encouragement from military leaders.

The preoccupation of the European general staffs with ground warfare left little time for building air strength or planning its use. Germany, with a first-line aircraft strength of more than 200, had almost twice as many planes as either France or England. The Germans had a marked superiority in airships, or lighter-than-air craft. These large airships, called Zeppelins after their creator, Graf Ferdinand von Zeppelin, carried out most of the German bombing attacks against England during the early years of the war.

The contending air forces had been trained and equipped primarily for observation, but it quickly became apparent that the airplane had other military uses. As the primitive aircraft on hand at the beginning of the war demonstrated their ability to perform also as fighters and bombers, the demand for specialized aircraft stimulated great progress in aeronautics. Airplanes grew steadily larger and heavier. Their performance characteristics—speed, altitude, firepower, range—improved greatly. Indeed, the changing fortunes of the air war between 1914 and 1918 were largely the result of aeronautical design developments, with first one side and then the other gaining a temporary advantage because of some new and advanced type of plane or piece of equipment. The simple technology of the day enabled new designs to be developed and made operational within six months, so that neither side was able to maintain its advantage for more than a few months at a time unless it could field an overwhelming force.

1. Equipment and Organization.—*Planes and Armaments.*—The immediate impact of operations in 1914 with its emphasis upon gathering intelligence caused a rapid development of special planes for different purposes. The fighter was a small biplane of sturdy construction fitted with the most powerful engine applicable. In order to be fully capable of dogfighting (aerial combat) it was given high speed, great maneuverability, and rapid climbing power. Though its shape, construction, and armament have changed over the years, the fighter has remained basically the same in principle. Then as now fighters have usually been single- or two-seaters.

Both on land and at sea commanders regarded observation as the primary purpose of aircraft. Such aircraft were generally equipped with two seats, accommodating a pilot and an observer who doubled as rear-gunner. On reconnaissance missions over land, aircraft reported the position of enemy forces and observed or spotted the fall of shells and sought out enemy guns. They took photographs and thus supplied more accurate information. Radio communications were developed to enable observers to communicate directly with commanders on the surface. Many air battles developed around observation planes.

Bombers were of many types and ranged in size from observation planes to giants designed especially to carry heavy loads great distances. Bombers were generally slower than fighters, but some, such as the German Gothas and the British Handley Pages, often operated at night. Bombloads varied with the distance of the target from the aircraft's base. By 1917 the German Gothas were able to bomb London in daylight; at the very end of the war the British were just beginning to produce the Handley Page V-1500, intended for the bombing of Berlin. In Italy Count Caproni produced a tri-motored bomber capable of lifting 3,000 kg. (6,600 lb.) of bombs.

BRITISH ARMSTRONG-WHITWORTH FIGHTER PURSUING A GERMAN PLANE IN WORLD WAR I

Both the Germans and the British developed a number of types of aircraft for use at sea. Some of these were adaptations of aircraft used by the armies, but many, especially in the Royal Naval Air Service, were specially designed. Seaplanes were mounted on floats and were generally single-engined biplanes capable of carrying a few bombs or a torpedo. Flying boats, which by 1917 were potent antisubmarine and occasionally anti-Zeppelin weapons, had a motorboat type of lower hull which enabled them to take off and land on water. They had a considerable range, were generally multiengined, and carried a crew of at least three. Various attempts to use such aircraft in conjunction with ships were not very successful, but they laid the groundwork for the task forces of World War II.

Airships were of three main types: the nonrigid (or blimp), the semirigid, and the rigid (or dirigible). Nonrigid airships were originally observation balloons that had been fitted with an airplane engine and fuselage. They obtained their lift from gasbags and their shape from air pressure. Semirigids were similar but also had a keel spar. Both types lost their shape when the gas was let out. The rigid airships, of which the Zeppelins were the principal examples, were generally about 650 ft. in length, approximately ten times larger than the other types, and had a rigid framework covered with fabric within which were the gasbags. Nonrigid airships were used primarily for antisubmarine warfare, and by the end of the war those of the British North Sea class were capable of staying at sea for nearly two days. Zeppelins, though designed originally for naval reconnaissance, became the original strategic bombers with raids starting in 1915. Whereas the blimps were low-altitude ships, Zeppelins were constructed to operate at 24,000 ft. so as to avoid British defenses.

For bombing to be effective, bombs, bombracks (bomb bays), and bombsights had to be developed. Early methods consisted simply in throwing some type of explosive weapon over the side of the aircraft. But gradually bombsights which took account of drift and altitude as well as speed were developed. In addition, bombs were evolved first from hand grenades and then from finned artillery shells, until finally streamlined bombs appeared which carried about half again as much explosive as an equivalent artillery shell. Early bombs were as small as ten pounds, but by the end of the war those weighing 250 lb. were becoming standard and types weighing 2,000 lb. were under development. Bombracks were standardized so that they could be attached to any aircraft.

Firepower soon became a requirement. From pistols and rifles, airmen moved to the use of machine guns. At first these could not fire through the propeller arc, so a number of early fighters, such as the Vickers Gunbus had a free-mounted machine gun forward of the pilot. Most fighters, however, had their machine gun mounted above the upper wing. In 1915 the French produced a primitive interrupter gear enabling a gun to be fired through the whirling propeller blades. The device fell into German hands and was quickly perfected by Anthony Fokker (q.v.). Thereafter, the Germans, and then in 1916 the British, developed fighters with one or more fixed guns firing forward so that the pilot could concentrate solely on aiming the aircraft as a gun platform.

Organization of Fighting Units.—Before World War I airplanes had been organized into units for administrative convenience, though the number of planes and the number of types in any unit might vary widely. Due to high casualty and accident rates (sometimes 66% a month), the number of planes in a unit might be very high.

The squadron was the smallest administrative unit during World War I and was charged with housing and maintaining men and aircraft. For fighting purposes it was divided into three or more flights of three aircraft apiece. As more squadrons became available and air battles became bigger, squadrons were joined together in organizations called groups (British wings) and were led by veteran commanders.

As the Allies concentrated and conserved their forces in 1918, so the French and Americans developed a larger unit, which they called a wing. Wings consisting of two or more groups were used by Billy Mitchell when he concentrated approximately 1,500 aircraft for the Saint-Mihiel offensive in September 1918. This is claimed to be the first major concentration of aircraft controlled as a unit as opposed to parceling them out to ground units.

2. Tactical Air Support.—During World War I air power was used primarily to support the land forces, and the subordinate

(TOP) SOPWITH CAMEL, BRITISH SINGLE-SEAT FIGHTER PLANE WITH TWO GUNS FIRING FORWARD THROUGH THE PROPELLER. (BOTTOM) FRENCH NIEUPORT BIPLANE, THE FIRST ALLIED SCOUT FIGHTER ABLE TO COMPETE WITH THE GERMAN FOKKER IN WORLD WAR I

air arms were, therefore, largely responsive to the demands of their parent services. In general, this meant that military priorities were dominant, the only exception being the British Royal Naval Air Service.

Ground commanders regarded airplanes as an extension of the reconnaissance functions of cavalry. The basic role of aircraft in their view was to locate enemy troop concentrations and movements and to spot for artillery. Because knowledge of the enemy's intentions was regarded as the key to battle, each commander was anxious to prevent his opponent from enjoying a similar knowledge of his own dispositions. Therefore, even by the end of 1914 fighting was beginning to take place in the air in order to attempt to deny such information to the enemy. Thus, both sides placed considerable emphasis upon fighters, some of which had been designed before the war. These aircraft gradually obtained greater speed, maneuverability, and firepower, and eventually developed into flying gun platforms with the mission of destroying enemy aircraft and gaining air superiority over the battlefield.

The first key development in air fighting was the redesign by Anthony Fokker of a French interrupter gear which had fallen into German hands, mentioned previously. The Allies were compelled to accelerate their search for a better plane, and a seesawing technological battle then ensued that lasted throughout the war.

At the same time, in 1915 formation flying came into being and by the time of the British Somme offensive in 1916 both sides were using large formations in their struggle for air superiority. Intensive fighting took place mainly over active ground areas, but interception was largely a matter of visual sighting by patrols of either enemy aircraft or of antiaircraft shell bursts. At the same time, bombing raids against railway facilities and airfields behind the lines were intensified.

The Germans brought improved types, the Albatross and the Halberstadt, into action during the summer and fall of 1916; they also organized formations of fighters known as flying circuses, which developed mobile tactics of fighting. The British and French countered by developing improved planes and continuing to increase the size of their fighter units.

During 1917 the air war grew steadily more intense, individual air battles sometimes involving as many as 100 planes. Operations against enemy air units, either in the air or on the ground, came to be the dominant feature of the air war as both sides strove to achieve aerial superiority. Fighter aces became popular heroes in the warring countries as their exploits were reported colourfully by the press. Outstanding among these aces were Georges Guynemer, René Fonck, and Charles Nungesser of France; Baron Manfred von Richthofen, Oswald Boelcke, Max Immelmann, Werner Voss, and Hermann Göring of Germany; Edward Mannock and Albert Ball of Great Britain; William A. Bishop of Canada; and Edward ("Eddie") Rickenbacker and Frank Luke of the United States.

Although the fighter plane continued to dominate the air war and the fighter aces captured the imagination of the public, progress was also made in the use of bombing, especially during the last year of the war. Army commanders began to see the advantages of striking enemy rail and supply centres behind the lines. Since the orders for these sorties came from army headquarters, they were regarded as strategic operations though limited to what in World War II were called tactical actions. The reason for this was that the bombers had neither the range, the defensive speed, nor the armament to attack targets located to the rear of the enemy's aerial defensive zone. It was this, coupled with strong reluctance on the part of the French politicians to expose their cities and industries to German counterattack, that limited bombing operations rather than that ground commanders could not see the value of hitting at targets more removed from the battlefields. When bombardment of rear areas did develop, it was in large measure as retaliation for the German bombing of Britain in the summer of 1917 and was made possible by the increasing Allied air superiority over the Western Front. In other areas long-range bombing was almost never undertaken, owing to the lack of both means and targets.

In the spring offensive of 1918 the Germans made a supreme

(ABOVE) DE HAVILLAND DH-4 LIGHT BOMBERS, REDESIGNED BY THE U.S., ON PATROL OVER BATTLE LINES, 1918. (BELOW) A SQUADRON OF GERMAN FOKKER TRIPLANES ON THE WESTERN FRONT IN WORLD WAR I

effort in the air, concentrating about 900 aircraft for attack on the Allied forces. But although they achieved some impressive bombing successes against supply depots and other tactical targets, they could not wrest control of the air from the French and British, now reinforced by Americans. Indeed, the numerical superiority of the Allies increased greatly in spite of heavy losses during the spring of 1918.

When the Allies launched their great offensive in the Somme area in August 1918, their air strength of almost 2,000 planes for the operation put them in a position to overwhelm the 365 German planes pitted against them. In September the Allies concentrated almost 1,500 planes in support of the successful campaign to flatten the German salient at Saint-Mihiel. The German Air Force remained in being until the end of the war, and although greatly outnumbered, it managed on occasion to gain local control of an area by concentrating its forces. But the steady offensive of the Allied air forces, sustained day after day, prevailed at all key junctures of the fighting.

Tactical air forces scored one notable success away from the Western Front. In Palestine British Field Marshal Edmund Allenby not only obtained air superiority over the Turks before the Battle of Megiddo but also used aircraft both to isolate Turkish headquarters from the battlefield and to harass and destroy the routed enemy.

3. Long-Range Bombing.—World War I also saw the beginning of long-range aerial attacks against centres of civilian population. The precedent for these lay in naval bombardments and in the strategic conception that the object of war is to destroy the enemy's will to fight. Although these operations in the 1914–18 war were on a small and sporadic scale, they had an enormous influence upon theory in the interwar years (1918–39) and upon practice in World War II. The British bombed targets in Germany during 1914, but the raids were carried out by only a few planes and were directed against military targets, particularly factories producing Zeppelins. The Germans had a number of these airships on hand at the beginning of the war. Their range made them a logical choice to carry out bombing raids against Great Britain.

In January 1915 Kaiser William II gave permission to attack London and other British targets. A few attacks on England had been made by German airplanes in December 1914 and there were a few more during 1915, but most of the raids during 1915–16 were made by Zeppelins. On Jan. 19, 1915, naval Zeppelins dropped bombs on villages in Norfolk, Eng., and killed five people.

In the first raid on London, May 26, 1915, a single airship dropped a ton of bombs, killing 7 people and injuring 35. During the latter months of 1915, London was bombed four more times.

To meet these attacks the British adopted a variety of measures. Guns and searchlights were installed around vital centres, and airplanes were stationed near the coast to intercept raiders and to guard cities. A blackout was adopted in the East Anglia area, and a mobile antiaircraft force was established. But these defenses had little success against the Zeppelins. At first the Admiralty controlled the air defense of Britain. But as it became a political issue together with several other aspects of air power, dissatisfaction caused it to be returned to the War Office and the Royal Flying Corps in February 1916. No significant change was observable until September, when three Zeppelins were shot down on British soil by a combination of guns and aircraft.

Eleven airships which attacked London on Oct. 1, 1916, caused only one death in the city. The defenders of London had now mastered the lighter-than-air attacks, and no German airships thereafter flew intentionally over the metropolis. British planes shot down additional German airships before the end of 1916, clearly indicating that the Zeppelins were highly vulnerable to attack. Thereafter, the Germans sharply reduced the number of Zeppelin attacks—from 22 in 1916 to 7 in 1917 and 4 in 1918. Even the German tactic of ascending to great altitudes did not stop the defense from defeating the Zeppelin.

Early in 1917 Germany began to form a squadron of Gotha G.IV airplanes for the systematic bombing of England. The squadron began its operations on May 25, 1917, and although the 23 airplanes dispatched did not reach London, they dropped bombs in Kent and demonstrated that the British defense against airplanes was not adequate. Raids by Gothas against London were made in daylight during June–August 1917, causing hundreds of casualties and necessitating diversion of Royal Flying Corps squadrons from France to England. These attacks were of great significance since they were witnessed by many people, including General Smuts. The public outcry for retaliatory raids on Germany could not be gratified owing to a shortage of suitable aircraft, to the demands of the Western Front, and to the recognition that unless these counterstrikes were heavier and more continuous than the German raids, they would only stiffen the German will to resist and bring greater harm to Britain. Thus the Germans were allowed to continue their raids, which they did in September with moonlight attacks. They dispatched their newest aircraft,

(ABOVE) FOKKER C2-3 TRI-MOTOR TRANSPORT BEING REFUELED IN THE AIR PRIOR TO ITS RECORD-BREAKING ENDURANCE FLIGHT OF 150 HR. 50 MIN. 40 SEC., JANUARY 1929. (BELOW) LIEUT. JAMES H. DOOLITTLE AND THE CURTISS R3C-2 RACER IN WHICH HE WON THE 1925 SCHNEIDER TROPHY WITH A RECORD SPEED OF 232.6 MPH

BY COURTESY OF (BELOW) THE AIR FORCE MUSEUM, WRIGHT-PATTERSON AIR FORCE BASE, OHIO; PHOTOGRAPH, (ABOVE) WIDE WORLD

the Giant, against London on Dec. 18, 1917, and followed with additional raids during 1918, using bombs weighing up to 660 lb. Both the Gothas and the Giants had relatively good speed and climbing characteristics and were difficult to intercept, especially at higher altitudes.

The Zeppelins began their last series of raids on England on the night of March 12, 1918, but because of the high altitudes from which they bombed, they did little damage. They made their last raid on the night of August 5–6, 1918, but did not succeed in dropping any bombs on land.

The last airplane raid, on the night of May 19–20, 1918, was made by 43 Gothas and Giants against London. Thirteen of the planes reached the city and caused considerable damage. The British defense, however, was alert and effective. Antiaircraft batteries shot down three German planes, and fighters brought down three more. This defensive success was final, and the German air force made no further attempt to bomb London with airplanes.

In these raids on England the Germans flew 208 airship and 435 airplane sorties, but dropped less than 300 tons of bombs with which they killed approximately 1,300 people and injured about 3,000. Property damage was moderate, the chief effects

of the raids being to slow down production and to create a fear of bombing. The latter in particular had important effects both during and after the war.

In the summer of 1917 the British government seriously considered the whole problem of air power. The German raids emphasized the need for effective air defenses and for the allocation of production to meet the air needs of both the Army and Navy and of home defense. Two German raids in early September merely emphasized the urgency of making changes. The task was given to the War Priorities Committee, which persuaded the Cabinet that an Air Ministry should be formed without delay; the Air Ministry came into being in January 1918 and the Royal Air Force (RAF), amalgamating the Royal Flying Corps and the Royal Naval Air Service, was formed on April 1, 1918. In the meantime the nucleus of a retaliatory air force had been organized as 41 Wing in October 1917, with the intention that it should bomb German industrial targets. It flew 57 sorties (from Feb. 1, 1918, as 8th Brigade) before June 6, when it was absorbed into the Independent Bombing Force. Its raids had the same effects on German cities as did German raids on British—light casualties but a slowing down of production. The latter was caused as much by false alarms as by actual raids. Sir Hugh Trenchard had been brought home from his command of the Royal Flying Corps in France to become Chief of the Air Staff. He was fired from this position in April and eventually persuaded to take the post of commander of the Independent Bombing Force. Trenchard did not believe in retaliatory strikes, and most of his force's efforts were devoted to hitting targets just behind the front. Attempts to strike into Germany were extremely costly. On July 31, 1918, for instance, only two of nine aircraft which set out to attack Mainz returned. On Oct. 26, 1918, Trenchard's command became the Inter-Allied Independent Bombing Force, but it had been known after June as the Independent Air Force and was really the creation of Sir Frederick Sykes, the new chief of the Air Staff. Owing both to French fear of retaliation and to the British Cabinet's distrust of Trenchard's interest in strategic bombing, the air command planned to open operations against Berlin from Norfolk, Eng. But at the war's end only three of the Super Handley Page V-1500's were available, and none flew on operations. In the meantime, the idea that the next war might open with a massive air blow against an enemy's capital city had been submitted by Sykes to the British War Cabinet in June 1918.

The influence of these developments upon future theory was very important. Billy Mitchell had contacts with both the British and with the Italians. It seems apparent that in Britain Sykes and Groves and in Italy Douhet and Caproni came to the same, but independent, conclusions about the future value of strategic bombing and together with Mitchell became crusaders for it.

4. Naval Aviation.—Conscious of the possibility that revolutionary technological developments being perfected in the early years of the 20th century might have a direct bearing on the safety of the kingdom, the British Admiralty under Adm. Sir John Fisher (q.v.) in March 1907 instructed Capt. Reginald Bacon to study aviation. In July 1908 Prime Minister Herbert Asquith, on the basis of a memorandum by Bacon supported by Fisher, told the Admiralty to go ahead and build a rigid airship. By 1909 the details were arranged and Vickers began construction of No. 1, known as "Mayfly." In 1911 the airship was tested unsuccessfully, and the Admiralty temporarily abandoned the idea. But almost at once the success of the Zeppelins and the advent of Winston Churchill as head of the naval service caused a reversal in policy. Under a large budget, in which aeronautical expenditures were easily concealed, Churchill proceeded to push the development of both lighter- and heavier-than-air craft. In Germany Zeppelins were being built in floating sheds on Lake Constance and in 1912 began to make their first patrols over the southern North Sea. At the same time, the British were developing seaplanes and flying boats and the necessary ancillary naval equipment to make use of them at sea. In all of this work Adm. Sir John Jellicoe and Adm. Sir David Beatty (qq.v.) took a strong interest. Further British development of rigid airships was not very successful since most of the designs were copies of captured German ships or plans,

and the British versions were much delayed in construction. On the other hand, nonrigid airships were developed rapidly, and attempts were made to use the more sophisticated models at sea with the fleet; however, their relatively low speed in a headwind made this impractical for other than antisubmarine work. To protect the fleet from both submarines and mines, kite balloons were towed by British warships whenever in the last years of the war the fleet was at sea. In Germany no such development took place, though Zeppelins were used to scout for the German Navy and also for independent patrols. However, much of their work was concentrated in strategic attacks against Britain. Small non-rigid airships were used around the British coasts both as convoy

(Above left) Vickers FB5 Jockey, British single-seat all metal fighter plane, 1933. (Above right) Boeing B-9, U.S. twin-engined all metal monoplane bomber, and Boeing P-26, first monoplane fighter produced for the U.S. Army Air Corps, 1932. (Below) Russian Policarpov I-16, first used in the Spanish Civil War, carried two cannon, two machine guns, and small bombs

escorts and on patrols against submarines, and a very low loss rate for merchant ships was achieved when they were operating in the vicinity. They were also employed on patrol in the Mediterranean.

Naval airplanes were also specially developed by Britain's Royal Naval Air Service (RNAS) and also to a much more limited extent by other nations. The first pilots were trained at Eastchurch in Kent starting in 1911. Nearby, Short Brothers had a factory where they specialized in manufacturing naval airplanes. Seaplanes were developed from ordinary landplanes fitted with floats. Operating at sea after being hoisted over the side of an "aircraft carrier," they were moderately successful in the calm Mediterranean but failed in the choppy North Sea.

Naval aircraft scored a first in the Dardanelles campaign of World War I when, on Aug. 12, 1915, an enemy ship was sunk by an aerial torpedo. RNAS airmen also pioneered in penetration raids deep into enemy territory, such as the attack upon Friedrichshafen to knock out Zeppelin production on Nov. 21, 1914, and the ship-launched strike on the Cuxhaven airship sheds on Dec. 25, 1914. As a result of the latter, special work upon aircraft carriers was undertaken which at the end of the war led to the evolution of the first fully flush-decked carrier. In the meantime, on Aug. 3, 1917, Squadron Comdr. E. H. Dunning had successfully landed on the foredeck of a moving ship. The first real aircraft carrier available to the Grand Fleet was "Argus," in which was embarked for the first time in October 1918 a full squadron of torpedo bombers. Another method was the towed lighter, from which in August 1918 Lt. S. D. Culley flew a Sopwith Pup and shot down Zeppelin L.53.

The activities of the RNAS were not limited to actions at sea. Apart from the Friedrichshafen raid, it undertook both fighter and bomber raids from its base at Dunkirk (Dunkerque), striking at Zeppelin and submarine bases. For this part of naval warfare the RNAS rather than the RFC developed the large Handley Page bombers and pioneered night-flying and bombing techniques. By the time of its absorption into the RAF in April 1918, the RNAS

had become the world's largest and best naval air force.

In the meantime, in the United States occurred a similar, if much more lethargic, development—long hampered by inadequate financial support. In September 1910 Capt. W. I. Chambers was assigned by the U.S. Navy to handle aviation affairs. And on Nov. 14, 1910, the first flight ever to be made from the deck of a ship took place when Eugene Ely flew a Curtiss biplane off a special platform over the bow of the cruiser "Birmingham" anchored in Hampton Roads, Va. On Jan. 11, 1915, Ely landed on the battleship "Pennsylvania" at San Francisco. Shortly afterward a naval officer at Annapolis, Md., attempted the first flight from a catapult. By August 1913 the U.S. Navy had nine qualified pilots, and at the end of the year Capt. Mark L. Bristol was placed in charge of naval aviation. Bristol concentrated on taking aircraft to sea, leaving Captain Chambers to undertake the equally important task of developing material. The Naval Yard at Pensacola, Fla., was developed as a base. However, not until the "navy second to none" program of 1916, was money plentiful, and even in July 1917 there were only 38 pilots and that number was only increased after the U.S. entered the war. By the end of the war U.S. naval aviation units were fighting alongside the RAF in France, helping to carry out antisubmarine patrols and strikes against submarine bases. But the group as a whole was only just really ready to fight when the war ended.

C. INTERWAR YEARS

1. Evolution of Separate Air Forces.—While for various reasons the British establishment in early 1918 of an Air Ministry and the RAF has been remembered, it is often forgotten that these were intended as temporary wartime measures. Both the British Army and Navy thought that they would recover their air services after the war ended. And indeed the fate of the RAF hung in balance until late 1922. The Air Ministry was safe because it was to supervise civil aviation (q.v.), but the RAF had yet to establish a role for itself. It was the intention of the government headed by David Lloyd George that it should be disbanded. But in early 1919 Trenchard, again Chief of the Air Staff, was able to show that the Air Force could garrison Iraq at about one-third of the cost of the Army there. Then in 1922 deteriorating Anglo-French relations, coupled with skilful propaganda by P. R. C. Groves, led to a fear that London would be bombed. The Balfour Committee noted that only the RAF could provide for air defense and in May 1923 the Salisbury Committee confirmed this judgment. The government under Prime Minister Stanley Baldwin at once began a five-year buildup, which was not, however, completed when rearmament in the face of the German threat began in 1934. In practice, the RAF devoted most of its energies to developing a colonial air force, for although the Home Defence Air Force was supposed to be a counterstrike deterrent force, it was not equipped with suitable airplanes. At the same time, aircraft used by the Navy were manned and serviced by RAF crews until 1924, when the Fleet Air Arm was established using naval personnel. The Fleet Air Arm did not achieve autonomy and revert to the Admiralty until mid-1937. The supply of aircraft remained largely an Air Ministry responsibility, and naval aircraft were largely inferior to contemporary land-based types until U.S. aircraft became available during World War II.

In 1936 the RAF was divided into three operational commands: Fighter, Bomber, and Coastal, with the latter being responsible for operations from shore bases. The reasons for the developments up to 1937 can be traced to the fact that officers for the postwar RAF were handpicked by Trenchard. Thus most ex-RNAS personnel were eliminated and the service was heavily dominated by former members of the RFC who had served in France. It was only in 1937, partly as a result of a memorandum by Capt. B. H. Liddell Hart, that the defense of Britain was transformed from a reliance on bombers to one on fighters so that the island base could survive as an arsenal. The correctness of this decision was made obvious by the results in the Battle of Britain of 1940–41.

Independent air forces developed slowly in other countries. The Italians under Benito Mussolini, influenced by Douhet and Caproni, established the *Regia Aeronautica* in 1923. The French followed in 1928 with an air ministry and later with the creation of an independent *Armée de l'air*. Denied an air force by the Versailles Treaty restrictions, the Germans gained their experi-

MARTIN B-10, U.S. MEDIUM BOMBER INTRODUCED IN 1932, FEATURED INTERNAL BOMB STOWAGE AND AN ENCLOSED, ROTATING FRONT GUN TURRET. TOP SPEED WAS 207 MPH, FASTER THAN ANY U.S. FIGHTER THEN IN SERVICE

ence abroad instructing Soviet fliers and operating airlines in Europe and Latin America. In 1935 the Versailles restrictions were unilaterally abrogated, and the German *Luftwaffe* came into being. With the death of Gen. Walter Wever in 1936, Hermann Göring (*q.v.*), Ernst Udet, and Field Marshal Milch tied the *Luftwaffe* closely to the German Army. None of the other major powers, the Soviet Union, the United States, or Japan removed their air forces from the control of the older military services. In both the latter two countries strong naval air arms were developed which would after 1941 battle for control of the Pacific. Their development was largely due both to naval realities and to intraservice rivalries. The Japanese naval air arm was trained in the early 1920s by ex-RNAS personnel, while in the United States the claims of the Army Air Force fostered the development of what would become naval carrier task forces. The possibility of an independent Japanese air force vanished when the Japanese were defeated. In the United States, the logical progress from recognition of the Army Air Corps, first implicitly in the Army Reorganization Act of 1920 and then in the Air Corps Act of 1926 and in the War Department's recognition of the General Headquarters Air Force in 1935, did not reach its conclusion until the United States Air Force was created in 1947. The latter, however, developed strictly from the old Army Air Corps and included no naval components. Nevertheless, early in World War II War Department Circular No. 59 (effective March 9, 1942) had made the Army Air Forces one of the autonomous and coordinate commands under the Army Chief of Staff. In effect, not only did the air forces achieve equal status with the ground forces, but

their commander, Gen. H. H. Arnold, not only ranked immediately under the Chief of Staff, Gen. George C. Marshall, but also sat with him on the Joint and Combined Chiefs of Staff.

2. Technological Developments.—The organizational problems described above were keenly fought within and between the armed services, but they had relatively little effect upon the development of the aircraft themselves. Since the rapidity of technological development depends upon the amount of time, effort, and money available, these were the real determining factors when coupled to the attitude of the political higher direction. Thus the French Air Force received substantial sums in the 1920s when fear of Germany was greatest, but was allowed to deteriorate in the 1930s when internal political squabbles and socialist domination resulted in uncertainties and the ultimate nationalization of the aircraft industry. In Britain and the United States progress was slow because of vast war surplus stocks on the one hand and an idealistic pacifism on the other. The chief spur to progress came from attempts on various world aviation records and from the Schneider Trophy seaplane races. The latter in particular saw intense competition between Italy, the United States, and Britain which raised the world air speed record from 111 mph in 1920 to 407 mph in 1931 and engine horsepower from 450 to 2,300. Though the air forces of the world successfully advanced the long-distance record from a few hundred miles to the RAF's successful 7,162 mi. in 1938, it was the airlines which pressed for economy and reliability until by 1938 they had machines which could safely cross both the Atlantic and the Pacific. The Schneider Trophy also had the effect of making metal a respectable and recognized aeronautical material, much more durable than wood and fabric. At the same time in Britain it rehabilitated the monoplane, which had been banned after a series of accidents in 1913. And not only were airframes and engines developed, but fuel research was also pressed in the 1920s. The result was that about 1930 there began a technical revolution in aeronautics. Variable and constant-speed metal propellers replaced fixed-pitch wooden ones. Engines were both air-cooled radials and liquid-cooled in-lines of increased reliability (up to approximately 100 hours as compared to the less than 3 hours of the engines of World War I). Streamlined metal airframes were being made of new lightweight alloys. Monoplanes were replacing biplanes, and flaps and retractable undercarriages were being incorporated. In many of these developments commercial airliners led, and the military followed. The first all-metal monoplane had been built by Hugo Junkers in 1915, and European airlines developed the idea after 1920. But not until 1939 were all-metal monoplanes becoming dominant in the military air forces of the world.

For military purposes there were three important lines of development: fighters, bombers, and transports. Fighters improved as a result both of the stimulus of racing and because of the development of engines of less frontal resistance. The first major breakthrough was the Curtiss liquid-cooled D-12, which made the engine less important than the needs of the pilot in determining the width of the fuselage. Responding to the challenge, radial-engine manufacturers developed better cowlings to make their engines competitive, and designers paid more attention to clean aerodynamic design. Speed, rate of climb, and maneuverability remained the basic considerations. Since most fighters were visualized as being interceptors, their range was strictly limited. It was the Japanese, perhaps influenced by Seversky's P-35, who were the first to fit long-range fuel tanks into operational fighters about 1940. Fighter armament changed little between 1919 and 1932, but at about that time it was quadrupled in strength. Bombers in the RAF were developed in the dual role of transports, but progress was slow since these aircraft were generally used outside of Europe and faced no opposition. The Handley Page V-1500 was not developed further nor was the U.S. Barling six-engined type of 1921, with the result that bomber design made small progress until the 1930s. Then the Italians and Germans produced a series of twin- and tri-motored machines that were used well into World War II. In Britain, despite the counterstrike deterrent theory, it was not until 1932 that bomber design was seriously pursued, starting with the Vickers Wellington and the

Handley Page Hampden. But in 1936 specifications were issued for four-engined aircraft with the range to strike Berlin, and these resulted in the Stirling, Lancaster, and Halifax, while the Sunderland maritime reconnaissance type was evolved from the civil Empire flying boat. Neither the Russians nor the Germans attempted to develop a four-engined bomber because the leading advocates of strategic bombing in those countries did not survive in the late 1930s. In the U.S. the Air Corps got its first all-metal bomber, the Martin B-10, in 1932. However, it was not until 1935 that the first real strategic U.S. bomber, the Boeing B-17, began to fly, and it had to be considerably modified for combat service in 1941–42. Neither the experimental B-15 nor the B-19 went into production, as both suffered from the fact that the engines available lacked sufficient power. In 1939 the U.S. began to develop a second bomber, the Consolidated B-24. The two most notable advances in the interwar years in transport aircraft were the German Junkers Ju 52 of 1932 and the U.S. Douglas DC-3 of 1936, both of which became the transport backbone of their air forces in World War II.

In regard to naval air forces the interwar years saw a number of important improvements. Apart from patrol flying boats, which showed a slow, but steady development, naval aircraft were almost exclusively single-engined. Thus, because engine failure meant ditching and possibly drowning, the emphasis was placed upon reliability. At the same time, the development of aircraft carriers, which had begun in the British fleet in 1914–18, progressed rapidly. The flight deck in the new carriers, the first of which was the British "Argus," ran the full length of the hull, and the funnels and the bridge were shifted to the starboard side. Since aircraft were airborne at very low speeds because of their light wing loadings, the principal problems were landing on the carriers and stowage. After a series of experiments, the modern hydraulically controlled transverse arrester wires were developed to aid in landing by 1933. To enable more planes to be carried, aircraft were fitted with folding wings to reduce the stowage space required below decks. At the same time aircraft types evolved in World War I, such as the torpedo bomber, were improved while the newer technique of dive-bombing was perfected, particularly by the United States Navy, which had commissioned its first carrier, the "Langley," in 1922. Both the British and U.S. navies converted large battle-cruiser hulls into aircraft carriers before designing carriers from the keel up, though the first such vessel was the British light carrier, "Eagle," also commissioned in 1922.

More important than the development of the carrier, was the evolution of the doctrine and technique of utilizing carriers. In this area, the U.S. Navy led with the Japanese not far behind. The first six years that the "Langley" was in commission aviators used it as a rigourous testing ground for aircraft and equipment, with the result that by 1928 when the "Lexington" and the "Saratoga," the first two U.S. fleet carriers, entered service, techniques and doctrines were well worked out. In maneuvers during 1929 the "Saratoga" managed to evade defenders of the Panama Canal and deliver a decisive simulated strike from 200 mi. offshore. In 1938 maneuvers were carried out which concluded with a simulated strike at the Mare Island Naval Base in San Francisco Bay, Calif. Much of the success of these operations was due to the improvements in navigation and to the perfection of the dive bomber, which enabled attacks to be delivered from 15,000 ft. Much of the progress was conditional on technological and industrial advances and upon money available. In order not to court criticism and restrictions, the U.S. Navy moved carefully and was only by 1939 finally beginning to standardize its types. In the meantime, in 1934 "Ranger" was commissioned, but it was only suitable for reconnaissance aircraft; it was not until the arrival of "Yorktown" in 1938 that the U.S. Navy had three assault carriers capable of carrying the requisite combination of fighters, torpedo carriers, and dive bombers which was the core of the fast carrier task force that played such an important role in the Pacific operations of World War II.

3. Interwar Air Defense Systems.—In countries threatened by air attack, it was natural also that there should be some con-

siderations of the problems of air defense. Despite the British experience with strategic bombing that had shown that defenses could succeed, the British government refused during the 1920s to do more than set up a secret committee to investigate. The government's attitude was dictated to a large extent by the RAF's determined pronouncements that aircraft would always penetrate any defenses. However, the French, faced with both an imagined German threat and a more real British one, went ahead and passed a law in 1927 establishing a system of civil defense against air raids. The British hesitated until 1935, when an Air Raid Precautions establishment came into being. In the meantime, little had been done to develop more than listening devices and some anti-aircraft guns and to consider the effects of incendiary, high-explosive, and gas bombs. It was not until 1936, with radar a possibility, that serious efforts were devoted to setting up an anti-aircraft section of the Army and Fighter Command of the RAF. In other countries much less was done, despite the lessons of the Spanish Civil War of 1936–39. The Germans did not take serious air raid precautions until after war began and bombs started to fall on their country. In the United States almost nothing was done until the advent of the so-called missile-gap issue of the 1960 elections. The armed forces were in many cases not much better off than the civil population. Though in the armies some anti-aircraft units were provided for tactical use in the field, the world's navies were generally badly underarmed and suffered seriously in the first years of the 1939 war from hostile air attack.

4. Use of Air Power.—None of the various disarmament conferences which met during the interwar years had any success in regard to aircraft, for air power was too new and too flexible, and the experts were unable to agree on any proportionate divisions or upon definitions. Thus air power remained at large and employable.

The British developed the use of air power as a means of pacifying and controlling colonial areas, notably in Iraq, in Aden, and along the northwest frontier of India. As such, it was an economical substitute for an army in controlling unruly colonial subjects. But the U.K.'s attempt to use air power as a strategic force in defense of the British Empire failed at Singapore and in Burma in 1941–42 due to lack of aircraft and supporting facilities.

More successful was the Italian use of the tactical air force against Ethiopia (1935), where experience in dropping supplies by parachute was gained. But the most important uses of air power in the interwar era were in Spain and the Far East. Supporting Gen. Francisco Franco in the Spanish Civil War (1936–39), the air forces of Italy and Germany soon dominated the skies and undertook attacks in support generally of ground operations. Their attacks upon cities, such as Barcelona and Madrid, and towns and villages were not always successful owing to the light weight of the bombs dropped and the stone construction of Spanish buildings. Italian bomber units operated from as far away as Italy itself. The German *Legion Condor* under Gen. Hugo Sperrle was the most effective force in the field, especially after the arrival of the Ju 87 Stuka dive-bomber, which did well in skies in which it faced no opposition. On the whole, the Germans gained more from the intervention in Spain than both the Italians, for the experience enabled them to work out both the tactics for use with ground forces in their blitzkriegs of 1940–41 and the technique of fighting in pairs against enemy fighters.

In the Far East the Japanese began military operations against China in 1931 as a result of the conflict between the two nations in Manchuria. Japanese men and equipment were superior in action to the Chinese, who lacked supplies. Although they faced light opposition, the Japanese continued to develop their equipment. Partly as a result of a defeat by the U.S.S.R. in 1939, Japan entered World War II with the finest light fighter of the day, the Zero. The clash with the Soviet Union also caused the Japanese to reorganize their tactics and equipment. But Japanese bombers, like their German and Italian counterparts, were ill-equipped for defense at the start of World War II, owing to the lack of opposition they had previously received, even when they attacked major targets such as Nanking and other cities in 1937.

By 1939 the world was aware that air power was a real threat.

GERMAN BOMBERS, WORLD WAR II

(Above left) Junkers Ju 87 Stuka, two-seater dive bomber, was used effectively in support of ground forces early in the war but sustained heavy losses during the Battle of Britain due to its low top speed of 210 mph. (Above right) Heinkel 111 medium bomber on a reconnaissance flight during German invasion of Norway, May 1940. (Below) Junkers Ju 88, twin-engined day or night fighter-bomber with a top speed of 280 mph, largely replaced the Ju 87

Hitler invoked the potential power of the German *Luftwaffe* to achieve some of his diplomatic goals prior to the beginning of World War II.

D. World War II

The threat of air power was important in the moves that led to World War II. It is now evident that Hitler intended his air force as a tactical weapon. Among the most important factors that influenced both Neville Chamberlain of the U.K. and Édouard Daladier of France at the Conference of Munich (*q.v.*) in 1938 were fear of massive German air strikes against London and Paris and their awareness of their own weakness. Not until 1961 were the real reasons known for what came to be regarded as appeasement. These were that the British had deluded themselves into believing that the Germans would strike, because this was what the British deterrent policy was based upon, and that studies started in 1936 and just available in September 1938 showed that the RAF could not hit Germany, let alone Berlin, in any strength. In addition to this, it was not until 1939 that the British had an effective home defense force of fighters controlled by a primitive radar. The French Air Force was in even worse condition, and the French were equally afraid of being bombed. The one hopeful sign on the Allied side by the time war broke out in September 1939 was that British aircraft production was just beginning to exceed that of Germany.

1. Strength of Air Forces.—At the outbreak of war in Europe the *Luftwaffe* and the RAF were the world's best-equipped air forces. The *Luftwaffe* had a strength of 500,000 men and 5,000 aircraft, while the British had about 100,000 men and 2,000 aircraft. On the whole, German equipment was more modern and better adapted to a tactical role. The French Air Force, which reached its peak at the end of the 1920s, had by 1939 deteriorated badly and had relatively little modern equipment. Despite purchases begun in the United States in 1938, it still had only about 600 first-line aircraft and lacked organization. The Poles had about 500 aircraft, but like the Italians, who entered the war in 1940, their machines were older. Neither of these powers was able to stand up to opponents with first-class equipment. The Soviet Union, which had been largely influenced by the Germans, had a large number of aircraft primarily for tactical operations.

The powers in the Pacific were Japan and the United States. At the end of 1941 the Japanese had a well-trained and experienced army air force which had been fighting in China for several years and which had absorbed the lessons of the defeat inflicted by the U.S.S.R. in 1938–39. In addition, there was an efficient naval air force. The combined total for both groups amounted to about 2,700 aircraft. On the American side, the U.S. Army Air Corps had about 2,900 first-line aircraft, many of which were obsolescent. However, the U.S. aircraft industry was already moving into high gear both to supply the British and to fulfill programs developed by the U.S. government. At sea, the U.S. Navy was developing new strength, but at the time of Pearl Harbor had only three air-

craft carriers to ten for the Japanese. During the war the U.S. Navy expanded from about 3,400 aircraft to more than 40,000. During the same period the U.S. Army Air Forces accepted delivery of approximately 159,000 aircraft, of which about 51,000 were bombers and 47,000 fighters. Other powers involved in the war in the Pacific were engaged elsewhere in 1941 and were able to spare only very small obsolete air forces to defend their possessions.

Throughout the war various additional factors played a serious part in the exercise of air power. Directly affecting the air forces were their arrangements for salvage and repair. Much neglected before the war, when writing off damaged aircraft was one of the few ways to acquire money for new ones, repair and salvage organizations became vital during the conflict. By 1943 the British were obtaining up to 50% of their new aircraft from this source. Both Germany and the U.S. made great use of transport aircraft, while the British, who had pioneered in this field, concentrated on fighters and bombers and had to wait to build an air transport system until a large number of U.S. aircraft were available to engage the Germans.

As important as machines were men. The British, the Americans, and the Germans all organized air/sea rescue units which attempted to pluck airmen out of the waters around Europe and in the Pacific. By the end of the war the Allied teams were especially proficient at this. In addition to antiaircraft defenses similar to those of World War I, the British in 1939 had a chain of 20 radar stations which replaced sound locators and, when coupled to Fighter Command sector control stations, enabled defending fighters to intercept accurately approaching hostile or unidentified aircraft. This development was of particular importance during the Battle of Britain in 1940 because it enabled the few British squadrons to remain on the ground until the last moment. The British also were leaders in the development of passive defense measures. Once the government overcame its initial fear of a public panic at the thought of war, actions were taken to provide community and home shelters and to set up a national territorial organization to handle the effects of bombing. Ultimately this organization grew to include 1,000,000 people. Gas attacks never developed. Incendiary bombs became the principal weapon against which action had to be taken, and fire fighting was organized on local levels. Civilian morale in Britain remained high. The measures employed proved able to counter adequately German attacks of 1940–41. Once the British began effectively to hit Germany in 1942, the Germans had to organize similar defenses. They had a more difficult job since the British were able, with the help of the U.S. later, to bring a far greater destructive weight to bear. The British also learned from the bombing of their own country of the great effectiveness of mixing high-explosive and incendiary bombs in order to hamper the work of fire fighters. The destruction of Hamburg in July 1943, using such a mixture, was accomplished by a fire which did more damage than either of the atomic bombs dropped on Japan.

Little was done about air defense in the U.S. other than studying the problems and setting up the Air Defense Command in 1940. The war years saw the establishment of about 75 radar sets and the manning of additional observation posts by civilians, but apart from those in Alaska and the Panama Canal areas, all were dismantled in 1943 when the danger of air attack passed. The Japanese began establishing their defense system after the U.S. bombing raid of Tokyo on April 18, 1942, and intensified it in the last years of the war when raids by both U.S. carrier- and island-based aircraft occurred with increasing tempo.

In contrast to the biplanes of World War I, aircraft in World War II were nearly all monoplanes of all-metal construction armed with multiple machine guns or cannons. During most of the war these aircraft were powered by reciprocating engines, but in the last months jet and rocket-engined planes became operational. Speeds rose from about 350 to nearly 600 mph for fighters, while bombers operated at closer to 200 mph. Armament increased from four .303 machine guns to 20-mm. cannon, and some special aircraft were fitted with guns as large as 75 mm. Most bombers were equipped with multiple-gun, power-operated turrets. Rockets were developed for aircraft and used by both fighter and strike aircraft, while missiles were developed by the Germans both in the form of the V-1 pulse-jet guided airplane and the V-2 pure ballistic rocket. Bomb loads varied from the 4½-lb. incendiary and the 500-lb. general-purpose bomb to 8,000-lb. "blockbusters" and special 22,000-lb. "Tallboy" armour-piercing superbombs. Special unarmed aircraft, developed for photographic reconnaissance, flew at altitudes up to 50,000 ft. and at speeds in excess of those of their standard fighter or bomber counterparts. Naval aircraft also followed these trends as did night fighters, which were in addition usually heavily equipped later in the war with radar so that they could duel in the dark. Aircraft of World War II were technologically in a period of transition between the biplanes of the 1920s and the supersonic jets of the 1960s. By the end of the war the new high speeds were producing such problems as metal fatigue; high speeds and high altitudes were responsible for the need to develop cooling and pressurization systems.

2. Campaign in Europe, 1939–40.—On Sept. 1, 1939, the German blitzkrieg was unleashed. It was a stunning combination of land and air mobility. The Polish Air Force was largely knocked out while still on the ground in the first few days of the attack, leaving the *Luftwaffe* free to perform its tactical role of destroying railways and supporting the advancing motorized infantry and tanks. Warsaw was bombed as a tactical target and fell to the German Army on Sept. 27, 1939. The German Stuka dive-bomber scored as much a psychological victory as a military one, a result true for the blitzkrieg as a whole.

After a long lull during the winter, the Germans in April 1940 spearheaded their attack on Norway by an aerial assault across the Danish straits, with parachutists playing a prominent part in the assaults on Oslo and Stavanger. They also used transport aircraft to supply their forces in the new campaign. Next the Germans rolled into the Netherlands, Belgium, and France. In these advances the command of the air over the battlefield was generally decisively obtained by superior German air power and equipment. Fighters cleared the skies and then helped demoralize the resistance by attacks on enemy columns, both military and refugee, which the Stukas had already dive-bombed. The Ger-

mans also employed paratroopers and glider-borne groups to take key points such as the Belgian Fort Eben Emael, an assault for which they had practised against a full-scale model in Germany before the campaign. Again a city, this time Rotterdam, was bombed for tactical reasons just as it was about to surrender in a revival of the technique of striking terror into others to weaken their resistance. Allied opposition in the air was made difficult by the rapidity of the German advance after a breakthrough. The Allies were unprepared for mobile war, and confusion rapidly developed as squadrons had constantly to pull back to new temporary fields on which they were always in danger of being overrun by German ground forces. Covered by the *Luftwaffe*, German troops drove forward to cut off the British and part of the French armies at Dunkirk, but they failed to prevent the evacuation, for the beaches were within fighter cover from British bases. This enabled about 300,000 troops to be evacuated between May 26 and June 3, 1940. Meanwhile, the Germans drove on westward, Paris was declared an open city and not bombed, and France surrendered on June 22.

The lessons of this campaign were taken to heart by Britain and used effectively in the invasion campaign four years later when the Allies had absolute air superiority for approximately 100 mi. behind the Normandy beaches.

3. Battle of Britain.—Immediately after the fall of France the Germans had to pause to regroup and to sort out their strategy. Hermann Göring, as head of the *Luftwaffe*, won the day with a proposal that the air force alone be allowed to defeat Britain. Hitler could not afford to wait while a submarine blockade became effective; therefore, he had to invade. However, the Germans had not the equipment for a seaborne invasion of Britain, and so Göring's proposal seemed a logical solution. Though it might have been, it was incorrectly applied. The *Luftwaffe* attempted a daylight battle of attrition against the RAF, but quit too soon. The British were reduced to a two-week reserve of aircraft. The *Luftwaffe* then undertook a night battle, but chose once again to stop too soon. Bombing of the ports, if continued a month longer, would very likely have brought Britain to starvation. Then the planned invasion of the Soviet Union in mid-1941 drew off German forces to the Eastern Front. The *Luftwaffe*'s failure was not so much one of equipment, though its tactical bombers were not designed for strategic use and its logistics were geared for short campaigns, but of insufficient intelligence and of the mistakes of the high command.

On the British side there were certain advantages throughout the battle. The British had well-established bases and the ability to withdraw aircraft out of range. Pilots shot down often parachuted safely over England. Above all, early-warning radar was tied to a fine fighter direction system which enabled Air Chief Marshal Sir Hugh Dowding to bring superior fighter forces against many German raiding groups.

The air battle began on July 10, 1940, when the Germans attempted to clear the English Channel of British convoys. In this they were partially successful since low-flying aircraft could not be detected on British radar. The second phase began on Aug. 8 with German attacks on British fighter airfields in southern Britain; these were countered by withdrawing the squadrons to airfields farther north and by Britain's refusal to commit all the aircraft available. The third phase started at the end of August

BY COURTESY OF (ABOVE) VICKERS-ARMSTRONGS, LTD.; PHOTOGRAPH, (RIGHT) WIDE WORLD

BRITISH FIGHTER PLANES, WORLD WAR II

(Above) Supermarine Spitfire Mark XII, single-engined, single-seat fighter with a top speed of 393 mph. (Right) Hawker Hurricane, first British fighter to exceed 300 mph. During the Battle of Britain, Hurricanes shot down more enemy aircraft than all other defenses combined

GERMAN FIGHTER PLANES, WORLD WAR II
Both the Focke-Wulf Fw 190 (top left) and the Messerschmitt Me 109 (left) were fast, heavily armed aircraft. (Above) 20-mm. cannon in the wing of an Me 109

with intensified attacks on airfields and with night raids throughout the kingdom. On Aug. 25 the Germans accidentally bombed London, and the British at once retaliated with a token attack on Berlin. Hitler and Göring then decided to break the morale of Londoners as they had that of the citizens of Warsaw and Rotterdam. On Sept. 7, 1940, began a series of raids on the capital city that *Luftwaffe* commanders believed would see the end of the RAF, for they hoped that Dowding would send all forces to defend London. The critical turning point was reached when the RAF on Sept. 15, 1940, claimed to have brought down 185 (actually 60) enemy aircraft. At the end of September Göring, having already lost more than 1,650 aircraft, changed to high-altitude night raids. The battle really ended in November, but night raids against Britain continued into 1941. In the meantime, not only had the RAF won the battle over Britain, but it had also defeated a project to invade Britain by sea by destroying the barges and landing craft that the Germans had been assembling. Above all, Dowding proved that an air force could, contrary to RAF doctrine, fight a successful defensive battle.

The night bombing of Britain during the winter of 1940–41 became known as the "blitz." The attacks on British cities were sporadic and, while they did cause temporary disruption of production, they never succeeded in completely stopping it, in part due to the long-established British "shadow" factory scheme in which industry had been spread throughout the countryside. Göring's forces, however, still had a chance to defeat Britain. The true British industrial heartland was not only its own Midlands but also the United States and Canada. The strategic bottleneck, where Britain was most vulnerable, was its port system and the railways leading from it. The Germans failed to realize this and thus were unable to knock Britain out before becoming embroiled with the Soviet Union. From 1941 to 1944 the British enjoyed a respite from heavy attacks, as the *Luftwaffe* concentrated its strength elsewhere.

4. The Mediterranean.—When Italy entered the war in June 1940, the British found their supply route through the Mediterranean severed and their forces in Egypt pinched between the Italians in Libya and Ethiopia. The RAF in the Middle East possessed poorer equipment than did the Italians, but nevertheless under Field Marshal Sir Archibald Wavell the British fought a

brilliant series of actions which cleared the Italians out of Ethiopia and pushed them back in Libya. Then for political reasons forces were dissipated to help the Greeks. The resulting disaster wasted precious equipment for no gain. The Germans then made special use of their superiority in the air to invade and capture Crete. Already skilled in airborne operations and thwarted in their seaborne invasion plans by the British Navy, the Germans landed paratroops outside the perimeters of British airfields and then mortared the runways. Thus they destroyed the British defensive air force. However, British and Commonwealth troops still proceeded to put up a stiff resistance. The result was ironical. The Germans won but concluded that airborne operations were too expensive to be pursued profitably. The British lost but were convinced that future offensive operations would have to include paratroopers and glider-borne infantry.

At the same time Field Marshal Erwin Rommel had arrived in the western desert (of Libya) to take command of the German ground forces and their Italian allies. Covered by the *Luftwaffe*, he pushed the British back into Egypt. The Germans also attempted to eliminate Malta, the British island base between Sicily and Tripoli. From this small island complex the British had maintained cruiser, submarine, and air offensives which were a perpetual nuisance to the Axis. Attempts to bomb Malta into submission, like the German attacks on Britain, failed. The key to the Battle of Malta was supply. For the first time in history new aircraft were delivered by flying them off carriers brought within striking range. Such operations and several desperately needed convoys enabled Malta to hold out until the offensive started at El Alamein brought it within range of fighter protection from British bases in North Africa. Throughout the period the island sent its aircraft to sink Axis ships.

In the seesaw battles in the desert, the British had been learning a great deal about highly mobile air warfare. Air Chief Marshal Sir Arthur Tedder, commanding the RAF in the Middle East, proceeded to develop not only a mobile logistical system but also the technique of leapfrogging squadrons from airfield to airfield so that he always had operational units while others were redeploying. Thus, when Gen. Bernard Montgomery's offensive broke out at El Alamein (October–November 1942), not only was the RAF already able to bomb enemy rear bases but it was also able to imitate earlier German tactics by providing air superiority over the advancing forces. This enabled Montgomery to make an almost nonstop run of 1,200 mi. to Tripoli with air supply for his advanced units. Meanwhile, an Anglo-American force had landed in November on the northwest coast of Africa using paratroops and at first carrier-borne air cover, which was, however, quickly replaced by aircraft operating from newly constructed or captured fields ashore. By early 1943 the Germans were being penned back into the Tunisian peninsula, and Allied aircraft of both the RAF Desert Air Force and the U.S. 9th and 12th Air Forces were joining to harass both the men on the ground and those attempting to flee to Italy by air. The final German collapse in Africa in May 1943 was in part a triumph of the new Allied tactical air power.

5. War in the Soviet Union.—When Hitler attacked the Soviet Union in June 1941, he was able to bring to bear a numerically inferior air force of about 3,000 aircraft against perhaps 7,500 Soviet machines. In equipment, training, and experience, however, the Germans were far superior. Not only had they had two more years of successful campaigning in conjunction with armoured and motorized armies, but they also had far superior technical equipment, especially for radio communication and reconnaissance. Thus the *Luftwaffe* quickly gained the upper hand and possibly destroyed as many as 5,000 Soviet aircraft in the first few months of the conflict. Though the Germans bombed Moscow in July and August 1941, neither side had a strategic bomber force. The German use of air power was hindered by the vast distances in the U.S.S.R., by the extensive dispersion of the ground forces, and by the demands of other battlefronts. In addition, when winter came, German mobility was seriously affected by failure to anticipate the problems of cold-weather lubrication, low visibility, and generally hazardous operational conditions; also at that time Soviet antiaircraft fire became highly effective. One result was that around Moscow the Germans lost 1,000 out of 1,500 aircraft engaged in the winter of 1941–42. By 1942 the U.S.S.R. had achieved equal strength with Germany and was getting more modern equipment. Both sides used their air power strictly on a tactical level, the Germans in particular making great use of air transport to keep supplies moving and to concentrate forces briefly for special offensive operations. In the battle for Stalingrad (Volgograd) the German transport fleet played a major role but at great cost to itself. The Soviet Air Force gradually gained the upper hand and sealed the fate of the Germans in that city.

Industrial centres were moved behind the Urals, and the Germans had no means of striking at Soviet aircraft production. The Soviets by 1943, therefore, were able to obtain air superiority over the whole front and to begin to make the same use of air-supported armoured forces that the Germans had so successfully exploited from 1939 to 1941. Though a Soviet long-range force was revived, its operations were largely in the form of token raids. It is not surprising that a force which rarely dispatched more than 100 aircraft on any one raid made little impact when the Allies in the West with much larger forces equipped with much more sophisticated systems also made relatively small impact on Germany until 1944. Soviet superiority was helped by the permanent withdrawal of one of the three German air fleets to meet the needs of the North African campaign of 1942–43 and by

the withdrawal of other units to help man the defenses at home. On the other hand, the Soviet high command misjudged the direction of the German thrust that was blunted at Stalingrad and concentrated their air force about Moscow to the north. It took them some time to reorient it to meet Göring's attack. At the same time the U.S.S.R. used air transport to move toughened troops into the Stalingrad area, an operation that the *Luftwaffe* could not disrupt because the Soviets had at last obtained modern escort fighters and because new attack aircraft were used against the German forward airfields. Weather, too, came to the aid of the Soviets. And, lastly, it must be recalled that the Allied attacks from the West on Germany tied 75% of German production of fighters to home defense. Thus for the last three years of the war the Soviets were given almost undisputed control of the air over their armies. Numerically, this meant that the Germans normally never had more than 2,000 aircraft on the Eastern Front with which to oppose 10,000 to 15,000 Soviet planes. In aircrew the situation was also virtually the reverse of that in 1941. Poorly trained Germans in badly maintained aircraft faced more and more experienced Soviets. In addition the Soviets, who had pioneered the use of rockets against armour, now were experts at that type of harassment.

In the last years of the war the U.S.S.R. had 18 air armies in action, supported by a well-drilled, flexible organization with a swiftly flowing supply stream from factories in the rear. The Germans increasingly began to find the skies over their airfields filled with Soviet bombers and fighters which had quickly followed earlier Soviet reconnaissance flights. Nevertheless, the Soviets still lacked radar and night-fighter equipment, with the result that the Germans were as late as 1944 able to raid Poltava, the shuttle base in the U.S.S.R. of U.S. Flying Fortresses that had flown over Germany from Britain. The last German air offensive was that in connection with the attacks near Kursk and Orel, and it failed. From then until the end of the war, the Soviet Air Force was the absolute master of the Eastern Front. But when the war ended no one on the Allied side really knew how well the Soviets could perform the much more complex businesses of strategic bombing and air defense, because they had never seriously

BY COURTESY OF (TOP LEFT AND RIGHT, BOTTOM RIGHT) THE AIR FORCE MUSEUM, WRIGHT-PATTERSON AIR FORCE BASE, OHIO; PHOTOGRAPH, (BOTTOM LEFT) SOVFOTO

LIGHT BOMBERS, WORLD WAR II

(Top left) Douglas A-20 U.S. light bomber carried seven 0.30-in. machine guns and 2,600 lb. of bombs. (Top right) Messerschmitt Me 110, German twin-engined, two-seat fighter-bomber. (Bottom left) Ilyushin IL-2 Stormovik, Soviet two-seat plane designed for ground attack, carried two 32-mm. cannon and four machine guns. (Bottom right) Potez 63, versatile French fighter and light bomber, could carry eight 124-lb. bombs at speeds up to 280 mph

undertaken these tasks. Theirs had been a tactical war.

6. Strategic Air Offensive Against Germany.—A major tenet of prewar British air power philosophy was that an enemy would be deterred by the threat of a counterstrike at his vitals. The theory presupposed the ability to deliver such blows in the event of war. In fact, no air force in 1939 was capable of undertaking such operations. It was not, in fact, until after five years of war that the means for striking devastating blows with conventional bombs existed in sufficient quantity and quality to become a serious threat to German production. The Germans had, it is true, almost succeeded against Britain, but Britain's was a much more vulnerable insular economy. To attack Germany effectively from the air it was necessary to have a considerable knowledge of the whole German economic organization. This was lacking, as also was an effective appreciation of the limited damage being done by the bombing which was undertaken. Indeed, it is not unfair to say that the RAF in 1939–42 was not suited to the offensive role it had to play against a Germany constantly expanding its economic resources and its productive machinery. It is significant that both the British and the German economies only reached their wartime peaks in 1944.

The British had assumed that their new aircraft, such as Wel-

BY COURTESY OF (BELOW) REPUBLIC AVIATION DIVISION, FAIRCHILD HILLER CORP.; PHOTOGRAPH, (ABOVE) WIDE WORLD

U.S. FIGHTER PLANES, WORLD WAR II

(Above) North American P-51 Mustang armed with four 20-mm. cannon. The addition of wing-drop tanks in 1943 gave the P-51 a range of more than 2,000 mi., making long-range bomber escort missions possible. (Below) Republic P-47 Thunderbolt was used both as a long-range escort and a fighter bomber. Shown is the P-47N, which could carry two 1,000-lb. bombs

The bomber aircraft employed at the beginning of the war were all twin-engined types capable of carrying up to 4,500 lb. of bombs on short raids and about 1,000 lb. when attacking objectives at longer distances. Powered by two 1,000-hp. engines, these partially fabric-covered aircraft could cruise at 180 mph and could operate effectively from a maximum altitude of about 18,000 ft. The four-engined aircraft which began to join Bomber Command in 1942 were epitomized by the end of the war by the all-metal Avro Lancaster, which could carry about 12,000 lb. of bombs approximately 900 mi. from bases in England to Berlin at a speed of 210 mph and drop them from about 23,000 ft. On occasion these aircraft could carry a 22,000-lb. "Grand Slam" earthquake bomb such as those used to destroy the Bielefield Viaduct (March 14, 1945). The U.S. daylight bombers entered the war over Europe with a .50-calibre machine-gun armament in contrast to the British .303. Both the Boeing B-17 and the Consolidated B-24 carried smaller bombloads than the equivalent British aircraft but had a much greater supply of ammunition and remained the mainstay of the U.S. Army Air Force throughout operations.

The British Spitfire, while an excellent fighter, even with drop tanks never developed a useful range for bomber escort operations against Germany. More-

lingtons, equipped with power-operated turrets and flying in close formation, would be able to operate in daytime. They were quickly disillusioned by German Me 109s whose cannons outranged the machine guns in the British aircraft. Early night operations were mostly leaflet raids, which allowed crews to learn night navigation over a blacked-out Europe. When bombs were carried, the crews, just as in the Zeppelin raids of World War I, came back with glowing reports of the damage done. It took until 1942 for photographic reconnaissance units to convince Bomber Command headquarters that most of the bombs were going at least five miles wide of their targets. By the end of the war, with the development of Pathfinder forces to mark targets and with radar as a guide, bombing accuracy was brought within 300 yd. Partly because of the weakness in navigation and aiming of bombs, targets were changed from precise to more general objectives.

The problems which afflicted the RAF Bomber Command in 1939–42 also troubled the U.S. Army Air Corps' 8th Air Force when it became operational in 1942. But the U.S. arrived at a different solution. While the British specialized in night operations and their aircraft flew singly within "streams," U.S. aircraft flew in tight defensive formations and undertook daylight precision bombing. But this type of operation was not successful until the development, at British suggestion, of a long-range escort fighter, the most successful of which was the P-51 Mustang. This aircraft, which together with the P-47 Thunderbolt fought the main battle of fighter attrition over Germany, was not available until early 1944. It was only from that date that a really effective round-the-clock bombardment of Germany went into effect.

over, night operations made the carrying of a radar operator essential. It was only after a large number of the sleek twin-engined de Havilland Mosquitoes became available that night fighters were employed defensively in the British bomber formations. In daylight, however, escort was quite a different matter. The U.S. extended the range of its strikes as longer-ranged escort aircraft became available and relay systems were worked out. The Mustang was ideal in that with drop tanks it had a range of 1,700 mi., a speed well over 400 mph, and six .50-calibre machine guns.

To meet the Allied strategic air offensive, the Germans relied primarily on heavy flak (antiaircraft) boxes around likely targets together with flak belts dispersed across bomber routes, especially over the Low Countries, and also on a variety of fighter forces. In the daytime the backbone of the German defense was the Me 109 and the Fw 190, both fast, maneuverable, single-seater fighters. These were supported by rocket-equipped, twin-engined aircraft and late in the war by the rocket-driven Me 163 and by a handful of new jet fighters, the first of their kind in the world. In the period before 1944 the bombers of the U.S. 8th Air Force had to strike beyond the range of their fighter escorts and suffered severe losses. But beginning in 1944 U.S. fighters were able both to escort their own bombers and to roam German skies looking for fights. As U.S. pilots became more experienced, German pilots were becoming less so due to a shortage of gasoline for training; German losses rose sharply, despite adequate fighter production up to September 1944. One counter to both ground and airborne radar defenses was the development of "window," metallic foil strips which fogged radar screens. Airborne jamming devices

BY COURTESY OF (LEFT) THE AIR FORCE MUSEUM, WRIGHT-PATTERSON AIR FORCE BASE, OHIO; PHOTOGRAPH, (RIGHT) "AEROPLANE"

(LEFT) FOCKE-WULF Fw 200 CONDOR, GERMAN FOUR-ENGINED RECONNAISSANCE BOMBER CONVERTED FROM A COMMERCIAL AIRLINER IN 1940. (RIGHT) AVRO LANCASTER I, FOUR-ENGINED BRITISH HEAVY BOMBER. DESIGNED FOR NIGHT BOMBING WITHOUT ESCORT, IT HAD A BOMB CAPACITY UP TO 22,000 LB.

were also used, but in a seesaw technical battle throughout the war first one side and then the other developed a measure or a countermeasure. To help identify friends, Allied aircraft were fitted with I.F.F. (Identification Friend or Foe) which gave a special signal on radar sets.

It was only in March 1940 that the British government began to allow RAF aircraft to bomb targets in Germany, and the first raid on Berlin was not carried out until Aug. 25, 1940. Thereafter, the RAF sought and was finally granted permission to engage in raids against cities when it became obvious that it was unable to hit specific targets and at a time when Britain had no other means of striking at Germany. Even after this much of the weakness of the British attack was due to lack of knowledge of the German industrial system and its vulnerable points, though many lessons learned from the German bombing of Britain were applied. RAF Bomber Command began to come into its own only after the appointment of Air Chief Marshal Sir Arthur Harris in 1942 at a time when heavy bombers such as the Lancaster and Halifax were becoming available. Attacks on German oil and attacks to undermine morale were the basis of the campaign from November 1940; they were not effective—the weight of bombs dropped was only 100 tons per raid. Moreover, aircraft were constantly being switched to the Battle of the Atlantic (see below). In 1941 the RAF Bomber Command proposed the revival of the plan to strike against German transportation, regarding this as the main bottleneck against which the power available would be most destructive and, therefore, effective. In July the British government agreed to couple the attack on transportation to that on morale. The next month a high-level British Cabinet study (the Butt Report) vindicated the reports that bombing of specific targets had been generally inaccurate, and area bombing was, therefore, adopted. That Churchill agreed to this was due primarily to the fact that this was the only way at the time that Britain could strike effectively at Germany. At the same time, an intensive search to make Bomber Command more effective led to a successful liaison between the operational scientists, or "boffins," and D. C. T. Bennett, a former RAF and airline pilot and a specialist in navigation who had returned to

active duty. Under Bennett, the Pathfinders were developed. These were selected crews who marked targets with coloured incendiary bombs and then circled the targets radioing instructions to arriving bombers. At the same time, the Butt Report led to the appointment of Air Marshal Sir Arthur Harris, who led the Bomber Command for the rest of the war. Harris at once initiated a series of raids, culminating in the 1,000-plane attack on Cologne (May 30, 1942). This raid was primarily conducted with twin-engined aircraft from both operational and training units, for the force at the time could usually operate only 500 aircraft on any given day. By the end of the war, however, the normal force was 1,000 four-engined heavy bombers. At the same time better liaison was established between the target experts in the Bomber Command and those in the Ministry of Economic Warfare.

Just as RAF Bomber Command was becoming effective, the first elements of the U.S. 8th Air Force began to undertake operations. Twelve aircraft attacked Rouen in daylight on Aug. 17, 1942, but, owing to the need to provide aircraft and crews for the 12th Air Force engaged in the North African campaign beginning in November 1942, the U.S. buildup for bombing Germany was slow. By 1943 about 100 aircraft were available daily and on Jan. 27, 1943, the first attack on Germany proper was undertaken in a raid on Wilhelmshaven. The range of raids was extended as escort fighters became available and on Aug. 17, 1943, the ball-bearing factory at Schweinfurt was struck. Casualties on those raids were high, especially in the second attack on Schweinfurt on Oct. 14, 1943, and the 8th spent much of the fall of 1943 reorganizing. Despite the directives from the Casablanca Conference, calling for unconditional surrender, all attempts by the air forces to give priority to the campaign in Germany were defeated by the necessities of the Battle of the Atlantic. (See further WORLD WAR II CONFERENCES, ALLIED.) Nor were there the necessary daylight escort fighters. So it was not until February 1944 that something like round-the-clock attacks on Germany could be undertaken, and then only when the weather over British bases was such that aircraft could make sorties even though radar-bombing equipment enabled attacks to penetrate cloud cover over Germany.

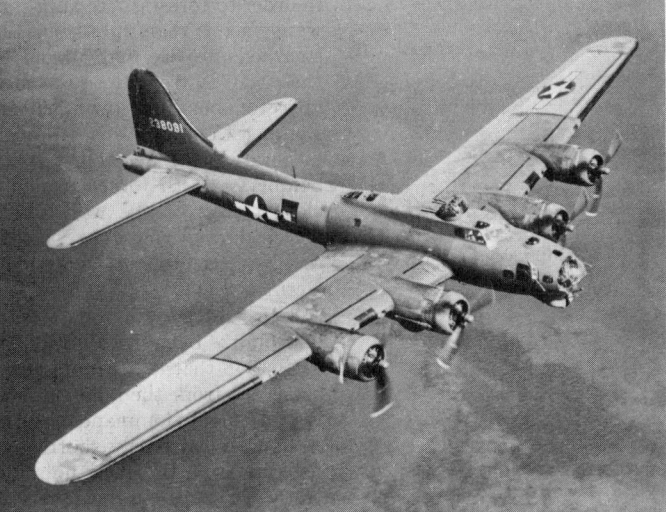

BOEING PHOTO

BOEING B-17 FLYING FORTRESS, FOUR-ENGINED HEAVY BOMBER USED BY U.S. AND BRITISH AIR FORCES. THE MODEL "G" SHOWN HERE CARRIED THIRTEEN 0.50-IN. MACHINE GUNS FOR DEFENSE AGAINST FIGHTER ATTACKS

While the British were beginning to lose the initiative in night raids in late 1943 due to increased effectiveness on the part of German night fighters, the U.S. was preparing to go over to offensive rather than evasive tactics. On Feb. 20, 1944, the 8th Air Force struck once again at Schweinfurt, but this time it was fully escorted all the way, forcing the *Luftwaffe* either to fly and fight or be destroyed on the ground. This began the air battle of Germany, a frank war of destruction of industry and of attrition in the air. Göring was reluctant to believe that the Allies could penetrate German airspace at will, but Gen. Adolf Galland, his fighter commander, took off to find out and was chased all the way back to Berlin by U.S. Mustangs. Losses of German fighters in one period during February 1944 approached 15%, causing Göring to order his fighters to attack only bombers and to avoid fighter escorts. In response to this, the U.S. bomber forces in March were routed along provocation tracks and the escorts were detached to fight any German planes that rose to battle. The Germans could not recover in the face of these tactics because they could not withdraw their forces, as Dowding had been able to do in the Battle of Britain, to fields beyond the range of U.S. forces. In the meantime, U.S. and British forces based in Italy had been for some time striking into Germany in addition to undertaking special raids, such as that against the Ploești oil fields in Rumania (Aug. 1, 1943) carried out by more than 170 B-24's. The entire effort was coordinated by U.S. Gen. Carl Spaatz, working with the RAF's Sir Charles Portal, the chief of the U.K. air staff.

Although the Germans could put up about 850 fighter planes on any given day, the results were far from what they would have been in 1940 due to the decline in quality of their pilots and their shortage of fuel. On both sides when losses in any unit began to exceed 5% per raid, the practice was to withdraw the unit, if possible, for rest, training, and reequipment. In part, in early 1944 the problem of losses to night fighters was hidden by the fact that the RAF Bomber Command was diverted to strike against targets in France, where the German night fighter force was not especially strong.

PHOTOGRAPHS (TOP) KEYSTONE, (BOTTOM) BOEING PHOTO

(TOP) DE HAVILLAND MOSQUITO, BRITISH FIGHTER AND LIGHT BOMBER, WAS THE FASTEST RAF AIRCRAFT UNTIL 1944. THE BOMBER VERSION COULD CARRY A 4,000-LB. BOMB LOAD, COMPARING FAVOURABLY WITH MOST MEDIUM BOMBERS, AND WAS EQUIPPED WITH NO DEFENSIVE ARMAMENT BECAUSE OF ITS HIGH SPEED. (BOTTOM) CONSOLIDATED PBY CATALINA, U.S. LONG-RANGE OCEAN-PATROL FLYING BOAT, WAS USED TO OBSERVE FLEET MOVEMENTS AND TO ATTACK SUBMARINES

After the Normandy invasion by the Allies on June 6, 1944, the Germans began to lose their advantage in two ways. First, the conquest of France and the Low Countries resulted in the loss of Germany's early-warning radar stations, and second, the conquest allowed the British to begin sending their own long-range night fighters over Germany. This resulted in an improved situation from the British point of view, but it was still a seesaw technical battle until the end of the war.

The preparations for the Normandy invasion involved some acrimonious disputes over strategy, which ultimately affected the battle over Germany by siphoning off Allied air strength to disrupt transportation in France and in effect to seal off the land battlefield. From March 1944 until September 1944 the U.S. 8th Air Force and RAF Bomber Command were placed with the Allied Expeditionary Air Forces under the supreme commander, Gen. Dwight Eisenhower, whose deputy, Sir Arthur Tedder, was responsible for the "communication plan," as the pre-D-Day program was called. This delayed the attack on German oil supplies but at the same time allowed the air weapon to be used as had been intended in 1918 as a supplement to tactical air forces when the occasion required. At the same time, with the outbreak of German V-1 (self-propelled jet-powered pilotless bomb) and V-2 (long-range ballistic rocket) attacks upon Britain, bombers were diverted to destroy the launching sites along the French, Belgian, and Dutch coasts. The real return to the oil strategy, probably the most correct of all the bomber objectives during the war, did not take place until September except by the units operating from Italy against Rumanian targets. But even by then it was the precision attacks in May 1944 which had drastically cut German oil production for June. These attacks, Albert Speer, the overseer of all German production, called decisive as far as the war was concerned. After them Germany had no hope of winning. For the rest of the war, and especially after the bombers were handed back to their commanders by Eisenhower in September 1944, Allied bombers ranged over Germany, attacking transportation and oil targets. In the final days of the war an argument arose on the western Allied side as to whether or not the bomber forces should be used to aid the Soviet forces or whether they should strike a blow which would make the German people realize that they had lost the war. The choice fell upon the latter. On Feb. 13–14, 1945, Dresden was attacked in what has since become probably the most controversial raid of the war. Apart from that one blow the Allied bomber force, then capable of dropping 134,000 tons a month with an accuracy within three miles, engaged in a major mine-laying campaign which hamstrung German coastal shipping and also disrupted German submarine training by strikes into the Baltic Sea. A considerable effort was also devoted to the destruction of German submarine building facilities and assembly lines in order to forestall the appearance at sea of the new models which were faster than most surface escorts. As the Allied armies smashed into Germany from the west and Soviet armies forced their way in from the east, the number of strategic targets available for bombing dwindled rapidly. On April 7, 1945, RAF Bomber Command discontinued area bombings, and on April 16 General Spaatz declared the strategic air war at an end for U.S. bombers. Both forces turned to assist the ground forces in the closing days of the war. Their final missions were errands of mercy during which they dropped food to the starving people of the Netherlands and evacuated liberated prisoners of war from Germany.

The strategic air offensive against Germany took a great time to mount. It was not until 1944 that it became effective and not until 1945 that it became truly disruptive with masses of refugees displaced from their homes both by the Soviet advances and by RAF Bomber Command's urban attacks. After mid-1944 the Germans were extremely short of oil and all their operations suffered severely from this lack, notably the Ardennes offensive at the end of the year. Though alone it did not bring Germany to defeat, the use of strategic air power brought home to the civilian population the fact that Germany had been defeated. During the course of the war against Germany, the Anglo-American air forces dropped almost 2,700,000 tons of bombs. At the same time, it must not be overlooked that the battle over Germany was intimately connected to the Battle of the Atlantic.

7. Battle of the Atlantic.— The ability of the Allied air forces to undertake offensive operations from defended bases in Britain was conditioned by the successful movement of supplies from the U.S. industrial heartland to Britain. This was a major logistical operation involving food, raw materials, and finished products, all of which were vital. It also encompassed problems of shipbuilding, repair, and the division of manpower between many vital services. For the Germans the problem was to find and destroy the convoys passing across the North Atlantic. In this latter task the Germans made relatively little use of air power apart from some long-range reconnaissance by Focke-Wulf Kurier aircraft after the conquest of Norway and France and attacks by torpedo bombers against Soviet convoys. In contrast, the British, and later in the war, the Americans, made

BY COURTESY OF U.S. AIR FORCE

U.S. CONSOLIDATED B-24 LIBERATOR BOMBERS ATTACKING OIL REFINERIES AT PLOEŞTI, RUM., MAY 31, 1944

great use of air power in the Battle of the Atlantic. Near the British coast antisubmarine and fighter patrols protected convoys. Gradually, as newer long-range aircraft became available to supplement the Short Sunderland flying boats, patrols were flown over the Atlantic at ever greater distances from bases in western England, Northern Ireland, Scotland, Iceland, and Canada. In April 1941 the British Admiralty was given operational control over RAF Coastal Command, and a strongly coordinated air-sea effort was put into effect. But by that time the Germans had been able to build bombproof shelters for their submarines, notably at Brest, France. Considerable effort by RAF Bomber Command did little damage to submarines in such shelters, but the Admiralty demand for such action hampered Bomber Command's attack on Germany. Late in 1941 British air patrols were reinforced with both very-long-range Consolidated Liberator (B-24) bombers and by the development of escort aircraft carriers. As the number of squadrons available for antisubmarine warfare increased, offensive measures were adopted. Increasingly, Coastal Command aircraft patrolled the Bay of Biscay, forcing German submarines to remain submerged while proceeding to and from their patrol areas. In this cat-and-mouse game much depended both on the alertness of air crews on flights of up to 18 hours and upon technical developments. Radar was used by both sides; the British developed the Leigh light to illuminate submarines on the surface at night, and also introduced de Havilland Mosquito aircraft, which were equipped with both rockets and 57-mm. cannon. The Germans countered by equipping their submarines with quadruple 20-mm. gun mounts and instructing them to fight on the surface. These measures resulted in a seesaw battle throughout the war. Among the major factors helping the Allies to win was the use of continuous air escort for convoys crossing the North Atlantic. Allied aircraft were responsible for destroying many German submarines.

The battle in the Atlantic was, however, only part of a complex logistical war. Throughout the conflict two schools of thought existed about the best way to deal with Germany's submarines. Logically the airmen were correct in advocating the destruction of submarine construction facilities and the harassment of crews under training, but they were unable to achieve those objectives. Thus in practical terms the Navy was correct when it argued that under the circumstances the convoys were the most vital element and that the correct method was to draw the submarines toward them, where they could be destroyed by the convoy escorts. The Admiralty alternated between these two courses of action and often requisitioned Bomber Command aircraft to undertake attacks on objectives of special interest to the Navy.

When the U.S. entered the war at the end of 1941, Germany quickly transferred many of its submarines to the U.S. coast, thus compelling the U.S. to organize air patrols. Of considerable influence among those were the U.S. Navy's nonrigid airships, which were able to undertake patrols of several days' duration and were particularly useful because they were slow enough to be able to stay above a submerged submarine.

8. Invasion of Fortress Europe.— For the liberation of Western Europe and the conquest of Germany the Allies gathered their most powerful forces. The RAF 2nd Tactical Air Force and the U.S. 9th Air Force were organized to provide support for the ground armies. In the months preceding D-day the tactical air forces used their thousands of medium and fighter bombers against airfields, radar, and V-weapon sites, locomotives and rolling stock, and gun emplacements in German-occupied France and the Low Countries. The strategic bombers joined in the assault against railroads and other targets. Before D-day, German access to the Normandy area by rail had been blocked as far back as the Seine River. Incessant attacks by the Allied air forces drove the German air units back from their bases in the west to the interior of France and even into Germany itself. Many fighter units were withdrawn to defend Germany against the devastating attacks of Anglo-American bombers. By D-day the Germans in the Normandy area had a total of 160 fighters, of which only 80 were operational.

On D-day the Allied air forces flew almost 15,000 sorties during a 24-hour period. The massive assault was begun during the night by thousands of transports and gliders, which dropped whole airborne divisions in the hedgerows of Normandy. Allied fighters ruled the air over the landing zone and deep inland for many miles. Allied heavy and medium bombers struck at every manner of target which might have a bearing on the battle— coastal batteries, beach defenses, railroad centres, bridges, airfields, depots. The weak German air units were able to dispatch only 250 planes against the landings, of which barely a dozen were fighter bombers. The complete success of the assault was made possible by the overwhelming air superiority of the Allies.

BY COURTESY OF U.S. AIR FORCE

U.S. PARATROOPS LANDING IN SOUTHERN FRANCE IN 1944

the months immediately preceding Germany's surrender May 8, 1945. The *Luftwaffe*, which only a few years before had been the world's most powerful air force, was knocked out and ceased to exist.

A notable feature of the land campaign in Europe was Allied use of airborne troops. First used offensively by the U.S.S.R. against Finland in 1939 and then most successfully by the Germans in their blitzkriegs until their victory at Crete in 1941, airborne operations were then taken up by the western Allies. The Germans developed glider and air-transport forces to provide airborne units with the necessary heavy equipment. But, in general, airborne units were intended to be used for rapid seizure of bridgeheads, and their maximum endurance was about four days. In July 1943 the British 1st Airborne Division seized vital bridgeheads about Syracuse, Sicily, and the U.S. 82nd Airborne Division was used in the main assault on Sicily. In the predawn darkness of D-Day in

The pattern of air domination established on D-day continued for the remainder of the campaign. Anglo-American fighter bombers spearheaded the breakthroughs which collapsed the German lines and sent their armies into headlong retreat. Allied heavy bombers helped prepare the way for the breakthrough at Saint-Lô, France, in July 1944 with a tremendous bombardment of the battle area. At Mortain, France, early in August, the fighter bombers of the U.S. 9th Air Force and the British 2nd Tactical Air Force ended German hopes of launching a counterattack which would sweep the Allied armies back into the ocean. The *Luftwaffe* was unable to offer any effective opposition in the air because of the pressure maintained by the superior Allied air forces. In one of the most remarkable events of the war, a large body of German troops trapped south of the Loire River in August 1944 insisted on surrendering to a representative of the U.S. 19th Tactical Air Command, which had so harried them from the air that they had lost all hope of escape even though they had not encountered any Allied ground forces.

On Aug. 15, 1944, U.S. and French forces landed in southern France and fought their way northward to a junction in eastern France with the Allied armies which had surged across France from Normandy. U.S. and French air units, organized as the 1st Tactical Air Force (provisional), provided air cover for this swift advance from the Mediterranean to the Swiss border near Belfort, France.

In the rapid sweep across France, the Allied tactical air forces kept on the heels of the retreating armies. By the end of September, the British and Americans had airfields in operation in central France and in Belgium, while the *Luftwaffe* had been flung back into Germany proper. Until December 1944 a comparative lull existed in the ground battle while the two exhausted armies girded themselves for the next round. The German attack in the Ardennes in December—the "Battle of the Bulge"—after an initial success was blunted and turned back once Allied air power came into full play.

The Allies resumed their offensive in February 1945. German resistance in the air was at an absolute minimum except for an occasional fierce attack on Allied heavy bombers, and the German armies were at the mercy of the Allied planes. The heavy bombers joined increasingly in the assault on tactical targets in

Normandy, the 6th British and the 82nd and 101st U.S. airborne divisions landed behind the beaches. Earlier in 1944 the 1st Allied Airborne Army had been created, and it was held in readiness for some months after D-Day. Its day came in the operations to open a corridor for Field Marshal Bernard Montgomery's 21st Army Group to seize the bridges across the Rhine River. U.S. airborne units successfully took Nijmegen and Eindhoven and held them until the ground forces broke through to their support. However, the most advanced group, the British who landed at Arnhem, was unsuccessful for reasons which clearly illustrated the problems of airborne operations. They were dropped too far ahead of the ground forces, which were delayed, and they landed on top of a German armoured division at rest, a unit of which Allied intelligence had been unaware. Resupply for the airborne troops was badly handled due to radio failures. Finally, bad weather prevented fighter support from providing vital antitank assistance. In March 1945 the largest airborne assault of the war took place under conditions the reverse of those at Arnhem. A total of 17,122 paratroopers, 614 jeeps, and 286 pieces of artillery plus tons of supplies were airlanded or dropped within two hours on the east bank of the Rhine near Wesel to seize a bridgehead; the operation was immediately supported by troops crossing the river in landing craft.

The war in Europe also led to the development of new uses for aviation by armies. The Germans developed the Fiesler Storch light observation aircraft for use by blitzkrieg commanders and artillery spotters. The British saw the effectiveness of this type of plane in the North African campaign and in 1940 developed their own system of aerial observation posts using aircraft of the Taylor Cub variety. U.S. observers saw these at the Royal Artillery School in 1941 and persuaded the U.S. War Department to adopt the idea. "Bird Dogs" as they eventually were named, became part of the U.S. Army in June 1942. They flew artillery spotting, liaison, and other missions close to the front lines.

9. Italian Campaign.—Although eventually overshadowed by the main arena of war in Western Europe, the campaign in Italy contributed greatly to the Allied victory. After the conquest of Tunisia in May 1943, the Allied bombers forced the surrender of the key islands of Pantelleria and Lampedusa, thereby making it unnecessary to fight what was expected to be a difficult ground campaign for their possession. In July and August 1943 the veteran British and U.S. air units drove the *Luftwaffe* and the Italian *Regia Aeronautica* out of the skies over Sicily and helped hammer the German and Italian ground forces in Sicily into submission.

The invasion of the Italian mainland in September met strong resistance at Salerno and might have failed but for the prompt and effective use of Allied bombers and fighters against the German efforts to destroy the beachhead. The Allied air forces, the RAF Desert Air Force and the U.S. 12th Air Force, paced the armies in their advance up the peninsula, until the Germans, aided by bad weather and rugged terrain, succeeded in halting the Allies. The amphibious landing at Anzio in January 1944, which was protected by Allied air power, pinned down a large portion of the German forces and helped make possible the resumption of the Allied advance in the spring. The retreating *Luftwaffe,* out-

BY COURTESY OF U.S. AIR FORCE

GERMAN CITY OF WESEL AFTER BOMBING DURING WORLD WAR II

numbered as much as ten to one, could not interfere effectively with Allied air or ground operations except by an occasional major effort. In the campaign which led to the capture of Rome in June and a sweep beyond to the north, the Allied air forces hammered systematically at German communication lines and supplies in Operation Strangle, which cut the German armies off from their supplies and forced them into what often became disorganized retreats.

After reaching the northern Apennines, the Allies bogged down in October 1944, partly as a result of having transferred a substantial portion of their strength to France. During the winter of 1944–45 the Allied air forces had the chief responsibility on the Italian front for maintaining constant pressure on the German forces. So complete was Allied air control that medium bombers usually flew without escort. Once again the Anglo-American fighters and bombers blocked German supply lines so thoroughly, especially at the Po River and the Brenner Pass, that when the Allied armies resumed their advance in April 1945, they met little opposition from the German forces, which surrendered on May 2.

10. Pilotless Aircraft and Rocket Campaign.—One of the most significant features of the air war in Europe was the use of pilotless aircraft and rockets by the Germans. Rumours of the impending use of new weapons against the U.K. had been current for some time before the British became convinced of their existence and took measures to counteract them in 1943. In August 1943 RAF Bomber Command attacked and heavily damaged the Peenemünde experimental station on the Baltic, where the V-weapons, as they became known, were being developed and tested.

German preparations for launching the weapons from sites in France were discovered during the summer of 1943, and the Anglo-American air forces quickly began a systematic campaign—known as "Crossbow"—against those sites. The campaign was extended to the factories producing the weapons and the plants manufacturing the hydrogen and liquid oxygen fuels which powered them. This bombing campaign lasted 13 months, during which Allied planes dropped 100,000 tons of bombs on "Crossbow" targets, 9% of the total tonnage dropped during that period. It was estimated by the Allies that the bomber attacks delayed the beginning of the German V-weapon campaign by about three to six months.

The German programs for development and production of the V-1 and the V-2 did not keep pace with established goals. Inter-

service rivalries, interference by Hitler, and Allied bombings delayed the beginning of the V-1 campaign until June 13, 1944, when the first V-1 fell in southern England. This weapon, which came to be known as the "flying bomb" and the "doodle-bug," was a pulse-jet pilotless aircraft with 2,000 lb. of explosives in its nose and a speed of nearly 400 mph. In all, about 8,000 V-1s were launched against England, most of them directed at the London area. The attacks against England killed 6,139 people and seriously injured 17,239, causing extensive damage in urban areas. However, Allied airplanes and antiaircraft guns proved successful in countering the V-1 threat during the height of the attacks against London in July and August 1944. After the loss of the continental coast to the Allied armies in the summer of 1944, the Germans switched to targets on the European continent held by the Allies, chiefly Antwerp, Belg., which received most of the additional V-1s launched.

By early September 1944 the V-1 threat had been greatly reduced because of the loss of the launching sites in France. But on Sept. 8, 1944, the first V-2 fell in the London area, and before the end of the war about 1,100 exploded in England and 1,675 on the continent, again chiefly in Antwerp. The V-2 was a ballistic missile. It was 46 ft. long and more than 5 ft. in diameter, carried a ton of explosives in its warhead, had a range of about 200 mi. and a speed of more than 3,000 mph, and was propelled by a liquid oxygen fuel. The Germans launched most of the V-2s from sites in the Netherlands. The rockets killed 2,855 and severely injured 6,268 people in England.

The V-weapon campaign did not significantly affect the conduct of the air war in Europe. To be sure, in order to counter the weapons, the Allies had to divert a substantial portion of their bombing effort from German targets and were also forced to use large numbers of troops and guns against the V-1s. But in producing and operating these weapons the Germans expended enormous resources which might have been used more effectively for other military purposes. The V-2, especially, carried fewer explosives than a conventional bomber and usually penetrated too deep on impact to have much effect. Since it could not be heard approaching, it lacked the psychological power of the V-1 whose point of potential impact was always a matter of uncertainty to those who could see or hear its approach. Nevertheless, the development and use of the V-2 rocket by the Germans ushered in the age of guided missiles and went far toward establishing patterns for the future. (See ROCKETS AND GUIDED MISSILES.)

11. Air War in the Pacific.—In the Pacific phase of World War II the Japanese, like the Germans in Europe, gained an early advantage by advance preparations and surprise attacks. At Pearl Harbor, on Dec. 7, 1941, Japanese naval aircraft temporarily crippled U.S. naval power in the Pacific. On Dec. 10, 1941, Japanese bombers sank two major British naval vessels off Malaya, eliminating British naval power from the Far East for some time to come.

Freed of serious naval opposition during this crucial early phase of the war, the Japanese Army and Navy, operating under an air umbrella, conquered the Philippines, Malaya, Burma, the Dutch East Indies (now Indonesia), and other islands in the Pacific. In its speed and effectiveness, the Japanese advance rivaled the German blitzkriegs in Europe. In the air they usually faced untried Allied pilots in obsolescent aircraft.

Stiffening Allied resistance eventually brought the Japanese advance to a halt in the Pacific, first at Midway, west of Hawaii, and then at Guadalcanal in the Solomon Islands and in the Owen Stanley Mountains of New Guinea. In Burma the situation became stabilized at the Indian frontier, and the Japanese were destined never to attain their dream of conquering India. The

BY COURTESY OF (ABOVE) COL. G. B. JARRETT (RET'D); PHOTOGRAPH, (BELOW) "AEROPLANE"

JET FIGHTERS, WORLD WAR II

(Above) German Messerschmitt Me 262, world's first operational warplane powered by turbojet engines, entered combat service in mid-1944. Antenna on plane's nose indicates radar equipment for night use. (Below) Gloster Meteor, British turbojet fighter, had a top speed of 585 mph. The Meteor was the only Allied jet aircraft used in World War II

headlong Japanese advance carved out an enormous empire rich in resources but with a fatal defect that soon became apparent. The conquering forces at the far ends of this empire had to be supplied and reinforced over sea-lanes, which soon became the hunting grounds of U.S. and British aircraft and submarines. The subsequent strain on Japanese shipping proved too great to be endured, and the perimeter of Japanese dominion in the Pacific shrank steadily after 1942.

Although the tide of Japanese conquest surged mightily during the first eight months of the war, the U.S. Army Air Forces and the U.S. Navy joined forces to bring the war home to Japan itself in a grim warning of the future. On April 18, 1942, Lieut. Col. James H. Doolittle led 16 Army Air Force B-25 bombers from the U.S. Navy aircraft carrier "Hornet" in a spectacular low-level attack against Tokyo and other Japanese cities. Although all of the planes were lost in bad weather over China, most of the crews were saved. In addition to the heartening psychological effect in the United States and in other Allied countries, the raid probably caused the Japanese to retain four army fighter groups in Japan during 1942 and 1943, when they were badly needed in the South Pacific. It appears also that the Doolittle

raid impelled the Japanese to push beyond their originally planned defensive perimeter, thereby increasing the vulnerability of their supply lines.

Burma and China.—In Burma the monsoon rains brought the Japanese advance to an end on the Indian frontier at the beginning of the summer of 1942. The fighters and tactical bombers of the RAF and the U.S. 10th Air Force played a dominant role in turning back Japanese attacks during 1943 and 1944. One of the most remarkable aspects of the war in Burma, and of World War II as a whole, was the supply of whole British armies by air for extended periods of time. During the Imphal campaign in the spring of 1944, an army of 150,000 men in contact with the enemy was maintained solely from the air by RAF and U.S. Army Air Force transport planes.

The great offensive of 1944–45 which reconquered Burma from the Japanese was also made possible by Anglo-American air power. Liberators struck Japanese depots and installations throughout southeast Asia. The Japanese could muster barely 50 planes to face more than ten times as many Allied aircraft, while on the ground they were constantly harried by the veteran Allied fighter and bomber groups. Air transports supplied the victorious British 14th Army of 300,000 men. The end of the war in Burma found the Japanese reduced to impotence on the ground and in the air.

In China the U.S. established under Maj. Gen. Claire L. Chennault an air task force, composed at first of the "Flying Tigers"—members of a civilian U.S. volunteer group that had been recruited before the war to fight for China against the Japanese. In March 1943 U.S. air units in China were organized into the 14th Air Force, which provided the Chinese armies with most of their air support during the remainder of the war and, although usually outnumbered, consistently carried the war to the Japanese, attacking targets as far away as Shanghai and preying on Japanese shipping off the coast of China.

For the greater part of the war the 14th Air Force was supplied by air from India. The U.S. Army Air Forces Air Transport Command carried out this remarkable long-range operation over the "hump" of the Himalayas, the highest mountains in the world. In spite of the great handicaps under which they laboured, Chennault's "Flying Tigers" compiled a brilliant record and made outstanding contributions to the development of tactics and techniques of aerial warfare.

Guadalcanal to the Philippines.—After the fall of the Philippines in April and May 1942, Allied forces were concentrated in Australia under the command of Gen. Douglas MacArthur. The strategic victory of the U.S. Navy over the Japanese in the Battle of the Coral Sea in May 1942 prevented the Japanese from taking Port Moresby in New Guinea, which could have served as a springboard for invasion of Australia. The respite afforded by this victory permitted a buildup of U.S. air strength in Australia, New Guinea, and the Solomon Islands. In August 1942 U.S. Marines began at Guadalcanal the long, drawn-out reconquest of the Solomons, which was not completed until 1944. U.S. Navy, Marine, and Army Air Force units provided the air support which was essential to the operation. Meanwhile, U.S. and Australian ground forces, under the constant protection of the U.S. 5th Air Force and the Royal Australian Air Force, won back New Guinea and New Britain in 1943–44. In March 1943 the Allied air forces performed one of the most striking aerial feats of the war in wiping out the greater part of a large Japanese convoy in the Bismarck Sea.

Allied strategy in the Pacific called for an island-hopping advance toward Japan always under the protective cover of shore-based or carrier-based air power. By the middle of 1944, U.S. air, ground, and naval forces in the southwest Pacific had attained the strength and strategic position to undertake long-range advances. In October came the landing on Leyte in the Philippines, and in January 1945 the landing on Luzon. The U.S. 5th and 13th Air Forces and naval air units smashed Japanese air and naval power in the Philippines and ruled the air over the battle areas and far behind the Japanese lines.

North and Central Pacific.—In June 1942 the Japanese occupied Attu and Kiska in the Aleutian Islands, but any hopes they had of exploiting their position were frustrated by the bombardments of the U.S. 11th Air Force. In 1943 U.S. Army forces reconquered Attu, and the Japanese abandoned Kiska. The 11th Air Force also carried the air war to the Japanese home islands with attacks against the Kurile Islands in 1943 and 1944.

In the central Pacific an island-hopping strategy under the cover of air power was also followed. Heavy bombers of the U.S. 7th Air Force and carrier task forces softened up the islands before they were assaulted by U.S. Marine and Army forces. Tarawa and Makin fell in the autumn of 1943, and in February 1944 the Marshall Islands were also taken. The Marianas, which could provide air bases from which the new heavy bombers could strike at the heart of Japan, were the next to fall. By August 1944, the main islands of the Marianas, Guam, Saipan, and Tinian, had been taken. The loss of the Marianas was the turning point of the war, for it allowed the penetration of the inner defenses of the Japanese empire and laid Japan open to devastating attacks by B-29 bombers.

The last great tactical campaign in the Pacific was at Okinawa, in the spring of 1945. There, Japanese kamikazes—suicide bomber pilots—caused great damage to U.S. naval vessels. Their technique of deliberately crashing explosive-laden aircraft into targets, especially ships, was a clear indication of the desperate position in which the Japanese Army and Navy air forces found themselves. In all, the Japanese flew 2,500 suicide sorties, of which 475 scored direct hits, sinking about 40 ships and seriously damaging many others. Many of these attacks were made during the Okinawa campaign, but the Japanese could not contest control of the air over Okinawa itself, and after the island was conquered in June 1945, it became the main base for the planned invasion of Japan. Fighters and bombers of the 5th Air Force attacked southern Japan from Okinawa, and bases were built on the island for B-29s to carry the war to Japanese industrial centres.

B-29 Campaign.—The U.S. developed the B-29 for the specific purpose of using it against the Japanese homeland. The first B-29 units operated from bases in India and China. They attacked Japan on June 15, 1944, striking steel mills at Yahata. A few other strikes against Japanese targets from Chinese bases followed, but owing to logistical problems of supply over "the hump," the force was moved to air bases in the Marianas when these became available. The total B-29 force was concentrated there under the U.S. 20th Air Force, which numbered almost 1,000 B-29s by the end of the war.

On Nov. 24, 1944, the first B-29 mission from the Marianas— 100 strong—left Saipan and bombed Tokyo for the first time since the Doolittle raid in 1942. The attacks on Japanese targets grew in size and intensity as the 20th Air Force received more B-29 units. In March 1945, Maj. Gen. Curtis LeMay, commanding the bombers, made one of the most important decisions of the war. He decided to use the B-29s in low-level night attacks with incendiary bombs against the highly vulnerable Japanese cities. On the night of March 9, 1945, 279 B-29s, bombing from altitudes ranging between 4,000 and 9,000 ft., burned out 15.8 sq.mi. of the heart of Tokyo. The pattern established by this attack was followed in striking other Japanese cities, and as a result Nagoya, Ōsaka, and Kōbe sustained tremendous damage. The climax of the bombing campaign came on Aug. 6, 1945, when the B-29 "Enola Gay" dropped the first atomic bomb on Hiroshima with devastating results. A second atomic bomb was dropped on Nagasaki on Aug. 9. Japan surrendered soon afterward.

In an exhaustive study after the war, the U.S. Strategic Bombing Survey found that the aerial bombardment, to which aircraft carrier strike forces had also contributed during 1945, had taken a terrible toll of Japanese industry, urban areas, and people. The incendiary-bomb campaign had already produced a decisive result by the time the atomic bomb brought the war to an end.

Also of decisive effect on the outcome of the war was the blockade of the Japanese home islands. The Japanese merchant fleet, under attack from Allied sea and air forces, had been reduced to little more than 20% of its original strength by the end of the war. That was achieved primarily by submarines of the U.S. Navy, but aircraft alone sank about 1,000,000 tons of Japa-

BY COURTESY OF LOCKHEED AIRCRAFT CORP.

LOCKHEED P-38 LIGHTNING, U.S. SINGLE-SEAT INTERCEPTOR AND FIGHTER-BOMBER, WAS USED IN EVERY COMBAT AREA OF WORLD WAR II

nese shipping in 1944. B-29s helped greatly in this campaign by mining the waters around Japan, dropping 1,000 tons of mines in the Shimonoseki Straits during the four days preceding the landings on Okinawa. *See* also WORLD WAR II: *The War in the Pacific.*

E. AIR POWER IN THE COLD WAR

The end of World War II saw conventional air forces provided with sufficient aircraft, technical navigational and bomb-aiming devices, and operational techniques to achieve some deterrent capacity. At the same time, the sudden advent of the atomic bomb meant that a much smaller force could deliver a far more destructive blow in a shorter space of time. The immediate reaction to U.S. possession of a monopoly of this power was to regard most conventional airplanes as likely to be obsolete. The battle in the U.S. in the 1920s between the Army and the Navy was revived in the late 1940s between the newly created U.S. Air Force and the Navy. The Soviet Union, which had ended the war without a strategic bomber force, feared a U.S. attack and thus accented air defense while working on its own nuclear deterrent. Much attention was paid to this aspect of air power, in part because strategic air force generals dominated the U.S. Department of Defense. At the same time, too little attention was paid to conventional warfare and requirements for it until the middle 1950s. The Korean War was at first regarded as an unusual limited war, but by the late 1950s it was becoming increasingly obvious that there probably would be more limited wars of that type, as the nuclear stalemate made massive war seem unthinkable. During

GRUMMAN TBF AVENGER, THREE-SEAT U.S. NAVY ATTACK PLANE, CARRIED A 2,000-LB. TORPEDO INSIDE THE LOWER PART OF THE FUSELAGE

BY COURTESY OF DEPARTMENT OF NATIONAL DEFENSE, CANADA

JAPANESE AIRCRAFT, WORLD WAR II

(Top) Mitsubishi Model 97 army reconnaissance bomber carried a 4,000-lb. bomb load and had a top speed of 248 mph. (Centre) Mitsubishi Zero, highly maneuverable, high-speed fighter plane. (Bottom) Baka, rocket-powered flying bomb, carried a kamikaze pilot and a 2,600-lb. explosive charge

and within it the U.S. Air Force. The secretary of the air force was subordinated to the secretary of defense, who became the only cabinet member representing the military establishment. The chief of staff of the U.S. Air Force became one of the three joint chiefs of staff at the top of the U.S. military structure. The creation of the Strategic Air Command, Tactical Air Command, and the Air Defense Command on March 21, 1946, had provided the fundamental framework of the air force with five supporting and five overseas commands. Foremost among the latter were the U.S. air forces in Europe and the Far East air forces. Important new commands added after 1947 were the Air Research and Development Command, the Continental Air Command, and the joint Military Air Transport Service. The Air Force Organization Act of 1951 established by law the organization which the air force had already achieved. Owing to interservice wrangling over roles and missions, a conference was called at Key West, Fla., in March 1948, at which the services agreed that the air force should have control of strategic bombing and also the responsibility for providing close and logistical air support to the army.

Although the Soviet Army and Navy have been represented sometimes by separate and sometimes by combined ministries, the air forces have never had their own ministry. On the other hand, the Soviet organization is distinctive in that all air forces, including naval, are for administrative purposes under one marshal of aviation, who has the status of a first deputy minister of defense. However, this officer has direct operational control only of the important tactical or "army" air force, termed "frontal aviation" of the air forces, which has the largest number of aircraft of any air command. The other operational commands, headed by "deputies" to the senior air officer, are the long-range air force, the fighters of the air defense forces, airborne troops, and naval aviation. As the Soviet Union has no aircraft carriers, its naval aviation is comparable to the British RAF Coastal Command.

The two great developments that affected air forces in the post-World War II period were the development of long-range guided missiles and the advent of nuclear bombs. The nuclear weapons at first had the effect of greatly increasing the relative importance of the strategic bombing forces because they quelled any doubts about the efficacy of strategic bombing. After the appearance of thermonuclear weapons in 1952, however, a trend started in the other direction. It was observed that strategic bombing with such weapons might be too effective to be borne, so long as there was any chance that the enemy would strike back in kind. Moreover, the very considerable problems of protecting civil populations had yet to be solved. Thus, an interest developed in attempting to keep wars limited, with nulear weapons either ruled out or kept to comparatively small sizes. In such limited wars, aircraft would very likely again serve in a role ancillary to the ground forces.

Despite the considerable development of jet-powered aircraft of all combat types during the post-World War II period, a development that greatly increased the cost of individual units, the coming of ballistic missiles threatened to diminish the role of aircraft even within the air forces. For the first time it appeared that the air forces would be operating vehicles that were not piloted by human beings with specialized flying training. In 1956 the U.S. secretary of defense decided that the U.S. Air Force should be responsible for intermediate and long-range missiles, limiting the Army, which at its Redstone Arsenal had made great progress under the direction of the German Wernher von Braun, to missiles of less than 200-mi. range.

the 1960s a more balanced conception of air power once again came to the fore. The war in Vietnam underscored a need for pilots and tactical aircraft.

1. Post-World War II Air Forces.—At the end of World War II only three nations had appreciable air power: the United States, the Soviet Union, and, falling increasingly behind in the ensuing race, the United Kingdom. The only important organizational change was in the status of the U.S. Army Air Forces, changed from an autonomous to a fully independent organization. Congress on July 26, 1947, created the Department of the Air Force

On both offensive and defensive operations the surface-to-air missile supplanted manned aircraft as the chief instrument for destroying enemy bombers. The high speeds and altitudes of modern jet bombers was thought to give the manned interceptor too little opportunity to maneuver into a good firing position; an interceptor at the end of the 1950s cost approximately $1,000,000, which made them relatively uneconomical as compared with defensive missiles. Against enemy long-range missiles the fighter-interceptor obviously had no value whatever, and was to be replaced by systems using anti-missile missiles.

2. Guided Missiles.—The launching of the first true guided missile, the German V-2, against the U.K on Sept. 8, 1944, and the dropping of the first atomic bomb on Hiroshima on Aug. 6, 1945, heralded the beginning of a new era of warfare. These two remarkable technological advances, occurring within 11 months of each other in the last year of World War II, provided the basic elements for the most destructive mode of warfare yet devised by man, but the principles of war still applied.

Although strategic bombing was only one of the means employed to defeat Germany and Japan during World War II, its result had been seen and its potential, with atomic bombs at its disposal, was terrible to contemplate. But there was still another step—the use of atomic warheads on long-range guided missiles—that promised even quicker and more decisive results than those achieved by bomb-carrying aircraft. Such missiles could travel many times faster than the fastest bomber, and defense against them would be extremely difficult. Opinion was divided about whether defenses could ever be adequate to preserve a civilian society.

The U.S. had begun guided missile research before 1944, but

BOEING PHOTO

BOEING B-29 SUPERFORTRESS, LARGEST U.S. BOMBER BUILT DURING WORLD WAR II, HAD A RANGE OF MORE THAN 4,000 MI. CARRYING 18,000-LB. BOMB LOAD

knowledge of the successful use of the V-1 and V-2 by the Germans led to an expansion and acceleration of such work by all three military services. During the first five years after the war, progress was slow; not until 1953 did the first U.S. Air Force missile, the Martin B-61 Matador, come into operational service. But the Matador was little more than an improved V-1, designed chiefly for short-range tactical use. Although the greatest emphasis continued to be placed on the long-range intercontinental ballistic missile (ICBM), a whole series of additional missiles of lesser range was also under development by the U.S. Army, Navy, and Air Force. In 1956 the U.S. Department of Defense placed a high priority on development of a missile of intermediate range— about 1,500 mi.

In the field of interceptor missiles, the Army's Nike came into use in the early 1950s and became the chief ground antiaircraft weapon for defense of U.S. cities. In 1955 the Air Force put into operation the Falcon, an electronically controlled missile launched from fighter airplanes against other aircraft at distances measured in miles. In the 1960s anti-missile systems such as Nike-Zeus were under development.

In the decade after World War II the Soviet Union made rapid progress in guided missile development with the aid of German scientists and engineers who had worked on the V-1 and V-2. The problem of designing warheads of sufficient power to make the missiles effective was solved by the successful military application of atomic and thermonuclear energy. The Soviet Union also worked to develop an intercontinental ballistic missile. In 1956 Khrushchev stated that the U.S.S.R. would soon be able to deliver missiles with thermonuclear warheads to any part of the world.

The intensive race between the U.S. and the U.S.S.R. for acquisition of guided missiles portended a capacity for destruction approaching total annihilation. By the late 1950s new systems were coming into being to make it harder to destroy the opponent's deterrent capacity. The U.S. Navy developed the solid-fueled Polaris missile system for launching ICBM's from submerged submarines. The Polaris had a range of 1,500 mi., later increased to 2,500. Mounted in nuclear submarines, which could remain submerged on patrol for 60 days at a time, Polarises were mobile

WIDE WORLD

MITSUBISHI AIRCRAFT FACTORY AT NAGOYA, JAPAN, AFTER A BOMBING RAID BY B-29S IN 1945. IN NINE MONTHS, B-29S BASED IN THE MARIANA ISLANDS DROPPED MORE THAN 170,000 TONS OF BOMBS ON JAPAN, ALMOST COMPLETELY DISRUPTING THAT NATION'S MILITARY INDUSTRIES

and could be hidden in the vast ocean reaches of the world. On land the United States went through a period of placing Titan and Minuteman missiles in underground silos placed throughout the country and thought to be protected against an initial enemy attack. That system was abandoned after the middle 1960s. At the same time, work went forward on air-launched missiles carried by Strategic Air Command (SAC) aircraft, which would not themselves have to penetrate into enemy airspace.

In the meantime the Soviets were also developing similar systems. A crisis occurred in 1962 when the U.S.S.R. attempted to implant some missiles in Cuba. U.S. Pres. John F. Kennedy demanded that the missiles be removed and the Soviets subsequently withdrew them. Meanwhile, other nations had also begun working on missiles. The British started and then abandoned the liquid-fueled Blue Streak ballistic missile. France and Communist China developed nuclear warheads, and the Japanese created small rockets for upper-attmosphere research. The awesome power of the new weapons acted as a deterrent to their use and tended to lend substance to the hope that war would become impossible because it invited mutual destruction. (*See* ROCKETS AND GUIDED MISSILES.)

Aircraft during the postwar era remained of great military value because of their ability to carry out armed reconnaissance—the pursuit of targets whose exact location is not well enough known to make them available for missiles—and also because of their greater bombing accuracy and greater load-carrying characteristics. Military planners assumed that planes would remain a military necessity for a considerable period in the future. They were looked upon as being especially necessary for limited wars, in which nuclear weapons were proscribed or under constraints, and also for the transport of ground troops.

3. Postwar Air Defense Systems.—During the early years of peace that followed the defeat of Germany and Japan, air defense seemed unnecessary. The victorious western Allies quickly demobilized and scrapped or stored most of their air defense weapons. However, by 1948 the cold war had begun and, as the split between the free world and the Communist nations widened, most governments began to rearm.

Basic to the U.S. air defense system, and all others, was early-warning radar equipment. Although restricted in its ability to "see" long distances because it operated on a line-of-sight principle and did not follow the curvature of the earth, radar in the air defense system of the 1950s was able to detect aircraft at distances of nearly 250 mi. and at heights of 50,000 ft. By the mid-1960s the distance had increased to about 3,000 mi., and radar could also detect missiles early in their trajectories. With a network of one or more lines of radar sets, a nation could hope for enough warning of approaching bombers to alert its defenses.

Because a serious limitation of radar is its inability to detect objects at low altitudes, all air defense systems continued for some years to rely upon ground observers to augment the radar networks. Ground observer posts were placed at points in the network where gaps in radar coverage existed or where the importance of the defended area warranted additional protection.

When unknown aircraft were detected by the early-warning radar network, the air defense system had to determine whether they were friendly or hostile. Since no reliable electronic means of identification existed, the United States adopted an elaborate system of correlating flight plans. Areas called air defense identification zones (ADIZ) were established around the nation's borders or vital areas. Each aircraft flying through an ADIZ was required to file a flight plan and to fly a prescribed course. Accurate identification depended upon correlation of data from the radar site with flight plan data from the air movements information section (AMIS) of the Civil Aeronautics Administration. Any variation of an aircraft from its prescribed course in an ADIZ called for investigation by the air defense forces. Unidentified objects were investigated by fighters operating from a ground-controlled interception station or an air defense direction centre. Once airborne, the interceptor's success largely determined the success or failure of the entire air defense system. With the electronic equipment carried by all-weather interceptors, it was possible for an interceptor pilot to complete his mission without seeing his target.

Backing up the interceptor force was the ground-based antiaircraft artillery (AAA). The primary role of AAA in the air defense system of the early 1950s was point defense (defense of a specific location, such as a city) since its armament consisted primarily of conventional guns such as the 120-mm. and the U.S. developed, radar-controlled, 75-mm. Skysweeper. The future of AAA in air defense depended upon the development of surface-to-air guided missiles, such as the U.S. Nike and its derivatives. AAA units, which in the U.S. military structure were assigned to the Army, were under the operational control of the air defense commander. When controlled by the air defense commander, AAA was an integral part of the air defense system.

North America.—To provide the greatest amount of early warning for North American defenses, the U.S. and Canadian governments cooperated in placing three radar lines in operation across Canada. Near the Arctic Circle was the distant early warning (DEW) line of more than 50 radar stations, completed in 1957. The DEW line was constructed and manned by the U.S. Backing up the DEW line was the Mid-Canada line, built and operated by Canada at about lat. 55° N. To the south was the joint Canadian-U.S. Pinetree line, which was integrated into the permanent U.S. radar system. To fill gaps in the radar coverage afforded by these lines, small automatic radar sets were installed at appropriate sites. To extend early-warning coverage seaward, airborne early-warning aircraft, suitably equipped ships, and "Texas towers" (stationary radar platforms resembling those used for well-drilling) were in operation. All of those radar sets were tied into the combat operations centre at the headquarters of the joint command at Colorado Springs, Colo.

In addition to the extensive North American radar network, which would alert the defensive forces of the United States and Canada, the U.S. Air Force provided or helped maintain radar networks in most of the world's non-Communist nations. Early-warning radar stations operated in such outposts as Greenland and Iceland as well as in Western Europe, the Middle East, and Japan. It was possible to foresee that someday all those radar stations might be integrated into a worldwide defense network.

Aiding the North American radar network were the ground observer corps of the U.S. and Canada. Scattered throughout the U.S. were approximately 16,000 ground observer posts manned by almost 400,000 unpaid volunteers. After 1952 a considerable portion of the ground observer corps was on 24-hour duty, called Operation Skywatch. In November 1958 the U.S. Air Force announced that its radar network had been developed to an extent that made continuance of the ground observer corps unnecessary.

To make full use of information gathered by the early-warning system, an extensive organization was established in the U.S. under the Continental Air Defense Command (CONAD) and the North American Air Defense Command (NORAD). CONAD, a joint command including Army, Navy, and Air Force personnel, was created in 1954 and was augmented by Canadian units. NORAD, an integrated headquarters designed to direct the air defense of North America, came into being in May 1958 when the U.S. and Canadian governments reached formal agreement. Headquarters of both organizations were in Colorado Springs, Colo. There were 16 Air Defense Control Centres in the United States, each the headquarters of a CONAD division area. The commander of each division area directed the operations of the interceptors and AAA units in his sector and was responsible for alerting civilian defense organizations. Each control centre was tied into a combat operations centre in one of the three CONAD regions. At the summit was the combat operations centre, which in 1966 moved into a large chamber blasted out of solid granite under Cheyenne Mountain near Colorado Springs.

Information concerning hostile aircraft was sent from the control centres to civil defense personnel through civilian-manned air defense warning centres, at least one in each state. One of three types of warning could be transmitted by the control centre or by higher headquarters: warning Yellow, which meant that an attack

BRITISH AVRO VULCAN, FIRST LARGE BOMBER TO UTILIZE THE DELTA WING CONFIGURATION. THE VULCAN ENTERED SERVICE WITH BOMBER COMMAND IN 1956

was likely; warning Red, indicating that an attack was imminent; or White, indicating "all clear." At the same time the military organizations would receive warnings through the military air-raid warning service. When warning Yellow was received, civil defense authorities would institute evacuation plans or alert civil defense workers to stand by for instructions. Upon receipt of warning Red, expected to be from one to three hours after warning Yellow, the public would be alerted and preplanned defense measures would be taken by military and civil defense organizations.

Once defense officials had been alerted, several actions were to be taken simultaneously. A plan for the security control of air traffic, known as SCAT, was to be placed in operation. The SCAT plan provided for the temporary diversion or grounding of all civil or military aircraft not essential for defense. When it was safe to allow air traffic to resume, the flow would be regulated on a priority basis.

In the mid-1950s the passive air defense program of the Federal Civil Defense Administration in the U.S. was based upon the principles of dispersion, evacuation, and shelter. A national policy for industrial dispersion, with federal financial aid, was announced in 1951. Evacuation—the movement of the population from threatened areas—was deemed necessary because of the great destructive power of thermonuclear weapons and the large resultant nuclear fallout area. However, because of the difficulties involved and in the face of much public criticism, emphasis was changed from evacuation to protection against fallout by shelters. Plans called for fully equipped fallout shelters for more than 100,-000,000 people residing in the more heavily populated areas. Little was achieved beyond marking shelter spaces in public and larger private buildings. Success of mass protection depended, principally, upon the amount of prior warning received from the air defense system and maximum use of the shelters. (*See* further CIVIL DEFENSE.)

By 1957 the U.S. Air Force had begun the installation of a system designed to cope with the problem of intercontinental supersonic bombers and guided missiles. By centralizing air defense functions, the semi-automatic ground environment (SAGE) system simplified air defense operations. Men continued to make the basic decisions, while the SAGE machines performed the complex tasks of computation.

The SAGE system consisted of a vast interconnected network of electronic computers into which information was fed by the various detection and control centres. Installed at various strategic locations, SAGE direction centre computers stored information, performed intricate calculations, and presented visual display of the results for use by human controllers. Based upon the data

fed into it, SAGE indicated to the controller the best solution to a particular air defense problem. It monitored the air situation so that the SAGE operator was able to follow action in the air at all times.

The prinipal advantage of SAGE was in the speed with which it could solve air defense problems and display results. The cost of the system was great, and only the U.S. and Canada had civilian communications networks capable of supporting such a system. (*See* further INFORMATION PROCESSING.)

The advent during the 1950s of intercontinental ballistic missiles and of the possibility of missiles launched from space vehicles marked the beginning of a new era in air defense. Many observers were at first filled with a feeling of hopelessness when confronted with the task of providing a defense against such weapons. A combination of a ballistic missile early-warning system (BMEWS) and a space detection and tracking system was established under NORAD, however. BMEWS was designed to provide warning of a missile attack on North America from the north. From detection stations in Alaska, Greenland, and England information was sent to NORAD, which, in turn, relayed the data to SAC forces. To detect and track space vehicles, a National Space Surveillance Control Center and a system to detect satellites operated under the control of NORAD. The former received data from detection facilities, while the satellite-detection system served as "an electronic curtain in the sky" for air defense against satellites.

Soviet Union.—At the end of World War II Soviet strategic air defense was weak. The Germans had never presented a long-range bomber threat, and the mild raids against Moscow in the summer of 1941 had been mastered in short order. Since the major Soviet air effort and air defense had been concentrated upon tactical operations, in 1945 the Soviet Union had no early-warning radar defense and few antiaircraft guns designed for use against high-flying aircraft. But the end of the war made it plain to Soviet leaders that jet aircraft armed with nuclear weapons could easily decimate Soviet industrial complexes in a few days. So making extensive use of captured German equipment and scientists, the U.S.S.R. set out to build up its air defenses, with the result that by 1950 a chain of defenses stretched along most boundary areas from the Black Sea to Alaska. But the defense did not exist in depth, and it was several years before it was sufficiently strong to provide ground-controlled interception of enemy aircraft. It was to test the efficiency and coverage of this system that American U-2 aircraft made high-altitude flights over the Soviet Union; one

BOEING B-47 STRATOJET, U.S. SWEPT-WING MEDIUM BOMBER WITH A TOP SPEED IN EXCESS OF 600 MPH, MADE ITS FIRST FLIGHT DEC. 17, 1947

such flight led to the May 1960 incident when one of those aircraft was downed in the U.S.S.R. At the same time, Soviet jet fighters that could climb to high altitudes were developed.

The Soviets had also taken over German antiaircraft rockets, but it was not until 1955 that development, manufacturing, and training difficulties had been overcome and that the first operational units were deployed to defend Moscow. By the end of the Korean War Soviet fighters were fitted with radar-gunsights and were under ground-controlled radar direction, where equipment existed. Real development took place after 1955 when the U.S.S.R. developed fighters that could reach supersonic speeds and when the antiaircraft and defensive missile command was raised to first-class status and given full control over policy, administration, and decision. But at the same time, despite Soviet space successes, the U.S. began to take the lead in intercontinental ballistic missiles (ICBM's). Yet as long as the Anglo-American bomber threat remained, the U.S.S.R. had to maintain a fighter force, which may have been as large as 5,000 aircraft supported by more than 10,000 radar-controlled antiaircraft guns. The development in the U.S. of the ballistic missile again in effect destroyed Soviet air defenses. The Soviet reaction at first seemed slow, but by the mid-1960s the U.S.S.R. appeared to have made great progress in developing long-range radar, antimissile missiles, and civilian shelters.

United Kingdom.—The leader in air defense during World War II, the U.K. maintained the nucleus of its wartime system during the postwar years. The peacetime system was concentrated around London with the radar network facing the continent of Europe. By World War II standards, the British air defense system was satisfactory.

Beginning in 1955, however, the U.K. adopted a new defensive concept. Realizing that the best air defense system it could develop with current resources would not be effective against supersonic bombers and guided missiles, Great Britain decided to abandon gradually its conventional defenses. The Antiaircraft Command was inactivated in 1955, and two years later the government announced that the fighter force would be phased out slowly. Until reliable guided missiles were developed, the U.K. would depend upon the deterrent effect of thermonuclear weapons, a limited early-warning network, and a shrinking fighter force. For

some years U.S.-made Thor ICBM's were based in Britain under joint control, but they were phased out in the 1960s. By the end of the 1960s it appeared that with the retirement of their V-bombers the RAF would no longer be a nuclear deterrent force, though the purchase of U.S.-built F-111 aircraft might still provide some capacity.

Long before the British decision was announced, the Western countries had come to depend more and more on the U.S. Strategic Air Command. Military plans of the non-Communist nations were based largely upon the retaliatory power of thermonuclear weapons carried by SAC intercontinental bombers.

F. Air Power in Limited Wars

Though the major emphasis in the postwar period was on strategic air power and the use as deterrents of ballistic missiles with nuclear warheads, air power continued to be used in limited and antiguerrilla conflicts. Notable in this respect was the British campaign in the Aden Protectorate, finally abandoned by the late 1960s. In the campaign to suppress guerrilla forces in Malaya in the late 1940s and early 1950s the British made extensive use of limited air power for strikes, and for the landing, supply, and recovery of combat units. Even conflicts involving major powers, such as the combined Israeli-Egyptian war and Anglo-French Suez attack in 1956 did not see the use of anything more than tactical air power. In fact, it was not, except for the Korean War, until 1965 that strategic bombers were used in war for the first time since 1945. And even then, strategic strikes were undertaken by fighter-bomber aircraft, while strategic bombers were confined to massive raids against minor targets. In addition to its traditional tactical role in limited operations, the latest, though not a new role for air power, has been the great use made of air transport in impassable country. Reminiscent of the Burma campaign of 1944 was the use of air transport in the war in Vietnam. In that conflict direct tactical use of air transport in the form of both conventional aircraft and helicopters took place. They were used, moreover, not only as supply vehicles, but also for battle casualty evacuation and, on occasion, for tactical redeployment of ground forces while actually in contact with the enemy.

One consequence of the new importance of tactical air power

BY COURTESY OF (BELOW) DOUGLAS AIRCRAFT CO., (RIGHT) REPUBLIC AVIATION DIVISION, FAIRCHILD HILLER CORP.; PHOTOGRAPH, (ABOVE) WIDE WORLD

COMBAT PLANES, KOREAN WAR

(Above) Soviet MiG-15, (below) U.S. Douglas AD-1 Skyraider attack bomber, (right) U.S. Republic F-84 Thunderstreak

was shortage of pilots. The pool of World War II aircrew available for the Korean War did not exist by the 1960s. At the same time, the very rapid growth of airlines brought on by the economic success of the jet airliner rapidly dried up other sources of trained pilots. The U.S. tactical air forces, while generally adequately supplied with transports and helicopters, found themselves also facing a shortage of aircraft; greater time was needed to build complex modern aircraft. An additional factor was the trend to build increasingly complicated and sophisticated aircraft to the neglect of simplified, easier-to-produce machines, and the failure to observe one of the fundamental rules of technological war, which is that numbers are also important. No matter how fast or how sophisticated a machine, it can only be in one place at one time. As a result by the late 1960s it seemed likely that there would be a move back to producing less sophisticated aircraft in large numbers. Limited wars also

KEYSTONE

BOEING B-52 STRATOFORTRESS, U.S. INTERCONTINENTAL JET BOMBER USED BY THE STRATEGIC AIR COMMAND FROM 1955. A PRE-PACKAGING SYSTEM CUT LOADING TIME FOR THE PLANE'S 54,000-LB. OF BOMBS TO LESS THAN ONE-THIRD THE TIME REQUIRED BY PREVIOUS METHODS

emphasized that except in areas where large military forces are concentrated and susceptible to attack by single concentrations of force, most classes of unmanned missiles are unusable. This in its turn placed a greater emphasis in undeveloped areas on the use of manpower and firepower on the ground, especially against guerrilla forces without air power.

In addition to the regular air force, increasingly after World War II army air forces appeared again. In the U.S. the Army's air arm had reached 1,200 aircraft and the same number of aircrew by the outbreak of the Korean War. By the end of that conflict the total had jumped to 5,000 aircraft, of which, by the later 1950s, about half were helicopters. At first it was the threat of nuclear warfare that caused the Army to plan for greater mobility on the battlefield than ground vehicles could provide. But both the Korean and the Vietnam wars emphasized the need to be able to move troops and their supplies to areas not easily accessible. In addition, the Army sought better means of reconnaissance, detection, location, and warning of enemy forces. Thus its aircraft became equipped with sophisticated airborne gear for battlefield surveillance.

At the same time, the Army developed the ability, as exemplified by the 1st Air Cavalry, to move rapidly to and about the battlefield. Casualty evacuation also became a major job of Army Air Force helicopters. In general, army aviation in all countries provided close liaison, support, and mobility for army commanders, while strike support generally came from air force units flying faster and heavier jet aircraft.

Most of the world's navies managed to maintain their own air components, usually because they operated aircraft carriers. Apart from the fact that naval aircraft are fitted with certain equipment to enable them to operate off aircraft carriers, after World War II they became increasingly similar to their land-based counterparts in speed, armament, and striking power. And just as the army air forces adopted the helicopter, so the marines and navies made great use of it. At sea helicopters were used extensively for antisubmarine warfare, rescue, and internal communications within fleets. In the U.S. and British navies the air component also played a large part in patrolling sea-lanes and oceans looking for enemy submarines and, in the Cuban crisis of 1962 locating ships carrying contraband.

The U.K. and the U.S. also used the aircraft carrier as a mobile

airfield secure from guerrilla attack. Some carriers were converted into mobile helicopter landing pads with their own complement of marine combat units. In addition, major carriers underwent vast modification and by the 1960s could carry not only a powerful tactical striking force with the ability to undertake operations in all weather but also could accommodate strategic strike aircraft equipped with major nuclear weapons. The pattern was originally developed in operations in the Pacific in World War II, was further refined during the Korean War, and was used effectively both as a deterrent off the Chinese coast in the late 1950s and operationally off the coasts of North and South Vietnam in the late 1960s.

1. Korean War.—In the decade after World War II, air power emerged clearly as the dominant mode of warfare. But in spite of the intense competition between the U.S. and the U.S.S.R., neither atomic bombs nor guided missiles were used in the Korean War.

Although it served as a testing ground for U.S. and Soviet aeronautical equipment between 1950 and 1953, the Korean War did not prove to be a preview of the strategic air warfare of the future. It was a limited war, requiring no all-out air effort by the United States, which carried the chief burden for the United Nations. The Soviet Union gathered valuable data from the experience of the North Koreans and Chinese who used Soviet aircraft. Soviet pilots also gained experience in jet warfare.

The U.S. 5th Air Force moved with most of its units from Japan to South Korea after the North Korean invasion of June 25, 1950. The 5th was still equipped chiefly with World War II planes—F-51 Mustangs and B-26 Invaders—and its only jet airplane was the F-80 Shooting Star, which was already on the verge of obsolescence. Reinforced by additional combat wings from the United States and a few squadrons from other UN countries, especially the U.K. and Australia, the 5th Air Force quickly won mastery of the air. During the first phase of the campaign, from July to October 1950, the UN air forces supported the ground armies and bombed enemy supply lines and production centres. Their attacks on the North Korean armies resulted in the deaths of an estimated 39,000 soldiers and destruction of approximately 76% of the total tanks destroyed by the UN forces.

During the UN retreat from the Yalu River in November and December 1950, after the large-scale intervention of Chinese Com-

U.S. ARMY HELICOPTERS LANDING INFANTRYMEN AND SUPPLIES IN VIETNAM, 1966. IN THE WAR IN VIETNAM HELICOPTER-BORNE GROUND FORCES LARGELY SUPERSEDED TROOPS LANDED BEHIND ENEMY LINES BY PARACHUTE AND GLIDER

The attacks provoked the largest air battles of the war, almost exclusively between U.S. F-86 Sabrejets and MiGs. This first large-scale combat between jet fighters in the history of warfare ended strongly in favour of the F-86s, which claimed the destruction of 800 MiGs as against a loss of only 58 Sabrejets. Much of the fighting took place in the vicinity of the Yalu, with the MiGs availing themselves of sanctuary on the Chinese side of the boundary when hard pressed by the F-86s.

2. Minor Conflicts.—The period between the Korean War and the operations in Vietnam witnessed a number of minor actions in which air power played an ancillary role. The French loss of Indochina in 1954 did not see any successful use of air power, though the defenders of Dien Bien Phu were supplied by air until the last moments and fought in defense of an airfield. Nor was the revolution in Cuba which brought Fidel Castro to power in 1959 accomplished by air power,

munist forces, the UN air forces slowed the Chinese advance, thereby permitting an organized withdrawal of the UN ground forces. The UN air forces, which operated in close support of the ground troops and harassed the Chinese supply lines by day, played a large part in frustrating the Chinese effort to destroy the UN forces. The pressure of the UN bombers and fighters forced the Chinese to fight and move supplies chiefly by night, though they never completely stopped trains from moving.

B-29 bombers from the United States flew to bases in Japan and Okinawa shortly after the outbreak of the conflict and carried on a steady campaign against North Korean targets. But the North Koreans, and later the Chinese, received their supplies and equipment from far beyond the Yalu River boundary, and North Korea offered no such strategic target systems as had Germany and Japan in World War II. The decision of the UN to localize the war and not to attack targets in China denied the B-29s targets more appropriate for their capabilities.

The greater part of UN air power continued to concentrate on support of the ground armies. Bombers and fighters, including jet F-84s and F-86s, took a heavy toll of the Chinese between November 1950 and June 1951, a period of heavy fighting. Still unable to move troops and supplies by day because of the constant air attacks, the Chinese could not mass sufficient supplies at the front to support a sustained offensive. Until the end of the war in 1953, UN air power played a major part in frustrating all major Chinese attacks. Most of the fighting for air supremacy was done by the U.S. Air Force with some Allied support, while U.S. Navy fliers from aircraft carriers offshore carried out tactical strikes against ground targets.

The UN control of the air, which helped to nullify the numerical superiority of the Chinese on the ground, could be broken only by superior air power. The Chinese Communist Air Force, supplied by the Soviet Union with MiG-15 jet fighters, made an effort to gain superiority late in 1950. Although safe from UN attacks on their bases beyond the Yalu, the Chinese found it difficult to dispute control of the air over the battlefield because of the short range of the MiGs. In late 1951 they began to build a chain of airfields in North Korea which would have permitted them to make much more effective use of their MiGs. UN planes attacked those bases as they neared completion and repeated the attacks again and again as the Chinese attempted to repair the damage.

though an unsuccessful attempt to overthrow Castro in 1961 was said by some observers to have failed in part because of lack of air support. In its attempts to control a revolutionary situation in Cyprus the U.K. made use of helicopters, but it was still basically a ground guerrilla war. The one operation in which air power played a significant part was that at Suez in 1956 in which the U.K. and France used carrier-based strike forces, medium bombers, and transports in an attempt to seize the canal. At the same time, the Suez operations helped provide air cover for the Israeli strike across the Sinai peninsula. In all these minor wars, including the peaceful U.S. landing in Lebanon and the interposition of the U.S. 7th Fleet between Communist China and Formosa, there was no aerial opposition.

3. War in Vietnam.—In 1961 the United States stepped into the conflict in South Vietnam between the Communist Vietcong insurgents and the government of South Vietnam. At first U.S.

MCDONNELL F-4B PHANTOM, U.S. NAVY TACTICAL JET BOMBER, BEING CATAPULTED FROM THE USS "CONSTELLATION" FOR A MISSION AGAINST NORTH VIETNAM, 1966. IN THE FOREGROUND ARE DOUGLAS A4DS

LOCKHEED C-130 HERCULES, U.S. AIR FORCE TROOP AND CARGO TRANSPORT, BEING LOADED FOR AN AIRLIFT IN VIETNAM, 1967. THE C-130 ACCOMMODATES 92 FULLY EQUIPPED TROOPS AND HAS A RANGE OF 3,400 MI. WITH 25,000 LB.

new STOL (short take-off and landing) aircraft were completed an a new COIN (counter-insurgency) light aircraft was also pushed to operations. Many of the types needed were, in fact, essential tactical aircraft neglected in the 1950s when SAC and the ICBM dominated military thinking. Only in Canada was there an industry geared to producing the kind of aircraft needed.

Perhaps by far the most significant new use of air power in Vietnam was the development of full air mobility for Army units (1st Air Cavalry). This was demonstrated in October 1965 when the relief of an outpost was accomplished not by road but by the arrival in helicopters of a whole division complete with its artillery. In a four-week campaign the division moved its guns 66 times by air and kept them supplied with ammunition (33,000 rounds); the helicopters also furnished about 13,250 tons of other types of supplies.

4. Summary.—The lessons for air power in the years after World War II seemed to be that a nation must always maintain a balance among the types of air power available to it. But in the complex technological and logistical realities of the modern world, and this is especially true of the aerospace industry and of air power, the enemy's moves have to be anticipated by as long as ten years if the needed doctrine and equipment are to be available to meet each challenge. Moreover, whereas in World War I pilots went into action with fewer than 20 hours of flying time, by the late 1960s they needed 400 hours and approximately 18 months of training. Yet while the U.S. Air Force increasingly moved toward higher educational requirements, the Israelis in the seven-day war of early June 1967 showed that by keeping everything as simple as possible high-school graduates could inflict a decisive defeat upon major enemies. The Israeli operations effectively illustrated the use of a counterstrike force in a tactical and strategic manner. The opposing air forces were knocked out of the air, but no attacks were made on cities or other controversial targets.

The war in Vietnam also appeared to prove that "compact" aircraft in large numbers were needed as much as were highly sophisticated, air-superiority fighters. Air power, like sea power, called for a delicate mix of manned and unmanned, and large and small aircraft and, to be effective, required a certain amount of specialization both in aircraft and in men. *See also* AIRPLANE; AVIATION, HISTORY OF.

BIBLIOGRAPHY.—*General Works: Jane's All the World's Aircraft* (annually); *Brassey's Annual; Journal of the American Aviation Historical Society; United States Naval Institute Proceedings; Air University Review; Air Power Historian; Air Force; Military Review; Jour-*

personnel acted as advisers to the South Vietnamese. The air support provided was primarily used to move supplies. In February 1965, the U.S. Air Force began to launch major air strikes into North Vietnam. By the end of 1966 the U.S. had lost more than 300 aircraft on those missions, though many of the crews had been saved by helicopter and amphibian rescue services. Attacks on Vietcong positions were undertaken by a combination of methods. SAC B-52s flew 2,200 mi. from Guam to bomb intensively valleys thought to hold the enemy; each plane carried fifty-one 750-lb. bombs. Supersonic F-4 Phantom fighter-bombers struck at targets reported by spotter planes, while F-105 fighter-bombers were used on all targets. As in Korea, aircraft carriers offshore provided heavy strike forces also. In general, planes flew above 3,500 ft. to avoid small arms fire, though the introduction around targets in North Vietnam of Soviet surface-to-air radar-guided missiles compelled attacking aircraft to come down to 1,500 ft. where they could escape the missiles but were vulnerable to light antiaircraft fire. By mid-1965 the war had become a curious tactical conflict in which strategic targets were often hit by tactical aircraft and tactical targets by strategic bombers. Slow-flying transports were used to defoliate jungle. The war in Vietnam was also the first in which aerial refueling was used as an essential part of the entire operation.

It was also a war in which slow-flying aircraft were needed. Stockpiles were searched for the old Skyraiders, which could carry a large load but fly slowly enough to bomb jungle targets. The old DC-3 (C-47) once again appeared, fitted with an 18,000 rounds-per-minute broadside machine-gun armament. Special

NORTH AMERICAN OV-10A, U.S. AIRPLANE DESIGNED FOR COUNTER-INSURGENCY WARFARE, CAN OPERATE FROM ROUGH TERRAIN IN FORWARD COMBAT AREAS; MISSIONS INCLUDE RECONNAISSANCE, HELICOPTER ESCORT, AND GROUND ATTACK

nal of the Royal Aeronautical Society; Royal Air Force Quarterly; Journal of the Royal United Service Institution.

Origins to the End of World War I: L. T. C. Rolt, *The Aeronauts: a History of Ballooning, 1783–1903* (1966). Charles H. Gibbs-Smith, *The Aeroplane: an Historical Survey* (1960), *The Invention of the Aeroplane* (1965); Arthur Marder, *From the Dreadnought to Scapa Flow,* IV (1968); René Chambe, *Histoire de l'Aviation* (1958); J. L. Nayler and E. Ower, *Aviation: Its Technical Development* (1965); David Divine, *The Broken Wing* (1966); P. K. Kemp, *Fleet Air Arm* (1954); A. D. Turnbull and C. L. Lord, *History of United States Naval Aviation* (1949); Charles deF. Chandler and Frank P. Lahm, *How Our Army Grew Wings: Airmen and Aircraft Before 1914* (1943); I. B. Holley, *Ideas and Weapons* (1953); Wilhelmine Burch *et al.,* *History of the U.S. Air Force, 1907–1957* (1957); Sir Walter Raleigh and H. A. Jones, *The War in the Air,* 6 vol. (1922–37); Hilary St. G. Saunders, *Per Ardua* (1945); Raymond Fredette, *The First Battle of Britain* (1966); George van Deurs, *Wings for the Fleet* (1966); Robin Higham, *The British Rigid Airship, 1908–1931* (1961); Douglas H. Robinson, *The Zeppelin in Combat* (1962); Geoffrey Norris, *The Royal Flying Corps: a History* (1965).

The Interwar Years: L. S. Howeth, *History of Communications—Electronics in the United States Navy* (1963); Eugene Emme (ed.), *The Impact of Air Power* (1959); Guilio Douhet, *Command of the Air,* Eng. trans. by D. Ferrari (1942); William Mitchell, *Winged Defense* (1925); Alfred F. Hurley, *Billy Mitchell: Crusader for Air Power* (1964); Andrew Boyle, *Trenchard: Man of Vision* (1962); Robin Higham, *The Military Intellectuals in Britain, 1918–1939* (1966) and *Armed Forces in Peacetime: Britain, 1918–1940* (1963); C. P. Snow, *Science and Government* (1961); Ronald W. Clark, *Tizard* (1965); Richard K. Smith, *The Airships Akron and Macon* (1965).

World War II: Denis Richards and Hilary St. G. Saunders, *Royal Air Force 1939–1945* (1953–54); Asher Lee, *The German Air Force* (1946), *The Soviet Air Force* (1950); U.S. Strategic Bombing Survey, *Over-all Report (European War)* (1945), *Over-all Report (Pacific War)* (1946); Air Ministry, *The Rise and Fall of the German Air Force* (1948); W. F. Craven and James L. Cate (eds.), *The United States Army Air Forces in World War II,* 7 vol. (1949–54); Sir Charles Webster and Noble Frankland, *The Strategic Air Offensive against Germany, 1939–1945* (1961); Derek Wood and Derek Dempster, *The Narrow Margin* (1961); Werner Baumbach, *The Life and Death of the Luftwaffe* (1960); Adolf Galland, *The First and the Last* (1954); David Irving, *The Mare's Nest* (1964), *The Destruction of Dresden* (1964); Ronald W. Clark, *The Rise of the Boffins* (1962); Hans Rumpf, *The Bombing of Germany* (1962); A. M. Prentiss, *Civil Defense in Modern War* (1951); T. H. O'Brien, *Civil Defense* (1955); C. F. Rawnsley and Robert Wright, *Night Fighter* (1957); Andrew Ten Eyck, *Jeeps in the Sky* (1946); James M. Gavin, *Airborne Warfare* (1948); Lynn Montross, *Cavalry of the Sky* (1954); George Chatterton, *The Wings of Pegasus: the Story of the Glider Pilot Regiment* (1962); S. L. A. Marshall, *Night Drop: the American Airborne Invasion of Normandy* (1962); I. B. Holley, *Buying Aircraft* (1964); E. B. Potter and Chester Nimitz (eds.), *Sea Power* (1960); Robert Sherrod, *History of Marine Corps Aviation in World War II* (1952); Sir William James, *Ark Royal, 1939–1941* (1957); Samuel Eliot Morison, *History of U.S.N. Operations in World War II* (1947–1962); Robert E. Futrell, "Airpower Lessons of World War II," *Air Force* (September 1965); R. N. Gale, *With the Sixth Airborne Division in Normandy* (1949); Sir Frederick Pile, *Ack-Ack: Britain's Defence Against Air Attack in the Second World War* (1949); Dudley Saward, *The Bomber's Eye* (1959).

After World War II: Robert F. Futrell, *The U.S. Air Force in Korea, 1950–1953* (1961); M. W. Cagle and F. A. Manson, *The Sea War in Korea* (1957); Edgar O'Ballance, *Malaya: the Communist Insurgent War, 1948–1960* (1966); David Wise and Thomas B. Boss, *The U-2 Affair* (1962); Frank Harvey, "The Air War in Vietnam," *Flying* (November 1966); Eldon W. Downs (ed.), *The U.S. Air Force in Space* (1966); Robert Strausz-Hupé and Stefan T. Possony (eds.), "Air Power and National Security," *The Annals of the American Academy of Political and Social Science,* vol. 299 (May 1955); *Semiannual Reports of the Secretary of the Air Force* (1948–); Robert Kilmarx, *A History of Soviet Air Power* (1962); M. G. Saunders (ed.), *The Soviet Navy* (1958); Asher Lee (ed.), *The Soviet Air and Rocket Forces* (1959); Raymond Garthoff, *Soviet Strategy in the Nuclear Age* (1958); Louis A. Sigaud, *Air Power and Unification* (1949); Bernard Brodie, *Strategy in the Missile Age* (1959); Herman Kahn, *On Thermonuclear War* (1960); P. W. Powers, *A Guide to National Defense* (1964). (R. Hᴍ.)

AIR PUMP: *see* Compressor; Vacuum.

AIR RAIDS: *see* Air Power.

AIRSCREW: *see* Aircraft Propulsion.

AIRSHIP, or dirigible balloon, a self-propelled aircraft that can be inflated with a gas lighter than air and can thus be sustained aloft by buoyancy. To distinguish it from the simple balloon, which has similar aerostatic characteristics but no propelling or steering system, the dirigible balloon is sometimes referred to simply as a dirigible.

Consisting of an elongated gas-filled streamlined hull, and possessing propulsive power, stabilizing surfaces, and altitude and directional control, an airship is classified by its structural type as nonrigid, semirigid or rigid. The body of a nonrigid airship, or blimp, consists of a fabric envelope highly impervious to lifting gas or air. The envelope maintains its streamlined form by the interior pressure of both the lifting gas and of air, the latter being contained in variable-volume compartments called ballonets which inflate and deflate to compensate for changes in lifting gas volume. The semirigid airship similarly depends upon internal gas and air pressure to maintain its envelope form but has, in addition, a supporting structural keel extending longitudinally along the bottom of the envelope.

Nonrigid and semirigid airships are known as pressure airships because of the pressure differential used to maintain envelope rigidity. This distinguishes them from the rigid airship, which maintains its shape through a rigid structural framework independent of internal gas pressure. This framework has an outer cover (generally fabric), and on the inside, individual lifting gas cells are placed throughout the ship's length, an installation that is comparable to the watertight compartmentation of water-borne vessels.

EVOLUTION OF THE AIRSHIP

Human flight was first made possible in 1783 by the invention of the free balloon, and there immediately followed a period of intensive balloon development (*see* Aviation, History of; Balloon Flight). Man's desire to contrive an aircraft which could be steered and propelled independently of the wind inevitably led to the airship. Thus, between 1783 and 1852, when the first airship was flown, numerous unsuccessful attempts were made to steer and propel balloons. These efforts failed primarily because of dependence upon primitive forms of manual power in the absence of suitable mechanical means of propulsion.

Finally, in 1851, Henri Giffard, the French inventor of the steam injector, overcame the airship power-plant problem by developing a 350-lb. steam engine of 3 h.p. which could drive a propeller 11 ft. in diameter at 110 r.p.m. The following year he constructed an 88,000-cu.ft. airship, 144 ft. long and 40 ft. in diameter, and mounted his engine on it. Giffard ascended in this hydrogen-filled craft on Sept. 24, 1852, from the Hippodrome in Paris and, at an estimated speed of 6 m.p.h., demonstrated in a light wind the first appreciable control ever exerted on a lighter-than-air craft.

Initial application of the internal-combustion engine to airship flight was made by the German engineer Paul Haenlein, who, in 1872, completed and flew an airship propelled by a gas engine which drew its fuel from the envelope. The French brothers Albert and Gaston Tissandier were the first to build an electrically powered airship; their 37,500-cu.ft. craft, powered by a 1.5-h.p. electric motor, made a successful initial flight on Oct. 8, 1883.

The first airship to possess control sufficient to enable it to return to the point of ascent was the electrically powered 66,000-cu.ft. "La France," constructed of an envelope of Chinese silk and a car of bamboo trelliswork. Powered by an 8-h.p. electric motor and piloted by its constructors, Charles Renard and A. C. Krebs, this French airship made its first trial flight on Aug. 9, 1884, at Chalais-Meudon, completing a circular flight of about five miles.

A 130,000-cu.ft. aluminum-hulled airship, built and tested in Germany in 1897 by David Schwarz, was the first of the rigid type. Having an aluminum framework covered by aluminum sheeting, it was also the first airship powered by a gasoline engine. Meanwhile, Alberto Santos-Dumont, a Brazilian living in Paris, had become interested in lighter-than-air flight and in 1898 completed his first of a series of 14 nonrigid, gasoline-powered airships. These small airships performed a number of record-making and unusual flights which won world-wide fame for their constructor. In 1905 Santos-Dumont abandoned airship development to turn his inventive genius to heavier-than-air craft.

Of great importance was the first Zeppelin airship (LZ-1), a rigid type, which made its initial flight from a floating hangar on Lake of Constance, near Friedrichshafen, Ger., on July 2, 1900. The 388,140-cu.ft. LZ-1 was 420 ft. long and 38 ft. in diameter.

Its designer was Count Ferdinand von Zeppelin, a retired German army officer, who, while serving as a balloon observer with the Union forces in the American Civil War, conceived the idea of placing a number of balloons in line within a streamlined structure which could be propelled and steered. The cigar-shaped aluminum frame of the LZ-1 consisted of 24 longitudinal girders, extending from nose to tail, set within 16 transverse frames or rings and braced by diagonal wiring. The entire framework was covered by a cotton cloth to protect the inner structure and to present a smooth outer surface. Inside the framework, between the transverse rings, were separate hydrogen-filled gas cells of rubberized cloth, while beneath the craft there was a keellike structure connecting two external cars. In each of the cars there was a 16-h.p. engine geared to two propellers. A sliding weight secured to the keel was designed to afford vertical control by raising or lowering the nose, while rudders were provided for horizontal control. Despite structural weaknesses, the LZ-1 proved the practicability of the Zeppelin design and attained speeds approaching 20 m.p.h.

AIRSHIP OPERATION AND CONSTRUCTION

Flight Principles.—The Archimedean precept (*see* MECHANICS, FLUID) is the fundamental principle of airship flight. Airships lighter than the air they displace experience a buoyant force tending to make them rise; those which are heavier will tend to descend. An airship or balloon floats in the air whenever the sum of the weight of the gas container and other weights appended to it, plus the weight of the lifting gas itself, is the same as the weight of the air displaced by the gas. The lift acquired by an airship from the buoyancy of its gas is known as static lift. When a lighter-than-air aircraft is buoyant, it is said to be light. When its weight and static lift are equal, it is in equilibrium. It is heavy when its weight exceeds its static lift. Airships and simple balloons are most accurately described as displacement aircraft.

An airship is also subject to aerodynamic or dynamic lift derived from its motion through the air, its body and horizontal surfaces or stabilizers producing an appreciable lifting effect when driven through the air at an inclination. The airship utilizes this dynamic lift to meet either a heavy or a light condition in flight, a heavy ship flying in a nose up attitude and a light one flying nose down. The static condition of an airship varies in flight, depending upon the amount of fuel consumed, the rain or snow loads acquired and the temperature of the lifting gas. Extreme heaviness can be remedied by jettisoning ballast, while excess lightness can be overcome by releasing lifting gas or by taking on sea water or other ballast. Large helium-inflated airships use equipment whereby water may be recovered from the fuel consumed to compensate for the weight of the latter.

Normal control of altitude by airships is maintained by putting the elevators (movable surfaces attached to the horizontal fins) in their up position or in their down position. Horizontal steering is similarly accomplished. The airship and the submarine are somewhat analogous in design and operational features.

Lifting Gases and Pressure Control.—In simple terms the buoyancy, or lift, equals weight of air minus weight of lifting gas. Under standard conditions (32° F., 29.92 in. pressure), 1,000 cu.ft. of dry air weighs 80.72 lb., 1,000 cu.ft. of pure helium weighs 11.14 lb. and the same quantity of hydrogen weighs 5.61 lb. Although coal gas is often used in sport ballooning, it is not light enough for airship use. Thus, under standard conditions 1,000 cu.ft. of pure hydrogen will lift 75.11 lb., while the same quantity of pure helium will lift 69.58 lb. Helium, therefore, possesses 92.6% of the lift of hydrogen. Under operating conditions 68 to 70 lb. for 1,000 cu.ft. of hydrogen and 62 to 65 lb. for 1,000 cu.ft. of helium are used as average lift values. The lesser lift of helium is offset by its complete noninflammability, an advantage which caused the U.S., in 1922, to adopt a "helium only" policy in airship operation.

Because the rigid airship is not dependent upon internal pressure to maintain its form, openings in the hull permit ready flow of air in and out to equalize internal and external air pressure. However, in the nonrigid and semirigid types, too much internal pressure places undue strain on the envelope or automatically releases

lifting gas; too little pressure might cause the envelope to fold or buckle. The fluctuations in gas volume (and hence pressure, the pressure of a gas being proportional to its volume at like temperatures) are compensated for by varying the air pressure in ballonets that are separated from the lifting gas by fabric diaphragms. There are generally two ballonets, one forward and one aft, so that they may also be used for trimming purposes (attitude control).

Construction Details.—Rigid airship structures were usually made of aluminum alloys. Outer cover fabrics were generally of cotton, with linen sometimes used on the fins and movable surfaces. Gas cells were originally lightweight cotton fabric lined with goldbeater's skin for gastightness, but synthetic materials replaced the latter.

Nonrigid airship envelopes originally consisted of long-staple cotton fabric impregnated with rubber, but synthetics, such as neoprene and Dacron, superseded the cotton-rubber combination. An aluminum-pigment paint on the outside reflects the sun and reduces the amount of heat absorption by the lifting gas. Battens of stiff material around the blimp's nose reinforce it against buckling at cruising speeds.

In rigid airships the control car and other cars containing the propulsion plants usually were hung beneath the hull. In the U.S. navy's "Akron" and "Macon," however, the engines were located within the hull, driving outside propellers by means of shafting. In blimps the latter practice was followed in a few designs, but generally both the engines and propellers were mounted as units on the car in outside nacelles. In early blimps, cars were suspended by wires leading from suspension patches on the outside of the envelope. This practice was later succeeded by a system of internal and external catenary curtains.

Personnel, armament, power plants and virtually all the equipment of a nonrigid airship are carried by its car, which is equipped with a retractable wheel to make possible running take-offs and landings. Airship cars provide space for excellent habitability and for communications, navigational and other equipment.

Airships are equipped with lines used in ground handling operations to steady the ship and hold it in position or to pull light craft to earth. At the extreme bow of the airship is a disk mounting a horizontal spindle to which a hinged cone is attached. Mooring is accomplished by drawing this cone into a cuplike device at the top of the mooring mast. With its nose held in this manner, the airship is free to rotate about the mast as the wind shifts, and if the mast is mobile, the airship can be docked, undocked and "walked" over the landing field.

DEVELOPMENT OF NONRIGID AND SEMIRIGID TYPES

Germany.—Despite the prominence of (rigid) Zeppelins in Germany, other types of airships also received attention there. Maj. August von Parseval, in 1906, constructed the first of about 28 Parseval pressure airships for the German army. In 1907 a semirigid airship was constructed by Maj. Hans von Gross and Nikolas Basenach; the last of four additional Gross-Basenach ships, completed in 1913, saw service with the German navy.

Great Britain.—Prior to World War I, Great Britain made little contribution to airship development, although a few private British experimenters, notably Henry Spencer, Dr. Barton and E. T. Willows, aroused sufficient interest to cause the government to begin airship construction in 1907. From that date to the outbreak of hostilities in 1914, about eight British pressure airships were constructed, varying in volume from 21,000 to 180,000 cu.ft., while an additional five were purchased from France and Germany. During the war period of 1914–18 seven nonrigid types were evolved for antisubmarine, antimine and coastal patrol duties. Great Britain built or used 207 nonrigid airships in 1914–18; of these, 56 were in active service from June 1917 to Oct. 1918. More than 9,000 patrol and 2,200 escort missions were made from 17 airship stations and 12 mooring-out sites. After the war, nonrigid activity ceased, but one commercial blimp, the 60,000-cu.ft. AD-1, was constructed in 1929.

France.—French interest lapsed considerably after Santos-Du-

mont demonstrated his series of airships. The first significant
modern airship of native French design was the Lebaudy brothers'
"Jaune" (1902). The Lebaudy success encouraged others. From
1904 until the outbreak of World War I, pressure airships for
private use and for export were constructed for the French government in appreciable numbers by the Astra, Clément-Bayard,
and Zodiac firms and by the government's factory at Chalais-
Meudon.

The French army abandoned its airship activity in 1917, transferring eight ships to the navy. With an additional 52 airships,
the French navy in 1917–18 performed more than 3,300 flights.
These airships attacked about 60 U-boats and sighted about 100
mines. French naval nonrigid and semirigid airship activity continued after the war until 1937. During that period the French
naval airship service operated an average minimum of two ships
from the main operating base at Rochefort.

All airships built during this period were constructed by the
sole remaining French airship manufacturer, Zodiac, which from
1924 to 1937 produced six nonrigid and four semirigid airships,
varying from the 130,000-cu.ft. Vedette to the 350,000-cu.ft. Es-
corteur. In 1936 Zodiac developed for the French army a 35,000-
cu.ft. motorized observation balloon with an attachable power and
control gondola. It went into production in May 1940, and 21
were completed. The termination of navy airship activity by government decree in 1937 and of similar army activity by the German
conquest in 1940 was made all the more complete by Allied bombings of airship hangars and by other war destruction.

Italy.—Italian airship construction embraced mainly the semirigid type. Several P- and M-type airships, 166,000 cu.ft. and
424,000 cu.ft., respectively, were designed and built by Gen. A.
Crocco and O. R. Ricaldoni prior to World War I; several Forlanini
semirigid airships had similarly been completed by the beginning
of hostilities. During the period 1914–18 additional types were
developed, primarily to increase altitude performance during bombing missions. In 1921 a 1,240,000-cu.ft. semirigid type, the
"Roma," was sold to the U.S. army; this 410-ft. airship was
shipped disassembled to the U.S., where it was re-erected. During
a test flight on Feb. 21, 1922, the "Roma" crashed and burned, resulting in the death of 34 persons.

The well-known N-type Italian semirigid airship, developed by
Gen. Umberto Nobile, was the last airship type undertaken under
government sponsorship. Italy officially terminated its airship
program in 1927. On May 11, 1926, the 654,000-cu.ft. "Norge"
(N-1), carrying an expedition headed by Roald Amundsen, Lincoln
Ellsworth and Nobile, left Spitsbergen, passed over the north pole
on May 12 and, continuing its 3,000-mi. flight, landed two days later
at Teller, Alaska, where it was dismantled. The N-3, third of the
Nobile series, was sold to Japan, where it was destroyed during
naval maneuvers in Oct. 1927. Using the "Italia" (N-4), Nobile
attempted another polar flight in May 1928, but after reaching
the north pole, the ship crashed on its homeward journey with the
loss of seven lives.

Russia.—Although Russia before World War I had shown an
interest in airships by purchasing semirigid types from France,
there was little concerted activity until about 1931, when a public
subscription of 15,000,000 rubles toward an airship program was
announced. The second five-year plan provided for the operation
of airships on civil air routes within the U.S.S.R., and the services
of General Nobile were secured. A number of small pressure airships were subsequently constructed, and in 1933 plans were announced to construct two larger commercial airships and a large
metal-clad airship.

The Dirigiblestroi (Dirigible Construction trust) in 1936 began
the 353-ft.-long, 882,829-cu.ft. semirigid DP-9. In 1937 a Russian
airship commission visited the United States to study American
airship efforts and expressed a desire to purchase the U.S. navy's
German-built rigid airship "Los Angeles." Russia operated a regular airline before World War II, using small airships in a service
connecting Moscow with Sverdlovsk. It has been stated that
Russia had 15 nonrigid and semirigid airships in operation and was
seriously considering larger craft of the rigid type.

A Soviet request for U.S. blimps on a lend-lease basis late in

World War II was refused by the U.S. In late 1945 it was disclosed that a small civil airship, the "Victory," had made an 80-hour
demonstration flight over the Black sea. In Nov. 1946 the existence of another Soviet airship, the "Patriot," was announced; this
150-ft.-long craft was reported to be dual engined and capable of
carrying 12 passengers with a one-man crew.

United States.—In the United States a few small privately
owned pressure airships were built and flown by Capt. Thomas S.
Baldwin, Lincoln Beachey and Roy Knabenshue immediately following the beginning of the 20th century. The first practical U.S.
airship was Baldwin's "California Arrow" (1903), while the first
U.S. government airship was a 19,500-cu.ft. craft purchased from
Baldwin by the U.S. army in 1908. Two unsuccessful attempts to
fly to the north pole were made in 1907 and 1909 by the explorer
Walter Wellman in his airship "America." Using the same craft,
Wellman in 1910 attempted a transatlantic flight which similarly
failed. In 1912 Melville Vaniman took off from Atlantic City,
N.J., for a transatlantic flight in the "Akron," but within 15 minutes
after departure the airship caught fire and was destroyed with the
loss of its entire crew of five.

U.S. naval airship activity began when the 175-ft.-long, 114,800-
cu.ft. DN-1 was contracted for in 1915. Erected in a floating
hangar at Pensacola, Fla., the DN-1 (later redesignated the A-1)
was completed in April 1917; the craft proved unsatisfactory because of excessive gas leakage and was abandoned after three flights.
In 1917 serious attention was given to the development of nonrigid airships for antisubmarine and coast patrol. The navy ordered 15 B-type airships (77,000 to 84,000 cu.ft.), which were
completed in 1917–18 by the Goodyear Tire and Rubber company,
Goodrich Tire and Rubber company and Connecticut Aircraft company. The B-class was followed by the 182,000-cu.ft. C-type, for
which 30 (reduced to 10 after the Armistice) were contracted with
Goodyear and Goodrich; the first C-ship was completed in Sept.
1918. During U.S. participation in World War I, U.S. navy blimps
were based at seven Atlantic coast air stations, ranging from
Chatham, Mass., to Key West, Fla., while other airships, acquired
from the French, were operated from Paimboeuf, France. In May
1919 the C-5 attempted a transatlantic crossing. After flying from
Montauk, Long Island, N.Y., to Newfoundland in 23 hours, the
blimp was lost and never again sighted when strong winds tore it
away crewless from the hands of the ground crew and blew it to
sea.

Five D-type airships (189,000 cu.ft.) were then built. A considerably modified D-ship, the D-6, was later produced for the
navy. In 1918 and 1919 two small, single-engined, nonrigid airships were built, designated the E-1 and F-1, and purchased by
the navy. A 400,000-cu.ft. "G" design was completed in 1919, but
no ships of this type were constructed. A later class of utility and
training ships (183,000 to 196,700 cu.ft.), which began with the
G-1 (ex-Goodyear "Defender"), was acquired in 1935. The only
navy semirigid airship was the O-1, erected at Cape May, N.J.,
in Sept. 1919. Imported from Italy, this craft saw only three
months' service. In 1921 the navy acquired the 43,000-cu.ft.
single-engined H-1 airship, which could be towed or used as a
kite balloon. The next naval airship type was the J-class, of
which the first unit was completed in 1922.

Meanwhile, the U.S. army, which also had flown both observation
(kite) balloons and blimps in Europe during World War I, proceeded with nonrigid and semirigid development from main airship
bases at Langley field, Va., and Scott field, Ill. To investigate the
semirigid design, the army purchased the "Roma" from Italy in
1921 and the 719,000-cu.ft. RS-1 from Goodyear four years later.
The hydrogen-filled "Roma" was destroyed by fire, with the loss of
34 lives, on Feb. 21, 1922, after striking an electric power line at
Langley field, Va. The RS-1, after several years of intermittent
service, was dismantled and the army concentrated thereafter on
nonrigid types and motorized balloons. Finally, in 1937, the army
terminated its airship program and turned over its nonrigid airships
to the navy.

In the period between World Wars I and II, United States civil
airship activity was primarily limited to the operation of commercial and advertising blimps by the Goodyear company, constructor

of virtually every significant U.S. airship after 1911. After experimenting with a small "pony blimp," Goodyear in 1925 began the operation of from one to six of its own nonrigid helium-inflated airships, which pioneered many airship flight and ground handling improvements. The capacity of these Goodyear blimps varied from 51,000 cu.ft. to 183,000 cu.ft. but was later standardized at 123,000 cu.ft., a size which carried six passengers. These craft were taken over by the U.S. navy for service in World War II. In civil employment through 1958, the Goodyear blimp fleet had carried more than 483,000 passengers and made over 178,000 flights without a single passenger injury or fatality.

In 1935, with rigid airship activity interrupted by the sinking of the "Macon" (see below), naval lighter-than-air efforts again centred about nonrigid development and operation of the 210,000-cu.ft. J-4, the 320,000-cu.ft. K-1 and the 202,000-cu.ft. ZMC-2. The J-4 was an open gondola ship completed in 1924, and the experimental K-1 was built in 1931. The ZMC-2, the first successful all-metal airship, was constructed in 1929 by the Metalclad Airship corporation of Detroit, Mich. Its hull consisted of 24 longitudinals and 12 circular frames to which an 0.0095-in.-thick outer cover of an aluminum-base alloy sheet was riveted. Although possessing certain rigid construction characteristics, the ZMC-2 was, nevertheless, a pressure airship, depending upon internal pressure to maintain hull strength in flight. Although the craft had a long successful life prior to dismantlement, no other metal-clad airships were built. The 183,000-cu.ft. Goodyear-owned "Defender" was acquired by the navy in 1935 and designated the G-1.

Increased airship strength was authorized as the entry of the United States into World War II drew near, and at the time of the Pearl Harbor attack the navy was operating four K-type patrol airships and three small L-type trainers (all built in 1938–41), as well as the G-1 and the ex-army TC-13 and 14. The airship building program was accelerated, and an improved G-type and new M-type ship evolved. During the war the navy operated a total of 134 K-type (425,000 cu.ft.) and 4 M-type (647,500 cu.ft.) patrol airships, 22 L-type training ships of 123,000-cu.ft. capacity and 8 G-type (196,700 cu.ft.) training and utility blimps.

Except for those used primarily for training and experimentation, U.S. navy airships of World War II were grouped into 14 U.S. fleet blimp squadrons, which, operating from more than 50 main and auxiliary bases, performed antisubmarine patrol and escort operations in a 3,000,000-sq.mi. area along the U.S. Atlantic, Gulf and Pacific coasts, in the Caribbean, along the South American coast from Panama to Rio de Janeiro and in the Mediterranean. A fleet blimp utility squadron operated similarly from five bases along the Atlantic seaboard. These 15 squadrons flew a total of 55,900 flights for 550,000 hours and escorted 89,000 ships without the loss of a single vessel to enemy action. Of the blimps assigned to fleet units, 87% were in operational readiness at all times, thereby establishing a record availability for military aircraft.

The first nonrigid airship transoceanic flight was made in 1944 when blimp squadron 14 was ordered based with six K-ships at Port Lyautey (now Kenitra), former French Morocco, for patrol of the Straits of Gibraltar. The blimps were ferried across the Atlantic in pairs from South Weymouth, Mass., via Newfoundland and the Azores. The first flight (3,145 mi.) was made on May 29–June 1, 1944, by the K-123 and K-130 in a total flight time of 58 hours. In 1945 two additional K-ships were flown to Port Lyautey from Weeksville, N.C., via Bermuda and the Azores; the 3,532-mi. flight was completed in a flight time of 62 hours.

Although antisubmarine operations were the main duties of U.S. navy airships during the war, their unusual flight characteristics were valuable in general utility missions. Used in shipping control to direct and facilitate the rendezvous, formation and breakup of merchant convoys, airships saved a great deal of shipping time. Torpedo recovery, aerial photography, observation, special equipment calibration, search operations, rescue work and other services requiring slow speed and low-altitude operations for extended periods of time were performed in great numbers and variety for fleet and shore units. In the Mediterranean, airships assumed unprecedented importance in mine sweeping operations by spotting and marking otherwise undetected mine fields and through saving a number of mine sweeping vessels by diverting them from collision courses with mines the mine sweepers could not see.

With the end of World War II, U.S. naval airship activity was materially reduced, only to be expanded upon the outbreak of the Korean war in 1950 and then reduced again. Various configurations of the K-patrol-type blimp were evolved, with increased volume up to 670,000 cu.ft. On Nov. 2, 1946, the 725,000-cu.ft. XM-1 (formerly the 647,500-cu.ft. M-1) completed a 170-hr. 17-min. world's aircraft endurance record for continuous unrefueled flight. In 1953 the first N-type blimp, subsequently designated the ZPG-2 type, was placed in service. This 1,000,000-cu.ft. ship resulted from a project begun late in World War II to achieve increased blimp performance mainly in amount of equipment carried. The ZPG-2W was a configuration intended specifically for airborne early warning service. On July 1, 1957, one airship squadron took its place in early warning service at sea and quickly demonstrated the airship's all-weather reliability, economy and high technical efficiency in such service. Other blimp units continued as part of the antisubmarine warfare team. In March 1957 a ZPG-2 airship completed an unrefueled flight of 264 hr. 14 min. for a new record distance of 8,216 nautical (9,448 statute) miles over the North Atlantic and the Caribbean. This also broke the 6,980-mi. nonstop record made by the airship "Graf Zeppelin" between Friedrichshafen and Tokyo in 1929. On July 21, 1958, the first of the ZPG-3W type of over 1,500,000-cu.ft. volume, largest blimp ever built, made its maiden flight. Its most unique feature was the installation within the envelope of a large radar antenna, giving this craft valuable early warning service capabilities.

DEVELOPMENT OF RIGID TYPES

Germany.—In the category of rigid airships Count Zeppelin's only competitors were Johann Schütte and Heinrich Lanz, who evolved a rigid design using a spirally disposed wooden girder type of construction. Their first ship, a 700,000-cu.ft.-capacity, 430-ft.-long, 60-ft.-wide craft, was completed in 1911 and attained a speed approaching 50 m.p.h. During World War I the Germans standardized on the Zeppelin type, and a total of only 20 Schütte-Lanz airships were built and flown. At four fabrication plants 88 Zeppelins were built, a production rate of one ship per two weeks being achieved. These ships operated with the German army and navy in bombing strategic areas and in North sea scouting and patrol (see AIR POWER). Their bombing activities, however, were gradually rendered ineffective by improvement of Allied defense measures, particularly the employment of incendiary devices for setting the Zeppelins' hydrogen afire. To get greater range and larger bomb loads and to fly higher and faster, the Zeppelins underwent remarkable improvements during this period. By 1918 their size had increased to 2,400,000 cu.ft., their speed to 80 m.p.h., their useful lift to 50 tons, and their ceiling to over 20,000 ft. They were armed with machine guns mounted in the cars and atop the hull for protection against airplanes. They also had a car or "spy basket" which could be lowered beneath the clouds to permit the observer in this car to navigate or direct bombing while the airship remained hidden above. Of German naval airship employment, only about 10% was in bombing raids, 90% having been on strictly naval missions. Zeppelin activity ceased temporarily with the capitulation of Germany in 1918. Existing Zeppelins were dismantled or delivered to France, Italy, England, Belgium and Japan. A few were sabotaged by their crews.

Success of the Zeppelin type had led to the formation in 1910 of the Delag, or Deutsche Luftschiffahrts-Aktien-Gessellschaft, which provided commercial and pleasure flights in airships up to the outbreak of World War I in 1914. During those five years, Delag's five small airships made 1,588 flights, carrying 34,228 passengers without injury. Two small commercial Zeppelins built immediately after the Armistice carried 2,380 passengers, all in safety, in 103 flights before being surrendered—the "Bodensee" to Italy, the "Nordstern" to France. Under Allied terms, later lifted, the Germans were prohibited from undertaking further airship construction.

The next Zeppelin airship was the 2,470,000-cu.ft. LZ-126, which was constructed as a war reparations payment to the U.S. Later christened the "Los Angeles," it was delivered to the U.S. in a transatlantic flight in Oct. 1924. The "Graf Zeppelin" (LZ-127), a 3,308,600-cu.ft. ship completed in Sept. 1928, saw nine years of successful continuous service. When decommissioned in 1937, the "Graf Zeppelin" had made 590 flights (including 144 ocean crossings) and had flown 1,053,391 mi., carrying 13,110 passengers and 235,300 lb. of mail and freight. In 1929 Hugo Eckener, successor to Count Zeppelin, who died in 1917, commanded the ship on a 21,255-mi. world flight that was completed in an elapsed time of 20 days 4 hr. 14 min.

The LZ-128 did not progress far beyond the blueprint stage and was followed by the 7,063,000-cu.ft. "Hindenburg" (LZ-129), completed in 1936. This 804-ft.-long airship, of conventional Zeppelin design with 36 longitudinal girders and 15 wire-braced main transverse frames, was powered by four 1,100-h.p. Mercedes-Benz diesel engines, giving it a maximum speed of 84 m.p.h. At a cruising speed of 78 m.p.h., the "Hindenburg," which contained accommodations for 50 passengers, had an 8,750-mi. range. In 1936 this airship inaugurated commercial air service across the North Atlantic by carrying 1,002 passengers on ten scheduled round trips between Germany and the U.S.; westbound crossings averaged 65 hours; eastbound, 52 hours. On May 6, 1937, while landing at Lakehurst, N.J., on the first of its 1937 schedule of North Atlantic crossings, the hydrogen-inflated "Hindenburg" burst into flames and was completely destroyed, with a loss of 36 lives—the first passenger fatalities in the history of commercial airship operation. The fire was generally attributed to a discharge of atmospheric electricity in the vicinity of a hydrogen leak; however, the possibility of sabotage cannot be overlooked.

The LZ-130, bearing again the name "Graf Zeppelin," was completed and tested in Sept. 1938. Designed for helium operation, this slightly modified sister ship of the "Hindenburg" was built for transatlantic commercial service, but the tense international situation at the time, together with the refusal of the U.S. to export helium, prevented the use of the ship for that purpose. Inflated with hydrogen, the LZ-130 made 30 exhibition and test flights for a total of 400 hours but saw no commercial or war service.

With the completion of the LZ-130 in 1938, work was begun on the LZ-131, but as the outbreak of World War II approached, the German government in July 1939 directed the Zeppelin company to discontinue all lighter-than-air manufacture. Finally, in April 1940, another Nazi directive ordered the dismantlement of the LZ-130, the old decommissioned "Graf Zeppelin" (LZ-127) and the main zeppelin operating terminal at Frankfurt am Main; the reason given was the war need for duralumin and steel. Later, in July 1944, Allied bombings of Friedrichshafen resulted in the destruction of the hangars, shops and production facilities of the Zeppelin company, then engaged in the production of miscellaneous war materials.

Great Britain.—In 1911 the British 660,000-cu.ft. "Mayfly," modeled along zeppelin lines, was completed but never flown; it broke in two while being brought out of its shed at Barrow. Rigid construction was not undertaken again until 1914 when work was begun on the R-9; this airship was completed three years later. Six rigid airships (two modified to abolish external keels) of the R-23 class were next laid down, followed by the R-31 and R-32, which were of wooden construction. None of these, however, equaled the products of the experienced Zeppelin designers and constructors. The German Zeppelin L-33, shot down in good condition over Essex in 1916, served as a model for the next British rigid airships, the R-33 and R-34. They were completed in 1919 and were of marked improvement; in fact, the R-34 made a transatlantic flight from East Fortune, Scot., to Mineola, N.Y., in July of the same year and returned to England, the first aircraft to cross the Atlantic nonstop from east to west and the first to complete a transatlantic round trip by air.

Two additional rigid airships, the R-80 and R-36, were launched in 1920 and 1921. They were followed by the 2,700,000-cu.ft. R-38, which was to be purchased by the U.S. navy. On its fourth flight, on Aug. 24, 1921, this craft, designed for high altitude operation, broke in two under severe handling at low altitude and fell into the Humber river, killing 44 British and U.S. officers and men.

The R-38 disaster brought British service airship activity to a halt, but in 1924 an empire communications scheme was undertaken, calling for British construction of two commercial 5,000,000-cu.ft. rigid airships, the R-100 and R-101. Both were completed in 1929, the former by the Airship Guarantee company at Howden and the latter by the Royal Airship Works at Cardington. The R-100, with accommodations for 100 passengers, was built on a modified Zeppelin design with six gasoline engines. Its two-year life was relatively uneventful, although in July 1930 it flew to Montreal, Que., in 78 hours, returning in 58 hours. The R-101, lengthened after completion to increase its lifting capacity, accommodated about 50 passengers and deviated substantially from Zeppelin practice by using steel girders and five diesel engines. During an attempted flight on Oct. 5, 1930, to India, the R-101 crashed into a hill near Beauvais, France, and burst into flames, killing 48 persons. (The unreadiness of the ship for such an undertaking had been no secret.) Following this disaster, the government scrapped the R-100 in 1931 and abandoned airship activity indefinitely.

France.—After the World War I Armistice considerable interest in rigid airships was shown by the French government. Only one of this type had previously been constructed in France, the none too successful "Spiess," a privately owned wooden type built by the Zodiac firm in 1912. Three Zeppelins, the L-72, LZ-113 and the small commercial "Nordstern," were turned over to France by Germany in 1920–21. The last two saw little active service prior to dismantlement, but the 2,470,000-cu.ft. L-72 (renamed the "Dixmude" by the French) established an endurance record of 118 hr. 41 min. in Sept. 1923.

In December of the same year the "Dixmude" was lost over the Mediterranean with its entire complement, ending rigid airship activity in France.

United States.—In 1919 the U.S. navy began construction of the 2,115,174-cu.ft. ZR-1. Fabricated at the Naval Aircraft factory, Philadelphia, Pa., and assembled at the Naval Air station, Lakehurst, N.J., this ship, christened the "Shenandoah," was largely a copy of the German Zeppelin L-49 design, modified mainly for mooring mast and helium operation. Her maiden flight on Sept. 4, 1923, was followed by a number of noteworthy flights, including a 9,000-mi. transcontinental round trip in Oct. 1924. On Sept. 3, 1925, the "Shenandoah" failed structurally in a thunderstorm near Ava, O., and 14 members of her crew of 43 were killed.

On Oct. 15, 1924, the German Zeppelin Airship Works delivered the 2,470,000-cu.ft. ZR-3, later christened the "Los Angeles," to Lakehurst, N.J., after a 5,000-mi. flight from Friedrichshafen, where the ship had been constructed as a war reparations payment to the U.S. This 658-ft.-long dirigible was used extensively for experimental work on flight and mooring problems and developed a means for hooking-on and releasing airplanes in flight. After 331 flights, consuming a total of 4,320 hours, the "Los Angeles" was decommissioned at Lakehurst in 1932 and dismantled seven years later.

The German Zeppelin patents and processes, together with the services of key Zeppelin personnel, were acquired in 1924 by the Goodyear Tire and Rubber company, which then formed a subsidiary, the Goodyear-Zeppelin corporation, in Akron, O. In 1928 Goodyear-Zeppelin (later Goodyear Aircraft corporation) began the construction of two 6,500,000-cu.ft. rigid airships for the navy. Both ships were 785 ft. long and 133 ft. in diameter, with a cruising range of 6,500 mi. and a maximum speed of 72 knots. The novel power plant installation consisted of eight 560-h.p. Maybach engines mounted in separate engine rooms within the hull and driving propellers so mounted on outriggers that they could be swiveled to produce a vertical lifting component. To compensate for weight lost through fuel consumption, water recovery apparatus was installed, with exhaust condensers mounted on the hull above the engine rooms. Each ship also carried a trapeze for the landing and launching of airplanes and had an internal hangar for five planes. The "Akron" (ZRS-4) was completed in 1931 but, after about 1,700 hours of service, crashed, with the loss of 73 lives, on April 4, 1933, in a storm off the New Jersey coast. Her sister ship, the "Macon" (ZRS-5), was launched the same month and operated primarily from the new airship base at Sunnyvale, Calif. On

Feb. 12, 1935, while returning from fleet maneuvers, the "Macon" suffered failure of her upper fin structure, resulting in loss of control. With severe gas leakage and accompanying structural collapse, the "Macon" settled to the sea and slowly sank off the California coast; all but two crew members were rescued. She had flown 1,798 hours.

The loss of the "Macon" left the navy without an operational rigid airship and led to numerous naval, governmental and civil investigations to determine the safety and practicability of rigid airships. Since the results of these investigations endorsed further dirigible construction, a 3,000,000-cu.ft. navy rigid airship was authorized in 1938. However, money appropriated by congress to begin its construction reverted to the treasury after delays in selecting the design and size; subsequent funds were not voted, and the ship never progressed beyond the drawing board stage.

BIBLIOGRAPHY.—*General:* A. Santos-Dumont, *My Airships* (1904); A. Hildebrandt, *Airships Past and Present* (1908); *Jane's All the World's Aircraft*, annual (1909 *et seq.*); G. Whale, *British Airships, Past, Present, and Future* (1919); E. M. Maitland, *The Log of H.M.A. R–34* (1920); E. Lehmann and H. Mingos, *The Zeppelins* (1927); C. Sprigg, *The Airship* (1931); C. J. Hylander, *Cruisers of the Air* (1931); H. Allen, *The Story of the Airship* (1931), *The Story of the Airship (Non-Rigid)* (1942); C. E. Rosendahl, *Up Ship!* (1931), *What About the Airship?* (1938); P. W. Litchfield and H. Allen, *Why? Why Has America No Rigid Airships?* (1945); U.S. Naval Air Station, Lakehurst, N.J., *Airship Operations in World War II* (1946); N. S. Norway, *Slide Rule: the Autobiography of an Engineer* (1954); J. Leasor, *Millionth Chance: the Story of the R. 101* (1958).
Technical: E. H. Lewitt, *The Rigid Airship* (1925); R. H. Upson and C. de F. Chandler, *Free and Captive Balloons* (1926); C. de F. Chandler and W. S. Diehl, *Balloon and Airship Gases* (1926); T. L. Blakemore and W. W. Pagon, *Pressure Airships* (1927); C. P. Burgess, *Airship Design* (1927); H. R. Cox and T. S. Collins, "Airship Design" in *Handbook of Aeronautics* (1931); K. Arnstein, W. Klemperer and M. Munk, "Performance and Aerodynamics of Airships" in *Aerodynamic Theory*, ed. by W. F. Durand, vol. vi (Jan. 1934). (J. G. V.; C. E. Ro.)

AIR SICKNESS: *see* MOTION SICKNESS.

AIR UNIVERSITY, U.S.A.F., a centre for the professional education of air force officers, was established in 1946 at Maxwell air force base near Montgomery, Ala. It includes three general service schools at Maxwell—the squadron officer school offering a 14-week course for company grade officers with approximately 5 years of service; the command and staff school offering a 9-month course for field grade officers with about 10 years of service; and the air war college offering a 10-month course for selected officers with 15 years of service. A warfare systems school offers instruction in the employment of aerospace vehicles and weapons. The air university is also the home organization for air force officers who instruct in, or attend as students, schools of the other armed services. Associated with the university is the school of aviation medicine at Randolph air force base, near San Antonio, Tex., which instructs medical officers and airmen and conducts research on the physiology of flight. Another associated activity is the air force institute of technology at Wright-Patterson air force base, near Dayton, O., an engineering school that offers some resident courses and sends selected officers to civilian colleges and universities for special instruction. The air force reserve officers training program (R.O.T.C.) in civilian colleges and universities is administered by the air university.

The extension course institute of the air university offers correspondence courses related to the resident courses of both the air university and the air force training command. The research studies institute includes the arctic, desert, tropic information centre, the documentary research division and the historical division. The air force reserve officers training program in civilian colleges and universities also has its headquarters at Maxwell air force base. The *Air University Quarterly Review* is a professional journal published at the air university. (J. C. SH.)

AIR WARFARE: *see* AIR POWER.

AIRY, SIR GEORGE BIDDELL (1801–1892), British astronomer, the seventh astronomer royal, who discovered an inequality in the motions of Venus and Earth and reorganized Greenwich observatory, was born at Alnwick, Northumberland, on July 27, 1801. He was educated at Colchester grammar school and at Trinity college, Cambridge, where he graduated as senior wrangler in 1823. He became a fellow of his college (1824), Lucasian professor of mathematics (1826) and then (1828) Plumian professor of astronomy and director of the new Cambridge observatory. Before long a mural circle was installed, and regular observations were instituted with it in 1833.

In the same year the duke of Northumberland presented the Cambridge observatory with a fine object glass of 12-in. aperture, which was mounted according to Airy's designs. Airy's writings during this time were divided between mathematical physics and astronomy. The former were for the most part concerned with questions relating to the theory of light, arising out of his professional lectures. Of his astronomical writings during this period the most important are his investigation of the mass of Jupiter and his memoir *On an Inequality of Long Period in the Motions of the Earth and Venus.*

Airy's discovery of a new inequality in the motions of Venus and Earth was a remarkable achievement. In correcting the elements of J. Delambre's solar tables he discovered an inequality overlooked by their constructor. Eight times the mean motion of Venus is so nearly equal to 13 times that of Earth that the difference amounts to only $\frac{1}{240}$ of Earth's mean motion, and from the fact that the term depending on this difference, although very small in itself, receives in the integration of the differential equations a multiplier of about 2,200,000, Airy was led to infer the existence of a sensible inequality extending over 240 years. The investigation leading to this result was probably the most laborious that had been made up to Airy's time in planetary theory, and represented the first specific improvement in the solar tables effected in England since the establishment of the theory of gravitation.

In June 1835 Airy was appointed astronomer royal in succession to John Pond. Under Airy's administration modern apparatus was installed, and the whole organization was placed on a scientific footing. No fewer than 8,000 lunar observations were rescued from oblivion and were, in 1846, placed at the disposal of astronomers in such a form that they could be used directly for comparison with the theory and for the improvement of the tables of the moon's motion. (*See* HANSEN, PETER ANDREAS.)

One of the most remarkable of Airy's researches was his determination of the mean density of the earth by means of pendulum experiments at the top and bottom of a deep mine. After some failures, successful experiments were made at the Harton pit, near South Shields, Durham, in 1854. Their immediate result was to show that gravity at the bottom of the mine exceeded that at the top by $\frac{1}{19.286}$ of its amount, the depth being 1,256 ft. From this Airy was led to the final value of 6.566 for the mean density of the earth as compared with that of water. At the age of 71 Airy embarked on a new method of treating lunar theory. It consisted essentially in the adoption of C. Delaunay's final numerical expressions for longitude, latitude and parallax, with a symbolic term attached to each number, the value of which was to be determined by substitution in the equations of motion. The work was published in 1886, when its author was 85 years of age. In 1881 Sir George Airy resigned the office of astronomer royal. He died at Greenwich on Jan. 2, 1892. The learned societies of his own and other countries conferred many honours on him.

See also references under "Airy, Sir George Biddell" in the Index.

See W. Airy (ed.), *Autobiography of G. B. Airy* (1896).

'A'ISHA ('AYSHAH, AYESHA, BINT ABI BAKR) (*c.* 614–678), wife of Mohammed, the founder of Islam, who after his death became an authority on his life and sayings and those of some of his companions, was born in Mecca, Arabia, about 614. Her father, Abu Bakr (*q.v.*), supported Mohammed. 'A'isha became Mohammed's child wife and favourite, whom he usually defended against political critics and harem rivals. She was a childless widow at 18, and Mohammed's widows, called "mothers of the believers," were not permitted to remarry. 'A'isha used her energies in family and social activities during the strong caliphates of her father and of Omar I. When reformers demanded the abdication of the weak and aged caliph Othman, 'A'isha intrigued, hoping to regain the caliphate for her family. However, the extremists in Medina demanded Othman's death, and 'A'isha withdrew to Mecca and into a questionable neutrality. Othman was assassinated and Ali ('Ali ibn Abi Talib), Mohammed's cousin and husband of his daughter Fatima (*q.v.*), won the succession. 'A'isha held Ali responsible for Othman's death, which she proposed to avenge. In the civil war that followed, 'A'isha's army was defeated near Basra in 656 in the battle of the Camel, so called after her mount. 'A'isha herself was captured but was released by Ali after promising to refrain from politics. She kept her promise, though her influence continued to be sought. Her oral statements and public speeches were later put into writing. She died on 17 Ramadan, A.H. 58 (July 13, 678). She is venerated by all Muslims, though her opposition to Ali is still resented by his followers, the Shi'ahs.

See Nabia Abbott, *Aishah, the Beloved of Mohammed* (1942).

(N. A.)

AISLE, in architecture, a term originally meaning the wing of a house, but more commonly used to indicate any long, narrow space separated from the remainder of the building by a line of piers, columns or arches. It is specially used to designate the side portions of a church or other large room in which interior supports occur. The term also has come to mean a passageway, especially a passageway between groups of seats, as in a church or theatre.

From the time of the early Christian basilica, the use of one or more side aisles flanking a central nave has been almost universal in church building, and church aisles are known as nave aisles, transept aisles or choir aisles from their position in relation to the nave, transept or choir. The choir aisle around the east end of a choir is known as an ambulatory. In the normal Romanesque or Gothic church the roof of the aisles is lower than the central nave; but in certain examples in southern France (*e.g.*, St. Nazaire, Carcassonne), in Spain (*e.g.*, Barcelona) and especially in Germany, where for the smaller churches it is almost normal, the nave and aisles are of the same height. A church with nave flanked by one aisle on each side is known as a three-aisle church; one with two side aisles on each side as a five-aisle church, and so on.

AISNE, a *département* of northern France. Area 2,868 sq.mi. Pop. (1962) 512,920. It touches the western end of the Ardennes (930 ft.) in the northeast, but its surface is all of younger sedimentary rocks. Outlying masses of rock, often with steep flanks, form important sites such as that of Laon, the capital, and the famous Chemin des Dames. The Aisne river enters the *département* from the east just as it leaves the chalk scarp and flows west to the Oise (*q.v.*), the other river of the *département* which has been canalized to include the deep Château-Thierry portion of the Marne valley, too far west to focus on Épernay or Reims and allied to the hill country farther north rather than to Paris on the west.

The *département* had a number of forests before World War I, when it was the scene of much fighting, but it lacks metallic ores, though quarries yield building stone, gypsum and clay. Mostly in the belt of rainfall 20–30 in. and well watered and sheltered, it contains rich cornlands in the south and west, with specialization in dairying toward the northeast in Thiérache.

Of the towns, Guise in the north is an agricultural and industrial centre and St. Quentin and numerous villages are well known for weaving of cotton, wool and silk. St. Gobain has made mirrors since the 17th century. Beet sugar has been an important crop and industry. There are good communications by rail and by navigable rivers (Aisne, Oise, Marne). Laon, Soissons (*qq.v.*), St. Quentin and Vervins give their names to *arrondissements* and are, with Château-Thierry (*q.v.*) and Hirson, the chief towns. This *département* and that of Oise were rich in architectural monuments, several of which were ruined in World War I, but the churches at Laon, Braine and Urcel (mainly 12th century) survived and the splendid *basilique* of St. Quentin was largely repaired, while the castle ruin (1400) of La Ferté-Milon did not suffer.

Soissons was made the seat of a bishop in the province of Reims. The *département* was placed in the educational province (*académie*) of Douai (*q.v.*).

The German offensive launched on May 27, 1918, against the Chemin des Dames ridge is sometimes referred to as the battle of

the Aisne (*see* CHEMIN DES DAMES, BATTLE OF THE). Historical aspects may also be found in ÎLE-DE-FRANCE, PICARDY and CHAMPAGNE, the old provinces of France, parts of which comprise Aisne.

(AR. E. S.)

AÏSSE (Turkish AISHA; also called HAIDÉE), MADEMOISELLE (*c.* 1694–1733), a Circassian girl distinguished in French literary history. Purchased as a slave in Istanbul by Charles de Ferriol, ambassador to Turkey, she was sent by him to France in 1698 to be educated by his brother's wife, a sister of Mme de Tencin (*q.v.*). Returning to France in 1711, Ferriol kept her as his mistress until his death in 1722. Meanwhile, however, she had made the acquaintance not only of literary people, including Voltaire, Fontenelle, Montesquieu, Mme du Deffand and, especially, Lord Bolingbroke, but also of the chevalier Blaise Marie d'Aydie, with whom she fell in love. She bore him a daughter secretly in 1721, but in 1727 refused his proposal of marriage. She died in Paris on March 13, 1733.

Aïssé's letters to Mme Calandrini (née Julie de Pellissary, an aunt of Bolingbroke's wife) provide valuable insights on the society in which she moved and give a moving analysis of her love and her anguish of conscience at its illicit nature. First printed in 1787, they were reprinted many times; *e.g.*, by E. Asse, *Lettres du XVIIe et du XVIIIe siècle* (1873).

BIBLIOGRAPHY.—Mrs. Campbell Praed, *The Romance of Mademoiselle Aïssé* (1910); H. Courteault, *Mlle Aïssé . . .* (1908); J. d'Ivray, *L'Étrange Destin de Mademoiselle Aïssé* (1935).

AISTULF (d. A.D. 756), king of the Lombards from 749 to 756, whose revival of the expansionist policy of King Liutprand led to the first important Frankish interventions in Italian and papal affairs (*see* ITALY: *History;* LOMBARDS; PAPACY). Having conquered the exarchate of Ravenna by 751, Aistulf turned against the duchy of Rome and in 753 was threatening Rome itself. As the Byzantine emperor gave no effective help, Pope Stephen II appealed to Pepin, king of the Franks. In 754, having failed to defeat the Frankish army at its entry into Italy near Mt. Cenis, Aistulf was besieged in Pavia. He promised to restore the conquered territories. After the Franks had left the country, however, he resumed his aggressive policy, and in Jan.–April 756 laid siege to Rome. A fresh appeal by the pope led to a second Frankish intervention. Again besieged in Pavia, Aistulf promised to pay an annual tribute to the Frankish king and did surrender his conquests, which Pepin, in accordance with promises made in 754, handed over to the pope. Aistulf died shortly after, in Dec. 756.

BIBLIOGRAPHY.—T. Hodgkin, *Italy and Her Invaders,* vol. vii (1899); L. M. Hartmann, *Geschichte Italiens im Mittelalter,* vol. ii, 2 (1903); O. Bertolini, article in *Miscellanea Giovanni Mercati,* vol. v (1946).

(N. R.)

AITKEN, ROBERT GRANT (1864–1951), U.S. astronomer, who was an authority on double stars, was born in Jackson, Calif., on Dec. 31, 1864. Aitken was educated at Williams college, Williamstown, Mass., from which he graduated in 1887, and received his M.A. in 1892. From 1888 to 1891 he was instructor of mathematics in Livermore college, and 1891–95 was professor of mathematics and astronomy in the College of the Pacific, Stockton, Calif. In 1895 he was appointed astronomer at Lick observatory, Mt. Hamilton, California, of which he was director 1930–35. There he specialized in the study of double stars, of which he discovered more than 3,000. For these discoveries, he was awarded in 1906 the Lalande prize by the Academy of Sciences of France and, in 1932, the gold medal of the Royal Astronomical society. He published *Binary Stars* (1918) and *New General Catalogue of Double Stars* (1932). He died Oct. 29, 1951.

AIX-EN-PROVENCE, a city of southeast France, in the Bouches-du-Rhône *département*, 19 mi. N. of Marseilles by road. Pop. (1962) 55,398. It is situated in a plain overlooking the Arc river about a mile from the right bank. The roads from the north of France to Italy and from Marseilles to the Alps cross there. It is the seat of an archbishop.

The Cours Mirabeau, a tree-lined avenue, divides the newer southern part of the town from the older northern part. Among the many ancient buildings are the 11th–13th century cathedral of St. Saviour with its triptych, the "Burning Bush," by Nicolas

Froment; the 13th-century church of St. John of Malta containing the tombs of the counts of Provence; and the 17th-century church of St. Mary Magdalene. The *hôtel de ville* (17th century) contains fine woodwork and a large library with valuable old manuscripts. There are many fountains and fine old houses. The Granet is the best known of several museums. Aix-en-Provence is one of the largest university centres in France and is the seat of Aix-Marseilles university.

Aix, which is served by the Marseilles-Grenoble railway, is a tourist centre and has hot mineral springs, which are recommended for diseases of blood circulation. The springs contain lime and carbonic acid. The best known is the Sextius spring.

The town is an important agricultural centre and has a market for olive oil and almonds. Its industries are the manufacture of jams, preserved fruits, sugared almonds, burnt almonds and some local cake specialities, *calissons* and *biscotins*.

When Gaul was conquered by the Romans, the proconsul, Sextus Calvinus, built a vast entrenched camp called Aquae Sextiae in the valley of the Arc about 123 B.C. There was fought the battle of Aix in 102 B.C. in which Marius routed the Teutones. Augustus Caesar made Aix a Roman colony, and in the 4th century it was the metropolis of Narbonensis Secunda. Occupied by the Visigoths in 477, and repeatedly plundered by Franks and Lombards, it was taken by the Saracens in 731. During the middle ages it was the capital of Provence (*q.v.*), governed by the counts and dukes of Anjou, of whom the most famous was René (1409–80), and reached its zenith after the 12th century when the houses of Aragon and Anjou made it a centre of art and learning. It became a university city in 1409 and passed with Provence to the crown in 1486, becoming the seat of *parlement*. It suffered from the wars of Charles V, the religious wars and the plague, yet remained a centre of political and intellectual activity in Provence until the 19th century. (P. Y. B.)

AIX-LA-CHAPELLE: *see* AACHEN.

AIX-LA-CHAPELLE, CONGRESSES OF. Three congresses or peace conferences have met at Aix-la-Chapelle (Aachen, Ger.)—in 1668, in 1748 and in 1818.

1. The treaty of May 2, 1668, which ended the War of Devolution, was the outcome of that of St. Germain signed on April 15 by France and the representatives of the triple alliance. The treaty of Aix-la-Chapelle left to France all the conquests made in Flanders during 1667, with all their *appartenances, dépendances et annexes,* a vague provision of which, after the peace of Nijmegen (1680), Louis XIV took advantage to occupy villages and towns adjudged to him by his *Chambres de réunion* as dependencies of the cities and territories acquired in 1668. On the other hand, France restored to Spain Cambrai, Aire and St. Omer, as well as Franche Comté. The treaty of Aix-la-Chapelle was placed under the guarantee of England, Sweden and Holland, by a convention signed at The Hague on May 7, 1669, to which Spain acceded.

2. On April 24, 1748, a congress assembled at Aix-la-Chapelle to end the War of the Austrian Succession. The definitive treaty was signed on Oct. 18. Its most important provisions were those stipulating (*a*) a general restitution of conquests, including Cape Breton to France, Madras to England and the barrier towns to the Dutch; (*b*) the assignment to Don Philip of the duchies of Parma, Piacenza and Guastalla; (*c*) the restoration of the duke of Modena and the republic of Genoa to their former positions; (*d*) the renewal in favour of Great Britain of the Asiento contract of March 16, 1713, and of the right to send an annual vessel to the Spanish colonies; (*e*) the renewal of the article of the treaty of 1718 recognizing the Protestant succession in the English throne; (*f*) the recognition of the emperor Francis and the confirmation of the pragmatic sanction, *i.e.,* of the right of Maria Theresa to the Habsburg succession; (*g*) the guarantee to Prussia of the duchy of Silesia and the county of Glatz (Klodzko).

The treaty was supplemented by that of Madrid (Oct. 5, 1750), by which Great Britain surrendered the Asiento right for a sum of £100,000. It left the main colonial disputes between Britain and France unsettled and Habsburg counterpoise to French power in Europe as effective as before the war.

3. The congress of Aix-la-Chapelle in 1818 was primarily a meeting of the four allied powers—Great Britain, Austria, Prussia and Russia—to decide the question of the withdrawal of the army of occupation from France and the consequent international relationships of the powers. The congress, which opened on Oct. 1, was attended by Alexander I of Russia, Francis I of Austria and Frederick William III of Prussia. Great Britain was represented by Lord Castlereagh and the duke of Wellington, Austria by Prince Metternich, Russia by Counts G. A. Capo d'Istria and Karl Vasilievich Nesselrode, Prussia by Prince Karl August von Hardenberg and Count Christian Günther Bernstorff. The duc Armand Emmanuel de Richelieu was present on behalf of France.

The evacuation of France was agreed to in principle at the first session, the consequent treaty being signed on Oct. 9. The rest of the time of the congress was mainly occupied in discussing the form to be taken by the European alliance against a fresh outburst on the part of France. The proposal of Alexander I, to establish a "universal union of guarantee" on the broad basis of the Holy alliance, broke down on the opposition of Great Britain; and the main outcome of the congress was the signature, on Nov. 15, of two instruments: (*a*) a secret protocol confirming and renewing the quadruple alliance established by the treaties of Chaumont and Paris (Nov. 20, 1815) against France; (*b*) a public "declaration" of the intention of the powers to maintain their intimate union, of which the object was to preserve peace on the basis of respect for treaties.

The congress also concerned itself with the questions of the suppression of the slave trade and the Barbary pirates. In neither case was any decision arrived at, because the other powers refused to agree with the British proposal for a reciprocal right of search on the high seas, and Great Britain objected to international action, which would have involved the presence of a Russian squadron in the Mediterranean. A great variety of lesser questions was considered. The congress represents the restoration of France to the status of a great power, and the highest point reached in the attempt to govern Europe by an international committee of the powers.

See also Index references under "Aix-La-Chapelle, Congresses of" in the Index volume.

BIBLIOGRAPHY.—H. Vast, *Les grands traités du règne de Louis XIV,* 3 vol. (1893–99); Comte G. de Garden, *Histoire générale des traités de paix,* 15 vol. (1847–87); W. Alison Phillips, *The Confederation of Europe,* 2nd ed. (1920); H. G. Nicolson, *Congress of Vienna: a Study in Allied Unity, 1812–1822* (1946). (W. A. P.; D. Tᴎ.)

AIX-LES-BAINS, a thermal spa and fashionable resort in eastern France, in the *département* of Savoie, lies 9 mi. N. of Chambéry along the Lac du Bourget at the mouth of a gap in the Préalpes used by the Mt. Cenis route to Italy. Pop. (1954) 12,799. The sulfur and alkaline springs have been used since Roman times, and there are the remains of Roman baths. The local museum lies within the site of a Roman temple. The tourist station on Mt. Revard at 4,578 ft., reached by aerial cableway, offers a fine panorama, and the lake and beach add to the amenities that attract many summer visitors; situated at the entry to the Alps, Aix also serves as a base for winter sports. (Aʀ. E. S.)

AJACCIO, the capital of Corsica (*q.v.*), lies on the west coast of the island. Behind the sandy beaches of Ajaccio bay the land rises up to the snow-covered Monte d'Oro (7,844 ft.). Pop. (1954) 28,732. It is the seat of a bishopric. The harbour to the east is protected on the south by a peninsula, where the citadel (1551) is situated. On the base of the peninsula is the old part of the town. Ajaccio is the birthplace of Napoleon and the association is emphasized by street names and statues. The Maison Bonaparte, where he was born, has been turned into a museum with many personal relics. The town hall has another Napoleon museum. The cathedral was completed in 1593 and its magnificent high altar came from Lucca, the gift of a sister of Napoleon. The Fesch palace contains a library and an art gallery. Apart from a few boulevards, Ajaccio has narrow streets. It is linked with the mainland of France by sea, and from Campo del Oro (5 mi.) air services connect it with France, north Africa and London, while railways and highways run to other parts of the island. It is a tourist centre, having a mild winter and a hot summer climate.

There are fetes, carnivals, horse racing and a regatta.

Macaroni, sails and a liqueur of citron and myrtle are manufactured in the town and there is shipbuilding. Timber, pit props, briar pipes, planks, dried fruit and almonds are exported.

The original Roman settlement of Ajax lay about 2 mi. N. of the present site, to which the town was transferred by the Genoese in 1492. Occupied in 1553 by the French, it again fell to the Genoese after the treaty of Cateau Cambrésis in 1559. The town finally passed to the French in 1768. In 1793 Corsica was divided into two *départements,* Golo and Liamone, Ajaccio becoming the capital of Liamone. In 1811 Corsica became a single *département* with Ajaccio as its capital. (F. Pe.)

AJANTA, a village in Aurangabad district, Maharashtra state, India, celebrated for its Buddhist caves and wall paintings. The site is reached by road, either from Jalgaon on the Delhi-Bombay main railway line (58 mi.) or from Aurangabad on the Manmad-Secunderabad metre-gauge line (66 mi.). The caves lie in a wooded and rugged ravine about 3½ mi. from the village. The ravine is that of the Wagura river, a tributary of the Tapti, which falls from the east over a bluff forming several waterfalls. There are about 30 caves excavated in the precipitous south side of the ravine. They are of two types, viharas (monasteries) and chaityas (meeting halls). The viharas reflect the plan of structural monasteries throughout India and essentially consist of a square hall surrounded by cells on three sides. The front has a broad veranda. In the back wall was placed a shrine which gradually came to dominate the structure. The chaityas are oblong with apsidal ends and pillared aisles. A stupa or dome-shaped memorial shrine was set in the centre of the apse. The oldest caves probably date from the 1st century B.C.–A.D. to the 3rd century. A second important group dates from the 6th–7th centuries. These contain inscriptions of the Vakataka dynasty of Berar (*q.v.*), the contemporaries of the Gupta dynasty of north India. The caves are unique in India for the quantity and quality of their fresco paintings. The earliest are thought to belong to the 1st or 2nd century A.D. but the majority are of the 6th–7th centuries. Strictly they are not frescoes, in that the surface was prepared with a cow-dung plaster and finished with white gypsum on which the paintings were done. Although many of them were in decay when discovered they have now been carefully conserved and form an important record of the wall-painting techniques and life of medieval India. *See* INDIAN ART; *see* also Index references under "Ajanta" in the Index.

BIBLIOGRAPHY.—J. Griffiths, *The Paintings in the Buddhist Cave Temples of Ajanta,* 2 vol. (1896–97); Lady Herringham, *Ajanta Frescoes* (1915); G. Yazdani, *Ajanta,* plates with explanatory text, 4 vol. (1930–55). (F. R. A.)

AJAX, the name of two figures in Greek legend.

1. AJAX THE GREATER, son of Telamon, king of Salamis, is described in the *Iliad* as being of great stature and colossal frame, second only to Achilles in strength and bravery. He engaged Hector in single combat and, with the aid of Athena, rescued the body of Achilles from the hands of the Trojans. In the competition between him and Odysseus for the armour of Achilles, Agamemnon, at the instigation of Athena, awarded the prize to Odysseus. This so enraged Ajax that it caused his death. According to a later story, accepted by Sophocles as the basis of his drama, Ajax' disappointment drove him mad. He rushed out of his tent and fell upon the flocks of sheep in the camp under the impression that they were the Greeks; on coming to his senses he slew himself with the sword that he had received as a present from Hector. From his blood sprang a red flower (*see* HYACINTHUS), which bore on its leaves the initial letters of his name, AI, also expressive of lament. He was the tutelary hero of the island of Salamis, where he had a temple and an image and where a festival called Aianteia was celebrated in his honour (described by Pausanias).

2. AJAX THE LESSER, son of Oïleus, king of Locris, was called the Lesser or Locrian Ajax to distinguish him from the son of Telamon. In spite of his small stature, he held his own among the other heroes before Troy; he was brave, next to Achilles in swiftness of foot and famous for throwing the spear. But he was boastful, arrogant and quarrelsome. Voyaging homeward, his ship was wrecked, but Ajax was saved by a rock. Boasting of his escape he

was cast by Poseidon into the sea and drowned. For his crime (not definitely mentioned by Homer) of dragging Cassandra from the statue of the goddess Athena, during the sack of Troy, and violating her, he barely escaped being stoned to death by his Greek allies. In addition, a plague fell upon the Locrians. Following an oracle they undertook 1,000 years' penance (which was still being observed in early Christian times) by which they sent yearly two girls chosen by lot to serve in the temple of Athena at Troy.

Ajax was worshiped as a national hero by the Opuntian Locrians (on whose coins he appeared), who always left a vacant place for him in their battle line.

BIBLIOGRAPHY.—L. R. Farnell, *Greek Hero Cults and Ideas of Immortality* (1921); A. Pauly and G. Wissowa, *Real-Encyclopädie der classischen Altertumswissenschaft;* W. Roscher, *Ausführliches Lexikon der griechischen und römischen Mythologie.* (T. V. B.)

'AJLUN, a town of the Hashemite Kingdom of Jordan. The town is situated on the mountains overlooking the Jordan valley a few miles west of Jarash. At the time of the 1961 census the population was 5,384. The town has an interesting early mosque with a square minaret, and on the mountain top to the west is the Arab castle called Qalat al-Rabadh, built by Aus al-Dyn Ausama, cousin of Saladin, in 1184 and enlarged in the 13th century. 'Ajlun *liwa'* (district) was renamed Irbid (*q.v.*) in 1964.

(G. W. L. H.)

AJMER (AJMERE; AJMIR), a large city in Rajasthan state, India, and the administrative headquarters of the district of the same name, is 275 mi. S.W. of Delhi on the Western railway. The population of Ajmer in 1901 was 73,839 and by 1961 it had risen to 231,240, making it the second largest city of Rajasthan (second only to Jaipur). It is on the lower slopes of Taragarh hill (3,000 ft.) in the Aravalli range. To the north of the city is a large artificial lake called the Ana Sagar constructed in the 11th century, and farther up the valley is a new lake, the Foy Sagar, from which the water supply of the city is derived.

The chief object of interest is the dargah, or tomb, of the famous Muslim saint Muin-ud-din Chishti (d. 1235). It consists of a group of white marble buildings without much pretension to architectural beauty. An ancient Jain temple, converted about A.D. 1200 into a mosque, is also on the lower slope of the hill. Although, with the exception of that part used as a mosque, it is largely in ruins, the architectural and sculptural remains are of considerable beauty. The summit of the hill is crowned by a fort, two miles in circumference, which can be approached only by steep, roughly paved paths.

The modern city is an administrative and railway centre. It is well laid out with wide streets and handsome houses, and does an active trade in salt, which is imported in large quantities from the Sambar lake (45 mi. N.E.) and Ramsur. The extraction of vegetable oil is also a profitable trade. Cotton cloths are manufactured to some extent, for the dyeing of which the city has attained a high reputation. The educational institutions include the Mayo Rajkumar college, opened in 1875 for training the sons of the nobles of Rajputana on the lines of an English public school, and five of the colleges of Rajasthan university, of which two are for women.

Seven miles west of Ajmer lies the lake of Pushkar, one of the most sacred pieces of water in India, where a pilgrim fair is held every autumn and where is found almost the only temple dedicated to Brahma in India.

AJMER STATE (called AJMER-MERWARA before 1950) was formerly administered by the government of India through a chief commissioner. It was divided into two isolated tracts, the larger comprising the subdivisions of Ajmer and Merwara; the smaller, to the southeast, being the Kekri subdivision. Of the Hindus, the Rajputs are largely landholders and the Jats and Gujars cultivators. The Jains are traders and moneylenders. The aboriginal Mers are partly Hindu, partly Muslim. The state became the Ajmer district of Rajasthan in 1956. Area 3,283 sq.mi.; pop. (1961) 976,547.

The distinguishing feature of the district is the Aravalli range (*q.v.*), running northeast-southwest between Ajmer and Nasirabad and marking the watershed of northern India. The district is on the border of the arid zone and the soil is generally sandy. The main crops are maize, millet, barley, cotton, oilseeds, wheat, chillies and onions; but Ajmer is not self-supporting in foodstuffs. There are cotton, textile and hosiery mills and factories for ginning and pressing cotton. Beawar and Kekri are the chief trading centres. Mica, steatite, beryl and asbestos quarries are worked. Ajmer city is connected by rail with Ahmedabad and Delhi.

Ajmer was founded by a Chauhan ruler, Ajayadeva, about the end of the 11th century A.D. It became an appanage of the crown of Delhi in 1193. Its internal government, however, was handed over to its ancient rulers upon the payment of a heavy tribute to the conquerors. It acknowledged the suzerainty of Delhi till 1365, when it was captured by the ruler of Mewar. Akbar took it back in 1556; and it continued in the hands of the Moguls, with occasional revolts, till 1770 when it was ceded to the Marathas, from which time up to 1818 the unhappy country was the scene of a continual struggle, being seized at different times by the Mewar and Marwar rajas, from whom it was so often retaken by the Marathas. In 1818 the latter ceded it to the British in return for a payment of Rs. 50,000. (C. C. D.; S. GL.; S. M. T. R.)

AKAN. The Akan are peoples who speak languages of the Twi branch of the Kwa subfamily of the Western Sudanic linguistic stock. These languages include Ahanta, Akwapim, Akyem, Agni, Asante, Asen, Bono, Brusa, Chakosi, Fante, Guan, Kwahu, Nzima and Wasa. The Akan inhabit the eastern part of Ivory Coast, the southern half of Ghana and parts of Togo. Only the Chakosi live in north Ghana, in the Dagomba district. The majority are in Ghana, where they settled in successive waves between the 11th and 18th centuries. The most powerful Akan states were Bono, Denkera, Akwamu, Akim and the Ashanti (q.v.) and Fanti (q.v.) confederacies which developed in the 17th and 18th centuries.

The Akans have certain common institutions. The basis of their social and political organization is the lineage of maternal kinsmen, in which inheritance and succession are based on matrilineal descent. A tribe consists of several lineages which form a political unit under the chief, elected from one of the lineages, and a council of elders, each of whom is the elected head of a constituent lineage. Besides public offices, land tenure is also vested in the lineage (see GHANA: *The People*).

The tribes are grouped into clans. Most accounts give seven: Aduana, Agona, Asenee, Asona, Bretuo, Ekona and Oyoko; but some count localized matrilineages and give more than these. Clans were exogamous and matrilineal, the members being united by belief in a common descent from a remote ancestress.

Though succession to property and public office is based on matrilineal descent, the Akan peoples recognized paternal descent also. Everyone belonged to one of a dozen Ntoro groups: Bosomafi, Bosomafram, Bosomakan, Bosomayesu, Bosomdwerebe, Bosomkonsi, Bosomkrete, Bosommuru, Bosompo (or Nketia), Bosompra, Bosomsika, Bosomtwe—membership of which derived from one's father. Common taboos, surnames, forms of etiquette and ritual lustrations linked members of the same Ntoro. Among some Akan peoples, such as the Fanti, there were also quasi-military groupings based on paternal descent.

The Akan have common religious beliefs and practices based on belief in a supreme deity who created the universe, in lesser deities who derive their power from the supreme deity and in spirits who have their abode in shrines, trees, rivers or rocks. But the most prominent aspect of Akan religion is the worship of ancestors. Periodical rites in which ancestors are commemorated are the most powerful sanctions of tribal unity and morality. The Akan are thus linked by bonds of language, social institutions and religion.

See also AFRICA: *Ethnography (Anthropology): West Africa*.
BIBLIOGRAPHY.—W. T. Balmer, *A History of the Akan Peoples of the Gold Coast* (1925); J. B. Danquah, *Akan Laws and Customs* (1928); M. Manoukian, *Akan and Ga-adangme Peoples of the Gold Coast* (1950); E. L. R. Meyerowitz, *The Sacred State of the Akan* (1951), *Akan Traditions of Origin* (1952), *The Akan of Ghana* (1958). S. G. Williamson, *Akan Religion* . . . (1965). (K. A. Bu.)

AKBAR (JALAL-UD-DIN MOHAMMED) (1542–1605), the greatest of the Mogul emperors in India, was born in Oct. or Nov. 1542 at Umarkot in Sind when his father, Humayun, driven from the throne of Delhi by the Afghan usurper Sher Shah, was escaping to Iran. It was not until 1555 that Humayun undertook to reconquer Hindustan and when he died in 1556 the Mogul empire was still only an idea. On succeeding his father, Akbar first overthrew all rivals, the chief of them being the Hindu minister Hemu, defeated at Panipat on Nov. 5, 1556. Akbar then embarked upon a career of conquest. By 1562 his kingdom embraced the Punjab and Multan, the basin of the Ganges and Jumna rivers from Panipat to Allahabad, Gwalior in central India, Ajmer and, in Afghanistan, the province of Kabul. Another 14 years of warfare resulted in the conquest of Malwa, Chitor, Ranthambhor, Kalinjar, Gujarat and Bengal. Between 1586 and 1595 he added Kashmir, Sind, Baluchistan, Kandahar and parts of Orissa to his dominions. With his power firmly established in the north he then crossed the Narmada (Narbada) river into the Deccan and annexed Khandesh, Berar and parts of Ahmednagar. By 1605 his empire comprised 15 subahs (provinces) and stretched from the Hindu Kush to the Godavari river and from Bengal to Gujarat.

Akbar did more than achieve Mogul political hegemony in northern India; he stabilized and prolonged it by giving it a framework of administrative and military institutions and a foundation of political and social principle. Moreover, he provided the inspiration as well as the opportunity for the burgeoning of a remarkable synthetic Mogul culture extending over art, architecture, literature, history, gastronomy, dress and pastimes, which dominated the imagination and engaged the sympathies of Indians of diverse communities until the 19th century. His system of provincial administration, still discernible in modern India and Pakistan, and drawn in its details from the experience of nearly 400 years of Muslim rule was based on the subah, sircar, or sarkar (administrative district), pargana and mahal (revenue division), the principal executive officers (whether financial or military) being appointed and transferred frequently from the centre.

Under vigorous management, such as Akbar himself provided, the military system of recruiting cavalry by *mansabdars* (imperial officers) provided an army loyal, effective and large enough for Indian conditions before the 18th century. The reform of the traditional method of land revenue collection, by which the state's demand for one-third of the gross produce was commuted into a cash payment scientifically assessed by reference to average local prices and yields, provided Akbar with the resources that his schemes of conquest required, without oppressing the cultivator.

Akbar deliberately founded his empire on an understanding with the Hindu Rajputs and on respect for Hindu religion and culture. In 1562 and 1570 he married Rajput princesses. He conferred important *mansabs* upon Rajput chiefs and appointed some to high positions in revenue departments. He set his face against a militant orthodox Islam by formally abolishing, in 1564, the *jizya* or poll tax on non-Muslims and by rescinding the taxes previously levied on Hindu pilgrims. He discouraged cow slaughter, participated in Hindu festivals and encouraged the study of Sanskrit classics, ordering their translation into Persian.

In his own personal religious life, too often regarded as purely opportunistic politically, Akbar stood at the confluence of many contemporary streams of thought, all militating against a strict Sunni orthodoxy and in favour of toleration. The famous *mahzar* or "declaration" of 1579, to which a group of religious scholars at his court subscribed, allowed Akbar certain powers of religious interpretation as a mujtahid of Islam in matters not already explicitly covered by a clear scriptural text or by agreement among the religious scholars (only ignorance of the character of religious authority in Islam or of the text itself, however, could suggest that the *mahzar* conferred "papal" powers on Akbar). In 1575 Akbar built an *ibadat-khana* (house of worship) at Fatehpur-Sikri in which Muslims of many hues, Jesuit fathers from Goa, Zoroastrians, Hindu pandits and yogis, discussed religion with Akbar himself. After 1582 he and his mentors at court formulated the *tauhid-i-ilahi* or divine monotheism compounded of ideas from Sufism and observances from Zoroastrianism, with Akbar himself as the adherents' *pir* or spiritual leader. Akbar did not compel adherence to his beliefs in the empire at large. As a sincere seeker after God and as a ruler, he would not have been true to himself had he acted otherwise. Akbar died at Agra on Oct. 16, 1605. See INDIA-PAKISTAN, SUBCONTINENT OF: *History*; see also references under "Akbar" in the Index.

BIBLIOGRAPHY.—V. A. Smith, *Akbar*, 2nd ed. (1927); Ibn Hasan, *The Central Structure of the Mughal Empire* (1936); P. Saran, *The Provincial Government of the Mughals, 1526–1658* (1941); Makhanlal Roychaudhuri, *The Din-i-Ilahi* (1941); Sri Ram Sharma, *The Religious Policy of the Mughal Emperors* (1940).   (P. H.)

AKEE, the West African name of a small tree (*Blighia sapida*) of the soapberry family (Sapindaceae), native to Guinea, and also of its important food fruit. Introduced in 1778 into Jamaica, which exports the fruit, its cultivation has spread throughout most of tropical America. The shrublike, stiff-branched tree, sometimes 20 ft. to 30 ft. high, bears handsome red or orange coloured fruits, about 3 in. long, in small clusters at the tips of slender branches. The fruit, which is a soft-walled capsule, splits when ripe into three sections, from apex to base, displaying round, shining, black seeds, attached to the base by large whitish or yellowish fleshy arils. When cooked the arils bear a resemblance to a fine omelette both in taste and in appearance. Ripe fruit may be eaten fresh by most persons without producing any untoward effects; unripe and overripe akees, however, may be decidedly unwholesome and even poisonous.

AKELEY, CARL ETHAN (1864–1926), U.S. naturalist, was noted for his taxidermy and sculpture of African big game, and for advances in museum methods helping to usher in a new era in exhibition—that of big habitat groups showing animals in natural surroundings. Born May 19, 1864, in Orleans county, N.Y., he served an apprenticeship in Ward's Natural Science establishment, Rochester, N.Y. During his productive years he was associated with the Chicago Natural History museum (1895–1909) and the American Museum of Natural History, New York city (1909–26). He wrote *In Brightest Africa* (1923).

The big game of Africa fascinated him, and he made five trips there to study and to collect living animals. He once killed barehanded an attacking leopard and another time was badly mauled by an elephant. He died Nov. 17, 1926, and was buried on Mt. Mikeno in Parc National Albert in central Africa, a sanctuary especially for gorillas, the establishment of which was one of the goals of the conservation-minded Akeley.

He devised a method of mounting big mammals by applying the skin to a finely modeled manikin, giving realistic results never before approached, which helped gain support for his vision: a panorama of Africa and its big game in U.S. museums.

His modeling led to sculpturing, with notable pieces showing elephants, lions and Nandi lion-spearers. Inventions that grew out of his work include the Akeley cement gun, from modeling, and the Akeley camera, from field photography.

See *Akeley Memorial Number, Nat. Hist., N.Y.*, vol. 27, no. 2, pp. 115–179 (1927).   (A. L. Rd.)

AKENSIDE, MARK (1721–1770), English poet and physician best known for his philosophical poem *The Pleasures of Imagination*, was born at Newcastle-upon-Tyne on Nov. 9, 1721. He went to Edinburgh university, intending to become a minister, but began to read medicine. His training was completed by a brief stay in Leiden in April and May 1744. His first poem, "The Virtuoso," a Spenserian imitation, appeared in the *Gentleman's Magazine* in 1737, and in 1738 he published *A British Philippic . . . Occasioned by the Insults of the Spaniards and the Preparation for War*. In 1744 his most celebrated work, *The Pleasures of Imagination*, appeared in three books. Akenside subsequently added a fourth book and extensively revised the poem, and his final version appeared in his collected *Poems* (1772) with the title *The Pleasures of the Imagination*. The work is an eclectic philosophical essay which takes as its starting point Joseph Addison's papers on the same subject in the *Spectator*. It is in Miltonic blank verse, and according to Akenside's preface he used Virgil's *Georgics* and Horace's *Epistles* as models. The influence of the *Georgics* is clear in the studied elevation of the language and the skill with which Akenside evolves a poetic style suitable for a subject not in itself poetical. There is, *mutatis mutandis*, something of the pleasure which Addison distinguishes as characteristic of the Georgic in Akenside's work, namely watching the poet "toss the dung about with an air of gracefulness," perceiving in this case how he endows the abstractions of philosophic thought with

poetic form. The Horatian influence is clear in the skillfulness of the transitions and the tact with which Akenside handles his subject. Later in 1744 Akenside turned to satire in *An Epistle to Curio*, a poem occasioned by the change of political attitude which had enabled William Pulteney, leader of the opposition to Walpole, to accept the earldom of Bath in Henry Pelham's ministry. In 1745 he published *Odes on Several Subjects*, and thereafter the ode was his favourite form. Akenside's willingness to consider himself as the English Pindar is satirized with other aspects of his character in Tobias Smollett's *Peregrine Pickle* (1751), where he appears as the physician in the continental scenes.

Meanwhile Akenside was making slow progress as a doctor. On his return from Leiden he had attempted unsuccessfully to establish practices first in Northampton and then in Hampstead. In 1747, however, his financial worries ended when his friend Jeremiah Dyson established him in a house in Bloomsbury square, London, and settled an allowance upon him. His reputation increased and he was eventually appointed physician to the queen. He delivered the Gulstonian lectures in 1755, the Croonian lectures in 1756, the Harveian oration in 1759. In 1746 he published his "Hymn to the Naiads" and "To the Evening Star"; he also contributed to R. Dodsley's periodical the *Museum*.

Akenside died in London on June 23, 1770.

See C. T. Houpt, *Akenside: a Biographical and Critical Study* (1944); Samuel Johnson's *Lives of the Poets*, iv (1781).   (JN. C.)

AKERSHUS, a *fylke* (county) of southeast Norway, surrounds Oslo and extends northward to Lake Mjösa. Area 1,895 sq.mi. Pop. (1960) 233,891. Forested hills of Precambrian bedrock in the east and south, and of plutonic granite in the west surround undulating lowland covered by submarine clay. Two big rivers, Vorma and Glomma, meet in Akershus and flow into Lake Öyeren to the south. Akershus was well populated even in prehistoric times. Eidsvoll in the north was an early religious and administrative centre; the constitution of Norway was drafted and sanctioned there in 1814. Lilleström at the head of Öyeren and Sandvika in the southwest are small industrial communities in the outskirts of the capital. The lowland is among the best agricultural regions of the country, producing milk, grain, potatoes, vegetables and fruits.   (L. H. HG.)

AKHENATEN: *see* IKHNATON.

AKHISAR (anc. THYATEIRA), a town in the Manisa *il* of Turkey, lies in a fertile plain on the Gurduk Chai (*Lycus*), 58 mi. N.E. of Izmir with which it is connected by railway. Pop. (1965) 47,-422. The area around is extensively cultivated; tobacco and grapes are the chief crops, and a cotton of excellent quality is grown. The town exports tobacco, cotton, wool, opium, cocoons, and cereals, and is celebrated for its scarlet dyes. Thyateira was an ancient town repeopled with Macedonians by Seleucus about 290 B.C. It became an important station on the Roman road from Pergamum to Laodicea, and one of the "Seven Churches" of Asia (Rev. ii, 18), but was never a metropolis, though made the centre of a *conventus* by Caracalla.   (N. Tu.; S. Er.; E. Tu.)

AKHMATOVA, ANNA (real name ANNA ANDREYEVNA GORENKO) (1888–1966), one of the finest Russian poets of the early 20th century. She was born in Kiev. In 1910 she joined the "Acmeist" writers (who rejected symbolism, aiming at a neoclassic purity of expression), wrote for their magazine *Apollon* (1909–17) and married the Acmeist poet Nikolai Gumilev, whom she divorced in 1918. The lyrics in her collections *Vecher* ("Evening," 1912), *Chetki* ("The Rosary," 1914), *Belaya Staya* ("The White Flock," 1917), *Podorozhnik* ("The Buckthorn," 1921) and *Anno Domini MCMXXI* (1922) are remarkable for their simplicity and intensity: many are love poems, all are profoundly personal, like her only long poem *U samogo morya* ("At the Edge of the Sea," 1921). She published no original verse from 1922 to 1940, when *Iz shesti knig* ("From Six Books") and *Iva* ("The Willow Tree") appeared. During World War II she published poems in magazines and in 1945 gave a popular series of readings from her own work; however, in Aug. 1946 her poetry was attacked by the central committee of the Communist party as "empty" and "bourgeois" and in Sept. 1946 she was expelled from the Soviet writers' union. Poems signed by her were published as *Iz tsikla "Slava Miru"* ("From the Cycle,

Glory to Peace") in 1950. After Stalin's death disapproval was relaxed, and she was also honoured abroad, in 1965 receiving an honorary doctorate of literature from Oxford University. Akhmatova died near Moscow on March 5, 1966.

BIBLIOGRAPHY.—Much of her verse was translated into English by N. S. Duddington as *Forty-Seven Love Poems* (1927). *See* also Gerald Shelley, *Modern Poems from Russia* (1942); L. I. Strakhovsky, *Craftsmen of the Word: Three Poets of Modern Russia* (1949).

AKHMIM (EKHMIM), a market town of Sawhaj governorate in the United Arab Republic, on the east bank of the Nile 66 mi. S. of Asyut by river and 4 mi. above Sawhaj on the west bank. Pop. (1957) 39,392. The town has several mosques and two Coptic churches. It maintains a weekly market and manufactures textiles from cotton and flax, particularly the pale blue galabia and check shawls favoured by the Egyptian peasantry.

Outside the walls are the scanty ruins of two ancient temples. In the time of Abulfeda (*q.v.*; 13th century A.D.) a very imposing temple still stood there. Akhmim was the Egyptian Apu or Khenmin, in Coptic Shmin, known to the Greeks as Chemmis (Khemmis) or Panopolis, capital of the 9th or Chemmite nome of upper Egypt. Herodotus mentions the temple dedicated to "Perseus" and asserts that Chemmis was remarkable for the celebration of games in honour of that hero, after the manner of the Greeks, at which prizes were given; but it is possible that he confused Coptos with Chemmis. Strabo mentions linen weaving as an ancient industry of Panopolis, and it is not altogether a coincidence that the cemetery of Akhmim is one of the chief sources of the beautiful textiles of Roman and Coptic age that are brought from Egypt. Monasteries abounded in this neighbourhood from a very early date. Nonnus, the Greek poet, was born at Panopolis.

AKHTAL, AL- (GHIYATH IBN HARITH) (*c.* 640–710), Arab poet of the Omayyad period, highly esteemed for his perfection of form, was born about 640 either at Hira, not far from Rusafa in Mesopotamia, or in the Syrian desert, and belonged to the Mesopotamian tribe of Taghlib. Like his fellow tribesmen he was a Christian, enjoying the freedom of his religion but not taking its duties very seriously. Al-Akhtal, Jarir and al-Farazdaq form a famous trio among the Arabs, but there is dispute as to their relative superiority. The celebrated philologist Abu 'Ubaida placed al-Akhtal highest of the three on the grounds that among his poems there were ten flawless qasidas ("odes") and ten more that were nearly so, and that this could not be said of the other two poets.

BIBLIOGRAPHY.—A. Salhani, *Diwan de Ahtal: Reproduction photolithographique du manuscrit de Bagdad, avec préface et variantes* (1905); E. Griffini, *Le Diwân d'al-Ahtal reproduit par la photolithographie d'après un manuscrit trouvé au Yemen, avec préface, glossaires* ... (1907). For a full account of the poet and his times *see* H. Lammens, *Le chantre des Omiades* (1895), a reprint from the *Journal Asiatique* for 1895.

AKIBA (AQIBA) **BEN JOSEPH** (*c.* 40–135), Palestinian teacher and rabbi, was one of the group known as tannaim whose teachings comprise the body of the Mishnah. An illiterate shepherd until 40, Akiba, after mastering the necessary rudiments, joined the great academy of scholars at Yabneh and rose to prominence there. Later he established his own academy at Bene Berak. Among his many students were those, like Rabbi Simeon ben Yohai and Rabbi Meir, who became the leading teachers of the following generation and through whom Akiba exerted a formative influence on the development of later talmudic thought. Akiba's genius was both legal and humanitarian. He was apparently the first to organize into a code, divided logically by subject matter, all the legal and ethical norms constituting the traditions of the various sages. He developed principles of biblical exegesis which formed the basis for all subsequent talmudic speculation. Maintaining that no letter or word in Scripture was superfluous but that each had its special meaning, he was able to find a scriptural basis for norms he felt to be vital to the needs of Jewish life in his time. Opposing the priestly interpretation of biblical law, Akiba tended to recognize the problems and views of the disadvantaged groups, the artisans and labourers. He tried to limit the prerogatives of the priests; to raise the status of women; and to foster the doctrine of peace as a fundamental political and religious ideal. Although Akiba recognized Bar-Cochba as a possible messiah, the usual view that he played an important part in Bar-Cochba's revolution seems erroneous. Nonetheless, Akiba was imprisoned by the Romans for continuing to teach Torah after that had been forbidden. According to tradition he was flayed alive in 135, after three years' imprisonment, and met his death with steadfastness and composure.

See Louis Finkelstein, *Akiba—Scholar, Saint and Martyr* (1936); and the biography of Akiba by Louis Ginzberg in *The Jewish Encyclopedia.*
(L. F.)

AKITA, Japanese prefecture on the Sea of Japan coast of northwestern Honshu. Area 4,483 sq.mi. Pop. (1960) 1,335,511. Most of the population is located on lowlands along the courses of the Yoneshiro (north) and Omono (south) rivers. Essentially agricultural, Akita produces large rice surpluses even though cultivation is restricted to the summer months; the winters are long, cold and snowy. Lumbering, based on large timber stands in the mountainous interior, ranks second in importance. Akita is Japan's leading petroleum producer and has small exploitable deposits of copper, sulfur, lead and manganese. Petroleum products and chemicals from Akita city and wood products from Noshiro are the principal manufactured items.

AKITA is the capital and largest city (203,643 in 1960) of Akita prefecture. It is located at the mouth of the Omono river. Formerly a castle town of the Satake clan, it is the prefecture's administrative, commercial, industrial, transportation and cultural hub. It is served by an outport, Tsuchizaki. (J. D. EE.)

AKKAD, the ancient name designating the northern part of the country in middle Iraq, which was the home of the Babylonian civilization (*see* BABYLONIA AND ASSYRIA). Geographically its boundaries are not clearly defined, even as against Sumer, the southern part of the country. From about 2000 B.C. rulers of the whole land called themselves "kings of Sumer and Akkad." Roughly, the location of Akkad was in that region where the Tigris and Euphrates rivers approach closest to each other, and its northern limit may be placed above the line of the modern Fallujah and Baghdad. The boundary on the Tigris between Akkad and its northern neighbour Assyria lay at about latitude 34° N., where the tributary Adhem joins the Tigris. The name of Akkad was taken from the city of Agade (*q.v.*), founded by the Semitic conqueror Sargon I, about 2300 B.C. At least from that time onward the inhabitants of this northern region were predominantly Semitic, and it is their speech (the oldest Semitic dialect to be preserved, in the cuneiform script) which was called by them, as by modern scholars, Akkadian (*see* AKKADIAN LANGUAGE). Within the area of Akkad lay some of the principal centres of Babylonian civilization, Babylon itself, Kish, Borsippa, Cuthah, Eshunna, Sippar and Akshak. (C. J. G.)

AKKADIAN LANGUAGE, one of the Semitic languages (*q.v.*), was the language of Mesopotamia (present-day Iraq) in the three thousand years before the Christian era. Assyrian is a dialect of Akkadian, but the entire language was once referred to as "Assyrian" because explorations of Mesopotamia in the early part of the 19th century brought to light inscriptional materials from Assyria long before the discovery of comparable materials in Babylonia. (*See* BABYLONIA AND ASSYRIA.)

Akkadian is often assigned to the eastern group of Semitic languages, in contrast to Hebrew, Phoenician, Amorite, Ugaritic, Aramaic (including Syriac), Arabic and Ethiopic, in the western Semitic group.

The oldest sources of Akkadian appear at the beginning of the third millennium B.C. in personal names and loan words occurring sporadically in inscriptions written in the Sumerian language (*q.v.*), the commonly used language of the period in southern Mesopotamia. With the rise of the Akkad dynasty under its great Semitic ruler Sargon, the Akkadian language spread widely over the whole expanse of the Sargonic empire, extending from the shores of the Mediterranean sea to the Persian gulf. After a short setback during the period of the Sumerian revival under the 3rd dynasty of Ur, at the beginning of the Old Babylonian period (*c.* 2000 B.C.), Akkadian became the only spoken language of Mesopotamia, while Sumerian continued in partial use as the written language of sacred literature.

The three earliest stages of Akkadian, attested in the pre-

Sargonic, Sargonic and Ur III periods, are generally included under the term Old Akkadian. After the fall of the 3rd dynasty of Ur, the Old Akkadian language broke into two dialects: Assyrian, spoken in Assyria, in the northern part of Mesopotamia; and Babylonian, spoken in Babylonia, in the southern part of Mesopotamia. Each of the two dialects is considered in three chronological subdivisions, Old, Middle and New.

Assyrian and Babylonian.—The Assyrian dialect was used extensively in the Old Assyrian period in correspondence and commercial records between the Assyrians and the natives of Asia Minor, and in historical inscriptions. In the Middle Assyrian period the code of laws, contracts and letters were written in the Assyrian dialect, but the historical inscriptions began to be written in the Babylonian dialect.

In the New Assyrian period, at the time when the Assyrians held sway over the whole near east, the Babylonian dialect took over almost entirely. In that period the official and historical inscriptions, belles-lettres and the religious literature were all written in Babylonian. However, the Assyrian dialect continued to be used in legal contracts and in letters.

The expansion of the Babylonian dialect outside Babylonia proper reached its height in the middle period, when Babylonian became the lingua franca of the near east. The correspondence archive of the Egyptian kings discovered at Tell-el-Amarna in upper Egypt testifies to the use of Babylonian in international relations between Egypt, Syria, Palestine, Asia Minor and Assyria. Babylonian was also used extensively in Elam, in the southern regions of what is now Iran. In the New Babylonian period, another Semitic language, Aramaic, gradually replaced Babylonian as the spoken and written language of the country, limiting the latter to learned literature of mathematics and astronomy. By the time of Christ, Babylonian had died out entirely, and all knowledge of it was lost until its recovery by decipherment in the first half of the 19th century.

Akkadian Writing.—In contrast to all other Semitic languages, which used writings consisting of a limited number of from 22 to 30 signs, all developed ultimately from a form of writing originating in Syria, the Akkadian language used a type of writing, called cuneiform (q.v.), which utilized about 600 word and syllable signs, developed from Sumerian.

Phonology.—The classical Akkadian has 20 consonantal phonemes. They are ', b, d, g, ḫ, j, k, l, m, n, p, q, r, s, ṣ, š. There are eight vowel phonemes, a, i, e, u, both short and long.

Morphology.—The noun has two genders, masculine and feminine; three numbers, singular, plural and dual; and three cases, nominative, genitive and accusative. The feminine is distinguished from the masculine by the addition of a morpheme -at- or -t- to the stem. The plural is usually formed by the prolongation of the gender vowel of the singular, as in kalbū (originally *kalbūm), "dogs," beside kalbu(m), "dog," or kalbātu(m), "bitches," beside kalbatu(m), "bitch." Later on the masculine plural was formed with the endings -ē and -ānu/i. The use of the old dual is limited in classical Akkadian to words denoting parts of the body. The case endings in the singular are -um in the nominative, -im in the genitive, and -am in the accusative; mimation had no function and disappeared in the later language. Characteristic of Old Akkadian only is the use of the case endings -iš for the dative and -ūm for the locative.

The verb has two tenses, preterit, as in iprus, "he decided," "he has decided," and present-future, as in iparras, "he decides," "he will decide." A tenseless stative (or permansive) has, in this verb, the form paris, which can be translated as "it is (was, will be) being decided." Of the four main stems, the first, the one in the above quoted examples, is called basic; the second stem, marked by the doubling of the second root consonant, denotes plurality or intensity of action or gives a causative meaning to intransitive verbs; the third stem, marked by an infix š, denotes a causative, as in ušapris, "he caused to decide"; the fourth stem, marked by an infix n, denotes the mediopassive, as in ipparis (from inparis), "it was decided." Each of the stems can appear with further infixes, t, tn (and even tt, ttn), to denote various shades of reciprocal, reflexive, iterative and other aspects. The

forms with t evolved into a new tense called perfect. The verb distinguishes also a subjunctive, an allative, an imperative, used with the second person only, an infinitive and participles.

See W. von Soden, Grundriss der akkadischen Grammatik (1952); R. Labat, Manuel d'épigraphie akkadienne (1948).   (I. J. G.)

AKLAN, a province in the Republic of the Philippines, occupying the northwestern portion of Panay Island. The province was created in 1955 from the western portion of Capiz province. Pop. (1960) 226,232. Most of the population reside in the valley of the Aklan river and along the north-facing coastal lowland, both rice-producing centres.

Kalibo, the provincial capital, had a population of 21,303 (1960) within the municipality. It is the province's main trading centre and transportation junction. The port of New Washington, 7 mi. E. of Kalibo, provides interisland shipping connections; Ibajay, 18 mi. W. of Kalibo, is the province's second trading centre.

(R. E. HE.)

AKOLA, a town in Maharashtra state, India, the headquarters of Akola district, is on the Murna tributary of the Purna river 140 mi. W.S.W. of Nagpur (158 mi. by rail). Akola proper is on the west bank, and Tajnapeth, containing the administrative buildings and most of the population, is on the east bank. Pop. (1961) 115,760. The town has walls built mainly by a Mogul feudatory about 1700 and a citadel built under Hyderabad rule in the early 19th century. It is on the national highway and main rail route from Calcutta to Bombay and at the junction of the Central railway broad-gauge route from Nagpur to Bombay via Bhusaval, and the metre-gauge route linking Khandwa with towns in the Godavari basin to the south. Akola is one of the cotton towns of Berar (q.v.) and has ginning factories and cotton presses. There is a government college affiliated to Nagpur university and an industrial school supported by a Protestant mission.

AKOLA DISTRICT is in general flat, the greater part being in the central valley of Berar. Pop. (1961) 1,189,354. Area 4,095 sq.mi. It is bounded on the north by the Melghat hills; and on the south by eastern outliers of the Ajanta hills, with summits rising to 2,000 ft., and by the fertile Washim (Basim) tableland, which slopes from 1,000 ft. southwestward into the valley of the eastward-flowing Penganga. North of the Ajantas the land is drained westward by the Purna (an affluent of the Tapti, q.v.) and its tributaries. The heat from April to mid-June is great (May maximum 107° F., mean 94° F.), but the nights are cool. Annual average rainfall is 34 in. In the north the Purna valley, where the elevation falls below 1,000 ft., has rich black loamy soil particularly suited to cotton. Almost all the district is cultivated, secondary crops after cotton being jowar and some wheat and oilseeds. The district's largest towns after Akola, Akot (31,459), Karanja (26,440) and Washim (26,494), are, unlike Akola, predominantly centres of agricultural population. Washim, 37 mi. S. of Akola, was the capital of a feudatory kingdom of the Hindu Vakataka dynasty in the 4th century A.D.   (S. M. A.)

AKRON, a city of Ohio, U.S., and seat of Summit county, is situated on the watershed which separates the tributaries of the Ohio river from the waters flowing north to Lake Erie. It is approximately 1,200 ft. above sea level and one of the highest points in the state. The name Akron was taken from a Greek word meaning "high." Akron was established in 1825, incorporated as a village in 1836, became the county seat in 1842 and was chartered as a city in 1865. It is about 35 mi. S.E. of Cleveland and has an area of 53.9 sq.mi. Pop. (1960) 290,351; standard metropolitan statistical area (Summit and Portage counties) 605,367. (For comparative population figures see table in OHIO: Population.) The city of Barberton adjoins Akron on the southwest. On the north is the city of Cuyahoga Falls (q.v.). North of Cuyahoga Falls are the residential communities of Stow and Silver Lake. Other villages near Akron in Summit county are Tallmadge, Hudson, Munroe Falls and Mogadore.

The Ohio and Erie canal linking Lake Erie with the Ohio river was opened in 1827; and the Pennsylvania and Ohio canal linking Akron with Pittsburgh and Beaver, Pa., was opened in 1840. These canals afforded Akron its most important means of transportation for 25 years, until the advent of the railroads. Water power supplied by the canals led to Akron's early development as an industrial centre. By 1840 there were flour and cereal mills, iron furnaces and plants making tile, brick and sewer pipe among other items. After the American Civil War, the manufacture of mowers and reapers was started, as well as plants producing matches and fishing tackle.

The ample water supply, the transportation afforded by two railroads and the financial assistance of a persuasive board of trade led B. F. Goodrich to move a small rubber factory to Akron in 1870. Other rubber companies were established during the next two decades. These companies first manufactured rubber hose, bicycle tires and solid rubber tires for buggies. The introduction of the automobile created a demand for pneumatic tires, and the existing companies expanded and several new ones were organized. The expansion of the rubber industry fostered Akron's rapid growth. Between 1910 and 1920 the population of the city tripled to 208,435. Thereafter Akron was known as the "rubber capital of the world."

Other products made in Akron include steam boilers, steel rims for trucks and tractors, metal stampings and military aircraft. Wood, plastic and synthetic rubber products number in the thousands. Chemical companies make ingredients for paints; sulfur is refined; salt, silica sand and clay are mined in the area. The many machine shops located in Akron, Barberton and Cuyahoga Falls, make machinery, molds, tools and other equipment used by rubber manufacturers and by the government. Synthetic rubber plants built during World War II and operated for the government were later purchased by private companies and expanded for increased production. Several large trucking companies have their headquarters in or near Akron.

Because of the dominating industries, Akron's population tended to have a preponderance of men, a large proportion of skilled and semiskilled labour, relatively high wages and a high percentage of men engaged in gainful occupations. The population was not congested, even after the period of rapid growth. Small detached or semidetached dwellings are most common. After mid-20th century approximately 70% of the homes were owner-occupied.

Metropolitan parks occupying more than 4,300 ac., about 12 lakes and reservoirs and several golf courses afford recreation areas. The University of Akron was created in 1913 when the city council accepted as a nucleus the plant and endowment of Buchtel college, founded in 1870 and named after its chief benefactor John R. Buchtel (1822–92), an Akron businessman. After mid-20th century, the university enrolled more than 5,000 students.

The old Portage trail, used by the Indians in carrying their canoes from the Cuyahoga river to the Tuscarawas in the journey from Lake Erie to the Ohio, runs through the city for about 7 mi. The Summit County Historical society has placed historical markers along the Portage trail and operates a house once occupied by John Brown, the abolitionist, as a historic house museum. (W. D. Ov.)

AKSAKOV, the name of a family of Russian writers.

Sergei Timofeevich Aksakov (1791–1859) was born Sept. 20, 1791, at Ufa, on the Russian steppelands, and brought up in patriarchal conditions on the estates purchased from the Bashkirs by his pioneering grandfather. He was educated in the 18th-century French pseudoclassical tradition at home, at school and at the newly founded university in Kazan (1804–07). He became a translator in the legislative commission of the civil service, resigning in 1811; served in the militia in the war of 1812; married in 1815; and in 1816 retired to the family estate. After a decade as a sporting country squire, with little talent for estate management, he returned to the civil service in Moscow and became literary censor (1826), inspector (1834) and, later, director of the college of land surveying. Inheriting money, he retired in 1839 and lived in and near Moscow, entertaining his friends, mainly writers and Slavophils. He died at Abramtsevo, April 30, 1859.

Before 1834, when his successful *Blizzard* was published, Aksakov's writings reflected outmoded literary tastes: translations of Boileau and Molière, undistinguished verse and articles on the theatre—the latter valuable source material. But he was in-

spired by his love for rural Russia in the days of serfdom, by his Slavophil sons and by Gogol, whose genius—though poles apart from his own—he admired, to set down the story of his grandfather, his parents and his own childhood recollected in tranquillity and transposed into realistic fiction in three books which have become classics: *Semeynaya Khronika* and *Vospominaniya* (both 1856), and *Detskie gody Bagrova vnuka* (1858). Though necessarily introspective, Aksakov unfolds his epic chronicle objectively in an unaffected style and simple language. Its interest lies in the Proustian illusion of reality and intimacy created by his vivid remembrance of the continuous past. These works, a cross between memoirs and the novel—a new genre in Russian literature—brought Aksakov fame. He is also one of the few Russian writers on shooting, fishing and butterfly collecting, and his reminiscences of Gogol are firsthand material on his friend's complex personality.

Bibliography.—His collected works were ed. by I. S. Aksakov (1886); other editions 1909, 1911 and 1916. For full bibliography *see* I. V. Vladislavlev, *Russkie Pisateli* (1924). There are English translations of *Semeynaya Khronika* by M. C. Beverley as *Chronicles of a Russian Family* (1924) and by J. D. Duff as *A Russian Gentleman*, in the "World's Classics Series" (1923); and of *Vospominaniya* as *The Autobiography of a Russian Schoolboy* (1917), and *Detskie gody Bagrova vnuka* as *Years of Childhood* (1916), both by J. D. Duff. (E. Hl.)

Aksakov's sons were also well-known writers and Slavophils.

Konstantin Sergeevich Aksakov (1817–1860), the Slavophil movement's principal theorist, was born April 10 (new style; March 29, old style), 1817, in Aksakovo, Orenburg. A keen student of Hegel, he became a literary critic, a grammarian, a historian and a political philosopher. In his interpretation of history a mystical conception of ancient "land" (*Zemlya*) was contrasted with the "state"—an alien idea imposed by Peter the Great, whose Europeanizing influence he deplored: he praised the traditional spiritual "conscience" of Russia and decried European legal values. For him "Holy Russia" literally was sacred. He died on the Greek island of Zante, Dec. 19 (N.S.; 7, O.S.), 1860.

His brother Ivan Sergeevich Aksakov (1823–1886) was born at Nadezhdin, near Yekaterinburg (Sverdlovsk), Oct. 8 (N.S.; Sept. 26, O.S.), 1823. He founded and edited the newspapers *Den* (1861–65) and *Moskva* (1867–69)—often suppressed and censored; and wrote the first Russian narrative poem on peasant life, *Brodyaga* ("The Tramp," 1852). Leader of the Panslavists during the Russo-Turkish War (1877–78), he was exiled for denouncing the treaty of Berlin (1878) but returned to found the influential journal *Rus* in 1880, editing it until his death in Moscow, Feb. 8 (N.S.; Jan. 27, O.S.), 1886.

AKSHAK, a powerful city of ancient Mesopotamia, on the northern boundary of Akkad, identified by some authorities with Babylonian Upi (Opis). About 2500 B.C. it was conquered by Eannatum, king of Lagash, who had previously worsted its ally Kish. About a century later, according to the king lists, Akshak established its hegemony over Sumer and Akkad, following on the 4th dynasty of Kish. The proposed location of this important city on the site of the later Seleucia (mod. Tall Umar on the west bank of the Tigris, south of Baghdad) is uncertain. The Mari documents (c. 1770 B.C.) indicate that it lay near Eshnunna in the Diyala valley. *See* further Babylonia and Assyria. (M. E. L. M.)

AKSUM (Axum), the ancient capital of Ethiopia and the spiritual home of Abyssinian religion and civilization to the present day. Aksum is situated in the Tigre province of northern Ethiopia, a few miles west of Adwa, at an altitude of 7,000 ft. (For the history of the Aksumite kingdom *see* Ethiopia or Abyssinia: *History.*)

Aksum had been known to classical and early Christian writers. In the *Periplus Maris Erythraei,* an anonymous 1st-century account of travel and trade in the Indian ocean, we encounter probably the first reference to "the city of the people called Auxumites"; *i.e.,* Aksum. A far more detailed story is told by Cosmas Indicopleustes in his *Christian Topography.* Cosmas had visited Aksum about the year A.D. 525 and had marveled at its churches and antiquities. Aksum is also mentioned in south Arabian and early Ethiopic inscriptions, and the city's ancient monuments have been meticulously studied by the German Aksum expedition

(1906), by U. Monneret de Villard (1937) and others. Earlier European travelers already had brought back descriptions of the Aksumite monuments which varied considerably in value and accuracy. The significance of the holy city of Aksum forms the centrepiece of the greatest work of Ethiopian literature (q.v.), the *Kebra Nagast* ("Glory of the Kings"), which describes the transference of the Ark of the Covenant from Jerusalem to Aksum, the new Zion, by Menelik, the son of the queen of Sheba and King Solomon.

The Ark (*tabot*—replicas are in every Ethiopian church) is alleged to be kept in the holy of holies of the most famous rectangular sanctuary in Ethiopia, the church of St. Mary of Zion at Aksum, which was known already in the 6th century. At the top of the flight of stairs leading to this church there is a throne and footstool, a characteristic feature of the Aksumite remains. The most notable achievements of indigenous art are the deservedly famous Aksumite obelisks which embody delicately executed ornamental designs of the story or window type. They are pre-Christian and served as gravestones and memorials. The perfection reached by the largest of these monoliths is expressed not only in the immense technical skill required in working, moving, and erecting these colossal single blocks of granite but especially in their beautiful sculpturing and rich decoration as well-proportioned multistory towers. The largest obelisk still standing at Aksum is nearly 70 ft. high, while the biggest of all, though broken through the force of its fall, measures about 110 ft. in height and is thus the largest (at one time upright) monolith in the world (exceeding the height of the Lateran obelisk by just over four feet).

BIBLIOGRAPHY.—For a detailed topographical, architectural and epigraphic account of the Aksumite monuments *see* the four volumes by E. Littmann, T. von Lüpke, D. Krencker, *Deutsche Aksum-Expedition* (1913); J. T. Bent, *The Sacred City of the Ethiopians* (1893); A. Dillmann, "Zur Geschichte des Axumitischen Reichs," *Abhandlungen der königlichen Akademie der Wissenschaften* (1880); E. Glaser, *Die Abessinier in Arabien und Afrika* (1895); *Guida dell' Africa Orientale* (1938); U. Monneret de Villard, *Aksum* (1938); E. Ullendorff, *The Ethiopians* (1960). (E. U.)

AKTYUBINSK, an *oblast* and town in the northwest of the Kazakh Soviet Socialist Republic, U.S.S.R. The *oblast* is bounded on the west by the Gur'yev and Ural'sk (formerly West Kazakhstan) *oblasts* of the Kazakh S.S.R., on the north by the Orenburg *oblast* of the Russian Soviet Federated Socialist Republic, on the northeast by the Kustanay *oblast* of the Kazakh S.S.R., on the east and southeast by the Karaganda and Kzyl-Orda *oblasts* of the Kazakh S.S.R., and on the south by the Kara-Kalpak Autonomous S.S.R. Area, 115,753 sq.mi. The population in 1959 was 401,049, of which 44% was urban and 56% rural. The three largest towns are Aktyubinsk (the capital), Temir, and Chelkar. There are 13 *rayons* (districts).

The *oblast* includes brown soil steppe in the north and desert in the south. The Caspian lowland (west) is separated from the Turgai tableland (east) by the Mugodzhar hills. The precipitation is low, varying from 10 in. in the south to 16 in. in the north, and the river network is therefore scanty. The main rivers are the Emba, which flows southwest toward the Caspian sea, and the Irgiz, which waters the eastern section and flows into the inland lake Chelkar-Tengiz.

Most of the *oblast* is devoted to livestock breeding (sheep, goats, camels), and agriculture is restricted to the north. There are rich nickel deposits near Batamshinski and chrome at Donskoye and Khrom-Tau, east of the town of Aktyubinsk. Coal is mined at Berchogur. Large phosphorite deposits round Kandagach south of Aktyubinsk are processed into fertilizers at the Alga Chemical works. Another chemical plant at Chelkar exploits the salt deposits from the Aral sea. The eastern section of the Emba oil deposits has its chief field at Shubar-Kuduk. The Transcaspian railway intersects the *oblast* northwest by southeast, crossing the Orsk-Gur'yev line at Kandagach. In the early 1960s there were more than 600 schools in the *oblast*.

The town of AKTYUBINSK (pop. [1959] 96,680) is situated on the Ilek river, a tributary of the Ural. It began its existence in 1869 as Ak-Tyube ("white hill" in Kazakh), a small fort. In 1878 the first Russian settlers arrived there and in 1891 it was established as the capital of an *uyezd* (district). It is one of the most important industrial centres of Kazakhstan and has electrotechnical engineering works, stockyards and flour mills. During World War II a ferroalloys plant was established near the town for working the nickel and chrome of the Mugodzhar hills. Educational establishments include a woman teachers' training college. (G. E. Wr.)

AKUTAGAWA RYŪNOSUKE (1892–1927), a Japanese writer of stories, plays and poetry, was born in Tokyo on March 1, 1892. As a boy he was sickly and hypersensitive, but excelled at school and was an omnivorous reader. He began his literary career while attending Tokyo university, where he studied English literature from 1913 to 1916. The publication in 1915 of his short story "Rashomon" led to his introduction to Natsume Soseki, the outstanding novelist of the day. Under Natsume's encouragement he began to write a remarkable series of stories, derived largely from 12th- and 13th-century collections of Japanese tales but retold with modern psychology in a highly individual style. Akutagawa's stories have a feverish, unhealthy intensity well suited to their often macabre themes and revealing much of his own highly strung sensibilities. It is easy to see resemblances between the artist described in his *Jigokuhen* (*Hell Screen*, 1917) who must witness with his own eyes scenes of horror before he can paint his gruesome masterpiece, and Akutagawa himself, who underwent constant mental agonies as a writer. In 1922 he turned away from medieval themes to devote himself mainly to thinly disguised autobiographical fiction. Akutagawa's modern stories lack the exotic if sometimes lurid glow of the older tales, a fact that may account for their comparative unpopularity. His last important work, *Kappa* (1926–27), a satirical fable about elflike creatures, is written, despite the subject, in the mirthless vein of his last period and reflects his depressed state at the time. Akutagawa committed suicide on July 24, 1927, leaving behind many works that were published posthumously.

English translations of Akutagawa's works include *Rashomon and Other Stories* (1952) and *Japanese Short Stories* (1961), both trans. by Takashi Kojima; *Exotic Japanese Stories: the Beautiful and the Grotesque,* trans. by Kojima and John McVittie (1964); *Hell Screen and Other Stories,* trans. by W. H. H. Norman (1948); *Kappa,* trans. by Seiichi Shiojiri (1951); and *Tu Tze-Chun,* trans. by Dorothy Britton (1964). (Dd. K.)

AKYAB, a municipality and district in the Arakan division of the Union of Burma. The district includes the confluence of the Mayu, Kaladan and Lemro rivers. The Arakan coast on the Bay of Bengal receives the full force of the southwest monsoon and Akyab has been built in a relatively sheltered site on the eastern side of a hilly ridge. In addition to the usual public buildings it has several rice mills and the chief export is rice. After the cession of Arakan to the British by the treaty of Yandabu in 1826, the old capital Arakan (on a small branch of the Kaladan river) now known as Myohaung ("old city") was abandoned as the seat of government, and Akyab on the sea coast selected instead. Trade restrictions were removed and Akyab rapidly grew from a small fishing village into a leading port of Burma. The population has varied but slightly since the census of 1881, and in 1931 it was 38,094. Of these, 4,049 were then classed as "adventitious" Muslim and Hindu labourers—Indians who came temporarily as labourers, leaving their womenfolk behind. Since the independence of Burma in 1948, the Indian population has greatly decreased. In 1962, the population was estimated at 86,451.

AKYAB DISTRICT, with an area of 5,252 sq.mi. and a population in 1962 of 665,305, forms the natural geographical hinterland of the port. Rice is grown on extensive alluvial plains and there is little settlement on the wet, forested hill ridges. *See also* ARAKAN. (L. D. S.)

ALA, in architecture, one of the side recesses which usually opened off the atrium (q.v.) of a Roman house. One was placed on each side in the corners off the back of and entirely open to the atrium. The term applies also to the wings, open their entire width in front, at each side of the cella in one of the Tuscan temple plans.

ALABAMA is called the "Yellowhammer state" because of its state bird, the "Cotton state" because of its chief agricultural product and the "Heart of Dixie" because of its location. The state is situated between 84° 51′ and 88° 28′ 03″ W. and 30° 13′ and 35° N., and is bounded north by Tennessee, east by Georgia, south by Florida and the Gulf of Mexico and west by Mississippi. The total area of Alabama is 51,609 sq.mi., of which 549 sq.mi. are inland water surface. It is the 29th state of the union in size. The state capital is Montgomery and the state entered the union on Dec. 14, 1819, as the 22nd state.

The southern pine has been adopted as the state's official tree and the camellia as the official flower. The state flag is a red cross of St. Andrew on a white field; square in shape, the flag is modeled upon the battle flag of the Confederacy. The name "Alabama" is of Choctaw origin and means "thicket-clearers" or "vegetation gatherers" and not "here we rest" as it is sometimes rendered.

PHYSICAL GEOGRAPHY

Physical Features.—North Alabama is a diversified region, entered by the Appalachian highlands. In the northeast, Lookout, Sand and Raccoon mountains are important physical features. The rugged Cumberland plateau, extending deeply into the state from Tennessee, is crossed from east to west by the fertile Tennessee valley. The highest point in Alabama is Cheaha mountain (2,407 ft.) in the northeastern corner of the state. The great Appalachian valley and the Piedmont plateau invade the state for a considerable distance from the Georgia line. The Coosa and the Tennessee rivers drain the highlands and provide an important source of hydroelectric power. The "black belt" is prairie country which crosses the central portion of Alabama generally from east to west. Farther south lies the Gulf coastal plain, which slopes gradually down to sea level in the south, where it touches the Gulf of Mexico.

The principal rivers of Alabama are the Tombigbee and Black Warrior in the west, the Alabama and the Coosa in the central portion, the Tennessee in the north and the Chattahoochee, which forms much of the Georgia boundary, in the east. The Alabama river flows to the southwest where it joins the Tombigbee; their waters then part to flow into Mobile bay as the Mobile and Tensaw rivers. Mobile bay averages about 12 ft. in depth, although there is a ship channel through the bay with a controlling depth of 36 ft. and a width of 400 ft.

Climate and Soil.—Alabama has a temperate climate. The average mean temperature for the state in winter is 46° F. and in summer 79° F. Snow falls only once or twice a year in the northern part. Alabama has abundant rainfall with a yearly average of 53 in. Heaviest rainfall is along the Gulf coast with about 65 in. per year, and the lightest is near the centre of the state with about 50 in. Rainfall and temperature account for the state's long growing season: 298 days in south Alabama, 198 days in the north.

There are four principal belts of soil. In the timber belt along the coast the soil is sandy. North of this lies the "black belt" ("black prairie" or "cotton belt"), approximately 13,000 sq.mi. in extent, which has black soil that is rich in limestone and marl formations, without sand or loam and is especially adapted to the production of cotton and grasses. Between the cotton belt and the Tennessee valley lies the mineral belt, the soils of which are of varied fertility. North of the mineral belt is the cereal belt in the Tennessee valley, containing red clays and dark loams.

Vegetation and Animal Life.—Plants and animals are both numerous and varied in the semitropical climate of Alabama. There are about 4,500 kinds of native plants. The approximately 125 varieties of trees include soft pines such as loblolly, shortleaf, longleaf and slash. In addition there are 22 kinds of oak trees, cedar (red and white), walnut, sweet gum, other gum trees, magnolia, tulip trees, dogwood, haw (20 kinds) and others. Examples of the state's abundant plant life include shrubs (more than 150 species), native grasses (more than 200 species) and many wild flowers, ferns, vines and mosses. Honeysuckle, Virginia creeper and smilax are common. Spanish moss grows on the coastal plain and the carnivorous pitcher plant is found in the forests.

Ornithologists have identified 325 species of birds in the state including quail (the most abundant game bird), turkeys, pintail ducks, mallards, geese, doves, robins, cardinals, mockingbirds, warblers, eagles, ospreys and yellowhammers.

Fresh-water fish of particular interest to fishermen include bream and catfish. Many Alabama farms have a private, stocked fishpond. Along the Gulf coast, the prevalence of salt-water fish such as tarpon and king mackerel promotes sport fishing, which is climaxed by an annual Deep Sea rodeo. Commercial fishermen catch red snapper, mullet, flounder, shrimp, crabs and oysters. Of 63 kinds of snakes found in Alabama, only the copperhead, the cottonmouth moccasin, the coral and the rattlesnake are poisonous. Alligators are found in the swamps and bayous.

Animals found in the forests include deer, bears, opossums, raccoons, wildcats, foxes (red and gray), coypu or nutria, mink, skunks, otters and beavers. The most numerous are rabbits and squirrels; gophers, moles and muskrats are common.

Parks and Monuments.—Alabama's state parks are administered by the state department of conservation which also has responsibility for parkways, historic sites and monuments and the state's public lakes. The largest is the Oak Mountain State park in Shelby county (9,940 ac.). Other major parks are De Soto (De Kalb county), Gulf (Baldwin county), Little Mountain (Marshall county), Cheaha (Clay-Cleburne-Talladega counties), Joe Wheeler (Lawrence-Lauderdale counties), Monte Sano (Madison county), Chewacla (Lee county), Ft. Morgan (Baldwin county) and Meaher (Baldwin county).

The state maintains a number of public lakes, the most popular of which is that in Tuscaloosa county.

Horseshoe Bend National Military park, near Dadeville and Alexander City, was created by an act of congress in 1956 to commemorate Andrew Jackson's victory over the "Red Stick" (Creek) Indians, March 27, 1814, during the War of 1812. The park is administered by the national park service which also administers the historic Natchez Trace parkway which crosses the northwestern corner of Alabama.

Conecuh National forest is in the extreme southern part of Alabama, while Black Warrior National forest is in the northwestern part of the state. The Choccolocco division of Talladega National forest is in eastern Alabama; the Okmulgee division is in central Alabama.

HISTORY

Early Indian Life.—Indians living in the area now designated as the state of Alabama left artifacts which yield a more detailed prehistoric record than other sites in North America. In 1956 the Smithsonian institution and the National Geographic society supported excavation work by Carl F. Miller who employed the radioactive carbon 14 method in excavating Russell cave in Jackson county in the northeastern corner of Alabama. The de-

EWING GALLOWAY

CYPRESS SWAMP IN SOUTHERN ALABAMA

BY COURTESY OF (LEFT) ALABAMA DEPARTMENT OF ARCHIVES AND HISTORY, (RIGHT) SMITHSONIAN INSTITUTION, (BELOW) ALABAMA BUREAU OF PUBLICITY AND INFORMATION

(LEFT) LITHOGRAPH OF THE BURNING OF THE CAPITOL AT MONTGOMERY, DEC. 14, 1849. (RIGHT) A HOME COTTON FACTORY IN ALABAMA ABOUT 1875. (BELOW) THE FIRST "WHITE HOUSE" OF THE CONFEDERACY, MONTGOMERY; JEFFERSON DAVIS LIVED IN IT AFTER HIS INAUGURATION AS CONFEDERATE PRESIDENT

tailed record of Indian life thereby uncovered extended over a period of nearly 9,000 years.

Prehistoric Indians developed their technical skill to the point of building remarkable mounds, many of which are still to be seen at various sites along the rivers of Alabama. Artifacts of the mound builders are exhibited by the state of Alabama in the museum at Mound State monument in Moundville, Hale county.

When Europeans came to the shore of Alabama, the principal Indian groups were as follows: Chickasaws (northwest Alabama), Cherokees (northeast Alabama), Muskogees, also designated Creeks (southeast and central Alabama) and Choctaws (southwest Alabama). Each of these groups extended beyond Alabama into the adjoining states. In the 1960s there remained only one Indian settlement in Alabama—that of about 500 Creeks in the southern part of the state.

Exploration and Early Settlement.—Into the lands of the Alabama aborigines there penetrated each of the European powers which became a major contender for dominance in North America. The first of the known explorers were Spaniards, including Alonzo Alvarez de Piñeda (1519), Pánfilo de Narváez (1528), Hernando De Soto (1540), Guido de las Bazares (1558) and Tristán de Luna (1559–61). Luna's men made several temporary settlements in Alabama, particularly at Mobile, Claiborne and on the Coosa river. The exploration of Alabama areas by De Soto was extensive—from north to south, from east to west and finally from south to north. The scene of one of the bloodiest battles between Europeans and Indians was at Mabila in Clarke county, where De Soto and his men fought the Indians under Chief Tuscaloosa, Oct. 18, 1540. The smallest figure set by the conflicting contemporary accounts of Indian casualties was 2,500.

In addition to the Spaniards, the English and the French also claimed the area which became Alabama. The English included the Alabama country in the Carolina charters of 1663 and 1665, and English traders from the Carolinas made numerous trips to the valley of the Alabama river prior to establishment of the first colony in the area by the French, who founded the first permanent European settlements in Alabama. Under the leadership of the Le Moyne brothers, Pierre Le Moyne, Sieur d'Iberville and Jean Baptiste Le Moyne, Sieur de Bienville, the French established Ft. Louis (1702, at Twenty-Seven Mile bluff), Port Dauphin (1702, Dauphin Island), Mobile (1711), Ft. Toulouse (1714, near Wetumpka) and Ft. Tombecbé (1736, in Sumter county). These settlements were parts of the chain of forts which stretched from the Gulf of Mexico, through the Mississippi valley to Canada for defense against the British.

The struggle of France against Great Britain in the Second Hundred Years' War (1689–1763) was reflected in campaigns in the Alabama country which involved the Indian allies of the European powers. The Choctaws were allies of the French while the Chickasaws were allies of the British.

Before Statehood.—The treaty of Paris (1763) removed the French and established British mastery in the Alabama country. During the American Revolution, Spanish forces under Bernardo de Gálvez seized portions of Alabama and also land farther along the fringe of the Gulf coast. This physical possession was confirmed in the treaty of Paris (1783), whereby Spain held Mobile and the coastal fringe, and the U.S. held the more northerly parts of Alabama. The dividing line between Spain and the U.S. in the Alabama country was the southern boundary of the U.S. at the time, but its exact location was not clear until Thomas Pinckney negotiated the treaty of San Lorenzo el Real (1795), establishing the boundary along the thirty-first parallel. This became known as the Dunbar-Ellicott line, named for Sir William Dunbar representing Spain and Andrew Ellicott representing the U.S., who surveyed the line. Spanish control of Baldwin and Mobile counties was not removed until the U.S. took possession of the area, claiming it to be a part of the Louisiana Purchase, in 1813, bringing all of Alabama under the U.S. flag.

War with the Creek Indians centred in the Alabama area and was closely woven into the War of 1812. The Shawnee chief, Tecumseh, persuaded a majority of the Creek Indians to take up arms against the American settlers while at the same time the Shawnees in the Great Lakes area were also resisting the advance of the American frontiersmen. In the early stages of the Creek War there occurred one of the bloodiest Indian massacres on the American frontier—the massacre of Ft. Mims, Aug. 30, 1813, in which more than 500 persons were killed. The most important engagement in the Creek War was the battle of Horseshoe Bend, March 27, 1814. Gen. Andrew Jackson's victory in this battle was a major step in a career which led to the presidency. The Creek War ended with the treaty of Ft. Jackson (1814). With the restoration of peace, the trickle of Anglo-Americans from nearby states, especially from Georgia, the Carolinas, Virginia and Tennessee, swelled into a flood which quickly populated the Alabama country. In 1817 the Alabama territory was created, with the capital at St. Stephens and William Wyatt Bibb as the governor. Alabama became a state in 1819, with the capital located successively at Huntsville (1819–20), Cahaba (1820–26), Tuscaloosa (1826–47) and Montgomery.

Ante-Bellum Problems.—The principal problems of ante-bellum politics centred about the state bank, Indian removal, education (see *Education*, below) and slavery.

The state bank, actually owned and operated by the state, was established in 1824 to provide money and credit which were much needed in the rapidly growing frontier state. The bank proved so profitable that all state taxation was abolished in 1836. The panic of 1837 placed too much strain on the bank, however, involved as it had become in politics, with bank officials elected annually. The bank was put out of business in 1843 after Benjamin Fitzpatrick was elected governor on the platform to abolish it.

The Indians were moved from Alabama by successive treaties of the federal government between the years 1814 and 1835.

Following the Mexican War (1846–48), political controversy stirred throughout the nation over the extension of slavery into the territories. This became a dominant theme in the history of Alabama. William L. Yancey was the author of the "Alabama platform," declaring that the federal government could not legally bar the extension of slavery to the territories. This issue was one of the prime reasons that a majority of Alabamians saw in the election of Abraham Lincoln to the presidency in 1860 adequate reason for secession. At a specially convened state convention, Alabama seceded on Jan. 11, 1861, by a vote of 61 to 39, with most of the antisecession votes coming from north Alabama.

Civil War and Reconstruction.—Montgomery became the first capital of the Confederacy, and there, on Feb. 18, 1861, Jefferson Davis was inaugurated president of the Confederate States of America. Military operations in Alabama included raids by Union forces: John B. Turchin, 1862; A. D. Streight, 1863; Lovell H. Rousseau, 1864; and J. H. Wilson, 1865. The battle of Mobile bay (1864) was won by Adm. David G. Farragut.

Estimates of the Alabamians in Confederate military service vary from 65,000 to 100,000. Thirty-nine generals in the Confederate army came from Alabama. Approximately 3,000 Alabamians served in the Union army.

The postwar reconstruction in Alabama had three distinct phases: (1) The presidential period of reconstruction (1865–67) which was marked by a constitution adopted in 1865 that ratified the 13th amendment abolishing slavery, nullified the ordinance of secession and provided for the election of state officers. Opposition to certain state laws by the radical Republicans in the national congress resulted in the denial of seats to Alabama's representatives and senators. (For the general background of this period *see* UNITED STATES [OF AMERICA]: *History: Civil War and Reconstruction, 1850–1876.*) (2) The second period of reconstruction (1867–68) was ushered in by the national acts of March 1867 making Alabama a part of the third military district. Maj. Gen. Wager Swayne of Ohio was appointed under presidential authority as military governor of Alabama and the radical Republicans took charge of the state's electoral processes. In Nov. 1867 another constitutional convention drafted a new constitution which, in accord with the aims of the radical Republicans, forced the adoption of the 14th amendment. (3) The "carpetbag-scalawag" era (1868–74) was the third phase of reconstruction. It was marked by corruption and extravagance on the part of numerous public officials and is generally regarded as the low ebb of the state's history. Between the terms of radical Republican governors William H. Smith (1868–70) and David P. Lewis (1872–74), the Democrats managed to elect Robert B. Lindsay (1870–72), but it was not until the term of Democrat George S. Houston in 1874 that self-government was restored to the state.

The period from 1874 to 1896, designated the "Bourbon era," was characterized by economy, retrenchment, conservatism and dominance of the Democratic party. Paradoxically this period was marked by progress in education and industry, as the state struggled to recover from the costly losses of 14 years of war and reconstruction. The general level of economic life was low, however, by comparison with the 20th century and also with ante-bellum times. Widespread poverty and depressed agricultural prices sparked the Populist revolt of the 1890s. This political group, using the designation "Jeffersonian party," nearly captured the governorship in 1890 and again in 1892. The farm revolt gradually subsided, but left a legacy of demands which were for the most part enacted into law during the 20th century.

The 20th Century.—Alabama started the 20th century with a new constitution—that of 1901 (see *Government*, below). The Democratic party remained dominant, but some counties of the hill area consistently voted Republican. Many Negroes also voted Republican, particularly in the period prior to 1936.

In 1948, when Pres. Harry S. Truman ran as the regular Democratic nominee against Thomas E. Dewey, Republican, Alabama's electoral votes were cast for J. Strom Thurmond, States' Rights Democrat. In 1952 Dwight D. Eisenhower proved popular but ran behind Adlai Stevenson and his running mate, Alabama Sen. John J. Sparkman. In 1956 Stevenson again carried Alabama over Eisenhower, with one electoral vote cast for Walter B. Jones of Montgomery. The Democratic slate won in 1960 but six unpledged electors voted for Sen. Harry F. Byrd of Virginia while five voted for John F. Kennedy. After the passage of the Civil Rights bill in 1964, Alabama, for the first time since 1872, gave its vote to a Republican presidential candidate, Barry Goldwater, in preference to Democratic candidate Pres. Lyndon B. Johnson.

Military installations in the state during World War II included Maxwell field, Camp Rucker, Ft. McClellan and Brookley field. There were increases in agricultural production, manufactures and commerce. One shipbuilding company pioneered in the construction of ships with welded hulls, promoting speed in wartime shipbuilding. Jan. 31, 1958, marked the orbiting of the first U.S. satellite, Explorer 1, which was developed at Huntsville in the U.S. army's ballistic missile centre, Redstone arsenal, which became the state's largest industrial enterprise. A National Aeronautics and Space administration (NASA) installation was located at Huntsville, Oct. 1, 1958, and the George C. Marshall Space Flight centre was dedicated there Sept. 8, 1960.

In the 1950s and 1960s Alabama was deeply involved in the conflict over racial segregation and the Negroes' struggle for civil rights, especially after the 1954 U.S. supreme court's decision that racial segregation in the public schools was unconstitutional. In the spring of 1961, mobs greeted busloads of "freedom riders" sponsored by the Congress of Racial Equality (C.O.R.E.) in Anniston, Birmingham and Montgomery. Gov. John Patterson declared martial law after federal marshals were sent into the state by U.S. Atty. Gen. Robert F. Kennedy.

In Sept. 1963 Gov. George C. Wallace who in his election campaign had promised "to stand in the schoolhouse doorway" to prevent integration, finally yielded to federal authority after attempting to block the admission of Vivian Malone and James A. Hood to the University of Alabama when that institution and various public schools in Birmingham, Mobile and Tuskegee acted under court orders to accept Negro students. Before 1963 the only Negro admitted to a state-supported college designated for white students only had been Autherine Lucy, at the University of Alabama in 1956, but other Negroes had attended certain privately supported colleges in the state.

Running as an avowed stand-in candidate for her husband, Gov. Wallace, who was barred by the state constitution from succeeding himself, Lurleen Wallace won the 1966 Democratic primary nomination for governor and won in the general election.

GOVERNMENT

The constitution of the state dates from 1901, earlier constitutions being those of 1819, 1865, 1868 and 1875. The constitution of 1901 comprises 18 articles and 139 amendments. It contained a suffrage clause that restricted the right to vote to those who could read and write any article of the constitution of the United States and who had been regularly engaged in some lawful employment, business or occupation, trade or calling, for the greater part of the 12 months preceding the time they offered to register, or who had paid taxes on property assessed at $300.

However, by what was called the "grandfather clause" or "permanent roll" those who had served in the army or navy of the United States or of the Confederate states in time of war, their

W. M. MASSEY FROM F.P.G.

VIEW OF BIRMINGHAM THROUGH SPRING FOLIAGE

the same election as the legislators, but unlike legislators is not eligible to succeed himself. The governor, however, is eligible for re-election to nonconsecutive terms. Since the ratification of the constitution, only two governors have actually served two terms: Bibb Graves (1927–31 and 1935–39) and James E. Folsom (1947–51 and 1955–59). The administrative organization of Alabama was streamlined under the leadership of Gov. Frank M. Dixon (1939–43), the culmination of efforts to this end dating back to the administration of Gov. Benjamin M. Miller (1931–35). Judges are chosen by popular election, and the larger burden of litigation falls upon the state circuit courts. The probate judge in each county has administrative and legislative duties as well as judicial functions. The probate judge is often considered the most influential official of an Alabama county.

Since the county is a subdivision of the state, the distinction between state and county government is not always clear either in law or in administrative procedure. The following are usually regarded as holding important county positions: the various county judges, the county engineer, county board of education and superintendent of education, also the sheriff, tax assessor and public health officer.

Alabama cities afford examples of all three of the principal types of city government found in the United States. The mayor-council plan, oldest of the three, is the one most widely used.

Finance and Taxation.—The state's revenue derives from nontax money (13%), federal funds (21%) and state taxes (66%). Annual receipts from all sources amount to more than $600,000,-000. Sales taxes, income taxes (both individual and corporate) and general property taxes are the chief taxes. Approximately 32% of the state's revenues are spent on education, about 25% on highways, nearly 13% on public welfare and slightly more than 6% on health and hospitals. The state's income, after World War II, increased about five times over the prewar figure, but the state's per capita income remained among the lowest in the union, usually about 47th among the states. In the 1960s the state's gross debt stood at about $300,000,000.

POPULATION

The population of Alabama in 1820, a year after it obtained statehood, was 127,901. Its population ranked 20th among the 27 states and territories that then comprised the union, and was classified at 100% rural. The next decade was the period of the most rapid growth in the state's history—the population increased by 142% between 1820 and 1830.

Immediately before the Civil War, in 1860, the state had a population of 964,201. Of this total 435,080 (nearly half) were Negro slaves. It had advanced to the 13th most populous state, and was about 95% rural in character. The next ten years had the slowest population growth in the state's history. In 1870 the population was only 3.4% greater than it had been in 1860.

At the beginning of the 20th century, the state had slipped to

lawful descendants in every degree, and persons of good character who understood "the duties and obligations of citizenship under a republican form of government" were relieved from the operation of this law, provided they registered prior to Dec. 20, 1902. Moreover, the new constitution stated that no person under 45 years of age might vote who had not paid, by Feb. 1 preceding an election, all poll taxes due from him to the state. Constitutional amendments of 1923, 1924 and 1944 exempted veterans of World Wars I and II from the latter provision. Since the various exemptions applied primarily to white citizens only, the effect of the restrictive clauses in the constitution was to prevent most Negroes from voting. Payment of poll or other taxes as a prerequisite for voting in federal elections was abolished by the 24th U.S. constitutional amendment in 1964, and in all elections by the U.S. supreme court in 1966.

The legislature meets biennially in regular session, and in special session when summoned by the governor. Members of the house and senate serve four-year terms, being elected in alternate, even-numbered years. The house of representatives comprises 106 members. In July 1962 Alabama became the first state to be reapportioned by a federal court order; based on the method of equal proportions, each county was given at least one representative with the largest county, Jefferson, receiving 17 (previously 7). The last apportionment had been made by the constitutional convention in 1901. The senate has 35 members, representing 67 counties, and the members are elected from districts comprising from one to three counties. Much of the business of the legislature is transacted by standing committees, of which there are 15 in the house and 30 in the senate.

The governor also serves a four-year term, and is chosen in

Alabama: Places of 5,000 or More Population (1960 Census)*

Place	Population				
	1960	1950	1940	1920	1900
Total state . . .	3,266,740	3,061,743	2,832,961	2,348,174	1,828,697
Albertville . . .	8,250	5,397	3,651	1,666	—
Alexander City . .	13,140	6,430	6,640	2,293	1,061
Andalusia . . .	10,263	9,162	6,886	4,023	551
Anniston . . .	33,657	31,066	25,523	17,734	9,695
Athens . . .	9,330	6,309	4,342	3,323	1,010
Atmore . . .	8,173	5,720	3,200	1,775	—
Attalla . . .	8,257	7,537	4,885	3,462	1,692
Auburn . . .	16,261	12,939	4,652	2,143	1,447
Bay Minette . .	5,197	3,732	1,763	1,092	—
Bessemer . . .	33,054	28,445	22,826	18,674	6,358
Birmingham . .	340,887	326,037	267,583	178,806	38,415
Brewton . . .	6,309	5,146	3,323	2,682	1,382
Chickasaw . . .	10,002	4,920	—	—	—
Clanton . . .	5,683	4,640	3,982	1,411	611
Cullman . . .	10,883	7,523	5,074	2,467	1,255
Decatur . . .	29,217	19,974	16,604	4,752	3,114
Demopolis . . .	7,377	5,004	4,137	2,779	2,606
Dothan . . .	31,440	21,584	17,194	10,034	3,275
Enterprise . . .	11,410	7,288	4,353	3,013	610
Eufaula . . .	8,357	6,906	6,269	4,939	4,532
Fairfield . . .	15,816	13,177	11,703	5,003	—
Florence . . .	31,649	23,879	15,043	10,529	6,478
Fort Payne . . .	7,029	6,226	4,424	2,025	1,037
Gadsden . . .	58,088	55,725	36,975	14,737	4,282
Greenville . . .	6,894	6,781	5,075	3,471	3,162
Guntersville . .	6,592	5,253	4,398	1,909	618
Hartselle . . .	5,000	3,429	2,584	2,009	670
Homewood . . .	20,289	12,866	7,397	—	—
Hueytown . . .	5,997	—	—	—	—
Huntsville . . .	72,365	16,437	13,050	8,018	8,068
Jacksonville . .	5,678	4,751	2,995	2,395	1,176
Jasper . . .	10,799	8,589	6,847	3,246	1,661
Lanett . . .	7,674	7,434	6,141	4,976	2,909
Leeds . . .	6,162	3,306	2,910	1,600	—
Mobile . . .	202,779	129,009	78,720	60,777	38,469
Montgomery . .	134,393	106,525	78,084	43,464	30,346
Mountain Brook .	12,680	8,359	—	—	—
Northport . . .	5,245	3,885	3,187	1,606	424
Opelika . . .	15,678	12,295	8,487	4,960	4,245
Opp . . .	5,535	5,240	3,178	1,556	—
Ozark . . .	9,534	5,238	3,601	2,518	1,570
Phenix City . .	27,630	23,305	15,351	5,432	4,163
Prattville . . .	6,616	4,385	2,664	2,316	1,929
Prichard . . .	47,371	19,014	6,084	—	—
Roanoke . . .	5,288	5,392	4,168	3,841	1,155
Russellville . .	6,628	6,012	3,510	2,269	1,602·
Scottsboro . . .	6,449	4,731	2,834	1,417	1,014
Selma . . .	28,385	22,840	19,834	15,589	8,713
Sheffield . . .	13,491	10,767	7,933	6,682	3,333
Sylacauga . . .	12,857	9,606	6,269	2,141	880
Talladega . . .	17,742	13,134	9,298	6,546	5,056
Tarrant City . .	7,810	7,571	6,833	734	—
Troy . . .	10,234	8,555	7,055	5,696	4,097
Tuscaloosa . . .	63,370	46,396	27,493	11,996	5,094
Tuscumbia . . .	8,994	6,734	5,515	3,855	2,348
West End Anniston	5,485	3,228	—	—	—

*Populations are reported as constituted at date of each census.
Note: Dash indicates place did not exist during reported census, or data not available.

18th in rank of population with a total of 1,828,697 persons by the 1900 census. It was still largely rural in character; 88% of the people were classified as nonurban dwellers. From 1900, the nonwhite population began a slow, but steady decline which continued through the 1960 census. In 1880 the nonwhite population was 47.5% of the total, but by 1960 had declined to 30%. The 1960 population showed a total of 3,266,740 persons. The rural population had declined to 45% of the total at that time. The six standard metropolitan statistical areas existing in 1960 (Birmingham, Mobile, Gadsden, Montgomery, Huntsville and Tuscaloosa) contained, in 1950, 39% of the total population.

By 1960 these metropolitan areas housed 44% of the total population. In 1960 Alabama had a population increase of 204,997 or 6.7% over 1950 compared with an increase for the U.S. of 18.6% during the same period, even though Alabama's birth rate is higher, and its death rate lower, than the nation as a whole. These figures point to migration from the state that is only in part countered by migration into the state. Twenty-one counties increased in population during the ten-year period and 46 counties sustained net losses of population, primarily the result of migration of agricultural workers into urban areas in addition to the migration of population from the state.

In 1960, for the first time in the history of Alabama, more than half of the population of the state was concentrated in ten counties.

The population per square mile in 1960 was 63.3, as compared with 49.6 for the United States as a whole. The 1960 urban population was 1,791,721 or 54.8% of the total, continuing the trend toward increasing urban residence.

EDUCATION

Among the earliest schools in Alabama were the John Pierce school at the boat yard on Lake Tensaw (1799), Washington academy at St. Stephens (1811) and Green academy at Huntsville (1812), all private schools. One of the most celebrated of the ante-bellum schools was the Greene Springs School for Boys (1847–82), founded and operated by Henry Tutwiler.

Altogether Alabama had an extensive system of private schools before any of its counties had a public-school system.

When Alabama became a state in 1819 the legislature provided that funds derived from the sale of the 16th section (640 ac.) of land in each township be allotted for public education, but a number of years passed before public schools actually operated. The first public education was at the college level, when the University of Alabama commenced operating in 1831. The Mobile public-school system was created in 1852, and two years later, through the efforts of A. B. Meek, chairman of the legislature's committee on education, a Public School act was passed which authorized public schools throughout the state. This system grew rapidly between 1854 and 1861 until about one-half of school-age white children were enrolled in schools.

After the Civil War and reconstruction, the constitution of 1875 made provision for public education, despite the state's unfavourable financial condition. Illiteracy decreased from 50.9% in 1880 to 34% in 1900, and by the second half of the 20th century the population was almost entirely literate.

The 1901 constitution made detailed provisions concerning public education. Most important was the provision that school money should be apportioned among the counties according to school population in order to provide school terms in the various counties of equal or nearly equal length. This provision was important because the distribution of children and of taxable wealth was not closely correlated. Equalization was not substantially achieved, however, until the equalization program of 1929, while Bibb Graves was governor.

Other outstanding acts of the 20th century affecting public education were the three mill tax, authorizing counties and school districts to increase local school taxes from one mill to three, the School Budget act, and acts for minimum school program, teachers' tenure and teachers' retirement. In 1938 the state appropriated about 8% of its income for educational purposes, but after World War II, four times as much was being spent.

In the second half of the 20th century Alabama had 14 senior colleges and 7 junior colleges for white students and 8 colleges for Negroes. State-supported senior colleges for white students were: the University of Alabama (1831, Tuscaloosa); Auburn university (formerly Alabama Polytechnic institute, 1872, Auburn); Alabama college (1895, Montevallo); and state teachers' colleges

SLAG POURING FROM A BLAST FURNACE INTO SLAG PIT, LEFT, AT ONE OF BIRMINGHAM'S OLDEST STEEL PLANTS

BY COURTESY OF (ABOVE LEFT) LOUISVILLE AND NASHVILLE RAILROAD, (ABOVE RIGHT) MOBILE CHAMBER OF COMMERCE; PHOTOGRAPH, (BELOW) THIGPEN

(ABOVE LEFT) FREIGHTER UNLOADING IN MOBILE HARBOUR. (ABOVE RIGHT) COURTYARD OF A HOUSE IN MOBILE COUNTY. (BELOW) THE CITY OF MOBILE WITH MOBILE RIVER DELTA AND THE STATE DOCKS IN BACKGROUND

blind at Talladega; hospitals for insane whites and Negroes at Tuscaloosa and one for Negroes at Mount Vernon; and a school for mental defectives at Tuscaloosa. All these institutions are under the management of trustees appointed by the governor.

Penal institutions include 5 prisons, 2 honour camps, about 30 road camps and 3 training schools for youthful offenders.

THE ECONOMY

Agriculture.—Nearly one-fourth of the employed population in Alabama works in agriculture, forestry or fisheries with most of them in agriculture. The comparable figure for the United States as a whole is approximately one-eighth in agriculture, forestry or fisheries. During and after World War II, there were trends in Alabama toward fewer farmers, fewer and larger farms, less total farm acreage, more mechanization, more rural electrification, fewer tenant farmers, less farm debt and more farm income.

Cotton remained the chief money crop, as it had been through most of the years since colonial times. Alabama ranked as the fourth state in the nation's total cotton production. Yet, for various causes, particularly the system of federal government allotments, the state's cotton acreage declined rapidly, especially between the years 1925 and 1947, when cotton acreage in Alabama was cut in half.

at Florence (1872), Jacksonville (1883), Livingston (1883), and Troy (1887).

The state had the following state-supported colleges for Negroes: Alabama Agricultural and Mechanical college (1873, near Huntsville); Alabama State college (1884, Montgomery); and Tuskegee institute (1881, Tuskegee). Tuskegee, supported only in part by state funds, has been well known since the days when Booker T. Washington and George W. Carver worked there for pragmatism in education.

Private senior colleges for white students were: Athens college (1822, Athens, Methodist); Spring Hill (1830, near Mobile, Catholic); Judson (1839, Marion, Baptist); Howard (1842, Birmingham, Baptist); Huntingdon (1854, Montgomery, Methodist); St. Bernard college (1892, Cullman, Catholic); and Birmingham-Southern (1856, Birmingham, Methodist). Junior colleges for white students included the following: Alabama Christian college (1942, Montgomery); Marion Military institute (1887, Marion); Snead college (1892, Boaz, Methodist); and Walker college (1938, Jasper).

Privately owned colleges for Negroes in Alabama were. Talladega college (1867, Talladega); Stillman college (1876, Tuscaloosa, Presbyterian); Selma university (1878, Selma, Baptist); Daniel Payne junior college (1889, Birmingham); and Miles college (1905, Birmingham, Methodist).

HEALTH, WELFARE AND CORRECTION

Alabama's various philanthropic institutions include an institution for white deaf and blind and a school for Negro deaf and

While cotton acreage was reduced from year to year, the acreage of forestry increased, as did diversification of farm production of row crops and livestock. Conversion of former cotton fields into permanent pasture for dairy and beef cattle was marked, particularly in some of the counties located in the Tennessee valley and in the "black belt."

The shift from cotton to cattle represented a full turn in the cycle of history, for cattle raising was the chief agricultural pursuit in Alabama prior to statehood and the growth of the cotton kingdom.

Manufactures.—The growth of manufactures was notable after World War II, although the history of manufactures actually extends into colonial days. In the 18th century manufacturing in Alabama consisted of hand processing of such products as indigo, naval stores and skins and furs. During the first half of the 19th century Alabama manufactures were usually produced on the farm and in small shops with extremely limited facilities of tools and power although some water power was used. Iron manufacturing, as noted previously, began in 1818. Sawmills, gristmills and boat yards were found in the state even earlier.

Before 1850 Alabama had a dozen cotton mills employing more than 700 persons and processing more than 5,000 bales of cotton yearly. In the same year the state had a total of 16 foundries, forges and furnaces. Crude as their methods were, ante-bellum ironmakers more than doubled the value of their raw materials through manufacturing. Owners of all manufacturing plants of Alabama in 1849 numbered 1,026 with a capital investment of $3,450,606; 4,938 persons were employed. The average factory employed five workers and represented an investment of $3,500. By 1860 the U.S. census showed that 56 items were being manufactured in the state. Average annual pay, however, was low. For example, in 1860 the coal miner averaged $344 and the cotton textile worker only $151 yearly.

As late as 1880, flour and gristmills led all factories in the value of their products, but iron products moved into first place during the 1880s. In 1880 and again in 1890 manufactures of lumber and timber ranked in second place in value of products. By 1900 Alabama had about 5,000 factories employing nearly 53,000 persons. The period after 1910 witnessed enormous strides in manufactures as the state succeeded in balancing agriculture with industry.

Of all employed persons, 21.8% worked in factories—a figure which nearly equaled the average for the United States (25.9%). This trend was gradual throughout the period, but accelerated after 1940 when Alabama experienced a faster relative growth of industry than the south as a whole and a faster rate than the nation.

The largest industry in the state by mid-20th century was the manufacture of primary metals. Rated according to value added by manufacture, the 12 leading industries in Alabama were: primary metals; textiles; chemicals; food; pulp and paper; apparel; transportation equipment; rubber and plastics products; fabricated metals; lumber and wood; stone, clay and glass; and printing and publishing. At that time the total value added by manufacture was more than $1,000,000,000 annually, an increase of 50% over the immediate post-World War II figure. With adjustments made for monetary inflation, the increase was nearly 28%.

Minerals.—Iron and coal have played starring roles in the drama of industry in Alabama. During the decade 1880–90 industries based upon iron and coal became dominant, but iron manufacturing began in 1818 when the Cedar Creek furnace started operating in Franklin county. Alabama coal received wide attention for the first time when in 1849, the British geologist Sir Charles Lyell, often called "the father of geology," published his *A Second Visit to the United States of North America*, in which he gave an account of his visit to the Warrior coal field.

In addition to the Warrior, largest of the Alabama coal fields, there are the Coosa field and the Cahaba field. In ante-bellum times coal production was measured by the bushel, but by 1870 Alabama coal production was 13,200 tons.

Alabama's first blast furnace began operating in 1880 and the first steel mill in 1888 and by 1891 the state had 53 blast furnaces and 9 rolling mills. Rapid expansion of the coal, iron and steel business depended upon close proximity in the state of large deposits of iron ore, coal and limestone—the three basic materials for steelmaking. Pig iron reached a record volume of production in Alabama in 1957, with 4,975,000 net tons. Coal production in Alabama reached a peak during 1926 of 21,001,000 net tons.

Measured by value of production, coal and iron account for a considerable part of the mineral wealth of Alabama. Yet the extent and variety of all minerals is noteworthy—coal, iron, clays, stone, limestone, sand, gravel, bauxite, greensand, gold, graphite, copper, barite, asphaltic sandstone, asphaltic limestone, salt, kaolin, fuller's earth, ocher, fluorite, silica (glass sand), lead, arsenic, manganese, lignite, dolomite, corundum, asbestos, marble, natural gas and petroleum.

Some of the Alabama deposits of these minerals are small, inaccessible or for some other reason have failed of commercial exploitation. Others have accounted for much of the wealth of Alabama.

The world's largest known deposit of white marble is found in the vicinity of Sylacauga. Natural gas has been produced in Fayette, Marion and Walker counties. Since 1944, when the first oil well in Alabama commenced producing, more than 1,000 wells have been drilled. Of these only a few have yielded gas in commercial quantities, but several hundred have yielded petroleum.

The oil fields of Alabama are Citronelle (Mobile county); East Gilbertown (Choctaw county); West Gilbertown (Choctaw county); Pollard (Escambia county); and South Carlton (Baldwin and Clarke counties). Mining is the occupation of 1.1% of all employed people in the state.

Transportation.—Alabama has 1,237 mi. of navigable rivers, as follows: Black Warrior-Tombigbee waterway (465 mi.); Tombigbee from Demopolis to the Mississippi boundary (107

BY COURTESY OF (BELOW LEFT) INTERNATIONAL HARVESTER CO.; PHOTOGRAPHS, (ABOVE) PHILIP GENDREAU, (BELOW RIGHT) THIGPEN

(ABOVE) WILSON DAM ON THE TENNESSEE RIVER IN NORTHWEST ALABAMA, COMPLETED 1924. (BELOW LEFT) MECHANICAL COTTON PICKER HARVESTING OPEN-BOLL COTTON IN ALABAMA. (BELOW RIGHT) PAPERMAKING PLANT IN SOUTHERN ALABAMA

mi.); Chattahoochee river (135 mi.); Alabama river (315 mi.); and that portion of the Tennessee river which is in Alabama (200 mi.).

The U.S. government spent millions of dollars on the elimination of obstructions in the rivers and on the improvement of Mobile harbour. Federal, state and city funds were used to improve the facilities of the port of Mobile. During 1920 the first vessel of a fleet of government-owned-and-operated self-propelled barges made its way down the Mississippi river to New Orleans and through the Mississippi sound to Mobile and then up the rivers to Birmingport and Cordova, in the heart of the Warrior coal fields, a system of locks and dams having canalized the Tombigbee and Black Warrior, making the latter navigable deep into the mineral region of the Cumberland plateau.

An act of the legislature at the session of 1923–24 provided for an issue of $10,000,000 of bonds for the Alabama state docks, which have played a dominant role in the increase in foreign commerce through the port of Mobile. All the large railroad systems of the southern states enter Alabama.

There are about 66,000 mi. of highway, of which more than 39,-000 are paved. In 1930, 277,146 motor vehicles were registered; 35 years later the number exceeded 1,600,000 of which almost 300,-000 were trucks.

At the same time, Alabama had more than 100 public and private airports. Among the cities served by one or more airlines are Birmingham, Mobile, Montgomery, Selma, Dothan, Gadsden, Tuscaloosa, Florence, Sheffield, Tuscumbia and Huntsville.

See also references under "Alabama" in the Index.

BIBLIOGRAPHY.—*Bibliographies:* T. M. Owen, *Annual Report of the American Historical Association for 1897* (1898); R. C. Ellison, *Check List of Alabama Imprints: 1807–1870* (1946).
General: Information regarding the resources, climate, population and industries of Alabama may be found in the reports of the U.S. Bureau of the Census; the publications of the U.S. Department of Agriculture and the U.S. Geological Survey; the bulletins of the Alabama Agricultural Experiment Station (1888 *et seq.*); the bulletins and reports of the Alabama Geological Survey; *Alabama Business* and other publications of the Bureau of Business Research of the University of Alabama. *See also* Writers' Program, *Alabama: a Guide to the Deep South* (1941); H. H. Chapman *et al., The Iron and Steel Industries of the South* (1953); M. H. Hawley, *Personal Income in Alabama Counties Since 1939* (1958); S. Berney, *Hand-Book of Alabama* (1892); J. M. Richardson and H. R. Padgett, *Alabama Almanac and Book of Facts* (1955); R. M. Harper, *Resources of Southern Alabama* (1920).
History: T. P. Abernethy, *The Formative Period in Alabama,* 2nd ed. (1965); C. G. Summersell, *Alabama History for Schools,* rev. ed. (1961), *Mobile: History of a Seaport Town* (1949); M. C. McMillan, *Constitutional Development in Alabama, 1798–1901* (1955), *The Alabama Confederate Reader* (1963); W. H. Brantley, *Three Capitals* (1947), *Banking in Alabama 1816–1860* (1961); M. C. Boyd, *Alabama in the Fifties* (1931); J. B. Clark, *Populism in Alabama* (1927); P. A. Brannon, *Milestones Along Alabama's Pathway* (1931); C. S. Davis, *The Cotton Kingdom in Alabama* (1939); J. F. Doster, *Alabama's First Railroad Commission, 1881–1885* (1949); F. L. Owsley, *Plain Folk of the Old South* (1949); W. L. Fleming, *Civil War and Reconstruction in Alabama* (1949); A. J. Going, *Bourbon Democracy in Alabama: 1874–1890* (1951); P. J. Hamilton, *Colonial Mobile* (1897), rev. ed. by Mrs. R. D. H. Cannon (1952); A. B. Moore, *History of Alabama* (1935); T. M. Owen, *History of Alabama and Dictionary of Alabama Biography,* 4 vol. (1921); A. J. Pickett, *A History of Alabama* (1851); J. B. Sellers, *The Prohibition Movement in Alabama, 1702 to 1943* (1943), *Slavery in Alabama* (1950); J. F. Sulzby, Jr., *Historic Alabama Hotels and Resorts* (1960). The *Alabama Official and Statistical Register* gives election returns and other data. The *Alabama Review* quarterly and the *Alabama Historical Quarterly* contain articles on Alabama history.
Government: W. V. Holloway and C. W. Smith, Jr., *Government and Politics in Alabama* (1941); W. Cooper, *Municipal Government and Administration in Alabama* (1940); C. B. Ransone and F. C. Roberts, *Civics for Alabama Schools* (1960).
Current statistics on production, employment, industry, etc., may be obtained from the pertinent state departments; the principal figures are summarized annually in the *Britannica Book of the Year.*

(C. G. SL.)

"ALABAMA" ARBITRATION, a notable example of peaceful settlement of a dispute between the United States and Great Britain, according to the treaty of Washington (1871). The dispute centred on the cruiser "Alabama," built in England and used by the Confederacy as a commerce destroyer during the American Civil War.

With the outbreak of the Civil War in 1861 it became necessary for the leading maritime powers of Europe to define their relations to the conflict. The blockade of the ports and coasts of the Confederacy by the Federal government under its declaration of April 19, 1861, automatically extended belligerent status to the Confederate government, yet the United States protested any foreign action having the same effect. The British government, in protection of its own interests, accorded the same status to the Confederacy through its proclamation of neutrality on May 14. Similar action on the part of other countries followed.

The Confederacy immediately set about building a navy to defeat the Union naval power and to destroy the mercantile marine of the United States. The principal instrument for destroying Union commerce on the high seas was the Confederate cruiser "Alabama," built by the Laird company of Birkenhead under contract with Capt. James D. Bulloch of the Confederate navy. Acting on evidence provided by the U.S. consul at Liverpool, Charles Francis Adams, U.S. minister to Great Britain, requested Earl Russell, the British foreign secretary, either to detain the vessel or to certify to its friendly character in respect of the United States. Subsequent representations to the foreign office, and reference of the question to lesser authorities, such as the commissioners of customs, had no immediate effect, but later, upon receipt of more convincing evidence, the British government issued an order of detention. However, before the order was received by the enforcement officers the "Alabama" set out to sea without clearance and did not return. She proceeded to the Azores, where she received armament and additional seamen from two British ships. Ably commanded by Capt. Raphael Semmes (*q.v.*) of the Confederate navy and superbly equipped, the "Alabama" virtually drove Union ships from the high seas for a period of almost two years until her destruction by the "Kearsarge" off Cherbourg, France, on June 19, 1864.

Angry feeling developed in the United States over the destruction and immobilization of the nation's merchant marine and over the maritime economic advantage which accrued to Britain as a result. As early as Oct. 23, 1863, Adams protested to Earl Russell that the "Alabama" had been built, armed and equipped with "one single criminal intent," with the main portions of the crime planned and executed within the lawful jurisdiction of Great Britain. He asserted that the British government must assume responsibility for damages to U.S. citizens sustained by depredations of the "Alabama" but stated that the United States would submit to any fair and equitable form of conventional arbitration. Earl Russell replied on Oct. 26, disclaiming responsibility for the acts of parties fitting out "a seeming merchant ship" and converting it into a vessel of war after leaving the jurisdiction of British courts. Expressing surprise that the U.S. navy had not captured the "Alabama," he observed that the object of Her Majesty's government was to perform the duties of neutrality fairly and impartially, and at the same time to maintain the spirit of British law and protect the shipbuilding industry. On Aug. 30, 1865, Earl Russell added further fuel to the flames of American feeling by declaring that the two questions involved—(1) the due diligence or good faith and honesty of the British government in maintaining their neutrality and (2) the proper understanding of the law officers of the Foreign Enlistment act in declining to advise detention of the "Alabama" and other ships—could not be put to a foreign government with any regard to the dignity and character of the British crown and nation. He finally agreed to refer to a commission all Civil War claims on which the parties could agree.

After prolonged negotiation between Reverdy Johnson, the new U.S. minister to Britain, and Lord Clarendon, the new British foreign secretary, the Johnson-Clarendon convention was signed, under which four commissioners would settle all outstanding claims where possible, and on irreconcilable questions would utilize an umpire. Sen. Charles Sumner attacked the treaty in a senate speech, charging the absence of any expression of regret by Great Britain, undue haste in negotiations and responsibility to Britain for a prolongation of the war. The treaty was rejected by a vote of 44 to 1.

A negotiating state of mind soon prevailed in both countries.

It was realized that something must be done to settle the disputes growing out of the Civil War, regarding the northeast fisheries and the San Juan water boundary. On Jan. 26, 1871, Sir Edward Thornton, British minister at Washington, suggested to Secretary of State Hamilton Fish that a joint high commission be set up to settle these and any other outstanding controversies between the two nations. The commission began its work in Washington, D.C., on Feb. 27, 1871. The United States was represented by Hamilton Fish and four others. Great Britain was represented by Earl de Grey and Ripon, together with four additional colleagues. On May 8, 1871, the treaty of Washington was signed. It provided for four separate and distinct arbitrations and was the most ambitious arbitral undertaking the world had experienced up to that time.

The principal arbitration, that of the "Alabama Claims," was to be held at Geneva, Switz. Following an unusual procedure, the United States named Charles Francis Adams and Britain named Sir Alexander Cockburn as their arbitrators. At the invitation of the parties, Italy named Count Frederic Sclopis, Switzerland named Jacques Staempfli and Brazil named Viscount D'Itajuba as additional arbitrators. The U.S. agent was J. C. Bancroft Davis and the British agent was Lord Tenterden. Both were supported by an imposing array of counsel.

Upon the insistence of the U.S. commissioners, the negotiators had agreed, in article 6 of the treaty, on three rules which would be the test of neutral duty that would apply to the case. By these rules a neutral government was bound:

First, to use due diligence to prevent the fitting out, arming or equipping, within its jurisdiction, of any vessel which it has reasonable ground to believe is intended to cruise or to carry on war against a power with which it is at peace; and also to use like diligence to prevent the departure from its jurisdiction of any vessel intended to cruise or carry on war as above, such vessel having been specially adapted, in whole or in part, within such jurisdiction to warlike use. (With substitution of "means at its disposal" for "due diligence," this rule was adopted in article 8 of the Hague convention, 1907.)

Second, not to permit or suffer either belligerent to make use of its ports or waters as the base of naval operations against the other, or for the purpose of the renewal or augmentation of military supplies or arms, or the recruitment of men.

Third, to exercise due diligence in its own ports and waters, and, as to all persons within its jurisdiction, to prevent any violation of the foregoing obligations and duties.

The United States, in asking the tribunal to award compensation for damages caused by the acts of the "Alabama" and other Confederate cruisers of British origin, set forth the following categories of claims:

1. The claims for direct losses growing out of the destruction of vessels and their cargoes by the insurgent cruisers.

2. The national expenditures in the pursuit of those cruisers.

3. The loss in the transfer of the American commercial marine to the British flag.

4. The enhanced payments of insurance.

5. The prolongation of the war and the addition of a large sum to the cost of the war and the suppression of the rebellion.

The tribunal rendered its award on Sept. 14, 1872. In regard to the first item, the "direct" losses, the tribunal, voting unanimously in the case of the "Alabama" and with some dissenting votes in the cases of other ships, found Britain legally liable for the direct losses caused by these ships, and awarded the United States $15,500,000, including interest. As to the second category of claims, i.e., that of the national expenditures in pursuit of cruisers, the tribunal decided that they could not properly be distinguished from general expenses of the war conducted by the United States, and by a majority of 3 to 2, denied any compensation to the United States. With respect to the third, fourth and fifth classes of losses, embracing "indirect" claims, Great Britain stoutly denied the jurisdiction of the tribunal on the ground that such claims were barred by the treaty. The United States insisted that the treaty embraced them. This difference, which threatened the success of the tribunal, was resolved by a pre-

liminary declaration by the tribunal that these claims, despite any view of the two governments regarding the competence of that body, did not, under international law, afford a good basis for compensation and should be excluded from consideration. Thus the "Alabama" arbitration was brought to an end.

This case has had a profound effect on the history, practice and procedure of arbitration, and on the progressive development of international law. It gave to the process of arbitration, latent for many years, a new impetus, both in practice and in theoretical discussion. Differences at first regarded as inviolate questions of national honour were eventually submitted to arbitration as ones of international interest and concern. The unusual procedure of including three arbitrators chosen by as many neutral governments contributed to a growing flexibility of arbitration as a process. The rather novel nature of the claims, from a legal standpoint, indicated the wide reach of arbitration to classes of disputes then scarcely deemed justiciable in their nature. The acceptance of the three rules of the treaty of Washington disclosed a readiness to supply the defects of unsettled rules of international law by means of a device legislative in character. The number and variety of private interests affecting a great number of American nationals gave the arbitration a genuine national character. The consummate diplomacy of the members of the joint high commission in planning the labours of a future board of arbitration demonstrated in a striking manner the importance of prior negotiation as an aid to arbitration. The arbitration was a triumph for diplomacy as well as for international law and arbitration.

BIBLIOGRAPHY.—Mountague Bernard, *A Historical Account of the Neutrality of Great Britain During the American Civil War* (1870); Caleb Cushing, *The Treaty of Washington, its Negotiation, Execution, and the Discussion Relating Thereto* (1873); J. C. Bancroft Davis, *Mr. Fish and the Alabama Claims: a Chapter in Diplomatic History* (1893); John Bassett Moore, *History and Digest of the International Arbitrations to Which the United States Has Been a Party*, vol. i, ch. xiv (1898); Thomas Walling Balch, *The Alabama Arbitration* (1900); F. W. Hackett, *Reminiscences of the Geneva Tribunal of Arbitration* (1911); E. D. Adams, *Great Britain and the American Civil War*, 2 vol. (1925). (C. E. M.)

ALABAMA RIVER, in Alabama, U.S., is formed by the Coosa and Tallapoosa rivers about 7 mi. N.E. of the city of Montgomery; its name is derived from a Creek Indian tribe, the Alibamu. The Coosa is navigable for about 200 mi. southward from Rome, Ga., largely within Alabama. Full navigation of the Tallapoosa (268 mi. long and originating in Paulding county, Ga.) is prevented by a 60-ft. fall at Tallassee, northeast of Montgomery.

The Alabama winds westward from Montgomery to the town of Selma and then flows southward. Its width varies from 600 to 900 ft. and its depth from 3 to 7 ft. Its length by steamboat measurement is 420 mi. and by U.S. survey, 315 mi. It drains about 22,600 sq.mi. of the state and is navigable through most of the year. Its chief tributary, the Cahaba (185 mi. long), rises near Birmingham and enters the Alabama at Cahaba, about 17 mi. below Selma; it is joined 44 mi. above Mobile by the Tombigbee river (about 450 mi. long, with a drainage of about 19,500 sq.mi. in Mississippi and Alabama) to form the Mobile and Tensaw rivers which flow into the Gulf of Mexico.

Until about 1900 the Alabama and its related waterways exerted a dominant influence upon economic developments in the state. Mobile and Montgomery became major cities largely because they were on the river. The Alabama is still an important carrier of cotton, cottonseed, fertilizer, cereals, lumber, naval stores, textile goods, iron products and automobiles. (W. T. Jo.)

ALABASTER (ARBLASTIER), **WILLIAM** (1567–1640), English poet, mystic and scholar in Latin and Hebrew, is the author of the Latin tragedy *Roxana* (1597, published 1632), which Dr. Johnson thought the finest Latin writing in England before Milton's *Elegies*. He was born in 1567 at Hadleigh, Suffolk, and matriculated at Trinity college, Cambridge, in 1584. As chaplain to the earl of Essex he accompanied him on the Cadiz expedition of 1596, and in 1597 was converted to Roman Catholicism. He suffered several terms of imprisonment in England on this account, but when visiting Rome in 1609 was denounced to the Inquisition because of his mystical writings. For the next eight years he wavered between Catholicism and Protestantism, finally becoming

Anglican and hence king's chaplain in 1618. In 1627 Alabaster was appointed rector of Little Shelford, Cambridgeshire. He died in April 1640.

Alabaster's unfinished Latin epic, *Elisaesis*, glorifying Elizabeth I, was praised by Spenser in 1591. His many spiritual sonnets and occasional poems in Latin, Greek and Hebrew, only a few of which have been printed, reveal his study of the Kabbala. His mysticism is apparent in the prose works *Apparatus in revelationem Jesu Christi* (1607) and *Ecce Sponsus venit* (1633), as well as in his commentaries on Revelation and the Pentateuch.

See L. I. Guiney and G. Bliss (eds.), *Recusant Poets* (1939); G. M. Story and Helen Gardner (eds.), *Alabaster Sonnets* (1959).

(M. H. D.)

ALABASTER. The alabaster of the ancients was really a marble; the alabaster of modern times is a granular form of the mineral gypsum. On the European continent the centre of the alabaster trade is Florence, where it is extensively used for statuary work and carving of ornamental objects. The best kind is pure white and translucent, but by careful heating in nearly boiling water it can be made nearly opaque, resembling marble. For discussion of the occurrence, composition and uses of alabaster *see* GYPSUM; MARBLE.

ALACA HUYUK, an archaeological site about 20 mi. N.E. of Bogazkoy, the old Hittite capital city of Hattushash, a few miles northwest of the Turkish market town of Alaca. The name "Eyuk," current in older sources, represents a haphazard transliteration of the old Ottoman spelling of *huyuk,* "mound."

The low but extensive mound near Alaca attracted the sporadic attention of archaeologists from the 19th century onward. Part of it was occupied by a modern village, and the only visible monuments were two colossal stone sphinxes forming part of a one-time city gate. After preliminary diggings by Georges Perrot (1861), Ernest Chantre (1863) and Hugo Winckler (1906), the excavations of Makridi Bey in 1907 revealed sections of buildings inside the gateway and a number of sculptures dating from the period of the Hittite empire. Yet the truly significant discoveries were reserved for the systematic explorations begun by the Turkish Historical society in 1935 under the direction of H. Z. Kosay and R. O. Arik. Inside the sphinx gate traces of a large building were discovered, reminiscent of the Hittite temples at Bogazkoy. In soundings undertaken between the houses of the modern village Kosay penetrated beyond the Hittite level to a layer of ashes and debris pointing to the catastrophic end of an earlier settlement.

At and below this level the excavators uncovered between 1935 and 1939 a royal necropolis of 13 tombs dating from the Central Anatolian "Copper Age" shortly after the middle of the 3rd millennium B.C. (*cf.* ASIA MINOR: *Archaeology*). Previously the same period was known from the earlier levels at Alishar Huyuk (*q.v.*), which pointed to a relatively primitive community of farmers and traders. The tombs of Alaca Huyuk, however, provide evidence of unique cultural accomplishment and refinement in their particular topographical and chronological setting.

The small intramural cemetery was located near the centre of the city, wedged in among the town buildings. The interments reflect a succession of occupation levels spanning a number of generations. Several tombs contained the remains of both a man and a woman. The standard type is a shallow rectangular shaft lined with stones, in which the individual body was placed on its side in a contracted position. Weapons, or ornaments and toilet articles, accompanied the man or the woman respectively. Facing the dead were found vessels and household goods, numerous objects, probably used for religious purposes, notably so-called solar disks, and various statuettes and figurines. The tomb pits were covered with wooden ceilings, clay and earth; the location was marked with another stone lining, next to which lay the skeletal remains of animals sacrificed as part of the funeral proceedings.

While the pottery is comparatively primitive in style, the tomb finds (now in the Ankara museum) offer eloquent evidence of the advanced accomplishments of Copper Age metallurgy. Filigree diadems, bracelets, anklets, buckles, pins, handles, bowls, jugs and chalices of gold were found, and sheet gold or gold wire was freely used in ornamentation. Vessels and bands of silver and bowls and statuettes of copper or bronze are freely represented. Alloys were used in mixing metals and incrustation with jade, electrum and diverse precious stones was common. A unique find was a dagger with an iron blade: iron was by far the rarest and most expensive metal of the time and still a rarity a whole millennium later.

The metal "solar disks" and animal statuettes (stag, ox) are frequently fitted to a narrow base obviously designed to be attached to the top of a staff and are hence referred to as "standards." The figurines are generally female "idols" with grotesquely accentuated sexual characteristics, probably early cult images of the typical Anatolian Mother Goddess.

There is nothing to indicate Mesopotamian inspiration or influence in the Alaca culture. While the ethnic identity of its preliterate bearers must remain obscure, it seems most plausible to assign them to the autochthonous pre-Indo-European "Hattic" population. From an archaeological point of view approximately contemporary parallels are available among Heinrich Schliemann's Trojan treasures from Troy II, from the Early Bronze Age at Cyprus and in a find of similar gold, silver and copper objects near Amasya, northeast of Alaca, in 1950.

See H. Z. Kosay, *Les Fouilles d'Alaca Hüyük* (1951); S. H. F. Lloyd, *Early Anatolia* (1956). (J. Pl.)

ALACALUF, almost extinct Indian tribe of Chile found in the islands of Patagonia, chiefly around Ración Sound in the 1960s. Formerly they were much more numerous, and their canoes might be seen southward from the Gulf of Peñas to Brecknock peninsula in Tierra del Fuego, including the Strait of Magellan. Their culture in general closely resembles that of the other canoe-using tribe of Tierra del Fuego, the Yahgan. The use of planked canoes by the Alacaluf has suggested the possibility of culture transference from Polynesia, but the Alacaluf planked canoe is demonstrably a local development.

See M. W. Holgate, "Man and Environment in the South Chilean Islands," *Geographical Journal,* vol. 127 (1961); J. Bird, "The Alacaluf," in J. H. Steward (ed.), *Handbook of South American Indians* (1963). (S. K. L.)

ALACOQUE, SAINT MARGARET MARY (1647–1690), French Visitandine nun and initiator of the modern practices of devotion to the Sacred Heart of Jesus, was born at L'Hautecour, Burgundy, on July 22, 1647. Having been cured of paralysis, as she believed by the Blessed Virgin, she entered the Visitation convent at Paray-le-Monial in 1671 and made her profession of vows in 1672. Leading a life of severe austerity and strict observance of rule, she testified that Christ had revealed to her his heart burning with love for mankind and bade her establish the practices of Holy Hour, communion on the first Friday of the month, and the feast of the Sacred Heart, to be observed on the Friday after the octave of Corpus Christi. Devotion to the Sacred Heart spread rapidly in the Catholic Church, and Margaret Mary, who died on Oct. 17, 1690, was pronounced blessed in 1864 and canonized in 1920. Her feast day is Oct. 17.

BIBLIOGRAPHY.—St. Marguerite Marie Alacoque's writings and autobiography are contained in *Vie et oeuvres par les contemporaines,* 2 vol. (1901); the autobiography was published again at Paray-le-Monial in 1918 and translated into English in 1930. See also E. Bougaud, *Life of St. Margaret Mary Alacoque* (1920); *The Letters of Saint Margaret Mary Alacoque* (1954). (L. Cn.)

ALAGÔAS, a small state in northeastern Brazil, bounded on the east by the Atlantic ocean, north and west by the state of Pernambuco and south and west by the states of Sergipe and Bahia, from which it is separated by the São Francisco river. It has an area of 10,707 sq.mi. The terrain in Alagôas slopes downward from a semibarren plateau through wooded ridges and fertile valleys to a narrow coastal plain. The climate is hot and dry in the interior and humid along the coast. The name of the state is derived from the many lakes (*lagôas*) formed near the coast by beach sands blocking the river outlets. The valleys and slopes are cultivated and produce sugar, cotton, tobacco, Indian corn, rice, manioc, fruit and castor beans. Hides and skins, mangabeira rubber, cabinet woods and rum are exported in moderate amounts. Cattle raising was formerly a prominent industry but has steadily declined in recent years. Manufacturing, which has been insignificant, was expected to expand as a result of the abundant electric power available from the Paulo Afonso hydroelectric project on the São Francisco river between Alagôas and Bahia. The capital, Maceió (pop. [1960] 153,305), is the chief commercial city of the state, and a modest foreign and coastwise trade is carried on through its port (Jaraguá).

Alagôas was a district of Pernambuco until 1817 when it became a captaincy. It became a province of the Portuguese empire in 1823 and a state of the republic in 1889. Transportation and communication links between Alagôas and the rest of Brazil have not expanded greatly under the republic, with the result that the state has not fully kept pace with political and social developments and the material progress achieved in other areas of the northeast. State politics are marked by periodic violence, and the literacy rate (14.7%) is the lowest in Brazil. Pop. (1960) 1,271,062.

(R. E. P.)

ALAIN (real name ÉMILE AUGUSTE CHARTIER) (1868–1951), French philosopher whose work profoundly influenced several generations of readers, was born on March 3, 1868, at Mortagne, Orne, and went to school there before proceeding to Alençon and Paris. Graduating in philosophy, he taught at *lycées* in a number of towns, including Rouen, where he became involved in politics and began contributing his daily *propos*, a short article of 600 words, to a Radical newspaper. The high literary quality of these *propos* soon attracted attention and they were collected and published (1908) in a book which came to be regarded as a classic. Appointed to teach philosophy at the Lycée Henri Quatre, in Paris, Alain became the mentor of most of the teachers of philosophy of the next generation in France. In defiance of public opinion he foretold and denounced World War I; on its outbreak, however, he enlisted in the artillery. Refusing promotion, he spent the whole war in the ranks; and it was in the front line or in battery telephonists' dug-outs that he wrote *Mars, ou la guerre jugée* (pub. 1921; Eng. trans. by D. Mudie and E. Hill, 1930), *Quatre-vingt-un Chapitres sur l'esprit et les passions* (1917) and *Système des beaux-arts* (pub. 1920). Subsequently he resumed his post at the Lycée Henri Quatre. His most important publications over the ensuing years were *Les Idées et les âges* (1927), *Entretiens au bord de la mer* (1931), *Idées* (1932), *Les Dieux* (1934), *Histoire de mes pensées* (1936) and *Les Aventures du coeur* (1945). When age and painful disease made it impossible for him to teach any longer, he retired to a little house in the neighbourhood of Paris, where his disciples could visit him. In 1951 he was awarded the Grand Prix National de Littérature, of which he was the first recipient; this was the only honour that he accepted. He died at Le Vésinet, near Paris, June 2, 1951.

Most contemporary French critics recognize Alain as a great writer, comparing him with his friend Paul Valéry. Like Socrates Alain tried to provoke thought by stimulating and shocking men's minds, not to impose a predigested system. At the same time he was like Descartes in wanting men to be capable both of doubt and of making a choice; and he was like Spinoza in regarding happiness not as the reward of virtue but as virtue itself. We must promise ourselves to be happy, he maintained: it is man, not the physical universe, who is to blame for the sufferings of humanity. Error is human and cannot be eliminated; it can however be transcended, and it is the source of all truth. In *Les Dieux* Alain presents the religions of the world as being not milestones in a horizontal progress (*étapes*) but complementary levels in a vertical construction (*étages*); and he reverently examines each one for the measure of truth that it contains. Similarly, his attitude to individual philosophers is that it is more important to understand their meaning than to refute their arguments. Practising always what he professed, he was indeed a true lover of wisdom, in the classic sense.

See A. Maurois, *Alain* (1949); H. Mondor, *Alain* (1953). (AÉ. M.)

ALAIN DE LILLE (ALANUS DE INSULIS) (*c.* 1128–1202), French theologian and poet, so celebrated for his varied learning that he was known as "the universal doctor," probably was born at Lille in about 1128 and studied and taught at Paris. He lived for some time at Montpellier and later joined the Cistercians, withdrawing to Cîteaux where he died in 1202.

Alain's eclectic scholasticism is both rational and mystical; his allegorical poetry is didactic and moral. In his apologetic works Alain endeavours to prove by reason the tenets of the faith in opposition to the opinions of unbelievers. His main theological treatise, *The Art of the Catholic Faith*, purports to present a rational demonstration of the faith in a mathematical manner; his *Treatise Against Heretics* essays to refute heterodoxy on rational grounds; and his *Maxims of Theology* assume that the principles of the faith are self-evident propositions. Alain is noted in the history of medieval Latin literature for two poems: his *Plaint of Nature*, a clever satire on human vices; and his *Anticlaudianus*, a lengthy allegory on the creation and perfection of the human soul by God and nature, theology and philosophy, the virtues and arts.

BIBLIOGRAPHY.—Alain de Lille's published works are in J. P. Migne, *Patrologia latina*, vol. 210; *see also* M. B. Hauréau, "Mémoire sur la vie et quelques oeuvres d'Alain de Lille," *Mémoires de l'Institut National de France, Académie des Inscriptions et Belles-Lettres*, vol. xxxii, pp. 1–27 (1886); M. Baumgartner, *Die Philosophie des Alanus de Insulis* (1896). (D. D. McG.)

ALAIN-FOURNIER (real name HENRI ALBAN FOURNIER) (1886–1914), French writer whose one novel, *Le Grand Meaulnes*, has become a classic, was born on Oct. 3, 1886. He was brought up in La Chapelle-d'Angillon (Cher), a quiet country village where his parents were schoolteachers, and completed his education at the Lycée Lakanal in Paris; after two years' military training he became first a reporter and then private secretary to a businessman. He was posted missing, presumed killed, after being ambushed on Sept. 22, 1914, during the first battle of the Marne.

Most of his writings were published posthumously; they include his early verse and prose, *Miracles* (1924), and his correspondence with his close friend Jacques Rivière. His fame, however, rests on his one completed novel, *Le Grand Meaulnes* (1913; Eng. trans. *The Lost Domain*, 1959) which was inspired by his own experiences and aspirations. The hero, an idealistic but forceful schoolboy, runs away from his village school and wanders into a children's party in a decrepit country house, where he meets a beautiful girl; the story of his search to rediscover the girl, the house and the mood of wonderment he had known there completes the novel, the outstanding quality of which is its atmosphere of other-worldly nostalgia, evoked against a realistically observed rural background.

See R. Gibson, *The Quest of Alain-Fournier* (1953). (R. D. D. G.)

ALAJUELA, a town in Costa Rica, located on the central plateau at an altitude of 3,141 ft. Its population in 1963 was 19,620. It is on the Inter-American highway and the Costa Rican railway. Alajuela, also known in Spanish colonial times as La Lajuela and Villahermosa, by the late 18th century had a population of only a few hundred people. The town was active in support of independence from Spain in 1821 and five years later suffered from a plot to restore Spanish control over Costa Rica. Alajuela was the capital of Costa Rica for a brief period in the 1830s. It was the home of Juan Santamaría, a Costa Rican soldier and hero of the defense against the invasion by William Walker (*q.v.*) in 1856. Costa Rica's coast-to-coast railway was begun in the 1870s with Alajuela the starting point and centre of much of the construction activity.

Alajuela is the capital of ALAJUELA PROVINCE, which has an area of 3,668 sq.mi. and in 1963 a population of 240,672. Next to San José it is the leading province in Costa Rica in livestock and in industrial and commercial activity. Alajuela produces about one-half of the nation's sugar cane and is a significant producer of coffee and fruits. (T. L. K.)

ALALAKH, an ancient city in the Orontes valley on an old trade route connecting Aleppo with the Mediterranean. This site, in southeastern Turkey northeast of Antioch, is marked by a mound named Atshana, which was excavated by Sir Leonard Woolley between 1936 and 1949. Eighteen main levels of occupation were defined, each accompanied by a distinctive architecture. The place was certainly occupied before 3200 B.C., but there are no buildings that need be dated before *c.* 2100 B.C. Remains of a massive palace with a mud-brick colonnade prove that the township was already rich in the 19th century B.C., and this preceded an even greater structure in level VII known as the palace of Yarim-Lim, a contemporary of Hammurabi of Babylon, of *c.* 1780 B.C. At this time Alalakh was the chief city of the district known as

Mukish and was incorporated within the kingdom of Yamkhad, of which Aleppo was the capital. The layout of the palace has something in common with Cretan architecture, but is in fact Syrian, and anticipates a type of building known as *bit hilani* more than 1,000 years later. Later levels included an important series of temples, houses and military buildings within powerful fortifications.

Even more grandiose was a towered palace in level IV occupied by several successive rulers, one of whom, Idrimi, ruled for 30 years and probably died about 1450 B.C. His magnesite statue with a long inscription records his seven-year exile and his return after coming to terms with the king of Mitanni. Extensive evidence of destruction by fire provides vivid proof of the dangers that beset this township, situated as it was in border country, on the fringes of the Egyptian, Hittite and Mitannian empires. The dominant element in a mixed population was Hurrian; in spite of many murderous raids the town was frequently rebuilt and remained a rich centre until its final destruction by the "Sea peoples" shortly after 1200 B.C. Luxury goods were common; pottery proves close contact with Cyprus and the Aegean. There was a squirearchy known as *Mariannu* who probably provided chariots in time of war, and an educated class of scribes. Inscribed tablets refer to a bazaar in which many different trades were plied. Husbandry was one of the chief sources of wealth. Silver and gold were abundant.

BIBLIOGRAPHY.—C. L. Woolley, *Alalakh, an Account of the Excavations at Tell Atchana in the Hatay, 1937–1949* (1955) and *A Forgotten Kingdom* (1959); Sidney Smith, *The Statue of Idri-mi* (1949); D. J. Wiseman, *The Alalakh Tablets* (1953). (M. E. L. M.)

ALAMANNI (ALEMANNI), a Germanic people first mentioned by Dio Cassius in connection with the Roman attack on them in A.D. 213 under Caracalla. In the following decades their pressure on the Roman provinces became severe, Italy itself being more than once threatened. They occupied the Agri Decumates (*q.v.*) *c.* 260 and maintained pressure on the Romans in eastern Gaul as long as the Western empire existed. Late in the 5th century they expanded into Alsace and northern Switzerland, thus making those regions German speaking. In 495 they were conquered by Clovis and incorporated in the Frankish dominions.

They were originally composed of fragments of several Germanic peoples and remained throughout a loosely knit confederation of tribes (*pagi*)—the Juthungi, the Lentienses, the Bucinobantes and others. These tribes found it difficult to combine, though several of them might put their military forces under the joint command of two leaders for the duration of a campaign; *e.g.*, in 357 when the Romans under Julian defeated them in the battle of Strasbourg. But they had nothing that could be called a central government; a tribe could undertake a campaign on its own initiative, and war between tribes may not have been unknown. The Alamanni remained pagan until the first half of the 8th century. *See* also Index references under "Alamanni" in the Index volume. (E. A. T.)

ALAMEDA, a city of Alameda county, Calif., U.S., located in San Francisco bay on an island 1 mi. wide and 4 mi. long with an elevation of 15 ft. It is separated from Oakland to the east by an estuary crossed by four bridges and an underwater tube. Pop. (1960) 63,855. (For comparative population figures *see* table in CALIFORNIA: *Population.*)

The city is widely known as the site of one of the largest naval air stations in the United States. Established in 1940, the base became a home for the navy's fleet and aircraft squadrons supporting the action in the Pacific ocean during World War II and the Korean war. These defense installations cover about 2,500 ac., with buildings, grounds and repair shops valued at more than $100,000,000. The naval air station employs a staff of approximately 15,000 military and civilian personnel.

During the early Spanish rancho era Alameda was a cattle-grazing region. Following the gold-rush days it became a residential district noted for its favourable climate, vegetable gardens, flowers and long stretches of sandy beach. The town was incorporated in 1854.

After 1900 the business and social life of Alameda was closely related to the entire east-bay metropolitan area which includes Albany, Berkeley, Emeryville, Piedmont, Oakland, San Leandro and Hayward. The city residential districts stand in contrast to the docks, warehouse terminals, shipbuilding ways and industrial plants scattered along the 14 mi. of water front. Manufacturing includes steel fabrication, lumber mills, paper products and food processing. Alameda adopted a council-manager form of government in 1917. (R. M. W.)

ALAMEIN, BATTLE OF: *see* EL ALAMEIN, BATTLE OF.

ALAMGIR I: *see* AURANGZEB.

ALAMGIR II (1699–1759), Mogul emperor from 1754 to 1759, was born in Multan on June 6, 1699, a younger son of the emperor Jahandar Shah (reigned 1712–13). He was placed on the throne by Imad ul-Mulk, the wazir who had deposed Ahmad Shah (*q.v.*). Since his father's murder, Alamgir had been secluded in the fort of Delhi, devoting himself to study and piety. Though he adopted Alamgir I (Aurangzeb, *q.v.*) as his exemplar in the public conduct of business, Alamgir II remained always the puppet of more powerful men. Provoked by Imad ul-Mulk's attempt to reassert control over the Punjab, Ahmad Shah Durrani (*q.v.*) occupied Delhi in Jan. 1757 and confirmed Alamgir as emperor of Hindustan. His withdrawal opened a struggle for the plundered capital between his agent Najib Khan and the Marathas (in alliance with Imad ul-Mulk). The Marathas seized Lahore from Ahmad Shah Durrani's son in April 1758, leading to another Durrani invasion in Oct. 1759. Fearing that Alamgir II would again be captured by the invaders and turned into a tool against him, Imad ul-Mulk on Nov. 29, 1759, had the emperor murdered.

See Sir Jadunath Sarkar, *Fall of the Mughal Empire*, vol. ii, 2nd ed. (1950). (P. H.)

ALAMO, a historic building in San Antonio, Tex., noted as the scene of a heroic defense by a small body of Texas volunteers against a Mexican army in Feb.–March 1836. The building was originally the chapel of the Mission San Antonio de Valero, founded between 1716 and 1718 by Franciscans. Before the end of the century the mission was abandoned and the buildings had fallen into partial ruin. After 1801 the chapel was occupied sporadically by Spanish troops. Apparently it was during this period that the old chapel became popularly known as "the Alamo" from the grove of cottonwood (Sp., *alamo*) in which it stood.

In Dec. 1835, at the opening of the Texas war for independence (*see* TEXAS: *History*), a detachment of Texas volunteers drove a Mexican force from San Antonio and occupied the Alamo. Some Texan leaders, including Sam Houston, counseled the abandonment of San Antonio as impossible to defend with the small body of troops available, but the volunteers at the Alamo refused to retire from their exposed position. On Feb. 23, 1836, a Mexican army, numbering about 4,000 and commanded by Gen. Antonio López de Santa Anna, arrived from south of the Rio Grande and immediately began a siege of the Alamo. The defending force was a small body of men—possibly 187 in all—commanded by Cols. James Bowie and William B. Travis and including the renowned Davy Crockett. For 12 days they held out, but on the morning of March 6 the invaders stormed through a breach in the outer wall of the courtyard and overwhelmed the Texans. Santa Anna had ordered that no prisoners be taken, and the defenders were all slain. The invaders suffered heavy casualties, with the number killed reliably estimated at from 1,000 to 1,600. These casualties and the time lost in reducing the Alamo dislocated Santa Anna's campaign long enough to permit Houston to perfect plans for the defense of Texas. The Alamo became for Texans a symbol of heroic resistance in the cause of freedom.

For many years after 1845 the Alamo was used by the U.S. army for the quartering of troops and the storage of supplies. In 1883 it was purchased by the state of Texas. In 1903 Texas acquired title to the remainder of the old mission grounds. The Alamo and adjacent buildings have been restored and are maintained as a historic site and as a memorial to the heroes of the 1836 siege.

BIBLIOGRAPHY.—Amelia Williams, "A Critical Study of the Siege of the Alamo," *Southwestern Historical Quarterly*, xxxvi–xxxvii (1933–34); J. M. Myers, *The Alamo* (1948); F. C. Chabot, *The Alamo: Altar of Texas Liberty* (1931). (H. W. BY.)

ALAMOGORDO, a city in southern New Mexico's Tularosa

basin, U.S., 80 mi. N.N.E. of El Paso, Tex., seat of Otero county. (For comparative population figures *see* table in NEW MEXICO: *Population.*) The name is from the Spanish and means "the big cottonwood tree." Founded in 1898 by the Southern Pacific railroad, Alamogordo until World War II was economically dependent upon the railroad and ranching, and upon the timber, recreational areas, and orchards and farms of the Sacramento mountains. The New Mexico School for the Visually Handicapped is located there. White Sands National monument, Lincoln National forest, Mescalero Indian reservation and Sacramento Peak observatory are nearby.

The first atomic bomb was exploded July 16, 1945, at the Alamogordo air force base. This base subsequently was converted to the Holloman Air Development centre for testing guided missiles and pilotless aircraft, and for aeromedical and space-biology research. (I. G. C.)

ALANBROOKE, ALAN FRANCIS BROOKE, 1ST VISCOUNT (1883–1963), of Brookeborough, British field marshal, one of the leading figures of World War II, was born at Bagnères de Bigorre, France, of north Irish stock, on July 23, 1883, and educated abroad. After serving in the royal artillery in World War I he became director of military training at the war office (1936–37) and held the antiaircraft and southern commands at home. In World War II, as commander of the 2nd army corps, he rendered outstanding service during the retreat to Dunkerque (Dunkirk) and commanded the reconstituted expeditionary force until the French armistice. In July 1940 Brooke became commander in chief of the home forces, and in Dec. 1941 he succeeded Sir John Dill as chief of the imperial general staff, a post he held until 1946. As chairman of the chiefs of staff committee he represented their views ably and firmly to the prime minister and to the United States and helped to direct Allied strategy. Brooke was also recognized as a brilliant commander in the field: it was his ill-fortune that none of the great overseas commands fell to him. Brooke was made a baron in 1945 and created a viscount in 1946. He died at Hartley Wintney, Hampshire, on June 17, 1963.

See Sir A. Bryant, *The Turn of the Tide* (1957), *Triumph of the West* (1959). (J. R. M. B.)

ÅLAND ISLANDS: *see* AHVENANMAA.

ALANI, a nomadic pastoral people who occupied the steppe region northeast of the Black sea. Their name first appears in Roman literature in the 1st century A.D. Later they frequently raided the Parthian empire and the Caucasian provinces of the Roman empire. Overwhelmed by the Huns c. 370, many fled westward and crossed into Gaul in 406 in company with the Vandals and Suebi. Some of these settled near Orléans and others near Valence, but most crossed to Africa with the Vandals. The official title of the Vandal kings in Africa was "king of the Vandals and Alans." Those Alans who remained under the rule of the Huns are said to be the ancestors of the modern Ossetians in the Caucasus, whose speech belongs to the Iranian group of Indo-European languages.

The Alans are described by Ammianus Marcellinus in the 4th century as a people to whom agriculture and slavery were unknown; they lived in wagons and moved from pasture to pasture with their herds, devoting particular attention to horse breeding. Warfare was their great delight. They had no temples or shrines but worshiped a naked sword stuck in the ground. (E. A. T.)

ALAPAYEVSK, a town of Sverdlovsk *oblast* of the Russian Soviet Federated Socialist Republic, U.S.S.R., is situated on the eastern flank of the Urals, on the Neyva river and on the north-south lateral railway, with a branch westward to Nizhni Tagil. A centre of iron and copper mining, it is one of the oldest metallurgical towns in the Urals, dating from 1703. There is an integrated iron and steel works, and copper smelting and machine building are carried on. There is a hydroelectric plant on the Neyva river. Pop. (1959) 47,103. (R. A. F.)

ALARCÓN, PEDRO ANTONIO DE (1833–1891), Spanish writer famous for his novel *El sombrero de tres picos* (*The Three-Cornered Hat*), was born at Guadix, March 10, 1833. He had achieved a considerable reputation as a journalist and poet when his play *El hijo pródigo* was hissed off the stage in 1857. The

failure exasperated Alarcón so much that he enlisted as a volunteer in the Moroccan campaign of 1859–60. The expedition provided the material for his brilliant *Diario de un testigo de la guerra de África* (1859), a masterpiece in its way as a description of campaigning life. On his return Alarcón served the liberal cause as editor of the periodical *El Látigo.* But in the years 1868–74 he ruined his political reputation by rapid changes of front. His literary reputation steadily increased, however. *El sombrero de tres picos* (1874; Eng. trans. 1918, 1935), a short novel inspired by a popular *canción*, lives for its skilful construction and pointed observation. It is a masterpiece of the *costumbrista* ("regional") manner and a pointer to later things. Manuel de Falla based his ballet of the same title on the story. His major novels are: *El final de Norma* (1855), *El escándalo* (1875), *El niño de la bola* (1880) and *La pródiga* (1882). These all show a picturesque, vivid style, often marred by high-flown rhetoric, characteristic of Spanish romantic writing. Alarcón died at Valdemoro, near Madrid, July 10, 1891. (I. M. G.-LL.)

ALARIC (c. 370–410), chief of the Visigoths from 395 to his death, conqueror of Rome, was born on the island of Peuce at the mouth of the Danube. A nobleman by birth, he entered the Roman empire in 376 with the rest of his people from their former homes in the region now known as Rumania and settled with them in Moesia between the Danube and the Balkan mountains in 382. On the death of the emperor Theodosius I in 395, Alaric, chosen as chief of his people, complaining that the Visigoths had not been paid the agreed subsidies, marched on Constantinople. Diverted by the prefect Rufinus, he turned on Macedonia and Thrace. He was met by Stilicho (q.v.) and a Western Roman army who, however, were rendered powerless by the machinations of Rufinus and the Eastern emperor Arcadius. Alaric and his men turned southward and devastated southern Greece. Thebes was saved but the Piraeus was plundered, and Corinth, Megara, Argos and Sparta were ravaged. In the spring of 397 Stilicho again brought a force to Greece and surrounded the Visigoths in Elis, but for unknown reasons did not force them to surrender. Alaric then plundered Epirus until Arcadius placated him, probably by appointing him *magister militum* (master of the soldiers) in Illyricum. In 401 Alaric appeared west of the Julian Alps and advanced to Aquileia. Stilicho withdrew his troops from the Rhine and from Britain and inflicted a reverse on the Visigoths at Pollentia (Pollenzo) on Easter Sunday, April 6, 402; but he allowed Alaric to leave Italy. In 403 Alaric again crossed the Julian Alps and threatened Verona, where he was defeated by Stilicho but was allowed once again to escape from Italy.

Little is known of him in the years that immediately followed. He intrigued with Stilicho against the Eastern empire, but in 407 obliged the Roman senate to pay him 4,000 lb. of gold. On the murder of Stilicho (Aug. 408) an antibarbarian party took power in Rome and incited the Roman troops to massacre the wives and children of the barbarian soldiers who were serving in the Roman army. These troops thereupon went over to Alaric and substantially increased his military strength. Although he was anxious to keep peace with Rome, his negotiations broke down; he invaded Italy, reached the walls of Rome and cut off the city's food supply. When the senate promised him a large sum of money and assistance in his negotiations with the emperor Honorius, Alaric raised the siege of the city, which had suffered severely from famine. Honorius remaining intransigent, however, Alaric in 409 marched again upon Rome, and again the city suffered from hunger as a result of his blockade. A rival emperor, Priscus Attalus, was set up and gave Alaric an important official position in the Roman service, that of *magister utriusque militiae* (master of both services), but refused to allow Alaric to occupy Africa. Alaric subsequently deposed him but again failed to reach agreement with Honorius. In 410 he laid siege to Rome for the third time. The city gates were treacherously opened to him on Aug. 24 and for three days his men occupied the capital, which had not been captured by a foreign enemy for nearly 800 years. Much wealth was plundered and some buildings were burned. But several stories were afterward told to illustrate the humanity of the Christian Visigoths while inside Rome, and there is no reason to attribute any extensive destruction of the buildings in the city to Alaric's men. When he withdrew from Rome, taking with him as a prisoner the emperor's sister Placidia, he planned to occupy Africa, the granary of Italy. He marched southward to Rhegium (now Reggio di Calabria), but the ships he assembled were wrecked in a storm and the enterprise had to be abandoned. The Visigoths turned northward again, but Alaric died at Consentia (Cosenza) and was buried with many treasures in the bed of the Busentus (Busento) river, where his body might never be found and desecrated. He was succeeded as leader of the Visigoths by his brother-in-law Ataulphus.

The chief event with which Alaric's name is associated, the capture of Rome in 410, was a symbol of one of the great processes of history, the fall of the Western Roman empire; yet few would refer to him as one of the "great men" of history, for in fact his career was a failure. Throughout his time as leader of the Visigoths his aim was to find land within the Roman empire on which his people could settle in security and peace and where he himself would be recognized as an important Roman dignitary. But he never achieved this aim, and all his marches and countermarches in Greece and Italy were ultimately futile. It is impossible to estimate in detail his qualities as a military leader, for no description exists of any of his battles. None of his major battles was a complete success, and his losses were often severe. He penetrated to Rome only when the Roman government had been disorganized by the murder of Stilicho and his followers. Yet in spite of his consistent lack of success his influence over the Visigoths appears to have been immense, for mention is rarely made of dissensions in his camp or of his men deserting to the Romans (though cases are not wholly unknown).

It is also impossible to form a picture of his personality, for the sources of information about him are very meagre and disjointed. But he does not appear to have been a mere rude barbarian. Throughout his career he moved on terms of some familiarity with members of the official aristocracy of the empire, and these Roman officials were able to exercise considerable influence over him in such important matters as the raising of the siege of Ravenna during the campaign of 409 and the deposition of his puppet emperor Attalus. In the opinion of the Gothic historian Jordanes, it was his farsighted policy to bring it about that Romans and Goths should live on such amicable terms that both might be considered to be a single people; and this policy was subsequently taken up by his successor Ataulphus, though it was never fully achieved.

Two anecdotes told about Alaric are perhaps revealing. When advised to withdraw from Italy in 402 he told his warriors that a clear voice had come to him from a grove, saying "Thou shalt penetrate to the city." And when a monk urged him to abandon his designs on Rome in 408, he is said to have replied that he was not acting of his own free will but was forced by some power which incessantly urged him to occupy Rome. He apparently believed that it was his destiny to capture the city. He was an Arian Christian, like the majority of his followers.

See J. B. Bury, *History of the Later Roman Empire*, vol. i (1923); E. Demougeot, *De l'Unité à la division de l'empire romain, 395–410* (1951). (E. A. T.)

ALARIC II (d. 507), king of the Visigoths, succeeded his father Euric on Dec. 28, 484. His dominions comprised Spain (except Galicia), Aquitaine, Languedoc and western Provence. Alaric, like his father, was an Arian Christian, but he mitigated the persecution of Catholics and authorized the Catholic council at Agde in 506. To provide a law code for his Roman subjects he appointed a commission to prepare an abstract of Roman laws and imperial decrees. This code, issued in 506, is generally known as the *Lex Romana Visigothorum* or *Breviary of Alaric* (q.v.).

Alaric tried to maintain his father's treaty with the Franks, but Clovis, the Frankish king, made the Visigoths' Arianism a pretext for war. In 507 the Visigoths were defeated in the battle of the Campus Vogladensis (Vouillé or Vouglé, in Poitou). Alaric is said to have been overtaken in flight and killed by Clovis himself.

ALAS, LEOPOLDO (pseudonym, CLARÍN) (1852–1901), Spanish novelist, an Asturian but born at Zamora, April 25, 1852, became by his periodical articles, sometimes called *paliques* ("chit-

chat"), the most feared and influential literary critic of Spain in the period 1887–1900. Among his friends were Menéndez y Pelayo, Armando Palacio Valdés and Miguel de Unamuno. His enemies were numberless. In two of the greatest novels of the century, *La Regenta* (1884–85) and *Su único hijo* ("An Only Son"; 1890), he transfixed with biting irony and brilliant characterization the intriguing, selfish bourgeois society of a provincial city, especially that of Vetusta (Oviedo), in which he spent his life as a professor of law. In his delightful and often humorous short stories are revealed his love for Asturias, the breadth of his reading and the richness of his personality. His early advocacy of anticlericalism, naturalism and Krausism considerably obscured his fame in Spain.

Alas died at Oviedo on June 13, 1901. (R. F. B.)

ALASEHIR (anc. PHILADELPHIA), a town in the Manisa *il*, Turkey, lies in the valley of the Kuzu Chai (Cogamus) at the foot of the Boz Dag (Tmolus), 83 mi. E. of Izmir (105 mi. by railway). Pop. (1960) 13,924 (urban), 48,680 including villages administered by the town. It is connected by railway with Afyon Karahisar and Izmir. Alasehir is poorly built but, as it stands above the wide fertile Hermus plain, the distant view is imposing. There are small industries and a fair trade. A mineral spring yields a heavily charged water, *eau de vols,* in great demand in Izmir. Tobacco, grapes and fruit are the main agricultural products; the town exports these and imports cereals, especially wheat to meet local demand.

Philadelphia was founded by Attalus II of Pergamum about 150 B.C., became one of the "seven churches" of Asia and was called "Little Athens" because of its festivals and temples. It was subject to frequent earthquakes. Philadelphia was an independent neutral city, under the Latin knights of Rhodes, when taken in 1390 by Sultan Bayezid I after a long resistance, when all other cities of Asia Minor had surrendered. Twelve years later it was captured by Timur, who built a wall with the corpses of his prisoners. (N. Tu.; S. Er.; E. Tu.)

ALASKA, largest state of the United States, occupying the extreme northwestern part of North America and including the adjacent islands. The name "Alaska" is an adaptation of the Eskimo *Alakshak,* meaning "mainland," though much popular belief, going back to the voyages of Captain Cook, gives it the meaning "the great country." Alaska is bounded on the north by the Arctic ocean; on the west by the Arctic ocean, the Bering sea and Bering strait; on the south and southwest by the Gulf of Alaska and the Pacific ocean; and on the east by the Yukon Territory and British Columbia.

The eastern limits of the state follow the U.S.-Canadian boundary along the 141st meridian from the Arctic ocean to within ten marine leagues of the Gulf of Alaska. A narrow strip of coast known as the Panhandle continues southeastward to Cape Muzon in latitude 54°40′ N. and the Portland canal and includes the islands of the Alexander archipelago. The international boundary follows the summit of the coastal mountains or parallels the coastline at a distance of not more than ten marine leagues.

The U.S.-U.S.S.R. boundary, which marks the western extent of Alaska, passes between the eastern and western Diomede Islands in the Bering strait. The two islands are a little over a mile apart. Other Alaskan islands in the Bering sea are St. Lawrence, St. Matthew, Nunivak and the Pribilof Islands.

Forming a southwestern arc from the Alaska peninsula, the Aleutian Islands separate the Bering sea from the Pacific and extend to Attu Island (173° E.–53° N.). The U.S.S.R. boundary passes midway between Attu and Copper Island off Kamchatka. The large Alaskan island, Kodiak, is east of the Alaska peninsula in the Pacific.

Alaska covers 586,400 sq.mi., an area equal to nearly one-fifth that of the rest of the United States. Admitted to the union as the 49th state in 1959, it is sometimes known as "the Last Frontier." The state capital is Juneau (q.v.); the state flower is the forget-me-not, the state tree is the Sitka spruce, the state fish is the king salmon and the state bird is the Alaska willow ptarmigan. Gold stars representing the Big Dipper and Polaris on a field of blue form the state flag.

PHYSICAL GEOGRAPHY

Alaska may be divided into three great regions on the basis of topography, drainage and climate: (1) mountainous southern Alaska; (2) the Interior, a broad area of low relief drained by the Yukon and Kuskokwim rivers; and (3) arctic Alaska, which is separated from the Interior by the Brooks range.

Southern Alaska.—This is a mountainous strip often 100 mi. wide comprising a number of exceedingly rugged ranges, crowned by Mt. McKinley, the highest of North American mountains. The sea-borne visitor approaches southeastern Alaska along the sheltered Inside passage through the evergreen-clad islands of the Alexander archipelago. Proceeding through Icy strait to the Gulf of Alaska, he may glimpse the most heavily glaciated area of Alaska, including the piedmont-type Malaspina and Bering glaciers, each as large as the state of Rhode Island. Along much of the coast, however, the ranges rise to great heights directly from the ocean. Toward the west, the mountains of the Alaska peninsula and the Aleutian Islands are lower and younger, having shown volcanic activity at least 47 times since 1760.

This region is an extension of the Coast range, a section of the great arc of mountains surrounding the Pacific basin and a part of the circumpacific volcanic belt and earthquake zone. Tilted sedimentary deposits of great depth are intermingled with volcanic rocks to form an exceedingly complex geological story. To the effect of repeated folding and uplifting has been added glacial action. Large areas were probably at one time under a continental sheet, and native legend suggests that glaciers may have been much larger within the past 1,000 to 2,000 years.

In consequence of its geological history, southern Alaska has short river valleys and limited amounts of level land. Hence agriculture is largely confined to limited areas around Palmer in the Matanuska valley and around Homer on the Kenai peninsula. A second consequence is the presence of minerals. Gold has been found at a number of places. An extremely rich copper mine was operated at Kennicott. Coal is known in a number of places. Oil has been produced commercially at Katalla and in the Cook inlet area. But because of extensive faulting, rich mineral prospects have not always demonstrated sufficient reserves to sustain commercial operation.

The Interior.—The Interior of Alaska is a broad area between the Alaska range to the south and the Brooks range to the north. It is a land of broad valleys and comparatively low ranges. Its dominant feature is the Yukon river, which rises in Canada and flows northwesterly to join the Porcupine at Fort Yukon (*see also* YUKON RIVER). It then flows southwesterly to the Yukon delta, where, near Russian Mission, it again swings northwest to the Bering sea. At the Canadian boundary a wedge-shaped projection of hills separates the Yukon from its southern tributary, the Tanana. The city of Fairbanks is located in the Tanana valley, the principal agricultural area of the Interior.

The wedge of hills converges near Livengood, broadening out only to be cut by the Yukon river as it tumbles through its narrow confines at Rampart. There the Ray mountains blend with the foothills of the eastern Brooks range, which are drained by the Koyukuk, the Chandalar and other streams whose names have become half forgotten since the gold rush of 1898.

In the southwest, the many-branched Kuskokwim river drains the foothills of the Alaska range, then flows through the Kuskokwim mountains to empty its waters in the great delta areas of the Yukon. Southwest of its upland plateau are a number of smaller rivers draining into Bristol bay.

To the northwest lies the mountainous Seward peninsula, terminating in Cape Prince of Wales at Bering strait. Gold, tin and platinum are among the minerals which have been recovered in commercial quantities from this area.

Arctic Slope.—The Brooks range separates the Yukon valley from the arctic slope. It is an extension of the Rocky mountain system. At the Canadian border it approaches the Arctic ocean, its peaks reaching an elevation of 9,239 ft.; toward Bering strait their elevation decreases to around 3,000 ft. The average width of the range is about 80 mi. The mountains are for the most part rugged and barren. A number of mountain groups compose the range. Anaktuvuk pass in longitude 151° W. is the principal means of access from the Yukon.

North of the Brooks range lies a foothills province which is about 20 mi. wide at the Canadian border and reaches its greatest width, 80 mi., near the Colville river, which flows easterly some distance through the foothills before turning north to the ocean. While the foothills break sharply from the mountains at an elevation of about 4,000 ft., their transition to the coastal plain is at times very gradual.

The arctic coastal plain forms a crescent, the tips of whose horns touch the Canadian border on the east and Cape Beaufort on the west. Its greatest breadth, about 90 mi., is south of Point Barrow. The plain is remarkable for the number of shallow lakes covering its northern portion. During the summer much of the area becomes so swampy as to be impassable. The plain is so flat that hummocks a dozen feet high may be seen at great distances. The coastal waters are shallow, with frequent sand bars and islands paralleling the coast. Occasionally the shore line consists of bluffs, seldom exceeding 25 ft. in height.

About 37,000 sq.mi. of the 76,000 sq.mi. north of the divide constitute the United States naval petroleum reserve number 4. From 1923 to 1926 the U.S. geological survey conducted reconnaissance surveys of the geology and topography of the region. A wartime effort to locate fuel resources was begun in 1944 and continued until 1953. At Umiat an oil field was located. Gas struck near Barrow was piped to that village for fuel. The principal gas discovery was the Gubic field. (*See also* ALEUTIAN ISLANDS; EARTHQUAKE; ARCTIC, THE; BERING SEA AND STRAIT; NORTH AMERICA; CANADA; GLACIER.)

Climate.—Alaska presents wide variations in climate, no error being greater than to assume that all areas are arctic, or that the heaviest glaciation is in the arctic areas.

Southern Alaska has an oceanic climate with no great extremes of temperature, the Japan current bringing both warmth and moisture. The southeast coast has a heavy rainfall, the amount varying sharply within a few miles, due to local factors. Juneau (*q.v.*), with an annual rainfall of about 90 in., is fairly typical. This rainfall is no greater than at Tillamook, Ore., although a greater proportion falls during the summer at Juneau. Juneau airport receives 25 in. less than the city. Ketchikan receives about twice the rainfall of Juneau. The south central coast tends to have less rain and more snow. Anchorage's annual precipitation is 18.6 in.

The great glaciers of Alaska lie principally between Glacier bay and Prince William sound, where the heights of the St. Elias, Wrangell and Chugach mountains, a number of which are 10,000 to 15,000 ft. high, intercept the moisture-laden winds from the Pacific. Other glaciers lie along the Alaska-Canada boundary of

MAC'S FOTO

BUSH PLANE BRINGS A LOAD OF SUPPLIES TO A TRAPPER AT HIS CAMP. RAISED CACHES ARE FOR STORING PELTS

(Left) Rocking for gold on the beach at Bluff City, one of the mining towns of the 1890s gold rush era; (right) prospectors transporting supplies by dog sled in the same period. (Below) Modern gold dredge at Ester near Fairbanks

the vegetable cover will cause pits to form, requiring repeated leveling for farm use or for construction purposes. Special engineering techniques protect buildings and airfield runways from sinking as the thaw progresses. Other problems created are sewage disposal, protection of groundwater supplies from contamination, piping of domestic water and fertilization.

Vegetation.—The Alaskan flora is varied. Wild flowers are alpine in size, colour and profusion. The timber of the Tongass National forest in southeastern Alaska is primarily hemlock. Other common varieties are Sitka spruce (*see* SPRUCE) and cedar. While that area has been described as "northern jungle," the timber of the Chugach National forest around Prince William sound is stunted and of little immediate commercial value. The western timber limit is on Kodiak

southeastern Alaska. Glaciers are reported to cover only 3% of the area of Alaska.

The Aleutian Islands are cool in summer, cold in winter and rainy at all times. Temperatures seldom exceed the range 0° to 70° F. (about −18° to 21° C.). The annual rainfall at Unalaska Island approximates 80 in., with 250 rainy days out of the year. The main plague of the navigator is fog.

The Interior has a continental climate, with an annual rainfall of about 20 in. The mean temperature for January at Fairbanks is comparable to that of Nebraska. Winter temperatures occasionally fall below −70° F. (about −57° C.), while the long hours of summer sunlight may send the temperature above 90° F. (32° C.). Along the Bering sea the tempering influence of the ocean currents practically disappears north of the Pribilof Islands, which are often within the edge of the midwinter ice fields.

The arctic slope is wind swept; the midsummer and early autumn temperatures are relatively mild.

Ice bars shipping from Point Barrow from October to August. On land, however, the spring and late autumn are the best seasons for movement of supplies by aircraft or motor vehicles.

Soils.—Two characteristic conditions of Alaskan soils are glacial gravels and permafrost. Permafrost (*q.v.*) is the condition in which the soil is frozen several feet below the surface throughout the year; it exists throughout the arctic slope and in roughly half the Yukon valley and in isolated spots in southern Alaska. During the summer the surface will thaw, the depth depending on latitude, vegetable cover, orientation to the sun and other factors. Where small bodies of ice have formed, removal of

Island. The Aleutian Islands are almost destitute of trees, although shrubs and berries grow, and grass is often lush and rank.

The woods of the Interior consist largely of spruce, with birch and balsam poplar intermixed. Thickets of alder and willows grow in wet places and on new-made land, while west of the spruce area aspens and large cottonwoods are common. Northward, the timber line follows the southern slope of the mountains from Kotzebue sound to a point eastward of Anaktuvuk pass, where the timber line crosses to the northern slopes.

On the arctic slope the willows shrink to shrubs. Several varieties of grasses are found. Most distinctive is the ubiquitous carpeting of mosses and lichens, varying in colour from the pure white and cream of the reindeer moss, a species of lichen, to the deep green and brown peat moss, all conspicuously spangled in the brief summer with bright flowers, heavy blossoms on stunted stalks.

Animal Life.—Alaska's rich and surprisingly varied animal life has not only been the economic base of Eskimo, Aleut and Tlingit cultures, but has proved the principal economic base of its development under Russia and the United States.

Most universally exploited of its fish have been the salmon, on which all its peoples have depended. Halibut remains a staple. The cod have almost disappeared. King and Dungeness crabs and smaller shellfish are marketed. The sea otter, whose fine pelt became the staple of the Russian-American company, was found all along the southern coast from the Aleutians eastward. After becoming almost extinct, the sea otter is again increasing in numbers. The sea lion, walrus and fur seal are found, the latter breeding on the Pribilof Islands. Big game along the south coast and in the Interior included bear, moose and elk. Great herds of caribou range the arctic slope and are occasionally seen in the Interior. Whale continue to provide food to the Eskimo, as well as commercial fats and proteins to modern whalers. Animals hunted for their fur include several varieties of fox, the sable, ermine, wolverine, mink, land otter, beaver and muskrat.

National Parks and Monuments.—Glacier Bay National monument (*q.v.*) is about 100 mi. N.W. of Juneau. Brought to public notice by the writings of John Muir, it is now accessible by air as well as by sea. It has been the site of many glaciological studies. Mt. McKinley National park (*q.v.*) is accessible from the Alaska railway and from the Alaska highway system via the Denali highway. Mt. McKinley rises to a height of 20,320 ft. The park is also a wildlife preserve. Katmai National monument on the Alaska peninsula was established after the eruption of Mt. Katmai in 1912 was found to have created a host of fumaroles in the Valley of Ten Thousand Smokes (*q.v.*) similar to those of Yellowstone. Although this volcanic activity has decreased sharply, the monument has become a Mecca for sports fishermen. Sitka National monument is a 54-ac. park on the site of the Indian fort destroyed by the Russians in 1804. Its notable totem pole collection came from old Haida (*q.v.*) villages in southern Alaska. Kodiak National Wildlife refuge was established in 1941.

Transportation Routes.—The principal sea routes to Alaska have been from Seattle through the Inside passage to southeastern Alaska ports, or from San Francisco directly to Cook inlet, Prince William sound or the Bering sea. Until 1898 the few bulk commodities that went to the Interior were usually shipped by river steamer up the Yukon. The White Pass and Yukon railroad, following a miners' trail, opened an alternate route through Canadian territory. Two routes to the Interior were opened through Alaskan territory, one from Prince William sound where a trail was developed into the Richardson highway, the other being the Alaska railroad's route from Cook inlet. The Alaska highway begins at Dawson Creek, B.C. It follows the course of the Tanana river. One may cross the mountains north of the Tanana to the Yukon by either the Taylor highway to Eagle, Alaska, or to Dawson, Yukon Territory, or travel the Steese highway to Circle, Alaska. Point Barrow was formerly accessible only by ship during late summer, or by dog sled. Regular air flights have been established to Point Barrow, as well as to Kotzebue.

HISTORY

Russian Period.—At approximately the same time that French fur traders and trappers were paddling up the Great Lakes, Russian traders and trappers were following the rivers of Siberia to the Pacific. Further exploration awaited Peter the Great's commissioning Vitus Jonassen Bering (*q.v.*) to determine whether Siberia and North America were linked. In Aug. 1728 Bering sighted St. Lawrence Island and entered the Arctic ocean, returning without having sighted the American mainland or having definitely proved it to be separated from Siberia.

Though probably sighted in 1732, effective discovery of Alaska, which came to be known as Russian America, and exploration of its southern coast awaited Bering's second voyage in 1741. On July 15 Alexei Chirikov, commanding Bering's second vessel, made a landfall, and on the next day Bering sighted magnificent Mt. St. Elias (18,008 ft.) on the southern coast. Bering's vessel was wrecked on Bering Island (one of the Commander group), where he died. The survivors brought pelts of the sea otter to Petropavlovsk, stimulating a demand which lured fur traders to the new coasts.

During the next six decades a host of traders and hunters purchased or stole peltries from the Aleuts, seized their women, massacred and enslaved them. (*See also* ALEUT; ALEUTIAN ISLANDS.)

Until 1775 no ensign other than the imperial Russian eagle had been seen along the Alaskan coast. However, in that year a tiny Spanish schooner commanded by Juan Francisco Quadra reached the site of Sitka. The British ensign was borne into the Gulf of Alaska by Capt. James Cook in 1778. Cook's landfall at Mt. Edgecumbe approximated Quadra's farthest penetration. Cook

continued westward, explored the inlet given his name, sailed through Bering sea and into the Arctic ocean in search of the northwest passage. On his return he made a three-week stay at Unalaska in the Aleutians, where he shared geographical data with the Russian explorer Gerasim Grigorievich Ismailov. The following year Cook's vessels again attempted the northwest passage. Failing, the vessels put into Canton, China, where the sailors received high prices for the furs they had bartered for trinkets. This casual trading is credited with having established the triangular trade, to the northwest coast for furs then to Canton for tea and Chinese luxuries, in which both British and American shipmasters engaged. While Cook's vessels retraced their path through Bering strait, a second Spanish expedition, commanded by Lieut. Ignacio Arteaga, explored the southeast coast from Prince of Wales Island to Cook inlet.

The fleur-de-lis was seen in 1786 when a French scientific expedition under Jean François de Galaup la Pérouse spent six weeks exploring the vicinity of Lituya bay. This expedition and reported Russian advances alarmed Spain, which renewed its explorations. An expedition under Estévan José Martínez and López de Haro visited the Russian settlements on Kodiak and Unalaska in 1788. Intimations that the Russians were planning to occupy a site on Vancouver Island led the viceroy of Mexico to order establishment of a Spanish settlement at Nootka sound in 1789.

Meanwhile, in 1785 and 1786, Capt. James Hanna had brought a British brig from Canton to trade along the northwest coast. In 1787 eight British vessels appeared, the "Nootka" under Capt. John Meares penetrating Cook inlet and Prince William sound. Although ordered away for infringing on a British company's monopoly, Meares was back at Nootka sound (King George's sound, Vancouver Island) in 1788 with two vessels under Portuguese registry. He put ashore 50 Chinese labourers with instructions to build living quarters and a vessel. On May 6, 1789, Martínez' Spanish squadron reached Nootka sound, expecting to find the Russians established. Instead, Martínez found the Meares settlement. He seized four of Meares's vessels as prizes of war, then released two provisionally and sent two to Mexico as prizes.

Great Britain considered this seizure a cause for war and hastily endeavoured to fit out its fleet. Spain sought and failed to obtain military support from France. After extended negotiations, Spain paid an indemnity, and each nation acknowledged the other's right to navigation of the North Pacific and use of Nootka sound. Of historical significance is the fact that by this act Spain relinquished its previous exclusive claims to the northwest coast. The first United States vessels reached the northwest coast in 1788. They were the "Columbia" under Capt. John Kendrick and the "Lady Washington" under Capt. Robert Gray. They wintered at Nootka sound and were not molested by Martínez. Gray reached China with a cargo of furs in the "Columbia," formerly under Kendrick. These were forerunners of Yankee vessels that traded along the Alaskan coast.

To close the controversy with Spain, the British government sent Capt. George Vancouver (*q.v.*) with two vessels to Nootka sound. He spent the summers of 1792, 1793 and 1794 in surveys along the coast, including the Alexander archipelago. Meanwhile, the settlement established at Kodiak in 1784 was the main centre of Russian activity until the headquarters of the Russian-American company were transferred to New Archangel (Sitka) in 1804. The competition between rival fur interests and the appearance of British and Spanish vessels along the coast led Grigori Shelekhov, one of the leading Siberian merchants, to recommend the formation of a trading monopoly. In 1799 Shelekhov's heirs obtained imperial consent to the creation of the Russian-American company, in which they held about one-third of the shares.

The Russian-American Company.—Before the imperial government had chartered the company, Aleksandr Baranov, Shelekhov's manager at Kodiak, had already moved to secure new fur country by establishing a post at Yakutat. He moved south in 1799, building a fort on Baranof Island. This the Tlingit attacked and burned in 1802. In 1804 Baranov retaliated by bombarding the Sitkan Indians' fortress and rebuilding his post, New Archangel, beside its ruins. There he ruled until 1818.

Under a succession of governors, of whom Baron Ferdinand von Wrangell, Adolph Etolin and Prince Matsoutov deserve mention, New Archangel developed a shipbuilding industry which launched about 25 vessels up to 1860. Its foundry cast not only steam engine parts, but church bells, some of which went to the Spanish California missions. A sawmill and machine shop were established. Nautical charts were engraved and printed. A magnetic observatory was established, which has operated since 1842. An Orthodox seminary existed for a short time.

Attempts to grow cereals in Russian America failed. After Count Nikolai Rezanov made a much-romanticized trip to San Francisco seeking famine relief in 1806, a fort with outlying farms was established in 1811–12 north of San Francisco. In 1841 this unprofitable operation was abandoned. Ft. Ross in California and the ill-starred efforts of Baranov's agent, Yegor Scheffer, to establish Russian influence in the Hawaiian Islands mark the extreme advance of the Russian-American company.

Russian exploration of the Interior dates from 1833, when the mouth of the Yukon was explored and St. Michael's redoubt was founded. In the succeeding decade the lower reaches of the Yukon and Kuskokwim rivers were traced and several posts were founded. From 1842 to 1844 Lieut. Lavrenti Alekseev Zagoskin made extensive explorations on the Koyokuk, Yukon and Kuskokwim. The Hudson's Bay company meanwhile was pressing westward from the Mackenzie watershed. In 1847 Alexander Murray descended the Porcupine to its junction with the Yukon and established Ft. Yukon in Russian territory. While the Interior thus became known, decades elapsed before the Indians opened the passes from the south coast to the whites.

International Conflicts, 1821–67.—Russia's policy was unsuited to its economic means. By a ukase of 1821, other nations were forbidden "the pursuit of commerce, whaling and fishery, and all other industry, within an area extending from Bering Strait south to 51° of north latitude on the American coast." Unfortunately for Russian interests, the colony repeatedly had to depend on the purchase of foreign cargoes for trade goods, and Russian naval forces were seldom present to enforce the order.

Both the U.S. and Great Britain protested against the ukase. After negotiations, Russia and the U.S. signed a treaty in 1824 which defined the southeastern boundary of Russian America as latitude 54° 40′ N., and granted the U.S. trading rights for ten years. The Russo-British treaty of 1825 defined more exactly the common boundary with British North America. Russia also abandoned its claims to sovereignty over the high seas north of 51°.

In 1834 Peter Skene Ogden of the Hudson's Bay company sought to pass up the Stikine river to establish a post in British territory, but was barred by the Russians. The British government presented a bill of damages at St. Petersburg, claiming infraction of the treaty. As a result, an agreement was reached by which Russia leased the mainland strip from Portland canal to Cape Spencer to the Hudson's Bay company. The agreement was in effect from 1839 to 1859.

American whaling vessels had appeared off Russian America about 1820. In 1842 and afterward Governor Etolin urged his government to drive American vessels from the Bering sea, which Russia considered to be enclosed territorial waters. Eventually more than 300 vessels were whaling in the area, of which the majority were American.

The outbreak of the Crimean War in 1854 placed Russia's Pacific colonies in a vulnerable position. A fictitious sale of the Russian-American company to a San Francisco firm was planned. Rumours of the negotiations with U.S. interests led to a pact between the two fur companies protecting the properties of both. This the British and Russian governments unofficially endorsed. The exposed position of Russian America led the imperial government to consider the possibility of a sale to the U.S. Further, a gold rush to British Columbia showed how word of any gold discovery in the Russian possessions would attract hosts of American prospectors. In 1857 the Russian minister to Washington was instructed to hint that Russia might sell its colony. Negotiations were undertaken in 1859, but the American Civil War delayed further consideration of the matter.

In Feb. 1867 the Russian minister to Washington returned to his post with instructions to enter into negotiations. One consideration was the possibility of embroiling Britain with the United States and diverting its attention from the straits at Constantinople. The treaty was completed in haste on March 30, the agreed sale price being $7,200,000. The treaty passed the senate on April 9, but the appropriation did not pass congress until July 1868. (*See* also SEWARD, WILLIAM HENRY.)

Alaskan Government, 1867–1912.—Transfer of control to the United States took place at Sitka on Oct. 18, 1867, and most of the full-blooded Russians departed. Administration of Alaska was placed under the department of war, and a collector of customs was appointed by the department of the treasury. The new American residents of Sitka organized a town council and opened a school. After five years of struggle, both expired.

In 1877 the last soldiers were withdrawn from Alaska to help suppress an Indian uprising in Idaho and administration was transferred to the department of the treasury. The collector of customs remained the sole official, until he, too, departed in 1878. Meanwhile the Indians were constantly becoming more threatening. When repeated appeals for a U.S. warship went unanswered, an appeal was made to the British government at Vancouver, and a ship was dispatched to Sitka. A short time afterward it was relieved by the U.S.S. "Jamestown." Until 1884 Alaska was under the treasury department, with a vessel of the revenue cutter service, a precursor of the coast guard, representing law and order.

With the discovery of gold in Juneau in 1880, a renewed demand came for a genuine government. To the voices of the miners was added that of the Rev. Sheldon Jackson, a pioneer of Protestant missions and later of public schools in Alaska. The Organic act of 1884 provided for a governor, a district court, a marshal and four commissioners who were to be mining registrars as well as perform functions of justices of the peace. Alaska was proclaimed a land district, and $25,000 a year was provided for education.

Between 1897 and 1901 several acts were passed concerning Alaska. Its homestead act was less generous than the act of 1862 applying to the surveyed public domain in the western United States. Civil and criminal codes were provided, judicial districts were created and provision was made for incorporation of towns and establishment of municipal schools. In 1906 Alaska was granted a nonvoting delegate to congress.

With the growth of the conservation movement during Theodore Roosevelt's presidential administration, it was natural that reservations of resources should be made in Alaska. However, by the way in which land laws were applied, economic development was retarded. A scandal arose when it appeared that certain coal-mining claims, supposedly granted to private individuals, were actually held by the Guggenheim-Morgan copper-mining syndicate. This resulted in a notable controversy between Richard A. Ballinger, secretary of the interior, and Gifford Pinchot, chief forester.

In 1911 bills were introduced into congress to create a territorial legislature. After 16 months of argument, the Organic act of 1912 was passed. This created a legislature that was more restricted than earlier U.S. territorial legislatures, especially in taxing and licensing powers.

Economic Development, 1867–95.—Speculators flocked from the United States to Sitka with the transfer of sovereignty. A San Francisco firm bought the warehouses and much of the trading stock at Sitka. A New London whaling firm bought the salt-houses and buildings on the Pribilof Islands, but found the San Franciscans and another firm already entrenched on the islands. These three drove off all other interests until, in 1870, congress authorized leasing of the sealing concession. The San Francisco interests, now called the Alaska Commercial company, obtained a 20-year lease. This company built a number of trading posts, had lobbyists in Washington and long dominated the economic and political life of the territory. However, when the lease came up for renewal in 1890, it was granted to the North American Commercial company. Upon expiration of the second lease the U.S. government undertook direct management of the seal islands.

The first known prospectors on the Alaskan Yukon were Arthur

Harper and Leroy McQuesten, who entered the territory in 1873. All gold discoveries, however, were in Canadian territory up to 1886 when a strike on Fortymile creek just within U.S. territory led to a small stampede. Meanwhile, the U.S. army detailed Lieut. Frederick Schwatka for an exploration of the Yukon in 1883. Reaching the Yukon from Lynn canal, he descended the river to its mouth. In 1885 Lieut. H. T. Allen reached the Yukon from Prince William sound via the Copper river.

Economic Development, 1896–1940.—By 1896 gold production in the Alaskan Yukon had reached about $700,000 a year. Then in Aug. 1896 gold was discovered on the Klondike in Yukon Territory. It was not until 1898 that miners reached the area in substantial numbers or that the richness of the mines was fully demonstrated. The record known pan of gold contained $212. Mining camps sprang up in the territory, notably at Dawson, while impatient miners filled Skagway and St. Michael, Alaska, on their way to the Interior. Northwest mounted police estimates indicate that no more than 4,000 miners were on the Klondike at any one time, although popular estimates of the numbers in the camps have run as high as 40,000. From 1897 to 1900 over $50,000,000 in gold was mined in the Klondike. The White Pass and Yukon railway was begun in midsummer 1898 and completed in 1900, eliminating the principal hazards of the trail.

The Nome gold rush followed hard on the heels of the Klondike excitement. Prospectors discovered gold on Anvil creek in 1898. In 1899 "claim jumpers," a ruthless element that sought to drive off many of the original prospectors, caused mounting tension at Nome. Discovery of gold in the beach sands, which none could claim but all could work, relieved the tension.

In 1900, when 18,000 people were estimated to be in the Nome (q.v.) area, Arthur H. Noyes arrived with an appointment as U.S. district judge, accompanied by his friend and accomplice, Alexander McKenzie. The conflicting mining claims provided Noyes with the opportunity to appoint McKenzie receiver and operator of the disputed properties. The two men defied a circuit court order to make restitution of all properties. Only in 1901 was Noyes finally removed from office. About $5,000,000 was mined annually from 1900 to 1906; in 1907 production reached $7,500,000. Thereafter large investments in dredges became increasingly necessary. Mining activity in the Nome area continued on a reduced scale for over half a century.

The year 1898 likewise saw the discovery of rich copper ore on the Copper river. Four mines were worked over a period of four decades, the last one closing in 1938. The Kennecott Copper company built the port of Cordova (q.v.), constructed a railway and acquired control of the Alaska Steamship company.

Several railway lines were begun in Alaska around the turn of the century. None succeeded in joining the southern coast to the Interior until in 1914 the congress authorized the construction of such a railroad. The rights and properties of the Alaska Central from Seward (q.v.) northward and the Tanana Valley railway were acquired. The port of Anchorage was built as a construction base. In 1923 the line was completed to Nenana. It was extended to Fairbanks a year later.

The 1920s were marked by the development of aviation in Alaska. With the most rudimentary aids, Alaska's "bush pilots" carried men and materials throughout the territory. Where roads were lacking, air transport opened a new era in communications. Radio eliminated the isolation of remote communities and reduced dependence on the mail carrier and his boat or dog sled.

The decade of the 1930s saw a new generation seeking the Alaskan frontier. Men who had lost jobs or businesses at home through the economic depression decided to try their luck in the fisheries and the mines. In 1935 the Federal Emergency Relief administration colonized 200 families in the Matanuska valley, a project which received much publicity but which failed to start a northwestward migration. Branches of various federal welfare agencies were established in Alaska during the decade. On the brink of World War II, Alaska had a population of 73,000, half of whom were natives. It was a frontier area showing steady but unspectacular growth.

Diplomacy Involving Alaska.—The Russo-British treaty of 1825 had provided that the boundary between Russian America and British North America should be the crest of the mountains, except where the crest lay more than ten marine leagues from the coast, in which case the line should run at that distance. In 1898, as miners were rushing through Skagway (q.v.) to the Klondike, Canada claimed that the boundary should be measured from the tips of the promontories rather than from the windings of the coast. In 1903 a convention was signed providing for arbitration by a board of six impartial jurists. After several months, a line was drawn recognizing the principle of the U.S. contention. The line followed the crest of the mountains for the most part, but the ports on Lynn canal were retained by the U.S.

Fur seals caused extended controversy between Canada and the U.S. These marine animals range widely over the North Pacific, but annually return to breed on the Pribilofs, the Russian Commander Islands and a Japanese island. On land it is possible to

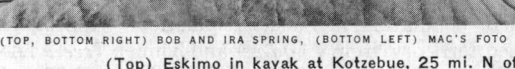

(TOP, BOTTOM RIGHT) BOB AND IRA SPRING, (BOTTOM LEFT) MAC'S FOTO

(Top) Eskimo in kayak at Kotzebue, 25 mi. N of Arctic Circle. (Bottom left) Eskimo walrus hunter's umiak is made of skin and powered by an outboard motor mounted in a well inside the boat. (Bottom right) An Indian artist using a handmade adz to carve a totem pole at Wrangell

BOB AND IRA SPRING

RAILROAD YARDS AT FAIRBANKS, ALONG THE CHENA RIVER

select the young males for their skins without reducing the breeding stock. On the sea, pelagic sealers must kill indiscriminately, losing up to half those killed, and also losing a pup and an unborn seal each time a female is destroyed. In 1886 the U.S. government ordered a revenue cutter to seize all vessels found sealing in the Bering sea. Three Canadian ships were seized and condemned. In 1887 six U.S. and six Canadian sealers were seized. To Canadian protests, the U.S. replied that the Bering sea had been a mare clausum, that is, a closed sea under the dominion of the state, under the Russians, and the U.S. had succeeded to the Russian rights.

An arbitration tribunal in 1893 sustained the Canadian claims and assessed $473,151 damages against the U.S. Only in 1911, when the seal herd had been reduced to about 125,000 from perhaps 3,000,000, did the U.S., Canada and Japan give effective protection to the seals under the North Pacific sealing convention. In 1941 Japan withdrew from the agreement, claiming that the seals were damaging its fisheries. A temporary agreement was arranged between the U.S. and Canada. In 1956 representatives of Canada, the U.S., Japan and the Soviet Union worked out a new convention.

The U.S. and Canada likewise found their interests in conflict over fisheries. A landmark was the establishment of a closed season under the North Pacific halibut treaty of 1923. During the 1930s Japanese boats fishing offshore produced several instances of violence. In 1954 the three nations organized the International North Pacific Fisheries commission as a permanent body sponsoring fisheries research and regulation. A sharp increase in the Japanese salmon catch along the Aleutians in 1957, with a decrease in the Alaskan salmon catch, created a serious problem of redefining fisheries rights and regulating fishing methods.

Impact of World War II.—From the turn of the century to 1940 mining and fisheries contributed about equally to Alaska's wealth. A new and potent force in its development entered in 1941 when the U.S. government began to make Alaska the northwestern bastion of North America's defenses. Kodiak Island became the site of Alaska's principal naval base. A major air base and fort were established outside Anchorage. Ladd field, later converted to Fort Wainwright, was established at Fairbanks on the air supply route to Siberia. Many secondary airfields were built and the communications network was strengthened. Construction of the Alaska highway provided an inland supply route, should control of the sea routes be lost to the enemy. The outbreak of war in Korea in 1950 produced a second military construction boom which stimulated Alaska's industries. This time many military personnel brought their families, thus increasing the civilian population.

Statehood.—Although Alaska was an organized territory from 1912 to 1958, it at no time received the full measure of powers that had been granted to older continental territories. Amend-

ments to the Organic act were proposed at every session of congress for 42 years, but only six were adopted.

The first bill for Alaskan statehood was introduced in 1916, when it had already appeared that territorial development was hampered by congressional unwillingness to give adequate consideration to Alaska's problems. Efforts to strengthen the territorial government took precedence, however, until 1943, when a statehood bill was again introduced in congress.

The statehood issue was debated extensively in congress during 1950. It was not allowed to die until statehood had been granted in 1958. Meanwhile, in 1956, a constitutional convention met on call of the territorial legislature. The draft constitution was approved by popular vote on April 24, 1956 (see *Government*, below). Following Tennessee's precedent, two senators and a representative were elected and appeared at Washington, but congress did not act in time for them to be seated. Proponents of statehood claimed that the development of Alaska had too long awaited local control of its resources. Arguments against statehood centred on possible increases in Alaska's taxes and loss of federal subsidies. Pres. Dwight D. Eisenhower signed the Alaska Statehood act on July 7, 1958. The required referendum approved the constitution and terms of admission 5 to 1. On Jan. 3, 1959, the president formally announced the admission of Alaska as the 49th state. After statehood was achieved the petroleum industry led Alaska's industrial advancement (see *The Economy* below). Final implementation of the state constitution was achieved in 1961 by a general law permitting the establishment of a borough form of local government, analogous with county government in most of the states.

On March 27, 1964, the state was struck by a major earthquake, ranked by some observers as more severe than the San Francisco earthquake of 1906 and among the largest ever recorded. Damage was extensive, amounting to hundreds of millions of dollars. The fishing industry was especially hard hit. The epicentre of the quake was placed by the U.S. geological survey at 61.1° N. and 147.7° W., near the shore of Prince William sound about 100 mi. E. of Anchorage, between Anchorage and Valdez. Damage was severe at Anchorage; much of the downtown district was destroyed; water, gas, sewer and electric lines were broken; and streets and airport runways were crumpled. Much of the damage at Anchorage resulted from consolidation of the soil which was a loose saturated glacial till. Seward, Valdez and Kodiak, on Kodiak Island, also suffered severe damage, especially from the tsunamis, or seismic waves, generated by the earthquake which wrecked docks, canneries and other waterfront properties; at Seward, fires fed by ruptured petroleum storage tanks added to the destruction. Tsunamis wrecked coastal areas in Canada, Oregon and California and reached Hawaii, Midway and Japan. The earthquake in Alaska also produced "in resonance" waves along the coast of the Gulf of Mexico. Property damage in Alaska amounted to millions of dollars. State and federal funds aided in reconstruction.

The centennial of the Alaska purchase was marked by statewide observances in 1967.

THE PEOPLE

Alaska's native races have been a constant and colourful element in its population. Approximately half have been Tlingit, Haida (*qq.v.*) and Tinneh (*see* ATHAPASKAN) Indians, the balance being Eskimos and Aleuts. The Aleuts declined sharply in numbers during the Russian occupation. Prior to World War II the Scandinavian element was conspicuous among the whites. A sprinkling of Russian names occurred. During and after World War II a Negro element was added to the population.

The Indians.—*The Tlingit.*—This tribe predominates along the southeastern coast. Their territory extends from Portland canal to Controller bay. A few Haidas dwell on Prince of Wales Island. A group of Tsimshians migrated to Metlakatla from British Columbia in 1887 with the Rev. William Duncan.

The Tlingit are the tallest of the coastal Indians. They are broadheaded, and may exhibit the Mongolian eye fold. Four clans and fourteen geographical divisions of the tribe are recognized.

All three tribes belong to the northwest coast cultural complex, based economically on fisheries. The relative abundance and seasonal appearance of the catch left time for cultivation of the arts. Wood carving is the predominant artistic medium of the culture. Basketry also plays an important role. Best known of the art objects are the totem poles. Stylized representations of the bear, wolf, beaver, killer whale, sea otter, salmon, raven and eagle form much of the art.

The Tinneh.—These Indians of the Yukon, also known as Dene, speak an Athabascan language. Their territory extends from the Mackenzie watershed to the Yukon delta, with a branch at Cook inlet and Copper river.

The Alaskan branch of the family has assimilated many of the elements of Eskimo culture. The tribes are without clans and have little cohesiveness.

Small birchbark canoes were used for transportation in summer, while dogs were depended on in winter. Dried salmon constituted the staple food, except for one group that depended on hunting Christian missions were in contact with most of the Tinneh before the close of the 19th century. The modern Tinneh divide their time between the fishing and hunting of their fathers and the construction gangs and other pursuits of the whites. (*See* also INDIANS, NORTHWEST COAST.)

Eskimos and Aleuts.—The Eskimos inhabit the coasts of the Arctic ocean, Bering sea and the Gulf of Alaska, villages having existed as far east as Prince William sound. The Aleutian Islands and the south side of the Alaska peninsula are the home of the Aleuts, the first of the native peoples to come under Russian domination.

The similarities in language, physical type and culture between the Aleuts and Eskimos are more striking than their differences. The Eskimo and Aleut tongues are related. Both groups are light yellowish-brown in colour; the hair is straight and black, the face broad, cheekbones high, the nose flat, eyes black and beards scanty, resembling north Asians. Blood-type tests indicate kinship between the Eskimos and Aleuts, although the parent stocks probably diverged centuries ago.

Archaeologists distinguish several layers of culture, both on the Aleutian Islands and around Bering sea. Radiocarbon dating indicates that the oldest known Aleutian culture existed on Anangula Island around 8,000 B.P. (Before Present). The Old Bering Sea Eskimo culture has been dated around 300 B.C. Archaeological and ethnological evidence relates these peoples to a Mesolithic, or Middle Stone Age, Lake Baikal culture of Siberia.

The Eskimo huts and Aleut barabara were crude sod houses with driftwood timbers supporting the roof. By mid-20th century these had been almost entirely replaced by small frame houses. The summer tupek of skins had given way to the canvas tent. Fishing and hunting of sea mammals—the seal, walrus, sea lion and whale—formed the basis of Eskimo and Aleut economy. A few inland Eskimos relied on the native caribou. Berries and roots formed a supplement to the flesh diet. Kayaks were used for the hunt. Umiaks, large open boats made of skins, were used for transport. Both have largely given way to the motorboat.

The Eskimos are noted for their manual dexterity. Their ivory carving is justly famous. Basketry is the most distinctive of the Aleut native crafts, Attu baskets being particularly prized. Aleuts and Eskimos have long been employed in commercial fisheries. Petroleum prospecting and military construction in the Alaskan arctic during the 1940s and later brought unaccustomed wealth to many Eskimo communities.

Reindeer, introduced into northwestern Alaska during the 1890s, once numbered 250,000 head. Eskimo herders were trained and a commercial outlet developed. A federal policy decision forced the commercial outlet to close in 1939, destroying the industry. By 1950 the herds numbered less than 30,000 head. (*See* also ALEUT; ESKIMO.)

Social Welfare.—The Alaska native service of the bureau of Indian affairs, a branch of the U.S. department of the interior, for long was responsible for the education, health and welfare of the natives. Despite schools in many of the villages, the educational level of the natives is about the fourth grade. Natives attend municipal high schools when available; for those from the villages there are boarding facilities at the federal Mt. Edgecumbe vocational boarding school and the Presbyterian-supported Sheldon Jackson high school and junior college, both at Sitka. In the 1950s the territorial government began taking over operation of the native service schools.

The hospitals were transferred to the U.S. public health service in 1955.

POPULATION

The federal census of 1960 showed a total population of 226,167 persons. At the time Alaska was admitted to statehood, it was estimated that there were about 211,000 persons, of whom 171,000 were whites. Natives numbered about 35,000, while the remaining 5,000 were mainly Negro and Filipino. Over half the total were in the age bracket 20–44, as against one-third in the U.S. as a whole.

When ceded to the U.S. in 1867, Alaska's population was estimated at 30,000, of whom no more than 1,000 were whites. The census of 1880 (unreliable) reported 33,426. Gold strikes on the Yukon and Klondike brought the total to 63,592 in 1900. During the next decade the peak was passed. By 1920 the total had fallen to 55,036. In 1939, 72,524 were reported. Nonwhites numbered 33,354; native-born whites, 30,384; foreign-born whites, 8,786. Of these, 42% were born in Norway and Sweden. The wartime peak of 1943 consisted of 75,000 civilians and 150,000 military personnel.

As a frontier area, Alaska has had a surplus of males. In 1910 there were five white men to every white woman. In 1950 the ratio was still 2 to 1; by 1960 it was 1.32 to 1.

Although only two Alaskan cities have a population (1960 census) of over 10,000, most communities serve a considerable trad-

LOGS BEING BROUGHT UP FROM THE WATER TO A SAWMILL AT JUNEAU

Alaska: Places of 5,000 or More Population (1960 Census)*

Place	Population				
	1960	1950	1939	1920	1900
Total state	226,167	128,643	72,524	55,036	63,592
Anchorage	44,237	11,254	3,495	1,856	—
Fairbanks	13,311	5,771	3,455	1,155	—
Juneau	6,797	5,956	5,729	3,058	1,864
Ketchikan	6,483	5,305	4,695	2,458	459
Spenard	9,074	2,108			

*Populations are reported as constituted at date of each census.
Note: Dash indicates place did not exist during reported census, or data not available.

ing area and their commercial facilities and social activities make them more cosmopolitan than their size suggests. *See* also separate articles on principal cities, as ANCHORAGE; JUNEAU; etc.

GOVERNMENT

Constitution.—The constitution of Alaska was drawn up by a convention which completed its work on Feb. 5, 1956. It was subsequently approved by a vote of the people and submitted to the U.S. congress for its approval. The document which sets the minimum voting age at 19 years, is a model for brevity, for a modern restatement of the Bill of Rights and for its creation of strong legislative, executive and judicial branches.

The house of representatives consists of 40 members elected from 19 districts for two-year terms. The senate consists of 20 members elected from 11 districts for four-year terms, with one-half of the senate membership elected every two years. The constitution provides for reapportionment and redistricting of both houses after each decennial census on the basis of the recommendations of an advisory board to the governor. The house was reapportioned on the basis of population in 1961 and both houses were reapportioned on the basis of population, effective 1966.

The governor and secretary of state are the two constitutional executive officers, all others being created by statute. A single vote cast for the two assures their being of the same party. The governor has broad powers of appointment and assignment of functions among the executive departments. He may veto any bill, and strike out or reduce any item in an appropriation bill.

The constitution vests details of administration in not more than 20 departments, with minor boards and regulatory bodies in addition. When the constitution became effective 16 major departments were in existence. Fiscal control rested with the department of finance. It prepared the budget, maintained central accounts, purchased all supplies, examined all claims, administered much state property, could reduce appropriations if revenues were insufficient to meet the budget, filed records of all corporations authorized to do business in Alaska and certified declarations of candidacy for state office.

The court system under the territorial government had consisted of a U.S. district court of four divisions which heard cases arising under both federal and territorial law. Appeals lay with the U.S. circuit court in San Francisco, and thence with the U.S. supreme court. The district court for the territory of Alaska, with its four divisions, was abolished and a single federal district court for the state of Alaska was created with provision for holding court at Anchorage, Fairbanks, Juneau and Nome. The Alaska constitution created a supreme court with a minimum of three justices. A superior court bench of five judges, increased by the first legislature to eight judges, later increased to nine judges, in four districts, was established as the trial court of general jurisdiction. Power to create lower courts was given to the legislature, which established a system of district and deputy magistrates. A judicial council with the chief justice as chairman was provided to lay down rules for all courts and to study the improvement of court administration.

Public Finance.—The fiscal system of Alaska underwent a pronounced change at the 1949 legislative session. Repeal by congress of the licence statutes of 1899 and 1900, under which the federal government pre-empted the licensing of certain occupations and industries, enabled the legislature to establish a new revenue structure. This included an income tax on persons and corporations, a business licence tax and taxes on the value of canned salmon, raw fish, fish traps, motor fuel, tobacco, fishermen's licences, automobile and drivers' licences and a general property tax. The former liquor taxes and head tax for schools were retained.

Revenues conferred upon the state of Alaska by the federal government under the admitting act included: 70% of the net proceeds of the sale of sealskins and sea otter skins; 5% of the net proceeds of the sale of federal public lands in Alaska; monies allocated to the territory for wildlife restoration. A substantial increase in federal funds for highway construction was realized after achievement of statehood.

Principal Federal Agencies.—From the days when a collector of customs, a small army force and, later, a warship represented U.S. authority, federal agencies have profoundly influenced Alaskan life. The geological survey has carried out detailed explorations and furnished technical advice to miners. The bureau of mines has been particularly interested in Alaska's coal resources. State and federal agencies serve all of the state's citizens; the bureau of Indian affairs, however, continues to exercise an important role in providing for the education, health and welfare of a substantial share of the population. The department of agriculture has had control over two huge national forests, and has furnished funds for agricultural research. The bureau of fisheries and the fish and wildlife service have regulated one of Alaska's greatest resources. During World War II policy affecting all phases of Alaskan life was made by the war, navy and defense departments.

Economic Research.—In 1945 the Alaska Resource Development board was created. The board, discontinued when Alaska became a state (1959), was composed of the governor, the president of the University of Alaska and the heads of the departments of fish and game, mines, highways and public works, aviation, agriculture, and lands. Its publications furnished economic and statistical data needed by settlers and investors. The Alaska Development corporation was established by the legislature in 1962.

EDUCATION AND WELFARE

When Alaska became a state, approximately 21,000 pupils attended 28 district schools; 5,800 pupils were in attendance at federally financed and territorially administered military base schools;

BOB AND IRA SPRING

HOMESTEAD AT HOMER ON KENAI PENINSULA

3,000 were in 68 rural territorial schools. Alaska native service day schools enrolled about 3,700, while about 750 were at Mt. Edgecumbe secondary and vocational boarding school at Sitka. About 1,200 were in other public and private schools. With statehood, the public schools were placed under borough control. Enrollments in the 1960s exceeded 60,000.

The University of Alaska, near Fairbanks, was founded in 1917 as a land-grant college and began instruction in 1922. Under the Community College Enabling act of 1953 the university cooperates with qualified high school districts in organizing community colleges of junior college level, which offer credits for transfer to the university as well as terminal and semiprofessional courses. Public community colleges organized under this act include Anchorage, 1954; Juneau-Douglas at Juneau, 1956; Ketchikan, 1954; Palmer, 1958; and Sitka, 1962. Sheldon Jackson junior college at Sitka is a Presbyterian institution; Alaska Methodist university at Anchorage was chartered in 1957 and began instruction in 1960.

The department of public welfare administers old-age assistance, aid to dependent children and aid to the blind. A licence system for foster boarding homes was established in 1956–57. The Alaska Pioneers home for aged residents of the state, located at Sitka, had accommodations for 250 persons, entrance requirements being five years' residence in Alaska immediately preceding application, and age 65. Welfare needs of fishermen were met from a special fishermen's fund. The health needs of the native population have been cared for in a measure by a system of federally supported hospitals. The dedication in 1962 of a 225-bed psychiatric institute in Anchorage marked the beginning of a state program for the care of the mentally ill. Tuberculosis treatment is carried out by contract at a sanatorium at Sitka. The state operates a youth camp but no penitentiaries or reformatories. A state jail is maintained at Ketchikan.

THE ECONOMY

The economy of Alaska has been founded on extractive industries. Fisheries have been its most constant source of revenue. Mining has rivaled fisheries in total value of product. Furs were Alaska's original commercial mainstay, and remain important. In the decade following 1945, increased attention was given to lumbering and wood pulp production, while military construction and service industries based on military personnel and their families gave an additional stimulus to the economy. The modern oil and gas industry began substantial expansion in the late 1950s. Forest products continued to grow in importance and the tourist industry expanded, especially with improvements in transportation in the 1960s.

Living Conditions.—In towns of even a few thousand population most personal services and all essential household needs are available. Despite a wide variety of occupations the comparatively small numbers employed in any one area makes job placement difficult at times. There are three mass employers of labour: fisheries and canneries, mines and dredges, and construction companies. As these industries often bring in seasonal labour from Seattle and San Francisco, opportunity is often furnished for employment while looking for a permanent position. The cost of living in Alaska has consistently been substantially higher than in the U.S. states to the south, usually ranging from 120% to 150%, as compared with Seattle, Wash., in Ketchikan, Sitka, Juneau, Anchorage and Fairbanks, for example, with Anchorage and Fairbanks at the top.

BOB AND IRA SPRING

WATERFRONT AT SITKA, LEFT. THE MOUNT EDGECUMBE VOCATIONAL BOARDING SCHOOL ON JAPONSKI ISLAND, RIGHT

Mining.—Between 1880 and the 1960s approximately $1,000,000,000 in minerals were mined in Alaska. Gold and copper led in value, accounting for more than $700,000,000 and more than $225,000,000 respectively; silver, about $15,000,000, was third.

As early as 1861 gold discoveries were made on the Stikine river; colourings along the Yukon were reported in 1866–67 and systematic prospecting of the upper river began about 1873. Juneau was founded in 1880 following placer gold discoveries; its famous quartz mines were opened later. Coarse gold was discovered on Fortymile creek in 1886, the first significant discovery in the Alaskan section of the Yukon valley. The excitement following these discoveries, however, was as nothing to the feverish rushes that followed the location of the first Klondike (*q.v.*) claims in Canadian territory and the discovery of gold at Nome (*q.v.*) in the 1890s.

Mineral explorations in the second half of the 20th century included surveys of iron deposits in southeastern Alaska, chromite in the Kenai-Moose range, tungsten and copper on Kodiak. Huge reserves of iron were found at the head of the Alaska peninsula in 1964. Deposits of other metals which have been exploited commercially include tin and platinum on the Seward peninsula, chromite on the Kenai peninsula and mercury at several points.

Alaska's fuels include coal, petroleum and gas. Known coal reserves amount to over 100,000,000,000 short tons, of which over 70,000,000,000 tons are subbituminous and lignite. They occur at many locations throughout Alaska. Bituminous and anthracite coals occur in the Bering river and Matanuska fields. The Anchorage and Fairbanks areas have made use of domestic coals over a number of years. Petroleum was produced and refined at Katalla, southeast of Cordova, until the refinery burned in 1933. Oil seepages on the arctic slope were reported in the 1880s. A naval oil reserve near Point Barrow was created in 1923, but exploratory drilling was not undertaken until 1944–53. A producing well was brought in at Umiat, while gas was struck near Point Barrow, and a find of substantial gas reserves at Gubic aroused the hope of supplying gas to the Yukon valley. During the late 1950s several major oil companies undertook petroleum explorations and had brought in two wells in south central Alaska by the close of 1958.

In the closing years of Alaska's territorial period, its mining industry experienced a shift to production of construction materials, explorations for a variety of minerals and growing excitement over the possibility of substantial petroleum discoveries. During the 1950s military and highway construction shifted mining interest to gravels, sands and clays. Thus while gold production averaged $8,400,000 annually in the 1950s, sand and gravel production rose to $8,800,000 by 1957. The total annual value of minerals produced in the decade 1948–57 rose, with minor fluctuations, from a low in 1948 of $13,000,000 to a high in 1957 of just under $29,-000,000. In subsequent years, while the value of gold production declined, marked increases in the value of petroleum and natural gas production after 1958 raised the state's total to more than $80,000,000 in the 1960s. Coal rose to third place after petroleum and natural gas, and sand and gravel.

Fisheries.—Alaska's fishing industry has been equal to mining in importance to its economy. Two salmon canneries were established at Sitka (q.v.) and Klawak in 1878, their first season's pack being valued at $16,000. In the second half of the 20th century there were about 170 wholesaling and manufacturing establishments which had a total annual production valued at more than $100,000,000.

Alaska's fish products, of which salmon are the most important, are handled in a variety of ways. King salmon command a premium price as fresh fish. Sockeye or red salmon supply the choice canning grades. Halibut are marketed fresh or frozen. Among the shellfish are shrimp, razor clams, Dungeness and king crabs. The shellfish industry achieved substantial growth in the 1960s.

Resident fishermen ordinarily operate trawlers or other small craft. Cannery corporations have invested substantial sums in fish traps: box nets supported on pilings with funnel nets inside to trap the fish. If the traps are set too close to the mouth of a stream, or operated continuously through a season, so few salmon escape to return to their spawning grounds that the catch is cut materially in future years of that particular cycle.

The industry suffered extensive damage from the earthquake and ensuing seismic waves of March 27, 1964. Much of the fishing fleet was damaged or destroyed. Docks, canneries, processing plants, freight handling equipment and other facilities were demolished or put out of commission. Especially severe damage was reported at Seward, Valdez and Kodiak.

Fur Industry.—Alaska had produced over $200,000,000 worth of furs between 1867 and the 1960s. Sealskins from the Pribilof Islands (q.v.) contributed half this total. Throughout Alaska trap lines have furnished a source of cash income to native peoples and whites alike.

By the 1920s fur farms were being established, particularly on the coastal islands which were well adapted to control and protection of the animals. About 300 farms were in operation prior to World War II; at the end of the war a quarter of them were still in operation. During the 1950s and 1960s the annual value of the fur seal harvest was ordinarily between $4,000,000 and $6,000,000. The value of other furs exceeded $4,000,000 in 1948, but averaged considerably less in succeeding years.

Agriculture.—Alaska's long hours of summer sunlight are adapted to the growing of many varieties of vegetables and cereals. Cabbage, lettuce, cauliflower, potatoes, beets and carrots grow well in certain areas, sometimes reaching enormous size. Grasses, clover, vetch and peas help to support the dairy industry. Wheat, oats, rye and barley may be grown in the Interior. Blueberries, raspberries and strawberries thrive. The dairy industry has been one of the most successful, being carried on in southern Alaska as far west as Kodiak and on the upper reaches of the Yukon.

Farming areas in southeastern Alaska are small and scattered, usually being located on the deltas of creeks or rivers. A large proportion are dairies or poultry ranches. In the Matanuska valley about 8,000 ac. are under cultivation, producing dairy products, meat, poultry, eggs and vegetables. Small grains grow well in the Interior. Hardy wheats have been introduced from Siberia, and much experimental work has been carried out. The Fairbanks area has been considered the best farming region of the Interior.

The annual value of Alaska's agricultural production was around $3,000,000 in the 1950s, rising to over $4,000,000 in the 1960s. Farming development has been encouraged by an agricultural extension service, a farm loan program and several agricultural research stations. By the second half of the 20th century soil surveys and classification had covered 1,900,000 ac.

Timber Production.—Most of Alaska's commercial timber is contained in the two great national forests, the Tongass in southeastern Alaska and the Chugach on Prince William sound. In the interior valleys are about 25,000,000 ac. of spruce and birch.

Estimates of the marketable timber in the Tongass forest run about 90,000,000,000 bd.ft., primarily western hemlock, with marketable quantities of Sitka spruce, western red cedar and Alaska cedar. Potential productivity has been estimated as high as 1,000,-000,000 bd.ft. a year. However, much of the timber is overripe, and yield estimates are uncertain.

In the mid-1950s the Tongass National forest was blanketed by timber leases for the production of pulpwood and saw timber. Mills had been established at Wrangell, Ketchikan, Sitka and Juneau. Value of timber products ran about $4,300,000 annually from 1950 to 1953. In 1956 it shot up to $34,400,000 and in the 1960s exceeded $50,000,000.

Power.—Electric power has been derived from a variety of sources: small thermo- and hydroelectric plants and diesel engines. The potential hydroelectric power production in several areas of Alaska is vast. The Juneau area is estimated to have a potential annual firm production of 9,800,000,000 kw.hr., with 8,800,000,000 in the Yukon flats area and a total for Alaska of 46,900,000,000 kw.hr. annually of firm power.

Communications.—For 60 years after 1867 mail steamers were the principal means of communication, supplemented by dog teams for winter mail in the arctic. Airmail was established in 1924, and by 1940 much of the mail was moving by air. The Alaska Communications system was established under the army signal corps in 1900 to carry governmental and commercial messages. It has developed cable, telegraph, telephone and radio links. Radiotelephone stations in remote areas were established by the territory and the Alaska native service. By the late 1950s "White Alice," an integrated microwave communications system, was providing high-quality service for all government agencies in Alaska.

Transportation.—High transportation costs have been a continuous factor in retarding Alaska's economic development. These costs have been justified to some extent by high insurance rates and a limited amount of cargo for back haul from Alaska. In other instances, charges have been clearly discriminatory. With statehood, Alaskans hoped to remedy the situation.

Coastal transportation has been built around the schooner, coastal steamer and smaller craft. The Inside passage provides sheltered communication along the southeast coast, but elsewhere navigation is hazardous. In part because of airline competition, the last American flag shipboard passenger service to Alaska was discontinued in 1954. Canadian steamers, however, continued the tourist run, and year-round ferry service was established by the state on the Inside passage in the 1960s. Ferry services also connect Cordova with Valdez and Kodiak with the mainland.

Commercial aviation developed rapidly in Alaska during the 1920s, proving invaluable in a region of few roads. Even before World War II, Alaskans flew 23 times as often and shipped 1,034 times as much air freight per person as other U.S. citizens. In the 1960s Alaska had more than 500 airports and Anchorage was rated among the top U.S. cities in volume of air traffic.

Alaska's principal highway prior to World War II linked Valdez (q.v.) on the coast with Fairbanks. During World War II the Alaska highway was opened from Dawson Creek, B.C., to Fairbanks. The principal routes from the United States run from Great Falls, Mont., through Edmonton, Alta., to Dawson Creek, and from Seattle to Vancouver and up the Fraser river to Dawson Creek. Normal driving time from Great Falls or Seattle to Fairbanks is six to eight days. Most of the road is macadam and is open at all seasons. Current information should be obtained from provincial authorities at Edmonton before planning a trip. Branch highways run to Haines (closed in winter), Anchorage, Palmer and neighbouring towns.

The federally owned Alaska railroad runs from Seward through Anchorage to Fairbanks, a distance of 470 mi. A branch runs to the port of Whittier. Passenger and freight service are provided. The narrow gauge White Pass and Yukon railway, running for 91 of its 111 mi. within Canada, connects the port of Skagway with Whitehorse, Yukon Territory. *See also* references under "Alaska" in the Index.

BIBLIOGRAPHY.—For a guide to the period up to 1924, *see* James Wickersham, *A Bibliography of Alaskan Literature* (1927). *Arctic Bibliography* (7 vol. to 1957) is exhaustive on scientific topics and covers many basic studies in other fields.

For general descriptions of Alaska, *see* U.S. Department of the Interior, *Mid-century Alaska* (1957); Herbert Hilscher, *Alaska Now* (1948), *Alaska, U.S.A.* (1959); B. W. Denison *et al.*, *Alaska Today* (1950); Merle Colby, *Alaska* (1940).

Outstanding on political and economic problems is Ernest Gruening, *The State of Alaska* (1954). *See* also the Governor of Alaska, *Annual Reports* (1910–58). *See* also Jeannette Paddock Nichols, *Alaska: a History of Its Administration, . . . During Its First Half Century Under the Rule of the United States* (1924; reprinted 1963).

For explorations, *see* John Muir, *Travels in Alaska* (1915); B. R. Hubbard, *Cradle of the Storms* (1935); A. H. Brooks, *Blazing Alaska's Trails* (1953). Reports of official explorations from 1867 to about 1900 are available in the congressional document series.

For Alaskan history, *see* C. C. Hulley, *Alaska, 1741–1953* (1953), which sheds new light on the gold rush while providing a competent summary of older materials, *Alaska, Past and Present,* 2nd ed. (1959); Ernest Gruening (ed.), *Alaskan Reader 1867–1967* (1966); S. R. Tompkins, *Alaska, Promyshlennik and Sourdough* (1945); H. H. Bancroft, *History of Alaska* (1886; reprinted 1959); W. H. Dall, *Alaska and Its Resources* (1870).

The U.S. Department of the Interior, *Alaska: Reconnaissance Report on the Potential Development of Water Resources in the Territory of Alaska,* House Document 197, 82nd Congress, 1st Session (Jan. 1952), goes far beyond water resources in describing the economy and physical geography of the region.

Current statistics on production, employment, industry, etc., may be obtained from the pertinent state departments; the principal figures, together with the current history, are summarized annually in the *Britannica Book of the Year.* (J. E. CL.)

ALASTOR, in Greek mythology, the name of a person and also of an idea.

1. Alastor in early mythology is the spirit of revenge that prompts the members of a family to commit fresh crimes to obtain satisfaction. Further acts of vengeance transmit the curse from generation to generation (*cf., e.g.,* the repeated murders in the house of Atreus [*q.v.*]).

The word is also used for a man's evil genius that drives him to sin; a man so driven is sometimes called Alastor. The epithet is applied to the Erinyes as the deities of revenge, and to Zeus when he is invoked as the "Avenger."

2. Alastor, a son of Neleus, whose wife, Harpalyce, was seized from him by her incestuous father, was killed by Heracles at the siege of Pylos. (T. V. B.)

ALA-TAU (variegated mountains) is the name given to the following ranges in Asiatic U.S.S.R.: (1) Terskei; (2) Kungei; and (3) Trans-ili (Zailiyski). All three link the Tien Shan (*q.v.*) and the Kirgiz ranges. (1) Lies south and (2) and (3) north of and parallel to Lake Issyk-Kul (*q.v.*). The average height is 6,000–7,000 ft. (Pik Talgar 16,243 ft.) and the snow line 11,000–11,700 ft. (4) Talasski Ala-Tau, also called Talastau, is west by south from the Kirgiz range. (5) Dzungarian or Dzhungarski Ala-Tau is a range bordering the Dzungarian gate, north of the Tien Shan, with an average height of 13,000 ft., maximum 14,642 ft. (6) Kuznet or Kuznetski Ala-Tau, between the upper Ob and the upper Yenisei, west of the Abakani mountains, has an average height of 6,000–7,000 ft. (G. E. WR.)

ALATRI, a town in Lazio, central Italy, in the province of Frosinone, lies in the valley of the Cosa river, 1,706 ft. above sea level. Pop. (1961) 20,543 (commune). It is said to have been founded in 1830 B.C. as Aletrium, mentioned by Strabo and Pliny; it belonged to the confederation of the Hernici (*q.v.*) of which it was the chief bastion in the struggle against Rome. Archaeologically it is most important. Its ancient origin is attested by traces of a great belt of Cyclopean walls (6th century B.C.), within which is the superb trapezoid "Pelasgian acropolis," the most beautiful and complete that has been preserved, whose walls are almost intact.

In the outer circle of walls, which extend about 4 km. (2½ mi.) and at intervals in which are fine medieval towers, are the Porta Civita with its monolithic architrave, the Porta Minore and the Nuova Porta, recently discovered. Other important monuments and buildings are the churches of Sta. Maria Maggiore, S. Francesco and S. Silvestro, all rich in frescoes; the palace of Cardinal Gottifredi "Casegrandi," now the civic museum, the bishop's palace, the episcopal seminary and the Conti Gentili college.

Alatri is a holiday resort 17 km. (10½ mi.) from Fiuggi, with quick, convenient and frequent connections with Rome (90 km. [56 mi.]) and Naples (235 km. [146 mi.]). It is a pleasant place because of its healthful air, the good quality of its agricultural products (cereals, wine, oil and vegetables) and the excellence of the water (there are two mineral water springs). A business centre, the city is expanding westward where the modern part of the town lies, augmented after World War II with imposing public and private buildings.

ÁLAVA, MIGUEL RICARDO DE (1771–1843), Spanish soldier and statesman, was Spanish commissary at the duke of Wellington's headquarters during the Peninsular War and was active in political life thereafter until 1837. Born at Vitoria in 1771, he was a member of the Bayonne assembly which in 1808 accepted Joseph Bonaparte as king of Spain. Shortly afterward, however, he joined the patriotic party fighting the French and was made an aide-de-camp to Wellington, being promoted brigadier general. Out of favour because of his liberal ideas on the restoration of Ferdinand VII, he was appointed ambassador to the Netherlands in 1815 and so came to be present at the battle of Waterloo. (Having previously been on board his uncle's flagship in the battle of Trafalgar, he is said to have been the only man present at both Trafalgar and Waterloo.) He became president of the *Cortes* in 1822, but the absolutist reaction of 1823 forced him into exile in London. Returning to Spain after Ferdinand VII's death (1833), he supported María Cristina against Don Carlos. He was ambassador to Great Britain in 1834 and to France in 1835. Having refused to take the oath to the constitution of 1837, he went into exile from Spain again and died at Barèges, France, in 1843.

(R. S. LL.)

ÁLAVA, one of the Basque provinces of northern Spain, flanks part of the upper Ebro valley and the southern Basque mountains. Pop. (1960) 138,934; area 1,177 sq.mi.; density per square mile 118.0. Formerly a lordship, Álava was incorporated in Castile in 1332. In the southern part of the province is the Treviño enclave (190 sq.mi.) which belongs to the province of Burgos.

As the Basque name of Álava (*araiiar,* "set among the mountains") implies, its core area is an intramontane basin (about 1,500 ft.). This basin is called the Llanada de Vitoria and is a continuation of the tectonic corridor in which Pamplona is situated. From the north the valleys of the Urquiola, Bayas and Omecillo rivers enter it and carry roads between the mountains of Aitzgorri, Peña de Gorbea and Peña Igaña, all of which rise above 4,500 ft. The Montes de Vitoria separate the Llanada de Vitoria from the enclave of Treviño, partly an ancient lake drained by the Ayuda river. To the south the mountain ranges of Cantabria and Toloño overlook the third and lowest plain, the Alavese Rioja, which goes down to the Ebro.

In many respects the province is transitional between the Basque lands to the north and Castile to the southwest. It shares the continental cold and summer drought of the Meseta. Its landscapes are much more open than those of the northern provinces, with bare or scrub slopes, fewer forests and extensive fields of cereals on the plains. Maize is grown only in the northern valleys with higher rainfall; wheat, barley and oats are grown elsewhere. The Alavese Rioja is famous for its vineyards. Few Spanish provinces have more mechanized farming, and sugar-beet production is very important in the Vitoria district.

The population is less scattered than farther north, and the hamlet is an ancient feature. Vitoria (*q.v.*) the capital (pop. [1960] 73,701) remained the only town with more than 3,500 inhabitants. Built in 1256 near the site of an ancient hamlet, its oval plan showed little growth and it was still a small market town of 15,569 in the mid-19th century. It grew rapidly thereafter, first with the advent of the railway and later with the establishment of new factories for agricultural machinery, sugar refining, furniture making, truck construction, etc. These industries are supplied with hydroelectric power from dams constructed on the upper courses of the Bayas, Urrunaga and Zadorra, and also from the Ebro dam near Reinosa in Santander. (J. M. Ho.)

ALB, a liturgical vestment, reaching from neck to ankles, worn by the officiants at Mass. Both the alb and its name are derived from the *tunica alba*, the white under-tunic that formed part of the ordinary dress in the Roman and Greek world. The date of its definite adoption as a liturgical vestment is uncertain; as late as the 9th and 10th centuries the *alba* was still an everyday as well as a liturgical garment. Its equivalent in the Eastern Churches is the sticharion. *See* VESTMENTS, ECCLESIASTICAL.

ALBA (ALVA), **FERNANDO ÁLVAREZ DE TOLEDO,** DUQUE DE (1507–1582), Spanish soldier and statesman, famous for his conquest of Portugal and notorious for his tyranny as governor general of the Netherlands, was born at Piedrahita (Ávila) on Oct. 29, 1507, of a rich family with a long record of service to the kings of Castile. In 1524 he joined the Spanish forces fighting the French at Fuenterrabía and so distinguished himself that he was appointed governor of the town after its capture. Subsequent campaigns made him the most thoroughly professional military commander of his age. He insisted on rigorous training and discipline for his troops and developed the tactical use of firearms. He was a master of logistics, and his greatest asset was unshakable self-confidence which enabled him to resist the rash counsels of his more impetuous officers. In 1546–47 Alba commanded the imperial armies against the German Protestant princes of the League of Schmalkalden. By his victory at Mühlberg (April 24, 1547), Alba placed the emperor Charles V at the pinnacle of his power. Alba was made commander in chief of the imperial forces in Italy in 1552 and, after the succession of Philip II of Spain, viceroy of Naples (1556). In the last phase of the Franco-Spanish war in Italy, he outmaneuvered the duc de Guise and forced Pope Paul IV to come to terms with Spain (1557).

After the peace of Câteau-Cambrésis (1559), Alba became one of Philip II's two leading ministers. In opposition to the other, Ruy Gómez de Silva, he pressed for a vigorous foreign policy. Following the popular movements of 1566, Philip sent Alba to the Netherlands with a large army to punish the rebels, root out heresy and re-establish the king's shaken authority (Aug. 1567). Alba arrested the comte d'Egmont and Philippe de Montmorency, comte de Horn, the rather halfhearted leaders of the opposition, and set up a new court, the Council of Troubles (soon to be known as the Council of Blood). This court set aside all local laws and tried and condemned thousands who had taken part in the religious and political opposition to the king. It was a deliberate policy of terror, and it worked in the short run. Not a single town rose to support William the Silent, prince of Orange, in his invasion of the Netherlands in 1568. Egmont and Horn were executed.

Alba was, however, unsuccessful in placing his government on a stable financial basis, independent of the estates. He proposed a 10% sales tax but this proved inoperable and he had to modify it. The opposition of the lower classes and the clergy was so strong that even this modified tax was never collected. In 1572 the Gueux (*q.v.*) captured most of Holland and Zealand, and the prince of Orange and his brother Louis of Nassau invaded the Netherlands from Germany and France respectively. Alba defeated the land invasions and recaptured part of Holland, where his troops committed terrible atrocities. Short of money and lacking adequate sea power to oppose the fleet of the Gueux, he failed to recapture the remainder of Holland and Zealand. (*See* also NETHERLANDS.)

Alba's failure and the intrigues of the Gómez party at the court induced Philip II to recall him (1573). In 1579 Alba was placed under house arrest on his estates after his son had defied the king in marrying against the royal wishes. In 1580 Cardinal Granvelle persuaded Philip to let Alba command the invasion of Portugal. Within a few weeks, in one of his most brilliant campaigns, Alba took Lisbon. Yet he never regained Philip's favour. He died at Lisbon on Dec. 11, 1582.

In Protestant countries Alba's name became a byword for cruelty and religious tyranny. Outside Spain he has never been forgiven for his disregard of legality, for his policy of terror and for the outrages committed by his troops in the Netherlands and in Portugal. Of the responsibility for these acts he cannot be exonerated nor were they universally accepted even by Catholic opinion in the 16th century. In Spanish history Alba is important as a representative of the old nobility, independent and proud of its rights and privileges yet willing to serve as the champion and defender of an absolute monarchy.

See Duke of Berwick and Alba, *The Great Duke of Alba as a Public Servant* (1947) and *Epistolario del III Duque de Alba,* 3 vol. (1952).
(H. G. Ko.)

ALBACETE, a town of Spain and capital of the province of Albacete, lies on the Balazote river where it unites with the Canal of María Cristina, 134 mi. S.E. of Madrid. Pop. (1960) 74,417 (mun.). The upper town, to the south, is the old quarter, while the lower town is modern. The principal church is dedicated to San Juan Bautista and there is a provincial museum containing pictures, sculpture and archaeological finds. Canalejas park is the chief open space. The aerodrome is at Los Llanos where there is an aviation school. Albacete has an annual fair with bullfighting. Flour and cutlery are made, and knives and daggers from Albacete are well-known throughout Spain. It is a market town for saffron, fruit and other agricultural produce. First mentioned in the 12th century when the district was being freed from Moorish domination, Albacete was founded in 1365 and became separate from neighbouring Chinchilla. It played an important part in the War of the Spanish Succession, the battle of Almansa being won near there by Philip V in 1707. During the civil war of 1936–39 Albacete remained in Republican hands.

ALBACETE PROVINCE covers an inland area of 5,737 sq.mi. Pop. (1960) 370,976. It is somewhat featureless except for the Sierra de Alcaraz in the west. The drainage is almost entirely to the Mediterranean by the Júcar and Segura rivers, but the rainfall is low and the province contributes little to these rivers except from the western sierras, where the snow lies for several months; elsewhere the climate is mild and healthful. The chief towns are the capital Albacete and Almansa and Hellín. Other towns are Alcaraz, Casas Ibañez, Chinchilla, La Roda and Yeste. The province is crossed by the main routes from Madrid to the plain of Valencia and the southeast. The railway from Madrid passes through Albacete southwest to Chinchilla where it divides, one branch going to Alicante and one to Murcia. A large part of the province is accessible only by road. Manufactures include the making of flour, coarse cloth, porcelain, earthenware and cutlery; hemp is spun and brandy is distilled. Albacete is a stock-raising province, but wheat-growing is increasing steadily with a corresponding decline in livestock. Of these, sheep of the large Manchigan breed are the most important. Cheese is sent to all parts of Spain; vines, which have suffered much from phyloxera, and olives are cultivated; the peaches of Cabriel and Júcar valleys supply canning factories in Valencia. Saffron, esparto grass and wood from the pine forests are traded.

ALBACORE (*Thunnus alalunga*), a large, edible oceanic fish allied to the tunas and mackerels (*qq.v.*) and placed with them in the family Scombridae.

ALBA FUCENS (mod. ALBE), an ancient town on a lofty site (3,347 ft.) at the foot of Monte Velino, 4 mi. N. of Avezzano in the modern Italian *regione* of Abruzzi e Molise. Originally a town of the Marsi, it was occupied by a Latin colony *c.* 303 B.C. It lay at the junction of the Via Valeria (the road from Rome to the Adriatic) with a road coming up the Liris valley from the south. It was situated just south of the Via Valeria on a hill with three distinct summits, all of which were enclosed within the walls. Its strong position made it important in the Social War (when it was perhaps captured; it was widely replanned thereafter) and in the civil wars; state prisoners of the Romans were often held there. The main circuit of walls, much of which survives, dates from *c.* 303 B.C. and is about two miles in circumference; the walls are of polygonal masonry, carefully jointed, with faces smoothed. Three gateways remain; they are so placed as to expose the right side of an attacking force. A stretch on the northwest side was later doubled by a second wall of similar construction but with smaller blocks. Early in the 1st century B.C. this part and the southeastern section also were strengthened. The acropolis in the northern corner (where the ruins of the village of Albe and the Orsini castle lie) had in addition a separate line of walls and thus formed an independent stronghold. Extensive excavations (from 1948) have revealed terra cottas which indicate the existence of a temple on the site by *c.* 500 B.C., while the town plan and streets of the later settlement have been recovered, together with buildings in the central area: a basilica, market place, baths, temples, theatre, shops and houses. The amphitheatre was built by the praetorian prefect Naevius Sertorius Macro (*c.* A.D. 40). Finds of marble statuary are numerous.

See the excavation reports in *L'Antiquité classique* (1954, 1955), *Fasti Archaeologici*, vol. iv (1951–); *Archaeology*, vol. xii (1959).
(H. H. Sd.)

ALBA IULIA (Ger. KARLSBURG; Hung. GYULA-FEHÉRVÁR), a town of former Transylvania, in the region of Hunedoara, Rumania, lies on the Mures, 73 mi. (117 km.) S of Cluj by rail. Pop. (1963 est.) 19,953. It consists of an upper town or citadel and a lower town, and was the seat of a Roman Catholic bishop. Its fine 13th-century cathedral, rebuilt in Gothic style (1443) by the Hungarian national hero John Hunyadi, contains his tomb.

Near the cathedral are the episcopal palace and Batthyaneum, founded by Count Batthyány in 1794, containing a valuable library with many incunabula and old manuscripts (including one of the *Nibelungenlied* and the 9th-century *Codex aureus*), an observatory and a museum of antiquities and minerals. The citadel was built in 1716–35 by the emperor Charles VI. Alba Iulia occupies the site of the 2nd-century Roman colony of Apulum and many Roman relics are in the museum. In the 16th century the town became the residence of the independent Transylvanian princes. From that period date the castle (now in ruins) and the buildings of the former university founded by Gabriel Bethlen, now used as barracks. Alba Iulia with Cluj was the Transylvanian centre of the Rumanian national movement. It was there in 1600 that Michael the Brave proclaimed himself prince of Transylvania, Walachia and Moldavia. In 1918 the union of Transylvania with Rumania was proclaimed at Alba Iulia and King Ferdinand of Rumania was crowned there in 1922.

ALBA LONGA, an ancient city of Latium, on the western edge of Lake Albano, probably situated where the modern Italian town of Castel Gandolfo stands, about 12 mi. S.E. of Rome. Founded traditionally by Ascanius, the son of the legendary Aeneas, *c.* 1152 B.C., it was said to be the oldest Latin city and to have founded others including Rome. It headed a Latin league of uncertain extent, until destroyed *c.* 600 B.C. by its daughter city Rome, whither some of its inhabitants were transported; others survived at Bovillae (*q.v.*). The name Albanum, from about 150 B.C. until the time of the emperor Constantine the Great, meant the imperial villa in the Alban territory. The emperors formed a single estate out of a considerable part of this district, including apparently the whole of the lake, and Domitian was especially fond of it. The imperial villa occupied the site of the present Villa Barberini at Castel Gandolfo, and considerable remains still exist. To the south a camp, with baths, an amphitheatre and a large water reservoir, was constructed by Septimius Severus for the Second Parthian legion, his bodyguard. The camp was given up in the time of Constantine, when the Civitas Albanensis (Albano) arose.

Of the pre-Roman Alba only the necropolis has been revealed. The earliest of its tombs are Villanovan (Early Iron Age). Later ones belong to the 7th century B.C.

The *lapis Albanus* is a green-gray volcanic stone with black and white grains in it (peperino), much used for building material in Rome and its neighbourhood.

See R. MacIver, *Italy in the Iron Age* (1927); B. Tilly, *Vergil's Latium* (1947).

ALBAN, SAINT (3rd century A.D. ?), the first British martyr, traditionally of Verulamium (St. Albans). According to Bede he served in the Roman army and was converted to Christianity by a fugitive priest whom he sheltered and exchanged clothes with, so that he was martyred in the priest's place. Gildas surmised, and Bede stated, that he suffered during the persecution of Diocletian (*c.* 286–303), but there is no certainty that this persecution extended to Britain. His feast day, properly June 22, is commemorated on June 17 in the Church of England because of a confusion between Roman numerals. The tomb of St. Alban was venerated by St. Germanus of Auxerre as early as 429, when a church had also been built. Later a monastery was founded, around which grew the town of St. Albans (*q.v.*).

See H. Thurston and D. Attwater (eds.), *Butler's Lives of the Saints*, 2:612–614 (1956); W. Levison, "Saint Alban and St. Albans" in *Antiquity*, 15:337–359 (1941). (PL. GN.)

ALBAN HILLS (MONTI ALBANI or COLLI ALBANI), a district of extinct volcanoes southeast of Rome, Italy, consists of an outer circle, approximately 6–8 mi. in diameter, and an inner circle, approximately 1½ mi. across. The highest point of the outer rim is Monte Peschio (3,081 ft.) and of the inner rim, Monte Faete (3,136 ft.). Lakes Albano and Nemi (*qq.v.*) occupy two of the ancient craters. Even before the emergence of Rome as a great power the Alban hills were a place sacred to the people of the Latium (Lazio) region, and Roman roads, temples, villas and theatres are still partially preserved there. Because of their coolness in summer and the absence of malaria the Alban hills have for centuries been a favourite summer residence of Romans, where they built such magnificent summer residences as the Villa Falconieri and Villa Mondragone. The Alban vineyards produce the wines known as those of the *castelli Romani*, the most popular of the Roman region. An electric suburban railway connects Rome with Frascati, Grottaferrata, Albano, Velletri, Genzano and Castel Gandolfo. (G. KH.)

ALBANI (ALBANO), **FRANCESCO** (1578–1660), Italian painter, whose exquisite compositions are distinctive among the works of the followers of the Carracci, was born at Bologna. His first master was Denis Calvart, with whom Guido Reni was at the same time a pupil. He was soon left by Calvart entirely to the care of Guido whom he followed to the school of the Carracci. Albani opened an academy in Rome, where he resided for many years. There he painted, after the designs of Annibale Carracci, the whole of the frescoes in the chapel of San Diego in the church of San Giacomo degli Spagnuoli. His best frescoes are those on mythological subjects.

ALBANIA, a People's Republic, officially styled REPUBLIKA POPULLORE E SHQIPERISE, is a small state of 11,100 sq.mi. Its local name Shqiperi means "eagles' country," which aptly reflects its mountainous nature and remoteness. It is situated on the Adriatic coast of the Balkan Peninsula bounded to the north by the Dinaric Mountains, to the east by the Macedonian Highlands, and to the south by the Pindus (Pindhos) Mountains. It has common boundaries with the Yugoslav republics of Montenegro, Serbia (Kosmet), and Macedonia to the north and east, and with Greece to the south. The population (1960 census) was 1,626,315. Albania has the highest birthrate in Europe. The capital is Tiranë.

Following are the main divisions of this article:

I. Physical Geography
II. The People
III. History
  1. The Despotate of Epirus
  2. The Serbian Occupation
  3. The Ottoman Invasion and Skanderbeg
  4. Under Turkish Rule
  5. The Independence Movement, 1878–1914
  6. The Settlement of 1921
  7. The Kingdom of Albania
  8. World War II
  9. Communist Supremacy
IV. Population
V. Administration and Social Conditions
VI. The Economy

I. PHYSICAL GEOGRAPHY

Structure and Relief.—Albania forms part of the Dinaric folded mountain system largely uplifted during the Tertiary Era. Some movement continued into the Quaternary, and minor earthquakes which still affect the region are a reminder of its inherent tectonic instability. The Dinaric system is characterized by northwest-southeast trend lines and these are strongly reflected in the relief of the country as a whole. Anticlinal and synclinal axes are as aligned as are lines of tectonic weakness to which most of the main rivers have succeeded in adjusting themselves. The axial plane of a massive overthrusting associated with the Ser-

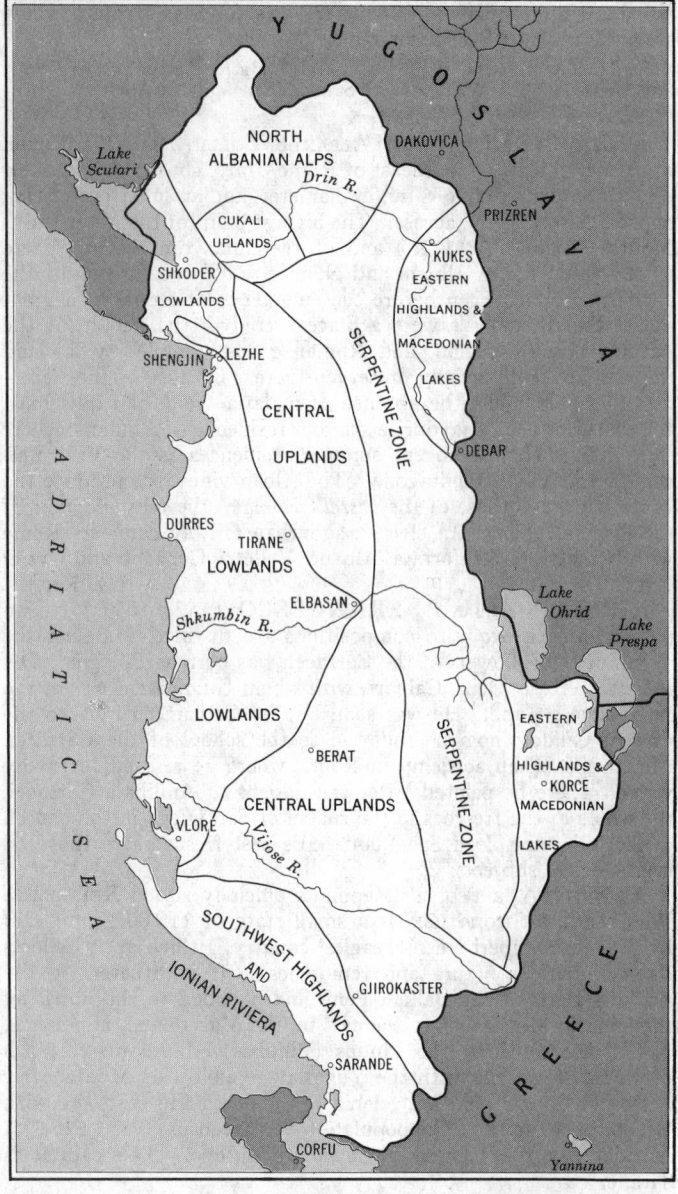

PHYSIOGRAPHIC REGIONS OF ALBANIA

characterized by the recurring theme of basin and gorge so widely prevalent in the country. Where local lithology has allowed slope wastage the river valleys are broader and shallower but otherwise they are deeply incised in narrow valleys. In consequence the rivers do not provide easy access to the interior, nor are their valleys easily crossed. The main water parting, or divide, between rivers flowing into the Adriatic on the one side and into the Black Sea and Aegean on the other is farther removed from the Adriatic in Albania than is the case in either Yugoslavia or Greece. The fast-flowing perennial rivers have brought down considerable quantities of detritus and have built out an extensive coastal plain into the Adriatic. Finally, during Quaternary times oscillations in sea level combined with periglacial action have resulted in the alternate deepening and aggregation of river courses, while in the North Albanian Alps features resulting from glacial erosion are found.

Geographic Regions.—*The North Albanian Alps* is a convenient name to describe an extensive series of high mountain ranges and plateaus varying between 5,000 to 8,000 ft. in the extreme north of the country adjoining similar territory in Montenegro (Crna Gora). Korab, the highest peak, attains 9,026 ft. Sandstones, limestones, conglomerates, and shales outcrop at the surface. The whole area has been uplifted and dissected by radial drainage. Glaciation has resulted in a deepening and widening of the valleys, and in fretted slopes and in arêtes. The slopes are heavily wooded and the high plateaus are clothed in alpine meadow. The whole area is isolated and sparsely populated.

The Cukali Uplands immediately to the north of the Drin River consist of a number of anticlines formed of Mesozoic shales, cherts, and limestones. The surface forms are more rounded and dome-like than those found in the Alps, the valleys shallower and the elevation, from 3,000 to 5,000 ft., is lower.

The Serpentine Zone of east-central Albania includes most of the extensive high plateau of Albania south of the Drin River. Rocks outcropping at the surface include various limestones, for example the *krasta* (karst) of the Golloborde Plateau (*see* KARST), as well as Tertiary marls, loams, and clays, but the prevalent and most distinctive rocks are the Serpentine, the largest complex of such metamorphic rocks in Europe. They give rise to bold rounded upland features; for the most part the rock is pervious and dry and once the original forest vegetation has been removed it is usually replaced by a poor scrub or heath. The Serpentine rocks are rich in chrome and copper ores and these are of some importance in the economy.

The Eastern Highlands and Macedonian Lakes include the deeply trenched valleys of the White and Black Drin, lakes Ohrid, Prespa, and Maliq (now drained), the Kenete depression, the basins of Korçë and Bilisht together with the associated highlands. All the lakes act as local collecting centres of inland drainage. Lake Prespa, which is shallow, drains underground into the deep Lake Ohrid which occupies a tectonic depression, and this lake in its turn is drained by the Black Drin northward. In this eastern area the mountain ranges are roughly aligned north-south and are formed for the most part of metamorphized rocks of Permocarboniferous and Triassic Age or of tabular limestone. The dazzling white peaks of the Korab Range composed of gypsum and marble and which attain a height of over 8,000 ft. are especially conspicuous. To the south extend the high mountains of the Mal' i Thate, the Morava and Gramos, for the most part composed of limestone. This eastern borderland of Albania is somewhat isolated by reason of its physical structure and drainage from the rest of Albania.

The Central Uplands comprise a very large area of central Albania stretching from the coast ranges in the north right through to the Greek boundary in the southeast. It is a zone with a relatively simple Dinaric structure where a series of parallel folds have given rise to successive anticlinal ridges and synclinal valleys aligned along a northwest-southeast axis. The physiography consists of an overburden of Lower Tertiary rocks (flysch) through which Serpentine and Cretaceous rocks outcrop. These outcrops often form lofty plateaus capped with limestone with well marked karst features. The most extensive surface rocks however constitute the so-called flysch (*q.v.*) which consists of friable beds of

pentine complex of rocks in eastern Albania is also roughly Dinaric in alignment; but the structural grain of the country is not everywhere so simple. It is complicated in the east by a north-south trend reflected in the rift valley of the Drin i Zi (Black Drin) and Lake Ohrid and in the western boundary fault of the Mal' i Thate. In central Albania there are traces of a southwest-northeast faulting diametrically opposed in direction to the Dinaric trend, and in the north overthrusting on an east-west axis combined with fracturing and imbrication, or shinglelike overlapping, complicate the structure still further. Block faulting is a feature in the extreme southwest of the country.

The solid geology of Albania ranges from the Upper Paleozoic, through Mesozoic and Tertiary to the deposits of the Quaternary Era. The resultant varied surface lithology is a factor in the multiplicity and diversity of land forms which owe their origin in part to differential weathering. In general the relief of Albania may be likened to an amphitheatre with lofty mountains and dissected plateaus fringing a coastal lowland. A series of long rivers traverse the country and debouch on a low marshy coastal plain. The drainage pattern has distinctly angular characteristics; the principal rivers have pronounced L-shaped bends; there are recurring deep gorges and rapids and the long profiles of the rivers are interrupted by a series of knickpoints or abrupt changes in gradient. A trellis pattern of drainage has developed

shale and marl with occasional sandy limestones and coarse conglomerates. These rocks are much softer than the Serpentine and Mesozoic tabular limestones and have been much eroded. Gullying is a feature on the upper slopes, and landslips are common in wet weather. The north coast mountain ranges with a characteristic Dinaric northwest-southeast trend are typical of the ranges of the central upland. They form an extension of the Dalmatian coastal ranges into Albania. South from Shengjin these mountains continue as the Krujë Ridge inland in the direction of Elbasan.

The Coastal Lowlands consist for the most part of relatively broad stretches of Tertiary sands, clays, and marls, separated by low ranges of rain-washed sandstone and pitted, limestone hills. Included in the lowlands are the diversified plains of Shkodër (Scutari), Tiranë (Tirana), and Elbasan, all with fertile pockets of soil and well populated in comparison with other parts of the country. The coast itself is fringed with dunes and recurring spits enclose reedy, marshy lagoons. In parts there are great spreads of gravel into which the rivers have incised their beds. Near the coast the rivers frequently change their courses; the Drin itself has so changed in historical times. Only small areas of the marshy plains, once plagued by malaria, have been reclaimed. Paradoxically the coast has been a barrier against rather than a link with the outside world.

The Southwest Highlands consist of a series of dissected block-faulted anticlines with a northwest-southeast axis. Limestone dominates but Triassic sandstones and soft Tertiary rocks are present as well. The most distinctive feature of this region is its sheltered coast where limestone cliffs and clear water justify the description of the Albanian or Ionian riviera, strongly contrasting with the low coast so characteristic of Albania north of Vlorë (Valona).

Climate.—In general Albania has a climate characterized by mild winters, hot summers, and moderately heavy rainfall. Marked regional contrasts in climate do occur however and only sheltered, lowland coastal districts enjoy typically Mediterranean weather. Inland diurnal and seasonal temperatures become progressively more extreme according to aspect, altitude, and distance from the coast. Since Albania experiences the passage of depressions, or low-pressure centres, not only from the Atlantic but also from the Mediterranean, and is additionally subject to cyclones originating locally in the Adriatic, weather tends to be wetter and more changeable than elsewhere in the Mediterranean. In the North Albanian Alps and other high mountains snowfall is frequent in winter and the summers are subject to rainstorms. High thermal and barometric gradients between the interior and the sea in winter give rise to the bora, strong dry winds, in all but sheltered coastal districts.

Vegetation.—The natural vegetation of Albania has been much influenced by man and his grazing animals and in part has been reduced to brushwood and rock-strewn, herbaceous communities. Except for lacustrine and coastal marshes, which have an interesting flora of their own, for a few skeletal soils, and for the alpine mat flora of the high mountains, the climax vegetation is predominantly forest. Oak-hornbeam, beech, or pine dominate according to local climatic and soil conditions. Near the coast maquis (tough scrub) is prevalent, consisting for the most part of evergreen brushwood ascending to about 3,000 ft. on the coastal ranges, typical species being the strawberry tree, juniper, holm oak, myrtle, wild rose, bramble, and thorny smilax. Inland, oak forest is widely prevalent in varying stages of degradation. Hairy, Turkey, and Macedonian oak form the chief varieties.

Apart from wild swine the oak forest has few animals but has been intensively used for grazing and for fuel. Where it has been cleared it is replaced by a secondary growth of deciduous shrubs with such plants as broom, dwarf juniper, hazel, and locally *çiblak*. The latter forms an impenetrable mass of thorny scrub with Christ's-thorn dominating. On the higher slopes a great deal of beech forest still survives, usually in the cloud belt 3,000–5,000 ft. above sea level. Because of its inaccessibility the beech wood has been put to little economic use. Above the beech zone, and also at lower altitudes in areas of dry soils, pine forest is dominant. Black pine and peuke pine occur in Serpentine rocks, for example, and

the white-barked pine on deep limestones. Above 5,000 to 6,000 ft. occurs the alpine mat plant community, rich in grass and flowering plants and affording pasture in summer. The area of alpine vegetation has been much extended downhill by grazing.

II. THE PEOPLE

Tribal Organization.—The character, manner, and outlook of the people of Albania cannot be understood without reference to their tribal organization, of paramount importance in the past and still influential. Even communism is unlikely to modify for some time the core of traditional behaviour which sprang originally from the strict observations of the customary ordinances collectively known as the Canon of Lek. Single tribes or clans (*fis*), usually grouped for the convenience of administration and intermarriage into *bajrak* (literally, "standard"), claimed male descent from a single male progenitor. Life was entirely prescribed by customary enactments and the more severe intertribal crimes were resolved by blood feud. Land and grazing rights were jealously guarded and kept within the tribe, and business was conducted by a council of elders. Tribal organization survived in its purest form in Albania north of the Shkumbin River and embraced both the Roman Catholic and Muslim population.

Language.—A common language has provided the unifying force in the development of the Albanian nation. For centuries after the destruction of the Roman frontier on the Danube, hordes of alien invaders pressed south from eastern Europe and Asia. Classical and contemporary languages in Illyria and Thrace survived only in remote places and Albanian is one such survival (*see* ALBANIAN LANGUAGE). It has a widespread distribution in the western Balkan Peninsula partly because of the outward migration of Albanians during the Turkish period. Thus there are more than 500,000 Albanian speakers in Yugoslav Kosmet, 100,000 in Macedonia, perhaps as many as 200,000 in modern Greece, and a substantial element in southwest Italy and Sicily.

Religion.—Both the Church of Rome and the Orthodox Church were instrumental in bringing Christianity to Albania. In general the north came under the influence of the former and the south of the latter. The Turks brought the Muslim faith into the country and the majority of people in central Albania accepted, or were forced to accept, Islam. The Turks proved more tolerant of the Orthodox Church but Roman Catholicism survived in the high mountains of the north. Today Roman Catholics constitute about 12% of the population and Orthodox Christians about 20%. The Orthodox Church became self-governing in 1937. The Muslims are mainly Sunnites but there is a strong element of the Bektashi sect (*see* BALKAN PENINSULA: *Ethnology: Turks*) of which the world headquarters is at Tiranë. (H. R. WI.)

III. HISTORY

For the early history of Albania to the Slavonic invasions of the Balkan peninsula, *see* ILLYRIA. When, at the beginning of the 8th century, the wave of Slavonic invasions subsided, the ethnological structure of the Balkans had been greatly modified. The lands of the Albanian-speaking people had been reduced to present-day Albania, Kosovo (in Yugoslavia), parts of western Macedonia and northern Greece. Until the overthrow of the West Bulgarian Empire by the Byzantines in the 11th century Slavs were occupying even the Drin and Devoll valleys in present-day Albania. The first recorded use of the name Albanians instead of Illyrians occurs in Anna Comnena's account of the resistance by her father, the Byzantine emperor Alexius I Comnenus, to the attack by the Normans from southern Italy under Robert Guiscard, who took Durazzo (Durrës) in 1082.

1. The Despotate of Epirus.—After the capture of Constantinople by the Latins of the Fourth Crusade and the substitution of the Latin empire for the empire of the Comneni (*see* BYZANTINE EMPIRE; CRUSADES), Michael Angelus Comnenus founded the despotate of Epirus (*q.v.*), which he ruled until 1214, maintaining himself against the Greek emperor of Nicaea. This despotate extended beyond the limits of present-day Albania. Michael's successor Theodore Angelus, however, proclaimed himself the only legitimate heir to the imperial throne, in opposition to the Latins, as well as to Nicaea. Having overthrown the elected Latin emperor Peter of Courtenay (who had landed at Durazzo on his way from the west to Constantinople) in 1216, Theodore had himself crowned emperor at Salonika in 1224 but was defeated on his way to Constantinople by the Bulgarian king Ivan Asen II. Ivan Asen could then claim to have extended his empire over Albania, Greece, and Serbia. After Ivan's death Michael II Angelus restored the despotate of Epirus, but was defeated by the emperor Michael VIII Palaeologus in 1264. Albania then became once more a dependency of the Byzantine Empire. After establishing his Angevin dynasty in southern Italy, Charles I of Naples resumed the quarrel that his Norman predecessors had had with Byzantium and took the title of "king of Albania," but was never able to consolidate his authority over the country.

2. The Serbian Occupation.—At the end of the 13th century the Serbs were already occupying parts of Albania, and in the first half of the 14th century the country was annexed to Stephen Dushan's short-lived empire. This disintegrated, however, after Stephen's death in 1355. Many Albanians meanwhile had fled south and founded colonies as far away as the Morea (Peloponnesus).

3. The Ottoman Invasion and Skanderbeg.—In the second half of the 14th century, when the Ottoman Turks were overrunning the Balkans, Albania was in the throes of feudal quarrels between a number of small principalities virtually independent of Byzantium. The chief dynasties were, from north to south: Balsha, Dukagjin, Thopia, Kastrioti, Muzaki, Arianit-Komneni, and Shpata. All were staunchly Catholic, strongly attached to the papacy—a tradition maintained since the early days of the Christian Church when Albanian bishops took a prominent part in ecumenical councils. Taking advantage of the rivalry between these princes, the Venetians had occupied Alessio (Lesh), Scutari, and Durazzo, and the Turks were able to make deep inroads into Albanian territory. The Albanian princes were forced one by one to capitulate and to pay the sultan tribute. Turkish garrisons were established in the main cities and in the fortified citadels such as Krujë, Kanine, and Sfetigrad.

In 1443 George Kastrioti, surnamed Skanderbeg (*q.v.*), rallied the Albanians and proclaimed holy war against the Turks. In 1449 the sultan Murad II sent an army under his best general to crush Skanderbeg, but it was defeated at the frontier. This Albanian victory won for Skanderbeg the felicitations of Christian rulers, but the war that it inaugurated was to last a quarter of a century. Invading Turkish armies appeared almost every year and were as regularly destroyed. Unable to continue the struggle singlehandedly, Skanderbeg in 1451 made an alliance with King Alfonso I of Naples (Alfonso V of Aragon), whose vassal he became, and a permanent Neapolitan garrison was installed in his fortress of Krujë. The misgivings of the other Albanian princes about this treaty were allayed by papal representations.

The popes did what they could to help the Albanians, but the other European princes were too deeply engaged in their own quarrels to support Skanderbeg. Pope Pius II's appeal fell on deaf ears. The climax came in 1466 with the siege of Krujë by 200,000 Turks led by the sultan Mohammed II, who had to return home unsuccessful. A second siege of Krujë by Mohammed in 1467 was likewise raised, but this was Skanderbeg's last triumph. A year later he died from fever, mourned by a whole nation. Krujë fell to the Turks in 1478 and the conquest of Albania was completed with the evacuation of Durazzo by the Venetians in 1501.

4. Under Turkish Rule.—As a result of the Turkish conquest Albania was devastated, and the destruction of the monuments of Latin and Christian civilization, begun during previous invasions, was intensified. Thousands of Albanians fled to Italy; many others, especially among the landowning class, embraced Islam. Turkish administration was established in the cities and the lowlands but the communities of the mountainous interior continued to enjoy their ancient autonomy, subject to the payment of tribute. For more than four centuries Albania suffered cultural stagnation and economic decadence. The land could not feed even a depleted population, and many Albanians left to seek fortune in other parts of the Ottoman Empire. Muslim Albanians, educated in Turkish schools, reached high positions in the army and in the administration, and hardy mountaineers joined the Turkish Army as professional soldiers. But national sentiment never died, and whenever Turkey went to war with European powers the Albanians seized the opportunity to revolt.

When the crisis of the Ottoman Empire began in the 19th century (*see* EASTERN QUESTION) administrative chaos and economic stagnation in Albania were at their worst. Two-thirds of the population had become Muslims, the remainder being Roman Catholics and Greek Orthodox. Muslim and Christian lived side by side without acute religious strife. Some of the Muslim landlords who had acquired their titles of bey or pasha by military service with the sultan acted as his local representatives, while the virtually independent highland communities of northern and eastern Albania were ruled by their *bajraktar* (standard-bearer) assisted by a council of elders.

The weakness of the central power encouraged ambitious local leaders. In the south, Ali (*q.v.*), son of a minor bey, rose to be pasha of Janina and made himself an independent ruler from the Shkumbin River to the Pindus Mountains. After a ruthless and efficient career, however, he was overthrown and killed at Janina in 1822.

In northern Albania three generations of the Bushati family strove to make themselves independent of Constantinople. The lands of Mehmet Bushati, in the 18th century, stretched from

MESI BRIDGE NEAR SHKODËR, PROBABLY BUILT IN THE 15TH CENTURY AT THE TIME OF THE TURKISH CONQUEST

Scutari to Tiranë, but his grandson Mustafa was captured by the Turks in 1831 in the Rosafat fortress at Scutari. Once their nominal authority had been reestablished over Albania, the Turks introduced the administrative and social reforms of the *tanzimat* (*see* ABDUL MEJID I) but their success was sporadic and limited.

5. The Independence Movement, 1878–1914.—At the Congress of Berlin (*q.v.*) in 1878, the European powers confirmed the cession to Montenegro of the Albanian districts of Gusinje and Plave and the ports of Antivari (Bar) and Dulcigno (Ulqinj), which Russia had snatched from Turkey by the Treaty of San Stefano. With the support of the Turkish authorities, the Albanians formed a national league at Prizren to resist this cession. The powers sent warships into the Adriatic to secure the ports at least for Montenegro. Then the Turks, aware that the Albanians were fighting for their own independence, turned against them and assisted the naval squadron. The loss of the two ports, however, greatly stimulated the Albanian independence movement.

The Albanians had to struggle against both the repression by the Turks and encroachments by their neighbours. Publications in Albanian were forbidden by the Turks since the national language and alphabet served as a unifying factor to counteract religious diversity. The League of Prizren was disbanded, but patriotic societies were formed in Constantinople and in the Balkan capitals and published the works of poets and writers which were secretly distributed in Albania. The national movement was intensified after the revolution of the Young Turks. A national congress at Monastir (Bitolj) in 1909 (which also adopted the unified Albanian alphabet) appointed a committee of national union, envisaging, as a first step toward complete independence, an autonomous Albania within the Ottoman Empire, including the four vilayets (provinces) of Scutari, Kosovo, Monastir, and Janina. The Young Turks however, though they owed much of their success to the Albanians, refused to acknowledge their right to self-government until a national uprising in 1912 culminated in the occupation of Shkup (Skopje) by Albanian mountaineers under the command of Isa Boletin. Thereupon the Young Turks yielded. The puppet chamber of deputies was dissolved and a Turkish delegation went to Pristina (Prishtina) to negotiate.

The neighbouring Balkan states resented the Albanians' success, since an independent Albania within its ethical frontiers would deprive them of the best part of the spoils of the Ottoman Empire which they coveted. With a view to partition of these areas they had signed a military alliance early in 1912, and they now had to go to war earlier than they had intended (*see* BALKAN WARS). The sudden collapse of the Turkish Army left the Albanians exposed to the onslaught of the Greek, Serbian, and Montenegrin armies. Nevertheless their national leaders gathered in Vlorë (Valona) to proclaim the independence of Albania on Nov. 28, 1912, and Ismail Qemal Vlora became the head of the first Albanian government.

The Serbs' advance toward Durazzo alarmed Austria-Hungary, just as the Greeks' declared aim of annexing southern Albania including Vlorë alarmed Italy. To prevent the war's leading to a general European conflagration, Sir Edward Grey called a conference of the powers in London. Russia took the Slav side, Austria-Hungary and Italy the other, but finally the principle of an independent Albania was accepted (December 1912). When it came to drawing frontiers, however, self-determination gave way to the balance of power, and Serbia was allowed to keep Kosovo, a province with more than 800,000 Albanians in it. The Greek frontier was left to be established on the spot by an international còmmission, which eventually drew it in the protocol of Florence (1913).

The great powers decided to appoint Prince William of Wied as ruler of the new state, assisted by an international control commission. After his long-delayed arrival in Durazzo a new government under Turkhan Pasha tried to establish its authority over the territory that was to become Albania. But Greece had turned southern Albania into the so-called autonomous Northern Epirus, Montenegro had occupied Scutari thanks to the treachery of Essad Pasha (*q.v.*), and a peasant revolt had spread in central Albania. Confusion and disorder were at their highest when World War I broke out. Albania was then occupied by the belligerents and became a battleground in spite of its declared neutrality.

6. The Settlement of 1921.—At the Conference of Paris after World War I, Italy joined Albania's Balkan neighbours in contending for the partition of the country, but Woodrow Wilson saved it from being sacrificed to diplomatic expediency. The Paris deliberations closed without solving the Albanian problem, which was passed to the so-called Conference of Ambassadors (*q.v.*). The Albanians, tired of waiting, held a national congress (1920) in the small town of Lushnje, despite the presence of Italian troops. A regency council was elected, a government formed under Sulejman Delvina and Tiranë chosen as the temporary capital. The Allied troops occupying Shkodër and Korçë handed these places over to the national government. An Albanian rising in Vlorë then forced the Italians to withdraw, the troubled state of affairs in Italy itself adding to their difficulties. In December 1920 Albania entered the League of Nations, and in November 1921 the Conference of Ambassadors at last reaffirmed the frontiers of 1913. The League intervened to induce the Yugoslavs to evacuate the Albanian territory that they had occupied.

7. The Kingdom of Albania.—From 1921 to 1924 the liberal intelligentsia of the new state tried in vain to set up a democratic regime. Ahmed Bey Zogu, prime minister from December 1922 to February 1924, was driven from the country in June 1924 by a national uprising, which led to the formation of a revolutionary government under Bishop Fan Noli. Six months later Ahmed Zogu, who was to rule dictatorially until the Italian invasion of 1939, came back to power with the backing of the conservative landlords and the highland chieftains and with help from the Yugoslavs.

Despite his obligation to the Yugoslavs, Ahmed Zogu aligned Albania with Italy by two treaties (1926 and 1927). Next, in 1928, he proclaimed himself king of the Albanians as Zog I (*q.v.*). The political and military alliance with Italy however was accompanied by concessions to Italian companies. Albania received a loan of 50,000,000 gold francs at a heavy rate of interest and, unable to pay the interest even for the first year, was to lose its freedom of action in the economic and eventually in the political field. Practically nothing was done to organize agriculture, the mainspring of the country's life, on a sound basis, and the great landlords were left to exploit their estates for their personal benefit. Grain had to be imported, and the balance of trade showed a constant deficit. Finally Italy had to subsidize the monarchy for purely political reasons.

Behind a constitutional facade Zog ruled as a dictator, buying support with patronage. Poverty was widespread and discontent acute among the peasants and the liberal intelligentsia. The lower strata of the educated class were already looking to Communism as a solution of the country's social problems. Several attempts at armed revolt proved to be costly failures and led to further repression. Yet the 11 years of Zog's monarchy formed the only period in modern times when Albania enjoyed political stability under a national government. Public administration and all the machinery of a modern state had to be created. The gendarmery organized by British officers was a model. Hundreds of boys and girls received scholarships to western universities and on their return many were appointed to administrative posts. In spite of Italian pressure Fascism was never introduced, so that public education and literary creation remained free from ideological regimentation. The main towns were linked by good roads, and for the first time in history the central government's authority was exercised in the remote mountain districts, so that national unity became at last a reality. Albania in the long run would have been able to free itself from Italian tutelage if the course of international affairs had been different.

Zog's marriage to the Hungarian countess Geraldine Apponyi in 1938 amid genuine popular rejoicing was the swan song of the Albanian monarchy. Hardly a year had passed before Mussolini, prompted by Germany's annexation of Bohemia and Moravia, decided to turn Albania into an Italian military outpost. His ultimatum to Zog, demanding a monetary and customs union and the installation of an Italian garrison on Albanian territory, was re-

GUNTHER REITZ—PIX FROM PUBLIX

STATUE OF JOSEPH STALIN IN SKANDERBEG SQUARE, TIRANË, WITH THE MINARET OF THE HAJI ETHEM MOSQUE (COMPLETED IN 1821) AND THE VENETIAN CLOCK TOWER SURMOUNTED BY THE COMMUNIST STAR

jected, and Mussolini chose Good Friday, 1939, to invade Albania with 100,000 troops backed by his Navy and Air Force. The Albanian government was unprepared, and such sporadic resistance as the invaders encountered came from local units fighting against overwhelming odds. Military occupation was followed by the transformation of the country into an Italian province with a puppet Albanian government. Victor Emmanuel III of Italy was proclaimed king of Albania, and supreme power was exercised by his lieutenant general, Francesco Jacomoni. Preparations for World War II were hastened, and the exploitation of Albania's natural resources began in earnest to increase Italy's supplies of essential raw materials (oil, iron, copper, etc.).

8. World War II.—Italy entered World War II in June 1940 and, on Oct. 28, invaded Greece from Albania, but instead of the triumphant advance on Athens that had been expected the adventure ended in military disaster. The Greeks occupied the Albanian districts of Korçë and Gjirokastër (Argyrokastron) and furthermore took the opportunity to revive their claim to Northern Epirus. Finally, Hitler rescued the Italians by sending his troops through Yugoslavia to Greece.

When the storm of invasion had died down Albanian nationalists began to organize secret resistance against the occupier. The Balli Kombetar (National Front), with members from all classes of society, was formed to restore independence under a democratic regime of equality, social justice, and personal freedom. Its armed bands, under army officers or civilian leaders, did much to hinder the Italian war effort, as did the Zogists of the Legality Party.

When the Germans invaded the U.S.S.R. in 1941 the Communists aligned themselves with the resistance. They numbered only a few scattered groups, mainly of petty-bourgeois intellectuals, but with the help of two emissaries sent by Tito from Yugoslavia they organized themselves into a party which was eventually recognized by the Comintern. To win popular support the party adopted the camouflage of the National Liberation Movement (L.N.C.), which at first issued an impeccably democratic program with only hints of future plans. The general course of the war after June 1941, moreover, led to the Communists' receiving more support and material help from the western Allies than was given to any other group in Albania. This, added to their ruthless methods and propaganda, ensured that they would remain the only organized political force in the country. Only after Mussolini's downfall did the Balli Kombetar and the nationalist Communists try to form a united front, but this agreement was denounced by the pro-Tito and the pro-Russian Communists, who then plunged the country into civil war. The nationalist movement was reduced to powerlessness.

9. Communist Supremacy.—Totalitarian communism was set up in November 1944 with the formation of a government led by Enver Hoxha (Hodja). A wave of terror swept the country. Thousands were summarily executed for alleged collaboration with the enemy and various crimes were invented by the new rulers to destroy their opponents. The Roman Catholic clergy suffered most heavily. The Communists then carried out their social revolution with ruthless efficiency. All properties belonging to the Italian government or to private citizens were nationalized. The landowning class was virtually wiped out and the large estates were distributed to the peasants who worked on them. Next the bourgeoisie was deprived of its assets through overwhelming taxation. Many of its prominent members, moreover, were put to death on political charges. Elections to a National Assembly took place in 1945.

Albania's mining of the Corfu Channel and firing on vessels passing through it (1946) led to a long dispute with Great Britain. The United States also broke off diplomatic relations.

From the end of World War II to 1948 Albania was a satellite of Yugoslavia with a customs and monetary union, and a series of mixed companies were formed to carry out economic development. This cooperation, however, had hardly begun when Yugoslavia was expelled from the Cominform, and the Albanian Communists were faced with a crucial choice. Koci Xoxe (Dzodze), a former tinker who had become organizing secretary of the Communist Party and head of the secret police, led a small pro-Yugoslav clique, but this was overpowered by the Stalinist faction, which had Hoxha as its political expert and Mehmet Shehu as its military strategist. Xoxe and his chief supporters were put to death as traitors.

Thenceforward, till 1961, Albania was a satellite of the U.S.S.R. In the elections for the National Assembly in 1950, when the Democratic Front, led by the Party of Labour (Communist), was modeled on the Communist and nonparty bloc in the U.S.S.R., official candidates won 99% of the votes—a pattern that has been regularly repeated. Although still geographically isolated from the Soviet bloc, Albania was included in the Warsaw Treaty Organization in 1955. Thousands of experts and all kinds of industrial equipment were sent to exploit the country's raw mineral resources, and preparations were made to turn Vlorë into a Soviet naval base. Russia's long-standing desire for an outpost on the Adriatic was fulfilled—ironically by a nation to whose creation the Russians before World War I had been implacably opposed.

The Albanian Communists maintained a Stalinist system of government while paying lip service to N. S. Khrushchev's new policies, and no relaxation of the police regime was felt in any quarter. The U.S.S.R., however, found it expedient to continue to support the Tiranë regime. The cancellation by the U.S.S.R. of an accumulated debt of 422,000,000 rubles was announced in 1957, together with the opening of a large new credit. An extended visit to Albania paid by Khrushchev in May–June 1959 was interpreted as signalizing Albania's status as a fully integrated member of the Soviet bloc. But from 1960 Albanian-Soviet relations deteriorated. Soviet economic aid dried up and Albania signed economic agreements with Communist China. Albanian hostility toward Yugoslavia was intensified, and propaganda attacks against Yugoslav revisionism followed the same line as those of China. After Khrushchev's denunciation of Albania's pro-Stalinism at the 22nd Congress of the Soviet Communist Party, the Soviet government severed diplomatic relations in December 1961.

Relations with China were consolidated by the first official visit of Chou En-lai to Albania (Dec. 31, 1963–Jan. 9, 1964). For the Chinese, Albania was a useful foothold in Europe and a faithful puppet-voice in support of their version of Communism. China supplied technicians and some equipment to assist Albanian industries, and a new high-powered radio transmitter was set up to broadcast the Chinese point of view; but real economic aid from China remained slight. Though barter agreements were concluded with some Communist countries and with a few Western countries and though diplomatic relations were developed with China's satellites and with some of the new African states, Albania remained largely isolated from the rest of the world, with a precarious economy. (T. Z.; D. R. O.-H.)

IV. POPULATION

The total population of Albania was 1,391,499 at the census of Oct. 2, 1955, and 1,626,315 at the census of Oct. 2, 1960. It was officially estimated at 1,889,800 in April 1966. In 1955 about 67.8% of the population had been engaged in agriculture or stock raising; 15.9% in construction or industrial labour; 11.8% in government employment; and the rest in crafts, commerce, or the professions.

The principal towns, in order of size in 1960, are Tiranë (Tirana; the capital), Shkodër (Scutari), Durrës (Durazzo), Vlorë (Vlonë or Valona), Korçë (Koritsa), Elbasan, Berat, Kavajë and Gjirokastër (Argyrokastron). The population of Tiranë (136,295 in 1960) is between three and four times as large as that of the next largest town.

V. ADMINISTRATION AND SOCIAL CONDITIONS

In 1946 the Communist government promulgated a Soviet-type constitution, which was revised in 1950. The National Assembly, elected by universal adult suffrage, with its Presidium, is nominally the sovereign body, but executive power lies with the Council of Ministers. In practice all decisions are taken jointly by the cabinet and the Central Committee of the Communist Party and simultaneously communicated to the district executive committees and the parallel party committees. There are 26 administrative districts (*rrethe*) and the city of Tiranë.

Taxation and Wages.—Taxation consists mainly of obligatory deliveries of produce and of indirect taxation from profits on state enterprises, covering almost all non-agricultural production. Direct taxes on lower incomes were abolished in 1967; total direct taxation came to only about 1% of revenues. After the revaluation of the lek, official retail price cuts were made for most essential foods and some manufactures.

Housing.—Housing in the towns is controlled; in the villages individuals are still free to build. By tradition southern village houses are mainly grouped together, but in the north sturdy, stone houses often stand alone on the farmer's land, from customary motives of independence and security against attack; the grouping of new houses is now encouraged.

Social Conditions.—In the past Albania was almost entirely an agricultural and pastoral country. Land was owned largely by families in the north, where the clan system persisted, and in

STREET IN DURRËS, THE MAIN PORT OF ALBANIA, LINKED BY RAIL WITH TIRANË AND ELBASAN. THE GREAT MOSQUE, BUILT IN 1939, APPEARS IN THE BACKGROUND

parts of the south where many men bought land with savings accumulated during emigration, principally in the United States. In central Albania (Tiranë, Elbasan, Berat, and Vlorë) land was chiefly owned by the beys and farmed by peasants on a partnership basis. Produce was brought into markets and freely sold. Large flocks of sheep and goats were grazed everywhere on communal pastures, often, especially by the Vlach shepherds of the south, on the mountains in summer and on the plains in winter. Sheep are milked and dairy products form the staple items of diet apart from bread. Meat was a luxury, chiefly for festive occasions, though more was eaten in the towns. The proportion of wheat to maize (corn) bread has been increasing, but since the 1913 frontier deprived Albania of substantial plains now in Yugoslavia the country has never been self-sufficient in cereals. Clothing of extreme durability, from wool and goats' hair in various local designs, was entirely handmade, as were the women's beautiful national costumes.

The Communist government has aimed at the central control and intensification of agriculture, the exploitation of mineral resources, and the creation of a substantial state-controlled manufacturing industry. Because a very large proportion of the agricultural as well as the mineral wealth is exported in return for machinery, equipment, etc., the condition of the individual peasant remains poor as in the past.

The development of industry has been artificially rapid and consequently skilled workers are at a premium, foreign technicians being indispensable. Women have been brought into industry, though the raising of families is also encouraged by tax concessions, grants, and public day nurseries. Many villages have electricity, and radio sets are widespread. The youth movement (*Rinija*) and the pioneer organization for the very young are strongly supported by the government. Sport is encouraged, as are the theatre, ballet, and music, and Tiranë has a film studio. These developments, accompanied by the general regimentation of the people, have radically changed the national life.

Justice.—The districts have tribunals of first instance, with elected magistrates, and there is a high court at Tiranë. An act concerning "personal crimes" was aimed at stamping out the traditional vendetta.

Welfare Services.—Medical care is free, and after 1945 there was a large increase of hospitals, sanatoriums, and maternity

Administrative Subdivisions

Districts	Area in sq.mi.	Population (1960 census)	Districts	Area in sq. mi.	Population (1960 census)
Berat	410	85,227	Mat	397	38,457
Durrës	335	126,606	Mirditë	266	17,318
Elbasan	580	105,142	Përmet	367	26,911
Ersekë	312	17,460	Peshkopi	609	77,833
Fier	460	112,123	Pogradec	279	35,899
Gjirokastër	439	44,185	Pukë	375	22,539
Gramsh	270	19,989	Sarandë	424	48,039
Korçë	843	139,271	Shkodër	978	128,235
Krujë	236	43,229	Skrapar	271	19,823
Kukës	604	47,521	Tepelenë	315	25,709
Lezhë	182	27,231	Tiranë*	446	58,625
Librazhd	391	35,718	Tropojë	403	20,615
Lushnje	277	65,475	Vlorë	621	100,840

* Excluding the city of Tiranë, pop. 136,295.

Albanian street scenes. (Above) Gjirokastër, southern Albania, possibly on the site of the ancient Hadrianopolis; (left) in the old quarter of Tiranë, the capital; (below) plumbers in Shkodër's main street

(ABOVE) THREE LIONS, (BOTTOM LEFT) DALMAS—PIX FROM PUBLIX, (BOTTOM RIGHT) © ALLAN CHAPPELOW, M.A., F.R.S.A.

political commissar was reintroduced. Albanian pilots operate aircraft originally supplied by the U.S.S.R. A paramilitary organization, SH.N.U.M. (Association for Assistance to the Army and Defense), trains volunteers of both sexes in marksmanship, communications, and nursing, and encourages physical fitness.

(D. R. O.-H.)

VI. THE ECONOMY

The deeply dissected, mountainous nature of the country, two-thirds of which is over 3,000 ft. in height, the marshy coastal plain, and the general difficulty of communications both internally and with the outside world have all been factors inhibiting the economic development of Albania in the past. At the beginning of the 20th century the population of Albania was largely illiterate, traditional, and generally oriental in outlook, and with a standard of living barely at subsistence level. Agricultural practices had remained unchanged for centuries; the resources of the country were unknown. The development of the modern economy only began after World War I, partly under Italian instigation. After 1944, when the Communist government came into power, plans for development were speeded up, but capital was lacking.

Help was sought from the Yugoslavs, but after the break with Yugoslavia in 1948 Albania relied almost entirely on the Soviet Union, both for technical advice and for capital loans, till the 1960s. An interim two-year plan was put into operation in 1949–50, followed by five-year plans. The government's aim to transform the whole of the social and economic life by the rationalization of agriculture and industrialization has meant a painful transition for the economy.

clinics, all state-owned. There are state life, crop, and stock insurance schemes.

Education.—Primary education is compulsory for four years for boys and girls from the age of seven. There are 8-year and 12-year schools, which include the primary classes, and kindergartens, evening schools, teachers' training schools, and technical schools, both industrial and agricultural. The State University of Tiranë, founded in 1957, incorporating six former institutes of higher learning, has faculties of law, economics, history and philology, engineering, medicine, natural sciences, and pedagogy. There is a high institute of agricultural and veterinary science. Increased adult education classes are claimed to have reduced illiteracy.

Defense.—Albania has an army, a navy and an air force, a frontier guard, and internal security forces, including police. The armed forces are manned mainly by conscripts; the system of rank in the armed forces was abolished in May 1966 and the function of

Agriculture.—The basis of the Albanian economy has long been agriculture. Arable cultivation is limited by lack of suitable land, and since World War II much effort has been made to increase the available area by land reclamation and irrigation projects, and by bringing more of the highlands into use. In the late 1960s of the total land area of 2,874,000 ha. (about 11,100 sq.mi.) about 44% was said to be under forest. Of the remaining suitable land, there was probably twice as much under pasture as under crops (including fruit, vine, and olive orchards). No precise figures, however, are issued, the improvements and production figures being regularly quoted in terms of percentages of previous periods.

Maize (corn) is Albania's chief crop, but wheat, rice, and potatoes have become increasingly important. Emphasis has been placed on crops that will engender industry, such as olives, cotton, tobacco, sugar beets, and sunflowers. Where conditions permit, oxen and wooden plows are being replaced by tractors, modern farm implements, and even combine harvesters. By the late 1960s there were said to be more than 7,500 tractors in the country.

As one might expect from the physical conditions, livestock raising has always been important, probably more so than crop farming. The total number of animals was just about back to prewar levels by the late 1950s, with about 2,500,000 sheep (grazed in state-owned "brigades") and goats and about 500,000 cattle; the number of cattle increased in the 1960s. A new development was the improvement in both quality and number of pigs: the number almost tripled after 1946, reaching at least 100,000 by the 1960s in spite of Muslim opposition to pig farming.

The freehold of cultivated land formerly owned by families was completely vested in the state by 1967 except for land devoted to state-run farms. Family plot-size was reduced in collectives, but milk and vegetables were supplied at less than the ruling prices and other incentives were provided. These measures and increased highland acreage were intended to make Albania self-supporting in grain and other foodstuffs, and to make larger surpluses of such specialized goods as table fruit, olives, and wine grapes available for export. Irrigation works were also considerably increased with the intention of providing water for more than half of all arable lands by the early 1970s.

Forestry.—Not all of the large area under forest is of particularly good quality. Some of the most valuable trees, such as walnut, were exploited and devastated before World War II, and some of the best timber is inaccessible in the mountains. There is much beech, fir, chestnut, oak, and lime. Extensive replanting took place after the war, and in the mid-1960s the emphasis in new planting was on poplar.

GUNTHER REITZ—PIX FROM PUBLIX

FERTILE PLAIN NEAR ELBASAN, ON THE NORTHERN BANK OF THE SHKUMBIN RIVER. ALBANIA IS MAINLY AN AGRICULTURAL NATION

Mining.—Although not rich in mineral wealth, Albania has important mineral resources. Bituminous coal is lacking, but brown coal is worked in central Albania as well as in the Memaliaj-Tepelenë district, the Korçë basin, and at Pogradec. Albania is an important producer of chrome. New deposits have been found in the northeast. The copper ores are worked both in the north and in the southeast at Vithkuq near Korçë. Other minerals worked include pyrites, iron nickel ore, arsenic ore, bauxite, gypsum, and limestone for cement, as well as oil, asphalt, and bitumen.

Even before World War II the Albanian oil fields were being exploited by foreign oil companies, mainly Italian. The chief fields are at Kuçovë (Qytet Stalin) and at Patos northeast of Vlorë. Drilling has proceeded there and in other localities. Before World War II crude oil was piped to Vlorë for export to Italy; since the war, much of it has been exported under barter agreements, while the rest goes to Cerrik refinery (near Elbasan), said to have an ultimate capacity of 300,000 tons, enough for most local needs. Natural gas is also an important source of fuel but is limited in use because of distribution problems.

Industry.—Before 1940 there were few industries in Albania apart from those associated with agricultural activities such as flour milling, brewing, and tobacco processing, together with cement, brickmaking, and carpentry. Heavy industry was nonexistent and the few consumer goods needed were imported. Under the fourth five-year plan (1966–70) industry was responsible for about 40% of the national income, and industrial production exceeded 56% of total production. The emphasis has been on the development of hydroelectricity as a major source of power. Thus, the advantages of the many perennial streams fed by heavy rainfall from the mountains are obvious, though high evaporation rates and seepage from storage basins present difficulties. The sparse population also makes distribution costly and inhibits really large capital schemes except at a few points.

The two largest plants are the Karl Marx at Ulzë, with an initial capacity of 125,000,000 kw-hr., ultimately to be expanded, and the Lenin plant near Tiranë, which supplies the capital with electricity and water. In 1967 a start was made on a hydroelectric plant on the Drin at Vau i Dejës, southeast of Shkodër. A large number of small power stations have been built to supply local needs.

Industrial plants established after World War II include textile combines at Tiranë and at Berat, cotton ginning works at Fier, brick and glass factories, metalworking plants at Tiranë (making machinery, spare parts, diesel engines, and farm implements), cement works and a rice mill at Vlorë, and sugar-beet refineries at Korçë and Maliq. Other developments include food processing and canning, and the production of leather, footwear, soap, chemicals and copper concentrates, plywood and furniture, rubber goods, paper and cement bags, fertilizers, copper wire, and domestic hardware. A steel mill was opened at Elbasan in 1966. Chinese technicians replaced those from the U.S.S.R. and local workers have been trained intensively.

Transport and Communications.—Albania has long been a backwater in southeastern Europe, and trade routes have tended to bypass it on either side. Italian and central European trade contacts with the eastern Mediterranean lands were easier and cheaper by sea, and Venetian and Ragusan ships ignored Albanian ports. Turkish caravan routes and, later, railways made use of the Vardar valley routeway through Macedonia. In fact, only two highways have traversed Albania in the past. The Via Egnatia was a road engineered by the Romans to link Italy directly with the Balkan provinces and to carry Roman troops and trade overland to Salonika. On the division of the Roman Empire into East and West this route fell into disuse. The Via Zenta, along the Drin valley, was developed by Ragusan merchants to tap the resources of the old Serbian Empire. The advent of the Turks, the eclipse of the medieval Slav empires, and the troubles which followed put an end to this trading enterprise, and Albanian caravan routes lost their importance.

The Turks had no interest in maintaining roads across Albania beyond those necessary for general administration, nor did the

SOVFOTO

KUÇOVË (QYTETI STALIN), ONE OF ALBANIA'S PRINCIPAL OIL FIELDS, DEVELOPED AFTER WORLD WAR II

primitive tribal economy of the country call for any elaborate system of communications, as its needs were met by mule and cart tracks focusing on small market towns.

Modern communications were constructed largely for strategic reasons, first by the Austrians and then by the Italians. As a result Albania still lacks an integrated pattern of communications, and many rural areas in north and central Albania are as distant as 10–15 mi. from the nearest road. Shkodër is the best road centre but is of peripheral importance to the rest of the country. Tiranë is linked by adequate roads not only with the port of Durrës and with Shkodër, but south with Elbasan and Korçë, and east with the hinterland.

There are probably not more than 3,000 mi. of modern roads and, although some have been excellently engineered through difficult country, the surfaces are poor because of the difficulty of maintenance. Several local roads have been built, but construction is costly because it calls for many bridges and elaborate engineering to overcome steep gradients.

Albania has few railways, and the building of normal-gauge lines was not begun till 1947. One line connects Durrës and Tiranë and has a northward branch in the direction of Milot; another line connects Durrës and Elbasan and has a short branch from Papër southward to Cerrik oil refinery and a longer branch (started in 1967) from Rrogozhinë southward to Fier. There is also the prewar narrow-gauge line from Vlorë to the bitumen workings at Selenicë.

Air services have been developed since the 1930s, with Tiranë as the centre. Albania and China maintain a jointly owned shipping line.

Albania has a reasonably extensive telephonic network. There are internal and external radio broadcasting services.

Finance and Trade.—Albania had no coinage of its own before 1925. Then the National Bank of Albania was founded with help from Italy. The monetary unit then established was the Albanian franc, divided into five leks and fixed at parity with the Swiss franc. An underdeveloped country with a shortage of capital for internal investment and with an adverse trading balance, Albania still depended heavily on Italy for finance; and in 1939, after the Italian occupation of the country, the Albanian franc was linked to the Italian lira at a ratio of 1 to 6.25.

In 1946–47, when Albania's financial ties with Western Europe were broken, a new currency was established, based on the lek at parity with the Yugoslav dinar; but after the break with Yugoslavia (1948) the currency was reorganized again, and the lek was linked to the Soviet ruble at a ratio, originally, of 100 to 8. After the break with the U.S.S.R., it was not until August 1965 that financial realities were faced, and the lek was devalued, 1 new lek representing 10 old leks. Foreign exchange rates were adjusted by the Albanian State Bank.

Currency changes make difficult any comparison between prewar and present revenue. After World War II, Albania depended heavily on subsidy and loans from the U.S.S.R. till 1961. The loss of this aid has been slightly offset by credits from China.

Investment is fixed according to the five-year plans, the target figures of which are annually drastically revised in the light of actual attainment. Industry, power projects, and technical education receive priority. The revenue is largely raised by indirect taxation, by a system of levies and quotas on the production of farms, and by the profits of state enterprises.

For export, Albania has a surplus of crude oil, bitumen, chrome and other ores, timber, fruit, vegetable oils, and other specialized agricultural products, and an increasing range of finished and semi-finished goods. From abroad mainly capital goods are needed. While the state has nominal agreements for barter with various Communist countries, as well as special trade agreements with China, geography dictates that in the long run trade can be profitably developed only with the countries of the Mediterranean and with central Europe. Consequently, Albania has contracted trade agreements with Italy, Austria, France, and Yugoslavia; but commerce remains inhibited by the difficulties of financial negotiation and the political climate.

See BALKAN PENINSULA; also references under "Albania" in the Index.   (H. R. WI.; D. R. O.-H.)

BIBLIOGRAPHY.—For general description *see* M. E. Durham, *High Albania* (1909); C. A. Chekrezi, *Albania Past and Present* (1919); J. Bourcart, *L'Albanie et les Albanais* (1921); H. Louis, *Albanien: eine Landeskunde vornehmlich auf Grund eigener Reisen* (1927); N. Heseltine, *Scarred Background: a Journey through Albania* (1938); S. Skendi(ed.), *Albania* (1957); E. B. Valev, *Albaniya* (in Russian; 1960); D. Cusack, *Illyria Reborn* (1966). For vegetation *see* F. Markgraf, *Pflanzengeographie von Albanien* (1932). For customs *see* M. Hasluck, *The Unwritten Law in Albania* (1954).

For general history *see* J. Swire, *Albania: the Rise of a Kingdom* (1929); T. Zavalani, *Histori e Shqipnis*, 2 vol. (1957–66); S. Skendi, *The Albanian National Awakening, 1878–1912* (1967). For World War II and later politics *see* J. Amery, *Sons of the Eagle* (1948); L. Gardiner, *The Eagle Spreads His Claws: a History of the Corfu Channel Dispute* (1966); H. Hamm, *Albania: China's Beachhead in Europe*, Eng. trans. (1963); W. E. Griffith, *Albania and the Sino-Soviet Rift* (1963).

For earlier works on Albania *see* E. Legrand, *Bibliographie albanaise* (1912).

Current history and available statistics are summarized annually in the *Britannica Book of the Year*.

ALBANIA, the ancient name of part of the Azerbaijan Soviet Socialist Republic, U.S.S.R., in the eastern Caucasus, extending along the left bank of the Kura (Cyrus) river from the hills west of the confluence of the Kura with the Alazan as far as the Caspian sea. The Albani, according to Strabo, were tall and well-built and, in character, simple and honest; they worshiped Zeus, the sun and, more especially, the moon. They lived on the produce of their fertile land but were less skilled in agriculture than their western neighbours, the Iberi. They became subject to Armenia after their defeat by Tigranes I *c.* 90 B.C. When in 65 B.C. the Romans under Pompeius Magnus invaded their territory, the Albani are said to have mustered 60,000 infantry and 12,000 cavalry in an unsuccessful attempt to oppose them. By the terms of Pompeius' general settlement of the near east in 62 B.C. the king of the Albani became nominally a vassal of Rome. Their king made submission to the emperor Trajan again in A.D. 114. Their territory was overrun by the Alani during the reign of Hadrian and passed under Sassanid suzerainty, at the latest, by A.D. 364. They were driven finally into Armenia by the Khazars and ceased to exist as a separate people.

See D. Magie, *Roman Rule in Asia Minor* (1950); A. E. Christensen, *L'Iran sous les Sassanides* (1936).   (E. E. D. M. O.)

ALBANIA, ORTHODOX CHURCH OF, an autocephalous Orthodox Church the members of which are a minority in a predominantly Muslim country. Its Orthodox metropolitans formerly were Greek bishops directly dependent upon the ecumenical patriarchate of Constantinople. Before World War I, however, with Albania newly become an independent state, strong separatist tendencies were revealed in ecclesiastical as well as political matters, and the Albanian government began to claim ecclesiastical independence for its Orthodox population (about 20% of the total). In 1937 this was finally granted by the ecumenical patriarch, whose honorary primacy is recognized by the Albanian Orthodox. The Albanian synod is formed by the archbishop of Tirane as president, and the bishops of Berat, Korce (Koritsa) and Gjirokaster (Argyrokastron). A seminary was founded to provide elementary ecclesiastical education for parish priests. Many of the Albanian bishops had received their education in Greek seminaries and at the University of Athens.

Under Italian rule during World War II, the Albanian Orthodox Church suffered considerably, and some of its bishops were sent into exile. The policy of the Communist regime is not much more favourable to it, though the church theoretically enjoys complete religious liberty under the Albanian constitution. There is practically no communication with other Orthodox churches except those behind the "iron curtain." The language used in both teaching and worship is Albanian, into which all the liturgical books have been translated from the original Greek. A small number of Orthodox Albanians live abroad (some for political reasons), especially in the U.S., where a small independent Albanian Orthodox Church was founded under Fan Noli (Albanian prime minister in 1924), who became its bishop. *See also* ORTHODOX EASTERN CHURCH. (H. S. AL.)

ALBANIAN LANGUAGE, an Indo-European language, is spoken by about 2,000,000 inhabitants of the eastern Adriatic coast, within the national boundaries of Albania, and in neighbouring Serbia (Kosovo-Metohija) west of a line from Pristina to Lake Ohrid. There are perhaps an additional 500,000 speakers in isolated villages and village groups in southern Italy (Abruzzi e Molise, Basilicata, Apulia, Calabria and Sicily) and southern Greece (Boeotia, Attica, Euboea, Andros and the Peloponnesus).

Origins both of the general name Albanian (attested since Ptolemy; Calabrian Albanian Arbresh, modern Greek Arvanit-is, Turkish Arnaut), which traditionally referred to a clan area in central Albania, and of the native official name Shqiperi which may be a totem name originating in the term for "eagle," are much disputed.

Dialects.—The two principal dialects, Gheg in the north and Tosk in the south, are bounded roughly by the Shkumbi river, which bisects Albania. Gheg has more marked subvarieties, the most striking of which are the northernmost, which include those of the city of Shkoder (Scutari), the neighbouring mountains, Kosovo-Metohija, and the isolated village of Borgo Erizzo, on the Croatian coast of Dalmatia near Zadar (about 2,000 speakers; founded in the early 18th century by refugees from near Bar, formerly Antivari). All the Italian and Greek enclaves are Tosk and seem to be related in dialect most closely to the extreme south of Albania, known as Camerija; they represent incompletely understood population movements of the 13th–15th centuries. A few isolated outliers in Bulgaria, Turkey and Bessarabia are of unknown date, provenience and vitality, though an extant Tosk enclave in the Ukraine appears to be of moderately recent settlement; the enclaves of Istria and Sirmia are extinct. Gheg and Tosk have been diverging for a millennium; their less extreme forms are mutually intelligible.

History.—The official language, written in a standard Roman-based orthography adopted only in 1909 at a congress in Monastir (Bitolj), was from the beginning of the Albanian state until World War II based on the south Gheg dialect of Elbasan and after that time on Tosk. Before 1909, the little literature that was preserved, apart from material scientifically recorded by 19th-century scholars, was written in local makeshift Italianate, Hellenizing or even Turco-Arabic characters and systems.

A few brief written records are preserved from the 15th century, such as a baptismal formula from 1462. The scattering of books produced in the 16th and 17th centuries originated largely in the Gheg (often Scutarene north Gheg) area and reflect Roman Catholic missionary activities. Much of the small stream of literature in the 19th century was produced by exiles in foreign cities. The earliest purely literary work is perhaps the 18th-century poetry of the Calabrian Gjul Variboba, of the enclave at S. Giorgio, Italy;

a trickle of literary production continued through the 19th century in the Italian enclaves. No similar activity is recorded in the Greek enclaves. All these documents show the language in general little different from what is found today.

Morphology.—The grammatical categories and form classes of Albanian are much like those of other European languages. Nouns show gender, number, and case (three or four of them); a unique feature is that nouns are further inflected obligatorily to show definite or indefinite meaning. Adjectives, except numerals and certain quantifying expressions, follow the noun and are remarkable in having a prefix agreeing with the noun. Verbs have roughly the number and variety of forms found in French or Italian, and involve considerable irregularities. In general mechanics Albanian is reminiscent of Serbian, modern Greek and Romance; in sounds, of Hungarian and Rumanian.

Classification.—Albanian is of clearly Indo-European origin; this fact was recognized by Franz Bopp in 1854, and the details of its main correspondences were elaborated by Gustav Meyer in the 1880s and '90s. A few etymologies suffice to illustrate this relationship, as later refined by other scholars, particularly H. Pedersen and N. Jokl (the asterisk denotes a hypothetical form): *pesë* "five" (from $*penk^we$), *zjarm* "fire" ($*g^whermos$), *natë* "night" ($*nok^wt$-), *gjumë* "sleep" ($*súpnos$), *gjarpën* "snake" ($*sérpŏn$-), *bjer* "bring!" ($*bhere$), *djeg* "I burn" ($*dheg^whō$), *kam* "I have" ($*kapmi$), *pata* "I had" ($*pot$-), *pjek* "I roast" ($*pek^wō$), *thom, thua, thotë* "I say, you say, he says" ($*kē(n)smi$, $*kēns$ . . . , $*kē(ns)t$ . . . .). The verb system includes many archaic traits: retention of distinct active and middle personal endings (as in Greek); change of a stem vowel *e* in the present to *o* (from $*ē$) in the past; and reflexes of Indo-European stem suffixes in the present. Because of the superficial changes in the shape of the language over two millennia, and because of its borrowing of words from diverse neighbouring cultures, the clear continuity of the Indo-European heritage in Albanian has been underrated.

Albanian shows no obvious close affinity to any other Indo-European language; it is plainly the sole modern survivor of its own subgroup. Of ancient languages, both Thracian and Illyro-Messapic have been claimed as its ancestor or next of kin, but this relationship is not yet settled. (*See* ILLYRIAN LANGUAGE.)

Vocabulary.—Among the host of interesting borrowings from its neighbours, Albanian shows exceedingly few evidences of contact with ancient Greek; one such is Gheg *mokën* (Tosk *mokërë*) "millstone." Obviously close contacts with the Romans gave many Latin loans: *e.g., mik* "friend," *këndoj* "sing, read" (for this association of senses *cf.* Turkish *okumak*). Furthermore, Albanian attests parallel developments in Balkan Latin to those reflected in Rumanian: Latin *palūdem* "swamp" became *padūlem* and then Rumanian *pădure*, Albanian *pyll* "forest." Conversely, Rumanian shares some apparently native terms with Albanian: Rumanian *brad*, Albanian *bredh* "fir." Thus these two languages reflect special historical contacts of early date. Early contacts with Slavs gave *gozhdë* "nail." Many Italian, Turkish, modern Greek, Serbian and Macedonian-Slav loans are easily referred to cultural contacts of the last half millennium with Venetians, Ottomans, Greeks (to the south), and Slavs (to the east). A fair number of features (*e.g.*, the formation of the future tense) are shared with other Balkan languages, but are of obscure provenience and development; Albanian or its earlier kin could easily be the origin for at least some of these.

BIBLIOGRAPHY.—L. Newmark, *Structural Grammar of Albanian* (1957), excellent annotated bibliography of descriptive studies; N. Jokl, "Albaner" in M. Ebert's *Reallexikon der Vorgeschichte*, vol. i, 84–94 (1924); G. Meyer, *Etymologisches Wörterbuch der albanesischen Sprache* (1891); C. Tagliavini, *L'albanese di Dalmazia* (1937), etymological glossary supplements Meyer; E. Hamp, "Albanian and Messapic" in *Studies Presented to Joshua Whatmough* (1957); E. Legrand, *Bibliographie albanaise* to 1900 (1912); N. Jokl et al., *Indogermanisches Jahrbuch*, vii. Abteilung (1916–), elaborately complete bibliography. (E. P. H.)

ALBANO, LAKE (LAGO DI ALBANO), a crater lake in the Alban hills southeast of Rome, Italy. The lake, eliptic in shape, formed by the fusion of two ancient craters, lies at 961 ft. above sea level. It is 2 mi. long with a maximum width of 1½ mi.; and its greatest depth is 558 ft. Among the towns on its banks, Castel

Gandolfo (*q.v.*), summer residence of the pope and probable site of Alba Longa (*q.v.*), is best known.

An outlet of Lake Albano was made in 398–397 B.C. because the Delphic oracle said that Veii (*q.v.*) could only be taken when the lake's waters reached the sea. This outlet, still in use, is 1 mi. long, 6 ft. high and 4 ft. broad, with vertical shafts and a sluice chamber.   (G. Kh.)

ALBANY, DUKES OF. The name Albany, which formerly designated those parts of Scotland lying north of the firths of Clyde and Forth, has on several occasions been attached to a dukedom. After the four dukes of the first two creations (1398 and c. 1458; *see* below), the dukedom of Albany was next bestowed upon Henry Stuart, Lord Darnley, in 1565 and passed from him to his son James VI of Scotland and I of England, who gave it to his second son Charles (I) at birth. Charles II in 1660 gave it to his brother James, duke of York (later king as James VII and II). King George I, however, in 1716, gave the title duke of York and Albany to his youngest brother, Ernest Augustus (1674–1728), bishop of Osnabrück, who died without heirs. Next, in 1760, Edward Augustus (1739–67), second son of Frederick Louis, prince of Wales, was created duke of York and Albany by George II, but he also died without heirs. Then in 1784 the same title was given to George III's second son (*see* YORK [AND ALBANY], FREDERICK AUGUSTUS, DUKE OF), but he likewise left no heir. For the creation of 1881 *see* below.

The First Creation.—ROBERT STEWART (c. 1340–1420), duke of Albany, regent of Scotland, was the third son of Robert II of Scotland and his first wife, Elizabeth Mure. He was made high chamberlain of Scotland in 1382 and won a military reputation in campaigns against England. Chosen guardian of Scotland by the estates in 1388, he retained the control of affairs after his brother John became king as Robert III in 1390. In April 1398 he was created duke of Albany. In 1399, however, his nephew David, duke of Rothesay, the heir to the crown, succeeded him as governor. Uncle and nephew soon differed, and in March 1402 the latter died in prison at Falkland. While Albany and the earl of Douglas were certainly responsible for the imprisonment of Rothesay, the cause of his death is unknown, though contemporary suspicion pointed to the uncle's guilt. Restored to the office of governor, the duke was chosen regent of the kingdom after the death of Robert III in 1406, because the new king, James I, was a prisoner in London. Albany continued, with vigour if with no great success, to prosecute the war with England, which had been renewed a few years before. He suppressed a formidable revolt led by Donald Macdonald, 2nd lord of the Isles, who claimed the earldom of Ross and was in alliance with Henry IV of England. Albany died at Stirling castle in Sept. 1420 and was buried in Dunfermline abbey. His son, MURDAC (or Murdoch) STEWART, succeeded him as duke of Albany and regent but was executed in 1425, when the dukedom became extinct.

The Second Creation.—ALEXANDER STEWART (c. 1454–1485), duke of Albany, the second son of James II of Scotland, was styled earl of March in 1455 and created duke of Albany before 1458. Both he and John, earl of Mar, quarreled with their brother James III, who imprisoned them in 1479. Mar died but Albany escaped to carry on a series of intrigues with the English, who supported his pretensions to the Scottish crown. He was lieutenant general of the realm during the winter of 1482–83, but was attainted in 1483 and defeated in another rising in 1484. Escaping to France, he died there in 1485.

JOHN STEWART (c. 1484–1536), duke of Albany, regent of Scotland, was the only son of Alexander Stewart by his second wife, Anne de la Tour. In 1515, at the request of the Scottish parliament, he came to Scotland from France. Inaugurated regent in July, he organized resistance to the English influence of Queen Margaret (*q.v.*) Tudor, whom he took prisoner at Stirling in August. Subsequently he suppressed the rebellion of the Home family, the earl of Angus (Margaret's second husband) and James Hamilton, earl of Arran. He was declared heir to the throne on Nov. 13, 1516. Returning to France in 1517 he concluded the treaty of Rouen, which renewed the alliance between France and Scotland and stipulated that a daughter of Francis I of France

should marry James V of Scotland. Returning to Scotland at the close of 1521 he immediately became the object of English attacks. He reconciled himself temporarily with Margaret, supported her cause against Angus and was accused by the English government of scheming to marry her himself. This was denied by the Scots, and the English demand for the regent's dismissal was refused. War with England broke out in Sept. 1522, but Albany had little success in the field and retired to France. Returning again in Sept. 1523 he failed once more and finally left Scotland on May 20, 1524. His regency was expressly terminated by the declaration of parliament later that year. From 1530 he acted as French ambassador in Rome. In 1533 he conducted Catherine de Médicis, his wife's niece, to France for her marriage to Henry (afterward Henry II of France). Thereafter much of his time was spent in protracted and fruitless negotiations for the marriage of James V. Albany died on June 2, 1536, leaving no legitimate heir.

A singularly unfortunate commander in the field, Albany was an honest, loyal and unselfish ruler and administrator. He regarded himself, however, essentially as the subject and servant of the king of France and so subordinated Scottish interests to French interests.

The Creation of 1881.—LEOPOLD GEORGE DUNCAN ALBERT (1853–1884), the youngest son of Queen Victoria, was born on April 7, 1853, and created duke of Albany in 1881. Distinguished for his interest in the arts, in science and in language and for his promotion of education, he died at Cannes on March 28, 1884. A posthumous son, LEOPOLD CHARLES EDWARD GEORGE ALBERT (1884–1954), born at Claremont in Surrey on July 19, 1884, succeeded to the dukedom of Albany and, on July 30, 1900, became duke of Saxe-Coburg and Gotha after the death of his father's brother Alfred. Deprived of his British titles in 1919 he later co-operated with the Nazis and was president of the German Red Cross. He died at Coburg on March 6, 1954.   (G. S. P.)

ALBANY, LOUISE MAXIMILIENNE CAROLINE, COUNTESS OF (1752–1824), was the wife of the "Young Pretender," Prince Charles Edward, and later became the mistress of the Italian poet and dramatist Alfieri. The elder daughter of Gustavus Adolphus, prince of Stolberg-Gedern, she was born at Mons in the Austrian Netherlands on Sept. 20, 1752. She entered the convent of Ste. Waudru in Mons, where as a canoness she was able to receive a good education despite the poverty in which her father's death at the battle of Leuthen had left her family. In 1772 she was married to Prince Charles Edward, self-styled count of Albany, who was 32 years older than she.

In Rome the countess was embarrassed by her husband's attempts to have her treated as a queen. After they had moved to Florence it became plain that she would not present him with an heir, his bouts of drunkenness returned and they became estranged. In 1780 she fled from him and placed herself under the protection of his brother Henry, cardinal duke of York. Charles Edward's ill-treatment of her was the reason given for this move, but the real cause was her liaison with Count Vittorio Alfieri (*q.v.*), who soon followed her to Rome. When this liaison became known to the cardinal he withdrew his support and had Alfieri banished. After some wanderings the couple settled in Florence, Louise having obtained a legal separation from her husband in 1784 through the intervention of Gustavus III of Sweden. On a visit to London the countess was received at court and obtained a pension from George III.

After Alfieri's death (1803) Louise continued to live in Florence in the company of the French painter François Fabre, to whom she bequeathed all her property. Her house on the Lung' Arno was frequented by scientists and men of letters and she enjoyed a reputation for wit. Her letters show a spiteful and uncharitable disposition with an undue preoccupation with her position as "legitimate" queen of England. She died at Florence on Jan. 29, 1824.

BIBLIOGRAPHY.—Vernon Lee, *The Countess of Albany* (1884); Marchesa Nobili-Vitelleschi, *A Court in Exile* (1903); H. M. Vaughan, *The Last Stuart Queen* (1910). *See* also the *Life* of Vittorio Alfieri, trans. by Sir H. McAnally (1953).   (B. F.)

ALBANY, a municipal town of Western Australia, lies on the northern shore of Princess Royal harbour in King George's sound on the most southerly stretch of the state's coast. It possesses a fine protected and deepwater anchorage. Pop. (1961) 10,526. Area 13 sq.mi. The population of the town increased 250% between 1946 and 1960. The town hall (1888) and St. John's Anglican church (1848) are on York street; other main business streets are Stirling terrace, Middleton road and Albany highway. Albany is 340 mi. distant from Perth by rail, 254 mi. by road and 241 mi. by air and is linked by regular services. It has government and commercial radio stations. Industries include woolen mills, fish and meat canning, superphosphate and brick works, whaling, dairying and fruit growing. The climate is mild, with an average summer maximum of 74° F. and an annual rainfall of 38 in.

Albany, the oldest settlement in Western Australia, was founded by an expedition sent by the New South Wales government, which landed at the site on Christmas day 1826. Capt. Matthew Flinders (q.v.) had landed at the same place in 1801. The first road to Perth was opened in 1841. Albany became a municipality in 1871.
(D. J. Su.)

ALBANY, a city and seat of Dougherty county, in southwestern Georgia, U.S., 170 mi. S.E. of Atlanta at the head of navigation of the Flint river. Founded in 1836 by Nelson Tift, who laid out broad streets in checkerboard fashion, it was incorporated in 1838 and early enjoyed a lucrative wagon trade from the surrounding cotton plantations. In 1857 the Southwestern railroad connected it with Macon. Later six other lines converged on the point to make it the principal transportation hub in southwestern Georgia. Cotton growing in the area declined after the entry of the boll weevil about 1915. A wide diversification of agricultural products followed, with emphasis on papershell pecans and Spanish peanuts, the processing of which became an important industry. Other industries included textiles, meat packing, candy, farm implements and pharmaceutical chemicals. Radium Springs, four miles south of the city, is an important recreation centre. In 1903 Albany State college, a coeducational teacher-training and liberal arts college, was founded there as a school for Negroes.

A council-manager form of government was adopted in 1924. Pop. (1960) city 55,890; standard metropolitan statistical area (Dougherty county) 75,680. For comparative population figures see table in GEORGIA: *Population.* (Js. C. B.)

ALBANY, capital city of the state of New York, U.S., on the west bank of the Hudson river, is 145 mi. N. of New York city and the junction of the water route from New York city to the Great Lakes, and to Montreal; it is the seat of Albany county and a port of entry. Albany has claims to being the oldest existing town in the 13 original American colonies, and is the second permanent settlement operating continuously under the original city charter. A rail, highway, waterway and air crossroads, it established the first municipal airport in the U.S. (1919). Ocean-going freighters using the 32-ft.-deep Hudson channel dock at the port of Albany.

Albany was first reached in 1540 by Frenchmen who, according to later Indian reports, constructed a small fort on Westerlo Island in the Hudson. It was rediscovered and claimed for the Dutch by Henry Hudson in 1609. In 1614 a new fort was constructed on Westerlo (then Castle) Island, and was used by agents of the United Netherlands company for three years as a trading post. In 1618 a new trading post was established on the mainland, but permanent colonization did not begin until 1624, when a group of Dutch Walloon families arrived and built Fort Orange near the site of the present capitol. The settlement around it was known as Beverwyck. In 1629 the Dutch West India company granted a large tract of land on both sides of the river to Kiliaen Van Rensselaer, a diamond merchant of Amsterdam. His grant, which included the area of Beverwyck, was named Rensselaerwyck, and attracted a sizable body of colonists. In 1652 Peter Stuyvesant, after a lengthy controversy with the director of Rensselaerwyck, established Beverwyck as an independent village. When Fort Orange surrendered to the English (Sept. 24, 1664), Beverwyck was renamed Albany, one of the titles of the duke of York (later James II). The Van Rensselaer family in the Netherlands attempted to obtain a patent from the duke of York which would restore their control of Beverwyck, but Thomas Dongan, one of

the first English governors, declined to grant it because he "did not think it convenient that the second town in the government should be in the hands of private men."

On July 22, 1686, Governor Dongan granted a city charter to Albany by which all vacant and unappropriated lands within its limits were vested in the mayor, aldermen and commonality of the city. Peter Schuyler (1657–1724) was appointed the first mayor.

At that time, Albany had about 200 families, according to the report of the Rev. John Miller, who described the city a few years later (1695). This represented a substantial increase over the 25 or 30 families reported by Father Isaac Jogues in 1643. The first federal census (1790) counted a population of 3,498; by 1850 it had reached 50,763; and by 1960, 129,726. In 1960 the population of the Albany-Schenectady-Troy standard metropolitan statistical area (Albany, Rensselaer, Saratoga and Schenectady counties) was 657,503. (For comparative population figures see table in NEW YORK: *Population.*)

As late as 1750, a Swedish naturalist, Peter Kalm, who wrote a vivid description of the city, found, although the dress was English style, the language and manners were Dutch. Early Dutch origins are reflected in street and park names and in the importance placed upon Dutch ancestry by many of the city's families.

Albany's strategic location made it a place of importance throughout the colonial period. Not only did it attract settlers, but it also developed as a meeting place for representatives from the other colonies. In 1689, in one of the first intercolonial conventions, delegates from Massachusetts Bay, Plymouth, Connecticut and New York met with Indian representatives of the five nations (the Iroquois confederation) to plan a system of defense. A more significant historical gathering took place in 1754 when the famous Albany congress met in anticipation of hostilities with the French. Among the delegates was Benjamin Franklin, who proposed a plan for "one general government" of the English colonies for purposes of common defense. Adopted by the congress, the "Albany plan," although disapproved by the English rulers and by the colonial governments, paved the way for the congress of 1765 and the continental congress of 1774. Migrating pioneers journeying west began to appear in the city as early as 1783, and by 1795, 500 oxcarts a day were making their way through the town. By 1825 the opening of the Erie canal had linked Albany to the Great Lakes; canal traffic increased the flow of migrants through the city and doubled its population. There were six-day lines to Michigan, and passage to the Northwest territory and the Mississippi could be booked on the pier at Albany. Many wagon trains made Albany their point of departure, forming and supplying themselves with provisions, before taking to the western road.

Albany, primarily known as a seat of government, became the permanent state capital in 1797. Industries include papermaking and the manufacture of felts and blankets, meat products, printing, stationery and paper products, dye stuffs, pharmaceuticals, chemicals and cleansers, industrial fabrics, machine tools, steel, foundry products and castings, brushes, baked goods and brewing.

There are a number of fine specimens of colonial and later architecture in the city. These include the Schuyler mansion (1761), a state historical monument; the State Bank of Albany (1803); the original Albany academy (now the Joseph Henry memorial); the Capitol, and the State Education building, which houses the State museum. Institutions of higher education include the State University at Albany (1844), a unit of the State University of New York (1948), also in Albany; the professional schools of Union university: Albany Medical college (1839), Albany Law school (1851), Albany College of Pharmacy (1881) and Dudley observatory; the Roman Catholic colleges of Saint Rose (women) and Siena (men); and Russell Sage Junior college. Albany provides an extensive public park and recreational system and is within easy travel distance of New York's upstate lakes and the Berkshires and Green mountains of New England.

A high point each year is the tulip festival. City parks and private gardens are ablaze with this flower, and descendants of the city's founders, dressed in ancient Dutch costumes, scrub down the main street of the community. (P. F. W.)

ALBANY CONGRESS, an intercolonial conference held June 19–July 11, 1754, at Albany, N.Y., on invitation from Lieut. Gov. James DeLancey at the behest of the British board of trade. The board's chief purpose in calling the conference was to conciliate the Iroquois whose loyalty was thought to be wavering. There were, therefore, 150 Indians present as well as 25 representatives of New York, Pennsylvania, Maryland and the four New England colonies. DeLancey took the lead in parleys with the Iroquois, placated them with promises of redress of grievances and dismissed them with presents and provisions.

In accordance with the board's broader purpose, the congress, led by Thomas Hutchinson from Massachusetts, forcibly drew public attention to French encirclement. It also made suggestions that produced practical results in the form of the royal appointment of superintendents for Indian affairs and in regulation of the westward push of the pioneers.

In the spirit, if not the letter, of the board's instructions the congress also proposed a colonial union based on a plan submitted by Benjamin Franklin. This plan called for parliament to create a federation with a central government consisting of a president general appointed by the king and a representative council chosen by the colonial legislatures. Parliament was to empower this government to regulate trade with the Indians and the sale and settlement of Indian lands. It was also to have authority to build forts, raise armed forces and levy taxes on the colonists to defray the expense of these measures. This plan, acceptable neither to the colonies nor the crown, foreshadowed, in its federal aspect, the constitution of the United States drawn up in 1787.

BIBLIOGRAPHY.—L. H. Gipson, *The British Empire Before the American Revolution,* vol. v (1942); Robert Newbold, *The Albany Congress and Plan of Union of 1754* (1955); D. M. Ellis *et al., A Short History of the State of New York* (1957).   (J. T. Ho.)

ALBANY REGENCY, the name given to a coterie of politicians who from about 1820 to 1854 largely controlled the machinery of the Democratic party in the state of New York. Among the members of this unofficial body, whose headquarters were at Albany, were Martin Van Buren, W. L. Marcy, Silas Wright and John A. Dix.

See also NEW YORK: *History.*

ALBANY RIVER of northern Ontario, Can., rises in Lake St. Joseph about 50° 55′ N. and 91° 25′ W. and flows 610 mi. eastward into James bay, descending 1,218 ft. It is navigable for nearly half its length to Martin's falls. The lower 150 mi., lined by a strip of forest, leads through flat, swampy country. Principal tributaries are the Ogoki, running parallel to the upper Albany, and the Kenogami, whose many branches rise north of Lake Superior. There are four Hudson's Bay company trading posts on its banks, including Fort Albany (established 1684) near its mouth. Hydroelectric power is generated at Rat Rapids.   (AN. KR.)

ALBATEGNIUS: *see* BATTANI, AL-.

ALBATROSS, a large, powerful-flying sea bird, any one of 13 species related to the petrels (*q.v.*) and constituting the family Diomedeidae in the order Procellariiformes. They have large heads, stout bodies, extremely long narrow wings and short or moderately long (*Phoebetria* species) tails. The bill, very stout and hooked, is covered with distinct horny plates; a short tube-like structure on either side of the upper beak houses the nostril. The legs are short and the feet webbed, with the hind toe (hallux) lacking or rudimentary. Plumage may be brown, black and white or almost wholly white; the sexes are alike in coloration except in the wandering albatross (*Diomedea exulans*).

Albatrosses inhabit southern oceans from about latitude 30° to Antarctica and are in northern Pacific waters to the Bering sea. Nine species are confined to colder parts of the southern hemisphere; one is equatorial but feeds mostly in temperate waters of the Humboldt current; and three belong to the North Pacific area.

When not breeding they range the high seas for months on end, seldom coming close enough to be seen from land. Masters of gliding flight, they are capable of remaining air-borne on virtually motionless wings for many hours and can breast the strongest winds with apparently effortless ease. Albatrosses customarily

(LEFT) WANDERING ALBATROSS (DIOMEDEA EXULANS) WITH CHICK; (RIGHT) BLACK-FOOTED ALBATROSS (DIOMEDEA NIGRIPES) IN FLIGHT

accompany ships long distances to feed on discarded refuse. But, contrary to popular belief, the same birds are rarely in attendance for more than a few days.

There is evidence that some albatrosses may circumnavigate the southern hemisphere one or more times between breeding seasons. A wandering albatross shot on the coast of Chile in 1847 bore a vial in which there was a note documenting a journey of 3,150 mi. during a period of only 12 days. Of much interest also was the capture near Cape Horn in 1916 of an albatross banded three years earlier at Kerguelen Island in the southern Indian ocean—a distance of 6,000 mi.

The phenomenal homing instinct of these oceanic birds is suggested by experiments in which 18 nesting Laysan albatrosses (*D. immutabilis*) were removed from Midway Island and sent by plane to be released at distant parts of the North Pacific. All but four returned to their nests, one having covered 4,120 mi. in 32 days and another 3,200 mi. in just over 10 days, at an average speed of 317 mi. per day.

The name albatross is a corruption of the Spanish word *alcatraz,* meaning a pelican. Various vernacular names are also applied by sailors, especially mollymawk (or mollyhawk, mollymoke, etc.) for the smaller species and gony or gooney for the larger forms, the latter designations being English dialect words for a simpleton or booby.

Seamen formerly held albatrosses in considerable awe: they believed that ill luck followed the bird's destruction—a superstition that became the theme of Coleridge's *Rime of the Ancient Mariner.* Despite this superstition generations of seafaring men amused themselves on long voyages by capturing albatrosses on baited hooks trailed in the water. The sailors fashioned albatross skins into feather rugs, feet webs into tobacco pouches and the long hollow bones into pipestems. But far more serious than the random destruction of albatrosses by seamen were the organized raids on breeding colonies by professional plume hunters. Their systematic slaughtering of the birds greatly diminished the North Pacific species and virtually exterminated the short-tailed albatross (*D. albatrus*), once the commoner of the two species to reach the offshore waters of western North America.

Although accustomed to the ceaseless movements of the sea, captive albatrosses nevertheless show the classic symptoms of seasickness when brought aboard a ship, and at all times they have the disagreeable habit of discharging musky oily fluid from the mouth and nostrils when disturbed.

Albatrosses feed on fish, squid and other marine animals. They drink sea water with impunity, the excess salt being discharged from the body by means of enlarged nasal glands. All breed in colonies on remote oceanic islands, sometimes in steep and virtually inaccessible sites. With the exception of the Galapagos or waved albatross (*D. irrorata*), which lays its eggs in May and June (late fall in the southern hemisphere), the breeding season for both the northern and far southern species is September to February. Both before and after mating some albatrosses indulge in elaborately stylized courtship performances accompanied by grunting, croaking and braying sounds. The nest may be either a hollow in the ground or a low mound of grass, moss and earth. The single white egg is extraordinarily large (equivalent to the volume of six chicken eggs), chalky and coarse in texture and sometimes speckled with brown. Incubation, shared by the parents, may in the larger species last 70 to 80 days. The young, fed by food regurgitated by the parents, soon become excessively fat. In some species the pure-white downy chicks remain in the nest eight months or longer, leaving only when finally deserted by their parents, who apparently breed at two-year intervals.

The largest and most famous species is the wandering albatross, which ranges over southern oceans and northward occasionally to the Tropic of Capricorn. Mainly white, but with black wing tips and mottled tail and wing coverts, it measures 44–53 in., weighs 15–18 lb. and may have a wingspread of $11\frac{1}{2}$ ft.—the greatest of any present-day bird. Immature birds are brown, becoming more white with each molt. Other essentially white species are the somewhat smaller royal albatross (*D. epomophora*), found off the coasts of southern South America and southward to New Zealand; and the short-tailed albatross, the only white species in the North Pacific but now almost extinct. (E. R. Be.)

ALBAY, one of the six provinces of the Bikol region of southeastern Luzon, Republic of the Philippines. Pop. (1960) 514,980, a density of 517 per square mile. The province is an area of volcanic soils derived chiefly from the debris of Mt. Mayon (7,943 ft.), the most perfect known volcanic cone. Destructive eruptions of Mayon have occurred from time to time. The most notable eruption occurred in 1815 when approximately 1,200 inhabitants were killed and much of the nearby area was buried under several feet of ashes, cinders and lava.

Albay is basically an agricultural province with a fertile soil and abundant rainfall throughout the year. Rice fields dominate the lowland landscape; abacá (Manila hemp) and coconuts are produced on the rolling uplands and lower mountain slopes. Rice is the food crop and abacá the principal money crop; the larger abacá plantations are in the Lagao-Iriga area and on the lower slopes of Mt. Mayon. Albay is noted for the manufacture of abacá rugs, place mats, slippers, bags and sinamay cloth. Coconut groves are important chiefly on the hillsides north and south of the Legaspi plain and along the shores of Tabaco, Bacacay and Libog. Minor crops are corn, sweet potatoes, cassava, fruits, vegetables and pili nuts. Minerals include coal on Batan Island and copper on Rapu-Rapu Island and at Lagao.

The principal towns are Legaspi City (pop. [1960] 60,593), the capital and chief port (formerly a chartered city); Tabaco (pop. [1960] 46,416), a copra and hemp port; Guinobatan, the site of an abacá experiment station; Lagao; and Iriga. (An. C.)

ALBEDO (from Lat. *albus*, "white"), "whiteness," a word used principally in astronomy for the measure of reflecting power. A body shining by reflected light is said to have albedo $\frac{1}{2}$ if it reflects (or scatters outward) half the light incident on it. The albedo for visual light of the cloud-covered planets (Venus, Jupiter, Saturn, Uranus, Neptune) ranges from 0.56 to 0.73; of Earth 0.43; Mars 0.15; Moon 0.07. See also METEOROLOGY: *Solar and Terrestrial Radiation*.

In nuclear physics albedo refers to the reflective coefficient defined as the fraction of neutrons reflected back to the source. See DIFFUSION: *Importance and Application of Diffusion*.

ALBEMARLE, GEORGE MONCK, 1ST DUKE OF: see MONCK, GEORGE, 1st Duke of Albemarle.

ALBEMARLE SOUND, a large sea-level bay on the Atlantic coast of North Carolina, U.S., separated from the ocean by a long, narrow barrier beach known as the Outer Banks. It was explored by Ralph Lane of Sir Walter Raleigh's Roanoke Island colony in 1585. The earliest permanent North Carolina settlements were made along its shores and tributaries in the 1660s. Originally called Bay of Albemarle or Albemarle river, it was named for George Monck, duke of Albemarle, one of the original lords proprietor of Carolina.

Albemarle sound extends in an east and west direction along the 36th parallel of north latitude for a total length of about 52 mi., and varies in width from $3\frac{1}{2}$ to 14 mi. At no spot deeper than 25 ft., it averages between 5 and 10 ft. in depth. It receives the water flow from a large mountainous area of western North Carolina and Virginia through the Chowan and Roanoke river systems at its western end, and discharges this flow at its southeastern end through the smaller Roanoke and Croatan sounds to Pamlico sound, and thence through Oregon, Hatteras and Ocracoke inlets to the sea.

A number of smaller bays, rivers and creeks branch off from Albemarle sound, draining the Dismal swamp on the north and other swamps and lakes on the south. It is connected with Chesapeake bay by the Dismal Swamp canal and the Albemarle and Chesapeake canal, and is crossed near its eastern end by the Intracoastal waterway. (Da. St.)

ALBÉNIZ, ISAAC (MANUEL FRANCISCO) (1860–1909), Spanish pianist and composer, one of the leaders of the Spanish nationalist school of musicians, was born at Camprodón, Catalonia, on May 29, 1860. He appeared as a piano prodigy at the age of four in Barcelona, and at seven in Paris; but being declared too young for admittance to the Conservatoire there he went to study in Madrid, only to run away when he was nine, and again later, to give concerts in various parts of Spain. He embarked for Costa Rica, played throughout the United States and returned via England to become a pupil at the Leipzig conservatory at the age of 14. Returning to Spain without funds, he was fortunate in obtaining a royal grant enabling him to study in Brussels. In 1878 he fulfilled a long-held ambition by going to Budapest for lessons from Liszt, whose influence on his style was considerable. He toured extensively as a virtuoso, often playing small romantic pieces of his own which he composed with great facility, among them several with a Spanish flavour such as *Córdoba* and his famous *Tango*. He then settled down to teach in Barcelona and Madrid.

Only in 1890 did he take up composition more seriously when, having moved to Paris, he came under the influence of Vincent d'Indy, Paul Dukas and other French musicians. In the following year the English banker Francis Burdett Money-Coutts offered him a handsome allowance on condition that Albéniz set to music various opera librettos of his. After the production in London of the comic opera *The Magic Opal,* libretto by Arthur Law (1893), Albéniz wrote the three-act *Henry Clifford* (Barcelona, 1895), but neither this nor *Merlin,* the first of a projected Arthurian trilogy, proved very congenial to him, and it was not until the one-act *Pepita Jiménez* (Barcelona, 1896) that he achieved a real stage success.

He developed Bright's disease (eventually to prove fatal), and after 1900 spent most of his time in Spain, where he worked at the Arthurian opera cycle and continued to write copiously for the piano. It is on his music for that instrument that his fame chiefly rests, particularly on *Iberia,* a collection of 12 scenes of Spanish (mainly Andalusian) life, written during 1906–09, coloured by the rhythms and harmonies of Spanish popular music, but highly virtuosic and complex in texture. He died at Cambo-les-Bains, Basses-Pyrénées, on May 18, 1909.

BIBLIOGRAPHY.—M. Raux Deledicque, *Albéniz* (1950); A. Sagardia, *Isaac Albéniz* (1951); H. Collet, *Albéniz et Granados,* 2nd ed. (1948). (L. Sa.)

ALBERDI, JUAN BAUTISTA (1810–1884), perhaps the most influential of 19th-century Argentine political thinkers, was born in the province of Tucumán on Aug. 29, 1810. He joined the liberal opponents of the dictator Juan Manuel de Rosas (q.v.) and in 1838 went into exile in Uruguay, where he took a law degree. In Uruguay, in Chile and in Europe, Alberdi studied and wrote voluminously about the reactionary condition of his country. After the defeat of Rosas (1852), Alberdi distilled his ideas into a book entitled *Bases and Starting Points for the Political Organization of the Argentine Republic,* which emphasized the need for a central, federalized government and urged immigration and foreign investment. His ideas influenced the constituent assembly which in 1853 wrote Argentina's enduring constitution. Certainly his writings helped to guide his countrymen toward a liberal era which, before Alberdi's death and in keeping with his motto "to govern is to populate," saw a vast expansion of Argentina's economy and population.

Appointed by Pres. Justo José de Urquiza to represent Argentina in Europe in the 1850s, Alberdi was not in the favour of Pres. Bartolomé Mitre and his successors after 1861. He spent his last years in semiexile in Europe, continuing his extensive and significant writing until his lonely death in Paris, Jan. 18, 1884.

(T. F. McG.)

ALBERONI, GIULIO (1664–1752), Italian cardinal and statesman, who as *de facto* prime minister of Spain from 1716 to 1719 played a major part in bringing about the revival of Spain after the War of the Spanish Succession, was born at Piacenza on March 21, 1664, the son of a gardener. Educated by the Jesuits, he took holy orders and by 1698 had been appointed to a canonry at Parma. In 1702 he was sent on a diplomatic mission from the Parmesan government to the duc de Vendôme, the commander of the French forces in Italy during the War of the Spanish Succession. Subsequently he accompanied Vendôme to France in 1706 and to Spain in 1711, acting as his secretary but remaining an agent of the duke of Parma. After Vendôme's death in 1712, Alberoni was ordered to remain at Madrid and in April 1713 he was made official Parmesan representative there. In this position he was responsible for negotiating, through the princesse des Ursins (*q.v.*), the marriage of Philip V of Spain with the duke of Parma's niece and step-daughter, Elizabetta Farnese. Under the protection of the new queen, Alberoni's influence at the Spanish court increased steadily during 1715 and by the beginning of 1716 he was exercising the powers of a prime minister.

Alberoni's domestic policy was largely a continuation of the administrative centralization and fiscal reform begun by Jean Orry. He also encouraged the establishment of industry by tariff reform and by the importation of foreign craftsmen. His greatest service to Spain, however, was the destruction of the power of the royal councils (which, though originally the chief executors of royal policy, had, by this time, become the centres of aristocratic opposition to reform), which he brought about by a series of decrees issued in Jan. 1717. His foreign policy was motivated by a desire to drive the Austrians from Italy and to safeguard Spanish trade with its American colonies. This policy was accompanied by the successful rebuilding of the Spanish navy, but the credit for this properly belongs to Alberoni's principal lieutenant, José Patiño. The Spanish military expeditions to Sardinia (1717) and Sicily (1718), which led to war with the quadruple alliance of Great Britain, France, Austria and the Netherlands, were regarded by Alberoni as premature and only resulted from a policy imposed on him by the queen. Nevertheless, the failure of the Spanish forces during the Franco-British invasion of Spain led to his banishment on Dec. 5, 1719.

Alberoni, who had been made a cardinal in 1717, went from Spain to Italy, where for a time he was forced to go into hiding. But he took part in the conclave which elected Pope Innocent XIII in 1721 and was later acquitted by a papal inquiry into the charges made against him by Spain. He became legate of Ravenna in 1735 and of Bologna in 1740. He died at Piacenza on June 16, 1752.

BIBLIOGRAPHY.—E. Bourgeois (ed.), *Lettres intimes de J. M. Alberoni* (1892); P. Castagnoli, *Il cardinale Giulio Alberoni*, 3 vol. (1929–32); S. Harcourt-Smith, *Alberoni* (1943).   (B. J. R.)

ALBERT, SAINT (called THE GREAT): see ALBERTUS MAGNUS, SAINT.

ALBERT I (1875–1934), king of the Belgians, was born in Brussels on April 8, 1875, the younger son of Leopold II's brother Philip, count of Flanders (1837–1905), and Princess Marie of Hohenzollern. The premature death of Prince Leopold, only son of Leopold II, on Jan. 22, 1869, made Albert's brother Baudouin (born 1869) heir presumptive to the Belgian crown, but on Baudouin's death on Jan. 23, 1891, Albert became next in the line of succession. He received his training in military matters at the École Militaire and served as an officer to the grenadier regiment. On Oct. 2, 1900, he married in Munich Elisabeth (1876–1965), second daughter of Charles Theodore, duke of Bavaria. Three children were born of this marriage: Leopold, duke of Brabant (the future Leopold III), 1901; Charles, count of Flanders, 1903; and Marie José, 1906.

On Dec. 23, 1909, Albert took the oath of fidelity to the Belgian constitution and became king under the name of Albert I. He was a patron of art and literature and occupied himself actively with the improvement of conditions in his country, interesting himself in various social and legal reforms and especially in the organization of the army. In May 1913 he gave his assent to a law designed to secure for Belgium an army of 350,000 men. On July 31, 1914, when World War I was breaking out, Albert wrote to the German emperor William II, reminding him of the respect due to Belgian neutrality. Germany replied by the ultimatum of Aug. 2, which was rejected. Hostilities then began. The king took command of the troops and established his headquarters first at Louvain and afterward in Antwerp. He directed in person the first advance from Antwerp toward Louvain with a view to relieving the French and British forces engaged with the German right wing. After the fall of Antwerp, the king and queen accompanied the retreating army until it came to a halt on the Yser river. From Oct. 17 to 24 the Belgian army, under the king's command, withstood the German invasion without any assistance. During the whole of the war he remained with his troops, exposed to the risk of enemy bombardment. He made continual visits to the front-line trenches from his headquarters at La Panne and even surveyed the enemy's lines from an aircraft.

When the general Allied offensive of Oct. 1918 was undertaken, Albert was appointed commander of the northern army group, consisting of both Belgians and French, which captured the forest of Houthulst, Thourout, Ostend and Bruges and forced the passage of the Lys. After the armistice the king asked the Allies for the abolition of Belgian neutrality and of the treaties of 1839, which had left Belgium open to invasion.

Albert also interested himself in the Belgian Congo and presided in person over the colonial congresses of 1920 and 1926. On Feb. 17, 1934, while rock climbing at Marche-les-Dames, near Namur, he fell and was killed.

BIBLIOGRAPHY.—P. Nothomb, *Le Roi Albert* (1934); E. Cammaerts, *Albert of Belgium* (1935); Gen. R. van Overstraeten (ed.), *The War Diaries of Albert of Belgium* (1954).   (JE. D.)

ALBERT I (*c.* 1255–1308), German king from 1298 to 1308, was the eldest son of King Rudolf I, of the house of Habsburg. He was invested with the duchies of Austria and Styria in 1282. After Rudolf's death (1291), the electors, determined to prevent the German crown from becoming a hereditary possession of the powerful Habsburgs, checked Albert's aspirations by choosing Adolf (*q.v.*) of Nassau as German king. Albert, however, drew the electors into an alliance (1297), engineered the deposition of Adolf and defeated him on July 2, 1298, at Göllheim. His election, proclaimed at Mainz before the battle, was repeated at Frankfurt, on July 27, and he was crowned at Aachen on Aug. 24.

Albert, after signing an alliance with Philip IV of France in 1299, claimed possession of Holland, Zealand and Frisia as vacant fiefs. This effort to obtain control of the mouths of the Rhine was opposed by the four Rhenish electors, who agreed at Heimbach on Oct. 14, 1300, to procure the eventual deposition of Albert. Albert, aided by the cities of the Rhineland, crushed the coalition in a series of savage campaigns between 1300 and 1302. He obtained confirmation of his election from Pope Boniface VIII on April 30, 1303, swore an oath of obedience to the pope and promised that none of his sons should be elected German king without papal consent. His attempt to place his son Rudolf on the vacant throne of Bohemia in 1306 was only momentarily successful, and his claim to Thuringia and Meissen, inherited from Adolf of Nassau, was checked by a defeat near Lucka in 1307. On May 1, 1308 Albert was assassinated in Brugg on the Reuss by his nephew John of Swabia, later called the "Parricide," from whom the king had unjustly withheld his inheritance.

See A. Hessel, *Jahrbücher des deutschen Reichs unter König Albrecht I von Habsburg* (1931).   (C. C. BA.)

ALBERT II (1397–1439), German king, king also of Hungary and Bohemia from 1438 to 1439 and, as Albert V, duke of Austria, was born in Aug. 1397, the son of Albert IV, duke of Austria. His father's early death was followed by a long regency (1404–11), but after this the young Albert began to show his capacities; *e.g.*, in the economic and military organization of his lands (there were Hussite invasions until 1434) and in his acceptance, in 1418, of full authority from Pope Martin V for the reform of the Austrian monasteries. After the death of the German king Sigismund (whose daughter Elizabeth he had married), Albert was in 1438 elected king of Hungary (Jan. 1), German king (March 18) and king of Bohemia (June 29). As German king he advocated a policy of neutrality for the princes of the empire with regard to the affairs of the Council of Basel and the crisis of the papacy. His death from dysentery, on Oct. 27, 1439, in Neszmély near Esztergom in Hungary, on his way home from a campaign against the Turks, cut short his plans for reform of the empire. His posthumous son was László V of Hungary. The Czech chronicler Bartosek calls him "good though German, bold and merciful."

See Wilhelm Wostry, "König Albrecht II," *Prager Studien aus dem Gebiet der Geschichtswissenschaft,* 12 and 15 (1906–07). (A. Lн.)

ALBERT (1828–1902), king of Saxony, was born in Dresden on April 23, 1828, the eldest son of Prince John, who succeeded to the throne in 1854. Commissioned as lieutenant in the artillery in 1843, Albert was at Bonn university in 1847–48. He served as a captain in the Schleswig-Holstein campaign of 1849 against the Danes. He married Caroline, granddaughter of Gustavus IV of Sweden, in 1853. In 1857 he was made general of infantry. He became a member of the upper chamber of the Saxon parliament in 1862. In the Seven Weeks' War of 1866 he commanded the Saxon army, effecting an orderly retreat when the Prussians invaded Saxony and holding his position with tenacity in the defeat at Königgrätz (Sadowa). Albert had always favoured the Prussian connection and on Saxony's entry into the North German federation he became commander of the 12th army corps, formerly the Saxon army.

In the Franco-German War of 1870–71, Albert's corps fought at Gravelotte and, with the Prussian guard, carried the attack on St. Privat, the conclusive action of the battle. In the march on Paris he commanded the 4th army, consisting of Prussian and Saxon troops, and played a vital role in the operations preceding the battle of Sedan. In the battle itself he conducted the envelopment of the French on the east and north. After the armistice of Jan. 28, 1871, he commanded the army of occupation from March 18 to June 8. On his return to Saxony he was made inspector general of the German army by the emperor (June 15) and field marshal by King John of Saxony (July 11).

Succeeding to the Saxon throne on Oct. 29, 1873, Albert concerned himself mainly with military affairs, but also approved the administrative reforms of his reign. Decrees of 1873 regularized local administration and education and instituted school inspectors, and in 1878 fiscal reforms based on a progressive income tax were introduced. Throughout the reign industrialization increased rapidly and the railways were nationalized in 1876.

A Catholic ruler of a Protestant country, Albert remained popular with his subjects. He died in Schloss Sibyllenort, near Öls (Olesnica) in Silesia, on June 19, 1902, leaving no children, and was succeeded by his brother George.

ALBERT (FRIEDRICH RUDOLF ALBRECHT), ARCHDUKE (1817–1895), Austrian field marshal, the son of the archduke Charles (Karl Friedrich), was one of the last of the colourful princeling generals who had commanded continental armies for so long but who were by his time already outmoded. Born in Vienna on Aug. 3, 1817, he was educated privately under the strict supervision of his father, before entering the Austrian army as a colonel of infantry in 1837. In 1839 he transferred to the cavalry. Six years later he became military governor of Austria. About this time he became a pupil of Radetzky in the art of war. This for the time being removed him from the ceremonial to the more practical and sterner side of soldiering. As a result of this association he fought as a volunteer under Radetzky throughout the Italian campaign of 1848 and was present at the action at Pastrengo and at the battles of Santa Lucia and Custoza. He then greatly distinguished himself as a divisional commander in the 2nd corps at Novara.

In 1850 he was promoted to the rank of general of cavalry and from 1851 to 1860 he was military governor of Hungary. Soon after the termination of this appointment he was made commandant in Vicenza, Venetia, and in 1863 he became a field marshal. When war became imminent early in 1866 the archduke took command of the field army in Italy. Although in a secondary theatre of operations, Albert soon showed his capacity as a commander by winning a decisive victory at Custoza on June 24, 1866. The fighting lasted for only eight days, but the defeat of the Italian army in this battle brought about its disintegration and enabled Albert to send most of his troops to Bohemia where the Austrians, hard pressed by the Prussians, were falling back on Vienna. On July 10, 1866 the archduke assumed command of the forces defending the capital, but peace intervened and his plans were never tested. (*See* SEVEN WEEKS' WAR.)

With the end of hostilities he became what was virtually inspector general of the Austrian army. By this time the advent of railways had made it possible to support much larger field armies and Albert's main task was to reorganize the Austrian forces on a short-service national basis. By conscripting men for a short period a large reserve was created, which could be mobilized quickly in the event of war.

The archduke Albert lived at a time of transition in military affairs. Railways and the general staff system had greatly increased the size of armies and the speed and efficiency with which they could be assembled and controlled. In the tactical field fire power had been vastly increased by the introduction of new weapons. Moreover, there was now no place for the princely sort of commander who, in Prussia, was on the point of being superseded by the dedicated and highly trained general staff officer, typified by the elder Moltke. The Austrians had lagged behind the Prussians in these new developments, with the result that in the Seven Weeks' War Austria was defeated in a very short time.

In the latter years of his life Albert edited the military works of his father and also wrote a few books of his own on military subjects. He died in Arco, Tyrol, on Feb. 18, 1895.

See Carl von Duncker, *F. M. Erzherzog Albrecht* (1897).
  (C. N. B.)

ALBERT OF SAXE-COBURG-GOTHA (1819–1861), the PRINCE CONSORT of Queen Victoria of Great Britain, was born in Rosenau, near Coburg, Ger., on Aug. 26, 1819, and was baptized as Francis Charles Augustus Albert Emmanuel. He was the second son of Ernest, duke of Saxe-Coburg-Gotha, by Princess Louise of Saxe-Gotha-Altenburg (d. 1831), from whom the duke was divorced in 1826. Albert's father's sister married the duke of Kent, whose daughter Victoria was born in the same year as her first cousin. He and his brother Ernest were educated privately, in Brussels, and at the University of Bonn, and in 1836 accompanied their father to England on a visit to the widowed duchess of Kent. Marriage between Victoria and Albert was the cherished plan of their uncle Leopold I of Belgium, but was opposed by William IV, who favoured Prince Alexander of Orange as Victoria's husband. Albert himself was "gloomy" of the outcome; nevertheless, after wintering in Italy with his mentor, Baron von Stockmar (*q.v.*), Leopold's former adviser, he returned to England in Oct. 1839. Betrothal swiftly followed. His future, he realized, was "high and brilliant but also plentifully strewn with thorns." Victoria and Albert were married on Feb. 10, 1840.

Politically, the role of the queen's husband was anomalous; but he received a "key to the secret boxes" during her first pregnancy (1840) and thereafter was effectively Victoria's private secretary and confidential adviser. The fall of the Melbourne government (1841) made way for Sir Robert Peel, with whom the prince had much in common: both were men of serious temper, remarkable ability and industry, happiest in their domestic circle and least at their ease with the English aristocracy. Albert thus became, in Russell's later phrase, "an informal but potent member of all cabinets." With the retirement too of the Baroness Lehzen, Victoria's former governess, who had come to rule the royal household, to Hanover in 1842 he had gained effective control of, and by 1844 had completely reorganized, the household. Further, he busied himself with the improvement of the queen's properties. He made the queen intensely happy, steadied her self-willed judgment and made her almost as hard-working as he was himself. A handsome, accomplished and serious-minded man, he was unable, however, to persuade many of her subjects to like him. The aristocracy still looked askance at the palace, perhaps the more readily for its new and severely domesticated moral tone; the prince, although he both shot and rode well, was too intellectual, too professorial, for the English gentleman, nor might every minister welcome the degree of consultation which his vigilance enjoined. "He had not the knack," said Walter Bagehot, "of dropping seed without appearing to sow it."

His public life may hardly be separated from that of the queen herself (see VICTORIA). Prejudice against him was never fully dissipated in his lifetime; if his understanding love and self-sacrificing labour were a benison to the queen, the value of his counsel, based on wide knowledge, pertinacity and caution, might scarcely be known beyond a very small circle. His especial political preoccupation was to maintain (it was wrongly believed that his aim was to extend) the influence of the crown as an increasingly nonpartisan agency in domestic government; and in foreign affairs to ascertain that the private intelligence available to a ruling family with a growing body of relatives throughout Europe was made available to, and taken into consideration by, a foreign office not eager, especially in Lord Palmerston's day, for this advantage. In 1846–47 the royal pair encountered a wave of unpopularity, in the main directed at the prince; on the eve of the Crimean War there was a strong rumour that he had been imprisoned in the Tower as a Russian (some said an Austrian) agent; and in 1854 there were newspaper attacks upon "the influence of the Crown." In fact, "under his care the Crown played the part reserved for it under a constitutional monarchy and played it well" (Gavin B. Henderson, "The Influence of the Crown," *Crimean War Diplomacy* [Jackson Son & Co. (Booksellers) Ltd., Glasgow, 1947]). His was an increasingly valuable second opinion. In 1856, for example, he showed the foreign secretary that his proposed dispatch to Prussia might suggest an ultimatum and Clarendon gratefully altered it; again, in 1861 it was Albert's characteristic changes (just before he died) in the dispatch addressed by Lord Russell to the U.S. government over the seizure of the confederate envoys on the English steamer "Trent" which opened up the possibility of the peaceful settlement which eventuated. Growing daily in his lifetime, perhaps his most important political influence came after it: what she imagined would have been his judgment remained his widow's ultimate criterion.

In critical and foreign surroundings he found his greatest satisfaction, outside his family, in encouragement of the arts (he was himself an erudite and accomplished musician) and in the application of science to manufacturing industry. In the face of fierce and sustained prejudice, not unmixed with personal abuse, he was the prime mover in the Great exhibition of 1851. His detailed perseverance as president was rewarded by success, the surplus realized going to endow the South Kensington (afterward renamed Victoria and Albert) museum. Similar activities found in him ready and learned support, and provided an opportunity to deliver speeches characterized by a firm grasp of English, of information and of purpose. To the education of his family and the cause of army reform he applied the same German thoroughness. In neither was he especially successful, but the domestic felicity of the royal family became proverbial and played its part in guaranteeing the continuity of the English monarchy, a regime by no means so assured on the queen's accession. In 1856 the queen drew attention to his equivocal position; he had received special precedence by letters patent but still held no titular rank by law. Even so, it was still thought wiser to avoid parliamentary (it did not offset newspaper) controversy and when he became prince consort in 1857 it was also by letters patent.

In 1861 he was busy with the projected international exhibition when he was seized with what proved to be typhoid fever and, congestion of the lungs supervening, he died at Windsor castle on Dec. 14. He had persistently lived on "the treadmill of never-ending business" and he did not "cling to life." The queen was overwhelmed and the universal sympathy was not unmixed, perhaps, with compunction for earlier want of appreciation.

Memorials were erected throughout the country, most notably the Albert memorial (1863–72) and the Royal Albert hall (1867–71) in London. His name was also commemorated in the queen's institution of the order of Victoria and Albert (1862) and of the Albert medal (1866) for gallantry in saving life.

BIBLIOGRAPHY.—By the queen's authority, her secretary C. Grey compiled *The Early Years of the Prince Consort* (1867), and *The Life and Letters of the Prince Consort*, 5 vol. (1877–80) was similarly edited by Sir Theodore Martin. His *Principal Speeches and Addresses*, with an introduction by Sir Arthur Helps, was also published (1862). *See also* C. F. von Stockmar, *Memoirs* (1872); *Letters of Queen Victoria*, 1st series (1907); G. B. Henderson, *Crimean War Diplomacy* (1947); Roger Fulford, *The Prince Consort* (1949). (E. T. Ws.)

ALBERT (1490–1568), last grand master of the Teutonic Order and first duke of Prussia, was born in Ansbach on May 16, 1490, the third son of Frederick of Hohenzollern, prince of Ansbach and Bayreuth, and Sophia, daughter of Casimir IV, king of Poland. On Jan. 3, 1511 Albert was made grand master of the Teutonic Order, which had held East Prussia under Polish suzerainty since 1466. In 1519 Albert was at war with his Polish suzerain, and though a truce was made in 1521 the dispute, which was referred to the Holy Roman emperor, remained unsettled. In addition there was the antagonism between the Teutonic knights and the local nobility. To overcome these difficulties, Albert decided in 1525 to follow Luther's advice given at Wittenberg two years earlier, to dissolve the order in Prussia and to transform the territory into a dukedom under Polish suzerainty. The agreement of Sigismund I of Poland was obtained in April 1525 at Cracow.

The new duke proceeded to further Protestantism in East Prussia. In 1530 the emperor Charles V ordered the return of Prussia to the Teutonic Order, but the knights were unable to recover the duchy. Albert was placed under the ban of the empire in 1531, but the ban was never enforced. To counteract the isolation brought about by his breaking away from the order's extensive organization, he was fairly active as a member of the leagues which German princes formed in opposition to Charles V's imperial policy; moreover, when Sweden and Denmark had become Protestant, he attempted to co-ordinate his politics with the actions of these Baltic powers. In internal affairs he secularized the centralized administration established by the order, but he had to concede to the landowning nobility, now a uniform body, a definite influence on the government of the land. The situation of the peasants deteriorated in his territory, as it did everywhere east of the Elbe. In 1544, in spite of some opposition, he founded a university at Königsberg, where he appointed his friend Osiander to a professorship in 1549, although he lacked the formal qualification of a theological degree. In addition Osiander's divergence from the doctrine of justification by faith, current in Wittenberg, involved him in a violent quarrel with Melanchthon, who had adherents in Königsberg, and these theological disputes soon led to an uproar in the town. The duke strenuously supported Osiander, and the area of the quarrel soon broadened. After Osiander's death in 1552, a preacher named Johann Funck, with an adventurer named Paul Scalich, exercised great influence over Albert. The turmoil caused by these disputes compelled Albert to consent to a condemnation of Osiander's teaching, and in 1566 the estates appealed to Sigismund II, king of Poland, who sent a commission to Königsberg. Scalich fled, and Funck was executed; the question of the regency was settled and a strict form of Lutheranism was declared binding on all teachers and preachers. A disappointed man, Albert died in Tapiau in East Prussia on March 20, 1568.

BIBLIOGRAPHY.—J. Voigt, *Briefwechsel der berühmtesten Gelehrten des Zeitalters der Reformation mit Herzog Albrecht von Preussen* (1841); K. Lohmeyer, *Herzog Albrecht von Preussen* (1890); E. Joachim, *Die Politik des letzten Hochmeisters in Preussen, Albrecht von Brandenburg* (1892); K. Forstreuter, *Vom Ordensstaat zum Fürstentum* (1951). (H. Lz.)

ALBERT III (ANIMOSUS or THE COURAGEOUS), DUKE OF SAXONY (1443–1500), the founder of the Albertine branch of the house of Wettin (q.v.), was born in Grimma on July 31, 1443, the younger son of Frederick II, elector of Saxony. In July 1455 Albert and his brother Ernest were abducted by Kunz von Kaufungen, a member of the lesser nobility, but on the way to Bohemia were rescued by workmen and were restored to their father. This incident, known as the *Prinzenraub,* was typical of the relations between the orders of society in 15th-century Germany and became famous in legend and literature. On their father's death (Sept. 1464) Albert and his brother became joint rulers of his territories.

Albert had married Sidonia, daughter of George of Podebrady (*q.v.*), in 1464, but his candidature for the Bohemian throne in 1471 was unsuccessful. In 1472, however, he purchased the lordship of Sagan in Silesia. Firmly loyal to the Habsburgs, Albert was marshal of the Holy Roman empire under Frederick III and imperial governor of the Netherlands from 1488 to 1493. He was made hereditary governor of Friesland in 1498.

In the Wettin lands, Albert centralized the financial administration and established a central high court at Leipzig in 1482, but it was his initiative which brought about the Leipzig partition of 1485. This ended the dual reign of Albert and Ernest and divided the Wettin lands between them. The partition, which resulted in the lasting separation of the Wettins into Ernestine and Albertine branches (*see* SAXONY), was not meant to be permanent and so was not based on geographical realities, though Albert's personal authority in his lands on the middle Elbe was strong enough. He died in Emden in lower Saxony on Sept. 2, 1500. In his will he attempted to establish primogeniture in his lands.

(HE. K.)

ALBERT I THE BEAR (*c.* 1100–1170), margrave of Brandenburg, was one of the main leaders of 12th-century German expansion in eastern Europe. The only son of the "Ascanian" Otto the Rich, count of Ballenstedt, and Eilika, daughter of Magnus Billung, duke of Saxony, he inherited the Saxon estates of his father between the Harz mountains and the middle reaches of the Elbe in 1123 and, on his mother's death in 1142, succeeded to possessions of the Billung dynasty in central Germany. The main inheritance, however, including the Saxon dukedom, went to the Welfs. Although Albert used every opportunity to attempt a reversal of this decision and to obtain a foothold in northern Germany near the seaboard and had for some time the support of Conrad III, the first German king of the Hohenstaufen dynasty, his Welf counterparts Henry the Proud and Henry the Lion prevailed during his lifetime. Albert's greatest achievement was in the east. After his services in Italy (1132) had been rewarded in 1134 by the investiture of the north mark, east of the junction of the Elbe and Havel rivers, he spent three years campaigning against the Wends and, by an arrangement made with Pribislav, prince of the Havelland, secured that district when the prince died in 1150.

Taking the title margrave of Brandenburg, he pressed the warfare against the Wends, extended the area of his mark and increased its population and prosperity by introducing Frisian and Saxon settlers. In this work of colonization based on forest clearance and drainage of swamps he had the help of the Premonstratensians and Cistercians; missionary work among the Slav population, which included the revival of the bishoprics of Havelberg and Brandenburg, was the other aspect of his policy.

A loyal supporter of the Italian policy of Frederick I Barbarossa, Albert may have been made archchamberlain of the empire, an office which afterward gave the margraves of Brandenburg the rights of an elector. He died on Nov. 13, 1170. His surname "the Bear" can be traced back to Helmold, the contemporary historian of the German expansion in the north.

See A. Krabbo, "Albrecht der Bär," *Forschungen zur Brandenburg-Preussischen Geschichte,* vol. 19, part 2 (1906); A. Jaster, *Geschichte der askanischen Kolonisation in Brandenburg* (1934). (H. Lz.)

ALBERT II ALCIBIADES (1522–1557), margrave of Brandenburg-Kulmbach, was born in Ansbach on March 28, 1522, a member of the Franconian branch of the Hohenzollern family. His father, Casimir of Brandenburg, died in 1527 and Albert was declared of age by the emperor Charles V in 1541. His restless nature marked him as a leader of mercenaries; and, having collected a small band of soldiers, he assisted the emperor in his war with France in 1543. Sharing in the attack on the Saxon electorate, Albert was taken prisoner at Rochlitz in March 1547 by John Frederick, elector of Saxony, but was released as a result of the emperor's victory at Mühlberg in April. He then followed the

fortunes of his friend Maurice, the new elector of Saxony, deserted Charles and joined the league which proposed to overthrow the emperor by an alliance with Henry II of France in 1552. Having extorted a large sum of money from the burghers of Nürnberg, he quarreled with Henry and offered his services to the emperor. Charles, who was attempting to reconquer Metz from France, assented to Albert's demands and ratified his possession of the lands taken from the bishops of Würzburg and Bamberg. But now Protestant and Catholic princes allied against Albert under the leadership of Maurice, whose forces defeated him at Sievershausen (July 9, 1553), though Maurice himself was killed. Outlawed by the imperial chamber at Speyer (Dec. 1, 1553), Albert had to seek asylum in France (June 1554). He returned in 1556 with plans of revenge, but died on Jan. 8, 1557, at the court of his brother-in-law, the margrave of Baden.

See O. Kneitz, "Albrecht Alcibiades . . . ," *Die Plassenburg Blätter für Heimatkunde und Kulturpflege* (1951). (H. Lz.)

ALBERT III ACHILLES (1414–1486), elector of Brandenburg from 1470 to 1486, surnamed Achilles because of his relentless energy, physical strength and bravery. Combining political shrewdness and enthusiasm for tournaments and chivalrous display, he was a German representative of a type most fully developed at the Burgundian court. He was born in Tangermünde on Nov. 24, 1414, the third son of Frederick I of Hohenzollern, elector of Brandenburg. On the division of territory which followed his father's death in 1440 he received the lands around Ansbach; on the death of his brother John in 1464 he inherited Bayreuth. During this period the city of Nürnberg remained a dangerous antagonist, so that Albert was never a friend of towns and their citizens. On Dec. 20, 1470, on the abdication of his brother Frederick II, he became elector of Brandenburg.

Family aggrandizement was his main object and the development of a coherent administration his main achievement. To provide their sons with appropriate positions and income was an important motive in the policy of territorial princes of the time, but Albert saw that division of the inheritance weakened a family's power. He therefore devised the famous *Dispositio Achillea* of Feb. 24, 1473, which decreed that the mark of Brandenburg should descend intact to the eldest son; two younger sons were to receive the Franconian possessions of the Hohenzollerns which at this time yielded a larger income. By this regulation Albert wished to emphasize the duty of his descendants to preserve the dynasty's inheritance intact. He did not establish the principle of primogeniture, but his disposition started a tendency in this direction. Albert was one of a small class of German magnates of the late 15th century who began to take seriously the administrative needs of their territories. He combated the banditry of the lesser nobles with effective legislation, paid his officials and regulated their methods. Under him an accounting system for the ducal administration was instituted. The separation from Franconia resulting from the *Dispositio Achillea* narrowed down the political activities of his successors in Brandenburg, especially in imperial affairs. Albert died in Frankfurt am Main on March 11, 1486.

BIBLIOGRAPHY.—*Das kaiserliche Buch des Markgrafen Albrecht Achilles,* ed. by C. Hoefler and J. von Minutoli, 2 parts (1850); *Quellensammlung zur Geschichte des Hauses Hohenzollern,* vol. i, ed. by C. A. H. Burkhardt (1857); *Politische Korrespondenz des Kurfürsten Albrecht Achilles, 1470–86,* ed. by F. Priebatsch (1894–98); D. B. Rogge, *Vom Kurhut zur Kaiserkrone,* vol. i (1892); E. W. Kauter, *Markgraf Albert Achilles,* vol. i (1911). (H. Lz.)

ALBERT (1490–1545), elector and archbishop of Mainz, attacked by Martin Luther over the sale of indulgences, was born on June 28, 1490, the younger son of John Cicero, elector of Brandenburg. He became archbishop of Magdeburg and administrator of the bishopric of Halberstadt in 1513 and archbishop and elector of Mainz the next year.

This pluralistic holding of episcopal dignities was contrary to canon law and Albert had to contribute a considerable sum toward the rebuilding of St. Peter's in Rome in order to induce Pope Leo X to overlook the irregularity. The money was borrowed from the banking house of Fugger, and to repay it Albert obtained permission from the pope to conduct the sale of a special plenary indulgence in the dioceses of Magdeburg and Halberstadt, half the proceeds of which were to go to him and half to the pope. To sell the indulgence Albert procured the services of the Dominican Johann Tetzel (q.v.), whose activities provoked Luther to publish his 95 theses in 1517, attacking Albert and through him the system of indulgences. In 1518 Albert was created cardinal.

During the imperial election of 1519 his vote was eagerly courted and he was well paid for the vote that he eventually cast for Charles V. At one time his well-known liberal outlook suggested he might support the Reformation; but after the peasants' war of 1525 he strenuously opposed it, though he was compelled to grant religious liberty to the inhabitants of Magdeburg in exchange for 500,000 florins, a sum he used to pay off his debts. During his later years he became less tolerant toward the Protestants, and by inviting the Jesuits to Mainz he helped to foster the Counter-Reformation in Germany.

Albert was a generous patron of art and learning and his large and liberal ideas won him the friendship of men like Ulrich von Hutten and Erasmus. He founded the Stiftskirche at Halle in 1528 and adorned it and the cathedral at Mainz in sumptuous fashion. His motto was *Domine, dilexi decorum domus tuae,* from Ps. xxvi, 8 (in the Authorized Version: "Lord, I have loved the habitation of thy house, and the place where thine honour dwelleth"). He died in Aschaffenburg on Sept. 24, 1545.

BIBLIOGRAPHY.—J. May, *Der Kurfürst, Kardinal und Erzbischof Albrecht II von Mainz und Magdeburg,* 2 vol. (1865–75); W. Schum, *Kardinal Albrecht von Mainz und die Erfurter Kirchenreformation* (1878); P. Redlich, *Kardinal Albrecht von Brandenburg, und das neue Stift zu Halle* (1900); P. Kalkoff, *W. Capito im Dienste des Erzbischofs A. von Mainz, 1519–1523* (1907). (D. G. D.)

ALBERT OF AIX (fl. *c.* 1130), canon and *custos* ("keeper") of the church of Aix-la-Chapelle (Aachen), author of a history of the first crusade and of the early years of the Latin kingdom of Jerusalem (to 1121), in 12 books. This work, entitled *Historia Hierosolymitanae expeditionis* or *Chronicon Hierosolymitanum de bello sacro,* was used by William of Tyre for the first part of his history of the kingdom of Jerusalem and was very widely read in the middle ages. Albert was not an eyewitness, but gathered his information from diverse sources. Writing at a time when the history of the crusade was beginning to be surrounded by legends, *c.* 1125 or later, he accepted some of these, especially those concerning Peter the Hermit. He was also particularly interested in the crusaders from lower Lotharingia (Lorraine) and the family of Godfrey of Bouillon. His work is, nevertheless, one of the best sources for the history of the crusade. First printed in 1584, the text was reprinted in the *Recueil des historiens des croisades,* vol. iv (1879).

See S. Runciman, *History of the Crusades,* vol. ii (1952) and works there cited. (J. B. R.)

ALBERT OF SAXONY (1316?–1390?), German scholastic philosopher especially remarkable for his investigations into physics, was born at Helmstedt in lower Saxony. He studied at Prague and then at Paris university, where he was a master of arts from 1351 to 1362 and rector in 1353. Most probably he is to be identified with the Albert of Ricmestorp or Rückmersdorf who was rector of Vienna university in 1365 and bishop of Halberstadt from 1366 until his death there in 1390. Albert based his logic on William Ockham, his physical theory on Jean Buridan, his mathematics on Thomas Bradwardine and his ethics on Walter Burley (rejecting Buridan's psychological determinism) and was at first respected more for clarity and exactness in exposition than for originality. The later scholastic logicians adopted many of the terminological distinctions first found in his works (*see* for instance A PRIORI AND A POSTERIORI), and he examined and classified 254 *sophismata* or logical paradoxes. In physics, he wrote at length on place, space and time, on the impossibility of a plurality of worlds and, in great detail, on the movement of bodies (Leonardo da Vinci seems to have been indebted to him on this subject). Albert gave particular attention to the problem of gravity, being perhaps the first thinker to distinguish the centre of gravity from the geometrical centre, and to that of the velocity of falling bodies, appreciating that the question was whether velocity was proportional to time or to space. He can also be regarded as a precursor of aerostatics, as he maintained that a light balloon would rise and remain suspended in the air if a particle of fire were enclosed in it. Finally, his search for mathematical formulas to express laws of nature foreshadowed the usage of modern physics.

BIBLIOGRAPHY.—P. Duhem, *Le Système du monde,* vol. vii–ix (1956–58); G. Heidingsfelder, *Albert von Sachsen (Beiträge zur Geschichte der Philosophie des Mittelalters,* vol. xxii, 1921); F. Dalla Zuanna, *Doctrina de spatio in schola nominalistica parisiensi saec. XIV* (1936); A. Maier, *Studien zur Naturphilosophie der Spätscholastik,* 5 vol. (1949–58). (F. SE.)

ALBERT L'OUVRIER ("the Worker"; real name ALBERT ALEXANDRE MARTIN) (1815–1895), the first industrial workingman to enter a government in France, was born in Bury, Oise, on April 27, 1815. A convinced socialist and republican, he played an active part in the Revolution of 1848 and was made a member of the provisional government, his name appearing on all documents as "Albert l'Ouvrier." He was subsequently appointed vice-president of the Commission du Luxembourg (an assembly of workers' delegates) under Louis Blanc (q.v.). Sentenced to life imprisonment for his part in the uprising of May 15, 1848, Albert was amnestied in 1859. He died in Mello, Oise, on May 28, 1895.

ALBERT, HEINRICH (1604–1651), German composer of a famous and popular collection of songs, was born in Lobenstein, Saxony, July 8, 1604. He was a cousin of Heinrich Schütz, with whom he studied composition at Dresden before taking a course in law at Leipzig, where his musical studies were encouraged by J. H. Schein.

In 1627 Albert set out for Königsberg to pursue a musical career; after being taken prisoner by a Swedish army he arrived in 1628. He was appointed cathedral organist (1631) and there published works from 1632. He died in Königsberg, Oct. 6, 1651.

Albert composed numerous festival pieces for the Brandenburg princes but is best known for his *Arien,* published by himself between 1638 and 1651. These settings of sacred and secular texts form the most characteristically German song collection of the 17th century. He also has a place in the early history of German opera; the scores have not survived, but two pieces from *Cleomedes* occur among the *Arien.* (C. P. Co.)

ALBERT, LAKE, is situated in equatorial Africa astride the boundary between Uganda and the Republic of the (former Belgian) Congo. It was named after Queen Victoria's consort, receiving the now discarded hybrid name of Albert Nyanza, from Sir Samuel White Baker (q.v.) who first reached the lake on March 14, 1864. The Lunyoro name is *Muitanzige* ("that which kills locusts" because of their unsuccessful attempts to cross it). Baker's exaggerated impression of its size was corrected by R. Gessi, who circumnavigated it in 1876. The length is 108 mi., the average width 19 mi. and the area approximately 2,075 sq.mi. Surface level is 2,034 ft. above sea level, but the height is liable to small seasonal changes and to greater periodic fluctuations. The lake is shallow, 168 ft. being its maximum depth, and in this respect it contrasts with Lake Tanganyika which is also situated in the western branch of the East African rift system.

With the gradual subsidence of the floor of the Albertine depression and with intermittent faulting from Pre-Miocene times onward, thousands of feet of sedimentary material were laid down in the trough under shallow water conditions. Most important among these deposits are the Lower Pleistocene Kaiso beds derived from sluggish streams which flowed across the landscape now represented by the gentler upper portion of the flanking scarps. A major movement of the boundary faults followed the deposition of the Kaiso beds, thus giving rise to the steep fault scarps which now dominate the scenery of the rift valley. The scarps are developed in the Basement system and they are marked by a hanging base line between the older and the newer elements of their morphology. Wild, wooded ravines form gashes in the scarps and fine cascades are a feature of this young tectonic landscape. The Congo and the Uganda sides of the trough are closely comparable, except that the scale is grander in the former.

In many places the walls of the rift rise directly from the lake, but elsewhere there are restricted patches of lowland at or near lake level, and especially on the southeastern shore there are well-developed sandspits and lagoons, at Buhuka, Kaiso, Tonya and Butiaba. In the southwest the Semliki river brings the waters of Lake Edward, of the Congo escarpment and of the rain-soaked massif of Ruwenzori into Lake Albert. In so doing it has built up a considerable alluvial plain and its ambatch- and papyrus-choked delta continues to encroach upon the shallow waters of the lake. North of Butiaba as the lake shore curves away from the straight edge of the escarpment, there declining in height, there is a considerable expanse of lowland at the northern end of which the Victoria Nile enters Lake Albert as a sluggish stream in a swampy delta. Almost immediately the lake narrows into the Albert Nile, through which the natural reservoir of Lake Albert maintains a constant supply of water to the White Nile.

The lake shores are hot and dry, with a mean annual temperature of 78° F. and a mean annual rainfall of just over 30 in. at Butiaba. There is a high rate of evaporation from the lake and its waters are distinctly saline. The vegetation of the flats consists of poor grasses and scattered drought-resistant trees and bushes. Game is abundant, especially in the Semliki plains and in the area adjacent to the Murchison Falls National park, elephant, buffalo, hippopotamus, crocodiles and various antelope being much in evidence. The population is scanty and the traditional settlements are fishing villages sited in relation to the sandspits and cusps. The fish fauna of the lake is very different from that of Lake Victoria, with the break coming at the 130-ft. drop of the Murchison falls. The main catch in the Uganda waters of Lake Albert comprises *ngara* (*Alestes* species), *mputa* (*Lates* species, "perch"), *ngassa* (*Hydrocyon* species, "tiger fish") and *ngege* (*Tilapia* species, "carp"). The fish caught in the Uganda section of the lake find their main market in the Congo. Steamship services provided by the East African Railways and Harbours administration connect Butiaba with Kasenyi (a fishing centre and a port for the Kilo-Moto mines) and with Mahagi port. The Pakwach-Butiaba service copes with a passenger traffic of migrant labour and Nile-route tourists and provides an outlet for West Nile cotton. The extension of the railway from Soroti to Gulu and ultimately to the Nile, after 1960, will inevitably draw traffic away from Lake Albert.

BIBLIOGRAPHY.—Sir S. W. Baker, *The Albert N'yanza,* 2 vol. (1866); H. E. Hurst, *The Lake Plateau Basin of the Nile,* parts i and ii (1925–27); E. B. Worthington, *A Report on the Fishing Survey of Lakes Albert and Kioga* (1929); "The Life of Lake Albert and Lake Kioga," *Geogr. J.,* 74:109–132 (1929); S. J. K. Baker, "Bunyoro: a Regional Appreciation," *Uganda J.,* 18:101–112 (1954); N. Harris, J. W. Pallister and J. M. Brown, *Oil in Uganda* (1956). (S. J. K. B.)

ALBERTA, a province of Canada, was created in 1905. Area 255,285 sq.mi. (land 248,800, water 6,485). On the south the 49th parallel separates Alberta from the United States and 800 mi. N. the 60th parallel separates it from the Northwest Territories. The province has an average width of 300 mi.; the boundary on the east is the 110th meridian, and on the west the crest of the Rocky mountains and the 120th meridian. The province of Saskatchewan lies to the east, British Columbia to the west. The capital is Edmonton (*q.v.*).

Physical Geography.—*Geology.*—Almost all of Alberta is in the Interior Plains physiographic region of North America, which consists of nearly flat-lying sedimentary rocks. Only in the extreme northeast do the crystalline rocks of the Canadian shield appear at the surface; in the southwest the generally subdued plains terrain is relieved by the spectacular ranges of the Rocky mountains which flank the province for about 420 mi. The basement Pre-Cambrian rocks which outcrop in the northeast have depths of 10,000 ft. below the surface in the western part of the plains, and are covered by layer after layer of Paleozoic and Mesozoic sediments. Most of the surface bedrock consists of Cretaceous sediments, though there are extensive areas of Tertiary deposits on top of these beyond the margins of the foothills of the Rockies. The Cretaceous and Devonian formations contain important coal and oil deposits respectively. The Rocky mountains, the eastern ranges of the western Cordillera, are carved out of a thick series of folded and faulted sedimentary of Paleozoic age. The foothills are formed of Mesozoic strata.

Physical Features.—The plains have an elevation of 4,000 ft. at the foothills on the west and gradually slope northward and eastward to an elevation less than 700 ft. in northeastern Alberta,

where they meet the shield. Within the plains there is considerable variation in terrain. Major streams flow in valleys that are as much as 400 ft. below the prairie surface and are from one to two miles wide. In the arid southern part of Alberta there are sharply dissected badlands along a few of the streams. Above the level of the plains there are a number of hills, mostly erosion remnants of the Tertiary deposits. The 4,810-ft.-high Cypress hills in southeast Alberta, rising to 1,200 ft. above the surrounding prairie, are the most prominent of these, but there are other lesser elevations above the plains in central and northern Alberta. Most of the present surface materials are the result of the Pleistocene continental glaciation. Gently rolling plains occur over wide areas; hummocky morainic deposits are also common, but they are not so extensive. The Peace river (*q.v.*) country toward the northwest is an area of relatively level glacial drift, together with some clay sediments deposited in a glacial lake. It is separated from the agricultural land to the south by a belt of poorly drained glacial drift. The Rocky mountains have a general elevation of 8,000–9,000 ft., but rise to occasional peaks that exceed 11,000 ft. Mt. Columbia, 12,294 ft., is the highest peak. Northern Alberta is drained to the Arctic ocean (via the Mackenzie river; *q.v.*) by the Hay, Peace and Athabasca (*q.v.*) rivers; central and southern Alberta to Hudson bay (via Lake Winnipeg and the Nelson river; *qq.v.*) by the North and South Saskatchewan rivers; and the extreme southern plains to the Gulf of Mexico (via the Missouri and Mississippi rivers) by the Milk river.

National parks and reserves include Jasper, Banff, with the re-

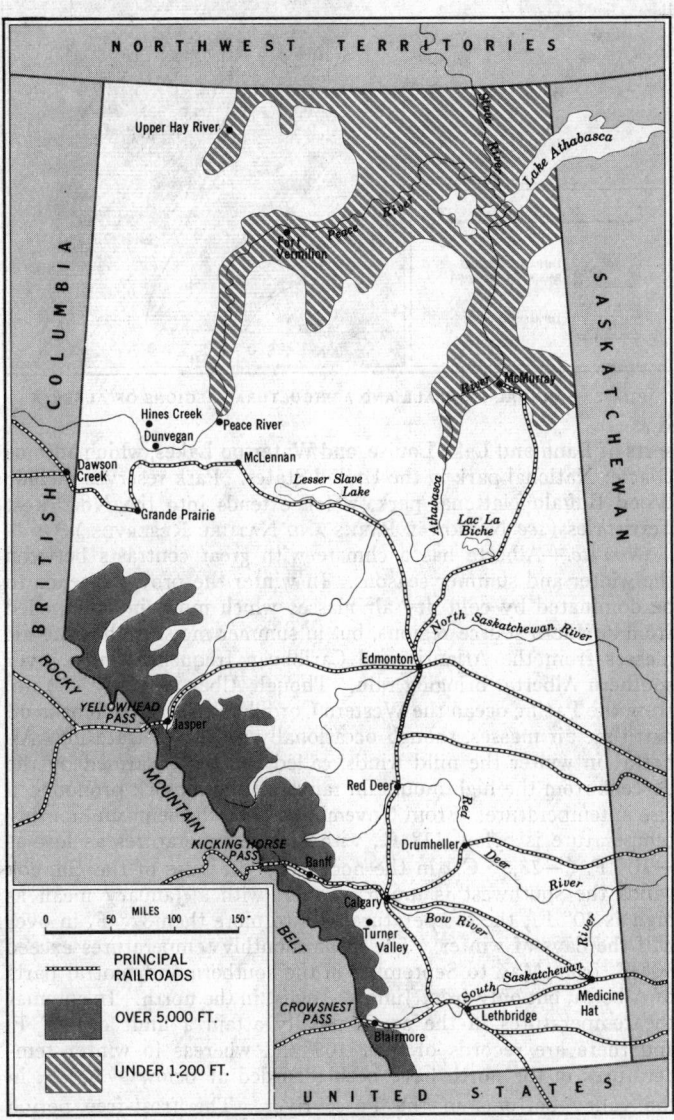

FIG. 1.—TOPOGRAPHY AND PRINCIPAL RAILROADS OF ALBERTA

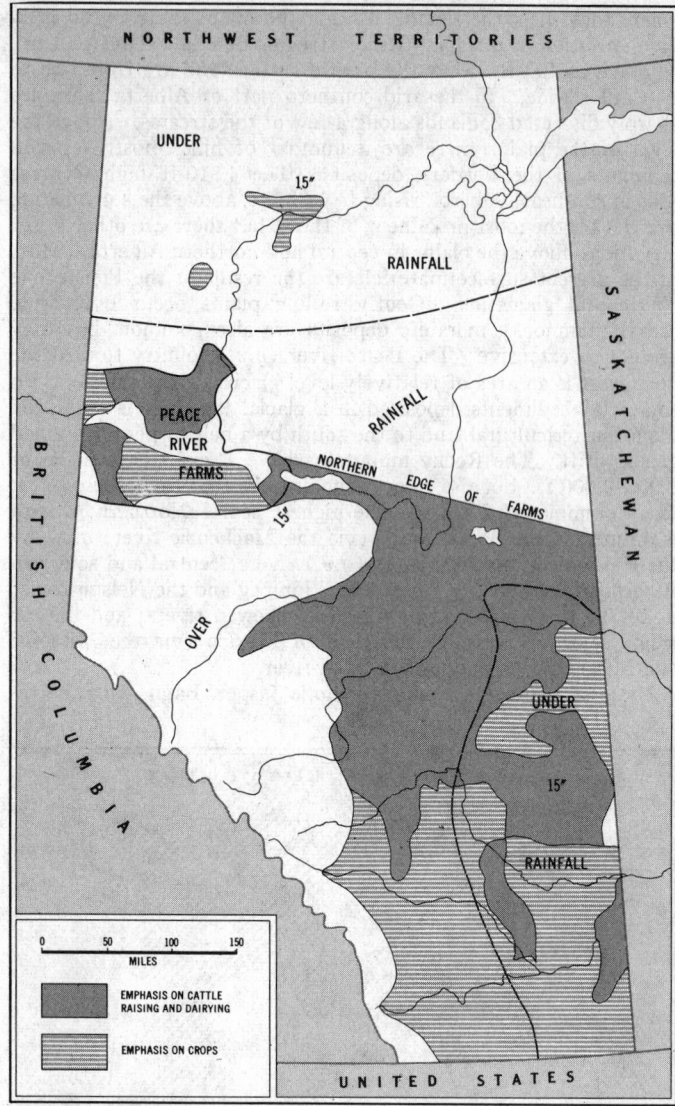

NORTHWEST TERRITORIES

UNDER

15"

RAINFALL

PEACE

RIVER

FARMS

NORTHERN EDGE OF FARMS

RAINFALL

15"

OVER

UNDER

15"

RAINFALL

BRITISH COLUMBIA

SASKATCHEWAN

0   50   100   150
MILES

█ EMPHASIS ON CATTLE
RAISING AND DAIRYING

▤ EMPHASIS ON CROPS

UNITED STATES

FIG. 2.—ANNUAL RAINFALL AND AGRICULTURAL REGIONS OF ALBERTA

sorts of Banff and Lake Louise, and Waterton Lakes, which adjoins Glacier National park in the United States. Park reserves include Wood Buffalo National park, which extends into the Northwest Territories (see NATIONAL PARKS AND NATURE RESERVES.)

Climate.—Alberta has a climate with great contrasts between the winter and summer seasons. In winter the province tends to be dominated by cold dry air masses which move in unimpeded from northern source regions, but in summer moisture-bearing air masses from the Atlantic and Caribbean frequently move over southern Alberta, bringing rain. Though Alberta is only 400 mi. from the Pacific ocean the Western Cordillera effectively blocks off maritime air masses, though occasionally some penetrate into Alberta; in winter the mild winds, called chinooks, warmed by the descent from the high mountain ranges, bring a quick pronounced rise in temperature. From November to March the mean monthly temperature is below 32° F., with mean temperatures as low as −10° F. (−23.3° C.) in the northeast. Because of the chinook winds the southwest is much warmer, with a January mean as high as 20° F.; the temperature rises to more than 32° F. in over half the days of winter. The mean monthly temperatures exceed 50° F. from May to September in the southern and central parts of Alberta, but only from June to August in the north. In summer the temperatures in the south usually attain a limit of 90° F. and there are records of over 105° F., whereas in winter temperatures in the north have been recorded at below −70° F. in the valley bottoms of the Peace river. The frost-free period ranges from an average of 111 days at Lethbridge (*q.v.*) to 100

days at Edmonton and to 65 days at Fort Vermilion in the north.

The precipitation increases from 14 in. in the northern plains to 18 in. in the central region, and then decreases to 13 in. in southeast Alberta, but near the foothills some areas average well over 20 in. annually. There is a strong summer maximum; the six months from May to October receive 70% of the precipitation. Snow contributes approximately 25%–30% of the precipitation. Precipitation varies considerably from year to year: Edmonton with a mean of 18.3 in. has recorded a low of 10.9 in. and a high of 27.8 in., and Medicine Hat in the dryer southeast has a mean of 13.3 in., with a low record of 6.7 in. and a high of 25.3 in. Along with the rest of the prairies, southern Alberta is the sunniest part of Canada, and sunless days are rare in summer. There is considerably less evaporation of moisture in the central and northern parts of the province, so that the precipitation is more effective than in the semiarid south.

Soils.—The soils of Alberta in general follow the vegetation divisions (*see* below). Shallow, brown grassland soils, which are liable to drift when cultivated, have developed in the southeast, but the grassland soils become darker, with added organic matter, as the moisture conditions improve northward and these are excellent wheat-producing soils. Between the prairie and the forest, in the park belt, are the black soils, with high humus content, considered to be one of the most fertile soils in Canada. Diversified agriculture is found on this soil. The forest soils of the north have a rather low percentage of arable land, except in the Peace river country, where there are some degraded black soils; the best of these are used for mixed farming.

Vegetation.—The variation in the effectiveness of the moisture is reflected in a gradual change of vegetation, from short grasses in the south through deciduous groves to coniferous woods in the north. In the southeast there is a true steppe vegetation with only a sparse cover of grass. To the north and west the grasses become taller and more luxuriant, and north of Calgary there is a parkland of tall grass interspersed with groves of trees, particularly aspen. From Edmonton north to the border, there is a continuous forest cover of deciduous and coniferous trees, with the exception of the Peace river country, which is an isolated area of parkland, and of a purely coniferous area to the northeast. Aspen and spruce are the chief trees in the mixed woods and the Peace river area, and spruce, balsam fir and tamarack in the coniferous zone. Along the flanks of the Rocky mountains there is another forest belt of Engelmann's spruce, lodgepole pine and alpine larch.

Animal Life.—Before settlement bison ranged over the prairies of Alberta; now they are preserved in a few parks. Other prairie mammals include the pocket gopher, badger, coyote and jack rabbit. In the forest area moose, mule deer, woodland caribou, black bear, timber wolf, lynx, beaver, muskrat, otter and fox are found, while in the Rocky mountains grizzly bear, mountain goat and mountain caribou also are present. Breeding birds are numerous in the province, including prairie chicken, sharp-tailed grouse, mallard and black duck.

History.—Alberta was originally a part of the Hudson's Bay territory granted by the charter of 1670 (see HUDSON'S BAY COMPANY). Pierre Boucher, sieur de Boucherville, following the lead of Pierre Gaultier de Varennes, sieur de la Vérendrye, visited the region in 1751, but it was not until the last quarter of the 18th century that the Northwest company and the Hudson's Bay company penetrated into the area for trading purposes. Both companies founded posts near Edmonton (1795) but the fur trade developed northward.

The transfer of the northwest on Nov. 19, 1869 from the Hudson's Bay company to the new dominion of Canada led to the "act for settlement" (1872) and, on completion of the Canadian Pacific railway (1885), to a continued influx of settlement from eastern Canada, from overseas and across the border. Settlement led to territorial government at first under the Northwest Territories act of 1875. An act of 1882 separated out four provincial "districts" (Assiniboia, Saskatchewan, Alberta, Athabasca) leaving west of Hudson bay the area north of 60° as Northwest Territories (*q.v.*). Alberta (southern half of the present province) was named for Princess Louise Alberta, daughter of Queen Victoria and Albert,

VIEW OF LAKE LOUISE IN THE CANADIAN ROCKIES

Lake Louise, viewed from a trail along the edge of the water looking toward Mt. Lefroy on the left, and Mt. Victoria in the centre, both crowned with glaciers. In the early morning perfect pictures of the glaciers are mirrored in the depths of the blue and green shaded waters

PLATE II

ALBERTA

PHOTOGRAPHS, (1, 5) PIX-HARMON FROM PUBLIX, (2) PIX FROM PUBLIX, (3, 4, 6) PAUL'S PHOTOS

VIEWS OF ALBERTA

1. A snow cornice in the Canadian Rockies
2. Skiers at a lodge in Banff
3. Bridge of the Banff-Jasper highway over Athabasca falls in Jasper National park. In the background is Mount Kerkeslin

4. Tongue of the Athabasca glacier (right) in Jasper National park
5. Lake Minnewanka, Banff
6. Airview of Calgary, looking northwest

the prince consort. At the census of 1901 Alberta and Athabasca (the area now Alberta) had a population of 73,022. The ensuing rapid settlement led in 1905 to the creation of the present province of Alberta and of its sister province Saskatchewan. The provinces had at once the status conferred by the British North America act of 1867 but, to facilitate settlement, the public domain remained under federal control until 1929. With grain growing and ranching as the economic basis, the population reached 374,295 in 1911 and 588,454 in 1921.

The government was at first conducted by parties formed on the standing model of conservatives and liberals. In 1921 agrarian interests (United Farmers of Alberta) formed the government, but were replaced by the Social Credit party in 1935 during the depression years. This party under the leadership of William Aberhart proposed to introduce a system of monetary reform that would solve the economic difficulties of the province and also construct a new society. Aberhart proposed to issue dividends (social credit) based upon the real wealth of the country to every person. The party was never able to implement its full program because its proposals were disallowed by the dominion cabinet. But the Social Credit party directed Alberta's developments along orthodox financial lines during the years that oil and natural gas strengthened its economy. As a result of this prosperity some dividends, Citizens' Oil Royalties, were paid in 1957 and 1958, but after that the government directed its surplus funds toward a five-year antirecession development program.

Government.—The Alberta legislative assembly, consisting of 61 members elected for a maximum term of five years, meets at Edmonton. There is an executive council, or cabinet, of 15 ministers selected from the party holding the majority in the assembly. This government has the right to make laws relating to education, natural resources, municipal government, property and other matters. The chief sources of revenue are licences and permits for developing natural resources, sales taxes (particularly gasoline taxes), corporation taxes, succession duties, revenue from liquor control and federal subsidies. Heaviest expenditure after World War II was to help municipal authorities provide services for an increasing population. Transportation facilities, health and social welfare services and education facilities particularly were improved.

For administrative purposes Alberta is divided into 38 municipal districts, 10 counties (where municipal districts and school administrative areas coincide), 49 improvement districts (sparsely inhabited areas) and 2 special areas.

Population.—Alberta's population in 1961 (1,331,944) had increased by 392,443 from 1951 as new resources and industries were developed that attract people from other parts of Canada and elsewhere. The increase has occurred in the urban areas; farm population is decreasing because of a trend toward fewer, larger and more mechanized farms. The proportion of people living on farms decreased more than 40% from 1931 to 1961.

From 1900 to 1910, when Alberta's farm lands were rapidly occupied, immigrants streamed in from many European countries, so that the people are extremely varied in cultural origin. In the second half of the 20th century 48.1% of the population was of British origin, 11.5% German, 9.3% Ukranian, 7.5% Scandinavian and 6.0% French; included in the balance of the population were

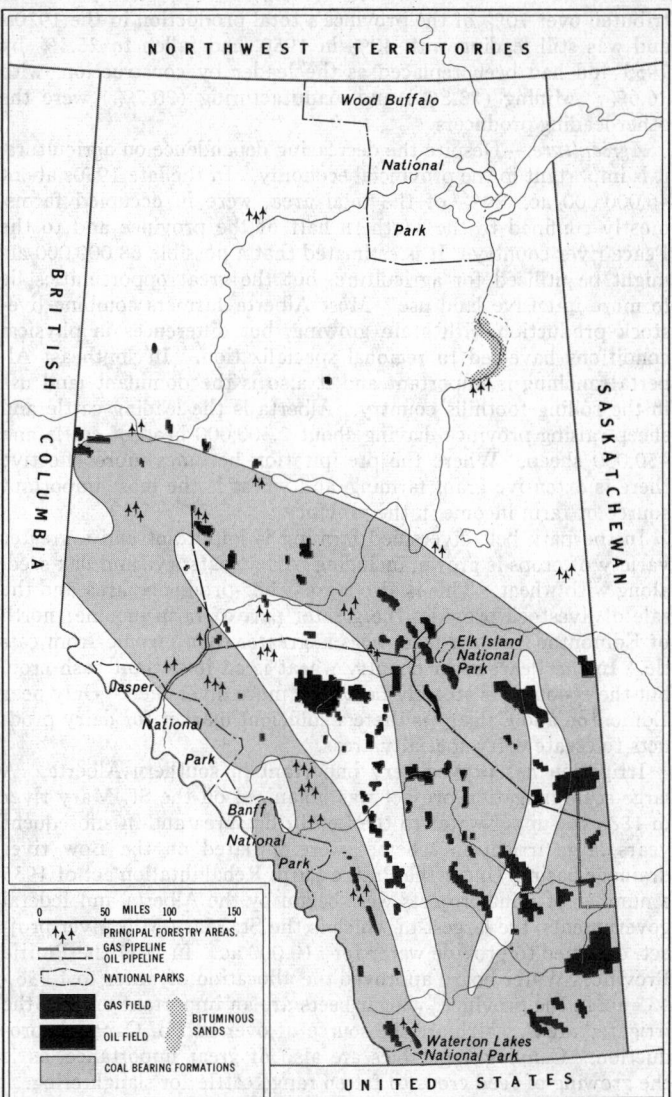

FIG. 3.—NATURAL RESOURCES AND NATIONAL PARKS OF ALBERTA

about 21,000 Indians and Eskimos, about 2.3% of the total population.

Population distribution follows the agricultural land use. South of the 55th parallel there is continuous agricultural settlement with its necessary trading towns, and also large cities. In the southeast the population density is generally less than four per square mile, but it increases to four to ten per square mile and even higher toward the foothills and toward Edmonton. North of the 55th parallel there is only one large area of continuous settlement, the Peace river country, where density is high. The remainder of the northern part of the province is sparsely inhabited.

Education.—In the 1960s approximately 22% of the population was enrolled in educational institutions in Alberta. The province has a 12-grade school system, in which centralization of school facilities resulted in great improvements. Revenue for the schools is obtained from legislative appropriation and a uniform requisition on all municipalities and is paid out by the department of education to each school authority in accordance with its needs and services. Vocational education is provided in public high schools, in the Provincial Institute of Technology and Art at Calgary and in schools maintained by the department of agriculture. There is one provincial university located at Edmonton, with a branch at Calgary, and three affiliated colleges. The university is very active in extension work and operates the Banff School of Fine Arts every summer.

The Economy.—The net value of production in Alberta represents about 8% of the Canadian total. Agriculture, which con-

Alberta: Places of 5,000 or More Population

Place	Population				
	1961	1956	1951	1941	1921
Total province . .	1,331,944	1,123,116	939,501	796,169	588,454
Beverly . . .	9,041	4,602	2,159	981	1,039
Bowness . . .	9,184	6,217	2,922	—	—
Calgary . . .	249,641	181,780	129,060	88,904	63,305
Camrose . . .	6,939	5,817	4,131	2,598	1,892
Edmonton . . .	281,027	226,002	159,631	93,817	58,821
Forest Lawn . .	12,263	3,150	1,079	899	—
Grande Prairie . .	8,352	6,302	2,664	1,724	1,061
Jasper Place . .	30,530	15,957	9,139	—	—
Lethbridge . . .	35,454	29,462	22,947	14,612	11,097
Medicine Hat . .	24,484	20,826	16,364	10,571	9,634
Montgomery . .	5,077	—	—	—	—
Red Deer . . .	19,612	12,338	7,575	2,924	2,328
Wetaskiwin . .	5,300	4,476	3,824	2,318	2,061

Note: Populations are reported as constituted at date of each census. Dash indicates place did not exist during reported census, or data not available.

tributed over 70% of the province's total production in the 1920s, and was still leading with 40% in 1950, had fallen to 25.3% by 1955 and had been replaced as the leader by construction, with 26.6%. Mining (23.8%) and manufacturing (20.7%) were the other leading producers.

Agriculture.—Despite the decreasing dependence on agriculture, it is important in the provincial economy. In the late 1950s about 46,000,000 ac., 29% of the total area, were in occupied farms, mostly confined to the southern half of the province and to the Peace river country. It is estimated that a possible 68,000,000 ac. might be utilized for agriculture, but the great opportunities lie in more intensive land use. Most Alberta farmers combine livestock production with grain growing, but differences in physical conditions have led to regional specialization. In southeast Alberta ranching is important and it also is the dominant land use in the rolling foothills country. Alberta is the leading cattle and sheep-raising province, having about 2,300,000 head of cattle and 450,000 sheep. Where the precipitation becomes more effective there is extensive grain farming, and wheat is the most important source of farm income in the province.

In the park belt diversified farming is important and a greater variety of crops is grown, including barley, oats, rye and flax seed, along with wheat. This is also a great hog-producing area and the sale of livestock provides the greater part of farm income; north of Edmonton, income from hogs is greater than income from cattle. In the Peace river country wheat is an important cash crop, but the economy is steadily becoming more diversified. Only near Edmonton and Calgary is there a sufficient market for dairy products to create dairy specialty areas.

Irrigation has proved very important in southern Alberta. A large-scale irrigation project was organized on the St. Mary river in 1883 to supply water to the Lethbridge area and in subsequent years large irrigation schemes were initiated on the Bow river drainage basin. Under the Prairie Farm Rehabilitation act of 1935 a number of joint projects were begun by the Alberta and federal governments, the largest of which is the St. Mary-Milk river project, designed to provide water for 510,000 ac. In 1957 the Prairie Provinces Water board approved the allocation of water to 1,256,435 ac. in the province. Sugar beets are an important crop in the irrigated areas, which are the source of over half of Canada's production. Canning vegetables are also of great importance, as is the growing of feed crops to fatten range cattle for slaughtering.

Within Alberta there is a great range in farm size, since land use varies from extensive ranching and grain growing to intensive irrigation agriculture, but the majority of the holdings are large: in the late 1950s the average area per farm was nearly 580 ac.

Forestry.—Alberta has an estimated 88,227 sq.mi. (36% of the total area) of productive forest out of a total forested area of 151,278 sq.mi. (60% of the total area). A program for placing the forests on a sustained yield basis is in effect. Formerly the main use of the forests was to supply timber for many sawmills scattered through the wooded part of the province, but in 1957 a large pulp mill was established at Hinton, and another company manufactures plywood in the Peace river area.

Mining.—Reserves of minerals, especially fossil fuels, indicate possibilities for great expansion of the industry. The province contains the largest reserves of coal in Canada, the coal area being estimated by the Geological Survey of Canada at 16,588 sq.mi., containing a possible reserve of 47,874,300,000 tons. The coal beds outcrop along the Rocky mountain foothills from the international border northward for 460 mi. and are mined where they are reached by railway lines at Crowsnest, Canmore, Luscar and other places. Coal-bearing formations also are found in the flat-lying Cretaceous sediments of Alberta, from the Peace river south through Edmonton to the border. These are mined at various places, including Drumheller, Lethbridge and Taber. Alberta produces all types of coals, including some anthracite; mostly, however, they are bituminous and subbituminous, with some lignite. The highest-ranking coals are found close to the Rocky mountains. Coal production declines, however, as competition from oil and natural gas increases. In the late 1950s Alberta contributed nearly 30% of Canadian coal production.

Crude oil after 1953 led all Canadian minerals in annual value, and Alberta accounted for about 85% of Canada's crude oil production by the 1960s. Oil was first brought into production in commercial quantities at Turner Valley in 1914 and this area remained Alberta's principal centre of production until 1947, when the Leduc field, south of Edmonton was discovered. Oil is obtained throughout all of southern Alberta. At first it was derived primarily from Devonian strata, but as drilling continued reserves were found throughout the geological sequences of the Alberta sedimentary rocks. The most important Canadian producing field is the Pembina field, southwest of Edmonton, but other important fields are found from the Peace river to the U.S. border. Pipelines from Alberta to Vancouver, on the Pacific coast, and to Sarnia, Ont., bring the petroleum to market.

For 70 mi. along the Athabasca river in northern Alberta there are great reserves of oil in oil-impregnated tar sands, but these have remained unexploited. Natural gas was used as a commercial fuel in Alberta as early as 1890, and enormous reserves have been located since then in the Peace river country and in southern Alberta. Gas also is brought by pipeline to markets in the densely settled parts of Canada.

Salt, gypsum, bentonite and clays suitable for baking are obtained from the sedimentary rocks of southern Alberta. Since the Canadian shield, rich in metallic ores, touches only northeast Alberta, there are no important deposits of metallic minerals in the province.

Power.—Though fossil fuels are important in electricity production, water power still provides more than 50% of the electricity generated. By the late 1950s installed capacity (less than 300,000 h.p.) represented only a small part of the estimated 1,258,000 h.p. available. Most of the hydroelectric power is obtained from installations on the Bow river in the southern Rocky mountains. It is likely that fuel electric power will increase in importance, since the hydroelectric potential is on the rivers of northern Alberta, away from the centres of population.

Manufacturing.—Alberta's manufacturing is based on the processing of primary raw materials, and after the resource base was widened by the oil and gas discoveries it increased rapidly in importance, since oil and gas provide both fuel and raw material. Alberta leads the prairie provinces in manufacturing. Food and beverages are of most importance, particularly slaughtering and meat packing, which account for nearly half of the province's manufacturing. Petroleum and coal products are in second place, large oil refineries being located in Edmonton, Calgary and lesser centres. These industries and the petrochemical industries dependent upon oil and natural gas are growing. Polyethylene plastics, fertilizers and inorganic products also are produced. Iron and steel products are manufactured for the gas and oil industries. Printing and publishing are important, and there are some important wood products industries. A potteries industry, based on local clays and utilizing natural gas as fuel, is located at Medicine Hat.

Transportation and Communications.—In the days of the fur trade, rivers were the important means of communication in Alberta, and for a time in the latter part of the 19th century they were used for steam navigation. They were rapidly replaced by the railway in southern Alberta, and waterways are important only on the Athabasca, which is the connecting link between rail transportation and the Mackenzie system. The Canadian Pacific (C.P.R.) railway line was constructed across present Alberta through Calgary by 1883, and remained the undisputed main railway line until 1915 when the Grand Trunk Pacific (later the Canadian National [C.N.R.]) was completed through Edmonton to the Pacific. In the meantime the C.P.R. had built a line to Edmonton from Calgary (1891) and another line to the Pacific via Crowsnest pass through southern Alberta. Within the agricultural part of Alberta an adequate railway network was quickly built up to serve the population's marketing needs. From Edmonton northward, branches were completed to the Peace river country in 1914, and to McMurray on the Athabasca in 1921. After 1929 these two branches were operated jointly by the C.N.R. and the C.P.R. as the Northern Alberta railways.

Market roads have long been available permitting farmers to

bring their produce to the trading centres, but Alberta also developed an extensive system of trunk highways. The main routes are the east-west Trans-Canada highway through Calgary and the north-south highway from Edmonton through Calgary to the U.S. border. The highway from Banff (*q.v.*) to Jasper national park in the Rocky mountains is an important scenic route that has helped develop Alberta's most important tourist attraction. The Alaska highway begins at the railhead in the Peace river country at Fort St. John, B.C., and the Mackenzie highway extends from Grimshaw on the Peace river to Great Slave lake.

Alberta is well supplied with air services. Transcontinental flights pass through Edmonton and Calgary, and there are local services within the prairie region to British Columbia and the Northwest Territories. Various air services connect with United States centres.

BIBLIOGRAPHY.—*Canadian Census; Canada Year Book* (annual); J. Blue, *History of Alberta* (1929); W. G. Hardy, *The Alberta Golden Jubilee* (1955); J. A. Irving, *The Social Credit Movement in Alberta* (1959); Ken Liddell, *Alberta Revisited* (1960); D. F. Putnam (ed.), *Canadian Regions: a Geography of Canada* (1952). Current statistics on production, employment, industry, etc., may be obtained from the pertinent provincial departments. (JN. H. W.)

ALBERT EDWARD NYANZA: see EDWARD, LAKE.

ALBERTI, the name of two families important in medieval Italy.

1. Members of the Tuscan feudal family of the Alberti are recorded as counts from the 10th century onward. The most important branch of this family was that of Prato. Next to the Guidi, the Alberti were the most powerful feudal lords of the country round Florence, and the territorial expansion of the Florentine commune brought them into frequent conflicts with that city. Support from the Holy Roman emperors provided only temporary relief, and in 1200 Count Alberto finally submitted to Florence. His newly built town Semifonte was destroyed on Florentine orders in 1202.

See R. Davidsohn, *Geschichte von Florenz,* vol. i (1896); P. Santini, "Studi sull' antica costituzione del Comune di Firenze," *Archivio storico Italiano,* series 5, vol. xxv and xxvi (1900).

2. The Alberti del Giudice were among the wealthiest Florentine merchant bankers for about 100 years from mid-14th century. They engaged in extensive international trade and in the second half of the 14th century played a leading role in financial transactions of the papacy. Political rivals of the Albizzi (*see* FLORENCE), they were nearly all deprived of civic rights in 1393 and all male members of the family were banished in 1402. They were allowed to return to Florence in 1428, but did not recover full civic rights until after the fall of the Albizzi in 1434.

See L. Passerini, *Gli Alberti di Firenze* (1869); A. Sapori, "La famiglia e le compagnie degli Alberti del Giudice," in his *Studi di storia economica . . . ,* vol. ii, 3rd ed. (1955). (N. R.)

ALBERTI, DOMENICO (*c.* 1710–1740), Italian musician, who achieved immortality unawares as the writer of a number of harpsichord sonatas in which the melody is supported by a familiar, but now little esteemed, formula of accompaniment, known as the Alberti bass and consisting of gently moving arpeggios in the left-hand part. His sonatas were plagiarized by the Italian singer and harpsichordist Giuseppe Jozzi. He was born in Venice, about 1710 and died in Rome, 1740.

See W. Wörmann, "Die Klavier-Sonate Domenico Albertis," in *Acta Musicologica,* vol. 27 (1955). (CS. CH.)

ALBERTI, LEON BATTISTA (1404–1472), Italian humanist, architect and principal founder of Renaissance art theory, was born in Genoa on Feb. 14, 1404, the illegitimate son of an exiled Florentine nobleman. While a student of law at Bologna he started his literary career with a Latin comedy, *Philodoxeus* (*c.* 1424), which his contemporaries mistook for a lost Roman work, and essays and dialogues on moral themes. In 1434 he became a papal secretary, and in this capacity worked in Florence, where the intense activity in the arts inspired his treatises on sculpture and painting. His *Della pittura* (1436), the first literary formulation of the aesthetic and scientific attitudes of Renaissance painting, proposed an idealized imitation of nature and provided a foundation for modern perspective. During the 1430s Alberti produced a major study on education and the ethics

of domestic life. *Della famiglia,* which reflected the new social and economic conditions of Italian Renaissance culture.

Alberti was most influential in the field of architecture. His treatise, *De re aedificatoria* (1452; first printed in 1485), modeled on manuscripts of the Roman architect Vitruvius, testified to a scholarly fascination with ancient architecture and learning. It also provided the Renaissance with an original program for architectural design based on employing new procedures in musical harmony and mathematical technique to produce a perfection of proportion in plan, elevation and the interrelationship of parts. In his buildings Alberti restored the monumentality of ancient architecture, reinterpreting the triumphal arch and the temple front for the façades of S. Francesco in Rimini and of S. Sebastiano and S. Andrea in Mantua—churches which also reflected Roman tombs and basilicas in plan. Alberti's concept of harmonic proportion is demonstrated by the façades of Sta. Maria Novella and the Rucellai palace in Florence.

Other subjects treated by Alberti in books and essays include domestic animals, religion and the priesthood, jurisprudence, politics, government, mathematics, mechanics, literature and language. He also composed poetry and fables, pioneered in the development of surveying and of the camera obscura and reputedly initiated the replanning of Rome.

In the refinement of his personality and works and in the vast breadth of his learning, Alberti was the prototype of the Renaissance man.

He died in Rome on April 25, 1472.

BIBLIOGRAPHY.—G. Mancini, *Vita di L. B. Alberti,* 2nd ed. (1911); P. Michel, *La pensée de L. B. Alberti* (1930); Sir K. Clark, *Leon Battista Alberti on Painting* (1945); R. Wittkower, *Architectural Principles in the Age of Humanism* (1950). The treatises on architecture and painting have been republished in English (1955). (J. S. A.)

ALBERTINELLI, MARIOTTO (1474–1515), Italian painter, was born in Florence on Oct. 13, 1474, and was a fellow pupil and partner of Fra Bartolommeo, with whom he painted many works. His chief paintings are in Florence, notably his masterpiece, the "Visitation of the Virgin" (1503) at the Uffizi palace.

Albertinelli died in Florence on Nov. 5, 1515.

ALBERTINI, LUIGI (1871–1941), Italian journalist distinguished as a liberal and as an opponent of fascism, was born in Ancona on Oct. 19, 1871. While studying labour problems in London, he acquired close knowledge of the organization of *The Times* (London). Having joined the *Corriere della Sera* of Milan in 1896, he became its business manager (1898) and editor (1900), developing it on modern lines, improving its technical services and equipment and making it one of the most widely circulated and authoritative dailies in Europe. It owed its prestige as an independent liberal paper to Albertini. A liberal with a conservative bias, he was always ready to defend both the freedom of the citizen and the authority of the state. In 1914 he entered the senate. He was in favour of Italy's entry into World War I, but was not an irredentist and disapproved Gabriele d'Annunzio's coup in Fiume (Rijeka) and the Italian annexations in Dalmatia. He supported the final agreements with Yugoslavia. He criticized the post-World War I governments for their weakness and opposed fascism from the start, being one of the few newspaper editors to stand up to the threats and blandishments of the Fascists until, in Nov. 1925, the owners of the *Corriere* removed him from the paper. He retired from public life and gave his time to historical studies and land reclamation on his model estate at Torrinpietra near Rome. He died in Rome on Dec. 29, 1941. (N. S. J.)

ALBERTUS MAGNUS, SAINT (ALBERT THE GREAT or ALBERT OF COLOGNE) (*c.* 1200–1280), scholastic philosopher, scientist and theologian, called *doctor universalis* for the very universality of his knowledge and of his thought, was born (not, as used to be alleged, as a count of Bollstädt) at Lauingen in Swabia. He joined the Dominican order at Padua in 1223. After teaching at several convents in Germany, lastly at Cologne, he was sent, before 1245, to the University of Paris, where he was graduated master in the theological faculty and acquired great fame by his theological and philosophical works. Roger Bacon, who was by no means friendly toward him, speaks of Albert as "the most noted of Christian scholars," who was cited in the schools as an authority in the same way as Aristotle, Avicenna and Averroës. He returned to Cologne in 1248 to organize the *studium generale,* where Thomas Aquinas was his chief disciple until he too was sent to Paris in 1252. From 1254 to 1257 Albert was provincial of "Teutonia" (the German province of the Dominicans); and during this period, in 1256, he was ordered by Pope Alexander IV to his court at Anagni to defend the Mendicants against the professors of Paris university, who were members of the secular clergy—especially against their spokesman William of St. Amour. By order of the same pope he accepted, in 1260, the bishopric of Regensburg, in spite of the instances of Humbert de Romans, general of the Dominican order; but Albert resigned after the pope's death in 1261. He then returned to his order, but as *episcopus quondam Ratisbonensis* he was in some part exempt from its control and could dispose of his time and even of his revenues. From 1263 to 1264 he was legate of the pope, preaching the crusade in Germany and in Bohemia; subsequently he lectured at Würzburg and at Strasbourg. In 1270 he settled definitively at Cologne, where again, as previously in 1252 and also in 1258, he made peace between the archbishop and this city. In 1274 he attended the council of Lyons, where he spoke in favour of acknowledging Rudolph of Habsburg as German king. Albert died in Cologne on Nov. 15, 1280. In 1931 he was canonized and proclaimed a doctor of the church. His feast day is Nov. 15.

Albert's works embrace the entire knowledge of his time not only in theology (represented by commentaries on many books of the Bible, on the *Sentences* of Peter Lombard and on all the works of Dionysius the Areopagite) but also in philosophy and in the natural sciences. He alone among medieval philosophers made commentaries on all the works of Aristotle, both genuine and spurious (for example *Liber de causis* and *De mineralibus*), mostly in a paraphrasing manner. His importance for medieval science essentially consists in his bringing Aristotelianism to the front against reactionary tendencies in contemporary theology. On the other hand, without feeling any discrepancy in it, he also gave the widest room to Neoplatonic speculation, which was continued by Ulrich of Strasbourg and by the German mystics of the 14th century. Above all it was by his writings on the natural sciences that he exercised the greatest influence until modern times. Though considerable gratitude may be owed to the elder Oxford school (Alfredus Anglicus, Robert Grosseteste and Roger Bacon) for its marked interest in those sciences, Albert must nevertheless be regarded as unique in his time for having made accessible and available the Aristotelian knowledge of nature (already enlarged by the Arabs) and for having enriched it by his own observations in all branches of nature. A pre-eminent place in the history of science must be accorded to him forever.

BIBLIOGRAPHY.—The complete edition of Albert's works undertaken by the Albertus-Magnus-Institut of Cologne includes for the first time his writings *De bono* (1951); *Super Isaiam* (1952) and the *Quaestiones super "De animalibus"* (1955). The earlier edition by P. Jammy, 21 vol. folio (1651), was reprinted by A. Borgnet, 38 vol. (1890–99). For studies *see* F. Ueberweg and B. Geyer, *Die patristische und scholastische Philosophie* (1928; reprinted 1951); M. Schwertner, *St. Albert the Great* (1932); Lynn Thorndike, *A History of Magic and Experimental Science,* vol. ii (1923); H. C. Scheeben, *Albertus der Grosse: zur Chronologie seines Lebens,* vol. 27, *Quellen und Forschungen zur Geschichte des Dominikanerordens in Deutschland* (1931), *Albertus Magnus* (1955); H. Ostlender (ed.), *Studia Albertina* (1952), Supplementband IV, *Beiträge zur Geschichte der Philosophie und Theologie des Mittelalters.* For further bibliography *see* the *Revue thomiste* (1931); *Angelicum* (1944).   (B. G.)

ALBI, a city of southwest France and capital of the *département* of Tarn, lies 47 mi. N.E. of Toulouse by road. Pop. (1962) 31,672. Albi is situated on both banks of the Tarn river where it leaves the Massif Central for the Garonne plain and is dominated by its fortress-cathedral of St. Cecilia (1277–1512), a brick building without transepts or aisles. The 13th- to 15th-century archbishop's palace of Berbie, by the river to the north, is fortified and contains a collection of paintings and drawings by Henri de Toulouse-Lautrec. The church of St. Salvi has a magnificent cloister (11th–15th centuries). The centre of the town is medieval.

There is a public library and park. The Tarn (*q.v.*) is spanned by two bridges, one modern and one dating from the 9th century. In the evenings from May 1 to Sept. 30, the history of Albi is presented through the medium of *Son et Lumière* and in March there is an important fair, or carnival show. International motor racing and *moto-cross* (cross-country motorcycle racing) also take place in May and June. Albi is a good centre from which to explore the Tarn gorges. There are dye works, cement works, coal mines, glassworks and flour mills. Hats, cloth, umbrellas, artificial silk and agricultural implements are also made and wheat, wine and prunes are produced.

Albi (Albiga) was the capital of the Gallo-Roman Albigenses, and later of the viscounty of Albigeois, a fief of the counts of Toulouse. From the 12th century its bishops encroached on the authority of the viscounts and, after the Albigensian War, lost their estates, which passed ultimately to the crown. By a convention (1264), the temporal power was granted to the bishops (archbishops after 1678) which lasted until the French Revolution. Albi, an active centre of Catharism (*see* CATHARI), gave its name to the Albigensian heresy, which led to the Albigensian crusade and later to the development of the Inquisition.   (J. M. ME.)

ALBIGENSES (ALBIGENSIANS), the name, derived from the city of Albi (*q.v.*), of a heretical sect in southern France in the 12th and 13th centuries, against which a crusade was launched (1209). For their doctrines and history *see* CATHARI.

ALBINISM, derived from the Latin *albus* for "white," refers to the absence of yellow, red, brown or black pigments in the eyes, skin, scales, feathers or hair. This condition is inherited in man and other vertebrates. Normal pigmentation serves as a light screen, for radiation protection and for protective coloration; albino animals therefore survive only rarely in the wild. Where natural selection against pigmentary deficiencies is relaxed, as in cave dwelling fishes, unpigmented races may evolve.

Pigment-producing cells in vertebrates originate in the neural crest during embryological development in close association with the developing nervous system and then migrate to their characteristic locations. If, during this critical period, these cells move into a hostile tissue environment, they fail to survive, and white spotting, or piebalding, results. This white spotting, also inherited, may extend over the whole body surface; in individuals in whom this occurs, only the presence of pigment in the eyes indicates that the individual is not a true albino.

Given a favourable genetic make-up and tissue and hormonal environment the pigment cells synthesize their coloured products. One class of pigments, the melanins, occur throughout the animal kingdom and the melanin-producing cells (melanocytes) account for all integumentary pigments in birds and mammals. Brown and black melanin synthesis begins with the oxidation of a colourless precursor, the amino acid tyrosine; hence the name tyrosinase for the enzyme that catalyzes the oxidative reactions. Pigment granules are formed when tyrosine oxidation products are polymerized and attached to colourless protein granules. Thus, in contrast to white spotting, the lack of pigment in albinos is due to an inherited defect in the metabolic machinery of colourless melanocytes. These cells are deficient in tyrosinase synthesis and may also suffer from other functional defects.

ALBINO GRAY SQUIRREL (SCIURUS CAROLINENSIS)

Environmental factors, such as sunlight and temperature, affect melanin production. Ultraviolet radiation in sunlight increases melanin synthesis (sun tanning), in part by destroying substances that normally inhibit tyrosinase action. Lowered temperature also plays a part; in the Himalayan rabbit and the guinea pig, albinos completely white at birth subsequently darken in the normally cooler body parts such as ears, snout and paw tips. Here the temperature effect involves a shift in the delicate balancing of rates of tyrosinase synthesis and destruction, as well as the rate of melanin production.

It is not yet known whether this temperature-controlled balance of pigmentary factors can account for seasonal variations in certain animals such as the arctic fox, ermine or ptarmigan. In these cases the fur or feathers are white in winter and pigmented during the warmer seasons. However, since melanin is not easily destroyed, it seems likely that such drastic pigmentary changes are accompanied by moulting and a new growth of pelage or plumage. (*See* Coloration, Biological.) (M. Fo.)

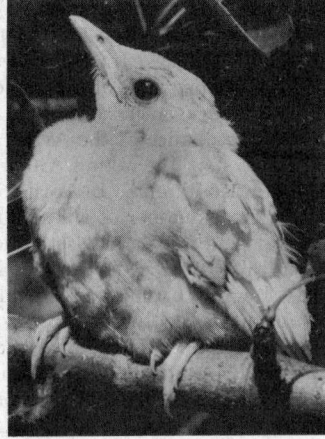

ALBINO AMERICAN ROBIN (TURDUS MIGRATORIUS)

Albinism in Man.—Albinism in the human is caused by the absence of melanin, the dark-brown pigment normally present in the skin, hair and eyes. At least three different grades or degrees of albinism occur, depending on the degree of lack of melanin. The forms are: (1) universal complete albinism, involving the skin, hair and eyes; (2) ocular albinism, in which only the eyes are affected; and (3) localized albinism, in which small areas of the body lack pigment (white locks, spotlings). All three forms are hereditary. Other types of pigment deficiencies, such as the graying of hair during aging, are not examples of albinism.

The universal complete albino has milk-white skin and hair, both of which may turn yellow with injury or aging. The iris of the eye typically appears pink. Some slight amount of iris pigment, which may be present at birth or may develop with age, may give the iris a yellowish or even blue colour. The pupil appears red from light reflected by blood in the unpigmented choroid. Defective vision results from inadequate screening of stray light. Photophobia and nystagmus, the rapid involuntary oscillation of the eye, are usually present. Universal complete albinism is recessively transmitted and therefore when it appears it does so in one out of four children, on the average, born of apparently unaffected parents. The parents and two-thirds of the unaffected children nevertheless carry an albinism gene, which has no detectable effect by itself. Instances are on record of marriages of two albinos, all of whose children were affected. The parents of albinos are often consanguineous since this increases the likelihood that both will possess the same rare gene. Universal complete albinism occurs in all races in about one in 20,000 persons. There are localized areas of higher incidence, such as the occurrence of 7 per 1,000 among the San Blas Indians of the Caribbean.

Ocular albinism is limited to the structures of the eye; *e.g.*, the iris and choroid. The visual defects are like those of complete albinism, but the pigmentation of hair and skin is normal. Ocular albinism is very rare; only a few, though extensive, family histories of the condition have been described. Its inheritance is sex-linked, being transmitted by unaffected mothers to affected sons in the same way as colour blindness. The unaffected females carrying the gene can be distinguished by clumps of pigment granules in the margins of their retinas, although they have no visual disturbances.

Localized albinism is the commonest form of albinism. The areas of affected skin, many of them near the midline of the body, resemble the skin of the complete albino. Elsewhere pigmentation is normal. Extensive pedigrees reaching from the middle ages are known with such spots occurring in remarkably constant locations in a given family. The spots are inherited dominantly, with half the members of each generation, on the average, of affected families being marked.

The number and density of the tiny sepia-coloured melanin granules normally present in the skin, iris and other sites account very largely for the range of skin colours seen in the different races of mankind, as well as for the various shades that occur in different structures of the same individual. Without these granules, as in albinos, the colour of individuals of all races is very similar because the pigments of the blood and internal organs that account for most of the residual colouring are unaffected by albinism. The residual colouring results from the red colour of oxygenated hemoglobin in the blood in the minute vessels near the skin, the yellow of carotenes in the cells and the whiteness caused by the reflection of all wave lengths of light by various cellular structures that are larger than 1μ in diameter. The melanin granules, when present, darken the tissues. They are less than 0.7μ in diameter and therefore selectively reflect the shorter (blue) light rays.

The three albinotic conditions arise from distinct hereditary interferences with the normal function of melanocytes. The melanocytes first appear in the neural crest and migrate from there to the structures that will become pigmented. At a later stage pigment production begins as a result of hormonal control. The pigment is formed by the oxidation of the normal cell constituent, tyrosine, to a complex polymer, melanin. This action is catalyzed by the enzyme tyrosinase located in the pigment cells. The melanin is bound to particles in the pigment cell that resemble mitochondria. Pigment deficiencies could therefore arise from abnormalities of several kinds: total absence of the pigment cells, exclusion of these cells from affected areas, lack of the hormonal stimulus for pigment production or subcellular abnormalities of the melanocyte, such as deficiences of the precursor tyrosine, of the active enzyme tyrosinase or of the particles into which melanin is normally bound.

See Genetics: *Physiological Genetics.* (W. E. K.)

Bibliography.—D. L. Fox, *Animal Biochromes* (1953); M. Gordon *et al.* (eds.), *The Biology of Melanomas,* special publication of New York Academy of Sciences (1948), *Pigment Cell Growth* (1953), *Pigment Cell Biology* (1959); A. B. Lerner, "Melanin Pigmentation," *J.A.M.A.* 19:902–924 (1955); C. C. Little, "Coat Color Genes in Rodents and Carnivores," *Quart. Rev. Biol.* 33:103–137 (1958).
(M. Fo.)

ALBINONI, TOMMASO (1671–1750), Italian composer chiefly remembered for his instrumental music. Born in Venice, June 8, 1671, he was the son of a wealthy paper merchant. Of independent means, he described himself as a *dilettante veneto* ("Venetian amateur"), although he was a fully trained musician and at one time held a professional post as chamber musician to the duke of Mantua. Little is known of his life, except for the production (1694–1740, mainly at Venice), of his 48 operas. He died in Venice, Jan. 17, 1750.

As well as many vocal works, now forgotten, Albinoni published nine sets of instrumental works, which achieved wide popularity: two of his themes were used as subjects for fugues by Bach. Several have been republished during the 20th century. Specially notable are the *Sinfonie e Concerti a 5* (Op. 2, 1707); the concertos for solo violin (Op. 5, 1710); and the concertos for one and two oboes in Op. 7 and Op. 9. As an instrumental composer he occupies a place between Corelli and Vivaldi, lacking the gracious serenity of the former and the fiery impetuosity of the latter, but with his own urbanity and charm.

See R. Giazotto, *Tomaso Albinoni* (1945). (Cs. Ch.)

ALBINOVANUS PEDO, Roman poet (fl. early 1st century A.D.), wrote a *Theseis,* referred to in a letter from his friend Ovid, epigrams which are commended by Martial and an epic poem on the military exploits of the Roman general Germanicus Caesar, Tiberius' adopted son, under whom he probably served. This may have been used as a source by Tacitus. All that remains of his works is a beautiful fragment, preserved in the *Suasoriae* of Seneca, describing the voyage of Germanicus (A.D. 16) through the Ems river to the Northern ocean.

Three elegies were formerly attributed to Pedo by Joseph Scaliger; two on the death of Maecenas (*In obitum Maecenatis* and *De verbis Maecenatis moribundi*), and one addressed to Livia (*Consolatio ad liviam de morte Drusi* or *Epicedion Drusi,* usually printed with Ovid's works); but it is now generally agreed that they are not by Pedo. The *Consolatio* has been put down as the work of a 15th-century Italian imitator, there being no manuscript and no trace of the poem before the publication of the *editio prin-*

ceps of Ovid in 1471. There is an English verse translation of the elegies by John Plumptre (1807).

BIBLIOGRAPHY.—M. Haupt, *Opuscula,* i (1875); E. Bährens, *Poetae Latini Minores* (1879) and *Fragmenta Poetarum Latinorum* (1886).

ALBINUS (2nd century A.D.), philosopher, a forerunner of Neoplatonism, was a pupil of Gaius and a teacher of Galen. His works comprise: (1) the work *On Incorporeal Qualities,* perhaps preserved as a work by Galen; (2) an introduction or "prologue" to Plato (mainly classifications of the dialogues); and (3) the *Didascalicus* or *Epitome,* formerly attributed in manuscripts to Alcinous. This last is a presentation of Plato's philosophy, which it combines with Peripatetic and Stoic doctrines and divides into three parts: logic; a theoretical part (subdivided in Aristotle's manner into mathematics, physics and theology, the last including much of Aristotle's "mind" theology and describing the way of negation among the approaches to the knowledge of God); and a practical part (ethics, economics, politics).

For the *Epitome* see the text ed. with Fr. trans. by P. Louis (1945); also H. Cary *et al.,* trans., *The Works of Plato,* vol. vi (1852). *See* further R. E. Witt, *Albinus and the History of Middle Platonism* (1937); E. Orth, "Les Oeuvres d'Albinos," *L'Antiquité classique,* vol. xvi (1947); R. le Corre, "Le Prologue d'Albinus," *Revue philosophique,* vol. lxxxi (1956).   (PP. M.)

ALBINUS, BERNARD SIEGFRIED (1697–1770), outstanding descriptive anatomist, was born at Frankfurt-on-Oder, and from 1718 to his death occupied the chair of anatomy, surgery and medicine at Leiden. He was the first to show by injections the connection of the vascular systems of the mother and the fetus.

He also edited with Hermann Boerhaave the works of Vesalius and Harvey. Albinus is chiefly famed for the excellent drawings in his *Tabula sceleti et musculorum corporis humani* (1747). His *De ossibus corporis humani ad auditores suos libellus* appeared at Leiden in 1726. Albinus died on Sept. 9, 1770.

ALBINUS, DECIMUS CLODIUS SEPTIMIUS (d. 197), Roman general, a candidate for the imperial title in the years 193–197, was born probably between A.D. 140 and 150, the son of well-to-do citizens of Hadrumetum in Roman Africa. The confused account of the *Augustan History* suggests that he began his public career in the equites and was made a senator in the last years of the emperor Marcus Aurelius. Soon after 180, Albinus distinguished himself in a campaign "beyond Dacia," perhaps under the generalship of his fellow townsman Salvius Julianus. Consul in the late 180s, he became an army commander on the Rhine and was then transferred to Britain, about 191, where he found the army disgruntled. Early in 193, after the murder of the emperor Pertinax, the guards in Rome proclaimed M. Didius Salvius Julianus (*q.v.*) emperor; some evidence argues that Albinus may have encouraged Didius, whose mother was a native of Hadrumetum and a relative of Salvius Julianus. The armies of the Danube and of Syria, however, proclaimed instead their respective commanders Lucius Septimius Severus (*q.v.*) and Pescennius Niger. After the murder of Didius, Severus entered Rome as emperor and came to an agreement with Albinus, acknowledging him as Caesar and heir; but after the destruction of Niger by Severus a rupture between the two remaining rivals was inevitable. In 197 Albinus, now proclaimed emperor, crossed to Gaul and advanced toward Rome with the army of Britain. Severus marched through southern Germany and came down from the Swiss passes upon Albinus' rear, defeating and killing him in a two-day battle outside Lyons. At least in retrospect, Albinus was "better liked by the senate than any other of the emperors." He appears as the candidate of the aristocracy of the Latin-speaking west, in contrast to Niger, candidate of the Greek-speaking east, and to Severus, candidate of the army and of the Balkans.   (JN. R. M.)

ALBION, the ancient name for the island of Britain. A Massiliote Periplus of the 6th century B.C. (quoted by Avienus) mentions "the island of the Albiones"; and other Greek geographies not only distinguish Albion from Ierne (Ireland) and from smaller "Britannic" isles but also say that Albion was the native name. The name has been translated as "white land"; and the Romans explained it as referring to the chalk cliffs of Dover (Latin *albus,* "white").

ALBITE: *see* FELDSPAR.

ALBOIN (d. 572), king of the Lombards and barbarian conqueror of northern Italy, succeeded his father Audoin about 565. The Lombards (*q.v.*) at that time occupied Noricum and Pannonia and were engaged in constant war with the Gepidae. Alboin obtained the alliance of the Avars and with their help destroyed the Gepidae, slew their king, Cunimund, in battle and married his daughter Rosamund. In April 568 Alboin had assembled his people with a great number of allies, among them 20,000 Saxons, to cross the Alps and form a new settlement in Italy. There appears to be no truth in the legend that the Lombards were invited to attack Italy by the Byzantine general Narses. This was in effect a migration rather than a mere invasion. The Roman defenses were overrun, Milan was occupied (Sept. 569) and Pavia was invested. Lombard rule was established in northern Italy. But Alboin was murdered in 572 at the instigation of Rosamund, whom Alboin had offended, so the story goes, by making her drink wine from her father's skull.

Apart from the ancient sources (Procopius, Paulus Diaconus and Agnellus of Ravenna), *see* Thomas Hodgkin, *Italy and Her Invaders,* vol. v (1916), with bibliography.

ALBORADA, literally a Spanish word meaning "dawn song" or *aubade* (*q.v.*), but specifically the name of a Spanish form of popular music heard in the northwest provinces of Spain and played on bagpipes and side drum. The alborada is in several sections or variations, improvised in free rhythms by the player on the bagpipes and accompanied by the drummer. The style of this folk music inspired the piano work, *Alborada del gracioso* ("The Jester's Dawn-Song"), the fourth in the set *Miroirs* (1905) by Maurice Ravel.

ALBORNOZ, GIL ÁLVAREZ CARRILLO DE (d. 1367), Spanish cardinal, notable both for his work in restoring the authority of the pope in the papal states and for his codification of laws for them, was born at Cuenca early in the 14th century. Noble connections combined with personal ability enabled him to rise rapidly to high office, first as royal councilor and then, from 1338, as archbishop of Toledo. His political achievements, especially in organizing resistance to the Moors, attracted the notice of the papal curia and in 1350 he was created cardinal. Then began the second and more memorable phase of his life, spent almost entirely in Italy, where he was twice sent as legate (1353–57 and 1358–67), with the task of restoring the authority of the Avignon popes in the states of the church so as to make possible the return of the papacy to Rome. In this capacity Albornoz accomplished more than any of his predecessors in subduing the feudatories and despots who exercised effective power in the papal states, but even his achievement was partial and impermanent. His resources were limited and, being poorly supported by the curia, he had partly to pay his mercenaries out of his own pocket. While he managed to expel certain of the despots, he had to accept others as allies, creating them vicars "in temporal matters" of the papal government. Neighbouring powers who were also hostile to a strengthened papacy further compromised his work, which was almost wholly undone by the brutal misgovernment of his successors and the disorders of the Great Schism. His most enduring monument, the legal code known as the *Constitutiones Aegidianae* (Gil = Lat. Aegidius), which he published at a parliament at Fano in 1357, remained in force in the papal states until the 19th century. He died in Italy, at Viterbo, on Aug. 23, 1367.

See F. Filippini, *Il cardinale Egidio Albornoz* (1933).   (P. J. J.)

ALBRECHTSBERGER, JOHANN GEORG (1736–1809), Austrian organist, composer and theorist, the teacher of Beethoven. Born at Klosterneuberg, near Vienna, Feb. 3, 1736, he studied the organ and thorough bass with Leopold Pittner, and became one of the most learned and skilful contrapuntists of his time. From 1755 to 1766 he held various posts as organist and in 1772 he was appointed deputy court organist in Vienna. From 1793 until his death he was chapelmaster at St. Stephen's cathedral. His fame attracted many pupils, among them Beethoven, who recommended him to Karl Czerny and Ferdinand Ries, J. N. Hummel, J. Weigl and others. Most of his compositions, which include many religious and chamber works, remain in manuscript. His main theoretical work was *Gründliche Anweisung zur Komposition* (1790). A collection of his theoretical writings on harmony was edited by his pupil, Ignaz Ritter von Seyfried (3 vol., 1826; Eng. trans., 1835, 1844 and 1855). A selection of his music, edited by O. Kapp, was published in *Denkmäler der Tonkunst in Österreich*, vol. xvi, no. 2 (1909). (Cs. Ch.)

ALBRET, the name of a family celebrated in French history, is derived from that of Labrit, a small village in the Landes of Gascony (on the main road from Bordeaux to Dax and Bayonne), which it owned in the 10th century. The lords (*sires*) of Albret gradually acquired more seigniories in the surrounding country, in Bazadais, Condomois and Bordelais and along the Adour river. Of the several branches of the family, the senior one remained the most important, reaching the height of its power in the 14th–16th centuries.

In the Hundred Years' War, Arnaud Amanieu (d. 1401), sire d'Albret, fought first for the English in Guienne. In 1368 he married Marguerite de Bourbon, sister-in-law of Charles V of France, and then fought for France. His son Charles I d'Albret (d. 1415), who was constable of France from 1403 to 1411, was killed in the battle of Agincourt. As a result of family alliances Charles I's greatgrandson, Alain d'Albret (1440–1522), became one of the chief territorial magnates in France, and because of this was called Alain the Great. His son Jean (d. 1516) in 1484 married Catherine de Foix-Grailly, queen of Navarre. After her death in 1517 their son became titular king of Navarre as Henry II. For him the patrimonial lands of Albret were made a peerage duchy of France in 1550.

Henry's daughter Jeanne d'Albret (1528–72), by her marriage to Antoine de Bourbon, duc de Vendôme, was the mother of the future Henry IV of France.

See A. Luchaire, *Notice sur les origines de la maison d'Albret* (1873) and *Alain le Grand, sire d'Albret* (1877); R. Boutruche, *La Crise d'une société* (1947). (R. Bo.)

ALBRIGHT, WILLIAM FOXWELL (1891–), U.S. biblical archaeologist and near eastern scholar, noted especially for his excavations of biblical sites, was born on May 24, 1891, in Coquimbo, Chile, the son of U.S. Methodist missionaries. His family returned to the United States in 1903. He obtained his doctorate in Semitic languages at Johns Hopkins university, Baltimore, Md. While there he studied under Paul Haupt, whom he succeeded in 1929 as W. W. Spence professor of Semitic languages, a position he held until his retirement in 1958.

Appointed fellow of the American School of Oriental Research, Jerusalem, in 1919, Albright served as the school's director for 12 years (1920–29, 1933–36). Among his excavations are Gibeah of Saul, Tell Beit Mirsim (Kirjath-Sepher), and, in association with others, Beth-zur and Bethel in Palestine and Baluah and Petra in Jordan. In 1950–51 he was chief archaeologist of excavations made by the American Foundation for the Study of Man at Wadi Bayhan (Beihan), Hajar Bin Humaid and Timna in Arabia. In addition, he undertook important archaeological explorations in Jordan and in Sinai. He was a pioneer in stressing the value of archaeology and of topographical and linguistic studies for biblical history, and in making pottery and potsherd identification a reliable scientific tool.

Albright's scientific writings, which considerably influenced the development of biblical and related near eastern scholarship, include, among others, *The Archaeology of Palestine and the Bible* (1932–35), *The Vocalization of the Egyptian Syllabic Orthography* (1934), *The Excavation of Tell Beit Mirsim* (1932–43), *From the Stone Age to Christianity* (1940–46) and *Archaeology and the Religion of Israel* (1942–46); *The Bible and the Ancient Near East* (1961).

Bibliography.—*An Indexed Bibliography of the writings of William Foxwell Albright*, ed. by Harry M. Orlinsky (1941); *American Spiritual Autobiographies*, ed. by Louis Finkelstein, pp. 156–181 (1948); B. Maisler (Mazar), "Prof. W. F. Albright," *Hadoar* (Hebrew), pp. 607–608 (June 8, 1951). *See* also the 70th birthday *Festschrift*, ed. by G. Ernest Wright (1961). (N. Gk.)

ALBULA PASS, in the Albula Alps in Switzerland, the principal route from northeast Graubünden to the upper Engadine, has been used since the 13th century. A carriage road (highest point, 7,585 ft.) was made across it in 1865, but for a long time it was not used as much as the Roman route over the Julier pass (7,493 ft.). The opening of the railway in 1903, however, greatly increased its importance. Starting from Chur the railway follows the Rhine to Reichenau (6¼ mi.), and then the Hinterrhein to Thusis (10½ mi.). It then runs through the deep Schyn gorge (cut by the Albula torrent) to Tiefencastel (7½ mi.), where it leaves the Julier route to the south and continues to follow the course of the Albula past Filisur and Bergün (12½ mi.) to the mouth (5,879 ft.) of the first of the three spiral tunnels (each ¾ mi. in length, highest point 5,987 ft.) before entering the 3¾ mi. long tunnel at Preda which was pierced below the pass. The railway then descends through the Bevers gorge to Bevers (2½ mi.) in the upper Engadine, about 5 mi. below St. Moritz, which is 56 mi. from Chur by this route. (A. F. A. M.)

ALBUMAZAR (Albumasar; also abu-Mashar) (805–886), a celebrated Muslim astrologer, was born in Balkh, Khurasan, Persia, flourished in Baghdad and died in Wasit, central Asia. His principal works were translated into Latin: *Introductorium in astronomiam* (1489); *De magnis conjunctionibus* (1489), plagiarized from al-Kindi; *Flores astrologici* (1488). He maintained in the second that the world, created when the seven planets were in conjunction in the first degree of Aries, will come to an end at a like conjunction in the last degree of Pisces.

Albumazar's name is used for the subject of *L'astrologo* by Giovanni Battista della Porta (1606), a play adapted in *Albumazar* by Thomas Tomkis, played before James I in 1615 and revived by John Dryden in 1668.

See G. Sarton, *Introduction to the History of Science*, vol. i (1945). (D. McK.)

ALBUMINS are a class of proteins characterized by heat coagulability and solubility in dilute salt solution. Among the best known are: ovalbumin (egg white), lactalbumin (in milk) and blood serum albumin. The last has the important function of maintaining the osmotic pressure of blood; thus human serum albumin is used medically for the treatment of shock. The molecular weight (69,000) and shape (ellipsoid, 150 Å long by 38 Å in diameter) of human serum albumin are ideally suited for osmotic regulation. (*See* Shock.)

The albumins of animal blood are similar to human albumin in gross chemical and physical properties. During World War II strenuous efforts were made to utilize albumin from bovine blood for the treatment of shock in humans, but anaphylactic reactions obtained in test subjects were adjudged too severe for safe usage. The resulting availability of highly purified bovine albumin, however, contributed to the remarkable postwar expansion of protein research.

See A. White *et al.*, *Principles of Biochemistry* (1954); H. Neurath and K. Bailey (eds.), *The Proteins: Chemistry, Biological Activity, and Methods* (1953–54). (W. F. Wh.)

ALBUMINURIA is the condition in which the urine contains abnormal amounts of the protein albumin. Other proteins and similar compounds such as albuminoses and proteoses occasionally also are found in the urine; these conditions are called proteinurias. Excessive loss of protein from the body produces serious physiologic changes, and the loss of even small amounts may profoundly affect metabolism. Therefore, the detection of albumin in the urine is of great diagnostic importance, for its presence may indicate serious pathologic changes in the body, particularly in the kidneys.

The urine may contain red blood cells or hemoglobin, a protein found in red blood cells, but these conditions are not classified as albuminuria. Protein also may appear in the urine as a result of injury or disease of parts of the urinary tract other than the kidneys, being referred to as "accidental," "false" or "postrenal" albuminuria.

See Urinary System: *Proteinuria and the Nephrotic Syndrome.*

ALBUQUERQUE, AFFONSO DE (1453–1515), known as the Great, the second viceroy of Portuguese India and the virtual founder of the Portuguese dominion in the Indian ocean, was born at Alexandria, near Lisbon, in 1453. He was already a veteran soldier when in 1503 he made his first expedition to India, where he obtained permission from the king of Cochin to build a Portuguese fort. He returned home in July 1504, and King Emmanuel gave him the command of a squadron of 5 vessels in the fleet of 14 which sailed for India under Tristão da Cunha. After a series of attacks on the Arab cities on the east coast of Africa, Albuquerque separated from Da Cunha and captured (Sept. 1507) the Island of Ormuz in the Persian gulf; he held the island, then one of the chief centres of commerce in the east, for some months.

He reached the Malabar coast at the end of 1508 and produced a commission from the king empowering him to supersede the governor Francisco de Almeida. The governor imprisoned him, and he was only released on the arrival of the grand marshal of Portugal with a large fleet.

The strategic operations which Albuquerque now set in motion were designed to secure four major fortified bases, Aden, Ormuz, Goa and Malacca, from which Portuguese power could control the commerce of the Indian ocean and southeast Asia. An unsuccessful attack upon Calicut in Jan. 1510 was immediately followed by the capture of Goa. Albuquerque abandoned the town in August and returned with reinforcements in November when he obtained undisputed possession. Following this, Albuquerque directed his forces against Malacca, which he subdued after a severe struggle. In 1512 he sailed for the coast of Malabar. On the voyage Albuquerque's vessel, the "Flor de la Mar," which carried the treasure that he had amassed in his conquests, was wrecked and he himself barely escaped with his life. In September of the same year he returned to Goa where he suppressed a serious revolt.

For some time Albuquerque had been under orders from the home government to undertake an expedition to the Red sea to secure it exclusively for Portugal. Accordingly he besieged Aden in 1513 but was repulsed and his voyage into the Red sea, the first ever made by a European fleet, had no substantial result. His last success was the recapture of Ormuz in 1515.

Albuquerque had several enemies at the Portuguese court. On his way home from Ormuz he met, at the entrance to Goa harbour, a ship from Europe bearing dispatches announcing that he was superseded by his personal enemy Lope Soarez. He died at sea on Dec. 15, 1515. Before his death he wrote a letter to the king vindicating his conduct and claiming for his son the honours and rewards due to himself. His body was buried at Goa and in 1566 was removed to Portugal; it is, perhaps, the most convincing proof of the justice of his administration that Muslims and Hindus used to go to his tomb to invoke protection against the injustice of his successors.

BIBLIOGRAPHY.—Affonso (Braz) de Albuquerque, *Commentarias do Grande Affonso d'Albuquerque* (1557), Eng. trans. by W. de G. Birch, 4 vol., Hakluyt Society (1875–84); *Cartas de Affonso de Albuquerque*, 7 vol. (1884–1935); Edgar Prestage, *Afonso de Albuquerque* (1929).
(R. A. Sn.)

ALBUQUERQUE, the largest city of New Mexico, U.S., seat of Bernalillo county, was founded in 1706 when 36 families settled at a ford on the Rio Grande opposite a pass between the Sandia and Manzano mountains to the east. The town, named for the duke of Alburquerque, then viceroy of New Spain, became an important trading centre on the Chihuahua trail from Mexico. After 1800, growing trade on the Santa Fe trail brought settlers from the states. After U.S. occupation (1846) an army post was established there. During the American Civil War the town was captured by the Confederates (1862), but remained loyal to the Union.

The original plaza was the town's centre until 1880 when the Atlantic and Pacific railroad (later the Atchison, Topeka and Santa Fe) laid its tracks one mile east of the plaza. The town quickly closed the gap with a streetcar line and began to spread eastward. By the time the "new town" was organized as a town (1885) the first "r" had been dropped from the name. Albuquerque was incorporated as a city in 1890 and adopted the commission-manager form of government in 1917. The characteristically Spanish "old town" of Albuquerque and the mission church of San Felipe de Nerí (1706) still survive.

The population of the town was 11,020 in 1910. As New Mexico's climate became favourably known for the treatment of tuberculosis, new citizens came and several sanatoriums were built. Numerous federal government agencies were established there in the 1930s and by 1940 the population was 35,449, after which the establishment of nuclear research centres was responsible for substantial population increases, to 96,815 by 1950 and to 201,189 by 1960. The population of the standard metropolitan statistical area, consisting of Bernalillo county, was 262,199 in 1960. (For comparative population figures *see* table in NEW MEXICO: *Population.*)

One year after the first atomic bomb, designed and assembled at Los Alamos as the Manhattan project, was exploded near Alamogordo on July 16, 1945, a branch laboratory was set up at Albuquerque. In 1949 the Sandia corporation was formed as a subsidiary of Western Electric company to take over the laboratory activities and, under a nonprofit contract with the Atomic Energy commission (A.E.C.), to conduct research, development and prototype production on the ordnance aspects of atomic weapons in close

THE CHURCH OF SAN FELIPE DE NERÍ, BUILT IN 1706 BY SPANISH PRIESTS, IS LOCATED IN THE "OLD TOWN" SECTION OF ALBUQUERQUE

support of the University of California's nuclear physics laboratories at Los Alamos and at Livermore, Calif. In the same year Kirtland air force base, established on the site of a municipal airport and used for flight tests of the Manhattan project, became the U.S. air force special weapons centre; it also served for flight tests for the A.E.C. In the early 1960s control of the field was turned over to the city, the air force remaining as a tenant.

Albuquerque also has numerous light industries and distributes supplies and material of all kinds to the sheep and cattle industry, to mining and timbering operations and to smaller cities and towns throughout the state. The Santa Fe maintains large railroad shops there.

Albuquerque is the seat of the University of New Mexico. The university, founded in 1889, was remodeled and enlarged in 1903 in an adaptation of the pueblo style of architecture, suggested by the nearby pueblo of Isleta.

The bracing climate and the large proportion of sunshiny days have given Albuquerque a reputation as a health resort. The city, in co-operation with the Middle Rio Grande Conservancy district, formed to drain marshes and develop irrigation for agriculture, established a natural park along the river with swimming beach and zoo. (E. Fe.)

ALBURY, a city of New South Wales, Austr., about 135 mi. S.W. of Canberra (*q.v.*). It lies on the north bank of the Murray river, approximately 1,470 mi. from its mouth, and on the border between New South Wales and Victoria. Pop. (1954) 16,726. The mean temperature is 60.7° F. and annual rainfall 27.65 in., of which 18.9 in. falls between April and October. The city's position on the flank of the eastern highlands and on the main connecting lines between Sydney (about 450 mi. N.E.) and Melbourne (about 200 mi. S.W.) contributes to its importance as a distributing and marketing centre. The Victoria and New South Wales railway systems join there. At the centre of the eastern Riverina (*q.v.*), Albury adjoins a rich agricultural and pastoral district producing sheep, wheat, fruit and dairy products, and has many light industries. The district provides fishing, boating and skiing as well as varied and beautiful scenery for tourists.

The Murray river was first crossed at this site by the explorers Hamilton Hume and William Hovell in 1824. The tributaries Mitta Mitta and Kiewa meet the Murray near Albury and the historic River Murray agreement (1914) resulted in the building of the nearby Hume reservoir to the east of the city. Albury became a municipality in 1859 and a city in 1946.

ALCAEUS (*c.* 620–*c.* 580 B.C.), Greek lyric poet born in Mytilene in Lesbos, wrote in local (Lesbian-Aeolic) dialect on diverse themes in an unprecedented variety of metres. He was a contemporary of Sappho. What remained of his work in the 2nd century B.C. was collected and edited in ten books, first by Aristophanes of Byzantium and later by Aristarchus. This edition did not survive and nothing of Alcaeus' poetry remained except a few brief quotations in other authors. In the 20th century, however, the stock was greatly increased (and the reputation of Alcaeus greatly enhanced) by the recovery of fragments of at least 21 different papyrus texts, all from the 1st to the 3rd centuries A.D.

Most of the fragments fall under four main headings, very diverse in tone, style and matter: (1) delicately phrased hymns in honour of divinities and legendary persons; (2) love poems (sparsely represented now, but attested by Cicero, Horace and others); (3) other songs for recitation at table, various in theme and mood; (4) political poems, reflecting the struggle for power in Mytilene, including vituperative attacks on enemies, especially Pittacus. Enough survives to indicate the broad outlines of Alcaeus' career. When the ancient hereditary kingship of Mytilene ended (mid-7th century B.C.), several groups of nobles competed for supremacy. Alcaeus, himself of good family, was a champion of one such group, and much of his life seems to have been spent in a vain struggle to obtain control of the state. His poems, supplemented by other scanty sources (themselves dependent on his authority) show, first, the brothers of Alcaeus together with Pittacus overthrowing a rival, Melanchrus; then Alcaeus himself fighting beside Pittacus against the Athenians at Sigeum (in this battle Alcaeus dropped his shield and ran); then the treachery of Pittacus, who broke his oath of loyalty to the group and joined the archenemy Myrsilus in control of Mytilene, leaving Alcaeus in exile; next, jubilation at the death of Myrsilus, and an appeal to the people to reject Pittacus despite which Pittacus was elected sole ruler. So far as is known, Alcaeus' party never came to power and the fragments afford no evidence about his career after the establishment of Pittacus as sole ruler (traditionally 590 B.C.).

All Alcaeus' poetry shows his natural, easy command of language and metre. He is concise, lucid and forceful in expression, using as a rule simple and apt words with very little embellishment or artifice. His poetry is straightforward and sincere, though never profound in thought, showing a keen eye for beauty, and a comprehensive range of loves and hatreds. Its political outlook is narrow and selfish.

BIBLIOGRAPHY.—Fragments ed. by E. Lobel (1927). Complete text (to date), together with Sappho, ed. by E. Lobel and D. L. Page in *Poetarum Lesbiorum Fragmenta* (1955). *See* also the companion volume by D. L. Page, *Sappho and Alcaeus* (1955), with Eng. trans., commentaries and further bibliography. (D. L. P.)

ALCAICS, a variety of Greek lyric stanza named after and presumably invented by the Lesbian poet, Alcaeus, and employed in Latin by Horace. The first two cola ("limbs") are of the same form: anceps (a long or short syllable), cretic ($-\cup-$), anceps and $-\cup\cup-\cup-$; *e.g.*,

Odi profanum ‖ vulgus et arceo.
favete linguis: ‖ carmina non prius

The third colon consists of anceps, cretic, anceps, cretic, anceps:

audita musarum sacerdos

and the fourth is a prosodiac (*see* PROSODY, CLASSICAL):

virginibus puerisque canto

Alcaeus sometimes permits a word to overlap from the third to the fourth colon, so that these must originally have been conceived as a single verse. Horace's alcaics are composed according to strict rules and differ in some ways from those of Alcaeus. Horace's ancipitia are usually long. In the first two cola there is caesura after the fifth syllable (as in his lines quoted above). Word-end occurs at this point in about two-thirds of Alcaeus' lines. In the third colon, word-end after the fourth syllable is avoided by both Alcaeus and Horace (with the exception of *Odes* I, xxvi, 11). Word-end after the fifth syllable, when long, is avoided by Alcaeus, but freely allowed by Horace.

Tennyson's *Milton* is an example of English alcaics.

(L. P. E. P.)

ALCALÁ (Arabic AL KALA, "fortress" or "castle"), is the name of 13 towns in Spain, founded and named by the Moors.

ALCALÁ DE HENARES, lies on the Henares river in the central plateau 29.5 km. (18 mi.) N.E. of Madrid by road. Pop. (1960 est.) 21,000 (mun.). It contains the unique Magistral Church of San Justo, called La Magistral because Pope Leo X in 1519 expected all its canons to have the degree of doctor or professor. The university buildings, now used as a school, include the college of San Ildefonso (1508) with a beautiful façade. The former archbishops' palace is a seminary. There are military quarters, an airfield and a bull ring. Known under the Romans as Complutum, Alcalá was destroyed in 1000 and rebuilt in 1038 by the Moors, who called it Al Kala en Nahr. It was reconquered in 1083 by Alfonso VI. Its university was founded in 1508 by Cardinal Francisco Jiménez de Cisneros (*q.v.*) who there ordered the production of the Complutensian Polyglot Bible (1514–17). In 1836 the university was moved to Madrid. The town was the birthplace of Cervantes, the emperor Ferdinand I and Catherine of Aragon. Products include chemicals, cotton goods, perfumes, pottery and the famous (iced) "almonds of Alcalá." (J. GA.)

ALCALÁ LA REAL, a municipality and city in the province of Jaén, lies on the Sierra de Parapanda, 76 km. (47 mi.) S. of Madrid. Pop. (1950) 30,062 (mun.). Its title, "la Real," was granted by its conqueror, Alfonso XI of Castile, in 1341. The town has a medieval appearance with stone houses having heraldic shields and interior patios. It had great strategic importance during the conquest of Granada from the Moors; parts of the walls remain. The surrounding land is fertile and well watered, producing grain, olives and pasture.

ALCALÁ DE LOS GAZULES lies on the Barbate river in the province of Cádiz. Pop. (1950) 10,340 (mun.). It takes its name from a famous Moorish family. Sheep and goats are raised, and there are about 23 sq.mi. of cork trees. Flour milling is also carried on.

ALCALÁ DE GUADAIRA lies on the Guadaira river 14 km. (8½ mi.) S.E. of Seville in Seville province. Pop. (1950) 25,049 (mun.). It is popularly known as Alcalá de los Panaderos because of the number (64) of its bakeries and its flour mills. The other big industry is connected with olives many of which are exported; oil from them is expressed and refined in the town. (M. B. F.)

ALCALÁ ZAMORA, NICETO (1877–1949), Spanish statesman, who was president of the second republic in Spain from

1931 to 1936, was born at Priego, Córdoba, on July 6, 1877. Elected to the *Cortes* in 1905, he became minister of works (1917) and minister of war (1922). In 1930 he declared himself a Republican and was sent to prison for his share in a military rising at La Jara. He headed the poll in Madrid in the municipal elections of April 1931 and, as leader of the revolutionary committee, demanded Alfonso XIII's abdication. After Alfonso's departure (April 14), he became prime minister of the provisional government. He resigned on Oct. 14, 1931, because of the acceptance by the *Cortes* of the anticlerical articles (no. 24 and 26) in the new constitution. Nevertheless, on Dec. 11, 1931, he was elected the first president of the second republic.

Behaving in strict obedience to the new constitution, with which, as a devout Roman Catholic, he himself was not fully in agreement, Alcalá Zamora attempted to exercise a moderating influence in politics. In fact, he was increasingly attacked by both right- and left-wing parties, and after the popular front victory of Feb. 1936, a motion for his deposition was passed by the *Cortes* by 238 votes to 5. Subsequently, Alcalá Zamora went into exile in France and, later, in Argentina. He died at Buenos Aires on Feb. 18, 1949.

ALCALDE (from Arabic *al-qadi*, "judge"), the Spanish title for the mayor of a town or village. Formerly the term was applied to local government officials whose functions were various but always included a judicial element. Types of alcalde were differentiated according to the specialized nature of their judicial functions: the *alcalde de corte* was a judge of the palace court, with jurisdiction in and about the residence of the king; the *alcalde mayor* assisted the judges (*corregidores*) appointed by the king in the towns. From the 19th century the alcalde has had the dual character of leader of the local council (*ayuntamiento*) and representative of the central government. His duties have become mainly administrative, with scarcely any judicial attributes.

ALCAMENES, a Greek sculptor perhaps from Lemnos, but domiciled in Athens. He was a younger contemporary of Phidias and noted for the delicacy and finish of his works, among which a Hephaestus and an "Aphrodite of the Gardens" were conspicuous. Pausanias says that he was the author of one of the pediments of the temple of Zeus at Olympia, but there are great chronological and stylistic difficulties in accepting this. At Pergamum there was discovered in 1903 a copy of the head of the "Hermes Propylaeus" of Alcamenes identified by an inscription.

See Gisela M. A. Richter, *Sculpture and Sculptors of the Greeks,* rev. ed., pp. 237–240 (1950).

ALCAMO, a town in the province of Trapani, Sicily, lies 51½ mi. W.S.W. of Palermo by railway. Pop. (1961) 42,524 (commune). The name comes from the Saracenic fortress of Alqamuh on Monte Bonifato. The present town was founded by the emperor Frederick II in 1233. The 17th-century Assunta church contains frescoes by Guglielmo Borremans and sculptures by Antonello Gagini (1511); the church of S. Tomaso has an elaborate 14th-century doorway.

ALCÁNTARA, a small agricultural town of western Spain in the province of Cáceres, is built on a rock above the left bank of the Tagus about 45 mi. N.W. by road of Cáceres and 7 mi. E. of the Portuguese frontier. Pop. (1950) 4,150 (mun.). The walled town was named after the six-arched Roman bridge (Arab. *al-kantara*, "the bridge") spanning the Tagus, built in A.D. 105–106 in honour of the emperor Trajan. Destroyed by the Moors in 1214, it was restored in 1543 and has been altered many times since. There is a small Roman temple where it joins the left bank and a triumphal arch in the centre. The church of Santa María de Almocobar dates from the 13th century; that of San Benito (1576) belonged to the now ruined convent and contains tombs of many grand masters of the knights of Alcántara. The town is served by buses to Cáceres and Ceclavín. It is doubtful whether there was a Roman town there, but it became famous about 1215 as the stronghold of the knights of Alcántara.

ALCATHOUS, in Greek legend, was a son of Pelops, brother of Atreus (*q.v.*). He slew the Cithaeronian lion, which had killed Euippos, son of King Megareus, and thereby won the king's daughter and succeeded to the throne of Megara. With the help of Apollo he rebuilt the walls of the city, which had been destroyed in the Cretan invasion (*see* NISUS), becoming a kind of refounder of the city. Games were celebrated in Alcathous' honour, as described in Pindar's *Isthmionikai,* and a *heroum* was dedicated to him in the city. (T. V. B.)

ALCÁZAR DE SAN JUAN, a town of central Spain in the region of New Castile and province of Ciudad Real, lies on the high Iberian plateau 2,135 ft. above sea level, 92 mi. S.S.E. of Madrid by rail. The old part of the town has many narrow streets in contrast with the wide avenues and tree-lined squares of the newer districts. The church of Santa María stands on the site of a pre-Christian temple of Hercules and nearby is the 14th-century tower of Don Juan of Austria and the municipal archaeological museum containing Roman mosaics of the 2nd and 3rd centuries. The main line south from Madrid divides at Alcázar de San Juan, one branch running southeast and the other southwest. There are railway works and ironworks. The town is the marketing centre of an agricultural and industrial district, its particular products being wines and cheeses, a cheese made from sheep's milk being a speciality. Pop. (1960) 24,963 (mun.).

Alcázar de San Juan was known to the Romans as Alces. The Arabs renamed it Al Kazar ("the palace"). The knights of St. John conquered it in 1186 and ruled it until 1292, when it was captured by King Sancho IV of Castile. It was the centre of the order of San Juan in the 14th, 15th and 16th centuries.

ALCAZARQUIVIR (KSAR EL KEBIR or AL QSAR AL KBIR, "The Great Fortress"), a town of Morocco, lies on the road from Rabat to Tangier. Pop. (1960) 34,035. It is at the centre of a wide cultivated plain crossed by the Lucus (Loukkos) river, and is essentially a rural market. The old Arab village was enlarged and surrounded with walls by Yakub al-Mansur (1184–99). In 1911 the Spanish found a sleeping town which they occupied and largely rebuilt. Near the town, by the banks of the Makhazan river, is the site of the "battle of the three kings," fought in 1578 between Dom Sebastian, king of Portugal, and the Moors under Abd al-Malek, in which the Moors were victorious, though both kings perished as well as the deposed Mohammed XI, who had called in the Portuguese to his aid. (G. L. M.)

ALCHEMY. In the strict sense, alchemy is the pseudo science which concerns attempts to transform base metals such as lead or copper into silver or gold. At all times, however, such attempts have involved purely chemical procedures, and the pseudo science has, for most of its existence, been closely connected with the development of chemistry itself. In fact, for many centuries the history of alchemy is the history of chemistry.

The close connection is shown in the name, which in the opinion of most scholars is derived from the Greek word *cheo,* "I pour" or "cast," and which refers to the activities of the metal workers who were the originators of alchemy. An alternative theory ascribes the word to the ancient name for Egypt, *Khem,* "the Black Land" (referring to the black soil of the country). This would indicate the Egyptian origin of alchemy. During the Arabic period, the Arabic article, *al,* was added to produce the word alchemy, and when chemistry emerged as an independent science, the article was dropped.

EARLY HISTORY AND PHILOSOPHICAL BASIS

The exact date at which alchemy began is not known. The first alchemical writings, at least in the western world, date from the 3rd or 4th centuries A.D., but they already represented a flourishing science and it is thought that the earliest alchemists were active during the 1st century. There is no doubt that alchemy originated in the Hellenistic culture of Alexandria in Egypt. Alexandria at this period was the centre of the learned world, and there met and mingled the three streams from which alchemy was formed. These were Greek philosophy, Egyptian technology and the mysticism of the middle eastern religions.

Greek philosophy always attempted to explain the nature of the entire physical world, though the Greek contempt for manual labour prevented any effort to check these explanations by experiment. The theories reached their culmination in the system of Aristotle, whose ideas for nearly 2,000 years remained the basis for all attempted scientific speculations. Certain of his ideas contributed directly to the theories of alchemy. Aristotle believed that there existed a prime matter which was the basis for all substances in the terrestrial world. Upon this prime matter a variety of forms could be impressed by suitable means. The interaction of matter and form gave rise to the four elements, fire, air, water and earth, which in turn through their various combinations produced all material objects. In a sense these elements represented what we today consider physical properties. A preponderance of earth in a body caused it to be solid; water tended to produce liquids, or at least substances which could be melted; air was a spirit, sometimes equated with the soul by the Stoics; and fire represented the principle of combustion. Changes in the proportions of these elements resulted in change in the form of the prime matter, and so, in theory, any substance could be changed into any other substance if the right conditions could be found.

Egypt had long had a class of skillful artisans who were especially adept in working with metals. The Hellenistic culture of Alexandria encouraged some of these artisans to speculate on the causes for the physical facts which they observed. Since they operated their own workshops, they had lost the old Greek contempt for work with the hands, but they now gained the philosophic viewpoint which had animated the Greek cosmologists. These men formed a class which in its combination of philosophy and technology approached more nearly the modern concept of a group of scientists than existed again until the Renaissance. Such men as Archimedes in his studies of hydrostatics or Hero in his mechanical inventions which used the power of steam are examples of these early scientists.

The first alchemists were typical members of this group. They were the metallurgical workers who not only prepared gold and silver objects for wealthy nobles, but also manufactured cheaper substitutes for poorer citizens. They naturally attempted to make these resemble true gold or silver as much as possible, while recognizing the inferior nature of their materials. In view of the Aristotelian theories, however, they knew of no reason why they could not make real silver or gold almost as easily as they could manufacture the obvious substitutes.

They were supported in this view by the astrological ideas which came chiefly from Mesopotamia. The astrologers believed in the coexistence of the macrocosm, the great world of stars and planets, and the microcosm, the small world of man. Events in the macrocosm were reflected in the microcosm, and vice versa. Thus, under the proper astrological influences a change of lead to gold might easily occur, and the proper way to bring this change about was to use the methods of the microcosm: growth and development. As men grew and changed, so could the metals grow and change; as the human soul perfected itself and passed through death and resurrection to the perfection of heaven, so could metals develop in the earth from the less perfect to the most perfect, gold. The artisan in his laboratory could perhaps hasten this process by careful nurture and long heating, by "killing" the metal and then reviving it in more perfect form until the ultimate perfection of gold was reached.

Thus copper could be "killed" by blackening it (converting it to the black oxide) and then revived by forming a silver-coloured alloy with mercury or arsenic, a whitening process. Other reagents produced yellow or red colours and represented the final steps in the process. This sequence of colours made a strong impression on the Alexandrian artisans, who besides their metallurgical work, were often dyers as well. They came to believe that the series of colour changes, black-white-yellow (later red), was essential to a successful transmutation, and that the stage of any such change could be determined by the colour at any given time. The sequence black-white-red became standard in all later alchemy, and many chemical discoveries resulted from attempts to produce the correct colour.

It can be seen then that the original alchemy was a practical series of chemical operations, guided by the accepted theory of the nature of matter, and in its actual operations directed by the astrological and religious ideas which circulated freely in Alexandria. This practical alchemy could be, and was, expressed symbolically in terms of the perfection of the human soul. This aspect

appealed to many who were in no way interested in actual laboratory operations. Almost from the first there occurred a split between the practical and the mystical alchemists, and this distinction existed throughout the entire history of the art.

The practical alchemists invented and used many types of laboratory apparatus which in modified form are used today. Stills, furnaces, water baths, flasks and beakers were in everyday use. Chemical reactions were their stock in trade. The alchemists were still essentially artisans, however, and did not wish to reveal their trade secrets. They therefore invented many concealing names for the materials with which they worked. Almost every piece of apparatus, every reagent, acquired a symbolic name. Astrological influences led to ascribing each metal to a heavenly body. Gold, the noblest metal, obviously belonged to the sun, and silver to the moon. There had to be five other metals, since there were five planets. In general, copper belonged to Venus, lead to Saturn, iron to Mars, tin to Jupiter, and mercury to the planet of that name. The metals were then represented in alchemical manuscripts by the astrological sign of their controlling body. Other reagents were given names such as "bile of the tortoise." Such reagents multiplied until the uninitiated could not understand the text at all. The writers usually ascribed their manuscripts to some god, hero, king or philosopher of olden time. Alchemical manuscripts were said to have been written by Isis, Moses, Aaron, Hermes, Solomon, Democritus and many others.

These confusing tendencies, initiated by the practical alchemists, were intensified as the mystically minded began to develop alchemical ideas. C. G. Jung has shown that the symbolism of alchemy appeals to basic psychological tendencies of the human mind, and so it is not surprising that many were attracted to alchemy by its symbolism and its search for perfection, without any knowledge of the practical chemistry upon which it was originally based. Their mystical writings tended still further to bring confusion to the subject. Even the earliest works which have come down to us, the *Physica et Mystica* by an author who wrote under the name of Democritus, but was probably a certain Bolos of Mendes, and the encyclopaedia of alchemy by Zosimus,

"THE ALCHEMIST." DETAIL FROM A PAINTING BY DAVID TENIERS THE YOUNGER (1610—90)

are very difficult to read. As Hellenistic philosophy shifted more and more from the technical scientific viewpoint to the emphasis on divine revelation of Gnosticism, Neoplatonism and Christianity, the alchemical writings became more and more mystical and allegorical. They often became mere commentaries on each other, adding nothing to what had already been said. The later Byzantine manuscripts are of this type.

Chinese Alchemy.—While these developments were occurring in the west, a similar alchemy was growing up in China. Based on the Taoist philosophy (*see* TAOISM) which sought to understand the "way" of nature (*tao* means "way" or "path"), Chinese alchemy like its western counterpart tried to perfect base metals into gold. In two respects, however, the Chinese form differed from the western. The Chinese alchemist made use of a "medicine," a substance which he added to mercury or other metals to bring about the transmutation. The gold thus prepared was valued less for its own sake than for the fact that the metal possessed the power of conferring immortality on anyone who ate it, or in less favourable cases, at least of prolonging life and curing illnesses.

As time passed, both in the west and in the east the mystical alchemists became dominant. Writings became more and more obscure; the alchemists separated themselves more and more from the laboratory. In China the art degenerated into a mass of superstitions and contributed nothing more to the intellectual life of the nation. In the west a different path was followed.

Arabian Alchemy.—The Nestorian Christians who broke away from the Orthodox Church in Byzantium in the 5th century spread their faith rapidly throughout Asia Minor. They founded schools in Edessa, Nisibis and Jundi-Shapur, and in these they taught the philosophy and science of their Hellenistic background. They translated all the available manuscripts of Greek learning into their own language, Syriac. Many alchemical works were included in these translations. In the 8th and 9th centuries the Nestorians came into close contact with the rising power of the Arabs, among whom a group centring around the court of the Caliph in Baghdad became deeply interested in Greek science. The manuscripts were again translated, this time from Syriac into Arabic.

A number of practical alchemists began to work among the Arabs, bringing the art of alchemy back to its origins in the laboratory. These included such famous physicians as Rhazes and Avicenna (*qq.v.*). The most active workers were to be found among the sect of the Isma'iliya (whose modern descendants follow the Agha Khan). This group published a large body of alchemical and mystical literature, most of which was attributed to a certain Jabir ibn Hayyan (*see* GEBER). Jabir may have actually lived in the 8th century and written alchemical books, but the great majority of the works said to have been written by him were certainly composed by members of the sect in the 9th and 10th centuries. Nevertheless the name of Jabir became the best known of all Arabic alchemists.

Arabian alchemy drew its chief ideas from the alchemy of Alexandria, but the Arabs were also in contact with China and they took over the two most characteristic ideas of eastern adepts. The Chinese "medicine" which had to be added to base metals to produce gold became the "philosopher's stone" of later European alchemy, and the idea of the healing power of gold was expanded into a belief that this philosopher's stone could not only heal "sick" (*i.e.*, base) metals by converting them to gold, but could also act as the elixir of life, in much the same way as the Chinese gold. The Arabian alchemists also modified the Aristotelian idea of the four elements by supposing that all metals were actually composed of two immediate constituents, sulfur and mercury, though these in turn were built up from the four elements. The sulfur and mercury were not the actual substances, whose properties were perfectly well known, but represented the basic principles of combustibility and liquidity which made possible burning or melting.

Arabic alchemists discovered important new classes of chemicals such as the caustic alkalies and improved such technical methods as distillation. After the 10th century, however, the same trend

AN ALCHEMIST HOLDING A SALAMANDER IN THE FIRE, AN ILLUSTRATION FROM AN ALCHEMICAL TREATISE, "THE BOOK OF LAMBSPRINCK." THE SALAMANDER WAS BELIEVED TO BE BORN IN FIRE AND CAPABLE OF WITHSTANDING ITS FLAMES

toward domination by mystical and allegorical thinking became apparent as had appeared in the west and in China. Again a new people stepped in to reverse this trend.

DEVELOPMENTS SINCE THE 10TH CENTURY

Almost all traces of Greek philosophy and science had been lost in western Europe after the fall of Rome. Alchemy completely disappeared. In the 11th and 12th centuries, however, a reawakening of interest in science led to a recognition of the value of the Arabic accomplishments. In Spain and Sicily, where Europeans and Arabs were in close contact, new schools of translation were set up. Many scholars devoted themselves to translating the works of Arabic physicians, philosophers and scientists into Latin. Works which had come from Greek through Syriac and Arabic now reached the west and through their Latin versions eventually were translated into all the major European tongues. Among these were many of the alchemical manuscripts.

These first translations were in no sense made by alchemists. Neither was their wider dissemination due to alchemical influence. In the 12th and 13th centuries a number of scholars, such as Arnold of Villanova, Roger Bacon, and above all Albertus Magnus, devoted themselves to compiling all phases of human knowledge into encyclopaedic works. The alchemical explanation of the nature of matter was naturally an important part of such books. This portion of their work was at once seized upon by the alchemically minded, and alchemy entered upon a new phase of vigorous activity.

As was to be expected, the practical and mystical branches of alchemy developed more or less separately. The practical alchemists were the earliest European chemists. The most influential of these was an author who wrote under the name of Jabir, or Geber in the Latin form, probably in order to benefit from the prestige of the great Arabic alchemist. It is likely that he was a practising Spanish alchemist of the 14th century. He used alchemical theory to explain his results, but the practical portions of his books are clearly the work of a man familiar with experimental laboratory operations.

The works of Geber became the textbooks of the alchemists, but their own books, which appeared in increasing quantity, began to show the familiar shift toward mysticism and allegory. The alchemist became a recognized figure in his society, usually regarded with some awe and not a little contempt, for it was soon realized that most of the professed members of this group were actually dishonest charlatans. This aspect of public feeling is reflected in the Canon's Yeoman's Tale of Chaucer and in Ben Jonson's play *The Alchemist*.

At the same time many honest men spent their lives and fortunes in the attempt to transmute base metals into gold. Nobles and kings, such as James IV of Scotland and Rudolf II, the Holy Roman emperor, often supported alchemists in the hope of augmenting their revenues, though frequently the unfortunate alchemists who failed to supply the promised gold lost their lives as a result.

The alchemy of the 15th to the 17th centuries produced little that was new, though much that was obscure. Alchemical symbolism and allegory became more and more complex. Many beautifully illustrated manuscripts were produced, but their texts were usually mere repetitions of what had gone before. Gradually the practical alchemists began to turn their attention to more useful purposes than the attempt to make gold. One of the greatest of such alchemists was Paracelsus (*q.v.*) who took for his purpose the manufacture of metallic medicines to cure ills with which the Galenic physicians of his day could not cope. He thus founded the school of iatrochemistry, the chemistry of medicines, the forerunner of modern pharmacology. He and his followers spoke in alchemical language, but in spirit they were true chemists.

The revival of classical scholarship in the 16th century led to a rediscovery of Greek atomism and a strong shift away from Aristotelian theory. The newer schools of physicists and chemists no longer accepted the possibility of transmutation. The chemical facts which had been accumulated by the alchemists were now reinterpreted and made the basis upon which modern chemistry was erected.

This did not mean that the alchemists vanished. The hope of gaining great wealth through conversion of cheap materials into gold did not die easily. Alchemists have existed until the present day, but they have sunk to the level of astrologers, numerologists, and other practitioners of what once were respectable sciences.

The discovery of the structure of the atom at the beginning of the 20th century has, in a sense, vindicated one of the oldest of alchemical theories, since the electron and nucleus of protons and neutrons might be considered the prime material, and their structural relations the form which confers individual properties on material substances. By suitable treatment the modern scientist has indeed been able to transmute one element into another, and even to "make gold," but such transformations are a far cry, both in method and purpose, from the attempts of the ancient alchemists. *See also* CHEMISTRY: *Emergence of Alchemy*. For the historical development of science from ancient time through the 20th century *see* SCIENCE, HISTORY OF.

BIBLIOGRAPHY.—J. Read, *Prelude to Chemistry* (1937) contains excellent colour reproductions of alchemical illustrations. Other good general studies of alchemy are J. Read, *Humour and Humanism in Chemistry* (1947); F. Sherwood Taylor, *The Alchemists* (1949); E. J. Holmyard, *Alchemy* (1957). Special fields are covered by A. J. Hopkins, *Alchemy, Child of Greek Philosophy* (1934); O. S. Johnson, *A Study of Chinese Alchemy* (1928); J. Needham, *Science and Civilisation in China*, vol. i (1954); P. Kraus, *Jabir ibn Hayyan. Contribution à l'histoire des idées scientifiques dans l'Islam*, 2 vol. (1942–43); C. G. Jung, *Psychology and Alchemy* (1953). The setting of alchemy in the history of chemistry is well discussed in J. M. Stillman, *The Story of Early Chemistry* (1924). The classic comprehensive works on alchemy are M. P. E. Berthelot, *Collection des anciens alchimistes grecs* (1888) and *La chimie au moyen âge* (1893); and E. O. von Lippmann, *Entstehung und Ausbreitung der Alchemie* (1919–31).   (H. M. L.)

ALCIBIADES (*c.* 450–404 B.C.), Athenian general and statesman who provoked the sharp political antagonisms which were the cause of Athens' final defeat in the Peloponnesian War (*q.v.*). He belonged to the family of the Alcmaeonidae and was a near relative of Pericles. He was very handsome and possessed great wealth, which he squandered in every sort of dissipation and extravagance, including the upkeep of a fine stud of horses. He was an admirer of Socrates, who saved his life at Potidaea (432), a service which Alcibiades repaid at Delium. In 421 Alcibiades came

to the fore in politics as the opponent of Nicias and the peace party and engineered an anti-Spartan alliance between Athens and the democracies of Argos, Mantinea and Elis. Sparta was thus placed in a critical position, and the policy might have succeeded if Athens had disregarded the opposition of Nicias and given it wholehearted support. But in 418 Alcibiades was not re-elected general and Sparta broke up the confederacy by the crushing victory of Mantinea. Alcibiades' most bitter enemies were the leaders of the radical democrats who inherited the policies of Cleon (*q.v.*) and resented Alcibiades' influence with the people; this bitterness was aggravated when Alcibiades unexpectedly allied himself with Nicias to secure the ostracism of the radical democrat Hyperbolus in 417. When Nicias had failed in Thrace (418–417), Alcibiades became the chief advocate of the Sicilian expedition, partly from policy and partly from private ambition, and was appointed commander jointly with Nicias and Lamachus. But shortly before the expedition was due to leave the *hermae* (numerous small effigies in the streets throughout Athens) were found to have been mutilated, and Alcibiades was accused of being the originator of the sacrilege (and also of having profaned the Eleusinian mysteries). Alcibiades demanded an immediate inquiry but his enemies, led by Androcles, obliged him to set sail with the charge still hanging over him. When he reached Sicily he was recalled to stand trial, but on the journey home he escaped to Sparta. Learning that he had been condemned to death in his absence, he openly joined the Spartans and persuaded them to send Gylippus to assist the Syracusans and to fortify Decelea in Attica (which they did in 413 B.C.), advice which proved the ruin of Athens. He then passed over to Asia Minor, induced many of the Ionic allies of Athens to revolt and procured an alliance for Sparta with the Persian satrap Tissaphernes. But in a few months he had lost the confidence of the Spartans and made an enemy of their king Agis (whose wife he had seduced). He therefore retired to the court of Tissaphernes (412) and, hoping to secure his reconciliation with Athens, advised the satrap to withdraw his active support from Sparta. At the same time he conspired with the oligarchic party at Athens who brought about a revolution in 411, with the aim of having Alcibiades recalled to Athens as the price of Persian support; Androcles and Hyperbolus were murdered but in the end Alcibiades was not recalled. He therefore attached himself to the fleet at Samos, which remained loyal to the democracy, and was at last recalled by Thrasybulus, but he did not at once return to Athens. Being appointed commander in the neighbourhood of the Hellespont, he defeated the Spartan fleet at Abydos (411) and Cyzicus (410) and recovered Chalcedon and Byzantium (408). These successes encouraged him to return to Athens, where he was welcomed with enthusiasm (407); proceedings against him were canceled and he was appointed general with full powers. But he was attacked by Cleophon who after the defeat at Notium (406) induced the Athenians to dismiss Alcibiades from his command. He thereupon retired to the Thracian Chersonese. After the final defeat of Athens he was exiled and took refuge in Phrygia with Pharnabazus, who was induced by the Spartans to have him murdered (404).

Alcibiades possessed great charm and brilliant political and military abilities but was absolutely unscrupulous. His advice, whether to Athens or Sparta, oligarchs or democrats, was dictated by selfish motives and the Athenians could never trust him enough to take advantage of his talents. He could not practise his master's virtues, and there is no doubt that the example of Alcibiades strengthened the charges brought against Socrates in 399 of corrupting the youth.

See J. Hatzfeld, *Alcibiade* (1940).   (R. ME.)

ALCIDAMAS (fl. 4th century B.C.), a prominent Greek sophist and rhetorician who taught in Athens, was born at Elaea in Aeolis. He was a pupil of Gorgias and a rival of Isocrates. His only extant work, *Peri Sophiston* ("Concerning Sophists"), stresses the superiority of extempore (though prepared) speeches over written ones. The oration attributed to him entitled *Odysseus* is spurious. Only fragments of his other works survive. Two papyrus fragments of his *Mouseion* are possibly part of an early version of the *Agon Homerou kai Hesiodou* ("Competition Between Homer and Hesiod") which is extant in a 2nd-century A.D. form.

Aristotle criticized Alcidamas for his improper and too frequent use of adjectives, and cited him as an example of frigidity of style.

BIBLIOGRAPHY.—For *Odysseus* and *Peri Sophiston* see F. Blass' ed. of Antiphon in the "Teubner Series" (1881). For fragments *see* C. Müller, *Oratores Attici*, vol. 2, pp. 316–318 (1858); T. W. Allen's ed. of Homer in the Oxford classical texts, vol. 5, p. 225 (1912); and G. S. Kirk, "The Michigan Alcidamas-Papyrus," *Classical Quarterly*, 44:149–167 (1950). See also E. R. Dodds, "The Alcidamas Papyrus Again," *Classical Quarterly*, 46:187–188 (1952); H. L. Hudson-Williams, "Impromptu Speaking," *Greece and Rome*, 18:28–31 (1949); M. J. Milne, *A Study in Alcidamas and His Relation to Contemporary Sophistic* (1924); G. Walberer, *Isokrates und Alkidamas* (1938).

ALCINOÜS, in ancient Greek legend, king of the Phaeacians, on the fabulous island of Scheria, son of Nausithoüs and grandson of Poseidon. His reception and entertainment of Odysseus (*q.v.*), who when cast by a storm on the shore of the island was rescued by the king's daughter Nausicaä, is described in the *Odyssey*. Scheria was identified in very early times with Corcyra, where Alcinoüs was reverenced as a hero; Homer relates that the ship in which Alcinoüs sent Odysseus home to Ithaca was transformed by Poseidon into a rock, which can still be seen as the island Pontikonisi in the harbour of Corcyra (Corfu).

In the Argonautic legend, Alcinoüs dwelt on the island of Drepane, where he received Jason and Medea in their flight from Colchis, pursued by her father's men who sought to compel her to return. Alcinoüs agreed to return Medea only if she were still single, whereupon (as related by Apollonius Rhodius) she and Jason were married. (T. V. B.)

ALCIPHRON (2nd century A.D.), Athenian rhetorician, was the author of a collection of fictitious letters, of which 124 (118 complete and 6 fragments) have been published; they are written in the purest Attic dialect and are considered models of style. The scene throughout is at Athens; the imaginary writers are country people, fishermen, parasites and courtesans, who express their sentiments and opinions on familiar subjects in elegant language. The "courtesan" letters are especially valuable, the information contained in them being chiefly derived from the writers of the New Comedy, especially Menander. Alciphron is believed to have been a contemporary and imitator of the sophist and satirist Lucian.

See M. A. Schepers (ed.), *Alciphronis rhetoris Epistularum libri iv*, in the "Teubner Series" (1905); *Letters From the Country and the Town, of Fishermen, Farmers, Parasites, and Courtesans*, trans. by F. A. Wright (1923).

ALCMAEON, of Argos, in Greek legend, was the son of Amphiaraus (*q.v.*) and Eriphyle. When his father set out with the expedition of the Seven against Thebes, which he knew would be fatal to him, he enjoined upon his sons to avenge his death by slaying Eriphyle (who had been bribed by Polyneices with the necklace of Harmonia [*q.v.*] to persuade her husband to fight) and undertaking a second expedition against Thebes. After the destruction of Thebes by the Epigoni (the sons of the Seven), Alcmaeon carried out his father's injunctions by killing his mother, as a punishment for which he was driven mad and pursued by the Erinyes from place to place.

On his arrival at Psophis in Arcadia, he was purified by its king, Phegeus, whose daughter Arsinoë (or Alphesiboea) he married, making her a present of the fatal necklace and the robe of Harmonia, which brought misfortune to all who possessed them. But the land was cursed with barrenness, and the oracle declared that Alcmaeon would never find rest until he reached a spot on which the sun had never shone at the time he slew his mother. Such a spot he found at the mouth of the Achelous river, where an island had recently been formed by the alluvial deposit. There he settled and, forgetting his wife, married Callirrhoë, the daughter of the river-god.

His new wife longed for the necklace and robe, and Alcmaeon, returning to Psophis, obtained possession of them, on the pretense that he desired to dedicate them at Delphi. When the truth became known he was pursued and slain by Phegeus and his sons. On his death, Callirrhoë prayed that her two young sons might grow to manhood at once and avenge their father. This prayer was granted; her sons, Amphoterus and Acarnan, slew Phegeus and, returning with the necklace and robe, dedicated them at Delphi.

After his death Alcmaeon was worshiped at Thebes; his tomb was at Psophis in a grove of cypresses. His story was the subject of an old epic and of several tragedies, none of which has been preserved, and of the modern parody, "A Fragment of a Greek Tragedy," by A. E. Housman. (T. V. B.)

ALCMAEON OF CROTONA (5th century B.C.), Greek philosopher and physiologist, may be regarded as a typical scientific researcher of the pre-Socratic period, before there was any clear division between philosophy and physiology (in which he had a special interest). He observed that "most things human are two" and made a "list of opposites" that bears a superficial resemblance to the Pythagorean list; but there is no clear evidence that he belonged to the Pythagorean community flourishing at Crotona in his time.

His doctrine was that health consisted in the "isonomy" of the components of the body (like a city whose citizens are all of equal standing); the "monarchy" of any one ingredient led to disease. A very similar theory is found in the Hippocratic treatise *On Ancient Medicine*, where health is said to lie in the equal "blend" of the bodily components or "powers." Alcmaeon is the first person known to have practised dissection (probably not vivisection) for scientific purposes; his aim was to discover the seat of the intelligence. He inferred that this was the brain from his observation that concussion of the brain resulted in injury to the intellect as well as to the senses; and his dissections showed "passages" connecting the brain with the eyes and ears. He also distinguished between sensation (in animals) and intelligence (in man only) and conducted research in embryology.

BIBLIOGRAPHY.—For fragments and testimonia *see* H. Diels and W. Kranz, *Die Fragmente der Vorsokratiker*, 6th ed. (1951–52). *See* also J. Wachtler, *De Alcmaeone Crotoniata* (1896); J. I. Beare, *Greek Theories of Elementary Cognition From Alcmaeon to Aristotle* (1906); J. Burnet, *Early Greek Philosophy*, 4th ed. (1930); W. A. Heidel, *Hippocratic Medicine* (1941); H. Erhard, article in *Sudhoffs Archiv für Geschichte der Medizin*, vol. xxxiv (1941); G. Vlastos on "Isonomy," *American Journal of Philology*, vol. lxxiv, pp. 337 ff. (1953).

(A. L. PK.)

ALCMAEONIDAE, a powerful Athenian family claiming descent from the legendary Alcmaeon, which played a leading part in the politics of the 6th and 5th centuries B.C. During the archonship of an Alcmaeonid Megacles (?632 B.C.) a certain Cylon unsuccessfully attempted to make himself tyrant and his followers were murdered when they had taken sanctuary. The Alcmaeonidae consequently incurred bloodguilt which was to be frequently raked up in later years for political reasons. The family was banished for the murder but returned by the time of Solon (archon in 594) and Alcmaeon, son of Megacles, led the Athenian contingent supporting Delphi in the Sacred War of *c.* 590. In the next generation another Megacles married Agariste, daughter of Cleisthenes, tyrant of Sicyon, and led a party in Athens which accepted the reforms of Solon.

When Pisistratus (*q.v.*) became tyrant in 561–560 the Alcmaeonidae, allied with the more conservative aristocrats, drove him out, but soon preferred to help him back to power at the price of a marriage alliance. The alliance broke down and Pisistratus was again driven out (556). When he returned to power after his second exile, the Alcmaeonidae again were exiled and plotted continually to return. Cleisthenes, son of Megacles, was recalled and made archon in 525 after the death of Pisistratus, but after the murder of Pisistratus' son Hipparchus in 514 he was again exiled by Hippias. He then led the Alcmaeonidae in an abortive invasion of Attica from their base in Boeotia. While in exile the Alcmaeonidae, whose great wealth may have been largely derived from friendly relations with the Lydian court, rebuilt Apollo's temple at Delphi more handsomely than the contract specified. They were rewarded when the Spartans, largely at the insistence of the Delphic oracle, drove out the Pisistratidae (510). When in 508 Cleisthenes (*q.v.*) adopted a radical program of constitutional reform, Sparta intervened and under the pretext of the bloodguilt expelled Cleisthenes and his supporters. The policy followed by this opportunist family during the next generation is obscure: they were suspected of Medism at the time of Marathon; the direct line was considerably less prominent after the Persian Wars, but Alcibiades and Pericles were members of the family on their mothers' side. The Spartan demand for the expulsion of the Alcmaeonidae recurred as a provocation directed at Pericles at the beginning of the Peloponnesian War. (R. Me.)

ALCMAN (active in Sparta in the second half of the 7th century B.C.), Greek poet, is traditionally held to have founded Dorian choral lyric poetry. He probably owes this reputation to the fact that earlier choral lyrics did not survive in any considerable quantity into Hellenistic times. His work is known mainly from quotations and references in later writers; but he was the first Greek lyric poet to benefit by papyrological discoveries. One papyrus fragment contains over 100 lines of a *parthenion* (song for a chorus of girls). Alcman's language, though strongly flavoured by epic and Laconian usages, is clear and simple, and so, except in one fragment, are his metrical schemes. His manner is light and gay and unlike the traditional idea of Sparta; hence it was disputed in antiquity whether he was a born Laconian or an "incomer" from Lydia. He had a sharp eye for a pretty girl and a fondness for good living, but there was more substance in his poetry than philandering and gastronomy.

BIBLIOGRAPHY.—A. Garzya (ed.), *Alcmane. I frammenti* (1954); E. Lobel *et al.* (eds.), *Oxyrhynchus Papyri*, vol. 24, no. 2387–2394 (1957); D. L. Page, *Alcman: The Partheneion* (1951). *See also* M. F. Galiano, "La lírica griega a la luz de los descubrimientos papirológicos," in *Actas del I congreso español de estudios clásicos*, pp. 128–130 (1958); and C. M. Bowra, *Greek Lyric Poetry*, 2nd ed. (1961). (Jn. A. D.)

ALCMENE, in Greek mythology, the daughter of Electryon, king of Mycenae, and wife of Amphitryon (*q.v.*). She was the mother of Heracles by Zeus, who assumed the likeness of her husband during his absence.

ALCOBAÇA, a town of Portugal, in the district of Leiria, lies at the confluence of the Alcoa and the Baça rivers in a fertile fruit-growing valley, 17 mi. S.S.W. of Leiria city. Pop. (1960) 5,174. Alcobaça is chiefly interesting for its Cistercian monastery (Mosteiro de Santa Maria), now used partly for administrative offices and partly for a college. It was founded by King Afonso I about 1148 and was rebuilt in the 13th century. During the middle ages it rivaled the greatest European abbeys in size and wealth. It was supplied with water by an affluent of the Alcoa, which still flows through the kitchen. The vast abbey church is early Gothic somewhat defaced by baroque and later additions. Portions of the library are preserved in the public libraries of Lisbon and Braga. Alcobaça is the marketing centre for the fruit (pears, plums, melons) grown in the district; some of the fruits are candied, and cotton materials and pottery are made there.

ALCOCK, JOHN (*c.* 1430–1500), English bishop and statesman who founded Jesus college, Cambridge, was born in Beverley, Yorkshire, and educated at Cambridge. In 1461 he was made dean of Westminster and thereafter his promotion was rapid in church and state. In 1462 he became master of the rolls and in 1470 was sent as ambassador to Castile. He became successively bishop of Rochester (1472), Worcester (1476) and Ely (1486). He also held the office of chancellor and conducted negotiations with James III of Scotland, besides filling other posts under both Edward IV and Henry VII. He died at Wisbech castle on Oct. 1, 1500. Alcock was a man of learning and an architect. Besides founding a charity at Beverley and a grammar school at Kingston-upon-Hull, he restored churches and colleges and founded Jesus college, Cambridge, on the site of the convent of St. Radegunda. His published works, most of which are extremely rare, are: *Mons perfectionis, otherwise in English, the Hill of Perfection* (1497); *Gallicantus Johannis Alcock episcopi Eliensis ad fratres suos curatos in sinodo apud Barnwell* (1498), a good specimen of early English printing and quaint illustrations; *The Castle of Labour* (1536), translated from the French; and various other tracts and homilies.

See F. Brittain, *A Short History of Jesus College, Cambridge* (1946). (X.; M. Dk.)

ALCOCK, SIR JOHN WILLIAM (1892–1919), English aviator who, on June 14–15, 1919, achieved fame by flying from Newfoundland to Ireland together with Lieut. Arthur Whitten Brown in the first nonstop transatlantic flight. Alcock was born in Manchester on Nov. 6, 1892, the son of a horse dealer. Before World War I he had been in possession of the aviation certificate

for two years, when he joined the royal naval air force as an instructor in 1914. In 1916 he was posted at no. 2 wing at Mudros. There he performed many famous exploits, including the bombing of Istanbul on Sept. 30, 1917.

He was forced to alight at sea near Suvla bay on his return from this expedition, and he and his companions swam ashore and were taken prisoners by the Turks. After leaving the air force in March 1919, he set the transatlantic record with Brown, flying from St. John's, Nfd., to Clifden, Ire., in 16 hr. 27 min. He was then created knight commander, order of the British empire. A week later Alcock was flying to Paris in an amphibian airplane when he crashed and sustained fatal injuries at Côte d'Evrard, Normandy, on Dec. 18, 1919.

See G. Wallace, *The Flight of Alcock and Brown* (1955).

ALCOFORADO, MARIANA (1640–1723), Portuguese nun, long believed to have written the famous *Lettres portugaises*, was born at Beja in 1640 (baptized April 22), and died there on July 28, 1723. She was professed at the convent of Nôtre Dame de la Conception in 1656, becoming mother superior in 1709.

The letters appeared in French in January 1669. In a preface, the publisher, Claude Barbin, claimed that they had been written to a "man of quality," but that he knew neither the name of the writer nor of the person to whom they were addressed. He gave no information about his sources, nor the name of the translator. The letters were extremely popular, partly because of the intrigue to which they referred. A French officer had seduced a nun of good family in a convent in the province of Alentejo; fearing the consequences, he had returned hurriedly to France. The letters describe the nun's betrayed faith and disillusionment.

They were generally accepted as authentic. In later editions (beginning with that at Cologne, 1669), the "man of quality" was identified as the "chevalier de C—" (taken to be the marquis de Chamilly), and the translator as "Guilleragues," *i.e.*, the vicomte de Guilleragues (*q.v.*). In 1810 the scholar J. F. Boissonade claimed to have found a copy of the first edition in which, in an unknown hand, the name of the writer was given as "Mariana Alcoforado." Later research proved that a nun called Maria Ana Alcoforada had been living at Beja at the right period, and, despite certain inconsistencies, it was assumed that she was the author, until, in 1926, F. C. Green found the original royal privilege (1668), which stated that Guilleragues was the author, not the translator, of the *Lettres portugaises*. Their effects, however, had been great: while thought genuine, they had been praised for sincerity and passion by many, including Saint-Simon (who brought evidence to support the identification of Chamilly), La Bruyère, and Sainte-Beuve; and they have influenced writers from Stendhal to Rilke.

BIBLIOGRAPHY.—*The Lettres portugaises* were widely translated: Eng. trans. 1678 and 1893. *See* F. C. Green, "Who Was the Author of the *Lettres Portugaises?*" in the *Modern Language Review*, xxi (April 1926); A. Gonçalves Rodrigues, *M. Alcoforado—história e crítica de uma fraude literária* (1944), with bibliography of editions and studies; M. Ribeiro, *Vida e morte de Madre Mariana Alcoforado,* with new Portuguese translation of the *Lettres* (1940).

ALCOHOL, without modifying adjectives, refers to a particular class of oxygen-containing organic chemical compounds. The term denotes as well one member of this class, ethyl alcohol (*q.v.*), known also as grain alcohol or spirits of wine, which is the physiologically active principle of beverages produced by fermentation. Ethyl alcohol has the chemical formula C_2H_5OH; it may be considered a derivative of water, HOH, in which one hydrogen atom has been replaced by the ethyl group, C_2H_5, or it may be described as a derivative of the hydrocarbon ethane C_2H_6, in which one hydrogen has been replaced by the hydroxyl group, OH. The class of alcohols comprises those organic compounds which, like ethyl alcohol, contain a hydroxyl group attached to a saturated carbon atom; *i.e.*, one in turn attached to three other carbon or hydrogen atoms. Since wide variation is possible in the carbon-containing portion of alcohols, a large number of compounds, including complex species such as sterols and carbohydrates, may be classed as alcohols. Compounds with a hydroxyl group attached to an unsaturated carbon atom, such as phenols, are not generally considered alcohols.

The generally accepted derivation of the word alcohol is from the Arabic *kuhl, koh'l* or *kohol,* meaning a "very fine powder." *Alkohol,* or the "fine powder," referred usually to a finely powdered antimony sulfide used in cosmetics to darken the eyelids. For a long time the word *alkohol* or *alcool* referred only to a fine powder. For example, *ferrum alcoholisatum* was finely powdered iron. Gradually the word came to mean "essence" and Paracelsus defined it in the 16th century as "the most subtle part of anything." It was in this sense that he wrote of *alcool vini,* the most subtle part of wine, but never *alcool* alone. Gradually *vini* was dropped, but it was not until the 19th century that the term alcohol came to be used generally for wine spirits. The limiting term "ethyl" refers to the fact that this particular alcohol can be converted to ether. The "-yl" suffix is derived from the Greek word "hyle" and was employed first by Justus von Liebig and Friedrich Wöhler in the sense of "stuff" or "material."

Important alcohols of commerce include: methyl or wood alcohol, better known as methanol, which is used as a solvent, radiator antifreeze and as a chemical intermediate, chiefly in the manufacture of formaldehyde; ethyl alcohol, occurring in beverages, which is important as a solvent and for the synthesis of such compounds as acetic acid, acetic anhydride, ethyl acetate and tetraethyl lead; *n*-butyl alcohol, a solvent and precursor of solvents; ethylene glycol, the nonvolatile antifreeze, which is also necessary to the preparation of synthetic polyester and polyurethane fibres and resins; glycerol or glycerin, required in manufacture of alkyd resins, nitroglycerin, and in the formulation of cosmetics, tobacco products, inks and other materials. Other alcohols produced on a large scale are isopropyl alcohol, allyl alcohol, propylene glycol, pentaerythritol, sorbitol and polyvinyl alcohol. Still other alcohols are used in smaller amounts in the preparation of perfumes, synthesis of pharmaceuticals and in other branches of the chemical industry.

Members of the alcohol group occur throughout nature, often combined as esters. The lower monohydroxy alcohols are frequently so found in the volatile oil of fruits; *e.g.,* ethyl acetate in the pineapple. Animal and vegetable waxes are mixtures of esters of long-chain monohydroxy alcohols with long-chain fat acids. Fats and oils are mixtures of esters of the trihydroxy alcohol glycerol (glycerides) with similar acids. Naturally occurring free alcohols are the sterols, high-molecular-weight alcohols with a complex hydrocarbon framework. Among these are cholesterol (*q.v.*), present in the blood and tissue of animals and related to the bile acids and steroid hormones, and ergosterol, a precursor of vitamin D obtained from yeasts. Vitamin A_1 is another complex alcohol occurring naturally. The extremely widespread and important carbohydrates, including the starch, cellulose and sugars, are polyhydroxy alcohols.

(*See* also Butyl Alcohols; Carbohydrates; Ethyl Alcohol; Glycerol; Glycols; Methyl Alcohol.)

Nomenclature.—Many of the structurally simple and common alcohols are named by modifying the word alcohol by a term descriptive of the nonhydroxylic portion of the molecule. Compounds containing two hydroxyl groups on different carbon atoms are known as glycols and may be named similarly. This method of nomenclature becomes impractical in most cases, however, and one of three more systematic approaches is used instead: (1) In the I.U.C. (International Union of Chemistry) or Geneva system, the suffix "-ol," plus an appropriate positioning number, is added to the name of the hydrocarbon from which the alcohol is derived. (2) The alcohol is named as a derivative of methyl alcohol, called carbinol. (3) In complex cases containing certain additional functional groups, the hydroxyl group is indicated by the use of a number plus the term hydroxy.

Because the properties of alcohols vary somewhat with the position of the hydroxyl group in the carbon skeleton, alcohols are also divided into three classes, depending on the number of carbon atoms attached to the hydroxyl-bearing atom. Where this number is one, as in ethanol and dodecanol-1, the alcohol is known as a primary alcohol; in cases such as propanol-2, the alcohol is secondary; and when three carbons are attached to the hydroxyl-bearing carbon, as in 2-methylpropanol-2, the alcohol is called

Examples of Alcohol Nomenclature

Formula	Common names	Geneva system	Carbinol system
CH_3OH . . .	methyl alcohol	methanol	carbinol
C_2H_5OH	ethyl alcohol	ethanol	methylcarbinol
$CH_3CHOHCH_3$	*iso*propyl alcohol	propanol-2	dimethylcarbinol
$CH_3(CH_2)_{10}CH_2OH$.	lauryl alcohol	dodecanol-1	
$CH_3CHOHCH_2OH$	propylene glycol	propanediol-1,2	
$CH_2OHCHOHCH_2OH$	glycerol	propanetriol	
$CH_3CHOHCOOH$	lactic acid	2-hydroxypropionic acid	
$(CH_3)_3COH$ . . .	*tertiary* butyl alcohol	2-methylpropanol-2	trimethylcarbinol

tertiary. Methanol, although by this definition not a primary alcohol, is often considered to be one. Other divisions of alcohols are made on the basis of the hydrocarbon portion of the molecule, *e.g.,* into aliphatic, alicyclic and araliphatic; or because of additional functional groups present in the molecule, *e.g.,* into amino alcohols, olefinic alcohols, keto alcohols, etc.

Physical Properties.—The lower monohydroxy alcohols containing less than three carbon atoms are completely miscible with water and most organic solvents. Alcohols of up to five carbon atoms are appreciably soluble in water, while higher monohydroxy alcohols are not. The water solubility of tertiary alcohols of given molecular weight is higher than that of primary or secondary alcohols; *e.g.,* 2-methylpropanol-2 is completely miscible with water but butanol-1 is only slightly soluble. Increasing the number of hydroxyl groups in the alcohol molecule increases the water solubility and decreases the solubility in organic solvents; glycerol, for example, is completely miscible with water but insoluble in such organic solvents as ether and carbon tetrachloride.

Alcohols boil at higher temperatures than the hydrocarbons of equivalent molecular weight; methanol, molecular weight 32, boils at 64° C. and propanol-1, molecular weight 60, boils at 97° C. although the corresponding hydrocarbons ethane (molecular weight 30) and butane (molecular weight 58) boil at −88° C. and 0° C. respectively. This phenomenon arises from the association of alcohol molecules in the liquid state through interaction of the highly polar hydroxyl groups. Boiling points for a given molecular weight range increase with the number of hydroxyl groups in the molecule: ethylene glycol, CH_2OHCH_2OH, boils at 197° C., 100° C. higher than propanol-1, the monohydroxy compound of approximately the same molecular weight.

With increasing chain lengths the liquid straight carbon chain alcohols become increasingly viscous; the first straight chain alcohol to be solid at room temperature is dodecanol-1. Chain branching, however, generally raises the melting points of alcohols, 2-methylpropanol-2 melting at 25° C., while butanol-1 melts at −80° C. Additional hydroxyl groups also raise the melting point, but polyhydroxy compounds have a marked tendency to supercool.

Chemical Properties.—The distinguishing feature of alcohols is the grouping –C–O–H, the reactions of which give rise to the characteristic chemical properties of alcohols. Many of the reactions of alcohols bear a resemblance to those of water.

Alcohols are very weak acids, about as acidic as water, but they do react with alkali metals and with amalgamated aluminum or magnesium to liberate hydrogen gas and form salts known as alkoxides, as illustrated by the reaction of ethyl alcohol and sodium,

$$C_2H_5OH + Na \longrightarrow C_2H_5O^-Na^+ + \tfrac{1}{2}H_2$$

Alkoxides are hydrolyzed by water to regenerate the alcohol and form a hydroxide,

$$C_2H_5O^-Na^+ + H_2O \longrightarrow C_2H_5OH + NaOH$$

Metal alkoxides are very strong bases and are used as condensing agents in organic synthesis. Certain of them, such as aluminum isopropoxide, are useful as reducing agents.

In addition to their acid properties, alcohols have weakly basic characteristics and in the presence of strong acids form oxonium salts,

$$CH_3CH_2CH_2CH_2OH + H^+ \longrightarrow CH_3CH_2CH_2CH_2OH_2^+$$

Because of this reaction many water-immisicible primary alcohols such as butanol-1 are soluble in concentrated aqueous acid. However, under these conditions, tertiary alcohols and, to a lesser extent, secondary alcohols undergo reactions in which the hydroxyl group is lost. On treatment with concentrated hydrochloric acid, 2-methylpropanol-2 is converted to 2-chloro-2-methylpropane:

$$(CH_3)_3COH + HCl \longrightarrow (CH_3)_3CCl + H_2O$$

and with aqueous sulfuric acid to the olefin 2-methylpropene (isobutylene),

$$(CH_3)_3COH \xrightarrow{H_2SO_4} (CH_3)_2C = CH_2 + H_2O$$

If conditions are properly chosen, alcohols can generally be made to form unsaturated compounds by loss of the elements of water, either by acid treatment or, more satisfactorily, by passing the alcohol vapour over a hot alumina surface.

Another reaction of alcohols brought about by anhydrous strong acid is the formation of ethers, as exemplified by the formation of ether (diethyl ether) itself by sulfuric-acid treatment, under proper conditions, of ethyl alcohol:

$$2C_2H_5OH \xrightarrow{H_2SO_4} C_2H_5OC_2H_5 + H_2O$$

This reaction was reported in the 16th century.

The preparation of esters by reactions of alcohol with acids is a general and exceedingly useful reaction. Alcohols can be made to form esters with inorganic acids such as nitric, sulfuric and phosphoric, as well as with organic acids. For example, glyceryl trinitrate, formed by reaction of glycerol with nitric acid in the presence of sulfuric acid,

$$\begin{array}{l} CH_2OH \\ | \\ CHOH \\ | \\ CH_2OH \end{array} + 3HONO_2 \xrightarrow{H_2SO_4} \begin{array}{l} CH_2ONO_2 \\ | \\ CHONO_2 \\ | \\ CH_2ONO_2 \end{array} + 3H_2O$$

is the important explosive more often called nitroglycerin. Pentaerythritol tetranitrate (PETN) is another member of this class. Cellulose nitrates, although extremely inflammable, have been used in the past as a base for photographic films and molded plastic products; certain grades are used to make guncotton.

Phosphate esters of alcohols are also of importance; triethyl phosphate, $(C_2H_5O)_3PO$, is used in the synthesis of insecticides and tributyl phosphate as a plasticizer in the formulation of plastics. These are esters prepared in the reaction of phosphorous oxychloride with the corresponding alcohols. Sodium dodecyl sulfate, $CH_3(CH_2)_{10}CH_2OSO_3Na$, a salt of the half ester of dodecyl or lauryl alcohol with sulfuric acid, is an important ingredient of detergent formulations.

With carboxylic acids (q.v.), again under acid catalysis, alcohols form carboxylic esters. Butyl acetate, solvent, can thus be formed by reaction of n-butyl alcohol with acetic acid in the presence of a strong acid such as sulfuric:

$$CH_3COOH + HOCH_2(CH_2)_2CH_3 \xrightarrow{H_2SO_4}$$
$$CH_3COOCH_2(CH_2)_2CH_3 + H_2O$$

Carboxylic esters may also be formed by the reaction of an alcohol with an anhydride, as illustrated by the formation of cellulose triacetate, an intermediate in the production of acetate rayon, photographic film and other plastic products:

cellulose

cellulose triacetate

Acyl halides may also be used to introduce the acid component. A further method of producing carboxylic esters, known as transesterification, involves the base catalyzed reaction of an alcohol with an ester to produce a new ester plus the alcohol of the first ester. By way of illustration, dimethyl terephthalate is converted to the hydroxyethyl ester of terephthalic acid, an intermediate in the production of polyethylene terephthalate fibres and films:

$$CH_3OCO \langle \bigcirc \rangle COOCH_3 + 2HOCH_2CH_2OH \xrightarrow{base}$$

$$HOCH_2CH_2OCO \langle \bigcirc \rangle COOCH_2CH_2OH + 2CH_3OH$$

In general both inorganic and organic esters may be hydrolyzed to the alcohol plus the acid (or its salt) in the presence of acidic (or basic) catalysts. Soaps are the sodium or potassium salts of the long-chain fatty acids obtained, in addition to glycerol, by alkaline hydrolysis (saponification) of animal or vegetable fat:

$$\begin{array}{l} CH_3(CH_2)_{14}COOCH_2 \\ CH_3(CH_2)_{14}COOCH \\ CH_3(CH_2)_{14}COOCH_2 \end{array} + 3NaOH \longrightarrow$$

glyceryl tripalmitate
tripalmitin

$$3CH_3(CH_2)_{14}COONa \qquad \begin{array}{l} CH_2OH \\ | \\ CHOH \\ | \\ CH_2OH \end{array}$$

sodium palmitate   glycerol

The esterification of alcohols and the saponification of their esters increase in difficulty in the order primary, secondary, tertiary.

Alcohols may be oxidized. Primary alcohols are converted to aldehydes:

$$CH_3CH_2OH + [O] \longrightarrow CH_3CHO + H_2O$$

or carboxylic acids:

$$CH_3CH_2OH + 2[O] \longrightarrow CH_3COOH + H_2O$$

while secondary alcohols are oxidized to ketones:

$$\begin{array}{l} CH_3 \\ \diagup \\ CHOH \\ \diagdown \\ CH_3 \end{array} + [O] \longrightarrow \begin{array}{l} CH_3 \\ \diagup \\ CO \\ \diagdown \\ CH_3 \end{array} + H_2O$$

Tertiary alcohols can be oxidized only with disruption of the carbon skeleton.

Several methods are available to bring about these reactions. In the laboratory, chromic acid is frequently used as the oxidant. The oxidations of ethanol to acetaldehyde and isopropyl alcohol to acetone are carried out on a large scale as dehydrogenation reactions in which the alcohol is passed over a copper catalyst at 250°–300° C.:

$$\begin{array}{l} CH_3 \\ \diagup \\ CHOH \\ \diagdown \\ CH_3 \end{array} \underset{Cu}{\overset{250° C.}{\rightleftarrows}} \begin{array}{l} CH_3 \\ \diagup \\ CO \\ \diagdown \\ CH_3 \end{array} + H_2$$

Characteristic of the hydroxyl function of alcohols is its replacement by a halogen when treated with phosphorus halides, thionyl chloride or, in the case of tertiary alcohols, simply halogen acids. This reaction proceeds with increasing ease in the order primary, secondary, tertiary, and is illustrated by the reaction of 2-methylpropanol-2 with hydrochloric acid, mentioned above, and the preparation of *n*-butyl bromide by treatment of butanol-1 with phosphorous tribromide:

$$3CH_3(CH_2)_2CH_2OH + PBr_3 \longrightarrow 3CH_3(CH_2)_2CH_2Br + H_3PO_3$$

Preparation.—Numerous methods are available for the preparation of alcohols, some used in the laboratory for the preparation of alcohols of complex structure, others for large-scale production.

Fermentation processes are important for the industrial synthesis of ethyl alcohol and n-butyl alcohol, the latter being formed in a process which also produces acetone. The substrates for the microbiological action are carbohydrates from molasses or grain.

A more general technique for the preparation of higher alcohols is the hydrogenation (reduction) of more highly oxidized hydrocarbon derivatives, particularly esters; *e.g.*,

$$CH_3(CH_2)_{10}COOC_2H_5 + 4[H] \rightarrow CH_3(CH_2)_{10}CH_2OH + C_2H_5OH$$

This transformation may be carried out by means of hydrogen gas under pressure in the presence of a metal or metal oxide catalyst. Other reagents used are sodium metal dissolving in a lower alcohol and metal hydrides such as lithium aluminum hydride, $LiAlH_4$. The reduction of esters yields primary alcohols from the acid portion of the ester. Aldehydes, RCHO, may be similarly reduced; when applied to ketones, these reactions produce secondary alcohols:

$$(CH_3)_2CO + 2[H] \longrightarrow (CH_3)_2CHOH$$

Carbon monoxide, reduced by hydrogen over an oxide catalyst, is the source of most methanol:

$$CO + 2H_2 \xrightarrow{ZnO, Cr_2O_3} CH_3OH$$

Alcohols are also prepared from olefins, hydrocarbons containing a double bond, by hydration, a reaction usually carried out with an aqueous acid such as sulfuric. Ethyl alcohol and isopropyl alcohol are produced in this way from ethylene and propylene:

$$CH_2 = CH - CH_3 + H_2O \xrightarrow{H_2SO_4} CH_3CH(OH)CH_3$$

In this reaction, the hydroxyl group is always introduced at the carbon which bears the fewer hydrogen atoms. When sulfuric acid is used as the catalyst, an intermediate is the sulfuric acid half ester with the alcohol; this ester is hydrolyzed to the alcohol and sulfuric acid.

Mixtures of higher alcohols are produced industrially by the "oxo" reaction of olefins, carbon monoxide and hydrogen, or by the reduction of aldehydes produced in this process.

The hydrolysis of alkyl halides provides a route to alcohols; C_5 alcohols (amyl alcohols) are prepared from a mixture of chlorinated pentanes, and allyl alcohol arises from allyl chloride:

$$CH_2 = CH - CH_2Cl + H_2O \longrightarrow CH_2 = CHCH_2OH + HCl$$

A number of alcohols are prepared by hydrolysis of their naturally occurring esters with various acids, the most noteworthy example being glycerol.

Industrially, the controlled oxidation of hydrocarbon provides a route to alcohols, as well as other organic compounds. Ethylene is oxidized over a silver catalyst to ethylene oxide, which may in turn be hydrolyzed to ethylene glycol:

$$CH_2 = CH_2 + O_2 \text{ (air)} \xrightarrow{Ag} \overset{CH_2CH_2}{\underset{O}{\diagup\diagdown}}$$

$$CH_2CH_2 + H_2O \longrightarrow CH_2CH_2$$
$$\underset{O}{\diagdown\diagup} \qquad \qquad \underset{OH\ OH}{|\ \ |}$$

Some alcohols are produced by the condensation of aldehydes or ketones with themselves or each other, usually followed by a step involving reduction. The variations on this method are manifold. An example may be noted in the synthesis of pentaerythritol from acetaldehyde and formaldehyde:

$$CH_3CHO + 3CH_2O \xrightarrow[\text{base}]{} (HOCH_2)_3CCHO$$

acetaldehyde　formaldehyde　not isolated

$$(HOCH_2)_3CCHO + CH_2O \xrightarrow[\text{base}]{} (HOCH_2)_3CCH_2OH + HCOOH$$

Organometallic compounds such as organolithium and organomagnesium compounds react with aldehydes to yield secondary alcohols and with ketones and esters to yield tertiary alcohols:

$$\overset{R}{\underset{R'}{\diagdown}} CO + \overset{R''MgCl}{\underset{R''Li}{\text{or}}} \xrightarrow[\text{by } H_2O]{\text{followed}} \overset{R}{\underset{R''}{\diagdown}} \overset{|}{\underset{|}{C}}OH + \overset{Mg(OH)Cl}{\underset{LiOH}{\text{or}}}$$

This reaction is used primarily in the laboratory.

See C. R. Noller, *Chemistry of Organic Compounds,* 2nd ed. (1957); R. E. Kirk and D. F. Othmer (eds.), *Encyclopedia of Chemical Technology* (1947–56). (K. D. K.)

ALCOHOLIC BEVERAGES, DISTILLED, are variously described under terms such as spirits, distilled spirits, liquors, etc.; among English-speaking peoples they include brandy, gin, rum, whisky and vodka. The excise, duty or revenue imposed upon distilled alcoholic beverages by all governments constitutes such an important part of the income of most national treasuries that distilling throughout the world is a carefully supervised and regulated industry. In most countries it is conducted under direct control and supervision of government excise or treasury agents. No still may be built or operated without a licence; and these licences are always precarious in nature, being subject to immediate cancellation if the distiller should infringe or violate a regulation. All operations and installations are subject to inspection by government agents at any time. Other regulations affect the labeling of various beverages, prohibit adulteration, etc.

Distillation and Components.—The principle of alcoholic distillation is based upon the different boiling points of alcohol (78.3° C.) and water (100° C.). If an alcohol-containing liquid is heated to a temperature above 78.3° C. but below 100° C., the alcohol will vaporize and separate from the original liquid and can be gathered and recondensed into a liquid of much greater alcoholic strength. Similar but cruder separation results can be obtained by inverting the process; *i.e.*, by freezing the alcohol-

Congener Content of Six Types of Distilled Spirits

Ingredient	American blended whisky	Canadian blended whisky	Scotch blended whisky	Straight bourbon whisky	Bonded bourbon whisky	Cognac brandy
Total congeners (wt./vol. %) . .	0.116	0.085	0.160	0.292	0.309	0.239
	Grams per 100 liters at 100 proof					
Fusel oil . . .	83	58	143	203	195	193
Total acids (as acetic acid) . .	30	20	15	69	63	36
Esters (as ethyl acetate) .	17	14	17	56	43	41
Aldehydes (as acetaldehyde) . .	2.7	2.9	4.5	6.8	5.4	7.6
Furfural	0.33	0.11	0.11	0.45	0.90	0.67
Tannins	21	18	8	52	48	25
Total solids . . .	112	97	127	180	159	698

Reprinted by permission from *Quarterly Journal of Studies on Alcohol*, p. 71 (March 1958).

containing liquid. The water will commence to freeze out at a temperature below 0° C. and may be separated from the alcoholic solution whose freezing point will progressively fall toward −114° C., the freezing point of ethyl alcohol.

The major components of distilled alcoholic beverages are ethyl alcohol (C_2H_5OH) and water. The combination of these two substances alone does not produce an attractive beverage. It is from small quantities of more complex constituents that alcoholic beverages obtain their individual characters.

The minor constituents, termed congeners or congenerics, include higher alcohols, aldehydes, ethers, esters, volatile acids, furfural and other organic compounds, whose influence on the character, aroma and flavour of the beverage is out of all proportion to their quantities. As they are too great or too small, they invest the liquor with fuller or feebler flavour than may be desired.

The aim of the distiller has always been to produce a spirit of satisfactory strength with sufficient flavouring agents to yield a palatable product. The variance in congeneric content of several types of whiskies and Cognac brandy is illustrated in the table above.

Distilling in Antiquity.—The evaporation of the alcohol out of the various beers, wines and such liquors and its reclamation in liquid form gave rise to interesting developments in the forms of distilling apparatus. Originally a cool surface was held in the hot vapours from the boiling liquor and periodically cleared of the fluid which collected upon it. Pliny mentions the hanging of fleeces over boiling resin to collect turpentine, and Alexander of Aphrodisias records that sailors boiled sea water and collected sweet water by hanging sponges in the steam. This expedient seems to have been superseded, for the sake of more efficient collection, by the use of a bowl filled with cold water, from the outer surface of which the condensate dripped into a vessel within the still pot (Tibetan and Bhutan style) or into a tube which transferred it to an external receiver (according to Peruvian practice).

By leading the vapours from the still pot through a pipe into a receiving vessel where they condensed naturally, the Kalmuck Tatars made another evolutionary step; the Sinhalese in their warmer climate augmented the effectiveness of this arrangement by immersing the receiver in cold water. The natives of Tahiti sought to chill the vapours before they reached the receiver by cooling the connecting pipe, and so invented the precursor of the Dariot or Liebig condenser, which

FIG. 1.—ANCIENT FORM OF STILL USED IN TIBET

has in modern times been modified into many ingenious forms. The Alexandrians elaborated the primitive cold surface into a more complex still head, or alembic, with an annular gutter by which the distillate was led to an external receiver; the addition of supplementary water cooling to this head exemplifies the form of the Mysore still, which was reinvented in later years in the guise of Kodak and Sheldon condensers.

Modern Types of Still.—Simple pot stills constructed on the lines of the Tahiti model are used even now in France for brandy and in Scotland and Ireland for whisky, but the pot is usually

FIG. 2.—ANCIENT FORM OF STILL USED IN PERU

surmounted by a bulbous head or capital for the purposes of freeing the rising vapours from spray, which would contaminate the distillate, and of avoiding the risk of priming or blowing liquid over with the vapour. In some Irish installations, however, the still is connected to the condenser through a cooled lyne arm which partially condenses the less volatile components of the vapour, these being returned to the still pot while the more volatile substances pass on to the condenser. This is a primitive type of fractionator or rectifier. Some of the French brandy stills have a two-compartment bulbous vessel between the still and the condenser: one compartment contains the next charge to be transferred to the still; while in the other the less volatile substances are partially condensed, as in the lyne arm of the Irish still, but the heat lost by the vapour in becoming liquid is gained by the wine about to be run into the pot. This heat interchanger is an economizer of fuel. The pot stills used in the whisky distilleries of Scotland become more complicated, with two or more vessels between pot and condenser; they are retorts (the "eggs" of Eduard Adam's patent of 1801, inspired by the Woulfe bottle) or rectifiers, which return less volatile components to the pot and pass on the lighter fractions toward the condenser. These operate by virtue of the latent heat liberated by the steam during its condensation, evaporating spirit out of liquid which has already condensed. Wash heaters or heat interchangers are also incorporated.

The idea of the charge heater of the French brandy still is not modern, for a similar design appears in a publication by H. Braunschwick in 1512 (see fig. 6) the arrangement being shown as surmounting the boiler; it thus appears as the precursor of the modern refluxing fractionating column or still head which, in all its complicated modifications, is designed to give the maximum separation of volatile components in the course of a single operation. These improvements have been so effective that fractionating columns have become quite useful instruments in an analyst's equipment.

It is by an easy progression from the fractionating column, via the designs of Louis Charles Derosne, J. H. L. Pistorius and J. J. Saint-Marc, that Aeneas Coffey's and other patent stills were developed; these offer an efficiency in industrial operations which is unattainable on the laboratory scale so far as economical operation is concerned. The subject of Coffey's patent of 1831 consists of two towers that are essentially large-scale fractionating columns and heat interchangers (see fig. 7). The first tower, called the analyzer, may or may not surmount a boiler and is a fractionating column into which steam is blown at the bottom and the alcoholic liquor or wash injected near the top. The tower is packed with perforated plates through which the steam blows, preventing the wash from passing from one plate to the next below through the perforations; when any upper plate carries sufficient liquor, the excess flows through a short pipe standing in a cup which rests on the plate below. This serves both as weir and as an obstruction to the steam, which can then rise through the tower only by bubbling through successive layers of liquid. The heat evolved in the condensation of some of this steam evaporates or strips the alcohol out of the wash; and the mixed vapours pass to the base of the second tower, or rectifier, which contains an arrangement of plates similar to that of the analyzer and a pipe lying in sinuous coils between each pair of plates. This pipe serves two purposes: it acts both as a heat interchanger, by warming the wash which passes through on its way to the top of the analyzer; and as a cooler, by causing partial condensation of the vapours passing through the column. Finally, the vapour issuing from the top of the column is condensed as high-strength spirit containing few impurities and known as plain, neutral, silent, velvet or Cologne spirit. It is used to dilute other alcoholic drinks which are too highly flavoured, to prepare compounded spirits and to fortify weak wines; the rest of it finds an outlet in industry.

Much industrial equipment has an important peculiarity: a refrigerator, which usually has the form of a simple worm condenser, is interposed between the condenser proper and the receiver; its purpose is to complete condensation and to chill the distillate, so

FIG. 3.—STILL OF ANCIENT TYPE AS USED IN TAHITI

reducing the vapour pressure of the latter that loss by evaporation is minimized.

Origin.—The history of distilled beverages is obscure, but the following brief tabulation shows the origin of some of them:

Date	Country	Raw material	Fermented liquor	Distillate
—	China	Rice and millet	Tchoo	Sautchoo
800 B.C.	Ceylon and India	Rice and molasses or palm sap	Toddy	Arrack
—	Asiatic Tatary	Mare's milk	Kumiss	Arika
—	Caucasia	Mare's milk	Kefir	Skhou
—	Japan	Rice	Sake	Sochu
A.D. 500	Britain	Honey	Mead	Mead distilled
1000	Italy	Grapes	Wine	Brandy
1100	Ireland	Oats and barley malt	Beer	Usquebaugh
1200	Spain	Grapes	Wine	Aqua vini
1300	France	Grapes	Wine	Cognac
1500	Scotland	Malted barley	Beer	{ Aqua vitae { Whisky

In general, the raw material is a sugar such as is to be found in honey, ripe fruit, sugar cane, beetroot, milk or a substance of an amylaceous nature which may be easily converted into a sugar. Fortunately this change is simply effected, for some of the active agent is already present in cereals containing the necessary starch or is easily developed in them; where it is absent, as in potato starch, a suitable cereal can be added.

Action of Enzymes.—The active agents which break down

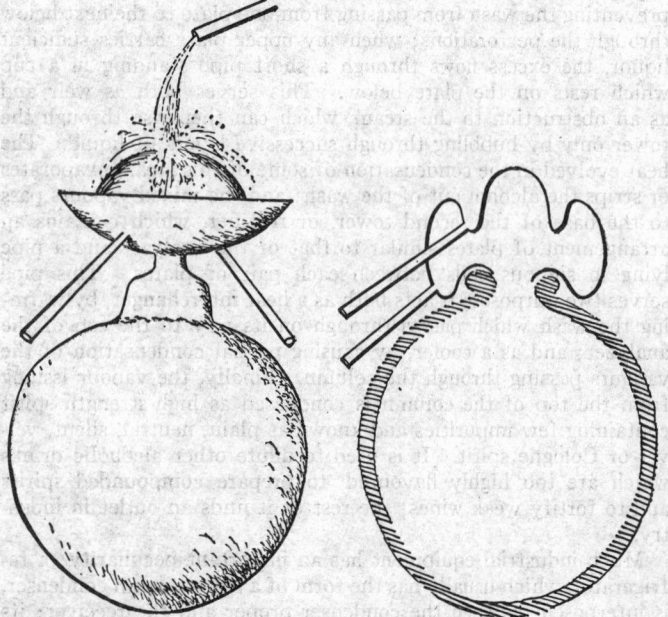

FIG. 4.—ANCIENT STILL USED IN SOUTHERN INDIA (MYSORE STILL)

starches into sugars and sugars into alcohol are known as enzymes; they are generally water-soluble nitrogenous compounds having something of the nature of albuminoids. They behave rather like catalysts in that a very little of them will cause a fundamental change in large quantities of the material being processed; they are easily poisoned by certain substances such as hydrocyanic acid, mercury salts and formalin, are sensitive to temperature variations (being rendered inactive in certain conditions), and are specific in action in that each is effective for certain classes of substance only. They convert complex insoluble material into simpler assimilable substances: the enzyme amylase, for instance, will reduce starch to dextrin and then to the sugar maltose; the enzyme maltase will reduce maltose to the simpler sugar dextrose; and, finally, the enzyme zymase will ferment the dextrose to alcohol and carbon dioxide. All of these changes take place easily in aqueous solution. The presence of amylase and maltase in cereals, particularly if germination has begun, and the presence of zymase in yeast ensure that all the necessary materials for the manufacture of spirit are readily and economically available. There are, of course, other enzymes—sucrase, present in yeast and malt, will break down cane sugar to invert sugar; lactase will hydrolyze milk sugar to simpler fermentable sugars; cytase will disintegrate cellulose; lipase will degrade fats, and so on.

Processing.—In the case of cereals, processing is begun by grinding the grain and heating it with water to gelatinize the starch and so form the mash. This is cooled to a temperature between 50° and 60° C. and saccharified by adding ground malt, a preparation obtained from a cereal such as barley which has been moistened, allowed to germinate, dried, kilned (over peat fires for Scotch whisky) and ground; in this meal there are sufficient amylase and maltase to break down not only the starch of the malted cereal but also that of the other amylaceous material. The liquid, now known as wort, is cooled to about 20° C. and pitched with yeast to initiate fermentation, a process which produces a wash ready for the stills.

Saccharine materials do not need the assistance of malt to prepare them for fermentation, and the simpler ones, such as honey and grape sugar, can be fermented without any preparation other than solution in water; but the more complex sugars, such as cane sugar (molasses), beet sugar and many fruit sugars, need to be simplified or inverted before the yeast can attack them. The enzyme effecting this change, invertase or sucrase, is fortunately present in yeast and malt, and its action can proceed simultaneously with fermentation.

Yeast, the fermenting agent, is a budding fungus or unicellular vegetable organism without chlorophyll belonging to the genus *Saccharomyces;* of its many kinds, those of interest to brewers and distillers are of the species *cerevisiae.* In this species there are many varieties that do not always contain the same enzymes and that behave differently toward various sugars. Charles Simmonds gives an interesting synopsis in his book *Alcohol.*

The whole story of yeasts and molds, their active principles and the manner of utilizing them, is a long and fascinating one that has occupied the attention of many investigators since the publication of the researches of Louis Pasteur (*q.v.*).

Maturing.—The wash or the wine is conducted to the stills where, in the case of the pot stills, two or more successive distillations are performed to produce a spirit of the desired strength; in the case of column- or patent-still distillates, the process is completed in one continuous operation. The resultant liquid is colourless and rather sharp or raw in aroma and taste, although the higher proof spirits distilled off at between 90% and 96% of alcohol are much less so. The lower the proof at which the spirit comes off the still, the higher its congeneric content will be, and for greater palatability, it must be matured.

Generally, distilled spirits mature best in barrels, casks or puncheons made of seasoned American white oak. Notable exceptions are cognac, which is aged in Limousin oak casks, and armagnac, aged in casks coopered from the black oak of Gascony. In the case of American straight whiskies, U.S. government regulations specify that the barrels must be new (unused) and charred internally. In other distilling centres the casks are not charred,

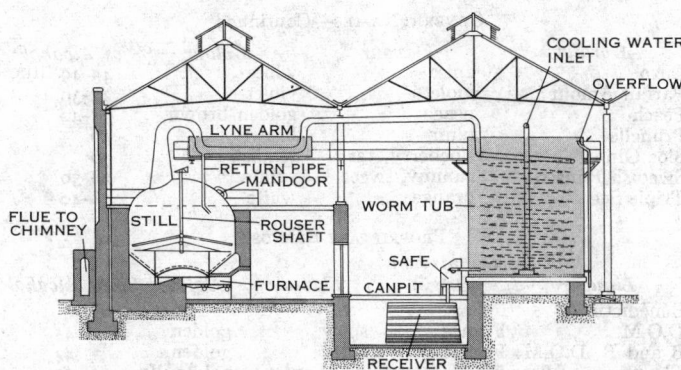

FIG. 5.—DIAGRAM OF SINGLE TYPE OF IRISH POT-STILL PLANT (JOHN JAMESON'S DISTILLERY, DUBLIN)

and casks that have previously been used to hold sherry or a spirit are preferred. When the liquid is barreled its alcoholic content is reduced by the addition of water. Barreling or filling strength practices vary from region to region. In the United States, whiskies are generally barreled at 103 proof (51½% alcohol); in Scotland, filling is usually at 124 proof (62% alcohol); while in Cognac the brandy is filled at 140 proof (70% alcohol), the proof at which it came off the still.

Maturing customs vary, but generally the barrels or casks are stored in warehouses where there will be no drafts and are placed in tiered racks that permit constant inspection for leakage. During the aging period marked changes occur in the liquid. The wood of the cask is sufficiently porous to permit air to penetrate, and at the same time to allow some of the liquid to escape through evaporation. In most cases more water is lost than alcohol, and the remaining alcohol proportion will be greater, i.e., the proof will increase, as occurs in American whiskies; in other cases, such as cognac, the reverse is true. At the same time other important changes take place among the secondary constituents. The volatile acids and the alcohols combine to produce an increased ester content, while the alcohols combine with air, primarily the oxygen, to form a larger quantity of aldehydes. The liquid also extracts tannins and additional furfural (which is an aldehyde) from the wood of the cask, acquiring colour meanwhile. The length of time required for optimum maturation varies with different distilled spirits. The lighter bodied spirits require less than the fuller bodied. Spirits mature more rapidly in a new charred oak barrel than in a re-used cask, and climatic conditions are still another determining factor. The minimum aging is two years but most aged spirits are matured in wood four years or more. If a spirit is kept in wood too long, it will absorb an excess of tannin and furfural and will acquire a sharp woody taste. Cognac brandy may be kept longer in wood than other distilled spirits, but it is

rarely kept over 50 years, and if kept that long it is periodically refreshed through additions of younger, fresher brandies. Distilled spirits do not mature in glass. Once bottled they will never become "older" than they are on the day of bottling.

Classification of Potable Spirits.—There are a number of classes of commercially produced distilled spirits:

Whisky (or whiskey) is a distilled spirit obtained from the distillation of a fermented mash of grain, suitably aged in wood. Whiskies are produced in many countries, but the principal ones, in order of importance, are the United States, Scotland, Canada and Ireland. It is spelled "whisky" in Scotland and Canada and "whiskey" in Ireland and the United States. U.S. whiskies are defined by government regulations as straight, bourbon, rye and blended whiskey. Scotch whisky is wholly a product of Scotland. Its distinctive peaty (smoky) taste is due to the use of peat to dry the freshly sprouted barley malt in open kilns and to the quality and character of the water found in Scotland. Irish whiskey is produced in a somewhat similar fashion, except that the malt is not kilned "in contact" with peat smoke, and the whiskey therefore has no peaty or smoky flavour. Canadian whisky distilling is similar to that of the U.S.

Vodka is an unaged distilled spirit, obtained from a fermented mash of any suitable raw material, filtered through vegetable charcoal and reduced to potable strength with water. In Russia and Poland more vodka is distilled from potatoes than from grain, but in the United States (the next largest market) practically all vodka is distilled from a fermented grain mash. The distilled spirit for vodka comes off at a very high proof, over 190 in the United States; this together with charcoal filtration assures a beverage "without distinctive character, aroma or taste."

Rum (Spanish *ron*, French *rhum*) is any distilled spirit obtained from fermented sugar-cane juice or its molasses. Wherever sugar cane grows a rum is distilled, almost always as the by-product of sugar manufacture. Rums can be classified into three basic groups: the dry, light-bodied, brandylike rums best exemplified by those of Puerto Rico and Cuba (rums of this type are also produced in Mexico, Brazil, Argentina and Paraguay); the rich, full-bodied, pungent rums such as those of Jamaica, Barbados, Demerara (British Guiana), etc.; and the brandylike but very aromatic rummy Batavia Arak from Java in Indonesia. In between are the brandylike yet full-flavoured Haitian and Martinique rums.

Brandy is a potable distilled spirit obtained from wine or a fermented mash of fruit, usually suitably aged in wood. The use of the term brandy by itself is generally accepted to mean grape brandy, i.e., the distillate of wine; the universally accepted preeminent brandy is that of Cognac, France. Other fruit brandies are distilled from the fermented mash of apples, plums, cherries, apricots, etc. In general these brandies are marketed and better known under specific names.

Slivovitz is the generic term employed to describe the plum brandy which is the national beverage of Hungary, Rumania and Yugoslavia, but the plum brandies of Alsace derive their names from the variety of plum used; i.e., Quetsch or Mirabelle. Hungary's Barat Palinka is a brandy obtained from the fine-flavoured Hungarian apricot. All of these brandies are matured in wood, are golden-brown in colour and possess the distinctive aroma of the fruit.

The cherry brandy which is called kirsch in France and kirschwasser in Germany and Switzerland, the three principal regions of production, is obtained from a small black cherry found in the Rhine basin. It is always colourless and is not aged. It possesses a fine clean cherry aroma and flavour, together with a slight bitter-almond undertone derived from the cherry stones which are partly crushed and remain in the mash during fermentation. For the same reason the bitter-almond undertone is characteristic of slivovitz, Barat Palinka and other fruit brandies, except apple brandy.

Other Distilled Spirits.—Tequila, the national distilled spirit of Mexico, is obtained from the heart-sap of the genus *Agave* of the amaryllis family, a cactus also known as the century plant or American aloe, termed *mezcal* (mescal) in Mexico. Both unaged

FIG. 6.—DESIGN FOR DISTILLING APPARATUS FROM BRAUNSCHWICK'S DAS BUCH ZU DISTILLIEREN (1512)

and four-year-old tequila are marketed at 86 to 100 proof in Mexico and the United States.

Okolehao or "oke" is an exotic Hawaiian contribution to distilled spirits. It is a distillate obtained from the fermented mash of the proper proportion of sugar-cane molasses, Koji rice lees and the juice of baked tiroot, to which water has been added. (Tiroot is the root of the taro or kalo plant—*Colocasia antiquorum*. It is also from tiroot that Hawaiians make one of their favourite foods, poi.) *Okolehao* is matured for several years in charred oak barrels and marketed at 80 or 90 proof. It is dark in colour and has a smoky aroma and flavour imparted by the baked tiroot. White *okolehao* is also produced by using coconut milk in place of tiroot and aging in uncharred barrels. It is almost colourless.

Ng ka py (whisky in Chinese) is a distilled spirit obtained from a fermented mash of millet, with various aromatic herbs added. It is slightly sweetened and has an aromatic aroma and flavour. *Ng ka py* is aged in wood and generally marketed at 96 proof.

Flavoured Spirits.—In the family of distilled spirits the next most important group is that which embraces the flavoured spirits, notably gin, aquavit, absinthe, zubrovka, etc. They are all obtained by redistilling a spirit in the presence of the flavouring agent or agents. Gin is the most universally produced and used. The primary flavouring of gin is the juniper berry, although many other "botanicals" are also used to lend subtle nuances of aroma and flavour.

The national distilled spirit beverage of the Scandinavian countries is aquavit or *akvavit*, which is produced in the same manner as gin. High-proof potato spirits are redistilled in the presence of the flavouring agents, the selection of which varies from one country to the other but which always includes caraway and cumin seeds. Danish *akvavit* is colourless and has the most pronounced caraway flavour, while the Norwegian and Swedish versions have a straw colour and sweeter spicier taste, and the Finnish variety has a cinnamon flavour. Scandinavian aquavits are marked at 83 to 90 proof.

Liqueurs.—Finally in the family of distilled spirits there is the group of brightly coloured, fragrantly flavoured and richly sweetened liqueurs or cordials. They were developed originally during the middle ages by physicians and alchemists as medicinal remedies, love potions, aphrodisiacs and general cure-alls. Through the centuries they have been known as elixirs, oils, balms, and ratafias as well as liqueurs and cordials. The variety of colours, flavours and combinations thereof is limitless; the one factor that makes them cordials is their sugar content. Under U.S. regulations a cordial must contain more than 2½% of sugar, but all cordials contain considerably more. They are divided into two groups: those with generic names, produced in all parts of the world; and those with proprietary brand names, which are produced by the trade-mark owner, such as Bénédictine or Chartreuse, and are made only at their places of origin. The list given below indicates the name, flavour, usual colour and alcoholic content of some of the better known cordials:

GENERIC NAMES

Cordial	Flavour	Colour	% of Alcohol*
Anisette	anise	white	27
Anis	anise	white	39-48
Apricot	apricot	brown	30
Blackberry	blackberry	dark-red	30
Cherry	cherry	bright red	30-32
Crème de Cacao	chocolate, vanilla	brown or white	25-27
Crème de Cassis	sweet currant	red	12-25
Crème de Framboises	raspberry	red	30
Crème de Menthe	mint	green, white, pink	30
Crème de Roses	roses	rose	30
Crème de Vanille	vanilla	brown	30
Crème de Violettes	violet	violet	30
Curaçao	orange	orange	30-42
Danziger Goldwasser	orange-spicy	white	38
Kümmel	caraway	white	39-46
Maraschino	cherry	white	30-32
Ojen	anise	white	42

GENERIC NAMES—Continued

Cordial	Flavour	Colour	% of Alcohol*
Ouzo	anise	white	45-49
Parfait Amour	violet	violet	27-30
Peach	peach	golden-brown	35-40
Prunelle	plum	brown	40
Sloe Gin	sloeberry, tart	reddish	30
Swedish Punsch	rummy, sweet	yellow	28-30
Triple Sec	orange	white	38-40

PROPRIETARY BRANDS

Liqueur	Country of Origin	Flavour	Colour	% of Alcohol
Bénédictine, D.O.M.	France	spicy	golden	43
B and B, D.O.M.	France	spicy	golden	43
Chartreuse yellow	France	spicy-anise	gold-yellow	43
Chartreuse green	France	spicy-licorice	green	55
Cherry Heering	Denmark	cherry	cherry-red	24½
Cordial Medoc	France	orange-cocoa	brown	44
Cointreau	France	orange	white	40
Crème Yvette	United States	violet	violet	33
Drambuie	Scotland	spicy-Scotch	golden	40
Falernum	Barbados	lime-almond	white	6
Forbidden Fruit	United States	orange-grapefruit	orange	35
Galliano	Italy	spicy	golden	40
Grand Marnier	France	orange	orange-red	40
Gilka Kümmel	Germany	caraway	white	43
Irish Mist	Ireland	spicy-honey	golden	40
Liqueur d'Or	France	spicy-lemon	light gold	43
Strega	Italy	spicy	light gold	42½
Tia Maria	Jamaica	coffee	brown	31½
Vieille Curé	France	spicy	golden	43

*Note: In the United States, the alcoholic strength of these beverages is always expressed in degrees proof, each of which is equal to ½ of 1%; therefore, 27% of alcohol is 54 proof.

For more detailed discussions of the different classes see the articles BRANDY; GIN; LIQUEURS; RUM; VODKA; and WHISKY. There are also articles on several of the liqueurs—BÉNÉDICTINE, D.O.M.; CHARTREUSE; etc.

General Properties of Distilled Beverages.—Apart from aroma, which is usually caused by small quantities, even traces, of strongly flavoured secondaries, essences or extracts, the general properties of distilled beverages are those of aqueous solutions of ethyl alcohol, a colourless mobile liquid with a slightly higher

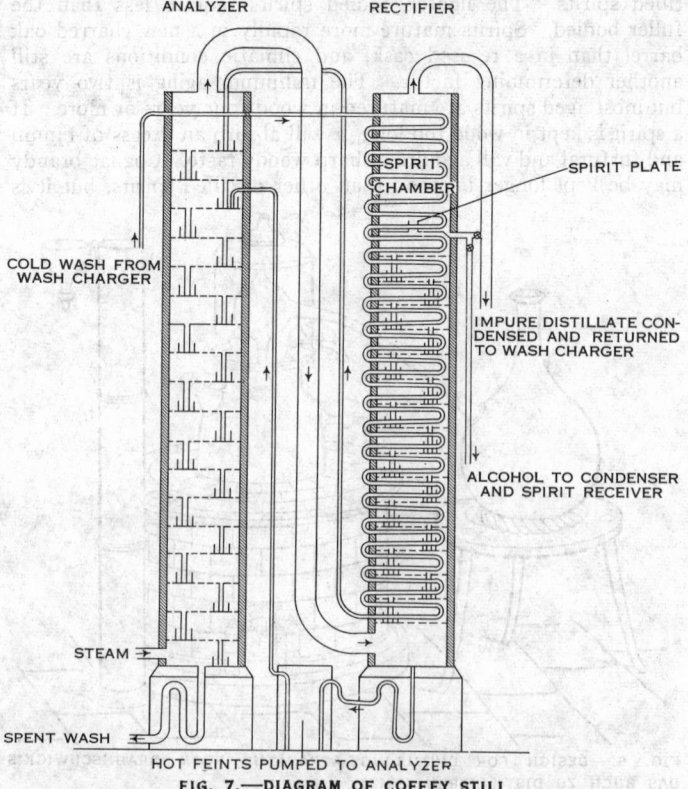

FIG. 7.—DIAGRAM OF COFFEY STILL

viscosity but a lower surface tension and a much lower electrical conductivity than water. It is neutral in character, but can act either as a base, by combining with acids to form esters or ethereal salts; or as an acid, by combining with strongly basic metals to produce ethylates. It can burn in air with a blue nonluminous flame and is decomposable in the absence of air at high temperatures, particularly in the presence of catalysts such as powdered aluminum, zinc dust, reduced nickel, thoria or alumina, releasing hydrocarbons and other simple compounds. On the other hand, contact with strong oxidants will result in the formation of aldehyde, acetic acid and even of carbon dioxide and water. Absolute alcohol is hygroscopic and miscible with water in all proportions, with an accompanying evolution of heat and a contraction in total volume that is most noticeable when 52 volumes of alcohol are mixed with 48 volumes of water at 20° C., to yield 96.3 volumes when temperature is restored to 20° again. Specific heat is about $\frac{2}{3}$, and thermal expansibility $5\frac{1}{2}$ times that of water at 20° C.; these characteristics, coupled with the possession of a low freezing point (−114° C.), render the liquid a suitable filling for certain ranges of thermometers. The boiling point of alcohol is 78.3° C.; heat of vaporization is only about $\frac{2}{11}$ of that of water; vapour pressure at ordinary temperatures is about $2\frac{1}{2}$ times as great: these facts are reflected in the relatively easy separation of alcohol from water by fractional distillation—up to a certain limit—and in the lesser known data of flash points. According to von Schwartz, the following temperatures may be taken as a guide to the flash points of various alcoholic liquors:

Ethyl alcohol 100%	10.6° C.
Ethyl alcohol 95%	13.9° C.
Rum, arrack and cognac	25° C.
Whisky	27.8° C.
Hollands gin	31.7° C.
Sherry and port wine	53.9° C.

These temperatures must be regarded with a certain amount of reserve, since they are dependent upon spirit strength, which has a considerable range of variation in each type of beverage. Aqueous mixtures at any given pressure boil at various temperatures, according to the alcohol content, but the lowest boiling point is that of a solution containing 4.43% of water, the mixture of constant boiling point; i.e., 79.15° C. at 760 mm. as against 78.35° C. for pure alcohol. This is an azeotropic mixture—one which distils at a constant temperature lower than the boiling points of its components, without change of composition, when the pressure is kept constant. Constitution varies with pressure, and at pressures below 70 mm. of mercury the alcohol-water azeotrope does not exist; it is therefore possible to obtain absolute alcohol by vacuum fractional distillation, although in practice the separation is not easily effected because of the small difference between the boiling points of the absolute and aqueous alcohols. The spirit produced from wash by any simple distillation process at ordinary atmospheric pressures can never be pure alcohol; but the latter may be obtained by drying out the water with powerful dehydrating agents before a final distillation, by vacuum fractional distillation or by adding to the aqueous alcohol a sufficient quantity of another liquid, such as benzene, or a chlorohydrocarbon to form a triple azeotrope boiling at a still lower temperature and fractionating. In this instance, first the triple azeotrope containing the undesired water, and then a double azeotrope containing the excess of the added substances are eliminated, leaving absolute alcohol as a residue or final distillate.

Mixtures of alcohol and water have values intermediate between those of the pure components for some of their physical characteristics, such as vicosity, heat of vaporization, specific heat, thermal expansion, vapour pressure, electrical conductivity, boiling point, refractive index and specific gravity. Although the variations may not be strictly proportional to the amount of alcohol present, they are nevertheless generally progressive for certain ranges, if not right through the scale of concentrations. This fact has provided some convenient physical means of determining spirit strength, and it is common practice to derive such information from the specific gravity. Provided that the liquid is free, or has been freed by distillation, from saccharine and other

matter which would interfere, the specific gravity is determined by immersing in it a hydrometer which may be graduated: (1) in terms of specific gravity; (2) with arbitrary scales (Great Britain, U.S.S.R.); (3) in percentages by volume of alcohol (Belgium, France, Italy, Norway, Spain, Sweden); (4) in percentages by weight of alcohol (Germany); (5) in percentages by volume of proof spirit (U.S.); and (6) with a scale based upon fractions of the volume of the instrument (Netherlands). In all cases these instruments are calibrated at standard temperatures; when the liquid to be tested is cooler or warmer (as it usually is), reference is made to tables to ascertain the true value for the spirit at the standard temperature.

Spirit strength may be designated in several ways—percentage by weight, weight per gallon, gallons per hundredweight or percentage by volume, all these having reference to absolute alcohol and water. But there are other standards in common use; e.g., U.S. proof spirit, which is 50% by volume of alcohol and water, and British proof spirit, which is of such a strength that at 51° F. its weight is $\frac{12}{13}$ of an equal volume of water; this solution contains 49.28% by weight or 57.10% by volume of alcohol at 60° F. The subject of alcoholometry is comprehensively described in Simmonds' *Alcohol*. See also ALCOHOL.

BIBLIOGRAPHY.—P. Duplais, *A Treatise on the Manufacture and Distillation of Alcoholic Liquors*, trans. and ed. by M. McKennie (1871); W. T. Brandt, *Practical Treatise on Distillation and Rectification of Alcohol*, 2nd ed. (1904); H. W. Wiley, *Beverages and Their Adulteration* (1919); *Report of Royal Commission on Whisky*, Cd. 4796, H.M.S.O. (1909); A. Harden, *Alcoholic Fermentation*, 3rd ed. (1923); R. Dodge and F. G. Benedict, *Psychological Effects of Alcohol* (1915); V. A. H. Horsley and M. D. Sturge, *Alcohol and the Human Body* (1915); Charles Simmonds, *Alcohol* (1919); Sydney Young et al., *Distillation Principles and Processes* (1922); Joseph Reilly, *Distillation* (1936); C. S. Robinson and E. R. Gilliland, *Elements of Fractional Distillation* (1939); R. Delamain, *Histoire du Cognac* (1935); W. B. Dick, *Encyclopedia of Practical Receipts and Processes* (1872); Edward R. Emerson, *Beverages, Past and Present* (1908); Philip Gee, *Scotch Whisky* (1957); Harold J. Grossman, *Grossman's Guide to Wines, Spirits and Beers*, rev. ed. (1955); Sir Robert Lockhart, *Scotch* (1951); Aeneas McDonald, *Whisky* (1934); W. H. Smith and F. C. Helwig, *Liquor, the Servant of Man* (1939); M. B. Jacobs (ed.), *The Chemistry and Technology of Food and Food Products*, vol. iii, ch. 5 (1951).

(R. Su.; H. J. Gn.)

ALCOHOLISM, better called chronic alcoholism, is a disease in which a person has an uncontrollable desire for alcohol. Once his craving is triggered he begins to drink steadily and excessively. A state of physiological dependence exists, and the true alcoholic may be considered to be addicted to alcohol. Not all persons who drink regularly or even excessively are alcoholics. Most drinkers, even including some who drink regularly or even to excess occasionally, are not addicted and are able to give up alcohol at will.

Chronic alcoholics are of two types, the spree drinker and the steady drinker. The spree drinker alternates periods of sobriety with periods, lasting for days or weeks, of drunkenness. The steady drinker consumes too much alcohol every day.

Alcohol (see ETHYL ALCOHOL), in moderate doses, is useful in relieving anxiety. On the other hand, alcohol addiction is an important public health problem in most Western countries.

Physiological Action of Alcohol.—After an alcoholic beverage is ingested it is rapidly absorbed in the gastrointestinal tract (stomach and intestines), because it does not undergo any digestive processes; thus, alcohol rises to high levels in the blood in a relatively short time. From the blood the alcohol is distributed to all parts of the body. It is absorbed until an equilibrium is attained between the alcohol in the blood and that in the various organs. Considerably more time is required to eliminate alcohol from the bloodstream. Some alcohol is still present in the bloodstream 18 hours after ingestion. This discrepancy between rapid absorption and slow removal is an important factor in determining the maximal level of alcohol in the blood (blood alcohol). It assures a relatively long stay of alcohol in the body, during which time it continues to exert its characteristic actions. The degree of intoxication reflects to a certain extent the concentration of alcohol in the blood.

The presence of food in the gut slows the rate of absorption of alcohol, and it is well known that alcohol exerts a greater effect when consumed on an empty stomach. All foodstuffs, however, are not equally effective in impeding absorption. Milk (actually the fat contained) and meat (protein) are particularly potent in this regard. The diminished degree of intoxication that results when alcohol is consumed with or after food must be imputed largely to the reduction of its maximum concentration in the blood and therefore in the brain. Though the amount of alcohol finally absorbed may be the same, the peak concentration is lower and occurs later.

Slow rate of drinking also reduces the maximal level of alcohol in the blood by slowing absorption. Dilution also influences the blood alcohol level. When the percentage of alcohol in a beverage is small, the amount of alcohol per volume of absorbed fluid is correspondingly low. On the other hand, in high concentration the irritating effects of alcohol on the lining of the gastrointestinal tract diminish absorption. Taking into consideration all the data, the most rapid rate of removal from the gastrointestinal tract occurs when alcohol is imbibed in 10% to 30% dilutions, in wines and highballs. For equal volumes of alcohol, beer (with dilutions ranging from 1% to 7½%) and neat whisky (43% to 53%) are less intoxicating than wines and highballs with alcohol in 20% dilution. When alcohol is taken in carbonated fluids the rate of absorption of the alcohol is increased, because carbon dioxide stimulates gastric motility, which hastens the passage of alcohol into the intestine, where its absorption is much more rapid than in the stomach. As for mixed drinks, the total effect depends primarily on the volume of alcohol ingested: the reputed increased intoxication occurring with mixed drinks may be ascribed, in large part, to their nonalcoholic constituents, which add to their untoward aftereffects.

Drinking while under the influence of barbiturates is hazardous. The depressant effects of this combination are not simply additive but greater than their sum taken individually, and there is correspondingly greater danger when excessive doses of either or both are taken together.

Social setting is important. When one is drinking alone, alcohol seems to be less intoxicating than in the presence of stimulating company; e.g., at a cocktail party. This may be illusory, however, for it is difficult to distinguish the effects of alcohol from the effects of exciting company.

Oxidation.—During the time when alcohol is being absorbed, metabolic factors are initiated that tend also to diminish its concentration; they continue to function until all alcohol is removed. A relatively small amount of alcohol, at most 10%, is eliminated in the urine, in the breath, and in perspiration. The remainder, 90%, is consumed in the body by oxidation. The rate of oxidation is slow, however: approximately one ounce of whisky per hour. There is some doubt as to whether the rate of oxidation is constant or whether the rate is slightly faster when the concentration is higher and somewhat slower as the concentration diminishes. But the central fact that the rate of combustion is slow, alcohol remaining in the body for a long period, is undisputed.

The process of oxidation yields carbon dioxide, water, and heat to the extent of seven calories for each gram of alcohol oxidized. Hence it must be regarded as a food which, in this sense, can take the place of carbohydrate, fat, or protein. There are three chief steps in the oxidation process: (1) the combustion of alcohol, chiefly in the liver, producing acetaldehyde, a chemical that appears in the blood only after alcohol is ingested; (2) the oxidation of acetaldehyde to acetic acid, taking place not only in the liver but in other organs as well; and (3) oxidation of the acetic acid to carbon dioxide and water, a reaction that takes place readily throughout the body.

At least two important peculiarities of alcohol combustion make it different from most other foodstuffs. Chiefly because of its slow rate of oxidation, limited mainly by the capacity of the liver, not more than 300 g. of alcohol can be oxidized in a single day. Such a caloric yield (2,100 calories) is sufficient for a sedentary person, but activity increases the energy need, and a person performing physical work could not live on alcohol, since the amount oxidized cannot be raised above the level of approximately 300 g. per day.

A second characteristic of alcohol as a food is that it is devoid of such dietary elements as vitamins, essential amino acids, essential fatty acids, and minerals. As a matter of fact, too-exclusive reliance on alcohol for calories results in a number of deficiency diseases which may complicate the course of alcoholism (*see* below).

Alcoholic Intoxication.—Since there is an equilibrium between the alcohol in the blood and that in the brain, it might be expected that there would be some relationship between the blood alcohol concentration and mental changes. To gauge the degree of intoxication by the symptoms alone is unsatisfactory, and even physicians fail to agree when using such a basis. Laboratory tests to determine the alcohol content in the blood afford an objective measurement of the severity of intoxication. Blood alcohol also can be estimated indirectly by its concentrations in the urine, saliva, or exhaled air in accordance with the following ratios:

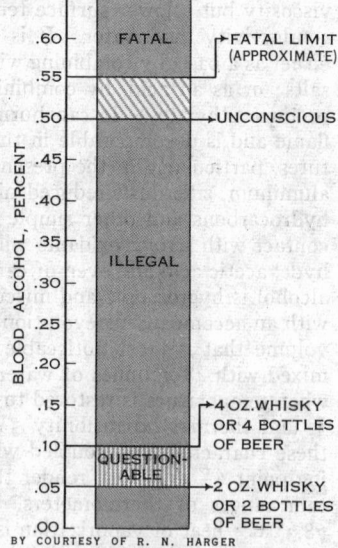

BY COURTESY OF R. N. HARGER

BLOOD ALCOHOL AS RELATED TO DRIVING (PERCENTAGE IN A PERSON WEIGHING 150 LB.)

Urine : blood :: 1.20–1.30 : 1
Saliva : blood :: 1.3 : 1
Alveolar air : blood :: 1: 2,100

The urine and saliva contain slightly higher concentrations of alcohol per given volume of fluid than does the blood, whereas air from the lungs (alveolar air) contains much less per given volume. Tests for mental impairment and muscular coordination show that abstainers and moderate drinkers exhibit undesirable changes when the levels of alcohol in the blood are between 0.05 and 0.1%, and even heavy drinkers habituated or accustomed to alcohol may show disabilities with values above 0.1%. Intoxication becomes obvious when the blood alcohol rises above 0.15%.

The American Medical Association and the National Safety Council made recommendations which in general indicate that persons with concentrations of less than 0.05% of alcohol in the blood should not be regarded as under the influence of alcohol. The interpretation of alcohol levels in the blood is necessarily questionable between the blood levels of 0.05 and 0.10% because the phenomena of tolerance and habituation must be taken into consideration in relation to the impairment of judgment and performance. Tolerance depends upon individual susceptibility or resistance to alcohol, and is inherent. Habituation differs from tolerance in that it is acquired by practice; there is good evidence that it is an adaptive change whereby the brain reacts to alcohol to a lesser degree as a result of previous exposure.

Blood alcohol values of 0.10% or more can be taken as legal evidence that the person is under the influence of alcohol. The accompanying diagram shows the volumes of whisky or beer necessary to produce levels of 0.05 and 0.10% respectively in a person weighing 150 lb. (68 kg.). In order to attain in the blood the amount of alcohol contained in four ounces of whisky it is necessary to have imbibed slightly over five ounces of whisky, because of the various processes, described above, that act to remove alcohol from the body.

The earlier standard of 0.15% as indicating the level of alcohol in the blood at which a person is considered a definite hazard on the road was too high. Actual field tests in automobiles and by laboratory experiments, however, led the National Safety Council to recommend that the standard be reduced to 0.10%, *i.e.*, a person having a blood alcohol level of 0.10% or higher should be considered under the influence of alcohol and therefore a dangerous driver. This standard, long accepted by many European countries, has now been generally adopted in many states of the U.S.

In the U.S., unlike some other countries, the drawing of blood samples from persons suspected of intoxication has met with resistance. There are, however, various devices (Alcometer, Breathalyzer, Drunkometer, Intoximeter, etc.) for the rapid analysis of alcohol in the breath, and apparently this method is more acceptable. The analysis depends on securing an entire sample of expired air or the last portion of it. Once the alcoholic content of the air is determined—usually in ten minutes or less—the alcohol content of the blood can be calculated in accordance with the ratio mentioned above.

Drug Action.—The above discussion reveals that alcohol in excess has a pronounced effect on the mind in terms of altering behaviour. It exerts a depressant action on the brain; it muffles the mind. It therefore belongs to the group of depressant drugs, of which ether and the barbiturates are representative. Under the influence of alcohol the functions of the brain are depressed in a characteristic pattern. The so-called higher or more complex functions rather than the semiautomatic ones are affected first (for example, a stenographer under the influence of alcohol may type at her usual speed but the errors become more numerous). The most complex actions of the brain—judgment, self-criticism, the inhibitions learned from earliest childhood—are thus depressed first, and the loss of this control results in a feeling of excitement in the early stages. For this reason, alcohol is sometimes thought of, erroneously, as a stimulant. Under the influence of increasing amounts of alcohol the drinker gradually becomes less alert, awareness of his environment becomes dim and hazy, muscular coordination deteriorates, and sleep is facilitated.

Finally, with increasing effects of alcohol, even the vital centres—those which control pulmonary ventilation, heart rate, and blood pressure—become impaired. If medical treatment is not initiated, death due to respiratory failure and shock associated with low blood pressure is imminent.

Ether exerts a similar graded pattern of depression. It can be used as an anesthetic because of the wide dosage margin between the depression of the higher activities of the brain and the lower vital ones. With large amounts of alcohol the depression of the vital centres occurs at doses relatively close to the lethal dose.

Causes of Alcoholism.—The stupor and forgetfulness which result from excessive doses of alcohol can become desired ends for the confirmed addict. But the earlier comforting action of alcohol which is sought by the inexperienced drinker is the depression of the higher centres and the reduction of anxiety. Occasionally an unpalatable compromise must be accepted. The discomfort accompanying such situations can be effectively allayed, temporarily, by alcohol. A drink or two before going to sleep can bring relief from useless and painful reviews of the day's events. This comforting action of alcohol is noted in the New Testament, where St. Paul advises Timothy, "No longer drink only water, but use a little wine for the sake of your stomach and your frequent ailments" (I Tim. 5: 23). The great physician William Osler said, "Alcohol does not make people do things better, it makes them less ashamed of doing them badly." Self-criticism is removed, self-doubt is eliminated, and inhibitions are stilled. When alcohol is used to the exclusion of other more realistic means to meet life situations, however, when the person relies on alcohol alone to relieve his anxiety and does not assay more appropriate methods of overcoming his difficulties, he starts a trend which under certain circumstances can lead to chronic alcoholism.

There must be additional contributing factors in the production of alcoholism, however, since many persons who drink regularly never become addicts. One of these factors is a personality characteristic in which a person has less than average tolerance for the anxiety caused, for example, by frustration or criticism. This type of person has a stronger push to recourse to alcohol than have others who are less sensitive.

There are also certain psychotic persons who can achieve reasonably satisfactory relations with others only through the aid of alcohol; though his difficulties may be imaginary, they are very real and compelling to the person who has them, and by blunting his mind he can effect a better rapport with those around him. With this aid, for example, a schizophrenic can make a marginal adjustment to the demands of society and even, in a small way, make a contribution to it. Such a person can fall a victim to

alcoholism more easily than can a person who is not psychotic.

The discussion of personality characteristics predisposing to alcoholism leads to an examination of the heredity factor. It has been suggested that individuals may inherit metabolic patterns (*e.g.*, impaired glucose metabolism or unusually large requirements for vitamins) which result in nutritional deficiencies that in turn give rise to a craving for alcohol. Other evidence does not support this viewpoint. Many alcoholics do have an alcoholic parent, and the normal expectancy of alcoholism is vastly higher among children of alcoholic parents as compared with the general population. But in a study in which 36 children of alcoholic parents were separated from the true parents and reared by nonalcoholic foster parents, none of the children became alcoholics. Such observations suggest that heredity alone cannot account for the choice of alcoholism as a way of escape from life's difficulties. Environmental influences seem much more important.

The accepted customs of the society in which a person lives have a strong influence on the attitude toward alcohol. For example, in the United States women are brought up to regard drunkenness more seriously than do males, and American male alcoholics outnumber women by five to six times. In a group that frowns on drunkenness, even though its members may frequently use alcohol in many forms, alcoholism may be practically unknown. One such group is represented by the Orthodox Jews, among whom drinking is used to draw the family together, to facilitate other interpersonal relationships and as part of the religious rituals. In this group drinking is not associated with strong emotion. There are no movements for total abstinence, and drunken parties are equally unknown. Violators of the rules followed by this group are punished in one way or another, and persons who succumb to drunkenness are scorned. In contrast, there are other groups among whom disapproval is applied irregularly and who drink together for fun, to escape from social pressures rather than as, in the preceding group, in conformity with accepted standards. Drinking may then be attended by a feeling of guilt, and may be exhibitionist or carried out secretly. In such groups alcoholism is not rare. Still others (for example, the Mormons) forbid alcohol, and usually it is an outcast who yields to drunkenness, which is regarded as immoral.

It must also be realized that the immediate cause of alcoholism is not known. The use of alcohol does not necessarily induce alcohol addiction. In the United States less than 10% of drinkers become alcoholics. Similarly all persons are subject to anxiety, but only a few succumb to alcoholism. Even in groups which tolerate drunken episodes, only 3% to 7% of users become addicts. Why one person in a setting favourable to alcoholism remains untouched while a second succumbs, and why others in similar situations develop ulcers of the stomach or become schizophrenic, cannot be explained.

Nature of Addiction.—Some of the mechanisms which trap the alcoholic and maintain his addiction are known, however, as is the fact that an addicted drinker is a changed person, both psychologically and physiologically.

Physiologic.—For the alcoholic, alcohol has become a necessity; it has assumed the characteristics of a food, and he is worse off without it than with it. There has occurred a profound change in the cells of his body, which have become adapted to alcohol and operate poorly in its absence.

This physiological change is evidenced by the fact that withdrawal of alcohol from the addict produces grave disturbances which affect not only the patient but those around him. In contrast, the nonaddicted drinker can stop drinking at any time without ill effects. The more moderate signs and symptoms seen after an addict is deprived of alcohol include an intense craving for it, weakness, tremor, perspiration, and an increase in anxiety (the last caused partly by the other withdrawal symptoms). The alcoholic deprived of his potion characteristically has the "shakes," or becomes tremulous, and a few drinks usually eliminate this symptom. More grave results of withdrawal are nausea and vomiting, fever and rapid heart rate, convulsions and hallucinations. Delirium tremens combines several of these withdrawal symptoms, including loss of awareness of the environment as well as an impairment of insight or understanding of the situation. Delirium tremens can also occur during a drinking bout (*see* DELIRIUM).

Continued excessive drinking produces a number of disagreeable physical symptoms that add to the alcoholic's anxiety and call for additional drinking. The lining of the stomach and intestines becomes inflamed so that food is not easily digested. Furthermore, morning nausea renders any food unpalatable, and the alcoholic therefore may take two or three drinks on arising in order to overcome his nausea and anxiety. With the loss of essential dietary constituents the alcoholic begins to show signs of food deficiencies.

His nerves, particularly those in his legs, may undergo degeneration, giving rise to pain and weakness. The liver suffers severe changes, grouped by physicians under the term cirrhosis. The organ is enlarged, the person's skin darkens as he becomes jaundiced, the abdominal cavity swells as it fills with fluid. Sometimes the patient dies in a coma as a result of failure of liver function. He suffers severe headaches, dizziness, nausea and vomiting, the well-known hangover symptoms. These symptoms are partly due to gastritis, or inflammation of the lining of the stomach, but they are also a direct effect of alcohol on the inner ear, the part of that organ that aids in regulating the equilibrium of the body. The characteristic thirst is ascribed to loss of fluids through perspiration, urination, and vomiting.

Psychologic.—While the alcoholic is undergoing these changes in his body he passes also through a series of behavioural patterns. At first, he utilizes alcohol for its anxiety-relieving action only occasionally. Later he imposes on alcohol for more continuous relief, and drinks daily. At this time he must drink greater quantities as he becomes habituated. Then he may become subject to blackouts, exhibiting a complete loss of memory in the morning for what he said or did the previous evening. He drinks surreptitiously and avidly. He is overcome with guilt feelings in regard to his drinking and avoids reference to alcohol in his conversation. Finally there is loss of self-control, and any drinking starts a chain reaction of further drinking based on intense craving. By now he is under severe pressure from his wife, his business employer, and his friends to reduce his drinking, and he seeks a series of alibis to explain it. Sometimes, in remorse, he has periods of total abstinence. Finally, he may become a confirmed alcoholic. He drops his friends, quits his job, and goes on prolonged binges. He suffers ethical deterioration and impairment of thinking, and even may become psychotic (*see* PSYCHOSES); at this time he may lose some of his tolerance and habituation to alcohol.

The alcoholic may also suffer mental deterioration, though degeneration of the brain probably is caused by the imperfect diet and is not a primary effect of alcohol. There is a growing incapacity for sustained attention, and memory as well as other mental functions become impaired. The alcoholic becomes careless of his personal appearance and neglectful of his family. Social responsibility disappears. Usually he is in carefree good humour, but any reproof may evoke a violent outburst of irritability. He is occasionally brutal, surly, and without shame.

Treatment.—*Acute Alcoholic Poisoning.*—Treatment of a patient suffering from acute alcoholic poisoning—that is, a drunken episode—is divided into two stages. For the earlier excitement, sedatives such as tranquilizing drugs or barbiturates (*qq.v.*) are used. The more dangerous deeper stage of coma, or alcohol anesthesia, is a serious medical emergency caused by the excessive presence of alcohol in the body. Treatment to speed up the elimination of alcohol is therefore required. It is impossible to administer medication by mouth to a patient in coma; it must be injected into the veins. Glucose, with or without insulin, fructose, amino acids, and vitamins may speed the combustion of alcohol. These substances are injected intravenously in saline fluids which the dehydrated patient sorely needs.

Delirium Tremens.—This is another acute episode in which tranquilizers and intravenous medications are necessary treatment. Most U.S. psychiatrists believe that in the treatment of delirium tremens alcohol should be withdrawn immediately and medication prescribed as for a comatose patient. Some physicians prefer a more gradual withdrawal of alcohol, a tapering-off process, logical

for patients in whom the delirium tremens was brought on by sudden abstinence.

Long-Term Treatment.—In contrast to treatment of these comparatively temporary conditions is the treatment of the alcoholic between drinking bouts, when attempts must be made to help him overcome his disease. This treatment is most difficult and meets with repeated failures. In an attempt to treat chronic alcoholism it is necessary to consider both the physical and psychological aspects of the disease.

The various physical disorders secondary to alcoholism and caused in part by an inadequate diet can be corrected by a return to better eating habits, with foods containing mostly proteins and only moderate amounts of fat. The B group of vitamins, as well as A and C, should be added to the diet. These dietary measures also apply to all the other complications of alcoholism.

Psychological factors are of greatest significance in the impelling motivation for alcoholism and hence of greatest significance in its treatment. The personality structure must be investigated. In a way the treatment should be regarded as a learning process, the desired result being to make the patient another kind of man who is better able to understand his condition (and thus reduce his anxieties) and to accept more readily the unavoidable stresses of everyday living. The role played by interpersonal relationships cannot be overemphasized. A possessive mother, a domineering father, a spouse who keeps the mate in a dependent position must be informed of their contributions to the patient's condition. In these efforts not only the psychiatrist, trained to treat alcoholism, but the general physician and the clergyman should be enlisted. The international organization of Alcoholics Anonymous (AA), which emphasizes spiritual aspects, has a membership of alcoholics and former alcoholics who meet to discuss their common problem. In the company of other persons who suffer from the same disease, the alcoholic realizes that others share his problems and have valuable suggestions for the maintenance of sobriety. The society, numbering over 6,000 chapters throughout the world, also recognizes the worth of a spiritual awakening as an aid in combating the craving for alcohol.

The motivation of the patient is of great importance in combating the illness. He must want treatment. He may say that he has realized his situation and has decided to stop drinking and, therefore, has no problem. He will cite previous instances when he has actually stopped drinking for a shorter or longer time. Yet, without a fundamental desire to change, eventually he will relapse to his former pattern of drinking. Thus, as the first step in the treatment of alcoholism, the patient must admit that he is a problem drinker. Frequently it requires some dramatic incident with high emotional content to cause the drinker to seek treatment. He must "hit bottom." Sometimes the threat of divorce or of dismissal from employment can cause him to face his problem. His motivation for treatment is highest immediately after the hangover, and the object of treatment is to maintain this motivation. One step in that direction is to allow the patient to speak freely. Conversations with the therapist can throw light on the particular series of events which forced him into the path of alcoholism. The therapist should withhold moral condemnation. Though an old viewpoint regards alcoholism as immoral, the current view is that it is a disease; hence the therapist's aim is to correct the causes rather than to lecture the patient.

Administration of Antabuse, or disulfiram, and Temposil, citrated calcium carbimide, can help the patient continue in the path of sobriety. These drugs increase the concentration of acetaldehyde in the body whenever alcohol is consumed, for they retard the oxidation of that substance to acetic acid. The accumulation of acetaldehyde in the body produces a series of changes which resemble those of the acute hangover. In fact, the patient feels so uncomfortable that fear of the results can strengthen any faltering determination to abstain from alcohol. After disulfiram has been taken, even the smallest amount of an alcoholic beverage can initiate almost unbearable effects. The drinker first has a feeling of warmth in his face; the face, neck, and chest are suffused with scarlet and the eyes become bloodshot. At the same time he is aware of palpitation of the heart and feels choked for want of air. Nausea and vomiting follow, and the intense flushing is replaced by pallor as blood pressure falls.

The patient's willingness to take this drug can be accepted as a sign, at least for the moment, that he is strongly motivated in his desire for relief from alcoholism. This treatment has other advantages; instead of fighting the craving for alcohol many times a day, the patient has to make his decision only once, at the time he is taking his disulfiram medication. Temposil is a weaker drug than Antabuse and therefore has less deterrent action against the drinking of alcohol, but it is correspondingly safer.

Another method is the aversion treatment, in which alcohol is administered with a drug that produces nausea and vomiting. If the patient successfully establishes an association between the physical discomfiture and drinking, an aversion to alcohol is created. Other methods that have been tried include hypnosis and the administration of the psychedelic drug *d*-lysergic acid diethylamide (LSD-25). Hypnosis may be of some value in allaying the anxiety that perpetuates the drinking habit, but attempts to induce an aversion to alcohol by this method frequently have been unsuccessful. Strong claims were made for LSD therapy in the late 1960s, but the experimental evidence seemed to be inconclusive. Furthermore, it is possible that one form of drug dependency is being substituted for another.

Outlook.—Alcoholism cannot be regarded as a curable disease. The best that can be hoped for is arrest of its progress. The patient must be disabused of the idea that he can take an occasional drink with impunity. For success in the treatment of alcoholism there can be no compromise with the principle of complete abstinence from all alcoholic beverages.

Public Health Aspects.—The foregoing discussion points up the complexity of the alcoholism problem, concerned as it is with multiple factors directly and indirectly related to the health and welfare of man. One of the means of attacking such a complex problem is the public health approach of which there are three chief facets: (1) the biological and medical, with the conception that the inability to control one's drinking is a disease and that there is an individual susceptibility to alcoholism; (2) the psychological, concerned not only with the personality of the addict but also with the interpersonal relationships between the addict and his fellows; and (3) the social and economic, the influence of the particular social circumstances of the drinker and of the culture in which he lives as well as of his economic status. Combining these three aspects we find that the stresses of society may sometimes render life almost unbearable; alcoholism is one way out. Alcoholism may therefore be regarded as a reaction of certain individuals to abnormal circumstances.

See also TEMPERANCE; DRUG ADDICTION; LIQUOR LAW; and references under "Alcoholism" in the Index.

BIBLIOGRAPHY.—G. N. Thompson (ed.), *Alcoholism* (1956); H. E. Himwich (ed.), *Alcoholism: Basic Aspects and Treatment* (1957); H. D. Kruse (ed.), *Alcoholism as a Medical Problem* (1956); O. Diethelm, *Etiology of Chronic Alcoholism* (1955); R. J. Gibbins, *Chronic Alcoholism and Alcohol Addiction* (1953); M. Keller and V. Efron, "The Prevalence of Alcoholism," *Quart. J. Stud. Alcohol.*, 16:619–644 (1955); American Medical Association, *Manual on Alcoholism* (1967); F. Todd, *Teaching About Alcohol* (1964); R. G. McCarthy (ed.), *Alcohol Education for Classroom and Community* (1964).

(HA. E. H.)

ALCOHOLOMETRY: *see* ALCOHOLIC BEVERAGES, DISTILLED.

ALCOTT, AMOS BRONSON (1799–1888), U.S. teacher, reformer and philosopher, associated with the Transcendentalists, was born in Wolcott, Conn., Nov. 29, 1799. After a brief schooling and several peddling tours in the south he began teaching children in accord with a theory which owed something to Pestalozzi but more to the examples set by Socrates and Jesus. His chief aim was to "awaken the soul" and stimulate original thought. In method his teaching was conversational and in manner uniformly courteous, gentle, and firm. Questions of discipline were referred to the class as a group, and punishment consisted only of requiring the pupil to strike the teacher's hand with a ruler.

These innovations were too bold for the time, and before he was 40 Alcott had to close his last school, in Boston. He continued his teaching on lecture platforms, bringing to adults as he had to children a doctrine of pure idealism. In 1842 he visited England, and there, while living at Alcott House, named in his honour, caught the contagion of reform. One result was his founding of a short-lived utopian community, called Fruitlands, in northern Massachusetts.

He was a vegetarian, an abolitionist, an advocate of women's rights, and a charter member of the Transcendentalist group. His thought was vague, lofty, consistent, and intensely spiritual. As a speaker he exerted a wide influence, wholly for good. His life was a deliberate imitation of Christ, whom he did not think divine. Always poor and in debt, he lived on the bounty of others. His wife and daughters adored him.

Ralph Waldo Emerson said that for pure intellect he had never seen Alcott's equal. Henry Thoreau said that Alcott was the sanest man he ever knew. Most of the reforms Alcott fought for eventually triumphed. Many who had laughed at his impracticality came to admire his serene wisdom. The literary success of his daughter Louisa May Alcott, whom he had educated, brought him financial security. Even the town of Concord, Mass., which had cold-shouldered him for many years, had to respect the Summer School of Philosophy, founded by him and held on his grounds.

He died in Boston, March 4, 1888. The best of Alcott's writing is available in *The Journals of Bronson Alcott* (1938), selected and edited by Odell Shepard.

Alcott's educational theory and practice are described by Dorothy McCuskey in *Bronson Alcott, Teacher* (1940). A comprehensive biography based upon original manuscripts is Odell Shepard's *Pedlar's Progress, the Life of Bronson Alcott* (1937). (O. SD.)

ALCOTT, LOUISA MAY (1832–1888), U.S. author well known for her children's books, especially *Little Women,* and the daughter of Amos Bronson Alcott (*q.v.*), was born Nov. 29, 1832, in Germantown, Pa., where her father was teaching at the time. She spent most of her life in Concord and Boston, Mass. Ralph Waldo Emerson and Henry Thoreau were her earliest friends; Nathaniel Hawthorne was her neighbour; and from childhood she was exposed to the conversation of Margaret Fuller, Oliver Wendell Holmes, William Ellery Channing, Henry James, Sr., and other scholars.

Louisa soon realized that her father was too impractical to provide for his wife and four daughters; after the failure of Fruitlands, his experiment in "consociate" living, her lifelong concern for the welfare of her family began. As a child she earned money making dolls' clothes; then she went on to other sewing, to teaching school (which she hated), to a brief period of domestic service, and to writing —at first potboilers, then books.

THE BETTMANN ARCHIVE

BRONSON ALCOTT, PHOTOGRAPHED ON THE STEPS OF THE ORCHARD HOUSE CHAPEL, CONCORD, MASS.

CULVER PICTURES, INC.

LOUISA MAY ALCOTT

Her first published book was a collection of fairy stories, *Flower Fables* (1855), originally told to Emerson's daughter Ellen.

An ardent abolitionist, Louisa volunteered as a nurse when the Civil War began. She contracted typhoid from unsanitary hospital conditions and was sent home. She was never completely well again, but the publication of her letters in book form, *Hospital Sketches* (1863), brought her the first taste of fame.

Her stories began to appear in the *Atlantic Monthly*, and she was asked by Roberts Brothers to write a book for girls. At first she refused, "not liking girls, preferring boys." But because family needs were pressing, she wrote the autobiographical *Little Women* (1868–69), an immediate success and one of the most popular books for girls ever written. In 1869 she wrote in her journal: "Paid up all the debts ... thank the Lord! ... Now I think I could die in peace."

Other books followed, drawn from her early experiences: *An Old-Fashioned Girl* (1870); *Aunt Jo's Scrap Bag*, 6 vol. (1872–82); *Little Men* (1871); *Jo's Boys* (1886); and others. Two serious novels, *Moods* (1865), her favourite, and *Work* (1873), were less successful, as was *A Modern Mephistopheles* (1877). They were almost all written under pressure when she was in ill-health.

The last years of her life, though free from financial worry, were shadowed by the deaths of Elizabeth (the "Beth" of *Little Women*), her mother, and her youngest sister, May, who left a little daughter for Louisa to rear. Tired and in constant pain, she sought peace in the home of her physician, Rhoda Lawrence, where she died, March 6, 1888. She was buried in Concord's Sleepy Hollow cemetery on Author's hill, near the graves of Emerson, Thoreau and Hawthorne.

Louisa May Alcott: her Life, Letters, and Journal was edited by Ednah Cheney (1889).

BIBLIOGRAPHY.—In addition to the *Life* by Miss Cheney, there are biographies by Marjorie Worthington (1958), Madeleine Stern (1950), Katharine Anthony (1938), and Belle Moses (1909).   (M. WT.)

ALCOY, a town of southeastern Spain, in the north of the province of Alicante, is situated on the small Serpis river 25 mi. N. of Alicante city. Pop. (1960) 51,096 (mun.). Standing on the foothills of the Penibético system, it has a high and irregular terrain. There was a town there before Roman times but the Moors founded the present Alcoy, giving it the name of Alcoyll after a city in Tunis. The narrow streets and juxtaposition of old and new buildings give the town a variegated appearance. A fiesta, held on the day of San Jorge, the town's patron saint, is a great tourist attraction. Alcoy is the terminus of a branch line from the Barcelona-Valencia-Alicante railway; the line to Gandía was constructed in 1893 by the English. The town is an important centre of the textile industry and as early as 1590 it had 140 looms. A Real Fábrica de Paños ("Royal textile factory") was established there in 1800 and it was the site of the first Spanish industrial school. The industry was mechanized about 1925. The principal manufactures include paper, especially cigarette paper. There is also some metallurgical industry.   (M. B. F.)

ALCUIN (c. 732–804), English scholar and ecclesiastic, born in or near York about 732, is of great importance for three reasons. First, he carried English learning to France, working as head of that Palace school established by Charlemagne at Aachen in which the king-emperor himself, his family, his friends and his friends' sons were taught in a centre of lively discussion and exchange of knowledge mingled with wit and sharp criticism. Second, as the loyal and devoted adherent of Charlemagne and his subjects, he fought heresy both by preaching and teaching and by his writings, and laid the foundation of the Roman Catholic missal. Third, he left more than 300 Latin letters, a valuable source for the history of his time.

Alcuin's life was divided into three periods. Fifty years were spent in Yorkshire, where he went as a pupil to the school of York, the most renowned of its day, under Egbert, archbishop of York, and Aelbert, master of studies. Then, after Aelbert became archbishop, Alcuin was made head of the school (778). In 781, when on a journey in Italy, he was invited by Charlemagne to become director of the Palace school of Aachen and accepted the call.

Probably shortly before he left York he wrote a long poem in hexameter verse telling of men of renown in York's history. His source here was largely Bede, but he describes much of interest from his own knowledge. In 796 he resigned his work at the court, to rule as abbot the monastery at Tours made famous by St. Martin. There he encouraged the work of his monks on the beautiful script known as Caroline minuscule which was to become ancestor of the modern Roman type. He died at Tours on May 19, 804.

His life throughout was marked by strong contrast, the result of an inner conflict of zeal with uncertainty and diffidence. He was a leader in church and state, and his leadership was to be remembered throughout the middle ages. Yet he remained but a deacon to his death, and his writings as teacher show no original mind. He loved England, but in the troubled 8th century he went to live permanently abroad. He loved Charlemagne, his king-emperor, as his letters show; but his fear was as great as his love. Medieval men looked back with gratitude to his work for the liberal arts. The church did not include him in the canon of saints, yet has ever held in reverence his labour for the liturgy.

Alcuin's position as a formative influence in the development of Roman Catholicism rests mainly on his revision of the liturgy of the Frankish Church, which was based partly on the Gregorian sacramentary received from Rome and partly on the so-called Gelasian sacramentary which combined Roman, Gallican and other practice. He was also responsible for the introduction of the sung creed; arranged votive masses for particular days of the week in an order still followed by Catholics; re-edited the Latin Vulgate; wrote works on education and encouraged study of the secular liberal arts for the better understanding of spiritual doctrine; and was the author of biblical commentaries and of studies in theology and philosophy.

Certain questions concerning Alcuin are of interest. Did Alcuin, who amid much mediocre verse wrote with charm on the nightingale and the cuckoo, herald of spring, write also those well-known poems "The Contest of Winter and Spring" and the "Farewell to My Cell"? What was his share in shaping for Charlemagne the document *De litteris colendis*, that general letter which commanded the abbots of his realm to hasten diligence in learning among their novices and pupils? Did he preside over the scholars of Charlemagne who met to compose the *Caroline Books*, sent forth in wrathful protest against action in the east and demanding a sane and sober reverence for the statues and images in churches east and west? And, finally, what part did he play in the events preceding the coronation of Charlemagne by Pope Leo III on Christmas Day, 800? Did he work to restore the Roman empire in the west? On these questions scholars differ and it seems unlikely that definite answers can soon be given.

BIBLIOGRAPHY.—For further details on Alcuin's life and writings and for bibliographies *see* C. J. B. Gaskoin, *Alcuin* (1904); S. J. Crawford, *Anglo-Saxon Influence on Western Christendom* (1933); C. H. Dawson, *The Making of Europe* (1932); A. Kleinclausz, *Alcuin* (1948); E. S. Duckett, *Alcuin* (1951); Gerald Ellard, S.J., *Master Alcuin, Liturgist* (1956); M. Deanesly, *A History of Early Medieval Europe* (1956). *See* also, on Alcuin's verses, F. J. E. Raby, *A History of Christian Latin Poetry*, 2nd ed. (1957); on the *De litteris colendis*, L. Wallach, *Speculum*, vol. xxvi (1951); on the *Caroline Books*, L. Wallach, *Traditio*, vol. ix (1953) and Ann Freeman, *Speculum*, vol. xxxii (1957); on the crowning of Charlemagne, W. Levison, *England and the Continent in the Eighth Century*, pp. 121 ff. (1946).   (E. S. DT.)

ALCYONE (HALCYONE), in Greek mythology, daughter of Aeolus and wife of Ceyx. For their insolence in calling themselves Zeus and Hera, Alcyone was changed into a diver, Ceyx into a kingfisher. In another story, Ceyx was drowned and his body cast on the shore. His wife found the body, and the gods, out of compassion, changed both into kingfishers. The winds ceased to blow during their brooding time, hence the expression "halcyon days," used in ancient and modern times to denote a period of calm and tranquillity.

ALDABRA ISLANDS, a group of islands lying in the Indian ocean 265 mi. N.W. of the northern point of Madagascar, 630 mi. S.W. of Mahé and 70 mi. W. of the Cosmoledo group. They were formerly part of the British colony of Seychelles. Pop. (1947) 47. The islands constitute an oval atoll about 1½ mi. broad which is 23 mi. long and 8 mi. wide and encloses a large but shallow lagoon. Channels divide the ring into four islands which rise from 20 to 80 ft. above the sea. Grande Terre or South island forms three-fifths of the circumference; the other islands are West island or Île Picard, Polymnie, Middle island, and several islets (e.g., Île Michel) in the lagoon. The total land area is about 6½ sq.mi. Cliffs of coral and limestone are in places replaced by sandy beaches and sand hills, and there is very little soil. Dense scrub covers most of the land, but the lagoon shore is bounded by mangrove swamps.

In common with the other islands of the Seychelles (which were visited by the John Murray scientific expedition in 1934), the Aldabra group seems to have been built up on the sunken surface of the old southern continent of Gondwanaland (or Lemuria, as it is sometimes called) by a deposit of foraminiferal remains, mostly coccoliths and rhabdoliths; it has never been joined to any other land. At Aldabra the coral foundation is totally above water; the coral is generally reddish, but runs from light yellow to chocolate brown. The coral limestone of the atoll is vitrified and gives out a ringing sound when struck or simply walked on.

In 1955 the islands were leased for the commercial exploitation of mangrove timber and fishing, under stringent safeguards for the rare flora and fauna. South island has been declared a nature reserve with absolute protection for animal and bird life. Rarities include a rail (Dryolimnas aldabranus), an ibis (Ibis abbottii) and a dove (Alectroenas sgazini). The giant land tortoise (Testudo elephantina) is found and the lagoon teems with hawksbill and edible turtles including the unique "blonde" hawksbill turtle. Oysters and large crabs also occur and a small mussel is found in enormous numbers. Besides mangroves, there are some endemic plants but both flora and bird life are predominantly derived from Madagascar brought by currents and winds.

Aldabra was visited by the Portuguese in 1511 but was already known to the Arabs, who named it. In the 18th century the islets became dependencies of the French establishments at Bourbon (Réunion). In 1810, with Mauritius, Bourbon (for a time), the rest of the Seychelles and other islands, Aldabra became British. In 1965 the islands became part of the British Indian Ocean Territory.

See W. B. Hemsley et al., "Flora of Aldabra," Kew Bull. (1919); W. B. Hemsley and W. B. Turrill, "Plants of Seychelles and Aldabra" J. Bot., Lond., vol. 55 (Oct. 1917); F. D. Ommaney, The Shoals of Capricorn (1952); W. Travis, Beyond the Reefs (1959).

ALDAN, a river in the U.S.S.R., the second largest tributary of the Lena (q.v.) by length and the largest by area of its basin, rises in the Stanovoi range and after taking a northward course, turns sharply to east-southeast and then swings in a giant curve to the north and west to join the Lena at Batamai (Ust-Aldan). It is 1,393 mi. long and drains more than 252,000 sq.mi. Its width varies from 160–270 yd. in its middle course to nearly 1,000 yd. in the lower reaches, where it divides into innumerable channels. The average annual discharge is 184,000 cu.ft. per second, but there is considerable variation both seasonally and annually. The river is frozen from mid-October to mid-May. The Aldan is navigable to Tommot, while the lower reaches of its major tributaries, the Maya and Uchur, are also navigable. The chief economic importance of its basin lies in the gold fields south of Tommot. (R. A. F.)

ALDANOV, MARK ALEKSANDROVICH (real surname LANDAU) (1889–1957), Russian émigré writer bitterly critical of the Soviet system, was born Nov. 7, 1889, in Kiev, where he took a university degree in chemistry. In 1919 he emigrated to France, which he left for the United States in 1941. He wrote an essay on Lenin (1921), a work comparing the Russian and French revolutions, Deux Révolutions (1921), and a scientific treatise, Actinochimie (1936), as well as many novels, most of which were translated into English, including a trilogy on revolutionary France, Myslitel (1923–25; The Thinker, 1924–28), an anti-Soviet satire, Nachalo kontsa (1939; The Fifth Seal, 1943) and Istoki (1947; Before the Deluge, 1948), a picture of Europe in the 1870s. He died in Nice, France, Feb. 25, 1957.

ALDEBARAN, officially designated as α Tauri, one of the 20 brightest stars in the sky, is in the constellation Taurus (q.v.). It is a reddish giant star having a diameter approximately 50 times that of the sun and is located at a distance of about 80 light-years. It is accompanied by a very faint companion star.

ALDEBURGH, a municipal borough on the coast of East Suffolk, Eng., lies 25 mi. N.E. of Ipswich by road. Pop. (1961) 3,007. Area 3.8 sq.mi. Formerly the coast extended farther east —the 16th-century Moot hall is now almost on the beach—and the Alde estuary formed a harbour of some importance to the medieval town. The river is diverted sharply southward a few yards from the sea at Slaughden, 1 mi. S., by a shingle bank extending for 12 mi. to Hollesley bay. Though there is still some fishing, Aldeburgh is chiefly a residential and holiday town with golf links and a lifeboat station. The annual summer Aldeburgh Festival of Music and Arts was inaugurated in 1948, the prime mover being Benjamin Britten (q.v.), several of whose works received their first performance there. The festival includes exhibitions of East Anglian artists' and craftsmen's work (e.g., printing, china). The manor, mentioned in Domesday Book, was bequeathed in 1155 by William Martel, together with the church, to the abbey of St. John at Colchester to endow what was soon to become an independent Austin priory at Snape. In the 16th century it came into the hands of Cardinal Wolsey and later it came into the possession of the Wentworth family. In the 16th century Aldeburgh was a place of considerable commercial importance; the earliest charter was conferred by Henry VIII in 1529 and the town was incorporated under Edward VI. The borough sent two members to parliament from 1572 until 1832 and three years after that the town was deprived of its charter, but it was newly incorporated in 1885. Elizabeth Garrett Anderson (q.v.), one of the first women doctors, was elected mayor of the town in 1908 and became the first woman mayor in England. In the Perpendicular parish church is a bust of the poet George Crabbe (q.v.) who was born in Aldeburgh and was curate there for a time.

ALDEHYDES AND KETONES, two important related classes of chemical compounds containing the carbonyl grouping, $C=O$. The aldehyde or ketone group is present in a number of natural products (e.g., carbohydrates, essential oils, perfumes, steroids) and aldehydes and ketones are intermediates in the manufacture of a variety of industrial products (e.g., resins, dyes, medicinals, solvents). Aldehydes are characterized by the general formula

$$R—\overset{\displaystyle H}{\underset{\displaystyle |}{C}}=O,$$

where R is either a second hydrogen atom or an alkyl (aliphatic) or aryl (aromatic) radical; ketones, on the other hand, are characterized by the general formula

$$R—\overset{\displaystyle R'}{\underset{\displaystyle |}{C}}=O,$$

where R and R' may be either the same or different (see also below), but neither can be a hydrogen atom. Since aldehydes and ketones differ in important ways, they are discussed separately.

ALDEHYDES

The group CHO which is to be found in all aldehydes contains the most active form of the carbonyl function known to chemists, and it is to the intense reactivity of this function that the aldehydes owe their importance as organic synthetic agents both in nature and in the chemical laboratory.

Aldehydes are generally named after the acids into which they are converted by oxidation; thus formaldehyde, acetaldehyde and benzaldehyde furnish formic, acetic and benzoic acids, respectively. The termination "al" is employed to denote aldehydic functions, according to the Geneva convention of chemists; thus geranial, the aldehyde of lemon-grass oil, is the oxidation product of the alcohol geraniol, contained in geranium oil (see TERPENES).

Many aldehydes are known. Some are produced artificially; numerous others are found in plants, either free (e.g., cinnamaldehyde in cinnamon oil) or combined in certain glycosides (e.g., benzaldehyde in amygdalin; see GLYCOSIDES, NATURAL).

Properties of Typical Aldehydes.—Formaldehyde, H—CHO, the simplest of the aldehydes, is a gas at the ordinary temperature (b.p. −19° C.) and is prepared by passing the vapour of methyl alcohol and air over heated copper gauze. The gaseous aldehyde is collected in water to form a 30–40% solution known commercially as Formalin. This solution on concentration yields a white amorphous solid known as paraformaldehyde, which is considered to be a complex mixture of substances of type formula $HOCH_2-(OCH_2)_nOCH_2OH$, with n possessing values up to about 100. When, however, formaldehyde is distilled from a 60% aqueous solution containing 2% sulfuric acid, it polymerizes to a crystalline modification termed α-trioxymethylene or trioxane, $(CH_2O)_3$. These polymeric forms are dissociated on heating into the gaseous monomeric formaldehyde.

Acetaldehyde, prepared by oxidation of ethyl alcohol (q.v.) or by hydration of acetylene (q.v.), is a volatile liquid boiling at 21° C. and miscible in all proportions with water. It is readily polymerized catalytically by traces of zinc chloride, hydrochloric acid, etc., at the ordinary temperature to para-acetaldehyde or paraldehyde (q.v.), $(C_2H_4O)_3$, a liquid boiling at 124° C. and only moderately soluble in water. Paraldehyde, employed medicinally as a sedative without action on the heart, is administered intravenously as an anesthetic or hypnotic. When the foregoing polymerization of acetaldehyde takes place in a freezing mixture, metaldehyde or meta-acetaldehyde, $(C_2H_4O)_4$, is produced as a white crystalline solid subliming at 112°–115° C. This substance when heated in a sealed tube at 100° C. is reconverted into the monomeric form. Metaldehyde has been recommended as a smokeless fuel.

The simultaneous chlorination and oxidation of ethyl alcohol leads to trichloroacetaldehyde which in its hydrated state is the well-known drug chloral hydrate (see CHLORAL).

Aldolization.—The transformation of formaldehyde and acetaldehyde into their polymeric forms is a chemical change which is readily reversible by thermal dissociation. In addition to this change, aldehydes have the capacity for undergoing a polymerization in which the carbon atoms of separate molecules become directly attached, so that β-hydroxyaldehydes are formed. This process also is often reversible, especially in the presence of a basic catalyst. This mode of polymerization, which is termed aldolization, is an important reaction in organic synthesis. Aldol (β-hydroxybutyraldehyde) is formed by a combining of two molecules of acetaldehyde:

$$CH_3—CHO + H—CH_2—CHO = CH_3—CH(OH)—CH_2—CHO$$

By loss of water aldol passes into the unsaturated crotonaldehyde, $CH_3—CH=CH—CHO$.

Resinification.—Acetaldehyde and certain of its homologues are converted into resins under the influence of alkalis. Acrolein, $CH_2=CH—CHO$, the simplest of the unsaturated aldehydes, is obtained by abstraction of water from glycerin by the agency of alkali bisulfates and phosphoric or boric acid. It is a colourless liquid boiling at 52.4° C. with a disagreeable, tear-exciting odour. In the presence of traces of acids, it readily undergoes polymerization to form a solid resinous material, metacrolein (see RESINS).

Aromatic Aldehydes.—Benzaldehyde, the most important commercially of the aromatic aldehydes, is usually made from the chlorinated derivatives of toluene. Benzyl chloride, $C_6H_5—CH_2-Cl$, heated with aqueous lead or cupric nitrate furnishes benzaldehyde, which is also prepared by heating benzal or benzylidene chloride, $C_6H_5—CHCl_2$, with aqueous calcium hydroxide. Benzaldehyde can also be prepared by the direct oxidation of toluene by chemical means (manganese dioxide and sulfuric acid) or by electrolytic means (in acetone-sulfuric acid solution with platinum electrodes).

Benzaldehyde is a colourless, highly refractive liquid boiling at 179°–180° C. with the characteristic odour of oil of bitter almonds of which oil it is the essential constituent, being derived from the hydrolysis of the glucoside, amygdalin, present in the almond. It readily absorbs oxygen from the air, becoming oxidized to benzoic acid. With aqueous caustic alkalies it undergoes the Cannizzaro reaction:

$$2C_6H_5—CHO + H_2O = C_6H_5—CH_2—OH + C_6H_5—CO_2H$$

yielding molecular proportions of benzyl alcohol and benzoic

acid. With alcoholic potassium cyanide, it gives benzoin, $C_6H_5-CH(OH)—CO—C_6H_5$. Benzaldehyde is also an intermediate in the production of colouring matters (see DYES AND DYEING).

Furfural (q.v.) (furfuraldehyde) is an example of a nonaromatic cyclic aldehyde manufactured in the U.S. by the action of steam and dilute acid on oat hulls and corncobs and cornstalks contained in large digesters. The volatile furfural (b.p. 160°–162° C.) is isolated and purified by fractional distillation.

General Methods of Preparation.—*Direct Synthesis.*—Arising from a study of chemical reactions under high pressure it has been found that when carbon monoxide and hydrogen are heated together at 360°–380° C. under a pressure of 200 atm. in the presence of a mixed catalyst consisting of the oxides of cobalt, copper, manganese and zinc, a mixture of aliphatic aldehydes is produced among which formaldehyde, acetaldehyde, propionaldehyde and higher aldehydes have been identified (see PRESSURE CHEMISTRY).

Action of Ozone on Olefines.—During an investigation of the action of ozone on various organic substances, C. D. Harries discovered that this active form of oxygen has a specific action on carbon compounds containing a double or ethylenic linkage. A molecular proportion of ozone attaches itself to the carbon atoms of the double bond, forming an ozonide, which on treatment with water yields an aldehyde and an aldehyde peroxide, the latter becoming transformed into an acid. In the simplest case of ethylene this gas furnishes an explosive ozonide which subsequently gives rise to formaldehyde and formic acid,

$$CH_2=CH_2 + O_3 \rightarrow CH_2—O—CH_2 \rightarrow CH_2O + CH_2O_2$$
$$\underset{O—O}{}$$

A similar ozonization applied to more complex olefines has led to aldehydes which are otherwise prepared only with difficulty:

$$C_6H_5—CH=CH—CHO + O_3 = C_6H_5—CO_2H + CHO—CHO$$

Cinnamaldehyde   Benzoic   Glyoxal
acid

Dehydrogenation of Primary Alcohols.—The primary alcohols may be dehydrogenated either thermally or by oxidation. It is from such transformations that the word "aldehyde" (alcohol dehydrogenatum) was originally derived by J. von Liebig. In the former process the alcohol is passed over a heated metallic catalyst, preferably copper, although nickel, palladium or platinum or such oxides as vanadium pentoxide, V_2O_5, may be employed. The oxidation of a primary alcohol to an aldehyde is generally effected by aqueous chromic acid (a solution of sodium bichromate and dilute sulfuric acid), but other oxidizing agents such as manganese dioxide and dilute sulfuric acid, or even atmospheric oxygen in presence of platinum black or bone black, may be employed.

Thermal Decomposition of α-Hydroxycarboxylic Acids.—This process, discovered by H. R. Le Sueur, has been worked out chiefly with the higher fatty acids. For example, stearic acid is converted successively into α-bromostearic and α-hydroxystearic acids. The latter acid, on heating at 270° C., yields margaric aldehyde, $C_{16}H_{33}—CHO$, and formic acid. Incidentally this method forms a means of passing from common acids such as stearic and palmitic acids, which are readily obtained from natural sources, to acids such as margaric acid, $C_{16}H_{33}—COOH$, which do not occur in nature.

Aldehydes From Calcium Formate and Salts.—This method depends on the heating together of an intimate mixture of calcium formate and the calcium salt of some other acid:

$$(CHO—O)_2Ca + (C_nH_{2n+1}—CO—O)_2Ca = 2CaCO_3 + 2C_nH_{2n+1}—CHO$$

Aldehydes From Grignard Reagents.—Grignard reagents (q.v.), with the general structure RMgX, react with disubstituted formamides $H—CO—NR'R''$ to give products which on hydrolysis yield the aldehydes RCHO; and with ethyl orthoformate $HC(OC_2H_5)_3$ to give the acetals $RCH(OC_2H_5)_2$, from which the aldehydes RCHO can be freed by the action of an aqueous acid.

Aldehydes by Reduction.—Acid chlorides, RCOCl, can be reduced catalytically with hydrogen and palladium to give aldehydes in good yields if the activity of the catalyst is reduced by the so-called poisoning (*see* CATALYSIS) of the catalyst with a sulfur-quinoline mixture to prevent overreduction to the alcohol.

Many useful aldehyde syntheses have been developed, based on the reduction of carboxylic acid derivatives with complex aluminum hydrides (*see* HYDRIDES). For example, acid chlorides are generally converted to the corresponding aldehydes on reaction with lithium tri-*t*-butoxyaluminum hydride, $LiAlH(OC_4H_9)_3$. Similarly, certain carboxylic acid amides, such as N-methylanilids, $RCON(CH_3)C_6H_5$, give good yields of aldehydes on reduction with lithium aluminum hydride, $LiAlH_4$. Complex boron hydrides, such as sodium trimethoxyboron hydride, have been successfully employed in the reduction of acid chlorides to aldehydes.

Aromatic Aldehydes From Phenols.—A long-known process for the conversion of phenols into hydroxy-aryl-aldehydes is associated with the names of C. L. Reimer and F. Tiemann. It consists in treating the phenolic compound with chloroform in presence of concentrated alkalis. With phenol itself the reaction proceeds as follows:

$$HO—C_6H_5 + CHCl_3 + 3NaOH = HO—C_6H_4—CHO + 3NaCl + 2H_2O$$

Two isomerides are produced, parahydroxybenzaldehyde and salicylaldehyde (orthohydroxybenzaldehyde). The latter isomeride occurs in the volatile oils of Spiraea and in the glucoside, salicin, of the willow.

Syntheses Catalyzed by Metal Halides.—The two syntheses described under this heading, which are due to L. Gattermann, are, like those of the preceding section, applicable only to the aromatic series. The first depends on the use of carbon monoxide, this gas and hydrogen chloride being passed into a solution of an aromatic hydrocarbon in a dry solvent in the presence of cuprous and aluminum chlorides. In the case of toluene the condensation gives rise to *p*-tolualdehyde. In all probability the carbon monoxide absorbed by the cuprous chloride forms an intermediate compound, H—COCl, with the hydrogen chloride and this unstable formyl chloride under the influence of aluminum chloride condenses with the hydrocarbon to give rise to the aldehyde:

$$CH_3—C_6H_5 + H—COCl = CH_3—C_6H_4—CHO + HCl$$

The second Gattermann synthesis involves the use of hydrogen cyanide (anhydrous prussic acid). The aromatic substance, which may be a hydrocarbon or a phenol, is dissolved in a dry solvent containing anhydrous aluminum or zinc chloride and to this mixture hydrogen cyanide is added while hydrogen chloride is bubbled in to saturation. The two hydrides interact potentially as $HN≡CHCl$:

$$HN≡CHCl + C_6H_5—OH = HN≡CH—C_6H_4OH + HCl$$

The aldehyde-imine thus formed as an intermediate product is hydrolyzed, when boiled with water, into ammonia and the corresponding aldehyde, $HO—C_6H_4—CHO$.

General Reactions of Aldehydes.—The aldehydes combine additively with sodium hydrogen sulfite to furnish bisulfite compounds, $R—CH(OH)—SO_3Na$. These compounds, being crystallizable and easily hydrolyzed by dilute acid, are frequently used in the purification of the aldehydes. Sodium hydrosulfite also interacts with aldehydes, giving rise to compounds of the general formula $R—CH(OH)—SO_2Na$. The formaldehyde compound is the important reducing agent Rongalite, employed in calico printing for discharging the colour of dyes.

Aldehydes react with hydrogen cyanide to form cyanohydrins, $R—CH(OH)—CN$, which are hydrolyzable to α-hydroxycarboxylic acids containing one more carbon atom than the original aldehyde. Aldehydes combine with hydroxylamine to form oximes (*q.v.*), with phenylhydrazine to phenylhydrazones and with semicarbazide to crystallizable semicarbazones. The action of active metals in the presence of acids reduces aldehydes to primary alcohols, whereas with Grignard reagents they are converted into secondary alcohols. Formaldehyde condenses with aqueous ammonia to form hexamethylenetetramine, $N_4(CH_2)_6$, a urinary antiseptic, urotropine, whereas the other aliphatic aldehydes combine with ethereal ammonia to give aldehyde-ammonias, which are usually assigned structures of the type $R—CH(OH)—NH_2$, but which are actually of uncertain composition and molecular weight; from these the aldehydes can be regenerated by distillation with dilute acid. Aldehydes in general are characterized by the colour reaction of H. Schiff, this being the reddish-violet coloration developed with a solution of magenta or fuchsine which has been decolorized by sulfurous acid.

KETONES

Ketones have the general formula R—CO—R' (*see* above). If the groups R and R' are identical, the ketone is called a simple ketone, of which the best known and simplest example is acetone (*q.v.*), used in large amounts during World Wars I and II as a solvent in the manufacture of the explosive cordite. If the groups R and R' are different, a mixed ketone results, and of this class acetophenone (*q.v.*), $CH_3—CO—C_6H_5$, may be cited as a typical representative. It has been used as a soporific under the name of "hypnone."

The lower members of the aliphatic ketones are liquids and are lighter than water; the higher members containing C_{12} and upward are solid. (For the initial member of the series *see* ACETONE.) Methyl ethyl ketone, $CH_3—CO—C_2H_5$, the simplest of the mixed ketones, occurs in the products of thermal decomposition of wood and is also prepared by the dehydrogenation of *sec*-butyl alcohol, $CH_3—CHOH—C_2H_5$ (*see* below). This ketone is employed in the preparation of dimethylglyoxime, a useful analytical reagent for nickel (*q.v.*). Pinacolone, or methyl *tert.*-butyl ketone, $CH_3—CO—C(CH_3)_3$, a liquid boiling at 106° C. and having a camphoraceous odour, is produced by the action of dilute sulfuric acid on pinacol (*see* GLYCOLS), this peculiar reaction being known as the "pinacol rearrangement." The aromatic ketones may be either partly aliphatic or totally aromatic. The simplest and most important examples of these two types of substances are given respectively, by the already mentioned acetophenone and by benzophenone (*q.v.*), $C_6H_5—CO—C_6H_5$.

General Methods of Preparation.—(1) from secondary alcohols, either by oxidation or by thermal dehydrogenation in the presence of catalysts, such as heated-reduced copper: $(CH_3)_2CHOH—2H=(CH_3)_2CO$; (2) hydration of derivatives of acetylene, preferably in the presence of sulfuric acid and of mercuric salts, $C_6H_5—C≡CH + H_2O = C_6H_5—CO—CH_3$; (3) the interaction of acid chlorides and organo-zinc or organo-cadmium compounds, *e.g.*, $C_6H_5—COCl + Cd(CH_3)_2 = C_6H_5CO—CH_3 + CH_3CdCl$; (4) the Friedel-Crafts reaction is applicable to ketones containing one or two aromatic radicals; *e.g.*, acetyl chloride with benzene gives acetophenone; carbonyl chloride or benzoyl chloride with benzene gives benzophenone.

General Reactions.—*Oxidation and Reduction.*—Ketones are relatively resistant to oxidizing agents. However, they are easily reduced to secondary alcohols by hydrogen and a platinum, palladium or nickel catalyst, and to mixtures of secondary alcohols and pinacols (*see* GLYCOLS) by aluminum, sodium or magnesium amalgams.

Addition Products.—Such products are formed less readily by ketones than by aldehydes. Nevertheless, ketones and mercaptans form addition compounds, the mercaptols, such as $(CH_3)_2C(SC_2H_5)_2$ from acetone and ethyl mercaptan. This mercaptol on oxidation furnishes the drug sulfonal. Grignard reagents (*q.v.*) add to ketones, and the products when decomposed by water give rise to tertiary alcohols. Hydrogen cyanide and ketones give rise to hydroxynitriles hydrolysable to hydroxycarboxylic acids, and a few ketones unite with sodium hydrogen sulfite, yielding bisulfite compounds from which the ketone can be regenerated by aqueous sodium carbonate.

Condensation Products.—Ketones condense with hydroxylamine, giving ketoximes, although not always so readily as aldehydes give aldoximes. With a mixed ketone, R—CO—R', two oximes, R—CR'=NOH, are often obtained, the isomerism of which is explained by assuming a different spatial arrangement of the groups R, R′ and OH about the doubly linked residue

$$-C=N-$$ (A. R. Hantzsch and A. Werner, 1890). In studying the stereoisomeric oximes (*see* STEREOCHEMISTRY: *Stereochemistry of Nitrogen*), considerable use has been made of a characteristic chemical change undergone by ketoximes, known as the Beckmann rearrangement (1886), which results in each of these isomeric oximes, R—CR′=NOH, changing into the corresponding amide, R—CO—NHR′ or R′CO—NHR (*see* OXIMES). This change is effected by phosphorus pentachloride, benzenesulfonyl chloride or warm concentrated sulfuric acid. Ketones condense with phenylhydrazine and other hydrazines to yield characteristic hydrazones which are useful for the purposes of isolation and identification. Ketones condense with ketones and esters under the action of catalysts. Thus, acetone reacts with itself to give diacetone alcohol, $(CH_3)_2C(OH)CH_2-CO-CH_3$, and mesityl oxide, $(CH_3)_2C=CH-CO-CH_3$.

Diketones.—Compounds containing in their molecules two ketonic groups are termed diketones, and the group is divisible into subgroups depending on whether the two carbonyl groups are adjacent or separated by one or more carbon atoms.

Diacetyl, $CH_3-CO-CO-CH_3$, the simplest member of the 1,2- or α-diketones, is a yellowish-green liquid boiling at 88° C. and of specific gravity 0.9734 at 22° C. It is found in the aqueous distillates of many essential oils; for example, bay, cedarwood, iris and sandalwood oils, to which it communicates its colour and odour. It occurs also in butter, for the characteristic odour of which it is largely responsible. Diacetyl is made from methyl ethyl ketone by treatment of this ketone with amyl nitrite and subsequent hydrolysis of the resulting diacetyl-monoxime with dilute sulfuric acid. Diacetyldioxime or dimethylglyoxime is prepared by treating methyl ethyl ketone successively with amyl nitrite in presence of hydrogen chloride and with hydroxylamine hydrochloride.

Acetylacetone, the simplest member of the 1,3- or β-diketones, is a colourless pungent liquid boiling at 139° C. It is regarded as an equilibrium mixture of two isomeric forms, $CH_3-CO-CH_2-CO-CH_3$ and $CH_3-C(OH)=CH-CO-CH_3$, the latter predominating. Acetylacetone is prepared by adding successively ethyl acetate and acetone to sodium wire under dry ether.

See J. F. Thorpe and M. A. Whiteley, *Dictionary of Applied Chemistry,* 4th ed., vol. vii (1946); O. Bayer, *Die Methoden der organischen Chemie,* 4th ed., vol. vii (1963). (G. T. M.; G. W. Wᴅ.; X.)

ALDEN, JOHN (1599?–1687), one of the Pilgrims who in 1620 emigrated to America in the "Mayflower," founded the Plymouth colony. He was a settler of Duxbury, Mass., where he lived for most of his life. From 1633 until 1686 he was an assistant to the governor of the colony, frequently acting as governor. At the time of his death on Sept. 12, 1687, he was the last male survivor of the "Mayflower" company.

He is remembered chiefly because of a popular legend, put into verse as "The Courtship of Miles Standish" by Henry W. Longfellow, concerning his courtship of Priscilla Mullins, whom he married in 1623, after having wooed her first for his friend Myles Standish.

ALDER, KURT (1902–1958), German chemist, was awarded the 1950 Nobel prize for chemistry jointly with Otto Diels for the development of the diene synthesis, one of the outstanding achievements of modern organic chemistry. Born at Königshütte (Chorzow) on July 10, 1902, he studied chemistry in Berlin and Kiel, where he received his doctor's degree in 1926. He was professor at Kiel (1934–36) and worked in the research laboratories of I. G. Farben at Leverkusen (1936–40). In 1940 he became professor of chemistry and director of the chemical institute at the University of Cologne. He died in Cologne, June 20, 1958.

The diene synthesis consists essentially of the addition of substances containing two conjugate double bonds, such as the butadienes, to substances such as maleic acid or quinones. Diels and Alder published their first paper on the reaction of dienes with quinones in 1928. Similar additions had been recorded by others, but it was Diels and Alder who provided the first experimental proof of the nature of the reaction and who demonstrated

its application to the synthesis of a wide variety of ring compounds.

A remarkable feature of the diene synthesis is the ease with which it can be effected without the use of powerful chemical reagents. Study of the reaction has contributed greatly to the knowledge of polymerization processes by which valuable plastic materials have been obtained. The discovery is of considerable theoretical interest, because many plant products are probably formed in nature by diene additions. (W. J. Bᴘ.)

ALDER (*Alnus*), the name given to a group of shrubs and trees belonging to the birch family (Betulaceae), comprises about 30 species distributed through the north temperate zone. In the new world a few extend south over the mountains of Central America and the South American Andes to Peru and Chile. They are readily distinguished from the birches by their stalked, valvate, winter buds, and cones (strobiles) with thick woody scales which persist on the branchlets long after their small winged fruits (nutlets) have been released.

JOHN MARKHAM

ALDER (ALNUS GLUTINOSA): (LEFT) YOUNG MALE CATKINS; (CENTRE) RIPENING CONES; (RIGHT) DRIED CONES

The black alder (*A. glutinosa*), the most important old-world species, is widespread on wet sites in Europe, Asia and northern Africa, and has become naturalized in the eastern United States. It is the only alder indigenous to Great Britain, where it attains a height of 75 ft. and a diameter of 30 in. The soft, light-brown wood is used for many purposes including furniture, piling and charcoal manufacture. The speckled or hoary alder (*A. incana*), usually a large shrub, is found in Europe and northern Asia and in swamps of eastern United States and Canada. The green alder (*A. viridis*), a small shrub of Europe and Asia, is also found in eastern North America.

The alders of the Rocky mountain region and Pacific slope often become large trees. Among these are the red alder (*A. rubra*), the Sitka alder (*A. sinuata*) and the white alder (*A. rhombifolia*).

The red alder, which attains a height of 120 ft. and a diameter of 40 in., is the most valuable. The wood is soft, works well and is largely used in the manufacture of inexpensive furniture.

In mountain regions alders are among the first woody plants to appear in areas denuded by avalanches and in the rubble around the edges of receding glaciers.

Many alders are prized ornamentals, especially horticultural varieties of the black and speckled alder and the Japanese alder (*A. japonica*), which is one of the largest and most beautiful members of the genus. (E. S. Hʀ.)

ALDER FLY, the name given to insects of the family Sialidae of the order Neuroptera; they are characterized by long filamentous antennae and four large wings, of which the hind pair has the anal area folded fanwise when at rest. They are dark-coloured, sluggish insects, one inch or less in length, and are found only near fresh water. The eggs, often very numerous, are laid in clusters on plants, etc., close to the water. The larvae are aquatic, living in streams, large rivers or lakes; they have biting jaws and breathe by seven or eight pairs of filamentous abdominal gills. The pupae are found in soil, moss, etc., and there is no cocoon.

Sialis lutaria is the common alder fly of Great Britain. In North America there are 18 species, several of which are common and widely distributed.

See NEUROPTERA: *Suborder Megaloptera.*

ALDERMAN, a term indicating membership in the legislative body of a municipal corporation in England and the United States. The word alderman had an extended meaning in early English law, some authorities enumerating 11 classes of aldermen. Among the

Anglo-Saxons, earls, governors of provinces and other persons of distinction received this title; later the term was used to designate the chief magistrate of a county or group of counties.

In the American colonial period city councils resembled their British prototypes, in which aldermen and common councilors commonly sat together as one body under the chairmanship of the mayor. In most colonial boroughs both aldermen and councilmen were chosen by the voters, but in a few cases only councilmen were elected, the aldermen being selected by the councilmen as in England. In addition to their legislative duties as members of the council, aldermen in the colonial period also exercised judicial power in minor civil and criminal cases. The mayor, recorder and aldermen sat together to try important cases where they did not have jurisdiction when sitting singly.

Following the colonial period, all members of the council, including aldermen, were elected by popular vote. During the 19th century extensive use was made of the bicameral legislative principle by municipalities, one house being designated as the board of aldermen and the other as the common council. The bicameral principle was gradually abandoned and by the second half of the 20th century had practically disappeared. The members of this single house came to be referred to in the statutes and city charters of some states as councilmen or members of the council, but they were frequently referred to popularly as aldermen; and in some states the legal terminology as well as the popular designation was alderman. The term was generally reserved for members of the council in mayor- and council-governed cities, members of the council in commission-governed and council-manager cities being referred to both by law and popularly as commissioners or councilmen. Aldermen, as opposed to councilmen and commissioners, are usually elected by wards, and the term has come to have that implication.

By the English Municipal Corporations acts of 1835 and 1882, and by the Local Government act of 1933, the term was used to designate one type of membership in borough and county councils. While local government councils in England are unicameral in nature, county councils and those in county boroughs and municipal boroughs have two types of members—councilors and aldermen. The councilors are elected by the voters; a number of aldermen equal to one-third the whole number of councilors are then selected by the councilors. Under the London Government Act 1963 a Greater London council was to be established on April 1, 1965. The number of aldermen on this council was to be one-third, and on the London borough councils one-sixth, of the whole number of councilors. An alderman may be elected from among the councilors, when another councilor must be chosen to fill his place, or he may be anyone eligible to be a councilor. (*See* LONDON.) Aldermen serve for six years and councilors for three years. In Scotland the bailie corresponds to the alderman.

See Eugene McQuillin, *The Law of Municipal Corporations*, 20 vol. (1949–51). (C. M. KR.)

ALDERNEY (French, AURIGNY), the northernmost of the larger Channel Islands. It is 3½ mi. long from north-northeast to west-southwest, about 1 mi. wide and a little over 3 sq.mi. in area. The French coast is 9 mi. away across the Race of Alderney; the nearest English coast is about 55 mi. distant.

Physiography.—Alderney is a tableland cut partly in crystalline rocks and partly in sandstones. Granite and granulite in the southwest and syenite in the centre are thought to be of Pre-Cambrian Age; the coarse sandstone of the east, with its outlier on the south coast, belongs to the Lower Cambrian. Superficial deposits include weathering-products, loess, raised beaches and the blown sand which occurs north of Longy bay. The plateau, mostly over 200 ft. above sea level and just below 300 ft. at the highest, is very little dissected, but the terrain becomes lower and hillier in the east where it is additionally complicated by quarries. Steep cliffs between 175 and 275 ft. in height line the south and west coasts, while old cliffs rise behind raised beaches in the north and east. The two main inlets are Braye harbour, protected by a 1,000-yd. breakwater, on the north, and Longy bay, backed by an almost-filled lagoon, on the southeast.

Local tides are dangerous and strong. Races include the Swinge,

a narrow channel on the west which separates Alderney from the uninhabited Burhou, Ortac and smaller islets. Beyond these, the notorious Casquets carry a lighthouse. (G. H. D.)

History.—The earliest known inhabitants of Alderney were the builders of the megalithic tombs. The Bronze Age is well represented and the Romans appear to have built a small fort ("The Nunnery") on the island, possibly as part of the fortifications of the "Saxon Shore." Nothing is known of the island during the dark ages until it appears as part of the domain of the duke of Normandy early in the 11th century. Then and later the chapter of Coutances and Cherbourg abbey acquired important properties on the island. During the 13th and 14th centuries the administration of Alderney was similar to that of the other islands, on a reduced scale, the king's court being composed of a *prévôt* and seven jurats. (In the 13th century the chapter of Coutances claimed that it shared the lordship with the king and that the court was presided over alternately by the chapter's *prévôt* and the king's; but no evidence survives to support this claim.) The history of Alderney during the later middle ages is obscure. The island was occupied by the French from 1338 to 1340 and, though it never seems to have been left uninhabited as Sark was, it was frequently raided until late in the 16th century. In 1559 it was leased to George Chamberlain, and granted by letters patent to his brother John in 1584. John Chamberlain transferred the grant to the earl of Essex, whose descendants held it until the Civil War, though they never visited the island. From the Restoration, the government of Alderney was separated from that of Guernsey, being granted in 1660 to Edward de Carteret, who transferred it in 1661 to George de Carteret. George's widow sold it to Edmund Andros of Guernsey (*c.* 1682) from whom it descended to the Le Mesurier family, who held the island as hereditary governors until 1825, when it was reabsorbed into the government of Guernsey. During the 19th century Alderney was heavily fortified by the British government, which maintained a large garrison there until 1930. Immediately before the German occupation of June–July 1940, Alderney was completely evacuated. Repatriation of the Alderney community, which had been held together in England, was carried out between Nov. 1945 and July 1946. As a result, it has been necessary to re-create the island's economy and to make important changes in its government (1948–49). (*See* also CHANNEL ISLANDS.) (LE P.)

Population, Local Government and Communications.—The population (1961 census) was 1,472. The total has exceeded 1,000 since the late 17th century, except during the World War II evacuation and was above 1,500 at the censuses of 1921 and 1931. During the mid-19th century numbers were at times brought above 3,000 by a military garrison and by workers on the admiralty breakwater and war office forts constructed between 1845 and 1860. Exceptionally for the Channel Islands, settlement on Alderney is nucleated, most inhabitants living in the only town, St. Anne's, on the brow of the plateau overlooking Braye harbour. (Until the 16th or 17th century St. Anne's appears to have been called Sainte-Marie.) Newtown forms an appendage of St. Anne's at a lower level. Nucleation of settlement was associated with the holding of land in common; the cultivated area of the plateau top, the Blaye, is the common arable attached to St. Anne's; former common grazings, however, were distributed in 1831.

Alderney is included in the bailiwick of Guernsey (*q.v.*), but has its own local administration. Under the reformed constitution of 1949, the president and States of Alderney (nine members) are popularly elected; the Court of Alderney administers justice.

Communications are directed through Guernsey, to which Alderney is linked by air and shipping services. In addition to regular sailings of passenger and cargo vessels between the two islands, there are excursions in the summer season.

Production and Economy.—With external traffic delayed by transit through Guernsey, Alderney is poorly placed to share in the cropping for export which distinguishes the two largest Channel Islands. Tillage declined steeply between the two world wars, dairying becoming the leading type of farming and much of the Blaye being put to ley grass. Dairy farming and the tourist trade are the bases of the present economy. Little fishing is practised and the stone quarrying which flourished during the 19th century has almost ceased. (G. H. D.)

See L. L. Clarke, *The Island of Alderney* (1851); articles in *Transactions of La Société Guernesiaise,* esp. vol. xvi, A. H. Ewen, "The Town of St. Anne, Alderney"; *Report of the Committee of the Privy Council on the Island of Alderney* (1949: Cmd 7805); for general works see CHANNEL ISLANDS. (Le. P.)

ALDERSHOT, a municipal borough in the Aldershot parliamentary division of Hampshire, Eng., 34 mi. S.W. of London by road. Pop. (1961) 31,225. Area 6.5 sq.mi. Aldershot was a mere village until 1854 when a permanent military camp was established there on the advice of Lord Hardinge, commander in chief of the British army. He had already formed a temporary training camp on Chobham ridges, north-northeast of Aldershot, in 1852. During World War II Aldershot became a district and part of Southern command.

The borough, incorporated in 1922, is governed by 35 council members, 3 of whom are directly appointed by the secretary of state for war, in which respect Aldershot is unique. The military area in the immediate vicinity of the town is more than 4 sq.mi., including training grounds adjacent to the buildings. The borough, now entirely built up, has extended its houses over the county boundary into Surrey. There are several recreation grounds covering an area of more than 153 ac. The industries include printing and the manufacture of briar pipes and cosmetics.

On a hill to the west of the town is an equestrian statue of the duke of Wellington which was brought there from London in 1885.

ALDFRITH (d. 704), king of Northumbria from 685 to 704, was notable as a patron of literature. An illegitimate son of Oswiu, he succeeded to the throne when his brother Egfrith was killed at the battle of Nechtansmere, after which Bede says that "he nobly restored the ruined state of the kingdom, though within narrower bounds." Aldfrith was educated for the priesthood, probably studying at Malmesbury and in Ireland. Bede, Eddi (Eddius) and Alcuin praised his learning and Aldhelm dedicated to him, under the name of Acircius, his work on Latin metres. He was visited by Adamnan, abbot of Iona, whose work on the Holy Places he caused to be copied and he gave to the monastery of Wearmouth a large estate in exchange for a work on cosmography brought from Rome by Benedict Biscop. Stimulated by his interest, Northumbrian scholarship flourished, producing the conditions under which Bede was educated. Aldfrith resisted Bishop Wilfrid's claims to the whole of Northumbria as his see and expelled him in 691; in 702 he held a council at Austerfield on this question, but, although Wilfrid appealed to Rome, he was not restored in Northumbria until after Aldfrith had died, in Driffield, on Dec. 14, 704.

BIBLIOGRAPHY.—Bede, *Historia Ecclesiastica,* bk. iv, ch. 24, bk. v, ch. 12, 15, 18 ff., 21; Eddius, *Life of Bishop Wilfrid,* ed. by B. Colgrave (1927); *Anglo-Saxon Chronicle;* F. M. Stenton, *Anglo-Saxon England,* 2nd ed. (1947). (D. Wk.)

ALDHELM (*c.* 639–709), abbot of Malmesbury in Wiltshire, Eng., the most learned teacher of 7th-century Wessex, a pioneer in the art of Latin verse among the English and author of numerous writings in Latin in both verse and prose which are still extant, was born about 639 in southwest England, of the royal house of the west Saxons. His education gave him training both in Celtic-Irish scholarship, then eagerly sought by the Saxons, and in knowledge from continental sources. As a boy of about 15 he entered the monastic enclosure which had been established at Malmesbury, where he learned Latin, with something of the Latin Bible and its interpretation by the Latin Fathers, from Maelduib (Mailduif), Malmesbury's Irish founder. Soon after he was 30 he went on to study in the famous School of Canterbury under Theodore of Tarsus, consecrated archbishop in 668, and Hadrian, once abbot of a monastery near Naples, who was head of the abbey of St. Peter and St. Paul.

There Aldhelm studied biblical and patristic writings and canon and civil law. He read widely in Latin poetry and prose, pagan as well as sacred, he learned Greek, he followed the arithmetic and the astronomy of his day, and he worked hard at the varied forms and intricacies of metrical science. But these secular studies were to him but handmaids in the service of the church. Eventually he returned to Malmesbury, where, about 675, he succeeded Maelduib as abbot. From this time until 705 he carried on a threefold work, as monk and priest, as encourager of learning, and as Latin poet.

His work as monk and priest was both pastoral and concerned with the development of the west Saxon church. At Malmesbury he trained Saxon youths as novices in the rule of St. Benedict, then making its way into English houses of religion; he built three churches; and he taught the people of the surrounding countryside. A pleasant story tells that he was skilled in his native Anglo-Saxon song, and that on Sunday mornings he would stand on the bridge over the Avon to try to attract by his singing lazy peasants who had stolen out of church before the sermon which followed the liturgy. He also founded a monastery at Bradford-on-Avon, in Wiltshire, and another at Frome in Somerset. About 693 he journeyed to Rome as a pilgrim at the invitation of the pope and brought back for the monasteries under his control a written privilege of exemption from papal control. At the request of the Saxon bishops he composed a letter of remonstrance addressed to the British king and the clergy of Devon and Cornwall, exhorting them to give up their stubborn adherence to their own Celtic dating of Easter and to their Celtic tonsure in favour of the Roman discipline, which was followed by Canterbury.

As scholar and teacher Aldhelm's influence was chiefly exerted through the aid and encouragement he gave to other scholars by his vigorous letters. Those still extant show evidence of his Celtic training. They are written in an almost unreadable Latin: a mixture of words foreign, hybrid, artificial, piled one on another in long, alliterative sequences, in swollen, bombastic sentences. Such concoction of "Latin" prose was the delight of many Celtic scholars in the early middle ages. In similar prose he also wrote a lengthy treatise on the celibate life for the nuns of Barking in Essex. Its flood of learning and its difficult style so delighted the community that he promptly proceeded to make a version in Latin hexameters.

For it was on metrical science that Aldhelm spent the time he could spare from his duties as abbot and counselor. The riddles of Symphosius, a 5th- or 6th-century Latin poet, inspired him to compose 100 brief poems of the same kind in Latin hexameters; these he inserted as illustrations in a treatise on metrics sent to his friend Aldfrith, king of Northumbria from 685 to 704. Usually of four or five lines, they describe everyday objects both natural and man-made in riddles and double acrostics intended to puzzle and delight the reader. There are pictures in verse of sun, clouds, wind, fire and water; of beast, bird and insect (lion, elephant and camel; eagle, nightingale and swallow; spider, caterpillar and bee); of household utensils and tools (candle, spindle, bellows, even a "double cooker"); of pen and writing tablets; and of an organ. Finally all is summed up in 83 lines praising the Lord who created all.

At the end of his treatise Aldhelm asked Aldfrith to study and to defend this new venture in writing: "no one of Saxon race has toiled in this way before myself." In the 8th century Saxon writers—Tatwine, archbishop of Canterbury; Eusebius, probably abbot of Wearmouth in Durham; St. Boniface, apostle of Germany—found in Aldhelm's work inspiration for their own Latin riddles.

In 705 Aldhelm was consecrated bishop for the region west of Selwood forest: Somerset and parts of Dorset and Devon, with his seat at Sherborne in Dorset. He died in 709 at Doulting in Somerset. Its church bears his name, as do those of Broadway in Somerset and Bishopstrow in Wiltshire.

The best edition of Aldhelm's work is *Aldhelmi S. Opera,* by R. Ehwald, in *Monumenta Germaniae Historica, Auctores Antiquissimi,* xv (1919). There is also an edition by J. A. Giles, *Patres Ecclesiae Anglicanae,* i (1844), reprinted in J. P. Migne, *Patrologia Latina,* lxxxix, 87 ff.; it includes a *Vita S. Aldhelmi* (by Faricius, abbot of Abingdon, d. 1117).

BIBLIOGRAPHY.—Leo Bönhoff, *Aldhelm von Malmesbury* (1894); W. Bright, *Chapters of Early English Church History* (1897); E. von Erhardt-Siebold, "Die lateinischen Rätsel der Angelsachsen," in *Ang-*

listische Forschungen, lxi (1925); E. S. Duckett, *Anglo-Saxon Saints and Scholars* (1947); Archer Taylor, *The Literary Riddle Before 1600* (1948); F. J. E. Raby, *A History of Christian-Latin Poetry,* 2nd ed. (1953); M. L. W. Laistner, *Thought and Letters in Western Europe,* 2nd ed. (1957). (E. S. DT.)

ALDOBRANDESCHI, in medieval Italy, a Tuscan feudal family, which was probably descended from a Count Hildebrand recorded in the late 9th century. The period of the Aldobrandeschi's greatest power was in the 11th and 12th centuries, when their lands extended from Colle di Val d'Elsa near Siena to the lake of Bolsena and included the Tuscan Maremma, Mt. Amiata and the towns of Grosseto and Pitigliano. While the size and situation of their lands enabled the Aldobrandeschi to hold out against the communes longer than most other feudal families of Tuscany, they gradually yielded ground to Siena and Orvieto, being much weakened after 1208 by the division of their lands among the four sons of Count Aldobrandino. After 1216 Orvieto gained control of the territory situated south of the Albegna river, and Siena, to which the Aldobrandeschi had submitted in 1221, captured Grosseto in 1224. In the course of the 13th century Orvieto and Siena increased their effective hold over the Aldobrandeschine lands. The division of these between the Aldobrandeschi of Santa Fiora and those of Sovana-Pitigliano became definitive in 1274. The lands of the Aldobrandeschi of Sovana-Pitigliano passed to the Orsini in the following century.

See G. Ciacci, *Gli Aldobrandeschi nella storia e nella "Divina Commedia"* (1935); D. Waley, *Mediaeval Orvieto* (1952). (N. R.)

ALDRED (EALDRED) (d. 1069), Anglo-Saxon archbishop of York who played an important part in politics at the Norman conquest. He became bishop of Worcester in 1046 but was made to relinquish this see in 1062 by the pope, having become archbishop of York at Christmas 1060. He nevertheless retained for some time all but 7 of the Worcester estates and kept 12 until his death. He unsuccessfully claimed jurisdiction over Lindsey against the bishop of Dorchester. He was prominent even before his elevation to York and in 1054 he went to Germany to negotiate the return of the heir to the throne, Edward, son of Edmund II "Ironside." He administered the see of Ramsbury (Wiltshire) from about 1055 to 1058, and that of Hereford from 1056 to 1060. In 1058 he made a pilgrimage to Jerusalem. As archbishop, he established prebends at Southwell and added to the buildings there and at York and Beverley, which he enriched with treasures. He was a friend of Earl Godwin's sons, and it was probably he who crowned Harold as king. After the battle of Hastings he was among those who wished to elect Edgar the Atheling, but soon after he submitted to William at Berkhamsted. He crowned William on Christmas day 1066. He died in York on Sept. 11, 1069.

BIBLIOGRAPHY.—*Anglo-Saxon Chronicle; Historians of the Church of York,* ed. by J. Raine, vol. i, pp. 239–242, vol. ii, pp. 344–354 (1879–94); *Vita Wulfstani,* ed. by R. R. Darlington (1928); F. M. Stenton, *Anglo-Saxon England,* 2nd ed. (1947). (D. WK.)

ALDRICH, NELSON WILMARTH (1841–1915), U.S. senator and financier, was born in Foster, R.I., Nov. 6, 1841. Highly competent in politics and business, he rose from the Providence common council through the Rhode Island legislature to the U.S. congress (representative 1879–81, senator 1881–1911), meanwhile amassing a modest fortune through investments in banking, electricity, gas, rubber, sugar and traction. A member of the small inner coterie setting Republican legislative policy, he was distinguished for his great skill in handling both friendly and unfriendly individuals. Attackers could not disturb his equipoise. He was exceptionally free from presidential ambitions, political resentments and oratorical compulsions. He quietly and effectively implemented conservative Republican doctrines, shouldering much of the labour in securing the rising rates in the tariffs. Through his influence the Interstate Commerce act of 1887 and the Sherman Anti-Trust act of 1890 were modified in a conservative direction. By his work on the Aldrich-Vreeland Currency act of 1908 and his chairmanship of the national monetary commission, 1908–12, he helped to prepare the way for the Federal Reserve act of 1913 (*see* FEDERAL RESERVE SYSTEM). He died in New York City, April 16, 1915.

See N. W. Stephenson, *Nelson W. Aldrich, a Leader in American Poli-*

tics (1930). (J. P. N.)

ALDRICH, THOMAS BAILEY (1836–1907), U.S. author and editor, was born on Nov. 11, 1836, in Portsmouth, N.H., a town portrayed in his popular classic *The Story of a Bad Boy.* His education was interrupted at the age of 13, when his father died, and shortly after he became a merchant's clerk in New York city. He began to contribute to various newspapers and magazines. After publication of his first book of verse, *The Bells* (1855), he became junior literary critic on the *New York Evening Mirror,* and later subeditor of the *Home Journal.* For the remainder of his life he devoted himself to literary work. He acted as adviser to various publishing houses, but his chief work was as a contributor to and editor of various magazines. He was editor of the *Atlantic Monthly* (1881–90).

The cultural atmosphere of New England and his frequent European tours were the most influential factors in ripening his art. Few poets have so ruthlessly discarded early poems in later editions. His verse is therefore better studied in later volumes such as *Cloth of Gold* (1874), *Flower and Thorn* (1877), *Mercedes and Later Lyrics* (1884), *Windham Towers* (1890), and the various collected editions. These show him to be a poet of lyrical skill and felicitous conceit. His long narrative and dramatic poems are less successful.

His best-known prose works are the autobiographical *The Story of a Bad Boy* (1870), and *Marjorie Daw and Other People* (1873), a collection of short stories. His effective use of the surprise ending influenced the development of the short story. He died in Boston, Mass., March 19, 1907.

Aldrich's writings were collected in 1897 and in 1907 (Ponkapog edition). *See also* Ferris Greenslet, *Life of Thomas Bailey Aldrich* (1908), and Lilian W. Aldrich, *Crowding Memories* (1920).

ALDRIDGE, IRA FREDERICK (called the AFRICAN ROSCIUS) (1804–1867), U.S. Negro tragedian, considered one of the finest actors of his time, probably was born in New York City. Little is known of his early life; he may have begun his acting career at the African Theatre in New York. He went to England around 1824 and made his English debut in 1825. He appeared in such roles as Othello, Lear, Macbeth, and Rolla. It is debatable whether he ever returned to the United States; if so, it was in an unsuccessful engagement at Baltimore, Md., during the 1830s. After 1853 he played primarily on the European continent where he amassed a considerable fortune and received many honours, including tributes from the emperor of Austria and the king of Prussia. In 1863 he became an English citizen.

While on a trip to Russia Aldridge died, on Aug. 7, 1867, at Lodz, Poland.

See Herbert Marshall and Mildred Stock, *Ira Aldridge, the Negro Tragedian* (1958). (O. G. B.)

ALDRIDGE, an urban district in the Walsall South parliamentary division of Staffordshire, Eng., lying about 10 mi. N. of the centre of Birmingham. · Pop. (1961) 51,046. Area 1.5 sq.mi. The district comprises the parishes or villages of Aldridge, Great Barr, Pelsall, Pheasey, Rushall and Streetly. At the time of Domesday Book in the 11th century Aldridge (Alrewic) and Great Barr (Barre) were both held by the knight, Robert, from William Fitz Ansculf of Dudley castle. Later Aldridge became a separate manor. In the 12th century Aldridge was included in the royal forest of Cannock, while Great Barr was in Sutton Chase. In the later middle ages Great Barr was a charcoal-burning centre. This "Colefield"—a lawless district—stretched northward and eastward to Sutton and Aldridge. The destruction of trees left a waste or common for sheep, which was enclosed in 1795; on this former common is the 700 ft. high ridge, Barr beacon, which served as a signal point from Tudor times. The park on the summit is a World War I memorial. Until the 19th century Aldridge and Barr were largely agricultural, but from 1880 to 1936 coal mining was the chief occupation at Aldridge. Limestone beds at Rushall were quarried from the 13th century to 1939; local ironstone maintained an iron industry there from the later middle ages.

Notable buildings are Great Barr hall (now St. Margaret's hospital) and the timber-framed Old hall. Local products include bricks and tiles, especially the Staffordshire blue brick, while machinery making, metallurgy and general, electrical and light engineering are the chief industries in the local authority's industrial estate. Considerable expansion in industry had taken place by the early 1960s, but the convenient distance of the district from Walsall and Birmingham helped to preserve its residential character.

ALDROVANDA (*Aldrovanda vesiculosa*) is a small carnivorous (insectivorous) plant that traps and digests insects. *See* also CARNIVOROUS PLANTS.

ALDROVANDI, ULISSE (1522–1605), distinguished Italian naturalist and author of a famous work on natural history, was born at Bologna. He became page to a bishop, then to a merchant at Brescia and subsequently went on a pilgrimage to Spain. Returning to Bologna he studied law both there and at Padua but eventually changed to medicine. In 1549 he was accused of Lutheranism and arrested and sent to Rome but was conditionally released by the Inquisition. He returned to Bologna and after becoming doctor of medicine in 1553, took up the study of botany and became professor of natural history and logic at the university in 1560. Aldrovandi persuaded the senate to found a botanical garden and was its first director. He was also inspector of drugs and pharmacies and incurred the enmity of local apothecaries who tried to have him dismissed, but his appointment was confirmed by Pope Gregory XIII. His book *Antidotarii Bononiensis epitome* (Bologna, 1574) is a model for subsequent pharmacopoeias. He formed a museum at Bologna, still in existence. He employed artists and engravers for more than 30 years in connection with the production of his immense compilation on natural history. Only four volumes of this great work appeared during his lifetime but another ten volumes were prepared from his manuscripts by his pupils at the expense of the senate of Bologna university and even this represents only a part of the material he had accumulated. In addition Aldrovandi wrote an account of various ancient statues in Rome (*see* L. Mauro, *Le Antichità della città di Roma, etc.* [Venice, 1556]). (ED. HE.)

ALE: *see* BEER.

ALEANDRO, GIROLAMO (HIERONYMUS ALEANDER) (1480–1542), Italian cardinal and humanist, who was an important opponent of the Lutheran Reformation, was born at Motta di Treviso, near Venice, on Feb. 13, 1480. A remarkable scholar, particularly of classical languages, he was in his youth closely associated with Erasmus. He lectured at Venice, Orléans and Paris where he was appointed rector of the university. In 1520 Pope Leo X sent him to Germany to lead the opposition against Luther at the Diet of Worms. This brought about his break with Erasmus. The edict against Luther, which was adopted by the Diet, was drawn up and proposed by Aleandro, and in Brussels it was Aleandro who was responsible for the death of the first martyrs of the Reformation. In 1523 Clement VII sent him as nuncio to the court of Francis I with whom he was taken prisoner at the battle of Pavia (1525). He was subsequently employed on various papal missions, especially to Germany, but was unable to check the progress of the new doctrines. He was created cardinal in 1538 by Paul III, and died at Rome on Feb. 1, 1542.

Apart from Latin verses and a scholastic work on Greek grammar, Aleandro's chief work is his unfinished treatise, *De habendo Concilio*, setting out his views on the Council of Trent of which he was the ardent supporter. This and other documents of Aleandro in the Vatican library, relating to his opposition to Luther, were used in Sforza Pallavicino's *Istoria del Concilio Tridentino* ("History of the Council of Trent"; 1656).

See also J. Paquier, *L'Humanisme et la Réforme* (1900); J. Paquier (ed.), *Lettres familières de Jérôme Aléandre* (1909).

GIROLAMO ALEANDRO (1574–1649), the grandnephew of the cardinal, was a poet, scholar and antiquarian. He was a founder of the Roman Academy of Humorists and wrote scholarly works on archaeology, ancient costumes and religion.

ALEARDI, ALEARDO, CONTE (1812–1878), whose life and work are typical of the 19th-century Italian poet patriots. Born at Verona, Nov. 4, 1812, he was brought up to resent Austrian rule. He was associated with the poet Giovanni Prati in pub-

lishing a political journal, *Il Caffè Pedrocchi*, and for his part in the revolutionary movements of the 1840s and 1850s was twice imprisoned and finally exiled. His best political poems are the ode *Le città italiane marinare e commercianti* (1856) and *I Tre Fiumi* (1857). He also wrote popular love poems, *Lettere a Maria* (1847). Returning to Verona after the expulsion of the Austrians, he became professor at the academy of fine arts, and published his *Il canto politico* (1862). He sat in the Italian parliament and was eventually made a senator. He died at Verona, July 17, 1878. A collection of his poems, *Canti scelti di Aleardo Aleardi*, was edited by L. Grilli (1918).

See V. Primavera, *Aleardi e la sua fortuna* (1929).

ALECSANDRI, VASILE (1819 or 1821–1890), Rumanian lyric poet and dramatist, was the first collector of Rumanian popular songs and one of the leaders of the movement for the union of the Rumanian principalities. Born at Bacău in Moldavia, he was educated at Jassy and subsequently in Paris (1834–39). He published his first collection of folk songs in 1844 and was also active in the Rumanian revolutionary cause. His lyrical poems, *Doine şi Lăcrimioare*, appeared in Paris in 1853 and during 1852–53 he published at Jassy two volumes of ballads and songs. In 1867 he published his descriptive poems of landscapes entitled *Pasteluri*. As a playwright he created Rumanian social comedy, but his most important contributions to the theatre were his poetic dramas: *Despot Vodă* (1879), *Fântâna Blanduziei* (1884) and *Ovidiu* (1885). In later life Alecsandri played an important part in his country's affairs. As minister for foreign affairs (1859–60), he went to London as Prince Alexander Cuza's special envoy to seek British recognition of the United Rumanian Principalities. In 1885 he was appointed Rumanian minister in Paris. He died at Mirceşti, on Aug. 22, 1890. (G. NS.)

ALEGRÍA, CIRO (1909–   ), Peruvian novelist, was born in Sartimbamba, Nov. 4, 1909. He is Spanish America's foremost writer of the Indianist novel, for which he draws on firsthand knowledge acquired in his native province of Huamachuco. From 1930 to 1934 active in the Aprista party's program of social reform, he was twice jailed and finally exiled to Chile. His best novel, *El mundo es ancho y ajeno* (1941) (English trans. by H. de Onís, *Broad and Alien Is the World* [1941]), the story of an Indian tribe struggling to survive against the greed of land-hungry white men, won first prize in an international competition judged at New York. In that same year he came to the United States and remained until 1948. All his novels have to do with the Peruvian Indians, sympathetically portraying them as communities engaged in conflict with an unfriendly environment. Accurate observation of folkways and a flexible, simplified style contribute to the powerful effect. *La serpiente de oro* (1935) (English trans., *The Golden Serpent* [1943]) tells of the diversified human life along the Marañón river; *Los perros hambrientos* (1938) concerns the difficulties faced by sheepherding Indians of the highlands.

See Jefferson Rea Spell, *Contemporary Spanish-American Fiction*, pp. 253–268 (1944).

ALEKHINE (ALJECHIN), **ALEXANDER** (originally ALEKSANDR ALEKSANDROVICH ALEKHIN) (1892–1946), champion chess player, was born in Moscow on Nov. 1, 1892. He displayed precocious ability as a chess player, and in 1910 he did well at the Hamburg tournament at the age of 17. When World War I broke out in 1914 he was playing at the Mannheim tournament and escaped from internment to serve in the Red Cross division of the Russian army. After the Revolution he became a naturalized Frenchman, and studied law at the University of Paris. The victor in many international tournaments, he won the world championship for blindfold chess in 1924, 1925 and 1933. In 1927 he won the world championship from Capablanca (champion since 1921), lost it in 1935 to Max Euwe, but regained it from Euwe in 1937.

Alekhine died March 24, 1946, in Estoril, Port.

See his book, *My Best Hundred Games* (Eng. trans., 1927).

ALEKSEEV, MIKHAIL VASILIEVICH (1857–1918), Russian general, a leading champion of the White cause in the civil war following the Russian Revolution, was born in Tver on Nov. 15 (new style; Nov. 3 old style), 1857, the son of a private soldier. Entering the army in 1876, he graduated in 1890 from the staff college and became a general in 1904. In World War I, as chief of staff to the southwest army group, he planned the successful Russian offensive into Galicia (1914). After five difficult months in command of the northwestern front he became chief of the general staff in Aug. 1915 and assumed control of all Russian armies in the European theatre. As a strategist he was capable, but was reluctant to delegate responsibility. His task was hampered by the growing isolation of the court from public opinion, and in the autumn of 1916 he prepared a somewhat desperate plan whereby the emperor Nicholas II was to be presented with an ultimatum and forced to grant reforms. But Alekseev's intentions became known; he fell ill and was suspended from duty.

In March 1917 he helped to bring about Nicholas' abdication and was appointed commander in chief; but, considering the provisional government insufficiently resolute in combating the dissolution of the army, he resigned his post on May 21. Subsequently he sympathized with Gen. L. G. Kornilov and attempted to effect a compromise between him and A. F. Kerenski. After the Bolshevik revolution Alekseev escaped to the Don, where he started to organize an anti-Bolshevik volunteer army. Command of this force, however, soon passed to Kornilov, succeeded on his death by A. I. Denikin, while Alekseev retained control of political affairs. He died in Ekaterinodar (now Krasnodar) on Oct. 8, 1918.

(J. L. H. K.)

ALEMÁN, MATEO (1547–1614?), Spanish picaresque novelist, a master stylist and rhetorical moralizer, was born at Seville, the son of the physician to the royal prison. His forebears were Jews forcibly converted to Catholicism, and consciousness of this background coloured his life's work. Alemán graduated at Seville in 1564. He studied medicine at Salamanca and Alcalá for four years but never practised. In 1580 he was imprisoned for debt. His literary career began with the publication of a prologue to a book of moral proverbs in 1598. The first part of his chief work, *Guzmán de Alfarache*, the quintessential example of the picaresque novel, appeared in 1599, and had the most immediate success of any Spanish classic. There were 23 editions (50,000 copies) in five years and translations into several languages, including English (1624; mod. ed. 1924); since almost all the editions were pirated, the financial position of the author was not improved, and he was again imprisoned for debt. The second part of *Guzmán* appeared in Lisbon in 1604. Aleman's view of humanity was one of suspicious pessimism. He made two important journeys: to Italy and to Mexico, where he died, probably in 1614. (Ay. K.)

ALEMÁN, MIGUEL (1902–   ), Mexican political figure, president of Mexico from 1946 to 1952, was born on Sept. 29, 1902, in Sayula, Veracruz, where his father was a village shopkeeper and subsequently a revolutionary general. He was educated in Mexico City and in 1925 entered the National Autonomous university to study law. At the age of 26 Alemán set up practice in Mexico City, specializing in labour cases. In 1930 he entered politics. He was appointed senator from Veracruz and in 1936 became governor of his native state. In 1940 he resigned to manage the successful presidential campaign of Manuel Ávila Camacho (*q.v.*), who rewarded him with the powerful post of minister of *gobernación* ("interior"). Alemán became the official candidate for the presidency (Partido Revolucionario Institucional, or Revolutionary Institutional party) in 1946 and easily defeated Ezequiel Padilla. His administration saw a slowdown in Mexico's agrarian reform, but greatly accelerated industrial development. Though there were charges of extensive graft and corruption in government, nonetheless, economic progress was marked during Alemán's term of office. *See* Mexico: *History.*

(R. E. Q.)

ALEMBERT, JEAN LE ROND D' (1717–1783), French mathematician and philosopher is remembered for his enunciation of "D'Alembert's principle," a basic concept in mechanics, and for his work in connection with Diderot's *Encyclopaedia.* He was born in Paris in Nov. 1717. He was a foundling but it afterward became known that he was the illegitimate son of the Chevalier Destouches and Madame de Tencin. Destouches, without disclosing his identity, provided for the boy, who was educated at the

Mazarin college under the Jansenists.

Having studied law, he was admitted as an advocate in 1738, but did not enter upon practice. He next devoted himself to medicine; but within a year he resolved to give his whole time to mathematics. In 1741 he received his first public distinction in being admitted a member of the Academy of Sciences, to which he had previously presented several papers, including a *Mémoire sur le calcul intégral* (1739). In his *Mémoire sur la réfraction des corps solides* (1741) he was the first to give a theoretical explanation of the phenomenon which is witnessed when a body passes from one fluid to another more dense in a direction not perpendicular to the surface which separates the two fluids. In 1743 he published his *Traité de dynamique,* a work famous as developing the mechanical principle, known as "D'Alembert's principle," first enunciated in 1742. In 1744 D'Alembert applied this principle to the theory of the equilibrium and the motion of fluids, *Traité de l'équilibre et du mouvement des fluides,* and all the problems before solved by geometricians became in some measure its corollaries.

This discovery was followed by that of the calculus of partial differences, the first trials of which were published in his *Réflexions sur la cause générale des vents* (1747). In 1747 he applied his new calculus to the problem of vibrating chords. In 1749 he furnished a method of applying his principles to the motion of any body of a given figure; and in 1754 he solved the problem of the precession of the equinoxes, determined its quantity and explained the phenomenon of the nutation of the earth's axis. In 1752 he published an *Essai d'une nouvelle théorie sur la résistance des fluides,* which contains a large number of original ideas and new observations. In 1746 and 1748 he published in the *Memoirs* of the Academy of Berlin "Recherches sur le calcul intégral," a branch of mathematical science which is greatly indebted to him. In his *Recherches sur différents points importants du système du monde* (1754–56) he perfected the solution of the problem of the perturbations of the planets, which he had presented to the academy some years before.

D'Alembert's association with Diderot in the preparation of the *Dictionnaire Encyclopédique* led him to a wider range of work. He contributed the *Discours préliminaire* on the rise, progress and affinities of the various sciences. He also wrote several literary articles for the first two volumes of the encyclopaedia, and to the remaining volumes he contributed mathematical articles chiefly. Of D'Alembert's works on other than mathematical subjects the most important is the *Éléments de Philosophie* (1759) in which he discussed the principles and methods of the different sciences. D'Alembert was much interested in music both as a science and as an art, and wrote *Éléments de musique théorique et pratique* (1779).

D'Alembert died in Paris on Oct. 29, 1783.

BIBLIOGRAPHY.—The scientific works of D'Alembert have never been published in a collected form. The most important of them have been mentioned above, with the exception of the *Opuscules mathématiques* (1761–80). His literary and philosophical works were collected and edited by Bastien (1805). A better edition by Bossange was published at Paris in 1821. *See* J. L. F. Bertrand, *D'Alembert* (1889).

ALEMBIC, an apparatus for distillation (*q.v.*) used chiefly by the alchemists, and now superseded by more convenient forms of still, both in the laboratory and in the factory. It consisted essentially of three parts: a vessel containing the material to be distilled and called, from its gourdlike shape, the cucurbit, or mattrass; a vessel to receive and condense the vapour, called the head, capital or alembic proper; and a receiver for the distillate, connected by a pipe with the capital. The entire apparatus was sometimes constructed of glass, but more usually the cucurbit was of copper or earthenware, and the capital alone of glass.

ALENÇON, DUCS D'. The French peerage duchy of Alençon was created in 1415, when the countship of Alençon was raised to that rank. The town of Alençon in Normandy (now in the French *département* of Orne), is known to have been held as a seigniory by the house of Bellême at least from the time of Guillaume I (d. 1028). By the marriage of Guillaume's granddaughter Mabille (d. 1082) to Roger de Montgomery, who first took the title of count, Alençon passed to a new line, but the last heiress of this line sold her rights to Philip II of France about 1220. Louis IX of France in 1268 granted the countship as an appanage to his fifth son, Pierre, who held it until his death in 1284. It was next, in 1293, granted to Charles of Valois, on whose death in 1325 it passed to his second son Charles (killed at the battle of Crécy in 1346). This Charles's grandson, Jean (1385–1415), was created duc d'Alençon on Jan. 1, 1415 (new style; 1414 old style) but did not long enjoy his duchy, as he was killed the following October in the battle of Agincourt. His son and successor Jean II (1409–76), who was at first dispossessed of Alençon by the English but recovered it in 1449, conspired first against Charles VII of France on behalf of the future Louis XI, then against Louis on behalf of the English, with the result that he spent many years in prison. The last duc of the first line, Jean II's grandson Charles (1489–1525), disgraced himself when Francis I of France was taken prisoner at the battle of Pavia, and died soon afterward leaving no heir. His widow Margaret of Angoulême (Francis I's sister, later queen of Navarre) then held the duchy until her death in 1549, whereupon it was reunited to the French crown. Catherine de Médicis, to whom it was granted for her lifetime in 1559, transferred it in 1566 to her youngest son François Hercule (1554–84), later duc d'Anjou, who is remembered for his intrigues under Charles IX and Henry III, for his persistent wooing of Elizabeth I of England (1579 and 1581–82) and for his campaign in the Spanish Netherlands (1582–83) with a view to securing the duchy of Brabant for himself. On his death it passed back again to the French crown. Louis XIV's uncle, Gaston, duc d'Orléans, to whom the appanage was granted in 1646, transferred it to his daughter Elizabeth (1646–96), who married Louis Joseph, duc de Guise. On the death of their son François Joseph, duc de Guise, in 1675, Alençon again returned to the crown. Louis XIV's grandson, Charles, duc de Berry, had the appanage from 1710 to his death in 1714 and Louis XVI's brother, the future Louis XVIII, received it in 1785. The title duc d'Alençon was revived for Ferdinand (1844–1910), second son of Louis d'Orléans, duc de Nemours, and passed from him to his son Emmanuel (1872–1931), who was also duc de Vendôme.

ALENÇON, a town and prefecture of Orne *département* in northwest France, lies 30 mi. N. of Le Mans by road at the confluence of the Sarthe and Briante rivers and in the centre of a plain surrounded by wooded hills. Pop. (1954) 19,427. Of the castle of the dukes of Alençon, taken by William of Normandy in 1048, a pepperpot tower and a 15th-century fortified gateway remain; the 18th-century law courts incorporate the living quarters. In the church of Notre Dame (13th–18th century) Thérèse Martin (St. Thérèse de Lisieux), born at Alençon in 1873, was baptized. The town hall (1783) contains an art gallery and an exhibition of Alençon lace, and the 15th-century Maison d'Oze contains historical documents. The municipal library is in the former Jesuit chapel (16th-century). There is an airfield for local services at Valframbert, about 2 mi. N.E. The chief industry is lacemaking, especially *point d'Alençon*, copied from Venice and introduced by Jean Baptiste Colbert in the mid-17th century. Printing, dyeing and the manufacture of household goods and sewing machines are also carried on, and Alençon is an agricultural market centre. It was the capital of the county and duchy of Alençon and passed to the French crown in 1549. Heavily damaged in World War II, it was the first town to be liberated by Gen. Jacques Philippe Leclerc in 1944. (A.-M. JA.)

ALENI, GIULIO (1582–1649), Italian Jesuit missionary, author of a Chinese *Life of Christ* used even by Protestant missionaries, was born in Brescia. He landed at Macao in 1610 and penetrated into China three years later. During his more than 30 years residence in China he adopted the dress and manners of the country, was the first Christian missionary in Kiangsi and built several churches in Fukien. In addition to the *Life of Christ* (8 vol., 1635–37; often reprinted), he wrote a cosmography (*I che fang wai ki Hang-chow*, 6 vol., 1623) which was translated into Manchu under the title *The True Origin of 10,000 Things*. A copy was sent from Peking to Paris in 1789. Aleni died in Foochow on Aug. 3, 1649.

ALENTEJO, an ancient province of southern Portugal, lies mostly south of the Tagus valley, and is bounded on the east by the Guadiana river, which forms part of the Portuguese-Spanish frontier. Pop. (1950) 780,610. Area 10,152 sq.mi. It is a vast, rolling plain, four-fifths of it at 300–600 ft., rising gradually to 900–1,500 ft., in the south and the northeast. It has a monotonous landscape of large, open fields with cereal crops, isolated in the poorer lands by wastes of gum cistus or woodlands of cork and evergreen oaks. Prevalently poor schistose soils and the traditions of latifundia explain the low densities of population, 10–70 per square mile.

In 1933 Alentejo was divided into two provinces, Alto Alentejo (*q.v.*) in the north whose capital is Evora (pop. 25,409) and Baixo Alentejo (*q.v.*), of which Beja is the capital (14,028).

(J. M. Ho.)

ALEPPO (Arabic, HALEB or HALAB), a city and administrative district of Syria, stands on a series of limestone hills at 1,220 ft. above sea level, and on a small stream, the Kuwaik (anc. Chalys). It is the largest city in Syria and the mercantile centre of the country. Pop. (1960) 957,000. The inhabitants are mainly Muslims, but there are large Christian-Arab, Armenian and Kurdish communities. The climate is healthful and bracing, though of continental type; in summer maximum temperatures of between 110° and 115° F. are tempered by breezes. The region has always suffered from severe earthquakes; the town was damaged in 1157 and partially destroyed in 1822 and 1830.

After World War II Aleppo expanded considerably, particularly to the north and west of the old square town which frames the citadel. In the new quarters there are many fine streets shaded with trees and modern buildings of cement and stone, including banks, hotels, hospitals and factories. Water is piped from the Euphrates. Part of the University of Syria, including the engineering faculty, is housed there, and the new museum, with its important collection from Ras Shamra (anc. Ugarit) and Mari, is centrally situated. The old quarter has the most famous covered bazaars in the middle east, extending over 15 mi., and many khans, mosques and merchants' houses. These are all stone built, many dating from the 16th or 17th centuries. The most spectacular building is the citadel, on a semiartificial mound dominating the city. The present building, erected on the site of earlier fortifications of Byzantine date, was constructed in the 12th century A.D. and restored in the 16th. Its gate bears an inscription of the Mameluke sultan Khalid, who restored it after the sack of the city by the Mongols in 1258. The earliest remains excavated under the citadel are Hittite; on top is a mosque dedicated to Abraham, on the site of a Byzantine church. Five of the original nine gates of Aleppo were still visible in the second half of the 20th century, the best preserved being the Bab al-Hadid ("the Iron gate"), 15th century, the Bab al-Antakya ("the Gate of Antioch"), 12th century, and the Bab Kinnesrin. The city walls, built in the

AUTHENTICATED NEWS

12TH CENTURY TURKISH CITADEL IN ALEPPO, AROUND WHICH THE OLD CITY WAS BUILT

Hellenistic period and reconstructed first in the 12th century and again in the 15th, were also still partially intact.

There are many mosques: the largest is the Jami Zakariyah (the Great Mosque), built in 715 on the site of the Christian cathedral and named after Zacharias, the father of John the Baptist. Its finest feature is the minaret, of Seljuk workmanship, built in 1090. The mosque was destroyed twice by fire and rebuilt (in 1159 and in 1258). The oldest mosque is the Jami Tut ah, mid-7th century. South of the main town is the madrasah and mosque of Al-Firdaus ("the School of Paradise"), founded by the widow of Al-Zahir Gazi, as a monument to him, the finest surviving piece of medieval architecture in Syria. The theological schools include the madrasah Hallawiyah, built on the site of the 5th-century Byzantine cathedral, a foundation of the empress Helena, and converted into a mosque in the 12th century, and also the Sultaniyyah and the Sharafiyah, the latter containing a fine library of Arabic manuscripts. Nearby is the Khan al-Gumruk ("Inn of the Customs"), the 16th-century headquarters of the European merchants. The largest khan is that of the vizier (16th century), well decorated in black and white stone, and the most ornamental is the khan al-Sabun, early 16th century. Houses in the older quarters, often fine examples of 17th- or 18th-century building, with open courtyards surrounding a pool with shady trees and with beautifully carved interior woodwork, have in many cases been transformed into schools or orphanages.

Aleppo is situated on the Istanbul-Baghdad railway and is also linked by rail with Beirut and with Tripoli, Lebanon, and by narrow-gauge line with Damascus, Syria. It is a focal point for transdesert routes to Mosul and Baghdad in Iraq, and is linked by motor roads with Antakya (Antioch), in Turkey, Latakia and Damascus. There is an airfield, 2 mi. S.E., at Nerab. The town is an important centre for the textile trade; its chief industries are silk weaving and cotton printing, and subsidiary industries include wool, hides, dried fruit and nuts. There are cement and cotton-ginning factories.

History.—Haleb (Halpa) is believed to be a place where Abraham grazed his cows; it is said to derive its name from the Semitic term for milk. It is first mentioned in the 3rd-millennium texts of the Agade period, but the existence of an earlier settlement is indicated by the remains of prehistoric Tell Halaf pottery of the 6th millennium B.C. on the hills now incorporated within the city boundary. The presence of the Islamic citadel on the ancient hill of Aleppo precluded extensive excavations, but material from the 2nd millennium B.C. has been unearthed. According to the Mari letters of that period the city in the 18th century B.C. had a powerful ruler in Yarim-Lim of Yamkhad, who rivaled Hammurabi and was followed into battle by 20 subsidiary kings. To the Hittites this Amorite city linking the vital trade routes was of considerable importance strategically; it was sacked by Mursilis, and again by Tudhalyias in 1596 B.C. After the decline in Hittite fortunes Halpa became part of the Hurrian confederacy, and during the 15th and 14th centuries it fell intermittently within the Egyptian, Mitannian and Hittite spheres of influence. It was finally conquered by the Hittite king Suppiluliumas (c. 1375–35), who placed his son Telepinus on the throne. Later relations between the Hittites and Aleppo are referred to in the preamble to the treaty between Muwatallis (1306–1282 B.C.) and Rim-Sharma, king of Aleppo, found in the Boğazköy archives. One of the Hittite allies in the battle of Kadesh (c. 1286 B.C.) against the Egyptians was the king of Halpa. After the fall of the Hittite empire Halpa became an independent kingdom until its conquest by Assyria in 853 B.C. For a short time it was in the hands of Sarduris, king of Urartu, but was reconquered in 743 by the Assyrians and appears to have been held by them until their fall in 612. During the Assyrian period it was known as Halman.

The city subsequently fell into the hands of the Neo-Babylonians, Persians and Seleucids. It was largely rebuilt by Seleucus Nicator (312–280 B.C.), who renamed it Beroea after a Macedonian city. It became a first-ranking city of the Hellenistic period and, after the destruction of Palmyra, the great commercial entrepôt between the Mediterranean region and the lands further to the east. By the 4th century A.D. it had developed as an important

Christian centre and the seat of an archbishopric, but Chosroes II of Persia reduced the town to ashes and in 638 it fell without resistance into Arab hands. The city then reverted to its old name, Haleb, and prospered under the Ummayads, for whose cause it was to pay dearly on the Abbasid conquest. The house of Hamdan next established itself in Aleppo as an independent principality and fought with varying success against the Byzantines, who captured the town, but not the citadel, in 962. Of this period the best-known ruler is Saif al-Daula, who had a brilliant court and surrounded himself with poets and men of letters. After this golden age Aleppo fell successively under the Fatimids in 1015 and the Seljuk Turks from 1086 to 1117. It was besieged by the crusaders in 1124 and again the following year, later submitting to the prince (atabeg) of Mosul, Imad al-Din Zengi, under whom it became a centre for Muslim resistance against the crusaders. After the death of his son, however, the city became part of the Ayyubite dominion Iliitz under Al-Zahir Gazi, son of Saladin, who rebuilt it and made it Saladin's northern base. In 1260 it was taken by the Mongols under Hulagu and its inhabitants massacred. After an interval of several centuries under the Mamelukes Aleppo surrendered to the Turks in 1516, and with the exception of seven years under Egyptian control in the 19th century it formed part of the Ottoman empire until 1918. In 1920 it was independent for a short time, before becoming part of the Syrian mandated state under French control, an arrangement which came to an end in 1941.

The Aleppo administrative district has an area of 8,849 sq.mi. and a population (1953 est.) of 1,094,447. It comprises several *kazas* or subdistricts, under the administration of kaimakams, responsible to the governor of Aleppo. It is a rich agricultural area, extending to the banks of the Euphrates on the east and to the Bab al-Hawr ("Gate of the Winds"), the frontier with Turkey on the west. There are several small towns and a number of large villages, the average population of which is between 4,000 and 5,000 inhabitants. The main products of the region are grapes, wheat, barley, cotton, fruit, nuts and sesame.

BIBLIOGRAPHY.—Kamal ed-Din, *Histoire d'Alep,* trans. by G. Bouchet (1900); *Revue Archéologique Syrienne* (1935); G. M. Haddad, *Fifty Years of Modern Syria and Lebanon* (1950); S. Saouaf, *Alep* (1951); S. Runciman, *History of the Crusades,* 3 vol. (1951–54).

ALÈS, a town in the Gard *département* of southeastern France, lies 27 mi. N.N.W. of Nîmes at the foot of the Cévennes on the left bank of a loop of the Gardon d'Alès river. Pop. (1954) 20,259. Vauban's fortress (1788), containing a museum and library, stands on a hill dominating the town and round it are the Bosquet gardens. The cathedral of Saint Jean and the town hall were built in the 18th century. The narrow streets in the centre of the town are being replaced by modern roads and squares with gardens, and new suburbs have been built. Alès is on the main railway line from Paris and Clermont-Ferrand to Nîmes. It is the chief industrial town in southeastern France and a tourist centre for exploring the Cévennes (*q.v.*). There are commercial houses, metallurgical workshops, coal mines and factories for making ovens and underwear.

In the 10th century B.C. the Phoenicians settled at Alès, giving it the name Alest (Phoenician word for "industry"). The Romans called it Alestium. It received its charter in 1200 and was made part of the French kingdom by Louis IX in 1243. It suffered in the religious wars of the 16th century and in 1629 the Grâce of Alais, the treaty which ended the last War of Religion, was signed there. Little affected by the French Revolution, it became industrialized 100 years later. In 1926 the name was changed from Alais to Alès. (Ru. M.)

ALESIA (on Mont Auxois, above the village of Alise-Sainte-Reine in the *département* of Côte d'Or, France) was a hill-fort town of the ancient Gallic tribe of the Mandubii, succeeded on the same site by a Roman town. It is famous for the siege of Vercingetorix by Julius Caesar in 52 B.C., decisive in his conquest of Gaul. Vercingetorix, who had raised a widespread revolt in Gaul against Caesar, withdrew after some successes and reverses into the prepared fortress of Alesia. Caesar invested the position, surrounding it with lines of contravallation (ten miles in perimeter) and, outside these, building lines of circumvallation against relieving forces of the Gauls. When the Gauls gathered in large numbers they were repulsed, being inadequately organized; and a sortie by Vercingetorix was equally ineffectual. A final attempt at relief was made at the weakest spot on the northwest (which could not be enclosed by the lines of circumvallation), but this also failed, and Vercingetorix was forced to surrender from lack of supplies.

Excavations sponsored by Napoleon III in 1861–65 revealed siege works fitting Caesar's detailed description. Napoleon III also erected the statue of Vercingetorix on Mont Auxois. Excavations in the 20th century (notably from 1942 onward) revealed a mixture of Gallic and Roman elements: traces of the Gallic town and wall, with circular and rectangular huts, together with evidence of metalworking. Remains of the Roman town include the forum, a three-apsed basilica, a theatre, a temple and other sanctuaries.

BIBLIOGRAPHY.—T. R. Holmes, *Caesar's Conquest of Gaul* (1911), *The Roman Republic*, vol. ii (1923); J. Toutain, *Alésia Gallo-romaine et chrétienne* (1933) and articles in *Gallia*, vol. i, ii and vi (1944–49).
(H. H. Sd.)

ALESSANDRIA, a town in Piemonte, Italy, capital of Alessandria province, lies 35 mi. E.S.E. of Turin. Pop. (1961) 94,502 (commune). Situated 342 ft. above sea level at the confluence of the Bormida and the Tanaro rivers and at the junction of railways and important highways, its previous domination of the valley of the Alpine passes gave rise to its military importance. As a stronghold it could not expand beyond its defensive works. These were destroyed in the time of the Napoleonic empire but were restored during the War of Independence. Expansion outside them is of recent date. The historic churches and civil edifices were for a long time built to comply with military need.

The cathedral church of Sta. Maria del Castello and the Carmelite church date from the 13th century; the latter, built on the hexagonal ground plan of a basilica, contains a 15th-century register of prelates. The episcopal palace is of the 15th century and there are the Ghilini, Cuttica, Guasco and Sambuy palaces. There are a museum, picture gallery and library. The chief industries are hatmaking (especially the Borsalino), the manufacture of foodstuffs, coloured leads, textiles and chemicals and ironworking and machinemaking. The leading commercial activity is marketing agricultural products, especially wines.

Alessandria was founded in 1168 by the Ghibelline marquis, Guglielmo del Monferrato, who called it first Civitas Nova and later Cesaria. It pursued an anti-imperial policy, took part in the struggles against the communes and Frederick Barbarossa, and was named Alessandria in honour of Pope Alexander III, head of the Lombard league. It has been an episcopal see since 1175. After resisting Barbarossa the town was left defenseless by its confederates and was ceded to the emperor, adopting once again the name of Cesaria. On achieving its freedom as a commune it was transferred to the Visconti in the 14th century, and in 1702 passed to Savoy. After the battle of Marengo it was subject to Napoleon I, and when he fell it suffered damage at the hands of the Austrians. It was the centre of the movement for freedom in Piedmont in 1821 and of the conspiracy of Giuseppe Mazzini in 1833. A vital stronghold, it was garrisoned by the Austrians after their victory at Novara (1849).

See C. Patrucco, *Perché e come fu fondata Alessandria* (1927); G. Jachino, *Storiografia Alessandrina* (1938).   (M. T. A. N.)

ALESSANDRI PALMA, ARTURO (1868–1950), Chilean president and statesman, was born near Linares, the son of an Italian immigrant, Dec. 20, 1868. He graduated in law from the University of Chile in 1893 and four years later was elected to the chamber of deputies. During a political career that spanned more than 50 years he was minister of industry, minister of finance, congressman (elected six times), senator (elected twice) and president (1920–25, 1932–38). He won his reputation as a liberal and the title "Lion of Tarapacá" by defending the working groups, especially the nitrate miners of the north. His concern for the less-privileged elements during the years before 1920 permitted him to capitalize upon the rapidly expanding working and middle-class vote.

Alessandri was elected president of Chile in 1920 as the candidate of a liberal coalition. He was forced into exile in 1924 by the military forces but was recalled the following January with the understanding that the constitution would be rewritten to give the president greater power. This was done. Alessandri returned to the presidency in 1932 as a strict constitutionalist. Before the end of his term he had come to depend primarily upon the political right. This helped to promote economic recovery from the depression but alienated most of his labour and middle-class supporters who joined the Popular Front, which had communist affiliations. In 1946 Alessandri was elected to the senate for a second time and as a senator he again displayed liberal leanings. He died Aug. 24, 1950.   (J. J. J.)

ALESSI, GALEAZZO (1512–1572), Italian architect, was born at Perugia and was probably a pupil of Caporali. He was an enthusiastic student of ancient architecture, and his style gained for him a European reputation. Genoa is indebted to him for a number of magnificent palaces, and his art may be studied in the churches of San Paolo and Santa Vittoria at Milan, in certain parts of the Escorial, and in numerous churches and palaces throughout Sicily, Flanders and Germany.

ÅLESUND (AALESUND), a town on the northwest coast of southern Norway, lies 185 mi. N. of Bergen. Pop. (1960) 18,-942. It was rebuilt in stone after the old wooden town was destroyed by fire in 1904. Ålesund has a history dating back to Rollo (Rolf) the Ganger, who in the 9th century was expelled from Norway by Harald Fairhair (Harald I; q.v.) and settled with his followers in the lower Seine valley in what is now Normandy. The winters are mild and the temperature seldom falls below zero. The economy of the town depends on fishing and sealing in northern and arctic waters and on its position as a market for agricultural produce, chiefly milk and fruit, from the surrounding districts. There is an airport, opened in 1958. There is no railway, but there are good land and sea connections with the rest of the country.

ALEURITES, tropical and subtropical trees of the genus *Aleurites* (Euphorbiaceae), producing apple-sized fruits containing large seeds or nuts rich in drying oils, used in the manufacture of many products. Five species are known: *A. cordata*, Japanese woodoil tree; *A. fordii*, tungoil tree; *A. molluccana*, candlenut tree; *A. montana*, mu-oil tree; and *A. trisperma*, soft lumbang. The first two are the most valuable, since they produce the best oils. Orchard planting in the U.S. began about 1910. Extensive plantings were made thereafter in states from Florida west to eastern Texas. Important planting began about 1925 in Argentina, Australia, Brazil, New Zealand and Nyasaland.

ALEUT, a native of the Aleutian Islands and western portion of the Alaska peninsula. With the closely related Eskimos (q.v.) they constitute the Eskimo-Aleut stock sharing basic similarities in language, race and culture. At the time of their discovery in 1741 they occupied all the Aleutian Islands and the western part of the Alaska peninsula to a line running from Port Moller on the north side to Kupreanof point on the south side where they met their Eskimo-speaking neighbours, the Koniags, who also occupied Kodiak Island. Linguistically they comprise three mutually intelligible dialect groups. Aleut, though having diverged from Eskimo about 4,600 years ago, can no longer be understood by an Eskimo. Structurally the languages are still much the same but share less than 25% of their vocabulary. (*See* ESKIMO-ALEUT LANGUAGES.)

Racially Aleuts, like Eskimos, are most similar to Siberian peoples and easily distinguishable from American Indians. They possess straight black hair, eye folds, long trunks and relatively short legs, small hands and feet, large head and face with small nose. One of the largest skulls in the world is that of a mummified Aleut from Kagamil Island with over 2,000 c.c. cranial capacity. Serologically they possess a large proportion of blood group A, close to 50%, and varying amounts of group B, very low frequencies of type N, and all are Rh positive. Blood group B is not found in American Indians but is found in Asia. Physically the western Aleuts of Attu Island (the westernmost) and Atka show more traces of the earliest people who moved into the islands from the Alaska mainland about 4,000 years ago. The earliest people, termed Paleo-Aleuts, were more narrow headed than the later. Like their Koniag neighbours the present Aleuts are more broad headed.

The rich animal and plant life of the area was skilfully exploited by the Aleut hunters and explains their high population, conservatively estimated at 16,000, and their early exploitation by Russian traders. Sea otters, the most valued of pelts, were hunted by harpoon cast with throwing board from kayaks (one-man skin boats also known as bidarka). Whales, sea lions, seals and, in the eastern area, walrus were also hunted from the kayak. The Russians employed Aleut hunters transporting many to Fort Ross in California, the northern Kurils, the Pribilof Islands and the Commander Islands of Russia. The large open skin boat (Eskimo umiak) was extensively used. Nets, spears and hooks were also employed. The annual runs of salmon were trapped, then sundried and stored in containers made of the stomachs of seals and sea lions. While the bow and arrow was little used in the islands it was more commonly used on Unimak Island and the peninsula for caribou and bear hunting.

From their earliest appearance in the islands, about 2,000 years B.C., they had a rich material culture with many things made of stone: lamps, chipped knives and points; bone: harpoon heads, fish hooks, wedges for splitting driftwood; and ivory: lip decorations (labrets), figurines and needles. These are found in the old village middens, particularly in the refuse under the semisubterranean houses, often situated at mouths of the salmon streams.

The Aleuts possess an exceptional knowledge of human anatomy based upon extensive butchering of sea mammals and use of ordinarily discarded parts (intestines, pericardia) for fabricational purposes (waterproof parkas); comparative anatomy of sea otter; dissection of deceased persons to find out why they died; rational medicine and health practices; and true mummification (removal of intestines) of distinguished persons such as whalers.

In the last half of the 20th century about 500 Aleuts occupied 11 villages in the islands and on the Alaska peninsula, another 500 lived in the Pribilof Islands and approximately 300 lived on the Russian Commander Islands. Most are members of the Russian Orthodox Church. A small amount of the famous fine grass basketry is still made and many of the native foods are still eaten.

See also ALEUTIAN ISLANDS; ESKIMO.

BIBLIOGRAPHY.—Knut Bergsland, "Aleut Dialects of Atka and Attu," *Trans. Amer. Phil. Soc.*, vol. 49, part 3 (1959); Ales Hrdlicka, *The Aleutian and Commander Islands and Their Inhabitants* (1945); Waldemar Jochelson, *History, Ethnology and Anthropology of the Aleut*, Carnegie Institution of Washington, D.C., Publication 432 (1933); W. S. Laughlin and G. H. Marsh, "A New View of the History of the Aleutians," *Arctic*, vol. 4, no. 2, pp. 74–88 (Sept. 1951); W. S. Laughlin, "Neo-Aleut and Paleo-Aleut Prehistory," *Proceedings of the 32nd International Congress of Americanists* (1956–58), "Eskimos and Aleuts: Their Origins and Evolution," *Science*, vol. 142 (Nov. 1963); D. E. Dumond, "On Eskaleutian Linguistics, Archaeology, and Prehistory," *Am. Anthrop.*, vol. 67 (Oct. 1965).   (W. S. LN.)

ALEUTIAN ISLANDS, a chain of small islands situated in the North Pacific ocean, and extending about 1,200 mi. westward from the extremity of the Alaskan peninsula toward the peninsula of Kamchatka; they constitute a district (6,821 sq.mi.) of the state of Alaska. The islands, also called Catherine archipelago, comprise four groups—the Fox, Andreanof, Rat and Near islands—all between 52° and 55° N. and 172° E. and 163° W.

The axis of the archipelago near the mainland of Alaska has a southwest trend, but near the 179th meridian its direction changes to the northwest. This change of direction corresponds to a curve in the line of volcanic fissures which have contributed their prod-

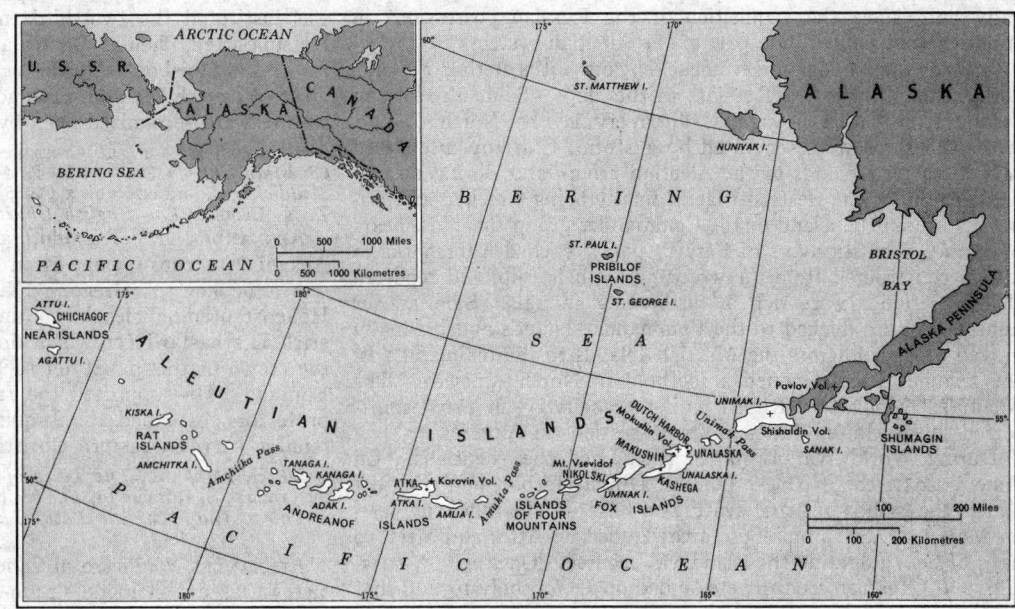

THE ALEUTIANS AND NEIGHBOURING ISLANDS IN THE BERING SEA

ucts to the building of the islands. The island chain, a segment of the circumpacific earthquake (*q.v.*) belt, is a western continuation of the Aleutian range on the mainland. The great majority of the islands bear evident marks of volcanic origin, and there are numerous volcanic cones on the north side of the chain, some of them active; many of the islands, however, are not wholly volcanic, but contain crystalline or sedimentary rocks, and also amber and beds of lignite. The coasts are rocky and surf worn and the approaches are exceedingly dangerous, the land rising immediately from the coasts to steep, bold mountains.

The climate of the islands is oceanic, with moderate and fairly uniform temperatures and heavy rainfall. Fogs are almost constant. The summers are much cooler than on the mainland at Sitka, but the winter temperature of the islands and of southeastern Alaska is very nearly the same. The mean annual temperature for Unalaska, the most important island of the group, is about 38° F. The growing season lasts about 135 days, from early in May till late in September, but agriculture is limited to the raising of a few vegetables. The islands are practically destitute of trees, but are covered with a luxuriant growth of herbage, including grasses, sedges and many flowering plants. Attempts have been made to raise sheep and reindeer on the islands, but the industry is still in its infancy with some uncertainty as to future results. The principal occupations of the native Aleuts (*see* ALEUT) have always been fishing and hunting, and the women weave basketry of exquisite fineness. From the end of the 18th century the Russian fur traders had settlements there for the capture of the seal and the sea otter and the blue and the Arctic fox. After the U.S. purchase of Alaska, seal fishing off the Aleutians, save by the natives, was declared illegal, but the rapid depletion of animals threatened the Aleuts with starvation. In later years the raising of foxes, especially of blue fox, was conducted quite extensively throughout the islands and with a fair measure of success. This industry furnished employment to many natives. Fish and sea fowl are extremely abundant.

It is stated that before the advent of the Russians there were 25,000 Aleuts on the archipelago, but that the barbarities of the traders nearly extinguished the native population. In 1885 it was estimated that there were 2,950 Aleuts. The total population of the archipelago in 1950 was 5,600, there being 3,892 Aleuts mainly in the Aleutians. In 1960 the population was 6,011. The principal settlements are on the Unalaska Islands. Of these Unalaska, the oldest, settled in 1760–75, has a customhouse, a Russian-Greek church and a Methodist mission and orphanage; it is the headquarters for a considerable fleet of United States coast guard vessels which patrol the sealing grounds of the Pribilofs. Adjacent is Dutch Harbor, where a U.S. naval base was established in 1941.

The Commander Islands group near the Asiatic coast is geographically but (since the acquisition of the Russian possessions in America) not politically a part of the Aleutian system.

In 1741 the Russian government sent out Vitus Bering, a Dane, and Alexei Chirikov, a Russian, in the ships "Saint Peter" and "Saint Paul" on a voyage of discovery in the North Pacific. After the ships were separated by a storm, Chirikov discovered several eastern islands of the Aleutian group, and Bering discovered several of the western islands, finally being wrecked and losing his life on the island of the Commander group that now bears his name. The survivors of Bering's party reached Kamchatka in a boat constructed from the wreckage of their ship, and reported that the islands were rich in fur-bearing animals. Siberian fur hunters at once flocked to the Commander Islands and gradually moved eastward across the Aleutian Islands to the mainland. In this manner Russia gained a foothold in North America. The Aleutians belonged to Russia until that country, in 1867, transferred to the United States all its possessions in America.

During World War II Japan threatened the Aleutians. On June 3, 1942, the Japanese bombed Dutch Harbor, and they occupied the islands of Attu, Agattu and Kiska. The following year, on May 11, U.S. amphibious forces landed on Attu, and after 19 days of heavy fighting the island was secured. On Aug. 15, 1943, U.S. and Canadian troops were landed on Kiska, only to find that the Japanese had evacuated the island. After the war Aleutian radar stations became an important link in the air defense net surrounding North America.

ALEWIFE, a fish (*Alosa pseudoharengus*) of the Clupeidae family, which also includes herring, shad and sardines. Alternative common names for the alewife are sawbelly, grayback, gaspereau and branch herring. During the spring, the alewife spawns in ponds and sluggish rivers of eastern North America between Newfoundland and Florida. Except for a few landlocked populations, the rest of the life history is spent in the sea, where the alewife congregates in large schools. The adults usually return to their native stream after three or four years in the ocean, and those that survive will return in subsequent years. Their food is chiefly plankton. They grow to a length of one foot and are an important food fish. (C. Hu.)

ALEXANDER, the name of eight popes.

St. Alexander I "followed this Euarestus" (Evaristus), according to St. Irenaeus in his *Against Heresies,* and was the fifth pope after St. Peter. His rule of approximately ten years (105–115 or 109–119) is attested by Eusebius. The *Book of Popes* (*Liber Pontificalis,* edited by L. Duchesne) confirms the foregoing. (J. M. F. M.)

Alexander II (Anselm of Lucca) (d. 1073), pope from 1061 to 1073, was a native of Milan. As bishop of Lucca he worked for the abolition of simony and the enforcement of clerical celibacy. Though he was elected pope, the German court nominated Peter Cadalus of Parma as Honorius II. But in 1062 the antipope was dropped by the German regents and the schism ceased to be important. In co-operation with Hildebrand (later Gregory VII, q.v.) and Peter Damian (q.v.), Alexander laid the foundations of the reform movement which reached its climax under Gregory VII. It was his deposition of the imperial bishop of Milan for simony which led to the investiture struggle between papacy and empire. (R. E. McN.)

Alexander III (Roland Bandinelli of Siena) (d. 1181), one of the outstanding popes in history, occupied the throne from Sept. 7, 1159, to Aug. 30, 1181. As theologian and canonist, Roland was a celebrated professor at Bologna, and as cardinal (1150) and papal chancellor (1153–1159), he was the adviser of Adrian IV, whom he succeeded. An open opponent of the universal claims of Emperor Frederick I, Alexander was opposed by three imperial antipopes during a 17-year schism. Seldom in Rome, Alexander in exile became the symbol and leader of Italian resistance to German domination, and Frederick's final defeat by the Lombard league at Legnano made possible the Peace of Venice (1176) with the pope and his Italian confederates. (*See* also Frederick I Barbarossa.)

First of the great lawyer-popes, Alexander convoked the third Lateran council (1179) to repair the schism, and at this council was instituted the two-thirds majority rule for papal elections. He supported Thomas Becket and imposed penance on Henry II for the archbishop's murder. His reign furthered the development of church law and papal government. His merits and moral stature were recognized even by his adversaries.

Bibliography.—F. L. Cross (ed.), *The Oxford Dictionary of the Christian Church* (1957); H. K. Mann, *The Lives of the Popes in the Middle Ages,* 2nd ed., vol. x (1925); M. Pacaut, *Alexandre III* (1956); Z. N. Brooke, *The English Church and the Papacy,* reprint (1952).

Alexander IV (Rinaldo, family of the counts of Segni of Anagni) (d. 1261), pope from Dec. 12, 1254, to May 25, 1261, was a nephew of Gregory IX. Following Innocent IV's anti-Hohenstaufen policies, he continued war on Manfred (q.v.), Frederick II's bastard (crowned king of Sicily in 1258), and offered the crown of this papal fief to Henry III of England for his son Edmund. He supported the friars at Paris against the secular professors, extended the Inquisition in France and worked for reunion between eastern Christians and Rome.

See H. K. Mann, *The Lives of the Popes in the Middle Ages,* vol. xv (1929); S. Runciman, *The Sicilian Vespers: A History of the Mediterranean World in the Later Thirteenth Century* (1958). (J. J. Rn)

Alexander V (Pietro di Candia or Petros Philargos) (c. 1339–1410) was an antipope (1409–10) unanimously elected by the invalid Council of Pisa in 1409. Of Greek parentage, Alexander became a Franciscan theologian, then archbishop of Milan. He was 70 years old at the time of his election and reigned only ten months.

See Philip Hughes, *A History of the Church,* vol. iii (1947); Ludwig Pastor, *The History of the Popes . . . ,* vol. i (1891).

Alexander VI (Rodrigo Borgia) (1431–1503), pope from 1492–1503, was one of the worst of the Renaissance popes. Born Jan. 1, 1431, at Xativa, Spain, he studied law at Bologna and then served for 35 years at the papal court, where he proved himself an able administrator. As pope, Alexander became deeply involved in the political turmoil in Italy, the struggles of Italian families like the Orsini, della Rovere and Colonna for power and wealth, the conflict between France and Spain for control of Italy and his own efforts to endow his children—he had at least four before he became pope—with estates in Italy.

When Charles VIII (q.v.) of France invaded Italy, seized Rome and Naples, Alexander helped organize an alliance with Milan, Venice, Spain and the Holy Roman empire which forced Charles to leave Italy. When Alexander's son the duke of Gandia sought to punish the Orsini for having sided with the French he was mysteriously murdered. The pope then abetted the marriage of his infamous son Cesare Borgia (q.v.) to a French princess, annulled the marriage of Louis XII of France and Jeanne Valois and thus won an ally in France and aid for Cesare's attempt to win Romagna and to punish Borgia enemies. Alexander's neglect of the spiritual interests of the church worsened the prestige of the papacy. *See* also Savonarola, Girolamo.

Bibliography.—Philip Hughes, *A History of the Church,* vol. iii (1947); Ludwig Pastor, *The History of the Popes,* vol. vi (1923); A. Fliche and V. Martin, *Histoire de l'Eglise,* vol. xv, R. Aubenas and R. Ricard, *L'Eglise et la Renaissance* (1951). (J. A. Ct.)

Alexander VII (Fabio Chigi) (1599–1667), pope from 1655 to 1667, was born at Siena on Feb. 13, 1599. He served the church as nuncio at Cologne between 1639 and 1651. During the negotiations leading to the Peace of Westphalia (1648) he urged the Catholic princes not to sacrifice the rights of the church. They, however, were tired of war and yielded to France and the Protestants. Secretary of state to Innocent X in 1651 and made cardinal in 1652, Chigi was elected pope on April 7, 1655. His pontificate was marked by disputes with the Catholic powers, especially with France. When Alexander resisted the French claims, Louis XIV forced him to accept the humiliating peace of Pisa (1664) by a threat of war. Alexander took measures against the Jansenists who failed to submit (*see* Jansenism). He died on May 22, 1667.

Alexander VIII (Pietro Ottoboni) (1610–1691), pope from 1689 to 1691, was born at Venice on April 22, 1610. Made cardinal in 1652, he was elected pope on Oct. 6, 1689. Alexander tried to make a settlement with Louis XIV and succeeded in initiating the measures which led eventually to a solution. He maintained the condemnation of the Gallican articles of 1682 (see GALLICANISM) and opposed Jansenism. He died on Feb. 1, 1691. See also PAPACY.　(E. A. R.)

ALEXANDER (870–913), Byzantine emperor from 912 to 913, was the third son of Basil I of the Macedonian dynasty. He was crowned co-emperor about 879 but came to power only on the death of his brother Leo VI (May 12, 912), when the latter's son Constantine VII was a minor. Alexander then acted as senior emperor, using the title "autocrator" on his coins. He was vicious and irresponsible, and his foolish policy aggravated tension at home and abroad. He replaced Leo VI's ministers with his own friends, and Zoë, the dowager-empress, was banished from the palace. Leo's opponent, the deposed Nicholas Mysticus, was restored to the patriarchal throne, which Euthymius was forced to vacate. Alexander's refusal to pay the annual tribute owed to the Bulgars by the treaty of 896 precipitated war with Simeon, their powerful and aggressive king. Alexander's rule was brought to an early end by his death on June 6, 913. He left a divided front at home and the empire threatened with invasion by Simeon, who coveted the imperial throne.

BIBLIOGRAPHY.—G. Ostrogorsky, *History of the Byzantine State*, p. 207, p. 231 (1956); A. Rambaud, *L'Empire grec au Xe siècle: Constantin Porphyrogénète* (1870); S. Runciman, *The Emperor Romanus Lecapenus and His Reign* (1929).　(J. M. Hy.)

ALEXANDER I (ALEKSANDR PAVLOVICH) (1777–1825), emperor of Russia, son of the grand duke Pavel Petrovich (afterward Paul I) and Maria Fedorovna (Sophia Dorothea of Württemberg), was born on Dec. 23 (new style; Dec. 12, old style), 1777. The strange contradictions of his character make Alexander one of the most interesting as well as most important figures of the 19th century. Autocrat and Jacobin, man of the world and mystic, he was to his contemporaries a riddle which each read according to his own temperament. Napoleon thought him a "shifty Byzantine." To Metternich he was a madman to be humoured. Castlereagh gave him credit for "grand qualities," but said that he was "suspicious and undecided." His complex nature was the outcome of the complex character of his early education. Reared in the free-thinking atmosphere of the court of Catherine II, he had imbibed from his Swiss tutor, Frédéric César de La Harpe, the principles of J. J. Rousseau's gospel of humanity and from his military governor, Count N. I. Saltykov, the traditions of Russian autocracy, while his father had inspired him with his own passion for military parade. These contradictory tendencies remained with him through life and were revealed in the fluctuations of his policy.

When, upon the murder of his father, of which he had had knowledge in advance, Alexander succeeded to the throne on March 24 (N.S.; 12, O.S.), 1801, he was young, impressionable, well-meaning and egotistic and plunged with all the ardour of youth into the task of realizing his political ideals. While he retained for a time the old ministers who had served and overthrown his father, one of the first acts of Alexander's reign was to appoint a secret committee, called ironically the "committee of public safety," consisting of young and enthusiastic friends of his own— Viktor Pavlovich Kochubei, Nikolai Nikolaevich Novosiltsev, Pavel Aleksandrovich Stroganov and Adam Jerzy Czartoryski— to draw up a scheme of internal reform. Their aims were far in advance of the possibilities of the time, and even after they had been raised to regular ministerial positions little of the group's program could be realized. Russia was not ripe for liberty, and Alexander was—as he himself said—but " a happy accident" on the throne of the tsars. He spoke bitterly of "the state of barbarism in which the country had been left by the traffic in men." "Under Paul," he said in 1807 to A. J. M. Savary, the French ambassador, "three thousand peasants had been given away like a bag of diamonds. If civilization were more advanced, I would abolish this slavery, if it cost me my head." But the universal corruption, he complained, had left him no men, and the filling of the government offices with Germans and other foreigners merely accentuated the sullen resistance of the "old Russians" to his reforms. That his

reign, which had begun with so large a promise of amelioration, ended with the Russian people still more firmly oppressed was, however, mainly due to the defects of the tsar himself.

His love of liberty, though sincere, was in fact unreal. It flattered his vanity to pose before the world as the dispenser of benefits, but his theoretical liberalism was mated with an autocratic will which brooked no contradiction. Moreover, with this masterful temper was joined an infirmity of purpose which seized upon any excuse for postponing measures the principles of which he had publicly approved. Codification of the laws initiated in 1801 was never carried out during his reign, nothing was done to improve the status of the Russian peasantry, and the constitution drawn up by M. M. Speranski (q.v.) and passed by the emperor remained unsigned. Alexander experimented in the outlying provinces of his empire, and the Russians complained that, not content with governing through foreign instruments, he was conferring on Poland, Finland and the Baltic provinces benefits denied to themselves. In Russia, too, certain reforms were carried out; but they could not survive the suspicious interference of the autocrat and his officials. The newly created council of ministers and the senate, endowed for the first time with certain theoretical powers, became in the end slavish instruments of the tsar and his favourites of the moment. The elaborate system of education culminating in the reconstituted or new-founded universities of Dorpat (Tartu), Vilna (Vilnius), Kazan and Kharkov was strangled in the supposed interests of "order" and of orthodox piety, while the military colonies which Alexander proclaimed as a blessing to both soldiers and state were forced on the unwilling peasantry and army with pitiless cruelty.

Alexander's grandiose imagination was, however, more strongly attracted by the great questions of European politics arising from the French Revolutionary and Napoleonic wars than by attempts at domestic reform. Immediately after his accession he reversed his father's policy, denounced the League of Neutrals, made peace with England (April 1801) and opened negotiations with Austria. Soon afterward, at Memel, he entered into a close alliance with Prussia. The development of this alliance was interrupted by the short-lived peace of Oct. 1801, and for a while it seemed as though France and Russia might come to an understanding. Carried away by the enthusiasm of Frédéric César La Harpe, who had returned to Russia from Paris, Alexander began openly to proclaim his admiration for French institutions and for the person of Napoleon Bonaparte. Soon, however, came a change. La Harpe, after a new visit to Paris, presented to the tsar his reflections on the true nature of Bonaparte's life consulship, which, as Alexander said, revealed Bonaparte as "the most famous tyrant the world has produced." His disillusionment was completed by the murder of the duc d'Enghien, and diplomatic relations with Paris were broken off.

The tsar's attitude during the war that followed was governed by his vision of the future history of Europe. In opposing Napoleon, "the oppressor of Europe and the disturber of the world's peace," Alexander believed himself to be fulfilling a divine mission. In his instructions to Novosiltsev, his special envoy in London, he elaborated the motives of his policy as directed toward a general treaty for collective security that would govern the relations of states in a "European confederation," provided that at the conclusion of the general war it were possible to establish on clear principles the prescriptions of the rights of nations. Napoleon, however, never gave up hope of detaching Alexander from the coalition. He had no sooner entered Vienna in triumph than he opened negotiations with him. He resumed them after Austerlitz. Russia and France, he urged, were "geographical allies"; there was between them no true conflict of interests; together they might rule the world. But Alexander was still determined "to persist in the system of disinterestedness in respect of all the states of Europe which he had thus far followed," and he again allied himself with Prussia. The campaign of Jena and the battle of Eylau followed, and Napoleon, though still intent on the Russian alliance, stirred up Poles, Turks and Persians to break the obstinacy of the tsar. A party in Russia itself was clamorous for peace, but Alexander, after a vain attempt to form a new coalition, summoned the Russian nation to a holy war against Napoleon as the enemy of the Orthodox faith. The outcome was the Russian defeat in the battle of Friedland (June 1807). Napoleon saw his chance and seized it. Instead of making heavy terms, he offered to the chastened autocrat his alliance and a partnership in his glory.

The two emperors met at Tilsit on June 25. Alexander, dazzled by Napoleon's genius, was completely won. Napoleon knew well how to appeal to the imagination of his new-found friend. He would divide with Alexander the empire of the world; as a first step he would leave him in possession of the Danubian principalities and give him a free hand to deal with Finland; afterward, they would together drive the Turks from Europe and march across Asia to the conquest of India. A program so stupendous awoke in Alexander's impressionable mind an ambition to which he had hitherto been a stranger. The interests of Europe were forgotten. "What is Europe?" he exclaimed to Savary: "Where is it, if it is not you and we?"

It was not long before the first enthusiasm of Tilsit began to wane. Napoleon promised much and performed little. The French remained in Prussia, the Russians on the Danube. Each accused the other of breach of faith. Meanwhile, however, the personal relations of Alexander and Napoleon were cordial, and it was hoped that a fresh meeting might adjust all their differences. The meeting took place at Erfurt on Oct. 12, 1808, and resulted in a treaty which defined a common policy. But Alexander's relations with Napoleon none the less changed. He saw that Napoleon had never intended his proposed "grand enterprise" seriously and had only used it to preoccupy the mind of the tsar while he consolidated his own power in central Europe. From this moment the French alliance was for Alexander also an affair of pure policy. He used it, in the first instance, to remove "the geographical enemy" from the gates of St. Petersburg by wresting Finland from the Swedes (1809), and he hoped by means of it to make the Danube the southern frontier of Russia. Events were in fact rapidly tending to the rupture of the Franco–Russian alliance. Alexander, indeed, assisted Napoleon in the war of 1809, but he declared that he would not allow Austria to be crushed, and Napoleon complained bitterly of the inactivity of the Russian troops during the campaign. The tsar in his turn protested against Napoleon's encouragement of the Poles. In the matter of the French alliance he knew himself to be practically isolated in Russia, and he declared that he could not sacrifice the interest of his people and empire to his affection for Napoleon. He complained that the treaty of Vienna (Oct. 14, 1809), which added largely to the duchy of Warsaw, had "ill requited him for his loyalty," and he was only mollified for the time by the Franco–Russian convention of Jan. 4, 1810, declaring that "the kingdom of Poland will never be restored."

But if Alexander suspected Napoleon, Napoleon was no less suspicious of Alexander; and, partly to test his sincerity, he sent an almost peremptory request for marriage with the grand duchess Anna, the tsar's youngest sister. After some delay Alexander returned a polite refusal. Napoleon's answer was to refuse to ratify the convention of Jan. 4 and to announce his engagement to the Austrian archduchess Marie Louise. Relations between the two emperors were further embittered by Napoleon's seizure of Oldenburg (the ducal house there being closely linked with the Romanovs) and by the ruinous effect of Napoleon's "continental system" on Russian trade. An acid correspondence followed, and ill-concealed preparations for war, which culminated in the summer of 1812 in Napoleon's invasion of Russia. Yet, even after the French had passed the frontier, Alexander still protested that his personal sentiments toward Napoleon were unaltered. It was the occupation of Moscow and the desecration of the Kremlin, the sacred centre of Holy Russia, that changed his sentiment into passionate hatred. In vain the French emperor, within eight days of his entry into Moscow, wrote him a letter revealing the desperate straits of the invading army and appealing to "any remnant of his former sentiments." Alexander returned no answer.

The campaign of 1812 was the turning point of Alexander's life. Its horrors, for which he felt himself largely responsible, overset still more a mind never too well-balanced. At the burning of Moscow, he declared afterward, his own soul had found illumina-

tion and he received the divine revelation of his mission as the peacemaker of Europe. He tried to calm the unrest of his conscience by correspondence with the leaders of the evangelical revival and sought for guidance in texts of Scripture. It was not, however, according to his own account, till he met the baroness Barbara Juliane von Krüdener (q.v.) at Basel, in the autumn of 1813, that his soul found peace. From this time a mystic pietism influenced his policy.

Such was Alexander's mood when the downfall of Napoleon left him the most powerful sovereign in Europe. With the memory of Tilsit still fresh in men's minds, it was not unnatural that to cynical men of the world like Metternich he merely seemed to be disguising "under the language of evangelical abnegation" vast and perilous schemes of ambition. The puzzled powers were, in fact, the more inclined to be suspicious in view of other, and seemingly inconsistent, tendencies of the emperor, which yet seemed all to point to a like disquieting conclusion. At the congress of Vienna Alexander's attitude accentuated this distrust. Castlereagh, whose aim was the restoration of "a just equilibrium" in Europe, reproached the tsar to his face for a "conscience" which suffered him to imperil the concert of the powers by keeping his hold on Poland in violation of his treaty obligation.

Yet Alexander was sincere. The Holy alliance (q.v.) was the pet offspring of his pietism and seemed to him the only means of placing the "confederation of Europe" on a firm basis of principle. So far from its being directed against liberty, he declared roundly to all the signatory powers that "free constitutions were the logical outcome of its doctrines." To the other powers, however, it seemed at best "verbiage" and "exalted nonsense," at worst an effort of the tsar to establish the hegemony of Russia on the good will of the smaller signatory powers. To liberals, it was clearly a hypocritical conspiracy against freedom.

From the end of the year 1818 Alexander's views began to change. A revolutionary conspiracy among the officers of the guard and a foolish plot to kidnap him on his way to the congress of Aix-la-Chapelle are said to have shaken the foundations of his liberalism. At Aix he came for the first time into intimate contact with Metternich, who was swift to take advantage of the psychological moment. From this time dates the ascendancy of Metternich over the mind of the Russian emperor and in the councils of Europe. It was, however, no case of sudden conversion. Though alarmed by the revolutionary agitation in Germany, which culminated in the murder of his agent, the dramatist August von Kotzebue (q.v.), Alexander approved of Castlereagh's protest against Metternich's policy of "the governments contracting an alliance against the peoples," as formulated in the Carlsbad decrees in 1819. He still declared his belief in "free institutions, though not in such as are forced from feebleness, nor contracts ordered by popular leaders from their sovereigns." "Liberty," he maintained, "should be confined within just limits. And the limits of liberty are the principles of order."

It was the apparent triumph of the principles of disorder in the revolutions of Naples and Piedmont, combined with increasingly disquieting symptoms of discontent in France, in Germany and among his own people, that completed Alexander's conversion. In the seclusion of the little town of Troppau (Opava in Silesia), where in Oct. 1820 the powers met in conference, Metternich found an opportunity for cementing his influence over Alexander which had been wanting amid the turmoil and feminine intrigues of Vienna and Aix. The issue was momentous. In the preceding January Alexander had still upheld the ideal of a free confederation of the European states, symbolized by the Holy alliance, and had still protested against the claims of collective Europe to interfere in the internal concerns of the sovereign states. On Nov. 19 he signed the Troppau protocol, which consecrated the principle of intervention and wrecked the harmony of the concert (see TROPPAU, CONGRESS OF).

At Laibach (Ljubljana), whither in the spring of 1821 the congress had been adjourned, Alexander first heard of the revolt of the Greeks. From this time until his death his mind was torn between his anxiety to realize his dream of a confederation of Europe and his traditional mission as leader of the Orthodox crusade against the Turks. At first, under the careful nursing of Metternich, the former motive prevailed. He directed his foreign minister, Count I. A. Kapodistrias, (*q.v.*), himself a Greek, to disavow all sympathy of Russia with the Greek enterprise; and, the next year, a deputation of the Greeks of the Morea on its way to the congress of Verona was turned back by his orders. He made, indeed, some effort to reconcile the principles at conflict in his mind. He offered to surrender the claim that the affairs of the east were the "domestic concerns of Russia" and to march into Turkey, as Austria had marched into Naples, "as the mandatory of Europe." Metternich's opposition to this first opened his eyes to the true character of Austria's attitude toward his ideals. Once more in Russia, far from the fascination of Metternich's personality, the immemorial spirit of his people drew him back into itself; and when, in the autumn of 1825, he took his dying empress for change of air to the south of Russia, in order—as all Europe supposed—to place himself at the head of the great army concentrated near the Ottoman frontiers, his language was no longer that of "the peace-maker of Europe," but of the Orthodox tsar determined to take the interests of his people and of his religion "into his own hands." Before the momentous issue could be decided, however, Alexander died at Taganrog on Dec. 1 (N.S.; Nov. 19, O.S.), 1825, "crushed," to use his own words, "beneath the terrible burden of a crown" which he had more than once declared his intention of resigning.

Modern history knows few more tragic figures than that of Alexander. His early years had been full of brilliant promise, and he had countenanced a crime in order to obtain the power to realize his ideals; but in the end he left a terrible legacy to Russia: a principle of government which, under lofty pretensions, veiled a tyranny supported by spies and secret police; an uncertain succession; an army permeated by organized disaffection; an armed Poland, whose hunger for liberty the tsar had whetted but not satisfied; the quarrel with Turkey, with its alternative of war or humiliation for Russia; an educational system rotten with official hypocrisy; a church in which conduct counted for nothing, orthodoxy and ceremonial observance for everything; economical and financial conditions scarce recovering from the verge of ruin; and serfdom.

In private life Alexander displayed many lovable qualities. All authorities combine in praising his handsome presence and the charm of his address. His personal friendship, too, once bestowed, was never lightly withdrawn. By nature he was sociable and pleasure-loving; he proved himself a notable patron of the arts and took a conspicuous part in all the gaieties of the congress of Vienna. In his later years, however, he fell into a mood of settled melancholy and, though still accessible to all who chose to approach him with complaints or petitions, withdrew from all but the most essential social functions and lived a life of strenuous work and of Spartan simplicity. His gloom had been increased by domestic misfortune. He had been married on Oct. 9 (N.S.; Sept. 28, O.S.), 1793, without his wishes being consulted, to the beautiful and amiable Louise of Baden-Durlach (Elizaveta Alekseevna), a political match which proved the misfortune of both. Their second and only surviving child, a daughter, died on May 12, 1808, and their common sorrow drew husband and wife closer together. Toward the close of his life their reconciliation was completed by the wise charity of the empress in sympathizing deeply with him over the death of Sophia, his second daughter by his mistress Maria Antonovna Naryshkina (née Princess Czetwertynska). For portrait *see* article RUSSIAN HISTORY.

BIBLIOGRAPHY.—*General:* Comtesse S. de Choiseul-Gouffier, *Mémoires historiques sur l'empereur Alexandre* (1829) and *Réminiscences sur l'empereur Alexandre Ier* (1862); Joseph de Maistre, *Mémoires historiques et correspondance diplomatique* (1859); Prince Adam Czartoryski, *Mémoires et correspondance avec l'empereur Alexandre Ier* (1887); S. S. Tatishchev, *Alexandre Ier et Napoléon d'après leur correspondance inédite* (1891); P. Bailleu (ed.), *Briefwechsel König Friedrich Wilhelms III. und der Königin Luise mit Kaiser Alexander I.* (1900); F. C. de La Harpe, *Le Gouverneur d'un prince* (1902). *Lives:* M. I. Bogdanovich, *Istoria tsarstvovaniya imperatora Aleksandra I*, 6 vol. (1869–71); Theodor Schiemann, *Kaiser Alexander I und die Ergebnisse seiner Lebensarbeit* (1904); K. Waliszewski, *Le Règne d'Alexandre Ier*, 3 vol. (1923–25); G. M. Paléologue, *The Enigmatic Czar* (1938); L. I. Strakhovsky, *Alexandre I of Russia* (1949).
(W. A. P.; G. A. LN.)

ALEXANDER II (ALEKSANDR NIKOLAEVICH) (1818–1881), emperor of Russia from 1855 to 1881, was born in Moscow on April 29 (new style; April 17, old style), 1818, the eldest son of the emperor Nicholas I. Up to the time of his accession in 1855, no one imagined that he would be known to posterity as a great reformer. In so far as he had any political convictions he seemed to be animated with the reactionary spirit which at that time was suppressing all freedom of thought and all private initiative. Educated so as to have a smattering of a great many subjects and a good practical acquaintance with the chief modern European languages, he lived the life of an officer of the guards modified by the ceremonial duties incumbent on him as heir to the throne. His natural kindliness and his disposition for a military life, however, had been fostered by his tutor V. A. Zhukovski, the amiable humanitarian poet, and they remained with him all through life. On April 28 (N.S.; April 16, O.S.), 1841, he married the daughter of the grand duke Louis II of Hesse, Marie, thenceforward known as Maria Aleksandrovna, who bore him six sons and two daughters. Though his father, in his desire to exclude western ideas from Holy Russia, disapproved of foreign tours and could not encourage in his own family what he tried to prevent among the rest of his subjects, Alexander was allowed to visit England in 1839 and, in the years immediately preceding his accession, was entrusted with several missions to Berlin and Vienna.

At his father's death Alexander succeeded to the throne, March 2 (N.S.; Feb. 18, O.S.), 1855, during the Crimean War. The peace treaty of Paris was signed in the following year, and then began a period of radical reforms, recommended by public opinion and carried out by the imperial government. The policy of Nicholas I of sacrificing all other interests to that of making Russia an irresistibly strong military power had been discredited by the war. A new system had, therefore, to be adopted. All who had any pretensions to enlightenment declared loudly that the only way of restoring Russia to its proper position in Europe was to develop its natural resources and to reform thoroughly all branches of the administration.

Basically a conservative, Alexander nevertheless appreciated the necessity for reforms. At first he moved so slowly that the impatient reformers began to murmur. Important changes, however, were made in the legislation concerning industry and commerce, and the new freedom thus accorded produced a large number of limited liability companies. At the same time a great network of railways was planned, partly for economic and partly for military purposes.

Further progress was blocked by a great obstacle, the existence of serfdom, and Alexander grappled with this dangerous problem. Taking advantage of a petition presented by the Polish landed proprietors of the Lithuanian and Belorussian provinces, praying that their relations with the serfs might be regulated better, he authorized the formation of committees "for ameliorating the condition of the peasants" and laid down the principles on which the amelioration was to be effected. Without consulting his ordinary advisers, he then ordered a copy of these instructions to be forwarded to the provincial governors of European Russia and suggested that perhaps the landed proprietors of other provinces might express a similar desire. In all provinces where serfdom existed emancipation committees were formed. Emancipation meanwhile was bound to affect the economic, social and political future of the nation profoundly, the main question being whether the serfs should become agricultural labourers dependent economically and administratively on the landlords or be transformed into a class of independent communal proprietors. The emperor gave his support to the latter project. On the numerous other questions submitted to him he began by carefully consulting the conflicting authorities and, while leaning as a rule rather to the liberals, never went so far as they desired and always sought some middle course. On March 3 (N.S.; Feb. 19, O.S.), 1861, the emancipation law was signed and published.

Other reforms followed in quick succession during the next five or six years: army and navy organization; a new judicial administration on the French model; a new penal code and a greatly simplified system of civil and criminal procedure; an elaborate scheme of local self-government for the rural districts and the large towns, with elective assemblies possessing a restricted right of taxation; and a new rural and municipal police under the direction of the minister of the interior. These new institutions were better than the old ones which they replaced, but they did not work such miracles as inexperienced enthusiasts expected and had, in fact, many real defects. Hence arose a general feeling of disappointment which showed itself in different natures in different ways. In the educated classes two extreme groups appeared: on the one hand, the discontented conservatives, who recommended a return to a more severe disciplinarian regime; and on the other, the discontented radicals, who would have been satisfied with nothing less than the adoption of a socialist program. Between the two extremes stood the discontented liberals, who grumbled freely without knowing how to remedy the state of things. For several years the emperor held the balance fairly between the two extremes, but when radicalism assumed more and more the form of secret societies and revolutionary agitation he felt constrained to adopt repressive measures.

Revolutionary agitation was confined to a section of the educated classes and emanated from the universities and higher technical schools. At the beginning of the reform period there had been much enthusiasm for scientific as opposed to classical education, on the ground that the country needed practical scientists capable of developing its natural resources. The government, in agreement with this view, had encouraged scientific studies until it found cause to believe that there was some mysterious connection between natural science and revolutionary tendencies. Thereafter the zealous guardians of political order were in conflict with the youthful, hotheaded partisans of revolutionary physical science, whose nihilism (q.v.) eventually assumed the form of terrorism and aimed at the assassination of prominent officials and even of the emperor himself. The natural result of this was that the reactionary tendencies of the government were strengthened.

In foreign policy Alexander followed a course dictated by circumstances. When he came to the throne the Crimean War was still going on, but he concluded peace with the allies when the impossibility of continuing the war became clear. Prince A. M. Gorchakov (q.v.) for 15 years avoided foreign complications, while national pride and ambition were gratified by the expansion of Russian power in Asia. Twice, indeed, during that period Gorchakov ran the risk of provoking war—first in 1863, when the western powers seemed inclined to interfere in the Polish question and Russia declared categorically that no interference would be tolerated; then during the Franco-German War of 1870–71, when the Russian government declared that it considered itself no longer bound by the Black Sea clause of the Paris treaty of 1856. On both occasions hostilities were averted because the western powers were unwilling to take up the challenge. Between these two occasions, in 1867, Alexander visited the emperor Napoleon III in France where on June 6 an unsuccessful attempt on his life was made by a Polish nationalist, Antoni Berezowski.

In 1875, however, when Hercegovina rose in insurrection against the Turks, Alexander found himself in a more delicate position. Though he still had no wish to provoke a European war, he had inherited the claim that his predecessors had sporadically made to be the protectors of the Orthodox Christians of the Ottoman empire, he came forward as the champion of oppressed Slav peoples and he also hoped to be able to take advantage of the situation in order to recover, with Austria-Hungary's diplomatic support, the part of Bessarabia that had been taken from Russia by the treaty of Paris (see EASTERN QUESTION). Gradually, then, he allowed himself to drift into a position from which he could not retreat without obtaining some tangible result. Supposing that Turkey would yield to diplomatic pressure and make some reasonable concessions, he delivered on Nov. 10 (N.S.; Oct. 29, O.S.), 1876, his famous Moscow speech, in which he declared that if Europe would not secure a better position for the oppressed Slavs he would act alone.

Diplomatic pressure failed and war became inevitable (see RUSSO-TURKISH WARS). While it lasted he refused to yield to extremes. He would not listen to those who began to despair and

advised him to conclude peace on almost any terms, but when more headstrong advisers urged him to insist on terms which would probably have produced a conflict with Great Britain and Austria-Hungary, he resolved, after some hesitation, to make the requisite concessions. The discovery during the war that he could not rely on support from Germany made him waver in his devotion to the German alliance, which had been the main pivot of his foreign policy; but his personal attachment to the emperor William I and the pressure of powerful partisans of the German alliance in the Russian foreign service prevented his adopting a hostile attitude toward the German empire that he had helped to create. His surprising support of Pan-Slavism during the Turkish war proved but a passing fad; it ended with the abandonment of the treaty of San Stefano and the substitution of another treaty at the congress of Berlin (q.v.).

The patriotic excitement produced by the war did not weaken the revolutionary agitation. The struggle between the terrorists and the police authorities became more and more intense, and attempts at assassination became more and more frequent. Alexander succumbed by degrees to the mental depression produced originally by the disappointments which he experienced in his home and foreign policy; and in 1880, when he had reigned 25 years, he entrusted to Count M. T. Loris-Melikov (q.v.) a large share of the executive power. In that year the empress died, and a few weeks afterward he married Princess Ekaterina M. Dolgoruky, with whom he had entertained intimate relations for many years. Early in 1881, on the advice of Loris-Melikov, he determined to try the effect of some moderate liberal reforms on the revolutionary agitation, and for this purpose he caused an ukaz to be prepared creating a special commission, on which the zemstva and the municipal councils were to be represented, to examine legislative bills. On the very day on which this ukaz was signed—March 13 (N.S.; March 1, O.S.)—he fell victim to a plot sponsored by the executive committee of an organization called Narodnaya Volya ("People's Will"). When driving in one of the central streets of St. Petersburg, near the Winter palace, he was mortally wounded by the explosion of some small bombs and died a few hours afterward.

BIBLIOGRAPHY.—Marquis A. de Ségur, *Alexandre II* (1892); S. S. Tatischev, *Imperator Aleksandr II* (1903); F. Charles-Roux, *Alexandre II, Gortchakoff et Napoléon III* (1913); E. Daudet, *Soixante années du règne des Romanoff: Nicolas Ier et Alexandre II* (1919); B. H. Sumner, *Russia and the Balkans, 1870–1880* (1937); M. T. Florinsky, *Russia: A History and an Interpretation*, vol. ii (1953); V. Laferté (Princess E. M. Dolgorukaya), *Alexandre II: détails inédits sur sa vie et sa mort* (1882); G. M. Paléologue, *The Tragic Romance of Alexander II of Russia* (1926).   (D. M. W.; M. T. F.)

ALEXANDER III (ALEKSANDR ALEKSANDROVICH) (1845–1894), emperor of Russia, second son of Alexander II and of Maria Aleksandrovna (Marie of Hesse), was born in St. Petersburg on March 10 (new style; Feb. 26, old style), 1845. In natural disposition he bore little resemblance to his softhearted, impressionable father and still less to his refined, philosophic, sentimental, chivalrous, yet complex granduncle, Alexander I. He rather gloried in the idea of being of the same rough texture as the great majority of his subjects. His straightforward, abrupt manner savoured sometimes of gruffness, while his direct, unadorned method of expressing himself harmonized well with his roughhewn, immobile features and somewhat sluggish movements. His education was not fitted to soften these peculiarities. During the first 20 years of his life he had no prospect of succeeding to the throne, because he had an elder brother, Nicholas, who seemed of a fairly robust constitution. Alexander received only the perfunctory and inadequate training usually given to grand dukes of that period, which did not go much beyond primary and secondary instruction, practical acquaintance with French, English and German and a certain amount of drill. When he became heir apparent by the death of his elder brother in 1865, he began to study the principles of law and administration under K. P. Pobedonostsev (1827–1907), who influenced the character of his reign by instilling into his mind hatred for representative government and the belief that zeal for Orthodoxy ought, as an essential factor of Russian patriotism, to be specially cultivated by every right-minded tsar.

The tsarevitch Nicholas, on his deathbed, had expressed a wish that his affianced bride, Princess Dagmar of Denmark, thenceforward known as Maria Fedorovna, should marry his successor. The marriage was celebrated on Nov. 9 (N.S.; Oct. 28, O.S.), 1866, and the union proved a most happy one to the end. During those years when he was heir apparent—from 1865 to 1881—Alexander allowed it to become known that he had certain ideas of his own which did not coincide with the principles of the existing government. He deprecated undue foreign influence in general and German influence in particular. His father, however, who had strong German sympathies, occasionally ridiculed the exaggerations of the Slavophils and based his foreign policy on the Prussian alliance. The antagonism between father and son first appeared publicly during the Franco-German War, when the tsar sympathized with Prussia and the tsarevitch with the French. It reappeared in an intermittent fashion during the years 1875–79, on the Eastern question (q.v.). At first the tsarevitch was more Slavophil than the government, but any of the prevalent popular illusions that he may have imbibed were soon dispelled by personal observation in Bulgaria, where he commanded the left wing of the invading army in the Russo-Turkish War. He did not, however, make himself conspicuous during the campaign, but fulfilled his military duties in a conscientious and unobtrusive manner. After many mistakes and disappointments the army reached Constantinople and the treaty of San Stefano was signed; but much that had been obtained by that important document had to be sacrificed at the congress of Berlin (q.v.), when Bismarck failed to do what the Russians had confidently expected of him. To this disappointment, moreover, Bismarck shortly afterward added the German alliance with Austria for the express purpose of counteracting Russian designs in eastern Europe. Although the existence of the Austro-German alliance was not disclosed to the Russians until 1887, the tsarevitch reached the practical conclusion that for Russia the best thing to do was to prepare for future contingencies by a radical scheme of military and naval reorganization. In accordance with this conviction he called his father's attention to the grave disorders and corruption in the army. His representations were not favourably received.

On March 13 (N.S.; March 1, O.S.), 1881, Alexander II was assassinated, and the following day autocratic power passed to his son. In the last years of his reign, Alexander II had been much exercised by the spread of Nihilist conspiracies. On the very day of his death he signed an *ukaz* creating a number of consultative commissions which might have been transformed eventually into a representative assembly. Alexander III at once canceled the *ukaz* before it was published and in the manifesto announcing his accession to the throne let it be clearly understood that he had no intention of limiting or weakening the autocratic power which he had inherited. Nor did he afterward show any inclination to change his mind. All the internal reforms which he initiated were intended to correct what he considered as the too liberal tendencies of the previous reign. In his opinion Russia was to be saved from anarchical disorders and revolutionary agitation, not by the parliamentary institutions and so-called liberalism of western Europe, but by the three principles enunciated by Count S. S. Uvarov (minister of education from 1833 to 1849) and the elder generation of the Slavophils; viz., Orthodoxy, autocracy and *narodnost,* or belief in the Russian people.

Alexander's political ideal was a nation containing only one nationality, one language, one religion and one form of administration, and he did his utmost to prepare for the realization of this ideal by imposing the Russian language and Russian schools on his German, Polish and Finnish subjects, by fostering Orthodoxy at the expense of other confessions, by persecuting the Jews and by destroying the remnants of German, Polish and Swedish institutions in the outlying provinces. In the other provinces he sought to counteract the liberalism of his father's reign. For this purpose he clipped the feeble wings of the *zemstvo* (an elective local administration resembling the county and parish councils in England) and placed the autonomous administration of the peasant communes under the supervision of landed proprietors appointed by the government. At the same time he sought to strengthen and centralize the imperial administration and to bring it more under

his personal control. In foreign affairs he was emphatically a man of peace, but not at all a partisan of the doctrine of peace at any price. Though indignant at the conduct of Bismarck toward Russia, he avoided an open rupture with Germany, and even revived for a time the Three Emperors' alliance. It was only in the last years of his reign, especially after the accession of William II as German emperor in 1888, that Alexander adopted a more hostile attitude toward Germany. The initiative of the termination of the Russo-German alliance in 1890 came from G. L. von Caprivi, the new German chancellor, and drove Alexander reluctantly into an alliance with France, a country which he strongly disliked as the breeding place of revolutions. The Franco-Russian alliance was signed in St. Petersburg on Dec. 31, 1893 (N.S.). With regard to Bulgaria the tsar exercised similar self-control. The efforts of Prince Alexander and afterward of Stefan Stambulov to destroy Russian influence in the principality excited his indignation, but he persistently vetoed all proposals to intervene by force of arms. In central Asian affairs he followed the traditional policy of gradually extending Russian domination without provoking a conflict with Great Britain, and he never allowed the bellicose partisans of a forward policy to get out of hand.

As a whole Alexander's reign cannot be regarded as one of the eventful periods of Russian history; but it is arguable that under his hard, unsympathetic rule the country made some progress. He died at Livadia, in the Crimea, on Nov. 1 (N.S.; Oct. 20, O.S.), 1894, and was succeeded by his eldest son, Nicholas II.

BIBLIOGRAPHY.—N. A. Notovich, *L'Empereur Alexandre III et son entourage* (1893); E. Daudet, *L'Avant-dernier Romanoff, Alexander III* (1920); A. D. Popov, *Imperator Aleksandr III* (1908); K. P. Pobedonostsev, *Mémoires politiques, correspondance officielle et documents inédits relatifs à l'histoire du règne de l'empereur Alexandre III* (1927); Baron B. E. Nolde, *L'Alliance franco-russe* (1936).
(D. M. W.; M. T. F.)

ALEXANDER (1893–1920), king of the Hellenes from 1917 to 1920, was born in Athens on Aug. 1, 1893, the second son of King Constantine and Queen Sophia. He came to the throne of Greece on the deposition of his father (June 12, 1917) during World War I. The government itself was for the time in the hands of Eleutherios Venizelos, who had the confidence of the Allies, and Venizelos' diplomatic triumphs at the peace conference and treaty of Sèvres (Aug. 10, 1920) seemed to offer the new king the prospect of being the ruler of that "Greater Greece" to which national aspirations had long been directed (*see* GREECE: *History*). These hopes were cut short by his death at the Tatoi palace on Oct. 25, 1920, through blood poisoning from the bite of a pet monkey.

In Nov. 1919, Alexander had made a morganatic marriage with an Athenian lady, Aspasia Manos; after his death a daughter was born to her in Paris on March 25, 1921. On Oct. 12, 1922, the daughter became his legal heir, though she did not thereby acquire any rights in respect to the throne. (B. S.-E.)

ALEXANDER III, called THE GREAT (356–323 B.C.), king of Macedonia, who overthrew the Persian empire, carried Macedonian arms to India, and laid the foundations for the Hellenistic world of territorial kingdoms. He was born at Pella in Macedonia, the son of Philip II (q.v.) and Olympias, daughter of Neoptolemus of Epirus. From age 13 to 16 he was taught by Aristotle (q.v.), who inspired him with an interest in philosophy, medicine, and scientific investigation; but he was later to advance beyond his teacher's narrow precept that non-Greeks should be treated as slaves. Left in charge of Macedonia in 340 during Philip's attack on Byzantium, Alexander defeated the Maedi, a Thracian people; two years later he commanded the left wing at the Battle of Chaeronea, in which Philip defeated the allied Greek states, and displayed personal courage in breaking the Sacred Band of Thebes. A year later Philip divorced Olympias; and after a quarrel at a feast held to celebrate his father's new marriage, Alexander and his mother fled to Epirus, and Alexander later went to Illyria. Shortly afterward father and son were reconciled and Alexander returned; but his position as heir was jeopardized.

In 336, however, on Philip's assassination, Alexander, acclaimed by the army, succeeded without opposition. He at once executed the princes of Lyncestis, alleged to be behind Philip's murder, along with all possible rivals and the whole of the faction opposed to

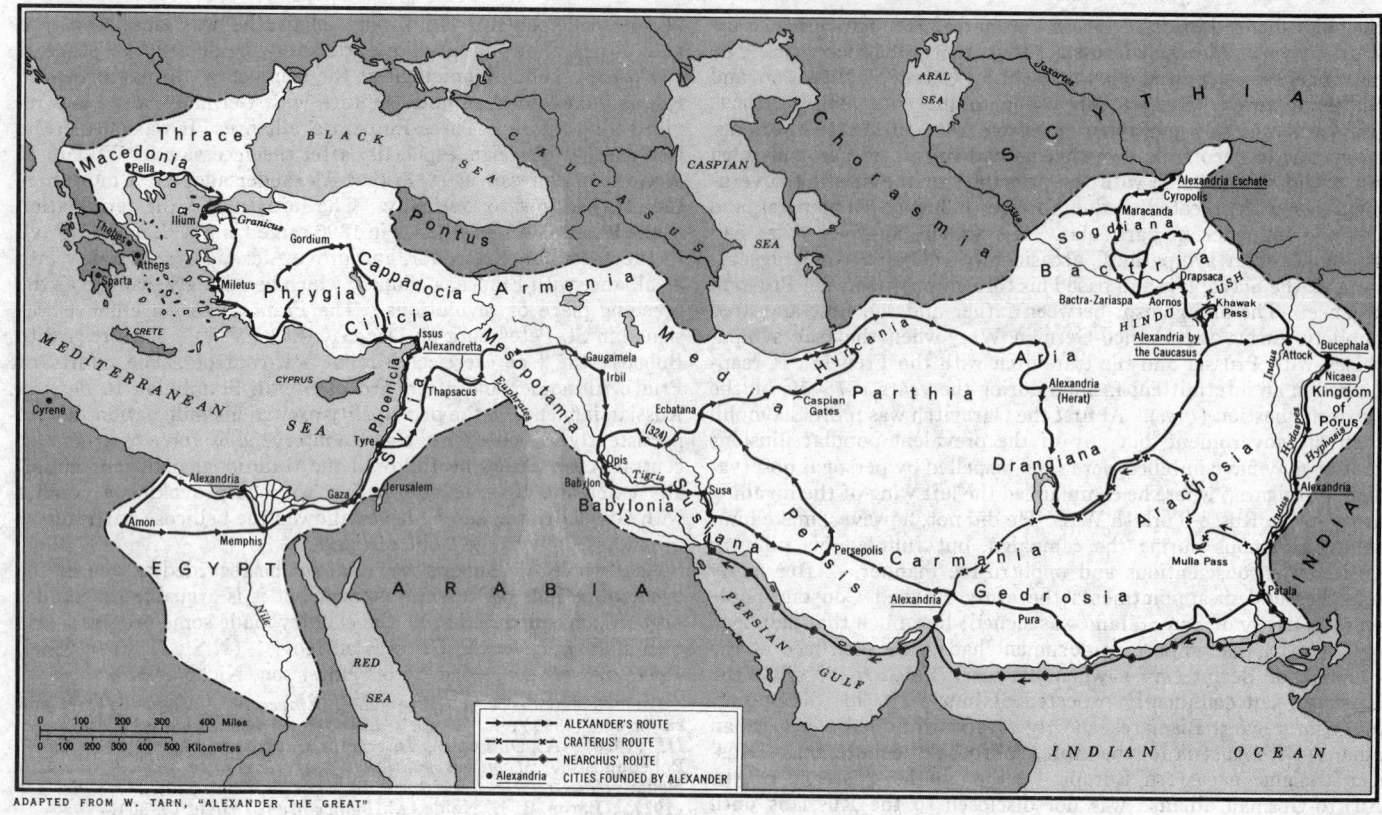

ADAPTED FROM W. TARN, "ALEXANDER THE GREAT"

THE EMPIRE OF ALEXANDER THE GREAT

him. He then marched south, recovered a wavering Thessaly, and at an assembly of the Greek League at Corinth was appointed generalissimo for the forthcoming invasion of Asia, already planned and initiated by Philip. Returning to Macedonia by way of Delphi (where the Pythian priestess hailed him "invincible"), he advanced into Thrace in spring 335 and, after forcing the Shipka Pass and crushing the Triballi, crossed the Danube to disperse the Getae; turning west, he then defeated and shattered a coalition of Illyrians who had invaded Macedonia. Meanwhile a rumour of his death had precipitated a revolt of Theban democrats; other Greek states favoured Thebes, and the Athenians, urged on by Demosthenes, voted help. In 14 days Alexander marched 240 mi. from Pelion (near modern Korce, Albania) in Illyria to Thebes. When the Thebans refused to surrender, he made an entry and razed their city to the ground, sparing only temples and Pindar's house; 6,000 were killed and all survivors sold into slavery. The other Greek states were cowed by this severity, and Alexander could afford to treat Athens leniently. Macedonian garrisons were left in Corinth, Chalcis, and the Cadmea (the citadel of Thebes).

Beginnings of the Persian Expedition.—From his accession Alexander had set his mind on the Persian expedition. He had grown up to the idea. Moreover, he needed the wealth of Persia if he was to maintain the army built by Philip and pay off the 500 talents he owed. The exploits of the Ten Thousand (*see* XENOPHON) and of Agesilaus (*q.v.*) of Sparta, in successfully campaigning in Persian territory, had revealed the vulnerability of the Persian empire. With a good cavalry force Alexander could confidently expect to defeat any Persian army. In spring 334 he crossed the Dardanelles, leaving Antipater as his deputy in Europe with over 13,000 men; he himself commanded about 30,-000 foot and over 5,000 cavalry, of whom nearly 14,000 were Macedonians and about 7,000 allies sent by the Greek League. This army was to prove remarkable for its balanced combination of arms. Much work fell on the light-armed—Cretan and Macedonian archers, Thracians, and the Agrianian javelin men. But in pitched battle the striking force was the cavalry, and the core of the army, should the issue still remain undecided after the

cavalry charge, was the infantry phalanx, 9,000 strong, armed with 13-ft. spears and shields, and the 3,000 men of the royal battalions, the hypaspists. Alexander's second-in-command was Parmenio, who had secured a foothold in Asia Minor during Philip's lifetime; many of his family and supporters were entrenched in positions of responsibility. The army was accompanied by a vast organization of surveyors, engineers (for building siege engines), architects, scientists, court officials, and historians; from the outset Alexander seems to have envisaged an unlimited operation.

After visiting Ilium (Troy), a romantic gesture inspired by Homer, he confronted his first Persian army, led by three satraps, at the Granicus (modern Kocabaş) River, near the Sea of Marmara (May/June 334). (*See* GRANICUS, BATTLE OF THE.) The Persian plan to tempt Alexander across the river and kill him in the melee almost succeeded; but the Persian line broke, and Alexander's victory was complete. Darius' Greek mercenaries were largely massacred, but 2,000 survivors were sent back to Macedonia in chains. This victory exposed western Asia Minor to the Macedonians, and most cities hastened to open their gates. The tyrants were expelled and (in contrast to Macedonian policy in Greece) democracies were installed. Alexander thus underlined his panhellenic policy, already symbolized in the sending of 300 panoplies (sets of armour) taken at Granicus as an offering dedicated to Athena at Athens by "Alexander son of Philip and the Greeks (except the Spartans) from the barbarians who inhabit Asia"—a formula noteworthy for its omission of any reference to Macedonia. But the cities remained *de facto* under Alexander, and his appointment of Calas as satrap of Hellespontine Phrygia reflected his claim to succeed the Great King of Persia. When Miletus, encouraged by the proximity of the Persian fleet, resisted, Alexander took it by assault; but, refusing a naval battle, he disbanded his own costly navy and announced that he would "defeat the Persian fleet on land," by occupying the coastal cities. In Caria, Halicarnassus resisted and was stormed; but Ada, the widow and sister of the satrap Idrieus, adopted Alexander as her son, and expelling her brother Pixodarus he restored her to her satrapy. Some parts of Caria held out, however, until 332.

Asia Minor and the Battle of Issus.—In winter 334/333

Alexander conquered western Asia Minor, subduing the hill tribes of Lycia and Pisidia; and in spring 333 he advanced along the coastal road to Perga, passing the cliffs of Mt. Climax, thanks to a fortunate change of wind. The fall in the level of the sea was interpreted as a mark of divine favour by Alexander's flatterers, including the historian Callisthenes. At Gordium in Phrygia tradition records his cutting of the Gordian knot, which could only be loosed by the man who was to rule Asia; but this story may be apocryphal or at least distorted. At this point Alexander benefited from the sudden death of Memnon, the competent Greek commander of the Persian fleet. From Gordium he pushed on to Ancyra (modern Ankara) and thence south through Cappadocia and the Cilician Gates (modern Külek Boğazi); a fever held him up for a time in Cilicia. Meanwhile Darius with his Grand Army had advanced northward on the eastern side of Mt. Amanus. Intelligence on both sides was faulty, and Alexander was already encamped by Myriandrus (near modern Iskenderun) when he learned that Darius was astride his communications at Issus (autumn 333). Turning at once, Alexander found Darius drawn up along the Pinarus River. For the battle that followed, *see* ISSUS, BATTLE OF. Alexander won a decisive victory. The struggle turned into a Persian rout and Darius fled, leaving his family in Alexander's hands; the women were treated with chivalrous care.

Conquest of the Mediterranean Coast and Egypt.—From Issus Alexander marched south into Syria and Phoenicia, his object being to isolate the Persian fleet from its bases and so to destroy it as an effective fighting force. The Phoenician cities Marathus and Aradus came over quietly and Parmenio was sent ahead to secure Damascus and its rich booty, including Darius' war chest. In reply to a letter from Darius offering peace, Alexander replied arrogantly, recapitulating the historic wrongs of Greece and demanding unconditional surrender to himself as lord of Asia. After taking Byblos and Sidon he met with a check at Tyre, where he was refused entry into the island city. He thereupon prepared to use all methods of siegecraft to take it, but the Tyrians resisted, holding out for seven months. In the meantime (winter 333–332) the Persians had counterattacked by land in Asia Minor, where they were defeated by Antigonus, the satrap of Greater Phrygia, and by sea, recapturing a number of cities and islands.

While the siege of Tyre was in progress Darius sent a new offer: he would pay a huge ransom of 10,000 talents for his family and cede all his lands west of the Euphrates. "I would accept," Parmenio is reported to have said, "were I Alexander"; "I too," was the famous retort, "were I Parmenio." The storming of Tyre in July 332 was Alexander's greatest military achievement; it was attended with great carnage and the sale of the women and children into slavery. Leaving Parmenio in Syria, Alexander advanced south without opposition until he reached Gaza on its high mound; there bitter resistance halted him for two months, and he sustained a serious shoulder wound during a sortie. There is no basis for the tradition that he turned aside to visit Jerusalem.

In November 332 he reached Egypt. The people welcomed him as their deliverer, and the Persian satrap Mazaces wisely surrendered. At Memphis Alexander sacrificed to Apis and was crowned with the traditional double crown of the pharaohs; the native priests were placated and their religion encouraged. He spent the winter organizing Egypt, where he employed Egyptian governors, keeping the army under a separate Macedonian command. He founded the city of Alexandria near the western arm of the Nile on a splendid site between the sea and Lake Mareotis, protected by the island Pharos, and had it laid out by the Rhodian architect Deinocrates. He is also said to have sent an expedition to discover the causes of the flooding of the Nile. From Alexandria he marched along the coast to Paraetonium and from there inland to visit the celebrated oracle of Amon (at Siwah); the difficult journey was later embroidered with flattering legends. On his reaching the oracle in its oasis, the priest gave him the traditional salutation of a pharaoh, as son of Amon; Alexander consulted the god on the success of his expedition but revealed the reply to no one. Later the incident was to contribute to the story that he was the son of Zeus and so to his "deification." In spring 331 he returned to Tyre, appointed a Macedonian satrap for Syria, and prepared to

HEAD OF ALEXANDER ON A COIN OF LYSIMACHUS

advance into Mesopotamia. His conquest of Egypt had completed his control of the whole eastern Mediterranean coast.

Gaugamela to the Death of Darius.—In July 331 Alexander was at Thapsacus on the Euphrates. Instead of taking the direct route down the river to Babylon, he made across northern Mesopotamia toward the Tigris, and Darius, learning of this move from an advance force sent under Mazaeus to the Euphrates crossing, marched up the Tigris to oppose him. The decisive battle of the war was fought on the plain of Gaugamela between Nineveh and Arbela; for this, *see* GAUGAMELA, BATTLE OF. Alexander pursued the defeated Persian forces for 35 miles to Arbela, but Darius escaped with his Bactrian cavalry and Greek mercenaries into Media.

Alexander now occupied Babylon, city and province; Mazaeus, who surrendered it, was confirmed as satrap in conjunction with a Macedonian troop commander, and quite exceptionally was granted the right to coin. As in Egypt the local priesthood was encouraged. Susa, the capital, also surrendered, releasing huge treasures amounting to 50,000 gold talents; here Alexander established Darius' family in comfort. Crushing the mountain Ouxians, he now pressed on over the Zagros range into Persia proper and, successfully turning the pass of the Persian Gates, held by the satrap Ariobarzanes, he entered Persepolis and Pasargadae. At Persepolis he ceremonially burned down the palace of Xerxes, as a symbol that the panhellenic war of revenge was at an end; for such seems the probable significance of an act which tradition later explained as a drunken frolic inspired by Thaïs, an Athenian courtesan. In spring 330 Alexander marched north into Media and occupied its capital Ecbatana. The Thessalians and Greek allies were sent home; henceforward he was waging a purely personal war.

As Mazaeus' appointment indicated, Alexander's views on the empire were changing. He had come to envisage a joint ruling people consisting of Macedonians and Persians, and this served to augment the misunderstanding which now arose between him and his people. Before continuing his pursuit of Darius, who had retreated into Bactria, he assembled all the Persian treasure and entrusted it to Harpalus, who was to hold it at Ecbatana as chief treasurer. Parmenio was also left behind in Media to control communications; the presence of this older man, one of Philip's generals, had perhaps become irksome.

In midsummer 330 Alexander set out for the eastern provinces at a high speed via Rhagae (modern Ray near Teheran) and the Caspian Gates, where he learned that the Bactrian Bessus had deposed Darius. After a skirmish near modern Shahrud, the usurper had Darius stabbed and left him to die. Alexander sent his body for burial with due honours in the royal tombs at Persepolis.

Campaign Eastward, to Central Asia.—Darius' death left no obstacle to Alexander's claim to be Great King, and a Rhodian inscription of this year (330) calls him "lord of Asia"—*i.e.*, of the Persian empire; soon afterward his Asian coins carry the title of king. Crossing the Elburz Mountains to the Caspian, he seized Zadracarta in Hyrcania and received the submission of a group of satraps and Persian notables, some of whom he confirmed in their offices; in a diversion westward, perhaps to modern Amol, he reduced the Mardi. He also accepted the surrender of Darius' Greek mercenaries. His advance eastward was now rapid. In Aria he reduced Satibarzanes, who had offered submission only to revolt, and he founded Alexandria of the Arians (modern Herat). At Phrada in Drangiana (either near modern Nad-i-'Ali in Seistan, or farther north at Farah) he at last took steps to destroy Parmenio and his family. Philotas, Parmenio's son, commander of the elite Companion cavalry, was implicated in an alleged plot against Alexander's life, condemned by the army, and executed; and a secret message was sent to Cleander, Parmenio's second-in-command, who obediently assassinated him. This ruthless action excited widespread horror but strengthened Alexander's position relative to his critics and those whom he regarded as his father's men. All Parmenio's adherents were now eliminated and men close to Alexander promoted. The Companion cavalry was reorganized in two sections, each containing four squadrons (now known as hipparchies); one group was commanded by Alexander's oldest friend, Hephaestion, the other by Cleitus, an older man. From Phrada Alexander pressed on during the winter of 330–329 up the valley of the Helmand River, through Arachosia and over the mountains past the site of modern Kabul into the country of the Paropamisadae, where he founded Alexandria by the Caucasus.

Bactria and Sogdiana.—Bessus was now in Bactria raising a national revolt in the eastern satrapies with the usurped title of Great King. Crossing the Hindu Kush northward over the Khawak Pass (11,650 ft.), Alexander brought his army, despite food shortages, to Drapsaca (sometimes identified with modern Banu [Andarab]; probably farther north at Qunduz); outflanked, Bessus fled beyond the Oxus (modern Amu-Darya), and Alexander, marching west to Bactra-Zariaspa (modern Balkh [Wazirabad] in Afghanistan), appointed loyal satraps in Bactria and Aria. Crossing the Oxus, he sent his general Ptolemy in pursuit of Bessus, who had meanwhile been overthrown by the Sogdian Spitamenes. Bessus was captured, flogged, and sent to Bactra, where he was later mutilated after the Persian manner (losing his nose and ears); in due course he was publicly executed at Ecbatana.

From Maracanda (modern Samarkand) Alexander advanced by way of Cyropolis to the Jaxartes (modern Syr-Darya), the boundary of the Persian empire. There he broke the opposition of the Scythian nomads by his use of catapults, and after defeating them in a battle on the north bank of the river pursued them into the interior. On the site of modern Leninabad (Khojent) on the Jaxartes he founded a city, Alexandria Eschate, "the farthest." Meanwhile Spitamenes had raised all Sogdiana in revolt behind him, bringing in the Massagetae, a people of the Saka confederacy. It took Alexander until the autumn of 328 to crush the most determined opponent he had to meet. Later in the same year he attacked Oxyartes and the remaining barons who held out in the hills of Paraetacene (modern Tadzhikistan); volunteers seized the crag on which Oxyartes had his stronghold, and among the captives was his daughter, Roxana. In reconciliation Alexander married her, and the rest of his opponents were either won over or crushed.

Progress Toward Absolutism.—An incident which occurred at Maracanda widened the breach between Alexander and many of his Macedonians. He murdered Cleitus, one of his most trusted commanders, in a drunken quarrel; but his excessive display of remorse led the army to pass a decree convicting Cleitus posthumously of treason. The event marked a step in Alexander's progress toward Eastern absolutism; and this growing attitude found its outward expression in his use of Persian royal dress. Shortly afterward, at Bactra, he attempted to impose the Persian court ceremonial, involving prostration (*proskynesis*), on the Greeks and Macedonians too; but to them this custom, habitual for Persians entering the king's presence, implied an act of worship and was intolerable before a man. Even Callisthenes, whose ostentatious flattery had perhaps encouraged Alexander to see himself in the role of a god, disappointingly refused to abase himself. Macedonian laughter caused the experiment to founder, and Alexander was wise enough to abandon it. Shortly afterward, however, Callisthenes was held to be privy to a conspiracy among the royal pages and was executed (or died in prison; accounts vary); resentment of this action alienated much sympathy from Alexander within the Peripatetic School, with which Callisthenes had close connections.

Invasion of India.—In early summer 327 Alexander left Bactra with a reinforced army under a reorganized command. If Plutarch's figure of 120,000 men has any reality, however, it must include all kinds of auxiliary services, together with muleteers, camel drivers, medical corps, peddlers, entertainers, women, and children; the fighting strength perhaps stood at about 35,000. Recrossing the Hindu Kush, probably by Bamian and the Ghorband Valley, Alexander divided his forces. Half the army with the baggage under Hephaestion and Perdiccas was sent through the

Khyber Pass, while he himself led the rest, together with his siege train, through the hills to the north. His advance through Swat and Gandhara was marked by the storming of the almost impregnable pinnacle of Aornos, the modern Pir-Sar, a few miles west of the Indus and north of the Buner River, an impressive feat of siegecraft. In spring 326, crossing the Indus near Attock, Alexander entered Taxila, whose ruler, Taxiles, furnished elephants and troops in return for aid against his rival Porus, who ruled the lands between the Hydaspes (modern Jhelum) and the Acesines (modern Chenab). In June Alexander fought his last great battle on the left bank of the Hydaspes. (*See* HYDASPES, BATTLE OF THE.) He founded two cities there, Alexandria Nicaea (to celebrate his victory) and Bucephala (named after his horse Bucephalus, which died there); and Porus became his ally.

How much Alexander knew of India beyond the Hyphasis (probably the modern Beas) is uncertain; there is no conclusive proof that he had heard of the Ganges. But he was anxious to press on yet further and he had advanced to the Hyphasis when his army mutinied, refusing to go further in the tropical rain; they were weary in body and spirit, and Coenus, one of Alexander's four chief marshals, acted as their spokesman. On finding the army adamant, Alexander agreed to turn back.

Return from India.—On the Hyphasis he erected 12 altars to the 12 Olympian gods, and on the Hydaspes he built a fleet of 800 to 1,000 ships. Leaving Porus he then proceeded down the river and into the Indus, with half his forces on shipboard and half marching in three columns down the two banks. The fleet was commanded by Nearchus and Alexander's own captain was Onesicritus; both later wrote accounts of the campaign. The march was attended with much fighting and heavy, pitiless slaughter; at the storming of one town of the Malli near the Hydraotes (Ravi) River Alexander received a severe wound which left him weakened.

On reaching Patala he built a harbour and docks and explored both arms of the Indus, which probably then ran into the Rann of Cutch. He planned to lead part of his forces back by land, while the rest in perhaps 100 to 150 ships under the command of Nearchus made a voyage of exploration along the Persian Gulf. Local opposition led Nearchus to set sail in September (325), and he was held up for three weeks until he could pick up the northeast monsoon in late October. In September Alexander too set out along the coast through Gedrosia, but he was soon compelled by mountainous country to turn inland, thus failing in his project to establish food depots for the fleet. Already Craterus had been sent off with the baggage and siege train, the elephants, and the sick and wounded, together with three battalions of the phalanx, by way of the Mulla Pass, Quetta, and Kandahar into the Helmand Valley; from there he was to march through Drangiana to rejoin the main army on the Amanis (modern Minab) River in Carmania. Alexander's march through Gedrosia (modern Baluchistan) proved disastrous; waterless desert and shortage of food and fuel caused great suffering, and many, especially women and children, perished in a sudden monsoon flood while encamped in a wadi. At length, at the Amanis, he was rejoined by Nearchus and the fleet, who had also had losses and many adventures.

Political Developments.—Alexander now proceeded further with his policy of replacing senior officials and executing defaulting governors, on which he had already embarked before leaving India. Between 326 and 324 over a third of his satraps were superseded and six were put to death, including the Persian satraps of Persis, Susiana, Carmania, and Paraetacene; three generals in Media, including Cleander, the brother of Coenus (who had died a little earlier), were accused of extortion and summoned to Carmania, where they were arrested, tried, and executed. How far the rigour which from now onward Alexander displayed against his governors represents exemplary punishment for gross maladministration during his absence and how far the elimination of men he had come to distrust (as in the case of Philotas and Parmenio) is debatable; but the ancient sources generally favourable to him comment adversely on his severity.

In spring 324 he was back in Susa; the story of his journey through Carmania in a drunken revel, dressed as Dionysus, is embroidered, if not wholly apocryphal. He found that his treasurer,

Harpalus, evidently fearing punishment for peculation, had absconded with 6,000 mercenaries and 5,000 talents to Greece; arrested in Athens, he escaped and was later murdered in Crete. At Susa Alexander held a feast to celebrate the seizure of the Persian empire, at which, in furtherance of his policy of fusing Macedonians and Persians into one master race, he and 80 of his officers took Persian wives; he and Hephaestion married Darius' daughters Barsine (also called Stateira) and Drypetis respectively, and 10,000 of his soldiers with native wives were given generous dowries.

This policy of racial fusion brought increasing friction to Alexander's relations with his Macedonians, who had no sympathy for his changed concept of the empire. His determination to incorporate Persians on equal terms in the army and the administration of the provinces was bitterly resented. This discontent was now fanned by the arrival of 30,000 native youths who had received a Macedonian military training and by the introduction of Orientals from Bactria, Sogdiana, Arachosia, and other parts of the empire into the Companion cavalry; whether Orientals had already previously served with the Companions is uncertain, but if so they must previously have formed separate squadrons. In addition, Persian nobles had recently been accepted into the royal cavalry bodyguard. Peucestas, the new governor of Persis, gave this policy full support to flatter Alexander; but most Macedonians saw it as a threat to their own privileged position. The issue came to a head at Opis (324), when Alexander's decision to send home Macedonian veterans under Craterus was interpreted as a move toward transferring the seat of power to Asia. There was an open mutiny involving all but the royal bodyguard; but when Alexander dismissed his whole army and enrolled Persians instead, the opposition broke down. An emotional scene of reconciliation was followed by a vast banquet with 9,000 guests to celebrate the ending of the misunderstanding and the partnership in government of Macedonians and Persians—but not, as has been argued, the incorporation of all the subject peoples as partners in the commonwealth. Ten thousand veterans were now sent back to Macedonia with gifts, and the crisis was surmounted.

In summer 324 Alexander attempted to solve another problem, that of the wandering mercenaries, of whom there were thousands in Asia and Greece, many of them political exiles from their own cities. A decree brought by Nicanor to Europe and proclaimed at Olympia (September, 324) required the Greek cities of the Greek League to receive back all exiles and their families (except the Thebans), a measure which implied some modification of the oligarchic regimes maintained in the Greek cities by Alexander's governor Antipater. Alexander now planned to recall Antipater and supersede him by Craterus; but he was to die before this move had been carried out.

The Last Year.—In autumn 324 Hephaestion died in Ecbatana, and Alexander indulged in extravagant mourning for his closest friend; he was given a royal funeral in Babylon with a pyre costing 10,000 talents. His post of chiliarch (grand vizier) was left unfilled. It was probably in connection with a general order now sent out to the Greeks to honour Hephaestion as a hero that Alexander linked the demand that he himself should be accorded divine honours. For a long time his mind had dwelt on ideas of godhead. Greek thought drew no very decided line of demarcation between god and man, for legend offered more than one example of men who, by their achievements, acquired divine status. Alexander had on several occasions encouraged favourable comparison of his own accomplishments with those of Dionysus or Heracles (Hercules). He now seems to have become convinced of the reality of his own divinity and to have required its acceptance by others. There is no reason to assume that his demand had any political background (divine status gave its possessor no particular rights in a Greek city); it was rather a symptom of growing megalomania and emotional instability. The cities perforce complied, but often ironically: the Spartan decree read, "Since Alexander wishes to be a god, let him be a god."

In the winter of 324 Alexander carried out a savage punitive expedition against the Cossaeans in the hills of Luristan. The following spring at Babylon he received complimentary embassies from the Libyans and from the Bruttians, Etruscans, and Lucanians of Italy; but the story that embassies also came from more distant peoples, such as Carthaginians, Celts, Iberians, and even Romans, is a later invention. Representatives of the cities of Greece also came, garlanded as befitted Alexander's divine status. Following up Nearchus' voyage, he now founded an Alexandria at the mouth of the Tigris and made plans to develop sea communications with India, for which an expedition along the Arabian coast was to be a preliminary. He also dispatched Heracleides to explore the Hyrcanian (*i.e.,* Caspian) Sea. Suddenly, while busy with plans to improve the irrigation of the Euphrates and to settle the coast of the Persian Gulf, he was taken ill after a prolonged banquet and drinking bout; ten days later, on June 13, 323, he died in his 33rd year; he had reigned for twelve years and eight months. His body, diverted to Egypt by Ptolemy, the later king, was eventually placed in a golden coffin in Alexandria. Both in Egypt and elsewhere in the Greek cities he received divine honours.

No heir had been appointed to the throne, and his generals adopted Philip II's half-witted illegitimate son, Philip Arrhidaeus, and Alexander's posthumous son by Roxana, Alexander IV, as kings, sharing out the satrapies among themselves, after much bargaining. The empire could hardly survive Alexander's death as a unit. Both kings were murdered, Arrhidaeus in 317 and Alexander in 310–309. The provinces became independent kingdoms and the generals, following Antigonus' lead in 306, took the title of kings (*see* HELLENISTIC AGE: *Outline of Political History*).

Alexander's Achievement, Generalship, and Character.—Of Alexander's plans little reliable information survives. The far-reaching schemes for the conquest of the western Mediterranean and the setting up of a universal monarchy, recorded in Diodorus, are probably based on a later forgery; if not, they were at once jettisoned by his successors and the army. Had he lived, he would no doubt have completed the conquest of Asia Minor, where Paphlagonia, Cappadocia, and Armenia still maintained an effective independence. But in his later years Alexander's aims seem to have been directed toward exploration, in particular of Arabia and the Caspian. Whether eventually conquest would have followed is unknown.

In the organization of his empire Alexander had been content in many spheres to improvise and adapt what he found. His financial policy is an exception; though the details cannot be wholly recovered, it is clear that he set up a central organization with collectors perhaps independent of the local satraps. That this proved a failure was partly due to weaknesses in Harpalus' character. But the establishment of a new coinage with a silver standard based on that of Athens in place of the old bimetallic system current both in Macedonia and in Persia helped trade everywhere, and combined with the release of vast amounts of bullion from the Persian treasuries gave a much-needed fillip to the economy of the whole Mediterranean area.

Alexander's foundation of new cities—Plutarch speaks of over 70—initiated a new chapter in Greek expansion. No doubt many of the colonists, by no means volunteers, deserted them, and marriages with native women led to some dilution of Greek ways; but the Greek (rather than Macedonian) influence remained strong in most of them, and since the process was carried further by Alexander's Seleucid successors the spread of Hellenic thought and customs over much of Asia as far as Bactria and India was one of the more striking effects of Alexander's conquests.

His plans for racial fusion on the other hand were a failure. The Iranian satraps were perhaps not efficient, for out of 18, ten were removed or executed—with what justice it is no longer possible to say. But, more important, the Macedonians, leaders and men alike, rejected the idea, and in the later Seleucid empire the Greek and Macedonian element was to be clearly dominant.

How far Alexander would have succeeded in the difficult task of coordinating his vast dominions, had he lived, is hard to determine. The only link between the many units that went to make up an empire more disparate than that of the Habsburgs, and far larger, was his own person; and his early death came before he could seriously tackle this problem.

What had so far held it all together was his own dynamic personality. He combined an iron will and ability to drive himself and his men to the utmost with a supple and flexible mind; he knew when to draw back and change his policy, though he did this very reluctantly. He was imaginative and not without romantic impulses; figures like Achilles, Heracles, and Dionysus were often in his mind, and the salutation at the oracle of Amon clearly influenced his thoughts and ambitions ever afterward. He was swift in anger, and under the strain of his long campaigns this side of his character grew more pronounced. Ruthless and self-willed, he had increasing recourse to terror, showing no hesitation in eliminating men whom he had ceased to trust, either with or without the pretense of a fair trial. Years after his death, Antipater's son Cassander could not pass his statue at Delphi without shuddering. Yet he maintained the loyalty of his men, who followed him to the Hyphasis without complaining and continued to believe in him throughout all hardships. Only when his whim would have taken them yet farther into unknown India did he fail to get his way.

As a general Alexander is among the greatest the world has known. He showed unusual versatility both in the combination of different arms and in adapting his tactics to the challenge of enemies who commanded novel forms of warfare—the Saka nomads, the Indian hill tribes, or Porus with his elephants. His strategy was skilful and imaginative and he knew how to exploit the chances that arise in every battle and may be decisive for victory or defeat; he also drew the last advantage from victory by relentless pursuit. His use of cavalry was so effective that he rarely had to fall back upon his infantry to deliver the crushing blow.

Alexander's short reign marks a decisive moment in the history of Europe and Asia. His expedition and his own personal interest in scientific investigation brought many advances in the knowledge of geography and natural history. His career led to the moving of the great centres of civilization eastward and initiated the new age of the Greek territorial monarchies; it spread Hellenism in a vast colonizing wave throughout the Near East and created, if not politically, at least economically and culturally, a single world stretching from Gibraltar to the Punjab, open to trade and social intercourse and with a considerable overlay of common civilization and the Greek *koine* as a lingua franca (*see* GREEK LANGUAGE: *Koine and Byzantine*). It is not untrue to say that the Roman empire, the spread of Christianity as a world religion, and the long centuries of Byzantium were all in some degree the fruits of Alexander's achievement.

Even in his lifetime fabulous stories were being told of Alexander, and later he became the hero of a full-scale legend bearing only the sketchiest resemblance to his historical career. For the developments of this in Greek, Latin, European, and Eastern literatures *see* ALEXANDER ROMANCES.

BIBLIOGRAPHY.—*General:* J. G. Droysen, *Geschichte Alexanders des Grossen* (1833; reprinted 1933, 1942); K. J. Beloch, *Griechische Geschichte*, 2nd ed., vol. iii and iv (1922–25); H. Berve, *Das Alexanderreich auf prosopographischer Grundlage*, 2 vol. (1926); W. W. Tarn in *Cambridge Ancient History*, vol. vi, ch. 12–13, with bibliography (1927), *Alexander the Great*, 2 vol. (1948); G. Radet, *Alexandre le Grand* (1931); U. Wilcken, *Alexander der Grosse* (1931), Eng. trans. (1932); G. Glotz and R. Cohen, *Histoire grecque*, vol. iv, part 1 (1938); A. R. Burn, *Alexander the Great and the Hellenistic Empire* (1947); F. Schachermeyr, *Alexander der Grosse, Ingenium und Macht* (1949); H. Bengtson, *Griechische Geschichte*, 2nd ed. (1960), with critical bibliography.
Ancient Sources: Arrian (based mainly on Ptolemy) is the most reliable; Plutarch, *Alexander;* Diodorus Siculus, book xvii; Curtius Rufus; Justin. For discussion *see* W. W. Tarn, *Alexander the Great*, vol. ii; L. Pearson, *The Lost Histories of Alexander the Great* (1960); E. Badian, "The Eunuch Bagoas," *Classical Quarterly*, new series, 8:144 ff. (1958); P. A. Brunt, "Persian Accounts of Alexander's Campaigns," *ibid.*, new series, 12:141 ff. (1962).
Army: J. F. C. Fuller, *The Generalship of Alexander the Great* (1958); E. W. Marsden, *The Campaign of Gaugamela* (1964); A. R. Burn, "Notes on Alexander's Campaigns, 333–330 B.C.," *Journal of Hellenic Studies*, 72:81 ff. (1952); P. A. Brunt, "Alexander's Macedonian Cavalry," *ibid.*, 83:27 ff. (1963); G. T. Griffith, "A Note on the Hipparchies of Alexander," *ibid.*, 83:68 ff. (1963).
Administration and Ideas: E. Meyer, "Alexander der Grosse und die absolute Monarchie," *Kleine Schriften*, vol. i, 283 ff. (1910); W. W. Tarn, *Alexander the Great*, vol. ii, 378 ff. (on the "world-kingdom"), 399 ff. (on the "brotherhood of man"); J. P. V. D. Balsdon, "The 'Divinity' of Alexander," *Historia*, 1:364 ff. (1950); E. Badian, "Alexander the

Great and the Unity of Mankind," *ibid.*, 7:425 ff. (1958), "The First Flight of Harpalus," *ibid.*, 9:245 f. (1960), "The Death of Parmenio," *Transactions of the American Philological Association*, 91:324 ff. (1960), "The Death of Philip II," *Phoenix*, 17:244 ff. (1963), "Harpalus," *Journal of Hellenic Studies*, 81:16 ff. (1961), "Alexander the Great and the Loneliness of Power," *Studies in Greek and Roman History*, 192 ff. (1964).
Reviews of Recent Literature: R. Andreotti, "Il problema di Alessandro Magno . . . ," *Historia*, 1:583 ff. (1950); G. Walser, "Die Weltmonarchie Alexanders des Grossen . . . ," *Schweizer Beiträge zur allgemeinen Geschichte*, 14:156 ff. (1956).   (F. W. WA.)

ALEXANDER I (*c.* 1080–1124), king of Scotland, probably the fifth son of Malcolm III and Margaret (later St. Margaret), succeeded to the throne on the death of his brother Edgar in 1107. He relinquished Strathclyde and the area between the Lammermuir hills and the river Tweed to David, his brother and heir. Alexander probably ruled as vassal of Henry I of England; he married Henry's illegitimate daughter Sibylla and in 1114 led a Scottish contingent in Henry's Welsh campaigns. Alexander founded an Augustinian priory at Scone *c.* 1115 and planned to found others; but he quarreled with Turgot, bishop of St. Andrews, and with Eadmer, elected to succeed Turgot, and he did little to revive the secular church. Alexander died, probably at Stirling, in April 1124.
(A. A. M. D.)

ALEXANDER II (1198–1249), king of Scotland, only legitimate son of King William (later called "the Lion"), was born on Aug. 24, 1198, and succeeded to the throne in 1214. Hoping to regain territory in northern England he supported the English baronial rebellion against King John, but after its collapse in 1217 he did homage to Henry III whose sister, Joan, Alexander married in 1221. She died childless in 1238 and a year later Alexander married Mary de Coucy. Their son (afterward Alexander III) was betrothed to Henry's daughter Margaret in 1242. The friendly relationship between the kings was strained by Henry's claim of suzerainty over Scotland and by Alexander's claim to the northern counties of England which he only abandoned in 1237 in return for some English estates. Renewed friction in 1244 nearly precipitated a war. About that time Alexander tried unsuccessfully to buy the Isle of Man and the Hebrides from Norway. In Scotland he exterminated a rival line in 1230, and suppressed disorders in Caithness in 1222 and in Galloway in 1235. He was on an expedition to Argyll when he died at Kerrera on July 8, 1249.

See A. O. Anderson, *Early Sources of Scottish History A.D. 500 to 1286*, vol. ii (1922).

ALEXANDER III (1241–1286), king of Scotland, was born at Roxburgh on Sept. 4, 1241, the only son of Alexander II, whom he succeeded in 1249. Henry III of England tried to take advantage of Alexander's youth to obtain suzerainty over Scotland, but he failed to obtain the support of Pope Innocent IV and at the marriage in 1251 of Alexander to Henry's daughter Margaret, Alexander evaded doing homage for Scotland. In 1255 Henry's nominees secured the regency of Scotland until Alexander should be of age, but they lost it through conciliar changes made in 1257 and 1258 partly because Gamelin, bishop of St. Andrews, persuaded Pope Alexander IV to excommunicate them. When in 1278 Alexander attended the court of Edward I, who had succeeded his father Henry III in 1272, he did homage for his English estates only.

Alexander's rumoured intention to annex the Hebrides in 1263 provoked Haakon IV of Norway to lead a force to Scotland. After inconclusive campaigning and a repulse at Largs in Ayrshire, Haakon withdrew to Orkney where he died in Dec. 1263. By the treaty of Perth (1266) his son Magnus VI (IV) ceded the Isle of Man and the Hebrides to Alexander in return for a down payment and an annual rent.

Alexander's first wife died in 1275 and all their children predeceased him. In 1285 the king married Yolande, daughter of Robert, count of Dreux. Riding to join her at Kinghorn in Fife on the night of March 18–19, 1286, he was thrown from his horse and killed. His grandchild, Margaret, was proclaimed queen of Scotland, but died in 1290. Alexander left Scotland independent, united and prosperous, and in the troubled years that followed the extinction of his line his reign was remembered as a golden age.

See A. O. Anderson, *Early Sources of Scottish History A.D. 500 to 1286*, vol. ii (1922).

ALEXANDER (ALEKSANDAR OBRENOVICH) (1876–1903), king of Serbia from 1889 to 1903, was born in Belgrade on Aug. 14 (new style; Aug. 2, old style), 1876, the only child of Milan (*q.v.*) Obrenovich and his consort Natalie. After his father's abdication he succeeded, on March 6 (N.S.; Feb. 22, O.S.), 1889, as king of Serbia, under a regency. He dismissed the regency council on April 13 (N.S.; April 1, O.S.), 1893, and proclaimed himself ruler before attaining his majority.

In order to govern through the Liberals and Progressives, whose parties were in decline, or through politically neutral governments at a time when the Radical party was at its peak in Serbia, Alexander in 1894 abolished the liberal constitution of 1889 and restored the constitution of 1869. Cabinets came and went. Alexander appointed his father commander in chief (1898–1900). In 1900, however, while his prime minister and his father were abroad, he announced his engagement to Draga Masin, née Lunjevica (1866–1903), ten years his senior, a childless widow with a dubious past, former lady in waiting to his mother. His government then resigned, and Alexander had great difficulty in forming the new one, which was composed mainly of civil servants. The Russian tsar Nicholas II agreed to act as best man at the wedding, which took place on Aug. 5 (N.S.; July 23, O.S.), 1900. Alexander then tried to placate the political parties by granting a more liberal constitution (1901) and by instituting a senate as a second chamber. In 1903, however, he suspended the constitution for only a few hours in order to dismiss some senators appointed by him for life, to remove some irremovable judges and to grant a new electoral law which would enable his supporters to get a majority. To spare the country from further disaster, members of an already existing conspiracy thereupon decided to act, and on June 11 (N.S.; May 29, O.S.), 1903, Alexander and Draga were assassinated. The Obrenovich dynasty was extinguished.

Torn since childhood between his parents, who were divorced in 1888 after years of quarreling, Alexander's loyalty was divided. Save in his last three years, he was always under the influence of one or the other of them. His father pushed him toward Austria–Hungary and authoritarian rule, his mother toward Russia and the Radical party. His ten years' personal rule was but a succession of four *coups d'état* and 17 governments. Nevertheless the conversion of the national debt, the appointment of Serbian instead of Greek bishops in Macedonia, the reorganization of the army and his attempt to revive the Balkan alliance go to the credit of his reign.

See C. Mijatovich, *A Royal Tragedy* (1906); S. Jovanović, *Vlada Aleksandra Obrenovića*, 2 vol. (1929–31). (K. St. P.)

ALEXANDER I (1888–1934), king of the Serbs, Croats and Slovenes from 1921, of Yugoslavia from 1929 to 1934, was born at Cetinje on Dec. 16 (new style; Dec. 4, old style), 1888, the second son of Peter Karageorgevich (*q.v.*) and of Zorka of Montenegro. He spent his early childhood at Geneva with his exiled father. Sent to St. Petersburg in 1899, he entered the Russian imperial corps of pages in 1904. In 1909 he returned to Serbia, where his father had been reigning since 1903. Incidents provoked by the fiery temper of his elder brother George resulted in the latter's renouncing his right of succession (March 28, 1909) so that Alexander became the heir to the throne. On the outbreak of the first Balkan War (1912) he assumed command of the Serbian 1st army and won fame at the battle of Kumanovo (Oct. 24, 1912), subsequently distinguishing himself in the second Balkan War (1913). His father, being in poor health and advanced in years, appointed him regent of Serbia (June 24, 1914), and Alexander then became commander in chief of the armed forces. During World War I, Alexander remained permanently at army headquarters, returning in triumph to Belgrade (Oct. 31, 1918).

The kingdom of the Serbs, Croats and Slovenes was proclaimed on Dec. 1, 1918, with Alexander as regent. A new constitution was passed by the constituent assembly on June 28, 1921. As he was returning from the *skupstina* after taking the oath to this constitution an attempt was made upon his life. On his father's death (Aug. 16, 1921) Alexander succeeded as king of the Serbs, Croats and Slovenes. On June 8, 1922, he married Marie (1900–61), second daughter of Ferdinand I of Rumania. An heir was born (Sept. 6, 1923) who received the name of Peter; a second son (1928) received the Croatian name Tomislav and a third (1929) the Slovenian name Andrei.

Political conditions were somewhat unsettled, as centralist tendencies prevailed among the Serbs while the Croats were federalist or even separatist, and on June 20, 1928, two Croatian leaders were shot dead and three wounded on the floor of the *skupstina* by a Serbian member from Montenegro who felt that he had been deeply insulted by one of them. Although the crime was unanimously condemned by the Serbs, the Croatian members withdrew from the *skupstina*. Alexander, convinced that the very existence of the state was threatened, abolished the constitution (Jan. 6, 1929), assumed full powers in order to reduce tension, changed the name of the country to Yugoslavia (Oct. 3, 1929) and proclaimed a new constitution (Sept. 3, 1931). He tried to establish friendly relations with neighbouring countries, but met with bitter enmity in Italy and Hungary. A second attempt upon his life, planned abroad in 1933, was prevented, but on a state visit to France he was murdered at Marseilles (Oct. 9, 1934) by hired assassins who had been trained at Janka Puszta (Hungary) and at Borgo di Taro (Italy). He was succeeded by his eldest son, Peter II, under a regency.

A soldier-statesman who never avoided responsibilities, authoritarian whenever he considered that firmness was needed, immensely popular with the army and among the Serbian peasantry, disliked by a minority, and respected by all, Alexander was the strongest ruler of his country since the rebirth of Serbia in the 19th century.

See A. R. Dimitrijević, *Naš veliki kralj* ("Our Great King") (1936); S. Graham, *Alexander of Yugoslavia* (1938). (K. St. P.)

ALEXANDER (ALEKSANDAR KARAGEORGEVICH) (1806–1885), prince of Serbia from 1842 to 1858, was born at Topola on Oct. 11 (new style; Sept. 29, old style), 1806, the third son of Karageorge (*q.v.*) and of Yelena Yovanovich. Alexander went into exile with his father in 1813, but in 1842, after the deposition of Michael Obrenovich, he was elected prince of Serbia. The validity of this election was contested by Russia, but at a second election next year he was chosen again. During the Hungarian revolution of 1848–49 he helped the Serbs and Croats of the Austrian empire against the Hungarians. Under Russian pressure he dismissed his pro-western prime minister Iliya Garashanin (*q.v.*) in 1853, but despite the pro-Russian majority in his council he maintained neutrality in the Crimean War. As a reward, the treaty of Paris (1856) placed Serbia's autonomy within the Turkish empire under the collective guarantee of the European powers. During Alexander's reign the embryo of a university, a national library and museum (1844), a supreme court (1846) and the first code of civil law were established and more than 200 schools were opened.

Well-intentioned but weak and impulsive, Alexander had to share power with a council of members appointed for life. A struggle for supremacy ensued, and after the discovery of a plot against his life (1857) Alexander overthrew the oligarchy. In 1858, however, he was compelled to abdicate. He died in exile at Temesvar (Timisoara) in the Banat on May 3 (N.S.; April 21, O.S.), 1885. By his marriage in 1830 with Persida Nenadovich (1813–75) he had ten children, one of whom, Peter, became king of Serbia in 1903. (K. St. P.)

ALEXANDER of APHRODISIAS, Greek philosopher, who wrote commentaries on most of the Aristotelian works, was born in Aphrodisias in Caria and was a pupil of Aristocles of Messene. Toward the end of the 2nd century A.D. he became head of the Lyceum at Athens. His commentaries were intended to restore the pure doctrine of Aristotle and free the tradition of the Lyceum from the syncretism of Ammonius. His commentaries on the *Prior Analytics I*, on the *Topics*, on the *Meteorologica*, on the *De sensu* and on the *Metaphysics I–V* are extant; and fragments of his lost commentaries are found in all later commentaries. In antiquity his commentaries constituted the most influential section of his writings, causing him to be styled, by way of preeminence, "the expositor"; but in the middle ages it was rather for his original works that he was known, both to Arabic and to Christian philosophers. The most important of these later works are *On Fate,* in which he defends free will against the Stoic doctrine of necessity, and *On the Soul,* in which he tries to explain Aristotle's doctrine of the soul and the intellect. Reason, being the form of the body in man, is mortal and may be called material intellect as it may become all things, or virtual intellect, because of its potentiality of thinking. This mortal intellect has to be actualized by the active intellect, which comes from outside and is identical with God. This doctrine, revived by Averroës, was warmly debated in the 13th century, as it raises the problem of personal immortality.

BIBLIOGRAPHY.—Alexander's works are printed in *Commentaria in Aristotelem Graeca,* vol. i–iii, and in vol. ii of the supplement (1883–1901); the Latin translations appeared in 16th-century editions. See also P. Moraux, *Alexandre d'Aphrodise* (1942); H. Thery, *Alexandre d'Aphrodise* (1926); P. Wilpert, "Reste verlorener Aristotelesschriften bei Alexander von Aphrodisias," *Hermes,* vol. 75 (1940), "Die Ausgestaltung der aristotelischen Lehre vom Intellectus agens," *Beiträge zur Geschichte der Philosophie und Theologie des Mittelalters,* suppl. 3 (1935). (P. A. W.)

ALEXANDER OF BATTENBERG (1857–1893), prince of Bulgaria, was born at Verona, Italy, on April 5, 1857, the second son of Prince Alexander of Hesse and Julia the Countess von Haucke, his morganatic wife (*see* BATTENBERG). In 1877 he served with the Russian forces in the war with Turkey, which resulted in the autonomy of Bulgaria (*see* RUSSO-TURKISH WARS). The emperor Alexander II of Russia, who had married a sister of Alexander of Hesse, showed much interest in his nephew Alexander and gave decisive support to his election on April 29, 1879, as prince of Bulgaria. The prince, however, who was impulsive and not particularly shrewd by nature, had little chance of success in his new position after the assassination of Alexander II (1881), as he soon lost the favour of the new emperor Alexander III. Germany, moreover, under Bismarck, supported Russian policy in Bulgaria; both deterred Austria-Hungary from helping the prince and frustrated British efforts to do so.

On July 8, 1879, the prince took the oath to the Bulgarian constitution. This constitution, however, was ill-suited to conditions in a new country. The two political parties (one pro-Russian, the other anti-Russian) were in violent conflict, and the opposition soon became so obstructive that Alexander dissolved the national assembly on Nov. 24, 1880. In May 1881, he suspended the constitution, declared that fresh elections were to be held on a new basis and assumed plenary powers for seven years. This policy was approved by the new national assembly in June 1881, and Alexander appointed a government headed by Gen. J. C. Ehrnroth, a Finn in the Russian service. Russia reacted strongly against Alexander's unlimited powers, particularly in military matters, and Ehrnroth was recalled. Alexander then went to St. Petersburg to negotiate a modus vivendi with the Russians. A new Bulgarian government was appointed with the Russian generals L. N. Sobolev and A. I. Kaulbars as ministers of the interior and war so that they could keep Bulgaria in the Russian fold and restrict the prince's control of the army. By their political ineptitude and arrogance they caused such resentment that the two Bulgarian parties temporarily united behind the prince. The constitution of 1879 was restored in Sept. 1883 and Sobolev and Kaulbars were dismissed—to Alexander III's great indignation.

Alexander of Battenberg was now in open opposition to Russia, and the breach was widened when Bulgaria annexed Eastern Rumelia, in Sept. 1885 without consulting Russia. The Russian emperor denounced this *fait accompli,* had the prince's name removed from the Russian army list and recalled all Russian officers in Bulgaria. The Serbs invaded Bulgaria, with Austria-Hungary's connivance, in Nov. 1885 but were driven back, and the Bulgarian army's advance into Serbia was halted only by strong pressure from Vienna (*see* SERBO-BULGARIAN WAR). Bulgaria gained nothing from the war, and disappointment and propaganda against the "German" prince prepared the ground for a *coup d'état.* In the night of Aug. 20–21, 1886, Bulgarian officers forced Alexander to abdicate, abducted him and delivered him to the Russians at Reni (Ismail province, Rumania). Two weeks later, however, he was back in Bulgaria at the insistent request of the people. Before assuming power, he sent a telegram to St. Petersburg incautiously

putting his crown at the Russian emperor's discretion. This altered nothing of the emperor's hostility, and the prince abdicated for good on Sept. 8, 1886. Assuming the title of Graf von Hartenau, he took service as a general in the Austrian army. He died at Graz on Oct. 23, 1893, leaving two children by his marriage (Feb. 6, 1889) with the opera singer Johanna Loisinger.

See A. Koch, *Prince Alexander of Battenberg* (1887); E. C. Corti, *Alexander von Battenberg* (1955). (N. I. M.)

ALEXANDER OF HALES (*c.* 1170 or 1185–1245), English theologian and philosopher, known to the scholastics as *Doctor irrefragabilis,* was born at Hales in Gloucestershire. He studied and taught in Paris (master of arts before 1210, of theology in 1229), was archdeacon of Coventry in 1235, became a Franciscan *c.* 1236 and then founded in Paris the Schola Fratrum Minorum, thus being the first holder, possibly until his death, of the Franciscan chair in that university. Much of the teaching of such theologians as St. Bonaventure and John of La Rochelle developed from this master's doctrine. The *Summa Theologica* for centuries ascribed to him ("Summa Fratris Alexandri," ed. by the Bonaventure institute, Quaracchi, 1924–48) is largely the work of followers, among them William of Milton; Roger Bacon had already denounced the wrong attribution. Only the most general features of Alexander's theology and philosophy have been made clear: basically an Augustinian, he had taken into account, to some extent, the psychological, physical and metaphysical doctrines of Aristotle, while discarding popular Avicennian tenets.

The "Franciscan" theories of matter and form in spiritual creatures, of the multiplicity of forms and of illumination combined with experience are probably Alexander's adaptations of similar theories of the Augustinian and other traditions.

Alexander's original works, apart from sections of the *Summa* and of an *Expositio Regulae,* include a commentary on the *Sentences* (ed. by the Bonaventure institute, Quaracchi, 3 vol., 1951–54); *Quaestiones antequam esset frater* (some of them, on matrimony, ed. by K. F. Lynch in *Franciscan Studies,* xi, pp. 131–139); *Quodlibeta;* sermons; and a treatise on difficult words, *Exoticon.*

BIBLIOGRAPHY.—Apart from the *Prolegomena* to vol. iv of the *Summa* and to vol. i of the commentary on the *Sentences,* see V. Doucet, "Alessandro di Hales," *Enciclopedia Cattolica,* vol. i (1949); I. Herscher, "A Bibliography of Alexander of Hales," *Franciscan Studies,* xxvi, pp. 434–454. (L. M.-Po.)

ALEXANDER (NEVSKI) (1220–1263), Russian grand prince and canonized a saint of the Russian Orthodox Church in 1380, was a son of Yaroslav Vsevolodovich, who for a time was ruler of Novgorod. Alexander's greatest achievements took place early in his life, in defense of Novgorod's frontiers. First, in 1240, he defeated the Swedes on the Neva (hence the name Nevski), but then he quarreled with the princes of Novgorod and went to Pereyaslavl. In 1241, however, he returned at the urgent request of the Novgorodians, who were being hard pressed by the knights of the Teutonic Order (*q.v.*). Having freed all Russian districts which had been captured by the knights, he carried the war into German-occupied Estonia and, in April 1242, defeated the knights on the ice of Lake Peipus. The grand master of the order then renounced all previous conquests in Russia. This was not the end of aggression against Russia from the west, but the wave of enemy attack was stemmed at its most dangerous moment. At the same time, by his decisive action against the Lithuanians, Alexander secured relative peace in the west and was able to turn his attention eastward.

When Yaroslav Vsevolodovich, who had become grand prince of Vladimir and Kiev in 1243, died in 1246, Alexander and his brother Andrei were sent by Batu Khan to Karakorum in Mongolia. There Andrei was appointed grand prince of Vladimir; Alexander became prince of Kiev. But when Andrei was crushed by the Mongols for disobedience (1252), Alexander became grand prince. Henceforth his policy was marked by cautious collaboration with the Mongols and profound mistrust of the west. By his conciliatory attitude to the Golden Horde (*q.v.*) he managed to avert further disastrous attacks. He did what he could to assist Mongol officials carry out a census of the population; in Novgorod he even arrested his son and quelled a rebellion in order that the census might be peaceably completed. After a general uprising in Suzdal in 1262 he managed to persuade Berke Khan not to take punitive measures. He died in Nov. 1263 at Gorodets, on the Volga, returning from the Golden Horde. Stalin pronounced him one of the great national heroes in 1941 and in 1942 there was established by the supreme soviet of the U.S.S.R. the order of Alexander Nevski.

See George Vernadsky, *Kievan Russia* (1948). (J. L. I. F.)

ALEXANDER THE PAPHLAGONIAN (2nd century A.D.), a celebrated impostor and worker of false oracles, was born at Abonouteichos (mod. Inebolu) in Paphlagonia. The vivid narrative of his career given by his contemporary Lucian (*q.v.*) is corroborated by certain coins of the emperors Lucius Verus and Marcus Aurelius and by Athenagoras, also writing in the 2nd century, who mentions that a statue of Alexander stood in the forum of Parium in Phrygia. Alexander succeeded in establishing an oracle of Aesculapius at his native town, having staged a "rebirth" of the god in the form of a snake which he called Glycon. His usual methods were those of the numerous oraclemongers of the time, of which Lucian gives a detailed account. The reputation of the oracle spread, and Alexander set up an intelligence bureau in Rome, instituted mysteries like those of Eleusis, from which the Christians and Epicureans were alike excluded as profane, and celebrated a mystic marriage between himself and the moon. Lucian's own close investigations into Alexander's methods of fraud led to a serious attempt on the writer's life. Alexander lived to be 70 and amassed great sums of money.

ALEXANDER OF PHERAE (d. 358 B.C.), despot of Pherae in Thessaly from 369 B.C., whose tyranny caused the intervention of a number of states in Thessalian affairs. The other Thessalian cities, refusing to recognize him as *tagos* or head magistrate in succession to his father Jason, led by the Aleuadae of Larissa, appealed first to Macedonia and later, in 368, to the Thebans, who sent Pelopidas (*q.v.*) to their assistance. Alexander, who had procured an alliance with Athens, imprisoned Pelopidas, and the Thebans had to send Epaminondas with a large army to Thessaly to secure his release. In 364, under Pelopidas, the Thebans defeated Alexander at Cynoscephalae, Pelopidas being killed in action. Alexander was at last compelled by Thebes to acknowledge the freedom of the Thessalian cities, to limit his rule to Pherae and to join the Boeotian league. He was finally murdered at his wife's instigation in 358.

See N. G. L. Hammond, *A History of Greece* (1959).

ALEXANDER OF TRALLES (ALEXANDER TRALLIANUS) (525?-605?), widely traveled Byzantine physician who practised and taught in Rome, was among the most famous medical writers of his day. His most important work, a pathology and therapy of internal disease in 12 books, indicates that he was the only one of the Byzantine medical compilers who displayed distinct originality. Although he made careful use of the writings of the established authorities and avowed his agreement with the theories of Galen, his independence in practical questions is obvious and his opinions were clearly based on his own observations. The diseases described by him in the order "from head to foot" include those of the nervous system (including psychoses), the eye, the respiratory tract, the genitourinary system and gout. Although his anatomical and physiological knowledge was scanty, his disease descriptions and his discussion of general pathology and therapeutics reveal him as a physician of wide experience and a talented writer. His writings, translated into Arabic and Latin (*Libri duodecim de re medica*), served as a basis for instruction long after his death. Greek, Latin and Greco-Latin editions were printed throughout the 16th century.

BIBLIOGRAPHY.—*Alexander von Tralles,* Original Text and Übersetzung . . . . von Theodor Puschmann, 2 vol. (1878-79); E. Milward, *Trallianus Reviviscens* (1734).; M. Neuburger, *History of Medicine,* vol. i (1910); T. C. Allbutt, *Greek Medicine in Rome* (1921).
(I. V.)

ALEXANDER, JEROME (1876-   ), U.S. chemist, best known for his work in physical and colloid chemistry applied to semibiological problems and industrial medicine. He was born Dec. 21, 1876, in New York city, and graduated in 1896 from the College of the City of New York, from which he received a master of science degree in 1899. For 25 years he was a chemist for companies manufacturing glues, sizing and chemical specialties.

From 1922 he was a consulting chemist and chemical engineer. Alexander was an early expert with the ultramicroscope in the United States. He published *Colloid Chemistry* (1919; 4th ed., 1937); *Glue and Gelatin* (1923); *Life, Its Nature and Origin* (1948); was editor of seven volumes of *Colloid Chemistry, Theoretical and Applied* (1926); and in 1909 translated Richard Zsigmondy's *Colloids and the Ultramicroscope.* (V. Bw.)

ALEXANDER, JOHN WHITE (1856-1915), U.S. painter, was a leading portrait and figure painter of the academic style. He was born in Allegheny, Pa., Oct. 7, 1856. From magazine illustration he proceeded in 1877 to study painting in Europe. After 1890 his manner of sweeping curves and suffused light popularized his portraiture and figure painting, but proved imaginatively inadequate for his extensive mural decorations in Carnegie institute, Pittsburgh, Pa. He executed six lunettes for the library of Congress. As adviser to Maude Adams on lighting and colour, he contributed much to the distinction of her stage productions. President of the National Academy of Design (1909-15), he was also active in many other art organizations. His honours included gold medals, many lesser prizes and the rank of chevalier of the Legion of Honour. He died in New York city May 31, 1915.

(Vl. B.)

ALEXANDER, NATALIS (properly NOËL ALEXANDRE) (1639-1724), French Dominican theologian and ecclesiastical historian, born at Rouen, Jan. 19, 1639, was doctor of the Sorbonne and regent of studies at Saint-Jacques, Paris. In 1701 he signed the *Cas de conscience,* a document allowing "silent submission" to a Jansenist asking for absolution, but when it was condemned by the pope he submitted to the latter. He appealed against the bull *Unigenitus* (1713), which condemned propositions of the Jansenist Pasquier Quesnel, but again later submitted to the pope. His chief work, *Selecta historiae ecclesiasticae capita,* 26 vol. (1676-86), was placed on the Index in 1684 and 1687 because of its defense of Gallican claims. Alexander brought out a revised edition entitled *Historia ecclesiastica veteris et novi testamenti,* 8 vol. (1699) but it was not until after his death that the edition with explanatory notes by C. Roncaglia (1734) was removed from the Index. Alexander died in Paris on Aug. 21, 1724.

See A. Hänggi, *Der Kirchenhistoriker Natalis Alexander* (1955).
(H. J. Cr.)

ALEXANDER, SAMUEL (1859-1938), one of the few British philosophers in the first half of the 20th century who produced a comprehensive metaphysical system, was born in Sydney, N.S.W., Austr., on Jan. 6, 1859. He was educated at Wesley college, Melbourne, at the University of Melbourne for two years and at Balliol college, Oxford, where he was a scholar. He read mainly in classics, philosophy and mathematics and gained the Green moral philosophy prize in 1888 for an essay published under the title *Moral Order and Progress* (1889).

As his interest in philosophy developed, he felt the need to connect it with the study of experimental psychology, still in its infancy in Great Britain. Accordingly he left his fellowship at Lincoln college, Oxford (he had been the first Jew to be elected to a fellowship at an Oxford or Cambridge college), and during 1890-91 studied experimental psychology in Germany under Hugo Münsterberg. In 1893, after a brief return to Oxford, he was appointed professor of philosophy at Owens college, Manchester, holding this chair until his retirement in 1924 and continuing to reside in Manchester until his death, which took place on Sept. 13, 1938. During the early part of his tenure he was one of a distinguished group of Manchester professors in the formative period in which Owens college, then a constituent college of the federal Victoria university, was turned into the independent University of Manchester.

In 1920 Alexander published *Space, Time, and Deity* (Gifford lectures), a comprehensive metaphysical system. Space time is represented as a cosmic matrix out of which different levels of organization emerge with the characteristic properties of matter, life and mind. Each level presupposes those preceding and shows a tendency or "nisus" toward a higher level, "deity" being the name given to the next level toward which the cosmic order is tending. Within this framework Alexander gave a detailed treatment of some of the main traditional philosophical problems, such as universals, the mind-body relation, values and the nature of knowing. In his last years his interest turned mainly to aesthetics. In *Beauty and Other Forms of Value* (1933) he described art as the expression of a constructive impulse turned contemplative.

Alexander was awarded the Order of Merit in 1930. A notable bust of him by Jacob Epstein stands in the entrance hall of the Arts building of the University of Manchester. *Philosophical and Literary Pieces*, a collection of occasional papers, with a memoir by John Laird, was published posthumously (1939).　(D. M. E.)

ALEXANDER AETOLUS (fl. *c.* 280 B.C.), Greek poet of Pleuron in Aetolia, was commissioned by Ptolemy Philadelphus to arrange the tragedies and satyric dramas in the library of Alexandria. In 276 he went to the court of the king of Macedonia. He was one of the Alexandrian Pleiad (a group of seven tragic poets), but only the title of one of his plays, *Astragalistae* ("The Dice Players"), survives. He also wrote short epics, epigrams and elegies. Two of the last are known, the *Apollo*, a collection of love stories with unhappy endings, and the *Muses*, dealing with literary criticism. Alexander's powers as a critic are further displayed by an appreciation of Euripides in anapaestic tetrameters (fr. 7).

For the fragments of his works *see* J. U. Powell (ed.), *Collectanea Alexandrina*, 121–130 (1925); Auguste Couat, *Alexandrian Poetry Under the First Three Ptolemies, 324–222 B.C.*, trans. by James Loeb, 109–115 (1931).　(E. A. B.)

ALEXANDER BALAS (d. 145 B.C.), ruler of the Seleucid kingdom from 150 to 145 B.C., was a native of Smyrna. His claim to the Seleucid throne on the ground that he was the son of Antiochus IV Epiphanes (d. 163) was sponsored by the kings of Pergamum and Egypt and supported by the Roman senate. Powerfully aided by the Egyptian king Ptolemy VI Philometor (whose daughter Cleopatra he later married), he defeated and killed Demetrius I in 150 and took over his kingdom. He proved a bad ruler, and Ptolemy eventually changed sides and supported Demetrius' son Demetrius against him. This led to Alexander's defeat and death after a short campaign. (*See* SELEUCID DYNASTY.)　(R. H. SI.)

ALEXANDER OF TUNIS, HAROLD RUPERT LEOFRIC GEORGE ALEXANDER, 1ST EARL (1891–　　　), British field marshal and prominent figure in World War II. Of North Irish stock and third son of the 4th earl of Caledon, he was born in London on Dec. 10, 1891, and educated at Harrow and Sandhurst. He joined the Irish guards (of which regiment he later became colonel) and served with distinction in World War I and on the Indian frontier. In World War II he held with uniform success a series of important commands at home and overseas. After commanding the rear guard at Dunkirk he showed remarkable coolness and skill in extricating British and Indian forces from Burma. He next reorganized the middle east command and coordinated the Allied advances from Egypt and Algeria which led to the German surrender at Tunis in May 1943. He then commanded the forces drawn from many Allied nations which drove the Germans from Sicily and southern Italy, forced the Italians to surrender, and finally liberated the whole of Italy. After the war Alexander served as governor general of Canada (1946–52) and later as minister of defense (1952–54) under Sir Winston Churchill. Alexander was created a viscount in 1946 and an earl in 1952.　(J. R. M. B.)

ALEXANDER POLYHISTOR, CORNELIUS (fl. *c.* 70–*c.* 60 B.C.), Greek polymath whose fragments provide valuable information on antiquarian and especially Jewish subjects, was born at Miletus, and became a Roman citizen in 82 B.C. after being taken prisoner in the Mithradatic war.

See F. Jacoby, *Die Fragmente der griechischen Historiker*, pt. 3A, pp. 96–121 (1940), and part 3a, pp. 248–313 (1943).

ALEXANDER ROMANCES. The personality and career of Alexander the Great (*q.v.*) led early to the development of legends about him, based partly on historical sources and partly on attribution to him of marvelous deeds. As with the romance cycles connected with other great figures, the stories about Alexander were retold with different emphasis and interpretation by each civilization and age. Thus, for example, some philosophers

of antiquity stressed his career as an illustration of the workings of the wheel of fortune; the early Christian fathers used it to justify the working out of God's judgments; the middle ages saw him as a pattern of knightly chivalry; and Jewish and eastern storytellers connected him with historical events in their own history.

Ancient Sources.—The first version of the Alexander Romance was written in Greek by a hellenized Egyptian in Alexandria during the time of the Ptolemies, *c.* 200 B.C. In its original form it is no longer known to us, since it was copied, rewritten, translated into more than 30 languages and expanded with fresh episodes until the original was completely lost sight of. Yet it is possible to reconstruct roughly the contents of the national Egyptian folk epic. It began by praising the wise Egyptians, skilled in astrology and magic, and went on to tell of the Egyptian king Nectanebes, who, fleeing from the enemies who had invaded his country, came to Macedonia, where he seduced with his magic arts Olympias, the wife of King Philip, and thus became the father of Alexander. An oracle had meanwhile proclaimed to the Egyptians that their departed king would return to them as a young man and would overcome their enemies, the Persians. When Alexander was grown up he immediately led his army through Italy to Africa. In the temple of Amon he was hailed as the son of the god; he founded Alexandria, after which he continued his march through Tyre to Persia, whose king, Darius, he defeated in two battles. When Darius was murdered by his own people, Alexander hunted down the murderers and had them executed. He next moved against Porus, king of India, and defeated him in a single battle. In India he talked with the wise Brahmans and also met the race of Amazons. Finally he returned to Babylon where he was poisoned at the instigation of Antipater.

This folk epic was considerably expanded in a number of early Greek versions and was sometimes attributed to the ancient Alexandrian historian Callisthenes, who, however, could not possibly have been its author. For this reason it later became known as the pseudo-Callisthenes. The episodes added to the original romance were taken partly from historical accounts and partly from reports of marvelous events which in the first romance had played only a subsidiary part. These reports were mainly contained in letters supposed to have been written by or to Alexander or other important persons in the story. Thus, for example, Alexander's visit to the palace of the Ethiopian queen, Candace, was developed into a major event, and a group of letters described more fully the marvels of the east, while a number of Jewish legends told of his visit to Jerusalem and his establishment of the Jewish quarter in Alexandria. That we can still follow the broad outlines of the romance from the Egyptian epic through to its Byzantine versions is due to the fact that we possess not only a considerable number of Greek manuscripts dated from the 11th century onward and a Byzantine epic of approximately the 13th century but also several earlier translations. These are: two Latin translations, one by Julius Valerius from the beginning of the 4th century A.D. (*Res Gestae Alexandri Macedonis*) and the other by the archpriest Leo of Naples from the 10th century (originally called *Nativitas et Victoria Alexandri Magni; see* below); an Armenian translation from the 5th century; a Syrian translation from the 7th century; and a very late Ethiopian translation, which, through the Arabic, leads back to the Syrian version. Some fragments of a Coptic version have also survived.

Besides the different recensions of the so-called pseudo-Callisthenes itself, there existed in Greek shorter accounts of Alexander's legendary exploits, as well as the letters already mentioned. Some of these existed also in Latin; for example, the *Epistola Alexandri ad Aristotelem de mirabilibus*, which played a considerable part in the development of the Alexander legend in the west during the middle ages. Further, there was a group of Indian tractates about the Brahmans, which, in Latin versions, were widely read during the middle ages, and an account of Alexander's last days, containing his testament, which is also found in pseudo-Callisthenes (III, 33). This text has also been preserved in Latin: it forms the second part of the so-called Metzer Epitome. Finally, among these secondary sources, reference must be made to the independent legend of Alexander's capture of the wild people of Gog and Magog, which occurs in several texts, the most important being the *Revelationes* of the pseudo-Methodius, and is frequently mentioned in both oriental and occidental literature.

Vernacular and Medieval Latin Versions.—These romance tales are the basic material from which all the stories subsequently told of Alexander both in the east and the west derive, and the historical person of the king was increasingly eclipsed by them. They found their way into history and re-emerged in a wide variety of literatures. In the west Old English was the first vernacular language in which comprehensive accounts of Alexander are found, in the translation, made during the reign of Alfred the Great, of Orosius' history of the world. In the section dealing with Alexander use is made of the romance and its derivatives as well as of historical sources, and mention is made of Nectanebes. In the 10th century the *Epistola Alexandri* was translated into Anglo-Saxon, and in the 11th appeared the Middle Irish Alexander romance, based on Orosius, Josephus, the *Epistola* and the letters purporting to have been written between Alexander and the Brahman Dindimus. The early Middle High German *Annolied*, in which some of Alexander's fabulous deeds are related, dates from *c.* 1100. Soon after, in the 12th century, during the time of the crusades, came the succession of great poems about Alexander, beginning with the French epic the *Roman d'Alexandre* begun by Albéric de Briançon (Besançon, or Pisançon), who takes the story up to the death of Darius, from which point it was later continued in other French verse romances. The first German Alexander epic, by "Pfaffe" Lamprecht, is based on Albéric, and it also was later revised and supplemented. To the end of the 12th century also belongs the Anglo-Norman epic by Thomas of Kent, *Le Roman de Toute Chevalerie*, which, *c.* 1275, was refashioned into the Middle English *Kyng Alisaunder*. At this period also, two historical sources for the life of Alexander, by Curtius and Justinus, came into prominence, particularly through the *Alexandreis*, the great Latin epic by Gautier de Châtillon (second half of the 12th century) which is based on them and which, in the 13th century, was translated into Spanish (*Libro de Alexandre*), Icelandic (by Brand Jónsson), Middle Dutch (*Alexanders Geesten*, by Jacob van Maerlant [*q.v.*]), German (by Ulrich von Eschenbach) and Czech. The German epic by Rudolf von Ems (*c.* 1230–55) also uses Curtius as its main source.

Besides the Alexander poems and prose tales in the vernacular, versions in Latin continued to appear. Thus the translation by the archpriest Leo was completely reshaped in a number of revisions, to form the *Historia de proeliis*, which in its turn has been translated into many European languages; world histories from that of Ekkehard of Aura (early 12th century) onward generally contained a version of the Alexander story; and the great succession of the Latin encyclopaedias, from Isidore of Seville to Vincent of Beauvais (*qq.v.*), followed the tradition established by Pliny and included fabled accounts of Alexander's career. New legends also came into being, such as that of Alexander's journey to Paradise which first appeared in the 12th-century *Iter ad Paradisum*.

In the 14th century the Italian Alexander romances began to appear, in both prose and verse, closely followed by the Swedish verse *Konung Alexander* and also by versions in Scots, Danish and, dating originally from a little earlier, in the Slavonic languages. These had been begun by the translation into Bulgarian of the pseudo-Callisthenes, on which are based the various Russian Alexander romances. In the Slavonic romances are found episodes unknown elsewhere, as for instance, in the works of the Polish chronicler Kadlubeck (d. 1223), and as late as the Renaissance period we find the first mention of the *Privilegium Slavicum* supposed to have been granted to the Slavonic peoples by Alexander.

Eastern Versions.—Alexander romances developed equally prolifically in the east. Besides the eastern translations of pseudo-Callisthenes already mentioned, particular emphasis was there given to the Christian legend based on Jewish traditions of Alexander's capture of Gog and Magog, which is told in prose in Syrian and later, in verse, by Jacob of Serugh (d. 521), and is also included in the Koran (Sura 18, 82ff.) The Arabs also translated the Syrian romance, expanded it, combined its contents with their own chronicles, and passed on these versions to the many peoples with whom they had contact, by conquest and trade, reaching as far as Java, where, in about the 16th century, a version of the romance was translated into Malay. Through them, too, it again entered Spain, where a partly new tradition was introduced, which in its turn was spread further in Latin, Hebrew, Spanish and other languages. The Arabs also carried the romance to Persia where the poets Firdausi (*c.* 935–1020) and Nizami (d. *c.* 1200) gave it new forms. The works of Nizami were, toward the end of the 14th century, translated into Turkish, and the sultan of that period, Bayazid, claimed descent from Alexander. His great grandson, Mohammed II, conqueror of Constantinople, modeled himself on Alexander, and poems about him were his favourite reading. With the revival of classical scholarship during the Renaissance, however, literature based on the various versions of the Alexander romance in both east and west gradually gave way to historical accounts, in which use was made of the more reliable sources of Plutarch, Arrian and Diodorus.

BIBLIOGRAPHY.—*General survey* (with texts): F. P. Magoun, *Gests of King Alexander of Macedon* (1929); G. Cary, *The Medieval Alexander* (1956). For the development of the Greek Romance *see* A. Ausfeld, *Der griechische Alexanderroman* (1907); F. Pfister, "Studien zum Alexanderroman," in *Würzburger Jahrbücher*, vol. 1 (1946); R. Merkelbach, *Die Quellen des griechischen Alexanderromans* (1954).

Editions of primary texts: Historia Alexandri Magni (Pseudo-Callisthenes), ed. by W. Kroll, vol. 1 (1926); H. van Thiel, *Die Rezension λ des Ps.-Callisthenes* (1959); *Julii Valerii res gestae* ed. by B. Kübler, in the "Teubner Series" (1888); F. Pfister, *Kleine Texte zum Alexanderroman* (1910), *Der Alexanderroman des Archipresbyters Leo* (1913) and *Eine jüdische Gründungsgeschichte Alexandrias* (1914); R. Raabe, *Die armenische Übersetzung der sagenhaften Alexander-biographie* (1896); E. A. T. W. Budge, *The History of Alexander the Great, being the Syriac Version* (1889) and *The Life and Exploits of Alexander, being a series of Ethiopic texts* (1896); O. von Lemm, *Der Alexanderroman bei den Kopten* (1903); W. Boer, *Epistola Alexandri ad Aristotelem* (1953); P. H. Thomas, *Epitoma rerum gestarum Alexandri* (1960), the so-called Metzer epitome; *Historia de proeliis*, ed. by O. Zingerle, *Die Quellen zum Alexander des Rudolf von Ems* (1903); A. R. Anderson, *Alexander's Gate, Gog and Magog, and the inclosed nations* (1932).

Later versions in east and west: Most of the editions are given in G. Cary (see above): see in particular A. Hilka, *Der altfranzösische Prosa-Alexanderroman* (1920); J. Storost, *Studien zur Alexandersage in der älteren italienischen Literatur* (1935); H. H. Ronge, *Konung Alexander* (1957); H. H. Bielfeldt, *Die Quellen der altschechischen Alexandreis* (1951); T. Nöldeke, *Beiträge zur Geschichte des Alexanderromans* (1890); P. J. Leeuwen, *De Maleische Alexanderroman* (1937); F. Pfister, *Alexander der Grosse in den Offenbarungen der Griechen, Juden, Mohammedaner und Christen* (1956); I. Friedlander, *Die Chadirlegende und der Alexanderroman* (1913). (F. Pf.)

ALEXANDERS (*Smyrnium olusatrum*, family Umbelliferae), a stout herbaceous plant with a furrowed, much-branched stem, one to five feet high, and large, dark-green, shiny compound leaves with broad sheathing stalks and broad cut segments. Small yellow-green flowers, in compound umbels (*see* UMBELLIFERAE), are pollinated by flies attracted in swarms by their heavy odour. The fruits are nearly black. The plant is native of the Mediterranean region and was formerly commonly cultivated as a vegetable. It is now found wild throughout the British Isles.

In the United States the name is applied to *Angelica atropurpurea,* and the name golden alexanders to *Zizia*, especially *Z. aurea*.

(MD. E. M.)

ALEXANDER SEVERUS (MARCUS AURELIUS SEVERUS ALEXANDER) (208–235), Roman emperor from A.D. 222 to 235, was born in Phoenicia in 208. His grandmother was sister-in-law of the emperor Septimius Severus, who died in 211 and whose son Caracalla was murdered in 217. Then, after the brief rule of Macrinus, the Syrian legions in 218 proclaimed Alexander's 14-year-old cousin Elagabalus emperor. Elagabalus was persuaded to adopt Alexander as his heir, and on the murder of Elagabalus (March 222) Alexander became emperor, also at the age of 14. In the words of Herodian, he "always did everything his mother told him." To advise his mother, Julia Mamaea, the senate appointed a regency council of 16, without whose vote "nothing was to be said or done." To Herodian the "form of government was changed from the excesses of tyranny to the type of aristocracy." He and Dio Cassius, the contemporary chroniclers of the reign, both combine general praise with an embarrassed lack of detail. The regency was unable to control the conflicts within the empire. The people of Rome fought a three-day street battle with the guards regiments, but people and guards united in dislike of the government; provincial armies elevated short-lived local emperors, while provincial civilians sheltered army deserters, runaway slaves and outlaws. The guards murdered their commander Ulpian, the chief minister of state, in the presence of the emperor and his mother, and the government could only take vengeance on the chief murderer by sending him to Egypt as governor and there assassinating him. Alexander is said to have wished to include Christ among the Roman gods.

Alexander's government survived its internal weakness; it was destroyed by its military incompetence. On the eastern frontier, the Arsacid dynasty of Parthia was overthrown by the Sasanians, who revived the ancient Persian claim to rule all Asia Minor and the eastern Balkans. A massive Roman counteroffensive, based on the co-ordination of three army groups, was disastrously defeated because the army under Alexander's personal command failed to advance. This failure was followed by operations on the Rhine, which Alexander ended by buying peace from the Germans, to the indignation of his army. His mother was hated for her fussing about small details, especially in matters of money. Early in 235 Alexander and his mother were murdered, the army of the Rhine proclaimed Gaius Julius Verus Maximinus emperor, and the "type of aristocracy" again gave way to the "excesses of tyranny." Senatorial pamphleteers of the 4th century, the writers of the *Augustan History* (q.v.), chose to found upon his inconspicuous person their picture of the ideal prince, gifted with a wide range of conflicting virtues and the supposed author of the governmental reforms that they themselves desired. (JN. R. M.)

ALEXANDERSON, ERNST FREDERIK WERNER

(1878–   ), Swedish-American electrical engineer and inventor, best known for his contributions in the field of radio communications, was born at Uppsala, Jan. 25, 1878. He graduated from Royal Institute of Technology at Stockholm and did graduate work in Berlin. In 1901 he went to the United States with an ambition to work with C. P. Steinmetz and the following year did start work under Steinmetz at the General Electric company at Schenectady, N.Y. During 45 active years with that company, he did pioneering work in railroad electrification, ship propulsion and electric motor control. In the field of radio communications he invented and developed the Alexanderson alternator for transoceanic communication as well as antenna structures and radio receiving and transmitting systems. In 1930 he demonstrated a complete television system, including projection of a large picture on a theatre screen.

The General Electric company loaned his services to the Radio Corporation of America to be its chief engineer for a few years following its organization in 1920. In that capacity he supervised the installation of a number of powerful Alexanderson alternator radio transmitters.

Alexanderson was decorated by King Gustavus V of Sweden and received the Valdemar Poulsen, John Ericsson, Cedergren and Edison medals. He wrote numerous technical articles and had more than 300 patents to his credit. (W. C. WH.; X.)

ALEXANDRA

ALEXANDRA (ALEKSANDRA FEDOROVNA) (1872–1918), empress of Russia, consort of Nicholas II (q.v.), was born at Darmstadt in Germany on June 6, 1872, the youngest daughter of the grand duke Louis IV of Hesse-Darmstadt. Her original name, Alix, was changed when she married the Russian emperor Nicholas II on Nov. 26 (new style; Nov. 14, old style), 1894, four weeks after his accession. Unpopular in court society because of her reserved temperament, she withdrew into embittered seclusion, seeking solace in religion and her immediate family circle. Her inclination toward mysticism was increased by her almost fanatical acceptance of Orthodoxy and the medieval doctrine of God-given autocracy; she conceived it as her sacred duty to assist Nicholas in resisting popular pressure and maintaining his powers intact for posterity. Her relations with her weak-willed husband, whom she dominated completely, were idyllic; she bore him four daughters and, in 1904, a long-awaited male heir. But the tsarevich Aleksei suffered from hemophilia, a disease hereditary in Alexandra's family. Her neurotic concern lest the slightest injury to the prince might prove fatal and imperil the future of the dynasty led her to seek the aid of a debauched "holy man" with hypnotic powers, Grigori Efimovich Rasputin (q.v.). She came to venerate Rasputin as a saint, sent by God to save the throne and "holy Russia," and as the true voice of the common people who, she believed, still preserved their traditional loyalty to the autocracy—unlike educated society, which she feared and despised. Rasputin's influence was a public scandal, but Alexandra silenced all criticism.

World War I widened the breach between the monarchy and Russian society. Alexandra, more convinced than ever of the need for autocracy, persuaded Nicholas to assume supreme command at the front (Aug. 1915), while she ruled the country in his stead. Distrusting the duma and even the loyally conservative government, she arbitrarily dismissed capable ministers, replacing them by nonentities or dishonest careerists who enjoyed Rasputin's favour. The administration was paralyzed, the whole regime discredited. Alexandra was widely, but erroneously, believed to be a German agent. Yet she disregarded all warnings; even Rasputin's assassination failed to shake her confidence. She was thus largely responsible for the collapse of the autocracy in March 1917; like a Greek tragic heroine, she destroyed all that she sought to preserve. After the Bolshevik revolution she acquitted herself with great courage. She was put to death, with Nicholas and their children, at Ekaterinburg (now Sverdlovsk) on July 17, 1918.

BIBLIOGRAPHY.—M. Paléologue, *Alexandra Feodorowna* (1932); Sir Bernard Pares (ed.), *Letters of the Tsaritsa to the Tsar, 1914–16* (1923); Sir Bernard Pares, *The Fall of the Russian Monarchy* (1939). (J. L. H. K.)

ALEXANDRA (1844–1925), queen consort of Edward VII of Great Britain, was born at the Gule palace, Copenhagen, on Dec. 1, 1844, and was christened Alexandra Caroline Maria Charlotte Louise Julia. Her father was heir to the Danish throne, which he ascended as Christian IX in 1863. With three brothers and two sisters, she was a member of a boisterous and carefree family circle which remained the abiding influence of her life. Alexandra became engaged to Edward, prince of Wales, on Sept. 9, 1862, when both were staying at Laeken palace, Brussels, as the guests of Leopold I of Belgium. They were married in St. George's chapel, Windsor, on March 10, 1863. The exceptional beauty and graceful manner of the princess made her an immediate and lasting favourite with the British public, and her affection for Denmark and dislike of Prussia were generally respected. She had six children—Albert Victor, George (afterward King George V), Louise, Maud (afterward queen of Norway), Victoria and John, who died in infancy. Alexandra devoted herself to her children by whom she was always known as "Mother-dear," and she regarded the calls of the official world as an unwelcome intrusion on her family life. This tendency was strengthened by a serious illness in 1867 which left her lame and accentuated a hereditary deafness. As queen she devoted much of her income and time to the poor and suffering; she founded the Imperial Military Nursing service in 1902, and started Alexandra Rose day for British hospitals in 1913. Although she did not share her husband's taste for fashionable society, and her incurable lack of punctuality offended his meticulous standards, he greatly admired her and one of the first acts of his reign was to admit her to the Order of the Garter, from which all the female relations of the sovereign had been excluded since Tudor times.

After King Edward's death in 1910 Queen Alexandra lived at Marlborough house, London, and at Sandringham in Norfolk, where she died on Nov. 20, 1925.

See Sir George Arthur, *Queen Alexandra* (1934); W. R. H. Trowbridge, *Queen Alexandra* (1921). (R. T. B. F.)

ALEXANDRETTA: see ISKENDERUN; HATAY.

ALEXANDRIA, the name of a number of ancient cities as well as the great Alexandria (q.v.) in Egypt, founded by Alexander the Great in the course of his campaigns from 334 to 323 B.C. Fifteen of these are listed here.

ALEXANDRIA TROAS, founded in 334 B.C. on a site about 15 mi. S. of Hisarlik, a mound in Turkey 4 mi. S.E. of the mouth of the Dardanelles which is identified with the site of ancient Troy.

ALEXANDRIA in Cilicia, founded after the battle of Issus in 333 B.C., the modern Iskenderun (*q.v.*) or Alexandretta in southern Turkey.

ALEXANDRIA, founded after the battle of Gaugamela in 331 B.C., the modern Irbil (*q.v.*) in northern Iraq.

ALEXANDRIA OF THE ARIANS, founded in Aria in 330 B.C., the modern Herat (*q.v.*) in northwestern Afghanistan.

ALEXANDRIA PROPHTHASIA, founded in 330 B.C., according to W. W. Tarn (*The Greeks in Bactria and India*, 1951) on an unidentified site on the Helmand lake in the Seistan region of eastern Iran and southwestern Afghanistan; others place it at Farah in the province of Farah in southwestern Afghanistan. The name *Prophthasia* ("anticipation") was probably an allusion to the detection and suppression in 330 B.C. of the conspiracy of Philotas.

ALEXANDRIA OF THE ARACHOSIANS, founded in 330–329 B.C. According to Tarn the site is at Ghazni (*q.v.*) in eastern Afghanistan; others identify it with Kandahar (*q.v.*) in southern Afghanistan.

ALEXANDRIA BY THE CAUCASUS, founded in 329 B.C. near the Paropamisus or Caucasus (the Hindu Kush), not far from the modern town of Charikar in the Kabul province of eastern Afghanistan.

ALEXANDRIA ESCHATE, that is, "the Farthest," founded in Sogdiana in 329 B.C. to mark the northeastern extremity of Alexander's conquests, the modern Leninabad (*q.v.*), or Khojent, in the Tadzhik S.S.R.

ALEXANDRIA on the Oxus (Amu-Darya) river, founded in 329 B.C. on an unidentified site southwest of Dushanbe in the Tadzhik S.S.R.

ALEXANDRIA IN MARGIANA, founded in 327 B.C. but destroyed soon afterward by nomads. The site is identified with that of Merv (*q.v.*) in Turkistan.

ALEXANDRIA on the Indus, founded in 325 B.C. near the confluence of the Indus river with the combined streams of the Hydaspes (Jhelum), Acesines (Chenab) and Hyphasis (Beas) rivers, perhaps identifiable with Uch in Bahawalpur (West Pakistan).

ALEXANDRIA OF THE SOGDI, founded in 325 B.C. at an unidentified site farther down the Indus than the above.

ALEXANDRIA in Gedrosia, founded in 325 B.C., the modern Bela, in southeastern Baluchistan.

ALEXANDRIA in Carmania, founded in 325 B.C., the modern Gulashkird, a village in southeastern Iran.

ALEXANDRIA on the Persian gulf, founded by Alexander in 324 B.C. and refounded with the name Antioch by Antiochus IV Epiphanes in the 2nd century B.C.; renamed as Charax when the provincial governor of Mesene revolted against Seleucid rule after the death of Antiochus VII Sidetes.

ALEXANDRIA (Arabic AL ISKANDARIYAH), a city, governorate (*muhafaza*) and the chief seaport of Egypt. For more than 1,000 years from its foundation it was the capital of the country. It lies on the Mediterranean 129 mi. N.W. of Cairo by rail.

The population of Alexandria in 1964 was estimated to be 1,742,-000. The nationality analysis of 1960 was 1,471,527 Egyptians, 6,398 Italians, 24,609 Greeks, 4,233 Syrian, Lebanese and other Arab nationalities and 9,467 others. Since the end of 1956 many of the European and Jewish inhabitants have departed.

In Alexandria the climate from December to March is variable with predominantly cool sunny days but occasional heavy falls of rain or hail, and stormy winds. The coldest month is January with a mean day temperature of 64° F. In summer the heat is moderated by sea breezes but there is much humidity; in August, the hottest month, the average day temperature is 87°.

The city is built on the strip of land separating the Mediterranean from Lake Mareotis (Maryut), and on a T-shaped promontory that forms harbours east and west. The stem of the T was originally a mole leading to the island of Pharos which formed the crosspiece. In the course of centuries this mole has been silted up and is now an isthmus half a mile wide. On it a part of the modern city is built.

The western end of the original Pharos Island is the cape of Ras al-Tin ("cape of figs"); the eastern cape is still known as Pharos. On the eastern point of Pharos Island stood the great lighthouse, one of the Seven Wonders of the World, reputed to be 400 ft. high. The first Ptolemy began it and the second completed it at a total cost of 800 talents. It is the prototype of all lighthouses in the world. The eastern cape is also known as Qa'itbay from the 15th-century fort and mosque.

The customs house and chief warehouses are by the western harbour, but the principal buildings of the city are in the eastern and southeastern quarters. One of the main features of modern Alexandria is a fine seacoast road (completed 1934), formerly called the Corniche but now Rue al-Geish (army avenue). It runs eastward for about 16 mi. and along most of its length are bathing beaches. A focal point of the city is the Mohammed Ali square with an equestrian statue of Mohammed Ali the Great. Known in the 19th century first as the Place des Consuls and then as the Grand square, it has always been colloquially called al-Manshia, but in 1952 its name was officially changed to Midan al-Tahrir (Liberation square). On its northern side is the Anglican church of St. Mark's built on land originally given to the British community by Mohammed Ali in 1839 as a free grant. Looking on to this tree-lined square, the starting point of the numerous buses and electric trams, are the cotton bourse and law courts. Further east and giving on to the sea is the Saad Zaghlul square called after the nationalist leader who died in 1927 and whose statue stands among grass plots in the centre. The chief hotel in the town, the Hotel Cecil, is here and close by is the middle east headquarters of the World Health organization.

Southeast from Mohammed Ali square is the shopping and commercial part of the town through which run Rue Sherif and Rue Tewfik. One of the main east-west streets is Rue Rosette (formerly Rue Fuad al-Awal), to the north of which is the Graeco-Roman museum, an excellent collection of antiquities. The Municipal library, formerly in Rue Rosette and now near the waterworks, houses about 65,000 volumes in Arabic and European languages. Beside it is an art gallery. There are two fine botanical gardens in the city, the Nouzha gardens and the Antoniades park, and near the railway station is a sports stadium to accommodate 25,000 spectators, where the Arab Olympic games are held. South from Rue Rosette is the mosque of Nebi Daniel containing the tomb of Said Pasha and other royal tombs. Nearer the western harbour is the Place Ibrahim, often called the Place Ste. Catherine from the Roman Catholic church there. St. Catherine was said to be martyred in Alexandria under orders of the emperor Maximinus. The northern quarter of Alexandria is oriental in style. It is crossed by Rue Ras al-Tin, leading to the promontory of that name. The smart Yacht club which overlooked the harbour at Ras al-Tin is now the Egyptian naval officers' mess, and the Yacht club has been moved to the eastern harbour. Also on the promontory is the palace built by Mohammed Ali, which since the abdication of King Faruk in 1952 has been open to the public.

The eastern bay is rocky and exposed, and is used only by fishing craft and yachts. The two ancient Egyptian obelisks now in London (Cleopatra's Needle) and New York city looked onto this bay.

In the district between Mohammed Ali square and the western harbour, one of the poorest quarters of the city, is an open space in the centre of which is Fort Caffarelli, so named because it was fortified by the comte de Caffarelli, Napoleon's engineer. This quarter has been pierced by several straight roads, one of which, crossing the Mahmudiya canal (built by Mohammed Ali in 1819) by Pont Neuf, leads to Gabbari, an industrial and manufacturing region. In the southern part of the city are the Arab cemetery, Pompey's Pillar and the catacombs. Pompey's Pillar (actually dedicated to Diocletian soon after A.D. 297), which stands on the highest spot in Alexandria, is about 88 ft. high including the pedestal with a diameter of 9 ft. at the base and 6½ ft. at the pinnacle. Close by are the famous Hadrianic catacombs of Kom al-Shugafa containing a very beautiful central tomb surrounded by many passages with loculi and a large triclinium.

East of Alexandria is the university (formerly the Faruk university); in 1956–57 it had 14,158 men and 1,519 women students.

Close by is the Mowassah hospital and school of nursing. This hospital is among the best equipped in Europe or the middle east. Two sports clubs, close to this district, comprise a race course, polo fields, golf links, tennis courts, etc. Farther down the coast is the boys' boarding school, Victoria college, where many past and present leaders of the middle east were educated. It has been under Egyptian management instead of British since the Suez conflict of 1956–57, but it is still run on English public school lines. There is a girls' college nearer the town. The great sea road Rue al-Geish ends at the former royal palace of Montaza. This is now a casino where only foreigners are admitted, but the royal gardens and bathing beaches are open to all on payment.

The Port.—The harbour is on the west of Pharos and is partly formed by a breakwater (built 1871–73 and prolonged 1906–07) two mi. long. Opposite is Ras al-Tin, on which is a lighthouse (180 ft.) built by Mohammed Ali. Another breakwater starts from the Gabbari side, the opening between the two being about half a mile. The enclosed water is divided into an outer and inner harbour by a mole 1,000 yd. long. The inner harbour ($\frac{3}{4}$ sq.mi. in area) is lined for 2$\frac{1}{2}$ mi. by quays, affording accommodation for ships drawing up to 28 ft. The outer harbour (2$\frac{1}{3}$ sq.mi.) has a graving dock, 520 ft. long, and quays and jetties.

The city is the headquarters of most of the merchants and companies engaged in the development of the delta. More than 80% of the total exports and imports of the country pass through the port. During 1958, 2,810 vessels of 6,000,000 tons aggregate, with 26,000 passengers, entered Alexandria harbour. The large suburb of al-Raml (Ramleh) stretches eastward from Alexandria in an unbroken line for about 16 mi.

Communications.—Alexandria is linked to other towns of Egypt by railway, telegraph and telephone lines, roads and air services. It also has good canal connection with the interior for merchandise. Two main roads run to Cairo, one through the western desert, passing by the salt-and-soda works of Wadi Natrun and the famous ancient Coptic monasteries, the other through the delta. Another road leads west along the coastal desert, past al-Alamein to the Libyan frontier, and connects with the north African coastal road. The civil airport is 1$\frac{3}{4}$ mi. south of the city. Electric trams and buses connect al-Raml with Alexandria and link different quarters of the town together. Buses go to outlying towns and along the coastal desert road to al-Sallum. There is also a train service to this Libyan frontier town. Motor coaches go to Cairo through delta and desert.

Industries.—The region of Gabbari contains asphalt works, oil, rice and paper mills. On either side of the canal are the warehouses of wholesale dealers in cotton, wool, sugar, grain, onions, etc. Close by is the Mina al-Bassal area with the important cotton exchange where the varieties are graded and valued. Beyond Gabbari to the southwest is al-Maks with considerable salt and tanning industries and stone quarries. The area south and southeast of Alexandria has been greatly developed as an industrial area. There are important cotton textile and dyeing works, as well as factories for ginning and pressing cotton; paper, chocolate and confectionery works; food processing and canning; leather, soap and soda works; plastics, pottery and car-assembly workshops. A Ford factory set up in Alexandria produced 7,000 cars and tractors in 1952. An oil refinery has been established and electric power available to the city has been much increased. In the Abis district an area of some 24,000 ac. was being drained and reclaimed from marsh in the mid-1950s. Model villages were built and landless peasants from overcrowded areas were given a new start. The resulting crops are marketed in Alexandria. In the desert to the west extensive agricultural experiments were also taking place and olives, vines, figs and tomatoes were successfully grown. By far the largest and most valuable export from Egypt via Alexandria is cotton, followed by cereals and vegetables. Tea, coffee, textiles, coal, fertilizers and machinery are imported. The inhabitants of Alexandria are mostly occupied in trade and transport of merchandise in all its branches, harbour work, industries, shipping and fishing.

History.—From about 1,500 B.C. there existed the pharaonic city of Rhacotis. When Alexander the Great came to Egypt (332

QA'ITBAY FORT ON THE EASTERN CAPE OF ALEXANDRIA; 15TH CENTURY

B.C.) he added a suburb called Neapolis to the west, Rhacotis and Neapolis being included under the general name of Alexandria. The great Macedonian intended the city to supersede Naucratis as a Greek centre in Egypt, and to be a naval base for his designs on Persia and a link between Macedonia and the rich Nile valley. Alexander occupied Pharos, and had a walled city marked out by Deinocrates on the mainland to include Rhacotis. A few months later he left Egypt for the east and never returned to his city; but his body was ultimately entombed there. His viceroy, Cleomenes, continued the creation of Alexandria. Inheriting the trade of ruined Tyre and becoming the centre of the new commerce between Europe and the Arabian and Indian east, the city grew in less than 100 years to be larger than Carthage; for several centuries it had to acknowledge no superior but Rome. It was a centre not only of Hellenism but of Semitism, and the greatest Jewish city in the world. Here the Septuagint (q.v.) was produced. The early Ptolemies fostered the development of its museum into the leading Greek university, and, as a free Greek city, it retained its own senate into Roman times. The famous Alexandrine libraries founded by Ptolemy I decreased in importance with the political decline of the city and were eventually destroyed. (See LIBRARY: *History: The Ancient World*.) In 80 B.C. it passed formally under Roman jurisdiction according to the will of Ptolemy Alexander, though it had been under Roman influence for more than 100 years previously. Julius Caesar dallied with Cleopatra in 47 B.C. and was mobbed by the rabble in Alexandria and his example was followed by Mark Antony, for whose favour the city paid dearly to Octavian (later Augustus), who placed over it a prefect from the imperial household.

Alexandria seems from this time to have regained its old prosperity, commanding as it did an important granary of Rome; in the Augustan age its free population was estimated at 300,000, in addition to an immense number of slaves. In A.D. 215 the emperor Caracalla (Marcus Aurelius Antoninus) visited the city, and, in order to repay some insulting satires that the inhabitants had made upon him, a general massacre was perpetrated. Notwithstanding this terrible disaster, Alexandria soon recovered its former splendour and for some time longer was esteemed the first city of the world after Rome, while it now acquired fresh importance as a centre of Christian theology and church government. Tradition has it that St. Mark had come in person and converted Alexandrians to Christianity. There Arianism was formulated and there Athanasius the Great, bishop of Alexandria (328–373), opponent of both heresy and pagan reaction, worked and triumphed. As native influences, however, began to reassert themselves in the Nile valley, Alexandria gradually became an alien city, more and more detached from Egypt; and, losing much of its commerce as the peace of the empire broke up during the 3rd century A.D., it declined fast in population and splendour. In 616 it was taken by Khosrau II, king of Persia; and in 646 by the Arabs, under Amr ibn al-As (*q.v.*), after a siege that lasted 14 months. The building of Cairo in 969 and, above all, the discovery of the route to the east by the Cape of Good Hope in 1498, nearly ruined Alexandria's commerce. The canal which supplied it with Nile water became blocked and although it remained a principal Egyptian port Alexandria played no great part in history until Napoleon's Egyptian expedition thrust it into prominence. The French troops stormed the city on July 2, 1798, and it remained in their hands until the arrival of the British expedition of 1801. Sir Ralph Abercromby defeated the French at the battle of Alexandria on March 21 of that year and the city surrendered to the British five months later.

By the beginning of the 19th century Alexandria had sunk to a small town of about 4,000 inhabitants; it owes its modern renascence to Mohammed Ali, who wanted a deep port and naval station for his viceregal domain. Being the starting point of the "overland route" to India, and the residence of the chief foreign consuls, it quickly acquired a European character. At Alexandria most of the negotiations between the great powers and Mohammed Ali were conducted; thence started the Egyptian naval expeditions to Crete, the Morea (Peloponnesus) and Syria. It was connected with Cairo by railway in 1855 and remained the real capital of Egypt till Said Pasha died there in 1863 and Ismail Pasha came into power. Though this prince continued to develop the city, giving it a municipality in 1866 and new (but inadequate) harbour works in 1871–78, he developed Cairo still more; and the centre of gravity definitely shifted to the inland capital. In 1881 a mutiny of soldiers occurred and in the following year the arrival of an Anglo-French fleet led to a rising under Arabi Pasha, in which many Europeans were killed. The rising was put down by the British and this action was followed by the British occupation of the whole country.

In World War I Alexandria was the chief Allied naval base in the eastern Mediterranean and it played the same role in World War II during which it was bombed many times by the Germans. The British forces left in 1946. Alexandria is an increasingly important base for the country's naval and mercantile fleets, and as a resort has gained much in general popularity with Egyptians. *See also* EGYPT: *History.*

BIBLIOGRAPHY.—S. R. K. Glanville (ed.), *The Legacy of Egypt* (1942); A. de Cosson, *Mareotis* (1935); E. M. Forster, *Alexandria* (1938); E. Breccia, *Alexandre ad Aegyptum* (1922); Mary Rowlatt, *A Family in Egypt* (1956); Alan Rowe, "The Temple Tombs of Alexander the Great and His Palace in Rhacotis," *Bulletin of John Rylands Library,* vol. 38 (Sept. 1955) and "The Great Serapeum of Alexandria," *Bulletin of John Rylands Library,* vol. 39 (March 1957); P. G. Elgood, *The Ptolemies of Egypt* (1938). (M. Ro.)

ALEXANDRIA, a city of Louisiana, U.S., on the south bank of the Red river, in the centre of the state; the seat of Rapides parish. (For comparative population figures *see* table in LOUISIANA: *Population.*) The city is on a level plain in the centre of extensive forests of longleaf pine, interspersed with various hardwoods. Corn, cotton, sugar, alfalfa and vegetables are the principal crops raised in the vicinity. There are about 100 factories in and near the city, including sawmills, a creosoting plant, foundries and machine shops, cottonseed oil mills, brickyards, an oil refinery, broom handle and talcum factories and railroad repair shops. Alexandria has a large wholesale and retail trade.

Free traffic bridges lead to the town of Pineville, on the north side of the river, where there is a national cemetery. A state hospital for the insane, Huey P. Long Charity hospital, Louisiana college (a Baptist coeducational institution which was opened in 1906), a U.S. veterans' hospital, the state industrial school for girls and the state colony for the feeble-minded are also near by.

Alexandria was named after Alexander Fulton, on whose grant from Spain the first settlement was made in 1785. In 1805 Fulton formally laid out the city at the rapids which then marked the head of navigation in the river. It was incorporated as a town in 1818 and received a city charter in 1882. The rich, level farm land to the south already produced cotton, sugar cane and cattle, and the city thrived on river commerce before the American Civil War. In May 1863 and again in March 1864 it was occupied by Union forces under Adm. David D. Porter and Gen. N. P. Banks. When finally vacated, May 12–13, 1864, the city was almost entirely burned and all city records were lost. Union gunboats, which had passed up the river toward Shreveport at high tide, were caught above the falls at Alexandria; Banks' forces, retreating from defeat at Mansfield, escaped entrapment when Lieut. Col. Joseph Bailey built wing dams to allow passage of the fleet. Railroad growth and exploitation of the dense pine and hardwood forests helped restore the city after the war. (W. M. Lo.)

ALEXANDRIA, a city and a port of entry in northern Virginia, U.S., on the west bank of the Potomac river below its falls, 6 mi. below Washington, D.C.; contiguous to, but independent of, Arlington county.

Alexandria is primarily a residential city, with quiet, shady streets. Many buildings date from the 18th century; Christ church (1773), in which George Washington and, later, Robert E. Lee worshiped; Carlyle house (1752), where Gen. Edward Braddock made his headquarters in 1755 while preparing for the ill-fated expedition to Fort Duquesne, and where, in the same year, the five royal governors met; Gadsby's tavern (1752), where Washington had his headquarters while recruiting rangers for the campaign of 1754; Alexandria academy (1785), first free school in northern Virginia; Friendship Engine house (1774); the home of "Light Horse Harry" Lee, father of Robert E. Lee; Presbyterian meeting house (1774), housing the oldest pipe organ in America; Ramsay house (1748); and many others. The *Alexandria Gazette* is one of the oldest daily newspapers in the United States, founded in 1784 and in continuous circulation since.

On the hill in the western part of the city is the George Washington Masonic National memorial which was dedicated in 1932. Just over the western boundary line is the Protestant Episcopal seminary of Virginia, opened in 1823.

Alexandria is the commercial centre for northern Virginia. A large plant for construction and repair of refrigerator cars is near the city. The products of the industrial plants in Alexandria include fertilizers, beverages, shirts, chemicals, sewer pipes and lumber products.

The first settlement was made in 1695. In 1731 Scottish merchants founded the community of Belhaven, which in 1749 was established as a town under the name of Alexandria in honour of John Alexander, who originally owned the land. It was incorporated as a city in 1779. Before the American Revolution the city reflected its loyalty to the British crown by giving its streets such names as King, Queen, Prince and Duke. George Washington helped lay out the town's streets and lots, drilled his troops there in 1754 before marching against the French and Indians and at-

CHRIST CHURCH, ALEXANDRIA, VA., 1773

tended its religious services, balls, fairs and political rallies. Alexandria enjoyed a flourishing trade with the interior and became an important port for the products of northern Virginia, shipping flour and tobacco to the West Indies and to Europe. Improved roads were built for wagon trains and "rolling roads" were constructed on which hogsheads of tobacco were rolled down from the plantations to the port. The city's economic development was checked, however, after Baltimore developed railroad connections with the west.

From 1791 to 1847 Alexandria was part of the District of Columbia, at first with a vague and uncertain status and later overshadowed by the development of the capital. It was ceded back to Virginia in 1847. At the outbreak of the Civil War its sympathies were with the Confederacy. But in May 1861, federal troops took possession of the city and occupied it for the duration of the war, making it a base for the invasion of Virginia. After the creation of the state of West Virginia (1863) and until the close of the war, it was the seat of the "Alexandria government" (*see* VIRGINIA). After the Civil War Alexandria resumed its normal existence whose quiet for the next half-century was broken only by the movements of the railroad establishing connections with Richmond and by the activities of the Potomac railroad yard.

A small town until the 20th century, Alexandria's population increased almost 500% in 50 years, from 15,239 in 1910 to 91,023 in 1960. Its rapid growth is attributable, in large measure, to the increasing settlement there of people employed in the nation's capital. The city is a part of the Washington, D.C.-Maryland-Virginia standard metropolitan statistical area. For comparative population figures *see* table in VIRGINIA: *Population*.

(F. B. S.)

ALEXANDRIA, GREEK ORTHODOX PATRIARCHATE OF. The pope and patriarch of Alexandria, generally called the Greek Orthodox patriarch of Alexandria, is regarded by the Eastern Orthodox as the successor of St. Mark the evangelist, the second in rank of the patriarchs after the ecumenical patriarch, and the head of the church in Africa. At the time of the Council of Nicaea (325), his jurisdiction was considered to extend over Egypt, Libya and the Pentapolis. He has the title of "judge of the world" (Gr. *Krites tes oikoumenes*), because in early Christian times Alexandria decided the date of Easter for the whole world. His see is regarded by the Orthodox as one of the sees of St. Peter, since St. Mark was the companion and interpreter of St. Peter. After the Council of Chalcedon in 451, the great majority of the Egyptian Christians refused to recognize the deposition of Dioscorus, patriarch of Alexandria, in that council and ceased to be in communion with the church of the Roman empire (*see* COPTIC CHURCH). The small minority that remained in communion with the other Orthodox Christians at the time of this separation consisted of Greeks living in Egypt. When Egypt came under Muslim rule in the 7th century this Greek minority became smaller still, but it continued to exist in the city of Alexandria and in Cairo as a minority group within the Christian minority after most people became Muslims.

In the 19th century the prosperity of Egypt caused thousands of Greeks and Syrians to settle there, and with these immigrants the Greek Orthodox Church in Egypt grew rapidly, although it remains much smaller than the Coptic or Egyptian Church. In the 20th century many Greeks and other Eastern Orthodox Christians settled in Sudan, Ethiopia, South Africa, Madagascar and elsewhere within the jurisdiction of the patriarch of Alexandria, so that Greek sees have been established in African countries outside Egypt. But in the middle of the century there was a rapid reduction in the Greek population of Egypt itself.

There are Greek Orthodox metropolitans in Egypt (Zagazig, Tanta, Mina and Port Said), at Tripoli in Libya, Addis Abbaba, Tunis, Khartoum and Johannesburg. The number of members in Africa is difficult to estimate, but by 1960 it was probably less than 150,000, including 12,000–15,000 Arabic-speaking "Egyptian national Orthodox," mainly of Syrian origin and sometimes described as Syrian Orthodox (Gr. *Syrorthodoxoi*) in Egypt, a small number of African congregations in Uganda that had become Orthodox

and a few Russians.

The patriarchs of Alexandria well known in history include St. Athanasius, St. Cyril, St. John the Almsgiver, Cyril Lucaris and Metrophanes Critopoulos. *See* ORTHODOX EASTERN CHURCH.

See J. Faivre, "Alexandrie," in A. Baudrillart (ed.), *Dictionnaire d'histoire et de géographie ecclésiastiques*, vol. ii, col. 289–369 (1914); C. Papadopoulos, *Historia tes ekklesias Alexandreias* (1935).

(E. E.)

ALEXANDRINA, LAKE, lies in South Australia, 40 mi. S.E. of Adelaide. With the associated Lake Albert and the long narrow Coorong lagoon it forms the outlet of the Murray river (*q.v.*). Although merely a large (220 sq.mi.) lagoon, after its exploration by Charles Sturt in 1830 it attracted attention (especially from South Australian publicists) as a possible maritime outlet for that river. It is unfitted for this purpose because its depth is only 5–15 ft. and the seaward approach is over an extremely difficult shifting sand bar. Later interest centred on the possibility of reclaiming portions of the lakes for agriculture. In 1940 barrages were built at the entrance to prevent the intrusion of salt water, which in times of drought penetrated well upstream. With increasing freshness, irrigation is developing along the estuarine shores. However, the lake's main interest may remain geomorphological.

(O. H. K. S.)

ALEXANDRINE VERSE. The Alexandrine is the leading measure in French poetry, and consists of a line of 12 syllables, rhyming in alternate masculine and feminine couplets. The name probably derived from the early use of the verse in the *Roman d'Alexandre*, a collection of romances compiled in the 12th century, of which Alexander of Macedon was the hero. Application of the name has been traced back to a text of 1432: "*sont dittes telles lignes alexandrines pour ce que une ligne des fais du roy Alexandre fu fait de ceste taille.*" Rarely used until the Renaissance, the Alexandrine was deliberately cultivated by the poets of the Pleiade (*q.v.*), especially Ronsard, and it has been said that three-quarters of French verse written after 1600 is in this measure.

The reason would seem to lie in the adaptability of the Alexandrine to a wide range of subjects and feelings. It has been condemned by foreign critics as monotonous. Walter Savage Landor compared its regular beats to "the handle of a pump" and said that the caesura "split it down the back like a mackerel." This is to ignore its structural metrical principle. It is based not on accentual feet, as is English verse, nor on quantitative feet as in Latin, but on stress according to the sense. There is indeed in the regular form of the line a caesura after the sixth syllable, but the secondary stress within each group of six can be on any syllable, and the charm of the Alexandrine to a French ear consists largely in this variety. Thus what Landor thought to be invariably 6:6 may be any two divisions of six: *e.g.*, 1,5:2,4, as in *Ah, ne puis-je savoir si j'aime ou si je hais*; 3,3:4,2, as in *Voulez-vous que je dise? Il faut qu'enfin j'éclate*; or even 1,5:5,1, as in *Rien ne me verra plus, je ne verrai plus rien*. Six syllables is as it happens a normal breath group. (A passage of prose by Bossuet has been analyzed into the normal pauses of a reading voice and yields the following consecutive groups of syllables: 6,6,7,4,4,6,3,7,5,5,8,7.) Thus the two halves of the Alexandrine lend themselves equally well to plain and ornate statement. The line may be made up of two short prose statements; *e.g.*, *Il ouvre un large bec, laisse tomber sa proie*. But in the hands of a poet the 12 syllables can be used to suggest all the emotions, from the sensuous *Tout m'afflige et me nuit et conspire à me nuire*, to the grand definition of an attitude, *Rome n'est plus dans Rome, elle est toute où je suis*, or Victor Hugo's description of the guard's last fight, *Puis à pas lents, musique en tête, sans fureur . . . La garde impériale entra dans la fournaise*.

The last example shows that even the caesura is not the fetter that quotations from Boileau have suggested. The classical French poets occasionally, and the 19th-century poets frequently, wrote a three-part line, known as *vers romantique* or *trimètre*: *Il vit un oeil tout grand ouvert dans les ténèbres*. Paul Verlaine perhaps went furthest in this loosening of structure: *Lamentable ami qui me cherches où je suis*.

The secret of the Alexandrine can perhaps be related to what may be described as the French approach to life: its greatest effects are those of balance, contrast, synthesis. The single line, it has been said, can be used to express logical form, tragic tension or unlimited suggestion. It is perhaps not surprising that it has not often been successfully used as a continuous form outside France. Michael Drayton (1563–1631) used it for his long topographical poem; *Polyolbion,* as did Browning for the shorter *Fifine at the Fair* (1872), and Robert Bridges in his *Testament of Beauty* (1927–29). It has also been successfully used, notably by Dryden, as an occasional variant in heroic and blank verse, and is perhaps seen at its best in English poetry as the concluding line of the Spenserian stanza. (W. G. Me.)

ALEXANDRISTS, the name given to those Renaissance philosophers who, in the controversy about personal immortality, followed the explanation of Aristotle's *De Anima* given by Alexander (*q.v.*) of Aphrodisias. The orthodox Thomism of the Roman Catholic Church maintained that Aristotle, who regarded reason as eternal, also regarded it as a faculty of the individual soul and so could be cited as believing the individual soul to be immortal. The Latin Averroists, on the other hand, evolved a doctrine of universal, as opposed to individual, immortality, holding the individual intellect to be reabsorbed after death into the eternal intellect which had been individualized in it. The Alexandrists, however, led by Pietro Pomponazzi (*q.v.*), denied that either the Thomist or the Averroist view could justly be attributed to Aristotle. Instead they held that Aristotle considered the soul as a material and therefore a mortal entity, operating during life only under the authority of universal reason and organically connected with the body, on the dissolution of which it would become extinct. *See* also AVERROISM, LATIN.

ALEXANDRITE, a variety of chrysoberyl (*q.v.*) discovered in the Urals in 1833, on the day set apart for celebrating the majority of the Russian tsarevitch, afterward the tsar Alexander II, in whose honour the stone was named. It is remarkable for being strongly dichroic (that is, exhibiting different colours depending on the direction from which it is viewed), generally appearing dark green by daylight and raspberry red by artificial light or by daylight transmitted through the stone. As red and green were the military colours of Russia, the mineral became highly popular as a gem stone.

ALEXANDROUPOLIS (Turkish DÉDÉAGATCH), a seaport of western Thrace, Greece, lies 10 mi. N.W. of the Maritsa (Evros, Meriç) estuary, on the gulf of Enos (Enez), an inlet of the Aegean sea. Pop. (1961) 18,712. Its Turkish name is derived from the settlement there of a Dervish community of the Dédé sect in the 15th century, but it remained a mere fishing village until 1871, when the products of its valonia oak woods were first marketed. The opening of the Istanbul-Salonika railway in 1896 increased its prosperity, but it was for a long time a bone of contention between Greece and Bulgaria. After the Balkan War in 1913 the town was ceded to the Bulgarians and provided them with an outlet to the Aegean sea until the end of World War I. The peace treaty granted it to Greece, and by the treaty of Lausanne (1923), which gave Enos to Turkey, Alexandroupolis became a Greek frontier town on the Maritsa river. In 1941 it was again occupied by Bulgarian troops but was restored to Greece in 1944. It is now the seat of the metropolitan bishop of Alexandroupolis–Samothrace, capital of Evros nome, and forms one of the principal centres of the import trade of mainland Greece; its chief export is tobacco. (D. M. N.)

ALEXIS (ALEKSEI MIKHAILOVICH) (1629–1676), tsar of Russia from 1645 to 1676, was born in Moscow on March 20 (new style; March 10, old style), 1629, the son of the first Romanov tsar, Michael. He came to the throne at the age of 16, having received a superficial education in reading, writing and church singing from his tutor, Boris Ivanovich Morozov. During the first three years of Alexis' reign, Morozov (who in Jan. 1648 became the tsar's brother-in-law) was actually in charge of affairs of state, but his friendship with foreign merchants and the government's attempt to raise revenue by increasing the salt tax led, in the summer of 1648, to violent popular disturbances in Moscow.

Alexis was compelled to grant most of the rebels' demands, to exile Morozov and to convene a land assembly (*zemski sobor*), which in 1649 produced a new code of laws (*ulozhenie*) for Russia. There were further disturbances, however, in Pskov, Novgorod and other cities in 1650. Morozov's place as the court favourite was taken first by Prince N. Odoevski and then by the metropolitan Nikon (*q.v.*). Russia accepted sovereignty over the Dnieper Cossacks in Jan. 1654 and, in the following May, entered into a drawn-out war with Poland. This also involved a conflict with Sweden from 1656, terminated by armistice in 1658 and by the peace of Kardis in 1661. By the treaty of Andrussovo (Jan. 1667), which ended the Polish war, Russia gained Smolensk, Kiev and the lands lying east of the Dnieper river.

Perhaps the most momentous event of Alexis' reign was the church schism. The tsar backed Nikon's efforts to revise Russian liturgical books and certain rituals which in the course of the preceding century had departed from their Greek models. Although before long he became estranged from Nikon, whose violent temper and authoritarian inclinations had earned him many enemies, the revisions which Nikon initiated were retained, and the opponents of the reform were excommunicated. After the disgrace of Nikon, A. L. Ordyn-Nashchokin (*q.v.*) was the tsar's principal adviser till A. S. Matveev took his place in 1671.

The reign of Alexis was characterized by some important legislative activity—the effects of which, however, were often unintentional. The duties and obligations of each estate of the realm were firmly defined; the peasants were tied to the land and to the landlord and thus finally enserfed; the land assemblies were allowed to fall into gradual disuse; the professional bureaucracy and regular army grew in importance. Foreign influences also began to crack the hitherto fairly solid wall separating Russia from its Roman Catholic and Protestant neighbours. Dissatisfaction with the reign centred in the cities (which chafed under the competition of foreigners and of the tax-free groups of the population) and in the peasantry (which was deprived of the last vestiges of freedom). The social dissatisfaction expressed itself in frequent rebellions, the most savage of which was the rising on the eastern borderlands led by Stenka Razin (*q.v.*) from 1667 to 1671. In general, the "middle classes"—the gentry and the wealthy merchants—fared best under this administration.

Virtually all the sources agree that Alexis was a gentle, warm-hearted and popular ruler. He was extremely pious and attached great importance to the strict fulfillment of all churchly (as well as courtly) rituals, so much so that some contemporaries called him a "little monk"; but there is also evidence that his religious sentiment had a deeper, more spiritual foundation. He was generous to his friends and, though occasionally short of temper, tended to err rather on the side of kindness. He liked falconry (for which he wrote a manual) and the theatre, which he introduced to the Russian court. By Russian standards of the time he was fairly well-read; his numerous extant writings display an unsophisticated humour and homespun philosophy. His main fault, in the opinion of contemporaries, was indolence. Indeed, through most of his reign matters of state were handled by favourites. Platonov characterizes Alexis as "interesting and pleasant, but more virtuous than effective."

He was married twice, first to Maria Ilinishna Miloslavskaya (who bore him two sons, the future tsars Fedor and Ivan, as well as several daughters), then to Natalia Kirillovna Naryshkina, whose son became Peter the Great. Alexis died in Moscow on Feb. 8 (N.S.; Jan. 29, O.S.), 1676.

See R. Nisbet Bain, *The First Romanovs* (1905); S. F. Platonov, *Tsar Aleksei Mikhailovich* (1913). (R. E. Pi.)

ALEXIS (ALEKSEI PETROVICH) (1690–1718), Russian tsarevich, son of Peter the Great and the tsaritsa Eudoxia (*qq.v.*), was born on Feb. 28 (new style; Feb. 18, old style), 1690. In 1698 Peter obliged Eudoxia to take the veil, and Alexis was temporarily entrusted to the tsarevna Natalia Alekseevna. Baron Heinrich von Huyssen was appointed tutor to the tsarevich in 1702, but the ambitious curriculum drawn up by him was never put into practice. In 1704, during the Great Northern War, Alexis took part in the siege of Narva. After the capture of the fortress from the

Swedes, Peter warned Alexis that he would disown him if he did not act in conformity with his wishes. Most of the next five years Alexis spent at Preobrazhenskoye near Moscow. Under the influence of a coterie centred round his confessor, Yakov Ignatiev, Alexis' estrangement from his father turned to hostility. In 1707, re-enlisted in Peter's service, Alexis took charge of fortifying Moscow against a possible Swedish attack. Though he showed administrative competence and worked conscientiously, Peter reproached him with lack of zeal. In Oct. 1709 he was sent to Dresden in Saxony to complete his education. His marriage with Princess Sophia Charlotte of Brunswick-Wolfenbüttel took place at Torgau in Oct. 1711. Alexis' frequent absence at the wars and his growing attraction to drink made the marriage an unhappy one, and the princess died on Nov. 2 (N.S.; Oct. 22, O.S.), 1715, ten days after giving birth to the future Peter II. On Nov. 8 (N.S.; Oct. 28, O.S.) Peter the Great's second consort, the future empress Catherine I, also gave birth to a son. On the previous day Peter had handed Alexis a letter accusing him of persistently burying his talents and calling on him to mend his ways or forfeit his right to the succession. Alexis chose the latter course, but Peter, knowing how strongly Alexis was imbued with the spirit of old Muscovy, as opposed to the westernization that the tsar was sponsoring, declared that he could not accept Alexis' renunciation, since one day the clergy might persuade him to change his mind and use him as their tool: Alexis should therefore reform or become a monk. The order to make his final decision followed in Sept. 1716. Leaving Russia for Austria with his mistress Afrosinya and a few servants, Alexis in November arrived in Vienna and placed himself under the protection of the Holy Roman emperor Charles VI, who gave him sanctuary first in the Tirolean fortress of Ehrenberg and later in the castle of Sant' Elmo near Naples. In Oct. 1717 Count P. A. Tolstoi, on Peter's instructions, prevailed on Alexis to go back on the understanding that he would be pardoned and allowed to marry Afrosinya. On Feb. 11 (N.S.; Jan. 31, O.S.), 1718, he arrived in Moscow. Three days later Peter qualified his promise with new conditions: Alexis must forswear the succession and denounce those who had assisted his flight. This done, the trial of Alexis' partisans began on the following day. The investigation, conducted with the utmost cruelty, revealed the existence of a potential movement of reaction for which Alexis might become a rallying point. On March 26 and 28 (N.S.) the principal accused were put to death; on March 29 Peter moved to St. Petersburg, taking Alexis with him. In mid-April Afrosinya was questioned and confronted with Alexis by Peter himself. In the tsar's eyes, Alexis' daydreams of his father's death, of rebellion aided by the Austrians and of a return to the Muscovite way of life amounted to high treason and released him from his promise of clemency. On June 28 Alexis was forced to confess his guilt before the senate. During the following week he was tortured and questioned; on July 4 a special tribunal condemned him to death; and on July 7 (N.S.; June 26, O.S.), 1718, he died in the SS. Peter and Paul fortress, in all probability under the knout.

See A. Brückner, *Der Zarewitsch Alexei* (1880). (L. R. Lr.)

ALEXIS (4th–3rd century B.C.), Greek poet of the Middle and New comedy, is said to have been Menander's uncle and to have written 245 comedies, of which 130 titles are preserved. The fragments (about 1,000 lines) attest his wit and poetic talent. Born at Thurii, he became a citizen of Athens. According to Plutarch he lived to the age of 106 and died on the stage while being crowned.

For the fragments of his work *see* T. Kock, *Comicorum atticorum fragmenta* (1880–88).

ALEXIS, WILLIBALD (pseudonym of GEORG WILHELM HEINRICH HÄRING) (1798–1871), a versatile and prolific German writer and critic best known for his historical novels. Born at Breslau on June 29, 1798, from his boyhood he lived in Berlin, where he attended the *Friedrich Werdersche Gymnasium*. After service as a volunteer in the campaign of 1815, he studied law at Berlin and Breslau, but abandoned his legal career for writing after the success of his literary hoax *Walladmor* (1824), an amusing parody of Scott published as "freely translated from the English of Walter Scott." The joke, detrimental to Alexis' literary reputation, was repeated in the more ambitious and original novel *Schloss Avalon* (1827). Although his home was in Berlin, where he edited the *Berliner Konversationsblatt* (1827–35) and contributed essays and reviews to literary journals, he traveled widely in Europe and recounted his experiences in some readable travel books; *e.g.*, *Herbstreise durch Skandinavien* (1828).

With *Cabanis* (1832), a story of the age of Frederick the Great, Alexis embarked on a cycle of novels with the aim of making known forgotten but significant periods of Prussian history. He was not content to abide by Scott's formula for the historical novel and was continually experimenting with methods of presentation. *Der Roland von Berlin* (1840) portrays the struggle for power in the 15th century between the municipal authorities of Berlin-Kölln and the ruler of Brandenburg; *Der falsche Woldemar* (1842) the rise and fall of a pretender a century earlier. In the first part of *Die Hosen des Herrn von Bredow* (1846–48) Alexis reveals outstanding qualities as a humorist and is unusually successful in organizing his material. The concluding section, describing the elector Joachim's ineffectual opposition to Luther's teaching, strikes a more serious note. Diffuseness spoils *Ruhe ist die erste Bürgerpflicht* (1852), in which the activities of criminals are presented as symptomatic of Prussian degeneracy in 1806. The sequel *Isegrimm* (1854) foreshadows a rebirth of patriotism.

Alexis was the first writer to reveal the poetic aspects of the Brandenburg landscape. His writing is uneven, passages of effective realistic description alternating with others in which romantic mystification predominates. His stories, poems and dramas are largely derivative. From 1842 until 1860 he edited, almost singlehanded, a remarkable collection of famous lawsuits, *Der neue Pitaval*. In 1856 he suffered a stroke and later retired permanently to Arnstadt in Thuringia, where he died, Dec. 16, 1871.

Alexis' novels were published as *Vaterländische Romane*, edited by L. Lorenz and A. Bartels (1912–25). His *Erinnerungen* ("Memoirs") were edited by M. Ewert (1900).

See L. H. C. Thomas, *The Life and Work of Willibald Alexis* (1952); *Goedekes Grundriss zur Geschichte der deutschen Dichtung*, vol. ix (1910), vol. xiv (1955). (L. H. C. T.)

ALEXIUS I (ALEXIUS COMNENUS) (1048–1118), Byzantine emperor from 1081 to 1118, was the third son of John Comnenus and nephew of Isaac I Comnenus, emperor 1057–59. Under Romanus IV Diogenes (1068–71) Alexius served with distinction against the Seljuk Turks. Under Michael VII Ducas (1071–78) and Nicephorus III Botaniates (1078–81) he was also employed, along with his elder brother Isaac, against rebels in Asia Minor, Thrace and Epirus. The Comneni, however, belonged to the military magnates who were opposed to the ineffective rule of the civil aristocracy, and, when Nicephorus III (though of the military nobility) proved incapable of restoring order, Alexius Comnenus emerged successful in the competition for the throne. In this he was supported by his brother Isaac and by his mother Anna Dalassena; he then placated the powerful Ducas family by marrying Irene Ducas. Nicephorus abdicated and Alexius I was crowned on April 4, 1081.

Alexius found the empire faced with disaster on all sides. In 1081 the Normans of southern Italy, led by Robert Guiscard, attacked Greece. They took Corfu and Durazzo and advanced in Epirus, Thessaly and Macedonia. With Venetian help, Alexius halted them, and the danger was temporarily removed by Robert's death (1085). On the northern frontier the empire was constantly threatened by the Pechenegs, who raided the Balkans and were supported by the dualist sects there, especially the Bogomils. In 1091 a crushing defeat was inflicted on the Pechenegs at Mt. Levunion (near Enos) in Thrace, with the help of their rivals, the Kumans. In the east Alexius faced the Seljuk Turks, who occupied the greater part of Asia Minor, but he had already come to terms with Sulaiman of Iconium (Konya) in 1081, and in 1091, by skilfully utilizing Muslim rivalries, he made a treaty with the latter's son Kilij Arslan. By 1095 Alexius could consider taking the offensive, but at this point he encountered his greatest danger, the first crusade (*see* CRUSADES).

Alexius had always been willing to use western mercenaries,

but he had not visualized an independent feudal force, nor an undisciplined pilgrim rabble such as accompanied Peter the Hermit. The crusaders came through Constantinople, where Alexius exacted from the western lords an oath of allegiance and a promise to restore former Byzantine territory. In the event, Alexius recovered control over much of western Asia Minor (as Nicaea, Smyrna, Ephesus and Sardis), but not over the Latin principalities established in Syria and Palestine. The real contention arose over Antioch, which was in the hands of Robert Guiscard's son Bohemund, the bitter enemy of Byzantium. Advancing toward Antioch, Alexius captured Adana, Tarsus and Mamistra, as well as towns farther south on the Syrian coast. Bohemund, under pressure both from the Byzantines and the Turks, returned to Italy, where he spread false reports of Alexius' perfidy toward the Latin crusaders. He then launched an offensive against the Byzantine empire, attacking Avlona (Vlonë or Valona in Albania) in 1107, but was defeated by Alexius and forced to agree to the treaty of Devoll (1108) whereby he recognized Alexius as overlord of Antioch. This treaty was not implemented. Alexius, however, had steadily restored Byzantine prestige and recovered much lost territory.

At home Alexius vigorously opposed the widespread dualist heresy of the Bogomils; he also had the scholar John Italus tried for heresy, perhaps from political motives. He tried to stabilize the currency and to build up Byzantine trade, but was forced to grant substantial trading privileges to Venice in return for naval help. He made no attempt to curb the great landed magnates. His reign appears to have seen the first instance of a grant in *pronoia* (see BYZANTINE EMPIRE) in return for military service. Alexius resisted the efforts of his wife Irene and his daughter Anna Comnena to get him to recognize the latter's husband Nicephorus Bryennius as his successor instead of his son John. He was an able general and a distinguished diplomat but could not permanently restore the Byzantine empire, though he temporarily checked its enemies.

BIBLIOGRAPHY.—F. Chalandon, *Essai sur le règne d'Alexis Ier Comnène* (1900); G. Ostrogorsky, *History of the Byzantine State* (1956); G. G. Buckler, *Anna Comnena* (1929); J. M. Hussey, *Church and Learning in the Byzantine Empire 867–1185* (1937).   (J. M. Hy.)

ALEXIUS II (ALEXIUS COMNENUS) (1169–1183), Byzantine emperor from 1180 to 1183, was the son of Manuel I Comnenus and Mary, daughter of Raymond, prince of Antioch. When his father died on Sept. 24, 1180, he became emperor at the age of 11, with his mother as regent. She unwisely entrusted the government to her favourite, the unpopular and incapable Alexius (Manuel's nephew), who had the title *protosebastus*. She was hated as a Latin, and there was widespread opposition to this regime, but the conspirators, including Alexius II's sister Mary and her husband John, failed to overthrow the regency. The victory lay with Andronicus I Comnenus, Manuel I's cousin, who advanced through Asia Minor and was waiting at Chalcedon when anti-Latin riots broke out in the capital (May 1182). The *protosebastus* Alexius was captured and blinded, and Andronicus entered the capital as the protector of Alexius II. He promptly had his opponents executed, including the dowager-empress Mary, whose death warrant her son Alexius had to sign. Crowned co-emperor in Sept. 1183, Andronicus soon after had Alexius strangled. He subsequently married Alexius' young widow Agnes, daughter of Louis VII of France.

See G. Ostrogorsky, *History of the Byzantine State* (1956).
                                                    (J. M. Hy.)

ALEXIUS III (ALEXIUS ANGELUS) (d. 1211 or later), Byzantine emperor from 1195 to 1203, was the second son of Andronicus Angelus, grandson of Alexius I. In 1195 he was proclaimed emperor by the troops; he captured his brother, the emperor Isaac II, at Stagira in Macedonia and had him blinded and imprisoned. Crowned in April 1195, Alexius III was a weak and greedy emperor and his *coup d'état* had disastrous results. Byzantine prestige declined in the Balkans, where his failure to aid his son-in-law Stephen Nemanya obliged the latter to turn to the Bulgars for help. Byzantine campaigns against the Bulgars ended in defeat (1195 and 1196), and intrigues and diplomacy were equally unsuccessful since the new Bulgarian ruler Kaloyan acknowledged

the pope's supremacy instead of that of Constantinople. Then the Hohenstaufen emperor Henry VI had designs on the Byzantine empire and had to be bought off by the heavy "German" tax. So depleted were imperial resources that Alexius was reduced to despoiling the imperial tombs of their ornaments.

The danger from the west was only temporarily postponed by Henry VI's death (1197). Shortly afterward the fourth crusade was launched (see CRUSADES). One factor which contributed to its diversion to Constantinople was an appeal for help from Isaac II's son Alexius, who had escaped to Philip of Swabia, his brother-in-law. In 1203 the crusaders succeeded in restoring Isaac II and his son (now crowned Alexius IV). Alexius III fled from the capital with what treasure he could collect and escaped to Mosynopolis in Thrace.

After an unsuccessful attempt to recover the throne he wandered about Greece and surrendered to Boniface of Montferrat, then master of a great part of the Balkan peninsula, but left his protection and then sought shelter with Michael Angelus, despot of Epirus. Finally he went to Asia Minor, where his son-in-law Theodore Lascaris was holding his own against the Latins. Alexius, joined by the sultan of Iconium (Konya), demanded Theodore's crown and, when it was refused, marched against him. Taken prisoner by Theodore in 1210, he was sent to a monastery at Nicaea, where he died on some date unknown.

BIBLIOGRAPHY.—J. M. Hussey in *Cambridge Medieval History*, new ed., vol. 4, ch. 4 (1963); G. Ostrogorsky, *History of the Byzantine State* (1956); E. Pears, *The Fall of Constantinople, being the Story of the Fourth Crusade* (1885).   (J. M. Hy.)

ALEXIUS IV (ALEXIUS ANGELUS) (d. 1204), Byzantine emperor from 1203 to 1204, was the son of the emperor Isaac II, whom Alexius III dethroned and blinded in 1195. Alexius IV, however, escaped in 1201 to Germany, where he persuaded his brother-in-law, Philip of Swabia, and Boniface of Montferrat, the leader of the crusaders, to divert the fourth crusade to Constantinople (see CRUSADES). In Aug. 1203 Isaac was restored, with Alexius IV as joint emperor, but they were unable immediately to fulfill the promises made to the crusaders to contribute men and money for the expedition to Jerusalem and to bring about the reunion of the Greek and the Latin church. At the beginning of 1204 quarrels broke out between the crusaders and the Greeks, who revolted under the leadership of Alexius Ducas Murtzuphlus, Alexius III's son-in-law. Proclaimed emperor as Alexius V in Jan. 1204, Murtzuphlus had Alexius IV strangled, while Isaac died of shock. On April 9 the crusaders stormed and captured Constantinople and elected Baldwin of Flanders as Latin emperor.

See G. Ostrogorsky, *History of the Byzantine State* (1956); E. Pears, *The Fall of Constantinople, being the Story of the Fourth Crusade* (1885).   (J. M. Hy.)

ALEXIUS V (ALEXIUS DUCAS MURTZUPHLUS) (d. 1204), Byzantine emperor in 1204, was related to the imperial family of Ducas and was a son-in-law of Alexius III Angelus, who had been deposed in 1203. He was brought to the throne late in Jan. 1204 by the revolution of the Greeks against Isaac II and Alexius IV, who owed their crowns to the Latins of the fourth crusade. As leader of the anti-Latin party in Constantinople, he conducted its defense with great bravery. When it became hopeless he fled (April 12) and joined the fugitive Alexius III, who blinded him. He was then captured by the crusaders, who put him to death as the murderer of Alexius IV by casting him from the top of a column in Constantinople.

See G. Ostrogorsky, *History of the Byzantine State*, Eng. trans. by J. M. Hussey (1956).   (D. M. N.)

ALFA or HALFA: see ESPARTO.

ALFALFA (LUCERNE or PURPLE MEDICK), known botanically as *Medicago sativa,* is a leguminous forage plant famed in the regions of its adaptation for its tolerance of drought, heat and cold; for the remarkable productivity and the quality of its herbage; and for its incidental value in soil improvement. It is grown primarily for hay, pasturage and silage. The plant is an erect, long-lived, tap-rooted, perennial herb with numerous thin, hollow and branching stems arising from a much-branched crown which is partially embedded in the surface layer of soil. As the plant develops, numerous stems bearing many trifoliolate leaves arise from the crown buds and attain lengths of from one to five feet. Racemes of small flowers arise from the upper axillary buds of the stems. The flowers of all commercial varieties are predominantly purple. This is particularly true of the types grown in Russian Turkistan and the regional strains of common alfalfa grown in North and South America. However, from 5% to 40% of variegated and yellow flowers occur in such well-known hardy commercial varieties as Vernal, Grimm, Cossack, Ladak and Canadian variegated. These were derived from crosses between the purple *M. sativa* and the wild yellow-flowered species, *M. falcata*. With approaching maturity, coiled pods containing from two to eight or more seeds develop abundantly in regions with much sunshine, moderate heat and dry weather.

Growth Characteristics.—The primary root of alfalfa attains great depths. When 20 or more years of age, this tap root may descend as much as 50 ft. or more where the subsoil is porous. This accounts for the unusual ability of the plant to tolerate drought. The roots of seedling plants are known to penetrate the soil for three feet at two months, and for six feet with plants five months of age. Not infrequently, newly established fields of alfalfa survive severe summer drought and heat when stands of red, alsike and white clover, and other members of the genus *Trifolium* may succumb, partly because the roots are much shallower and more branching.

Alfalfa has remarkable capacity for rapid and abundant regeneration of dense growths of new stems and leaves following cutting. This makes possible from one to as many as 13 crops of hay in one growing season. The frequency of harvest and the total seasonal yields are dependent largely on the length of the growing season, the adaptability of the soil, the abundance of sunshine, and especially the amount and distribution of rainfall or irrigation during the growing season. On nonirrigated lands, yields of from two to four tons per acre are common, but with long growing seasons and with irrigation as much as ten tons of dry hay per acre are obtained. Green leafy alfalfa hay is very nutritious and palatable, containing about 16% proteins and 8% mineral constituents. In addition it is rich in vitamins A, E, D and K.

Although alfalfa is highly tolerant to drought and heat, it utilizes very large quantities of water to produce forage. A yield of three tons of dry herbage per acre requires the absorption by the roots from the soil of approximately 2,490 tons of water, the equivalent of about 22 in. of rainfall. Such heavy utilization of water greatly reduces the reserves of subsoil moisture and yields may decline markedly unless the moisture supply is replenished adequately by rainfall, surface irrigations or subirrigation. Most all water utilized for growth is lost in transpiration, being evaporated through the leaf pores or stomates after passage through the stems and the veins of the leaflets. In the course of growth, some of the water is combined with carbon dioxide in the synthesis of sugar and numerous other organic compounds, of which the dry matter of the plant is largely constituted.

J. HORACE MCFARLAND CO.

ALFALFA, OR LUCERNE, IN FLOWER

Although a native of the old world, the acreage of alfalfa occurs primarily in the western hemisphere. Estimates vary, but in the second half of the 20th century more than 60,000,000 ac. of alfalfa were ordinarily grown in the world each year, of which nearly 50% was grown in the United States and about 40% in Argentina.

History of Cultivation.—It is likely that alfalfa had its origin in the dry, hot regions east of the Mediterranean. It occurs in the wild state in the Transcaucasian mountains of southern U.S.S.R. with many other species of *Medicago*. Historically, alfalfa has been grown for a longer period for forage than any other plant. Incident to the invasion of Greece it was introduced into that country by Medes and Persians about 400 B.C. It was grown extensively in Italy in the 1st century and the Romans introduced it into other parts of Europe. It is probable that the Moors also introduced alfalfa into Spain. It was the Spaniards who, coincident with their lure for gold, brought alfalfa to the new world, having introduced it into South America in the 16th century.

Alfalfa was introduced into eastern United States by the early colonists. George Washington and Thomas Jefferson attempted to grow it, but its culture met with but little success in this humid region with its leached and highly acid soils. In only a few areas of the eastern states, where soils derived from limestone were abundant in mineral residues, did the culture of alfalfa persist. While alfalfa may have been introduced into southwestern United States from Mexico through Spanish influence, it was the discovery of gold in California in 1848 which gave alfalfa culture its great impetus in the western states. The gold seekers from the eastern states brought alfalfa from Chile to California in 1854 where it became known as "Chilean clover" and later as Spanish or common alfalfa. Subsequently, alfalfa culture spread through the west as this vast territory was settled by the migrations of settlers from the eastern states.

In the western states, with arid or semiarid climates, soils were high in mineral residues containing calcium, phosphorus and potassium compounds and other sources of nutrients which are requisites for successful alfalfa culture. In addition, the climate with its abundant sunshine and favourable winters was, in the main, ideal for alfalfa culture. It is not surprising, therefore, that alfalfa culture was predominantly a western enterprise for more than 70 years after its introduction into California in 1854. In 1899, 2,000,000 ac. of alfalfa were harvested for hay and 97% of this was grown in the 17 western states, Nebraska, California, Kansas, Idaho, Oregon, Washington, Nevada, Utah, Arizona, New Mexico, Colorado, Wyoming, Montana, North and South Dakota, Oklahoma and Texas. In 1929 the total acreage of alfalfa harvested for hay was 11,500,000 ac., of which 71% was grown in the aforementioned western states. By this time, however, extensive researches, demonstrations and experience had established clearly the significant fact that alfalfa could be grown successfully in the northern humid states by adjusting the soil environment with applications of various forms of lime and of phosphate and potash fertilizers. These practices, along with the development of artificial cultures for the inoculation of seed with nitrogen-fixing bacteria; the improvement of seeding techniques; the establishment of proper managerial practices; and the utilization of winter-hardy varieties such as Vernal, Ranger, Narragansett, Grimm, Canadian variegated, Cossack and Ladak instead of the less hardy regional strains of American Common, presaged the remarkable eastward expansion of alfalfa culture. As a consequence, by mid-century the central states—Minnesota, Wisconsin, Michigan, Iowa, Illinois, Indiana, Ohio, Kentucky and Missouri—grew approximately 43% of the 28,000,000 ac. grown for hay in the U.S. compared with 45% for the 17 western states and 12% for the remaining eastern and southern states.

Alfalfa culture is widely distributed throughout the nations of the world, and particularly where arid and semiarid climates and irrigation prevail. In a sense, alfalfa is a crop par excellence for drylands. Its culture, however, increased in humid regions in the 20th century.

Diseases and Insects.—Like all crops, alfalfa is beset with hazards of climate, diseases and insects. Among the more serious of these are winterkilling, bacterial wilt disease, grasshoppers, spotted aphid and leafhoppers. In the humid and in the irrigated areas, stands three or more years of age have often become badly thinned by the infections from the soil-borne bacterial wilt organism, *Phytomonas insidiosum*. Severe damage is caused periodically by winter manifestations of the humid areas such as enduring and contacting sheets of ice, or protracted periods of extremely cold weather without the insulation of snow or vegetative cover or both, or long periods of alternate freezing and thawing which on heavy, water-saturated soils lift or "heave" the plants, exposing the crown to harmful aerial temperatures and desiccation. Such losses are greatly reduced through the selection of soils with good surface and underdrainage; through managerial treatments; and by the use of winter-hardy and wilt-resistant varieties such as the new synthetic varieties, Vernal and Ranger. Orestan, Ladak and Cossack alfalfas are winter-hardy and moderately resistant to wilt but Grimm and Canadian variegated, while winter-hardy, are very susceptible to the wilt disease. The tiny leafhoppers, *Empoasca fabae,* which cause stunting and yellowing of summer growths of alfalfa in warm humid areas, may be controlled by cutting management under some conditions.

See F. B. Morrison, *Feeds and Feeding* (20th ed., 1936); L. F. Graber, "A Century of Alfalfa Culture in America," *Agronomy Journal,* 42:11 (1950); *Climate and Man,* U.S. Dept. of Agriculture, yearbook of agriculture (1941). (L. F. G.)

ALFARO SIQUEIROS, DAVID: see SIQUEIROS, DAVID ALFARO.

ALFASI (AL-PHASI), **ISAAC BEN JACOB** (1013–1103), Jewish rabbi and codifier, known as Rif from the initials of Rabbi Isaac Fasi, was born near Fez, in north Africa, and died at Lucena, Spain.

His fame rests on his talmudic digest, which omitted all homiletical passages and also passages relating to religious duties practicable only in Palestine. He occupies an important place in the development of the Spanish method of studying the Talmud (*q.v.*). As opposed to the French rabbis, the Spanish sought to simplify the Talmud, and to free it from casuistical detail. Alfasi's digest was the forerunner of the great codes of Maimonides and of Joseph Caro.

ALFIERI, VITTORIO, CONTE (1749–1803), the greatest Italian tragic poet, was born of rich and noble parents at Asti in Piedmont on Jan. 16, 1749. Educated at the military academy of Turin, he left it in 1766 with the rank of ensign. He conceived, however, a strong distaste for the military profession and obtained leave to travel. After a tour of the principal cities of Italy (1766–67), he visited France, England and Holland (1767–68) and then set off, after a few months in Piedmont, to visit Germany, Denmark, Sweden and Russia, then England, Holland and France again and finally Spain and Portugal (1769–72). During these travels he indulged in a number of amorous adventures, several of them leading to duels, one culminating in an attempt at suicide by Alfieri (at The Hague in 1768) and another involving him in a divorce suit (London, 1771). Nevertheless, though much time was wasted in dissipation, he found in England the political liberty that became his ideal and in France the literature that influenced him most profoundly. He studied Voltaire, J. J. Rousseau and, above all, Montesquieu; and his reading confirmed in him that love of freedom and hatred of tyranny which were to dominate his thought.

On his return to Piedmont in 1772, Alfieri settled in Turin, where he continued his life of dissipation. After an illness at the end of 1773 he resigned his commission. Then, in 1774, to divert himself, he began to compose a play. The result was *Cleopatra,* a tragedy, which was performed with great success in 1775. Thereupon Alfieri, who had serious misgivings about the merit of his first work, decided to devote himself to literature.

To the fulfillment of his new ambition he brought all the energy that had previously driven him to wander from city to city in Europe. He began a methodical study of the classics and of the Italian poets and, having been accustomed to express himself mainly in French, the language of the ruling classes in Turin, decided to go to Tuscany to familiarize himself with pure Italian. After a visit in 1776, he returned for a longer stay in 1777. By the end of 1782 he had composed 14 tragedies as well as many poems (including four odes in the series *L'America libera,* on American independence, to which a fifth was added in 1783) and a political treatise in prose, *Della tirannide* (composed in 1777). Ten of the tragedies were printed at Siena in 1783.

Meanwhile, in Florence in 1777, Alfieri had met the countess of Albany, wife of the Stuart pretender to the English throne, Charles Edward. He fell in love with her and remained deeply attached to her for the rest of his life. Renouncing his Piedmontese prop-

erties (1778), he lived first in Florence, then in Rome (1781–83) and then, after a year of separation from the countess, mainly at Colmar in Alsace (1784–86). At the end of 1786 he moved with her to Paris, where a new edition of his tragedies was published (1787–89), containing 19 plays in all.

Alfieri hailed the French Revolution with an ode on the fall of the Bastille, *Parigi sbastigliata* (1789), but the later excesses of the populace disgusted him. After an excursion to England (1791), he and the countess left France in 1792, returning to Florence. Occupied to the last with his literary activity, particularly with his autobiography (which he had begun to write in 1790 and which he continued to the last year of his life) and with his six comedies (begun in 1800), Alfieri died in Florence on Oct. 8, 1803.

The Tragedies.—Alfieri's genius was essentially dramatic. His great aspiration was to act upon the society of his time. He sought to wage war against tyrants and he learned to use his lines of verse as a substitute for weapons. The conciseness of his style, his disdain for euphony and musicality, the power of his jarring words, even his strict adherence to the classical form of tragedy with its "unity of action" and its rejection of subordinate episodes and secondary characters—all are to be explained by his one preoccupation: to make the Italians accept his political ideas and his philosophy of life, to inspire them to "heroic deeds." Nearly always Alfieri's tragedies present the struggle between a champion of liberty and a tyrant. The hero has all the qualities of the heroes of Plutarch and is generally lost by his loyalty. The tyrant is evil personified, Machiavellian and reminiscent of some character from Tacitus. Love has little place in a world so shaken by political passions.

Alfieri had a systematic and conscientious method of composing his plays. Inspired by a theme, he would first draw up a plan, then draft a text in prose and then versify the text. Even then, the verse might be subjected to recurrent revisions. Moreover, he was usually engaged simultaneously on several works at varying stages of composition. The 19 tragedies which he finally approved for publication in the edition of 1787–89 were *Filippo, Polinice, Antigone, Virginia, Agamennone, Oreste, Rosmunda, Ottavia, Timoleone, Merope, Maria Stuarda, La congiura de' Pazzi, Don Garzia, Saul, Agide, Sofonisba, Bruto primo, Mirra* and *Bruto secondo.* The best are *Filippo,* in which Philip II of Spain is presented as a tyrant whose hatred for his liberal-minded son, Don Carlos, is exacerbated by jealousy; *Antigone* and *Oreste,* adaptations of themes handled by ancient Greek dramatists; and, above all, *Mirra* and *Saul.* In *Mirra* Alfieri deals with love, but the love is incestuous. *Saul,* his masterpiece, is the most powerful drama in the Italian theatre. The Godforsaken king of Israel who kills himself on the battlefield is much more than the usual tyrant: his character is a portrait of Alfieri himself and reflects the poet's own rage, the poet's own despair. Saul is a forerunner of Byron's heroes.

Other Works.—Alfieri's autobiography, published posthumously as *La vita di Vittorio Alfieri, scritta da esso* (1804), is his chief work in prose. He takes pleasure and pride in portraying his rise from provincial nobleman to poet, and the lifelong conflict between his generous, heroic ambitions and the weaknesses, whims and vanity of the man of the world. Some of his childhood recollections are affecting.

Alfieri's *Rime* (published 1804; mainly sonnets) is also a kind of autobiography, inspired by the various incidents of his life. He reveals lyrical feeling in the sonnets, expressing romantic loneliness, bitter pessimism and melancholy, but his style is always too concise for formal elegance and his prosody too rough to be musical.

In his comedies (*L'uno, I pochi, I troppi, L'antidoto, La finestrina* and *Il divorzio*), and in his 17 satires, Alfieri is concerned with the overthrow of tyrannies, with the defects of the new democracies or with the way in which Italian society should be reformed. These works, however, are less important than the *Misogallo* ("Francophobe"), a collection of epigrams and sonnets, with five prose pieces, chiefly inspired by resentment at the French occupation of Florence in 1799. In a section of the *Misogallo*

Alfieri turns from generalizations about freedom to make a direct appeal to the Italians to recover their own. By that appeal and by many of his lyrics and dramas he helped to revive the national spirit of Italy and so earned the title of precursor of the Risorgimento. For a portrait of Alfieri *see* ITALIAN LITERATURE.

BIBLIOGRAPHY.—For Alfieri's complete works *see* the collected edition by F. Maggini, 2 vol. (1940–41) or the critical edition by L. Fassò, F. Maggini *et al.* (1951–   ). There are English translations of the *Tragedies* by C. Lloyd (1815) and ed. by E. A. Bowring (1876) and of the *Life* by Sir Henry McAnally (1953). *See also* E. Bertana, *Vittorio Alfieri studiato nella vita e nel pensiero e nell'arte* (1903); B. Croce, *Poesia e non poesia* (1935); C. R. D. Miller, *Alfieri: a Biography* (1936); M. Fubini, *Vittorio Alfieri: il pensiero—la tragedia* (1937).

(F. Di.)

ALFONSO, the name of five kings of Aragon.

ALFONSO I (c. 1073–1134), called "the Battler," king of Aragon and of Navarre from 1104 to 1134, was the son of Sancho V Ramírez. Alfonso was a single-minded man of action and a very successful general, but a poor diplomat. He was persuaded by Alfonso VI of León and Castile to marry the latter's heiress, Urraca, widow of Raymond of Burgundy. In consequence, when Alfonso VI died (1109) the four Christian kingdoms were nominally united and Alfonso I took his father-in-law's imperial title. If the union had succeeded, the reconquest of Islamic Spain might well have been greatly accelerated and the fractionalist tendencies of the Christian-held territories might perhaps have been checked. It failed, however, because León and Castile felt hostility toward an Aragonese emperor; because Urraca disliked her second husband; because Bernard, the French Cluniac archbishop of Toledo, wanted to see his protegé, Alfonso Ramírez (infant son of Urraca and her Burgundian first husband), on the imperial throne; and probably because Alfonso handled all opposition too brusquely. At Bernard's prompting, the pope declared the Aragonese marriage void, but Alfonso continued to be involved in civil strife in the central kingdom until he eventually gave up his claims in favour of his stepson after the death of Urraca (1126). Despite these embroilments, he achieved spectacular victories against the Almoravids in the Ebro valley. Saragossa, capital of an important Moorish kingdom, fell to him (1118), as did many other places far to the south of the river. With these victories, Aragon ceased to be a Pyrenean kingdom. In 1125 Alfonso led a spectacular military raid far into southern Andalusia and returned with many thousands of Mozarab immigrants, whom he settled in the newly conquered territories. In his campaigns he received much help from the rulers of the counties north of the Pyrenees, and in 1116 the count of Toulouse became his vassal. This led to the political involvement of Aragon in the affairs of southern France. Alfonso was fatally wounded in battle at Fraga in 1134 and died in September. Despite his hostility to Cluny he was a deeply religious man, a supporter of the Cistercians and of the Templars and Hospitallers, and he bequeathed his kingdom to the two latter orders. His former subjects, however, refused to accept the donation.

ALFONSO II (1152–1196) was born in Barcelona, the son of Ramón Berenguer IV, count of Barcelona, and Petronilla, daughter of Ramiro II of Aragon. He succeeded his father as count of Barcelona in 1162 and his mother as ruler of Aragon in 1164. The two countries thus became associated under the house of Barcelona—a union which was destined to be permanent. Aragonese involvement in France became steadily greater in Alfonso's reign. Nevertheless, the conquest of Teruel (1171) opened the way for the conquest of Valencia and, in 1179, the pact of Cazorla with his ally, Alfonso VIII of Castile, fixed the future zones of reconquest for the two countries. Alfonso died in Perpignan in 1196. In his will he followed the Spanish custom of dividing his kingdom. Provence was thus lost to the Aragonese crown.

ALFONSO III (1265–1291) was the son of Peter III, whom he succeeded in 1285. A weak king, he was involved in an unsuccessful constitutional struggle with the Aragonese nobles. In 1287 he was compelled to grant the so-called "Privilegio de la unión," which handed over a number of important royal prerogatives in the old kingdom to baronial control. He died in Barcelona, June 18, 1291.

ALFONSO IV (1299–1336) was the son of James II, whom he succeeded on Nov. 2, 1327. He was well-intentioned, but weak. His reign was marked by a serious revolt in Sardinia, which led to war with Genoa, and by the establishment of diplomatic relations with the Moorish kingdoms of north Africa. The failure of the king to resist the efforts of his second wife to further the future of her sons at the expense of Alfonso's heir, Pedro, led to serious political disturbances. Alfonso IV died in Barcelona on Jan. 24, 1336.

ALFONSO V (c. 1396–1458), called "the Magnanimous," was the son of Fernando de Antequera (afterward Ferdinand I of Aragon), whom he succeeded on April 2, 1416. His military campaigns in the central Mediterranean made him one of the most famous men of his day. He subdued the refractory Sardinians (1420) and restored order in Sicily. In 1421 Joan II of Naples, her throne gravely threatened by Louis III of Anjou, made Alfonso her heir. His attempt to make good his claim to Naples involved him in hostilities with the papacy, Louis of Anjou, Genoa, Milan and other Italian rulers, and an immensely complicated diplomatic and military struggle followed in which Alfonso showed masterly understanding of Italian power politics. He was disowned by Joan in favour of René of Anjou and defeated at sea by the Genoese off Ponza (1435), being taken prisoner. He charmed his captor, the duke of Milan, into an alliance and, in 1442, Naples fell to him at last. He transferred his court there permanently in 1443, much to the annoyance of his Aragonese and Catalan subjects. Alfonso certainly established the basis of subsequent Spanish power in Italy and was much admired there for his skill as soldier and politician. Though he was friendly with a number of Italian humanists, the cultural significance of his court at Naples has probably been exaggerated. A restless, energetic person, he kept Italy in turmoil for years and was planning the conquest of Genoa when he died, in Naples, on June 27, 1458. His long absence from the Iberian peninsula was politically disastrous for his dominions there. In his will he left his Italian possessions to his illegitimate son, Ferdinand, so dissolving the empire that he had built up.

(P. E. R.)

ALFONSO, the name of 11 kings of Asturias, León and Castile.

ALFONSO I (693?–757), king of Asturias from 739 to 757, was probably the son-in-law of the first Asturian king, Pelayo. The rebellion of the Berber garrisons in Islamic Spain (741) and the civil strife there which followed gave him the opportunity to incorporate Galicia into his kingdom. He also campaigned far to the south of the Asturian mountains, but lack of manpower made it impossible to exert permanent control on the plains and, in his time, a wide, largely uninhabited no man's land came into being between Asturias and the settled territories of the amirate of Córdoba.

ALFONSO II (c. 759–842), king of Asturias from 791 to 842, was born at Cangas in about 759, the son of Fruela I. He had to face frequent and determined attacks by the armies of the amirate of Córdoba and was often defeated, but his doggedness saved Asturias from extinction. He built a new capital, Oviedo, on a strategic site in the mountains and set about giving the Asturian kingdom a national identity by restoring Visigothic tradition in its administrative and ecclesiastical life. He did not hesitate to make common cause with Muslim rebels against the authority of the amirs. He tried to enter into relations with Charlemagne, but although he seems to have failed to get Carolingian support, there are some traces of Frankish influence in Asturias. During Alfonso's reign the discovery of the supposed tomb of St. James the Apostle in Galicia made the kingdom the guardian of an important Christian shrine and this, too, helped to give it a national identity. Alfonso died in Oviedo in 842.

ALFONSO III (c. 838–910), "the Great," king of Asturias from 866 to 910, succeeded his father, Ordoño I, on May 26, 866. The political troubles in the amirate of Córdoba which followed the death of Mohammed I (886) gave Alfonso his chance to take the offensive. He occupied the line of the Duero, founded Burgos and extended his rule as far east as Osma. These new territories, especially in León, were settled largely by Mozarabic immigrants from the amirate. His reign saw a further development of neo-Visigothic traditionalism in Asturias, reflected in two contemporary chronicles (*Chronica Visegothorum* and *Crónica Albedense*), which claimed that the rulers of Asturias were direct descendants of the Toledan royal line and stressed their duty to proceed to the early and complete reconquest of Spain. Alfonso, like his predecessors, saw the wisdom of interfering to his advantage in the political troubles of the amirate when he could, and perhaps reached some sort of *modus vivendi* with the amirs themselves in the later years of his reign. He also did much to develop the cult of St. James at Santiago de Compostela. As his successors were so often and so disastrously to do, Alfonso II wished to divide his kingdom between his sons when he died. Given the position of the country in relation to Muslim Spain, this proposal reveals serious limitations in his political vision. As a result of it, his reign ended in internal confusion. He probably died on Dec. 20, 910.

Alfonso IV (d. 933), king of León and Asturias from *c.* 926 to *c.* 931, was the son of Ordoño II and the successor of Fruela II. He became a monk, abdicated and then thought better of it and tried to recover his throne. His short reign was, in consequence, one of political chaos, ending in about 931.

Alfonso V (994–1028), king of León from 999 to 1028, came to the throne when, because of the devastating campaigns of Almanzor (*see* Mansur, Al) against the Leonese kingdom (981–1002), his father, Bermudo II, had been forced to accept Almanzor's *de facto* suzerainty over León. This position continued under Almanzor's son, Abd-al-Malik al-Muzaffar. The Leonese were forced to take part in the latter's campaign (1003) against the Catalans, and invited Abd-al-Malik to mediate (1004) in a dispute between Count Sancho García of Castile and Alfonso's tutor, Menendo González. In 1005, supported by the Castilian count, the army of the Córdoban dictator penetrated far into northern León. The latter's death (1007) and the political troubles which continued until the fall of the caliphate (1031) relieved León of Islamic pressure, but Alfonso was soon faced by the growing power of Sancho III of Pamplona (Navarre). His marriage (1024) to Sancho's daughter Urraca ended this threat, and, in the last years of his life, he was able to undertake the reconquest of the Portuguese territories lost during Almanzor's time. He was killed at the siege of Viseu. Lack of adequate sources makes it difficult to interpret Alfonso's character and reign; emergence from subordination to Córdoba seems to have been made possible more by events there than by Leonese military recovery.

Alfonso VI (*c.* 1042–1109), king of León from 1065 and of Castile from 1072, was an outstanding personality among medieval Spanish kings. His vision and generalship at last established Christian hegemony in the peninsula. During his reign the isolation from the rest of Europe which had so far characterized the history of León and Castile was abandoned, though not until he had hesitatingly tried the possibility of setting up, under Christian political direction, a mixed Christian and Muslim state. Alfonso was the second son of Ferdinand I. The latter, who died in 1065, partitioned his realm, allotting León to Alfonso, whose elder brother, Sancho of Castile, regarded this as an affront and deposed him by force. Alfonso took refuge at the court of Yahia I, king of Toledo—an experience which gave him expert knowledge of His-pano–Moorish politics. Sancho's death at Zamora (1072) made Alfonso king of León and Castile. By 1077 he had assumed the title *imperator totius Hispaniae* ("emperor of all Spain"), in which role the other Christian kings accepted him. From 1072 to 1086 his military genius dominated Spain, and Toledo, the former Visi-gothic capital, fell to him (1085). The Moorish kingdom of Saragossa was already under the tutelage of Rodrigo Díaz de Vivar, the Cid, so that the effective frontiers of Muslim Spain were now pushed south of the Tagus. Moreover, the petty kingdoms (*taifas*) of Moorish Andalusia were forced to recognize his suzerainty and pay him tribute. Alfonso was inclined to grant a wide degree of tolerance toward the religion and culture of his new Islamic subjects—his son and heir was the offspring of his liaison with the daughter of the Moorish king of Seville—but this attitude was frustrated by the antagonism of the French

Cluniac monks, whom the emperor had brought into Spain to reform the Spanish church. Led by Bernard, archbishop of Toledo, these refused to allow toleration and insisted on liturgical and other reforms calculated to approximate Spanish religious life and attitudes more closely to those of the rest of Europe. Alfonso also committed the political error of putting too much financial pressure on the *taifa* kingdoms. These, in consequence, asked the Almoravid amir of north Africa to come to their aid. In 1086 Alfonso was routed at Sagrajas by an army of fanatical African tribesmen and the rest of his reign became a desperate struggle to survive a series of similar defeats. He was probably saved by the tendency of Almoravid armies to disintegrate when victory had been won, and by their rulers' political incompetence. Only in the east did defeat come to the Almoravids when the Cid captured Valencia (1094). In a new defeat at Uclés (1108) the emperor's heir was killed. It was characteristic of his indomitable spirit that he at once arranged for his daughter, Urraca, to marry Alfonso I of Aragon so that the battle against the Almoravids should be competently continued after his death, even if it meant that León and Castile would be ruled by an Aragonese prince.

Alfonso VI was long remembered for his success in establishing the rule of law throughout his dominions. Also very important for Spanish relations with northern Europe was the attention he gave to making the pilgrim road to Santiago both safe and easily passable. He died in Toledo on June 30, 1109.

Alfonso VII (*c.* 1104–1157), king of León and Castile from 1126 to 1157, was the son of Raymond of Burgundy and the grandson of Alfonso VI, whose imperial title he assumed. Though his reign saw the apogee of the imperial idea in medieval Spain and though he won notable victories against the Moors, he remains a somewhat hazy figure. His childhood was complicated by the struggle between his mother Urraca and her second husband, Alfonso I of Aragon, for control of Castile and León. Only on Urraca's death (1126) did his stepfather finally relinquish his claims. Alfonso was then formally accepted as emperor by the kings of Aragon and Pamplona (Navarre), by the count of Barcelona and by various Hispano-Moorish rulers. His capture of Almería (1147) from the Moors won him renown, as did other victories, but in the end these led to little expansion of territory. Almería was lost again in 1157 and Córdoba only remained in his hands for three years. In 1146 a new invasion of north African fanatics, the Almohads, began. Alfonso now allied himself with the Almoravids and devoted the rest of his life to a series of campaigns to check Almohad expansion in southern Spain. Despite the importance of the imperial idea at this time, peninsular fractionalist tendencies were by no means dormant. Alfonso was unable to prevent the establishment of Portugal as an independent kingdom (1140) and, in his will, he himself divided his realm between his two sons, Sancho III of Castile and Ferdinand II of León. This act finally destroyed the concept of empire in medieval Spain. Alfonso VII died in Fresnada in Aug. 1157.

Alfonso VIII (1155–1214), king of Castile from 1158 to 1214, was the son of Sancho III, whom he succeeded when 3 years old. His minority was troubled by internal strife and Navarrese intervention in Castilian affairs. In 1170 he married Eleanor (d. 1214), second daughter of King Henry II of England. His reign was characterized by a close alliance with Aragon and in 1179 he concluded the pact of Cazorla which settled the future line of demarcation between Castile and Aragon when the reconquest of Moorish Spain was completed. In 1188 Alfonso IX of León did homage to him—a dramatic demonstration of the fact that the ancient hegemony of León had now passed to Castile. The main task of Alfonso's reign was resistance to the Almohad invaders who, by 1172, had secured control over almost all the Moorish states. In 1195 they inflicted a great defeat on him at Alarcos while, in collusion with them, the kings of León and Navarre invaded Castile. Alfonso remained calm in this dangerous situation. Aided by Peter II of Aragon, he dealt with León and Navarre, forcing the king of León to marry his daughter and annexing Álava and Guipúzcoa from Navarre. In 1212, at Las Navas de Tolosa, he finally secured a great victory over the Almohad sultan which broke Almohad power in Spain. He died on Oct. 6, 1214.

ALFONSO IX (cousin of Alfonso VIII of Castile and numbered next to him as a junior member of the family) (1171–1230), king of León from 1188 to 1230, was a forceful personality who brought the restless nobles under firm control and favoured the power of the municipalities. His father was Ferdinand II of León. Alfonso IX was determined to recover Leonese territory lost to Castile and, despite the fact that he had done homage to Alfonso VIII, did not hesitate to ally himself with the Almohads to further this end. As a result, his kingdom was placed under papal interdiction and he was finally compelled to marry the Castilian king's eldest daughter. He refused, however, to join his father-in-law in the crusade against the Almohads in 1212 unless the lost lands were first restored by Castile. This was not done and the Leonese army was, therefore, absent from Las Navas de Tolosa. Nevertheless, operating on his own, Alfonso IX won important victories beyond the southern frontiers of León, taking Cáceres (1227) and Mérida and Badajoz (1230) from the Almohads. These victories opened the road for a future reconquest of Seville. He died at Villanueva de Sarria on Sept. 24, 1230.

ALFONSO X (1221–1284), "the Wise," king of Castile and León from 1252 to 1284, was "wise" as a patron of learning and literature but not as a politician. He was born at Burgos on Nov. 23, 1221, the eldest son of Ferdinand III. He was a farsighted lawmaker, as his great corpus of constitutional, civil and criminal law—the *Siete Partidas*—reveals, but his reign was inept. It was dominated by his costly and unpopular attempt to become German king and Holy Roman emperor. In 1257 he was actually elected German king, but the pope refused to accept the election and Alfonso fruitlessly pursued the matter for years. In 1275 his heir, Ferdinand (Fernando de La Cerda), died. According to the *Siete Partidas,* primogeniture had been established in the succession and the king recognized Ferdinand's son, Alfonso, as his successor. His own second son, Sancho, refused to accept this decision and, posing as the defender of the nobles against the crown, took up arms against his father, whose reign ended, with his death in Seville on April 4, 1284, in civil war. Despite these misfortunes he captured Cartagena and Cádiz from the Moors.

ALFONSO XI (1311–1350), king of Castile and León from 1312 to 1350, succeeded his father, Ferdinand IV, when he was only a year old. His minority was marked by violent strife between factions of nobles, but when he came of age (1325) he restored order with unprecedented vigour. He gave new powers to the municipalities and to the *cortes,* in exchange for their support against the nobles, and furthered the power of the crown by choosing officials without aristocratic affiliations. He then turned his attention to the Benemerín kings of north Africa, who had seized Gibraltar and routed the Castilian fleet at Algeciras (1340). He won, with the Portuguese, a great victory over the invaders at Río Salado (1340) and recaptured Algeciras (1344). On March 26, 1350, after promulgating important administrative and legal reforms in the ordinances of Alcalá de Henares (1348), he died of the plague while besieging Gibraltar. Alfonso was assiduously courted by both France and England, who wished for an alliance which would give them the support of his powerful fleet. He avoided committing himself to either party. Though a highly successful king, Alfonso left his heir, Pedro, an unfortunate legacy—his formidable mistress, Leonor de Guzmán, and a succession of ambitious and powerful bastard sons he had had by her.

(P. E. R.)

ALFONSO XII (1857–1885), king of Spain from 1874 to 1885, was born in Madrid on Nov. 28, 1857, the son of Isabella II. After his mother's deposition by the revolution of Sept. 1868, he accompanied her into exile, receiving his education at the Theresianum in Vienna, and at the Royal Military college, Sandhurst, in England. On June 25, 1870, Isabella abdicated her rights in his favour. Four years later (Dec. 29, 1874) Alfonso was proclaimed king of Spain by Gen. A. Martínez Campos at Sagunto. He landed in Barcelona on Jan. 9, 1875.

The two most urgent problems of the new reign, ending the Carlist war and drafting the constitution, were both settled in 1876; peace was also established in Cuba by the treaty of Zanjón (1878) and for most of Alfonso's reign Spain enjoyed an unaccustomed tranquillity. The pattern of political life was determined by Antonio Cánovas del Castillo (*q.v.*), prime minister from 1875 to 1881 and again from Jan. 1884. Alfonso XII, although politically inexperienced, showed himself to possess great natural tact and a sound judgment, which gave rise to hopes that the monarchy would not suffer if the democratic constitution enacted by Cánovas in 1876 was fully implemented in practice. Attempts made on the king's life (Oct. 1878 and Dec. 1879) and a military *pronunciamiento* against the regime (1883) were not indicative of any general discontent with the restored monarchy; on the contrary, Alfonso enjoyed considerable popularity. His early death, from tuberculosis, on Nov. 25, 1885, was therefore a disappointment to those who looked forward to a constitutional monarchy in Spain.

In Jan. 1878 Alfonso married María de las Mercedes, daughter of the duc de Montpensier, but she died six months later. He then married (Nov. 1879) a daughter of the archduke Charles Ferdinand, María Cristina, by whom he had two daughters and a son, born posthumously, who became king as Alfonso XIII.

ALFONSO XIII (1886–1941), king of Spain from 1886 to 1931, was born in Madrid on May 17, 1886, the posthumous son of Alfonso XII, and was immediately proclaimed king under the regency of his mother María Cristina. Alfonso proved a lively and intelligent boy, but was brought up by a doting mother in an ultraclerical and reactionary atmosphere. From an early age he reacted against the unexciting nature of court life and, encouraged in this by his military attachés, began his long-lasting attachment to the Spanish army. He began to rule in 1902 on his 16th birthday. (For details of the political history of his reign, *see* SPAIN: *The Later Bourbons, 1875–1931.*)

Alfonso was immediately seen to relish his position of authority. For a time the system, initiated by Antonio Cánovas del Castillo (*q.v.*) in 1876, of alternating Conservative and Liberal governments, based on "made" elections, continued, but the politicians depended upon the king for their ability to "make" elections and Alfonso began increasingly to intervene in politics. The result was instability—33 governments in Spain were formed between 1902 and 1923—and a steady discrediting of the parliamentary system. Inevitably some of this discredit was shared by the monarchy and the king's popularity began to decline. After the celebrated attempt on the life of Alfonso and his bride, Victoria Eugénie of Battenberg, on their wedding day (May 31, 1906), there was a constant succession of plots to assassinate the king. But at the same time, Alfonso's great personal courage in the face of these attacks won him considerable admiration.

After the failure of the government of Antonio Maura in 1909, the last hopes for the parliamentary regime seemed extinguished and the king's position grew more and more difficult. During World War I his conduct was irreproachable; he observed a scrupulous neutrality and rendered considerable services to humanitarian causes. In the postwar period he began to move toward a system of more personal rule and sought a means to rid himself of parliament. To this end the king intervened directly in the Moroccan war in 1921 with disastrous effect. A subsequent commission of inquiry placed the blame squarely on the king; a week before its report was due to be published, however, Alfonso was rescued from a humiliating situation by the *coup d'état* (Sept. 13, 1923) of Gen. Miguel Primo de Rivera (*q.v.*).

However, by directly associating himself with the overthrow of the parliamentary regime, the king linked his fortunes with those of the dictatorship and, when Primo de Rivera fell from power in Jan. 1930, the fall of the monarchy became a certainty. A temporary government under Gen. Dámaso Berenguer was brought in to attempt to save the king, and various expedients were tried by Alfonso to bring about a return to a constitutional regime without the risk of elections. Eventually he agreed to hold municipal elections (April 1931). The results, at least in the important towns, showed a landslide for the Republican parties. They demanded the king's abdication; the army withdrew its support and Alfonso, though refusing to abdicate, was forced to leave Spain (April 14, 1931).

He never returned in his lifetime, though Gen. Francisco Franco reinstated him as a Spanish citizen and, by a decree of April 24, 1939, restored his property which had been confiscated in 1932. He died in Rome on Feb. 28, 1941, and was buried there, in the church of S. Maria di Monserrato. On Jan. 15, 1941, he had abdicated his rights to his third son, Don Juan.

BIBLIOGRAPHY.—M. Fernández Almagro, *Historia del reinado de Alfonso XIII* (1933); R. Sencourt, *King Alfonso* (1942); Gerald Brenan, *The Spanish Labyrinth,* with full bibliography, 2nd ed. (1950).

ALFRED (AELFRED) THE GREAT (848 or 849–899), Anglo-Saxon king of Wessex (*q.v.*) from 871 to 899, was born at Wantage, the fifth son of King Aethelwulf and his wife Osburh. When Alfred was four or five his father sent him to Rome where Pope Leo IV stood sponsor to him at his confirmation and invested him with the honorary dignity of a Roman consul, in a ceremony misinterpreted as a kingly consecration by the writer of the *Anglo-Saxon Chronicle.* He went to Rome again in 855 with his father, who stayed there a year. Aethelwulf died in 858; his eldest son, Aethelstan, was already dead and the next sons, Aethelbald and Aethelberht, had short reigns. The fourth son, Aethelred I, succeeded in 865, the year of the great Danish invasion. The Danes were bought off from East Anglia and then destroyed the kings of Northumbria. King Aethelred and Alfred went to help King Burgred when the Danes invaded Mercia in 868, but the Danes avoided battle and the Mercians made peace. Late in 870 the Danes came to Reading in Wessex and nine battles were fought against them in the following year, although the *Chronicle* names only six. Ealdorman Aethelwulf defeated them at Englefield early in 871, but the king and Alfred failed to capture Reading four days later. Yet the English reassembled their forces in another four days and won the great battle at Ashdown on the Berkshire downs, where Alfred attacked the Danish earls while his brother, who was to oppose the division led by the Danish kings, was still attending divine service. One Danish king and five earls were killed and the Danes fled. A fortnight later, however, the king and Alfred were defeated at Basing and again two months later at a place called Merton (Meretun).

A great reinforcement joined the Danes at Reading and Aethelred died (soon after Easter 871). Alfred thus became king at a critical juncture. He was defeated at Wilton, and may at this time have fought some of the engagements unnamed in the *Chronicle.* The West Saxons then made peace; they may have purchased it, but the quality of their resistance explains their freedom from attack during the next few years. Alfred was not idle and he probably began at once to increase the fleet, as the surest defense for a long coast line. In 875 he went to sea with a fleet which repelled seven ships and captured one. The Danes marched across Wessex in 876, but Alfred surrounded them at Wareham, where they gave hostages and swore to leave Wessex; but they broke their oaths and occupied Exeter. Alfred pursued them and again they came to terms, the more readily because a storm had destroyed their fleet.

Early in Jan. 878 the Danes made a surprise attack, established themselves at Chippenham and almost conquered Wessex. Alfred withdrew to the Somerset marshes and harassed the enemy from a fort which he built at Athelney. In the seventh week after Easter he assembled a force from the surrounding shires, defeated the Danes at Edington in Wiltshire and besieged them in their stronghold for a fortnight until their king, Guthrum, promised to leave Wessex and to be baptized. This baptism took place at Aller on the river Parret, Alfred standing as sponsor, and Guthrum stayed 12 days with the king at Wedmore (Somerset), where the ceremony of the unbinding of the chrism took place and the details of the treaty were probably settled. This victory not only gave Alfred peace until 885 but ensured that the Danes never again overcame Wessex. In saving his own kingdom Alfred prevented England from becoming a Scandinavian country and retained a base from which the Danelaw (the area of Danish occupation) was later reconquered and Christianity re-established.

In 885 a Danish invasion of Kent was repelled and the next year Alfred occupied London and placed it under his future son-in-law Aethelred, ealdorman of the Mercians. As a result the English not under Danish rule, that is, those of southwest Mercia and perhaps those of Northumbria beyond the river Tyne, accepted Alfred's rule. The extant treaty between Alfred and Guthrum must be assigned to a date after this capture of London. Another large Danish force from the continent, which landed in Kent in 892, was constantly harried by the English and finally returned to France in 896 without gain, despite the support it had received from the Danes of East Anglia and Northumbria which caused Alfred to send an expedition as far as York in 896. Land and sea raids from these last two areas harassed Alfred in the years 896–899.

During his last years King Alfred reaped the benefits of his defensive measures. He reorganized the English levies to keep an army constantly in the field and established the burghal system to defend his kingdom with a ring of fortified centres, regularly maintained and garrisoned. Although this plan received inadequate support from Alfred's subjects and was not completed until his son's reign, the boroughs already built proved their value in the campaigns of 892–896. The reconquest of the Danelaw by his son Edward the Elder and daughter Aethelflaed after his death was probably planned by Alfred.

King Alfred's first biographer, Asser, a contemporary Welsh scholar, tells that the rulers of various parts of Wales sought Alfred's support against their rivals or against the Mercians. There was a Welsh contingent with the English forces in 893, and an entry in the Welsh annals mentions Englishmen in the army with which the Welsh king Anaraut raided a rival's territory in 894. There is evidence to support Asser's claim that Alfred's court was much visited by foreigners, and that he received letters and gifts from the patriarch of Jerusalem.

Alfred reorganized his finances and also the attendance of thegns (noble followers) at his court. He issued a code of laws after examining the legal principles implied in the book of *Exodus* and studying the codes of Aethelbert of Kent, Offa of Mercia (whose laws are lost) and Ine of Wessex. Many of his pronouncements are not found in earlier legislation; the more important defined the rights of sanctuary, regulated and limited the blood fued, and imposed penalties for breach of oath and pledge, stressing especially the enormity of treason to one's lord.

A decay of Latin scholarship in England had set in before the Danish invasions, and these accelerated it. To further his own studies and to raise the level of learning in his country by providing vernacular translations of "some books which may be most necessary for all men to know," Alfred first obtained help from Mercia, the western part of which had suffered little devastation. Thence came Waerferth, bishop of Worcester, Plegmund, who later became archbishop of Canterbury, and the priests Aethelstan and Werwulf. Then Alfred looked further afield. Asser probably first came to his court early in 886, and two continental helpers were Grimbald, of the monastery of St. Bertin at St. Omer, and John, a priest and monk from the land of the Old Saxons. According to Asser, on Nov. 11, 887, the king began to translate Latin and compile the lost "Handbook," apparently a collection of quotations. The first translation to be produced was Bishop Waerferth's version of the *Dialogues* of Pope Gregory the Great. The order of Alfred's translations is uncertain. They are Gregory's *Cura pastoralis,* a copy of which was sent to every see in his kingdom at a date not before 890; the *De consolatione philosophiae* of Boethius, which Alfred rendered entirely in prose, adding later a verse translation of the metrical portions; the *Historia adversus paganos* of Orosius, regarded as a textbook of universal history; and a free rendering of the *Soliloquies* of St. Augustine of Hippo, which was probably Alfred's last work. An Old English version of Bede's *Ecclesiastical History* was ascribed to Alfred a century later, but its vocabulary and syntax contain so many Mercian features that although it may have been planned by Alfred, it must mainly be the work of a Mercian writer. There is no evidence that Alfred had any hand in the writing of the *Anglo-Saxon Chronicle* (*q.v.*), but it is probable that the prose version of the Psalms in Old English in the Paris Psalter preserves part of the translation of the psalms attributed to him by writers after the Norman conquest. Although these works were translated as part of an educational scheme, there is no doubt that Alfred himself was keenly interested in their content, especially that of the Boethius and the *Soliloquies* of St. Augustine, and that he pondered deeply on the theological and philosophical problems which they raise.

Asser relates that Alfred caused children both of noble and of humble birth to be taught to read English and Latin at his court, and his preface to the *Cura pastoralis* outlined an education for the sons of all free men who could afford it; all were to learn to read English, and those destined for the church were to read Latin also. Alfred founded a nunnery at Shaftesbury and a monastery at Athelney, with John the Old Saxon as its abbot, but his attempt to revive monasticism received little support from his subjects.

Although Alfred's laws reveal a deep concern for the rights of the church, and Asser speaks of his generosity to it, the pope complained that he infringed its privileges. The reason for this complaint is unknown, but possibly Alfred refused to allow as much immunity as the church claimed from necessary defense works. The sources show him as a deeply religious man, who regarded the government of his kingdom as a divine charge.

Alfred died on Oct. 26, 899, and was buried at Winchester. Subsequent generations regarded him rightly as the saviour of his people from the Danes and as a lawgiver; many of his administrative reforms were permanent, and his books continued to be copied and read throughout the Anglo-Saxon period and beyond it. Many legends grew up about him, including the famous incident of his being reproved by a peasant woman for letting her cakes burn, which is recorded in the 11th century. The 12th-century *Proverbs of Alfred* calls him "darling of the English." There seems to have been a continuous oral tradition concerning him.

BIBLIOGRAPHY.—The main sources for Alfred's reign are the *Anglo-Saxon Chronicle;* Asser, *Life of King Alfred,* ed. by W. H. Stevenson (1959 reprint with chapter on recent work by D. Whitelock); *English Historical Documents,* vol. i, ed. by D. Whitelock, pp. 33 ff., 492, 501 ff., 810–820 (1955); F. L. Attenborough, *The Laws of the Earliest English Kings* (1922).

For his own works, see *King Alfred's West Saxon Version of Gregory's Pastoral Care* (1871) and *King Alfred's Orosius* (1883), both ed. by H. Sweet; *King Alfred's Old English Version of Boethius,* ed. by W. J. Sedgefield (text 1899, trans. 1900); *King Alfred's Old English Version of St. Augustine's Soliloquies,* ed. by H. L. Hargrove (text 1902, trans. 1904). The Old English version of Bede's *Ecclesiastical History* was edited by T. Miller (1890–98) and Waerferth's translation of Gregory's *Dialogues* by H. Hecht (1900).

Of biographies of Alfred, C. Plummer, *The Life and Times of Alfred the Great* (1902) and B. A. Lees, *Alfred the Great, the Truth Teller* (1915), still retain some value, but should be compared with F. M. Stenton, *Anglo-Saxon England,* 2nd ed. (1947) and *English Historical Documents,* vol. i. A popular account is given by E. S. Duckett, *Alfred the Great and his England* (1957).   (D. Wᴋ.)

ALFUR, a term applied to those people in the Celebes, Moluccas and other parts of the Lesser Sunda Islands who represent a transition-mixed type between the Malayan and the Papuan-Melanesian peoples of New Guinea. They are not a distinct cultural or physical type. The people in the Moluccas (Timor, Flores, Sumba, Ambon), who have often been called Alfur, according to Raymond Kennedy, are taller than the Malay, with features ranging from Mongoloid to the narrow faces and Semitic type of nose of the Papuan. *See also* HALMAHERA; ARU ISLANDS.

See R. Kennedy, *Islands and Peoples of the Indies* (1943); F. L. Cooley, "Ambonese Kin Groups," *Ethnology,* vol. 1 (1962).
                                                        (F.-C. CE.)

ALGAE include the pond scums of fresh water, the greenish stains on rocks and tree trunks, and the giant seaweeds of the oceans. They are primitive organisms claimed by botanists as plants and in part by zoologists as animals. Many of them superficially resemble higher plants but have no true leaves, stems, or roots, and no vascular system. Furthermore, while they may produce sex cells or gametes, they do so not in specialized sex organs as is the case in vascular plants.

Marine algae include all algae growing in the ocean and in brackish coastal waters. Freshwater algae include all nonmarine algae irrespective of whether they grow submerged in water or in habitats where they are not submerged. The distinction between marine and freshwater algae is ecologically sound because each of the approximately 18,000 species of algae normally is exclusively marine or exclusively freshwater. Taken together the marine and freshwater algae exhibit a diversity of form not found in any other group of plants, ranging from one-celled organisms as small as the largest bacteria through manifold colonial forms to simple or branched rows of cells (filaments) and onward to elaborate massive plants, such as the kelps, comparable in size with the flowering plants. As a general rule, freshwater algae are minute and can be distinguished from one another only with the help of a microscope. The great majority of species of marine algae are visible to the naked eye and readily recognizable when found growing or cast ashore on the beach.

While the algae form a reasonably cohesive group of primitive organisms, they are distinctive enough in technical details to be placed in several divisions, comparable to animal phyla: Chlorophyta (green algae); Euglenophyta (euglenoids); Pyrrophyta (cryptomonads and dinoflagellates); Chrysophyta (golden algae and diatoms); Phaeophyta (brown algae); Rhodophyta (red algae); and Cyanophyta (blue-green algae). Algologists (or phycologists) disagree over whether there should be as few algal divisions as five or as many as nine. Protozoologists recognize some of the motile flagellated forms as protozoa (*q.v.*)—especially the dinoflagellates, cryptomonads, chrysomonads, euglenoids, and volvocine flagellates. The nature of flagellar structure, bounding membranes, pigments, and reserve food materials speak convincingly (at least to botanists) of the plant affinities of these organisms. Some biologists prefer to group these lower organisms with bacteria, protozoa, and fungi in a separate kingdom, the Protista (*q.v.*). For this discussion, however, the algae are treated as plants and are arranged in the seven groups listed above.

GENERAL FEATURES

Significance in Nature.—Algae are invaluable in the economy of nature. In all but a few isolated cases they contain chlorophyll and are thus of great importance as primary producers of the food that ultimately sustains all aquatic animal life. The teeming marine planktonic algae, called the "grass of the sea," has been estimated to carry on about 90% of all the photosynthetic activity on earth. (For the significance of algae in aquatic food cycles *see* ECOLOGY; ANIMALS, DISTRIBUTION OF; and PLANKTON.)

Importance to Man.—Certain species of algae, especially the larger marine types, formerly constituted the basis of seaweed industries in Japan and China. For centuries sea coastal countries have harvested seaweed for local use as manure, medicine, and food, and for manufacture into many other products of industrial use. Since algae are common inhabitants of surface waters, they (especially some of the blue-greens, golden-browns, and dinoflagellates) often present a troublesome source of pollution in water supplies by producing disagreeable odours and "fishy" tastes and by clogging filtration machinery.

Several marine algae are used as food by man. The amount consumed in Europe and America is insignificant and is chiefly the utilization of the seaweed known as Irish moss in making blancmange and other puddings. In the orient, on the other hand, certain algae are highly esteemed as foodstuffs and are used both in the making of soups and as condiments. The most widely used for such purposes is the red alga *Porphyra.* Most of the *Porphyra* eaten in the orient comes from Japan. The yearly market value runs in the millions of dollars. Some is sold fresh, but most of it is sun-dried before reaching the consumer. The supply is obtained almost exclusively from plants cultivated on suitable tidelands. Kombu, a product made from various kelps, is one of the standard foods of Japan. Kelps harvested by fishermen are dried and then sent to manufacturers for conversion into kombu. The manufacturer boils the dried algae and then spreads them out in flat wooden presses where the whole mass is compressed, dried, and then shredded or powdered for the market.

There is great interest in the possibility that freshwater algae may be cultivated as a source of food for man and domestic animals. *Chlorella,* a one-celled green alga with spherical cells about 4/1,000 in. in diameter, has been used in studies on photosynthesis and mass cultivation. Its rate of multiplication is rapid, the increase per day in number of cells being about eightfold under the most favourable circumstances. Increase in number of cells may continue until there are about 1,000,000,000 cells per millilitre of liquid. *Chlorella* may be cultured in such a manner that the cells have either a high fat or a high protein content. The protein content may comprise more than 50% of the dry weight. Cultivation of *Chlorella* on a large scale out of doors involves many engineering problems. For one pilot plant it was estimated that when operated under optimum conditions the dry weight yield would be at the rate of 100 lb. per acre per day. This is at the rate of 17.5 tons per acre per year. The costs per pound of *Chlorella* for running pilot plants were so high that it was economically unprofitable.

The feasibility of using algae like *Chlorella* in a closed system like a space capsule has been proved with *Cebus* monkeys. *Chlorella pyrenoidosa* is especially promising since it is one of several one-celled algae that can be made into a palatable food for man. It could supply the needed oxygen for a spaceman and also utilize his waste products—expired carbon dioxide and urine and feces—as nutriment in which to grow. Such a system, however, presents special space and weight burdens that must be overcome before it proves practicable.

Products from marine algae have a wide variety of industrial uses. At one time kelps and rockweeds were of considerable importance as sources of potassium and iodine. The discovery of mineral deposits containing these elements has, however, made their recovery from algae unprofitable. Agar is a gelatinous substance obtained from the red alga *Gelidium* by a rather involved process of extraction. Most of the agar sold in world markets comes from Japan. The production of agar in the United States has increased significantly. The best-known use is that of a solidifying agent in media used in bacteriological cultures. It is also used as a stiffening agent in certain food products, as a sizing material, mucilage, and in clarifying liquids. The red algae *Chondrus crispus* and *Gigartina mamillosa,* both known as Irish moss or carrageen, are a source of a gelatinous substance widely used in industry. The algae are dried and bleached before being sold to manufacturers. Manufacturers use Irish moss as an agent that helps keep substances in suspension. Examples of this are various pharmaceutical preparations, especially hand lotions and chocolate milk, coating for photographic film, and paints. Irish moss is also used by brewers to clarify and to give body to beer. Alginates, salts of alginic acid, are jellylike substances obtained from the brown algae known as kelps. Alginic acid is used in the manufacture of rubber tires. Alginates sold in the United States are extracted from a giant kelp, *Macrocystis,* which grows in extensive stands along the coast of southern California. One widespread use of alginates is in the manufacture of ice cream. Alginates have also replaced the use of agar and of Irish moss in a considerable number of manufactured products.

The value of diatoms is treated in the articles DIATOMS and DIATOMACEOUS EARTH.

DISTRIBUTION AND OCCURRENCE

Freshwater Algae.—Many species of freshwater algae are found in all parts of the world, from the tropics to the polar regions, and in a variety of habitats. Other species are restricted to particular habitats, but even these may be found at stations thousands of miles apart.

Some of the freshwater algae, such as *Trentepohlia* and *Pithophora,* are more abundant in the tropics than in temperate regions, and a few genera are never found in colder regions. The best known of the latter are *Cephaleuros,* a green alga parasitic on leaves of several flowering plants, and *Compsopogon,* a red alga found in the southern part of the United States, the West Indies, Central America, and the Indian subcontinent.

The only group of freshwater algae in which there is striking evidence of geographical variation is that of the desmids (fig. 1E–F, G). A specialist shown a collection rich in species of desmids, but not told the source of the collection, would be able to tell whether it came from Europe, Australia, the Indo-Malay region, or the Americas.

Aquatic Types.—These include all algae growing permanently submerged and either attached (benthic) or free-floating (planktonic). Filamentous grass-green and blue-green algae predominate in the benthos and they grow attached to stones, twigs, aquatic seed plants, or other algae. The chief habitats of benthonic algae are flowing waters, ponds and lakes, pools and ditches, and bogs and swamps. Each of the foregoing types of habitat has characteristic species but the composition varies from lake to lake and from bog to bog.

Members of the plankton are chiefly unicellular or nonfilamentous colonial algae and are found in lakes, ponds, or slowly flowing streams. Many of the planktonic algae are structurally adapted to a free-floating life. Examples of this are the algae in which the colony is a flat plate (e.g., *Pediastrum,* fig. 1D; *Merismopedia,* fig. 4G), or as in *Golenkinia,* the cell bears numerous bristles. As a general rule, soft-water lakes are rich in numbers of species but the total number of individuals is small. The reverse condition is true of hard-water lakes. Here certain blue-green algae may suddenly become so numerous as to make "pea soup" of the water and cause what is known as "water bloom." Diatoms, blue-green algae, and grass-green algae predominate in the plankton; golden-brown algae and dinoflagellates are present in smaller numbers.

Aerial and Terrestrial Types.—Aerial algae are frequently defined as algae that obtain their water wholly or in large part from moisture in the air. However, it is difficult to draw precise limits between aerial algae that obtain all their water from moisture in the air and terrestrial algae that obtain their moisture partly from air and partly from groundwater. The primary feature distinguishing aerial from aquatic algae is their ability to endure drought without entering upon special resting stages; this, in turn, depends more upon the water-retaining capacity than upon the water-absorbing capacity of the cells. Strictly aerial algae are found on the bark and leaves of trees, woodwork, stones, and rocky cliffs. A familiar example is the greenish incrustation of *Protococcus* on the shaded (usually north) side of tree trunks, a growth popularly referred to as "moss." Aerial algae are more abundant in tropical than in temperate regions, and in humid tropical areas filamentous grass-green and blue-green algae form a felty coating on almost every stone and tree trunk.

Soil-inhabiting algae are more nearly aerial than aquatic, but all of them obtain a part of their moisture from the groundwater. Terrestrial algae may grow on the surface of the soil or a few feet below the surface. Those growing at the soil's surface may form a powdery or felty encrustation (e.g., *Vaucheria*) an acre or more in extent. Grass-green and blue-green algae predominate in this flora, and the particular species present at any given locality are in large part dependent upon the soil's texture and chemical composition.

The length of time that soil algae can withstand desiccation is remarkable; some are able to resume growth after being dry for more than 50 years. Terrestrial algae play an important role in the colonization of bare surface by plants. They aid in preventing erosion of exposed surfaces, their decay affords the first available supply of humus, and they afford a moisture-retaining substratum for spores and seeds of more advanced plants.

Forms of Unusual Habitats.—There is a surprisingly long list of algae restricted to unusual environmental conditions or to particular substrata. Certain of them are adapted to extraordinary conditions of temperature. *Chlamydomonas* grows in the snow and ice of polar regions or of high mountain peaks. These algae are found both in regions of perpetual snow and in snow fields at the top of mountains where the snow melts every summer. Most of them are grass-green algae and they may be present in sufficient abundance to colour the snow. This colour is usually red because practically all snow-inhabiting green algae have their chlorophyll masked by a red pigment (haematochrome). The algae growing in hot springs are in an environment directly antithetical to that of snow algae. Such algae are found in various parts of the world including Iceland, New Zealand, and the United States. The best known and most spectacular of all hot springs are those in Yellowstone National Park. Here algae have been found grow-

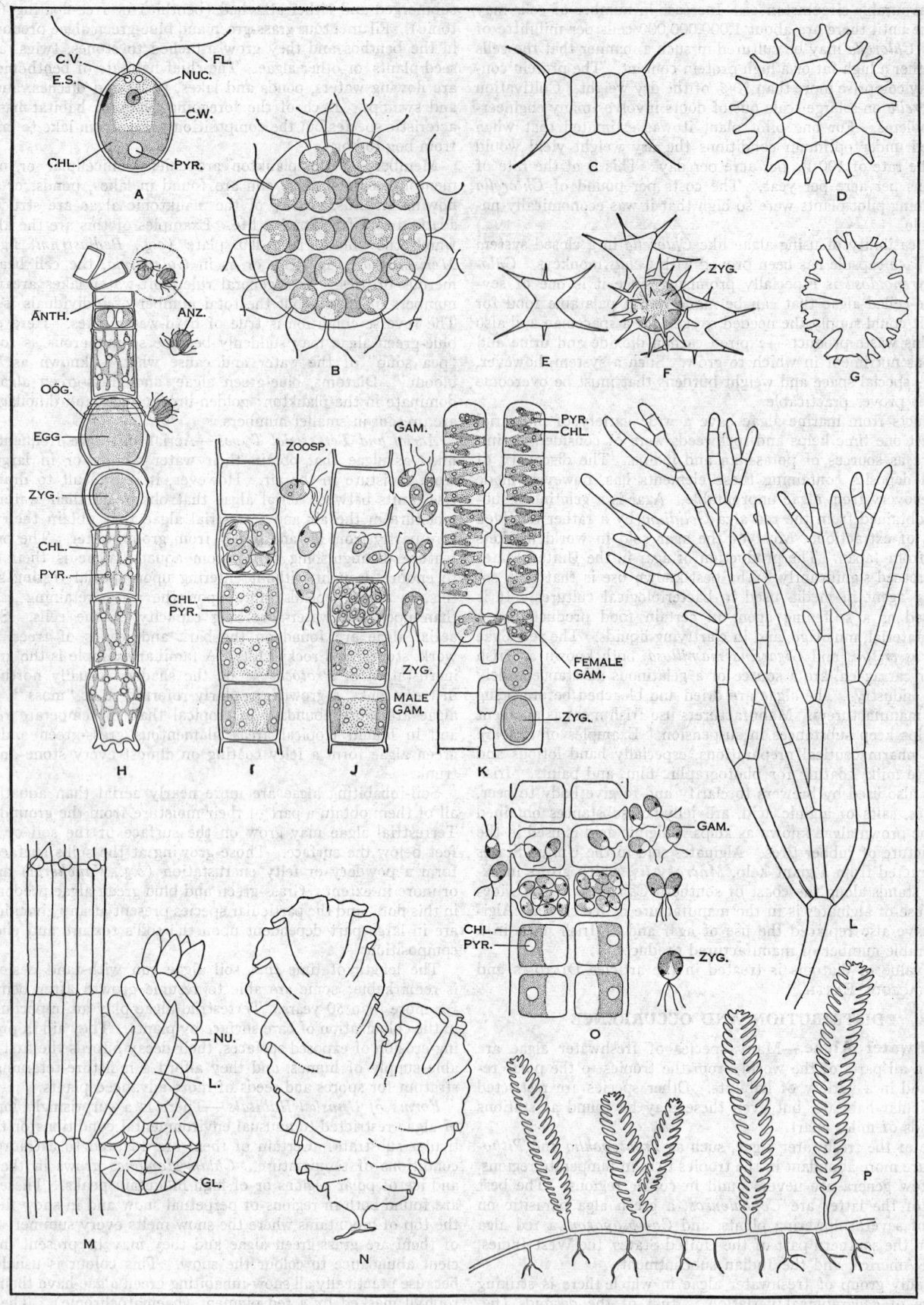

FIG. 1.—GRASS-GREEN ALGAE

A, Chlamydomonas; B, Eudorina; C, Scenedesmus; D, Pediastrum; E-F, Staurastrum; G, Micrasterias; H, Oedogonium; I-J, Ulothrix; K, Spirogyra; L, Cladophora; M, Chara; N-O, Ulva; P, Caulerpa. Anth., antheridium; Anz., antherozoid; Chl. chloroplast; C.V., con-tractile vacuole; C.W., cell wall; E.S., eye spot; Fl., flagellum; Gam., gamete; Gl., globule; L., "leaf"; Nu., nucule; Nuc., nucleus; Oög., Oögonium; Pyr., pyrenoid; Zoosp., zoospore; Zyg., zygote. All except N and P highly magnified

ing and multiplying in water as hot as 85.2° C (about 186° F). With a few exceptions all of the hundred or more algae recorded from hot springs are blue-greens.

The "brine lakes" found in arid regions of the United States and other countries represent another unusual type of environment with a distinctive algal flora. Most of the species in these lakes belong to the grass-green algae and, strange as it may seem, algae closely related to them are found in fresh waters instead of in the ocean. The ability of these algae to live in a salt solution 2 to 15 times stronger than that in the ocean seems to rest upon a different permeability to salts as compared with that of other freshwater or marine algae.

There are many freshwater algae found only in association with specific plants or animals. Most of the animals bearing particular algae live in or about the water but a few strictly land animals regularly harbour algae. The most striking of the latter is the three-toed sloth, which bears a *Protococcus*-like alga among its hairs, imparting a distinctly greenish coloration. Algae associated with aquatic animals may grow upon the surface of them, as is true of the filamentous green alga (*Basicladia*) found only on the backs of turtles; or the alga may grow within the tissues of the animal, as is the case with the unicellular green alga (*Chlorella*) found within *Hydra*. Algae associated with specific plants may likewise grow upon their surfaces or within their tissues. Those growing within tissues may be space endophytes or true parasites. The *Nostoc* growing within the liverwort *Anthoceros* is an example of a space endophyte. The best known of the parasites is *Cephaleuros,* which at times causes serious damage to certain cultivated tropical plants, notably tea and pepper.

Marine Algae.—The marine algal flora differs from the freshwater flora in that more than 95% of the benthic species are red or brown algae. Red algae predominate in warmer waters of the oceans, brown algae in the colder waters. Each ocean has its distinctive flora and a very large percentage of the species in any one of the oceans is not found in other oceans. Of the algae found along the shores of the United States less than 10% are found along both the Atlantic and the Pacific coasts. There is also a rather definite geographical distribution of species of a particular ocean and this distribution is correlated with average water temperatures during the warmest month of the year. When this temperature difference between two portions of the shore is 5° C (10° F) there are marked differences in composition of the flora. On the Pacific coast of North America the differences in temperature produce four distinct flora: the boreal, extending from Alaska to Puget Sound; the temperate, extending from Puget Sound to Point Conception, California; the subtropical, extending from Point Conception to Magdalena Bay, Mexico; and the tropical, extending from Magdalena Bay to the Isthmus of Panama.

At a given place along the shore of any ocean there is a distinct vertical distribution of benthic algae, especially of those growing between the high tide and low tide levels. The number of species growing at or just below high tide level is small because relatively few marine algae are able to withstand the periodic severe wilting produced by several hours exposure to air. The number of species increases progressively to extreme low tide level because of the progressive shortening of the period of intertidal exposure. Other factors, especially penetration of water by sunlight, affect the vertical distribution. The maximum depth at which algae grow is primarily dependent upon penetration of light into the water. In high latitudes the lowest depth at which algae occur is 105–180 ft. In tropical and subtropical seas, where the sun's rays are more nearly vertical, algae can grow at a depth of 300–600 ft. There is some evidence that certain algae grow at even greater depths, far deeper than the 1,000 ft. to which light penetrates. These forms are assumed to utilize the "rain" of decomposing matter from the lighted levels.

Plankton algae of the ocean are either diatoms or dinoflagellates but the number of strictly planktonic species is large. Most species are restricted to a single ocean and in many cases the distribution within an ocean is quite definite.

FORM AND FUNCTION

Cell Structure.—Cells of all algae except the blue-greens are essentially like those of more advanced plants. There is a distinct wall, and the protoplasm within the wall is differentiated into cytoplasm and nucleus. The chlorophyll and other pigments that give different algae their distinctive colours are localized in chromatophores of distinctive size and shape from genus to genus. The chromatophores that bear chlorophyll are called chloroplasts; they usually lie in the portion of the cytoplasm just within the cell wall (fig. 1A; 1H; 1I) but they may lie at the centre of the cell. Chromatophores of grass-green algae contain one or more rounded bodies, the pyrenoids (fig. 1A; 1H), which are concerned with the formation of platelets of starch.

Plant Body.—The simplest algae are one celled. The most primitive of these have threadlike extrusions (flagella) protruding through the cell wall. Flagella (fig. 1A) are motile organs that, by lashing backward and forward, propel the cell through the water. Nonmotile unicellular algae are usually of microscopic size and globose or angular. Certain unicellular algae are of macroscopic size and variously branched. The most highly differentiated of all macroscopic unicellular algae is *Caulerpa* (fig. 1P), and alga differentiated into leaf-, stem-, and rootlike branches superficially resembling the leaf, stem, and root of a seed plant.

When the plant body is composed of more than one cell, the cells may not have a definite orientation with respect to one another (*Gloeocapsa*) or they may be joined end to end in branched or unbranched filaments (*Ulothrix*, fig. 1I; *Ectocarpus*, fig. 2E). Branched filamentous algae may have the various branches free from one another, or have them compacted to form a plant body of characteristic macroscopic form. The great majority of red algae (*e.g., Chondrus,* fig. 4A) are of the compacted type; the plant body thus formed may be a foot or more in height. The largest and most complex plant bodies among algae are those of the kelps. These brown algae have a rootlike holdfast, a stemlike stalk (stipe), and one or more leaflike blades. Kelps of the Atlantic Ocean are rarely more than 5 ft. tall, but certain kelps found along the Pacific coast of North America and in the Antarctic Ocean attain a length of more than 100 ft. Kelps also have the highest differentiation of tissues found in any algae. Here the blades, stipe, and branches of the holdfast are internally differentiated into cortex and medulla. The cortex is composed of approximately cubical cells with chromatophores; the medulla is composed of colourless interwoven filaments. In a few genera, as *Nereocystis* and *Macrocystis,* certain of the filaments develop into sieve tubes similar to those found in flowering plants.

Reproduction.—Algae may multiply vegetatively by fragmenting into two or more parts, but in most cases they reproduce asexually by means of spores formed within and liberated from ordinary vegetative cells or from special cells (sporangia). Spores of red algae are of types peculiar to that group (*see* below); those produced by other algae are either flagellated self-propelling zoospores or nonflagellated passively transported aplanospores. Zoospores and aplanospores may be formed singly, in multiples of two, or in indefinite numbers within a cell or a sporangium. Liberation of the spores may be by rupture or gelatinization of the surrounding wall, or through a pore in the wall.

Sexual reproduction is effected by a fusion in pairs of gametes produced within ordinary vegetative cells or within special modified cells (gametangia). Sexual reproduction is of frequent occurrence among grass-green, brown, and red algae; it occurs very infrequently among yellow-green and golden-brown algae; and apparently not at all among blue-green algae. The most primitive type of gametic union is where both gametes of a fusing pair are motile and of equal size (fig. 1J). More advanced than such an isogamous union of gametes is that where both are motile but one small and active, the other large and sluggish. In such an anisogamous union of gametes the smaller gamete is male and the larger is female. Anisogamy, in turn, leads to the condition of oögamy, in which there is union of a small flagellated male gamete (antherozoid) with a large nonflagellated immobile gamete (egg) (fig. 1H). In oögamous algae the male gametangium

FIG. 2.—A-D, YELLOW-GREEN ALGAE; E-P, BROWN ALGAE

A, Chlorochromonas; B, Tribonema; C, Botrydium; D, Ophiocytium; E-G, Ectocarpus; H, Sphacelaria; I-J, Desmarestia; K-M, Laminaria, K, female gametophyte, L, male gametophyte, M, sporophyte; N, Postelsia; O, Nereocystis; P, Alaria. Anth., antheridium; Anz., anthero-zoid; Chr., chromatophore; Fl., flagellum; Gam., gametangium; Oög., oögonium; Un. S., unicellular sporangium; Zoosp., zoospore. All except J and M-P highly magnified

(antheridium) is usually much smaller than the female gametangium (oögonium) (fig. 1H). Antherozoids of oögamous algae may swim into the oögonium and unite with the egg or eggs within it; or the eggs may be discharged from an oögonium and the antherozoids swim to and unite with the eggs floating passively in the water.

Fusing gametes (whether isogamous, anisogamous, or oögamous) are devoid of a membrane but the resultant zygote soon secretes a wall. In most grass-green algae the zygote enters upon a dormant period and secretes a thick wall; in a few grass-green algae and in all brown algae there is no dormant period and the wall is always thin. A feature of deeper significance in the formation of a zygote is the union into a single nucleus of the two nuclei derived from the two gametes.

Life Cycle.—All plants more advanced than algae have a life cycle with two distinct phases or generations, a sexual (gametophytic) generation and an asexual (sporophytic) generation follow one another in alternate succession. Sexually reproducing algae may or may not have such an alternation of generations, depending on whether there is a reduction division (halving the chromosome number) of the zygote nucleus.

Zygotes of most grass-green algae secrete a thick wall and do not germinate until they have undergone a ripening period lasting weeks or months. All such algae have a reduction division of the zygote nucleus and, consequently, the development of a gamete-producing generation (gametophyte) when the zygote germinates. The life cycle of these algae consists of a succession of gametophytic generations with a one-celled phase, the zygote, intervening between successive generations. Many algae with this type of a life cycle have the gametophyte also producing zoospores or aplanospores. This results in a life cycle in which there is a reduplication of the gametophytic generation and not one in which there is an alternation of gametophytic and sporophytic generations.

A few grass-green algae and all brown algae except Fucales have an immediate germination of the zygote, no reduction division of the zygote nucleus, and the production of a generation in which each cell has the same number of chromosomes as a zygote. This generation is strictly asexual (sporophytic) and there is a reduction division of nuclei in the cells producing zoospores or aplanospores. These spores develop into sexual (gametophytic) plants. In these algae with an alternation of generations in the life cycle the two generations may be identical in size, shape, and vegetative structure, or the two may be markedly unlike. Certain algae (as *Dictyota* and *Laminaria*) have the two alternating generations following each other in regular sequence; other algae (as *Ectocarpus*) may have the regular alternation interrupted by a reduplication of either the sporophytic or gametophytic generations.

All red algae except Bangiales have an alternation of generations; Bangiales may have three generations in the life cycle, one gametophytic, the other two sporophytic.

SURVEY AND CLASSIFICATION

Green Algae (Chlorophyta).—Chromatophores of Chlorophyta are green with the same pigments as vascular plants. The chief food reserve is starch. All flagella of a motile reproductive cell are the same length and the number of flagella is two to eight. There are two classes: the Chlorophyceae (grass-green algae) and the Charophyceae (stoneworts).

Chlorophyceae.—The plant body of members of the Chlorophyceae never grows by means of an apical cell and the reproductive organs are always one-celled and without a sheath of vegetative cells. There are approximately 350 genera and 5,500 species of Chlorophyceae. Arrangement of the genera in major groups (orders) is primarily on the basis of cell structure, organization of the plant body, and structure of reproductive cells.

The most primitive order (Volvocales) includes all Chlorophyceae with motile vegetative cells. Most genera are freshwater and either unicellular (*Chlamydomonas,* fig. 1A) or colonial. The number of cells in a colony is a multiple of two and usually less than 128 (as in *Eudorina,* fig. 1B) but in *Volvox* it may be several thousand. Colonies with a small number of cells have all cells fertile; those with a large number of cells have reproduction restricted to a few greatly enlarged cells.

Somewhat advanced over the Volvocales are the Tetrasporales in which the cells are irregularly distributed through a colourless jelly. Vegetative cells of Tetrasporales may develop flagella at any time and temporarily live in the manner of a *Chlamydomonas* cell. The number of species in the order is about 100 and most of them are found in fresh waters.

Members of the Ulotrichales have uninucleate cells with a single band-shaped chromatophore and the cells are united end to end in filaments. There are approximately 80 genera and 450 species. Most genera are exclusively freshwater; a few are exclusively marine or have both marine and freshwater species. The filaments may be unbranched, as in *Ulothrix* (fig. 1I), or branched. Genera with branched filaments may have the branches standing free from one another (*Stigeoclonium*) or laterally compacted to form a solid disk (*Coleochaete*). A considerable number of genera are of microscopic size and epiphytic on coarse filamentous freshwater algae or endophytic within tissues of marine algae.

Ulvales have cells resembling those of Ulotrichales but have the cells laterally adjoined in flat sheets or in hollow tubes. The plant body is macroscopic and often several inches tall. There are approximately 100 species and the majority of them are strictly marine. Two genera, *Ulva* (fig. 1N; 1O) and *Enteromorpha,* are abundant in all oceans. These two genera have an alternation of generations; certain other genera (as *Monostroma*) do not have this type of life cycle.

The Schizogoniales include three genera in which the plant body is either filamentous or sheetlike. These genera differ from other Chlorophyceae in structure of chromatophore, and in reproducing exclusively asexually by aplanospores. *Prasiola,* the most widely distributed genus, usually grows only where the substratum is rich in soluble nitrogenous compounds; marine species of the genus are restricted to the high tide level of rocks covered with droppings from sea birds.

The Cladophorales have cylindrical multinucleate cells joined end to end in branched or unbranched filaments. The most widely distributed of the dozen genera is *Cladophora* (fig. 1L), a genus with more than 150 species. It is one of the branched algae and is common in both fresh and salt waters.

Oedogoniales are exclusively freshwater and are the only filamentous Chlorophyceae in which flagella of zoospores are numerous and arranged in a ring near one end. Sexual reproduction is oögamous and the antherozoids resemble the zoospores. There are 3 genera and approximately 350 species. *Oedogonium* (fig 1H), the genus with the largest number of species, is one of the commonest filamentous algae of pools and ditches.

Zygnematales are the only green algae in which sexual reproduction is by a union of two amoeboid gametes. In some genera this is by establishment of a tube connecting two cells (fig. 1K). The order includes approximately 40 genera and 3,000 species, all freshwater and a large majority strictly aquatic. Some genera have the cells permanently united in unbranched filaments; other genera are unicellular or have the cells only temporarily united in filaments. *Spirogyra* (fig. 1K), the most widely distributed genus of all freshwater algae, is representative of the permanently filamentous genera. The unicellular genera have cells constricted into two symmetrical halves (*Staurastrum,* fig. 1E; 1F; *Micrasterias,* fig. 1G). These algae, the desmids, have long been favourites of microscopists because of their symmetrical shapes.

Chlorococcales have approximately isodiametric cells that do not divide vegetatively and are algae in which an increase in number of cells is brought about by production of spores or gametes. The order is a large one and most of the species are freshwater. Some genera, as *Chlorella* and *Golenkinia,* are unicellular; other genera (*Scenedesmus,* fig. 1C; *Pediastrum,* fig. 1D) have the cells united in nonfilamentous colonies in which there is no increase in number of cells once a colony has been formed.

The Siphonales are unicellular, multinucleate branched tubes capable of indefinite elongation. Most of the 50 genera are marine and found in tropical or subtropical seas. Many marine Siphonales

FIG. 3.—A-I, BROWN ALGAE; J-N, RED ALGAE

A-C, Dictyota, A, thallus, B, section of gametophyte, C, section of
sporophyte; D-H, Fucus, D, thallus, E, antheridium, F, section through
conceptacle, G, liberation of eggs, H, fertilization; I, Sargassum; J-K,
Nemalion, J, thallus, K, section of thallus; L-N, Agardhiella, L, female
gametophyte, M, section through sporophyte, N, section through female
gametophyte. A.C., auxiliary cell; Anth., antheridium; Anz., antherozoid; Apl., aplanospore; Conc., conceptacle; Cpgn., carpogonium;
Cps., carposporangium; Gon., gonimoblast; Oöbl., oöblast; Oög.,
oögonium; Sp., sporangium; Spg., spermatangium; Spm., spermatium;
Tr., trichogyne; Ts., tetraspore; Tsp., tetrasporangium. All except
A, D, I-J, and L highly magnified

are of macroscopic size, freely branched, with the branches of different shape and free from one another (*Caulerpa*, fig. 1P), or with the branches alike and densely interwoven (*Penicillus*, *Codium*). Reproduction of many Siphonales is exclusively sexual and frequently anisogamous.

The Siphonocladales have multicellular thalli attached by a system of rhizoids. The cells are multinucleate and divide in a unique manner. There are about 18 genera and 150 species; all marine and usually restricted to warm seas.

The Dasycladales have an erect central axis bearing whorls of branches from top to bottom or only at the upper end. Some of the order are known only as fossils. Seven genera have living species. These are all marine and found only in warm seas.

Charophyceae.—The Charophyceae (stoneworts) have a multicellular plant body differentiated into nodes and internodes, and one in which terminal growth is initiated by an apical cell. The sex organs (antheridia and oögonia) are surrounded by envelopes of sterile cells. There is but one order, the Charales. Some genera are known only as fossils. The 6 genera with 200 living species grow submerged in fresh or brackish waters.

The plant body consists of a slender cylindrical axis bearing whorls of short branches ("leaves") separated at regular intervals by relatively long internodes. The plant surface is frequently encrusted with lime, hence the popular name stonewort.

Asexual reproduction is exclusively vegetative and usually by a shedding of special reproductive branches. Sexual organs are produced one above the other at the nodes, as in *Chara* (fig. 1M). The oögonium with its covering of 5 spirally twisted cells crowned by 5 or 10 small cells comprises the nucule. The antheridia are united in a branching filament and several antheridial filaments are surrounded by a globose envelope composed of 8 shield-shaped cells. The mass of antheridial filaments and the envelope surrounding them jointly constitute the globule. When the globule is mature the shield cells separate from one another and the antherozoids escape from the exposed antheridial filaments. They swim down through the apex of the nucule and unite with the egg. The zygote formed within the nucule develops a thick wall and ripens for several weeks before germinating to form a new plant.

Euglenoids (Euglenophyta).—The Euglenophyta have grass-green chromatophores with a pigmentation similar to that of Chlorophyta. The food reserves are either paramylum (an insoluble carbohydrate related to starch) or fats. Flagella differ from those of other major groups (divisions) in that they are inserted in a small interior chamber at the anterior end of a cell. Reproduction is by cell division but several genera are known to form thick-walled resting stages. Sexual reproduction is not definitely known for any species.

Euglenophyceae.—There is but one class, the Euglenophyceae, and most genera of this class are naked motile unicellular organisms similar to *Euglena* so frequently present in stagnant fresh waters. All genera with motile cells are placed in a single order, the Euglenales. One genus (*Colacium*) has nonflagellate cells organized in dendroid colonies similar to those of certain Tetrasporales. It is the sole member of the order Colaciales. (*See* also EUGLENA.)

Cryptomonads and Dinoflagellates (Pyrrophyta).—Members of this division are the only algae with yellowish to brownish chromatophores that store reserve foods as starch or starchlike compounds. Motile cells are biflagellate, usually with the flagella unequal in length and movement. The division has three classes (Cryptophyceae, Desmokonteae, Dinophyceae) primarily distinguishable by the structure of the flagella.

Cryptophyceae.—The Cryptophyceae (cryptomonads) include 12 genera: 10 unicellular and motile, and 2 with a colonial organization similar to that of *Tetraspora*. Cells of Cryptophyceae have one or two brownish-yellow chromatophores and granules of starch. Motile vegetative cells and zoospores are biflagellate with the two flagella alike except for slight differences in length. Some algologists exclude the Cryptophyceae from the Pyrrophyta and consider the class one of uncertain systematic position.

Desmokonteae.—Desmokonteae differ from other Pyrrophyta in having the cell wall vertically divided into two homogeneous halves (valves). Motile cells have two apically inserted flattened flagella that differ from each other in type of movement. All members of the class are rare organisms and most of them are marine.

Dinophyceae.—Cells of most Dinophyceae have numerous golden-brown to chocolate-brown chromatophores, but cells of certain species lack chromatophores. Motile cells and zoospores are encircled by a transverse groove—the girdle. The two flagella are inserted in or near the girdle; one of them encircles the girdle, the other extends vertically backward. The class includes about 120 genera and 950 species, almost all of which are marine and restricted to the plankton. Ninety percent of the genera are unicellular and motile; the remainder are either unicellular and immobile, or *Tetraspora*-like, or filamentous. Motile genera are placed in three orders: one (Gymnodiniales) without a wall, the other two (Peridiniales and Dinophysidales) with a wall and with one made up of a definite number of plates. The Peridiniales, as in *Glenodinium*, have a wall that is not longitudinally divided into two halves; the Dinophysidales have a wall longitudinally divided into two halves. Immobile genera have the cells regularly producing one or more *Gymnodinium*-like zoospores. According to organization of the plant body they are placed in the following orders: Dinocapsales, with nonflagellate cells irregularly distributed through a gelatinous matrix; Dinotrichales, with nonflagellate cells joined end to end in filaments; Dinococcales, with solitary nonflagellate sessile or free-floating cells. These three orders correspond, respectively, to the Tetrasporales, Ulotrichales, and Chlorococcales of the Chlorophyceae.

Golden Algae and Diatoms.—(Chrysophyta).—The Chrysophyta have yellowish-green to yellowish-brown chromatophores in which there is a preponderance of carotinoid pigments. The chief food reserves are leucosin (an insoluble carbohydrate of unknown composition) and oils. Cell walls are usually composed of two overlapping halves and are frequently impregnated with silica. Various types of spores are formed and sexual reproduction, when present, is usually by an isogamous fusion of zoogametes or aplanogametes. There are approximately 300 genera and 5,700 species, three-quarters of which are freshwater. The division has three classes—Xanthophyceae, Crysophyceae, and Bacillariophyceae.

Xanthophyceae.—The Xanthophyceae (Heterokontae), familiarly known as yellow-green algae, are almost exclusively freshwater. They have yellowish-green chromatophores and store foods as leucosin or as oils, never as starch. Motile stages are regularly biflagellate and with the two flagella markedly unequal in length (fig. 2A). Asexual reproduction by zoospores or aplanospores is of frequent occurrence; sexual reproduction very rarely occurs, and is definitely established for but few genera. Although the number of genera and species (about 75 and 200) is much smaller than in Chlorophyceae, the Xanthophyceae exhibit much the same range in form, and most orders of Chlorophyceae have their counterpart among the Xanthophyceae.

The nine genera with motile vegetative cells are placed in the Heterochloridales and all genera are unicellular. The Rhizochloridales with naked amoeboid cells united in colonies comprise an order without counterpart among the Chlorophyceae. All of the eight genera are exceedingly rare and most of them are freshwater. The Heterocapsales include a few rare freshwater genera with colonies similar to those of Tetrasporales. The Heterotrichales have cylindrical cells joined end to end in branched or unbranched filaments. *Tribonema* (fig. 2B), with unbranched filaments composed of cells surrounded by walls with two overlapping halves, is very common in freshwater pools during the spring months.

Similar to Chlorococcales, the Heterococcales have no vegetative cell division and are unicellular or with the cells united in nonfilamentous colonies. This is the largest order and all but a couple of the 45 genera are freshwater. *Ophiocytium* (fig. 2D) is the most frequently encountered genus of the order, but it is never found in abundance. The Heterosiphonales, an order corresponding to the Siphonales, have but three or four genera. *Vaucheria*, the commonest genus, is usually aquatic. It consists of a single, sparingly branched, tubular cell. *Botrydium* (fig. 2C),

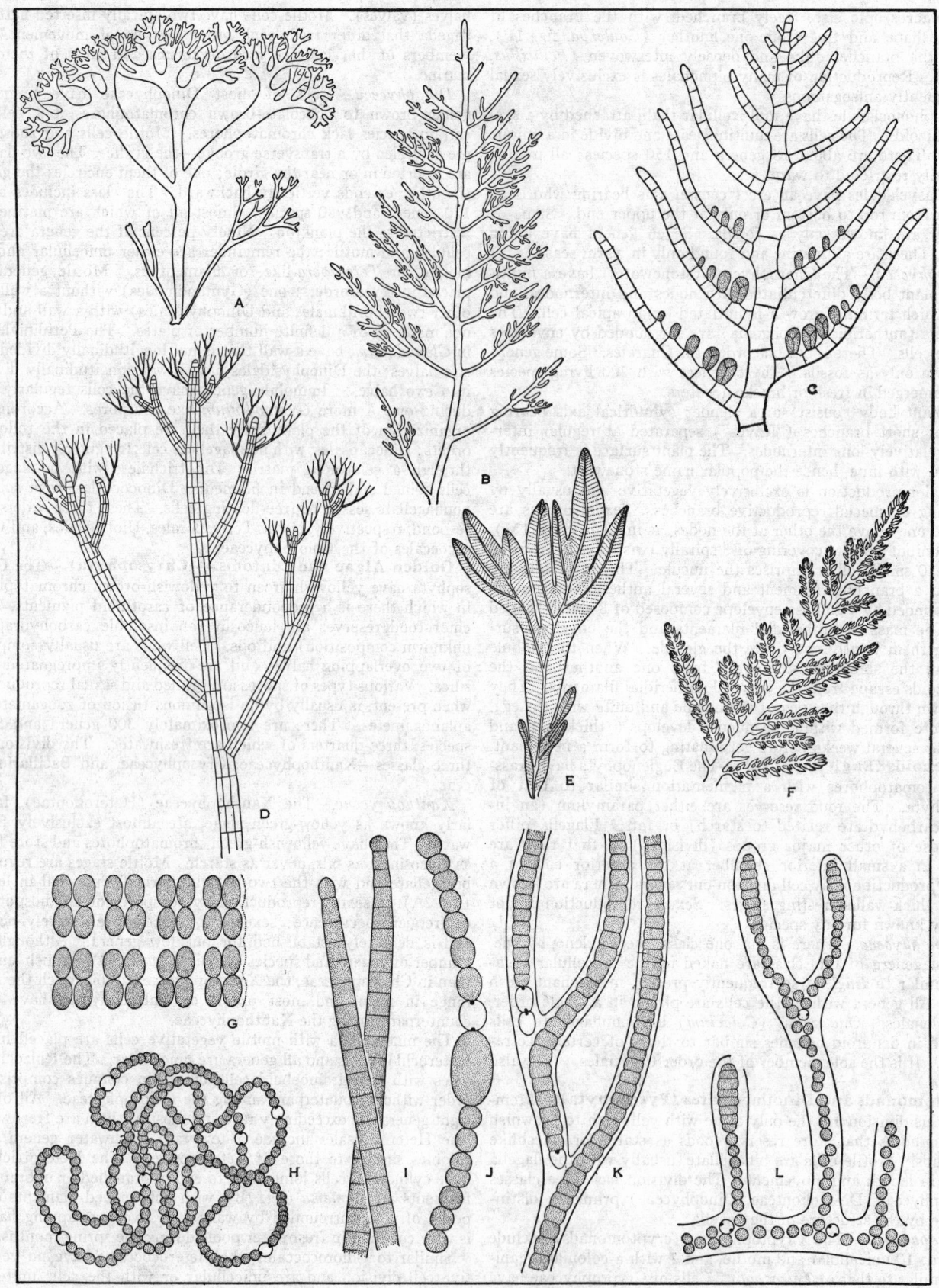

FIG. 4.—A–F, RED ALGAE; G–L, BLUE-GREEN ALGAE

A, Chondrus; B, Gelidium; C, Callithamnion; D, Polysiphonia;   latoria; J, Anabaena; K, Tolypothrix; L, Stigonema. All except
E, Membranoptera; F, Ptilota; G, Merismopedia; H, Nostoc; I, Oscil-   A–B and E–F highly magnified

the other common genus, is always terrestrial. The serial portion is spherical; the subterranean portion is tubular.

Chrysophyceae.—Typical Chrysophyceae have golden-brown chromatophores and a storage of reserve foods as leucosin or fats. They form a distinctive type of spore, the endospore. About half of the 70 genera belong to the Chrysomonadales, the only order in which the vegetative cells are motile. Cells of Chrysomonadales may be uni- or biflagellate and solitary or in colonies. The Rhizochrysidales have immobile amoeboid cells that may be naked or may have a wall-like envelope (lorica). All 12 genera of the order are freshwater; some are unicellular, others colonial. Members of the Chrysocapsales are colonial and with cells irregularly distributed through a colourless jelly as in Tetrasporales. There are ten genera, of which the most widely distributed is *Hydrurus*, an inhabitant of swiftly flowing coldwater streams.

The Chrysotrichales have cells united end to end in branched or unbranched filaments. Some of the branched genera have the branches standing free from one another; others, as *Thallochrysis*, have the branches laterally united. The five genera of the order are rare algae and are found in fresh water. The Chrysococcales correspond to the Chlorococcales of the Chlorophyceae. All six genera referred to the order are imperfectly known; and all, as *Chrysosphaera*, are found in fresh water.

Bacillariophyceae.—The Bacillariophyceae, or diatoms, have cell walls composed of two overlapping halves and a bilateral or radially symmetrical ornamentation of the wall. (*See* DIATOMS.)

Brown Algae (Phaeophyta).—Phaeophyta have chromatophores in which carotinoid pigments, chiefly fucoxanthin, predominate. The primary food reserve is a carbohydrate, laminarin, dissolved in the cell sap. Motile reproductive cells, whether zoospores or gametes, have two laterally inserted flagella of unequal length.

All but 3 of the 900 species are strictly marine. Brown algae predominate in the algal flora of colder seas, but certain brown algae, notably Dictyotales and *Sargassum*, are found only in tropical or subtropical waters. Marine Phaeophyta grow along rocky ocean shores and usually where the water is less than 50 ft. deep. All of the brown algae are multicellular and either filamentous or with a more complex plant body. In all except the Fucales there is an alternation of two free-living generations, but the gametophyte and sporophyte may be vegetatively similar. Gametophytes usually produce multicellular gametangia in which each cell contains a gamete but they may produce unicellular gametangia containing a single gamete. Gametic union ranges from isogamy to oögamy. The sporophyte produces unicellular sporangia containing spores in multiples of two (usually 64 or 128). In addition to unicellular sporangia, a sporophyte may also produce multicellular sporangia indistinguishable in appearance from gametangia. The reduction division of nuclei within a unicellular sporangium and the lack of this in a multicellular sporangium is of fundamental significance since it determines whether a plant growing from a spore is to be gametophytic or sporophytic.

The primary difference between the three classes of the Phaeophyta is in the life history. These differences are: alternation of similar generations in Isogeneratae; alternation of dissimilar generations in Heterogenerate; and lack of a gametophytic generation in the Cyclosporeae.

Isogeneratae.—The simplest Isogeneratae, the Ectocarpales, have a filamentous plant body. The type genus, *Ectocarpus* (fig. 2E–2G) is a common epiphyte on other marine algae. Its plant body is freely branched and it grows by division of cells a short distance back from each branch tip. The gametophyte produces multicellular gametangia and union of gametes may be isogamous or anisogamous. Sporophytes developing from a zygote typically produce unicellular sporangia and have the zoospores released from them developing into gametophytes. However, a sporophyte may also produce multicellular sporangia whose zoospores reduplicate the sporophytic generation.

Another one of the filamentous types are the Sphacelariales, which have a branched threadlike plant body with cells regularly arranged in transverse tiers. Growth of each branch is initiated by an apical cell (fig. 2H). Reproductive organs resemble those

of Ectocarpales and the life cycle is similar. The order has 15 genera and 175 species, most of which are restricted to the Atlantic Ocean. Tilopteridales have a freely branched plant body in which the lower portions are similar to *Sphacelaria* and the upper portions of the branches are *Ectocarpus*-like. The Cutleriales include two anomalous genera with filaments laterally compacted to form a blade- or disklike plant body. Gametophytes have multicellular gametangia borne in groups and gametic union is markedly anisogamous. Sporophytes produce unicellular sporangia only; hence there is a regular alternation of generations.

Members of the Dictyotales are branched ribbon- or fanlike algae (fig. 3A) with growth initiated by solitary or laterally adjoined apical cells. There are about 20 genera and 100 species. Dictyotales are the predominant brown algae of tropical seas and many of them grow in abundance. The gametophytes produce sex organs in patches (sori): female gametangia (oögonia) are one celled (fig. 3B) and the male gametangia (antheridia) are many celled. Unicellular sporangia of sporophytes are unique for brown algae both in the small number of spores (four or eight) and in the absence of flagella on the spores (fig. 3C).

Heterogeneratae.—Gametophytes of Heterogeneratae are always irregularly branched filaments; sporophytes may be filamentous, or of a modified filamentous construction, or nonfilamentous. Genera with a filamentous organization are placed in the subclass Haplostichineae; those with a nonfilamentous organization in the subclass Polystichineae. The Haplostichineae are grouped in three orders (Chordariales, Sporochnales, Desmarestiales) differing in organization of the sporophyte. Sporophytes of Chordariales and Sporochnales are obviously filamentous; those of Desmarestiales (fig. 2I; 2J) are obscurely so because the branches become covered with irregularly arranged cells. Gametophytes of Chordariales resemble irregularly branched gametophytes of *Ectocarpus;* those of the other two orders are oögamous and with both antheridia and oögonia, one celled.

The Polystichineae are also divided into three orders; two (Punctariales and Dictyosiphonales) without internal differentiation of tissues in the sporophyte; the third (Laminariales) with an internal differentiation of tissues. Sporophytes of Punctariales are of medium size and usually bladelike or saccate; those of Dictyosiphonales are profusely branched and threadlike. Sporophytes of Laminariales (kelps; fig. 2M) vary from 1 to more than 100 ft. in height. Most of the 30 genera of Laminariales are restricted to the North Pacific Ocean but certain genera, as *Laminaria* (fig. 2K-M), are found in all oceans. The sporophyte of *Laminaria*, which is rarely more than six feet tall, has a rootlike holdfast, a stemlike portion, and a single blade terminating the stem.

Many Pacific ocean kelps are notable for their complexity of external form and for their size. These "giant kelps" have numerous blades borne either at the apex of a branched stem (*Nereocystis,* fig. 2O) or at regular intervals along a branched stem (*Macrocystis*). Giant kelps grow where the water is 20–40 ft. deep and attain a length of 20–150 ft. Some are perennial; one is an annual that grows to a length of more than 100 ft. in a single season. Sporophytes of all kelps produce unicellular sporangia on the blade portion of the plant and have the sporangia grouped in sori. The gametophytes are microscopic irregularly branched filaments that rarely have more than 50 cells. Male gametophytes (fig. 2L) bear many antheridia, each containing a single antherozoid; female gametophytes (fig. 2K) have one to six oögonia, each containing a single egg.

Cyclosporeae.—The Cyclosporeae have a sporophytic plant body whose spores function as gametes instead of developing into gametophytes. Cyclosporeae differ from other brown algae in that the reproductive organs are borne in round cavities (conceptacles) within tips of the plant body. The single order, the Fucales, contains approximately 40 genera and 350 species. Fucales are worldwide in distribution but most genera are restricted to oceans of the Northern or the Southern hemispheres. Those growing on rocks high in the intertidal zone are often called rockweeds; one of them, *Fucus* (fig. 3D–H), is common rockweed along seacoasts of the temperate region of the Northern Hemisphere. Its leathery, repeatedly forked plant body is anchored to rocks by a disk-shaped holdfast.

Conceptacles are produced in abundance on somewhat inflated tips of branches. Each conceptacle contains many sex organs. In some species both antheridia and oögonia are borne in the same conceptacle, in other species the two are in separate conceptacles, in still others the two are borne on separate plants. Oögonia (fig. 3F) have 8 large nonflagellated eggs; antheridia (fig. 3E) have 64 small biflagellate antherozoids. Oögonia become detached from the side of a conceptacle, float out through the opening at the apex of a conceptacle, and then liberate their eggs (fig. 3G). Eggs liberated from oögonia become surrounded by many antherozoids (fig. 3H). The zygote produced by union of egg and antherozoid immediately begins to develop into a new plant.

Sargassum is the commonest genus in warmer portions of the oceans. Its plant body (fig. 3I) is differentiated into stemlike and leaflike branches. Many branches terminate in small air-filled bladders, and if a plant becomes detached, it floats freely. Gametic union is similar to that of *Fucus*. Some species, as the two growing free-floating in the Gulf Stream and the Sargasso Sea, multiply exclusively by fragmentation.

Red Algae (Rhodophyta).—The Rhodophyta have chromatophores in which the photosynthetic pigments are masked by a red pigment (phycoerythrin); sometimes there is also a blue pigment (phycocyanin). The chief food reserve is an insoluble carbohydrate, floridean starch. Sexual reproduction is unique in that nonflagellate male gametes (spermatia) are passively transported to female sex organs. Red algae also differ from all other except the blue-green algae in lacking flagellated asexual spores. All Rhodophyta are placed in a single class, the Rhodophyceae, with about 400 genera and 2,500 species. About 50 species, belonging to a dozen genera, are freshwater; all other red algae occur in marine environments.

Rhodophyceae.—Rhodophyceae predominate in the algal flora of tropical seas but they are present in all seas, including those of polar regions. Almost all marine species grow attached and the great majority of them grow at or a few feet below the intertidal levels. In northern portions of the Atlantic and Pacific oceans red algae rarely grow in water more than 100 ft. deep; in portions of these oceans nearer the Equator they have been dredged from a depth of 500 ft. Certain forms growing in fresh water, as *Batrachospermum*, are usually restricted to clear, cool, swiftly flowing streams.

The plant body is usually a simple blade, a much-divided blade (fig. 4E), or more complex and differentiated into stem- and bladelike portions (fig. 4A). None of the red algae attains a size comparable to that of the larger brown algae. The coralline red algae have their plant bodies heavily impregnated with lime. They have been shown to be of considerable importance in the formation of "coral" reefs and atolls.

The Rhodophyceae are divided into two subclasses, Bangioideae and Florideae. The Bangioideae have two distinctive characters: (1) cell division may take place anywhere in the plant body; and (2) the direct division of the zygote into carpospores. The single order (Bangiales) includes about 15 genera and 60 species. A few species are freshwater, the remainder are marine. The most conspicuous and abundant of the marine genera is *Porphyra*. Its plant body is a tough leathery blade one or two cells in thickness. *Porphyra* usually grows on rocks in the intertidal zone and its blades may be more than a foot in length.

All Florideae have a filamentous plant body in the majority of genera this is not obvious because the filaments are laterally compacted to form a structure of definite macroscopic form. Cell division is restricted to terminal cells of the branches. In Florideae the male sex organ (spermatangium) is unicellular and contains a single nonflagellate spermatium (fig. 3K). A spermatium liberated from a spermatangium floats to and lodges against a hairlike prolongation (trichogyne) of the one-celled female sex organ (carpogonium) (fig. 3K) borne at the apex of a carpogonial filament. Gametic union is followed by a development of special filaments (gonimoblast filaments) that bear sporangia (carposporangia) containing carpospores (fig. 3K). In some Florideae the gonimo-

blast filaments grow directly from the base of a carpogonium. In other Florideae fertilization is followed by growth of a delicate tube (oöblast) (fig. 3N) from the carpogonium to another cell of the plant. The zygote nucleus migrates to this auxiliary cell and then gonimoblast filaments grow from the auxiliary cell. The mass of gonimoblast filaments and carposporangia, whether growing from a carpogonium or an auxiliary cell, jointly constitute the cystocarp or "fruit" of the sexual plant. Many algologists interpret the cystocarp as a small asexual generation, the carposporophyte, that grows parasitically on the sexual plant (gametophyte). Each carposporangium of the carposporophyte liberates a single spore.

Primitive Florideae have a reduction division of the zygote nucleus and have the carpospores developing into gametophytes. More advanced Florideae have no reduction division of the zygote nucleus and produce carpospores in which the chromosome number is the same as that of the zygote. Carpospores of these Florideae develop into free-living asexual plants of the same size and vegetative structure as gametophytes. This asexual plant, the tetrasporophyte, bears sporangia (tetrasporangia) in which the single nucleus divides reductionally before the sporangial contents divide to form four tetraspores (fig. 3M). These tetraspores, upon liberation from a tetrasporangium, proceed to develop into gametophytes.

Classification of Florideae into orders is based on mode of development of the carposporophyte and on the presence or absence of a tetrasporophyte. The Nemalionales, the most primitive order, have no tetrasporophyte and usually have gonimoblast filaments developing from the carposporangium. There are approximately 35 genera in the order. All other orders have tetrasporophytes, and of these the Gelidiales, a small order with about six genera, are the only ones in which the gonimoblast filaments grow directly from the carpogonium. All other orders with tetrasporophytes have the gonimoblast filaments growing from an auxiliary cell. In Cryptonemiales, an order with 85 or more genera, the auxiliary cell is borne in a special filament resembling a carpogonial filament. In the 70 genera placed in the Gigartinales the cell functioning as an auxiliary cell is an ordinary vegetative cell of the plant body.

The two remaining orders, Rhodymeniales, with about 25 genera, and Ceramiales, containing about 160 genera, have a special auxiliary cell borne adjacent to the base of a carpogonial filament. Rhodymeniales have this cell developing before fertilization; Ceramiales have it formed after fertilization.

Blue-Green Algae (Cyanophyta).—The Cyanophyta are the only algae in which photosynthetic pigments are not localized in definite chromatophores and in which the nuclear substances are not localized in definite nuclei. In these regards, and in their lack of large, water-filled vacuoles and lack of mitochondria, the cells of blue-green algae resemble bacteria. The photosynthetic pigments are evenly distributed through the cytoplasm and are masked by a blue pigment (phycocyanin); sometimes, as in the blue-greens that colour the Red Sea, there is also a red pigment resembling phycoerythrin of Rhodophyta. Cyanophyta have no motile flagellated cells, either vegetative or reproductive, and no members of the division reproduce sexually. There are about 150 genera and 1,400 species, more than 80% of which are freshwater and are found in water or on the surface of moist rocks and soil.

Myxophyceae.—The division contains but one class, the Myxophyceae (Cyanophyceae). All members of the class are of microscopic size but in some cases (*e.g.*, *Nostoc*, fig. 4H) many plants may be aggregated to form a macroscopic mass of definite shape. Some genera are unicellular; the majority are multicellular and either filamentous or nonfilamentous. The most primitive order, the Chroococcales, has solitary cells or has them united in nonfilamentous colonies (fig. 4G). Some of the species occasionally produce spores but the usual method of reproduction is by vegetative division of cells and fragmentation of colonies. The order includes about 35 genera and 250 species, almost all of which are freshwater. Members of the Chamaesiphonales regularly have the contents of a cell dividing into a number of minute nonmotile endospores. The plant body is usually unicellular and epiphytic on other algae. There are about 30 genera and 130 species, most of which are marine. The Hormogoneales have their cells united end to end in filaments. There are approximately 90 genera and 1,000 species, the great majority of which are freshwater. The filaments may be unbranched (fig. 4H–4J) or branched (fig. 4L). Some genera have the filaments breaking at certain points and the ends growing out at the point of rupture. This results in a "false branching" of a filament (fig. 4K). Practically all genera multiply by fragmentation of a filament into short parts, each composed of a few cells. These hormogones then develop into long filaments. Many filamentous genera form special thick-walled cells with transparent contents. These cells, the heterocysts (fig. 4H; 4J–4L), are sporelike in nature but rarely germinate to form new plants. Filaments of some species regularly break into shorter filaments at points next to the heterocysts.

Genera with heterocysts also produce large spores (akinetes, fig. 4J) densely filled with protoplasm rich in reserve foods. Akinetes regularly germinate into new filaments.

See also references under "Algae" in the Index.

BIBLIOGRAPHY.—F. E. Fritsch, *The Structure and Reproduction of Algae* (1935–45); G. M. Smith, *Cryptogamic Botany,* 2nd ed., vol. 1 (1955), *Fresh-water Algae of the United States,* 2nd ed. (1950), *Marine Algae of the Monterey Peninsula* (1944), and (ed.), *Manual of Phycology* (1951); G. W. Prescott, *Algae of the Western Great Lakes Area.*(1951); G. S. West and F. E. Fritsch, *Treatise on the British Freshwater Algae* (1927); L. Newton, *Handbook of the British Seaweeds* (1931); W. R. Taylor, *The Marine Algae of Florida* (1928), *Marine Algae of the Northeastern Coast of North America* (1937); H. Gaffron, "Food from Algae," *Research,* 6 (1953); V. J. Chapman, *Seaweeds and Their Uses* (1950); G. E. Fogg, *Algal Cultures and Phytoplankton Ecology* (1965); D. F. Jackson (ed.), *Algae and Man,* sponsored by the NATO Advanced Study Institute (1964); G. W. Prescott, *How to Know the Fresh-Water Algae* (1964); C. M. Palmer, *Algae in Water Supplies,* Public Health Service Publication no. 657 (1959). (G. M. S.; X.)

ALGARDI, ALESSANDRO

ALGARDI, ALESSANDRO (1595–1654), after Bernini the most important Roman sculptor of the 17th century, was born at Bologna in 1595 and trained under Lodovico Carracci. After a short period of activity in Mantua (1622), he moved to Rome (1625), where he designed the stucco decorations in S. Silvestro al Quirinale and gained some success as a restorer of classical sculptures. With the monument of Cardinal Millini (d. 1629) in Sta. Maria del Popolo, the Frangipani monument in S. Marcello al Corso and the bust of Cardinal Laudivio Zacchia (Berlin), Algardi emerged as the principal rival of Bernini in the field of portrait sculpture. After the election of Pope Innocent X (1644), he superseded Bernini in papal favour, and between this date and his death in Rome on June 10, 1654, he produced some of his most celebrated works, among them the seated statue of the pope now in the Palazzo dei Conservatori (1645) and a colossal marble relief of the "Meeting of Attila and Pope Leo the Great" in St. Peter's (1646–50). At this time he also designed the Villa Doria Pamphili and a fountain in the Cortile di S. Damaso of the Vatican. Algardi's style was less ebullient and pictorial than Bernini's and, even in such characteristically baroque works as the tomb of Pope Leo XI in St. Peter's (1642–44) and the high altar of S. Paolo at Bologna (1641), the restraining influence of the antique is strongly felt.

See H. Posse, "Alessandro Algardi," in Jahrbuch der Königlichen Preussischen Kunstsammlungen, xxvi, pp. 169–201 (1905); J. Hess, Die Künstlerbiographien von Giovanni Battista (1934).

(J. W. P.-H.)

ALGAROTTI, FRANCESCO

ALGAROTTI, FRANCESCO, CONTE (1712–1764), Italian connoisseur of the arts and sciences, esteemed by the philosophers of the Enlightenment for his wide knowledge and elegant presentation of advanced ideas, was born in Venice on Dec. 11, 1712, and educated in Rome, Bologna and Florence. At the age of 20 he went to Paris, where his great physical beauty, his urbanity and his versatile intelligence quickly made an impression in intellectual circles. His *Newtonianismo per le dame* (1737; written 1733), a popular exposition of Newtonian optics, was highly praised by Voltaire. After a visit to England, Algarotti in 1739 went to Russia, whence he returned to England by way of Saxony. In 1740 he received a flattering invitation to Prussia from Frederick

the Great, which led to his staying more than nine years in Germany. Ill health eventually obliged him to return to Italy, to live first in Venice, then in Pisa, where he died of consumption on May 3, 1764. Frederick the Great caused a fine monument to be set up on his tomb, with the famous epitaph *"Algarottus non omnis"* ("[Here lies] Algarotti [but] not all").

Algarotti's many writings include several studies on classical themes and stimulating essays on architecture (1753), the opera (1755; Eng. trans. reprinted with essay by R. Northcott, *Francesco Algarotti,* 1917) and painting (1762). Lord Chesterfield, Lord Hervey, Thomas Gray, Metastasio, Voltaire, Maupertuis and Heinrich von Brühl were among his correspondents.

BIBLIOGRAPHY.—*Opere del conte Algarotti,* ed. by F. Aglietti with life by D. Michelessi, 17 vol. (1791–94); *Letters From Count- Algarotti to Lord Hervey and the Marquis Scipio Maffei,* with miscellaneous other works, Eng. trans. (1769). *See also* I. F. Treat, *Un Cosmopolite italien du XVIIIe siècle* (1913); F. Viglione, *L'Algarotti e l'Inghilterra* (1919); A. Ambrogio, *L'Estetica di Francesco Algarotti* (1925).

ALGARVE

ALGARVE, an ancient kingdom (established by Afonso III in 1253) and province in southern Portugal, now corresponds with the administrative district of Faro. Pop. (1960) 312,509. Area 1,958 sq.mi.

A fundamental distinction can be made between the interior hills bordering Baixo Alentejo and the limestone scarplands and coastal plain to the south, running about 85 mi. between Cape St. Vincent and the mouth of the Guadiana. The uplands, composed of Carboniferous slates, culminate in the Serra do Caldeirão (1,893 ft.) although the western massif of Monchique (2,959 ft.), composed of eruptive rocks, is the only mountainous area. Much of this zone is a waste of cistus scrub (*matorral*) only partially colonized, with seldom more than 10 to 20 persons per square mile. Only at Monchique (pop. [1960] 9,450) and Caldas de Monchique, a thermal spa, is the population denser. The coastal lands of Algarve are, however, densely populated, reaching 200–400 persons per square mile in areas of the coast. The scarplands and plateaus of the *barrocal,* composed of Jurassic limestones, are thickly covered with groves of figs, almonds, carobs, olives, and the alluvial lands along the coast have horticultural crops wherever irrigation from well supplies is possible. Maize is widely grown. East of Faro the coast called Sotavento is fringed for 30 mi. with sand bars and lagoons. Algarve (Arabic al-Gharb meaning "the west") is the most Moorish part of Portugal and hedges of prickly pear give it an African look. The whitewashed stone houses are elaborately decorated. Three-quarters of the urban population is concentrated in a series of 32 fishing and small seaports. Loulé and Silves are the only centres of note in the interior. Faro (*q.v.*), the capital, Olhão (pop. [1960] 15,711), Portimão (11,-930) and Vila Real de Santo António carry on coastal trade and tunny fishing. There is little industry apart from some cork manufactures, flour milling and mining. (J. M. Ho.)

ALGEBRA

ALGEBRA. To the layman, algebra means elementary algebra, that branch of mathematics in which one learns to calculate with variables instead of just the numbers of arithmetic and to solve polynomial equations. To the professional mathematician, however, as well as to increasing numbers of scientists in other fields, algebra means rather what is called modern, higher or abstract algebra. Loosely speaking, this is the study of abstract mathematical structures in which there are operations having the properties of addition or multiplication.

Essential to both elementary and higher algebra is the fact that the calculations should always involve only a finite number of quantities and end after a finite number of steps; in other words, processes in which the answers are obtained "in the limit" generally do not belong to algebra (*see* LIMIT). Thus

$$1 + x + x^2 + x^3 + \cdots + x^n = \frac{1 - x^{n+1}}{1 - x}$$

is algebra, but

$$1 + x + x^2 + x^3 + \cdots + x^n + \cdots = \frac{1}{1 - x}$$

is not.

A second characteristic of algebra is its abstractness. Even in elementary algebra calculations are made not with numbers but with letters that represent numbers. In higher algebra the letters may represent much more general objects, and the system of calculation is itself an abstraction of systems having similar properties. This abstract, general viewpoint has become closely associated with modern algebra, so that to the professional mathematician the word "algebraically" sometimes means only "abstractly and axiomatically."

The demands placed on algebra by other branches of mathematics have been the richest and most significant source of new results in algebra, while, at the same time, the axiomatic, abstract algebraic viewpoint has simplified and clarified work in other fields, providing techniques leading both to new results and to unexpected connections between work in widely separated fields. This "algebraization" of mathematics has been one of the most characteristic features of 20th-century mathematics. In this way the influence of algebra has actually been far greater than its results. At the same time, modern algebra has brought a clearer understanding of the processes of elementary algebra and has enabled mathematicians to "get behind" the calculations to an understanding of the principles that underlie them. A general, nonrigorous survey of both algebras is presented here. Detailed treatments of specific subjects are contained in the articles named as cross references.

ELEMENTARY ALGEBRA

Content.—Elementary algebra includes a miscellany of topics representing the accretions of several centuries (see ALGEBRA, HISTORY OF). Some of them can by no stretch of the imagination be called algebra, while others are included in algebra only out of hospitality because they have no other place to go.

The basic task of elementary algebra is the solution of polynomial, i.e., "algebraic," equations and the stepwise introduction of new types of numbers—negative, real and complex—to use in solving them. Some interest is added by applying equation-solving to verbal problems of varying degrees of removal from reality. There is also usually a great deal of drill in calculation with polynomials (q.v.) and letters—the binomial theorem (q.v.) and formulas for the sum of arithmetic and geometric progressions belong in this category. Determinants and matrices are devices for facilitating the solution of simultaneous equations and thus have their place (see DETERMINANT; MATRIX). The quadratic formula is the explicit solution of the quadratic equation, and so also merits attention. It is regrettable that the strong emphasis on drill often makes students equate "algebra" with "calculation"; the concentration on details of technique, short cuts for factoring, and so on, seriously obscures the logical outline of the subject.

Two traditional topics deserve mention. Permutations and combinations (typical problem: in how many ways can six men choose their wives from among six women, assuming no bigamy) are really elementary probability theory, but they use only algebraic arguments and the formulas are occasionally useful—the binomial coefficients, for instance (see COMBINATORIAL ANALYSIS). Exponentials and logarithms, on the other hand, are certainly not algebra, since they involve passage to the limit in their definition. Of course, the emphasis in elementary algebra is not on the precise definition of these functions but rather on the formal rules for operating with them, such calculation with formal rules being universally interpreted as "algebra."

Kinds of Numbers.—Elementary arithmetic uses only positive rational numbers (the natural numbers 1, 2, 3, . . . and common fractions such as $\frac{1}{2}$, $\frac{7}{3}$, . . .) and zero. These, however, do not suffice to solve even the simplest equation: $x + 3 = 0$, for instance. To solve such equations, negative rational numbers are introduced. To use these negative numbers, however, it is necessary to know how to calculate with them, and so the law $(-1)(-1) = 1$ is given. Where does this law come from? The answer is that the calculation rules for negative numbers are adopted so that the five rules or laws

1. $a + b = b + a$
2. $a + (b + c) = (a + b) + c$
3. $ab = ba$
4. $(ab)c = a(bc)$
5. $a(b + c) = ab + ac$

which are valid for positive numbers will continue to be valid for the larger system including the new negative numbers. Rule 5 gives

$$0 = -1(1 - 1) = (-1)1 + (-1)(-1) = -1 + (-1)(-1)$$

so that adding 1 to both sides gives $1 = (-1)(-1)$. In other words, this last result is to be interpreted as a consequence of the five laws viewed as axioms, an interpretation very much in the spirit of modern algebra.

The introduction of negative rational numbers suffices for the solution of linear equations, those of the form $bx + a = 0$, and for simultaneous linear equations:

$$ax + by = c$$
$$a'x + b'y = c'$$

to give an example of two equations in two variables x and y—there could be more variables and more equations, of course. It is inadequate, however, for solving equations of higher degree, such as the quadratic $ax^2 + bx + c = 0$. Two roads are open: one can develop methods for determining when an equation with rational coefficients does have a rational solution, or one can extend again the number system in the hope of solving more equations.

Following the second alternative, the extension is first made to the system of all real numbers. This permits the solution of some equations not solvable in rational numbers, $x^2 - 2 = 0$, for instance. Another extension leads to the set of complex numbers $a + b\sqrt{-1}$, where a and b are real (see COMPLEX NUMBERS). With each extension, it is necessary to explain how to calculate with the new types of numbers. For the real numbers this explanation is taken for granted, while for the complex numbers the familiar laws are given, again with the purpose of preserving the validity of the five previously given axioms. The employment of complex numbers makes the extension complete by virtue of the so-called fundamental theorem of algebra, which says that every polynomial equation with complex coefficients has a solution in complex numbers; it only remains, then, to describe processes and to give formulas when possible for actually finding the solutions.

Unfortunately, however, this fundamental theorem is not a theorem of algebra at all—indeed, it is never proved in algebra courses. The difficulty begins with the introduction of the irrational numbers. These are represented in the familiar way by the points on a line. Now the rational numbers, when plotted on the line, are dense on the line in the sense that any line segment, no matter how small, will always contain points representing rational numbers. Thus, constructing the irrational numbers from the rational numbers is essentially a process of filling in the gaps on the line, which, no matter how it is done, will involve notions of limit and therefore will not be describable in terms of a finite number of operations. For example, the most familiar way of describing an irrational number is as an infinite decimal: $\pi = 3.14159 \ldots$. But what this means is only that the infinite sequence of rational numbers 3, 3.1, 3.14, 3.141, . . . , is approaching π; to stop after a finite number of steps will not give the precise value of π.

The real numbers (and thus the complex numbers, also) being so defined by the use of nonalgebraic processes, a proof of the fundamental theorem must inevitably be achieved through some nonalgebraic argument. For example, the most "algebraic" proof known starts from the following result: a polynomial $x^n + a_1 x^{n-1} + \ldots + a_n$ of odd degree and with real coefficients has a real root. Now if the graph of such a polynomial is considered, the result is "self-evident," because for large positive values of x the graph of the polynomial always lies above the x-axis, whereas for large negative values of x it always lies below; therefore it must cross the axis somewhere in-between, and this is where the root will be. This argument assumes, however, that the graph is represented by an unbroken curve; and the careful explanation of just what this means, coupled with a careful proof of it and the foregoing statement about the necessity for crossing, can only be achieved by appealing to the infinite process of passing to a limit.

The fundamental theorem of algebra being of essentially nonalgebraic character, the same should be true of any of the well-known approximation methods for actually obtaining a solution, such as Newton's and Horner's methods. Yes and no: they are nonalgebraic because they must be infinitely repeated to obtain the exact solution, but algebraic insofar as that, at any finite stage, only algebraic arguments and techniques—simple additions and multiplications—are employed.

The other road that was mentioned, the determination of when a polynomial with rational coefficients does have a rational root, leads to the problem of factorization. If a is a root of the polynomial $f(x)$, then according to the factor theorem $f(x) = (x - a)g(x)$, where $g(x)$ is also a polynomial with rational coefficients, and there exist criteria for determining when such a factorization is possible. More generally, there is the problem of determining whether a given polynomial will factor into the product of two smaller ones. The important thing to observe here is that the problem is relevant only when the types of numbers to be available as coefficients are made clear. Thus $x^2 - 2$ does not factor if only rational coefficients are permitted, but it does if irrational coefficients can be used; and any polynomial of degree greater than one factors if complex coefficients can be used. In other words, the problem of factorization is connected with the process of extending the number system; how far one has gotten with the latter determines the success in factorization.

MODERN ALGEBRA

Modern algebra evolved from elementary algebra in a series of jumps beginning essentially with the work of Évariste Galois in 1830. It includes all of elementary algebra and a great deal more, but in an extensively generalized form; each topic of elementary algebra is thus viewable as the starting point of one of the theories of modern algebra. However, modern algebra is somewhat different in spirit and method, as the following example, carried out in some detail, will show.

Abstract Axiomatic Systems; Commutative Rings.—Take as a starting point the set of integers, including zero and the negative integers, with the operations of addition and multiplication obeying the five laws previously given. Division is forbidden, because the quotient of two integers is not usually an integer. Subtraction is permitted, because $a - b$ can be interpreted as the addition of a to $-b$; however, because there is nothing in the five laws that says that the negative integers are really in the set (the laws apply equally well, as has been seen, to just the positive integers), a sixth law must be added:

Rule 6. There exists an object 0 such that, for all a, $0 + a = a$, and there is a unique object $-a$ such that $a + (-a) = 0$.

Thus there is on hand a collection of objects (the integers) with two operations ($+$ and $\cdot$) which satisfy six laws. The viewpoint of abstract algebra is now: forget that this is a collection specifically of integers—what follows from these six laws without any further assumptions? This is the axiomatic viewpoint, for the laws are interpreted as the axioms that give the rules for calculation with the objects. Such a collection with two operations satisfying the given laws is called a commutative ring.

Another example of a commutative ring is given by the set of even integers. The polynomials in one variable with real coefficients form such a ring, if the operations are taken to be the usual polynomial addition and multiplication. The numbers from 0 to $n - 1$ form a ring which will be denoted by Z_n if one adds and multiplies as usual, but subtracts a multiple of n from the answer so as to make it a number between 0 and $n - 1$ again. For instance, to calculate in Z_6, $4 + 5 = 3$, $4 \cdot 5 = 2$, $2 \cdot 3 = 0$. Here 6 has been subtracted from the first answer, 3×6 from the second and 6 from the third. (This procedure is familiar in "casting out nines.") As a more bizarre example of a commutative ring, take as the objects of the collection all possible sets A, B, C, . . . of points in a plane; for instance, A might be the set of all points inside some circle, B might be a single point, C might be the set of all points on some line, and so on. Include in the collection also the empty set—the set with no points at all. Define the operations $+$ and $\cdot$ in this way: $A + B = $ all points in either A or B but not in both, while $A \cdot B = $ all points in both A and B. It can be shown that these operations do indeed satisfy the six axioms. The

empty set is the element 0, and one has the calculation rules $A + A = 0$, $A \cdot A = A$.

To be of value, the axioms must not be so peculiar and special that they reflect no significant mathematical reality, nor must they be so general that nothing very significant follows from them alone; in other words, the axioms must really summarize a large part of what is important in the systems being studied abstractly. Here one is on weaker ground, for it must be admitted that, although there are plenty of commutative rings in nature, usually their most significant properties do not follow just from their being commutative rings alone—some additional axiom is required.

For instance, although one cannot in general divide one integer by another, the integers are contained in a larger commutative ring in which division by any nonzero element is possible, namely the ring of rational numbers. Such a commutative ring admitting division is called a field. The ring of polynomials with real coefficients also has this property; it is contained in the field of rational functions $f(x)/g(x)$, where f and g are polynomials with real coefficients. The rings Z_2, Z_3 and Z_5 themselves turn out to be fields; for instance, in Z_5, $\frac{3}{4} = 2$, since $3 = 4 \cdot 2$. On the other hand, Z_4 and Z_6 are not contained in any field, nor is the ring of sets described above. On analyzing the matter, one can prove that the necessary and sufficient condition for a commutative ring to be contained in a field is that it satisfy a seventh axiom: whenever $ab = 0$, then either $a = 0$ or $b = 0$. One now can check that Z_n has this property exactly when n is a prime number; certainly the ring of sets does not have it, because if A and B are sets with no points in common, then $A \cdot B = 0$, although neither A nor $B = 0$. Commutative rings satisfying this additional axiom are called integral domains, and thus the statement that the integers are contained in the rational numbers generalizes to the statement that every integral domain is contained in a field.

Here is another example. What underlies and justifies the effort spent in factoring polynomials in elementary algebra is the result that any polynomial with, say, rational coefficients is in one and only one way (up to a constant factor) the product of irreducible polynomials with rational coefficients (those that cannot be further factored). There is an analogous result for the integers: a positive integer is in one and only one way the product of prime numbers.

One may ask now, in general, for which integral domains is there such a unique factorization theorem? This is not an easy question, and no universal criterion is known; there are, however, several reasonable axioms, any one of which will guarantee unique factorization. One that works for both the integers and the polynomial rings is the Euclidean axiom: if a and b are given, and $b \neq 0$, then one can divide a by b with a remainder r which is "smaller" (in a precise sense which shall not be described) than b; that is, $a = bq + r$. For integers, the size is to be measured by the absolute value, while for polynomials, by the degree. Thus, an integral domain satisfying the Euclidean axiom (such are called Euclidean domains) admits unique factorization.

Thus far the given set of axioms has been added to in order to obtain worthwhile results. A common practice is to drop axioms, or substitute weaker ones for them, and see what results. If axiom 3 is dropped, the resulting system is called a ring. If 3, 4 and 5 are dropped while 1, 2 and 6 are retained, there results a system with one law called an abelian group. Groups are of vast importance in modern algebra (see GROUPS; GROUPS, CONTINUOUS; GROUPS, TRANSFORMATION; GROUPS AND ALGEBRAS, REPRESENTATIONS OF).

To sum up, therefore, one gains by this process of abstraction great generality, because a theorem about an abstract commutative ring automatically holds for any specific example of such a ring and therefore need not be tediously proved for every special case. On the other hand, the process has its dangers, and the goal must always be the attainment of the richest consequences with the minimum number of assumptions.

To reiterate an earlier remark, there is an implicit limitation to those axiomatic systems whose operation laws involve only finite processes using a finite number of elements. Though there is in principle no objection to laws of infinite type, the resulting systems would be outside the domain of algebra.

Scope of Study.—Now that the type of object studied in modern algebra has been outlined, the scope of the study will be indicated in some detail. The scope will be divided, somewhat artificially, into three parts: first, some general comments about what sorts of results one tries to obtain for an abstract axiomatic system, then a brief survey of the existing types of systems and what is known about them, and, finally, a discussion of the interaction of algebra with other parts of mathematics and with science in general.

Classification of Systems.—Given an abstract system (such as a group, or a commutative ring) defined by operations satisfying certain axioms, the basic problem is to classify the different types of such a system. It may help the reader to consider an analogous classification problem in biology. To "classify all birds" would mean: to the list of properties that make an animal specifically a bird, add other distinguishing sets of properties—the species properties—so that each bird belongs to one and only one species and the birds of each species are essentially indistinguishable biologically. This is not quite enough; one would also like a specimen, or at least a picture, of a representative member of each species.

A similar situation exists in the classification of algebraic structures. One adds properties which narrow down the possibilities sufficiently, then seeks to obtain a specimen of each "species." For example, to classify all commutative rings is certainly a hopelessly formidable task—there are too many different kinds. If the category is limited to all integral domains, the class is still too wide. If, however, one asks for the integral domains with only a finite number of elements, they can be classified completely. In this case, the species are completely determined by telling how many elements they contain. Let this number of elements be designated by n. Then if n is a prime number, Z_n is a representative of the species; if n is not prime, no such integral domain exists.

To clarify the foregoing, the meaning of the term species must be explained: this should consist of a class of algebraic structures which are essentially indistinguishable. The relevant algebraic notion is that of isomorphism: two collections A and A' of objects with given laws of operations are isomorphic if one can associate each object of A with a definite object of A' so that all the objects in A' are associated with something in A and so that different objects in A are associated with different objects in A' (in short, make a one-to-one correspondence between A and A'), and so that the operation laws are preserved; i.e., if a and a' correspond, and b and b' correspond, then to $(a + b)$ should correspond $(a' + b')$, and so on. If A and A' are isomorphic, then their algebraic structures are indistinguishable; algebraically they differ only in that their objects have different names. It is easier to give examples of isomorphic groups than of isomorphic rings, since there is one less operation to worry about. The positive real numbers form an abelian group under multiplication, and the whole set of real numbers forms an abelian group under addition. These two groups are isomorphic, because if to each positive real number x one associates the real number $\log x$, then the correspondence is one-to-one, and the operation is preserved, because to xy corresponds $\log (xy) = \log x + \log y$; that is, addition in the second group corresponds to multiplication in the first group. Again, the additive group Z_6 that has been described is isomorphic to the group of rotations of a regular hexagon (where to "add" two rotations means to perform first one, and then to follow it with the other).

The explanation of the classification problem can now be completed in this manner: once there have been added enough additional properties to determine uniquely the species, designate a specimen of it; then the species consists of all systems isomorphic to the given specimen. Thus in the earlier illustration, the species whose members are all integral domains containing p elements has Z_p as a specimen, and any other such integral domain is isomorphic to Z_p.

Kinds of Algebraic Systems.—The principal abstract objects of study are groups, rings, fields, vector spaces and algebras. Groups have one operation (usually called addition if the group is abelian,

otherwise multiplication); rings have two; fields (*q.v.*) are commutative rings in which one can divide; vector spaces are additive groups in which there is a scalar multiplication by elements of some field; algebras (sometimes called linear algebras) are vector spaces with a multiplication law defined (*see* ALGEBRAS [LINEAR]).

Most of these abstract systems grew naturally out of elementary algebra. The theory of rings came, as has been seen, from study of the formal properties of integers and polynomials; a noncommutative ring differs from a commutative ring in that one drops axiom 3: $ab = ba$. Fields arose, as has been seen, from the attempts to provide solutions for algebraic equations. The proof that the equation of fifth degree could not be solved by a formula analogous to the quadratic formula gave rise to group theory. Finally, the solution of simultaneous linear equations in elementary algebra led directly to the theory of vector spaces and matrices; the square $n \times n$ matrices themselves give one of the most important examples of an algebra.

The classification problem has been solved most completely for several types of algebras. There are the famous Wedderburn theorems: if the algebra is a finite division algebra (has only a finite number of elements and always permits division by a nonzero element), then the multiplication law must be commutative, so that the algebra is actually a finite field, and it is not hard to classify all of these. If it is what is called a "central simple" algebra, then it is isomorphic to the algebra of all $n \times n$ matrices, whose entries come from a certain division algebra. Other algebras that have been classified are Lie algebras, Jordan algebras and division algebras over number fields.

For groups, the solution of the general classification problem is far from complete. If the group is finite, one general procedure is, first, to classify all of the simple groups (those without nontrivial normal subgroups), and then to describe how an arbitrary group is built out of simple subgroups. New simple groups are still being discovered, however, though it is now known that there are none with an odd number of elements, except for the groups Z_p (where $p \neq 2$). The study of infinite groups has not progressed far. Even the abelian ones can be very complicated—for instance, the additive group of rational numbers is one of the most difficult.

Every field contains a uniquely determined smallest field, called the prime field, which is isomorphic either to the field of rational numbers or to one of the finite fields of Z_p. This fact provides, therefore, a first basis for classifying them. The next step is to decide whether every element in the field is a root of some polynomial equation with coefficients in the prime field. If this is the case the field is called algebraic; if not, it often is possible to attach a number to the field (called its transcendence degree) which measures roughly how far away it is from being algebraic. The further classification of the algebraic fields is called algebraic number theory; the classification of fields with transcendence degree properly belongs to algebraic geometry.

Effect of Modern Algebra on Other Subjects.—In mathematical analysis, the influence of algebra has produced the so-called functional and abstract analysis. The subject matter of classical analysis is, more or less, the study of functions in ordinary real or complex Euclidean space, particularly on the line. One studies both the behaviour of the functions themselves and the properties of the integral and differential equations they satisfy. The algebraic viewpoint is that suitable classes of these functions form vector spaces satisfying certain additional axioms, generally of a nonalgebraic character (Hilbert spaces or Banach spaces, for example). The study of the integral equation or the differential equation may now be formulated as a study of the properties of a certain linear transformation on this vector space. From this point of view, the theory is the generalization to infinitely many dimensions of the theory of linear transformations on a finite-dimensional vector space; i.e., the theory of matrices. Many theorems bear a resemblance to the corresponding theorems about matrices, although, of course, they are far more difficult to prove. Again, the classical theory of periodic functions and trigonometric series, which is basically a theory of functions on the circle, is generalized to functions on more general groups, the topological groups; this, then, is abstract harmonic analysis. Although algebra has systematized and clarified many theorems here, it seems that the crux of any significant theorem always turns out to be a piece of "hard" analysis of the old-fashioned sort. (*See* ANALYSIS; ANALYSIS, ABSTRACT.)

The influence of algebra on geometry can be divided into applications to differential geometry, topology and algebraic geometry. Dominating much of differential geometry (*q.v.*) in the 20th century has been the theory of Lie groups, those groups in which the multiplication law is given "analytically" by differentiable functions; the group of all $n \times n$ matrices with real or complex entries is an important example. To each such Lie group one can associate an algebra (vector space with multiplication)—its Lie algebra—which in turn determines many of the properties of the group. The classification of Lie algebras is a purely algebraic problem, whose solution gives in turn a classification of Lie groups, or, at least, a wide class of them.

An even more striking example of the application of algebra to geometry is afforded by topology. This is the branch of mathematics that studies the properties of those geometric objects that remain invariant under continuous deformation ("stretching"). At first glance it might seem that the rigidity of the structures in algebra would have little light to shed on the elastic objects of topology, but this is not so. The basic method of algebraic topology is to associate with the geometric object (called a topological space) certain algebraic structures—groups and rings, for the most part—which remain unchanged by a deformation of the space. Properties of the spaces are then reflected in properties of the algebraic structures, and the goal is to find enough associated algebraic structures to effect a complete classification of topological spaces: two spaces can be deformed one into the other (the surface of a sphere and that of a sausage, for instance, or that of a teacup and a doughnut) if and only if their associated algebraic structures are isomorphic. (*See* TOPOLOGY, ALGEBRAIC; TOPOLOGY, GENERAL.)

As an example of such a structure, consider a point fixed in the space, and assume that all closed paths in the space begin and end at this point. If one does not consider two paths to be different if one path can be deformed into the other, the set of paths forms a group (to multiply two paths, first follow one, and then the other: the result is still a closed path) called the fundamental group of the space. The fundamental group of a cylinder, for instance, is isomorphic to the group of integers, since two paths which go around the cylinder the same number of times can always be deformed one into the other. The fundamental group alone is enough to classify all closed surfaces in three-dimensional space which have no edge and do not cross themselves. For instance, if the fundamental group consists of 0 alone, the surface can be deformed into the surface of a sphere. This group is also the main tool in describing when two knots in three-dimensional space can be deformed one into the other.

Perhaps the most intimate of all the influences of modern algebra on other branches of mathematics is the relation of algebra to algebraic geometry and algebraic number theory: indeed, in the works of some authors one gets the feeling that these last two subjects are only chapters in algebra. Algebraic number theory is the study of the properties of algebraic numbers—those complex numbers that are the roots of polynomials in one variable with rational coefficients. Algebraic geometry (*q.v.*) is the study of geometric loci in space defined by algebraic equations in several variables: algebraic curves, surfaces and similar objects in *n*-dimensional space, called simply "varieties." These are, then, the sets of points forming the zeros of a finite set of polynomials in *n* variables, with coefficients from some field (for example, the complex numbers).

In these studies, certain groups, rings and fields keep recurring constantly as the natural structures which summarize and characterize the properties of number fields and varieties. In algebraic number theory, for instance, the group of admissible permutations of the roots of an algebraic equation (*see* EQUATIONS, THEORY OF) plays a decisive role; it is called the Galois group. In algebraic

geometry, the field of all rational functions on the variety is one of the most important invariants of the whole variety. The geometric behaviour of the variety in the neighbourhood of a point p on it is described algebraically by the properties of the integral domain consisting of all rational functions that do not become infinite or undefined at the point p. For instance, whether the variety is or is not smooth around p (a cone would be smooth everywhere except at the vertex) can be expressed entirely in terms of this ring. The purely algebraic study of these integral domains (called local rings), which has become so popular, is a good example of the influence of other fields on algebra itself.

Most amazing of all perhaps has been the success of the so-called homological methods; these abstract algebraic methods of handling the groups which arise in algebraic topology (the homology groups) have turned out to be the natural way to describe the most advanced portions of algebraic number theory, and they are rapidly invading much of the rest of mathematics as well.

Finally, a word should be said about some of the applications of algebra to science other than mathematics. In theoretical physics, the theory of groups and their representations has played an important part in the development of quantum theory, particularly in connection with solid-state physics. The theory of Boolean algebras (the ring of point sets in the plane, described earlier, is an example of one) has been widely used in the design of computing machines. In the social sciences, psychology and economics are finding use for matrices and linear algebra in what is called linear programming. In all of these subjects, too, the introduction of algebra has stimulated algebra as well.

See also Index references under "Algebra" in the Index volume.

BIBLIOGRAPHY.—The classical works on algebra are: W. Weber, *Lehrbuch der Algebra,* vol. 1, 2, 3 (1898); M. Bôcher, *Introduction to Higher Algebra* (1907). For elementary algebra there are many textbooks, for instance, M. Knebelman and T. Thomas, *Principles of College Algebra* (1942). Somewhat more advanced are the books on theory of equations, for example: L. Weisner, *Introduction to the Theory of Equations* (1947); L. Dickson, *New First Course in the Theory of Equations* (1939). Some books on modern algebra, in increasing order of difficulty, are: M. Weiss, *Higher Algebra for the Undergraduate* (1949); A. Albert, *Introduction to Algebraic Theories* (1941); G. Birkhoff and S. MacLane, *A Survey of Modern Algebra* (1953); B. van der Waerden, *Modern Algebra* (1949). (A. P. M.)

ALGEBRA, HISTORY OF. Algebra separated from arithmetic early in the development of mathematics, probably in Babylonia when equations and methods for reducing them were introduced. A considerable number of cuneiform mathematical tables from the period of the Hammurabi dynasty (1800–1600 B.C.) deal with problems now classified as algebra. The calculations of the examples from this period are presented in a way that makes clear that the general methods, and not the numerical results, are the main goal. A mastery of quadratic equations is evident; often they were presented in the standard form $x + x^{-1} = a$, which could be solved by means of tables or by reduction to a square root extraction as at present. Another normal form for quadratic problems in two unknowns was $x \pm y = a$, $x \cdot y = b$. More complicated problems were reduced to these. Closely related to these questions are studies of the integral solutions of Pythagorean triangles, that is, determination of integers satisfying $x^2 + y^2 = z^2$. There occur instances of fourth degree equations reducible to quadratic equations and also special cases of cubic equations, presumably solved by tables. Summation of arithmetical progressions and the sums of squares of integers also were known.

The Egyptian knowledge of algebra seems to have been much more limited than that of Babylonia and may have developed under Babylonian influence. The problems as are known from the Rhind mathematical papyrus (copied by Ahmes, *c.* 2000–1800 B.C.) are in the main limited to linear equations. A first approach to formal algebra is the use of a standard symbol h (*aha, hau*), meaning quantity, to denote the unknown to be determined.

The cultures of Asia Minor and Babylonia influenced Greece strongly, and the Greeks undoubtedly received much of their basic knowledge of algebra from these sources. However, within Greek mathematics algebra took on a geometric aspect primarily, it is believed, because of the logical difficulties created by irrational numbers. In the geometric language, for instance, of Euclid's *Elements* (about 300 B.C.) the quantities were represented by lengths of lines, products of two quantities by the area of rectangles and products of three factors by volumes of rectangular solids. In this manner all problems appear in the form of homogeneous relations between quantities of the same dimension. Thus the quadratic equation can be written $b^2 = x(x \pm a)$ and the solution consists in finding a rectangle with sides x and $x \pm a$ whose area is equal to that of a given square b^2. The actual construction can be made by right triangles or mean proportionals. In line with this geometric view of algebra is the development of the theory of conic sections, which reached its zenith in the *Conica* by Apollonius of Perga (220 B.C.). The solution of such problems as the duplication of the cube and the trisection of the angle also were given in terms of the intersection of special curves.

The later Alexandrian period of Greek mathematics seems to have been closer to Babylonian sources. From the point of view of algebra the most noteworthy work is the *Arithmetica* of Diophantus (date uncertain, about A.D. 200). His problems are mostly of the so-called Diophantine type whose solutions are positive fractions or integers; usually the equations are linear or quadratic in several unknowns, but these are systematically reduced to a single unknown. Remarkable are the beginnings of algebraic notation or shorthand. The unknown is denoted by s (perhaps the final letter in the Greek *arithmos*, "number") with special terms for the first powers. Terms to be added are simply written together while a special sign is used for minus.

Concerning the development of algebra in the orient, in India, China and Japan there is still a good deal of dispute, partly with a nationalistic flavour. The very beginnings of algebra in all these countries seem to have been influenced by the Babylonian and Greek schools. Among the Hindu algebraists one should mention especially Brahmagupta (about A.D. 630), whose work on indeterminate equations in many ways goes beyond Diophantus. Somewhat later (about A.D. 1150) are the outstanding works of Bhaskara, the *Lilavati* and the *Vija-ganita*. Here one finds rules for dealing with negative quantities: a dot over a number was used to indicate minus. It was realized that square roots of positive numbers have two roots, and Bhaskara also mentions that there are no roots of negative numbers. Unknowns were denoted by the names of various colours. Powers and roots were indicated by the initial letters or first syllables in the corresponding words, giving a close approach to algebraic symbolism.

With the ascendancy of Mohammedanism the Arab world became the centre for mathematical studies. A number of Arab mathematicians wrote commentaries upon Greek works in the geometric tradition, but there also were notable original algebraic contributions. The cubic equation was a favourite topic for such writers as al-Mahani (about A.D. 850), Tabit ibn Korra (870), Alhazen (1000) and particularly the poet and mathematician 'Omar Khayyam (about 1100), who dealt with it extensively in his algebra; the solutions were obtained by intersections of conics.

The most influential algebraic work from this period was the *Kitab al jabr w'al-muqabala* of al-Khwarizmi composed in Baghdad (about 825). The title may be translated: "The Rules of Restoration and Reduction." The influence of the book on Europe was so great that its name became synonymous with equation theory. The unknown was called *shai*, "the thing"; otherwise al-Khwarizmi shows little tendency to algebraic symbolism.

Arab algebra was introduced to Europe, especially to Italy, in the 13th and 14th centuries. Most important in this process was Leonardo of Pisa's *Liber abaci* (1202) from which later Italian algebra books borrowed freely. Under the influence of Arab usage the unknown was called *res* in Latin, *cosa* ("the thing") in Italian, while algebra itself became known as *l'arte della cosa*, cossic art or the rule of coss. Occasionally algebra was termed the *Ars magna*, "the great art," in contradistinction to the lesser art of arithmetic.

Italian algebraists, for instance Fra Luca Pacioli (1494), had expressed the belief that the general cubic equation could not be solved algebraically (by means of radical expressions). Thus it was a remarkable achievement when around 1515 Scipione del Ferro, professor at the university of Bologna, succeeded in solving the cubic equation in the special form $x^3 + ax = b$. Del Ferro did not reveal his formula, but after his death it passed to his pupils. In a mathematical tournament with one of them, Niccolò Tartaglia from Brescia rediscovered the method and confided it to Girolamo Cardano, a physician in Milan, under promise of secrecy. In 1545 Cardano published his *Ars magna*, the most important algebraic work of the Renaissance. It contained the solution of the cubic equation, still erroneously called Cardano's formula, and also the method for solving fourth-degree equations discovered by Cardano's former servant and protégé, Lodovico Ferrari. The *Ars magna* contained novel ideas concerning the relations between roots and the coefficients of equations; Cardano even calculated formally with imaginary numbers. Publication of this work had a considerable influence on the rapid growth of algebra in Europe.

The presentation in the *Ars magna* is partly geometric in the Greek tradition and partly verbal with scant use of symbols. For problems as complicated as these, such form became very cumbersome, and evidently a stage had been reached at which effective simplification was required. It should be observed that some standard notations had already become common in arithmetic, for instance $\bar{p}$ and $\bar{m}$ were used for plus and minus. The latter symbol was reduced to the bar to denote minus while the present plus sign $+$ is a condensed form for the Latin *et*. The $\times$ sign for multiplication appeared in England around 1600; the radical sign $\sqrt{}$ may originally have been the letter r as an abbreviation for radix.

Cardano's compatriot Raphael Bombelli (about 1560) had made some attempts at simplified writing of algebraic formulas, but the credit for a first systematic effort to introduce an algebraic sign language must go to the French mathematician François Vieta. In his *Isagoge in artem analyticam* (1591) the quantities are denoted by letters, often vowels for the unknowns and consonants for given numbers. The powers of a number A were written Aq (*quadraticus*), Ac (*cubus*), Aqq (*biquadraticus*), and so on. The present usage of denoting unknowns by the last letters (x, y, z) of the alphabet and known quantities by the first letters (a, b, c) is attributed to Descartes (1637); he was the first to write powers with exponents in the modern form, although this notation had been used sporadically by earlier writers. John Wallis (1655) and Sir Isaac Newton (1669) introduced fractional exponents for roots. The equality sign is attributed to Robert Recorde (1557). From the middle of the 17th century the algebraic notations were close to the modern ones. Once initiated, the advantage of symbolic writing was obvious, and the development of an effective and logical mathematical sign language has since been a continuous process.

The rapid use of algebraic technique in the 16th and 17th centuries rendered obsolete some of the medieval algebraic methods, particularly the popular rule of false position inherited from the Arabs. This rule was used to solve linear problems by trying out one or two particular values and adjusting them to satisfy the given conditions. As Recorde states in his *Ground of Artes* (1542):

> Suche falsehode is so good a grounde
> that truth by it will soone be founde.

The idea of solving systems of linear equations by determinants seems to have been originated by Leibniz (1693) although Chinese and Japanese sources contain some indications of similar methods. The first systematic treatments of determinant theory were given by A. T. Vandermonde (1771) and Pierre Laplace (1772), but they were not commonly used until further phases of the theory had been developed by Augustin Cauchy (1812) and Karl Jacobi. A standard tool of algebra, the binomial theorem, is ancient and was quite well known by the middle of the 16th century. The more general multinomial theorem is usually ascribed to Leibniz. The interest in equation theory stimulated the study of symmetric functions of roots. The fundamental facts about them were developed particularly by Newton, Wallis, Edward Waring and other members of the English school of mathematicians studying combinatorial analysis.

The introduction of such new fields of mathematics as analytic geometry by Descartes and the calculus by Newton and Leibniz also contributed greatly to the development of algebra. For instance, one may say that the Greek idea of a geometric algebra was now reversed into an algebraic geometry. The study of algebraic curves advanced the field of algebra itself by introducing methods of reduction and elimination for general algebraic equations in several unknowns, together with the various concomitant concepts such as resultants and discriminants (Étienne Bézout, 1764).

The properties of algebraic equations indicated the desirability of recognizing complex numbers as roots on a par with real roots. Only then would the so-called fundamental theorem of algebra be valid. The theorem states that an equation of nth degree always has n roots. This was realized as early as Cardano for third- and fourth-degree equations. It was expressed by Albert Girard (1629) and Descartes. A fully rigorous proof was given first by Karl Gauss (1799) in his doctoral thesis. The representation of complex numbers graphically by co-ordinates in the plane is also sometimes ascribed to him, but the credit for this idea must be awarded to the Norwegian surveyor Caspar Wessel (1795).

Methods for numerical resolution of equations, in particular for extracting square and higher roots, were devised by all the ancient schools of mathematics. Leonardo of Pisa gives a numerical solution of a cubic equation with the root accurate to more than six sexagesimal places. The calculus facilitated the development of a large number of such methods; among them are those proposed by Vieta (1600), Newton and a method by W. G. Horner (1819) that is still in use. Various criteria were devised to determine the general locations of the roots, for instance, the number of positive roots or roots in an interval. Theorems of this kind were proved by Newton, Jean Fourier, Jacobi and others; most complete is a criterion by Jacques Sturm (1835).

The Renaissance discovery of methods for the solution of equations of third and fourth degree left open the puzzling question of whether similar radical expressions could be found for roots of fifth and higher degree equations. This was a central problem in algebra in the 17th and 18th centuries and many excellent mathematicians, notably Joseph Lagrange, expended much effort on it. A feeling that the problem was insoluble became widespread. A first proof was published by Paolo Ruffini (1803, 1805), but the proof by Niels Henrik Abel (1824, 1826) is generally regarded as the first rigorous one for what has come to be known as the Abel-Ruffini theorem which states: the general algebraic equation of degree higher than four cannot be solved by radical expressions. Abel attacked the general problem when an algebraic equation of higher degree can be solved by radicals.

His papers inspired Évariste Galois (1831) to his remarkable Galois theory of equations based upon the new and fundamental concept of group theory. Although the importance of Galois' work was not realized until long after his death, group theory now permeates all fields of mathematics and has become one of the most important branches of algebra.

The 19th century saw a great surge in algebraic research with the creation of several new branches of algebra. Introduced were such topics as invariant theory, originally inspired by the desire to determine those algebraic quantities of a curve that are independent of the choice of the co-ordinate systems; the theory of algebraic functions; the theory of algebraic numbers created by Ernst Kummer and Julius Dedekind, including the theory of ideals, one of the most fertile concepts of modern algebra; further extensions of the number concepts, first through the quaternions of Sir William Hamilton and later through the general hypercomplex numbers, which in turn are closely related to the theory of matrices, an all-pervading part of recent mathematics.

The algebraists of the 20th century have continued the work in these and many other domains. With increased knowledge in so many branches of algebra has come the realization that the various theories are related through certain general principles underlying them all. This has led to the development of a so-called abstract algebra with two chief aims: (1) A deduction problem comprised of the derivation of the properties of a system with given axioms. These axioms are of algebraic nature, and the operations on the elements correspond in some way to addition, subtraction, mul-

tiplication and division. (2) A completeness problem consisting of the construction and classification of all systems that can exist for a given family of axioms. A typical example of an analysis of the latter kind is a work by Ernst Steinitz (1910) deriving all types of fields; that is, an algebraic system in which all the ordinary axioms for the four basic operations are satisfied. The theory of rings has become equally fundamental, uniting the principles of many domains of algebra; this theory deals mainly with operations, corresponding to the first three fundamental ones. Finally, intense efforts have been made in the study of groups and grouplike systems with only one operation, sometimes called an addition but more often a multiplication.

See ALGEBRA; MATHEMATICS, HISTORY OF; ALGEBRAIC GEOMETRY.

BIBLIOGRAPHY.—*The Rhind Mathematical Papyrus*, ed. by T. E. Peet (1923) and by Chace and others (1927–29); O. Neugebauer, *Vorgriechische Mathematik* (1934), *The Exact Sciences in Antiquity* (1957); O. Ore, *Cardano: the Gambling Scholar* (1953); Florian Cajori, *History of Mathematical Notation*, 2 vol. (1928–29); D. E. Smith, *History of Mathematics* (1923–25); E. T. Bell, *The Development of Mathematics* (1940); D. J. Struik, *A Concise History of Mathematics*, 2 vol. (1948); B. L. van der Waerden, *Science Awakening* (1954).

(O. Oe.)

ALGEBRAIC FORMS: *see* ALGEBRAIC GEOMETRY: *Definitions;* INVARIANTS; NUMBERS, THEORY OF: *Representation by Forms;* TENSOR ALGEBRA.

ALGEBRAIC FUNCTIONS, a study of a class of functions associated with algebraic equations. *See* ELLIPTIC FUNCTIONS; FUNCTION; NUMBER: *Generalizations.*

ALGEBRAIC GEOMETRY, a branch of mathematics in which the properties of a geometrical structure are described by means of algebraic expressions.

The origins of algebraic geometry go back to the introduction of co-ordinates into geometry. It was not, however, until the early 19th century that the subject began to stand on its own, and indeed for nearly half a century after that its role was mainly to supplement the synthetic methods of dealing with projective geometry. Nevertheless, it is convenient to date the modern subject of algebraic geometry from the introduction of homogeneous co-ordinates into projective space by August F. Möbius and others. From this time onward algebraic methods of investigating figures and loci in projective space became of increasing importance, and during the great period in the history of projective geometry in the later 19th and early 20th centuries the use of algebraic methods was all-important. The achievements of this form of algebraic geometry belong, however, more properly to projective geometry.

Nevertheless this association with projective geometry is the basis on which all the modern developments in algebraic geometry are founded. One of the most usual methods of establishing algebraic geometry on a rigorous basis is to define first a projective space over an algebraic field and then to define algebraic varieties in it. The field may be any algebraic field, but it is usually assumed to be commutative. Further restrictions that are often imposed are that the field should be algebraically closed, or that it should be of characteristic zero; *i.e.*, if a is any nonzero element of the field, a, $2a = a + a$, $3a = 2a + a$, ... are all distinct. The case in which the field is the field of complex numbers is usually referred to as the classical case, and until quite recent times was the only one that had received thorough study. Since this article follows chronological order in general, it shall be assumed that the classical case is being discussed, until the section on *Developments After 1920.*

Definitions.—The following definitions are most convenient when approaching algebraic geometry from the classical point of view. Recent advances have shown that a more abstract approach is desirable, but this will be referred to only in later sections.

Let $(x^0, \ldots, x^n)$ be a co-ordinate system in a projective space P_n of n dimensions. The subset U of points whose co-ordinates satisfy a system of homogeneous polynomial equations,

$$f\alpha(x^0, \cdots, x^n) = 0$$

where α runs over some indexing system (not necessarily finite), is called an algebraic variety of P_n. It can be proved that any algebraic variety can be defined by a finite set of equations, and that a set of points that satisfies the definition of an algebraic variety in one set of co-ordinates in P_n does so in any other permissible co-ordinate system. If V is another algebraic variety in P_n, given by the equation

$$g^i(x^0, \cdots, x^n) = 0 \ (i = 1, 2, \cdots)$$

the intersection $U \cap V$ is defined to be the set of points satisfying the combined system of equations

$$f^\alpha(x^0, \cdots, x^n) = 0$$
$$g^i(x^0, \cdots, x^n) = 0$$

(all possible α, i); and the join $U + V$ of U and V is given by the equation

$$f^\alpha(x^0, \cdots, x^n) \ g^i(x^0, \cdots, x^n) = 0$$

(all possible α, i). A variety U is said to be irreducible if, whenever it is written as a join $U = V + W$, then either $U = V$ or $U = W$; and it is shown that every algebraic variety in P_n can be expressed in one and only one way as the join of a finite number of irreducible varieties.

Two irreducible algebraic varieties U and V are said to be in birational correspondence if there exists a correspondence (expressible by means of algebraic equations) between their points such that to a general point of U (or V) there corresponds just one point of V (or U). An elaboration of the definition of a birational equivalence makes it possible to define at least one point, but in general a locus of points, of V which corresponds to any point of U. Points that have a locus of corresponding points are called fundamental points of the correspondence.

The term algebraic geometry embraces the study of all general properties of algebraic varieties, as opposed to properties of special loci like planes, quadrics, and so on, which belong to projective geometry. The most highly developed part of algebraic geometry, called birational geometry, concerns the study of those properties common to all members of a class of birationally equivalent varieties.

Algebraic Curves.—In the case $n = 2$, the only irreducible algebraic varieties in the plane (x^0, x^1, x^2), other than the plane itself, are single points, or loci given by a single irreducible equation

$$f(x^0, x^1, x^2) = 0$$

Such a locus is called an irreducible plane curve; in general a plane curve is the join of a finite number of irreducible plane curves. The earliest investigations in algebraic geometry concerned the properties of plane curves. These deal with the notion of multiple point, bitangents and inflexions. (*See* CURVES.) A rigorous definition of the intersection multiplicities of plane curves is also possible, satisfying Étienne Bézout's theorem that the sum of the multiplicities of the intersections of two curves in a plane of orders m, n is mn. A slightly later development concerns the behaviour of a curve under a birational transformation of the plane into itself. The simplest such transformations are the collineations (projective transformations) of the plane. These have no fundamental points. But there is a much wider class of self-transformations of the plane into itself, namely the Cremona transformations, which can be shown to be generated by collineations and quadratic transformations of the type

$$x^0 y^0 = x^1 y^1 = x^2 y^2$$

An important theorem is that given any curve C in a plane there exists a Cremona transformation which transforms it into a plane curve D whose multiple points are ordinary singularities. An ordinary singularity is an r-fold point having r distinct linear branches through it with distinct tangents. If D is a curve of order n having ordinary singularities of multiplicity $r_1, r_2, r_3 \ldots$, the genus of D is defined to be

$$\tfrac{1}{2}(n - 1)(n - 2) - \tfrac{1}{2}\Sigma r_1 \, (r_1 - 1)$$

The orders and multiplicities of the singularities of the curve D with ordinary singularities obtained from C by Cremona transformations depend on the transformation used, but the genus of D

depends only on C and hence is called the genus of C. Two curves that are equivalent under Cremona transformations thus have the same genus.

Parallel with this theory of curves G. F. B. Riemann developed his theory of algebraic functions of a complex variable. His problem was to study a function w of the complex variable z defined by an irreducible algebraic equation

$$f(z, w) = 0$$

Since, if z, w are interpreted as nonhomogeneous co-ordinates in a plane, this is the equation of an irreducible curve and the problem is essentially the same as in algebraic geometry. Riemann's method consists in constructing a complex manifold, the Riemann surface of the curve, on which he studies the more elementary functions.

Two sets of points S_1 and S_2 on the Riemann surface are said to be equivalent if they are the poles and zeros, respectively, of a rational function on the surface. Given any set of points S on the surface the sets equivalent to S are S itself and the zeros of the rational function which have their poles at S: the aggregate of equivalent sets is called the complete linear system $|S|$ defined by S.

The celebrated theorem of Riemann-Roch asserts that the sets of points equivalent to a given set S can be represented by the points of a projective space of dimension

$$r = n - p + i$$

where n is the sum of the multiplicities of the points of S, p is the genus of the curve and i is an invariant of S called its index of speciality.

The properties of complete linear systems can be interpreted in geometrical terms on the curve C. Two sets S_1 and S_2 on C are then equivalent if and only if there exists a set S such that there exist two curves $\phi_1 \ (x^0, x^1, x^2) = 0$ and $\phi_2 \ (x^0, x^1, x^2) = 0$ whose intersections with C are $S + S_1$ and $S + S_2$ respectively. A system of curves

$$\sum_{i = 0}^{r} \lambda_i \phi_i(x^0, x^1, x^2) = 0$$

none of which contains C identically, which passes through a fixed set S cut C residually in a linear system of sets of n points, denoted by g_n^r, and the existence of a unique complete system containing a given set S is easily proved. By writing $\lambda_i = a_i\rho + b_i\sigma$ when ρ and σ are parameters, a one-dimensional system can be defined g_n^1. In this g_n^1 there is a finite number of sets in which a point counts twice; if the set of double points is denoted by J, the various "Jacobian" sets J which arise from different g_n^1 taken from the complete system g_n^r defined by S are all linearly equivalent, and the system $|K|$ which can be defined symbolically by $|K| = |J - 2S|$ is independent of the system S chosen and is an invariant system—the canonical system—on C. The sets of it, indeed, correspond to the zeros of the different differentials of the first kind.

Starting from these ideas a complete geometrical theory corresponding to the theory of rational functions on a Riemann surface can be built up. Now it is easy to show that if D is any curve (not necessarily plane) which is birationally equivalent to C, the sets of points on D cut by hyperplanes on D determine the sets of a linear system on C; and conversely, if g_n^r is a linear system on C

$$y^i = \phi^i(x_i x_1 x_2) \ (i = 0, \cdots, r)$$

determines a curve D in P_r which is, in general, birationally equivalent to C. Thus the theory of linear systems on a curve contains the theory of birational transformations of the curve. A result of particular importance is that there exists a linear system on C that transforms it birationally into a curve with no singular points.

Algebraic Surfaces.—M. Noether, A. Cayley, H. G. Zeuthen and others in different ways tackled the problem of constructing a theory of surfaces in P_3, but the systematic development of a general theory of surfaces was first undertaken, and largely carried through, by the Italian school of geometers, led by C. Segre, G.

Castelnuovo, F. Enriques and F. Severi. Their method was to generalize the idea of a linear system of sets of points on a curve to linear systems of curves on a surface. However, the generalization is not straightforward. One immediate difficulty is that while it is possible to analyze the nature of a curve in the neighbourhood of a singular point in complete detail, a similar analysis presents very great difficulties in the case of a singular point of a surface. The natural remedy for this is to try to obtain a surface birationally equivalent to the given one which has no singularities. Various attempts were made on this problem, but it was not until 1935 that R. J. Walker gave a proof on classical lines which has withstood all criticism. (Since then O. Zariski has given two proofs, based on advanced algebraic techniques.)

Even with the result that a surface can be transformed into one without singular points there is a further difficulty. Let F and F' be two nonsingular surfaces obtained from a given surface by birational transformations. F and F' are birationally equivalent to one another, but in the one-to-one correspondence between their points there may be fundamental points where the correspondence ceases to be one-to-one. For this reason the invariants of non-singular surfaces are divided into "absolute" invariants, unaltered for all birational transformations, and "relative" invariants, which are unaltered only for birational transformations in which there are no fundamental elements.

In practice, when it is desired to make use of projective properties of P_3 in proving theorems, it is convenient to project the nonsingular surface, from a generally chosen vertex, into P_3. The resulting surface has singularities consisting of a double curve and triple points which are also triple for the double curve. The surface is then said to have ordinary singularities. The situation is illustrated by the degenerate case of three planes; the double curve is of order three, consisting of the intersection of pairs of planes, and the common point is triple for the double curve and the surface. The procedure now is to take a surface in P_3 with ordinary singularities and to consider linear systems of curves on it. The relation between linear systems and birational transformations is as in the case of curves. Given any linear system $|C|$ of dimension at least three, a subsystem can be selected from it and a Jacobian curve can be defined of the subsystem. The various curves J that are obtained by taking different subsystems for $|C|$ are all equivalent and the complete system $|K|$ defined by $|J^* - 3C|$ is independent of $|C|$; here J^* means a Jacobian curve J if there are no curves on the surface having zero intersection with the general curve of $|C|$, but is J suitably modified by a combination of these curves where they exist. $|K|$ is called the canonical system. The number of linearly independent curves on $|K|$ is called the geometric genus (denoted by p_g) of the surface. It is an absolute invariant.

A Riemann-Roch theorem can be established for a complete system of curves $|C|$ on a surface, but in its classical form it appears as an inequality

$$r \geqq n - \pi + 1 + p_a - i$$

where r is the dimension of the complete system $|C|$, n is the intersection number $C \cap C$, π is the genus of C, p_a is an absolute invariant of the surface, called the arithmetic genus, and i is the index of speciality of $|C|$ defined in a similar way to the index of speciality on a curve. In comparing this formula with the Riemann-Roch theorem for a curve two points should be stressed. First, the relation is an inequality. A good deal is known about sufficient conditions for equality to hold, but until recent times, when other methods became available, no simple interpretation of the excess of the dimension over the expression given on the right was known. Second, p_a corresponds to the genus p which appears in the formula for curves and which also corresponds to the geometric genus p_g. In general, however, p_g is not equal to p_a, but $p_g \geqq p_a$ always. The invariant $p_g - p_a = q$ is called the irregularity of the surface and is of fundamental topological importance.

A number of other invariants play an important role in the theory of surfaces:

(1) The linear genus $\omega - 1$ is equal to the intersection number $K \cap K$ of two canonical curves.

(2) The Zeuthen-Segre invariant $I + 4$ is defined as follows: let $|C|$ be any one-dimensional linear system of curves on the surface, let $C \cap C = n$ and let δ be the number of curves of $|C|$ with double points (curves with higher singularities count an appropriate number of times), and let π be the genus of C. Then $I + 4 = \delta - n - 4(\pi - 1)$. Both $\omega - 1$ and $I + 4$ are relative invariants but

$$(\omega - 1) + (I + 4) = 12(p_a + 1)$$

is an absolute invariant.

(3) The bigenus of the surface P_2 is the number of linearly independent curves of the complete system $|2K|$.

A great deal of the literature on algebraic surfaces is devoted to the study of special surfaces, such as hyperelliptic surfaces, or to the classification of surfaces having given values of the invariants, particularly for low values of the invariants. Two results may be mentioned. First, if $p_g = p_a = P_2 = 0$, the surface is rational (that is, birationally equivalent to a plane). Second, if $p_g = 0$, $p_a < -1$, the surface is birationally equivalent to a ruled surface of genus $-p_a$.

On a curve a set of n points defines a unique linear system whose dimension is, in general, less than n, but clearly they belong to a system of sets which can be represented by the points of an algebraic variety of dimension n, namely the variety which represents all the sets of n points on the curve. This notion of algebraic systems on a curve is trivial, but when its generalization to surfaces is considered an important new field of investigation emerges. The problem is simply: do there exist systems of algebraic curves on a surface that are represented by points of an irreducible algebraic variety and are not all contained in a linear system? A consideration of the generators of a nonrational ruled surface shows that such systems may exist. The general result is that a complete linear system belongs to an algebraic system of systems represented by an algebraic variety of dimension $p_g - p_a$. (A modification of this statement is necessary when the given linear system is "virtually nonexistent"; e.g., when it is a combination of irreducible curves some of which are counted negatively.) Hence for a regular variety every algebraic system is contained in a linear system.

The existence of these algebraic systems of curves enables us to group the curves on a surface into wider equivalent groups, but this generalized notion of equivalence requires careful formulation. It is not sufficient to say that two algebraic curves C and D are equivalent in this wider sense if there exists a curve E and that $E + C$ and $E + D$ belong to the same irreducible algebraic system, for this relation may not be transitive. If this relation is defined by $C \equiv D$, two curves C, D have to be defined to be algebraically equivalent, $C = D$, if there exists a sequence $C_1, C_2, \ldots, C_r$ of curves such that

$$C \equiv C_1, C_1 \equiv C_2, \cdots, C_r \equiv D$$

Then the fundamental result is that the classes of algebraically equivalent curves on a surface form, under the addition of curves, a group which is the direct sum of a finite number ρ of infinite cyclic groups and a finite group (the torsion group). Let $C_1, \ldots, C_\rho$ be curves of the surface that define algebraic systems that are generators of the ρ infinite cyclic groups. Then any curve C on the surface satisfies as again

$$C = \lambda_1 C_1 + \cdots + \lambda_\rho C_\rho + \Gamma \quad (\Gamma \text{ in the torsion group})$$

Further, the $\rho \times \rho$ intersection matrix $(C_i C_j)$ is nonsingular. The curve $C_1, \ldots, C_\rho$ is called a base.

The theory of algebraic functions of two variables and their integrals, which is related to the theory of surfaces as the theory of the Riemann surface is related to the theory of curves, was developed about the same time by E. Picard. Most of the methods used have, however, been superseded by the new methods of topology and sheaves (see below).

Generalizations.—Attempts in the same manner to generalize the theory of curves and surfaces as outlined above to varieties of higher dimension will be briefly summarized.

The generalization of the theory of linear systems, as far as "sufficiently general" linear systems are concerned, was made by

Severi in 1907, who established the form of the Riemann-Roch theorem in suitably restricted cases. The same author later generalized in some measure the theory of the base to higher varieties. Of more significance, however, is the theory of systems of equivalence. In this theory, instead of considering linear systems of varieties of dimension $n - 1$ on a variety of dimension n, consideration is given to "systems of equivalence" of varieties of dimension r $(0 \leqq r \leqq n)$, so defined that when $r = n - 1$ a system of equivalence is a linear system. Severi established the existence of a relatively invariant system of equivalence of points on a surface closely related to the Zeuthen-Segre invariant. In the definition given above of the Zeuthen-Segre invariant δ is interpreted as the set of double points, n as the set of intersections and $2\pi - 2$ as a canonical set K on C; then $\delta - n - 2K$ is an invariant system of equivalence (the canonical system of points of the surface). This result of Severi's was generalized to varieties of three dimensions by B. Segre, and a complete set of canonical systems of equivalence of dimension r, for $r = 0, \ldots, n - 1$ on a variety of n dimensions was obtained by J. A. Todd. Similar results were obtained by other methods by M. Egar.

Developments After 1920.—Developments in algebraic geometry after 1920 merit special mention. In 1921 S. Lefschetz began using the new science of topology in the study of algebraic varieties (defined over the complex field). By making a direct study of the topology of a nonsingular algebraic variety he achieved his first objective of giving a simplified account of Picard's work on algebraic integrals associated with a surface and of generalizing the results to varieties of higher dimensions. In doing this, however, he did much more, and his work really forms the starting point of a great new field of research. His investigations of the topology of an algebraic variety established the existence of a large number of properties of the topology of an algebraic variety V of dimension m. Among these are the following properties: the pth homology group of V is isomorphic to the pth homology group of a prime section, if $p < m - 1$ and the $(m - 1)^{\text{th}}$ homology group of a prime section is epimorphic to that of V. The Betti numbers of odd dimensions are even, and those of even dimensions are at least one. Such properties are special to algebraic varieties but do not characterize them. (*See* TOPOLOGY, ALGEBRAIC; TOPOLOGY, GENERAL.)

A further contribution made by Lefschetz concerns the cycles defined by the algebraic subvarieties of V. Lefschetz's contribution was the theorem that on an algebraic surface a two-cycle is homologous to the cycle which represents a curve on the surface if and only if every nonsingular double integral $\int \int R(xyz)dxdy$ attached to the surface has no period on it. This result has subsequently been generalized to deal with two-cycles on V_m (W. V. D. Hodge) and $(2m - 2)$-cycles on V_m (K. Kodaira and D. C. Spencer). Lefschetz's investigation further led to a very simple and significant interpretation of the theory of the base for curves on a surface. The main result is that two curves on a surface are algebraically equivalent, in the sense just described, if and only if they are homologous as two-cycles. The additive group of algebraic systems is then isomorphic to a subgroup of the Betti group of two-cycles.

The foregoing investigations by Lefschetz form the starting point of the modern theory of complex manifolds (*q.v.*). A complex manifold of m dimension is a manifold (which is assumed in this article to be compact) with the property that it can be covered by a set of neighbourhoods each of which can be parametrized by m complex co-ordinates in such a way that where these neighbourhoods overlap the two sets of co-ordinates are analytically related. A nonsingular algebraic variety is the simplest example of a complex manifold, but not all complex manifolds are algebraic varieties. Various powerful methods have been developed for studying the properties of complex manifolds, such as the theory of harmonic integrals (W. V. D. Hodge and G. de Rham) and the theory of sheaves (or *faisceaux*) (H. Cartan and J. Leray). Using harmonic integrals, it is possible to show that a considerable number of Lefschetz's results on the topology of algebraic varieties follow from the fact that the complex manifold defined by an algebraic variety is a Kähler manifold; that is, it can be given a

hermitian metric that can be written in terms of local co-ordinates as

$$\Sigma_\alpha \Sigma_\beta a_{\alpha\beta} \, dz^\alpha \, d\bar{z}^\beta$$

whose associated differential form

$$\omega = ia_{\alpha\beta} \, dz^\alpha \cap d\bar{z}^\beta$$

is exact. Still more properties follow from the fact that on an algebraic manifold the Kähler matrix can be chosen so that the value of the integral of ω over any integral cycle is an integer; Kodaira has shown that this additional property is sufficient to ensure that the complex manifold arises from an algebraic variety. This is one of a series of results which go beyond the strict confines of algebraic geometry, dealing with the possible differential structures which can be imposed on a topological manifold.

Kodaira and Spencer (1952–55) systematically applied the theory of sheaves to investigate properties of algebraic varieties of dimension m. Their main task was the relation between linear systems of subvarieties of dimension $m - 1$ and simple analytic 1-vector bundles. (r-vector bundles are defined over any topological space: over an open set U the bundle is the direct product of U by a vector r-space, but when these local products are fitted together they are "twisted" in a certain way, so that the total bundle on the variety is not, in general, a direct product.) The system of tangent spaces at the points of an algebraic variety is an important example of a bundle, the tangent bundle. Associated with a complex analytic r-bundle are important cohomology classes, the Chern classes of the bundle.

In the case $r = 1$ there is only one Chern class, which is dual (in a certain sense) to the cycles representing the subvarieties of a complete linear system associated with the bundle.

Their most important contributions are as follows: (1) They developed the general form of the Riemann-Roch theorem for varieties of dimension $m - 1$. The form of the theorem obtained made it possible to express the dimension of a complete linear system in the form obtained by Severi for "sufficiently large systems" (this expression is called the virtual dimension) but including additional terms (index of speciality, etc.) that make it exact in all cases. These additional terms are expressed as dimensions of certain cohomology groups but can be given an interpretation in terms of classical algebraic geometry. (2) They obtained a very simple proof of Lefschetz's conditions (*see* above) for a $(2m - 2)$-cycle on a variety of m dimension to be algebraic. (3) They reconciled various definitions of the arithmetic genus of an algebraic variety whose equivalence had been conjectured by Severi.

The Chern classes of an r-bundle are dual to cycles representing varieties of dimension $m - 1, m - 2, \ldots, m - r$. In particular, the Chern classes of the tangent bundle define algebraic varieties of dimension $m - 1, m - 2, \ldots, 0$. These varieties vary in some way in systems, but except in the first case, where the varieties vary in a complete linear system, the exact nature is not known, though they are contained in systems of equivalence as defined by B. Segre and Todd. These systems are, indeed, the canonical systems of Todd and Egar. Using these notions F. Hirzebruch was led to a considerable generalization of the Riemann-Roch theorem for r-bundles. The "sections" of such bundles form a module over the complex field which in the case $r = 1$ is isomorphic to the set of subvarieties of the corresponding complete linear system. The Riemann-Roch theorem for r-bundles is represented by the equality of two expressions: one that gives the virtual division of the module of sections of the bundle and is equal to the effective dimension plus a series of terms that are the dimensions of a set of cohomology groups associated with the bundle, and the other is expressible entirely in terms of the intersection numbers of the varieties that represent the Chern classes of the r-bundle and those of the tangent bundle. A still wider generalization of the Riemann-Roch theorem is due to A. Grothendieck.

Another development in recent years of classical algebraic geometry is the formulation and development of the basic concepts in terms of modern abstract algebra. Here two distinct lines may be distinguished. In a series of papers (1931–39) B. L. van der Waerden gave a precise algebraic formulation of algebraic geometry over any field (the definition of an algebraic variety at the beginning of this article is based on his work) and led up to a rigorous definition of the central concept of geometry, the intersection of subvarieties. Zariski then made notable contributions by his analysis of the notion of a simple point of an algebraic variety and developed his general theory of birational transformations of varieties in which he made great use of the algebraic theory of valuations of a field. In addition to his proof that any algebraic surface may be birationally transformed into one without singularities, already referred to, he succeeded in proving a similar, but much more difficult, result for varieties of three dimensions. It seems probable that the problem for varieties of m dimensions is of the same order of difficulty, but a complete proof for values of m greater than three has not yet been given.

In the course of his investigations in valuation theory Zariski was led to introduce a topology into algebraic geometry. In this topology, now called the Zariski topology, the closed sets on an algebraic variety are the algebraic subvarieties, their complements being, of course, the open sets. This topology has proved fundamental in modern algebraic geometry. As a first instance of its use it enables us to extend the notion of sheaves to general algebraic varieties, and results of great generality have been achieved in this way by J. P. Serre, Grothendieck and others.

A parallel development is due to A. Weil, whose approach is rather different. While van der Waerden and Zariski began by considering varieties as subsets of projective space, and led on to the notion of the function field of an algebraic variety and the generic point of a representation of it, which subsequently plays a fundamental role in Zariski's work, Weil started from these notions, and his book *The Foundations of Algebraic Geometry* (1946) is to a great extent a chapter in the theory of algebraic fields. A minor difference is that originally he defined algebraic varieties in affine space instead of projective space, but this led to the very important concept of an abstract variety. A Zariski topology can be defined on a variety on affine space and is useful in defining open sets (as in the projective case). Weil then constructed an algebraic variety by piecing together open sets. Since two open sets meet in an open set, which is nearly the whole of an algebraic variety, the correspondence must be a birational one, but it is subject to an important restriction: if U_1 and U_2 are the two open sets, and if U_1' is that part of U_1 that has corresponding points on U_2 and U_2' that part of U_2 that has corresponding points on U_1, the birational correspondence between U_1' and U_2' must be one-to-one without exception. This makes it possible to identify U_1' and U_2' and so piece U_1 and U_2 together. Corresponding to the notion of a compact manifold is the notion of a complete variety: a variety is complete if any specialization (similar to a limit) of a generic point is represented by a point of at least one covering open set. Most of Weil's general theorems can be proved for abstract varieties; but many other results are proved only in the case of projective varieties; i.e., varieties defined as projective space by the van de Waerden methods. Clearly any projective variety can be regarded as an abstract variety: M. Nagata has shown by examples that there exist abstract varieties that cannot be represented as projective varieties.

See ANALYTIC GEOMETRY; GEOMETRY; SURFACES; ALGEBRA.

BIBLIOGRAPHY.—Books dealing with the general theory of algebraic varieties are B. L. van der Waerden, *Einführung in die algebraische Geometrie* (1939); A. Weil, *Foundations of Algebraic Geometry* (1947); W. V. D. Hodge and D. Pedoe, *Methods of Algebraic Geometry* (1947–54); S. Lefschetz, *Algebraic Geometry* (1953).

Books on algebraic curves include F. Enriques, *Teoria geometrica delle equazioni* (1915–34); F. Severi, *Vorlesungen über algebraische Geometrie* (1921); R. J. Walker, *Algebraic Curves* (1950). On algebraic surfaces, *see* F. Enriques, *Superfici algebriche* (1932); O. Zariski, *Algebraic Surfaces* (1935).

For an account of systems of equivalence, *see* B. Segre, *Géométrie sur une V_s algébrique* (1936); F. Severi, *Serie, sistemi d'equivalenza e corrispondenze algebriche sulle varietà algebriche* (1942).

The original book dealing with the applications of topology to algebraic geometry is S. Lefschetz, *L'Analyse situs et la géométrie moderne* (1923). An account of the applications of harmonic integrals to algebraic geometry is given in W. V. D. Hodge, *Theory and Applications of Harmonic Integrals* (1952). For another account of harmonic integrals, *see* G. de Rham, *Variétés différentiables* (1955). The treatment of al-gebraic varieties as complex manifolds will be found in A. Weil, *Variétés Kähleriennes* (1958). For the theory and applications of sheaves (*faisceaux*), *see* R. Godemont, *Théorie des faisceaux* (1958).

(Wi. Ho.)

ALGEBRAIC NUMBERS: *see* NUMBERS, THEORY OF: *Generalizations of Arithmetic.*

ALGEBRAS (LINEAR), also called hypercomplex systems, may be described as vector spaces in which a multiplication of vectors can be performed that behaves like the ordinary multiplication of numbers. More precisely, an algebra over a field F (*see* FIELDS) consists of a set of elements (which may be thought of as "numbers" and, in the older literature, are actually called "hypercomplex numbers") and three operations that may be performed on these elements, *viz.*, addition, multiplication and multiplication by elements of F. Moreover, it is necessary that the first and third of these operations satisfy the postulates for a vector space, that the first and second satisfy the postulates for a ring and that the second and third satisfy the condition $\alpha(ab) = (\alpha a)b = a(\alpha b)$ for every a and b in A and every α in F. Even more general systems are sometimes called algebras, especially those in which F is allowed to be any commutative ring, and the nonassociative algebras discussed later.

According to the theory of vector spaces, there can always be found a basis of the algebra, *i.e.*, elements $u_1, \ldots, u_n$ in the algebra such that every other element is uniquely expressible in the form $\alpha_1 u_1 + \ldots + \alpha_n u_n$ for suitable $\alpha_1, \ldots, \alpha_n$ in F. Here n, the number of elements in the basis, is the same for every basis and is called the dimension of the algebra. (Algebras need not be finite dimensional; however, the most extensive theory has been developed for algebras of finite dimension.) Using the multiplication in the algebra reveals that every product $u_i u_j$ of basis elements is again an element in the algebra. The n^2 product elements $u_i u_j$ ($i, j = 1, \ldots, n$) comprise a multiplication table of the algebra. Once it is specified, the product of any two elements in the algebra is determined because of the postulated relations among the three algebra operations:

$$(\Sigma \alpha_i u_i)(\Sigma \beta_j u_j) = \underset{i\ j}{\Sigma} \alpha_i \beta_j (u_i u_j)$$

Conversely, given a basis $u_1, \ldots, u_n$ of an n-dimensional vector space over F and a multiplication table, there is a multiplication defined in the vector space by the preceding equation. This multiplication will make the vector space an algebra if the associative law $(u_i u_j)u_k = u_i(u_j u_k)$ is satisfied for all i, j, k.

Examples.—*Zero Algebras.*—Any vector space can be made into an algebra by defining all products to be zero.

The Algebra of Complex Numbers.—Let F be the field of real numbers and A the set of all complex numbers. The ordinary addition and multiplication of complex numbers and multiplication by real numbers make A a two-dimensional algebra over F. To describe this algebra by a multiplication table, choose the usual basis $u_1 = 1$, $u_2 = \sqrt{-1}$; the multiplication table is then $u_1 u_1 = u_1$, $u_1 u_2 = u_2$, $u_2 u_1 = u_2$, $u_2 u_2 = -u_1$.

The Algebra of Quaternions.—The quaternions (discovered by W. R. Hamilton in 1843) form a four-dimensional algebra over the field of real numbers with a basis $1, i, j, k$ and a multiplication table defined by the conditions $ij = k$, $jk = i$, $ki = j$; $ji = -k$, $kj = -i$, $ik = -j$; $ii = jj = kk = -1$; and $1a = a1 = a$ for every a. The multiplication of quaternions, like that of real and complex numbers, has the property that division is uniquely possible, except by zero: given quaternions a and b with $a \neq 0$, there always exist unique quaternions x and y such that $ax = b$ and $ya = b$. This fact is expressed by saying that the quaternions form a division algebra. In 1878 G. Frobenius proved that there are no n-dimensional division algebras over the field of real numbers (with $1 \leq n < \infty$) other than the real numbers, the complex numbers and the quaternions. Unlike the multiplication of real or complex numbers, the multiplication of quaternions is not commutative; *e.g.*, $ij \neq ji$.

Matrix Algebras.—The set of all n by n matrices with entries from a field F forms an n^2-dimensional algebra over F, using the ordinary definition of addition of matrices, multiplication of matrices and multiplication of matrices by elements of F (see MATRIX). This algebra is often denoted by F_n. The most usual basis consists of the matrices e_{ij} ($i, j = 1, 2, \ldots, n$), which have all entries equal to zero except for an entry 1 in the ith row, jth column. The multiplication table is $e_{ij}e_{kl} = 0$ if $j \neq k$, and $e_{ij}e_{jl} = e_{il}$. More generally, the n by n matrices with entries from another algebra A form an algebra which is denoted by A_n. If A has dimension k, then A_n has dimension kn^2.

Homomorphisms.—If A and B are algebras over the same field F, a homomorphism from A to B is a function f associating to each element a of A a single element $f(a)$ of B in such a way as to preserve the three algebra operations. That is, for a function f to be a homomorphism, whenever f sends a in A to b [$= f(a)$] in B, and sends a' in A to b' in B, then f must send $a + a'$ to $b + b'$, aa' to bb' and αa to αb for every α in F. If every element of B corresponds to some element of A by the homomorphism, B is said to be a homomorphic image of A. A homomorphic image of A may be thought of as a condensed version of A. If there is no condensation, i.e., if each element of B corresponds to exactly one element of A so that f is a one-to-one correspondence, the homomorphism f is called an isomorphism, and B is an isomorphic image of A. For many purposes an isomorphic image of A may be considered to be identical to A.

One measure of how far a homomorphism f is from being an isomorphism is the kernel of f; i.e., the subset of A consisting of all elements that f sends to zero in B. If the homomorphism is an isomorphism, its kernel consists of zero alone; otherwise its kernel contains nonzero elements. An ideal in an algebra A is a subset of A that is the kernel of some homomorphism; a subset I of A is an ideal if and only if it is a vector subspace and contains all products of elements of I with elements of A.

Direct Sums.—The direct sum of two algebras A_1 and A_2 is an algebra, denoted by $A_1 \oplus A_2$, consisting of all pairs (a_1, a_2) with a_1 ranging over A_1 and a_2 ranging over A_2. The algebra operations are performed componentwise: $(a_1, a_2) + (a_1', a_2') = (a_1 + a_1', a_2 + a_2')$, $(a_1, a_2)(a_1', a_2') = (a_1 a_1', a_2 a_2')$, and $\alpha(a_1, a_2) = (\alpha a_1, \alpha a_2)$. The direct sum of n algebras $A_1 \oplus A_2 \oplus \ldots \oplus A_n$ is defined similarly as the set of n-tuples $(a_1, a_2 \ldots, a_n)$ with componentwise operations.

Structure Theory.—The aim of the structure theory of algebras (as of any structure theory in mathematics) is to give a list of concrete examples of algebras which shall contain one and only one isomorphic image of every algebra. For finite-dimensional algebras, this aim is approached fairly closely, as follows.

An algebra is termed simple if every homomorphism from the algebra either is an isomorphism or sends every element to zero. The first structure theorem asserts that the algebra of all n by n matrices with entries from a division algebra (see *The Algebra of Quaternions*, above) is a simple algebra and, conversely, that every simple algebra is an isomorphic image of such a matrix algebra.

Next, for an arbitrary finite-dimensional algebra A, the radical of A is defined as the set of elements of A that are sent to zero by all homomorphisms from A to simple algebras. The second structure theorem asserts that there is a single homomorphism whose kernel is exactly the radical of A and such that the corresponding homomorphic image of A is the direct sum of simple algebras. This homomorphic image is uniquely determined by A. If the multiplication in A is commutative, the homomorphism and direct-sum statements can be interchanged: A is isomorphic to the direct sum of algebras $A_1 \oplus \ldots \oplus A_n$ and each A_i has a simple homomorphic image, with the kernel of the homomorphism being the radical of A_i.

Finally, the radical N of an algebra is itself an algebra and is nilpotent, meaning that for some positive integer k, $N^k = 0$; i.e., all products of k elements of N are zero. (This is a generalization of the zero algebras mentioned above.)

These theorems reduce the structure theory to three problems: (1) to what extent an algebra is determined once its radical N and the corresponding direct sum S of simple algebras are given; (2) the structure theory of nilpotent algebras; and (3) the structure theory of simple algebras, which the first structure theorem has already reduced to the structure theory of division algebras.

A partial answer to (1) is the principal Wedderburn theorem: if F contains the ordinary integers, then the algebra is an isomorphic image of an algebra consisting of all pairs (s, n) with s ranging over S and n ranging over N, with addition of pairs and multiplication of pairs by elements of F defined componentwise, as in the direct sum $S \oplus N$. However, multiplication of these pairs is only partly componentwise: $(s, n)(s', n') = (ss', nn' + f)$, where f is a function of s, s', n and n' which is zero if n and n' are zero. The lack of complete information about f is the reason for calling this a partial answer.

Little is known concerning problem (2). The answer to (3) varies, depending on the field F. If F is the field of complex numbers, the only division algebra is F itself, thus the only simple algebras are the matrix algebras F_n. If F is the field of real numbers, the Frobenius theorem asserts that there are exactly three division algebras. If F is the field of rational numbers, or, more generally, a field algebraic over the rational numbers, every division algebra over F is a cyclic algebra, which is a specific kind of generalization of the algebra of quaternions.

This last theorem is due to the combined efforts of R. Brauer, E. Noether, H. Hasse and A. A. Albert (1932–33). The proof involves the theory of numbers in an essential way. The other theorems were proved by J. H. M. Wedderburn in 1907. (In the special case where F is the field of complex numbers, they had already been proved by É. Cartan in 1898 and, somewhat less completely, by T. Molien in 1893.) The first three structure theorems were generalized to a theory of rings with suitable finiteness conditions by E. Artin in 1928 and E. Noether in 1929. Since then, more or less close analogues of these Wedderburn-Artin theorems have been proved for some infinite-dimensional algebras and for arbitrary rings.

Tensor Products.—The tensor product $A \otimes B$ of two algebras A and B over the same field F (also called the direct product or the Kronecker product) is an algebra consisting of all the formal finite sums of expressions $a \otimes b$ with a in A and b in B, manipulated according to the rules $a \otimes \alpha b = \alpha a \otimes b = \alpha(a \otimes b)$ and $(a \otimes b)(a' \otimes b') = aa' \otimes bb'$, for all a, a' in A, b, b' in B and α in F. If $a_1, \ldots, a_m$ form a basis of A and $b_1, \ldots, b_n$ form a basis of B, then the elements of $A \otimes B$ are uniquely expressible in the form $\alpha_{11} a_1 \otimes b_1 + \ldots + \alpha_{mn} a_m \otimes b_n$ (i.e., the set of all $a_i \otimes b_j$ forms a basis of $A \otimes B$). If A is an algebra over F, then $A \otimes F_n$ is just A_n (see *Matrix Algebras*, above). Similarly, $F_m \otimes F_n$ is F_{mn}. This construction is as vital to the theory of algebras as is the direct sum. Some instances of its use are as follows.

The centre of an algebra A is the subset consisting of all elements c such that $ca = ac$ for every a in A. An algebra is called central if there is a one-to-one correspondence between the centre and F such that when c and α correspond, then $ca = \alpha a$ for every a in A. Two algebras A and B are termed similar if $A \otimes F_n$ is an isomorphic image of $B \otimes F_m$ for some matrix algebras F_n and F_m. The similarity classes of central simple algebras then form a group with $\otimes$ as the group operation. This group is called the Brauer group of F. Its structure both depends on and illuminates many properties of the field F. If A is a central simple algebra over F, there is a normal extension field K such that $A \otimes K = K_n$. This gives rise to the theorem that every central simple algebra is similar to a crossed product, a specific type of algebra generalizing the cyclic algebras mentioned earlier.

The tensor product $V \otimes W$ of two vector spaces V and W is defined in the same way as the tensor product of algebras, except, of course, that no attempt is made to define a multiplication in $V \otimes W$. The infinite direct sum of the vector spaces F, V, $V \otimes V$, $V \otimes V \otimes V$, ... is denoted by T; its elements are merely polynomials in a basis $v_1, \ldots, v_n$ of V with coefficients in F, except that in writing and multiplying polynomials, the v's are not assumed to commute; e.g., $v_1 \otimes v_2 \neq v_2 \otimes v_1$. Now define the product $(a_1 \otimes \ldots \otimes a_r)(b_1 \otimes \ldots \otimes b_s)$ to be $a_1 \otimes \ldots \otimes a_r \otimes b_1 \otimes \ldots \otimes b_s$ whenever the a's and b's are in V, and define the products of other elements of T in terms of these special products by using the distributive laws. This transforms T into an infinite-dimensional algebra generated by the elements of V, called the tensor algebra of V. Every algebra whose dimension is the dimension of V, or which is generated by a subspace of this dimension, is a homomorphic image of T. The elements of $V \otimes \ldots \otimes V$ (with r factors) are called tensors of rank r, or homogeneous elements of degree r. (*See* TENSOR ALGEBRA.)

The homomorphic image of the tensor algebra T which is obtained by setting $a \otimes b$ equal to $-b \otimes a$ when a and b are elements of V is called the exterior algebra (or Grassmann algebra) of V. When this equality is assumed, all homogeneous elements of degree $n+1$ or more are forced to be zero, so that if V is n-dimensional, the exterior algebra of V has finite dimension (in fact, exactly 2^n). This algebra was first introduced by H. G. Grassmann in 1844 for geometric purposes; the linear manifolds of dimension r in projective n-space are best described by the homogeneous elements $a_1 \otimes \ldots \otimes a_{r+1}$ in the exterior algebra of an n-dimensional vector space.

Nonassociative Algebras.—A vector space with a multiplication satisfying all the postulates for an algebra except the associative law of multiplication is called a nonassociative algebra (*see* A. A. Albert, "Non-Associative Algebras," *Annals of Mathematics,* 43:685–723 [1942]).

Undoubtedly the most important nonassociative algebras are the Lie algebras, in which two postulates provide a substitute for the associative law: $aa = 0$ and $a(bc) + b(ca) + c(ab) = 0$ for every a, b, c in the Lie algebra. The set of vectors in three-space with cross product as multiplication form a Lie algebra. The structure theory for Lie algebras over the real and complex fields is as complete as that of associative algebras. The importance of Lie algebras stems from their connection with Lie groups (*see* GROUPS AND ALGEBRAS, REPRESENTATIONS OF; GROUPS, CONTINUOUS). With each Lie group is associated a Lie algebra which reflects essentially all the local properties of the group.

Nonassociative division algebras over the field of real numbers are of importance in topology; the existence of such an algebra of dimension n gives a continuous vector field on the $(n-1)$-dimensional sphere. H. Hopf proved in 1940 that the only possible values of n are powers of 2. For $n = 2$ there is the algebra of complex numbers, and for $n = 4$ the algebra of quaternions (both are associative). For $n = 8$ there is a nonassociative algebra discovered by A. Cayley in 1843 called the algebra of Cayley numbers and defined from the quaternions much as the quaternions can be defined from the complex numbers. In 1958, using topological results of R. Bott, J. Milnor and M. A. Kervaire each proved that there are no nonassociative division algebras of dimension 16 or higher over the real numbers.

BIBLIOGRAPHY.—A. A. Albert, *Structure of Algebras* (1939); E. Artin, C. Nesbitt and R. M. Thrall, *Rings with Minimum Condition* (1944); N. Bourbaki, *Algèbre,* vol. 8 (1960); C. Chevalley, *Construction and Study of Certain Important Algebras* (1955); N. Jacobson, *Theory of Rings* (1943), *Structure of Rings* (1956); B. L. van der Waerden, *Modern Algebra,* 4th ed., vol. 2 (1960). (D. Z.)

ALGECIRAS, a town and seaport in the province of Cádiz, Spain, lies at the extreme south of the country, 6 mi. W. of Gibraltar on the opposite (western) side of the Bay of Algeciras. Pop. (1960) 66,317 (mun.). In Arabic the name means "the island," from the Isla Verde which stands at the entrance to the port. The town has a mild and healthful climate which attracts tourists and invalids. It was perhaps the Roman Portus Albus, but was probably refounded in 713 by the Moors, who held it until 1344; it was then taken by Alfonso XI of Castile after a famous siege of 20 months. It was reoccupied in 1704 by Spanish colonists from Gibraltar and in 1760 rebuilt by Charles III on the present rectangular plan. The Algeciras conference (*q.v.*), held in 1906, introduced effective administration in Morocco and a new alignment of the powers in Europe. The modern town is without great interest, though there is a splendid view of Gibraltar across the bay. A little way inland along the railway, which runs northeast to Córdoba, are several arches of a Moorish aqueduct. The main commercial activity is that connected with the port, which is a stopping place for transatlantic liners and handles many passengers, especially from the ferry services to and from north Africa; there are also ice-making and preserving plants. (M. B. F.)

ALGECIRAS CONFERENCE, an international conference that opened on Jan. 16, 1906, to discuss France's relationship to the government of Morocco. Two years earlier an entente cordiale, signed by Great Britain and France, had provided, among other things, for British support of French special interests in Morocco. France's attempt to implement the agreement by presenting the Moroccan sultan with a program of economic and police "reforms" brought the indignant German kaiser to Tangier in March 1905. The kaiser challenged French intentions by affirming the sovereignty of the sultan and demanding the retention of the "open door" for commerce.

Tension was relieved as U.S. Pres. Theodore Roosevelt was prevailed upon by the kaiser to help bring about the 1906 conference in Algeciras, Spain. Contrary to German expectations, only Austria-Hungary supported Germany's views; Italy, Russia and, more significantly, Britain and the United States lined up behind France. On the surface, nevertheless, the convention, signed April 7, 1906, appeared to limit French penetration. It reaffirmed the independence of the sultan and the economic equality of the powers, and provided that the French and Spanish police officers were to be under a Swiss inspector general.

The real significance of the conference is to be found in the substantial diplomatic support given France by Britain and the United States, foreshadowing their roles in World War I, of which the Moroccan crisis was a prelude. *See also* MOROCCO: *History.*

See Joseph B. Bishop, *Theodore Roosevelt and His Time Shown in His Own Letters* (1920); Eugene Anderson, *The First Moroccan Crisis, 1904–1906* (1930). (W. SY.)

ALGER OF LIÈGE (known also as ALGER OF CLUNY and ALGERUS MAGISTER) (1060?–1131?), French priest who had, in his time, a wide reputation for learning and ecclesiastical writing, was born in Liège about 1060. He was first a deacon of the church of St. Bartholomew at Liège and was appointed (*c.* 1100) to the cathedral church of St. Lambert. He declined many offers from German bishops and finally retired to the monastery of Cluny, where he died about 1131.

His *History of the Church of Liège* and many of his other works are lost. The most important of those extant are: *De misericordia et justitia,* a collection of biblical and patristic extracts with a commentary, an important work for the history of church law and discipline, in the *Anecdota* of Martène, vol. v; *De sacramentis corporis et sanguinis Domini,* a treatise in three books against the Berengarian heresy, highly commended by Peter of Cluny and Erasmus; *De gratia et libero arbitrio,* in B. Pez's *Anecdota,* vol. iv; and *De sacrificio missae,* in the *Scriptorum veterum nova collectio* of Angelo Mai, vol. ix, p. 371.

See J. P. Migne, *Patrologia Latina,* vol. clxxx, pp. 739–972; article by S. M. Deutsch in Herzog-Hauck, *Realencyklopädie für protestantische Theologie.*

ALGER, HORATIO (1832–1899), the most popular author in the U.S. in the last 30 years of the 19th century and without doubt the most influential author of his generation, was born Jan. 13, 1832, in Revere, Mass. He was the son of an extremely conservative Unitarian minister, who personally undertook the supervision of his son's early life and saturated him with prayer, study, and discipline. By the age of nine "Holy Horatio," as he came to be known, was reading Plato and early showed an interest in writing. His formal education began at Gates Academy, and at Harvard he distinguished himself in the Classics and in French.

Alger attempted to earn his living after graduation from Harvard in 1852 as a private tutor and as a newspaperman. He eventually gave in to his father's pressure and in 1855 enrolled in the Harvard Divinity School. He graduated in 1860, but instead of entering the ministry as his father wished, he took an unexpected inheritance and went to London and Paris where he spent a year living the life of a bohemian. He returned to America, and after several futile tries at enlisting in the Union Army at the outbreak of the Civil War, again succumbed to the arguments of his father and in 1864 was ordained a minister of the Unitarian Church in Brewster, Mass.

At the invitation of William T. Adams, a publisher and author of juvenile literature, Alger resigned his pulpit at Brewster and moved to New York to pursue a literary career. Alger by this time had published several works, but nothing in particular had come of them: *Bertha's Christmas Vision* (1856); *Nothing to Do; a Tilt at Our Best Society* (a narrative poem published anonymously in 1857); *Frank's Campaign, or What Can a Boy Do* (1864); and *Helen Ford* (1866; unique among Alger's works in that the principal character is a girl). It was, however, with the appearance of *Ragged Dick, or Street Life in New York,* published in 1867, that Alger found the vein he was to work the rest of his life. The success of *Ragged Dick* had consequences that were to play an important part in Alger's life. Charles O'Conner, a New York social worker, suggested that Alger visit the Newsboys' Lodging House, a home for foundlings and runaway boys. Not only did Alger come to use the home as a base of operations, but he identified himself with the lodging house and for the next 30 years became the benefactor, champion, and hero to the boys of the institution.

At the suggestion of his publisher Alger traveled in the West to gather material for his stories. From this tour came *The Young Miner* and *Both Sides of the Continent.* Returning east he settled in Peekskill, N.Y., where at the age of 63 he met and fell madly in love with a married woman. The lady's husband found them out and he took her away to France. Alger, in financial difficulty and unable to follow, took to his pen and in 27 days wrote *Frank and Fearless* and *Upward and Onward.* With an advance from his publisher he booked passage to Europe. In Paris, however, Alger was rejected and he suffered a severe nervous breakdown. After his recovery he returned to the U.S. and to the lodging house. After the death of O'Conner, his only close friend in life, Alger retired to live with his sister in Natick, Mass., where he died on July 18, 1899.

It was in the atmosphere of the lodging house that Alger began to write those stories of poor boys who rose from rags to riches, which would make him famous and contribute the "Alger hero" to the American language. In a steady succession of books, all alike except for the names of the characters, he preached that by honesty, cheerful perseverance,

THE BETTMANN ARCHIVE

TITLE PAGE FROM ALGER'S "LUCK AND PLUCK" SERIES

and hard labour, the virtuous lad would have his just reward (even though the just reward was almost always precipitated by a stroke of good luck). The Alger hero fired the imagination of millions of impressionable readers because, with his pluck and luck, he embodied a whole constellation of popular aspirations. With the exception of the western frontiersman, no other myth figure has exerted so powerful an influence on American culture. Particularly popular during Alger's lifetime and on into the 20th century were the "Ragged Dick," "Luck and Pluck" and "Tattered Tom" series.

See Herbert R. Mayes, *Alger, a Biography Without a Hero* (1928); J. Tebbel, *From Rags to Riches* (1963); R. D. Gardner, *Horatio Alger: or, The American Hero Era* (1964). (K. S. LN.; X.)

ALGER, RUSSELL ALEXANDER (1836–1907), U.S. businessman, soldier, and Republican politician, was born in Medina County, O., Feb. 27, 1836. He practised law in Cleveland for a few months in 1859, then moved to Grand Rapids, Mich., and entered the lumber business. At the outbreak of the American Civil War in 1861 he enlisted as a private and by 1864 had risen to the rank of colonel. He resigned that year and was later brevetted major general. Alger then returned to his Michigan lumber business and accumulated a large fortune. He served one term as governor of Michigan, 1885–87; was Michigan's "favourite son" candidate for the presidential nomination in 1888; and served as national commander of the Grand Army of the Republic, 1889–90. Alger's gift of $10,000 to Gen. Philip Sheridan drew criticism from Charles Dana of the *New York Sun,* who claimed to have discov-

ered irregularities in Alger's discharge papers. Though Dana and others later exonerated him, the disclosure nullified his presidential chances in 1892. As secretary of war in 1897–99 Alger was criticized and ridiculed for inefficiency of the supply services and for other errors during the Spanish-American War. More recently, scholars have noted that, although Alger undoubtedly lacked initiative and resolution, the chief fault lay with the American people and the nation's moribund military establishment. In 1902 Alger was appointed to the U.S. Senate to fill the vacancy caused by the death of Sen. James McMillan, and was elected in 1903. He died on Jan. 24, 1907, in Washington, D.C.

See Margaret Leech, *In the Days of McKinley* (1959). (L. L. S.)

ALGERIA (French ALGÉRIE), an independent republic in North Africa, formerly under French dominion, is bounded north by the Mediterranean, east by Tunisia and Libya, south by Niger, Mali and Mauritania, and west by Morocco. Algeria proper has an area of 113,912 sq.mi. (295,032 sq.km.), measures over 600 mi. (950 km.) east to west and 160–250 mi. (250–400 km.) north to south. The two Saharan *départements* to the south (known as the Southern Territories from 1902 to 1958) legally belong to the republic, but under the Évian agreements (1962) France retained certain economic and military concessions (see *History,* below). Their area is 805,679 sq.mi. (2,086,711 sq.km.) and their southernmost point is 1,200 mi. from Algiers, the republic's capital. The population of Algeria in 1966 was 12,093,203.

PHYSICAL GEOGRAPHY

Geology and Structure.—The two physical divisions of Algeria are the Sahara, an ancient platform or shield, locally disturbed, against which the Atlas were forced, and the Atlas, folded chains of Tertiary Age, including remnants of ancient massifs. The Saharan shield is of peneplained Precambrian rocks overlain by Paleozoic deposits (exposed in the Ahaggar), the whole frequently masked by the later limestones of shallow Cretaceous seas. The Atlas lands of northern Algeria consist of a former geosyncline squeezed and folded into mountain chains by pressure from the two flanking continental masses of Tyrrhenia to the north and the Saharan shield. The mountain building epoch lasted throughout the Tertiary Period, the two chief stages being the Pyrenean (Cretaceous-Eocene) and Alpine (Miocene). Thick limestone deposits, mainly of Jurassic, Cretaceous, and Eocene Ages, mingled with sandstones and conglomerates, form the bases of the Atlas ranges. Archean and Paleozoic rocks are little represented except where remnants of Tyrrhenia, such as the Djurdjura (Jurjura) range, provide mountain fastnesses with cores of Archean and Precambrian schists and gneisses.

Relief and Drainage.—Articulated Alpine structures dominate northern Algeria where two series of young fold mountains, the Maritime Atlas and the Saharan Atlas, are separated by a less disturbed plateau zone, the trend being southwest to east-northeast. In the north is the Tell, comprising discontinuous coastal hills and inland ranges of the Maritime Atlas. The coastal hills average 1,500 ft. (450 m.) in the west but attain 7,572 ft. (2,308 m.) in the crystalline Djurdjura east of Algiers. Between them and the Maritime Atlas lie a series of discontinuous valleys and plateaus extending from Ouahran to Bejaïa. The broken mountains of the Maritime Atlas include the Tessala and Ouarsenis and extend from eastern Morocco into Tunisia.

To the south, between the Maritime Atlas and the Saharan Atlas, lies the undulating steppe land of the High Plateaus with an average altitude of 3,500 ft. (1,050 m.). Numerous muddy salt flats (*shatts* or *chotts*) are characteristic, notably Chott ech Chergui (100 mi. in length), Zahrez Gharbi and Zahrez Chergui, salt lakes almost dry in summer, and Chott al Hodna (1,283 ft.), now almost entirely a salt marsh. The Saharan Atlas, in a vast sweep from the High Atlas of Morocco to the Aurès Mountains and the Tunisian boundary, shuts off northern Algeria from the Sahara proper. In the southwest the Ksour Mountains attain 7,333 ft. but toward the east-northeast altitude diminishes, denudation is more intensive and the mountains practically merge into the High Plateaus, their tops projecting like islands from an accumulation of debris. The Zab Mountains south of Chott al Hodna drop to 1,500 ft., offering useful passes north to the Algerian Tell. Immediately to the east rise the Aurès (q.v.) Mountains of folded Jurassic and lower Tertiary sediments weathered into a formidable terrain of peaks and gorges, containing the highest mountain in Algeria, Djebel Chélia, 7,648 ft. In the Aurès, spurs of the Maritime Atlas meet the Saharan Atlas and the mountains, high above the Sahara, permit the vegetation of the Tell to continue south toward Biskra. The Algerian Sahara presents an undulating plateau surface, rising in the south to the crystalline Ahaggar massif. In the north, Cretaceous limestones are overlain with a veneer of sands and pebble beds. The area is not entirely barren; depressions in the limestone plateaus make accessible water-bearing strata sustaining palm groves and oases.

The limited amount of rainfall and its seasonal regime and the porous nature of much of the rock accounts for the paucity of surface drainage. Most of the wadis (oueds) are periodic; even those flowing from the Maritime Atlas to the sea, the Sig, Isser, and Soummam, are feeble trickles in summer. Only four streams from the High Plateaus break through to the Mediterranean: the Chéliff, Bou Sellam, Rhumel (Rummel), and Seybouse. They flow strongly in their lower courses in winter, but in summer they are practically dry. In the southern High Plateaus and the Sahara interior drainage within closed basins prevails. The coastline, about 620 mi. (1,000 km.) long, trends with the ranges. It is little indented, frequently steep and rocky to the shore, and offers few good port sites

Climate.—Algeria's position between the Mediterranean and the Sahara causes a marked seasonal contrast in climate. In winter depressions passing eastward along the Mediterranean (then a region of low pressure) bring considerable rainfall to the north. In summer low pressure systems develop over the Sahara and High Plateaus, drawing in dry winds from the northeast. Winters are cool and wet, summers hot and dry; sunshine is plentiful in all months. On the coast winter temperature averages 10°–12.2° C (50°–54° F), summer temperature 23.9°–26.1° (75°–79°), and rainfall 30 in. (762 mm.). Away from the coast continental conditions become very marked. On the High Plateaus winter temperature averages 3.9°–5.6° (39°–42°) with much frost, summer temperature averages 25.6°–28.3° (78°–83°) with maxima near 35° (95°) or even 40.6° (105°) in the Sahara; rainfall 8–16 in. (203–406 mm.). Biskra on the edge of the desert records January 11.7° (53°), July 33.3° (92°), annual rainfall 7 in. (178 mm.). The desert itself is virtually rainless.

Vegetation and Animal Life.—In northern Algeria as far as the southern edge of the Saharan Atlas the vegetation is largely Mediterranean. Of 3,500 species only 500 are peculiar to the country. Vegetation becomes progressively poorer with diminishing rainfall from north to south and develops greater African characteristics. Evergreen trees and shrubs predominate: olives in the coastal hills and depressions, the Aleppo pine, cork oak, cedars, thuja on higher areas. Thick brushwood undergrowth of plants such as rosemary, lentisk (mastic plant), buckthorn, myrtle, strawberry tree, and various woody climbers clothe the lower slopes. Steppe communities are abundant on the poorly watered High Plateaus where alfa or esparto grass (*Stipa tenacissima*) is widespread, with occasional woods of red juniper in the higher parts and drinn grass on the sandier soils. The Saharan region has a poor xerophilous, or drought-resistant, vegetation of which many species grow rapidly after rain; the oases are characterized by the date palm; the sand dunes and *ergs*, or deserts of shifting sands, have drinn steppe; the gravelly areas support dwarf perennials including a number of herbs (chenopods and crucifers) and grasses; the rock deserts (hammada) are practically devoid of vegetation.

The animal life is similar to that of other Mediterranean countries but has been considerably modified within historic times, mainly through the disappearance of old forms. The elephant and lion have become extinct; the panther and hyena are rare. A single variety of monkey (*Pithecus innuus*) occurs. Jackal and wild boar are abundant where there is cover and there are various antelopes (gazelles). Birds of prey include several varieties of eagle, vulture, and hawk; ostrich, becoming scarce, is found on the

Saharan border. In the desert horned vipers and scorpions are fairly common. Five of the 31 species of freshwater fish are peculiar to Algeria.

Geographical Regions.—Algeria may be divided into five distinctive regions: the Tell, the High Plateaus, eastern Algeria, the Saharan Atlas, and the Sahara.

The Tell comprises the hills and plains adjacent to the coast, the series of ranges and plateaus inland forming the Maritime Atlas, and the intermediate valleys and basins. There is considerable diversity of geology, soils, and relief. The climate is characteristically Mediterranean, although frequently modified by local position and aspect. The climatic and geological affinities with southern France, the proximity of the coast and ports, relative ease of movement along the valleys, and the poverty and harshness of the rest of the country caused the Tell region to become the principal area of French settlement and the most productive part of Algeria. The soils of the Tell are poorer in humus than comparable soils in northern Europe. Upland soils are thin and contrast markedly with the deep alluvial soils and loams of the plains. Agricultural development is most marked in the Sahel of Ouahran, the Mitidja (the Algiers plain), and the plain of Bejaïa, alluvial plains exposed to rain-bearing winds where magnificent vineyards, citrus groves, and flowers for perfume making surround the substantial modern buildings of European farms. Some interior valleys (*e.g.*, the Chéliff) are poorly developed because of aridity and excessive heat in summer. The mountains, of limestones, sandstones, and much dissected clays and marls, support brushwood, evergreen oaks, and pine forests. Occasional springs near their base provide sites for settlement and agriculture. This region supports nearly 90% of the total population and contains practically all the towns.

The High Plateaus are undulating steppe lands, here and there varied by ridges and rocky outcrops and with a chain of chotts, brackish lakes, and marshes. Ruins of agricultural and irrigation

PALM TREES GROWING NEAR IN-SALAH OASIS IN THE ALGERIAN SAHARA; THE DUNES ARE PLANTED WITH HEDGES IN AN ATTEMPT TO STABILIZE THE SAND

works suggest a more pluvial and prosperous period in the Middle Ages. The sparse rainfall (10–12 in.) now supports a steppe vegetation including tufts of alfa. Sheep range widely over these pastures along regular tribal routes and the alfa is collected for export or weaving into baskets, ropes, and mats. The scanty population is mainly nomadic.

Eastern Algeria differs from western in being a compact massif, much dissected into mountains, plateaus, and basins not paralleling the coast. Spurs from the Maritime and Saharan Atlas stretch out to become the formidable Aurès massif, providing an effective termination to the High Plateaus. The coastal mountains from Bejaïa eastward are higher than to the west and provide the best-watered parts of Algeria (over 40 in.) with abundant forests of cork oak and cedar. Population is sparse, communications difficult.

Inland a number of former lake basins provide upland plateaus, such as the plains of Sétif where cereal crops survive under near-steppe conditions or the more saline marshes of the Constantine chotts which offer good grazing. Nearer the Tunisian border the scanty population is related to mineral working, particularly hematite and phosphate, along the Souk-Ahras–Tébessa railway.

For discussion of the Saharan Atlas and Sahara *see* ATLAS MOUNTAINS and SAHARA.   (A. B. M.)

HISTORY

The early history of Algeria, which derives its name from *Al Jazair*, Arabic for "the islands" (*i.e.*, the small islands in the roadstead of Algiers), cannot clearly be distinguished from that of northwestern Africa as a whole (*see* AFRICA: *History: North Africa* and *Sahara and Sudan*), since the territory unified by the French under the name Algérie extends from the Mediterranean coast and its immediate hinterland—of which there is recorded history since the beginning of classical times—far into the south across the Sahara, which does not emerge from prehistory until very much later. (For the history of Mediterranean Algeria from the time of the Phoenician or Carthaginian settlements to the end of the Roman Empire and the Vandal kingdoms *see* AFRICA, ROMAN PROVINCE OF; MAURITANIA, ISLAMIC REPUBLIC OF; NUMIDIA.)

Arabs and Berbers.—Muslim armies (*see* CALIPHATE) had begun their westward advance from Egypt in A.D. 647, but their conquest of northwestern Africa or Barbary—so named because of its predominantly Berber (*q.v.*) population—was not completed until 711. The eastern part of what is now Algeria, in particular the Aurès Mountains and the surrounding area, under the leadership of two Berbers, Kosaila (Kusayla), and the chieftainess Kahenna (al-Kahina), was the main centre of resistance to the invaders. The Muslim conquest did not, however, lead to the settlement of the country by Arabs. While Arab leaders and soldiers were installed in small numbers in the towns (in Tunisia, moreover, to a greater extent than in Algeria), the rural areas remained Berber, and the problems posed by the introduction and evolution of Islam (*q.v.*) were decided among the Berbers themselves.

Barbary was at first a province of the Omayyad caliphate, which ruled from Damascus in Syria, but by 742 almost the whole of Barbary, under the influence of a Muslim heresy, Kharijism (*see* KHARIJITES), had freed itself from eastern control. Several Berber and Kharijite kingdoms were founded in Algeria, the most important being that of the Rostemids at Tahert (in the region of Ouahran). The eastern border area, however, remained under the rule of the Aghlabids (*q.v.*), who made Kairouan, Tunisia, their capital, an active centre of orthodox Islamic thought, which gradually spread westward again and, during the 9th–11th centuries, supplanted Kharijism.

It was the support of the Kabyles, a confederation of Berber tribes in eastern Algeria, that made possible the rise of the Arab dynasty of the Fatimids (*q.v.*), who were Shi'ites, at the beginning of the 10th century. Zeiri and his son Bulukkin, moreover, founders of the Berber dynasty of the Zeirids, with their capital at Achir, held the central area round Algiers as vassals of the Fatimids. Western Algeria, however, remained almost continually

under groups of the Zenata Berbers (enemies of the Fatimids and allies of the caliphs of Córdoba in Spain) until, in the second half of the 11th century, an orthodox Berber dynasty, the Almoravids (*q.v.*), added the whole country as far as Algiers to their empire, which they governed from Marrakech in Morocco.

The Zeirids, who moved their capital to Kairouan in 972, and the Hammadids, who early in the 11th century had set up another dynasty at Qalaa (in the Constantine region), reverted to orthodox beliefs under pressure of opinion in the mid-11th century and broke with the Fatimids of Egypt, who, to avenge themselves, sent three Arab tribes, the Beni Hilal, the Beni Sulaim, and the Beni Maqil, against them. These Bedouins impoverished Barbary by ruining its peasant economy and profoundly disturbed its social organization by spreading nomadism at the expense of settlement. Though they did little to change the religious state of the country, they brought the Arabic language to the plains and steppes. Within 100 years they had spread over the whole of eastern Algeria.

Western Algeria received the Spanish-Moorish civilization under the Almoravids, and the Almohads (*q.v.*), another Berber dynasty, who overthrew the Almoravids in the middle of the 12th century and extended their authority over the whole of Barbary, brought this civilization to the towns of eastern Algeria also, checking the Bedouin menace. In the 13th century, however, the Almohad Empire began to break up, and Barbary was partitioned between three new Berber powers, the Marinids of Fès, the Abd-al-Wadids of Tlemçen, and the Hafsids of Tunis.

Turkish Conquest.—The Christian reconquest of Spain was followed, in the first years of the 16th century, by the Spanish occupation of places on the Algerian coast (Mers el Kébir, Ouahran, Bejaïa, and the island part of Algiers itself) and by the levying by Spain of tribute from other cities. The Abd-al-Wadid sultan accepted a Spanish protectorate. The Muslim population then appealed to Turkish pirates for help (*see* BARBAROSSA), and these pirates in turn appealed to the Ottoman sultan, who sent strong forces to their support (1518). This led to the expulsion of the Spaniards from Algiers (1529), to the fall of the Abd-al-Wadids (1554), and to the reduction of Algeria to a vassal state of the Ottoman Turkish Empire.

The Barbary pirates (*q.v.*) made Algiers a flourishing city in the 17th century but were less active in the 18th and in the early years of the 19th, when Algiers, weakened also by epidemics, declined in importance.

Turkish Algeria was theoretically governed by a dey nominated by the officers of the militia. The country was divided into three provinces under beys and subdivided into cantons under *caïds*, who were in most cases chosen from the heads of tribes. Both beys and *caïds* enjoyed a large measure of autonomy, and Algeria was never really unified under the control of the central government.

Revolts by tribes and Marabout groups gradually weakened the power of the deys, who by 1830 were exercising effective authority over only a small part of the country.   (H. L. E. T.)

French Conquest.—The government of the deys was brought to a violent end by French intervention in 1830. A claim by two Algerian citizens for payment for wheat delivered to France under the Directory had been outstanding since the end of the 18th century. In April 1827 an altercation arose over this between the dey Hussein and the French consul during an audience. The dey threatened to withdraw the concession by which the French maintained a fortified trading post, named the Bastion, near Annaba, and, becoming exasperated at the consul's rudeness, flicked him with his fly whisk. To avenge this insult to France the government of Charles X instituted a naval blockade; this had little result beyond causing the loss of the Bastion. A naval and military expedition was then sent under Adm. Baron Victor Duperré and Marshal Comte Louis de Ghaisnes de Bourmont. The expedition landed at Sidi Farruj on June 14, 1830, and the dey, after his forces had been defeated, capitulated on July 5. The enterprise was presented by the French as one of common interest to the civilized world in that it put an end to Algerian privateering. This, however, had already ceased to be a serious menace, and the desire for prestige and for the maintenance of a privileged trading position was the basic motive.

(ABOVE) CARAVAN SILHOUETTED AGAINST THE DAWN SKY. (BELOW) WITH THE AID OF METAL MATS A TRUCK LADEN WITH DATES HAS BEEN EXTRICATED FROM SAND IN THE DESERT SOUTH OF TAMANRASSET

Eventually the French retained Algiers, and by degrees a sort of protectorate (without the name) was established over the coastal areas. Resistance to the French appeared wherever there was a leader to organize it. The beys of Ouahran and Titeri submitted, but the bey of Constantine, Ahmed, held out, and it was only after seven years that the city fell (Oct. 13, 1837). In the west resistance was organized by Abd-el-Kader (*q.v.*). In 1834 the French government appointed a governor-general of French possessions in North Africa. The same year was marked by the signing of an abortive treaty with Abd-el-Kader; this was followed by the more important Treaty of Tafna (May 30, 1837). Seeing, however, that this did not put an end to French progress, Abd-el-Kader proclaimed a holy war on Nov. 18, 1839.

In 1840 the French government finally decided on the conquest and colonization of the whole country. This task was entrusted to Gen. (later Marshal) T. R. Bugeaud de la Piconnerie (*q.v.*), who was the real creator of the army of Africa. Abandoning the system of blockhouses, Bugeaud sent out columns in all directions, seizing cattle and crops and often destroying the olive and other fruit-bearing trees. Abd-el-Kader's arsenals at Takdempt, Saïda, and Boghar were destroyed and Mascara and Tlemçen occupied by 1842, and part of his *smala* or movable capital (with a population of 50,000) was captured in May 1843. When the sultan of Morocco gave his support to Abd-el-Kader, the French bombarded Tangier and Mogador and defeated the Moroccan Army at Isly (Aug. 15, 1844). It was not, however, until Dec. 23, 1847, that Abd-el-Kader finally surrendered. His disappearance marked the end of the main resistance, but many further campaigns were necessary. From 1884 until 1954 there was no serious challenge to French authority.

French Colonization.—Two major changes took place in Algeria under French rule between 1830 and 1954. First, a new Algerian people, of European outlook, was created, numbering 800,000 by 1954. Of these, half were of Spanish, Italian, Maltese, or other non-French origin. The Algerian Jews, numbering 150,-000, were completely assimilated to this group politically. Second, the Muslim population increased from 3,000,000 to 9,000,000. The guiding threads of Algerian history during this period are therefore to be sought in the development of European settlement on the one hand and the subservient status of the conquered Muslim inhabitants on the other.

The first major impulse to colonization was given by Marshal Bertrand Clauzel in the 1830s and by Bugeaud while he was governor-general (1840–46). At Bugeaud's retirement, 40,000 Europeans, largely ex-soldiers, had been settled. Settlement of individuals was the practice also under the second republic and was to be so under the third. The second empire, on the other hand, granted large concessions and sought to attract capital on a large scale. Colonization received a fresh impulse after the 1871 uprising led by Mohammed al-Moqrani, which was followed by the confiscation of much tribal land, while an act to reduce communal holdings facilitated the acquisition of land by Europeans. By 1881 the European population was 376,000, of whom 140,000 lived in rural areas. The maximum European settlement in rural districts (234,000) was reached about 1926. By 1954 migration to the towns had reduced it to 196,000.

During the conquest the government was military. The second republic moved toward civil administration. In 1848 Algeria was declared French territory. The three former provinces of the Turkish regency were made *départements,* each headed by a prefect. Napoleon III aroused the indignation of the settlers by two letters which he published after visiting Algeria. "Algeria," he said, "is not a colony properly so-called, but an Arab kingdom . . . I am just as much emperor of the Arabs as I am of the French." Administration, which had been entrusted in 1858 to a minister in Paris, was subsequently given back to the military authorities. These tended to act as arbitrators between the settlers and the Muslims and to be less under the influence of the settlers than was the civil administration. A Senate decree (1865) declared that the native Muslim was a Frenchman. In fact he became a French subject rather than a French citizen, having no political rights and being subject to special police regulations.

On the fall of the second empire civil administration was set up. Where settlers were numerous the community was administered by an elected mayor, as in France (*commune de plein exercice*); where the settlers were few, it was administered by an appointed official (*commune mixte*). From 1881 to 1896 each administrative service worked under the relevant ministry in Paris; then they were again placed under the governor-general. By 1900 the administrative and budgetary autonomy of the government general was complete, the budget being voted by *délégations financières*, of whom one-third were Muslims elected by their coreligionists. These changes, however, had little bearing on the Muslims' legal status. In 1936 the Blum-Violette proposals, which would at once have given the vote to 21,000 Muslims on equal terms with the Europeans, were defeated by settler opposition.

Beginnings of Nationalism.—By 1936 two political tendencies had become apparent among the Muslims. One, connected with the name of Ferhat Abbas (*q.v.*), aimed at the complete assimilation of the Muslims through education and the franchise. The other, the Mouvement pour le Triomphe des Libertés Démocratiques (MTLD), under an Algerian working-class leader, Messali Haj, was an Algerian nationalist movement. Both movements derived momentum, within the general Arab renaissance, from the fact that in the 1930s the immigrant Christian minority enjoyed a standard of living as high as that of Western Europe, while the Muslim majority was underemployed and undernourished, with a school-age population of about 2,500,000, of whom only one in eight could find a place in a primary school.

In February 1943 Ferhat Abbas, disillusioned with assimilation, presented to the French and Allied authorities in North Africa a manifesto embodying Algerian claims. In December of that year Gen. Charles de Gaulle declared that the loyalty of French territories during World War II had put France under an obligation to them, particularly in the case of the Muslims of North Africa. Accordingly an ordinance of March 7, 1944, extended citizenship to certain categories of Muslims, and in 1946 a law granted them 15 deputies in the National Assembly and 7 senators in the Council of the Republic. Meanwhile, however, in May 1945 demonstrations at Sétif in celebration of the Allied victory in Europe had led to a scuffle between the police and demonstrators carrying Algerian Nationalist flags. This developed into an unorganized uprising in which 88 French lost their lives. Repression by the French authorities in the villages in the Sétif area resulted—according to French official statements—in the deaths of 1,500 Muslims. Qualified observers, however, claimed that the figure was as high as 5,000 or even 10,000. The massacre and the reprisals were a great shock to French as well as to Muslim opinion, and many proposals were put forward.

Nevertheless the French Constituent Assembly later refused even to discuss a proposal by Ferhat Abbas for the creation of an autonomous Algerian state federated with France. Instead, after long discussion, it passed, with the 15 Algerian deputies abstaining, the Statute of Algeria (Sept. 20, 1947). This declared Algeria to be "a group of *départements* endowed with a civic personality, financial autonomy, and an organization of its own." An Algerian assembly was created, far-reaching reforms were promised, and 58,000 Algerians with high qualifications were allowed to vote with the European electoral college which elected one-half of the 120 members of the assembly. The other 60 members were to be elected by Muslims possessing only local status. An important proviso stated that for any legislation there must be a two-thirds majority whenever this was demanded by at least 30 members. During the succeeding years the promised reforms were in general not implemented, as the assembly failed to pass the necessary legislation.

The Nationalist Uprising.—On the night of Oct. 31–Nov. 1, 1954, a concerted uprising began. Organized by a group of activists who had seceded from the MTLD, this uprising had been in preparation probably since 1947. In the first place it consisted of coordinated attacks on such establishments as police posts and forest guard posts in the Aurès Mountains and in the Kabyle country, causing several deaths. The rebels took the name of Front de Libération Nationale (FLN) and issued a manifesto. This stated that their objective was the restoration of a sovereign Algerian state, of which any resident of Algeria could become a citizen with full rights provided that he was prepared to adopt Algerian nationality. A second more extensive outbreak occurred on Aug. 20, 1955. A massacre of French near Skikda (then named Philippeville) had as its sequel large-scale executions of Muslims in the stadium of that city. Reforms proposed by the new governor-general of Algeria, Jacques Soustelle, were not sufficiently striking to win over hesitant Muslims, and during 1956 nearly all the outstanding Muslim political leaders, who had at first held back, left the country and joined the rebels' political headquarters in Cairo.

On Jan. 31, 1956, a Socialist prime minister, Guy Mollet, came into power in France with a program of peace in Algeria. Having announced the appointment of the liberal Gen. G. Catroux as minister resident in Algeria, he went himself to visit Algiers (Feb. 6, 1956), where he was greeted by the Europeans with hostile demonstrations. Catroux resigned and was replaced by Robert Lacoste. It was proposed to secure a cease-fire by force of arms and then to hold elections and to negotiate with the elected representatives of

THE MODERN CITY OF ALGIERS, CAPITAL AND CHIEF SEAPORT OF ALGERIA, STRETCHING 10 MI. (16 KM.) ALONG THE BAY OF ALGIERS

the Algerian people; meanwhile, certain reforms were to be introduced, as far as the fighting permitted. This policy involved the dispatch of large numbers of soldiers to Algeria to deal with the increasing military and political activity of the rebels. *Sections administratives spéciales* (SAS) were established wherever possible. These corresponded to the original *bureaux arabes* and had the task of promoting Muslim village welfare wherever rebel influence could be eliminated. For this purpose 1,250,000 villagers were resettled under the supervision of the army. Another 150,000 took refuge in Tunisia and Morocco.

In October 1956 an aircraft chartered by the Moroccan government to convey five Algerian rebel leaders, led by Ahmed ben Bella, from Rabat, where they had been the guests of the sultan of Morocco, to a conference at Tunis was diverted to Algiers and the five men were arrested by the French. Widespread terrorism in Algeria was suppressed early in 1957 by the use of parachute troops and, it seemed, by the use of torture to extract information from prisoners. In spite of French objections the subject of Algeria was discussed at the United Nations General Assembly in February 1957 and on subsequent occasions. The activities of the rebels were much hindered by fortified fences on the Tunisian and Moroccan frontiers.

The discovery of important oilfields in southern Algeria led to the creation, on Jan. 11, 1957, of an Organisation Commune des Régions Sahariennes (OCRS) which included the two southern Algerian *départements,* Oasis and Saoura, detaching them from Algeria proper. The OCRS was administered directly from Paris by a minister for the Sahara.

In May 1958 suspicions on the part of the settlers that the French government intended to negotiate with the rebels led to demonstrations in Algiers on May 13 and to a political crisis in France which ended with the assumption of power by General de Gaulle. De Gaulle ignored a *loi-cadre,* laboriously passed by the French National Assembly, which provided for the setting up of regional assemblies in Algeria. He also showed no favour toward the idea of integration but seemed to be working for a self-governing Algeria associated with France. Army control was sufficiently effective to permit a referendum to be held (Sept. 26–28, 1958) which gave a large majority for the new French Constitution. On Oct. 3 De Gaulle announced a vast plan for Muslim economic and educational betterment. On Oct. 23 he offered to discuss the terms of a cease-fire with what he called an "external organization"; *i.e.,* the FLN. This had meanwhile constituted itself in Tunis into a Gouvernement Provisoire de la République Algérienne (GPRA) on Sept. 19 with Ferhat Abbas as prime minister. No response being forthcoming, fighting continued. By the early 1960s there were about 500,000 French troops stationed in Algeria.

On Sept. 16, 1959, De Gaulle announced that Algerians would, within four years of the restoration of peaceful conditions, settle their future by a free vote. They could choose between association with France and secession. If they voted for association they would have a choice between complete integration or association as a separate entity. An insurrection of Europeans broke out in Algiers in January 1960 in protest against De Gaulle's Algerian policy, but quickly collapsed. De Gaulle visited Algeria in March and December 1960 but unrest continued, culminating in a second revolt, this time initiated by army officers, which began on April 22, 1961. It was led by four generals (Maurice Challe, André Zeller, Edmond Jouhaud, and Raoul Salan) but collapsed on April 25–26 after De Gaulle assumed extraordinary powers.

The Cease-Fire and Independence.—On Aug. 27, 1961, Ferhat Abbas resigned and was succeeded as prime minister of the GPRA by Ben Yusuf Ben Khedda. His foreign minister, Belkacem Krim, started secret negotiations with Louis Joxe, the French minister for Algerian affairs. On March 18, 1962, a cease-fire in Algeria was signed at Évian-les-Bains, and on the same day a series of official statements was agreed upon between the two delegations. First, the two governments fixed the principles for agreement which included economic and social cooperation and the right of France to maintain for five years experimental rocket and nuclear testing sites (at Reggane and elsewhere) in the Sahara;

THE AHAGGAR MOUNTAINS, SOUTHEASTERN ALGERIA

second, they agreed about the referendum to be held in all 15 Algerian *départements* (including the two Saharan, which put an end to the OCRS).

Ben Bella and four other Algerian leaders detained in France were relased on March 18, 1962. Two days later they were in Rabat, Morocco, where they attended the first public meeting of the GPRA. The provisional executive, consisting of nine Muslims (including six FLN members) and three Europeans was officially installed on April 7, 1962, at Rocher-Noir, the administrative headquarters established in 1961 about 40 mi. E of Algiers. The following day the people of France proper approved the Évian agreements by 90.7% of the valid votes.

In order to render the implementation of the Évian agreements impossible the French Nationalist OAS (Organisation de l'Armée Secrète) started a terrorist activity, killing Algerian Muslims and blowing up town halls, schools, and even hospitals. The OAS leader was the former General Salan, who was captured in Algiers on April 20, 1962. Ignoring the OAS order to stay, the great majority of the French population of Algeria started a mass exodus immediately after the cease-fire agreement; by the end of September only about 250,000 Frenchmen remained. The referendum in Algeria was held on July 1; by 5,975,581 votes to 16,534 the people declared themselves for an independent Algeria in cooperation with France. Two days later President de Gaulle recognized the independence of Algeria. In the meantime the OAS was defeated and its leaders fled to France and other European countries.

On July 3, 1962, Ben Khedda moved with his ministers from Tunis to Algiers, where they were enthusiastically greeted by the Muslim population; his deputy prime minister Ben Bella, however, remained in Morocco. On July 22, at Tlemçen, Ben Bella formed a seven-member political bureau of the FLN, as an organ of supreme power in Algeria. On Aug. 4 Ben Bella arrived in Algiers and explained in a press interview that he differed from Ben Khedda mainly in his attitude toward "neo-colonialism": the Politburo considered that the Algerian revolution must continue on socialist lines. As the local rebel commander introduced a military censorship of all of Politburo communications, Ben Bella on Aug. 25 left for Ouahran (then called Oran). From there he ordered on Aug. 30 the march of the Algerian People's Army on Algiers. This army consisted of units formed in Morocco and Tunisia under the command of Col. Houari Boumédienne (*q.v.*). Some fighting took place between these units and the guerrillas of the Algiers area under Col. Si Hassan, but Boumédienne on Sept. 9 entered Algiers, where his 7,000 soldiers were greeted by Ben Bella.

CAMERA PRESS—PIX FROM PUBLIX

THE PERREGAUX BRIDGE SPANNING THE OUED RHUMEL IN CONSTANTINE;
THE MÉDERSA (MUSLIM COLLEGE) IS IN THE BACKGROUND

Arabic language. The Berbers have preserved their national temperament and customs, and whereas the Arabs remain essentially tent-dwelling herdsmen, the Berbers are highlanders and cultivators, living in towns and villages. Berber dialects survive in western Kabylia (see KABYLE; KABYLIA), in the Aurès Mountains, and among the Tuareg (q.v.). Muslim peoples increased rapidly under French rule, from about 2,310,000 in 1856 to 9,240,000 in 1958.

In 1957 about 835,000 Muslims (9%) lived in the Southern Territories. The urban element (1958) in the Muslim population was about 15%. In 1958 (before the massive exodus of the French population) Europeans (mostly French), with other non-Muslims, numbered 1,033,000, one-fourth of whom lived in Algiers and 18,000 in the Southern Territories. In 1959 the crude birth rate per 1,000 of the Muslim population was 47, and the crude death rate 11 per 1,000. The rapid increase in the Muslim population has raised many social and economic problems. One-half of the Muslim population is under 20 years of age. The majority of Europeans are Roman Catholics under the archbishop of Algiers.

The chief towns are Algiers, Ouahran (Oran), Constantine, Annaba (Bône), Sidi Bel Abbès, Mostaganem, Sétif, Tlemçen, Skikda (Philippeville), Blida, and Bejaïa (Bougie) (qq.v.).

Election of the 196-seat Constituent Assembly was fixed for Sept. 20, 1962, but Ben Khedda and many of his supporters were dropped from a single list of candidates revised by the Politburo. Of the electorate (6,000,000), 85% cast their votes. The National Assembly convened on Sept. 26, electing Ben Bella as prime minister. He formed a provisional Algerian government comprising a 17-member cabinet, with Boumédienne as minister of defense, and on Sept. 29 received a vote of confidence by 159 votes to one, with 19 abstentions. On Oct. 8 Algeria became a member of the United Nations. (N. BA.; X.)

During 1963 French properties, including farms, left vacant since 1962 were taken over by workers' management committees, together with some large agricultural estates still under French management. In September of that year the electorate approved a presidential type of constitution (see below, Administration and Social Conditions). Ben Bella was elected president on Sept. 15 and introduced further socialist measures.

On June 19, 1965, Ben Bella was overthrown by his defense minister, Boumédienne, in a bloodless coup d'état. Boumédienne slowed down nationalization schemes; cooperation with France improved; and an important Franco-Algerian oil agreement was signed on July 29. Algeria broke off diplomatic relations with Britain on Dec. 18, alleging failure on Britain's part to deal adequately with Southern Rhodesia's unilateral declaration of independence.

During 1966 Algeria regained much of the diplomatic prestige it had lost after Ben Bella's overthrow. Ben Bella himself continued to be held at a secret place of detention. A border dispute with Morocco was referred by the latter to the Organization of African Unity. When war broke out between Israel and Egypt on June 5, 1967, Algeria declared war on Israel. On June 6 the Algerian government joined with the governments of other Arab states in banning oil supplies to the United States and Britain. (X.)

POPULATION

The major indigenous element in the population is Berber (q.v.), affected in varying degrees by Arab influences. There are few pure Arabs in the country, the Arab invasions having had little influence upon ethnic types although spreading Islam and the

ADMINISTRATION AND SOCIAL CONDITIONS

Government.—Algeria was not a French colony in the usual sense. Because of the early desire of the French colonists to be ruled by the home government rather than by military authorities, a very close connection with France developed whereby Algeria came to be regarded as an integral part of France, sending representatives to the French National Assembly. Assimilation, however, was never complete and a considerable measure of autonomy was exercised. Under the Statute of Algeria (1947) the country became a group of three départements: Algiers, Ouahran, and Constantine. In 1956 these became regional prefectures, being subdivided into départements. By a further administrative reorganization in 1958 the country was divided administratively into two parts: Northern Algeria and the Saharan départements. Northern Algeria comprises 13 départements divided into 76 arrondissements. There are two Saharan départements divided into 5 arron-

Algeria: Area and Population

Départements	Area (sq.mi.)	Population (1960 census)	Density (per sq.mi.)
Northern Algeria*			
Algiers	1,310	1,560,000	1,190.8
Batna	14,863	567,455	38.2
Annaba (Bône)	9,794	761,233	77.7
Constantine	7,683	1,410,522	183.6
Médéa	19,433	757,181	39.0
Mostaganem	4,382	696,015	158.8
Ouahran (Oran)	6,378	1,020,339	160.0
El Asnam (Orléansville)	4,732	693,656	146.6
Saïda	23,210	193,908	8.4
Sétif	6,720	1,081,747	161.0
Tagdempt (Tiaret)	10,038	320,884	32.0
Tlemçen	3,127	382,622	122.4
Tizi-Ouzou	2,242	751,178	335.0
Saharan départements			
Oasis (capital Ouargla)	500,791	421,445	0.8
Saoura (capital Colomb-Béchar)	304,888	166,124	0.5
Total	919,591	10,784,309	11.7

*Départements in Northern Algeria are named for their capitals.

dissements (*see* Table). The *arrondissements* are subdivided into *communes*.

On Sept. 8, 1963, a new constitution for the republic of Algeria was approved by national referendum. This provided for a presidential regime with a single parliamentary assembly, the candidates for which would be nominated by the FLN.

Living Conditions.—The rapid increase in the Muslim population after World War II contributed to unemployment problems in town and country, to a movement from country to town in search of work and to political unrest.

Styles and types of housing are influenced by the way of life. In the scantily peopled districts used by pastoral nomads, mainly the Sahara and steppe of the High Plateaus, the tent, made of material woven from wool, goats' hair, and esparto grass, predominates. In the Tell the seminomad owns fields as well as herds, and the stone or clay hut or gourbi is common, standing alone near the fields and used only while crops are sown or reaped. The poorer permanent dwellings, clay-walled and flat-roofed, stand in groups, usually on hilly defensive sites, often terraced. Their owners cultivate tree crops and live permanently near their orchards. These occur in the Aurès, the Maritime Atlas, and the Djurdjura. Tiled houses similar to those of the French peasant are found in parts of the Djurdjura and Babor mountains. Houses of European style are confined principally to the main towns.

Land Tenure.—At the French occupation in the 1830s three main types of land tenure were operative: *beylik, arch* (*arsh*), and *melk*. The *beylik* lands were the property of the state; the *arch* lands belonged to tribes in communal tenure and were most common in the east; *melk* included all forms of freehold in land and was most common in the mountain areas. French colonization and the necessity of defining boundaries led to private ownership supplanting the traditional system, and in 1863 the tribes were declared owners of the land they had been using and private ownership was recognized by the issue of title deeds for *melk* land. In 1873 the conversion of tribal and family property into freehold was legalized; this was reinforced by subsequent laws in 1897 and 1926, but not all Muslims have taken advantage of these opportunities. Wherever crops could be grown, however, collective ownership has given way to private ownership since 1926. To the French citizen free grants of land with obligatory residence had been the rule. The decree of 1904 recognized four modes of land transfer: sale at a fixed price at a public office, sale by auction under public control, sale by private treaty, and free concession with a ten-year period of obligatory residence. A decree of 1924 lengthened the latter period to 20 years and the period during which the lands might be transferred only to French colonists from 20 to 40 years. The proportion of colonization land reserved to Muslims was increased from one-third to one-half. In 1950 there were about 5,650,000 ha. (mostly in the Tell) under the French system; European property covered 2,690,000 ha. (50% in the *département* of Ouahran). Of this, the official colonizing schemes accounted for 1,680,000 ha.; private colonization, 1,010,000 ha.

Justice.—Muslim common law was administered by justices of the peace and cadis, with appeal to French courts. Criminal justice was organized as in France. There are 17 courts of first instance in the *arrondissements* and appeal courts at Algiers, Ouahran, and Constantine.

There are also commercial and industrial dispute courts.

Education.—From 1882 primary instruction for Europeans and Jews was compulsory, with the establishment of schools for the Muslims at the discretion of the governor general. Early attempts at mixed French and Muslim primary and secondary schools had little success, but improvement was marked after 1920 and in 1949 French and Muslim primary schools were amalgamated. In 1958 only 12% of the children of all communities attended school, but a huge program of elementary education was designed to have two-thirds of Algeria's children in school by 1963. Few Muslims go beyond the primary schools, but secondary education by means of *lycées* and the former Muslim *médersas* can lead to the University of Algiers. There are also special high schools for commerce, fine arts, agriculture, and hydrography. The University of Algiers (1879) has faculties of law, medicine, science, and letters.

THE ECONOMY

The greater part of Algeria is of limited value for agriculture and not exceptionally well-endowed with mineral wealth. Most of the agricultural wealth accrues from the limited area of highly fertile valleys and basins near the coast where farming is up-to-date and on a commercial scale. Elsewhere the mountains and plateaus offer forests and grazing rather than farming. With subsistence cultivation most of the Muslim population is poor.

Production: *Agriculture.*—The area under cultivation totaled about 4,100,000,000 ac. (16,600,000 ha.), one-third of which was farmed by Europeans before independence. Cereals (wheat, barley, and oats) form the chief crops. The best cereal-growing regions are the Tell and the high plains of Constantine around Sétif, Constantine, and Guelma. Grapes, the principal commercial fruit, are limited to a belt about 65 mi. wide along the coast. The expansion of vineyards was particularly rapid from 1865 to 1870 when the grape phylloxera (an insect) ruined the French vines and led to the emigration of many growers to Algeria. Viticulture is related to European settlement and is most important in Ouahran *département*. France is the chief market for wine. Olives are common, mostly in Kabylia, but other fruits grow in abundance, particularly citrus, figs and apricots, almonds, and, in the south, dates. The mildness of the winter along the coast has led to the growing of early vegetables and their export, particularly to France. Local farmers produce two-thirds of the tobacco crop,

(LEFT) ERNEST RATHENAU—PIX FROM PUBLIX, (RIGHT) CAMERA PRESS—PIX FROM PUBLIX

(LEFT) MAN READING IN A STREET IN ALGIERS. (RIGHT) CORNER OF A MARKET PLACE IN THE KASBAH THAT DOMINATES THE OLD TOWN OF ALGIERS

chiefly in Constantine *département*. Irrigated crops are limited by the paucity of water resources. Dams and reservoirs supply about 38,000,000 ac. (155,000 ha). In the Saharan *départements* about 5,500,000 date palms are in production.

Stock raising is especially important among the Muslims, and large flocks belonging to nomadic and semi-nomadic tribes traverse the High Plateaus to the Maritime Atlas during the summer.

Forestry.—The area of state forests in the early 1960s was more than 620,000,000 ac. (2,500,000 ha.). Much is of little value, but particularly in the east there are valuable stands of Aleppo pine, evergreen oak, cedar, and cork oak. Timber is cut for firewood, railway sleepers, telegraph poles, etc., and cork is the main commercial forest product.

Mining and Power.—The principal mining takes place in the east (Constantine *département*). The phosphate workings at Djebel-Kuif (Jbel Kouif) near Tébessa, which for many years produced more than 500,000 tons annually, were nearly depleted by the mid-1960s. Large but lower-grade reserves exist farther inland at Djebel-Onk (Jbel Onck). Iron ores with an annual output exceeding 3,000,000 tons are mined near the Tunisian frontier (Djebel Ouenza, Djebel bou Kadra), in the Miliana region (Djebel Zaccar) and near Ouahran (Béni-Saf). Iron content averages 55%. There are also large iron ore reserves at Gara-Djebilet near Tindouf. Zinc and lead ores are widely present and mainly worked in the east. Coal is almost entirely produced from one small coal field at Kenadsa, 20 mi. W of Colomb-Béchar.

Rich discoveries of petroleum (including natural gas) have been made in the northern Sahara, and wells at Hassi-Messaoud and Edjélé in eastern Algeria began production in 1958. A third Sahara oil installation was opened in 1966. Oil pipelines operate between Djanet, Hassi-Messaoud, and Bejaïa and between Edjélé and As Sukhayrah (in Tunisia). A gas pipeline was completed from Hassi-Messaoud via Hassi-R'Mel to Ouahran–Arzew–Algiers. Under the Évian agreements of March 1962 French-Algerian co-operation was assured in the exploitation of the Saharan subsoil. Extraction of crude petroleum in the mid-1960s exceeded 26,000,000 metric tons and that of natural gas 809,000,000 cu.m. annually.

Production of electricity in the 1960s was about 1,300,000,000 kw.hr. annually, of which about one quarter was produced by hydroelectric power and most of the remainder by steam power.

Fisheries.—There are extensive fisheries for sardines, anchovies, tunny, shellfish, and whitefish. Much of the annual catch is used by the local canning factories.

Industries.—World War II, with the isolation of North Africa from France, gave an impetus to the rise of varied industries, which has since continued. The country, however, remains essentially agricultural; there is virtually no export of manufactured goods, whereas the import trade in them is heavy. The principal industries include food processing, notably flour milling, fish canning, wine and oil manufacture, the preserving of fruit and vegetables, tobacco, leather, and textile manufacturing. Other industries produce fertilizers, fats, soaps, matches, glass, paper, bricks and tiles, and telephone equipment, and there are metal-rolling works. Local craftsmanship is of little importance except for such products as carpets and leather goods.

Trade and Finance.—From 1835 onward France granted Algeria preferential treatment and from 1867 there was complete reciprocity in customs dues. The greater part of the imports consists of products required for industry and agriculture (machinery, metal manufactures, and fuel) followed by food products (25%, including sugar, dairy produce, oils, and fats) and textiles. Principal exports include crude oil, wine, and citrus fruits.

The monetary unit is the dinar, at par with the French franc.

Transport and Communications.—A good road network exists in the Tell and there are established routes and motor transport for both passengers and freight across the Sahara. There are about 2,670 mi. (4,300 km.) of railway lines. A central line runs from the Moroccan to the Tunisian frontier with branches to the chief ports as well as lines southward to Crampel and Kenadsa from Ouahran; to Burdeau and Djelfa; to Touggourt from Skikda through Biskra; and to Khenchela and Tébessa. The major port, Algiers, is almost entirely artificial. Annual imports through the

port of Algiers amount to about 1,800,000 metric tons; exports average 1,500,000 metric tons. Ouahran's imports average about 1,000,000 tons and exports (mainly wine) just over 1,000,000 tons annually. Annaba is the principal mineral port of eastern Algeria.

Algeria provides essential airfields on routes between Europe and farther Africa and between the Americas and the East.

See also references under "Algeria" in the Index. (A. B. M.)

BIBLIOGRAPHY.—Sir R. Lambert Playfair, *A Bibliography of Algeria from the Expedition of Charles V in 1541* (1888; with supplement 1898); C.-A. Julien, *Histoire de l'Afrique du Nord, Tunisie, Algérie, Maroc.*, vol. ii, 2nd ed. rev. (1952); N. Barbour (ed.), *A Survey of North West Africa*, 2nd ed. (1962); S. Gsell, *Les Monuments antiques de l'Algérie* (1901); G. Marçais, *Les Arabes en Berbérie du XIe au XIV siècle* (1914); H. D. de Grammont, *Histoire d'Alger sous la domination turque* (1887); E. Plantet, *Correspondance des deys d'Alger avec la cour de France* (1889); P. Masson, *Histoire des établissements et du commerce français dans l'Afrique barbaresque* (1903); Sir Godfrey Fisher, *Barbary Legend* (1957); G. Esquer, *Les Commencements d'un empire: la prise d'Alger* (1930); P. Azan, *Récits d'Afrique. L'Émir Abd-el-Kader* (1925); J. Cambon, *Gouvernement général de l'Algérie* (1918); A. Bernard, *L'Algérie* (1929); C.-A. Julien, *L'Afrique du nord en marche* (1953); G. Tillion, *L'Algérie en 1957* (1957); P. Bourdieu, *Sociologie de l'Algerie* (1958); C. H. Favrod, *La Révolution algérienne* (1959); R. and J. Brace, *Ordeal in Algeria* (1960).

Documents algériens (weekly); E. Guernier (ed.), "Algérie-Sahara," *Encyclopédie coloniale et Maritime*, 2 vol. (1946); *Guide bleu: Algérie-Tunisie* (1955); J. Despois, *L'Afrique du nord* (1949); M. Larnaude, *Algérie* (1950); P. Cornet, *Le Pétrole Saharien* (1961); J. Blottière, *L'Algérie*, (1955); J. Kraft, *The Struggle for Algeria* (1961); current history and statistics are summarized annually in *Britannica Book of the Year*. (A. B. M.; N. Ba.)

ALGIERS (Fr. ALGER; Arabic AL JAZAIR), the capital and chief seaport of Algeria, stretches for 10 mi. along the west side of the Bay of Algiers. It is built on the slopes of the Sahel hills which run parallel to the coast and rise to 1,353 ft. in Mt. Bouzaréa behind the town. The city faces east and north, offering from the sea a view of dazzling white terraces below green-topped hills. The population of Algiers, in particular the Muslim population, increased rapidly after World War II. Pop. (1966) 903,530; including the seven suburbs of Bouzaréa, Al Biar, Hussein Dey, St. Eugène, Maison-Carrée, Kouba and Birmandreis, which are continuous with the town, 1,134,209, of whom more than one-half were of European stock.

The City.—Turkish Algiers was a town of nearly 100,000 people in the 17th century, with the kasbah, or citadel, forming the apex of a triangle of which a line of rocky sea cliffs, now the Boulevard de la République, formed the base. The highest part, on steeply scarped hills, has best preserved its native character with its maze of high buildings with balconies overhanging very narrow lanes. Through the old town two roads, the Rue Randon and the Rue Marengo, have been cut. The kasbah, 387 ft. above sea level, still dominates the old town. Built in the 16th century, it was the residence of the two last deys. It was there that the dey Hussein struck the French consul with a fly whisk on April 30, 1827, an incident which led to the end of Turkish rule and the capture of the city by the French in 1830.

French Algiers grew piecemeal around the Muslim town. The three main thoroughfares are a long street with different names (part of it is the Boulevard de la République) running north-south from St. Eugène along the sea front, through the harbour to Maison-Carrée; the Rue Charles-Péguy, a narrow street carrying the main north-south city traffic; and the tortuous Boulevard du Telemy which runs from the Gouvernement Général to the Summer palace. Along the shore some corsairs' houses built in the 18th century have been preserved. Wide, handsome boulevards skirt the port 45 ft. above the quays. The chief official and commercial buildings of Algiers are on these boulevards. At the base of the old town is the Place du Gouvernement. This was long the centre of the town with several important roads starting from it. One of these, the Rue Bab Azoun, leads south to Opera House square, Rue Charles-Péguy and the University of Algiers (1879) at the modern city centre. The university's 12 specialized institutes include an institute of Islamic studies and a nuclear research centre. To the west of the Place du Gouvernement is the modern cathedral (1845–60) built on the site of a mosque. Nearby are the old palace of the archbishops, formerly the Jénina or palace

COURT OF THE GREAT MOSQUE, 1322–23, IN THE OLD TOWN OF ALGIERS

of the dey, and the Winter palace, now used as an office building, which was for long the residence of the governor general. In the vicinity of the cathedral is the ancient National library in one of the finest Moorish houses in Algiers (1798). There are several learned societies, including the Pasteur institute and an astronomical observatory.

To the north is the suburb of St. Eugène, dominated by the basilica of Notre Dame d'Afrique. Mustapha, once a southern suburb, grew greatly after the fortifications between it and Algiers were demolished, and the two are now continuous. The lower part of Mustapha is the industrial area while up the hillside are residential villas and a number of skyscrapers. After World War II many houses were built in the outskirts of the town.

The airport, Maison Blanche, is $12\frac{1}{2}$ mi. from the city.

The Port.—Khair ed-Din (Barbarossa) created the old Turkish port by building a jetty in 1529 from the mainland to an islet, one of several called in Arabic Al Jazair ("the islets"), corrupted to Algiers. (The others have disappeared under harbour works.) On this island are a lighthouse and the admiralty buildings. In the shallow pool to the north fishing and pleasure boats are moored; to the south lies the modern port. The heavy merchandise traffic includes imports of vehicles, petroleum products, wheat, cement, metal products, cotton cloth, sugar and coffee; the main exports are wine, potatoes and other vegetables, citrus and dried fruits, olives, vegetable fibre, iron and phosphate.

History.—The islet of Algiers was occupied by the Phoenicians, who called it Icosim (meaning, probably, the gulls' island). In Roman times a small town named Icosium existed where the marine quarter of the city is located and there were Roman cemeteries near the present streets of Bab Al Oued and Bab Azoun. Bishops of Icosium are mentioned as late as the 5th century. The Muslim city was founded toward 950 by Bulukkin ben Zeiri, the founder of the Zeirid-Sanhaja dynasty, which was overthrown by Roger II of Sicily in 1148. (See FATIMIDS.) The Zeirids had before that date lost Algiers, which in 1082 was occupied by the Almoravids, and in 1152 by the Almohads and in the 13th century came under the dominion of the Abd-al-Wadid sultans of Tlemcen. Nominally

part of the sultanate of Tlemcen, Algiers had a large measure of independence under amirs of its own, the chief seaports of the Abd-al-Wadids being Oran, Rashgun and Honain. The islet in front of the harbour, subsequently known as the Peñón, had been temporarily occupied by the Spaniards as early as 1302. Thereafter, a considerable trade grew up between Spain and Algiers, which, however, remained comparatively unimportant until after the expulsion from Spain of the Moors, many of whom sought an asylum in the city. In 1510, following their occupation of Oran and other towns on the coast of Africa, the Spaniards reoccupied and fortified the Peñón. In 1516 the amir of Algiers, Salim-et-Teumi, invited the brothers Aruj and Khidr to expel the Spaniards. Aruj went to Algiers, had Salim assassinated and seized the town. Khidr succeeded Aruj, who had been killed by the Spaniards in 1518, took the name Khair ed-Din and placed himself under the authority of the Ottoman sultan. He drove the Spaniards from the Peñón in 1529 and was the founder of the pashalik (afterward deylik) of Algeria. (See also BARBAROSSA.) Algiers from that time became the chief seat of the Barbary pirates. In Oct. 1541 the Holy Roman emperor Charles V sought to capture the city but was defeated owing to a storm which destroyed most of his ships in the bay.

Repeated vain attempts were later made by various nations to quell the pirates and in 1816 the British and Dutch burned the corsair fleet. But the piracy continued, though much weakened, until 1830, when a French army captured the city.

From Nov. 1942 until Aug. 1944 Algiers was the headquarters of the Allied forces in north Africa and the seat of the French Committee of National Liberation.

See ALGERIA; see also Index references under "Algiers" in the Index volume. (R. LE T.; X.)

BIBLIOGRAPHY.—H. de Grammont, *Histoire d'Alger sous la domination turque (1515–1830)* (1887); Gabriel Esquer, *Les Commencements d'un Empire: La Prise d'Alger 1830,* 2nd ed. (1930); *Alger et ses environs* (1950); Y. Laye, *Le port d'Alger* (1951); *Documents algériens* published by the Government General of Algeria, no. 55, 56, 82, 83 (1951) and 62 (1952).

ALGIRDAS (Polish OLGIERD) (d. 1377), grand prince of Lithuania from 1345 to 1377, made his country one of the largest European states of his time (see LITHUANIA: *History*). One of the seven sons of Gediminas (Gedymin), he came to power when his brother Kestutis put him in possession of Vilnius, the capital, in the place of their incapable younger brother Jaunutis.

Algirdas planned to consolidate all Lithuanian lands. In the west his plan to eliminate the rival power of the Teutonic Order (*q.v.*) in the Baltic area by diverting it to the Ukraine (where it might protect his Slavonic subjects from the Tatars) failed, but kept the order from increasing its hold on Lithuania, despite continual attacks. In the east and in the south Algirdas won considerable successes, chiefly by matrimonial alliances. Himself twice married to Russian Orthodox princesses (Maria of Vitebsk and Yuliana of Tver), he acquired a number of Russian principalities by placing most of his 12 sons in Slavonic lands and by marrying his 7 daughters to Russian and Polish princes. The area of Smolensk came under his control in 1351, Rzhev in 1355, Bryansk in 1356 and Chernigov and Novgorod Seversk soon after. His victory over the Tatars at Sinie Vody (the Sinucha river, a tributary of the Southern Bug) in 1362 gave him possession of all the fertile lands of Podolia and the steppes north of the Black sea to the Dnieper in the east. He annexed the grand principality of Kiev in 1363. In the north, Algirdas was on friendly terms with the republic of Novgorod.

Desiring to reduce the growing power of the grand princes of Muscovy, Algirdas fought them three times. In 1368 he defeated the Muscovite army at the Trostna river and left Moscow in flames. Dimitri Donskoi was forced to withdraw from the principality of Tver, whose prince, Michael, was Algirdas' ally and brother-in-law. In 1370, after a victory at Volokolamsk, Algirdas held Moscow's *kreml* for eight days until an armistice was made. Finally in 1372 he again helped Michael against Dimitri. Thereafter the German danger made him refrain from intervening between Tver and Moscow.

Algirdas did not accept Christianity from the Teutonic Order.

He was convinced that the Germans wanted Lithuanian lands and were not concerned for the souls of their inhabitants. He was, however, quite tolerant about religion and permitted the Orthodox faith in all the Russian lands that he controlled.

Algirdas died a pagan in 1377 and was cremated with 18 horses near Vilnius. He was an able diplomat and a clever leader.

See T. Chase, *The Story of Lithuania* (1946); C. Jurgela, *History of the Lithuanian Nation* (1948); J. Deveiké, "The Lithuanian Diarchies," *The Slavonic and East European Review* (1950); H. Paszkiewicz, *The Origin of Russia* (1954).　　　　　　　　　　　　　(MA. G.)

ALGOL (β Persei) is the second brightest star in the constellation of Perseus and is the prototype of a large class of variable stars called eclipsing binaries. Its variation in light, which was noted in 1670 by G. Montanari of Italy, was closely watched by the English amateur astronomer John Goodricke, who found (1782) that it repeated itself every 2 days 20 hr. and 49 min. Goodricke suggested that the variation might be caused by partial eclipses of the star by a dark body, a hypothesis that was proved correct in 1889, when spectroscopic observations of its velocity in the line of sight showed that the bright star was traveling round an orbit in the period given above. Further, the reduction of light occurs when the bright star is most remote from the earth; that is, just at the time when the dark companion passes between the earth and the bright star. Algol remains of almost constant brightness for 59 hr., the remaining 10 hr. of its cycle being occupied by the eclipse. The comparatively long duration of the eclipse shows that the dimensions of the two stars are by no means small in comparison with the distance between them. Accurate observations show that the light is not absolutely constant even during the 59 hr., because the dark component reflects (or reradiates) light from the bright star, and thus goes through phases like the moon. Accordingly, after the eclipse is over, the total light still continues to increase a little because the "moon" is progressing from new to full. In the middle of the 59-hr. interval the light dips again when the bright star is hiding its companion.

Small fluctuations in the period of the light variation of Algol can be partly explained by assuming that, besides the eclipsing binary, the system contains two other stars for which the periods of orbital revolution are 1.873 years and 188.4 years; these stars take no part in the eclipses. The presence of a companion with a period of 1.873 years was confirmed by spectroscopic observation, but the presence of the fourth star had not been confirmed by the late 1950s. From analysis of the light variation of Algol, combined with the spectroscopic observations, the following dimensions for the system have been deduced: radius of Algol, 3 × sun's radius, and of eclipsing companion, 3.2 × sun's radius; mass of Algol, 5 × sun's mass, of eclipsing companion, 1 × sun's mass, and of star with 1.873-year period, 1.5 × sun's mass; density of Algol, 0.16 (water = 1), and of eclipsing companion, 0.01; separation of eclipsing stars, 6,000,000 mi.　　　　　(O. J. E.)

ALGONKIAN TRIBES. A widely dispersed series of North American Indian groups which, although diversified in their aboriginal mode of life and speaking many mutually unintelligible languages, can, nevertheless, be identified as a unit because the basic structure of their speech indicates affiliations linking them together as members of a single linguistic family. The name applied to this group of languages is of Indian origin. It is derived from a small ethnic group of Indians called Algonkin by the French when first encountered on the Gatineau river, east of Ottawa. While the significance of the name remains uncertain, it has been said to mean "at the place of spearing fish and eels from the bow of a canoe." Subsequently spelled in various ways, "Algonquian" being the form adopted by the Bureau of American Ethnology, the name came, in time, to be applied to linguistically related groups and finally, as a consequence of systematic scholarly work, to a family of languages comparable in degree of relationship to the Romance or Germanic languages of Europe. Tribes belonging to the Algonkian linguistic stock were found to occupy a more extensive geographical area than any other linguistic family on the continent in aboriginal times. In American colonial history Algonkian tribal groups played a prominent role in the relations between Indians and whites and some aspects of Algonkian culture and language influenced the earliest settlers. Many Indian leaders, such as King Philip, Powhatan, Tecumseh and Pontiac, captured the imagination of American historians, dramatists, poets and novelists.

In Canada, southwest, south and east of Hudson bay were to be found the Cree-Montagnais-Naskapi. It is likely that the Beothuk of Newfoundland, who became extinct in the 18th century, also spoke an Algonkian tongue. So did the Indians of the maritime provinces and New England; *e.g.*, the Micmac, Malecite, Passamaquoddy and Penobscot. The Puritans met Algonkian speakers, tried to convert them and fought them. The first Bible printed in the colonies (1663) was in an Algonkian language (Natick), a translation by John Eliot. In the conflict between whites and Indians the redoubtable Wampanoag sachem, King Philip, became the most notorious of all New England Indians. Algonkian-speaking groups extended southward down the Atlantic seaboard to Cape Hatteras, the Lenape (Delaware) and the Virginia Algonkians, made famous by Powhatan and Pocahontas, being the best known. In the Ohio valley, among other tribes were the Miami, Peoria and Illinois. There Tecumseh, a Shawnee, failed in uniting the Indians for a last stand against the whites when this region was becoming a new frontier. In the area of the Great Lakes were found the Sauk and Fox, Menominee, Kickapoo, Potawatomi, Ojibwa and the Ottawa whose leader Pontiac also achieved fame in frontier history. On the Great Plains, Algonkian-speaking tribes were represented by the Arapaho, Cheyenne and the aggressive Blackfoot, whose languages comprise distinct subdivisions of the family and were mutually unintelligible although their mode of life was similar. Far across the mountains in California, the Wiyot and Yurok have, in recent years, been shown conclusively to belong to the Ritwan subgroup of the Algonkian family. And, it now appears that there is likewise a genetic relation between the Muskogean family of languages, which once prevailed in the Gulf states, and the Algonkian family.

The Algonkian tribes which occupied the forests in Canada, north of the Great Lakes and in the Labrador peninsula, were food gatherers and hunters. They were among the first Indians to come into contact with the men of the Hudson's Bay company and to become involved in the fur trade. It was from these Indians that the use of the birch bark canoe was learned by whites. The Algonkians of the Great Plains were typical buffalo hunters. They lived in tepees and belonged to a culture area distinct from that of their linguistic kinsmen in the woodlands. South of the Great Lakes and on the eastern seaboard, a sedentary existence, combined with the occasional hunting and fishing, was adopted. Maize was the staple crop of these Algonkians and it was from them, both at Jamestown (1609) and later in New England, that the early colonists learned to plant and raise corn. From these Indians, too, the whites learned to make hominy and johnnycake and to use maple syrup. From the same source were derived the earliest Americanisms—words for animals, plants, food products, utensils, clothing—unfamiliar to the first settlers. Indian words in American English are predominantly Algonkian words. A. F. Chamberlain compiled a total of 132, of which about 30, dating back to 17th-century borrowings, are still current; *e.g.*, hickory, hominy, moccasin, moose, opossum, persimmon, raccoon, sachem, skunk, squash, squaw, terrapin, tomahawk, totem, wigwam and woodchuck.

See also references under "Algonkian Tribes" and other tribal names in the Index.

Bibliography.—Leonard Bloomfield, "Algonquian" in Harry Hoijer *et al.* (eds.), *Linguistic Structures of Native America*, Viking Fund Publications in Anthropology, No. 6 (1946); Alexander F. Chamberlain, "Algonkian Words in American English: a Study in the Contact of the White Man and the Indian," *Journal of American Folk-Lore*, pp. 240–267 (1902); Mary A. Haas, "Algonkian-Ritwan: the End of a Controversy," *International Journal of American Linguistics*, 24:159–173 (1958), "A New Linguistic Relationship in North America: Algonkian and the Gulf Languages," *Sthwest. J. Anthrop.*, 14:231–264 (1958); "Algonkin" and "Algonquian Family," F. W. Hodge (ed.), *Handbook of American Indians North of Mexico* (1959); C. Callender, *The Social Organization of the Central Algonkian Indians* (1962); C. F. Hockett, "What Algonquian Is Really Like," *International Journal of American Linguistics*, vol. 32 (Jan. 1966).　　　　　　(A. I. H.)

ALGORITHM (ALGORISM), in modern mathematics, a set of operations reduced to a uniform procedure for solving a specific type of problem, for example, the algorism of continued fractions. In the middle ages, the name was applied to arithmetic employing the Indo-Arabic numerals. (*See* ALGEBRA, HISTORY OF, for al-Khwarizmi, who wrote *Liber algorism*, "the Book of al-Khwarizmi.") In the middle ages the abacists computed on the abacus (*q.v.*), while the algorists computed by algorism. Robert Recorde wrote in his *Ground of Artes* (c. 1542): "Some call it Arsemetrick, and some Augrime. . . . Both names are corruptly written: Arsemetrick for Arithmetick, as the Greeks call it, and Augrime for Algorisme, as the Arabians found it" (1646 edition).

ALGUAZIL (from Arabic *al-wazir*, "vizier"; mod. Sp. *alguacil*), a Spanish title originally applied to the official responsible for the local administration of justice. Often, he was also the governor of a town or fortress. Later, however, the term came to be applied to subordinate officers of the court, entrusted with the service of writs and certain police duties. The title is also given to inspectors of weights and measures in market places, and similar officials, and to an official of the bull ring, who is charged with communicating the orders of the president to those taking part in the fight.

ALGUM (ALMUG TREE). The Hebrew words *Algummin* or *Almuggim* are translated Algum or Almug trees in the authorized version of the Bible (*see* 1 Kings x, 11-12; 2 Chron. ii, 8, and ix, 10-11); *almug* is an erroneous form. The wood of the tree was very precious, and was brought from Ophir (probably some part of India), along with gold and precious stones, by Hiram, and was used in the formation of pillars for the temple at Jerusalem, and for the king's house; also for the inlaying of stairs, as well as for harps and psalteries. It is probably the red sanders or red sandalwood of India (*Pterocarpus santalinus*). This tree belongs to the large family Leguminosae, suborder Papilionaceae. The wood is hard, heavy, close-grained and of a fine red colour. It is different from the white fragrant sandalwood, which is the produce of *Santalum album*, a tree belonging to another family, the Santalaceae.

ALHAMBRA, a city of Los Angeles county, Calif., U.S., 8 mi. N.E. of Los Angeles, at the western entrance to the San Gabriel valley. Its population totaled 54,807 in 1960. (For comparative population figures *see* table in CALIFORNIA: *Population*.) It was named after the Moorish palace in southern Spain by Benjamin D. Wilson when he set aside a tract for a city out of his vast ranch holdings. Wilson (after whom Mt. Wilson was named) and his son-in-law, J. de Barth Shorb, were primarily responsible for the city's development in the 1870s. They brought to Alhambra the first piped water in southern California, making possible an early diversification of agriculture, with vineyards, apple and apricot orchards and orange groves. The city was incorporated in 1903 and adopted a commission-manager form of government in 1914. By the second half of the 20th century commercial agriculture had given way to industrial and residential development. Alhambra's inhabitants work in Los Angeles or in the numerous light industries in the city. Products manufactured include plastics, oil refinery machinery, steel equipment, paper materials, furniture and precision instruments. Although it is a part of the Los Angeles metropolitan area, Alhambra retains its identity as a small community with its own school system, library, parks and commercial recreational facilities. On the outskirts of Alhambra is the San Gabriel mission (founded 1771 by the Franciscans). (J. A. Sz.)

ALHAMBRA, THE, an ancient palace and fortress of the Moorish monarchs of Granada, in southern Spain. Its plateau, which measures about 2,430 ft. in length by 674 ft. at its greatest width, extends from west-northwest to east-southeast, and covers an area of about 35 ac. It is enclosed by a strongly fortified wall and 13 towers. The Darro river, which foams through a deep ravine on the north, divides the plateau from the Albaicín district of Granada. The name Alhambra, signifying in Arabic "the red," is probably derived from the colour of the sun-dried tapia, or bricks made of fine gravel and clay, of which the outer walls are built.

History.—(For an account of the period to which the Alhambra belongs, *see* GRANADA [city].) The palace was built chiefly between 1238 and 1358, in the reigns of Al Ahmar and his successors. The splendid decorations of the interior are ascribed to Yusuf I, who died in 1354. After the expulsion of the Moors in 1492, the open work was filled up with whitewash, the painting and gilding effaced, the furniture soiled, torn or removed. Charles V (1516–1556) rebuilt portions in the modern style of the period, and destroyed a part of the Alhambra to make room for an Italian palace by Pedro de Machuca in 1526. In 1812 some of the towers were blown up by the French under Count Sebastiani, and the rest of the buildings narrowly escaped the same fate. In 1821 an earthquake caused further damage. The work of restoration undertaken in 1828 by the architect José Contreras was endowed in 1830 by Ferdinand VII; and after the death of Contreras in 1847 it was continued by his son Rafael (d. 1890) and his grandson Mariano.

Description.—The situation of the Alhambra is one of rare natural beauty. The park (Alameda de la Alhambra), was planted by the Moors with roses, oranges and myrtles; its most characteristic feature, however, is the dense wood of English elms taken there in 1812 by the duke of Wellington.

The Moorish portion of the Alhambra included a castle, a palace and a residential annex for subordinates. The Alcazaba or citadel, its oldest part, is built on the precipitous foreland on the northwest. Only its massive outer walls, towers and ramparts are left. Beyond the Alcazaba is the palace of the Moorish kings, or Alhambra properly so-called, and beyond this is the Alhambra Alta (Upper Alhambra), originally tenanted by officials and courtiers.

The lower entrance to the park is the Puerta de las Granadas (Gate of Pomegranates), a massive triumphal arch dating from the 16th century. A steep ascent leads past a fountain erected in 1554 to the main entrance of the Alhambra. This is the Gate of Judgment, a horseshoe archway, surmounted by a square tower, and used by the Moors as an informal court of justice.

The present entrance through the Oratory leads to the Patio de los Arrayanes (Court of the Myrtles). This court is 140 ft. long

C. J. BROWN

PRINCIPAL COURTS OF THE ALHAMBRA: (LEFT) PATIO DE LOS LEONES (COURT OF THE LIONS); (RIGHT) PATIO DE LOS ARRAYANES (COURT OF THE MYRTLES)

by 74 ft. broad, and in the centre there is a large pond set in the marble pavement, full of goldfish, and with myrtles growing along its sides. There are galleries on the north and south sides; that on the south is 27 ft. high, and supported by a marble colonnade.

The Sala de los Embajadores (Hall of the Ambassadors) is the largest in the Alhambra, and occupies all the Torre de Comares. It is a square room, the sides being 37 ft. in length, while the centre of the dome is 75 ft. high. This was the grand reception room, and the throne of the sultan was placed opposite the entrance.

The Patio de los Leones (Court of the Lions) is an oblong court, 116 ft. in length by 66 ft. in breadth, surrounded by a low gallery supported on 124 white marble columns. A pavilion, perhaps modeled upon a Cistercian lavabo, projects into the court at each extremity, with filigree walls and light domed roof. The square is paved with coloured tiles, and the colonnade with white marble, while the walls are covered 5 ft. up from the ground with blue and yellow tiles, with a border above and below enameled blue and gold. In the centre of the court is the Fountain of Lions, a magnificent alabaster basin supported by the figures of 12 lions in white marble, emblems of strength and courage.

The Hall of the Abencerrages derives its name from a legend according to which Boabdil, the last king of Granada, having invited the chiefs of that illustrious line to a banquet, massacred them there. This room is square, with a lofty dome and trellised windows at its base. The roof is exquisitely decorated in blue, brown, red and gold. Opposite to this hall is the Sala de las dos Hermanas (Hall of the Two Sisters), so-called from two large white marble slabs laid as part of the pavement. There is a fountain in the middle of this hall, and the roof—a dome honeycombed with tiny cells, all different, and said to number 5,000—is an example of the stalactite vaulting of the Moors. The original furniture of the palace is represented by a splendid vase dating from 1320, and belonging to the first period of Moorish porcelain.

Of the outlying buildings, the foremost in interest is the Generalife (the Moorish *Jennat al Arîf,* or "Garden of the Builder"). This villa probably dates from the end of the 13th century, but has been several times restored. The Villa de los Mártires (Martyrs' Villa), on the summit of Monte Mauror, commemorates by its name the Christian slaves who were employed to build the Alhambra, and confined there in subterranean cells.

See also references under "Alhambra, The," in the Index.

BIBLIOGRAPHY.—T. Gowry and Owen Jones, *Plans, Elevation, Sections and Details of the Alhambra,* 2 vol. (1842 and 1845), gives the best pictorial representation of the Alhambra; Rafael Contreras, *La Alhambra, El Alcázar, y la gran Mezquita de Occidente* (1885); *The Alhambra,* by Washington Irving, was written in 1832, and rewritten in 1857; Albert F. Calvert, *The Alhambra* (1907); L. Torres Balbás, *Ars Hispaniae,* vol. iv, p. 83–140 (1949), gives the best archaeological account, based upon excavations; Frederick P. Bargebuhr, "The Alhambra Palace of the Eleventh Century," *Journal of the Warburg and Courtauld Institutes,* 19:192–258 (1956); L. Torres Balbás, *La Alhambra y el Generalife* (1952), gives the best general guide, containing an English language summary. (G. A. Kr.)

ALHAZEN (Arabic ABU-'ALI AL-ḤASAN IBN AL-HAYTHAM), Arabian mathematician, was the first great discoverer in optics since the time of Ptolemy. He was born at Basra and died at Cairo in 1038. He is distinguished from another Alhazen who translated Ptolemy's *Almagest* in the 10th century. Having boasted that he could construct a machine for regulating the inundations of the Nile, he was summoned to Egypt by the caliph Hakim; but, aware of the impracticability of his scheme, and fearing the caliph's anger, he feigned madness until Hakim's death in 1021.

According to Giovanni Battista della Porta, Alhazen was the first to explain the apparent increase in size of heavenly bodies near the horizon, although Roger Bacon gives the credit for this discovery to Ptolemy. His treatise on optics was translated into Latin by Witelo (1270), and afterward published by F. Risner in 1572, with the title *Opticae thesaurus Alhazeni libri VII, cum ejusdem libro de crepusculis et nubium ascensionibus.* Works on geometrical subjects were found in the Bibliothèque Nationale de Paris in 1834 by E. A. Sédillot; other manuscripts are preserved in the Bodleian library at Oxford and in the library of Leiden.

ALHUCEMAS (AL HOCEIMA; AL KHUZAMA), the name of a bay, islands, and a small port on the Mediterranean coast of Morocco, about 50 mi. W of Melilla. The bay, about 9 mi. wide and 5 mi. long (14 by 8 km.), lies between Cape Nuevo, which is of Triassic limestone, and the Miocene volcanic hills of Cape Quilates. Its sandy bottom is an extension of the alluvial plain of Wadi Nekor. The coast is dry but misty in summer.

At the southwest of the bay are three small islands: Land Island and Sea Island are low, rocky and uninhabited; the Peñón of Alhucemas is a limestone rock 88.6 ft. high, separated from the coast by a channel 1,422 yd. wide, and on it is the building of the former Spanish presidio. The presidio was occupied by a small garrison and a few families from 1673 to 1961; provisions and water were brought from Spain. The three islands form part of the Spanish "plazas" on the Moroccan coast which have been claimed by Morocco.

On the mainland the settlement of Al Hoceima (called Villa Sanjurjo by the Spanish) contained 11,262 inhabitants in 1960, the majority of whom were still Spanish. (J.-J. Ds.)

ALI ('ALI IBN ABI TALIB) (c. 600–661), fourth caliph of the Muslim Arab empire and Mohammed's cousin and son-in-law (*see* CALIPHATE). His father, Mohammed's uncle, Abu Talib, was for a time chief of the clan of Hashem of the tribe of Quraysh at Mecca. Ali, living in Mohammed's household when Islam was first proclaimed, became one of the first Muslims though still a boy. Soon after the Hegira (Mohammed's migration to Medina), in 622, he married Mohammed's daughter Fatima (*q.v.*), who bore him two sons, Hasan and Husain (*q.v.*). Ali is said to have been a brave fighter and to have taken part in nearly all of Mohammed's expeditions and battles. He led an important expedition to the Yemen in 632 but otherwise was not prominent in Mohammed's lifetime nor under the first three caliphs. To the rebels against Othman he apparently gave encouragement but no active support.

On the assassination of Othman (June 656), the Muslims in Medina recognized Ali as caliph. Two leading Meccans, Talha and al-Zubayr, along with 'A'isha, daughter of Abu Bakr and widow of Mohammed, organized armed opposition at Basra, but, when Ali moved against them from Kufa, were defeated (Dec. 656) at the "battle of the Camel" (ridden by 'A'isha).

More serious was the refusal of Mu'awiya (*q.v.*), governor of Syria, to recognize Ali. Demanding vengeance for his kinsman Othman, he led the Syrian army against that of Ali from Iraq. An indecisive battle at Siffin (657) in Syria was followed by the "arbitration," at which a representative of each of the rivals tried to reach agreement. The accounts of this series of events have been falsified by later propaganda, but Ali, disappointed, apparently denounced the decision. No further battle took place against Mu'awiya, but the latter gained control of Egypt and launched raids of increasing severity against Iraq. Meanwhile Ali had to fight against former supporters who opposed his policies. The annihilation of a body of these at Nahrawan (July 658) did not extinguish this Kharijite movement (from *khariji,* "outgoer"). Ali had lost control of Khurasan to local rebels by 659 and of the Hejaz by 660. In Jan. 661 he was assassinated by a Kharijite, Ibn Muljam, outside the mosque in Kufa.

The real personality is hidden in the mass of legend that has gathered round Ali, but he seems to have been genuinely religious though not highly gifted as a statesman. The legends are due to those Muslims who sought a superhuman or charismatic leader and found him in Ali or his descendants. These are the Shi'ites (collectively Shi'ah; *i.e.,* "the party" [of Ali]). Round his supposed tomb near Kufa they have formed the town of Al Najaf. From Ali the charismatic leadership, which he supposedly received from Mohammed, passed to his sons Hasan and Husain (or to another son Mohammed ibn al-Hanafiya), then to the descendants of Husain.

Among some of the strange sects on the fringes of Islam, Ali is regarded as an incarnation of God. *See* SHI'ISM; FATIMIDS.

(W. M. Wt.)

ALI (called THE LION OF JANINA) (1741–1822), Turkish brigand who became pasha of Janina in 1788 and eventually established within the Ottoman empire his authority over much of Albania and

Macedonia, Epirus, Thessaly and the Morea. His father, Veli, bey of Tepeleni, died a poor man when Ali was 14. His ferocious mother, Khamco, formed a brigand band to restore the political and material fortunes of the family. Ali respected his mother, learned her ways and became a notorious brigand leader. After service with the pasha of Negropont (Euboea) he joined the wealthy pasha of Delvino whose daughter, Eminé, he married in 1768. He turned treachery and murder to his own account, neglecting the interests of his father-in-law. Becoming lieutenant to the derbend-pasha of Rumelia, he policed the highroads, enriched himself and sent presents to Constantinople. At length he was rewarded with the pashalik of Trikkala and after a series of murders and intrigues obtained that of Janina. His son Veli took over Trikkala and later the Morea; while another son, Mukhtar, became pasha of Lepanto. Though constantly thwarted by the Christian Souliots, whom he finally subdued in 1803, Ali obtained control of the Gulf of Arta and took the ports of Butrinto, Preveza and Vonitsa. He also gained control of the pashaliks of Elbasan, Delvino, Berat and Valona (Vlore).

All this time, by murders and extortions, he increased his wealth and by intriguing with Greeks and Albanians extended his authority over beys and townships. Though appointed viceroy of Rumelia, he repeatedly failed to carry out the orders of the sultan, to whom he sent plausible excuses and many presents. Indeed, he acted as an independent sovereign and was treated as such by the British and French, with whom he intrigued, hoping to found a sea power. Aiding first one and then the other, he tried in vain to obtain possessions in the Ionian Islands; and he coveted the mainland dependency of Parga which, through British help, he ultimately obtained in 1819. By that time the sultan, Mahmud II, who intended to centralize the government of his empire, was determined to remove Ali; and Ali's old enemy, Ismail Pasho Bey, was plotting his immediate downfall. Assassins sent by Ali to Constantinople to murder Ismail were caught (Feb. 1820) and made to disclose their master. Ismail was appointed to Janina and ordered to remove Ali. He found the task beyond him and was replaced by Khurshid Pasha. Ali might have bid for the support of the Greeks who were planning insurrection, but he knew instinctively that his power could not be based on the Greeks, who had separatist aims. He therefore tried to save himself by his old methods but was deserted by his sons and allies. His end came on Feb. 5, 1822, when (according to tradition) he was shot by Khurshid's men at a small island monastery in the lake of Janina.

In Ali's time, Janina was the foremost centre of Greek culture, for Ali employed Greeks and founded Greek schools. His court (described by Lord Byron, J. C. Hobhouse [Lord Broughton], T. S. Hughes, W. M. Leake, Sir Henry Holland, C. R. Cockerell and F. C. H. L. Pouqueville) was one of barbarous refinement and bestial cruelty. Ali ruled by cunning, by bribery and by ample intelligence upon which, whether true or false, he acted ruthlessly and swiftly. From those who survived his capricious rule he received loyal service; and even the liberated Greeks looked back upon him with some respect.

BIBLIOGRAPHY.—W. C. F. Plomer, *Ali the Lion* (1936), with bibliography including the works of the travelers. For Ali's dealings with Great Britain and France, *see* J. W. Baggally, *Ali Pasha and Great Britain* (1938); and G. Remérand, *Ali de Tébélen* (1928). (D. Dn.)

ALICANTE, a city of southeastern Spain in the region of Valencia and capital of the province of the same name, lies on the centre of Alicante bay 113 mi. S. of Valencia by road. Pop. (1960 est.) 111,875 (mun.). Situated on the amphitheatre formed by the Santa Pola and Huerta headlands, Alicante is dominated by Benacantil hill (721 ft.) and the citadel of Santa Bárbara, whose earliest foundations date from 230 B.C. Arrabal Roig, the old quarter, dominates the sea from its Balcón del Mediterráneo. The modern city has wide streets and a three-coloured marble pavement along the esplanade. The town hall (1701) and the church of Santa María (14th century) are baroque; the cathedral of San Nicolás (18th century) is in Renaissance style. Alicante is the commercial port of Madrid. Its mild climate makes it a winter resort and the beaches of Costa Blanca attract summer tourists. Alicante is on the railway from Murcia to Valencia; another line runs inland to Albacete and Madrid. Steamers ply to Barcelona, Valencia, Marseilles, the Balearic Islands, Algiers, Oran and the Canary Islands. There are air services to Madrid, Oran and Algiers. Wine, tomatoes, bricks and tiles, cigarettes, fertilizers, aluminum utensils, diesel motors, furniture and embroideries are the main products. Founded as Acra-Leuca ("white summit") by the Phocaeans in 325 B.C., the city was captured by the Romans in 201 B.C. who called it Lucentum. Moorish domination lasted from 718 to 1249, when it was named Al-Akant. Besieged by the French in 1709 and the federalists of Cartagena in 1873, it was under Republican control during the civil war of 1936–39.

ALICANTE PROVINCE is a seaboard province formed (1833) from parts of the provinces of Valencia and Murcia. Pop. (1960 est.) 660,312. Area 2,264 sq.mi. In the north and west there are mountain ranges cut by deep ravines; farther south the land is flatter and more fertile. The 168-mi.-long coast has salt marshes, beaches at Calpe, Benidorm, San Juan, Alicante, Guardamar, and *huertas* (market gardens) at Denia and Alicante. The only large river is the Segura, flowing from the highlands of Jaén and Albacete through Murcia and Orihuela. The scanty but torrential rainfall makes irrigation from wells and the Segura with its canals important. The principal towns are Alicante, the capital (pop. [1960 est., mun.] 111,875), Alcoy ([1958 est.] 51,900), Crevillente (13,964), Denia (12,256), Elche (69,091), Orihuela (46,040), Torrevieja (9,451), Villajoyosa (10,565) and Villena (21,070). The dialect is a variety of Valencian. The tourist trade is rapidly becoming important; Denia, Calpe, Altea, Benidorm and Alicante are well-known summer and winter resorts of the Costa Blanca. Half the province is cultivated, 33% is forest and 17% unproductive. The principal products are wine and liquors, fruits and vegetables, fish, almonds, fertilizers, textiles, embroideries, cement, bricks and tiles, salt, products of the palm, *turrones* (nougats), toys, cigarette paper, marble, rubber shoes, carpets, medicinal or industrial herbs. Almonds and *turrones* have made the names of Alicante, Alcoy and Jijona world-famous.

See F. Figueras Pacheco, *Geografía general del reino de Valencia, prov. de Alicante* (1920); José Pastor de la Roca, *Historia general de la ciudad y castillo de Alicante* (1854). (F. F. Gu.)

ALICE SPRINGS, a town of Northern Territory, Austr., lies at an altitude of 1,900 ft. virtually in the centre of the continent among the beautiful scenery of the Macdonnell ranges. Its main importance has been as a telegraph station on the overland route from Adelaide to Port Darwin. The temperature range is from 19° to 117° F., but is seldom above 80° from May to October. Annual rainfall (average 10.55 in.) varies from 4.3 in. to 28.37 in. Pop. (1954) 2,785. There are Anglican and Roman Catholic churches and the John Flynn Memorial (United) church, a hospital, schools, banks, hotels and motel camps. Radio school courses were begun in 1951. To the west are reserves for the native peoples, and Hermannsburg, about 80 mi. W. on the Finke river, is the home of aboriginal artists. Alice Springs is the railhead for the line from Adelaide (981 mi.), opened in 1929, and is linked by road with the northern railway at Birdum and so with Port Darwin (1,105 mi.). The principal train is still known as "the Ghan" after the Afghan camel drivers who helped to develop the route before the line was built and whose descendants still live there. The airport links the town with north and south and the flying doctor service operates from there for a radius of about 500 mi. Besides cattle raising the district has mines for gold, copper, wolfram, mica, etc.; and citrus fruits, grapes and dates are grown. There are light industries for local needs.

The town was formerly known as Stuart after John McDouall Stuart who first crossed the continent near there in 1860. From 1926 to 1931 it was the capital of the short-lived territory of Central Australia. About 1930 the official name was changed to the more popular one of Alice Springs, the water hole found in 1871 which made the town's existence possible and which was named after the wife of Sir Charles Todd, then superintendent of telegraphs.

ALIEN. Numerous passages in the Old Testament command equitable treatment of the alien—*e.g.,* "Love the sojourner therefore; for you were sojourners in the land of Egypt" (Deut. 10, 19)

ALIEN

and "You shall have one law for the sojourner and for the native" (Lev. 24, 22). The alien was to be protected, the German neo-Kantian philosopher Hermann Cohen has said, "not because he was a member of one's family, clan, religious community; but because he was a human being. In the alien, therefore, man discovered the idea of humanity."

In the early history of the human race, the tendency was to look upon the alien as an enemy and to treat him as a criminal or outlaw; the legal or religious expression of the idea of humanity as exemplified in the alien is a relatively modern development.

The biblical commandment of just treatment of the alien sojourner summarizes the universal tension created by the stranger—on the one hand, to hate and abuse him; on the other hand, to welcome him as a fellow human being, to respect in him "the idea of humanity." This tension between the feeling of enmity and the sentiment of charity has nowhere at any time been wholly resolved.

Aliens in Antiquity.—Aristotle, probably in this instance reflecting the view that obtained generally in the ancient world, conceived of non-Greeks as barbarous peoples who were slaves "by nature." He advised Alexander to make a sharp distinction between Greeks and barbarians, and to be to the former as a leader and to the latter as a master. To Aristotle there was no room in the *polis* or city-state for foreigners except as "natural" slaves. But Alexander envisioned an empire in which he would be the ruler equally of Greeks and of non-Greeks, in which persons belonging to different nations would intermarry and would render common military service. Alexander in fact displaced the *polis* with a *cosmopolis,* a world state in which there was equality between Greek and barbarian. The Stoics began to teach the equality of all men; and Plutarch, writing four centuries after Aristotle and Alexander, said that one should reckon all men as his fellow citizens, "and there should be one Life and one order (*cosmos*), as it were one flock on a common pasture feeding in common under one joint law."

At the same time St. Paul preached that in the universal church there was "neither Greek nor Jew, . . . barbarian, Scythian, bond nor free." This was the idea of the *cosmopolis,* founded on the ideals of equality and fraternity embracing all men, subject to a common law of God or of nature; yet when Paul was arrested in Jerusalem and treated roughly, the centurion and the tribune restored his liberty when he disclosed that he was a Roman citizen (Acts 22)—the alien and the citizen obviously did not enjoy equality before the law.

Later Attitudes.—The rise of national states and their development from the 16th century on left the alien even more exposed to mistreatment, for imperial demands ceased to exist, and the creation of national churches under Protestantism tended to confine the universal ideals of religion to those who could claim membership in the same state and church. The alien with a different citizenship or religion was an enemy or a heretic.

But the idea that the alien has rights was not altogether lost or destroyed. Many factors favoured the idea: improvements in facilities for travel; large migrations of peoples and intermarriage; the Judaeo-Christian idea of the unity of mankind; the *jus gentium,* that Roman law which was applied both to citizens and foreigners; international law writings, especially of Francisco de Vitoria, Samuel Pufendorf, Emeric de Vattel; the spread of diplomatic agents and their efforts to protect nationals of their countries; treaty provisions providing for the reciprocal fair treatment of aliens; the ideal of cultural pluralism; international forums for the public expression of grievances against a country charged with mistreatment of aliens, such as the League of Nations, the United Nations and the International Labour organization; international press services and the reporting of events by newspapers and other communication mediums.

Against these liberalizing influences are factors that tend to place the alien in an unfavourable economic and social position: intense national feelings; religious intolerance; ideas of racial superiority; fear of the alien as a possible enemy agent or as a subversive radical; the desire to maintain the "purity" of the country's culture; the desire to protect citizens in their jobs, professions and businesses against unemployment and competition; fear that aliens may lower the standard of living; the feeling that a country's natural resources are for the use and enjoyment of its citizens exclusively; the notion that aliens are not to be entrusted with the conduct of enterprises that may be turned against social interests; the idea that a state may go far in its efforts to protect the public interest in health, safety, morals and the general welfare.

Concept of Juristic Natural Rights and Treaty Arrangements.—As sovereign national states began to develop in modern times, founders of international law asserted against these states juristic natural rights that were vested in all persons, without regard to citizenship or alienage, of which they ought not to be deprived by civilized societies or their governments. There was no general agreement on the content or scope of these rights as they affected aliens; but the existence of some minimum standard of civilized treatment was asserted. The minimum standard, however, did not include the right of the alien to own realty or to enter gainful professions. To meet this situation, states entered into treaties that provide that each of the contracting states will treat the nationals of the other state on an equal footing with its own nationals in the admission into trades and professions, ownership or possession of property, access to courts, enjoyment of liberty of conscience and freedom of worship; but some treaties will purport to extend rights to aliens unless the rights are, by municipal law, reserved exclusively to nationals of the country, thus making municipal law, rather than conventional international law, controlling.

Common economic needs of nations, however, have had some liberalizing effects on the status of aliens; *e.g.,* the treaty constituting the European Coal and Steel Community (signed in 1951) binds the member states to renounce restrictions, based on nationality, against employment in the coal and steel industries of qualified workers who possess the nationality of one of the member states, and prohibits discrimination in remuneration and working conditions between nationals and aliens. This treaty may in time serve as a model to raise the so-called minimum standards in the treatment of aliens.

English Law.—The emergence of higher juristic standards may be illustrated from the history of English and U.S. law. As England in the 13th century lost most of its continental possessions, insular prejudices led to the view that aliens, though protected by the king, were virtually without rights. They had no capacity to hold official positions or franchises. They could not hold land; an alien's inheritance or purchase of land was a nullity, and his land could be seized by the king. This harsh law was justified in Calvin's case (1609) by the statement that, were the law otherwise, "the secrets of the realm might thereby be discovered. The revenues of the realm . . . should be taken and enjoyed by strangers born. It should tend to the destruction of the realm." The prohibition on the alien's acquisition of land, and the right of the king to seize the alien's land, ended in 1870.

As to personal rights, Sir Thomas de Littleton in the 15th century wrote that an alien could bring no legal action, real or personal. This meant that the alien was rightless, that he had no remedy for the vindication of any rights he might assert. Sir William Holdsworth asserts that Littleton was mistaken except as to actions affecting land; according to Holdsworth, aliens had rights in the courts of England.

Magna Carta asserted that "all merchants shall have safe and secure . . . entry to England, with the right to tarry there and to move about . . . for buying and selling by the ancient and right customs . . ."—a provision which implies personal rights essential to a merchant. (These rights were, however, curtailed by the privileges of boroughs.)

As the law merchant was absorbed into the common law, the rules made for the alien merchant were extended to all aliens, so that by the end of the 16th century an alien could bring personal actions and could own personal property. An exception was made, however, in the case of the alien enemy, who continued to be rightless.

The Status of Aliens act, 1914, not repealed by the British

Nationality act, 1948, provided that real and personal property of every description might be taken, acquired, held and disposed of by an alien in the same manner in all respects as by a British subject; but acts of parliament provide that no alien may be appointed to any office or place in the civil service; there are restrictions on his employment on ships; without express official permission, he may not use any name other than that by which he is ordinarily known; and, from 1920, aliens must register. Restrictions on aliens are, however, sometimes varied by administrative action; and international conventions and treaties affect the rights and freedoms of aliens.

U.S. Law.—Although feudalism was not imported into the American colonies from the mother country, phases of feudal real-property law were imported as part of the common law. The supreme court in *Fairfax Devisee* v. *Hunter's Lessee* (1813) recognized the feudal real-property law as obtaining in the United States insofar as it affected aliens. An act of congress, adopted in 1887, restricted the ownership of land by aliens in the District of Columbia and in territories of the United States. Most states, however, by statute accorded aliens the same rights with respect to real property as those enjoyed by citizens. States on the west coast had laws which radically restricted the rights to own or lease land by aliens who were ineligible for citizenship; these laws affected particularly Chinese and Japanese immigrants; but the legal base of these state enactments was removed by acts of congress of 1943, 1946 and 1952, which wiped out all racial bars on naturalization. Beginning in 1940, on the other hand, all aliens had to register.

The supreme court in *Truax* v. *Raich* (1915) held that the equal protection clause of the 14th amendment applies to aliens as well as to citizens; that a state may not deny to aliens the ordinary means of earning a livelihood; that if a special public interest is shown with respect to a particular business in which the employment of aliens might reasonably be shown to be a peril to the public welfare, a state may prohibit employment of aliens in that particular business. Notwithstanding constitutional limitations, many states restrict the employment of aliens. There is no consistent pattern among the states, nor is there a consistent formula to rationalize the restrictive legislation within any state.

Constitutionally, said Justice Robert H. Jackson in a case decided by the U.S. supreme court in 1952, the alien in the United States is afforded a large measure of economic opportunity; he may invoke the writ of habeas corpus; in criminal proceedings he is entitled to the guaranties of the Bill of Rights; and his property cannot be taken without just compensation. But to remain in the country "is not his right, but is a matter of permission and tolerance"; the government has the power to terminate its "hospitality," for his domicile is held by a "precarious tenure"—the power to deport him is "inherent" in the United States as a sovereign state. This has been and continues to be the law of the United States. As long as the alien is in the U.S., the constitution is his protection; but congress, not the constitution, decides whether or not he is to remain. Justices Black and Douglas dissented from the latter proposition and urged that the deportation process be made subject to the limitations of the Bill of Rights.

BIBLIOGRAPHY.—Marcus Lee Hansen, *The Immigrant in American History* (1940); Oscar Handlin, *The Uprooted* (1951); Clive Parry, *British Nationality* (1951); John Mervyn Jones, *British Nationality Law and Practice*, 2nd ed. (1955); Andreas Hans Roth, *The Minimum Standard of International Law Applied to Aliens* (1949); Milton R. Konvitz, *The Alien and the Asiatic in American Law* (1946), *Civil Rights in Immigration* (1953); United Nations Secretariat, *Compilation of Laws on the Legal Status of Aliens (1941–54)*; United Nations, *Laws Concerning Nationality* (1954–); UNESCO, *The Positive Contribution by Immigrants* (1955); John Higham, *Strangers in the Land* (1955); I. Foighel, *Nationalization: a Study in the Protection of Alien Property in International Law* (1957); W. Preston, *Aliens and Dissenters* (1963). (M. R. K.)

ALIENATION, in law, the act of transfer of property by voluntary deed and not by inheritance. In regard to church property the word has come to mean a transfer from religious to secular ownership (*see* REAL PROPERTY AND CONVEYANCING, LAWS OF). For the term as applied to mental derangement, *see* INSANITY. A discussion of alienation of affection, one of the grounds for which

divorce may be granted, can be found in DIVORCE.

ALIEN PROPERTY, a term used to describe foreign-owned property located in the United States or its possessions that has been vested, *i.e.*, seized, by the United States government under wartime authority granted by the Trading With the Enemy act. The vesting of property results in ownership by the government subject to a return of the property, or the proceeds of its liquidation, upon a judicial or administrative finding that the former owner is not an enemy as defined in that act.

World War II vesting action was generally limited to the property of enemy powers and their nationals. Legislation enacted after the end of hostilities made the victims of persecution by those powers eligible for return regardless of their enemy nationality. Other postwar legislation disposed of additional enemy assets as follows: virtually all assets of Italy and its nationals were returned; assets of Germany, Japan and their nationals were devoted to the compensation of Americans mistreated by enemy forces; certain assets of Bulgaria, Hungary, Rumania and their nationals were devoted to the compensation of U.S. claimants against those countries, and the remainder was made subject to return.

Vested property held by the United States is administered by the office of alien property, department of justice.

See also NATIONALIZATION; LAWS OF WAR. (S. LM.)

ALIGARH, a town, and headquarters of the district of the same name, lies in Uttar Pradesh, India, about 80 mi. S.E. of Delhi on the Grand Trunk road. It has rail connections with Delhi, Calcutta and Bombay, but the city itself lies west of the railway and is generally called Koil or Kol, Aligarh being the name of a fort beyond the civil station east of the railway. The population (185,020 in 1961) greatly increased after about 1940.

The town of Koil has a handsome appearance, the centre being occupied by the lofty site of the old Dorfortress (1524), now crowned by a mosque, built early in the 18th century, which was repaired during 1898–99 at a cost of more than Rs. 90,000 subscribed by residents in the district. A pillar erected in 1253 to commemorate the victories of Sultan Nazir-ud-din Mahmud was pulled down in 1862. In and about the town are several tombs of Muslim saints. Koil contains a civil general hospital and a women's hospital; the Lyall library, opened in 1889, is known as Malviya library. A large part of the city is built on swampy land around the fort; there are a number of good metaled roads. Its principal manufactures include locks, metal works and cotton rugs and carpets.

Aligarh town has a number of degree colleges but it is chiefly celebrated for the Aligarh Muslim university, founded by Sir Sayyid Ahmad Khan. The university consists of a number of allied institutions of which the engineering college, the polytechnic and the Opthalmic institute are outstanding. The Opthalmic institute is the only one of its kind in Asia. The Azad library, named after the central education minister, Maulana Abul Kalam Azad, has a fine building in the heart of the university campus.

ALIGARH DISTRICT has an area of 1,941 sq.mi. Pop. (1961) 1,765,275. It contains a farm owned by the state government, and butter forms an important article of export. There is a glass factory at Sasni, and locks are also exported; sugar, rice, piece goods, metals and timber form the chief imports. (S. M. T. R.)

ALIMENTARY CANAL: *see* GASTROINTESTINAL TRACT.

ALIMONY, maintenance and support refer, in general, to the payments that a man is obligated to make, after separation or divorce, to the woman who is, or formerly was, his wife. The terms are also applied to the payments that under modern statutes a woman may have to make to her present or former husband. The more precise legal meanings of these terms differ in England and the commonwealth on the one hand and in the United States on the other.

The United States.—In the United States, alimony usually refers to the payments a court may order a party to a divorce or a judicial separation, usually the husband, to make for the other party's support. Alimony must thus be distinguished from separate maintenance, which one of the parties to a marriage may be ordered to pay to the other while they are living apart but not divorced. The payments that a parent, before or after divorce from his spouse, may have to make for the maintenance of a child are known as child support. During the pendency of a suit for divorce, one spouse may be ordered to pay temporary alimony (alimony *pendente lite*); in addition, a husband may be ordered to pay suit money to give the wife the funds necessary to pursue or defend a divorce suit. In a suit for divorce, judicial separation or separate maintenance, it may be necessary also to decree a property settlement; *i.e.,* an allocation of the parties' property.

In a broader sense, the term alimony may cover all the various provisions just stated.

Alimony in both the strict and the broader senses has come to serve a number of different functions. Where, as under the common law, marriage gave a husband title to all personal property and to all income from real property of his wife, it was necessary in the case of a separation that the husband be ordered to provide her with the means to live. Where, as in the official law of many states, divorce is treated as the privilege of an innocent party to cast out a spouse who has committed an unforgivable act of misconduct, alimony tends to assume the character of damages to be granted to the innocent party for the loss of marital support at the home, but is refused altogether to a guilty party or fixed at a minimum subsistence level which keeps that party, from becoming a burden on the taxpayers. Where courts do not clearly distinguish between alimony and child support, the award made to a wife having child custody tends to combine support for both mother and children. Where, as in many U.S. courts, alimony is awarded in a lump sum to be paid either at once or in fixed installments, it tends to merge with property settlement and to afford the court an opportunity to grant the wife a portion of the property that she has helped the husband to accumulate and that she would have inherited had the marriage lasted until the husband's death. Courts can thus produce results similar to those of community property, which prevails (in Anglo-American countries) only in a few jurisdictions of the United States and in a few parts of the commonwealth.

The different purposes served by alimony are reflected in the variety of statutory rules and the even greater variety of judicial practices. While in one jurisdiction alimony is strictly refused to a guilty party without regard to need, in another it is awarded to a party in need without regard to guilt. Traditionally, alimony is ordered to be paid in periodic installments, the amount of which may be revised by the court in accord both with changing need and changing ability to pay.

In accord with the mores of a time in which men were the breadwinners and women were supposed to live on their husbands' incomes, alimony was once a privilege of women. Gradually the law is realizing not only that women are able to earn their own living but also that a man may be dependent for his livelihood on the income of his wife. But even where the law allows an alimony award to be made to a husband, the courts are inclined to limit the exercise of that power to cases where he is without means of his own and is too handicapped to earn a living.

The obligation to pay money under a judicial award of alimony can, as a general rule, be enforced like any other money judgment; *i.e.,* by attaching the debtor's property or by garnishing his bank account, his claim for wages or his other claims. In addition to these generally available remedies, the payment of alimony can also be enforced by imprisoning the one who fails to pay or earn the necessary money although he is able to do so.

A judicial award for alimony will, as a general rule, not be made unless it has been applied for. It was estimated in the 1950s that applications for permanent alimony were made in no more than about 10% of the divorces pronounced in cases in which no provision had to be made for children. In some of the remaining 90% of these cases, the parties may have made an alimony agreement out of court. But in the majority of cases it seems that alimony was not asked for, either because early remarriage was contemplated by the wife, or out of pride or absence of need, for other personal reasons, or because the husband's income and earning capacity were regarded as too low to allow a realistic expectation of payments.

English Law.—In English law, alimony refers to the payments a husband may be ordered to make to his wife by a decree of the high court rendered in formal proceedings of judicial separation, a decree that does not dissolve the tie of marriage. Payments, however, ordered by the high court in a decree of divorce, by which the marriage is terminated, are called maintenance. The same term also applies to the payments a husband may be ordered to make to his wife by a separation or maintenance order issued by magistrates in informal proceedings in which a marriage cannot be dissolved. These three forms of matrimonial relief differed at one time not only in procedure but also with respect to the circumstances under which they would be granted and the amounts to be paid. These differences have gradually disappeared, except that under the legislation in force in 1960 the maximum amount of maintenance obtainable in a magistrates' court was limited to £5 a week for a wife and 30 s. a week for a child. In general, however, the determination of the amount of alimony or maintenance is left to the discretion of the court. In a case before the divorce court the husband may be ordered either to make periodic payments to the wife, to set aside a special fund for her support, or both. This order may be altered from time to time in accord with changing circumstances. The divorce court may also grant maintenance to a wife found guilty of marital misconduct; in a magistrates' court the power to grant maintenance is limited in cases where the wife has been guilty of adultery, and no alimony can be granted to the wife in a decree of judicial separation obtained by the husband on the ground of adultery.

A wife is under a duty to provide for the maintenance of a husband only if she divorces him on the ground of incurable insanity. She may generally be ordered, however, to reimburse the National Assistance board for any sums it had to pay as assistance to her husband, just as a husband may be ordered to reimburse the board for sums paid to his wife.

In addition the court may adjust property rights arising out of a divorce or separation settlement, and this power may be exercised in favour of the husband and the children.

See also DIVORCE; ANNULMENT.

BIBLIOGRAPHY.—E. L. Johnson, *Family Law* (1958); J. L. Burton, "The Enforcement of Financial Provisions" in *A Century of Family Law, 1857–1957,* ed. by R. H. Graveson and F. R. Crane, pp. 352 ff. (1957); W. T. Nelson, *Divorce and Annulment,* 2nd ed., pp. 5 ff. (1945–58); C. G. Vernier, *American Family Laws,* vol. 2, sec. 104 ff. (1932–38); M. Ploscowe, *The Truth About Divorce* (1955); W. J. Goode, *After Divorce,* pp. 158–162 (1956); M. B. Virtue, *Family Cases in Court,* pp. 92–93 (statistics) (1956); F. H. Kuchler, *Law of Support,* "Legal Almanac Series," No. 12, 2nd ed. (1958). (M. Rⁿ.)

ALI PASHA, MOHAMMED EMIN (1815–1871), Ottoman Turkish grand vizier distinguished for his liberal policies, was born in Istanbul on March 4, 1815, of a poor family. He had no regular education, but learned French and obtained the post of secretary to the divan (council) of the Sublime Porte. After being ambassador in London (1841–44), he became foreign minister under Mustafa Reshid Pasha and took part in the congresses of Vienna (1855) and Paris (1856). He was five times grand vizier (1852, 1855–56, 1858–59, 1861, 1867–71). He resisted attempts by the sultans to take away the powers of the Sublime Porte; he settled the troubles in Serbia and in Moldavia-Wallachia by peaceful measures; and, in 1868, he pacified the Cretan revolt by the grant of a measure of local self-government. He was one of the most zealous advocates of westernizing reforms and of friendship with France and Great Britain during the reigns of the sultans Abdul-Mejid I and Abdul-Aziz. He was also a devout Muslim but nevertheless forced the sultans to allow men of all creeds to hold public office. He died in Istanbul on Sept. 7, 1871. (E. Z. K.)

ALIQUIPPA, a borough of Pennsylvania, U.S., situated on the Ohio river, approximately 18 mi. N. of Pittsburgh, is the largest municipality in Beaver county. (For comparative population figures *see* table in PENNSYLVANIA: *Population.*)

The legal incorporation of Aliquippa dates from Jan. 22, 1894. In 1900 there were only 620 inhabitants in the community; the town developed rapidly with the expansion of the Pittsburgh district steel industry in the early part of the 20th century. About two-thirds of the working force of the borough, which is an integral part of the Pittsburgh industrial complex, is engaged in steel production. (P. R. J.)

ALIQUOT PART, an exact divisor of a number or quantity (that is, a divisor giving an integral quotient). For example, 2 is an aliquot part of 10, $33\frac{1}{3}$ is an aliquot part of 100, a line $2\frac{1}{2}$ in. long is an aliquot part of one that is $7\frac{1}{2}$ in. long, and $\frac{1}{3}$ is an aliquot part of 1; but $\frac{2}{3}$ is not an aliquot part of 1, the quotient of 1 divided by $\frac{2}{3}$ not being an integer.

ALISHAR HUYUK. The mound known as Alishar Huyuk is situated on a river plain between Yozgat and Bogazliyan in north-central Turkey, about 50 mi. S.E. of the ruins of the Hittite capital Hattushash at Bogazkoy. It was the scene of thorough and extensive excavations by an expedition of the Oriental institute of The University of Chicago, led by H. H. von der Osten and E. F. Schmidt, between 1927 and 1932. From a technical point of view this undertaking represented a new departure in Anatolian archaeology: in contrast with the hitherto largely limited and haphazard excavations of European scholars at other sites, the resources of the U.S. team enabled it to submit every habitation layer of the mound to exemplary archaeological scrutiny.

The Alishar excavation, then, was the first systematic stratigraphic investigation on the Anatolian plateau. The finds justified the enterprise, and the field work, the recording and the publication of the results were all of remarkable quality. It had been hoped, however, that another great Hittite metropolis, complete with archives comparable to those of Bogazkoy, would be uncovered. Yet in the long succession of archaeological strata revealed at Alishar—from Chalcolithic to Phrygian (*cf.* Asia Minor: *Archaeology*)—the only era that was not represented was in fact the Hittite, from the 17th to the 13th century B.C., so that it seems clear that the mound was not inhabited in that period.

In addition to the stratigraphic discontinuity created by this gap, a further complication was the irregular shape of the mound itself, consisting of an off-centre top elevation, known as the citadel, and a sloping terrace. Irregular habitation of one or both of these sections at various periods made collations of occupation levels extremely difficult; the designations applied by the excavators were subject to frequent revisions in successive reports and considerable controversy persisted for a long time regarding the proper inclusion of the Alishar periods in a wider framework of Anatolian stratigraphy. On the basis of Osten's final report the archaeological history of Alishar may be summarized.

The deepest and earliest phase is called "Neolithic" by Osten, but it more probably comprises layers from the late Chalcolithic and early Copper Age. The most conspicuous finds are large jars and bowls of dark clay on footed stems (so-called "fruit-stands"). Metal (copper, then bronze) first appears in the succeeding layers, showing dried-brick walls on stone foundations, which represent the Copper Age. Then follow two controversial, more or less contemporaneous, phases in parallel layers from the full Bronze Age, one of which is represented chiefly on the citadel and is characterized by the sudden appearance of brightly painted polychrome pottery known as "Cappadocian ware." It may point to an intrusion of foreign invaders, possibly Indo-European Hittites or related tribes, whose culture was subsequently rapidly assimilated to the more continuous native Anatolian tradition represented by the elegantly shaped monochrome pottery of the other, probably somewhat later, phase. The latter has yielded a number of "Cappadocian tablets," best known as records of Old Assyrian merchant colonists at Kultepe (*q.v.*) farther south, and datable to the 19th century B.C. At that time strong fortifications surrounded both the citadel and the sprawling community below it. Besides bronze, stone and bone implements were still used. The dead were buried in huge clay jars.

At the end of that period the occupation of Alishar was interrupted. At least five or six centuries later, however, the emplacement of the pre-Hittite citadel mound was chosen as the site of a Phrygian fortress, with a walled section on the slope below. Some centuries later the walls were extended to include additional new inhabited areas in the immediate vicinity. The settlement perhaps survived down to the time of Lydian hegemony in the 6th century B.C. In the end the citadel was destroyed by fire.

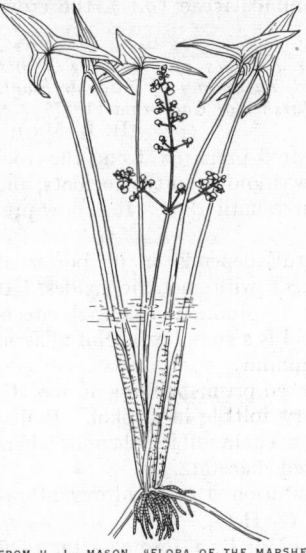

FROM H. L. MASON, "FLORA OF THE MARSHES OF CALIFORNIA," UNIVERSITY OF CALIFORNIA PRESS

FIG. 1.—ARROWHEAD (SAGITTARIA LATIFOLIA), SHOWING SUBMERGENT RHIZOMES AND EMERGENT FLOWERS AND LEAVES

In conclusion, Alishar has provided little of conspicuous epigraphic or architectural interest. Its importance lies in the ample and detailed scope of its general archaeological testimony rather than in any specific find of intrinsic significance.

See H. H. von der Osten, *Discoveries in Anatolia 1930–31* (1933) and *The Alishar Hüyük Seasons 1930–32* (1937); S. H. F. Lloyd, *Early Anatolia* (1956). (J. Pl.)

ALISMACEAE (Alismataceae), the water plantain family of plants belonging to the monocotyledonous order Alismales, of which the water plantain (*Alisma plantago*), arrowhead (*Sagittaria*) and burhead (*Echinodorus*) are of frequent occurrence. They are typically marsh plants and often occur as weeds in rice paddies. Although most species are perennial, any may behave as annuals, producing an abundance of seed the first year. Some produce several radiating, stolonlike rhizomes or rootstocks which develop a corm at the end and from which a new plant is generated the following year. Leaves are produced basally. Often when submerged they are linear with little or no development of a blade. Usually, however, the leaves are emergent from the water and there is a distinct arrow-shaped, triangular or elliptic blade on a long slender stalk or petiole, often very variable in a species. Flowers are usually bisexual or with stamens and carpels in different flowers, often showy, in whorls in simple or compound inflorescences that are usually taller than the leaves. They are regular with three green sepals and three showy, white, pink or sometimes purple, spotted petals; stamens are six to many, carpels six to many and free. The fruit is a head of achenes or less commonly follicles, sometimes (as in *Damasonium* and *Echinodorus*) burlike.

Pollination is by insects. About 11 genera and 75 species occur in warm and temperate regions of both hemispheres. The largest group is the arrowheads (*Sagittaria*), with about 40 or more species.

See Arrowhead.

Entire plants are eagerly sought after and eaten by migrating waterfowl; for that reason, some wildlife refuges provide plantings of arrowheads. Corms of *Sagittaria sinensis* are cultivated for food in the orient; *S. latifolia* is the "wapato" of northwest American Indians, who gathered the large corms for food. Some taxonomists point to the differentiated perianth and free carpels of Alismaceae as possible evidence of an evolutionary connection of the monocotyledons

FROM H. L. MASON, "FLORA OF THE MARSHES OF CALIFORNIA," UNIVERSITY OF CALIFORNIA PRESS

FIG. 2.—ALISMACEAE, REPRESENTATIVE SPECIES

(A) American water plantain (*Alisma plantago-aquatica*: (left) flower; (centre) flower with petals removed showing swollen sepals; (right) ring of mature achenes. (B) Starfruit (*Damasonium californicum*); bud, flowers and maturing fruit. (C) Burhead (*Echinodorus cordifolius*); maturing fruits

with the dicotyledonous family Ranunculaceae (*q.v.*), the crowfoots.

BIBLIOGRAPHY.—J. Hutchinson, *The Families of Flowering Plants*, vol. ii (1926–34); G. H. M. Lawrence, *Taxonomy of Vascular Plants* (1946); H. L. Mason, *Flora of the Marshes of California* (1957).
(H. L. MN.)

ALIZARIN, a vegetable dyestuff prepared from the root of the madder (*Rubia tinctorum*), was known to the ancients, and was prepared entirely from this source until 1868. It is now prepared synthetically.

The value of alizarin as a dyestuff depends on its power of forming insoluble compounds (lakes) with metallic oxides. It is in the form of these lakes that it produces coloured effects on textile fibres. Alizarin red on wool is a complex lake of alizarin with the oxides of calcium and aluminum.

The pure substance crystallizes in red prisms melting at 290° C. It is insoluble in water, and not very soluble in alcohol. It dissolves readily in caustic alkalis on account of its phenolic character, and it forms a yellow-coloured diacetate.

Alizarin has the chemical constitution 1.2 dihydroxyanthraquinone and the molecular formula $C_{14}H_8O_4$.

AL JAZIRAH, a *liwa* (province) of Iraq, formed after 1947 by reconstitution of a geographically distinctive unit formerly divided between the older *liwas* of Dulaim and Mosul. Area 9,670 sq.mi. Jazirah means "island," here referring to the rolling and irregular plateau (800–1,500 ft.) lying between the Euphrates and Tigris rivers, and defined to the north by the Jabal Sinjar. The region is dissected by now dry river valleys trending mainly southward to the Euphrates and there are several closed drainage basins with salt marshes. Most is desert, but there is a remarkable spring vegetation; hence the Jazirah is occupied almost entirely by nomads of the Shammar Jarba and Dulaim tribes. The former are "camel" nomads, the latter chiefly shepherds who also include an increasing number of semisettled groups.
(W. B. FR.)

ALKALI. In modern chemistry the term alkali is specifically applied to the very soluble hydroxides of lithium, sodium, potassium, rubidium and cesium which are known as the alkali metals. An alkali is distinguished from an acid or a neutral substance by its characteristic action on litmus, phenolphthalein and other indicators.

The term is shared by the less soluble hydroxides of the alkaline earth metals, calcium, strontium and barium, also by ammonium hydroxide and thallous hydroxide. Industrially the term is extended to include other compounds which are soluble and which behave actively as bases. (*See* ALKALI MANUFACTURE.)

The term was originally applied to the ashes of plants from which the carbonates of sodium and potassium were lixiviated or leached. The conversion of these "mild" alkalis into "caustic" alkalis by treatment with lime was practised in Pliny's time and was utilized in the manufacture of soap, the ashes of sea plants yielding a hard soap and those of land plants a soft one. The distinction between the two components of this fixed alkali was made by the French chemist, Henri Louis Duhamel du Monceau, who in 1736 established that the ashes of sea plants contain the same base as is found in natural deposits of sodium salts or mineral alkali, and that this substance was different from the vegetable alkali obtained from the ashes of land plants (potashes). Later, Martin Heinrich Klaproth, who found the vegetable alkali in certain minerals, proposed the name potash. The symbol for potassium, K, was taken from the modernized Latin word *kalium* (from the Arabic word for "calcined").

See also Index references under "Alkali" in the Index volume.
(J. B. Ps.)

ALKALI MANUFACTURE. The manufacture of alkali, which in an industrial sense refers usually to soda ash (Na_2CO_3, or sodium carbonate) and caustic soda (NaOH, or sodium hydroxide), is one of the most important activities of chemical industry. At mid-20th century, the production of almost every manufactured consumer item depended on the use of alkali at some stage. Alkali was essential to the production of glass, soap, miscellaneous chemicals, viscose rayon and cellophane, paper and pulp, cleansers and detergents, textiles, water softeners, certain metals (especially aluminum), bicarbonate of soda, and gasoline and other petroleum derivatives. Per capita annual consumption of alkali at mid-20th century ranged from 9 to 110 lb., the highest rates of consumption being in the heavily industrialized countries.

Man has been using alkali for centuries, obtaining it first from the leachings (water solutions) of certain desert earths. Near the end of the 18th century, the leaching of wood or seaweed ashes became the chief source of alkali. Shortcomings of cottage industry methods induced the French Academy of Sciences in 1775 to offer monetary prizes for new manufacturing methods. The prize for soda ash was awarded to Frenchman Nicolas Leblanc, who in 1791 patented a salt conversion process that dominated world production until late in the 19th century. Following World War I the Leblanc method was completely supplanted by a salt conversion process introduced in 1863 by Ernest Solvay of Belgium after the method had failed earlier in both England and France.

Late in the 19th century, electrolytic methods for the production of caustic soda appeared and grew rapidly in importance until by the mid-1940s more than half of all caustic was produced by electrolysis.

Solvay Process of Soda Ash Manufacture.—By the early 1960s the Solvay process (also called the ammonia-soda method) was being employed in approximately 65 factories in 24 countries. The Solvay factories had a range of daily production capacity from about 100 to 2,000 tons, with the larger ones able to produce more efficiently and economically than the smaller ones. Ten factories in North America, with a combined capacity of more than 6,000,000 tons annually, accounted for nearly half the world's soda ash production. Comparatively little soda ash was being handled in international trade, mainly because the importing countries were buying products made from soda, rather than soda itself.

In the Solvay process, common salt in saturated brine, usually obtained from wells drilled into underground deposits of rock salt, is chemically treated to eliminate calcium and magnesium impurities and then is saturated with recycling ammonia gas in towers originally of the bubble-cap type but now more often tile-packed. The ammoniated brine is carbonated in a different type of tower with carbon dioxide gas at pressures of three to four atmospheres. Both these gas absorption processes evolve considerable heat and require precise cooling control and considerable investment in water pumping equipment and heat transfer surfaces.

Ammonia absorption proceeds readily as the brine showers down the tower through a rising stream of gas. In contrast, carbonation requires pressure as a driving force to bubble the gas up through the tower full of liquid, thus enabling crystals of sodium bicarbonate, while in suspension, to grow to filterable size. This kind of carbonation equipment is often called a "Solvay" tower, and its development laid important groundwork for theories concerning the chemical behaviour of liquids falling through rising streams of gases under conditions of continuous feed and discharge.

The carbonator discharge stream, consisting of a slurry of crystals of sodium bicarbonate, is filtered continuously on rotary vacuum filters, although several European plants use continuous centrifuges. The filter cake is then continuously heated at atmospheric pressure to decompose bicarbonate to monocarbonate and simultaneously to drive off water and ammonia. The need for a high degree of recovery of undiluted ammonia (NH_3) and carbon dioxide (CO_2) and the inherent caking and scaling tendency of crude bicarbonate combine to make the calcination (roasting) step the most difficult one in the process. Originally, this procedure was carried out in stationary pans with stirrers over direct fire. Later, externally fired rotary kilns were used. At mid-20th century, steam-heated rotary driers were the rule, especially in the U.S. The trend appeared to be for future factories to calcine under pressure sufficient for direct carbonation, possibly using the fluidized solids techniques of the petroleum industry.

Gases produced during calcination are recycled to the NH_3 and CO_2 absorption steps; other CO_2 required for the process comes from the burning of limestone in coke-fired kilns controlled to effect high carbonate decomposition without excess fuel or combustion air. The kiln gas is compressed for the carbonators. The lime produced is used to decompose the ammonium chloride while heating the mother liquor resulting from the bicarbonate filtration. This distillation returns the ammonia to the absorption process already described. The resultant calcium chloride solution or "distiller waste" is sent to waste or (in small part) to refinement and dewatering for market.

Electrolytic Production of Caustic Soda.—This process also begins with a saturated and purified salt brine. Electrolytic cells of two main types and many subtypes are used most of which have graphite anodes and steel cathodes. Diaphragm cells use an asbestos diaphragm to keep chlorine gas separate from the sodium hydroxide solution obtained at the cathode by the interaction of the sodium ion with water in the brine. The resulting caustic solution is of the order of 130 to 150 g. of caustic soda per litre and must be concentrated in large evaporator equipment from which unreacted salt is recycled to the cell. Mercury cathode cells react sodium amalgam with water in a separate compartment of the cell, giving a salt-free solution generally of 750 g. of sodium hydroxide per litre. Both diaphragm and mercury cathode cell types produce about a ton of caustic per ton of chlorine, but, because chlorine is expensive to store and hazardous to dispose of as waste, the process is limited and scheduled according to chlorine sales.

Refining Natural Alkali.—In a few places in the world there are substantial deposits of the mineral form of soda ash, or "natural alkali." The mineral usually occurs as sodium sesquicarbonate or trona ($Na_2CO_3.NaHCO_3.2H_2O$), which contains soluble and insoluble impurities. In the U.S., soda ash is produced commercially from trona deposits at dry bed lakes in California and from underground mines in Wyoming. Soda ash also is produced from wet surface lakes in Kenya, and minor amounts are mined or refined in Egypt, Mexico, Turkey, Chile, South Africa, Canada and elsewhere. At mid-20th century, natural alkali production comprised only 5% of total alkali production but was increasing at a faster rate than production from the Solvay process.

Marketing.—The soda ash and caustic soda now being produced are extremely pure compounds that meet rigid specifications. Most soda ash is shipped in bulk by barges and boxcars. When bagged, it usually is shipped in single-trip multiwalled paper sacks. Caustic soda is usually shipped in tank cars as a 50% or 70% solution; anhydrous caustic soda is shipped in steel drums, either in the flaked or solid condition.

Soda ash is marketed either as "light," a fine powder weighing about 35 lb. per cubic foot, or as "dense" (65 lb. per cubic foot), a much coarser grain material made especially for glassmakers by recrystallization or mechanical densification. Some soda ash is converted to other carbonates and hydrates, such as sodium bicarbonate for the baking and pharmaceutical industries and sodium sesquicarbonate for laundering compounds, and also to the monohydrate. The decahydrate, or old-fashioned "crystal soda" ($Na_2CO_3.10H_2O$), is fast disappearing. Some briquettes and fused soda ash, and mixtures of various carbonates and hydroxides, have important markets in small tonnages.

See CHEMICAL INDUSTRY: *Foundation of the Chemical Industry, Solvay Process, Electrolysis;* CHLORINE: *Electrolytic Process;* GLASS MANUFACTURE: *Properties; Manufacture;* SOLVAY, ERNEST; SOAP; DETERGENTS AND WETTING AGENTS; ALKALI.

BIBLIOGRAPHY.—Te-pang Hou, *Manufacture of Soda,* rev. ed. (1942); F. W. and D. B. Osterwald, *Wyoming Geological Survey Bulletin,* no. 45 (1952); R. E. Kirk and D. F. Othmer, *Encyclopedia of Chemical Technology,* 1:358–430 (1947). (Z. G. D.)

ALKALINE EARTHS. By the early chemists, the term earth was used to denote those nonmetallic substances which were insoluble in water and were unaffected by strong heating; and since some of these substances (*e.g.,* lime) were found to be very similar in properties to those of the alkalies, they were called alkaline earths. Lime, strontia and baryta were assumed to be elements until 1807, when Sir Humphry Davy showed that they were oxides, respectively, of the metals calcium, strontium and barium. These elements and the other members of Group IIa of the periodic system, beryllium, magnesium and radium, are now known as the alkaline earth metals, or the alkaline earths. The metals are never found in the uncombined condition, but occur most often in the form of carbonates and sulfates; they form oxides of the type RO, and peroxides of the type RO_2. The oxides of type RO are soluble in water, with generation of heat (*e.g.,* the slaking of lime); the resulting solution possesses a strongly alkaline reaction because of the presence of the hydroxide $R(OH)_2$, which rapidly absorbs carbon dioxide on exposure. These oxides and hydroxides are basic in character and dissolve readily in acids with the formation of the corresponding salts. As the atomic weight of the elements increases, it is found that the solubility of the hydroxides in water increases although that of the sulfates decreases.

The metals calcium, strontium and barium oxidize rapidly on exposure. Their salts usually crystallize well, the chlorides and nitrates dissolve readily in water, while the carbonates, phosphates and sulfates are either sparingly soluble or insoluble in water.

(J. B. Ps.)

ALKALOIDS, complex compounds in plants that may produce pronounced physiological effects when consumed by or administered to man and animals. Examples of alkaloids are morphine, quinine, nicotine, strychnine and reserpine.

Although it is virtually impossible to frame a definition for which there are no exceptions, alkaloids are usually understood (1) to be of plant origin; (2) to possess a basic, salt-forming, ammonialike character, a property from which they derive their name (alkaloid means alkali-like); (3) to contain nitrogen; and (4) to produce physiological effects on man and animal.

History.—Man has from very early times made use of natural drugs for medicinal or spiritual purposes. However, his knowledge about the active constituents of such plant preparations or extracts, which may contain alkaloids, glycosides or other components, is of relative late date. The first reported attempt to isolate an alkaloid dates back to 1803 when Charles Derosne observed that a sirupy extract of opium, when diluted with water, deposited crystalline matter, which he separated and tried to purify and so prepared the first alkaloid, probably impure narcotine. When he added alkali to the diluted opium sirup he obtained a different substance that undoubtedly contained the alkaloid morphine. About the same time A. Séguin obtained impure morphine by a similar procedure.

But the credit for first isolating a typical alkaloid in a pure state and describing its properties in unmistakable terms was reserved for F. W. A. Sertürner, who in 1806 announced he had isolated morphine, a new organic base that apparently was related to ammonia. He prepared a number of salts and was able to demonstrate the physiological activity of the alkaloid. In 1810 B. A. Gomes treated an alcoholic extract of cinchona bark with alkali and obtained a crystalline precipitate that he called cinchonino. Subsequent work on this material by Pierre Pelletier and J. B. Caventou resulted in the discovery that it was a mixture of two alkaloids, which were separated and called quinine and cinchonine. In the years between 1820 and 1840 a large number of alkaloids were isolated and purified and their properties described in the literature. Important alkaloids discovered during that period are veratrine, strychnine, piperine, berberine, coniine, atropine, codeine, thebaine, hyoscyamine, curarine, emetine, quinidine, aconitine and colchicine. Because of the complex chemical structure of most of these alkaloids very little progress was made during the 19th century in the difficult task of elucidating their molecular structure. Only after the theory and technique of organic chemistry had developed to a sufficiently high level could this problem be attacked successfully. By the early 1960s the structure of almost all important alkaloids had been established. A large number of them had also been synthesized by that time. New alkaloids were being reported in the chemical literature almost every month, and the establishment of their structure constituted an important part of natural-product chemistry.

Classification.—More than 900 alkaloids are known, but they are comparatively restricted in their distribution among plants. They occur chiefly in Rubiaceae, Papaveraceae, Fumariaceae, Solanaceae, Leguminosae and Apocynaceae and to a lesser extent in the Rosaceae, Graminaceae, Labiatae and Compositae. It has been generally observed, although there are exceptions, that the same genus, and in some cases related genera, yield the same or at least structurally related alkaloids; *e.g.*, seven distinct genera of Solanaceae yield the alkaloid hyoscyamine, the optically active form of atropine. Because of this observed distribution of chemically related alkaloids in related plants there is some similarity between the two commonly used systems that classify alkaloids either according to the plant genera in which they occur or on the basis of similarity in molecular structure. Examples of important groups of alkaloids containing generically related members are strychnos alkaloids, opium alkaloids, cinchona alkaloids, lupine alkaloids, ephedra alkaloids, aconitum alkaloids and rauwolfia alkaloids. Names for alkaloid groups that are classified for chemical reasons are usually derived from the name of that part of the molecule that all members of any given group have in common. Thus, members of the pyrrolidine group contain the heterocyclic ring system pyrrolidine, whereas indol alkaloids are more or less complex derivatives of indol. Other examples of this classification include quinoline alkaloids, isoquinoline alkaloids and pyridine alkaloids.

Pharmacology.—Physiological actions of some alkaloids are widely known; *e.g.*, quinine is usually associated with the treatment of malaria, morphine with the relief of severe organic pain, cocaine with minor surgical operations and atropine with the work of the ophthalmologist. Although almost all alkaloids exert a distinct physiological action on higher animals and man, only about 20 are used for medicinal purposes. The large majority of alkaloids produce either no favourable effect at all or are too toxic to be useful drugs. Similar to many other drugs, those alkaloids that are used in medicine are not free from undesirable side effects. For example, morphine, which is still unsurpassed as an analgesic drug, is strongly habit-forming and may lead to addiction. Codeine and cocaine suffer from the same drawback. It is the aim of the pharmaceutical chemist to modify the chemical structure of these alkaloids in such manner that the resulting drug is superior to the natural product by maintaining the desired activity but producing less severe side effects.

Although very little is known about the biochemical action of the various alkaloids when administered to man, it is possible to divide them into groups whose members produce similar effects by acting upon the same part of the central nervous system. Examples of some of these groups with representative members are pressor alkaloids (ephedrine, gramine), which are capable of raising the blood pressure; cardioactive alkaloids (quinidine, erythrophleine), capable of altering some function of the heart; respiratory stimulants (nicotine, atropine), acting upon the respiratory system; uterine stimulants (ergotamine, quinine), causing increased activity of the uterus; and phrenotropic alkaloids (reserpine, mescaline), drugs that influence the function of the mind and the affective behaviour. Many alkaloids show activity in two or more of these groups; *e.g.*, reserpine, which can be listed as a hypotensive agent, a central nervous depressant or sedative, in addition to being a phrenotropic agent.

An important factor of physiological activity of alkaloids is the dose in which they are administered. Strychnine, for example, is used in small doses as a heart stimulant but can cause death in larger doses. The alkaloids of curare, the deadly arrow poison of the South American Indians, can be useful drugs for treatment of cerebral palsy when administered in small doses.

Detection and Preparation.—The processes by which alkaloids are obtained from plants depend upon the complete extraction of the dry ground material (bark, roots, leaves or seeds) with a suitable solvent, usually alcohol or slightly acidified water. The solvent is then distilled off under vacuum and the resulting extract diluted with water, made distinctly acidic and left to stand to deposit impurities. It is next made alkaline, preferably with sodium carbonate or ammonia; the bulk of the alkaloid is then usually precipitated and can be filtered off. If the alkaloid is soluble in water, other procedures involving the use of immiscible solvents (*i.e.*, liquids that, when shaken with watery fluids, will remove soluble substances therefrom and then form a separate layer) and sometimes special precipitants or absorbents have to

be adopted. These processes almost invariably yield a mixture of alkaloids, since the latter rarely occur singly in plants. The separation of these mixtures into their components can generally be achieved by fractional crystallization of the bases or their salts with suitable acids. More efficient processes for separation of alkaloid mixtures are adsorption or partition chromatography or countercurrent distribution between two solvents. Final purification of the alkaloids is usually carried out by repeated recrystallization from selected solvents.

Each kind of alkaloidal plant requires different treatment; the preparation process has been greatly simplified for most of the alkaloids produced on a large scale for use in medicine, though the standard of purity is constantly rising. The criteria of purity for alkaloids are the same as those for any other organic compound, viz., determination of physical constants such as melting point or boiling point (for liquids), optical rotation and the chemical composition as determined by ultimate analysis. The use of infrared and ultraviolet or visible absorption spectra has become quite common as additional means for control of purity.

The analytical work of the toxicologist in connection with alkaloids is important. The methods by which poisonous alkaloids are extracted from viscera and stomach contents do not differ in principle from those for the extraction of alkaloids from plant material, but in these cases the problem is greatly complicated by the smallness of the quantities of alkaloids to be recovered. Again, spectroscopic methods have proved to be quite useful in this field in the detection and identification of alkaloids. Other methods for detecting and identifying micro quantities of alkaloids are colour tests, which most of the alkaloids give with certain reagents, and in a few cases special pharmacological tests; these methods give quite satisfactory results in the hands of experts.

Determination of Molecular Structure.—A few of the alkaloids are liquid and volatile, but most of them are colourless crystalline solids. If a new alkaloid has been isolated and obtained in a pure state the rather complicated process of elucidating its structure is usually started by determining its molecular formula. By quantitative analysis for the elements present (always carbon, hydrogen and nitrogen and in most cases oxygen as well), the chemist derives the ratio at which these elements are present in the molecule. Determining the molecular weight enables him to write the molecular formula that expresses the number of carbon, hydrogen, nitrogen and oxygen atoms that comprise the molecule.

Next, the chemist may direct his work to obtaining information about the nature of the nitrogen atoms in the compound. Since the alkaloids can be regarded as extensively substituted ammonias, those containing two atoms of nitrogen may be expected to be capable of forming salts derived from two molecules of monobasic acids. This is true with some alkaloids such as quinine ($C_{20}H_{24}O_2N_2$) but quite frequently, as in the case of strychnine, only one of the two nitrogen atoms is capable of binding one molecule of acid whereas the second nitrogen is not basic enough to form a salt. This difference in basicity of the two nitrogen atoms must be taken into account in assigning a structural formula to such alkaloids. In most cases, the nitrogen atoms are tertiary; that is, each is united to three carbon atoms, one of which is frequently in a methyl group. Qualitative and quantitative procedures are available for recognizing the presence of such a grouping. Sometimes, a secondary nitrogen group is present, in which only two of the hydrogen atoms of ammonia have been replaced by carbon linkages. The hydrogen of a secondary nitrogen group can be easily detected by infrared spectroscopy and chemical tests.

By similar means it is possible to discover how the oxygen atoms in an alkaloid are built into the molecule. Most frequently they are present as hydroxy (—OH), methoxy (—OCH₃), acetoxy (—OCOCH₃) or benzoxy (—OCOC₆H₅) groups. Occasionally a carboxyl group (—COOH) is present, and this, together with the basic nitrogen, may form a betaine. Frequently this carboxyl group occurs as its methyl ester. There are well-established methods of ascertaining the presence or absence of these groups. Spectroscopic methods (infrared, ultraviolet, visible, nuclear magnetic resonance) are employed to supplement the chemical tests.

Next, the chemist has to ascertain how the alkaloid nucleus, the carbon-hydrogen skeleton to which these groups are attached, is built up and to determine the position at which each functional group is joined to this framework. No general scheme exists for this phase of the work. Success depends strongly on the skill and ingenuity of the chemist. The most frequently followed approach is to break up the alkaloid into small pieces by suitable reactions, to examine each piece in the same way as the parent alkaloid was examined and to continue with this process until a recognizable fragment, which may be any of the thousands of known organic compounds, is found. With that first clue to guide him and within the limits rigidly prescribed by all he knows regarding the composition and reactions of the alkaloid, the chemist can then proceed to visualize a structural formula.

This breaking-down process is generally accomplished by carefully regulated oxidation with such reagents as potassium permanganate, chromic acid or nitric acid—substances that burn off a few carbon atoms at a time and leave products that generally become simpler in character. Exhaustive methylation is another example of a valuable reaction that is frequently used to eliminate the nitrogen atom from a molecule and to leave a simpler compound that may be more easily recognized. The final part of an elucidation of structure is usually concerned with obtaining information as to the stereochemistry of the alkaloid, viz., deriving a complete three-dimensional expression for the arrangement of the atoms in the molecule. The structural formulas of the more important alkaloids are usually confirmed by total synthesis of the natural product from simple chemicals.

Biogenesis of Alkaloids.—Because of the complicated structure of most alkaloids, the question of their synthesis in the plant is of general interest. In addition, any knowledge of their biosynthesis may also give valuable information about the function of the alkaloids in the living plant. Therefore, chemists and biologists have speculated on this subject and developed many theories about biosynthetic schemes for various alkaloids. The concept with the widest support maintains that alkaloids are derived from amino acids, the building blocks of proteins. This idea is supported by the observation that the structure of most alkaloids can be derived from one or more simple derivatives of the naturally occurring amino acids, which are linked together by well-known chemical reactions. Some of the less complicated alkaloids have been synthesized in the laboratory in accordance with such biogenetical theories from derivatives of amino acids under physiological conditions (room temperature and neutral reaction media). With the advent of isotopically labeled compounds these theories became subject to experimental tests. For example, it has been demonstrated that morphine is produced in the plant from the common amino acid tyrosine. When opium poppy was grown in water containing isotopically labeled tyrosine, the extracted morphine had the isotopic atoms located at the same positions as expected from the biogenetic theory that maintains morphine is built from two molecules of tyrosine. Several other alkaloids (hyoscyamine, nicotine and ergotamine) have been shown by similar techniques to be products derived from amino acids.

Very little is known about the function of alkaloids in plants. Any theory concerned with this subject has to take into consideration that about 90% of all plants manage very well without ever producing alkaloids. Suggested theories, however, without much experimental evidence, are based on the idea of protection against higher animals, of the function of alkaloids as regulating agents in such activities as growth, general metabolism and reproduction, and finally of their function as detoxicating agents that eliminate substances whose accumulation might otherwise cause damage to the plant.

See CHEMISTRY: *Organic Chemistry; see* also references under "Alkaloids" in the Index.

BIBLIOGRAPHY.—T. A. Henry, *The Plant Alkaloids*, 4th ed. (1949); R. H. F. Manske and H. L. Holmes, *The Alkaloids: Chemistry and Physiology*, vol. i–vi (1950–59); F. E. Hamerslag, *The Technology and Chemistry of Alkaloids* (1950); H. G. Boit, *Fortschritte der Alkaloid-Chemie seit 1933* (1950); K. W. Bentley, *The Chemistry of the Morphine Alkaloids* (1954); Supplements no. 138 and 165 to U.S. Public Health Reports, viz.: L. F. Small *et al., Studies on Drug Addiction* (1938); H. Krueger, N. B. Eddy and M. Sumwalt, *Pharmacology of the Opium Alkaloids*, parts i and ii (1944); R. E. Woodson, Jr., *et al., Rauwolfia: Botany, Pharmacognosy, Chemistry and Pharmacology* (1957). See also *Annual Reports on the Progress of Chemistry; Annual Reports on the Progress of Applied Chemistry.* (G. L. C.)

ALKAN (real name CHARLES HENRI VALENTIN MORHANGE) (1813–1888), French pianist and composer of virtuoso works for the piano, was born in Paris, Nov. 30, 1813. He was a pupil at the Paris conservatoire of P. Zimmermann, and became known as a pianist and, later, as a teacher. As a composer, he displayed considerable imagination and ingenuity in advancing keyboard virtuosity; Busoni considered him, in this respect, second only to Liszt and Brahms, and César Franck paid homage by transcribing, for the organ, several of his preludes (*Préludes et Prières de Ch.-V. Alkan*, 1889). His numerous works include sets of both preludes and studies in all the major and minor keys; 12 pieces, *Les Mois;* the sonata, *Les Quatre Ages;* the Piano Concerto in C sharp minor; and the *Duo Dantesque* for piano and violin. He died in Paris, March 29, 1888. (F. E. G.)

ALKMAAR, a town in the province of North Holland, Neth., is situated several miles from the coastal dunes in flat country 25 mi. by road north-northwest of Amsterdam. Pop. (1960) 43,-606 (mun.). Alkmaar is a colourful town with canals and red-brick houses. It is a marketing centre for cattle, eggs and vegetables and is world-famous for its Friday cheese market, held from May to October in the Kaasmarkt. The weighhouse (rebuilt from a 14th-century chapel in 1582) has a tower with a carillon added in 1595–99 and is just north of the main street, Langestraat, in which are the public library, the town hall (1520, west part 1694) and museum (1873). St. Lawrence's church (1470–1520) has one of the oldest organs in the Netherlands (1511). In Laat is St. John's chapel (1443). Other old buildings include Sonoy court (16th century), the New Doelen (Archery house, *c.* 1600) and several almshouses. There is a park with a monument to the town's resistance to the Spanish siege of 1573. Industries include the manufacture of church organs, railway signaling apparatus, yachts, furniture, clothing and foodstuffs. In the 8th century Saints Willibrord and Adalbert from England preached Christianity in the district. The original charter was dated 1254; charters of Philip the Good of Burgundy established an oligarchy. Much damage was done in wars between the Hollanders and Frisians, the Gelderlanders and Frisians capturing the town in 1517. Alkmaar acquired an important trade after the reclamation of the surrounding swamps from 1564 onward. In 1799 it gave its name to a convention by which the Russo-British army evacuated Holland. In World War II Alkmaar was in German hands from May 1940 until May 1945.

ALLAH, the Arabic word for God, used by Christians as well as by Muslims and known to Arabs even in pre-Islamic times. The probable etymology is the contraction of *al-Ilah,* "the God," although the Aramaic *Alaha* also has been proposed.

The one and only God is the pivot of the Muslim faith. The Koran constantly preaches Allah, his inaccessible mystery, his names and his actions on behalf of his creatures. Three themes preponderate: (1) God is creator, judge and rewarder; (2) he is unique (*wahid*) and inherently one (*ahad*), "He begets not, nor is he begotten"; (3) he is omnipotent and all-merciful, the "Lord of the Worlds," the most high, "nothing is like unto him," and this in itself is to the believer a request to adore him as protector and to glorify his powers of compassion and forgiveness.

God, says the Koran, "loves those who do good," and two texts (iii, 31 and v, 54) express a mutual love between God and man; but the precept of love in its absolute cast, "thou shalt love thy God with all thy heart," is nowhere formulated. The emphasis is rather on his inscrutable sovereignty, to which one must abandon oneself. God speaks to man through his prophets, and the "surrender to God" (*islam*) is the religion (*din*) itself (Koran v, 3).

Many verses require "reflection on the signs of the universe" through which appear the "signs of God." Guided by him, human reason will find in transitoriness a testimony to the necessary and transcendental existence of the creator: "All must perish save his visage."

The Koran proclaims the "most beautiful Names" that are the

glory of God. He is One and Only, the Living One, the Subsisting, the Real Truth, the Sublime All-high, the Redoubtable, the Light and the Light of Lights, the Wise, the Omnipotent, the Absolute and Unceasing Creator, the One who is unlike all else, the Hearer, the Seer, the Omniscient, the Witness, the Giver, the Protector, the Generous, the Benefactor and the Merciful, the constant Remitter, the Compassionate, the Benevolent, the Best of Judges. Muslim piety has collected, in the Koranic text and in tradition, the 99 "fairest names," which it loves to repeat and meditate upon.

At all times there have been freethinkers in Islam, but rare indeed are those who have denied the existence of God. The profession of faith by which a person is introduced into the Muslim community is the affirmation that God is one and that Mohammed is his envoy. This is the *shahada* or "testimony," the first phrase of which proclaims "There is no god but God," *la ilah illa' Allah.* According to Koranic doctrine, the *shahada* uttered in sincerity is a means of salvation.

At the beginning of any obligatory action or one bringing merit, the pious Muslim invokes the divine name; thus, each chapter of the Koran opens with *bismillah al-Rahman al-Rahim,* "In the name of God, the Merciful, the Compassionate"; in everyday life it often appears in the shortened form *bismillah.*

Every contemplated action and every hope are subject to the divine will, hence the frequent use in daily speech of the formula *in sha' Allah,* "if God wills"; this use is known to Christian tradition also (*cf.* James iv, 15: "if the Lord will"). In Islam it is the reminder of an ever-present divine intervention in the order of the world and the acts of men. This is not in fact fatalism, as one might at first sight suppose, but a keen realization that nothing happens and nothing is performed unless it is by the will or commandment of God. Muslim schools pose the question: should one add *in sha' Allah* to "I believe"? Most agree that this should be so.

The treatises of religious knowledge devote long chapters to God and his existence and attributes. Briefly summarized, the personal attitude of a Muslim believer (*mu' min*) is and must be a complete and confiding submission, in the dark, to God "whom one does not question," but whom one knows according to his (Koranic) word to be the fair judge, at once formidable and benevolent, and the supreme help. It is this above all that is in the Muslim's mind when he names Allah.

See H. A. R. Gibb (ed.), *Encyclopaedia of Islam,* 2nd ed., vol. i, pp. 406–417 (1956), pp. 714–717 (1958), pp. 1084–85 (1959); and H. A. R. Gibb and J. H. Kramers (eds.), *Shorter Encyclopaedia of Islam* (1953). (L. Ga.)

ALLAHABAD, a city in Uttar Pradesh, India, is located at the confluence of the Ganges and Jumna (*qq.v.*) rivers, 110 mi. S.S.E. of Lucknow and 365 mi. S.E. of Delhi. It is the headquarters of Allahabad district and division and seat of the state judicature. Pop. (1961) 431,007. Allahabad was raised from municipality to city corporation status in 1959.

Allahabad is divided into two parts by the railway: to the north are the military cantonment and the "civil lines" (the administrative and professional quarter); to the south the city proper. The latter is congested and its streets are narrow, except for a few that were widened after World War II. The civil lines and cantonment are well planned with a rectangular pattern of good straight roads lined with single-story residences. Apart from historic monuments (*see* below), there are several modern buildings of note: Government house (built for the city's former role as provincial capital), Anglican and Roman Catholic cathedrals, the Juma Musjid or "great mosque," Mayo hall (a civic memorial to a 19th-century British viceroy) and the museum.

The university, founded in 1887, comprises central teaching departments and a number of constituent and associated institutions including colleges of agriculture, engineering and medicine. There are two open spaces, the Khusru Bagh (*see* below) and Alfred park.

The Grand Trunk road connecting Calcutta with Delhi and Amritsar passes through Allahabad, and other main roads link it eastward with Mirzapur and southward with the Varanasi-Cape Comorin national highway. It is at the junction of the Delhi-Calcutta railway with the line from Bombay. The city is mainly an educational, administrative and legal centre, but there is some industry, including the manufacture of steel trunks and the canning of guava products. Development of an industrial estate was begun on the south side of the Jumna in 1958.

History and Monuments.—Allahabad is on the site of the ancient Prayag, "place of sacrifice," a holy city comparable in fame with Varanasi (Benares) and Hardwar (*q.v.*). Its religious and commercial importance in the Buddhist period is attested by inscriptions of 243–232 B.C. on the pillar of Asoka (*q.v.*) standing within Allahabad fort. Its religious importance persists: in the month of Magh (December–January) each year a religious fair is held at the river confluence. Every 12th year this Magh Mela is replaced by the great Kumbh Mela during which an estimated 500,000 persons come from all over India to bathe simultaneously at the confluence. The Kumbh of 1954 was the scene of disaster when about 500 people were killed during the rush to bathe.

The present city owes its origin to the Mogul emperor Akbar (*q.v.*), who in 1583, with an eye to the strategic position of the confluence, began the great fort and named the settlement Al-Ilahbad, "city of God." Allahabad became the capital of a *suba,* or province, of the Mogul empire. From 1599 to 1604 it was the headquarters of the rebellious prince Salim (later the emperor Jahangir, *q.v.*); and in 1622 it became the burial place of his ill-starred son Prince Khusru, whose domed tomb in a garden—the Khusru Bagh—is still a popular resort.

With the decline of the Moguls, Allahabad changed hands many times before it was finally ceded by the nawab of Oudh to the British in 1801, in commutation of the subsidy paid for protection. Allahabad was the scene of a great massacre during the 1857 revolt against the British, but in general it prospered under their rule. Until 1888–89 it was at the focus of the only rail routes linking Delhi, Calcutta and Bombay. From 1901 to 1949 it was the capital of the United Provinces (now Uttar Pradesh). It was a notable centre of the Indian national movement before 1947 and the home of the Nehru family.

ALLAHABAD DISTRICT comprises an area of 2,800 sq.mi. spread over the confluence of the Ganges and Jumna rivers. These rivers divide the district into three regions. The Doab (*q.v.*), the western region between the rivers, is agriculturally the most productive, while the trans-Ganges region to the north contains many small lakes and is less fertile. The trans-Jumna region to the south extends into the Vindhyan hill tract. About 80% of the district's population (2,422,558 in 1961) depend on agriculture. Rice, wheat, barley, millets, gram and oilseeds are the main crops.

ALLAHABAD DIVISION comprises the districts of Etawah, Farrukhabad, Fatehpur, Kanpur (*qq.v.*) and Allahabad. Total population (1961) 8,339,947. Area 10,096 sq.mi. (M. N. K.)

ALLAN, SIR HUGH (1810–1882), Canadian financier and a figure in the so-called Pacific scandal, was born on Sept. 29, 1810, at Saltcoats, Ayrshire, Scot. He immigrated to Canada in 1826 and in 1831 entered the employ of the chief shipbuilding and grain-shipping firm of Montreal, of which he became a junior partner in 1835. In 1853 he organized the Allan line of steamships, plying between Montreal, Glasgow and Liverpool. Until his death he was closely associated with commerce, and in 1871 was knighted in recognition of his services. In 1872–73 he headed the Canada Pacific Railway company of Montreal and obtained from the Canadian government a charter for building a transcontinental railway, outmaneuvering a rival Toronto company that was also seeking a charter. It was subsequently disclosed that Allan was associated with a Chicago financial syndicate and that he had contributed about $300,000 to the Conservative campaign of 1872. This "Pacific scandal" led to the overthrow of the government and the dissolution of Allan's railway company. He died in Edinburgh on Dec. 9, 1882. *See* CANADA: *History.*

See Donald Creighton, *John A. Macdonald, the Old Chieftain* (1955); J. C. Dent, *Canadian Portrait Gallery* (1881). (P. G. Co.)

ALLBUTT, SIR THOMAS CLIFFORD (1836–1925), British physician, who made important contributions in several areas of medicine, invented the short clinical thermometer and was, in addition, a distinguished historian of medicine. He was born on July 20, 1836, at Dewsbury, Yorks. He received his M.B.

in 1861 (Cambridge) and his M.D. in 1868. Among his teachers were Sir George Humphrey, Sir George Paget, Henry Bence Jones and Armand Trousseau. Allbutt settled in Leeds, becoming in 1864 physician to the Leeds General infirmary. In 1892 he became regius professor of physic at Cambridge, where he remained for the rest of his life. Allbutt was elected a fellow of the Royal society in 1880; in 1878 he gained membership of the Royal College of Physicians, of which he was elected fellow in 1883. He delivered the Goulstonian lectures in 1884 (on "Visceral Neuroses"), and in 1891 gave the Harveian lecture (on "Common Neuroses"). He was created a knight commander of the Bath in 1907, and in 1920 was made a privy councilor. He died at Cambridge on Feb. 22, 1925.

While working as a clinical clerk under Bence Jones in 1860, Allbutt became interested in acute aortitis, working later with J. A. Lockhart in microscopic neurology. He invented the short clinical thermometer in 1866. In 1868 he gave the first description of the histologic changes in syphilitic disease of the cerebral arteries. In 1885 he introduced surgery of tuberculous glands in the neck. His monograph *On the Use of the Ophthalmoscope in Diseases of the Nervous System and of the Kidneys* appeared in 1871, his *Diseases of the Arteries Including Angina Pectoris* in 1915. His excellent study on *Greek Medicine in Rome* was published in 1921. Allbutt's chief work, however, was his *System of Medicine*, 8 vol. (1896–99).

ALLEGHENY MOUNTAINS or The Alleghenies, a name formerly applied to all the Appalachian mountains (q.v.), and now, sometimes, to all that system lying west and south of the Hudson river, being steep and narrow-crested in Pennsylvania (1,500–1,800 ft.), in Maryland, Virginia and West Virginia rising to 4,860 ft. (Spruce Knob) and with broader crests. It is also used to include the ridges (the Allegheny ridges) parallel to the Blue ridge; the northwestern part of this region is called the Allegheny Front, and is characterized by a bold southeastward facing escarpment and a gentle northwestward slope. The Allegheny plateau is the northwesternmost division of the Appalachian system; it is an eroded mass of sedimentary rock sloping northwestward to the Lake plains in the region of the Great Lakes and reaching southwest from the Catskill (see Catskill Mountains) region of New York state to the Cumberland plateau region in Tennessee. The Alleghenies, which once formed a barrier to western communication, have long since been crossed by numerous railways and highways which follow the lower elevations or the "water gaps" of the eastward-flowing streams.

ALLEGHENY RIVER, a river of western Pennsylvania and southern New York and a major headwater of the Ohio river, whose source is the confluence of the Allegheny and Monongahela rivers at Pittsburgh. The Allegheny rises in the high, hilly plateau region of Potter county, Pa., at an elevation of about 2,250 ft. above sea level. From its source it flows in a general northwesterly direction about 80 mi., crossing into New York, to a point 11 mi. N. of the state line. There it turns abruptly southwest and continues in this direction for 120 mi. to the central part of Venango county, Pa. It then turns to the southeast and again southwest to its confluence with the Monongahela at Pittsburgh. Its total length is about 325 mi. and it drains an area of 11,410 sq.mi. The average fall of the river is 2.2 ft. per mile, making the stream a potential source of water power. The chief tributaries of the Allegheny are Kiskiminetas, Clarion and Conemaugh rivers, and Red Bank, Oil and French creeks. The drainage basin has resources of coal, oil and natural gas. The Allegheny once served as an important highway for keel-boat navigation before the beginning of railway competition. Between 1903 and 1938 nine dams were completed to make the river navigable with a 7-ft.-deep channel for 70 mi. from Pittsburgh to East Brady. Because of periodic flooding of the Allegheny, flood control dams have been built on many of its major tributaries. (E. W. Mi.)

ALLEGIANCE: see Loyalty.

ALLEGORY is the intentional conveying, by means of symbol and image, of a further, deeper meaning than the surface one. Allegory may thus be said to be extended metaphor, worked out in many relationships. It is of greater length and complexity than

parable or fable and is imaginative where analogy is rational. The chief application of the word is to literature, both theological and secular.

Most languages are known to use allegory to convey difficult or metaphysical truths. Allegorical layers of meaning were used extensively in the Hindu and Buddhist scriptures and in ancient Persian and Arabian heroic legends. The Christian scriptures used allegorical symbols in the Song of Solomon, the Revelation and Psalm 80; medieval scholars, influenced undoubtedly by the writings of the ancient east, propounded a fourfold allegorical interpretation of the Christian scriptures. This attempt to relate the outer world of phenomena to the inner world of man's aspiration became stylized, and Prudentius (A.D. 348–c. 405) in his *Psychomachia* ("the battle of the soul") describes a series of combats in which faith conquers idolatry, patience anger, shame passion, and humility pride. This has been called the first allegory.

At the Renaissance, allegory came to mean the intellectual substitution or interpretation of one symbol or image by another. Thus distinction grew between religious and secular allegory; Dante (1265–1321) applied the theological fourfold interpretation to his own poetry. But St. Thomas Aquinas (c. 1225–74) made a clear distinction between the two kinds. In 1477 Plato was said to have taught "his sapyence by allegorye." Little allegory can be found in Latin classical writing, but that of the belly and its members in Livy and in Plutarch's *Life of Coriolanus* are worth mentioning.

The 13th and 14th centuries saw the composition of many allegories, both religious and secular, in Europe. Guillaume de Lorris began and Jean de Meun completed the *Roman de la Rose,* an elaborate secular allegory of the quest in the garden of life for the desired rose of love's happiness. William Langland wrote *The Vision of Piers Plowman,* a religious allegory which may be interpreted, though not consistently, as a vision of Christ on earth as Everyman. Chaucer's *Parlement of Foules* (1382?) is a humorous allegory of man's similarities to and kinship with the birds. The *Faerie Queene* (1596) of Edmund Spenser is a threefold allegory of physical and spiritual chivalry. Jonathan Swift's *Tale of a Tub* (1704) and *Gulliver's Travels* (1726) are satirical allegories. But perhaps the most widely read is John Bunyan's *Pilgrim's Progress* (1678), the story of the perils and burdens of man until he sees the light of Christian faith.

Allegory has been less often used in the 19th and 20th centuries, but George Orwell's *Animal Farm* (1945) may be said to belong to the genre, and C. S. Lewis's *Pilgrim's Regress* (1933) is subtitled "An allegorical apology for Christianity, reason and romanticism."

See also references under "Allegory" in the Index.

See G. Highet, *The Classical Tradition* (1949); C. S. Lewis, *The Allegory of Love* (1936). (J. W. T.)

ALLEINE, JOSEPH (1633–1668), English Nonconformist minister, regarded by contemporaries as second only to Richard Baxter (q.v.) in sanctity and scholarship and one of those ejected under the Act of Uniformity of 1662. Born at Devizes, Wiltshire, in 1633, he went to Oxford in 1649 and after graduation (1653) was appointed chaplain of his college, Corpus Christi. In 1655 he was ordained by the presbyters as assistant to George Newton, vicar of St. Mary Magdalene, Taunton, where he was as much respected for his wide learning as loved for his gentle piety. Ejected in 1662, he suffered hardship as a wandering preacher, often in hiding and in prison. He died on Nov. 17, 1668. His *Alarme to Unconverted Sinners* (1672) became a classic of evangelical appeal and his lost treatise, *Theologia philosophica,* was highly praised by Baxter.

ALLELOMORPH, in biology, the name applied to the alternative forms of a gene (q.v.). *See* also Heredity; Genetics.

ALLEMANDE (Fr. "German"), a German dance in 3/4 time, a forerunner of the waltz; and an 18th-century German national dance in lively 2/4 time. It is also the name of a slow, stately dance in 4/4 time, first appearing about 1550. After introduction at the French court it became the only court dance in which partners held both of each other's hands and performed flowing *enchaînements* while walking and balancing. Likewise, the music freely employed flowing 16th notes in its melodic structure. After 1620 it became the opening movement of the suite, occasionally preceded by a prelude. *See* COURANTE; DANCE. (L. HT.)

ALLEN, ETHAN (1738–1789), American soldier, frontiersman, author of several books and pamphlets and Vermont folk hero, was born in Litchfield, Conn., Jan. 21, 1738 (new style; Jan. 10, 1738, old style), of humble backwoods stock. Little is known of his early life other than that he was preparing for college when his father died in 1755, that he had military service during the French and Indian War and that he came under the intellectual influence of Thomas Young, an erudite, unorthodox rationalist. By 1769 Allen's enterprising nature led him into the New Hampshire grants, an area then claimed by both New Hampshire and New York. Allen and his brothers formed the nucleus of the Green Mountain Boys, an irregular but effective force for resistance to the "Yorkers." Superb propagandists as well as efficient soldiers, they exploited the grievances the backwoodsmen had against lower New York and identified the cause of the land speculators with the cause of the settlers. (*See* VERMONT: *History*.) When the news of Lexington and Concord arrived, Ethan Allen's energies were turned toward the larger conflict. Following instructions from the Connecticut assembly he raised a force and with considerable skill and dispatch took the British fort at Ticonderoga on May 10, 1775, as Allen reported "in the name of the great Jehovah and the Continental Congress." What might have been a brilliant military career for this bold and impulsive man was thwarted when he was captured during a foolhardy attempt to capture Montreal in Sept. 1775. He was held prisoner until an exchange could be arranged on May 6, 1778. The following year he published his *Narrative of Colonel Ethan Allen's Captivity*. Congress gave him the brevet rank of colonel with back pay, but he did not serve in the revolutionary forces after his release. He devoted his time to local affairs in Vermont and to the struggle with New York. Allen was unsuccessful in presenting the Vermont claim for separate statehood to the congress in Sept. 1778. He then entered into a correspondence with Gen. Frederick Haldimand, British commander at Quebec, to see upon what terms Vermont could rejoin the British empire. Allen's apologists have insisted that these actions were a ruse to bring the continental congress to terms. Modern scholars are of the opinion that his actions were at first purely opportunistic and that finally in disgust with the continental congress he threw himself into a wholehearted move to make Vermont a British province. The generous peace treaty wrecked the province scheme and Vermont had to wait until 1791 for statehood. Allen did not live to see this. He died on Feb. 11, 1789, at Burlington.

Ethan's youngest brother, IRA ALLEN (1751–1814), was born at Cornwall, Conn. His career was closely connected with that of his brother. He was less a military man and more the politician and negotiator. He was a member of the convention that declared Vermont's independence (1777), and served as a member of the council of safety (1776–86), assemblyman, surveyor general and treasurer of Vermont. He endowed and was the virtual founder of the University of Vermont. During the Anglo-French struggle following the French Revolution, Ira Allen belonged to a Vermont faction that allied itself with France to wrest Canada from England. He was captured with a cargo of arms and held in Britain for prolonged litigation. During his absence his lands were sold for taxes and he was forced to spend the rest of his life in Pennsylvania to avoid debtors' prison. In 1798 he published in London his *Natural and Political History of the State of Vermont*.

BIBLIOGRAPHY.—J. B. Wilbur, *Ira Allen, Founder of Vermont*, 2 vol. (1928); John Pell, *Ethan Allen* (1929); S. H. Holbrook, *Ethan Allen* (1940); Chilton Williamson, *Vermont in Quandry: 1763–1825* (1949). (RA. MU.)

ALLEN, SIR HUGH PERCY (1869–1946), English musician who exerted a far-reaching influence upon the musical life of his time, especially in education, was born at Reading, Berkshire, Dec. 23, 1869. He received his early training at Chichester as an articled pupil of Frederick Read, organist and composer, and at Cambridge, where in 1892 he became organ scholar at Christ's college. Appointments as organist at Ely cathedral (1898) and

New college, Oxford (1901), gave outlet to his uncommon vision, energy and initiative, and led to his appointment (1919) as director of the Royal College of Music, London. As conductor of the Bach choirs in Oxford (from 1901) and London (1907–20), he did much for English choral music, particularly by performance of Bach's works, and of those of Sir Hubert Parry and Vaughan Williams.

In 1918 he became professor of music at Oxford, a position which enabled him to persuade a conservative university to admit music to its proper position in the curriculum and to make more adequate provision for research and teaching. These developments at Oxford had wide influence elsewhere. Allen's studies in the music of Heinrich Schütz and J. S. Bach, though unpublished, stimulated musicians and scholars. As a conductor he gave many distinguished and inspiring performances. He was knighted in 1920. He died at Oxford, Feb. 20, 1946.

See C. Bailey, *Hugh Percy Allen* (1948). (TH. A.)

ALLEN, SIR JAMES (1855–1942), New Zealand statesman, chiefly distinguished as minister of defense from 1912 to 1920, was born near Adelaide, South Australia, on Feb. 10, 1855. His parents settled in New Zealand a year later. He was educated in England at Clifton college, Bristol, and at St. John's college, Cambridge, and afterward studied at the Royal School of Mines, London. Returning to New Zealand, he was, in 1887, elected a member of the house of representatives. He was minister of finance, defense and education from 1912 to 1915. He continued as minister of defense in the national coalition government of 1915–19, when he was responsible for making the New Zealand expeditionary force a first-class fighting body. In the absence from the country of his chief, W. F. Massey, during and after 1917, he was acting prime minister. He remained minister of defense in 1919–20, after the end of the coalition government, when he was also minister of external affairs and finance. He was high commissioner for New Zealand in London from 1920 to 1926, his long political experience making him a useful man on committees and at conferences. On returning to New Zealand he was appointed to the legislative council. He was knighted in 1917. He died at Dunedin, New Zealand, on July 28, 1942. (J. C. BE.)

ALLEN, JAMES LANE (1849–1925), U.S. novelist of Kentucky, was born Dec. 21, 1849, on a small plantation near Lexington, Ky., where he passed most of his early life. He studied at Transylvania college, Lexington, Ky., was professor of Latin and English at Bethany college, Bethany, W.Va., and taught languages in various preparatory schools. He began his literary career by writing poetry and criticism but soon shifted to the tales and novels of an idealized plantation society for which he is best known. These include *Flute and Violin* (1891), *The Blue-Grass Region of Kentucky* (1892), *A Kentucky Cardinal* (1894), and its sequel, *Aftermath* (1895). *A Summer in Arcady* (1896) marks his turn to the contemporary problems, particularly of sex, that dominated his subsequent novels.

Allen died in New York city, Feb. 18, 1925.

See G. C. Knight, *James Lane Allen and the Genteel Tradition* (1935).

ALLEN, RICHARD (1760–1831), U.S. Negro clergyman, a founder and first bishop of the African Methodist Episcopal Church, was born of slave parents in Philadelphia, Pa., in 1760. Soon after his birth his parents were sold and moved to Delaware. At 17 he joined the Methodist Episcopal Church and when 22 years old was licensed to preach. Four years later (1786) he purchased his freedom for $2,000, continental money, and returned to Philadelphia. There he joined St. George's Methodist Episcopal church in which he was permitted to preach to Negroes at 5 o'clock meetings. Dissatisfied with the restrictions placed upon those who attended these meetings, he decided to withdraw. He purchased a lot at the corner of 6th and Lombard streets and moved onto it an old blacksmith shop which he refurbished as a house of worship. There he organized in 1787 the first church for Negroes in the United States. His followers were called Allenites. Despite opposition and a series of obstructive lawsuits, a charter was secured from the general assembly of Pennsylvania. A new church building, erected and opened in 1794, was dedicated by Bishop Francis Asbury (*q.v.*) and called Bethel. In 1799 Allen became the first

Negro to be regularly ordained in the ministry of the Methodist Episcopal Church and in 1816, upon the organization of the African Methodist Episcopal Church, he was elected bishop. He died in Philadelphia on March 26, 1831.

See *Centennial Encyclopaedia of the African Methodist Church* (1916).

ALLEN, VIOLA (1869–1948), U.S. actress, was born in Huntsville, Ala., Oct. 27, 1869, the daughter of C. Leslie and Sarah (Lyon) Allen, actors. She was educated in Boston, Toronto and New York city and made her debut at 13, succeeding Annie Russell in the title role of *Esmeralda* at the Madison Square theatre, New York city. In 1884 she appeared with John McCullough, and at the opening of the Lyceum theatre in New York in 1885 she played Madeleine in *Dakolar*. Engagements with Tommaso Salvini and with Joseph Jefferson followed. In 1889 she created the role of Gertrude Ellingham in Bronson Howard's *Shenandoah,* the success of which established Charles Frohman as a producer. From 1893 to 1898 Miss Allen was a member of Frohman's Empire theatre stock company, where she enhanced her reputation in a variety of leading roles in comedy and drama. She left to star in the role of Gloria Quayle in Hall Caine's *The Christian* (1898). From 1903 to 1907 she played Viola, Rosalind, and both Hermione and Perdita in *A Winter's Tale.* For eight years she starred in modern plays, but in 1915 returned to Shakespeare as Lady Macbeth opposite James K. Hackett. She last appeared in 1916 as Mistress Ford in *The Merry Wives of Windsor.* In 1906 she married Peter Duryea. She died May 10, 1948, in New York city. (B. Ht.)

ALLEN, WILLIAM (1532–1594), English cardinal and scholar who founded the English college at Douai, was born at Rossall, Lancashire, and educated at Oxford. He became principal of St. Mary's hall but was deprived for refusing the oath of supremacy, and in 1561 he moved to Louvain, Belg. He returned to England in 1562, but left finally in 1565 for Mechelen, where he was ordained priest and lectured in theology in the Benedictine college. He was principally responsible in 1568 for setting up a college at Douai for training Englishmen as "missionary priests." This college, of which he was president and lecturer until 1585, gave its name to the Reims-Douai translation of the Bible into English, in which project the translator, Gregory Martin, worked under Allen's direction. Allen was also on the Sixtine commission for the revision of the Vulgate. In 1576 he supported the foundation of the English college in Rome. The college at Douai withdrew to Reims in 1578, and Allen spent seven years at Reims. In 1585 he went to Rome where he spent the rest of his life. In 1587 he was made cardinal at the request of Philip II of Spain. In 1589 he supported the foundation of the English seminary at Valladolid, Spain. He died in Rome on Oct. 16, 1594. Allen has been criticized for political intrigue; he undoubtedly encouraged the intervention of Spain in English affairs, but in the seminaries his rule against political discussions or planning was rigorously observed.

See Martin Haile, *An Elizabethan Cardinal, William Allen,* with bibliography (1914). (M. Dk.)

ALLEN, BOG OF (Móin Almhaine), a group of peat bogs between the Liffey and Shannon rivers in the counties of Kildare, Offaly, Laoighis (Leix) and Westmeath, Ire. They occupy an area (about 370 sq.mi.) of confused drainage behind the great terminal moraine of debris left after the Ice Age. The higher ground on the eskers and moraines carries strips of cultivation between bogs so that the latter really occupy only half the area. Much peat has been cleared and the land used for grazing. The Grand canal, cut through the bog, carries considerable traffic, but the Royal canal is disused. (T. Her.)

ALLENBY, EDMUND HENRY HYNMAN ALLENBY, 1st Viscount (1861–1936), British field marshal, whose campaign in Palestine in World War I showed his genius for war and served as a classic example of the military art, was born at Brackenhurst, near Southwell, Nottinghamshire, on April 23, 1861. Joining the Inniskilling dragoons in 1882, he took part in the Bechuanaland expedition (1884–85) and in the South African War (1899–1902). He commanded the 5th lancers (1902–05) and on the outbreak of World War I in 1914 took the cavalry division to France. After periods in command of the cavalry and the 5th corps, he became commander of the 3rd army in Oct. 1915 and was prominently engaged in the battle of Arras (April 1917). His efforts to achieve surprise by improving on the then accepted tactical methods of position warfare were unfavourably regarded by general headquarters. In June 1917, Allenby took command of the Egyptian expeditionary force. The strength of his personality created a new spirit throughout the army, and after careful preparation and reorganization he gained a decisive victory over the Turks at Gaza (Nov. 1917), which led to the capture of Jerusalem (Dec. 9, 1917). Further advances were checked by calls from France for his troops, but after receiving reinforcements from elsewhere he struck the enemy decisively at Megiddo (Sept. 1918) and, using his cavalry to exploit the victory, captured Damascus and Aleppo. This brought about the capitulation of Turkey. He was created a viscount in Oct. 1919. As high commissioner for Egypt from 1919 to 1925 Allenby steered that country firmly but impartially through a succession of political disturbances. It was during his tenure of office that Egypt was recognized as a sovereign state in 1922. He died in London on May 14, 1936, and his ashes were interred in Westminster abbey.

See A. P. W. Wavell, *Allenby, Soldier and Statesman* (1946). (R. G. Th.)

ALLENTOWN, a city in eastern Pennsylvania, U.S., is located on the Lehigh river about 55 mi. N.W. of Philadelphia and 93 mi. W. of New York; it is the seat of Lehigh county. The population was 108,347 in 1960. The population of the Allentown-Bethlehem-Easton standard metropolitan statistical area, comprising Lehigh and Northampton counties in Pennsylvania and Warren county in New Jersey, was 492,168 in 1960. (For comparative population figures *see* table in Pennsylvania: *Population.*) The city derives its name from its founder, William Allen, a chief justice of Pennsylvania, who acquired the land in 1735, erected a hunting and fishing lodge on it in the 1750s, and eventually, in 1762, laid out the town. His settlement was incorporated as the borough of Northampton in 1811 and became the seat of Lehigh county the following year when the latter was separated from Northampton county. In 1829 the construction of a canal along the Lehigh and Delaware rivers, linking Philadelphia with the northern coal regions, brought new economic opportunities to the borough of Northampton. An iron industry was started in 1847, a cement plant in 1850 and a rolling mill in 1860—all of these presaged an important industrial future. Anticipating this future, Allentown was incorporated as a city in 1867.

Allentown owes its steadily expanding prosperity to the rich mineral deposits and the fertile farm land of the surrounding countryside. Although iron ore, slate and zinc have contributed to its economy, limestone has made Allentown the centre of the greatest concentration of the cement industry in the U.S. After mid-20th century there were more than 300 manufacturing establishments employing about 30,000 workers. The largest of these industries produced electronic equipment, automobile trucks, cotton textiles, food products, machinery and machine tools. One-fifth of the inhabitants migrated originally from eastern and central Europe. The descendants of the Germans, who came to Pennsylvania during the first part of the 18th century, form the dominant segment of the population; they cling to their Pennsylvania Dutch dialect—a frontier mixture of German and English.

Muhlenberg college was founded in 1848 as Allentown seminary, and later came under the management of the Lutheran Church. In 1867 the Evangelical and Reformed Church founded Cedar Crest college for women. These two church-affiliated colleges reflect the prominence of the Lutheran and the Evangelical and Reformed (now the United Church of Christ) denominations in a city of many churches.

Trexler-Lehigh county game preserve, north of the city, contains the largest herd of buffalo in eastern United States and also large herds of elk and deer. The buffalo were originally native to the territory but were driven west by the early settlers. When the game preserve was created the animals were brought back to their original habitat. (R. G. Co.)

ALLEPPEY, a seaport and district in Kerala state, India. The town is on a narrow spit between the Arabian sea and a great backwater, the Vembanad "lake," 34 mi. S. of Cochin (q.v.). Municipal area 12.5 sq.mi.; pop. (1951) 116,278. It is the seat of two colleges affiliated with Kerala university. There is no railhead, but Alleppey is on the main road from Cochin to Trivandrum, and there is considerable barge traffic on the backwater and by canal north to Tirur and south to Trivandrum. Alleppey is a roadstead port, with a safe anchorage protected by a mud bank about a mile offshore. Alleppey's main industry and commerce stem from the coconut, the district's chief product: coconut oil is milled, coir ropes, mats and carpets manufactured and copra exported. Lesser exports include pepper and ginger.

The port was opened to foreign trade by the British in the late 18th century to end the commercial supremacy of the Dutch factory at Porkad, 10 mi. away.

ALLEPPEY DISTRICT (711 sq.mi.) was formed in 1958 by transferring six *talukas* (subdivisions) from Quilon district and one from Kottayam district. Pop. (1961) 1,809,530.   (G. Kn.)

ALLERGY AND ANAPHYLAXIS are terms describing the exaggerated reactivity of a living organism to foreign substances that sometimes occurs following exposure to those substances. The terms have different historical origins and slightly different connotations but refer to essentially the same phenomenon. The word allergy was first proposed by Clemens von Pirquet in 1906 as a broad term to cover all specifically induced changes in reactivity, but with time its meaning has become more and more restricted. It is now generally used to describe only increased (i.e., not decreased) reactivity occurring following exposure to foreign substances, or any increased reactivity (hypersensitivity), whether inherited or acquired. It is also frequently used by laymen to refer to a specific symptom, as when a patient refers to his asthma as his allergy.

The term anaphylaxis was introduced by Charles Richet in 1898 to describe the sometimes fatal reaction of an animal to a second injection of eel serum. Since a first injection of this serum did not produce any noticeable reaction, Richet used the term anaphylaxis to signify a state that was the antithesis of prophylaxis, the latter being a condition of immunity commonly produced by injections of bacterial toxins. Anaphylaxis is a technical term generally used to describe severe reactions of animals following immediately on the second injection of a foreign protein. Allergic and anaphylactic reactions occur in both animals and men under a wide variety of circumstances and with a wide variety of manifestations. All of these may be considered as phenomena of the adaptation of an individual to his environment.   (D. W. Te.)

The Anaphylactic Reaction.—The anaphylactic reaction is characteristic for the species of animal in which it occurs and is not determined by the foreign protein that produces it. If, for example, a guinea pig is injected with horse serum, egg albumin or other protein substance, it gradually becomes sensitized to the protein injected, so that, after an interval (called incubation period) of 10 to 14 days, the reinjection of this protein produces anaphylactic shock. Within a period of a few minutes after reinjection the animal sneezes, scratches its nose, becomes restless, usually discharges urine and feces and has great difficulty in breathing. The latter may increase until the animal dies from asphyxia as the result of inability, in spite of violent effort, to ventilate its lungs effectively. The difficulty in respiration is caused by an intense spastic contraction of the smaller air passages, or bronchioles. In the dog the prominent phenomena are vomiting, defecation, fall in blood pressure, collapse and incoagulability of the blood. In the rabbit the prominent phenomena are alternate and fleeting reddening and pallor of the ears, discharge of urine and feces, weakness, cardiac irregularities and collapse. Many minor phenomena—e.g., decrease in the number of circulating white blood cells and increase in the formation of lymph—also occur in these animals. If an animal survives, it is for a short time (one to two days) refractory to a subsequent injection of the foreign protein and is said to be antianaphylactic as the result of the desensitization produced.

Anaphylactic phenomena occur in various isolated tissues taken from sensitized animals; e.g., the isolated uterus or a small portion of the intestine from guinea pigs, when suspended in an oxy-

genated and warm saline bath, contracts markedly when minute amounts of the foreign protein are added to the bath. This reaction, referred to as the Schultz-Dale test, is so delicate and specific that fractions of a milligram of foreign protein can be detected by it.

Localized anaphylactic phenomena are seen in some animals. When the specific foreign protein is injected under or into the skin of a sensitized rabbit, there may result within the ensuing 48 hours swelling, hardening and gangrenous slough at the site of the injection. This local reaction was first described by Maurice Arthus and is referred to as the phenomenon of Arthus.   (C. A. Dt.)

Manifestations of Allergy.—In contrast to the classical anaphylactic reactions of animals, allergic reactions of human beings are seen in a great variety of forms. Hay fever, asthma and eczema are typical, but fever, hives, rashes, headaches, abdominal cramps, diarrhea and a great variety of other symptoms also may have an allergic basis. Serious illnesses such as nephritis and rheumatic fever may be considered as allergic reactions to streptococcal products. The manifestation of allergy in any particular case depends on at least three factors: (1) the mode of contact, or portal of entry; (2) the localizing character of the foreign substance (allergen); and (3) the responding tendencies of the individual. For example, ragweed pollen most commonly produces symptoms in the nose and eyes, where it first makes contact with the body fluids. Some persons, however, respond to ragweed by developing asthma without hay fever, and an occasional patient may have headache or hives. Allergic reactions to foods (e.g., fish, peanuts, fruit) commonly manifest themselves as hives or rashes of the skin, although the food makes first contact with the body in the gastrointestinal tract. The same person may have hay fever when exposed to ragweed pollen or hives when he eats fish, and may break out in a rash if he is given phenobarbital. The only characteristic feature common to all these reactions is that the manifestation of the allergy to a given substance is qualitatively different from the toxic or pharmacological response of most individuals of the same species. For example, the pharmacological response to phenobarbital is drowsiness. The allergic response may be a rash.

Diagnosis of Allergy.—The problem is twofold: (1) to determine whether a given reaction is allergic in nature; and (2) to identify the causative agent or allergen. The first question cannot be answered with certainty without the second. Allergy may be suspected because of the nature of the reaction (e.g., hives) or because of frequent recurrences separated by periods of complete freedom from symptoms. However, a diagnosis of allergy cannot be made with certainty without identifying the allergen. The reason for this difficulty is that a living organism is a reacting system with a relatively small number of ways of reacting. Just as a rubber ball is likely either to bounce or to roll regardless of what force is applied to it, so a human being may respond to many different stressful and injurious stimuli in exactly the same way. For example, typical asthmatic symptoms may be produced by ragweed allergy, inhaling cold air, coughing, bronchial infection, heart disease, emotional stress or tumours pressing on the bronchus. In fact, several of these factors frequently operate in the same person.

Since identification of the allergen is essential to the diagnosis of allergy, it is important to know something of the types of foreign substances likely to induce allergy. The most important are drugs, pollens, molds, lints, animal danders, dandruff, cosmetics, industrial chemicals, bacteria and food. While this list includes nearly everything a person is likely to contact, considerable information is obtained from observing the nature and course of the allergic reaction. In fact, a clear and complete history is the most important factor in a correct diagnosis. Allergy to inhalants such as pollens, molds, lints and danders is most likely to give symptoms in the eyes, nose and bronchus. Cosmetics affect the face and hands. Allergy to pollens is noted only in season; i.e., spring for trees, early summer for grasses and late summer for weeds. Allergy to an occupational contact will diminish during a vacation.

Testing Procedures.—The purpose of all testing procedures is to obtain more history by exposing the person suspected of allergy to a variety of substances to which he might be allergic. It is important that the testing procedure be rigidly controlled and reproduce as nearly as possible the conditions of natural exposure. If a suspected allergen is a skin contactant, such as lipstick it is possible to apply some of the allergen to an unaffected portion of skin and observe the developments. A food may be added to or withdrawn from the diet. For this purpose, careful food diaries should be kept. In some cases it is necessary to use strict elimination diets consisting of only a few items of rarely allergenic foods. Suspected foods are then added one at a time. Difficulties arise because there is sometimes a lag of several days between exposure to the allergen and the allergic reaction. In the case of food allergies this may require long periods of dieting. In the case of skin contactants, the allergen may be applied on an adhesive patch and left for several days. With inhalant allergens it is impractical and frequently dangerous actually to inhale a sample of each suspected allergen. In this case, solutions or extracts of the allergens are applied to the skin through a small scratch or directly into the outer layers of the skin with a hypodermic syringe and needle. Unfortunately, these two methods are not very reliable.

Mechanism of the Allergic Reaction.—A large number of theories have been advanced to explain the allergic reaction, but no single one has been found satisfactory to account for all the observed phenomena. It seems likely that a great variety of things happen as a result of the introduction of allergen into a sensitive person. One of these is the liberation of histamine, a powerful substance that causes smooth muscle contraction, capillary dilatation and fall in blood pressure. Other substances liberated probably include acetylcholine, heparin and serotonin. It is probable that many more such substances are liberated by the cells of the body when they are injured. The mechanism by which the cells are injured is equally obscure. It is generally believed, however, that the basis of allergy is a reaction between the allergen and a body protein called an antibody.

Allergy and Immunity.—The usual response of a person to infectious disease is the production of protein substances called antibodies that circulate in the blood. Antibodies give immunity (protection) against second attacks of the disease that stimulated their production. Antibodies are highly specific; e.g., the antibody to the measles virus does not provide immunity to chicken pox. Antibodies act by first combining with the corresponding virus or bacterium and then destroying it with the aid of other bodily substances or cells. The production of antibodies may be stimulated by dead virus or bacterial particles and by their toxic products, and this fact provides the basis for many immunization procedures. Antibodies are also produced against completely harmless substances when they find their way into the body's tissues. As a result the antibody response, which is an adaptive response necessary for survival, sometimes causes the unpleasant side effects known as allergy. This is partly due to the body's inability to distinguish between harmful and harmless substances. It is also due to the fact that against harmful bacteria and toxins allergic symptoms may be important for survival by warning the invaded person and stimulating his other bodily defenses. (See also IMMUNITY AND IMMUNIZATION.) (D. W. TE.)

Treatment.—Whenever the specific factor can be identified, the patient should avoid it. To remove the cat or dog, to change the kapok ("silk floss") pillow, to clean house and remove the dusty rug or the old stuffed sofa may be all that is necessary, and the clue lies in the clinical history. When elimination is not possible, then desensitization, by a series of injections of small doses of the specific allergen, can be attempted, but the technique is difficult. In hay fever, particularly, where the large number of patients makes it easy to compare one with another, the results are good. Moreover, the study of the same patient in successive years has made it possible to reduce greatly the number of doses and sometimes to omit them entirely.

Beginning about 1945, a series of useful antihistaminic drugs was discovered and developed. In addition, in May 1949, Philip S. Hench, Edward C. Kendall and their associates at the Mayo clinic

announced the discovery of cortisone and ACTH—hormones derived from the adrenal cortex and the pituitary gland, respectively. These extraordinarily active substances are concerned with the defense of the body against the damages of stress and strain. They can relieve the symptoms of many diseases, including the so-called allergic diseases, as long as they are administered in adequate doses. The allergic reaction is not inhibited, but the effects of it are modified in some way. When continued for too long a time, however, these drugs may lead to serious complications and they do not represent the final answer to the problem of allergy. *See* IMMUNITY AND IMMUNIZATION and articles on such conditions as ASTHMA; HAY FEVER; *see* also references under "Allergy and Anaphylaxis" in the Index. (F. M. RN.)

BIBLIOGRAPHY.—S. M. Feinberg, *Allergy in Practice*, 2nd rev. ed. (1946) and *Allergy: Facts and Fancies* (1951); R. A. Cooke, *Allergy in Theory and Practice* (1947); D. W. Talmage, "Allergy and Immunology," *Ann. Rev. Med.*, 8:239–256 (1957). (D. W. TE.)

ALLERTON, ISAAC (1586–1659), born in England, was one of the Pilgrims who came to America on the "Mayflower" in 1620. He was one of those to sign the "Mayflower Compact," and upon arrival at Plymouth took a leading part in the affairs of the colony. He journeyed to England as a representative of the community and aided in the negotiations of the settlers with the Indians. But in 1631 Allerton broke with the governing powers in Plymouth and took up residence in the Massachusetts Bay colony. He later moved to New Amsterdam (now New York city) where he was made a member of the governing council in 1643. He died in New Haven, Conn., in 1659. His daughter Mary, who died in 1699, was the last survivor of the original Plymouth colony.

See William Bradford, *History of the Plymouth Plantation* (1856); and Edward Beaman Patten, *Isaac Allerton, First Assistant of Plymouth Colony* (1908). (E. E. R.)

ALLESTREE (ALLESTRY), **RICHARD** (1619–1681), English theologian who was regius professor of divinity at Oxford from 1663 to 1679 and provost of Eton college from 1665 until his death, was born at Uppington, Shropshire, in March 1619. He was educated at Christ Church, Oxford, and took up arms on behalf of Charles I in the English Civil War. During the Commonwealth, by which time he had taken holy orders, he frequently carried dispatches between the exiled Charles II and the English royalists. He was imprisoned for a brief period after one of these missions. At the Restoration he became canon of Christ Church, D.D., city lecturer at Oxford and chaplain to the king, before gaining his appointment as regius professor. As provost of Eton from 1665, he introduced order into the disorganized finances of the college and procured the confirmation of Archbishop Laud's decree, which reserved five of the Eton fellowships for members of King's college, Cambridge. His additions to the college buildings were less successful, for the Upper school, constructed by him at his own expense, was falling into ruin almost in his lifetime and had to be rebuilt in 1689. Allestree died on Jan. 28, 1681, and was buried in the college chapel at Eton.

Allestree's writings include many controversial tracts. It is possible that he had a share in the composition of the books published under the name of the author of the *Whole Duty of Man* (Nichols' *Literary Anecdotes*, ii, 603).

ALLEYN, EDWARD (1566–1626), English actor and founder of Dulwich college, London, was born in London on Sept. 1, 1566, the son of an innholder. By 1586 his name was on the list of the earl of Worcester's players, and he was eventually rated as the foremost actor of his time, especially in Christopher Marlowe's plays. Ben Jonson bestowed unstinted praise on Alleyn's acting (*Epigrams*, no. 89); Thomas Nashe expressed, in *Pierce Penilesse*, his admiration of him; while Thomas Heywood called him "inimitable," "the best of actors," "Proteus for shapes and Roscius for a tongue." After his marriage on Oct. 22, 1592, to Joan Woodward, stepdaughter of the theatrical manager Philip Henslowe, Alleyn became part owner in Henslowe's ventures and, in the end, sole proprietor of several playhouses and other profitable pleasure resorts in London. Among these were the Rose theatre at Bankside, the Paris garden and the Fortune theatre in St. Luke's—the last occupied by the lord admiral's company, of which Alleyn was the head.

He filled, too, in conjunction with Henslowe, the post of "master of the king's games of bears, bulls, and dogs." On some occasions he directed the sport in person, and John Stow, in his *Chronicles,* gives an account of how Alleyn baited a lion before James I at the Tower.

Alleyn's connection with Dulwich began in 1605, when he bought the main part of the manor of Dulwich from Sir Francis Calton. The landed property, of which the entire estate had not passed into Alleyn's hands until 1614, stretched from the crest of that range of Surrey hills on whose summit the Crystal Palace stood to the crest of the parallel ridge, 3 mi. nearer London, known in its several portions as Herne hill, Denmark hill and Champion hill. He began the task of building and endowing in his own lifetime the College of God's Gift at Dulwich. Tedious delays over the charter or deed of incorporation occurred in the Star Chamber, but the college was founded and endowed under letters patent of James I, dated June 21, 1619. In 1623 Alleyn's first wife died and he married Constance, daughter of John Donne.

Alleyn died in Nov. 1626 and was buried in the chapel of the college he had founded. *See also* DULWICH.

See George Hosking, *Life and Times of Edward Alleyn* (1952).

ALL FOOLS' DAY: *see* APRIL FOOLS' DAY.

ALLIANCE, a city of Stark county, Ohio, U.S., on the Mahoning river, 55 mi. S.E. of Cleveland. (For comparative population figures *see* table in OHIO: *Population.*) Among the manufactured products are electric traveling cranes, first invented and produced at Alliance, ladle and soaking pit cranes, steel forgings and castings, railroad equipment, steel bathtubs, rubber bands, subfractional horsepower electric motors, tools and seamless tubing.

Mount Union college, a coeducational school of the Methodist Church, was founded in 1846 and received its charter as a college in 1858; Scio college (1857) was merged with it in 1911. Alliance was settled and laid out in 1838, incorporated as a village in 1854 and as a city in 1888. It was named for the junction and crossing of the New York Central and Pennsylvania railroads.

(E. T. HE.)

ALLIANCE. In a state system of multiple sovereignties, such as that of modern times which encompasses the whole world, those of the ancient Greek city-states or the principalities of Renaissance Italy, those of China in the "Spring and Autumn" period (722–481 B.C.) or of the Indian state system of Kautilya's *Arthasastra* (*c.* A.D. 325), it is almost a law of nature that one's enemy's enemy is one's own ally. Although Rome in a series of wars was able to establish its ascendancy over the ancient Mediterranean world, characteristically the aspirant for leadership, or hegemony, in a multistate system finds alliances formed against it long before the hegemony can be established. Thus, Louis XIV overreached himself and provoked the formation of a grand alliance against France. Napoleon's ambitions were thwarted by a series of coalitions formed against him. Ideology need not play the primary role in such coalitions. The Catholic Francis I of France made common cause in 1541 with the infidel Turks against the Catholic Charles V whose possessions almost encircled France. Protestant Sweden and Catholic France were able to act together in the Thirty Years' War.

In a state system in which none is able to establish hegemony, it follows that none is strong enough to stand completely alone against the united strength of the remaining states in the system. Threatened by any power or combination of powers greater than itself, a state may supplement its capacity for self-protection by pooling its strength with others. The end point of the alliance-building process may come when the great powers of a given era are formed into opposing armed camps, and conflict involving any two of them carries with it the threat of general war. The European great powers of the pre-World War I period, divided as they were into the triple alliance and the triple entente, typify the "two-camp" pattern.

Alliances are often designed to deter a would-be aggressor as well as to defeat the aggressor if the effort to deter fails. Secret agreements of alliance have the disadvantage of misleading the state which is the "target" of the agreement. British diplomacy

before 1914 is sometimes criticized for having, by military staff conversations, created an obligation of honour toward France in the event of a German attack without making it clear to Germany that Great Britain would range itself alongside France in the event of war. It has also been asserted that a commitment by the United States to support Great Britain and France might have discouraged Germany from embarking on either World War I or II.

Smaller states, when their geographical situation permits, often seek to avoid being aligned while the bipolar alliance pattern is being formed in periods of international tension. Thus, the Low Countries, the Scandinavian states, Switzerland and Spain avoided alliance commitments with either side before World Wars I and II. Other small states, perhaps making a virtue of necessity when they were clearly dependent for their security on a powerful neighbour, have entered into alliances in which they have for all practical purposes surrendered their policy-making initiative to their great-power partner. In the post-1945 era, in which the two great superpowers, the United States and the Soviet Union, dominated the world scene, such alliances became common. Within the Soviet-dominated world particularly, the alliance relationship seemed to have become a satellite relationship. (*See* WARSAW TREATY ORGANIZATION.)

Alliance by Treaty.—An alliance, under circumstances carefully defined in the treaty on which it is based, provides for combined action on the part of two or more independent states. The most critical clauses in a treaty of alliance are those which define the *casus foederis,* that is, the circumstances under which an ally becomes obligated to aid a fellow ally. Alliances are almost always defensive in form, although agreements among revisionist powers may obligate an ally to aid its partner even if that partner is the aggressor.

The North Atlantic treaty (1949), by which the United States and 15 other signatories in the post-1949 period committed themselves to support each other against attack in the North Atlantic-Mediterranean areas, is an outstanding example of an alliance which is meant to deter. As military technology has lengthened lead times in rearming and shortened the prospective period of decisive fighting in a general war, alliances have had to be supported by detailed military planning and co-ordinated protracted peacetime mobilization if the alliance is to be both credible in its objective of deterrence and effective if war should come. This is the explanation for the elaborate political and military organization created to put teeth in the North Atlantic treaty. Two years earlier the Inter-American Treaty of Reciprocal Assistance, "the Rio treaty," had provided "that an armed attack against an American state shall be considered as an attack against all American states." (*See* NORTH ATLANTIC TREATY ORGANIZATION.)

United States.—Although an alliance with France in 1778 helped the infant North American republic make good its challenge to Great Britain in the American Revolution, the government of the United States was not again to enter into a treaty of alliance until after World War II. It followed for more than a century and a half a diplomacy of "no prior commitment," although it did not thereby escape participating in any of the general wars of Europe which occurred after 1776. The Jeffersonian shibboleth, "entangling alliances with none," reflected, however, prevailing U.S. belief that alliances would get the country into "other people's wars" without any compensating advantage. The country. it was believed, had more than enough power to protect itself against its new world neighbours or against the forces which any of the European nations could safely spare from the power struggle in Europe for a new world adventure.

Collective Security Agreement.—A collective security agreement differs from a treaty of alliance in a number of ways. It is more inclusive in its membership. The target of the agreement is an unnamed aggressor who may be one of the signatories. The object of the agreement is to deter the aggressor by the prospect that preponderant power will be organized against him. The threats to security after 1945 seemed so identifiable and precise that regional alliances and collective defense agreements underpinned by detailed military planning, as exemplified by the North Atlantic Treaty organization, supplemented, if they did not displace, the collective security provisions of the charter of the United Nations. *See* COALITION; BAGHDAD PACT; SOUTHEAST ASIA TREATY ORGANIZATION; WAR; AGGRESSION. (W. T. R. F.)

ALLIBONE, SAMUEL AUSTIN (1816–1889), U.S. bibliographer and librarian is best known for his monumental three-volume *Critical Dictionary of English Literature and British and American Authors* (1854–71). He was born in Philadelphia, Pa., April 17, 1816, of French Huguenot and Quaker ancestry. He was privately educated and for many years was engaged in mercantile business in his native city. He, however, acquired a very unusual knowledge of English and American literature and compiled various anthologies and indexes. From 1867 to 1873, and again in 1877–79, Allibone was book editor and corresponding secretary of the American Sunday School union; and from 1879 to 1888 he was librarian of the Lenox library, New York city. He died at Lucerne, Switz., Sept. 2, 1889.

A two-volume supplement to his *Critical Dictionary* by John Foster Kirk was published in 1891.

ALLIER, a *département* of central France on the northern margin of the Massif Central, formed from the old province of Bourbonnais. Pop. (1962) 380,221. Area 2,850 sq.mi. It is bounded on the north by Nièvre, east by Saône-et-Loire, southeast by Loire, south by Puy-de-Dôme, southwest by Creuse and northwest by Cher. The *département* consists mostly of the foreland of the Massif Central and is traversed from south to north by the Allier river. The Loire river forms most of the eastern boundary, and the Cher flows parallel to the Allier across the west. The heights of the Forez region in the southeast are wet, with severe winters. The basin of the Allier, east of its tributary the Sioule, within the *département*, is a northward continuation of the Limagne in Puy-de-Dôme, and is known as the Limagne Bourbonnaise. It is less fertile, however, with ill-drained hollows and much heath, though reclamation has increased the farmland since the middle of the 19th century. Farming is concerned especially with fattening cattle and with production of pigs, poultry and fruit on small holdings.

There are scattered outcrops of coal in the area west of the Allier, especially at Commentry. The local coal, and iron ore brought from Berry by canal, provided early ironworks at Montlucon. Specialized metalworking industries, glass, pottery and chemical works, and a large rubber factory are active, but coal mining has greatly declined. Vichy (*q.v.*), in the south on the Allier, is the best-known spa in France.

Moulins (the capital), Montluçon (*qq.v.*) and Lapalisse are towns that give their names to the constituent *arrondissements*. The *département* is also the diocese of Moulins under the archbishop of Bourges. Its court of appeal is at Riom (*q.v.*), famous for the trials of statesmen of the third republic during World War II. Apart from Moulins, there are noteworthy medieval buildings at Souvigny (Cluniac priory), St. Menoux, Ebreuil, Gannat, Veauce and Ygrande (Romanesque churches), Huriel (castle and fine 11th-century church) and St. Pourçain-sur-Sioule (11th–18th-century church). The castle at Bourbon-l'Archambault was the seat of the first lords of Bourbon (*see* BOURBONNAIS). (AR. E. S.)

ALLIER RIVER (anc. ELAVER), in central France, flows into the Loire (*q.v.*), and is 255 mi. in length, 153 mi. of which are navigable. Its basin has an area of 5,573 sq.mi. Rising in the *département* of Lozère, its upper course is mostly through deep gorges following structural lines of weakness between the mountains of the Margeride and those of the Velay. It then traverses the basins of Langeac and Brioude, receives torrents from the mountains of Dore and Dôme and flows through a wide but shallow channel in the fertile wheat-growing plains north of Clermont-Ferrand, being joined by the Sioule above Moulins (*q.v.*), the chief town on its banks. It enters the Loire, 4 mi. W. of Nevers. (AR. E. S.)

ALLIGATOR, common name for large, long-snouted, cylindrical reptiles that along with caymans comprise the family Alligatoridae. Alligators, crocodiles, gavials and caymans are all crocodilians (*see* CROCODILIA) which live in and along swamps, rivers and lakes of the tropics and subtropics. Two species are still living: *Alligator mississipiensis*, of the southeastern United States, averaging ten feet in length, and the Chinese *A. sinensis*, along the Yangtze Kiang, reaching five feet. *See* also references under "Alligator" in the Index.

ALLIGATOR GAR: *see* GAR.

ALLIGATOR PEAR: *see* AVOCADO.

ALLISON, WILLIAM BOYD (1829–1908), U.S. senator from Iowa, was born near Ashland, O., March 2, 1829. He studied at Wooster academy, Allegheny college and Western Reserve college and then read law in Wooster, O. He practised law in Ashland, 1852–57. He was first a Whig, then in 1855 a member of the convention that founded the Republican party in Ohio, and a year later a delegate to the national Know-Nothing convention. In 1857 he moved to Dubuque, Ia., where he joined the Iowa Republicans. Elected to the house of representatives from Iowa in 1862, he served until 1871. He attained recognition on the committee on ways and means and was known as a friend of the railroad interests, narrowly missing involvement in the Crédit Mobilier (*q.v.*) scandal. In 1870 he was defeated in his campaign for the senate but won in 1872 and continued to represent Iowa in the senate until his death. A contender for the Republican presidential nomination in 1888 and 1896, he received and declined offers of the treasury portfolio in 1881 and 1889 and the department of state in 1897. Allison, Nelson W. Aldrich, Orville H. Platt and John C. Spooner ("The Four") dominated the senate in the early 1900s. Best known for the Bland-Allison act of 1878, he deserves more credit for his chairmanship of the senate committee on appropriations and his aid to Pres. Theodore Roosevelt in passing a railroad rate regulation bill in 1906 over Aldrich's opposition. Renominated in Iowa's first senatorial primary, he died two months later, Aug. 4, 1908, at Dubuque.

See also Leland L. Sage, *William Boyd Allison: a Study in Practical Politics* (1956). (L. L. S.)

ALLITERATION, the repetition of words with the same initial letter or sound for emphasis or stylistic effect. Like rhyme, it aids the memory, as may be seen in such proverbial phrases as "time and tide," "kith and kin." It is frequently used in titles of books and plays, in names of commercial products, athletic teams and nicknames. Purists in prose style frown upon it, but in fanciful prose, such as that of Robert Louis Stevenson, it is often used for decoration. In poetry it is regarded as legitimate embellishment. Thus A. E. Housman in "The Chestnut Casts His Flambeaux" underscores his bitterness: "*W*hatever *b*rute and *b*lackguard made the *w*orld." *See* also ALLITERATIVE VERSE. (G. W. A.)

ALLITERATIVE VERSE. Although alliteration, the poetic device of beginning two or more words in a line of verse with the same sound, occurs in the poetry of many nations, the ancient Germanic races alone among Indo-Europeans developed a verse using it continuously as a main principle. (In Celtic poetry it was from the earliest times an important, if subordinate, principle, always remaining so in the Gaelic strict metres, while in Welsh it was developed very intricately as Cynghanedd [*q.v.*].) Such verse is extensively preserved in Old Norse, Old English (*e.g.*, *Beowulf* [*q.v.*]) and Old Saxon (*i.e.*, Old Low German), and there are considerable traces of it in Old High German. Practically all this surviving poetry represents developments of the common Germanic verse by Old English and Old Saxon monastic poets and Old Norse professional poets (scalds). Yet the Old High German *Hildebrandslied* and the Old English *Fight at Finnsburg* appear to have extensive remains of ancient Germanic heroic lays, which provide evidence for the antiquity of the broad essentials of the alliterative technique as seen elsewhere.

The Germanic alliterative line consisted of two parts. Effective alliteration fell on accented syllables only: unaccented syllables were not effective, even if they began with the alliterating letter. In the first half line, there might be one or two alliterating letters, in the second only one:

wuldres wealdend	*woroldare forgeaf* (*Beowulf*, 1.17)
Wedera leode	*on wang stigon* (*Beowulf*, 1.225)

However, alliterative verse also has severe rules of accent and quantity. Eduard Sievers by statistical analysis determined that half lines are of five main rhythmic types (see *Bibliography*). This variety of rhythm disturbed many, for it leaves doubt how the verses are to be spoken. One theory is that every half line begins effectively from the first accented syllable, any unaccented syllable preceding that syllable being anacrusis. Another is that a half line not beginning with an accented syllable really begins with an initial stress, not in the words but in the musical accompaniment.

In Low German, alliterative verse is not known to have survived after 900 at the latest and in Old High German, rhymed verse was by that time already replacing it, especially in the great gospel poem *Evangelienbuch* of Otfrid (*q.v.*). In English, strict alliterative verse is not found after 1066, but alliterative jingling became common in prose and to judge from rough verses inserted in the Old English *Chronicle,* such as those on Prince Alfred's death (1036), was used in popular poetry together with rhyme and parallelism. From such poetry Layamon (*q.v.*) derived his metrical technique and a fund of traditional diction for *Brut,* his epic on the legendary history of Britain (*c.* 1200). He lived in Worcestershire and alliterative verse survived mainly in western England, for in the 14th century much was produced, often associated linguistically and by internal allusions with the west. The best known poems are *Piers Plowman* and *Sir Gawain* (*see* ENGLISH LITERATURE). The tradition spread through the north midlands to Scotland, where it was still practised by Alexander Montgomerie (*q.v.*) and Sir Patrick Hume of Polwarth under James VI.

This late alliterative poetry often uses rhyme as well. Sometimes all the verses rhyme; sometimes the succession of alliterative verses is broken by rhymed verses grouped at roughly regular intervals. In the *Pearl,* the main principle seems to be rhyme, but the sonnet-like 12-line stanzas are heavily ornamented with alliteration. Many poems, however, are purely alliterative. The metrical structure of the lines is less restricted than in the early Germanic languages. The alliteration also is freer: the second half line can contain more than one alliterating word, and restrictions on alliterating finite verbs are no longer regarded. Although the rhythm was very free, the second half line practically always had a feminine ending until the great loss of unaccented syllables in the 15th century. James VI, who had no doubt heard alliterative verses recited by their authors, called them "tumbling verse," as having extreme metrical freedom, but he regarded their basic rhythm as anapaestic. In England the tradition died earlier and the last alliterative poem is usually held to be *Scottish Field,* which deals with the battle of Flodden (1513).

In Old Norse, the Germanic alliterative verse survived least altered in the metre known as *Fornyrthislag,* but there are also much modified developments of it, especially *Malahattr* and *Ljothshattr.* But at least from 900, Norse poets combined many forms of rhyme and assonance with alliteration, and developed many strophic forms. After 1000, the practice of this verse became practically confined to Icelanders, among whom it continued, so that modern Icelandic poetry may be said to be directly descended from Germanic alliterative verse. *See* ICELANDIC LITERATURE.

BIBLIOGRAPHY.—E. Sievers, *Altgermanische Metrik* (1893); J. Schipper, *A History of English Versification* (1910); A. Heusler, *Deutsche Versgeschichte,* vol. i (1925); J. C. Pope, *The Rhythm of Beowulf* (1942); A. J. Bliss, *The Metre of Beowulf* (1958); D. Everett, *Essays on Middle English Literature,* ch. 2 and 3 (1955); D. Slay, "Some aspects of the technique of composition of Old English verse," *Transactions of the Philological Society, 1952,* pp. 1–14 (1953); Sir W. A. Craigie, "The Scottish alliterative poems," *Proceedings of the British Academy,* vol. xxviii, pp. 217–236 (1943).   (AL. C.)

ALLIUM (Lat. for "garlic"), a genus of plants of the family Liliaceae with about 325 species, found in central and south Europe, north Africa, the dry country of west and central Asia and North and Central America. The plants are bulbous herbs, with flat or rounded radical leaves and a central naked or leafy stem, bearing a head or umbel of small flowers, with a spreading or bell-shaped white, pink, red, yellow or blue perianth. Several species afford useful foods such as onion (*Allium Cepa*), leek (*A. Porrum*), shallot or eschallot (*A. ascalonicum*), garlic (*A. ursinum*) and chives (*A. Schoenoprasum*).

See CHIVES; GARLIC; LEEK; ONION; SHALLOT.

In North America there are about 70 native species, most numerous in the Rocky mountain region and in California where the majority are found. Among about ten species occurring in the eastern United States and Canada are the meadow garlic (*A. canadensis*), formerly used for food by the Indians; the wild leek (*A. tricoccum*), found in rich woods; the wild chive or rush garlic (*A. sibiricum*), found from Maine to Alaska; the nodding wild onion (*A. cernuum*), with inverted clusters of handsome flowers; and the prairie wild onion (*A. stellatum*), of rocky banks in the interior. The field garlic (*A. vineale*) of Europe, widely naturalized in meadows and pastures, is a troublesome weed tainting the flavour of butter.

ALLOA, a small burgh and the administrative centre of Clackmannanshire, Scot., lies on the north bank of the river Forth, 8 mi. E. of Stirling and almost equidistant from Edinburgh, Glasgow and Perth. Pop. (1961) 13,896. Much of the material of the 17th-century church, of which only the spire remains, was used in the construction of the 19th-century Gothic parish church of St. Mungo. To the southeast are the ruins of Alloa tower (13th century), once the stronghold of the powerful family of Erskine, descendants of the earl of Mar. Mary, queen of Scots, and James VI of Scotland spent part of their youth at Alloa tower which, in 1566, Mary revisited with Lord Darnley.

The chief industries of Alloa are yarn spinning, brewing, electrical and general engineering, ship repairing, iron founding and the manufacture of hosiery, glass containers, agricultural implements, tiles and bitumen. In the vicinity of the town are two distilleries, a yeast factory, a tanning works and paper mills. Alloa is connected to Stirling and Dunfermline by rail and above the town the Forth is crossed by a railway bridge. Immediately adjoining Alloa are New Sauchie to the northeast and Tullibody to the northwest. Coal mining in the district is extensive.

ALLOBROGES, an ancient Celtic tribe living in the northeast of Gallia Narbonensis; *i.e.,* in the part of southeastern France bounded by the Rhône to the north and west, the Isère to the south and the Graian Alps to the east, and in the part of Switzerland around Geneva. If the name is rightly interpreted as meaning "aliens," they would seem to have driven out the original inhabitants. Their chief towns were Vienna (Vienne), Genava (Geneva) and Cularo (later Gratianopolis, whence Grenoble). The Allobroges are first recorded in history when Hannibal passed through their territory in 218 B.C. After the subjugation of the Salluvii by the Romans in 123 B.C., the Allobroges were attacked and finally defeated (121 B.C.) at the junction of the Rhône and the Isère rivers by Q. Fabius Maximus, who was therefore called Allobrogicus. They were incorporated in the new province of Transalpine Gaul.

Roman extortions at length provoked a brief revolt in 61 B.C., but they refused to listen to the overtures of Catiline (63) or of Vercingetorix (52) and were protected by Julius Caesar against Helvetian attack in 58. Thereafter they remained loyal.

ALLOCUTION, before Pius XII, was a term reserved almost exclusively to the address made by the pope in the course of a secret consistory (*q.v.*). With Pius XII (1939–58), however, addresses (*allocutiones*) to various congresses and conventions— of doctors, scientists, jurists, sodalities, sociologists, labourers, etc.—became the occasion of significant papal declarations on points of moral theology especially pertinent to the respective audiences.   (J. J. RE.)

ALLOPHANE: see CLAY AND CLAY MINERALS.

ALLORI, CRISTOFANO (sometimes called BRONZINO) (1577–1621), Italian portrait painter, among the foremost exponents of the mannerist late Florentine school, was the son of Alessandro Allori (1535–1607). Cristofano, who was born at Florence, received his first lessons in painting from his father, but becoming dissatisfied with the hard anatomical drawing and cold colouring of the latter he entered the studio of Gregorio Pagani (1558–1605), who was one of the leaders of that later Florentine school which endeavoured to unite the rich colouring of the Venetians with the correct drawing of Michelangelo's disciples. His technical skill is proved by the fact that several copies he made after

Correggio have been taken to be duplicates made by Correggio himself.

The finest of all his works is his "Judith and Holofernes," in the Pitti palace. The model for the Judith was his mistress, the beautiful Mazzafirra, who is also represented in his Magdalene; and the head of Holofernes is generally supposed to represent his own.

ALL-OR-NONE LAW in physiology relates response to stimulus in excitable tissues. It was first established for the contraction of heart muscle by H. P. Bowditch in 1871. Describing the relation of response to stimulus, he stated, "An induction shock produces a contraction or fails to do so according to its strength; if it does so at all, it produces the greatest contraction that can be produced by any strength of stimulus in the condition of the muscle at the time." It was believed that this law was peculiar to the heart and that the other highly specialized and rapidly responding tissues—skeletal muscle and nerve—responded in a different way, the intensity of response being graded according to the intensity of the stimulus. This impression arose because nerves and muscles are composed of hundreds or thousands of individual fibres, and since some of these do not respond to a weak stimulus the total response of the organ is apparently subject to such gradation. It has been established, however, that the individual fibres of both skeletal muscle and nerve respond to stimulation according to the all-or-none principle. This does not mean that the size of response is immutable. Functional capacity varies with the condition of the tissue. The response to a stimulus applied during recovery from a previous response is subnormal. But the size of response is independent of the strength of stimulus, provided this be adequate. These facts show that the functional response is essentially alike in these specialized tissues—heart, skeletal muscle and nerve; its precise nature is not known, but it resembles an explosive reaction in that it depletes for a time the available store of energy on which it depends. (A. Fo.)

ALLOSAURUS, a large carnivorous dinosaur of the Jurassic period (from 160,000,000 to 230,000,000 years ago). Fossils from North American rock strata show it to have been over 30 ft. long (including its counterbalancing tail) and to have progressed on its hind legs.

See DINOSAUR.

ALLOTT, ROBERT (fl. 1600), was probably the editor of a book of "elegant extracts" of Elizabethan poetry entitled *Englands Parnassus* (1600). Nothing more is known of him, except that he compiled a prose anthology called *Wits Theatre of the Little World* (1599). *Englands Parnassus* is a collection of quotations, arranged alphabetically under various subject headings, from the works of contemporary poets. Allott assigns each excerpt to its author, though not always correctly. Although as an editor he was neither scrupulous nor accurate, his work succeeds in preserving some poetry of merit, in identifying the authors of a number of books and in giving an indication of contemporary taste. The best modern edition is that of Charles Crawford (1913), who gives reasons for attributing the work to Allott.

ALLOUEZ, CLAUDE JEAN (1622–1689), French Jesuit missionary to New France, who has been called the founder of Catholicity in the west, was born at St. Didier on June 6, 1622. He entered the Society of Jesus at Toulouse, was ordained priest in 1655 and sailed for Quebec in 1658. He was stationed at settlements along the St. Lawrence river until his appointment in 1663 as vicar-general of the northwest. He traveled extensively, preaching to the Indians and establishing missions, chiefly in the territory to the southwest of the Great Lakes. His own accounts of his activities are frequently quoted in *The Jesuit Relations.* He was a predecessor and later a colleague of Jacques Marquette (*q.v.*), for whom he wrote a book of prayers in Illinois and French. Allouez's last years were spent mostly among the Miamis of the St. Joseph river in southeast Michigan, and he died in one of the Ottawa missions near the site of Niles, Mich., on the night of Aug. 27–28, 1689.

BIBLIOGRAPHY.—R. G. Thwaites (ed.), *The Jesuit Relations,* 73 vol. (1894–1901) especially vol. 44–62; C. Fennelly, "Father . . . Allouez S.J.," *Records of the American Catholic Historical Society of Philadelphia,* 62:12–24 (1941); F. J. Nelligan, "The Visit of Father Allouez to Lake Nipigon in 1667," *Report of the Canadian Historical Association,* pp. 41–52 (1956). (P. Cn.)

ALLOWAY, a hamlet in Ayrshire, Scot., $2\frac{1}{4}$ mi. S. of Ayr, is famous as the birthplace of Robert Burns (*q.v.*). The thatched cottage where he was born in 1759 became the property of the Burns trust in 1881, and in 1900 a museum was built adjacent to it where many Burns manuscripts and relics are kept. A Grecian round temple with nine fluted Corinthian columns was built in 1820 as a monument to Burns, and inside are the Bibles exchanged by Burns and "Highland Mary," Jean Armour's wedding ring and other mementos of the poet. Figures of "Tam o'Shanter" and "Souter Johnnie" stand in a grotto in the garden.

ALLOYS have been defined as metallic substances which contain more than one chemical element. Logically this definition is unsatisfactory because no metallic element can be obtained in a condition of absolute purity, and if applied strictly the definition would result in all nominally "pure" metals being classed as alloys. The definition may be accepted on the understanding that, when dealing with nearly pure metals, there is no sharp dividing line between an impure metal and an alloy.

Most alloys consist essentially of two or more metallic elements and are classed as binary, ternary, quaternary or more complex according to the number of constituent elements. Nonmetallic elements may also be present, notably carbon, nitrogen, oxygen, phosphorus and sulfur. These are often accidental impurities introduced from the original ore or during the production of the alloy. In some cases, however, such as that of carbon in steel or cast iron, the nonmetallic element is an essential constituent, the presence of which determines the properties of the alloy.

Industrial alloys are classed as ferrous (iron base) and nonferrous; the first named, having iron as the main constituent, form the larger group. The most important ferrous alloys are those of iron and carbon, and where the carbon content is less than 1.3% by weight they are known as steels, while cast iron and malleable iron contain 2% to 5% carbon by weight. (*See* IRON AND STEEL INDUSTRY; STEELS, ALLOY; CAST IRON.) The terms "alloy steel" and "special steel" are used to describe steels in which metals other than iron are present in relatively large amounts. Thus stainless steel (*q.v.*) contains chromium (*q.v.*) and nickel, a common composition being 18% chromium and 8% nickel by weight.

Of the nonferrous alloys, those of copper have been known since the Bronze Age. The brasses (*see* BRASS) are essentially alloys of copper and zinc; the copper content usually varies between 57% and 70% by weight. The bronzes (*see* BRONZE) are essentially alloys of copper with 5% to 10% tin by weight. In early writings the distinction between these two classes of alloy is not always clear, and the word "brass" is used to describe what were really impure bronzes. The original copper-base coinage alloys were impure bronze.

Coinage bronze (95% copper, 4% tin and 1% zinc) was adopted by France in 1851; the 20th-century copper coins of Great Britain are made of a copper alloy containing 95.5% copper, 3% tin and 1.5% zinc. (*See* also COBALT.)

The expansion of the aircraft industry during 1910–40 led to the development of light alloys, of which those of aluminum (*see* ALUMINUM: *Alloys and Uses*), having densities of the order 2.7 g. per cubic centimetre, are the most important. With magnesium-base alloys (*see* MAGNESIUM) the density can be reduced to 1.81 g. per cubic centimetre, but the mechanical properties of these alloys are not, in general, so good as those of aluminum alloys. The melting points of aluminum (660° C.) and magnesium (650° C.) are relatively low, and the strength of their alloys falls rapidly between 300° and 400° C. The increasing speed of flight of airplanes means that these temperatures may be exceeded as the result of friction between the air and the wing of the airplane, and this stimulated the search for new constituent materials. Great interest was attached to the use of titanium (*q.v.*) which has a melting point of 1,660° C., and a density of 4.5 g. per cubic centimetre, though it appeared unlikely that titanium-base alloys could be used above 500° C.

The following discussion deals with the more technical aspects of the preparation of alloys, their structure and their electrical properties.

For more general information about manufacture, uses, etc., *see* articles on various alloys, as BABBITT'S METAL; BRASS; BRONZE; etc., and on processes, as ANNEALING; HEAT-TREATMENT; SURFACE HARDENING; etc. For discussion of the various concepts and theories of structure and properties referred to, *see* CRYSTALLOGRAPHY; METALLURGY; MINERALOGY.

PREPARATION OF ALLOYS

The most common way of preparing alloys is by the melting together of the constituent metals. If the melting points of the metals differ widely, or if one is relatively very reactive, it may be convenient to prepare first a master alloy, portions of which are then melted with the remaining metals. According to the nature of the alloy, the melting process may be carried out in furnaces fired by gas, coke or oil. Electrical heating, by resistance, induction or arc-melting methods, is also used. A few alloys are prepared directly by the process in which the metals are extracted from their ores.

Thus pig iron is prepared by the reduction of iron ore in the blast furnace, and steels are prepared by the further purification of pig iron (*see* BLAST FURNACE; CAST IRON; IRON AND STEEL INDUSTRY; CONVERTER STEEL). Alloys may also be prepared by mixing finely divided powders of the constituent metals, and compacting the mixture under high pressure, followed by sintering of the compact.

For further details of the preparation of alloys, *see* under the names of the constituent metals (*see* also FURNACE, METALLURGICAL; POWDER METALLURGY; etc.).

STRUCTURE OF ALLOYS

The properties of alloys depend upon their structure, and are best understood by considering the structures of pure metals. Solid metals are crystalline in the sense that, although they may not exhibit external plane faces, their constituent atoms are arranged in definite three-dimensional patterns or lattices. The great majority of the metals crystallize in one or more of the three typical metallic structures shown in fig. 1. In the body-centred cubic structure the unit cell is a cube with one atom at the centre, and one at each corner. In the face-centred cubic structure, the unit cube has one atom at each corner, and one at the centre of each face. In the close-packed hexagonal structure the atoms are arranged in hexagonal layers (fig. 1) stacked so that the third layer is vertically over the first; the axial ratio is equal to the height of the cell divided by the length of the side of the hexagon. Each of the three typical structures gives rise to a characteristic X-ray diffraction pattern (*see* CRYSTALLOGRAPHY; X RAYS) from which the size of the unit cell can be calculated. The "atomic diameter" of an element may be defined as the closest distance between two atoms in the crystal of the element concerned, and these atomic diameters play an important part in determining the structure of alloys.

Solid Solutions.—The process of solidification of an alloy is such that cast alloys seldom exist in a state of true thermodynamic equilibrium; *i.e.*, the state of lowest free energy (*see* THERMODYNAMICS; CHEMICAL EQUILIBRIUM). When, however, a cast alloy is heated or annealed at a temperature not too far below the melting point, atomic rearrangement occurs and the equilibrium state is gradually approached. (It should be said here that the term annealing was originally used to describe the process in which a metal was heated and allowed to cool slowly in a furnace, and in industrial ferrous metallurgy it is used in this sense. In scientific metallurgy the term is used to describe the heating of an alloy.) If the alloy is then rapidly cooled or quenched (*e.g.*, by immersion in cold water) it is sometimes possible to retain the structure of the higher temperature. Examination then shows that in an alloy of two metals, A and B, the first small additions of B to A result in the formation of a homogeneous alloy whose X-ray diffraction pattern is of the same type as that of the metal A. This implies that the essential structure of the alloy is the same as that of the metal A, and such alloys are called primary or terminal solid solutions. A polished and etched section of such an alloy shows a number of polygonal grains (fig. 2), each of which is a single crystal containing, as do single crystals of pure metals, dislocations and other imperfections. (*See* CRYSTALS, DISLOCATION OF.)

Solid solutions are of two main types. In the interstitial solid solutions the solute atoms occupy the holes or interstices between the solvent atoms, and in this kind of solid solution there is nearly always an expansion of the solvent lattice. Interstitial solid solutions are formed only if the solute atom is very much smaller than that of the solvent metal. Hydrogen, boron, carbon, nitrogen and oxygen are the main elements which dissolve in metals in this way. The solid solution of carbon in face-centred cubic or γ-iron is stable only at high temperatures, but its existence determines the structure and many of the properties of steels (*see* CAST IRON).

For further discussion of solid solutions *see* BRASS; METALLOGRAPHY: *Metals and Alloy Structure*. Many minerals occur in nature as solid solutions: for example, *see* FELDSPAR. *See* also GEOCHEMISTRY: *Crystallization of Magma*; PETROLOGY: *Habit of Igneous Rocks* and *Plutonic Complexes*.

When the two kinds of atom are more nearly equal in size, the solid solution is of the substitutional type, and the atoms of the solute replace those of the solvent so that the two occupy a common lattice.

The extent of a primary solid solution may vary from complete miscibility of two or more metals in the solid state (*e.g.*, silver and gold) to a solubility which is too small to be detected by ordinary methods. Complete miscibility in the solid state is possible only if the metals concerned have the same crystal structure, although a difference between the axial ratios of close-packed hexagonal metals does not prevent the formation of continuous solid solutions between two metals (*e.g.*, magnesium and cadmium).

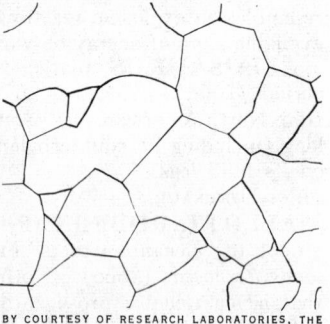

FIG. 2.—SINGLE PHASE SUPER-PURITY BASE Al-1.25% Mg ALLOY SOFT SHEET, ELECTROPOLISHED AND ETCHED TO SHOW GRAIN BOUNDARIES

The fitting together of different atoms on a common lattice is possible only if their sizes do not differ too greatly. If the atomic diameters of two metals (as defined above) differ by more than about 15%, the size factor is unfavourable, and the primary solid solutions are usually restricted to a few atomic per cent. Where the atomic diameters are more nearly equal, the size factor is favourable, and wide solid solutions may be formed, provided that other factors are also favourable, but considerations of size factor alone do not permit the prediction that a wide solid solution must be formed.

When two metals differ greatly in electrochemical characteristics there is a general tendency for the primary solid solutions to be restricted, and for stable intermetallic compounds to be formed.

Thus, with magnesium as solvent, the size factor for antimony is favourable, but antimony is so electronegative compared with magnesium that an extremely stable compound, Mg_3Sb_2, is formed, and the primary solid solutions in magnesium and antimony are very restricted.

When the proportion of solute is less than the solubility limit at a particular temperature, the alloy will be homogeneous after

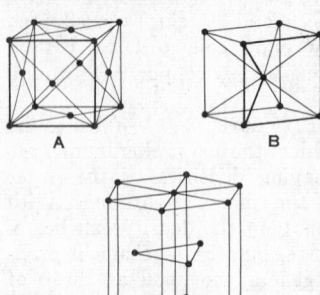

FIG. 1.—THREE METALLIC STRUCTURES SHOWING (A) FACE-CENTRED CUBE; (B) BODY-CENTRED CUBE; (C) CLOSE-PACKED HEXAGONAL STRUCTURE WITH AXIAL RATIO 1:633

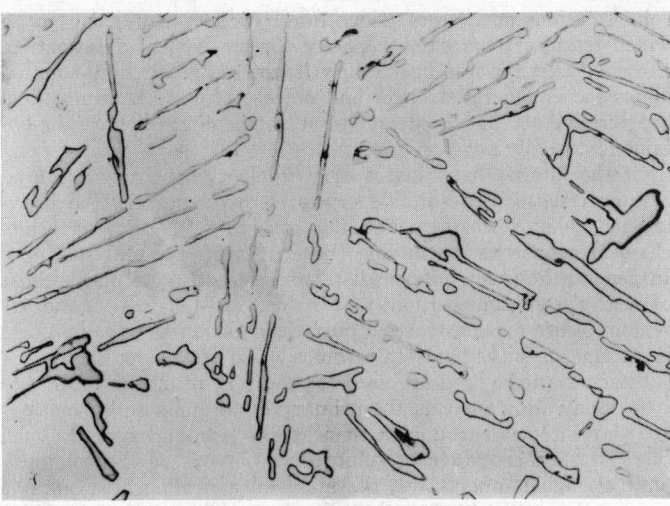

FIG. 3.—SUPERPURITY BASE Al-11.7% Si ALLOY, UNETCHED (× 200)

annealing to equilibrium at this temperature. When the percentage of solute exceeds the solubility limit a second phase appears and, after polishing and etching, a microstructure will show two phases (in certain alloys the structure is revealed without etching; see fig. 3). In some alloy systems (e.g., copper-silver) the only solid phases formed are the two primary solid solutions. In other alloys (e.g., copper-zinc) intermediate phases with characteristic crystal structures are formed, and on exceeding the limits of the primary solid solution, the alloy consists of a mixture of the primary solid solution and of the intermediate phase.

Short-Range and Long-Range Order: Superlattices.—The formation of a substitutional solid solution is accompanied by distortion and strain of the lattice of a solvent, A, by a solute, B. Primary solid solutions are often said to have a random arrangement of the two kinds of atom on a common lattice, but in most solid solutions there is a tendency for solute atoms to avoid being closest neighbours because in this way the strain energy is lowered. This tendency for there to be fewer B-B neighbours than is required by a random arrangement is said to give rise to "short-range order." In a few alloys (e.g., aluminum-zinc) the reverse effect is found, and solute atoms tend to cluster together to a greater extent than required by a random arrangement.

In many alloys where a wide solid solution is formed but the size factor is not too favourable, solid solutions of some compositions show short-range order at high temperatures but, on annealing at low temperatures, atomic rearrangement takes place so that the different atoms form a definite pattern on the lattice. Thus copper and gold are both face-centred cubic metals and form continuous solid solutions at high temperatures. On annealing the alloy of composition Cu_3Au at low temperatures the atoms rearrange themselves to form the structure of fig. 4. If the distinction between the atoms is ignored this structure is face-centred cubic, but the long-range ordered structure or superlattice of fig. 4 is such that no two gold atoms are closest neighbours, and this arrangement lowers the strain energy of the alloy.

Intermediate Phases and Intermetallic Compounds.—In many alloy systems the only solid phases found are the primary solid solutions, with superlattices in some cases. In other systems some alloys of intermediate composition, after annealing to equilibrium, are homogeneous but with crystal structures different from those of the constituent metals. Such phases may be of fixed or variable composition, and in the early days of metallography it was thought that all such phases were based on definite chemical compounds of the two metals. It was later recognized that, although in some cases intermediate phases may correspond with the existence of definite compound molecules, many or most intermediate phases are structures in which the atoms are held together by electron-sharing similar to that existing in pure metals, and involving no more chemical combination than exists between the atoms in a crystal of a pure metal. Some writers use the term

intermetallic compound to describe those intermediate phases whose compositions are only very slightly variable, and the term intermediate phase to describe those of variable composition (see INTERMETALLIC COMPOUNDS).

When one metal is very electropositive and the other very electronegative, intermediate phases may be formed whose compositions correspond with those expected from the normal valencies of chemistry (e.g., Mg_3Sb_2, Mg_2Sn). Some intermediate phases are readily understood as examples of covalent bonding (see VALENCE). Thus the well-known diamond structure involves a tetrahedral arrangement of atoms in which each atom completes an octet of electrons by sharing one electron with each of four neighbours (e.g., diamond, silicon, germanium and grey tin). In combinations such as gallium-arsenic, zinc-selenium or copper-bromine there are eight valency electrons to two atoms (i.e., an

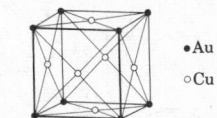

FIG. 4.—Cu_3Au SUPERLATTICE STRUCTURE

average of 4:1) and although these do not form the diamond structure, they do crystallize in structures in which each atom has four neighbours arranged tetrahedrally. Some of these covalent phases have valuable properties as semiconductors (see ELECTRICITY, CONDUCTION OF: Semiconductors).

Most normal chemical compounds are insulators because all the electrons exist in stable groups. The normal valencies are an expression of the way in which these stable groups may be formed by electron-sharing (covalency) or electron-transference (ionic compounds) (see VALENCE). Most intermediate phases in alloys are conductors of electricity and this implies that some electrons are left free, and consequently the atomic ratios are in general different from those expected from the normal valencies. (This description is oversimplified and the full explanation involves the Brillouin-zone characteristics.)

In alloys of copper, silver and gold with elements of the B subgroups and the short periods of the periodic table (see PERIODIC LAW: The Transition Elements) intermediate phases of definite crystal structures often occur at characteristic ratios of valency electrons to atoms. Thus in copper-zinc, copper-aluminum and copper-tin alloys intermediate phases of variable composition are found whose homogeneity ranges include the atomic ratios CuZn, Cu_3Al and Cu_5Sn respectively. Using the normal valencies (copper 1, zinc 2, aluminum 3, tin 4) these all correspond to a ratio of 3 valency electrons to 2 atoms, i.e., to an electron concentration of 3:2.

Phases of a characteristic γ-brass structure occur at an electron concentration of 21:13 (e.g., Cu_5Zn_8, Cu_9Al_4). Such phases are known as electron compounds or Hume-Rothery phases, and they are usually of variable composition, and do not entail the formation of compound molecules—the formulas given above are merely to indicate the compositions involved. Ternary electron compounds can be obtained in which the characteristic structure is retained, provided that the composition is adjusted to maintain the required electron concentration.

Electron compounds are formed only when the size factors are not too unfavourable, and the electrochemical factors are small. In some alloy systems where the sizes of the atoms differ appreciably, intermediate phases exist whose structures are determined by characteristic ratios of the atomic diameters of the constituent atoms. Thus the intermediate phases Cu_2Mg, Au_2Bi and KBi_2 have the same Cu_2Mg-type of crystal structure, and if the formulas are regarded as of the AB_2 type, all are characterized by the ratio of the atomic diameters being of the order 1.2. Such phases are called Laves phases. Ternary phases also exist whose structures are determined by the relative sizes of the atoms concerned.

The above examples are of the simplest type of intermediate alloy phase. In most cases all three factors (size factor, electron concentration and electrochemical factor), together with others not yet understood, control the stability of the phase, and the science of alloy structures is correspondingly complex.

See SOLID STATE PHYSICS: Physical Properties of Solids.

PROPERTIES OF ALLOYS

Electrical Properties.—The metallic elements are electronic conductors of electricity, whose electrical resistivities diminish with falling temperature and become zero at the absolute zero. The perfectly free motion of electrons in the strictly periodic field of the crystal of a pure metal is the result of the wavelike properties of the electron (*see* QUANTUM MECHANICS: *Wave Mechanics*) and anything which tends to destroy the perfect periodicity (*e.g.*, increasing amplitude of thermal vibrations with rise of temperature) tends to increase the electrical resistance.

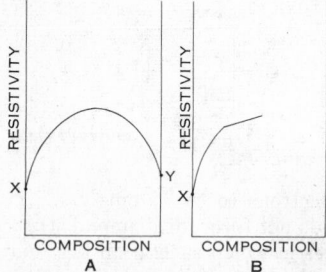

FIG. 5.—ELECTRICAL RESISTIVITY/ COMPOSITION CURVE FOR (A) TWO METALS, X AND Y, WHICH FORM CONTINUOUS SOLID SOLUTIONS AND (B) A SOLID SOLUTION OF LIMITED EXTENT

The lattice distortion accompanying the formation of a solid solution therefore produces an increase in the resistivity.

Where two metals form a continuous solid solution, the typical resistivity/composition curve has the inverted-U shape of fig. 5(A), and where partial miscibility occurs, the relation is of the type of fig. 5(B). The kink in the curve in fig. 5(B) occurs at the boundary of the solid solution, and the subsequent line may slope upward or downward according to the resistivity of the second phase which appears when the limit of the solid solution is exceeded.

The temperature coefficient of electrical resistance of a pure metal is lowered by the formation of a solid solution, and for this reason solid-solution alloys such as Manganin, a copper-base alloy of manganese and nickel (82% Cu, 15% Mn, with FeNi), are used for instruments whose electrical resistances are required to vary as little as possible with changing temperature.

In the formation of a superlattice (*see* above) the irregular structure of the solid solution is replaced by an ordered structure, and the change is therefore accompanied by a fall in the resistivity, and an increase in the temperature coefficient of resistance.

Intermediate phases of fixed, or almost fixed, composition have their characteristic resistivities which are generally higher than that of at least one constituent metal, and in some cases are very much higher than those of both constituents. Where an intermediate phase is of variable composition, the resistivity varies with the composition, and if ordering of the atoms (superlattice formation) occurs, the resistivity may have a minimum value at the composition concerned.

Other electrical properties (*e.g.*, thermoelectric power) show analogous behaviour, in that intermediate phases of fixed composition have characteristic values of the property concerned; in phases of variable composition there is a continuous variation with composition, while maximum or minimum values may occur if long-range ordered structures are formed at particular compositions.

Mechanical Properties.—From the earliest times it has been known that many alloys are harder and stronger than pure metals. By far the greatest use of alloys is for construction purposes, and most work on alloys is ultimately directed toward the improvement of mechanical properties.

The weakness of pure metals is the result of the facts (1) that the three typical crystal structures (fig. 1) are such that deformation of the crystal can take place by the slipping of planes of atoms over one another and (2) that real metallic crystals do not possess a perfectly regular arrangement of the atoms, but contain imperfections known as dislocations (*see* CRYSTALS, DISLOCATION OF) whose presence enables the slipping process to take place relatively easily. When a solid solution is formed the slipping process is hindered because the solute atoms interact with the dislocations, and the lattice distortion makes slip more difficult. Solid solutions are, thus, stronger and harder than their constituent metals. The increase in hardness of a solid solution is generally accompanied by a decrease in ductility. There are, however, some solid solutions such as cartridge brass (copper 70%, zinc 30%) which retain a remarkable capacity for mechanical deformation. Provided that the loss in ductility is not too great, solid-solution alloys are in general stronger and more useful mechanically than are pure metals, but the degree of strengthening which can be obtained is usually not very great.

Of the intermediate phases of variable composition in alloys, a few of those with suitable crystal structures (*e.g.*, the body-centred cubic β-brasses containing 40% to 50% zinc) have mechanical properties resembling those of primary solid solutions. In general, however, intermediate phases, and particularly those of nearly fixed composition, tend to be hard but brittle, and are seldom of use for construction purposes. Sometimes the hardness is extreme, as in the tungsten carbides which are among the hardest substances known, and are used for the tips of cutting tools.

In many alloy systems the primary or terminal solid solutions are of greater extent at high than at low temperatures. In such cases, if the percentage of solute does not exceed the solubility limit at high temperatures, the alloy on annealing at a suitable temperature will become a homogeneous solid solution, and this structure may be retained on quenching (*e.g.*, in cold water). The resulting alloy is said to be "homogenized," and although harder than a pure metal, it may be sufficiently soft and ductile to undergo the severe deformations which occur in the industrial processes of rolling, pressing, etc. If the product is then reannealed at a temperature sufficiently low for the solid solution to be supersaturated, but sufficiently high for atomic movement to take place, precipitation of the excess of solute will occur with the production of an alloy consisting of small particles of a solute-rich phase embedded in a matrix of solid solution. A polyphase alloy of this kind is in general harder than the same alloy in the form of a homogeneous solid solution, because the small particles of the disperse phase interfere with the slipping process which accompanies plastic deformation. The process is known as precipitation hardening, and in alloys of low melting point the mere holding of the homogenized specimen at room temperature may result in precipitation gradually taking place. The phenomenon was discovered in certain alloys of aluminum, notably duralumin (*q.v.*), which were found to undergo increase in hardness on standing at room temperature, and the process was called age-hardening or aging. Later work showed that, although precipitation of a phase from a solid solution was usually accompanied by an increase in strength and hardness, the greatest hardness did not correspond to complete precipitation. The precipitation process was found to occur in definite stages, and the greatest hardness usually corresponded to an intermediate structure in which distortion and strain of the lattice of the solid solution made the slipping process more difficult. The phenomenon of age-hardening is thus complicated, and the details vary from one alloy to another.

In many alloys the structure stable at high temperatures is different from that stable at low temperatures and, on slow cooling, transformation from one structure to another will occur, while rapid cooling or quenching may retain the high-temperature structure. In some cases even the most rapid cooling may not be able to prevent structural changes from taking place, and intermediate structures of great hardness may be formed. Thus in plain carbon steels, carbon is almost insoluble in body-centred cubic or α-iron which is stable at low temperatures, but is slightly soluble in the face-centred cubic or γ-iron which is stable between 910° C. and 1,389° C.; the solid solution, austenite, is of the interstitial type (*see* IRON AND STEEL INDUSTRY: *Steel Metallurgy: Slowly Cooled Steels*). If the alloy is homogenized in the austenitic region, and then slowly cooled, the iron matrix changes from the face-centred cubic to the body-centred cubic form, and the carbon is converted into iron-carbide Fe_3C, cementite. If the alloy is quenched, the matrix transforms almost instantaneously by a shear mechanism, and the carbon atoms have no time in which to diffuse to form cementite, but are retained in the body-centred modification of iron whose structure is distorted from body-centred cubic to body-centred tetragonal (*see* CRYSTALLOGRAPHY). The resulting structure, martensite, is in a state of great strain, and is extremely hard. If it is reheated or tempered at a comparatively

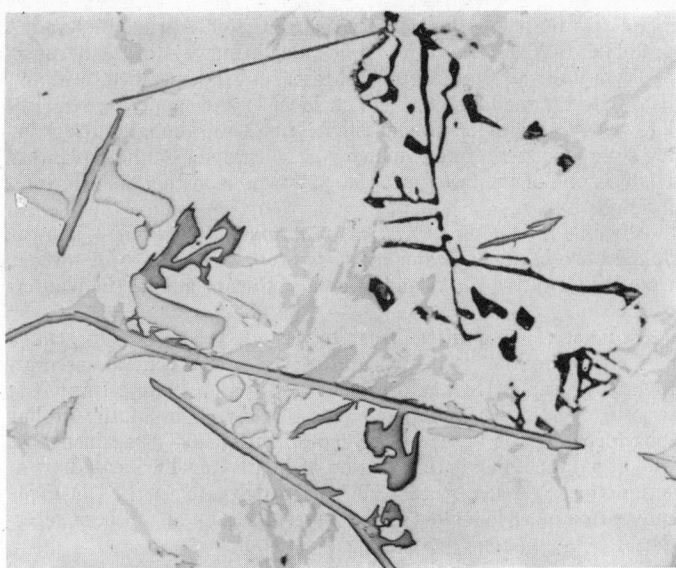

BY COURTESY OF RESEARCH LABORATORIES, THE BRITISH ALUMINIUM CO. LTD.

FIG. 6.—COMPLEX STRUCTURE IN 1% Fe, 6% Cu, 6% Si, 3% Mg ALLOY, UNETCHED (× 200)

Mg_2Si tarnished black; silicon medium tone in relief; β (Cu-Fe) light needles in relief; $CuAl_2$ light, slightly in relief; λ (Al-Cu-Mg-Si) very flat, slightly darker than $CuAl_2$

low temperature, change to the stable structure (α-iron + cementite) begins to occur, but the process is not simple and usually involves the formation and decomposition of intermediate phases. Analogous changes are found in many alloys (*e.g.*, copper + 10% aluminum) in which a phase which is stable at high temperatures decomposes into more than one phase on cooling.

The structures of cast alloys are often very complicated (*see* fig. 6). In relatively simple cases they can be understood by reference to what are called constitutional or equilibrium diagrams. Such diagrams refer only to conditions of true equilibrium. They are not concerned with the arrangement of the constituents in the alloy, but show the temperature-composition ranges over which different phases, or mixtures of phases, are stable. Thus, fig. 7 shows a hypothetical equilibrium diagram of two metals, A and B. The primary solid solution of B in A is α, and β that of A in B, while γ is an intermediate phase. The curves aechb give the temperature composition limits above which the alloy is totally liquid. The line ae is the liquidus curve, representing the beginning of solidification of the solid solution α, and ad is the solidus curve, representing the end of solidification, provided that the rate of cooling is sufficiently slow for equilibrium conditions to be maintained. The corresponding liquidus and solidus curves for the solidification of the solid γ phase of composition between f and c are ce and cf. The liquidus curves ae and ce meet at the minimum or eutectic point e, and at this temperature liquid of composition e is in equilibrium with solid α of composition d and solid γ of composition f. On cooling below this temperature the liquid of composition e solidifies to a mixture of the two solid phases. The lines dl and fm are the solid solubility curves of the α and γ phases, and alloys within the field adlk consist of homogeneous α-solid solution. Alloys within the field defml consist of a mixture of solid α and solid γ, and an alloy x contains α-phase of composition y together with γ-phase of composition z. Similar constructions give the compositions of phases in equilibrium in other two-phase fields.

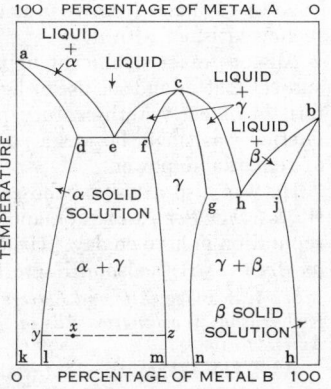

FIG. 7.—HYPOTHETICAL DIAGRAM OF THE EQUILIBRIUM OF TWO METALS, A AND B

Diagrams such as fig. 7 refer to equilibrium conditions, and a consideration of the above description will show that when an alloy is cooled, equilibrium will in general only be maintained if diffusion takes place in the solid phases. Since diffusion is a slow process, the structures of cast alloys tend to show a wider range of constituents and compositions than would result from cooling under equilibrium conditions. Nevertheless, diagrams of this nature are of great value in understanding the structure of cast alloys.

For ternary systems the equilibrium diagram requires two dimensions to represent the composition and a third dimension for the temperature.

The mechanical properties of an alloy depend greatly on the spatial arrangement of the particles of the different phases. They are also profoundly altered by mechanical deformation, but these effects are not shown on the equilibrium diagram. *See* FUSIBLE ALLOYS; *see* also Index references under "Alloys" in the Index volume.

BIBLIOGRAPHY.—W. Hume-Rothery and G. V. Raynor, *Structure of Metals and Alloys* (1954); E. C. Rollason, *Metallurgy for Engineers* (1949); C. S. Barrett, *Structure of Metals* (1952); A. R. Bailey, *Textbook of Metallurgy* (1954); C. H. Desch, *Metallography* (1942); F. N. Rhines, *Phase Diagrams in Metallurgy* (1956); A. H. Cottrell, *Theoretical Structural Metallurgy*, 2nd ed. (1955); R. H. Greaves and H. Wrighton, *Practical Microscopical Metallography*, 4th ed. rev. (1957). For numerical data reference may be made to the following books which contain much useful information: C. J. Smithells (ed.), *Metals Reference Book* (1955); American Society for Metals, *Metals Handbook* (1948), *Supplement* (1955). (W. H.-Ry.)

ALLOY STEELS: *see* STEELS, ALLOY.

ALLPORT, GORDON WILLARD (1897–   ), U.S. psychologist, noted for his work in the theory of personality, was born in Montezuma, Ind., on Nov. 11, 1897. Trained at Harvard university (B.A., 1919; Ph.D., 1922), he taught psychology there after 1930.

Although Allport made important contributions to the analysis of prejudice (*The Nature of Prejudice*, 1954), he is most respected for his creative work in the theory of personality (*Personality: a Psychological Interpretation*, 1937; *Becoming*, 1955).

Best known is his theory of functional autonomy of motives; *i.e.*, that adult motives develop from, but become independent of, infantile drives, an important shift from Freudian theory. His approach favours emphasis on the present problems of an adult personality as against infantile emotions and experiences. In *Becoming* he stressed the importance of the self and the uniqueness of the adult personality, in contradistinction to behaviourist and Freudian views. The self, he holds, is an identifiable organization within each individual, available for scientific study by suitable methods. As such it accounts for the unity of personality, for the higher motives and for the continuity of personal memories. By showing that a psychology of self need not be mystical, Allport greatly influenced mid-20th-century theorizing about personality.

(R. SR.)

ALL SAINTS, FESTIVAL OF, on Nov. 1, commemorates all the saints of the church, both known and unknown. Its origin cannot be traced with certainty, and it has been observed on various days in different places. A feast of all martyrs was kept in the east by Ephraem Syrus (d. *c.* 373) on May 13, which may have determined the choice of May 13 by Pope Boniface IV when he dedicated the Pantheon in Rome as a church in honour of the Blessed Virgin and all martyrs in 609. The first evidence for the broadening of the festival to include all saints as well as all martyrs and for its celebration on Nov. 1 is the dedication on that day by Pope Gregory III (731–741) of a chapel in honour of all saints at St. Peter's, Rome. In 800 the *solemnitas* of all saints was kept by Alcuin on Nov. 1, on which day also it appears in a 9th-century English calendar. In 837 Gregory IV ordered its general observance, and in 1480 Sixtus IV gave it an octave.

Eastern Christendom honours all saints on the first Sunday after Whitsunday. In medieval English usage the festival was known as All Hallows, and its eve is still called Halloween (*q.v.*). *See* also CHURCH YEAR.

BIBLIOGRAPHY.—H. Delehaye *et al.*, *Propylaeum ad acta sanctorum decembris,* pp. 488–489 (1940); I. Schuster, *The Sacramentary,* vol. v, pp. 208–213 (1931); H. Thurston and D. Attwater (eds.), *Butler's Lives of the Saints,* vol. iv, pp. 232–235 (1956).   (L. C. S.)

ALL SAINTS BAY (BAHIA DE TODOS OS SANTOS), a landlocked bay and natural harbour on the eastern coast of Brazil, named by its discoverer, Amerigo Vespucci, who, it is said, first entered the bay on All Saints day, Nov. 1, 1501. It has been an important Brazilian naval base since colonial times. The bay is about 20 mi. wide and 23 mi. long and is situated about 738 mi. N.E. of Rio de Janeiro. Salvador or Bahia (pop. [1960] 630,878), the principal seaport and capital of the state of Bahia, is on the peninsula that separates the bay from the Atlantic, at 13° S. and 38° 30′ W. The harbour at Salvador is protected by two detached breakwaters, one 1,300 yd. long and the other about 1,000 yd. long. The main channel is dredged from the 2-mi.-wide Atlantic entrance between Salvador and the island of Itaparica to the port of São Francisco do Conde, outlet for the petroleum refinery at Mataripe. Brazil's only producing oil field is on the northeast shore of the bay between Candeias and Lobato.
(R. E. P.)

ALL SOULS' DAY (Nov. 2, or Nov. 3 if Nov. 2 is Sunday), the day appointed in the Roman Catholic Church for a special commemoration of all the faithful departed, those baptized Christians who are believed to be in a state called purgatory because they have died with the guilt of lesser sins on their souls. Catholic doctrine holds that the prayers of the faithful on earth will help cleanse these souls in order to fit them for the vision of God in Heaven.

From antiquity certain days were devoted to intercession for particular groups of the dead. The institution of a day for a general intercession on Nov. 2 is due to Odilo, abbot of Cluny (d. 1048). The date, which became practically universal before the end of the 13th century, was chosen to follow All Saints' day, Nov. 1 (*see* ALL SAINTS, FESTIVAL OF). Having celebrated the feast of all the members of the church who are believed to be in heaven, the church on earth turns on the next day, Nov. 2, to commemorate the deceased members whose souls are believed to be suffering in purgatory.

Black vestments are worn, the office of the day is that of the dead and the Roman liturgy permits every priest to celebrate three Requiem Masses, one for the intention of the celebrant himself, one for all the faithful departed and one for the intention of the pope.

The feast was abolished in the Church of England at the Reformation but has been revived in Anglo-Catholic churches. Among continental Protestants its tradition was more tenaciously maintained, even without ecclesiastical sanction.   (G. L. D.)

ALLSPICE, the dried, nearly ripe berry of the pimento or allspice tree (*Pimenta officinalis*) of the myrtle family. The tree, which attains a height of 25–30 ft., is native to the West Indies and Central America. This highly aromatic spice, widely used in baking and always present in mincemeat and mixed pickling spice, takes its name from the fact its flavour resembles a combination of cloves, cinnamon and nutmeg. Early Spanish explorers, mistaking it for a type of pepper, called it *pimenta,* hence its botanical name and such terms as pimento and Jamaica pepper. The first record of its import to Europe was in 1601, supposedly as a substitute for the spice cardamom. The name is applied also to other aromatic shrubs, especially to one of the sweet shrubs, the Carolina allspice (*Calycanthus floridus*), a handsome flowering shrub native to southeastern United States and often cultivated in England; to the Japanese allspice (*Chimonanthus praecox*), native to eastern Asia and planted for ornament in England and the United States; and to the wild allspice or spicebush (*Lindera benzoin*), a lauraceous shrub of eastern North America, with aromatic berries, reputed to have been used as a substitute for spice.
(M. W. N.)

ALLSTON, ROBERT FRANCIS WITHERS (1801–1864), U.S. planter and governor of South Carolina, provided an important source of information about the agriculture and the political and social history of the south by his papers, *South Carolina Rice Plantation.*

He was born in All Saints' parish, S.C., on April 21, 1801. A graduate of West Point in 1821, he aided in surveys of the harbours of Plymouth and Provincetown, Mass., and the entrance to Mobile bay. He resigned his commission in 1822 and, applying scientific knowledge of agriculture and engineering to draining and reclaiming swamp country, rose to a high position among southern planters. His was one of the last great rice plantations in the Atlantic coast lowlands.

Allston's *A Memoir of the Introduction and Planting of Rice in South Carolina* (1843) and *An Essay on Sea Coast Crops* (1854) were authoritative works and of great influence among the planters of the time.

Also active in politics, Allston was elected surveyor general of South Carolina (1823–27) and served in the general assembly for many years. He was president of the state senate from 1847 to 1856. As the secession movement of 1847–52 in South Carolina took form, Allston favoured the "co-operationists" as against those who urged the immediate secession of South Carolina regardless of action by any other state. He was a delegate to the Nashville convention of 1850, called in the hope of a general southern secession.

Elected governor by the legislature for the term 1856–58, he did much for the development of agriculture and the improvement of the public schools.

Allston died near Georgetown, S.C., on April 7, 1864.

South Carolina Rice Plantation was edited by J. H. Easterby (1945).

ALLSTON, WASHINGTON (1779–1843), U.S. painter and author, the first important U.S. romantic painter, was born on Nov. 5, 1779, on his family plantation on the Waccamaw river in South Carolina. He was educated at Newport, R.I., and at Harvard, where he graduated in 1800.

In London he studied at the Royal academy, where he learned the colouristic technique destroyed on the continent by neoclassicism. Study at the Louvre in Paris (winter of 1803–04) and in Italy (1804–08) acquainted him with the Venetian and Roman masters upon whom he based his own development. Also during this period he formed his friendships with S. T. Coleridge and Washington Irving.

He returned to Boston in 1808, spent seven fruitful years in London from 1811, settled in Boston in 1818 and finally in Cambridgeport, Mass., in 1828.

Before his final return to the United States, Allston's art was dramatic and large in scale; he delighted in the supernatural. "Dead Man Revived by Touching the Bones of the Prophet Elisha" (1811–13), "The Angel Liberating St. Peter From Prison" (1812) and "Belshazzar's Feast" (1817–43) are memorable works of this phase of romanticism. His dramatic landscapes "The Deluge" (1804), "Diana in the Chase" (1805) and "Elijah in the Desert" (1818) are the first important achievements of American landscape.

After his return to Boston in 1818 Allston's art became quieter, striking a new note of reverie and fantasy. "Moonlit Landscape" (1819) and "The Flight of Florimell" (1819) are the chief works of a period before he became preoccupied with "Belshazzar's Feast," brought unfinished from London. He worked on this from 1820 to 1828 and from 1839 until his death on July 9, 1843, never feeling satisfied with it.

Allston was a significant figure in the experiments in dramatic subject matter and the use of light and atmospheric colour, characteristic of early 19th-century painting. Although his life's production was small, he was a painter of distinction and at his best of remarkable power.

He was also a writer whose verse, *The Sylphs of the Seasons With Other Poems* (1813), and prose, *Monaldi* (1841) gave him a reputation in his own day. His theory of art, published as *Lectures on Art* (1850), is also of interest.

See J. B. Flagg, *Life and Letters of Washington Allston* (1892); E. P. Richardson, *Washington Allston, a Study of the Romantic Artist in America* (1948).   (E. P. R.)

ALLUVIUM, the material deposited by rivers. It is usually most extensively developed in the lower part of the course of a river, forming flood plains and deltas, but may be deposited at any point where the velocity of a river is checked; for example, where it runs into a lake. Alluvium in the true sense consists mostly of silt, sand and gravel, without much true clay; it often contains a good deal of organic matter and therefore yields very fertile soils. Some of the great alluvial deposits of the world are: the flood plain of the Mississippi, the deltas of the Nile, of the Ganges and Brahmaputra, and of the Hwang Ho in China. Owing to elevation of the land and consequent deepening of the river channel, patches of alluvium are often left forming terraces on the sides of valleys. On such terraces much of London is built.

In some regions alluvial deposits contain gold, platinum or gem stones, and the greater part of the world's supply of tin ore comes from similar sources.

See GEOLOGY: *Stratigraphy;* RIVER: *Physical Characteristics of Rivers.* (R. H. RA.)

ALMA, BATTLE OF THE, a victory won by Franco-British forces, with some Turkish support, over the Russians on Sept. 20 (new style; Sept. 8, old style), 1854, during the Crimean War (*q.v.*). About 36,000 Russian troops under Prince Aleksandr Menshikov took up position on the heights above the Alma river in the southwestern Crimea, thus blocking the way to Sevastopol. This formidable barrier was threatened by about 58,000 men commanded by Lord Raglan and Marshal Armand de Saint-Arnaud. With their right against the sea, and supported by the guns of the allied fleet, the French attacked first. Ascending difficult but lightly defended territory swiftly, they awaited British support. After a delay the British assaulted the Russian centre frontally, moving over the Alma and up the naturally defensible slope in the face of fierce artillery and musket fire. The light division gained the first plateau only to be thrown back because the reserves were slow in coming to its support. The Russians, however, were alarmed and withdrew their artillery, and the next attack by the Guards brigade, in splendid formation and firing disciplined volleys, decided the issue. The Russians retreated toward Sevastopol. Impatient allied cavalry were not permitted to pursue them. Generalship was lacking on the allied side, and the victory was attributable to the disciplined nature of the British infantry. The Russian losses were estimated at about 5,700, the British at about 2,000. The French claimed to have suffered 1,340 casualties.
(D. M. Sc.)

ALMA-ATA (formerly VERNY), an *oblast* of the Kazakh Soviet Socialist Republic, U.S.S.R., extends along both sides of the Ili river, from Lake Balkhash to the borders of Sinkiang Uigur Autonomous Region, China. In June 1959 its area was more than doubled to 87,876 sq.mi. (227,600 sq.km.) by the addition of the former Taldy-Kurgan *oblast.*

The population (1,402,625 in 1959) was 675,684 urban and 726,941 rural. Two-thirds was said to be Kazakh. Other nationalities included Russians, Uigurs (Uygurs), Ukrainians, Uzbeks, Tatars and Belorussians. It is very mountainous in the south (Trans-Ili or Zailiyski Alatau, Ketmen and Dzungarski Alatau ranges), and there is a sandy desert southeast of Lake Balkhash and along the lower Ili river. The climate is variable, being continental, with a very cold winter in the north but milder in the foothills. The economy is predominantly agricultural except for important lead and zinc mines and a refining plant at Tekeli. There is a great variety of irrigated crops on the southern mountain slopes, the main ones being wheat and sugar beets, but there are also tobacco, opium and rubber, as well as medicinal plants. The fruit industry is very important.

Near Lake Balkhash, sheep are raised, and saxaul trees are processed for local fuel. Industry consists mainly of food processing (sugar refining, flour milling and fish canning). The Turksib railway crosses the *oblast* from northeast to west. Air transport is used extensively, and the Ili river is used for the transport of goods.

Apart from Alma-Ata, the capital, the principal towns or "settlements of town type" are Burundai, Fabrichny, Imeni Panfilova, Ili and Taldy-Kurgan. In the early 1960s there were more than 880 schools in the *oblast.* Most of the cultural activity is concentrated in the capital. (G. E. WR.)

ALMA-ATA, the capital of Alma-Ata *oblast* in the Kazakh Soviet Socialist Republic, U.S.S.R., was founded in 1854 as a fortress with the name of Verny. The population grew from 45,600 in 1926 to 456,481 in 1959. Situated in the picturesque foothills of the Trans-Ili, or Zailiyski Alatau, it is entirely surrounded by apple orchards and is considered one of the most beautiful cities of the U.S.S.R. It has a heavy-machine-building industry (including railway shops), a spinning mill, fruit-preserving and meat-packing plants, wine and tobacco factories, tanneries and sawmills.

There are a number of educational and cultural establishments, including the Kazakh S. M. Kirov State university (established 1928), institutes of foreign languages, agriculture, medicine, zootechnic and veterinary sciences and pedagogy, a music conservatoire, a large library, Kazakh and Russian opera houses, theatres and museums. Alma-Ata is the seat of the Kazakh Academy of Sciences. (G. E. WR.)

ALMADÉN, a Spanish town in the province of Ciudad Real, lies 67 mi. from the city of Ciudad Real. Pop. (1960) 13,443 (mun.), an increase of 6% since 1950. In Arabic *almaden* signifies "mine . . . ," an allusion to the historic exploitation of the local deposits of mercuric ores, which were known to the Romans, although the identification of Almadén with the Roman Sisapo is doubtful. The seams of mercuric ore are found in quartzite occurring in three ridges. The mineral was deposited by internal thermal waters carrying a solution of mercuric and sodium salts. The town, after being captured from the Moors by Alfonso VII in 1151, was given to the Order of Calatrava which exploited the mines. The king of Spain, Charles I (Holy Roman Emperor Charles V), granted them to the Fugger (*q.v.*) family as security for a loan. From the middle of the 17th century the mines were worked by the royal exchequer. (M. B. F.)

ALMAGEST, the Arabicized name for *The Great Treatise,* the Greek astronomical and mathematical encyclopaedia written in the 2nd century A.D. by Claudius Ptolemy, of Alexandria. The work was the ultimate authority on astronomy (the Ptolemaic system) until the time of Copernicus, A.D. 1543. The *Almagest* contains a catalogue giving the ecliptical coordinates and the magnitudes of more than a thousand stars, based on the lost catalogue by Hipparchus of the 2nd century B.C.; it preserves, therefore, the oldest accurate Greek description of the stars and constellations.

See PTOLEMY: *Astronomical Work.* (A. Po.)

ALMAGRO, DIEGO DE (*c.* 1475–1538), a Spanish soldier and conquistador. He was abandoned as an infant at Almagro, a town near Ciudad Real, Spain. He is believed to have joined Pedrarias Dávila in the new world, in 1524, following service in the Spanish army. In Panamá he became a close friend of Francisco Pizarro (*q.v.*) and joined him, together with Hernando de Luque, in the conquest of Peru (1533). Almagro considered himself poorly rewarded after the first attempt, and the friendship between the two men ceased.

Almagro, nevertheless, co-operated in the subsequent conquest and in 1534 was named *adelantado* of the territory just south of Peru by Emperor Charles V. He organized an expedition to Chile but found it barren and lacking in gold.

Disappointed in this venture, he marched to Cuzco, Peru, then under Indian siege, seized control of the city and jailed the two brothers of Francisco Pizarro. A war with the Pizarro brothers followed, in which Almagro was defeated by Hernando Pizarro at Las Salinas. Convicted of treason, Almagro was executed in Cuzco, in 1538. (J. L. TR.)

ALMANAC, a book or table containing a calendar of the days, weeks and months of the year, a register of ecclesiastical festivals and saints' days and a record of various astronomical phenomena, often with weather prognostications and seasonal suggestions for the countryman.

The first printed almanac bears the imprint 1457, but almanacs have appeared in some form since the beginnings of astronomy. For example, a crude kind known as clog almanacs were the original calendar of the Norwegians and Danes; they consisted of square blocks of hard wood, about eight inches in length, with notches along the four angles corresponding to the days of the year. The clog almanacs were in use in some parts of England as late as the end of the 17th century. J. J. Lalande, an investigator of early astronomical works, did not find any express mention of almanacs before those published by Solomon Jarchus in A.D. 1150. Probably

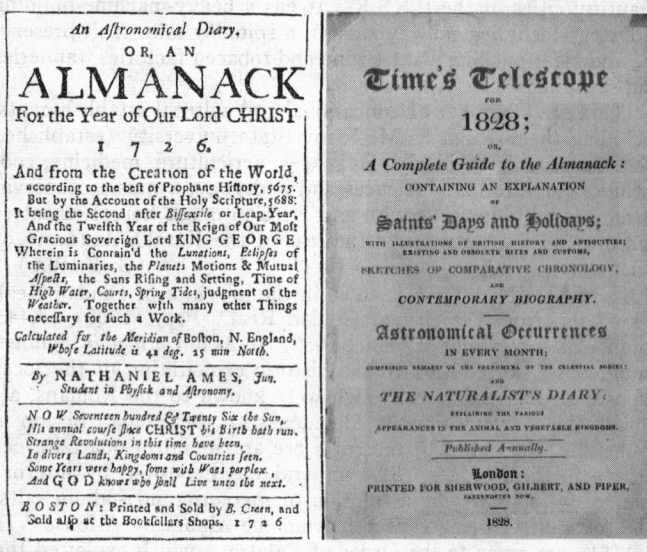

An Astronomical Diary,
OR, AN
ALMANACK
For the Year of Our Lord CHRIST
1726.

And from the Creation of the World, according to the best of Prophane History, 5675. But by the Account of the Holy Scripture, 5688: It being the Second after Bissextile or Leap-Year, And the Twelfth Year of the Reign of Our Most Gracious Sovereign Lord KING GEORGE Wherein is Contain'd the *Lunations, Eclipses* of the Luminaries, the *Planets* Motions & Mutual *Aspects,* the Suns Rising and Setting, Time of High Water, Courts, Spring Tides, judgment of the Weather. Together with many other Things necessary for such a Work.

Calculated for the Meridian of Boston, N. England, Whose Latitude is 42 deg. 25 min North.

By NATHANIEL AMES, Jun.
Student in Physick and Astronomy.

N O W Seventeen hundred & Twenty Six the Sun, His annual course since CHRIST his Birth hath run. Strange Revolutions in this time have been, In divers Lands, Kingdoms and Countries seen. Some Years were happy, some with Woes perplext, And G O D knows who shall Live unto the next.

B O S T O N : Printed and Sold by B. Green, and Sold also at the Booksellers Shops. 1 7 2 6

Time's Telescope
FOR
1828;
OR,
A Complete Guide to the Almanack:
CONTAINING AN EXPLANATION
OF
Saints' Days and Holidays;
WITH ILLUSTRATIONS OF BRITISH HISTORY AND ANTIQUITIES; EXISTING AND OBSOLETE RITES AND CUSTOMS,
AND
SKETCHES OF COMPARATIVE CHRONOLOGY,
AND
CONTEMPORARY BIOGRAPHY.
Astronomical Occurrences
IN EVERY MONTH;
COMPRISING REMARKS ON THE PHENOMENA OF THE CELESTIAL BODIES;
AND
THE NATURALIST'S DIARY;
EXPLAINING THE VARIOUS APPEARANCES IN THE ANIMAL AND VEGETABLE KINGDOMS.
Published Annually.
London:
PRINTED FOR SHERWOOD, GILBERT, AND PIPER, PATERNOSTER ROW.
1828.

(LEFT) COVER OF FIRST AMES ALMANAC, PUBLISHED IN NEW ENGLAND, 1726; (RIGHT) COVER OF TIME'S TELESCOPE, PUBLISHED IN LONDON, 1828

the earliest almanacs now extant are those in manuscripts of the early 12th century, examples of which are to be found in the libraries of the British museum and Cambridge and Oxford universities. The Savilian library at Oxford contains a manuscript copy of an almanac published by Petrus de Dacia in about the year 1300. The first standard almanacs, such as those produced by John Somers (1380) and Nicolas de Lynne (1386), were issued at Oxford.

Most English almanacs were published by the Stationers' Co., the most famous of them being the *Vox Stellarum* of Francis Moore (1657–1715?), the first number of which was completed in July

PAGES FROM THE FARMER'S ALMANAC, PUBLISHED IN NEW ENGLAND, 1835

1700 and contained predictions for 1701. Its publication has been continued under the title of *Old Moore's Almanac.*

Scotland pioneered astrological almanacs during the 1500s and 1600s. Notable was *Edinburgh's True Almanack, or a New Prog-*

nostication (begun in 1683), a format which in 1837 became *Oliver and Boyd's New Edinburgh Almanac,* the standard reference for Scottish affairs.

The first American almanacs were printed in Cambridge, Mass., under the supervision of Harvard college; the first book issued from the college press was *An Almanac for New England for the Year 1639,* compiled by "William Pierce, mariner." Until nearly 1700 an almanac was printed yearly from this press.

One of the American myths is that Philadelphia cradled the American almanac and even that Benjamin Franklin founded it. Franklin's brother James printed *The Rhode Island Almanac* in 1728, and Benjamin Franklin (under the nom de plume of Richard Saunders) started his *Poor Richard's Almanack* in Philadelphia five years later. *Poor Richard's* was America's most famous almanac, but Nathaniel Ames of Dedham, Mass., ran a close second with his *Astronomical Diary and Almanack,* which he published from 1726 to 1764 when he died. The business was continued by his son until 1775. It reached an annual circulation of 60,000 copies, far exceeding that of *Poor Richard's.*

During the 1700s and 1800s in America there were about 2,000 almanacs printed for various trades, organizations, businesses, military and religious groups and finally as an advertising medium.

The 18th-century almanac was actually the forerunner of the modern magazine, departing from newspaper format which until the late 1800s was one sheet of paper folded twice. The earliest magazines were similar, but the almanacs were composed of ten or more sheets stitched together. With the almanac as a guide, the farmer could reset a stopped clock, tell the time of day and estimate the proper season for all farm chores. It also furnished much incidental information—instructive and entertaining as well— which made it greatly appreciated where other reading matter was scarce.
(E. Sl.)

ALMANZOR: see MANSUR, AL-.

ALMA-TADEMA, SIR LAWRENCE (1836–1912), British painter of popular historical idyls and genre, was born Jan. 8, 1836, at Dronrijp, near Leeuwarden, Neth., the son of a notary. Originally intended for medicine, he studied art at the Antwerp academy from 1852–56, under E. C. G. Wappers and later under Baron Hendrik Leys, the medieval history painter, whom he assisted in 1859 with the frescoes in the Stadhuis, Antwerp. He exhibited his first picture, a medieval subject, at the Brussels salon in 1857 and gained a gold medal at Amsterdam in 1862.

During a visit to Italy in 1863, Alma-Tadema became interested in Greek and Roman antiquity and in Egyptian archaeology; thereafter he depicted subjects drawn almost exclusively from these sources. His first paintings exhibited at the Royal Academy in 1869 included "The Pyrrhic Dance" (Guildhall art gallery, London). A year later, following the death of his first wife, he left Brussels for England, and in 1871 married the painter Laura Epps. He became a naturalized British subject in 1873, settling in St. John's Wood, London, in a pseudoantique style house.

His work is remarkable for its clarity of colour, exactness and smoothness of finish; he imagined a Rome of sunlit skies and gentle sentiment. Immensely successful during his lifetime, his repute did not survive; in a later era his gifts might have been employed in creating vast biblical film sets. Elected associate of the Royal Academy in 1876, he became a full academician in 1879, was knighted in 1899 and was awarded the Order of Merit in 1905. He died in Wiesbaden, Ger., on June 25, 1912; a posthumous exhibition of his work was held in London in 1913. Five representative works are in the Tate gallery, London.

See Helen Zimmern, "L. Alma-Tadema, His Life and Work," *Art Annual,* 1886; C. Monkhouse, *British Contemporary Artists* (1899).
(D. L. Fr.)

ALMEIDA, FRANCISCO DE (c. 1450–1510), the first viceroy of Portuguese India, was born in Lisbon about the middle of the 15th century. In March 1505 Manuel I appointed him viceroy of the newly conquered territory in India, and he set sail from Lisbon in command of a large and powerful fleet. In July he arrived at Quiloa (Kilwa) which he took almost without a struggle. Mombasa was destroyed and its great treasures went to strengthen Almeida's resources. At the island of Angediva, near Goa, and at Cananor he built forts and adopted measures to secure

Portuguese supremacy. Upon his arrival in India he took up residence in Cochin, where a Portuguese fort had been built by Affonso de Albuquerque in 1503.

The most important events of Almeida's brief but vigorous administration were the conclusion of a commercial treaty with Malacca and the discoveries made by his son Lourenço who acted as his lieutenant. The latter was probably the first Portuguese to visit Ceylon, where he established a settlement, and Fernão Soares, captain of a squadron of his fleet, appears to have been the first European to sight Madagascar. In 1508 Lourenço was killed at Chaul in a naval engagement with the Egyptians, who at this time attempted to dispute Portuguese supremacy in the Indian ocean. Affonso de Albuquerque (q.v.) then arrived in Cochin and presented a commission empowering him to supersede Almeida in the government. Almeida refused to recognize Albuquerque's commission and put him in prison.

Almeida then avenged Lourenço's death on the Arabs and their Egyptian allies. Sailing along the coast, he pillaged and burned various ports, including Goa and Chaul, and finally he encountered the enemy's combined fleet off Diu in Feb. 1509 and destroyed it completely. On his return to Cochin, he held out for a few months against Albuquerque's claims, but in Nov. 1509 he was compelled to yield. He sailed for Europe on Dec. 1 with an escort of three vessels. On the voyage he called at Table bay, then known as Saldanha bay, for water, and there he was killed (March 1, 1510) in an attack upon the Hottentots, during which he showed great personal courage. In this fight, which took place on the site of Cape Town, 65 Portuguese were killed including 12 captains. Almeida's body was recovered on the following day and buried on the spot where he fell.

See João de Barros, *Decadas da Asia*, ii (1553); Franz Hümmerich, *Die erste deutsche Handelsfahrt nach Indien, 1505–06*, Historische Bibliothek, Bd. 49 (1922).　　(R. A. Sn.)

ALMEIDA, JOSÉ VALENTIM FIALHO DE (1857–1911), Portuguese short story writer and pamphleteer, was born on May 7, 1857, at Vila-de-Frades, Alentejo. After leaving the primary school, and not without financial sacrifices on the part of his parents, he went to Lisbon to take a course in pharmacy. Soon captivated by the literary and artistic life of Lisbon, he remained there even after the death of his father; and, intent on becoming a doctor, he registered as a student in the Escola Médico-Cirúrgica in 1878, finishing the course in 1885. He supported himself in Lisbon with difficulty, by contributing to newspapers and magazines. Meanwhile, in 1881 he published his *Contos* and in the following year, *A cidade do vício*, which established him as one of the most forceful of Portuguese storytellers, despite the unevenness noted by critics. Almeida's efforts to achieve independence quickly wearied him, and, not meeting with any official patronage, perhaps because of his undisciplined and bohemian temperament, he gave vent to his rancour in a publication called *Os gatos* ("The Cats," 1889–94). Its pages included some great literature—*e.g.*, "O entêrro de D. Luís" (on the burial of the king Don Luís); "O violinista Sérgio" (on the violinist Sérgio); "Tragédia de um homem de génio obscuro" (the tragedy of an unknown genius); "Descrição de uma manhã no Tejo" (description of a morning in the Tejo)—but there were many vehement attacks as well, especially on the political institutions of the country and on the persons of the royal family, including the king.

These attacks, which greatly contributed to the downfall of the monarchy, finally made him unacceptable in official circles and caused him, in 1893, to return to the Alentejo where he married a rich heiress who died shortly afterward. Almeida was left master of an important farmstead and devoted the greater part of his time to its administration, seldom going to Lisbon and only at long intervals writing for newspapers and magazines. In 1907 he accepted the dictatorship of João Franco and after the assassination of the king and the heir apparent he severely criticized the Republican party, thus making himself unacceptable to the republic which was formed in 1910. He died at Vila-de-Frades on March 4, 1911.

As well as the works already mentioned, Almeida wrote *Pasquinadas* (1890), *Lisboa galante* (1890), *Vida irónica* (1892), *O país*

das uvas (1893) and *A esquina* (1903). Many of his articles were collected posthumously in such volumes as *Barbear, Pentear* (1911); *Saibam quantos* (1912); *Figuras de destaque* (1924); and *Vida errante* (1925).

The dramatic, poetic and fantastic aspects of Almeida's talent as a storyteller are exemplified in "A Ruiva" (*Contos*), "Madona do Campo Santo" (*A cidade do vício*), "O sineiro de Santa-Agata" (*Aves migradoras*) and "Ceifeiros" (*À esquina*). His liking for themes of social pathology is seen in "O roubo" (*A cidade do vício*) and "Três cadáveres" ·(*O país das uvas*). His language suffers from excessive subordination to French influence and to the stylistic niceties of French realism introduced into Portugal by Eça de Queirós; and his independence of linguistic tradition is confirmed by his capacity to create new words, unequalled by any other 19th-century Portuguese writer.

See Alvaro J. da Costa Pimpão, *Fialho, Introdução ao estudo da sua estética* (1945).　　(A. J. da C. P.)

ALMEIDA GARRETT, JOAO BAPTISTA DA SILVA LEITÃO, Visconde de: *see* Garrett, João Baptista da Silva Leitão de Almeida.

ALMELO, a town in Overijssel province, Neth., lies at the junction of the Overijssel canal and the branch of the Twente canal, 9 mi. N.W. of Hengelo. Pop. (1964 est.) 54,603 (mun.). Among the chief buildings are the 17th-century Dutch Reformed church; the 16th-century town hall, now a tourist office; and the Weigh house, an art gallery. Almelo is on the main railway from Amsterdam, Rotterdam and The Hague to the German border via Deventer. The town shared in the rapid development of the Twente district and has many modern buildings. Its chief manufactures are cotton and metal.

The lordship of Almelo belonged to the lords of Heeckeren, who acquired the barony of Rechteren by marriage in 1350 and the countship of Limpurg in 1711. A branch of the family still holds the seat.　　(H. F. He.)

ALMERÍA, a city and seaport of southern Spain, capital of the province of the same name and in the region of Andalusia, lies 103 mi. (165 km.) S.E. of Granada by road (via Guadix). Pop. (1960) 86,808 (mun.). Facing south over the gulf of Almería below steep mountains, the town has an architecture and a dazzling brightness which gives it a Moroccan rather than a European appearance. The streets of the shopping centre are wide and tree lined, with gardened squares. The principal thoroughfares are the Paseo del Generalísimo Franco and the Calle de Reina Regente leading to the park of José Antonio, which extends along the shore of the bay. Among the chief buildings are the Gothic cathedral (1524–43), built in the form of a fortress, the bishop's palace and seminary and the Alcazaba (773), built by the amir of Córdoba Abd-al-Rahman I. The dismantled Castillo de San Cristóbal overlooks the city and harbour, which is sheltered and equipped with modern facilities. The town has an archaeological museum, an institute of historical research, an art school and the Francisco Villaespesa cultural institute, which houses the municipal library. The mild and sunny climate, which makes bathing possible all the year round, gives Almería its claim to be the great city of the Costa del Sol. Almería is the terminus of a railway from Linares and Madrid and lies on the coastal highway, with a branch road to Granada. There is manufacture of chemicals, metalworking, fish canning and salting. The port is especially busy from August to December because of the export of oranges and grapes.

Known to the Romans as Urci or Portus Magnus, Almería was one of their chief harbours after 19 B.C. It received its name from the Moors, who held it, with one brief interlude, until its reconquest by Ferdinand V and Isabella in 1489.

Almería Province was formed in 1833. Pop. (1960) 360,777; area 3,388 sq.mi. This most easterly part of Upper Andalusia is crossed by sierras in which terminate successive zones of the Sistema Penibético. The Sierra de Gádor and Sierra Alhamilla form part of, or continue, the Alpujarra system (*see* Alpujarras, Las); the Sierra de los Filabres continues the Nevada core of the cordillera, while the enveloping crystalline of the Málaga zone is represented in the Sierra de las Estancias. The intervening valleys of the rivers Adra, Andarax-Almería and

Almanzora provide the only fertile land. The annual rainfall is below 8 in. in the east of the province, and the supply of water for irrigation is most irregular. Nevertheless, several important irrigation systems were inaugurated, resulting in a considerable increase in the area of land under cultivation. Fruitgrowing is the principal agricultural activity, and large quantities of the world famous oranges and white grapes are exported. Olive oil, cane and beet sugar, almonds and esparto are also produced. Livestock is raised, especially sheep. Almería has important mineral resources, including deposits of iron, lead and gold, and fine marble is quarried in the Sierra Nevada. There is a flourishing ceramics industry at Níjar. The mountainous character of the area prevents good communications, but road improvements have been made. The province is served by the railway from Almería to Madrid and by the coastal road westward toward Málaga and the highway from Murcia and the northeast. A road links Almería with Granada and there are some minor roads. The port is well served by shipping services, and there is an airport. The principal towns (1960 mun. pop.) are Almería, the capital (86,808), Adra (15,669), Berja (12,732), Cuevas de Vera (9,073), Huércal Overa (14,302), Níjar (11,559) and Garrucha (2,559). (J. S. CA.)

ALMOGÁVARES (from Arabic *al-Mughāwir*, "raider"), the historical name of a class of Spanish soldiers who came originally from the Pyrenees and were in later times recruited mainly in Navarre, Aragon and Catalonia. They were frontiersmen and professional foot soldiers who wore no armour, dressed in skins, were shod with brogues (*abarcas*) and carried the same arms as the Roman legionaries—two heavy javelins (Spanish *azagaya*, the Roman pilum), a short stabbing sword and a shield. In the war between the houses of Aragon and Anjou for the possession of Naples and Sicily after the Sicilian Vespers (1282), the Almogávares formed the most effective element of the Aragonese army. When the war ended in 1302 they went with their commander Roger de Flor (*q.v.*) to Constantinople as mercenaries, under the name of the Grand Catalan company, for the Byzantine emperor Andronicus II against the Turks. In 1304 they successfully relieved the Turkish siege of Philadelphia (modern Alasehir, Turk.), but their lust for plunder made them as dangerous to their Greek employers as to the Turks. The emperor recalled them to Europe after they had attacked the Byzantine town of Magnesia (modern Manisa, Turk.) and settled them at Gallipoli, but in April 1305 their leader Roger was assassinated at Adrianople and they embarked on a war of vengeance against the Greeks. They devastated Thrace for two years before marching into Macedonia. They pillaged the monasteries of Mt. Athos, but failed to take Thessalonica (1308) and made their way south into Thessaly. Engaged as mercenaries by the Frankish duke of Athens, Walter of Brienne, they turned against him and in March 1311 defeated and killed him in the battle of the Cephissus, by Lake Copais in Boeotia. Frankish rule in central Greece then gave place to the Catalan duchy of Athens, which in 1312 the Almogávares placed under the protection of the king of Sicily. Though Thebes, their first capital, fell to the Navarrese company in 1379, the duchy survived until 1388, when Athens was occupied by the Florentine lord of Corinth, Nerio Acciajuoli (see GREECE: *History*).

The name Almogávares died out in the 16th century, but it was revived for a short time in the civil wars of the reign of Ferdinand VII.

See Ramon de Muntaner, *Chronicle*, Eng. trans. by Lady Goodenough (1920); K. M. Setton, *Catalan Domination of Athens, 1311–1388* (1948). (D. M. N.)

ALMOHADS (AL-MUWAHHIDUN, "the Unitarians") was the name taken by a Berber confederation which ruled at Marrakech in Morocco from 1147 to 1269. It was based on the Masmuda tribe from the High Atlas mountains and had its origin in a movement for religious reform inspired by Mohammed ibn Tumart, a Berber from the Anti-Atlas. It succeeded in founding the greatest empire known in the Muslim west.

Ibn Tumart, who had studied in the Muslim east, formulated a doctrine which demanded puritanical moral reform and at the same time presented a very strict concept of the unity of God. To this orthodox teaching, however, he added certain Shi'ite elements,

proclaiming himself mahdi and "sinless *imam*," absolute master in both spiritual and temporal spheres. He taught without much success in Tunisia and Algeria, gathering only a few faithful disciples, one of whom was a Zenati from the Tlemçen region, Abd-al-Mumin. In Morocco, for preaching against the Almoravid sultans, Ibn Tumart was forced to flee to the Atlas mountains. There he quickly roused his fellow tribesmen, the Masmuda, and, with Tinmel as its centre, founded a strange Berber state in the form of a confederation of tribes united by their Islamic beliefs. Ibn Tumart, who had failed in an attack on Marrakech, died in 1129. He was succeeded by Abd-al-Mumin, who after 18 years of bitter fighting conquered the Maghreb from the Almoravids. Marrakech, which fell in 1147, was retained as capital by the Almohads, who made it more flourishing than ever before. In two campaigns (1151–52 and 1159) Abd-al-Mumin conquered North Africa as far east as Tripolitania and brought all the Berbers under one rule. With the title of caliph, he brought Berber Islam to its zenith. Though he defeated a coalition of Arab tribes at Setif in 1152, these tribes were later to prove themselves the dynasty's worst enemies. Abd-al-Mumin had to intervene in Spain where the Andalusian amirs had been independent since the fall of the Almoravids and the Christians were gaining ground, but it was his son Abu Yaqub Yusuf (1163–84) who succeeded in conquering the territories of Spanish Islam.

The Almohad empire kept its original tribal hierarchy as a political and social framework, the founders and their descendants forming a ruling aristocracy, but a Spanish form of central government was superimposed on this Berber organization. Abd-al-Mumin soon forgot the puritanical outlook of Tinmel. Like the Almoravids, he had costly monuments built by Andalusian artists, and the ornamentation of some of his mosques was of a truly classical elegance. His successors continued his patronage of the arts in all their domains.

Under the second and third caliphs the Almohad empire remained powerful, although throughout the reign of Abu Yusuf Yaqub al-Mansur (1184–99) serious Arab rebellions devastated the eastern provinces. In Spain the Christian threat remained despite Al-Mansur's brilliant victory at Alarcos (1196). The fourth caliph, however, Mohammed al-Nasir (1199–1213), suffered a shattering defeat by a Christian coalition at Las Navas de Tolosa (1212). Thereafter the fortunes of the Almohad dynasty declined, and their empire gradually broke up. The Hafsids seized power at Tunis (1236), the Abd-al-Wadids at Tlemçen (1239) and the Marinids, a Zenati dynasty, at Marrakech (1269).

The movement for religious reform did not survive. The Almohad kings did not restrain the great mystical movement which was revolutionizing the outlook of western Islam, and they protected the great philosophers of their time, Ibn Tufail and Averroës (*qq.v.*). In all their territories they were, like the Almoravids, the devoted servants of Spanish-Moorish civilization. *See also* ISLAM.

BIBLIOGRAPHY.—E. Fagnan, *Histoire des Almohades d'Abd el-Wah'id Merrakechi* (1895); I. Goldziher, *Mohammed ibn Toumert* (1903); Al-Umari, *Masalik al-Absar*, vol. i, with French trans. by M. Gaudefroy-Demombynes (1927); E. Lévi-Provençal, *Documents inédits d'histoire almohade* (1928); H. Basset and H. Terrasse, *Forteresses et sanctuaires Almohades* (1932); H. Terrasse, *Histoire du Maroc*, vol. i (1949).
(H. L. E. T.)

ALMON, JOHN (1737–1805), English parliamentary reporter and political writer, who was keenly involved in the 18th-century struggle between press and parliament. He was born in Liverpool, Dec. 17, 1737. When he arrived in London (*c.* 1758), freedom of expression in political matters was in hazard. He became known for his *A Review of Mr. Pitt's Administration* (1761) and other pamphlets. He was a friend of John Wilkes (*q.v.*) and was himself one of the most industrious writers in the Whig cause. In 1763 he opened a bookseller's shop in Piccadilly, which became a centre for the dissemination of political publications. In 1765 he was unsuccessfully prosecuted for publishing *Juries and Libels* but in 1770 was fined for reprinting Junius's letter to George II in *The London Museum*. The result was the bitter letter of Junius to Lord Mansfield (see JUNIUS). The following year, believing that the country had the right to know what was going on in parliament, he used his notes on proceedings in the commons in his paper the *London Evening Post.* Other papers followed this example and the failure of the action by the commons against eight newspapers marks the beginning of the tacit acknowledgment of the right to publish parliamentary proceedings. In Nov. 1774 he began publishing *The Parliamentary Register,* a monthly record of proceedings, which continued until July 1813. He had meanwhile become a marked man and in 1773 John Miller, the publisher of the *London Evening Post,* had been fined the crippling sum of £2,000 for publishing his article accusing the notorious earl of Sandwich of selling an office of trust. At one point Almon was imprisoned for libel and at another was forced to leave the country. It is not surprising that he once wrote that "A man had better make his son a tinker than a printer or a bookseller. The laws of tin he can understand, but the law of libel is unwritten, uncertain, and undefinable. It is one thing to-day and another to-morrow. No man can tell what it is." His publications include *Memoirs of John Almon, Bookseller in Piccadilly* (1790), *Anecdotes of William Pitt . . .* (1792), *Biographical, Literary and Political Anecdotes . . .* (1797), *The Correspondence of John Wilkes,* vol. iii (1805) and an edition of *The Letters of Junius . . .* (1806), wrongly identifying their author as Hugh Boyd. He died at Boxmoor, Hertfordshire, Dec. 12, 1805.   (J. H. Ja.)

ALMOND, the tree, nut or seed of *Prunus amygdalus,* an important food-producing species appearing to be native to southwestern Asia. The nuts are of two distinct types, sweet and bitter. The sweet are the well-known edible almonds of the world's market. The kernels of the bitter almonds are as inedible as peach kernels. They contain about 50% of a fixed oil, which occurs also in the sweet almond, together with a ferment emulsin, which in the presence of water acts on the glucoside amygdalin, yielding (1) glucose, (2) prussic (hydrocyanic) acid and (3) the essential oil of bitter almond, benzaldehyde (*q.v.*). When freed from prussic acid, the oil of bitter almonds is used in the manufacture of flavouring extracts. The sweet almond is cultivated extensively in certain favoured regions between 28° and 48° N. and between 20° and 40° S. Sweet almonds are eaten as nuts, or are used in confectionary or as a source of almond oil or almond meal. Leading exporting countries of shelled almonds during the late 1950s were Italy (half the production from Sicily), Spain, the United States, Iran, Portugal and Morocco.

The almond tree greatly resembles the related peach (*q.v.*), with which it occasionally hybridizes. While dormant, it is nearly as hardy as the peach, but ordinarily flowers much earlier, from late January to early April north of the equator. This causes crops of nuts to be uncertain wherever frosts are likely to occur during flowering. Sweet almonds mature only occasionally in climates like that of southern England. Ridenhower and other hard-shelled varieties which are self-fertile and otherwise indicate peach hybrid ancestry in their foliage, nut shell grooves and poor kernel flavour, have matured fairly regularly in such areas as Illinois and Pennsylvania, but are of no commercial promise.

The almond tree grows somewhat larger than the peach and lives longer. It is strikingly beautiful when in flower. The growing fruit resembles the peach until it approaches maturity, but its outer flesh then does not enlarge and become sweet and edible as in the peach. In ripening, the leathery outer covering, called the hull, splits open along the suture line, curls outward and discharges the nut.

The old-world almond industry was characterized by small plantings; trees interplanted with other crops; great variability in age, condition and bearing capacity of individual trees; and hand labour, often with crude implements. To a great extent production was primarily for food to be used by the family, and exports represented small surpluses from many small plantings. Modern Italian and Spanish growers pay more attention than they once did to the asexual propagation of improved varieties. But sales are by type rather than by variety in the horticultural sense of a clone. Thus two of the best-known type names are Jordan and Valencia from Spain. Neither is a true variety, as each includes many clones producing nuts similar in appearance and general character. The kernels of both are excellent for certain

(LEFT) BY COURTESY OF CALIFORNIA ALMOND GROWERS' EXCHANGE, (RIGHT) J. HORACE MC-FARLAND CO.

ALMOND (PRUNUS AMYGDALUS); FLOWERS AND FRUIT

purposes, particularly for making glacé almonds. However, the shells of both types are hard, the trees are light bearers, and neither has been found profitable to grow elsewhere.

Almond growing in the United States is confined almost wholly to California, where interior valleys and hillsides are protected from cold Pacific air movement by mountains near the coast. Production is mainly from orchards, often several hundred acres in extent. The trees are of similar age throughout an orchard, and of carefully selected varieties of California origin. As cross-pollination is required, a few special pollinizing varieties are systematically placed in all plantings, and colonies of bees are placed in strategic positions while the trees are in flower. Among leading varieties are Drake, I. X. L., Ne Plus Ultra, Nonpareil, Peerless and Texas. Newer varieties with better combinations of late flowering and high kernel quality, obtained through controlled breeding, were introduced in the early 1960s.

Orchard heating and other protective measures are frequently employed when subfreezing temperatures appear imminent during still nights when California almonds are flowering. By use of such measures it is often possible to save the major portion of a crop which otherwise would be lost during one or more nights of frost. Special wind machines and sometimes helicopters are used to drive cold air from low levels and allow it to be replaced with warmer air from slightly higher levels. Irrigation water, either flooded or applied by sprinkler to the tree tops, also is frequently useful in preventing much freeze damage to flowers or small almond fruits, unless temperatures drop to excessively low levels. The California Almond Growers exchange maintains standards of size, appearance and general quality.   (J. C. Mc D.)

ALMONER, originally an officer charged with the distribution of alms, primarily for a religious house. Almoners attached to the French court appear early, but the title of grand almoner of France first appears in 1486. The office, which acquired great importance through its control of preferments, was suppressed in 1790, revived by Napoleon I and again by Napoleon III, but was abolished in 1870. In England the offices of hereditary grand almoner (a sinecure held by the marquess of Exeter) and lord high almoner still exist. The latter, usually a bishop or other prelate, distributes the royal alms of silver pennies on Maundy Thursday (*q.v.*).

In modern times the word is used in Britain for a professionally trained social worker, usually a woman, qualified to work in a medical setting (the corresponding term in the United States is medical social worker). The almoner, co-operating with the doctor, helps the patient and his family to make constructive use of medical care. To do this she makes an appraisal of the social and other problems of a patient's illness, establishes a firm and trusting relationship with him and where indicated helps to make and carry through plans for the future. Almoners are employed by most hospitals and an increasing number of public health departments.

ALMORA is a town and district in Uttar Pradesh, India. The town lies about 170 mi. N.E. of Delhi on a ridge of the Himalayas,

5,494 ft. above sea level. Pop. (1961) 16,004; cantonment 598. There are road connections with Delhi via Moradabad. It has a degree-granting college affiliated to Agra university, named after Sir Henry Ramsay, and several schools.

Almora was captured in 1790 by the Gurkhas, who constructed a fort on the eastern extremity of the ridge. Another citadel, Ft. Moira, is situated 2 mi. away at the other end of the ridge. Almora is also celebrated as the scene of the British victory which terminated the war with Nepal in 1815.

ALMORA DISTRICT was constituted in 1891, together with Nainital, by a redistribution of the two former districts of Kumaon and the Tarai. Bordering Tibet on the north and Nepal on the east, it lies almost entirely within the Himalaya mountains and about one-third of it lies above the snow line. In the northern parts elevations reach to about 20,000 ft. and peaks of the Nandakot and Panchachuli group are noteworthy. The upper waters of the Ganges and the Kali, which flows along its eastern boundary, drain the slopes, which abound in oak, deodar and pine.

With an area of 2,713 sq.mi., it had a population of 633,407 in 1961. The only other town of any size is Ranikhet (pop. [1961] 10,600), 29 mi. W. of Almora. Because of its rugged topography, only about 15% of the area is cultivated. Rice, wheat and small millet (raggee) are the main cereals and tea is grown in small quantities. Magnetite deposits are found at Jakhera and large deposits of copper ore also occur. (S. S. BH.)

ALMORAVIDS (AL-MURABITUN, "the people of the ribat"), rulers of northwestern Africa and Muslim Spain in the 11th and 12th centuries, were a confederation of Saharan Berbers—Lamtuna, Goddala, Massufa—belonging to the Veiled Sanhaja, closely akin in their way of life to the modern Tuareg. They acquired about A.D. 1040 a new cohesion and strength when their leader Yahya ibn Ibrahim, returning from the pilgrimage to Mecca, brought back with him a Moroccan Berber scholar, Abdullah ibn Yasin, to improve their rather sketchy knowledge of Islamic doctrine. Onto this movement for religious reform, which had started in a Senegalese hermitage (ribat), a great military enterprise was grafted, and the Veiled Sanhaja under their amir Abu Bakr were thrown into the conquest of Morocco.

Abu Bakr was later replaced by his cousin Yusuf ibn Tashfin, amir from 1062 to 1106. He founded Marrakesh, established the Almoravid movement in Morocco and continued the great enterprise.

The conquest of Morocco and western Algeria (1063–82) required strenuous efforts. Algiers was included in the Almoravids' African empire, but they halted before the kingdoms of the Sanhajan Zeirids and Hammadids who were of the same people as the Veiled Sanhaja. Ibn Tashfin did not assume the caliph's title *amir al-muminin* ("commander of the faithful") but that of *amir al-muslimin* ("commander of the Muslims") and paid homage to the Abbasid caliph in Baghdad.

In Spain, meanwhile, the provincial rulers who, at the beginning of the 11th century, had divided among themselves the territories of the old caliphate of Córdoba were retreating before the Christians. When Toledo was retaken by Alfonso VI of Castile and León in 1085, Ibn Tashfin was called in to help. At the battle of Zallaka or Salaca (Sacralias, north of Badajoz) in 1086 he halted a dangerous advance by the Castilians. Having established his position, he later extended his rule over the whole of Muslim Spain except the kingdom of Valencia, which retained its independence under Rodrigo Díaz (the Cid; *q.v.*) for some time.

A new situation thus developed. Spain and northwestern Africa (the Maghreb) became parts of the same empire, and with the help of the Almoravids the civilization of Andalusia took root in African towns. In the reign of Ibn Tashfin's successor, Ali ibn Yusuf (1106–42), the union between Spain and Africa was consolidated. The administrative machinery of the Almoravids was Spanish in pattern; writers and artists crossed the straits; and the great monuments raised by Ibn Yusuf in the Maghreb were triumphs of pure Andalusian art with all its richness and subtle beauty.

But the Almoravids, despite the courage of their leaders and their astonishing adaptability, suffered from one great weakness:

they were only a Berber clan at the head of a Spanish-African empire in which they were always a foreign minority. They tried to hold Spain with Berber troops and Maghreb with a strong Christian guard; but with the fall of Saragossa in 1118 the tide of Christian reconquest started to advance and in 1125 the rebellion of the Almohads (*q.v.*) broke out in the Atlas mountains. After 22 years of fighting the Almohads were victorious; Marrakesh fell in 1147, and thereafter Almoravid leaders survived only for a time in Spain and the Balearics.

The achievements of the Almoravids, though incomplete, were of considerable importance. Their reign marked the political zenith of one of the great Berber clans, the Sanhaja. Moroccan territories were for the first time united under a single ruler and, although in matters of religion they followed the sterile Malikite school, the Almoravids were, especially in Africa, the devoted and efficient servants of Spanish-Moorish civilization.

See also ISLAM.

BIBLIOGRAPHY.—W. M. de Slane, *Histoire des Berbères,* French trans. from Ibn Khaldun's history, 2nd ed., 3 vol. (1925–34); R. Dozy, *Histoire des Musulmans d'Espagne,* 2nd ed. (1932); E. Lévi-Provençal, *Islam d'occident* (1948); H. Terrasse, *Histoire du Maroc,* vol. i (1949) and "Les Conséquences d'une invasion berbère: le rôle des Almoravides dans l'histoire de l'Occident," *Mélanges L. Halphen* (1951).
(H. L. E. T.)

ALMQVIST, CARL JONAS LOVE (1793–1866), Swedish writer, an interesting representative of mid-19th-century romanticism, was born at Stockholm on Nov. 28, 1793. After studying at Uppsala university he entered the department of ecclesiastical affairs in Stockholm. In 1823 he gave up his position and went to western Sweden to lead with a group of friends an idealized peasant existence. Two years later he returned to Stockholm and from 1829 to 1841 he was rector of an experimental secondary school. In 1851 he fled to the U.S. after being accused of fraud and attempted murder. He returned to Europe in 1865 and died at Bremen, Ger., on Sept. 26, 1866.

Almqvist was little known until the mid-1830s when he began to publish a stream of works in prose and verse. Most of these—novels, short stories, poems and verse dramas—were included in a series called *Törnrosens bok* ("The Book of the Briar Rose," 13 vol., 1832–40; vol. 14, 1851; 2nd series, 1839–50). Particularly important were *Amorina* (written *c.* 1821; pub. 1839) and *Drottningens juvelsmycke* ("The Queen's Diamond Ornament," 1834), a historical novel whose heroine, the mysterious, hermaphroditic Tintomara, is Almqvist's most fascinating character and a central symbol in his creative writings. *Det går an* ("It will do," 1839; Eng. trans., *Sara Videbeck,* 1919) is a brilliant, realistic story pleading for the emancipation of love and marriage. Almqvist was also a musician and set some of his short lyrics to music.

In both his life and his writings Almqvist showed an astonishing versatility. His vast literary output is a strange mixture of bizarre romanticism and bold realism. He attacked conventional matrimony, satirized the beliefs of the Lutheran Church (although he took orders in 1837) and as a radical journalist and in many of his creative writings fought for moral and social reform. But there were in his nature strong tendencies toward egocentric indifference and separatism, and the core of his personality remained dominated by Christian mysticism and Swedenborgian other-worldliness. Although uneven, his work contains brilliant passages and greatly influenced the development of Swedish literature.

An unfinished edition of his collected writings was published in 21 volumes (1920–38).

BIBLIOGRAPHY.—The literature on Almqvist is extensive. A standard modern work is Henry Olsson, *Carl Jonas Love Almqvist till 1836* (1937). *See also* Olsson's chapter on Almqvist in *Ny illustrerad svensk litteraturhistoria,* part 3, *Romantiken. Liberalismen* (1956), with a bibliographical survey. (G. SDT.)

ALMUCANTAR (also written ALMACANTAR), an astronomical term for a small circle of the celestial sphere parallel to the horizon; when two stars are in the same almucantar, they have the same altitude. The term also refers to instruments of a pattern invented by S. C. Chandler to determine the latitude or the time by observing the times of transit of stars across a fixed almucantar.

ALMUCE (Amice or Amess), a hooded cape of fur, or fur lined, worn as a choir vestment; not to be confused with the amice worn by the priest when celebrating the Eucharist. It is known to have been worn as early as the 12th century, and by the 16th it had become definitely established as the distinctive choir vestment of canons, often being carried over the left arm as a symbol of office. *See* Vestments, Ecclesiastical.

ALNAGE or Aulnage, a term describing the system for standardizing the size and quality of woolen cloth maintained by the English government for about 600 years. The word also denoted the fee charged by officials who measured cloth. This early state regulation of industry was designed, as a commission of 1622 put it, to prevent "the false and deceitful making, dyeing and dressing of our cloth and stuffs, which disgraceth it in foreign parts." It also protected English buyers from like deceit by foreign manufacturers whose cloth was sold in England.

The assize of cloth, first promulgated by Richard I in 1197, prescribed statutory dimensions for all salable cloth. It was reaffirmed in Magna Carta and by 1280 was enforced by special officers called aulnagers, who examined cloth for quality and dimensions, sealing what was sound and confiscating what was defective. The effort to enforce standard dimensions broke down during the 14th century through the increasing variety in overseas demand, but the drive for standard qualities continued. Aulnagers, however, often sealed cloth without scrutiny, only asking their fees.

An act of 1552 provided searchers to assist the aulnagers in every borough, a device extended to the counties by statutes of 1598 and 1601. In 1594 the finer fabrics made in England by refugees from the Spanish Netherlands were brought within the aulnage. By 1699, when it was abolished, the system was in evident decay. However, local efforts to regulate quality through searchers persisted in the Yorkshire woolen industry until 1765.

(Gy. T.)

ALNWICK, a market town in Northumberland, Eng., lies 34 mi. N. of Newcastle by road. Pop. (1961) 7,482. Area 7.5 sq.mi. It is on the south bank of the river Aln, in undulating wooded country between the Cheviots and the sea. The town is dominated by the castle which, although extensively restored, occupies the same area as when founded in the 11th century; the shell-keep of Eustace Fitz-John (*c.* 1157) still forming its central building. In 1309 it was bought and enlarged by the Percy family and acquired great strategic importance during the Border wars. It has remained the principal seat of the earls and dukes of Northumberland (*q.v.*) ever since. After 1750 the first duke transformed it into a palace, Gothic outside and Italianate within, while the gardens were laid out by Lancelot "Capability" Brown (1765). The castle houses a museum and is open to visitors during the summer.

Ruins remain of St. Leonard's hospital (*c.* 1200) and, in Hulne park, of the Gatehouse of Alnwick abbey (1147) and parts of the Carmelite Hulne priory (1240). The church of St. Michael was rebuilt in Perpendicular Gothic about 1464, and from the 15th-century parts of the town wall (notably the Hotspur tower), the old grammar school and a chantry chapel still survive.

(Mi. G. C.)

ALOADAE (Aloidae), Otus and Ephialtes, in ancient Greek legend, the twin sons of Aloeus or Poseidon, celebrated for their extraordinary stature and strength. According to the *Odyssey*, they made war upon the Olympian gods and endeavoured to pile Pelion upon Ossa in order to storm heaven itself, but Apollo destroyed them before they reached manhood. In the *Iliad* Ares is imprisoned by them but delivered by Hermes. They sought Artemis and Hera in marriage, whereupon Artemis appeared between them in the shape of a stag, which they endeavoured to kill, but slew each other.

ALOE, a genus of plants belonging to the family Liliaceae, with about 180 species growing in the dry parts of Africa, especially Cape Colony, and in the mountains of tropical Africa.

The plants are apparently stemless, bearing a rosette of large, thick, fleshy leaves, or have a shorter or longer (sometimes branched) stem, along which, or toward the end of which and its branches, the generally fleshy leaves are borne. They are

WILLIS PETERSON

ALOE VERA

much cultivated in the warm parts of the world as ornamental plants, especially in public buildings and gardens, for their stiff, rugged habit. The leaves are generally lance-shaped with a sharp apex and a spiny margin, but vary in colour from gray to bright green, and are sometimes striped or mottled. The rather small tubular yellow or red flowers are borne on simple or branched leafless stems and are generally densely clustered.

The juice of the leaves of certain species yields a medical substance called aloes. In some cases, as in *Aloe venenosa,* the juice is poisonous. The American aloe, *Agave americana* (see Agave), belongs to a different family, viz., Amaryllidaceae.

Aloes is used medicinally as a purgative and produced from various species of aloe, such as *A. vera, A. barbadensis, succotrina, chinensis,* and *perryi.* Several kinds of aloes are distinguished in commerce—Barbadoes, Socotrine, hepatic, Indian and Cape aloes. The first two are those commonly used for medicinal purposes. When the leaves are cut the juice flows out and is collected and evaporated. From the juice active principles termed aloins are extracted by water.

The lign-aloes is quite different from the medicinal aloes. The word is used in the Bible (Num. xxiv, 6), but as the trees usually supposed to be meant by this word are not native in Syria, it has been suggested that the Septuagint reading in which the word does not occur is to be preferred. Lign-aloe is a corruption of the Lat. *lignum-aloe,* a wood, not a resin. Dioscorides refers to it as *agallochon,* a wood brought from Arabia or India, which was odoriferous but with an astringent and bitter taste. This may be *Aquilaria Agallocha,* a native of east India and China, which supplies the so-called eaglewood or aloeswood, which contains much resin and oil.

ALONSO, AMADO (1896–1952), Spanish philologist who applied to his native language several harmoniously fused methods of analysis, was born in Lerín, on Sept. 13, 1896. Trained as a linguist in Madrid and Hamburg and variously associated with Madrid's Centro de Estudios Históricos, Alonso rose to fame as professor at the University of Buenos Aires and director of its Instituto de Filología (1927–46). Later he taught at Harvard university. Alonso was a brilliant lecturer, dynamic teacher, demanding editor (*Revista de filología hispánica,* 1939–46) and imaginative organizer. Noteworthy among his writings are the miscellaneous *Estudios lingüísticos* (1951–53), the essays included in vol. i of *Biblioteca de dialectología hispanoamericana* (7 vol., 1930–49), the torso of an inquiry into early modern Spanish pronunciation (1955–) and monographs on the historical novel (1942) and on P. Neruda's hermetic poetry (2d ed., 1955). Alonso died at Arlington, Mass., on May 26, 1952. (Y. M.)

ALOR ISLANDS: *see* Solor and Alor Islands.

ALPACA (*Lama pacos*), a fleece-bearing, cud-chewing mammal, one of four new world relatives of the camel. The alpaca and the llama (*q.v.*) are each distinct species probably saved from extinction through domestication by Indians in the lofty Andes. Two other *Lama* species (lamoids) exist more or less in the wild state, the vicuña and the guanaco (*qq.v.*). Alpacas are readily distinguished from llamas (*Lama glama*) by their smaller size (about three feet high at the shoulders) and rounded, rather than squarish, body. Also the alpaca usually appresses its tail close to the body, whereas the llama usually holds its curled tail somewhat erect. The shaggy hair varies in colour from the usual black or brown through lighter shades to pale yellow and occasionally white. Rarely are alpacas multicoloured, and blotched individuals with alpacoid characteristics are mostly hybrids resulting from crosses with llamas. Present distribution is restricted to southern Peru, adjacent Bolivia and northern Argentina. Alpacas are the most limited in range and the most specialized of the four lamoids, being adapted to marshy ground at altitudes from 14,000 to 16,000 ft. In adaptation to the reduced oxygen content of the air, red blood corpuscles are exceptionally numerous—20,000,000 per cubic millimeter, as against 6,000,000 to 8,000,000 per cubic millimeter in man at high altitudes. Alpacas are the most important of the lamoids for wool production. During the Inca civilization, alpaca and vicuña wools were reserved for the higher classes and royalty.

BY COURTESY OF NEW YORK ZOOLOGICAL SOCIETY

ALPACA (LAMA PACOS)

Two breeds, the common and the suri, were developed in pre-Columbian time. If the hair of the suri breed is allowed to grow, it reaches the ground, making the animal look like an overgrown poodle. Hybrids between alpaca and llama are common, but they do not breed true and in time revert to the parental types.

Although the alpaca has been crossed with the vicuña since Inca time to establish a hybrid (paco-vicuña) with the exquisite silky wool of the vicuña and the high wool production of the alpaca, success has never been achieved. After the first shearing, the fleece of the paco-vicuña loses its fine quality and the coarse hairs increase. Furthermore, succeeding generations revert to alpaca or vicuña types. To hybridize the alpaca and vicuña, a baby male vicuña is disguised with the skin of a baby alpaca and given to a lactating alpaca. Only in this way will the foster mother accept the vicuña, and only a vicuña reared by an alpaca will be accepted by a female alpaca as a mate.

When an alpaca reaches its third year, the oldest hairs begin to shed individually at various times, not all at once during a particular period of each year, as in sheep. From the age of two years onward, an alpaca is sheared every other year. Hair growth in two years is about 12 in. in the common breed and 24 in. in the suri. When maximum yield is achieved at five years of age, each shearing yields about 6 lb. of wool. Individuals are considered old at about seven years, though longevity is much longer, and they are killed for meat.

The wool has excellent qualities in being remarkably light in weight, strong, lustrous, high in insulation value and resistant to rain and snow. It is used in parkas, sleeping bags and fine coat linings.

Peru leads in production with an estimated 2,000,000 alpacas producing annually over 3,000 tons of wool, most of which is marketed in Arequipa, where it is sorted into seven grades by Indian women. The Peruvian government has established a breeding station to improve the quality of the wool and increase production.

Although the fleece of alpaca has been used in making clothing since the Inca civilization, it was considered unworkable material for textiles until Sir Titus Salt developed ingenious techniques to enable successful manufacture of alpaca cloth for European use. *See* also TYLOPOD. (H. K. B.)

ALP ARSLAN, MOHAMMED IBN DA'UD (c. 1030–1072), whose Turkish name Alp Arslan means "the lion hero,"

was the second sultan of the Great Seljuk line (*see* SELJUKS). He succeeded his father Da'ud Chaghri Beg as ruler of Khurasan *c.* 1060 and his uncle Togrul Beg as sultan in western Iran and Mesopotamia (1063), thus uniting under his rule the whole of the Seljuk empire except Kerman. Alp Arslan's fame rests mainly on his victories against the Byzantine empire. He invaded Armenia in 1064 (capturing Ani, the old capital) and Georgia in 1068. In 1071, while marching against Aleppo on his way to attack the Fatimids in Egypt, he was diverted by an attack of the Byzantine emperor Romanus IV Diogenes, who penetrated deep into Armenia. Alp Arslan was forced to turn back, and the armies met in the battle of Manzikert (*q.v.*) in Aug. 1071. The Byzantine army, deceived by the Turkish tactic of simulated flight, was to-

tally defeated and Romanus taken prisoner. As a result of the battle, the Byzantine army was rendered powerless and the Turkomans were enabled to effect a permanent settlement in Asia Minor, thus laying the foundations of modern Turkey.

Alp Arslan died in late Nov. 1072 at the hand of a prisoner captured during an expedition against the Qarakhanids of central Asia. Christian writers represent him as interested neither in administration, which he left in the hands of his great vizier, Nizam al-Mulk, nor in intellectual life; yet it was for him that an anonymous author wrote the *Maliknameh,* the sole source of information on the origins of the Seljuk dynasty.

BIBLIOGRAPHY.—W. Barthold, *Turkestan Down to the Mongol Invasion,* an Eng. trans. from the Russian made with the assistance of H. A. R. Gibb, "Gibb Memorial Series," new series no. 5, 2nd. ed. (1928); Paul Wittek, "Deux Chapitres de l'histoire des Turcs de Roum," *Byzantion,* vol. xi (1936); C. Cahen, "La Campagne de Mantzikert" and "La Première Pénétration turque en Asie Mineure," *Byzantion* vol. ix (1934) and vol. xviii (1948); G. Ostrogorsky, *History of the Byzantine State,* Eng. trans. by J. M. Hussey (1956). (CL. CA.)

ALPES-MARITIMES, a *département* in the extreme south-

east of France, formed in 1860 out of the county of Nice (till then a possession of the house of Savoy) with the addition of the districts of Grasse (formerly in the *département* of Var) and Menton (purchased from the prince of Monaco). A frontier strip (202 sq.mi.), ceded by Italy under the terms of the Franco-Italian peace treaty of 1947, was also acquired and extended the border northward along the crest of the Maritime Alps. It is bounded northeast by Italy, south by the Mediterranean sea and west by the *départements* of Var and Basses-Alpes. Pop. (1962) 618,265. Area 1,659 sq.mi. Alpes-Maritimes surrounds the rocky promontory of Monaco (*q.v.*) which, with Monte Carlo adjoining, forms an independent principality.

Most of the *département* consists of rugged limestone mountains, with peaks approaching 10,000 ft. inland. The mountains extend right to the coast in a succession of rocky headlands, such as Cap Ferrat and Cap d'Antibes. The former shelters the naval base of Villefranche (*q.v.*), and the ancient port of Nice (Gr. Nicea) also lies in the shelter of a limestone promontory. Most of the *département* lies within the basin of the Var river and its main tributaries, the Tinée and Vésubie, which often flow in deep gorges; there is little coastal lowland.

The coast itself, from Cannes in the west to the Italian frontier in the east, sheltered by the Alps and bathed in Mediterranean sunshine, has developed as a great tourist region, known as the Côte d'Azur or French Riviera. Along the coast is a succession of fashionable resorts, including Cannes, Antibes, Nice, Monte Carlo, Menton (*qq.v.*) and Juan-les-Pins (*see* also RIVIERA). Slightly inland is Grasse (*q.v.*), famous for its scent industry. Lavender cultivation, together with vineyards, olive groves and fruit orchards extend up the alpine valleys. Between the main urban areas the coastlands are dotted with innumerable villas and are served by good roads, including the Corniche system at three levels between Nice and the Italian frontier. They provide magnificent views of the coast and of ancient perched villages such as Èze and La Turbie.

The *département* is divided into the *arrondissements* of Nice and Grasse. It forms the bishopric of Nice, dating back to the 4th century. (AR. E. S.)

ALPHA AND OMEGA (A and Ω), the first and last letters

of the Greek alphabet used as the self-designation of God, denoting his eternity and infinitude, and of Christ. The New Testament references are Rev. i, 8; xxi, 6; and (of Christ) xxii, 13. The usage is based on passages such as Isa. xliv, 6 ("I am the first and I am the last") and Ps. xc, 2 ("from everlasting to everlasting thou art God"). In rabbinic literature the first and last letters of the Hebrew alphabet are similarly used. The word *Emeth* ("truth"), composed of the first, middle and last letters of the Hebrew alphabet, is the seal of God.

ALPHABET, strictly defined, indicates by written symbols a set of speech sounds. The alphabet was a Greek invention based upon North Semitic (proto-Canaanitish) writing which indicated only consonants, a procedure suitable enough for a Semitic language but not for an Indo-European one. The word itself is derived from the names (of Semitic origin) of the first two letters of the Greek alphabet, alpha and beta, and the definition is of quite a general character, as is easily seen in the case of the first letter of the English alphabet, which represents different sounds in the words "father," "man" and "take." Even when a letter represents a single sound, it does so roughly, taking no account of intonation, stress or pronunciation, which vary not only between speakers but also within the speech of an individual according to the position of the sound in a word or phrase and the nature of the phrase.

An alphabet is a highly developed, artificial form of writing. The connection between sound and character is conventional and not essential. This is not the case with all forms of writing. Pictographs, ideographs and hieroglyphs bear an essential relationship to what they represent. Such methods constitute an earlier stage of writing than syllabaries and alphabets.

Alphabetic writing is the most convenient and adaptable form of writing. It is learned in childhood with ease, which is not the case with the Chinese script, for instance. The alphabet may also be passed from one language to another without difficulty. It has changed surprisingly little in nearly 3,000 years, despite the introduction of printing and the typewriter. (The history of writing, from its earliest forms to the development of the alphabet, is discussed in WRITING AND PALAEOGRAPHY. Nonalphabetic forms of writing and communication are treated in CUNEIFORM; HIEROGLYPHS; LOGOGRAM AND SYLLABARY; and PICTOGRAPHY.)

Origin.—The oldest known Greek inscriptions of the 2nd millennium B.C., found in Greece near Pylos, at Mycenae, and elsewhere, and in Crete, are written in a syllabary (see MINOAN LINEAR SCRIPTS). They are some centuries older than Greek inscriptions written in the Greek alphabet, which is now thought to be derived from a Canaanitish variety of North Semitic script that came to the Greeks through Phoenician traders as intermediaries.

The story of the alphabet from the time it is first found employed in Greek inscriptions is not hard to trace. It is its pre-Greek history that is still disputed. The Greek names for its letters, alpha, beta, gamma, delta, etc., demonstrate its Semitic origin, for though the names may not in every case have a Semitic etymology, they correspond closely with the Semitic names (cf. the Hebrew aleph, beth, gimel, daleth). Two questions have remained unanswered. How did the Greeks obtain it from the Semites? And what was its pre-Semitic history?

In 1929 an epoch-making discovery of cuneiform texts of the 15th century B.C. was made at Ras Shamra (ancient Ugarit) on the Syrian coast opposite Cyprus. This cuneiform script seems to have been derived from the North Semitic by people who were accustomed to the use of clay and stylus, since it combines the idea of an alphabet for consonantal writing with the use of wedge-shaped elements arranged in simple combinations. Other important documents, discovered at Byblos (now Jebeil, Lebanon) in 1929, 1933 and following years, are written in a pseudohieroglyphic syllabary; its symbols bear some resemblance to Egyptian hieroglyphs and may be of the 22nd century B.C.

Until the second decade of the 20th century the earliest known examples of the Semitic alphabet were found in the Moabite stone (an inscription of Mesha, king of Moab, dating from the 9th century B.C.) and in a votive inscription to Baal-Lebanon discovered in Cyprus. Various theories have been current as to the origin of the Semitic alphabet, the earliest being the view of Lenormant, published by De Rougé in 1874, that Egypt was its starting place. Others attempted to connect it with Babylonian cuneiform, with the Cyprian syllabary or with the Minoan writing of Crete. This was the view of Sir Arthur Evans, who, in his *Scripta Minoa*, developed the theory that the alphabet was taken from Crete to Palestine by the Philistines and from them borrowed by the Phoenicians. The Egyptian view was revived in 1916 by Alan Gardiner in a paper dealing with certain inscriptions discovered in 1906 by Sir W. Flinders Petrie in the Sinai peninsula, which exhibit a stage of writing intermediate between Egyptian hieroglyphs and the Semitic alphabet. The script appears to be alphabetic, and the date of the inscriptions is not later than 1500 B.C. These inscriptions have also been dealt with by Hans Bauer, who saw in the script a prototype of the Semitic alphabets, independent of Egypt.

Advocates of this view appeal to the evidence of the four South Semitic alphabets. These are known as Sabaean, Lihyanic, Thamudenic and Safahitic. Inscriptions in these South Semitic alphabets were discovered in considerable numbers during the course of the 19th century. Those in the Sabaean alphabet came from the district of Yemen in South Arabia, the Lihyanic from El-Ola in the north of the Hejaz. The Thamudenic inscriptions are from northwestern Arabia, and the Safahitic inscriptions came from rocks in the district of Safah near Damascus. Most of the South Semitic inscriptions read from right to left but a few are written boustrophedon, i.e., from right to left and left to right in alternate lines. There are 29 letters in the Sabaean alphabet. The date of the earliest Sabaean inscriptions appears to be about the 6th century B.C., and most of those who have noticed them are agreed that this alphabet descends not from that of the Moabite stone but from an older source common to both. Gardiner saw this source in the alphabet of the Sinai inscriptions. Two or three of the signs, notably that for *beth* ⊏ in Sabaean, for *phe* ◊ in Sabaean and for *thau* ✝ in Thamudenic and Safahitic, resemble symbols of the Sinai script. But there are strong objections to the theory, which is now generally abandoned.

	SABAEAN	LIHYANIC	THAMUDENIC	SAFAHITIC	EARLY ETHIOPIC
'	⋔⋔	⋔⋔⋎	⋔⋔⋉⋊	⋊⋊⋉ΚΚ	⋔⋔
b	∏⋒	∏⋒	∏∏⋑⊏ ⊓ ○	)(⊂⊃⋒	∏⋒
g	⌐	⌐	◻◻◻⌐	∧∩○○◻	⌐⌐
d	⋈⋈	⋈⋈⋈⋈	✗⋎⋏⋎✗	⋏⋎⋏	⋈
d	⋈⋈	⋔⋔	⋔⋔⋔⋒	⋔⋔⋔	⋓⋔⋔
h	Ψ⋔ΨΥ	⋏⋌⋌⋌	ΥΥ⋌Υ⋌	Υ⋌⋌ⵏ	⋁⋁∪Υ
w	⊕∞	⊕⋄∇	⊕⊖⊕⊞	⊕⊖⊘⊖⊖	∇∇∞∞
z	⋈✗⋈✗	⋈⋈	Τ⋀⋀Τ	Τ⋀⋀Υ⋏	⋈⋈ⵂ
ḥ	⋏⋎	∧∧∧⋏	⋏϶⋒Ε⋎	∧⋎⋲⋒⋎	ⵀ
h	Ψ⋔⋎	⋏⋏⋏⋏	✗	✗ ✗	⋎⋎
t	⋛⋛⋛	⋇⋇⋇	⅃⋁⋏ (?)	∪⋏∩∪⋏	
ṭ	⊞	⊞	⧻⧻⧻⧻⋒	⊞⋏⋏⋏	⊓⊓
y	♀	♀ ♀♀	⅃♂⅃	⅃⋏⋏⋏	♀⋔Υ♀
k	⋒⋒⋒	⋒ ⋒ ⋎	⋔ ⋔⋔⋌	⋎⋎⋎⋎⋲	⋔⋔⋔⋔
l	⅃⋀	⅃⋀⋀⋀	⅃⋀⋀⊏⋲	⸀⸀⸀⸀⸀	∧
m	⊠⋎⋎	⋎⊙⊙⊙⋎⋎⋅	⋎⊡⋎⋎⋎	⊠⊙⊡∇⋎⋎	∇∇⊞⋎
n	⅃⋏⋏⋎	⋲⋲⋲⋲	⋎⋏⋅⋎⋅⋎⋎⋎	⋲⋲⋲⋅⋎⋎⋎	⋎⋎⋎
s	∏✗	∏⋎⋎∇⋎	⋎⋈⋅⊐	∧∨⋲⋎⋒	∏⋎
ġ	⋒⋒	⋎⋎∇	⋛⋎⋲	⋛⋛⋲	
ʿ	○○	○○	○⋅⋰	○⋅○⋅○⋀	○○∇
p	◊♦○	⋀∩∩	⋎⋎⋀Ε⋀	⋛⋛⋛	⋲⋌⊄⋌
ḍ	⊟		⧻⊠⊟	⊠⊟	
ṣ	⋛⋛⋛⋛⋒⋀	⋒⋒	⋛⋛⋎⋎⋎⋛	⋛⋛⋲⋌⋎⋎	⋀⋎⋒⋒
q	◊◊	◊◊	◊◊◊	⋛⋛⋛	◊◊⋎
r	)⋛⊂	))	)⋅⊂)(⋎⋐	⋛⋛⋛)⊂(	⋲⋲⋲)⋲⋲
š	⋛⋛⋛	⋛⋛⋛⋛	⋛⋛⋛⋛	⋛⋛	⋎⋎⋎⋎∪
t	⋛	✗ ✗	⋛⋛	⋛⋛⋐⋛⋛	
t	✗✗	✗	✗✝	✝✗	✝✗✝✗✝

FIG. 1.—SOUTH SEMITIC ALPHABETS

	HEBREW NAME OF LETTER	APPARENT MEANING	GREEK NAME	ETHIOPIC NAME	ARABIC NAME	CRETAN	SINAITIC	MOABITE	PALESTINIAN	ARAMAEAN (ZENJIRLI)	BYBLUS	N. SYRIA	CYPRUS
1	ĀLEPH (ALF)	OX	ALPHA	ALF (13)	ALIF (1)								
2	BĒTH (BĒT)	HOUSE	BĒTA	BĒT (9)	BĀ (2)								
3	GIMEL ‡	CAMEL	GAMMA	GAML (20)	JĪM (5)								
4	DĀLETH (DELT)	(FOLDING) DOOR	DELTA	DANT, DENT (19)	DĀL (8)								
5	HĒ	LATTICE WINDOW (?)	EI	HŌI (1)	HĀ (26)								
6	WĀW	HOOK, NAIL	△	WAWĒ (15)	WĀW (27)								
7	ZAYIN	WEAPON, OLIVE (?)	ZĒTA	ZAI (17)	ZĀ (11)								
8	ḤĒTH (ḤĒT)	FENCE, BARRIER (?)	(H) ĒTA	ḤAUT (3)	ḤA (6)								
9	ṬĒTH (ṬĒT)	A WINDING (??)	THĒTA	ṬAIT (21)	ṬĀ (9)								
10	YŌD	HAND	IŌTA	YAMAN (18)	YĀ (28)								
11	KAPH	BENT HAND	KAPPA	KĀF (14)	KĀF (22)								
12	LĀMED (LAMD)	OX-GOAD	LAMBDA	LAWE (2)	LĀM (23)								
13	MĒM	WATER	MU	MĀI (4)	MĪM (24)								
14	NŪN	FISH	NU	NAHĀS (12)	NŪN (25)								
15	SĀMEK (SAMK)	PROP (?)	XEI	SĀT (7)									
16	'AYIN	EYE	OU	'AIN (16)	'AIN (18)								
17	PĒ	MOUTH	PEI	ĀF (25)	FĀ (20)								
18	ṢĀDĒ	FISH-HOOK (?)	(see no. 7)	ṢADAI (23)	ṢĀD (14)								
19	ḲŌPH	EYE OF NEEDLE (?)	KOPPA	ḲĀF (8)	ḲĀF (21)								
20	RĒSH	HEAD	RHŌ	RE'ES (6)	RĀ (10)								
21	SHIN, SIN	TOOTH	SIGMA, SAN	SHAUT (5)	SHĪN (13) SĪN (12)								
22	TAW	MARK	TAU	TAWE (10)	TĀ (3)								
23					THĀ (4)								
24				KHARM (11)	KHĀ (7)								
25					DHĀL (9)								
26				ḌĀPPA (28)	ḌĀD (15)								
27					ẒĀ (17)								
28					GHAIN (19)								
29			U										
30			PHEI										
31			KHEI										
32			PSEI										
33			Ō										
	1	2	3	4	5	6	7	8	9	10	11	12	13

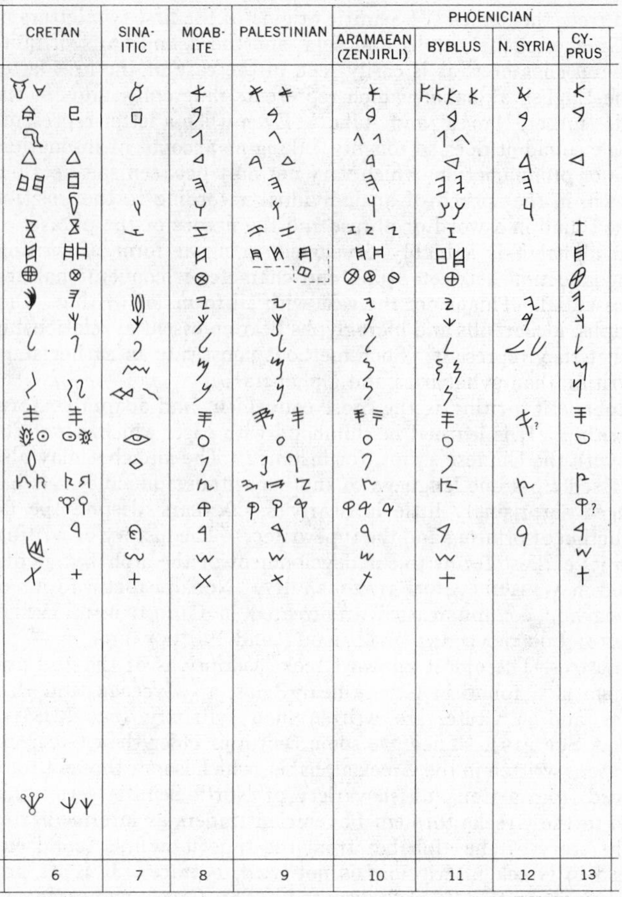

ADAPTED FROM TABLE OF ALPHABETS, "CAMBRIDGE ANCIENT HISTORY," VOL. III; CAMBRIDGE UNIVERSITY PRESS

FIG. 2.—COMPARATIVE TABLE OF ALPHABETS. THE FIGURES IN COLUMNS 4 AND 5 INDICATE THE ORDER OF THE LETTERS IN MODERN ETHIOPIC AND
△ VAU (DIGAMMA)

A different view of the origin of both the Phoenician and Greek alphabets was offered by Flinders Petrie. He argued that both these alphabets, together with those of Asia Minor, the South Semitic, Cyprian and certain Egyptian scripts, developed from a series of conventional marks or signs employed for commercial purposes throughout the Mediterranean area from earliest times. But he was practically alone in supposing that the early marks to which he referred had any certain significance, and his theory of the development of various local alphabets from such marks has not found general acceptance. Too many links are missing in the chain of proof. The fact that identical alphabetical symbols occur in widely distant regions of the Mediterranean area, which he stressed, is capable of other explanations.

The most important fact ignored by any theory that would derive the Greek and Phoenician alphabets independently from a source older than either is that the names of the letters, as far as they have a known etymology or meaning, are Semitic. The Semitic names are all words in the Semitic languages. The Greek names are meaningless in Greek. It has indeed been argued that the Greek names were the original ones, meaningless, and taken in the first instance simply from the sounds represented by the letters; and that the Phoenicians took over the alphabet together with the names from the Greeks and adapted the names by the process known as folk etymology. But the Sinai inscriptions, discussed above, have rendered this theory untenable. If they do not represent a link between the hieroglyphic system of Egypt and the Phoenician alphabet, they represent a prototype of the latter, appearing at a date and at a place that render any theory of borrowing from Greek sources highly improbable. It is reasonably certain that the Greeks derived their alphabet from Semitic sources, taking over the names with the letters. The names are not identical. The Greek names end with a vowel—alpha for *aleph,* beta for *beth,* etc. The vocalization has been explained merely as being more in agreement with Greek morphology, and this is a very satisfactory explanation.

The Greek Alphabet.—The two forms of the Greek alphabet, Chalcidic and Ionic, generally known as western and eastern, represent two different borrowings, but the theory of any direct borrowing from Phoenician sources may probably be ruled out. The tradition that this was so came from Herodotus, who referred only to Boeotia, and it is probable that the name *Phoenices* was a vague term for eastern foreigners. The Achaeans were a naval power settled in the eastern Aegean in the 15th century B.C. There is therefore no difficulty in concluding that they borrowed the alphabet from peoples with whom they were in close contact in western and southern Asia Minor at a considerably earlier date than has generally been supposed; or that, independent as Greek states were, there were separate borrowings and separate adaptations.

The inscriptions of the Bronze Age discovered in Palestine in the third decade of the 20th century have simplified the problem considerably even though there is still no complete agreement. These texts, conveniently described as being in an early Canaanitish script, are thought to provide a transition between Sinaitic and those North Semitic forms which include early "Phoenician" forms that the oldest Greek alphabet resembles so closely as to make it commonly asserted that the Greek alphabet is of Phoenician origin. All authorities accept the relationship as proved beyond question. But the Phoenician is only one variety of North Semitic (*i.e.* ultimately Canaanitish) writing and the Greek alphabet therefore must be regarded as of North Semitic origin, probable as it is that the Phoenicians were the intermediaries through whom the Greeks obtained their alphabet.

The North Semitic varieties of writing concerned are shown on the accompanying chart.

The chief adaptations made by the Greeks were the allocation of certain of the 22 Semitic letters to vowel sounds and the addition of certain letters. The oldest extant inscriptions written in the Greek alphabet are those found in 1896 on the island of Thera, which date from the 8th, possibly even the 9th, century

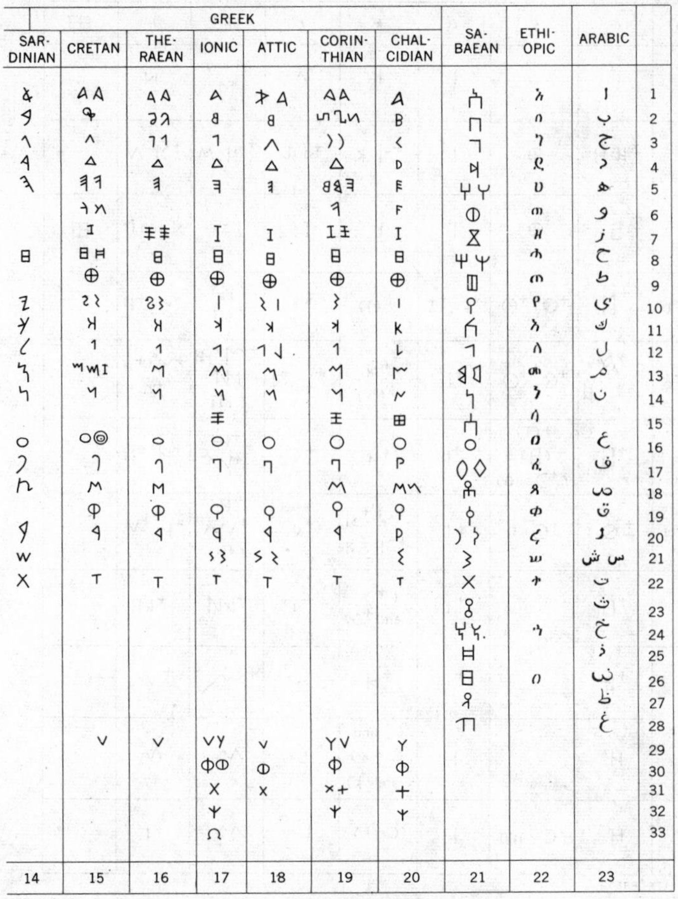

SAR-DINIAN	CRETAN	THE-RAEAN	IONIC	ATTIC	CORIN-THIAN	CHAL-CIDIAN	SA-BAEAN	ETHI-OPIC	ARABIC	
GREEK										

(Columns numbered 14–23 across the foot; line numbers 1–33 down the right side. The cells contain ancient Sardinian, Greek, Sabaean, Ethiopic and Arabic letter-forms.)

ARABIC ALPHABETS GIVEN IN COLUMNS 22 AND 23. ‡ (GAML, GIML);

more usually represented the short vowel alone. In addition to this, however, it was occasionally used throughout to represent the long close *ē* (the long *ē* represented by eta was open), which in Attic was written $\epsilon\iota$, since this diphthong had become *ē*. The Corinthian alphabet was peculiar in using (up to the 6th century and later in outlying regions) the sign **B** or **B** to represent *e*, the long close vowel being written **BS**. Sicyon used a symbol with the form **X**. Semitic *cheth* (Greek eta) was used, as has been seen, in the east generally speaking as a vowel, in the west as the rough breathing. In the Theran inscriptions it occurs in both capacities. The semivowel *i* (resembling the sound of English initial *y*) had disappeared from the Greek language in prehistoric times, degenerating into a rough breathing, so that Semitic *yod* was adapted in Greek to represent the vowel ι (iota). Koppa (**Q**) had disappeared in the eastern alphabets by the 5th century B.C., its place being usurped by kappa (**K**), but it lingered in the west and was introduced into the Italic alphabets, as will be seen.

The digamma (**F**, representing the *w* sound) was of Semitic origin. *Vau*, the sixth letter of the Semitic alphabet, was taken by the Greeks for use as a vowel, exactly as they had taken *yod*, and placed at the end of the alphabet following tau. But whereas the consonantal *i* sound did not exist in Greek, the consonantal *u* sound (akin to *w*) survived till classical times in certain dialects and needed a symbol to represent it. But the digamma also kept both the place of *vau* in the order of the alphabet and the value of consonantal *u*, and its old numerical value ("six").

The treatment of the sibilants of the Semitic alphabet by the Greeks is complicated. *Zain* was taken over as zeta, though its

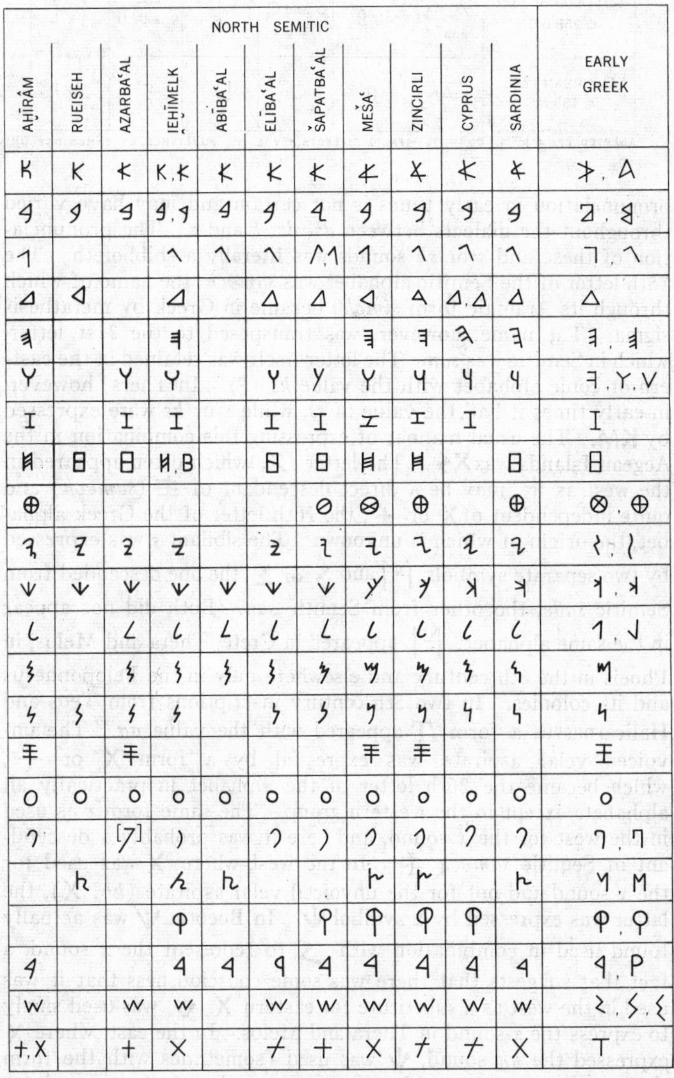

B.C.; the inscriptions from Abu Simbel in upper Egypt, dating from the 7th century; a Corinthian and an Athenian inscription of the 6th century; and some vase inscriptions still older. In Thera the oldest inscriptions are written from right to left, others are boustrophedon, others still later read from left to right. In the Lydian alphabet, known from inscriptions found at Sardis at the beginning of the 20th century, these symbols also represent vowels. Most Greek states developed local variations either in the forms of certain letters or in the representation of sounds not represented by any of the 22 letters taken over. The two main divisions, eastern and western, however, remained till the 4th century B.C., when, in the main, uniformity of alphabet (eastern) was attained throughout Greece. The early inscriptions from Thera show a remarkably close resemblance to the forms of the Semitic alphabet as represented on the Moabite stone or the Baal-Lebanon inscription from Cyprus. The alphabet of Abu Simbel was of the Ionic type. Alphabets derived from, or related to, the Greek (*e.g.*, Carian, Iberian and Etruscan) sometimes show clear traces of syllabic, as distinguished from purely alphabetic, writing.

The two main divisions, eastern and western, again subdivided into two, the cities of Asia Minor and the adjacent islands with their colonies using forms showing in some cases slight differences from those in use in the Cyclades and in Attica. Again, the alphabets of Megara, Corinth, Sicyon, Phlius and western Argolis with their colonies differed from the rest, which included Euboea, Boeotia, Phocis, Locris, Thessaly and the remainder of the Peloponnesus. Throughout all Greek alphabets the Semitic letters *aleph*, *he* and *'ayin*, which represented breathings, were adapted to represent vowels. Alpha (*aleph*) was consistent throughout. The letter corresponding to Semitic *he* (later epsilon) represented both the short and long vowel *e* in those cases where eta (H, η and ' from **Ͱ**) represented the rough breathing. Generally speaking, eta represented the vowel sound in the eastern alphabet, the breathing in the western. Thus in the west the symbol **F** or **E** was used for the two sounds represented in Attic by ϵ and η; in the east it

	NORTH SEMITIC											EARLY GREEK
	AḤIRĀM	RUEISEH	AZARBA'AL	IEḤĪMELK	ABIBA'AL	ELIBA'AL	SAPATBA'AL	MESĀ'	ZINCIRLI	CYPRUS	SARDINIA	

(The grid below the header shows North Semitic and Early Greek letter-forms arranged in rows.)

ADAPTED FROM I. J. GELB, "A STUDY IN WRITING"

FIG. 3.—NORTH SEMITIC AND EARLY GREEK SCRIPTS

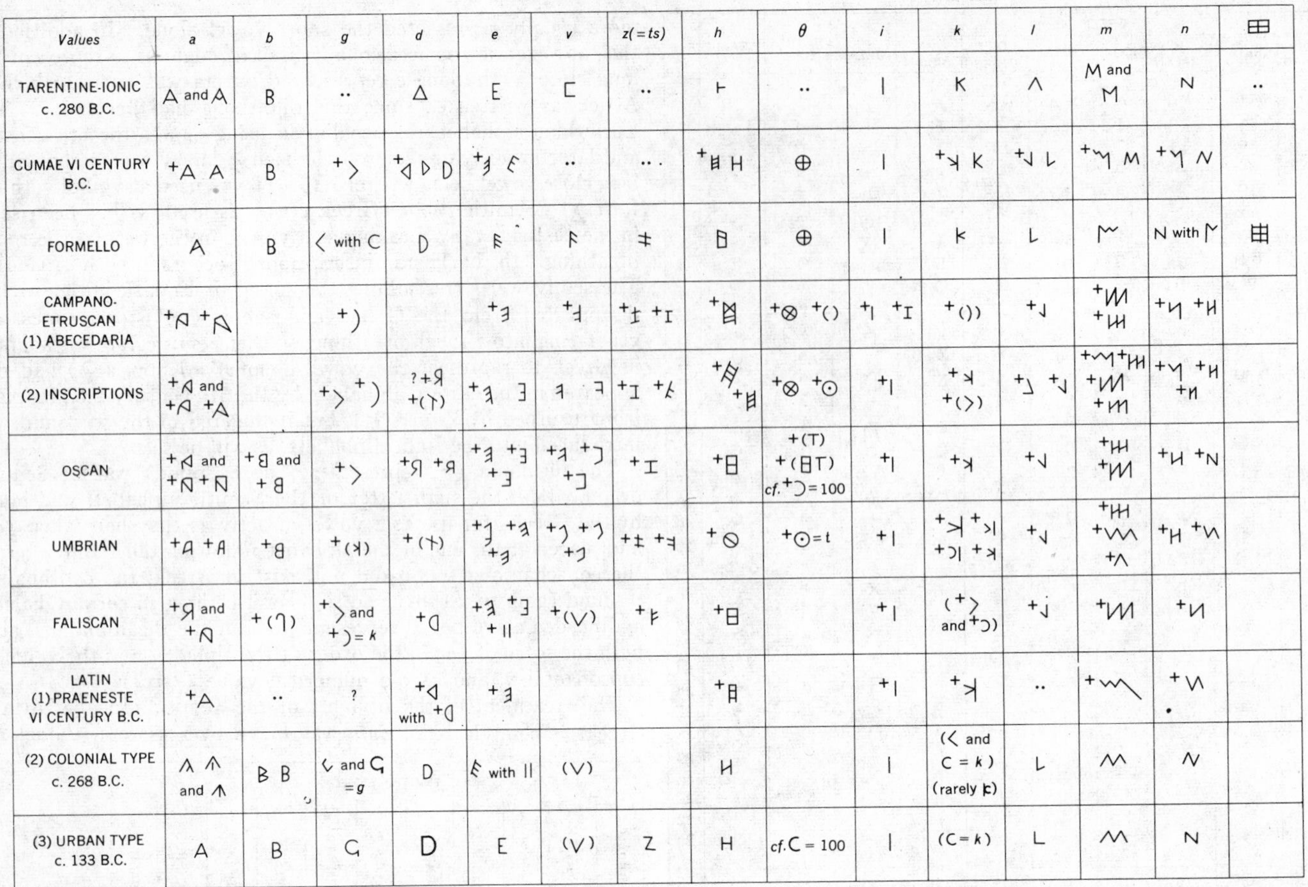

Values	a	b	g	d	e	v	z (= ts)	h	θ	i	k	l	m	n	⊞
TARENTINE-IONIC c. 280 B.C.	A and Λ	B	··	Δ	E	Ϲ	··	⊢	··	I	K	Λ	M and Ϻ	N	··
CUMAE VI CENTURY B.C.	+Λ A	B	+⟩	+◁ D D	+Ϟ Ɛ	··	···	+⊟ H	⊕	I	+⤓ K	+⤓ L	+ᛗ M	+ᛝ Ṇ	
FORMELLO	A	B	⟨ with Ϲ	D	Ϟ	Ϝ	≠	⊟	⊕	I	L	Ⳑ	ᛉ	N with Ⳑ	⊞
CAMPANO-ETRUSCAN (1) ABECEDARIA	+Ↄ +Ↄ		+⟩		+Ɛ	+Ⅎ	+⊥ +I	+⊠	+⊗ +()	+I +I	+()	+⤓	+ᛗ +ᛉ	+ᛝ +ᛡ	
(2) INSCRIPTIONS	+Ↄ and +Ↄ		+⟩ +()	?+Я +(Ɣ)	+Ɛ Ɛ	Ⅎ Ⅎ	+Ⅎ	+⊠ +⊠	+⊗ +()	+I	+⤓ +(⟩)	+⤓ +⤓	+ᛗ +ᛉ +ᛗ	+ᛝ +ᛡ +ᛝ	
OSCAN	+Ↄ and +Ↄ +Я	+B and +B	+⟩	+Я +Я	+Ɛ +Ɛ +Ɛ +Ɛ	+Ⅽ +Ⅽ	+I	+⊟	+(T) +(⊟T) cf. +Ↄ = 100	+I	+⤓	+⤓	+ᛞ +ᛗ	+ᛡ +N	
UMBRIAN	+Ↄ +Ↄ +Я	+B	+(K)	+(T)	+Ɛ +Ɛ +Ɛ +Ɛ	+Ⅎ +Ⅎ	+I +Ⅎ	+⊘	+⊙=t	+I	+⤓ +⤓ +⤓ +IↄЯ	+⤓	+ᛞ +ᚢ +Λ	+ᛡ +ᛝ	
FALISCAN	+Я and +Ↄ	+(Ɣ)	+⟩ and +)=k	D+	+Ɛ +Ɛ +II	+(∨)	+⫟	+⊟		+I	(+⟩ and +Ↄ)	+⤓	+ᛞ	+ᛡ	
LATIN (1) PRAENESTE VI CENTURY B.C.	+Ↄ	··	?	+◁ with +Ↄ	+Ɛ	+Ɛ		+⊟		+I	+⤓	··	+ᛗ	+ᚢ	
(2) COLONIAL TYPE c. 268 B.C.	Λ Λ and Λ	B B	⟨ and Ɡ =g	D	Ϟ with II	(∨)		⊦		I	(⟨ and C = k) (rarely ⋵)	L	ᛉ	N	
(3) URBAN TYPE c. 133 B.C.	A	B	Ɡ	D	E	(∨)	Z	H	cf. C = 100	I	(C = k)	L	ᛉ	N	

FIG. 4.—TABLE OF ITALIC ALPHABETS. + INDICATES

pronunciation in early times is not certain and may have varied throughout the dialects between *dž, dz, ž* and *z*. The pronunciation of these and *s* or *sh* sounds was literally a shibboleth. The 15th letter of the Semitic alphabet was *samech*, the name of which through its Aramaic form *simcha* became in Greek by metathesis sigma. The name, however, was transposed to the 21st letter, which in Semitic was *san*. The letter itself was retained in the eastern or Ionic alphabet with the value *ks* (ξ). In Thera, however, in early times it had the value of *ss*, while *x* or *ks* were expressed by **KM**. The usual manner of expressing this combination in the Aegean Islands was **Xϟ**. The letter **X**, which often appeared in the west as **+**, may be a direct descendant of **⧻** (*samech*) and quite independent of **X** or **+**, the 26th letter of the Greek alphabet, the origin of which is unknown. The sibilant *s* was expressed by two separate symbols, **Ϻ** and **ϟ** or **Σ**, the one descended from Semitic *sade*, the other from Semitic *san*. Both did not appear in the same alphabet. **Ϻ** appeared in Crete, Thera and Melos, in Phocis in the 6th century and elsewhere only in the Peloponnesus and its colonies. In two 5th-century inscriptions from Teos and Halicarnassus a form **T** appeared with the value $\sigma\sigma$. The unvoiced velar aspirate was expressed by a form **X** or **+**, which became the 26th letter of the alphabet in practically all alphabets except in the western group. The same form was used in the west for the *x* sound, and here it was probably a descendant of Semitic *samech* **⧻**. In the west where **X** was used for the *x* sound and not for the unvoiced velar aspirate (*kh*, **X**), the latter was expressed by a symbol **Ψ**. In Boeotia **Ψ** was actually found used in combination with **ϟ** to represent the *x* sound, a fact that suggests that there was some consciousness that it was used in the west as a substitute for eastern **X**. **Ψ** was used singly to express the *x* sound in Thera and Melos. In the east, where **X** expressed the *kh* sound, **Ψ** was used (sometimes with the form **Ψ**) to express the combination *ps*, a use in which it was later standardized by the spread of the Ionic alphabet.

Other symbols not derived from Semitic were: (1) ϕ (phi), used to express the unvoiced labial aspirate (*ph*); and (2) Ω the last letter of the Greek alphabet, probably differentiated from **O**. In the west this symbol appeared very seldom. In the east it represented the long open *o*. In the Cyclades, by a phonetic change, it frequently expressed the close vowel, whether long or short (*o* or *ov*), while **O** represented the open sound. The origin of the symbols ϕ and **Ψ** is unknown. In the case of **X** or **+** it is probable that **X** derived from **⧻** and standing for *x* should be differentiated from **X** standing for *kh*. The origin of the latter is, however, obscure. It is possible that these signs were adapted in Asia Minor from the Cypriote syllabary.

Various local alphabets that were parallel to the Greek were in use in Asia Minor. The Lydian alphabet for instance is known from inscriptions dating from the 4th century B.C. A few of these were discovered in the 19th century, 36 were found by a U.S. expedition in Sardis between 1910 and 1913, the rest by J. Keil and Von Premerstein and others in various parts of ancient Lydia since 1906. Another U.S. expedition began excavations in Sardis in the early 1960s.

The Lydian alphabet consisted of 26 symbols. The parallelism of the Greek and Semitic alphabets is clear but there are additional symbols the sound of some of which is uncertain in the absence of a completely certain interpretation of the language of the inscriptions. The most interesting fact about this alphabet is the identity of the symbol for *f*, which is **8**, with the Etruscan and Italic symbol for the same sound.

The Latin Alphabet.—The western Greek or Chalcidic alphabet was brought to Italian soil by the Etruscans and by the Greek colonies of Magna Graecia; it was once confidently held that the Latin alphabet was derived from this Chalcidic alphabet by contact with the Greek colonies of southern Italy. Too little was made of the influence of Etruria because too little was known of that country and its people. Over a dozen Italic alphabets are known. The Messapic is purely Greek in origin and was used by a people who were isolated in Calabria and spoke an Illyrian dialect.

o	p	San	ϙ	r	s	t	u	x	φ	ψ	f	i̯	u̯	d̯ (ř)	ç (š)	j (ž)	z (voiced s)
see under u̯ (ů)	Π			P	ς ; Σ and C	T	Y and (OY)	X = x	Φ	Ψ = ψ and (ΠΣ)	+S ς (Φ) (O H?) (B)	(EI)	?Y O ∩ and (OY)				(Σ)
o O	Π and Γ		+Q	+٩ P P	+ς +ς	T	V	+ = x	Φ	Ψ = x							
⊙	P	M	٩ and ٩	P	3 and ξ	T	Y with ৮	+ with X = x	Φ	Ψ = x							
+⅄ +⅄	+⋈ +(I)	+Ο	+٩	+Δ	+ς +ς	+⊤	+V +V		+Φ +(٦)	+Ψ = x	+8 +8						
+Π +٦ +٦ and +٦	+⋈		+Ο	+Δ and ? +٩	+ς +ς and ? +ς	+X +Y +ᚷ +⊤	+V +Y +Y			+⊦ = x +(Ħ)+	+8 +(Ħ٦)						
see under u̯ (ů)	+Π +Π	+Π		+Δ +٩ +Δ	+ς +ς	+⊤ +⊤	+Y +Y +V	+(кς) = x cf. +X = 10	+(BΠ)	+(кς) cf. +Ψ	+8 +8 +8 and +8	+⊦ +⊦	+Y +y +V +V				+(ς)
see under u̯ (ů)	+٦	+M		+Δ +Δ	+ς	+⊤ +٦ +٦	+V	+(кς) = X cf. +X = 10		+8	+(I) +(3) and +(I3)	+(V)	+٩	+d	?+(I)	
+Ο	+٦		+ℛ and ℛ	+ς +ς +S	+Y	+V	+X = x		+⋀							
+Ο	..	..	..	+ς	+V	..		+(Ħ٦)								
∧ ∩ and Γ	Γ Γ and Γ		ℛ and ℛ ℛ and ℛ	ς ς ς and S	⊤ and ⊤	V	..			F and I'			⊃			
O	٦ with P		Q	R	S	⊤ ⊤ and ⊤	V V	X = x	cf. CI⊃ = 1000	(CH) = x (Pael.)	F	(I)	see under o	(RS) (Umb.)	ς (Umb.) ٩	(S) Ꝺ (Pael.)	Z (Osc.)

RETROGRADE DIRECTION, THAT IS, RIGHT TO LEFT

The Umbrian, Oscan and various subalpine alphabets are derived from the Etruscan. The district in which the Umbrian alphabet was used was east of the Apennines. The Oscan was in Campania. Thus the Latin and Faliscan alphabets were bounded on all three sides by the Etruscan and alphabets derived from it. In these circumstances Etruscan must have exercised a strong influence upon the Latin alphabet, following the impact of Etruscan civilization upon Roman in other directions.

The Etruscan alphabet is known from certain tomb inscriptions, from part of an Etruscan book that was used as the wrapping of a mummy and from several alphabets or abecedaria. It has **F** (digamma) and retains forms corresponding to all three Phoenician sibilants, *samech, san* and *sade*. It has **X** representing *ks*, φ for *ph* and **Ψ** as *kh*. On one tomb inscription of the 8th century B.C., **8** is found representing *f*, identical with the same character used for the same sound in the Lydian alphabet (*see above*). The view now usually held as to the origin of the Etruscan alphabet is that it was brought by its users to Italy when they migrated from Asia Minor probably in the 9th century B.C., and that they had received it while still in Asia Minor or in the Aegean Islands from Greek sources at a period prior to the division of the Greek alphabet into eastern and western. The Etruscan names for the letters of the alphabet are the same, in the main, as the Latin, which had borrowed them. There is nothing impossible, or even improbable, in the view of the derivation of the Etruscan alphabet from Greek sources in the Aegean at an early date since inscriptions found on the island of Lemnos show them in possession of it.

The oldest extant records of the Latin alphabet are first the inscription known as the Dvenos inscription (it begins **DVENOS MED FECED**), found in 1880 in Rome upon an earthenware vessel with three separate branches and dating from the first half of the 4th century B.C. In the second place is the Praeneste fibula, dating from the 6th or 5th century, the inscription upon which runs from right to left. It reads **MANIOS MED FHEFHAKED NUMASIOI** and is remarkable as illustrating the device of com-bining the letters **F** (digamma) and **H** (aspirate) to represent the sound of *f* which was common in Latin but did not occur in Greek. In the Dvenos inscription **F** alone is used, a later development, for the Romans had the *w* sound in their language, but instead of using **F** to represent it, they rather clumsily allowed **V** to represent both this and the vowel sound *u*. The third instance of early Latin is an inscription upon a column, written boustrophedon, found in the Roman forum and dating probably from the 5th century. In it **K** is in ordinary use for *k*, and **Q** for *q* or *qu;* and the word **RECEI** occurs where **C** has still the force of *g*.

The third letter of the alphabet, Γ, < and C, which represented in Greek the voiced velar stop (the sound of *g*), came in Latin to represent the unvoiced stop. The reason for this is obscure, but Etruscan influence cannot have been absent for the voiced stops were unrepresented in the Etruscan language. Latin did not lose the voiced stop but adapted a symbol **G** from **C** to represent it, which it placed in the position of **I** (zeta) for which it had no use. **C** thus took the place of **K**, which fell out of ordinary use, remaining only as the initial of archaic or official words. **C** also remained with the force of *g* in the initials of proper names. **F** (digamma) was used at first in combination with **H** to represent the *f* sound. Later the **H** was dropped, again probably under Etruscan influence. When after the conquest of Greece Greek words began to be borrowed by the Latin language, the symbols **Y** and **Z** were adapted from Greek for use in such words and placed at the end of the alphabet. There were no sounds in Latin to correspond to the three aspirates. ⊙ (theta) was retained to represent the numeral 100 and became modified to **C** and identified with the initial letter of the number (centum). Φ (phi) written (I) was used to represent 1,000 and became identified with **M**, the initial letter of *mille.* Ψ (chi) became ⊥, then **L**, and was used for 50.

The Latin alphabet of 23 letters (including **Y** and **Z**) became extended during the course of the middle ages to the English alphabet of 26 by the division of **I** into *i* and *j* and the tripartite division of V into *u, v* and *w*. *J* developed in the 15th century as an initial (more ornate) form of *i*, and as the consonantal sound occurred more at the beginning of words as well as in the middle, *j* became specialized to represent the consonant wherever it came in the word. The history of *u* and *v* is precisely similar except that it took place five centuries earlier. *W* arose, as its name implies, out of a combination *uu* or *vv*, which about the 11th century came to represent in Old English the *w* sound, previously represented by a rune.

Other Alphabets.—The alphabets of India derive from two sources, Kharosthi and Brahmi. Though attempts have been made to show that the Brahmi alphabet was developed in India itself without connection with outside sources, this contention cannot be maintained. It has a manifest kinship with the Semitic alphabets. Its origin is obscure, but there seems little doubt that it derives from the South Semitic group of alphabets through contact with Sabataean traders. The Brahmi alphabet is the parent of all modern Indian alphabets. Kharosthi is an adaptation, to the needs of the Indian languages, of the Aramaic alphabet, in use in northwest India in the days of Persian rule. Inscriptions in it first appear in the 3rd century B.C. None has been found of a date subsequent to the 5th century A.D. By the 3rd century A.D. it had spread to Chinese Turkestan. It was superseded in all districts by Brahmi.

The alphabets in use in Persia, at least from the time of the Arsacid dynasty onward, are based upon the Aramaic. Cuneiform was the writing of the Achaemenidae empire, but after the Greek conquest Aramaic was introduced and became general. The Pahlavi is the alphabet of the Sassanid kings. The Arsacid and Sassanian alphabets are found together in the liturgical inscription of Hadji-abad, as well as in the Paikuli inscriptions dating from about 300 B.C.

Modern Arabic writing has developed from a form of Aramaic used in the land of the Nabataeans, an Arabian people. The oldest record of it now extant is a stele from Tema, in northwest Arabia, dating from the 5th century B.C. or perhaps earlier. Distinctively Nabataean inscriptions are from a period beginning about the mid-

dle of the 1st century B.C.; the script was standardized in the early Christian era. The graffiti on the rocks of Mt. Sinai carry the record of the development of this alphabet down to the 3rd century A.D. In the early Islamic period two types of Arabic writing existed, known as the Kufic and the Naskhi. The former was discontinued except for formal purposes, where cursive writing could not be employed. The Naskhi is the parent of modern Arabic writing, in which many characters have become so similar owing to the degeneration of the cursive script that it is necessary to distinguish them by diacritical points.

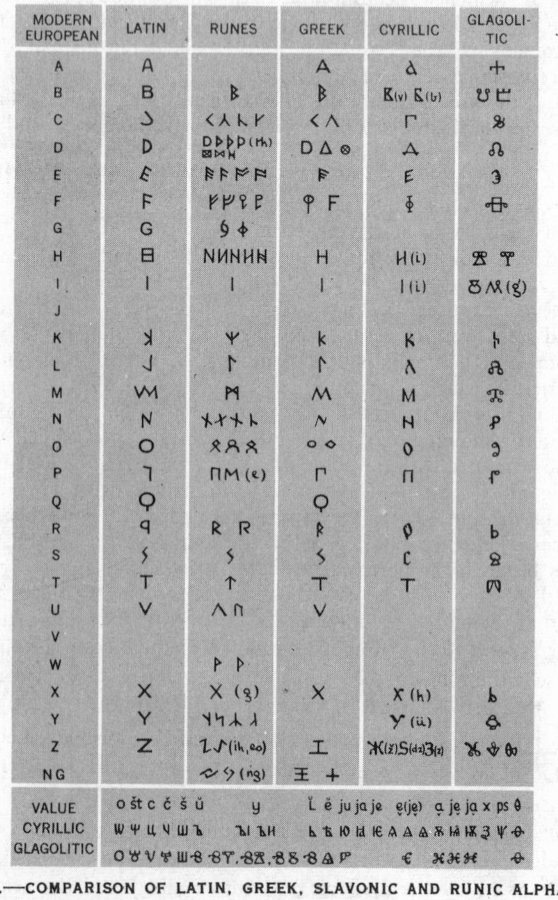

Persian, Turkish (until recently) and a few other languages have used the Arabic alphabet. But there has been a marked trend in modern times to take over the Latin or Roman alphabet, as was done in Turkey in 1930. The Latin alphabet has also been adapted to some languages in the U.S.S.R., Africa and elsewhere.

The earliest records of Aramaic go back to about 800 B.C. and were found at Sindjirli in northern Syria. The alphabet at this time differed little from that of the Moabite stone. Aramaic became by far the most important and widespread of the North Semitic alphabets. It was used in Assyria as a cursive script by side with cuneiform. It is marked by two distinct tendencies: (1) the opening of the heads of the letters, *beth* ( ) becoming , *daleth* ( ) and *resh* ( ) . became , then ; (2) angles became rounded and ligatures developed. These tendencies were completed during the Persian period and they are emphasized in the Aramaic writing on papyrus employed in Egypt between 500 and 200 B.C. Other developments of Aramaic are modern square Hebrew and the alphabet of Palmyra.

A group of alphabets arose in Asia Minor during the first half of the 1st millennium B.C. deriving from a common source, which was also akin to the source of the Greek alphabet. The Carian alphabet was one of these, the Lycian another. Both seem parallel to Greek, not offshoots of it. The Phrygian, on the other hand, seems to be derived from the Greek and from the western variety.

The Armenian alphabet owes its origin to Bishop Mesrob late in the 4th century A.D., who adapted it from Greek for the use of a rising Armenian Christian literature. A few Persian characteristics that appear are the influence of the dominating political power.

In all Germanic countries are found inscriptions in the alphabet known as runic (*see* RUNE). The affinities of this alphabet with the Greek are apparent, but there has been dispute whether or not it is derived directly from Greek or through an Italic alphabet. Comparison with subalpine alphabets (of Etruscan origin) and the fact that the oldest runes are found just north of the eastern end of the Alps supports the latter view.

The cryptographic Ogham writing was employed by Celtic peoples in Britain and Ireland (*see* OGHAM WRITING). In this the several letters of the alphabet were represented by strokes differing in number (from one to five) and in position on either side, or on both sides, of a straight horizontal line. The symbols are indicative of binary choices in origin. The bulk of the Ogham texts, both in Ireland and in Wales belong to the 3rd to 5th centuries A.D.

Finally must be mentioned the two Slavonic alphabets, Cyrillic and Glagolitic, both according to tradition the invention of Cyril, the missionary to the Slavs, in the 9th century. Each is taken from the Greek alphabet of that period, Glagolitic from the cursive writing, Cyrillic from uncial, when the value of **B** had become the spirant *v*, that of **H** *i*, of Φ *f* and of **X** the sound of Scotch *ch*. Several additional symbols were invented to express those sounds of the Slavonic language which could not be comprised within the compass of the Greek alphabet. Glagolitic survived in Croatia till the 17th century. Cyrillic has for long been the alphabet in which the Slavonic languages are normally expressed.

See articles on specific languages and letters of the alphabet; *see* also references under "Alphabet" in the Index.

BIBLIOGRAPHY.—D. Diringer, *The Alphabet*, 2nd rev. ed. (1951); J. Février, *Histoire de l'écriture* (1948); I. J. Gelb, *A Study of Writing* (1952); G. R. Driver, *Semitic Writing from Pictograph to Alphabet* (1948); Marcel Cohen, *La grande invention de l'écriture* (1958); current bibliography in *Bibliographie linguistique* (Comité International Permanent des Linguistes, since 1939). Of older works, only the more important are listed below. The detailed bibliography given by

FIG. 5.—COMPARISON OF LATIN, GREEK, SLAVONIC AND RUNIC ALPHABETS

Diringer should be consulted for specialist works also not repeated here.

On the early Canaanitish texts, *see* Frank M. Cross, Jr., "Evolution of the Proto-Canaanite Alphabet," *American Schools of Oriental Research Bulletin*, 134:15–24 (April 1954).

Sinai Inscriptions: Alan H. Gardiner, "The Egyptian Origin of the Semitic Alphabet," *Journal of Egyptian Archaeology*, 3:1 ff. (1916); Hans Bauer, *Zur Entzifferung der neuentdeckten Sinaischrift* (1918).

Origin of Phoenician Alphabet: A. H. Sayce, in *Proceedings of the Society of Biblical Archaeology*, vol. xxxii, pp. 215–222 (1910); Sir W. Flinders Petrie, *The Formation of the Alphabet* (1912).

Greek: A. Kirchhoff, *Studien zur Geschichte des griechischen Alphabets*, 4th ed. (1887); E. S. Roberts, *Introduction to Greek Epigraphy*, pt. i (1887), with E. A. Gardiner, pt. ii (1905); W. Larfeld, "Griechische Epigraphik," *Handbuch der klassischen Altertumswissenschaft* (1914). On the Greek alphabet, E. Schwyzer, *Griechische Grammatik*, vol. i, pt. i, pp. 137–150 (1934); C. D. Buck, *Greek Dialects*, pp. 17–19 and 347–349 (1955); L. H. Jeffery, *The Local Scripts of Archaic Greece* (1961); on Minoan writing, S. Dow in *American Journal of Archaeology*, 58:77–129 (1954).

Lydian: Pauly-Wissowa, *Real-Encyclopädie*, vol. xiii, article "Lydia," p. 2157 ff. (1927). On the Italic alphabets, J. Whatmough, *Foundations of Roman Italy* (1937), and *The Prae-Italic Dialects of Italy*, vol. ii, pp. 501–543 (1934), for the subalpine origin of the runes, *see* p. 505. *Indian:* Cambridge History of India, vol. i, p. 62, ed. by E. J. Rapson; G. Bühler, *Indische Palaeographie, Grund. d. indo-ar. Phil.* (1896; Eng. trans., *Indian Palaeography*, ed. by J. F. Fleet, 1904). *Pahlavi:* Ernst Herzfield, *Paikuli* (1924). (B. F. C. A.; J. Wh.)

ALPHA PARTICLES, also called α-rays, the positively charged particles that are ejected by certain radioactive substances. (*See* RADIOACTIVITY.) They are the nuclei of helium atoms (*i.e.*, normal atoms of the isotope He^4), which, however, are without their usual complement of two exterior electrons (*i.e.*, doubly ionized helium-four, He^{4+}). (*See* ATOM; ELECTRON.) These may also be produced by an electric discharge through this gas. *See* also references under "Alpha Particles" in the Index.

(H. B. Lm.)

ALPHEGE (AELFHEAH), **SAINT** (954–1012), English archbishop and martyr. His early life is obscure, but he was a monk at Deerhurst and later a hermit at Bath, where followers are said to have flocked to him, electing him abbot. He was a friend of St. Dunstan, through whose influence he was named bishop of Winchester in 984. In 1006 he succeeded Aelfric as archbishop of Canterbury. Alphege was captured by the Danes in the sack of Canterbury in 1011 and held for ransom for seven months. When he refused to pay he was stoned to death at Greenwich. He was first buried at St. Paul's but was removed to Canterbury in splendour in 1023. From the earliest years after his death he was venerated as a martyr. His feast day is April 19.

See J. P. Migne (ed.), *Patrologia Latina*, vol. cxxxix. (T. L. C.)

ALPHEUS (mod. Gr. ALFIOS), the chief river of Peloponnesus, Greece. The Alpheus proper is 68 mi. long and rises near Asea in central Arcadia (Arkhadhia), but its passage there by subterranean channels from the Tegean plain, and its union with the Eurotas are probably mythical (W. Loring, *Journal of Hellenic Studies*, vol. xv, p. 67). The shallow and rapid stream occupies but a small part of its broad, stony bed. Leaving the plain of Megalopolis by a rugged gorge, it receives above Olympia two large tributaries, Erimanthos and Ladhon, from the northeast and empties into the Ionian sea. In late Tertiary times the plain of Megalopolis was occupied by a lake, and the lower Alpheus represents the overflow channel by which it was drained. Pliny states that it was navigable for six Roman miles from its mouth. Alpheus was recognized as the typical river god in the Peloponnesus, as was Achelous (*q.v.*) in northern Greece. His waters were said to pass beneath the sea and rise again in the fountain Arethusa at Syracuse. (Wm. C. B.)

ALPHONSE I (1103–1148), count of Toulouse, son of the crusading count Raymond IV by his third wife, Elvira of Castile, was born in the castle of Mont-Pèlerin at Tripoli in the Lebanon and was surnamed Jourdain, having been baptized in the Jordan. He was taken to France in 1107 and, on the death of his brother Bertrand (1112), succeeded to the whole countship of Toulouse and marquisate of Provence, which had been first divided between Bertrand and him. Dispossessed of the countship of Toulouse by William IX, duke of Aquitaine, in 1114, he recovered part of it in 1119 and the rest in 1123. He next fought against Raymond Berengar I (Ramón Berenguer III of Barcelona) for the sover-

eignty of Provence, and by a peace reached in Sept. 1125 became master of most of the country north of the Durance. He occupied Narbonne in 1134 and held it till 1143.

Alphonse did much to reduce his vassals to obedience and to protect the towns (charters of 1141 and 1147 to Toulouse); his great work was the founding of Montauban (1144). In Spain he arbitrated several times between princes. In 1141 he was attacked by Louis VII of France, who besieged Toulouse, on the pretext of rights due to his wife Eleanor of Aquitaine. After being twice excommunicated (in 1123 for interfering with the abbey of Saint-Gilles and in 1142 because of a dispute with Montpellier), he took the cross in 1146 at Vézelay and embarked for Palestine in Aug. 1147, reaching Acre in 1148. He was poisoned at Caesarea, Palestine, in April 1148, at the instigation either of Eleanor or of Melisande, mother of Baldwin III of Jerusalem.

ALPHONSE (1220–1271), count of Poitiers and of Toulouse, notable for his administration of Languedoc, was born on Nov. 11, 1220, the fifth son of Louis VIII of France, under whose will he received Poitou and Auvergne in appanage. He married Joan, daughter of Raymond VII of Toulouse, in 1237. While he was in Egypt with his brother Louis IX of France, during the seventh crusade, he inherited the countship of Toulouse on Raymond's death (1249). Returning to France (1250), he was joint regent with Charles of Anjou from 1252 till Louis IX's return in 1254. In his lands in southern France he repaired some of the damage done in the Albigensian War, created and developed privileged settlements of the type known as *bastide* (*q.v.*) and tried to keep the peace between the various orders of society in the towns. By working through a large administrative staff in Paris he helped to prepare the way for the final reunion of the countship of Toulouse with the French crown. In 1270 he went to Tunis for the disastrous eighth crusade. On his way home he died in Italy, probably at Savona, on Aug. 21, 1271. There is an edition of his administrative correspondence by A. Molinier, 2 vol. (1884–1900).

ALPHONSINE TABLES, astronomical tables prepared in Toledo, Spain, about 1272 (for the epoch 1252), under the direction of King Alfonso X, by Judah ben Moses and Isaac ibn Sid. The Alphonsine tables superseded the Toledan tables prepared in the 11th century by al-Zarqali (Arzachel); they served the European astronomers for several centuries in several Latin versions. With the gradual introduction of the Copernican system and the publication of Reinhold's *Prutenicae tabulae* (1551) and of Kepler's *Tabulae Rudolphinae* (1627), tables based on the Ptolemaic system became useless.

See ASTRONOMY: *History of Astronomy*. (A. Po.)

ALPHONSO, an English form of a Christian name derived from the ancient Germanic Adalfuns (*adal*, "nobility," *funs*, "eager"). The French form is Alphonse, the Spanish (Castilian) Alfonso, the Portuguese Afonso. The widespread use of the name in Spain and Portugal seems to have originated in some association with that of the 7th-century archbishop of Toledo, St. Ildefonsus (Sp. Ildefonso), the latter name representing perhaps an old patronymic meaning "son of Adalfuns," Sp. *hi(jo) de Alfonso*. The name has been borne in the form Alfonso (*q.v.*) by 11 kings of Asturias, Castile and León, by 5 kings of Aragon the last of whom was also king of Naples, and by 2 kings of all Spain, as well as by another king of Naples alone; and in the form Afonso (*q.v.*) by 6 kings of Portugal.

ALPHORN (German, *Alpenhorn*), the wooden trumpet of Alpine herdsmen and villagers, sounded for intercommunication and at daily ceremonies and seasonal festivals. It is carved or bored in wood and overwound with birch bark. Some instruments are straight, reaching 12 ft. in length, with a curving bell; others, mainly in the eastern Alps, have the shape of a trumpet. The alphorn is often played in trios and quartets, with the same compass and notes as a natural French horn in F. (A. C. Ba.)

ALPINI, PROSPERO (1553–1616), Italian physician and botanist, best known for his observations on the pollination of the date palm, was born at Marostica in the Veneto, on Nov. 25, 1553. He accompanied the Venetian consul, Giorgio Emo, to Egypt as medical adviser and made full use of his three years' stay there to study the flora. He stated that "the female date-trees or palms do not bear fruit unless the branches of the male and female plants are mixed together; or, as is generally done, unless the dust found in the male sheath or male flowers is sprinkled over the female flowers." He saw the coffee plant growing in Cairo and his account of it is said to be the first published in Europe. In 1593 he was appointed professor of botany at Padua (the oldest botanical chair in Europe) and cultivated many Egyptian plants in the university garden. He died at Padua on Nov. 23, 1616. His best-known work is *De plantis Aegypti* (1592). He also wrote *De Medicina Aegyptiorum* (1591) and *De Plantis exoticis* (1627), published by his son, ALPINO ALPINI (1592–1637), who succeeded to the chair in 1633, and died in 1637.   (J. RM.)

ALPS, the collective name for one of the great mountain systems of Europe stretching from the Gulf of Genoa to Vienna, and rising between the plains of northern Italy and of southern Germany. The Alps do not present so continuous a barrier as the Himalayas, the Andes or even the Pyrenees. They are less extensive than the Urals or the Scandinavian highlands. They are formed of numerous ranges, divided by comparatively deep valleys. This mountain mass forms a broad band, convex toward the north, while most of the valleys lie between the directions west to east and southwest to northeast. Many deep transverse valleys intersect the prevailing direction of the ridges and facilitate the passage of man, animals and plants, as well as of currents of air which mitigate the contrast that would otherwise be found between the climates of the opposite slopes. The derivation of the name alps is uncertain; in all parts of the great chain itself the term alp (or alm in the Eastern Alps) is strictly applied to the high mountain pastures, and not to the peaks and ridges of the chain. The name alps has been applied to other ranges in the world, notably the Australian Alps and Japanese Alps.

Limits of the Alps.—Merely to distinguish the Alps from minor ranges the best limits are on the west (strictly speaking, south), the Sella di Altare or Colle di Cadibona (1,427 ft.), leading from Turin to Savona and Genoa, Italy, and on the east the line of the railway over the Semmering pass (3,215 ft.) from Vienna, Austria, to Marlbor, Yugoslavia, in the Mur (Mura) valley, and on by Ljubljana, Yugoslavia, to Trieste. An Italian commission in 1926 placed the limit on the east at a line from Vienna through Graz to Rijeka, Yugoslavia. But if the term is confined to those parts where the height is sufficient to support perpetual snow, the limit to the west will be the Colle di Tenda (Col de Tende) (6,135 ft.), leading from Cuneo (*Coni*) to Ventimiglia, Italy, while on the east the line will be the route over the Radstädter Tauern (5,702 ft.) and the Katschberg (5,384 ft.) from Salzburg, Austria to Villach in Carinthia, and thence by Klagenfurt to Maribor and so past Ljubljana in Yugoslavia on to Trieste.

On the north side, the Alps (in either sense) are definitely bounded by the Rhine from Basel to Lake Constance, Switzerland, the plain of Bavaria and the low foothills from Salzburg to the neighbourhood of Vienna. The waters of the northern slope of the Alps run either into the North sea through the Rhine, or into the Black sea by means of the Danube, none reaching the Baltic sea. On the south side the mountains from near Turin to near Trieste subside into the great plain of Piedmont, Lombardy and Venetia. The true west section of the Alps runs from near Turin to the Colle di Tenda, in a southerly direction, then bends east to the Sella di Altare, which divides it from the Apennines.

Divisions.—The Alps consist of a main chain, with ramifications, and of several minor chains. They form a single connected whole as contrasted with the plains at their base, the only breaks in them being mountain passes at high altitudes. For the sake of convenience the best marked passes have long been used to serve as limits within the chain, whether to distinguish several great divisions or to break up these into smaller ones. Coolidge's system of division considers only topographical aspects (*see* COOLIDGE, WILLIAM AUGUSTUS BREVOORT). The divisions given lie between the Colle di Tenda and the route over the Radstädter Tauern. Three main divisions are generally distinguished: the Western Alps, extending from the Colle di Tenda to the Simplon pass; the Central Alps, extending from the Simplon pass to the Passo di Resia (Reschen Scheideck); and the Eastern Alps, ex-

PRINCIPAL CITIES AND PHYSICAL FEATURES OF THE ALPS

tending from the latter to the Radstädter Tauern route, with a bend outward toward the southeast in order to include the higher summits of the southeastern Alps. Assuming these divisions, it is found convenient to subdivide the whole mountain system into 18 smaller groups—5 in the Western Alps, 7 in the Central Alps and 6 in the Eastern Alps. These, with the limits of each subdivision, are as follows:—

Western Alps.—The Maritime Alps (from the Colle di Tenda to the Col de l'Argentière). The Cottian Alps (from the Col de l'Argentière to the Mont Cenis pass and west to the Col du Galibier). The Dauphiné Alps (from the Col du Galibier, westward and southward). The Graian Alps (from the Mont Cenis to the Little St. Bernard pass). These are usually divided into three groups, the Central (the watershed between the two passes named), the Western or French, and the Eastern or Italian. The Pennine Alps (from the Little St. Bernard pass to the Simplon pass).

Central Alps.—The Bernese Alps (from Lake Geneva to the Furka pass, the Reuss valley and Lake Lucerne). The Lepontine Alps (from the Simplon to the Splügen and south to the Furka and the Oberalp passes). The eastern portion of this range is sometimes named the Adula Alps (from the St. Gotthard to the Splügen pass). The Tödi range (from the Oberalp to the Klausen pass). The Glarus Alps (north of the Klausen pass). The Bernina Alps (from the Maloja to the Resia and the Giogo dello Stelvio, south and east of the Val Bregalia and of the Engadine [q.v.] and north of the Valtellina [q.v.]). The Albula range (from the Splügen to the Fluela pass, north and west of the Val Bregaglia and of the Engadine). The Silvretta and Rhätikon ranges (from the Fluela to the Passo di Resia and the Arlberg pass).

Eastern Alps.—The Alps of Bavaria. Vorarlberg and Salzburg (north of the Arlberg pass, Innsbruck, the Pinzgau and the Enns valley). The central Tirol Alps (from the Brenner to the Radstädter Tauern pass, north of the Drave valley and south of the Pinzgau and the Enns valley). This includes the Zillertal and the Tauern ranges. The Ortler, Stubai and Ötztal (from the Passo di Resia and the Stelvio to the Brenner pass, south of the Inn valley, and north of the Tonale pass). The Lombard Alps (from Lake Como to the Adige valley, south of the Valtellina and the Aprica and the Tonale passes). This division includes the Adamello, Presanella, Brenta and Bergamasque ranges. The Dolomites of south Tirol (from the Brenner to the Passo di Monte Croce Carnico, and south of the Pustertal). The southeastern Alps (east of the Monte Croce Carnico). This division includes the Julian, Carnic and the Karawanken Alps.

In 1926 an Italian commission considered the subdivision of the Alps and their suggestions embodied several modifications of the above. (*See* L. W. Freshfield, *Geogr. J.*, p. 37, Jan. 1928.)

Geology and Structure.—The Alps form but a small portion of a great zone of crumpling which stretches in a series of curves from the Rif mountains of Morocco to beyond the Himalayas. The whole group of mountains may be conveniently called the Alpine-Himalayan group. Within this zone the crust of the earth has been ridged up into a complex series of creases and folds, out of which the great mountain chains of southern Europe and Asia have been carved by agents of weathering and erosion. Superficially, the continuity of the zone is broken at intervals by gaps of greater or less extent; these are due in part at least to the subsidence of portions of the folded belt and their subsequent burial by more recent accumulations. Such a gap is that between the Alps and the Carpathians.

This mountain system, which stretches a quarter of the way across the globe, is formed not of a single fold of the crust but of a number of such, often parallel to one another and to the general direction (trend) of the chain. The mountains of southern Europe are an exception to the last statement, for there are five great mountain systems radiating from the Alps themselves. One arm stretches east through the Carpathians and another to the southeast through the Dinaric Alps. The latter passes through Candia and Rhodes into the Taurus mountains, where it is joined by the continuation of the Carpathian branch, and east into the Iran plateau and the Himalayas. This arm appears to cross southern China while there is a loop to the south forming the Burmese-Malayan arc. The third arm stretches west from the mountains of Provence into the Pyrenees and the northern Spanish highlands; a fourth through Liguria, Corsica, Elba, the Apennines, Sicily, the Balearic Islands, the Baetic Cordillera (Cordillera Penibética), across the Strait of Gibraltar and into the Rif mountains of Morocco. This latter demarcation of the fourth arm is according to R. Staub, but L. Kober considers the Baetic Cordillera as part of the Provence-Pyrenees branch, and thinks that the Apennines branch continues by way of Sicily directly into the Rif mountains. A fifth narrow chain stretches from Grenoble into the Jura mountains. These several chains, forming one great mountain system, were uplifted during the same period of earth movement and by the same set of causes. Each branch is in a certain sense a separate unit but each is represented in the Alps which is the narrowest portion of the whole mountain belt, and in consequence every aspect of the geology of the Alps is of paramount importance when the whole chain is considered.

Sedimentary rocks form a large part of the Alps. These range from the Trias to the Miocene, but older rocks (Permian, Carboniferous, Devonian, Silurian and possibly Cambrian) also occur and are of considerable importance, especially in the Eastern Alps. Crystalline gneisses and schists and igneous rocks also occur. There are many rock types of local importance which need special mention. Here are found characteristic Tertiary rocks, Molasse, Nagelfluh and Flysch. The former consists of a remarkably uniform series which crops out along the northern border of the Alps in the Swiss plateau. To the south of this is the Flysch zone which attains more important dimensions in the east than in the west. Other types which have commanded universal interest are the Gossau beds, Verrucano and Schistes Lustrés.

The Alps stand upon the site of a geosyncline which, from late Carboniferous times, through the whole of the Mesozoic period until the Miocene period, existed between the Eurasian (Foreland) land mass to the north and the African (Hinterland) land mass to the south. The sea which occupied this depression was called by Eduard Suess (*q.v.*) and others the "Tethys." Great thicknesses of deposits were laid down in it, causing the floor to sink and thus enabling the sediments to be deposited at approximately the same depth below the sea level. P. Termier compared this geosyncline to a huge vise, the jaws of which moved slowly inward concurrently as deposition was taking place between them. The Hinterland moved northward toward the Foreland. E. Argand has suggested that, by this movement two geanticlines (arches) arose within the geosyncline, thus bringing about the following subdivision:—the Valais geosyncline (north), the Briançonnais geanticline, the Piedmont geosyncline, the Dolin geanticline and the Canavese geosyncline. The two geanticlines continued to increase in size as compression proceeded during the whole of the Mesozoic period until the culmination of the movement in the Miocene. The compression was so great that the geanticlines rose completely out of the Tethys and were driven northward on to the Foreland in the form of huge recumbent folds, to which the name of "nappes" was given. The geanticlines can now be identified in the Pennine Alps as the Great St. Bernard nappe and the Dent Blanche nappe. Further, the rise of these two structures also brought about the formation of other structures within the Alpine geosynclines; the Great St. Bernard nappe forcing upward and forward the three Simplon nappes which lie beneath it, and the Dent Blanche nappe similarly bringing into being the Monte Rosa nappe. There are thus in the Pennine Alps six major tectonic elements which arose from the Alpine geosyncline.

Apart from these, the Foreland and the Hinterland both played important roles and large tracts of the mountains belong to these divisions. Sedimentary rocks were laid down in epicontinental seas upon the peneplained Hercynian surfaces of these continental masses and these rocks, as well as the fundamental crystalline rocks, were affected by the Alpine earth movements. The northward movement of the Hinterland was so great that portions of it were driven completely over the geosynclinal rocks on to the Foreland itself. Sedimentary rocks of the same age belong to the Foreland, the Hinterland and the Geosyncline, but there are distinct differences in facies between them as well as differences within each group. Recumbent folding and overthrusting are common throughout the whole of the Alps, but the particular type of structure found in any locality depends upon the nature of the rocks and their location in one or other of the main divisions.

From a geological point of view it is convenient to divide the Alps into Western Alps and Eastern Alps along the Rhine line (a north-south line through Lake Constance, Chur and the Septimer pass). The following is a summary of the chief tectonic divisions:—

Western Alps.—(1) The Jura mountains; (2) the Swiss plateau of Tertiary rocks; (3) the Prealps, with exotic Paleozoic, Mesozoic and Tertiary rocks; (4) the zone of the High Calcareous Alps of Switzerland (the Helvetide zone of R. Staub); (5) the zone of Mont Blanc in which are the crystalline Hercynian massifs, Mercantour, Pelvoux and Belledonne, Mont Blanc and the Aiguilles Rouges, Gotthard, Aar and Gastern-Erstfeld (the Autochthonous massifs of Heim); (6) the Pennine zone, in which occur the Pennine nappes (Pennides of R. Staub); (7) the zone of the "Inner Roots," containing the roots of the Pennine, Austride and Dinaride nappes.

Eastern Alps.—(1) The Swiss plateau with Tertiary rocks; (2) the northern Flysch zone (the East Alpine equivalent of the zone of the High Calcareous Alps); (3) the zone of the Eastern Alps; (*a*) the northern Limestone zone of Triassic, Jurassic and Cretaceous rocks; (*b*) the Greywacke zone of schists and limestones of Paleozoic Age; (*c*) the central zone, forming the chief mountain tracts of the Eastern Alps and built up chiefly of Austride nappes; (*d*) the Pennine "windows" which occur within the central zone and in which Pennine nappes are found; (4) the Dinaride zone in which the Dinaride nappes occur and which is formed of Paleozoic and Mesozoic rocks and several plutonic intrusions.

Of these divisions the Jura mountains, the Swiss plateau, the zone of the High Calcareous Alps, the northern Flysch zone and the zone of Mont Blanc belong to the Foreland; the Pennine zone, the Pennine "windows" and part of the zone of the "Inner Roots" belong to the Alpine geosyncline, while the northern Limestone zone, the Greywacke zone, the central zone, the Prealps, part of the zone of the "Inner Roots" and the Dinaride zone belong to the Hinterland.

Although the Foreland acted as a single unit during the Alpine earth movements it did not possess a simple homogeneous structure. Some portions of it (*e.g.*, the central plateau of France, the Vosges, the Black Forest, the Bohemian mountains and the massifs of the zone of Mont Blanc) resisted the northward advance of the folds, and the effect of this is well seen in the trend of the chain. There were two sets of obstructions, an outer group comprising the Maures-Esterel massif, central plateau of France, Vosges-Black Forest and Bohemian massifs; and an inner group, the zone of Mont Blanc. The outer group, well within the Foreland, determined the trend of the chains of the Basses and Dauphiné Alps, the Jura mountains and Swabian Alps. The effect of the zone of Mont Blanc, nearer the southern edge of the Foreland, is seen in the Pennine and Eastern Alps. Here R. Staub has identified ten distinct arcs, five in the Eastern Alps and five in the Western Alps. The latter are more distinct than those east of the Rhine line, for the massifs of the zone of Mont Blanc all occur in the Western Alps, but the occurrence of arcs farther east indicates the presence of similar massifs buried beneath the Austrides. The presence of these is further indicated by the occurrence of culminations, which are portions of the true nappe mountains in which the lower elements have been forced to high altitudes, having been driven over elevated portions of the Foreland. Denudation, especially river action, has brought about the removal of much of these upper structures and has revealed different lower units in different districts. Vertical movement, during and since the orogenic period, has made this type of segmentation more marked. Between two culminations a tectonic depression occurs in which, owing to downward sagging, the uppermost tectonic elements have been preserved from denudation. Staub has identified eleven culminations and eleven depressions in the Alps, and in the Western Alps the culminations occur in each case directly behind the individual massifs

of the zone of Mont Blanc.

The massifs of the zone of Mont Blanc are, generally speaking, large granitic intrusions (batholiths), surrounded by crystalline schists and gneisses with sedimentary rocks more or less highly metamorphosed. In the Aar, Mont Blanc and Pelvoux massifs "fan" structure has been identified, the granitic rocks being subdivided longitudinally by steep-sided synclines of crystalline schists. The larger massifs of the zone, namely, the Aar-Gotthard, Mont Blanc, Pelvoux and Mercantour, form an inner arc, while the smaller ones, namely, the Gastern-Erstfeld, Aiguilles Rouges and Belledonne, form an outer arc. Both arcs are open to the south and adjacent massifs are separated by zones of sedimentary rocks, many of which have been so highly metamorphosed as to be reduced to paragneisses. The Lötschental zone (paragneisses), the Chamonix sedimentary zone and the zone between the Pelvoux and the Belledonne occur between the two arcs. In the two former zones and in the adjacent massifs the roots of the nappes of the High Calcareous Alps are located. The sedimentary cover of the Aiguilles Rouges and the Gastern massifs has been called the Autochthon. This term is also applied by some authorities to all that portion of the sedimentary cover of the Hercynian peneplained surface which has not suffered acute folding, such as is found in the zone of the High Calcareous Alps. A. Heim further calls the massifs of the zone of Mont Blanc the autochthonous massifs. The Autochthon (in its wider sense) has not suffered acute folding such as is found in the other parts of the Alps, but the rocks are in contact with the surface upon which they were originally deposited.

In the High Calcareous Alps six nappes have been identified. These are called the Helvetides by R. Staub, but simply the nappes of the High Calcareous Alps by L. Collet and others. They are named as follows (from the highest to the lowest):—(6) The Oberlaubhorn nappe, (5) the Mont Bonvin nappe, (4) the Plaine Morte nappe, (3) the Wildhorn nappe, (2) the Diablerets nappe, (1) the Morcles nappe.

The Morcles nappe lies as a great recumbent fold upon the Autochthon, and has its roots in the zone of Chamonix. It is composed of sediments ranging from the Trias to the Eocene. Above it lies the Diablerets nappe, the roots of which probably lie in the Mont Blanc massif. This nappe does not possess a reversed limb, this and much of the upper limb having been replaced by a "slide" (E. B. Bailey). The Wildhorn nappe is the greatest of this group and is characterized by a number of digitations in the front of the structure, by disharmonic folding, and a large "involution." Its roots probably occur on the south side of the Mont Blanc massif. The three higher nappes (the Ultra-Helvetian nappes of Heim) crop out in a belt 16 mi. long on the south side of the Wildhorn-Wildstrubel range, and again on the north side of the High Calcareous Alps in the zone of cols, where they form the Internal Prealps. In eastern Switzerland (*i.e.*, east of the Hasli-Tal) the following units occur:—The Säntis-Drusberg unit, the Axen unit, the Glarner-Mürtschen unit, the Parautochthonous nappes.

The upper unit (Säntis-Drusberg) is an eastward extension of the Wildhorn nappe, the Glarner-Mürtschen unit is homologous to the Diablerets nappe, and the Parautochthonous nappes rest upon the Autochthon and are homologous to the Morcles nappe. The Axen unit is not represented in west Switzerland. Three nappes, digitations of one structure, are distinguished in the Säntis-Drusberg unit, four in the Axen unit and two in the Glarner-Mürtschen unit.

With the exception of the Prealps, the Swiss plateau bounds the High Calcareous Alps on the north. The plateau is underlain by Tertiary rocks, covered by glacial, fluvio-glacial and alluvial deposits. It forms a wide syncline between the Jura mountains and the Western Alps, and in it are gentle flexures, the most important of which is a central anticline which passes from Lake Constance to Lake Geneva. The sedimentary rocks of the Jura mountains are continuous with those of the Autochthon beneath the Tertiary rocks of the great Swiss plateau, but they do not show the same facies. They have been folded into anticlines and synclines, the trend of which is parallel to that of the Alps, but the folds are bunched together in the neighbourhood of the central plateau of France and the Vosges-Black Forest massifs. In the eastern part of the mountains the folding is complicated by block faulting. This portion is known as the Jura tableland while the remainder is called the Folded Juras. The folding has only a superficial character, for it dies out downward, the Anhydrite group (Middle Muschelkalk) not being folded. The beds of this latter horizon acted as a plane along which the folding took place, so producing a *décollement*. A study of the tectonics of the Jura mountains reveals a remarkable association between them and the Alps.

The Pennine nappes (Pennides of R. Staub), being great recumbent folds which arose out of the Alpine geosyncline, consist of Paleozoic rocks as crystalline cores, with envelopes of newer sedimentary rocks now highly metamorphosed and known as *schistes lustrés*. The evidence for the age of the *schistes lustrés* is sufficient to prove that they range from the Lower or Middle Trias to the Nummulitic limestone (Eocene). They occur in the synclinal structures between the crystalline cores of the nappes and also along the frontal archbends of the latter. The three Simplon nappes, Monte Leone (III), Lebendun (II), Antigorio (I), crop out in the Ticino district, in the Lepontine culmination brought about by the obstacle of the Aar massif. (The figures I, II, etc., after the names of the nappes indicate the relative position of the structures, I to VI being Pennine nappes and VII–X Austrides.) The nappes pass round the culmination and are directly connected in the south with their roots. The *schistes lustrés* associated with them are not so thick as elsewhere in the Pennine Alps. The Great St. Bernard nappe (IV), which arose from the Briançonnais geanticline, occurs above the Simplon nappes, the latter being regarded as major digitations of the higher structure. The Great St. Bernard nappe is the most extensive of the Pennine units and stretches in an almost unbroken outcrop from the Gulf of Genoa to the Simplon pass. *Schistes lustrés* mark the front of it and also separate it from the crystalline core of the Monte Rosa (V) nappe, which forms the massifs of Monte Rosa, Grand Paradis, Ambin and Dora Maira and is in fact a major digitation of the highest Pennine nappe. The Dent Blanche (VI) nappe, which arose from the Dolin geanticline, has suffered considerable denudation and its main outcrop in the Dent Blanche-Weisshorn mountain mass is now isolated from the roots. Here the nappe is in contact with the Great St. Bernard nappe, for the Monte Rosa nappe does not reach so far north and the Great St. Bernard has suffered backward folding.

The country east of the Rhine line belongs principally to the Hinterland. In it are found several tectonic units, named the Austrides by R. Staub, who also recognizes two divisions in the group, the Upper (Tirolides) and the Lower (Grisonides), both so named because of the location of their main outcrops. This is R. Staub's scheme, but L. Kober uses the name East Alpine nappes for the Austrides and recognizes in them four main divisions. The Austrides overlie the Pennine nappes in the Eastern Alps, for where denudation has been great the lower structures are exposed beneath the Austrides in what are known as "windows." In the Lower Engadine window, *schistes lustrés* occur surrounded by Grisonide elements, while in the Hohe Tauern window are tectonic elements correlated by R. Staub with the Monte Rosa and the Dent Blanche nappes as well as *schistes lustrés*. (L. Kober considers that the lowest elements here are homologous with the higher Simplon nappes.) In the Semmering window, denudation has revealed the Grisonides beneath the Tirolides.

The Grisonides are divided into two major structures, the Campo (VIII) nappe and the Err-Bernina (VII) nappe, each of which has several digitations in its frontal portion. The lower of the two rests on the Margna (VI) nappe, which is homologous to the Dent Blanche nappe. The Grisonides consist of crystalline cores surrounded by sedimentary rocks, the latter being peculiar in age and facies to each nappe. In the Rhätikon the Grisonides show *schuppen* structure (*i.e.,* slices overthrust one upon another) and parts of them exhibit interesting sedimentary types, which are important in a study of the Prealps. The Tirolides are similarly divided into two major structures, the Ötztal

(X) nappe and the Silvretta (IX) nappe. The latter nappe is the greatest East Alpine structure and, being the lower of the two Tirolide elements, will occur to the north of the Ötztal nappe in the root region, but the sedimentary cover of the latter has been driven over the Silvretta nappe and forms the northern Limestone zone. The main outcrop of the Ötztal nappe is in the Mur Alps of Styria, while the other forms the Silvretta mountain mass. The northern Limestone zone forms a wide belt from the Rhine line to Vienna and has the structure of a great pile of overthrust masses of rocks ranging from the Trias to Cretaceous, the dolomite of the Trias being the principal member of the group. North of this zone is the northern Flysch zone, which is the eastern representative of the High Calcareous Alps.

Austride elements occur west of the Rhine line, in the Prealps, which lie between the Swiss plateau and the High Calcareous Alps and between the Arve river and the Lake Thun. The following tectonic elements have been identified in this region: the External Prealps forming the northern portion and being overthrust upon the Molasse of the Swiss plateau; and the Internal Prealps on the southern margin. The Internal and External Prealps are probably connected and completely underlie the basinlike structure filled by the higher elements of the Prealps. In these two zones the higher units of the High Calcareous Alps occur. Above the Internal Prealps is the Niesen nappe (chiefly sandstones and conglomerates), which shows Pennine affinities; while above the External zone there are similar sandstones, etc., forming the zone of Gurnigel which is considered by some to represent the Niesen nappe. The Median Prealps nappe occurs above the zones mentioned and forms the greater part of the Prealps. Above it are the Simme nappe and the Brèche nappe. These structures seem to show Austride affinities, and the association between them and the Austrides is further established by the occurrence of *Klippen* (*i.e.,* frontal portions of nappes isolated by erosion) which have the character of a connecting link, resting upon the Mesozoic rocks of the High Calcareous Alps in the central Swiss region. According to Argand the roots of the Simme nappe occur in the zone of Canavese, south of the Lepontine culmination. These also are west of the Rhine line, but they are continuous with the roots of the other Austride elements farther east. In the zone of Canavese the Dent Blanche nappe is rooted together with the Austrides, and in consequence of this Kober considers that this nappe must belong to the East Alpine group (Austrides) and not to the Pennine chain.

The roots of the Pennine nappes (the "inner roots") lie in a zone which stretches eastward from near Ivrea, through Locarno. The roots of the Austrides are in contact with these but on the south side of them. The nappes are vertical in this zone or even overturned toward the south. To the south again are the Dinaride nappes. The boundary between the Austrides and the Dinarides (the Dinaric boundary) passes from the neighbourhood of the Italian lakes to Merano, then east through the Drau range to the southeast end of Bacher mountains, where it disappears beneath the Hungarian plain. The tectonics of the Dinarides are comparatively simple. The term "nappes" is still used here by some authorities to designate the tectonic units; but the latter are very different from the nappes of other parts of the Alps, being essentially thrust masses. The extent of the thrusting is never very large. Moreover the units are not so strikingly different from one another in facies as is the case in other parts of the Alps. L. Kober recognizes four zones here, the Outer zone (Adriatic), the Lower Dinaric nappe, the Upper Dinaric nappe and the High Dinaric nappe. The stratigraphy of the Dinaric zone shows an important development of Upper Paleozoic rocks, Silurian, Devonian, Carboniferous, Permian and Trias. Jurassic, Cretaceous and Flysch are also important in some units. This southern belt of the Alps is noted for its rich development of calcareous rocks. *Klippen* (outliers) of Dinaride elements occur resting upon the Oetztal nappe in the Mur Alps district. The tectonics of the structures south of the Dinaric boundary show a southward direction of movement. This reverse direction of movement probably indicates one of the latest phases of the Alpine movements. There has been considerable igneous activity in this region, but the intrusions are not all of the same age. The following are affected by Tertiary movements and must therefore belong to an earlier period:—the Kreuz, Iffinger, Brixen, and Riesenferner intrusions. The "Peri-Adriatic Intrusion zone" (W. Salomon) contains the following igneous bodies:—Ivrea, Baveno, Bergeller, Adamello, the tonalite of Eisenkappel and the granites of the Bacher mountains. These were not affected by Alpine movements and are, by many authorities, thought to be of slightly later date than those movements.

Main Chain.—Several important mountain groups are situated on one or other side of the watershed of the Alps and form almost independent ranges, connected with the main chain by a kind of isthmus: such are the Dauphiné Alps, the Eastern and Western Graians, the entire Bernese Oberland, etc. The Alps, therefore, are not composed of a single range but of a great "divide," flanked on either side by other important ranges.

Starting from the Col d'Altare or Colle di Cadibona (west of Savona), the main chain extends first southwest, then northwest to the Colle di Tenda, though nowhere rising much beyond the zone of coniferous trees. Beyond the Colle di Tenda the direction is first west then northwest to the Rocher des Trois Évêques (9,422 ft.), just south of the Mont Enchastraye (9,698 ft.), several peaks of about 10,000 ft. rising on the watershed, though the highest of all, the Punta Argentera (10,817 ft.) stands a little way to its north. From the Rocher des Trois Évêques the watershed runs due north; of the two loftiest peaks of this region, one, the Aiguille de Chambeyron (11,155 ft.), is just to the west and the other, the Monte Viso (12,602 ft.), to the east of the watershed. From the head of the Val Pellice the main chain runs northwest and diminishes much in average height till it reaches the Mont Thabor (10,-505 ft.), which forms the apex of a salient, which the main chain here presents toward the west. Hence the main watershed extends east, culminating in the Aiguille de Scolette (11,509 ft.) but makes a great curve to the northwest and back to the southeast before rising in the Rochemelon (11,607 ft.), a re-entering angle in the great rampart by which Italy is guarded. Thence the direction taken is north as far as the east summit (11,873 ft.) of the Levanna, the watershed rising in a series of snowy peaks, though the loftiest point of the region, the Pointe de Charbonel (12,306 ft.), stands a little to the west. Once more the chain bends northwest rising in several lofty peaks (the highest is the Aiguille de la Grande Sassière [12,323 ft.]), before attaining the considerable depression of the Little St. Bernard pass (7,178 ft.). Thence for a short way the direction is north to the Col de la Seigne (8,245 ft.), and then northeast along the crest of the Mont Blanc chain, which culminates in the peak of Mont Blanc (q.v.; 15,771 ft.), the loftiest in the Alps. A number of high peaks crown the watershed before it attains the Mont Dolent (12,542 ft.). Thence after a short dip southeast, the chain takes near the Great St. Bernard pass (8,100 ft.) the general easterly direction that it maintains throughout the Pennine Alps till it reaches Monte Rosa, whence it bends north, making one small dip to the east as far as the Simplon pass. In the Pennine Alps the main chain maintains a greater average height than in any other part, but, though it rises in a number of lofty peaks, such as the Mont Velan (12,251 ft.), the Matterhorn (q.v.; 14,688 ft.), the Lyskamm (14,691 ft.), the Nord End of Monte Rosa (15,131 ft.) and the Weissmies (13,199 ft.), many of the highest points such as the Grand Combin (14,153 ft.), the Dent Blanche (14,294 ft.), the Weisshorn (14,780 ft.), the true summit or Dufourspitze (15,203 ft.) of Monte Rosa itself, and the Dom (14,911 ft.) rise on its northern slope and not on the main watershed. The chain between the Great St. Bernard and the Simplon sinks at barely half a dozen points below a level of 10,000 ft. Eastward from the Simplon (6,578 ft.) through the Lepontine Alps so far as the St. Gotthard (6,916 ft.) the divide runs northeast, all the higher summits (including the Monte Leone, 11,657 ft., and the Pizzo Rotondo, 10,472 ft.) rising on it, a curious contrast to the long stretch just described. From the St. Gotthard to the Maloja (5,955 ft.) the watershed between the basins of the Rhine and Po runs east as a whole, though making two great dips toward the south first to near the Vogelberg (10,558 ft.) and again to near the Pizzo Gallegion (10,203 ft.), so that it presents a broken

and irregular appearance. Its highest point is the Rheinwaldhorn (11,161 ft.).

From the Maloja pass the main watershed dips southeast for a short distance, and then east and nearly over the highest summit of the Bernina group, the Piz Bernina (13,284 ft.) to the Bernina pass (7,621 ft.). Thence to the Passo di Resia (4,947 ft.) the main chain is ill-defined, though on it rises the Corno di Campo (10,833 ft.), beyond which it runs slightly northeast, past the sources of the Adda and the Frael pass (6,414 ft.), sinks to form the depression of the Ofen pass (7,050 ft.), soon bends north and rises once more in the Piz Sesvenna (10,515 ft.). The break in the continuity of the Alpine chain marked by the deep valley, the *Vintschgau,* of the upper Adige (q.v.) is one of the most remarkable features in the orography of the Alps. The chief source of the Adige is the little Reschen lake, which is only 13 ft. below the Passo di Resia (4,947 ft.) and but 5 mi. from the Inn valley. East of this pass the main chain runs northeast to the Brenner pass along the snowy crest of the Ötztal and Stubai Alps, the loftiest point on it being the Weisskugel (12,257 ft., Ötztal), for the highest summits both of the Ötztal and of the Stubai districts, the Wildspitze (12,382 ft.) and the Zuckerhütl (11,539 ft.), stand a little to the north.

The Brenner (4,501 ft.) is almost the lowest of all the great motor road passes across the main chain, and has always been the chief means of road communication between Germany and Italy. For some way beyond it the watershed runs east over the Hochfeiler (11,516 ft.), the highest crest of the Zillertal Alps. A little farther, at the Dreiherrenspitze (11,480 ft.), we have to choose between following the watershed south, or keeping due east along the highest crest of the Greater Tauern Alps. (1) The latter course is adopted by many geographers. The watershed (though not the chief Alpine watershed) continues east through the Greater Tauern Alps, culminating in the Gross Venediger (12,054 ft.), for the Gross Glockner (12,457 ft.) rises to the south. The chain bends northeast near the Radstädter Tauern pass (5,702 ft.) and preserves that direction through the Lesser Tauern Alps to the Semmering pass (3,215 ft.). (2) On the other hand, from the Dreiherrenspitze the true main watershed of the Alpine chain dips south, passes over the Hochgall (11,270 ft.), the culmination of the Rieserferner group, and then sinks to the Sella di Dobbiaco (3,966 ft.) but a little east of the great Dolomite peak of the Drei Zinnen (9,839 ft.) it bends east again and rises in the Monte Cogliano (9,121 ft., the monarch of the Carnic Alps). Soon after the watershed makes a last bend to the southeast and culminates in the Triglav (9,393 ft.), the highest point of the Julian Alps, though the Grintovec (8,392 ft., the culmination of the Karawanken Alps) stands more to the east. Finally the watershed turns south and ends near the great limestone plateau of the Birnbaumerwald, between Ljubljana and Gorizia.

Principal Passes.—The Alps have never formed an impassable barrier. The spots at which they are crossed are the points at which the great chain sinks to form depressions. Hence the oldest name for such passes is *Mont* (still retained in cases of the Mont Cenis (q.v.) and the Monte Moro); it was long before this term was especially applied to the peaks of the Alps, which, with a few rare exceptions (e.g., the Monte Viso was known to the Romans as Vesulus), were simply disregarded. The native inhabitants of the Alps were naturally the first to use the alpine passes, but to the outer world these passes first became known when the Romans traversed them in order to conquer the world beyond. For obvious reasons the Romans, having once found an easy pass did not trouble to seek for harder routes. The passes known to them were comparatively few: they are, in topographical order from west to east, the Col de l'Argentière, the Col de Genèvre (Montgenèvre pass), the two St. Bernard passes, the Splügen, the Septimer, the Brenner, the Radstädter Tauern, the Sölkscharte, the Plöcken (Croce Carnico) and the Pontebba (or Saifnitz). The Col de Genèvre and the Brenner were the most frequented, while it will be noticed that in the Central Alps only two passes (the Splügen and the Septimer) were certainly known to the Romans. The Simplon is first certainly mentioned in 1235, the St. Gotthard (without name) in 1236, the Lukmanier in 965, the San Bernardino in 941. Even the Mont Cenis (from the 15th to the 19th century the favourite pass for travelers) is first heard of in 756 only. In the 13th century many hitherto unknown passes came into prominence, even some of the easy glacier passes. In the Western and Central Alps there is but one ridge to cross, to which access is gained by a deep-cut valley, though often it would be shorter to cross a second pass in order to gain the plains, *e.g.*, The Col de Genèvre, that is most directly reached by the Col du Lautaret. In the Eastern Alps it is generally necessary to cross three distinct ridges between the north and south plains, the central ridge being the highest and most difficult. The passes which crossed a single ridge, and did not involve too great a detour through a long valley of approach, became the most important and the most popular, *e.g.*, the Mont Cenis, the Great St. Bernard, the St. Gotthard, the Septimer and the Brenner. As time went on the travelers who used the great alpine passes could not put up any longer with the bad old mule paths. A few passes (*e.g.*, the Semmering, the Brenner, the Tenda and the Arlberg) can boast of carriage roads constructed before 1800, while those over the Umbrail and the Great St. Bernard were not completed till the early 20th century. Many of the carriage roads across the great alpine passes were constructed in the 19th century, largely due to the impetus given by Napoleon. As late as 1905, the highest pass over the main chain that had a carriage road was the Great St. Bernard (8,100 ft.). By mid-20th century railway lines had been carried over or through the chain—there being the Brenner and Pontebba lines, both over passes, and the Colle di Tenda, Mont Cenis, Simplon, St. Gotthard, Lötschen, Arlberg, Albula and Pyhrn through tunnels. Road tunnels were constructed (1960) under the Mont Blanc massif and under the Great St. Bernard pass.

See also Albula Pass; Brenner Pass; Lötschen Pass; Mont Cenis Pass; Saint Bernard Passes; Saint Gotthard Pass; Semmering; Simplon Pass; Splügen Pass; Resia, Passo di.

Glaciers.—Because the Alps were explored and studied earlier than the other mountain systems of the world, the type of glaciation found there has received the name "Alpine type." It is similar to that of parts of the Himalayas, Andes, Rockies and the mountains of New Zealand but is different from that of Spitzbergen, Greenland, Alaska and the Polar regions (*see* Glacier). The main characteristics of the Alpine type consist of an elevated "catchment area" from which valleys pass down to lower altitudes. The highest peaks do not necessarily form the centres from which the largest glaciers radiate, but these latter arise where the topography of the mountain masses is that of numerous depressions and wide hollows separated by rounded snow-capped peaks, as Mont Blanc or by steep-sided frost-eaten peaks and ridges as the Aiguilles. Snow accumulates in these hollows and is compacted into ice which differs in appearance and internal structure from ice formed in the normal way by freezing. It is known as *névé* (Fr.) or *firn* (Ger.). This ice is forced downward by the weight of the accumulated snow above, or falls down as avalanches into the valley below, forming the valley glaciers characteristic of the Alps. The boundary between the *névé* and the valley glacier (the *firn* line) is marked by a change in the character of the surface of the ice. Above the *firn* line precipitation is greater than melting and so snow covers the surface, but below it the reverse is the case and the ice is exposed. In summer the *firn* line is quite distinct, but generally some hundreds of feet below the limit of perpetual snow.

It is estimated that there are 1,200 separate glaciers and *névé* fields in the Alps, but many are mere accumulations of snow in small hollows which really form part of larger basins. The largest glacier in the Alps is the Aletsch glacier which is 16 mi. long and with its *névé* and catchment area covers an area of over 50 sq.mi. The lowest point reached by glaciers varies considerably; it is as low as 3,200 ft. above sea level at Grindelwald, but the height is more often quite 1,000 ft. higher than this. The line of perpetual snow lies between 8,000 ft. and 9,500 ft. Its exact position varies locally; regions which rise above these limits form centres for the radiation of valley glaciers. The largest of such centres are in the Mont Blanc group, the Bernese Oberland (from Blumlisalp to the Wetterhorn) and in the Pennine Alps (from the Grand Combin

to the Mischabel). The main chain boasts of more glaciers and *névé* than the subsidiary chains. Nevertheless, the three longest glaciers of the Alps, the Greater Aletsch (16 mi.) and the Unteraar and the Viescher (each 10 mi.), are in the Bernese Oberland. The longest glaciers in the main chain are the Mer de Glace and the Gorner (each 9¼ mi.).

During the Pleistocene Ice Age the whole chain was more than once covered by an ice sheet above which perhaps the main peaks stood out. A. Penck infers four ice maxima. One of the intervals, it is generally agreed, witnessed a return of warm temperate conditions. The final retreat of the Pleistocene Ice Sheet proceeded by stages, and it has been suggested there was a serious regrowth of glaciers in early centuries of the last millenium B.C. Each stage was marked by a continuous retreat of the ice front to higher altitudes, no movement or perhaps even a temporary advance occurring in the intervals. During historical times the movement of the fronts has not been very marked. In 1918 a general forward movement was noticed in most Alpine glaciers, the previous great advance commencing in 1818 and finishing in 1822. The smaller glaciers will, of course, show movement more quickly than the larger. This is illustrated in the case of the Aletsch glacier, which has maintained the same position of its front for many years. In 1823 this glacier suddenly dropped its level (for reasons not understood) causing the level of Lake Märjelen, which is formed by the glacier obstructing the mouth of a tributary stream, to fall.

Lakes and Water Power.—The lakes of the Alps are of several types. (*See* Lake.) Lakes of the barrier type are formed in various ways, principally by terminal and lateral moraines, in rarer cases by land slides, alluvial fans or a glacier. Lake Zürich (*q.v.*) shows interesting phases of damming by various moraines; Lake Mattmark is formed by a lateral moraine; Lake Märjelen is a classic example of a glacier acting as a dam. Examples of lakes of tectonic origin are Lake Joux, in the Jura region, which occurs in a syncline, and Lake Fählen near Säntis. Lakes formed by the solution of calcareous rocks are of two types: the "polje" and the "doline" types. Frequently the depressions occupied by these lakes were the sites of former glaciers, as proved by the lining of glacial clay which the lakes now possess. Lakes of these types are quite frequent in the limestone areas and examples are Lakes Dauben, Mutten and Seewli (the latter also being in a corrie). Lakes in depressions in water-bearing strata occur on moraines or on fluvioglacial material. No rivers feed them and they have no visible effluents. Examples of the formation of two small lakes from a large one by a lacustrine delta are the lakes of Thun (*q.v.*) and Brienz and of Sils and Silvaplana.

By mid-20th century the Alps had become a most important source of hydroelectric power for industry, railway transport and lighting, and the amount of coal used is diminishing. Nowhere, even in the limestone districts, is the amount of water so small as to warrant the exclusive use of coal or other fuels. As the water is derived from melting snow and ice, there is no fear of summer shortage, but a winter stoppage may occur. Most of the great lakes of the subalpine region are used as sources of supply, as also are many of the smaller ones; in the latter cases the level of water is frequently raised by a dam. The water is drawn from the bottom of the lake in order to ensure a constant supply in winter. Reservoirs are also constructed in suitable places. The choice of site depends upon several factors, *e.g.*, the impermeable nature of the rocks forming the basin, an adequate supply of water, a minimum amount of deposition of sediment within the basin and the geographical position. Old lake basins have been transformed into reservoirs, *e.g.*, the Barbarine, and many deep gorges have been so utilized. Electric power and lighting are to be found in remote villages. Many of the valleys in the French Alps have become industrial districts as a result of the availability of electric power; bauxite is refined, and numerous electro-chemical and electro-metallurgical industries are active.

In the Alps are the sources of the great rivers of western Europe—the Po, Rhône, Rhine and Danube (the actual source of the latter is in the Black Forest, but its main tributaries rise in the Alps). These rivers drain the south, west, north and east slopes respectively, and the Danube also drains the north slope. There exists a very close connection between the direction of the river valleys in the Alps and the geological structure. Most of the valleys are either parallel to or at right angles to the trend of the chains. Examples of the former are the Isère, the Upper Rhône and the Upper Rhine, and of the latter the rivers of the Pennine Alps. (J. I. P.; F. J. M.)

Minerals.—Mineral deposits in the Alps are generally small and scattered, and there were only a few mines of economic significance in the 1960s. The Swiss Alps provide no minerals of any commercial importance apart from minor deposits of lead, zinc and copper in Valais. Coal has in times of necessity been produced from Valais, but the quality is very poor. The principal minerals extracted from the Austrian Alps consist of iron ore (there are very large reserves of good quality in Styria), lignite, magnesite (the Veitch mines are the richest), salt (important in the Salzburg area), and some minor deposits of lead, zinc and copper. In the past, gold was mined in the Hohe Tauern. In the Italian section of the Alps some anthracite is obtained from the Aosta region, together with iron and copper pyrites; there is also a small production from scattered deposits of antimony, zinc, lead and manganese. The alluvium of several rivers was washed for gold, and numerous small gold mines opened in the past in the Monte Rosa area and elsewhere, but little gold is extracted. The principal mineral worked in the French Alps is bauxite, in the extreme south near Brignoles; this area produces about three-quarters of the total output of bauxite in France. Near La Mure (south of Grenoble), and elsewhere, there are some small coal deposits, but these supply less than 1% of France's coal production. Limestone is found widely in the Alps, and is quarried for cement. (C. Em.)

Climate.—It is well known that with the rise from the sea level into the upper regions of the atmosphere the temperature decreases. Mountain chains cause the prevailing winds to rise to higher altitudes, thus frequently bringing about the precipitation of snow or rain principally upon the windward side. The vast mass of snow, converted into glaciers, maintains a gradation of very different climates within the narrow space that intervenes between the foot of the mountains and their upper ridges; it cools the breezes that are wafted to the plains on either side, but its most important function is to regulate the water supply of the large region traversed by Alpine streams. Nearly all precipitation during six or seven months is in the form of snow, gradually released by melting in the course of the succeeding summer; even in the hottest and driest seasons the reserves accumulated in the form of glaciers maintain the regular flow of the greater streams. Nor is this all; the lakes that fill several main valleys on the south side are somewhat above the level of the Lombardy plain, and afford inexhaustible water for that system of irrigation to which it owes its proverbial fertility.

Six regions or zones, which are best distinguished by their characteristic vegetation, are found in the Alps. They are (1) the olive region; (2) the vine region; (3) the mountain region or the region of deciduous trees; (4) the subalpine region or the region of coniferous trees; (5) the Alpine region; (6) the glacial region. Local conditions of exposure to the sun, protection from cold winds or the reverse, as well as height above sea level, are of primary importance in determining the climate and the corresponding vegetation.

1. The great plain of Upper Italy is colder in winter than the British Isles which has mean winter temperature of about 40° F. The olive and the characteristic shrubs of the north Mediterranean coasts do not thrive in the open, but olives ripen in sheltered places at the foot of the mountains and along the deeper valleys and the lake shores. The evergreen oak grows wild around Lake Garda, and fruit is cultivated on a large scale, with partial protection in winter.

2. The vine is far more tolerant of cold than the olive, but to produce tolerable wine it demands, at the season of ripening, not much less warmth than the olive, about 68° F. average. These conditions are satisfied in the deeper valleys of the Alps, and up to a considerable height on slopes exposed to the sun. Winter snow covering helps the plant to resist severe and prolonged frosts.

3. So many varieties of grain are grown under various climatic conditions that their limits of cultivation are less useful for determining zones than are those of the chief deciduous trees—oak, beech, ash and sycamore. These do not reach exactly to the same elevation, nor are they often found growing together; but their upper limit corresponds accurately enough to the change from a temperate to a colder climate. This limit lies about 4,000 ft. above sea level on the north side of the Alps, but on the southern slopes it often rises to 5,000 ft., sometimes even to 5,500 ft. The interference of man has in many districts almost extirpated these trees. Their place has been occupied by the Scotch pine and spruce, which suffer less from goats, the worst enemies of trees. The mean annual temperature differs little from that of the British Isles which is about 50° F.; but snow usually lies for several months, till it gives place to a spring and summer considerably warmer than the average of British seasons.

4. The subalpine is the region which mainly determines the manner of life of the farming population of the Alps. Of the space lying between the summits of the Alps and the low country on either side roughly one-quarter is available for cultivation of which about one-half may be vineyards and cornfields, while the remainder produces forage and grass. About another quarter is utterly barren, consisting of snow fields, glaciers, bare rock, lakes and the beds of streams. There remains about one-half, which is divided between forest and pasture, and it is the produce of this half which mainly supports the relatively large population. For a quarter of the year the flocks and herds are fed on the upper pastures; but the true limit of the wealth of a district is the number of animals that can be supported during the long winter, and while one part of the population is engaged in tending the beasts and in making cheese and butter, the remainder is busy cutting hay and storing up winter food for the cattle. The larger villages are mostly in the mountain region, but in many parts of the Alps the villages stand in the subalpine region at heights varying from 4,000 ft. to 5,500 ft. above sea level, more rarely extending to about 6,000 ft. Coniferous trees, where they have not been artificially kept down, form vast forests. They protect the valleys from destructive avalanches, and, retaining the superficial soil by their roots, they mitigate the destructive effects of heavy rains. On very steep slopes avalanches have frequently torn up the trees, leaving long avenues of varying width through the forests. In such places and in valleys where they have been rashly cut away, and the waters pour down the slopes unchecked, every tiny rivulet becomes a raging torrent, that carries away the soil and subsoil from the grassy slopes and devastates the floor of the valley, covering it with debris and gravel. The prevailing species are the common spruce, the silver fir, the larch and the Scotch pine. The Siberian fir is also found. In the northern Alps the pine forests rarely surpass the limit of 6,000 ft. above the sea, but on the south side they commonly attain 7,000 ft., while the larch, Siberian fir and mughus often extend above that elevation.

5. Throughout the Teutonic region of the Alps the word *alp* is used specifically for the upper pastures where cattle are fed in summer, but this region is held to include the whole space between the uppermost limit of trees and the first appearance of permanent snow. Here the characteristic vegetation of the Alps is developed in its full beauty and variety. Shrubs are not wanting. Three species of rhododendron give masses of red or pink flowers; the common juniper rises higher still, along with three species of bilberry; and several dwarf willows attain nearly to the utmost limit of vegetation, the so-called limit of perpetual snow.

6. On the higher parts of lofty mountains more snow falls in each year than is melted on the spot. A portion of this is carried away by the wind before it is consolidated; a larger portion accumulates in hollows of the surface, and, gradually converted into glacial ice, descends slowly into the deeper valleys, to swell perennial streams. As on a mountain the snow does not lie in beds of uniform thickness, and some parts are more exposed to the sun and warm winds than others, are commonly found beds of snow alternating with exposed slopes covered with brilliant vegetation; and to the observer near at hand there is no appearance in the

least corresponding to the term *limit of perpetual snow*, though the case is otherwise when a high mountain chain is viewed from a distance, for the level at which large snow beds show themselves along its flanks is approximately horizontal, in so far as conditions are similar. On the opposite sides of the same chain, exposure to sun or to warm winds may cause a wide difference in the level of permanent snow; but in some cases the increased fall of snow on the side exposed to moist winds may more than compensate increased influence of the sun's rays. Still, even with these reservations, the so-called line of perpetual snow is not fixed. In some parts of the Alps the limit may be set at about 8,000 ft. above the sea, while in others it cannot be placed much below 9,500 ft. As very little or no snow can rest on rocks that lie at an angle exceeding 60°, some steep masses of rock remain bare even near the summits of the highest peaks, but as almost every spot offering the least hold for vegetation is covered with snow, few flowering plants are seen above 11,000 ft. It is, however, want of soil rather than climatic conditions that checks the upward extension of the alpine flora. Increased direct effect of solar radiation compensates for the cold nights, and in the few spots where plants have been found in flower up to a height of 12,000 ft., nothing has indicated that the processes of vegetation were arrested by the severe cold which they must sometimes endure. The climate of the glacial region has often been compared to that of the polar regions, but they are widely different. Here, intense solar radiation by day, which gives the surface when dry a temperature approaching 80° F., alternates with severe night frost. There, a sun which never sets sends feeble rays that maintain a low equable temperature rarely rising more than a few degrees above the freezing point. Hence the upper region of the Alps sustains a far more varied and brilliant vegetation. (J. I. P.;. F. J. M.)

Vegetation.—The alpine flora in general belongs essentially to the middle belt of the European high mountain flora, and contains numerous significant species common to all these mountains. The flora of the western parts of the Alps shows connections with that of the Pyrenees, while the flora of the eastern parts shows a closer relationship to that of the Carpathians. The Alps, however, have a considerable number of species that occur nowhere else, the so-called endemic species. It is difficult to find a border line within the Alps between the east and west, since the distribution of the vegetation does not correspond with the geographical borders between the eastern and western Alps. The differences in the two floras here mainly derived from the destruction of plants in the Ice Age and the postglacial plant migrations in the thickly glaciated middle part of the Alps. The easiest way to describe the present distribution is to divide the transverse mountain chains of the middle and eastern Alps (Helveto-Norican province, from Geneva to Vienna and Trieste) from the longitudinal ones of the southwestern Alps (Gallic province, from Geneva to the Riviera). The middle and eastern Alps with their great transverse valleys are characterized, among other things, by such outstanding communities as those of *Pinus mugo* (mountain pine) and *Rhododendron hirsutum* (alpine rose); the region of the southwestern Alps is characterized by *Hugueninia (Sisymbrium) tanacetifolia, Scutellaria alpina, Saxifraga diapensioides, Artemisia glacialis*, etc. The latter region, in contradiction to the former, is marked by great longitudinal valleys which allow the Mediterranean flora to intrude far into the inner parts of the Alps. In some respects the southern limestone Alps (from Lake Maggiore to the Karawanken), belonging to the transverse mountain chains but favoured by a very good climate, are similar to the Gallic province; therefore they are often designated as a region of their own within the Helveto-Norican province.

History.—The "old-oceanic" element is the most ancient representative of the recent alpine flora. It consists mainly of very ancient mosses of tropic-oceanic distribution (*Rhacomitrium* heaths, *Hookeria* and *Brotherella* in subalpine mixed woods). The presumably oldest flowering plants of the Alps are restricted to the lower situations (submontane region) such as ravines (*Phyteuma comosum, Saxifraga paradoxa*), to mountain forests and the edges of woods, (*Wulfenia carinthiaca, Pedicularis acaulis*) and to the subalpine vegetation of tall perennial herbs (*Gentiana*

lutea, Rhaponticum scariosum [Centaurea rhaponica], Sanguisorba dodecandra). These forms which were already developed during the folding of the Alps apparently did not produce high alpine descendants; on the other hand the ancestors of the original high-alpine-flora (certain species of *Primula, Gentiana* and *Saxifraga*) which had been growing once in lower situations, died out long ago. The real alpine plants (oreophytes), making up the Tertiary stock, can be divided into two elements: the arctico-tertiary group of high Asiatic origin, only growing in a narrow climatic region (*Saxifraga, Primula, Androsace, Gentiana, Pedicularis*), and the Mediterranean, eurythermic group, adapted to a broad belt of different climates (*Campanula, Phyteuma, Achillea, Sempervivum, Viola*). During Tertiary times (and possibly caused by the periodic folding of the different parts of the Alps) many species were split into parallel species, vicariads, such as *Pinus mugo* and *P. uncinata (mugo rostrata), Gentiana clusii* and *G. kochiana*. The glacial periods obliterated many ancient Tertiary elements, mainly the subtropical ones of the lowlands and the rich, Tertiary deciduous forests; but the main part of the truly alpine elements succeeded in surviving in refuges on the unglaciated borders of the Alps. There are a great number of plants that have migrated to the Alps from the north during these periods of cold climate; among them are not only purely arctic species and those of northern Europe but a number of Asiatic species. Besides many plants of bogs and moors (*Juncus, Carex, Scirpus*), there are plants of the dry alpine meadows and rock heaths (altaic-alpine elements, alpine steppe: *Callianthemum, Hedysarum, Astragalus, Lloydia, Leontopodium*). Many of the alpine plants that seem to be characteristic (*e.g.*, the well-known edelweiss) have become inhabitants of the Alps only in relatively recent times. In the postglacial periods the re-afforestation of the Alps that took place led to the structure of vegetation that is found there now.

Vegetation Zones.—In the Alps the following zones of vegetation are usually distinguished: (1) colline zone (up to the upper limit of vine culture, 1,800–4,000 ft.); (2) montane zone (to the limit of the decidous woods, 2,600–5,600 ft.); (3) subalpine zone (to the limit of the coniferous woods and the "fighting" zone, 5,200–7,900 ft.); (4) alpine zone (the region of the mountain pine, followed by dwarf shrubs and alpine meadows, 5,600–9,200 ft.); and (5) snow zone (above the climatic snow line, the region of pioneer-grass-heath communities, cushion plants and cryptogams). Over the whole range of the Alps the zones and the plant sequences within the several regions can be very different, depending on their geographical situation. Moreover, regional divisions in separate parts of the area can be recognized; for instance, in the forest region of Switzerland there is a northern zone of beech, a central zone of pine and a south alpine zone of chestnut; in the eastern Alps, to the north and to the south, a bordering zone of deciduous forest, a zone of mixed forest and an inner zone of coniferous forest are to be found. The most outstanding factor everywhere is the forest and tree limit (and between them the "fighting" zone); these limits are not only caused by low temperatures, but by the short growing season and by the lack of appropriate soils. In the oceanic marginal areas of the Alps the forest limit consists of spruce, but in the more continental areas of the central and parts of the southern Alps cembra pine and larch grow in the highest places. Above the tree limit there is the region of the true oreotrephes showing various adaptations to this special climate: the short growing period is overcome by perennial growth, evergreen foliage and early flowering; high transpiration, caused by intensive sunlight, is diminished by cushion growth, a dense cover of hairs and alterations in the structure of the leaves (leathery, needle-shaped or succulent leaves). Many alpine plants can bear freezing and melting; others, the less hardy ones, are found only in places where they are sheltered by snow during the winter. Another sharp separation is caused by the fact that many species are only able to grow on soil with a certain degree of acidity; a limestone substratum will not produce soils of very high acidity so the limestone floras (calcicole) are mostly very different from the silicate floras (calcifuge) of the acid soils of the crystalline rocks. The splitting into separate species, subspecies or varieties was often combined with their separation in calcicole and calcifuge races (*Pulsatilla alpina* and *P. apiifolia*, *Rhododendron hirsutum* and *R. ferrugineum*).

Plant Associations.—The following is a list of the chief plant associations of perennial dicotyledons with examples found in each: rock crevices (*Potentilla caulescens*, *Androsace multiflora*), shale and gravel (*Thlaspi rotundifolium*, *Androsace alpina*), tall perennial herbs (*Adenostyles*), late-snow-patches (*Salix herbacea*, *Arabis coerulea*); in all these cases there is a clear division into calcicole and calcifuge plants. There are also associations, mainly dominated by monocotyledons, chiefly sedges and grasses, of the shallow moors and transition moors (*Carex fusca* and *C. davalliana*), of the rich meadows and pastures (*Trisetum flavescens*, *Poa alpina*), of dry, rich grass heaths (*Sesleria*, *Elyna*) and of the sour, poor grass heaths (*Nardus*, *Carex curvula*). The tree- and shrub-associations can be divided into the following zones (excluding the associations of the deciduous trees, which are mostly restricted to the lowest zones): coniferous trees (spruce and fir), subalpine shrub-associations (*Pinus mugo*, *Alnus viridis*) and dwarf shrubs (*Rhododendron*, *Loiseleuria*, *Vaccinium*). (HE. M.)

Animal Life.—The fauna of the Alps includes both invertebrates and vertebrates. The invertebrates are geologically more ancient than the vertebrates and the details of their distribution markedly different. The birds and mammals, zoologically the most recent, have evolved rapidly and show a different distribution, one that can be more clearly distinguished as alpine.

In the mountains of the northern hemisphere generally may be found species of birds and mammals typical of the cold plains further north. As compared with the mountain ranges of Asia, those in Europe show a smaller number of species and the individuals of these species are most sparsely distributed. Some of these species represent relics of the Ice Age, left behind on "islands" as the glaciers retreated north. Others belong to species that enjoy a wide distribution elsewhere but have found a congenial habitat in the Alps also. Among birds, the chaffinch is an example of a species widely distributed that also lives in the Alps wherever there are trees. The skylark, typically an inhabitant of low-lying pastures, will be found on alpine pastures provided the slope is not too steep. The wheatear occurs locally in the Alps, and other mountainous regions, but is also found on shores, moors and heaths, wherever there are large stones or rocky outcrops.

When these and the other ubiquitous species, found in the lowlands, hilly country and mountains, are ignored, the birds of the Alps can be divided into three groups: (1) those belonging more properly to the coniferous forests of the Siberian taiga and its outliers further west; (2) those common to the Alps and to the mountain ranges of central Asia; and (3) those common to the Alps and the arctic tundra.

The species included under (1) are such as the capercaillie, black grouse and hazel hen, the black and the three-toed woodpecker, the nutcracker, the crossbill, Tengmalm's owl and the pigmy owl. These are all birds of the cold forests and although their distribution has been effected by climatic changes during the Pleistocene period they are not markedly separated from their main centre of distribution in the north, and are not therefore typically alpine.

The birds grouped under (2) are most distinctly mountain birds and represent a few of the species that have their main centre of distribution in the Tibetan mountains. These typically Asiatic species become more rare as one travels west, until in the Alps they are represented only by the lammergeier, rock partridge, alpine chough, water pipit, wall creeper, alpine accentor and snow finch. Mountains, being inaccessible, often serve as the last refuges from persecution by man. This has not saved the lammergeier or bearded vulture, which has been exterminated in the Swiss Alps and occurs there now only as a very rare vagrant, at the most. Like all the other birds listed under (2) it is adapted to a rocky biotope, nesting on precipices. The rock partridge flourishes in wooded rocky country, the alpine chough nests in rocky clefts, sometimes in ruins that simulate cliffs, always at great altitudes. The water pipit is a race of the rock pipit which breeds near the shore, but the water pipit breeds in mountainous areas, nesting in crevices. The wall creeper inhabits rocky ravines and earth cliffs, breeds in crevices on inland cliff faces, in rocks or, occasionally,

on buildings, from 6,000 ft. to the snow line. All these move down in winter to the rocky valleys and the foothills. The snow finch breeds on bare mountain tops above 6,000 ft. coming lower in winter.

Like the varying hare, the birds listed under (3) are distinctly isolated from their main area of distribution in the north. They constitute small islands of the arctic fauna, left behind by the retreating ice, and are characteristic elements of the glacial relict fauna. They include the ptarmigan and the dotterel, the latter being localized and of irregular occurrence in the Alps.

The mammals are less numerous than the birds, both in species and in populations. Only one of them represents a true relict of the glacial fauna. This is the varying hare, living at 4,500 to 9,000 ft. It is known in England under a variety of names: Scottish, blue, variable or mountain hare. It is intermediate in size between the common rabbit and the brown hare, and is unlike either of these in changing from a summer to a winter coat. There are other varying hares, all restricted to the northern regions except for this one isolated form in the Swiss Alps.

The beasts of prey are represented by the fox, weasel and stoat. So far as the fox is concerned there is some evidence that individuals living on mountains are slightly larger in size than the lowland foxes. This is to be expected, since the large bulk gives a relatively smaller surface area thus reducing the loss of body-heat, the usual response to living in a colder climate.

Two rodents are characteristic of the Alps. The marmot is a relative of the ground squirrels. There are several species, mostly mountain dwellers, in northern Europe, northern Asia and North America as far north as Alaska. The common marmot of the Swiss Alps, about two feet long, lives among piles of rocks. It exists elsewhere only in the Carpathians but has recently been introduced into the Pyrenees. The second rodent is the snow vole, with a curiously discontinuous distribution in the Alps. It is a large vole with a grey coat and is found on rocky islets protruding through the glaciers at 12,000 ft. It also occurs in suitable habitats down to sea level.

The alpine ibex, in the Alps of Switzerland, France, Italy and Austria, is a small animal less than three feet at the shoulder, with horns up to 35 in. It is believed to have been exterminated as a wild animal but has been re-introduced to many of the valleys where it interbreeds freely with the domestic goat, so that it is doubtful whether there is any pure blood left. The well-known chamois, one of the goat antelopes, lives in the Alps and a few other mountain ranges in southern Europe as well as in Asia Minor. It is preserved as a sporting animal and is usually found at the upper edge of the tree line, going higher up into the mountains in summer. (MA. BU.)

The People.—The Alps have been inhabited since prehistoric times, but their population has never been a homogeneous one; the uniqueness of their surroundings has not produced any ethnic unity among the people. The races, languages and religions, with only slight modifications, are those of the European countries that share the Alpine chain. The Alps, therefore, so closely associated with the history of Europe, do not constitute a region apart.

The peopling of the Alps began during Paleolithic times with raids by hunters; it was completed in the Neolithic Age (when the last Quaternary glaciers melted) by cultivators and herdsmen. In the Iron Age the copper and iron workings of the Alps drew further numbers of people. Hallstatt (*q.v.*) where the first Iron Age was determined, lies in the calcareous Alps of Austria, southwest of Salzburg. Salt (from Salzkammergut, in Austria), and alpine pasture above the tree line were other sources of attraction. The people in the western Alps with the most distant origins are the Ligurians (see LIGURIA), who came from the shores of the Mediterranean, and in the central Alps the Raeti or Rhetae (see RAETIA), who possibly originated in the Dinaric region. The Celts or Gauls mingled with both groups a short time before the Roman conquest. The Romans were the only people to unify the Alps under one system of administration, which depended on a network of roads and military posts. They created towns, notably Augusta Pretoria (Aosta), lying at the junction of the routes to the Great and Little St. Bernard. The Germanic invasions of the first centuries of the Christian era—Burgundians in the west, Alemanni in the centre and Bavarians in the east—changed the population of the central and eastern Alps and penetrated as far as the Italian side. Slavonic peoples infiltrated the southwestern corner of the Alpine chain.

The languages spoken in the Alps are mainly German (Austria, Bavaria, eastern Switzerland), French (western Switzerland, France), Italian on the southern side and Croatian in the southeastern corner. In the heart of the Alps, in the vast canton of Graubünden (Grisons), Ladin or Raeto-Romance, a Latinized form of the language of the ancient Raeti, is still used (see RAETO-ROMANCE DIALECTS). The linguistic boundaries do not correspond to those on the map; French is spoken on the Italian side, in the eastern Briançonnais part (which belonged to France until 1713) and in the Valle d'Aosta; German has been maintained in the southern Tirol (an Austrian possession until 1919), chiefly in the valley of the Alto Adige. Even the Swiss Valais is shared linguistically between German and French, the boundary passing through Sierre (Ger. Siders).

The boundary between Roman Catholics and Protestants in no way corresponds to linguistic boundaries. Protestants, very much in the minority, are predominant only in a few Swiss cantons (Bern, Glarus, Graubünden). The French and Piedmontese Alps, where the Waldenses were numerous, have now only small groups of Protestants. The French Alps, like the Italian Alps, Valais, Ticino, and the Bavarian and Austrian Alps, are Catholic.

The original customs and various types of culture of the inhabitants of the Alps are retreating before the invasion of modern civilization. The costumes, which are the modified and fossilized forms of the old costumes of the plains, are interesting only as relics of the past, except in Bavaria and the Tirol; the costumes of the women were often uncomfortable and heavy. The houses have remained more faithful to tradition. In the Germanic Alps of Bavaria, Austria and Switzerland (with the exception of a part of Graubünden) wood is used for building. Apart from a few places stone dwellings are preferred in the French, Italian and Croatian Alps. Quite often an attic of wood is built on top of a ground floor of stone and on the roofs corrugated iron, tiles and slate have replaced thatch and stone. In the French and Italian Alps houses are grouped into villages and hamlets, but are more widely dispersed in the Germanic Alps. In the case of the former this has been detrimental to property holding, land being split up into fragments following successive divisions. Forests and pasture land are generally owned by the community, the right of use being regulated by different customs. Direct ownership of the soil is very ancient except in the neighbourhood of the towns and convents. The mountain people often own vineyards at low altitudes; they move about in order to work their land at the different levels, going up to the pastures in the spring and summer and returning in the autumn to the village, where they spend the winter. They have several houses in which they live in turn. The problem of overpopulation was at one time dealt with by seasonal migrations (itinerant tradesmen, chimney sweeps, agricultural workers, cab drivers, etc.), but it is now taken care of by permanent emigration. The western Alps have lost a good part of their population, more so than the eastern Alps. Industry based on electrical power, timber, in some cases iron (Austria) and the tourist trade—at first in summer and then both in winter and summer—have changed conditions of life in much of the Alps. Tourism is one of the chief sources of income and many Alpine resorts such as Chamonix, St. Moritz, Davos, Garmisch-Partenkirchen, Cortina d'Ampezzo and Zermatt (qq.v.) are internationally known. Towns have grown up which are the regional centres of intellectual life and economic vitality. (P. VE.)

Exploration of the High Alps.—About 20 glacier passes were certainly known before 1600, about 25 more before 1700 and another 20 before 1800. Though the attempt of P. A. Arnod (an official of the duchy of Aosta) in 1689 to "re-open" the Col du Géant may be counted as made by a non-native, no further cases of this kind occurred until the last quarter of the 18th century. Among the earliest recorded ascents of high peaks made by non-natives were those of the Rochemelon in 1358, in fulfilment of a

vow, and of the Mont Aiguille in 1492 by order of Charles VIII of France, in order to destroy its reputation for inaccessibility. In 1555 Konrad von Gesner (q.v.) climbed the lowest of the seven summits of Pilatus. The first two men who really explored the regions of ice and snow were Horace Benedict de Saussure (q.v.; 1740–99, the Pennine Alps), and the Benedictine monk of Disentis, Placidus à Spescha (1752–1833), most of whose ascents were made before 1806 in the valleys at the sources of the Rhine. The ascent of Mont Blanc in 1786 by M. G. Paccard (1757–1827) and Jacques Balmat (1762–1834) was the first great milestone in the development of the sport of mountaineering. In the early 19th century the Meyer family of Aarau conquered the Jungfrau (q.v.) (1811) and the Finsteraarhorn by deputy (1812, though this is disputed and the first ascent may not have been made until 1829) beside several glacier passes, all in the Bernese Oberland. Their work was continued by a number of Swiss, particularly Gottlieb Studer (1804–90) of Bern, and Edouard Desor (1811–82) of Neuchâtel. In 1787 Mark Beaufoy (1764–1827) made the first English ascent of Mont Blanc, a mountain to which his fellow countrymen devoted themselves rather exclusively, with notable exceptions such as J. D. Forbes (q.v.; 1809–68), A. T. Malkin (1803–88) and John Ball (1818–89). Around Monte Rosa the Vincent family, Josef Zumstein (1783–1861) and Giovanni Gnifetti (1801–67) explored in the period from 1778 to 1842, while in the Eastern Alps the Archduke John (1782–1859) and P. J. Thurwieser (1789–1865) were pioneers worthy of note. The spread of railways in Europe in the 1850s made access to the Alps much easier and British climbers became especially active. The second half of the century saw a systematic exploration of the Alps, in particular by F. F. Tuckett (1834–1913), W. A. B. Coolidge (q.v.; 1850–1926), Edward Whymper (q.v.; 1840–1911), W. M. Conway (1856–1937) and D. W. Freshfield (1845–1934). The English Alpine club was founded in the winter of 1857–58, followed in 1862 by the Austrian Alpine association, in 1863 by the Italian and Swiss Alpine clubs and in 1874 by the French Alpine club. In 1874 the Austrian Alpine association was fused with the German Alpine association, founded in 1869, but they were later separated. These clubs have explored the peaks, built huts, trained guides and published journals and guidebooks. (See also MOUNTAINEERING.)

The two subjoined lists give the dates of the initial conquest of about 50 of the greater peaks (apart from those already noticed) achieved before and after Jan. 1, 1858.

Before Jan. 1, 1858: Titlis (1744), Mont Vélan (1779), Rheinwaldhorn (1798), Gross Glockner (1800), Ortler (1804), Tödi (1824), Altels (1834), Gross Venediger (1841), Wetterhörner (1844–45), Mont Pelvoux (1848), Piz Bernina (1850), Fletschhorn (1854), Monte Rosa (1855), Laquinhorn, Allalinhorn (1856) and Pelmo (1857).

After Jan. 1, 1858: Dom, Eiger (1858), Aletschhorn, Bietschhorn, Rimpfischhorn, Grand Combin (1859), Grand Paradis, Grande Casse (1860), Weisshorn, Monte Viso, Gross Schreckhorn, Lyskamm (1861), Dent Blanche, Monte Della Disgrazia, Täschhorn (1862), Dent d' Hérens (1863), Presanella, Barre des Écrins, Mont Dolent, Zinal Rothorn (1864), Matterhorn, Ober-Gabelhorn, Aiguille Verte, Piz Roseg (1865), Grandes Jorasses (1868), Langkofel (1869), Cimon della Pala, Ailefroide (1870), Aiguille de Blaitière, Rosengartenspitze (1874), Monte di Scerscen, Aiguille Noire de Peuterey, Meije (1877), Aiguille du Dru (1878), Aiguille du Grépon (1881), Aiguille du Géant (1882), and Aiguille Blanche de Peuterey (1885).

See also references under "Alps" in the Index.

(T. S. BL.)

BIBLIOGRAPHY.—A. Heim, *Geologie der Schweiz*, 2 vol. (1919–22); R. Staub, "Der Bau der Alpen," *Beitr. Geol. Schweiz*, vol. lii (1924); L. Kober, *Bau und Entstehung der Alpen* (1923); L. W. Collet, *The Structure of the Alps* (1927); E. Argand, "Sur l'arc des Alpes Occidentales," *Ecologae Geologicae Helvetiae*, vol. xiv (July 1916); A. Penck and E. Brückner, *Die Alpen im Eiszeitalter* (1927); H. Gams and R. Nordhagen, "Postglaziale Klimaänderungen und Erdkrustenbewegungen in Mitteleuropa," *Mitt. geogr. Ges. Münch.*, vol. xvi (1923); W. B. Wright, *The Quaternary Ice Age*, 2nd ed., ch. 9 (1937); H. Christ, *Das Pflanzenleben der Schweiz* (1876); M. Jerosch, *Geschichte und Herkunft der schweizerischen Alpenflora* (1903); R. Pampanini,

Essai sur la géographie botanique des Alpes et particulier des Alpes sudorientales (1903); L. Diels, "Genetische Elemente in der Flora der Alpen," *Englers Bot. Jb.,* vol. 44 (1910); J. Braun-Blanquet, "Über die Genesis der Alpenflora," *Verh. Naturf. Ges. Basel,* vol. 35 (1923), "La végétation alpine et nivale des Alpes françaises," *VIIIᵉ Congr. Int. de Bot. Paris-Nice* (1954); C. Schröter, *Das Pflanzenleben der Alpen,* 2nd ed. (1926), *Taschenflora des Alpenwanderers,* 25th ed. rev. by W. Lüdi (1940), *Flora des Südens,* ed. by E. Schmid (1956); H. Gams, "Das ozeanische Element in der Flora der Alpen," *Jb. Ver. Schutze Alpenpfl.,* vol. 3 (1933), "Das Alter des alpinen Endemismus," *Ber. schweiz. bot. Ges.,* vol. 42 (1933), "Der tertiäre Grundstock der Alpenflora," *Jb. Ver. Schutze Alpenfl.,* vol. 5 (1933), "Die nacheiszeitliche Geschichte der Alpenflora," *Jb. Ver. Schutze Alpenfl.,* vol. 7 (1938); R. Scharfetter, *Die Pflanzenwelt der Ostalpen* (1938); H. Merxmüller, "Untersuchungen zur Sippengliederung und Arealbildung in den Alpen," *Jb. Ver. Schutze Alpenfl.,* vol. 17 (1952), with J. Poelt, "Beiträge zur Florengeschichte der Alpen," *Ber. bayer. bot. Ges.,* vol. xxx (1954); L. Fenaroli, *Flora della Alpi* (1955), with V. Giacomini, *La Vegetazione. I. L'Italia alpina* (1957); C. Favarger, *Flore et végétation des Alpes,* 2 vol. (1956–58); H. Pitschmann and H. Reisigl, *Bilderflora der Südalpen* (1959); G. Hegi, *Alpenflora,* 15th ed. by H. Merxmüller (1959); R. Blanchard, *Les Alpes et leur destin* (1958), *Les Alpes Occidentales,* 13 vol. (1944–56); J. E. Tyler, *The Alpine Passes* (1930); J. Tyndall, *Hours of Exercise in the Alps* (1871); E. Whymper, *Scrambles Amongst the Alps* (1871; 6th ed. 1936); Leslie Stephen, *The Playground of Europe* (1871; reprint 1946); W. M. Conway, *The Alps from End to End* (1895); A. F. Mummery, *My Climbs in the Alps and Caucasus* (1895; reprint 1946); C. E. Mathews, *The Annals of Mont Blanc* (1898), G. W. Young, *Mountain Craft* (1920; 7th ed. 1949) and *On High Hills* (1927; 5th ed. 1947); R. L. G. Irving, *A History of British Mountaineering* (1955); Arnold Lunn, *A Century of Mountaineering* (1957). (HE. M.; T. S. BL.)

ALPS, AUSTRALIAN: *see* AUSTRALIAN ALPS.

ALPS, ROMAN PROVINCES OF THE, small provinces established in the Western Alps under the Roman empire occupying areas in modern France, Italy and Switzerland. Around most of the Alpine barrier Italy was regarded as extending to the mountain summit and the defense of the passes could be provided by the adjoining military provinces, Pannonia, Noricum and Raetia (*qq.v.*). But Gaul was by the time of the empire practically demilitarized, and the vital passes from the Great St. Bernard to the coast needed special treatment.

1. The Alpes Maritimae were made a province, administered by a procurator, probably in 14 B.C., and included Pedo (Borgo San Dalmazzo in Piedmont) in the Italian foothills as well as Cemenelum (Cimiez, adjoining Nice) on the Gallic side of the summit. The coastal towns were still regarded as Italian, but the procurator's main duty was clearly to protect the Via Julia Augusta (the Riviera road on which they lay).

2. Adjoining the Alpes Maritimae near the Col de l'Argentière was the province of the Alpes Cottiae, with its capital at Segusio (Susa in Piedmont) and extending west to take in Ebrodunum (Embrun). Cottius, king of this region, had kept his tribes loyal to Augustus and was left in charge of them as prefect (*praefectus civitatium*), though both he and his son are sometimes called rex. The son died about A.D. 65 and was replaced by a procurator.

3. Further north was a province in Savoy, called variously Alpes Graiae or Atrectianae or Ceutronicae, with capital at Forum Claudi Ceutronum (Aime). There the province was wholly on the transalpine side of the Little St. Bernard (Alpis Graia), since in Italy the colony of Augusta Praetoria Salassorum (Aosta) had already been founded in 25 B.C. with a territory extending to the passes. Similarly the Great St. Bernard (Alpis Poenina) was the frontier of Italy: beyond it the Vallis Poenina (the Swiss canton of Valais) was first grouped with Raetia, but in the 2nd century A.D. was detached and added to the Alpes Graiae. All these border areas contained cities which attained Latin rights, a status formally accorded to the whole of the Alpes Maritimae in A.D. 63.

See D. Gribaudi, *Il Piemonte nell' antichità classica* (1928); G. E. F. Chilver, *Cisalpine Gaul* (1941). (G. E. F. C.)

ALPUJARRAS, LAS, a district of southern Spain in the provinces of Granada and Almería, stretches northward from the towns of Motril and Almería to the foothills of the Sierra Nevada. It is in fact a trough between the coastal mountains—the Sierra la Contraviesa and the Sierra de Gádor—and the Sierra Nevada. The rivers Guadalfeo to the west and Andarax to the east, as well as smaller streams, have cut gorges and flow through beautiful fertile, secluded valleys. Frequently the villages are on ledges overhanging the gorges and it is to these villages exclusively that the name Alpujarras is often applied.

A centre of repeated Moorish rebellions, the inhabitants of Moorish descent were finally evacuated in 1570 and were replaced by colonists from Extremadura and Galicia; however, not all of the 165 Moorish villages were repopulated. Although they were little experienced in irrigation the new colonists cleared much of the land for dry cereal cultivation, but because of the steep slopes erosion was severe. In consequence, new deltas have appeared on the coast, notably at Adra.

The district has a range of vegetation unparalleled in Europe: from sugar cane and palm on the coast, it extends through belts of citrus, vine, olive, chestnut and oak to alpine flora on the heights. This poverty-stricken region was first developed by the fruit and vegetable industry and in the mid-20th century it was further developed by new roads. Lanjarón (pop. [1950] 5,029) has become a notable mineral spa. The district has a population of about 50,000.

See J. Sermet, "Le relief de la Sierra Contraviesa," *Bol. Soc. esp. Hist. nat.* (1934), "Un cas de morphologie littorale heritée sur la côte de Grenade" (1954). (J. M. Ho.)

ALSACE (Ger. ELSASS), a region of Europe, corresponding to the modern French *départements* of Haut-Rhin and Bas-Rhin and Territoire de Belfort (*qq.v.*) bounded by the Vosges mountains and the historic Lorraine on the west, the German *Land* Rhineland-Palatinate on the north, the middle Rhine river on the east and Switzerland on the south.

Alsace is an area in which many races have come into collision and many civilizations met. Occupied by the Romans during Julius Caesar's conquest of Gaul in the 1st century B.C., it had been profoundly romanized by the time of the invasion of the Alamanni (*q.v.*) in the 5th century A.D. The Alamanni, however, were soon conquered by the Franks under Clovis. In the Frankish duchy of Alsace Christianity prospered, and many ecclesiastical foundations were made. Incorporated in Lotharingia (*see* LORRAINE) by the treaty of Verdun in 843, Alsace was united with the German territories of the Carolingians by the treaty of Mersen (870) and so remained part of the Holy Roman empire for 800 years. During that period its territory was divided into a number of ecclesiastical or secular lordships and municipalities, whose boundaries varied in the course of time but whose influence persisted until the French Revolution. The period was also marked by the growing importance of the cities, as these, with the support of the emperors, were able to emancipate themselves from their feudal overlords. The burghers of Strasbourg, for example, expelled their prince-bishop after their victory at Oberhausbergen (1262), and many cities in upper Alsace freed themselves from the control of Habsburg princes. Ten Alsatian cities, Haguenau, Landau, Colmar, Sélestat, Wissembourg, Obernai, Rosheim, Kaysersberg, Turkheim and Munster, formed a union (*decapolis*) in 1354, under the protection of the Holy Roman emperor, who appointed a *Landvogt* (resident) with his seat at Haguenau. This lasted till Louis XIV's time and did much to give unity to the country.

The Reformation transformed Alsace profoundly, its political mosaic being complicated by a religious one. Strasbourg, where the reformer Martin Bucer came into especial prominence, became in a way the capital of Alsatian Protestantism, and the *Gymnasium* of Strasbourg was a centre of humanist learning for the Rhineland. Strasbourg's Protestantism, however, was countered by the resolute Catholicism of the Habsburgs, who after suppressing the Peasants' War (1525) eradicated heresy in upper Alsace.

French influence began to be felt in Alsace later in the 16th century, during the Wars of Religion (Calvin moreover spent two years in Strasbourg before returning to Geneva in 1541). This influence became stronger during the Thirty Years' War, when the Alsatian cities, seeing both their political and religious freedom threatened by Austrian Catholicism and by Swedish Protestantism alike, appealed to the king of France for help. The war left Alsace exhausted, but the peace of Westphalia (1648) made the French king, in rather ambiguous terms, either the sovereign or the protector of the Alsatian lands.

Under the French Bourbon monarchy, from 1648 to 1789, the

territorial unit of Alsace was further consolidated. The policy of *chambres de réunion,* whereby cities on the frontier declared themselves reunited with France, culminated in the French occupation of Strasbourg (1681), which then became the capital of Alsace, its cathedral being restored to the Catholics. The administration of justice, police and finance passed into the hands of *intendants* and Colmar was made the seat of a *conseil supérieur.* In the peaceful years of the 18th century the population of Alsace increased and its economy prospered, chiefly the result of the transit trade (Alsace remaining outside the French customs system), agricultural development and increased exploitation of the textile and metallurgical industries. The people continued to speak a German dialect, but French spread among the upper classes.

The French Revolution and the Napoleonic era brought further changes to Alsace. The Protestants, who had been insecure though never persecuted under the kingdom, enjoyed complete freedom, the peasants were released from the arbitrary domination of the local territorial lords, and the towns exploited the increased facilities for trade up and down the Rhine. Alsace was included in the French customs area, enterprising *préfets* (as, for instance, Adrien Lezay-Marnézia) took the place of the *intendants,* a court of appeal was set up at Colmar, and the two *départements* of Haut-Rhin and Bas-Rhin, into which the country was divided, were both included for ecclesiastical purposes within the diocese of Strasbourg. The administrative reorganization was followed by a road-building program and increased industrialization. Neither the merchants of Bas-Rhin nor the manufacturers of Haut-Rhin, however, took much interest in acquiring large estates, so the number of peasant proprietors grew. The first teachers' college was founded in Strasbourg in 1810.

From 1815 to 1870 Alsace actively participated in the French national life. The introduction of universal suffrage (1848), the building of railways and the development of other communications and information services all contributed to bind France and its eastern frontier province more closely together. These links, however, were shattered at the end of the Franco-German War when Alsace was detached from France and annexed to the German empire. For its subsequent history *see* ALSACE-LORRAINE.

(G. LI.)

ALSACE-LORRAINE (Ger. ELSASS-LOTHRINGEN), the name given to the 5,607 sq.mi. of territory ceded by France to Germany in 1871 after the Franco-German War, retroceded to France in 1919 after World War I, ceded again to Germany in 1940 during World War II and again retroceded to France in 1945. It comprised the French *départements* of Haut-Rhin and Bas-Rhin, namely the former province of Alsace (*q.v.*), together with two *arrondissements* (Château-Salins and Sarrebourg) from the former *département* of Meurthe and five (Metz, Thionville, Boulay, Forbach and Sarreguemines) from the original *département* of Moselle, the two latter *départements* having been part of the ancient Lorraine (*q.v.*). As the French had formed the *département* of Meurthe-et-Moselle from what was left to France of Meurthe and of Moselle in 1871, the modern *département* of Moselle was formed to comprise all the parts of Lorraine retroceded in 1919.

The population of the area is predominantly Roman Catholic. Pop. (1954) 1,986,969. The majority speak German or dialects of German as well as French, a minority German alone. (*See* BAS-RHIN; HAUT-RHIN; MOSELLE.)

History.—Annexed to the newly founded German empire by the treaty of Frankfurt in May 1871 after the Franco-German War (*q.v.*), Alsace-Lorraine was constituted as a *Reichsland* or condominium of all the states of the empire, instead of being attached to Prussia or to any of the states individually. The population, however, was enthusiastic for the new French republic and had sent a delegation to the French national assembly to protest against the transfer to Germany. Its first delegation to the German *Reichstag,* in 1874, likewise carried a protest, and until 1890 practically every such delegation was unanimously opposed to the German regime. Many irreconcilables left the region and went to France or other countries. The German chancellor, Prince Otto von Bismarck, seems to have had high hopes for an early assimilation of the German-speaking majority, but under the circumstances

he was practically compelled to govern Alsace-Lorraine as a conquered province. A local consultative committee (*Landesausschuss*) was granted in 1874 and in 1877 was given some power to initiate legislation, but in 1879 a *Statthalter* or resident representing the chancellor was appointed, with powers to declare martial law whenever he thought fit. Consequently there could be no effective self-government until 1902, when these special powers were withdrawn from the *Statthalter.* From the time of the Dreyfus case onward, however, the French government pursued an increasingly anticlerical policy that alienated many of the inhabitants of Alsace-Lorraine. By 1905 the anticlerical legislation had been passed in France and the clerical party, the strongest single party in Alsace-Lorraine, sought a new orientation. Bismarck (despite his *Kulturkampf*) and the German statesmen who succeeded him after 1890 never interfered with the functioning in Alsace-Lorraine of the concordat of 1801 between France and the papacy. The eventual German compromise with the church appealed to the clericals more than French anticlericalism. After 1900 the clericals in Alsace-Lorraine looked forward to an autonomous Alsace-Lorraine within the German empire.

By 1911 a new constitution was granted which opened the way for the *Reichsland* to become an equal among the members of the empire. Provision was made for a bicameral *Landtag* and a vote in the imperial federal council. There was much dissatisfaction, but the first election seemed to indicate that the government party had the majority. Feelings of sympathy for Germany, however, were soon counteracted by a new trend of events. After the fall of Bismarck, German statesmen had moved in the direction of pan-Germanism and imperialism. The new policy called for a tremendous increase in the military and naval budgets and these were opposed by the members of the *Reichstag* from Alsace-Lorraine. The inhabitants of the region saw nothing to be gained and much to be risked by war. As an exposed part of the empire, they were heavily garrisoned. Clashes between the civilians and the military authorities were inevitable. The most notorious was the incident at Saverne (Zabern) in Nov.–Dec. 1913, when a German lieutenant provoked a riot by insulting Alsatian recruits (29 people were arrested). The local diet, under the presidency of Eugen Ricklin, a leading autonomist, placed the blame for this directly on the military authorities. Such incidents caused the tide to turn against the German regime although it was not until 1916, two years after the outbreak of World War I, that the majority were against the government. To meet this situation it was proposed to dismember the province and partition it among several German states, but the course of the war led to the abandonment of this project. Instead the Germans decided that Alsace-Lorraine was to have a more autonomous government. The local politicians, however, were too shrewd to attempt to form a cabinet.

The treaty of Versailles in 1919 recognized "the moral obligation to redress the wrong done by Germany in 1871 both to the rights of France and to the wishes of the population . . . ," but little consideration was given to the extent to which these wishes might have changed since 1871, especially with regard to the Alsatian areas. The tumultuous welcome given to the French (Nov. 1918) was the result, in a measure at least, of war weariness. French officers had made it clear that traditions and liberties would be respected, but French officials almost immediately began to speak of assimilating the reconquered provinces to France. A commissioner-general for Alsace-Lorraine was appointed with one commissioner for each of the three resurrected *départements,* but no sovereign power was recognized except the central government of France. Even the functions of the transitional commissariat-general were transferred to Paris in 1925. Then Edouard Herriot's ministry (1924–25) declared for the introduction of "the whole of the republican legislation" into Alsace-Lorraine, and the implication that the status of the confessional schools was to be changed was seen as a threat of the concordat of 1801.

At that stage, Eugen Ricklin founded a newspaper and the Heimatbund ("League for Home Rule") calling for complete autonomy "within the French state." The issue was between centralization and particularism. The French premier Raymond Poincaré in 1926 resorted to drastic action, suppressing newspapers on the ground that they were in a foreign tongue, although German was the written language of 75% of the population, and on Christmas Eve 1927 wholesale searches, seizures and arrests were made. Two of those held were elected to the chamber of deputies before their trial, but were denied the right to their seats on their being convicted, whereupon a second election gave the voters the opportunity to elect two other autonomists. These events induced the French government to adopt a more conciliatory policy, which, however, did not cause the autonomists to disband.

In World War II the collapse of France in 1940 was followed by the annexation of Alsace-Lorraine to Germany. Part of the territory was then incorporated in Baden, part in the Westmark, and about 18,000 Alsatians perished in the German armies on the eastern front, but attempts to germanize Alsace-Lorraine were a failure.

In 1945 Alsace-Lorraine became French again. Problems subsequently became much less acute. The local legislation and particularly the concordat remained in force. The autonomist movement disappeared. If most of the people would still call themselves Alsatian, few, if any, would accept being labeled Germans. By the wish of the majority, some German was reintroduced in the elementary schools, but basic teaching was given in French.

See also references under "Alsace-Lorraine" in the Index.

See H. Stegemann, *The Struggle for the Rhine* (1927); G. Zeller, *L'Alsace française de Louis XIV à nos jours* (1945).

ALSBERG, CARL LUCAS (1877–1940), U.S. biochemist, who specialized in food chemistry, was born in New York city on April 2, 1877. He graduated from Columbia university in 1896 and from the College of Physicians and Surgeons in 1900. Following study in Germany in 1900–03, he was an assistant and instructor at Harvard university until 1908. From 1908 to 1912 he was chemical biologist in the bureau of plant industry and was chief of the bureau of chemistry in the U.S. department of agriculture from 1912–21.

In 1920 Alsberg was made director of the Food Research institute, Stanford university, Stanford, Calif., and in 1937 director of the Giannini Foundation of Agricultural Economics, University of California, Berkeley.

Alsberg's research included investigations on pure foods and drugs, the biology and toxicology of molds, cyanogenesis in plants, poisonous plants, phosphoric acid, metabolism, nucleic acids, proteins, cystinuria and enzymes. He also studied problems of population growth and food supply.

Alsberg died on Nov. 1, 1940, at Berkeley, Calif.

ALSIKE CLOVER, the common name of *Trifolium hybridum*. It is of agricultural importance for hay, pasture and soil improvement in cool humid climates of North America and Europe. Botanically, alsike clover is a perennial, but under many agricultural conditions it behaves as a biennial. The flower colour is white or pinkish white. A native of Europe or Asia Minor, alsike clover has become widely naturalized in the United States, since the first known seed introductions in 1839. It is probable that it had been previously introduced by chance.

ALSOP, VINCENT (*c.* 1630–1703), English Nonconformist minister, a leader of those ejected under the Act of Uniformity of 1662. He was born in Northamptonshire about 1630, and after being ordained deacon, became a schoolmaster, but was converted from his "rollicking ways" and reordained by the presbyters. Ejected from Wilby, Northamptonshire, in 1662, he was licensed as a Congregational teacher, preaching privately and gaining fame as a hard-hitting and witty pamphleteer, particularly by his *Antisozzo* (1675), a defense of Nonconformist theology against William Sherlock's attacks. He became minister of the Presbyterian congregation in Tothill street, Westminster, in 1677 and was subsequently appointed to several lectureships. He was a leader in the so-called "happy union" of Presbyterians and Congregationalists (1691). He gained some favour with James II, who pardoned his son's "treasonable practises," and he continued to write and preach with undiminished vigour until his death in London, May 8, 1703.

ALSTON, JOSEPH (*c.* 1779–1816), U.S. lawyer and gover-

nor of South Carolina during the War of 1812. The precise date and place of his birth are not known. As a rice planter in South Carolina he lived at "The Oaks" on Waccamaw river, adjoining "Brookgreen" plantation of William Alston and his son Washington, the celebrated painter. Alston was educated at Princeton, but left in his senior year to study law under Edward Rutledge. Elected to the state legislature in 1802, he served until 1812, being speaker from 1805 to 1809. In 1801 he married Theodosia Burr, brilliant daughter of Aaron Burr (*q.v.*), thereby becoming involved in the Burr conspiracy. How much he knew of Burr's plans is uncertain, but he assisted with funds and personal participation, and he defended Burr during his trial in Richmond. These activities did not promote Alston's political fortunes, yet he was elected governor in 1812 and vigorously supported the war against England. During this year his only son died, and in 1813 Theodosia was lost at sea. Three years later, on Sept. 10, 1816, Alston died and was interred at his plantation.   (T. P. A.)

ALT, ALBRECHT GEORG (1883–1956), one of the most important Old Testament scholars of the first half of the 20th century, was born on Sept. 20, 1883, in Stübach, Bavaria. He was *Privatdocent* and professor in Greifswald from 1909 to 1914, then professor in Basel (1914–21), Halle (1921–22) and Leipzig (1922–56). He was also head of the Deutsches Evangelisches Institut für Altertumswissenschaft des Heiligen Landes (German Evangelical Institute for Archaeology of the Holy Land) in Jerusalem from 1921 to 1923 and remained thereafter its spiritual and organizational leader. He died in Leipzig on April 24, 1956.

His chief field of study was Palestinian history and archaeology and the history of ancient Israel in its relationship to the history of the near east. He specialized in the legal and political institutions of ancient Israel, and also shed light on the religion and worship which lie behind the Old Testament traditions. His most important papers are *Die Landnahme der Israeliten in Palästina* (1925), *Die Staatenbildung der Israeliten in Palästina* (1930), *Der Gott der Väter* (1929) and *Die Ursprünge des israelitischen Rechts* (1934). He laid the foundation for a new and soon widely accepted view of the history of Israel and decisively influenced Old Testament studies throughout the world.

BIBLIOGRAPHY.—Collected edition of most of Alt's writings in *Kleine Schriften zur Geschichte des Volkes Israel*, vol. 1–3 (1953–59); list of 243 of his works in his *Festschrift, Geschichte und Altes Testament* (1953); M. Noth, memoir in *Zeitschrift des deutschen Palästina-Vereins*, vol. 72, pp. 1–8 (1956).   (M. N.)

ALTAI, a complex mountain system of central Asia, at the junction of the boundaries of the Union of Soviet Socialist Republics, Outer Mongolia and China. The Altai, which means "gold" in Mongolian, extends from 48° to 53° N. latitude and from 81° to 90° E. longitude. Most of the mountain system is situated within the Gorno-Altai autonomous *oblast* of the U.S.S.R., with the outer slopes extending into the Tuva autonomous *oblast* and the Khakass autonomous *oblast* in the northeast, the Altai *krai* in the northwest, the East Kazakhstan *oblast* in the west, China's Sinkiang Uigur autonomous region in the south and the western portion of Outer Mongolia in the southeast. The mountain system of the Altai may be divided into four subranges fanning out from the mountain hub of Kuiten (14,388 ft.) situated near the junction of the Soviet, Chinese and Mongolian borders. These four major subranges or groups of ranges are the south Altai, extending to the west, the central Altai, to the northwest, the east Altai, to the northeast, and the Mongolian Altai, to the southeast. The south Altai, which forms the watershed between the upper Irtysh and Bukhtarma rivers, is known as the Narym range at its western end. The south Altai reaches an elevation of 12,700 ft. in its highest point. Mountain spurs on its southern slope enclose the lake Marka Kul. The central Altai, which consists of parallel elongated ranges extending to the northwest, contains snow-capped mountains known in Russian as *belki*. The most important of these ranges, the Katun, reaches 14,783 ft. in Mount Belukha, the highest point in the Altai. The east Altai forms the watershed between the Ob and Yenisei river systems. It begins at the Tabun Bogdo hub as the Saylyugem range (14,288 ft.) and continues northward as the Shapshal range before linking up with the mountain systems of the west Sayans and the Kuznestk Ala-tau. The picturesque Teletskoye mountain lake (1,066 ft. deep) lies on the western slopes of the east Altai subrange. The Mongolian Altai extends about 900 mi. southeast into Outer Mongolia (Mongolian People's Republic), where it gradually breaks up into lower ranges that disappear in the Gobi desert. The Mongolian Altai reaches an elevation of 13,881 ft. in the Munku-Khayrkhan.

Geology.—From the point of view of historical geology, the Altai system is divided into two parts: the Altai proper, which includes the larger northeastern portion of the system, and the so-called Rudny (or mineralized) Altai in the southwest. The Rudny Altai emerged during the Upper Paleozoic (Variscan) period of mountain forming, while the Altai proper was subjected to the most intense folding during the Lower Paleozoic (Caledonian) revolution. The Altai proper consists of Paleozoic rocks extending to the Upper Devonian period, when the last marine transgression took place. In the Rudny Altai, on the other hand, marine sediments have been found through the Lower Carboniferous period. The long duration of the continental phase, which began in the Lower Carboniferous and in many places even earlier, led to the wearing away by erosion of the entire Altai, which did not exist as a mountain system during the Tertiary period. At the end of the Tertiary and the start of the Quaternary, extensive faulting took place, creating the configuration of the present Altai. This is characterized by the predominance of plateaus of varying elevations, sometimes half worn away by erosion. Many of these watershed plateaus are quite flat and allow poor drainage. Streams drain at first with a barely perceptible gradient, then cut deep gorges at the points where they empty into the main rivers. Such are the upper courses of the Katun and Biya rivers, the two headstreams of the Ob. Other rivers rising in the Altai are the Bukhtarma, a tributary of the Irtysh, and the Kobdo in Outer Mongolia. Most of these rivers rise in small glaciers, but glaciation is relatively limited in the Altai. The total glacier area is 230 sq.mi., far less than in the Tien Shan.

Climate.—The Altai is situated near the centre of Asia far from the moderating influence of the sea and its climate is sharply continental. Dry south and southwest winds prevail in winter, and moist northwest and west winds in summer. Most of the annual precipitation of about 40 in. occurs in July and August. The western Altai, directly in the path of the moisture-laden winds from the Atlantic ocean, receives most of the precipitation. Valleys on the leeward side of the ranges are quite dry. On moist slopes the snow line lies at an elevation of about 8,000 ft.; on dry slopes at 10,000 ft.

Vegetation.—The steppes that adjoin the Altai are suitable for agriculture, which can be carried on up to an elevation of about 3,500 ft. The forest zone, which extends in places to 8,000 ft., consists mainly of conifers, such as the larch, stone pine, fir and spruce. Deciduous stands (birch, aspen, mountain ash) are of secondary importance. After a transitional zone of stunted shrubs, such as the dwarf arctic birch and dwarf willows, the alpine meadows begin.

Settlement and Economy.—The indigenous Altaic tribes (formerly called Oirat) are of mixed Mongol-Tungus descent. In ancient times they developed a well-rounded economy, including agriculture, stock raising and metal working. However, when the first Russian settlers reached the foothills of the Altai in the 17th century, they found the Altaic peoples engaged only in hunting and primitive stock raising. Under Russian rule, the Altai passed through an early silver-mining phase, which lasted from the early 18th century until the second half of the 19th. This was followed by more intensive agricultural settlement of the Altai piedmont in the late 19th and early 20th centuries. Under Soviet rule, the Altai has played an important role both as a mining region and a piedmont farming area (wheat, sunflowers, sugar beets). Mining is carried on primarily in the mineralized section of the Altai (Rudny Altai), which corresponds to the East Kazakhstan *oblast* of the Kazakh Soviet Socialist Republic. This area is one of the Soviet Union's most important lead and zinc producers, with mines and smelters at Leninogorsk, Ust-Kamenogorsk and Zyryanovsk.

Other minerals mined in Altai include tungsten, tin, copper and mercury. Railroad spurs of the Soviet rail system serve both the rich wheat lands of the Altai piedmont and the mining area of Kazakhstan. In the mountains themselves, transportation relies on motor highways, such as the Chuya valley road, which connects the Soviet Union with Outer Mongolia.   (T. Sᴅ.)

ALTAIC PEOPLES, on the basis of their linguistic affinity, comprise the Turks, the Mongols and the Manchu-Tungus. These peoples have been grouped on a linguistic basis since 1730, when F. J. von Strahlenberg first proposed the genetic relationship of these languages. He further suggested their inclusion in a larger family of Ural-Altaic languages (*q.v.*), including the Finnic, Hungarian, Samoyedic and other peoples. The Ural-Altaic relationship was accepted more or less through the 19th century, came under sharp attack during the first part of the 20th century, and today is the subject of careful consideration by scholars. This article deals only with the Turkic, Mongolic and Manchu-Tungusic peoples.

The largest of the three divisions of Altaic peoples is the Turkic. There are about 50,000,000 Turkic-speaking peoples in the countries of Asia and Europe. Turkic-speaking peoples of the Soviet Union number about 20,000,000; about 1,000,000 live in eastern Europe; 18,000,000 live in Turkey; about 4,000,000 live in China; and the remainder live in Iran, Afghanistan and neighbouring countries (northern Iraq and Syria). The Turkic peoples are divided into four main subdivisions: (1) *Northwest:* Kazakh, Kirghiz and Kara-Kalpak in central Asia; Nogai, Karachai, Balkar and Kumyk in the north Caucasus; Tatar, Mishar, Tepter, Bashkir in European Russia; Karaim in Poland; Siberian Tatar; (2) *Northeast:* Tuvinian (Soyot, Urianghai) in Tuva and southern Siberia; Karagas; Shori, Khakass and lesser languages of the Sayan mountains; Saryg Uighur of China; Altai mountain Turkic; Baraba dialects; (3) *Southeast:* Uighur or Turki of Chinese and Russian Turkestan; Uzbek of Russian Turkestan and Afghanistan; and (4) *Southwest:* Turkish and related Anatolian dialects of Turkey; Azerbaijani of the Soviet Caucasus and Iran; Turkmen of Russian Turkestan, Iran and Afghanistan; Gashgai, and Ainalu of southwest Iran; Balkan Turkish of Yugoslavia, Greece, Bulgaria and Rumania (Gagauz); Crimean Tatar. Two distantly related Turkic languages are Chuvash of European Russia and Yakut of northeast Siberia. Yakut has a general relationship to the Siberian Turkic dialects, including the Dolgans, a group of Tungus who have become Yakutized.

The Mongols are classified into three subdivisions, the eastern, western and northern. The eastern Mongols include the Mongols of Outer Mongolia (Khalkha Mongol) and Inner Mongolia (Ordos, Urat, Tumut, Kharchin, Chahar, Chipchin). Monguor of Kansu (China) and Dagur of the Amur basin are separately classified. Western Mongol includes Mogol of Afghanistan, Oirat of Sinkiang and western Mongolia, Volga Kalmyk (including Sart Kalmyk of Kirgizia). The northern Mongols include the Buryats.

The largest number of Mongols live in China (1,500,000 in 1953); of these the majority live in Inner Mongolia (1,100,000) the remainder are distributed in north and northwest China. The Mongols of Outer Mongolia number about 750,000. The Buryats number 253,000, the Kalmyks 106,000 (1959). The remainder of the Mongol groups are fewer in number. A small number of Kalmyks settled in the United States after World War II. The total of all Mongols in the world is 2,500,000 to 3,000,000.

The Manchu-Tungusic peoples live in China proper, Manchuria and eastern Siberia. A small number are settled in Inner and Outer Mongolia and Sinkiang. The most powerful group were the Manchus who conquered all of China in the 17th century; since then many Manchus have been absorbed into Chinese culture. The census of mainland China of 1953 counted 2,400,000 Manchus. However, many of these are only nominally Manchus and live scattered among the Chinese. The Manchu-Tungusic peoples are divided into a northern and southern branch. The northern branch includes the eastern Siberian Tungus proper (Evenki or reindeer Tungus and Lamut or coastal Tungus), and Negidal of the Amur region. The southern branch includes the Manchus proper; and the river tribes of Manchuria: Nanai or Gold, Ulchi, Orochi, Ude and Oroki. These tribes number only a few thousand. The largest of the Manchu-Tungusic peoples other than the Manchus are the Evenki, who number 24,000 (1959).

The Turks and Mongols live in a zone of aridity: desert, steppe desert and steppe. The traditional economy of the earliest of these peoples, the Huns (Hiung-nu), Juan-Juan, Sien-pi and Avars, was nomadic pastoralism; that is the raising of stock and pasturing them in a fixed round of annual movement. Today, Mongols of Inner and Outer Mongolia and the Turks of Iran and Afghanistan still nomadize in the traditional fashion. Most of the other Turks and Mongols, once nomads, have become sedentarized.

The traditional habitat of the Manchu-Tungusic peoples is the Siberian forest and the Amur drainage to the south. They are pastoralists of a simpler type: they raise but one animal. The Evenki raise reindeer, as do many Turk-speaking peoples of Siberia, the Yakut, Dolgan and Sayan mountain Turks. Some Tungus and Manchus raise pigs. The remainder hûnt and fish.

The Turks and Mongols were called Tatars in the olden sources of the Chinese and Russians. The nomad Tatars lived in a complex interrelationship of raiding, trading and tribute exchange with their sedentary neighbours, at times erupting into great conquests (Jenghiz Khan, Timur [Tamerlane], Ottomans). These conquests succeeded when the indigenous sedentary dynasties of China and interior Asia were weakened internally. *See also* TATAR; MONGOL; TUNGUS; TURKIC PEOPLES.

BIBLIOGRAPHY.—W. Barthold, *Histoire d'Asie Centrale* (1948) Mme Donski's adaptation; Lawrence Krader, "Feudalism and the Tatar Polity of the Middle Ages" in the *Comparative Studies of Society and History,* vol. i, no. 1 (1958), "The Cultural and Historic Position of the Mongols," vol. iii, no. 2 (1952), "Principles and Structures . . . of the Asiatic Steppe-Pastoralists," vol. xi, no. 2 (1955), "Ecology of Central Asian Pastoralism," *Southwestern Journal of Anthropology,*" vol. xi, no. 4 (1955); N. N. Poppe, *Introduction to Comparative Mongol Studies* (1955); G. J. Ramstedt, *Studies in Korean Etymology* (1949); M. Räsänen, *Materialien zur Lautgeschichte der türkischen Sprachen* (1949); S. A. Tokarev, *Etnografiya Narodov SSSR* (1958); D. Sinor (ed.), *Aspects of Altaic Civilization* (1963).   (L. K.)

ALTAI KRAI, a territory of the Russian Soviet Federated Socialist Republic, U.S.S.R., covers an area of 101,042 sq.mi., almost wholly in the basin of the upper Ob (*q.v.*) and its headstreams, the Biya and the Katun. The northern and northwestern parts consist of rolling plain and mountain foreland with steppe and forest-steppe vegetation. The southern part, which forms the Gorno-Altai Autonomous *oblast* within the *krai,* consists of mountain ranges and high plateaus, with wide intermontane basins and deeply incised valleys. The mountains and plateaus are forested, the basins are under steppe vegetation. The 1959 population was 2,683,231, of whom 882,624 were urban. The chief towns are Barnaul, the capital (305,046), Bisk (146,416) (*qq.v.*), Rubtsovsk (111,357), Slavgorod and Gorno-Altaisk (27,534). Of the 157,161 inhabitants of the Gorno-Altai Autonomous *oblast,* about one-fourth were Altai, a Turkic people related to the Tuvinians.

The *krai* is one of the most important areas in western Siberia, both agriculturally and industrially, lying close to the Kuznetsk basin. The northern steppes are almost entirely under cultivation, with wheat, oats and maize (corn) the chief crops, together with sunflowers, flax, hemp and sugar beet. In the mountains there are large herds of cattle and sheep. Nonferrous ores, copper, zinc, lead, silver, mercury, barium, tungsten and gold are mined, chiefly around Zmeinogorsk, and salts are obtained from the lakes of the Kulunda steppe. Light engineering, mostly agricultural machinery, chemical industry and timber working are developed in the main towns. The north is served by a railway net focussed on Barnaul, while the Bisk-Mongolia highway crosses the mountains.

Once part of the khanate of Dzungaria (*q.v.*), the *krai* was colonized by the Russians from the 18th century, following the overthrow of the khanate. Its early importance lay in silvermining, but with the coming of the Turksib railway the lower north was opened up to agriculture.   (R. A. F.)

ALTAIR, the brightest star in the constellation Aquila (*q.v.*), and, because of this, also known as α Aquilae. It is the middle member of the group β, α, γ in the constellation, and is of the first magnitude, being one of the nearest and brightest stars. Its distance from the solar system is about 16 light-years. It is a white star having a size somewhat greater than that of our sun and giving out about ten times as much light.

ALTAMIRA CAVE, famous for its magnificent prehistoric paintings and engravings, is situated 2 km. (1 mi.) from Santillana-del-Mar, a small town 30 km. (19 mi.) W. of Santander in northern Spain. The opening of the cave, at the summit of a limestone cliff, was discovered by a hunter in 1868. In 1875 it was visited by Marcelino de Sautuola, an engineer from Santander, who found animal bones and flint implements there. He returned in the summer of 1879, and on one visit was accompanied by his little daughter Maria; it was she who, looking at the roof, noticed paintings of "bulls." With Vilanova y Piera, professor of geology of Madrid university, they went back to the cave, and the geologist examined the finds, which included bones engraved with animal figures. Both men were convinced of the antiquity of the paintings. As early as 1880 Sautuola reproduced them in his booklet *Breves apuntes sobre algunos objetos prehistóricos de la provincia de Santander,* and in the same year Vilanova y Piera made them known to an international congress held in Lisbon. Both Spanish and foreign experts reacted unfavourably; the paintings were dismissed as recent forgeries or as the work of Roman soldiers taking part in the Cantabrian war of 26 B.C. to 19 B.C. Sautuola died in 1888 and Vilanova in 1893. Shortly after, the repeated discoveries of small carved objects created a more favourable atmosphere, and the engravings which came to light in the cave at La Mouthe (Dordogne) in 1895 prepared the way for the acceptance of Altamira. Finally, the discovery in 1901 of paintings in the caves of Combarelles and Font-de-Gaume (Les Eyzies, Dordogne) made the truth manifest. The French scholar Émile Cartailhac thereupon wrote his famous article *Mea culpa d'un sceptique* (1902) and went to Altamira with the abbé Henri Breuil, who made copies of the paintings. These were published by the Institut de Paléontologie Humaine in 1908. A second edition, in English and Spanish and with new copies, was brought out by the Real Academia de la Historia in 1935.

The Altamira cave is 270 m. long. In the vestibule numerous archaeological remains belonging to the Aurignacian (Perigordian), upper Solutrian and lower or middle Magdalenian periods (*i.e.,* between approximately 30,000 B.C. and 10,000 B.C.) were found, including ceremonial staves and engraved animal shoulder blades. At some time after the middle Magdalenian a rock fall closed the cave, around which Abbevillian, Acheulian and Mousterian tools have been discovered. The great lateral chamber which contains most of the paintings measures 18 m. by 9 m., the height of the vault varying from 1.15 m. to 2.65 m.

The roof of the chamber is covered with paintings, chiefly of bison, executed in a magnificent, vivid polychrome of red, black and violet tones. The animals are in various positions, protuberances of the rock having been utilized to assist in rendering their poses. There are in addition two wild boars, some horses, a hind 2.25 m. in length and some other figures in a simpler style (*e.g.,* a perfectly executed bull's head in black); also eight engraved anthropomorphic figures and various hand prints and hand outlines. The other galleries contain numerous black-painted or engraved figures, especially of horses, deer, wild cattle and goats; tectiforms (wedge-shaped markings resembling a sloping roof) and other signs which are indecipherable; finger-drawn lines and bear tracks. In the last gallery there are an engraved antelope and a figure which may represent a wolf. At the very back of the cave is a row of six engraved heads of hinds. The number of figures discerned totals 150.

Abbé Breuil and H. Obermaier assign them to various periods of culture as follows: the silhouettes, hands, tectiforms and other markings to the Aurignacian; the monochromes in semi-relief to the lower Magdalenian; the beautiful polychromes to the upper Magdalenian. Spanish authorities are dubious of this scheme; they prefer to allot the light silhouettes and monochromes to the Solutrian period, preceding the Magdalenian. Steps have been taken to preserve this magnificent assemblage which Joseph Déchelette called the Sistine chapel of Quaternary art.   (L. P. G.)

ALTAMURA, a city of southeast Italy in the region of Puglia, and the province of Bari, is situated on the side of the Murge

Salentine hills at 1,543 ft. above sea level 27 mi. by road S.S.W. of Bari. Pop. (1961) 42,951 (commune). The town is elliptical in shape and surrounded by a high medieval wall from which it takes its name. The Romanesque cathedral of the Assumption, begun in 1232 by Frederic II of Swabia, has been restored several times. Its façade, flanked by two Romanesque belfries, has a beautiful central rose window; the west door rests on two marble lions. The Pulo d'Altamura, about 4 mi. away, is a large limestone abyss, 1,640 ft. across and 246 ft. deep. Cattle and cereals are the chief products from the district and almonds and vines are cultivated. There is a wool market in the town. Altamura was founded about 1200 by Frederick II who created several new towns in Apulia, attracting Saracens and Jews with privileges to help him in his struggle against the barons. In World War II Altamura was captured by the Allies in Sept. 1943.

(M. T. A. N.)

ALTAR is the name given to a surface at or on which sacrifice is offered. In primitive religious observances, a natural rock, a stone or heap of stones, or a mound of earth probably sufficed for this purpose. With the development of the institution of sacrifice in sanctuaries and temples, more elaborate structures were built of stone or brick on which the victim was killed and its blood channeled off or its flesh burned. A trench or pit often was used for offerings to the dead, to chthonian divinities, and to the heroes, as, for example, in Greek temples; or the altar might take the form of a table on which food was placed for the deity. In some religions no altars are used, the sacrifice being simply placed on the ground, thrown into water, etc. Where an altar is used it is set apart as holy, and regarded as a place of contact with the deity, whether it serves as a table of sacrifice to him, a hearth for burnt offerings, or a grave ditch where oblations are made to the dead.

NON-CHRISTIAN RELIGIONS

Egypt.—A bowl, tray, or censer sometimes stood on a pillow-shaped upright stand of stone or wood for offerings of incense. Oblong tables (*hotep*) with a spout in front were a development of the mat on which the sacrificial gifts were laid for the gods or the deceased. The great rectangular altars occasionally found in solar temples are rare, and those approached by a flight of steps, as in the temple of Hatshepsut at Dayr al Bahri, are of the period of the New Kingdom.

Mesopotamia.—The archaic altars depicted on Babylonian seals are small portable constructions carved out of stone or built of large flat bricks or stones placed one upon another, triangular in shape, with a fire pan on the top. Others are of clay in the form of houses, hollow and approached by steps, and ornamented with doves, lions, and serpents, or of hourglasses, candlesticks, and stands for flower vases. Tables of offerings frequently are depicted; in Assyria these were fashioned in bronze with molded legs joined to one another by horizontal bars.

Syria and Palestine.—Banks of earth or heaps of unhewn stones were piled up to represent mountains on which sacrifices were offered. In a sanctuary an unhewn stone pillar (*mazzebah*) was erected on which oil was poured sacrificially, as in the story of Jacob at Bethel (Gen. 28:18 ff.), the pillar being regarded as the abode of the indwelling deity. The simplest artificial constructions apart from these mounds, cairns, and menhirs were rock-cut altars, often rounded at the top, with a square base and steps cut in the stone at the corners or, as at Petra, approached by a flight of steps on the east side. Such altars had a hollow, used as a fire pan, on the top, and conduits through which the blood was carried into basins.

Ancient Hebrews.—When the Hebrews occupied Palestine they continued the Canaanite practice of erecting altars of earth and of unhewn stone (Ex. 20:24–26). After the centralization of worship at Jerusalem, Solomon is alleged to have incorporated a bronze altar (II Chron. 4:1; II Kings 16:14) on three levels (Ezek. 43:13–17) like the Babylonian temple towers, perhaps under the influence of Mesopotamian cosmic ideas transmitted from Phoenicia. That the normal equipment of the earlier Semitic sanctuaries, or "high places," survived during the monarchy in Israel is shown by the efforts of Hezekiah and Josiah to destroy the *mazzebah* (I Kings 14:23; II Kings 17:10). (*See* HIGH PLACE.) The old Canaanite sites, such as Taanach, Gezer, Schechem, and Megiddo, with their altars, standing stones, sockets for the sacred poles, and remains of infant victims which have survived to the present day, were still places of sacrifice as late as the 8th century B.C. Indeed, it was not until after the exile 200 years later, when the Priestly document was compiled (*see* PENTATEUCH), that altars were erected in the post-exilic temple on what was alleged to have been the pattern of the tabernacle (*q.v.*) in the wilderness. As these altars were required for burnt offerings, however, they could hardly have been made of acacia wood overlaid with bronze and gold, as is asserted (Ex. 27); this seems to have been a fanciful correlation on the part of the priestly writers. The earlier sanctuaries were brought within the tradition of Israel, for instance by assigning Bethel to Jacob (Gen. 28:18 ff.), the altar on Mt. Ebal to Joshua (Josh. 8:30), and representing the altar set up by the tribes of Reuben, Gad, and the Manasseh group east of the Jordan as a witness of their solidarity with the rest of Israel and not as a place for sacrifice (Josh. 22:9–34). Thus, the altar, reinterpreted, was preserved as a legitimate centre of worship.

Similarly, in the Second Temple (I Macc. 4:47) and in Herod's Temple the altar was again constructed after the same model and dimensions as the original. (*See* TEMPLE, JEWISH.) According to Josephus' book on the Jewish war, the altar in Herod's Temple was 15 cubits high and 50 cubits square with corners like horns and approached by a slight slope, to evade the prohibition of steps in Ex. 20:26; the talmudic tractate *Middoth* gives rather different measurements. Use of iron tools in construction of the altar was strictly forbidden in order to preserve its archaic character. The altar had "horns" (protuberances) at the four corners (Ex. 27:2); these were later regarded as its holiest part, so that any one clinging to them was immune from molestation (*cf.* I Kings 1:50, 51; 2:28).

Before the veil separating the holy of holies from the holy place stood an altar overlaid with gold, perhaps a so-called altar of incense (Ex. 30) used for burning incense or fat, though no description is given of its form (I Kings 6:22; 7:48). It was removed from the Temple at Jerusalem by Antiochus Epiphanes and subsequently restored (or rebuilt) by Judas Maccabaeus (I Macc. 1:21–23; 4:35–49). A table, made of acacia wood overlaid with gold (Ex. 25:23–30), on which the shewbread (*q.v.*) was laid, stood in the holy place; but it was not an altar.

Greece and Rome.—The Greeks had both domestic altars for family use and public altars such as the city altar on which fire continually burned and the temple altar dedicated to the god concerned. Altars varied greatly in shape and size, but were generally made of stone and often decorated with relief work. Roman altars were very similar to those of the Greeks. Usually they were rectangular, though some of the older ones were round or oval like the earth mounds on which they were modeled. In Hellenistic times small circular altars used for burning incense and for libations and gifts of fruit and flowers were common. Larger altars for animal sacrifice were erected on terraces approached by steps. The altar of Zeus at Olympia is said by Pausanias to have been 22 ft. (6.7 m.) high, 125 ft. (38.1 m.) in circumference on its lowest platform, and 32 ft. (9.4 m.) on the altar proper. That at Pergamum had a platform of 20-ft. circumference and a total height of 40 ft. These lofty structures were particularly suitable for sky gods such as Zeus (Jupiter); for the earth and for domestic deities such as Vesta, Demeter, and the Erinyes low altars were more suitable. But Roman temples usually stood on eminences with steps in front of which were altars, often decorated with allegorical and ceremonial scenes in the form of reliefs and with naturalistic garlands carved in the marble.

In the home, since the hearth was the centre of the domestic cult and the kitchen the principal room, the shrine frequently was located near the kitchen hearth, as may be seen at Pompeii. But sometimes a special room was provided for the altar. When the temple of Vesta became the hearth of the city, with its vestal virgins continually in attendance upon the sacred fire, the divine personification of the hearth fire was worshiped by the Senate in the *atrium Vestae* on the Forum. Small altars were placed in the streets in niches with pictures of the gods to whom they were dedicated; such altars served as places of refuge for suppliants who were under the protection of the god to whom the altar belonged.

Iran and India.—Altars are not mentioned in the Avesta or in Zoroastrian inscriptions, but in Iran during the Achaemenian period the sacred fire burned continually in urns on altars supported by pedestals and set upon mountains and eminences; later the altar was surmounted by a baldachin with four arches. Portable altars containing the fire were carried in processions. From Sasanian times (3rd century A.D.) animal sacrifices were strictly forbidden. The Parsees of India, among whom the religion of Zoroaster survives, continue to use the fire altars, priests performing before them the prescribed rites.

Behind this reverence for fire lies the very ancient cult of Agni (*q.v.*) in the Indo-Iranian background of Zoroastrianism. It is found also in Hinduism, in which the building of the fire altar in seven layers in the form of a falcon representing the body of Agni was a repetition of creation. In the midst of the construction a fire pan was fashioned as a ritual act by which the creation of the universe was reproduced, and the sacred flame rekindled by the fire sticks of the priests recreated the life pervading the universe. Each type of offering had its own distinctive altar, constructed according to carefully prescribed dimensions, symbolizing in its form and construction its purposes and significance.

China.—From early times the Chinese offered burnt sacrifices to the god of heaven on mountaintops. In the Ming period (A.D. 1368–1644) a magnificent marble altar dedicated to Heaven was erected on three circular terraces in a park on the south side of Peking; the enclosure occupied more than a square mile and was approached by flights of steps located at the four points of the compass. The lowest terrace was 210 ft. (64 m.) in diameter, the second 150 ft. (45.7 m.), and the third 90 ft. (27.4 m.). At this altar the emperor offered the sacrifice to imperial Heaven at the winter solstice each year until the fall of the empire in 1911. At midsummer he repaired to the smaller altar of Earth in the northern suburb to sacrifice for the purpose of inducing the earth to produce "the balmy wind and sweet rain." Local sacrifices to the earth were offered on mounds about five feet square and a foot high. In both Confucian and Buddhist temples stands a rectangular stone table, used as an ancestral altar, on which are two candlesticks, a censer, and sometimes a pair of bronze porcelain or stone vases. Altars in front of tombs received sacrifices to the spirits of the dead, and most private houses contained miniature altars where food offerings and incense were presented to deceased relatives or to a particular minor divinity.

America.—Altars were in common use among the Indian tribes of North America. In the chief village of the Natchez of Louisiana stood a large temple in the centre of which a fire burned perpetually on an altar; behind the altar was a raised platform on which were laid baskets containing the bones of some of the "suns" who formed the governing caste (*see* NATCHEZ). This practice was adopted by the surrounding tribes. In the mounds area east of the Mississippi altars of clay, or very occasionally of stone, in various shapes and sizes, were situated near the centre of the mound, seldom more than a few inches above the ground (*see* MOUND BUILDERS). Basin-shaped hollows filled with ashes have been found at the tops of these mounds, and on one mound an oval altar six feet in length with charcoal and fragments of charred human bones was found, suggesting that it was used for burnt offerings or mortuary rites.

The most elaborate Indian altars, however, are those built by the Hopi and other Pueblo peoples of the southwest, constructed of sand to resemble animals (*e.g.*, snake or antelope). Behind the sand altars are reredoses made of wooden slats placed horizontally and vertically, decorated with symbolic pictures of rain and cloud. The Zuñi in western New Mexico have similar altars composed of a picture on the floor in coloured earths with reredoses of carved and painted symbolic slats.

In Central America every home had its domestic altar, but it was in the temples that human sacrifice was practised. Thus, in the great temple of Huitzilopochtli, the Aztec warrior god, in Mexico City, the heart of the sacrifice was extracted on a jasper stone. The ancient Mayans and Guatemalans had sculptured altars of similar shape and proportions with grooves at the top to receive the blood. Sometimes they were erected on the graves of the dead, but generally they were placed at a considerable elevation on a pyramid.   (E. O. J.)

CHRISTIAN RELIGION

Early Christian apologists insisted that they, unlike other people, had neither temple nor altar. Christ had said, "The hour is coming when neither on this mountain nor in Jerusalem will you worship the Father" (John 4:21), and the stress in Christianity was to be on "worship in spirit and truth." Thus, the true temple would be the body of Christ (*i.e.*, the church) and the true altar Christ himself. Even today, in the ceremony for the ordination of the subdeacon in the Roman rite, it is stated that "Christ Himself is the altar of holy Church."

Paul refers to "the table of the Lord" (I Cor. 10:21) on which the Eucharist was celebrated and which signified the table of the Lord's Supper, the table on which the new paschal lamb was placed. Accordingly, in all developments of the Christian altar, it is never overlooked that the altar of the New Covenant is basically a table.

Development of the Christian Altar.—Since Paul had also referred to Christ as the Rock (I Cor. 10:4), it was only natural that the eucharistic table, in the course of time, would be made of stone. Indeed, after the period of persecution, the remains of the martyrs were often reburied under altars. As tombs, these were appropriately made of stone. By the 6th century the Western Church insisted on this requirement, and the same prescription is found in the most recent Roman Catholic code of rubrics (1960). However, since it often proved difficult to have the entire altar made of stone, and because altars sometimes had to be moved, the stone element was reduced to a minimum, the altar stone, a small square slab of stone containing relics and placed on that part of the altar where the chalice and host were to stand. In the Eastern Church altars are commonly made of wood, and the antimension, a small precious cloth containing relics and adorned with icons of Christ's passion, corresponds to the Western altar stone.

In the course of time, liturgical elaboration was reflected in increasing ceremony surrounding the altar. As a holy place, it was removed from the people into the sanctuary. In the Eastern Church, even today, the priest alone may approach the altar, which is normally hidden from view by the iconostasis. In the West, as early as the time of Constantine (early 4th century), the altar was covered by a canopylike structure, the baldachin (*q.v.*) or ciborium, resting on columns placed around the altar. The altar was further ornamented by the reredos, a screen or wall covered with painted or sculptured images.

In the Western Church during the Middle Ages side altars began to appear, especially in larger churches. These provided for a multiplication of Masses, sometimes celebrated simultaneously, for special intentions of benefactors or for the repose of the faithful departed. During the Middle Ages, too, greater stress was placed on the reservation of the blessed sacrament (which had originally been a practice for the benefit of communion of the sick outside the eucharistic celebration). Customs in this regard varied widely, from the use of suspended pyxes or doves to reservation in a cupboard in a room adjoining the sanctuary. In the 15th century the tabernacle, a metal or stone box of reservation, was commonly placed on the main altar; this practice, while never universal, became increasingly widespread.

Reformed Churches.—In the churches of the Reformed traditions the altar has usually been omitted or much simplified. Much depends on the particular church's understanding of the Eucharist. Broadly stated, those churches deriving from John Calvin and possessing a strong evangelical tradition tend to place the stress on the pulpit, using a communion table (not called an altar), de-

Model of an Egyptian copper altar table (*hotep*) from Abydos; 6th Dynasty, *c*. 2300 B.C. The top is in the shape of two loaves of bread on a reed mat; hieroglyphs on the front represent the priest's name and titles

Hebrew limestone horned altar from Megiddo; period of the Israelite monarchy, 10th–9th centuries B.C.

Part of a triangular bronze fire altar, probably from Mesopotamia; 1st– 2nd centuries A.D.

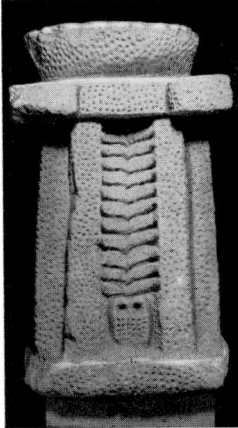

Neolithic limestone altar slab, originally painted red, from Hagar Qim, Malta

Pre-Islamic incense altar, probably of limestone, with goats and astral symbols carved in relief around the top; from southern Arabia

Altar 'Q' at Copán, Honduras, an ancient Mayan altar with carved figures of representatives from 16 Maya centres. The date inscribed on top of the altar corresponds to A.D. 776

Remains of the lower part of the Bactrian fire altar of the south temple at Surkh-Kotal, site of worshipers of Mazdak, Afghanistan; 1st–2nd centuries A.D.

Ruins of a large rectangular Hellenistic sacrificial altar in the Athenian Agora; 4th century B.C.

ANCIENT ALTARS

PLATE II

ALTAR

Three-legged table set with bread and wine, an early representation of an altar from a fresco in the catacomb of St. Calixtus, Rome; late 2nd century A.D.

High altar in the church of S. Ambrogio, Milan, Italy; Byzantine, A.D. 835. The reliefs are silver and gold, decorated with enamel and jewels

Baldachin over papal altar in St. John Lateran, Rome; 14th century

Carved stone reredos behind the chapel altar in All Souls college, Oxford, England; 15th century, restored 19th century

Altar of Mercy in the pilgrimage church of Vierzehnheiligen, Germany; 18th century

Tapestry reredos by Fernand Léger behind the altar in Notre Dame des Pauvres, Audincourt, France; mid-20th century

Altar in All Saint's, Basel, Switzerland; mid-20th century

CHRISTIAN ALTARS

PHOTOGRAPHS, (TOP LEFT, TOP RIGHT) MANSELL—ALINARI, (CENTRE LEFT) ALINARI, (CENTRE) THOMAS PHOTOS, OXFORD, ENG., (CENTRE RIGHT, BOTTOM LEFT AND RIGHT) G. E. KIDDER SMITH

prived of symbolic significance, strictly for the time of communion. Churches of the Anglican and Lutheran traditions have commonly kept the altar, though not always the term.

Liturgical Movement.—In the 20th century several developments have occurred, in the Roman Catholic and many Protestant churches, associated with the liturgical movement. A deeper understanding of eucharistic theology on all sides having led to ecumenical rapprochement, many contemporary Roman Catholic and Protestant church buildings and altars or communion tables have come to resemble one another. A return to earlier traditions, before the Reformation, is taking place.

For the Roman Catholic Church the Constitution on the Sacred Liturgy promulgated at the second Vatican Council (Dec. 4, 1963) calls for the "worthy and well-planned construction of sacred buildings," including the functional shape and construction of altars and a "moderate" use of images, with "their relative positions reflecting right order" (Nos. 128 and 125). The subsequent appendix to the constitution insists on the primacy of the main altar, roughly in the middle of the church and "decorated in a noble simple style," with no interference from any side altars. This obviously provides for a return to the early practice in which the priest at the altar faces the people rather than turns his back to them, as had been common since the Middle Ages; it also does away with excessive ornamentation. A subsequent instruction (Oct. 16, 1964) from the Sacred Congregation of Rites is even more explicit in providing "that the celebration may take place facing the people." One problem treated in both documents, but not given a definitive rubrical solution, is the placing of the tabernacle for reservation of the blessed sacrament. Accordingly, in churches constructed around mid-20th century or after it is sometimes found on the main altar, but low enough so that the priest may be seen by the people; sometimes on a side altar; sometimes in a special chapel; and sometimes in a shrine within or near the sanctuary wall. Provision is also made for a cross and for candles on or near the altar. The trend appears to be toward variety and flexibility, provided the central meaning of the altar is not obscured.

(C. J. McN.)

BIBLIOGRAPHY.—See articles on the altar in J. Hastings (ed.), *Encyclopaedia of Religion and Ethics,* vol. i (1908); H. Bonnet (ed.), *Reallexikon des ägyptischen Religionsgeschichte* (1932); T. Klauser (ed.), *Reallexikon für Antike und Christentum,* vol. i (1950); Pauly-Wissowa, *Real-Encyclopädie der classischen Altertumswissenschaft,* vol. i (1894); K. Galling (ed.), *Die Religion in Geschichte und Gegenwart,* vol. i, 3rd ed. (1957). *See* also K. Galling, *Der Altar in den Kulturen des alten Orients* (1925); K. Erdman, *Das iranische Feuerheiligtum* (1941); H. H. Bancroft, *Native Races of the Pacific States of North America,* vol. iv (1878); F. W. Hodge (ed.), "Handbook of American Indians North of Mexico," pt. i, Bureau of American Ethnology, *Bulletin 30* (1907); T. A. Joyce, *Central American and West Indian Archaeology* (1916); S. Pedersen, *Israel, its Life and Culture,* vol. iii–iv (1942); C. G. Yavis, *Greek Altars* (1949). The classic work (somewhat dated) on the Christian altar is J. Braun, *Der christliche Altar,* 2 vol. (1924); *see* also R. K. Seasoltz, *The House of God* (1963); articles by A. M. Roguet in *La Maison-Dieu,* No. 63; J. F. White, *Worship and Church Architecture* (1964); M. Marx, "The Altar of the Sacrifice Banquet," in *The Challenge of the Council* (1965).

(E. O. J.; C. J. McN.)

ALTARPIECE. The altarpiece, or retable, is a structure above the altar table, adorned with holy personages, saints and biblical subjects. The term "reredos" is used for structures not directly attached to the altar table but affixed to the wall behind it. The predella is a low, decorated strip intended to raise the main part of the altarpiece to a height where it is readily visible from a distance. A diptych is an altarpiece consisting of two panels; the triptych consists of three panels; and the polyptych of still a greater number of panels. A winged altarpiece is one equipped with wings which can be opened and closed over a fixed central part. It allows various representations to be exposed.

Painting, relief and sculpture in the round have been used in altarpieces, either separately or in various combinations. The art work cannot be fully understood divorced from its original context. The structure connecting the altarpiece with the altar proper may be a simple picture frame or it may consist of the most elaborate architectural elements.

Painted altarpieces were originally in tempera on wooden panels.

In the 15th century oil became the more widely used technique, and in the 16th century canvas became the preferred surface. Some early, relatively small altarpieces were made in low relief of gold, silver or gilded copper over wooden cores, and decorated with precious stones. Reliefs, as well as figures in the round, were carved in stone. Carvings in wood, usually coloured and gilded, were very popular in 15th-century Germany. Bronze was rarely used before the 17th century. Coloured and gilded stucco became a favoured material in the 18th century in Germany and Austria.

The architectural framework for painted panels or wood sculptures was carved in wood and gilded. The simpler frames for large Renaissance paintings were done in the same technique. Where stone sculpture was used, the architectural parts were also in stone. The baroque, with its large, stagelike structures, used a good deal of stucco with imitation marble effects for some of the architectural parts.

Middle Ages.—The practice of erecting a structure above the altar and adorning it with paintings and sculptures reaches back at least to the 11th century. The earlier custom of having a hanging or an image on the wall behind the altar was very likely one of the sources of this development. The new devotional spirit of the Gothic and the improved social and economic conditions of the medieval city-states also contributed. The reversal of the position of the priest in relation to the congregation was still another factor. In the early church the priest stood behind the altar and faced the congregation. The introduction of the altarpiece necessitated a change of the position of the celebrating priest who would otherwise have been covered by the altarpiece. This change took place in the 12th or 13th century but was never canonized. It is for this reason that a return to the original position of the priest has become possible today. (*See* below.)

The earliest altarpieces were rather small and often were not permanently connected with the altar. They were made of precious materials and this is one reason so few have survived. The *pala d'oro* of St. Mark's, Venice, whose earliest parts are from the 10th century, is a good example.

One of the oldest known painted panels is the triptych of the "Savior Between the Virgin and St. John" in the Cathedral of Tivoli, Italy, which is possibly of the 11th century. This piece was painted in the so-called Byzantine tradition of Italy which lasted through the 13th century. Many important pieces painted in this manner are now in museums (*e.g.*, "St. Magdalen," late 13th century, Accademia delle Belle Arti, Florence). These works, many of which were by anonymous masters, attest to the widespread use of painted altarpieces in Italy by this time.

Outside Italy, painted altarpieces seem to have been rare before the 15th century. After the great achievements of Gothic sculpture in the 13th century, sculpture was more popular in the north. Among the early large altarpieces in sculpture is that in the church Unserer Lieben Frauen (1308) in Oberwesel, Ger. Numerous saints appear in individual niches in an elaborate Gothic structure. More restrained in the over-all composition, even if profuse in the movements of the single figures, is the marble altar at Lucca by the Italian Jacopo della Quercia, of 1424. Mention should also be made of the free-standing sculptures created by Donatello for the high altar of the Santo in Padua (1450).

The greatest carved altars are those of the German school, marking the end of the middle ages in the 15th century. Outstanding are the violently expressive forms of the "Altar of Mary" (1477–89), by Veit Stoss, in Cracow, Pol., and the more quietly moving figures of the "Blood Altar" in Rothenburg-ob-der-Tauber, by Tilman Riemenschneider, which was finished in 1505.

Renaissance.—In all of Europe except Germany, sculpture was overshadowed by painting until the baroque period. In 14th-century Italy two contrasting tendencies developed side by side. In the first, which was strongly influenced by the Gothic and centred in Siena and Venice, the architectural framework was very elaborate and polyptychs were quite frequent (*e.g.*, the triptych of the "Annunciation" (1333), by Simone Martini, Uffizi, Florence). The second, which centred in Florence and favoured single, monumental paintings with simple frames, represented the more progressive tendencies of the Renaissance; an outstanding example of this truly great style is Giotto's "Madonna" in the Uffizi, Florence, of the early 14th century.

In 15th-century Italy, altar painting was simply a branch of the general development of painting. An outstanding example is Piero della Francesca's "Nativity" in the National gallery, London. A characteristic transformation of the Gothic triptych with elaborate architectural framework is Giovanni Bellini's altar (1488), in the Frari church in Venice. The intricately carved frame represents the arched nave of a church with one bay on each side. The perspective of the painting continues the architecture of the frame into the depth of the picture.

Outside Italy, altar painting began only in the early 15th century, with its centre in the Netherlands. The famous polyptych with movable wings (1432), by the Van Eyck brothers, is the outstanding example of this group. Some of its panels are no longer conceived as individual representations or scenes. In the "Annunciation" for instance, four panels are drawn together to represent the room where the event takes place; the partitions of the frame are like windows through which one can look into space. Retarded in style but often very expressive and refined are the great polyptychs of the 15th century in Germany; e.g., the "Altar of Mary" by Konrad of Soest, in Dortmund.

In Renaissance Italy, the polyptych had been all but eliminated in favour of large single paintings. The elaborate architectural framework of the Gothic was replaced by a relatively narrow gilded frame, the prototype of the frame that remained an integral part of all easel painting until the 20th century. Characteristically, the increased importance of the picture, as against the frame, was particularly favoured by the great painters of Venice. The paintings themselves had become very large; for instance, Titian's "Assumption" in the Frari church, Venice, is over 22 ft. high. Michelangelo's huge fresco of the "Last Judgment" (1534–41), in the Sistine chapel, even though technically not an altarpiece, should not be omitted in this context. For all practical purposes it functions as a reredos. The last great altarpieces in which painting was the dominant factor were by 17th-century masters such as Caravaggio and Rubens.

The end of the middle ages in Germany witnessed a splendid combination of sculpture and painting. Painted wings closed over boxlike cores with elaborate sculptures carved in wood, gilded and coloured. The greatest work of this type is Matthias Grünewald's "Isenheim Altar" (about 1516).

Baroque.—Gothic altars were still essentially pieces of church furniture, whether they were freestanding or attached to a wall. During the Italian Renaissance, on the other hand, there was an increasing tendency to integrate the whole altarpiece with the architecture of the church. This aim, however, was hardly ever accomplished because the church and its interior equipment were rarely planned and executed together during the short period of the High Renaissance. It was only with the baroque that a complete integration of the various components was accomplished. The essential distinction between the architecture of the church, the architecture of the altarpiece, and the sculptural and painted portions disappeared. However, with some notable exceptions, the artistic quality of painting and sculpture declined in connection with this change. Interest in the ensemble overshadowed interest in the components. Even the altar proper became more and more an adjunct to the altarpiece, and lost much of its original, independent significance.

As a consequence of this tendency to merge all the arts, the baroque excelled in large stagelike ensembles. The great architect-sculptor Bernini made the most creative contributions toward this development. His "Cathedra Petri Altar" (1657–66), in St. Peter's, Rome, is an outstanding example. This altar is no longer a piece of church furniture; its components are a direct extension of the architecture, integrating even the sources of light into the general composition. Bernini's "Altar of St. Teresa" became the prototype of German 18th-century altarpieces in which the design of building and altar originated together. The high altar of the church of the Monastery in Weltenburg, Bavaria, by the brothers Asam is an outstanding example. The altar proper, populated with many painted sculptures, is simply an extension of the

architecture of the nave. It opens into an arched stage with the figures of St. George and the Dragon indirectly lighted by an unseen window. The background of this stage is taken up by a painting which blends with the colours of the sculptural and architectural parts in front.

A Spanish variant of the baroque altarpiece was transplanted to the Americas in the 18th century. It is of the reredos type, which, in Spain, was already favoured during the Gothic period.

19th and 20th-Century.—In the 19th century, following the use of various historical styles in church architecture, the design of altarpieces degenerated into pure eclecticism. Interesting attempts to revive the altarpiece were made in the 20th century. Examples by such great contemporaries as Matisse and Bonnard are in the church of Assy, France. A reredos in the form of a huge stained glass window by Emil Frei is in St. Ann's church, Normandy, Mo. The general tendency of the 20th century, however, seemed to be toward the reintroduction of the unadorned altar table combined with a return to the early position of the priest behind the altar.

BIBLIOGRAPHY.—Karl Kunstle, *Ikonographie der Christlichen Kunst* (1926–28); Joseph Braun, *Der Christliche Altar* (1924); Hans Huth, *Künstler und Werkstatt der Spätgotik* (1923); Francis Bond, *The Chancel of English Churches* (1916).   (P. M. L.)

ALTA VERAPAZ, a department in north-central Guatemala. Its area is 3,354 sq.mi., and its population (1964) was 259,873. Its capital is Cobán. Most of the inhabitants are in the highlands east of the Río Chixoy where there are coffee plantations. Other crops include maize, beans, sugar cane, cacao; much of the land is used for beef cattle. From the forests of the north come chicle, vanilla and wood. The main route of access is by road and rail to the Río Polochic and Lago de Izabal to the port of Livingston.   (P. E. J.)

ALTAZIMUTH, an astronomical telescope of a pattern similar to a theodolite but on a much larger scale. It is used principally to observe positions of the moon before first quarter and after last quarter, when the moon passes across the meridian in daylight. In order to secure more favourable nocturnal observations at such times it is necessary to have an instrument which can be turned out of the meridian but in other respects is used similarly to a meridian circle.

ALTDORF, the capital of Uri canton, Switz., is on the Reuss river where it is joined by the Schächen torrent, 490 m. (1,607 ft.) above sea level, 74 km. (46 mi.) by road south of Zürich. Pop. (1960) 7,477, mostly Roman Catholic and German-speaking. In the centre of Altdorf a bronze statue of William Tell by Richard Kissling of Zürich stands on the spot where, according to tradition, Tell shot the apple from his son's head. In 1899 a theatre was opened for the performance of Schiller's play *Wilhelm Tell*. Near Altdorf is Bürglen, where Tell is said to have been born and later drowned. In the village is a Tell museum in an ancient tower. The town is on the Saint Gotthard railway from Zürich and Lucerne to Lugano and Italy. The main road from north to south also passes it, the part to the north, the famous Axenstrasse, being partly in tunnel cut out of the mountainside above Lake Lucerne. There are rubber and cable works and an ammunition factory. Altdorf was burned down four times, completely in 1400 and 1799 and half of it in 1488 and 1692, with loss of historical documents.   (HA. GA.)

ALTDORFER, ALBRECHT (?1480–1538), German painter, engraver and architect, among the earliest European artists to stress the romantic aspects of landscape, became a citizen of Regensburg in 1505 and remained there all his life, aside from occasional visits to Austria. In later years, he was official architect of the city and held a seat in its inner council. Altdorfer was the guiding spirit of the Danube school. He was the first European painter to probe the mysteries of impenetrable forests ("St. George," 1510, Munich), of sunset moods ("Danube Landscape Without Figures," Munich), and of picturesque ruins in twilight ("Nativity," Berlin). For Altdorfer, man was part of a strange symphony of trees, plants, rocks, mountains and clouds, and often resembled their weird, primeval forms. He disregarded the Italian concepts of rational organization which occupied his great con-

Jesus Christ, centre detail of the *pala d'oro* in St. Mark's, Venice, Italy; 10th-century Byzantine gold work inlaid with jewels

Painted and carved wood polyptych of the high altar in the monastery church of Blaubeuren, Germany, by Michael and Gregor Erhart; 1493–94

"Adoration of the Lamb," bottom centre panel of the interior of the polyptych of St. Bavon, Ghent, Belgium, attributed to Hubert and Jan van Eyck; 1432

ALTARPIECES OF THE 10TH AND 15TH CENTURIES

ALTARPIECE

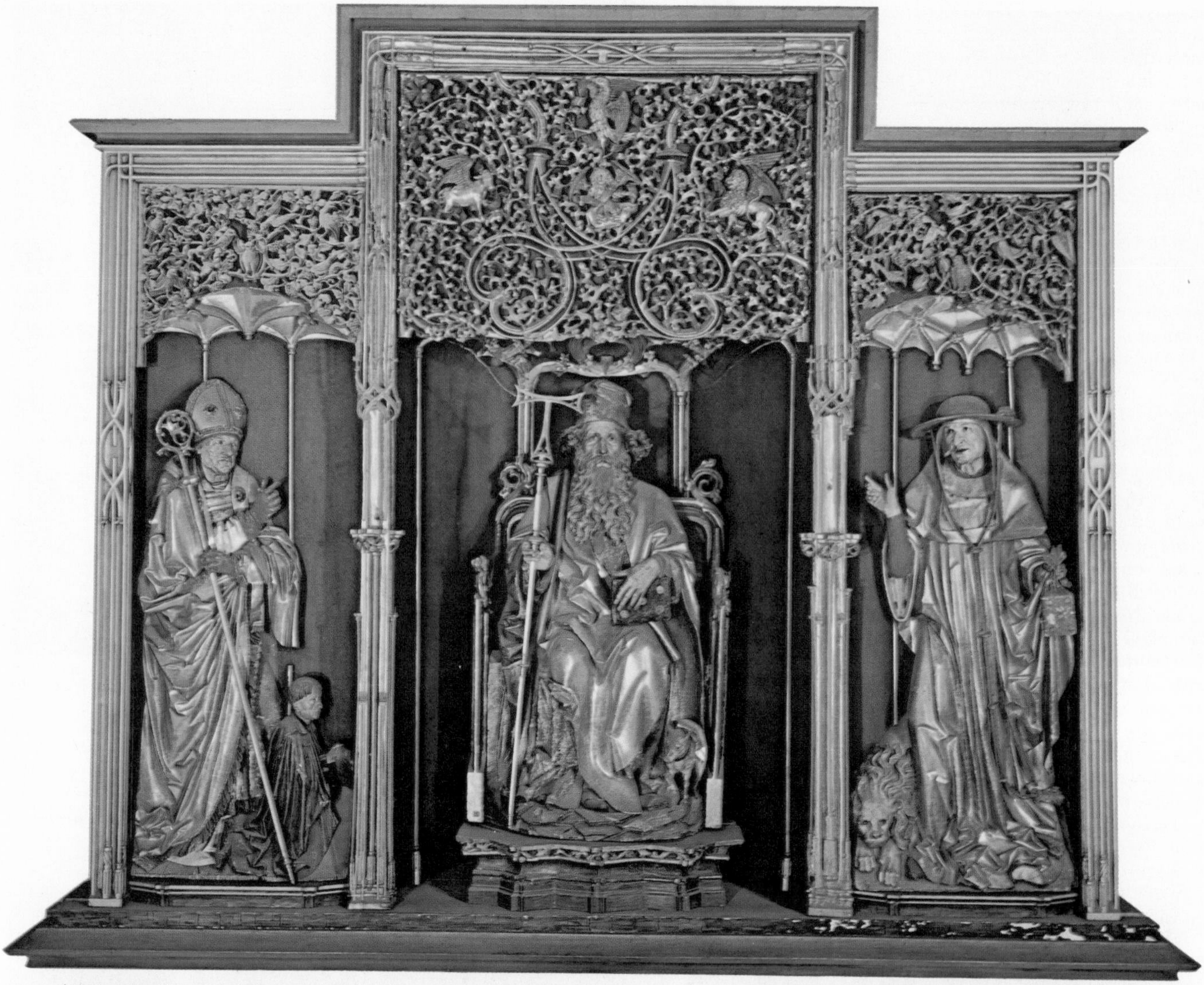

Interior of centre panel of the Isenheim altarpiece carved by Niklaus Hagnower; 1505. In the Colmar museum, France

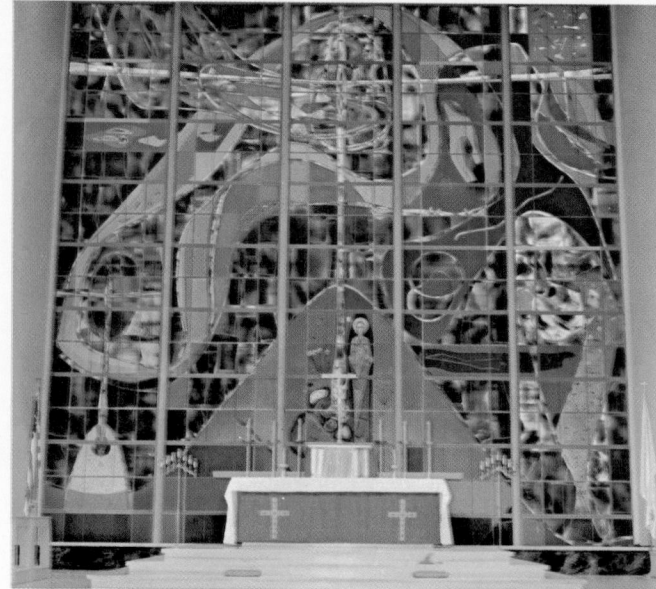

Reredos in the form of a 38-ft. stained-glass window in St. Ann's church, Normandy, Mo. Designed by Emil Frei; mid-20th century

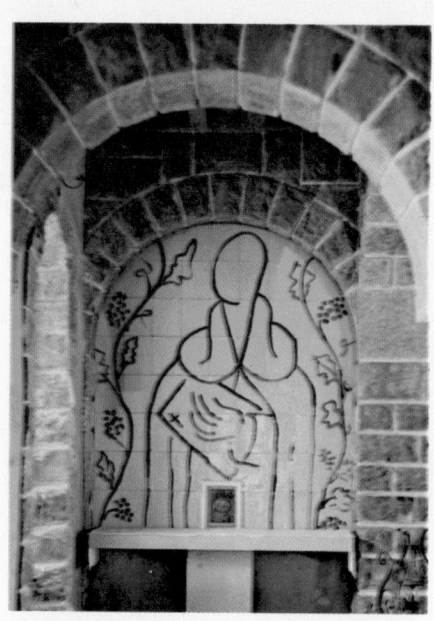

St. Dominic, ceramic tile altarpiece by Henri Matisse, church of Assy, France; mid-20th century

16TH- AND 20TH-CENTURY ALTARPIECES

PHOTOGRAPHS, (TOP) ERIC SCHAAL, "LIFE," (BOTTOM LEFT) JOHN H. GERARD, (BOTTOM RIGHT) W. RUBIN

temporary, Albrecht Dürer. Of the masterful altar panels in St. Florian near Linz (1518), depicting the Passion of Christ and the martyrdom of St. Sebastian, several are night scenes illuminated by torches or a distant twilight—a new venture then. His masterpiece in dramatic illumination is the "Battle of Alexander at Issus" (1529, Munich).

The fantastic element appears most unrestrained in his drawings, most of which are in black and white lines on brown or blue-gray tinted papers. His engravings and woodcuts are generally of miniature size, but their playful imaginativeness distinguishes them from the more pedantic production of the "Little Masters" of engraving. His most important woodcuts are the 40 plates called "The Fall and Redemption of Man." About 1530, he used the new medium of etching in nine exquisite landscapes as well as a series of fanciful tankards, intended as work models for goldsmiths.

Bibliography.—William M. Ivins, Jr., "The Woodcuts of Albrecht Altdorfer," *Print Collector's Quarterly*, vol. iv, pp. 31–60 (1914); Max J. Friedlander, *Albrecht Altdorfer* (1923); Emil Waldmann, *Albrecht Altdorfer,* catalogue of engravings and etchings (1923); Otto Benesch, *Der Maler Albrecht Altdorfer* (1938); Franz Roh, "Altdorfer," *The Selective Eye,* pp. 28–39 (1955). (H. Jm.)

ALTENBURG, a town in the Leipzig district of Germany, lies on the southern edge of the central German brown coal deposits about 30 mi. S. of Leipzig. Pop. (1964) 113,377. The town is known as the birthplace of the card game skat (*q.v.*). The former ducal castle, built in the 10th century and several times destroyed, was restored in the 19th century and contains a playing-card museum. The fountain is decorated with sculptures of skat players. The Lindenau museum contains a large collection of art objects. Altenburg is noted for its manufacture of playing cards, and the nationally owned playing-card factory exports all over the world. Sewing machines (also a nationally owned enterprise) are exported and hats are made. Altenburg has the only drum-skin tannery in east Germany, a private concern with an extensive export program. A teachers' training school and schools for papermakers and railwaymen are located there.

The town arose in 1130 as a trading centre. It served the emperor Frederick Barbarossa as a royal residence and he founded an Augustinian monastery there. Altenburg was a principality from 1603 to 1672, and from 1826 to 1918 it was the residence of the dukes of Saxe-Altenburg.

ALTERNATING CURRENT, electric current which grows to a maximum value, decreases, changes its direction (with respect to a datum line), reaches a maximum value in the new direction (which is equivalent to a minimum value for the original direction), and returns to its original value, whence it repeats this cycle an indefinite number of times. The interval between the attainment of a definite value on two successive occasions is called the period, and the number of cycles or periods per second is the frequency of the alternating current. High-frequency currents have several thousand cycles per second. The amplitude is the deviation of the maximum (or of the minimum) from the datum line. *See* ELECTRICITY: *Induced Electromotive Forces; see* also references under "Alternating Current" in the Index.

ALTGELD, JOHN PETER (1847–1902), governor of Illinois in the 1890s, famous for his pardon of convicted Haymarket rioters. He was born in Prussia, Dec. 30, 1847, and as a child was brought by his parents to a farm near Mansfield, O. He had little formal education. At the age of 16 he served for a short time in an Ohio volunteer regiment during the Civil War. After the war he moved west and studied law. In 1869 he went to Savannah, Mo., where in 1874 he won his first political race and became county prosecuting attorney. He resigned this office the next year and moved to Chicago. He entered politics again in 1884, running as Democratic candidate for congress, but he was not elected. The same year he published a book, *Our Penal Machinery and Its Victims,* which reflected his deep resentment against injustice. From 1886 to 1891 he was superior court judge in Chicago. Meanwhile he had accumulated a fortune in real estate. In 1892 he won his party's nomination for governor and was elected by farm and labour votes, the first Democratic governor of the state since the Civil War.

As governor he promoted reform programs, especially social legislation. Early in his term as governor he was urged by Clarence Darrow, labour leaders and others to pardon three of the men convicted of complicity in the Haymarket riot (*see* CHICAGO: *History*) that had occurred in Chicago in 1886. He signed the pardons in June 1893, and at the same time released a statement charging that the men had not been given a fair trial. The anticipated storm then broke. Altgeld was denounced by the press and employers as the friend of anarchists. A year later, Altgeld's protest to President Cleveland against the use of federal troops during the Pullman strike produced further attacks, and in 1896 he was defeated for re-election. He became an advocate of free silver and supported Bryan in 1896 and 1900.

Altgeld had published a book entitled *Live Questions* in 1890; an expanded edition appeared in 1899. Another book, *Cost of Something for Nothing,* was published posthumously in 1904. He died on March 12, 1902.

See: Harry Barnard, *Eagle Forgotten; Life of John Peter Altgeld* (1938); Raymond Ginger, *Altgeld's America* (1958); Henry M. Christman (ed.), *The Mind and Spirit of John Peter Altgeld* (1960). (H. F. Tt.)

ALTHING, the legislative assembly of Iceland (*q.v.*).

ALTICHIERO (ALDIGHERO) **DA ZEVIO** (*c.* 1330–after 1390), Italian painter, was the effective founder of the Veronese school. He was born, according to Vasari, at Zevio, a village near Verona. Nothing is known of his early work in Verona. He migrated to Padua about 1370, perhaps at the invitation of Francesco I Carrara, painting frescoes (destroyed) in the Sala dei Giganti and, with Guariento, in the Palazzo del Capitano del Popolo. His main surviving works are two fresco cycles; one, with the "Crucifixion" and "Scenes from the Legend of St. James," in the chapel of S. Felice in the basilica of S. Antonio (completed 1379), and the other, with "Scenes from the Legends of St. George and other Saints" (*c.* 1384), in the Cappella di S. Giorgio nearby. In the latter cycle Altichiero was assisted by an associate, Jacopo Avanzo: the respective shares of the two artists in the work have not been satisfactorily ascertained. Altichiero returned to Verona, probably about 1390, executing (before 1396) a votive fresco over the Cavalli monument in Sta. Anastasia.

Altichiero's frescoes, in which elements deriving from Giotto are combined with a courtly style that anticipates Pisanello, had a profound influence on Veronese painting in the early 15th century.

(J. W. P.-H.)

ALTIMETRY. Altimetry is the process of determining the altitude above mean sea level of a point in the atmosphere, usually by measurement of the air pressure with an aneroid barometer. The relationship between pressure and altitude varies in space and time with varying weather conditions and is determined at known elevations on the surface of the earth with mercurial barometers. However, for points above the surface of the earth it must usually be calculated by assuming the hydrostatic equation, which expresses the fact that the rate of decrease of pressure with altitude is such that the difference in pressure on the bottom and top of a unit volume of air is equal to its weight. The weight of the air depends on its pressure, temperature and water-vapour content, the values of which are measured in the upper air with radiosondes or aeroplanes. The hydrostatic equation can be expected to be in error by less than 0.1% except in extreme weather conditions such as hurricanes or thunderstorms. Meteorological charts are used to interpolate the pressure-height relationship between observation points and for making forecasts of future conditions. (*See* METEOROLOGY.)

Altimeters, which are aneroid barometers used for altimetry, are marked in terms of a special pressure parameter, the pressure altitude, which is the height in a standard atmosphere at which a given pressure occurs. As an example, the U.S. standard atmosphere is defined as one in which the pressure at sea level is 760 mm. of mercury and in which the temperature is 15° C. at sea level and decreases with altitude at the rate of 6.5° C. per kilometre until it becomes equal to −55° C., above which point the temperature remains constant. The standard atmospheres have been chosen to represent average atmospheric conditions so that the numerical pressure indications are approximately equal to the altitude. The difference between the actual altitude of a point and the pressure altitude at that point is called the altimeter correction and thus varies in both space and time. The maximum spatial variations of the altimeter corrections are observed to be about plus or minus 2,000 ft., while the time variations at a given point during periods of a few days are usually considerably less than this amount.

In order to obtain direct indications of altitude most altimeters are constructed so that the pressure-measuring apparatus can be adjusted with respect to a separate altitude scale in such a way that the appropriate altimeter correction is mechanically added to the measured pressure altitude. The amount of adjustment is usually indicated by an altimeter setting scale. The altimeter setting is defined as being the pressure corresponding to that pressure altitude which is equal to the negative of the altimeter correction.

From 1938 radio altimeters had been developed which measure the height of an aircraft above the surface of the earth by measuring the time for a radio signal generated in the aircraft to be reflected from the earth's surface back to the aircraft. With such instruments the altitude above mean sea level can be determined directly without a knowledge of the pressure distribution when flying over oceans. However, when flying over land, rapidly varying altitude of the underlying terrain, the elevation of which many times cannot conveniently be determined from the aircraft, limits the usefulness of these instruments for determining altitudes above mean sea level. (J. C. By.)

ALTITUDE AND AZIMUTH, two readings useful in astronomy, navigation, gunnery and other fields for describing the position of an object above the earth. Altitude in this usage is defined as the distance of the object above the ground or sea level and usually is expressed as the angular elevation (up to 90°) above the horizon. Azimuth (or bearing) is the number of degrees (up to 360°) clockwise from north, or (up to either 90° or 180°) east or west of a north-south base line. Altitude and azimuth readings can be made with radar or with special telescopic devices such as the theodolite (q.v.) or altazimuth (q.v.).

OBJECT WITH AZIMUTH OF 40° EAST OF NORTH AND ALTITUDE OF 30°

For purposes such as aerial gunnery in which exact position is needed, a third factor must be known—the range, or distance from the object to the observer. See diagram for the position of an object with an azimuth of 40° east of north and an altitude of 30°.

See also ALTIMETRY; COMPASS: Azimuth Instruments; SEXTANT; SURVEYING: Units of Measure Used in Surveying.

ALTMAN, BENJAMIN (1840–1913), U.S. merchant, art collector and philanthropist, established one of the world's great department stores. Born on New York city's lower east side on July 12, 1840, he had little formal schooling, but at the age of 25 he was able to open his first dry goods store, and in 1906 moved it to the uptown section, pioneering the movement of business there. With additions in 1913–14, the store occupied the entire block bounded by Madison and Fifth avenues and 34th and 35th streets. Known for his organizing ability and his promotion of medical service, rest and other benefits for his employees, he set up a foundation for their welfare and for other philanthropic purposes.

An astute art collector, Altman also built up a valuable art library. He had extensive collections of Chinese porcelains, crystals, rugs and other objects of art. Among his paintings were 13 Rembrandts and canvasses by Botticelli, Holbein and Filippo Lippi. The entire collection, appraised at $20,000,000, was bequeathed, with $150,000 for its care, to the Metropolitan Museum of Art.

Altman's estate of $35,000,000 included a substantial gift to the National Academy of Design to encourage American painting. He died in New York city Oct. 7, 1913.

ALTO, a musical term meaning "high" (Ital., from Lat. altus) and used of certain types of voice—the countertenor in men and the contralto in women (see VOICE). It is also the term in Italian and French for the viola which used to take the highest part in works for strings (see VIOLIN FAMILY), and is used as part of a compound (e.g., alto trombone) for instruments of high pitch.

ALTO ALENTEJO, a province of southern Portugal, was created in 1933 to include the two districts of Évora and Portalegre. Pop. (1960) 377,626. Area 5,128 sq.mi. It comprises a series of high plateaus at 600–1300 ft. forming the watershed between the Tagus (Port. Tejo) and Guadiana rivers. The province is divided naturally into four regions: the Évora plateau to the south, the Campo de Benavila drained by the Sado river to the west, the Elvas-Estremoz plateau on the east and the Serra de S. Mamede (3,363 ft.) to the northeast. Most of the land consists of ancient crystalline rocks with poor soils. The province is sparsely populated and in summer is exposed to the rays of a torrid sun. Extensive stock raising and cereal production on large properties of 100 to 1,000 ac. are typical, and rich cereal lands are found where the diorite weathers into deep, black soils around Elvas, Campo Maior and Alter do Chão, and especially where the soils of syenite origin occur around Évora. There are famous olive groves and fruit orchards in the Elvas and Estremoz districts.

Évora (q.v.), the capital, has much fine architecture dating from the 17th century. Elvas (11,672), Estremoz (9,942) and Portalegre (11,073) are noted agricultural centres but, apart from food processing and marble quarries, there is little industry.

(J. M. Ho.)

ALTON, an urban district and market town of Hampshire, Eng., lies among the downs on the river Wey, 18 mi. N.E. of Winchester by road and 20 mi. by rail. Pop. (1961) 9,159. In the church of St. Lawrence, which is Perpendicular with a Norman tower, fierce fighting took place between parliamentarians and royalists in 1643. Eggar's grammar school was founded in 1642 and there are many Georgian buildings. William Curtis, the botanist, was born at Alton in 1746 and the Curtis museum was founded in 1855. Within the urban district are the Lord Mayor Treloar Orthopaedic hospital, the 20th-century abbey of the Order of St. Paul and the village of Holybourne, where Mrs. Elizabeth Gaskell died in 1865. During 1809–17 Jane Austen lived at Chawton, 1 mi. S., and in 1588 George Wither was born at Bentworth, 3½ mi. N.W. The village of Selborne (q.v.), where Gilbert White lived, lies 4½ mi. E.S.E. Alton was granted an annual fair by Edward II; it is now biannual. Hops are grown in the district and the chief industries are brewing and the making of artificial limbs.

ALTON, a city of Madison county, Ill., U.S., on the Mississippi river, about 5 mi. above the mouth of the Missouri and 25 mi. N. of St. Louis, Mo. (For comparative population figures see table in ILLINOIS: Population.)

Named after Alton R. Easton, a son of the St. Louis lawyer politician who platted the townsite in 1817, it was organized as a town in 1833 and in 1837, when the population was about 4,000, it was incorporated as a city.

While Alton never realized its early ambition of commercial greatness, it enjoyed steady economic development as a part of the industrial arc that reaches down the Mississippi to East St. Louis. Locally, glass, paper, metal and canvas products, building materials, cereal foods and oil refining industries are important. Alton is divided by bluffs, some of which rise abruptly to a height of more than 200 ft. In the lower town, industrial establishments fill the river plain. Residential Alton lies away from the river on the bluffs. In some sections the wide, brick-paved streets and architectural styles convey the flavour of the 19th century.

Shurtleff college (Baptist) founded at Alton in 1827, and Monticello seminary for girls, founded in 1835 at the village of Godfrey, 5 mi. N., were among the earliest educational institutions in the Mississippi valley. Southern Illinois university operates a campus on the site of Shurtleff college. Historical monuments commemorate abolitionist newspaper editor Elijah P. Lovejoy, who was killed by a pro-slavery mob in 1837, and the scene of the last Lincoln-Douglas debate in 1858. (R. E. M.)

ALTONA, a suburb of Hamburg, in the north of Germany, is situated on the right bank of the Elbe. Until 1938 it was administered as a separate town, with a charter dating from 1664. Altona is built on cliffs above the Elbe and lies 5 km. (3 mi.) W. of the centre of Hamburg, with which it is connected by railway and buses. The industries are similar to those of Hamburg. The name may have come originally from *allzu-nah* ("all too near") which was the Hamburger's designation for an inn which lay too close to their territory, and which for a long time was the only building. Altona was a small fishing village called Altwasser when captured by the Danes in 1640 but soon became a formidable rival to Hamburg. It passed to Prussia in 1866. *See* Hamburg.

ALTOONA, a city of Blair county, Pa., U.S., 99 mi. E. by N. of Pittsburgh. It is located in the rugged terrain of central Pennsylvania, on the eastern slopes of the Allegheny front which separates the Atlantic from the Mississippi valley watersheds. The city was named for Altona, an important river port in Schleswig-Holstein, Ger.

The Altoona region has always functioned as a transportation and communication centre between the eastern and western states. The first settlements in the area were made before the American Revolution. Fort Roberdau was established in the region in 1778 to protect lead deposits used by the patriot army. In 1787 the Frankstown trail (connecting the Susquehanna and Ohio river systems) was surveyed. Shortly after 1800 that highway was extended to Pittsburgh. During the canal building boom of the 1830s the most spectacular of all canal links, the Portage railroad, was developed to span the 36-mi. divide between the Juniata and Connemaugh rivers. Using railroad flat cars, the canal barges were hauled up a series of inclined planes and lowered by similar stages down the western slopes.

The city of Altoona proper was founded in 1849 by the Pennsylvania Railroad company. It soon became the major centre for the construction and repair of railroad rolling stock, still the city's chief occupation after mid-20th century. The city's population declined, from a peak of 82,054 in 1930, to 80,214 in 1940, to 77,177 in 1950 and to 69,407 in 1960, largely as a result of the conversion from steam to diesel locomotives and a general decline in railroad activity.

The population of the standard metropolitan statistical area (Blair county) was 137,270 in 1960. (For comparative population figures *see* table in Pennsylvania: *Population*.)

Pennsylvania State university has an undergraduate centre at Altoona. Nearby points of interest include surviving portions of the Portage railroad and Horseshoe Curve park. (R. L. Le.)

ALTO PARANÁ, the easternmost department of Paraguay, was named after the river which bounds it for 150 mi. and separates it from Brazilian Paraná and Argentine Misiones. Area 7,817 sq.mi. It forms part of the Paraguayan extension of the Brazilian plateau, dissected by eastward-flowing tributaries of the Paraná. In the northeastern corner occur the Guaíra (Sete Quedas) falls. Although as large as Wales, its population was estimated at only 13,745 in 1960, mainly recent European immigrants. Its economic development was awaiting transport links, the first of which would be a trunk road connecting Asunción with Foz do Iguaçú in Brazil. The only significant settlement is Hernandarias, the capital, previously named Tacurupucú.

(G. J. B.)

ALTO-RILIEVO: *see* Relief.

ALTRINCHAM, a municipal borough of Cheshire, Eng., lies 8 mi. S.W. of Manchester. Pop. (1961) 41,104. About 1290 Altrincham was granted by charter of Hamon de Massey a court leet, market and annual fair, the latter being replaced from 1319 to 1895 by the "Sanjam" held on the eve, fast and morrow of St. James's day. The court leet regulated the town's affairs, appointing officials such as constables, market lookers and dog muzzlers, until the middle of the 19th century. The town was incorporated in 1937 and the market is now biweekly. The 18th-century Dunham Massey hall, seat of the earl of Stamford, stands in a fine deer park. The old town hall, built by the 7th earl in 1849, now forms part of a hotel; the new town hall was opened in 1901. The Stamford hall serves as a social centre. Altrincham's commercial expansion began with the construction of the Bridgewater canal, started in 1760. In the mid-19th century the spinning of linen thread and bobbin turning were its two industries, and market gardening the chief occupation of its inhabitants, but early in the 20th century engineering of various kinds became the main local industry, and many residents travel daily to work in Manchester. Manchester airport is situated at Ringway, 3½ mi. S.E.

ALTRUISM, a philosophical term used in ethics (*q.v.*) for the theory of conduct which regards the good of others as the end of moral action. It was invented by Auguste Comte and adopted generally as a convenient antithesis to egoism. As a theory of conduct, its adequacy depends on the interpretation given to the term good. If the good is taken to be pleasure and the absence of pain, altruism would seem a reasonable principle. Most men would agree that a moral agent has an obligation to further the pleasures and alleviate the pains of other people, while it would seem contrary to ordinary usage to say that a man has a duty to further his own pleasure or to spare himself pain or is to be blamed for not doing either of these things. The same arguments hold if happiness is taken as the end of life. But if good is used more widely to include knowledge, aesthetic experience, virtue of character and personal holiness, then altruism fails as a complete theory of morals, for a moral agent has a duty of self-improvement in these fields, as well as his duties to others.

Some utilitarians (*e.g.*, Herbert Spencer and Sir Leslie Stephen; *see* Utilitarianism) held that these distinctions between self and others were unsatisfactory. Both egoism and altruism conceived society as an aggregate of units. The true moral aim was the welfare neither of others nor of self but of society (the social organism). This view claimed the support of evolutionary theory. Society was thought of as preserved and developed by the harmonious co-operation of the individuals composing it, just as an organism is by the harmonious interaction of the cells of which it is made up. This analogy was dangerous for two reasons: it does not seem possible to speak of the good of a society except in terms of the goods of its individual members; and these theories do not make clear whether the society to which individual actions are referred is one society or many. In ordinary usage there are many societies, each with its own members, but it is not an adequate theory of morals to limit the moral agent's duties to actions serving the particular society to which he belongs.

The principle of altruism recalls the Christian maxim "Do unto others as you would they would do unto you." But "others" in this maxim means not "other Englishmen" or "other Christians" but "other men regardless of the particular societies to which they happen to belong." (J. D. M.)

ALUDEL, a pear-shaped pot generally made of fire clay and open at both ends. The aludels are arranged in series, the neck of one fitting into the base of the next, to form a condenser. They were used by the early chemists in sublimation and, at Almaden in Spain, the aludel or bustamente furnace has long been employed for the extraction of mercury from its ores.

(J. B. Ps.)

ALUM is the name commonly applied to a hydrated double salt, usually consisting of aluminum sulfate, water of hydration and the sulfate of another element. In more specific chemical terminology, alum refers to a whole series of hydrated double salts resulting from the hydration of the sulfate of any one of a number of triple-valence (+3) ions, including aluminum, and the sulfate of a single-valence (+1) ion.

The alums collectively have many important uses, including the production of medicines, textiles, sugar, paper, paints, matches and deodorants. They also are used in baking powder, styptic pencils, fire extinguishers, as a mordant (binder) in dyeing, as a flocculating agent in water purification and for waterproofing paper. The alum of greatest commercial importance is aluminum potassium sulfate, also known as potassium alum or potash alum.

Aluminum sulfate also can form alums with the sulfates of the singly charged (valence of 1) ions of sodium, ammonia, cesium, silver, rubidium, thallium, hydrazine, hydroxylamine, many organic amines and possibly lithium. These sulfates of singly charged ions, in addition to combining with aluminum sulfate, also can form alums with the sulfates of trivalent iron, chromium, manganese, cobalt, gallium, titanium, vanadium, iridium, rhodium, indium and others. Many of the alums theoretically possible have not yet been prepared.

Alums generally are produced by precipitating them from solution. For instance, in producing aluminum potassium sulfate, aluminum sulfate $(Al_2[SO_4]_3)$ and potassium sulfate (K_2SO_4) are dissolved in water and then on evaporation the alum is caused to crystallize out of solution. The formation of each formula weight of alum requires one formula weight of aluminum sulfate, one formula weight of potassium sulfate and 24 molecules of water. The resulting hydrated double salt can be written either as $K_2SO_4.Al_2(SO_4)_3.24H_2O$ or as $KAl(SO_4)_2.12H_2O$. In general, the ease of alum formation increases (i.e., the solubility decreases) as the size of the singly charged ion increases and that of the trivalent ion decreases. Thus, the largest of the singly charged metal ions, cesium, forms alums with all the triply charged ions listed, while for the smallest, lithium, only the aluminum alum has been reported and the supporting evidence for it has been questioned.

The list of alums is considerably extended by substituting selenate ion for part or all of the sulfate ion. Similar compounds have been prepared in which sulfate has been replaced by fluoroberyllate $(BeF_4{}^{2-})$ or chlorozincate $(ZnCl_4{}^{2-})$.

Nature of Alum Crystals.—The alums crystallize in the regular system, usually in octahedra; however, from a basic solution of ordinary alum, the cube tends to predominate. An octahedral crystal immersed in a slightly basic solution at room temperature will gradually be converted to the cubic form, the composition remaining unaltered. Owing to the symmetry of the crystal form, perfect single octahedra of large size may be obtained by slow crystallization at room temperature. A crystal weighing 125 lb. has been grown in this way in a period of about two years.

Studies of alum crystals by X-ray analysis have shown that the triply charged ion is in union with six water molecules, which occupy the corners of an octahedron, with the metal ion at the centre. The other six molecules of water serve to link these octahedra to the ions of the singly charged ion and the sulfate ions. Because the various singly charged ions differ markedly in size, the ions do not pack together in quite the same way in crystals of different alums. This gives rise to three distinct types of alums, which show different crystal shapes and can often be distinguished by outward appearance. The alums containing medium-sized singly charged ions have a structure designated as α, those of large ions as β, and those of small ions as γ. For aluminum alums, sodium forms the γ modification; ammonium, potassium and rubidium, the α; and cesium, the β. Some alums can be induced to crystallize in more than one form, but in general the classes are not isomorphous and do not combine to form mixed crystals. Consequently, fractional crystallization furnishes a means of separating rubidium (α alum) from cesium (β alum). The nature of the triply charged ion also has some influence on determining the type of alum formed, as is shown by X-ray studies of chromium alums. The rubidium alum of this series forms β crystals rather than the α type formed in the aluminum series. Of the other chromium alums studied, potassium and ammonium are α, while cesium, thallium, and methyl ammonium are β.

Properties.—Potash alum, as is true of most alums, has an astringent and acid taste. It is colourless, odourless and exists as hard, transparent crystals or white crystalline powder. Potassium and ammonium aluminum alums are stable in air, but the sodium salt effloresces and disintegrates. The alums melt in their water of hydration between about 37° C. for thallous ferric alum and 117° C. for cesium aluminum alum. By careful heating in a current of air, ordinary alum can be dehydrated at 100° C. If heated rapidly, it swells and forms a light bulky mass of "burnt alum." When ammonium alum is heated at much higher tempera-

tures, it yields pure aluminum oxide.

The solubilities of alums in water vary widely. The quantities (parts) of some of the aluminum alums dissolved by 100 parts of water (15° C.) are as follows: cesium alum, 0.35; potassium alum, 9.59; ammonium alum, 12.66; sodium alum, 51 (16° C.). Water dissolves several times its own weight of potassium alum at 90° C. The aqueous solutions act as weak acids.

Mixtures of chromium and aluminum alum are used to produce and measure the lowest temperatures yet achieved. In this application, the alum is cooled with liquid helium, magnetized with a strong magnetic field, then insulated from its surroundings, and the magnetic field removed. Work is done by the alum during its spontaneous demagnetization and the energy required is obtained at the expense of heat energy, so that the temperature falls. By this method, temperatures are obtained well within a tenth of a centigrade degree of the theoretical lower limit of temperature (absolute zero).

Manufacture.—The early history of the manufacture of alum is unknown. Potassium alum, aluminum sulfate and iron sulfates occur native in varying degrees of admixture and purity, and the *alumen* mentioned by Pliny in chapter 15, book 35 of *Natural History* would appear to include a number of salts and mixtures. In the 15th century, the Turkish Mediterranean trade in dyed fabrics and wool, in which alum was employed as mordant, amounted to a considerable sum. About 1460, John di Castro, after learning the alum manufacturing process at Constantinople, began to make alum at Tolfa, Italy, from a local deposit of alunite (a basic sulfate of aluminum and potassium) that was still being used in the 20th century. The introduction of the manufacture of alum into Italy (where it shortly afterward became a papal monopoly) was announced as a victory over the Turks. In England, preparation of alum from the schists of Yorkshire was begun about 1600.

Manufacture of alum from both alunite and alum schists was carried on without addition of sulfuric acid, the production of which did not assume importance until about 1800. In 1845, the manufacture of alum in England was radically altered by the substitution of aluminous shales for the schists. These shales contained more aluminum and less iron, and after being heated were reasonably soluble in sulfuric acid, from which alum could be crystallized. With the change to shales, the weight of alummous material required to produce a ton of alum was reduced from about 100 tons to two-thirds of a ton; the time required also was greatly shortened, and so the old process was gradually abandoned.

Potassium alum is largely obtained from the Italian mineral, leucite, a double silicate of aluminum and potassium or sodium. After crushing, grading, and an electromagnetic separation of gangue, the leucite meal is treated with sulfuric acid. The resulting solution contains aluminum and potassium in almost equimolar mixture, and the alum can be crystallized out and purified. In the United States alum is obtained by treatment of bauxite or clay with sulfuric acid, followed by addition of potassium sulfate to the solution. The alum crystallizes when the solution cools. Iron alum (ferric ammonium sulfate) is manufactured to a small extent, but the only other alum of commercial importance is the chromium potassium sulfate obtained as a by-product from the reduction of potassium dichromate in the manufacture of alizarin.

BIBLIOGRAPHY.—Lucien Geschwind, *Manufacture of Alum, and the Other Salts of Aluminum and Iron* (1901) ; Julian Eisenstein, *Rev. Mod. Phys.*, 24:74–78 (1952) ; M. C. Sneed and R. C. Brasted, *Comprehensive Inorganic Chemistry*, vol. vi, pp. 161–165 (1957). (R. A. PL.)

ALUMBRADOS (Sp. "enlightened"), the name given to followers of a pseudo-mystical movement current in Spain during the 16th and 17th centuries. Its adherents, who began to attract the attention of the Inquisition, especially in Andalusia, at the end of the 15th and beginning of the 16th centuries, claimed that the human soul, having attained a certain degree of perfection, was permitted a vision of the divine and could enter into direct communication with the Holy Spirit. From this state the soul could neither advance nor retrogress; consequently intercession of the saints, good works and observance of the exterior forms of religious life were unnecessary for those who had received the "light." The *Alumbrados* came especially from among the reformed Franciscans and the Jesuits (St. Ignatius Loyola was charged in 1527 with sympathizing with them); the extravagant claims made for their visions and revelations caused them to be relentlessly persecuted. The Inquisition issued edicts against them on three separate occasions (1568, 1574 and 1623), and it is principally from these that knowledge of the beliefs of the *Alumbrados* is derived. *See also* ILLUMINATI.

BIBLIOGRAPHY.—M. Menéndez y Pelayo, *Historia de los heterodoxos españoles*, vol. ii (1880); P. Pourrat, *La Spiritualité Chrétienne*, vol. iii (1927); H. Brémond, *Histoire littéraire du sentiment religieux en France*, vol. viii (1928).

ALUMINA, the oxide of aluminum, occurs as corundum which is a hard crystalline mineral. The dark variety of corundum contains magnetite and is known as emery (*q.v.*); clear transparent crystals, tinted by other metallic oxides, are gem stones such as ruby and sapphire. Alumina may be prepared by the ignition of aluminum hydroxide, ammonium alum, etc., and from the various natural hydrated oxides of aluminum which occur in the minerals bauxite and gibbsite. Alumina is used in the manufacture of metallic aluminum, in the manufacture of synthetic gems, as an abrasive, and in the manufacture of refractory materials. It is polymorphous, existing in a number of crystalline forms, is close to the diamond in hardness and has the chemical formula Al_2O_3. *See* ABRASIVE; ALUMINUM; CORUNDUM; CORUNDUM, ARTIFICIAL; GEM; *see* also Index references under "Alumina" in the Index volume.

ALUMINUM or ALUMINIUM is the most modern of the common metals, having been first isolated in 1825 and introduced to the public in 1855 at the Paris exposition. Its name is derived from the Latin *alumen*—a naturally occurring aluminous sulfate, probably a crude potash alum. Crude salts of this sort were used as astringents and mordants at least as early as the 5th century B.C. In the 13th century, men began to purify these crude salts into crystalline alum. The first mention of the production of alum from clay occurred in the 17th century, and in the 18th century its earthy base was differentiated from lime, shown to exist in clay, and given a name (*terre argilleuse*). It was suspected that it had a metallic base, but this was unproved until Sir Humphry Davy showed, in 1809, that an aluminum-iron alloy could be produced by the electrolysis of fused alumina in a hydrogen atmosphere, and that, on dissolving this alloy, aluminum oxide could be recovered from the solution. Davy suggested the name aluminum for this metal, a name which has been retained in North America but modified to aluminium in England and in most European countries. Its chemical symbol is Al, atomic weight 26.98 and atomic number 13.

Occurrence and Ores.—Because of its chemical activity, aluminum never occurs in the metallic form in nature, but its compounds are present to a greater or less extent in almost all rocks, vegetation and animals. In fact, aluminum is the third most abundant element on the earth's surface, being exceeded in amount only by oxygen and silicon. It is estimated that the outer ten miles of the earth's crust contain about 8% by weight of aluminum, or about 15% of aluminum oxide (alumina). The aluminum present in the original igneous rocks on the earth's surface (chiefly as feldspar and mica in the granites, basalts, etc.) is relatively insoluble in the weathering process by which soil has been formed out of these rocks. Therefore, it largely remains in this soil in the form of an aluminum silicate (clay), or when the weathering was more extensive much of the silica of the aluminum silicate was also dissolved by the percolating water, and the alumina and most of the oxides of iron and titanium present in the rock were deposited in the hydrated form as laterites or bauxites. (*See* BAUXITE; BOEHMITE; CLAY AND CLAY MINERALS.) These may contain up to 60% or even 70% of aluminum oxide, and are the principal commercial sources of aluminum and its compounds. In a few igneous rocks, deposits of crystalline alumina (corundum or emery) occur, and are mined for the production of natural abrasives. In some places aluminum sulfate, alum or alunite (*q.v.*) have been formed in weathered aluminous rock under the influence of sulfur-bearing gases or solutions. Cryolite (*q.v.*), the double fluoride of sodium and aluminum, oc-

curs in a great dike in Greenland, and is of commercial importance.

PRODUCTION OF THE METAL

Unlike the other common industrial metals (iron, copper, zinc, lead) pure aluminum is not produced by the direct smelting of its ores. In the first place, its affinity for oxygen is so much greater than that of the principal metallic impurities in the ore (iron, silicon, titanium) that their oxides are more readily reduced to the metallic state than is alumina. Therefore, if smelting conditions were chosen which would reduce the alumina, the other oxides would also be reduced and the resulting alloy would be too impure for use. In the second place, the temperature at which pure aluminum oxide is reduced by smelting with carbon is so very high that the greater part of the aluminum produced is lost, mostly as vapour with the gaseous carbon monoxide, unless there is considerable less-volatile metal such as iron or copper present to absorb it, or enough excess carbon to convert it into aluminum carbide. The production of alloys of aluminum with iron, copper and silicon has, however, been carried out commercially by such electrothermal smelting processes.

The earliest methods of producing metallic aluminum involved chemical reactions between purified aluminum compounds and metallic sodium or potassium. Hans Christian Oersted was the first to produce the metal (in 1825) by causing dilute potassium amalgam to react with an excess of anhydrous aluminum chloride. By distilling the mercury away from the resulting aluminum amalgam, a residue of slightly impure aluminum was obtained. In 1827, Friedrich Wöhler described the production of aluminum as a powder by the direct reaction of potassium upon anhydrous aluminum chloride. In 1845, he was able to make slightly larger amounts of the metal (some of the particles being as large as big pinheads) and determine some of its physical properties, such as specific gravity, ductility, colour, etc. In 1854, H. Sainte-Claire Deville improved Wöhler's method by using the cheaper sodium instead of potassium, forming a fusible double salt ($NaCl.AlCl_3$) flux, which allowed the aluminum globules to coalesce. This developed into a successful (but expensive) commercial process which was practised in France and several other countries until the advent of the cheaper electrolytic process.

Aluminum cannot be produced by the electrolysis of aqueous solutions of its salts, hydrogen and aluminum hydroxide being formed at the cathode instead of aluminum. In 1854, Robert Wilhelm von Bunsen showed that the metal could be produced by the electrolysis of molten anhydrous sodium aluminum chloride, but as batteries were the only available source of electricity, the development of this process was impractical.

The modern electrolytic method of producing aluminum was discovered almost simultaneously by Charles Martin Hall, in the United States, and Paul L. T. Héroult, in France, in 1886. The development of the dynamo had then reached the point where currents of several hundred amperes were commercially available, thus making electrolytic methods of production practical.

The essentials of the Hall and Héroult processes were identical and are the basis of the modern aluminum industry. Purified alumina (Al_2O_3) is dissolved in molten cryolite and electrolyzed with direct current. The mixture is contained in a carbon-lined steel box which acts as the cathode (negative pole) while carbon rods or blocks dipping into the molten bath form the anode or positive pole. Under the influence of the current, the oxygen of the Al_2O_3 is deposited upon the anode, which is thereby burned, while the molten aluminum is deposited on the carbon lining of the cell (cathode). Since molten aluminum is slightly heavier than molten cryolite at the operating temperature (about 950° C.) the metal accumulates in the bottom of the cell. Additional alumina is stirred into the electrolyte from time to time and the molten metal removed. Most commercial cells for the production of aluminum use currents of 50,000 to 100,000 amp. Since each cell requires only five to six volts, it is customary to connect a large number (often 100 or more) of such cells in series, and supply the necessary power from a group of rotary converters, mercury arc rectifiers or large direct current generators. In many plants, large Söderberg self-baking electrodes (one or two per cell) are used instead of the numerous smaller prebaked carbon anode blocks or rods which are employed in the older plants.

The steel box for 50,000-amp. cells may be 20 ft. long, 6 ft. wide and about 3 ft. deep, made of steel about 0.5 in. thick. Such cells are arranged in a line or several lines in suitable buildings (often 700 ft. or more in length) supplied with equipment to remove and collect the fumes and minimize the effect of the radiated heat. The gross power consumption may be 8–10 kw.hr. and the gross carbon consumption 0.6–0.8 lb. per pound of metal produced. Aluminum fluoride is added to the molten electrolyte from time to time to neutralize the soda in the alumina (derived from the Bayer process), and some cryolite is added to make up for the absorption by the cell lining, losses caused by spillage, etc. The total of such additions is usually less than 0.1 lb. per pound of metal produced, while the alumina required is somewhat more than 1.9 lb. per pound of metal.

An upward trend in world production of aluminum, which began in 1947, continued into the second half of the 20th century, with world capacity reaching about 5,000,000 short tons by 1960. The United States and Canada produce more than half the world total.

ALLOYS AND USES

In general, small to moderate amounts of aluminum may be added to certain other metals to improve their properties for special uses (*e.g.*, in the case of aluminum bronzes and most magnesium base alloys), or small to moderate amounts of other metals and silicon can be added to aluminum to form the so-called aluminum-base alloys, which because of their improved castability and higher strength, are better adapted than pure aluminum for most industrial applications.

Strictly speaking, ordinary commercial aluminum (99.0%–99.6% pure) should be considered as an alloy of pure aluminum with small amounts of iron and silicon. These definitely change the properties of the pure metal, markedly increasing its strength and decreasing its resistance to corrosion. For practical reasons, iron is generally considered as an impurity to be controlled, while silicon may be either an impurity or a major alloying ingredient. The other major alloying ingredients are copper, magnesium, manganese, zinc and nickel. Moderate amounts of tin, cadmium, lead, bismuth and cobalt may be used in special alloys; small amounts of chromium and titanium (usually less than 0.3%) and still smaller amounts of vanadium, zirconium, boron, beryllium and sodium are also sometimes used for special purposes, such as grain refinement (*see* ALLOYS).

Casting Alloys.—Pure aluminum, like most pure metals, can only be made into commercial castings with considerable difficulty. A pure molten metal freezes quite sharply at a definite temperature, and consequently it is difficult to arrange "risers" and other devices to feed molten metal into the casting during freezing, and make up for the solidification shrinkage. The alloys used for making castings, on the other hand, freeze through a considerable range of temperature, passing through a mushy stage in which the crystals of more or less pure aluminum are mixed with the still-liquid concentrated alloy. This permits the metal from the gates and risers to flow into the casting until the solidification (and therefore the shrinkage) is nearly complete, and minimizes the formation of shrinkage cavities, which are objectionable in the finished castings. One of the advantages of the presence of a considerable percentage (5%–20%) of silicon in aluminum-base casting alloys is that silicon actually expands on freezing or crystallizing out of molten aluminum, and consequently tends to counteract the solidification shrinkage of the aluminum itself.

In the early days of the industry, up to about the outbreak of World War I, the alloys used in the United States were of the aluminum-copper type, while those used in England and in Europe were largely of the aluminum-zinc type, but often contained some copper. Shortly after the war, the aluminum-silicon alloys were introduced and became quite popular. The 12% silicon alloy (containing a small amount of sodium to "modify" the silicon)

largely displaced the aluminum-zinc alloy in England and Europe, while a 5% silicon alloy became popular in the United States for architectural and other castings, where good casting properties and high resistance to corrosion were important and high strength was not required. Alloys containing about 10% copper were used quite largely throughout the world after World War I, to make pistons for internal combustion engines, being generally cast for this purpose in iron molds (so-called permanent molds). Most of the aluminum alloy castings made in the United States up to the time of World War II continued to be made of alloys containing 7%–10% copper, although heat treated alloys containing about 4.5% copper or 10% magnesium were extensively employed where higher strength and ductility were required.

The heat treatment of castings requires a relatively long heating (6–24 hr.) at temperatures of 700°–1,000° F.—the exact temperature and time depending on the alloy composition and type of casting (sand or permanent mold). This is followed by "quenching" the casting in hot or cold water or oil, with subsequent aging at either room temperature or a temperature somewhat above the boiling point of water. The purpose of the "solution heat treatment" at 700°–1,000° F. is to put into "solid solution" as much as possible of the alloying elements, particularly copper, magnesium and zinc.

The reason for the long time of heat treatment is inherent in the structure of the castings. When a casting is made from an aluminum-base alloy containing copper, for example, the crystals which form first during the freezing process are nearly pure aluminum. Most of the copper remains in the liquid phase, and as the crystals grow the concentration of the copper in the liquid increases, although small amounts of it are deposited in the outer layers of the crystal. Since increasing the proportion of copper in aluminum lowers its freezing point, this process continues as the casting cools, until the temperature is reached at which the eutectic (lowest melting mixture) of aluminum and copper (containing 33% copper) freezes. Meantime, however, the crystals have grown until they almost touch one another, so that when the eutectic freezes it fills the small intergranular spaces and acts as a cement between the crystals. Aluminum can hold approximately 4.3% of copper in solid solution at the heat treating temperature (about 950° F.) but only a small fraction of this is actually in solid solution "as cast"; the rest being in the intergranular eutectic. In order to obtain a nearly saturated solid solution in the aluminum, it is necessary to hold the casting at high temperatures long enough for the copper to diffuse from the grain boundaries and distribute itself throughout the grains or crystals. Naturally, the larger the grains the longer this takes. Consequently, fine-grained castings (such as those cast in permanent molds) require a shorter heat treating time than coarse-grained castings, and wrought material (where the eutectic has been broken up and mechanically dispersed) a much shorter time. (*See* also HEAT TREATMENT.)

If the article is now suddenly cooled or quenched to room temperature, we have a supersaturated solid solution, since the solid solubility of copper in aluminum at room temperature is about 0.25%. Unless some accelerating metal, such as magnesium, is present, this solid supersaturated solution only changes and precipitates slowly through a long period of storage at room temperature. However, if the temperature is raised to the boiling point of water or higher, the mobility of the atoms of copper in the alloy is sufficiently increased so they are able to get together in a few hours and apparently precipitate in the form of submicroscopic particles of the compound $CuAl_2$. With longer heating and at higher temperatures, these particles may grow large enough to become visible under the microscope upon a polished and properly etched surface of the alloy. They are found to be arranged in quite definite patterns along certain planes in the individual crystals. Apparently the effect of these minute particles of hard constituent is to "key" these slip planes, just as a stack of sheets of paper would be keyed against a sidewise thrust by particles of fine sand between each sheet and the next. The precipitation process thus increases the tensile strength and yield strength of the alloy but decreases its ductility. In the presence of 0.5% magnesium, this precipitation occurs spontaneously in a few days at room temperature. Such precipitation at room temperature is spoken of as "natural aging," while precipitation induced by heating at elevated temperatures is spoken of as "artificial aging."

In the binary aluminum-magnesium alloys the solid solubility of magnesium at the heat treating temperature and at lower temperatures is considerably greater than that of copper, but the phenomena of heat treating, quenching and aging are similar. The solubility of silicon varies little with temperature, so that a solution heat treatment of a binary aluminum-silicon alloy has little effect on its properties. However, if magnesium is present, a magnesium silicide (Mg_2Si) is formed which has an appreciable solid solubility at heat treating temperature, and precipitates by natural aging after quenching. A heat treatable casting alloy of this type may contain about 5% silicon, 0.5% magnesium and 1–1.5% copper. Its tensile properties are lower than those of the heat treated copper or magnesium alloys, but it has much better casting properties, and is used for difficult castings.

The physical properties of castings vary greatly, depending not only upon the composition but also on the casting conditions. Thin sections generally show a somewhat higher tensile strength in pounds per square inch than do thick sections. Heat treated alloys generally show higher strength and ductility than those not heat treated. Typical strengths for ordinary sand cast alloys are in the range 19,000–30,000 lbs. per square inch (p.s.i.), while heat treated alloys may show 30,000–45,000 p.s.i. As a general rule, an alloy cast in permanent (metal) molds will show tensile strengths 5,000–10,000 p.s.i. higher than when sand cast.

Wrought Alloys.—Contrary to the situation in the casting field, the pure metal is the easiest form of aluminum to use in producing wrought articles. This is because of its softness and high ductility, which permit it to be rolled, forged, drawn, extruded, etc., with a maximum of ease and a minimum of scrap. Alloying elements cause the pure metal to become stronger, harder and less ductile, although these increases are not necessarily directly proportional to the amount of the added alloying ingredients. The higher strength naturally imposes a greater burden upon the fabricating machinery, and the lower ductility increases the tendency of the metal to crack or tear when worked severely.

The first step in the production of wrought articles is the casting of the ingot which is to be worked. Because of the tendency of pure aluminum to crystallize out first and leave the liquid portion enriched in the alloying ingredients (as explained above) the tendency of some of the alloying metals to segregate into certain areas during the freezing of the ingot is increasingly troublesome as the amounts of alloying ingredients increase. Rather elaborate special mechanical arrangements are therefore required to produce satisfactory ingots of such alloys. The basic principle of such ingot production is to chill the metal vigorously and cause it to freeze rapidly, preferably from the bottom up, so that the primary grains may be as small as possible and the distribution of the eutectic (which solidifies last) may be as uniform as possible throughout the whole ingot.

As indicated, commercial aluminum may be considered to be an alloy of pure aluminum with small amounts of iron plus silicon and traces of other elements, particularly copper and manganese. As the simplest of the aluminum alloys, it stands next to pure aluminum in ease of working. Ordinary commercial "pure aluminum" sheet contains 99.0%–99.4% aluminum. Foil is generally made of somewhat higher purity material, ranging up to 99.99% for foil used in electrolytic condensers. Ordinary pure aluminum tubing has about the same composition as sheet aluminum, but the so-called "collapsible tubes," made as containers for tooth paste, shaving cream, etc., are usually made of 99.5%–99.8% aluminum to reduce their stiffness. Wire for electrical conductors is usually 99.5%–99.7% aluminum. With this purity of metal, the conductivity is 60%–62% of the international annealed copper standard.

In the manufacture of wrought aluminum articles, maximum ductility and minimum strength are produced by annealing the cold worked article, usually by heating for some time at a temperature of about 650° F.

The hardening and strengthening effect of even small amounts of alloying ingredients is clearly seen on comparing the typical properties of commercial annealed aluminum sheet with those of similar sheet made of 99.99% aluminum. The typical tensile strength of about 7,000 p.s.i. for 99.99% metal increases to 13,000 p.s.i. for commercial aluminum sheet, while the yield strength increases from 1,800 p.s.i. to 5,000 p.s.i. (The yield strength of aluminum is defined as the load in p.s.i. which produces a permanent elongation or "set" of 0.2% in 2 in.). At the same time the elongation in 2 in. is reduced from about 50% to 35%. Cold working (rolling, forging, drawing through dies, etc., at ordinary temperatures) hardens the metal, increasing both tensile and yield strength. This effect increases with the amount of cold work. The magnitude of the changes involved is seen from the fact that a typical tensile strength for hard rolled commercial aluminum sheet would be 24,000 p.s.i. with a corresponding yield strength of 21,000 p.s.i. and an elongation of only 5% in 2 in. Intermediate amounts of cold working produce intermediate tempers designated as quarter-, half-, and three-quarters hard. In general, annealed or quarter-hard sheet is chosen as the starting point for such operations as the production of cooking utensils by drawing or spinning, and the production of other drawn articles. Aluminum electrical conductors, on the other hand, are practically always delivered in the full-hard condition, because high strength is desired.

Next to commercial aluminum, the simplest wrought aluminum alloy is the one made by adding about 1.25% of manganese to commercially pure aluminum. This alloy has been widely employed under various designations, both in Europe and in the United States, for uses such as the manufacture of cooking utensils, where a somewhat higher strength than that of commercial aluminum is desired. It is slightly more difficult to work (draw, spin, etc.) than commercial aluminum, as would be expected from its higher strength.

Another group of relatively simple aluminum-base alloys includes those in which magnesium (2%–9%) is added to commercial aluminum, with or without small amounts of chromium, manganese or zinc. The most common type contains about 2.5%–3.5% magnesium and either about 0.5% manganese or 0.2% chromium. It has a considerably higher strength in the annealed and cold worked conditions than the manganese alloy, together with excellent resistance to sea water corrosion. An alloy containing 2.5% magnesium and 0.25% chromium would have typical tensile and yield strengths in the annealed condition of 29,000 and 12,000 p.s.i., and in the hard rolled condition of 41,000 and 36,000 p.s.i., with elongations of 25% and 7% respectively. With 5.2% magnesium and 0.1% each of manganese and chromium, these figures become 42,000 and 20,000 p.s.i., respectively, in the annealed condition, and 58,000 and 48,000 p.s.i. in the hard worked condition. Somewhat higher physical properties may be obtained by further increasing the magnesium and manganese contents, at the risk of producing alloys which may be subject to a marked acceleration of their rate of corrosion under the influence of stresses, particularly in the hard worked condition.

The heat treated strong alloys of aluminum form an important and characteristic group. Their importance may be seen from the fact that after 1938 substantially all the structural parts of military and larger civilian airplanes were made of them. The earliest and most important group of these is popularly known as duralumin (q.v.) and contains 4%–5% copper, 0.6%–1.2% magnesium and 0.6%–1.2% manganese. Their heat treatment has been discussed above, under casting alloys.

The important copper-free heat treatable alloys containing magnesium silicide (Mg_2Si) with a slight excess of silicon were first developed and commercially exploited in the United States in the early 1920s. Their somewhat inferior strength, compared with the duralumin type alloy, was offset by greater workability, both hot and cold, and consequently lower fabricating cost. The use of these alloys gradually spread to other lands, where they were given distinctive local designations.

Great difficulty was found in the early days in producing satisfactory forgings of the duralumin type alloys, because of their high strength and tendency to crack under the hammer. Along with the magnesium silicide type alloys, therefore, there was developed and commercialized in the United States a special forging alloy which differed from duralumin in omitting the magnesium. This facilitated fabrication, and the resulting forgings, after solution heat treatment and quenching, could be artificially aged to substantially the properties of duralumin. This made it practical to produce commercially aluminum propellers for the multitude of aircraft which were needed in World War II, and most of the metal propellers used before and during this war were forged out of this alloy.

After the obstacles to the fabrication of the standard duralumin had been overcome, intensive research and development work in both Germany and the United States brought forth a stronger variety of this alloy in which the copper and magnesium were both increased appreciably, and yet the composition was so adjusted that it was still possible to fabricate it commercially into sheet and other forms. This variety (first commercialized in the United States and known throughout the English-speaking world as 24S or 2024) had, roughly, 10% higher tensile and yield strengths than its predecessor.

A further increase in physical properties was accomplished near the end of World War II, by the practical introduction of aluminum base alloys in which the magnesium-zinc compound $MgZn_2$ was the principal hardening agent. These alloys had been originally developed and patented in Germany in the early 1920s, but their practical use had been prevented because of their susceptibility to stress corrosion. After many years of work, the modifying effects of copper and small amounts of chromium, vanadium and other elements on this sensitiveness to stress corrosion were worked out and commercially stable alloys developed. The alloy of this type commercialized in the United States in 1944 contained about 5.75% zinc, 2.5% magnesium, 1.6% copper and a little chromium. Heat treated extrusions of this alloy showed a typical strength of 88,000 p.s.i. and a yield strength of 80,000 p.s.i., with an elongation of 10% in 2 in. It was also used in what is known as the "alclad" sheet form, where its tensile properties were somewhat reduced by the presence of a thin layer of a weaker alloy on each surface of the sheet. Even then, in the heat treated state the tensile strength was typically 76,000 p.s.i. and yield strength 66,000 p.s.i., with 11% elongation.

The problem of protecting alloys of the duralumin type from corrosion is not serious when only relatively thick pieces are involved, but when the aircraft industry began to require large quantities of very thin sheet (0.01–0.02 in. thick) it became apparent that even slight superficial corrosion might be serious and must be prevented. The advantage of protecting the surfaces of such sheet with a thin integral coating of pure aluminum (which not only mechanically protected the surface from corrosion, but also electrolytically protected the cut edges, just as zinc does in the case of galvanized iron) was first demonstrated and a practical method for producing such sheet worked out in 1926, in the United States. The production and use of such alclad sheet spread throughout the aluminum-producing countries of the world during the next ten years, and the use of such sheet for wing covering and other purposes on airplanes became substantially standard for civilian planes and most military planes by the beginning of World War II. Pure aluminum is satisfactory as a cladding layer for alloys of the duralumin type, but in some countries (and for other types of alloys) alloys containing small amounts of magnesium silicide or zinc, with or without manganese, are preferred.

Standard specifications for the various types of wrought and cast aluminum alloys have been developed and published by official and semiofficial bodies in the United States, England, Germany, France and Italy, and should be referred to in connection with the literature of the producers for specific information as to alloys available in the different countries.

Other Uses.—High thermal and electrical conductivity, together with light weight and excellent resistance to corrosion, were the basis of most of the early tonnage uses of aluminum, as in the field of cooking utensils and electrical conductors. In cooking utensils, high thermal conductivity of the metal is especially important in conducting the heat laterally and spreading it uniformly over the bottom of the utensil which is in contact with the flame or other source of heat, thus avoiding local hot spots which might cause the food to burn.

Although considerably weaker than hard-drawn copper conductors, pure aluminum wire was made to compete economically for transmitting electric power at high voltages over long distances by stranding it about a strong galvanized steel wire core to make "aluminum cable steel reinforced." The use of aluminum bar, cable and wire for secondary electrical distribution systems employing moderate voltages, and for motor, generator and transformer windings, became important about 1950.

With the development of stronger and better cast and wrought alloys in the period between World War I and World War II, aluminum became increasingly important as a structural material, particularly in the transportation industry. The original and most important early use of the wrought alloys of the duralumin type was in the framework of the Zeppelin airships which were used by the Germans in World War I. Aluminum castings were used in airplane engines in that war, and the Germans made a beginning in the use of duralumin type alloys in the structural parts of the planes themselves. In the period between World War I and World War II, wood (which had been the principal structural material for planes prior to that time) was almost completely replaced by metal (chiefly strong aluminum alloys of the duralumin type) in the form of sheet, extrusions and tubing. At the same time increased experience and the reduction in cost of producing and fabricating such alloys resulted in their rapid introduction in many other industrial fields where strength was required but light weight was advantageous. Buses and trucks used for long distance hauling were increasingly provided with aluminum bodies, crankcases and other parts. Aluminum tank trucks and trailers for hauling gasoline and milk were found to be economically advantageous, and railway tank cars were constructed of aluminum for the shipment of hydrogen peroxide, high strength (95 + %) nitric acid, organic solvents and other special materials. Deluxe high speed trains were built of aluminum alloys, and considerable aluminum was used in the construction of passenger automobiles.

The light weight, attractive appearance and resistance to atmospheric influences displayed by aluminum accounted for its introduction and popularity in the architectural industry, beginning about 1926. Aluminum spandrels, windows, doors, ornamental railings and grillwork, roofing, store fronts and miscellaneous hardware became increasingly popular both before and after World War II. Exterior walls of aluminum sheet, backed with light concrete, fashioned in attractive patterns, either anodically oxidized (and often coloured) or enameled, became popular for large buildings about 1954. By 1960 the building and construction industry had become the largest consumer of aluminum.

Because of its resistance to many rather corrosive chemicals, and the colourless and nontoxic character of its corrosion products, aluminum has been extensively used in the chemical and allied industries for tanks, piping, reaction vessels and miscellaneous equipment. Its use is particularly important in the synthetic acetic and nitric acid industries and in the manufacture of formaldehyde, hydrogen peroxide and various organic chemicals. For similar reasons, it has been widely used in the brewing industry for brewing kettles, storage tanks, fermenters and other equipment, and for beer barrels. The use of light aluminum drums was an important and successful application during World War II for the shipment of aviation gasoline by air from India to bases in China.

In this war, the use of aluminum for military and naval purposes other than aviation was limited as strictly as possible because the tremendous demands of the aircraft industry taxed the producing and fabricating capacity. It was, however, extensively used for mess kits, canteens and other articles carried by the men, and for various parts of the superstructure and furniture of naval vessels. Similar uses in merchant vessels were extensive after the war.

An aluminum powder, used as a pigment for paint and ink, is produced by a stamping or grinding operation. It has the form of minute thin flakes, coated with a little stearic acid which makes the flakes "leaf" or come to the surface of the paint coat. This phenomenon and the complete opacity of the metal flakes protect the dried and hardened vehicle in the paint layer from deterioration caused by sunlight, air and rain, giving the paint a long life, even in the tropics, and a good reflecting power for radiant heat from the sun. A similar powder, compacted into ingots and fabricated by extrusion or rolling, gives a product (called SAP or APMP) which retains its strength exceptionally well, for aluminum, at elevated temperatures. Its commercial use began about 1955.

Because of its higher strength and lower cost, aluminum foil largely replaced tin foil as a wrapping material for chocolate bars and other candies, cheese and other foodstuffs. Laminated with thermoplastic resins, it became widely used during World War II in the manufacture of small "heat sealed" packages for foodstuffs, medicines, etc. Large tonnages of aluminum foil are also used for electrical condensers in radio and radar equipment, and small strips of foil were scattered from aeroplanes to confuse enemy radar. Aluminum foil and thin aluminum sheet have been used to a large extent in the manufacture of closures for milk bottles and other bottles containing foods and drinks.

Aluminum castings have been used for a great variety of applications, the largest being probably in connection with internal combustion engines (pistons, crankcases, cylinder heads, etc.) and domestic appliances such as washing machines and vacuum cleaners. They are made by techniques similar to those employed with other nonferrous metals.

Extrusions are made by forcing the solid metal (hot or cold) through a suitable die under heavy pressure. Collapsible tubes for toothpaste and the like are made by "impact extrusion" in which a blank of cold metal placed in a suitable die is struck a sudden blow by a plunger in a press. The diameter of the plunger is just a little less than the diameter of the hole in the die, so that the metal is forced back up as a thin tube between the plunger and the die, while a part of the metal remains in the die to form the head of the tube. Most extrusions are, however, made by using hot ingots (700°–950° F.) 6–18 in. in diameter and of suitable length, placed in a hydraulic "extrusion press." They are then subjected to high pressures and forced through dies, from which they emerge in the desired form as rods, structural shapes, heavy walled tube "blooms," special moldings for window frames and other construction, etc. These extrusions may be of pure aluminum or of any of the aluminum alloys. Most of the extrusions used in the aircraft industry are made of high strength aluminum alloys and heat treated. Tube "blooms" are reduced to tubing by cold drawing.

Forgings are made with air or steam hammers or suitable forging presses, from "forging stock," which is usually a rod or bar of high strength aluminum alloy. Tremendous numbers of such forgings have been used in aircraft, several hundred being used on each large plane. The manufacturing technique resembles that employed in forging steel articles of similar size.

Joining Aluminum.—In building aluminum structures such as buses, cars, aircraft and the like, and in many simpler articles, it is necessary to join together various pieces of aluminum, with or without pieces of other metal. As in steel structures, riveting may be employed. Untold millions of small, strong aluminum alloy rivets were used in the construction of aircraft in World War II. During that war, however, electric spot welding and seam welding made marked progress and were increasingly used, particularly with alclad sheet. Torch welding, with a suitable welding flux, has been extensively used since before World War I for joining articles of pure aluminum or nonheat treated alloys, and was supplemented just before World War II by arc welding, with either metallic or carbon electrodes. Later, argon or helium arc welding became common practice. Aluminum may

also be soldered, but the joint should usually be protected against moisture.

While many improvements have been made in solders, the demand for this type of joint has largely been met by the brazing process, in which the metal used for uniting the two aluminum surfaces is an aluminum base alloy (generally containing silicon) melting at a convenient interval below the melting point of the articles to be joined. By the use of a suitable flux, articles may thus be joined by the use of a torch or by passing them through a furnace at a controlled temperature. More intricate assemblies (such as an intercooler for an airplane) may be brazed by immersing the article for a few minutes in a bath of molten flux maintained at the proper temperature. Brazing is often facilitated by using sheet metal having a thin layer of brazing alloy on one or both sides, similar to the protective layer in the alclad strong alloy sheet. Brazing became of commercial importance at about the beginning of World War II. Brazed joints are in general as resistant to corrosion as the rest of the article. Inserts of copper, brass or iron may be united with aluminum by the brazing process.

PROPERTIES

Physical.—Aluminum is a silvery ductile metal which is one of the lightest of those used structurally, being only about one-third as heavy as an equal volume of iron, brass or copper. The table shows many of its physical properties. It crystallizes in the cubic system (face centred cubic lattice) and when it is deformed by working (rolling, forging, drawing, etc.) slip within the crystals occurs predominantly on the octahedral planes. Upon melting, the solid metal expands about 7% in volume, the solidification shrinkage being 6.6% of the liquid volume.

Physical Properties of Aluminum

Density (g./c.c.) at 20° C. (68° F.)	2.70
Melting point (° C.)	660.2
Melting point (° F.)	1,220.4
Boiling point (° C.)	2,477±50
Boiling point (° F.)	4,491±90
Specific heat at 100° C., cal./g.	0.2241
Latent heat of fusion cal./g.	96.4
Heat of combustion ($2Al+3O = Al_2O_3$) kg. cal.	400.0
Heat of vaporization at b.p., B.Th.U. per pound	4,670
Thermal expansivity 20–100° C., per degree	23.86×10^{-6}
Thermal expansivity 20–200° C., per degree	24.58×10^{-6}
Thermal expansivity 20–300° C., per degree	25.45×10^{-6}
Thermal expansivity 20–400° C., per degree	26.49×10^{-6}
Thermal expansivity 20–500° C., per degree	27.68×10^{-6}
Thermal expansivity 20–600° C., per degree	28.6×10^{-6}
Electrical resistivity (vol.) at 20° C., microhm-cm.	2.6548
Electrical conductivity (vol.) at 20° C., percent of international annealed copper standard	64.94
Temperature coefficient of resistance at 20° C.	0.00429
Thermal conductivity—cal./sec./sq.cm./cm./° C.	0.5
Thermal emissivity at 100° F., percent	3
Reflectivity for light, tungsten filament, percent	90
Reflectivity for radiation at 2,500 Å.U.	85
Reflectivity for radiation at 10,000 Å.U.	95
Magnetic susceptibility, c.g.s. units.	0.61×10^{-6}
Atomic radius, Å.U.	1.431
Ionization potential, volts.	5.98,18.8,28.5
Oxidation-reduction potential (calc.), volts	1.67
Electron structure	$1s^2, 2s^2, 2p^6, 3s^2, 3p^1$
Radioactive isotopes (mass numbers)	24, 25, 26, 26*, 28, 29

The strength of aluminum depends upon its purity and the thermal and mechanical treatment to which it has been subjected. Pure aluminum (99.996%) is quite soft and weak in the cast or annealed condition, with a tensile strength of only about 7,000 p.s.i. By alloying and proper thermal and mechanical treatment, however, tensile strengths as high as 100,000 p.s.i. may be obtained. Silicon and most of the common metals (copper, iron, zinc, tin, manganese, magnesium) readily dissolve in molten aluminum, but sodium and potassium are almost completely insoluble, and the solubility of titanium, vanadium, boron and chromium is low. Hydrogen is about the only gas which is appreciably soluble in molten aluminum: its solubility increases with temperature but becomes nearly zero when the metal freezes.

Chemical.—Ordinarily aluminum is trivalent, although there is evidence that it may be monovalent and possibly bivalent at elevated temperatures under some conditions. Its oxide, Al_2O_3, is amphoteric; i.e., it may act as a base to form salts with acids, or as a weak acid to form salts with strong alkalies. Its heat of formation is high (400,000 cal. per gram molecule) and aluminum is therefore able to reduce most metallic oxides, in the thermit process (see THERMITE). A freshly cut surface of metallic aluminum is immediately oxidized and covered with a thin, transparent coating of Al_2O_3, about 0.00000025 in. thick, which protects it from further oxidation and reaction, except with substances which can dissolve the oxide. The surface of molten aluminum is also covered with a similar oxide coating which protects it from burning. However, finely divided metallic aluminum is rather easily inflammable and, when mixed with air and ignited, will produce a violent explosion. Protective coatings of aluminum oxide may be produced by anodic oxidation of aluminum in certain electrolytes such as dilute sulfuric or chromic acids. These coatings are adsorbent and may be impregnated with dyes or mineral pigments to produce pleasing finishes, or with salts of chromic acid to improve their protection against corrosion. Thinner, impervious coatings of Al_2O_3, produced anodically in boric or phosphoric acid or their salts, are important in aluminum condensers and electrolytic rectifiers.

Aluminum is slowly attacked by most dilute acids, especially the mineral acids. Concentrated hydrochloric acid dissolves it rapidly, $2Al + 6HCl = 2AlCl_3 + 3H_2$. On the other hand, concentrated nitric acid (95%–100%) has so little effect on it that aluminum drums and tank cars are used for shipping this chemical. Strictly anhydrous organic acids often attack aluminum vigorously, but the presence of a few tenths of a percent of water will greatly retard this reaction. The rate of attack by dilute acids is largely reduced as the purity of the aluminum is increased, and is slow for metal with a purity more than 99.95%. Alkalies, on the other hand, attack it rather vigorously irrespective of its purity; sodium and potassium hydroxide dissolve it rapidly with the formation of the corresponding aluminates, $2Al + 2OH^- + 2H_2O = 2AlO_2^- + 3H_2$. Sodium carbonate solution attacks and corrodes it more slowly, and this reaction may be largely prevented by the addition of a suitable amount of sodium silicate. Lime also corrodes it. Distilled water at ordinary temperatures has almost no action on aluminum, but water containing dissolved salts (especially common salt) allowed to stand for a long time in contact with commercial aluminum, may gradually attack and corrode it to an extent depending upon both the kind and amount of salts present and upon the kind and amount of alloying elements or metallic impurities present in the aluminum. High purity aluminum and certain aluminum-magnesium alloys are, however, resistant to corrosion, even by sea water, for many years.

Because of its great affinity for oxygen, finely divided aluminum, if ignited, will burn in carbon monoxide or carbon dioxide with the formation of a mixture of aluminum oxide and carbide; it will also burn in nitrogen to form the nitride (AlN). The carbide (Al_4C_3) is substantially insoluble in molten aluminum, so that only a superficial film of it is formed when the molten metal stands in contact with carbon. It is easily formed by the electrothermal reduction of the oxide in the presence of an excess of carbon at temperatures above about 1,800° C. Aluminum combines vigorously with the halogens at slightly elevated temperatures but is inert to sulfur at temperatures up to red heat. Phosphorus does not react with aluminum at ordinary temperatures, and aluminum phosphide is substantially insoluble in molten or solid aluminum.

Most of the metals which are soluble in molten aluminum form compounds with it, which crystallize out when the metal freezes, and can be identified under the microscope on a polished surface, particularly after etching. Silicon alone forms no binary compound with aluminum, and crystallizes out as such upon cooling the binary aluminum-silicon alloy. It does, however, form ternary compounds with aluminum and iron or manganese, when they are present. The study and identification of these constituents and their behaviour in the aluminum alloys is an important part of the metallography of aluminum. In addition to the amount of alloying metal which combines with the aluminum to form the precipitated compounds, a certain amount remains in "solid solution" in the solid aluminum. The solid solubility of some of these

metals (copper, zinc, magnesium) may be considerable at elevated temperatures, but is markedly lower at room temperature.

Physiological.—Metallic aluminum and its oxide and hydroxide are completely nontoxic, and generally inert as far as living organisms are concerned. Thus, in contrast to copper and iron, the metal has no bactericidal effect. Animal experiments have shown that small amounts of aluminum dust inhaled with silica dust into the lungs prevent the development of the typical lesions of silicosis (q.v.) by coating the silica particles with a thin layer of aluminum hydroxide, which apparently makes them inert. Inhalation of small amounts of aluminum dust has also been reported to have a beneficial effect in allaying some of the symptoms of human silicosis. Colloidal aluminum hydroxide, administered as a nasal drip or by mouth, has been found to exert a marked healing effect in cases of stomach ulcer. Water soluble aluminum salts (such as the chloride and sulfate) are used in medicine and in cosmetics as astringents.

CHEMICAL COMPOUNDS

Aluminum Oxide and its Hydrates.—Aluminum oxide exists in several different crystallographic forms. The one which occurs in nature (corundum, q.v.) is designated as the alpha form, and is characterized by a high specific gravity (4.0), a high melting point (about 2,015° C. or 3,660° F.) and great insolubility. Its high hardness (hard enough to scratch glass) makes it one of the most useful of natural or artificial abrasives (q.v.). Commercially pure aluminum oxide is made by calcining the purified hydrate at temperatures about 2,000° F. and is chiefly used as a raw material for the production of the metal. Its principal impurities are soda (0.1%–0.6%), iron oxide and silica (usually less than 0.03% each). It is an important raw material for the manufacture of certain articles such as insulators and spark plugs, "Alundum" laboratory ware (tubes, crucibles, etc.) and pure fused alumina for certain types of abrasive wheels. Rubies and sapphires are crystalline, nearly pure varieties of alpha alumina, the colours being the result of small amounts of impurities. Synthetic rubies and sapphires are made on a commercial scale by fusing a mixture of high purity Al_2O_3 with traces of the necessary colouring agents, in an oxyhydrogen blowpipe flame (see GEM: *Synthetic Gems*). Most of the material thus produced is cut up into jewels for watches and other precision instruments.

When the alumina hydrates are heated to gradually increasing temperatures up to about 1,000° F., they are decomposed and lose most of their water. The aluminum oxide formed goes through a series of physical changes as the temperature increases, and some of the products are interesting and commercially important. At the lower temperatures, water is driven out without appreciable shinkage of the granules; so that the result is a porous structure. The area exposed in the pores when the water has been driven out can be measured by physicochemical means, and may be as high as several hundred square metres per gram. This surface is extremely active and has the power of adsorbing water vapour and some other gaseous molecules upon it. The product (commercially known as activated alumina) is important in drying gases and some liquids, and as a catalyst carrier in certain reactions such as the production of toluene from the vapours of other hydrocarbons at high temperatures. The affinity of the alumina surface for water vapour is such that air may be dried by it as completely as with phosphorus pentoxide.

The hydrous forms of alumina (often called alumina hydrates) may contain either one (monohydrate) or three (trihydrate) molecules of water per molecule of Al_2O_3. Each is known in two distinct modifications (alpha and beta). In both cases the alpha variety is the more common one. The alpha trihydrate (gibbsite or hydrargillite) is the principal constituent of the bauxites found in North and South America, and in the East Indies. The alpha monohydrate (boehmite) is the principal constituent of European bauxites. The beta monohydrate occurs in nature as the mineral diaspore.

Alpha trihydrate is the variety sold commercially as hydrated alumina. It is the raw material out of which commercial alumina is prepared by calcination, and is produced by the Bayer process.

The first step in this process involves dissolving the alumina hydrate out of bauxite or laterite in superheated caustic soda (sodium hydroxide) solution under pressures of 60–200 p.s.i. The solution is then filtered from the residue (red mud) containing the impurities. The filtered solution (sodium aluminate) is cooled to a little above room temperature and becomes supersaturated with respect to alumina hydrate. Upon now agitating this solution with "seed" of the finely divided crystalline trihydrate, the excess (about two-thirds of the total) of the alumina crystallizes out. The solution, after some evaporation, is used to extract more alumina from a new charge of bauxite. The precipitated hydrate is washed and dried, or else calcined if the oxide is to be the finished product. This trihydrate is a fine crystalline powder (specific gravity about 2.4), soluble only to the extent of less than one part per million in water but readily soluble in dilute mineral acids, sodium hydroxide or potassium hydroxide. Aside from the production of the various forms of alumina, its principal use is for the production of pure aluminum sulfate and alums (q.v.).

Beta alumina trihydrate may be made by neutralizing sodium aluminate solution with carbon dioxide under certain carefully controlled conditions. It is unstable, rather readily converted to the alpha monohydrate by heating in water.

The alpha monohydrate may be produced from the trihydrate by heating it cautiously in air or under pressure with water containing some sodium hydroxide. It is less easily dissolved in dilute acid and alkalies than the trihydrate; consequently monohydrate bauxites are not as suitable for the manufacture of alum, and require a higher temperature and a higher sodium hydroxide concentration than the trihydrate bauxites in the Bayer process.

Salts.—Various sulfates and double sulfates are the commonest of the aluminum salts. Alums (q.v.) are soluble double sulfates of aluminum with potassium, sodium or ammonium. Alunite (q.v.) is an insoluble basic alum. The normal aluminum sulfates are quite soluble in water, and are discussed under sulfuric acid (q.v.).

Aluminum chloride and aluminum nitrate are also soluble, and are discussed under the corresponding acids.

See also Index references under "Aluminum" in the Index volume.

BIBLIOGRAPHY.—For detailed information on alloy compositions, forms, uses, fabrication methods, etc., reference should be made to trade literature and pamphlets issued by all of the important producers and fabricators of this metal. General references: J. W. Mellor, *Comprehensive Treatise on Inorganic and Theoretical Chemistry,* vol. 5 (1924) on the chemistry of aluminum compounds; J. D. Edwards, F. C. Frary and Z. Jeffries, *The Aluminum Industry,* a general survey, 2 vols. (1930); D. B. Hobbs, *Aluminum, Its History, Metallurgy and Uses, with Projects for the School and Home Shop* (1938) is a more popular discussion. Swiss practice is described by A. von Zeerleder, *The Technology of Aluminum and its Light Alloys,* tr. by A. J. Field (1936). For special fields, A. Jenny, *Anodic Oxidation of Aluminum and Its Alloys,* tr. by Winifred Lewis (1940); J. D. Edwards, *Aluminum Paint and Powder* (1936); Aluminum Company of America, *Structural Aluminum Handbook* (1945). For a discussion of the economics of the industry, see N. H. Engle, H. E. Gregory and R. Mossé, *Aluminum, an Industrial Marketing Appraisal* (1945). Current statistics on world production and prices are summarized annually in the *Britannica Book of the Year.* (F. C. F.)

ALUMINUM BRONZE, the name given to copper-base alloys containing aluminum as the main alloying constituent. They have strength comparable with mild steel, and good resistance to oxidation at high temperatures and to corrosion, particularly by dilute acids.

Alloys with up to about 8% aluminum have a simple homogeneous structure and can be cold-rolled into sheet or drawn into tubes. Such alloys, which may also contain small amounts of iron, nickel and manganese, are used in chemical plants, oil refineries, etc., for pressure vessels and heat exchangers.

Alloys containing more than 8% aluminum are capable of only limited cold working, although they can be readily hot-rolled, extruded or forged. Iron is an essential constituent and manganese is also usually added. The strongest and most corrosion-resistant alloy of the group contains nickel and has the nominal composition 80% copper, 10% aluminum, 5% nickel, 5% iron. Typical properties for forgings are: 0.1% proof stress, 25 tons per square inch; tensile strength, 45 tons per square inch; elongation, 15%. This alloy has good resistance to creep up to 250° C. (in lightly stressed parts it can be used at much higher temperatures) and to fatigue and corrosion-fatigue, and has been used for gas turbine compressor blades. The alloys containing about 10% aluminum have excellent casting characteristics, although special running systems must be used to avoid entrapment of the tenacious oxide film present on the molten metal. They are used for gravity die-casting small high-strength components such as gear selector forks as well as for sand casting. Many marine castings, including large ships' propellers, are made from an aluminum-nickel bronze.

Aluminum bronzes can be welded by the metallic arc process and can be brazed, with special fluxes. Other applications are pickling crates and parts of plants dealing with dilute sulfuric, hydrochloric and hydrofluoric acids; papermaking machinery; in the electrical industry for brush holders and clamps for welding machines; heavy-duty gear wheels, worm wheels, metal forming dies and machine guides; nonsparking tools and nonmagnetic chains and anchors. Because of their golden colour and high resistance to tarnishing the alloys are also used for jewelry and in architectural work. (E. C. M.)

ALUNDUM, a hard material belonging to the class of abrasives (q.v.), also used for the manufacture of laboratory apparatus. It is obtained by fusing bauxite (q.v.) in an electric furnace.

ALUNITE or ALUM STONE, a hydrated basic aluminum and potassium sulfate mineral which has alternately served as a source of potash (during World War I) and as a source of alumina (during World War II). In Europe it was once used extensively to make potash alum, being mined for this purpose since its first recognition at Tolfa, near Rome, in the 15th century (see ALUM). Alunite occurs as pockets or seams in volcanic rocks such as rhyolites, trachytes and andesites, presumably formed by their chemical reaction with escaping sulfurous vapours. Large deposits occur near Beregszász, Hung., Almería, Spain, and Bullah Delah in New South Wales, Austr. In the United States alunite has been mined at Marysvale, Utah, and Sulphur, Nev. Common colours are white, gray or reddish buff. The composition of alunite is $KAl_3 (SO_4)_2 (OH)_6$. Its hardness of 3.5 to 4 on Mohs' scale may be increased by admixtures of quartz and feldspar.

(F. D. B.)

ALVAR, from a Tamil word implying absorption in devotion, designates a class of southern Indian saints, wandering singers intensely devoted to Vishnu, the second member of the Hindu trinity. Their earliest representatives lived in the 2nd century A.D. and the latest in the 10th. The Alvars, inspired by the teaching of Vishnuism, which traveled southward from the north, composed and sang poems in Tamil. Their doctrines, similar to the *bhakti* (love, or devotion) mysticism of the Bhagavata Purana and the Bhagavad Gita, were embodied in psalms rather than philosophical treatises, and some of their hymns rate high in the world's treasury of devotional literature. Describing his insatiable love for God, Nam Alvar said:

> My heart for his wonderful grace melts
> How then can I my restless love suppress?

In the 7th and 8th centuries 12 Alvars wandered through the south, and the attractiveness of their school was strongly instrumental in the defeat and absorption of Buddhism in India. Theistic interpretations of the Vedanta Sutra (*see* INDIAN PHILOSOPHY: *Vedanta*), advanced by the passionate devotional hymns of the Alvars, culminated in the philosophy of Ramanuja, according to whom *bhakti* was the essential teaching of the Vedanta.

See K. W. Morgan (ed.), *The Religion of the Hindus,* pp. 36–37, 39–40 (1953); Surendranātha Dāsa-Gupta, *Hindu Mysticism,* pp. 149–150 (1927). (E. J. Ju.)

ALVARADO, PEDRO DE (1485?–1541), one of the conquerors of Mexico and Central America, was born at Badajoz, Spain, about 1485. He commanded one of the ships of Juan de Grijalva that were sent from Cuba in 1518 to explore Yucatán, and in Feb. 1519 he accompanied, also from Cuba, Hernan Cortés' army that was to conquer Mexico. Alvarado was placed in charge of Tenochtitlán, or Mexico City, after its first occupation, and in 1522 he became the city's first alcalde mayor, or principal magistrate. When the Spaniards, because of Aztec hostilities, were forced to retire temporarily from the city on June 30, 1520 (la Noche Triste), Alvarado was in command of the rear guard. It has been said that during the flight of the Spaniards, Alvarado, with the use of his spear, vaulted across a broad opening in one of the city's causeways. This was the famous *Salto de Alvarado*, one of the several fables of the conquest.

In 1523, leading an army of Spaniards and Indian allies, Alvarado marched south from Mexico and conquered the Quichés and Cakchiquels of Guatemala. In the following year he founded the town of Santiago de los Caballeros de Guatemala, later capital of the captaincy general of Guatemala, which was to include much of Central America and to be governed for a time by Alvarado. In the same year, 1524, he carried the conquest into El Salvador.

In 1534 Alvarado led a fleet to Ecuador with the intention of conquering the area, but for 100,000 pesos, given to him by Diego de Almagro, one of Francisco Pizarro's captains, he agreed to forego this venture. Two years later Alvarado returned to Spain, where his contract for discovery in the Spice Islands, which he had received in 1527, was renewed, together with the privilege of sharing whatever discoveries Viceroy Antonio de Mendoza of New Spain (Mexico) might make on the northern borderlands of his viceroyalty. Alvarado thus became one of Mendoza's rivals in the search for the Seven Cities of Cíbola. Alvarado did not live to share in either the northern discoveries of New Spain or in the Spice Islands, for he died in 1541 in or near Guadalajara as the result of a fall from a horse during the Mixton War.   (R. C. E.)

ÁLVAREZ, JUAN (1790–1867), Mexican revolutionary patriot of Indian blood, was born at Concepción de Atoyac (now Ciudad Álvarez, Guerrero). He participated in many of the revolutionary movements between 1810 and 1855, creating for himself a sphere of influence in his native state. In 1811 Álvarez joined José María Morelos (*q.v.*) in the unsuccessful campaign for independence from Spain. He had a prominent part in the revolt of Antonio López de Santa Anna in 1822–23 which overthrew Agustín de Iturbide, and in 1847 he served in the war with the United States. Álvarez began his civil career in 1849 as the first governor of the new state of Guerrero, ostensibly as a liberal. He was sufficiently flexible, however, to accommodate himself to the revived dictatorship of Santa Anna in 1853 and 1854. Melchor Ocampo and Benito Juárez refused to do so and were exiled, but Álvarez tolerated the dictatorship as long as Santa Anna did not threaten his hegemony in Guerrero. When in 1854 Santa Anna moved against Guerrero, Álvarez declared himself in rebellion, launching the movement at (famous plan of) Ayutla. With the defeat of Santa Anna, Álvarez became provisional president, but his inability to provide strong national leadership led to his resignation in 1855. The movement he had begun, however, flowered in the liberal reform and in the constitution of 1857. Álvarez died on Aug. 21, 1867. *See* MEXICO: *Independent Mexico*.   (R. E. Q.)

ÁLVAREZ DE PEREIRA Y CUBERO, JOSÉ (1768–1827), Spanish sculptor, whose best works are portrait busts of stylized neoclassical realism, was born on April 23, 1768, at Priego, Córdoba, famous for its rococo sculpture. Álvarez studied at Madrid. Between 1799 and 1826 he lived in Paris, where Napoleon rewarded him, and in Rome, where he was befriended by Antonio Canova. His academic art imitated in correct modeling and cold perfection the classical style, as in his marble group the "Defense of Saragossa" (Nestor and Antilochus), in the garden of the Museum of Modern Art in Madrid.

He died in Madrid on Nov. 26, 1827. Once renowned, his art is almost forgotten in the 20th century.

See María Elena Gómez Moreno, *Breve historia de la escultura española* (1951).   (M. S. S.)

ÁLVAREZ QUINTERO, the name of two brothers, SERAFÍN (1871–1938) and JOAQUÍN (1873–1944), Spanish dramatists, whose plays are based upon direct observation of Andalusian life. Both were born at Utrera, Seville, Serafín on March 26,

1871, and Joaquín on Jan. 21, 1873. Writing in the traditional style of the 16th-century playwright, Lope de Rueda, and of González del Castillo (1763–1800), they produced comedies remarkable for the vivacity of their dialogue, though lacking depth. Among the most popular of their works were *Los Galeotes* and *El Patio* (both 1900), *Las de Caín* (1908), *Malvaloca* (1912), *La Calumniada* (1919) and *Cancionera* (1924).

The success of some of their plays in London and New York—*Fortunato, El Centenario* (1909; *A Hundred Years Old*) and *La Puebla de las mujeres* (1912; *The Women Have their Way*)—owed much to the fine translations by Helen and Harley Granville-Barker, which were published in 1928. Both brothers died at Madrid, Serafín on April 12, 1938, and Joaquín on June 14, 1944.   (W. F. S.)

ALVEAR, MARCELO TORCUATO DE (1868–1942), president of Argentina (1922–28), was descended from a distinguished and wealthy family. He was born at Buenos Aires, on Oct. 4, 1868. He joined the Radical (democratic) party at its inception (1889–91), became congressman in 1912 and minister to France from 1917 to 1922, during the presidency of the Radical leader, Hipólito Irigoyen. Advanced by Irigoyen as his successor in office, Alvear was elected as president in 1922. During his term of office his policies diverged from those advocated by Irigoyen; a complete break occurred between the two, leading to the establishment by Alvear of the Anti-Personalist Radical party. Despite the alliance of the Anti-Personalists with the conservatives, Irigoyen was elected to a second term in 1928. When Irigoyen's presidency was ended by a conservative revolution (1930), Alvear returned to the party and later to its leadership, but the Radicals were unable to regain the presidency prior to Alvear's death, on March 23, 1942.   (T. F. McG.)

ALVERSTONE, RICHARD EVERARD WEBSTER, 1ST VISCOUNT (1842–1915), lord chief justice of England, who represented Great Britain on several international boundary commissions. He was born in London on Dec. 22, 1842, and died Dec. 15, 1915, at Cranleigh, Surrey. Educated at King's college and Charterhouse schools and Trinity college, Cambridge, he was called to the bar in 1868 and became a queen's counsel only ten years later. His practice was chiefly in commercial, railway and patent cases until (June 1885) he was appointed attorney general in the Conservative government. He sat in the house of commons first for Launceston and then for the Isle of Wight. Except for two brief periods of Liberal government Webster was attorney general from 1885 to 1900. During 1888–90 he was leading counsel for the *London Times* in the Parnell inquiry; in 1893 he represented Great Britain in the Bering sea arbitration and in 1898 in the matter of the boundary between British Guiana and Venezuela. In 1903 he was one of the members of the Alaska Boundary commission.

In 1900 he became master of the rolls, being raised to the peerage as Baron Alverstone, and in October of the same year succeeded Lord Russell of Killowen as lord chief justice. He retired in Nov. 1913, when he was created a viscount.   (W. T. Ws.)

ÄLVSBORG, a *län* (county) of southwest Sweden, is bounded by Lake Vänern (east), Göteborg och Bohus *län* along the coast (west), the Norwegian frontier (north) and Småland (south). Pop. (1950) 358,988. It thus straddles the Göta river which drains over 19,000 sq.mi. and whose falls and rapids are harnessed for electricity, though a canal is necessary for navigation. The *län* is a district of poor soils and three-quarters remains forested. The main wealth lies in industry. Borås (*q.v.*) is a textile and clothing centre, and Trollhättan (*q.v.*) is a hydroelectric centre with locomotive works. Dalsland, with a declining population, is the northern part and has the Dalsland canal, important when opened in 1868 but now little used. Vänersborg is the administrative centre of the *län*.   (A. C. O'D.)

ALWAR, a city and district in northeast Rajasthan, India. The city (pop. 1951, 57,868) lies 98 mi. S.W. of Delhi on the Western railway. It was the capital of the former princely state of the same name founded in 1771 by Maharaja Pratap Singh of the Kachawa clan of Rajputs. Alwar is dominated by a fort on a conical hill, and is backed by a range of hills. A steep ascent leads to the fort behind which stands a monument to the founder of the town. The palace, separated from the base of the hill by a picturesque tank or *sagar,* consists of a group of buildings in different styles. The museum which occupies a portion of this palace has a collection of Hindi, Sanskrit and Persian manuscripts, while the picture gallery has a valuable collection of Mogul and Rajasthani paintings.

ALWAR DISTRICT (area 3,241 sq.mi.) had a population of 1,089,-333 in 1961. Its eastern part is open and highly cultivated; the western is diversified by the hills which are a continuation of the Aravalli range. These hills run in rocky and precipitous parallel ridges, in some places upward of 2,200 ft. in height. The Sabhi and Ruparel are the only streams of importance.

Alwar was the first princely state to accept a currency, struck at the Calcutta mint, of the same weight and assay as the imperial rupee, bearing the head of the British sovereign. Under British paramountcy it was controlled through the Jaipur subagency of the Rajputana agency. After India became independent it joined the Matsya union (March 18, 1948) and the union was merged with Rajasthan on May 15, 1949. (S. M. T. R.)

ALYATTES (7th–6th centuries B.C.), king of Lydia from 617 at the earliest to 560 B.C., was the son of Sadyattes, of the house of the Mermnadae (*see* LYDIA). On succeeding his father, he carried on the war against Miletus for five years. He next came into conflict with the rising power of Media; but after a pitched battle had been interrupted by an eclipse of the sun, a peace was concluded, through the mediation of the kings of Babylon and Cilicia, which fixed the Halys river (mod. Kizil Irmak) as the boundary between the two kingdoms. Alyattes drove the Cimmerians (*q.v.*) from Asia, subdued the Carians and captured Smyrna. His son Croesus succeeded him.

The tomb of Alyattes, described by Herodotus, still exists in the plain between the Gygaean lake (Marmara Gölü) and the Hermus (mod. Gediz) river in western Turkey, about 7 mi. N. of Sardis. A large mound of earth, with a substructure of huge stones, it was first excavated by H. Spiegelthal in 1854, who found that it covered a large vault of finely cut marble blocks approached from the south by a flat-roofed passage of the same stone. The site was further explored after 1910 by the American Society for the Excavation of Sardis, whose reports are published (from 1922) in the periodical *Sardis.*

ALYPIUS (c. A.D. 360), Greek writer on music whose *Introduction to Music* describes the 15 transcriptions of the scale in vocal and instrumental music in the diatonic and chromatic systems, and nine transpositions in the enharmonic system, with tables of their method of notation.

The treatise was published by I. Meursius in 1616, and by M. Meibom (with the tables of notation) in 1652. The authoritative edition is by K. von Jan in *Musici scriptores Graeci* (1895).
(E. J. Wz.)

ALYSSUM, SWEET: *see* SWEET ALYSSUM.

ALZON, EMMANUEL MARIE JOSEPH MAURICE DAUDE D' (1810–1880), French ecclesiastic, founder of the order of Augustinians of the Assumption or Assumptionists, was born Aug. 30, 1810, at Le Vigan, Gard, the scion of one of the richest families of southern France. He was educated privately and at St. Louis and Stanislas colleges in Paris. In 1831 he entered Montpellier seminary and in 1832 continued his studies in Rome, where he was ordained on Dec. 26, 1834. He was named canon and vicar-general of his diocese of Nîmes, and retained this position under four bishops until his death.

In 1842, after a few years of preaching and other ministry, he acquired Assumption college in Nîmes. There also he founded, in 1845, the Congregation of the Augustinians of the Assumption, dedicated to education, missionary and social work. In 1863 he sent his first missionaries to the near east, especially to Bulgaria. To help in this work he also founded a congregation of women, the Oblates of the Assumption. He attended the Vatican council of 1869–70 as theologian to his bishop and was active in preparing the definition of papal infallibility. On Aug. 28, 1871, he started the Alumniates, apostolic schools for the ecclesiastical education of poor boys. He died at Nîmes on Nov. 21, 1880.

The Assumptionists are organized into seven provinces, spread through 27 countries, including the United States, Canada and Mexico. Their main apostolic works are colleges, journalism (La Bonne Presse, Paris) and pilgrimages. (A. A. DE.)

AMADEO (1845–1890), king of Spain from 1870 to 1873, was born at Turin, Italy, on May 30, 1845, the second son of Victor Emmanuel II (the future king of Italy) and was originally known as Amedeo, duke of Aosta. He married Maria Vittoria dal Pozzo della Cisterna in 1867. His candidature for the Spanish throne (vacant after the deposition of Isabella II in Sept. 1868) was supported by Juan Prim and Francisco Serrano (*qq.v.*) and triumphed on Nov. 16, 1870, when he was elected and proclaimed king by the *Cortes.* His arrival in Spain (Dec. 30, 1870) coincided with the assassination of Prim, his principal supporter, and his first public function was a visit to Prim's lying-in-state. Notwithstanding the king's good intentions, the political situation remained unstable and there was a succession of short-lived ministries. In 1872 a Carlist rising took place in the north of Spain, republican agitation increased and a large number of influential people made known their support for a petition asking Alfonso de Borbón (afterward Alfonso XII) to proclaim himself king. Abandoned by his supporters and attacked on all sides, Amadeo abdicated the throne on Feb. 11, 1873. He then returned to Italy and settled at Turin. The duchess Maria Vittoria having died in 1877, he married his niece Marie Létitia Bonaparte (daughter of his sister Clotilda and Jérome Bonaparte's son Napoleon Joseph Charles) in 1888. He died at Turin on Jan. 18, 1890. (R. S. LL.)

AMADÍS DE GAULA, a famous Spanish romance of chivalry. The first known edition appeared in 1508. Its publication gave the medieval chivalresque romance of Celtic origin and French elaboration a further lease of life in a new and idealized form. Immediately followed by sequels and imitations in Spanish and Portuguese, it was widely read, adapted, and translated into French, Italian, German, Dutch and English and for four centuries exerted an influence that makes it one of the most important works in the history of the European novel and indeed of European sensibility.

Origins of the Work.—The authorship, date of composition and even the original language of the romance are in doubt. The 1508 edition was "corrected and emended" by Garci Rodríguez de Montalvo. Montalvo, apparently writing shortly after the conquest of Granada in 1492, states that the work was already circulating in corrupt versions. The only extant remnants of any earlier text, however, are fragments of an early 15th-century Spanish manuscript. The earliest recorded reference to *Amadís de Gaula* occurs in a minor Spanish poet, Pero Ferrús, about 1380. From internal evidence, however, the novel was probably in circulation in the early 14th or even the 13th century. In book i of the novel we read that Prince Afonso of Portugal had a change made in one episode of the story. The prince in question could be none later than the son of King Dinis, who succeeded as Afonso IV in 1325. Further, in book ii there is a free translation of a poem (referring to one of the characters) known to be the work of the 13th-century Portuguese troubadour João de Lobeira. This fact only came to light with the discovery in the 19th century of the early Portuguese lyric and lends some support to a Portuguese tradition, first recorded about 1460 by the Portuguese chronicler Gomes Eanes de Zurara, that the novel was of Portuguese origin, though Zurara calls the author Vasco de Lobeira and states that he wrote in the time of King Ferdinand (1367–83). Zurara's statement remained unpublished until 1792, but the same belief is recorded in the 16th century by the Portuguese historian João de Barros and by Miguel, the son of the poet António Ferreira. Learned opinion has been fairly evenly divided on whether the extant Spanish text derives from a Portuguese original or not. It would be rash to dismiss the Portuguese claim, particularly since Zurara's reference to the novel is slightly disparaging and cannot be attributed to literary chauvinism; nevertheless the evidence remains inconclusive.

Character of the Work.—*Amadís de Gaula* owes much to the French romances of the Arthurian cycle on which it was modeled. Nevertheless it is distinct from the Arthurian romances, is not based on any particular set of legends and in Montalvo's version exalts a new concept of chivalry which caught the imagination of polite society all over Europe. Amadís is the most handsome, upright and valiant of knights and the most constant of lovers, devoted to Oriana (daughter of Lisuarte, king of Great Britain) whom he eventually marries and who is his constant inspiration. Throughout the work his incredible feats of arms alternate with expressions of tender and often lachrymose sentiment. Amadís is more idealized and less human than such heroes as Lancelot and Tristan and needless to say, far more chaste. In the Arthurian legends (*q.v.*) the disruptive eroticism of the Celtic tales had been palliated by the courtly veneer their French elaborators gave them; with the Spanish *Amadís* medieval chivalry achieved complete respectability.

A certain Renaissance spirit can be discerned in the work. Amadís, himself a royal prince, only discovers this fact after he has established his fame by his own prowess. As in Renaissance pastoral, there is no particular sense of place or time, but rather a vague unspecified field for the interplay of idealized human relationships. Similarly, the concept of kingship is in accord with the new age. The anarchic individualism of earlier knights-errant reflects feudal society; the authority with which monarchy is invested in *Amadís* heralds the advent of absolutism.

Influence.—This new style of chivalresque romance was immediately and extraordinarily successful both in the Iberian peninsula and in Europe as a whole, particularly in France where the work became a textbook of chivalresque deportment and epistolatory style; the numerous editions, translations and adaptations of the work down to the 20th century prove its enduring influence. Among early readers were Charles V, Francis I, the humanist Juan Luis Vives, St. Teresa, Ignatius Loyola, Montaigne and Cervantes. In the 16th century there appeared in Spain and Portugal about 50 inferior sequels and feeble imitations; and though this literary fashion was given the deathblow by parody in *Don Quixote,* Cervantes himself held *Amadís* in high esteem, and much of its idealism was integrated into his own masterpiece. Cervantes indeed took the subject a stage further and in Don Quixote's character showed the idealized, oversimplified chivalry of Amadís in conflict with the realities of modern life; in the resultant clash, modern life as much as idealism came in for criticism. Thus the spirit of *Amadís de Gaula* was an important stimulus and an essential ingredient in the first great modern novel.

The first English adaptation appeared in 1567; the best English translation is Robert Southey's abridged version, first published in 1803.

BIBLIOGRAPHY.—*Amadís de Gaula,* ed. by Pascual de Gayangos, *Biblioteca de Autores Españoles,* vol. xl (1857; reprinted 1950); ed. by E. B. Place (vol. i, including bibliographical study, 1959); E. Baret, *De l'Amadis de Gaule et de son influence sur les moeurs et la littérature au XVIe et au XVIIe siècle* (1853, 1873); M. Menéndez y Pelayo, *Orígenes de la novela,* vol. i (1905); H. Thomas, *Spanish and Portuguese Romances of Chivalry* (1920); A. Rodríguez-Moñino *et al., El primer manuscrito del Amadís de Gaula* (1957).　　　(T. P. W.)

AMADOU, a soft tough substance once frequently used as tinder, derived from *Fomes fomentarius* (L.) Gill, a fungus belonging to the group Basidiomycetes and growing upon old trees, especially birch and beech. For use as tinder, the fungus is cut into slices and then steeped in a solution of nitre. Amadou is prepared on the continent of Europe, chiefly in Germany, but the fungus is a native of Britain and America. *Fomes igniarius* (L.) Gill and other species are also used, but yield an inferior product.

AMAGASAKI, Japanese industrial city contiguous to Osaka (*q.v.*) on the Inland sea coast of southeastern Hyōgo prefecture. Pop. (1960) 405,962. Once a feudal period castle town, in the 20th century it attracted many large, modern factories that produce the full range of iron and steel goods, machinery, heavy chemicals and such consumer items as foodstuffs and textiles. The main industrial belt lies along the coast on a river delta, where the threat of water damage necessitated the construction of costly protective dikes. The city has large electric plants, superb railroad facilities and canals and strong economic ties with Osaka.

　　　　　　　　　　　　　　　　　　　　(J. D. Ee.)

AMAKUSA-RETTŌ, group of Japanese islands off western Kyushu, administered by Kumamoto prefecture. The archipelago is formed by more than 90 islands, among which are Shimo, and Kami (separated by Hondo strait, which is only 218 m. wide) and Ōyano. There is little farming because of the rough mountainous terrain, but forestry and offshore fisheries are actively pursued. Excellent quality bituminous coal is mined on the main islands and good pottery clay deposits are also worked. Hondo (pop. 41,896 in 1960) and Ushibuka (pop. 34,704 in 1960), both on Shimo Island, are the largest cities.　　　(J. D. Ee.)

AMAL, the name of the royal family among the Ostrogoths, of which Theodoric (*q.v.*) the Great (d. 526) was the most famous member. The family is said to have been pre-eminent even in the 4th century A.D., but this may be a fabrication designed to flatter the 6th-century Ostrogothic kings.　　　(E. A. T.)

AMALARIC (died 531), king of the Visigoths, son of Alaric II (*q.v.*), was a child when his father fell in battle against Clovis, king of the Franks (507). He was carried for safety into Spain, which country, with southern Languedoc and Provence, were thenceforth ruled by his maternal grandfather Theodoric (*q.v.*) through his vice-regent, an Ostrogothic nobleman named Theudis. On Theodoric's death in 526, Amalaric assumed full royal power in Spain and a part of Languedoc, relinquishing Provence to his cousin Athalaric. He married Clotilda, daughter of Clovis, but his disputes with her, he being an Arian and she a Catholic, brought on a Frankish invasion, in which he lost his life in 531.

AMALASUNTHA (AMALASUENTHA) (498–535), queen and regent of the Ostrogoths, daughter of the Ostrogothic king of Italy Theodoric the Great. She married Eutharic in 515 and had a son, Athalaric, and a daughter, Matesuentha, by him, but he died soon after. When Athalaric became king in 526, Amalasuntha became regent. An educated woman, brave and intelligent, she favoured the Roman population in Italy, sought to remain on good terms with the emperor and the church, and gave her son a more civilized and literary education than the Ostrogoths at large approved. Her foreign policy favoured the Byzantines and was opposed by many Ostrogoths. Conscious of her unpopularity, she banished and afterward put to death three Ostrogothic nobles whom she suspected of intriguing against her, and also opened negotiations with the emperor Justinian with a view to transferring herself and the Gothic treasure to Constantinople if her position in Italy should become untenable. When Athalaric died on Oct. 2, 534, she invited her cousin Theodahad to share the throne, but he failed to support her. Either by his orders or with his connivance, she was banished to an island in the Tuscan lake of Bolsena, where in the spring of 535 she was murdered in her bath by the relatives of the Goths whom she had slain. According to Procopius, Theodora, wife of Justinian, intrigued to bring about the crime.

See J. B. Bury, *History of the Later Roman Empire,* vol. ii (1923).

　　　　　　　　　　　　　　　　　　　　(E. A. T.)

AMALEKITES, an ancient tribe or collection of tribes, of the nomadic type, familiar from their relations to Israel. Though Hebrew ethnology made them a subordinate branch of Edom (Gen. xxxvi, 12), and even connected them closely with the tribe of Ephraim in Judg. xii, 15, they are uniformly represented as enemies of Israel. They harried the fugitives as they escaped from Egypt at the exodus (Deut. xxv, 17–19); were included among the foes through whom a passage must be forced into southern Palestine from Kadesh (Num. xiv, 43–45); attacked Israel at Rephidim, where they were utterly defeated by Joshua (Ex. xvii, 8–16); formed part of the coalition which Eglon, king of Moab, used to oppress Israel (Judg. iii, 13); were included among the hordes of nomadic raiders defeated by Gideon (Judg. vi, 3, 33); and were condemned to annihilation by Samuel (I Sam. xv), though King Saul incurred the anger of Yahweh by sparing Agag and the cattle. Enough of them survived to raid Ziklag in David's absence and to be overwhelmed by his vengeance (I Sam. xxx); their remnant is reported to have been destroyed in the time of Hezekiah (I Chron. iv, 43). The Amalekites were made the object of a perpetual curse (Ex. xvii, 14–16; Num. xxiv, 20; Deut. xxv, 17–19).

The district over which the Amalekites ranged lay south of Judah, extending probably into northern Arabia; they may at times have been located farther east. The association of their name with "Canaanites" suggests that it may have been used at times for an indistinct group that constituted an enemy of Israel in the early period. Even in one of the Psalms (lxxxiii, 7) Amalek is mentioned among the foes of Israel, and the same feeling is reflected in the book of Esther, where Haman the Agagite is pitted against Mordecai the Benjamite. The name of Amalek is celebrated in Arabian tradition, but the confused and conflicting stories are, for historical purposes, practically worthless.

(J. P. Hy.)

AMALFI, a town and archiepiscopal see in Campania, Italy, in the province of Salerno, lies about 12 mi. west-southwest from Salerno city on the north coast of the Gulf of Salerno. Pop. (1961) 6,907 (commune). This picturesque old town and popular tourist resort lies in the ravine of the Valle dei Molini amid splendid coastal scenery. The cathedral of S. Andrea (begun 11th century) is in Lombard-Norman style with a façade in black and white stone, magnificent bronze doors executed at Constantinople before 1066, and a campanile (1276). The body of St. Andrew rests in the crypt. Above Amalfi and slightly to the west is the old Capuchin monastery (founded 1212), with fine cloisters. Partly destroyed by a landslip in 1899, it was remodeled as a hotel.

Although it was known in the 4th century, Amalfi had no importance until the middle of the 6th century. As a naval power in the 9th century it shared with Venice and Gaeta the Italian trade with the east, and in 848 its fleet went to the assistance of Pope Leo IV against the Saracens. It was then an independent republic with a population of about 70,000, but in 1131 it was subdued by King Roger II of Sicily. In 1135 and 1137 it was taken by the Pisans, and rapidly declined in importance, though its maritime code, known as the *Tavole Amalfitane*, was recognized in the Mediterranean until 1570. It now has no harbour. There are water-driven paper mills in the Valle dei Molini.

AMALGAM, an alloy composed of mercury and one or more other metals. Pliny in the first century said that all things float in mercury except gold which combines with it. Actually mercury (*q.v.*) will combine with many metals to form amalgams. Most amalgams are crystalline in structure and those with a large proportion of mercury are liquid. Amalgams of gold and silver have been found occurring in nature. Amalgams may be formed by one of four methods: (1) by direct contact of a metal with mercury; (2) by electrolysis of a mercurial salt solution using the metal to be amalgamated as the cathode; (3) by immersing the metal to be amalgamated in a solution of a mercurial salt; and (4) by bringing mercury into contact with a metallic salt whose amalgam is desired. The most common use of amalgam is in the silver fillings used by dentists, which are composed of filings of an alloy of silver (65%), copper (6%), zinc (2%) and tin (25%) (approximate proportion), mechanically mixed with mercury.

During their formation, most amalgams (*e.g.*, those of mercury with such metals as zinc, thorium, tellurium, silver, magnesium, gold, cadmium, arsenic, and antimony) exhibit little exothermic activity; *i.e.*, they release minimal amounts of heat energy. In the case of amalgamation with tin, lead, or bismuth, the reaction is endothermic (*i.e.*, measurable quantities of heat energy are absorbed). Notable exceptions as far as thermal effects are concerned are amalgams of potassium and sodium. When these are formed, they generate substantial amounts of heat energy, elevating the temperature of their surroundings considerably. In this regard, they represent a definite safety hazard, and inexperienced persons are cautioned to avoid unsupervised experimentation in the preparation of sodium or potassium amalgams. These two metals are dangerously reactive, not only with mercury, but with many other common substances (including water). For example, a bit of sodium dropped on the skin may react with scarring effect.

BIBLIOGRAPHY.—William L. Dudley, *The Nature of Amalgams*, pp. 146–160 (1889); T. W. Richards, J. H. Wilson and R. N. Garrod-Thomas, *Electrochemical Investigations of Liquid Amalgams of Thallium, Indium, Tin, Zinc, Cadmium, Lead, Copper, and Lithium* (1909); Eugene W. Skinner, *The Science of Dental Materials*, p. 316 (1943); I. D. Gainsford, *Silver Amalgam in Clinical Practice* (1965).

(W. J. Mr.)

AMALGAMATION, in metallurgy, is the once widely used process of extracting gold and silver from their ores by means of mercury. It depends on the fact that mercury, or quicksilver, "wets" and adheres to metallic gold and silver and penetrates them, forming pasty amalgams of a silvery colour. Particles of amalgam readily adhere to each other, and the aggregates become large and heavy enough to sink in running water which carries away sand and other earthy materials. Pieces of gold, if not too small, sink perfectly well of themselves and adhere to mercury or amalgam lying at the bottom, and gold ores have been widely amalgamated on this principle. Coarse gold can be saved without the aid of mercury but finely divided gold is more likely to escape. Grains of silver naturally settle also, but most silver ores do not contain metallic silver. They contain compounds such as silver sulfide, which will not settle in water and must be decomposed to set free the silver before it can be amalgamated.

In amalgamation, ores are crushed in water and mixed with mercury with violent agitation in order to break up the mercury into minute globules and disperse them throughout the mass, and so enable them to be brought into contact with the gold or silver. Afterward by dilution with water and gentle stirring, or by a running stream of water, the amalgam and surplus mercury are induced to coalesce and settle to the bottom, where they are caught in a pool of mercury or on the surface of copper plates to which they adhere. When the earthy matter has been washed away, the mixture of metals is put into filter bags and squeezed to remove the surplus mercury. The liquid mercury passes through, containing a minute quantity of gold and silver dissolved in it, and pasty amalgam containing from 25 to 50% gold remains in the bag. The amalgam is heated in retorts (fig. 4), the mercury driven off as vapour and condensed for reuse, and the gold and silver are melted down and cast into bars. Since all gold ores contain some silver and silver ores some gold, the bars consist of a mixture of gold and silver which is afterward parted (*see* GOLD). The process is a very old one. The extraction of gold by mercury is mentioned by Pliny in his *Natural History*, and descriptions of amalgamation processes for both gold and silver are to be found in various 16th-century treatises. The history of the process was given in detail by John Percy in *Silver and Gold* (1880).

Mercury may, however, become so excessively subdivided, as the result of too violent agitation or pounding, especially when mixed with grease or certain kinds of ore, that it becomes "floured" or "sickened." Floured mercury is a white powder, although under the microscope it is seen to consist of minute globules of apparently ordinary mercury, heaped together. The globules will not coalesce and are carried away and lost in the tailings or refuse. They are generally separated only by films of air, and may be made to coalesce by the action of acids or in other ways entailing expense or loss. Again, although earthy matter and mercury have no action on each other, mercury attacks and amalgamates copper, lead, zinc, and some other metals, especially when they are present in the metallic state. The amalgam thus becomes debased and powdery so that part is lost and the remainder is costly to refine. Also there are ores which do not yield a reasonable percentage of their values when treated by amalgamation; these are called refractory and those which are amenable to amalgamation are described as free-milling.

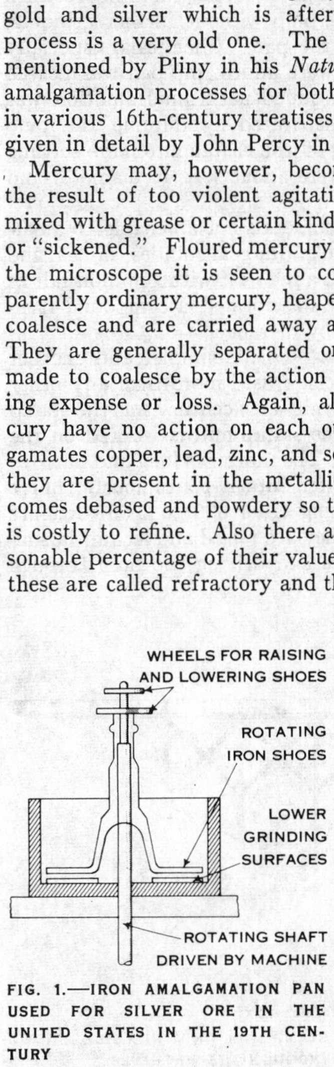

Patio or Mexican Process.— In Pachuca (*q.v.*), Mex., in the 16th century silver ore was ground by mule power in arrastras or shallow circular pits paved with stone. Large blocks of stone attached by beams to a central rotating post were dragged round the arrastra and reduced the ore to fine mud which was taken out and spread over a courtyard or patio in low heaps. It was then sprinkled with mercury and chemicals (common salt and copper sulfate) and mixed by mules which were driven over every

FIG. 1.—IRON AMALGAMATION PAN USED FOR SILVER ORE IN THE UNITED STATES IN THE 19TH CENTURY

WHEELS FOR RAISING AND LOWERING SHOES
ROTATING IRON SHOES
LOWER GRINDING SURFACES
ROTATING SHAFT DRIVEN BY MACHINE

part of the heaps. Complicated chemical reactions took place, never fully understood, the effect of which was to free the silver from its compounds and enable it to be taken up by the mercury. The heaps were trodden by the mules every day or two until the amalgamation was complete, which might require a month. Lastly the material was agitated with water in large tubs and the mud run off through the plug holes. The amalgam found at the bottom was collected and treated as already described. The process was especially suitable for the silver ores of the dry barren districts of Mexico, where water and fuel are scarce, and was not finally displaced by the cyanide process (*q.v.*) until early in the 20th century. It was used in the production of a large proportion of the world's silver for 350 years.

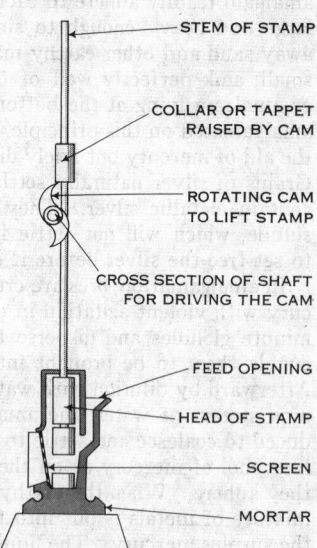

FIG. 2.—CALIFORNIA STAMP MILL, AN IMPROVED FORM OF THE OLD GERMAN TYPE OF 1556

Labels: STEM OF STAMP / COLLAR OR TAPPET RAISED BY CAM / ROTATING CAM TO LIFT STAMP / CROSS SECTION OF SHAFT FOR DRIVING THE CAM / FEED OPENING / HEAD OF STAMP / SCREEN / MORTAR

Pan Amalgamation Process.—The process was used for silver ores, especially in the United States, in the latter half of the 19th century and was superseded by the cyanide process and by smelting. Silver ore was ground to a fine paste with water in iron pans (fig. 1) by rotating iron shoes. The shoes were then raised a little, so as to agitate the pulp without further grinding, and mercury was sprinkled into the pan. Chemicals, especially common salt and copper sulfate, were added, the pan was heated with steam and agitation was continued until amalgamation was completed. The amalgam was separated by diluting the pulp and stirring and finally by running off the charge into large settling tanks. The amalgamation pans were about 5 ft. in diameter and the charge was 2,000 or 3,000 lb.

Complex silver ores containing minerals not amenable to amalgamation (such as the arsenical and antimonial sulfides, galena, and blende) were roasted in furnaces at a red heat with common salt as a preliminary, when silver chloride was formed, a compound from which the silver can be extracted by mercury.

Amalgamation of Gold Ores.—This is simpler and cheaper than that of silver ores. The machine used more than any other for the reduction of gold ores after mid-19th century was the stamp mill or battery (fig. 2 and 3). The stamp mill is worked on the principle of the pestle and mortar. The mortar is long and narrow, and ore, water, and mercury are fed into it continuously. Five heavy steel stampers, each weighing from 800 to 2,000 lb., are ranged in a row in one mortar. They are raised and let fall in succession, crushing the lumps of ore and driving the pulp through

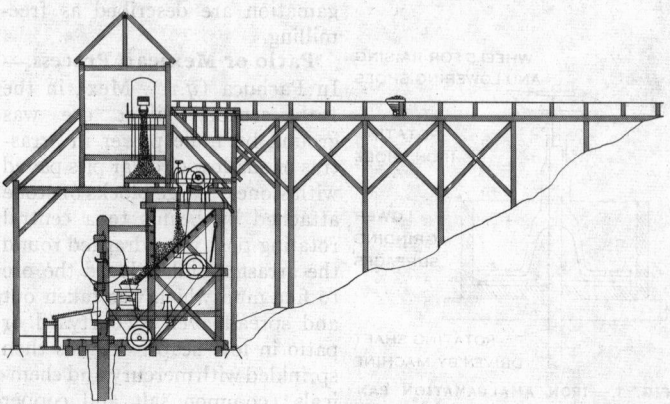

BY COURTESY OF FRASER AND CHALMERS ENGINEERING WORKS
FIG. 3.—GENERAL SECTION OF A GOLD STAMP MILL ON A HILLSIDE, SHOWING SUPPLY OF ORE AND ITS PASSAGE THROUGH THE MACHINES

screens set in one side of the mortar. The old-fashioned wire screens were later replaced by perforated steel plates. The pulp coming from the screens is still further reduced by grinding in tube mills (rotating cylinders half filled with large pebbles, or lumps of unbroken ore) and then flows over sloping electro-silvered copper plates or tables, whose surface is amalgamated by rubbing with mercury. In older practice the copper plates were placed just outside the screens (fig. 3). The particles of gold adhere to the surface of the plate. Earlier still, amalgamated plates were fixed inside the mortar. The size and weight of stamps in the 20th century caused excessive loss of mercury by flouring and the addition of mercury and the fixing of plates in the mortars were given up, the battery reverting to its original use as a mere crushing machine. Stamps forced down by springs or by power applied in various ways are sometimes used instead of gravity stamps and rotating crushers of various kinds (ball mills, tube mills, etc.) replaced them in some plants.

The cleanup takes place at intervals of a fortnight or a month. The stamps are hung up, the sand is washed away, the amalgamated plates are scraped, and the amalgam after careful cleaning is squeezed and retorted (fig. 4). The percentage yield of gold varies with the conditions and the nature of the ore. Coarse gold is easily caught, but finely divided gold escapes in great part. Generally about 60% of the gold in the ore was recovered by amalgamation, and the remainder by cyanide. Ores containing only one-fourth of an ounce of gold or even less per ton of ore have been treated at a profit.

On the Rand in South Africa, amalgamation on copper plates had been generally discarded by 1925, because of the difficulty of preventing the theft of the amalgam and the danger from mercury poisoning. Instead of passing the crushed ore from the tube mills

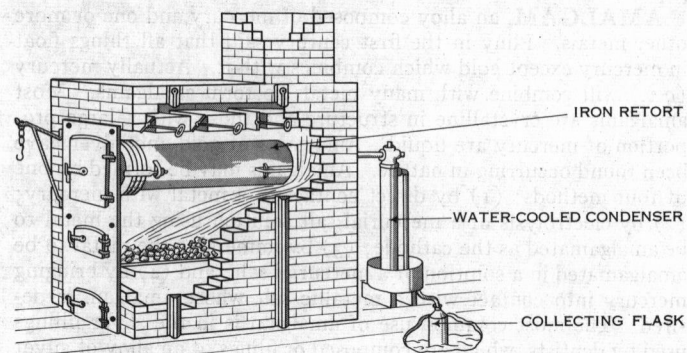

FROM ROSE, "METALLURGY OF GOLD," BY PERMISSION OF C. GRIFFIN & CO., LTD.
FIG. 4.—CUTAWAY VIEW OF AN AMALGAM RETORT FOR SEPARATING GOLD FROM MERCURY

Labels: IRON RETORT / WATER-COOLED CONDENSER / COLLECTING FLASK

The amalgam of gold and mercury is placed in the retort and heated to redness. The mercury is separated and as vapour passes to the condenser and then to the collecting flask. The gold remains in the retort

over amalgamated plates it is concentrated on a surface of corduroy, which retains the heavy particles including all coarse gold. This is a reversion to the primitive practice of the gold diggers of California in 1849 who used their blankets in concentrating gold sands. At intervals the corduroy is taken up and washed in boxes and the coarse gold is extracted from the contents of the boxes by further concentration. The fine gold left in the ore is extracted in the cyanide plant. The corduroy also catches osmiridium and other valuable metals of the platinum group which had previously been lost.

The method of extracting gold from ores by solution in aqueous solutions of sodium cyanide which became increasingly used after 1900 has almost completely replaced amalgamation. The only important exception into the second half of the 20th century was its use at the Homestake Mine, Lead, S.D. In South Africa and a few other fields amalgamation plays a minor role for cleanup and recovery of gold from gravity concentrates.

Amalgamation of Other Metals.—Although historically the use of mercury in metallurgy has been confined almost exclusively to amalgamating gold and silver, it is well known that numerous other metals form amalgams and the use of mercury for extracting such metals from ores or secondary products has frequently been suggested.

Technical success has been reached in some instances; for example, light metal scrap was refined by an amalgam process in Germany, but in general such methods have seldom attracted commercial interest.

A procedure having considerable merit was announced in 1957 by the U.S. Bureau of Mines in which mercury was used for recovering zinc from drosses and other by-products resulting from galvanizing operations. Material such as chloride skimmings in which the zinc is water soluble are leached and the resulting solution is used as electrolyte in an electrolytic cell with an insoluble anode and mercury cathode thus producing a zinc amalgam. This is maintained in a liquid condition and continuously circulated by pumping to an adjacent recovery cell where it becomes the anode with an aluminum cathode and zinc sulfate electrolyte. Zinc is deposited on the cathode in the solid state.

In treating by-products containing zinc in the metallic state, mercury is used to amalgamate and remove the zinc which is then recovered in a pure state in an electrolytic cell similar to the second cell referred to above.

In both of the above procedures zinc of high purity is obtained and there is little loss of mercury.   (T. K. R.; C. R. H.)

BIBLIOGRAPHY.—T. K. Rose, *The Metallurgy of Gold* (1915); D. M. Liddell, *Handbook of Nonferrous Metallurgy* (1945); A. F. Taggart, *Handbook of Mineral Dressing, Ores and Industrial Minerals* (1945); J. V. N. Dorr and F. L. Bosqui, *Cyanidation and Concentration of Gold and Silver Ores*, 2nd ed. (1950); C. R. Hayward, *Outline of Metallurgical Practice*, 3rd ed. (1952).

AMALRIC I (d. 1174), king of Jerusalem, was the son of Fulk and Melisinda of Jerusalem and succeeded his elder brother, Baldwin III, in 1163. He was twice married: by his first wife, Agnes of Edessa, he had issue a son and a daughter, Baldwin IV and Sibylla; while his second wife, Maria Comnena, bore him a daughter, Isabella, who ultimately carried the crown of Jerusalem to her fourth husband, Amalric of Lusignan (Amalric II; *q.v.*). The reign of Amalric I was occupied by the Egyptian problem. It became a question between Amalric and Nureddin which of the two should control the discordant viziers who vied with one another for control of the decadent caliphs of Egypt. For some five years a contest was waged between Amalric and Shirquh, the lieutenant of Nureddin, for the possession of Egypt. Thrice (1164, 1167, 1168) Amalric penetrated into Egypt; but the contest ended in the establishment of Saladin, the nephew of Shirquh, as vizier—a position which, on the death of the puppet caliph in 1171, was turned into that of sovereign. The extinction of the Latin kingdom then seemed imminent, and anxious appeals for assistance were made both to Byzantium and the west. But though in 1170 Saladin attacked the kingdom and captured Aila on the Red sea, the danger was not so great as it seemed. Nureddin was jealous of his overmighty subject, and his jealousy bound Saladin's hands. This was the position of affairs when Amalric died, in 1174; but, as Nureddin died in the same year, the position was soon altered and Saladin began the final attack on the kingdom. Amalric I, the second of the native kings of Jerusalem, had the qualities of his brother Baldwin III (*q.v.*). Like him, he fostered the Byzantine alliance. He was something of a scholar, and it was he who set William of Tyre to work. He was more of a lawyer; he knew the *Assises* better than any of his subjects.

William of Tyre is the original authority: *see* xix, 2–3, for his sketch of Amalric. *See also* R. Grousset, *Histoire des croisades*, vol. ii (1935); and G. Schlumberger, *Campagnes du roi Amaury I en Égypte* (1906).

AMALRIC II (d. 1205), king of Jerusalem and Cyprus, was a son of Hugh the Brown of Lusignan and the brother of Guy of Lusignan. His second wife was Isabella, daughter of Amalric I, and he became king of Jerusalem in right of his wife in 1197. In 1198 he was able to procure a five years' truce with the Muslims, thanks to the struggle between Saladin's brothers and his sons for the inheritance of his territories. The truce was disturbed by raids on both sides, but in 1204 it was renewed for six years. Amalric died in 1205. The kingdom of Cyprus, which he had inherited from his brother, passed to Hugh, his son by his first

wife, Eschiva; while that of Jerusalem fell to Mary, the daughter of Isabella by her previous marriage with Conrad of Montferrat.

AMALTHAEA, in Greek (originally Cretan) mythology, the foster mother of Zeus. She is sometimes represented as the goat that suckled the infant god in a cave in Crete, sometimes as a nymph of uncertain parentage who brought him up on the milk of a goat. This goat having broken off one of its horns, Amalthaea filled the horn with flowers and fruits and presented it to Zeus, who placed it, together with the goat, among the stars. According to another story, Zeus himself broke off the horn and gave it to Amalthaea, promising that it would supply in abundance whatever she desired. Amalthaea gave it to Achelous (her reputed brother), who exchanged it for his own horn, which had been broken off in his contest with Hercules for the possession of Deianira. Speaking generally, it was regarded as the symbol of inexhaustible riches and plenty, and became the attribute of various divinities and of rivers as fertilizers of the land. Cretan coins represent the infant Zeus being suckled by the goat; other Greek coins exhibit him suspended from its teats; others, carried in the arms of a nymph.

AMAMBAÍ, SERRA DE (Sp. SIERRA DE AMAMBAY), the range of heights forming the divide between the tributaries of the Paraguay river and those of the Paraná in southwest Mato Grosso, Brazil. The range forms the western side of the Brazilian plateau, held up by resistant diabase sheets which spread over a wide area of this part of South America. It is not properly described as a mountain range although its average elevation is 1,312 ft. above sea level. This high margin of the plateau extends about 200 mi. S.S.W. from Campo Grande. Its southern end forms a part of the border between Brazil and Paraguay.   (P. E. J.)

AMAMBAY, the northeastern department of Paraguay, is separated from Brazil by the Río Apa and the Serra de Amambaí, the western flanks of which provide Paraguay's highest terrain (over 2,000 ft.). Drained to the Paraguay river, it forms part of the Paraguayan extension of the Brazilian plateau, with important forest resources. The population in 1962 was 33,782. The department produces cattle and maté, and practises subsistence agriculture. There are several links with communities across the Brazilian frontier, and a road from Pedro Juan Caballero, the capital, connects the department with the river port of Concepción, 125 mi. to the southwest.   (G. J. B.)

AMANITA, a genus of mushrooms, important because of its deadly poisonous species. It is doubly dangerous because it contains fine edible species such as *Amanita caesarea* and *A. rubescens*. Amateur collectors should rigidly avoid collecting any species of *Amanita* for the table (*see also* MUSHROOM).

The brilliant colours of amanitas have attracted people since the dawn of history. Amanitas can be recognized by the following combination of characters: the presence of a universal veil; lamellae (gills) free from the stipe (stalk); white spore deposit; and bilateral gill trama. The universal veil is a thin protective layer covering the entire young fruiting body. It becomes ruptured as the pileus expands. If it is membranous and tough, a cup ("death cup") remains around the base of the stipe. If it is fragile, it breaks into warts or powdery particles which adhere for a time on the cap and around the base of the stipe. The lamellae are thin plates of tissue on the underside of the pileus.

Over 100 species are known. The poisons of a variety of *A. muscaria* have been used by primitive peoples to produce intoxication. Muscarine is the principal active compound. *A. phalloides* and *A. verna* are deadly poisonous.   (AR. H. S.)

AMANULLAH KHAN (1892–1960), king of Afghanistan from 1919 to 1929, was born at Paghman on June 1, 1892, the third son of the amir Habibullah Khan. When Habibullah was assassinated on Feb. 20, 1919, Amanullah was acting as his regent at Kabul. Taking advantage of his possession of the capital, he declared himself amir, ignoring the claim of his uncle Sirdar Nasrullah Khan, which was supported by his eldest brother, Inayatullah Khan. Established on the throne, he declared Afghanistan independent in both internal and external affairs, thus fulfilling the long-cherished desire of his people, and demanded recognition of this status by the government of India. The resulting negotiations led to war with the British, which broke out, undeclared, on May 3, 1919. The fighting, however, was sporadic and inconclusive, and peace was signed at Rawalpindi on Aug. 8, 1919, Great Britain recognizing Afghanistan's independence. Amanullah assumed the title of king. In internal affairs Amanullah tried to introduce social reforms based on western models with a view to preparing his people for the requirements of modern international life, but in this he met strong opposition from reactionaries. Soon after his return from an extensive tour of Europe, tribal risings broke out, and in Dec. 1928 a notorious bandit named Habibullah took advantage of the chaotic situation to seize Kabul. Amanullah abdicated on Jan. 14, 1929, and, after an unsuccessful attempt to regain the throne, left Afghanistan for Europe in the following May, never to return. He died in Zürich, Switz., on April 25, 1960.

(Md. A.)

AMAPÁ, one of five federal territories in Brazil, the others being Acre, Fernando de Noronha, Rio Branco and Rondônia (formerly Guaporé). Formerly a part of the state of Pará, Amapá was created by decree law in 1943. It has an area of 53,013 sq.mi., and a population (1956 est.) of 53,000. Located on the equator in the north central part of Brazil, it is bounded on the north by a small bit of Surinam and by French Guiana, on the northeast by the Atlantic ocean, on the southeast by the north channel of the Amazon river, and on the southwest by the state of Pará. Its boundary with French Guiana is along the Oiapoque river. Its western boundary is the Jarí river. Amapá includes an area of tropical rain forest with patches of savanna along the coast, an area that has long remained very scantily populated. The chief town and capital, Macapá is located on the bank of the Amazon (pop. [1950] 9,748). The chief products are cabinet woods, medicinal plants, skins of wild animals, rubber, Brazil nuts and fish. Gold is found in the stream gravels. Chief importance of the territory is the large deposits of manganese discovered during World War II inland from Macapá, now reached by rail from that port.

(P. E. J.)

AMARAH (Al Amarah), a town of Iraq and capital of a *liwa* (province) of the same name, stands on the left bank of the Tigris, 90 mi. above Qurnah and 126 mi. below Kut al Imara, on a low ridge enclosed between the Tigris on the west and the Masharah and Kahla' canals on the north and east. Pop. (1957) 53,311. Since the middle of the 19th century it has developed as the principal market and river port on the Tigris south of Baghdad. With the growth of irrigation, agriculture greatly expanded, and Amarah is a market for grain, fruit and vegetables, and for pastoral products (live sheep and cattle, wool, hides, etc.). These have usually been sent by river to Baghdad, though much of the river traffic has been diverted to road and rail as the result of the construction of a standard-gauge line between Baghdad and Basrah via Amarah. There is also some manufacturing: weaving of Arab dress and rugs, and the making of silverware, for which Amarah is widely known in the middle east. The population is mixed, consisting of an Arab majority but with numbers of Sabians, some Persians, Christians and Lurs.

The *liwa* (pop. [1957] 329,647; area 7,095 sq.mi.) corresponds closely to the boundaries of the Ottoman sanjak (district) and comprises the large irrigated area on both sides of the Tigris mainly south of Amarah town. Water is supplied by six major channels: the Masharah, Kahla' and Michariyah on the east bank, and the Butairah, Tabar and Mijar al Kabir on the west. There are also adjoining expanses of swamp, grazing areas and unused desert.

(W. B. Fr.)

AMARANTH (Amarant), a name chiefly used in poetry, and applied to certain plants which, because they do not wither rapidly, typified immortality (from the Gr. *amarantos,* "unwithering").

The plant genus *Amaranthus* (of the family Amaranthaceae) contains over 50 species of annuals, mostly weedy, and some well-known garden plants, chiefly of tropical origin. Love-lies-bleeding (*A. caudatus*) is a showy everlasting and a vigorous hardy annual, with dark-red flowers crowded in handsome drooping spikes. Another species, prince's-feather (*A. hybridus hypochondriacus*), has deeply veined lance-shaped leaves, purple on the under face, and deep crimson flowers densely packed on erect spikes. One of

the finest is Joseph's-coat (*A. tricolor*), a coarse annual two to four feet high, with variously coloured foliage. All the above are easily cultivated as garden annuals in rather sandy loam; richer soils produce larger leaves but less colour. Seeds should be sown one-fourth inch deep in full sun.

Globe amaranth belongs to an allied genus, *Gomphrena,* and is a native of the old world tropics. It is an annual about 18 in. high, with solitary round heads of flowers; the heads are violet, red, pink, white or yellow from the colour of the bracts which surround the small flowers. It is one of the best of the everlastings, if its chaffy blooms are picked in mid-August.

In North America more than 30 species of amaranth occur, chiefly in the southern and southwestern United States, several of them being introduced weeds, mostly from the tropics. Among the most widely distributed are the green amaranth or wild beet (*A. retroflexus*), the red amaranth or pigweed (*A. hybridus*), the thorny amaranth (*A. spinosus*), the prostrate amaranth (*A. graecizans*) and a tumbleweed (*A. albus*). In ancient Greece the amaranth (also called *chrysanthemon* and *elichrysoe*) was sacred to Ephesian Artemis. It was supposed to have special healing properties and as a symbol of immortality was used to decorate images of the gods and tombs.

In legend, Amarynthus (a form of Amarantus) was a hunter of Artemis and king of Euboea; in a village of Amarynthus, of which he was the eponymous hero, there was a famous temple of Artemis Amarynthia or Amarysia.

(N. Tr.)

AMARAPURA, a former capital of Burma, is now a suburb of Mandalay, Union of Burma. The Burmans call it Taung-myo, "the southern town," and Mandalay, Myauk-myo, or "northern town." Amarapura has long been famous for its silk-weaving industry, producing the colourful *longyis* (skirts for both sexes) in a distinctive heavy silk. Another famous industry is casting in bronze (actually bronze and lead), especially of statues of Buddha, bells and gongs. The work is extensively exported. Founded in 1782 by King Bodawpaya as a new capital about six miles northeast of Ava, it was estimated in 1810 to contain 170,000 inhabitants; but a fire in that year and the removal of the court back to Ava in 1823 caused a decline to about 30,000 by 1827. Tharrawaddy (1837–46) took the capital back to Amarapura but an earthquake in 1839 destroyed much of the city, which was finally abandoned in 1860, when King Mindon occupied Mandalay. Amarapura was laid out on much the same plan as Ava. The ruins of the city wall, long overgrown with scrub, show it to have been a square with a side about three-quarters of a mile long. At each corner stood a solid brick pagoda about 100 ft. high; a celebrated temple with 250 pillars of gilt wood contained a colossal bronze statue of Buddha. Amarapura has now little to show except the tombs of Bodawpaya and his successor Bagyidaw, both inscribed in English. The Burmans know the old fortified city as Myohaung, "the old city." It has a station on the Rangoon-Mandalay railway, and is the junction for Lashio and for Myitkyina. (L. D. S.)

AMARA SIMHA (*c.* 4th–6th centuries A.D.), Sanskrit lexicographer, who wrote the *Amara-kosa* ("Thesaurus of Amara"), a list of synonyms in verse containing about 13,000 words. Memorizing the *Amara-kosa* came to be an important part of the training of Sanskrit poets, and this kept the work popular despite its numerous imitations. Amara Simha was a Buddhist. He probably drew on earlier compilations, later lost, especially for his botanical and medical terms.

Of the many editions of the Sanskrit text perhaps the handiest is that with the commentary of Ksirasvamin edited by Krishnaji Govind Oka (1913). (D. H. H. I.)

AMARAVATI, a ruined Buddhist site on the south bank of the Krishna river in the Guntur district of Andhra Pradesh, India. It stands on the outskirts of the ancient Dhanyakataka, a provincial capital of the Satavahana empire (2nd century A.D.) and of the early Pallavas and a Buddhist centre for many centuries. The great *stupa* (Buddhist memorial mound) of Amaravati was richly adorned with sculptured stone slabs dating from the 1st century A.D. (early phase) to the 3rd (late phase). These are now mainly housed in the Madras museum and in the British museum, London.

See D. Barrett, *Sculptures from Amaravati in the British Museum* (1954); C. Sivaramamurti, *Amaravati Sculptures in the Madras Government Museum* (1942). (F. R. A.)

AMARILLO, a city of northwest Texas, U.S., in the Texas Panhandle; seat of Potter county. Pop. (1960), city 137,969; standard metropolitan statistical area (Potter and Randall counties) 149,493. (For comparative population figures *see* table in TEXAS: *Population.*) The name Amarillo probably came from the Spanish word for yellow, the colour of nearby clay deposits; for the geography of the region *see* LLANO ESTACADO.

Amarillo's origins can be traced to a construction camp of the first railroad built across the region in 1887. Population in 1890 was only 482 and there was no organized government until 1899. About 1900 wheat growing became important in the Panhandle and during the 1920s an oil and gas industry grew rapidly. In the 1930s general economic depression and prolonged drought restricted growth. After 1940, however, extensive irrigation from underground water enlarged the region's agricultural output, especially in grain sorghums.

U.S. government installations in and around the city include a major helium plant, an air force base and an atomic energy project. In addition to various city recreation facilities, there is a large state park, containing the Palo Duro canyon, about 16 mi. S. of Amarillo. The city established a council-manager form of government in 1913. (C. C. TN.)

AMARNA TABLETS: *see* TELL EL AMARNA.

AMARYLLIDACEAE, the amaryllis family, a numerous group of monocotyledonous plants (those with a single seed leaf), closely allied to the lily family (Liliaceae). Familiar representatives are the daffodil, jonquil, snowdrop, tuberose (*qq.v.*) and snowflake. The family comprises about 86 genera and 1,050 species, found chiefly in tropical and subtropical regions. Many are bulbous plants of arid lands, leafing only in spring or after rains. A large number bear handsome lilylike flowers, often popularly called lilies, as Amazon lily (*Eucharis grandiflora*), spider lily (*Hymenocallis* sp., *Pancratium* sp.) and zephyr lily (*Zephyranthes* sp.).

Among the larger genera are *Agave, Crinum, Hippeastrum, Hypoxis* and *Narcissus.* Various species of *Agave* yield valuable fibres, as henequen, pita and sisal hemp; the bulbs of some species are used in medicine, while those of the South African belladonna lily (*Amaryllis belladonna*) and the buphane (*Buphane disticha*) are highly toxic, the latter furnishing a Kaffir arrow poison. Representatives of more than 40 genera are grown as ornamental plants in greenhouses and gardens. In North America there are more than 40 native species; these are found chiefly in the southern and the southwestern United States and belong mostly to the genera *Agave, Hymenocallis* and *Zephyranthes.* Of those native to the eastern United States, the best known are the atamasco lily (*Zephyranthes atamasco*), cultivated for its handsome flowers, and the yellow star grass (*Hypoxis hirsuta*), the only representative extending northward into Canada. Native plants of the family in the British Isles are the yellow daffodil (*Narcissus pseudo-Narcissus*), the snowdrop (*Galanthus nivalis*) and the summer snowflake (*Leucojum aestivum*).

See AGAVE; AMARYLLIS; HEMP; HIPPEASTRUM; LILIACEAE; NARCISSUS; SISAL FIBRE.

For a treatment of the genera *see* F. Pax and K. Hoffmann, "Amaryllidaceae"; Engler and Prantl, *Die natürlichen Pflanzenfamilien,* 2nd ed., 15a: 391–430, fig. 163–187 (1930).

AMARYLLIS. Many lilylike plants, notably *Crinum, Hippeastrum* (including the Barbados lily), *Brunsvigia* (Josephine's-lily), *Sprekelia* (St.-James's-lily) and *Lycoris* (the hardy amaryllis), are often called Amaryllis by gardeners. The name refers to the genus *Amaryllis* which has a single species, the belladonna lily (*A. belladonna*), a South African bulbous plant of great beauty and widely cultivated. It has an enormous bulb and strap-shaped leaves which appear after the flowers have withered. The showy, fragrant flowers are lilylike, crowded in a terminal cluster (umbel) on a stout solid stalk. The perianth is funnel-shaped, about three and one-half inches long, typically rose-red, but blush, pink, purple or white-striped in horticultural

J. HORACE MCFARLAND CO.

BELLADONNA LILY (AMARYLLIS BELLADONNA)

varieties. The culture of the belladonna lily and of all the above-mentioned amaryllis is essentially the same (except for *Lycoris*). They need greenhouse culture (or outdoors in frostless regions) and have a decided resting period. The bulbs should be planted in January or February in a rich soil, in large pots and kept well watered, in a temperature of 65° F (18° C). When bloom is finished, watering should be continued until the leaves have matured, and thereafter diminished until the leaves wither. Bulbs should then be taken out of the pots and stored over the winter. (N. TR.)

AMASIS: *see* AHMOSE.

AMASYA (AMASIA), the chief town of the *il* (province) of the same name in northern Turkey, is beautifully situated on the Yesil Irmak (Iris) river. Pop. (1965) 33,129. It is a trade centre on the Samsun-Sivas road (about 90 mi. N.W. of Sivas and 50 mi. S.W. of Samsun) and railway. Unusually well-built, it has a good bazaar and khans (inns or lodging places), a clock tower and extensive fruit gardens. Amasya was one of the chief towns of the kingdom of Trebizond and of the Seljuks, under whom it was enriched with fine buildings and the castle restored, enabling it to withstand a seven months' siege by Timur. It was much favoured by the early Osmanli sultans, and Bayezid II built a fine mosque. The ancient town has left little trace except on the castle rock, where the acropolis walls and some rock-cut tombs are found, described by Strabo (who was born at Amasya) as those of the kings of Pontus. The last king to reign there was the father of Mithradates VI Eupator, "the Great"; the latter however used it as a base for his operations against the Romans from 89 to 67 B.C. Pompey made it a free city in 65.

The *il* of Amasya (pop. [1965] 285,348; area 2,131 sq.mi.), lying between the Black sea and inner Anatolia, contains fertile plains crossed by the Yesil Irmak, Cekerek and Tersakan rivers. The principal products are cereals, tobacco, poppy and sugar beet. Fruit growing is important; apples and grapes are the chief exports. Amasya ochre has long been famous. (N. TU.; S. ER.; E. TU.)

AMATEUR. The word "amateur" (Fr. *amateur* from Latin *amatorem,* "one who has a taste for anything") came into use in France in the middle of the reign of Louis XIV (1643–1715) to denote a connoisseur of the fine arts. The term was first recorded in Britain in 1784, again referring to one who appreciated the polite arts of painting and music. Its earliest sporting connotation is in a reference to ringside prize fight spectators as gentlemen amateurs in 1801. The original meaning of the word, indicating one who participates in any art, craft, game, sport or other activity solely for pleasure and enjoyment, has been largely supplanted by an acquired secondary meaning indicating a person of inferior or superficial skill, ability or proficiency, as compared with others who specialize in and are expert in any field.

In the first half of the 19th century the distinction in sport in Great Britain between an amateur and a professional was not so much financial as social; *e.g.,* in 1831 the teams of Oxford and the Leander club rowed at Henley for £200 a side yet there was no question of professionalism, for indeed such oarsmen underlined their amateurism by showing that they, unlike artisans, could well afford to lose. Conversely as late as 1871 the Henley committee declined a local entry for the Wyfold cup on the grounds that the crew included people who were or had been mechanics, artisans and labourers. There was no question of their having rowed for money but merely that they were not gentlemen amateurs.

With the formation of the Football association (1863) and the Amateur Athletic club (1866), sport ceased to be a gentleman's preserve. Though mixed games of players and gentlemen had been successfully played in cricket for over a century, an incursion of artisans into other sports brought a number of abuses including disorderly gambling, bribery and impersonation. The gentlemen amateurs, now merely amateurs, reacted against this: since they could not apply social sanctions against corruption and the threat of being outclassed by whole-time performers, they resorted to monetary ones, so that by 1880 the distinction between amateurs and professionals had generally, though not in rowing, become a financial one. The social stigma of being a professional may, however, be said to have persisted in Great Britain until the conferring of knighthoods upon Jack Hobbs in cricket and Gordon Richards in horse racing in 1953.

It is in the realm of athletics, where both amateurs and professionals coexist, that the meaning of the word most often comes into question, as participation in amateur sports (which include the Olympic games and other international competitions as well as the national and collegiate championships of most nations) must obviously be confined to amateurs. However, the fact that the various sports federations and bodies governing national sports have adopted different definitions (and often different interpretations) of what constitutes an amateur has on occasion led to confusion and controversy.

There is no problem with respect to the outright professional, who participates in professional competitions as his sole or principal means of livelihood and thus presumably can and does devote most of his time and energies to perfecting his athletic skills. He is never eligible to participate in amateur competitions in his own sport and, with few exceptions, neither is he eligible for amateur competitions in any other sport. However, even without becoming an outright professional as above, there are various acts by which an athlete may nevertheless render himself ineligible for further competition as an amateur. The word "non-amateur" would better characterize such athletes than the word "professional."

The basic distinction between the amateur and the non-amateur in athletics is that the amateur, according to the International Amateur Athletic federation, is "one who competes for the love of sport and as a means of recreation, without any motive of securing any material gain from such competition." The Amateur Athletic Union of the United States defines the amateur as "one who engages in sport solely for the pleasure and physical, mental or social benefits he derives therefrom, and to whom sport is nothing more than an avocation." The Amateur Athletic Association of England defines him as "one who has never competed for a money prize or monetary consideration in any Athletic Sport or Game—who has never engaged in, assisted in or taught any athletic exercise for pecuniary consideration, or in any way exploited his athletic ability for profit."

The principal acts by which an athlete may render himself ineligible for amateur competition include: (1) competing, coaching or officiating for money; (2) demanding or receiving excessive or improper expenses; (3) fraud or grossly unsportsmanlike conduct in connection with any competition; (4) selling or pawning of prizes; (5) entering into an agreement for professional competition, which may be evidenced by permitting his name to be used for advertisement of any specific professional competition; (6) knowingly competing with or against ineligible persons without special permission; (7) capitalization of athletic fame, including employment where the athlete's sole or chief value is the publicity given to his athletic fame; (8) permitting use of name or photograph for advertising any product; (9) participation, without special permission, in radio or television broadcast for advertisement of any product; (10) selling or soliciting sale of sporting goods, prizes, trophies, etc., used chiefly in or in connection with sports.

An athlete competing away from his home territory may be reimbursed for his actual traveling expenses, lodging and meals. In international competitions he may receive a pocket-money allowance equivalent to $2.00 per day. Under the rules of the Amateur Athletic Union of the United States the allowance for lodging and meals in addition to traveling expenses may not exceed a total of $15.00 per day, though upon special application showing actual necessity an additional allowance up to $5.00 per day may also be permitted.

After 1946 a new element entered international sport with the arrival of the state amateur. In the U.S.S.R. and other eastern European countries a sport is run by government agencies and is the subject of political control. In such planned societies every permitted activity has a political significance and the distinction between the professional and the amateur becomes meaningless. Since sport has been officially acknowledged as "an excellent vehicle of propaganda in capitalist countries" and one which "helps in the work of foreign diplomatic missions and trade delegations," it is a simple matter for the state committee for sport and physical culture to command leave of absence for any athlete to prepare himself adequately.

Hundreds of athletes each year voluntarily relinquish their amateur status, most of them because they desire in one way or another to profit by their athletic skills or reputations. It is usually only the case of the athlete who desires both to retain such benefits and at the same time retain his status as an amateur that reaches the controversial stage and receives any publicity. The great all-round athlete, Jim Thorpe, lost his amateur status and thereby forfeited the Olympic gold medals won at Stockholm in 1912 because he had admittedly previously received pay for playing with a professional baseball team, an act permanently depriving an athlete of his amateur standing under any rules.

Many of the publicized cases of prominent athletes who have been deprived of their amateur status have been based upon proof of their having demanded or accepted payments in the guise of grossly excessive "expenses." Such was the case with Paavo Nurmi of Finland, Jules Ladoumege of France, Gunder Hägg and Arne Andersson of Sweden and Wes Santee of the United States. The latter's attempt, by court action, to enjoin the Amateur Athletic union from enforcing its rules pertaining to amateurism was emphatically rejected by the supreme court of the state of New York, on May 15, 1956.

The celebrated and oft-cited case of swimming star Eleanor Holm, while often incorrectly referred to as one involving amateur status, in fact involved only her suspension by the U.S. Olympic committee from the 1936 Olympic team for infraction of training rules. No question of amateurism was involved and, until she subsequently embarked upon a professional career, Miss Holm could have competed as an amateur in other competitions.

Suspension of an athlete for some of the above violations, where not involving acceptance of money for competing or coaching, or an act of fraud, etc., may under certain circumstances and conditions be lifted, but usually not prior to a designated period after commission of the last disqualifying act.

Formerly all teachers in any sport were disqualified from amateur competition, but by the second half of the 20th century even physical education teachers who coach athletes for competition were eligible provided they were not paid, directly or indirectly, for such coaching. Similarly lifeguards, playground attendants, camp counselors, etc., who formerly, even if they did not coach or instruct in athletics, were ineligible for amateur competition until after a specified time after termination of such employment, were eligible if not capitalizing upon their athletic fame or ability. The most controversial unresolved issue was that of so-called broken-time payments; i.e., compensatory payments for time lost from business while training for, traveling to and from, or competing in any competition. Such payments remained forbidden, but there were recurrent efforts to relax this rule.

So long as regulation of the rules of amateurism in sport is primarily the responsibility of the bodies governing separate sports in each separate nation, it will obviously remain difficult to obtain a single, uniform, hard and fast code of interpretation and enforcement in each nation, much less throughout the world. *See* also OLYMPIC GAMES; BOXING; CRICKET; ROWING; TRACK AND FIELD SPORTS; etc.   (N. D. McW.; Ps. Sr.)

AMATHUS, an ancient city founded by the Phoenicians about the middle of the 2nd millennium B.C. on the south coast of Cyprus, on a site about 30 mi. S.W. of Larnaca and 6 mi. N.E. of Limassol, among sandy hills and sand dunes, which perhaps explain its name

(Gr. *amathos,* "sand"). The earliest remains found there date from a period soon after the beginning of the Iron Age (*c.* 1500 B.C.). Amathus maintained strong sympathies with the Phoenician mainland and refused to join the revolt of Cyprus against Persia (500–494 B.C.). Similarly, in conjunction with the cities of Citium and Soli about 385–380 B.C., it opposed Evagoras of Salamis who was in revolt against Persia. When, after the death of Alexander the Great, the rest of Cyprus was annexed to Egypt, Amathus resisted annexation. It derived its wealth from grain and from copper mines, of which traces can be seen inland. The rich necropolis has yielded valuable works of art, but the city itself had by the middle of the 20th century not been fully excavated. Its temple of Adonis and Aphrodite was famous in Roman times, hence the Latin epithet "Amathusia" applied to Venus. The city still flourished in the 7th century A.D. but was almost deserted by the 12th.

See C. D. Cobham, *Excerpta Cypria* (1908); E. Gjerstad *et al., The Swedish Cyprus Expedition,* vol. ii (1935). (P. Ds.)

AMATI, the name of a family of celebrated Italian violin makers in Cremona in the 16th and 17th centuries.

ANDREA (*c.* 1520–*c.* 1578), the founder of the Cremona school of violin making, was perhaps originally influenced by the work of slightly earlier makers from Brescia. His earliest known violins are dated about 1564. In essentials, they set the style for all the models made by later members of the family and, with the modifications introduced by Antonio Stradivari (*q.v.*), for the modern violin. Andrea, like his descendants, made violins in two sizes, the larger of which later became known as the "grand Amati." He also introduced the characteristic amber varnish. Like all the family he was born and died in Cremona.

His two sons ANTONIO (*c.* 1550–1638) and GIROLAMO (Hieronymus) (1551–1635) worked together until the latter's death, and are known as the brothers Amati.

NICOLO (1596–1684), the son of Girolamo, was born on Sept. 3, 1596, and died on Aug. 12, 1684. The most famous of the family, he produced instruments notable for beauty of workmanship and tone, and was the master from whom Stradivari and Andrea Guarnieri (*q.v.*), among others, learned their craft. He was succeeded by his son GIROLAMO (1649–1740), who was born on Feb. 26, 1649, and died on Feb. 27, 1740. Although the instruments made by him are as fine as those of his father and grandfather, they suffered in comparison with those made by Stradivari.

The great contribution of the Amatis to the development of the violin was their evolution of the flat, shallow model, which, as improved by Stradivari, proved the fittest to survive in modern concert conditions by reason of the brilliant soprano tone of which it is capable. See also VIOLIN FAMILY. (E. HA.)

AMAUROSIS, a term for loss of vision, limited chiefly to those diseases not directly involving the eye, or involving the optic nerve.

AMAZON, in Greek mythology, one of the fabulous women warriors. The etymology is uncertain, the ancients fancifully deriving the word from the Greek for "breastless," it being said that they destroyed the right breast of their children to prevent it from getting in the way of the bowstring.

The only plausible explanation of the story of the Amazons is that it is a variety of the familiar tale of a distant land where everything is done the wrong way about; thus the women fight, which is man's business. The habitat of the Amazons becomes more remote as Greek geographical knowledge develops. In Homer's *Iliad* they are in Phrygia and Lycia, where Priam and Bellerophon respectively meet them; they are also associated with various legends of Ionia. In the cyclic *Aethiopis* their queen Penthesileia brings a contingent from Thrace to help Priam, and is slain by Achilles.

When the Black sea was colonized by Greeks, this region became the usual Amazon district, the precise place being Themiscyra on the Thermodon river. As there were in fact no Amazons there, it was necessary to explain what became of them, and one of the traditional labours of Hercules was an expedition to get the girdle of their queen for Eurystheus, as a result of which he conquered and expelled them. Subsidiary tales grew up, as that

the Amazons mated with men of another people, kept the female children and sent the males away to their fathers (Strabo, *Geography* xi, 5, 1; *see* the whole chapter for more legends and Herodotus iv, 110 ff. for an earlier form of the story; clearly it is meant to explain why, if the whole nation consisted of women, it did not die out in a generation).

Later than the story of Hercules, an Attic imitation of it arose, in which Theseus attacks the Amazons either with Hercules or independently. The Amazons in turn invade Attica but are finally defeated; at some point in the story Theseus marries one of them, Antiope. Latest of all, in Hellenistic times, the Amazons are associated with Dionysus, either as his allies or, much more commonly, as his opponents. Since the conquests of Dionysus are largely modeled on those of Alexander, it is not surprising that the latter meets an Amazonian queen, who claims to be the noblest of women and wants a child by the noblest of men.

ALINARI PHOTO
GREEK SCULPTURE OF AN AMAZON. VATICAN MUSEUM

In works of art, combats between Amazons and Greeks are placed on the same level as, and often associated with, combats of Greeks and centaurs. Their arms were the bow, spear, light double ax, a half shield, nearly in the shape of a crescent, called *pelta,* and in early art a helmet, the model before the Greek mind having apparently been the goddess Athena. In later art they approach the model of Artemis, wearing a thin dress, girt high for speed; while on the later painted vases their dress is often peculiarly Persian— that is, close-fitting trousers and a high cap called the *kidaris.*

The battle between Theseus and the Amazons is a favourite subject on the friezes of temples (*e.g.,* the reliefs from the frieze of the temple of Apollo at Bassae, in the British museum), vases and sarcophagus reliefs; at Athens it was represented on the shield of the statue of Athena Parthenos, on wall paintings in the Theseum and in the Stoa Poikile.

In the 16th century the Spanish explorer Francisco de Orellana asserted that he had come into conflict with fighting women in South America on the Marañón river which was named after them the Amazon, or river of the Amazons, although others derive its name from the Indian *amassona* (boat destroyer), applied to the tidal phenomenon known as the bore. The existence of "Amazons" (in the sense of fighting women) in the army of Dahomey in Africa in modern times is certain, but they are said to have died out during the French protectorate.

BIBLIOGRAPHY.—G. Grote, *History of Greece,* part i, ch. xi; L. Whibley, *Companion to Greek Studies,* 4th ed. (1931); Plutarch, *Greek Questions,* trans. by W. R. Halliday (1928). (H. J. R.; X.)

AMAZON (AMAZONAS), the greatest river of South America and the largest river in the world in volume and in the area of its drainage basin. While the name Amazon, or Amazonas, is popularly employed for the whole of the main stream, in Peruvian and Brazilian nomenclature it is properly applied only to sections of it. In Peru the upper stream, from its source to Iquitos, is called Marañón (Port., Maranhão) and from there to the sea, Amazonas. In Brazil the name Solimões is used from Iquitos to the mouth of the Negro river and Amazonas only from the Negro river to the sea.

In 1500, Vicente Yáñez Pinzón, in command of a Spanish expedition, discovered and ascended the principal mouth of the Amazon to a point about 50 mi. from the sea. He called it the Río Santa María de la Mar Dulce, which soon became abbreviated to Mar Dulce. The companions of Pinzón, in giving evidence in 1515, mention it as El Río Marañón, a name originally applied to the mouth of the Pará south of Marajó Island and later to the upper part of the main stream.

The first descent of the river from the Andes to the Atlantic

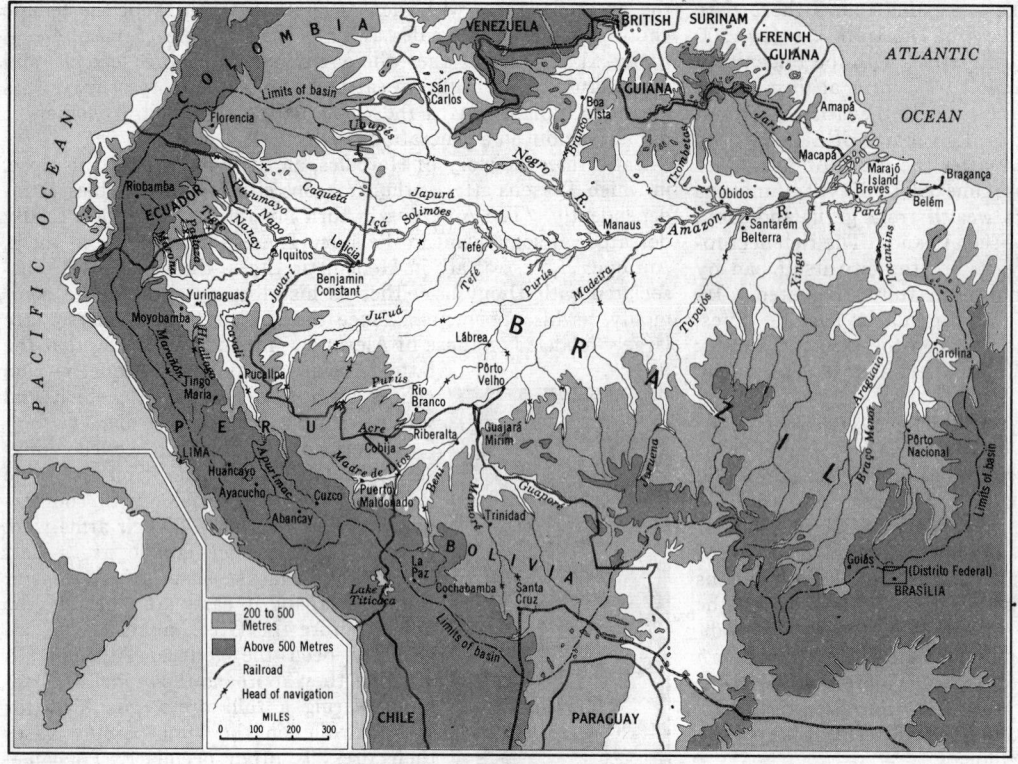

AMAZON RIVER BASIN AND DRAINAGE SYSTEM

The Amazon is less a single river than a network of rivers draining the largest area of equatorial rainy climate in the world. Seventeen of its tributaries have lengths in excess of 1,000 mi. Beginning with the lower river the major tributaries to the main stream will be discussed in order, beginning with the southern or larger affluents.

TRIBUTARIES

The TOCANTINS is not really a branch of the Amazon. It is the central fluvial artery of Brazil, running from south to north for a distance of 1,677 mi. It rises in the Planalto Central, near the city of Goiás and the site of the new capital of the republic at Brasília. Its more ambitious western affluent, the Araguaia, has its headwaters even farther south and flows 1,366 mi. before its junction with the parent stream, which appears almost to equal it in volume. Above the junction of the Araguaia with the main stream the Tocantins is interrupted in many places by rapids and sand bars. It is navigable only in its lower course. The Pará river, generally called one of the mouths of the Amazon, is really the estuary of the Tocantins, linked with the Amazon by the navigable Breves channel.

The XINGU, the next large river west of the Tocantins, was first explored by Karl von den Steinen in 1884–87. The river is formed at about 14° S. latitude, on the northern slopes of Brazil's Planalto Central, about 150 mi. northeast of Cuiabá. For most of its length of 1,304 mi. the Xingu is marked by a succession of falls and rapids that are serious obstacles even to canoe navigation.

The TAPAJÓS pours into the Amazon 500 mi. above Belém and is about 807 mi. long. Its headwaters are just to the west of the headwaters of the Xingu at 14° 25′ S. latitude. Near this place a number of streams unite to form the Arinos river. The Arinos, the Alto Tapajós and the Tapajós to the last rapid, the Maranhão Grande, is a continuous series of formidable cataracts and rapids; but from the Maranhão Grande to its mouth, about 188 mi., the river can be navigated by large vessels.

The MADEIRA has its junction with the Amazon 870 mi. by river above Belém, and almost rivals it in the volume of its waters. It has a length of 2,013 mi. and is navigable for 807 mi. It rises more than 50 ft. during the rainy season, and the largest ocean steamers may ascend it to the Falls of Santo António, 663 mi. above its mouth; but in the dry months, from June to November, it is navigable for the same distance only by craft drawing from 5 to 6 ft. of water. The Madeira begins where the Beni joins the Mamoré. The major tributary of the Mamoré is the Guaporé. The Guaporé has its headwaters almost in contact with the great Pantanal, probably the largest swamp in South America, which is part of the Paraguay-La Plata river system. Santo António is the first of a formidable series of cataracts and rapids, 19 in number, which, for a river distance of 263 mi., obstruct the upper course of the Madeira until the last rapid, called Guajará Mirim (small pebble), is reached, about 120 mi. below the union of the Guaporé with the Mamoré. The Madeira-Mamoré railroad circumvents these rapids. The Beni and the Mamoré join at the Madeira rapids, a stretch of nearly 5 mi. of reefs, whirlpools and rapids, about 40 mi. below the Guajará Mirim rapids. From the Guaporé, Mamoré and Beni rivers the Madeira receives the drainage from the whole of the eastern and northeastern slopes of the Andes from the southernmost sources of the Rio Grande

ocean was made in 1541 by Francisco de Orellana (q.v.), who reached the main stream by way of the Napo river. It is rather generally accepted that the name Amazonas was given to the river by Orellana after a battle with the Tapuyan Indians in which he believed that the women of the tribe fought side by side with the men. The first ascent of the river was made in 1638 by Pedro Teixeira, a Portuguese, who reversed the route of Orellana and reached Quito by the Napo.

The Amazon river has a drainage area of about 2,722,000 sq.mi. if the Tocantins river is included. This is nearly twice as large as the area drained by any of the other great rivers of the earth. It drains four-tenths of South America, including the world's largest continuous block of tropical rain forest, and gathers its waters from 5° N. to 20° S. latitude.

The source of the Amazon has long been the subject of speculation on the part of geographers and explorers. The main stream rises in a chain of glacier-fed lakes near the western edge of the Andes in central Peru about 100 mi. from the Pacific ocean, and flows for 3,915 mi. across Peru and Brazil to enter the Atlantic on the equator. The Ucayali-Apurímac-Amazon system, which heads near Lake Titicaca, is somewhat longer, but not long enough to challenge the 4,157-mi. Nile for the title of world's longest river.

The discharge of the Amazon has never been accurately measured, but on the basis of the amount of precipitation falling on its drainage area it is believed to exceed 4,200,000 cu.ft. per second, seven times that of the Mississippi. During the rainy season it probably exceeds 7,000,000 cu.ft. per second. Its discharge is detectable 200 mi. at sea and tides are felt upriver 600 mi., as far as Óbidos. It has been estimated that the Amazon carries nearly one-fifth of all the fresh water that runs off the earth's land surface. This tremendous volume results from the fact that the Amazon and its tributaries drain an area of equatorial lowlands where rainfall ranges from 70 to 120 in. annually. More than two-thirds of the immense Amazon basin lies within Brazil, but it also embraces large areas of Peru, Bolivia, Ecuador, Colombia and Venezuela. The main stream is navigable for large ocean-going vessels as far as Iquitos, 2,300 mi. from the sea, and for smaller ships 486 mi. further to the Pongo de Manseriche. With its tributaries, many of which approach the size of the main stream, it composes a fluvial net unequaled in the world.

(a tributary of the Mamoré) at about 20° S. latitude to the northernmost sources of the Madre de Dios river (tributary of the Beni) at about 12° S. latitude, the whole of the southwestern slope of the Brazilian Mato Grosso, and the northern slope of the Sierra de Chiquitos in the Gran Chaco. All of the upper branches of the Madeira flow across open, almost level plains, which are yearly flooded to an average depth of three feet for a period of from three to four months.

The PURUS, a very sluggish river of 1,995 mi., enters the Amazon about 230 mi. W. of the Madeira, which it parallels as far as the falls of the latter stream. It is practically a great drainage ditch for the half-submerged, lake-flooded district it traverses. It is one of the most crooked rivers in the world, its length in a straight line being less than half that by its meanders.

The JURUÁ is the next great southern affluent of the Amazon west of the Purús and traverses the same sort of low, half-flooded country as the latter. It rises in the highlands east of the Ucayali which carry the Peru-Brazil boundary and is navigable for a distance of 621 mi. above its junction with the Amazon.

The JAVARÍ (656 mi.), the boundary line between Brazil and Peru, is another Amazon tributary of importance. It is navigable by canoe only from above its mouth to its sources among the Ucayali highlands, but only a fraction has been found suitable for navigation by larger boats. The Brazilian Boundary commission ascended it in 1866 to the junction of the Shino with its Javarí branch. The country it traverses in its extremely sinuous course is very level, similar in character to that of the Juruá.

The UCAYALI is among the major tributaries of the Amazon. Its headwaters drain a great section of the Peruvian plateau from the source of the Vilcanota river only 70 mi. N.W. of Lake Titicaca to the sources of the Mantaro west of Cerro de Pasco. The lower 500 mi. of the main channel is bordered by large islands formed by numerous side channels, the whole being very low and flooded in the rainy season. The Ucayali is navigable for light draft launches as far as the Tambo-Urubamba junction. Large steam vessels reach as far as the Peruvian city of Pucallpa (pop. about 20,000), which is the terminus of the trans-Andean highway from Lima, and after Iquitos, the largest city in the Peruvian Oriente. South of Pucallpa, on the Pachitea river, a left bank tributary of the Ucayali, lies the Ganzo Azul oil field and the Tournavista agricultural colony, the latter a North American settlement venture.

The HUALLAGA, which joins the Marañón about midway between the Pongo de Manseriche and the mouth of the Ucayali, has its true source in the Yanahuanca river, a stream flowing from a series of glacier-fed lakes northwest of the famous mining centre of Cerro de Pasco. The name Huallaga is applied, however, to a more easterly and much less important headwater tributary which rises a short distance east of Cerro de Pasco. The whole stream is deeply entrenched and from the town of Huánuco to the mouth of the river much of its course is impeded by rapids and gorges.

The MARAÑÓN river rises in Lake Lauricocha, the northernmost of a chain of glacier-fed lakes about 100 mi. N.N.E. of Lima and flows northward in a deeply eroded valley. It is because of this and other deeply entrenched longitudinal valleys, cut by the tributaries of the Amazon, that the erroneous conception of the Peruvian Andes as three separate mountain ranges has arisen. At about 5° 30′ S. latitude the river makes a great bend toward the northeast and, after passing through a succession of narrows or *pongos* and no less than 35 formidable rapids, it breaks through the easternmost range of the Andes to the Amazon plain by a great canyon known as the Pongo de Manseriche. This canyon is about 2,000 ft. deep and narrows in places to a width of only 100 ft. Through this dark canyon the Marañón flows, at times, at a rate of over 12 mi. an hour. Beyond the *pongo* the river receives several large tributaries from the north and spreads out into a broad stream with numerous channels and islands.

From the north the Amazon receives many tributaries, but their total volume of water is not nearly so great as that contributed to the parent stream by its affluents from the south. The part of Brazil lying between the Amazon and French, Dutch and British Guiana, and bounded on the west by the Negro, is known as

Brazilian Guiana. It is the southern slope of the Guiana highlands, geologically a part of the larger Brazilian highland which lies south of the Amazon.

The TROMBETAS is the first river of importance on the northern side when ascending the Amazon. Its confluence with the Amazon is just above the town of Óbidos. It has its sources in the Guiana highlands, but its long course is frequently interrupted by violent currents, rocky barriers and rapids. The river is navigable for 149 mi. above its mouth.

The NEGRO, the great northern tributary of the Amazon, has its sources along the watershed between the Orinoco and the Amazon basins, and also receives some of the water from the upper Orinoco by way of the Casiquiare canal. The Negro is navigable in the dry season for 423 mi. above its mouth for vessels of 4-ft. draft, but it has many sandbanks and minor obstructions. In the wet season it overflows its banks, in places to a width of 20 mi. Its lower course is very wide and full of long islands and intricate channels. The main headwater affluent of the Negro is the Uaupés. Its principal affluent from the north is the Branco formed by the union of the Uraricoera and Tacutú which, with their tributaries, drain a large section of the southerly slopes of the Guiana highlands which separate Brazil from Venezuela and British Guiana. The Branco flows nearly straight south for 350 mi. to the Negro which it enters by numerous channels similar to those of the lower course of the latter.

The Casiquiare canal which connects the upper Orinoco, about 18 mi. below the old mission site of Esmeralda, with the Negro, a tributary of the Amazon, near the village of San Carlos, is a natural waterway, the only one of its kind known in the world. The Negro is in the process of capturing the upper Orinoco. According to data obtained by the Rice expedition, which made a survey of the canal in 1919, the length of the canal is 204 mi. Its width at its beginning in the Orinoco is 758 ft.; but this rapidly narrows down to 150 ft. and widens again to 2,150 ft. at its mouth in the Negro. The level of the water at the Orinoco end was found to be 283 ft. and, at the Negro end, 212 ft., giving the canal an average slope toward the Negro of 7.2 in. per mile.

The JAPURÁ or CAQUETÁ. West of the Negro the Amazon receives three imposing streams from the northwest—the Japurá, the Içá or Putumayo and the Napo. The first was formerly known as the Yapurá, but its Brazilian part is now called the Japurá, and its Colombian portion the Caquetá. Jules Crevaux, who descended it, describes it as full of obstacles to navigation, the current very strong and the stream frequently interrupted by rapids and cataracts. It rises in the Colombian Andes, nearly in touch with the sources of the Magdalena.

The IÇÁ or PUTUMAYO rises in the Colombian Andes east of Pasto, flows through the rain forest along the Colombia-Ecuador and Colombia-Peru border to join the Amazon at Santo António do Içá, Braz. Most of its nearly 1,000 mi. length is navigable for shallow-draft vessels.

The NAPO rises among the volcanoes of the eastern border of the Andes in northern Ecuador. Its headwater tributaries in the Ecuadorian Oriente flow through one of the least known areas of the eastern border of the Andes. The Coca, which has its source on the slopes of Cayambe volcano close to the equator, and the Aguarico, an important river with headwaters between Cayambe and the Colombian frontier, join it from the north. The Curaray, transecting an area rich in rubber, joins it from the south about 200 mi. from its mouth. The Napo is navigable for river craft to this point and by canoes to the mouth of the Coca. The Curaray-Coca section of the river is little known.

The NANAY, TIGRE, PASTAZA and MORONA are the major Amazon tributaries between Iquitos and the Pongo de Manseriche. Above the Pongo two important tributaries, the Santiago and the Chinchipe, join the Marañón from the north.

THE MAIN RIVER

Physical Characteristics.—The Amazon valley is a great structural depression, a subsidence trough filled with Tertiary sediments, which flares out to its greatest dimension in the upper reaches. It lies between two old and not very high crystalline plateaus, the rugged Guiana massif on the north and the lower Brazilian massif, lying somewhat farther from the main river, on the south. The Amazon valley was occupied by a great fresh-water sea during the Pliocene period. Sometime during the Pleistocene an outlet to the Atlantic was established and the great river and its tributaries became deeply entrenched into the Pliocene surface.

The modern Amazon and its tributaries occupy a great drowned valley. With the rise in sea level that followed the melting of the ice caps the steep-sided canyons that had been eroded into the Pliocene surface during the lower sea stand were flooded. The old lake surface is the soil of the terra firma on which much of the Amazon forest has developed. In the upper part of the valley, in the Peruvian and Bolivian Oriente, more recent outwash from the Andes has covered many of the older surfaces.

At the Óbidos narrows, where the river is constricted to a width of a little more than a mile, the average depth of the channel below the mean water level is 300 ft.; in most of the Brazilian part of the river its depth exceeds 150 ft. Yet at the Peruvian border, 2,500 mi. from the Atlantic, the elevation above sea level is less than 300 ft. The maximum free width (without islands) of the river's permanent bed is 8½ mi., upstream from the mouth of the Xingu. During great floods, however, when it completely fills the flood plain, it spreads out in a band 35 mi. wide or more. The average velocity of the Amazon is about one and one-half miles an hour, a speed that increases greatly at flood time.

The great river gradually rises from November to June, and then falls until the end of October. The rise of the Negro branch does not occur at the same time, for the steady rains do not commence in its valley until February or March. By June the Negro is full, and then it begins to fall with the Amazon. The flood levels are in places from 40 to 50 ft. above low river. Taking four roughly equidistant points, the rise at Iquitos is 20 ft., at Tefé 45, near Óbidos 35, and at Belém 12.

The Amazon does not meander in the fashion of the Mississippi but for the most part follows a remarkably straight course. It is still in the process of refilling its broad river-cut valley by its own alluvium, depositing silt into settling basins on a massive scale during each flood season. The size of the flood plain is moderate when compared with the volume of the river. The zone of active alluviation is typically 12–30 mi. wide and is bordered by steep cliffs (*barrancas*), often capped by a horizon of laterite rock (*canga*). Where these cliffs are being undercut by the river they produce the *terras caidas* or "fallen lands" so often referred to by Amazon travelers.

The so-called "black-water" tributaries of the Amazon, the Xingu, Tapajós, Negro, Tefé and Trombetas, carry little or no silt, in part because of the bleached sandy character of the country at their headwaters. The Tapajós and Xingu are in reality a bright emerald-green, for they lack the strong solution of humic matter that characterizes the Negro. Where such streams enter the main river they are blocked off to form true fresh-water lakes and resemble in form, width and depth marine rias.

The first highland met in ascending the river is on the north bank, opposite the mouth of the Xingu, and extends for about 150 mi. up, as far as Monte Alegre. It is a series of steep, table-topped hills, in part of Devonian and Carboniferous Age, interrupted by diabase intrusions. On the south side, above the Xingu, a line of low bluffs extends in a series of gentle curves with hardly any breaks nearly to Santarém. The line is a considerable distance inland, bordering the flood plain, which is many miles wide. Then the bluffs bend to the southwest, and, abutting upon the lower Tapajós, merge into the bluffs which form the terrace margin of that river valley. The next highland on the north side is Óbidos, a bluff 56 ft. above the river, backed by low hills. From Itaquatiara, nearly opposite the river Madeira, to near the mouth of the Negro, the banks are low. Approaching Manaus there are rolling hills; but from the Negro, for 600 mi., as far up as the village of Canaria, at the great bend of the Amazon, only very low land is found, resembling that at the mouth of the river.

On the south side, from the Tapajós to the river Madeira, the banks are usually low, although two or three hills break the general monotony. From the latter river to the Ucayali, a distance

of about 1,500 mi., the forested banks are just out of water, and are inundated long before the river attains its maximum flood line. Thence to the Huallaga the elevation of the land is somewhat greater; but not until this river is passed, and the Pongo de Manseriche approached, does the swelling ground of the Andean foothills raise the country above flood level.

The width of the mouth of the river is usually measured from Cabo Norte to Ponta Tijoca, a distance of 207 statute miles; but this includes the ocean outlet, 40 mi. wide, of the Pará river, which should be deducted, as this stream is only the lower reach of the Tocantins. It also includes the ocean frontage of Marajó, an island about the size of the kingdom of Denmark lying in the mouth of the Amazon. Following the coast, a little to the north of Cabo Norte, and for 100 mi. along its Guiana margin up the Amazon, is a belt of half-submerged islands and shallow sandbanks. There the tidal phenomenon called the bore, or pororoca, occurs, where the soundings are not more than four fathoms. It commences with a roar, constantly increasing, and advances at the rate of from 10 to 15 mi. an hour, with a breaking wall of water from 5 to 12 ft. high. Under such conditions of warfare between the ocean and the river, it is not surprising that the Amazon finds it impossible to build up a delta. Most of the 3,000,000 tons of sediment that the Amazon discharges daily into the sea is carried northward by coastal currents to be deposited along the Guiana coast.

Vegetation.—In diversity of forms and profusion of individuals the plant life of the Amazon river basin is probably the richest on the globe. Within the area drained by this river system, species of practically every ecological type find homes. Most of the idiosyncrasies of the plant kingdom are in evidence, for this enormous territory presents a myriad-faced environment, and each face has its own peculiar complement of plant inhabitants.

The dominant feature of the area is the Amazonian rain forest or selva, one of the most extraordinary vegetation panoramas on earth. It widens from a 200 mi. front on the Atlantic to a belt 1,200 mi. wide where the lowlands meet the Andean foothills, interrupted only by the rivers and, especially below Parintins, by local areas of campos or grassland.

The massiveness and continuity of the great forest, which covers almost the entire geographical area of Amazonia, is above all a reflection of the high rainfall, high humidity and monotonously high temperatures which prevail. Man's imprint on the natural landscape is singularly inconspicuous. The forest itself is, in a sense, a great plant museum, for it is considered by botanists to represent perhaps the oldest vegetation formation on earth, essentially unchanged from Tertiary times.

The most striking characteristics of these vast woods are: the comparative absence of pure stands of any tree species; the paucity of forest giants in large groups; the division of the vertical height of the forest into stories or floors; the multitudes of very different types, both as to form and habit, jumbled together, often in the most tangled confusion; the general absence of seasonal leaf fall and flowering time; the small percentage of soft woods; the number of tree forms with prop roots or buttressed trunks; the long distance between the forest floor and the first branches; the absence of great masses of floral colour and, comparatively speaking, the light colour of the bark.

In the middle latitudes, solid forests of one or a few species are characteristic, so that they are designated under the name of their dominant species, such as oak or pine forests. On an acre of Amazon forest, in most regions, scores of species occur, but only a few individuals of each, although there are considerable areas that might be called laurel forests.

Palms, myrtles, laurels, acacias, bignonias, cedrelas, cecropias, rosewoods, Bombacaceae, Brazil-nuts, rubber trees, figs, purplehearts and dozens of others often grow on one small area. Within a half-mile square, Louis Agassiz counted 117 different woods. In some regions, particularly rain forest on certain mountain slopes, tree ferns add to the variety. Legumes constitute the most important of all the families as much for their great number of species as for the high economic value of their woods. Conifers are absent.

Seen from the air the equatorial forest looks like an immense and continuous carpet with a spongy surface, uniform and monotonous. The abundant evergreen foliage of its canopy unites the crowns of its tallest trees at approximately the same level, usually from 100 to 150 ft. above the surface of the ground. The forest that grows on the flood-plain lands (*várzea*) of the Amazon and its tributaries and subtributaries can be distinguished from that occurring on the older, higher surfaces, terra firma, that stand above the level of the highest floods.

The *várzea* forest is the classical rain forest as described by early Amazon travelers who of necessity restricted their movements largely to the water courses. It has a greater botanical diversity than does that on higher ground, perhaps in part because of the quantity and variety of the seeds carried by the annual floodwaters and deposited on the rich soil of the flood plain. On the flood plain the so-called "white" or soft woods predominate; among them the Pará rubber tree (*Hevea brasiliensis*). One of the more typical trees is the *sumaúma* (*Ceiba*) or kapok whose thick, whitish trunk and tall, spreading crown have led it to be called the "queen of the *várzea*." On the upper Amazon and its tributaries, but not on the Negro and other black-water rivers, large areas of the *várzea* are dominated by the tall-plumed cane grass, *cana brava* (*Gynerium*). On the lower river and on Marajó Island the arborescent relative of the calla lily, *Montrichardia arborescens,* is a conspicuous element of the riverine formation. The giant water lily (*Victoria regia*) grows in the shallow backwater lagoons. The lower parts of the *várzea*, which are longest flooded, are the sites of extensive grasslands (*campos de várzea*) located along the edges of permanent or seasonal lakes and behind the natural levees, but this is true only from about Parintins downstream to the mouth of the Xingu. On the black-water rivers the *várzea* is usually replaced by overhanging cliffs or, as on the Tocantins, white sand beaches. Small streams of this character are often completely arched by the tangle of high forest and lianas.

The drier Tertiary surfaces above the flood plain typically support species with a higher density that are more valuable as construction timber. These include the *mogno* (*Swietenia mahogani*), *acapú* (*Vouacapoua americana*), *andiroba* (*Carapa guianensis*), *cedro* (*Cedrela*), *massaranduba* (*Mimusops huberi*), *pau rosa* (*Aniba rosaeodora*), *pau d'arco* (*Tecoma*) and an infinity of other species. The *castanheiro* (*Bertholletia excelsa*), source of the Brazil nut of commerce, also makes good construction lumber and is typically found on higher lands, as is the latex-yielding *caucho* (*Castilla*). So are several of the palms that produce nuts of economic value.

The region of the Amazon basin richest in flowers and colour is the little-explored, lichen-choked cloud forest or *ceja de la montaña*, home of the Cinchona, that fringes the tree limit on the eastern flanks of the Andes. Many of the plants recall the middle latitudes, although the species are generally different. Lupines, gentians, barberries, fuchsias, viburnums, lycopodiums, buddleias, raspberries and clematis are typical.

Some of the most valuable economic plants are indigenous to the Amazon valley. In addition to those already cited, the valley contains quinine, cacao, cassava (*Manihot utilissima*) from which tapioca is derived, sarsaparilla, ipecacuanha (the source of ipecac), copaiba, tonka beans for flavouring tobacco, annotto (*Bixa orellana*) for colouring butter and cheese, Pará rubber (*Hevea*), balata, rosewood, snakewood, guava, calabash, coca from which cocaine is derived, *guaraná* (*Paullinia cupana*) and, in the highlands, another long list headed by the white potato.

One of the most noteworthy features of the vegetation of the middle and lower parts of the Amazon valley, and one not fully appreciated until the advent of the airplane, is the considerable extent of scrub brush and short grassland (campos) on the higher regions between the main rivers. Palm and leathery-leaved, drought-resistant trees such as the *caimbé* (*Curatella americana*) are typically scattered over the surface of these poorly drained prairies. In most of the lower Amazon below Manaus, though not in the immediate vicinity of Belém, there is a fairly well-marked dry season with bright weather and only occasional thundershowers from July to September that permits annual burning. The

physical and chemical properties of the soils of these long-weathered surfaces also have had a marked effect on the vegetation in many areas, as on the sandy lower terrace behind Santarém and the plateau of Monte Alegre. The largest continuous areas of campos vegetation are to be found on the north side of the Amazon, especially the Rio Branco and Trombetas drainage, on the coast of Amapá province north of the Amazon mouth, and on Marajó Island.

Fauna.—Although the fauna of the Amazon valley is noteworthy for the variety and number of its genera and species, it is very deficient not only in species of the larger mammals but also in the individuals of these comparatively few species. In contrast with other regions of the world, a large percentage of the mammals are tree dwellers. None of them will attack man unprovoked, under ordinary circumstances. The monkeys are all arboreal and are common below 3,000 ft. altitude. The best known are the red howlers or *guaribas,* which make the great forest resound with their morning and evening choruses. Other common species are the spider, night, saki, marmoset, titi and squirrel monkeys. A scarlet-faced, almost tailless species occurs near Tefé. All forms are hunted and eaten by the aborigines. There are six species of the cat family, among which are the jaguar, puma or cougar, and the ocelot.

This region is particularly rich in rodents. The largest rodent species in the world, the capybara, is indigenous and common along the stream banks. It is said to attain a length of over four feet and a weight of over 50 kg. (100 lb.). Other common rodents are the paca (*Coelogenys*), cutia or agouti (*Dasyprocta*), *sauia* or spiny rat, *toro* (*Loncheres*), several species of squirrels, rats and mice, and two species of porcupines. Paca meat is highly esteemed, but the capybara and a number of other animals are also eaten.

The largest animal is the *anta* or tapir, which makes its home in the giant canebrakes along the streams. There are two species of peccary (*Dicotyles*). One of these, the *queixada* or *porco de matto,* lives in bands of 100 or more.

Five species of armadillos or *tatú* occur, both the giant and the pygmy species being represented. The former reaches a length of three feet. Of the three species of anteaters, two of them are tree-dwelling, while the giant anteater or *Myrmecophaga tridactyla* is generally a savanna animal. The two-toed sloths are both forest forms, and one species lives largely on Cecropia leaves, while the other has a more varied plant diet of foilage and fruit. The flesh of the latter recalls mutton.

Four species of deer are found on the savannas and neighbouring woods, and thousands of hides are exported. The three species of opossums range in size from the *mucura,* as large as a cat, to the mouse-dimensioned *mucura chichica* with large eyes.

Bats by the million fan the Amazon night air, and represent numerous species and genera. Among them are the bloodsucking vampires (*Dysopes, Phyllostoma*), although these are by no means as dangerous as travelers' tales would lead one to believe.

The sea cow or manatee is common in the lakes and is hunted for its meat, which resembles pork. It is one of the most peculiar mammals of the region, with its cowlike face, its small eyes and its two large, well-developed pectoral mammae.

The area is exceedingly rich in bird life. The great valley teems with species, genera and individuals. Vultures, the universal scavengers, are always alert for work. Morning and evening the parrots and macaws, two by two, in brilliant aerial processions, fly to and from their feeding grounds, their gorgeous plumage flashing in the sun, and their raucous voices calling out their presence. Toucans cry at sundown a discordant plaint from some tall, trailside tree. Through the day the hangnests or caciques quarrel in trees where their nests swing by dozens. Doves of various species dolorously coo through the hot afternoons. Hawks and eagles scream from dead tree stumps. The forest aisles ring with the clear, silvery, metallic notes of the *uirá purú* (*Pachysilvia*). At sundown *perdiz* or tinamous call out as do the quail. At night the air vibrates with the *correos* of the goatsuckers and whippoorwills. Early morning is full of the clattering music of the pheasantlike Pavos. Hoatzins screech in noisy flocks from streamside brush.

There is always the twittering of legions of small birds, the sound of busy woodpeckers and the guttural noises of various waterbirds. Parakeets fly about in great flocks, more common than sparrows in the United States.

One of the principal food supplies of the valley is the river turtle or tartaruga (*Podocnemis*). In former times millions of turtle eggs were annually gathered from the river sand bars at low water to be dried and rendered into an illuminating and cooking oil. Their numbers are now much reduced. The swamps, sluggish streams and lakes usually contain one or more species of cayman. Lizards of various sizes and colours dart back and forth across the trails. The snakes are not numerous, relatively speaking, but representatives of both poisonous groups occur. The constrictors reach huge proportions, 18 to 20 ft. not being rare. Snakes, however, are not a prominent feature of Amazon life; perhaps the poisonous varieties observed are not more than one in 20 or 30.

The number of fish species of the Amazon has been estimated at about 500 to 2,000, but only a few of them are of economic importance. Of these, the pirarucu is the most sought after. The scales of one species are utilized for making artificial flowers. In the half-covered forest pools, the electric eel is at home. Most of the streams are well stocked with the bloodthirsty piranha (*Serrasalmo*). Giant catfish are common and sting rays are present.

Insects are numerous in the Amazon. Countless multitudes of ants work night and day. Their work varies with the species. Some, like the saubas or leaf cutters, are farmers; others are always on marauding expeditions; while still others live in certain types of trees, and sting as well as bite. Termites, the so-called white ants, abound and cause great destruction to nearly anything of wood. Fireflies with yellow, red and green light make toy fairylands of little brooks, while a host of other insects by various devices, depending on the region, turn a paradise into purgatory. The bees are stingless, but hornets and wasps are plentiful. *Titanus giganteus*, one of the largest beetles known (5 to 6 in. long), is native. The larvae of some of the palm beetles are relished when fried. Cockroaches are everpresent. Part of the afternoon and evening music is furnished by several species of cicadas, one of which sounds like a shrill steam whistle. Centipedes, scorpions, ticks, red bugs and giant spiders are often encountered. Finally, there are the moths and butterflies, hundreds of kinds and thousands of individuals, in marvelous assortments of brilliant colours and patterns. Within an hour's walk of Belém, 700 species have been collected; around Tefé, Henry W. Bates collected 8,000 species of insects, of which 550 were species of butterflies.

Navigation.—On Sept. 6, 1850, the emperor Dom Pedro II sanctioned a law authorizing steam navigation on the Amazon, and confided to an illustrious Brazilian, Barão Mauá (Irineu Evangelista de Sousa), the task of carrying it into effect. He organized the "Companhia de Navigação e Commercio do Amazonas" at Rio de Janeiro in 1852; and in the following year it commenced operations with three small steamers, the "Monarch," the "Marajó" and "Rio Negro." At first the navigation was principally confined to the main river; and even in 1857 a modification of the government contract required the company to provide only monthly service between Belém and Manaus, with steamers of 200 tons cargo capacity, a second line to make six round-trip voyages a year between Manaus and Tabatinga and a third, two trips a month between Belém and Cametá. The government paid the company a subvention of £3,935 monthly. Thus, the first impulse of modern progress was given to the dormant valley. The success of the venture called attention to the unoccupied field; a second company soon opened commerce on the Madeira, Purús and Negro; a third established a line between Belém and Manaus; and a fourth navigated some of the smaller streams. Meanwhile the Amazonas company had largely increased its fine fleet. The latter was bought out in 1874 by an English group and, reorganized as the Amazon Steam Navigation company, continued its increasingly profitable operations as the rubber trade began to expand. The Amazon historically had been closed to foreign traffic. Pressure was strong from both Washington and London to internationalize it. The visit of Professor Louis Agassiz and the emperor's interest in his work powerfully aided the movement. On Dec. 7, 1866, a decree by Dom Pedro opened the river and certain tributaries to the ships of the world. Peru under an earlier treaty had been granted access to the sea, but now Bolivia, Ecuador and Colombia were similarly relieved from a dependence on trans-Andean trails to reach outside markets.

Rubber.—From 1872 to 1910 the economic life of the Amazon region was focused on the production of rubber from trees growing wild in the forest. Although crude rubber was sent from the Amazon as early as 1827, it was not until Charles Goodyear (*q.v.*) invented the vulcanizing process in 1839 that the annual exportation attained commercial importance. With the remarkable increase in the demand for rubber, prices rose, and gatherers in the forests were sent further afield.

In 1910, however, the increasing competition of low-cost plantation rubber from Malaya and Sumatra brought a disastrous decline of the prices. The whole system of rubber gatherers and traders collapsed, and many families were left stranded in remote places. Many towns were abandoned to the forest.

In 1927 the Ford Motor company established a Brazilian subsidiary to experiment with plantation rubber. Two plantations of 2,500,000 ac. and 600,000 ac., respectively, were established on the Tapajós river. The experiment was not successful because of the scarcity of workers. After World War II the plantations were given to the Brazilian government, which undertook their operation. The original Fordlandia plantation has been abandoned, but at Belterra, where growing conditions are more favourable, some 2,500,000 trees were growing in 1957. Only one out of three was of bearing age.

Trading Spheres.—The vast network of rivers is organized under the control of a hierarchy of traders. Since travel away from the rivers is virtually impossible, the people scattered in small communities along the river banks are dependent for their connections with the outside world on the launch of the trader to whom they are in debt. The largest trading companies are at Belém and Manaus; many smaller traders are controlled by the big companies, each of which occupies a strategic point at a river junction and controls all upstream communications. From many small villages comes a considerable movement of goods downstream, including such products as Brazil nuts, rotenone, cabinet woods, skins and substantial quantities of rubber. In return the traders supply foodstuffs, tools and firearms. The trader acts as purchasing agent for the special needs of his people; through the traders new medicines and drugs, new tools and machines, and even new ideas trickle into the vast region.

Air lines, radio and telegraphy offer connections between the larger towns along the main stream and the world outside. Almost all the towns have small electric light systems, and some are supplied with water from wells. Three railways were in operation in 1957: the Madeira-Mamoré railway, which runs for 226 mi. around the falls of the Madeira (opened in 1912, it never actually was completed to the Bolivian town of Riberalta on the Beni); the railway from Belém to Bragança; and the 126-mi. Amapá railroad completed in 1956 from a new river port near Macapá to the Serra do Navio manganese mine, one of the world's largest.

Exploration.—The unparalleled richness and diversity of the Amazon's fauna and flora and the scantiness of the human population in its unmapped vastness have attracted a steady succession of scientists and explorers. Outstanding among them have been the great naturalists such as C. M. de La Condamine, Alexander Humboldt, Karl von Martius, Robert Schomburgk, Prince Adalbert of Prussia, A. R. Wallace, H. W. Bates, Richard Spruce and Louis Agassiz, all of whom contributed importantly to the scientific knowledge of the area. The expeditions of Lieut. W. L. Herndon of the U.S. army (1851–52) and Lieutenants Henry Lister Maw (1827) and William Smyth (1835) of the British Royal Navy were also important milestones in Amazonian exploration.

Among the later and better-equipped expeditions the one of Theodore Roosevelt and Col. Cándido Rondón, which explored the Amazon, Tapajós and Madeira and their tributaries, was outstanding. It was initiated on the retirement of Roosevelt from the presidency of the United States in the autumn of 1913 and terminated in Belém in May 1914. The Rice expedition, sponsored by the Harvard Institute of Geographical Exploration, carried on diverse scientific activities from 1910 to 1924. Expeditions have also been sponsored by the American Geographical society and various United Nations organizations. Brazilian scientists have increasingly concerned themselves with the Amazon region. This is especially true of scientists associated with the Instituto Agronômico do Norte and the Museu Goeldi de História Natural e Etnografia, both located in Belém, the Conselho Nacional de Geografia, and the Instituto Nacional de Pesquisas da Amazônia, established in 1954, in Manaus.

Population.—The dense Indian population reported by Orellana along the river's banks suffered an early and catastrophic decline. Large-scale immigration, chiefly from the drought-stricken northeast (Ceará) area, was especially associated with the rubber bonanza period between 1850 and 1910, but it has continued sporadically to the present. The Amazon *caboclo* population has a large Indian component and the Indian contributed more to the culture of the Amazon region than to any other part of Brazil. Until well into the 19th century the *lingua geral,* a modified form of the Tupi-Guaraní tongue, was the most spoken language of the area.

The Amazon basin is one of the great demographic vacuums of the world. The Brazilian government estimated the population of the six federal units making up the Brazilian Amazon to be 2,321,-000 in 1960 (1,844,655 by the 1950 census) of which about 320,000 lived in Belém and another 170,000 in Manaus and vicinity. The population of that part of Amazonia falling within Bolivia, Peru, Ecuador, Colombia and Venezuela probably did not exceed 400,000, with 52,000 of these in Iquitos, capital of the Peruvian oriente. The relative emptiness of the Amazon has intrigued people for many years. That the region is unbearably hot is a myth. Temperatures of 100° F. are unknown and temperatures below 60° F. are rare. The humidity, especially near the river, is monotonously high, but this is compensated for on the lower river by a persistent easterly breeze. The increasing effectiveness of malaria control, improved diets and sanitation measures and increased ease in transportation are all making the Amazonian region more attractive for human settlement. Political indifference contributed its share to the cultural and economic stagnation of the basin, which is ruled by six governments. Since World War II, Brazil, Peru and Bolivia have all initiated schemes for the development of the Amazon through programs of public works and agricultural research.

Perhaps the most important lesson learned from the Ford plantation experiment was that workers could live in the Amazon, do hard work, and yet thrive and maintain good health. What is needed is money to provide medical and health services, proper housing and clothing, and the technical skill to provide a properly balanced diet. Yet the region remains empty, and life for the inhabitants of the scattered small villages is not easy. The answer, in part, is that the soils outside the flooded areas are among the poorest in the world; they are heavily leached and contain little humus. Trees grow well enough, but shallow-rooted crops and grasses do not thrive. Most of the agriculture of the region is carried out on soils that are not flooded, for the use of the flood plain would require vast and expensive flood control works. Government-subsidized agricultural colonies have been most successful where they have had access to markets for their produce, as adjacent to the Lima-Pucallpa highway and in the neighbourhood of the Amazonian metropolis of Belém. Japanese colonists since World War II have succeeded in growing jute and black pepper, in both of which Brazil has become self-sufficient. This success encourages the belief that other specialty crops might be found that are similarly adaptable to Amazonian conditions. But the problems of soil fertility on the upland surfaces remain unsolved, as witness the Zona Bragantina along the Belém-Bragança railroad, opened up in 1900 to agricultural settlement and 30 years later largely abandoned to second-growth forest (*capoeira*) because of the deterioration of the soils under permanent tillage. The *várzea*

lands and the foot slopes of the Andes are the most promising for agricultural development. The discovery of small quantities of oil at Ganzo Azul, on the Ucayali near Pucallpa, and at Nova Linda near the mouth of the Madeira river has given new hope to the valley. The large-scale colonization of the leached and poorly drained terra firma surface, however, which comprises 95% of the valley, seems unlikely in the foreseeable future.

See also Index references under "Amazon" in the Index volume.

BIBLIOGRAPHY.—A. R. Wallace, *A Narrative of Travels on the Amazon and Rio Negro* (1853); W. L. Herndon, *Exploration of the Valley of the Amazon* (1854); H. W. Bates, *The Naturalist on the River Amazons* (1863); P. Le Cointe, *L'Amazonie brésilienne* (1922); W. L. Schurz et al., *Rubber Production in the Amazon Valley* (1925); G. MacCreagh, *White Waters and Black* (1926); E. P. Hanson, *Journey to Manáos* (1938); P. Gourou, *Observações geográficas na Amazônia* (1949–50); L. Clark, *The Rivers Ran East* (1953); C. Wagley, *Amazon Town* (1953); C. P. Haskins, *The Amazon, Life History of a Mighty River* (1943); L. de Castro Soares, *Amazonia Guidebook,* xviii International Geographical Congress, (1956); H. Sioli, *Uber natur und mensch im Brasilianische Amazonas gebiet* (1956).
(O. E. W.; P. E. J.; Js. J. P.)

AMAZONAS, the extreme northwestern and largest state of Brazil, bounded north by Colombia, Venezuela and the territory of Roraima (*q.v.*), east by the state of Pará, south by the state of Mato Grosso, and the territories of Acre and Rondônia (formerly Guaporé), and west by Peru and Colombia. Originally a more extensive area, various reorganizations have reduced the size of the state to 604,032 sq.mi.; pop. (1960) 721,215. Approximately two-thirds of the inhabitants are Indians who are subject only in small part to government control. In the humid tropics, the state occupies an immense plain, densely wooded and traversed by innumerable rivers, whose flood plains are subject to extensive annual inundations.

The principal commercial products are rubber, cacao, jute and nuts; cattle are raised on the grassy plains of the north, west and southwest; curing fish and collecting turtle eggs for their oil give occupation to many people on the rivers. Maize, cassava (manioc), rice and various fruits are produced for domestic needs.

The capital, Manaus, is the only city and port of general commercial importance in the state; it is situated on the Rio Negro, 10 mi. above its junction with the Amazon, about 1,000 mi. from the sea. Manaus became a centre of population during the rubber boom which ended in 1910, and maintained its population in spite of the collapse of the industry. In 1960 the population was 154,-040.

Transportation depends largely upon the Amazon river and its tributaries, the Madeira, the Purús, the Jutaí, the Juruá, the Rio Negro and others, a total of about 7,500 mi. of navigable waterways. There is also a local air service.

Up to 1755 all the Portuguese territory on the Amazon formed part of the *capitania* of Pará. The upper districts were then organized into a separate *capitania,* called S. José do Rio Negro, to facilitate administration. When Brazil became independent in 1822, Rio Negro was overlooked in the reorganization into provinces, and reverted, notwithstanding the protests and an attempted revolution (1832) of the people, to a state of dependence upon Pará. In 1850 autonomy was voted by the general assembly at Rio de Janeiro, and on Jan. 1, 1852, the province of Amazonas was formally installed. In 1889 it became a federal state in the Brazilian republic. A governor is chosen by direct election for five years and is ineligible for immediate re-election. A single-chambered legislature of 24 members elected for three years exists. For purposes of internal administration the state is divided into 25 municipalities.

The increased demand for rubber during World War II revived the wild rubber industry of the Amazon basin, and thousands of rubber workers entered the region by way of Belém and Manaus. *See* also AMAZON; BRAZIL. (Js. J. P.)

AMAZONAS, a montaña department of northern Peru (pop. (1958 est.) 122,447; area 15,945 sq.mi.), bounded north by Ecuador, west by Cajamarca, south by La Libertad, southeast by San Martín, and northeast by Loreto. The department is composed of alternate mountain and valley; the mountains of the central cordillera are intersected by the deep valleys of the Marañón and its tributaries. The Marañón forms the boundary between Amazonas and Cajamarca for more than half the west side of the department, and then flows in a northeast direction. It is largely a region of equatorial rain forest with considerable rain, heat and humidity, particularly in the lowlands of the north. The main economic resources are forest products: rubber, quinine, hardwoods, nuts and coca. Agricultural products grown in the valleys include cacao, coffee, sugar, tobacco and cotton. Gold mines and placer gold exist there and rock salt is found at Chiliquin. The population, chiefly Indian and mestizo, is mainly in the south. Chachapoyas (pop. [1958 est.] 8,228), capital of the department, lies at 7,600 ft. above sea level on the Río Utcubamba, a tributary of the Marañón. It is the seat of a bishopric and industrial centre of the department; "Panama" hats are the principal manufacture. Chachapoyas may be reached by air and by motor road from Cajamarca. Transportation is otherwise conducted by river, on canoes or rafts or by trail. (J. L. TR.)

AMAZONAS, a vast territory, 67,857 sq.mi., forming the southernmost part of Venezuela, adjoins the Brazilian state of Amazonas. It lies partly within the drainage basin of the Orinoco and partly within that of the Río Negro, mighty northern tributary of the Amazon. The territory contains a maze of intricate watercourses, one 204-mi. stretch, the Casiquiare, links the Orinoco and the Río Negro. The Casiquiare is navigable for good-sized launches except at times of lowest water—January to March. Amazonas includes the western outliers of the Guiana highlands. The area has experienced only two periods of comparative prosperity: (1) in the 18th century when the Spaniards established military posts and (2) in the first decade of the 20th century when rubber prices were booming. The 1961 census showed Amazonas with a population of 11,757 (excluding Indians).

The capital is Puerto Ayacucho on the Orinoco river.

(L. WE.)

AMAZON STONE (AMAZONITE), named from the Amazon river, is an attractive bright green mineral sometimes used in jewelry. It is a variety of microcline feldspar obtained from the Ural mountains, U.S.S.R., and at Pikes peak, Colorado, and on the island of Madagascar.

See MICROCLINE; FELDSPAR.

AMB, the smallest of the frontier states that acceded to Pakistan, apart from the tiny khanate of Phulra (former state) in Hazara district, lies along the west bank of the Indus river some 25 mi. N.W. of Abbottabad, Peshawar division, West Pakistan. Apart from Amb, the principal township, it contains only a few villages and its population in 1961 was 5,073. Formerly it also included the feudal upper Tanawal across the Indus, but this was merged with Hazara district soon after the establishment of Pakistan in 1947, and after the merger the state was left with an area of 27 sq.mi. The residence of the ruler (nawab), formerly at Amb, is at Darband, the administrative headquarters. The village of Ashra is the trading centre for the state and adjoining territories.

The land rises to about 4,500 ft. and the main occupation is agriculture, with wheat, barley and maize as the chief subsistence crops. Many sheep and goats are kept and communication routes are restricted to mule tracks and footpaths. There is a small arms factory at Amb where guns, rifles and ammunition are made by hand. (K. S. AD.)

AMBALA, a city in Punjab state, India, headquarters of Ambala district and division, is situated in the plain 3 mi. E. of the Ghaggar river and 115 mi. N.N.W. of Delhi (124 mi. by rail). Pop. (1961) 76,204. The city has narrow, tortuous streets along which houses are disposed haphazardly. It has four degree-granting colleges affiliated to the Punjab university. Ambala city commands a prosperous agricultural area and has considerable trade in grains and sugar. Its industries include flour milling, glassmaking and papermaking and the manufacture of scientific instruments. Four miles southeast of the city is Ambala cantonment. Pop. (1961) 105,543. The cantonment is well laid out and, apart from its military origin, is a commercial centre. It has two Punjab university degree-granting colleges and the administrative offices of the divisional commissioner.

Ambala city and cantonment are on the Grand Trunk road and Northern railway main line between Delhi and Amritsar. Other railway lines link Ambala northward with Kalka and the hill metre-gauge line to Simla, and eastward with Saharanpur. The cantonment has a military airfield.

AMBALA DISTRICT lies between the Sutlej and Jumna rivers and southwest of the Siwalik hills. Immediately below the hills there is a strip of gently sloping land which is badly eroded by the *chos* or turbulent streams rushing down the Siwaliks. The rest of the district is an alluvial plain gradually sloping away from the Siwaliks. Drainage is provided by the numerous *chos* and by the nonperennial Ghaggar, the district's principal stream. The landscape of Ambala district, dotted with olive-green mango trees and with the Himalayan background beyond the Siwaliks, is impressive. The district has sufficient rainfall and only 10% of the cultivated area is irrigated; 65% of the district's area (2,134 sq.mi.) is cultivated. Wheat, sugar cane, maize, gram and peanuts are the main crops. Agriculture is the main occupation of the population, which was 1,373,477 in 1961. Chandigarh (*q.v.*; 89,321), the Punjab state capital inaugurated in 1953, is in the district, 27 mi. N. of Ambala city. Other centres of local trade in the district are Rupar (14,136), Jagadhri (32,637) and Kalka (18,068).

AMBALA DIVISION comprises the districts of Gissar, Karnal, Rohtak, Simla (*qq.v.*), Gurgaon and Ambala. (O. P. B.)

AMBARVALIA, an annual religious procession of the ancient Romans, occurring in May, usually on the 29th, the object of which was to secure the growing crops against harm. The priests probably were the Arval brothers (*q.v.*), who conducted the victims—ox, sheep and pig—in procession with prayer to Ceres around the boundaries of the *ager Romanus*. As the extent of Roman land increased, this could no longer be done, and in the *acta* of the Arval brothers, which date from the reign of Augustus, this procession is not mentioned; but in Virgil's *Georgics* and in Cato's *De re rustica* full details and the text of the prayers used by the Latin farmer in thus "lustrating" his own land are given.

The Christian festival that seems to have taken the place of these ceremonies is Rogation or gang week. The perambulation or beating of bounds is probably a survival of the same type of rite. *See* BOUNDS, BEATING THE; LITANY.

See W. W. Fowler, *Roman Festivals* (1899).

AMBASSADOR, the highest rank of diplomatic representative sent by one government to another. At the congress of Vienna, 1815, three classes of diplomatic agents were recognized, and a fourth was added by the congress of Aix-la-Chapelle, 1818: (1) ambassadors, including papal legates and nuncios, who are deemed to represent the person and dignity of the sovereign and are entitled to personal access to the sovereign to whom they are accredited; (2) ministers plenipotentiary and envoys extraordinary, including papal internuncios, who are accredited to the head of the state but do not represent the person and dignity of the head of their own state; (3) ministers resident, who are accredited to the head of the state but rank below the previous class; and (4) chargés d'affaires, who are accredited by the foreign minister to the foreign minister and may be appointed *ad hoc* (for a specific purpose) or *ad interim* (temporarily).

It was also agreed that agents of the same class should take precedence according to the date of presentation of their credentials, but in Catholic countries (except in France since the abrogation of the concordat) precedence is usually given to the papal legate.

The senior ambassador is the dean of the diplomatic corps and sees that diplomatic privileges and immunities are observed. These rules ended the undignified rivalries between ambassadors that were common in earlier centuries.

Ambassadors were originally accredited only to states enjoying royal honours. Later they were also sent to republics regarded as of equal rank. The United States, however, did not appoint ambassadors until 1893. In 1914 the great powers—Austria-Hungary, France, Germany, Great Britain, Italy, Japan, Russia and the United States—exchanged ambassadors with each other and with Spain and Turkey. The United States exchanged ambassadors with Argentina, Brazil, Chile and Mexico. Between

1919 and 1939 Belgium, China, Poland and Portugal were raised to ambassadorial status, and after 1945 this process was accelerated, especially among the Latin-American states and the new states in Asia. Some representatives to the UN, NATO and the Organization of American States also rank as ambassadors.

The privilege of an ambassador to see the head of the state to whom he was accredited declined in importance as sovereigns became constitutional monarchs or figurehead presidents; in Britain the sovereign is attended by a minister when receiving an ambassador. Before 1914 Emperor William II and Tsar Nicholas II often received ambassadors; so later did Adolf Hitler. In Washington ambassadors present their credentials to the president and thereafter are occasionally received by him on business, with the secretary of state usually present.

Originally ambassadors were entrusted with large, even plenary powers, but after the coming of the telegraph and the telephone they tended to become spokesmen of their foreign offices. Rarely does an ambassador enjoy extensive discretion; his duty is to obey instructions. On the other hand, his personality and prestige may play an important part in making the views of his government understood, and he can always make suggestions to his government. Probably the chief function of an ambassador in modern times is to report about the country to which he has been sent. For the immunities and privileges of ambassadors, see DIPLOMACY; EXTERRITORIALITY.

See Sir E. Satow, *A Guide to Diplomatic Practice*, 4th ed. by Sir Nevile Bland (1957). (B. E. S.)

AMBASSADORS, CONFERENCE OF.
This term has been used to denote the sessions or reunions of ambassadors at a certain centre, generally for the period of the execution of a treaty. The best example is perhaps the Ambassadors' conference which sat at Paris and Vienna during 1815–26. After World War I a similar conference meeting at Paris became one of the organs concerned with the execution of the Versailles treaty. It consisted of the representatives of Great Britain, France, Italy and Japan, with the U.S. ambassador attending in the capacity of a spectator after 1921.

The Ambassadors' conference as such had, of course, no special powers and it could only take unanimous decisions previously agreed upon between the respective governments. Such, for instance, was the case when on March 15, 1923, the conference recognized the Polish-Soviet frontier fixed by the treaty of Riga (March 18, 1921).

The most important function performed by the Ambassadors' conference was undoubtedly in Oct. 1921, when the former emperor Charles for the second time returned to Hungary with the intention of regaining his crown. The little entente (Czechoslovakia, Yugoslavia and Rumania) threatened very strong measures against Hungary. But, largely as a result of the ambassadors' intervention, Charles was deposed and extradited, and a law was passed by the Hungarian parliament which abrogated his sovereign rights (Nov. 4). In 1923 the conference was appealed to by the Polish government to settle the Polish-Lithuanian dispute over Vilna and on March 15 the conference awarded title to Poland.

Its action in 1923, in connection with the Corfu incident (*see* CORFU), brought the conference into some discredit, and shortly after he became prime minister, Ramsay MacDonald announced that its powers would be limited to the execution of the Versailles treaty. It was dissolved in 1931. Its chairman from its inception to the end was Jules Cambon of France.

AMBATO
(ASIENTO DE AMBATO), a city in the highlands of Ecuador, capital of the province of Tungurahua, 70 mi. S. of Quito with which it is connected by rail and by the Inter-American highway. Pop. (1959 est.) 44,300. It is located in an intermont basin at an elevation of about 8,400 ft. near the northeast foot of Mt. Chimborazo. The city is the commercial centre of one of the clusters of people in the highlands, and from it a trail passes over the eastern cordillera and descends to El Oriente. In the vicinity are numerous fruit growers, producing strawberries, peaches, apples, pears, grapes and oranges. Nearby are sugar cane plantations and farms that produce maize, wheat, barley and potatoes. In the city there is a variety of manufactures: tanneries, leather works, canneries, flour and textile mills, wineries, a rubber goods plant, and factories making furniture, buttons and other small items. The suburb of Miraflores is a favourite resort centre for the wealthy people of Guayaquil. The city has been frequently damaged by volcanic eruptions and earthquakes; about three-fourths of the buildings in the city were destroyed. (P. E. J.)

AMBEDKAR, BHIMRAO RAMJI
(1893–1956), untouchable leader, and law minister of the government of India, 1947–51, was born in April 1893, of an untouchable mahar family of western India. His father was a subhedar-major in the Indian army, but the boy was humiliated by his high-caste schoolfellows. After he had graduated from Elphinstone college, Bombay, he was awarded a scholarship by the Gaekwar of Baroda, and studied at universities in the United States, Great Britain and Germany. He was awarded doctorates for his *Evolution of Provincial Finance in British India* (1925) and his *Problem of the Rupee* (1923). He then entered the Baroda state service at the Gaekwar's request, but, again ill-treated by his high-caste colleagues, he turned to legal practice and to teaching and examined in economics and law for the University of Bombay. He soon established his leadership among the untouchables (*q.v.*), founded several journals on their behalf and did much to encourage them to improve their position. In his evidence before the Simon commission (1928–29) he demanded separate electorates for the untouchables. When this was conceded Gandhi began a "fast unto death" in protest. Ambedkar reluctantly yielded to this pressure and in the Poona pact (1932) agreed to a compromise whereby a panel of candidates would be chosen by untouchable voters for each untouchable seat, one member of the panel then being elected by a joint constituency of Hindus and untouchables. Ambedkar always contested Gandhi's claim to speak for the untouchables and expressed his views vigorously in *What Congress and Gandhi Have Done to the Untouchables* (1945).

Member for labour in the viceroy's executive council from 1942, Ambedkar became law minister in 1947. He took a leading part in the framing of the Indian constitution and skillfully steered it through the assembly. He resigned in 1951 disappointed at his lack of influence in the government. In Oct. 1956, finally despairing of the elimination of untouchability from Hinduism, he became a Buddhist, together with about 200,000 fellow untouchables, at a ceremony at Nagpur. He died in New Delhi on Dec. 6, 1956.

See Dhananjay Keer, *Dr. Ambedkar: Life and Mission* (1954). (KE. A. B.)

AMBER,
a deserted Indian city 5 mi. N.N.E. of Jaipur, ancient capital of a state in Rajasthan, was reputedly founded by the Minas, an aboriginal tribe. Its name was known to the Greek geographer Ptolemy in the 2nd century A.D. It was held by the Kachwaha Rajputs from 1037 to 1728, when the modern city of Jaipur supplanted it as the royal residence. Amber is celebrated for its scenery—mountain gorge and lake—and for its architecture. A range of hill fortresses defends the palace of Man Singh I (1600), extended in the mid-17th century by Jai Singh I, and comprising, beside the maharaja's apartments, a fine hypostyle *dīwān-i ām* (audience-hall), three temples and the *sukh niwās* (pleasure house) with its central water-channel, all grouped around an imposing courtyard. The *dīwān-i ām* shows the influence on the Rajput craftsmen of the early Mogul style; the fine palace entrance has closer affinities with the later Mogul buildings at Lahore, except that tempera painting replaces encaustic tilework. The ceilings are inlaid with coloured and mirror glass. (J. B.-P.)

AMBER.
True amber is a fossil resin of extinct coniferous trees that flourished along the Baltic coast in Tertiary (Eocene) times, from 60,000,000 to 70,000,000 years ago. The name came from the Spanish *ambar*, a rendering of the Arabic *anbar*. Succinite, the mineralogists' term for amber, was taken from the Latin name *succinum*, from *soccus* ("gum").

According to Greek myth, amber was the congealed tears of Phaëthon's sisters, who were turned to trees while weeping for his death. Since Aurignacian times in the Old Stone Age, or about 9000 B.C., amber has been used not only for ornaments but as a cure for countless illnesses such as asthma, rheumatism and internal disorders. Amulets of amber were worn by Roman women as a protection against witchcraft. Amber has been found in ancient European lake dwellings, at Stonehenge and in Mycenean tombs. In the Bronze Age and during Greek and Roman times amber was traded regularly across Europe to the Adriatic and Black seas. The history of its trade and acquisition, from crude and dangerous fishing in the sea in early times to modern mining techniques of digging and dredging, is a fascinating study. Equally interesting is the information obtained from the many hundreds of species of fossil insects and plants found as inclusions in amber (*see* PALEOBOTANY: *Means of Preservation;* PALEOENTOMOLOGY).

Amber occurs as irregular nodules, rods or droplike shapes in all shades of yellow to yellowish-brown. Light-coloured opaque material is known as "bone amber." The turbidity of certain kinds of amber is due to the inclusion of great numbers of minute air bubbles. Deeply coloured translucent to transparent amber is prized as a gem material. Though amber and amberlike resins have been found all over the world, true amber, or succinite, characterized by its yield of from 3% to 8% of succinic acid (*q.v.*), comes only from the shores of the Baltic, and in greatest amount from the glauconite sands or "blue earth" of the Samland peninsula in the Leningrad *oblast,* Russian Soviet Federated Socialist Republic, U.S.S.R. Other ambers contain little or no succinic acid. Simetite is a deep ruby or garnet-red amber from Sicily; some of it is coloured blue or green. The material found near Mt. Etna contains organic sulfur; it is a little softer than succinite. Rumanite, from Rumania, has a wide colour range of yellow, rose-red and dark smoky-gray. It contains many cracks, giving an iridescent effect, and is highly fluorescent. It gives off hydrogen sulfide when heated and has a slightly higher melting point than succinite. Burmite, a deep red amber from Burma, is a little harder than succinite and takes a brilliant polish.

Ornamental carved objects, beads, rosaries, cigarette holders and pipe mouthpieces, are made from amber. Ambroid, or "pressed amber," is obtained by softening fragments or shavings of amber and pressing it into flat sheets, which may be bored or worked into inexpensive articles. Small pieces of amber are used to make a very hard varnish. Synthetic succinic acid has replaced the succinic acid formerly obtained commercially by the distillation of amber. Bakelite, a common synthetic imitation of amber, may be distinguished by its higher refractive index and specific gravity. Celluloid, another synthetic, gives off an odour of camphor when vigorously rubbed.

X-ray investigations by the German crystallographer Friedrich Rinne demonstrated the amorphous, or noncrystalline, structure of amber. Its hardness is only 2.5 and it can be scratched by a copper penny. Though it is easily fractured it is not brittle, and can be carved, worked or bored easily. Its specific gravity ranges between 1.05 and 1.10. Amber will sink in distilled water and will just float in a saturated salt solution. There is variation of the refractive index according to specimen, but the average values are 1.53 and 1.55. Chemically, amber is a mixture of resins and a bituminous substance, approaching the formula $C_{10}H_{16}O$. Finely powdered amber is soluble in cold sulfuric acid; it completely decomposes in hot nitric acid; and is partially soluble in alcohol, ether, chloroform and turpentine. Between 280° and 290° C. amber will melt, throwing off white fumes of oil of amber and succinic acid, which are aromatic but irritating to the throat. A black residue, the bituminous material, is the main ingredient in what is commercially termed amber varnish. Amber is highly resistant to the flow of electricity (*see* INSULATING MATERIAL [ELECTRICAL]). From the Greek name *electron* for this material, an allusion to the sunshine colours of amber and its property of developing a negative electrical charge by friction, evolved the word "electricity." Amber fluoresces dull grayish-white or olive-green to bright yellowish-green in long-wave ultraviolet light. *See also* RESINS.

BIBLIOGRAPHY.—Karl Andrée, *Der Bernstein* (1937); Henry E. Briggs, *An Encyclopedia of Gems* (1944); Sydney Ball, *A Roman Book on Precious Stones* (1950); Leopold Schmid, *Bernstein* (1931); G. C. Williamson, *The Book of Amber* (1932); Herbert P. Whitlock, *The Story of the Gems* (1936). (J. W. FL.)

AMBERG, a town of Germany, which after partition of the nation following World War II was located in the *Land* of Bavaria, Federal Republic of Germany. It lies on both banks of the Vils, 41 mi. (66 km.) S.E. of Nürnberg, on the railway line from Nürnberg to Furth im Wald, the border station for Czechoslovakia. Pop. (1961) 42,493. It is a medieval walled town with four town gates, and it was the capital (until 1810) and ducal residence (until 1621) of the Upper Palatinate. It is first mentioned in records in 1034. The presence of a mint was recorded from 1274 to the end of the 18th century, and of ore mining from 1326. In the 14th, 15th and 16th centuries it was a court town, with considerable trade (in iron and tinplate) and industry, with many trading and shipping privileges. It was considered to be one of the strongest fortified towns in medieval Germany. Frederick V (*q.v.*) was born in Amberg and lived in the ducal castle for several years with his wife, Elizabeth Stewart. In 1796 the Austrians under Archduke Charles decisively defeated the French under Marshal Jean Baptiste Jourdan there; the battle is recorded on the Arc de Triomphe in Paris. The Gothic town hall is of the 15th century and the ducal castle is now the administrative centre of the rural district. The Jesuits transformed St. George's church from Gothic into baroque in the 18th century; St. Martin's church (begun in 1420) contains pictures by Caspar Crayer and has a tower 300 ft. high; the convent church of the former Salesian sisters is a rococo building; and the former church of the Pauline order is now the Evangelical-Lutheran parish church. The Mariahilfberg (393 ft. high) has been a place of pilgrimage since 1634. The state archives for the whole of the Upper Palatinate as well as the municipal archives are held there, and there is a provincial library, with beautiful ceiling paintings and furniture, founded in 1730. Amberg is a flourishing industrial and commercial centre, with large industries, iron-ore mining, blast furnaces and a foundry; machines are made and there are glass-grinding works, an enamel factory, cold storage plants, breweries, and a brickworks. The surroundings are rural, with cereal crops and potatoes, forestry and pisciculture. In the district there are lignite deposits and open-cast mines of kaolin, with summer skiing facilities on kaolin. Christoph Amberger, the painter and engraver, was born there about 1500 (there is a wooden bust by him in the National gallery, London, Eng.). Martin Merz, the great artillery expert of his time (d. 1501), is buried in Amberg.

(R. RE.)

AMBERGRIS is a concretion (whether normal or pathological is still debated) formed in the intestinal tract of the sperm whale. It is believed by some to have its origin in an intestinal irritation caused by the indigestible horny portions of the squid and cuttle-fish on which the whale feeds. Fresh ambergris is soft in consistency, black in colour, and has a disagreeable odour. Exposed to sun, air and sea water, however, the material hardens, its colour fades to a light gray, and it develops a subtle and pleasing fragrance.

Ambergris has been cast up on the shores of China, Japan, India, Africa, Ireland, the Americas and the islands of the tropical seas. The Bahamas have been a particularly rich collecting ground. In addition to this salvage supply from the sea, important amounts have rewarded the labours of the whale hunters. Pieces of ambergris rarely weigh more than a few ounces, but finds weighing up to 100 lb. have been reported.

Known from the days of antiquity, ambergris was long prized in the east as a perfume and a drug. In medieval Europe it was recommended for its fragrance and restorative powers. Its modern usage in the east is chiefly to spice foods and wines, while in the west it is used in the manufacture of perfumes.

The chemical structure of ambergris has not been precisely determined. It is known to contain alkaloids, acids and a fatty substance, ambrein. Ambergris commonly is used in the form of a tincture. It is ground in a mortar and placed in dilute solution with cold alcohol. The tincture is stored for about six months and then filtered. Introduced into fine perfumes, ambergris adds to the scent of essential flower oils its own suave and long-lasting bouquet. (E. L. Y.)

AMBIDEXTERITY, the ability to use both the right and the left hand with equal ease. *See* HANDEDNESS.

AMBLESIDE, a parish and town of Westmorland, Eng.,

nearly a mile north of Waterhead at the head of Lake Windermere and in the centre of the Lake district (*q.v.*) national park. Pop. (1961) 2,562. It is beautifully situated among the bare hills surrounding the richly wooded valley of the Rothay. The hills are Wansfell pike on the east, Loughrigg fell on the west, and Rydal fell and the ridge below Snarker pike (2,096 ft.) to the north. The landing stage of Ambleside is at Waterhead and nearby there are remains of a Roman camp (Borrans Field); in Ambleside is a museum of Roman antiquities. A charter for a market was granted to the town in 1650 and in 1688 James II granted a similar one and power to collect tolls for the poor. During the last week-end of July a rushbearing festival is held. The town was an urban district from 1895 to 1935, when it was combined with Grasmere (*q.v.*) and five parishes to form the Lakes urban district. Catering for tourists is the main industry.

AMBLYGONITE, an important source of lithium, was first discovered in Saxony in 1817, and later at Montebras, Creuse *département*, France, and at Hebron, Me. It occurs in pegmatite veins with other phosphates and other lithia-bearing minerals, especially spodumene and lepidolite. It is mined commercially near Keystone, S.D., in San Diego county, Calif., at Cáceres, Spain, and at Karibib and Tsumeb, South-West Africa. Canada began exporting small quantities to the U.S. in the 1950s. The mineral is found in cleavable, compact masses, occasionally in indistinct large crystals. It is translucent with a vitreous lustre, usually white, but varies to pale shades of yellow, green, gray or violet. It is readily distinguished from feldspar by its greater specific gravity (3.0) and its chemical properties. It is an aluminum and lithium fluophosphate, $LiAl(PO_4)F$, with part of the lithium replaced by sodium and part of the fluorine by hydroxyl. For uses and methods of extraction *see* LITHIUM.

(Ru. R.; Da. R.)

AMBLYOPIA means dimness of vision of one or of both eyes. It varies in degree and duration and is generally applied to those cases where there is no demonstrable structural defect in the eye itself. Amblyopia may occur suddenly or develop slowly as the result of functional disorders such as hysteria; it also may result from dietary deficiencies and from toxic substances, including various drugs, alcohol, tobacco, wood alcohol, quinine and arsenic. It may also occur as the result of kidney disease in uremic conditions or in the toxemias of pregnancy. The term is also used with reference to colour blindness and night blindness and may result from exposure to brilliant light or to long-continued darkness. It may be transient or permanent and progressive, in which case it may result in blindness. *See* BLINDNESS; EYE, HUMAN; VISION.

(F. L. A.)

AMBO (OVAMBO, AVAMBO), a southwest African people, many of whom live in southern Angola; the number residing in northern South West Africa, the former German colony and mandate to South Africa, is estimated at 150,000 (1960s). Politically they were divided into 13 autonomous units.

There are about 40,000 Ndonga, 17,000 Kwambi, 9,000 Nganjera, 7,000 Kwaluthi, and 4,000 Eunda and Nkolonkathi living in South West Africa. The Kwanyama have about 62,000 in South West Africa and more in Angola, and the Mbalantu have 10,000 in the former and a small number in the latter. The Esinga, Mbanja, Kashima, Evale, and Ehanda are in Angola. The Ndombothola of Angola are sometimes included as a 14th Ambo subgroup.

Formerly these political groups were ruled by kings, who also acted as rainmakers, and whose positions were hereditary within exogamous matrilineal lineages. The Ndonga, Kwambi, Nganjera and Kwaluthi are still ruled by hereditary kings, but the others are governed by councils of local headmen under the supervision of European administrators.

Millet and sorghum, the original staples of the Ambo, are still the most extensively cultivated crops, not only of the Ambo but of neighbouring peoples. Of equal importance to the economy of the Ambo is animal husbandry (herding), supplemented by fishing, hunting, and gathering. Cattle, sheep, goats, and dogs are owned by all of the tribes; cattle being of particular importance for marriage payments (*see* BRIDEWEALTH) as well as for milk and butter yield.

Sculpture is minimal, but they make pottery and coiled basketry, and smelt and work iron and formerly, copper. Clothing consisted of leather aprons of ox stomach supported by a broad leather belt, with women wearing an additional back covering of ox skin plaited into the hair. The men now wear what European clothes they can afford. Houses are circular with peaked roofs, and are arranged in an intricate circular pattern centred around the meeting place with the hearth for the sacred fire.

The sacred fire cannot be used for cooking, except for the meal of a departing warrior, or for warmth. It is kept alive by the principal wife or daughter of the king or the local chief, and its extinction is an omen of the impending destruction of all his subjects. Local chiefs and headmen light their sacred fires from those of their superiors.

See B. Stefaniszyn, *Social and Ritual Life of the Ambo of Northern Rhodesia* (1964). (Wi. B.; X.)

AMBO, the reading desk of the early Christian church, was originally small and movable but was afterward made of large proportions and fixed in one place.

By the 6th century the ambo was established as an important and stationary piece of great decorative value. In the Byzantine and early Romanesque periods it was an essential part of church furniture. From the 12th century, and earlier than that outside Italy, the ambo was gradually superseded by the pulpit and lectern. Even in Italy it passed out of liturgical use, except in the Abrosian rite in Milan.

The position of the ambo was not absolutely uniform; sometimes it was placed in the central point between the sanctuary and the nave, sometimes in the middle of the church and sometimes at one or both sides of the chancel. The normal single ambo consisted of a raised platform in three levels, reached by steps and protected by railings. Each level was consecrated to a special part of the service. The uppermost level was reserved for the deacon who read the Gospel; for promulgating episcopal edicts; for reciting the names inscribed on diptychs (*q.v.*); for announcing fasts, vigils and feasts; for reading ecclesiastical letters or acts of the martyrs celebrated on that day; for announcing new miracles for popular edification, professions by new converts or recantations by heretics; and for preaching sermons by priests and deacons. The middle level was for the deacon who read the Epistle and the lowest for the subordinate clergy who read other parts of Scripture. Later, a separate ambo was built at each side of the church and the various functions divided between them.

Ambos were usually composed as part of the choir screen. In finer churches they were made of marble and frequently decorated with mosaics and carving. A normal type is represented by those in S. Clemente at Rome which date from at least the beginning of the 12th century. Those of Sta. Maria in Ara Coeli, Sta. Maria in Cosmedin and S. Lorenzo, all at Rome of the 12th or 13th centuries, are rich with fine-scaled geometric mosaic known as Cosmati work. Fine examples are found in southern Italy, notably at Ravello and Salerno. There it was the rule to have the ambos supported on spiral columns; in Rome the base was usually solid.

In Russian Orthodox usage ambo usually designated the steps leading to the platform in front of the iconostasis (*q.v.*). In the Greek church the ambo retains its earlier form and is placed at one side of the church. In the Greek Catholic Church, the ambo is a table before the doors of the iconostasis.

AMBOINA (AMBON, AMBOYNA), an important island in the province of the Moluccas, Indonesia, lies southwest of Ceram Island, from 3° 29' to 3° 48' S. latitude and 127° 54' to 128° 25' E. longitude. It is 32 mi. in length and 11 mi. in width; two oblong peninsulas rise parallel from the sea and are united by a narrow alluvial isthmus not more than a mile long. Pop. (1957 est.) 72,679; area 314 sq.mi.

The island is subject to damage from earthquakes, as are the neighbouring isles to the east, the Uliasers. Amboina is a Tertiary (Miocene) formation and is traversed by mountain ranges (highest peaks are Salhatu, 3,360 ft., and Wawani, 3,010 ft.) of fine-grained granite, with serpentine, magnesite, etc. The chalk cliffs around

Amboina bay have stalactite caves. The rivers are small and un-navigable, and there are hot springs and *solfataras* but no active volcanoes. The climate of Amboina is comparatively healthful and not unpleasant, the mean maximum temperature being 84.6° F. and the mean minimum 73.4°. The hottest time is in February, the wettest in June and July (the east monsoon with very strong winds), and the average yearly rainfall is more than 135 in.

Vegetation and Animal Life.—The profuse vegetation varies on different sides of the island. Damar and copal resins are collected. Amboina wood, very hard and knotty, and of great value for ornamental woodwork, was obtained from Ceram and exported. The indigenous mammals of Amboina are few, but birds include a fine racquet-tailed kingfisher, *Tanysiptera galatea,* described by A. R. Wallace as "the largest and handsomest" of this family. The island also has a crimson lory, *Eos rubra,* and a brush-tongued parrot of vivid crimson colour, and it is rich in insects, particularly Lepidoptera, and in shells. There are 700 varieties of fish in the Bay of Amboina, under which, at the eastern end, are very fine marine gardens.

The People.—The Ambonese (or Amboinese) are mainly of the Melanesian racial type, with dark skin, curly to frizzy hair, flat nose and thick lips. Beside Amboina, they live on the adjacent Uliaser Islands (Saparua, Haruku and Nusa Laut) and the nearby coast of Ceram. Although there are many Muslims, chiefly in the northern part of Amboina, the dominant group is Christian. In 1935 the autonomous Moluccan Protestant church was organized, at which date it had 180,000 members, mainly in Amboina and surrounding islands. The language is a lingua franca Malay with many Portuguese and Dutch words.

The Economy.—Farming is insignificant. Some rice, maize, coffee and root crops are produced, mainly on shifting plots in the forest. The staple food is sago, derived from wild and planted groves, especially on Ceram. Cloves, once important, are still produced, but their export is less than 2% of the world trade. Copra, from the orchards of coconut palms that fringe the coasts, is another export item. Homemade wine, from the aren palm, is a popular drink. Hunting and fishing provide the animal protein in the meagre diet of many. A number of Ambonese, educated in Christian schools, served in the Dutch administration and army, and identified themselves with the colonial power. After independence their social and economic position became precarious.

History.—The clove trade of Amboina led the Portuguese to the island in 1512. They gave the place its name, and founded a settlement in 1521. The Dutch arrived in 1599 and in the next decades succeeded in wresting the monopoly of the spice trade from the Portuguese. In 1615 a British settlement was formed on the other side of the island at Cambello (the Dutch were on the Amboina town site), and the British remained there until 1623, when the Dutch claimed to have discovered British participation in a native revolt in Ceram and in the Bandanese island of Run and massacred the settlers. In 1796 the British captured the island, but it was restored in 1802, retaken in 1810, during the Napoleonic War, and once again restored to the Dutch in 1814.

Japan occupied the former district of Amboina in 1942. When Indonesia gained its independence in Dec. 1949 its structure was agreed to be on the federal principle. Amboina and surrounding islands were one of the constituent autonomous areas. When, a few months later, the central Indonesian government abolished the federation in favour of a unitary, centralized state, the Ambonese seceded and proclaimed an independent South Moluccan republic (April 1950). The movement was suppressed in Ambon by military action of the central government, but guerrilla warfare continued thereafter in Ceram, and a government-in-exile carried on, insisting that the United Nations, which sponsored the independent federated republic of Indonesia, should hear its complaint. In the meantime, a great number of Ambonese found refuge in the Netherlands.

Amboina District and Town.—Amboina was also the name of the former district of the residency of the Moluccas. This is now called Maluku Tenga (central Moluccas), covering an area of 11,-438 sq.mi. and including the islands of Amboina; the Uliasers; Buru (capital, Kajeli); Ceram (capital, Kairatu); and the Banda

Isles.

Amboina (or Ambon), the town, and residence of the governor of the province of the Moluccas, is a well-built place with wide streets, often tree-lined, and with many houses and business premises of stone. Ft. Victoria was built in the early 17th century and restored later. A church dating from the earliest settlement, a hospital, barracks (within the fort) and many government buildings were erected there. Most of these were destroyed in World War II.

The town and port is on the eastern side of the bay, a mile short of the narrow entrance to the inner harbour and about 8 mi. from the outer entrance. The depths in the outer bay are great, and anchorages are few but safe. The port, formerly well equipped with wharves and warehouses, served as an auxiliary naval base. It has regular connections with the rest of the archipelago, and is the chief centre for the shipment of Moluccan produce and for the distribution of imports from Europe and America. In 1956 the population was estimated to be 40,477. There are roads sufficient for local needs, a government radio station and a telephone system. G. E. Rumpf, the naturalist, lived and died in Amboina, and a monument commemorates the fact.

(J. O. M. B.)

AMBOISE, GEORGES D' (1460–1510), French cardinal and chief minister of state under Louis XII, was the son of Pierre d'Amboise, seigneur de Chaumont, chamberlain to Charles VII and Louis XI and ambassador at Rome. Georges received the bishopric of Montauban when only 14 and was appointed an almoner of Louis XI. As a young man under Charles VIII he suffered imprisonment for the cause of the duc d'Orléans (the future Louis XII), but he was elevated to the archbishopric of Narbonne and then to that of Rouen (1493) when Orléans was restored to favour. On the appointment of Orléans as governor of Normandy, Georges became his lieutenant general. When Orléans became king in 1498, Georges was made cardinal and first minister of the crown.

His domestic policy was prudent. He made economies and reduced taxation. By the *ordonnances* of 1499, his most important work, he improved the administration of justice. He was interested, too, in ecclesiastical reform, particularly in that of the monastic orders. Abroad, he sought to increase French power in Italy and supported the campaign begun in 1499 for the conquest of Milan. In 1500 he was named lieutenant general in Italy and charged with the organization of the conquest. On Pope Alexander VI's death (1503) he aspired to the papacy. With French troops at the gates of Rome he could easily have frightened the conclave into electing him, but he was persuaded to trust to his influence and prestige. The troops were dismissed, and an Italian was elected as Pius III. Again, on the death of Pius within a month, another Italian, Julius II, was chosen. The cardinal d'Amboise received in compensation the title of legate for life in France and in the Comtat Venaissin. He was one of the negotiators of the disastrous treaties of Blois (1504) and of the League of Cambrai against Venice (1508).

The cardinal again accompanied Louis XII into Italy in 1509. On his way home he died at Lyons on May 25, 1510. His body was moved to Rouen, and a magnificent tomb, on which he is represented kneeling in prayer, was erected in the cathedral there.

AMBOISE, a town in the *département* of Indre-et-Loire in central France, is situated on both banks of the Loire 16 mi. by road east of Tours. Pop. (1962) 7,332. Amboise is dominated by the magnificent château built on a rock between the main Loire valley and the side valley of the Amasse. This castle consists of a three-story building with a fine façade, whose top windows are dormer, flanked by two enormous squat towers, the tour des Minimes on the Loire side and the tour Hurtault on the side of the Amasse. The most important part of the château is the *Logis du Roi*, or King's house, the work of Charles VIII. There is an inclined plane up which horses and carriages may ascend. Straddling the ramparts is the small chapel of St. Hubert. The *hôtel de ville* (early 16th century), with a museum, is on the side of the Loire below the château and nearby is the 15th-century gateway called the Porte d'Horloge, which has a carillon. The 12th-century church of St. Denis to the west contains curious carved capitals to the columns and 16th-century carving representing the burial of Christ. On the Île d'Or in the Loire there is a large camping ground and a public park. Southeast of the town is Le Clos Lucé, formerly called the castle of Cloux, a 15th-century manor where Leonardo da Vinci lived for a short time and died (1519), now a museum. Two miles to the south is the seven-tiered Pagoda of Chanteloup. Amboise is on the main railway line from Paris to Bordeaux. Fishing tackle, shoes, wine presses, caravans, motor bodywork, photographic materials, metalwork, mill wheels, optical instruments, bedding and plastic goods are produced. Wine production is important.

The first mention of the town, then known as Ambatia, was when Alaric, king of the Goths, met Clovis, king of the Franks, between 498 and 506 on the Île St. Jean (now the Île d'Or). In the 11th century Amboise was a lordship under the counts of Anjou and the castle was improved by Fulk Nerra (see FULK). United to France in the middle of the 15th century, Amboise became a favourite residence of French kings. The discovery in 1560 of the "conspiracy of Amboise," a plot of the Huguenots to remove Francis II from the influence of the house of Guise, was avenged by the death of many members of that party. In 1563 Amboise gave its name to a royal edict, due to Catherine de Medici and proclaimed by her son, Charles IX, allowing freedom of worship to the Huguenot nobility and gentry. The château was frequently used as a state prison, Abd-el-Kader (q.v.) being incarcerated there from 1848 to 1852. In 1872 it was restored by the National assembly to the house of Orléans. Amboise was in German hands for a short time in 1870–71 and in World War II from June 1940 to Aug. 1944.

(R. Go.)

AMBRACIA (modern ARTA in the *nomos* of Arta in northwestern Greece), an ancient Corinthian colony in Epirus about 7 mi. inland from the Ambracian gulf (Gulf of Arta), on the navigable Arachthus river in a fertile wooded plain. It was founded between 650 and 625 B.C. by Gorgus, son of the Corinthian tyrant Cypselus. After the expulsion of Periander (q.v.) its government developed into a strong democracy. Early features were loyalty to Corinth, a consequent aversion from Corcyra and frontier disputes with Amphilochians and Acarnanians. It took a prominent part in the Peloponnesian War until its defeat by the Amphilochians and Acarnanians, aided by the Athenians, at Idomene (426). In 338 B.C. it surrendered to Philip II of Macedonia.

Ambracia subsequently (294 B.C.) became the capital of Pyrrhus, king of Epirus. It ultimately joined the Aetolian league. The city fell to Rome after a stubborn siege in 189 and never recovered. The foundation by Augustus of Nicopolis Actia (q.v.), into which the remaining inhabitants were drafted, left the site desolate. In Byzantine times a new settlement took its place under the name of Arta (q.v.).

AMBRIDGE, a borough of Beaver county, Pa., U.S., lies on a wide plain overlooking the Ohio river, 17 mi. N.W. of Pittsburgh. (For comparative population figures *see* table in PENNSYLVANIA: *Population.*)

An important industrial centre, Ambridge is the home of the largest bridge and structural steel plant in the world. Other products manufactured include wrought iron, cold finished steel, seamless pipe, electrical equipment and building materials.

Within the boundaries of Ambridge is the former village of Economy, founded in 1825 by the Harmony society, under its leader, George Rapp. The Rappites migrated to North America from the kingdom of Württemberg, Ger., at the beginning of the 19th century because of religious persecutions. In 1825 the Rappites, who had settled at Harmony, Pa., and New Harmony, Ind. (q.v.), established Economy on a 3,000-ac. tract of land extending five miles along the Ohio river. Under Rapp and his successor, R. L. Baker, Economy prospered for about 50 years and then began to decline because of the practice of celibacy and the lack of fresh converts. In 1906 the society was disbanded. Many of the original buildings were still standing after mid-20th century, including the Great House which was taken over by the state of Pennsylvania in 1919 and maintained as a historical museum.

In 1903 the American Bridge company purchased 2,500 ac. of land from the Harmony society as a site for the construction of a bridge works and a town. In 1905 the town was incorporated as a borough and named after the American Bridge company. It adopted a council-burgess form of government in 1905.

(M. R. Wo.)

AMBROS, AUGUST WILHELM (1816–1876), Austrian musicologist, best-known for his history of music. Of German-Czech parentage, he was born at Vysoké Myto, near Prague, Nov. 17, 1816. He studied law and entered the civil service in 1840. A keen, well-trained musician, he established himself as a brilliant writer on music, and his pamphlet *Die Grenzen der Poesie und der Musik* (1856), answering E. Hanslick's *Vom musikalischen Schönen,* was an important contribution to a heated aesthetic controversy. In 1869 he became professor of music at Prague and in 1872 professor of musical history at the conservatory in Vienna, where he died, June 28, 1876.

His main work is his comprehensively planned *Geschichte der Musik.* He published three volumes (1862–68); two more were compiled from his notes by C. F. Becker and G. Nottebohm (1878; rev. by H. Leichentritt, 1909), and by Otto Kade (1882), who also enlarged and revised vol. iii (1893). W. Langhans produced a continuation up to the 19th century, 2 vol. (1883–86). (H. Ga.)

AMBROSE (AMBROSIUS), **SAINT** (340?–397), bishop of Milan, one of the great doctors of the western church, was born in Trèves of a Roman senatorial family about 340. His father, prefect of Gallia Narbonensis, died while Ambrose was still a youth and the family returned to Rome where Ambrose and his brother Satyrus were educated as young nobles toward government careers. The family was Christian, and during Ambrose's teen years his sister Marcellina received the consecration of a virgin at the hands of Pope Liberius and his mother probably began the life of a dedicated Christian widow, two events which were reflected in his later interest in these forms of life (5 of his extant 35 treatises deal with these topics).

Around 365 Ambrose and his brother went to Sirmium to begin their government careers and were appointed advocates to the praetorian court; in 368 they were appointed to the council. In 370 Ambrose was made governor of Aemilia-Liguria with the seat of government at Milan, which was also the imperial city. He soon won popular favour for the honesty and fairness with which he dispensed justice and preserved the peace of the province.

In 374 the Arian bishop of Milan, Auxentius, died and, since the Catholic bishop had already died in exile, a new bishop had to be chosen. Each party was determined to obtain the bishopric, and it devolved on Ambrose to see that peace was maintained. Addressing the crowd gathered in the cathedral, he was interrupted by the acclamation, "Ambrose, bishop!" He tried every subterfuge to escape the office, but when even the emperor approved the choice he yielded. He was only a catechumen at the time but within a week he received baptism and the various orders, culminating in the episcopacy on Dec. 7. He insisted that he would receive the sacraments only at the hands of a Catholic bishop, thus indicating one of the salient features of his life; he was to be a firm and uncompromising foe of the Arians, although the imperial court favoured them.

As bishop of the imperial city he was thrown into close relationship with the court, and he exerted his influence to the utmost to defend the rights of the Catholics against the attacks of the Arians and the resurgence of paganism under Symmachus. At one time he even barricaded himself and the Catholic community in the cathedral to foil an attempt of the court to seize the church for the Arians. Although his staunch Catholicism earned the undying enmity of the dowager empress Justina, his influence was recognized and he was employed by the court on diplomatic missions on several occasions. Ultimately, he won over the young emperor, Valentinian II, to the Catholic side, but Valentinian died before Ambrose could baptize him.

Despite Ambrose's great political influence, especially in the field of church-state relationships, it is chiefly for his theological contributions that he is remembered. He was not a great speculative theologian, having neither the time nor the interest to develop such a theology. However, he took his episcopal duties seriously and devoted himself assiduously to the instruction of the people committed to his care. For this task he prepared himself to the best of his ability. He began his episcopal career without any foundation in the theological sciences, and so he devoted the first three years to serious study. Because he had had a good classical education he was fluent in Greek and turned to the writings of the Greek theologians for his training. Among these theologians the most noteworthy influences were found in Origen and Basil of Caesarea, though he was familiar with most of the writings of the great Greek writers of the 3rd and 4th centuries. He made frequent use of the material gleaned from these writers in his own sermons and writings, to such an extent that he has justly been credited with introducing the thought of the east into the Latin church. Perhaps his most important theological contribution to the west was the influence he exerted on the thought of Augustine, particularly in the doctrines of original sin and grace.

The repute in which Ambrose was held as an orator led the rhetorician Augustine to attend the services in Milan. The sermons he heard solved some of the difficulties he found in the Scriptures, and it was only a short time until he was received into the church by Ambrose. (*See* AUGUSTINE, SAINT.)

Ambrose died at Milan on April 4, 397. His feast day is Dec. 7.

Ambrose's writings cover a wide field. In addition to the treatises on virginity and widowhood mentioned above, he left several exegetical treatises. Most of these deal with the Old Testament: the patriarchs (*Hexaemeron, De paradiso*, etc.), the Psalms and a fragmentary commentary on Isaiah. One work on the New Testament, a commentary on Luke's gospel, is extant. He also left ethical treatises (*De Tobia, De Nabuthe*, etc.), an instruction for the clergy of his diocese (*De officiis*) and many important theological works (*De fide, De spiritu sancto, De mysteriis, De sacramentis, De paenitentia*). Most of his writings were first given as sermons to his people, and there remain three funeral orations, in addition to his treatises, from which a good idea of his sermon technique can be derived.

The Ambrosian corpus is completed by 91 letters and several hymns, although only a few of the latter can be attributed to him with any certainty.

See also references under "Ambrose, Saint" in the Index.

See, for the only fairly complete study of Ambrose in the English language, F. Homes Dudden, *The Life and Times of St. Ambrose*, 2 vol. (1935). This work contains a brief but good bibliography of other works. (O. T. W.)

AMBROSE (AMVROSY; in the world ANDREI STEPANOVICH ZERTIS-KAMENSKY) (1708–1771), archbishop of Moscow (1768–71), born on April 17, 1708, in Nezhin, was a typical supporter of the Enlightenment in the Russian hierarchy of the 18th century. He roused the charitable organization of the church to fight poverty in Moscow and did valuable work for church restoration there. During a plague in 1771 the people crowded round a miraculous icon of the Virgin which Ambrose then secretly removed to prevent the spread of infection. On Sept. 16 the enraged mob broke into the monastery where he was living and put him to a cruel death. Ambrose translated the Hebrew Psalter and many of the Greek and Latin Fathers.

See Brockhaus-Efron, *Entsiklopedichesky slovar*, vol. 1, p. 621 (1890). (F. v. L.)

AMBROSE (*c.* 1190), Norman poet and chronicler of the third crusade, a minstrel who accompanied Richard I of England on that expedition. Nothing more is known of him than that he was probably a native of Evreux and was a noncombatant making the pilgrimage to Jerusalem. His account of the crusade is preserved in the *Estoire de la guerre sainte*, a poem of 12,352 lines extant in an Anglo-Norman manuscript; but the *Estoire* is only an adaptation of Ambrose's work. It was, moreover, the original poem, not the *Estoire*, which was used by Richard, a canon of Holy Trinity, London, as the source for his *Itinerarium regis Ricardi*. The *Estoire* has not much literary merit, but its use of Ambrose's poem makes it a valuable historical source for the events of 1190–92, even though it is biased in favour of Richard.

For the text of the *Estoire* see the critical edition by Gaston

Paris (1897). There are English translations by M. J. Hubert and J. L. La Monte, *The Crusade of Richard Lion-Heart* (1941), in verse, with full bibliography; and by E. N. Stone, *Three Old French Chronicles of the Crusades* (1939), in prose. (J. B. R.)

AMBROSE, ISAAC (1604–1663/64), English Nonconformist minister and a leading figure among those ejected under the Act of Uniformity of 1662, was born in May 1604 at Ormskirk, Lancashire. He was educated at Brasenose college, Oxford, and became vicar of Castleton, Derbyshire, in 1627. He attracted the attention of the duke of Bedford and became one of the king's preachers for Lancashire in 1631 and, by the patronage of Lady Margaret Hoghton, vicar of Preston in 1640. Suffering many vicissitudes during the Civil War, he took part in the subsequent establishment of presbyterianism in Lancashire and Yorkshire. After his ejection from Garstang, to which he had moved in 1654, he retired to Preston, where he died in Jan. 1663/64. His piety and evangelizing zeal won general admiration and his writings show a vivid imaginative power reminiscent of Bunyan. His *Looking Unto Jesus* (1658) was often reprinted. He recommended the keeping of a diary as a pathway to the devout life and fragments of his own are included in his complete works (published 1812).

AMBROSIA AND NECTAR, in Greek mythology, sometimes the food, sometimes the drink, of the immortals. Probably the two terms were not originally distinguished; but usually, both in Homer and in later writers, nectar is the drink and ambrosia the food. On the other hand, in Alcman nectar is the food, and in Sappho and Anaxandrides ambrosia the drink. Each is also used in Homer as a fragrant unguent (*Iliad*, xiv, 170; xix, 38). The word ambrosia has generally been derived from the Greek for "not" and "mortal." A. W. Verrall, however, denied that there is any clear example in which the Greek word *ambrosios* necessarily means "immortal," and explains it as "fragrant," a sense which is always suitable. If so, the word may be derived from the Semitic *ambar* (ambergris), to which eastern nations attributed miraculous properties. W. H. Roscher thought that both nectar and ambrosia were kinds of honey. The name "ambrosia" was also later applied by Dioscorides and Pliny to certain herbs and has been retained in modern botany for a genus of plants from which it has been extended to the group of dicotyledons called Ambrosiaceae, including *Ambrosia* (ragweed), *Xanthium* and *Iva*, all annual herbaceous plants represented in America. *Ambrosia maritima* and some other species occur also in the Mediterranean regions. (T. V. B.)

AMBROSIAN CHANT is the term for the kind of plainsong (*q.v.*) sung in the diocese of Milan and the churches under its influence, which in the middle ages reached as far as Bavaria. It is still used in Milan and by some churches in Lugano and the Swiss canton of Ticino.

It was introduced probably by Auxentius, a Cappadocian, who was bishop of Milan from 355 to 374, and derived from Antioch. According to St. Augustine (*Confessions*, ix, 7) St. Ambrose (*q.v.*), who succeeded Auxentius, made use of the Syrian practice of singing in alternate choirs, but adapted it in a special way. When he and his followers were besieged in their church by the armies of the Arian empress Justina, he raised their spirits by teaching them to sing psalms "in the oriental manner." From his own account (*Hexameron*, iii, 25) it may be deduced that this meant that the whole congregation joined in the singing of strophic hymns and in responding to each verse of the psalm by a refrain taken from the first line. This way of singing soon spread to all the churches in the west. St. Ambrose was long considered to have introduced the chant which bears his name; though this is no longer thought to be so, he is still accepted as the author of some of the Latin metrical hymns known as "Ambrosian hymns."

Adherence to Ambrosian chant and to the use of the Ambrosian liturgy (*see* LITURGY) by the churches of Milan was often challenged, notably by Charlemagne, who attempted to discourage, and indeed to destroy, all music and ritual not in conformity with the Roman practice. Many of the chants were, however, gradually adapted to, or replaced by, Gregorian melodies. As no manuscripts containing Ambrosian chant written earlier than the 12th century are extant, it is impossible to estimate how much of what survives has the character of the chant in its original form. It may be assumed that the *ambitus*, or range, of the Ambrosian melodies is smaller than that of Gregorian chant proper, that the texture is looser, and that a definite preference for the interval of the fourth (as opposed to the Gregorian fifth) is noticeable. There are, however, some melodia, obviously of a later date, consisting of a number of freely recurring melodic phrases, indicated by roman numerals (*e.g.*, I II III IIII V III IIII V III IIII). Such structure and numbering is a feature of Ambrosian chant. These melodies may either represent forerunners of the sequence melodies or later imitations.

BIBLIOGRAPHY.—The main source for the study of Ambrosian chant are three manuscripts of which the Codex Add. 34209 in the British Museum, London, is published in *Paléographie Musicale*, vol. v (facsimile) and vol. vi (transcription). On the basis of these manuscripts Dom G. M. Suñol re-edited the chants for Mass (1935) and Vespers (1939). *See also* M. Magistretti, *La Liturgia della chiesa milanese nel secolo IV* (1899); Introduction to *Paléographie musicale*, vol. v (1896); "Fonti e Paleografia del canto Ambrosiano," in *Archivio Ambrosiano*, vii (1956). (E. J. Wz.)

AMBROSIASTER, a commentary on St. Paul's epistles, "brief in words but weighty in matter," and valuable for the criticism of the Latin text of the New Testament, long attributed to St. Ambrose. Erasmus in 1527 threw doubt on the accuracy of this ascription, and the author is usually spoken of as Ambrosiaster or pseudo-Ambrose. Owing to the fact that Augustine cites some parts of the commentary on Romans as by "Sanctus Hilarius" it has been ascribed by various critics at different times to almost every known Hilary.

See A. Souter, *The Earliest Latin Commentaries on The Epistles of St. Paul* (1927).

AMEBA: see AMOEBA.

AMEGHINO, FLORENTINO (1854–1911), noted Argentine paleontologist, whose contributions of discovery, description and ordering of sequences of fossil mammals are of major importance to the science, was born Sept. 18, 1854, probably in Luján. Although he was a teacher and administrator, his studies of extinct mammals and the development of man in Argentina were his chief interests. Nearly 200 monographs and memoirs are a monument to his productivity as a scientist.

He began his investigations before he was 20 years old and, except for three years' study spent in Europe, devoted his career to Argentina. From 1902 he was director of the museum of natural history in Buenos Aires.

Ameghino's views of the origin of mammals and especially races of man were radical, and precipitated considerable controversy among his contemporaries. One of his contentions was that all mammals of the world as well as man had their beginnings in Argentina (and other parts of South America). Some of these views, however, were put forward in the face of overwhelming contrary evidence. Severe criticism served to intensify his support of these unorthodox ideas that tended to discredit his extremely valuable, purely factual contributions.

He died at La Plata on Aug. 6, 1911, a controversial figure whose studies, in the light of later evidence, are only now being seriously reappraised by the paleontological world.

His complete works are collected in *Obras Completas y Correspondencia Científica de Florentino Ameghino*, 24 vol. (1913–36). (E. C. O.)

AMEN, an old Hebrew word used in worship by Jews and Christians and to a lesser degree by Muslims. The basic meaning of the Semitic root from which it is derived is "firm," "fixed" or "sure," and the related Hebrew verb also means "to be reliable" and "to be trusted." As a religious term amen expresses agreement, confirmation or desire. The Greek Old Testament usually translates amen as "so be it" (*genoito*); in the English Bible it may be rendered as "verily" or "truly."

1. In its earliest use the amen occurs initially, referring back to the words of another speaker with whom there is agreement. It usually introduces an affirmative statement (I Kings i, 36; Jer. xi, 5; xxviii, 6; *cf.* Rev. vii, 12). Sometimes the amen stands

alone and the expected complementary sentence is suppressed and can be inferred only from the context (Deut. xxvii, 12–26; *cf.* Rev. v, 14). For emphasis, as in solemn oaths, the amen may be repeated (Num. v, 22; Ps. xli, 13; Neh. viii, 6). Such double amens are particularly common in the Fourth Gospel (25 times), even in cases in which other Gospel parallels have the singular form (compare, for example, John xiii, 38 and Mark xiv, 30).

Jewish tradition indicates that in temple liturgy the response was not a simple amen but an extended formula, such as seems to be preserved in Ps. xli, 13; lxxii, 18–19; lxxxix, 52. But the use of amen as a response by the people at the close of a doxology or prayer uttered by a priest seems to have been current as early as the time of the Chronicler; who appends an amen to extracts quoted from Ps. xcvi and cvi (I Chron. xvi, 36; *cf.* Neh. viii, 6). The liturgical use of amen developed in the synagogue was adopted by the Christians, as was the Jewish practice of enunciating the amen with full power of the voice. Justin (*c.* A.D. 150) indicates that amen was used in the liturgy of the Eucharist in his day; and it was later introduced into the baptismal service.

2. The use of initial amen ("verily" or "truly"), single or double in form, to introduce solemn statements of Jesus in the Gospels (52 times in the Synoptic Gospels and 25 times in the Fourth Gospel) has no parallel in Jewish practice. Seldom do such amens relate to a preceding speech with which they mark agreement. They rather express the certainty and truthfulness of the statement that follows.

3. A final amen, added by the speaker who offers thanksgivings or prayers, public or private, to sum up and confirm what he himself had said, developed naturally from the earlier usage in which others responded with the amen (*see* 1, above). Such use is found in the detached doxologies in Ps. lxxii, 18–19; III Macc. vii, 23; and IV Macc. xvii, 24, and final amens, with no change in speaker, are common in the New Testament from the epistles onward. The use of amen to conclude prayer was common among Jews in ancient times (Tob. viii, 8); and Christians closed every prayer with it; with the growing popularity of hymns the use of the final amen has been extended.

As early as the 1st century A.D. Jews used amen in response to a good wish; and in the middle ages they added an amen to every possible expression of a desire. Prayers were concluded with such expressions as "and let us say amen" or "Amen; may this be the will [of God]." In reaction to Christian usage (*c.* A.D. 400) Jewish leaders placed restrictions on the use of amen in their liturgy; but it is still used in synagogue services.

4. Although amen is used as an impersonal substantive in II Cor. i, 20 and the Hebrew text of Isa. lxv, 16, the personal use of "the Amen" as a designation of the Christ in Rev. iii, 14 is unique. It is interpreted by the words "the faithful and true witness," added immediately in apposition, which guarantee the certain truth of the revelation given by him.

Although amen is but little used among Muslims it is universally employed among them after every recital of the first sura.

BIBLIOGRAPHY.—G. Dalman, *The Words of Jesus*, pp. 226–229 (1902); L. Gillet, "Amen," *Expository Times*, 56:134–136 (1944–45); H. W. Hogg, "Amen; Notes on Its Significance and Use in Biblical and Post-Biblical Times," *Jewish Quarterly Review*, 9:1–23 (Oct. 1896); E. Nestle, "The Last Word in the Bible," *Expository Times*, p. 190 ff. (Jan. 1897). (RD. A. B.)

AMENDMENT, a change of some document or written or oral statement, by substitution, omission or addition, or by a combination of these methods of change. The change or proposed change may intend improvement or correction by the one proposing the amendment, but improvement or correction are not essential elements.

The word "amendment" is used in many transactions, such as the amendment of federal and state constitutions and statutes, and of municipal ordinances; of bills in the course of their passage by congress or state legislatures; of indictments in criminal cases; of pleadings and records in civil and criminal proceedings, and in briefs filed in such cases; of trusts; of the charters of private corporations and of numerous other papers representing private transactions; and of oral motions that may be made in meetings of public bodies and private organizations (*see* RULES

It is difficult to generalize about the function of amendments to governmental constitutions or charters. In the 17th century John Locke drafted his "Fundamental Constitutions" intended to "remain the sacred and unalterable form and rule of government of Carolina forever." In the 18th century, this attitude toward immutability was abandoned and the United States constitution of 1789 provided for its own amendment. (*See* UNITED STATES [OF AMERICA]: *Administration and Social Conditions*.) However, the difficulty of amendment, with other reasons, led to reliance on judicial review (*q.v.*) as the primary means of adjusting the U.S. constitution to new developments. Among democratic nations, no other constitution is so difficult to alter by formal amendment as that of the United States.

Beginning in the 19th century, constitutions provided for somewhat easier amendment procedures. Among U.S. state constitutions, amendment is often so easy as to give the total result the likeness of a statutory code. (*See* also LEGISLATION; and for motions to amend, RULES OF ORDER.)

Many legislative enactments take the form of amendments to existing law. Thus, in England, for example, the 1949 provision reducing the powers of the house of lords was titled "An Act to amend the Parliament Act of 1911." In the United States, among many examples, Trade Agreements Extension acts are regularly enacted by congress to amend the Tariff act of 1930.

Legislative rules governing amendments vary. Most require that amendments be "germane" or pertinent to the subject of a bill, but this may raise difficult questions of interpretation. An amendment may sometimes be a "substitute motion" introduced in place of pending business, which, if passed, would kill the original measure by supplanting it. Another form of amendment is the "rider"—a provision tacked onto a bill—which its sponsor hopes to get through more easily by including it in other legislation. Riders are also aimed at making the original bill so unattractive as to defeat it.   (W. F. D.; C. E. V.)

AMENDOLA, GIOVANNI (1882–1926), Italian journalist who became one of the foremost opponents of fascism, was born in Rome on April 15, 1882. As a young man he contributed articles on philosophical and literary subjects to various reviews and also published several books. He was for a time a lecturer in philosophy at the University of Pisa. Turning to political journalism, he was successively Rome correspondent of the *Resto di Carlino* and of the *Corriere della Sera*. He campaigned for Italy's entry into World War I, in which he fought as a volunteer. After the war he devoted himself entirely to politics as a Democratic Liberal and favoured a policy of *rapprochement* with the Slavs. First elected to parliament in 1919, he was in 1922 minister for the colonies in Luigi Facta's cabinet. After Mussolini's advent to power he became a leader of the opposition and attacked the new regime through the columns of his newspaper *Il Mondo*. After the murder of G. Matteotti he was one of the deputies who withdrew from the chamber in the "Aventine secession" (*see* ITALY: *History*). In spite of threats against his life during the election campaign of 1924, he declared the fascist electoral law to be unconstitutional. He died at Cannes, France, on April 6, 1926, as a result of injuries received when a gang of fascists attacked him in the Italian spa of Montecatini.

See G. Carocci, *Giovanni Amendola* (1956); F. Rizzo, *Giovanni Amendola e la crisi della democrazia* (1956).

AMENEMHET (AMUN-EM-HET; Gr. AMMENEMES), the name of four pharaohs of the 12th dynasty of Egypt and several of the 13th. The first three were the most notable.

AMENEMHET I (reigned *c.* 1991–1962 B.C.), the first pharaoh of the 12th dynasty, is perhaps to be identified with the vizier Amenemhet who held office under the last 11th-dynasty king, Mentuhotep S'ankh-ka-Ra; if so he must have usurped the throne. To him was due the recovery of administrative efficiency and economic prosperity after a long period of civil war, and it was probably he who moved the capital from Thebes to Al Fayyum (oasis), where large irrigation schemes were inaugurated. He secured the northern frontier of Egypt against Asiatic incursions and extended the southern as far as Korusko. A collection of maxims

on wise government, purporting to be addressed by the king to his heir Senusret I, hints in the preamble at an attempt on his life which may have been successful. He was buried in the north pyramid at Lisht.

AMENEMHET II (NUB-KAU-RA), grandson of Amenemhet I, reigned from *c.* 1929 to 1895 B.C. Under his administration agriculture was fostered and the Red sea trade with Punt (probably the Somali coast) reopened. He was buried in the "white pyramid" at Dahshur. In the smaller nearby pyramids of his princesses were found some of the finest examples of Middle Kingdom jewelry.

AMENEMHET III reigned from *c.* 1842 to 1797 B.C. To his long and prosperous reign are attributed large-scale works of drainage and irrigation in Al Fayyum (planned and begun by his predecessors) and the great building known to the Greeks as the Labyrinth, which was probably his mortuary temple. Amenemhet III built two pyramids, one at Dahshur which was abandoned in favour of a larger at Hawara, near the Labyrinth. *See* EGYPT: *History*.   (M. S. DR.)

AMENHOTEP (AMUN-HOTPE, "Amun is pleased"; Gr., AMENOPHIS or AMENOPHTHIS), the name of four pharaohs of the 18th dynasty and of numerous private persons in ancient Egypt.

AMENHOTEP I (DJESER-KA-RA), was the son of Ahmose I, the Liberator. The length ascribed by Manetho to his reign, namely 20 years and 7 months, is probably correct; it is dated to *c.* 1546–1526 B.C. by a recorded rising of the star Sothis in his 9th year. He extended Egyptian rule over the Libyan oases and southward beyond the second cataract of the Nile and appointed a viceroy over Nubia. Much of his reign was spent in reorganizing the administration of Egypt and in building temples; he was later worshiped as patron of the Theban metropolis.

AMENHOTEP II (AA-KHEPERU-RA), the son of Thutmose III and Queen Meryt-Ra Hatshepsut, reigned from *c.* 1450 to *c.* 1425 B.C. His upbringing was strenuous; he prided himself on his strength and physical prowess, and his monuments refer repeatedly to feats of horsemanship and chariot driving, rowing and archery and to his personal bravery in battle. Succeeding to the throne as a youth he carried on his father's policy of ruthless aggression in Asia and made Napata the boundary of his Nubian empire. Remains of his mortuary temple have been found in west Thebes; his tomb (no. 35) in the valley of the tombs of the kings is well preserved.

AMENHOTEP III (NEB-MA'ET-RA'), sometimes called "the Magnificent," was the son and successor of Thutmose IV. During his largely peaceful reign, *c.* 1417–1379 B.C., Egypt was at the height of its prosperity, and skilful diplomacy, as the Amarna tablets show, maintained the pharaoh's prestige at the Babylonian, Assyrian, Mitannian and Hittite courts. Amenhotep employed his great wealth in the building and embellishment of temples and palaces throughout the land. Of his funerary temple in west Thebes, probably the largest of its kind, virtually nothing is now left but the huge monolithic statues known as the Colossi of Memnon. South of it was the royal palace, or complex of palaces, covering 80 ac., and the vast pleasure lake which he made for his chief wife, Tiy (who appears to have been influential in affairs of state). On the opposite bank of the Nile he greatly enlarged the temples of Karnak and built a temple at Luxor. His mummy and portraits show that his declining years were marred by ill-health.

AMENHOTEP IV, son of Amenhotep III, is better known as Ikhnaton (*q.v.*).

AMENHOTEP, THE SON OF HAPU (Amenhotep the Wise) was chief architect and adviser to the pharaoh Amenhotep III. He was responsible for erecting the colossi mentioned above and other large public works and was awarded the unique privilege of a mortuary temple next to the king's own. In Ptolemaic times he was worshiped as a god in various temples, his father Hapu being identified with Apis (Hapi). *See* EGYPT: *History*. (M. S. DR.)

AMENORRHEA, the absence of the menstrual flow, is normal before puberty, during pregnancy and lactation, and after the menopause; otherwise not. After conception the first expected period is usually missed, but sometimes a flow, usually light or only spotting, is noticed at this time. Occasionally, however, there is a flow after conception that is mistaken for a typical menstrual period. In such cases the termination of the pregnancy is calculated from what is really the second month, and consequently labour sets in a month sooner than expected. *See* MENSTRUATION.

(G. W. B.)

AMERCEMENT (AMERCIAMENT), in English law, an arbitrary pecuniary penalty, inflicted in former days on an offender by the peers or equals of the party amerced. The word has in modern times become practically a poetical synonym for fine or deprivation. But an amercement differed from a fixed fine, prescribed by statute, by reason of its arbitrary nature; it represented a commutation of a sentence of forfeiture of goods, while a fine was originally an arrangement agreed upon between the judge and the prisoner to avoid imprisonment. Articles 20 to 22 of Magna Carta regulated the assessment of amercements. *See* MAGNA CARTA; ENGLISH LAW.

AMERICA FIRST COMMITTEE, a noninterventionist foreign policy pressure group organized in the United States in Sept. 1940. It opposed Pres. Franklin D. Roosevelt's policy of extending all aid short of war to the victims of Axis aggression. Its leaders feared such aid would involve the United States unnecessarily and unwisely in World War II. The founder and national director of the America First committee was R. Douglas Stuart, Jr., a Yale university law school student. Gen. Robert E. Wood of Sears, Roebuck and company was national chairman. Other spokesmen included Charles A. Lindbergh (*q.v.*), Burton K. Wheeler, Gerald P. Nye and John T. Flynn. The committee enrolled over 800,000 members. It was accused of getting support from Nazi sympathizers, but its leaders tried to bar such persons from membership.

America First battled against passage of the Lend-Lease act, use of the navy for convoys and repeal of provisions of the Neutrality act in 1941. It was defeated in its major campaigns and failed to prevent entry of the U.S. into World War II. But the noninterventionist strength it represented discouraged President Roosevelt from moving further and faster to aid Great Britain against Nazi Germany. After the Japanese attack on Pearl Harbor on Dec. 7, 1941, the committee dissolved and urged its members to support the war effort.

See Walter Johnson, *The Battle Against Isolation* (1944); Wayne S. Cole, *America First: the Battle Against Intervention, 1940–41* (1953).

(W. S. Co.)

AMERICAN ABORIGINAL LANGUAGES. The term "American aboriginal languages" (or, more commonly, "American Indian languages") is a convenient designation for the languages spoken by the original inhabitants of the new world and their modern descendants. It has no other significance. The American Indian languages do not form a single historically interrelated stock (as do the Indo-European languages), nor are there any structural features (in phonetics, grammar or vocabulary) whereby American Indian languages can be distinguished as a whole from languages spoken elsewhere.

Number and Distribution of Languages.—We have no precise knowledge of the number of American Indian languages spoken in the aboriginal period, *i.e.*, before discovery and European contact, nor of the size of the population which spoke these languages. Estimates of new world population, based in large part on reports of 16th- and 17th-century contacts between Indians and Europeans, vary widely. The population has been put as low as 8,400,000 and as high as 50,000,000. J. H. Steward in 1949 suggested 15,500,000, an estimate which appeared to meet general agreement. This population probably spoke more than 2,000 languages; the precise number cannot be determined.

During the aboriginal period (before about A.D. 1500), the American Indian languages covered both continents and the islands of the West Indies. There were, however, considerable differences in the distribution of the languages and language groups, and in the size of the populations which spoke these languages.

In America north of Mexico, where the Indian population was thinly spread, there were a number of language groups, *e.g.*, the Eskimoan, Algonkian, Athabascan and Siouan, which covered large

territories and included a score or more of closely related idioms. Other language groups, however, were smaller and the areas containing them correspondingly more diverse in language. In California, for example, more than 20 distinct language groups were represented. These, according to Edward Sapir, exhibited greater and more numerous linguistic extremes than may be found in all of Europe. America north of Mexico, taken as a whole, had about 300 distinct languages, spoken by a population estimated at about 1,500,000.

Mexico and Central America had a much larger Indian population—estimated at about 5,000,000—which spoke about the same number of languages, 250 to 300, as were spoken north of Mexico. Some of these languages, *e.g.*, of the Aztecs of central Mexico and the Maya of Yucatan and Guatemala, belonged to large and complexly organized empires and probably accounted for most of the native population. Others were far more restricted in area and numbers of speakers. The area of greatest linguistic diversity appears to have been in southern Mexico and the region now occupied by the Central American republics.

South America, according to J. Alden Mason (1950), had both the largest aboriginal population of the three regions mentioned and the greatest diversity of languages. Here there were probably 9,000,000 people and in excess of 1,400 languages. The bulk of the population was in the Andean region, where there was also a powerful Indian empire, that of the Incas. Their conquests spread the Incas' Quechuan languages far beyond their original homeland in the southern Peruvian highlands and unquestionably resulted in the extinction or reduction of many other Indian tongues. The area of greatest linguistic diversity in South America was in the tropical lowlands of Venezuela, the Guianas and Brazil. Languages of three South American groups spread northward: the Chibchan (centred in Colombia) to parts of Central America, and the Cariban and Arawakan (both mainly in Brazil) to the West Indies.

Indian Languages Still Spoken at Mid-20th Century.—European conquest and colonization ultimately led to the disappearance of many American Indian language groups and to radical changes in the lives of the groups which survived. A number of languages became extinct: in the West Indies the aboriginal languages have almost entirely disappeared, and in America north of Mexico, according to C. F. Voegelin (1941), nearly one-half of the aboriginal languages had become extinct. The situation is somewhat different in Central and South America. There, although precise figures are not available, fewer languages had disappeared and a greater number were still spoken, some of them by large populations.

Of the American Indian languages still spoken, many by the mid-1950s had only a bare handful of speakers. In America north of Mexico, more than 50% of the surviving languages had fewer than 1,000 speakers each, and of these, more than 70% had less than 500 speakers each (Voegelin, 1941). In communities as small as these, most people were bilingual, and the younger people, educated in English, often had little more than a superficial command of the native idiom. In short, even though the Indian population north of Mexico was actually increasing (1950 census), most of the aboriginal languages were slowly dying out. Only a few languages were flourishing: Navaho, spoken in New Mexico and Arizona by nearly 80,000 people; Ojibwa, in northern United States and southern Canada, by about 32,000; Cherokee, in Oklahoma and North Carolina, by more than 50,000; and Dakota-Assiniboin, in the northern portions of midwestern United States, by more than 42,000. Even in these groups, however, there was a high proportion of bilingualism and it was unlikely that the native languages would long survive in competition with the obviously more useful languages (English and Spanish) of European origin.

In parts of South and Central America there were still a number of widespread and flourishing language groups. Quechuan was one of these: it was estimated that this group of closely related dialects had several million speakers in Ecuador, Peru and parts of Bolivia and Argentina. One of these still-living languages, the dialect of Cuzco, Peru, was the principal language of the Inca empire, conquered by Pizarro in 1533. The Indians of Mexico and Central

America also still spoke languages which go back to the time of the Spanish conquest (about A.D. 1500): Nahuatlan (or Aztecoid), a group of languages in central and parts of southern Mexico with about 750,000 speakers; the Mayan languages, spoken in Yucatan, Guatemala and adjacent territories by about 500,000 people; and Otomian of central Mexico with about 300,000 speakers. All three of these were languages of Indian empires before 1500, and both the Maya and Aztec peoples had a system of writing similar in kind to (but not derived from) the early Egyptian writing.

One other persistent Indian language group of South America deserves mention, Tupi-Guarani of eastern Brazil and Paraguay. During the aboriginal period, languages of this group were spoken by a large and widespread population. Tupi of Brazil became, after the conquest, the basis of a lingua geral, the medium of communication for Europeans and Indians throughout the Amazonian region. Guarani similarly became a general language medium for much of Paraguay. Tupi was by the mid-20th century gradually being replaced by Portuguese, but Guarani remained an important second language of modern Paraguay, and was even the vehicle of an extensive folk literature.

Classification of Languages.—Linguists classify languages by grouping them into linguistic stocks or families, each of which contains 2 to 20 or more distinct but related tongues. The relationship between languages belonging to the same stock is historical—these languages are derived from a single protolanguage, real or hypothetical, which was spoken at some time in the past. Thus, French, Spanish, Portuguese, Rumanian and a few other so-called Romance languages belong to one stock because of their common derivation from Latin, a protolanguage of which we have actual documentary record. A similar relationship obtains between English, German, Dutch and the Scandinavian languages, which are derived, however, from a hypothetical language called Proto-Germanic. In this case, as in many others, there is no documentary record of the protolanguage; it is assumed on the basis of the many systematic resemblances in sound feature, grammar and vocabulary that exist in the languages belonging to the stock.

To determine whether or not two or more languages belong to the same stock, it is necessary to compare them in some detail. If such comparison reveals the systematic resemblances mentioned above, then the languages are of the same stock. If it does not— that is, if the languages compared reveal only random similarities or similarities which are clearly the result of words and phrases borrowed by one language from another, then the languages are considered to be unrelated, that is, members of different stocks. Close relationships between languages are easy to uncover; it requires, for example, little skill to discover the many resemblances which connect English and German or Spanish and Portuguese. The remoter relationships are more difficult to discover; it is only the expert who can determine the links which unite such diverse tongues as English, Gaelic, Russian, Greek and many others into the large and widespread Indo-European family of languages.

The application of the comparative method to the American Indian languages, and the resultant classification of these languages, presents many difficult problems. For instance, only two American languages were written, and in these (Aztec and Maya) the written records are too few to be of aid to historical studies. Dependence must be placed alone on relatively modern forms (i.e., after 1500) of the languages compared, the records taken by linguists and others since first contact was made with the American aborigines. Some of these records, and in particular those made before 1850, are wholly or in large part inadequate for comparative studies. They were made for more practical reasons, as aids to missionaries and others who had reason to learn to speak and understand the aboriginal languages. Scientifically accurate recordings came for the most part after 1850 and then only for relatively few languages. There were in the mid-1950s a large number of Indian languages, particularly in Latin America, for which there were no adequate recordings at all, to say nothing of the considerable data required for purposes of classification.

As a result, the task of classifying American aboriginal languages is far from complete. Most is known about the languages north of Mexico, somewhat less of the languages of Mexico and Central America, and very little about the languages of South America and the West Indies. At mid-20th century the linguistic stocks so far established were numerous but tentative; further research would undoubtedly both reduce their number and clarify many remoter relationships which were then obscure. One fact was clear, however: the languages of the Americas are too diverse to be derived from a single source. They belong rather to a large number of stocks, which differ fundamentally from each other in sound features, grammar and vocabulary.

The precise number of linguistic stocks in the Americas was not yet determined. Conservative estimates, however, enumerated about 40 for North and Central America and between 80 and 100 for South America. In North and Central America, where linguistic studies by the late 1950s were further advanced, the latest work suggested a drastic reduction in the total number of stocks, perhaps to as few as 15 or 20. Many of these hypotheses, which consisted of attempts to link smaller language families into larger ones, were debatable; the more remote relationships which had been suggested were not supported by a great deal of evidence. In South America it seemed quite clear that the number of stocks estimated was too large; this number resulted mainly from the fact that too little was known of the South American languages to permit an adequate classification. (For details of the classification of the American Indian languages, see CENTRAL AND NORTH AMERICAN LANGUAGES; SOUTH AMERICAN LANGUAGES.)

Relations Between American Indian Languages and Languages Outside the Americas.—Although there is little doubt that the American Indians came originally from Asia, there is no clear evidence relating the languages of the Americas to those of Asia or elsewhere in the old world. Several such relationships had been proposed by the late 1950s: (1) between the Eskimo-Aleut languages and the proposed Ural-Altaic stock of Asia; (2) between the Nadene languages of North America and the Sino-Tibetan languages of Asia; (3) between the Hokan languages of North and Central America and the Malayo-Polynesian of Oceania; and (4) between the Chonan languages of southern Argentina and the languages of Australia. None of these hypotheses had been verified, and the evidence for all of them was extremely slender. Far more research was needed, on both the American Indian groups concerned and on the language stocks of Asia and Oceania, before any profitable examination of the proposed relationships could be made.

Linguistic Structures of Native America.—A linguistic structure, as the linguist defines it, is made up of two parts: (1) the phonology of the language, which includes not only its distinctive sounds (phonemes) but also the patterns whereby these combine in speech; and (2) the grammar of the language, the meaningful arrangements whereby its words, phrases and sentences are constructed. Each language has also a lexicon, or stock of morphemes. Morphemes are the basic meaningful units of linguistic form: where many words, and all phrases and sentences may be divided into sequences of two or more meaningful units, morphemes may not. Some morphemes function also as words (for example, in English, "cat," "dog," "horse")—these are called free morphemes. Others function only as parts of words: examples are such prefixes as the in- of "in-active" or suffixes like the -er of "farm-er"; these are bound morphemes.

The American Indian tongues exhibit a wide diversity of structure, one so wide that it is quite impossible to speak of the general presence or absence among them of particular structural features. It is also true that structural features evidenced by American Indian languages are only rarely restricted to them. Most of the structural peculiarities found in one or another American language may be paralleled, more or less precisely, in languages outside the Americas.

Finally, it should be noted that there is nothing "primitive" or "undeveloped" about American Indian linguistic structures. All of these structures, whether of the languages of the culturally advanced Maya, Aztec and Quechua peoples, or of the languages of the less advanced Eskimo, Paiute or Ge-speaking peoples, have a fully developed phonology and grammar, as rigidly perfected and systematized as those of the languages which, like French, English or Spanish, have become the vehicles of a world civilization.

To give some notion of the character and variety of American Indian linguistic structures, we shall describe and illustrate, in the following paragraphs, a few items of phonology and grammar. The languages chosen for illustration are mainly from America north of Mexico, simply because more is known of these languages than of those in Central and South America.

Phonology.—Like languages everywhere else, those of the American Indian vary greatly in phonology, with respect both to the number and kind of the phonemes employed and to the ways in which these may be combined. Some languages have relatively few phonemes: Greenlandic Eskimo has only 17, and Tonkawa, a nearly extinct language of Texas, 25 (as compared with 46 in most English dialects). In Navaho, however, we find 47 phonemes, and the same number is found in Nootka, a language of Vancouver Island.

Some phonemes, particularly consonants, apparently occur more frequently in American Indian languages than in languages elsewhere. One of these is the glottal stop, a sound (often written ') made by closing momentarily the vocal cords in the larynx. This consonant is rather widespread in the Americas, particularly in western North America, but occurs less frequently in the languages of Europe and Asia. In America, too, we find the so-called glottalized consonants, which are formed by making simultaneous closures in the mouth and in the larynx and releasing the two together. The sounds *t* and *k,* and affricates like the *ch* of English "church," are frequently so modified. In Navaho, for example, a clear distinction is made between ordinary *t, k* and *ch,* and *t, k* and *ch* with accompanying glottal closure. Navaho also modifies continuants, *e.g.,* sounds like *m, n* and *y,* by glottalization. This feature occurs elsewhere in the Americas but appears to be rare in other parts of the world.

Other unusual consonantal features found in American Indian languages include: (1) a voiceless and spirantized (fricative) *l* (written ł and similar to the Welsh *ll*), which contrasts with voiced *l* (as in English "light") and, in some languages, with an *l* that is neither voiced nor spirantized; (2) the distinction, in many languages, between aspirated consonants (followed by a puff of air, as in the *p* and *t* of "put" and "take") and consonants which are not aspirated (these are similar to the *p* and *t* of French *père* and *tu,* respectively); (3) the distinction, found in the Eskimo languages, among others, between a palatal *k* (roughly as in English) and one articulated farther back in the throat (the back-velar *k*); and (4) the occurrence, particularly common among the languages of the North Pacific coast, of many consonant clusters; *i.e.,* sequences of two to as many as five consonants without an intervening vowel.

Vowel systems are often quite simple in the languages of the Americas. Greenlandic Eskimo has only three distinctive vowels: *i, u* and *a* (compare the relatively complex scheme of most English dialects, which usually have nine distinctive vowels). Other American Indian languages, however, have more complex vowel systems: Navaho has 8 vowels, Tonkawa 10, and an Otomi dialect of Temoaya, Mex., has 12.

Nasalized vowels (similar to those of French) are found in some languages: of the eight Navaho vowels, four are nasalized. In the Otomi dialect mentioned above, the vowels *i, a* and *u* contrast with nasalized *i, a* and *u,* but the remaining six vowels are all without nasalization. Taos (a language of New Mexico) has 11 vowel phonemes: *a, e, i, o* and *u,* nasalized *a, e, i, o* and *u* and one vowel, phonetically written ə, which is unnasalized.

In some American Indian languages, as in English, stress accent plays an important role. This is true, for example, of Taos, Delaware (an eastern Algonkian language) and Tunica (a language of Louisiana). Other languages are characterized by pitch accent (rising and falling tones), better known for their occurrence in Chinese, or by complex accentual systems in which both stress and pitch play a part. Navaho is a pitch language (stress plays no role) where each syllable must be either high or low in pitch relative to others in the same utterance. Thus, *bini'* means "his nostril" if both syllables are high in pitch, "his face" if both have the low tone, and "his waist" if the first is low and the second high.

Grammar.—American Indian languages are sometimes called polysynthetic, to indicate that the words of these languages are in general made up of long series of bound morphemes. An example of polysynthesis is found in Yana (a language of northern California), in the word *yābanaumawildjigummaha 'nigi,* "let us, each one (of us), move indeed to the west across (the creek)!" This form contains seven bound morphemes: the stem *yā-* "several people move"; formal suffixes of mode (*-ha'* hortatory) and person (*-nigi* "we"); and the modifying suffixes *-banauma* "everybody," *-wil* "across," *-dji* "to the west" and *-gumma* "indeed."

Polysynthesis is not found in all American Indian languages, although it does exist in a number, notably the languages of the Eskimo-Aleut and Algonkian stocks. Other American Indian languages, like Takelma (of southwestern Oregon) and Yokuts (of California), have less complex word structures (much like those of Latin or modern German), and still others (*e.g.,* Coos of the Oregon coast) have even simpler word structures, comparable to those of modern English. In grammar, as in phonology, there is no simple typological category which encompasses all American Indian languages and sets them off from languages spoken elsewhere.

The paragraphs which follow illustrate some aspects of grammar in a few American Indian languages; these, as the reader will note, are by no means general or exclusive to the Americas.

1. Gender, as illustrated by the masculine, feminine and neuter noun categories of many European languages, is rare in the Americas. It is, however, found in the Chinookan languages of the Oregon coast. An equivalent system, which divides nouns into animate and inanimate categories, is fairly widespread in North America, particularly in the languages of the Algonkian stock. Oneida, an Iroquoian language, distinguishes a kind of gender in the third person pronoun. These pronouns are four in number: neuter (for inanimate things and abstract notions), feminine-zoic (in the singular for adult, female persons or general or indefinite reference to any animal; in the dual and plural for groups composed entirely of females, any group of animals, and for inanimate dual and plural objects which are in motion), masculine (in the singular for a male person or animal; in the dual and plural for any group of persons whether these are all males, of mixed sex or their sex is unknown) and feminine indefinite (used in the singular only for a young female or old woman, or in reference to an indefinite person or persons in general).

2. Noun cases, analogous to the nominative, accusative, dative and genitive of modern German, are found in some American Indian languages (notably Yokuts and Wintun of California), but a majority of American languages (at least in the region north of Mexico) are as innocent of case distinctions as modern French or English. Greenlandic Eskimo is exceptional in having a complex system of noun inflection for both case and number.

Singular, dual and plural are distinguished for most nouns, as are two purely syntactic cases, absolutive and relative, and six adverbial cases: locative, ablative, allative, perlative, instrumental and simulative. Details of this system are too complex for inclusion here. (See *Handbook of American Indian Languages,* part i, p. 1010 ff.)

3. Plurality of the noun is often expressed as precisely as in English or French—and sometimes, as noted above for Eskimo, with greater precision. But there are many Indian languages where the noun has the same form in both singular and plural, just as with some English nouns; *e.g.,* "sheep" and "deer." In Navaho, for example, the word *tsé* may mean "stone" or "stones"; the interpretation is made from the context in which the word appears.

In some American languages, verbs may be inherently singular or plural. This is best illustrated by Navaho verbs having reference to movement of one kind or another. There is, for example, no verb which precisely parallels our verb "to go"; there are, instead, three quite distinct forms: *-yá* "one person goes," *-'ààs* "two persons go" and *-káàh* "several persons go." Transitive verbs are frequently altered to reflect the singularity or plurality of the object. Thus, *-γé* "to kill one" but *-γán* "to kill many" and *-tsèèd* "to slay, slaughter (a great many)."

4. Verb forms, in many American Indian languages, tend to be

far more complex in structure than words belonging to other form classes. In Navaho, for example, nouns have but one paradigm (declension, in nouns, or conjugation, in verbs), the possessive, whereas verbs are generally conjugated in seven. These conjugations do not emphasize tense, as in many European languages, but centre rather on aspect (indicative of the progress of the action) and mode (indicative of the manner of the action). Of the seven Navaho verb conjugations, only one expresses tense—the future. Four are aspectual: the imperfective, which denotes an action moving toward completion, the perfective, one which has been completed, the progressive, one in progress, and the iterative, one which is repeated over and over again. The remaining two conjugations are mainly modal: the customary, which denotes an action performed by reason of habit or custom, and the optative, expressive of a desire that an action be performed.

Tense distinctions are made, however, in some American Indian languages. In Wishram, a Chinookan dialect, we find six tenses: present, future and four preterit tenses which differ from each other in the remoteness of time from the moment of speaking. The Takelma language, on the other hand, distinguishes only two tenses: aoristic or indefinite, which may refer either to the present or the past, and the future.

5. An interesting feature of verb structure, which is found in a number of Indian languages, is noun incorporation, a technique of including noun stems (or some variant form of the stem) within the verb. Noun incorporation has been observed in the Nahuatlan languages of Mexico, Southern Paiute (western United States), Yana, Takelma, the Iroquoian languages (of northeastern United States and southeastern Canada) and Pawnee (of the southern plains region of the United States). We list a few examples from Yana: *k'ut-xai-sindja* "I am thirsty" (*k'ut-* "to want, desire"; *-xai-* incorporated form of *xana* "water"); *k'ut-au-sindja* "I want fire" (*k'ut-* "to want, desire"; *-au-* incorporated form of *auna* "fire"); *bui-djalilaihgadu-isiwandja* "he kicks my calf (of leg)" (*bui-* "to kick"; *djalilaihgadu* "calf of leg"); *haik'u-dal-sindja* "I am sick-handed (have a hurt hand)" (*haik'u-* "to be sick"; *-dal-,* incorporated form of *dalla* "hand").

6. Personal pronoun systems exhibit a considerable diversity in the Americas. In Navaho we find a relatively simple system, made up of: *ší*, first person singular; *nì*, second person singular; *bí* and *xó*, third person; and *nàxí,* first or second person dual. The two third person forms are differentiated as follows: *bí* has reference to persons psychologically close to the speaker, *e.g.,* his friends, relatives or fellow tribesmen; *xó* to persons psychologically remote, *e.g.,* nonrelatives or strangers. Gender distinctions, as in English "he," "she" and "it," are not made in the Navaho pronoun. Note, too, that there is only one plural form, the dual *nàxí* which refers to either the first or the second person and is also used in speaking directly to a second person in very formal discourse. No true plural is expressed in the Navaho pronominal system but *bí, xó* and *nàxí* may take a prefix *dà-*, which defines a distributive plural: *dà-bí, dà-xó* "they, each one of them" and *dà-nàxí* "we, you (pl.), each one of us, you."

Oneida possesses a far more complicated scheme. Taking into account only the subject pronouns (expressed by prefixes to the verb), we find the following distinctions in the singular (here given only in translation; the actual Oneida forms are too complicated to describe briefly): first person, second person, third person feminine-zoic gender, third person masculine and third person feminine-indefinite. The dual forms are: we two (someone and I), we two (you and I), you two and dual third persons for the feminine-zoic and masculine genders. Plural forms are similarly organized: we (they and I), we (you plural and I), you plural third persons for the feminine-zoic and masculine. The distinction between dual and plural inclusive (you and I, you plural and I) and dual and plural exclusive (someone and I, they and I) is an interesting and rare one, even in the Americas.

7. Demonstrative pronouns (like English "this," "that," "these," "those") also reveal wide variation in American languages. In Kwakiutl (of southern British Columbia) the word "that" of the expression "that house" must be translated by one or another of the following six forms (indicated in translation by a phrase; the native form is a single word): the (house) visible near me, the (house) invisible near me, the (house) visible near thee, the (house) invisible near thee, the (house) visible near him, the (house) invisible near him. All of these are indifferently singular or plural. In contrast, the Navaho system of demonstratives is relatively simple, although it is still very different from that found in English. Here we find five forms: *díí,* which is roughly the same as English "this" or "these" (no distinction is made for number), *'éí* "that nearby (close to the speaker and visible)," *nà-γáí* "that (near the one spoken to and visible)," *ńléí* "that (away from both speaker and spoken to but visible)" and *'èí* "that (remote and invisible)."

Structural Survey.—Sapir (1929) divided the American Indian languages north of Mexico (and some spoken in Mexico and Central America) into six major groups, and summarized the major structural characteristics of each group. This characterization, although it does not include the many other languages of Central and South America, nonetheless provides the best general survey of American Indian structural types available. (For a detailed statement of the languages included in the six groups, *see* CENTRAL AND NORTH AMERICAN LANGUAGES; INDIAN, NORTH AMERICAN: *Language.*)   (H. HR.)

1. The Eskimo-Aleut languages are polysynthetic and inflective; use suffixes only, never prefixes, reduplication, inner-stem modification or compounding of independent stems; have a great elaboration of the formal aspect of verb structure, particularly as regards mode and person; and make a fundamental distinction between the transitive and intransitive verb, to which corresponds the nominal case distinction of agentive-genitive and absolutive (or objective).

2. The Algonkian-Wakashan languages, too, are polysynthetic and, especially as regards Algonkian, inflective; make use of suffixes, to a much lesser extent, particularly in Algonkian and Ritwan, of prefixes, including reduplication; have important inner-stem modifications, including reduplication; have a weak development of case; and illustrate to a marked degree the process of building up noun and verb themes by suffixing to stems local, instrumental, adverbial and concretely verbalizing elements.

3. The Nadene languages, probably the most specialized of all, are tone languages and, while presenting a superficially polysynthetic aspect, are built up, fundamentally, of monosyllabic elements of prevailingly nominal significance which have fixed order with reference to each other and combine into morphologically loose words; emphasize voice and aspect rather than tense; make a fundamental distinction between active and static verb forms; make abundant use of postpositions after both nouns and verb forms; and compound nominal stems freely. The radical element of these languages is probably always nominal in force and the verb is typically a derivative of a nominal base, which need not be found as such.

4. The Penutian languages are far less cumbersome in structure than the preceding three but are more tightly knit, presenting many analogies to the Indo-European languages; make use of suffixes of formal rather than concrete significance; show many types of inner-stem change; and possess true nominal cases, for the most part. Chinook seems to have developed a secondary polysynthetic form on the basis of a broken-down form of Penutian; while Tsimshian and Maidu have probably been considerably influenced by contact with Mosan and with Shoshonean and Hokan respectively.

5. The Hokan-Siouan languages are prevailingly agglutinative; tend to use prefixes rather than suffixes for the more formal elements, particularly the pronominal elements of the verb; distinguish active and static verbs; and make free use of compounding of stems and of nominal incorporation.

6. The Aztec-Tanoan languages are moderately polysynthetic; suffix many elements of formal significance; make a sharp formal distinction between noun and verb; make free use of reduplication, compounding of stems and nominal incorporation; and possess many postpositions. Pronominal elements, in some cases nouns, have different forms for subject and object but the subject is not differentiated, as in types 1 and 4, for intransitive and transitive constructions.   (E. SA.)

Dictionaries and Texts.—American Indian languages probably have smaller vocabularies than the languages, like English, French and Spanish, which are mediums of expression for world-wide civilizations. But Indian vocabularies are not as small as some reports indicate; most of them, if adequately studied, contain thousands, rather than simply hundreds or scores, of words.

It would be a mistake to regard a small dictionary as evidence of a primitive linguistic structure. The vocabulary of a language is geared to the social and cultural requirements of the people who speak it. When a society is small and its culture relatively simple, the vocabulary is shorter than in the larger societies which possess relatively more complex cultures. American Indian groups which have, since European contact, become culturally more advanced, and which have at the same time retained their languages, have increased the native vocabulary to meet the new needs imposed by cultural change. Linguistic structures, wherever found, appear to be capable of such expansion whenever it may be demanded by an altered cultural milieu.

The truly wide differences in both structure and vocabulary which separate Indian languages from those of modern Europe and America result in considerable difficulties when translation is attempted from languages of one group to those of the other. These difficulties are sometimes interpreted as evidence that Indian languages are somehow less expressive, or even incapable of reproducing the finer nuances of meaning commonly employed in the languages of great civilizations.

But this is only a half-truth, at best. The fact is that translation is as difficult when we go from an Indian language to English (or another European tongue) as when we go in the opposite direction. This point may be illustrated by a very simple example: the English phrase "his house" is translated roughly by either of two Navaho expressions: *bì-kìn* or *hà-kìn*, the former employs the familiar third person possessive *bì-*, the latter the more formal pronoun *hà-*. But neither *bì-* nor *hà-* adequately translate "his," because this form implies the gender distinction between "his," "her" and "its," and also denotes a single person. But *bì-* and *hà-*, on the other hand, substitute for all nouns, regardless of gender (which is not expressed in Navaho) and may be used of either a singular or a plural referent.

If we now try to translate *bì-kìn* into English, we encounter difficulties of the same order, for *bì-* conveys the notion of a possessor psychologically close to the speaker (the familiar third person) and ignores the distinction of gender and number; no English pronoun conveys precisely this meaning. Moreover, the noun *kìn* refers to a special kind of house, one made in the modern manner and not necessarily a dwelling. The form which denotes a dwelling or home (modern or in the aboriginal style) is expressed by quite a different word, and the distinction between the two is not paralleled by any two items of the English vocabulary. The inevitable conclusion is that no language response can be separated from the cultural milieu in which it occurs, and that no two languages, providing that the cultures of the people who speak them differ, are precisely translatable one into the other.

Indian languages have of course no literature, as this term is ordinarily understood. But American Indian groups do possess oral folk literatures, the anonymous creations of many generations. These stories and poems or song texts, told and retold by expert raconteurs and sung in frequent rituals, illustrate an artistry of expression comparable to that found in the older European literature, much of which, like the Norse sagas, was derived from an earlier oral tradition. To give only one example—a Navaho song text, which comes from a ritual designed in part to aid the growing crops, and which in translation retains some of the flavour of the original:

> Growing things grow with me,
> Growing things grow with me,
> Growing things grow with me.
> Big corn grows with me.
> From beneath its feet, it grows with me,
> At the ends of its leaves, it grows with me,
> The dew of the plants, it grows with me,
> The corn flowers, they grow with me,
> The corn silk, it grows with me,
> The kernels of the corn, they grow with me,

> Beautifully, all grows with me.
> Growing things grow with me,
> Growing things grow with me,
> Growing things grow with me.

The Study of American Indian Languages.—Most, and probably all, American Indian languages are doomed to extinction; it does not seem likely that these languages will ever attain the status and importance of the modern world languages of European and Asiatic origin. One does not therefore study Indian tongues for their practical usefulness, or, since they are unwritten, to gain a better understanding of a great literary tradition. But these languages, like all others, are valuable to the science of language, for they present a variety of linguistic structures not to be found elsewhere. They provide, in fact, a laboratory for linguistic science, and it is safe to say that the science of language and general linguistic theory would not be so far advanced as it is were it not for the existence of this laboratory. To understand human language, it is not enough to know only those which are widely used; we must also have evidence from the languages of the more obscure and exotic societies of the world to complete the picture of the whole.

See also Index references under "American Aboriginal Languages" in the Index volume.

BIBLIOGRAPHY.—Franz Boas, *Handbook of American Indian Languages,* U.S. Bureau of American Ethnology *Bull. 40,* part 1 (1911), part 2 (1922), part 3 (1933–38); Harry Hoijer *et al., Linguistic Structures of Native America,* Viking Fund Publications in Anthropology, vol. 6 (1946); J. Alden Mason, "The Languages of South American Indians," vol. 6, pp. 157–317 of *Handbook of South American Indians,* U.S. Bureau of American Ethnology *Bull. 143* (1950); Edward Sapir, "Central and North American Indian Languages" in *Selected Writings in Language, Culture, and Personality,* ed. by David G. Mandelbaum (1949); J. H. Steward, "The Native Population of South America," vol. 5, pp. 655–668 of *Handbook of South American Indians,* U.S. Bureau of American Ethnology *Bull. 143* (1950); C. F. Voegelin, "North American Indian Languages Still Spoken and Their Genetic Relationships" in *Language, Culture, and Personality,* ed. by L. Spier *et al.* (1941).

(H. Hr.)

AMERICAN ACADEMY IN ROME, THE, situated on the Janiculum in Rome, Italy, comprises schools of fine arts and classical studies. Founded in 1894 under the leadership of Charles F. McKim, it is administered by a director and staff in Rome, and a president and board of trustees in New York city. The school of fine arts includes departments of architecture, painting, sculpture, landscape architecture, musical composition and creative writing, and the school of classical studies includes departments of classical studies and art history. Mature students of advanced attainment are chosen, through annual competitions, as fellows, for a term of one or more years. Residence and studio are provided in the academy without charge, and stipends are granted to cover the cost of living and travel. There is no formal instruction, but work and travel in classical lands are prescribed, and an excavation is conducted for the benefit of the students in archaeology. Results of research are published in the *Memoirs, Papers* and *Monographs* of the American Academy in Rome. By giving its selected artists and scholars opportunities for intimate association through study and travel in an atmosphere of art and amid the inspiration of masterpieces, the academy aims to contribute toward the elevation of American art and letters.

AMERICAN ASSOCIATION FOR THE ADVANCEMENT OF SCIENCE was established by scientists in 1848 to further the work of scientists, to improve the effectiveness of science in the promotion of human welfare, and to increase public understanding of the importance and promise of science in human progress. The association includes 70,000 individual members and has as formal affiliates 247 national and regional scientific societies and 47 state and regional academies of science.

All fields of science are included, and the association is divided into 18 sections; *e.g.,* physics, chemistry, geology and geography, zoology, psychology, engineering, medical sciences, etc. The association publishes the weekly magazine *Science* and a series of symposium volumes. A large annual meeting is held during the week following Christmas. Three divisions (Alaska, the Pacific coast, and the southwestern and Rocky Mountain area) also meet annually. Various special meetings and conferences are held on special topics. Other activities include work on the improvement of science teaching, the distribution of traveling libraries of science books to elementary and secondary schools, and the administration of awards to encourage research in selected areas and to encourage excellence of science reporting in the public press.

(D. W.)

AMERICAN BAR ASSOCIATION: *see* LEGAL PROFESSION.

AMERICAN CIVIL WAR, a conflict lasting four years between the United States federal government and 11 southern states that asserted their right to leave the Union. The total population (free and slave) of the southern states that seceded was slightly less than half the population of the northern states that remained in the Union. At the opening of the conflict the seceding states set up an independent government named the Confederate States of America (*q.v.*). The Civil War began when the guns of the South fired on the Federal Ft. Sumter on April 12, 1861; it ended with the surrender of Gen. *Robert E. Lee* at Appomattox Court House, Va., on April 9, 1865, and of Gen. *Joseph E. Johnston* at Durham Station, N.C., on April 26, 1865. (General *Johnston* had signed an armistice on April 18, but its terms were not acceptable to Gen. Ulysses S. Grant.) Approximately 4,000,000 troops took part in the war, which has been described as the first "modern" or "total" war—that is, a war in which the industrial potential of the victor determined the outcome. Total casualties exceeded 617,000 dead (North, 359,000; South, 258,000) and 375,000 wounded (North, 275,000; South, 100,000). The war resulted in the preservation of the Union and brought about important alteration in the U.S. constitution, the abolition of slavery and far-reaching social and economic changes.

For the sake of clarity, the names of Confederate statesmen, soldiers and ships are in italics. The article is organized according to the following outline:

I. The Outbreak of War
  1. Charleston Harbour, 1860–61
  2. The Call to Arms
  3. The Military Outlook
II. Military Operations, 1861
  1. The Opening Moves
  2. McClellan in Supreme Command
  3. Confederate Plans and Problems
  4. War in the West
III. Military Operations, 1862
  1. The Federal Offensive in the West
  2. McClellan's Peninsular Campaign
  3. The Confederate Offensive in the East
  4. The Confederate Offensive in the West
  5. The Federals Resume the Offensive
IV. Military Operations, 1863
  1. Chancellorsville
  2. Gettysburg
  3. Vicksburg and Chattanooga
V. Military Operations, 1864–65
  1. Grant in the East
  2. Sherman in the West
  3. Collapse of the Confederacy
VI. The Navies and the Blockade
VII. Concluding Observations on Military Aspects
VIII. Politics, Economics and Foreign Affairs
  1. Northern Politics
  2. Confederate Politics
  3. Economics of the War
  4. Foreign Affairs

I. THE OUTBREAK OF WAR

1. Charleston Harbour, 1860–61.—During the last months of Pres. James Buchanan's term a succession of events occurred that brought the contending sections to the verge of armed conflict. (For the earlier history of events leading to the Civil War *see* UNITED STATES (OF AMERICA): *History. See* also separate entries on battles and leaders and on major topics such as ARMY; ARTILLERY; CONFEDERATE STATES OF AMERICA; CONSCRIPTION; SMALL ARMS, MILITARY.) Soon after the election of Abraham Lincoln in Nov. 1860, the state of South Carolina called a convention that passed an ordinance of secession (Dec. 20, 1860), and Gov. *Francis Pickens* sent commissioners to Washington to claim possession of the forts in Charleston harbour and all other U.S. property in his

state. Maj. Robert Anderson, commanding the Federal garrison at Charleston secretly transferred his two weak companies from Ft. Moultrie, which was untenable against a land attack, to Ft. Sumter in the mouth of the harbour (Dec. 26). *Pickens* seized the arsenal and other forts and began throwing up batteries against Sumter while his commissioners at Washington demanded the recall of the Federal troops from Charleston. This demand Buchanan refused. He had already (Dec. 3) in his message to congress denied the right of secession, but he asserted that the constitution gave him no right to attempt coercion. He hoped for compromise, and a committee of congress considered various proposals for adjustment. A peace conference, called by Virginia, also met in Washington and suggested amendments to the constitution that would satisfy southern grievances. Lincoln and the leaders of the Republican party refused to accept the adjustments that the southerners demanded. Meantime, Buchanan sent an unarmed commercial steamer, "Star of the West," with supplies and reinforcements to Sumter, but it turned back when fired upon in the harbour on Jan. 9, 1861.

Between Jan. 9 and Feb. 1 six other states (Mississippi, Florida, Alabama, Georgia, Louisiana and Texas) followed South Carolina's example. Without attempting negotiation, their governors seized all the forts and arsenals in their respective states except Ft. Pickens in Pensacola harbour. Delegates from the seceding states met at Montgomery, Ala., organized the Confederate States of America and set up a provisional government with *Jefferson Davis* as president. Davis' inauguration took place on Feb. 18. The Confederate government then assumed control of the negotiations about Sumter. Neither Buchanan nor *Davis* was eager to precipitate a crisis. The former's fervent desire apparently was to leave the solution of the whole problem to his successor; *Davis* was chiefly concerned to get his own administration in working order. He sent Gen. *P. G. T. Beauregard*, an engineer officer of distinction, to Charleston to complete the defenses of the harbour. The day after *Beauregard* reached Charleston, Lincoln was inaugurated at Washington, D.C. (March 4, 1861).

A difficult problem confronted the new president. Seven slave states had seceded, but eight still remained in the Union. Any attempt at coercion would throw all these states, except Delaware (which practically counted as a northern state), into the arms of the Confederacy. At this stage neither side wanted war; certainly not the North, where a strong feeling was growing in favour of "letting the erring sisters depart in peace"; the South assumed a defensive role, that of a newborn nation asking only to be left alone. Lincoln's inaugural speech was really addressed to the slave states still in the Union; to the Confederate states it sounded like a declaration of war. But they sought to avoid the responsibility of striking the first blow.

The South hoped to force Lincoln's hand over Sumter. Anderson's position there was daily growing more difficult. He would have gladly evacuated the fort to avert a civil war. But his duty as a soldier compelled him to sit with folded hands while the enemy were completing their preparations. His provisions would be exhausted by mid-April. The Confederate batteries had made such progress that he doubted whether it was still possible to relieve the fort unless possession of the whole harbour were secured, and for that purpose he estimated that 20,000 men would be required. The whole U.S. army numbered only about 17,000 men, most of whom were scattered in small posts on the Indian frontier, whence they could not be hastily withdrawn.

Only on March 5 did Lincoln learn that Anderson might be starved into surrender. Gen. Winfield Scott, his chief military adviser, urged evacuation on military grounds. But Lincoln had pledged himself "to hold, occupy and possess the property and places belonging to the Government." It would be fatal to the prestige of his administration to start by going back on his word. Evacuation might seem a virtual recognition of the Confederacy. Against the advice of a majority of his cabinet he determined to send a relief expedition, carrying only food supplies, to Sumter. If the Federal flag should be fired on, that would constitute a *casus belli,* and the responsibility for beginning the war would rest on the Confederates.

Although he did not inform Anderson, Lincoln gave *Pickens* precise information of his intention. He must have foreseen the actual event. By war the Union could be restored and the North, which was not agreed on policy, could be united. *Pickens* promptly informed the Montgomery government, and *Davis* ordered *Beauregard* to reduce Sumter. On Anderson's refusal to evacuate, the batteries opened fire at 4:30 A.M. on April 12. The next afternoon Anderson agreed to surrender and evacuated the fort at noon on the 14th. The Confederate leaders' ready acceptance of Lincoln's challenge may have been due to a fear that without a collision the ardour of the southern people, many of whom had opposed secession, might abate. Neither Lincoln nor *Davis* could have foreseen the dimensions the war would assume.

2. The Call to Arms.—The fall of Sumter "fired the Northern heart." Democrats united with Republicans in denouncing this crowning insult to the national flag. Lincoln called for 75,000 militia for three months' service (April 15)—not that he underrated his task, but he intended to start by treating secession as an act of insurrection. To suppress insurrection was a constitutional function of the militia, but this force could be held only for three months' service outside its own state. The free states enthusiastically responded to the call, but the governors of the seven slave states still in the Union, except Gov. Thomas H. Hicks of Maryland, refused to raise their contingents.

The Virginia convention passed an ordinance of secession on April 17. Gov. *John Letcher* immediately seized the Harpers Ferry arsenal and Norfolk navy yard, and without waiting for popular confirmation of the convention's action entered into a military alliance with the Confederacy. North Carolina, Arkansas and Tennessee took the same course. If they had to choose between fighting for and against the Confederacy, they unhesitatingly threw in their lot with their sister states of the South. But western Virginia beyond the Allegheny mountains, which had its own grievances against the eastern section of the state and belonged geographically to the Ohio valley, repudiated the ordinance of secession and prepared to join the North. In Maryland there was a strong secessionist minority, chiefly concentrated in Baltimore, where a riot occurred (April 19) while the 6th Massachusetts regiment was passing through to Washington. For three weeks Washington was cut off from direct railway communication with the North. But troops were brought around by water to Annapolis, and thence to the capital. No help came to Baltimore from Virginia, and Governor Hicks outmaneuvered the local leaders of insurrection by pretending to yield to their demands until Gen. B. F. Butler with a small force made a sudden dash at the city and occupied it unopposed (May 13).

In Kentucky the parties were fairly equally divided. There was widespread sympathy for the South, but also a genuine devotion to the Union. The governor favoured secession but a small majority in the legislature was opposed to it. His refusal to supply Lincoln with troops met with no protest from the Unionists, who at first concentrated upon keeping the state neutral. But neutrality could not be a permanent attitude. It gave too great an advantage to the Confederates, who drew food supplies from Kentucky and were sheltered from invasion along their western front from the Alleghenies to the Mississippi. Sooner or later the Federal armies must occupy Kentucky as a base for an offensive campaign. But a premature movement would drive Kentucky into secession and to lose Kentucky would be "nearly the same as to lose the whole game," in Lincoln's judgment. Understanding the feeling of his fellow Kentuckians better than any of his counselors at Washington, he handled the critical situation with consummate tact. It was worth suffering some temporary disadvantage to win Kentucky in the end. The legislature steadily refused to summon a convention, which might declare for secession. The governor was too good a Kentuckian to overstep the constitutional limits of his office. In August a new legislature was elected with an overwhelming Unionist majority and Kentucky declared for the North in September.

In Missouri, Gov. *Claiborne F. Jackson* was a violent secessionist, eager to take his state out of the Union, and the legislature seemed ready to support him. But when a convention was summoned it proved to be overwhelmingly Unionist. An extreme section of Unionists, led by F. P. Blair, Jr. (whose brother was in Lincoln's cabinet) and largely recruited from the Germans in St. Louis, was ready to meet violence with violence. The St. Louis arsenal, the best equipped in all the slave states, was too rich a prize to be allowed to fall into *Jackson's* hands. But in February Scott had placed in it a sufficient Federal force to secure it against sudden surprise, and in March the convention had passed a resolution against secession. A large majority of the people favoured neutrality, and a policy of conciliation would probably have preserved peace within the state, as in Kentucky. But Lincoln allowed himself to be guided by the Blairs. Their agent was the fanatical Capt. Nathaniel Lyon, who broke up (May 10) a militia camp close to St. Louis on the ground that *Jackson* was plan-

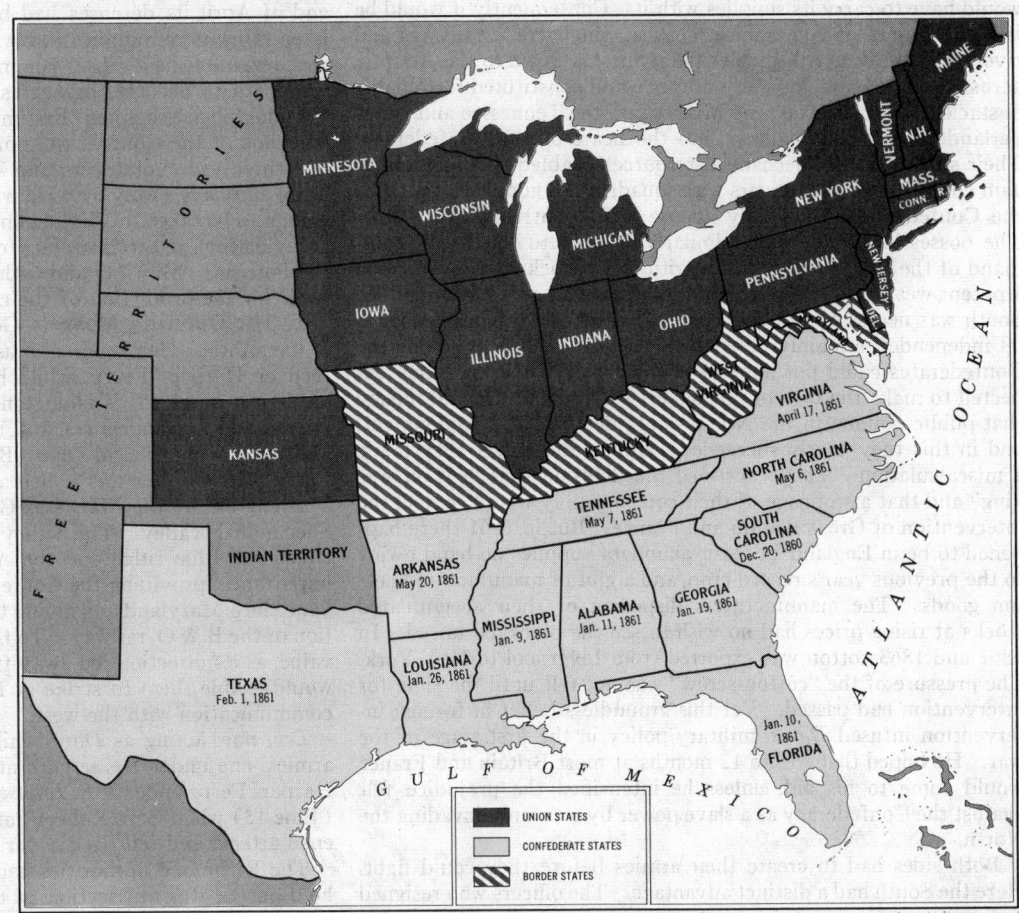

FIG. 1.—THE UNION AND THE CONFEDERACY, 1860–61, SHOWING DATES OF ADOPTION OF ORDINANCES OF SECESSION BY SOUTHERN STATES. BORDER STATES ARE THOSE SLAVE STATES WITH POPULATIONS OF DIVIDED ALLEGIANCE. TWO LOYAL STATES, CALIFORNIA AND OREGON, WERE TOO DISTANT TO BE OF MAJOR IMPORTANCE IN THE CONFLICT

ning an attack on the arsenal. His return to the city with his prisoners caused a riot with considerable loss of life. This premature appeal to force and the use of Federal troops caused a revulsion of feeling in the state. Civil war became inevitable when Lyon was appointed temporary commander of the Missouri department. He promptly ascended the Missouri river with a small force, occupied the state capital, Jefferson City (June 15), and routed a body of secessionist militia at Boonville (June 17). After this defeat *Jackson* fled to the Arkansas border.

3. The Military Outlook.—Twenty-three states (including Kentucky and Missouri) were now arrayed against 11, and the white population of the former (22,000,000) was four times that of the latter (5,500,000). But the 3,500,000 slaves in the South, so far from being a danger to the southern cause, proved of great assistance, supplying the labour required for the production of food and construction of fortifications. Over two-thirds of the officers and all the men of the U.S. army were on the side of the North; so, too, was the navy. In material resources and business capacity the North was overwhelmingly superior. All the manufacturing centres were within its borders, all the shipping in its hands. The South was dependent upon it for practically everything except food. But in spite of these advantages the North was likely to find its strength taxed to the utmost. To restore the Union the South would have to be conquered piecemeal and resistance crushed throughout the whole region, which was "30,000 sq.mi. larger than the combined areas of Austro-Hungary, Germany, France and Italy, with Belgium, Holland and Denmark thrown in." Neither a few victories in the field nor the capture of the Confederate capital would end the struggle, but only the permanent occupation of great stretches of southern territory. The country in which the invading armies must operate was sparsely inhabited, with few cities, poor railways and worse roads. Except in a few favoured districts an army could not find subsistence but would have to carry its supplies with it. Consequently it would be tied to its lines of communication, viz., single-track railways and rivers. East of the Alleghenies the rivers ran down to the Atlantic across the line of the invader's advance and constituted formidable obstacles, but to the west the Mississippi, the Tennessee and Cumberland rivers opened a way into the heart of the Confederacy. Their superiority in mechanical resources enabled the Federals to gain command of these rivers with squadrons of gunboats, to which the Confederates could only oppose a few untrustworthy craft. The possession of the navy similarly secured to the North command of the sea. In a war of attrition the blockade proved to be a potent weapon. The role of the North seeking to reconquer the South was necessarily offensive; that of the South fighting to win its independence mainly defensive. Against such heavy odds the Confederates could not hope to conquer the North, but they expected to make the task of reconquest so costly in life and money that public opinion in the North would demand its abandonment, and in this they nearly succeeded. But at the outset they made a miscalculation. They cherished the delusion that "cotton was king" and that a stoppage of their cotton supply would compel the intervention of Great Britain and France. But in 1861 there happened to be in England, at least, abundant supplies on hand owing to the previous year's record crop, and a glut of manufactured cotton goods. The manufacturers disposing of their accumulated stocks at rising prices had no wish to see the blockade raised. In 1862 and 1863 cotton was exported from Liverpool to New York. The pressure of the "cotton-screw" was not felt until the time for intervention had passed. Yet this groundless belief in foreign intervention infused *Davis'* military policy in the first stage of the war. He hoped that within 12 months at most Britain and France would come to his aid, unless he intensified the prejudice felt against the Confederacy as a slave power by wantonly invading the North.

Both sides had to create their armies before they could fight. Here the South had a distinct advantage. The officers who resigned their commissions contained a disproportionately large number of the ablest men in the old army; the two *Johnstons* and *Lee* had been pre-eminent in their profession. *Davis* was a graduate of West Point, had served seven years in the regular army, had won

distinction as a volunteer in the Mexican War, had been secretary of war in the 1850s and was chairman of the military committee in the senate until just before the outbreak of the Civil War. He could be trusted to appoint the best officers to command his armies and to see that the first steps in military organization were wisely taken. Lincoln lacked military experience, had no knowledge of the professional merits of his officers and personal acquaintance with but a few, including George McClellan, and no business training. His appointments were often made for political reasons. Nathaniel P. Banks, Benjamin F. Butler and John C. Frémont were flagrant instances. Again, the southerners could be more quickly trained as soldiers. There was in the South an aristocracy accustomed to rule, and another class of whites who recognized the aristocracy's claim to leadership. Southerners were accustomed to an open-air life, and were trained to the use of gun and horse. The North, except in the west, did not provide such good fighting material. The Federal armies were uniformly more successful in the west, where the troops on both sides were much of the same class and the North's superior resources turned the scale, whereas in the east townsmen and European immigrants were fighting against country-bred men. But, given time, the northern troops improved and throughout the war the advantage of superior numbers would be theirs. But this advantage was least felt in the first months of the war. The initial problem of both governments was not how to raise men, but how to equip them. There were more volunteers than could be armed. The stocks in the arsenals were quickly exhausted. The South had its fair share of weapons and *Davis* was purchasing arms in England. But the meagreness of his order (10,000 rifles) indicates that he did not anticipate a lengthy war.

II. MILITARY OPERATIONS, 1861

In the first days of the war the city of Washington, shut in between Virginia and Maryland, had been in danger, but by the end of April its defenses had been strengthened and a fortnight later railway communication with the North through Baltimore was re-established. *Lee,* commanding the Virginia state forces, was loath to become the aggressor and refrained from attacking Washington or helping Baltimore. Lincoln had proclaimed a blockade of the Confederate ports (April 19), and called for 42,-000 three-year volunteers and 40,000 more men for the regular army and navy (May 3). He was awaiting the result of the referendum to be taken in Virginia on May 23 and scrupulously avoided any violation of Virginian territory, though Federal troops crossed the Potomac (May 24) and without opposition occupied the south bank for the protection of the capital.

1. The Opening Moves.—Gen. Winfield Scott had little faith in the militia. He proposed to use them to defend Washington and recover Harpers Ferry, while he trained the volunteers for an autumn campaign. Washington was served by two railways, the Orange and Alexandria (O. & A.) running southward to Lynchburg and the Baltimore and Ohio (B. & O.) passing through Harpers Ferry. The former was joined at Manassas junction, 30 mi. from Washington, by the Manassas Gap railway from Strasburg in the Shenandoah valley. The Valley (as it was commonly called) between the Blue ridge and the Alleghenies was of great strategic importance, providing the Confederates with a covered line of advance into Maryland and giving them control of a considerable section of the B. & O. railway. To the Federals it was of less offensive value, as its direction led away from Richmond, but its possession would enable them to strike at Richmond's direct line of railway communication with the west.

Lee, now acting as *Davis'* military adviser, was gathering two armies, one under *Beauregard* at Manassas junction, the other at Harpers Ferry under *J. E. Johnston.* The latter evacuated his post (June 15) when Gen. Robert Patterson with a larger force threatened attack, and fell back covering the Manassas Gap railway.

The Richmond authorities had vainly attempted to retain their hold on the western section of the state. Having failed to raise recruits from the district itself for its defense, they sent a small force to hold the crests of the Alleghenies; but McClellan crossed the Ohio and overwhelmed it (July 11–13) at Rich mountain and Carrick's ford. Meanwhile a convention at Wheeling had repudiated secession and set up "a restored government of Virginia." West Virginia's defection was a serious blow to the Confederates, losing them the Ohio river, which they intended to make their line of defense, and the western portion of the B. & O. railway.

At Washington there was a demand that *Beauregard* should be attacked before the term of the militia's service expired. "On to Richmond," the new capital of the Confederacy, was the popular cry. On political grounds a plausible case could be made out for overruling Scott's advice. Gen. Irvin McDowell, whom Scott, too old and infirm for service in the field, had appointed commander of the forces south of the Potomac, submitted a plan of operations (June 24). With 30,000 men he proposed to drive *Beauregard's* 20,000 back behind the Rappahannock, provided that Patterson prevented *Johnston* from joining *Beauregard*. The plan was approved and McDowell advanced from Alexandria (July 16) and the next day *Johnston* rushed troops (part of the way by rail) to aid *Beauregard*. The opposing armies met (July 21) at Bull Run (*q.v.*), where after several hours' fighting the Federals left the field. Their retreat became a panic-stricken flight, which carried them back to the Potomac. The Confederates were too disorganized to conduct an immediate pursuit. Presently they advanced to Centreville, where they established their main position and waited for the Federals to make the next move. Washington quickly recovered from its alarm. McClellan was summoned from West Virginia and started to organize a fresh army. The first pitched battle of the war had been an alarming defeat for the North but was barren of decisive results.

In the west a neutral Kentucky interposed a barrier between the combatants, but there was some fierce fighting in southwest Missouri. Lyon pursued *Jackson* as far as Springfield, where he halted to await reinforcements. Ex-governor *Sterling Price*, commanding the state militia, raised a fresh force and being joined by Gen. *Benjamin McCulloch's* troops from Arkansas advanced against Lyon, who, being left unsupported, was defeated and killed at Wilson's creek (Aug. 10). This battle, too, lacked decisive results. *McCulloch,* having entered Missouri without orders from the government, retired after his victory into Arkansas, leaving *Price* to continue the struggle.

2. McClellan in Supreme Command.—The defeat at Bull Run was followed by "the second uprising of the North." Congress authorized the enlistment of 500,000 three-year volunteers. McClellan excelled as an organizer and within three months added 100,000 men to the army of the Potomac, whose discipline and training rapidly improved under his command. But in October public confidence in him began to abate. Confederate batteries on the lower Potomac, which closed its navigation, were left undisturbed, and at Ball's bluff (Oct. 21) four Federal regiments, ferried over the Potomac to make a reconnaissance toward Leesburg, were driven back into the river with the loss of over half their numbers. Nevertheless, on Scott's resignation McClellan, only 34 years of age, was appointed general in chief (Nov. 1). He was expected to open an offensive campaign while the roads in Virginia were still hard and dry. But though his forces were twice as strong as *Johnston's* at Centreville, he accepted the report of his secret service, which was double *Johnston's* actual numbers. Moreover, in his new post he was engaged, as will be seen, in organizing the military resources in all theatres of war and dispatching expeditions against the Confederate coast. Appreciating the value of sea power he was already contemplating the transfer of his army by water next spring to some point where he would be nearer to Richmond than *Johnston*. But he treated Lincoln with great lack of consideration in keeping his plans a secret from him. In December he contracted typhoid fever and was absent from duty for several weeks.

3. Confederate Plans and Problems.—The Confederate generals at Centreville had been vainly pressing *Davis* for reinforcements that they might enter Maryland. They realized the danger of prolonged inaction, while McClellan's army was daily growing stronger. If *Davis* could reinforce them with 20,000 trained men, they proposed to cross the Potomac and by threatening the communications of Washington force McClellan to risk a pitched battle, before he had time to train his raw levies. *Davis* in conference with his generals (Oct. 1) said that he had no reinforcements to spare; he could not withdraw troops from the coast, which was itself threatened with attack. Though the Confederate coastline extended 3,000 mi. the Federals could make the blockade practically effective by sealing up the few important harbours and getting possession of the North Carolina sounds. The forts guarding Hatteras inlet had been captured (Aug. 29); those protecting the entrance to Port Royal, S.C., fell to another and larger force (Nov. 7); and a third expedition on a still larger scale under Ambrose E. Burnside was being equipped against Roanoke Island, whose capture would complete the conquest of North Carolina's inland waters.

What, however, chiefly decided *Davis* to refuse his generals' request was his determination to stand strictly on the defensive.

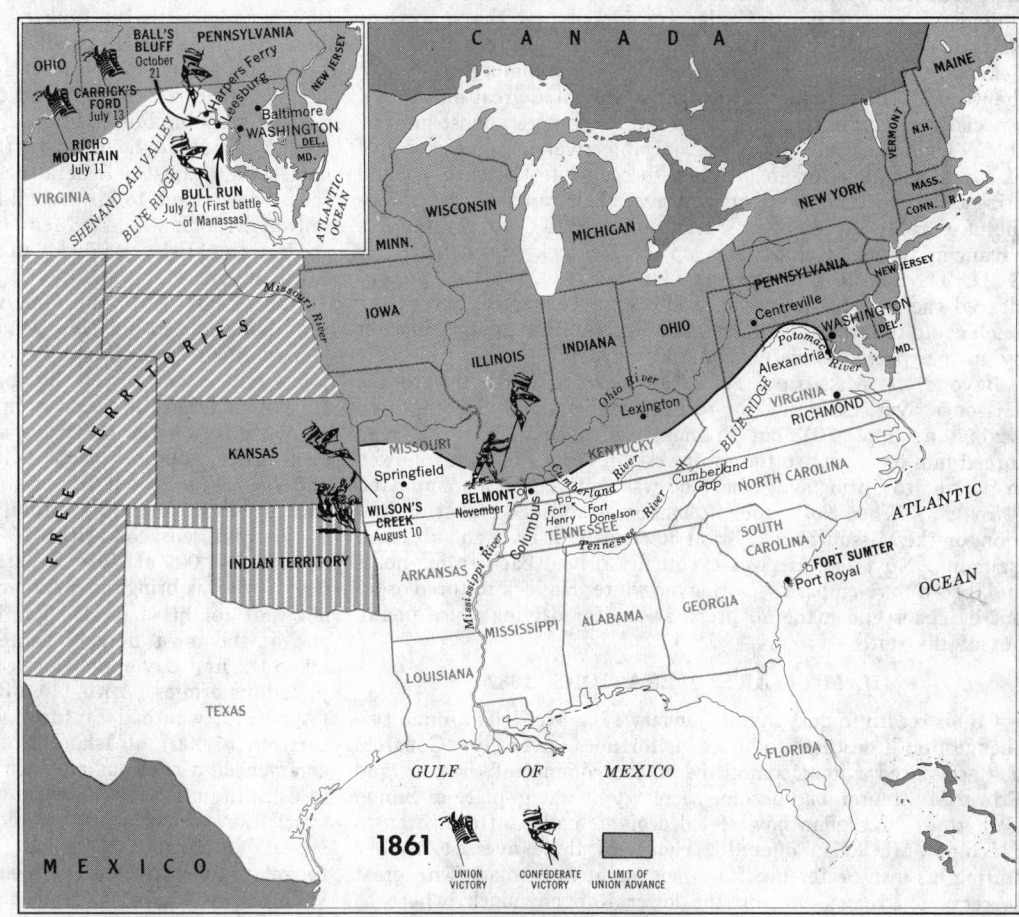

FIG. 2.—MAJOR BATTLES AND APPROXIMATE AREAS UNDER UNION AND CONFEDERATE CONTROL AT THE CLOSE OF MILITARY OPERATIONS FOR THE YEAR 1861. WINNERS OF BATTLES ARE SHOWN BY THEIR RESPECTIVE FLAGS. INSET AT UPPER LEFT SHOWS DETAIL OF MAJOR BATTLES IN VIRGINIA

Even in West Virginia, where William S. Rosecrans, McClellan's successor, was pushing forward into the Kanawha valley, no real counteroffensive was attempted. After Bull Run, *Lee* was sent to co-ordinate the operations of four separate detachments acting independently of each other. But he failed to produce an effective combination, and after his return to Richmond in October the loss of West Virginia was regarded as inevitable.

4. **War in the West.**—In the west, Confederate encroachments upon Kentucky's territory forced that state into the war. Frémont, commanding in Missouri, was threatening an expedition down the Mississippi, which would involve the occupation of the Kentucky shore. Therefore *Leonidas Polk*, general and bishop, early in September seized Hickman and Columbus, which afforded strong defensive positions on the river, while Grant, one of Frémont's brigadiers, promptly replied by occupying Paducah and Smithland at the mouths of the Tennessee and Cumberland. *Polk's* refusal to withdraw his troops, unless Grant set the example, ended Kentucky's neutrality. A new theatre of war was opened up, the great extent of which offered immense possibilities to either side. McClellan on becoming general in chief set up in the west two military departments, that of the Missouri embracing all Kentucky west of the Cumberland under Henry W. Halleck, and that of the Ohio including the rest of Kentucky under Don Carlos Buell. *Davis* appointed *A. S. Johnston*, one of his ablest generals, to supreme command in the west. *Johnston* advanced into Kentucky and took up a position with his left at Columbus and his right at the important railway junction of Bowling Green, while Forts Henry and Donelson in the centre guarded the approaches up the Tennessee and Cumberland rivers. At the outset the Federals were ill prepared to take the offensive. In Missouri, Frémont had left everything in confusion. The troops from the free states north of the Ohio had been largely diverted to West Virginia or Missouri. Lincoln and McClellan pressed Buell to advance into east Tennessee, Lincoln wishing to send relief to the distressed Unionists there, while McClellan considered that the success of his campaign in Virginia depended upon the capture of the East Tennessee railway, Richmond's direct line of communication with the west. But the proposed movement presented great difficulties, especially so late in the year, when the roads were almost impassable. There was no railway or navigable river to serve as a line of communication for an invading force, while the enemy could bring up troops from east or west over their railway. Buell was therefore reluctant to move. Meanwhile a small Confederate force advancing through Cumberland gap into Kentucky was defeated by G. H. Thomas at Mill Springs (Jan. 19, 1862). This victory cleared the way for an advance into east Tennessee, but before Buell could follow it up, his attention was called to another quarter by an unexpected move on Halleck's part.

Beyond the Mississippi *Price* had marched north toward the Missouri river, gathering up recruits as he went. He captured Lexington (Sept. 20), but Frémont's advance with 40,000 men forced him to retreat to the southwest border. Frémont followed in pursuit to Springfield, where he was relieved of his command (Nov. 2). When *Polk* from Columbus established a post at Belmont on the Missouri bank, Grant descended the river and attacked Belmont (Nov. 7). He was eventually driven back to his boats and forced to re-embark. During the winter Halleck restored order out of chaos and made all preparations for driving *Price* finally out of the state.

III. MILITARY OPERATIONS, 1862

On his return to duty in mid-January 1862 McClellan found two changes, both destined to affect his fortunes adversely. Congress had appointed a joint committee on the conduct of the war, and Edwin M. Stanton had become secretary of war in place of Simon Cameron. McClellan now revealed his new plan of campaign to Lincoln. McClellan offered a choice of three overseas routes, stating his own preference for a movement to be made with great secrecy to Urbana, Va., on the lower Rappahannock, where he would be within 50 mi. of Richmond. He expected by a rapid advance from that base to cut off a Confederate force in the Yorktown peninsula and capture Richmond, before *Johnston* could

intervene. Lincoln did not see how the preparations could be kept secret, and was sure that McClellan would still find *Johnston* between himself and Richmond. He objected to any movement that uncovered Washington and withdrew McClellan from interposing between the capital and *Johnston*. He gave, however (Feb. 27), a grudging assent to an overseas movement without specifying the actual point of disembarkation. Finally he forbade the Urbana plan and left McClellan his choice between landing at Ft. Monroe at the end of the Yorktown peninsula, the route which McClellan considered the worst of the three, and making an overland campaign. McClellan chose the first alternative. Probably the withdrawal (March 9) of *Johnston* behind the Rappahannock reconciled him to the sacrifice of his Urbana plan. Throughout these discussions Lincoln demanded adequate protection for Washington, and McClellan undertook to leave ample forces for the purpose.

1. **The Federal Offensive in the West.**—The weak point in *A. S. Johnston's* line was at the centre, where the Memphis and Ohio railway, which formed the link between his two wings, crossed the Cumberland and Tennessee so close to Forts Donelson and Henry that the capture of these forts would sever his line of communication with the Mississippi. The Tennessee was navigable as far as Tuscumbia in north Alabama, and the Cumberland up to Nashville. The Confederates had no gunboats on these rivers, and if these forts fell there was nothing to oppose the Federal advance to the Memphis and Charleston (M. & C.) railway, the direct line of communication between east and west. Halleck, without orders from McClellan or arrangement for co-operation with Buell, ordered Grant (Feb. 1) with 15,000 men and Andrew H. Foote's gunboats to ascend the Tennessee, capture Ft. Henry and destroy the railway bridge. Ft. Henry surrendered to the gunboats (Feb. 6), the garrison escaping to Ft. Donelson. *Johnston* evacuated Bowling Green, sending half his army to Ft. Donelson and retiring with the other half to Nashville. This division of forces proved fatal. The concentration of 18,000 men at Ft. Donelson did not prevent its surrender with the bulk of its garrison to Grant (Feb. 16). *Johnston* abandoned Nashville, which was occupied by Buell (Feb. 24), and took up his position at Murfreesboro, and *Beauregard*, sent from the east to command on the Mississippi under *Johnston*, evacuated Columbus (March 2) after removing its armament to New Madrid and Island No. 10, where he intended to make the next stand against a Federal descent of the river. *Johnston* was thus thrown back to his second line of defense along the M. & C. railway with his wings at Memphis and Chattanooga and his centre at Corinth, Miss. Halleck's unauthorized movement had proved a brilliant success.

Halleck now sent John Pope with 20,000 men down the Mississippi bank to capture New Madrid and Island No. 10, and summoned Buell from Nashville to Savannah on the Tennessee to join Grant encamped on the opposite bank at Pittsburg Landing. He assumed that the recent campaign had thrown the Confederates permanently on the defensive and that the concentration of his own forces would be effected without interruption. But *Johnston* and *Beauregard*, well served with information by local sympathizers, seized their opportunity. By calling up Gen. *Braxton Bragg* from Pensacola with 10,000 men they concentrated an army of nearly 40,000 at Corinth before the end of March. Gen. *Earl Van Dorn* was bringing 15,000 men from Arkansas, but they could not wait for his arrival. The battle of Shiloh (April 6–7) was one of the most fiercely contested in the war. *Johnston* was killed the first day and *Beauregard* retreated to Corinth. Halleck joined his armies (April 11) and having been reinforced by Pope (April 21), who had captured with the help of the gunboats the garrison (7,000) of Island No. 10 with all its guns and stores, commenced a cautious advance on Corinth. *Beauregard* held on to Corinth until May 30, when he retreated to Tupelo, Miss. The evacuation of Corinth was followed by that of Ft. Pillow below Island No. 10 and Memphis (June 3). The Federal squadron fought and destroyed a Confederate flotilla at Memphis (June 6). With the capture of Corinth and Memphis the Federal offensive virtually ended. They had cleared Kentucky and west Tennessee of the enemy, established themselves on the M. & C. railway and opened the Mississippi to Vicksburg. But the Confederate army

Abolitionist John Brown, whose raid on the arsenal at Harpers Ferry, Va., Oct. 16, 1859, increased the tension on both sides in the last months before secession and the war

Harpers Ferry. Building at left is the engine house where Brown and his small band of whites and Negroes held their hostages and fought off local militia and U.S. marines commanded by Robert E. Lee. After surrendering, Brown was tried, convicted of treason, and hanged Dec. 2, 1859

Abraham Lincoln, photographed by Mathew Brady Feb. 23, 1861, a few days before Lincoln's inauguration as 16th president of the U.S.

Jefferson Davis, Mississippi statesman who was elected president of the Confederate States of America Feb. 9, 1861

Confederate flag flying over Ft. Sumter, S.C., April 14, 1861. The garrison, cut off from food and supplies, surrendered April 13 after being shelled by artillery units under the command of Gen. *P. G. T. Beauregard.* This engagement marked the opening of the war

BACKGROUND AND BEGINNING OF THE WAR, 1859–61

PLATE II   AMERICAN CIVIL WAR

Robert E. Lee. Offered command of the Federal forces, Lee refused and became *Davis'* military adviser. Later he took the field as commander of the army of northern Virginia and in 1865 as commander of all Confederate forces

Remains of the Stone Bridge, destroyed by fleeing Federal troops after their defeat in the first battle of Bull Run, or Manassas, July 21. This was the first pitched battle of the war and both armies were inexperienced and disorganized

Federal generals: Left, Winfield Scott, commander in chief and Lincoln's military adviser at the outbreak of the war. Right, George B. McClellan, Scott's successor. Organizer of the army of the Potomac, McClellan served off and on as its commander until November 1862. He ran against Lincoln in the election of 1864

Group of young Confederate volunteers posing before the first battle of Bull Run. The Confederate congress had authorized 100,000 troops; Lincoln had called for 75,000. By the end of the war approximately 4,000,000 men saw action

Confederate generals: Left, *P. G. T. Beauregard,* who captured Ft. Sumter, fought at Bull Run and later at Shiloh, Charleston and Richmond. Right, *Joseph E. Johnston,* senior field officer at the beginning of the war, was also the last army commander to surrender, April 26, 1865

1861: RECRUITMENT AND THE FIRST MEETING OF THE ARMIES

Federal gunboats of the "Monitor" type, so-named for the ironclad which battled the Confederate "Merrimack" in March. Monitors were used on rivers and in harbours to attack coastal batteries

Build-up of Federal guns and troops at Yorktown, Va., in May as McClellan prepared for his peninsular campaign and an attack upon Richmond. He was defeated by *Lee* in the Seven Days' battle

"Burnside's Bridge" after the battle of Antietam or Sharpsburg, Sept. 17. Defense of the bridge by Gen. Ambrose Burnside halted the advance of Gen. *T. J. ("Stonewall") Jackson* in a bloody battle

Federal commanders: Left, Adm. David G. Farragut, whose ships ran past the Confederate forts on the Mississippi river to capture New Orleans in April. Right: Gen. Henry W. Halleck, who replaced McClellan as general in chief in July and has been held responsible for several Federal defeats in Virginia

Confederate generals: *A. S. Johnston* (left) and *T. J. ("Stonewall") Jackson*, two of *Lee's* best commanders, were killed early in the war: *Johnston* as he was within reach of victory at Shiloh April 6, 1862, and *Jackson* as Federal troops were routed at Chancellorsville in May 1863

1862: LAND AND SEA OPERATIONS

The dead along the Sunken road on Marye's heights, defending Fredericksburg, after the charge of Federal troops under the command of Gen. John Sedgwick, May 3. Burnside had failed in a similar attempt to take Fredericksburg the preceding December

Left, Gen. *George E. Pickett*, whose name was given to the famous charge against the Federal position at Gettysburg on July 3. Right, Gen. George G. Meade, commander of the Federal armies. His victory at Gettysburg ended *Lee's* invasion of the north and was a turning point in the war

Opponents in Tennessee: Left, Gen. *Braxton Bragg* who won a decisive victory at Chickamauga, Sept. 19–20, and besieged the Federal troops at Chattanooga. Right, Gen. G. H. Thomas whose defensive stand at Chickamauga prevented a Federal rout and earned him command of the Army of the Cumberland

Dugouts in a hill behind the centre of the Federal lines during the siege of Vicksburg, May–July. The campaign was a brilliant victory for Gen. U. S. Grant and completed the conquest of the Mississippi river

General Grant (left) on Lookout mountain after the "battle above the clouds" Nov. 23. Appointed commander of all the western forces after his victory at Vicksburg, Grant quickly developed a plan to free the troops from Chattanooga and resume the offensive

1863: FADING OF CONFEDERATE HOPES FOR VICTORY

Pontoon bridge across the James river where Grant's army crossed in June in a flanking maneuver from Cold Harbor to attempt an attack upon Petersburg and to cut the Confederate rail connections to Richmond

General Grant at Cold Harbor. He had been given command of the Federal armies in March and moved his headquarters to Virginia to supervise the campaign against *Lee*

Confederate defensive works in front of Atlanta. The two houses in the foreground have been stripped to construct the palisade. Despite a strong defense and counterattack by the Confederate armies under General *Hood*, the city fell on Sept. 2 to General Sherman who then began his march to the sea

A group of Col. *John S. Mosby's* rangers, a guerrilla band formed from the 43rd Virginia cavalry, which effectively harassed the army of General Sheridan during the Shenandoah valley campaign

Federal generals: Left, William T. Sherman, leader of the march to the sea, who reached Savannah in December and turned north to aid Grant. Right, Philip H. Sheridan, whose conquest and laying waste of the Shenandoah valley crippled the food supply of *Lee's* armies in Virginia

Confederate generals: Left, *Jubal A. Early,* Sheridan's opponent in the Shenandoah who made a spirited defense but was badly outnumbered. Right, *John B. Hood,* given command of the army of Tennessee in July, moved north after losing Atlanta in a futile attempt to make Sherman pursue

1864: CONQUEST IN THE SOUTH AND THE MARCH TO THE SEA

PLATE VI

AMERICAN CIVIL WAR

The ruins of Richmond, capital city of the Confederacy. Much of the business district was burned by garrison troops before they evacuated the city on the night of April 2. The objective of the first Federal thrust in 1861, Richmond had held until the end although a distance of only about 100 mi. separated it from Washington, D.C.

A battery of Parrot rifles used to reduce Ft. Sumter to rubble in February, thus bringing the war back to where it had begun

Federal troops resting before the final assault on Petersburg, which fell April 2 after a siege of 10 months. The ability of the north to provide a constant flow of fresh troops, well fed and equipped, made victory inevitable despite the frequent blunders of strategy during the war

The house of Wilmer McLean, Appomattox Court House, Va., where *Lee* surrendered the army of northern Virginia to Grant on April 9. *J. E. Johnston* surrendered at Durham Station, N.C., April 26, ending the war in which almost 1,000,000 men were killed or wounded

1865: END OF THE WAR

of the west had escaped and would presently take the offensive.

West of the Mississippi Halleck had scored another success. *Price* had been driven out of southwest Missouri by Gen. Samuel R. Curtis, who followed him into Arkansas. *Van Dorn,* commanding in the newly formed trans-Mississippi department, reinforced *Price,* and their combined forces attacked Curtis at Pea Ridge (or Elkhorn Tavern), Ark., but suffered a severe defeat (March 7–8). Still farther west the Confederates had suffered another reverse. A small expedition under Col. *Henry H. Sibley* had been sent up the Rio Grande to secure Arizona and New Mexico with a view to bringing California into the Confederacy. *Sibley* occupied Santa Fe in March, but was forced by Col. E. R. S. Canby in April to make a disastrous retreat to Texas, and the whole of the territory, which he had overrun, was secured permanently by the Federals. But of all the disasters suffered in the west by the Confederates in the spring of 1862 the greatest, because irreparable, was the loss of New Orleans. Flag Officer David G. Farragut with the Gulf squadron ran past the forts guarding the lower Mississippi and appeared next day before the city (April 24–25), which, abandoned by its garrison, surrendered to the fleet, and was formally occupied by Gen. B. F. Butler's troops (May 1).

2. McClellan's Peninsular Campaign.—The sensational appearance of the ironclad *"Merrimack"* in Hampton Roads, at the mouth of the James river (March 8), had threatened the collapse of McClellan's oversea campaign, but next day the "Monitor" proved more than her match, and the naval authorities gave a doubtful assurance that they could cover the landing. (*See* "Monitor" and "Merrimack," Battle of.) The embarkation began on March 17; McClellan himself reached Ft. Monroe on April 2. On taking command in the field of the army of the Potomac he had been relieved of his duties as general in chief. For the next four months Lincoln and Stanton were responsible for the "higher strategy." McClellan began his advance (April 4), expecting to move rapidly up the peninsula to the neighbourhood of Richmond, where he would fight and win the decisive battle, and capture the Confederate capital. He knew that Yorktown and Gloucester on opposite banks of the York river were fortified, but he counted on the co-operation of the navy to capture Yorktown and intended to land McDowell's corps, which had not yet arrived, on the left bank for the reduction of Gloucester. But the navy could give no help as long as the *"Merrimack"* was afloat; Lincoln detained McDowell for the protection of Washington on the ground that McClellan had not kept his promise of leaving it absolutely secure. McClellan was held up before Yorktown for a

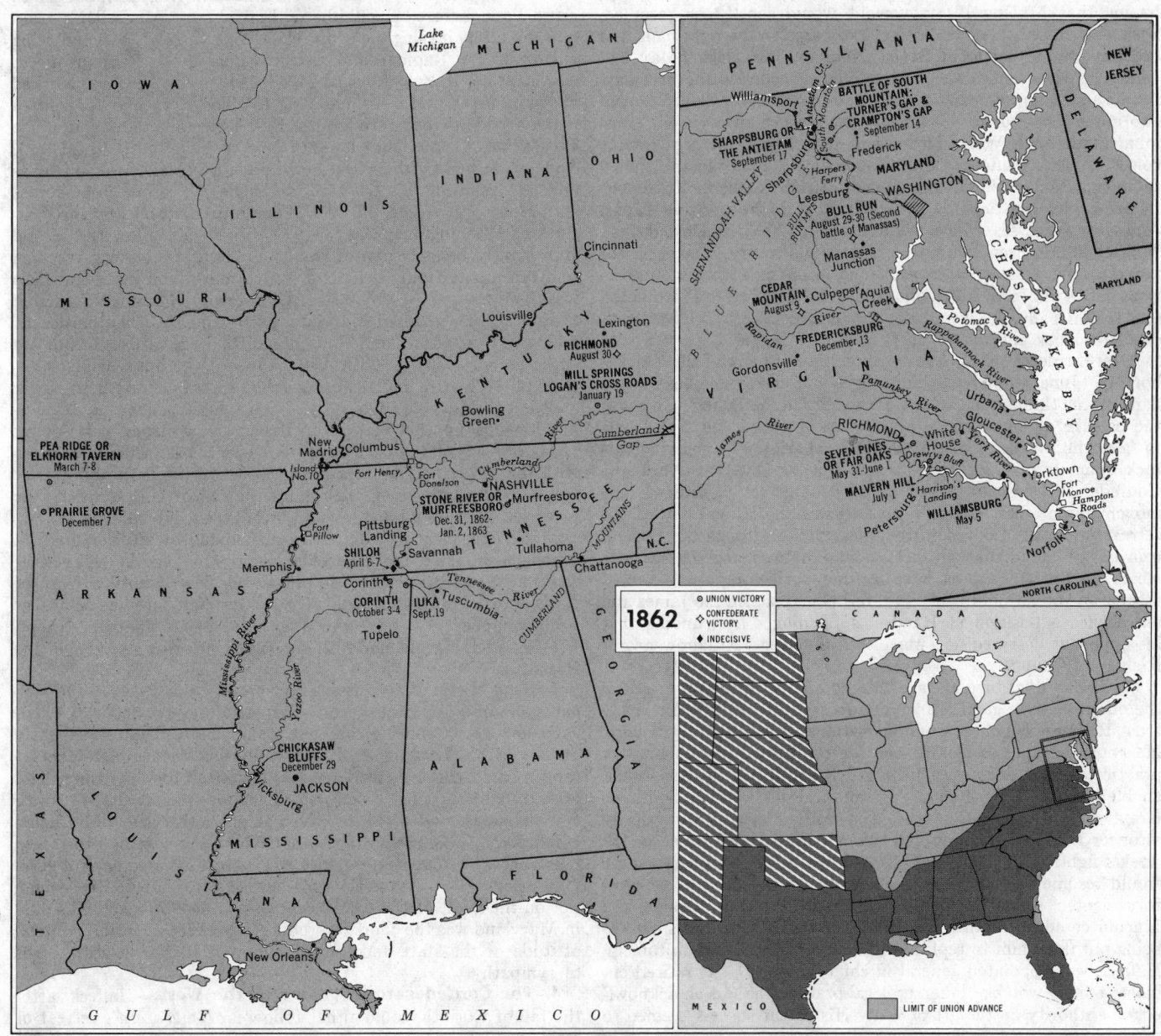

FIG. 3.—MAJOR BATTLES DURING 1862. INSET AT LOWER RIGHT SHOWS APPROXIMATE AREA OF UNION PENETRATION INTO CONFEDERATE TERRITORY

month (April 5–May 3).

J. E. Johnston, who had brought his army to the peninsula and assumed command at Yorktown (April 17), slipped away just as McClellan was about to open fire with his siege batteries. A sharp rearguard action took place at Williamsburg (May 5), and an attempt to intercept Johnston's retreat by sending a force up the York river failed. McClellan established his headquarters at White House on the Pamunkey river (May 16). He had succeeded in bringing over 100,000 men (organized into five corps) within striking distance of Richmond, and only 60 mi. away on the Rappahannock opposite Fredericksburg lay McDowell's corps, now under orders to advance on Richmond on May 26. McClellan would have transferred his base from the York to the James, now open to the Federal war vessels as far as Drewrys Bluff, as the Confederates after the evacuation of Yorktown had abandoned Norfolk and destroyed the "Merrimack," which was unable to ascend the river. But, informed by Stanton that he was to be reinforced, he advanced to the Chickahominy (May 20) and sent two corps across in preparation for the advance on Richmond, keeping three on the left bank to join hands with McDowell. He retained this position with his wings divided by the Chickahominy, although he learned (May 24) that McDowell's advance was suspended because of "Stonewall" Jackson's operations in the Valley, hoping that McDowell's movement would shortly be resumed. Johnston concentrated against the two corps on the right bank and brought on the battle of Seven Pines or Fair Oaks (May 31–June 1). He was beaten off, and himself wounded the first day. Lee on assuming command withdrew the troops. McClellan moved two more corps to the right bank, leaving one to cover his communications with White House and still hoping for McDowell's coming. Lee's plan was to continue using Jackson in the Valley to prevent McDowell from moving south, and at the right moment to bring him to Richmond to take part in the decisive battle. Jackson's successes (June 8–9) served to hold McDowell fast. McClellan had been waiting for the ground to dry, that he might move his siege batteries to the front. On the 25th his outposts were only 4 mi. from Richmond, and he telegraphed to Washington that the final advance was about to begin. He was too late. Next day Lee struck and the Seven Days' battle began.

After the defeat of his one corps on the left bank of the Chickahominy (June 27), McClellan decided to "change his base" by a flank march through the White Oak swamp to the James. To cover the passage of his trains he was forced to stand and give battle to Lee, who sought to destroy the Federal army by a combined attack upon its rear and right flank. But, as at Seven Pines, the Confederate commander and his staff failed to co-ordinate the movements of their troops. June 30 was the critical day of the retreat, when the Confederates almost broke through the Federal centre, but failed through lack of support to reach the road on which McClellan's trains were moving. After repulsing a final assault at Malvern hill (July 1), McClellan reached the James and entrenched a position at Harrison's Landing. Lee, finding that his opponent designed no immediate movement, withdrew nearer Richmond (July 8).

McClellan's "change of base" placed him in a position to renew the offensive with good chance of success. He was farther away from Richmond, but his communications were absolutely secure. He could advance on either side of the river. Petersburg lay practically defenseless within his reach and its occupation would enable him to cut Richmond's communications with the South, as Grant was to do in 1864–65. His army was still numerically stronger than Lee's, which had suffered the heavier losses in the week's fighting. It was at first assumed at Washington that he would resume the advance on Richmond when he received reinforcements. But McClellan demanded 100,000 fresh troops, and Lincoln could not find more than 20,000. Political pressure was being put upon him to replace McClellan. To solve the problem, Halleck was appointed general in chief (July 11). A retired engineer officer, who had taken up legal practice, he was an acknowledged authority on the art of war. His recent success seemed to mark him out as McClellan's natural successor, but he served only as Lincoln's military adviser. He visited McClellan's army (July

25) and committed his first blunder by ordering the withdrawal of the army of the Potomac to Aquia creek, where it could unite with Pope's army of Virginia on the Rappahannock for an overland advance on Richmond (Aug. 3).

Jackson's Valley campaign is described elsewhere. Here it may be noted that on three separate occasions Jackson caused McDowell's corps to be withdrawn from McClellan. His attack at Kernstown (March 23) alarmed Lincoln and was partly the cause of his detaining McDowell in the first instance at Washington. Throughout the campaign Lee worked upon Lincoln's anxiety for the safety of Washington to break up the threatened combination against Richmond.

3. The Confederate Offensive in the East.—Pope was summoned (June 26) from the west to command an army composed of the forces on the Rappahannock and in the Valley. Jackson's campaign had taught Lincoln that one general is better than three. Pope's immediate task was to lighten the pressure upon McClellan by threatening the Virginia Central railway. Lee dispatched (July 13) Jackson in time to save Gordonsville from Pope's cavalry. Jackson advancing toward Culpeper to prevent the concentration of Pope's scattered forces defeated Banks at Cedar mountain (Aug. 9), but fell back when Banks was reinforced. Lee, joining Jackson with James Longstreet's command (Aug. 15), sought to crush Pope, before he could be reinforced from McClellan's army now definitely leaving the peninsula. Pope narrowly escaped being cut off on the Rapidan and retreated behind the Rappahannock. Lee, learning that portions of McClellan's army had disembarked at Aquia creek and were marching to Pope, detached Jackson to make a wide detour through the Bull Run mountains and strike Pope's line of communications at Manassas junction (Aug. 25–27). Pope, mystified by this movement, made a succession of mistakes and Lee, reuniting his army on the battlefield, drove Pope across Bull Run (q.v.) (Aug. 29–30). Pope retired within the fortifications of Washington (Sept. 3). Lee would not allow the second Bull Run to be as barren of results as the first. Having received reinforcements from Richmond, which more than made good his losses, he crossed the Potomac at Leesburg and occupied Frederick (Sept. 7). He entered Maryland partly to "shift the burden of military occupation from Confederate to Federal soil." But his objective was partly political, to influence the approaching elections in the North, impress Europe with a sense of southern power and detach Maryland from the Union. Finding his line of communications up the Valley threatened by a strong garrison at Harpers Ferry, he divided his forces (Sept. 10), sending Jackson with the larger half to capture that post, while he withdrew the rest behind South mountain. After the fall of Harpers Ferry he proposed to reunite his army and invade Pennsylvania.

McClellan, placed by Lincoln in command of all the forces in Washington, again took the field (Sept. 7). Not knowing what Lee's next move might be, he advanced slowly, until a copy of Lee's order for the division of his army fell into his hands at Frederick (Sept. 13). He forced the South Mountain passes (Sept. 14). Lee fell back behind Antietam creek covering a ford over the Potomac.

Jackson with three divisions had crossed the Potomac at Williamsport and appeared before Harpers Ferry on Sept 13. The garrison (12,500), being completely surrounded, capitulated early on the 15th. Leaving A. P. Hill's division to complete the arrangements for the surrender, Jackson started for Sharpsburg and after a night march rejoined Lee on the morning of the 16th with two divisions, and a third arrived later in the day. McClellan reached the Antietam on the 15th, devoted the next day to reconnaissance and fought the battle of Sharpsburg or the Antietam (q.v.; Sept. 17). At the close of the day Lee still held his ground, but on the night of the 18th he recrossed the Potomac. His stay in Maryland was too short to produce any effect upon the political attitude of the state and the inhabitants had shown scant signs of sympathy.

4. The Confederate Offensive in the West.—Halleck, after the fall of Corinth, could either follow up Beauregard's retreat or strike at Vicksburg or Chattanooga. Pursuit should have ended in the annihilation of the sole Confederate army in the west; the capture of Vicksburg would open the Mississippi to its mouth and cut the Confederacy in two; the occupation of Chattanooga would further Lincoln's policy of sending relief to the Unionists in east Tennessee. Halleck limited his offensive to sending Buell's army alone toward Chattanooga, and wasted three weeks by forcing him to use as his line of supply the M. & C. railway, which was exposed to cavalry raids. At the end of June, Buell gained permission to transfer his base to Nashville. As no movement was made toward Tupelo, *Bragg*, who had succeeded *Beauregard* (June 27), left *Van Dorn* and *Price* to check Grant. On Halleck's appointment as general in chief at Washington, Grant had been left in command of the department of the Tennessee. *Bragg* sought the co-operation of *Edmund Kirby-Smith*, commanding in east Tennessee, in an advance on Nashville, but yielded to the other's confidence in the political results of an invasion of Kentucky and agreed to march to the Ohio. Buell, whose advance from Nashville on Chattanooga was twice suspended in consequence of cavalry raids upon his communications, took up a defensive position at Murfreesboro covering Nashville.

Kirby-Smith "turned" Cumberland gap, swept aside an extemporized force, which faced him at Richmond, Ky. (Aug. 30), and occupied Lexington (Sept. 2), threatening Louisville and Cincinnati. *Bragg*, concentrating behind the Cumberland mountains, appeared on Buell's front (Sept. 5). Then ensued a race to Louisville, in which Buell got the worst of the start, as he dared not uncover Nashville, and reached Bowling Green (Sept. 14) to find *Bragg* planted squarely across the railway between him and Louisville. Buell could not risk an offensive battle with so much at stake; *Bragg* would only fight on the defensive. He moved out of Buell's path because of lack of supplies (Sept. 21) to make connection with *Kirby-Smith*, who had collected a large depot of stores at Lexington. Buell entered Louisville (Sept. 25) and having reorganized his army marched out (Oct. 1) to find and fight the invaders. Their generals were more occupied with the inauguration of a provisional governor at Frankfort (Oct. 4) than with the need for concentrating their forces. An accidental encounter with indecisive results occurred at Perryville (Oct. 8) between Buell's and *Bragg's* left wings. *Bragg* and *Kirby-Smith* now united their armies, but only to retreat through Cumberland gap into east Tennessee. The Confederate invasion of Kentucky was barren of political results. The provisional governor was chased out of his capital immediately after his inauguration.

5. The Federals Resume the Offensive.—After issuance of the Emancipation Proclamation, McClellan was urged to cross the Potomac and force another battle, but he demanded time to reorganize his army. Five weeks passed before he began his advance along the east side of the Blue ridge. Then *Lee*, bringing *Longstreet* to Culpeper, again interposed. McClellan was relieved of his command (Nov. 7), and his successor, Burnside, adopted a new plan of campaign, to transfer his base to Aquia creek, cross the Rappahannock at or below Fredericksburg and march straight on Richmond. But delay in forwarding a pontoon train from Washington prevented his crossing until *Lee* had taken up a position on the Fredericksburg heights. Though the element of surprise was lost, Burnside persisted in crossing the river and, attacking *Lee*, was repulsed with terrible slaughter (Dec. 13).

In the west, Buell was replaced (Oct. 30) by Rosecrans, who as Pope's successor under Grant had gained the credit of defeating *Price* at Iuka (Sept. 19) and *Van Dorn* at Corinth (Oct. 3–4). Before renewing the advance upon Chattanooga he determined to make himself temporarily independent of the railway by accumulating a reserve of 2,000,000 rations at Nashville. The government chafed at the delay. Rosecrans refused to be hurried. He commenced his advance against *Bragg* (Dec. 26), who since returning from Kentucky had established himself at Murfreesboro, where he expected to pass the winter. The battle of Stones River or Murfreesboro (Dec. 31–Jan. 3) ended with *Bragg* abandoning the battlefield, evacuating Murfreesboro and falling back to Tullahoma. Rosecrans occupied Murfreesboro and settled down for the winter.

After *Van Dorn's* defeat Grant moved against Vicksburg. Gen. William T. Sherman, starting down the river from Memphis, was to land his troops at the mouth of the Yazoo, seize the bluffs north of Vicksburg and attack the city from the rear. Meanwhile Grant, who was already advancing along the Mississippi Central railway toward Jackson, Miss., would hold Gen. *John C. Pemberton, Van Dorn's* successor, fast and prevent his sending help to Vicksburg. But Grant had to retire when his supply depot was destroyed by a cavalry raid (Dec. 20), and Sherman was forestalled by *Pemberton*, who was kept informed by spies of the Federal movement, and defeated at Chickasaw Bluffs, 6 mi. N. of Vicksburg (Dec. 29). In northwest Arkansas *Thomas C. Hindman* was organizing a fresh invasion of Missouri but was anticipated by James G. Blunt and Francis J. Herron, who crossed the frontier and defeated him at Prairie Grove (Dec. 7).

IV. MILITARY OPERATIONS, 1863

In the east, after "the horror of Fredericksburg" the two armies passed the winter facing each other across the Rappahannock. Gen. Joseph Hooker replaced Burnside (Jan. 26) and quickly restored the shaken morale of his army. *Lee* found great difficulty in feeding his troops, and by direction of the war department *Longstreet* with two divisions was sent to the south bank of the James to collect provisions in the vicinity of Suffolk, which Federal troops occupied. *Longstreet* surrounded Suffolk and at the moment when his divisions were urgently needed on the Rappahannock was engaged in a futile siege 120 mi. away.

1. Chancellorsville.—Both *Lee* and Hooker were eager to take the offensive. *Lee* had been considering with *Jackson* an invasion of Pennsylvania, but in the absence of *Longstreet's* divisions had to resign the initiative to Hooker. The latter aimed at forcing *Lee* out of his entrenchments by a wide turning movement over the upper fords of the Rappahannock above its junction with the Rapidan, and sent his newly organized cavalry corps to destroy the railways in *Lee's* rear and intercept his retreat. He thus deprived himself of "the eyes of his army," and to the absence of his cavalry (except one brigade) was largely attributable the failure of the Chancellorsville campaign.

Hooker, who outnumbered *Lee* by fully two to one, concentrated the larger half of his army about Chancellorsville (April 30), while John Sedgwick crossed the Rappahannock below Fredericksburg. *Lee,* leaving 10,000 men to check Sedgwick, threw Hooker on the defensive (May 1), outflanked and rolled up his right wing with *Jackson's* corps (May 2), drove him out of his entrenchments to a fresh defensive position (May 3), turned on Sedgwick, who had captured the Fredericksburg heights, and forced him back over the river (May 4) and then countermarched to Chancellorsville to strike another blow at Hooker. But the latter retreated across the Rappahannock on the night of May 5. *Lee's* victory was dearly bought at the price of *Jackson's* life (May 10). He now reorganized his army into three corps under *Longstreet, Richard S. Ewell* and *A. P. Hill* and prepared to carry out his plan of invading Pennsylvania.

2. Gettysburg.—*Longstreet* had proposed a plan for the relief of Vicksburg, now in dire straits. *Lee* should leave the army that had fought at Chancellorsville to "contain" Hooker on the Rappahannock, and with *Longstreet's* two divisions join *Bragg* in Tennessee. *Johnston's* troops should be brought from Mississippi and *Simon B. Buckner's* from east Tennessee to the same point. The united forces under *Lee's* command could then take the offensive against Rosecrans, overwhelm him and then invade Kentucky and threaten Louisville and Cincinnati—forcing Grant to raise the siege of Vicksburg. But *Lee* was unwilling to leave Virginia or divide his army.

Lee's objectives in Pennsylvania were much the same as those that had prompted his invasion of Maryland in 1862, and in particular he hoped to levy much-needed supplies of food and clothing from a free state and prevent the sending of reinforcements to Grant before Vicksburg. He commenced his movement on June 3. His plan of campaign was to transfer his army to the Valley, cross the Potomac and march to the Susquehanna. He could count upon Lincoln's anxiety for Washington's safety to keep Hooker from attacking any of his widely separated corps before they were concentrated in Pennsylvania. A cavalry battle at Brandy Station

(June 9) warned Hooker that *Lee* was on the move. Being refused permission to march on Richmond, he began to fall back toward Manassas (June 13). *Hill* marched to the valley covered by *Longstreet,* who advanced east of the Blue ridge. *Ewell* captured Winchester (June 15) and crossed into Maryland, pushing his cavalry forward into Pennsylvania. *Longstreet* passed into the valley in *Hill's* rear and their two corps were crossing the river on June 23–24. Hooker began crossing on June 25 and concentrated at Frederick, threatening *Lee's* line of retreat. *Hill* and *Longstreet* were at Chambersburg, *Ewell* on his way to Harrisburg with two divisions at Carlisle and one at York (June 27). But the absence of *"Jeb" Stuart's* cavalry, which was on a raid around the Federal army and did not rejoin until July 2, left *Lee* in ignorance of Hooker's movements. He did not learn until the night of June 28 that Hooker had crossed into Maryland and was threatening his communications. He at once ordered a concentration of all his forces at Cashtown to keep the Federals east of South mountain by threatening Baltimore. Gen. George G. Meade, who had meanwhile replaced Hooker (June 28), was moving his army northward to prevent *Lee* from crossing the Susquehanna. A chance encounter on June 30 at Gettysburg (*q.v.*) brought on the famous battle.

Hill advancing from the west and *Ewell* coming down from the north had defeated two Federal corps and occupied Gettysburg (July 1). Neither *Lee* nor Meade expected a battle so soon, but *Lee* could complete his concentration first, and the chance of defeating his opponent in detail urged him to assume the offensive. But he could not get his corps commanders to work together as a team. No attack was delivered (July 2) until 4 P.M., and though the Confederates gained some ground on both flanks and for a moment broke through the Federal centre, at nightfall Meade still held Cemetery ridge and had his whole army concentrated. *Lee* made his final assault (July 3) with two divisions against the enemy centre, but again concert of action was lacking, and *George E. Pickett's* charge, being unsupported, was a costly failure. *Lee* began his retreat (July 4) through the South Mountain passes. He was held up at Williamsport for a week waiting for the river to run down, but on the night of the 13th withdrew his army and trains into the Valley before Meade, who had appeared on his front the day before, could make up his mind to attack.

Lee gradually fell back behind the Rapidan and Meade followed him across the Rappahannock as far as Culpeper. Both armies were weakened in September by sending heavy detachments to Tennessee. In October and November the two generals engaged in a campaign of maneuver, which had no decisive result and left

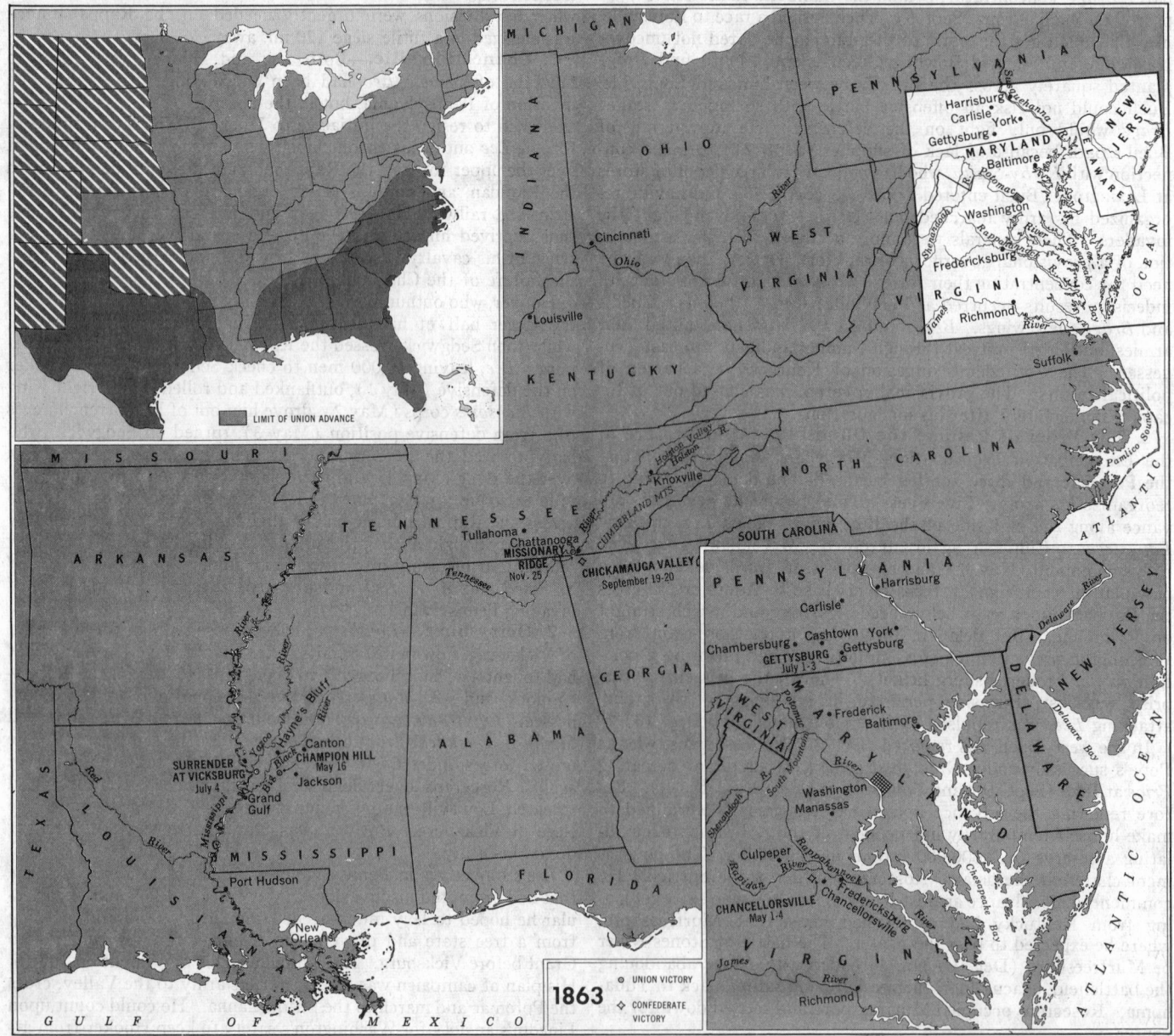

FIG. 4.—MAJOR BATTLES DURING 1863. INSET AT LOWER RIGHT SHOWS DETAIL OF PENNSYLVANIA AND MIDDLE ATLANTIC STATES; INSET AT UPPER LEFT SHOWS APPROXIMATE LIMIT OF UNION ADVANCE

them in their original positions on the Rapidan and Rappahannock respectively.

3. Vicksburg and Chattanooga.—In 1863, as in 1862, it was in the west that decisive results were obtained. By the capture of Vicksburg and Port Hudsón the Federals gained complete control of the Mississippi, and in east Tennessee they captured Chattanooga and Knoxville. Grant's Vicksburg (*q.v.*) campaign was one of the most brilliant operations of the war, though he owed much to his opponent's mistakes.

The problem was to transport his army from the right bank of the Mississippi to the high ground in the rear of Vicksburg. After four unsuccessful attempts (Feb.–March) to open up a water route, by which the enemy's flanks might be turned, Grant in April, when the winter floods had begun to subside, moved two corps by land to a point below Grand gulf, the extreme left of the Confederate defenses. Part of the Federal fleet had run past the Vicksburg batteries by night (April 16), bringing with them two transports, and five more transports got past six nights later. Grant began crossing the river on April 30. *Pemberton,* who as commander of the department of Mississippi and east Louisiana was responsible for both Vicksburg and Port Hudson, had been so mystified by Grant's demonstrations on the north side of Vicksburg that he had only four brigades available to meet his advance south of the Big Black river. Grant defeated these (May 1) and established a temporary base at Grand gulf. Having been joined by Sherman with further supplies, he advanced (May 7) against the Vicksburg-Jackson railway, on which *Pemberton* depended for supplies and reinforcements. But suspecting after the engagement at Raymond (May 12) that a considerable force was collecting at Jackson, Grant cut loose from his base and marched with his whole army on Jackson, living off the country until he could work around to the north of Vicksburg and establish a new base on the Yazoo. *J. E. Johnston,* commander in chief in the west, had been ordered (May 9) to assume personal command of the troops in Mississippi. He reached Jackson from Tullahoma (May 13) but found only two brigades there. Next day, after fighting a delaying action at Jackson, he retreated up the Mississippi Central railway to Canton. Grant then fell upon *Pemberton's* field force at Champion hill (May 16) and drove it into the fortifications of Vicksburg, occupying Haynes's Bluff two days later. The fate of Vicksburg was now sealed, for *Johnston* was unable to collect a force strong enough to create a diversion, and *Pemberton* capitulated (July 4).

Butler's successor at New Orleans, Gen. N. P. Banks, was equally successful in reducing Port Hudson, 200 mi. below Vicksburg (July 9). Farragut with two warships had run past the Port Hudson batteries (March 14), and by closing the mouth of the Red river deprived the garrison of its main source of supplies. Banks commenced siege operations (May 24), and the Confederates were on the verge of starvation when they surrendered.

In middle Tennessee, Rosecrans was urged by the government to take the offensive against *Bragg* to prevent him from sending reinforcements to Mississippi. But Rosecrans maintained that, while he remained on *Bragg's* front, the latter would not risk the loss of middle Tennessee by detaching troops elsewhere. *Bragg* did in fact send some reinforcements to *Johnston.* Rosecrans was really afraid that Grant might be defeated and was unwilling to commit himself to a fresh movement while the issue at Vicksburg remained unsettled. At last he advanced (June 23) and in nine days of incessant rain maneuvered *Bragg* out of two strong positions in succession and forced him to retreat behind the Tennessee river. He resumed his advance (Aug. 16) in co-operation with Burnside, who advanced from Kentucky and occupied Knoxville (Sept. 2). Rosecrans, feinting at *Bragg's* right, as if he intended to cross the Tennessee above Chattanooga and join Burnside, moved the bulk of his army across well below Chattanooga (Sept. 4) and advanced over the mountain ranges south of the river against *Bragg's* line of retreat. This maneuver forced *Bragg* to evacuate Chattanooga (Sept. 8), but he retreated only 25 mi. to Lafayette, where he covered the railway; waiting for a chance to defeat Rosecrans' army in detail. Rosecrans, imagining *Bragg* to be in full retreat, fell into the trap and pressed forward with three columns so widely separated that no two were within supporting distance of

each other. But *Bragg* failed to close the trap. Two chances of overwhelming isolated portions of the Federal army were lost by his lieutenants. Rosecrans reconcentrated his army (Sept. 18), and *Bragg,* having received considerable reinforcements, including five brigades under *Longstreet,* from Virginia, attacked and defeated him (Sept. 19–20) in Chickamauga (*q.v.*) valley and drove him back into Chattanooga, where the Federal army was practically besieged and in danger of starvation. Grant was now appointed to the supreme command in the west and reached Chattanooga (Oct. 23), where Hooker with reinforcements from the army of the Potomac had already arrived. Grant substituted Thomas for Rosecrans in command of the army of the Cumberland and averted all fear of starvation by opening a short line of communication with Bridgeport by way of two ferries over the Tennessee. *Bragg* now weakened himself by sending *Longstreet* with a large detachment against Burnside (Nov. 3). Grant, on the arrival of four divisions of the army of the Tennessee under Sherman, took the offensive and stormed *Bragg's* position on Missionary ridge, which overlooked Chattanooga (*see* CHATTANOOGA, BATTLE OF) (Nov. 25). In his anxiety for Burnside's safety Grant ceased his pursuit of *Bragg's* retreating army (Nov. 28) and dispatched Sherman to Knoxville, where *Longstreet* was besieging Burnside. After failing in an assault upon the Federal works (Nov. 29), *Longstreet* raised the siege (Dec. 4) on Sherman's approach and retreated up the Holston valley. The greater part of east Tennessee was now in Federal hands.

V. MILITARY OPERATIONS, 1864–65

Halleck having failed during 18 months to co-ordinate from Washington the movements of the Federal armies, Grant was commissioned (March 9) lieutenant general, a grade revived by congress, and appointed general in chief to command in the field. Deeming his presence more urgently needed in the east, he attached himself to the army of the Potomac, retaining Meade in actual command. Sherman succeeded him in the west. The presidential election was due in November. The North was war-weary, and Lincoln's chance of re-election would be small unless speedy victory were in sight.

When the Republican or National Union party convention met in Baltimore it renominated Lincoln but found it expedient to add to the ticket a "war Democrat," Andrew Johnson of Tennessee. The Democrats late in the summer nominated General McClellan for president and George H. Pendleton of Ohio for vice-president. The Democratic platform called for immediate cessation of hostilities and the restoration of peace. Although McClellan repudiated this plank, his candidacy gained much from the antiwar sentiment in the North, which was promoted by the "copperheads" (*q.v.*).

1. Grant in the East.—Grant's was a policy of attrition, aiming at the exhaustion of the only two enemy armies of considerable size still in the field, viz., *Lee's* in Virginia and *Johnston's* in Georgia, by concentrating against them all the force available. The objective for Meade's army was not Richmond, but *Lee's* army. Grant planned to force *Lee* out of his entrenchments behind the Rapidan and wear him down by continuous hammering. He could afford to lose two men to *Lee's* one, because southern manpower was nearly exhausted. But he also sought to create a diversion by threatening Richmond and its railway communications on both flanks. Columns were ordered to march on Staunton and Lynchburg, and then unite for a movement against Richmond; the army of the James was to advance up the south bank of the James river. But in allowing Butler to command this army, Grant made a grievous mistake. Butler, a criminal lawyer and influential politician, had shown no military capacity in his various commands, but he was a dangerous man to alienate in a presidential election year.

Grant crossed the Rapidan (May 4). After two days' battle in the Wilderness he moved by the left flank to Spotsylvania and continued this side-stepping maneuver until close to Richmond. But in these 40 days he never got *Lee* into the open. On the Po, North Anna and Totopotomoy rivers and at Cold Harbor he found *Lee* entrenched across his path. No diversion came from Butler, who missed the opportunity of capturing Bermuda Hundred in the first week and was bottled up by *Beauregard* (May 16). The other subsidiary movement was nearly as unsuccessful.

Grant's defeat at Cold Harbor (June 3) cost him about 7,000 casualties to probably less than 1,500 for the Confederates. The three Federal corps (II, VI and XVIII) advanced through devastating frontal and enfilade fire and were stopped within a matter of minutes before reaching their objective. The battle represented one of the worst defeats suffered by the Union forces and is often cited as an example of poor generalship.

After Grant's defeat at Cold Harbor *Lee* detached *Jubal A. Early's* corps to save Lynchburg from David Hunter, who had already captured Staunton. Hunter retreated into West Virginia, leaving the Valley open to *Early*, who marched down it, crossed the Potomac, defeated a small force on the Monocacy (July 9) and appeared before Washington (July 11). Grant sent back one corps for the protection of the capital. But *Early* withdrew (July 12) and retired into the Valley, having given Washington and Baltimore a sudden fright, but without seriously deranging Grant's plans.

Grant's finest achievement was the transfer of his army across the Chickahominy and James rivers unopposed under *Lee's* nose (June 12–15), but he lost the chance of capturing Petersburg (June 15–18), which *Lee* was slow to reinforce. The ensuing siege of Petersburg was trench warfare and a siege in name only, as *Lee's* army was never invested. Grant's aim was to extend his lines to his left so as to get possession of the railways from the south and southwest to Petersburg and Richmond, while making demonstrations on the north bank of the James and "feeling" the Richmond defenses. The fiasco of the "Burnside mine" (July 30)—when a mine was successfully exploded under a salient in the Confederate lines, but the assaulting troops, because of mismanagement, were repulsed with heavy loss—warned him against frontal attacks on *Lee's* lines around Petersburg. He secured a considerable section of the Weldon and Petersburg railway, but at the end of the year *Lee* still held the Petersburg and Lynchburg and Danville lines. The only Federal successes in the east this year were won by Gen. Philip H. Sheridan in the Shenandoah valley (*see* SHENANDOAH VALLEY CAMPAIGNS). Sent by Grant to drive out *Early,* he won three victories in a month (Sept. 19–Oct. 19) and completely devastated the Valley, which had become the granary of Richmond. Sheridan made excellent use of his cavalry during this campaign and defeated the Confederates in the engagements at Winchester, Fishers Hill and Tom's Brook. These victories, coupled with Sherman's capture of Atlanta (Sept. 2), secured Lincoln his overwhelming triumph over General McClellan in the election of 1864.

2. Sherman in the West.—Sherman, with three armies under Thomas, James B. McPherson and John Schofield, confronted *Johnston,* who had taken command of *Bragg's* beaten army. The Richmond government had wished *Johnston* to effect a junction with *Longstreet* and invade middle Tennessee, but *Johnston,* finding his army in no condition to take the offensive, remained at Dalton, where he occupied a strong defensive position. Grant's instructions to Sherman were "to move against *Johnston's* army, to break it up and to get into the interior of the enemy's country as far as you can." Atlanta, *Johnston's* base, was at the junction of four important railways. In Sherman's words, it was "full of foundries, arsenals and machine-shops. Its capture would be the death-knell of the Confederacy." Eventually Sherman captured Atlanta but the Confederate army escaped. He had about the same superiority of numbers as Grant had, roughly 100,000 against 60,000, and was as far from Atlanta as Grant was from Richmond. But as compared with Grant he had one great disadvantage. He was practically tied to the railway and could not be continually shifting his base. Grant had intended that Banks should effect a diversion in Sherman's favour by a movement on Mobile in co-operation with Farragut's fleet. But Banks was not available, having previously gone up the Red river on an expedition primarily designed to bring out cotton.

The campaign opened on May 4. *Johnston's* policy was to delay Sherman's advance as much as possible, withdrawing from his successive positions before he could be drawn into a pitched battle except upon his own terms. He was prepared to fall back as far as Atlanta, which he regarded as impregnable, "too strong to be taken by assault and too extensive to be invested." Sherman's general plan of campaign was to keep Thomas' army in the centre to contain *Johnston's* army, for which it was in itself a match, and use the other two to turn his flanks. With McPherson's army he outflanked *Johnston's* left and forced him to evacuate Dalton (May 13) and Resaca (May 15).

In the comparatively open and rolling country between the Oostanaula and the Etowah rivers *Johnston* expected to be able to make a stand and give battle, but his corps commanders dissuaded him. Retreating across the Etowah (May 20) he took up a strong position in the mountain pass at Allatoona.

By temporarily cutting loose from the railway and marching on Dallas, Sherman turned the Allatoona pass and by shifting McPherson over to the left flank gradually forced *Johnston* to contract his lines around Marietta (*q.v.*). Wishing to save his troops the fatigue of yet another flank movement over roads rendered almost impassable by continuous rain, Sherman attacked *Johnston's* lines on Kennesaw mountain (June 27), but was repulsed with heavy loss. Resuming the outflanking movement around *Johnston's* left he maneuvered him out of the Marietta position (July 2), and a week later *Johnston* withdrew his whole army behind the Chattahoochee, after Schofield had crossed above his right flank. Though in this protracted duel only the engagement at Kennesaw mountain ranks as a battle, skirmishing never ceased, often developing into hard fighting, especially during the operations around Dallas. During May and June Sherman's casualties amounted to about 17,000, and *Johnston's* were relatively, if not actually, greater. *Johnston* was preparing to fall upon Sherman's columns as they crossed the Peach Tree creek, the only natural obstacle between the Chatta-

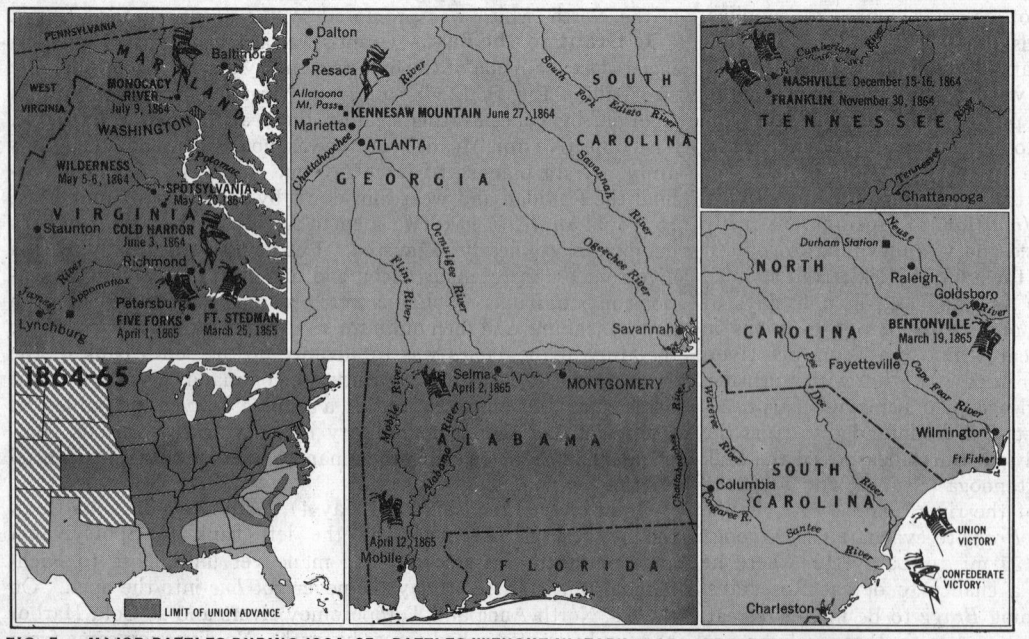

FIG. 5.—MAJOR BATTLES DURING 1864–65; BATTLES WITHOUT VICTORY FLAGS CONSIDERED INDECISIVE. INSET AT LOWER LEFT SHOWS APPROXIMATE AREA UNDER UNION CONTROL AT CLOSE OF THE WAR

hoochee and Atlanta's northern defenses, when he was superseded by *John B. Hood* (July 17).

Davis was tired of *Johnston's* Fabian tactics and believing that he would abandon Atlanta without a battle, put a fighting general in his place. *Hood* promptly fought three battles before the end of July, but was defeated in them all, and evacuated Atlanta (*q.v.*) (Sept. 2). Sherman waited for *Hood's* next move. *Hood* crossed the Chattahoochee (Sept. 29) and striking first at Sherman's communications marched to Gadsden, Ala., drawing Sherman in pursuit more than 100 mi. from Atlanta as far as Gaylesville (Oct. 20). When *Hood* moved still farther west to cross the Tennessee, Sherman started back to Atlanta to execute his long-cherished plan of marching through Georgia to the coast. He left Thomas to deal with *Hood*. But the force assigned to Thomas was barely sufficient for the purpose. In actual numbers superior to *Hood's* army, it was made up of widely separated commands; one corps was still in Missouri, and until its arrival at Nashville (Nov. 30) Thomas can hardly be said to have had an army at all. Sherman could easily have spared another 12,000 men, and this addition to his strength would have made Thomas' position absolutely safe.

Hood's plan was to destroy Thomas' forces before they could concentrate, capture Nashville, invade Kentucky, threaten Cincinnati and then march through east Tennessee to join *Lee*. But a three weeks' delay at Florence to collect supplies proved fatal. Schofield with 23,000 men had time to take position at Pulaski and delay his advance while Thomas was concentrating his other forces at Nashville. Having failed to envelop Schofield on the Duck river, *Hood* attacked him furiously but unsuccessfully at Franklin (Nov. 30) and appeared before Nashville (Dec. 2). In spite of the severity of his losses and the fact that he was confronted by an army superior to his own, *Hood* was still bent on retaining the offensive and detached his cavalry against the Federal lines of communication. He remained before Nashville in the vain hope of receiving reinforcements promised from Texas, until Thomas marched out and defeated him in one of the most decisive battles of the war (Dec. 15–16). *Hood* escaped over the Tennessee, but his army as a fighting force practically ceased to exist.

Sherman started from Atlanta (Nov. 15) on his 300-mi. march with 60,000 men and without encountering any organized resistance reached the outskirts of Savannah (Dec. 10), feeding his army off the country. His purpose was to demonstrate "the hollowness" of the Confederacy and by ruining the railway system of Georgia, now the granary of the South, prevent food reaching Richmond. Georgia was left undefended except by *Joseph Wheeler's* cavalry and the state militia. Sherman, having destroyed 160 mi. of the Georgia Central railway, established communication with the fleet in Ossabaw sound. Savannah was evacuated (Dec. 20). Sherman was now free to join Grant by sea or land.

Though the Confederates still held Mobile, its value as a port was gone. Farragut had forced an entrance into the bay (Aug. 5) and captured the forts guarding the harbour mouth. Only in the trans-Mississippi region had the Confederates gained any success. Bank's Red River expedition proved a complete failure and he retreated to New Orleans. But the Federals retained their hold upon northern Arkansas, including Little Rock, the state capital. *Price* made a last raid into Missouri in September and October.

3. Collapse of the Confederacy.—In the early months of 1865 Richmond's fall was near at hand. Grant's next advance would plant him on the Petersburg and Lynchburg railway. *Lee* did not have sufficient troops to hold a further extension of his lines. Desertion was thinning his ranks; conscription had broken down. Wilmington, the last Confederate port, was closed by the capture of Ft. Fisher (Jan. 15). A peace conference held in Hampton Roads failed (Feb. 3) because *Davis* still insisted on the recognition of southern independence. Congress forced *Davis* to appoint *Lee* (Feb. 9) commander in chief of all the Confederate forces. But this step came too late; *Lee* could only appoint *Johnston* to command such troops as could be mustered to meet Sherman. For Grant, having decided that to the army of the Potomac should fall the honour of capturing Richmond, ordered Sherman to march up through the Carolinas. To provide him with a base on the coast,

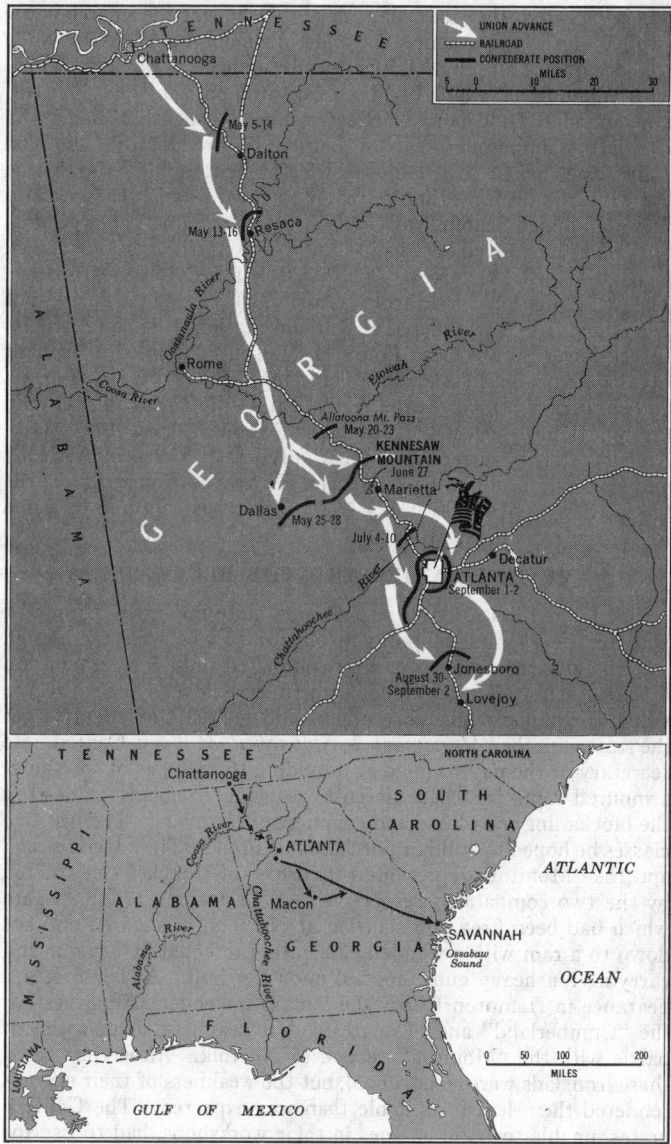

FIG. 6.—GENERAL SHERMAN'S INVASION OF GEORGIA, 1864: (TOP) UNION ADVANCE ON ATLANTA, SHOWING MAJOR MILITARY ENCOUNTERS; (BOTTOM) GENERAL LINE OF ADVANCE OF ENTIRE GEORGIAN INVASION, SOMETIMES REFERRED TO AS SHERMAN'S "MARCH TO THE SEA"

Grant brought Schofield from Nashville to North Carolina to capture Wilmington. Sheridan with 10,000 cavalry moved from the Valley to White House (March 19) in time for Grant's next advance. *Lee* had determined to withdraw his army to Danville and effect a junction with *Johnston* against Sherman. But his artillery horses and transport animals were in no condition for hard work, until the roads improved. To prevent Grant extending to the left, *Lee* attempted a diversion by attacking Ft. Stedman (March 25) on the right of the Federal lines. After the repulse of this sortie Grant ordered a general advance by the left flank. Sheridan's victory at Five Forks (April 1), beyond the extreme right of *Lee's* lines, where with his cavalry and Gouverneur K. Warren's corps he defeated *Pickett's* division and *Fitzhugh Lee's* cavalry, gave the Federals possession of the Petersburg and Lynchburg railway. Next morning Grant broke through *Lee's* lines on a broad front, driving him back into the suburbs of Petersburg. That night *Lee* commenced his retreat. Richmond surrendered on April 3. *Lee*, having been forced by Sheridan from the Danville road to the north bank of the Appomattox, surrendered on April 9.

Sherman advanced (Feb. 1) and occupied Columbia (Feb. 17). A large area of the city was burned, whether by Federals or Confederates or by accident has never been determined. Charleston was evacuated the following day. Although the march over swollen rivers and swamps was most arduous, Fayetteville, N.C., was occupied (March 11), where communication was established with Wilmington, which had been captured on Feb. 22. Sherman now aimed at Goldsboro to effect a junction with Schofield, who had left Wilmington for New Bern. To prevent this junction *Johnston* attacked Sherman's left wing at Bentonville (March 19), but withdrew his forces and retreated to cover Raleigh (March 21). Sherman joined Schofield at Goldsboro (March 23). From Goldsboro Sherman moved out against *Johnston* (April 10) and occupied Raleigh (April 13). Next day *Johnston* asked for an armistice. The assassination of Lincoln (April 14) caused a delay, but *Johnston* finally surrendered at Durham Station, N.C., on April 26. In the lower South, Gen. James H. Wilson conducted a brilliant cavalry campaign in Alabama, defeating Gen. *Nathan B. Forrest* and capturing Selma (April 2), the last Confederate arsenal, and Canby, Banks's successor, captured Mobile (April 12). Gen. *Richard Taylor* surrendered the Confederate forces in Alabama and Mississippi to him (May 4), and *Kirby-Smith* surrendered the trans-Mississippi forces (May 26). *Davis* was captured by some of Wilson's cavalry (May 10).

VI. THE NAVIES AND THE BLOCKADE

The United States navy in 1861 was quite unprepared for war. Half of the 34 steamships available for service were on foreign stations and the home squadron comprised only 7 steamers and 5 sailing ships. The navy department was slow to recognize the value of armour plate for warships and let the Confederates get the start with the *"Merrimack."* Stephen R. Mallory, Confederate secretary of the navy, aimed at providing three types of warships: armoured rams for coast defense, seagoing ironclads to destroy the blockading squadrons and commerce destroyers. The last two classes he hoped to build or purchase in Europe. The *"Merrimack"* and the "Monitor" represented the types of ironclad constructed by the two combatants respectively. The former, a U.S. frigate which had been fired and scuttled at Norfolk, was raised and cut down to a ram with a wooden casemate, protected by armour and carrying ten heavy guns, erected upon her hull. At her first appearance in Hampton Roads she sank two wooden sailing vessels, the "Cumberland" and "Congress," but next day, after a drawn battle with the "Monitor," retired to Norfolk. Altogether 12 of these ironclads were constructed, but the weakness of their engines rendered them less formidable than was expected. The Confederates, unable to build engines in their workshops, had to use for their ironclads either the old ones or those they took out of other steamers. The main features of the "Monitor," designed by John Ericsson to counter the *"Merrimack,"* were the revolving turret, the low freeboard and the projecting overhang. She drew less water and was more easily handled. The Federals built a large number of monitors, which, though more than a match for the rams, were comparatively ineffective against forts, as was proved by the failure of the naval attack on the Charleston forts (April 7, 1863). The river ironclads, which fought in the waters of the west, were gunboats constructed by James B. Eads with a partially armoured casemate. To the original nine, five more were added in 1863, more heavily armoured and powerfully armed. Three single-turret ironclads of light draught were specially constructed for the Red River expedition.

Two powerful ironclads were built in England for the Confederates, but the British government kept them from sailing. One ironclad built in France passed into southern hands, but reached Havana too late to take part in the war. Three commerce destroyers built or purchased in England did great damage to the Federal mercantile marine. Having auxiliary sail power they could economize on coal. The *"Alabama,"* during her 22 months' cruise, never put into a Confederate port. She captured 68 prizes in the Atlantic, Indian ocean and China sea, sank the Hatteras gunboat off Galveston but was herself sunk off Cherbourg, France, by the sloop of war "Kearsarge" (June 19, 1864). The *"Shenandoah's"* objective was the whaling fleet in the North Pacific, which she destroyed (June 1865), having no official news that the war was over. The *"Florida"* raided northern commerce from 1862 to 1864, when she was captured and sunk. The Geneva arbitration (1872) found Great Britain responsible for the losses inflicted by these three cruisers to the amount of $15,500,000. (*See* "ALABAMA" ARBITRATION.)

The Federal navy concentrated upon blockading the seven principal southern ports. Lincoln had proclaimed a blockade of the southern coast on April 19, 1861. But for many months it was little more than nominal for lack of ships to enforce it. An attempt to close Charleston harbour by sinking stone-laden hulks in the entrance proved a failure. Not until the middle of 1862 could the blockade be regarded as even moderately effective. Then with the export of cotton at last unrestricted and an increasing demand in the English market, vessels specially adapted for blockade-running were built in the English shipyards, and in spite of the Federal navy blockade-running only ceased to be a profitable speculation when the ports were actually in Federal hands. Savannah had been practically closed since the capture of Ft. Pulaski (Dec. 12, 1862). The loss of Charleston and Wilmington left the Confederacy without an Atlantic port, and reduced the armies of *Lee* and *Johnston* to a state of destitution.

VII. CONCLUDING OBSERVATIONS ON MILITARY ASPECTS

The collapse of the Confederacy was so sudden and complete that it took Europe by surprise. Sherman's "march to the sea" first opened foreign eyes to the probability of southern defeat. But as early as 1863, when *Lee* had suffered defeat at Gettysburg and *Bragg* had finally lost Chattanooga, and the Federals had recovered the Mississippi between Vicksburg and Port Hudson, ultimate defeat stared the Confederacy in the face. The sole remaining hope was that the North, through sheer war-weariness, might throw away the victory already won. When it appeared that Grant had been fought to a standstill by *Lee* around Richmond in the summer of 1864, and when *Johnston's* army remained still unbeaten between Sherman and Atlanta, the North very nearly reached the limit of its endurance. The Democrats put forward a program, the first article of which pronounced the war a failure. Lincoln despaired of re-election. But the fall of Atlanta and Sheridan's triple victory over *Early* in the Valley came in time to turn the scale in favour of the government. Gradually, too, the significance of Grant's position in front of Petersburg came to be realized. *Lee* had lost the power to maneuver when he was shut up in Richmond and Petersburg, and could not force Grant to relax his hold. Yet once more the North was filled with alarm when *Hood* crossed the Tennessee and, with Sherman far away in Georgia, threatened an invasion of Kentucky. Grant himself was on his way to take command at Nashville when he heard the news of Thomas' crowning victory. Sherman could now present Lincoln with Savannah as a Christmas gift, and the one organized army of the Confederacy in the west was definitely broken up.

The South made a great mistake during the first winter of the war, when the North was organizing its military strength and the Confederates took no countermeasures. Their government, counting on European recognition to be followed by peace, left *A. S. Johnston* in the west with an entirely inadequate force to hold Kentucky and Tennessee. At the first onset the Federals broke through his line of defense; his counterstroke failed; Kentucky and a great part of Tennessee were permanently lost; New Orleans fell; and the Federals gained control of great stretches of the Mississippi. Then the Confederate government awoke from its dream. The first Conscription act (April 1862) retained in service the 148 regiments of one-year volunteers and by encouraging voluntary enlistment enabled *Lee* to save Richmond, but the ground lost in the west was never recovered.

The Confederacy had one inherent weakness. It was composed of sovereign states, which would temporarily sacrifice their "state rights" for the success of their revolution, but demanded that the central government should provide for their protection, and if it failed in that duty, would take their own measures for self-defense. The state governors were always a thorn in *Davis'* side. From the first they required delicate handling and, when things began to go wrong, became refractory. This state patriotism combined with geographical conditions to isolate the different sections of the country and prevented the Confederates from taking proper advantage of their "interior lines." Only once did troops from the trans-Mississippi region come to the aid of their countrymen on the other side of the river. *Van Dorn* moved from Arkansas to *Beauregard's* aid at Corinth, but his men were very reluctant to cross the river, and it is significant that no attempt was made to bring reinforcements to Vicksburg in 1863 from that department. Only once were considerable reinforcements sent from the east to the west, when *Longstreet* with two divisions was sent to *Bragg's* aid, and the victory of Chickamauga (*q.v.*) was the result.

The west was the really decisive theatre of war. In the east *Lee's* victories did not alter the strategical position. The end of each campaign found the army of the Potomac on the Rappahannock, still menacing Richmond. But the fall of Vicksburg cut the Confederacy in two; the loss of the food supplies, especially cattle, from across the Mississippi was sorely felt, and the capture of Chattanooga and Knoxville not only cut off another section of territory, but opened the way to Georgia, the granary of the South. That *Lee's* and *Johnston's* armies were reduced to starvation was due to the loss of Georgia's supplies. Grant indeed captured Richmond and *Lee's* army, but had he chosen he might have brought Sherman's army by sea from Savannah to the James, and it could have been there two months before he began his final move.

In final analysis the North's naval superiority must be reckoned a decisive factor. It made possible the conquest of the Mississippi and Sherman's march through Georgia. The capture of New Bern by the Burnside expedition (March 1862) provided the Federal land forces with a base from which they could threaten an advance on Richmond, and caused the permanent retention in North Carolina of a considerable Confederate force which might have been profitably employed elsewhere, notably at the time of *Lee's* invasion of Pennsylvania. The blockade threw the South upon its own resources, which proved inadequate, especially in the matter of munitions of war and medical stores. It was not lack of food, but the difficulty of transport that reduced the Confederate armies to the verge of starvation. The southern railways were not equal to the strain of a four years' war. The rolling stock could not be replaced when worn out or the permanent way kept in working order as a result of the lack of iron rails.

VIII. POLITICS, ECONOMICS AND FOREIGN AFFAIRS

1. Northern Politics.—The military events of the war were played out against a background of political affairs, and politics influenced many military decisions. The Republican party had little internal unity. It was a composite of state parties with varying interests. There were elements of the old Whig party, former Free-Soilers and Liberty party men, Anti-Nebraska Democrats, free-trade westerners and Pennsylvanians who advocated a high protective tariff. The Democratic party, disrupted by internal dissensions, had still considerable strength in the states and in the federal congress. The firing on Ft. Sumter brought momentary unity to the Republicans, and sharpened division of the Democrats into two groups. War Democrats supported the administration in prosecuting the war, while peace Democrats continued to demand a negotiated peace and opposed conscription, arbitrary arrests, the suspension of habeas corpus and financial measures designed to support the war. Lincoln used patronage to create unity, and gave civil and military appointments to the war Democrats.

Factional divisions soon developed among the Republicans: a moderate group was content to follow Lincoln and prosecute the war in order to restore the Union, while "radical" Republicans enlisting the support of the old abolitionists, were determined to destroy slavery, punish the South, and reorder southern economic life for the benefit of northern industrial and financial interests. A congressional committee on the conduct of the war, dominated by the radicals, investigated and harassed Democratic generals, and became the fountainhead of propaganda demanding vigorous prosecution of the war, complete subjugation of the South, emancipation of slaves and eventually, enfranchisement of the freedmen and punishment of rebels. The committee waged a persistent

warfare against McClellan, a Democrat, and was largely responsible for his eventual removal. Closely allied to the committee were Secretary of the Treasury Salmon P. Chase and Secretary of War Edwin M. Stanton.

From the beginning Lincoln faced problems in handling the government. Congress was not in session when Ft. Sumter was fired on and Lincoln proceeded without immediate congressional sanction to call for troops, to increase the size of the navy and to authorize the enlistment of volunteers. He gave support to the Unionist faction in western Virginia, which was moving toward the creation of a new state; he suspended the writ of habeas corpus in Maryland and other places where dangerous disaffection developed. When congress assembled in July, it approved his actions.

More troublesome were the problems growing out of slavery. Lincoln insisted that he waged the war only for the preservation of the Union, and the day after the battle of Bull Run, congress declared that the federal government had no intention of interfering with slavery. However, fugitive slaves escaping into Union lines constituted a continuing problem for commanders in the field, some of whom returned them to their masters. In Virginia, however, Gen. B. F. Butler declared them "contraband of war" and put them to work on fortifications. In Missouri Gen. J. C. Frémont issued a proclamation confiscating the property of rebel sympathizers, declaring their slaves free. Since Lincoln believed this action would jeopardize the Unionist cause in Kentucky, he rescinded the order and removed Frémont. Radical Republicans denounced Lincoln and demanded an emancipation proclamation, but Lincoln countered with proposals for compensated emancipation in the loyal states. Congress provided for compensated emancipation in the District of Columbia, but not in the border states. In Aug. 1861 and July 1862 acts confiscating the property of rebels provided for freeing the slaves so expropriated. Radicals continued their pressure to make emancipation a war aim, and the movement was strengthened by the desire to use Negro soldiers in the northern armies. Lincoln resisted the pressure. In July 1862 he discussed an emancipation proclamation with his cabinet but determined to wait until a Federal victory furnished a propitious occasion. Late in August he asserted, replying to an editorial in the *New York Tribune,* "My paramount object in this struggle is to save the Union, and is not either to save or to destroy slavery. . . . What I do about slavery and the colored race, I do because I believe it helps save the Union, and what I forbear I forbear because I do not believe it would help save the Union." Within a month of this statement, however, two events hastened the announcement of a preliminary emancipation proclamation. One was the repulse of *Lee* at Antietam, and the other the assembling of northern governors at Altoona, Pa., where they were planning to demand emancipation and the use of Negro soldiers. On the eve of the governors' conference Lincoln issued the proclamation which effectively forestalled the governors' demand but changed the purpose of the war from the preservation of the Union to the emancipation of the slaves. The proclamation itself (issued Sept. 22, 1862, to take effect on Jan. 1, 1863) had no immediate effect, for it applied only to states that were in rebellion and therefore beyond Federal control. Lincoln continued to urge compensation for loyal masters. Slavery was not abolished until congress adopted the 13th amendment to the constitution and sent it to the states to be ratified. It was ratified and proclaimed in Dec. 1865.

The Emancipation Proclamation, arbitrary arrests and limited military success had political reactions, and in the state and congressional elections of 1862 Democrats gained strength. The regular Democrats took courage and began opposing the administration with increasing vigour. Seizing upon the arbitrary acts of the government, the Democrats proclaimed themselves the defenders of liberty and wore copper one-cent pieces which bore "liberty heads" to signify their position. Republicans vigorously denounced the "copperheads" (*q.v.*) and encouraged the formation of Union leagues, which carried on a consistent campaign for the "true" Republican principles of the radicals. In 1863, C. L. Vallandigham (*q.v.*) campaigned for governor of Ohio with copperhead support. General Burnside arrested him and a military commission sentenced him to imprisonment. Lincoln commuted the sentence to banishment to the Confederacy, but Vallandigham made his way to Canada and continued his campaign. Ohio troops suppressed disorders on election day and Republicans retained control of the state.

By the election of 1864 Lincoln had sufficient strength in his party to secure his renomination. Radicals, however, nominated Frémont, and for a time threatened to split the party. Democrats were seriously divided. They nominated General McClellan, but he repudiated their platform, which declared the war a failure. Negotiations resulted in Frémont's withdrawal and the fall of Atlanta contributed to Republican success. Lincoln won reelection by a vote of 212 to 21 in the electoral college.

2. Confederate Politics.—In the Confederacy, as in the North, there was a constant interaction of civil and military affairs. The Confederate constitution differed little from that of the United States, but there were distinct differences in the organization of political parties. *Davis* was not the choice of a party for the presidency, and there was no organized national party of opposition. There were, however, serious differences of opinion on policy and resulting factionalism. Fundamentally, the conflicts involved the issue of state rights as opposed to southern nationalism. *Davis* attempted to create a national army and administration, but met the opposition of state politicians who represented state interests. The issue became apparent on the question of conscription, which the governors of Georgia and North Carolina, with the support of Vice-Pres. *Alexander H. Stephens*, considered an invasion of state rights. In congress a faction opposing *Davis* questioned his judgment in conducting the war and singled out Secretary of State *Judah P. Benjamin* as the object of repeated attacks. Other matters that caused difficulty were taxation, loans and attempts of the government to fix prices. In 1863 opponents of *Davis* won control of congress and most of the state governments were unco-operative. The result of the declining popularity of *Davis* was lowered morale both in and out of the Confederate armies. Even before the final military campaigns began, the Confederacy, rent by internal divisions, had lost the will to fight.

3. Economics of the War.—In the final analysis, the North's victory was the result of its industrial and financial power. Essentially the conflict was between two different economic societies, and the northern economy proved better able to sustain itself in every way. In actual money the United States spent about $5,000,-000,000, while the Confederacy spent about $3,000,000,000. On both sides the war effort was financed by taxation, loans and the issue of paper money. Northern customs duties provided revenue, and successive tariff acts raised duties to 47%, the highest in the history of the country. An internal revenue act of 1862 imposed taxes on thousands of items. The income tax was first used in 1861. Loans, however, provided the greater part of the cost, while legal tender notes, inflating the currency, met immediate and pressing expenses. Partly to facilitate the sale of bonds and partly to destroy the confusing system of state banking, the National Bank act of 1863 was passed, creating a new national system of banking. In the Confederacy the government soon exhausted the available credit for its bonds and early resorted to paper money and inflation. When the declining value of currency brought hardship, the government levied a tax in kind to raise supplies.

In the North the financing of the war was accompanied by a series of acts that brought far-reaching economic changes in the nation. The Homestead act of 1862 gave western lands to actual settlers; the Morrill act in the same year made provision for establishing agricultural colleges; extensive grants of bonds and lands were given to aid the construction of railroad lines to the Pacific. Industrial development was stimulated by war contracts, by new sources of raw materials and by the widespread use of agricultural machinery. While the inhabitants of the Confederacy suffered from the exhaustion of their accumulations and severe shortages in supplies of every description, the people of the North generally enjoyed an unprecedented prosperity.

4. Foreign Affairs.—The Confederates, with a weak financial system, placed too much reliance on European aid, which they hoped to influence by controlling cotton. The Confederate govern-

ment expected recognition of its independence, and there was much sympathy for the southern cause in England and France. Early developments, in fact, seemed to presage aid from Europe. The United States was irritated when Queen Victoria, taking advantage of Lincoln's proclamation of a blockade of the southern ports, issued a proclamation recognizing the belligerent status of the Confederacy. A few months later a U.S. warship seized two Confederate emissaries, *James M. Mason* and *John Slidell,* from a British mail ship, the "Trent," and the incident threatened to cause a break in diplomatic relations. The good judgment of President Lincoln and of the Prince consort, Albert, calmed excitement, and the United States eventually surrendered *Mason* and *Slidell. Mason* made no headway in England, though he established a newspaper, the *Index,* and furnished aid and encouragement to Confederate sympathizers. The U.S. ambassador, Charles Francis Adams, watched carefully lest England give aid to the Confederates. He was unable to prevent the sailing of commerce destroyers from British ports, but he succeeded in stopping ironclad rams, being built in the Laird shipyards, from putting to sea. In France, *Slidell* was better received by Napoleon III, and a Confederate loan, supported by promises of payment in cotton, was floated on the Paris market. Despite widespread sympathy, however, the French did not recognize the Confederate government and gave it only sporadic, nongovernmental aid. *See also* references under "American Civil War" in the Index.

BIBLIOGRAPHY.—J. G. Randall, *Civil War and Reconstruction* (1937); Allan Nevins, *War for the Union,* 3 vol. (1959 ff.); T. Harry Williams, *Lincoln and His Generals* (1952); W. B. Hesseltine, *Lincoln and the War Governors* (1948); R. N. Current, *The Lincoln Nobody Knows* (1958); Kenneth Williams, *Lincoln Finds a General,* 5 vol. (1949–59); K. M. Stampp, *And the War Came* (1950); Douglas Southall Freeman, *R. E. Lee,* 4 vol. (1934–35), *Lee's Lieutenants,* 3 vol. (1942–44); Bruce Catton, *Mr. Lincoln's Army* (1951), *Glory Road* (1952), *A Stillness at Appomattox* (1953), *This Hallowed Ground* (1956); T. L. Livermore, *Number and Losses in Civil War* (1901); Mark M. Boatner III, *The Civil War Dictionary* (1959); Bell I. Wiley, *The Life of Johnny Reb* (1943), *The Life of Billy Yank* (1952); R. U. Johnson and C. C. Buel (eds.), *Battles and Leaders of the Civil War* (1887); R. M. Ketchum (ed.), *The American Heritage Picture History of the Civil War* (1960). The official documents are found in Richard Rush *et al.* (eds.), *Official Records of the Union and Confederate Navies in the War of the Rebellion,* 30 vol. (1894–1914); R. N. Scott *et al.* (eds.), *War of the Rebellion: a Compilation of the Official Records of the Union and Confederate Armies,* 130 vol. (1880–1901).   (W. B. Wo.; W. B. He.)

AMERICAN COLLEGE OF PHYSICIANS, founded in 1915, is an organization of specialists in internal medicine, including pediatricians, psychiatrists, neurologists, bacteriologists, pathologists, dermatologists, roentgenologists, medical teachers and investigators, tuberculosis and public health specialists. Its purposes are: (1) to maintain and advance standards in medical education, medical practice and clinical research; (2) to perpetuate the history and best tradition of medicine and medical ethics; and (3) to maintain both the dignity and efficiency of internal medicine in its relation to public welfare. Members are elected from all parts of North America.

Activities and functions of the college include the following meetings: an annual session; postgraduate courses held at several different medical schools each year; and approximately 30 regional meetings in as many states each year. The college publishes the *Annals of Internal Medicine,* a scientific journal; the *Bulletin,* a news magazine concerning the members; and a directory of membership. To promote medical education the college sponsors research fellowships, loan funds for young men in training and, in association with the W. K. Kellogg foundation, Latin-American fellowships. In maintaining high standards of medical practice the organization participates with other medical organizations in the Joint Commission on Accreditation of Hospitals and the Joint Commission on Professional and Hospital Activities. Headquarters are in Philadelphia, Pa.   (E. R. Ld.)

AMERICAN COLLEGE OF SURGEONS was organized in 1913 by leading surgeons of the United States and Canada. It is the largest and most active surgical organization in the world, having by 1960 more than 23,500 fellows in 70 countries. The college is dedicated solely to improvement of the care of the surgical patient, which purpose it fulfills through postgraduate education of surgeons, accreditation of various agencies in the field of medical care, financial support of research in surgery, enforcement of ethical principles in the relationship of its fellows with patients and co-operation with other national and international agencies in programs of public welfare.

The college furthers postgraduate education of surgeons by means of scientific meetings, five or six each year, at which programs of the latest developments in surgery are presented; by a library of medical motion pictures which are made available to professional groups; by a program for proper care of injured patients, which includes training of nonmedical persons such as policemen, firemen and ambulance attendants. It is one of four organizations composing the Joint Commission on Accreditation of Hospitals (founded by the college in 1917) which greatly elevated the standard of hospitals in the United States and Canada. The college is the sole agency in the United States which surveys and approves cancer programs which meet certain minimum standards for diagnosis and treatment of cancer. The cancer control program is supported in part by grants from the National Cancer institute and the American Cancer society. One of the major efforts of the college is toward the elevation of moral and ethical standards in dealing with surgical patients; it has conducted public campaigns against such practices as buying and selling of patients, unjustified surgical operations, ghost surgery and the charging of exorbitant fees. The college publishes *Surgery, Gynecology and Obstetrics;* the *Bulletin,* devoted to information to the fellowship; and a triennial *Directory of Fellowship,* with supplements in the intervening years. (P. R. Hy.)

AMERICAN COLONIES (U.S.). Thirteen English colonies were established in the area that is now a part of the United States during the 17th and early 18th centuries. They grew both geographically and numerically from the time of their founding to the American Revolution (1775–81). Their settlements had spread far beyond the Appalachians and extended from Maine in the north to the Altamaha river in the south when the Revolution began, and there were at that time about 2,500,000 Americans. Despite the fact that they had been, and still were, much occupied with physical tasks, they had also progressed culturally.

The colonists were remarkably prolific. Economic opportunity, especially in the form of readily available land, encouraged early marriages and large families. Bachelors and spinsters could not live very comfortably, and were relatively few; widows and widowers needed partners to maintain homes and rear children, and so remarried quickly. The social diseases were less common in America than in Europe; divorce was almost unknown; and birth control was seldom practiced. Accordingly, most adults were married, children were numerous and families containing ten or more were common. Despite heavy losses by disease and hardship, the colonists multiplied. Their numbers were also greatly increased by continuing immigration from Great Britain and from that part of Europe west of the Elbe river, for in England and in Europe the colonies were looked upon as a land of promise. Moreover, both the mother country and the colonies encouraged immigration, offering inducements to those who would venture beyond the ocean. They particularly welcomed foreign Protestants. In addition, many were sent to America against their will—convicts, political prisoners and Negroes. The American population doubled every generation.

In the 17th century the principal element in the colonies was English; the second largest was formed by the Negroes. German and Scotch-Irish immigrants arrived in large numbers during the 18th century. Other important contributions to the colonial bloodstock were made by the Netherlands, Scotland and France. New England was almost entirely English; in the southern colonies the English were the most numerous of the settlers of European origin; in the middle colonies the population was much mixed, but even Pennsylvania had more British than German settlers. Except in Dutch and German enclaves, which diminished with the passage of time, the English language was used everywhere and English culture prevailed. The "melting pot" began to boil in the colonial period, so effectively that Gov. William Livingston, three-quarters Dutch and one-quarter Scottish, described himself as an Anglo-Saxon. As the other elements mingled with the English, they became increasingly like them; however, all tended to become different from the inhabitants of "the old country" and to become American. By 1763 the word "American" was commonly used on both sides of the Atlantic to designate the people of the thirteen colonies.

While life was hard for the early settlers and for all those who made their homes on the frontier, the colonists generally lived in increasing comfort, by the European standards of their time. The log cabins of the middle and southern colonies were gradually replaced by sturdy and attractive homes of wood or brick; clapboard houses superseded the huts of the first settlers in New England; and many mansions appeared before 1776. Food was relatively abundant and varied, the products of tillage being generously supplemented by rich fisheries and plentiful game. Wines, sugar, coffee, tea and spices were eventually imported in quantity. Clothing was substantial, and that of the well-to-do became fine, being imported from England, although common folk continued to wear linsey-woolsey and buckskin. More leisure time became available, notably for wealthy planters, merchants and lawyers.

Social gradations were brought from England and existed in the colonies from the beginning. In 17th-century New England, for example, the gentleman was distinguished from the goodman. During the 18th century there was an American aristocracy based on the possession of land and slaves in the southern colonies, on the ownership of land and success in commerce in the middle and northern colonies. To this aristocracy belonged families such as the Rutledges and Pinckneys of South Carolina, the Randolphs and Lees of Virginia, the Livingstons and Schuylers of New York, and the Saltonstalls and Vassalls of Massachusetts. Hereditary titles were uncommon, and this aristocracy was gentry rather than nobility. Social distinctions became sharper as one moved from north to south, wealth being much more evenly divided in New England than it was in the plantation areas of the Chesapeake bay region and the low country of the Carolinas and Georgia. Most of the American aristocrats were of middle-class origins; few were descended from great English or European families.

The typical American was a landowning farmer. With him in the middle of society were mechanics, artisans, shopkeepers, teachers and other professional folk. The south already had its "poor whites," not yet called so; similar people were not unknown above the Mason and Dixon line. A special group of whites which did not endure was that of the bond servants, persons who contracted to work for a master for a period of years in return for passage money from Europe. Some of them were convicts who had chosen transportation to America in lieu of execution in England. It is likely that a majority of the colonists began their lives in the new world as servants of one sort and another. At the bottom of the social scale were the Negroes, who, in the 18th century, numbered about 20% of the whole; Negroes were most numerous in the southern colonies, forming about 40% of the population of Virginia and about half that of South Carolina. They were principally employed in field labour but some performed household duties. Almost all of them were slaves, although the first Negroes brought to Virginia were technically servants.

The colonists were generally Protestant, either by church affiliation or tradition. Roman Catholics were few, even in Maryland, which was founded in some part as a haven for them. Here and there were Sephardic Jews, notably at New York, where a synagogue was founded as early as 1654. Although scholars frequently say that the percentage of Protestant Church membership in the American population has greatly increased since the colonial time, Protestantism was relatively stronger in America during the colonial period than later. In colonial days it was much more difficult than afterward to secure and to retain church membership, and backwoods people found it hard even to attend services. We may safely assume that tens of thousands whose names were not on church registers were Protestants sufficiently orthodox, and it is clear enough that the clergymen were more influential than afterward, although they had lost much of the power they had exercised in 17th-century New England. As the Revolution approached, the Congregational Church was dominant and was officially established throughout New England, except in Rhode Island. The Anglican Church was established in all the colonies from Maryland southward, and also in three counties of New York. However, the Anglican Church probably did not have the allegiance of a majority of the people in any colony. Presbyterians were numerous in the middle and southern colonies, and Baptists were to be found everywhere. The Friends (or Quakers) and various sects of German origin were important in Pennsylvania, as was the Dutch Reformed Church in New York and New Jersey.

In the 18th century, the orthodox churches were threatened and weakened in several ways. The Anglican Church, frowning upon "enthusiasm" and not very aggressive, lost attractiveness for many who desired fervour rather than cerebral exercise. The Puritan Churches of New England, with their appeals to Biblical Law and logic, also suffered because they failed to offer a sufficiently emotional type of Christianity. The scholars of the Presbyterian pulpits similarly lost favour. In the Great Awakening of the 1740s and 1750s, in which even the distinguished Rev. Jonathan Edwards (q.v.) briefly participated, evangelism and emotional piety flourished, especially in the interior settlements. The orthodox churches were also attacked from a very different quarter, from the world of science. Some intellectuals, considering the universe in the light of Newtonian science, turned toward deism, trying to find the Creator through the laws of Nature rather than the revelations of the Scriptures. Others were satisfied with Unitarianism. The greater prosperity and security which the colonists enjoyed in the 18th century, pushing hardship and death away, lessened the terrors of the afterlife and encouraged doctrinal heresy. Orthodox Congregationalists founded Yale in 1701 because they believed Harvard had become heretical. It should be said, however, that American Christianity was altered rather than vitally weakened. Puritanism, in New England and also in the middle and southern colonies, continued to be a mighty force. On the other hand, the way was opening for the substantial separation of church and state and for a greater religious freedom. Discrimination on the score of religion existed in every colony in greater or lesser degree but was substantially ended during the Revolutionary period.

The rise of more liberal views regarding religion in the colonies was accompanied by and was in some part based upon a wider diffusion of knowledge, achieved principally through schools. It is well known that New England—except for Rhode Island—early took the lead in education and long held it both in quality and quantity. Massachusetts was in the forefront, its general court by a law of 1642 requiring every town to see to it that its children were taught to read. Another more important and famous statute of 1647 ordered every town containing 50 or more families to hire a master to teach children to read and write, or to pay a fine of five pounds. While many towns chose to pay the fine rather than to found a school, elementary instruction became widely available in Massachusetts. In 1647 the general court also called for the establishment of a Latin grammar school, and in the 18th century provided for several academies which gave instruction on the secondary level. Harvard college was founded in 1636, primarily to train clergymen. The example of Massachusetts was substantially followed in Connecticut and New Hampshire. The ability to read and write was fairly common, at least among men, in New England at the close of the colonial period. By that time four colleges had been founded east of the Hudson; in addition to Harvard and Yale, Brown was established as Rhode Island college in 1764, and Dartmouth as a school for Indian and white boys in 1769.

The need for education was recognized also in the middle and southern colonies. The Dutch and the Scotch-Irish, like the Puritans, were fond of learning. The Quakers were at first opposed to education on the grounds that it had a corrupting influence. Although there were public schools in New Netherland, reliance for elementary instruction in the middle colonies was placed in private schools, which were rather numerous. A few secondary institutions also sprang up, including the Philadelphia academy which later became the University of Pennsylvania. Princeton university appeared as the College of New Jersey in 1746, Columbia as King's

college eight years later and Rutgers university as Queen's college in 1766. Less active in the field of education were the southern colonies, although the College of William and Mary was established in 1693, eight years before Yale. A few public elementary schools appeared, and many private schools. Secondary education was reserved for young men of wealthy families that could afford to hire tutors or to send their sons to public schools in England. Such young men also attended the College of William and Mary, the College of New Jersey, and British and European universities. Illiteracy was somewhat more common in the south than elsewhere. The Negroes were not ordinarily allowed to learn to read and write.

The diffusion of learning was not, to be sure, confined to the achievements of the schools. Newspapers, of which there were 37 by 1776, served to spread information. Almanacs and private libraries served the same purpose. Colonial leaders were often well read in law, the classics and history. Blackstone's *Commentaries* was a favourite.

The colonists, as might be expected, were not so remarkable for their contributions to learning, science and the arts. Benjamin Franklin found England to be crowded with men of genius and talent as the American Revolution approached and the great spaces of America to have relatively few. However, the contributions of Franklin himself to science and literature were major; his autobiography remains a classic. If Jonathan Edwards did not push back intellectual frontiers in philosophy or theology, he was at least a genuinely competent scholar. There are those who claim that Edward Taylor (q.v.) of Massachusetts was one of the great metaphysical poets, second only to John Donne, and the most gifted American poet before the 19th century. Since his writings were not published until the 20th century was well under way, his achievements have not been assessed with any certainty. Cotton Mather (q.v.) was a fine scholar who presciently declared that disease was caused by animals too small to be seen. The charming sketches of William Byrd II, classicist and frank diarist, retain their attraction. The Bartrams, John and William, of Pennsylvania and Alexander Garden and John Lining of South Carolina were respectable scientists. In New York the royal official, Cadwallader Colden (q.v.), not only wrote a history of the Iroquois but delved into mathematics and physics, erroneously conceiving that he could correct Newton. As the colonial period drew to its close, America excelled in political philosophy and produced painters of stature, notably Benjamin West and John Singleton Copley (qq.v.). American culture then was clearly more creative and less derivative than it had earlier been. However, American cultural dependence upon England continued after the colonies had become politically independent. *See* AMERICAN FRONTIER; AMERICAN REVOLUTION; NEW ENGLAND; SOUTH, THE; UNITED STATES (OF AMERICA): *History; see* also Index references under "American Colonies" in the Index volume.

BIBLIOGRAPHY.—Louis B. Wright, *The Cultural Life of the American Colonies, 1607–1763* (1957) and *The First Gentlemen of Virginia* (1940); Moses Coit Tyler, *A History of American Literature During the Colonial Period, 1607–1765* (1878); Fiske Kimball, *Domestic Architecture of the American Colonies and of the Early Republic* (1922); Brooke Hindle, *The Pursuit of Science in Revolutionary America, 1735–1789* (1956); Carl Bridenbaugh, *Cities in the Wilderness* (1938) and *Cities in Revolt* (1955); Michael Kraus, *The Atlantic Civilization: Eighteenth-Century Origins* (1949); Samuel E. Morison, *The Founding of Harvard College* (1935) and *Harvard College in the Seventeenth Century* (1936); Marcus L. Hansen, *The Atlantic Migration, 1607–1860* (1940); William W. Sweet, *Religion in Colonial America* (1942); Thomas J. Wertenbaker, various books, including *The Founding of American Civilization*, vol. 2, *The Old South* (1942); Richard B. Morris, *Government and Labor in Early America* (1946); Marcus W. Jernegan, *Laboring and Dependent Classes in Colonial America, 1607–1783* (1931); Perry Miller, *The New England Mind* (1939) and *The New England Mind: From Colony to Province* (1953).   (J. R. AL.)

AMERICAN ENGLISH is the English language of the United States as distinguished from that used elsewhere; more narrowly, it pertains to any word or expression that originated in the U.S. Americanisms are of four chief kinds: (1) forms or meanings surviving in current American use though no longer current in British use; (2) foreign loanwords taken into the English language in America; (3) new meanings developed in America for

English words; and (4) new words coined in America. A fifth may be legitimately added: certain pronunciations and spellings are Americanisms in contrast to their standard British counterparts. (*See also* ENGLISH LANGUAGE; LANGUAGE; LINGUISTICS; GRAMMAR; and SLANG.)

1. Survivals.—*Fall*, a local word in England, was displaced by the foreign *autumn*, but in America the old word had a new growth and by 1700 had become the standard term. *Quit* will hardly be encountered in England outside of legal usage; in America it is on everybody's lips—to *quit* work, a game, almost any activity, and its offspring include *quitting time* and the vigorous *quitter*. *I guess* was the Englishman's comic stereotype for Yankee speech until an English scholar pointed out that Chaucer had used it regularly. So simple a word as the universal American *maybe* was described by *The Oxford English Dictionary* in 1906 as "archaic and dialectal," the English usage being *perhaps*. Americanisms of this first kind, though not numerous, illustrate the conservatism of language in colonies.

2. Loanwords.—Speakers of English in America adopted loanwords from all the important languages they met. Indian names for plants and foods include *squash, succotash, pecan, hickory, hominy, pone* and *tamarack;* for animals and fish: *moose, skunk, terrapin, raccoon, opossum* and *muskellunge* (the last three also shortened to *coon, possum, muskie*); for other things: *moccasin, mackinaw, toboggan.* All these have long been standard and hardly suggest their origin any more. Some that have not reached this status are *cayuse* (an Indian pony), *Podunk* (symbolic of an out-of-the-way small town) and *hooch*, for what used to be *firewater*. Others retain the association with Indians: *squaw, wigwam, tomahawk, tepee, wampum.* The Indians' ceremonies impressed themselves early upon American political life in such words as *powwow, sachem, mugwump* and *Tammany.*

French loans came in through early exploration; one of the most essentially American words is *prairie. Portage, butte, cache, chute, levee* and *rapids* are all reminiscent of the vast inland area which the French were the first white men to penetrate. Other Americanisms of the same source are *calumet, chowder, shivaree* (noisy serenading of a newly married couple), *depot* and *à la mode* (applied to *pie* or other pastry, and meaning "topped with ice cream"). The decimal money terms, *mill, cent* and *dime*, are French.

Though Spanish has contributed more loans than French many are limited to the west; *e.g.*, topographical terms: *canyon, mesa, arroyo;* names of animals: *alligator, coyote, cockroach, mosquito, tuna;* names of plants: *alfalfa, marijuana, locoweed;* a number associated with cattle herding: *ranch, buckaroo, rodeo, lariat, bronco, corral, mustang* and the more recent *palomino* horse. Yet others are *pickaninny, tornado, cafeteria* and the rather slangy *bonanza, calaboose, hoosegow* and *vamoose.* From Mexico new terms continue to trickle in.

The Dutch of New Amsterdam and the Hudson valley furnished such basic Americanisms as *Yankee* (a nickname meaning John Cheese), *Santa Claus, bakery, cole slaw* (often naturalized as *cold slaw*, to which has been added the counterpart *hot slaw*), *cookie, scow* and *sleigh*, all standard; in addition, the colloquial *boss* (which has gone around the world), *cruller, dope, stoop* (a small porch), *snoop* (to pry into people's affairs), *spook, caboose* and *poppycock.*

To the very large German immigration are due such words as *pretzel, delicatessen, pinochle, sauerkraut, wiener* and *hamburger*, as well as the colloquial or slang *dumb* (stupid), *bum* (a tramp, or as a verb, to act the tramp, beg), *loafer, dunk, hex* and *dingus* (a thingamabob). The 19th-century influence of Germany on American education is reflected in *kindergarten* (becoming naturalized as *kinder-garden*), *seminar, semester* and others less commonly used.

Other miscellaneous loanwords fully adopted as Americanisms are the African *voodoo, yam, okra, banjo* and *gumbo*, all standard; the regional *tote* (to carry), *goober* or *pinder* (peanut); and the more recent *juke* joint, with its *jukebox* (a coin-in-the-slot record player). *Tycoon* (a person of power or importance) appears to be the only Americanism from Japanese. *Chop suey* is from Chinese words, though the dish was concocted and given its name in the U.S. Some slang terms are *shebang*, of Irish origin, and *kosher, kibitzer* and *mazuma* of Jewish (Yiddish) origin. Though interesting, foreign loans account for a relatively small number of Americanisms, and the period of their internal adoption virtually ceased with the end of mass immigration.

3. New Meanings.—The altered conditions of colonial life, and later those of the new nation, led to the use of English words in countless new senses. In England *lumber* meant rubbish; in America it came to mean timbers and boards; *corn* had included grain in general (wheat, rye, oats), but became specifically Indian corn or maize; a *creek*, at first an inlet from the sea, turned into a small fresh-water stream; a *bug*, still specifically meaning a bedbug in England, is the general American word for insect. On the other hand the busy *bee* became the symbol of communal activity in America, with *bees* for everything from quilting to spelling. *Pioneer*, after acquiring meanings literal and powerfully metaphorical, has gone back to England. Other words with new American senses are the topographical terms *crotch, divide, sink* and *bluff;* also *bleachers* (unshaded seats at *ball games* and other spectacles), *gondola* (a type of *freight car*), a *bureau* of government and thousands more, for this is the second commonest kind of Americanism.

4. Coinages.—New formations generally follow the established patterns of the English language. There are numerous derivatives such as *auctioneer, Americanism* itself and Thomas Jefferson's *belittle.* Compounds, a very large group, include *corn bread, cocktail* (of disputed origin), *jackpot, hand-me-down, grab bag, deadwood, know-how* (supposed to be extremely American) and *pipeline* (which is acquiring interesting metaphorical uses). Many words have fathered an immense progeny of compounds: *land*, for example, begins about 80 new combinations (*land bank, land-hungry, land shark, land sakes!*) and ends another 150 (*bottom land, crawfish land, Yankeeland*).

Echoic and sound-symbolic words include *fizzle, honk, bingo, gooey* (sticky) and its noun *gooyum, the jitters* (nervousness) and *jittery*—the latter few still colloquial. Back-formations such as *enthuse* (from *enthusiasm*), *orate* (from *oration*) and some others are traditionally condemned, yet *jell* (from *jelly*) and *peeve* (from *peevish*) have achieved some acceptance. *Donate* was one of the first Americanisms to stir derision in Britain, yet it has long been standard.

New words produced by lopping off either end are common: *gas* (gasoline), *fan* (fanatic), *gym* (gymnasium) and the more recent *copter* (helicopter), which defies etymological division. *Acute* was beheaded to make *cute*, at first in the sense of sharp, clever, even tricky; now it is a counterword, a word with no exact meaning, used to show approval of almost anything and much favoured by women. Words made directly from proper names include *lynch, maverick, buncombe* (with its expressive shorter form *bunk*) and the immortal *bloomers. John Hancock*, the first signature affixed to the Declaration of Independence, means any signature (though it is changing to *John Henry*). Examples of folk etymology are *woodchuck* (from Algonkian *wejack*) and probably *hoecake* (from Narraganset *nokehick*), *carryall*, a light carriage (from French *carriole*), and more recently the Spanish *temblor*, an earthquake, has turned into *trembler.*

Very numerous are functional shifts from one part of speech to another without change of form: to *corner* the market, a *combine* in business or as an agricultural machine, to *feature* or *star* an actor or actress, to *service* machinery. A *mammoth exhibit* illustrates both noun converted to adjective and verb converted to noun (unless *exhibit* is simply a lopped form of *exhibition*). The adjective *real* has become a popular adverb (*real* good, nice, sweet) exactly as *very* did five centuries ago in England. Blend-words may be exemplified by *Amerindian* (American Indian), *motel* (motorist hotel), *smog* (smoke fog) and initial-words by *G.O.P.* (Grand Old Party, at first applied to the Democratic, later to the Republican party), *O.K.* (*q.v.*) and *m.c.* or *emcee* (master of ceremonies). Of the various kinds of Americanisms, new formations are by far the most numerous.

5. Pronunciations and Spellings.—A few individual words differ from British use. Examples are *corollary* and *laboratory* (accented on the first syllable in the U.S., the second in England), *trait* (the final *t* pronounced in the U.S., silent in England). In England the noun *slough* rhymes with *now,* in the U.S. with *too*—in fact, it is also spelled *slew* or *slue.* England clings to *plough* and *axe;* America simplifies to *plow* and *ax.* America also simplifies the double consonants of *traveller, woollen, waggon,* etc. The most regular difference of spelling is in the *color, honor, labor* group in the U.S., where Britain favours *-our.* British *aluminium* and *speciality* hold to the original French spellings; American *aluminum* and *specialty* are more fully naturalized.

6. Tendencies in Development.—Americanisms have come into being from every sphere of life, but among the most striking are those concerned with establishment of the colonies and, later, settlement of the continent. The new weather conditions produced *blizzard, Indian summer* and *cyclone.* Pioneering and the frontier gave *blockhouse, sod fence, Conestoga wagon, six-shooter, batteau* and *corduroy road;* life in the settlements contributed *breaking plow, crazy quilt, overalls* and *pieplant.* From agriculture and cattle raising have come *corncrib, dry farming, irrigate, share cropping, range, dogie* and *rustling.*

New religious developments are responsible for *Mormon, revivalist, Christian Science, amen corner* and many more. The widespread education accompanying democracy has been an active source of words: *schoolma'am, grade school, lyceum, campus, co-education* (and its colloquial abbreviation *coed*—a girl in a coeducational college), *commencement* and *valedictorian;* the classical element is evident.

Business terms, though numerous, are less original; yet *boom, boost, merger, gilt-edged, margin, greenback, emporium* and *crook* may be mentioned. American inventiveness is illustrated in *baseball, bifocals, chewing gum, cotton gin, lightning rod, submarine, typewriter, refrigerator* and many another, the words generally being adopted wherever the inventions themselves go.

Probably the most prolific sphere for new and striking words, however, has been that of government and politics: *democrat, caucus* (once thought to be an Indian word, but probably Greek), *congress,* both *gubernatorial* and *governmental, abolitionist, secession, spoils system, band wagon* and *Uncle Sam* himself. Later additions to the list include *suffragist, antisaloon, prohibition,* Teddy Roosevelt's *big stick* and Franklin Roosevelt's *New Deal* (adapted from Mark Twain). Politics produced or gave currency to a number of forms obviously relished for their grotesqueness: the *locofoco* party, the *gerrymander* (like a salamander), to *boondoggle* (put effort into useless activity), *globaloney* (which derides internationalism) and *snollygoster* (a term of insult).

Americanisms have always included words intended to avoid strong language, or embarrassing or unpleasant topics. Some early euphemisms were *darn, tarnation, doggone,* as mild oaths; *gentleman cow* instead of the sex-suggesting *bull.* A madhouse became a *sanatorium* and a coffin a *casket.* More recently undertakers have become *morticians* and their establishments *funeral homes;* the poor have become the *underprivileged* and an *exceptional child,* surprisingly, is one of subnormal intelligence. Closely connected with this is grandiloquence, the application of high-sounding terms to ordinary things, as *sanitary engineer* (plumber), *janitor* or *custodian* (caretaker) and many more. A discharged soldier, no matter how short a time he was in the service, is a *veteran.* To call an automobile "second-hand" is anathema; it is *used, reconditioned* or (a triumphant creation) *preowned.*

Like their linguistic ancestors of Elizabethan England, Americans enjoy new words and coin them freely at all levels of usage. This inevitably produces ugly, jargonish and ill-made words along with many very effective ones that win rapid adoption and even world-wide use. Especially characteristic are humorously exaggerated metaphors: *prairie schooner* (pioneer covered wagon), *panhandle* (a strip of land running off from the main body—as in Texas), *bulldozer* (something which intimidates, hence a powerful earth-working machine), *bootlegger* (seller of illicit liquor, who originally carried it in the leg of his boot), to *eat crow* (swallow something unpleasant, hence admit one's mistake), *ghost writer* (one who anonymously writes a speech, or the like, for a well-known person). Many are colloquial or slangy: *crowbait* (worthless meat, usually an old horse), *eye opener* (something surprising),

rubber check (one which "bounces" because there is no money in the bank to cover it) and the more recent *hot rod* (an old car used for racing) and *wetback* (a Mexican who enters the U.S. illegally by crossing the Rio Grande river).

The taste for novelty leads to many unconventional formations. From *cafeteria* the last syllables are detached and used to form *groceteria, gasateria, washateria* and so on for establishments in which, as in a cafeteria, one serves oneself. *Hamburger* is falsely split, *burger* comes to mean a sandwich made with a round bun, then *cheeseburger, steakburger, snakeburger* and many others follow. The *Ikeburger,* however, is honorific, not cannibalistic. Other unconventional suffixes are *-rama* (detached from *panorama*) as in *motorama, aquarama, futurama*—all used for exhibitions or elaborate shows; and *-oree* (*-aree, -eree*), from the Americanism *jamboree,* as in *fisheree, percharee, camporee* (contests or celebrations involving fishing, catching perch and camping).

The ordinary *-er* which makes nouns of agent has been much favoured, as in *squatter* (one who settles on a piece of land without legally owning it), *schooner* (a sailing vessel that skims over the water) and *cutter* (a sleigh that moves rapidly and easily). But there is a more characteristic *-er* which suggests the possession of some quality: *carpetbagger* (carrier of a carpetbag, an opportunistic speculator), *forty-niner* (one who approved the 49th parallel as a boundary between the Oregon territory and Canada or who rushed to California for gold in 1849), *fourflusher* (one who pretends to have five cards of the same suit but has only four, a *bluffer* or deceiver). Many of these creations begin as slang but move up rapidly into colloquial and even written use.

Yet another American predilection is for adding adverbs to verbs, sometimes without clearly affecting the sense—*beat up, close up, lose out, start in, test out*—but often with a decided change of meaning—*call down* (scold), *call up* (telephone), *get behind* (be delayed), *lay off* (discharge), *pass up* (fail to take), *put across* (do successfully), *turn down* (refuse).

7. American and English.—Americanisms, looked upon at first as deplorable deviations from the mother speech of England, were much condemned by some and as warmly defended by others (*see* H. L. Mencken, *The American Language,* ch. 1, and Supplement I, ch. 1). In the course of time attitudes have changed: Americans are less apologetic and Englishmen less disdainful—indeed, in the 20th century borrowing across the Atlantic in both directions is the normal state of affairs. The trade flows, if anything, more actively from west to east, with the influence of American literature, journalism, movies, radio and television making itself strongly felt. The man in the street is hardly aware whether new words are American or English in origin, and even the literary man must examine the evidence closely before he can be sure. The English language is a common possession to which many contribute.

A few examples of Americanisms adopted into standard English usage in the 20th century are: *ballyhoo* (noisy artificial publicity), *blurb* (a piece of overblown praise), *boost* (to "push" commercially or otherwise), *chore* (an unpleasant task), *doodle* (to scribble in a random way when one is abstracted), *hindsight* (the contrary of foresight), *quiz* (a set of questions to test one's knowledge), *routine* (in the sense of normal), the very useful noun *setup* (an arrangement of things) and so seemingly ordinary a term as *executive.*

Down the centuries hundreds of everyday Americanisms have quietly entered English usage—indeed, they have gone wherever the language is used (*see* H. W. Horwill). Nevertheless, variants persist. A partial list of contrasting terms follows; the American term appears first, followed by its English equivalent.

alumni—old boys (girls)
ash can—dust-bin
asman—dustman
baby carriage—pram
baggage car—luggage van
billboard—hoarding
brakeman—brakesman, guard
bumper (automobile)—buffer
burlap—hessian
calendar (court)—cause-list

call up (on the telephone)—
   ring up
can (container)—tin
candy—sweets
car (railroad)—
   carriage, van, waggon
carom (billiards)—cannon
catalogue (university)—calendar
checkers (game)—draughts
cheesecloth—butter muslin

chicken yard—fowl-run
chief of police—chief constable
collar button—stud
commencement (university)—
    graduation or degree cere-
    mony
cookie—small sweet cake, biscuit
corn—maize, Indian corn
counterfeiter—coiner
cowcatcher—fender, plough
cracker—biscuit
crystal (watch)—watch-glass
cuffs (trouser)—turn-ups
cute—quaint, attractive, dainty
daylight-saving time—
    summer time
derby (hat)—bowler
dime novel—penny dreadful
dishpan—washing-up bowl
drugstore—chemist's shop
dry-goods store—draper's shop
elevator—lift
enlisted man—private soldier
excelsior—wood-wool
express train—nonstop train
faucet—tap
fender (automobile)—
    wing, mud-guard
firecracker—squib
fire department—fire brigade
floorwalker—shop-walker
fraternal order—friendly society
freight—goods
freight car—goods waggon
gasoline—petrol
grade (railroad)—
    gradient (railway)
grain—corn
grain broker—corn factor
hardware dealer—ironmonger
headliner (stage)—topliner
hogpen, pigpen—sty, piggery
hood (automobile)—bonnet
huckster—
    barrow-boy, costermonger
hunting—shooting
installment plan—
    hire-purchase plan
internal revenue—inland revenue
janitor—caretaker
kerosene—paraffin
laborer—navvy
legal holiday—bank holiday
letter box—pillar-box
locomotive engineer—
    engine driver
long-distance call—trunk call
lumber—timber

molasses—treacle
movie—cinema, film
orchestra (seats)—stalls
outbuildings (farm)—offices
patrolman (police)—constable
pocketbook—handbag
poorhouse—workhouse
postpaid—post-free
prepaid—carriage paid
Rhine wine—hock
roast (of meat)—joint
roll call (in legislative assembly)—
    division
round-trip ticket—return ticket
shoeshine—boot polish
sidewalk—pavement
silverware—plate
sled—sledge
snoop—pry into others' affairs
soft drinks—
    minerals and squashes
sponge (surgical)—wipe
stockholder—shareholder
stocks—shares
store fixtures—shop-fittings
streetcar—tram
street railway—tramway
subway—tube, underground
suspenders (men's)—braces
switch (noun, railroad)—points
switch (verb)—shunt
tavern—public house (pub)
taxes (local)—rates
tenderloin (beef)—
    undercut, fillet
tenpins—ninepins
thumbtack—drawing-pin
ticket office—booking-office
tie (railroad)—sleeper
to run for (congress)—
    to stand for (parliament)
transom (door)—fanlight
transportation—transport
trolley car—tram
truck (vehicle)—lorry
tube (radio)—valve
tuxedo—dinner jacket
undershirt—vest
vest (men's)—waistcoat
warden (of prison)—governor
washrag—facecloth
washstand—wash-hand stand
wastebasket—
    wastepaper basket
windshield (automobile)—
    windscreen
witness stand—witness-box
wrench (tool)—spanner

Object	Northern	Midland	Southern
container for milk	pail	bucket	bucket
frying pan	spider	skillet	(mixed)
dragonfly	darning needle	snake feeder	mosquito hawk
seesaw	teeter (-board)	seesaw	seesaw
call to a cow	come boss!	sook!	co-wench!
roller shades	curtains	blinds	mixed
zigzag rail fence	rail fence	worm fence	rail fence
small firewood	kindling	kindling	lightwood
noise a cow makes	moo	moo	low

Numerous subregional and local variants exist for these and thousands of other terms. Pronunciation features are similarly distributed. Most elements of U.S. dialect derive ultimately from the British Isles. *See also* DIALECT GEOGRAPHY.

BIBLIOGRAPHY.—The principal authorities in the field of American English are *A Dictionary of American English on Historical Principles*, ed. by W. A. Craigie and J. R. Hulbert, 4 vol. (1938–43), and *A Dictionary of Americanisms on Historical Principles*, ed. by M. M. Mathews, 2 vol. (1951). The first is more comprehensive, using "American" inclusively and showing better the continuity of English in the new world; the second gives prominence to those words originally American, has some earlier and later evidence and many helpful illustrations. Both dictionaries, being historical, give dated citations to support every entry. Useful for background material is M. M. Mathews, *The Beginnings of American English* (1951). Rich in miscellaneous human and philological interest is H. L. Mencken, *The American Language*, 4th ed. rev. and enl. (1936) and its two supplements (1945–48), with thorough indexes and useful bibliographies. A short but valuable study is H. W. Horwill, *American Variations*, Society for Pure English Tract, 45 (1936). Two general studies are Thomas Pyles, *Words and Ways of American English* (1952) and A. H. Marckwardt, *American English* (1958). For current treatments of usage and word origins probably the best source is the quarterly magazine *American Speech*. *See also* "Words and Meanings, New," Encyclopædia Britannica *Book of the Year* (1944 *et seq.*).

For studies of American dialects *see* American Dialect Society, *Dialect Notes* (1890–1939) and *Publications* (1944 *et seq.*); Hans Kurath, *A Word Geography of the Eastern United States* (1949); Harold Wentworth, *American Dialect Dictionary* (1944); Hans Kurath and Raven I. McDavid, Jr., *The Pronunciation of English in the Atlantic States* (1960). (F. G. Cy.)

AMERICAN FARM BUREAU FEDERATION, largest U.S. farm organization, was an outgrowth of the county farm bureau movement. Shortly before World War I, the idea of using county demonstration agents, agricultural experts or extension workers to provide farmers with the results of scientific study was adopted in a number of areas. In many localities these agents were supported by local groups of farmers who constituted county committees or bureaus. Before the end of the war the county farm bureaus in several states had formed state organizations.

In Nov. 1919 representatives of the state farm bureaus met in Chicago, Ill., and completed plans for the organization of the American Farm Bureau federation. Prior to this meeting, education for better production had been emphasized, but post-World War I conditions were already bringing to the fore the need of a business organization to represent farmers. The purposes of the federation were stated in its constitution: "to promote, protect and represent the business, economic, social and educational interests of the farmers of the nation, and to develop agriculture."

Although the federation grew out of county and state farm bureaus organized to sponsor educational activities, it quickly became active in sponsoring a wide variety of measures to improve farmers' economic welfare. In the early 1920s it supported legislation to strengthen farmer co-operatives and make additional credit available to farmers. Later the federation supported the McNary-Haugen bill to increase prices of the major export crops; the bill was passed by congress in 1927 and 1928, but vetoed each time by Pres. Calvin Coolidge. It continued to press for legislative action for farmers and took a major part in formulating and obtaining passage of the Agricultural Adjustment acts of 1933 and 1938. During World War II the federation opposed price controls and objected to many of the administrative decisions that prevented price ceiling adjustments for farm products. Following World War II the federation supported measures to reduce government participation in economic activities. Through-

8. American Dialects.—The widespread notion that a dialect is a decayed form of a language is false. Historically all standard languages of today began as local dialects but became elevated through their use by a leading class or group to a position of prestige, their sister dialects suffering a corresponding loss of esteem.

In the U.S. there is no one "standard" pronunciation, though the language as printed is consistent in most respects. Standards in the spoken language go by broad regional divisions, whose subordinate variants, when they form localized types, may be called dialects. Since dialect survives only through some kind of isolation, geographic or social, and since there is much mixture, movement and intercommunication of the U.S. population, dialect as distinct from regional speech is virtually limited to coastal strips, mountain areas or those communities within large cities which have remained relatively homogeneous for some time.

Three regional divisions are now recognized: northern (including New England, New York city and the area north of a line drawn through the middle of Ohio, Indiana and Illinois, westward to the Pacific coast); midland (the wedge-shaped area between northern and southern, having Philadelphia at its apex and widening southward and westward to include most of the southwest and south Pacific states); and southern (including the south Atlantic states up to the Blue Ridge, the lowlands of the Gulf states and eastern Texas). A few characteristic terms are:

out the 1950s it advocated measures to reduce government farm price supports and return the direction of the farm economy more largely to commercial markets.

Membership in county and state farm bureaus slumped from between 400,000 and 500,000 in the early 1920s to less than 200,000 in the early 1930s. The more successful state farm bureaus sponsored affiliated co-operatives for the purchase of farm supplies and co-operative insurance companies. The practice of sponsoring affiliated co-operatives spread to most states, and membership in the farm bureau increased rapidly in the late 1930s and early 1940s. Membership exceeded 1,000,000 in the mid-1940s and stabilized a little above 1,500,000 in the second half of the 20th century.

Elected delegates from the county farm bureaus elect the state officers and formulate policies of the state farm bureaus. Delegates from the state farm bureaus elect the officers of the American Farm Bureau federation and formulate the policies of the federation in resolutions which they formulate and adopt annually. *See also* AGRICULTURAL ORGANIZATIONS.

BIBLIOGRAPHY.—Walter W. Wilcox, *Social Responsibility in Farm Leadership* (1956); F. A. Shannon, *American Farmers' Movements* (1957); Orville M. Kile, *Farm Bureau Through Three Decades* (1948); David E. Lindstrom, *American Farmers' and Rural Organizations,* ed. by Herbert McNee Hamlin (1948).   (E. E. Es.; W. W. Wx.)

AMERICAN FEDERATION OF LABOR-CONGRESS OF INDUSTRIAL ORGANIZATIONS, U.S. federation of labour unions formed in 1955 by the merger of the A.F. of L. and C.I.O. The A.F. of L., established in 1886, originally represented the principle of organizing workers in craft unions such as the United Brotherhood of Carpenters and Joiners, though its member unions were never all of this type. The C.I.O., which had broken away from the A.F. of L. between 1936 and 1938, represented the principle of industrial organization, sometimes called vertical organization, including in one union, such as the United Mine Workers of America, all employees in a given industry. Each union retained its autonomy under the new federation and was therefore free to work out its own policies in accordance with its own needs. In general, the new federation followed the policies of the predecessor federations, which are described below. By 1960 the membership of the federation totaled approximately 14,000,000, about 1,000,000 less than the total membership at the time of the merger. (*See also* LABOUR [TRADE] UNION: *United States.*)

Early Moves Toward Federation.—Largely as a result of efforts by the International Typographical union, a conference of labour organizations was called in Terre Haute, Ind., for Aug. 2, 1881. Only 21 delegates from 15 organizations attended. In view of the small attendance, the delegates did not deem it expedient to set up an organization. Instead they decided to call a national labour congress in Pittsburgh, Pa., on Nov. 15, 1881. The call declared the "time has now arrived for a more perfect combination of labor—one that will concentrate our forces so as to more successfully cope with concentrated capital." In addition, the call pointed to the need for the establishment of a legislative committee on the order of the parliamentary committee of the British Trade Union congress to protect the interests of the worker. The meeting was attended by 108 delegates, 50 of whom were members of the Knights of Labor, and the remaining ones from trade unions and central labour councils. The large contingent from the Knights resulted from the desire to prevent the emergence of a rival. After drawing up a preamble, the convention declared its opposition to child labour and Chinese immigration and demanded the establishment of an eight-hour workday and enactment of a mechanic's lien law. A new organization, the Federation of Organized Trades and Labor unions of the United States and Canada was established, and a legislative committee, made up of a secretary, treasurer, president and two vice-presidents, was chosen.

The new federation did little in its first year. It was virtually without funds and appointed no full-time officer. The trade unions which it had sought to rally did not respond, and the skimpy support the federation received never enabled it to do much more than issue an annual statement to its sparsely attended conventions.

It appeared for a time that a federation of trade unions, independent of political and reform parties, would not be established. However, a change in the attitude of many trade unions toward a federation was brought about by the activities of the Knights of Labor which greatly expanded its membership during the 1880s. Devoted to the view that it represented all labour, the Knights of Labor sought to set up organizations competing with many trade unions. These efforts inevitably aroused the resistance of those organizations whose jurisdictions were invaded. Consequently a number of trade unions decided to seek a common defense against these encroachments.

In the spring of 1886 a confidential circular signed by a group of leading trade unionists suggested a meeting of heads of unions to seek to devise a policy for preventing the continued invasion by the Knights of Labor. Twenty unions sent 22 delegates to a conference in Philadelphia on May 17, 1886. In addition, a number of trade unions which failed to send representatives approved the purpose of the meeting. After a two-day conference, a "treaty" was drawn up and submitted to the Knights of Labor. The treaty would have required the Knights of Labor to refrain from organizing trade unions whenever a national or international union was functioning and from admitting those who had been expelled or suspended from a trade union; and to avoid interfering with the activities of trade unions in any manner. In return, the trade unions offered to urge their members to join the Knights of Labor, which was to confine itself to educational work. As the Knights of Labor had just then experienced a great increase in membership and was at the height of its power, it naturally rejected the demands. Thereupon the trade unions called a convention for Dec. 1886, in Columbus, O., which established the American Federation of Labor, with which the Federation of Organized Trades and Labor unions of the United States and Canada merged.

American Federation of Labor.—In contradistinction to the older federation, the A.F. of L. had, from the beginning, the support of many trade unions. It also established a full-time salaried post of president, to which Samuel Gompers (*q.v.*) was elected. In the first years of its existence, the A.F. of L. had to struggle against the opposition of the Knights of Labor and the suspicion of the national and international trade unions that it might encroach upon their authority. As a matter of fact, the A.F. of L. was given no power over the national and international unions. The latter were independent and autonomous, and free to work out their own rules, policies and attitudes toward their members and their employers. Consequently, the A.F. of L. had within its ranks, craft and composite or industrial organizations, conservative and socialist unions, all of which tolerated each other.

By the end of the 1890s, the shrinking Knights of Labor was no longer a serious rival to the A.F. of L., which gradually became the economic spokesman for the U.S. labour movement. In time, virtually all unions, except the brotherhoods, whose members were employed in the service trades on the railroads, affiliated with the A.F. of L.

Throughout its history, the A.F. of L. was forced to develop policies governing the relations of its affiliates to the federation, and of the latter toward government and public issues. By refusing to charter unions whose jurisdiction bordered too closely on that of an affiliate, the federation frequently prevented the growth of narrow craft organizations without an adequate jurisdictional base. The federation also encouraged the amalgamation of closely related unions, so that they would have a broader membership and jurisdiction. Unions were also allowed to expand their jurisdictions so that they would be able to recruit the less skilled, and sometimes even the unskilled, in their industries into their organizations.

Despite the efforts to avoid conflict between labour organizations, jurisdictional disputes developed. Not only did some unions, which preceded the A.F. of L., have overlapping jurisdictions, but changing materials and processes in industry made inevitable conflict over which union would have the authority to organize a specific group of workers. Under the constitutional principles developed by the A.F. of L., every union affiliated with it had the exclusive right to organize the workers in its trade, which constituted its jurisdiction. When jurisdictional disputes first came before the executive council and convention of the A.F. of L., it was hoped that they would not become a serious source of difference and that they would be settled by conference and mutual concession. Instead the number and severity of these disputes increased. In 1900 the A.F. of L. faced a dilemma as a result of a conflict over the jurisdiction of the United Mine Workers of America. That union had, from its inception, organized all workers in and around the coal mines in an industrial union. Several craft unions—machinists, patternmakers, boilermakers, carpenters and others—insisted that the mine workers' union surrender the craftsmen it had recruited, and turn them over to the respective craft unions. As the United Mine Workers refused to agree to such a step, the A.F. of L. faced a serious crisis, which the convention of 1901 met by promulgating the "Scranton Declaration." The declaration recognized the desirability of the coal miners being organized in an industrial union because of the isolation of coal mining communities and the absence of virtually all other industries in coal mining areas. Consequently, it was held necessary, in this instance, to overlook the doctrine of exclusive jurisdiction of a particular union over the workers it had been allowed to organize.

Beginning in 1897, the unions affiliated with the A.F. of L. gained in membership and in influence, and they continued to progress until 1904. Simultaneously they were confronted with an elaborate and well-organized attack from employers so that some unions lost positions they had held for many years. Employer attacks were accompanied by proceedings in the courts against the use of the boycott, which culminated in the Danbury Hatters' suit and the prosecution of leading officers for violation of the restraining order against a boycott of the Buck's Stove and Range Co.

Little progress was made by organized labour between 1904 and 1910, but in the latter year unions were established in the men's and women's clothing industries. With the beginning of World War I in Europe, the unions began their upward march again. Several million members were gained in both the older organized industries and in some of the major unorganized industries such as steel and meat-packing. Union organization was aided by labour shortages and by the more favourable attitude of the federal government. The federal government not only found it desirable to deal with organized labour in the industries which came directly under its influence, but it established the National War Labor board, which in a limited sense protected the right of workers to organize.

Following World War I the A.F. of L. was confronted by attacks both from the right and the left. Steps were taken by employers to reduce the power and influence of labour unions by a concerted open-shop drive which had for its objective the elimination of organized labour from many plants and even industries. Many employers, among them the giant steel companies, refused to deal with unions. Such refusal precipitated strikes, but in the end the unions were usually defeated. On the left, the A.F. of L. faced opposition from elements which had become dissatisfied with its traditional policies. These groups demanded greater militancy on the industrial field and a change in political tactics. The A.F. of L. had followed a program of endorsing political candidates of both parties who supported labour and welfare legislation, a policy epitomized in the slogan "Reward your friends and punish your enemies."

On the other hand, there were always some within the federation who wanted the A.F. of L. to promote independent political activity by supporting a labour party. The leadership of the A.F. of L. modified its position in the campaign of 1924 when it endorsed the independent candidacy of Robert La Follette for the presidency. The step was taken, however, only because of the unacceptability of the candidates of the two major parties. In 1952 the convention endorsed the Democratic candidate, Adlai Stevenson.

After 1924 the A.F. of L. lost a large part of the membership gained during World War I. Even though employment was high during the 1920s, the A.F. of L. failed to gain in strength. With the onset of the depression in 1930 its major strongholds in the building trades suffered severe losses in membership. While the outlook seemed bleak for the A.F. of L. and its affiliated unions, there was an almost instantaneous change in their fortunes once the first Roosevelt administration took office in 1933. Section 7(a) of the National Industrial Recovery act, which guaranteed to labour the right to organize and bargain collectively through representatives of its own choosing, was of great aid in stimulating workers to join unions. Many organizations of the A.F. of L. greatly expanded during this period, and in some instances, as in bituminous coal mining, re-established themselves on a greater scale than ever. (*See also* UNITED STATES [OF AMERICA]: *History*.)

Emergence of the C.I.O.—At the same time, the A.F. of L. faced an internal crisis which its leaders could not solve. For the first time in history, there were widespread attempts of the workers in the mass production industries to form unions. These workers had, in the overwhelming majority of cases, never belonged to a labour organization and were not conversant with the constitutional procedures or the laws which governed jurisdictional rights within the A.F. of L. As the majority of the workers in these industries were semiskilled operatives, they sought to establish industrial unions. Such attempts encroached upon the jurisdictional rights of the older A.F. of L. craft unions. Despite the fact that the older unions had virtually no members in the mass production industries, they continued to insist that those who were eligible for membership in their organizations must be transferred from the mass production industrial unions into the craft or semicraft unions. Several efforts were made to compromise the conflicting claims, but none succeeded. When the resolutions for allowing the mass production industries to organize on an industrial basis were defeated at the A.F. of L. convention of 1935, eight unions organized the Committee for Industrial Organization, soon commonly known as the C.I.O. Under the leadership of John L. Lewis (*q.v.*), the C.I.O. raised large sums for organizing purposes and succeeded in establishing union recognition in the mass production industries. The success of the C.I.O. forced the A.F. of L. to expand its organizing activities and to recognize that in manufacturing industry the concept of exclusive jurisdiction could not be strictly followed. Once the A.F. of L. began to organize on a large scale, it succeeded in recruiting many more workers to its ranks than the unions of the C.I.O. In the meantime, the latter organization, whose member unions had been expelled (1936) from the A.F. of L., transformed itself into the Congress of Industrial Organizations (1938) and became a permanent rival to the A.F. of L. This step led to the withdrawal of one of its founding unions, the International Ladies' Garment Workers' union from the C.I.O. Eventually that union returned to the A.F. of L.

Reconciliation.—Once the A.F. of L. recognized in fact that unions in manufacturing would have to be allowed to function as industrial unions wherever the needs of the workers and the industry made such structural form necessary, the initial differences that divided the A.F. of L. and the C.I.O. were virtually extinguished. Yet the bitter rivalry and the personal animosity between the two bodies were not easy to overcome. Committees to unify the two organizations were elected a number of times, but their meetings did not lead to fruitful results. One important barrier was the attitude of some leaders of the A.F. of L. who regarded the C.I.O. as an erring offspring and constantly pleaded for a "return home." The presence of several Communist-dominated unions in the C.I.O. was also a complicating factor. These unions were expelled in 1949 and 1950.

The need of a common front before government and the public, especially during wartime, forced the two organizations to cooperate. With the death or retirement of some of the leading participants in the division of the trade unions, an approach to unity was made easier. The United Labor Policy committee which functioned during the Korean war was a first step. This group dissolved in 1951, but labour groups in 1953 appointed a joint A.F. of L.–C.I.O. unity committee to explore the possibilities of organic unity. A first step, the no-raiding agreement, was signed by the presidents and secretary-treasurers of the A.F. of L. and C.I.O. on Dec. 16, 1953. An overwhelming majority of affiliates of both federations accepted the proposal. This important step helped to eliminate competitive organizing and raiding, which usually led to irritation and promoted antagonisms between unions.

The next step was the working out of a merger agreement under which each national and international union, federal labour union, local industrial union and organizing committee holding a charter or certificate of affiliation from either federation was to retain its place in the merged federation. Each affiliate would retain its integrity and its right to existence and affiliation within the merged federation. Such a policy meant that duplication and overlapping of unions were inevitable. However, wherever such duplication or overlapping existed the affiliates were to be urged to eliminate the possibilities of conflict by agreement, merger or consultation. The merged federation recognized both craft and industrial unions as appropriate and necessary in a trade union federation, and thereby all ideological dissensions arising from differences on the structural question were automatically eliminated. The form of organization thereby became a purely practical problem to be determined by the needs of a particular group of workers.

At the first constitutional convention held in Dec. 1955, and in accordance with the merger agreement reached Feb. 9, 1955, the executive officers of the merging federation, president and secretary-treasurer were initially selected from the A.F. of L. The first president was George Meany and the first secretary-treasurer, William F. Schnitzler. On the other hand, the director of organization was appointed from the ranks of a union affiliated with the C.I.O. An executive council of 27 vice-presidents, with the 2 executive officers, was elected, 17 of the vice-presidents being chosen from A.F. of L. unions and 10 from C.I.O. unions. This council was to meet at least three times each year. An executive committee made up of the two executive officers and six vice-presidents, chosen by the executive council, was to meet bimonthly with the executive council and discuss policy matters. In addition a general board, consisting of the executive council, and a principal officer of each affiliated national and international union was to meet at least once annually and decide all policy questions submitted by the executive officers and executive council. The convention was to remain the seat of all authority, meeting every two years, but subject to special call. National and international unions and organizing committees were to pay a per capita tax, in an amount to be decided by the conventions, for the maintenance of the merged federation.

The merging federation established a department of organization to assist the affiliated unions in planning the federation's organizing work. This department was headed by a director appointed by the president, with the approval of the executive council.

In addition to the above structure a number of standing committees and staff departments were to be appointed by and under the direction of the president, also subject to the authority of the council. Standing committees appointed at the time of merging, as determined by the needs and problems facing the federation, included those on legislation, civil rights, political education, ethical practices, international affairs, education, social security, economic policy, community services, housing, research, public relations, veterans affairs and safety and occupational health.

A.F.L.–C.I.O.—In the first five years of its existence, the new federation (hereafter known as A.F.L.–C.I.O.) launched no major organizing drives, nor did it break any new ground except in the area of ethical practices. At the merger convention of 1955, the protection of the labour movement "from any and all corrupt influences" was declared to be one of the "objects and principles of this Federation." Investigations by the executive council at the request of the president or by any other member of the council were authorized and the committee on ethical practices was given "the duty and responsibility to assist the Executive Council in carrying out the constitutional determination of the Federation to keep the Federation free from any taint of corruption . . ." Codes of ethical practices were later drawn up. In 1956 and 1957 the conduct of six international unions was investigated; all were directed to change some of their policies and practices. Three,

the Allied Industrial Workers of America, the Distillery Rectifying and Wine Workers' International union and the United Textile Workers of America, agreed to introduce the reforms recommended and were placed on probation. Three others, the Laundry Workers' union, the Bakery Workers' union and the Teamsters' union were expelled. Other unions were chartered in place of the Bakery and Laundry organizations, but no steps were taken to challenge the Teamsters' union. The newly established A.F.L.–C.I.O. unions in the bakery and laundry industries made substantial progress, but the outlook for challenging the control of the Teamsters' union leadership was obviously not regarded as favourable.

By the federation's third convention in 1959, it was obvious that the merger was working. Friction appeared at several points in the disputes over jurisdiction between the old A.F. of L. and C.I.O. unions, but differences among affiliates were seldom fatal and had, in fact, usually existed when the A.F. of L. was an independent entity. In 1959 the International Longshoremen's union, which had been expelled by the old A.F. of L. before the merger, was readmitted to the A.F.L.–C.I.O. Several mergers of unions took place, the most important being in the paper manufacturing industry. Several unions of operating railroad workers, including the important Trainmen and Firemen's unions, joined the federation. The A.F.L.–C.I.O. promoted co-operation between the formerly warring seagoing unions but on the whole no significant gains in this area took place.

See also Index references under "American Federation of Labor–Congress of Industrial Organizations" in the Index volume.

BIBLIOGRAPHY.—John R. Commons *et al.*, *History of Labour in the United States* vol. 1, 2 (1921) and 4 (1935); Lewis Lorwin and J. A. Flexner, *The American Federation of Labor* (1933); Philip Taft, *The A.F. of L. in the Time of Gompers* (1957), *The A.F. of L. From the Death of Gompers to the Merger* (1959); Saul Alinsky, *John L. Lewis* (1949); Edward Levinson, *Labor on the March* (1938).   (P. Tt.)

AMERICAN FRONTIER. The term "frontier" has been defined in various ways and used by historians in even more ways. Webster's *International Dictionary,* in 1890, described it as "that part of a country which fronts or faces another country or an unsettled region; . . . extreme part of a country." The historian Frederick Jackson Turner early noted that, "especially in the United States," the term referred to "those outlying regions which, at different stages of the country's development," were "but imperfectly settled and constituted the meeting ground of savagery and civilization." To him it referred to that "belt of territory sparsely occupied by Indian traders, hunters, miners, ranchmen, backwoodsmen and adventurers of all sorts" which formed "the temporary boundary of an expanding society at the edge of substantially free lands."

Others have thought of it as "a form of society," "a state of mind," "the edge of the unused," "the first stage in the process of transforming the simplicity of the wilderness into modern social complexity." Some have used the terms "frontier" and "west" interchangeably as referring to an area having geographical location only in relation to a particular period of time and changing constantly as population had advanced. The U.S. census, on the other hand, has considered it a place where the inhabitants number two to the square mile, and on this basis marked the frontier line on a series of maps for each decade.

Yet, amid all this confusion in the use of terms, there remains the simple fact that the history of the United States, up to the beginning of the 20th century, was that of a people moving steadily forward to the occupation of a vast, raw continent. This involved not only recurring physical advances into new geographic basins where life had to be lived on simple, elemental levels for a time, but also constant social evolution from a simple hunting-trading stage to varying degrees of urban complexity and interdependence.

For 300 years this went on. For three centuries some Americans were leaving the older settlements and beginning over again on the frontier. For the same length of time, those who lived in what had become old and established centres were conscious of the fact that there remained an open door to free, unused lands where place and fortune were yet to be won. Thus as a reality for some and as a symbol for others, the frontier became a vital factor in shaping American life and American character.

The First Frontier.—Thus understood, the American colonies along the Atlantic coast were Europe's frontier, and their gradual drift away from European patterns was the first manifestation of frontier influence. They began the conquest of the wilderness; they took the first steps in crossing the continent; they became Americans. This, however, was only the beginning. Scarcely had the colonies themselves become firmly established before the western push began anew. Out from old centres, the dissatisfied, the restless, the adventurous made their way into the back country, there often to crowd the Indian into open resistance but ultimate retreat and to lay the foundations for a new society. Sometimes they moved to secure more room for themselves and their cattle; sometimes they moved because of "the strong bent of their spirits." Well before the American Revolution they had brought a new west into being—in upper New England, in the Mohawk valley, in the great valley of Pennsylvania and above the fall line and out into the ridges and valleys of the south. Already a few had crossed the mountains and opened the way for an even greater west.

This first west differed sharply from the original colonies which had already begun to reproduce the old world social and economic patterns with their class distinctions. It was a "democratic, self-sufficing, primitive agricultural society in which slavery and indentured servants played little part," and in which poverty and toil went along with a scarcity of social accumulations. As population spread and increased, differences between coast and interior became increasingly apparent and strife often developed over taxes, representation, internal improvements and religious matters. Bacon's rebellion, the Regulator movement and soon Shays's rebellion and the Whisky rebellion were all expressions of an east-west conflict produced by expansion.

The Second Period.—The second great westward push carried the frontier across the Alleghenies and deep into the heart of the continent. By 1800 Kentucky and Tennessee had entered the union as states, and Ohio was soon to follow them. The great migration, however, was to come in the years following the War of 1812. A traveler wrote in 1816 that "the Atlantic States seem to have had their day," and that the more active and enterprising, "the people who partake of youth, enterprise and hardihood . . . are looking more and more to the West." A year later another, himself on the road, noted that "Old America seems to be breaking up and moving westward."

The travelers were right. Within their life span (1840) settlement had spread across the lower south along the Gulf to the Mississippi and up the Red river, crowding the Indians out and creating the kingdom of cotton; spread along the Great Lakes into Michigan and Wisconsin, Indiana and Illinois to carry wheat and corn and hogs with it; and out in the centre, from Kentucky and Tennessee, it had crossed the Mississippi and reached the great bend of the Missouri from which the traders and trappers made their way on westward.

Characteristics of the First Frontiers.—Both of these two first frontiers were primarily agricultural in character. Here and there, where timber or minerals were found, lumbering and mining developed, but the main advance was always that of the farmer. Opening the way for him was the lone trapper and trader with the army and the missionary sometimes playing a part in dealing with the Indians. None of these made any great change in the wilderness. That was to come with the pioneers who wanted land and, at least, a temporary home.

The frontier process by which the well-wooded, well-watered regions east of the Mississippi river were settled is described in J. M. Peck's *A New Guide for Emigrants to the West* (1836). He speaks of "three classes, like the waves of the ocean," that had rolled along one after the other. First came the pioneer who lived "largely upon the natural growth of vegetation" and "the proceeds of hunting." He built a crude cabin, cleared a patch of ground by girdling the trees and moved on when "his neighbors' smoke vexed his eyes" and their voices disturbed his sleep.

The second wave of settlers bought these half-developed acres, cleared the roads, bridged the streams, built houses with glass windows, planted orchards, erected mills, schoolhouses and, as Peck puts it, soon exhibited "the picture and forms of plain, frugal, civilized life."

The final wave was composed of "men with capital and enterprise." They built houses of brick and stone, increased the agricultural surplus well above immediate needs and looked for wider markets in which to sell. They were the permanent settlers who brought the communities to maturity and created the towns with their general stores, their newspapers, their professional men and their politicians. They soon made their influence felt in national affairs.

Early Roads.—Access to the frontier at first was by way of Indian trails and waterways. Trappers and traders followed these in their wanderings and, in time, settlers on their way west pounded the trails into crude roads. Each group of pioneers evidently cleared, for their own passage, bits of whatever road they traveled. Trees were cut and the underbrush cleared away. In low, swampy places logs were placed side by side to form a corduroy road; where streams could not be forded, crude bridges were constructed. Stumps and the larger trees were left standing, and the drainage was so poor that travel was not possible in wet weather. Travelers usually found it best to make their journey when the ground was frozen. Roads to the west were improved only gradually and heavy traffic kept them in bad shape. Yet they tied the regions of unrest to the promised lands and helped to shape the character of both.

In the period before 1812 a system of wagon roads, following the old Indian trails, connected the eastern seaboard with Kentucky, Tennessee, southern Ohio and upper New York. Settlers in Kentucky and Tennessee came largely from the old south and from Pennsylvania. They followed one road that ran south and west from Richmond, Va., and another, known as the Great Valley road, that joined it near Ft. Chissel. From this junction the famous Wilderness road cut by Daniel Boone and his men ran through the Cumberland Gap and across Kentucky to Louisville. A branch road, west of Ft. Chissel, led south and west to Knoxville and on to Nashville. It was joined east of Knoxville by the Jonesboro road that stretched across North Carolina from New Bern on the coast.

Settlers from the middle states had a choice of three roads to the west. They could follow the Great Valley road or make use of one or the other of two military roads built during the French and Indian War—the Forbes road connecting Philadelphia with Pittsburgh, Pa., and Braddock's road running from Baltimore, Md., to Pittsburgh. Both had been recently improved by state action.

New Englanders of this period found a single road running west from Boston. It divided at the Connecticut river and sent one branch northward to join the Mohawk turnpike and the Great Genesee road, which were creeping across northern New York toward Lake Erie, and the other branch southwest to connect with the Catskill road leading to the headwaters of the Susquehanna river.

More important than any of these roads was the Cumberland or National road. In the Ohio Enabling act of 1802 a fund from the sale of public lands was set aside for road construction. In 1811 the federal government began work on the first section of a hard-surface (macadamized) road reaching from Cumberland, Md., to Wheeling, Va. (now W.Va.) on the Ohio river. Other sections were completed by 1833 to Columbus, O., at which point the state was forced by the opponents of national internal improvements (as roads and canals were known) to take over the "preservation and repair" of the road within its borders. Tollgates were then set up to provide funds for this purpose and to ensure the extension of the road farther to the west. The National road was not only highly beneficial to western settlement but it also pioneered the building of permanent roads with hard surfaces; it decided the question as to who was to build and maintain the public roads; and it showed the rich possibilities in east-west trade.

The "great migration" that came with peace in 1815 brought a new period of road building, especially along the Great Lakes and into the lower south. In New York the Genesee turnpike reached

Buffalo where new roads followed the south shore of Lake Erie across the Western Reserve and on to Chicago and beyond. From Detroit roads reached the eastern shore of Lake Michigan and a stage coach trail soon rounded the lake into Chicago. The National road had, meanwhile, crossed the new state of Indiana and reached Vandalia in Illinois. All along its course local roads branched out to carry farther inland and to contribute their share to the flood of humanity and goods that filled the main stream. Plank roads as well as roads with crushed rock surfaces were tried here and there, but dirt roads still predominated. Bad weather turned them into quagmires and thus stimulated western efforts at canal and railroad developments.

The opening of cotton lands in the lower south along the Gulf stimulated road building throughout the section. Migrants to the cotton kingdom came largely from the up-country of the old south and from the now mature Kentucky-Tennessee world. Those from the old south took either the Upper road which followed the piedmont from Virginia to Columbus, Ga., or the Fall Line road at the head of tidewater which also reached Columbus. From there the Federal road ran on to Mobile, Ala., and Natchez, Miss. Those who came from Kentucky and Tennessee found a network of roads that linked Lexington, Ky., Nashville and Knoxville with Memphis, Tenn., Natchez, Tuscaloosa and Florence, Ala., and New Orleans, La. None of these roads was first class, but when they were impassable, the abundant southern rivers were filled to overflowing and provided transportation.

Thus by the time the frontier reached the plains, roads were to be found wherever they were necessary. The railroad had reduced the need for roads on long hauls, but the improved road still served local needs and the Conestoga wagon was still an important American institution. *See* also OREGON TRAIL; PONY EXPRESS; SANTA FE TRAIL.

The Third Period.—The third and last frontier advance carried population across the remaining reaches of the continent to the Pacific and then turned back to fill in the areas passed over in the first forward drive. It began around 1840 and lasted to 1890 and beyond, when the federal census announced the frontier at an end. This is usually referred to as the trans-Mississippi frontier.

The region faced by the American pioneer in this last advance was strangely different in character from anything that he had met before, and the frontiers that emerged were more varied and more colourful than any earlier environments had produced. Beyond the first stretches of prairie lands lay the dry, treeless plains where rainfall was too scant for the accustomed agricultural crops and methods. Its nutritious grasses, however, had supported immense herds of buffaloes, and the settlers, after pushing old crops well beyond their limits, gave way to the cattlemen with their picturesque ranch houses, their cow towns and their carefree cowboys. It was a new kind of frontier, where capital and colour went together to stir the imagination of those whose lives were cast in more prosaic times and places.

Beyond the plains were the Rocky mountain ranges, with inland basins sometimes as large as an eastern state and with fur and mineral riches that brought the trapping frontier and the mining frontier to their fullest development. California and Oregon, on the Pacific coast, with their mines, their trading posts, their missions and their international complications, brought the frontiersman to the end of his journey and turned him back to the half-finished continent.

These last frontiers were unique in many ways. Vast distances and greater physical difficulties to be overcome created problems that the individual alone could not solve. Group action, government aid and outside capital were required to carry forward the necessary irrigation projects, to build the transcontinental railroads and to develop the mines and the timber resources. Everything was on a larger scale; everything was exaggerated. Settlement often came by rushes, not by a slow steady advance. There was more of waste, more of lawlessness, more of colourful incident. Hardships were greater and rewards were in proportion. All that any frontier had meant in the past to American life in terms of optimism, waste, lawlessness, abundance and progress were there magnified at the very time that the physical frontier was coming to an end.

Significance of the Frontier.—In his famous essay on "The Significance of the Frontier" (1893), Frederick Jackson Turner insisted that "the peculiarity of American institutions is, the fact that they have been compelled to adapt themselves to the changes of an expanding people—to changes involved in crossing a continent, in winning a wilderness, and in developing at each area of this progress out of the primitive economic and political conditions of the frontier into the complexity of city life." It was this unique American experience which reshaped inherited patterns into native ones. It created "a new product that is American." It explains "American development."

The fact that the frontiersman had to look to the national government for his land, often for protection and generally for aid in securing markets and ways to market served as a nationalizing tendency. "On the tide of the father of Waters," says Turner, "North and South met and mingled into a nation."

The part which the frontier played in promoting democracy has been subject to considerable questioning. The difficulty seems to be largely one of emphasis. Turner believed that the necessity of doing things for oneself and standing alone much of the time against difficulties developed a peculiar kind of individualism in the American, and at the same time strengthened his co-operative attitudes toward neighbours who faced the same problems. He saw no contradiction in the fact that a man might think that a fool can put on his own coat better than a wise man can do it for him and, at the same time, always be ready to take his part in the house-raising, the husking bee and the community moves for schools, churches and rapid urban development. This kind of individualism was "antisocial" but it led the new frontier states to grant democratic suffrage and to demand equal representation because their citizens believed in the individual's ability to care for himself. As long as opportunity remained in free lands, competency had its chance and democracy would result. Thus, argued Turner, the peculiar type of American democracy "came out of the American forest"; it was not a European importation.

Critics, however, have insisted that much of democracy came out of the old world and much of it resulted from conditions in American society that had nothing to do either with free lands or the frontier. Opportunity and abundance wherever found created a fluid social-economic condition which produced democracy. There was as much of these in the rising urban-industrial east as on the frontier. And besides, neither the Spanish nor the French frontiers showed democratic tendencies. For these reasons, say the critics, too much has been claimed for the frontier.

On the influence of the frontier in creating certain American intellectual traits there is more agreement. A practical, inventive quality in dealing with material things; an idealism that merges into an incurable belief in progress; a conservative approach that is mixed with a willingness to try new things when the accepted fails—these were frontier traits that have become American traits. With them has gone a rather unusual emphasis on the simple virtues of courage, loyalty, energy and physical strength; a larger respect for women; and a rather marked indifference to things abstract. European travelers, commenting on the American and his ways, have stressed these things and found them more common to the west and the newer regions than to the east.

The Frontier and Politics.—Out of the frontier and the west which it left behind it came a goodly share of the nation's problems and not a few of its most bitter conflicts. The steady advance of population produced a recurring Indian problem. Wars and treaties and ultimate removal of the Indians to reservations were a logical outcome of the frontiersman's determination to possess the whole continent.

The same steady advance kept the land problem alive. From pre-emption and graduation to the passage of the Homestead act and the heavy grants to railroads, the settler had his way against those who would use the public domain for revenue purposes. His insistent demands forced every public man to offer some land policy suitable to the people he represented.

Cheap lands on which to produce a surplus carried with them the demand for internal improvements and aid to markets. The part which government should play in the building of roads, canals and railroads and its right to pass protective tariffs, in part to create markets, occupied almost as much of congress' time for two generations as did the land policies themselves. All were related to the matter of finances. To migrate to the frontier and to establish a farm in the west was not something which every American could afford to do. It has been estimated that in the mid-19th century it took something like $1,500 to clear and stock an 80-ac. farm in the new west. Most settlers had to borrow money, and thus a hostility to banks which restricted credit and a general debtor attitude which favoured inflation characterized most frontiers. From Andrew Jackson to William Jennings Bryan such western attitudes played an important part in U.S. politics.

Westward expansion ultimately carried the settler across the border into Texas, and the idea of "manifest destiny," born out of three centuries of forward movement, led through the Mexican War to the acquisition of New Mexico and California. The moves to organize this vast, new territory became tangled with the slavery issue and altered its entire character. Where before the struggle had revolved about the merits of the institution itself, it now broadened into one over the expansion of slavery into the territories. The character of western settlement and the kind of institutions which were to be developed had become a part of a power struggle between the north and the south. The effort to shape the future of a frontier in Kansas brought the "cold war" between the sections to open bloodshed. The settlers at Massachusetts Bay, in Utah and elsewhere had attempted to maintain the unique character of their society but there for the first time rival civilizations fought for frontier control.

In no way did the frontier advance affect American life to a greater degree than in the creation of sections and sectional conflicts. Each forward movement into a new geographic area meant the formation of a new society which might be under the political dominance of some older state or in territories just beginning their careers in national life. In either case, its needs and attitude did not always agree with those of the more mature groups in the state or the nation. The result was conflict, and much of American history, local and national, is made up of the struggles and adjustments which resulted. State capitals have been moved, constitutions rewritten and legislative programs remade to satisfy contending interests, old and new, east and west. One American state has been divided. New western states have been created out of lands once claimed by older parent states. In one case, frontiersmen, who had formed their state of Franklin, had to give way to the demands of North Carolina. One need only recall the part played by the young west in the American Revolution and in the War of 1812 to understand the frontier's part in early national affairs. The dominant role which it played in the economic struggles and in the slavery controversy in the years from 1815 to 1860 has already been noticed. Even more significant as expressions of western as against eastern attitudes were the Granger, Populist and Nonpartisan drives of the late 19th century. Each revealed a marked democratic quality; each showed bitterness against eastern neglect; each bore a debtor flavour; and each tried to say that America stood for something which they represented and which, they thought, was being lost.

The Frontier Role of Women.—Women played an important but not spectacular part on the frontier. They never equaled men in numbers and were seldom found with the trapper and trader and not often in the early mining and lumber camps. Only when the settler came to clear a bit of land and to establish a home did the woman find a permanent place at the pioneer's side. Then she proved her ability to uphold her end of the load even where physical endurance was required. She bore the children, cared for them in sickness and often taught them to read and cipher. She tended her garden, cooked the family's food and preserved what she could for the winter. From the skins of wild animals or from homespun cloth she fashioned clothing for her men and children, and when danger from wild beasts or Indians threatened she proved herself capable in the use of a gun.

Disappearance of the Frontier.—During the final decade of the 19th century the open frontier disappeared from the map. Scattered areas still remained to be settled, but the building of the continental railroads had given them easy contact and means of communication with the rest of the nation. The physical frontier was at an end. Its influence had not come to an end, however. It was to remain, in picture and in story, as a colourful reminder of the American tradition of individualism, of freedom, of opportunity and of daring.

BIBLIOGRAPHY.—Frederick Jackson Turner, *The Frontier in American History* (1921), *The Significance of Sections in American History* (1932); R. A. Billington and J. B. Hedges, *Westward Expansion: a History of the American Frontier* (1949); F. L. Paxson, *When the West Is Gone* (1930); W. P. Webb, *The Great Frontier* (1952); A. P. Whitaker, *The Spanish-American Frontier: 1783–1795* (1927); J. D. Hicks, *The Populist Revolt* (1931). (Ay. Cn.)

AMERICANISM CONTROVERSY, centred about the French adaptation of the biography of Isaac Thomas Hecker (*q.v.*) by Walter Elliott in 1897, concerned doctrines ascribed to certain Roman Catholics, chiefly Father Hecker, founder of the Paulist Fathers; Archbishop John Ireland of St. Paul; Bishop John J. Keane, rector of the Catholic university; Monsignor Denis O'Connell in Rome; and Abbé Felix Klein of Paris. Pope Leo XIII in a letter, *Testem Benevolentiae*, Jan. 22, 1899, condemned as "Americanism" certain proposals that the church modify her doctrines to suit modern civilization and grant more freedom to individuals by rejecting external spiritual direction, by extolling natural over supernatural and active over passive virtues, and by eliminating vows in religious life. Ireland and Keane denied that they held the condemned doctrines, but Ireland's critics, Archbishop Michael Corrigan of New York and the German bishops of Wisconsin, thanked the pope for condemning the proposals.

(T. T. McA.)

AMERICANIZATION, in its narrowest meaning, describes those activities which are specifically designed to prepare foreign-born residents of the United States for full participation in citizenship. It aims not only at the achievement of naturalization but also at an understanding of and commitment to the fundamental principles of American life.

The analysis of this aim raises basic questions concerning national character and cultural change, and the term "Americanization" therefore broadens out as the discussion of its goal becomes more sophisticated.

The task of assimilating vast numbers of immigrants has not been unique to the United States, but no other nation has had as much experience or has faced the issues more squarely over as long a period of time.

Development of the Movement.—Before the outbreak of World War I in 1914, the American public generally took it for granted that the constant flow of newcomers from abroad brought strength and prosperity to the country. The metaphor of the melting pot had been introduced and enthusiastically accepted to symbolize the mystical potency of the great democracy, whereby people from every corner of the earth were fused into a harmonious and admirable blend. When the war began, however, American reactions to European hostilities revealed to everyone the fact, long known to a few, that the population contained many people who, in spite of long residence in the United States, were still completely foreign in sympathy, loyalty and general social and emotional affiliations. They thought and felt as Germans, Italians, English or Irish. To those who considered themselves true Americans, the sudden awareness of the aliens in their midst produced a profound consternation. If assimilation was not being produced by natural, spontaneous forces, then it must be achieved by deliberate, purposeful means.

The Americanization movement which came into being was primarily a program of education. Committees to promote the work were formed and public authorities at every level of government became active in the development of curriculums and the teaching of classes. The idea won immediate popularity. Throughout the country, Americanization agencies and activities in great variety sprang up, unified only by their common conception of the problem. The logic was simple. These unassimilated foreigners lacked some of the important characteristics of genuine Americans. This was dangerous for the U.S. Therefore they must be taught the missing qualities. To achieve this end, public schools organized classes, state departments of education formed special divisions, universities and city governments appointed Americanization directors, and both private industry and voluntary associations, such as the international institutes of the Young Women's Christian association, established their own activities or lent their support to the public programs. The teaching of foreigners became a favourite form of patriotic service, particularly after the entry of the United States into the war.

In its earliest days, the program was directed toward the correction of the most obvious deficiencies. The core of the curriculum was the English language, American history and the governmental structure of the United States, all necessary for naturalization (see NATURALIZATION LAWS: *United States*). Those who were interested in teaching other subjects began to capitalize on the popularity of the movement. Soon the offering included courses in millinery, cooking, social amenities and the care of children, all presented, of course, as essential elements of American culture.

Enthusiasm for Americanization persisted throughout World War I and was prolonged into the postwar period. Gradually, however, popular interest diminished. The broad adult education movement began its growth and many of the activities which had formerly been justified on the grounds of Americanization appeared worthy in their own right (see ADULT EDUCATION: *United States*). Many of the leaders and the programs which had formerly served foreigners broadened their scope of operations to include everyone. Wartime apprehensions subsided and new legislation severely limited the influx of immigrants. Before long Americanization became no more than a fairly obscure but continuing effort to prepare people for naturalization by teaching them English, civics and history, or even English alone. In this latter case, classes often included native illiterates.

During the great depression of the 1930s, there was some recurrence of popular concern with Americanization. Many Americans had come to assume that the foreigners had all been assimilated, but the conditions revealed by the economic crisis soon showed how false was that belief. A new fear of subversion arose and gave impetus to new efforts to inculcate American beliefs. Educational programs were sponsored by the various federal relief agencies, most notably the Works Progress (later Work Projects) Administration (WPA), and a stronger emphasis was placed on education by the various public and private immigration and naturalization services. These latter efforts were intensified in the period of worry about foreign influences which began with the outbreak of World War II in 1939.

Changing Concepts.—Meanwhile, however, there had been a thorough re-examination of the concept of Americanization. The early belief that all foreigners should be transformed into typical Americans began to appear naïve as soon as the tensions of World War I disappeared. Who is the typical American? Are American cultural habits (as defined in any particular curriculum) necessarily better than the way of life with which the foreign resident is familiar? Are there not many truly loyal and thoroughly assimilated Americans who are ignorant of much which the foreigner was required to learn? The United States was built by people who came from many backgrounds; is not the effort to impose conformity itself un-American? These and other questions proved hard to answer in the cynical 1920s. Moreover, even the most enthusiastic workers had found the task of assimilating aliens extraordinarily complex and difficult. The solutions proposed during the war years now seemed far too easy. So deeply did the disillusionment penetrate that within less than a decade after the armistice "Americanization" was a term to be shunned, not used. In the years that followed, it never quite regained its earlier lustre.

Instead of the old idea of supplanting all foreign traits by a standard pattern, there grew up the idea of cultural pluralism. Nationality groups continued to flourish and, particularly in the cities, to possess a political power which had to be reckoned with by the slate makers of every party. It was argued by some that assimilation in its accepted sense was not a desirable goal, but that the United States would reach its highest pinnacle by preserving many separate cultures side by side within its boundaries. Still others contended that this pluralism would gradually disappear over the years, that the American character was still in the process of formation and that as it gradually emerged, it would have been enriched by the harmonious blending of the admirable features of the various foreign nationalities.

The early faith in formal education as the only way to achieve assimilation also disappeared. The process involved represented a prolonged and difficult reaction to a social environment much more vital, involved and inclusive than that of a classroom. Special programs of education for the foreign-born became a permanent part of the work of public-school systems, particularly in the cities, and of many private religious and welfare organizations. English, history and civics remained the central themes, although the development of better methods and materials made possible great improvement in the quality of the teaching. These special classes aided their students to make their primary adjustment to life in the United States, but, both then and later, they were also conditioned by all those forces which mold their fellow citizens, including, of course, the widely available general provisions for adult education.

The problem of loyalty, which created the first interest in Americanization and which caused it to be re-emphasized in the depression and in World War II, still remained. Now, however, the focus was no longer primarily on the foreign-born but on the whole citizenry, and the term "Americanism" was increasingly used by legislative committees, militant associations and others to refer to the protection and inculcation of traditional American values.

BIBLIOGRAPHY.—Virtually all of the discussions about Americanization are presented in terms of the basic issues and problems concerned, such as immigration policy, security clearance, health, welfare, housing and education. On this latter subject, always central to the study of Americanization, one of the most useful publications is "Eight Measures for Evaluating Educational Programs for the Foreign-Born," U.S. Office of Education, *Circular 357* (1952).   (C. O. H.)

AMERICAN LABOR PARTY, a minor U.S. political party in New York state. It was organized in April 1936 by labour union leaders Sidney Hillman (Amalgamated Clothing Workers of America), David Dubinsky (Ladies' Garment Workers union), G. L. Berry (Pressmen's union), liberal Democrats and old-line Socialists. At first over 200 labour unions were associated with the party and all officers were unionists. It was hoped that the party could hold a balance of power between the Democratic and Republican parties in New York. As a pressure group it endorsed candidates who advocated social legislation. The party opposed Tammany Hall (*q.v.*) but generally endorsed Democrats. It also endorsed a few Republicans and occasionally ran its own candidates, winning five seats on the city council in 1936 and five seats in the assembly in 1937. It polled from 75% to 90% of its vote in New York city and never gained strength outside the city.

The party polled 274,924 votes for Franklin D. Roosevelt in 1936. It helped re-elect Fiorello LaGuardia mayor in 1937 and Herbert H. Lehman governor in 1938. It ran its own candidate, Dean Alfange, for governor in 1942 and endorsed Roosevelt for president in 1940 and 1944. Its largest vote, 509,000, went to Henry A. Wallace in 1948. The party was well organized with old-fashioned clubs and precinct workers.

From the first there were factional fights between the left and right wings. When the Communists failed to qualify on the ballot in 1938 they infiltrated the American Labor party and in the convention of 1940 rioted against the endorsement of Roosevelt. When the Communists gained control of the party in the primary of 1944, Dubinsky and many other founders of the party withdrew and organized the Liberal party (*q.v.*). Support of Wallace in 1948 drove more members from the party. In the election for mayor in 1950 the party's vote dropped to 147,000 votes. Its endorsed candidate for president in 1952, Vincent W. Hallinan, received only 64,000 votes.

After 20 years of stormy history, unable to reconcile the differences in personalities, composition of its membership and conflicting objectives, the state committee voted to dissolve the organization on Oct. 2, 1956.   (H. F. Tt.)

AMERICAN LAW. Speaking in a technical sense there is no American law. Except within a field constitutionally restricted, there is no national supreme tribunal to unify legal doctrine. Neither is there a common law of the United States as a sovereign state. Each of the states has its own common law, unrestrained otherwise than by certain provisions of the federal constitution; and none of these necessarily tends to produce unity of law except the clause requiring that "Full Faith and Credit shall be given in each State to the public Acts, Records, and judicial Proceedings of every other State"; a provision which does somewhat tend to unify doctrines respecting the conflict of laws.

For a period of nearly a century it was believed that unity would be promoted through the power of the federal courts to develop an independent body of national doctrine in the field of "general commercial law," which the state courts would be inclined, though not bound, to follow. However, the degree of uniformity produced in this way was disappointing, and any remaining hopes for progress along these lines were ended by the supreme court's decision in *Erie R.R. Co.* v. *Tomkins*, 304 U.S. 64 (1938), requiring the federal courts to apply the laws of the several states. A more significant approach to the ideal of uniformity has been through the uniform acts prepared by the National Conference of Commissioners on Uniform State Laws for adoption by the states. These statutes illustrate the sense in which there does exist an American law—there is a great body of judicial tradition and a vast mass of legislation embodying the rules and standards by which the American people, regardless of state lines, are content to guide their lives; and all this law presents broad features of unity. Indeed, nothing is more astonishing than the rapid spread of statutes, in a few years, into dozens or even scores of states—thus evidencing popular convictions nationally dominant; nothing more certain than the slower spread of a judicial doctrine that is felt to have adjusted justice to new conditions.

Of the civil law that once prevailed in territory subject to France and Spain, little trace remains except in Louisiana and in the variant marital community systems in a few other states.

In the sense just explained, American law is marked by four periods of development: (1) to 1776; (2) 1776–1828; (3) 1828–68; and (4) after 1868.

Colonial Law.—It is a traditional judicial tenet that the colonists brought with them as a birthright, along with English political traditions and precedents, the common law, its concepts of property, liberty and justice and such of its rules as fitted colonial conditions. They did indeed claim the general liberties of Englishmen. They did not claim or desire the common law; they had suffered too much from governmental tyranny which they deemed part and parcel of that system. All of the New England colonies, by practice or explicitly, denied its binding character. Half a dozen of the other colonies endeavoured to follow it from an early date. All the colonies, however, had codes, some notably complete, that covered their essential needs, so that at best the common law was but a subsidiary system; and in several even this position was accorded not to that law but to the Scriptures. Only three colonies gave statutory recognition to the English law in the colonial period.

For these reasons, and because the colonies were isolated and imperial control was slight, the 17th century in particular was a period of experiment and creativeness. The colonists were well aware of the proposals of reform and codification made by Lord Bacon and under the Commonwealth, and some of their codes were prepared in England by men who evidently sympathized with those proposals. Dozens of striking innovations—some of them of singularly modern semblance—were made upon the common law; some persisted into the later law—the most important was perhaps the recording of conveyances.

For two reasons, however, the history of this period, although profoundly interesting in itself, must be regarded as apart from the general legal development of the country. In the first place, its practices were too divergent from the tradition of the common law. There were almost no lawbooks—original, reprinted or imported. In most of the colonies there were extremely few trained lawyers and even the chief justices were rarely lawyers; the highest courts were legislative or executive. Laymen administered a sort of natural equity. In the second place, most of the valuable innovations were abandoned as soon as a reception of the common law began.

In the 18th century something like an independent judiciary developed. Imperial control became a reality; colonial statutes were disallowed (400 of them) for departures from established law; judicial appeals to England became steadily more numerous. A professional bar—for which there was evidently no place in the preceding century—gradually developed. Many of its leaders studied in the Inns of Court (perhaps 50 before 1760; 115 between 1760 and 1783), and to a very remarkable degree it was composed, otherwise, of graduates of American colleges. When the American Revolution came it was entirely dominant, and this pre-eminence it retained for a century.

This period was one of absorption of the English law, marked by the disappearance of older innovations and the development of few new ones. That it is in the truest sense an integral part of American legal evolution could be illustrated in many ways. Two instances are sufficient. The first, in the field of procedure, is its system of courts, the most characteristic feature of which—the multiplication of local tribunals that brought justice near to every man, instead of a circuit system—persisted (for reasons born of frontier conditions and self-government). The second, in substantive law, is the origin of the American doctrine that in libel truth (subject indeed to commentary for which there is no room) is a defense.

The whole of colonial experience was of course continuous and so the spirit of the earlier century lived on through the later. Demonstrably, various of its positive innovations, clearly adapted to colonial conditions, persisted against the English reception. As for many innovations of omission, doubtless "mere ignorance had freed the colonies of a great mass of antiquated and useless rubbish" (32 N.H. 231), but what was once overlooked in ignorance must later have been excluded in wisdom.

From 1776 to 1828.—Formal adoption of the common law, after the Revolution, as the basis of American law—but in all the states, explicitly or in judicial practice, only so far as suited to American conditions—set an ideal which the next period was reasonably well to realize. The present continued to be essentially one of reception of the English law. This was inevitable. There was still no independent body of American law; the first volume of American reports was published in 1789; less than a dozen volumes were in print in 1800. When James Kent was appointed to the New York bench in 1798 there were no reports of that state. "English authority," he says, "did not stand very high in these early feverish times, and this led me a hundred times to bear down opposition or shame it by exhaustive research and overwhelming authority."

Free from hampering precedents, in his 25 years as judge and chancellor he not only gave form to the entire law of that state but made an unrivaled contribution to the law of the whole country. In this his *Commentaries* (1826–30) played a large part; by universal consent they are worthy of comparison with Blackstone's. He set himself the task of establishing the common law and he succeeded. That he had not a reformer's spirit is shown by his sigh over "the piles of learning," "the profound logic, skilful criticism and refined distinctions" doomed to destruction by the New York statute abolishing the Rule in Shelley's Case. He did, however, reject the doctrine of market overt, extended replevin to any wrongful taking and lauded the establishment of the lien theory in mortgages.

Notable statutes of the period are fairly numerous: permitting grants in fee without mention of heirs; granting powers *in rem* to courts of equity; legitimizing children by subsequent marriage of their parents; abolishing entails and the Rule in Shelley's Case; abolishing primogeniture and establishing inheritance equally by all children; modifying the law of devises in favour of after-born children and the issue of predeceased children; conferring limited liability upon corporations; providing a general law under which corporations might freely organize. Pennsylvania—"the first of civilized countries to do so"—provided in 1776 for a penitentiary, presumably under the influence of the marchese di Beccaria, whose book had already been published in America and was soon to be found on the remotest frontiers. At the same time Pennsylvania introduced relief for insolvent debtors, and within a generation they were "scheduling out" of jail in remote western territories. New York in 1827 made a complete revision of its statute book, altering fundamentally the law of realty and providing a system later adopted by various states. Notable also were reforms due to popular disuse, such as the dying out of feoffments, fines and recoveries, all of which were used in colonial times and were provided for in the statutes of this period. These illustrations sufficiently indicate the experimental spirit of the time. It was not displayed in equal degree by the judiciary. Preferable to Kent's lament was the denunciation of demurrers, by a contemporary farmer-judge, as "an invention of the bar to prevent justice . . . a cursed cheat!"

From 1828 to 1868.—Almost as distinctly as in political history, the triumph of frontier democracy in the elections of 1828 marked the transition to a new era in the law. It was a period great for its critical spirit. Also, although individualism was the dominant notion of the contemporary world in politics and in economics, and though the frontier influence might have been expected to exalt its influence, it was a period remarkable for its social spirit. Both judicial and legislative improvements reveal its originality. What John H. Wigmore said of the law of evidence could be said of other fields of law: "Partly because of the lack of treatises and reports, partly because of the tendency to question important rules and therefore to defend on grounds of principle and policy whatever could be defended, partly because of the moral obligation of the judiciary, in new communities, to vindicate by intellectual effort its right to supremacy over the bar, and partly, also, because of the advent, coincidently, of the same rationalizing spirit which led to the reformatory legislation—this very necessity of restatement led to a finely reasoned system." Very important in this period, rivaling the influence of Kent in the preceding, was the work of Joseph Story, who in 13 years (1832–45) published nine remarkable textbooks, which in succeeding editions had a profound effect on forming American law.

Thus, in the law of evidence, "the period from 1840 to 1870 saw the enactment, in the various jurisdictions in this country, of most of the reformatory legislation which had been carried or proposed in England," and the promulgation of a body of opinions "superior (on the whole) to the judgments uttered in the native home of our law."

Notable innovations were the repudiation of the merger of torts in crimes and of postponement of the civil action; repudiation of the doctrine of ancient lights (impossible in a new country); introduction of apportionability of rent; the first decisions permitting suits upon a contract by the beneficiary (now the general doctrine); the first decisions treating divorce as a proceeding *in rem* and recognizing a woman's separate domicile for purpose of divorce; notable decisions—though with precedents "from the first colonization" (Chief Justice Morrison Waite)—upholding the regulation of private business "affected with a public interest"; and the first of many decisions forbidding the malicious use of a landowner's privileges.

Many changes plainly reflect the special conditions of the country. Examples of such were the substitution of navigability for the tidal test of admiralty jurisdiction, thus adapting it to the inland seas and rivers of the country; the introduction of the doctrine of "colour of title" in adverse possession, and other minor changes in that subject due to frontier conditions; fence laws reversing the common-law duties respecting trespass by animals; decisions concerning grain elevators that made novel changes in the law of bailments and confusion of goods. American deeds began to assume forms suitable to the simple description and titles of the country; quitclaim deeds became primary and original conveyances; disseizees acquired the right to make conveyances. Great modifications were made in equitable doctrines of laches and forfeitures in specific performance of contracts for the purchase of land on installments—modifications due to the fact that in America land has always been a subject of commerce, as Kent had pointed out. The amazing persistence of benefit of clergy down

to (and indeed through) this period was certainly due to the illiteracy of even prominent citizens in frontier society. A remarkable adoption of frontier customs in this period (though mainly by statute) was that of the mining and water laws developed in western mining camps.

Even more distinctive than the work of the courts was the legislation of this period. At this time reform by statute became, and remained, the primary characteristic of American government and law. "The establishment of self-government on a new soil realized the idea of the people as the source of political power as it had not been realized in historic times" (Ernst Freund); and on a scale equally unique they proceeded to illustrate the dictum that democracy relies on laws rather than on men. Religious and property qualifications for voting, officeholding and jury services were swept away by the middle of the century. To these triumphs of liberalism a third was added in the creation of a public-school system before the American Civil War.

A prelude to the use of the police power in the following period appears in the elaborate constitutional provisions, beginning before 1850, respecting banks, railroads and canals, and in statutes requiring periodical or cash payments of wages. Income taxes of the modern sense were adopted in the 1830s and 1840s in six states. A great moral movement in the political field—for prohibition, antislavery and women's rights—and an altruistic effort on a vast scale in favour of the poor and defective marked the entire period. Exemption laws (which had come down from colonial times) became general and liberal. Notable was the appearance of the homestead (1836) and its inclusion in the exemption statutes. Save for slight vestiges, imprisonment for debt was everywhere abolished.

The narrow protection in property rights accorded married women by equity was widened by statutes which placed them on an equality with their husbands, although not until 1913 were the disabilities of coverture abolished in the last state. Judicial liberalism supplemented this legislation; *e.g.*, in recognizing a wife's right in the society of her consort. It was recognition of woman's equal participation in the hazards and hardships of frontier life that wrote this entire chapter of the law. Children were protected against parental cruelty by imposing criminal responsibility; reformatories were established for minor delinquents, but their criminal liability was not much altered. In the law of property, rules of inheritance were greatly changed in favour of parents, surviving spouses, the half-blood and illegitimate children. Heirs and next of kin became generally identical. However acquired, and whether from the paternal or maternal side, estates were made to descend in the same manner. All real estate became liable to execution and administration assets for payment of debts with few preferences. The fictions of ejectment disappeared. In this whole field, however, legislative reform was always partial, casual and unsatisfactory. Variations from state to state remained innumerable. The distinctions between realty and personalty and between legal and equitable estates continued to be fundamental. The doctrines of tenure and the devices to evade them that fill the law of future interests remained untouched in most states except by fragmentary tinkerings. Entails are still theoretically possible in various states. Shelley's Case continued to have life in about half the states.

Equity, on the other hand, was developed with relative consistency. The erratic state of the property law continued to extend, however, to mortgages, which were hardly the same in any two states, although everywhere the legal incidents tend toward obsolescence. The equitable doctrine of priorities has from colonial days been fundamentally modified by the recording system. For historical reasons the spread of the equity system was delayed in various states, proceeding piecemeal by statutory grant; this was notably true, for example, in Massachusetts and Pennsylvania. The infiltration of equity into law, in such states, was a unique detail of American legal experiment. No American court exercises the full jurisdiction of English courts of chancery, its administrative portions having been given to separate tribunals. The development of probate courts was a noteworthy feature of the period before the Civil War. During it, also, the equitable jurisdiction was generally entrusted to courts of double jurisdiction (in a few states they continued to remain distinct and some others maintained distinct chancery terms). Under the codes of civil procedure adopted since 1848 in many states the administrative fusion has been complete, the common-law actions and the distinction between law and equity being abolished in the sense that rights and reliefs formerly "legal" or "equitable" are all enforced in one "civil action." This reform was accomplished for the federal courts with the adoption in 1938 of the federal rules of civil procedure, promulgated by the U.S. supreme court under authority of an act of congress. These rules, not only in their complete fusion of law and equity but in their thoroughgoing simplification of practice and procedure, were a major achievement in law reform and constituted a model for the states. The result was not to weaken equitable principles but to give them new vigour and applicability.

The adoption of these codes of civil procedure is the most remarkable feature of the third period and, on the whole, the most ambitious systematic reform yet undertaken in American law. The ideals of these codes were only imperfectly realized. For various reasons (not the least of which was the hostility of the courts when the codes were first created), their construction was once hardly less balefully technical (and perhaps less certain) than the old common-law system. Constant legislative tinkering increased uncertainty and resulted in monstrosities of bulk and complexity. While their fundamental reforms would doubtless never be abandoned, there was, later, a strong agitation for the regulation of strictly procedural matters by rules of court—the principle established in 1938 for the federal courts.

In some ways popular control in this period debased the judiciary. Of particularly evil consequence was a tendency to restrict the power of the trial judge in charging the jury, forbidding more than a bare restatement of the evidence. This remained general practice. Down to 1798 all the judges were appointed by the governor or elected by the legislatures; by 1840 popular election was characteristic, and thereafter it became increasingly predominant. A tendency to shorten the term of tenure sprang from democratic distrust of irresponsible authority. The powers of practically any judge to declare legislation unconstitutional and to issue injunctions kept such distrust alive. Elective terms, however, have always been long as compared with those of other officials, and no frontier state ever made judicial tenure so short and precarious as did two of the oldest states in New England. In the 20th century there has been a decided tendency to re-elect worthy judges and to make their salaries adequate. Few leaders of the bar can be drawn from practice by any feasible salary unless under tenure for good behaviour; but the rising level of judicial ability and the many instances of brilliant men who have already served on the bench justify the belief that judicial competence is obtainable under the elective system. The gravest charge that can be brought against the frontier democracy of the period before the Civil War is that it greatly lowered the standards of admission to the bar.

The bench was both able—in some states, notably in the south, brilliant—and liberal. The legislatures were characterized by rationalism and enlightenment. The bar, whatever its defects, dominated the legislatures and formerly enjoyed in general a social and political prestige that was to diminish in later years. On the whole, the period was one of contradictions but also of substantial accomplishment.

After 1868.—The ultimate protection of private rights rests upon guaranties in the federal constitution. No state may deprive any person "of life, liberty, or property without due process of law," "deny to any person within its jurisdiction the equal protection of the laws" or pass any law "impairing the Obligation of Contracts." The 14th amendment of 1868, containing the first two of these provisions, profoundly altered the relation between the state and federal courts and distinctly marked the beginning of a new period in the legal development of the country. Attempts to define due process and the police power made the federal courts the battleground of the social legislation which stemmed from the complex economic and industrial conditions developed after the Civil War. Many important cases involving corporations (which were for decades parties to approximately half of all litigation) were also thrown into the same tribunals, for they are "persons" under these clauses and "citizens" for purposes of federal jurisdiction, and their charters are contracts with the state. And as corporations carry on most of the business and own a very large percentage of all the property in the country (Justice Stephen Field of the supreme court estimated it as four-fifths in 1890), the matter has immense social significance.

The establishment of unbridled 19th-century democracy only slightly affected the treatment of industrial property. "For at least 60 years after the adoption of universal suffrage the tendency was all in the other direction—to legislate for the property owner rather than against him; to strengthen the powers of capital rather than diminish them. . . . The small protection given to the rights of man, as compared with that which was accorded to the rights of property, is a salient feature in the early history of every American state—and sometimes of its later history also" (A. T. Hadley).

The explanation of this fact lies undoubtedly in the loose economic framework of society. Cheap land created a people of freeholders without class distinctions, among whom any man who aimed high might rise high. Radicalism, in such a society, could gain no headway. That came with the development of great urban centres and an industrialized society. The rural population was nine-tenths of the total in 1800, and little less in 1850, but considerably less than half by mid-20th century.

Industrial regulation of the modern type began about 1870 with the railroads, and its assertion "shook the foundation of state and national politics for a generation." The subsequent increase of administrative commissions with investigative powers and subject to only limited judicial review is perhaps the most striking phenomenon in modern legislation. There is a tendency to standardize procedure and there is developing in this way a great field of administrative law. Trade regulation began to increase rapidly only in the late 19th century; for example, pure-food laws, later to become universal, began in 1892.

The purely legal status of the American industrial worker is unique. The exemption statutes lessened the effectiveness of the law's remedy of damages; the 13th amendment of the federal constitution, prohibiting "involuntary servitude," makes specific performance impossible, even were equity inclined to try it. Yet these immunities were relatively worthless so long as the worker was unprotected against unfair agreements secured through his economic needs. The tendency was strongly toward increasing restriction upon "freedom" of contract and "right" to labour. As late as 1905 the supreme court held unconstitutional a law regulating the hours of bakers, but the case soon lost its vitality; it was killed by a dissenting epigram of Justice Oliver Wendell Holmes—"the 14th Amendment does not enact Mr. Herbert Spencer's Social Statics." In the field of tort nothing had been done up to 1900 beyond limitations upon the rules of fellow servant, contributory negligence and assumption of risk, sometimes through and sometimes outside of employers' liability laws, thus leaving wholly unprovided for at least half of all industrial accidents. After 1910, however, all the states adopted workmen's compensation acts (first, 1902) entitling the injured employee to compensation without reference to common-law notions of fault.

The range of other social legislation became immense. Much was purely moralistic (against gambling, racing, cigarettes, liquor, sexual sin, etc.). The treatment of women merits, perhaps, special mention. Within the family the married woman was placed in substantial equality with her husband. In industry the attempt to give her special protection was a storm centre of agitation. But generally women came to enjoy such protection and to some extent a favoured position in property and domestic relations. Divorce is allowed in all states; causes run from adultery only to a score and more, including mental cruelty and incompatibility. Such causes are in many instances a cover for mutual consent. In 1942 the supreme court abrogated its former rule on interstate recognition of ex parte divorces (according to which a woman, though lawfully divorced in one state, might be convicted of bigamy in another upon remarriage), and announced that all states must recognize a divorce granted by the state of domicile of either spouse (*Williams* v. *North Carolina*, 317 U.S. 287). However, since a state could still withhold recognition on the basis of a finding that there was no domicile in fact in the divorcing state, "migratory" divorces of this type continued to confer only a somewhat precarious status. Suits for breach of promise to marry and for alienation of affection (both almost exclusively brought by women) are curiosities of American law. Common-law marriage still exists in many states. Desertion of wife or children, a very common offense, is generally a crime and a score of states have adopted a uniform act on this subject prepared by the National conference. There has been considerable eugenic legislation restraining freedom of marriage.

Defects of the System.—Dissatisfaction with the legal profession increased in the first third of the 20th century. The bar lost its onetime leadership because it ceased to lead, to make a social contribution commensurate with its political pre-eminence. In the first three decades of the century the judges, acting with a sense of duty but seldom guided by a liberal appreciation of expanding public interests, invalidated many popular legislative reforms. "Most of the common law has developed in that atmosphere of indifferent neutrality which has enabled courts to be impartial but also keeps them out of touch with vital needs" (Freund). Even the intelligent layman in America rarely knows anything of law except through the newspaper. There he reads only of constitutional questions—seemingly mere matters of policy of which any man may judge and which often seem irrational; of criminal cases which blazon all the vices of criminal procedure; of crowded dockets and delayed justice in spite of judicial work schedules which, at least to the layman, appear leisurely indeed. Hence the discontent which precipitated at one time the demand for the recall of judges and judicial decisions by popular vote and for limitations upon the power of divided courts to invalidate statutes, all of which demands became law in a few states. The administration of justice became a paramount problem in national life. Not only in many cities were the trial dockets filled for two to four years ahead; even in rural jurisdictions the same was sometimes true. General verdicts are the basis for repeated retrials of the facts. The reports of representative states show that at one time appellate decisions turned on pleadings in from 5% to 25% of all cases —and the higher number was much the nearer to the mean. Reversals for all causes are given in a large proportion of all cases appealed. Innumerable reversals are based, even in civil cases, upon errors that could not affect substantial rights, although this came to be statutorily prohibited in about two-thirds of the states. The efforts of reformers were directed toward strengthening the authority of the trial judge; re-establishing the original practice at common law of permitting the appellate court, even on writs of error, to render final judgment on the facts without ordering a new trial, as in appeals in equity; regulating procedure in higher courts by rules of court, as in England, in place of the legislative enactments, sometimes of infinite detail, which had been the almost exclusive system and prolific of delay and appeals; and abolishing appellate reversals for immaterial defects. As regards the last there was a marked improvement in the attitude of appellate judges. A great reform was the declaratory judgment; by the early 1960s more than 35 states had adopted the uniform act drafted by the National conference. Statutes of congress and of various states made arbitration agreements specifically enforceable. Much was also accomplished in expediting and cheapening the petty litigation of great urban centres by reorganizing them into appropriate branches under a simplified procedure. In a number of cities legal-aid societies were established to dispose of a vast amount of litigation substantially without charge. Regular courts for small claims and poor litigants were also set up.

All the evils of procedure present in civil suits exist in more aggravated form in criminal cases, with many others in addition. Homicides alone are estimated by many authorities as being in the thousands yearly. That many kinds of urban crime are on an organized business basis seems to be unquestionable. That lawyers are essential to, when not part of, this business, prepared with every legal device to delay and evade justice for their criminal clients, is often manifest. Equally alarming is the actual inequality of men, rich or poor, before the law, in consequence of its de-

lays, and of those rich or poor in influence in being brought before it. In 1909 Pres. William Howard Taft declared the administration of the criminal law in all the states, with possibly "one or two exceptions," to be "a disgrace to our civilization." Frequently hundreds, sometimes thousands, of veniremen are examined before a jury is secured; usually days, sometimes months, are thus utilized. Delays in trial are even greater than in civil cases. Indictments are still found deficient in appellate courts, though here there was great improvement, for flaws of unbelievable triviality. The defendant is nowhere compelled to testify. Punishments for the same crime vary amazingly from state to state. In some states the jury has large discretion in fixing the punishment; in many it is judge of both the law and facts. The requirement of unanimous verdicts is universal in criminal cases.

Legislation, however, became extremely active in remedying many of these evils. Some states adopted habitual-criminal acts which, among other things, impose life imprisonment upon a defendant with a record of a small number (usually four) of earlier convictions. Minors were also given greater protection after 1900 by raising the age of criminal responsibility (to 16 or 18) and establishing special courts to deal with the younger delinquents, subjecting these to the state's guardianship somewhat as under the old doctrines of equity. In the field of punishment notable reforms were introduced: suspended and indeterminate sentences, commutations for good behaviour and parole. But even these were perverted. Weak or calculating judges abused the first with a leniency so excessive that it approached immunity; the second appeared plainly to be overgenerous to hardened offenders. The most vicious of criminals were often paroled. The primary cause was probably politics; indubitably so in some states, where every step—whether or not an arrest should be made, the defendant held to the grand jury, the case dismissed, the convict paroled—seemed to be seriously entwined with political corruption.

For these evils, and equally for the evils in trial and appellate courts, in civil and criminal cases, springing from a deep-rooted attitude toward litigation as a mere game of wit, there is no cure except in an increased power and awakened conscience of the bench and a general betterment in the moral tone of the bar. At least as regards intellectual improvement much was accomplished. The university law schools acquired distinguished excellence and a high professional prestige. Higher standards of education were enforced through requirements for admission to the bar—the American Bar association advocating a minimum prelegal education of three years in college and a minimum professional training of three years in law school—but not all states meet these standards. Disbarment is in the hands of the courts and has been sparingly used. A few states incorporated their bars as self-governing bodies with exclusive power over admission and discipline.

Codification.—The process of codification, after the period of activity which began before the Civil War, temporarily ceased, but began again in a new form during the first half of the 20th century. Five codes of penal and of the substantive civil law, 30 codes of civil procedure and about 30 of criminal procedure were mainly the products of the earlier movement. The American Bar association, acting with state commissioners, had prepared more than 90 uniform acts by the early 1960s. Of these, five in the commercial field (on negotiable instruments, warehouse receipts, bills of lading, sales and stock transfers) were adopted in from half to all jurisdictions. An American Law institute, in which teachers of law are dominant, has prepared a restatement of various branches of the substantive law and a model code of criminal procedure, all designed to promote uniformity in essential principles. The "complete" or "revised" statutes existing in every state of course merely supplement the unenacted law, but in many states it would be hazardous to say which of the two is of greater scope. Legislative drafting bureaus (the earliest of 1890) came to exist in practically every state.

The impulse to codification came from the unmanageable bulk of judicial law and the consequent uncertainty of legal knowledge. The number of annual volumes of American reports is in the thousands. The cases cited by the court in any volume run into hundreds and frequently into thousands, from many jurisdictions. The law is beyond the power of any layman to discover or to comprehend.

Very much has been wisely said on the necessity of guiding legislation and judicial decision by the functional test of social utility, but no efficient instrumentality has existed through which to supply objective evidence of the relative working of substantive legal rules. On the other hand, it was expected that precisely this would be accomplished in the procedural field by the judicial councils created after 1922 in many states for the consistent study and improvement of judicial organization and procedure. Altogether, the immense significance of the new spirit manifest in the profession could not be doubted. Most important of all was the fact that the revolt against unsocial law created by the labour struggle had spread to social workers, social scientists, the law schools and even to the bar. It opened a new epoch in the law of the country.

BIBLIOGRAPHY.—S. E. Baldwin (ed.), *Two Centuries' Growth of American Law, 1701–1901* (1901); R. Pound, *The Spirit of the Common Law* (1921), *An Introduction to the Philosophy of Law* (1922); B. N. Cardozo, *The Nature of the Judicial Process* (1925); E. Freund, *Standards of American Legislation* (1917); M. Storey, *The Reform of Legal Procedure* (1911); J. Willard Hurst, *The Growth of American Law; the Law Makers* (1950); *Law: a Century of Progress, 1835–1935*, ed. by the New York University School of Law, 3 vol. (1937); Lewis Mayers, *The American Legal System* (1955); Robert W. Millar, *Civil Procedure of the Trial Court in Historical Perspective* (1952); René A. Wormser, *The Law* (1949); Max Radin, *The Law and Mr. Smith* (1938). (F. S. P.; B. Ce.)

PUBLIC LAW

The public law of the United States largely revolves around: (1) the federal system; (2) the written constitution; and (3) the judicial construction of written constitutions. These three elements are closely related, for the United States supreme court has from an early day been the final arbiter to determine the respective powers of the United States and of the states under the written constitution of the nation; and the state courts (each within its own territory) are the final arbiters of state governmental power under the written constitutions of the states.

The Federal System.—Plans of colonial federation were several times proposed before the period of the American Revolution. The movement that finally led to independence forced some degree of unity, and the first continental congress assembled in Philadelphia in 1774 was the outward symbol of unity of political action. What political direction there was of the revolutionary movement came through the continuance of such an organization, without any formal written instrument of union, and this system was highly inefficient. It was replaced by the Articles of Confederation in 1781.

The Articles of Confederation established a loose union, with little in the way of a national government and with no power in that government to raise revenue or to enforce its orders by action directed immediately toward the citizens of the United States. The confederation had authority to ask the states to act, but not to compel action either by the state or its citizens. It had power to make treaties but no power to enforce state observance of such treaties. Each state had power to impose restrictions upon trade with other states, and a state with the geographical advantages of New York was in a position to impose and did impose burdensome restrictions upon the commerce of the neighbouring states of New Jersey and Connecticut.

Such conditions could not long continue. They led to the assembling of the federal convention of 1787 and to the framing and adoption of the constitution of the United States, under which the government was instituted in 1789. The constitution was framed with specific reference to the difficulties presenting themselves before its adoption. A governmental organization was set up independent of that in the states, and with power to enforce its commands directly upon the citizens of the states. Large powers were conferred, the most important of which were the powers to control interstate and foreign commerce, to levy taxes and to raise federal revenues independently of the states and the control of foreign relations. Thus a central government was constituted with real authority. The history of the federal system since 1789 is to a large extent a history of the expansion of the importance and authority of the national government under this constitution. This expansion has been accomplished in several ways: (1) by a broadened construction of the original provisions of the constitution of 1787; (2) by amendment of this constitution; (3) by the development of means of transportation and communication which enormously increased the number of transactions in interstate and foreign commerce, subject to national control; (4) by the increased number of states, the larger portion of which were created out of territory belonging to the national government.

Construction of the National Constitution.—The constitution of the United States has been authoritatively and finally construed by the United States supreme court, an organ of the national government. In substantially all matters this court determines the limits of national power on the one hand and of state power on the other. No matter how impartial such a tribunal may have sought to be, it has almost of necessity tended to favour the government of which it is an organ. Under the chief justiceship of John Marshall (1801–35) it was an essential factor in establishing broad national authority. *McCulloch* v. *Maryland*, 4 Wheat. 316 (1819), determined that the nation had not only the powers expressly conferred upon its legislative, executive and judicial departments, but also all authority "appropriate" to carry such powers into execution. The constitution uses the words "necessary and proper," but the court held that there was no need to show actual necessity in order to uphold national power.

Under the chief justiceship of Roger Brooke Taney (1836–64) there was an occasional tendency in dicta of the court to regard state power as of greater importance, but no actual reduction of national power took place. In fact, two of the broadest extensions of national power were made under Taney through reversals of views taken under Marshall. In one of these cases admiralty jurisdiction was extended to all navigable waters (*Genesee Chief* v. *Fitzhugh*, 12 How. 443 [1851]). In the other the federal courts acquired an extensive jurisdiction in corporate matters (*L.C. & C.R.R. Co.* v. *Letson*, 2 How. 497 [1844]).

Although the powers of the national government under the constitution were expanded, the supreme court at the same time sought to prevent the destruction of state powers by construction. Although in mid-20th century W. W. Crosskey advanced a revolutionary thesis that the powers of the national government were originally intended to be plenary, the orthodox view to the contrary remained settled law, and the national government one of enumerated powers, residual powers being reserved to the states. While the nation's powers were extended, there remained a large sphere of state power upon which the nation may not encroach. No national power exists except as it is found in the terms of the written constitution, and the supreme court can expand such powers only as they may be derived from the terms of the written constitution. The terms of this document are broad and expansible, yet judicial construction of these terms has definite limits.

Amendment of the National Constitution.—By constitutional amendment the terms of the written constitution may be changed. Twenty-four amendments to the constitution of the United States had been adopted through 1964. The first ten of these amendments are limitations upon the national government, but in no material respect do they narrow the powers exercisable by that government. The 11th amendment safeguards the states against suits; the 12th, with reference to the election of the president, does not affect governmental power. The 13th affirmed the judgment of war that slavery should be abolished. As now construed by the courts, the "due process of law" and "equal protection of the laws" clauses of the 14th amendment have transferred the protection of individual rights from the states to the national government. The 15th, 19th and 24th amendments, and to some extent the 14th, limit the determination by the state as to who shall have the right to vote. The 17th, providing for popular election of senators, somewhat diminishes the importance of the states as units in the federal system. The 18th amendment, until repealed by the 21st, brought the government into closer contact with the lives of citizens. The 16th gave the national government a new source of revenue and made possible a system of subsidies through which the government gained increased control of state policy. The 20th set the dates for presidential and congressional terms and made provisions for succession in case of death of the president-elect. The 22nd prohibited a third elective presidential term. The 23rd granted residents of the District of Columbia the right to vote in national elections for president and vice-president.

Increased Contacts of a National Character.—In 1789 transactions in interstate commerce were few, and the means of conducting such commerce slow and cumbersome. As new agencies of commerce developed, the federal regulatory power was applied to them. With the transition from the horse and the stagecoach to the steamboat, the railroad, the telegraph, the telephone, the radio, television and the airplane, portions of the country once distant were brought into closer relationship, and the transactions controllable by the national government were infinitely multiplied. These changes necessarily brought increased exercise of national power.

Federal regulation of interstate railroad rates and service came in 1887 and expanded rapidly. The relations between interstate commerce and purely domestic commerce within a single state are necessarily close when both transactions are handled by the same agency. And so by legislation and by judicial decision, the federal government came largely to control the railroad rates for domestic transportation within the states, as an incident to the control of interstate commerce (*Railroad Commission of Wisconsin* v. *C.B. & Q. R.R.*, 257 U.S. 563 [1922]). In the same manner the nation has come to control safety appliances of railroads in both interstate and domestic commerce (*Southern Ry. Co.* v. *U. S.*, 222 U.S. 20 [1911]).

Congress began in 1890 the regulation of combinations in restraint of interstate commerce, and in this field largely replaced state action. The commerce power also became the basis of the Labor-Management Relations act, under which the regulation of important labour relations was largely transferred from the states to the national government, acting through the National Labor Relations board. By the expansion of the national banking system and the creation of the federal reserve system, the federal government largely controls the banking business of the country. There is extensive national control of industry, banking, labour, railroads and the protection of individual rights.

These expansions of national authority were natural and to be expected, but they made the national system differ materially from any that could have been thought of in 1787.

Increased Number of States.—The national government was created by a small number of states which were the creators of the nation. States as units in a federal system were naturally more important when their number was 13. The influence of increased numbers becomes more important when it is considered that 24 of the additional states were wholly created out of territory acquired by the nation and were never a part of the original states. These states, forming more than half of the area of the country, are in a very real sense creatures rather than creators of the national government. With the increased importance of interstate relations, state boundaries largely became artificial lines, and national consciousness, greatly strengthened by the Civil War, became politically dominant, since general elections are usually held in all the states upon the same day as national elections.

Yet, though the states came to be less important politically as units in a federal system and lost all political status in international affairs, they came, with increased complexity of social and economic needs, to have a heavier burden of governmental tasks than ever before. For upon them fall the burdens of administering criminal and civil justice in the daily affairs of life and the tasks of more detailed regulation of industry, as well as the conduct of schools, the administration of charities and the protection of persons and property.

The Written Constitution.—The written constitution is an essential element of the federal system in the United States, for there must be some authoritative statement of the respective powers of nation and states. The written constitution is not an essential device of state government in the United States, but each state has from its beginning had such a constitution.

The national constitution is a relatively brief document, as are a few of the earlier state constitutions. But the typical state constitution came to be a lengthy document that not only organizes and imposes limitations upon the state government, but also contains a great mass of detailed legislation. This legislative detail is frequently altered by state constitutional amendments. In theory the national government has only such powers as are granted to it by the national constitution, and a state government has all powers not denied it by the national constitution and the constitution of the state. This might naturally imply a strict construction against national powers and a liberal construction in favour of state legislative authority. But with long and detailed state constitutions, the opposite results. Under broad constitutional grants of national authority, the United States supreme court has, from the first, been liberal in the construction of national power. Under detailed state constitutions, hedging about the powers of state legislatures, the tendency of state courts has been toward a narrow construction of such powers.

Judicial Construction of Written Constitutions.—Some device is necessary in a federal system to preserve the barriers between federal and state powers. The United States supreme court serves as this agency. In addition it serves as the final agency in other cases for the determination of the powers of congress under the constitution; and the highest court of each state serves as the agency to determine the powers of its state legislature under the written constitution of that state. The courts of both state and nation decline to pass upon certain questions that they term political, but apart from this they construe the written constitutions of state and nation. The power of the courts to determine the constitutionality of legislation was first asserted in New Jersey in 1780, and has been generally recognized since the decision of the United States supreme court in *Marbury* v. *Madison,* I Cranch, 137 (1803).

The more detailed the constitutions and the greater the tendency to exercise governmental power to meet new industrial and social needs, the more often are the courts called upon to construe written constitutions. With numerous restrictions imposed on legislative action by constitutional texts, practically every important federal and state legislative enactment comes to the courts for the determination of its validity. This gives to judicial decisions an emphasis proportionately greater than they deserve in the constitutional system of the United States, for in most cases the courts reach results not dissimilar from those in the countries where legislative determinations are final. But in the United States the courts have the last word, and this often leads to an emphasis upon the technical issues of constitutional construction rather than upon the actual merits of legislation. Problems of constitutional construction have become increasingly important in the fields of administrative law and the administration of criminal law.

New economic and social problems necessitated the delegation of wide authority to permanent federal and state boards. National and state constitutions organize governments into three departments, and impliedly forbid the delegation of legislative authority. The courts must answer the questions as to what are the functions of each department and what are legislative powers that may not be delegated. Under pressure of practical need, the courts have found it possible to sustain wide delegations of rule-making power to administrative bodies, and also wide authority in such bodies to make determinations that may appear judicial in character. These results have been obtained through the construction of broad constitutional provisions, and have been wise ones, though the logical devices employed to distinguish later from earlier cases have often been amusing.

In the administration of criminal law the result has not been so satisfactory. Many constitutions contain detailed provisions regarding the grand jury, the jury, bail and the conduct of cases, and a number designate the precise words with which indictments shall terminate. These provisions promote technicality in judicial proceedings and retard progress, and although a number of constitutions are easy to change, others are difficult if not impossible to amend. The courts cannot ignore these constitutional provisions, but must enforce them, though something is accomplished by liberal judicial construction. For example, the constitution of Missouri required that indictments conclude with the words "against the peace and dignity of the State." The Missouri supreme court at first said that the omission of the second "the" was fatal to an indictment, but later took the opposite view (*State* v. *Campbell*, 210 Mo. 202 [1908]; *State* v. *Adkins*, 284 Mo. 680 [1920]). But however liberal the courts may be, simplification of criminal procedure is retarded by placing regulations as to such matters in the text of the state constitution.

The problems faced by the courts in constitutional construction are well illustrated by the developments in administrative law and in the administration of criminal law. Constitutional provisions creating three departments of government and providing that each shall exercise separate powers are general and vague in character. A court may and does construe these provisions to permit what the present needs require, even though earlier decisions may have taken a different view. The only harm done by such action, if it is a harm, is the occasional use of bad logic in the effort to harmonize judicial decisions that are obviously not capable of reconciliation. The specific constitutional provisions as to criminal procedure do not give a court as great a latitude of construction, though even where a constitution requires certain precise language the courts may permit some variation of that language.

The year 1937 witnessed a marked change in the attitude and function of the United States supreme court in constitutional litigation, especially as regards the validity of federal and state regulation of economic activities. For several decades prior to the election of Pres. Franklin D. Roosevelt in 1932, the court had generally, but not consistently, adhered to a narrow construction of the powers of congress in important areas. Thus, although the commerce clause was construed as affording a fairly broad basis for the regulation of railroads with respect to rates, safety appliances and injuries to employees, and even of business practices in stockyards, it was not regarded as authorizing the regulation of "production" as distinguished from "commerce"; and congress was denied power to prohibit the interstate shipment of products of child labour. Likewise, a tax on the employment of child labour was held invalid as an attempt to regulate matters reserved to the states and as an illegitimate use of the revenue powers. In the same period the court generally, but again not consistently, took a narrow view of state regulatory powers as restricted by constitutional provisions, notably those of the 14th amendment. Thus, while upholding state laws establishing maximum hours of work for minors and for women, as well as municipal zoning ordinances regulating the use of land, the court held unconstitutional a Pennsylvania statute prohibiting the mining of coal in such a way as to remove support from surface structures, a New York statute limiting hours of work in bakeries, a Kansas statute outlawing yellow-dog contracts (in which an employee agrees as a condition of employment that he will not become or remain a member of a labour union), New York statutes regulating prices charged by enterprises not "affected with a public interest," and a District of Columbia law establishing minimum wages for women and minors. In general, these restrictive attitudes were carried over into the period 1934–37, when state and federal governments alike were attempting to cope with the problems of severe economic depression. There were two notable exceptions: in 1934 the court sustained Minnesota's mortgage moratorium law against the charge that it impaired the obligation of contracts, and, by upholding a New York milk control law, established the general power to regulate prices. But the court again denied the power of government to establish minimum wages, and in a series of cases struck down one important piece of New Deal legislation after another: the National Industrial Recovery act on the ground that it was an unconstitutional delegation of legislative power to the president and an unpermitted regulation of intrastate transactions; the Railroad Retirement act, establishing a pension system for employees of interstate railroads, on the grounds that it denied due process

of law and was not within the commerce power; the Bituminous Coal Conservation act on the ground that it was not authorized by the tax, commerce and general welfare clauses; and the Agricultural Adjustment act on the ground that it was an unauthorized use of the tax and commerce powers. Widespread resentment by the New Deal of these decisions culminated in President Roosevelt's recommendation, shortly after his re-election in 1936, of legislation to reorganize the federal courts. If it had been enacted, this would have authorized increasing the membership of the supreme court from 9 to as many as 15, through appointment of an additional justice for every one who, on reaching retirement age, did not retire. Despite wide dissatisfaction with the court's decisions, this proposal, known as the court-packing plan, encountered strong opposition because of its threat to the independence of the judiciary and its disingenuousness. But within a few weeks the balance of opinion on the court shifted. Overturning its earlier decisions, the court upheld state minimum wage laws, and, despite the restrictive tendency of the precedents, sustained the National Labor Relations act. The reorganization bill, shorn of its defeated and obsolete purpose, was finally passed as a noncontroversial regulation of procedure in constitutional cases. Other New Deal legislation was upheld, notably in decisions which recognized the power of congress, under the commerce clause, to establish national policy with respect to conditions of employment (including child labour) and agricultural production. The Social Security act was sustained as an appropriate exercise of national fiscal power. Rationing and rent- and price-control measures during World War II were sustained without serious question. After 1937 decisions by the supreme court invalidating acts of congress became extremely rare, and decisions invalidating state economic regulation only slightly less so.

This change in attitude was no mere yielding to considerations of expediency, nor was it an abdication of the function of judicial review. It reflected primarily the court's acceptance of a principle of self-restraint which had long been urged upon it by dissenting justices. There was increased awareness of the need for a philosophy of constitutional construction which would not paralyze the agencies of government in their attempts to deal with changing conditions; there was increased tolerance for change and for distasteful economic policy. Above all, there was increased deference to the constitutional function of the legislative branch, a willingness to recognize that the courts are not the sole guardians of the constitution and that they are not the agency best equipped to determine the appropriateness of the means chosen for accomplishment of a legitimate governmental end. Implicit in the new attitude was the conviction that political processes, where available, must constitute the first line of protection against legislative error or excess. The function of the court in constitutional cases nevertheless remained a significant one, involving a considerable degree of independent judgment, especially in cases where political restraints are inadequate, as where the impact of state legislation is upon national interests or upon the interests of minorities.

Thus the court has occasion, from time to time, to protect interstate commerce from undue interference by state regulatory and tax measures. In 1952 it upheld the supremacy of congress in the legislative sphere by holding unconstitutional Pres. Harry S. Truman's seizure of the steel mills to avert a strike. In an important series of decisions it established minimum standards for fair trial in criminal cases, involving such matters as the right of the defendant to representation by counsel and to an impartial jury, the use of forced confessions and the use of illegally obtained evidence. In 1955 it invalidated a section of the Code of Military Justice purporting to authorize military tribunals to try civilians for offenses they had committed while in military status. Another series of decisions strongly reinforced the constitutional guaranties of freedom of speech and religion.

National security legislation was in general upheld after careful scrutiny, but state laws concerning picketing, the use of streets and parks, house-to-house canvassing and the distribution of handbills, motion-picture censorship, compulsory flag salutes and the use of public-school facilities for religious instruction were frequently found to abridge the rights of free expression and free exercise of religion. The court's decisions dealing with racial discrimination were far-reaching. The right of Negro citizens to vote was made a legal reality; labour unions operating under federal regulation were forbidden by judicial decision to discriminate against Negro members of their crafts; racial restrictive covenants, a device for accomplishing by private action the segregation in housing which the states are forbidden to impose, were held unenforceable, with visible results especially in metropolitan areas. In the field of public education, after years of adherence to its 1896 doctrine that the furnishing of "separate but equal" facilities was a fulfilment of the state's obligation to provide "equal protection of the laws," the court first intimated that separate facilities could hardly be equal in graduate professional schools, and finally declared the inherent inequality of segregation throughout the public-school system.

In American constitutional law there is a tendency to decide the specific case before the court, without affording much guidance as to the law applicable to similar cases in the future. And the constitutional law of the United States is found not so much in the texts of written constitutions as in the judicial decisions construing such constitutions.

Judicial review in America does not amount, as superficial observers have commented, to "government by the judges." The power to declare legislation unconstitutional is, of course, not the same as the power to initiate laws; it is called into play only as the exigencies of adversary litigation require; it does not extend to matters which are purely "political"; and it is appropriately exercised with restraint and deference to legislative judgment. It is, nevertheless, a power of great significance. As Alexis de Tocqueville (q.v.) wrote after his mission to America in 1831, "Within these limits the power vested in the American courts of justice of pronouncing a statute to be unconstitutional forms one of the most powerful barriers that have ever been devised against the tyranny of political assemblies." (Alexis de Tocqueville, *Democracy in America*, ed. by Phillips Bradley, vol. i, p. 103, Knopf, 1945.)

See also Index references under "American Law" in the Index volume.

BIBLIOGRAPHY.—W. W. Crosskey, *Politics and the Constitution in the History of the United States* (1953); Milton R. Konvitz, *Bill of Rights Reader* (1954); Paul A. Freund, *On Understanding the Supreme Court* (1949); Robert R. Bowie and Carl J. Friedrich, *Studies in Federalism* (1954); Zechariah Chafee, Jr., *Free Speech in the United States* (1941); Charles G. Haines, *The American Doctrine of Judicial Supremacy* (1954); Edward S. Corwin, *The Constitution and What It Means Today* (1954); Charles P. Curtis, *Lions Under the Throne* (1947). (W. F. D.; B. Ce.)

AMERICAN LEGION, an organization of U.S. war veterans founded in Paris, France, March 15–17, 1919, by delegates from combat and service units of the American Expeditionary Force assembled in response to a call by a committee headed by Lt. Col. Theodore Roosevelt, Jr. A national charter was granted by congress on Sept. 16, 1919; the charter was amended in 1942 to admit World War II veterans and again in 1950 to include veterans of the Korean war. Nonpolitical and nonsectarian, the American Legion's membership requirement is honourable service and an honourable discharge. Its annual conventions are among the largest volunteer group meetings in the United States. They provide opportunities for airing the organization's special interests in education, labour and industry, and for government officials and candidates for office to express their views.

One of the Legion's major concerns has always been care of disabled and sick veterans; it was instrumental in establishing hospitals and other services for World War I veterans, services which have been expanded to meet the needs of veterans of later wars. During the 1920s the Legion supported proposals for paying a bonus to veterans. It champions compensation and pensions for the disabled and for widows and orphans, but does not favour further federal bonus payments nor all-inclusive general pension legislation. Measures successfully sponsored include many national defense programs, systems of security training for youth and the creation of the U.S. Veterans administration. In 1944 it played

an important role in the enactment of the G.I. Bill of Rights for World War II veterans, and later in supporting similar legislation for Korean war veterans. These measures afforded college or vocational training for more than 10,000,000 veterans, and enabled more than 5,600,000 veterans to purchase homes under the loan provisions of the act.

In its child welfare program the Legion expended more than $150,000,000 between 1925 and 1960 in emergency aid to needy children of veterans, mostly for food, clothing and medical treatment. The program was financed in part from the income from a $7,000,000 endowment fund, initiated in 1925. The Legion has helped to raise the standard of juvenile court procedure, child adoption, guardianship and the rights of children through federal and state legislation. The Americanism and youth programs include projects known as "boys' state" and "boys' nation" where groups of young people are given practical instruction in the functions of democratic government. It also includes sponsorship of 4,300 Boy Scout troops, junior baseball leagues with approximately 1,000,000 boys under 17 playing each year, and high school oratorical contests. A continuing program to combat subversive influences is carried on nationally. At the end of the 1950s the total membership of the Legion was 2,800,000 enrolled in 17,000 local posts. The national headquarters is in Indianapolis, Ind.

BIBLIOGRAPHY.—Marquis James, *A History of the American Legion* (1923); Richard Seelye Jones, *A History of the American Legion* (1946); Annual reports to congress; *Summary of the Proceedings of the National Conventions* (issued annually); *The American Legion Magazine*. (B. B. St.)

AMERICAN LITERATURE. Like other national literatures, American literature was shaped by the history of the country which produced it. For almost a century and a half, America was merely a group of colonies scattered along the eastern seaboard of the North American continent—colonies from which a few hardy souls tentatively ventured westward. After a successful rebellion against the motherland, America became the United States, a nation. By the end of the 19th century this nation extended southward to the Gulf of Mexico, northward to the 49th parallel and westward to the Pacific. By the end of the 19th century, too, it had taken its place among the powers of the world—its fortunes so interrelated with those of other nations that inevitably it became involved in two world wars and, following these conflicts, with the problems of Europe and the far east. Meanwhile, the rise of science and industry, as well as changes in ways of thinking and feeling, wrought many modifications in men's lives. All these factors in the development of the United States molded the literature of the country.

17th CENTURY

American literature at first was naturally a colonial literature, by authors who were Englishmen and who thought and wrote as such. An instance is that soldier of fortune, John Smith, who is credited with initiating American literature. His chief books included *A True Relation of such occurrences and accidents . . . as hath hapned in Virginia . . .* (1608); *Description of New England* (1616); and *The Generall Historie of Virginia, New-England, and the Summer Isles* (1624). Although these volumes set forth much in praise of their far from modest author, they were written avowedly to make known to Englishmen colonizing opportunities in the new world. In time, each colony was similarly described in one or more books: John Hammond's *Leah and Rachel* (1656) was subtitled *or, The Two Fruitfull Sisters Virginia and Mary-Land;* Daniel Denton wrote a *Brief Description of New York* (1670); William Penn, *Some Account of the Province of Pensilvania* (1681); Thomas Ashe, *Carolina* (1682)—and these were only a few of many works praising America as a land of economic promise for English colonists.

Such early writers tacitly acknowledged British allegiance. Others, however, wrote works which stressed some of the differences of opinion which spurred the colonists to leave their homeland—works which attacked certain doctrines of opposing sects and defended doctrines of their own. More important (according to modern thought, at least), they argued the questions of government, ordinarily questions which involved the relationships between church and state. The attitude which most of the authors attacked was jauntily set forth by Nathaniel Ward of Massachusetts Bay in a quaint book, *The Simple Cobbler of Aggawam in America* (1647). Here Ward amusingly defended the *status quo* and railed at colonists who sponsored newfangled notions. He was, for instance, against tolerance: "He," wrote Ward, "that is willing to tolerate any unsound opinion, that his own may also be tolerated, will for a need hang God's Bible at the Devil's girdle." A variety of counterarguments to such a conservative view were published. Stern John Winthrop's *Journal,* covering the years 1630 to 1649, told sympathetically of the attempt of Massachusetts Bay colony to form a theocracy —a state with God at its head and with its laws based upon the Bible. A theocracy, Winthrop thought, was "a mixed aristocracy"; a democracy, he believed, was "the meanest and worst form of government." Later defenders of the theocratic ideal were Increase Mather (1639–1723) and his son Cotton (1663–1728). William Bradford, in *The History of Plymouth Plantation,* told the story to 1646, of another colony. His history revealed that, unlike Winthrop's Puritan group, who merely wished to purify the Anglican Church, Bradford's Pilgrim companions—Separatists—broke completely with Anglicanism. More radical than the Puritans, they conceived of their government as a covenant, as evidenced by the Mayflower compact in which the Pilgrims agreed to "covenant and combine ourselves together into a civil body politic . . . and by virtue hereof to enact . . . such just and equal laws . . . as shall be thought most meet and convenient for the general good of the Colony, unto which we promise all due submission and obedience." Even more radical than Bradford was Roger Williams who left the Separatists to become a Baptist, the Baptists to become a Seeker. Williams, in a series of controversial pamphlets (1643–52) advocated concepts such as the separation of church and state, the vesting of power in the people and the tolerance of different religious beliefs. Although Williams' writings made very dull reading they contained important ideas, many of which were put into practice in the colony which he founded—Rhode Island, the first democratic commonwealth in America.

The factual or utilitarian writings of the 17th century included many sorts—not only promotion tracts, controversial works and autobiographies, but also biographies, treatises, accounts of voyages and sermons—and there were many works of each of these kinds. In this practical period of strenuous colonizing, belles-lettres loomed small. Yet there were some achievements in this field—not in drama or fiction, since there was a deep and widespread prejudice against these forms which Cotton Mather and others held were shelved in "the library of the powers of darkness," but rather, in the field of poetry. There was some very bad poetry in such works as the famous *Bay Psalm Book* (1640) which literally translated the psalms, and in Michael Wigglesworth's popular summary in doggerel verse of Calvinistic belief, *The Day of Doom* (1662). But there was some poetry, at least, of a higher order. Anne Bradstreet of Ipswich and North Andover, Mass., wrote some lyrics, published in her book, *The Tenth Muse,* (1650), which movingly conveyed her feelings concerning religion and her family. Engaging though some of her poems were, modern critics rank above her a poet whose works were not discovered and published until 1937. This shy poet was Edward Taylor (1644?–1729), an English-born minister and physician who lived in Boston and Westfield, Mass. Less touched by gloom than the typical Puritan, Taylor wrote conceit-filled lyrics which showed his delight in Christian belief and experience—poems which still have power to charm the reader.

All 17th-century writings, not surprisingly, are in the manner of British writings of the same—or even an earlier—period. John Smith wrote in the tradition of the geographical literature of the day; Bradford echoed the cadences of the King James Bible; the Mathers and Roger Williams, dissimilar as they were in their beliefs, wrote bejeweled prose typical of the day. Anne Bradstreet's poetic style derived from a long line of British poets, among them Spenser, Sidney, Quarles and Sylvester. Taylor was in the tradition of such metaphysical poets as Herbert, Donne and Crashaw; and he seems clearly to have been influenced by at least the first of these British poets. Both the content and form of the literature of this 1st century in America were thus markedly English.

18th CENTURY

In the early years of the 18th century, some writers carried on the older traditions. Cotton Mather, for instance, produced his huge *Magnalia Christi Americana* in 1702, his vigorous *Manuductio ad Ministerium* in 1726. Both these learned books were defenses of old beliefs, reiterations of ancient Puritan convictions. More effective as an advocate for old attitudes was Jonathan Edwards, born in Connecticut in 1703 and educated at Yale—an influential preacher in Massachusetts. Though a frail and intellectual man, Edwards was feverishly active as a religionist. He initiated the Great Awakening, a revival which stirred the eastern seacoast for many years. And he wrote much in behalf of his burning belief in Calvinistic doctrine—of the concept that man, born totally depraved, could attain virtue and salvation only through God's grace. Supporting this old belief, he wrote some truly great philosophical treatises, notably the one on *The Freedom of the Will* (1754). This philosopher's philosopher supported his claims by relating them to a complex and poetic metaphysical system, by reasoning brilliantly and by stating his thoughts in clear and often beautiful prose.

But Mather and Edwards were defending a doomed cause. Such liberal New England ministers as John Wise (1652–1725) and Jonathan Mayhew (1720–66) showed in their writings a movement away from the older beliefs and toward a less rigid religion. In other ways, Samuel Sewall (1652–1730), a magistrate and merchant of Boston, heralded a change in his famous and amusing *Diary* which covered the years 1673–1729. Sincerely religious though Sewall was, he showed in his daily records how life in commercial New England led him to love the more worldly things—to modify rigid Puritanism into what Parrington has called a "tradesman's conception of religion." Again, there was the *Journal* of another Bostonian, Mme Sarah Knight, comically detailing a journey she took to New York in 1704. Mme Knight, a woman with a keen eye for life and character along the way, wrote vividly of what she saw and commented upon it from the standpoint of an orthodox believer. But there was a quality of levity in her witty writings—even when some jocose impieties were involved—which showed that she was much less fervent than the Pilgrim founders had been.

In the south, a short time afterward, William Byrd II of Westover plantation, Va., showed how aristocratic plantation living had wrought to create an urbane and witty author who contrasted sharply with gloomier predecessors. His record of a surveying trip in 1728, *The History of the Dividing Line,* and his account of a visit to his frontier properties in 1733, *A Journey to the Land of Eden,* were his chief works. That this American's years in England, on the continent and among the social gentry of the south had created gaiety and grace of expression is evident in these sparkling journals. Although a sincerely devout Anglican, Byrd was far from being obsessed by religion; on the contrary, he was as playful as the Restoration wits whose works he clearly admired.

The wrench of the American Revolution emphasized differences which had been growing, perhaps without being voiced, between American and British political concepts. As the colonists moved to the belief that rebellion was inevitable, as they fought the bitter war and as they worked to found the new nation's government, their thoughts, feelings and actions were influenced by a number of very effective political writers.

Important in the early stages of the war were such authors as Samuel Adams (1722–1803) of Boston, Mass., John Dickinson (1732–1808) of Philadelphia, Pa., both of whom favoured the colonists—and Loyalist Joseph Galloway (1731–1803) of Philadelphia. But two figures loomed above these—Benjamin Franklin and Thomas Paine.

Franklin, born in Boston in 1706, had started to publish his writings in his brother's newspaper as early as 1722. This newspaper, the *New England Courant,* which championed the cause of the Leather Apron man and the farmer, had attempted to appeal by using easily understood language and by using practical arguments. The style of writing probably had wielded its influence from the first upon this Yankee who took naturally to the idea that practical common sense was a good guide. The influence at any rate had been clear in the popular *Poor Richard's Almanack,* which Franklin edited between 1733 and 1758, annually filled with prudent and witty aphorisms purportedly written by uneducated but experienced Richard Saunders. The influence had been clear also in the author's *Autobiography,* written between 1771 and 1788, a record of his rise from humble circumstances which offered his descendants worldly-wise suggestions for future success.

Franklin had been molded by other family and social forces, and he had been a wide reader. His culture, though self-attained, was deep and wide, and it gave substance and skill to the varied articles, pamphlets and reports which he wrote concerning the dispute with Great Britain and which were extremely effective in stating and shaping the colonists' cause.

Thomas Paine, an Englishman, was a failure when he sought out Franklin in London to propound a scientific question. "Impressed," as Franklin explained, "by those wonderful eyes of his," Franklin persuaded Paine to try his fortunes in the new world. Paine went to Philadelphia, became a magazine editor and then, about 14 months later, the most effective propagandist for the colonial cause. His pamphlet, *Common Sense* (Jan. 1776), probably did more than any other agency to influence the colonists to declare their independence. His series, the *Crisis* papers (Dec. 1776–April 1783) spurred Americans to fight on through the blackest years of the war. One reason for the effectiveness of both works was the fact that the papers, based upon the simple deistic beliefs of Paine, showed the conflict as a stirring melodrama in which the angelic colonists arrayed themselves against the forces of evil. Such white and black picturings here, as often before, were highly effective as propaganda. Another reason for his success was the fact that Paine's poetic fervour found expression in impassioned words and phrases, many of which were long to be remembered and quoted.

An author of the war period who did not engage actively in the controversy was French-born Michel Guillaume Jean de Crèvecoeur. After serving in the French army in Canada, settling in New York and becoming a farmer and a naturalized citizen, Crèvecoeur wrote and published *Letters From an American Farmer* (1782). These commentaries picture the lives of Americans, at times idyllically, and at other times voice many of the advanced ideas afloat in tumultuous days of change.

The New Nation.—When the postwar period came, some of these eloquent men were no longer able to win a hearing. Thomas Paine and Samuel Adams, for instance, lacked constructive ideas which appealed to those interested in forming a new government. Others fared better, for example Franklin, whose tolerance and common sense showed themselves in addresses to the constitutional convention. A different group of authors, however, became leaders in the new period—the talented writers of the *Federalist* papers and Thomas Jefferson.

The Federalist was a series of 85 essays, published in 1787 and 1788, urging the virtues of the new constitution. They were written by Alexander Hamilton (1755–1804), James Madison (1751–1836) and John Jay (1745–1829). More distinguished for their insight into problems of government and for their cool logic than for their eloquence, these works became a classic statement of American governmental theory. At the time they were highly effective in influencing legislators who voted on the new constitution. Hamilton, who wrote the bulk of the series (perhaps as many as 51 essays), became, with John Adams (1735–1826), a leader of the Federalist party. A series of messages which Hamilton wrote as first secretary of the treasury (1789–95) were influential in increasing the power of national government at the expense of the state governments.

Thomas Jefferson, like Franklin, was a writer on politics who was influential both during the war and the postwar period.

The merits of his great summary, the Declaration of Independence, consisted, as Madison pointed out, "in a lucid communication of human rights, a condensed enumeration of the reasons for such an exercise of them, and in a style and tone appropriate to the great occasion, and to the spirit of the American people." After the war this philosophic statesman—probably the most cultured of the 18th-century American political thinkers—formulated in more detail the exact tenets of his faith. In various papers, but most richly in his letters and his inaugural addresses, he stated a belief at odds with that of Hamilton. Where Hamilton urged strong federal government, Jefferson urged individual freedom and local autonomy—decentralization. Thus far his life upon the frontier shaped his creed. Yet, being a Virginian, he had faith in aristocrats as leaders, and he thought that "a natural aristocracy" with "virtue and talents" should be trusted with high governmental positions. Though he held that all men are created equal, Jefferson did not hold that all are equally qualified as leaders. Jeffersonian democracy was a transitional stage between aristocratic belief and Jacksonian democracy.

Poets and Poetry.—Poetry became a weapon during the American Revolution, with both Loyalists and Continentals urging their forces on, stating their arguments and celebrating their heroes in verse. Some of the songs of wartime, such as "Yankee Doodle," "Nathan Hale" and "The Epilogue," are lively pieces, and most have more polish, say, than *The Bay Psalm Book* or "The Battle of the Kegs." Most, however, were set to popular British melodies of the time, and were in manner like the British poems of the period.

The period also was productive of a school of poets, a group centred in Hartford, Conn., and called the Hartford Wits. Most famed were John Trumbull (1750–1831), Timothy Dwight (1752–1817) and Joel Barlow (1754–1812). Most were Federalists in politics, and all tended to be as conservative in their methods of poetic composition. They wrote many satires, mock heroic poems and several dull epics. In general the poems show that these authors, adept though they were, were nothing more than skilled imitators of their contemporaries in England. One poet in the group, on one occasion, did better than the rest. This was Joel Barlow, who in 1793 composed "Hasty Pudding." Though this was a mock heroic poem in Popeian couplets and hence in general form like other imitative poems, it contained lively and vivid descriptions of rural New England scenes which gave it a momentary native flavour if not a completely native quality.

The most memorable poet of the period was Philip Freneau (1752–1832), a native New Yorker of Huguenot ancestry who became interested in writing while a student at Princeton. His first well-known poems were Revolutionary War satires which were effective propaganda, but later he turned to various aspects of the American scene. Although he wrote much in the stilted manner of the neoclassicists, such poems of his as "The Wild Honey Suckle," "To a Caty-did" and "On a Honey Bee" were romantic lyrics of real grace and feeling which were forerunners of a literary movement which was to be important in the 19th century.

Drama and the Novel.—In the years toward the close of the 18th century, both dramas and novels of at least some historical importance were produced. Despite the fact that theatrical groups had long been active in America, the first American comedy presented professionally was Royall Tyler's *The Contrast* (1787). This drama was full of echoes of Goldsmith and Sheridan, but it contained a Yankee character (the predecessor of many such in years to follow) who brought something native onto the stage. Tyler wrote only this one important play, but William Dunlap (1766–1839) wrote many dramas and encouraged other dramatists to try their skill.

William Hill Brown wrote the first American novel, *The Power of Sympathy* (1789), which showed authors how to overcome ancient prejudices against this form by following the preachy, sentimental novel form which had been invented by Samuel Richardson. A flood of sentimental novels followed, down to the end of the 19th century. Shortly H. H. Brackenridge followed other models—Cervantes and Fielding—with some popular suc-

AMERICAN LITERATURE

PLATE I

U.S. AUTHORS OF THE 18TH, 19TH AND 20TH CENTURIES

1. Benjamin Franklin (1706–90). 2. Washington Irving (1783–1859). 3. James Fenimore Cooper (1789–1851). 4. Ralph Waldo Emerson (1803–82). 5. Nathaniel Hawthorne (1804–64). 6. Henry Wadsworth Longfellow (1807–82). 7. John Greenleaf Whittier (1807–92). 8. Edgar Allan Poe (1809–49). 9. Oliver Wendell Holmes (1809–94). 10. Harriet Beecher Stowe (1811–96). 11. Henry David Thoreau (1817–62). 12. James Russell Lowell (1819–91). 13. Herman Melville (1819–91). 14. Walt Whitman (1819–92). 15. Emily Dickinson (1830–86). 16. Mark Twain (Samuel Langhorne Clemens) (1835–1910). 17. Henry James (1843–1916). 18. Edwin Arlington Robinson (1869–1935). 19. Edgar Lee Masters (1869–1950). 20. Stephen Crane (1871–1900). 21. Theodore Dreiser (1871–1945). 22. Robert Frost (1875–1963). 23. Sherwood Anderson (1876–1941). 24. Willa Cather (1876–1947). 25. Carl Sandburg (1878–   )

PLATE II

AMERICAN LITERATURE

BY COURTESY OF (4) ROBINSON JEFFERS AND SADIE ADRIANI, (6) HARPER & BROTHERS, (7) ARTHUR B. LONG (8, 13) CHARLES SCRIBNER'S SONS, (15) THE VANGUARD PRESS, INC.; PHOTOGRAPHS (1, 3, 10, 11) WIDE WORLD, (2) UNDERWOOD & UNDERWOOD, (5) PINCHOT, (9, 12, 14) UNITED PRESS

20TH CENTURY U.S. AUTHORS

1. Nicholas Vachel Lindsay (1879–1931). **2.** Sinclair Lewis (1885–1951). **3.** Van Wyck Brooks (1886–1963). **4.** Robinson Jeffers (1887–1962). **5.** Eugene O'Neill (1888–1953). **6.** Edna St. Vincent Millay (1892–1950). **7.** Katherine Anne Porter (1894–   ). **8.** Francis Scott Key Fitzgerald (1896–1940). **9.** John Dos Passos (1896–   ). **10.** William Faulkner (Falkner) (1897–1962). **11.** Stephen Vincent Benét (1898–1943). **12.** Ernest Hemingway (1899–1961). **13.** Thomas Clayton Wolfe (1900–38). **14.** John Steinbeck (1902–   ). **15.** James Thomas Farrell (1904–   )

cess, in *Modern Chivalry* (1792–1815), amusing because of its satire on democracy and interesting for its portrayal of frontier life. Gothic thrillers were nationalized to some extent at least in Charles Brockden Brown's *Wieland* (1798), *Arthur Mervyn* (1799–1800) and *Edgar Huntly* (1799). But all such works were more interesting as beginnings rather than as outstanding artistic achievements.

EARLY 19th CENTURY

In a commencement poem at Princeton in 1771, young Philip Freneau, celebrating "The Rising Glory of America," urged his compatriots to create a literature of their own. The prologue to *The Contrast,* in 1787, boasted that the play was one which the people of the nation "might fairly call their own." After the American Revolution, and increasingly after the War of 1812, writers were exhorted to produce a literature which was truly national. Although the most ambitious dramas were Elizabethan in form (if not in excellence), some dramas began to depict native characters. But this was not to be a great period in the American theatre. Nevertheless, to satisfy the demand for national writing, four authors of very respectable stature appeared. William Cullen Bryant, Washington Irving, James Fenimore Cooper and Edgar Allan Poe initiated a great half century of literary development.

Bryant (1794–1878), a New Englander by birth, attracted attention in his 23rd year when the first version of his poem, "Thanatopsis," appeared. This early poem showed, as later ones did, that his first training had been in the 18th-century school of poetry. Later, under the influence of Wordsworth and other romantics, he wrote nature lyrics which vividly represented the New England scene. In such poems as "To a Waterfowl," "A Forest Hymn," "Robert of Lincoln" and "The Prairies," he achieved truly impressive expressions of thought and feeling. Turning to journalism, he had a long career as the fighting liberal editor of the *Evening Post.* As a member of the so-called Knickerbocker Group Bryant overshadowed such earlier poets as Joseph Rodman Drake (1795–1820) and Fitz-Greene Halleck (1790–1867). He himself was overshadowed, in renown at least, by a native-born New Yorker, Washington Irving.

Irving, the youngest member of a prosperous merchant family, joined with some of the other gay young leaders of the town in producing *Salmagundi* papers (1807–1808) which took off on the foibles of Manhattan's citizenry. This was followed by *A History of New York* by "Diedrich Knickerbocker" (1809), a burlesque history which mocked pedantic scholarship and sniped at the old Dutch families. Irving's models in these works were obviously such neoclassical Englishmen as Addison, Steele, Goldsmith and Swift, from whom he had learned to write in a polished, bright style. When the family business was in dire straits in 1815, Irving went abroad to do what he could to save it. The business failed but Irving, having met Scott and having become acquainted with some of the imaginative German literature, introduced a new romantic note in *The Sketch Book* (1819–20), *Bracebridge Hall* (1822) and other works. He was at his best in essaylike narratives wherein his fancy and his charming personality were gracefully set forth. Irving was the first American writer to win the ungrudging (if somewhat surprised) respect of the British critics.

James Fenimore Cooper, born six years after Irving, won even wider fame. The son of a prosperous squire, he lived as a boy on Otsego lake in New York, then attended Yale briefly, went to sea briefly and settled down to be a country squire himself. Almost by accident he turned to the writing of fiction. Following the pattern of the Waverley novels, he did his best work in the Leatherstocking tales (1823–41) a five-volume series celebrating the career of the great frontiersman Natty Bumppo. His skill in weaving history into inventive plots and in characterizing his compatriots brought his acclaim not only in America and England but on the continent as well. He also wrote novels of the American Revolution, of life upon the sea and several novels of social purpose which embodied his vigorous social and political beliefs.

Edgar Allan Poe, reared in the south, lived and worked as an author and editor in Baltimore, Md., Philadelphia, Richmond, Va., and New York city. A neurotic and somewhat theatrical personality, he was the sort of figure about whom legends naturally tended to develop; his poems and stories, many of them weird and strange, were associated by many with his unhappy career. His work instead was shaped largely by his analytical skill which showed clearly in his role as an editor: time after time he gauged the tastes of readers so accurately that the circulation figures of the magazines under his direction soared impressively. It showed itself in his critical articles, wherein he lucidly explained and logically applied his criteria. His Gothic tales of terror were written in accordance with his findings when he studied the most popular magazines of the day. Moreover, his masterpieces of terror—"The Fall of the House of Usher" (1839), "The Masque of the Red Death" (1842) and "The Cask of Amontillado" (1846) and others—were written according to a carefully worked out psychological method. So were his detective stories such as "The Murders in the Rue Morgue" (1841), which historians credit as the earliest of the genre. As a poet, too, Poe wrote with a careful artistry—and at least some of his songs had melody and suggestive imagery of a high order. In general his methods and effects were too obviously contrived, but in his rather limited sphere he was an impressive craftsman.

Two southern novelists were also outstanding in this period: John Pendleton Kennedy and William Gilmore Simms. Kennedy, a citizen of Maryland, came to know Virginia when he visited his mother's family there. He wrote delightfully—if somewhat idyllically—of life on the plantations in *Swallow Barn* (1832); and in *Horse-Shoe Robinson* (1835) he told an interesting story of Virginia and the Carolinas during the Revolution. William Gilmore Simms of Charleston started his career in fiction with a melodramatic novel in 1833, then in 1834 he found his real bent. His forte was the writing of historical novels, like those of Scott and Cooper, which treated the history of the frontier and South Carolina. *The Yemassee* (1835) and a series of Revolutionary romances (1835–56) showed him at his best—particularly when he portrayed (usually in minor roles) a group of amusing rogues.

AMERICAN RENAISSANCE (1829–70)

The lives of the authors just discussed overlapped those of others who came into prominence in the 1830s and were active until about the end of the Civil War. But the new group—the humorists, the classic New Englanders, Herman Melville, Walt Whitman and others—were of a new breed. In various ways they were influenced, as their predecessors had been, by the literature of other lands. But they did their work in a new spirit and their achievements were of a new sort. Partly this was because all of them in one way or another were influenced by the broadening democratic concepts which in 1829 triumphed in Jackson's inauguration as president. Partly it was because, in this romantic period of emphasis upon native scenes and characters in many literatures, they put much of America into their books.

Particularly full of vivid touches were the writings of two groups of American humorists whose works appeared between 1830 and 1867. One group created several down-east Yankees who used common-sense arguments to comment upon the political and social scene. The most important included Seba Smith (1792–1868), whose chief figure was Jack Downing; James Russell Lowell (1819–91) who quoted the rhymed remarks of pious Hosea Biglow and rascally Birdofredum Sawin; and Benjamin P. Shillaber (1814–90), creator of Mrs. Partington and her nephew Ike. Despite their concern with preachments, these authors caught the talk, the characters, the ways of living in New England at the time as no one else did. In the old southwest, meanwhile, such writers as Davy Crockett (1786–1836), Augustus Baldwin Longstreet (1790–1870), Johnson J. Hooper (1815–62), Thomas Bangs Thorpe (1815–78), Joseph G. Baldwin (1815–64) and George W. Harris (1814–69) drew lively pictures of the people of the ebullient frontier. Though less interested in preachments than their New England counterparts, and though rather more boisterous and masculine, these authors accomplished the same sort of realistic sectional portrayal. All showed the kind of interest in the common man which was a part of Jacksonian democracy.

New England Brahmins.—Although one of their members, Lowell, for a time joined the writers of a native humour, the group of New England writers who were associated with Harvard and Cambridge in this period—the Brahmins, as they came to be called—were at an opposite extreme. Henry Wadsworth Longfellow (1807–82), Oliver Wendell Holmes (1809–94) and Lowell were all aristocrats, all steeped in foreign culture, all active as professors at Harvard. They wrote genteel literature which was at times touched by pedantry, at other times too close to foreign models. Yet each, through his travels and study and his interest in the American scene, had valuable gifts for his countrymen. Longfellow adapted European methods of storytelling and versifying to narrative poems dealing with American history, and a few of his less didactic lyrics perfectly married technique and subject matter. Holmes, in his occasional poems and his Breakfast Table series (1858–91) brought touches of urbanity and jocosity to a perhaps oversober polite literature. And Lowell, in poems descriptive of the out-of-doors in America, and in his *Biglow Papers* (1848, 1867) put much of his homeland into verse. His odes—particularly the "Commemoration Ode" (1865)—gave fine expression to noble sentiments. His chief importations from abroad were a set of critical standards and a method of criticism which made him one of America's most readable as well as incisive critics.

The Transcendentalists.—Concord, Mass., a village not far from Cambridge, was the home of the leaders of another important New England group. The way for this group had been prepared by the rise of a theological system, Unitarianism, which early in the 19th century had replaced Calvinism as the faith of a large share of the New Englanders. Ralph Waldo Emerson, the most famous of the Concord philosophers, started as a Unitarian minister but found even that liberal doctrine too confining for his broad beliefs. He became a Transcendentalist who, like other ancient and modern Platonists, trusted to insights transcending logic and experience for the revelations of the deepest truths. He was not, however, a perpetual dweller in cloudland for, as Lowell pointed out, if he had a "Greek head," it was set on "right Yankee shoulders." His scheme of things ranged all the way from the lowest objects and the most practical chores to soaring flights of imagination and inspired beliefs. He had theories too of writing which helped him phrase his thoughts in simple and concrete words, so that his prose was dotted with aphorisms. His *Essays* (1841, 1844), *Representative Men* (1850) and *English Traits* (1856) were thoughtful and poetic explanations of his beliefs; and his roughhewn lyrics, packed with thought and feeling, were as close to 17th-century metaphysical poems as any produced in his period.

An associate of Emerson with a salty personality of his own and an individual way of thinking was Henry David Thoreau. A sometime surveyor, labourer and naturalist, Thoreau was closer to the earthy and the practical than even Emerson was. He also was more of a humorist—a dry Yankee commentator with a flair for paradoxical phrases and sentences. Finally, he was a learned man, widely read in the western classics and the books of the orient. These qualities gave distinction to *A Week on the Concord and Merrimac Rivers* (1849) and to *Walden* (1854). The latter was a record of his experiences and ponderings during the time he lived in a hut by Walden pond—a defense of his belief that modern man should simplify his demands if need be to "suck out all the marrow of life." In his essay, "Civil Disobedience" (1849), Thoreau expounded his anarchistic views of government, insisting that if an injustice of government is "of such a nature that it requires injustice to another [you should] break the law [and] let your life be a counter friction to stop the machine." The concept of American individualism here reached one of its climaxes.

Associated with these two major figures were such minor Transcendentalists as dreamy Amos Bronson Alcott (1799–1888), George Ripley (1802–80), Orestes Brownson (1803–76), Margaret Fuller (1810–50) and Jones Very (1813–80). Margaret Fuller, a brilliant bluestocking, was for a time the editor of the organ of the movement, the *Dial* (published 1840–44) wherein some of the best writings by minor Transcendentalists appeared. Her *Woman in the Nineteenth Century* (1845) was historically important in the feministic movement.

New England Reformers and Historians.—The world-wide movement for change which exploded in the revolutions of 1848 naturally attracted numerous Americans. Reform was in the air, particularly in New England, and even the aloof Brahmins at times were drawn into the controversies raging during the period. Several Transcendentalists allied themselves with workers for change: not only Thoreau but also Alcott (at Fruitlands) and Ripley (at Brook Farm) experimented with anarchistic, socialistic or communistic schemes for living. Suffrage for women, better conditions for workers, temperance for all and even modifications of dress and diet all had their fiery defenders. And the advocates of the abolition of slavery made their mark upon U.S. history.

William Lloyd Garrison (1805–79), ascetic and fanatical, was the moving spirit in the fight against slavery; his weekly newspaper, *The Liberator* (1831–65), despite its rather small circulation, was its most influential organ. A contributor to the newspaper (who was more famous, however, as an eloquent lecturer) was aristocratic Wendell Phillips (1811–84). Still another contributor—probably the greatest writer associated with the movement—was John Greenleaf Whittier. His simple but emotional poems in behalf of abolition were collected in such volumes as *Poems Written During the Progress of the Abolition Question . . .* (1837), *Voices of Freedom* (1846) and *Songs of Labor* (1850). These had the melodramatic quality of rhetoric and therefore lacked excellence as poetry; his less controversial poems, some of them written after the war, were to have a more lasting appeal. The outstanding novelist of the movement—so far as effect was concerned—was Harriet Beecher Stowe. Her *Uncle Tom's Cabin* (1852) combined the elements of contemporary humour and sentimental fiction to dramatize the plight of the Negro. Probably no other American literary work, in that period or later, had so widespread an effect.

One other group of writers—and one great novelist—contributed to the literature of New England in this period of its greatest glory. The group consisted of several historians who combined scholarly methods learned abroad with vivid and dramatic methods of narration. These included George Bancroft, author of an impressive (though somewhat overpious) *History of the United States* (completed in 10 vol. in 1875), and John Lothrop Motley, who traced the history of the Dutch republic and the United Netherlands in nine fascinating volumes (1856–74). The greatest member of the group was Francis Parkman, descendant of a prominent Boston family who, in a series of books (1851–92), wrote as a historian of the fierce contests between France and England which marked the advance of the American frontier. His record of his own westward journey, *The Oregon Trail* (1849), is an absorbing picture of life along the trail and of a sojourn among the Sioux.

Hawthorne.—History also figured in the tales and romances of the leading New England fictionist of the period, Nathaniel Hawthorne. He was convinced, as he said, that such a writer as he succeeded best if he located his fictions in "a neutral territory . . . where the Actual and the Imaginary may meet, and each imbue itself with the nature of the other." Therefore many of his tales and longer works; *e.g.*, his masterpiece, *The Scarlet Letter* (1850), and "The Minister's Black Veil" were set against the background of colonial America with emphasis upon their distance from 19th-century New England. Others; *e.g.*, *The House of the Seven Gables* (1851), dealt with the past as well as the present. Still others, *e.g.*, "The Birthmark," "Rappaccini's Daughter" and *The Marble Faun* (1860), were set in distant countries. Remote though these narratives were at times from what Hawthorne called "the light of common day," they showed deep psychological insight and probed into complex ethical problems. Weaving allegory and symbolism firmly into the texture of his poetic fables, Hawthorne made them rich commentaries upon such subjects as the nature of sin and the relationship between the individual and his fellow men.

Melville and Whitman.—Another great fiction writer, for a time a neighbour and associate of Hawthorne, was New York-born

Herman Melville. After relatively little schooling, Melville went to sea; a whaling ship, as he put it, was his "Yale College and his Harvard." His first books were fiction in the guise of factual writing based upon his experiences as a sailor—*Typee* (1846) and *Omoo* (1847); so were such later works as *Redburn* (1849) and *White Jacket* (1850). Between 1846 and 1851, however, Melville's reading in philosophy and the literary classics, as well as in the writings of Hawthorne, gave him new literary interests and ambitions. The first sign of this interest was *Mardi* (1849), an uneven and disjointed transitional book which used allegory after the model of Rabelais to comment upon all sorts of ideas afloat in the period—nations, politics, institutions, literature and religion. The new interest came to its finest fruition in *Moby Dick; or The White Whale* (1851), a richly symbolic work, complex but brilliantly integrated, which gave the pursuit of the white whale by mad Ahab and his crew significant philosophical meanings. Only in short stories, "Benito Cereno"—a masterpiece of its genre—and others, in the psychological novel, *Pierre* (1852), and in the novelette, *Billy Budd* (1890?) was Melville again to show sporadic flashes of the genius which created *Moby Dick*.

Another New Yorker and one of the most ardent singers of the praise of Manhattan, Walt Whitman saw much less of the dark side of life than Melville did. He was a great optimist, and hence a voice for a period of general hopefulness. He was, in addition, a believer in Jacksonian democracy, in the splendour of the common man. Inspired by the romantic concept of the poet as prophet and also by the Transcendental philosophy of Emerson, Whitman in 1855 published the first edition of *Leaves of Grass*. As the years passed, nine other editions of this singular work were published, always with the revision of old poems and the adding of new ones. This autobiography in verse was intended to show the ideas, beliefs, emotions and experiences of the common man in this great period of American individualism. Whitman had a hard time winning a following, because he was frank and unconventional in his Transcendental thinking, because he used free verse rather than rhymed or regularly metred verse and because his poems were not conventionally organized. Nevertheless (assisted somewhat by enthusiastic friends), this poet steadily gained the approval of the critics and in time came to be recognized as one of the great poets of America. Modern critics see form where some of Whitman's contemporaries saw only chaos—in such fine poems as "Crossing Brooklyn Ferry," "Out of the Cradle Endlessly Rocking," "When Lilacs Last in the Dooryard Bloom'd" and "Passage to India." With the passage of time, too, readers came to be less shocked by Whitman's frankness, his thought, his strange diction and his irregular rhythms.

Southern Poets and Orators.—In the south, meanwhile, the authors tended to be overshadowed by their New England neighbours. The humorists of the southwest, to be sure, were unsurpassed, and Poe (who considered the south his home) wrote within certain limits important stories, poems and critical works. But, with one exception, other southern writers of significance were quantitatively and qualitatively surpassed. Henry Timrod (1828–67) and Paul Hamilton Hayne (1830–86) were the best of the poets. The former, in particular, achieved memorable expressions in behalf of the south in poems such as "Ethnogenesis," "Ode" and "The Cotton Boll." The south's best answer in poetry to the abolitionist songs of Whittier was William J. Grayson's "The Hireling and the Slave" (1854) wherein, in heroic couplets often very well turned, the author stated the case for slavery.

More noteworthy in a period of great oratory, were the orators of the south. New England, of course, had as its spokesman the "godlike" Daniel Webster whose eloquence many considered unsurpassed. But the southerners held with some reason that they had finer representation in the halls of congress than the north had managed to produce. John Randolph of Roanoke (1773–1833), a picturesque aristocrat, found the best expression for his flamboyant personality in his stirring addresses. Henry Clay (1777–1852), who was born in Virginia but represented Kentucky in Washington, D.C., was at the time esteemed as the greatest of the orators; doubtless his speeches did much to bring about the adop-

tion of his various proposals for compromise. More to the taste of later readers (and admired at the time) was John C. Calhoun (1782–1850) of South Carolina. His simplicity of style, his grasp of history and his sharp logic made the most impressive case possible for his beloved south.

Abraham Lincoln.—Kentucky and Illinois produced the one orator, Abraham Lincoln, who managed to speak to future generations in utterances which rose above the bitterness of wartime. His prewar speeches, including the famous debates with Stephen Douglas in 1858, were more effective upon the immediate audience than upon later readers. There were speeches even after his nomination for the presidency which, though historically important, were ephemeral in thought and form. But at least four of his speeches—"Farewell to Springfield" (1861), "First Inaugural Address" (1861), "The Gettysburg Address" (1863) and "Second Inaugural Address" (1865)—whether or not one agrees with their interpretation of history, were great utterances. Lincoln was able thus to stir listeners beyond his own times because he was at this stage in his career a sincere believer in democracy and a man profoundly aware of the sorrow and the suffering of war. He was also a devoted reader of two literary classics which molded his simple but eloquent style—Shakespeare and the King James version of the Bible. He was, finally, a man of real poetic ability who took great pains to seek out the words, the images and the rhythms which best expressed his thought and emotion.

THE CIVIL WAR TO 1914

Like the Revolution and the election of Andrew Jackson, the Civil War marked a turning point in U.S. history. To some degree a result of certain changes under way in the prewar decades, to some extent an accelerator of those changes, the Civil War marked the beginning of new ways of living. Industry became increasingly important as factories rose and cities grew and agrarian pre-eminence declined. Science contributed to the growth of industry, influenced men's thinking about philosophical problems and wrought great changes in everyone's life. The frontier, which always before had been an important factor in the economic scheme, moved steadily westward, and toward the end of the 19th century vanished. All these changes brought modifications in the ethical and political beliefs of many Americans. The rise of modern America was accompanied, naturally, by important mutations in literature.

Literary Comedians.—American humour, the type of writing which appealed most directly perhaps to popular taste, shortly embodied important changes. Although they continued to employ some of the devices of the older humorists, the group of comic writers which now rose to prominence was different in important ways from the older group. Charles Farrar Browne (1834–67), David Ross Locke (1833–88), Charles Henry Smith (1826–1903), Henry Wheeler Shaw (1818–85) and Edgar W. Nye (1850–96), wrote, respectively, as Artemus Ward, Petroleum V. (for Vesuvius) Nasby, Bill Arp, Josh Billings and Bill Nye. Appealing to a national audience, these authors forsook the sectional characterizations of earlier humorists and assumed the roles of literary comedians. This meant that the characters they pretended to be became blurred or unlocalized—that instead of writing in the roles, say, of Yankee farmers, Georgia planters or Tennessee mountaineers, they wrote (to use Samuel Clemens' phrase) as "genial idiots" whose characteristics were not particularized. In such guises they could often comment obliquely and amusingly upon current affairs. In such guises, too, they could use all sorts of verbal devices—slang, bad spelling, poor grammar and anticlimactic sentences, incongruously combined with learned allusions and Latinate words for humorous effects. The nature of the humour thus shifted from that of character portrayal to that of diction. Most that they wrote wore badly, but thousands of Americans in their time and some in later times found these authors vastly amusing.

Fiction and Local Colourists.—Since the achievements of short-story writers and novelists were to be both historically important and aesthetically appealing, the pre-eminent form in this period was destined to be fiction. The first group of fiction writers to become popular—the local colourists—took over to some extent the task of portraying sectional groups which had been abandoned by writers of the new humour. Bret Harte, the first of these writers to achieve great success, admitted indebtedness to the prewar sectional humorists, as did some others; and all showed resemblances to the earlier group. Some, it is probable, went to school to more respectable poets and novelists of the early 19th century. Whittier, for instance, before the war had written much poetry which authentically pictured New England life, and now was to write more including his masterpiece "Snow-Bound" (1866). Too, Cooper and innumerable other writers in the tradition of Scott had before the war pictured hundreds of characters with clearly displayed sectional traits.

Whoever their antecedents were, the local colourists quickly became pre-eminent. Within a brief period, books by pioneers in the movement appeared—Harriet Beecher Stowe's *Oldtown Folks* (1869) and *Sam Lawson's Oldtown Fireside Stories* (1871), delightful vignettes of New England; Bret Harte's *The Luck of Roaring Camp and Other Sketches* (1870), humorous and sentimental tales of California mining camp life; and Edward Eggleston's *The Hoosier Schoolmaster* (1871), a novel of the early days of the settlement of Indiana. Down into the 20th century, short stories (and a relatively small number of novels) in patterns set by these three appeared. In time, practically every corner of the country had been portrayed in local colour fiction. Additional important writings were the depictions of Louisiana creoles by George Washington Cable (1844–1925), of Virginia Negroes by Thomas Nelson Page (1853–1922), of Georgia Negroes by Joel Chandler Harris (1848–1908), of Tennessee mountaineers by Mary Noailles Murfree (1850–1922), of tight-lipped folk of New England by Sarah Orne Jewett (1849–1909) and by Mary E. Wilkins Freeman (1852–1930), of the people of New York city by Henry Cuyler Bunner (1855–1896) and by William Sydney Porter ("O. Henry") (1862–1910). The avowed aim of some of these writers was to portray realistically the lives of various sections and thus to promote understanding in a united nation. The stories as a rule were only partially realistic, though, because: (1) the authors often set their narratives in the past or, if they showed the contemporary scene, winnowed out the less glamorous aspects of life in their section; (2) they were often too much coloured by sentiment or humour, or (typically) by both; (3) they exploited the picturesque or the quaint rather than the typical. Some have suggested that the authors tended to revisit the past instead of portraying their own time, because of their nostalgia for an America which had disappeared. Touched by romance though they were, these fictional works were transitional to realism, for they did portray common folk sympathetically; they did concern themselves with dialect and mores; and some at least avoided the older sentimental or romantic formulas.

Mark Twain.—Samuel L. Clemens (Mark Twain) was allied with the literary comedians and the local colourists. As a printer's apprentice on his brother's newspaper in Hannibal, Mo., he knew and emulated the prewar sectional humorists. He rose to prominence in the days when Artemus Ward, Bret Harte and their followers were the idols of the public. His first books, *The Innocents Abroad* (1869) and *Roughing It* (1872), like several of later periods, were travel books in which the affiliations with the postwar professional humorists were clearest. *The Adventures of Tom Sawyer* (1876), *Life on the Mississippi* (1883) and *The Adventures of Huckleberry Finn* (1884), his best works, which recreated the life of the Mississippi valley in the past, were closest to the work of the older humorists and the local colourists. Even in his best work, however, he succumbed now and then to the temptation to play the buffoon or sink into burlesque.

Despite his flaws, Mark Twain was one of America's greatest writers. He had more skill than his teachers in selecting rich details of the life in his section; he had a genius for creating character; he had unusual inventive powers and he was master of a poetic and masculine style.

William Dean Howells.—The local colourists and Mark Twain thought of themselves as portrayers of life as it really was, although they frequently let a nostalgic haze blur actuality.

Nearer to the later concept of realism were some of the books of a long neglected New Englander, John William De Forest—*Miss Ravenel's Conversion From Secession to Loyalty* (1867) which told truths about the Civil War and which portrayed some very lifelike characters, and *Honest John Vane* (1875), a novel whose theme was the Crédit Mobilier scandal. Even nearer to the later concept were three novels produced in the middle west in the 1880s—E. W. Howe's *The Story of a Country Town* (1883), which showed the pinched life of a midwestern village, and Joseph Kirkland's *Zury, the Meanest Man in Spring County* (1887), a rather grim picture of the Illinois frontier. Howe was unaware that he was influenced by anybody; but Kirkland gladly acknowledged his indebtedness to the English realist, Thomas Hardy. A greater writer and a more conscious realist than any of these was another midwesterner, born and raised in Ohio, William Dean Howells.

Howells went abroad for consular service, then returned to live in the east. An avid reader from childhood, he apparently became enthusiastic about realistic writing when, in Italy, he encountered the plays of 18th-century Carlo Goldoni; but as the years passed he learned lessons from other authors as well. And as an influential editor and as an author, he was the most effective advocate of the new mode of fiction writing.

At the start, Howells conceived of realism as the truthful portrayal of ordinary facets of life—with some limitations; he preferred comedy to tragedy, and he tended to be reticent to the point of prudishness. The formula was displayed at its best in *Their Wedding Journey* (1872), *A Modern Instance* (1882) and *The Rise of Silas Lapham* (1885). Howells preferred later novels written after he had encountered Tolstoi's writings, and had been persuaded by them, as he said, to "set art forever below humanity." In such later novels as *Annie Kilburn* (1889), *A Hazard of New Fortunes* (1890) and *The World of Chance* (1893), he chose his characters not only because they were commonplace but also because the stories he told about them were commentaries upon society, government and economics.

The Naturalists.—Other writers toward the close of the 19th century moved toward naturalism, a more advanced stage of realism. Hamlin Garland was one whose writings marked some aspects of this development. When this young midwesterner called on Howells for the first time in 1885, his views were much like those of the older writer. In his short stories and novels, however, he departed from the practices of the Howells of the pre-Tolstoi period: he made his narratives vehicles for philosophical and social preachments; and he was franker than Howells in treating some aspects of life—the harsher details of the farmer's struggles and the subject of sex. His *Main-Travelled Roads* (1891) and *Rose of Dutcher's Coolly* (1895) displayed Garland's particular talents. These and his critical manifesto for the new fiction, *Crumbling Idols* (1894), were his effective contributions to the developing movement. He was to live well into the 20th century and to produce, in a new period, fine autobiographical works, notably *Son of the Middle Border* (1917) and *A Daughter of the Middle Border* (1921).

Garland thought of himself as a "veritist." Other authors of the same period or slightly later were avowed followers of the group of French naturalists led by Émile Zola (1840–1902). Theodore Dreiser, for instance, treated subjects which had seemed too daring to the earlier realists and, like other naturalists, illustrated his own beliefs by his depictions of characters and his unfolding of plots. Holding that men's deeds were "chemical compulsions," he showed characters unable to direct their actions. Holding, also, that "the race was to the swift and the battle to the strong," he showed characters defeated by stronger and more ruthless opponents. His important books included *Sister Carrie* (1900), *Jennie Gerhardt* (1911), *The Financier* (1912), *The Titan* (1914) and—much later—*An American Tragedy* (1925).

Dreiser did not bother with—or did not care for—some of the niceties of style such as were found in some French naturalistic works. Frank Norris and Stephen Crane were more concerned with such matters. As a result, they embodied many symbolic details in their writings. In his short novels *Maggie: A Girl of the Streets* (1893) and *The Red Badge of Courage* (1895) and in some of his short stories, Crane was an impressionist who made his details and his setting forth of them embody his conception of man overwhelmed by circumstance and environment. Frank Norris, who admired Crane's "aptitude for making phrases—sparks that cast a momentary gleam upon whole phases of life," himself tried to make phrases, scenes and whole narratives cast such gleams in *McTeague* (1899), *The Octopus* (1901) and *The Pit* (1903). Both Norris and Crane died young, their full abilities undeveloped, but their experiments foreshadowed later achievements in the 20th-century novel.

Henry James.—In the books of Henry James, born in New York but later an expatriate in England, fiction took a different pathway. Like the realists and naturalists of his time, he thought that fiction should reproduce reality. He saw reality as fiction presented it, however, as twice translated: (1) through the author's peculiar experiencing of it; and (2) through his depicting of it. Deep insight and thorough experience were no more important, in his thinking, than the highly complicated and delicate task of the artist. His *The Art of Fiction* (1884), his essays on novelists and his brilliant prefaces to his collected works showed him struggling very thoroughly and consciously with the problems of his craft. Together, they formed an important body of discussion of fictional artistry.

Excellent as a short-story writer, James nevertheless was chiefly important for novels in which his doctrines found concrete embodiment. Outstanding were *The American* (1877), *The Portrait of a Lady* (1881), *The Spoils of Poynton* (1897), *What Maisie Knew* (1897), *The Wings of the Dove* (1902), *The Ambassadors* (1903) and *The Golden Bowl* (1904). The earliest of these were international novels wherein conflicts arose from the relationships between Americans and Europeans—each group with its own characteristics and morals. As time passed, he became increasingly interested in the psychological processes of his characters and in the rendering of their limited insights, their perceptions, their emotions, in subtle and complex but interesting and true narratives. His later novels, in particular, fascinated the readers and critics who, beginning in the 1930s, gave James a higher place in U.S. fictional history than he had achieved during his lifetime.

Critics of the Gilded Age.—Writers of many types of works contributed to a great body of literature which flourished between the Civil War and 1914—literature of social revolt. Novels attacked the growing power of business, the growing corruption of government and some novelists outlined utopias. In 1873 Mark Twain and Charles Dudley Warner produced a chaotic novel, *The Gilded Age*, which featured the growth of corruption in government. The same theme, as well as political inefficiency, figured in Henry Adams' novel *Democracy* (1880). Edward Bellamy's *Looking Backward* (1888) was both an indictment of the capitalistic system and an imaginative picturing of a utopia achieved by a collectivist society in the year 2000. Howells' *A Traveler From Altruria* (1894) pleaded for an equalitarian state in which the government regimented men's lives. The year 1906 saw the publication of Upton Sinclair's *The Jungle*, the first of a library of novels and treatises by that author which criticized U.S. economic and political life and which urged socialism as the remedy.

Two poets became famous for the criticisms which they embodied in songs. Edwin Markham, a California schoolteacher, in 1899 published "The Man With the Hoe," protesting against the exploitation of labour and vaguely threatening revolution; it immediately stimulated nation-wide interest. A year later William Vaughan Moody's "An Ode in Time of Hesitation" denounced growing U.S. imperialism as a desertion of earlier principles. "On a Soldier Fallen in the Philippines" (1901) even more effectively developed the same theme.

With the rise of the journalistic magazines, a group of journalists became important as critics of America—the group dubbed "the muckrakers" by Theodore Roosevelt. Ida M. Tarbell's *History of the Standard Oil Company* (1904) and Lincoln Steffens' *The Shame of the Cities* (1904) were typical contributions by two members of a large group of journalistic crusaders.

Henry Adams.—One of the most devastating as well as one of the most literate of the attacks on modern life was the autobiography of a scion of an ancient New England family, the Adamses. Educated at Harvard and abroad, Henry Adams was a great teacher and a great historian (*History of the United States* [1889–91] and *Mont Saint-Michel and Chartres* [1904]). His *The Education of Henry Adams* (1906), however, complained that his lifelong hunt for some sort of order in the world, some sort of faith for man, in the end left him completely baffled. The quiet, urbane style served well to underline, in an ironic way, the message of this pessimistic book.

Poetry.—The latter 19th century and the early years of the 20th century were a poor period for poetry; yet (in addition to Moody) two poets of distinction wrote songs which survived long after scores of minor poets had been forgotten. One was southern-born Sidney Lanier, a talented musician who utilized the rhythms of music and the thematic developments of symphonies in such fine songs as "Corn" (1874), "The Symphony" (1875) and "The Marshes of Glynn" (1878). Distressed, like many of his contemporaries, by the changes in U.S. life, he wove his doubts, fears and suggestions into his richest poems.

The other poet was a New Englander, Emily Dickinson, probably the outstanding U.S. woman poet. A shy, playful, odd personality, Miss Dickinson allowed practically none of her writings to be published during her lifetime. Not until 1890, four years after her death, was the first book of her poems published, to be followed at intervals by other collections. Later poets were to be influenced by her individual techniques—the use of imperfect or eye rhymes, the avoidance of regular rhythms, the tendency to pack her brief stanzas with cryptic meanings. Like Lanier, she rediscovered the value of conceits for setting forth her thought and feeling. Such poems as "The Snake," "I Like to See It Lap the Miles," "The Chariot," "Farther in Summer than the Birds" and "There's a Certain Slant of Light" represented her unusual talent at its best.

FROM 1914 TO 1945

Looking back after several years, literary historians could see that modern movements in drama, poetry, fiction and criticism took form in the years before, during and after World War I. The eventful period which followed left its imprint upon books of all kinds, for it was a time when writers were much concerned with the life about them. World War I, the peace that followed it, the prosperous 1920s, the depression beginning in 1929, the New Deal, the drift to World War II, and World War II itself all shaped literary expression.

The literary forms of the period were extraordinarily varied, but one thing was true of every genre: in drama, poetry and fiction the leading authors tended to experiment with radical innovations in technique. So many deviations from older techniques occurred that some members of the reading public found the new literature, at first, beyond their comprehension. In time, however, the most startling innovations tended to disappear, and readers tended to approve of some of the changes.

Experiments in Drama.—U.S. drama in the 19th century had not been a pre-eminent form. During the American Renaissance the outstanding dramas had been grandiloquent blank verse tragedies such as Robert Montgomery Bird's *The Gladiator* (1831) and George Henry Boker's *Francesca da Rimini* (1855). The extraordinarily popular dramatizations of *Uncle Tom's Cabin* (1852) and Dion Boucicault's melodramas; *e.g.*, *The Octoroon* (1859), dated even more obviously. Nor did the post-Civil War stage fare much better. James A. Herne's *Hearts of Oak* (1878), *Margaret Fleming* (1890) and *Shore Acres* (1892) were praised as realistic plays, but were more stagey than lifelike. Bronson Howard (1842–1908), Augustus Thomas (1857–1934) and Clyde Fitch (1865–1909) were successful playwrights each of whom was, in his day, much admired. The works of these writers, however, in retrospect appear to have been rather shallow, good theatre rather than good drama.

No type of writing embodied wider experimentation than the new drama which arose as a result of a rebellion against the glib commercial stage. In the early years of the 20th century many young Americans, traveling abroad, found a vital theatre flourishing in Europe. Returning to their homeland, these young men and women became active in founding a little theatre movement in every corner of the country, experimenting with dramatic forms and methods of production free from commercial limitations. In time the movement supplied producers, actors and playwrights trained in community playhouses and college classrooms. And some little theatre groups became important commercial producers; *e.g.*, the Washington Square Players, founded in 1915, became the Theatre Guild in 1919. The drama which resulted was marked by a spirit of experimentation and by a new seriousness and a new maturity.

Eugene O'Neill, by general consent America's greatest dramatist in the period, was a product of the movement. Having been trained in George Baker's drama class at Harvard university, he worked with the Provincetown Players before his plays were commercially produced. His dramas showed a remarkable range of experimentation. Some, such as *Beyond the Horizon* (1920), *Anna Christie* (1922), *Desire Under the Elms* (1924) and *The Iceman Cometh* (1946), were naturalistic. Some used expressionistic techniques; *e.g.*, *The Emperor Jones* (1920) and *The Hairy Ape* (1922). He made use of a stream-of-consciousness dramatic form in *Strange Interlude* (1928) and of psychological analysis in *Mourning Becomes Electra* (1931). All his best plays, however, set forth O'Neill's tragic view of life in words of real poetic power.

Although no other dramatist was as generally praised as O'Neill, many others wrote plays—often in the same experimental spirit—which were of a high order. Marc Connelly collaborated with George S. Kaufman in writing the expressionistic *Beggar on Horseback* (1924) and himself wrote touching fantasy in a Negro folk Biblical play, *The Green Pastures* (1930). Elmer Rice wrote *The Adding Machine* (1923), an expressionistic drama, and the naturalistic *Street Scene* (1929). Maxwell Anderson began as a realist, then turned to poetic dramas such as *Elizabeth the Queen* (1930) and *Winterset* (1935), then to a musical comedy satire, *Knickerbocker Holiday* (1938). Robert Sherwood wrote distinguished plays in the forms of comedy; *e.g.*, *Reunion in Vienna* (1931); melodrama, *The Petrified Forest* (1935); historical chronicle, *Abe Lincoln in Illinois* (1938); and tragedy, *There Shall Be No Night* (1940). Clifford Odets, in *Waiting for Lefty* (1935), a plea for labour unionism, utilized the auditorium as well as the stage for action, and in *Awake and Sing* (1935) wrote in the vein of naturalism. Thornton Wilder used stylized settings and poetic dialogue in *Our Town* (1938) and turned to fantasy in *The Skin of Our Teeth* (1942). These dramatists and others were thus alike in their catholicity of form and their eagerness to make their plays, of whatever sort, convey significant commentaries.

The New Poetry.—*Robinson and Frost.*—In form, poetry ranged between older sorts of versification and sorts which departed greatly from the older procedures. Two New England poets who did not diverge from Victorian methods of writing won both critical and popular acclaim in the new period. Edwin Arlington Robinson, whose first book had appeared in 1896, found sonnets, ballad stanzas and blank verse satisfactory to set forth his thought; yet, in the 1920s, he won three Pulitzer prizes—for his *Collected Poems* (1922), *The Man Who Died Twice* (1925) and *Tristram* (1928). Like Robinson, Robert Frost used established stanzas and blank verse. His first book, *A Boy's Will* (1913), was followed by such volumes as *North of Boston* (1914), *Mountain Interval* (1916), *New Hampshire* (1923), *A Further Range* (1936) and *Masque of Reason* (1945). Both Robinson and Frost were admired because their concepts and emotions chimed with those of the time. Both saw tragic aspects of life, both commented upon the complexities of human existence and both were skeptical about pat solutions.

Midwestern Poets.—Just as modern U.S. drama had its beginnings in little theatres, modern U.S. poetry took form in little magazines. Particularly important was *Poetry: a Magazine of Verse* founded by Harriet Monroe (1860–1936) in Chicago in 1912. The region around Chicago—the midwest—soon became

prominent as the home of three poets. One was Vachel Lindsay, born and reared in Springfield, Ill. Adapting legendary lore and native oratory to irregular odelike forms, Lindsay wrote poetry in a style well adapted to oral presentation. His lively reading on lecture tours contributed to the success of such books as *General William Booth Enters Into Heaven, and Other Poems* (1913) and *The Congo, and Other Poems* (1914). Carl Sandburg of Galesburg, Ill., wrote Whitmanesque free verse about life on the prairies and in the cities, which appeared in such volumes as *Chicago Poems* (1916), *Cornhuskers* (1918), *Smoke and Steel* (1920) and *The People, Yes* (1936). Edgar Lee Masters, a native Kansan, was in Chicago when he wrote his very popular *Spoon River Anthology* (1915), free verse monologues of the village men and women most of whom spoke bitterly of their frustrated lives. All these poets experimented with new forms; all commented upon the ironic or bitter aspects of life; all were concerned in one way or another with the changes wrought by the rise of science and industry.

Changing Forms, Changing Ideas.—Modern readers, it soon developed, were hospitable to poets who experimented with new forms, or who expressed new attitudes, or who did both. Sara Teasdale (1884–1933) and Edna St. Vincent Millay (1892–1950) wrote traditional sonnets and brief, personal lyrics which were unusually frank (according to old standards) for women poets. Three fine Negro poets—James Weldon Johnson (1871–1938), Langston Hughes (1902–1967) and Countee Cullen (1903–46) told of the problems of their race in poetic forms which were only on rare occasions radically experimental. These typified a number of poets who found old molds satisfactory for new ideas.

Other poets tried a great range of experiments. Amy Lowell (1874–1925) was spokesman for the Imagists, a group with radical theories about the diction, the rhythms and the imagery (though not the subject matter) of poetry. Conrad Aiken (1889–   ) experimented with poetical imitations of symphonic forms often mingled with stream-of-consciousness techniques. Marianne Moore (1887–   ) invented and employed brilliantly a different kind of free verse. E. E. Cummings (1894–1962) abolished capital letters, used unusual punctuation and divided his lines in a novel fashion to produce poems which often had surprisingly fresh impacts. Stephen Vincent Benét (1898–1943), though ordinarily a rather conventional poet, ranged through many forms, from the ballad stanza to free verse: many of these he wove into his stirring novel in verse, *John Brown's Body* (1928). Robinson Jeffers (1887–1962) used violent imagery and interestingly modified Whitmanesque and blank verse lines to express what were perhaps the most bitter views of any major poet writing in the period.

The Metaphysicals.—The most complex modern poets proved to be a varied group who were strongly influenced by the 17th-century British poets, especially John Donne. Like Donne, these poets used unusual figures—conceits—and freighted their lines with philosophical thought, often of an obscure sort. Their ideas and emotions were unusual for poetry, and their lines often harshly departed from romantic rhythms and melodies. Lovers of poetry found them difficult to read, but often agreed that an understanding was worth the trouble.

The giant of the group and the acknowledged master of many of its members was T. S. Eliot. Eliot, himself, was much indebted to an unstable genius, Ezra Pound (1885–   ), whose critical ideas and fragmentary poetical works provided a great stimulus to Eliot and others. But, beginning with *The Waste Land* (1922) Eliot rapidly progressed in general esteem; and such volumes as *Ash-Wednesday* (1930), *The Rock* (1934) and *Four Quartets* (1943)—as well as his brilliant critical studies—led to the greatest respect. Not only was his style rich and complex; his thoughts and feelings were shared by many who, like him, moved from complete despair in a world that seemed chaotic to a faith of some sort.

The influence of Eliot was very clear in the writings of Archibald MacLeish (1892–   ); his earlier poems were similar both in manner and thought to *The Waste Land,* and in later poems he voiced a positive belief—a belief, however, in social advance rather than in the religious attitude advocated by Eliot. A number of southern poets showed affiliations, though not so clearly— John Crowe Ransom (1888–), Donald Davidson (1893–) and Allen Tate (1899–); their poems were particularly concerned with the south—its past and its problems. Hart Crane (1899–1932) was similar in manner but had matter of his own. Others of the metaphysicals with individual qualities of thought and method were Louise Bogan (1897–), Léonie Adams (1899–), Muriel Rukeyser (1913–), Delmore Schwartz (1913–66) and Karl Shapiro (1913–).

Fiction.—The little magazines which helped the growth of poetry were also influential in the growth of modern U.S. fiction. Not only did they print short stories which diverged from the older patterns; they also published attacks upon the established writers and stressed the merits of unconventional fiction. The *Dial* (1880–1929), the *Little Review* (1914–1929), the *Seven Arts* (1916–1917) and others encouraged rebellion (*see* LITTLE MAGAZINE). More potent than any of these were two magazines edited by that ferocious but humorous journalist-critic, H. L. Mencken (1880–1956)—*Smart Set,* which he edited from 1914 to 1923, and *American Mercury,* under his charge from 1924 to 1933. Mencken published short stories in the new manner, attacked established U.S. beliefs and institutions and praised fiction writers who were unconventional in thought and manner. A powerful influence, he helped launch the new fiction.

The trend was indicated by one of Mencken's favourites, James Branch Cabell. Cabell, who had been writing since 1905, sprang to fame with *Jurgen* (1919)—a novel which attacked America's orthodoxies and institutions by telling a cynical story full of Freudian symbolism. Other authors whom Mencken favoured launched "a revolt against the village," pointing out the narrow, frustrated qualities of life in rural communities; *e.g.,* Zona Gale (1874–1938) and Ruth Suckow (1892–1960). The most famous of the village writers was Sherwood Anderson. His *Winesburg, Ohio* (1919) and *Triumph of the Egg* (1921) were collections of short stories which showed villagers suffering from all sorts of phobias and suppressions. Anderson in time wrote several novels of superior quality, the best being *Poor White* (1920), which treated both a frustrated character and the impact of industry upon American living.

In 1920, critics noticed that a new school of fiction had risen to prominence with the success of books such as F. Scott Fitzgerald's *This Side of Paradise* and Sinclair Lewis' *Main Street.* Thereafter, fiction took on new qualities related to the modern period. Writers tended toward realism and naturalism—frank portrayals of contemporary life. There was a trend, however, from completely documented realism toward the selection of detail. The novelists' portrayal of characters and motives, and even their selection of detail, consistently were much influenced by the psychology of Freud and others.

And the novel tended to be particularly concerned with problems of the day. In the decades which followed, fiction voiced reactions to changing times: novels of the 1920s voiced disillusionment and protest against established institutions and ideologies. Some of those of the 1930s protested against the economic and political system; others advocated remedies of some sort—told of new-found hope and faith. The drift toward World War II and the war itself led many novelists to see qualities of excellence in American life not before realized, to voice patriotic enthusiasm. Some authors wrote works which fell into one or two of these periods; others ran the gamut from disillusion to the acquisition of a new faith. The number of competent—even superior— novelists was huge, so large that the following study can discuss only a few of those who generally were felt to be outstanding.

Critics of Society.—F. Scott Fitzgerald's *This Side of Paradise* (1920) showed the disillusionment, the moral disintegration of post-World War I America. The book initiated a career of great promise which found its finest fruition in *The Great Gatsby* (1925), a more poignant and more unified development of the same theme. These two books of criticism of American society were destined to be Fitzgerald's best achievements. Like Fitzgerald, Sinclair Lewis was best as a social critic. His onslaught against the "village virus," *Main Street* (1920); against average businessmen, *Babbitt* (1922); against materialistic scientists, *Arrowsmith* (1925); and against the racially prejudiced, *Kingsblood Royal* (1947) were satirically sharp and thoroughly documented. Similar careful documentation, though little satire, characterized James T. Farrell's naturalistic *Studs Lonigan* trilogy (1932–35), all of which indignantly underlined social inequalities. Similar in pattern were Richard Wright's books which protested against the position of the Negro—*Uncle Tom's Children* (1938) and *Native Son* (1940). A number of authors wrote proletarian novels attacking capitalistic exploitation; *e.g.,* Albert Halper wrote *The Foundry* (1934) and *The Chute* (1937). Satire, directed against some of the aristocratic New England groups, featured the rather lighter indictments of J. P. Marquand, *The Late George Apley* (1937) and *Wickford Point* (1939).

Particularly admired as a novelist of protest was John Dos Passos, who first attracted attention with an anti-World War I novel, *Three Soldiers* (1921). His most sweeping indictments of the modern social and economic system, *Manhattan Transfer* (1925) and the *U.S.A.* trilogy (*42nd Parallel* [1930]; *1919* [1932]; *The Big Money* [1936]), used various distinctive devices; *e.g.,* "The Camera Eye" and "Newsreel," to attack from the left. Later, after he had undergone changes in belief, he wrote *Adventures of a Young Man* (1939), *Number One* (1943), and *Midcentury* (1961), attacks upon the leftists.

Hemingway, Faulkner, Steinbeck.—Three authors whose writings showed the shift from disillusionment were Ernest Hemingway, William Faulkner and John Steinbeck. Hemingway's early short stories and his first novels, *The Sun Also Rises* (1926) and *A Farewell to Arms* (1929), were full of the disillusionments of the lost generation concerning both war and peace. The Spanish war, however, led him to believe in the possibility of collective action to solve social problems, and his novels *To Have and Have Not* (1937), *For Whom the Bell Tolls* (1940) and *The Old Man and the Sea* (1952) embodied the new belief. At his best, Hemingway showed a power to select and arrange details and to write simple, hard-hitting prose which critics found most effective.

Less controlled but equally distinctive, at its best, was the prose of William Faulkner. His handling of point of view, his use of stream-of-consciousness techniques and even some of his descriptions of backgrounds and actions all at times led to the puzzlement of the reader. But such novels as *The Sound and the Fury* (1929), *As I Lay Dying* (1930), *Light in August* (1932) and *The Hamlet* (1940) overcame handicaps of occasional obscurity. Many of his short stories and novels were parts of the unfolding of a history of Yoknapatawpha county, a mythical Mississippi community, which showed his convictions about the decadence of the south. The picture as a whole was grim and dark, but Faulkner had convictions about the solutions to the problem which became increasingly clear. These were set forth most clearly and explicitly in *Intruder in the Dust* (1948).

Steinbeck's career—marked by uneven achievements—began with a historical novel, *Cup of Gold* (1929), wherein he voiced the distrust of society, the glorification of the anarchistic individualist typical of the rebellious 1920s. Later, however, he appeared to move toward a belief in the possibilities of collectivist action as a pathway to man's salvation. Such, at least, was the implication of *In Dubious Battle* (1936) and *The Grapes of Wrath* (1939), generally considered to be his best books. The latter was a narrative, interrupted by prose poem interludes, of the migration of a dust bowl family to California. Their great discovery, symbolically set forth, was the necessity for co-operation between the poor and downtrodden for the betterment of the lot of men.

Lyric Fictionists.—One of the interesting developments in fiction was a movement in the direction of poetry. The increased tendency to select details and to endow them with symbolic meaning, the tendency to set down the thought processes and emotions of the characters and the tendency to make use of rhythmical prose gave fiction more of a lyrical quality than it had had. In varied ways, Crane, Norris, Cabell, Dos Passos,

Hemingway, Steinbeck and Faulkner all showed the trend—in passages, in short stories, even in entire novels. Faulkner showed the trend at its worst in *A Fable* (1954) which, ironically, won a Pulitzer prize.

Lyricism bulked increasingly in the writings of Willa Cather. *O Pioneers* (1913), *The Song of the Lark* (1915) and *My Antonia* (1918) contained poetic passages about the disappearing frontier and the creative efforts of frontier folk. *A Lost Lady* (1923) was elegiac in form, and *Death Comes for the Archbishop* (1927) was an exaltation of the past and of spiritual pioneering. Katherine Anne Porter, whose works took the form of novelettes, wrote more in the style of the metaphysical poets. Her use of the stream-of-consciousness method in *Flowering Judas* (1930) and *Pale Horse, Pale Rider* (1939) had the complexity, the irony and the symbolic sophistication characteristic of this group.

Another leading poetic fictionist was Thomas Wolfe, the author of four large novels which in effect were one long lyrical recording of the author's life—of his strivings, his thoughts and his feelings turned into fiction. *Look Homeward, Angel* (1929), *Of Time and the River* (1935), *The Web and the Rock* (1939) and *You Can't Go Home Again* (1940) dealt with a figure much like Wolfe—his youth in the south, his young manhood in the north and his eternal search to fulfill a vision. The memories of the author of details of his past and his contemplations upon the significances and meanings of his experiences were set forth in prose reminiscent of Walt Whitman's poetry. The books, despite their chaotic qualities (or perhaps because of them) were essentially lyrical achievements.

Criticism.—Some historians, looking back over the first half of the 20th century, were inclined to think that it was particularly noteworthy for its achievements in literary criticism. Beyond doubt, it was true that criticism thrived as it had not for several generations, that it was an important influence on the shaping of literature and that it quickened the perceptions of readers.

The period began with a battle between a group who called themselves the Humanists—a group which stood for the older values in judging literature—and a group who urged that old standards be overthrown and new ones adopted. The Humanists, allied in some ways with the earlier Brahmin critics of New England, were led by Irving Babbitt, Harvard university professor, whose scholarly books included *The New Laokoön* (1910), *Rousseau and Romanticism* (1919), *Democracy and Leadership* (1924) and *On Being Creative* (1932). In these books and in vigorous essays Babbitt preached his belief that man has a tendency toward the good, the true and the beautiful and a contrary tendency toward evil. The application of this scheme was that modern writers with their tendency toward naturalism—the base in man's nature—were a vicious influence. Such associates of Babbitt as Paul Elmer More (1864–1937), Norman Foerster (1887–   ) and Stuart Sherman (1881–1926) upheld this claim. The leader of the opposition was the pugnacious H. L. Mencken, who doubted that the values of the Humanists existed and who claimed that, regardless, the duty of writers was to present "the unvarnished truth" about life. His magazine articles and books of *Prejudices* (1919–27) shouted this claim, as did the writings of his associates, a number of figures of lesser fame. In the end, the results were the liberation of literature from a number of ancient restrictions and the progress of naturalism.

Socio-Literary Critics.—In this period of social change, it was natural for a number of critics to consider literature in its relationships to society and to politics. Their study took many forms, but consistently this group judged books: (1) as reflections of society; or (2) as expressions of social truth. Van Wyck Brooks and V. L. Parrington illustrated the two chief approaches. Brooks, who wrote numerous studies which embodied such an interest, in *America's Coming of Age* (1915) and *The Ordeal of Mark Twain* (1920) scolded the U.S. public for making it all but impossible for an author to realize his genius fully. Later books by him presented rather different pictures, but developed from similar interests: *The Flowering of New England* (1936), *New England: Indian Summer* (1940), *The World of Washington Irving* (1944), *The Times of Melville and Whitman* (1947) and *The Confident Years* (1952) showed how in the past many authors expressed their time and their locality. Parrington, in *Main Currents in American Thought* (1927–30) re-evaluated American literature in terms of its adherence to the tenets of Jeffersonian democracy.

The growth of Marxian influence upon thinking in the 1920s and 1930s was shown in several books. V. F. Calverton set forth the general principles of Marxian evaluations of literature in *The Newer Spirit* (1925), and in *The Liberation of American Literature* (1932) he judged literary figures on the basis of their representation of life and their implementation of the rise of the proletariat. Granville Hicks's *The Great Tradition* (1933) applied similar yardsticks. Many writers for a time followed the same lines of thinking, but beginning in 1939, as enthusiasm for communism waned, many (including Hicks) renounced the dogmas of the party. Some critics, however, found that some Marxian suggestions for critical procedures could be adapted and amended so as to be of service. Two outstanding critics in this group were Edmund Wilson (1895–   ) and Kenneth Burke (1897–   ).

Moral-Aesthetic Critics.—But Wilson and Burke, like many critics of the time, were interested in other matters than the relationships between literature and society; they were interested in both analyzing and evaluating literary creations. In a sense, they, like other moral-aesthetic critics, were eager to see in detail how a literary work was constructed; but they were equally eager to assess the sensitivity which the literary work embodied. Morton D. Zabel (1901–64), himself a leading critic and scholar of modern criticism, suggested that Henry James had aptly formulated the aim of this group when he said, "The critic's judgment, being in the best analysis an estimate of the artist's quality of mind, is at once moral and aesthetic." The group was distinguished, as a result, for its close attention to the creative process involved in a work and for care in ranking the work.

As in poetry, T. S. Eliot here proved a leader. In essays and books; *e.g.*, *The Use of Poetry and the Use of Criticism* (1933), he subjected writings and writers to careful analyses, and developed the thesis that "the 'greatness' of literature cannot be determined solely by literary standards; though we must remember that whether it is literature or not can be determined only by literary standards." Others used various ways of discussing relationships between form and value—R. P. Blackmur in *The Double Agent* (1935), Allen Tate in *Reactionary Essays on Poetry and Ideas* (1936), John Crowe Ransom in *The World's Body* (1938), Yvor Winters in *Maule's Curse* (1938) and Cleanth Brooks in *The Well Wrought Urn* (1947). This new school greatly advanced ways of discussing literary structure; it also distinguished and applied contrasting methods of evaluation. Like other groups, it therefore did much to advance the understanding and appreciation of literature. (W. BL.)

AFTER WORLD WAR II

The United States emerged from World War II as a world superpower, and its literature correspondingly took on a new, worldwide interest. Three of the nation's leading novelists received Nobel Prizes—Faulkner in 1949, Hemingway in 1954, and Steinbeck in 1962—and in each instance the award was presumed to have been made on the strength of work done in earlier decades. As the period began, many established writers were still on the scene: besides the above-named novelists there were, notably, the poets Robert Frost, Wallace Stevens, Marianne Moore, E. E. Cummings, William Carlos Williams, and (in a Washington, D.C., madhouse after years of self-imposed exile) Ezra Pound. But the most interesting work of all these writers already seemed to lie behind them. Several of them, in fact, soon were gone: the 1955–65 decade, for example, saw the death of both Hemingway and Faulkner as well as of Frost, Cummings, Stevens, and Williams. The deaths of such figures—writers who had given modern American writing its very tone and quality—made Americans realize how rich a literary era they had lived through; it also made them aware that that era was gone and done, revocable only in the boneyard of literary history.

Impending for postwar writing in the U.S., then, was a changing of the guard. To be sure, there was little in the way of consensus as to the old guard's successors or the qualities of the new era—a lack of consensus that extended from fiction through poetry to drama. Characteristic of American literature during the postwar period was its great diversity: of style, temperament, goals, and accomplishments.

Fiction.—In the middle 1960s the novelist and critic, George P. Elliott, noted that "a vast variety of fiction is being written in the United States. . . . Issues of high importance are being dealt with seriously. Both social criticism in the form of satire and psychological investigation in forms of autobiography are flourishing." There was multiplicity; and out of this multiplicity had come a great deal that was distinctly new in the American dream. In 1949 the critic Philip Rahv had delivered a stunning indictment of American literature for what he considered to be its split personality. Viewing American writing historically in a famous essay titled "Paleface and Redskin," Rahv placed the nation's major writers in two camps: the "Redskins," epitomized by the coarse-grained, naturalistic poet Walt Whitman, and the "Palefaces," typified by the cerebrally genteel novelist Henry James. In Rahv's view most American writing, major and minor, down to the time of his own essay, fell into one or the other of these two camps—to no good effect. He showed why no love was lost between the two traditions, and predicted that if they were not somehow reconciled American fiction was doomed to remain less than fully mature.

Yet much of the sting seems to have gone out of Rahv's indictment. For the two apparently divergent strains in American writing have made large strides toward reconciliation, and nowhere more impressively than in the work of two of America's most highly regarded novelists: Saul Bellow (1915–) and Ralph Ellison (1914–). Each has used elements of both the paleface and redskin traditions to produce powerful imaginative works.

Bellow's subject—most notably in *The Adventures of Augie March* (1953) and *Herzog* (1964)—is modern man in urban America. His heroes are generally Jewish intellectuals sent forth by their creator on an odyssey of the world of the 20th century. Beset by all the problems of modernity, Bellow's heroes resolutely refuse to settle for easy solutions; instead, they struggle to make sense of a complex and often cruel world and, in the process, to find their place in it. Bellow's novels are marked by wit, intelligence, sympathy, a high comic sense, and extraordinary craftsmanship. Essentially, they all ask the same question: How should a good man live?

Ellison's subject is the travail of the Negro in America, searching for "his place in history." Yet, unlike other American Negro writers, Ellison does not write of travail alone; he insists, in fact, that to picture the Negro as a mere sponge soaking up punishment and indignities, to exclude the joy and often heroic dignity that are an integral part of Negro life, is to diminish the Negro as a human being. Aside from some short stories and a volume of essays, Ellison has thus far written only one novel, *Invisible Man* (1952), but it has attained the standing of a contemporary American classic and is considered by many American critics to be the most successfully executed novel written in the U.S. since World War II. As with Bellow, what lifts Ellison above most of his fellow novelists—in addition to a superior craftsmanship—is his disdain for easy solutions, his appreciation of the complexity of life, and his concern for the dignity of men.

Bellow and Ellison are not alone among American writers in sensing that modern man exists in a state of crisis in the world. There has been a general awareness among American novelists that the categories, styles, and modes of thought traditional to American literature no longer apply with the old force. Those novelists whose work has not been touched by this awareness have had little or no serious effect on U.S. readers in the postwar period. Thus, while a number of new talents have emerged, there have also been casualties among novelists of established reputation. John Dos Passos, James T. Farrell, John O'Hara, and John Steinbeck, to name a few, continue to produce novels but fail to find a serious readership. On the other hand, the largely autobiographical novels of Henry Miller (1891–), an expatriate who did most of his writing in Paris in the 1930s, gained wide popularity. That most American novelists appear to be perceiving the world in radical flux is illustrated particularly well in the work of Norman Mailer (1923–). Although regarded one of the nation's most talented novelists, Mailer has been called a genius who has not yet found his subject. Since Mailer has written four novels—*The Naked and The Dead* (1948), *Barbary Shore* (1951), *The Deer Park* (1955), and *An American Dream* (1965)—on four different subjects in four utterly different styles, there would seem to be some truth to the remark. Two other important writers of Mailer's generation are James Jones (1921–) and William Styron (1925–). Jones in *From Here to Eternity* (1951) and Styron in *Lie Down in Darkness* (1951) produced remarkable first novels; and while their succeeding efforts were not up to the high mark set by their first novels, critics held to the hope that both might develop into major American novelists.

If the postwar period in American fiction can be said to have any dominant style, that style is irony. Joseph Heller (1923–), in *Catch 22* (1961), launched a searing attack on the stupidity of military bureaucracy and the inhumanity of war with irony perhaps the sole weapon in his arsenal. In *Goodbye, Columbus* (1959) Philip Roth (1933–), a writer whose most admirable talents are comical, took the brickbat, again utilizing irony, to those of his fellow American Jews who, though heirs to an altogether too long history of persecution, have closed their hearts to the suffering of others. Bruce Jay Friedman (1930–), whose first novel, *Stern*, was published in 1962, has shown how the middle-class dream of a peaceful life in the suburbs can turn into a nightmare. J. P. Donleavy (1926–), in *The Ginger Man* (1955), which is set in Dublin, presents a hero who, from all appearances, is totally irrational; but then the novel gradually reveals an entire world—with its wars, its frantic pace, the clutter of its creature comforts—that is itself more than a little mad. Once this is recognized, Donleavy's hero comes to seem much more sensible. After all, this satiric novel asks, in an insane world who is to say who the sane man is?

An even more extreme reaction has been registered by two American writers who, over the past decade, have established reputations as fantasists: Hubert Selby (1928–) and William Burroughs (1914–). In *Last Exit to Brooklyn* (1964), Selby's collection of stories, the modern world is portrayed as one vast, unrelieved hell. Burroughs' first book, *The Naked Lunch* (1959), is made up of obscene fragments from the fantasy life of a dope addict. There has even arisen among American novelists a group of writers—prominent among them are Terry Southern (1924–), Thomas Pynchon (1937–), and Kurt Vonnegut, Jr. (1922–)—whom the critics have labeled Black Humorists. Essentially satirists all, their basic novelistic strategy is to turn humour on its head and wring comedy out of the bleakest of situations.

But the content of American fiction during the postwar period has proved as various as the form of fiction itself. J. D. Salinger (1919–), John Updike (1932–), John Cheever (1912–), John Barth (1930–), and Flannery O'Connor (1925–64), to cite five instances, are novelists who fit conveniently into no group or category. Not a greatly productive writer, Salinger has published a novel, *Catcher in the Rye* (1951), and collections of short stories that include elaborately interwoven episodes in the life of an unusual New York family named Glass. At the centre of all Salinger's fiction are children, teen-agers, or young people on the edge of adulthood—characters who have neither lost their spontaneity nor been corrupted by the world of their parents. Updike has long been considered one of America's most promising novelists; his verbal gifts are dazzling. In *Rabbit, Run* (1960), *The Centaur* (1963), and *Of the Farm* (1965) Updike deals with such traditional themes as adolescence, marriage, and the family, but his lyrical treatment of them, aglitter with well-turned metaphor and polished simile, sets him apart from his contemporaries. Cheever is a writer who appears more at home in the short-story form, though he has produced two novels, *The Wapshot Chronicle* (1957) and *The Wapshot Scandal* (1964). He does a great many things well, but perhaps his claim to uniqueness is to be found in his treatment of middle-class, suburban America: he has an extraordinary ability to endow the lives of rather humdrum characters with a mythical element that produces a vividness and excitement one would hardly have thought possible. Barth, in *The Floating Opera* (1956), *The End of the Road* (1958), and *Giles Goat-Boy* (1966), has established a reputation as America's leading novelist of ideas. What is so impressive about Barth's work is the ingenious imaginative structures he develops to house his sophisticated, often quite subtle ideas. In *The Sot-Weed Factor* (1960) he produced a novel whose subject matter and syntax were 18th century in tone and feeling; the book is perhaps the greatest imaginative tour de force of the postwar period.

Flannery O'Connor died in 1964 at age 39. Her last book, a collection of stories, *Everything That Rises Must Converge* (1965), demonstrated her continued growth as a wholly original talent: all of her work was of a brilliance rare in any era. Miss O'Connor lived almost all her life in Georgia. A devout Roman Catholic, she combined immense comic gifts with an essentially religious concern with corruption in the human heart. "She wrote best in the short story," one critic noted after her death, "and has left a handful of them at least that are likely to last as long as literacy."

Miss O'Connor's Catholicism recalls the fact that the postwar period has seen the emergence of the minority-group writer as a force in American literature. To be sure, Jews, Negroes, and other representatives of minorities have always published novels in the United States, but during this period their work is for the first time being widely read; for the first time, too, they seem not merely in the mainstream of American fiction but absolutely central to it. Ralph Ellison, for example, as a Negro writer deals with explicitly Negro themes. Another prominent Negro writer is James Baldwin (1924–), whose novels, *Go Tell It on the Mountain* (1953) and *Another Country* (1962), and collections of essays, *Notes of a Native Son* (1955) and *The Fire Next Time* (1963), have served as a stimulus for the civil rights movement.

In addition to Bellow, Friedman, and Roth, other writers who treated of specifically Jewish subject matter were Bernard Malamud (1914–) in such novels as *The Assistant* (1957) and *The Fixer* (1966), and Herbert Gold (1924–) in *Love and Like* (1960) and *Fathers* (1967). The stories of J. F. Powers (1917–) and his novel *Morte d'Urban* (1962) are concerned almost exclusively with Catholics in the Middle West. Harry Mark Petrakis (1923–) writes of the Greek neighbourhoods of Chicago.

Strangely enough, in the midst of this profusion of talent and variety of works one of the more insistent literary questions of the period has been: Is the novel a dying form? Those who believe that it is argue that sociologists have taken over much of what was once the exclusive domain of the novelist—namely, the description of manners and milieu and the topical investigation of values. Moreover, they point to the great interest that has been aroused by nonfiction—essays, autobiographies, polemics—produced by American writers, and to the paucity of fictional masterpieces to have come out of the same period. (*See* below, *Literary and Social Criticism.*) Further grist for their argument was provided by the appearance, early in 1966, of *In Cold Blood*, a work of reportage that utilizes fictional techniques. The book is a chronicle, written with scrupulous regard for detail, of the murder of a Kansas family, and of the thoughts, lives, and, finally, the capture of the killers, two young ex-convicts who were eventually hanged for the crime. Its author, Truman Capote (1925–), himself a practising novelist of 20 years' standing, called *In Cold Blood* a "non-fiction novel" and claimed he had created a new genre. The implication (though Capote himself has not drawn it) is that this new genre has made the novel, indeed fiction itself, obsolete. The point will remain academic, of course, as long as novelists continue to turn out work of high quality.

Poetry.—The poetry of the postwar period also exemplified the theme of diversity in American literature. Although they greatly respected their predecessors of the early decades of the 20th century (especially Eliot and Pound) the poets who came to literary maturity after World War II moved in a different direction—or, to be more precise, in a number of different directions.

One group of poets—it would be incorrect to designate them a movement—tended to forsake the obscurantism, the surrealism, the free forms of previous American poetry and sought, instead, dramatic or dialectical organization. Some cultivated the epigram, the poetry of wit; most tended to be more rigid in versification, with a strong return to the use of rhyme. Poets who had anticipated these developments now came into their own: for example, Stanley Kunitz (1905–), little appreciated heretofore, won a Pulitzer Prize in 1959 for *Selected Poems 1928–1958*. Karl Shapiro (1913–), who was later to change his style decisively, was a Pulitzer prizewinner for *V-Letter and Other Poems* in 1945; Robert Lowell (1917–) for *Lord Weary's Castle* in 1947; Richard Wilbur (1921–) for *Things of This World* in 1957; W. D. Snodgrass (1926–) for *Heart's Needle* in 1960; Alan Dugan (1923–) for *Poems* in 1962; Louis Simpson (1923–), for *At the End of the Open Road* in 1964; and John Berryman (1914–) for *77 Dream Songs* in 1965. Two other distinguished poets in this group, Randall Jarrell (1914–65) and Theodore Roethke (1908–63), died prematurely; many critics thought Roethke, a Pulitzer winner in 1954, the ablest poet of his generation. In 1959 Lowell published *Life Studies,* of which Kunitz remarked that it gave him "the sense . . . of witnessing a preliminary breakthrough into the poetry of the next decade" since it "recaptured a good portion of the territory that poetry has for so long yielded to the novel." The poems in *Life Studies* show a loosening of form and combine the extremely personal with a concern with the surface of life—a concern more often found in fiction. To some degree such poetry was foreshadowed by Gwendolyn Brooks (1917–) in *Annie Allen,* the Pulitzer Prize volume for 1950, a largely autobiographical work recounting a Negro girl's life in the urban ghetto from childhood to maturity. Robert Penn Warren (1905–), similarly, experimented with what might be called the versified novel in *Brother to Dragons* (1953). In the 1960s, Anne Sexton (1928–) and Snodgrass were also publishing verse narrative; but the genre had not yet produced a recognized masterwork.

All the above-named poets, however different in temperament and style, could be said to represent the poetry Establishment in postwar American literature. The prestigious teaching jobs, the literary prizes, the grants, publication in the widely-read magazines, went to them. But there were also other forces at work in American poetry. There was, for example, something of a Midwest renaissance, evidence for which was supplied by the appearance in 1967 of an anthology entitled *Heartland: Poets of the Midwest.* Allied with this trend was a rather loosely organized movement, if one could call it that, led by the poet Robert Bly (1926–), which disdained English verse models and called for an image-driven poetry written in a wholly American idiom. The late William Carlos Williams proved an influence on a group known as the Black Mountain School (from a short-lived college of that name in North Carolina); its reigning doyen was Charles Olson (1910–) and its leading younger light was Robert Creeley (1926–). On the West Coast, mostly in and around San Francisco, a group known as the Beats began to be heard from in the mid-1950s; their work showed the influence of Walt Whitman, along with that of the recent American writers Kenneth Rexroth (1905–), a poet, critic, and translator; Kenneth Patchen (1911–), a surreal novelist and poet; and the prose writer Henry Miller. The wild rash of publicity the Beats attracted made any sort of serious appraisal of their work difficult. But when the noise died down and the movement, as such, seemed to have fallen away, two poets among the Beats were still highly regarded: Allen Ginsberg (1926–) and Lawrence Ferlinghetti (1919–). A good deal of poetry reflecting the Beats' freedom of form and thought continued to be written. Much of this later poetry was of a private, almost subterranean nature, and much of it was closely allied with protest movements.

Drama.—Perhaps because of ever-increasing costs of production, which permitted only "smash hits" to prosper, most dramatic writing in the postwar period was unexperimental and, by and large, unexceptional. Symptomatic were Pulitzer awards in 1950 and 1960 to authors of musical comedies and in 1958 and 1961 to dramatizations of novels. Furthermore, the best young literary minds showed a decided lack of interest in the theatre, many preferring to write for the films or television. So marked was this apathy that the Ford Foundation, in the early 1960s, began to offer grants to novelists and poets to study with a theatre company, in the hope they would one day write for the stage. The only significant theatre to come out of the project was Robert Lowell's anthology piece *The Old Glory* (1964), which included "Benito Cereno," from Melville's story; it was produced off Broadway. A hopeful sign was the establishment of several repertory companies—notably Tyrone Guthrie's Minneapolis group and the company at the Lincoln Center for the Performing Arts, in New York—though for the most part repertory companies tend to produce actors and directors rather than dramatists.

Over the postwar period two playwrights, both fairly successful at the box office, predominated: Tennessee Williams (1914–   ) and Arthur Miller (1915–   ). Williams' experimentation in *The Glass Menagerie* (1944), which used a narrator, unorthodox settings, and poetic dialogue, continued in *A Streetcar Named Desire* (1947), *Cat on a Hot Tin Roof* (1955), *Orpheus Descending* (1957), *Suddenly Last Summer* (1958), and *The Night of the Iguana* (1962). Miller was experimental in a variety of ways in *All My Sons* (1947), *Death of a Salesman* (1949), *The Crucible* (1953), and *A View from the Bridge* (1955). By the 1960s, however, there were signs that the talents of both playwrights were wearing rather thin. Williams began revising some of his work; and Miller's *After the Fall* (1964), a largely autobiographical play about his experience of McCarthyism and his marriage to the movie actress Marilyn Monroe, was deemed a failure. Yet at their best both Williams and Miller wrote plays that are classics of the American theatre.

The situation among younger American playwrights was quite fluid. One of the most promising, Lorraine Hansberry (1930–65), whose *A Raisin in The Sun* (1959) centred on Negro family life in Chicago, died young. Several younger dramatists seemed likely to have noteworthy careers: Jack Gelber, Frank Gilroy, and Jack Richardson, among others. Edward Albee (1928–   ), after early critical successes off-Broadway, established his reputation firmly with *Who's Afraid of Virginia Woolf?* (1962), an acidly witty play about the married life of intellectuals.

From a literary point of view, not only did the greatest share of the excitement of American dramatic writing after the war shift from Broadway to off-Broadway but indeed, in many cases, from off-Broadway to "off-off-Broadway." Much avant-garde theatre in the 1960s was produced in lofts and cabarets. One such group, the American Place Theater, went so far as to issue no invitations to critics, thus knowingly eschewing an opportunity for financial success. Improvisation, shock, and the Absurd were features of a good deal of "off-off" writing; the inspiration for it came not from American but older European playwrights—Beckett, Ionesco, Brecht—whose plays were much in vogue in the U.S. after 1945. Although purely American drama had undoubtedly fallen from the heights attained by such playwrights as Odets and O'Neill, the hope for its revival rested with young dramatists who were attempting, in the 1960s, to bring a special American quality to plays of a kind pioneered by the preceding generation in Europe.

Literary and Social Criticism.—The poet Randall Jarrell once described the postwar era in American literature as the Age of Criticism. At no other time in American literature, indeed, had so much criticism, both literary and social, been written. For the most part, literary criticism was centred in the universities. Freudians, Marxists, Symbolists, Archetypal Mythists—criticism of every stripe flourished. Perhaps for the first time anywhere, in America young men went off to college intending to become literary critics, in much the way a young man might set out to study dentistry. Yet, even given this institutionalization, not much changed in criticism itself. Yvor Winters, John Crowe Ransom, Cleanth Brooks, and others who had made their mark in an earlier era (*see* above, *From 1914 to 1945: Criticism*) still predominated; many fostered disciples who spread the master's word to other campuses.

In literary scholarship, three American critics turned out biographies that were acknowledged masterworks. In the first three volumes of his intended four-volume study of Henry James (*Henry James: Untried Years 1843–1870* [1953]; *Conquest of London 1870–1881* [1962]; *Middle Years 1882–1895* [1962])

Leon Edel produced a work that was at once subtle, masterly, and provocative. Ernest Samuels' three-volume biography of Henry Adams (*Young Henry Adams* [1948]; *The Middle Years* [1958]; *The Major Phase* [1964]) demonstrated a cultivated and refined literary craftsmanship rare in any era. Richard Ellmann's biography of James Joyce (*James Joyce* [1959]) was widely, and properly, regarded as definitive.

Alongside the more traditional critics, whose work was generally anchored in theory and doctrine, critics of another kind arose in the U.S. after the war. These tended to eschew the highly theoretical, preferring to deal with each new book, movement, or other literary phenomenon in a direct, topical, and often personal way. Nor did they restrict themselves to the exclusively literary. History, social theory, and politics, as they saw it, also fell within their purview. Thus, Irving Howe (1920–   ) established his reputation with *Politics and the Novel* (1957). Alfred Kazin (1915–   ), after producing a history of American literature, *On Native Grounds* (1942), turned to autobiography, which he used as a vehicle for investigating the social and cultural atmosphere of the 1930s. Norman Podhoretz (1930–   ), editor of the intellectual journal *Commentary*, perhaps went further than either Howe or Kazin when, in *Doings and Undoings* (1964), he flatly announced that the issues brought to the surface by authors interested him as much as, and sometimes more than, their books.

Bridging the two critical traditions—the scholarly and the intellectually committed—was Edmund Wilson, whose position on the postwar scene was reminiscent of Samuel Johnson in 18th-century England. Critic, historian, playwright, novelist, social reporter, travel writer, chronicler—Wilson was the complete man of letters. When, in 1963, Wilson was awarded the Presidential Medal of Freedom, the accompanying citation read: "Critic and historian, he has converted criticism itself into a creative act, while setting for the nation a stern and uncompromising standard of independent judgment."

Among others who turned away from an exclusive interest in literature was the Negro novelist James Baldwin, whose *Notes of a Native Son* (1955) and *The Fire Next Time* (1963) combined autobiography and radical social criticism in some of the most elegant and powerful essays of the postwar period. Paul Goodman (1911–   ), originally a novelist and poet, became best known for his study of the young in America, *Growing Up Absurd* (1960), and his other polemical and utopian writings. Norman Mailer, in *The Presidential Papers* (1963) and *Christians and Cannibals* (1966), wrote some of the most stunning political reportage in that genre's history. The novelist and poet Robert Penn Warren took time out from his literary work to compose *Who Speaks for The Negro?* (1965), one of the most forceful and intelligent books on the civil rights movement. Indeed, many of the problems and issues to arise in postwar America seemed so abrasive and urgent that literary men often found themselves stepping out of their conventional role and dealing with them directly in social criticism.

See also references under "American Literature" in the Index.

(J. Ep.)

BIBLIOGRAPHY.—For bibliographies see *Literary History of the United States,* vol. iii, comp. by Thomas H. Johnson (1948), and supplement, ed. by Richard M. Ludwig (1959); *Eight American Authors,* ed. by Floyd Stovall (1956). The periodicals *American Literature* (1929–   ) and *American Quarterly* (1949–   ) both have current bibliographies. A comprehensive descriptive bibliography of American authors from 1780 to 1950 is J. Blanck (comp.), *Bibliography of American Literature,* which began to appear in 1955.

History and Criticism: For general surveys, *see* the introductory chapters in *The Literature of the United States,* an anthology ed. by W. Blair, T. Hornberger and R. Stewart, 2 vol. (1953); *Literary History of the United States,* ed. by Robert E. Spiller and others, 2 vol. (1949); V. L. Parrington, *Main Currents in American Thought,* 3 vol. (1927–30); Leon Howard, *Literature and the American Tradition* (1960). *For the Early Period:* M. C. Tyler, *A History of American Literature During the Colonial Period, 1606–1765,* 2 vol. (1878), *The Literary History of the American Revolution, 1763–1783,* 2 vol. (1897). *For the 19th Century:* F. O. Matthiessen, *American Renaissance* (1941); F. L. Pattee, *A History of American Literature Since 1870* (1915). *For the 20th Century:* Willard Thorp, *American Writing in the Twentieth Century* (1960); Alan S. Downer, *Fifty Years of American Drama, 1900–1950* (1951); Joseph Warren Beach, *American Fiction, 1920–1940* (1941); Frederick J. Hoffman, *The Modern Novel in America,*

1900–1950 (1951); Louise Bogan, *Achievement in American Poetry, 1900–1950* (1951); Morton D. Zabel (ed.), *Literary Opinion in America* (1951).
(W. BL.)

AMERICAN MEDICAL ASSOCIATION.

The American Medical association was founded on May 5, 1847, when 250 delegates representing more than 40 medical societies and 28 colleges met in the hall of the Academy of Natural Sciences in Philadelphia, Pa. The objective of the association is the promotion of the science and art of medicine and the betterment of public health. It is a physicians' organization existing to serve the public and its physician members and their interests.

The association's first president was Nathaniel Chapman of Pennsylvania. Each year a new president succeeds to office, a position which he holds without pay and to which he is elected by the members of the house of delegates. This body consists of delegates mainly from state medical associations. Each state medical association is permitted a delegate for each 1,000 physician members of the A.M.A. or fraction thereof. This body meets twice each year to consider and determine the basic policies by which the association shall operate. Between meetings of the house the affairs of the association are governed by a board of trustees, the members of which are elected by the house for five-year terms of office.

Headquarters are at Chicago, Ill. In Washington, D.C., is another office which serves as a point of information for those seeking data on problems of interest to doctors, their patients and their national association. In the headquarters office are various departments concerned with a wide variety of medical topics, including geriatrics, maternal and child care, hospital facilities, medical education, nutrition, drugs, insurance plans, scientific exhibits, health in rural areas, medical films, medical books and journals, mental health, cost of medical care and health of industrial workers. There are other offices of similar importance which aid in the work of the association. Also located at the headquarters are chemical laboratories and other laboratories for testing physical devices.

Much of the work is done under the guidance of committees and councils, the membership of which is either elected by the house of delegates or appointed by the board of trustees. Other work is undertaken in departments. All offices have executive heads who are responsible for administrative activities. The council on medical education and hospitals was created in 1904, the council on pharmacy and chemistry (after 1957 the council on drugs) in 1905, the bureau of investigation (which looks into harmful health practices) in 1906, the chemical laboratory in 1906, and the bureau of health education in 1910.

Publications of the association include the *Journal of the American Medical Association* (weekly); nine journals issued monthly and devoted to medical specialties such as surgery and diseases of children; *Today's Health* (formerly *Hygeia*), a monthly magazine for the general public; and books relating to drugs, uniform nomenclature for illnesses and operations and other special medical subjects.

The American Medical association aids in the development of standards for the improvement of medical care. It does not develop or enforce laws; it has no legal power. Its effects, far reaching in many aspects of medical care, are possible because of the desire of its members and others to follow standards or worthwhile suggestions. Thus any improvements in drug therapy, insurance coverage, medical education standards, medical care in rural areas, or other act on which the A.M.A. may have had an effect stems from moral persuasion and not from legal enforcement.
(A. E. SH.)

AMERICAN MISSIONARY ASSOCIATION, THE,

was incorporated in 1846 by merger of three antislavery societies, worked for the abolition of slavery, and developed educational opportunities for freed Negroes in the South. The interdenominational organization at first supported several foreign missions in addition to many home missionaries, but gave up overseas work after the Civil War. When the Union armies began freeing slaves during the Civil War, the AMA opened schools for them. It cooperated for several years with the Freedman's Bureau, organized by the U.S. Congress, and absorbed the Bureau's assets when it was disbanded. The AMA eventually founded more than 500 schools in the South. While concentrating on the education of freed slaves, the schools were open to all and often operated as integrated institutions during the Reconstruction period. As the South recovered from the war and developed public school systems, the AMA gave their grade and secondary schools to the public systems and concentrated on improving and expanding colleges for Negroes in the South. Colleges supported by the AMA had integrated faculties and were open to all, but were attended primarily by Negroes. In the late 1960s it controlled Talladega and LeMoyne colleges, retained an interest in Hampton Institute, Fisk University, and Atlanta University, and contributed to the support of Dillard, Huston-Tillotson, and Tougaloo. The primary support of the AMA came from the Congregationalists. In 1937 it voted to have the Congregational Board for Home Missions (now the United Church Board for Homeland Ministries) act as fiscal agent. It remains a separate corporation.

AMERICAN REVOLUTION

(1775–1781), known also as the American War of Independence. This war, by which the British colonies along the Atlantic seaboard definitely separated themselves from the mother country, began with the skirmish at Lexington in Massachusetts, on April 19, 1775, and was virtually ended by the capitulation of Cornwallis at Yorktown, Va., on Oct. 19, 1781. In this article the progress of the war itself is alone considered; its other aspects are treated under UNITED STATES (OF AMERICA): *History* and related articles such as DECLARATION OF INDEPENDENCE; WASHINGTON, GEORGE. From a military standpoint it was a conspicuous and instructive conflict. It was conspicuous as being the most famous struggle in history where colonial dependencies defeated their mighty parent state, though the powerful aid of France, Spain and Holland must never be forgotten. It was instructive as presenting exceptional conditions and consequent errors in the attempt to put down the revolt. The reasons for Great Britain's failure appear in the progress of the war, which assumed two distinct stages: operations in the north, followed by operations in the south. In point of time and energy, military activity was about equally divided between these two fields. As the naval operations in connection with the war have a European interest as well, they are dealt with in a separate section.

LAND CAMPAIGNS

To strike at the rebellion first in the north was a natural move. To King George and his ministry, Massachusetts was the hotbed of disloyalty, the head and front of opposition to their colonial policy, and there coercion should begin. It was also a convenient point for a prompt display of authority, as the town of Boston was the headquarters of Gen. Thomas Gage, recently appointed royal governor of Massachusetts and commander of the king's troops in North America. He had with him four regiments of regulars, the initial force with which to overawe the restless and defiant population in his vicinity.

Lexington and Concord.—While Gage is to be credited with advising his government that not less than 20,000 men would be necessary for the work in hand, he proceeded after some delay to suppress warlike preparations near Boston. His first determined effort brought about the skirmish of April 19, 1775 (*see* LEXINGTON), in which a detachment sent to seize some military stores collected at Concord suffered heavily at Lexington, Concord and other places, at the hands of the surrounding militia. This encounter roused the New England colonies, and in a few days about 16,000 of their townsmen marched in small bands upon Boston to protest against and resist further incursions: and in this irregular body we have the nucleus of the colonial forces which carried the war through. A noteworthy incident of the Lexington affair, and characteristic of the attitude which the provincials had maintained and continued to maintain for another year, was the official representation to the king that the regulars were the first to fire, and that the colonials returned the fire and fought through the day in strict defense of their rights as Englishmen. Who actually fired the first shot immortalized as "the shot heard round the world,"

"THE LANDING OF THE BRITISH FORCES IN THE JERSEYS," UNDER GENERAL CORNWALLIS, NOV. 20, 1776. DRAWING ATTRIBUTED TO LORD RAWDON, BRITISH OFFICER, A MEMBER OF THE LANDING PARTY

no man knows. The colonists repeated their professions of loyalty to his majesty and the principles of the English constitution. Conscious, nevertheless, that a struggle impended, they instantly sent word to all the other colonies, whose Whig elements sympathetically responded to the alarm. The war had opened.

Siege of Boston.—The home government extended its precautions and preparations. Gen. Sir William Howe, who succeeded Gage in the chief command in October, and Gen. Sir Henry Clinton and Gen. John Burgoyne were sent out at once with reinforcements. Cornwallis followed later. These four generals were identified with the conduct of the principal operations on the side of the British. The force at Boston was increased. The continental congress at Philadelphia, acting for the 13 colonies, voted general defensive measures, called out troops and appointed George Washington of Virginia commander in chief. Before he reached the camp forming around Boston, a second and more important collision took place. On June 17, 1775, occurred the battle of Bunker hill (*q.v.*), in which, although victorious, the British suffered heavily, losing one-third of their force in storming the hastily constructed lines of the rebels. In moral effect the battle proved anything but a defeat to the Americans, who drew a cordon of works around Boston, hemming Howe's army in a contracted, and, as it proved, untenable, position. On July 3, Washington took command of the American forces at Cambridge, Mass., and attempted to train and organize them on a sound basis. He also proceeded with what is known as the siege of Boston, which was marked by no special incident, and closed with the American seizure of Dorchester heights and the evacuation of the town by the British on March 17, 1776, Howe sailing to Halifax, Nova Scotia.

Ticonderoga and Quebec.—While the main interest centred at this point, the year 1775 was marked by two enterprises else-

where. Fort Ticonderoga, the key to the passage of Lakes George and Champlain to Canada, was surprised and taken on May 10 by a small band under Col. Ethan Allen, yielding a valuable supply of cannon. Col. Benedict Arnold headed an expedition through the Maine woods to effect the capture of Quebec, where Sir Guy Carleton commanded. Gen. Richard Montgomery joined Arnold when he was near the city, and the combined force assaulted Quebec on Dec. 31, only to meet with complete defeat. Montgomery was killed and many of his men taken prisoners. Demonstrations against Canada were soon discontinued, and Arnold drew off the remnant of his army in May 1776.

Campaign of 1776.—The events of 1775, though partly favourable to America, were but a prelude to the real struggle to come. For the campaign of 1776 both sides made extensive preparations. To the home government the purely military problem, although assuming larger dimensions and more difficulties, still seemed to admit of a simple solution, namely, to strike hard where the rebellion was most active and capable of the longest resistance. Defeated there, it would quickly dissipate in all quarters. As more than one-half of the population and resources of the colonists lay north of Chesapeake Bay—New England alone having an estimated population of over 700,000 persons—it was only a question as to what point in this area should be made the future base of operations. Largely upon the representations of Howe, Burgoyne and others, it was determined to shift the field from Boston to New York city, from there to hold the line of the Hudson river in co-operation with a force to move down from Canada under Carleton and Burgoyne, and thus effectually to isolate New England.

Upon this plan the new campaign opened in June 1776. Howe, heavily reinforced from home, sailed on June 10 from Halifax to New York and on July 5 encamped on Staten Island. Washington, anticipating this move, had already marched from Boston and fortified the city. His left flank was thrown across the East river beyond the village of Brooklyn, while his front and right on the harbour and North or Hudson river were open to a combined naval and military attack. The position was untenable since the British absolutely dominated the waters about Manhattan. Howe drove Washington out of New York, and forced the abandonment of the whole of Manhattan Island by three well-directed movements upon the American left. On Aug. 22 he crossed the narrows to the Long Island shore with 15,000 troops, increasing the number to 20,000 on the 25th, and on the 27th surprised the Americans, driving them into their Brooklyn works and inflicting a loss of about 1,400 men. (See LONG ISLAND.) Howe has been criticized, rightly or wrongly, for failing to make full use of his victory. Washington skilfully evacuated his Brooklyn lines on the night of the 29th, and in a measure relieved the depression which the defeat had produced in his army. On Sept. 15, Howe crossed the East river above the city, captured 300 of the militia defending the lines and occupied the city. Washington had withdrawn his main army to the upper part of the island. A skirmish, fought the next day, opposite the west front of the present Columbia university, and known as the affair of Harlem heights, cost the British a loss of 70 of their light infantry. Delaying until Oct. 12, Howe again moved forward by water into Westchester county, and marching toward White Plains forced another retreat on Washington. In the fight on Chatterton hill at White Plains, on Oct. 28, an American brigade was defeated. Instead of pressing Washington further, Howe then returned to Manhattan Island, and, Nov. 16, captured Fort Washington with nearly 3,000 prisoners. This was the heaviest blow to the Americans throughout the war in the north. The British then pushed down through New Jersey with designs on Philadelphia. Washington, still retreating with a constantly diminishing force, suddenly turned upon Lieut. Col. Johann Rall's advanced corps of Hessians at Trenton on Dec. 26, and captured nearly 1,000 prisoners. This brilliant exploit was followed by another on Jan. 3, when Washington, again crossing the Delaware, outmarched Cornwallis at Trenton, and marching to his rear defeated three British regiments and three companies of light cavalry at Princeton, N.J. Marching on to Morristown, Washington encamped there on the flank of the British advance in New Jersey, thus ending the first campaign fought on the new issue of American independence, which had been declared on July 4, 1776.

The Decisive Year of 1777.—While these closing successes inspirited the Americans, it was undeniable that the campaign had gone heavily against them. Having raised a permanent force called the Continental line, they awaited further operations of the enemy. Following up the occupation of New York, Howe proceeded in 1777 to capture Philadelphia. Complete success again crowned his movements. Taking his army by sea from New York to the head of the Chesapeake, he marched up into Pennsylvania, where Washington had repaired to watch him, and on Sept. 26 entered the city. The Americans attempted to check the advance of the British at the Brandywine river, where an action occurred on the 11th resulting in their defeat (see BRANDYWINE, BATTLE OF); and on Oct. 4, Washington directed a well-planned attack upon the enemy's camp at Germantown on the outskirts of the city, but failed of success. (See GERMANTOWN.)

Howe's victorious progress in Pennsylvania was neutralized by disasters farther north. Indeed his whole expedition to seize "the enemy's capital" was nothing less than an abandonment of an expedition from the north with which he was expected to co-operate. Clinton, whom he left at New York, protested against this folly to the last. Lord George Germain in England was only in part to blame. Burgoyne marched from Canada in June 1777, with a strong expeditionary force, to occupy Albany and put himself in touch with Howe who was expected to come up the Hudson. Driving the Americans under Gen. Arthur St. Clair out of Ticonderoga, and making his way through the deep woods with difficulty, he reached the Hudson at Fort Edward on July 30. Gen. Philip Schuyler, commanding the Americans in that quarter, retreated to Stillwater, 30 mi. above Albany, barricading the roads and impeding Burgoyne's progress. Unjustified dissatisfaction with his con-

duct led congress to replace Philip Schuyler by Gen. Horatio Gates. On Aug. 13, Burgoyne dispatched a force to Bennington, Vt., under the German colonel, Friedrich Baum, to capture stores and overawe the country. On the 16th Baum was attacked by Gen. John Stark with the militia from the surrounding country, and was overwhelmed. Colonel Breyman, marching to his relief, was also routed. The misfortune cost the British 1,000 men. Equally unfortunate was the fate of an expedition sent under Col. Barry St. Leger to co-operate with Burgoyne by way of the Mohawk valley. On Aug. 6 he was met at Oriskany by Gen. Nicholas Herkimer and forced to retreat. Despite these disasters Burgoyne pushed south to Stillwater, where he was defeated by Gates's improvised army of continentals and militia in two battles on Sept. 19 (Freeman's farm) and Oct. 7 (Bemis's height). On the 17th he was forced to surrender. (See SARATOGA, BATTLES OF.) This disaster was followed by the alliance between America and France in 1778, and later by the addition of Spain and Holland to England's enemies—events of far-reaching importance.

Northern Campaigns, 1778-80.—A noteworthy movement, in 1778-79, was the expedition of George Rogers Clark, under the authority of the state of Virginia, against the British posts in the northwest. With a company of volunteers Clark captured Kaskaskia, the chief post in the Illinois country, on July 4, 1778, and later secured the submission of Vincennes, which, however, was recaptured by Gen. Henry Hamilton, the British commander at Detroit. In the spring of 1779 Clark raised another force, and recaptured Vincennes from Hamilton. This expedition did much to free the frontier from Indian raids, gave the Americans a hold upon the northwest, of which their diplomats probably took advantage in the peace negotiations, and later, by giving the states a community of interest in the western lands, greatly promoted the idea of union.

In 1778 Sir Henry Clinton succeeded Howe in the chief command in America. With fewer resources than his predecessor, he could accomplish practically nothing in the north. In June 1778, he evacuated Philadelphia, with the intention of concentrating his force at New York. Washington, who had passed the winter at Valley Forge, overtook him at Monmouth, N.J., and in an action on June 28 both armies suffered about equal loss. Thereafter (except in the winter of 1779, at Morristown) Washington made West Point on the Hudson the headquarters of his army, but Clinton avowed himself too weak to attack him there. In 1779 he attempted to draw Washington out of the highlands, with the result that in the maneuvers he lost the garrison at Stony Point, 700 strong, the position being stormed by Gen. Anthony Wayne with the American light infantry on July 16. During the summer Gen. John Sullivan marched with a large force against the Indians (all the Iroquois tribes except the Oneidas and part of the Tuscaroras siding with the British during the war) and against the Loyalists of western New York, who had been committing great depredations along the frontier; and on Aug. 29 he inflicted a crushing defeat upon them at Newtown, on the site of the present Elmira. In addition several Indian villages and the crops of the Indians were destroyed in the lake region of western New York.

Meanwhile the co-operation of the French became active. In July Comte de Rochambeau arrived at Newport, R.I., occupied by the British from 1776 to the close of 1779. An unsuccessful attempt was made to drive them out in 1778 by the Americans assisted by the French admiral Charles Hector d'Estaing and a French corps. The year 1780 is also marked by the treason of Gen. Benedict Arnold (q.v.), and the consequent execution of Maj. John André (q.v.). Minor battles and skirmishes occurred until in Aug. 1781 Washington undertook the project of a combined American-French attack on Cornwallis at Yorktown, Va., the success of which was decisive of the war.

Campaign in Georgia.—The inadequate results of the British campaigns against the northern colonies in 1776 and 1777 led the home government to turn its attention to the weaker colonies in the south. Operations in the north were not to cease, but a powerful diversion was now to be undertaken in the south with a view to the complete conquest of that section. Success there would facilitate further movements in the north. An isolated attack on

"THE BATTLE OF LEXINGTON," APRIL 19, 1775. COLONIAL MILITIA DISPERSES AFTER VOLLEY FROM MAJOR PITCAIRN'S BRITISH REGULARS. ENGRAVING BY AMOS DOOLITTLE, CONNECTICUT MILITIAMAN

Charleston, S.C., had been made by Sir Henry Clinton and Sir Peter Parker as early as June 1776, but this was foiled by the spirited resistance of Gen. William Moultrie; after 1778 the southern attempts, stimulated in part by the activity of the French in the West Indies, were vigorously sustained. On Dec. 29 of the same year Col. Archibald Campbell with an expeditionary corps of 3,500 men from Clinton's army in New York, captured Savannah, Ga., defeating the American force under Gen. Robert Howe. In the following month he pushed into the interior and occupied Augusta.

Gen. Benjamin Lincoln, succeeding Howe, undertook to drive the British out of Georgia, but Gen. Augustine Prevost, who had commanded in Florida, moved up and compelled Lincoln to retire to Charleston. Prevost, making Savannah his headquarters, controlled Georgia. In Sept. 1779 he was besieged by Lincoln in conjunction with a French naval and military force under Admiral d'Estaing, but successfully repelled an assault (Oct. 9), and Lincoln again fell back to Charleston. In this assault Count Casimir Pulaski, on the American side, was mortally wounded.

The prestige thus won by the British in the south in 1779 was immensely increased in the following year, when they victoriously swept up through South and North Carolina. Failing to achieve any advantage in the north in 1779, Sir Henry Clinton, under instructions from his government, himself headed a combined military and naval expedition southward. He evacuated Newport, R.I. (Oct. 25), left New York in command of the German general Wilhelm von Knyphausen, and in December sailed with 8,500 men to join Prevost of Savannah. Cornwallis accompanied him, and later Lord Rawdon joined him with an additional force. Marching upon Charleston, Clinton cut off the city from relief, and after a brief siege compelled Lincoln to surrender on May 12. (*See* CHARLESTON.)

The loss of this place and of the 5,000 troops included in the surrender was a serious blow to the American cause. The apparent submission of South Carolina followed. In June Clinton returned to New York, leaving Cornwallis in command, with instructions to reduce North Carolina also. Meanwhile an active and bitter partisan warfare opened. The British advance had been marked by more than the usual destruction of war; the Loyalists rose to arms; the Whig population scattered and without much organization formed groups of riflemen and mounted troopers to harass the enemy. Little mercy was shown on either side. The dashing rider, Col. Banastre Tarleton, cut to pieces (April 14, 1780) a detachment of Lincoln's cavalry, and followed it up by practically destroying Buford's Virginia regiment near the North Carolina border.

On the other hand, daring and skilful leaders such as Francis Marion and Thomas Sumter kept the spirit of resistance alive by their sudden attacks and surprises of British outposts. Hanging Rock, Ninety-Six, Rocky Mount and other affairs brought their prowess and devotion into notice. By the month of Aug. 1780, with the main British force encamped near the North Carolina line, the field seemed clear for the next advance.

The threatening situation in the Carolinas alarmed congress and Washington and measures were taken to protect the distressed section. Before Cornwallis could be brought to bay he was faced successively by four antagonists, the generals Gates, Nathaniel Greene, La Fayette and Washington. They found in him the most capable and dangerous opponent of the war. Greene called him "the modern Hannibal." With Lincoln's surrender of nearly all the Continental soldiers in the south, a new force had to be supplied to meet the British veterans. Two thousand men, mainly the Maryland line, were hurried down from Washington's camp under Johann de Kalb; Virginia and North Carolina put new men into the field, and the entire force was placed under command of General Gates. Gates marched towards Camden, S.C., and on Aug. 16 encountered Cornwallis near that place. Each army by a night march attempted to surprise the other, but the British tactics prevailed, and Gates was utterly routed. The reputation he had won at Saratoga was ruined on the occasion by overconfidence and incompetence; De Kalb was killed in the action. Gen. Greene, standing next to Washington as the ablest and most trusted officer of the Revolution, succeeded Gates. Cornwallis marched leisurely into North Carolina, but before meeting Greene some months later he suffered the loss of two detachments sent at intervals to disperse various partisan corps of the Americans. On Oct. 7, 1780, a force of 1,100 men under Major Patrick Ferguson was surrounded at King's Mountain, S.C., near the North Carolina line, by bands of riflemen under Col. Isaac Shelby, Col. James Williams, Col. William Campbell and others, and after a desperate fight on the wooded and rocky slopes, surrendered. Ferguson himself was killed.

On Jan. 17, 1781, Gen. Daniel Morgan was attacked at Cowpens, southwest of King's Mountain, by Colonel Tarleton with his legion. Both were leaders of repute, and a most stirring action occurred in which Morgan, with Col. William Washington leading his cavalry, practically destroyed Tarleton's corps. Despite the weakening his army suffered by these losses, Cornwallis marched rapidly through North Carolina, giving Greene a hard chase nearly to the Virginia line. On March 15 the two armies met at Guilford courthouse (near the present Greensboro, N.C.) and a virtually drawn battle was fought. The British, by holding their ground with their accustomed tenacity when engaged with superior numbers, were tactically victors, but were further weakened by a loss of nearly 600 men. Greene, cautiously avoiding another Camden, retreated with his forces intact. With his small army, less than 2,000 strong, Cornwallis declined to follow Greene into the back country, and retiring to Hillsborough, N.C., raised the royal standard, offered protection to the inhabitants, and for the moment appeared to be master of Georgia and the two Carolinas. In a few weeks, however, he abandoned the heart of the state and marched to the coast at Wilmington, N.C., to recruit and refit his command.

At Wilmington the British general faced a serious problem, the solution of which upon his own responsibility unexpectedly led to the close of the war within seven months. Instead of remaining in Carolina he determined to march into Virginia, justifying the move on the ground that until Virginia was reduced he could not firmly hold the more southern states he had just overrun. This decision was subsequently sharply criticized by Clinton as unmilitary, and as having been made contrary to his instructions. To Cornwallis he wrote in May: "Had you intimated the probability of your intention, I should certainly have endeavoured to stop you, as I did then as well as now consider such a move likely to be dangerous to our interests in the Southern Colonies." The danger lay in the suddenly changed situation in that direction; as Gen. Greene, instead of following Cornwallis to the coast, boldly pushed down towards Camden and Charleston, S.C., with a view to drawing his antagonist after him to the points where he was the year before, as well as to driving back Lord Rawdon, whom Cornwallis had left in that field. In his main object, the recovery of the southern states, Greene succeeded by the close of the year; but not without hard fighting and repeated reverses. "We fight, get beaten, and fight again," were his words. On April 25, 1781, he was surprised in his camp at Hobkirk's hill, near Camden, by Lord Rawdon and defeated, both sides suffering about an equal loss. On May 22 he attempted to storm the strong British post at Ninety-Six but was repulsed; and finally on Sept. 8 he fought the last battle of the war in the lower southern states at Eutaw Springs, S.C. In the first part of the action Greene was successful after a desperate conflict; in the pursuit, however, the Americans failed to dislodge the British from a stone house which they held, and their severe loss in both engagements was over 500 men. The British lost about 1,000, one-half of whom were prisoners. Better success attended the American partisan operations directed by Greene and conducted by Marion, Sumter, Andrew Pickens, Henry Lee and William Washington. They fell upon isolated British posts established to protect the Loyalist population, and generally captured or broke them up. Rawdon found himself unable with his diminishing force to cover the country beyond Charleston; and he fell back to that place, leaving the situation in the south as it had been in the early part of 1780. On the American side, Greene was hailed as the deliverer of that section.

Virginia Campaign.—Cornwallis, meantime, pursued his Virginia project. Leaving Wilmington, N.C., on April 25, 1781, he reached Petersburg on May 20. There he found British detachments, 2,000 strong, composed of troops whom Clinton had sent down separately under Gen. Benedict Arnold and Gen. William Phillips to establish a base on the Chesapeake, as a diversion in favour of the operations of Cornwallis in the Carolinas. Virginia at the moment presented a clear field to the British, and they overran the state as far north as Fredericksburg and west to Charlottesville. At the latter place Jefferson, governor of the state, barely escaped capture by Tarleton's men. A small American force under La Fayette, whom Wayne reinforced during the summer, partially checked the enemy. At Green Spring, near Jamestown Island, La Fayette boldly attacked his antagonist on July 6, but had to save himself by a hasty retreat. Early in August Cornwallis retired to Yorktown to rest and await developments. There he fortified himself, and remained until the American-French military and naval combination appeared and compelled his surrender on Oct. 19. (*See* YORKTOWN.)

With this event war operations ceased. Preliminary articles of peace, signed on Nov. 30, 1782, were followed by a definitive treaty concluded on Sept. 3, 1783. Charleston, S.C., was evacuated late in 1782; New York on Nov. 25, 1783. The reasons of Great Britain's misfortunes and failure may be summarized as follows: Misconception by the home government of the temper and reserve strength of her colonists, a population mainly of good English blood and instincts; disbelief at the outset in the probability of a protracted struggle covering the immense territory in America; consequent failure to dispatch sufficient forces to the field; the safe and Fabian generalship of Washington; and finally, most decisive of all, the French alliance and European combination by which at the close of the conflict Britain was without a friend or ally on the continent. (H. P. J.; C. H. VAN T.)

BIBLIOGRAPHY.—J. W. Fortescue, *History of the British Army,* vol. iii (1902); C. H. Van Tyne, *American Revolution* (1905); George O. Trevelyan, *American Revolution* 4 vol. (1909–12); Edward Channing, *A History of the United States* vol. iii (1905–25); John C. Miller, *The Triumph of Freedom, 1775–83* (1948); Willard M. Wallace, *Appeal to Arms, a Military History of the Revolution* (1951); Lynn Montross, *Rag, Tag and Bobtail, the Story of the Continental Army, 1775–83* (1952); Christopher Ward, *The American Revolution* 2 vol. (1952); John R. Alden, *The American Revolution, 1775–83* (1954).

THE WAR AT SEA

The American Revolution took on a prominently maritime aspect in its early phases. Heavily in debt from recent wars, England was also faced with a constantly increasing demand for overseas markets and marine expansion, because of the industrial revolution through which she was then passing. Beginning in 1764 parliament passed a series of laws to raise revenue through taxing the sea-borne imports of the colonies, and to favour English maritime trade by discriminations against colonial shipping. Laws looking solely to the latter object had been in existence for many years, but custom had given them little attention. A large and prosperous colonial merchant marine had grown up on a technically illegal trade and had become an important element in the economic life of the colonies. Consequently the enforcement of these Navigation acts was the cause of much hardship and resentment in America. As early as 1764 a British schooner so engaged was fired on in Rhode Island waters. In 1769 the sloop "Liberty," similarly employed, was seized and burned at Newport. Such incidents became more common as British coercive measures increased, and when war finally broke there was a popular uprising on the sea quite comparable to that on land.

The onset of the Revolution found the colonies with no naval forces whatever but with a large maritime population and many merchant vessels employed in domestic and foreign trade. This merchant service was familiar not only with the sea, but also with warfare. Colonial ships and seamen had taken a prominent part in the large naval expeditions against Cartagena and Louisburg, had engaged in privateering during the more recent French war, and even during peace had habitually gone armed as a protection against pirates. In 1775 it was therefore natural that considerable numbers of colonial merchant vessels should turn to privateering. This practice was continued on a large scale until the close of the war under legal authorization of individual colonies and of the continental congress. Records are incomplete but indicate that well over 2,000 private armed vessels were so employed during the course of the war, carrying more than 18,000 guns and 70,000 men. In addition, several of the colonies organized state navies which also engaged in preying upon hostile commerce. These operations were on such a scale that they must be regarded as a primary American military effort of the war. Together with the operations of a few continental vessels they constituted the only sustained offensive pressure brought to bear by the Americans which materially affected the attitude of the British people towards peace. Such injury was done British commerce as to increase insurance rates to unprecedented figures, to seriously reduce available sources of revenue and to alarm the seacoast population.

In its military-naval aspect the war followed two distinct phases, the first ending when France allied herself with the colonies in 1778, until which time Britain had no foreign enemy, and was free to concentrate her whole strength against the Americans. In the second phase England ultimately had to contend against the fleets of France, Spain and Holland, and her consequent inability to meet the naval necessities in American waters was a major influence in the final and decisive campaign ending at Yorktown. With the large navy available during the first three years of the Revolution it was repeatedly urged by Viscount Barrington, the British secretary of war, that: "Conquest [of the colonies] by land is unnecessary when the country can be reduced first by distress, and then to obedience by our marine totally interrupting all commerce and fishery, and even seizing all ships in the ports with very little expense and less bloodshed." Instead of adopting such strategy the British naval forces were used primarily in direct support of army operations and in the protection of their own maritime commerce.

The pressing lack of munitions for the colonial army was the chief impulse in the creation of regular American naval forces. This need caused Benedict Arnold, formerly a sea captain, to march from the siege of Boston, and in association with Ethan Allen to make a surprise capture of the well-stocked stronghold of Ft. Ticonderoga on Lake Champlain, May 10, 1775. This seemingly minor event had far-reaching results. Not only were munitions obtained, but the prompt seizure of all lake watercraft also gave to the colonies control of the only practicable line of communications from the St. Lawrence river to the Hudson valley. A few weeks after he took command of the Continental army besieging Boston, Washington organized a naval force to prey upon the British water communications of that port, and in this way essential munitions were obtained. In Oct. 1775 congress voted funds for the first units of a small fleet of eight vessels which sailed from the Delaware on Feb. 17, 1776, under Com. Esek Hopkins (q.v.). The objective was Nassau in the Bahama Islands, where a quantity of powder was stored. This was captured on March 3, and the valuable munitions taken in to New London. Meantime the British army under Howe had evacuated Boston and gone by sea to Halifax. Correctly estimating the future probabilities, Washington marched to New York and also provided for the defense of Lake Champlain. For the campaign of 1776 the British plan was to isolate New England by capturing and holding the line of the Hudson river. With this end in view, Howe, heavily reinforced, sailed in June for New York, while other forces undertook an advance via Lake Champlain. Here Arnold had retreated after an unsuccessful attack on Quebec, and had begun the construction of a fleet to retain control of the lake.

During the summer a British army of nearly 13,000 men advanced from Quebec to the lake but was compelled to halt until a sufficient naval force could be constructed to cope with Arnold's rapidly growing fleet. This they were able to do after some months through the assistance of artisans from their ships in the St. Lawrence river, and by reassembling on the lake a large vessel whose dismantled parts had been transported in small boats from Quebec. In a series of naval actions on Oct. 11, 12 and 13, Arnold's fleet of 15 vessels was destroyed. Meantime Howe had gained possession of the lower Hudson, but the season was now so late that the British command on Lake Champlain decided to abandon further operations until spring, and retreated into Canada. When in June 1777 Burgoyne renewed the advance from the north, Howe had shifted his operations by sea for the vicinity of Philadelphia, and Burgoyne was forced to surrender at Saratoga (Oct. 17, 1777) from lack of support. Thus had Arnold's fleet, by delaying the British army for nearly a year, contributed largely to the decisive battle of Saratoga which proved to be a turning point in the war.

Impressed by the evidence of American strength given at Saratoga, and wishing to recover her losses to England in previous wars, France entered into a treaty of alliance with the United States in Feb. 1778. The event marked the beginning of an entirely new phase in the war. Henceforth naval power was to be employed on a great scale and to vitally affect military operations in America, as well as the course of European history, and the fate of valuable possessions from the West Indies to the East Indies.

A French fleet under Admiral d'Estaing sailed from Toulon in April 1778, bound for America. Advance news of its coming caused a hasty evacuation of the Delaware by the British fleet then acting in support of the army occupying Philadelphia. Fearing to risk the loss of the army in the event of meeting a superior French fleet at sea, the British command decided to march the troops, bereft of their line of supply, by land to New York, where a junction with the fleet was again made. D'Estaing appeared off the port a few days later, but having missed the opportunity of a decisive victory in the Delaware, he sailed for Newport in accordance with an understanding made with Washington. While preparations were in progress at Newport for a joint attack by Americans and French upon the British garrison of 6,000 troops, the British fleet approached, having been reinforced from England. D'Estaing hastily abandoned the land operations and put to sea to meet them. A partial engagement ensued, followed by a gale which so damaged the ships as to persuade the French admiral to

BY COURTESY OF YALE UNIVERSITY ART GALLERY

"SURRENDER OF GENERAL BURGOYNE," OCT. 17, 1777. BURGOYNE PROFFERS SWORD TO GENERAL GATES AT SARATOGA. PAINTING BY JOHN TRUMBULL

"SURRENDER OF CORNWALLIS AT YORKTOWN," OCT. 19, 1781. GEN. BENJAMIN LINCOLN LEADS BRITISH OFFICERS BETWEEN FRENCH AND AMERICAN GENERALS. PAINTING BY JOHN TRUMBULL

go to Boston for extensive repairs (Aug. 1778). Because of this the American army before Newport was withdrawn. Meantime a second and more powerful French fleet had been fitted out at Brest with the object of indirectly assisting their overseas naval forces by holding the main strength of the British navy to its home waters. In July 1778 a large but indecisive fleet action was fought off Ushant. Under cover of these major operations Capt. John Paul Jones (q.v.) of the Continental navy with a small squadron based on French ports, carried on a series of raids against British coastal shipping.

At this period of history considerations of weather during the winter season usually caused the transfer of naval operations from the western hemisphere to the West Indies, which held the further attraction of being the richest of the world's commercial regions in value of products. Therefore when D'Estaing sailed from Boston in Nov. 1778 his destination was the Caribbean sea, for which locality most of the British fleet in America also sailed on the same day. The latter took 5,000 troops with them, thus greatly reducing the land forces opposed to the Continental army. During the next four years the West Indies were the scene of a large-scale naval war, the forces on each side being often augmented from home, and in the case of the French fleet, by Spanish reinforcements.

Meantime in the autumn of 1778 the British had sent a small expedition from New York, under naval convoy, to Savannah, which place was taken. These operations were extended to the neighbourhood of Charleston during the following year, and attracted the attention of D'Estaing. Arriving off Savannah from the West Indies with his whole fleet in Aug. 1779, he failed in an attempt to retake the place. Nevertheless, upon receiving news of the Savannah affair, General Clinton at New York was so concerned over the safety of his diminished army in the north that he abandoned Newport in order to concentrate his forces against possible French attack.

The summer of 1779 also saw the ill-starred Penobscot expedition. A British military-naval force having occupied what is now Castine, Me., the Massachusetts government undertook to dislodge it. A fleet of 40 vessels including three of the Continental navy and 20 transports, in all carrying 200 guns and 3,000 men, sailed from Boston and began its attack on the British position on July 25. Fighting continued afloat and ashore until Aug. 13, when a superior British naval squadron arrived from New York

and put Americans to rout.

John Paul Jones, operating from French bases with a small squadron, made a cruise around the British Isles from Aug. to Oct. 1779. Many prizes were taken and the British frigate "Serapis" was captured after a memorable duel with the American flagship "Bon Homme Richard." The success of these operations was greatly aided by the fact of the absence in distant waters of practically the whole naval strength of Great Britain, and by the operations in the English channel of a large combined French and Spanish fleet in support of a threatened invasion of England from France.

On the American coast the year 1780 saw the inception of the British policy of conquering the Carolinas which involved such a division of forces as to bring about the ultimate loss of the war. An army detachment escorted by naval forces was sent from New York and captured Charleston in May. These operations were placed in some jeopardy by the arrival of a French squadron with 6,000 troops at Newport in July, but this was offset by British naval reinforcements reaching New York.

Not meeting with the success which had been anticipated, Cornwallis, commanding the southern British army in America, decided upon a movement into Virginia where naval support could be utilized to better advantage. Meantime on the James river, Benedict Arnold (then under British allegiance) had been ravaging the country, and at the request of Washington the French squadron at Newport had proceeded to the Chesapeake; but after an indecisive action with a British squadron (March 1781), had returned to Newport. Cornwallis joined Arnold on March 20, at Petersburg, with the intention of undertaking vigorous offensive operations in Virginia. But the commander in chief, General Clinton, who was at New York, felt that the forces available were insufficient for such an undertaking, and ordered Cornwallis to intrench himself in a strong position which would control a fleet anchorage. Cornwallis complied by moving to Yorktown, where he arrived on Aug. 22 with 7,000 troops.

After the alliance with France the most important development on the American side was the emergence of General Washington as a master of military-naval strategy. The astonishing evacuation of Philadelphia by the British in great haste (1778) merely because of the probable arrival of a superior French fleet made a profound impression upon Washington. Thereafter he undertook only minor land operations for nearly three years, holding his army in readiness for joint action with a fleet, which he constantly sought. When D'Estaing attempted the capture of Savannah (Sept.–Oct. 1779), Washington vainly urged him to come north and attack New York jointly with the American army. Upon arrival of the handsome reinforcement of Rochambeau's army, July 1780, he held it inactive for nearly a year until De Grasse's fleet was expected. Summing up his operations for the year 1780 Washington wrote Franklin in Paris, "Disappointed . . . especially in the expected naval superiority, which was the pivot upon which everything turned, we have been compelled to spend an inactive campaign, after flattering prospects at the opening of it."

Washington finally got a fleet through sending his aide to Paris. When Adm. François de Grasse sailed from France for the West Indies he had orders to co-operate with Washington's armies in a joint operation. Exchanging messages by fast frigate, the general and admiral concerted a plan for a junction of fleet and armies for action against the British in lower Chesapeake bay. Later Cornwallis entrenched at Yorktown to facilitate receiving critically needed logistic aid from the British fleet. Thus Yorktown became the primary objective of the Franco-American military-naval forces upon their arrival in that locality.

In conformity with the agreed plan Rochambeau's army joined Washington north of New York and the two marched for northern Chesapeake bay down which they were to go principally by water transport, under cover of French naval vessels upon their arrival. Concurrently De Grasse sailed from his Haitian base, wisely deferring the dispatch of a large merchant convoy in order to take north his full force of 28 ships-of-the-line and 3,300 troops. Meanwhile, Adm. Samuel Hood of the British West Indies fleet became concerned for the security of New York. Although not aware of De Grasse's departure for the north, fearing such a move Hood started north five days after De Grasse, with 14 ships-of-the-line.

With faster ships following a more direct route, Hood was the first to reach the Chesapeake. Finding no sign of French ships he hastened to the protection of New York, where he was joined by five ships-of-the-line under Adm. Thomas Graves. The latter being senior took command of the whole force. Soon information was received of the sailing from Newport of eight ships-of-the-line under Admiral De Barras. Correctly assuming that this Newport squadron was bound for Chesapeake bay, Graves sailed with his 19 capital ships in ample time to intercept it. When Graves reached the Chesapeake entrance De Barras had not yet arrived, but a startling sight greeted him,—the forest of masts of the great fleet of De Grasse from the West Indies, at anchor just inside Cape Henry. The French admiral was equally astonished as he had not been aware of Hood's presence in northern waters.

This mutual surprise, Sept. 5, 1781, seems to have shaken the judgment of both admirals. De Grasse hastily got underway and stood out to sea in a long column, thus exposing his fleet to piecemeal destruction as it emerged from the harbour. Instead of exploiting such a golden opportunity, Graves deliberately awaited the exit of the French, outnumbering him 24 to 19, before attacking from his advantageous "weather gauge." The poorly executed British attack resulted only in leading squadrons of the two fleets being engaged in the late afternoon. For three days the two fleets were becalmed, and, within sight of each other, drifted nearly 100 mi. southward. One damaged British ship was abandoned and sunk by her crew. When a breeze sprang up the French got it first and hastened back to the Chesapeake where De Barras had arrived meanwhile. With this French reinforcement, the British were decisively outnumbered and Graves sealed the fate of Cornwallis by sailing for New York. In the opinion of the British naval historian, Sir William M. James, this was "the decisive battle of the war."

Washington's armies, aided by water transportation down Chesapeake bay under French naval protection, did not arrive before Yorktown until Sept. 28. Within a few days Cornwallis received a message from General Clinton in New York, stating that a reinforced British fleet of 26 ships-of-the-line and 5,000 troops would sail from New York about Oct. 5 for his relief. With hopes thus buoyed, Cornwallis continued resistance. On Oct. 13 he tried a retreat across the York river, hoping to reach a position more favourable to a relieving fleet for supplying him. Failing in the attempted retreat and in urgent need of supplies, he surrendered on Oct. 19, it being apparent that Clinton had been overly optimistic and that the indispensable relief by water could not possibly reach him in time.

In retrospect the American Revolution is seen to have developed from small beginnings into one of the greatest naval wars in history. During its progress the early issues of colonial maritime rights and independence became subordinated in European eyes to that of the control of the then commercially very valuable West Indies, and other objects. The fleet operations which in a few weeks decided the fate of Yorktown, and of the American cause, were merely incidental to the vast naval campaign carried on over a period of five years in Caribbean, European and Indian waters.

See also references under "American Revolution" in the Index.

BIBLIOGRAPHY.—Alfred T. Mahan, *The Major Operations of the Navies in the War of American Independence* (1913); Gardner W. Allen, *A Naval History of the American Revolution,* 2 vol. (1913); Sir W. Laird Clowes, *The Royal Navy: A History,* 7 vol. (1897–1903); Geoffrey A. Callender, *The Naval Side of British History* (1924); Sir William M. James, *The British Navy in Adversity* (1926); Louis Edouard Chevalier, *Histoire de la Marine française pendant la Guerre de l'Indépendence Américaine* (1877); Dudley W. Knox, *The Naval Genius of George Washington* (1932), and *A History of the United States Navy* (1936; rev. ed. 1948). (D. W. K.)

AMERICANS FOR DEMOCRATIC ACTION, a liberal independent political organization operating on national, state, and city levels in the United States. ADA was formed in January 1947 by labour leaders, civic leaders, representatives of the national congress and state legislatures, intellectuals and academicians who were liberal in national affairs, international in world outlook, and anti-Communist by conviction. It is devoted to the propagation of liberal ideas, the election of liberal public officials, and the passage of liberal legislation. The headquarters of the organization are in Washington, D.C., and the membership numbers about 50,000.

The organization was vigorously attacked by both the extreme right and the extreme left for some positions it took, among them the successful fight led by ADA for a strong civil rights platform in the 1948 Democratic convention, ADA's exposure of the Communist domination of the Progressive Party, and its vanguard battle against Sen. Joseph R. McCarthy and various right-wing movements residual from McCarthyism. With the election of John F. Kennedy as president of the United States in 1960, many ADA leaders and members were appointed to key positions in the new administration. Americans for Democratic Action believes that planned, reasoned processes of government can be used to bring about necessary social and economic changes and at the same time to protect individual rights and liberties. It sought to focus attention on the paramount issues of the day and to bring them from the discussion stage into the arena of practical political decision and action. (R. R. N.)

AMERICAN STATES, ORGANIZATION OF. On April 30, 1948, the 21 republics of the Western Hemisphere at the ninth conference of American states at Bogotá, Colombia, signed the charter of their new organization, replacing the Union of American Republics (*see* PAN-AMERICAN CONFERENCES). Ratification of the charter by the 14th state took place on Dec. 13, 1951, giving formal legal validity to the treaty which had been in practical effect since its signature.

Like the charter of the United Nations, the charter of the Organization of American States begins by stating the general nature and purposes of the organization, which do not differ substantially from the traditional objectives of the Union of American Republics. The two succeeding chapters of the charter set forth the principles of the organization and the fundamental rights and duties of member states, constituting a valuable summary of the basic law of the inter-American regional system, supplemented by provisions for the pacific settlement of disputes and for collective security in accordance with the provisions of the Treaty of Reciprocal Assistance signed at Rio de Janeiro in 1947.

The charter next sets forth the organs of the organization. The International Conference of American States, described as the Inter-American Conference, was made the supreme organ of the organization, functioning on the basis of the legal equality of the members, and holding its meetings every five years. Supplementing the conference, and equal in authority to it, is the meeting of consultation of foreign ministers, to be held to consider problems of an urgent nature and of common interest to the American republics. The meeting of foreign ministers was given the further duty of serving as the organ of consultation in the event of an armed attack or an act of aggression within the territory of an American republic, bringing into effect the provisions of the Treaty of Reciprocal Assistance. The third organ, in permanent session, is the Council, successor of the former governing board of the Pan American Union, composed of one representative of ambassadorial rank from each member state and acting as a sort of executive committee of the organization, supervising the activities of its central permanent secretariat, the Pan American Union (which name had hitherto been used popularly for the larger Union of American Republics), and having at its service three advisory councils, dealing respectively with economic and social, juridical, and cultural matters. In addition the Council of the organization supervises the work of the specialized conferences called from time to time to deal with special technical matters and of the various specialized organizations of a permanent character.

While the charter described the Organization of American States as a regional agency within the United Nations, in actual fact the organization was completely independent, merely subordinating its measures of enforcement to the obligations of its members as members also of the United Nations. Close cooperation, however, was maintained between the two organizations, particularly in respect to the work of their technical organs.

The collective security provisions of the Treaty of Reciprocal Assistance represented the general acceptance by the American states of the principle underlying the Monroe Doctrine (q.v.), that an attack upon an American state by a non-American state would be considered as an attack upon all, each state being obligated to assist in meeting the attack while awaiting measures of collective action by the whole group. The "continentalization" of the Monroe Doctrine, as it has been called, thus created obligations for the other American states without restricting the right of the U.S. to take immediate action in self-defense.

The adoption of the charter of 1948 not only established a system of regional collective security but created new agencies for the promotion of the economic and social welfare of the American states. An Economic and Social Council was created to assist in the development of the natural resources, agriculture, and industry; a separate Cultural Council was established to bring about greater mutual understanding through the exchange of teachers and students and the diffusion of educational material. The work of these agencies was greatly stimulated by the adoption in August 1961 of the Charter of Punta del Este establishing an Alliance for Progress, by which, under the leadership of the United States, the American states engaged in what was described as "a vast effort to bring a better life to all the peoples of the continent." The objectives of the Alliance included a more equitable distribution of the national income, acceleration of industrialization, increase of agricultural productivity, elimination of illiteracy, improvement of housing, stable price levels, measures of economic integration, and the stability of foreign exchange. The United States on its part agreed to provide the major part of the estimated $20,000,000,000 of external financing over the coming ten years; the Latin-American states were to provide the internal financing and to undertake the reforms required to achieve the objectives of the Alliance. A special Committee of the Alliance for Progress (CIAP) was formed to supervise its activities. Economic integration, after the manner of the Common Market in Europe, showed encouraging results, particularly in Central America; and industrialization made rapid progress. Of special significance in the activities of the Alliance for Progress were the measures of fiscal and agrarian reform and of public administration, looking to a fairer distribution of the national wealth and to cooperation on the part of the local communities in carrying out the projects agreed upon by the Committee of Experts.

In May 1965, after the United States had sent troops to the Dominican Republic to help restore order following an attempted military coup, the U.S. government proposed that the OAS create a peace force to take charge of the Dominican situation. Early in June a three-man OAS peace commission was formed to work out an amicable settlement, and by September a provisional president for the Dominican Republic was agreed upon by both sides. The Inter-American Peace Force remained in the island to prevent further violence.

See C. G. Fenwick, *The Organization of American States* (1963); Pan American Union, *Annual Reports of the Secretary General* (1964–).   (C. G. Fᴋ.)

AMERICAN TELEPHONE AND TELEGRAPH COMPANY, THE. The first telephone company was formed in 1876 when Alexander Graham Bell (q.v.) assigned his first two telephone patents to the Bell Patent Association. On July 9, 1877, this association was succeeded by the Bell Telephone Company, first as a trusteeship, and later as an incorporation. The Bell Telephone Company was succeeded in 1879 by the National Bell Telephone Company, and later by the American Bell Telephone Company, organized March 20, 1880. On Dec. 30, 1899, assets of the latter company were transferred to the American Telephone and Telegraph Company by an exchange of stock.

The American Telephone and Telegraph Company thus became the central organization of the Bell system. Through 20 principal telephone subsidiaries it provides the bulk of the telephone service in the United States. Revenues from telephone service make up more than 90% of the total operating revenues of the company and its principal associated companies. The company operates a network of wire and radio circuits and related equipment for intercommunication between and through territories of subsidiary companies and other telephone companies, and for interconnection between U.S. telephone systems and those in many other parts of the world. In 1882 the Western Electric Company was acquired as the system's manufacturing and supply unit. In 1925 the Bell Telephone Laboratories was established as the system's research and development organization.

In 1915 the first transcontinental telephone line was opened between New York and San Francisco. In 1927 New York and London were linked by radiotelephone. Three decades later, more than 120 countries and territories could be reached from the United States by radio and underocean telephone cable. The first undersea telephone cable was opened across the North Atlantic in 1956. Other cables subsequently linked the U.S. mainland with Alaska and Hawaii.

Various communication services furnished by the Bell system have been expanded over the years. Teletypewriter exchange service, a written form of public message communication, and private line systems are used extensively by industry, finance, the press, and government. Radio network service, started in the 1920s, grew greatly in the following years. In the 1940s, development of coaxial cable and radio relay made practical the transmission of intercity television programs.

During World War II, the telephone industry contributed greatly to the war effort, particularly in electronic developments such as radar. More than 1,200 military projects were completed. From 1942 through 1945, Western Electric supplied over $2,000,000,000 worth of specialized equipment to the government.

The Bell system's most extensive construction and expansion program followed World War II. Billions of dollars were invested in new buildings and equipment, to meet the demand for service.

The Bell system continued, primarily through Western Electric, to contribute to the nation's defense after the war. Bell Laboratories' inventions such as the transistor (q.v.) found ready use in both military and civilian capacities. For continental defense, the Bell system developed and produced the U.S. Army's "Nike" guided missile. In the far north, the DEW (Distant Early Warning) line of radar stations was constructed for the U.S. Air Force. Related military communications facilities were installed in Alaska. Western Electric played a major role in the construction of the U.S. Air Force's air warning and control system, known as the SAGE (Semi-Automatic Ground Environment) system. This included handling the project's engineering and administrative work, and designing and supervising construction of key buildings. Bell and independent telephone companies provided interconnecting communication facilities for this air warning system.

See also TELEPHONE.   (F. R. K.)

AMERICAS, THE. America, or the Americas, is the term by which the two continents of the western hemisphere are known. Differences between the two are marked, however, because of their relation to the earth's equator. The broad northern portion of North America has a subarctic climate, its mountains in the northwest bear huge glaciers, and much of the rest is covered with ice. In contrast, the northern part of South America, crossed by the equator, lies wholly within the tropics and has a torrid flora and fauna, while its southern end reaches a narrow point at Cape Horn and is characterized by cold waters and glaciers.

"AMERICA OR THE NEW WORLD, A NEW DESCRIPTION," FROM THEATRUM ORBIS TERRARUM, 1570, BY ABRAHAM ORTELIUS

The two continents reach their narrowest link at the Isthmus of Panama, where they are separated by the Panama canal. Linguistic and cultural divisions, however, do not correspond with the geographical. In these respects, there are two Americas: Latin America, which, broadly defined, includes Mexico, Central America, most of the West Indies, and all of South America; and Anglo-America; *i.e.*, the United States and Canada. The term Middle America is sometimes used to designate Mexico, Central America and the West Indies, collectively.

Christopher Columbus inaugurated the "Age of Discovery" by his epochal voyage of 1492 when he sailed westward and landed on what has been generally identified as Watlings (or Watling) Island in the Bahamas, on Oct. 12, 1492. The Indians called it Guanahani, but Columbus changed this to San Salvador (Holy Saviour). Norse explorers touched the North American mainland before this time, but their discoveries had no permanent results.

On his great voyage, Columbus was searching for and thought he had found a new route to India—and had thus reached the fabled orient, which Marco Polo had described for Europeans. Hence he spoke of the lands he had discovered as "the Indies," which long continued to be Spain's official name for her American possessions.

The name "America" is derived from that of the early explorer and friend of Columbus, Amerigo Vespucci (*q.v.*), who made several voyages to the new world and, perhaps just as important, described his travels in letters to friends in Italy. One of these letters, published in 1504, used the term *Mundus Novus* ("New World") in referring to South America. The letter circulated from hand to hand; the eye-catching title of *Mundus Novus* excited popular fancy. When a copy reached Martin Waldseemüller in Germany, he (apparently unaware of Columbus' voyage of 1498

during which he discovered the continent of South America) included some of Vespucci's writings in his *Cosmographiae Introductio* (1507).

Waldseemüller observed that "Another fourth part (of the inhabited earth) had been discovered by Americus Vespucius . . . ," and he suggested that the new land be called America. Waldseemüller's book was a best seller, and in time his proposal became universally accepted.

For further historical and geographical material *see* COLUMBUS, CHRISTOPHER and LATIN AMERICA; also, CENTRAL AMERICA; MIDDLE AMERICA; NORTH AMERICA; SOUTH AMERICA; WEST INDIES; GREENLAND; ICELAND; and articles on other regions and countries of the western hemisphere. *See* also references under "Americas, The" in the Index.

See E. G. Bourne, *Spain in America,* "American Nation Series" (1904); Harold Lamb, *New Found World, How North America Was Discovered & Explored,* "Mainstream of America Series" (1955).

(G. P. HD.)

AMERICIUM, a synthetic chemical element, has the symbol Am and atomic number 95. It is the sixth member of the actinide series in the periodic system (*see* PERIODIC LAW; TRANSURANIUM ELEMENTS). Americium was the fourth transuranium element to be discovered, following by a few months the discovery of the next higher element, curium. It was discovered by G. T. Seaborg, R. A. James, L. O. Morgan, and A. Ghiorso late in 1944 at the wartime Metallurgical Laboratory of The University of Chicago. These investigators observed the production of the isotope Am^{241} as the result of successive neutron-capture reactions by plutonium isotopes in a nuclear reactor according to the following reactions:

$$Pu^{239}(n,\gamma)Pu^{240}(n,\gamma)Pu^{241}\xrightarrow{\beta^-}Am^{241}$$

They suggested the name americium, after the Americas, since its rare-earth homologue, europium, had been named after Europe. The element was first isolated (as Am^{241}) by B. B. Cunningham in the form of a pure compound, the hydroxide, in the fall of 1945 at the Metallurgical Laboratory.

Production.—Americium can be prepared in kilogram amounts through the intensive slow neutron bombardment of Pu^{239} according to the reactions described above. This element is entirely synthetic in origin, and the amount which might be present in nature is too small to make its detection likely.

Since the isotopic composition of any given sample of americium depends on its source, the concept of atomic weight has no meaning in the ordinary sense. Because the isotope Am^{241} can be prepared in relatively pure form by extraction as a decay product, over a period of years, from strongly neutron-bombarded plutonium containing Pu^{241}, and because this has been a practical source of americium for many chemical investigations, it may be convenient to use 241 (more precisely 241.0567) as the atomic weight (on the scale C^{12} = 12.0000).

The isotope Am^{243} has proved more convenient for chemical investigations in view of its longer half-life (7,700 years as com-

Isotopes of Americium

Isotope*	Half-life	Type† and energy of radiation (Mev)
Am^{237}	~1.3 hr.	EC
		α(0.005%) 6.01
Am^{238}	1.9 hr.	EC
Am^{239}	12 hr.	EC
		α(4×10^{-3}%) 5.78
Am^{240}	50 hr.	EC
Am^{241}	433 yr.	α5.534 (0.35%), 5.500 (0.23%), 5.477 (85%), 5.435 (12.6%), 5.378 (1.7%)
Am^{242m_1}	152 yr.	IT 0.049
		β$^-$(<2% of IT)
		α(0.48%)
Am^{242m_2}	0.014 sec.	SF
Am^{242}	16.01 hr.	β$^-$(84%) 0.667, 0.625
		EC (16%)
Am^{243}	7,700 yr.	α5.339 (0.17%), 5.308 (0.16%), 5.266 (87%), 5.224 (11.5%), 5.169 (1.1%)
Am^{244m}	26 min.	β$^-$(>99%) 1.50
		EC (4×10^{-2}%)
Am^{244}	10.1 hr.	β$^-$0.387
Am^{245}	2.07 hr.	β$^-$0.91
Am^{246}	25 min.	β$^-$2.10, 1.60, 1.31

*The symbol m placed after the mass number refers to an isomeric form of isotope.
†EC=electron capture; IT=isomeric transition; SF=spontaneous fission; α=alpha particle; β$^-$=negative beta particle.

pared with 433 years for Am^{241}) and should assume greater importance as it becomes more available. A mixture of the isotopes Am^{241}, Am^{242}, and Am^{243} can be prepared by intensive slow neutron irradiation of Am^{241}. Nearly isotopically pure Am^{243} can be prepared by slow neutron irradiation of Pu^{242} according to the reactions:

$$Pu^{242}(n,\gamma)Pu^{243}\xrightarrow{\beta^-} Am^{243}$$

Fairly pure Pu^{242} for this purpose can be prepared by intensive slow neutron irradiation of Pu^{239} as the result of successive neutron capture reactions:

$$Pu^{239}(n,\gamma)Pu^{240}(n,\gamma)Pu^{241}(n,\gamma)Pu^{242}$$

Chemical Properties.—Americium is a basic element like the other actinide elements, and the reduction to the metal can be effected only with powerful reducing agents. The metal can be prepared by the reduction of americium trifluoride with barium at a temperature of 1,000° to 1,200° C. The metal produced in this manner is silvery white and appears to be more malleable than uranium and neptunium prepared in the same manner. It tarnishes slowly in dry air at room temperature. Its structure as determined by X-ray diffraction is hexagonal close-packed; a face-centred cubic form is also known. The corresponding calculated density at room temperature is 13.8 g/cc, and the melting point appears to be about 1,000° C. The surface of the metal reacts with oxygen or hydrogen to form AmO and AmH$_2$. There is some evidence for the existence of divalent americium in certain salt matrices. Americium metal is much more volatile than its neighbours plutonium and curium; this also suggests a tendency toward a dipositive character.

Much early chemical investigation of americium was done by use of the tracer technique, using the isotope Am^{241}, followed by work with weighable quantities, first using Am^{241} and then, more

and more, Am^{243}. The III oxidation state is very stable in aqueous solution, in line with the tendency toward the stabilization of the lower oxidation states in going from uranium to plutonium. The element exists in acidic aqueous solution in the III, V, and VI oxidation states with the ionic species corresponding to Am^{+3} (pink), AmO$_2^+$, and AmO$_2^{+2}$. The simple Am^{+4} ion is unstable and does not exist in aqueous solution, except as a fluoride complex ion. As a solution species simple americium IV disproportionates, yielding americium III and americium V. The oxidation potentials in acidic aqueous solution are summarized as:

$$
\begin{array}{c}
\overset{+2.32\text{v.}}{\overbrace{\boxed{<2.7\text{v.} \quad >1.5\text{v.}}}} \quad \overset{-1.69\text{v.}}{\overbrace{\boxed{-2.75\text{v.} \quad -0.75\text{v.} \quad -1.60\text{v.}}}} \\[4pt]
\text{Am}\longrightarrow\text{Am}^{+2}\longrightarrow\text{Am}^{+3}\longrightarrow\text{Am}^{+4}\longrightarrow\text{AmO}_2^+\longrightarrow\text{AmO}_2^{2+} \\[4pt]
\underset{-1.74\text{ v.}}{\underline{}}
\end{array}
$$

The potentials are in volts relative to the hydrogen-hydrogen ion couple as zero.

As the potentials indicate, americium can be oxidized to the V or VI state only with strong oxidizing agents, and this can be used to separate it from the other actinide elements.

Americium may be more readily oxidized in alkaline solution. Americium V can be precipitated readily in the form of an insoluble compound by oxidizing americium III in carbonate solution using sodium hypochlorite, ozone, or peroxydisulfate. This compound has been shown, for example, to have the composition KAmO$_2$CO$_3$ or RbAmO$_2$CO$_3$ when the only cation present is potassium or rubidium. Hexapositive americium occurs in such solid compounds as NaAmO$_2$(CH$_3$COO)$_3$ and AmO$_2$F$_2$. The simple fluoride, AmF$_6$, has not been prepared.

Adsorption and elution from columns packed with ion-exchange resins are used to separate americium from the other tripositive actinide elements. Americium can be separated from the rare-earth elements by exploiting its tendency to form strong complex ions with species such as chloride ion in connection with ion-exchange or solvent-extraction separation methods.

In its precipitation reactions americium III is very similar to the other tripositive actinide elements and to the rare-earth elements. Thus, the fluoride and the oxalate are insoluble and the phosphate and iodate are only moderately soluble in acid solution, while the other halides and the nitrate, sulfate, sulfide, and perchlorate are all soluble.

The absorption lines of solid americium compounds at low temperatures are extremely sharp—of the order of 1–10 Å wide, which is a width comparable to the sharpest rare-earth spectra. Some compounds exhibit fluorescence under certain conditions.

When americium III is precipitated as the insoluble hydroxide from aqueous solution and heated in air, a black oxide is formed which corresponds almost exactly to the formula AmO$_2$. This may be reduced to Am$_2$O$_3$ through the action of hydrogen at elevated temperatures. The AmO$_2$ has the fluorite type of structure, isostructural with UO$_2$, NpO$_2$, and PuO$_2$. The orange-red Am$_2$O$_3$ has both the hexagonal and the cubic sesquioxide structure typical of early members of the rare-earth series. As in the case of the preceding actinide elements, oxides of variable composition between AmO$_{1.5}$ and AmO$_2$ are formed, depending on the conditions. Am(OH)$_4$ is also known.

All four of the trihalides of americium have been prepared and their molecular structure identified: AmF$_3$ (hexagonal), AmCl$_3$ (hexagonal), AmBr$_3$ (orthorhombic), and AmI$_3$ (orthorhombic). These are prepared by methods similar to those used in the preparation of the halides of other actinide elements. In addition, AmF$_4$ can be prepared by the reaction of fluorine gas at 500° C with americium III, IV, or V compounds. Numerous tetrapositive fluoride compounds with alkali metals, such as K$_2$AmF$_6$, are also known.

Uses.—The isotope Am^{241} has a number of important industrial uses because of its 60-kev gamma ray; e.g., in fluid-density gauges, thickness gauges, aircraft fuel gauges, and distance-sensing devices. Through neutron irradiation it is a source of Cm^{242}, which has applications as an isotopic power source.

BIBLIOGRAPHY.—G. T. Seaborg and J. J. Katz (eds.), *The Actinide*

Elements, "National Nuclear Energy Series," div. iv, vol. 14A (1954); E. K. Hyde, I. Perlman, and G. T. Seaborg, *The Nuclear Properties of the Heavy Elements,* vol. i and ii (1964); J. J. Katz and G. T. Seaborg, *The Chemistry of the Actinide Elements* (1957); G. T. Seaborg, *The Transuranium Elements* (1958) and *Man-Made Transuranium Elements* (1963); R. A. Penneman and T. K. Keenan, *Radiochemistry of Americium and Curium* (1960); M. Haissinsky *et al.,* "Transuraniens," in *Nouveau Traité de Chimie Minérale,* series ed. by Paul Pascal, vol. xv, Troisième Fascicule (1962). (G. T. Sg.)

AMERIND or AMERINDIAN, a word coined by J. W. Powell, director of the Bureau of American Ethnology, to designate the aboriginal inhabitants of the American continent. The term "American Indian" was frequently abbreviated to "Indian," thereby leading to confusion with the inhabitants of India.

See INDIAN, NORTH AMERICAN.

AMERSFOORT, a town in the province of Utrecht, Neth., lies 12 mi. E.N.E. of Utrecht, on the Eem river. Area 10 sq.mi. Pop. (1960) 67,254. The walled centre of the city has a street pattern dating from the middle ages with two water gates and 15th- to 16th-century wall houses, built in the city walls. St. George's church (12th-16th century) has mural paintings and an organ loft and tombs by Jacob van Campen; the Gothic tower of Our Lady (*c.* 1450), 295 ft. high, was the bell tower of a church destroyed in 1787. Amersfoort has a regional museum, a government archaeological research station and a school for bell ringers. There was rapid development of light industry, chiefly metals, chemicals and foodstuffs, after World War II, with a corresponding increase in population.

AMERSHAM, a town in Buckinghamshire, Eng., 26 mi. N.W. of London by road, lies at the foot of the Chiltern hills, there thickly wooded, where the river Misbourne emerges from its valley. Pop. (1961) 14,612. The wide high street of the old town, with its inns, timbered buildings and 17th-century town hall, is very attractive. The parish church of St. Mary dates from the 13th century. Market gardening, turkey and pheasant raising, woodworking, light engineering and the manufacture of instruments, bricks and cosmetics are carried on in the district. In the newer part of the town there is a centre for the distribution of radioactive isotopes. Amersham and Chesham Bois railway station lies on the main line from London through Aylesbury to the north. Amersham, formerly a borough by prescription, returned two members to parliament from 1624 to 1832, when it lost its privileges. The fair has taken place annually since 1200. Amersham forms part of the Chiltern Hundreds (*q.v.*).

AMERY, LEOPOLD CHARLES MAURICE STENNETT (1873–1955), British politician who was a persistent advocate of imperial preference and tariff reform, and did much to promote the constitutional advance of colonial territories, is chiefly remembered for his part in bringing about the fall of the Chamberlain government in 1940. He was born at Gorakhpur, India, on Nov. 22, 1873, and educated at Harrow school and Balliol college, Oxford. He was elected a fellow of All Souls college, Oxford, in 1897. In 1899–1900 he was chief correspondent of the *Times* from the South African War and remained on the staff of that paper until 1909, editing *The Times History of the South African War,* 7 vol. (1900–09). He entered parliament in 1911 as Unionist member for the South (later Sparkbrook) division of Birmingham and held this seat until 1945. During World War I, he served abroad with the British army in 1914–16, but from 1917 he was on the staff of the war cabinet in London and of the inter-Allied war council at Versailles. He became undersecretary of state for the colonies in 1919 and was moved to a junior post at the admiralty in 1921. During this period he was a leader of the "undersecretaries' revolt" which contributed to the fall of the Lloyd George coalition government in 1922 and to the Conservatives' return to power.

He was made a privy councilor in 1922 and thereafter, apart from a term as first lord of the admiralty (1922–24), he spent the rest of his career as a minister in imperial departments. He was secretary of state for the colonies (1924–29) and also for the dominions (1925–29), and created in 1925 the dominions office which later became the commonwealth relations office. He was excluded from office by the national government (1931–40) and was a sharp critic of the Munich agreement with Hitler and Mussolini. Despite his industry, integrity and passionate advocacy of his own causes, he never dominated the house of commons, but in 1940 his voice was influential in breaking the Chamberlain government to which he applied Cromwell's injunction to the Long parliament: "In the name of God, go!" From 1940 to 1945 he was secretary of state for India and Burma. In 1945 he was made a companion of honour. He died in London on Sept. 16, 1955.

Amery's works include *Thoughts on the Constitution* (1947) and *My Political Life,* 3 vol. (1953–55). (J. F. B.)

AMES, FISHER (1758–1808), U.S. congressman, orator and essayist, was born at Dedham, Mass., on April 9, 1758, and entered Harvard college at the age of 13. After graduation in 1774 he remained at home, gaining more maturity through reading and studying, until 1781 when he began a successful law practice. Convinced by Shays's rebellion of 1786–87 (*see* MASSACHUSETTS: *History*) that stern measures must be taken to deter attacks upon property and authority, he turned to politics. As a member of the Massachusetts convention that ratified the federal constitution in Feb. 1788, he argued strongly in favour of the clause in the constitution providing for biennial rather than annual elections for the house of representatives. Ames was a Federalist member of the house during Washington's administration (1789–97). On April 28, 1796, he overcame Republican opposition by his spellbinding oratory and secured passage of the appropriation bill for Jay's treaty.

Ames agreed with Hamilton's vision of a vigorous federal government guided by men of means and virtue. Although not in congress during the Adams and Jefferson administrations, Ames shared the view of the Essex junto—a group of New England Federalists who urged a friendly policy toward Britain and a strong campaign against France. He hoped the Sedition act of 1798 would control the French revolutionary doctrines. After his retirement Ames continued to state his views in more than 25 essays and numerous letters. He died at Dedham on July 4, 1808.

(H. I. Be.)

AMES, JOSEPH (1689–1759), English bibliographer and antiquary, whose *Typographical Antiquities* (1749) is a valuable account of printing in England from 1471 to 1600. Later editions were published with added information by William Herbert (1785–90) and T. F. Dibdin (1810–19). Ames is variously described as a ship chandler, a patten maker, a plane-ironmaker, and an ironmonger. He led a prosperous life at Wapping, and amassed valuable collections of antiquities. He died on Oct. 7, 1759.

AMES, OAKES (1804–1873), U.S. industrialist and congressman, one of the builders of the first transcontinental railroad and key figure in the Crédit Mobilier scandal of 1872–73, was born Jan. 10, 1804, in Easton, Mass. He went to work as a youth in his father's shovel factory and helped develop a business valued at $4,000,000 on the eve of the American Civil War. Ames, a Republican, was elected in 1862 to the first of five consecutive terms in the national house of representatives. In 1865 he and his brother Oliver (1807–77) became associated with the Union Pacific railroad. Ames also obtained control of the Crédit Mobilier of America, a company organized by promoters of the Union Pacific for the purpose of securing to themselves the enormous profits expected from the building of the road. For details of the scandal, *see* CRÉDIT MOBILIER OF AMERICA. Ames became something of a scapegoat for the sins of a railroad-building generation, which, in condemning him, convicted itself. He died on May 8, 1873, at North Easton, Mass. (D. E. F.)

AMES, WILLIAM (known as AMESIUS) (1576–1633), English Puritan theologian and controversialist, a champion of Calvinism as opposed to Arminianism during the Remonstrant controversies, was born at Ipswich, Suffolk, in 1576. Ames was educated at Christ's college, Cambridge, and became a fellow there. In 1609, following a sermon in which he denounced the heathenish debauchery attending the feast of St. Thomas, he was obliged to leave England and spent the rest of his life in the Netherlands. He was aided in leaving England by wealthy English merchants who wished him to convert the supporters of the English church in Leiden. At Rotterdam, wearing the fisherman's habit donned for the passage, he opposed Grevinchovius (Nicholas Grevinckhoven, d. 1632), minister of the Arminian or Remonstrant church, in a debate. (See ARMINIANISM.) The fisherman-controversialist made a considerable stir and became known throughout the Low Countries. Subsequently Ames entered into a controversy in print with Grevinchovius on universal redemption and election and cognate problems. His views were brought together in his *Coronis ad collationem hagiensem,* prepared for the synod of Dort (*q.v.*), 1618–19, a book which figured largely in Dutch church history.

He was for a short time chaplain to Sir Horatio Vere in Holland, then professor of theology at Franeker, Friesland, from 1622 to 1633. In the latter year he moved to Rotterdam where he undertook pastoral work. Ames did not long survive this move and died in Rotterdam in Nov. 1633. His *Fresh Suit Against Ceremonies*—the book which is said to have made Richard Baxter (*q.v.*) a Nonconformist—was published posthumously. His other works include *Medulla theologiae,* a manual of Calvinistic doctrine for his students; *De conscientia eius iure et casibus;* and Latin commentaries on the Psalms and the Epistle of St. Peter.

See the *Life* by M. Nethenus, prefixed to the collected edition of his Latin works (1658).

AMES, WINTHROP (1871–1937), U.S. theatrical producer, was born in North Easton, Mass., on Nov. 25, 1871. He graduated from Harvard in 1895 and spent the following year in special study at the university. For eight years he edited and published art and architectural works in Boston, Mass., followed by a year abroad, where he studied the continental drama. In 1905 he became manager, in association with Lorin F. Deland, of the Castle theatre, Boston, where for three years they conducted a very notable stock company. In 1908 Ames became director of the New theatre (later the Century) in New York city, where he made an attempt to establish a repertory theatre. With the passing of the New theatre, he began, in 1912, independent production and management, erecting two theatres, the Little and the Booth. He contributed a wide variety of productions, among them *Snow White,* the first play given in New York city especially for children. He also produced the Gilbert and Sullivan operas.

Ames died in Boston on Nov. 3, 1937.

AMES, a city of Story county, central Iowa, U.S., 33 mi. (53 km.) N of Des Moines. The site of Ames was purchased in 1864 by Mrs. Cynthia Duff who was acting in secret for John I. Blair, a railroad promoter. Blair, who planned to construct a depot for the Cedar Rapids and Missouri railroad (later the North Western), named the town after Oakes Ames, one of the owners of the railroad. As the railroad developed and the slough and marshes of Ames were drained, the town prospered. By 1865 the population was 300. It was incorporated in 1870, and adopted the council-manager form of government in 1920. (For comparative population figures, *see* table in IOWA: *Population.*)

Ames is the seat of the Iowa State University of Science and Technology (formerly the Iowa State College of Agriculture and Mechanic Arts) established in 1858 as a "state agricultural college and model farm." The central campus of 781 ac. is a beautiful park. An inner plaza of 20 ac., containing a campanile with a chime of 36 bells cast in Loughborough, Eng., is surrounded by stately buildings of white Bedford stone. The university's college of veterinary medicine, founded in 1879, is the oldest in the United States and the U.S. department of agriculture's animal disease research laboratory is located in Ames. The Institute for Atomic Research, established at the university in 1945, became one of the major research centres of the U.S. Atomic Energy commission.

Toys, water purifiers and electronic and chemical instruments are manufactured in Ames.   (J. T. Sc.)

AMESBURY, a town in Wiltshire, Eng., lies in the rich and well-wooded valley of the Avon amid the chalk downs of Salisbury plain, 8 mi. N. of Salisbury. Pop. (1961) 5,611. The immediate neighbourhood is rich in remains of prehistoric man, among which Stonehenge (*q.v.*), 1½ mi. W., is the greatest surviving megalithic structure in the British Isles. On a hill overlooking the town is a large earthwork, the Ramparts, which perhaps marks an earlier settlement. At Amesbury (Ambresberia, Aumbresbery) a witena-

gemot (Anglo-Saxon national council or parliament) was held in 932, and about 980 Aelfthryth, queen dowager of Edgar, erected a nunnery there in expiation of the murder of her stepson. At the time of Domesday (1086), Amesbury was a royal manor. From the 12th century the nunnery was attached to the abbey of Fontevrault in Anjou, France, and was enriched by royal charters and private gifts. A weekly market (no longer held) and fair were granted in 1317. The church of St. Mary is largely Early English, with richly decorated windows. Pipe clay abounds in the neighbourhood and in the 17th century Amesbury was famous for its pipes. Its interests are largely agricultural, frequent sheep fairs being held. The town profits from the permanent army camps in the vicinity (particularly from Larkhill) and from the tourist traffic visiting Stonehenge and other objects of interest on the plain. Amesbury lies on one of the two main roads between London and Exeter and is served by a branch railway line for freight traffic.

AMESBURY, a town of Essex county, in northeast Massachusetts, U.S., on the Merrimack river, 43 mi. N. of Boston, at the New Hampshire border. (For comparative population figures *see* table in MASSACHUSETTS: *Population.*)

Amesbury was first settled in 1642 as part of Salisbury. It became practically independent in 1654 although not legally a township until 1666. In 1667 it was named for the English town in Wiltshire. In 1693 the hysteria of the Salem witch trials swept the town. Susanna (Goody) Martin of Amesbury was condemned in those trials and was hanged as a witch on July 19 of that year. The legends of Amesbury are rich in tales of the supernatural: the loom of Goody Whitcher, another Amesbury witch, weaved long after her death; in the early days headless men wandered the streets late at night; and nearby Barrow Hill was often the site of witches' routs and sabbats in the early years. Quaker settlers arrived there in 1701. Josiah Bartlett (1729–95), a signer of the Declaration of Independence, was born there.

The early agriculture was soon supplemented by shipbuilding and the making of barrel staves. Amesbury was an important shipbuilding centre until the decline of wooden sailing vessels. Other early industries included the manufacture of iron, begun in 1710; hats, 1769; nails, 1796; and carriages, 1800. The water power of the Merrimack and Powow rivers attracted the textile industry in 1812.

Modern manufacturing is varied in nature and provides the largest source of employment in the industrial area. Amesbury was the home of John Greenleaf Whittier from 1836 to 1876 and many of his poems describe the surrounding country and the life of the community.   (CA. M. C.)

AMETHYST, a violet or purple variety of quartz (*q.v.*) used as an ornamental or gem stone (*see* also GEM). The name is generally said to be derived from the Greek for "not intoxicating," expressing the old belief that the stone protected its owner from strong drink. It was held that wine drunk out of a cup of amethyst would not intoxicate. The colour of amethyst is usually attributed to the presence of manganese, but as it is capable of being much altered and even discharged by heat it has been referred by some authorities to an organic source. On exposure to heat, amethyst generally becomes yellow, and much of the cairngorm or yellow quartz used in jewelry is heat-treated amethyst.

The amethyst was used as a gem stone by the ancient Egyptians, and was largely employed in antiquity for intaglios. It later was used for episcopal rings. It is a very widely distributed mineral, but fine, clear specimens fit for cutting as ornamental stones are confined to comparatively few localities. Such crystals occur either in cavities in mineral veins and in granitic rocks, or as a lining in hollow agate nodules or geodes. Many of the hollow agates of Brazil and Uruguay contain a crop of amethyst crystals in the interior. Much fine amethyst comes from the U.S.S.R., especially the Sverdlovsk area.

AMETROPIA: *see* VISION: *Image Formation: Abnormalities in Refraction.*

AMHARA, the name of one of the former central provinces of Ethiopia, stretching roughly from the river Abbai or Abay (Blue Nile) on the west to Lake Hayk in the east, but later including

Begamedr (Begemdir) and Lake Tana. It has ceased to be an administrative unit, having been replaced by Shoa (Shewa) to the south. Amhara in early times was a kingdom ruled, under the king of Ethiopia, by a subking whose title was *tsahafalam*. This title first appears in documented history in the reign of King Amda Tseyon (1312–42), but appears to have lapsed by 1520, when the Portuguese embassy which included the chaplain Francisco Alvares came to Ethiopia. As late as 1689, however, the governor of Amhara was eighth in the official order of precedence. In 1646 Manoel de Almeida described Amhara as the most mountainous part of Ethiopia and as very fertile. From Amhara is derived the name of the modern official and literary language of Ethiopia, Amharic, spoken by 3,000,000 to 5,000,000 people over central Ethiopia almost from the eastern to the western border, though not as a lingua franca. It has developed from Ge'ez; the earliest known specimens belong to the 14th century A.D. *See* also ETHIOPIA: *History.*

BIBLIOGRAPHY.—C. F. Beckingham and G. W. B. Huntingford, *Some Records of Ethiopia, 1593–1646* (1954; for Almeida's description of 1646), *The Prester John of the Indies* (1961; for F. Alvares' descriptions of 1540); E. Ullendorff, *The Ethiopians* (1960); G. A. Lipsky *et al., Ethiopia* (1962).   (G. W. B. H.)

AMHARIC, the national language of Ethiopia probably since the 12th century, originally was spoken in the province of Amhara, hence its name; it is the language of the central and southern highlands of Ethiopia. The oldest Amharic documents are songs from the 14th century. In the late 16th and early 17th centuries, Jesuits used Amharic against the Monophysite Ethiopians. Amharic is one of the Semitic languages (*q.v.*), but has been greatly modified by Cushitic influence. Amharic uses the Ethiopic syllabary with additional signs; it has 33 characters. Each character has seven forms representing a consonant followed by different vowels.

In relation to proto-Ethiopic the features of Amharic are the following: In phonology the loss of the laryngeals and the palatalization of the dentals and sibilants are notable. In morphology the characteristic features are: the loss of -*t* as feminine marker; the disappearance of the mark -*a* of the accusative and of the construct state; and the usage of the external plural (-*oč*) with elimination of the internal plural. The verb developed derived stems for actions not found in proto-Ethiopic. Syntax and vocabulary are strongly influenced by Cushitic, especially by Galla and Sidamo.

BIBLIOGRAPHY.—C. H. Armbruster, *Initia Amharica. An Introduction to Spoken Amharic*, part 1: Grammar (1908); I. Guidi, *Grammatica elementare della lingua amariñña*, 4th ed. (1935); M. Cohen, *Traité de langue amharique* (1936); W. Leslau, *Ethiopian Argots* (1964); E. Ullendorff, *An Amharic Chrestomathy* (1965).   (W. LU.)

AMHERST, JEFFREY AMHERST, BARON (1717–1797), British soldier, who was commander of the army which captured Canada between 1758 and 1760, was born at Sevenoaks, Kent, on Jan. 29, 1717. He received a commission in the foot guards in 1731 and was selected as aide-de-camp first by Lord Ligonier and then by the duke of Cumberland. Pitt and Ligonier selected him for the Canadian command in 1758. With a force of 14,000 men he besieged and captured Louisburg, and was promoted to chief command in America. He then drew up a plan for a concentric advance on Montreal by three columns, one moving westward up the St. Lawrence river and capturing Quebec, the second northward from Albany by Ticonderoga and Crown Point, and the third westward from Fort Niagara. The first under James Wolfe captured Quebec late in 1759 and the final offensive was launched in 1760, when Montreal surrendered and Canada passed into British hands. Amherst remained in Canada as governor general till 1763, quelling the Indian rising under Pontiac in 1761. He acted as commander in chief of the British army almost continuously from 1772 to 1795, but though he suppressed the Gordon riots in 1780, his tenure of office was not a successful one, being marred by failure in the war with the American colonies and by the growth of serious abuses in the army.

He was created a baron in 1776, a field marshal in 1796, and died at Sevenoaks, Kent, on Aug. 3, 1797.

See Amherst, J. A., *Journal*, ed. by J. C. Webster (1931); J. C. Long, *Lord Jeffery Amherst* (1933).   (E. W. SH.)

AMHERST, WILLIAM PITT AMHERST, EARL (1773–1857), British diplomat whose tenure of the governor generalship of India (1823–28) was notable mainly for the conduct of the first Burmese War. He was born at Bath on Jan. 14, 1773, the nephew of Jeffrey, Baron Amherst (*q.v.*), to whose title he succeeded in 1797. Amherst served from 1809 to 1811 as British envoy at the court of Naples, where he acquired some reputation as a diplomatist. In 1815 he was sent to China to conduct negotiations on commercial questions, but achieved nothing because of his refusal to perform the *kowtow* ceremony or accept inferior diplomatic status. On his return journey he visited Napoleon at St. Helena (1817). In London he received more credit for his firmness than censure for the failure of his mission. On the resignation of Lord Hastings, Amherst was appointed governor general of India in 1823, against the rival candidacy of Lord William Bentinck. George Canning, who managed the appointment, called it, in a letter to William Huskisson, "as good a *barren* choice as could have been made."

So in fact it proved. Within a month of his arrival Amherst was confronted by aggression from Burma, which precipitated the first Burmese War (1824–26). Despite some mismanagement (including the dispatch of Indian troops by sea, which caused the Barrackpore mutiny in 1824), the war was brought to a conclusion with the annexation of the jungle coastal strips of Arakan and Tenasserim to Great Britain in 1826. For his services during the Burmese War, Amherst received an earldom in 1826. He died on March 13, 1857.

See A. T. Ritchie and R. Evans, *Earl Amherst* (1894).   (T. G. P. S.)

AMHERST, one of the four districts of the Tenasserim division of Burma. After the creation of the Karen state (*q.v.*) it was reduced to a narrow coastal strip, mainly of forested hills, running southward along the Gulf of Martaban from the mouth of the Salween. Its headquarters are at Moulmein (*q.v.*), an important town and port, but it takes its name from the town of Amherst, named in honour of a viceroy of India and planned as an outpost of Moulmein, though it failed to develop as such.

(L. D. S.)

AMHERST, a town of Hampshire county, Mass., U.S., in the central part of the state. (For comparative population figures *see* table in MASSACHUSETTS: *Population.*) The town was settled as a precinct of Hadley about 1730, and recognized as a district under the name of Amherst in 1759; it was named for Jeffrey Amherst (*q.v.*), a British general in the French and Indian War. It was incorporated as a town in 1775. Originally an agricultural area, it became an industrial village in the 18th century and for more than a century produced carriages, bricks, textiles, paper, tools and hats. In the 19th century industry gave way to farming: large dairy herds and apple orchards, some poultry and tobacco.

Amherst is, however, pre-eminently an academic town. Prior to the establishment of public high schools (1861) Amherst academy and other private schools provided training for young people, many from out-of-town. Amherst college, a men's college affiliated with the Congregationalist church, was founded in 1821; before 1871 more than 40% of its graduates entered the ministry. Its annual enrollment is approximately 1,000. Among its founders were Noah Webster, the lexicographer, and Samuel F. Dickinson, grandfather of the poet, Emily Dickinson.

Academic facilities include, in addition to classrooms and laboratories, Converse library, the Mead Art centre (with a distinguished collection of early American paintings), Kirby theatre, Pratt Museum of Natural History, an observatory and a special laboratory for radioactive research. The college administers the Merrill Center for Economics at Southampton, N.Y., and the Folger Shakespeare Memorial library in Washington, D.C. The University of Massachusetts (originally the Massachusetts Agricultural college and later Massachusetts State college) was incorporated in 1863 and admitted its first students in 1867. The campus comprises 700 ac. about 1 mi. N. of the village centre, and a demonstration forest of 755 ac. 6 mi. farther north. Helen Hunt Jackson and Emily Dickinson were born in Amherst, and Noah Webster lived in the village (1812–22) while working on his dictionary.

(F. P. RA.)

AMHURST, NICHOLAS (1697–1742), English satirical poet and editor of the *Craftsman,* was born at Marden, Kent, on Oct. 16, 1697. He was expelled from St. John's college, Oxford, in 1719, probably because of his outspoken Whig principles and because of the satire against the university in his poems.

Amhurst settled in London, and in 1721 began a series of satirical papers called *Terrae Filius.* He became prominent among the pamphleteers hostile to Sir Robert Walpole's government, and edited the famous *Craftsman,* the Whig paper which Lord Bolingbroke and William Pulteney had founded and to which they contributed. The paper had unprecedented popularity for a political journal, and published articles by Tory as well as Whig writers. In 1737 it printed a letter, supposedly from Colley Cibber, attacking the new act for licensing plays, and for this suspected libel both Amhurst and the printer, Richard Francklin, were imprisoned for a short time.

When Pulteney and his political friends came to terms with the government after Walpole's downfall, Amhurst was forgotten, and the end of his life was apparently spent in poverty and obscurity. He died at Twickenham, Middlesex, on April 12, 1742.

AMICABLE NUMBERS (also known as AMIABLE NUMBERS or, less commonly, as AGREEABLE NUMBERS), two integers each of which is equal to the sum of the aliquot parts (exact divisors) of the other. For example, 220 and 284 are amicable numbers, for the aliquot parts of 220 are 1, 2, 4, 5, 10, 11, 20, 22, 44, 55 and 110, the sum of which numbers is 284.

Similarly, the sum of the aliquot parts of 284 (that is, of 1, 2, 4, 71 and 142) is 220. These two numbers are mentioned by the Greek arithmetician Iamblichus (*c.* 325). Mathematicians have discovered 389 other pairs.

See E. B. Escott, "Amicable Numbers," *Scripta Mathematica,* vol. 12, pp. 61–72 (1946).

AMICI, GIOVANNI BATTISTA (1786–1863), Italian astronomer and microscopist, was born March 25, 1786, at Modena and died at Florence, April 10, 1863.

His name is best known for the improvements he effected in the mirrors of reflecting telescopes and in the development and construction of the microscope.

AMICUS CURIAE, a term used primarily in law, means, literally, "a friend of the court." An *amicus curiae* is a stranger to a law suit who assists the court by furnishing information or advice regarding questions of law or fact. He differs from an intervenor in that the latter has a direct interest in the outcome of the law suit and therefore is permitted to intervene as a party.

An *amicus curiae* normally may not participate except by leave of the court, and most courts seldom permit persons to appear as *amicus curiae.* However, the supreme court of the United States permits federal, state and local governments to submit their views in any case without obtaining the consent of either the court or the parties. Private persons may appear as *amicus curiae* in the supreme court either if both parties consent or if the court grants permission. (J. R. B.)

AMIDES (ACID AMIDES), chemical compounds which may be considered as derived from ammonia by replacement of one or more of its hydrogen atoms with acyl residues. (An acyl residue is the characteristic group of an acid, from which it may be derived by removal of the acidic hydroxyl group or groups.) Certain amides of the sulfonic acids, or derivatives of them, comprise the "sulfa drugs," of great importance in medicine. Sulfanilamide was the first of these drugs to be widely used; it may be considered the parent substance from which the remaining drugs are derived by structural modifications. (*See* SULFONAMIDES.)

A few amides of inorganic acids are known, such as nitramide, $H_2N.NO_2$ (from nitric acid), and sulfamic acid, $H_2N.SO_3H$ (from sulfuric acid), but the great majority are derived from organic acids. Of these latter compounds, the amides of the type $R.CO.NH_2$, which are derived from the carboxylic acids, are the most important, the group $.CO.NH_2$ being called the amido group. They may be prepared by the dry distillation of the ammonium salts of the acids (A. W. von Hofmann), by the partial hydrolysis of the nitriles, by the action of ammonia or ammonium carbonate on acid chlorides or anhydrides, or by heating the esters (*q.v.*) with ammonia. They are solid crystalline compounds (formamide excepted); the lower members of the series are soluble in water, the solubility, however, decreasing as the carbon content of the molecules increases. They are easily hydrolyzed, breaking up into organic acids and ammonia when boiled with acids or alkalies. Nitrous acid decomposes them, with elimination of nitrogen and the formation of the corresponding acid:

$$RCO.NH_2 + ONOH = R.COOH + N_2 + H_2O.$$

When distilled with phosphoric anhydride they yield nitriles. By the action of sodium hydroxide and either bromine or chlorine on the amides, they are converted into amines containing one carbon atom less than the original amide:

$$R.CONH_2 + R.CONHBr \rightarrow RNH_2 + Na_2CO_3 + NaBr$$

This reaction possesses great theoretical importance (A. W. von Hofmann), and is also of industrial interest in the Badische synthesis of indigo (*q.v.*), for in accordance with Hofmann's reaction phthalimide is converted by alkali hypochlorite into anthranilic acid.

Formamide, $H.CONH_2$, is a liquid readily soluble in water, boiling at about 210° C. with partial decomposition. Acetamide, $CH_3.CONH_2$, a white deliquescent crystalline solid, which melts at 82–83° C. and boils at 222° C., is usually prepared by distilling ammonium acetate. Benzamide, $C_6H_5.CONH_2$, crystallizes in leaflets which melt at 130° C.

The amides of the sulfonic acids are only slightly less important than those of the carboxylic acids discussed above. They may be prepared by the action of ammonia upon the corresponding sulfonyl chlorides:

$$RSO_2Cl + 2NH_3 = RSO_2NH_2 + NH_4Cl$$

Among the important derivatives of the amides are those in which one or more of the hydrogen atoms attached to nitrogen have been replaced by alkyl or aryl groups.

AMIEL, HENRI FRÉDÉRIC (1821–1881), Swiss writer whose *Journal intime* is a masterpiece of self-analysis, was born at Geneva on Sept. 27, 1821. After studying for seven years in Italy, France, Belgium and Germany, he was appointed professor of aesthetics in 1849 and of moral philosophy in 1854 at the academy in Geneva. Disappointments in his youth, followed by what he felt to be failure at the academy and as a poet—only his "Roulez, tambours" achieved success, becoming the national anthem of the French-speaking part of Switzerland—drove him into himself. He found his real life in the diary which he kept from 1847 until his death in Geneva on May 11, 1881. Parts of the 16,900 pages of this *Journal intime* were published during 1883–84. It gained a European reputation and was translated into English, Russian, German and other languages. It remains a fascinating document of a sensitive, rich mind desperately struggling for values in an age of growing scepticism and pessimism.

BIBLIOGRAPHY.—*Fragments d'un journal intime,* ed. by B. Bouvier, 3 vol. (1923) and by L. Bopp (1939–   ); B. Bouvier, *La jeunesse d'H.-F. Amiel* (1935); A. Thibaudet, *Amiel ou la part du rêve* (1929); E. Merian-Genast, "H.-F. Amiel im Spiegel der europäischen Kritik, 1881–1931," in *Neuere Sprachen* (1931); Van Wyck Brooks, *The Malady of the Ideal* (1913). (A. Bx.)

AMIENS, principal city of Picardy (region of northern France) and capital of the Somme *département,* lies in the marshy valley of the Somme river below its confluence with the Avre, 81 mi. N. of Paris by road. Pop. (1962) 101,677. It is the seat of a bishop.

The town is dominated by the cathedral of Notre Dame, one of the finest Gothic churches in France. Begun in 1220 on the plans of Robert de Luzarches it was finished about 1270; though the lateral chapels, the towers on each side of the façade and the rose window were added later. It is 469 ft. long by 216 ft. wide, the nave being nearly 140 ft. in height. There are aisles, a transept with aisles and a choir (with deambulatory) ending in an apse surrounded by chapels. The façade, flanked by two towers of unequal height added in the 14th and 15th centuries respectively, has three decorated portals. The central one has a 13th-century statue of Christ, while the right hand one contains a figure of the Virgin and other statuary and the left is devoted to St. Firmin. The portals are surmounted by two galleries, the upper one containing 22 statues of the kings of Judah in its arcades, and by a fine rose window. A slender spire rises above the crossing. The interior of the cathedral contains beautifully carved stalls and a flamboyant choir screen, and is remarkable for the high nave and the boldness of the columns supporting the vaulting.

The busy part of the city, largely reconstructed after extensive damage in the two world wars, lies between the railway to the south and the Somme on the north. The old quarter straddles the seven branches of the river and the new parts spread out to the north. The line of the former ramparts is followed by a series of boulevards, and there is another ring of boulevards beyond. Opposite the railway station is the 30-story Perret tower, 341 ft. high, built by Auguste Perret, architect of the station, after World War II. The town hall, built in the 17th century and almost entirely rebuilt in the 19th, stands in the centre of the old town. To the north is the 15th-century church of St. Germain, to the south the Picardy museum with collections of archaeological finds, paintings and sculpture and to the east the Louis XVI façade of the ancient theatre.

Amiens is on the main railway from Paris to Calais, and other main lines run northeastward to Dunkerque and Lille and southeastward to Laon, Reims and Switzerland. Secondary lines run to Rouen, Beauvais, Compiègne and St. Pol. There is an important railway marshalling yard at Longueau (1 mi. E.). The textile industry, famous since the middle ages, includes velvet, cotton, wool, silk, hemp and flax spinning, hosiery and a variety of mixed fabrics. Manufactures of machinery, chemicals and tires, and printing and dyeing are also carried on. Amiens is a market for the produce of the allotments and small market gardens (*hortillonnages*) in the fertile land between the many branches of the Somme and Avre, which cover a considerable area mainly to the east of the city. Amiens also trades in grain, sugar, wool, oilseeds, and in the duck pasties and macaroons for which it is renowned. The vegetable market is held on board the many small boats which bring the produce from the *hortillonnages,* and a fair for all types of merchandise is held every year.

In pre-Roman days Amiens was known as Samarobriva, capital of the Ambiani, from which it derives its modern name. Settled by the Romans at the beginning of the Christian era, Christianity was brought there in the 4th century by St. Firmin, its first bishop. Its territory became the medieval countship of Amienois and early in the 12th century the citizens gained a charter, profiting from the rivalry between count and bishop. The fief became a dependency of the French crown in 1185. By the treaty of Arras it went to the dukes of Burgundy in 1435 and remained theirs until 1477. Surprised by the Spaniards in 1597, the city was recaptured from them by Henry IV after a long siege. Until 1790 it was the capital of the government of Picardy. The treaty between Great Britain, France, Spain and Holland which made a short pause in the Napoleonic War was signed there in 1802. During the Franco-German War Amiens fell to the Prussians on Nov. 28, 1870, after a battle to the east of the city.

During World War I the city was captured by the Germans on Aug. 30, 1914, but after a few days they withdrew when the front was established about 20 mi. to the east, where it remained until 1918, when, during their final offensive, the Germans advanced to within 8 mi. of the city. In World War II Amiens was occupied by the Germans on May 21, 1940, and recaptured on Aug. 31, 1944.

See also references under "Amiens" in the Index.

(Be. Bo.)

AMIENS, BATTLE OF, the name commonly given to the opening stage of operations in Picardy in 1918, Germany's last bid for victory on the western front in World War I (*q.v.*).

Encouraged by the collapse of Russia, the German general Erich Ludendorff planned an offensive with the initial object of capturing the important communication centre of Amiens and thereby separating the British and French armies. The main attack started early on March 21, 1918, on a front of 60 mi. between Arras and Laon, held by British forces. The 71 German divisions were opposed by 29 British. Helped by fog, the attackers advanced rapidly, mainly on the front held by the British 5th army (Gen. Sir H. Gough). On March 26, however, when the French general Ferdinand Foch assumed control of all Allied forces, French reinforcements began moving up. By April 5 the Germans had advanced about 25 mi. and were within 10 mi. of Amiens, but the attack had spent its force. Amiens remained in Allied hands.

British casualties amounted to 163,493, French to about 77,000, Germans to about 250,000. Later German attacks on other parts of the front were without any solid success.

See Sir James E. Edmonds, the official British *History of the Great War,* vol. i and ii (1935 and 1937). (C. N. B.)

AMIN AL-HUSAINI (1893–), mufti of Jerusalem from 1921 to 1937, outstanding for his anti-British role in Arab politics. A Palestinian Sunni Muslim, he was educated in Jerusalem, at al-Azhar university, Cairo, and in Istanbul and was commissioned in the Turkish artillery (1910). He began recruiting for the Arabs of the Hejaz in their rising against Turkey in 1917, became *persona grata* in Arab nationalist circles and—after a brief imprisonment for anti-Zionist agitation—was made mufti of Jerusalem by the high commissioner, Sir Herbert Samuel, in 1921. He became president of the supreme Muslim council in 1922. As head of the important Palestine Arab party and later of the militant Arab Higher committee, he was an Arab nationalist party leader, the most extreme and least scrupulous spokesman and organizer of anti-Zionist activities in Palestine. He moved to Lebanon in 1937 and to Iraq (where he exercised considerable anti-British influence) in 1939. Fleeing from Iraq on the failure of Rashid Ali's movement (1941), he took refuge in Iran and then in Berlin, where from 1942 to 1944 he acted as wholehearted Nazi propagandist. From Germany he proceeded to France in 1945 and then in 1946 to Egypt, where he was received by King Faruk and re-elected as president of the Higher Arab committee for Palestine. From 1947 onward he lived at Heliopolis, outside Cairo, paying more than one visit to Pakistan as member, or president, of Muslim conventions. His titular position as head of the "government of all-Palestine" was meaningless after the partition of that country between Israel and Jordan (1947–49). Despite his wide pretensions, he had few followers in the 1950s. (S. H. Lo.)

AMINES, in chemistry, derivatives of ammonia (*q.v.*) in which one or more of the three hydrogen atoms are replaced by alkyl or aryl groups. The replacement of one hydrogen atom by one alkyl or aryl group gives rise to primary amines; of two hydrogen atoms by two groups to secondary amines; of three hydrogen atoms by three groups to tertiary amines. The tertiary amines possess the power of combining with one molecular proportion of an alkyl iodide to form quaternary ammonium salts.

The structural relations of these compounds may be shown thus:

$$NH_3$$
ammonia
$$NH_2R$$
primary amine
$$NHR_2$$
secondary amine
$$NR_3$$
tertiary amine
$$NR_4I$$
quaternary ammonium iodide

Aliphatic Amines.—An amine is said to be an aliphatic one if each carbon atom that is joined directly to the amino nitrogen atom is saturated. This is true even if aromatic rings are present in more distant parts of the molecule. (*Cf.* benzylamine, below.) The compounds of this type possess properties very similar to those of ammonia. The lowest members of the series are combustible gases and are readily soluble in water. The next higher members of the series are liquids of low boiling point and are also readily soluble in water, the solubility and volatility, however, decreasing with the increasing carbon content of the molecule. The highest members of the series are odourless solids of high boiling point and are insoluble in water. They are all moderately strong bases, readily forming salts with the mineral acids. They are ionized in aqueous solution to a somewhat greater extent than ammonia. The quaternary ammonium bases, NR_4OH, as distinct from the amines, are solids that are soluble in water; they are much more strongly basic than ammonia or any of the amines, and, in fact, are comparable in strength with sodium and potassium hydroxides.

Many methods have been devised for the preparation of primary amines. Methylamine was isolated in 1849 by C. A. Wurtz on boiling methyl isocyanate with potassium hydroxide, $CH_3.NCO + 2KOH = CH_3NH_2 + K_2CO_3$. Further methods of preparation include the reduction of nitriles with alcohol and sodium; the hydrolysis of the alkyl phthalimides (S. Gabriel, 1887); and the action of bromine or chlorine and a strong base on the amides of carboxylic acids (A. W. von Hofmann, 1885).

The secondary amines are prepared, together with the primary and tertiary, by the action of ammonia on the alkyl iodides (see below) and also in numerous other ways.

By the action of ammonia on the alkyl iodides a complex mixture of primary, secondary and tertiary amines, along with a quaternary ammonium salt, is obtained, the separation of which is difficult. A method was worked out by von Hofmann in 1850 for the ethylamines but has not been widely extended. A more general method devised by O. Hinsberg (1890) consists in treating the mixed bases with benzene sulfonyl chloride (or p-toluene sulfonyl chloride). The primary base gives an acidic derivative, $C_6H_5.SO_2.NHR$, soluble in aqueous alkali, the secondary base furnishes the compound $C_6H_5.SO_2NR_2$, insoluble in alkali, whereas the tertiary base does not react. The process is applicable to both aliphatic and aromatic amines.

The primary, secondary and tertiary amines may be distinguished by their behaviour with various reagents. Primary amines when heated with alcoholic sodium hydroxide and chloroform yield isonitriles, which are readily detected by their offensive odour. The secondary and tertiary amines do not give this reaction. With nitrous acid, the primary amines yield alcohols (usually accompanied by olefines), the secondary amines yield nitrosamines and the tertiary amines do not react. The condensation with benzene sulfonyl chloride in the presence of alkali also furnishes a method of diagnosis (see above).

Methylamine, CH_3NH_2, occurring in the herb *Mercurialis perennis*, in bone oil and herring brine, is also a decomposition product of many alkaloids. At ordinary temperatures it is a gas with a strong ammoniacal smell, burns readily and is exceedingly soluble in water. Dimethylamine, $(CH_3)_2NH$, found in Peruvian guano, is a heavy vapour which liquefies at 7° C. and has a strong fishlike smell. Trimethylamine, $(CH_3)_3N$, is a vapour very similar to dimethylamine, but liquefies at 3.2°–3.8° C. It is usually obtained from vinasse, the residue from the distillation of beet sugar alcohol. The three methylamines can be obtained from ammonia and formaldehyde solution and a suitable separation for each of the three was devised by E. Werner (1917).

Tetramethylammonium iodide, $N(CH_3)_4I$, the final product obtained by the action of methyl iodide on ammonia (Hofmann), crystallizes in quadratic prisms and has a bitter taste. By warming its aqueous solution with an excess of silver oxide it is converted into tetramethylammonium hydroxide $N(CH_3)_4OH$, which crystallizes in hygroscopic needles, and has a very alkaline reaction. On dry distillation it is decomposed into trimethylamine and methyl alcohol. If the nitrogen atom in a quaternary ammonium salt is in combination with four different groups, then the molecule is dissymmetric, and the salt can be resolved into optically active enantiomorphous isomerides (W. J. Pope and S. J. Peachey, 1899 [see STEREOCHEMISTRY]).

Benzylamine, $C_6H_5.CH_2NH_2$, although it contains the phenyl group C_6H_5, is a typical aliphatic primary amine (see above). It can be obtained together with di- and tribenzylamines by the action of ammonia on benzyl chloride (S. Cannizzaro, 1865) and in other ways. It is a liquid which boils at 183° C., has an alkaline reaction and is miscible in all proportions with water, alcohol and ether.

Diamines.—The diamines contain two amino groups. Two of them are identical with the so-called ptomaines, which are produced by the putrefactive action of bacteria on albumen and other related substances. Tetramethylenediamine (putrescine), $NH_2.(CH_2)_4.NH_2$, is prepared also by reducing ethylene dicyanide (succinonitrile) with sodium in absolute alcoholic solution (A. Ladenburg, 1886). It melts at 27° C. and is easily soluble in water. Pentamethylenediamine (cadaverine), $NH_2.(CH_2)_5.NH_2$, is prepared by reducing trimethylene cyanide in ether solution by zinc and hydrochloric acid (Ladenburg, 1883). Cadaverine is a sirup at ordinary temperatures and boils at 178°–179° C. It is readily soluble in water and alcohol, but only slightly soluble in ether.

Aromatic Amines.—The aromatic amines are those in which the amino nitrogen atom is joined directly to at least one aromatic ring. These substances in some respects resemble the aliphatic amines, since they form salts with acids and also distill without decomposition. On the other hand, they are much weaker bases than the aliphatic amines, their salts undergoing extensive hydrolysis in aqueous solution. The primary aromatic amines may be prepared by the reduction of the nitro-hydrocarbons, the reducing agents used being frequently tin and hydrochloric acid, or on the manufacturing scale iron and water acidified by hydrochloric acid. They may also be obtained by the action of sodium hydroxide and either chlorine or bromine upon the amides of aromatic carboxylic acids, and on the manufacturing scale by treatment of aryl chlorides with ammonia at high temperatures and pressures in the presence of a catalyst.

The primary aromatic amines are colourless liquids or crystalline solids which are sparingly soluble in water but readily soluble in the common organic solvents. When heated with alkyl or aryl iodides they are converted into secondary and tertiary amines. When heated with concentrated sulfuric acid they become sulfonated. They form condensation products with aldehydes, and they form anilides when heated with organic acids. They give the isonitrile reaction (see above) when warmed with chloroform and a caustic alkali. When warmed with a solution of nitrous acid, they are converted into phenols; if, however, nitrous acid be added to an ice-cold solution of a primary amine in excess of mineral acid, a diazonium salt is formed (see ANILINE; AZO COMPOUND; DIAZO COMPOUNDS).

The secondary amines may be of two types—namely, the purely aromatic amines and the mixed secondary amines, which contain an aromatic residue and an alkyl group. The purely aromatic amines are obtained by heating the primary amines with their hydrochlorides and, in some cases, by heating a phenol with a primary aromatic amine and a catalyst (anhydrous zinc chloride or 1% of iodine). The mixed secondary amines are prepared by the action of alkyl iodides on the primary amines, or by heating salts of the primary amine with alcohols under pressure. (See ANILINE.) The mixed secondary amines have basic properties, but the purely aromatic secondary amines are only very feeble bases.

The tertiary amines may also be of two types, the purely aromatic and the mixed type. The mixed tertiary amines are produced by the action of alkyl halides on the primary amines. The simplest aromatic tertiary amine, triphenylamine, is prepared by the action of bromobenzene on sodium diphenylamine (C. Heydrich, 1885). Purely aromatic quaternary ammonium compounds are not known. The mixed quaternary hydroxides, such as trimethylanilinium hydroxide, $C_6H_5N(CH_3)_3OH$, are as strong bases as their purely aliphatic analogues.

Diphenylamine, $(C_6H_5)_2NH$, the simplest representative of the true aromatic secondary amines, crystallizes in white plates, which melt at 45° C., and it boils at 302° C.

Aromatic Diamines.—The simplest aromatic diamines are prepared by reducing the three nitranilines. Ortho-phenylenediamine, $C_6H_4(NH_2)_2$, crystallizes from water in plates, which melt at 102°–103° C. and it boils at 256°–258° C.

The three classes of aromatic diamines may be distinguished by their behaviour toward nitrous acid. The ortho compounds are transformed into benzotriazoles, the meta compounds yield azo dyestuffs and the para compounds yield bis-diazo compounds of the type $XN_2.C_6H_4.N_2X$. *See* DIAZO COMPOUNDS; *see also* Index references under "Amines" in the Index volume.

BIBLIOGRAPHY.—J. F. Thorpe and M. A. Whiteley, *Thorpe's Dictionary of Applied Chemistry*, vol. i, p. 305 (1937); N. V. Sidgwick, *The Organic Chemistry of Nitrogen*, rev. and rewritten by T. W. J. Taylor and W. Baker (1937); Louis F. and Mary Fieser, *Organic Chemistry*, 3rd ed. (1956). (G. T. M.; X.)

AMINO ACIDS, a class of organic acids containing the amino ($-NH_2$) group and forming the chief constituent of proteins. *See* PROTEINS; *see also* Index references under "Amino Acids" in the Index volume.

AMIOT (AMYOT), **JEAN JOSEPH MARIE** (1718–1793), French Jesuit missionary who provided a key to the thought and life of the far east by his *Dictionnaire tartare-mantchoufrançais*, was born at Toulon in Feb. 1718. He entered the Society of Jesus in 1737 and was sent in 1750 as a missionary to China. He soon won the confidence of the emperor Ch'ien Lung and spent the remainder of his life at Peking, where he died Oct. 9, 1793. Other than the *Dictionnaire* (1789), his writings are to be found chiefly in the *Mémoires concernant l'histoire, les sciences et les arts de Chinois* (1776–91). The *Vie de Confucius*, the 12th volume of that collection, is complete and accurate.

See, for full bibliography, C. Sommervogel, *Bibliothèque de la Compagnie de Jésus*, i, pp. 294–303 (1890–1932); for his works on Chinese music *see* F. J. Fétis, *Biographie universelle des musiciens* (1837–44).

AMIR, also spelled EMIR, a title common in the Muslim east (Arabic *amir*, "commander," from the root *'mr*, "command").

The word originally signified any military commander but was subsequently applied to governors of provinces and other high military officers. The title of *amir al-mu'minin*, "commander of the faithful," was assumed by the second caliph, Omar, and was adopted in later times by most of the various dynasties that claimed the caliphate (*q.v.*). In the 10th century the commander of the caliph's armies at Baghdad was styled *amir al-umara*, which is translated "supreme commander" or "generalissimo." In later use amir was applied as a title of dignity to the descendants of the Prophet.

Amir was also used in combination with other terms, to denote office (as in *amir al-hajj*, "leader of the pilgrimage"). It was adopted also by the rulers of several independent states in central Asia, notably those of Bukhara and Afghanistan. As applied to naval commanders it is the origin (through medieval Greek and Italian) of the English "admiral."

AMIR ALI, SEYYID (1849–1928), Indian-Muslim jurist, leader and thinker, was born at Cuttack in Orissa on April 6, 1849. He traced his descent from the eighth Shi'ite imam, Ali al-Riza. After graduating in Calcutta, he came to England and was called to the bar of the Inner Temple in 1873. Thereafter he began to practise law in Calcutta. A member of the Bengal legislative council in 1878, chief presidency magistrate in 1879, a legislative member of the governor general's council, he became a judge of the Calcutta high court in 1890. Permanently resident in England from 1904, he was appointed to the judicial committee of the privy council in 1909. He died in Sussex on Aug. 3, 1928.

A founder of the National Mohammedan association (1877) which was intended to give Indian Muslims experience in western political techniques and to protect their interests, Amir Ali supported British rule in India, believing that the alternative was Hindu domination masquerading as Indian nationalism. In 1909 he helped to secure communal electorates for Muslims under the Morley-Minto proposals (*see* INDIA-PAKISTAN, SUBCONTINENT OF: *History*). He sought also to reinterpret Islam in and to the modern world and his *Spirit of Islam* (1891) remains a modernist Muslim classic.

See "The Memoirs of the Late Rt. Hon'ble Syed Ameer Ali" in *Islamic Culture* (Oct. 1931 and Oct. 1932). (P. H.)

AMIR KHUSRAU (1253–1325), Persian poet and historian, known as "the parrot of India," and regarded as the greatest writer in Persian to be born outside the motherland, was born in 1253 at Patiala in northwest India. He was the son of a Turkish officer, who had joined the service of Iltutmish, sultan of Delhi. He showed a precocious gift for poetry, and was encouraged by

Balban, sultan of Delhi during 1266–86, and his son Mohammed Khan of Multan. In 1287 he was in Delhi when Bughra Khan advanced to expel his son the sultan Kai-Qubad; he witnessed their reconciliation, which provided him with the theme of his first historical epic, *Qiran al-sa'dain* ("Conjunction of the Two Stars"). Enjoying the patronage of Kai-Qubad and his successors, he composed a further series of epic poems celebrating the military exploits of his royal masters, ending with the *Tughlak-nama* on Ghiyas ud-Din Tughlak's victory in 1320 over the usurper Khusrau Khan. In the short span 1298–1301 he wrote a group of five long idylls in emulation of the *Khamsé* ("Five") of Nizami (*q.v.*). In addition he published no fewer than five collections of odes and lyrics, from *Tuhfat al-sighar* ("The Present of Youth") in 1272 to *Nihayat al-kamal* ("Ultimate Perfection") in 1325. In prose too he composed abundantly: a history of sultan Ala ud-Din Khilji's victories, a biography of the saint Nizam ud-Din Auliya whose disciple he was, and the *I'jaz-i Khusravi*, a massive collection of elegant compositions and model letters.

See Mohammed Wahid Mirza, *Life and Works of Amir Khusrau* (1935); A. J. Arberry, *Classical Persian Literature*, pp. 273–282 (1958). (A. J. AY.)

AMIS ET AMILES, an Old French epic written about 1200, concerns two men predestined to eternal friendship. When Amis is smitten with leprosy, Amiles kills his children so that his friend can be healed by bathing in their blood. The children are miraculously restored to life after the cure of Amis. The poem, written in assonanced decasyllabic verse, is stylistically one of the finest Carolingian epics. There were probably two earlier Old French epics on this subject; if they existed, both are lost. There are later versions in most European literatures.

See J. Bédier, *Les Légendes Épiques*, 4 vol., 2nd ed. (1914–21); J. A. Asher, *Amis et Amiles* (1952). (J. A. AR.)

AMISH, OLD ORDER, a conservative body of Mennonites characterized particularly by their distinctive dress and by their nonconformed way of life. Numbering about 17,500, they are found chiefly in Lancaster county, Pa.; Holmes county, O.; and Lagrange and Elkhart counties, Ind. *See* MENNONITES.

AMITABHA (Jap. AMIDA, "immeasurable light," or AMITAYUS, "immeasurable life"), the hero of the Sukhavativyuha Sutra (the fundamental scripture of the Pure Land, or Pure Realm, Buddhist faith), also host of the Pure Land. Besides the historical Buddha, Mahayana Buddhists conceived many Buddhas as their ideals, the most attractive figure among these being Amitabha. According to the sutra, long ago a monk named Dharmakara made a series of vows, the 18th of which reads: "If, after my obtaining Buddhahood, all beings in the ten quarters, who desire in sincerity to be born into my Buddha country, cannot be born thereto by only adoring me ten times, may I not take the enlightenment." His vows have been accomplished, he has become a Buddha and now lives in the Pure Land. This very Buddha is Amitabha. He acquired many followers in India and the far east, especially Japan, where the majority of Buddhists believe that by adoring Amida they will be born into the Pure Land. *See also* BUDDHISM.

See "The Larger and the Smaller Sukhavati-vyuha," trans. by F. Max Müller in *Sacred Books of the East*, vol. xlix (1883). (F. MA.)

AMMAN, JOST (1539–1591), Swiss painter and print maker, was one of the most prolific book illustrators of the 16th century. Born at Zürich on June 13, 1539, and educated there, he worked for a short time in Basel, where he designed glass paintings for prominent families. About 1560–61 he moved to Nürnberg, but retained his citizenship of Zürich until 1577. No paintings by Amman are known, but in his numerous drawings, such as the "Entry of Maximilian II Into Nürnberg in 1570," he reveals himself as a brilliant and witty recorder of contemporary events. His etchings include historical portraits, such as those of the kings of France, heraldic designs, title pages, scenes of warfare, hunting and pageantry. Most of his energy was consumed in the production of thousands of woodcut illustrations for the publisher Feirabend of Frankfurt. Most popular were those for the Bible, *Reynard the Fox*, *The Art of Riding* and the *Book of Animals*.

See Adam Bartsch, *Le Peintre graveur*, vol. ix, pp. 351–383 (1866). (H. JM.)

AMMAN, capital and administrative centre of the Hashemite Kingdom of Jordan, lies about 47 mi. E. of the Jordan river at an altitude of 2,400 ft. Amman *liwa'* (district) includes the subdistrict of Zerka (Az Zarqa'), and has an area of about 962 sq.mi. (2,491 sq.km.). Pop. (1961) city 246,475; *liwa'* 433,618.

The city is built on a series of hills and in their valleys, in one of which is the source of the Wadi Zerka (Jabbok). It almost trebled in size in the 15 years after 1945. Extending westward in the direction of Wadi Syr and eastward to the airport, it contains the royal palaces and many fine government and administrative buildings, law courts, hospitals, parliament building, etc. On the ancient citadel is the archaeological museum, displaying artifacts of all periods of the country's ancient history. A few miles to the southeast are quarries of coloured marble, which is used extensively for floors, dadoes, tables and other decorative purposes. Most buildings are constructed of local white limestone, a beautiful building material.

Amman is connected by railway with Damascus and Beirut in the north and Ma'an in the south; there is a modern airport with connections with all other middle eastern countries. It is the commercial heart of the country and provides a shopping centre; there is also a small market which caters to the needs of the desert dwellers and peasants. Chief exports include phosphates, building stone, vegetables, fruits and other vegetable products; imports include vehicles, liquid fuels, sugar, flour, fabrics, etc.

Amman is the site of the biblical Rabbath Ammon (*see* AMMONITES), though apart from some tombs excavated in the vicinity there are practically no remains of the ancient town. It was at the gate of Rabbath Ammon that Uriah the Hittite was placed in the forefront of the battle by order of David to meet his death. In Hellenistic times Ptolemy Philadelphus (283–246 B.C.) captured and rebuilt the city, renaming it Philadelphia, by which name it was known in Roman and Byzantine times. It was one of the cities of the Decapolis (*q.v.*). After the collapse of Byzantium in the 7th century A.D. the old name returned to use again. It became the capital of Transjordan when the amir Abdullah (later King Abdullah) established his government there soon after World War I.

There are many remains of the Roman city, in particular a fine theatre seating about 6,000, a much ruined nymphaeum on the river bank, and remains of a temple (probably of Hercules) on the citadel. Also on the citadel is a small square building attributed to either the Ghassanids or the Omayyads (6th or 8th century A.D.). (G. W. L. H.)

AMMANATI, BARTOLOMMEO (1511–1592), Florentine sculptor and architect, one of the most competent artists of the generation after Michelangelo, was born in Settignano on June 18, 1511. He executed works in Venice, Padua and Lucca as well as papal commissions in Rome and many designs for the archdukes of Tuscany in Florence.

Ammanati is distinguished for the precision, control and elegance of such structures as the bridge over the Arno known as the Ponte della Trinita (destroyed 1944, rebuilt 1957) and the Palazzo Giugni, both in Florence, and for the sober dignity of such portraits as those of the Del Monte tomb, S. Pietro in Montorio, Rome. His talents and limitations are clearly revealed in the Neptune fountain, Piazza della Signoria, Florence. The colossal central figure of Neptune seems a constrained and flaccid imitation of Michelangelo's heroic figures but the accompanying bronze figures of nymphs, satyrs and sea creatures are superbly wrought; a lively, inventive sequence executed with the ease and skill justly esteemed by Ammanati's aristocratic patrons. He died in Florence on April 22, 1592. (E. D. B.)

AMMETER: *see* INSTRUMENTS, ELECTRICAL MEASURING: *Indicating Instruments.*

AMMIANUS MARCELLINUS (*c.* 330–after 391), the author of a history of the later Roman empire from 353 to 378, was born into a Greek noble family at Antioch. Entering the army at an early age he served under Ursicinus, the *magister equitum* of Constantius II, first in the east against the Persians (353), then in Gaul against the Franks, and again in the east, where he barely escaped from the capture of Amida (now

Diarbekr) by the Persian king Shapur II in 359. Ammianus may have shared in Ursicinus' loss of favour with Constantius, but under Julian, Constantius' successor, he fought against the Persians, and on Julian's death (363) he took part in the retreat of his successor Jovian as far as Antioch, where he was living in 371. He visited Egypt and Greece. Eventually he settled in Rome, where at an advanced age he wrote (in Latin) a history of the Roman empire from the accession of Nerva to the death of Valens (96–378), thus continuing the work of Tacitus.

This history, *Rerum gestarum libri,* was originally in 31 books, of which the last 18 only have survived, covering the period from 353 to 378. It is a clear, comprehensive and honest account of events by a contemporary of soldierly qualities, independent judgment and wide reading. Roman history no longer turned on the city of Rome but was played out in the various theatres of imperial policy from west to east, and Ammianus made full use of his own experience. He gives excellent pictures of the social and economic problems of the empire, which go far to explain subsequent developments.

A pagan and religiously tolerant, he took an impartial view of the intellectual trends of his day. His judgment in political matters was limited only by his own straightforward attitude. In his literary composition he used the regular techniques of later Roman historiography: rhetoric in his speeches, ethnographical digressions, biographical conventions in character sketches, along with a fondness for literary allusion. Above all, he wrote with dramatic power in conscious imitation of Tacitus. His style is unequal and often overloaded with metaphor and ornament, but the effect is vivid and striking.

BIBLIOGRAPHY.—*Rerum gestarum libri,* ed. by C. U. Clark, 2 vol. (1910–15) and by J. C. Rolfe in the "Loeb Series" with Eng. trans., 3 vol. (1935–39). Eng. trans. by Philemon Holland (1609). *See also* S. Dill, *Roman Society in the Last Century of the Western Empire* (1898); T. R. Glover, *Life and Letters in the Fourth Century* (1901); E. A. Thompson, *The Historical Work of Ammianus Marcellinus* (1947).
(A. H. McD.)

AMMINES, in chemistry, compounds resulting from the addition of ammonia, NH$_3$, to metallic salts or other chemical compounds. The term is applied in a broader sense to compounds containing organic amines in place of part or all of the ammonia. It should not be confused with amines (*q.v.*). *See* CO-ORDINATION COMPOUNDS.

AMMONIA is a colourless alkaline gas, lighter than air, with a characteristic pungent odour. Ammonia and its salts have a wide range of applications in commercial products and processes, including use as fertilizer; in the manufacture of explosives; in refrigerating and air-conditioning equipment; in the manufacture of synthetic fibres and dyes; in the synthesizing of sulfa drugs; and (in conjunction with chlorine) in the purifying of water supplies.

The chemical formula of ammonia is NH$_3$.

In 1902 Wilhelm Ostwald, seeking to make Germany independent of Chilean nitrates, patented his process for producing nitric acid from ammonia. Much of the world's supply of nitrates is now derived from ammonia.

The ammonia clock, the first atomic timekeeping device, was developed in 1948 at the U.S. bureau of standards. Its design is based on the oscillation of the nitrogen atom in the ammonia molecule. It was the most accurate of all clocks until the development of another atomic timekeeper, the cesium clock.

Sal ammoniac (ammonium chloride) was an article of commerce in antiquity, and is mentioned by Pliny. It was first derived from organic material containing nitrogen by heating either camel's dung or a mixture of salt and urine. During the middle ages ammonia was obtained in aqueous solution by distilling the horns and hoofs of oxen; thus, its alchemical designation as "spirits of hartshorn."

Joseph Priestley (1774) prepared ammonia gas, which he called "alkaline air," by heating sal ammoniac with lime. Karl Wilhelm Scheele (1777) showed that ammonia contained nitrogen, but it remained for C. L. Berthollet (1785) to ascertain its exact composition.

Occurrence and Preparation.—Ammonia is found in small

traces in the atmosphere and in rain water, usually as the carbonate. It is formed when nitrogenous animal and vegetable matter undergoes putrefaction. It is found in humus-rich soils, in sea water and in plant and animal liquids (such as urine). It also occurs in variable but limited quantities in the vapours of lavas and in other volcanic effusions, in crater gases and is occasionally concentrated in the form of ammonium salts in the mineral incrustations adjoining fumaroles.

Ammonia is present to the extent of about 0.1% in the vapours of the *soffioni* (natural steam vents) at Larderello (province of Tuscany), Italy, and is actually recovered on a commercial scale from this source.

The more important laboratory methods for the preparation of ammonia include: (1) the action of alkaline hydroxides upon ammonium salts (usually the chloride or the sulfate), $NH_4Cl + NaOH = NaCl + NH_3 + H_2O$; and (2) the hydrolysis (decomposition by water) of nitrides such as magnesium nitride, $Mg_3N_2 + 6H_2O = 3Mg(OH)_2 + 2NH_3$. Large tonnages of ammonia and of ammonium sulfate are obtained as by-products in the manufacture of coke and gas from coal.

For many purposes, however, synthetic ammonia is preferred. The latter is made directly from the elements by the Haber process, or a modification thereof, involving use of high pressures ranging from 200 to 1,000 atm., temperatures between 400° and 500° C. and a variety of catalysts (*see* NITROGEN, FIXATION OF). The synthetic ammonia process is one of the most important industrial chemical processes now in operation and accounts for more than 85% of the total of ammonia production. An older process based upon the hydrolysis of calcium cyanamide is now used only to a limited extent.

Properties.—The density of air being taken as 1, the relative density of ammonia is 0.589. It is easily liquefied either by cooling to the normal boiling point, −33.42° C., or by compression. The most important physical properties of ammonia are given in Table I.

TABLE I.—*Physical Properties of Ammonia*

Melting point	195.36° K. (−77.74° C.)
Boiling point	239.68° K. (−33.42° C.)
Density of liquid at triple point	0.735 g./ml.
at boiling point	0.682 "
at critical temperature	0.234 "
Density of solid at triple point	0.81 "
Vapour pressure at triple point	45.58 mm.
at −40° C.	538.3 "
at 0° C.	3,221.0 "
at 30° C.	8,749.0 "
at critical temperature	112.3 atm.
Critical temperature	406.0° K. (132.9° C.)
Specific heat at boiling point	1.07 cal./g.
at freezing point	1.05 "
Heat of fusion	1,352 cal./mol.
Heat of vaporization (at boiling point)	5,581 cal./mol.
Ebullioscopic constant (observed)	0.34
Cryoscopic " (observed)	0.97
Dielectric constant at −60° C.	26.7
at 5° C.	18.94
at 25° C.	16.26
Refractive index, $\lambda = 0.5899\mu$ at 16° C.	1.325

The ammonia molecule has been shown to possess a pyramidal structure with the nitrogen atom resonating between two equally stable positions at a distance of 0.360 Å (Å, angstrom unit = 10^{-8} cm.) above and below the plane occupied by the three hydrogen atoms. Its electronic structure is represented by three normal covalent bonds between the three hydrogen atoms and the nitrogen atom, leaving the latter with an unshared pair of electrons. This structure accounts for many of the properties of ammonia (and of its derivatives), such as its tendency to act as a proton (hydrogen ion) acceptor to form the ammonium ion,

$$H:N:+H^+ = \left[H:N:H \right]^+ \text{ or } [H_3N \rightarrow H^+]$$

and its ability to form co-ordination compounds, such as the metal ammines, also designated as ammoniates; *i.e.*, compounds containing ammonia of crystallization. The latter vary widely in stability, some, such as $AgCl.3NH_3$, losing ammonia readily on heating, while others such as the cobalt and chromium ammines— *e.g.*, $[Co(NH_3)_6]Cl_3$ and $[Cr(NH_3)_6](NO_3)_3$—being stable (*see* CO-ORDINATION COMPOUNDS). It is of interest to note that Michael Faraday liquefied ammonia for the first time (1823) by heating the compound $AgCl.3NH_3$ in a sealed, two legged-tube, one leg of which was cooled in an ice-salt mixture to effect more ready condensation of ammonia vapour.

Ammonia undergoes thermal dissociation in the presence of certain catalysts to give nitrogen and hydrogen. Ammonia is therefore used as a convenient means for transporting hydrogen in the combined form since the gaseous mixture obtained by its decomposition contains 75% by volume of hydrogen and 25% by volume of nitrogen. Decomposition into the elements can also be effected by photochemical means and by passing a silent electrical discharge through the gas. Traces of hydrazine are obtained when such decomposition is brought about at low pressures, or when a highly heated tungsten filament is immersed in liquid ammonia.

Oxidation.—Ammonia does not support combustion, but it will burn when mixed with oxygen to give a variety of products, principally nitrogen and water with some oxides of nitrogen. Ammonia has been prominently mentioned as a constituent of various types of fuels, both for internal-combustion engines and for jet propulsion. A liquid mixture consisting of a solution of ammonium nitrate in liquid ammonia is stated to be a self-sustaining fuel combination requiring no addition of an oxidant, such as air.

The controlled oxidation of ammonia by air using platinum gauze as the catalyst is a technical process of great importance since it results in the formation of nitric oxide, this being the first step in the manufacture of synthetic nitric acid by the Ostwald process (*see* NITRIC ACID AND NITRATES). Mixtures of nitrous oxide and ammonia, especially in the volume ratio of 3:2, can be made to detonate with violence, yielding nitrogen and water as the reaction products: $3N_2O + 2NH_3 = 4N_2 + 3H_2O$. Ammonia reacts at higher temperatures with some metallic oxides, such as cupric oxide, to effect their reduction to the metals; in other cases, nitrides are formed. The hydrogen atoms of ammonia may be partially or completely replaced by metals to give either amides or nitrides. When ammonia is bubbled through molten sodium or potassium there are formed sodium amide, $NaNH_2$, and potassium amide, KNH_2, respectively; magnesium, on the other hand, is transformed into the nitride, Mg_3N_2.

Chemical oxidation of ammonia in aqueous solution usually causes formation of nitrogen gas. Chlorine reacts with ammonia (in excess) to give ammonium chloride and either nitrogen or chloramine, NH_2Cl. If chlorine is used in excess, the highly explosive nitrogen trichloride, NCl_3, is also produced. Iodine yields a violently explosive substance commonly referred to as nitrogen triiodide. This black crystalline product was shown by D. Chattaway and O. Silberrad to have the composition $NI_3.NH_3$. The commercial procedure for the manufacture of hydrazine is based upon the oxidation of aqueous ammonia by sodium hypochlorite solution, a process which appears to be successful only if a large excess of ammonia is employed together with certain catalytic materials which inhibit the decomposition of hydrazine: $2NH_3 + NaClO = N_2H_4 + NaCl + H_2O$. (*See* HYDRAZINE.)

Ionization.—The phase diagram of the system, ammonia-water, reveals the existence of two solid hydrates, $NH_3.H_2O$ and $2NH_3.H_2O$, both melting at approximately −79° C. It is doubtful if either one of these is capable of existing at room temperature, even though the solubility of ammonia in water is high. At 20° C. and normal pressures about 700 vol. of ammonia gas dissolve per volume of water. Ammonia gas may be expelled completely from the aqueous solution by boiling.

Since ammonia is a proton acceptor (combines with the hydrogen ion), that is, acts as a base, it undergoes reaction with water in accordance with the following equation: $NH_3 + H_2O \rightleftharpoons NH_4^+ + OH^-$. It is highly improbable that any appreciable concentration of molecular ammonium hydroxide, NH_4OH, exists in aqueous solution, even though water solutions of ammonia are generally referred to as "ammonium hydroxide." Ammonia is a weak base and therefore reacts with the solvent water only to a limited extent to produce ammonium and hydroxide ions. A decinormal solution of ammonia (0.17% NH_3) in water reacts only to the extent of about 1% to form NH_4^+ and OH^- ions, the dissociation constant, K_b, for aqueous ammonia as a base being $K = 1.65 \times 10^{-5}$ at 25° C.

The ammonium ion, NH_4^+, is a univalent radical resembling the alkali metal ions. Ammonium salts, for instance, are crystallographically similar to the corresponding potassium and rubidium salts. The ammonium radical may take the place of the alkali metals in such double salts as those represented by the type formula $CuSO_4.M_2SO_4.6H_2O$ and in the alums $MAl(SO_4)_2.12H_2O$, where M represents NH_4 or some alkali metal. Many attempts have been made to prepare the free ammonium radical, but the evidence for its existence is at best circumstantial. H. H. Schlubach and F. Ballouf allowed potassium and ammonium chloride to interact in liquid ammonia at −70° C. and obtained only one-third of the theoretical quantity of hydrogen. They therefore assumed the existence of free ammonium in such a solution; at −40° C. the remainder of the hydrogen was evolved. The addition of sodium amalgam to a cold concentrated aqueous solution of ammonium chloride gives a spongy mass which resembles the amalgams of the alkali metals in some respects but not in others; this product decomposes readily into ammonia and hydrogen.

Ammonium Salts.—Preparation of ammonium salts is by direct combination of gaseous or aqueous ammonia with the desired acids; thus, combination of ammonia with hydrochloric acid yields ammonium chloride (sal ammoniac), with nitric acid, ammonium nitrate. Ammonium salts of practically all acids, both inorganic and organic, have been isolated and characterized. The ammonium salts of strong acids dissolve in water to give an acid reaction, hydrolysis being caused by the fact that the following equilibrium is established: $NH_4^+ + H_2O \rightleftharpoons NH_3 + H_2O.H^+$. Rise in temperature shifts this equilibrium to the right as is evidenced by the fact that some ammonia is lost when solutions of ammonium salts are heated to boiling. Some ammonium salts, such as ammonium chloride, do not melt on heating but dissociate into their components in accordance with the equation: $NH_4X = NH_3 + HX$; others, such as ammonium nitrate and ammonium sulfamate, have definite melting points and are stable at the melting point.

Ammonium salts have been shown by L. F. Audrieth and co-workers to behave as acids at higher temperatures. Ammonium chloride has long been used as a fluxing agent for removal of oxide films from metal surfaces prior to soldering; ammonium sulfate has been employed in the "opening up" of ores; fused ammonium nitrate reacts directly with many metallic oxides to give the corresponding nitrates. Characterization of ammonium salts as acids, per se, is accounted for by the fact that the ammonium ion is capable of releasing the proton; i.e., can in accordance with the modern concept of acidity behave as an acid. Ammonium salts behave as acids when dissolved in liquid ammonia.

Ammonium salts have found wide application technically, but only the most important ones will be mentioned here.

Ammonium chloride, NH_4Cl, also long known under the trade name sal ammoniac, is made commercially by the neutralization of hydrochloric acid with aqueous or gaseous ammonia. It is purified by sublimation. It is extensively used as a constituent of galvanizing, tinning and soldering fluxes, since it reacts readily at higher temperatures with metal corrosion products, thus serving as a metal cleaner. In galvanizing operations a double salt with zinc chloride, either $ZnCl_2.2NH_4Cl$ or $ZnCl_2.3NH_4Cl$, is usually employed to serve first as a liquid protective layer over molten zinc; second, as a metal cleaner for the material to be coated with zinc; and third, to dry and preheat the work (sheet or article) which is to be coated with zinc. As a soldering flux it is employed either by itself or in aqueous solution or in admixture with rosin, paraffin waxes or oils, organic surface active agents and/or other acids. Ammonium chloride also finds use (1) as a pharmaceutical, being a common constituent of many proprietary cold and cough medicines; (2) in dry cells; (3) in the manufacture of a number of dyes and as a weakly acid constituent of dyeing baths; and (4) in the manufacture of iron cements and other ammonium salts.

Ammonium nitrate, NH_4NO_3, is the most important nitrogenous fertilizer. The commercially available "fertilizer grade" (FGAN) contains 33% available nitrogen. Due to its hygroscopicity (tendency to pick up moisture) it is manufactured in the form of pellets or balls ("prills") covered by a small amount of claylike conditioning material. When properly bagged and stored, it reaches the farmer in a form satisfactory for application to the soil with customary farm machinery. Mixed ammonium nitrate fertilizers are also produced commercially containing calcium phosphate, limestone, dolomite, ammonium sulfate or soluble potassium and phosphate ingredients. Ammonium nitrate is capable of explosive decomposition, especially in the confined state, and acts as a powerful oxidizing agent since it will support combustion in a fire with combustible material even in the absence of air. Because of these potential hazards special shipment and storage precautions have been imposed by government regulation to prevent disastrous explosions, such as those that occurred at Oppau, Ger. (1921), and Texas City, Tex. (1947), with attendant loss of life and destruction of property. Ammonium nitrate also finds widespread technical application as a constituent of various military high-explosive and propellant compositions, in dynamites and blasting explosives and as a source of nitrous oxide, since it decomposes on heating in accordance with the equation $NH_4NO_3 = N_2O + 2H_2O$.

Other Ammonium Salts.—Ammonium sulfate, $(NH_4)_2SO_4$, is produced in large amounts as a by-product in the manufacture of coke and gas from coal. It is one of the more important nitrogenous fertilizers, but also finds use in fireproofing fabrics and to a limited extent as a medicinal. Ammonium thiocyanate, NH_4SCN, can be obtained from carbon disulfide and ammonia. It isomerizes to thiourea on heating; if fused in the presence of desulfurizing agents such as lead oxide, PbO, it can be converted into a guanidine compound:

$$NH_4SCN = CS(NH_2)_2 \xrightarrow[PbO]{NH_4SCN} C(NH)(NH_2)_2.HSCN$$

Thiourea   Guanidine thiocyanate

Both thiourea and guanidine are valuable industrial raw materials in the manufacture of rubber accelerators, plastics and medicinals.

Three ammonium phosphates, known respectively as the mono-, di- and triammonium phosphates, or as the monobasic, dibasic and tribasic salts, are obtainable by interaction of phosphoric acid with the requisite quantities of ammonia. The solid triammonium phosphate, $(NH_4)_3PO_4$, loses ammonia quite readily to go over into the diammonium salt, $(NH_4)_2HPO_4$. The monoammonium phosphate, $NH_4H_2PO_4$, is an important ingredient of baking powders. Both the monobasic and dibasic salts are used extensively in flameproofing of paper, wood and textiles, in the formulation of nutrient solutions and in the production of special fertilizer mixtures as, for instance, for use in the practice of hydroponics (soilless agriculture).

Ammonia and carbon dioxide react to give ammonium carbamate, $NH_2COOH.NH_3$, which is formed as an intermediate product in the high-pressure synthesis of urea, $CO(NH_2)_2$. Ammonium carbamate hydrolyzes in water solution to form ammonium hydrogen carbonate, NH_4HCO_3. Commercial ammonium carbonate, $(NH_4)_2CO_3$, is usually a mixture of the normal carbonate and the hydrogen carbonate. Ammonium perchlorate, NH_4ClO_4, is of interest chiefly because it can be made to react with concentrated nitric acid to give nitrous oxide and perchloric acid. It is one of the less soluble ammonium salts. The ammonium salts of high molecular weight fatty acids, such as ammonium stearate, $RCOOH.NH_3$, find use as detergents, emulsifying agents, textile assistants and as surface active agents of the anionic type.

The Ammonia System of Compounds.—Particular reference is made to the fact that ammonia resembles water in many of its physical properties. This similarity is even more striking when consideration is given to the fact that ammonia occupies an anomalous position with respect to the other hydrogen compounds of the fifth group of the periodic system just as water is different from the remaining hydrides of the sixth group. Its boiling point, dielectric constant and heat of vaporization are abnormally high, as compared with phosphine, arsine and bismuth hydride, indicating that liquid ammonia consists of molecular aggregates, rather than of simple NH_3 molecules. Like water, liquid ammonia is not only an excellent solvent for many inorganic and organic compounds, but has been found to serve as a useful medium for carrying out a wide variety of chemical reactions.

Related to its interesting properties as a solvent is the fact that ammonia may be looked upon as the parent substance of the "ammonia" or "nitrogen" system of compounds. Nitrogen compounds, both inorganic and organic, can be regarded as derivatives of ammonia much as the oxygen compounds may be considered as derivatives of water. The prefix "ammono" has been applied to these nitrogen compounds to distinguish them from the analogous "aquo" compounds derived from water as the parent substance. This concept has not only been helpful in classifying nitrogen compounds but has received experimental confirmation by the study of behaviour of nitrogen compounds in liquid ammonia and other nonaqueous solvents. Typical ammono compounds are listed in Table II together with the analogous aquo compounds. The relationship of these to the corresponding oxygen compounds is evident from a consideration of related groups derived from each parent solvent.

From water: HOH OH^- O^{2-}
From ammonia: HNH_2 NH_2^- NH^{2-} and N^{3-}

Compounds containing the $-NH_2$ group have been shown to behave in ammonia as solvent in the same way that substances containing the OH group react in water.

The true character of many nitrogen compounds becomes self-evident from this point of view. Such mercury compounds as $HgNH_2Cl$ and $HgCl_2.2NH_3$, known as the "infusible" and "fusible white precipitates," represent an ammono basic compound and a compound containing co-ordinated ammonia, respectively (see MERCURY). Sulfamic acid, H_2NSO_3H, and sulfamide, $SO_2(NH_2)_2$, are both analogues of sulfuric acid as becomes obvious from the following structural relationship:

HO\   H₂N\   H₂N\
   >SO₂   >SO₂   >SO₂
HO/   HO/   H₂N/
Sulfuric acid   Sulfamic acid   Sulfamide

Sulfamic acid is now a commercially available chemical and has found widespread use as a nonhygroscopic, crystalline compound which in solution behaves as a strong acid. Ammonium sulfamate, $NH_4SO_3NH_2$, is an effective flame retardant and an outstanding herbicide. Sulfamide resembles urea and like the latter is used technically for the production of thermosetting polymers. Potassium nitridotrisulfate, $N(SO_3K)_3.2H_2O$, and the imidodisulfate, $HN(SO_3K)_2$, are salts of acids derived from sulfamic acid. They undergo hydrolysis in boiling water to give the sulfamate, KSO_3NH_2. Reaction of sulfur trioxide with ammonia gives mixtures of the ammonium salts of imidodisulfuric and nitridotrisulfuric acids.

TABLE II.—Ammono Compounds

Formula	Name	Character	Aquo analogue
KNH_2	potassium amide	ammono base	KOH
Hg_3N_2	mercuric nitride	anammonide	HgO
$K_2Zn(NH)_2$	potassium ammono zincate	amphoteric amide	K_2ZnO_2
$SO_2(NH_2)_2$	sulfamide	ammono sulfuric acid	$SO_2(OH)_2$
$C(NH)(NH_2)_2$	guanidine	ammono carbonic acid	$CO(OH)_2$
$CO(NH_2)_2$	urea	ammono carbonic acid	$CO(OH)_2$
H_2NCN	cyanamide	ammono carbonic acid	$CO(OH)_2$
CH_3NH_2	methylamine	ammono alcohol	CH_3OH
$(CH_3)_3N$	trimethylamine	ammono ether	$(CH_3)_2O$
CH_3CONH_2	acetamide	ammono acetic acid	CH_3COOH
$CH_3CONHNa$	sodium acetamide	salt of ammono acetic acid	CH_3COONa
$CH_3CONHCH_3$	N-methylacetamide	ammono ester	CH_3COOCH_3
$CaCl_2.8NH_3$	calcium chloride-8-ammonia	compound containing ammonia of crystallization	$CaCl_2.6H_2O$

Reactions With Halogen Compounds.—Ammonia is capable of converting active halogen compounds, such as the nonmetallic halides, thiohalides and oxyhalides, into the corresponding nitro-

gen compounds. These reactions of "ammonolysis" are similar to those effected by water (reactions of hydrolysis) as the following parallel equations demonstrate:

$$PCl_3+3H_2O=H_3PO_3+3HCl$$
$$PCl_3+6HNH_2=P(NH_2)_3+3NH_4Cl$$

The nitrogen content of products obtained by these reactions depends upon conditions, particularly the temperature. While phosphorus (III) triamide, $P(NH_2)_3$, is obtained and appears to be stable at $-33°$ C., the product loses ammonia at room temperature to yield diphosphorus (III) triimide, $P_2(NH)_3$, and undergoes complete deammonation (analogous to dehydration) at $550°$ C. to give phosphorus (III) nitride

$$P(NH_2)_3 \xrightarrow[25°]{-NH_3} P_2(NH)_3 \xrightarrow[550°]{-NH_3} PN$$

Table III gives a list of compounds obtained when specific nonmetallic halides react with ammonia.

TABLE III.—Reaction Products of Nonmetallic Halides With Ammonia

Compound treated with ammonia	Substance formed and conditions
BCl_3	$B(NH_2)_3$ ($-23°$, $0°$ C.)
BBr_3	$B_2(NH)_3$ ($-10°$, $+20°$ C.)
$SiCl_4$	$Si(NH_2)_4$ ($-50°$ to $0°$ C.)
	$Si(NH)_2$ ($20°$ C.)
$SiSCl_2$	$Si(NH)_2$
Si_2Cl_6	$[Si(NH)NH_2]_2$ (low temperatures)
$GeCl_4$	$Ge(NH)_2$ ($-80°$ C.)
$SnCl_4$	$2Sn(NH_2)_3Cl.NH_4Cl$ ($0°$ C.)
$TiBr_4$	$TiNBr.xNH_3$
PCl_5	$PN(NH_2)_2$ ($-70°$ C.)
PCl_3	$P(NH_2)_3$ plus $P_2(NH)_3$
$TaCl_5$	$Ta(NH_2)_2Cl_3.3NH_3$
SO_2Cl_2	$SO_2(NH_2)_2$ ($-33°$ C.)
$POCl_3$	$PO(NH_2)_3$
$VOCl_3$	$VO(NH_2)_3$ ($-80°$ C.)

Attention is directed to the fact that only partial replacement of halogen is effected in the case of the halides of tin, titanium and vanadium under the given reaction conditions. The reaction between phosphorus pentachloride and ammonia can also be made to stop at an intermediate stage, especially when ammonium chloride is used to effect ammonolysis. Here again parallel equations may be given to show the similarity between reactions of ammonia and water

$$PCl_5+NH_3(HCl) = PNCl_2+4HCl$$
$$PCl_5+H_2O = POCl_3+2HCl$$

Partial replacement of halogen in phosphorus pentachloride results in the formation of the phosphonitrilic chlorides, $(PNCl_2)_x$, where $x=3$, 4, 5, 6, 8 and n. The lower members of this series undergo polymerization on heating to the "inorganic rubber" $(PNCl_2)_n$, a substance which resembles the better known natural and synthetic elastomers in its physical properties.

Hydrolysis of the phosphonitrilic chlorides yields the corresponding phosphonitrilic acids, also known as the metaphosphimic acids; as represented by the type equation:

$$(PNCl_2)_x+2xH_2O=[PN(OH)_2]_x+2xHCl$$

These ammonophosphoric acids are related to amido- and diamidophosphoric acids, $(HO)_2PONH_2$ and $HOPO(NH_2)_2$, which were first isolated by H. N. Stokes. They constitute the simplest members of a large and interesting group of nitrogen derivatives of phosphoric acid.

Organic Derivatives of Ammonia.—Ammonia finds wide application in organic chemistry as a synthetic agent. It reacts with the alkylhalides to form the alkylamines, RNH_2 (primary), R_2NH (secondary), R_3N (tertiary); with ethylene dihalide to yield ethylenediamine, $H_2NCH_2CH_2NH_2$, diethylene triamine, $H_2NCH_2CH_2NHCH_2CH_2NH_2$, together with the higher members of this series; with ethylene oxide or ethylene chlorohydrin to give the mono-, di- and triethanolamines, $H_2NC_2H_4OH$, $HN(C_2H_4OH)_2$ and $N(C_2H_4OH)_3$. Under special conditions alcohols can be caused to react with ammonia in the presence of dehydrating catalysts such as activated alumina to yield the corresponding primary, secondary or tertiary amines, depending upon the ratios of the reactants and upon the temperature. The amines are basic in character and form salts which in many respects resemble the corresponding ammonium salts. Tertiary amines, R_3N, combine with alkylhalides to form the quaternary or tetraalkylammonium salts: $R_3N+RX=R_4NX$. These compounds resemble the alkali metal salts even more strongly than do the ammonium salts.

The tetraalkylammonium hydroxides are almost completely ionized and behave as strong bases in aqueous solution. The relative stability of the quaternary ammonium radical is further illustrated by the fact that the corresponding amalgams are much more stable than that of ammonium. H. N. McCoy and W. C. Moore obtained a tetramethylammonium amalgam which did not decompose below 10° C. Electrolysis of tetramethylammonium iodide in liquid ammonia results in the formation of a blue coloration in the cathode region. Since the alkali and alkaline earth metals produce this coloration in ammonia, it seems highly probable that the tetramethylammonium radical is actually discharged and thus capable of existence for a limited time. When all four alkyl groups of a quaternary ammonium salt are different, the compound can be resolved into optical isomerides.

Esters and acid chlorides react with ammonia to form amides:

$$RCOCl+2NH_3=RCONH_2+NH_4Cl$$
$$RCOOR'+NH_3=RCONH_2+R'OH$$

At high temperatures and in the presence of dehydrating catalysts it is possible to convert the fatty acids of high molecular weight, such as those derived from fats and oils, into the corresponding nitriles:

$$RCOOH+NH_3=RCN+2H_2O$$

The nitriles can be converted by various indirect procedures into the amidines, involving essentially addition of ammonia:

$$RCN+NH_3=RC(NH)(NH_2)$$

Of great technical importance is the high-pressure synthesis of urea from carbon dioxide and ammonia. Urea is, in fact, a carbonic acid derivative of ammonia and is related to such compounds as guanidine, cyanamide, cyanic acid and carbamic acid as indicated in the accompanying schematic diagram.

Some ammonia derivatives of carbonic acid. The compounds cyanic acid and cyanamide are desolvation products, whereas cyanuric acid and melamine are polymerization products of simpler units.

Hydronitrogens.—Ammonia is the simplest hydronitrogen, the latter being defined as one of a series of compounds containing only hydrogen and nitrogen. The hydronitrogens, like the hydrocarbons, may be divided into several homologous series, but unlike their carbon analogues only a few (ammonia, hydrazine and hydrazoic acid) have actually been isolated in the free state. Most of them are known only in the form of their organic derivatives, but these constitute a large and variegated group of compounds. (*See* also AMIDES; ANILINE; CYANAMIDE, CALCIUM; DIAZO COMPOUNDS; GUANIDINE; HYDRAZINE; UREA; URETHANE.)

Detection and Estimation.—Solutions of ammonia and ammonium salts, even if dilute, give a distinct yellow or yellowish-

TABLE IV.—*The Hydronitrogens*

Item	Empirical formula	Structural formula	Name
N_nH_{n+2} series .	NH_3	NH_3	ammonia and its derivatives
	N_2H_4	$H_2N—NH_2$	hydrazine and its derivatives
	N_3H_5	$H_2N—NH—NH_2$	triazane, prozane
	N_4H_6	$H_2N—NH—NH—NH_2$	tetrazane, buzane, hydrotetrazone
N_nH_n series .	N_2H_2	$HN=NH$	diazene, diimide, azo compounds
	N_3H_3	$HN=N—NH_2$	triazene, diazoamino compounds
	N_4H_4	$H_2N—N=N—NH_2$ $HN=N—NH—NH_2$	tetrazene, tetrazone isotetrazene, diazohydrazine, buzylene
N_nH_{n-2} series .	N_3H	$HN=N=N$	hydrazoic acid, azoimide, hydronitric acid
N_nH_{n-4} series .	N_5H_3 N_6H_4	$HN=N—NH—N=NH$ $HN=N—NH—N=$ $N—NH—N=NH$	bisdiazoamine octazotriene, octazones

brown coloration with Nessler's solution, because of the formation of a complex iodide, $NHg_2I.H_2O$, which is obtained as a precipitate from stronger solutions; this is also the basis of a colorimetric method for estimating minute traces of ammonia in drinking water.

Larger quantities of ammonia or its salts can be detected by evolution of the characteristic smell of free ammonia on heating with caustic alkalis or lime. Quantitative estimation may be effected by (1) distillation of salts or ammoniacal liquors with sodium or potassium hydroxide and absorption of the liberated ammonia in an excess of standard sulfuric acid, the excess being titrated by alkali; (2) by absorption of ammonia in hydrochloric acid and precipitation as the chloroplatinate, $(NH_4)_2PtCl_6$; or (3) by the addition of neutral formaldehyde to a neutral solution of an ammonium salt, whereby hexamethylenetetramine is formed and the acid originally in combination with the ammonia is set free and may be titrated: $4NH_4Cl + 6CH_2O = (CH_2)_6N_4 + 4HCl + 6H_2O$.

See ETHANOLAMINES; HYDRAZOIC ACID; NITRIDES; REFRIGERATION; *see* also references under "Ammonia" in the Index.

BIBLIOGRAPHY.—J. F. Gmelin, *Handbuch der Anorganischen Chemie,* 8th ed., vol. 4 (nitrogen), vol. 23 (ammonia) (1936); E. C. Franklin, *The Nitrogen System of Compounds* (1935); F. Raschig, *Schwefel- und Stickstoffstudien* (1924); L. F. Audrieth and J. Kleinberg, *Non-Aqueous Solvents* (1953); M. Goehring, *Ergebnisse und Probleme der Chemie der Schwefelstickstoffverbindungen* (1957); N. V. Sidgwick, *The Organic Chemistry of Nitrogen,* rev. and rewritten by T. W. J. Taylor and W. Baker (1937); L. F. Audrieth and B. A. Ogg, *The Chemistry of Hydrazine* (1951); R. N. Shreve, *The Chemical Process Industries* (1956); W. L. Faith, D. B. Keyes and R. L. Clark, *Industrial Chemicals,* 2nd ed. (1957). (L. F. A.)

AMMONIACUM or GUM AMMONIAC, a gum resin (*q.v.*) exuded from the stem of the perennial herb *Dorema ammoniacum* growing in Iran. Upon incision or injury, the plant oozes a milky juice which hardens to what is called in commerce tears or mass. This substance was formerly used medicinally as a stimulant, carminative and laxative. (R. H. DH.)

AMMONITE, any member of a group of extinct Mollusca belonging to the class Cephalopoda. They possessed an external shell that was coiled in a flat spiral and divided into chambers very similar to that of the modern nautilus. Many reached a

BY COURTESY OF WARD'S NATURAL SCIENCE ESTABLISHMENT, INC.

UPPER CRETACEOUS AMMONITE (PLACENTICERAS); DIAMETER, ABOUT 2 FT.

great size, the largest, *Pachydiscus seppenradensis*, from the Cretaceous of Westphalia, having a shell six feet eight inches in diameter.

The Ammonites appeared in the Carboniferous period (285,000,-000 to 235,000,000 years ago) and became extinct at the end of the Cretaceous (about 70,000,000 years ago).

AMMONITES, a Semitic people of ancient Transjordan. Their land was north of Moab, and their chief city, Rabbath Ammon (later Philadelphia, the modern Amman [*q.v.*], capital of the Hashemite Kingdom of Jordan), stood on the banks of a tributary of the Jabbok. In the Old Testament they are almost always referred to as "the sons of Ammon."

The Ammonite kingdom was not established until the 13th century B.C.; before then Transjordan was inhabited by wandering nomads. The original Ammonite kingdom apparently lay in a small strip east of the Jabbok river where it flows from south to north, extending to the desert. At times they spread westward to the Jordan river. Their civilization flourished from the 13th to the 6th century B.C., being very similar to that of Moab and Edom (*qq.v.*), and oriented to Syria and Arabia as well as Israel.

The Ammonites were defeated by the judge Jephthah and by Saul, and were subdued by David. They had regained their independence by the time of Shalmaneser III, who records that they furnished soldiers for the battle of Karkar in 853 B.C. (*See* AHAB.) Several Assyrian kings from Tiglath-pileser III through Ashurbanipal received tribute from kings of Bit-Ammanu, "the House of Ammon." Ammonites were allied with bands of Chaldeans, Syrians and others in an attack on Judah in the reign of Jehoiakim, but later, in the time of Zedekiah, were involved in plans for rebellion against Babylonia (Jer. xxvii). They may have taken some Judaean territory at the time of the Babylonian capture of Jerusalem, as the Edomites did. Several Hebrew prophets denounced them at various times (Amos i, 13–15; Jer. xlix, 1–6; Ezek. xxv, 1–7; Zeph. ii, 8–11). The Judaean governor, Gedaliah, was assassinated at the instigation of a king of Ammon. When Nehemiah attempted to restore the purity of the Judaean community, a bitter opponent was Tobiah the Ammonite. The Ammonites were defeated by Judas Maccabaeus (I Macc. v, 6–8). They still formed a community in the days of Justin Martyr.

Little is known of the religion and culture of the Ammonites. One of their gods was Milcom. They combined pastoral life with the limited amount of agriculture that is possible in the region east of the Jordan. Archaeology has shown that they had several fortified towns in the period from the 13th to the 6th century B.C.

(J. P. Hy.)

AMMONIUM is a positive univalent ion, NH_4^+, whose salts resemble those of potassium and univalent thallium in solubility and crystalline form. The free ammonium radical has been prepared as an amalgam. *See* AMMONIA.

AMMONIUS HERMIAE (*i.e.*, Ammonius son of Hermias) (fl. 5th century A.D.), Greek philosopher, who was one of the most influential of commentators on Aristotle. He studied under Proclus at Athens and later was appointed head of the Alexandrian school.

He was a sober, unprejudiced expositor, free from mysticism and well informed in the science of his day. The commentaries which survive are concerned with logical subjects. In the Berlin Academy's *Commentaria in Aristotelem Graeca* are to be found his commentaries on Porphyry's *Isagoge*, on the *Categories* and on the *De Interpretatione* (ed. by A. Busse, 1891) and also his commentary on the *Prior Analytics I* (ed. by M. Wallies, 1899). These works were much studied down to the time of the Renaissance and were printed in Latin versions.

The literary activity of Ammonius was more extensive than this. Expositions both of the *Organon* and of the physical treatises of Aristotle seem, from coincidences evidently pointing to a common source, to contain much that is derived from him. From internal evidence it appears that he did not himself prepare his commentaries for publication. A life of Aristotle which is ascribed to him in some manuscripts is full of errors and is evidently not his work.

(D. J. A.)

AMMONIUS SACCAS (*c.* A.D. 175–242), the teacher of Plotinus, was a self-taught Alexandrian philosopher who, according to Porphyry as reported by Eusebius, had been brought up a Christian and later became a pagan. His pupils, besides Plotinus, included the rhetorician and philosopher Longinus, the pagan philosopher Origen and perhaps also the Christian Origen. He left no writings, and his pupils were pledged to secrecy about his teaching; consequently next to nothing is known about his doctrines, the allusions to them in Nemesius and in Photius' extract from Hierocles giving no clear or reliable information. All that is certain is that he deeply influenced Plotinus, though there seems no way of establishing with certainty how much in the latter comes from Ammonius and how much is original. (A. H. Ag.)

See the article "Plotinus" in Pauly-Wissowa, *Real-Encyclopädie der classischen Altertumswissenschaft*, vol. xxi, pp. 477–481.

AMMUNITION, ARTILLERY, a term that includes projectiles, fuzes and propelling charges for guns, howitzers, mortars and recoilless rifles. Bombs, grenades, mines, rockets and guided missiles are also sometimes placed in this category, but are not included here as they are discussed in separate articles (*see* GRENADES; ROCKETS AND GUIDED MISSILES).

There is no hard and fast line separating artillery ammunition from small-arms ammunition but, in general, cartridges with projectile elements one inch or more in diameter are classified as artillery and the smaller sizes as small arms. In practice, ammunition of calibre .60 ($\frac{60}{100}$ in. in diameter) has usually been considered the largest of the small-arms types.

With small-arms ammunition, all the components of a single round are normally assembled into a compact unit which includes a metal (usually brass) case containing the propellant (often called smokeless powder or gunpowder), a projectile or bullet affixed to one end of the case and a primer inserted in the other end. The smaller calibres of artillery ammunition are assembled in the same manner and are known as fixed ammunition. Semifixed ammunition differs from fixed ammunition in that its projectile may be detached from the case to permit increasing or decreasing the propelling charge and thus adjusting the range. In the third type, known as separated ammunition, the projectile is separated from the case, but the case is sealed so that no adjustment can be made in its propelling charge. A fourth type, known as separate-loading ammunition, is employed for pieces of medium or large bore and permits adjustment of the propelling charge. As the name suggests, with this type of ammunition each element—projectile, propellant and primer—is loaded into the weapon separately. First the projectile, usually very heavy, is rammed into the chamber, then the desired number of bags of propellant are put in place (without a cartridge case) and the primer is separately inserted into its seat in the breechblock. No matter what its form (fixed, semifixed, separated or separate-loading), the combination of one full set of the elements (propellant, projectile and primer) necessary for a single firing of a piece is known as a complete round of ammunition.

Following are the divisions of this article:

I. General Terminology
II. History of Ammunition
  1. Early Ordnance Projectiles
  2. Round Shot
  3. Canister
  4. Explosive Shell
  5. Miscellaneous Types
  6. Early Fuzes
  7. Rifled Guns
  8. Confusion in Nomenclature
  9. Improved Fuzes
  10. Improved Shells
  11. Ammunition in World War I
III. Artillery Ammunition After World War I
  1. HE Shells
  2. Chemical Shells
  3. Armour-Piercing Projectiles
  4. Mortar Ammunition
  5. Recoilless Rifle Ammunition
  6. Canister
  7. Pyrotechnics
  8. Cartridge Cases
  9. Fuzes

10. Propellants and Explosives
11. Atomic Shells

I. GENERAL TERMINOLOGY

Fig. 1 indicates some of the standard terms employed to describe the many elements of a typical round of artillery ammunition. The tapered point of the standard high-explosive (HE) projectile

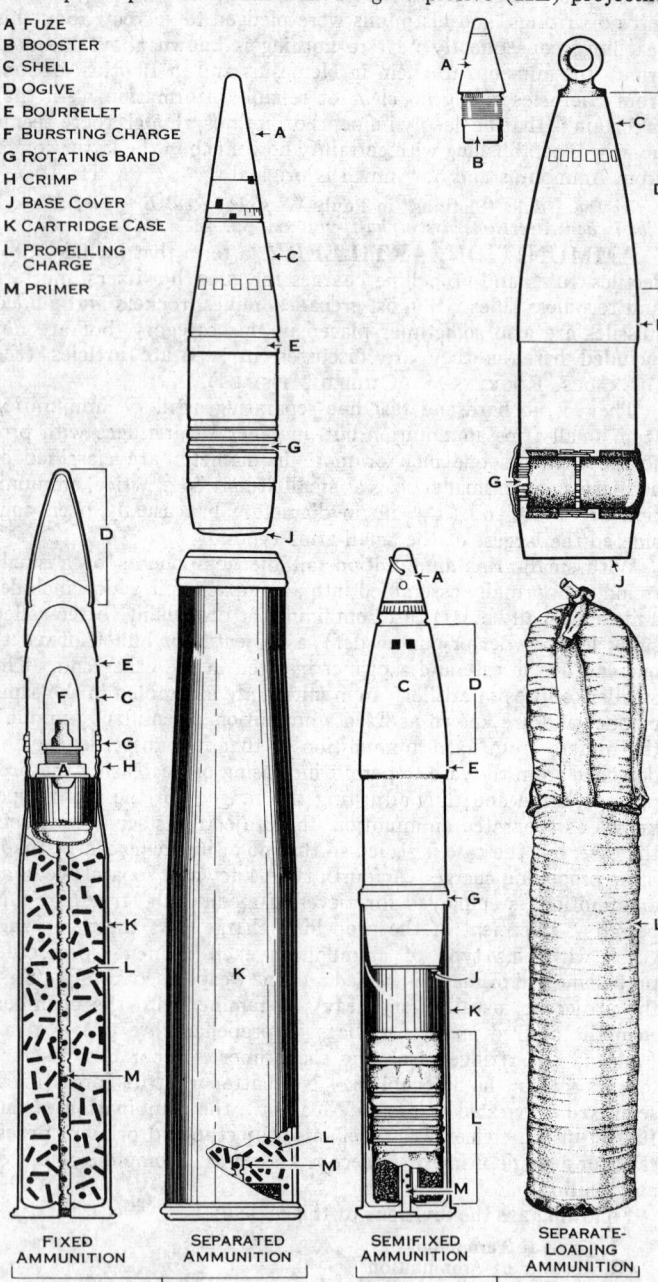

A FUZE
B BOOSTER
C SHELL
D OGIVE
E BOURRELET
F BURSTING CHARGE
G ROTATING BAND
H CRIMP
J BASE COVER
K CARTRIDGE CASE
L PROPELLING CHARGE
M PRIMER

FIXED AMMUNITION   SEPARATED AMMUNITION

NONADJUSTABLE-CHARGE AMMUNITION
DRAWN FROM A U.S. ARMY PHOTOGRAPH

SEMIFIXED AMMUNITION   SEPARATE-LOADING AMMUNITION

ADJUSTABLE-CHARGE AMMUNITION

FIG. 1.—TERMS USED TO IDENTIFY THE PRINCIPAL PARTS OF TYPICAL KINDS OF ARTILLERY AMMUNITION

is referred to as the ogive. It usually contains a fuze of one type or another, though with armour-piercing (AP) rounds the fuze may be at the base of the shell. Wherever placed, its function is to set off at the proper moment the explosive charge carried within the steel walls of the projectile. The *bourrelet* is an accurately machined section of the shell body, at the point where the body begins to taper. Slightly greater in diameter than the body of the projectile, it rides smoothly on the lands of the rifling and centres the forward end of the projectile as the rotating band centres the back end. The rotating band (or driving band) is a ring of comparatively soft material, such as gilding metal, pressed firmly into a groove near the base of the projectile.

When the weapon is fired and the projectile moves down the tube, the rotating band engages the lands of the bore and causes the projectile to rotate. As the rotating band is cut into, or engraved, by the lands it fills the grooves of the rifling and prevents escape of propellant gases. The part of the projectile back of the rotating band may be tapered somewhat to improve its flight characteristics and is then described as boat tailed. If not tapered, the shell is said to be square based. HE shells have their bases securely protected by a steel disk, known as a base plate or base plug, designed to keep powder gases from finding their way into the cavity containing the explosive through possible defects in the base of the shell.

The metal container for the propelling charge of fixed, semifixed or separated ammunition is the cartridge case, formerly made of brass but now commonly made of steel. Within the cartridge case is a metal tube known as a primer or artillery primer that contains a small quantity of sensitive explosive needed to bring about complete ignition of the propellant. The primer runs through the centre of the propellant charge and when fired spreads flame evenly throughout the charge. A common type, the percussion primer, is fired when struck by the weapon's firing pin. The electric primer is fired by heat generated when an electric current passes through a resistance wire. Still another type is fired by friction.

Within the typical HE shell is a high-explosive filler such as T.N.T. (trinitrotoluene) or RDX (cyclonite), and a booster containing a small quantity of some high explosive such as tetryl that is more readily detonated than the main charge. The latter, for reasons of safety in manufacture and handling, is always composed of a material that is insensitive to any but the most violent activators. In addition to the booster there is a primer, sometimes called the fuze primer to distinguish it from the primer that initiates the propellant. It is extremely sensitive but not very powerful. Next to the primer is the detonator which, when acted upon by the primer, amplifies the weak primer flash and transmits it to the booster. The whole arrangement, from fuze primer to detonator to booster to explosive charge, is known as the explosive train, and its functioning may be compared to the act of lighting a coal fire. First comes the striking of the match, which compares to the striking of the primer, but as the match will not itself set fire to a lump of coal it is applied first to crumpled paper or other readily inflammable material in much the same way that the primer is applied to the detonator. The burning paper in turn causes the wood kindling to take fire, just as the detonator ignites the booster; and the steady burning of the wood eventually ignites the coal in the same way that the booster sets off the explosive charge of the shell. The act of lighting a coal fire is slow, of course, while the explosive train of a shell acts with lightning speed and shattering effect.   (H. C. T.)

II. HISTORY OF AMMUNITION

1. Early Ordnance Projectiles.—The introduction of instruments employing gunpowder to project missiles dates from early in the 14th century (*see* ARTILLERY). The necessary propellant (black powder) had been described a full half century earlier by the English friar Roger Bacon, but he apparently remained unaware of its manifold military applications. The first ordnance projectiles were obviously adaptations of those already used in contemporary weapons (crossbow and longbow), being nothing more nor less than iron darts "feathered" with brass, their shafts wrapped with stuffings of leather to lessen leakage of powder gases. These projectiles could hardly have been large or heavy, for ancient records quoted by Napoleon III in his famous work on artillery, *Études sur . . . l'artillerie*, disclose the fact that there existed at the royal arsenal at Rouen in 1338 a *pot-de-fer* (cannon) the weight of a dart for which he estimates at not over $6\frac{2}{3}$ oz., the propelling charge therefore being about $\frac{2}{3}$ oz. of black powder. But some accounts speak of bolts weighing 200 lb.

2. Round Shot.—Though the dart was ballistically unsound, it and similar missiles continued occasionally to be discharged from firearms for centuries. As inventive minds cast about for something better they soon fastened on the sphere, a form of ammunition destined to rule supreme until the general introduction of rifled weapons in the 19th century. Stone was selected as the material for spherical projectiles because it was readily available and had been used in engines of war (q.v.) for ages past. References to stone spheres are found in France in 1346, in Italy in 1364 and in England in 1378. But because stone shot tended to break when it struck a stone wall, other materials were adopted to assure penetration. Thus iron shot is mentioned as early as 1350, though it apparently did not come into general use until the reign of Charles VIII of France (1483–98). Iron shot was designed originally for use in hand and shoulder weapons but it was soon applied to artillery.

Two ancient texts of the period 1400–50 recommend that small-arms balls be heated red hot when fired against troops sheltered in wooden structures. Hot shot is said to have been used in cannon as early as the siege of Cherbourg in 1418. It is probable that it would have been employed earlier but for the lack of adequate insurance against the propelling charge being set off ahead of time by the heat of the projectile. That problem was partially solved for artillery pieces by interposing a thick wad of moist clay, wet straw or other insulating agent between powder and shot. Naval hot shot became obsolete in the 19th century when navies adopted armour plate and when improved incendiary shells appeared.

Bronze shot enjoys an antiquity equal to that of the stone projectile, for it is mentioned by Petrarch (1344 or earlier) as in use among the Italians of his day. The same is true of leaden missiles, for Napoleon III quotes from 14th-century records to show that these were in use in France in 1345. For a period, metal shot of all three types just mentioned (iron, bronze, lead) appears to have been used indiscriminately. Thus the Venetians employed some of each in their action against the French at the battle of Taro (1491). Strange as it may appear, the material which survived most successfully the many field tests to which cannon missiles of the time were being subjected was stone. Such a choice was based on two very good reasons, viz., stone balls, even though their method of fabrication was painfully slow (gradual chipping into spherical form, with hammer and chisel, from rough blocks), were still cheaper than those of metal, for human labour commanded pitifully small recompense, and stone missiles, being lighter than metal ones of equal size, were started up the bore of a piece with smaller charges of powder, hence with less strain upon the fragile cannon of the period. Under the circumstances, it is easy to see that the life of one of the contemporary cannon, rudely fashioned as it was, was very likely to be more prolonged when balls of stone were fired from it than when those of metal were employed.

The same held for the crews that served them. The bursting of guns was a not unusual occurrence, as evidenced by a contemporary manuscript which says that: "A cannoneer must always love and serve God, for every time he fires a gun or makes powder, he may be killed." Each master gunner was then his own powder mixer, the art of incorporating the ingredients of this compound in such a manner that they would not separate on handling not having been developed. In separating, the heaviest ingredient, sulfur, settled to the bottom, while the lightest, carbon (charcoal), rose to the top, the result being a marked reduction in the potency of the product which, at best, was feeble and uncertain in action. Hence it became the practice to convey the components to the battlefield in separate containers and stir them together on the spot. And the danger undergone by him who undertook this was far from remote, for the glowing matches of any musketeers who happened about offered ready means for igniting the deadly brew before it could be gotten from mixing bowl to gun chamber.

3. Canister.—Round (spherical) shot proved satisfactory for battering walls and buildings and, in the smaller sizes, as used in hand and shoulder weapons, against personnel. But a single cannon ball, no matter how large, was of limited effectiveness against troops, because only those directly in its path were endangered. Hence, as the use of ordnance became more general, attention was directed toward devising means whereby a considerable number of small projectiles rather than a single large one could be fired simultaneously into hostile ranks. This end had already been

attained in a measure by the introduction and rather wide use of ribaudequins, which consisted in effect of a large number of shoulder pieces, or sometimes just the barrels, mounted like so many organ pipes on a cart and discharged simultaneously or in sizable numbers at the enemy. But such contrivances were clumsy and slow in operation and, once all the barrels had been emptied, practically impossible to reload and fire again before the fate of the day had been decided. Hence the early development of canister or case shot for great guns, consisting of a cylindrical metal container of bore diameter, filled with small projectiles of whatever nature happened to be handy—not infrequently simple pebbles of stone. The container burst and released its deadly burden shortly after leaving the muzzle.

The use of such projectiles is reliably reported as early as 1410 and they figured prominently in the siege of Belgrade three decades later. The ribaudequin slowly disappeared from the scene, though the idea persisted through the ages and took new life during the U.S. Civil War in the Billinghurst and Requa "machine gun," which, in the last analysis, was nothing more than a row of musket barrels mounted on a wheeled carriage.

4. Explosive Shell.—The next development in artillery ammunition was, quite logically, the shell, originally—and for centuries thereafter—a simple, hollow sphere of cast iron, filled with explosive (black powder), with a hole drilled through its wall into the explosive cavity and, fitted into this hole, a fuze of some sort to ignite the powder. W. W. Greener in *The Gun and Its Development* ascribes this invention to the Netherlands. Other authors state that the Venetians (1376) antedated the Hollanders in the employment of shell in cannon, and assert that the invention would have come still earlier had means for preparing satisfactory fuzes been available. After its introduction, the shell soon came into wide use for land operations among all great nations and eventually became and has remained, with certain periodic fluctuations in the degree of favour enjoyed, the most important projectile available to the artillerist.

On the sea, however, the firing of explosive or incendiary missiles was long held too dangerous (to the user) to be considered. But one captain, a Frenchman named Deschiens, appears to have defied convention and employed shells horizontally from his long guns. (Practice on land countenanced their use only for high-angle fire from mortars.) The efficacy of this tactic was attested in an engagement in 1690 wherein his vessel was beset by four British ships. Employing shells of his own contrivance he readily dispersed the British, and in a later exchange with two Dutch ships he sank one and disabled the other. But apparently he was far ahead of his time, for none undertook to follow the precedent he established. Toward the close of the 18th and the commencement of the 19th centuries, however, all nations began to realize that something must be done to make naval ordnance more effective. One incident which drove this fact keenly home was the battle of Trafalgar—in which not a single vessel was sunk by gunfire. Naval authorities began to look about for a remedy. They had not far to seek, for an excellent example lay before them.

In 1788 an Englishman, Sir Samuel Bentham, who had risen to high places in the naval service of the tsar of Russia, had fitted out a flotilla of longboats, mounting brass cannon and amply supplied with shell, carcasses (incendiary projectiles) and solid shot. Attacking with these minuscule vessels a very considerable Turkish squadron, he gained a notable victory. His shell not only tore gaping holes in the sides of the enemy ships but started conflagrations which resulted in the destruction of the entire Turkish fleet. As not infrequently happens, however, Bentham's countrymen studiously ignored the lesson thus delivered. So it fell to France to exploit the new agency, or rather the new adaptation of an old one. This it did assiduously over several decades, its efforts culminating in the development by Gen. Henri Paixhans (1822) of a comprehensive system of naval armament based upon a fleet of steam vessels especially designed to mount shell guns of high muzzle velocity and considerable range. Thenceforward the place of the shell in naval operations was assured.

The latter part of the 18th century also witnessed the adoption of the shell for horizontal fire in land operations, tests in England toward that end having been conducted as early as 1760 but discontinued when a number of the projectiles exploded in the bore. But the idea would not down, and was revived during the siege of Gibraltar (1779–83) when the British fired mortar shell from long 24-pounders into the Spanish lines. At about the same time Lieut. (later Gen.) Henry Shrapnel was making the first official demonstrations of the spherical case shot of his invention, adopted by the British army in 1803. This differed from ordinary case in that it was fuzed and filled with musket balls plus a small charge of black powder just sufficient to disrupt the container. When the fuze acted, the sphere was cleft open, and the balls continued forward in an ever-widening sheaf, laying low all enemy personnel in their path. As originally designed, no additional velocity was acquired by the musket balls when they left the shell beyond that possessed by the sphere at the instant of rupture. In later forms of shrapnel an elongated shell was used and an added velocity of about 350 ft. per second was imparted by the powder charge embodied in the missile.

5. Miscellaneous Types.—Other types of projectile once widely used (but now long obsolete) include the carcass, grape, bar shot, chain shot, etc. The first-named was an iron shell filled with inflammable materials which, ignited by the flash of the propelling charge, served to set afire wooden buildings or other vulnerable objects within enemy lines. Easier to manipulate than hot shot (which had to be heated to redness in a special furnace), it was handier to use and to transport (being naturally lighter than solid shot of equal diameter) but, by the same token, less far ranging.

A round of grape comprised a number of iron spheres, usually twice or more the diameter of the conventional musket ball as found in canister and shrapnel, and commonly arranged in three layers separated by metal plates. This composite projectile fell apart shortly after leaving the muzzle and was fearfully effective when fired at short ranges against assaulting troops, constituting, as it were, a sort of oversize canister.

Bar shot was employed in naval operations, and consisted of two spheres or two hemispheres of cast iron connected by a bar of the same material. Fired into the rigging of hostile vessels, they flew crazily through the air and caused great damage—provided they found their targets.

Chain shot, designed for a similar purpose, embodied two hollow hemispheres linked by a section of stout chain, the two portions of the globe being fitted together before firing, with the chain nested into the cavity so formed. Shortly after leaving the muzzle the hemispheres flew apart to the length of the connecting chain. As may be imagined, the effect on the spars, ropes and sails of an enemy vessel was considerable.

6. Early Fuzes.—The shell had in the first half of the 19th century come into its own, as had shrapnel. Neither of these, however, could attain full stature until the crude time fuzes of the period had undergone material improvement, and until the detonating powder developed by Alexander Forsyth in 1807 and the years immediately following, harnessed in percussion caps and other devices, permitted the construction of a missile that would explode on the shock of striking its target; i.e., the concussion or percussion shell. The time fuze was no novelty, for it required little ingenuity to pack a train of slow-burning powder into a wooden or metal tube and, knowing the distance traveled over varying periods of time by the shell in which this was to be used, and the burning rate of the powder train, to mark the tube surface with graduations corresponding to different ranges.

This device was now driven into a fuze hole in the shell, first having been cut off, or otherwise set, for the range at which firing was to take place. If all went well, the missile burst at the point intended. When the projectile was rammed home, the fuze faced toward the muzzle of the piece, being situated on the side of the shell opposite that which rested on the propelling charge. It was nevertheless ignited by the flash from the propellant, for the projectile was always sufficiently smaller in diameter than the bore of the gun firing it to permit a considerable portion of the incandescent-powder gases to escape past it and perform this important function. Obviously this clearance between projectile and bore resulted in the waste of a large percentage of the gases generated and a consequent reduction in the energy expended on propelling the missile. But this was considered a necessary evil and no serious steps were taken to remedy it until rifled pieces came upon the scene. This latter development, which was beginning to take place in the mid-19th century, had long been awaited, indeed foreseen. But the same difficulties that beset the infantryman in his search for a suitable rifled weapon operated in the case of artillery.

7. Rifled Guns.—A projectile small enough to pass readily down the bore of a piece to its seat in the chamber was, by the same token, not large enough to expand into and acquire a motion of rotation from a set of rifling grooves leading from that point to the muzzle. Further, such rotation increased the effectiveness of a round missile so little that it hardly justified the expense and trouble involved. It did increase enormously the range and accuracy of an elongated (cylindroogival) bolt; indeed, projectiles of this form could not be made to function properly save in a rifled piece. Elongated projectiles were obviously much heavier than spherical shot of equal diameter and called for greatly increased powder charges, which the older types of cannon were unable to withstand.

During the fourth, fifth and sixth decades of the 19th century, however, improvements in black powder and the materials and methods of gun construction made possible the building of ordnance capable of handling these charges. Coincidentally, inventors in widely separated parts of the world were developing systems of rifling and projectiles adapted to them which, while not at once wholly successful, presaged the early introduction of a new era. Among these systems may be mentioned that of Charles Lancaster, which involved the use of a projectile, oval in section, fired from a gun similarly bored (the oval spiraling from breech to muzzle); of Joseph Whitworth, who used a six-sided missile delivered from a tube the bore of which was a hexagon twisted upon itself (both of these designs were British); and the French system in which a series of studs that engaged the rifling grooves of the gun were screwed into the surface of the projectile. Another variation, which perhaps reached its highest degree of perfection in the U.S. Sawyer projectile, involved casting on the surface of the shell a series of longitudinal ribs or flanges, corresponding in number, position, angle and dimensions to the grooves of the gun bore.

All of these devices suffered from one of the chief faults of the smoothbore system: clearance between the surfaces of bore and missile was so considerable (and necessary, to permit easy loading) that much of the force of the powder charge was wasted in the gas that escaped past the projectile. To remedy this, scores of devices were employed, the commonest being a disk of some soft metal attached to the base of the shell, its edge curving slightly backward (toward the powder charge) all around its perimeter, exactly as though a pie pan had been nailed to the bottom of the missile. When the powder was ignited, the free edge of this disk was forced forward and outward by the pressure of the burning gases, sealing the bore more or less effectively. But at best these were makeshift solutions, and it required the perfection of the breech-loading gun to provide a really satisfactory answer to the problem of gas leakage.

This type of piece was as old as artillery itself, but had never proved practicable, not because of gas escape along the bore, but at the breech. However, during the 19th century breech-loading systems, each slightly better than its predecessor, followed one another in rapid succession; e.g., those of G. Cavalli (Sardinia), Baron Wahrendorff (Sweden), W. Armstrong (England), A. Krupp (Germany), R. de Bange (France), etc. It now became possible to introduce, at the breech of a piece, a projectile part or all of which was of "groove diameter"; i.e., equal in over-all thickness to the distance measured from the bottom of one groove to the bottom of that facing it on the opposite side of the bore. This meant that the lands, or elevated surfaces between the grooves, bit deeply into the outermost layer of the missile, forcing it to follow the spiral of the rifling. To avoid needless friction and unnecessary wear, those portions of the projectile which were machined to groove (maximum) diameter were fabricated of some relatively soft material. The Armstrong shell, for instance, was shrouded in a lead envelope. The body of the missile never measured more on its transverse axis than the distance across the lands; i.e., from the top of one land to the top of that opposite—technically known as bore diameter as contrasted with the groove diameter described above. It was soon found, however, that satisfactory rotation could be effected by encircling the projectile near its base with a single narrow band, rather than a full-length envelope, of ductile metal (copper), of groove diameter. The surface of the shell (which was of bore diameter) rode, as it were, the tops of the lands, while the latter cut into the copper rotating band to a depth equal to that of the grooves adjacent. Thus was finally evolved the basic form of projectile thenceforward to find employment in ordnance of every size and type.

8. Confusion in Nomenclature.—With the general adoption of rifled cannon and elongated projectiles, there occurred a confusion in nomenclature that was for a time quite disconcerting. During the centuries in which the round (cast-iron) sphere seemed best, guns had been classified according to the weights of the balls they carried. And since the specific gravity of the metal remained a constant, everyone knew that a 6-pounder was a gun with a bore of about 3.67 in., since a cast-iron shot weighing 6 lb. had a diameter of 3.55 in., and it was customary to make the bore of a gun slightly larger than the missile it was designed to project. Similarly a 12-pounder had a bore of 4.62 in.; an 18-pounder, 5.3 in.; a 24-pounder, 5.82 in.; a 32-pounder, 6.4 in.; and a 42-pounder, 7 in. But with the advent of the cylindroogival missile, a 10-lb. shell (as in the Parrott rifle) came to be fired from a 3-in. gun, whereas had it been a solid sphere it would have required a bore diameter of at least $4\frac{1}{3}$ in. to handle it. A 12-in. cast-iron shot weighed about $229\frac{1}{4}$ lb., while the solid elongated projectile fired in the U.S. 12-in. rifle, model 1874, weighed 700 lb. Obviously, to describe this piece as a "700-pounder" came far from giving an idea of its actual dimensions, for only the ordnance expert knew the length and shape of the missile it fired. (Had this been spherical, it would have called for a bore of more than 17 in.) The result was that designations in pounds, after struggling hard for survival, finally went by the board, being replaced by others wherein the calibre of the piece was indicated by its bore diameter in inches or millimetres.

9. Improved Fuzes.—As artillery ammunition improved in range and effectiveness, the old wooden and metal tubes stuffed with slow-burning black powder, which had served so long as fuzes, gave way to more efficient, if more elaborate and more complicated, types wherein the rate of burning and the instant of explosion could be more accurately controlled. It had long been recognized that any fuze containing black powder as a component was likely to be erratic in action by just so much as this ingredient might be affected by external influences (moisture content of the air, barometric pressure, etc.). Under ordinary conditions, these factors played insignificant parts, but in World War I it was discovered that the rate of burning of the powder train varied markedly with the altitude to which an antiaircraft shell was fired, thus adding just one more correction to those the gunner had to make. This discovery stimulated interest in a mechanical time fuze, the operation of which would obviously be independent of altitude effects, and such fuzes were developed and adopted, although their complexity and cost of manufacture placed them distinctly in the luxury category among war munitions.

The era of rifled ordnance resulted, as has been seen, in the introduction of tight-fitting, cylindroogival projectiles, the rotating bands of which sealed the bore so perfectly that almost none of the burning-powder gases escaped past them. But this set up a new problem for the ammunition maker, as it meant that the fuze was no longer inflamed by the flash of discharge, and that some other means to effect this must be contrived. The solution was simple. A striker was located in a hole drilled in the long axis of the fuze body which capped the shell. At the base of this hole was a percussion cap and below this a powder train. On firing, the cap was carried forward with the mass of the shell to impact against the striker which, floating freely in the drill hole, tended to remain stationary while the shell about it gathered momentum. The resulting flash ignited the powder train. This mechanism, technically known as setback, has been widely employed in fuzes of many types. As originally designed, it lacked safety factors, for if the shell were accidentally dropped, detonation of the cap was likely to result. To correct this defect, devices were later installed which interposed a block between striker and cap until disengaged by the centrifugal force developed from rotation of the missile in the bore. Such fuzes are known as bore safe, a number of rotations being required to arm the fuze, i.e., put it in a position to function, so that the missile has traveled an appreciable distance from the muzzle before the fuze is free to act. Some such safety mechanism is of necessity embodied in all types of shell. (See GUNS, SPORTING AND TARGET.)

10. Improved Shells.—As rifled pieces increased in power and range and suitable breech-loading mechanisms were perfected, the materials used in the fabrication of both guns and ammunition underwent corresponding changes. Solid and hollow missiles of cast iron began to give way to other types such as the Armstrong segment shell. This shell consisted of a thin outer casing of cast iron surrounding six layers, of seven segments each, of the same material, these in turn bordering a central cavity containing an explosive charge of black powder. This shell, in addition to incorporating a time fuze, was fitted with one of the percussion type. In this a detonating cap at the forward end of an axially located tube received the impact, when the shell was suddenly arrested in its flight, of a striker at the rear, which slid forward as the mass about it came to a stop—the action reversing that of setback described above. This arrangement, like the setback, later figured quite generally in shell design. Such a shell was found most effective when used against personnel, but was obviously impotent against fixed fortifications or armoured vessels, which used wrought-iron plates of increasing thickness as early as the 1850s. In order to render cast-iron projectiles effective against these, the shell was cast in a mold, as before, but the nose (point) cooled rapidly through contact with a cast-iron chill, the body proper radiating its heat more slowly in a bed of sand. This cooling resulted in greatly increased hardness and crushing strength at the point without otherwise modifying the characteristics of the projectile, and such bolts proved highly successful. But the defense now countered with the substitution of steel for wrought iron—a measure which would have been adopted sooner had the means for producing this material of good quality and at reasonable price been available earlier. Against steel, the cast-iron shell proved unavailing, and the offense was forced to steel missiles before it could make further headway. Thus projectiles of forged steel were already in common use by the late 1880s. Projectiles of cast steel had been experimented with, but not successfully.

As the shell body improved, so did its bursting charge and its propellant. The explosive properties of guncotton and of picric acid and certain of its salts had long been known, and such substances were the subject of numberless experiments attempting to produce them in forms suitable for use as shell fillers. Until the mid-1880s, however, none of these was attended with much success. But by 1886 the French had managed to control picric acid to a point where they commenced to employ it (under the name of melinite) in this capacity. The British followed with lyddite, the Japanese with shimose—all different names for the same substance. From this time, black powder saw less and less use as an explosive agency in shells, though it retained its place for this purpose in shrapnel. The only thing now lacking to bring artillery ammunition to the state of technical development which it enjoyed when World War I engulfed an amazed civilization was a smokeless propellant. This came about coincidentally with the introduction of high explosives as bursting charges and was largely the work of the French chemist P. Vieille (1884). Ballistite, a smokeless powder made of nitrocellulose and nitroglycerin, was introduced by Alfred Nobel (q.v.) in 1888. At the same time the British government adopted a similar compound known as cordite.

Some time elapsed, however, after smokeless powders were functioning satisfactorily in small arms before suitable types could be developed for heavy ordnance. Indeed, the Spanish-American War of 1898 was fought, so far as artillery matériel was concerned, chiefly with black powder, but this was the last major conflict in which it played an important part.   (C. Gᴅ.; H. C. T.)

11. Ammunition in World War I.—In World War I, artillery played an important role and, along with machine guns, reached a high point of development. Thunderous barrages were fired from hundreds of guns to demoralize the enemy, hamper his communications, destroy barbed wire and prepare the way for advancing infantry. The rate of fire of Allied field guns in 1918 ranged from 30 to 35 rounds per gun per day as compared with about 4 rounds per gun per day in the U.S. Civil War and the Russo-Japanese War. To seek protection from such concentrated fire, armies were forced to go underground, and a condition of stalemate resulted.

The main types of artillery ammunition employed in this conflict were explosive shell, shrapnel and canister, all of which have been previously discussed. Some shells were of the low-explosive type, filled with black powder; others were high-explosive, filled with T.N.T., amatol (a mixture of T.N.T. and ammonium nitrate), explosive D (ammonium picrate) or picric acid, widely used by the French. In the ordinary HE shell the weight of the explosive was about 10% that of the shell, but in armour-piercing varieties it amounted to only about 2%, for armour penetration called for projectiles with thick walls. Shell bodies were normally made of common steel, forged and machined to shape, though semisteel (practically a high grade of cast iron) was successfully used as a substitute. Chemicals of various types figured prominently as shell fillers, both for the purpose of producing screening effects (smokes) and producing casualties. Other special-purpose types of ammunition included incendiary shells filled with Thermit or phosphorus, plus a bursting charge just large enough to rupture the containing walls; illuminating or star shells for night operations; and tracer shells which marked their path by the emission of smoke or flame, thus enabling the gunner to alter his aim if incorrect.

A new use for artillery appeared during World War I—firing on hostile aircraft—but the development of special antiaircraft (AA) guns and ammunition was barely begun. At the same time, shrapnel was passing from the scene.

World War I was the last major conflict in which shrapnel was used, but the term continued in popular writing, erroneously applied to shell fragments. Shrapnel had proved useful against large infantry units in the open but of less value against dispersed and protected troops.

Whatever the design of a projectile, the problem of shooting it from the gun tube depends primarily upon the nature of the propellant, the modern term that is applied to chemical compositions that have taken the place of the earlier types of gunpowder or black powder. As noted above, so-called smokeless powder had first been introduced in the latter part of the 19th century and was generally adopted by the time of World War I. Oddly enough, smokeless powder was neither entirely smokeless nor a powder, but the term, nevertheless, gained wide currency. The two main types were single base, of nitrocellulose alone; and double base, nitrocellulose plus nitroglycerin. The U.S. forces favoured the former and British forces the latter, giving it the name cordite. Charges for fixed ammunition were loaded loose into the cartridge case while those for other types were prepared in silk bags that could be placed loose in the gun or in cartridge cases at the time of firing.

WATERPROOF COVER
21-SECOND COMBINATION FUZE   HEAD
INNER TUBE
BOURRELET
CENTRAL TUBE
BALLS
CASE
MATRIX (RESIN)
FIBRE
PAPER CUP
CLOTH DISK
DIAPHRAGM
ROTATING BAND
BASE CHARGE (LOOSE BLACK POWDER)

BY COURTESY OF U.S. DEPT. OF DEFENSE
FIG. 2.—75-MM. SHRAPNEL

A CLOSING CAP
B VENTS
C CONCUSSION PLUNGER
D RESISTANCE RING
E CONCUSSION PRIMER
F CONCUSSION FIRING PIN
G UPPER TIME-TRAIN RING
H POWDER TRAIN
J CHANNEL
K BODY
L PERCUSSION PRIMER
M MAGAZINE CHARGE (BLACK POWDER)
N POWDER PELLETS
O PERCUSSION FIRING PIN
P PERCUSSION PLUNGER
Q LOWER OR GRADUATED TIME-TRAIN RING
FROM A U.S. DEPT. OF DEFENSE DRAWING
FIG. 3.—21-SEC. COMBINATION FUZE

Raw silk was chosen as the material for the bags because it was almost entirely consumed on firing and left no smouldering remains in the bore.

III. ARTILLERY AMMUNITION AFTER WORLD WAR I

During the quarter century following World War I, artillery ammunition went through a period of rapid development, with improvements being made in all elements—fuzes, explosives, shell bodies, propellants and methods of manufacture. These developments were stimulated chiefly by the appearance in World War I of two new classes of weapon, the tank and the airplane, and they were aided by technological advances in metallurgy, chemistry and electronics. In turn, the development of new and improved ammunition types had an influence on military tactics, making World War II a far different type of conflict from its predecessor. World War II was a war of movement with the two standard elements, mobility and firepower, combined to an unprecedented degree. The HE shell continued to play a leading role on the battlefield, though for certain purposes aerial bombs were more effective. Anglo-American forces expended vast quantities of artillery ammunition to prepare the way for the advance of ground troops or to break up an enemy attack. Conventional HE ammunition was supplemented by hypervelocity armour-piercing (HVAP) ammunition for attacking armoured vehicles, fortifications or ships. A wide variety of chemical shells appeared, some yielding clouds of smoke to blind the enemy and others containing white phosphorus that burned the enemy as it gave off smoke.

Pyrotechnics were widely used for illumination or signaling, and the familiar canister was occasionally employed against personnel. Rockets and shells containing a new type of shaped-charge explosive proved exceptionally valuable for penetrating tank armour. For antiaircraft fire, and for attacking troops in the open, the VT or proximity fuze that detonated its explosive when the shell came within range of its target was a revolutionary new device.

By mid-20th century, before the possibilities for full employment of nuclear weapons had been realized, conventional artillery ammunition—that fired from guns, howitzers, mortars or recoilless rifles—held a commanding position in warfare. "The artillery projectile," wrote one U.S. officer in World War II, "has been the great instrument which has spread death and destruction among the enemy forces." It was the settled doctrine of U.S. and British commanders to pre-

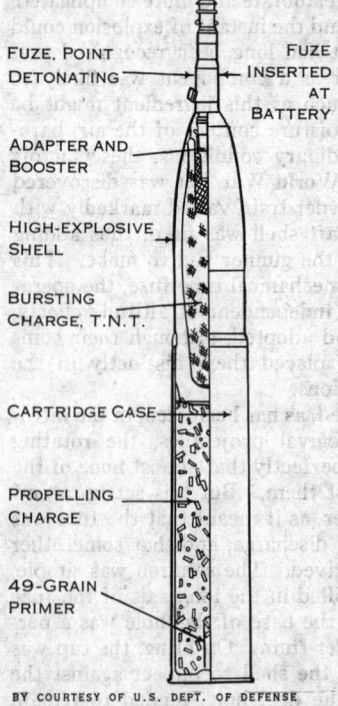

FUZE, POINT DETONATING
FUZE INSERTED AT BATTERY
ADAPTER AND BOOSTER
HIGH-EXPLOSIVE SHELL
BURSTING CHARGE, T.N.T.
CARTRIDGE CASE
PROPELLING CHARGE
49-GRAIN PRIMER

BY COURTESY OF U.S. DEPT. OF DEFENSE
FIG. 4.—ASSEMBLED ROUND OF 75-MM. AMMUNITION

pare the way for the advance of infantry troops by lavish expenditure of artillery ammunition. In the European theatre, U.S. forces fired, during the single month of Dec. 1944, over 3,000,000 rounds of 105-mm. howitzer ammunition. In Korea, where United Nations forces were outnumbered by the enemy, artillery ammunition was fired at previously unheard-of rates to hold back the enemy or break up his attacks.

1. HE Shells.—The typical HE shell of World War II and the Korean war was of the familiar cylindroogival shape and was made of forged steel with comparatively thin walls. The shell carried a large bursting charge of T.N.T., amatol, explosive D, RDX or other high explosive. It was equipped with a fuze designed to cause detonation of the explosive at the proper time, whether upon impact with the target, upon approaching the target or after a certain lapse of time. The standard HE shell came in a wide range of calibres, from the smallest to the largest guns, and was used against personnel, vehicles, buildings, bridges or fortifications. It achieved its end in part by the blast effect of the explosion and in part by filling the air with flying steel fragments.

The most widely used U.S. HE shell in World War II was that for the 105-mm. howitzer. Its projectile weighed about 33 lb. and had a maximum range of 12,500 yd. The armour-piercing round for the 155-mm. gun was far heavier, its projectile weighing 100 lb. and its range exceeding 25,000 yd. The still larger 8-in. howitzer fired a 200-lb. projectile containing over 35 lb. of T.N.T. The huge 240-mm. howitzer threw a 360-lb. shell containing 54 lb. of T.N.T. to a range of 25,250 yd.

2. Chemical Shells.—These were similar to HE shells in general construction but contained a military chemical rather than a high-explosive charge. One of the best-known types was the smoke shell containing white phosphorus. As noted above, it not only concealed troop movements and blinded the enemy but also served as an antipersonnel round by scattering pieces of burning phosphorus. Various types of poison-gas shells were available to the warring nations but were not used in combat. One type of chemi-

Data on Representative Ammunition Types of World War II

Calibre of weapon	Approx. weight of projectile in lb.	Approx. maximum range in yds.
37-mm. gun (U.S.)	1½	9,500
60-mm. mortar (U.S.)	3	2,000
75-mm. pack howitzer (U.S.)	14	9,760
25-pounder gun-howitzer (British)	25	13,400
105-mm. howitzer (U.S.)	33	12,500
150-mm. gun (German)	95	27,000
155-mm. gun (U.S.)	95	25,700
170-mm. gun (German)	140	32,000
7.2-in. howitzer (British)	200	16,900
8-in. howitzer (U.S.)	200	18,500
210-mm. howitzer (German)	249	18,260
240-mm. howitzer (U.S.)	360	25,250

cal shell contained a narrow burster tube filled with tetryl that served to rupture the shell and allow the chemical filler to escape without excess dispersion. Another type ejected its smoke canisters through the base of the shell while another emitted smoke from a hole in the base.

3. Armour-Piercing Projectiles.—This type of ammunition, long employed in the naval service, made great strides during World War II as designers of tanks and designers of antitank ammunition competed with each other. As tanks were built with thicker and tougher armour, ammunition makers were forced to devise new means of penetrating such armour—or "defeating" it, to use the language of the ordnance engineer. The term AP shot described a solid steel projectile—not a shell—without an explosive charge or a fuze. It was made of high-carbon alloy steel specially heat-treated to penetrate armour. A pointed nose or windshield of steel or aluminum was usually added to improve its ballistic performance. A similar type, fired at high velocity and known as HVAP, contained an extremely hard core of tungsten carbide. The U.S. army's 90-mm. HVAP round could penetrate many inches of homogeneous armour. The term AP projectile described a somewhat similar type that had a small cavity holding an explosive charge and a base-detonating fuze; i.e., a fuze that exploded the shell after it had penetrated the tank armour. For attacking face-hardened armour, the blunt nose of this type of shot or projectile

was sometimes enclosed in a cap of forged alloy steel, heat-treated so that it had a hard face and a comparatively soft core. On impact, the hardened face of the cap penetrated the hardened surface of the armour while the softer portion protected the core for further penetration. This type was known as armour-piercing-capped or APC ammunition, and sometimes also had a thin-walled windshield.

The most significant new type of antitank ammunition to appear in World War II was the so-called HEAT (high-explosive antitank) round based on the shaped-charge principle. An explosive such as pentolite, formed around a thin metal cone, with the base forward, achieved remarkable armour penetration by focusing the explosive effect on one spot, as a magnifying glass focuses the sun's rays. This type of ammunition was based on the so-called Munroe effect noted by the U.S. chemist Charles E. Munroe in the 1880s. Munroe had discovered that a cavity in the side of a block of explosive facing the plate to be penetrated increased the degree of penetration. Demolition engineers had applied the principle for years, and it is said that safe-crackers had long been familiar with it. Shaped-charge or HEAT ammunition differed from other types of AP ammunition in one important respect—its power of penetration was not a function of its velocity. For this reason it was first introduced in rifle grenades and in rocket launchers such as the bazooka (q.v.), both of which had a low velocity. In addition, the shaped-charge projectile lost some of its effectiveness when rotated as were other rounds fired from guns or howitzers. It was therefore necessary to devise special HEAT rounds that did not rotate, or rotated very slowly, and were stabilized by metal fins rather than by their rotation—fin stabilized rather than spin stabilized. Such ammunition was capable of penetrating the thickest armour known to be used on tanks in World War II and the Korean war. It was also effective against log bunkers and concrete fortifications.

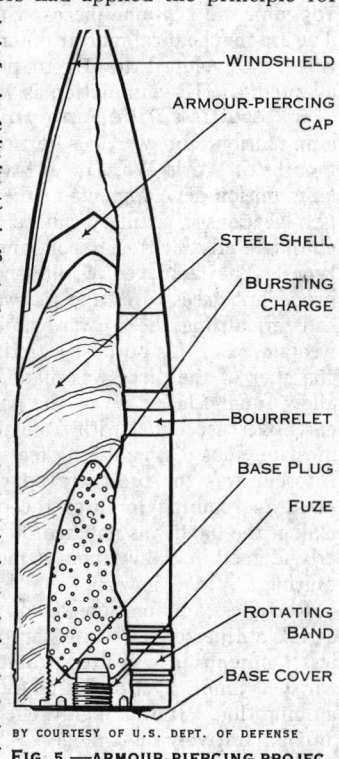

WINDSHIELD

ARMOUR-PIERCING CAP

STEEL SHELL

BURSTING CHARGE

BOURRELET

BASE PLUG

FUZE

ROTATING BAND

BASE COVER

BY COURTESY OF U.S. DEPT. OF DEFENSE

FIG. 5.—ARMOUR-PIERCING PROJECTILE

When the HEAT round struck its target, the shaped charge directed a jet of metallic particles from the cone liner against the target at very high velocity, on the order of 30,000 ft. per second, higher even than the detonation velocity of the explosive. This jet stream was followed by a slug formed of the remaining bits of the cone. Two requirements had to be met before the shaped charge achieved its full effect: the explosive charge had to be detonated from the rear, and it had to be detonated at a certain distance from the target, known as stand-off. (See also MINE, LAND.)

4. Mortar Ammunition.—This type differs from other forms of artillery ammunition in that it is ordinarily designed to be fired from smoothbore pieces, though rifled mortars are by no means unknown. Mortars are relatively light, simply constructed weapons that can easily be carried by front-line troops and quickly set up in firing position. Because they are usually smooth-bore weapons, mortars fire fin-stabilized projectiles. The typical mortar round has either a teardrop or cylindrical shape with a fuze in the nose and metal fins in the tail, the latter to keep it from tumbling end over end in flight. The propelling charge is placed within the fin assembly and may be adjusted in the field to yield the proper range. A mortar round is fired by dropping it, fins first, into the muzzle of the weapon, whereupon its ignition charge strikes the firing pin and inflames the propellant. Mortar ammunition is characterized

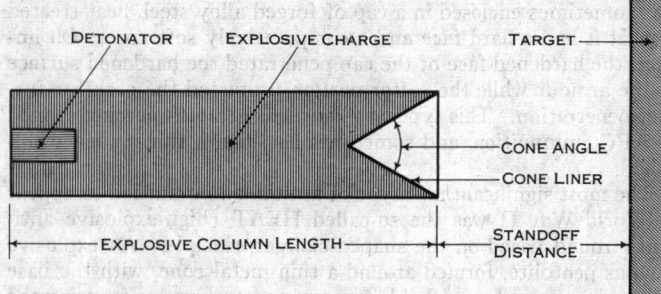

FROM A U.S. DEPT. OF DEFENSE DRAWING
FIG. 6.—SHAPED CHARGE AND TARGET

by its low muzzle velocity, high trajectory and short range. The most common types in World War II, and in the years that followed, were the 60-mm. and 81-mm. ranges extending from 200 yd. up to 2,000 or 3,000 yd. Larger rounds were developed for 105-mm. and 155-mm. pieces, with correspondingly greater ranges. The 4.2-in. chemical mortar differed from other types in that it was rifled. Developed at first to project smoke shells, it was later adapted for HE ammunition as well.

5. Recoilless Rifle Ammunition.—This special new type of ammunition, and weapons to fire it, appeared during the closing months of World War II. It was one of the most interesting new ammunition developments of the 1940s. The U.S. army produced two weapons of artillery calibre, 57 mm. and 75 mm., designed to eliminate all "kick" or recoil, and other nations developed similar types. They achieved recoillessness by permitting a portion of the propellant gases to escape rearward through vents in the breech, thus equalizing the forward and backward forces acting on the weapon. For this purpose, cartridge cases were perforated and the chamber of the piece was made larger than the cartridge case to allow room for escape of the gases to the rear. The perforated cartridge case, lined with paper to retain the propellant, was the most obvious distinguishing feature of recoilless rifle ammunition. Another was the pre-engraved rotating band. To eliminate the pressure required to force the copper rotating band against the rifling, the band was notched or pre-engraved so that, when properly aligned in the weapon, it moved easily through the tube, acquiring a spin as it went.

Recoilless ammunition was produced in a variety of types, such as HE antipersonnel, white phosphorus and HE antitank. Recoilless ammunition was fired from lightweight rifles (about 100 lb. for the 75 mm.), yet possessed the explosive power of light artillery ammunition. It was highly effective against tanks and pillboxes at comparatively short range. When designed to fire shaped-charge projectiles, for which spin is undesirable, recoilless ammunition was fin stabilized.

6. Canister.—Though an old type, canister proved valuable in the wars of the mid-20th century, particularly for use against troops concealed in the foliage of jungle areas. It consisted of a quantity of lead or steel balls embedded in a resinous matrix, the whole encased in a cylindrical metal container. The number of balls in each case varied from less than 50 to several hundred, depending upon the model and calibre. The canister round contained neither fuze nor explosive but burst automatically soon after leaving the muzzle. It was most effective at comparatively short ranges.

7. Pyrotechnics.—Under this heading are classed those forms

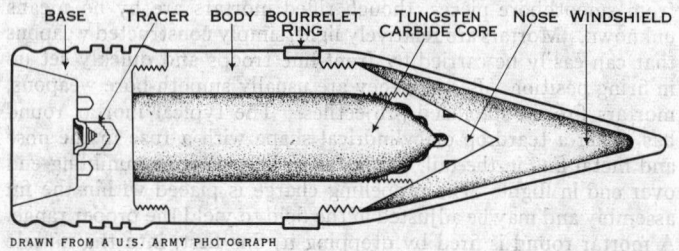

DRAWN FROM A U.S. ARMY PHOTOGRAPH
FIG. 7.—HYPERVELOCITY ARMOUR-PIERCING SHOT WITH TUNGSTEN CARBIDE CORE

of military ammunition used for producing light for illuminating enemy positions or smokes and lights for signaling. They consist mainly of flares, signals, photoflash cartridges and illuminating shells. Only the latter type clearly falls within the category of artillery ammunition. The standard illuminating shell of the U.S. army in the 1950s had an exterior design similar to that of standard HE shells, but its body enclosed a different set of elements. Most important of these elements was the illuminant, sometimes called the candle, consisting of powdered aluminum or magnesium along with an oxidizing material. Attached to the candle was a parachute that opened when the expelling charge of black powder forced it out through the base of the shell. The usual burning time for the larger types was about 60 sec. and the light was sufficient to illuminate a circle 400 yd. in diameter.

8. Cartridge Cases.—One of the most significant technological advances in ammunition during the 1940s was the development of cartridge cases made of steel rather than brass. The limited supply of copper, and the great demand for copper for other purposes, forced this development during World War II. But it was attended by many difficulties. Brass was an excellent material for cartridge cases because it could be easily worked, did not rust and had the necessary elasticity to expand at the moment of firing and instantly contract for easy extraction from the gun. Limited quantities of steel artillery cases were produced in the United States during World War II, and by the time of the Korean war they were in quantity production.

Meanwhile an entirely new approach to the cartridge-case problem was made by ordnance researchers working toward the production of combustible cases. Made of material that would burn rapidly and completely, leaving no residue in the chamber, combustible cases were seen to offer significant advantages for tank and aircraft guns because they would eliminate the need to dispose of fired cases.

9. Fuzes.—During World War II the U.S. army employed about 150 different types and sizes of fuzes, the three main classifications being point-detonating, base-detonating and time. As its name implies, the point-detonating fuze functioned when the point of the projectile, wherein the fuze was inserted, struck its target. It was commonly shipped separately from the projectile and inserted just before the shell was loaded into the gun. It came in several forms such as superquick, which caused instantaneous detonation; short delay, which held off the detonation for .05 sec.; and long delay, which held it off for .15 sec. Base-detonating fuzes were normally used in shells designed for penetrating armour or concrete against which a point fuze might have been crushed and rendered inoperative on impact. Time fuzes were used chiefly in antiaircraft shells and could be set to explode a shell in flight after it had reached the estimated altitude of the enemy plane. Time fuzes, as noted above, were of two types: the 21-sec. powder-train type or the mechanical time fuze with clockwork mechanism.

By far the most revolutionary development in fuzes in modern times came with the appearance of the VT or proximity fuze in World War II. This electronic marvel contained a miniature radio transmitting and receiving oscillator which, while the projectile was in flight, sent forth a continuous radio signal. When this signal was reflected back to the fuze by a solid object, whether airplane, ship or ground, the fuze detonated the projectile. The fuze was set with such precision that the shell would explode only when it was within lethal range of its target. Proximity to the target was the key to its functioning.

One of the most highly prized Allied secrets in World War II, the VT fuze was not at first used on land for fear the enemy would recover a specimen, learn the secret of its construction and turn similar ammunition against the fleets of Allied bombers that were pounding German and Japanese cities. Its first use was at sea in antiaircraft fire from the U.S. cruiser "Helena" in Jan. 1943. From that time on it was regularly employed by the British and U.S. navies and helped greatly to provide naval vessels with an effective means of defense against air attacks, which became particularly menacing as the Allied fleets closed in on the Japanese home islands.

The first land use of the proximity fuze for antiaircraft fire was in the defense of London against the German "buzz bombs" in 1944. Late in the autumn of 1944 the Allied high command released the VT fuze for unrestricted use by field artillery and it played a part in repulsing the German counteroffensive of Dec. 1944. It was very effective against troops in the open or in trenches and against truck convoys on the road, for it caused shells to explode in the air. Aerial bombs equipped with VT fuzes were dropped on the island of Iwo Jima in early Feb. 1945. In aircraft rockets or cannon it greatly increased the effectiveness of plane-to-plane fire and air-to-ground attacks.

10. Propellants and Explosives.—In the years following World War I much attention was devoted to two problems: (1) development of a propellant that would be as flashless as possible and would thus not reveal the location of guns employing it, particularly during night operations; and (2) development of non-

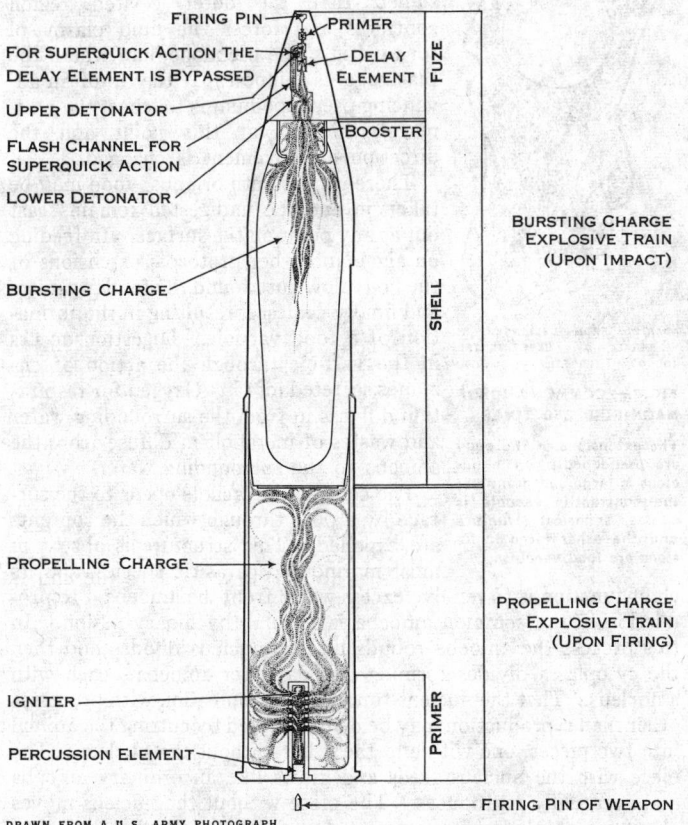

FIRING PIN
PRIMER
FOR SUPERQUICK ACTION THE
DELAY ELEMENT IS BYPASSED
DELAY ELEMENT
UPPER DETONATOR
FUZE
FLASH CHANNEL FOR
SUPERQUICK ACTION
BOOSTER
LOWER DETONATOR
BURSTING CHARGE
EXPLOSIVE TRAIN
(UPON IMPACT)
SHELL
BURSTING CHARGE

PROPELLING CHARGE
PROPELLING CHARGE
EXPLOSIVE TRAIN
(UPON FIRING)

IGNITER
PRIMER
PERCUSSION ELEMENT
FIRING PIN OF WEAPON

DRAWN FROM A U.S. ARMY PHOTOGRAPH
FIG. 8.—FUNCTIONING OF A TYPICAL ROUND OF AMMUNITION

hygroscopic propellants; i.e., without a tendency to absorb moisture. Considerable success attended these efforts and so-called flashless nonhygroscopic (FNH) propellants came into use. But achievement of all the desired characteristics in one propellant proved impossible. Reduction of smoke usually caused increased flash, and vice versa. The propellants in general use had a nitrocellulose base and were commonly known as smokeless powder. Their usual form was that of small cylindrical pellets, perforated to improve their combustion.

The standard explosive filler for HE shells during the first half of the 20th century was either T.N.T. or amatol. T.N.T. was a particularly satisfactory military explosive because it was sufficiently insensitive to withstand both the shock of setback when the projectile was fired and the shock of impact at the target. It was cheap, easy to manufacture and safe to handle—all very important practical considerations. And, unlike picric acid, it did not corrode metals or form dangerous compounds.

Ordnance scientists, however, continued to seek improved explosives, particularly those with greater brisance or shattering effect. Tetryl was more brisant than T.N.T. but was also more sensitive, so it was most often employed as a booster to detonate T.N.T. Another explosive, sometimes called cyclonite by the U.S.

and RDX by the British, gained wide acceptance in World War II. though it was so sensitive it had to be mixed with oils, waxes or other explosives to form a usable composition. Another new explosive was ethylenedinitramine, shorted to EDNA, developed largely by a U.S. chemist, George C. Hale, for whom it was named haleite. A fourth was PETN, the shortened name for pentaerythritol tetranitrate, and its derivative, pentolite (half T.N.T. and half PETN), which became the standard filler for high explosive anti-tank rounds. These and others were combined in many ways in a never-ending search for an ideal shell filler.

Military explosive charges are made in many different shapes and sizes to form a special class of ammunition known as demolition materials. Their main purpose is to destroy fortifications, railroads, bridges, dams or buildings, or to clear mine fields. Common forms are dynamite sticks, blocks of T.N.T., ammonium nitrate or nitrostarch and shaped-charge devices. The shaped-charge device used to blast holes in steel or concrete usually consists of a cylindrical block of high explosive with a conical cavity in its lower end and a blasting cap in the top end. The whole block rests upon metal legs that provide the necessary standoff for maximum effect. Small explosive charges may be connected to doors or windows so that they will explode when the doors or windows are opened or closed; others may be wired to attractive items to form booby traps that explode when the item is picked up. The bangalore torpedo is another type of explosive device used to clear a narrow path through mine fields or wire entanglements. It consists of lengths of explosive-filled steel tubes that may be used singly or joined together.

During World War II the appearance of the shaped charge, described above, helped solve the armour-penetration problem, and after the war an entirely new and infinitely more powerful element came into the picture, the atomic shell.

11. Atomic Shells.—The most spectacular development in artillery ammunition came in the decade following World War II with announcement by the U.S. army that it had produced a 280-mm. atomic shell. The first firing of this devastating new shell (about 11 in. in diameter) took place at the Atomic Energy commission's proving ground near Las Vegas, Nev., on May 25, 1953. Its range was announced as being approximately 20 mi. As the 280-mm. gun was a huge 85-ton weapon with limited mobility, work went forward in compressing atomic explosives into rounds of smaller calibre and by 1957 the existence of an 8-in. shell was announced by the U.S. army. Whether employed in artillery shells, bombs, demolition charges, rockets or guided missiles, nuclear energy held a dominant position in the military realm. See ROCKETS AND GUIDED MISSILES.

BIBLIOGRAPHY.—H. W. L. Hime, *Gunpowder and Ammunition* (1904); B. Crowell, *America's Munitions, 1917–18* (1919); Thomas J. Hayes, *Elements of Ordnance* (1938); A. Marshall, *Explosives,* 3 vol. (1917–32); T. L. Davis, *Chemistry of Powder and Explosives* (1943); Jules Bebie, *Manual of Explosives, Military Pyrotechnics, and Chemical Warfare Agents* (1943); T. C. Ohart, *Elements of Ammunition* (1946); James Phinney Baxter, *Scientists Against Time* (1946); C. M. Green, H. C. Thomson and P. C. Roots, *The Ordnance Department: Planning Munitions for War* (1955). (H. C. T.)

AMNESIA is a hysterical symptom, classified as a dissociative reaction, characterized by disturbances of memory. Amnesia may be general, in which case all functions of memory are involved; or partial, in which case only certain groups of ideas, proper names, the meanings of words, events and their associations, and the like are screened from memory. *See* HYSTERIA.

AMNESTY (oblivion of injuries), which may be declared by treaty or national authority, manifests a determination to forget past wrongs and animosities, to restore conditions of amity and to refrain from prosecuting persons guilty of political offenses. Generally cited as the first historical example of amnesty is the act by which Thrasybulus of Athens proclaimed an amnesty in 404 B.C., expressly excluding the 30 tyrants and a few others from its operation. In Roman law, the principle of *restitutio in integrum* amounted in practice to an amnesty.

In modern treaties an amnesty clause implies an obligation of the parties to regard their enmity as terminated and to renounce it as a pretext for a new war. The treaty of Osnabrück between the emperor on the one hand and Sweden and the Protestant states of Germany on the other (1648), and that of Oliva between the emperor, Sweden, Poland and the elector of Brandenburg (1660) provided not only that mutual wrongs should be consigned to oblivion but that property should be restored to all persons who had been dispossessed during the war. The final act of the congress of Vienna in 1815 extended amnesty to Poles and Swedes, and the treaty of Frankfurt between France and Germany in 1871 limited amnesty provisions to the inhabitants of the territory ceded by France to Germany, though this was subsequently extended by special negotiations. The treaty of San Stefano, between Russia and Turkey in 1878, contained the unusual provision requiring Turkey to extend amnesty to its own subjects compromised during the war. The peace of Vereeniging ending the Boer War in 1902 provided amnesty for Boers who accepted British nationality with exception of a list of Boer officers who were to be tried for violations of the law of war. Some peace treaties have not included an amnesty clause, but amnesty is said to be implied except in so far as express provision is made to the contrary.

National amnesties following civil strife are regarded as acts of grace by the sovereign. That proclaimed by Charles II on his restoration in 1660 excluded persons who had taken part in the execution of his father. The last British amnesty was that of 1747 extending to participants in the second Jacobite rebellion. Napoleon's amnesty of March 13, 1815, excluded Talleyrand and a dozen other eminent persons. Pres. Andrew Johnson issued a proclamation on May 29, 1865, which granted full pardon to all former Confederates (except certain leaders) who took an unqualified oath of allegiance to the United States; these provisions were modified in subsequent proclamations issued in 1867 and 1868.

The treaties ending the two world wars of the 20th century did not contain general amnesty clauses, but in some cases provided for the waiver of claims of certain types beyond those specified in the treaty. These treaties discriminated between the victorious allies and their enemies in respect to the restoration of sequestrated property. They provided explicitly for the return of prisoners of war and interned civilians, except those of enemy nationality subject to trial for war crimes or other offenses. France, Germany, the Netherlands, Norway, Belgium and Japan have declared amnesties for persons engaged in compromising activities during World War II, in the case of Japan including 1,300,000 persons. After prosecuting thousands of war criminals, the western Allies declared in 1949 that they would hold no further war crimes trials in either Europe or the far east. Opinion in Germany and Japan demanded clemency for convicted war criminals and, after the Japanese peace treaty went into effect in 1952, a clemency board was set up and large numbers of war criminals were paroled. In Germany a large proportion of war criminals held by the western powers had been released by 1953, but the Soviet Union still retained custody of an unknown number of prisoners of war and war criminals estimated at over 100,000. Some of these subsequently were released.   (Q. W.)

AMOEBA, the genus as well as the common name given to certain microscopic unicellular animals characterized by the ability to form temporary extensions of the body, called pseudopodia or false feet. The well-known amoeba of fresh-water ponds and streams, *Amoeba proteus,* is a fascinating object of study which may be found on decaying bottom vegetation. Each amoeba is a small mass of jellylike material, slightly grayish in appearance. Although apparently simple in gross structure, it carries on many of the vital functions of higher animals—metabolism, growth, reproduction, locomotion and response to stimuli.

The protoplasm of an amoeba is differentiated into a thin outer plasma membrane; a layer of stiff, clear ectoplasm just beneath the plasma membrane; and the central granular endoplasm. Located in the endoplasm are a granular nucleus, a clear contractile vacuole and numerous food vacuoles.

Amoeboid movement, characterized by the formation of pseudopodia, is considered to be the most primitive type of animal locomotion. This type of locomotion is also exhibited by certain cells

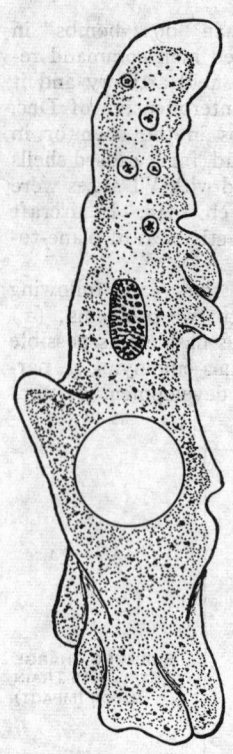

ADAPTED FROM DELLINGER IN "JOURNAL OF EXPERIMENTAL ZOOLOGY" (WISTAR)

FIG. 1.—COMMON AMOEBA MAGNIFIED 260 TIMES

The extensions of the body are pseudopodia. The nucleus is large and granular; the contractile vacuole is a clear spherical structure and the other large inclusions are food vacuoles

of higher animals, for example, white blood corpuscles. By watching the movements of the granular endoplasm one can see some of the factors involved in amoeboid movement. The outer, more viscous region of the ectoplasm is called the plasmagel, whereas the inner more fluid region is known as the plasmasol. A pseudopodium starts to form at a point where the outer gelated region of the amoeba liquefies, thus presenting a weakened region through which the adjacent plasmasol flows. As the plasmasol flows "forward," it turns back and becomes part of the plasmagel. At the temporary posterior of the amoeba, plasmagel changes into plasmasol. It is assumed that the outer gelated region contracts and forces the fluid plasmasol forward into the pseudopodium where the plasmagel is thinnest. If the tip of an advancing pseudopodium is touched, the plasmagel thickens at this point and the direction of movement is changed.

There is no mouth or anus; food may be taken in and the undigested remains cast out at any point on the surface. In feeding on algae and other protozoa, extensions of the body flow out around the food organism and finally coalesce, resulting in the formation of a food vacuole. Digestion occurs in the vacuole through the action of enzymes secreted into it. Oxygen for respiration diffuses in from the surrounding water and wastes of metabolism diffuse from the amoeba to the surrounding water.

The contractile vacuole opens to the surface by a pore through which the contents are expelled. This structure is absent in most marine and parasitic species, and its chief function is to remove excess water from the amoeba. Reproduction in the common amoeba is asexual, by binary fission. In this process the amoeba rounds up, the nucleus divides and then the cytoplasm divides forming two daughter amoebae, each with a nucleus. That the nucleus functions in connection with processes other than reproduction may be demonstrated by cutting the animal into two pieces, one with and the other without the nucleus. The piece with the nucleus feeds and grows like an ordinary amoeba and eventually reproduces. The piece without the nucleus moves about for a time but it cannot feed or digest food and it dies after the reserve food in its protoplasm has been used up.

During periods of adversity many kinds of amoebae are able to survive by encysting. In this process the amoeba rounds up, gives off a large amount of its water content and secretes a protective envelope or cyst membrane. Such cysts may be dispersed by air currents or other agencies; if they fall into a suitable environment, the envelope ruptures and the contained amoeba emerges.

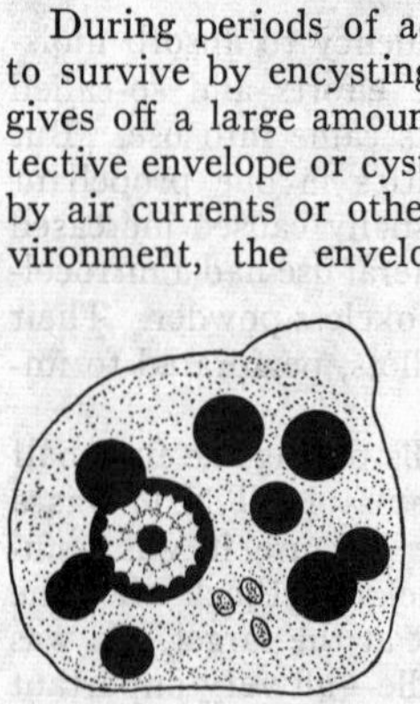

There are numerous species of parasitic amoebae. Of the six species of amoeba that may live in man's alimentary tract, one, *Entamoeba histolytica,* is pathogenic, causing amoebic dysentery. *E. histolytica* can penetrate the lining of the intestine and produce a characteristic ulceration in the intestinal wall. In some cases they are carried in the blood to the liver where they produce abscesses. This amoeba ingests red blood corpuscles. Transmission is by the cyst stage and numerous cysts may be present in the feces of infected individuals. Infection occurs through the drinking of contaminated water or the eating of un-

ADAPTED FROM DOFLEIN

FIG. 2.—DYSENTERY AMOEBA MAGNIFIED 2,250 TIMES

The dark circles are red blood corpuscles; the other circle with a beaded periphery is the nucleus

cooked contaminated food. Excystment, or emergence from the cyst, occurs in the intestine of man. The obvious control of *E. histolytica* is proper sanitation.

Amoebae, widely studied in zoological laboratories as examples of protoplasm, have also been used extensively in cell research in determining the relative functions and interactions of nucleus and cytoplasm.

See PROTOZOA. For more details on amoebic dysentery *see* DYSENTERY: *Amoebic Dysentery*. (W. H. J.)

AMOEBIASIS (AMEBIASIS), in general, means any infection with amoebae, but the term is most commonly used to describe infection with *Entamoeba histolytica,* including amoebic dysentery, amoebic liver abscess, etc. *See* PARASITOLOGY; AMOEBA; DYSENTERY.

AMON (AMUN, AMANA; Greek AMMON), Egyptian god, was originally one of eight gods (the ogdoad) of Khmun (Latin Hermopolis Magna, modern El Ashmunein) in middle Egypt, where they personified the mysterious invisibility of the primeval ocean. In circumstances unknown his cult reached Thebes shortly after that town became the capital of the united country (*c.* 2100 B.C.). There he assumed features of other gods, especially of the fertility god Min of Coptos, and was identified with the Heliopolitan sun-god Re as Amon-Re. His priesthood claimed for him the titles of "king of the gods" and "lord of the thrones of the two lands" (*i.e.,* of upper and lower Egypt), and two local deities were associated with him, the goddess Mut and the moon-god Khonsu.

Under the 18th dynasty (from 1580 B.C.) Amon was believed to have granted to the pharaohs the victories leading to the formation of their empire in Asia. At the same time his cult was introduced into Napata in Nubia, and a little later to the new royal residence at Pi-Ramesse and into the oases. The religious revolution of King Ikhnaton (*q.v.*) was chiefly directed against Amon and his priests, but after Tutankhamen's reaction (*c.* 1350 B.C.) his two Theban temples at Karnak and Luxor greatly increased in wealth; under the 21st dynasty (*c.* 1100 B.C.) Amon's high priest headed a sacerdotal state at Thebes. This soon began to decline, and the Assyrian sack of Thebes about 663 B.C. reduced Amon to mere local importance. His famous oracle at Oasis Siwa in the Libyan desert remained, however, to welcome Alexander the Great as the son of a god.

Amon was represented in human form, sometimes with a ram's head; his sacred animals were the ram and the Nile goose. The Greeks identified him with Zeus. *See* also references under "Amon" in the Index. (J. Cy.)

AMONTONS, GUILLAUME (1663–1705), French physicist, best known for his work in friction and in thermometry, was born in Paris on Aug. 31, 1663. In 1687 he presented to the Academy of Sciences a hygrometer of his own invention, and in 1695 he published his *Remarques et expériences physiques sur la construction d'une nouvelle clepsydre, sur les baromètres, thermomètres et hygromètres*. He also published some investigations on friction (1699) and several other papers on physical and mechanical subjects, the most notable being two papers on thermometry in 1702–03. He died in Paris on Oct. 11, 1705.

AMORA (meaning literally "speaker" or "interpreter"; pl. amoraim), one of four different types of Jewish postbiblical teachers, the others being Sofer, Tanna and Gaon (*q.v.*). The amoraim, working at academies in Palestine and in Babylonia, beginning about A.D. 200, were authors of the Gemara section of the Talmud, in the main a legal interpretation of and commentary on the Mishnah. Their work was completed with the compilation of the Babylonian Talmud about A.D. 500. *See* TALMUD.

AMORGOS, an island of the Cyclades (*q.v.*), Greece, is long and narrow—about 20 mi. from southeast to northwest. Area 45 sq.mi. Pop. (1961) 2,096. It is very mountainous but supports a dwindling agricultural community, notably in the Catapola plain, where there is the only good anchorage. Amorgos was a great centre in the Early Bronze Age, but in classical times had only three cities, Arcesine, Minoa and Aegiale. An important industry in antiquity was the production of *amorgina:* fine, transparent fabrics made from locally grown flax or cotton. The Romans used the island as a place of banishment. Visitors land at Catapola on the west coast, four hours traveling from Amorgos, the principal village. (J. Bo.)

AMORITES. The term Amorite, referring to a people of the ancient near east, encompasses the manifold aspects of race, language, territories occupied and even social status. Considered in the light of changes in historical conditions and semantic range during a period of more than 2,000 years, this subject is one of the most debatable in the history of the near east. The Amorites are known from cuneiform sources and from the Old Testament; these sources are here dealt with separately.

Generally speaking, the name Amurru or Amorite is, on the one hand, connected with northern Arabia and, on the other hand, with a Semitic group called Canaanites. At about 1600 B.C., the term Amorite lost all connection with Arabia and became instead the geographic term used to designate the land of the west; at the same time, the term Amorite lost all value for denoting a language.

Cuneiform Sources.—*Period I: c. 2400–2000 B.C.*—It is only a hypothesis that the earliest Amorites spoke the same language as the Akkadians. Some centuries later, when personal names and a few of their tribe names appear in the sources, at least a part of the Martu (the Sumerian equivalent of Amorite) spoke a language different from Akkadian, one that was perhaps between Akkadian and the language of the west Semitic group discussed below (*Period II*). From the oldest sources, the Martu, or Amurru as the Akkadians called them, were equated with the west wind and the west, though their true place of origin was most likely in Arabia, not Syria. In the Ur III period, three kinds of Martu were distinguished: (1) those dwelling in Arabia proper who made contacts with the kings of Ur (*e.g.,* King Ipiq-reum of Yamat, a region which later sources identify with Aḥlamu, meaning Arabia); (2) those tribes that crossed the two rivers to the eastern hills; (3) those Martu who were dispersed among the Sumero-Akkadian population as labourers but who perhaps still maintained their tribal organization; they were called Martu/Amurru and were distinct from the rest of the population.

The Martu of this period was described as one who ate raw meat, who knew no house, who was not buried when he died. They came down from the mountains, probably east of the Tigris, to encroach upon the civilized; they were one of the causes of the downfall of the Ur III empire. In this entire period, no Martu/Amurru is attested for the mid-Euphrates region or for Syria.

Period II: c. 2000–1600 B.C.—About a century after the end of period I, a large-scale migration of great tribal federations from Arabia resulted in the occupation of Babylonia proper, the mid-Euphrates region and Syria-Palestine. The language of these tribes was a dialect of the family of Semitic languages called Canaanite, best known from the Hebrew dialect. Because of this obvious affinity with Canaanite, some scholars apply the name Eastern Canaanite, or Canaanite, to the population that invaded Babylonia and the mid-Euphrates; other scholars name this distinct wave of population Amorites, thereby denying the basic difference between this stock and the people treated in period I above.

Although the local kings in Babylonia belonged to this stock almost without exception, they quickly assimilated to the basic population. Some tribes maintained their old sheikh system but recognized the local kings as chieftains. The same situation prevailed in the mid-Euphrates, well documented by the archives of Mari (Tall al Hariri). Farther west, the political centre of these Canaanites was the city of Ḥalab (Aleppo); in this area, as well as in Palestine, they were thoroughly mixed with the Hurrians (*q.v.*). The tribal federation to which the rulers of Mari and Aleppo belonged was that of the Haneans. There existed also other main tribe groups (*e.g.,* the "Sons of the North" and the "Sons of the South") whose relationship with the Haneans remains obscure. Clearly distinct from these "civilized nomads" were the wild nomads of Arabia and the Syrian desert, the Suteans. The region then called Amurru was northern Palestine with the centre at Hasor, and the neighbouring Syrian desert comprised of four independent kingdoms. This region was a centre of horse breeding whence both horses and personnel were brought.

Three great conquerers of this period bore Canaanite names:

Hammurabi of Babylon, Shamshi-Adad of the mid-Euphrates and Yarim-lim of Aleppo. In the Old Assyrian documents the term Amurru apparently covered a wider range of meaning than it did elsewhere, but why or to what extent has not been determined.

Period III: c. 1600–1100 B.C.—In the dark age that followed period II, the term Amurru as well as the Canaanite language disappeared completely from Babylonia and the mid-Euphrates, while it became dominant in Syria and Palestine. In the Amarna letters (*c.* ± 1360; *see* TELL EL AMARNA) the term Amurru is relegated to a tiny state that extended from the port of Arvad to the Lebanon; it was first under Egyptian, then Hittite control. At the same time, the bedouins, now called Aḫlameans, were still emigrating from Arabia. (*See* CANAAN; PHOENICIA.)

Period IV: 1100–500 B.C.—In the Assyrian inscriptions from 1100 on, the use of the by then purely literary term Amurru (*i.e.,* no Amorite kingdom, region or population still existed) was meant to designate part of Syria and the whole of Phoenicia and Palestine. Though Palmyra (Tadmor) still belonged to Amurru, the Arabian peninsula is no longer so called. In addition, the name Ḫatti came to be used almost synonymously with Amurru; this shift of meaning for these two historical terms is paralleled by the use of the terms Emori and Ḫitti in the Old Testament.

Old Testament.—The pentateuchal source called the Elohist (dating perhaps from the 8th century B.C.) named as Amorites the population (spread out in many small kingdoms) that was conquered by the Israelites. The Jahvistic source (*c.* 900 B.C.) applied instead the term Canaanites, so that the two terms must have been synonymous. But the table of nations in Gen. x (which is not assigned to either of the above-mentioned sources) lists Emori as one of the 11 sons (cities or tribes) of Canaan. The passage Judg. i, 29–36, in dealing with the remnants of the old population not conquered by the Israelites, distinguishes between Canaanites in the south and Amorites in the north of Palestine. A further historical reminiscence which may contain a sound tradition is found in Num. xxi, where Sihon the "king of the Amorites" is said to have dwelt at Heshbon, in a kingdom situated east of the Jordan between the Arnon and Jabbok rivers, in the country later known as Moab. The semimythical reference to the Amorites as a race of giants in Deut. iii, 11, Amos ii, 9 may be noted. *See also* SEMITIC LANGUAGES: *Amorite.*

BIBLIOGRAPHY.—B. Landsberger, *Zeitschrift für Assyriologie,* 35:236–238 (1924), and in *Journal of Cuneiform Studies,* 8:56 (1954); T. Bauer, *Die Ostkanaanäer* (1926); S. Smith, *Early History of Assyria* (1928); H. Frankfort, *Orient. Inst. Commun.,* 13:25–39 (1932); A. Poebel, *American Journal of Semitic Languages,* 48:20–26 (1931–32), and in *Journal of Near Eastern Studies,* 1:253–258 (1941); A. Goetze, *Language,* 17:127–138 (1941); J. R. Kupper, *Les Nomades en Mésopotamie au temps des rois de Mari* (1957); H. Klengel, *Zeitschrift "Das Altertum,"* 5:195–205 (1959) and *Zeitschrift der Humboldt-Univ. zu Berlin,* 8:211–227 (1959); I. J. Gelb, *Journal of Cuneiform Studies,* 15:27–47 (1961).   (B. LA.)

AMORTIZATION. In finance, amortization means the systematic repayment of a debt; in accounting, it means the systematic writing off of some account over a period of years. An example of the first meaning is a mortgage on a home that may be repaid in monthly installments that include interest and a gradual reduction of the principal obligation. Another is a bond issue of a business corporation or a governmental body that may be amortized by annual or semiannual payments. These payments may be used to repurchase bonds or held in a sinking fund to retire the debt at some date in the future or the bond issue may have serial maturities so that a portion of the issue comes due and requires repayment each year. Systematic annual reduction increases the safety factor for the investor by imposing a small annual burden rather than a single large final obligation that might be a threat to the solvency of the debtor. There is also the logic of repayment during a period not greater than the useful life of the property financed by the given debt.

In the second, or accounting sense, the amortization, or writing off, of an asset, such as a building, a machine or a mine, over its estimated life has the effect of reducing its balance sheet valuation and charging its cost into the expenses of operation. Such expense is called depreciation or, for exhaustible natural resources, depletion. In some instances the asset to be amortized may, like good will or organization expenses, be regarded as having an indeterminate life. Management often prefers to eliminate such intangible assets as a matter of conservatism but wishes the process to be gradual. Some items, like property that is abandoned or lost in some catastrophe, may continue to be carried among the firm's assets until its extinction is achieved by gradual amortization.

A corporation selling its own bonds at a price other than the face amount will nevertheless show the bond liability at the face, or par, value. Any excess proceeds over par will appear among the liabilities as "premium on bonds"; any deficiency, on the asset side as "discount on bonds." These two accounts are amortized over the life of the debt, unless prior repayment requires earlier extinction. The annual amortization of discount becomes an addition to the current interest payments as a part of the cost of the borrowed funds; premium amortization serves as a reduction of the interest costs. Investors, on the other hand, ordinarily enter such bonds in their accounts at their cost rather than at par value and treat the premium or discount as capital loss or gain when the bond is paid at par. A few investors, however, like life insurance companies, amortize the difference between cost and par over the life of the bond and are said to carry bonds at "amortized value" in their balance sheet. Some commercial banks carry discount bonds at cost until maturity or resale but charge off all premiums paid at the time of purchase as a matter of conservatism.

Taxation.—During World War II, business concerns in the United States were permitted to amortize the cost of defense facilities over a five-year period for income tax purposes when proper certificates had been issued. Any unamortized balance could be written off in the last year of the war. After the war, this principle of accelerated amortization was extended to encourage business to expand productive facilities which would serve the national defense. Because such plant and equipment would normally be acquired only if it had some peacetime use as well, the American Institute of Certified Public Accountants recommended that in published statements, "normal depreciation" should be employed rather than the accelerated amortization used in income tax returns. But such normalization of depreciation, if reported along with the reduced income taxes, would give an appearance of unusually high earnings during the five-year period of accelerated amortization followed by depressed earnings in the succeeding years when income taxes would appear above normal because of the absence of any deduction for depreciation or amortization. A recommendation was therefore made that with "normalized depreciation" should go a "normalized income tax expense" and that any amount of the income tax not being paid currently should be set up as a deferred income tax liability. At the end of the period of accelerated amortization, when income tax payments rise, the excess over normal is charged against this liability account so that the tax expense account shows only the same amount as in the preceding years. This normalization runs counter to the accounting theory which opposes introducing speculative figures into the accounts. The procedure assumes that future income tax rates will be like those of the present. On the other hand, the argument for normalization is that it improves the income statement as a basis for judging earning power and recognizes that income tax accounting does not always constitute the best measure of financial performance.

The advantage of accelerated amortization for tax purposes does not lie in any reduction of taxes paid but in their deferment. The drain of income taxes is reduced for the business during the early years when amortization is accelerated. It thus releases more funds for the repayment of any obligations incurred in financing the property. The financial problem arises in the subsequent years when, in addition to paying the normal income taxes, the business must earn enough to pay the additional income tax resulting from the absence of any deduction for depreciation.

Some public utility and railroad commissions have required companies subject to their rule to report normal depreciation rather than accelerated amortization but to report income taxes in the amounts currently being paid without any normalization. The income statements in these fields consequently require special analysis to ascertain the basis employed and the significance of the figures as measuring earning power on some uniformly comparable basis. (H. G. Gₙ.)

AMORY, THOMAS (1691?–1788), British writer of Irish descent known for his autobiographical *John Buncle*. It is believed that he lived in Dublin where he knew Swift. Later he lived at Westminster and also Hounslow. He was a staunch Unitarian and a student of medicine, geology and antiquities. He published two books, the *Memoirs* (1755) dealing with the life of an imaginary lady, Mrs. Marinda Benlow, and *The Life of John Buncle, Esq.*, 2 vol. (1756 and 1766), written in the form of an extravagant autobiography. The hero, "an odd compound of a man," marries seven wives in succession, each embodying one of his ideals of womanhood. Something of the spirit of Rabelais and of Dickens informs Amory's eccentric works. He died Nov. 25, 1788.

See J. C. Walters, *John Buncle, a Curio of Literature* (1919).

AMOS, BOOK OF, one of the books in the collection of 12 prophets (or minor prophets) in the Old Testament. In the original Hebrew text and in the Vulgate it is placed third, in the Septuagint second, but chronologically it is the earliest of the twelve.

Contents.—Amos was a pattern for later prophetic books. It contains: (1) oracles, often very short, which were gathered into groups by the prophet himself or by the traditionists; (2) short passages giving features from the life of the prophet, related by himself or by disciples or by later "historians"; and (3) later additions by disciples or traditionists. These three groups also can be found in other prophetic books of the Old Testament. It is not known whether Amos' oracles of doom were also patterns for contemporary and later prophets, or if this reaction from the prophets was a spontaneous one during this period.

The nine chapters of the book of Amos, which are mainly written in poetry, begin with an introductory prose verse indicating the period of the prophet, his profession and his habitat. His profession is given as that of a herdsman or shepherd, but his stylistic ability and his knowledge of the ancient traditions of his people show that he was no ordinary one. The second verse is a superscription and motto, while i, 3–ii, 16 is a composite composition, consisting of oracles against neighbouring peoples, Judah and Israel. The other oracles are built in the same way, and they are grouped together according to ancient near eastern patterns. It is probable that the prophet himself was responsible for the arrangement, for any compiler not only must have possessed great rhetorical and stylistic ability but also must have reshaped some of the oracles. The two first chapters and ix, 7 indicate clearly that God in the eyes of Amos was not nationally limited; here are glimpses of universalism like those found later in Deutero-Isaiah.

In ch. iii–vi the prophet pronounces a series of oracles against Israel, with arguments to show why the doom of Israel was necessary. It is here that he speaks of the day of the Lord as a day of lamentation, darkness and destruction (v, 16–20). The people of Israel had forgotten their ancient social solidarity; they suppressed the poor and put their trust in elaborate worship in the temple of Bethel and Gilgal (v, 4 ff). Therefore the doom had to come. In vii, 1–9, 10 several visions of the prophet are declared, interrupted by the narrative of the incident when the priest Amaziah turned Amos out of the king's sanctuary in Bethel (vii, 10–17). The two first visions, of locusts and of fire, in vii, 1–6 are supposed by some scholars to be from an early stage in the preaching of Amos, because in them Yahweh holds his doom back. There are, however, no suggestions in the text to support this theory. The last part of the book (ix, 11–15), which speaks about the restoration of the Davidic kingdom and the return of the exiles, is considered by many scholars to be an addition to the original text, but opinions diverge on this point.

Amos v, 25 is quoted by Stephen (Acts vii, 42), and Amos ix, 11–12 (the passage at the end about the rebuilding of the fallen booth of David) is quoted by James at the Council of Jerusalem (Acts xv, 16–18), but in neither case is Amos named. In later ages Amos was remembered for his prophecies of doom and for the oracle of the rebuilding of the house of David. In the eyes of the church fathers all his prophecies had been confirmed. Modern interpreters have first and foremost seen Amos as the first prophet of doom, who showed a way for his contemporaries and for later prophets.

Authorship and Date.—The book contains the words of the prophet Amos, who in the introductory verse is said to have had his visions two years before the earthquake, in the days of Uzziah, king of Judah, and of Jeroboam II, the son of Joash, king of Israel. King Uzziah, also called Azariah, reigned from *c.* 783 to *c.* 742 B.C. and Jeroboam II from *c.* 786 to *c.* 745 B.C. It is generally supposed that Amos acted as a prophet only for a short period, most probably beginning *c.* 760 B.C. From many of his words and especially from ch. vii it can be seen that he worked in Israel, the northern kingdom, although he had previously lived at Tekoa near Bethlehem, in the southern kingdom of Judah.

Amos' words were preserved by temple circles in Jerusalem, and thus reached their established place in the Old Testament. His oracles were most probably not written down as soon as they were uttered, nor were they ever written by the prophet himself, although he may have been able to write. Oral transmission was the usual one for oracles like his. Several features in the book indicate this, one of them being the way in which the narrative about the visit of Amos to the temple of Bethel has been inserted among the visions in ch. vii. Probably before the northern kingdom was destroyed by the Assyrians in 722 B.C. it was found necessary to have the oral traditions written, and thus the words of Amos were conveyed to Judah.

Bibliography.—A. Weiser, *Die Profetie des Amos* (1929); R. S. Cripps, *A Critical and Exegetical Commentary on the Book of Amos*, 2nd ed. (1955); J. Morgenstern, "Amos Studies I–III," *Hebrew Union College Annual*, vol. xi (1936), vol. xii (1937–38), vol. xv (1940); A. S. Kapelrud, *Central Ideas in Amos* (1956); N. H. Snaith, *Amos, Hosea and Micah* (1956); J. D. W. Watts, *Vision and Prophecy in Amos* (1958). (A. S. K.)

AMOSITE: *see* Asbestos.

AMOY (or Hsia-men), formerly also Ssu-ming, one-time treaty port in the province of Fukien (*q.v.*), on the highly indented southeast coast of China (24° 27′ N., 118° 05′ E.). Amoy's population (1953) of 224,300 made it the second largest city in Fukien. The city is on the southwest arm of hilly Amoy Island, about 45 sq.mi. in area, at the head of a wide bay at the mouth of the Chiu-lung river. Its deepwater anchorage is well protected from late summer typhoons and is one of the finest on the coast. The city's natural hinterland was long confined to southeast Fukien where tea for Europe attracted British and Dutch traders in the 18th century, and from whence Chinese traders and overseas settlers set out for T'aiwan (Formosa), the Philippines and Malaya. By the treaty of Nanking, 1842 (*see* China: *History*), Amoy was opened as one of the five original treaty ports, with westerners residing in the international settlement on Kulangsu Island, one-half mile to the west; in 1943 both the United States and Great Britain relinquished their special privileges. With the decline of tea exports in the late 19th century, Amoy stagnated commercially except for shipments of native paper, fishing nets, pottery ware, canned fruits and sea foods to the Chinese in southeast Asia. Remittances from Chinese living abroad have been locally important, as have been such activities as the founding of Amoy university by K. K. Tan, an Amoy man in Malaya, and the planning of the modern water reservoir by Homer Ling.

During the 1950s the area became increasingly important in the economic and military planning of the government of the Chinese People's Republic. On Dec. 9, 1956, the first train steamed into Amoy city, marking the completion of a 433-mi. railway from Ying-t'an, northern Kiangsi, and requiring 3.1 mi. of filled causeway from Chi-mei on the north. A branch to Foochow joined at Nan-p'ing, Fukien. This line provided a means for tapping the interior resources such as coal, iron, lumber and sugar; it also had military value because of its proximity to the Nationalist-held islands of Quemoy (Chin-men) and T'aiwan. (Te. H.)

AMPELOPSIS, a genus of about 20 species of woody, climbing, tendril-bearing vines of the grape family, Vitaceae. Strongly resembling the grapevine in habit, native to Asia and North America, some of them are cultivated as ornamental climbers. They have inconspicuous flowers, but showy, coloured berrylike fruits. The pepper vine (*A. arborea*), somewhat shrubby, with pinnate leaves is found in the southern United States and Mexico. The simple-leaved ampelopsis (*A. cordata*) occurs in the southern United States. The ampelopses are of easy cultivation in a variety of soils, but as they lack the sucking disks of the Virginia creeper, these vines need tying to their supports. All are hardy in England and the United States.

The Virginia creeper and the Boston or Japanese ivy were once placed in this genus but are now considered as belonging to *Parthenocissus*. (N. Tr.)

AMPÈRE, ANDRÉ MARIE (1775–1836), French physicist, who pioneered in electromagnetism, was born at Polémieux, near Lyons, Jan. 22, 1775. From about 1796 he gave private lessons at Lyons in mathematics, chemistry and languages; and in 1801 he removed to Bourg, as professor of physics and chemistry, leaving his ailing wife and infant son at Lyons. His wife died in 1804 and he never recovered from the blow. In 1809 he became professor of mathematics at the École Polytechnique in Paris. There he continued his scientific researches and multifarious studies with unabated diligence. He was admitted to the Institut National in 1814.

It is on the service that he rendered to science in establishing the relation between electricity and magnetism and in developing the science of electromagnetism, or, as he called it, electrodynamics, that Ampère's fame mainly rests. On Sept. 11, 1820, he heard of H. C. Oersted's discovery that a magnetic needle is acted on by a voltaic current. On the 18th of the same month he presented a paper to the Académie des Sciences, containing a far more complete exposition of that and kindred phenomena.

The whole field thus opened up Ampère explored with characteristic industry and care, and developed a mathematical theory which not only explained the electromagnetic phenomena already observed but also predicted new ones. Late in life he prepared a remarkable *Essai sur la philosophie des sciences,* and wrote many scientific papers, including two on the integration of partial differential equations (*Jour. École Polytechn.,* x, xi). He died at Marseille on June 10, 1836. *See also* MAGNETISM: *History.*

AMPÈRE, JEAN JACQUES ANTOINE (1800–1864), French critic, scholar and traveler who introduced works of foreign literature to France. The son of André Marie Ampère (*q.v.*), he was born at Lyons on Aug. 12, 1800. His life was largely dominated by his platonic love for Mme Récamier with whom he long corresponded. On his first journey to Germany, in 1826, he was greatly esteemed by Goethe, as later he was in France by Sainte-Beuve. In his wide knowledge of foreign civilizations, on which he lectured, as well as in his theories of the environmental influences on history, he was a precursor of H. A. Taine. He was a professor at the Sorbonne, at the Collège de France, and in 1848 he was elected to the French academy. Later, in the company of Prosper Mérimée, he traveled to the near east, and in 1852 to the United States and Mexico where he predicted the cutting of the Panama canal.

Among Ampère's works of research are his *Histoire littéraire de la France avant le 12e siecle,* 3 vol. (1839–40) and his *Histoire de la langue française* (1841). His major historical work is *L'Histoire romaine à Rome,* 4 vol. (1861–64). He died at Pau on the night of March 26/27, 1864.

BIBLIOGRAPHY.—C. A. Sainte-Beuve, *Nouveaux lundis,* vol. xiii and *Portraits littéraires,* vol. ii (1870); A. M. and J. J. A. Ampère, *Correspondance et souvenirs recueillis,* 2 vol. (1875); L. de Launay, *Un amoureux de Mme. Récamier* (1927); P. Mérimée, *Portraits historiques et littéraires* (1928); H. E. F. Haufe, *Jean-Jacques Ampère. Ein Kritiker der Frühromantik* (1935); L. Mallez, *Le Roman d'amour de Jean-Jacques Ampère* (1937).

AMPERE METER or AMMETER, an instrument for measuring electric currents. Ammeters used for the measurement of direct current are moving iron or moving coil low resistance galvanometers. For measuring alternating current, the instrument is, in general, a form of dynamometer, measuring the current flowing through two sets of coils which are connected in series. *See* INSTRUMENTS, ELECTRICAL MEASURING.

AMPERSAND, the name of the sign, *&* or *&,* which is a combination of the letters *e, t,* of the Lat. *et,* and; a corruption of the mixed English and Latin phrase, "and *per se* and," of which dialect forms are, "ampussyand," or "amperseand."

AMPHETAMINE, introduced commercially as BENZEDRINE, is one of a series of synthetic drugs with pronounced stimulatory actions on the central nervous system. It is a colourless, mobile, slowly volatile liquid, with an acrid taste and a slight odour of geranium leaves. The most widely used preparation of the drug is amphetamine sulfate, a white, odourless powder with a slightly bitter numbing taste. Other members of this series include dextroamphetamine (Dexedrine) and methamphetamine (Desoxyn).

In adequate doses, these drugs partially overcome the effects of anesthetics, narcotics, hypnotics and alcohol. All cause profound psychic effects, including wakefulness and mental alertness, increased initiative and elevation in mood, enhanced confidence, euphoria or elation, lessened sense of fatigue, talkativeness and increased ability to concentrate.

The stimulating effects of amphetamine make it useful for the symptomatic treatment of certain mild nervous depressions and, to a lesser extent, the more severe depressions accompanying some forms of mental disorder. In chronic alcoholism, the drug is of value as an aid to psychological suggestion in helping patients abstain. It is also useful for the management of narcolepsy, a condition marked by an uncontrollable desire for sleep. In that form of Parkinson's disease (shaking palsy) occurring after brain inflammation, the administration of amphetamine in conjunction with other therapeutic agents may relieve muscle rigidity. Amphetamine effectively dulls the appetite when taken before meals, and therefore is widely used as an adjunct to dietary restriction in weight reduction.

Amphetamine can produce undesirable effects, the commonest of which is overstimulation with restlessness, inability to sleep, tremor, tenseness and irritability. Abdominal cramping with nausea, vomiting and diarrhea also may occur. Large doses, sometimes taken with suicidal intent, can produce loss of consciousness, collapse and death.

Indiscriminate use of amphetamine to overcome fatigue and sleepiness or to provide increased energy and alertness is common, particularly among truck drivers, athletes and students. The council on drugs of the American Medical association in *New and Nonofficial Drugs, 1958,* pp. 189–190 (J. B. Lippincott Co., Philadelphia) has commented as follows regarding the use of the drug in normal persons:

The use of amphetamine to alleviate sleepiness and fatigue by persons not under medical control is to be condemned. The dangers lie in the elimination of the warning signal of fatigue in individuals who are overdoing, the possibility of habit formation on continued use, and undesirable circulatory effects. Collapse has occurred in some such cases. Except when administered under the strict supervision of the physician, its use is not recommended for developing a sense of exhilaration, increased energy and capacity for work; nor as a "pick-me-up" following temporary alcoholic overindulgence.

Although amphetamine can be obtained legally in the United States, as in Great Britain and most other countries, only on the prescription of a physician, illicit sale and distribution is common and constitutes one of the major grounds for prosecution under the Federal Food and Drug laws.

Because of its vasoconstrictive action, which is similar to that of epinephrine (adrenaline), amphetamine has been used by inhalation to produce shrinkage of the nasal mucous membrane in hay fever, asthma, acute sinusitis and similar conditions. Excessive improper use of Benzedrine inhalers has given rise to serious toxic effects, and U.S. and British manufacturers no longer make inhalers containing amphetamine.

Addiction to amphetamine can occur after prolonged use, but this is much milder in form than is addiction to narcotic drugs. The severe abstinence syndrome characteristic of the morphinelike drugs does not develop when amphetamine is withdrawn abruptly, although tremor, depression, weakness and gastrointestinal symptoms have been observed. Except in Japan, where amphetamine addiction became fairly common soon after World War II, the number of amphetamine addicts is probably small, certainly far smaller than the number of narcotic drug addicts. Despite its relative uncommonness and mildness, however, amphetamine addiction is a serious problem to the person concerned, since profound personality defects always underlie the tendency to drug abuse. In the United States, amphetamine addiction frequently is associated with similar abuse of barbiturates or alcohol. (J. C. Bn.)

AMPHIARAUS, a celebrated seer and prince of Argos, son of Oicles (or Apollo) and Hypermnestra. He took part in the voyage of the Argonauts and in the chase of the Calydonian boar. He foresaw the disastrous issue of the war against Thebes and at first refused to share in it, but his wife, Eriphyle, bribed by Polynices with the fatal necklace of Harmonia, persuaded him to set out on the expedition. Knowing his doom, he bade his sons, Alcmaeon and Amphilochus, avenge his death upon their mother.

On the defeat of the Seven, Amphiaraus, pursued by Periclymenus, would have been slain had not Zeus opened a chasm into which the seer, with his chariot and horses, disappeared. Thereafter he was numbered with the immortals and worshiped as a god. Near Oropus, on the supposed site of his passing, his sanctuary arose, with healing springs and an oracle famous for its interpretation of dreams. There was another temple dedicated to him on the road from Thebes to Potniae, and here was the oracle of Amphiaraus consulted by Croesus and Mardonius.

AMPHIBIA, a class of backboned animals sometimes known as the Batrachia. In the general classification of the animal kingdom, Amphibia are placed between the fish and reptiles. Living Amphibia include the frogs, toads, salamanders and caecilians, all of which have a smooth or rough but not scaly skin. Like the fish and reptiles, they are cold-blooded (poikilothermic or ectothermic); *i.e.,* their body temperature is related to the temperature of their environment.

Most Amphibia have four legs and live on land, but unlike other tetrapods they respire largely through their skin. Most of them lay their eggs in water; as the young develop they pass through a larval aquatic stage in which breathing is accomplished by external gills; the gills are lost during metamorphosis into the adult stage. The egg, even when laid on land, is without a shell and does not develop the amnion or allantois (egg membranes) of reptiles, birds and mammals.

Modern Amphibia are readily distinguished from reptiles by many skeletal differences, but the fossil forms were so similar that no sharp distinction can be made between them. Fossil remains have also tended to bridge the gap between Amphibia and fishes.

The living groups of Amphibia are a small remnant of what was once a larger and more successful class; the fossil and extinct types of Amphibia outnumber the living types. The ancestors of the amphibians were the internal nared fishes of the Devonian period. From the ancestral amphibians arose a great diversity of fossil forms. These forms survived until the Triassic period. From these ancestral fossil amphibians the living orders of frogs, salamanders and caecilians are descended. (For chart showing geological eras *see* GEOLOGY: *Historical Geology.*)

KINDS OF LIVING AMPHIBIANS

Frogs.—Among the living Amphibia the frogs, or Salientia, are the best known. Members of this group are also called toads, tree frogs, tree toads and spring peepers. Characteristically, they are modified for jumping by having enlarged hind legs, shortened forelegs and no tail.

From the eggs, which usually are laid in water, develop larvae commonly known as tadpoles, or polliwogs. The tadpoles are usually herbivorous whereas the adults are usually insectivorous or carnivorous. The duration of the tadpole stage varies according to the adaptations of the species and environmental conditions. After the larval development there is a period of metamorphosis during which gills are abandoned, lungs become functional and limb development is completed. Many frogs have modified this pattern by eliminating the free-swimming tadpole stage.

The approximately 2,000 species of frogs are widely distributed on all continents, although more than 80% of the species are found in the tropics. In Europe, one species is found as far north as 71° latitude, and in North America one species gets just above the Arctic circle. Frogs are known from the southern limits of Africa,

UNITED PRESS INTERNATIONAL
FIG. 1.—(LEFT) BULLFROG (RANA CATESBEIANA) AND (RIGHT) NORTHERN LEOPARD FROG (RANA PIPIENS PIPIENS)

Tasmania, Australia, New Zealand and South America.

The ancestors of the frogs appeared in the Triassic period about 200,000,000 years ago, but the modern frogs appeared in the Jurassic period about 160,000,000 years ago.

Salamanders.—The second best-known group of Amphibia are the salamanders, also known as newts, efts, spring lizards, water dogs, mud-puppies, hellbenders, tritons, congo eels and sirens. These amphibians characteristically have four legs and a tail, but some, for example the congo eels and sirens, have lost or reduced their appendages.

Many salamanders lay their eggs in water; from the eggs develop gilled larvae that later metamorphose into lung-breathing and/or skin-breathing adults. Some salamanders have evolved special types of eggs in which the larval stage develops; in others, the eggs are retained within the female, who gives birth to living young.

The approximately 200 species are found in Europe, North America, northern South America and eastern Asia. There are no salamanders in Australia, Central and South Africa, central and southern Asia, the Indo-Australian archipelago or the islands of the Pacific.

Salamanders date from the Upper Jurassic period (about 140,-000,000 years ago).

Caecilians.—The caecilians, or Apoda, are the least known of the living Amphibia. They are tropical, burrowing, wormlike creatures that lack legs. They are always found in moist places and usually lay their eggs near or in water. Some are ovoviviparous (*i.e.,* the eggs develop and hatch inside the female) with reduced larval stages; some have gilled larval stages of long duration. About 75 species are known from tropical Central and South America, Africa, Asia and the tropical Asian islands.

EVOLUTION

Descended From Fishes.—The first Amphibia made their appearance about 350,000,000 years ago, but their ancestry lies among the early internal-nared fishes belonging to the rhipidistian branch of the Crossopterygii, or lobe-fin fishes. These fishes lived in the large, continental fresh-water swamps and seas of the Devonian

ISABELLE HUNT CONANT
FIG. 2.—FIRE SALAMANDER (S. SALAMANDRA TAENIATA)

and Carboniferous periods. They were fusiform fish covered with an armour of cosmoid scales, with lobe fins and a heterocercal tail. These fish had functional lungs and an internal narial system that was probably complemented by gill breathing. The paired pectoral and pelvic fins had bony elements similar to elements in the primitive amphibian limb. The teeth were of the labyrinthodont type.

In the transition from rhipidistian fish to primitive amphibian many major anatomical and physiological changes had to take place. Probably due to the desiccation of the great fresh-water swamps, natural selection favoured those fishes that were best adapted to traversing short areas of dry land in order to get to the next pond, lake or other water body. The rhipidistian fish gave rise to the earliest amphibian fossils known —those belonging to the Ichthyostegalia.

These first amphibians had many skull features similar to the ancestral fish, but the opercular bones and probably the gill apparatus were reduced in the adult. The olfactory area in the anterior portion of the skull was enlarged and the posterior part was reduced, a reversal of the condition in the ancestral fish. The vertebral elements were only slightly better developed than in the ancestral fish with a slight increase in bony elements and a decrease in notochordal elements. In general the vertebral plan foreshadows the type found in the Rhachitomi. The pectoral and pelvic girdles and probably the limbs were well developed. The primitive amphibian probably carried his body well off the ground. A fishlike tail was retained with some dermal rays.

Early Adaptations.—The transition from crossopterygian fish to ichthyostegian amphibian enforced stringent selection on the early land vertebrate populations. Accommodation had to be made to the new environment. The buoyancy of the water no longer supported the body, and the vertebral column and the limbs had to support the body against gravity. The ancestral amphibian was no longer bathed continuously by water, and as a consequence the water conservation mechanisms in the skin and kidneys slowly evolved with increasing terrestrialism. The return to the water for fertilization and egg-laying by the ancestral amphibian was a return to his ancestral habitat. Here external fertilization took place and the larval gill forms (the branchiosaurs) underwent their metamorphosis, as evidenced by the fossilized remains of

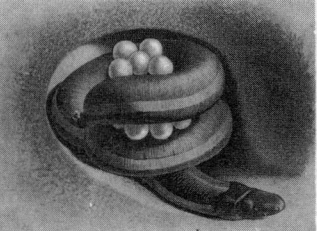

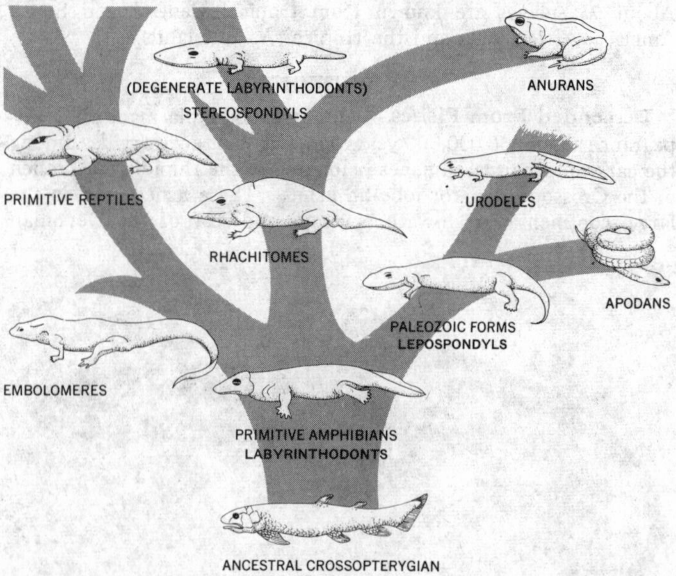

FROM F. AND P. SARASIN

FIG. 3.—CAECILIAN (ICHTHYOPHIS GLUTINOSUS) IN BURROW GUARDING EGGS

these larval forms.

Among the earliest derivatives of the Ichthyostegalia are the Embolomeri that appeared in the Carboniferous period. These were still aquatic or partially aquatic forms with a vertebral column strengthened by well-developed interlocking articulations (zygapophyses) and two equally developed central bony elements (pleurocentrum and intercentrum) over which rode the neural arch. The skull was relatively broad and flat with the orbits placed dorsolaterally. The skull was highly ossified but the limbs relatively weak. This line of amphibians was definitely tending toward terrestrial life although still highly aquatic. A closely related order, the Seymouriamorpha, has been placed sometimes among the reptiles and sometimes among the Amphibia. Many features of the skull of seymouriamorphs, such as the skull roof, clearly indicate relationship with the embolomeres. By the Permian period the embolomeres became extinct.

Rhachitomi and Stereospondyli.—An early and most successful derivative of the first amphibians were the Rhachitomi. These amphibians appeared in the Carboniferous and became extinct by Triassic times. These relatively terrestrial amphibians had a well-developed vertebral column with two bony elements— a large intercentrum and a smaller pleurocentrum—in the vertebrae. (This condition bears a distinct resemblance to the Ichthyostegalia.) The skull was very broad and flattened with orbits turned dorsad. The limbs were developed. Some of these rhachitomes grew to a length of at least six feet and had the general appearance of a modern crocodile.

By the end of the Permian or beginning of the Triassic, another group, the Stereospondyli, evolved from the Rhachitomi. These were secondarily aquatic amphibians with reduced ossification in the skull, weak limbs and a weak vertebral column. The skull became very flat and the vertebral centra became reduced to a single intercentral element. By the Triassic period this group was the dominant group of amphibians but became extinct shortly thereafter.

Lepospondyli.—By the early Carboniferous (Mississippian) period there appeared another major group of amphibians, the subclass Lepospondyli. Although not as abundant as the beforementioned groups of the Apsidospondyli, they still present an abundant fossil record in some cases. This group is characterized by the development of vertebrae as a bony cylinder around the notochord. It is the apparent similarity of the vertebrae of the Aistopoda, Nectridia and Microsauria with that of the Urodela and Apoda that places these groups in the same subclass. The Aistopoda were small snakelike forms with many vertebrae. The Nectridia were snakelike or peculiar aquatic forms with hornlike extensions of the skull and relatively weak bodies. The Microsauria were relatively unmodified in general appearance and build.

Frog Ancestry.—Among the living Amphibia the most successful group are the frogs. Their primary adaptation is the one for jumping, which involves loss of the tail, reduction of the vertebral column, elaboration of the pelvic girdle and enlargement of the pelvic limbs with shortening of the forelimbs. The jumping mechanism may have developed because it enabled the frog to escape from his enemies by outjumping them on land and outswimming them in the water.

The ancestry of the frogs is not yet clearly understood, but it most probably lies either among the Rhachitomi or the primitive Embolomeri. *Protobatrachus* of the Proanura has a froglike skull but little else indicating the major frog adaptation. There is no evidence of the frog's ancestry between the above Triassic form and the first frog remains from the Upper Jurassic (about 140,-000,000 years ago). It is plain that by the Upper Jurassic the frogs had developed their primary adaptation, the jumping mechanism, as is evidenced by the pelvic girdle.

The fossil history of the modern frogs is still fragmentary. Those families (Montsechobatrachidae, Notobatrachidae, Leiopelmidae) that are provided with nine or more presacral vertebrae, ribs, amphicoelous vertebral articulation and a supposedly primitive, weakly joined, pectoral girdle are considered primitive. The modern frogs appeared in the Cretaceous and were probably first represented by a leptodactylid type. From this type most

(DEGENERATE LABYRINTHODONTS)
STEREOSPONDYLS

ANURANS

PRIMITIVE REPTILES

URODELES

RHACHITOMES

APODANS

PALEOZOIC FORMS
LEPOSPONDYLS

EMBOLOMERES

PRIMITIVE AMPHIBIANS
LABYRINTHODONTS

ANCESTRAL CROSSOPTERYGIAN

FROM ALFRED S. ROMER, "THE VERTEBRATE STORY"; © THE UNIVERSITY OF CHICAGO

FIG. 4.—FAMILY TREE OF THE AMPHIBIA. THE THREE SURVIVING GROUPS ARE SHOWN AT UPPER RIGHT

of the advanced families are descended.

Caecilian Ancestry.—The caecilians and salamanders are believed to be related most closely to the other lepospondylous groups of Amphibia. This belief is based primarily on the development of the vertebral centra. There are many students of this problem, however, who believe that the very definite anatomical resemblance between salamanders and frogs may indicate a closer relationship.

On the basis of skull anatomy the caecilians are believed most closely related to a lepospondylous form such as *Lysorophus*. Since there is no fossil record for the caecilians the comparisons must be made between the living forms and their fossil relatives. Caecilians are characterized by a wormlike body that is divided into many external segments. These are primarily burrowing forms that feed on small invertebrates. Embedded in their skin are small dermal plates homologous to the dermal armour of ancient fossil Amphibia. All the living genera are placed in a single family that is circumtropical in distribution.

Salamander Ancestry.—The ancestry of the salamanders is poorly understood, although parts of the salamander fossil record are complete. The first salamanders are known from the Lower Cretaceous of Europe and North America and the Upper Jurassic

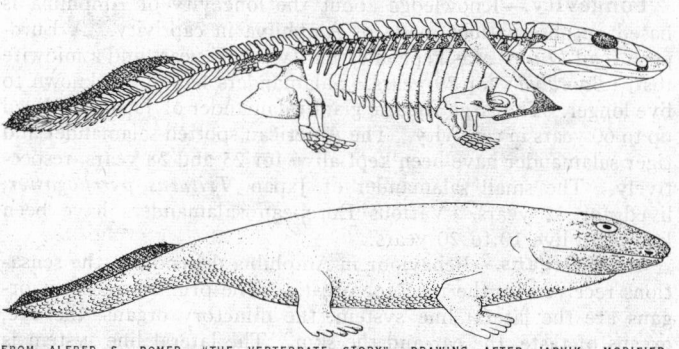

FROM ALFRED S. ROMER, "THE VERTEBRATE STORY"; DRAWING AFTER JARVIK, MODIFIED.
© THE UNIVERSITY OF CHICAGO, 1959

FIG. 5.—RESTORATION DRAWING OF A LABYRINTHODONT, ONE OF THE PRIMITIVE AMPHIBIANS, FROM THE LATE DEVONIAN OF EASTERN GREENLAND

of North America.

It is generally believed that the most primitive living salamanders are the Hynobiidae of Asia and eastern Europe. These salamanders are characterized by their method of external fertilization. The Cryptobranchidae, which developed from the primitive hynobiidlike ancestral type, are represented by two living genera, *Cryptobranchus* of the eastern United States and *Megalobatrachus* of China and Japan. These are essentially gill-breathing, giant derivatives of the hynobiids and are probably examples of a type of neoteny (the development of sexual maturity in the gilled larval stage). The Cryptobranchidae are like the Hynobiidae in having external fertilization. The fossil record for the genus *Megalobatrachus* is rather complete and is represented in the Tertiary period (about 70,000,000 to 1,000,000 years ago) of Europe by the genus *Andrias*.

From this basal group have evolved the higher salamanders, all of which have an internal fertilizing mechanism whereby the female picks up the sperm from the spermatophore produced by the male. In North America there is the family Ambystomidae with four or five living genera. In this family the development of neotenic forms is quite common. Another large family is the Salamandridae, with similar reproductive adaptations. This family, now found both in the new world (two genera) and in the old world, had already appeared by the beginning of the Tertiary and probably will be known from Cretaceous deposits; they probably gave rise to several other groups. The Amphiumidae or congo eels, a group of large eellike salamanders with reduced limbs, are restricted to the swamps of southeastern United States.

The Proteidae (sometimes regarded as two separate families, the Necturidae and Proteidae) is a family of two neotenic genera, *Proteus* and *Necturus*. The ancestry of *Proteus* is known to be

from a Middle Eocene form, *Palaeoproteus*, of Germany. The relatively reduced skeleton and musculature is due to neoteny and the general similarity to larvae of salamanders in general. The family Plethodontidae is one of the successful derivatives of the salamandroid complex and is characterized by the loss of lungs and related parts of the pulmonary circulation. These losses probably represented an early adaptation to mountain-stream life with later diversification into more aquatic and terrestrial habitats. The family has been reported from the beginning of the Tertiary era. It is found today primarily in the new world with one species, *Hydromantes italicus*, from France and Italy. Many genera still inhabit the primitive mountain-stream habitats but others have become terrestrial and have invaded the leaf mold of the forest floor. Others have become aquatic through neoteny, reaching such extreme cases as shown in the genera *Typhlomolge* and *Haideotriton*. Members of a section of this family have invaded the moist cool forest of Central America and are the only salamanders that now inhabit the tropics. These salamanders breathe primarily by cutaneous respiration and like all salamanders are restricted to moist terrestrial conditions. In general this group is more sensitive to water loss and heat than the equally successful Salamandridae.

The family Sirenidae is one of the most isolated of the salamander families. Studies based on blood serum and anatomy indicate it is only distantly related to the other salamandroid salamanders. Its fossil record is rather well known and apparently goes back to the Early Cretaceous (130,000,000 years ago). Its known past and present distribution is completely within North America. Today these gill-equipped salamanders are restricted to the swamps of the eastern United States and range in length from several inches to two or three feet.

MODERN AMPHIBIANS

Habitat.—*Physiological Limitations.*—The living members of the class Amphibia have reached all the continents, continental islands and most of the oceanic islands. They have achieved this in spite of limitations inherent in their physiology.

One major limitation is the ease with which they lose water, either as a result of simple desiccation or by being placed in salt water. Few amphibians ever live under true desert conditions, and those that do are able to survive only because they associate themselves closely with whatever water is available. The amphibians (usually frogs and not salamanders) that occur under such situations made their way into the desert under more pluvial conditions or were introduced by humans.

Many frogs have shown great ability to colonize oceanic islands, despite their inability to tolerate salt water. Experimental studies have shown frogs are unable to survive in water whose salt content is equal to that of sea water. Yet many anurans have successfully colonized such oceanic islands as those of the Antilles, Polynesia and Micronesia. This they have done by floating on or in logs or fallen trees that are carried in currents or by storms. It is possible that during and immediately after tropical storms enough fresh water is present on the surface of the sea to reduce the effect of the salt water on the frogs. Salamanders, by way of comparison, have been completely unsuccessful in this type of colonization.

Introduction by Humans.—Some amphibians have been distributed through human agency. The common marine toad, *Bufo marinus*, has been used as an enemy of various types of insects such as those in the sugar fields. This species has been introduced into the West Indies, Bermuda, Hawaiian Islands, tropical Australia, New Guinea, the Solomons and other Pacific islands. It is native only in tropical America. The American bullfrog, *Rana catesbeiana*, and the European edible frog, *Rana esculenta*, have been introduced for food.

Natural Range.—Frogs generally occur farther north than salamanders. *Rana temporaria* reaches 71° N. in Scandinavia and probably farther north in Asia. *Rana sylvatica*, the wood frog, gets above the Arctic circle in northwestern North America. *Hynobius keyserlingii* gets above the Arctic circle in Siberia, but no other salamanders approach this elsewhere. The salamanders of northern Europe (*Salamandra* and *Triturus*) do not get farther north than 63°. In North America the genus *Plethodon* reaches 55° N. in eastern Canada and the genus *Ambystoma* reaches 59° N. in Alaska. In the southern hemisphere, only frogs reach the tips of the southern continents.

Salamanders are found only on continental islands, such as the British Isles, Japan, the Ryukyus and Formosa. Caecilians mainly inhabit only the continental tropics but get to such continental islands as Ceylon, Sumatra, Java and Trinidad, and to such isolated islands as the Philippines. Frogs are on all continental islands and get to such isolated oceanic islands as the Seychelles, Madagascar, New Zealand, the Indo-Australian archipelago, the Philippines, the Solomons, Palau, the Fiji Islands and the West Indies.

The frogs are the most versatile of the living Amphibia in ability to adjust to climate. The caecilians are almost completely tropical, barely entering the edges of the temperate zone in Australia and South America. Salamanders are practically restricted to the north-temperate zone. The Salamandridae barely gets into the Asiatic tropics, whereas the Ambystomidae ranges into the tropical zones of Mexico but at high altitudes. The Thoriinae, one branch of the lungless salamanders (Plethodontidae), has invaded the tropics in Central America and northern South America. Such genera as *Bolitogloasa*, *Chiropterotriton*, *Magnadigitata*, *Oedopina* and *Pseudoeurycea* have invaded the tropics but primarily in special, localized cool habitats.

In peculiar habitats such as caverns, caves and isolated water holes many salamanders and frogs manage to survive by becoming specialized, although frogs rarely invade deep into caves because their visual equipment prevents them from passing semidarkness. Salamanders often adapt to cave life by losing their pigmentation and eyes, as in *Typhlotriton*, *Typhlomolge*, *Proteus* and *Haideotriton*. Salamanders that become associated with deep underground waters often become sexually mature in a larval stage, as in *Typhlomolge*, *Haideotriton* and *Proteus*. Under severe aridity or other conditions that make land surface uninhabitable, many other species of salamanders also become neotenic. Such is the case in western North America, where the genera *Ambystoma* and *Eurycea* have many isolated populations that are neotenic, probably because of reduced flow of thyroxine, the hormone produced by the thyroid gland. The metamorphosis steps seen in *Ambystoma* and *Eurycea* probably represent equivalent stages in the evolution of the perennibranch (permanent gills) salamanders, such as *Necturus*, *Proteus*, *Typhlomolge*, *Haideotriton* and *Siredon*.

Life History.—Most Amphibia lay their eggs in water, where they hatch into larvae or tadpoles destined to spend a more or less extended period in this element before metamorphosing into terrestrial adults similar to their parents. The larval state seems to be an inheritance from their crossopterygian fish ancestors. Even primitive Amphibia underwent a metamorphosis, as is proved by fossil remains of larval labyrinthodonts.

Metamorphosis represents a period of tremendous change in both the morphology and physiology of Amphibia. It is marked by such external changes in salamanders as the reduction of the external gills, the loss of the tail fin, the shedding of the larval skin, the formation of eyelids, etc. Fundamental changes in skull form and throat musculature also take place. In frogs metamorphosis is indicated by a freeing of the forelimbs by autolysis of local areas in the operculum, by radical changes in the shape and structure of the head and by absorption of the tail.

Certain groups of salamanders, as mentioned previously, fail to metamorphose. This phenomenon appears as a variation in the life history of many of the salamanders that normally metamorphose, particularly in species that pass their larval period in deep, cold water. Neoteny in the latter case is due to the failure of the thyroid to function, but the causes of arrested development in the case of groups unknown as metamorphosed individuals is more complex. Neoteny is not a new development in the Amphibia. It is found even in the Permian *Dvinosaurus*.

Some salamanders and many tropical frogs produce large yolked eggs which they lay on land, although a few retain them within the oviducts until the young are born, more or less fully developed. Only one genus of frogs is ovoviviparous; it includes two

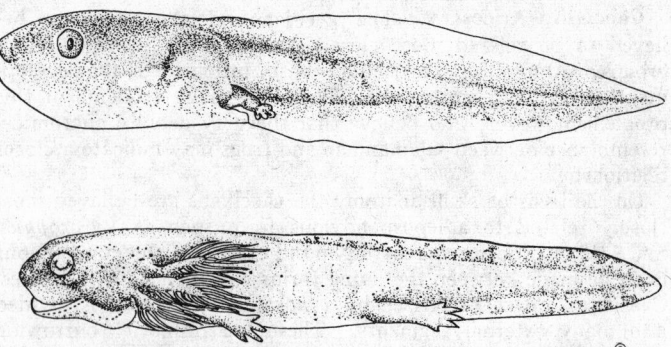

FROM ALFRED S. ROMER, "THE VERTEBRATE STORY"; DRAWING AFTER NOBLE. © THE UNIVERSITY OF CHICAGO, 1959

FIG. 6.—TWO AMPHIBIAN LARVAL TYPES. (ABOVE) FROG TADPOLE HAS GILLS COVERED BY FLAP OF SKIN; (BELOW) SALAMANDER LARVA HAS FEATHERY EXTERNAL GILLS

African species (*Nectophrynoides tornieri* and *N. vivipara*). The breeding habits of the Amphibia are often elaborate and one may trace within the group a gradual evolution in many of the instincts associated with courtship and egg-laying.

Longevity.—Knowledge about the longevity of Amphibia is based on observations made of Amphibia in captivity. A European toad (*Bufo*) was kept in captivity for 36 years and a midwife toad (*Bombina*) for 29 years. Salamanders have been known to live longer. The large aquatic giant salamander of Japan has lived up to 60 years in captivity. The American spotted salamander and tiger salamander have been kept alive for 25 and 28 years, respectively. The small salamander of Japan, *Triturus pyrrhogaster*, lived for 32 years. Various European salamanders have been known to live 10 to 20 years.

Sense Organs.—Behaviour in Amphibia depends on the sensations received by the receptor organs. The primary receptor organs are the lateral line system, the olfactory organs, the eye, organs of taste, the ear and the skin. The lateral line system is located, as in the fish, in deep pits in the skin along either side of the head and body. These pits, lined by sensory cells with nerve connections, respond primarily to changes in pressure and to vibrations in water. The lateral line is found in the aquatic larval stages of most Amphibia and in most aquatic adult salamanders and some aquatic adult frogs. The organs of olfaction are poorly developed in most Amphibia but are fairly well developed in the salamanders. Some can use the sense of smell to locate their prey. Caecilians possess a tentacle on either side of the snout that is a tactile as well as an olfactory organ. The sensation of taste is primarily centred in the mouth region. Isolated groups of taste buds are distributed over the palate, jaws and tongue.

Frogs and salamanders are visually oriented animals and can perceive colours. They are extremely sensitive to movement within their visual field but have only slight ability to distinguish shape and size. The eye in caecilians is small and lies under a transparent patch of skin. It is sensitive to light intensity and direction, a response that is associated with the caecilians burrowing mode of existence. In general the eyes become reduced in cave dwelling and burrowing forms. Light-sensitive cells are present in the skin of all Amphibia, and frogs may react to light after the eyes are removed.

The sense of hearing is best developed in the frogs, due in large part to the well-developed tympanum. Frogs can hear sounds over a range of 50 to 10,000 vibrations per second. Some females are extremely sensitive to the call of the male of their species and can distinguish their call from the calls of males of related species. Hearing is poorly developed in salamanders and caecilians. Sounds from the water or ground are transmitted to the inner ear through the soft tissues and bones.

Tactile sensations are perceived principally through the skin. The skin is also a chemoreceptor and is sensitive to heat, cold and moisture. For example, the skin on the soles of the feet of toads is highly sensitive to differences in moisture content of the

Green tree frog (*Hyla cinerea*) found in swampland and on the edges of lakes and streams in southeastern U.S.

Bullfrog (*Rana catesbeiana*), largest frog of the U.S., found throughout the eastern states and in most of the south. Grows to a length of six inches

A young Great Plains toad (*Bufo cognatus*), found chiefly in the north central plains states and in the southwestern U.S.

Southern leopard frog (*Rana pipiens sphenocephala*). Together with the northern and Rio Grande leopard frogs, also a subspecies of *R. pipiens*, this is the most widely distributed true frog in North America

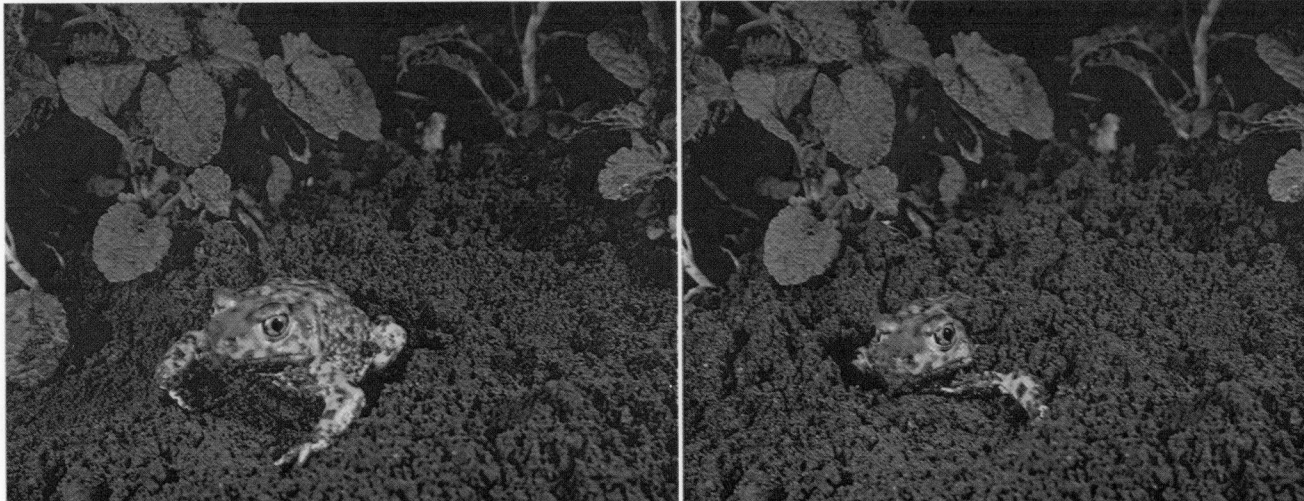

Two pictures taken less than one minute apart, showing the ability of the Couch spadefoot toad (*Scaphiopus couchi*) to bury itself by digging a burrow in the soil. Found in the southwestern U.S.

COMMON FROGS AND TOADS

PHOTOGRAPHS, (TOP LEFT, TOP RIGHT, CENTRE RIGHT) JOHN H. GERARD, (CENTRE LEFT, BOTTOM LEFT, BOTTOM RIGHT) WILLIS PETERSON

São Tomé caecilian (*Schistometopum thomense*). Caecilians are primitive limbless amphibians found in tropical climates

Two-lined salamander (*Eurycea bislineata*), lives in small brooks and streams of eastern U.S.

Tiger salamander (*Ambystoma tigrinum*). This is one of the mole salamanders, so-called because most members of this genus are found underground except during breeding season

Slimy salamander (*Plethodon glutinosus*), a large woodland salamander found in ravines or on hillsides in most of the eastern and southern U.S.

European fire salamander (*Salamandra salamandra*), a common and widely distributed species which breeds in woodland ponds in the early spring

A CAECILIAN AND FOUR COMMON SALAMANDERS

substratum.

Behaviour.—The behaviour of Amphibia is more stereotyped than that of higher vertebrates. Their response to environment depends on the ability of their sense organs to perceive sensations. As a result frogs and toads are more visually oriented than salamanders and caecilians. Frogs and toads have a strong sense of location and have a homing reaction. They can learn and find their way out of mazes and can remember this for as long as a month. The home territory of frogs and toads is greater than that of salamanders, who may spend their entire lives within a few square yards. Complex breeding migrations are made by many frogs and salamanders. In most of these the males precede the females to a body of water that may be a pond, spring or stream. Complex prenuptial behaviour patterns occur in many salamanders.

Voice.—During the breeding season, which usually occurs at the end of winter hibernation, frogs congregate in ponds and pools. Here the males call until the females come to the water to mate and lay their eggs. In some species there is only one median balloonlike vocal sac under the lower jaw. In others there are two, one on each side.

Salamanders have very rudimentary vocal powers. Occasionally they emit a gargling sound or a small cry probably associated with defense, not with reproduction.

Each species of frog has a distinct call, ranging from the high-pitched "peep" of the spring peeper to the deep-throated croak of the bullfrog. To produce the sound, the frog forces air out of the lungs, past the vocal cords and into vocal sacs. The mouth is kept closed and the air is sent back and forth between the vocal sacs and the lungs, producing sound each time it passes over the vocal cords.

Enemies.—Amphibia have many enemies, including man, fish, birds, mammals and invertebrates. The enemies may eat the larvae, the eggs or the adults. Some invertebrates parasitize Amphibia; molds and bacteria also may attack them.

Economic Value.—Toads, because they feed indiscriminately on insect life, are of great use to farmers. During insect plagues toads feed on the dominant insect and tend to restore the balance of nature. Frogs and toads are used for food in many parts of the world, but successful frog farms are rare. Frogs require from two to five years to reach maturity, and large quantities of living insect food are needed during this period. Hence, in America almost the entire frog crop is obtained in the wild state.

Dried frogs and salamanders are used for medicinal purposes in various parts of the world, particularly in the orient. Their value as a cure is chiefly psychological. Probably the greatest use of Amphibia to humanity is their martyrdom to science. Frogs and salamanders, both in adult and young stages, have long been recognized as ideal laboratory animals. Some of our most fundamental discoveries in experimental embryology, endocrinology and general physiology have been made with amphibian material.

GENERAL MORPHOLOGY

Integument.—The skin of modern Amphibia may be rough and dry or smooth and moist, but it is never covered with scales as in nearly all reptiles. Many caecilians, however, have rings of minute scales hidden in the transverse folds of their skin. Aquatic or fossorial Amphibia, which rely to a large extent on their skin for respiration, usually have a thinner and smoother integument than terrestrial forms, but many exceptions to this rule occur, particularly in the Pipidae and Bufonidae. The fossil labyrinthodonts and lepospondyls were frequently well armoured with scales, especially on the ventral surface where these scutes of varying shapes and sizes were arranged, for the most part, in orderly rows converging toward the mid-line. In a few salamandrids and many tropical Salientia a secondary deposit of bone forms in the deeper dermal tissues and may produce encrustations ankylosed to the underlying bones. The bizarre casques of *Pternohyla*, *Triprion*, *Diaglena*, etc., are of this character. Less conspicuous bony covers on the skull appear in the spadefoot toads and various hylids, particularly the marsupial frogs. Similar bony growths extend to the skin of the back in various Salientia and in rare instances (*Brachycephalus*) may be ankylosed to the vertebrae. The epider-

mis covering warts or spines may be more or less cornified (horny) in various Urodela (*Desmognathus*, *Necturus*, etc.). In a few hynobiids thick horny pads occur on the palms and soles, while in the larvae of others the epidermis of the digits is extended into pointed claws. Similar horny claws occur on the three inner toes of the African pipids and may have been found on all the digits of some extinct Amphibia, for in one of the most primitive labyrinthodonts the terminal phalanges have the form of curved claws.

The integument of modern Amphibia is further distinguished from that of reptiles in being highly glandular. There are two main types of glands: the granular and the mucous. The granular may be broadly distributed over the dorsal surfaces or massed in folds or warts on the sides of the body. Its secretion is creamy, very irritating to mucous membranes and poisonous when taken internally. The mucous glands are more uniformly distributed over the body. They produce a slime less irritating to the nasal passages and conjunctiva but, nevertheless, toxic when injected into lower animals. Amphibia differ enormously in both the quantity and kind of integumentary secretion. Some species, such as the toads, secrete only when mistreated, while others, such as *Dendrobates*, *Bombina* and particularly the American *Plethodon glutinosus*, produce a copious irritating or sticky secretion when handled. Closely related species may differ considerably in their secretions. The South American *Ceratophrys americana* has a virulent poison while the much larger and more brightly coloured *C. dorsata* possesses an innocuous skin secretion. Frequently the secretions are odorous, certain closely related forms of *Rana*, *Bufo* and *Hyla* being readily distinguished by their odour alone.

The skin of the larva differs from that of the adult in that the glands are unicellular and the epidermis consists of only two layers of cells. Larvae approaching metamorphosis and most perennibranchs have a thicker epidermis equipped with multicellular glands. The superficial layer of epidermis is periodically shed by the adults, usually in one piece. The first shedding of the entire epidermis occurs normally at metamorphosis.

Pigmentation.—The coloration of Amphibia is due in part to a diffuse pigment distributed throughout the integument but chiefly to a number of cellular elements of which three main types may be recognized: first, white cells that owe their colour to a dense deposit of guanine (a pigment allied to the urates); secondly, the yellow cells that contain droplets of oil; and thirdly, the dark brown cells filled with melanin.

White cells are often clumped together in small areas under the epidermis, producing the white flecks on the backs of many salamanders or the white spots in some tree frogs. Other guanine-filled cells lie closely associated with the yellow and brown cells directly under broad areas of the epidermis and give the characteristic ground colour of these regions. Green is a mixed colour due to the blue rays of light reflected from the small guanine or "turbid cells" mixing with the yellow tone in the overlying yellow cells to produce a green. The blue reflections of the turbid cells are swamped by the white reflections of the subjacent tissues when the melanophores or dark cells are contracted. Brown is produced by the complete enclosure of the turbid cells by the expanded melanophores. The latter expand to surround the turbid cells when stimulated by cold, moisture and rough surfaces, or by hormones produced by the pars intermedia of the pituitary gland. The colour tone of a frog or toad at any one time may be due to either stimulations received through the skin or eyes or to the emotional state of the individual toad or frog.

Organs of Nutrition, Circulation and Reproduction.—Larval Amphibia suck on plant material with cornified papillae situated around the mouth.

As the larvae develop, teeth are formed. But not all Amphibia have teeth. Frogs have teeth only in the upper jaw. Some salamanders and caecilians have teeth on several bones of the jaws. Normally the teeth are used only to catch and hold the prey, not to chew.

The tongue may be attached to the front, rear or floor of the mouth. In some Amphibia the tongue secretes a sticky substance that helps hold the prey. In others the tongue is prehensile with an identical effect.

Adult Amphibia eat all kinds of animals: insects and their larvae, myriapods, mollusks, worms, small crustacea, arachnids, fish, other Amphibia, small reptiles, birds and even small mammals. They can be voracious eaters. An American toad kept in captivity ate 9,936 different insects in a three-month period. A marine toad ate 52 mosquitoes in one minute. Some Amphibia are discriminating in their choice of food and will feed only on one kind of insect, such as ants or termites.

Although the Amphibia have not evolved from the dipnoans, they show many similarities in their venous and arterial systems. The hearts of salamanders show various modifications according to the extent the lungs are used in respiration.

Fertilization in the Amphibia may be external or internal. Most female salamanders, except in the Hynobiidae and Cryptobranchidae, are equipped with a spermatotheca, a series of tubules in the roof of the cloaca where the sperm remain after copulation until the time of fertilization. In these salamanders the sperm mass is emitted by the males in the form of spermatophores, small tufts of sperm attached to a gelatinous base. Courtship in the salamanders is primarily directed toward exciting the female sufficiently to ensure her picking up the spermatophore with the cloacal lips. The sperm then make their way into the spermatotheca by their own efforts. The Apoda are equipped with a protrusible cloaca that is used as an intromittent organ. The male American leiopelmid frog, *Ascaphus,* has a movable extension of the cloaca. In these forms, as well as in certain little-known African frogs that have no special apparatus for transmitting sperm, fertilization is internal. The gonads are variously modified in different groups to permit a greater freedom of the seminal ducts from the kidneys.

Skeleton.—Once vertebrate life was established on land it reverted not once but many times to the aquatic habitat long before the modern Amphibia appeared. Despite the frequent change of habitat the skeletal organization of the first Amphibia continued to evolve steadily in definite directions with time. In recent Amphibia, too, the fundamental structure has changed slowly while the various groups may show the widest adaptations. Ranids may be arboreal, aquatic or fossorial; plethodontids may be the same.

Skull.—The first tetrapods inherited a skull very similar to that of their fish ancestors. It consisted of a cartilaginous box, or chondrocranium, covered completely above by dermal bones that replaced the cartilage in part. This skull, the prototype of all tetrapod skulls, differed remarkably from that of modern Amphibia by the far greater number of skull elements it contained, by the greater ossification of the chondrocranium and by its reptilelike form.

The skull of the primitive Labyrinthodont agreed in most details with that of the osteolepid fishes. The skull roofs were similar except for a cluster of small bones in the nasal region in osteolepids. The distribution of the lateral line canals in both skulls facilitates the identification of lachrymal, prefrontal, jugal, postorbital, postfrontal, supra- and intertemporals. The spiracular notch of *Osteolepis* has become the otic notch and the elements bordering this and the orbit may be readily homologized. The palates agree remarkably in the small size of the interpterygoid vacuities and the almost identical position of the palatal and jaw bones. The distribution and replacement of the large teeth are identical in fish and tetrapod. An internal naris is present in all osteolepids and is identical in position, size and borders with that of primitive Amphibia.

The lower jaw of the first tetrapods differed greatly from that of modern Amphibia in the far greater number of elements it contained. It was, however, identical with that of the osteolepid jaw. The brain cases of osteolepids and primitive Amphibia were very similar but not identical.

Once this highly ossified and complex skull of the ancestral fish became established in land forms, it underwent enormous specialization. Very soon there began a progressive fenestration, the bones tending to segregate along lines of greatest stress. The solid domelike skull roof progressively lost various dermal elements until in the modern frogs only the premaxillary, maxillary, nasal, quadratojugal, squamosal, frontal and parietal are left. The more primitive salamanders still retain a lachrymal and prefrontal in

addition to the frog's equipment. The quadratojugal, although appearing as a separate element during ontogeny in the Urodela, later fuses with the quadrate. This loss of elements was perhaps largely due to a shortening of the skull. The second great change that developed as the tetrapod series evolved was the gradual flattening of skull. The third fundamental change was a progressive weakening of the bony organization of the skull with the result that the brain case became progressively less well ossified.

The most reduced part of the modern amphibian skull is the lower jaw. The primitive Amphibia inherited a complex mandible of many pieces. In primitive salamanders the only sections left were a dentary, a prearticular and articular and an angular. Coronoids are present in the larvae of most salamanders. The angular is fused with the prearticular in all members of this group above the Cryptobranchoidea. In caecilians a very early fusion of the jaw elements occurs in most genera, but the resulting element probably contains a coronoid as well as the dentary, articular and prearticular; two rows of teeth are present in many forms. In the Salientia the reduction is carried to an extreme, for only the dentary and prearticular are recognizable. The articular ossifies in very few Salientia and is then fused to the prearticular. The anterior end of Meckel's cartilage ossifies as a pair of distinct elements in some Ranidae, Hylidae and Bufonidae.

The osteolepid ancestors of the Amphibia had five branchial arches, while the modern Amphibia have at most four. The latter possess, however, a pair of laryngeal cartilages that may or may not represent the fifth branchial arch. The gill arches in the adult salamander or frog are modified by reduction and fusion.

Vertebrae.—The vertebrae of the Amphibia are often used as the basis for classifying the different subclasses, orders and suborders. Their history can be traced from the ancestral crossopterygian fish through the different groups of Amphibia and on to the amniote classes of vertebrates.

In the earliest amphibians and their ancestors, three separate elements can be recognized in the adult vertebrae: the neural arch, the pleurocentrum and the hypocentrum with its associated ventral arch and rib. In the rhipidistian ancestors of the early Amphibia the vertebrae are weaker in construction than in the Amphibia because the primary element, particularly in the centre of the vertebral column, was the notochord, although two thin, weak, bony elements, the pleurocentrum and hypocentrum, lie alongside the notochord under each neural arch. Such an arrangement gave little strength to the vertebral column, but this was efficient enough for an aquatic organism in which buoyancy was an important factor. These bony structures did not hinder the functioning of the axial skeleton as a flexible rod, which is so important in the more or less sinuous movement of the fish.

In the Ichthyostegalia the condition was intermediate between the rhipidistian fish and the earliest amphibian. In all later Amphibia the notochord is at least partially destroyed but may remain as an intervertebral element. The Ichthyostegalia have a modified rhipidistian plan with expanded hypocentrum (the larger centrum element) and pleurocentrum, plus erect large neural spines and zygapophyses. The pleurocentrum and hypocentrum of the rhipidistian fish have increased in thickness and compressed the notochord until it is but a narrow channel running through the middle of the vertebrae.

The Rhachitomi have taken this plan and elaborated it by developing a double centrum made up of two interlocking wedges, the intercentrum and pleurocentrum.

The Stereospondyli further developed the rhachitomous plan by reducing the size of the pleurocentrum (or eliminating it) so that in effect a single central element became the main supporting element of the vertebra. The Embolomeri have developed a double centrum with two equally developed elements, the hypocentrum (intercentrum of others) and pleurocentrum. Probably this primitive type of vertebra gave rise to the dominant, pleurocentrum type of vertebra of the seymouriamorphs and the amniotes.

The lepospondyls appear abruptly in the fossil record, and the intermediate condition is not known. But from a study of living forms it appears that the vertebra has a single spoollike centrum developed directly from bone, although on the basis of embryological evidence this centrum would be in the position of the pleurocentrum.

The origin of frog vertebrae is not yet clear, but they apparently can be derived from embolomerous, prerhachitomous or rhachitomous types of vertebra. Since the hypocentral elements are reduced in the frogs, there seem to be five basic types of centra in the Amphibia: (1) ichthyostegalian and rhachitomous; (2) embolomerous; (3) stereospondylous; (4) lepospondylous; and (5) anuran.

Ribs.—The ribs of primitive amphibians and reptiles articulate with all vertebrae, at least as far back as the middle of the tail. In phylogeny the sacral ribs become fused to the vertebrae first, then the caudals, next the lumbars, the cervical and finally the thoracic. In elongate salamanders the ribs have become reduced in number. *Siren* and *Amphiuma* have only the anterior thoracic vertebrae still retaining the ribs. In frogs the reductions have reached an extreme. Discoglossids retain three, leiopelmids retain only two ribs in the adult. The pipids have two ossified ribs in the larva, but these fuse later to the diapophyses. The bits of cartilage on the ends of the diapophyses of the higher frogs have been considered homologues of the ribs. This is perhaps a matter of definition. No ossified ribs appear as the distinct elements in the development of any Salientia above the Pipidae.

The ribs are shortest in the frogs and the long-bodied perennibranchs, longest in the primitive salamandrids. In *Tylototriton* and its close relative *Triturus waltl* the tips of the ribs may be long, pointed and actually protruding through the skin.

Pectoral Girdle.—The pectoral girdle of the first tetrapod was similar to that of the primitive bony fish except that a new dermal element, the interclavicle, had been added to its ventral surface in the mid-line.

The Salientia have retained the pectoral girdle of the more terrestrial primitive Amphibia. The interclavicle has been lost and a new structure, the omosternum, has arisen. The broadened ventral ends of scapulocoracoid bars have become fenestrated. The posterior rim ossifies as a separate centre, the coracoid, while the mesial and anterior part usually remains cartilaginous. The anterior rim is called the procoracoid, and the mesial part is called the coracoid cartilage. The sternum was possibly cartilaginous in the labyrinthodonts and branchiosaurs, although it is never found fossil in these groups.

The Urodela are specialized in the complete loss of the dermal elements. As if in compensation for this loss the coracoid cartilages are usually broadly dilated. The salamanders are primitive in that the scapulocoracoid usually ossifies as a single piece.

Pelvic Girdle.—The pelvic girdle of the first tetrapods has advanced beyond the conditions found in fishes in that a pubis, ischium and ilium are present, meeting in the acetabulum in a triradiate suture. The ilium, however, was not firmly attached to the sacral ribs. The ilium soon gained a firmer support to the sacral ribs.

Modern Amphibia have inherited the platelike pelvis of the primitive labyrinthodonts. The pubis is usually unossified, as in the higher labyrinthodonts. In a few Salientia the pubis region is ossified, but it rarely forms a separate bone. The pubis cartilage is of variable extent in the different families of Urodela, being more extensive in aquatic than in terrestrial forms.

Many salamanders exhibit at the anterior end of the pubis a Y-shaped cartilage called an epipubis or an ypsiloid apparatus; this structure serves to assist in controlling the shape of the lungs in those forms that use this structure as a hydrostatic organ. It seems to be a neomorph in the salamander group.

Limbs.—The Amphibia arose from some generalized crossopterygian. The skeletons of the paddles of only two of these primitive types of fishes are known. These fin bones are leglike in that they consist of a proximal element or humerus subtending two distal elements, a radius and ulna. The outer row of elements, however, are more numerous than the supporting elements in the hands or feet of tetrapods. The fundamental plan of single-proximal, double-median and multiple-distal elements was already well established in the fish ancestors of the tetrapods.

The chief problem in establishing the origin of the typical modern vertebrate limb concerns the distal segment. How many digits were present on the limbs of the first land vertebrates, and how many carpal and tarsal elements formed their support? *Diplovertebron* had five well-developed digits, as in the case of the oldest reptiles.

All modern Amphibia had only four digits in the hand. *Eryops* apparently had a stout prepollex (early form of thumb), a rudiment of the fifth finger (postminimus) and a cartilaginous block representing a sixth. In modern Salientia the prepollex is almost universally present and often hypertrophied in the male to ensure a better grip in amplexus. In Urodela, even in forms that are not known to practise amplexus, the prepollex is sometimes present and even bony. The modern Amphibia inherited a prepollex, four digits and a rudiment of a fifth digit in the hand.

In the foot of modern Amphibia there are five digits, as in *Diplovertebron*, but in most Salientia there is also a prehallux (early form of first toe); and in some primitive Urodela there are both a cartilaginous prehallux and a postminimus. In burrowing Salientia the prehallux is greatly enlarged to form the core of a "spade."

Numerous fusions and losses have occurred in the carpus and tarsus of modern forms. The Hynobiidae, Ambystomidae and Cryptobranchidae approach most closely the primitive condition. Salamanders with a reduced number of digits have suffered the greatest number of fusions. The Salientia have also diverged considerably from the primitive type. The tarsus of the Salientia is peculiar in the great elongation of the two proximal elements (astragalus and calcaneum) and in the loss or fusion of all the other elements except three or four that articulate with the bones of the "toes." This elongation of the proximal series gives the frog's hind leg the appearance of having three long segments instead of the usual two. Such a specialization is undoubtedly an adaptation to jumping, although various species living today have given up that habit.

CLASSIFICATION

The great array of living and fossil forms of Amphibia are classified below, with the living groups placed in their approximate phylogenetic position in relation to the fossil forms. The classification of the living forms is taken down to families to show the general diversity in these groups.

Subordinal groups are not included under the orders Anura and Urodela because of the general lack of agreement regarding this level of classification.

Subclass Apsidospondyli (amphibians with vertebrae preformed in cartilage and later changed to bone)
  Superorder Labyrinthodontia (ancestral and fossil amphibians with generally heavy, low, depressed skulls, relatively primitive limbs and labyrinthine teeth; began their history in the late Paleozoic era)
    Order Ichthyostegalia (among the most primitive amphibians, being intermediate between the ancestral lobe-fin fishes, the Crossopterygii, and the more advanced Amphibia; known from the Devonian to the Pennsylvanian periods)
    Order Rhachitomi (fossil amphibians with rhachitomous vertebrae; appeared in the Mississippian period and became very abundant during the Permian period)
    Order Stereospondyli (fossil group of primarily aquatic amphibians derived from the Rhachitomi; originated in the Early Triassic and became extinct by the earliest Jurassic period)
    Order Embolomeri (fossil amphibian group that appeared in the Pennsylvanian and continued into the Permian period; members of this group are intermediate between the primitive amphibians and the first reptiles)
  Superorder Salientia (frogs and their relatives)
    Order Proanura (ancestral type with froglike skull but with limbs not modified for jumping; known from the Triassic period)
    Order Anura (frogs and their relatives with hind limbs and pelvic girdle modified for jumping)
      Families of frogs:
        Montsechobatrachidae (primitive fossil frogs from the Jurassic of Europe and North America)
        Notobatrachidae (primitive fossil frogs of South America)
        Leiopelmidae (primitive living frogs from New Zealand and western North America)

Discoglossidae (the midwife toad, the fire-bellied toad or unken, the ribbed frog of Europe, Asia, North Africa and the Philippine Islands)

Pipidae (aquatic frogs lacking tongues; Surinam toads of South America and the clawed frog of Africa)

Rhinophrynidae (small burrowing frog of Central America and Mexico)

Pelobatidae (fossorial or partially fossorial spadefoot toads of North America and Eurasia)

Pelodytidae (group of frogs similar to the preceding but lacking spadefoot and called "mud divers"; known from Eurasia)

Palaeobatrachidae (modern type of fossil frog known from the Miocene of Europe)

Leptodactylidae (modern type of frog found abundantly in South America, Central America, West Indies, Australia; known in the United States as the white-lipped frog, barking frog, robber frog and cave frog)

Bufonidae (group similar to the above but lacking teeth on the upper jaw; commonly known as toads. Many species in North America; two species, the common toad and natterjack, in the British Isles; group occurs all over the world, partially by human introduction)

Dendrobatidae (brightly coloured poisonous tree frogs of South America)

Atelopodidae (brightly coloured tree frogs of Central America)

Pseudidae (paradox frogs of South America)

Hylidae (commonly known as the true tree frogs, usually with adhesive discs at the end of the digits that aid in climbing; usually arboreal but not always; practically a cosmopolitan group with many species in North America but unsuccessfully introduced into the British Isles)

Ranidae (commonly known as the true frogs of the old and new worlds; the green frogs, gopher frogs, meadow frogs, wood frogs, river frogs of North America and the common frog of Great Britain; found all over the world; common laboratory frog in United States and Great Britain)

Hyperolidae (Asiatic and African frogs and tree frogs closely related and similar to the preceding family)

Microhylidae (the narrow-mouth toads of the Americas, Africa, southern and eastern Asia, Indo-Australian archipelago and Australia)

Phrynomeridae (a single genus of frogs similar to the above family; found in Africa south of the Sahara)

Heleophrynidae (a single genus of toadlike frogs limited to South Africa)

Subclass Lepospondyli (amphibians with vertebrae not preformed in cartilage)

Order Aistopoda (group of late Paleozoic amphibians that are snakelike in form)

Order Nectridia (generally elongate or snakelike aquatic or subaquatic amphibians of the late Paleozoic era)

Order Microsauria (elongate, weak-limbed amphibians of the late Paleozoic era)

Order Urodela (salamanders or living tailed amphibians with appendages)

Families of salamanders:

Hynobiidae (Asiatic land salamanders with external fertilization; eastern Europe, and western and central Asia)

Cryptobranchidae (hellbender of the eastern United States and giant salamanders of Japan and China; aquatic forms with external fertilization)

Ambystomidae (tiger, spotted and burrowing salamanders of North America with internal fertilization)

Salamandridae (newts, efts and salamanders of Europe, Asia and North America with internal fertilization)

Amphiumidae (large snakelike salamanders with reduced limbs; called congo eels in the southeastern United States; with internal fertilization)

Plethodontidae (lungless salamanders of the new world and Europe; with internal fertilization)

Proteidae (the olm of Yugoslavia and the mud puppies of eastern North America; external gilled salamanders with internal fertilization)

Sirenidae (dwarf sirens, mud sirens and great sirens of the southeastern United States; with internal fertilization)

Order Apoda (wormlike amphibians of a single circumtropical family, Caeciliidae)

See also references under "Amphibia" in the Index.

Bibliography.—General Works: G. K. Noble, Biology of the Amphibia (1931); F. Angel, Vie et Moeurs des Amphibiens (1947); H. Gadow, Amphibia and Reptilia (1901); J. Rostand, La Vie des Crapauds (1941); F. Werner, Brehms Tierleben, "Lurche und Kriechtiere" (1912); G. Boulenger, Tailless Batrachians of Europe (1897); A. S. Romer, Vertebrate Paleontology (1945), The Vertebrate Story (1959); J. A. Oliver, The Natural History of North American Amphibians and Reptiles (1955); M. A. Freiburg, Vida de Batracios y Reptiles Sudamericanos (1948); P. Darlington, Zoogeography (1957).

Regional Works: R. Conant, A Field Guide to Reptiles and Amphibians (1958); R. C. Stebbins, Amphibians of Western North America (1951), Amphibians and Reptiles of Western North America (1954); A. H. Wright and A. A. Wright, Handbook of Frogs and Toads of the United States and Canada (1949); S. C. Bishop, Handbook of Salamanders (1943), Salamanders of New York (1941); J. S. Bleakney, A Zoogeographical Study of the Amphibians and Reptiles of Eastern Canada (1958); K. P. Schmidt, A Check List of North American Amphibians and Reptiles (1953), Amphibians and Land Reptiles of Porto Rico (1928); H. M. Smith and E. H. Taylor, An Annotated Check List and Key to the Amphibia of Mexico (1948); E. H. Taylor, The Frogs and Toads of Costa Rica (1952), The Salamanders and Caecilians of Costa Rica (1952); D. M. Cochran, Frogs of Southeastern Brazil (1955), The Herpetology of Hispaniola (1941); W. G. Lynn and C. Grant, Herpetology of Jamaica (1940); R. Mertens and L. Muller, Die Amphibien und Reptilien Europas (1940); M. Smith, The British Amphibians and Reptiles (1951); F. Angel, Faune de France (Reptiles and Amphibians) (1946); R. Mertens, Die Lurche und Kriechtiere des Rhein-Main-Gebietes (1947); P. Terentyev and C. Chernov, Handbook of the Reptiles and Amphibians of the U.S.S.R. (in Russian) (1949); G. F. de Witte, Batraciens et Reptiles du Parc National Albert (Congo Belge) (1941); W. Rose, The Reptiles and Amphibians of Southern Africa (1950); P. Kirtisinghe, The Amphibia of Ceylon (1957); R. Bourret, Les Batraciens de L'Indochine (1942); C. C. Liu, The Amphibians of Western China (1950); Y. Okada, Tailless Batrachians of the Japanese Empire (1931); I. Sato, The Tailed Batrachians of the Japanese Empire (1943); R. Inger, Philippine Zoological Expedition, 1946-1947 (1954); P. van Kampen, The Amphibia of the Indo-Australian Archipelago (1923).

Anatomy: E. Gaupp, Ecker and Wiedersheims' Anatomy of the Frog (1904); E. T. B. Francis, The Anatomy of the Salamander (1934); J. E. W. Ihle, Vergl. Anat. der Wirbeltiere (1927); L. Bolk, Handbuch der vergl. Anat. der Wirbeltiere (1931).

Systematic Studies: A. S. Romer, Review of the Labyrinthodontia (1947); E. R. Dunn, Salamanders of the Family Hynobiidae (1923), The Salamanders of the Family Plethodontidae (1926); H. W. Parker, A Monograph of the Frogs of the Family Microhylidae (1934).
(M. K. He.)

AMPHIBIAN PLANE: see Seaplane.

AMPHIBIOUS WARFARE, a term applied to military operations characterized by attacks launched from the sea by naval and landing forces against hostile shores. The principal form is the amphibious assault which may be conducted for any of several purposes. It may be a prelude to further combat operations ashore, it may be to seize a site required as an advanced naval or air base, or it may be to deny the use of the site or area to the enemy.

The Allied counteroffensive in World War II (with the exception of the Russian front) was predicated upon a series of amphibious operations required to give re-entry into Axis-held territory. In the European theatre these operations were generally called invasions because they were carried out against large land masses and were followed by extensive land campaigns. In the Pacific theatre, because of the insular nature and limited land area of most of the Allied objectives, particularly in the central Pacific, the term seizure was commoner. Tarawa, Eniwetok, Kwajalein, Peleliu and Iwo Jima are classic examples of amphibious seizures. On the other hand, operations against the larger islands, such as the Solomons, New Guinea, the Marianas, the Philippines and Okinawa, shared many of the characteristics of an amphibious invasion of a large land mass. (See Korean War; Tactics: World War II; World War II.)

Other forms of amphibious warfare, which differ from the amphibious assault in that they do not require the firm establishment ashore of the landing force, are the amphibious withdrawal, the amphibious demonstration and the amphibious raid.

An amphibious withdrawal is the evacuation of forces from a hostile shore by sea. The evacuation of the British expeditionary force from Dunkirk, France, in 1940 and of the United Nations force from Hungnam, Korea, in 1950 were both large-scale amphibious withdrawals.

An amphibious demonstration is a show of amphibious force for the purpose of deceiving the enemy. For example, such a demonstration was made against the southern beaches of Okinawa on April 1, 1945, to mislead the Japanese as to the site of the true landings.

An amphibious raid is a landing from the sea involving the temporary occupancy of the objective area. It is unique in that it ordinarily includes a planned withdrawal. Amphibious raids historically have had a variety of uses: to inflict loss or damage upon the enemy; to secure information; to create a diversion; or even for reasons of morale and training. Dieppe and Makin Island are noteworthy examples of World War II amphibious raids.

Early Historical Development.—The hydrography and geography of the Mediterranean have been particularly conducive to the conduct of amphibious operations, a fact which throughout recorded history is periodically reaffirmed. The battle of Marathon (490 B.C.), for instance, can be considered a successful counterattack by the Greeks against the beachhead established by the invading Persian host. The distinction between invasion and raiding was established very early. The requirement for specially trained troops was also soon perceived. The Romans, as early as the Punic Wars, employed specially trained legionnaries as marines. Julius Caesar, in particular, demonstrated his grasp of this form of warfare in his Mediterranean campaigns as well as in his two invasions of Britain.

The dark ages, following the decline of the Roman empire, are interesting from the viewpoint of amphibious warfare chiefly because they repeatedly demonstrated the vulnerability of western Europe and of Britain to the amphibious incursions of the barbarians from the north. These Norse amphibious techniques were combined successfully with French chivalry in William the Conqueror's invasion of England in A.D. 1066.

The middle ages, with warfare dominated by the armoured knight and the fortified castle, and with military thinking circumscribed completely by the laws of feudalism and the rules of chivalry, generated little in the way of amphibious innovations. An exception to this generalization can be found in certain of the waterborne crusades. For example, in Louis IX's crusade against Egypt (1249) the Genoese shipbuilders, going back perhaps to Roman designs, developed ramped galleys which could carry and launch through stern doors three or four smaller landing craft.

The Hundred Years' War (1338–1453), although marked by the repeated invasion of the Low Countries and France by the English, contributed little to amphibious knowledge. In almost every case the English had conveniently friendly territory in which to land so that there was no necessity to plan or execute an amphibious assault.

The maritime wars between the Dutch and the English in the 17th century are of amphibious interest in that both sides saw fit to establish permanent corps of marines. The duke of York and Albany's maritime regiment of foot was formed in 1664 and although there were subsequent reorganizations and interruptions in service this date is accepted as that of the founding of the present day royal marines. The Netherlands marine corps, with a similar history, was organized in 1665 by Adm. Michael de Ruyter. (*See* MARINES.)

The 18th century with its wars of colonial expansion paid considerable attention to conjunct operations and littoral warfare, as amphibious operations had come to be called. However, in practice, 18th-century amphibious warfare was more notable for its reverses than for its successes. Adm. Edward Vernon in his Caribbean venture, for instance, failed with 12,000 troops to take Cartagena in 1741 and later in the same year failed again at Santiago de Cuba. The capture of Quebec in 1759 by Gen. James Wolfe (*q.v.*) was one of the most striking successes of the Seven Years' War, illustrating the importance of combining surprise with strong ground and water-borne forces.

Napoleonic Era.—Napoleon's failure to carry out an invasion of England is cited frequently as a classic example of the inability of a strong continental force lacking in sea power to project its strength over even the narrowest of seas. Napoleon's preparations for the invasion reached a peak in 1805 when he had 100,000 troops encamped at Boulogne and over 500 transports at his disposal. But his crossing required that he control the Channel, and this

control his admirals could not give him. When Villeneuve was destroyed by Nelson at Trafalgar all chance of a successful invasion of England by the French disappeared. (*See* NAPOLEONIC WARS.)

The outstanding amphibious success of the Napoleonic Wars was probably the landing of Sir Ralph Abercromby on March 8, 1801, near Aboukir, Egy. Careful preparation and co-ordination enabled Sir John Moore, the landing force commander, to land 5,500 troops almost simultaneously. The remainder of the British troops were put ashore the same day, losses were only 600 killed and wounded, and the expedition successfully moved to the capture of Alexandria.

This success can be contrasted with the failure of Lord Chatham at Walcheren in 1809. Chatham, with 400 ships and 40,000 troops, the largest expedition to put out from England up to that time, landed successfully on the miasmic Lowlands island but ultimately foundered because of lack of strategic purpose, inertia and malaria, which alone caused 4,000 deaths.

19th-Century Amphibious Experience.—Amphibious doctrine of the 19th-century, as it had evolved from 18th-century and Napoleonic era successes and failures, was simple, direct and, within its limitations, effective.

Gen. Winfield Scott's capture of Veracruz during the Mexican War is typical. Avoiding the defenses of the city itself, he put his 12,000 soldiers and marines ashore in an unopposed landing on an open beach three miles south of the city. Then through a co-ordinated effort of the fleet and the army, the city was brought under siege, subjected to 500,000 lb. of shot and shell, and on March 29, 1847, capitulated.

Amphibious operations in the American Civil War are obscured by the more sanguinary campaigns fought in Virginia and the west, but by the end of the war the Federal forces had a well-developed amphibious capability as was demonstrated at Ft. Fisher. This fort was the key Confederate defensive position guarding the seaward approaches to Wilmington, N.C., which, by mid-1864, was the last Atlantic port accessible to blockade-runners. The conjoint attack aimed at its reduction had as its naval leader, Adm. David D. Porter, and, initially, as its expeditionary force commander, Maj. Gen. Benjamin F. Butler.

In the first attack against the fort, Porter landed Butler with 6,500 men on Christmas day, 1864. The Confederate scheme of defense was classic: light defense of the landing beaches, stubborn defense of the key feature (Ft. Fisher itself), and a strong mobile reserve (Hoke's division). After two days' ineffective maneuvering, Butler ordered his troops re-embarked. He was replaced by Maj. Gen. Alfred H. Terry, who on Jan. 13, 1865, landed with 8,000 men. Two days later a co-ordinated assault was made and Ft. Fisher was successfully taken.

The amphibious lessons of the Civil War had to be in large part relearned in the Spanish-American War of 1898. Adm. George Dewey, after his decisive defeat of the Spanish fleet in Manila bay, had no landing force at his disposal with which to exploit his victory and the eventual occupation of the city had to be delayed three months. On the other hand, Adm. William T. Sampson, in his operations in Cuban waters, was able to land a battalion of marines at Guantánamo bay and thus seize a base which contributed materially to the blockade of the Cuban north coast and the eventual destruction of the Spanish fleet at Santiago.

World Wars I and II.—Gallipoli, or the Dardanelles campaign, was the principal amphibious experiment of World War I. (*See* DARDANELLES CAMPAIGN.) Fostered by Winston Churchill, then first lord of the admiralty, the campaign had as its purpose the turning of the strategic flank of the central powers by knocking Turkey out of the war and reopening the Black sea route to tsarist Russia. The first naval attack began on March 18, 1915; the final evacuation took place on the night of Jan. 8, 1916. Of the 410,000 British and 79,000 French who were engaged, 252,000 became casualties.

After this disaster, world military opinion was almost universal in dismissing the future of amphibious operations, at least so far as the large-scale, daylight assault on a well-defended position was concerned. An exception to this thinking was to be found in a

WIDE WORLD
FRENCH EXPEDITIONARY FORCES LOADING TANK INTO U.S. LST (LANDING SHIP, TANK) IN NORTH AFRICA DURING WORLD WAR II

small group of U.S. marine and naval officers who, in a series of theoretical studies carried out primarily at Quantico, Va., dissected the Gallipoli landings and concluded that future amphibious assaults were feasible if certain conditions were met. These conditions included the requirements for a specially trained landing force; an integrated naval and landing force command; adequate ship-to-shore communications; adequate air cover; suitable amphibious transports, landing craft and amphibian vehicles; and many contributory techniques such as the combat loading of amphibious shipping and workable shore-based control of naval gunfire and close support aircraft.

As a result of these studies and the fleet exercises which tested their findings, the United States entered World War II with a well-developed amphibious theory and doctrine that was eventually adopted by all the major Allied powers. Conversely, the failure of Germany to develop an adequate amphibious doctrine or capability was a major contributory cause of Hitler's ultimate defeat. Hitler's unexpectedly swift victory over France in 1940 and Britain's decision to continue the war alone found the Germans unprepared for an invasion of England. In this respect, the similarity between Napoleon's position in 1805 and Hitler's in 1940 is obvious.

Korean War.—The outstanding example of amphibious warfare in the Korean war (1950–53) was the landing at Inchon on the west coast of Korea in Sept. 1950. A difficult and daring operation, it achieved complete success and resulted in the destruction of the North Korean army with a loss of more than 100,000 prisoners. This operation illustrated the point that under modern conditions amphibious landings can be made successfully only when the attacker has command of both sea and air, and only when the element of surprise is employed effectively. (*See* Korean War.)

Current Amphibious Doctrine.—Modern amphibious warfare integrates virtually all forms of land, sea and air operations. An amphibious operation's greatest advantage rests in its mobility and flexibility; concentrations of strength can be applied with great selectivity against the enemy's shore line; surprise is of great importance. An amphibious operation's greatest limitation is that the attacker must build up his strength ashore from an initial zero. The tactics and techniques by which the amphibious operation's advantages are exploited and its disadvantages overcome make this one of the most complicated and sophisticated forms of modern warfare. An amphibious operation, from its inception until its completion, usually passes through six recognizable phases: planning, embarkation, rehearsal, movement to the objective area,

assault and termination.

Planning begins with the decision that the landing be made and continues until the termination of the operation. Some of the factors which complicate amphibious planning are the necessity to co-ordinate naval and landing forces, the special problems of amphibious logistic support, the unique command relationships, and the requirement for precise timing in air, naval gunfire and artillery support.

Before detailed planning can proceed certain basic decisions must be made. Climatic and seasonal conditions as well as the strategic and tactical situation are factors in the determination of the date and time of landing. Similarly, geographic and hydrographic conditions, as well as the concept for operations ashore, affect the place of landing.

In the embarkation phase men and matériel are assembled and embarked in a manner designed to support the scheme of maneuver ashore. The key technique is combat loading of the amphibious shipping. Combat loading, which includes several methods of stowage and cargo handling, is designed to facilitate the rapid and selective unloading of troops, equipment and supplies.

World War II saw the development of a highly specialized family of amphibious ships. In the U.S. service, the principal types at mid-20th century were the AGC or amphibious force flagship, the AKA or attack cargo ship, the LSD or landing ship dock and the APD or high-speed transport, usually a converted destroyer type. Some use has also been made of transport submarines, for example, in the marine raid against Japanese-held Makin Island (1942).

An even more specialized form of amphibious shipping were the landing ships, based for the most part upon an amalgamation of American and British designs. These ships were unique in that they had a beaching capability. Best known and most versatile was probably the LST or tank landing ship. Other landing ships developed during World War II include the LSM or medium landing ship, the LSIL or infantry landing ship large, and the LSSL or support landing ship large.

Post-World War II developments in amphibious ship construction were directed at faster, more versatile ships, including a capability of operating helicopters. The LPH or amphibious assault ship, for example, combined many of the characteristics of an aircraft carrier with those of an assault transport.

The rehearsal phase includes the conduct of one or more exercises, under conditions approximating the impending operation, to test the planning, the timing, the communications and the combat readiness of the forces involved.

The movement to the objective area embraces the departure of the ships from the loading points (sortie), the passage at sea and the arrival in the objective area (entry).

The assault phase is distinguished by the ship-to-shore movement of the landing force. Much of the Allied amphibious success in World War II depended upon the development and large-scale production of landing craft and amphibious vehicles. The most widely used ramp-bowed landing craft were the 36-ft. LCVP (landing craft vehicle, personnel) and the 50-ft. LCM (landing craft, mechanized). Both were based on designs developed by Andrew

WIDE WORLD
AMPHIBIOUS ASSAULT FROM LCVP (LANDING CRAFT VEHICLE, PERSONNEL) BY U.S. TROOPS; NORMANDY, FRANCE, JUNE 1944

Higgins, a New Orleans boatbuilder. Two distinct types of amphibious vehicles appeared during World War II: the LVT or amphibian tractor developed for the marine corps and the army-sponsored duck (DUKW) or amphibious truck. The LVT, a track-laying vehicle which superficially resembled a tank, was based on the "alligator" invented by Donald Roebling of Florida. The duck, on the other hand, moved on rubber tires while ashore and was propeller-driven afloat.

At mid-20th century military opinion recognized that the great concentrations of shipping and the congested beachheads of World War II would be suicidal against a nuclear-equipped enemy. To eliminate this congestion, helicopters and other vertical-rising or short-take-off aircraft were replacing the slow landing craft and amphibian vehicles of the past. Helicopters, operating from high-speed amphibious assault transports such as the LPH, were to converge on the objective area from many miles at sea. At the same time they were to avoid the beach defenses by flying inland. *See also* COAST DEFENSE.

BIBLIOGRAPHY.—Holland M. Smith, "The Development of Amphibious Tactics in the U.S. Navy," *Marine Corps Gazette* (June 1946–March 1947); Alfred Vagts, *Landing Operations* (1946); Jeter A. Isely and Philip A. Crowl, *The U.S. Marines and Amphibious War* (1951); Alan Moorehead, *Gallipoli* (1956); Frank O. Hough, Verle E. Ludwig and Henry I. Shaw, Jr., *Pearl Harbor to Guadalcanal* (1958).

(E. H. SI.)

AMPHIBOLE, a large and important group of common rock-forming minerals. Most of the amphiboles are darkly coloured with various shades of green, brown and black predominating. Generally, the darker the colour, the higher the iron content. Magnesium-rich amphiboles can be nearly colourless. Sodium-rich amphiboles can have a distinct bluish colour if it is not masked by a high iron content.

The amphiboles are metasilicates (inosilicates). They are characterized by two planes of well-developed prismatic cleavages which intersect at angles of about $124°$ and $56°$. Many of the amphiboles develop elongate crystals, some becoming needlelike and fibrous. Other members of the group form short, stubby crystals and thus, all gradations can occur. Crystal faces, or traces of them, are commonly present on the individual grains, especially those faces which parallel the cleavage directions.

Amphiboles, as a group, form over most of the temperature range observed in the earth's crust. For example, amphiboles can be present in volcanic rocks, metamorphic rocks and as overgrowths on detrital grains in slightly metamorphosed sediments. Amphiboles can be found in most of the igneous rocks as minor and major constituents and form the major constituent in many metamorphic gneisses and schists. Hornblende schist, anthophyllite schist and cummingtonite schist are the commonest. Amphiboles form gangue (waste) minerals in certain ore deposits, and contact metamorphic deposits often include some of the amphiboles.

Some of the fibrous forms of the amphiboles, tremolite, anthophyllite and riebeckite, are often used in commercial asbestos. Some of the jade used in carvings and jewelry is a variety of tremolite called nephrite.

Composition and Classification.—The amphiboles are characterized by a large variation in composition including sodium (Na), calcium (Ca), magnesium (Mg), iron (Fe), aluminum (Al), silicon (Si), oxygen (O), hydrogen (H) and fluorine (F); the general formula is:

$$(Na,Ca)_{2-3}(Mg,Fe^{2+},Fe^{3+},Al)_5(Si,Al)_8O_{22}(OH,O,F)_2 \text{ or:}$$
$$(Mg,Fe^{2+},Fe^{3+},Al)_7(Si,Al)_8O_{22}(OH,O,F)_2.$$

Potassium is the only abundant element in the earth's crust that is not included as a major constituent. In mineral groups of such variable composition, species names are generally applied to idealized pure compositions called end members. These end members are capable of mixing with other end members to form single homogeneous solid solutions. Consequently, most of the natural minerals can be considered as being composed of various mixtures of these end members.

Mineral names are also given to ranges of compositional variation. In general, the amphiboles form two distinct groups: (1) those crystallizing in the orthorhombic system; and (2) those crystallizing in the monoclinic system. The more important end members are listed below.

Orthorhombic amphiboles

Anthophyllite	$(Mg,Fe)_7Si_8O_{22}(OH)_2$
Gedrite	$(Mg,Fe)_5Al_2(Si_6Al_2)O_{22}(OH)_2$

Monoclinic amphiboles

Cummingtonite	$(Fe,Mg)_7Si_8O_{22}(OH)_2$
Tremolite	$Ca_2Mg_5Si_8O_{22}(OH)_2$
Tschermakite	$Ca_2Mg_3Al_2(Si_6Al_2)(OH)_2$
Edenite	$NaCa_2Mg_5(Si_7Al)O_{22}(OH)_2$
Glaucophane	$Na_2(Mg_3Al_2)Si_8O_{22}(OH)_2$
Riebeckite	$Na_2(Fe_3^{2+}Fe_2^{3+})Si_8O_{22}(OH)_2$

The calcium-containing amphiboles listed above have iron equivalents: for these, the mineral name is prefixed with ferro-, as, ferrotremolite. If the iron content in the orthorhombic series exceeds a certain amount, the mineral becomes monoclinic; and also, magnesium-rich cummingtonite is unknown. It is apparent that the amphibole group can accommodate a wide variety of compositions and concentrations. It is also obvious that a chemical analysis is needed to identify the individual species. For this reason, the noncommittal name hornblende is generally applied to all of the calcium-rich amphiboles. Microscopic work is required to distinguish the orthorhombic amphiboles and cummingtonite from hornblende. At high temperatures such as occur in lava flows, hydrogen can be driven off and the ferrous iron oxidized to ferric iron, resulting in the oxyhornblendes.

The variation in composition allowed in the amphiboles is best explained by the following diagram. Instead of single chains for the form of the silicate anions (negative ions) as in the pyroxenes (*q.v.*), endless double chains occur:

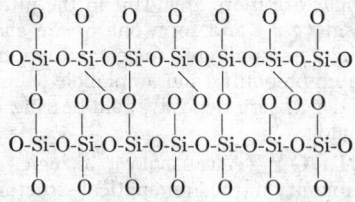

These double chain groups are parallel to the elongated direction of the crystal and are bonded to parallel adjacent double chains by the Na,Ca and Mg,Fe^{2+}, Fe^{3+},Al ions of the crystal. There are only small differences between the ionic sizes of Mg, Fe^{2+}, Fe^{3+} and Al so that those positions in the crystal which are occupied by Mg can also be occupied by these similarly sized ions; *i.e.*, they can substitute for each other. The ionic sizes of Ca and Na are similar enough that they can substitute for each other. The ionic size of Al is also close enough to the size of Si that a limited Al substitution for Si occurs. Thus, any combination of the one, two, three and four valent metal cations (positive ions) and any mixtures of similarly charged cations that will satisfy the remaining charge demands on the oxygen anions (plus the two OH [hydroxyl] groups) and at the same time will be accommodated in the seven atomic positions for the one, two and three valent cations and the eight atomic positions for the Si and Al cations (per 24 O's, as indicated in the diagram) can form as an amphibole. (G. W. DEV.)

AMPHIBOLITE, a rock composed of one of the amphibole (*q.v.*) minerals. Technically, amphibolite means that only amphiboles are present, but rocks composed of only one mineral are rare and it is customary to include rocks that are predominantly composed of amphiboles in the term amphibolite. The term is restricted to rocks of metamorphic origin, but this is not a complicating restriction inasmuch as amphibole-rich rocks are nearly always metamorphic. A planar or sheetlike structure or foliation is commonly present in such rocks and its presence is denoted by the term schist added to the rock name. Hornblende schist forms one of the commoner amphibolite rock types in metamorphic terrains. Anthophyllite schists, cummingtonite schists and glaucophane schists can also be important rock types in such an area.

The mineralogy of the amphibolites is relatively simple. Plagioclase feldspar of about andesine composition and quartz are the commonest minerals present with the amphiboles in amphibolite. Other minerals such as garnet, biotite, pyroxene and epidote may or may not be present. Except for the tremolite and anthophyllite schists which are often light coloured, the amphibolites are usually dark green or black. The elongate amphibole crystals are often oriented parallel to each other in the schistose rocks, but sometimes are intertwined together in nonschistose rocks.

The origin of the amphibolites and amphibole schists and the manner in which they are formed is not clearly understood. Classically, a large variety of different rocks which have chemical compositions similar to the amphibolites such as graywackes, shales, impure limestones, certain volcanic ash beds, basaltic lava flows, diabases and gabbros have been considered to be altered and recrystallized to form the amphibolites; i.e., the chemical composition of the original rock is preserved in the resulting metamorphic rock.

In addition to simple recrystallization, amphibolites can be formed if material of amphibolite composition is introduced into rocks not of amphibole composition. Such material can be introduced by a diffusion mechanism or solution transfer. The introduced material, by reacting with the material present in pre-existing minerals to form amphiboles or by dissolving the pre-existing minerals and simultaneously precipitating amphiboles, could transform the original rock into an amphibolite or amphibolite schist. The criteria to distinguish these two methods of formation are not clear-cut or even generally accepted. Because intermediate stages of transformation are often absent, it is sometimes impossible to determine the character of the original rock and the manner of formation of the amphibolite schist. The amphibolite schists are more abundant in the intermediate grades of metamorphism (q.v.) and form one of the characteristic rock types in the epidote-amphibolite facies and amphibolite facies.

Although the amphibolites and amphibole schists are not commonly associated with ore deposits, gold-bearing quartz veins are occasionally found.   (G. W. DeV.)

AMPHIBOLOGY (AMPHIBOLY), in logic, a verbal fallacy arising from ambiguity in the grammatical structure of a sentence. It occurs frequently in poetry, because of the alteration for metrical reasons of the natural order of words; as an example, the line from Shakespeare, *Henry VI,* is often quoted: "The duke yet lives that Henry shall depose." The success of ancient oracles was largely due to skill in amphibology.

AMPHICTYONY (AMPHICTIONY), in ancient Greece, meant an association of neighbouring states (from Gr. *amphictiones,* "dwellers around"), holding festivals accompanied by fairs. The term is restricted to associations based on a religious centre and is not used of political alliances. The most important such associations in the Greek world were the Delian and Delphic amphictyonies and, in the archaic period, the Calaurian (comprising states around the Saronic gulf).

The Delian amphictyony reached the height of its splendour early in the 7th century B.C. A hymn to the Delian Apollo composed about that time celebrates the gathering of the Ionians at the shrine of their god on the island of Delos, to worship him with music, dancing and gymnastic contests. Pisistratus, carrying out a purification of Delos in the 6th century to win the favour of Apollo, seems to have used the sanctuary as a means of extending his political influence; but the fall of the Athenian tyrants, the decline of Ionia and the growing danger from Persia led to the abandonment of the festival. When, after the Persian Wars, the Aegean cities united in a league they chose as its centre the temple of the Delian Apollo and the league's council met at Delos. The removal of the treasury to Athens in 454 B.C. deprived Delos of political importance, but Athenian commissioners controlled the treasury of Apollo, and in 426 the Athenians revived the festival and added horse racing. At the end of the Peloponnesian War Athens was deprived of Delos, but it appears to have regained control after the victory of the Persian fleet over the Spartans at Cnidus (394 B.C.). The affairs of the temple were managed by a board of five Athenian amphictyons, accompanied for a short period by five Andrians and assisted by some Delian officials. At

this time the amphictyony is known to have embraced both the Athenians and the inhabitants of the Cyclades; but a strong Delian party bitterly opposed Athenian rule, which came to an end with the supremacy of Macedonia. The dissolution of the amphictyony soon followed.

Far more famous is the Delphic amphictyony. It was originally composed of 12 tribes dwelling round Thermopylae—the Thessalians, Boeotians, Dorians, Ionians, Perrhaebians, Magnetes, Locrians, Oetaeans, Phthiotes, Malians, Phocians and Dolopians. The name of the council (*pulaia*) and of one set of deputies (*pulagorai*), together with the importance of the temple of Demeter at Anthela, near Thermopylae, suggests that this shrine was the original centre of the association. How and when Delphi became the centre is uncertain. The council of the league included deputies of two different kinds—*pulagorai* and hieromnemones. The latter were 24 in number, two from each tribe. Originally made up of neighbours, the league in time admitted the Dorians of the Peloponnese and the Athenians. After the Sacred War of 355–346 B.C. Macedonia took the place of the Phocians, and the Delphians partially displaced the Perrhaebians and Dolopians.

In the following century the Aetolians gained such dominance in the amphictyony as to convert the council into an organ of their league. They were never formally admitted to membership but maintained their supremacy in the council by controlling the votes of their allies. They made no material change in its composition, which, accordingly, after the dissolution of their league by the Romans is found to be nearly as it was after the Sacred War of 355–346. A few minor changes were introduced under the supremacy of the Roman republic. The emperor Augustus increased the number of votes to 30 and distributed them according to his pleasure. In the age of the Antonines the association was still in existence.

The hieromnemones of the Thessalians, who held the presidency, were elected, but the office was ordinarily, as at Athens, filled by lot. As a rule they were renewed annually. Each hieromnemon was accompanied by two *pulagorai,* elected semiannually. The hieromnemones were formally superior but, being usually mediocrities, readily became the tools of the *pulagorai,* who were orators and statesmen. The latter are rightly given credit for the acts of the council and had a right to propose measures and to take part in the deliberations. The hieromnemon, however, cast the vote of his community, though in the record his two *pulagorai* were made equally responsible for it. The council decided all questions which fell within its competence. Matters of greater importance, as the levy of an extraordinary fine on a state or the declaration of a sacred war, it presented in the form of a resolution to an assembly, composed of the deputies, the amphictyonic priests and any other citizens of the league who chanced to be present. This assembly was relatively unimportant, however.

The amphictyons met both in the spring and in the autumn at Delphi and at Thermopylae. The meeting at Thermopylae followed that at Delphi. The primary function of the council was to administer the temporal affairs of the two shrines. The duty of the hieromnemones was to inspect periodically the sacred lands, to punish those who encroached and to see that the tenants rendered their quota of produce; and the council held the states responsible for the performance of such duties by their deputies. Another task of the council was to supervise the treasury, to protect it from thieves, to increase the capital by investment and to control the expenditure. It contracted for the rebuilding of the Delphic temple after it had been destroyed by the fire of 548 and there are mentions of its adorning the interior with statues and pictures, inscribing the proverbs of the Seven Sages on the walls, bestowing crowns on benefactors of the god, preparing for the Pythian games, awarding the prizes and issuing coins. One law imposed an oath upon the members of the league not to destroy an amphictyonic city or to cut it off from running water in war or peace and enjoined them to wage war upon those who transgressed this ordinance and punish any others who sought to injure the god. In this regulation can be seen one of the origins of Greek interstate law. It was also unlawful to levy tolls on pilgrims to the shrines. Other regulations were made to secure peace at the time of the festival, and occasionally the council was called upon to arbitrate in a dispute, but no provision was made to compel arbitration.

The council furthermore had judicial power. As jurors the deputies took an oath to decide according to law or, in cases not covered by law, according to their best judgment. The earliest known penalty inflicted was the destruction of Crisa for having levied tolls on pilgrims. This offense was the cause of the first Sacred War (c. 590 B.C.); the Sacred Wars of 355–346 and 339–338 were declared by the amphictyons against the Phocians and the Amphissaeans respectively for trespassing on the sacred lands.

The judgments of the council were sometimes considered unfair, and were successfully defied by the states affected. The inability of the council to enforce its resolutions was chiefly due to its composition; the majority of the communities represented were even in combination no match for individual cities like Athens, Sparta or Thebes; the support of the great powers was necessary if more than moral influence was to be employed.

See W. A. Laidlaw, *A History of Delos* (1933); H. W. Parke and D. E. W. Wormell, *The Delphic Oracle* (1956).

AMPHILOCHUS, in Greek legend, a famous seer, son of Amphiaraus and Eriphyle and brother of Alcmaeon. According to some, he assisted in the murder of Eriphyle, which, according to others, was carried out by Alcmaeon alone. He took part in the expedition of the Epigoni against Thebes and in the Trojan War. After the fall of Troy he founded, in conjunction with Mopsus, another famous seer, the oracle of Mallos in Cilicia. The two seers afterward fought for its possession, and both were slain in the combat. Amphilochus is also said to have been killed by Apollo.

According to another story, he returned to Argos from Troy, but, being dissatisfied, left it for Acarnania, where he founded Amphilochian Argos on the Ambracian gulf. He was worshiped at Oropus, Athens and Sparta.

AMPHINEURA, a class of marine mollusks (phylum Mollusca) comprising two subclasses, the Aplacophora, wormlike animals without shell plates, and the Polyplacophora, flattened elliptical forms having eight shell plates on the dorsal surface. The Amphineura are world-wide in distribution, ranging from the intertidal zone to great depths. This article will deal only with the Polyplacophora, or chitons; for a discussion of the Aplacophora *see* MOLLUSK.

The Polyplacophora, also known as Loricata, Crepipoda or, more commonly, chitons, range in length from a fraction of an inch to 12 to 14 in. In most forms the shell plates are held together in part by a girdle which surrounds the edges of the plates. In others the plates may be completely imbedded in the tissue, as in the adult but not the young of *Cryptochiton*, or partially imbedded, as in *Cryptoplax*. The girdle may be smooth, scaly or armed with limy spicules or tufts of chitinlike hairs. On the ventral surface is a large, flat foot which is developed for creeping and for adhering by suction to the surface of rocks. The gills are located in a groove, the pallial or mantle groove, on either side of the foot between the foot and the mantle. The number of gill filaments varies greatly in the different groups. There may be only a few, near the posterior end of the animal, or many, extending nearly to the head.

The mantle covers the dorsal side of the animal, producing the shell plates dorsally and the covering of the muscular girdle at its margin. The overlapping plates and the many muscles attached to them give a chiton a great deal of flexibility which allows it to fit snugly into the irregularities of the substratum or to curl up into a ball as a pill bug, or wood louse (q.v.), when removed from the rocks. Because of the habit of curling, chitons are known as sea curbs in the Bahama Islands. They can adhere so firmly to a rock surface that it is usually necessary to use a knife or other tool to pry them loose.

Chitons feed by scraping off the surface film on rocks or other surfaces on which they might be living. They feed mainly on algae, diatoms, small hydroids, decaying seaweeds and the like. Most species feed only at night, wandering a short distance during the process but returning to their "home site" in the morning. Although some species remain on exposed rocks during the day,

most of them retreat to the underside of rocks or into crevices when exposed to sunlight.

Although world-wide in distribution, chitons are very much more abundant, both as to numbers of species and individuals, in tropical and warm temperate waters. Most species, particularly in warm areas, are found in shallow water, often in the intertidal zone, whereas in colder areas the proportionate number of species occurring in deeper water increases. A few species are found at great depths, some having been taken from over 2,000 fathoms. Fourteen species are listed for New England, only two of which, both small, may be collected in the intertidal zone, the remainder being obtained only by dredging. The eastern Pacific is rich in species and it is there that *Cryptochiton stelleri*, the largest known species (reaching a length of about 14 in.) is found; it ranges

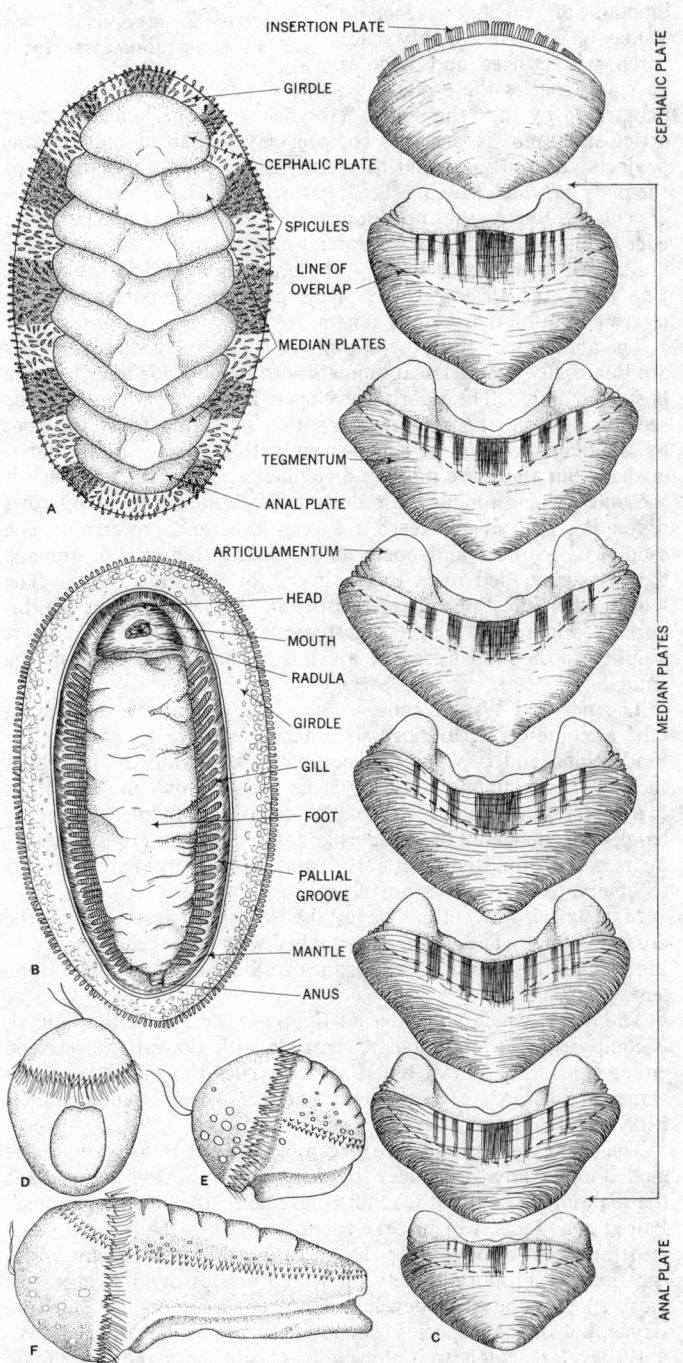

(D, E, F) ADAPTED FROM HEATH, "DEVELOPMENT OF ISCHNOCHITON," IN "ZOOLOGISCHEN JAHRBÜCHERN" (1899)

FIG. 1.—REPRESENTATIVE CHITON (ACANTHOPLEURA GRANULATA)
(A) Dorsal view; (B) ventral view; (C) disarticulated shell; (D) trochophore larva; (E, F) intermediate stages in development

from Alaska to California. The most varied and most beautiful chiton fauna is found in Australian and New Zealand waters. In this region, isolated plates of chiton shells, because of their shape, sculpture and beautiful colouring, are often referred to as butterfly, sunset or toenail shells.

The shell plates of a chiton are composed of two layers. The outer layer, or tegmentum, is porous and composed largely of conchilin with a relatively small amount of calcium carbonate. It may be smooth or highly sculptured with ridges and nodules. In many species these plates are penetrated by the "shell-eyes" (*see* below). The inner layer, or articulamentum, is a hard, compact layer that in most forms projects anteriorly beyond the tegmentum. It is this portion of the plate to which the muscles are attached. The extension of the articulamentum on the anterior edge of the head plate, the posterior edge of the anal plate and the lateral margins of the median plates are known as insertion plates. These are imbedded in the girdle. The characteristics of these plates are very important in the classification of the various genera.

The anatomy of the Polyplacophora is relatively simple. They are bilaterally symmetrical animals with an anterior mouth and a posterior anus. The poorly developed head region can only be seen by turning the animal over; it is separated from the foot by a narrow groove. A short snout with a mouth at its end is evident, but there are no eyes or tentacles. Within the mouth is the long rasping tonguelike radula that is armed with many rows of teeth; some of the teeth are very large and powerful. The esophagus is short and opens into a large, thin-walled stomach that is surrounded by a large "liver," or digestive gland. The long, coiled intestine, characteristic of all plant feeders (herbivores), is imbedded in the digestive gland. It opens on a short nipple into the pallial groove, which is at the posterior end of the animal.

The nervous system consists of a ring around the esophagus (the circumesophageal ring) with nerves running forward to the head region and two pairs of nerve cords running the length of the body, two running ventrally (the pedal cords) and the other two running laterally (the pallial cords). The ventral nerve trunks are connected in a ladderlike fashion by numerous connecting nerves. From the main nerve trunks small nerves are given off to innervate the various organs.

Many groups of chitons have "shell-eyes," or aesthetes, on the dorsal surface. These eyes are supplied with nerves that penetrate the shell plates. In some groups the eyes have a definite crystalline lens.

The heart, which is located at the posterior end of the animal, is composed of a long median ventricle with elongate auricles on either side. The dorsal blood vessel carries the blood from the ventricle forward to the various organs. Lateral blood vessels carry the blood from the gills back to the heart.

The elongate reproductive organ, or gonad, is located in the medial dorsal area just under the shell plates. Sexes are separate; the male organ is usually reddish in colour, the female greenish. Paired gonoducts, which carry sperm or eggs to the outside, open into the pallial groove near the posterior end of the body. The eggs may be produced singly, in jellied masses or in strings. In most species the eggs develop into free-swimming trochophore larvae, but in some species they are held within the pallial groove until development is well along. In *C. viviparus* the developing eggs are held within the gonoducts of the female, and there is no free-swimming stage. A very large number of eggs may be produced by a single female, the estimate being as high as 200,000 in some species. As is true throughout the animal kingdom where

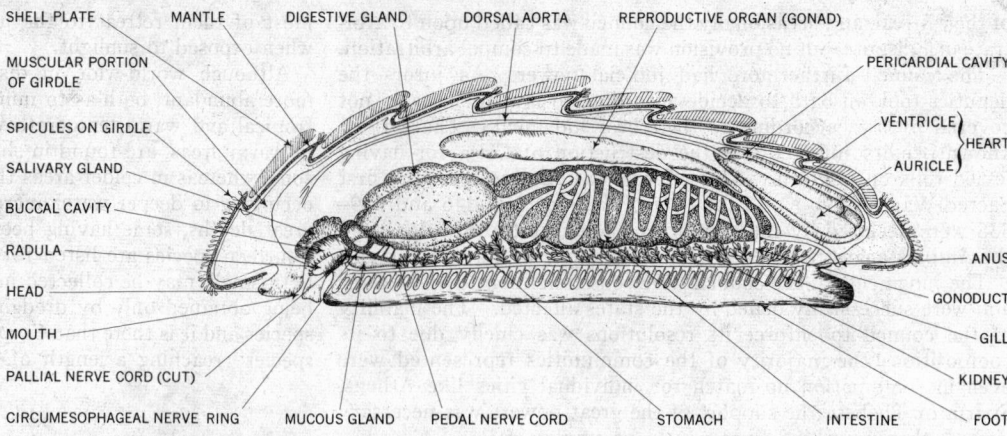

FIG. 2.—LONGITUDINAL SECTION THROUGH A CHITON SHOWING POSITION AND RELATIONSHIP OF PRINCIPAL ORGANS

such large numbers of eggs are produced very few ever reach maturity.

Chitons are not an economically important group. Although they may have been eaten by poorer classes of people at an earlier time, it was not a common practice. In the Bahama Islands chitons along with a variety of other mollusks not generally eaten may be gathered and made into a stew if food becomes scarce. Chitons are a source of food, however, for some carnivorous snails, and the tremendous numbers of free-swimming young released during the breeding season are an important element in the plankton on which many marine animals feed.

CLASSIFICATION

The classification of living Polyplacophora is based on whether or not insertion plates are present. There are two orders in this subclass: the Paleoloricata, which are fossil forms known only from the Upper Cambrian to the Upper Cretaceous; and the Neoloricata, which are known from the Upper Cambrian to the Recent. There are three main suborders in the Neoloricata. The suborder Lepidopleurina contains three families that usually lack insertion plates, but if plates are present, they are simple and without slits. The suborders Ischnochitonia with nine families and the Acanthochitonina with one family have insertion plates with slits. The numerous genera and more than 600 species belonging to these groups are classified mainly on the characteristics of the girdle and insertion plates, the sculpturing of the shell and the gill arrangement.

The fossil record for chitons is poor; about 100 species have been described. Unfortunately almost all of them have been based on isolated plates. Chitons are known to have occurred as far back as the Upper Cambrian (over 400,000,000 years ago).

BIBLIOGRAPHY.—Vera Fretter, "The Structure and Function of the Alimentary Canal of Some Species of Polyplacophora," *Trans. Roy. Soc. Edinb.*, 59:119–164 (1937); T. Iredale and A. F. B. Hull, "A Monograph of the Australian Loricates," *Royal Zoological Society of New South Wales*, pp. 1–168 (1927); H. A. Pilsbry, "Monograph of the Polyplacophora," *Manual of Conchology*, vol. 14, pp. i–xxiv, 1–350, vol. 15, pp. 1–132 (1892–93); Allyn G. Smith, "Amphineura" in *Treatise on Invertebrate Paleontology: Part I, Mollusca 1*, pp. 141–176 (1960).
(R. D. T.)

AMPHION and **ZETHUS,** in Greek mythology, the twin sons of Zeus by Antiope. When children, they were exposed on Mt. Cithaeron, but were found and brought up by a shepherd. Amphion became a great singer and musician, Zethus a hunter and herdsman. After punishing Lycus and Dirce for cruel treatment of Antiope (*q.v.*), they built and fortified Thebes, huge blocks of stone forming themselves into walls at the sound of Amphion's lyre. Amphion married Niobe, and killed himself after the loss of his wife and children.

AMPHIOXUS (LANCELET), the common name for small marine somewhat eellike animals (genera *Branchiostoma* and *Asymmetron*) of great interest to zoologists because of their primitive chordate characteristics (*see* CHORDATE). The term *Amphioxus* was formerly the accepted genus name of *Branchiostoma.*

Figure label callouts (Fig. 2): SHELL PLATE · MANTLE · DIGESTIVE GLAND · DORSAL AORTA · REPRODUCTIVE ORGAN (GONAD) · MUSCULAR PORTION OF GIRDLE · PERICARDIAL CAVITY · SPICULES ON GIRDLE · VENTRICLE · HEART · AURICLE · SALIVARY GLAND · BUCCAL CAVITY · RADULA · HEAD · ANUS · GONODUCT · MOUTH · GILL · PALLIAL NERVE CORD (CUT) · KIDNEY · CIRCUMESOPHAGEAL NERVE RING · MUCOUS GLAND · PEDAL NERVE CORD · STOMACH · INTESTINE · FOOT

Amphioxus lives in clean sand and moderately shallow water where there is a good flow of current. It ranges throughout the temperate and tropical regions and is especially abundant at the Straits of Messina (off the toe of Italy) and also off the China coast near Amoy, where the only amphioxus fishery in the world has existed for hundreds of years.

Its biological significance arises from its structure, which is clearly related to that of vertebrates in spite of the fact that it lacks a true head and backbone. Any theory concerning the origin of the vertebrate class as a whole, and therefore by inclusion man's own ancient origins, must rest heavily upon the nature of amphioxus, even though this animal is still a living contemporary and may or may not have changed since its origin.

General Structure.—Amphioxus is a slender, pinkish-white translucent creature about two inches long, pointed at both ends and flattened from side to side. It lives normally in the sand with its mouth more or less flush with the surface and its body almost completely buried, feeding upon minute particles filtered from the surrounding water. This method of feeding is associated with a sedentary existence. It is capable of quickly wiggling backward into the sand when disturbed and is further equipped with the basic locomotory apparatus characteristic of a fish, even though it lacks such control mechanisms as a brain and sense organs. Thus the whole organism is somewhat paradoxical, and in this combination of a sedentary filter-feeder mechanism, fishlike musculature and support, and virtual headlessness, its fascination and mystery lie.

The adult amphioxus has what every embryo, from fish to man, has to start with: a supporting rod of turgid cells known as the notochord. In vertebrates the vertebral column is built around the notochord, but in amphioxus the notochord persists alone. Above the notochord lies the nerve cord in the form of a hollow tube, the spinal cord, again similar to that of vertebrates. Along each side of these axial structures lie the long series of segmental muscle bands, arranged like chevrons on a sergeant's sleeve. These

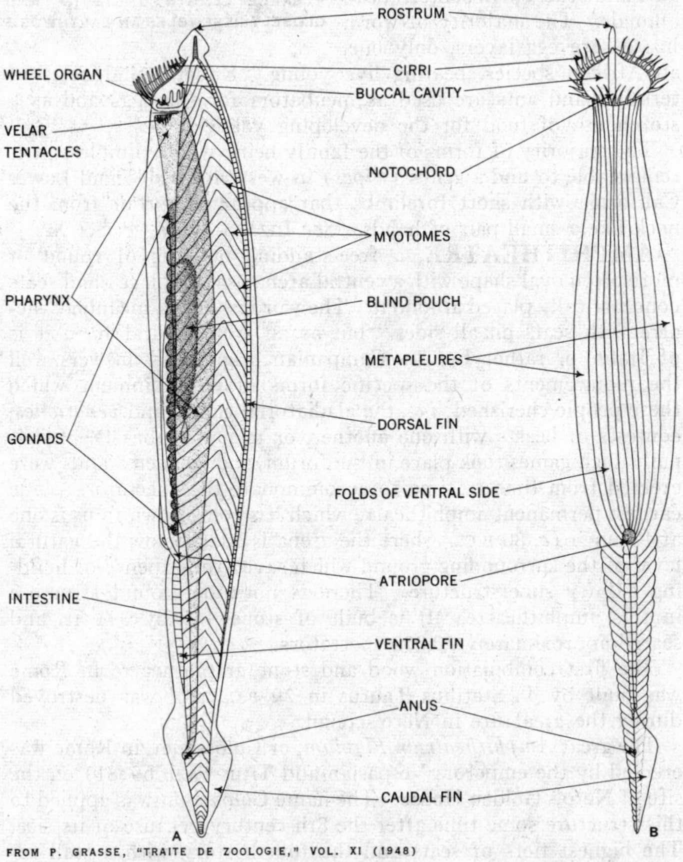

muscles, supplied by segmental nerves from the spinal cord, give rise by successive contraction to the quick undulating swimming movements that this animal can perform. This basic supporting structure and neuromuscular organization is the fundamental plan of vertebrates as well.

Amphioxus also possesses a cuticular vertical fin extending the length of the body, like an upper keel, and a ribbed underside, like rows of small bilge keels, all serving to stabilize movement through water. It is consequently remarkable that the spinal cord fails to expand in front to form any kind of brain and that there are no discernible organs for sight and balance, or even smell. Everything that is necessary to swim like a fish is present; there is, however, no guidance system, which suggests that in this sense amphioxus may be degenerate. As a swimming chordate animal, however, amphioxus is in other ways primitive rather than degenerate, for example, in the absence of paired fins.

Feeding Mechanism.—Amphioxus feeds by means of a highly elaborate and delicate mechanism, the endostylar feeding apparatus, which is almost identical with that of tunicates (*see* TUNICATE) and is also remarkably similar to that of the ammocoete larva of the lamprey, a true vertebrate. There is every reason therefore to regard this apparatus not only as an interesting mechanism in itself but as the primitive feeding mechanism for the chordate group as a whole, a mechanism which vertebrates in general discarded when they evolved jaws and became predators.

The mechanism is primarily a filtration system whereby minute food particles are filtered out of relatively large quantities of water taken in through the mouth. The digestive canal itself is a straight tube running from mouth to anus, but in the throat region it dilates as an extensive gill system. There is no liver or obvious digestive glands, except for a blind pouch where a liver or pancreas might be expected. The entire side walls of the throat, or pharynx, however, are pierced by a paired series of long narrow gill slits lined with powerful lashing cilia, or protoplasmic hairs. The combined action of these cilia is to draw water in through the mouth and to pass it out again to the exterior so that the large quantity of water taken in does not enter the digestive region of the intestine. The flow of water emerging through the gill slits on each side of the body does not however escape directly to the exterior; it enters an enclosed space known as the atrial cavity, or atrium, the outer enclosing wall of which serves to protect the delicate gill structure and to increase the efficiency of the outgoing water current. The atrium, which extends far back along the body, opens to the exterior only at the small atriopore situated a short distance in front of the anus. All the water drawn into the capacious pharynx is forcibly propelled out as a jet near the hind end of the body. This alone could serve as a means of gentle locomotion if the animal left the protection of the sand for a more hazardous existence in the sea above, which is actually the case during the night for at least one species. Otherwise the jet serves to flush the surrounding sand.

In amphioxus, as in the tunicates, water enters the front end into a vestibule, or buccal cavity. What part of it actually constitutes the mouth is a question of opinion. The outer opening is fringed by stiff processes, or cirri, which can bend outward to open the buccal cavity or can bend inward to form a protective grating to keep out sand and mud. Inside the cavity lies a second circlet, consisting of highly sensitive tentacles. These operate in such a way that only food or other particles below a certain minute size actually enter the pharynx behind the mouth. Within the pharynx lies the food-trapping mechanism which consists of a ventral groove or endostyle, diverging in front to pass up each side of the mouth to the dorsal side. The tissue lining the grooves secretes mucus that moves as a thin sheet forward and upward and backward, and on to which the fine food particles adhere. At the dorsal side of the pharynx the mucus sheet with its contained particles is passed along another groove and into the intestine. This extraordinarily efficient and intricate filter system is essentially the same in tunicates and the larval stage of lampreys.

It is remarkable, from a purely human standpoint, that in the lamprey larva part of the endostyle groove transforms at the time of metamorphosis into the thyroid gland of the adult; and in some-

ROSTRUM
WHEEL ORGAN
CIRRI
BUCCAL CAVITY
VELAR TENTACLES
NOTOCHORD
MYOTOMES
PHARYNX
BLIND POUCH
METAPLEURES
GONADS
DORSAL FIN
FOLDS OF VENTRAL SIDE
INTESTINE
ATRIOPORE
VENTRAL FIN
ANUS
CAUDAL FIN
A
B

FROM P. GRASSE, "TRAITE DE ZOOLOGIE," VOL. XI (1948)

FIG. 1.—AMPHIOXUS (BRANCHIOSTOMA LANCEOLATUM)
(A) left lateral and (B) ventral views

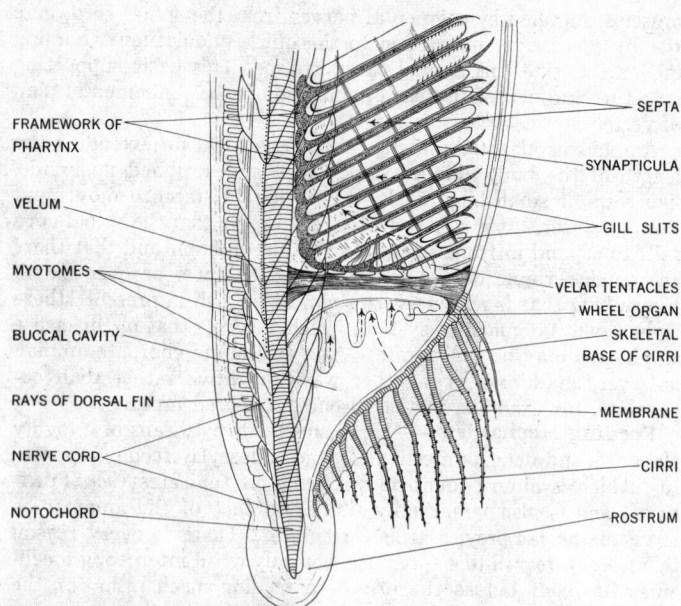

FRAMEWORK OF PHARYNX

VELUM

MYOTOMES

BUCCAL CAVITY

RAYS OF DORSAL FIN

NERVE CORD

NOTOCHORD

SEPTA

SYNAPTICULA

GILL SLITS

VELAR TENTACLES
WHEEL ORGAN
SKELETAL
BASE OF CIRRI

MEMBRANE

CIRRI

ROSTRUM

FROM P. GRASSÉ, "TRAITÉ DE ZOOLOGIE," VOL. XI (1948)

FIG. 2.—ORGANIZATION OF DIGESTIVE TUBE IN ANTERIOR REGION OF B. LANCEOLATUM. ARROWS INDICATE MOVEMENT OF FOOD AND WATER

what like manner in the human embryo, as in other vertebrates, the gland originates from a pocket in the floor of the pharynx. Similarly, the pituitary gland of vertebrates can be traced to a small structure, the wheel organ in amphioxus and tunicates, lying behind the mouth and below the floor of the nerve cord.

This unique feeding system has led to the large, complex gills of fishes and to their derivatives in higher vertebrates, the middle ear cavity of all land-living forms, and the two most important hormone-producing glands in the vertebrate body.

Reproduction and Development.—The sexes are separate in amphioxus, unlike the hermaphroditic condition in tunicates, and in both male and female the reproductive glands (gonads) are present as a paired series corresponding to the series of muscle segments of the middle part of the body. Each small gland, whether ovary or testis, bursts when ripe into the atrial cavity, and the released eggs or sperm pass to the exterior through the atrial pore, fertilization taking place in the water. The minute, transparent eggs develop in a manner essentially like that of many vertebrates. A flat plate of the outer embryonic layer folds inward to form a tube which in amphioxus becomes the spinal cord but in vertebrates becomes both cord and brain.

Amphioxus larvae hatch shortly after fertilization and spend many subsequent weeks, and perhaps months, drifting with the ocean currents. Surprisingly, they do not swim horizontally like a fish but drift head up and tail down as though they were already imbedded in the sand on the sea floor. Finally they do sink to the sea floor, at which time they transform from curiously asymmetric larva into symmetrical adults.

Classification.—Two genera are commonly recognized: *Branchiostoma (Amphioxus)*, which has a series of gonads along each side of the body; and *Asymmetron*, which has a series of gonads on one side only, recalling somewhat the asymmetrical nature of the larval type. Species of both genera are widely distributed. These genera constitute the nonvertebrate subphylum Cephalochordata of the phylum Chordata.

See also references under "Amphioxus" in the Index.

BIBLIOGRAPHY.—A. Willey, *Amphioxus and the Ancestry of the Vertebrates* (1894); P. Drach, "Anatomie et Physiologie des Cephalocordes," *Traité de Zoologie*, ed. by P. P. Grassé (1948); T. G. Chin, "The Biology of the Amoy Amphioxus," *Philadelphia Journal of Science*, vol. 75 (1941); W. J. Leach, "The Archetypal Position of Amphioxus and Ammocoetes, and the Role of Endocrines in Chordata Evolution," *Amer. Nat.*, vol. 78 (1944); E. G. Conklin, "The Embryology of Amphioxus," *J. Morphol.*, vol. 54 (1932). (N. J. B.)

AMPHIPOLIS (mod. AMFIPOLIS in the province of Macedonia), an ancient city of Macedonia, lies on the east bank of the Strymon (Strimon) river, about 3 mi. from the Aegean sea. Originally a Thracian town, known as *Ennea Hodoi* ("Nine Roads"), it was colonized by Athenians with other Greeks under Hagnon in 436 B.C., previous attempts—in 497, 476 and 465—having been unsuccessful. In 424 it surrendered to the Spartan Brasidas without resistance; Thucydides, the historian, who was with the fleet at Thasos, was too late in coming to the rescue. In 422 Cleon led an unsuccessful expedition to recover it; both he and Brasidas were slain. It was to have been restored to Athens by the peace of Nicias (421) but remained long independent. In 357 Philip II of Macedonia occupied it in spite of Athenian opposition. The importance of Amphipolis was due to its command of the bridge over the Strymon and the route from northern Greece to the Hellespont; it was a depot for the gold and silver mines of Pangaeus and for ship timber. Under the early Roman empire it became the headquarters of the governor of Macedonia, though itself a free city. Many inscriptions, coins, etc., have been found there, and traces of ancient fortifications and a Roman aqueduct are visible.

AMPHISBAENA, the genus name for one of the "worm lizards" (Amphisbaenidae), a family of elongate forms included among the lizards, though there is some doubt as to their actual kinship. The group is represented in Florida and Lower California, Mexico, Spain, north Africa and southwestern Asia, but most of its members are found in tropical America and Africa.

In these "lizards" the body is of nearly the same thickness throughout, the tail being very short. The various species range from about six inches to two feet in length. The head (in which the eyes are beneath the scales of the head) is blunt like the tail. Worm lizards feed on termites, ants and other small subterranean animals. The majority of worm lizards are egg layers, only one,

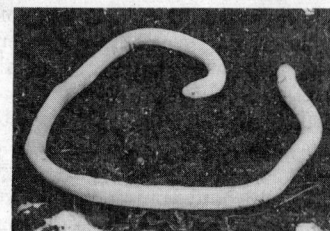

NEW YORK ZOOLOGICAL SOCIETY

RHINEURA FLORIDIANA, THE ONLY SPECIES OF AMPHISBAENA NATIVE TO THE UNITED STATES, ATTAINS AN AVERAGE LENGTH OF 12 IN. AND CLOSELY RESEMBLES AN EARTHWORM

an African species, bearing live young. Underground nests of termites and ants are used as incubators for the eggs and as a storehouse of food for the developing young.

The majority of forms of the family being wholly limbless, it is remarkable to find a genus (*Bipes*) in western Mexico and Lower California with short forelimbs that appear to sprout from the neck like a small pair of hands. *See* Lizard. (K. P. S.; X.)

AMPHITHEATRE, a free-standing building of round or more often oval shape with a central arena (sandy place) and seats concentrically placed around it. The word is Greek, meaning "theatre with seats on all sides," but as an architectural form it is of Italic, or rather Etrusco-Campanian origin, and answers well the requirements of the specific forms of entertainment which these people cherished; *i.e.*, the gladiatorial games and *venationes*, contests of beasts with one another, or men with beasts. Originally such games took place in the forum, and wooden stands were erected from time to time to accommodate the spectators. The earliest permanent amphitheatre which has come down to us is one at Pompeii (*c.* 80 B.C.) where the arena is sunk below the natural level of the surrounding ground which saved the expense of building a lofty superstructure. There is no underground structure in this amphitheatre. It is built of stone 445 by 341 ft. and seated approximately 20,000 spectators.

The first combination wood and stone amphitheatre in Rome was built by T. Statilius Taurus in 29 B.C., and was destroyed during the great fire in Nero's reign.

The great *Amphitheatrum Flavium*, or Colosseum, in Rome was erected by the emperors Vespasian and Titus (A.D. 69–81) on the site of Nero's Golden House. The name Colosseum was applied to this structure some time after the 8th century because of its size. The highest tiers of seats and the fourth story with a wall relieved by pilasters were rebuilt in the 3rd century. The Colosseum was seriously damaged by lightning and earthquakes in late

Amphitheatre at Pompeii; *c.* 80 B.C. The earliest permanent structure of its kind, it seated about 20,000 persons

Amphitheatre at Verona; built near the end of the 1st century A.D. The auditorium accommodated about 25,000 persons

The Colosseum (*Amphitheatrum Flavium*), Rome, built by emperors Vespasian and Titus on the site of Nero's Golden House; A.D. 69–81. Its over-all size was 620 by 513 ft., and its estimated seating capacity about 50,000

ROMAN AMPHITHEATRES

Plate II

AMPHITHEATRE

The amphitheatre at Arles, France; dating from the first and second centuries A.D.

Remains of the amphitheatre at Thysdrus (El Djem) in Africa near Carthage, Tunisia; erected 3rd century A.D.

ROMAN AMPHITHEATRES IN FRANCE AND AFRICA

PHOTOGRAPHS, (TOP) YAN—RAPHO GUILLUMETTE, (BOTTOM) G. E. KIDDER SMITH

antiquity and during the Middle Ages. All the marble seats and decorative materials have been taken from this edifice which was treated for hundreds of years as if it were a quarry. It measured in overall dimensions 620 by 513 ft. with a height of 160 ft.; the arena was 287 by 180 ft. and its capacity is estimated at about 50,000.

Other great examples of the ancient Roman amphitheatres are: the amphitheatre at ancient Capua (mod. Santa Maria Capua Vetere) second in size to the Colosseum, 560 by 460 ft., and 95 ft. high, built in the 1st century; that at Verona, 502 by 403 ft., and 98 ft. high, built near the end of the 1st century; that at Pozzuoli, 482 by 383 ft., and, outside Italy, Nîmes and Arles in France, Pola in Istria (Yugoslavia); and Thysdrus (El Djem) in Africa. The arenas were about 200 to 300 ft. long and about 115 to 200 ft. wide. Beside these mentioned, fragmentary remains in varying states of preservation and amounts of more than 75 Roman amphitheatres have been found in widely scattered areas throughout the provinces of the Roman empire. The best-preserved in England is the Roman amphitheatre at Caerleon in Monmouthshire where the seats were placed largely on banked-up earth.

In the majority of the Roman amphitheatres below the arena surface was an elaborate structure containing passages, the *media via* for scenery, others for elevators and machinery for lifting the animals and scenery used, rooms for gladiators, all ingeniously arranged to connect by means of many trap doors with the arena above. Around this arena, and separated from it by a high wall with a metal screen on top of it to prevent the animals from leaping over it, arose the seats of the spectators. These were divided by passageways running around the amphitheatre into several sections (*maeniana*): the lowest, known as the podium, where, in the centre section above the arena, the emperor and his retinue had a special box; while around him and on the opposite side the vestal virgins, consuls, praetors, ambassadors, priests, and other distinguished guests were seated. The rest of the first gallery contained senators and those of the equestrian rank. The second gallery was reserved for the patricians, and the third for the plebeians who sat or stood, and the fourth, uppermost, gallery for women, who were seated in boxes. Each of these galleries was divided into wedge-shaped sections (*cunei*) by radial walks and from them many exits (*vomitoria*) led down to the passages below the seats and so to the street.

The seats were supported on walls running radially to the exterior between which the exit stairs were most ingeniously arranged so that the enormous crowds were distributed evenly to the exit arches which surrounded the ground story. An awning (*velum* or *velarium*) manipulated by sailors sheltered the spectators from the sun. In addition, vaulted corridors ran elliptically around the outside, connecting the various radial elements; the arcaded exterior was therefore a necessary and logical expression of the construction.

In modern usage the word amphitheatre is sometimes used for a theatre or concert hall whose seats surround the central area, as, for example, the Albert Hall, London, and both the new and the old Madison Square Garden in New York.

Modern open amphitheatres also exist, particularly in connection with sports. *See* STADIUM. (Js. H. Br.)

AMPHITRYON, in Greek mythology, son of Alcaeus, king of Tiryns. Having accidentally killed his uncle Electryon, king of Mycenae, Amphitryon was driven out by another uncle, Sthenelus. He fled with Alcmene, Electryon's daughter, to Thebes, where he was cleansed from the guilt of blood by Creon, his maternal uncle, king of Thebes. Alcmene, who had been betrothed to Amphitryon by her father, refused to marry him until he had avenged the death of her brothers, all of whom except one had fallen in battle against the Taphians. Amphitryon accordingly took the field against the Taphians, accompanied by Creon, who had agreed to assist him on condition that he slay the Teumessian vixen, which had been sent by Dionysus to ravage the country. The Taphians, however, remained invincible until Comaetho, the king's daughter, out of love for Amphitryon, cut off her father's golden hair, the possession of which rendered him immortal (*cf.*, the story of Nisus [*q.v.*]). Having defeated the enemy, Amphitryon put Comaetho

to death and handed over the kingdom of the Taphians to Cephalus. On his return to Thebes he married Alcmene.

The more famous portion of the myth of Amphitryon concerns his wife. When Amphitryon was once absent at war, Alcmene became pregnant by Zeus, who, disguised as her husband, visited her during a long night (contrived by Apollo); she became pregnant again by her real husband on his return. Of these unions were born twin boys, of whom Iphicles was the son of Amphitryon, Heracles the son of Zeus.

The stories of the absolutely faithful wife deceived by a disguise, and of the hapless husband displaced by a paramour bearing his own name and form, have obvious dramatic possibilities. A number of ancient dramatists presented the theme, notably Plautus, whose comedy *Amphitruo* still survives (*cf.*, the sophisticated *Amphitryon 38* of Giraudoux).

The modern use of Amphitryon in the sense of a generous host is derived from Molière's comedy on the subject.

(T. V. B.)

AMPLIFICATION, the process by which the strength (current, voltage or power) of an electrical signal is increased. This process is accomplished by a device called an amplifier. Amplifying action can be provided by electromechanical devices such as transformers and generators, feed-back circuits, vacuum tubes and transistors (*see* AMPLIFIER, ELECTRONIC; AMPLIFIER, MAGNETIC; TRANSISTOR).

The ratio of the output (current, voltage or power) to the input, where both are expressed in the same units, is a measure of the amplification and is termed the gain. The term amplification factor, inherent where vacuum tube amplifiers are concerned and usually applied to a single tube, is defined as the ratio of a change in the plate voltage to a change in grid voltage that will produce no change in plate current. Both the gain and the amplification factor are pure numbers since they express ratios of similar quantities (*see* ELECTRON TUBE: *Grid Control of Electron Streams in High Vacuum*).

A single amplifier employed to perform an amplifying task is called a stage of amplification. The amplification resulting from a single stage is often insufficient to raise the output to the desired level. In such cases the output of the first stage is fed into a second stage, whose output is fed to a third stage, and so on, until the output level is satisfactory. The result is cascade, or multistage amplification. Long-distance telephone, radio, television, electronic control and measuring instruments, radar and countless other devices all depend on this basic process of amplification. The over-all amplification of a multistage amplifier is the product of the gains of the individual stages.

There are various schemes for coupling of cascading electronic amplifiers depending upon the nature of the signal involved in the amplification process. If the output of one stage is directly coupled to the input of a second stage, the term direct-coupled is applied. Such coupling is used, for example, where zero frequency (that is D.C.) signals are to be amplified. When a capacitor is used as the coupling device (a resistor is also necessary) between stages, the term R-C coupled is used. Should a transformer be used between stages, the amplifiers are said to be transformer coupled. The method of coupling employed is one scheme of amplifier classification.

An important aspect of the amplification process is the ability of an electronic amplifier to produce a magnified output signal, identical in every respect to the input signal. This is linear operation. If the output is altered in shape after passing through the amplifier, amplitude distortion exists. This type of distortion is usually measured by the percentage of harmonic content of the amplified signal in relation to the applied signal. If the amplifier does not amplify equally at all frequencies, frequency distortion or discrimination results. When the phases of some frequencies are shifted more than those of other frequencies, phase distortion exists. Frequency distortion usually results in phase distortion.

When the power level required from the output of the amplifier is so large as to preclude the use of electronic devices, dynamo-electric and magnetic amplifiers find wide application.

(A. L. Sy.)

AMPLIFIER, ELECTRONIC, a device designed to take a small signal (voltage, current or power) from some source and produce a much larger output signal that contains the essential wave-form features of the input signal. The output signal may be proportional to the input signal, or input and output may be related in quadratic, logarithmic or other nonlinear fashion when the amplifier is performing a function other than the simple multiplication of the original signal in amplitude (*see* Amplification).

Amplifier action can be utilized in electronic circuits in a number of ways, depending upon the results desired. The purpose for which the amplifier is used is responsible for a scheme of classifications for amplifiers descriptive of their properties and operation.

Amplifiers are classified as power, current or voltage amplifiers if they are designed to develop maximum power, current or voltage at the output. They are further classified with regard to the frequency range over which they are designed to operate. Direct-current amplifiers, audio-frequency amplifiers, radio-frequency amplifiers, video-frequency amplifiers, ultrahigh-frequency amplifiers and very high-frequency amplifiers are standard classifications.

Direct-current amplifiers amplify D.C. and low-frequency A.C. signals. Audio-frequency amplifiers respond to frequencies of about 20 to 20,000 cycles per second. Video-frequency amplifiers cover a range from well down in the audio range up to 5 megacycles and higher. Amplifiers designed to operate in and amplify any frequency range above the audio range are classified as radio-frequency, ultrahigh-frequency or very high-frequency amplifiers depending on the actual range of frequencies covered.

Four classes of electronic amplifier operation, applied particularly to power amplifiers, are class A, class AB, class B and class C. This scheme of classification is based primarily on the fraction of the input cycle during which plate current is expected to flow under full-load conditions. These terms are defined as follows (in *American Standard Definitions of Electrical Terms,* American Institute of Electrical Engineers [1941]):

Class A.—A class A amplifier is an amplifier in which the grid bias and alternating grid voltages are such that plate current in a specific tube flows at all times.

Class AB.—A class AB amplifier is an amplifier in which the grid bias and alternating grid voltages are such that plate current in a specific tube flows for appreciably more than half but less than the entire electrical cycle.

Class B.—A class B amplifier is an amplifier in which the grid bias is approximately equal to the cut-off value so that the plate current is approximately zero when no exciting grid voltage is applied, and so that plate current in a specific tube flows for approximately one-half of each cycle when an alternating grid voltage is applied.

Class C.—A class C amplifier is an amplifier in which the grid bias is appreciably greater than the cut-off value so that plate current in each tube is zero when no alternating grid voltage is applied, and so that plate current flows in a specific tube for appreciably less than one-half of each cycle when an alternating grid voltage is applied.

In all four classifications, the subscript 1 may be added to the letter or letters of the class identification to denote that grid current does not flow during any part of the input cycle. The subscript 2 is used to denote that grid current flows during some part of the cycle.

Other miscellaneous amplifier classifications such as wide band, narrow band, tuned and untuned are also sometimes used.

Electronic amplifier design requires consideration of the following factors: (1) amount of amplification required; (2) type of input signal; (3) desired frequency range; (4) impedance of source or pickup device connected to the amplifier input; (5) impedance of the load; (6) requirements for stability; (7) possible selectivity of amplification of certain frequencies; (8) type of coupling where several stages are used; (9) phase relation of output signal to input signal; and (10) power supply available.

In general, when the signal of interest is very small, or involves rapid changes or high frequencies, thermionic tube amplifiers are used almost exclusively. In cases where the power level required is so large as to preclude the use of electronic devices, dynamoelectric and magnetic amplifiers are used (*see* Amplifier, Magnetic).

Direct-current generators may be considered to be power amplifiers in that small changes in the value of the excitation can produce relatively large changes in the power output. Also, in a sense, voltage and current amplification is performed by the step-up transformer, but, in contrast to electronic and dynamoelectric amplifiers which draw power from a source other than the input signal, the transformer demands an even greater input power than it produces at the output.

For many high-power applications, particularly in the control of heavy machinery, specially constructed rotating electrical machines such as the amplidyne (essentially a two-stage amplifier) can be used as amplifiers; these have the advantage of simplicity and high power amplification. Frequently, electromechanical amplifiers of this type are used in conjunction with thermionic tube amplifiers.

See also Electron Tube; High-Fidelity Sound Systems; Radio; Telephone; Transistor.   (A. L. Sy.)

AMPLIFIER, MAGNETIC, a device using saturable reactors to secure amplification and control in alternating-current circuits (*see* Magnetism: *General Description of Magnetism*). Fig. 1(A) shows schematically a simple saturable reactor consisting of an iron core linked by two windings. With no signal applied, the magnetic core flux alternates about zero over a range of high permeabilities; in these conditions the load winding has a high reactance and the load current is small. The direct-current signal shifts the centre of the flux alternations from zero; low permeabilities prevail at some time in the cycle, and the load current becomes larger. Undesirable voltages are induced by transformer action in the control circuit of fig. 1(A); these voltages are repressed in the two-core reactor of fig. 1(B).

Among the earliest developments in electric control, saturable reactors were employed, for instance, to vary the brightness of lights in theatres. The electric power spent in the control circuit is much smaller than the power supplied to the bank of lamps; in other words, power amplification is obtained. E. F. W. Alexanderson used saturable reactors as amplitude modulators in transoceanic radiotelephony before the invention of suitable electron tubes.

The technological importance of magnetic amplifiers in modern automation and instrumentation is due largely to the development of core materials with sharp saturation characteristics; in these materials the differential permeability $\mu = \dfrac{dB}{dH}$ is extremely high when the magnitude of the induction is within a certain range, and drops abruptly, almost to zero, beyond this range (*see* Magnetism: *The Magnetization Curve*).

The introduction of rectifying elements in the circuit is a further development resulting in higher amplifications. Fig. 2 shows an elementary amplifier of the so-called self-saturating type. At the beginning of a positive half-cycle of the alternating supply voltage the core flux is at a certain ϕ_0. In the initial part of the half-cycle the supply voltage is balanced by the rate of change

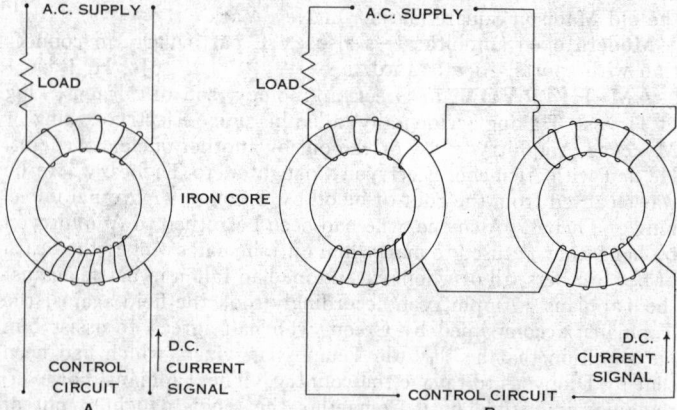

FIG. 1.—SCHEMATIC DRAWING OF SATURABLE REACTORS SHOWING (A) SINGLE-CORE REACTOR (BURGESS AND FRANKENFIELD, 1901); AND (B) TWO-CORE REACTOR (ALEXANDERSON, 1912)

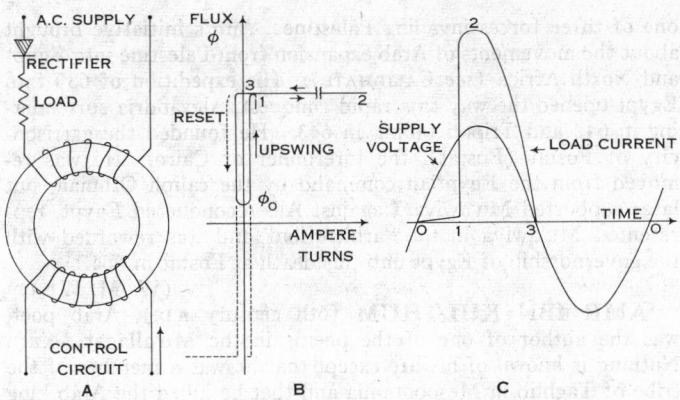

FIG. 2.—SELF-SATURATING MAGNETIC AMPLIFIER SHOWING (A) HALF-WAVE AMPLIFIER CIRCUIT; (B) HYSTERESIS LOOP OF THE CORE, FOR A CERTAIN VALUE OF SIGNAL; (C) LOAD CURRENT VERSUS TIME

of the rising core flux, and only a small current flows through the load. This unsaturated interval terminates when the magnetic induction reaches the saturation value, and then, for the remaining part of the half-cycle, the supply voltage appears transferred directly at the load terminals. In negative half-cycles the rectifier blocks the supply voltage and the flux is reset, from saturation to the level ϕ_0, under the influence of the signal. Essentially the duration of the unsaturated interval depends on the value of ϕ_0 and, in turn, ϕ_0 is dictated by the signal. Combinations of two or more of these half-wave components are used in more complex amplifiers, single-phase or polyphase, single-ended or in push-pull. Multistage amplification is possible, and positive or negative feedbacks can be introduced. A proper amount of positive feedback leads to a bi-stable type of operation in which the amplifier behaves like an on-off relay, without moving contacts. Amplifiers that detect signal powers of 10^{-10} w., and even less, are in industrial usage under severe environmental conditions. On the other hand, an application is known in which an output power of 1.7 megawatts is controlled by magnetic amplifiers, at 60 cycles per second. Smaller weights, as well as higher performance, result from the use of higher supply frequencies (400 to 10,000 cycles per second or higher).

The basic phenomena described can be exploited for many other purposes where power amplification is not the primary aim. Magnetic amplifier components are used to perform analytical and logic operations in analogue and digital computers. Signal integrators, pulse counters, timers, static frequency multipliers and dividers, modulators and choppers converting direct-current signals into alternating current, constant-current references and regulated power supplies, are further examples of the versatility of these magnetic devices. Structural simplicity, reliability and ruggedness are the essential advantages of the magnetic amplifier. Some disadvantages are seen in the peculiar wave forms of output voltage and in certain unavoidable delays, of one or more half-cycles, that occur between a change of signal and the corresponding readjustment of output.

See also AMPLIFIER, ELECTRONIC.

For a complete bibliography *see:* J. G. Miles, "Bibliography of Magnetic Amplifier Devices and the Saturable Reactor Art," *Trans. Amer. Inst. Elect. Engrs.*, vol. 70, pt. ii, pp. 2104-23 (1951); "Magnetic Amplifier Bibliography, 1951-56" A.I.E.E. Committee Report, *Trans. Amer. Inst. Elect. Engrs.*, vol. 77, pt. i, pp. 613-627 (1958); "1957 Magnetic Amplifier Bibliography," A.I.E.E. Committee Report, *Trans. Amer. Inst. Elect. Engrs.*, vol. 77, pt. i, pp. 1051-1057 (1958).
(L. A. F.)

AMPTHILL, ODO WILLIAM LEOPOLD RUSSELL, 1ST BARON (1829-1884), British diplomat, who was outstandingly successful as the first British ambassador in Berlin after the creation of the German empire. The third son of Maj. Gen. Lord George William Russell and of Elizabeth Anne, daughter of the Hon. John Rawden, he was born in Florence, Italy, on Feb. 20, 1829. His eldest brother, Hastings, became 9th duke of Bedford, and his brother Arthur represented Tavistock in parliament for many years. His mother held original views on education, and

Odo's linguistic talent, fully developed by private tuition and wide travel, made him a master of French, German and Italian. At the age of 20 he became attaché at Vienna: with his genial temper, integrity of mind and social gifts, he was assured of success in a diplomatic career. A period in the foreign office and experience in Paris, Constantinople and Florence was followed by special service in Rome from 1858 to 1870; there, in 1868, he married Lady Emily Theresa Villiers, third daughter of Lord Clarendon. In 1869-70, during the Vatican council (*q.v.*), the pope, appreciating Russell's discretion, granted Cardinal Manning a special dispensation to disclose secret information to him so that his government might be kept authoritatively informed. Recalled to become assistant undersecretary for foreign affairs, he was soon assigned another diplomatic mission, this time to Versailles. The Franco-German war was raging, and his appointment to the German headquarters, where he conferred with Bismarck on the critical situation created by Russia's denunciation of the Black sea clauses of the 1856 treaty of Paris, had important consequences. Though Gladstone feared he went beyond his instructions by threatening that Great Britain would be forced to go to war "with or without allies" if Russia persisted, Lord Granville reminded the prime minister that war had been a possibility after the last British note. The direct result of Russell's mission was a peaceful solution of the immediate problem through the London conference in Jan. 1871 and indirectly it led to his appointment to Berlin (Oct. 1871).

As ambassador, Russell worked wholeheartedly for good relations. Where internal policy was concerned he was prudent. His private conviction that the *Kulturkampf* must fail did not influence the objectivity of his reports, nor was his constant kindness to friends who incurred Bismarck's displeasure ever tainted by any suspicion of intrigue. While the crown princess found in the embassy a second home, and Count von Arnim (*q.v.*) learned that his disgrace did not affect Odo Russell's attitude, the cordial relations established with Bismarck at Versailles remained unimpaired.

Called to the privy council in 1872, Russell was made a knight grand cross of the Bath on Gladstone's resignation in 1874. During the near eastern crisis of 1875-76, he avoided adding to the excitement, acting with prompt tact upon his instructions. His appointment as third British plenipotentiary at the Berlin congress in 1878 was recognition of his patient services behind the scenes. Following that, he alone represented the government on the conference delimiting the Greek frontier. His creation as knight grand cross of St. Michael and St. George in 1879 was followed by elevation to the peerage in 1881, after Gladstone's return to power. Germany's colonial policy now began to create new problems, and Lord Ampthill's untimely death at Potsdam on Aug. 25, 1884, was a calamity for both countries. In Bismarck's own words, "England might give a successor to the ambassador that she had lost, but could not expect to replace him."

His eldest son, ARTHUR OLIVER VILLIERS RUSSELL (1869-1935), succeeded him as 2nd baron. After being private secretary to Joseph Chamberlain, he was governor of Madras, 1899-1906, acting as viceroy of India during Lord Curzon's absence in 1904.

See P. Knaplund, *Letters From the Berlin Embassy 1871-1874, 1880-1885* (1944); W. A. Taffs, *Ambassador to Bismarck* (1938).
(W. A. T.)

AMPUTATION means removal of any part of the body, but commonly the term is restricted to mean surgical removal of a part of or an entire limb, either upper or lower extremity. The reasons for surgical amputation in general are injury, infection, tumour, diabetes or insufficient blood supply (arteriosclerosis); occasionally surgical amputation is performed on nonfunctioning or grotesquely deformed limbs. Persons born without a limb or limbs are said to have suffered congenital amputation. Surgical amputation may be a lifesaving measure in the severely injured patient, suffering from both loss of blood and infection; in patients with diabetic or arteriosclerotic gangrene, in whom amputation may be the only method of preventing spread of the gangrene; and in patients suffering from malignant tumours of soft tissue or bone.

Modern reconstructive surgery makes possible the rehabilitation of many badly damaged limbs without amputation, and experience gained in World War II of early and thorough treatment of the severely injured, particularly the use of blood and plasma, has saved many extremities. Furthermore, modern prostheses, particularly for amputations in the lower extremity, have reduced the handicap to the amputee. The congenital amputee seldom requires any corrective surgery but is benefited by prosthetic replacement. There is no definitely known causative factor for congenital amputation, but it probably is not a hereditary deformity. *See* also PROSTHETICS. (C. N. L.)

AMRAM BEN SHESHNA (d. 875), a famous Gaon (*q.v.*) or head of the Jewish academy of Sura, Persia, whose prayer book, *Siddur Rab ʻAmram,* was the foundation of most of the extant rites in use among the Jews. He was author of many responses, (*i.e.,* interpretations of talmudic law), but his chief work was liturgical. He was the first to arrange a complete liturgy for the synagogue. The *Siddur* was published in Warsaw in two parts (1865).

AMRAVATI (formerly AMRAOTI), a town and district in Maharashtra state, India. The town, 85 mi. W.S.W. of Nagpur, is an important cotton-processing and marketing centre. Pop. (1961) 137,875. It is the seat of six colleges associated with Nagpur university. It is also the headquarters of the Shri Shivaji rural university and there is a fine government polytechnic built of basalt. It is the terminus of a branch line from Badnera on the Central railway's Nagpur-Bombay main line.

AMRAVATI DISTRICT (area 4,723 sq.mi.; pop. [1961] 1,232,780) is an undulating lava tract on the Berar plain. The average elevation is 1,000 ft. above sea level, except in the northwest where the Gawilgarh hills, a long spur of the Mahadeo (east-central Satpura) hills, intrude southwestward. These hills rise to 3,000 ft. between the Tapti river and its tributary the Purna to the south. The basaltic nature of the district's terrain yields rich black cotton soil; the main crops are cotton and jowar, grown in rotation. In Melghat subdivision on the Tapti, the shallow red soils are cultivated for grains by the Korkus. These aboriginal tribespeople speak one of the Munda languages (*q.v.*), but most inhabitants now speak the regional language, Marathi. Their main occupations are forestry and stock raising.

After Amravati the most important town is Achalpur (Ellichpur), a cotton-weaving centre with a population of 36,538 (1961), on another Central railway branch. Captured from the Hindu Yadava king Ramachandra in 1296 by ʻAla ud-Din Khalji (later usurping emperor of Delhi), it remained an important Muslim regional capital until the decline of the Moguls in the 18th century. A relic of this past is the stately *idgah* or prayer hall (1347) of Imadul-Mulk, nephew of the Delhi emperor Mohammed Tughluq. In the Gawilgarh hills are Gawilgarh fort, one of whose governors, Fathullah, proclaimed an independent Berar sultanate (1484–*c.* 1574), and the beautiful hill resort of Chikhalda. (D. G. NA.)

AMRELI (ancient AMARAVALLI), a town and district in Gujarat state, India. The town is in the Kathiawar (Saurashtra) peninsula, 125 mi. S.W. of the state capital, Ahmedabad (153 mi. by Western railway metre-gauge). Pop. (1961) 34,699. The chief industries are oil crushing and the manufacture of *khadi* (coarse cotton cloth). There is an airfield but no regular service. Amreli has a children's museum built in 1955.

AMRELI DISTRICT comprises the Kathiawar possessions of the former Baroda state (acceded to India in 1949) and Gogho mahal (subdivision), formerly in Ahmedabad district, with (from Aug. 1, 1959) the addition of seven mahals from adjacent districts and the exclusion of Okhamandal on the western tip of the peninsula. The 1959 reorganization was to help obviate the former scattered nature of the district. Area 1,545 sq.mi. (4,002 sq.km.). Pop. (1961) 667,823. The chief crops are millet, peanuts, cotton, wheat and pulses. (V. A. M. J.)

AMR IBN AL-AS (d. A.D. 664), the Arab conqueror of Egypt, was born in Mecca, possibly *c.* A.D. 580. He belonged to the tribe of Quraish (Koreish) in Mecca and was an opponent of Mohammed until his conversion in 629. Soon after becoming a Muslim and going to Medina he was given a series of military commands. In 633 the caliph Abu Bakr put him in charge of

one of three forces invading Palestine. Amr's initiative brought about the movements of Arab expansion from Palestine into Egypt and North Africa (*see* CALIPHATE). His expedition of 639 into Egypt opened the way to a rapid conquest, Alexandria surrendering in 642 and Tripoli falling in 643. He founded the garrison-city of Fostat (Fustat), the forerunner of Cairo. He was removed from the Egyptian command by the caliph Othman, but later supported Muʻawiya I against Ali, reconquered Egypt, represented Muʻawiya in the "arbitration" and was rewarded with the governorship of Egypt until his death at Fostat in 664. (W. M. WT.)

ʻAMR IBN KULTHUM (6th century A.D.), Arab poet, was the author of one of the poems in the Muʻallaqat (*q.v.*). Nothing is known of his life except that he was a member of the tribe of Taghlib in Mesopotamia and that he killed the Arab king of Hira, ʻAmr ibn Hind, who is violently attacked in his poem, for an insult offered to his mother.

AMRITSAR, a municipal city and district of Punjab, India. The city is about 16 mi. from Wagah, the outpost of the India-Pakistan border on the main road from Delhi to Lahore. It is the largest and most important city in Punjab, and in 1961 had a population of 384,287. It is the centre of Sikhism and the site of the Sikh's principal place of worship, the Golden temple. On a site granted by the emperor Akbar, the city was founded by Ramdas, the fourth Guru, who also ordered excavation of the sacred tank or Amrita Saras ("pool of nectar") from which the city derives its name. In the middle of this tank on a small island, the fifth Guru, Arjan, built a temple. During the reign of Ranjit Singh (1780–1839) the upper part of the temple was decorated with a gold-foil-covered copper dome and since then it has been known as the Golden temple, alternately called the Darbar Sahib ("court divine") by the Sikhs.

Nearby is an octagonal seven-story tower (150 ft. high) in memory of Baba Atal Rai, son of Hargobind, the sixth Guru. About two furlongs from the Golden temple is a spacious park, the famous Jallianwala Bagh where, in 1919, government troops fired on the participants of a political meeting, killing several hundred persons. The site of this massacre was declared a national monument after the country became independent.

Hall bazaar is the main shopping centre, while Guru bazaar is the centre for articles of jewelry. Bazaar Mai Sewan is famous for books and pictures of the Sikh religion. Near the Lohgarh gate is the Durgiana temple, built in recent times by Hindus. Just outside the city is Rambagh, a large well-kept park which contains the summer palace of Maharaja Ranjit Singh. Khalsa college (established 1899), a Sikh institution 3 mi. west of the city, Glancy medical college, a separate dental college and four other colleges are all connected with the Punjab university. The city is a centre for the textile and chemical industries and for the manufacture of electric fans, rolling mills and cycle parts. Other items of manufacture include carpets, silk, embroidery and brocade.

AMRITSAR DISTRICT (area 1,978 sq.mi.) is an almost level plain sloping slightly from northeast to southwest and drained by the Ravi and the Beas rivers that flow for some distance along its western and eastern boundaries respectively. In 1961 it had a population of 1,534,916.

Towns other than Amritsar are Taran Taran (20,961), Patti (15,833), Jandiala (11,915), Chheharta (13,760), Majitha (6,973), Khemkaran (7,142).

The district depends on agriculture and owes its prosperity to irrigation, mainly from the Upper Bari Doab canal (constructed in 1859). The main crops are wheat, pulses and maize with some cotton, sugar cane and oilseeds. There are cotton ginning and pressing factories. The Northern railway and Grand Trunk road cross the district from west to east. (S. S. BH.)

AMROHA, a municipal town and *tehsil* (subdivision) of Moradabad district, Rohilkhand division, Uttar Pradesh, India, lies about 81 mi. E. of Delhi on the Delhi-Moradabad section of the Northern railway. Pop. (1961) 68,965. It is on the left bank of the Sot river, on a low site among mango groves, and is noteworthy for the shrine of Sheikh Saddu, a Muslim saint. Three intermediate colleges are connected with Agra university. Carpet weaving and ornamental pottery making are its chief industries, and there is a sugar mill.

AMROHA TEHSIL has an area of 383 sq.mi. and a population (1951) of 293,198. (S. S. Bh.)

AMSDORF, NIKOLAUS VON (1483–1565), German Protestant reformer who was one of Luther's most determined and active supporters, was born at Torgau on Dec. 3, 1483. He was educated at Leipzig and then at Wittenberg, where he became a professor of theology in 1511. With Luther he attended the Leipzig conference (1519) and the diet of Worms (1521), and was in the secret of Luther's Wartburg retreat. He assisted the first efforts of the Reformation at Magdeburg (1524), where he became superintendent, Goslar (1531), Einbeck (1534) and the Schmalkalden debates (1537). In 1539 he opposed Luther by speaking out strongly against the intended bigamous marriage of Philip (q.v.), landgrave of Hesse. In 1542 he was made evangelical bishop of Naumburg by John Frederick I, elector of Saxony, and Luther, in opposition to the chapter. His position was a painful one, but under Luther's persuasion he remained until he had to yield place to the Roman Catholic bishop, J. Pflug, in 1547.

After 1547, as an exile at Magdeburg and (1550) a counselor of the Saxon dukes at Eisenach, he superintended the Jena edition of Luther's works and continued to fight for the purity of his doctrine. He opposed the Augsburg Interim, urged the separation of the High Lutheran party from Melanchthon and got the Saxon dukes to oppose the Frankfurt Recess (1558). Many of his letters and other short works are extant. He died at Eisenach on May 14, 1565. He became famous through his opinion on good works, which he held to be dangerous for faith. An inflexible character and a faithful Lutheran, he was more the type of an orthodox theologian than a representative of Luther's theological school.

BIBLIOGRAPHY.—Amsdorf's *Ausgewählte Schriften,* ed. by O. Lerche (1938); O. H. Nebe, *Reine Lehre. Zur Theologie des Niklas von Amsdorff* (1935); H. Stille, *Nikolaus von Amsdorf, 1483–1542* (1937); P. Brunner, *N. von Amsdorf als Bischof von Naumburg* (1961).
(E. Bi.)

AMSTERDAM, the capital of the Netherlands, and one of its chief ports, which also gives access from the Rhine waterways to the sea, is situated in the province of North Holland, at the mouth and on the south side of the Y or IJ, an inland arm of the Zuider Zee (called, since it has been largely drained, the IJsselmeer), and connected by canal with the North sea. Founded among swamps and stretches of water, the city has always been built on piles and methodically planned. Called by Luigi Guicciardini "the Venice of the North," its architectural style has inspired the planning of other cities, notably St. Petersburg (Leningrad), U.S.S.R., and Recife, Brazil. It is divided by the canalized river Amstel into two main sections, joined by a sluice dam (hence its name; originally Amstelredam or Amstel Dam), and subdivided by 50 mi. of canals into 70 islands, connected by 500 bridges.

The old part of the town owes its charm to its 17th- and 18th-century red brick houses, with high, pointed step-gables, and to the elm and linden trees that border the canals. The development of a distinctive modern style of architecture (the Amsterdam school) has ensured, however, that the newer districts are as beautiful as the old, and as characteristically Dutch. Pop. (1964 est.) 868,445 (mun.).

Plan and Development.—The medieval town, which had developed on both sides of the Amstel, is situated at the centre of the city, around the dam, in an area enclosed by the semicircular Singel (ditch or moat), outside which are the three main canals, constructed when the town's first big planned development took place in the 17th century: the Heren-, Keizers- and Prinsengracht. Within this area are two smaller canals running north–south; two others were filled in at the end of the 19th century. Two towers of the old fortifications are still standing: the Schreierstoren and the Sint Anthonieswaag (St. Anthony's weighing-house), now a historical and medical museum.

In this old part of the city are many ancient buildings. The

THE OUDE ZIJDS VOORBURGWAL, ONE OF THE OLDEST CANALS IN AMSTERDAM. IN THE BACKGROUND IS THE DOME OF SINT NICOLAAS-KERK, 1886

Oude Kerk (Old church) of St. Nicolas (1300) contains good 16th- and 17th-century glass; the Nieuwe Kerk (New church, 1408; rebuilt 1645), a fine building in which the sovereign of the Netherlands is invested during a session of the general assembly of the states general, stands near the dam. Next to it is the royal palace, built in classical Palladian style as a town hall by Jacob van Campen, 1648–55, and used as a palace after 1808, outside which stands the monument to those who died in World War II. Other notable old buildings are the Munttoren (Mint tower), the upper part of which was superimposed by Hendrik de Keyser in 1618 on to the remains of a medieval gate; the Zuiderkerk (1611), also by Hendrik de Keyser, in which is a permanent town-planning exhibition; the Trippenhuis (1662), originally the home of the patrician Trip family, now the Royal Academy of Science; the Westerkerk (1631), with the highest tower in Amsterdam (282 ft.), where Rembrandt is buried, which stands on the edge of the Jordaan, an old working-class district with a distinctive character; and the main building of the municipal university, the Oudemanhuispoort (Oldman's house gate). There are also good later buildings in this area: the Sint Nicolaas-Kerk (1886), the Centraal station (1889), the Exchange building (by H. P. Berlage, 1903) and the Shipping house, a good example of the Amsterdam school of architecture (1916). From early times the Jewish population has been concentrated in the east of the old town. The famous Portuguese synagogue (1670) and the house where Rembrandt lived and worked, now a museum containing many of his drawings and etchings, are located there. The three main squares of the old town are the Dam; the Leidseplein, where the Stadsschouwburg (city theatre) and the artists' *café,* the American, stand; and the Rembrandtsplein containing many cinemas and restaurants. The canals are lined with fine 17th- and 18th-century patrician houses.

The 17th-century development of the city (begun in 1612, completed in 1658, 1700) saw the enclosure of the town with the three canals, which were ringed by the Buitensingel, a moat with 26 bastions, now the Nassaukade, Stadhouderskade and Mauritskade. Building outside the Buitensingel began in the last quarter of the 19th century, when further extension was made necessary by rapid economic expansion, especially after the unification of Germany in 1871. Notable buildings in this area are the Rijksmuseum (1876–85); the Concertgebouw (concert hall, 1888), home of the famous Concertgebouw orchestra; and the municipal and shipping museums (1895 and 1922). Development at this stage was somewhat haphazard and a new systematic plan was adopted in 1907. After World War I the need for new houses became acute and a plan to increase the municipal territory fourfold was put into operation in 1921; this led to the development of the Amsterdam school of architecture, building mainly in brick. Several garden cities on the outskirts, in which low buildings predominate, belong to this period. The plan of 1928–34 laid down the main lines of the city's development to the year 2,000, envisaging the growth of population to approximately 1,000,000. Public buildings finished before World War II included the Royal Tropical institute (1916–26); the Olympic stadium, with 60,000 seats (1928); the nine-story State Insurance bank (1939); and the Amstel station (1939). Post-World War II buildings included a telephone exchange, a tax office 136 ft. high, the highest building in Amsterdam, and several interesting modern churches in the suburbs. Urban development took place chiefly toward the west.

There are several parks in the old part of the town, of which the best known is Vondelpark, named after the poet Joost van den Vondel. Between the Olympic stadium and the airport is the Amsterdamse Bos (the Forest park, 2,000 ac.). Started in 1928 it is 12 ft. below sea level and drained by 180 mi. of pipes. It contains a 2,200-m. rowing course used for international championships.

Amsterdam is the commercial, financial and cultural centre of the Netherlands and its stock exchange (*Beurs*) has achieved considerable importance. It is the seat of the Bank of the Netherlands, of the University of Amsterdam (1632) and of the Free Reformed university (1880). It is also the home of many scientific and learned societies, and of the state theatre and a national opera company. The city council awards annual prizes in literature, music, architecture, etc.

Communications, Shipping and Trade.—From Amsterdam communications radiate over the Netherlands and western Europe: roads connect it with The Hague, Rotterdam, Haarlem and North Holland; electric railways carry internal and transcontinental express traffic; the airport at Schiphol, 4½ mi. from the town, rebuilt after complete destruction in World War II, is one of the most modern in Europe. Amsterdam is also a centre of inland navigation, and the starting point of 245 truck-transport services and of 30 internal and trans-European bus services.

For centuries Amsterdam has been one of the chief outlets for the Rhine. At first the maritime route crossed the Zuider Zee, but as the entrance to the harbour gradually silted up, a 50-mi. canal through North Holland was opened (1824). In 1876 more direct communication with the North sea was established with the building of the 15-mi. North sea canal. At the sea end at IJmuiden there are huge locks. A new canal, the Merwede, was begun in 1892 and enlarged in 1952. It has one of the biggest inland sluices in Europe. After World War II new harbour installations for wood and oil developed west of the town and a power station, built in 1953, formed the centre of a growing industrial area.

Amsterdam had always been a piece-goods port, importing and processing goods from the east (tobacco, tea, rubber, cacao, spices). Industrial development between and after World Wars I and II brought changes, and in postwar traffic, greater in the late 1950s than in the 1930s, bulk goods played an important part. Annual traffic in the port averaged 7,000 ships.

The principal industries, employing more than 150,000 in the 1950s, of whom 25% were women, are those relating to metal, clothing, building, foodstuffs and beverages, chemicals, printing, leatherware, timber, paper and diamonds.

History.—Amsterdam originated in the 13th century as a small fishing village, held in fee by the lords of Amstel from the bishops of Utrecht. Its development began with the building of a dam to keep out the sea by Gisbertus III and it is first mentioned as a town in 1275, when a charter of Floris IV, count of Holland, exempted it from certain taxes. In 1296 it passed out of the hands of the lords of Amstel, because of the part played by Gisbertus IV in the murder of Count Floris V, and was bestowed by Count John (d. 1304) on his brother, Guy of Hainaut, who granted its first charter in 1300. In 1343 more extensive privileges were granted by Count William IV. It was walled in 1482.

During the 15th century Amsterdam developed into one of the most important trading centres of northern Europe. In 1367 it had joined the Confederation of Cologne, and its position as port for the Rhineland towns ensured its prosperity. In the religious wars of the 16th century it benefited from the influx of refugees from Antwerp and Brabant; because of its trading interests, it did not join the other towns in their revolt against Spain until 1578. However, its adherence to the nationalist Protestant side (against Catholic Spain) did not adversely affect its prosperity; it gained from the fact that Antwerp, another great trading centre, remained in Spanish hands. The Dutch voyages of discovery, and the founding (1602) of the Dutch East India company, enlarged its sphere of influence, and the policy of religious toleration in the northern Netherlands brought in new waves of refugees with their special skills—Jews from Spain and Portugal, merchants from Flanders, Huguenots from France. This led to a fourfold extension of the city at the beginning of the 17th century. In the 17th and 18th centuries it played a leading part in Dutch policy and this led to conflicts with the government, which had its seat at The Hague, although Amsterdam was the commercial capital. In 1650 it withstood attack by William II of Orange and in 1672 was defended by Stadtholder William III when attacked by Louis XIV, but in 1787 it was occupied by the Prussians and in 1795 the French commander Charles Pichegru was able to capture it because the exceptional cold froze the surrounding water into ice. It was then made capital of the Batavian republic, and in 1806 became capital of the kingdom of Holland established by Napoleon under the rule of his brother Louis. In 1810, when Holland was incorporated into the French empire, Amsterdam was designated its third city, after Paris and Rome. It became capital of the kingdom of the Netherlands when independence was proclaimed in 1813, sharing the status with Brussels until the separation of Holland and Belgium in 1830. During World War II, from 1940 to 1945, it was occupied by the Germans, and almost all the Jewish population (10% of the total) was deported. After the war Queen Wilhelmina granted it the use of the motto *Heldhaftig, Vastberaden, Barmhartig* ("Heroic, Resolute, Merciful") under its coat of arms, in recognition of the conduct of its people during the occupation.

See also Index references under "Amsterdam" in the Index volume.

See H. Brugmans, *Geschiedenis van Amsterdam*, 8 vol. (1930–33); P. J. Mijksenaar, *Amsterdam, Verleden, Heden, Toekomst* (1951).

(P. J. M.)

AMSTERDAM, city of Montgomery county, in eastern New York, U.S., lies on the north and south shores of the Mohawk river, about 31 mi. N.W. of Albany.

Amsterdam was settled by Albert Veeder of Schenectady in 1783 although other settlers were reported there as early as 1775. It was called Veedersburg until 1804, when its present name was adopted. It was incorporated as a village in 1830 and chartered as a city in 1885. Amsterdam grew in importance after the opening of the Erie canal in 1825 and the coming of the first railroad in 1836. A principal factor in its growth was its location on the low-level Mohawk river route through the Appalachian mountains. Through this natural corridor passed settlers headed west, many of whom stayed in the area. Once an important centre for the manufacture of rugs, carpets and other textiles, beginning with establishment of the carpet industry in 1838, the city began to shift to the manufacture of other goods in the 1950s. These included plastics, automotive, electronic and communications equipment, textiles and leather goods. For comparative population figures *see* table in NEW YORK: *Population*. (P. F. W.)

AMU-DAR'YA (ancient OXUS; Arabic JAYHUN) is the largest river of Soviet Central Asia, exceeding its nearest competitor, the Syr-Dar'ya (*q.v.*) by about two to three times in volume of flow. The headwaters rise in the lofty mountain ranges of Soviet Tadzhikistan and northern Afghanistan at elevations of up to 16,000 ft. In its upper, mountain-girt basin the Amu-Dar'ya follows a westerly course and, together with its upstream extensions, the Pyandzh (Panj) and the Pamir, constitutes the international frontier between the U.S.S.R. and Afghanistan. The river receives the name Amu-Dar'ya only below the confluence of the Pyandzh river with the Vakhsh, a tributary feeding into the main stream from the north. After leaving the highland zone, the Amu-Dar'ya veers to the northwest and crosses the desert expanses of the Turanian lowland to its mouth on the Aral Sea. In the lowland zone it forms the boundary between the Kara-Kum desert to the west and the Kyzyl-Kum desert to the east.

The upper, or ancient, delta begins at a point 240 mi. from the river's mouth, and the lower, or contemporary, delta 100 mi. from the mouth. In the lower delta the Amu-Dar'ya branches into a number of distributaries. Total length of the river from source to mouth is about 1,578 mi., of which almost one-half is in the mountain zone. Approximate area of the Amu-Dar'ya's basin is 180,000 sq.mi.

In ancient times the Amu-Dar'ya flowed into the Sary-Kamysh depression, a large dry basin to the west of the upper delta, rather than into the Aral Sea as at present. Part of the water in the Sary-Kamysh depression followed the channel of the Uzboy westward and discharged into the Caspian Sea near Krasnovodsk. The Uzboy dried up 2,000–3,000 years ago. The Turkmen Canal scheme, authorized in 1950 but subsequently abandoned, envisaged the diversion of water along this route for the irrigation of large acreages in western Turkmen Soviet Socialist Republic.

Hydrologically, as well as physiographically, the Amu-Dar'ya's basin consists of two units: the mountainous zone of nourishment and the lowland zone of depletion. In the upper basin, tributary streams flowing off the mountain slopes swell the main river as it wends its way westward along the international frontier. Major tributaries entering the river from the north, or Soviet, portion of the basin, are the Gunt, Bartang, Kyzyl-Su, Vakhsh, Kafirnigan, and Surkhandar'ya. The two main tributaries from the south, or Afghan, portion of the basin, are the Kokcha and Kunduz. Although 40% of the zone of nourishment lies within Afghanistan, a smaller share, not likely exceeding 25%, of the Amu-Dar'ya's runoff originates in that country. In its middle and lower courses across the Turanian lowland no tributaries enter the river and it is rapidly depleted through irrigation, seepage, and evaporation. The total average annual discharge of the river at Nukus, at the head of the lower delta, is about 38,000,000 ac.ft. (52,500 cu.ft. a second); at Kerki, 500 mi. upstream, the mean annual discharge is 52,500,000 ac.ft.

About 60% of the Amu-Dar'ya's runoff is concentrated in the four-month period from May to August. The river is fed to a large extent by meltwater from high perennial snow fields and alpine glaciers, and flows remain at a high level throughout the entire summer, peak discharges being recorded in July. In its lower course the Amu-Dar'ya is ice-covered for a period of two to two and one-half months; farther to the south, in its middle reaches, it rarely freezes. It is navigable up to the mouth of its tributary the Kokcha, or for a distance of almost 900 mi.

Irrigation has been practised in the basin of the Amu-Dar'ya since ancient times. The irrigated acreage of field crops in the Soviet portion of the basin expanded from about 1,000,000 ac. in the late 1920s to an estimated 1,500,000 ac. by the mid-1950s. About 65% of the irrigated land is in the delta region, 15% along the west bank of the middle course (between the Soviet-Afghan frontier and the delta) and 20% in the upper basin, primarily in the valleys of the Vakhsh, Surkhandar'ya and Kafirnigan. Cotton is the principal crop.

Several schemes have been proposed for diverting water westward to irrigate vast tracts between the Amu-Dar'ya and Caspian Sea. Construction of the Kara-Kum canal along the southern edge of the Kara-Kum desert was begun in the late 1940s and, after an interruption of several years, resumed in 1954. The scheme ultimately envisages a canal 550 mi. in length from the Amu-Dar'ya to a point west of Ashkhabad, irrigating an area of up to 1,100,000 ac. The abandoned Turkmen Canal scheme was planned to skirt the northern edge of the Kara-Kum desert.

Only a minor fraction of the Amu-Dar'ya's water resource is yet utilized for irrigation. It represents the last major source of surface water which can be tapped for irrigation expansion in Soviet Central Asia.

Hydroelectric development is confined to a few installations, of small to medium capacity, on upstream tributaries. (N. C. F.)

AMULET, an object, whether natural or made by man, believed to be endowed with special powers of protection or of bringing good fortune. In the latter capacity an amulet may also be called a talisman, or in modern usage a charm or mascot (though mascot is a wider term which can also include animals). Amulets are carried on the person or kept in the place which is

ANCIENT GEM AMULETS. (LEFT) AGATE AND (RIGHT) GREEN PORPHYRY FROM LATE MINOAN AND MYCENAEAN PERIODS; (CENTRE) BABYLONIAN GLAZED FAIENCE

the desired sphere of influence, for example, on a roof or in a field.

Natural amulets can be of many kinds: precious stones, metals, teeth and claws of animals, plants, etc. Man-made amulets are equally varied: for instance, small models of animals or of objects, medallions bearing religious pictures or inscriptions (such as invocations to deities, the tetragrammaton, texts from the Bible or the Koran), and lockets containing such inscriptions on paper or metal.

CARL G. DIEHL

AFRICAN AMULET FROM TANGANYIKA; MADE FROM THE GALL BLADDER OF A DOG

Amulets have been and are widely used by both primitive and civilized people, though as receptacles of superstitious belief and magical properties they have always incurred the disapproval of the Christian church.

Amulets are thought to derive power from their connection with natural forces, from religious associations (as for instance of a holy image or inscription) or from being made in a ritual manner at a time of favourable planetary influence out of material and in a shape suiting the purpose. An Indian advertisement in 1943 gave a list of 12 purposes (with three degrees of effective power for each) including financial gain, the cure of diseases, finding employment and getting married.

BIBLIOGRAPHY.—E. A. W. Budge, *Amulets and Superstitions* (1930); M. J. Marquès-Rivière, *Amulettes, talismans et pantacles* (1938); C. Bonner, *Studies in Magical Amulets, Chiefly Graeco-Egyptian* (1950). (C. G. Di.)

AMUNDSEN, ROALD (1872–1928), Norwegian explorer who must be regarded as one of the greatest in the field of polar exploration, discoverer of the south pole, was born at Borge, on July 16, 1872, a few miles south of Oslo. He studied medicine for a while and then took to the sea. In 1897 he joined a Belgian expedition as mate. The ship, the "Belgica," was the first to winter in the antarctic and Amundsen, with the American physician-explorer F. A. Cook, was largely responsible for bringing the crew through severe attacks of scurvy. In 1903 he made plans for conquering the northwest passage in a sloop of 47 tons named the "Gjöa." With a crew of six he sailed secretly to escape creditors. He was the first man to take a ship through the passage, and it focused his attention on the spectacular in polar exploration. His next plan, to drift across the north pole in F. Nansen's old ship, the "Fram," was affected by the news that Robert E. Peary, the American explorer, had reached the pole in 1909, but he continued his preparations. When he left Norway in June 1910 no one but his brother knew that he was heading for the south pole instead of the north. He sailed the ship direct from the Madeira Islands to Ross sea and there set up a base 60 mi. nearer the pole than Captain R. F. Scott, the English explorer. It was vital that he should be first at the pole and this he did in an amazing journey by dog sledge with four companions. With funds from this dramatic journey he successfully took up the shipping business and then built a new ship, the "Maud," with which to carry out his original plan. He left port in 1918, again secretly, so as to avoid German submarines and made the northeast passage to Bering strait. There things went wrong and he abandoned his plan in favour of trying to reach the north pole by air. In 1925 he made an adventurous journey with the American explorer Lincoln Ellsworth and got to within 170 mi. of it. In 1926 he tried once more, in the dirigible "Norge," and succeeded, jointly with Umberto Nobile of Italy, crossing from Spitsbergen to Alaska. Disputes arising over who should be credited with this flight embittered his later years.

Amundsen was lost over the arctic seas when on June 18, 1928, he joined in the attempt to rescue Nobile who had crashed in the dirigible "Italia." No trace of Amundsen's airplane was found.
　　　　　　　　　　　　　　　　　　　　　　　　(F. De.)

AMUR, an *oblast* of the Russian Soviet Federated Socialist Republic, U.S.S.R., was formed in 1932 from Khabarovsk *krai;* its present boundaries were established in 1948, giving it an area of 140,425 sq.mi. The *oblast* occupies the basins of the middle Amur and its tributary the Zeya, extending up to the crest of the Stanovoi range. The southern part is the fertile black-earth lowland of the Zeya-Bureya plain, which until the advent of the plow was covered by a steppe-like vegetation. The higher north and east is almost all forest-covered.

The population was 717,514 in 1959, most of which was of Russian or Ukrainian stock. The largest of the 16 indigenous groups are the Yakuts and Evenki of the north. The chief town and administrative centre is Blagoveshchensk (*q.v.*).

Agriculture is concentrated in the lowland and where virgin land has been plowed. Grain, chiefly spring wheat, occupies nearly three-quarters of the cultivated area, and maize has also been introduced. Soybeans and sunflowers are the main industrial crops. Opencast coal of low quality is mined at Raichikhinsk. In the north gold is mined.

Timber production for matches, telegraph poles and pit props is important but not fully developed. The main arteries of communication are the navigable Amur and the Trans-Siberian railway, which has feeders to the Amur river at Blagoveshchensk and elsewhere.

Russians first reached this area in the 17th century, but by the 1689 treaty of Nerchinsk yielded it to the Chinese. In the 19th century Russian colonization recommenced and in 1858 the area was incorporated in Russia.　　　　　　　　　　(R. A. F.)

AMUR (Chinese Hei-lung chiang), a river of eastern Asia, forming part of the Soviet-Chinese frontier. The Amur is formed by the confluence of the Shilka and the Argun. The Shilka, in turn, is formed by the junction of the Ingoda, rising near Mt. Sokhondo in Soviet Transbaikalia, and the Onon, which flows from Outer Mongolia. The Argun, known as the Hailar in its upper course, rises on the western slopes of the Khingan mountains and is connected by an intermittent channel with the lake Dalai Nor (Hu-lun ch'ih), which receives the Kerulen river from Outer Mongolia. The Amur river flows to Amur bay of the Tatar strait, which separates the island of Sakhalin from the Siberian mainland and connects the Sea of Okhotsk with the Sea of Japan. Counting the Shilka-Onon system, the Amur river has a length of 2,705 mi.; the Amur proper, from the Argun-Shilka confluence, is 1,768 mi.

long.

The Chinese name Hei-lung chiang means Black Dragon river; another Chinese name is Hei Ho (Black river). The origin of the name Amur is disputed. Some authorities link it to Mamu, a name given to the river in its lower reaches by local tribes; others derive the name Amur from Khara-muren (Black river), a Mongol-Tungus designation of the river. The Amur river flows past the cities of Blagoveshchensk, centre of the Zeya-Bureya agricultural plain, and Khabarovsk and Komsomolsk, Soviet industrial centres, and the fishing port of Nikolayevsk. The principal tributaries are the Zeya and Bureya rivers on the left and the Sungari and Ussuri (also a Soviet-Chinese border stream) on the right. The Amur proper is navigable in its entire length during the ice-free season, which lasts from May to October. During this season the Amur reaches its high-water stage due to summer monsoon rains. The river carries grain, salt and manufactured goods downstream, and crude and refined oil, fish and timber upstream. The Soviet bank of the Amur, which is paralleled by the Trans-Siberian railroad and is relatively well developed economically, contrasts sharply with the sparsely settled Chinese bank.

The Russians first appeared on the banks of the Amur in 1644, when Vasily Poyarkov's Cossacks reached the river from Yakutsk. Another Russian, Yerofey Khabarov, explored the Amur valley in 1649–51. By the treaty of Nerchinsk (1689), the Argun became part of the Russian-Chinese boundary and the Chinese retained both banks of the Amur. By the treaty of Aigun (1858), confirmed by the treaty of Peking (1860), the Chinese ceded all lands north of the Amur and east of the Ussuri to the Russians. In 1956 Soviet and Chinese experts began to formulate long-range plans for joint utilization of the hydroelectric, transportation and economic potential of the Amur river basin.　　　　　(T. Sd.)

AMUSEMENT TAX. By the early 1960s the U.S. federal government, over two-thirds of the states and a number of localities imposed amusement taxes or taxes on admissions. All but a few of the state taxes were either applications of general sales taxes to admissions or special levies on admissions to racing and other sporting events. State rates varied in the 2% to 5% range, but most were 3%. Local taxes, confined to about one-fourth of the states, were usually 5% or less. The federal tax, after 27 years at 10%, was raised to 20% in 1944 and then cut to 10% in 1954 except for admissions to cabarets. By 1960 admissions costing less than $1 were exempt from the federal tax. Most of the yield came from admissions to motion-picture showings.

Events sponsored by or for religious, educational, governmental, charitable, symphony, opera and other nonprofit organizations had become widely exempted, but details varied. Federal taxes such as those on club dues and bowling alleys, and state and local licence taxes or charges on theatres or places of amusement are not strictly admissions taxes. The pure amusement tax is almost always quoted separately and presumably shifted to the buyer of the ticket.

The common justification for singling out this form of consumption for special taxation is that entertainment is not a necessity and that spending on recreation evidences somewhat more than ordinary taxpaying ability. Such views, however, seem to many economists and others to be far removed from modern notions of psychology, the sources of mental health and the economics of consumption above the most elemental level.　　　(C. L. H.; X.)

Great Britain.—The entertainment duty, which was introduced by the Finance (New Duties) act of 1916 and amended by subsequent finance acts before its repeal by the Finance act of 1960, was chargeable on all payments for admission to any exhibition, performance, amusement, game or sport in which the person being admitted was a spectator and not a participant; for instance, no duty was chargeable for admission to a whist drive. There were three scales of duty: (1) on performances in which the performers were actually present and their words or actions constituted the entertainment (*e.g.*, a play, concert, lecture or circus); (2) on entertainment including racing, games or exhibitions; (3) on entertainment which consisted of reproductions of words or actions of performers not actually present (*e.g.*, a film show).

Duty was generally paid by tickets of admission which had to be stamped to show that the duty had been paid. In certain cases admission through a barrier or turnstile was authorized. In some cases also the proprietor of the entertainment, who was responsible for payment of the duty, furnished returns of payments for admission.

Certain entertainments were entirely or partially exempt from duty, and these exemptions were gradually extended by successive finance acts in the 1950s. In 1955 a number of entertainments received exemption, including wholly educational entertainments, indoor entertainments in rural areas or in buildings holding not more than 400 persons, and a wide range of entertainments given by charitable or nonprofitmaking organizations. In 1957 the Finance act provided that entertainments duty should not be chargeable except in respect of entertainments consisting wholly or partly of a motion-picture or television show.

In 1958 the Entertainments Duty act consolidated the previous enactments on this subject. Finally this act itself was repealed, and any entertainments duty unpaid at the passing of the Finance act in 1960 and chargeable on a payment for admission to an entertainment given after April 9 of that year was remitted, by virtue of section 4 of the act. The duty was thus abolished.
(W. T. Ws.)

AMYL ACETATE, the collective term applied to the acetic acid esters of any amyl alcohol or mixture of amyl alcohols. All of the amyl acetates are colourless, neutral, mobile liquids having pleasant fruitlike odours, hence the use of certain amyl acetates as essences in perfumery and cosmetics. Of the eight possible isomeric amyl acetates (empirical chemical formula $CH_3CO_2C_5H_{11}$), six are produced in commercial quantities. Amyl acetate is also known as banana oil.

The amyl acetates are powerful solvents, and with the exception of the small amounts used by the perfume and pharmaceutical industries, their commercial importance depends upon this quality. Production of amyl acetates in the U.S. declined rapidly after the peak years of 1944 and 1945. (D. G. Z.; N. C. S.; X.)

AMYL ALCOHOLS. There are eight of these alcohols theoretically possible. All are known, and the most important is isobutyl carbinol (or isoamyl alcohol), the chief constituent of fermentation amyl alcohol and consequently present in fusel oil (*q.v.*). It can be extracted from fusel oil by shaking this with strong brine, discarding the brine layer and collecting the portion boiling between 125° and 140° C. By shaking this product with hot aqueous calcium hydroxide, separating the oily layer, drying it with calcium chloride and collecting the fraction boiling between 128° and 132° C., a further degree of purification may be effected. A mixture of amyl alcohols that is used as a solvent for pyroxylin lacquers is manufactured by the chlorination of pentanes from petroleum and subsequent hydrolysis of the resulting amyl chlorides.

All eight amyl alcohols have the general formula $C_5H_{11}OH$, the differences being caused by the different ways in which the carbon atoms are linked together and by the different positions of the hydroxyl groups (OH). All have been obtained synthetically by the standard methods of organic chemistry.

AMYL NITRITE (ISOAMYL NITRITE), a liquid which finds application in medicine, since it dilates the blood vessels and gives quick relief from attacks of angina pectoris. It is used also to some extent in the preparation of diazonium and isonitroso compounds. It is prepared by passing nitrous fumes (from starch and concentrated nitric acid) into warm isoamyl alcohol; or by distilling a mixture of 26 parts of potassium nitrite in 15 parts of water with 30 parts of isoamyl alcohol in 30 parts of sulfuric acid. It is a yellow-coloured liquid of specific gravity 0.877, boiling at about 95°–96° C., of characteristic penetrating odour and having the composition $C_5H_{11}ONO$. It is insoluble in water, but dissolves readily in alcohol, ether, glacial acetic acid, chloroform or benzene. It is easily reduced by metal-acid combinations, with the formation of ammonia and isoamyl alcohol; and on hydrolysis with potassium hydroxide it forms potassium nitrite and isoamyl alcohol. When the liquid is dropped on fused potassium hydroxide, it forms potassium valerate. (F. L. A.)

AMYMONE, in ancient Greek legend, daughter of Danaüs. With her sisters, she had been sent to look for water, the district of Argos being then parched through the anger of Poseidon. Amymone, having thrown her spear at a stag, missed it, but hit a satyr asleep in the brake. The satyr pursued her, and she called for help from Poseidon, who threw his trident at the satyr. Where it fell a spring arose, which received her name. Aeschylus wrote a satyric drama on the subject. By the god Amymone became the mother of Nauplius, the wrecker. Her meeting with Poseidon at the spring is frequently represented on ancient coins and gems.

AMYNTAS II or **III** (d. 370 B.C.), king of Macedonia from *c.* 393 to 370 B.C., came to the throne at a time of confusion and disorder which had persisted since the death of the strong king Archelaus in 399. Externally he was beset by the Illyrians and by the Chalcidian league of Greek cities; the threat from the latter was removed when Sparta's intervention led to the league's being disbanded (379). Later he entered into alliances with Athens and with Jason of Pherae, the ruler of Thessaly, and played a minor role in Greek international politics. Philip II, who first made Macedonia a great power, was the youngest of his three sons.
See F. Geyer, "Makedonien bis zur Thronbesteigung Philipps II," *Historische Zeitschrift,* Beiheft xix (1930). (R. H. Si.)

AMYOT, JACQUES (1513–1593), French bishop and classical scholar, famous for his translation of Plutarch's *Lives* (*Vies des hommes illustres*), was born at Melun, near Paris, on Oct. 30, 1513. He was educated at Paris university and at Bourges, where he became professor of Greek and Latin and translated Heliodorus' *Aethiopica,* the romance of Theagenes and Chariclea. For this Francis I gave him the abbey of Bellozane. Amyot then went to Italy to study the Vatican text of Plutarch, on the translation of whose *Lives* (1559; 1565 ff.) he had been engaged for some time. He also undertook a mission to the Council of Trent. On his return to France he was appointed tutor to the sons of Henry II. Both favoured him on accession, Charles IX making him grand almoner in 1560. Amyot was made bishop of Auxerre in 1570, and spent the rest of his life there, troubled by insubordinate clergy but continuing to perfect his translations. He died at Auxerre on Feb. 6, 1593.

Amyot translated seven books of the historian Diodorus Siculus (1554), the *Daphnis et Chloé* of Longus (1559) and the *Opera Moralia* of Plutarch (1572), as well as the *Lives.* Idiomatic and lively in style, so that it reads like an original work, the *Vies des hommes illustres* was translated into English by Sir Thomas North (1579), and supplied Shakespeare with material for his Roman plays. The personal method of Plutarch appealed to a generation fond of memoirs, so that Amyot's book won immense popularity and exercised great influence upon several generations of French writers. Amyot took great pains to find out and to interpret correctly the best authorities, but the appeal of his translations lies in the simplicity and purity of language.
See A. de Blignières, *Essai sur Amyot et les traducteurs français au XVIe siècle* (1851); *Vies des hommes illustres* (1914).

AMYOTROPHIC LATERAL SCLEROSIS. Progressive muscular atrophy (PMA), amyotrophic lateral sclerosis (ALS) and progressive bulbar palsy (PBP) are all variations of a single disease process often referred to as "motor system disease." The outstanding feature is a progressive paralysis caused by an unexplained degeneration of the motor neurones in the spinal cord (PMA), spinal cord and cerebral cortex (ALS) and medulla oblongata (PBP).

The first symptom may be a weakness of a few of the muscles in the hand or arm or of the tongue, pharynx and larynx, the latter presenting itself as a difficulty in speech or swallowing. Twitchings of parts of muscles (fasciculations) and cramps are common. Later other muscles are involved. The limbs become either stiff with overly active reflexes or slack with reduced reflexes, depending on whether cortical or spinal motor neurones are predominantly affected. The senses are unimpaired and the intellect remains sound.

The onset is insidious, usually occurring in the fifth and sixth decades of life, and the course is usually progressive to a fatal termination in two to six years. The disease is rare and, as a rule, nonfamilial. The cause is unknown and there is no effective treatment. (R. D. A.)

ANABAPTISTS, called among themselves more commonly "Christian Brethren," constituted the massive radical or left wing of the Reformation. Their most distinctive tenet was adult baptism. In the first generations of the movement converts exposed themselves to the charge of submitting to a second baptism and were liable to capital punishment according to provisions against rebaptism in the Theodosian and Justinianic codes which were revived to cope with them.

The Anabaptists themselves, of course, denied that they were rebaptizers, for they repudiated their own baptism in infancy as a blasphemous formality. They considered their entry into "the covenant of a good conscience with God" in the public avowal of sin and faith, sealed by adult baptism, as the only proper implementation of the apostolic ordinance. They refused to consider the baptism of children, practised by classical Protestants in continuation of Catholic usage, as containing any of the essential elements of the true ordinance such as repentance, experiential faith and a responsible pledge to lead a Christian life. In their insistence on personal faith and accountability ("the Christian life is not child's play"), the Anabaptists held that the Protestant equation of circumcision under the Old Covenant and infant baptism under the New was a monstrous distortion of the gospel. Likewise they repudiated the interrelated doctrines of original sin and predestination on which this postulate of equivalence was theologically grounded (*e.g.*, by Zwingli). They held instead that Christ's atoning work had wiped out the consequences of Adam's fall for all mankind and that therefore infants were henceforth not punishable for sin until an awareness of good and evil emerged within them, whereupon by the exercise of their own free will (as against Luther's conception of the bondage of the will in respect to one's decision for salvation) they might appropriate the remedy instituted by Christ for the burden of personally committed sins, namely, the rite of believers' repentance and baptism.

In keeping with their distinction between circumcision and baptism, between the Old Testament and the New, the Anabaptists also on principle separated the church, which to them was the community of the redeemed, from the state, which for them was ordained solely for the punishment of sinners. This principle they defended with their lives in thousands of fiery, bloody or watery martyrdoms, thereby testifying to their conviction that no magistrate, whether a reforming Protestant or a defender of the Catholic order, had competence in the sphere of Christian regeneration nor any right to use coercion in the mysterious realm of faith and conscience. Most Anabaptists, indeed, opposed the use of the sword by Christians alike in the maintenance of social order and in the conduct of a just war, even in the defense of Christendom against the Turks. In their strict compliance to the laws of Christ they also refused to swear the civil oath.

Unlike the classical or magisterial Protestants, who on principle made use of the magistrate to implement their Reformation, the Anabaptists were not aiming at reform of the medieval church. They were determined instead to restore the institutions and the spirit of the primitive church in their utter confidence that they were living at the end of all ages. Hence they readily recognized in their leaders divinely summoned prophets and apostles. Hence also all converts, including women, the peers of men, stood ready to give a full account of their faith before the magistrates. In their restorationist urge, they identified their suffering with that of the martyrs and confessors of the first three Christian centuries.

Northwestern Europe.—Anabaptism was first organized in separate conventicles in the canton of Zürich in Jan. 1525 under the leadership of the young patrician Conrad Grebel (*q.v.*), erstwhile associate of Zwingli. The first to receive rebaptism was the former priest George Blaurock of Grisons. This radical evangelical movement spread rapidly like a revival with itinerant evangelists into the other cantons and thence into south Germany, there winning a notable convert in Balthasar Hubmaier, the reformer of Waldshut. The Swiss movement formulated some of its more distinctive convictions in the seven articles of the Con-

fession of Schleitheim drawn up in 1527 under the leadership of Michael Sattler.

A second and apparently independent hearth of Anabaptism was Augsburg, where Hans Denck, formerly of Nürnberg, rebaptized Hans Hut, who had once been a follower of the radical spiritualist Thomas Münzer (*q.v.*). Denck, more contemplatively inclined than Hut and inspired by the mysticism of Johann Tauler (*q.v.*), by young Luther's spiritualism and by Münzer's passion for social justice, stressed the redemptive importance of imitating Christ's suffering in patient abandon to the will of God (*Gelassenheit*) and the attendant purification of the will in preparation for the acceptance of the baptismal "covenant of a good conscience." Denck's disciple Hut carried over from Münzer more of the sense of the imminence of the Latter Days and the judgment of God and became the main apostle of Anabaptism in the upper valley of the Danube.

In Austria and the Tyrol and particularly in Moravia (which, under tolerant lords eager for enterprising colonists, quickly became an asylum for the persecuted Anabaptists from all parts), a third type of Anabaptism emerged which stressed the community of goods on the model of the primitive church in Jerusalem and under the influence also of an epistle (IV Clement) wrongly attributed to Clement I of Rome. Under the leadership of the charismatic Tyrolean Jakob Hutter, who imposed his will with the authority of a latter-day apostle, the burgeoning communistic colonies assumed his name. Hutterites survive to this day, mostly in the western states and provinces of the United States and Canada.

A fourth major regional variant of Anabaptism arose under the leadership of the former Lutheran evangelist turned radical apocalyptist, the furrier-prophet Melchior Hoffman (*q.v.*). In Strasbourg, where he was converted to Anabaptism, he came to espouse the view, shared in one form or another also by Kaspar von Schwenckfeld and Michael Servetus (*qq.v.*), that Jesus Christ's human nature derived not from the substance of Mary his mother but from God the Father and was brought with him from heaven, a celestial flesh identical with the manna which sustained the children of Israel in the desert. The doctrine was thus not only christological but also eucharistic and was the theological basis for a perfectionist conception of the church, to which the convert was admitted by believers' baptism, in which he was sustained by progressive incorporation into the eucharistic body, and from which, by a communally exercised ban, he could be excluded at the slightest infraction of the stern code of the disciples of Christ. Melchior Hoffman was the apostle of the lower Rhine and the Netherlands, beginning in 1530.

Hoffman was himself imprisoned on a return journey to Strasbourg in 1533. His eschatological fervour was misappropriated by the Dutchmen Jan Mathijs and later John of Leiden (Jan Beuckelson), who converted the radical reformation of Münster under Bernard Rothmann, a former Lutheran, into a communist, polygamous, Maccabean theocracy (1534–35). Over this community John ruled as the Anabaptist king with pretensions to global sway in preparation for the second coming of Christ and the Fifth Monarchy (the millennium).

The excesses of the bellicose Münsterites confirmed the evil reputation of all Anabaptists in the eyes of the classical Protestants and the Catholics. Both Protestants and Catholics henceforth, with little discrimination between the belligerent minority centred in Münster and the pacifistic majority elsewhere, intensified throughout central Europe the mandates and judicial procedures against what seemed to be an omnipresent conspiracy, at once seditious and blasphemous, on the part of the lower classes. The pacifistic Netherlands and north German Anabaptists now rallied under the leadership of the former priest Menno Simons (*q.v.*) and his lieutenant Derck Philips. They have survived in large numbers to the present day under the name of Mennonites (*q.v.*).

With the collapse of the Münsterite kingdom, Anabaptism extended as a movement of the people from Hull to Danzig, from Brussels to Venice.

Italy and Eastern Europe.—In the Po valley and particularly in Venetia and the Italian-speaking valleys within the jurisdiction of the relatively tolerant confederation of the Three Leagues of Raetia (Graubünden or Grisons), another regional variant developed under the influence of Servetus, an immersionist, and particularly of Camillo Renato. The distinctive features of Italian Anabaptism were a distrust of the Nicene formulation of the doctrine of the Trinity; a stress on the doctrine of election for salvation which attenuated the covenantal and ecclesiological significance of believers' baptism; and a widespread adherence to psychopannychism (the belief that the soul at death sleeps or even perishes altogether, to be resurrected with the body for the last judgment and eternal life with Christ). A large synod at Venice in 1550 articulated these views along with an adoptionist Christology which went much further than Servetus in the abandonment of the dogma of the Trinity.

Anabaptism in Poland and the grand duchy of Lithuania—though originally Mennonite, Silesian and Moravian and centred in the Dutch colonies in the marshy delta of the Vistula and related areas in ducal Prussia—at length transcended the language barrier, working within the radical sector of the Reformed Church to emerge as an important regional variant of the movement. Here its distinctive features were tritheism changing into ditheism and then unitarianism. Baptism was by immersion (instead of by pouring as with most other Anabaptists). Many members of the Polish gentry on becoming converts renounced the use of the sword and freed their serfs. Petrus Gonesius in 1558 was the first Pole to avow his adhesion to the Hutterite-Servetian version of Anabaptism before a duly convoked Reformed synod. Martin Czechowic and Gregor Pauli were other leaders. Vilna (Vilnius) in Lithuania (1563–66), Lublin, Cracow, Pinczow and the communistic colony at Rakow in Little Poland, beginning in 1569, were notable centres. Under the leadership of Faustus Socinus (see SOCINUS), a decade later, the Polish and Lithuanian Brethren were gradually converted to Socinianism, in which most of the typical Anabaptist characteristics, except for pacifism and adult baptism, were attenuated.

On their flight from Poland in the next century the Socinians introduced into Holland their practice of baptism by immersion, which was adopted by the Arminian Collegiants and by such liberal Mennonites as the Waterland *Doopsgezinden* (baptism-minded). In turn the practice of immersion was taken over by the English General Baptists exiled in their midst. English (Calvinistic) Baptists, however, were only indirectly connected with the Melchiorite (Hoffmanite) Anabaptists in England under Henry VIII and Elizabeth I, though the name Anabaptist with its Münsterite connotations was used of the Baptists by their foes in both old and New England into the 18th century.

Relationship with Baptists and Other Protestants.—Modern scholarship—still divided in assessing the genetic and theological relationship of 16th-century Anabaptism to normative or magisterial Protestantism on the one hand and, on the other, to the demimonde of late medieval piety and speculation—has variously characterized the movement as, at one extreme, a radical variant of authentic Protestantism, at the other as a Protestantized version of medieval conventicular dissent (Waldensianism, Hussitism, Sacramentism). Anabaptism was surely in one sense a radical sectarian version of the earlier Netherlands, Saxon and Swiss sacramentarian movement, represented by Cornelis Hoen, Karlstadt (*q.v.*) and Zwingli. It assimilated also and carried through, unambiguously or undialectically, such central Protestant affirmations as salvation by faith alone and the pre-eminence of the Bible over tradition, creed and canon law.

Precisely because of their evangelical fervour and biblicism, the Anabaptists were a continuous challenge to the more sensitive or conscientious leaders of classical Protestantism. Thus extended public disputations were as much a part of the 16th-century history of the movement as judicial hearings and persecutions. The most notable disputations, synodal and epistolary, within the radical Reformation itself were the Nikolsburg disputation in 1526 between Hubmaier and Hut over the legitimacy of using the sword; the debate in 1542 between the spiritualizer Kaspar Schwenckfeld and Pilgram Marpeck, the latter by then the principal organizer of south German Anabaptism; and the synod in Strasbourg in 1555 between the Netherlanders and the upper Germans over excommunication and Christology. The most notable confrontations with the classical Reformers, including Zwingli, Heinrich Bullinger (*q.v.*), Martin Bucer (*q.v.*) and Jan Laski (*see* LASKI), were the disputations of Zürich in 1525, Zofingen in 1532, Strasbourg in 1533, Berne in 1538, Worms in 1557, Frankenthal in 1571 and Emden in 1578.

More than was realized at the time on either side, the testimony and the stubbornness of the Anabaptists helped to build up the institutions and theology of classical Protestantism. Modern Protestantism, moreover, has in the perspective of the years come to see the Münsterite episode as an aberration of a movement some of the principles of which Protestantism has unconsciously assimilated or indeed openly espoused, notably the principle of the separation of church and state and the voluntary basis of church membership. *See also* REFORMATION: *Other Countries of Europe* and *Radicals, Anabaptists and Spiritualists; see* also references under "Anabaptists" in the Index.

BIBLIOGRAPHY.—R. J. Smithson, *The Anabaptists* (1935); John Horsch, *The Mennonites of Europe* (1942); Franklin Littell, *The Anabaptist View of the Church,* 2nd ed. (1958); G. H. Williams, *The Radical Reformation* (1962); *The Mennonite Encyclopedia,* 4 vol. (1955–59). (G. H. Ws.)

ANACARDIACEAE, the cashew family containing about 70 genera and 600 species of dicotyledonous trees and shrubs of both hemispheres, chiefly tropical. In North America *Rhus* and *Toxicodendron* (combined as one genus, *Rhus,* by some authors) are widely distributed and represented by about 20 indigenous species known as sumac, poison oak and poison ivy. Two other native genera *Metopium* and *Cotinus* are represented by the poison tree (*Metopium toxiferum*) of Florida and the smoke tree (*Cotinus americanus*) found from Tennessee to Texas.

The family is important for the edible nuts of the cashew (*Anacardium occidentale*) and pistachio (*Pistacia vera*); for the fruit of the mango (*Mangifera indica*), mombin (*Spondias* species) and Kafir plum (*Harpephyllum caffrum*); for resins, oils and lacquers obtained from the varnish tree (*Toxicodendron vernicifluum*) and the mastic tree (*Pistacia lentiscus*); for a few ornamentals (*Rhus* and *Cotinus* species); and for much of the commercial supply of tannic acid, obtained from the wood of the quebracho (*Schinopsis* species). *See* CASHEW; MANGO; MASTIC; POISON IVY; SUMAC; VARNISH TREE.

ANACHARSIS (? early 6th century B.C.), a legendary Scythian prince included in some ancient lists as one of the Seven Wise Men and extolled as a type of primitive virtue. Herodotus (iv, 76–77) describes how, after extensive travels abroad in quest of knowledge or as an ambassador, Anacharsis returned home and was killed by the Scyths either because he wanted to introduce the cult of the Great Mother of the Gods or because of his attachment to Greek customs. Later authors, however, offer more details, crediting Anacharsis with numerous aphorisms and citing an interview between him and Solon (*see* the "life" by Diogenes Laërtius, i, 101–105; also Lucian, *Scytha*). The Cynic philosophers represented Anacharsis as a "noble savage," to be contrasted with the degenerate Greeks. Ten letters anciently ascribed to him are obviously not authentic.

ANACHRONISM, a neglect or falsification, whether intentional or otherwise, of chronological relation (Gr. *ana,* "back," and *chronos,* "time"). Its commonest use is in the antedating of events, circumstances or customs; *i.e.,* in the introduction, especially in works of imagination that rest on a historical basis, of details borrowed from a later age. Anachronisms originate in disregard of the different modes of life and thought that characterize different periods, or in ignorance of the progress of the arts and sciences and other varying facts of history. Only since the close of the 18th century has this kind of misrepresentation jarred the general intelligence.

Anachronisms abounded in the works of Raphael and Shakespeare. Artists tended to represent characters in terms of their own nationality and time. The Virgin was pictured both as an Italian peasant and as a Flemish housewife; Alexander the Great appeared on the French stage in the full costume of Louis XIV down to the time of Voltaire. Modern realism, the progress of archaeological research and the scientific approach to history came to make an unconscious anachronism an offense. On the other hand, anachronisms may be introduced deliberately to achieve a burlesque or satirical effect; by contrasting contemporary customs or morals with an alien age the writer or artist re-evaluates the past or present, or both.

Thus Mark Twain wrote of a Connecticut Yankee visiting King Arthur's court, and James Ensor painted Christ entering Brussels.

ANACLETUS (Cletus), **SAINT,** the third pope, who occupied the papal chair 76–88 or 79–91. According to Epiphanius and Rufinus, he directed the Roman Church with Lindus, successor to St. Peter, during Peter's lifetime. He died probably as a martyr during the reign of Domitian. His feast day is April 26.

ANACONDA, a city in southwestern Montana, U.S., about 26 mi. N.W. of Butte; the seat of Deer Lodge county. Copperopolis was suggested as the name for the town, which was laid out under the direction of Marcus Daly in 1883. Anaconda was chosen since another Daly mining camp had the name of Copperopolis. The city marks its effective beginnings from 1884 when Daly located a copper smelter on Warm Springs creek, the closest source of a good water supply to his Butte mines. Large plant expansions in 1892 and 1902 and subsequent modernization made it one of the world's largest nonferrous and reduction works, which rank it still held after mid-20th century. The plant employed about 4,000 smelter workers after mid-20th century. The plant's smokestack, the largest of its kind, stands 585 ft. high and dominates the landscape. The manufacture of phosphate products is also an important industry.

Daly had hoped to make Anaconda the capital of Montana. His Montana hotel was one of the most ornate in the nation at the end of the 19th century, and his newspaper, the *Anaconda Standard,* had a plant as modern as any in New York city at the time, although the population was less than 5,000. (For comparative population figures *see* table in Montana: *Population.*)

Nearby recreational areas include Georgetown lake and adjacent fishing streams, as well as the rugged mountains adjoining the federal Pintlar Primitive area (145,000 ac. in the Deer Lodge, Beaverhead and Bitterroot forests), which provide excellent hunting in season.   (M. G. Bu.)

ANACONDA (*Eunectes murinus*), an aquatic boa (*q.v.;* family Boidae), inhabiting the swamps and rivers of Brazil, northeastern Peru and the Guianas in South America. The nonvenomous anaconda is the largest of American snakes and rivals the reticulated python (*q.v.*) as the largest snake in the world. Early travelers told exaggerated tales of its size and swallowing capacity, but the largest known do not exceed 30 ft. in length. There is great dread of this snake among the Indians, though authenticated cases of its having attacked man are few.

The general colour of the anaconda is olive-brown, with large oval black spots arranged in two alternating rows along the back, and with smaller white-eyed spots along the sides. The belly is whitish, spotted with black. The head is elongate, flat and very distinct from the neck. The nostrils are situated between three large shields.

ARTHUR W. AMBLER FROM NATIONAL AUDUBON SOCIETY

ANACONDA (EUNECTES MURINUS)

The anaconda feeds chiefly at night upon birds and other animals, which it kills by constriction. Good-sized caymans are regularly killed and eaten by anacondas. In contrast to the boa constrictor, the anaconda spends most of its time in the water, lying submerged with only a small part of its head above the surface, waiting for any suitable prey. Only seldom does it establish itself in the branches of trees as the boa does.

The young, born alive, are about 36 in. long at birth. A brood of 72 has been recorded.

A smaller species of anaconda, *Eunectes notaeus,* inhabits Paraguay and the northern part of Argentina. Other species have been described from northern South America.

See also Snake.

ANACREON (b. *c.* 570 B.C.), after Archilochus the most important writer of personal lyric poetry in the Ionic dialect of Greek, was born at Teos in Ionia (now Sighalik in Turkey). There is no direct evidence in his poetry that he accompanied the Teians to Abdera on their evacuation of Teos before the Persian advance (*c.* 545). His working life is associated mainly with the courts of "tyrants," the great patrons of art and literature in the 6th century. He appears first at the court of Polycrates of Samos (*c.* 539–522), and after the assassination of Polycrates by the Persian governor of Sardis, Anacreon is said to have been brought from Samos to Athens in a warship on the orders of Hipparchus, son of Pisistratus, the "tyrant" of Athens. It is not certain how long he survived the assassination of Hipparchus (514 B.C.), but his poems suggest that he lived to a considerable age, and his later popularity at Athens (attested by quotations and references in 5th- and 4th-century writers and Pausanias' statement that his statue stood on the acropolis beside that of Xanthippus, father of Pericles) allows the inference that he lived long

ALINARI

IDEALIZED REPRESENTATION OF ANACREON AFTER THE ANTIQUE. VILLA BORGHESE, ROME, ITALY

enough to ingratiate himself with at least some elements in the Cleisthenean "democracy" (perhaps even into the 5th century).

Pausanias describes the attitude of the statue mentioned above as "such as might be that of a man singing when in liquor"; and Anacreon's reputation throughout antiquity was that of a man for whom almost anything might be "an excuse for a glass," and any glass would inspire him to love and song. Few, if any, of his poems have been preserved complete; and it may be that those who have quoted short snatches of his poetry have done him an injustice by omitting the serious poems which there is reason to believe that he wrote, but it is true that most of the fragments which have survived deal with wine and love (and his beloved objects were of both sexes). His language and his metres are alike smooth and simple; and his technique is all but perfect. It is no wonder that many people in later times tried their hand at imitating him (whence the large collection of poems which go under the name of Anacreontics).

Bibliography.—Complete edition of fragments by B. Gentili (1958); most fragments ed. by J. M. Edmonds with Eng. trans. in *Lyra Graeca,* 2:120–221, Loeb series (1924). *See* also M. F. Galiano, "La lírica griega a la luz de los descubrimientos papirológicos," in *Actas del I congreso español de estudios clásicos,* pp. 111–119 (1958); C. M. Bowra, *Greek Lyric Poetry,* ch. 7 (1936); Freya Stark, *Ionia,* ch. 4 (1954).
           (Jn. A. D.)

ANACREONTICS are poems written in the metre and from the supposed outlook of Anacreon (*q.v.*). In Greek the metre is ◡◡–◡–◡––, and in modern European literature the line has seven or eight syllables with three or four main stresses. The

Anacreontic outlook is one of ironic enjoyment of life.

Greek Christian writers such as Clement of Alexandria, Gregory of Nazianzus and Sophronius wrote religious verse in the Anacreontic metre, but the best-known Anacreontics are the *Anacreontea,* a collection of about 60 short poems composed at various dates in the post-Classical period of Greek literature, first published by Henri Estienne as the work of Anacreon in 1554. These had a great influence on the Renaissance school of French poetry and were translated by Ronsard (1555) and Rémy Belleau (1556).

The word Anacreontiques was first used in England in 1656 by Abraham Cowley, who gives free translations of 11 *Anacreontea.* The following is an example:

> Oft am I by the Women told
> Poor Anacreon thou grow'st old.
> Look how thy hairs are falling all;
> Poor Anacreon how they fall.
> Whether I grow old or no,
> By th' effects I do not know.
> This I know without being told
> 'Tis Time to Live if I grow old.

There have been many translations of the *Anacreontea* into English, and Robert Herrick, William Oldys and William Shenstone, among others, tried original Anacreontics in English. Thomas Moore translated 60 *Anacreontea* and 19 "fragments," calling them "Odes of Anacreon," into English verse in 1800. The *Anacreontea* also had an influence on Italian and German literature.

See J. M. Edmonds, *Elegy and Iambus,* vol. 2, Loeb series (1931) for the *Anacreontea* with verse translation. (J. W. T.)

ANADYOMENE (Gr. *anaduomenē,* "emerging"). By a legend as old as Hesiod, Aphrodite was born from the sea. Hence in a famous picture by Apelles she was represented as having just emerged from the sea and in the act of wringing her tresses. This painting was executed for the temple of Asclepios (Aesculapius) at Cos, from which it was taken to Rome by Augustus, in part payment of tribute, and set up in the temple of Caesar. In the time of Nero, because of its dilapidated condition, it was replaced by a copy made by the painter Dorotheus.

ANADYR, a gulf of the Bering sea, a river and a town of the U.S.S.R. The gulf is in the extreme northeast of the Soviet Union on the coast of the Chukot National Okrug of the Russian Soviet Federated Socialist Republic, U.S.S.R. It lies between Cape Chukotski to the north and Cape Navarin to the south.

The river rises in the Anadyr plateau and follows a tortuous course of 694 mi. to the gulf of the same name; it drains about 57,915 sq.mi. and its average discharge is 5,000 cu.ft. per second. It is navigable to the village of Markovo. Its basin is bleak, thinly populated tundra but coal was discovered and is mined in small quantities.

The town lies on the south shore of the estuary of the Anadyr, centre of the Chukot National Okrug and a port on the Northern Sea route. It is a centre of fishing and reindeer-herding and since 1929 has produced small amounts of coal. A meteorological station of the Northern Sea Route administration is located there. (R. A. F.)

ANAGNI, a town of central Italy in the province of Frosinone in Lazio (Latium), is on a hill above the Sacco valley, 38 mi. by road E.S.E. of Rome. Pop. (1961) 15,740 (commune). The cathedral (1074) with its separate campanile is on the top of the hill and has a fine triple apse. The 13th-century Casa Barnekow stands at the entrance to the town. The Palazzo Communale and the palace of Boniface VII are 12th- and 13th-century buildings. The ancient city walls still stand. Buses connect with the station (6 mi. S.W.) on the Rome–Cassino–Naples railway. The Via Casiliana from Rome to Naples, and the Autostrada del Sole from Milan to Naples pass below the town. Anagni is an agricultural centre, and there are distilling, gas and rubber industries. In classical days as Anagnia it was capital of the Hernici (*q.v.*), losing its independence to Rome in 306 B.C. It was besieged by the Saracens in A.D. 877. Its leading medieval families were the Conti and Caetani. Four popes came from Anagni: Innocent III, Gregory IX, Alexander IV and Boniface VIII, who was captured there in 1303 (*see* BONIFACE). Damaged during World War II, Anagni was taken by the Allies in June 1944. (G. VI.)

ANAGRAM, the transposing of the letters of a word or group of words so as to produce other words that possess meaning. The construction of anagrams is of great antiquity, its invention being ascribed without authority to the Jews, probably because the later Hebrew writers, particularly the Cabalists, were fond of it, asserting that "secret mysteries are woven in the numbers of letters." Anagrams were known to the Greeks and also to the Romans, although the known Latin examples of words of more than one syllable are nearly all imperfect. They were popular throughout Europe during the middle ages and later, particularly in France, where a certain Thomas Billon was appointed "anagrammatist to the king."

The transposed word or words should, ideally, bear a logical relation to the original. The making of anagrams was an exercise of many religious orders in the 16th and 17th centuries, and the Angelical Salutation *Ave Maria, gratia plena, Dominus tecum* ("Hail Mary, full of grace, the Lord is with thee") was a favourite base; it was transposed to hundreds of variations, as, for example, *Virgo serena, pia, munda et immaculata* ("Virgin serene, holy, neat and immaculate").

Among other anagrams is that from Florence Nightingale into "Flit on, cheering angel." The pseudonyms adopted by authors are often anagrams. Some of the scientists of the 17th century—for example, Galileo, Christian Huygens and Robert Hooke—embodied their discoveries in anagrams with the apparent design of avoiding the risk that, while they were engaged in further verification, the credit of what they had found out might be claimed by others. In the 20th century, anagrams were frequently used in crossword puzzles, both in the clues and the solutions.

See H. B. Wheatley, *Of Anagrams* (1862); Archer Taylor, *A Bibliography of Riddles* (1939).

ANAH, a town of Iraq, lies on the Euphrates river 192 mi. below Dayr az Zawr and 119 mi. above Hit. Pop. (1957) 11,070, mostly Sunni Arabs. It retained its name at least from the beginning of the 2nd millennium B.C., but the actual site seems to have changed slightly. As late as the early 14th century A.D. it was on an island in the Euphrates, where the remains of a fortress and a minaret could still be seen in the middle of the 20th century. During the 17th century it lay on both banks of the river and was the residence of amirs of the al-Mwali tribe, which controlled the right bank from the territory of Tadmor to Hit. The town was sacked by the Persians shortly before 1629, became increasingly subject to raids from the desert and declined in size and prosperity. Alois Musil in 1912 reported the population as 700 Muslim and 500 Jewish families. Anah was confined 50 years later to a single, long street on the right bank of the river. Until the coming of motor transport it remained a staging post of some importance on the Euphrates valley route, which was joined at Anah by the desert route from Tadmor; but the modern road from Baghdad to Amman and the desert track to Damascus leave the Euphrates at Fellujah, and Anah became a local market town. It was formerly known for its wine and later for its palm groves; its products include butter and wool, and the strip of fertile land along the river yields cereals, fruit and dates. (E. E. D. M. O.)

ANAHEIM, a city of Orange county, Calif., U.S., 25 mi. S.E. of Los Angeles, in the fertile plain of the Santa Ana river. The area produces oranges, lemons, avocados, walnuts and vegetables. Anaheim is the largest industrial centre in the county.

Anaheim was the first co-operative settlement in southern California. In 1857, 50 Germans organized an association in San Francisco, bought 1,165 ac. of land and prepared it for occupancy. The tract was then divided into 20-ac. shares, which were distributed among the members by lot, with bonuses and rebates to equalize the differences in value. The town took its name from "Ana," the name of the river and "heim," the German word for home. The town was incorporated in 1870 and received a city charter in 1888; in 1950 a council-manager form of government became effective. The town grew steadily, to 14,556 by 1950. In the following decade the population increased more than 500%

chiefly because of the arrival of new industries and the rapid annexation of contiguous territory, and in 1960 the population was 104,184. In 1963 Orange county was designated a separate standard metropolitan statistical area (Anaheim-Santa Ana-Garden Grove), pop. (1960) 703,925. (For comparative population figures *see* table in CALIFORNIA: *Population*.)

In addition to local recreational facilities (the city has established a park site adjacent to each elementary school playground), the southern California beach, mountain and desert resorts are within short driving distances of the city. Disneyland, the amusement park, was opened in Anaheim in 1955.　　(WM. H. K.)

ANÁHUAC, a historical-geographic district of Mexico with indefinite boundaries. This was the heartland of Aztec Mexico, and in Nahuatl (Aztec) the name means "land by the water." In colonial times Anáhuac designated that part of New Spain which in 1821 became independent Mexico. The original Anáhuac of the Aztecs was the central plateau valley of Mexico, an area about 50 mi. long by 30 mi. wide, in which present-day Mexico City is located. When the Spaniards arrived in 1519 the valley contained five large interlocking lakes: Zumpango, Xaltocan, Texcoco, Xochimilco and Chalco. The Aztec capital Tenochtitlán (modern Mexico City, *q.v.*) was situated on islands in the middle of this series of lakes. Its streets were Venicelike canals and three long causeways connected the city to the mainland.

In 1607–08 the engineer Enrique Martínez dug a ditch and tunnel northward to the headwaters of the Pánuco river system and drained off much of the water of the five lakes. In the 20th century shrunken Lake Texcoco was further drained. Its salt marshes still remain, as do Xochimilco's "floating gardens," but the vast water area is now gone. Saline deposits made the reclaimed land almost unfit for agriculture. The lake beds also gave Mexico City a very unstable subsoil which necessitates the use of deep foundation piles in the construction of heavy buildings.

The Pánuco system drains the valley into the Gulf of Mexico, and the Lerma river drains the contiguous basin of Toluca (just west of Anáhuac) into the Pacific. The average elevation of Anáhuac is 7,500 ft., and its mean temperature is 60° F. May is the warmest month (65°) and January is the coldest (54.3°). Rainfall is heaviest in July (4.5 in.) and lightest in January (0.2 in.). *See also* MEXICO: *Physical Geography*.　　(J. A. CW.)

ANALCITE, sometimes referred to as analcime, is a common mineral of the zeolite group that usually occurs, associated with other zeolitic minerals, as beautiful glassy crystals lining amygdaloidal or vapour cavities in basic volcanic rocks such as basalt and melaphyre. Crystallizing in the cubic system, the common form is the icositetrahedron, either alone or in combination with the cube; it is often perfectly colourless and transparent with a brilliant glassy lustre, but sometimes it is opaque and white or pinkish-white. The Tertiary basalts of the north of Ireland frequently contain cavities lined with small brilliant crystals, and larger crystals of the same kind are found in the basalt of the Cyclopean Islands, Sicily. Large opaque crystals of the pinkish-white colour are found in cavities in melaphyre at the Seisser Alpe in southern Tirol. Analcite occurs in other zeolite areas, as in New Jersey and Nova Scotia, and good crystals have been found in copper mines in the upper peninsula of Michigan and at Table mountain, Colorado. Chemically, analcite is a hydrated sodium and aluminum silicate, $NaAlSi_2O_6 + H_2O$. The hardness is 5 to 5.5, and the specific gravity, 2.25. Before the blowpipe the mineral readily bubbles and gives up water, as other zeolites, and fuses to a colourless glass. It is decomposed by acids with separation of gelatinous silica. *See* ZEOLITE.

ANALGESIA is the name given to the loss of the sensation of pain, and is the result of an interruption of the nervous pathway between skin and brain. Different forms of sensation from one area of skin, such as touch, temperature and pain, travel to the spinal cord by different nerve fibres in the same nerve bundle. Hence any injury or disease affecting such a nerve would abolish all forms of sensation in the area supplied by it. However, when the sensory nerves reach the spinal cord their fibres separate and pursue different courses on their way upward to the brain. Thus it is possible for certain forms of sensation to be lost, while

others are preserved, in diseases which affect only certain areas in the spinal cord. Since the sensations of pain and temperature travel the same path, they are usually lost together. Diseases of the cord which may cause analgesia without loss of the sensation of touch are *tabes dorsalis*, syringomyelia and tumours of the cord. Analgesia may also be a manifestation of hysteria. The term is used for types of pain relief induced by the giving of various drugs. The term is used extensively in obstetric practice. *See* ANESTHESIA AND ANESTHETICS; OBSTETRICS.

ANALOGY. The term analogy (*ana logon*, "according to a ratio") was originally used by the Greeks to mean similarity in proportional relationships. Thus in Euclid's *Elements*, books v–vi, the word is used for a proportionate resemblance between two or more quantities. This may be a similarity between two figures (*e.g.*, triangles) which differ in scale, or a formula by which it is possible to calculate an unknown quantity if it is known that it stands in a relation to another quantity similar to that in which two other known quantities stand.

Thus, if $2:4::4:x$, it can be seen that $x = 8$. Another form of analogy noted by the Greeks was that of similarity of function performed by two elements in their respective contexts. (This kind of inference is now commonly known by psychologists as "educing the correlate," and the ability to perform it is held to be one of the tests of intelligence.) Aristotle (*Topics*, i, 17) states the formulas of these two kinds of analogy: "As A is to B, so C is to D"; and "As A is in B, so C is in D."

Plato makes particular use of analogies in the sense of arguments from similarity of function, of which the similes in his *Republic*, book vi, are among the most famous: for instance, the Idea of the Good is said to fulfil a function in making knowledge possible in the intelligible world similar to that performed by the sun in making vision possible in the perceptible world. A relationship not yet understood is indicated as analogous to one which is already familiar.

In the middle ages widespread use was made of arguments from analogy, on the belief that the universe formed an ordered structure of such a kind that the macrocosmic pattern of the whole was reproduced in the microcosmic pattern of the parts, so that it was possible to draw inferences from the one to the other. This belief underlay the mediaeval conception of the law of nature, in which the juridical sense of law, prescribing the fitting order of human relationships, could be assimilated to the physical sense of law, describing what was held to be the order obtaining in the natural world. The natural world was held to exhibit hierarchical degrees of subordination, from which it was argued that the proper ordering of human relationships should exhibit degrees of subordination, such as those of the patriarchal family as described in Aristotle's *Politics*.

Arguments which may seem purely allegorical can be seen to be built on this belief in an identity of pattern in different contexts, both as between the macrocosm and microcosm and as between the structure obtaining in one part of the world and that obtaining in another. Such parallels were held to constitute arguments and not merely allegorical illustrations; for instance, it was contended that, as there are two luminaries to light the world, the sun and the moon, and two authorities set over man, the spiritual authority of the papacy and the temporal authority of the empire, as the moon's light is reflected from the sun, so the imperial authority must be derived from the papal. Dante in his *De Monarchia*, while arguing against this particular analogy and claiming that the most that it could show is that the empire derives *light*, which is grace, and not *authority* from the papacy, nevertheless accepts the principles on which such arguments were built.

Analogy in Theology.—A uniquely important case of analogy was the comparison between God and His creatures, since no statement could be made about the Divine Nature which did not involve it. The classical treatment of the theological use of analogy is to be found in St. Thomas Aquinas (*Summa contra Gentiles*, I, xxxxxiv). He asks how we can use the same terms of God and creatures. They cannot be used univocally (in an identical sense), or we ignore the difference between infinite and finite being; they cannot be used equivocally (in quite unconnected senses), or we say nothing meaningful about God by using them. Nor should they be used only metaphorically, as when it is said that God may be imagined for purposes of illustration as doing something like what a creature does (*e.g.*, "the name of *lion* applied to God means only that God manifests strength in His works as a lion in his": St. Thomas, *Summa Theologica*, I, i, qu. 13, art. 6).

They must be used analogically, that is, in such a way as to say something positive about the Divine Nature while at the same time recognizing the distinction between the way in which God exists and the way in which creatures exist. Aristotle had already remarked (*Metaphysics*, vii, 1) that "being" is a term which is used in different senses in different categories: when we say that a quality exists, "exists" is not used in just the same sense as when we say that a substance exists.

According to St. Thomas, God is not in any category, therefore to say that He exists will not mean that He exists as a being in the same sense as a man or a material substance exists. He exists as infinite being itself.

The theological analogy which seeks to explain, *e.g.*, "God is wise," has the form called "analogy of proportionality." God's wisdom is said to be related to His infinite being in a way similar to that in which our wisdom is related to our finite being. It will be seen that there is here a double analogy: (1) the relation between God's infinite being and our finite being; and (2) the relation between the way in which God's wisdom is related to His infinite being and the way in which our wisdom is related to our finite being.

The analogy between the meaning of "wise" as applied to God and as applied to us rests therefore on there being a prior analogy between the meaning of "being" as applied to God and qualified by "infinite" and the meaning of "being" as applied to us and qualified by "finite" (*analogia entis*). So unless we know how God's existence stands to ours, we cannot determine the meaning of His wisdom.

To say what any term used of God may mean, it is therefore necessary first to be able to say something about the distinction between finite and infinite being and the relation between them. The distinction is drawn by appealing to the notion of perfection. Finite being is perfectible, while infinite being is perfect. So terms used of God must be used in a sense which expresses perfection, and not all creaturely attributes can be used analogically of God. Thus, it is held, we can say that the infinite existent is good and that it is not corporeal.

While the distinction in the analogy between the meaning of terms applied to infinite being and the meaning of terms applied to finite was drawn by qualifying them through the notion of perfection, the ground for the belief that terms so qualified can be used of God on analogy with what they mean when used of creatures was sought by looking for a positive relation between finite and infinite being to provide a basis for the analogy. This relation was that of the dependence of finite on infinite being. That infinite being exists and that finite being has this relation of dependence on it was claimed to be shown by the "argument from the contingency of the world."

This argument begins by stating that it is always possible in the case of finite beings to say that they might not have existed and goes on to maintain that their actual existence can only be explained by their causal dependence on an infinite being, which, if it existed at all, would exist necessarily; *i.e.*, a being such that it would not make sense to say that as a matter of fact it exists, but it might not have done so.

The argument, then, claims to establish not only the existence of infinite being, but also that finite beings are dependent on it as effects are dependent on cause and will resemble it insofar as they tend to perfection. (The connection between the notions of "infinite," "necessary" and "perfect" as applied to being is here assumed.)

Kant and certain 20th-century logicians have questioned this use of the conceptions of "necessary" and "cause." They hold that to speak of infinite being as "cause" of the world as a whole is not to use the word "cause" in the same sense as when we speak

of causes of contingent facts within the world which are themselves also within the sequence of contingent facts. The legitimacy of this extended use of the term is questioned; and if it is itself an analogy, how can it be appealed to as the basis on which analogies are based? Similarly, the notion of "necessary" is held to apply properly to propositions, and its meaning when applied to "being" is questioned. The problem of the justification of theological analogy is thus not solved but is referred one stage further back. (*See* Kant, "Transcendental Dialectic," *Critique of Pure Reason*; and C. D. Broad, in *Journal of Theological Studies*, vol. xl [1939]. For attempts to restate the argument, see A. M. Farrer, *Finite and Infinite* [1943]; and E. L. Mascall, *Existence and Analogy* [1949].)

It is likely that most forms of theological and metaphysical thinking, where language has to be used beyond its normal contexts, will make use of analogies, and the problem of their justification will be debated. Joseph Butler's *Analogy of Religion* (London, 1736) was, however, so entitled not for this reason but because it sought to show the likeness between religion, natural and revealed, and the course and constitution of nature, both being held to exemplify the same principles and to give rise to similar problems.

Analogy in Science.—In scientific thinking, analogy may be used in inductive arguments to suggest hypotheses. Resemblances between different sets of phenomena may be taken as suggesting, not mere accidental likeness, but the existence of some law or principle common to both sets. This is held to be especially probable where a comparison can be made between the functions of elements in two systems. Sometimes a relationship observed in one context may suggest a clue as to how another sought-for relationship is to be conceived, as when observation of the moons or satellites of Jupiter suggested by analogy the modern conception of the solar system. T. R. Malthus' argument that populations, if left uncontrolled, would tend to increase in numbers beyond the means of their subsistence suggested to Charles Darwin the hypothesis of natural selection as an evolutionary mechanism, whereby only the fittest to their environment survived out of large numbers. The fruitfulness of such analogies for scientific inquiries depends on whether consequences can be deduced from them which can be tested or observed, and this is likely to depend on whether the resemblance selected as analogous is of a fundamental or merely of a superficial kind. Resemblances of a functional kind are more likely to be fundamental than are qualitative resemblances such as those of colour. If structural relations can be reproduced in a simplified form in a different medium, a model may be constructed. For instance, an atom may be portrayed as if the elementary particles revolving round a nucleus were like a miniature solar system. But it would not be legitimate to conclude from this that, for example, the process of nuclear fission is similar to the process by which new planetary systems may be formed or disrupted. (*See* also INDUCTION.)

In social and political discussion, analogies often are used because of their persuasive power in bringing home some unfamiliar point in terms of what is more familiar. Thus biological analogies have frequently been used to suggest that the relation of members of a community to one another is an "organic" relationship in a "common life." Such analogies may be useful in so far as they suggest the mutual dependence of parts fulfilling different functions. They are misleading in so far as they omit the fact that individual members of the community also have purposes, rights and responsibilities of their own. An analogy is never an absolute likeness; it points to a similarity in certain respects, shown in contexts which will differ in other respects. In cases where appeal is made to analogy it should therefore be possible to show that the resemblances noted bear relevantly on the point to be established, while the differences are irrelevant for this purpose and can safely be ignored. In many cases it is difficult to be sure of this, and arguments from analogy are therefore precarious unless supported by considerations which can be established independently.

BIBLIOGRAPHY.—St. Thomas Aquinas, *Summa Theologica*, I, i, quaestio 13, and *Summa contra Gentiles*, I, xxix–xxxiv; M. Penido, *Le Rôle de l'analogie en théologie dogmatique* (1931); H. W. B. Joseph,

Introduction to Logic, 2nd ed., ch. xxiv (1916) ; L. S. Stebbing, *Modern Introduction to Logic,* ch. xiv (1930). (D. M. E.)

ANALYSIS (IN PHILOSOPHY), sometimes called "logical" analysis, has long been regarded as at least part of the philosopher's task. It was described by Kant as the process of stating, clearly and explicitly, what is already contained, though "covertly," in our concepts. In the 20th century, however, many philosophers have come to hold that analysis is the whole business of philosophy —that philosophy does not consist, as do other sciences, in the attempt to extend our knowledge but consists rather in the activity of making clear what we know already, removing problems and perplexities which are the result not of ignorance of fact but of conceptual confusion and misunderstanding. This view was at one time combined with the metaphysical doctrine that both facts and language could be resolved into their ultimate, absolutely simple elements and that all else could be exhibited systematically as a "construction" founded upon this ultimate basis. But philosophical analysis would now more commonly be regarded as a procedure of conceptual clarification to be pursued until the air is clear enough for one's present purpose or until some particular perplexity has been resolved, and not to be thought of as tending toward any metaphysically ultimate terminus. There is, however, no generally accepted doctrine about actual techniques of clarification; it would probably be denied that any general doctrine could be usefully formulated; and partly for this reason, many philosophers would regard the assertion that analysis is the proper business of philosophy as too vague to merit either acceptance or dissent. But the widespread verbal agreement on this point may serve to emphasize the markedly unmetaphysical character of most contemporary philosophy in English. It should be added that the predicate "analytic," as applied to propositions, is commonly used to distinguish a particular class of necessary truths.

ANALYSIS is one of three main divisions of mathematics, the other two comprising (1) geometry and topology and (2) algebra and arithmetic. In extent, analysis is the largest; it comprises subdivisions which are nearly autonomous and which are easier to describe than the division as a whole.

MEANING OF ANALYSIS

Relation to Science.—Greek mathematics had a geometrical tenor, as the works of Euclid, Archimedes, Apollonius of Perga and Pappus testify. It did initiate some durable topics of analysis, but the organized creation of analysis began only around A.D. 1600. Analysis then came into being in stages, growing up in intimacy with mechanics and theoretical physics. This is not to say that other mathematics does not enter into science, too; in fact, all mathematics does. The two great innovations in physics in the 20th century, relativity and quantum theory, had to rely heavily on existing mathematical tools of geometric and algebraic provenance. But whenever work in basic physics instigated a topic in mathematics spontaneously it was largely in analysis. Thus, differential and integral calculus, ordinary differential equations and the calculus of variations have arisen from mechanics; Fourier series from acoustics and thermodynamics; complex analysis (*q.v.*) from optics, hydrodynamics and electricity; and partial differential equations from elasticity, hydrodynamics and electrodynamics. And even mathematical probability, which falls under analysis, although born from problems of gambling and human chance, drew much of its syllogistic strength in the 19th century from statistical theories of mechanics and thermodynamics.

Derivatives.—Geometry deals with spaces and configurations, topology with spatial deformations, algebra with the general nature of the basic operations of addition, subtraction, multiplication and division, and arithmetic with additive and multiplicative properties of general integers. Analysis also deals with specific operations, namely with differentiation and integration. But it is more appropriate to say that it deals with the mathematical "infinite" in many of its aspects, such as those of an infinite multitude, the infinitely large, infinitely small, infinitely near, infinitely subdivisible. Its first objects and concepts, introductory and yet actively basic, are infinite sequence, infinite series, a function $y = f(x)$, continuity of a function, derivative of a

function $y' = df/dx'$, and integral of a function. The mathematical concept of the derivative is a master concept, one of the most creative concepts in analysis as well as in all of human cognition. Without it there would be in scientific investigation no velocity or acceleration or momentum; no density of mass or electric charge or any other density; no gradient of a potential and hence no concept of potential in any part of physics; no wave equation; no mechanics, no physics, no technology, nothing. The formal textbook definition of the concept took more than 150 years to evolve, but even to the untutored it will be rewarding to savour Isaac Newton's own description of it under the name of "ultimate ratio":

> For those ultimate ratios with which quantities vanish are not truly the ratios of ultimate quantities, but limits towards which the ratios of quantities, decreasing without a limit, do always converge: and to which they approach nearer than by any given difference, but never go beyond, nor in effect attain to, until the quantities have diminished *in infinitum.*

Newton's generation was literate enough to listen to a recondite mathematical definition, all in words, without symbols; and the marquise du Châtelet, woman of the world, could undertake to translate Newton's formidable *Principia* from Latin into French, ultimate ratios and all.

The semantic structure of the quoted sentence was well within reach of Greek natural philosophy. Similar sentences can be found in Euclid and Archimedes, and, outside of mathematics, in Thucydides. Now, if the inspiration of Greek thinking had been such as to be able to bring about the cognitive content of this sentence as well, then undoubtedly Aristotle would have devoted much of his "metaphysics" to it or even written a special treatise "On the Art of Derivation," and Archimedes might truly have discovered the 17th-century mathematics and physics which he had been dimly perceiving all his life.

Real Numbers.—Mathematical information of scientific statements introduces a peculiar kind of lucidity and precision into them and it suggests and establishes logical and cognitive relations between them. It also introduces challenging analogies and unifications. For instance, most phenomena of propagations of waves, whether in acoustics, hydrodynamics, electricity or optics, are assumed to be governed at the outset by virtually the same set of differential equations. Thus for a while the theories run parallel, until the actual differences of aim must be begun to be accounted for.

The most basic trait of unification is the fact that ultimately all specific and tangible information in science is quantitative; that is, it may be expressed in ordinary real numbers. Every physical magnitude, whatever its own unit of dimension (simple or composite) may be, is measured by one or perhaps several real numbers, and all these numbers come from the same joint supply. Without this fact, there would be no conservation laws in physics; the law of the conservation of energy, for example, could not be enunciated or even conceived. Space extensions, time intervals, noises, colours, tactile impressions and emotions—all these things are in the end valued quantitatively. The "meaning in depth" of formulas, equalities and inequalities in science comes to life by accompanying interpretations. But the transmittable specific information is all in numbers, whether on graphs or on punched cards or on tape.

This all-pervading arithmetization in physics and mathematics was begun systematically in the 17th century, and in mathematics its manifest outcome was first of all the "analytic" or "co-ordinate" geometry. Mathematics is less insistent than physics on its exclusiveness. To the contrary, 20th-century mathematics abounds and delights in ever introducing and rarely discarding concepts and objects which need not be numerical. But it somehow frequently comes back to numbers, and the effect of the 17th-century arithmetization of space on the course of mathematics cannot be overstated.

Magnitudes.—The Greeks never introduced the system of real numbers as the ultimate quantitative measure for geometry, and in science (excepting astronomy) only a few of their results became unmistakably quantitative at all. Instead, in mathematics, they tried to operate directly with the concept of a general "magnitude" which somehow was always geometrical. In the fifth book of

Euclid's *Elements* the technical term for "magnitude" is the noun *megethos*. In Homer, this noun still means personal greatness or stature (of a hero, say); and it is remarkable that in the French noun *grandeur* and the German noun *Grösse*, for instance, the two meanings of personal greatness and of mathematical magnitude likewise reside simultaneously. Twentieth-century mathematics has "magnitudes" on various levels of generality, but it has them in addition to and not instead of real numbers. The Greek attempt of bypassing real numbers altogether was amazingly mature, but in retrospect it appears to have been too mature. The Greeks took a giant stride, stopped and advanced no further.

STAGES OF DEVELOPMENT

Irrational Numbers.—In the 5th and 4th centuries B.C. the Greeks gave the first known satisfactory solution to a problem in analysis. In a square whose side has length 1, the diagonal has length $\sqrt{2}$. The decimal expansion of $\sqrt{2}$ is the nonterminating quantity 1.4142 ..., so that $\sqrt{2}$ is the sum of the infinite series

$$1 + \frac{4}{10} + \frac{1}{100} + \frac{4}{1,000} + \frac{2}{10,000} + \cdots$$

Now, the Greeks proved that $\sqrt{2}$ is not a rational number, that is, not a quotient p/q for integers p,q. But they apparently found for $\sqrt{2}$ an approximate representation by certain rational numbers, or rather they found for the diagonal of the square approximations by segments which are commensurate with the side of the square. The approximate numbers were what were later called the partial sums of the continued fraction for $\sqrt{2}$, and apparently it was from the study of this problem that there was evolved the so-called Euclidean algorithm. The deepest achievement in this entire context was the development of a general theory of irrational numbers, or rather of incommensurate ratios of certain types of "magnitudes" and of proportions between ratios. The fifth book of Euclid which contains this theory was much admired by the scholar and statesman Isaac Barrow, predecessor to Newton in the Lucasian professorship at Cambridge university, from which post Barrow resigned in favour of Newton in order to devote himself to statesmanship entirely.

Areas and Volumes.—The Greeks also investigated the number $\pi = 3.14159 \ldots$, which is the area of a circle of radius 1, and the problem of squaring the circle was so widely known to the Athenian public that Aristophanes could allude to it in his comedy *The Birds*. Computations of other areas and volumes and of centres of masses are known from the works of Archimedes, and these results taken cumulatively can be viewed as a precursor to the 17th-century theory of integration. But these "direct" Greek calculations of many particular areas and volumes by circumscribed and inscribed approximating figures, when compared with the procedures of the integral calculus proper, are heavy, tiring and tiresome.

Set Theory.—The Greeks were also puzzled by the fact that the ordinary number 1 is the sum of the geometric series

$$\frac{1}{2} + \frac{1}{4} + \frac{1}{8} + \frac{1}{16} + \cdots + \frac{1}{2^n} + \cdots \qquad (\text{I})$$

and this was for them part of a range of problems relating to "infinitely small" and "infinitely large." The preoccupation with such problems is reflected in the paradox of "Achilles and the Turtle" put forward by Zeno of Elea, and in the distinction between "potential" and "actual" infinite as proposed by Aristotle. Partly in order to refute this distinction, the 19th-century mathematician Georg Cantor developed his set theory or theory of aggregates, the beginnings of which go back even to Galileo. This theory not only strengthened the logical framework of analysis, but soon became a basic innovation in all of mathematics and in all the speculations about its essence and its general background.

Analytic Geometry.—The Greek achievements in analysis were but a prelude. A notable step was taken in the 14th century by Bishop Nicolas Oresme. He discovered the logical equivalence between tabulation and graphing, more or less, and in a way he proposed the use of a graph for plotting a variable magnitude whose value depends on that of another.

However, the systematic theoretical basis for this possibility evolved only later from the work of René Descartes, who in 1637 laid the foundation for analytic geometry; that is, a geometry in which everything is reduced to numbers. In this geometry a point is a set of numbers which are called its co-ordinates. A figure is viewed as an aggregate of points, but it is usually described by formulas, equations and inequalities. This approach to geometry is the basis for the maps, graphs and charts which have penetrated into all walks of life, and for the mathematical concept of a function $y = f(x)$ which, first intended only for analysis, has eventually penetrated into all corners of mathematics and into all areas of rational thinking as well.

Later in the 17th century the culminating event took place when Newton and Leibniz introduced derivatives and laid the foundation for calculus and mechanics. Archimedes had been uneasily groping for the concept of a derivative, especially in his book on spirals, but he could never hit upon it, although otherwise he would have been as well equipped for dealing with it as anyone in the 16th and 17th centuries. The 17th and 18th centuries produced much mathematics in all directions, but analysis was the underlying theme.

Developments in the 19th and 20th Centuries.—In the 19th century, topology, algebra and arithmetic were emerging as independent divisions of mathematics, rivaling analysis in attention; but analysis continued to proliferate and, by sheer bulk, to predominate. Many French treatises on general mathematics simply bore the title *Cours d'analyse*. But by a peculiarity of usage, in memory of the fact that Euclid's *Elements* were always being viewed as a book in geometry, in these same treatises a mathematician in general was frequently referred to as *un géomètre*, especially when he was *illustre*.

Only in the 20th century were topology and algebra beginning to achieve a status approximating that of analysis. At the same time the lines of demarcation between the main divisions of mathematics were becoming more flexible and uncertain. After the 1930s, on the one hand analysis penetrated into geometry and arithmetic further than ever, and on the other hand topology and algebra began to fit tighter and more streamlined structural schemes on the large body of analysis. Duplications and redundancies could be reduced by syllogistic identifications and assimilations, and in some areas an increase of the substance offered itself naturally (*see* ANALYSIS, ABSTRACT). Furthermore, digital computing machines injected into analysis a certain algebraization, if only marginally. The structure of the machines and the problem of coding both involve algebra of logic, and in computational assignments from analysis, limiting processes must be replaced by approximations within certain maximal numbers of steps.

FUNCTIONS

Higher Derivatives.—A function $y = f(x)$, for real numbers x,y, is equivalent with a graph in an (x,y) co-ordinate system. A graph looks like a curve, but a curve is a figure on ordinary paper whereas a graph is a figure on graph paper; and graph paper represents a Euclidean plane into which some fixed co-ordinate system has been introduced beforehand.

The derivative df/dx, at a value x, is the limit of the difference quotient $\Delta f/\Delta x$ as Δx tends toward 0. It is defined for the numerical function but has an interpretation for the graph as a figure, namely, as the slope of the straight line which is tangent to the figure at the given point with abscissa x. However, the numerical value of the slope does depend on the co-ordinate system given. This dependence becomes more emphatic when one introduces the second derivative of $f(x)$, that is, the derivative of the derivative:

$$\frac{d^2f}{dx^2} = \frac{d}{dx}\left(\frac{df}{dx}\right)$$

In order to form the second derivative one must view—no matter how inarticulately or deficiently at first—the first derivative itself as a new function, and then form the derivative of this new function in turn. Second derivatives were in the forefront of Newton's mechanics. They defined the kinematic concept of acceleration as the instantaneous rate of change of the velocity function, and then, by an interpretative correlation with it, the dynamic concept of force. The Greeks knew no functions or accelerations, and only varying notions of force.

General Functions.—A comprehensive concept of function was beginning to emerge only in the first half of the 19th century, at first only for numbers x, y and gradually for more general objects x, y. In the case of general objects x, y one also uses instead of the word function the words functional or operator, especially when functions for various types of objects are used in the same context simultaneously. For "working" mathematics, that is, when problems relating to foundations of mathematics are not at issue, the following unsophisticated description of a function $y = f(x)$ in general seems sufficient.

There are given two aggregates of mathematical objects, an aggregate X and an aggregate Y. Let x denote an element of X and y an element of Y. With each element x of X there is associated a certain element y of Y and a single one only. But the same element y may be associated to several different elements x, and on the other hand it is not necessary that each element y shall appear as an associate to some element x. For instance, it is admissible that all elements x have as associates the same element y, in which case the function is called a constant. In general the element y associated to x is denoted by a symbol like $y = f(x)$. It is also called the image of x, or the value of f at the "point" x. The entire object $y = f(x)$ is called a function from X into Y or, more explicitly, from the aggregate X into the aggregate Y.

Syllogistically, a mathematical statement is a certain conclusion drawn from particular assumptions and previous statements. A function in general, as just described, is not sufficiently tangible to start making statements about, even if X and Y are real numbers (except if one of them is a finite set). Rather, in order to start, it is necessary to impose on the functions some restrictions or qualifications, that is, to single out classes of functions with some particular features that may be analyzed. Together with the general notion of function there also began emerging certain over-all descriptive properties with which classes of functions could be singled out: continuity, differentiability, integrability, bounded variation, etc. But before that, especially in the 17th century, it was taken for granted, expressly or not, that a function is a "formula" or "expression" that is a tangible prescription for finding y if x is given. Certain functions, then familiar, were taken as known, being basic, as it were; for instance, $x, x^2, \ldots,$ $\sin x,$ $\tan x,$ $\arctan x,$ $e^x,$ $\log x;$ and a formula arose by taking one or several such functions and performing a finite number of "natural" operations, such being primarily the four arithmetical basic operations, but including also extraction of roots and, what is important, the substitution of one function into another.

However, there soon appeared in the manipulations certain expressions in which an infinite or unending succession of operations was involved: certain infinite series, infinite products and infinite continued fractions. Of these the infinite series proved the most important by far, and two types of such series have advanced into positions of leadership and command which no phase of development has seriously impaired since, although there have been cases of evasion from authority, half in mathematical sport and a little in earnest. These two are power series and Fourier series.

Power Series.—The simplest power series is the geometric series

$$\frac{1}{1-x} = 1 + x^1 + x^2 + x^3 + \cdots$$

and in a broad sense it is very ancient, since, for instance, Zeno's series (1) is a case of it for $x = \frac{1}{2}$ if one subtracts the number 1 from both sides. The general power series has the form

$$a_0 + a_1 x^1 + a_2 x^2 + \cdots + a_n x^n + \cdots \qquad (2)$$

in which $a_0, a_1, a_2, \ldots$ are fixed numbers and x is a variable which for the present we assume to be real-valued. Now, if such a series is convergent for all x in an interval $-R < x < R$, where R is some positive number, and if one denotes the sum by $f(x)$, then this function has "very good" properties. It is continuous, even differentiable, and in fact it has a second derivative, third

derivative, etc. Furthermore, if one knows the values of all those derivatives at one point, namely at the origin $x = 0$, then the coefficients a_n of the series (2) can be computed. They are

$$a_0 = f(0), \quad a_1 = \frac{1}{1} f'(0), \quad a_2 = \frac{1}{1 \times 2} f''(0), \cdots,$$

$$a_n = \frac{1}{1 \times 2 \times \cdots \times n} f^{(n)}(0)$$

(Brook Taylor, 1715). Also, it is possible to shift the origin $x = 0$ into any other fixed point $x = h$ by starting out with a series

$$a_0 + a_1(x - h) + a_2(x - h)^2 + \cdots + a_n(x - h)^n + \cdots$$

If this series converges in some interval $x_0 < x < x_1$, which contains the "special" point h, say in an interval $(-R + h) < x < (R + h)$, and if one denotes the sum function again by $f(x)$, then it has derivatives of all orders in the interval; and, moreover,

$$a_0 = f(h), \quad a_1 = \frac{1}{1} f'(h), \cdots, \qquad (3)$$

$$a_n = \frac{1}{1 \times 2 \times \cdots n} f^{(n)}(h), \cdots$$

In order to compute all these derivatives only for the point h, it suffices to know the function $f(x)$ in some partial interval containing the point h, no matter how small this partial interval may be, and the coefficients $a_0, a_1, a_2, \ldots,$ are already determined thereby. If, therefore, we consider the class of functions $f(x)$ which can be represented as sums of power series, we obtain the following uniqueness property: if two such functions are equal in some small interval, then they are equal in any larger interval containing it. Investigators in the 18th century were very impressed with this property because it agreed with a scientific presumption that if a closed mechanical system has been known for a certain time interval, then this knowledge ought to determine it for later time as well. J. L. Lagrange especially claimed, with more insistence perhaps than self-conviction, that mechanics, physics and even "significant" analysis in general ought to be able to do with such functions exclusively. He firmly attached to these functions the name "analytic" (probably already current before) which they have borne since, and in his works he tried to use them in an exclusive sense.

Piecewise Analytic Functions.—However, this exclusiveness still allowed for a certain generalization which Lagrange (like others) was taking for granted due to the following situation: If one throws a ball against a wall and it hits it at the time t_0, then in the time interval $0 < t < t_0$ the components of position and velocity and other quantities for the ball are analytic functions of the time variable and of each other. After colliding with the wall at the time point t_0, the ball flies on its rebound during a certain time interval $t_0 < t < t_1$. During the rebound the functions are again analytic, as they were before, but at the instant of collision itself this is not so. For instance at $t = t_0$ the velocity components are not even continuous, let alone analytic. Such "instantaneous" interruptions of analyticity, when the "instants" were only finitely many, were acceptable to Lagrange and others. Their occurrence was taken for granted, and viewed as a necessary generalization of the demand on analyticity if not of its basic definition.

In the 20th century such functions were called "piecewise" analytic, and this manner of generalization became important to many contexts. There are functions which are piecewise continuous, piecewise differentiable, etc. An indispensable method in algebraic topology, which was initiated in 1911 by L. E. J. Brouwer, is built on approximating to continuous functions in several variables by piecewise linear ones.

Fourier Series.—In physics and technology many phenomena are viewed as "waves" (under which "vibrations" and "oscillations" also fall), and there are waves in acoustics, hydrodynamics, electricity, optics, etc. In each context there is a certain first type of wave, not yet too complicated and yet already important, and the interpretations and names that are associated with it are closely analogous from context to context. There is always a certain decomposition of the general wave within that type into a series of component waves which themselves are no longer decomposable. The first in the series is the "basic," "lowest," "primary," etc.; the later ones are "refinements," "higher," "secondary," etc., and they are supposed to decrease in effect and in influence the later they come in the series. Also, each of these components has certain fixed attributes, such as (wave) length, frequency, phase, amplitude.

This analogy in the phenomena is simply due to the identity of the mathematical instrument used for their "decomposition." Invariably, a certain function of one variable x in $-\infty < x < \infty$ is being represented as a so-called Fourier series, and the attributes of the phenomena are simply attributes of this series.

This function is then a periodic function, that is, there is a fixed number p such that $f(x + p) = f(x)$. We are normalizing it by putting $p = 2\pi$ so that $f(x + 2\pi) = f(x)$, and its Fourier series is then an expansion

$$f(x) = \frac{1}{2}a_0 + (a_1 \cos x + b_1 \sin x) + (a_2 \cos 2x + b_2 \sin 2x) + \cdots \quad (4)$$
$$+ (a_n \cos nx + b_n \sin nx) + \cdots$$

in which $a_0, a_1, a_2, \ldots$; $b_1, b_2, \ldots$ are certain constants. The first coefficient is written with the coefficients $\frac{1}{2}$ in order to make the following formulas uniform

$$a_n = \frac{1}{\pi} \int_{-\pi}^{\pi} f(x) \cos nx \, dx \quad b_n = \frac{1}{\pi} \int_{-\pi}^{\pi} f(x) \sin nx \, dx \quad (5)$$

All terms in the series (4) have period 2π; however, for the computation of the coefficients a_n, b_n by the formulas (5) it suffices to know the function $f(x)$ only in the interval $-\pi < x < \pi$. This agrees with the fact that if a function $f(x)$ is given in the latter interval to start with, then it can be extended to a periodic function by repeating it successively in the intervals $(\pi, 3\pi)$, $(3\pi, 5\pi)$, ... to the right and similarly in the intervals $(-3\pi, -\pi)$, $(-5\pi, -3\pi)$, ... to the left.

For purposes of theoretical reasoning and of applications in physics it is appropriate to rewrite the series (4) into two more forms. The first is the "complex" version

$$f(x) = c_0 + (c_1 e^{ix} + c_{-1} e^{-ix}) + \cdots + (c_n e^{nix} + c_{-n} e^{-nix}) + \cdots$$

which arises by the substitution

$$\cos nx = \frac{e^{inx} + e^{-inx}}{2} \quad \sin nx = \frac{e^{inx} - e^{-inx}}{2i}$$

and in this version

$$c_m = \frac{1}{2\pi} \int_{-\pi}^{\pi} f(x) e^{-imx} dx$$

for all integers m, positive and negative. The second form arises if, for $n \geq 1$, we introduce the number $\rho_n = (a_n^2 + b_n^2)^{\frac{1}{2}}$ and an angle θ_n for which $a_n = \rho_n \cos \theta_n$, $b_n = \rho_n \sin \theta_n$. The series then becomes $f(x) = \frac{1}{2}a_0 + \rho_1 \cos(x - \theta_1) + \rho_2 \cos(2x - \theta_2) + \cdots$

$$+ \rho_n (\cos nx - \theta_n) + \cdots$$

In physical applications it is frequently pertinent to replace x by $x - at$, where t is time and a is the velocity of the wave; and the result is $f(x - at) = \frac{1}{2}a_0 + \rho_1 \cos(x - at - \theta_1) + \cdots$

$$+ \rho_n \cos(nx - nat - \theta_n) + \cdots$$

The constant term $\frac{1}{2}a_0$ does not represent anything "wavy" and it is frequently zero. However, the next term

$$f_1(x - at) = \rho_1 \cos(x - at - \theta_1)$$

represents the lowest indecomposable component of the wave, and the successive terms

$$f_n(x - at) = \rho_n \cos(nx - nat - \theta_n) \quad (6)$$

the higher ones. Also $2\pi/n$ is the length of (6), $na/2\pi$ its frequency, θ_n its phase and ρ_n its amplitude. The interpretation of the amplitude attaches itself to an important relation, called the Parseval equality. It states that for any Fourier series (4) one has

$$\frac{1}{\pi} \int_{-\pi}^{\pi} (f(x))^2 dx = a_0^2 + (a_1^2 + b_1^2) + \cdots (a_n^2 + b_n^2) + \cdots$$
$$= a_0^2 + \rho_1^2 + \rho_2^2 + \cdots + \rho_n^2 + \cdots$$

For some wave phenomena the quantity

$$\frac{1}{\pi} \int_{-\pi}^{\pi} (f(x))^2 dx$$

represents a certain volume of energy associated with the propagation of the wave. Now, ρ_n^2 is the volume of energy for the component wave $f_n(x)$. Therefore, if one ignores the neutral term a_0 then the Parseval equality states that this energy for the whole wave is the sum of the energies for all component waves.

Analytic Theory of Numbers.—The trigonometric expansion (4) is named after J. B. J. Fourier largely because he found a counterpart to it in which the sum is replaced by an integral. It is the pair of formulas

$$g(y) = \int_{-\infty}^{\infty} f(x) e^{2\pi i y x} dx \quad (7)$$
$$f(x) = \int_{-\infty}^{\infty} g(y) e^{-2\pi i x y} dy$$

and they belong together in the following sense. For certain classes of functions $f(x)$ in $-\infty < x < \infty$ the first integral exists for all y in $-\infty < y < \infty$, so that a function $g(y)$ arises. With this function one can form the second integral (7) and the resulting function $f(x)$ is the one from which the process started. This pair of formulas has given rise to a theory of "duality" in abstract analysis.

S. D. Poisson and others before him found a formula which combines the Fourier series with the Fourier integrals, and the simplest case of it is

$$\sum_{m=-\infty}^{\infty} \int_{-\infty}^{\infty} f(x) e^{2\pi i m x} dx = \sum_{n=-\infty}^{\infty} f(n)$$

It became one of the most important tools in the analytic theory of numbers when P. G. L. Dirichlet used it in 1837 for giving a new proof for the so-called Gauss reciprocity law. In number theory, the greatest master of this so-called Poisson summation formula was Erich Hecke (1887–1947).

Least-Square Approximation.—There is an amplification to the Parseval theorem which has shaped many conceptions in physics.

Let $f(x)$ be a function in $-\pi < x \leq \pi$. For a fixed integer $n \geq 1$ take any real numbers $A_0, A_1, \ldots, A_n$; $B_1, \ldots, B_n$ and set up the trigonometric sum

$$\sigma_n(x) = \frac{1}{2}A_0 + (A_1 \cos x + B_1 \sin x) + \cdots$$
$$+ (A_n \cos nx + B_n \sin nx)$$

A particular case of this sum is the nth partial sum

$$s_n(x) = \frac{1}{2}a_0 + (a_1 \cos x + b_1 \sin x) + \cdots \quad (8)$$
$$+ (a_n \cos nx + b_n \sin nx)$$

of the Fourier series (4); that is, it is, among the sums $\sigma_n(x)$, the one which arises if one chooses for the coefficients A_m, B_m the numbers a_m, b_m which are given by the formulas (5). But now form the difference $f(x) - \sigma_n(x)$ and ask for which choice of the coefficients A_m, B_m this difference will be a "least possible" one. A good answer to this question arises if one measures the size of the difference by a certain "average" of it, namely by the value of the integral

$$\frac{1}{\pi} \int_{-\pi}^{\pi} |f(x) - \sigma_n(x)|^2 dx \quad (9)$$

This quantity is always greater than or at best equal to

$$\frac{1}{\pi} \int_{-\pi}^{\pi} |f(x) - s_n(x)|^2 dx \quad (10)$$

so that it is smallest if the trigonometric sum (8) is the corresponding partial sum of the Fourier series for $f(x)$. Furthermore, the function $f(x) - s_n(x)$ has itself a Fourier series which arises by cutting off from the entire series (4) the partial sum $s_n(x)$, thus yielding

$$a_{n+1} \cos(n+1)x + b_{n+1} \sin(n+1)x + \cdots$$

Therefore, by Parseval equality, the integral (10) has the value

$$a_{n+1}^2 + b_{n+1}^2 + a_{n+2}^2 + b_{n+2}^2 + \cdots \quad (11)$$

and altogether the following result arises. If the degree of approximation is measured by the integral (9), and if $\sigma_n(x)$ is a trigonometric polynomial of prescribed degree n, then the best approximation is brought about by the partial sum of the Fourier series and its size is that given by (11).

This result is not restricted to expansions in which the "simple" functions are cos nx, sin nx, but it holds if they are a so-called complete orthonormal system, and in this way it broadens into a comprehensive proposition in many settings.

Functions of Real Variables.—The uniqueness property for analytic functions is indicative of great regularity of structure. Given a small piece of the function—that is, given the function in a small interval—it thence acquires a natural growth into a larger interval, and uniquely so. Also, if one places the x line on which it is defined as an x axis into the plane of the complex variable $z = x + iy$, then it spreads in a unique manner from the one-dimensional interval on the x axis into a two-dimensional domain of the plane. Syllogistically the decisive phenomenon of this spread is the fact that if a power series (2) is convergent on a real interval $-R < x < R$, and if one replaces the real variable x by the complex variable $z = x + iy$, then the power series with the same coefficients $a_0 + a_1 z^1 + a_2 z^2 + \dots$ will also converge in the entire disk $|x + iy| < R$.

The complex analytic functions thus arising lead to a theory of great structural variety and beauty. The mathematicians of the 19th century loved and admired it all. They gave it their best, and molded into it all the glamour of the "Victorian era" then regnant everywhere and in everything. Around 1900 and later a number of books on such functions bore the generic title "Theory of Functions" in the expectation that the "other" functions would identify themselves expressly; and so they did, by calling themselves functions of a "real" variable or, of real variables.

The theory of the latter functions somehow was also growing into a compound of many parts, and in the 20th century it was even beginning to gain an ascendancy of interest over the complex analytic area. But then the complex analytic functions started to revitalize themselves by branching out from one into several variables, and a balance of evenly divided interest was establishing itself.

Fourier series are intimately related to the theory of functions of real variables, although not to all of it, and yet they were a great ferment for the development of the theory in all its parts. We will cite the high points and refer for details to INTEGRATION AND MEASURE; SERIES; FOURIER SERIES. Functions of bounded variation arose from a paper of Dirichlet giving the first nonobvious convergence criterion for Fourier series. B. Riemann developed the theory of his integral in a paper on trigonometric series and Cantor, by pursuing a problem raised in that paper, was led to constructing the first part of his theory of sets, namely the theory of point sets in Euclidean space. The theory of summability of divergent series, originally designed as an aid for analytic continuation of power series, became lastingly indispensable when L. Fejér applied it to Fourier series. The importance of the Lebesgue integral was recognized when it led to the Riesz-Fischer theorem for Fourier series and to the Plancherel theorem for Fourier integrals; and the Stieltjes integral, originally designed for the so-called moment problem, acquired its stature when it entered Fourier analysis in the theory of probability.

ANALYSIS AND SPACE

Conformal Mapping.—In the plane of Cartesian co-ordinates (x,y) one can introduce the polar co-ordinates

$$\rho = (x^2 + y^2)^{\frac{1}{2}} \qquad \theta = \arctan \frac{y}{x} \qquad (12)$$

in the following way. On the half line which issues at the point of origin $(0,0)$ and passes through the point (x,y), the quantity ρ is the distance between the two points and θ is the angle between the positive half of the x axis and this half line. From (ρ,θ) the numbers (x,y) can be reobtained by

$$x = \rho \cos \theta \qquad y = \rho \sin \theta \qquad (13)$$

There are some complications in the use of (ρ,θ). First, the origin

itself, called the pole, is a singularity in the sense that no specific θ can be assigned to it; and second, even omitting the pole, the angle θ cannot be assigned continuously to the entire plane, but only for any sector of the plane, say, the positive quadrant $x > 0$, $y > 0$. These difficulties are familiar from the use of latitude and longitude in measurements on the earth. The earth is spherical, not planar, and due to that feature there are two poles at which no longitude is definable; and if one starts measuring longitude continuously eastward, say from Greenwich, then, on returning to Greenwich, the accumulated longitude is 360°, not 0° as at the start.

Coming back to the relations (12) and (13), we replace the letters ρ,θ by "neutral" letters u,v, and rewrite these relations thus:

$$u = \phi(x,y) \qquad v = \psi(x,y) \qquad (14)$$

$$x = A(x,y) \qquad y = B(x,y)$$

There are other possibilities for choosing functions ϕ,ψ together with A,B, and each choice creates a so-called curvilinear co-ordinate system, of which polar co-ordinates are a particular instance. In three-dimensional space many kinds of curvilinear co-ordinate systems are useful to computations in mechanics and physics.

The pair of functions (14) can also be interpreted entirely differently. In addition to the given (x,y) plane we introduce another Euclidean plane with co-ordinates u,v, this one also Cartesian, and we view (14) as a mapping which associates with each point $P : (x,y)$ of the first plane a point $Q : (u,v)$ of the second plane. Such a mapping falls under the general concept of function as formulated under *General Functions*, above, and the word mapping is meant to recall the map in geography that results when the points of a region of the earth are transferred into a certain co-ordinate system on a sheet of paper or on a globe.

Two particular types of mapping are dominant in the geometry of Euclid, congruences and similarities. In traditional geometry two triangles are congruent if, in modern parlance, there is a certain one-to-one mapping of the entire Cartesian plane into itself which carries one triangle into the other. Euclid's geometry characterizes these mappings by certain axiomatic requirements, but in terms of co-ordinate transformations they are

$$u = a + \alpha x + \beta y \qquad u = b + \gamma x + \delta y$$

where a,b are any real numbers and $\alpha,\beta,\gamma,\delta$ are real numbers for which

$$\alpha^2 + \beta^2 = 1 \qquad \gamma^2 + \delta^2 = 1 \qquad (15)$$

$$\alpha\gamma + \beta\delta = 0$$

It follows automatically that $\alpha\delta - \beta\gamma$ is either $+1$ or -1. If it is $+1$ then the transformation is sense preserving and can be brought about by a rigid motion of the plane; if it is -1 then a change of sense (replacing "clockwise" by "counterclockwise") has to be superimposed.

A Euclidean similarity arises if, more generally, instead of (15) one has

$$\alpha^2 + \beta^2 = c^2 \qquad \gamma^2 + \delta^2 = c^2$$

where $c > 0$ is any real number. This c measures the size of the dilation in the similarity.

Such analytic formulations of congruence and similarity suggest the introduction of more general transformations, and prominent among such is conformal mapping which is defined as follows: if one takes any point (x_0,y_0) and all "small" triangles having this point as one of the vertices, then, in the limit, their images are similar to them, but the size of the local dilation may vary with the point (x_0,y_0); that is, conformal mapping preserves angles but not distances. Two statements are indicative of the importance of such mappings. First, if one also demands that the sense of the angles be preserved, then conformal transformations are the same as complex analytic functions in the following manner: if a pair of functions (14) constitutes a conformal mapping, and if one introduces the complex variables $z = x + iy$, $w = u + iv$, then there is a complex analytic function $w = f(z)$ such that $f(z) = \phi(x,y) + i\psi(x,y)$; conversely, for any complex analytic function, its real and imaginary parts constitute a sense-preserving conformal transformation. Second, if one takes in the plane a region bounded by one curve only, then it can be mapped conformally into the interior of a circle, and this also holds if the region is on a sphere or on any two-dimensional surface in space. Thus, for any plot of land on the earth which can be enclosed by one continuous fence one can make a conformal (that is angle-preserving) mapping into the interior of a circle on a flat sheet of paper. The oldest conformal mapping is the stereographic projection of Hipparchus (c. 150 B.C.) and Ptolemy (c. A.D. 150), and its name is due to F. Aguilonius (1613).

Degrees of Freedom.—A point P in space has three co-ordinates (x,y,z). If there are given N points P_n, $n = 1, \ldots, N$, if the co-ordinates of the nth point are denoted by (x_n, y_n, z_n), and if the points constitute a mechanical system in motion, then at any given time the system is described by the $3N$ numbers (x_n, y_n, z_n), $n = 1, 2, \ldots, N$. It suggests itself to introduce a Cartesian space of $3N$ dimension, a point of which is an arbitrary set of $3N$ real numbers, and if one places the mechanical system into this space then the motion of the system reflects itself in an "orbit" of the space. Now, there may be constraints operative in the system. For instance, two of the points, say $P_1 : (x_1, y_1, z_1)$ and $P_2 : (x_2, y_2, z_2)$ may be linked by a rigid rod of length l so that always

$$(x_1 - x_2)^2 + (y_1 - y_2)^2 + (z_1 - z_2)^2 = l^2$$

In this case it is economical to eliminate one of the co-ordinates, say by putting

$$x_1 = x_2 + [l^2 - (y_1 - y_2)^2 - (z_1 - z_2)^2]^{\frac{1}{2}}$$

so that only $3N - 1$ "free" parameters are left. The physicists then say that the "true" number of degrees of freedom for the system is (at most) $3N - 1$, and it is sometimes preferable to interpret the motion of the system in a space of (at most) $3N - 1$ dimensions. If there are two restraints present, and if they are independent, then there are (at most) $3N - 2$ degrees of freedom, etc.

In mechanics, the theory of degrees of freedom was initiated by Lagrange, and the mathematical aspects of the phenomenon of dependence between functions and the subsequent reduction of the total dimension were put on a sure footing by K. G. J. Jacobi (1804–51) and A. Cayley (1821–95). These studies gradually led to the emergence of a precise concept of dimension and of (topological) manifold. The general public became aware of such possibilities at a rather advanced stage of the development, namely with the introduction in the 1920s of the theory of relativity of A. Einstein, which featured two interlocking hypotheses. It merged the three-dimensional "ordinary" space with the time variable into a physically inseparable four-dimensional space, and it allowed this total space to be a topological manifold which was no longer a Euclidean space in its entirety.

The advance of algebraic topology was especially stimulated by a formula due to L. Kronecker (1823–91), the so-called Kronecker integral, which represents the number of joint solutions of three independent functions

$$u = f(x,y,z) \quad u = g(x,y,z) \quad w = h(x,y,z)$$

in a region of three-dimensional Euclidean space, and similarly for higher dimensional space. The formula subsumes the so-called Cauchy formula in complex analysis and related formulas which are more familiar than Kronecker's formula itself.

Tensorial Functions.—Let a differentiable function $g(u,v)$ denote the height of a building erected over a domain D in the (u,v) plane as base. If one introduces a transformation of co-ordinates (14) then the height becomes

$$f(x,y) = g[\phi(x,y), \psi(x,y)]$$

Such a function is called an absolute scalar. Now, the "sky line" of the building—that is, the shape of its roof—is appropriately described by the two functions

$$\frac{\partial g}{\partial u} \qquad \frac{\partial g}{\partial v} \qquad (16)$$

In the co-ordinates x,y the corresponding functions

$$\frac{\partial f}{\partial x} \qquad \frac{\partial f}{\partial y} \qquad (17)$$

are linked to the functions (16) by the relations

$$\frac{\partial f}{\partial x} = \frac{\partial g}{\partial u} \frac{\partial \phi}{\partial x} + \frac{\partial g}{\partial v} \frac{\partial \psi}{\partial x}$$

$$\frac{\partial f}{\partial y} = \frac{\partial g}{\partial u} \frac{\partial \phi}{\partial y} + \frac{\partial g}{\partial v} \frac{\partial \psi}{\partial y}$$

so that in order to obtain either one of the two functions (17) both functions (16) must be known. In this sense the pairs (16) and (17) cannot be separated. In general, over manifolds with local co-ordinate systems, there are many types of groups of functions which must be kept together organically for purposes of finding their values under changes of co-ordinates. Such groupings of functions are called tensors, and the name first arose in elasticity to describe tensors whose components are strains and stresses in different directions. In the topology of manifolds, tensorial functions are vector bundles, more or less.

A very important tensor is the curvature tensor introduced by Riemann and anticipated by C. F. Gauss. It has inaugurated a new era in geometry, and although its adequate description is rather technical, it is a very unifying concept nonetheless. It brings together geometry proper, analysis, topology and even a branch of analytic theory of numbers (automorphic functions in several variables). Also, there would hardly be a general theory of relativity without it. (SN. B.)

ANALYSIS, ABSTRACT, a term almost synonymous with functional analysis and used to designate that part of mathematics which has resulted from axiomatizing and generalizing classical analysis. Abstracting what appear to be the essential elements in various branches of the latter subject, one sets up axiom systems and proves theorems which include the classical ones as special cases. Often several analogous classical results, as well as concrete results previously unformulated, appear as special cases of a single abstract theorem. Moreover, the process of abstraction has a clarifying effect in removing extraneous elements and revealing unsuspected relationships. The clarification thus achieved not only leads to a deeper understanding of previously known results but often paves the way for further progress.

In addition to its organizing and clarifying role with respect to classical analysis, abstract analysis is concerned with numerous problems of its own. It happens again and again in mathematics that a notion or concept introduced to help solve or clarify some problem suggests an array of questions about itself having little to do with the original problem. The notions of abstract analysis are no exception. Many of these are obtained from notions of abstract algebra by introducing an abstract notion of limit and replacing finiteness assumptions by assumptions about the behaviour of limits. Thus many problems in abstract analysis are generalizations of problems in abstract algebra and have an at least formally similar character. This part of abstract analysis is sometimes called topological algebra and is regarded by many algebraists as a part of algebra as well. In a somewhat similar fashion, abstract analysis overlaps with point set topology and, in general, has no sharp boundary lines.

It is sometimes asserted by enthusiastic abstract analysts that analysis, properly looked at, is just a synthesis of algebra and topology, and one might define abstract analysis as that part of mathematics in which this viewpoint is systematically adopted. On the other hand, it should be pointed out that many classical analysts are unimpressed with the usefulness of the abstract outlook and would regard the above account as a rather optimistic one. It cannot be denied that the more detailed and refined results of classical analysis still have a tendency to pass through the sieve of the abstraction process.

The Central Notions of Abstract Analysis.—Let R denote the set of all real numbers and let $C(R)$ denote the set of all continuous, complex valued functions f defined on R which are identically zero outside of some finite interval depending on f. For each f in $C(R)$ let $||f||_0$ be the least number such that $|f(x)| \leq ||f||_0$ for all x, let $||f||_1 = \int_{-\infty}^{\infty} |f(x)| dx$ and let $||f||_2 = (\int_{-\infty}^{\infty} |f(x)|^2 dx)^{\frac{1}{2}}$. It is easy to see that $\lambda f + \mu g$ is in $C(R)$ whenever f and g are in $C(R)$ and λ and μ are complex numbers, and that the two operations of addition and multiplication by complex numbers obey the formal laws laid down in the definition of a *vector space* over the complex numbers (*see* ALGEBRAS, [LINEAR]). It is also easy to see that whether $a = 0$, 1 or 2, $||f||_a$ behaves like the absolute value of a number in the sense that for all f and g in $C(R)$ and all complex numbers λ we have

$$||f + g||_a \leq ||f||_a + ||g||_a$$
$$||\lambda f||_a = |\lambda|\, ||f||_a \text{ and } ||f||_a = 0$$

if and only if $f = 0$.

Abstracting from these properties of $C(R)$ a *complex normed vector space* is defined as a vector space X over the complex numbers together with a nonnegative real valued function $f \rightarrow ||f||$ having the properties defined above. A *real normed vector space* is defined similarly. In any normed vector space (real or complex) the "distance" $\rho(f,g)$ between two elements f and g is defined to be $||f - g||$. With this distance the normed vector space becomes a "metric space," as defined in TOPOLOGY, GENERAL. As such one can speak of its convergent sequences, of whether or not it is complete, of continuous functions from it to another metric space, etc. A complete normed vector space is called a *Banach space*. $C(R)$ is not complete with respect to any of the three norms described above. However, in each case it may be "completed" by adding certain functions or classes of functions. For example, it becomes complete with respect to $||\ ||_2$ when all measurable functions f such that $\int_{-\infty}^{\infty} |f(x)|^2\, dx < \infty$ are added, provided that we identify two functions whenever they differ only on a set of Lebesgue measure zero.

As is shown in TOPOLOGY, GENERAL, many of the properties of metric spaces depend only upon the family of open sets defined by the metric and not on the metric itself. Taking the notion of open subset as basic undefined entity and introducing appropriate axioms, one defines the notions of *topological space* and *Hausdorff space*. A Hausdorff space is a special kind of topological space and every metric space is also a Hausdorff space. Generalizing the notion of normed vector space in a similar fashion, one defines a *topological vector space* to be a vector space (over the real or complex numbers), which is at the same time a Hausdorff space in such a manner that the operations of addition and multiplication by numbers are continuous in both variables simultaneously. The most important topological vector spaces are locally convex in the sense that in every open set containing 0 there is a smaller open set which contains 0 and every point on the line segment joining any two of its points.

Abstracting from the notions of scalar product in classical vector analysis and integral of the product of two functions, one defines an *inner* or *scalar product* in a real or complex vector space X as a real or complex valued function $f,g \rightarrow (f \cdot g)$ defined on pairs of elements f and g of X and having the following properties:

$$(f_1 \cdot g) = \overline{(g \cdot f_1)}$$
$$(\lambda f_1 + \mu f_2 \cdot g) = \lambda(f_1 \cdot g) + \mu(f_2 \cdot g)$$
$$(f \cdot f) > 0$$

for all f, f_1, f_2 and g in X with $f \neq 0$, and all real or complex numbers λ and μ (the bar over a number denotes its complex conjugate). It is easy to show that $\sqrt{(f \cdot f)}$ is a norm for X. A Banach space whose norm is so derivable from an inner product is called a *Hilbert space*. The completion of $C(R)$ with respect to $||\ ||_2$ is an example of a Hilbert space. Hilbert spaces have many properties not shared by Banach spaces in general.

A function T from one vector space to another is said to be linear if $T(\lambda f + \mu g) = \lambda T(f) + \mu T(g)$ for all f and g in the first space and all λ and μ in the appropriate number field. The most important examples are the linear integral and differential operators of classical analysis. If X and Y are normed vector spaces and T is a linear operator from X to Y, then T is continuous if and only if it is bounded in the sense that $||T(f)||/||f||$ is bounded as f varies among the nonzero elements of X. The least upper bound of these numbers is called the norm of T and is denoted by $||T||$. The set of all bounded linear operators from X to Y is a vector space itself under the obvious operations and is a normed vector space $B(X,Y)$ with respect to the norm just

defined. This space is complete and hence is a Banach space whenever Y is. When Y is the one-dimensional Banach space of all members of the underlying number field, $B(X,Y)$ is called the *dual* or *conjugate* of X and is denoted by X^* or $\overline{X}$. Its members are then called *linear functionals*. When X is a Hilbert space there corresponds to each member T of X^* a unique member g of X such that $T(f) = (f \cdot g)$ for all f in X. In this sense a Hilbert space is self-dual. If $X = Y$ and both spaces are complete then $B(X,Y) = B(X,X)$ is not only a Banach space but has further structure as well. Given T and S in $B(X,X)$, we define their product TS as the linear operator $f \rightarrow T(S(f))$ and verify at once that $||TS|| \leq ||T||\ ||S||$. $B(X,X)$ is an example of a *Banach algebra*; that is, a Banach space in which there is also a "multiplication" $f,g \rightarrow fg$ defined for all pairs f and g in X and having the following properties: (1) the multiplication satisfies the associative and distributive laws and so converts X into a *ring* in the sense of abstract algebra; (2) $(\mu f)g = f(\mu g) = \mu(fg)$ for all f and g in X and all real or complex numbers μ; (3) $||fg|| \leq ||f||\ ||g||$ for all f and g in Y. Banach algebras are sometimes called *normed rings*. Completing $C(R)$ with respect to the norm $||\ ||_0$ and defining multiplication of functions in the usual manner, we obtain an important example of a Banach algebra which is commutative in the sense that $fg = gf$ for all f and g. $C(R)$ becomes a commutative Banach algebra in rather a different way if multiplication is defined as "convolution": $f*g(x) = \int_{-\infty}^{\infty} f(x - y)g(y)dy$, and the space is completed with respect to the norm $||\ ||_1$.

Abstracting from the notions of "measurable set" and "measure" in the theory of the Lebesgue integral on the line and in n space, a *measure space* is defined as a set S together with a family M of subsets of S and a function μ from M to the nonnegative numbers and the symbol ∞ such that: (1) if E_1, E_2, ... are in M then the set $E_1 \cup E_2 \cup \ldots$ of all elements in at least one of E_1, E_2, ... is also in M; (2) if E is in M then the set $S - E$ of all elements not in E is in M; (3) if E_1, E_2, ... are members of M, no two of which have any elements in common, then $\mu(E_1 \cup E_2 \cup \ldots) = \mu(E_1) + \mu(E_2) + \ldots$; (4) the empty set O is in M and $\mu(O) = 0$. If $S = E_1 \cup E_2 \cup \ldots$ where $\mu(Ej) < \infty$, the measure space is said to be σ-finite. For real or complex valued functions defined on σ-finite measure spaces, one can define measurable functions and develop the theory of integration of such functions in fairly complete generalization of the classical theory of Lebesgue.

One feature of the classical theory which does not generalize to measure spaces is the important fact that the underlying space S is a commutative group, and that the Lebesgue measure of a set is invariant under group translation. This feature is recaptured in the theory of integration on locally compact topological groups. Generalizing from the continuous groups of S. Lie (considered globally rather than locally), one defines a topological group as a group which is at the same time a Hausdorff space, the topology and the group operations being so related that $x,y \rightarrow xy^{-1}$ is a continuous function of both variables together. Let G be a topological group which as a topological space is separable and locally compact. Let M denote the smallest family of subsets of G which contains all the open sets and satisfies (1) and (2) in the definition of measure space, above.

According to a celebrated theorem of A. Haar, there exists a measure in G defined on M which is finite on all compact sets, invariant under translation from the left by members of G and not identically zero. This measure is essentially unique in the sense that any measure with these properties is a constant multiple of any other. It is called the (left invariant) *Haar measure* for the group. There is, of course, also a right invariant Haar measure. Moreover, one can drop the hypothesis that G is separable, but only at the cost of complicating somewhat the statement of Haar's theorem.

Some Central Topics and Results.—Consider the following two important results of classical analysis.

1. If $K(x,y)$ is a symmetric continuous function defined on the square $0 \leq x \leq 1$, $0 \leq y \leq 1$, there exists a complete set of eigenfunctions for the integral operator $T_K : T_K(f)(x) = \int_0^1$

$K(x,y)f(y)dy$; that is, a set of functions $\psi_1, \psi_2, \ldots$, such that $T_K(\psi_j) = \lambda_j \psi_j$ where each λ_j is a real number and every square-summable function on $0 \leq x \leq 1$ has a unique expansion in the form $c_1\psi_1 + c_2\psi_2 + \ldots$, where the c_j are constants and the series converges in the mean.

2. Every function on the real line which is periodic of period 2π and square-summable on the interval $-\pi \leq x \leq \pi$ may be expanded in a Fourier series $\sum_{m=-\infty}^{\infty} c_n e^{inx}$ where again the c_j are constants and convergence is in the mean.

The first result may be interpreted as stating that the operator T_K may be decomposed as a "direct sum" of operators which are constant multiples of the identity. The second may be interpreted in almost exactly the same way except that now a family of operators is involved. For each n the function e^{inx} is carried into a multiple of itself by *all* translation operators $f(x) \rightarrow f(x + a)$. A rather large part of abstract analysis is devoted to showing that operators and families of operators may be decomposed into simpler ones in a manner analogous to (but often more complicated than) that of these examples, and to studying the properties of these decompositions.

An abstract generalization of result 1 states that a linear operator T from a Hilbert space H into itself has a "basis" of "eigenvectors" when it is *self-adjoint* in the sense that $(T(f) \cdot g) = (f \cdot T(g))$ for all f and g in H, and completely continuous in the sense that the unit sphere is mapped into a set whose closure is compact. The complete continuity implies the discreteness of the decomposition. When this hypothesis is dropped one has a generalization of 1, in which the summation is replaced by an integration. This generalization can be formulated and proved for operators which are not even bounded or everywhere defined, provided that they are still (in a suitable sense) self-adjoint. It is known as the *spectral theorem*. It leads at once to an "operational calculus" for self-adjoint operators; that is, to the possibility of making sense of such expressions as $f(T)$ where T is a self-adjoint operator and f is a Borel measurable function of a real variable. It plays a central role in the theory of linear differential equations—both ordinary and partial—and in the rigorous formulation of quantum mechanics.

On the other hand, one can drop the requirement that T be self-adjoint and that it acts in a Hilbert space and draw important conclusions from the fact that T is completely continuous. In particular, one can show that such a T behaves in important respects like an operator in a finite dimensional vector space and apply the results of linear algebra.

The translation operators appearing in example 2 are neither completely continuous nor self-adjoint. However, they are normal in the sense that they commute with their adjoints. The adjoint of a bounded operator T in a Hilbert space is the unique operator T^* such that $(Tf \cdot g) = (f \cdot T^*g)$ for all f and g. The spectral theorem can be extended without much difficulty to hold for all normal operators.

The Fourier expansion theorem and the theory of Fourier series in general have a considerable generalization in which functions of period 2π on the line are replaced by functions on a locally compact abelian group G and integration is carried out with respect to the Haar measure of the groups. The set of functions $\{e^{inx}\}$ is replaced by the set of all continuous complex valued functions $\aleph$ on G which satisfy the identity $\aleph(xy) = \aleph(x)\aleph(y)$ for all x and y in G—the so-called "characters" of G. When G is compact there is an expansion theorem just as in example 2, but when G is only locally compact the summation is replaced by an integration. The resulting formula reduces to the classical Fourier integral when G is the additive group of the real line. The general theory unifies Fourier series and Fourier integrals in one or more dimensions. Important features of this theory arise from the fact that the set of all characters of a locally compact abelian group G can itself be made into such a group in a natural way. It is called the *dual* or *character group* of G. The word dual is justified since G is in a natural way the character group of its character group—locally compact abelian groups occur in dual

pairs. The integration that occurs in the expansion theorem is with respect to the Haar measure in the dual group. This reduces to a summation when G is compact because then the dual is discrete.

The possibility of defining the convolution $f*g(x) = \int_{-\infty}^{\infty} f(x - y)g(y)dy$ of two functions of a real variable depends only upon the fact that the real numbers form a locally compact group under addition. The notion may be extended to functions defined on any locally compact group G and permits one to convert the Banach space $L^1(G)$ of all complex valued functions which are summable with respect to Haar measure into a Banach algebra. This Banach algebra is called the group algebra of G and is commutative if and only if G is commutative. When G is commutative the Fourier expansion theorem sets up a correspondence $f \rightarrow \hat{f}$ between functions on G and functions on the dual $\hat{G}$ of G. In particular, members of $L^1(G)$ correspond to continuous functions on $\hat{G}$ in such a manner that $(\widehat{f * g})$ is the ordinary product of $\hat{f}$ and $\tilde{g}$. More generally, let A be any commutative Banach algebra. The set M of all "regular maximal ideals" in A may be given a locally compact topology and A may be mapped into the algebra of all continuous complex valued functions in M in such a manner that $(f + g) = f^o + g^o$ and $(fg)^o = f^o g^o$ whenever f and g are in A and h^o denotes the continuous function on M corresponding to h. When $A = L^1(G)$ and G is commutative, M may be identified with the dual $\hat{G}$ of G and f^o with $\hat{f}$. Many classical theorems in Fourier analysis turn out to be specializations of theorems about the mapping $f \rightarrow f^o$ in commutative Banach algebras. That part of abstract analysis which studies Fourier analysis on groups and commutative Banach algebras is usually called abstract harmonic analysis.

The Fourier analysis of functions defined on locally compact commutative groups may be further generalized by allowing the group to be noncommutative and changing the domain of the functions from the group G itself to some space S on which the G acts as a group of transformations. For example, the group of rotations about 0 in Euclidean three-space transforms the surface S_2 of the unit sphere onto itself. This transformation is *transitive* in the sense that for each p and q in S there exists x in G such that $x(p) = q$. When one attempts to analyze complex valued functions in S_2 as sums of functions having simple properties under rotation, one is led to the classical spherical harmonics.

More general transitive transformation groups lead to theories of generalized spherical functions. In general, one assumes that S is a measure space and that the measure μ is invariant under the action of G. When S is finite it is always possible to write it as a union of disjoint subsets on each of which G acts transitively. In the infinite case this is not always true—even if one permits continuous summation processes. One is forced to consider a weaker kind of transitivity. The action of G on S is said to be *metrically transitive* or *ergodic* if, whenever E is a measurable subset of S such that each member x of G maps it into a set $x(E)$ differing from E by a set of measure zero, then E is either of measure zero or differs from S by a set of measure zero.

Whether or not G is in some sense transitive on S one can introduce the Hilbert space $L^2(S,\mu)$ of all measurable complex valued functions f on S such that $|f|^2$ has a finite integral. For each $x \epsilon g$ the "translation" operator $T_x : (T_x(f)(y) = f([y]x))$ is *unitary* in the sense that $T_x^* = T_x^{-1}$. Moreover, $T_{x_1 x_2} = T_{x_1} T_{x_2}$ for all x_1 and x_2 in G and $(T_x(f) \cdot g)$ is continuous in x for all f and g in $L^2(S,\mu)$. We have, in short, what is known as a *continuous unitary representation* of G. The classical theory of the representation of finite groups by matrices has a generalization to a theory of continuous unitary representations of locally compact groups. The "irreducible" representations of G play the role of the characters in the commutative theory. They may be infinite dimensional. Of course the direct sum decompositions of the classical theory give way to continuous direct sums or direct integrals. In addition there are certain new phenomena which have no classical counterpart. Their existence is closely related to that of metrically transitive transformation groups.

Via the group algebra there is a close connection between the classical theory of group representations and the classical theory of linear associative algebras. This connection persists in the infinite locally compact case. However, there are several different generalizations of the group algebra. Structure theorems for noncommutative Banach algebras generalizing the classical finite theorems of J. H. M. Wedderburn have been most thoroughly studied when the Banach algebra is a so-called *von Neumann algebra;* that is, a subalgebra of the Banach algebra of all bounded linear operators on some Hilbert space which contains the adjoint of each of its elements and is such that $(A')' = A$. Here A' denotes the set of all T such that $ST = TS$ for all S in A. Again one must deal with continuous direct sum decompositions and with certain new phenomena related to the existence of metrically transitive but intransitive transformation groups. These new phenomena manifest themselves in the existence of certain infinite analogues of full matrix algebras whose idempotent elements can have "fractional dimension"—the so-called factors of type II.

When G is the additive group of the real line, the theory of the unitary representations of G can be reduced at once to the theory of self-adjoint operators via a fundamental theorem of M. H. Stone according to which $T_x = e^{ixH}$ sets up a one-to-one correspondence between continuous unitary representations T of G and self-adjoint operators H. The operator iH is called the *infinitesimal generator* of the group. In particular this theorem allows one to apply the spectral theorem to the analysis of the one-parameter transformation groups which one gets by integrating the differential equations of classical mechanics. This connection with mechanics and its application to certain questions in statistical mechanics has led to the branch of abstract analysis known as *ergodic theory.*

The connection between one-parameter unitary groups and their infinitesimal generators can be considerably generalized. The operator T_x need not be unitary and may act in Banach spaces more general than Hilbert spaces. Moreover, the operator T_x need only be defined for $x > 0$. The resulting *theory of one-parameter semigroups* has important applications to the theory of partial differential equations.

The consideration of Banach spaces more general than Hilbert spaces and of topological vector spaces which are not Banach spaces raises many technical questions. Hilbert spaces have very many special properties not possessed by topological vector spaces in general but possessed by some which are not Hilbert spaces. An important branch of abstract analysis is devoted to exploring the logical interconnections between these properties and to deciding which spaces arising in practice possess them. Of course there are also spaces with useful properties not possessed by Hilbert spaces. Similar classification problems are studied for Banach algebras and the other objects of abstract analysis.

An important aspect of certain applications of abstract analysis to classical analysis is the introduction of "generalized functions" of various sorts. A space whose elements are concrete functions with regular properties may often be imbedded in a natural way in a larger space whose elements are of a more abstract character—this larger space being one in which the operations of analysis may be carried out more freely and in which the theorems take on a simpler and more elegant form. A particularly highly developed theory of this character is the theory of distributions of Laurent Schwartz. The space D of all distributions on Euclidean n space includes the space of all locally summable complex valued functions and every distribution has partial derivatives of all orders. D is one of the most important examples of a topological vector space which is not a Banach space.

BIBLIOGRAPHY.—Extensive bibliographies of the earlier literature will be found in these introductory treatises: F. Riesz and B. Sz. Nagy, *Leçons d'analyse fonctionnelle,* 3rd ed. (1955); L. H. Loomis, *An Introduction to Abstract Harmonic Analysis* (1953). For somewhat more recent work and topics not mentioned in the above, the following may be consulted: M. M. Day, *Normed Linear Spaces* (1958); E. Hille and R. S. Phillips, *Functional Analysis and Semi-groups,* rev. ed. (1957); J. Dixmier, *Les algèbres d'opérateurs d'ans l'espace Hilberten* (1957); L. Schwartz, *Théorie des distributions* (1950); N. Dunford et al., *Linear Operators* (1958); N. Bourbaki, *Éléments de mathématique,* part i, books v, vi (1953, 1955, 1957). (G. W. M.)

ANALYSIS, CHEMICAL: see CHEMISTRY: *Analytical Chemistry.*

ANALYSIS, COMPLEX, is that branch of mathematics which arose historically from the study of analytic functions of one or several complex variables. Beginning with B. Riemann's fundamental discoveries in the middle of the 19th century, there was a gradual but continual shift of emphasis toward the investigation of global properties of analytic functions by topological and algebro-geometrical methods, with the result that complex analysis became rather intricately interwoven with the other principal mathematical disciplines and could be viewed only against the background of mathematical development as a whole, which is characterized in the 20th century by a remarkable synthesis of ideas.

Analysis of the properties of functions of one complex variable (complex analysis in one dimension) had a remarkable growth during the second half of the 19th century as a result of the brilliant research of Riemann and, afterward, of H. Poincaré, F. Schottky, H. A. Schwarz, K. Weierstrass, C. Neumann and others. Shortly after 1900 the general principle of uniformization, conceived by F. Klein and Poincaré, was established by P. Koebe. These developments were presented as a unified theory in 1913 by H. Weyl.[1]

During the latter part of the 19th and the beginning of the 20th century, the theory of functions of several complex variables made its appearance, as did algebraic geometry, especially the theory of algebraic surfaces founded by M. Noether, E. Picard, Poincaré and, last but not least, the Italian geometers G. Castelnuovo, F. Enriques and, somewhat later, F. Severi. In 1895 P. Cousin[2] investigated certain global properties of analytic functions on domains in complex n-space and brought to the attention of mathematicians two problems which were later to bear his name; the study of these and related problems led to some of the most important developments of complex analysis during the first half of the 20th century.

In the years following the publication of Weyl's book, the geometrical concepts, first introduced into complex analysis by Riemann, were studied for their own sake and vastly generalized as a result of the growth of topology as a branch of mathematics. S. Lefschetz made a profound study of the topological properties of algebraic surfaces in his tract,[3] which exerted considerable influence on the later development of complex analysis, topology and algebraic geometry. E. Cartan developed and applied systematically the theory of exterior differential forms which merged with topology in the fundamental theorem proved by G. de Rham in 1932 and helped give birth to the concept of cohomology in algebraic topology. S. Bergman[4] discovered an important type of hermitian metric on subdomains of complex n-space which was subsequently generalized by E. Kähler and became known as a Kähler metric. Beginning about 1932, W. V. D. Hodge[5] generalized the theory of harmonic functions on Riemann surfaces to harmonic differential forms on higher dimensional compact Riemannian manifolds, and on complex manifolds which possess Kähler metrics. Hodge's theory was developed and perfected during the 1940s by K. Kodaira,[6] who also generalized the theory to open manifolds and introduced systematically the method of orthogonal projection in Hilbert space.

Simultaneous with the development of the theory of harmonic differential forms, an intensive investigation of questions related to the Cousin problems was made by K. Oka, H. Behnke, H. Cartan, K. Stein and others. Although the methods used by these investigators differed somewhat from those of Hodge, Kodaira and De Rham, the time was becoming ripe for a remarkable confluence of ideas and this took place shortly after 1950 with the introduction into complex analysis of new notions from algebraic topology, namely, fibre bundles and cohomology with coefficients in sheaves. The idea of a fibre bundle was first recognized during the period

[1]H. Weyl, *Die Idee der Riemannschen Fläche* (1913).
[2]P. Cousin, "Sur les fonctions de *n* variables complexes," *Acta Math.,* vol. 19, pp. 1–62 (1895).
[3]S. Lefschetz, *L'Analysis situs et la géométrie algébrique* (1924).
[4]S. Bergman, "Zur Funktionentheorie zweier komplexen Veränderlichen," *Jahresbericht der Deutschen Mathematiker Vereinigung,* vol. 41, *Jahresversammlung in Bad Elster,* pp. 78–80 (1931).
[5]W. V. D. Hodge, *The Theory and Applications of Harmonic Integrals* (1941).
[6]K. Kodaira, "Harmonic Fields in Riemannian Manifolds (Generalized Potential Theory)," *Ann. Math.,* vol. 50, pp. 587–665 (1949).

1935–40 while the notion of a sheaf was introduced into topology a few years later by J. Leray (similar concepts, never precisely defined, had occurred earlier in various special contexts). The introduction of these concepts had an explosive effect on the development of complex analysis during the following years.[7]

A third advance of great importance in complex analysis, which took place during the period 1935–50, was the development, principally by C. L. Siegel,[8] of the theory of automorphic functions of several complex variables.

An important generalization of the uniformization principle was provided early in the 1930s by independent solutions of the plateau problem by J. Douglas and T. Rado and by the subsequent investigations of the plateau problem by R. Courant and M. Shiffman. A further important outgrowth of the uniformization principle was the intensive investigation of the family of normalized univalent functions in the unit disk.

In this article the scope of complex analysis will be illustrated by describing briefly a few of the concepts and techniques mentioned above.

Complex n-Space, Functions, Maps.—Denote the set of complex numbers by C; i.e., the numbers $z = x + iy$ where x, y are real numbers and $i^2 = -1$. The addition of the complex numbers and multiplication by an arbitrary complex number impart to C the structure of a complex vector space of complex dimension 1. Generalizing, we obtain complex n-space, denoted by C^n, where n is a positive integer; it is the n-dimensional complex vector space of n-tuplets $(z^1, z^2, \ldots, z^n)$ of complex numbers $z^1, z^2, \ldots, z^n$. Addition of $(z^1, z^2, \ldots, z^n)$ and $(w^1, w^2, \ldots, w^n)$ is defined by $(z^1, z^2, \ldots, z^n) + (w^1, w^2, \ldots, w^n) = (z^1 + w^1, z^2 + w^2, \ldots, z^n + w^n)$, and multiplication of $(z^1, z^2, \ldots, z^n)$, by a complex number w, is defined by $w \cdot (z^1, z^2, \ldots, z^n) = (wz^1, wz^2, \ldots, wz^n)$.

For simplicity we write $z = (z^1, z^2, \ldots, z^n)$ where $z^1, z^2, \ldots, z^n$ are the co-ordinates of the "point" z. The conjugate $\bar{z}$ of $z = (z^1, z^2, \ldots, z^n)$ is defined to be $\bar{z} = (\bar{z}^1, \bar{z}^2, \ldots, \bar{z}^n)$ where z^α denotes the complex conjugate of z^α; i.e., $\bar{z}^\alpha = x^{2\alpha-1} - ix^{2\alpha}$ if $z^\alpha = x^{2\alpha-1} + ix^{2\alpha}$. The scalar product of z and w is $z \cdot \bar{w} = z^1 \cdot \bar{w}^1 + z^2 \cdot \bar{w}^2 + \ldots + z^n \cdot \bar{w}^n$, and the length $|z|$ of z is the square root of $z \cdot \bar{z}$. The distance between z and w is $|z - w|$.

An *open set* D of C^n is a set of points of C^n such that, for any z of D, all points w of C^n whose distance from z is sufficiently small also belong to D. For example, the ball consisting of all z with $|z| < 1$, and the polycylinder consisting of all points $z = (z^1, z^2, \ldots, z^n)$ with $|z^1| < 1, |z^2| < 1, \ldots, |z^n| < 1$, are open sets of D of particularly simple type. An open set D of C^n is called a domain if it is connected; i.e., if any pair of its points can be joined by a polygonal arc lying entirely in D. The ball and the polycylinder are connected and are therefore domains.

Let D and $\tilde{D}$ be open sets of C^m and C^n respectively, and denote the co-ordinates of C^m by $(z^1, z^2, \ldots, z^m)$, those of C^n by $(w^1, w^2, \ldots, w^n)$. A map $F : D \to \tilde{D}$ assigns to each point z of D a point w of $\tilde{D}$. Referring this map to the co-ordinates of C^n, F can be expressed in the form $F = (f^1, f^2, \ldots, f^n)$ where $w^\alpha = f^\alpha(z)$ is a complex-valued function defined over D. The map F is continuous if each "component" f^α of F is a continuous function; it is differentiable if each component f^α is differentiable, etc.

Let f be a complex-valued function on the open set D of C^n which has continuous partial derivatives of the first order. Let $z^1, z^2, \ldots, z^n$ be the co-ordinates of C^n, write $z^\alpha = x^{2\alpha-1} + ix^{2\alpha}$, and define

$$\frac{\partial f}{\partial \bar{z}^\alpha} = \frac{1}{2}\left(\frac{\partial f}{\partial x^{2\alpha-1}} + i\frac{\partial f}{\partial x^{2\alpha}}\right)$$

where $\partial f/\partial x^{2\alpha-1}, \partial f/\partial x^{2\alpha}$ denote the partial derivatives of f in the usual sense of calculus. The function f is said to be *holomorphic* (analytic) on D if $\partial f/\partial \bar{z}^\alpha = 0$ for $\alpha = 1, 2, \ldots, n$ (Cauchy-Riemann equations). A map $F : D \to \tilde{D}$ is said to be holomorphic if each component f^α of F is a holomorphic function on D.

A topological space is a set on which the notion of open set is given. Hence, on a topological space, the notion of a continuous function is defined. A map of one topological space onto another is said to be bicontinuous, or to be a homeomorphism, if it is one-one, continuous, and the inverse map is also continuous. Two topological spaces are said to be homeomorphic if they are connected by a homeomorphism. Homeomorphic spaces are topologically equivalent; i.e., their intrinsic topological properties are the same. For example, the ball and the polycylinder of C^n are homeomorphic. On the other hand, the domain $1/2 < |z| < 1$ of C^n is not homeomorphic to the polycylinder of C^n.

A map of one open set of C^n onto another is said to be biholomorphic if it is one-one and holomorphic (which implies that the inverse is also holomorphic). The ball of C^n cannot be mapped biholomorphically onto the polycylinder of C^n if $n > 1$. Thus topologically equivalent domains are not generally holomorphically equivalent, except under certain circumstances in the case $n = 1$.

Conformal Maps.—The study of conformal maps arose historically from the necessity of constructing geographic maps. Since the surface of the earth is approximately a sphere, it is readily seen that it cannot be represented on a flat surface with preservation of the proportion of all distances; indeed the same is true for any substantial portion of the earth's surface. The next best property to be preserved is the relative shape of configurations in the neighbourhood of each point; this, in a more precise mathematical formulation, amounts to preservation of the magnitude and sense of angles at each point. Such a map is called conformal. Examples are the familiar Mercator and stereographic projections. In a conformal map of one open set of the plane onto another, it is a simple matter to verify that the map is given locally by a biholomorphic transformation of one complex variable.

On the other hand, a biholomorphic map of one open set of C^n onto another is not generally conformal if $n > 1$. We therefore suppose throughout this section that $n = 1$.

The preceding local characterization of a conformal map disposes only of the most trivial aspect of it since it gives no information concerning the existence of a conformal map of one given plane domain onto another. Since it is impossible, except in the most trivial cases, to construct conformal maps explicitly, attention has centred mainly on the problems of proving their existence and of determining their properties.

A necessary condition in order that there should exist a biholomorphic (one-one conformal) map of one plane domain onto another is that there should exist a bicontinuous map (homeomorphism) of the one domain onto the other, and it is a remarkable fact that this necessary condition is in some cases sufficient.

Riemann Mapping Theorem.—Let D be a domain of C which is not the whole of C, and suppose that D is homeomorphic to the unit disk $|z| < 1$. Then, given an arbitrary point z_0 of D and a direction at z_0 (vector issuing from z_0), there exists a unique biholomorphic (one-one conformal) map of D onto the unit disk $|z| < 1$ such that z_0 goes into the centre of the disk and the given direction at z_0 transforms into the direction of the positive real axis.

Although the whole plane C is homeomorphic to the unit disk, it is impossible to map it conformally onto the unit disk; this is a consequence of a classical theorem of J. Liouville.

Denote by S the class of functions f of the complex variable z which are holomorphic in the unit disk, which map it one-one conformally onto domains of C, and which are normalized by the condition that their power series in z, convergent for $|z| < 1$, are of the form

$$f(z) = z + a_2 z^2 + a_3 z^3 + a_4 z^4 + \ldots + a_n z^n + \ldots$$

In his proof of the general uniformization principle (of which the Riemann mapping theorem is a special case), Koebe introduced the class S and studied some of its properties. This class quickly attracted the attention of a number of mathematicians, including L. Bieberbach, C. Carathéodory, G. Faber, T. H. Gronwall and P. Montel. If the class S is suitably "topologized," then,

[7]H. Weyl, "Address of the President of the Fields Medal Committee," *Proceedings* of the International Congress of Mathematicians, Amsterdam, vol. i, pp. 161–174 (1954).
[8]C. L. Siegel, "Analytic Functions of Several Complex Variables; Lectures Delivered at the Institute for Advanced Study, Princeton" (Mimeographed notes) (1948).

for each integer $n > 1$, the map $F^n : S \to \mathbf{C}^n$ which sends the function f of S into the point $(a_2, a_3, \ldots, a_{n+1})$ of $\mathbf{C}^n$, determined by the n coefficients $a_2, a_3, \ldots, a_{n+1}$ in the power series development of f, is continuous. Denote by B^n the image of S under the map F. The set B^n, homeomorphic to the closed unit ball $|w^1|^2 + |w^2|^2 + \ldots + |w^n|^2 \leq 1$ of $\mathbf{C}^n$, is called the nth coefficient region of S. The structure of the class S is completely determined by a knowledge of these coefficient regions and the maps F^n. In 1916 Bieberbach proved that B^1 is the region $|a_2| \leq 2$ and, soon thereafter, posed the problem of investigating the regions B^n for all n. He further conjectured that $|a_n| \leq n$ for all n (Bieberbach conjecture). This problem and conjecture were followed by an intensive study of the class S.

In 1923 K. Löwner[9] approximated an arbitrary function of S by a subclass of functions of S satisfying a differential equation in one real parameter and, in this way, proved that $|a_3| \leq 3$. Next, H. Grötzsch developed a method based on the characteristic conformal invariant (modulus) of a doubly connected domain and proved numerous "distortion theorems" for the class S. L. Ahlfors and A. Beurling developed a "method of extremal length" which systematized and generalized certain aspects of the work of Grötzsch. A variational calculus, which began with a paper[10] by M. Schiffer in 1938, was perfected and applied to the class S by Schiffer and other authors during the following years.[11] Variational methods were used by A. C. Schaeffer and D. C. Spencer[12] in determining explicitly the region B^2 and in investigating the properties of B^n, $n > 2$. In particular, they proved that a function of S maximizing the absolute value of its nth coefficient maps $|z| < 1$ onto the whole plane minus a single analytic slit extending from some finite point to "infinity." P. Garabedian and Schiffer, using variational methods, showed in 1954 that $|a_4| \leq 4$. O. Teichmüller, in a series of papers from 1938 to 1944, developed the theory of "quadratic differentials";

BY COURTESY OF A. C. SCHAEFFER AND D. C. SPENCER

ONE-HALF OF THE 3-DIMENSIONAL SECTION OF THE 4 REAL-DIMENSIONAL REGION B^2 FOR WHICH a_3 IS REAL

The three lines represent the co-ordinate axes of real Euclidean 3-space. The vertical line is the co-ordinate for the real part of a_2; the two horizontal axes represent a_3 and the imaginary part of a_2 (the latter pointing toward viewer). The total section is obtained by reflection of the portion shown on the horizontal plane. The boundary of B^2 consists of two 3-dimensional surfaces whose parametric equations are given by different formulas. One of these surfaces appears as the disconnected portions of the boundary (dark areas in the illustration). To each point of the boundary there corresponds a unique extremal function of the class S

these differentials occur in the variational method, namely, the nonlinear differential equations satisfied by extremal functions of the class S are equations connecting a pair of quadratic differentials. J. A. Jenkins, in 1954, proved a "general coefficient theorem"

which incorporates those aspects of quadratic differentials bearing on extremal problems and provides a systematic method of investigating the class S.[13]

Finally, the class S is a subclass of a wider class of functions, the so-called multivalent functions, which have been studied intensively by W. K. Hayman.[14] As a corollary of Hayman's investigations, the Bieberbach conjecture for a fixed function f of S and all sufficiently large n has been established, namely: for each f of S there exists a positive integer $n_0(f)$ such that $|a_n| \leq n$ for all n exceeding $n_0(f)$.

Complex Analytic Manifolds.—Riemann surfaces, as conceived by Riemann, are multisheeted coverings of the plane $\mathbf{C}$, or of the sphere obtained by compactifying $\mathbf{C}$ with the adjunction of a "point at infinity," and arose from the analytic continuation of multivalued functions over $\mathbf{C}$. It was a natural step, first taken by Klein, to introduce the notion of an abstract Riemann surface as a surface (in the topological sense) every point of which has a neighbourhood which is homeomorphic to an open set of $\mathbf{C}$, this homeomorphism defining on the neighbourhood a local complex co-ordinate z (or local uniformizing parameter). The transformation from one complex co-ordinate to another is biholomorphic (one-one conformal). A Riemann surface is a complex manifold of complex dimension 1.

The concept of a Riemann surface has a natural generalization to that of a complex (analytic) manifold of arbitrary (finite) complex dimension. Namely, a complex co-ordinate manifold of complex dimension n is a topological space together with a covering $\{U_i\}$ of it by overlapping open sets U_i and a system $\{h_i\}$ of homeomorphisms h_i of U_i onto open sets D_i of $\mathbf{C}^n$. For a point p of U_i, the homeomorphism h_i defines $z_i = (z_i^1, z_i^2, \ldots, z_i^n) = h_i(p)$ as a system of local complex co-ordinates on U_i, and the transformations from one system of local complex co-ordinates to another must be biholomorphic. Two systems $\{U_i, h_i\}$ and $\{U_i', h_i'\}$ of "co-ordinatizations" of the given topological space are said to be equivalent if the inverse map of h_i followed by h_j' is biholomorphic (where defined). A complex manifold, or complex structure on a topological space, is an equivalence class of complex co-ordinatizations.

It is usual to impose the further topological condition that the underlying topological space is "paracompact," that is: (1) any two distinct points of it have disjoint neighbourhoods; (2) from any covering of the topological space by open sets, a "locally finite" covering can be extracted, where a locally finite covering is one such that each point has a neighbourhood belonging to only finitely many open sets of the covering. These topological restrictions are important only in that they eliminate from consideration manifolds of a pathological nature.

A complex manifold is compact if, from *any* covering of it by open sets, a *finite* covering can be selected.

Complex n-space $\mathbf{C}^n$ is the simplest example of an open (*i.e.*, noncompact) complex manifold; it is covered by a single system of complex co-ordinates. It can be compactified in a natural way to give a compact complex manifold called complex projective n-space, denoted by $P_n(\mathbf{C})$. Namely, denote by $(z^0, z^1, \ldots, z^n)$ the complex co-ordinates on $\mathbf{C}^{n+1}$. Remove from $\mathbf{C}^{n+1}$ the origin $(0, 0, \ldots, 0)$ and call the resulting (complex) manifold W. Given a point p of W with the co-ordinates $(z^0, z^1, \ldots, z^n)$, the set of points defined by $c \cdot (z^0, z^1, \ldots, z^n) = (cz^0, cz^1, \ldots, cz^n)$, as c ranges over all nonzero complex numbers, is called a *complex line* through p. The points of complex projective n-space $P_n(\mathbf{C})$ are the complex lines of W. As homogeneous co-ordinates on $P_n(\mathbf{C})$ we may take $(z^0, z^1, \ldots, z^n)$ where $z^0, z^1, \ldots, z^n$ are not all zero, and where $(z^0, z^1, \ldots, z^n)$ and $c \cdot (z^0, z^1, \ldots, z^n)$ correspond to the same point of $P_n(\mathbf{C})$. Let U_i be the open set of $P_n(\mathbf{C})$ composed of points whose ith homogeneous co-ordinate z^i does not vanish. Then $U_0, U_1, \ldots, U_n$ cover $P_n(\mathbf{C})$ and $(z^0/z^i, \ldots, z^{i-1}/z^i, z^{i+1}/z^i, \ldots, z^n/z^i)$ is a system of complex co-ordinates covering U_i. It is easily verified that the transformation from the co-ordinates covering U_i to those covering U_j is biholomorphic.

[9]K. Löwner, "Untersuchungen über schlichte konforme Abbildungen des Einheitskreises. I," *Math. Ann.*, vol. 89, pp. 103–121 (1923).
[10]M. Schiffer, "A Method of Variation Within the Family of Simple Functions," *Proc. Lond. Math. Soc.* (2), vol. 44, pp. 432–449 (1938).
[11]M. Schiffer and D. C. Spencer, *Functionals of Finite Riemann Surfaces* (1954).
[12]A. C. Schaeffer and D. C. Spencer, "Coefficient Regions for Schlicht Functions," *Colloq. Publ. Amer. Math. Soc.*, vol. 35 (1950).

[13]J. A. Jenkins, "Univalent Functions and Conformal Mapping," *Ergebn. Math.*, new series, 18 (1958).
[14]W. K. Hayman, "Multivalent Functions," *Camb. Tracts Math.*, no. 48 (1958).

$P_n(\mathbf{C})$ is a *compact* complex manifold. The set of points of $P_n(\mathbf{C})$ for which $z^0 = 0$ is a hyperplane E_0, which is itself a complex projective space of dimension $n - 1$, and $P_n(\mathbf{C})$ is obtained from U_0, which is equivalent to $\mathbf{C}^n$, by adding to U_0 the hyperplane E_0 at "infinity," which compactifies it.

The complex projective line $P_1(\mathbf{C})$ is often called the complex-number sphere. In fact, $P_1(\mathbf{C})$ is topologically homeomorphic to a sphere since it is obtained from the plane by adding one point at infinity.

A "nonsingular" compact, complex analytic submanifold of $P_n(\mathbf{C})$ is called a *projective manifold*. For example, the complex plane E_0 is a projective manifold of complex dimension $n - 1$. A (possibly singular) subvariety of $P_n(\mathbf{C})$ defined by finitely many polynomial equations, homogeneous in the co-ordinates $z^0, z^1, \ldots, z^n$, is called a *projective algebraic variety*. It follows from a general theorem of W.-L. Chow that a projective manifold is a nonsingular projective algebraic variety. The projective manifolds are the commonest compact complex manifolds. For example, the equation $(z^0)^2 + (z^1)^2 + (z^2)^2 + (z^3)^2 = 0$ defines a nonsingular surface in $P_3(\mathbf{C})$. The study of projective algebraic varieties, from the algebraic point of view, constitutes "algebraic geometry" in the classical sense of the term.

Not all compact complex manifolds are projective. Indeed, in 1958 M. Nagata[15] showed that, to each projective manifold (variety) of dimension $n \geq 3$, there is associated a "birationally equivalent" nonprojective manifold (variety). The condition $n \geq 3$ is essential, as follows from fundamental results of Chow and Kodaira.[16]

Uniformization.—The theorem on uniformization established by Koebe may be stated as follows:

General Uniformization Principle.—Any Riemann surface which is homeomorphic to some subdomain of the complex sphere $P_1(\mathbf{C})$ can be mapped biholomorphically (one-one conformally) onto a canonical domain of $P_1(\mathbf{C})$, each boundary component ("connected piece of boundary") of which is either a point or a straight-line segment parallel to the real axis (canonical domain of D. Hilbert).

Given any compact Riemann surface V, there is associated to it another (generally open) Riemann surface $\tilde{V}$, called its "universal covering surface," which, if open, has the property that it is homeomorphic to the unit disk $|z| < 1$ of $\mathbf{C}$. Hence, by the uniformization principle, $\tilde{V}$ (if open) can be mapped conformally onto $\mathbf{C}$ (parabolic case), or onto $|z| < 1$ (hyperbolic case). We shall discuss briefly the hyperbolic case. In this case the points of $\tilde{V}$ "lying over" one and the same point of V are mapped into a set of points in $|z| < 1$ which is generated from any one point in the set by a "discontinuous group" G of analytic automorphisms of $|z| < 1$ (biholomorphic maps of $|z| < 1$ onto itself). The Riemann surface V corresponds to a fundamental domain of G in $|z| < 1$ which is the interior of a polygon whose sides are arcs (interior to $|z| < 1$) of circles orthogonal to the circumference $|z| = 1$, these sides being identified in pairs to form a compact surface. The Riemann surface V is entirely determined, up to isomorphisms, by the group G of automorphisms of $|z| < 1$, and the meromorphic functions on V are represented by meromorphic functions in $|z| < 1$ invariant under G—the so-called automorphic functions. The theory of automorphic functions, founded by Poincaré, is one of the most beautiful chapters in the theory of functions of one complex variable.

A compact complex manifold of complex dimension greater than 1 cannot in general be "uniformized"; *i.e.*, represented as a fundamental domain of a discontinuous group operating analytically on a subdomain of $\mathbf{C}^n$. However, examples of complex manifolds represented as fundamental domains of a discontinuous group operating analytically on a subdomain of $\mathbf{C}^n$, n larger than 1, have been constructed by Siegel using deep methods.[17]

Further results in the theory of automorphic functions of several

variables have been contributed by W. L. Baily, S. Bochner, F. Hirzebruch, I. Satake, A. Selberg, A. Weil and others.

Distribution of Values of Meromorphic Functions; Meromorphic Curves.—One of the most important contributions to the theory of functions of one complex variable in the first half of the 20th century was the theory of the value distribution of a meromorphic function on an open Riemann surface, which was originated by R. Nevanlinna and developed by Ahlfors and other members of the Finnish school. This theory was later generalized to "meromorphic curves" (analytic curves in projective n-space), whose parameter domain is an open Riemann surface, by Weyl,[18] who investigated the asymptotic behaviour of these curves as the parameter point approaches the boundary of the Riemann surface. Weyl's theory was further perfected by Ahlfors in an important paper.[19] A generalization of this theory to functions of several complex variables has been given by W. Stoll.[20]

Cohomology With Coefficients in Sheaves.—An n-dimensional complex analytic manifold V may be covered by a finite or (countably) infinite set $\mathfrak{U} = \{U_i\}$ of open sets U_i. Denote their nonempty intersections by $U_{ij} = U_i \cap U_j$ (where $U_i \cap U_j$ signifies the intersection of U_i and U_j), $U_{ijk} = U_i \cap U_j \cap U_k, \ldots$. Cochains with coefficients, or values, in the complex numbers, of dimensions 0, 1, 2, ... are defined by associating to each U_i, U_{ij}, U_{ijk}, ... complex numbers c_i, c_{ij}, c_{ijk}, ... depending skew-symmetrically on the indices. Consider, for purposes of illustration, a 1-cochain $c = \{c_{ij}\}$ (cochain of dimension 1). Its *coboundary* δc is a 2-cochain defined by associating to each U_{ijk} the number $(\delta c)_{ijk} = c_{ij} + c_{jk} + c_{ki}$. A cochain c is a *cocycle* if its coboundary vanishes. The coboundary of a $(q - 1)$-cochain is a q-cocycle (cocycle of dimension q) and it is said to be *cohomologous* to zero. The vector space of q-cocycles *modulo* the q-coboundaries defines the cohomology of the "nerve" of the covering $\mathfrak{U}$ with coefficients in the complex numbers and it is denoted by $H^q(\mathfrak{U}, \mathbf{C})$. The cohomology $H^q(\mathfrak{U}, \mathbf{C})$ depends on the covering $\mathfrak{U} = \{U_i\}$ of V by the overlapping open sets U_i but, by passage to finer coverings or by a suitable "normalization" of the covering, it can be made independent of the choice of the covering and the result is the q-dimensional cohomology of V with coefficients in the complex numbers $\mathbf{C}$, which is denoted by $H^q(V, \mathbf{C})$.

Now suppose that we replace c_i, c_{ij}, c_{ijk}, ... by holomorphic functions f_i, f_{ij}, f_{ijk}, ... on U_i, U_{ij}, U_{ijk}, ... We then obtain cochains with coefficients in the holomorphic functions and the resulting cohomology is called the cohomology of V with coefficients in the "sheaf" Ω of holomorphic functions; this cohomology, of dimension q, is denoted by $H^q(V, \Omega)$. Over any point of V the sheaf Ω consists of all functions f which are holomorphic in some neighbourhood, depending on f, of the point. In defining this cohomology we have used the fact that holomorphic functions can be added, their sum being again a holomorphic function. More generally, the cohomology can be defined with coefficients in any sheaf of "abelian groups."

Without attempting to define sheaves in general, we remark that various types of cohomology can be defined with coefficients in sheaves related, in various ways, to the complex analytic structure. Further examples will be indicated in the following section.

Complex Line Bundles; Complex Vector Bundles.—A divisor on a complex manifold V is defined by assigning, to each open set U_i of a covering $\{U_i\}$ of V, a meromorphic function f_i on U_i such that $f_i/f_j = f_{ij}$ is a nonvanishing holomorphic function on $U_{ij} = U_i \cap U_j$. Clearly $\{f_{ij}\}$ defines a 1-cocycle in the multiplicative sense, namely $f_{ij} \cdot f_{jk} \cdot f_{ki} = 1$. Hence a divisor defines an element (class) of the cohomology $H^1(V, \Omega^*)$ where Ω^* denotes the multiplicative sheaf of nonvanishing holomorphic functions. This class is trivial if there exists a 0-cochain $\{g_i\}$, with coefficients in Ω^*, satisfying $f_{ij} = g_j/g_i$; then $f = f_i \cdot g_i = f_j \cdot g_j$ in U_{ij} defines a meromorphic function f on V whose divisor is equal to the given one. The cohomology class of the 1-cocycle $\{f_{ij}\}$ cor-

[15]M. Nagata, "Existence Theorems for Non-projective Complete Algebraic Varieties," *Illinois Journal of Mathematics*, vol. 2, pp. 490–498 (1958).
[16]W.-L. Chow and K. Kodaira, "On Analytic Surfaces With Two Independent Meromorphic Functions," *Proc. Nat. Acad. Sci., Wash.*, vol. 38, pp. 319–325 (1952); K. Kodaira, "On Compact Analytic Surfaces, I," *Ann. Math.*, vol. 71, pp. 111–152 (1960).
[17]C. L. Siegel, *op. cit.*

[18]H. Weyl, "Meromorphic Functions and Analytic Curves," *Ann. Math. Stud.*, no. 12 (1943).
[19]L. Ahlfors, "The Theory of Meromorphic Curves," *Acta Soc. Sci. Fenn.*, new series A, 3, no. 4 (1941).
[20]W. Stoll, "Die beiden Hauptsätze der Wertverteilungstheorie bei Funktionen mehrerer komplexen Veränderlichen," part i, *Acta Math.*, vol. 90, pp. 1–115 (1953), part ii, *ibid.*, vol. 92, pp. 55–169 (1954).

responds to a class of complex analytically equivalent complex line bundles (complex analytic fibre bundles whose fibre is $\mathbf{C}$). A bundle F of this class may be constructed by taking the "products" $U_i \times \mathbf{C}$ whose points are pairs (z_i, ζ_i), where z_i is a point of U_i, ζ_i a point of $\mathbf{C}$, and identifying the points (z_i, ζ_i), (z_j, ζ_j) of $U_i \times \mathbf{C}$, $U_j \times \mathbf{C}$, respectively, if z_i and z_j are the same point Z of U_{ij} and $\zeta_i = f_{ij}(Z) \cdot \zeta_j$. The functions f_{ij} are called the *transition functions* of the bundle F over V. There is a holomorphic map $\pi : F \to V$ which is induced by the projection $U_i \times \mathbf{C} \to U_i$ sending (z_i, ζ_i) into z_i.

A holomorphic section s of the line bundle F over an open set U of V is a holomorphic map $s : U \to F$ such that s followed by π is the identity map of U. Since the holomorphic sections of F over U form a complex vector space, the cohomology of V with coefficients in the sheaf of sections of a complex line bundle F over V is defined; this cohomology, of dimension q, will be denoted by $H^q(V, F)$.

A complex line bundle is a special case of a complex (analytic) vector bundle. The fibre of a complex vector bundle is $\mathbf{C}^m$ and its transition functions f_{ij} are $(m \times m)$-matrices of holomorphic functions with nonvanishing determinant at each point of U_{ij}. Cohomology with coefficients in the sheaf of holomorphic sections of an arbitrary complex vector bundle F is defined since the sections form a complex vector space. For each q, the cohomology $H^q(V, F)$ is a complex vector space, which is finite dimensional if V is compact.

The Riemann-Roch Theorem.—Let F be a complex line bundle, over a compact Riemann surface V, defined by a divisor which is given by meromorphic functions f_i in each open set U_i of a covering $\{U_i\}$ of V. Since f_i/f_j is a *nonvanishing holomorphic function* in the intersection U_{ij} of U_i and U_j, a point in U_{ij} which is a zero (pole) of f_i of a certain order is also a zero (pole) of f_j of the same order. The finitely many points of V where the functions $f_i, f_j, \ldots$ have zeros or poles are therefore defined, and to each zero or pole there is assigned an integer, positive if the point is a zero and negative if it is a pole, whose absolute value defines the order of the zero or pole. The sum of all these integers is a topological invariant of the line bundle F which is called its characteristic class; it will be denoted by $c(F)$.

A compact Riemann surface is homeomorphic to the (topological) surface obtained from a sphere by cutting g pairs of holes in it and attaching to each pair of holes a "handle," forming a total of g handles, where g is an integer $0, 1, 2, \ldots$. The nonnegative integer g, a topological invariant of the Riemann surface, is called its *genus*. For example, the sphere with one handle, topologically the same as a torus, has genus equal to 1.

The classical Riemann-Roch theorem, expressed in the language of sheaf cohomology, asserts that

$$\dim H^0(V, F) - \dim H^1(V, F) = c(F) - g + 1$$

where $\dim H^q(V, F)$ signifies the dimension of the cohomology $H^q(V, F)$. The term $H^0(V, F)$ is the (vector) space of holomorphic sections of F. Since $\dim H^1(V, F)$ is a *nonnegative integer*, we obtain the Riemann-Roch inequality

$$\dim H^0(V, F) \geq c(F) - g + 1$$

In particular, if $c(F) \geq g + 1$, then $\dim H^0(V, F) \geq 2$ and there exist at least two linearly independent holomorphic sections s_1, s_2 of F over V whose ratio s_1/s_2 is a nonconstant meromorphic function f on V. Thus the Riemann-Roch theorem, for a Riemann surface, yields information concerning the existence of meromorphic functions with given divisor on V.

In 1954 Hirzebruch[21] generalized the Riemann-Roch theorem to complex analytic vector bundles F over projective manifolds V of arbitrary complex dimension. Introduce the Euler-Poincaré characteristic $\chi(V, F)$ of the cohomology of V with coefficients in the sheaf of holomorphic sections of the complex vector bundle F, namely,

$$\chi(V, F) = \dim H^0(V, F) - \dim H^1(V, F) + \cdots + (-1)^n \dim H^n(V, F)$$

We note that the Riemann-Roch theorem, for a complex line bundle F over a compact Riemann surface V, expresses $\chi(V, F)$ in terms of topological invariants of V and F. The Riemann-Roch theorem of Hirzebruch expresses $\chi(V, F)$ in terms of topological invariants of V and F called characteristic classes, or Chern classes of V and F (after S. S. Chern, who first gave a precise definition of these classes).

Hirzebruch's proof of his theorem, which is based on a deep and remarkable theory of R. Thom,[22] is nonalgebraic in character. A formulation of the Riemann-Roch theorem which contains Hirzebruch's theorem as a special case has been proved by A. Grothendieck[23] using only algebraic methods.

We remark that a knowledge of the value of $\chi(V, F)$ yields less information, concerning the existence of holomorphic sections of F, as the complex dimension n of V becomes larger.

Intrinsic Characterization of Projective Manifolds.—An intrinsic characterization of projective manifolds has been given by Kodaira,[24] which is a profound generalization of the classical theorem that every compact Riemann surface is projective. The theorem of Kodaira states that a compact complex manifold is projective if and only if there exists over it a "positive" complex line bundle, that is a complex line bundle F whose characteristic class $c(F)$, an element of the 2-dimensional cohomology of V with integer coefficients, can be represented by a positive-definite hermitian form of degree 2 (Hodge metric).

The proof is based on a "vanishing theorem," due to Kodaira also,[25] which states that the cohomology with coefficients in the sheaf of sections of a complex line bundle vanishes in the positive dimensions if the line bundle is sufficiently positive. The vanishing theorem, a generalization of earlier results of Bochner,[26] provides a criterion for the existence of holomorphic sections of vector bundles.

Stein Manifolds and Holomorphically Complete Spaces.—Beginning in the 1930s, K. Oka[27] made a deep investigation of questions connected with Cousin's problems and related topics in the theory of functions of several complex variables, and proved fundamental theorems which strongly influenced the work of others in this field. In particular, the notion of a "coherent analytic sheaf," an extremely important concept formulated by H. Cartan, has roots in some of Oka's work.

Shortly after 1950 a remarkable unification, by Cartan and J. P. Serre,[28] of certain aspects of the work of Oka and of that of Behnke, Stein and others was achieved with the use of sheaf cohomology. Numerous results of the theory of functions of several complex variables were subsumed in two main theorems of Cartan formulated in the language of cohomology with coefficients in coherent analytic sheaves. During the next decade, H. Grauert[29] and R. Remmert, using cohomological methods combined with various refined techniques, discovered profound generalizations of some of Oka's work. Other aspects of Oka's work were generalized by H. Bremermann and others of the Münster (Ger.) school of complex function theory, founded several years earlier by Behnke.

Since much of this work is highly technical in nature, explanations will be confined mainly to Cartan's second main theorem.[30] Although the theorem is easily stated in the language of sheaf cohomology, it should be emphasized that its proof is difficult.

[21] F. Hirzebruch, "Neue topologische Methoden in der algebraischen Geometrie," *Ergebn. Math.*, new series, 9 (1956).

[22] R. Thom, "Quelques propriétés globales des variétés différentiables," *Comment. Math. Helvet.*, vol. 28, pp. 17–86 (1954).

[23] A. Grothendieck: *see* articles by A. Borel and Serre, and by Grothendieck, in *Bulletin de la Société Mathématique de France*, vol. 86, pp. 97–154 (1958).

[24] K. Kodaira, "On Kähler Varieties of Restricted Type (an Intrinsic Characterization of Algebraic Varieties)," *Ann. Math.*, vol. 60, pp. 28–48 (1954).

[25] K. Kodaira, "On a Differential-Geometric Method in the Theory of Analytic Stacks," *Proc. Nat. Acad. Sci., Wash.*, vol. 39, pp. 1268–73 (1953).

[26] S. Bochner, "Curvature and Betti Numbers," part i, *Ann. Math.*, vol. 49, pp. 379–390 (1948), part ii, *ibid.*, vol. 50, pp. 77–93 (1949), "A New Viewpoint in Differential Geometry," *Canad. J. Math.*, vol. iii, pp. 460–470 (1951).

[27] K. Oka, "Sur les fonctions analytiques de plusieurs variables, II. Domaines d'holomorphie," *J. Sci. Hiroshima Univ.*, series A, 7, pp. 115–130 (1937), "Sur les fonctions analytiques de plusieurs variables, VII. Sur quelques notions arithmétiques," *Bull. Soc. Math. Fr.*, vol. 78, pp. 1–27 (1950).

[28] H. Cartan, *Séminaire de l'École Normale Supérieure, 1951–1952*; "Variétés analytiques complexes et cohomologie" in *Colloque sur les fonctions de plusieurs variables, tenu à Bruxelles*, pp. 41–55 (1953); J. P. Serre, "Quelques problèmes globaux relatifs aux variétés de Stein," *ibid.*, 57–68.

[29] H. Grauert, "Holomorphe Funktionen mit Werten in komplexen Lieschen Gruppen," *Math. Ann.*, vol. 133, pp. 450–472 (1957); "Analytische Faserungen über holomorph-vollständigen Räumen," *ibid.*, vol. 135, pp. 263–273 (1958).

[30] *See* Theorem B in H. Cartan, "Variétés analytiques complexes et cohomologie," *op. cit. See also* Serre, Exposé XX in Cartan, *Séminaire de l'École Normale Supérieure, 1951–1952, op. cit.*

The nature of the theorem will first be illustrated by an example. Let D be a subdomain of complex n-space $\mathbf{C}^n$. Suppose that there are given a covering $\{U_i\}$ of D by open sets U_i and, in each U_i, U_j, $\ldots$, meromorphic functions f_i, f_j, $\ldots$ where $f_j - f_i = f_{ij}$ is a holomorphic function in each intersection U_{ij} of U_i and U_j. The first problem of Cousin is that of determining a meromorphic function f on D such that $f - f_i$ is holomorphic in each U_i. The functions f_{ij} define a 1-cocycle with values in the sheaf Ω of holomorphic functions and hence determine a cohomology class of $H^1(D,\Omega)$. There exists a solution f of the first Cousin problem if and only if this class is trivial; i.e., if the 1-cocycle $\{f_{ij}\}$ is cohomologous to zero. In fact, if the desired meromorphic function f exists, then $g_i = f_i - f$ is holomorphic in U_i and $g_j - g_i = f_{ij}$; i.e., $\{f_{ij}\}$ is cohomologous to zero, and conversely. In particular, Cousin's first problem is solvable on D for arbitrary "Cousin data" $\{U_i, f_i\}$ if and only if $H^1(D,\Omega) = 0$. It was known that Cousin's first problem is always solvable on certain special subdomains of $\mathbf{C}^n$ called holomorphy domains, where a holomorphy domain is a domain of $\mathbf{C}^n$ on which there exists at least one holomorphic function which cannot be continued analytically (as a holomorphic function) into some larger domain. In the language of sheaf cohomology, the holomorphy domains are characterized by the property that the 1-dimensional cohomology, with coefficients in the sheaf of holomorphic functions, vanishes!

By introducing more general sheaves, namely coherent analytic sheaves, Cartan and Serre were able to characterize the Stein manifolds, previously defined by Stein in a purely function-theoretic way, as those complex manifolds V such that $H^1(V,\Phi) = 0$, or equivalently $H^q(V,\Phi) = 0$ for $q > 0$, for every coherent analytic sheaf Φ. Topological spaces with the property that the cohomology, with real or integer coefficients, vanishes in the positive dimensions, are called *acyclic*. The simplest acyclic spaces are those homeomorphic to a ball. In Cartan's general theorem, complex analysis found an analogue of the acyclic spaces of topology.

Theory of Deformation of Complex Analytic Structures. —Deformation of the complex structure of a compact Riemann surface (1-dimensional complex manifold) is an idea dating back to Riemann who, in 1857, calculated the number of independent parameters on which the deformation of the structure of a compact Riemann surface depends and called it the "number of moduli." The questions centring around the deformation of the complex structure of a Riemann surface have never lost their interest. The theory of quadratic differentials and extremal quasi-conformal maps was developed by Teichmüller in the years 1938–44 in order to give a systematic theory of the deformation of Riemann surfaces. Teichmüller's methods were perfected during the following years by Ahlfors, E. Rauch, L. Bers, Weil and others.

The deformation of the complex structure of higher dimensional complex manifolds seems to have been considered first in 1888 by Noether, who calculated the number of moduli for a class of algebraic surfaces in projective 3-space. However, in contrast to the case of complex dimension 1, the deformation of the structure of higher dimensional complex manifolds was neglected during the 70 years following Noether's work until the subject was taken up by A. Frölicher and A. Nijenhuis[31] and by Kodaira and Spencer.[32]

A more or less systematic theory of deformation of the complex structure of higher-dimensional, compact, complex analytic manifolds was given by Kodaira and Spencer,[33] and we now describe it briefly. They defined a differentiable family of compact complex manifolds as a fibre space $\mathcal{U}$ over a connected differentiable manifold M whose fibre V_t over the point t of M has a complex structure depending differentiably on the point t. Assume, for simplicity, that M is one dimensional and let U be a sufficiently small interval containing the point $t = 0$ in its interior. Then there exists a covering $\{U_i\}$ of the portion of $\mathcal{U}$ over U by open sets U_i where U_i is covered by the co-ordinates $(z_i,t) = (z_i^1, \ldots,$

$z_i^n, t)$. Denote by $z_i = h_{ik}(z_k,t)$ the biholomorphic co-ordinate transformations which determine the complex structure of V_t; i.e., $z_i^\alpha = h_{ik}^\alpha(z_k,t)$ where α ranges from 1 to n. Letting $\theta_{ik}(t) = (\theta_{ik}^1(t), \ldots, \theta_{ik}^\alpha(t), \ldots, \theta_{ik}^n(t))$, where $\theta_{ik}^\alpha(t) = \theta_{ik}^\alpha(z_i,t) = \partial h_{ik}^\alpha(z_k,t)/\partial t$, we obtain a 1-cocycle $\{\theta_{ik}(t)\}$ which defines a cohomology class $\theta(t)$ of the 1-dimensional cohomology $H^1(V_t,\Theta_t)$ of V_t with coefficients in the sheaf Θ_t over V_t of holomorphic vector fields. The class $\theta(t)$, called the "infinitesimal deformation" of V_t, measures the dependence of the complex structure of V_t on the parameter t. In the case where the fibres V_t are compact Riemann surfaces, $H^1(V_t,\Theta_t)$ is isomorphic to the vector space of quadratic differentials of the surface, in the sense of Teichmüller.

Proceeding in this fashion, a generalization of Riemann's concept of "number of moduli" was obtained. However, in contrast to the case of Riemann surfaces, this number is not defined for all compact complex manifolds. Particular examples of complex manifolds V_0, of complex dimension exceeding 2, show that not all cohomology classes of $H^1(V_0,\Theta_0)$ are the infinitesimal deformations of actual deformations of the structure of V_0. In fact, some classes of $H^1(V_0,\Theta_0)$ may be "obstructed," the obstructions occurring as classes in $H^2(V_0,\Theta_0)$. If $H^2(V_0,\Theta_0) = 0$, then any class of $H^1(V_0,\Theta_0)$ is the infinitesimal deformation corresponding to a deformation of finite magnitude.[34]

A classical problem[35] in algebraic geometry concerning the "completeness of characteristic systems" is to show that all "infinitesimal displacements" correspond to finite deformations of a complex analytic submanifold of a fixed algebraic manifold. A condition introduced by Severi[36] for the case of curves in algebraic surfaces was reformulated by Kodaira and Spencer in the language of sheaves and shown to be sufficient for completeness; i.e., for the existence of a finite deformation of the submanifold corresponding to any given infinitesimal displacement of it.

Finally, E. Calabi and E. Vesentini,[37] in a paper published in 1960, proved that a compact complex manifold, which is uniformized by an irreducible Cartan domain of at least two complex dimensions, is (locally) rigid; i.e., the number of its moduli is equal to zero. This result again underscores the difference between Riemann surfaces and complex manifolds of higher dimension.

(D. C. SR.)

ANALYSIS SITUS (POSITION ANALYSIS): *see* TOPOLOGY, ALGEBRAIC; TOPOLOGY, GENERAL

ANALYTIC GEOMETRY, the representation of the points in space by ordered sets of numbers called co-ordinates. For instance, any position on the earth can be specified by its latitude, longitude and height above sea level.

The one-dimensional case is well illustrated by a thermometer. There is a certain point on the line associated with the number 0; the positive integers 1, 2, 3, $\ldots$ are evenly spaced in one direction away from 0, the negative integers $-1, -2, -3, \ldots$ in the opposite direction, and the fractional numbers are interpolated in the ordinary manner. The displacement from one point x to another point x' is the positive or negative number $x' - x$.

In the two-dimensional case, the position of a point in a plane may be specified by its distances from two fixed perpendicular lines, the axes. The notion can be traced back to Archimedes of Syracuse (287–212 B.C.) and Apollonius of Perga (about 20 years later) or even to the ancient Egyptians; but it was first developed systematically by two Frenchmen, Pierre de Fermat (1601–65) and René Descartes (1596–1650). In their formulation the two distances were taken to be positive or zero. The important idea of allowing one or both to be negative was supplied by Sir Isaac Newton (1642–1727), and it was Leibniz (1646–1716) who first called them co-ordinates.

For some purposes it is just as easy to use *oblique* axes, as in

[31]A. Frölicher and A. Nijenhuis, "A Theorem on Stability of Complex Structures," *Proc. Nat. Acad. Sci., Wash.*, vol. 43, pp. 239–241 (1957).
[32]K. Kodaira and D. C. Spencer, "On the Variation of Almost-Complex Structure" in R. H. Fox *et al.* (eds.), *Algebraic Geometry and Topology* (1957).
[33]K. Kodaira and D. C. Spencer, "On Deformations of Complex Analytic Structures, I–II," *Ann. Math.*, vol. 67, pp. 328–466 (1958).

[34]K. Kodaira, L. Nirenberg and D. C. Spencer, "On the Existence of Deformations of Complex Analytic Structures," *Ann. Math.*, vol. 68, pp. 450–459 (1958).
[35]F. Severi, "La géométrie algébriques italienne: sa rigueur, ses méthodes ses problèmes" in *Colloque de géométrie algébrique*, pp. 9–55 (1949).
[36]F. Severi, "Sul teorema fondamentale dei sistemi continui di curve," *Ann. Mat.*, iv, vol. xxiii, pp. 149–181 (1944).
[37]E. Calabi and E. Vesentini, "On compact locally symmetric Kähler manifolds," *Ann. Math.*, vol. 71, pp. 472–507 (1960).

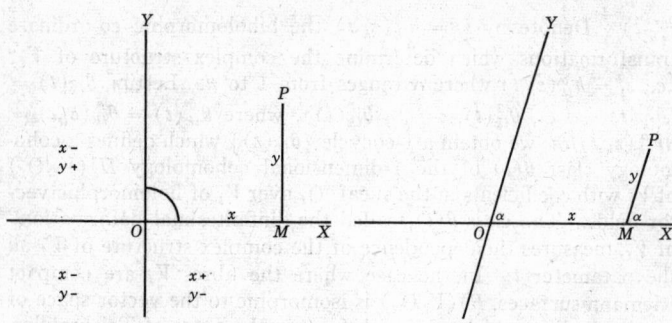

FIG. 1.—CARTESIAN CO-ORDINATES, RECTANGULAR AND OBLIQUE

the second part of fig. 1. Starting from the origin O, where the axes intersect, we reach the general point (x, y) by going a distance x along the x-axis OX and then a distance y along a line parallel to the y-axis OY. The x-axis is said to have the equation $y = 0$ because every point $(x, 0)$ satisfies this equation; similarly, $x = 0$ is the equation of the y-axis. On any other line through the origin, consideration of similar triangles shows that the ratio y/x is constant; thus any line through the origin $(0, 0)$ may be expressed as $ax + by = 0$, where a and b are arbitrary constants.

To obtain the equation for any other line, we take a point (x_1, y_1) on it. In terms of new co-ordinates x', y', derived by "translating" the origin from $(0, 0)$ to (x_1, y_1), the line may be expressed as $ax' + by' = 0$. Since $x' = x - x_1$ and $y' = y - y_1$, the same line, in terms of the original co-ordinates, is $a(x - x_1) + b(y - y_1) = 0$, or, say, $ax + by + c = 0$. Thus every line has a linear equation, and every linear equation determines a line. In particular, the line that makes intercepts x_0 and y_0 on the axes is $(x/x_0) + (y/y_0) = 1$, for this equation is linear and is satisfied by both $(x_0, 0)$ and $(0, y_0)$. Lines $ax + by + c = 0$ which have the same a/b and various values of c are parallel. The point of intersection of two nonparallel lines is obtained by solving the two simultaneous equations for x and y.

The equation $ax + by + c = 0$ with $b \neq 0$ may be solved for y in the form $y = -(ax + c)/b$. More generally, points whose co-ordinates satisfy an equation $F(x, y) = 0$ or $y = f(x)$ can be plotted by giving values to x and calculating the corresponding values of y. This procedure is particularly convenient when $f(x)$ is a one-valued function of x. In other cases it may be preferable to express the graph by parametric equations, giving x and y as functions of a single variable (or parameter) t. For instance, if P_1 denotes the point (x_1, y_1), any line through P_1 has parametric equations $x = x_1 + lt$, and $y = y_1 + mt$, where l and m depend on the direction of the line.

Sometimes, for the sake of symmetry, the single parameter t is replaced by two parameters, t_1 and t_2, related by an auxiliary equation. For instance, the general point (x, y) on the line through two given points P_1 and P_2 is given by

$$x = t_1 x_1 + t_2 x_2 \qquad y = t_1 y_1 + t_2 y_2 \qquad t_1 + t_2 = 1$$

This point P, dividing the distance $P_1 P_2$ in the ratio $t_2 : t_1$, is the centroid (or centre of gravity) of masses t_1 at P_1 and t_2 at P_2. Positions outside the interval from P_1 (where $t_2 = 0$) to P_2 (where $t_1 = 0$) are covered by allowing t_2 or t_1 to be negative (while still satisfying $t_1 + t_2 = 1$); we may justify this by calling them "electric charges" instead of "masses."

Distance.—For problems involving the distance between two points or the angle between two lines, it is often advisable to use rectangular axes, so that the distance from the origin to (x, y) is the square root of $x^2 + y^2$, and the distance between (x_1, y_1) and (x_2, y_2) is the square root of $(x_1 - x_2)^2 + (y_1 - y_2)^2$. Multiplication of the expression $p = ax + by + c$ by a suitable number enables us to normalize the equation $p = 0$ of the general line so that $a^2 + b^2 = 1$. Writing $p = 0$ in the form

$$(x - x_1 + 2p_1 a)^2 + (y - y_1 + 2p_1 b)^2 = (x - x_1)^2 + (y - y_1)^2$$

where $p_1 = ax_1 + by_1 + c$, we recognize it as the locus of points

equidistant from $(x_1 - 2p_1 a, y_1 - 2p_1 b)$ and (x_1, y_1); in other words, the line $p = 0$ serves as a mirror which interchanges these two points by reflection. It follows that the foot of the perpendicular from P_1 to $p = 0$ is $(x - p_1 a, y - p_1 b)$, and that the distance from P_1 to the line is $\pm p_1$ (provided $a^2 + b^2 = 1$). In particular, the distance from the origin to $p = 0$ is $\pm c$.

The locus of points at unit distance from the origin is the circle $x^2 + y^2 = 1$, which has the parametric equations $x = \cos\theta$, $y = \sin\theta$; or, with $t = \tan\frac{1}{2}\theta$,

$$x = (1 - t^2)/(1 + t^2) \qquad y = 2t/(1 + t^2)$$

Polar Co-ordinates.—For problems involving directions from a fixed origin (or pole) O, we often find it convenient to specify a point P by its polar co-ordinates (r, θ), where r is the distance OP and θ is the angle that the direction of r makes with a given initial line, which may be identified with the x-axis of rectangular Cartesian co-ordinates. When the complex number $x + yi = r\cos\theta$ is represented by the point (x, y), as in fig. 2 (the Argand diagram), the polar co-ordinates of the same point appear as the modulus and argument of the complex number $(q.v.)$. Of course, the point (r, θ) is the same as $(r, \theta + 2n\pi)$ for any integer n. It is sometimes desirable to allow r to be negative, so that (r, θ) is the same as $(-r, \theta + \pi)$.

Given the Cartesian equation for a curve, we can deduce the polar equation for the same curve by substituting

$$x = r\cos\theta \qquad y = r\sin\theta$$

For instance, the circle $x^2 + y^2 = a^2$ has the polar equation $(r\cos\theta)^2 + (r\sin\theta)^2 = a^2$, which reduces to $r = a$. (The positive value of r is sufficient, if we allow θ to take all values from $-\pi$ to π or from 0 to 2π.) Similarly, the line $y = x\tan\alpha$ has the polar equation $\sin\theta = \cos\theta\tan\alpha$, which reduces to $\theta = \alpha$. (The other solution, $\theta = \alpha + \pi$, can be discarded if we allow r to take negative values.)

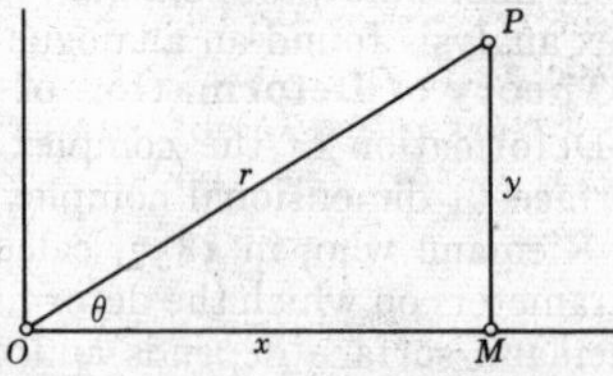

Transformation.—Two triangles are said to be similar if their sides are proportional, or if they have the same three angles. Their relationship can be extended to a transformation of the whole plane into itself. Such a similarity transforms every line segment AB into a line segment $A'B'$ which is μ times as long, where μ is a constant positive number (called the ratio of magnification). If $\mu \neq 1$ (and sometimes also if $\mu = 1$), there is a unique invariant point; i.e., a point that is transformed into itself. For instance, if two maps of the same country on different scales are drawn on tracing paper and superposed at random, there is always just one place that is represented by the same spot on both maps (even if one of the maps is turned over before it is superposed on the other). Taking the invariant point as the pole for polar co-ordinates, we find that the similarity transforms each point (r, θ) into $(\mu r, \alpha \pm \theta)$, where α is a constant angle (the same for all points). Taking the upper sign in "$\alpha \pm \theta$," we have a spiral similarity, including as special cases a rotation through α (given by $\mu = 1$) and a dilatation or "enlargement" (given by $\alpha = 0$). Taking the lower sign (as when one of the two maps is turned over), we have a dilative-reflection, including as a special case (when $\mu = 1$) a simple reflection in the line $\theta = \frac{1}{2}\alpha$.

The rotation $r' = r$, $\theta' = \theta + \alpha$ may be expressed in terms of Cartesian co-ordinates by writing $r\cos\theta = x$, $r\sin\theta = y$, so that, by the familiar formulas for the cosine and sine of $\theta + \alpha$,

$$x' = r\cos(\theta + a) = x\cos a - y\sin a$$
$$y' = r\sin(\theta + a) = x\sin a + y\cos a$$

In particular, rotation through a right angle is given by $x' = -y$, $y' = x$; and the condition for two lines

$$ax + by + c = 0 \qquad\qquad a'x + b'y + c' = 0$$

to be perpendicular is $aa' + bb' = 0$.

The Area of a Triangle.—If P_i has polar co-ordinates (r_i, θ_i),

FIG. 2.—CARTESIAN AND POLAR CO-ORDINATES (THE ARGAND DIAGRAM)

the area of a triangle OP_1P_2 is taken to be positive if $\theta_1 < \theta_2$, negative if $\theta_1 > \theta_2$. With this convention, the area is

$$\frac{1}{2}r_1r_2 \sin(\theta_2 - \theta_1) = \frac{1}{2}r_1r_2(\sin\theta_2\cos\theta_1 - \cos\theta_2\sin\theta_1)$$

or, in Cartesian co-ordinates,

$$\frac{1}{2}(x_1y_2 - x_2y_1) = \frac{1}{2}\begin{vmatrix} x_1 & y_1 \\ x_2 & y_2 \end{vmatrix}$$

To find the area of any triangle $P_1P_2P_3$, choose new axes parallel to OX, OY and passing through P_3. Since the new co-ordinates of P_i ($i = 1$ or 2) are $(x_i - x_3, y_i - y_3)$, the area of any triangle $P_1P_2P_3$ is

$$\frac{1}{2}\begin{vmatrix} x_1 - x_3 & y_1 - y_3 \\ x_2 - x_3 & y_2 - y_3 \end{vmatrix} = \frac{1}{2}\begin{vmatrix} x_1 & y_1 & 1 \\ x_2 & y_2 & 1 \\ x_3 & y_3 & 1 \end{vmatrix}$$

It follows that a necessary and sufficient condition for P_1, P_2, P_3 to be collinear is that this three-rowed determinant should be zero. The equation for the line P_1P_2 may be derived from this condition by writing (x, y) for (x_3, y_3).

Circles.—The circle with centre (p, q) and radius a, being the locus of points (x, y) distant a from (p, q), is $(x - p)^2 + (y - q)^2 = a^2$. Thus $x^2 + y^2 + 2gx + 2fy + c = 0$ is a circle with centre $(-g, -f)$ whenever $g^2 + f^2 \geq c$, degenerating to a "point circle" (radius zero) when $g^2 + f^2 = c$. If P_1 lies on the circle, the tangent at this point is $x_1x + y_1y + g(x + x_1) + f(y + y_1) + c = 0$, or $(x_1 + g)x + (y_1 + f)y + (gx_1 + fy_1 + c) = 0$, for this line passes through P_1 and is perpendicular to the diameter

$$(x + g)/(x_1 + g) = (y + f)/(y_1 + f)$$

The circle $x^2 + y^2 + 2gx + 2fy + c = 0$ is orthogonal to another circle

$$x^2 + y^2 + 2g'x + 2f'y + c' = 0$$

if, for a suitable P_1, the centre of each lies on the tangent at P_1 to the other. Adding

$$(x_1 + g)g' + (y_1 + f)f' = gx_1 + fy_1 + c$$

to the analogous relation with primed and unprimed letters interchanged, we see that the orthogonality of the two circles implies

$$2gg' + 2ff' = c + c'$$

Conversely, any two circles that satisfy this relation are orthogonal. In particular, the circles

$$x^2 + y^2 + 2gx + c = 0 \qquad x^2 + y^2 + 2fy - c = 0$$

whose centres lie on the x- and y-axes respectively, are orthogonal. Keeping c constant and allowing g or f to take various values, we obtain two orthogonal pencils of coaxal circles. If c is positive, the first pencil consists of nonintersecting circles, including two point circles ($\pm\sqrt{c}$, 0), called the limiting points of the pencil; the second pencil consists of all the circles that pass through both these points. If $c = 0$, each pencil consists of all the circles that touch one of the axes at the origin.

Barycentric and Areal Co-ordinates.—The centroid of m masses t_i at P_i is the point $(\sum t_ix_i/\sum t_i, \sum t_iy_i/\sum t_i)$. When $m = 2$ this is, as we have seen, a point on the line P_1P_2. But when $m = 3$, suitable values of t_i will place it anywhere in the plane. A. F. Möbius (1790–1868) called these three masses (t_1, t_2, t_3) the barycentric co-ordinates of the centroid with respect to the triangle of reference $P_1P_2P_3$. They are homogeneous co-ordinates since, for any $k \neq 0$, masses kt_1, kt_2, kt_3 have the same centroid as t_1, t_2, t_3. The barycentric co-ordinates of P are proportional to the areas of the three triangles PP_2P_3, PP_3P_1, PP_1P_2. Accordingly, when normalized so that $t_1 + t_2 + t_3 = 1$, they are called areal co-ordinates.

Projective Geometry.—The German astronomer Johannes Kepler (1571–1630) conceived the idea of extending the Euclidean (or affine) plane by postulating a line at infinity whose points lie on pencils of parallel lines. The plane so extended is called the projective plane. In terms of barycentric co-ordinates, the line at infinity has the equation $t_1 + t_2 + t_3 = 0$. General projective co-ordinates (x_1, x_2, x_3) are derived by the substitution $t_i = k_ix_i$, where the coefficients k_i are three constants. The line at infinity is now $k_1x_1 + k_2x_2 + k_3x_3 = 0$, and any other homogeneous linear equation represents an ordinary line. The transition to projective geometry is completed by waiving the distinction, so that a point at infinity is treated just like any other point. This vital step was taken by another distinguished German, K. G. C. von Staudt (1798–1867). It enables us to define the points of the projective plane as the ordered triads of numbers (x_1, x_2, x_3), not all zero, with the convention that (kx_1, kx_2, kx_3) is the same point for all nonzero values of k.

Given two points (x_1, x_2, x_3) and (y_1, y_2, y_3), or, more concisely, (x) and (y), we may express an arbitrary point collinear with them in the form $(x + ty)$, meaning $(x_1 + ty_1, x_2 + ty_2, x_3 + ty_3)$. In this notation, two triangles in perspective from (u) may be expressed as $(x)(y)(z)$ and $(x + u)$ $(y + u)$ $(z + u)$. Corresponding sides of the triangles meet in the three collinear points

$$(y - z) \quad (z - x) \quad (x - y)$$

in agreement with the two-triangle theorem of Gérard Desargues (1593–1662).

The general homogeneous linear transformation $x_i' = \sum c_{ij}x_j$ (summed over j), where $\det(c_{ij}) \neq 0$, transforms collinear points into collinear points; i.e., it is a collineation. For instance, the collineation

$$x_1' = x_1 \qquad x_2' = x_2 \qquad x_3' = kx_3$$

is a homology which leaves invariant every line through the point $(0,0,1)$ and every point on the line $x_3 = 0$.

Line Co-ordinates and Envelope Equations.—Julius Plücker (1801–68) provided an analytic expression for the principle of duality by defining co-ordinates not only for points but also for lines: the line $X_1x_1 + X_2x_2 + X_3x_3 = 0$ has co-ordinates $[X_1, X_2, X_3]$. The equation $\sum X_ix_i = 0$ now appears as the incidence condition for the line $[X]$ and the point (x). If (x) is a fixed point while $[X]$ is a variable line through it, the same equation $\sum x_iX_i = 0$ appears as the envelope equation of the point. Most problems involving envelopes of lines are conveniently treated by line co-ordinates and envelope equations.

A one-to-one correspondence between all the points A and lines a (in the real projective plane) is called a polarity if B lies on a whenever b passes through A. Following J. D. Gergonne (1771–1859), we call A the pole of a, and a the polar of A. If (x) and $[X]$ are related in this manner, we have $X_i = \sum c_{ij}x_j$ and $x_i = \sum C_{ij}X_j$, where $||c_{ij}||$ and $||C_{ij}||$ are inverse symmetric matrices. In terms of the pair of adjoint quadratic forms

$$(xx) = \sum\sum c_{ij}x_ix_j \qquad [XX] = \sum\sum C_{ij}X_iX_j$$

we see that the incidence condition for (x) and $[X]$ may be expressed either as $(xx) = 0$ or as $[XX] = 0$. If the quadratic forms are definite, this condition is never satisfied. If the forms are indefinite, the locus of points that lie on their polars, and the envelope of lines that pass through their poles, is a conic, which thus appears as a curve whose equation (in either point or line co-ordinates) is of the second degree. Such curves were obtained by Menaechmus (about 340 B.C.) as sections of cones. When the special role of the line at infinity is restored, we can distinguish between ellipses such as $x = a\cos t$, $y = b\sin t$, parabolas such as $x = at^2$, $y = 2at$, and hyperbolas such as

$$x = a\sec t, y = b\tan t$$

Three Dimensions.—Almost all the above remarks extend easily from two dimensions to three or more. In ordinary space a point has three Cartesian co-ordinates (x, y, z), a plane has a linear equation $ax + by + cz + d = 0$, and a line may be specified in various ways; e.g., as the intersection of two planes, or as the join of two points, or as proceeding from a given point in a given direction.

The last aspect yields the parametric equations

$$x = x_1 + lt \qquad y = y_1 + mt \qquad z = z_1 + nt$$

Polar co-ordinates have two spatial counterparts: cylindrical co-ordinates (r, θ, z), where r and θ are related to x and y in the usual way, and spherical polar co-ordinates, which consist of distance from the origin, latitude (or colatitude) and longitude. Barycentric (and other projective) co-ordinates are referred to a tetrahedron $P_1P_2P_3P_4$. The projective theory of collineations extends in a natural manner. The plane $\Sigma X_i x_i = 0$ has "co-ordinates" $[X_1, X_2, X_3, X_4]$. The first result that could not have been anticipated by simple analogy is that the matrix for a polarity (relating points and planes) is not necessarily symmetric ($c_{ji} = c_{ij}$): it may instead be skew-symmetric ($c_{ji} = -c_{ij}$), in which case every point lies on its own polar plane, and the lines that coincide with their polar lines form a very remarkable system called a linear complex.

The co-ordinates of three points may be arranged as a matrix having three rows and four columns. If the points are noncollinear, the matrix is of rank 3. By deleting the four columns in turn, we obtain four determinants, respectively equal to X_1, $-X_2$, X_3, $-X_4$, where $[X_1, X_2, X_3, X_4]$ are Plücker's co-ordinates for the plane determined by the three points. If, instead of three points, we take just two, say (x) and (y), we have a matrix of rank 2 with two rows and four columns. The six determinants $\{p_{14}, p_{24}, p_{34}, p_{23}, p_{31}, p_{12}\}$, where $p_{ij} = x_iy_j - y_ix_j$, are called the co-ordinates of the line.

The same co-ordinates, in a different order, can be derived by the dual procedure from two planes $[X]$ and $[Y]$ which pass through the line. The six p's are not arbitrary but always satisfy the quadratic equation

$$p_{14}p_{23} + p_{24}p_{31} + p_{34}p_{12} = 0$$

The above-mentioned linear complex consists of those lines which satisfy (also) the linear equation $\Sigma \Sigma c_{ij}p_{ij} = 0$, where

$$c_{14}c_{23} + c_{24}c_{31} + c_{34}c_{12} \neq 0$$

BIBLIOGRAPHY.—D. M. Y. Sommerville, *Analytical Geometry of Three Dimensions* (1934), *An Introduction to the Geometry of n Dimensions* (1929); A. Robson, *An Introduction to Analytical Geometry*, 2 vol. (1940, 1947); W. Blaschke, *Analytische Geometrie* (1954); H. S. M. Coxeter, *The Real Projective Plane*, 2nd ed., ch. 12 (1955), *Non-Euclidean Geometry*, 3rd ed., ch. 4 (1957).   (H. S. M. C.)

ANALYTIC MECHANICS: see MECHANICS: *Analytical Composition of Forces.*

'ANAN BEN DAVID (8th century), Persian Jew, founder within Judaism of the Karaite sect. *See* KARAISM.

ANANDA, one of the principal disciples of the Buddha, known as his "beloved disciple" and devoted companion, was a cousin of the Buddha. He entered the order of monks in the second year of the Buddha's ministry, and in the 25th year was appointed his personal attendant. According to the Vinaya texts, he persuaded the Buddha, much against the latter's own inclination, to allow women to become nuns. Of the Buddha's intimate disciples, Ananda alone had not attained enlightenment (arhatship) when the Buddha passed away. He attained it, however, just before the first council (*c.* 544 or *c.* 480 B.C.), at which he repeated the Discourses (Suttapitaka). He is represented as being interlocutor in many discourses and the actual author of several. A collection of verses is ascribed to him in the Theragatha. According to tradition, he lived to the age of 120 years.   (T. R. V. M.)

ANANIAS, the Greek form of Hananiah or Ananiah, the name of several persons mentioned in the Bible. The most prominent are: (1) A member of the first Christian community who, with his wife Sapphira, was punished by Peter with sudden death for falsehood (Acts v, 1–10). (2) A disciple at Damascus in the story of the conversion and baptism of Paul (Acts ix, 10–17; xxii, 12–16). (3) Son of Nedebaios, a high priest who presided during the trial of Paul at Jerusalem (Acts xxiii, 2; xxiv, 1–5). He was high priest A.D. 47–59 and, having been accused of acts of violence, was sent to Rome for trial (A.D. 52), but was acquitted by the emperor Claudius. As a friend of the Romans he was murdered by the people at the beginning of the Jewish war of revolt.

ANANKE (ANANGKĒ), in Greek literature, necessity or fate personified. In Homer the personification has not yet been achieved, although even the gods admit that they are limited in their freedom of action. She is fairly prominent in post-Homeric literature and theological speculation, particularly Orphic, but is definitely known to emerge into cult only at Corinth, where she was worshiped with Bia (might, force). There are one or two faint and dubious traces of her cult elsewhere, but because of her unalterable nature it was pointless to render her offerings or sacrifice—"Nothing is stronger than dread Necessity" was a Greek byword.

In literature she is associated with Adrasteia, the Moirai (or Fates, of whom she was the mother, according to Plato in the *Republic*) and similar deities. In Italy she does not appear to have been worshiped at all; the famous description of Necessitas (Ananke) in Horace's *Carmina,* which makes her attendant on Tyche, is purely literary.

See W. Roscher, *Ausführliches Lexikon der griechischen und römischen Mythologie.*   (T. V. B.)

ANANTAPUR, a town and district in Andhra Pradesh, India. The town lies 117 mi. N. of Bangalore (Mysore state) on the Hyderabad-Bangalore main road and on the Guntakal-Bangalore metre-gauge branch of the Southern railway. Population (1961) 52,280. It has a large college of science and arts and an engineering college, both affiliated to Sri Venkateswara university at Tirupathi.

Anantapur was built by a dewan of Vijayanagar (*q.v.*) who is said to have named it after his wife Ananda.

ANANTAPUR DISTRICT (7,385 sq.mi.; pop. [1961] 1,767,464) is part of the northern rim of the Mysore plateau, sloping from 2,200 ft. in the south to 1,000 ft. across the Pennar river in the north. On the east are the Errakondas ("red hills"). Anantapur is one of the driest districts of south India, and has often been the victim of serious famine. Much of it is a barren undulating plain of red soils, broken by long ridges of equally barren hills, but there are two important agricultural tracts of black cotton soil: one in the northeast ringed by ridges of the Errakondas; the other around Gooty, 30 mi. N. of Anantapur. The main crops are jowar and other millets, gram and other pulses and peanuts, followed by smaller areas of rice and cotton. Granitic formations in dome-shaped masses of great boldness and beauty occur throughout the district.

Potentially economic mineral deposits include widely dispersed corundum and steatite pockets, and diamonds at Wajrakarur, 30 mi. N.W. of Anantapur.

The area of the modern district was within the nucleus of the empire of Vijayanagar, Gooty (Gutti) being taken by the future kings, Harihara and Bukka, in 1336. Penukonda (Punugonda), 41 mi. S. of Anantapur, was the Vijayanagar capital in *c.* 1570–85, following the decline of the empire. Both had important hill fortresses (now ruined).

Subsequently the district passed to local and imperial Muslim regimes; to Tipu Sultan (*q.v.*); and to the Nizam of Hyderabad, who ceded it to the British in 1800. The district's first British collector (magistrate) was Major (later Sir Thomas) Munro, who introduced the ryotwari land-tenure system, thereby eliminating the intermediate rent collectors or zamindars. Munro's memory as a humanitarian official, and later as governor of Madras, is still cherished by the local people.   (G. KN.)

ANANTNAG (formerly ISLAMABAD), a town in Jammu and Kashmir, India, on the north bank of the Jhelum river, 35 mi. S.E. of Srinagar. Population (1961) 21,087.

The second town in the Kashmir valley and originally its capital, it is now decaying. There is an old summer palace, overshadowed by plane trees, and a fine mosque and shrine. There are many springs; below the town is a reservoir fed by one of these called the Anant Nag, slightly sulfurous, from which volumes of gas continually rise; the water swarms with sacred fish.

ANAPAEST, a metrical foot, basically $\smile\smile-$ or $\smile\smile\prime$. The Greek anapaestic metron consists of four bicipitia (*see* PROSODY, CLASSICAL). It is not, however, usual for two consecutive bicipitia to take the double-short form ($\smile\smile\smile\smile$). Thus the metron may take the forms $\smile\smile-\smile\smile-$, $\smile\smile--$, $--\smile\smile-$, $----$, $-\smile\smile--$, $-\smile\smile-\smile\smile$, $\smile\smile--\smile\smile$, the most common forms being those which do not involve reversal of anapaestic rhythm (*i.e.,* –◡◡ instead of ◡◡–). A metron ending with double short can only be followed by a metron beginning with a long; *e.g.,* –◡◡–◡ | –◡◡– . The anapaestic was a marching rhythm. Early Spartan marching songs were composed in sequences of catalectic anapaestic dimeters, also called "paroemiacs": ◡◡◡◡ ◡◡| ◡◡––. In Attic drama anapaests appear in "systems," sequences of full dimeters occasionally diversified by monometers and rounded off by paroemiacs. To keep the marching rhythm clear, there is usually diaeresis (word-end) between the two metra of the dimeter. The anapaestic tetrameter catalectic, a verse compounded of a full dimeter and a paroemiac, is used in comedy, especially in debates and in the parabasis. Passages in anapaests also occur in the lyric of tragedy, especially the monodies of Euripides. Lyric anapaests are characterized by spondaic rhythm (spondee: – –), presence of occasional proceleusmatics (◡◡◡◡), absence of diaeresis between metra, consecutive paroemiacs.

In English verse pure anapaestic rhythm produces a galloping effect; *e.g.* (from Byron): "And his cohorts were gleaming in purple and gold."

(L. P. E.)

ANAPHYLAXIS: *see* ALLERGY AND ANAPHYLAXIS.

ANARCHISM is the belief that it is practicable and desirable to abolish all organized government, laws and machinery for law enforcement. Anarchists aim at a stateless society in which harmony is maintained by voluntary agreements among individuals and groups. They envisage a social order without prisons, armies, police or other organized force to maintain property rights, collect taxes or enforce such personal obligations as contracts, debts or alimony.

Government, anarchists believe, is only needed to defend injustice. Without state support, they expect that unjust social arrangements will quickly disappear and be replaced by fair and equitable agreements freely accepted and maintained by all.

Some Basic Attitudes of Anarchism.—Man, as anarchists see him, is good. He can be trusted without government, or, at least, he will do less evil without government than with it.

Industrial society, they believe, can and should be run by means of a network of agreements among individuals and groups, associating freely on the basis of locality, region and industrial specialization. The seeming need of society for government, they say, is caused only by the injustice and unreasonableness of the social order, which should be abolished. Anarchists thus believe in radical social change. They wish to see property and class distinctions abolished, so as to leave more room for individual differences based on personality and accepted by consent.

Most anarchists consider themselves, therefore, socialists, but they differ radically from most socialists and liberal reformers by their refusal to work through legislation or government. Most consider themselves revolutionaries, but they differ in the methods they are willing to employ. Some are pacifists who will work only through example, persuasion, nonviolent resistance and civil disobedience, in the tradition of Henry David Thoreau, Lev Tolstoi and Mohandas K. Gandhi. Others are willing to support militant group action, including violence in revolution or civil war. Anarchists of this persuasion are often willing to accept the "spontaneous justice" meted out by revolutionary crowds or committees, but would refuse to let these develop into permanent courts or laws. Anarchosyndicalists rely on labour unions ("syndicates") as the main instrument for the revolutionary struggle and for the hoped-for stateless industrial society. (*See* SYNDICALISM.)

Anarchosyndicalist views were long favoured by some labour unions in some economically underdeveloped regions, particularly of Latin culture, where the workers in the few seaports and industrial centres saw little hope of persuading the large peasant majority to support reform legislation or nationalization measures favourable to wage earners. Anarchosyndicalists wanted a "syndicate" of workers and professional personnel in each industry or service to take over installations from the owners, private or public, and to administer production of its goods or services. In each town or region, councils of representatives of all local syn-

dicates were to agree on local economic policies, and a council of representatives of the national syndicates was expected to agree on similar policies at a national level.

Anarchosyndicalists are confident that members of a syndicate controlling a vital service, such as a hospital or power station, would not use their greater bargaining power to the disadvantage of other workers. Similarly, they feel that the syndicates of geographically or industrially favoured regions will not use their superior bargaining power to the detriment of others. As evidence for their contentions, they point to the relatively brief experience of anarchosyndicalist rule in Catalonia during the early stages of the Spanish civil war in 1936-37.

A minority of anarchists have favoured direct action by individuals, including acts of terrorism and assassination against representatives of governments that they considered oppressive. Between 1894 and 1901 such acts claimed the lives of M. F. Sadi Carnot, president of France; Elizabeth, empress of Austria; Humbert I, king of Italy; and William McKinley, president of the United States. Such acts of terrorism did much to establish an image of the bearded, bomb-throwing anarchist in the minds of generations of newspaper readers.

In fact, however, most adherents of anarchism were never terrorists. Where anarchist terrorism developed, it grew from conditions that also favoured terrorist response from extreme nationalists or members of aggrieved minorities: extreme social or economic deprivation, despair of legal remedies, a mutually reinforcing interplay of provocation and reprisal and fear and resentment of police brutality. After the 1920s and early 1930s, individual anarchist terrorism almost disappeared.

Anarchists of all persuasions refuse to organize political parties or to present candidates for elections. In promoting their beliefs and interests, however, they often play a role in politics through propaganda, manifestoes, demonstrations, strikes and other forms of action; and they are active in founding and leading labour unions, co-operative societies and other voluntary organizations.

History of Anarchism.—Forerunners of anarchism include the Greek philosopher Zeno and some Hussite and Anabaptist religious reformers. Anarchist ideas were expressed by the French writers Rabelais and Fénelon, and were familiar to 18th-century French intellectuals.

The first major modern exposition of anarchism was given by the English writer William Godwin in his *Enquiry Concerning the Principles of Political Justice* (2 vol., 1793). Godwin did not use the word "anarchism" but advocated a stateless society of small autonomous communities and a communist distribution of property, with the substance going "to him who most wants it." In 1796, in a second edition of his work, Godwin modified his communist views.

The name "anarchists" had been used as a term of reproach during the French Revolution by the moderates—the Girondists—for those radicals who continued to press for economic and social changes after the overthrow of Louis XVI. Only in 1840 was the term "anarchism" adopted by an anarchist writer, Pierre Joseph Proudhon, in his *Qu'est-ce que la propriété?* ("What Is Property?"). Proudhon answered, "property is theft," referring to property in its Roman-law sense of the irresponsible right to use and abuse; in its stead he advocated limited rights of possession in a no-government state of society which he called anarchy. Roman-law-type property was to be abolished not by expropriation but by wiping out interest and profits through a new system called mutualism. Under this system, a national bank was to be based on the mutual confidence of wage earners and other producers, who would exchange only strictly equivalent goods and services, reckoned in units of labour. Similar ideas of mutualism had been expressed earlier, in England by William Thompson, John Gray and J. F. Bray and in the U.S. by Josiah Warren.

In Germany, anarchist ideas gained adherents in the 1840s, when such left-wing Hegelians as Moses Hess and Karl Grün advocated anarchism. An extreme individualistic version of anarchism was developed by Max Stirner (Kaspar Schmidt) in his work *Der Einzige und sein Eigentum* ("The Unique Man and His Own"). Later echoes of individualistic anarchist attitudes may be discerned in the writings of the philosopher Nietzsche, who called for a superbly individualistic "superman" and despised the state as a "cold monster."

The politically most effective versions of anarchism were labour oriented and collectivist in emphasis. In the 1870s an alliance of labour groups with anarchist and mutualist views, principally in the Latin countries—Spain and Italy—and in Belgium and France, split off from the Marxist-influenced International Workingmen's association (see INTERNATIONAL, THE). After calling themselves federalists and antiauthoritarians, they eventually developed the doctrines of modern anarchism and accepted the name anarchists. An anarchist international was reorganized in 1881, and international meetings were held thereafter.

An outstanding leader in this development was the Russian Mikhail Bakunin (q.v.), a contemporary and opponent of Karl Marx. Major contributions to anarchist thought were made later by Prince Peter Kropotkin (q.v.) in Mutual Aid: a Factor in Evolution, The Conquest of Bread and other works. A third Russian writer, Count Lev Tolstoi (q.v.), without naming himself an anarchist, adopted on religious grounds an anarchist position toward property and government in such works as The Kingdom of God in Yourselves.

Anarchism and Communism.—In revolutions and civil wars, communists and anarchists sometimes started as allies but usually ended as adversaries. The anarchist headquarters in Moscow, for example, were attacked by artillery in April 1918, on Trotski's orders, and all anarchist activity was suppressed.

An international anarchist conference representing almost all major revolutionary syndicalist organizations, held at Berlin in Dec. 1922, repudiated explicitly the Leninist theory of the dictatorship of the proletariat. "Revolutionary syndicalism," it declared, ". . . has not for its object the conquest of political power, but the abolition of every state function in social life." The strongest anarchist movements at that time were those of Spain—the Federación Anarquista Ibérica (F.A.I.) and the syndicalist labour union, Confederación Nacional del Trabajo (C.N.T.), the latter claiming 2,500,000 members—and of Italy—the Unione Anarchica Italiana and the Unione Sindacale Italiana. These movements were driven underground by the dictatorships of Primo de Rivera and Mussolini, but with the fall of the De Rivera regime, the Spanish movement re-emerged.

During the Spanish civil war of 1936–39, anarchists and communists both sided with the government of the Spanish republic against the rebellion led by Gen. Francisco Franco, but eventually hostilities broke out between communists and anarchists, ending in the suppression of the latter and contributing significantly to Franco's victory.

Anarchism in the United States.—In 1882 the anarchist John Joseph Most founded in New York city the German weekly paper Die Freiheit. In the following year, an anarchist-led section of the International Workingmen's association was founded at Pittsburgh, Pa. By 1885 this federation claimed 80 sections, totaling 8,000 members. In addition to Most's weekly in New York, its adherents published a German daily newspaper, the Arbeiter Zeitung, and an English weekly, Alarm, in Chicago, Ill.; the Voice of the People in St. Louis, Mo.; and the Anarchist in Boston, Mass. The anarchists, with the exception of Most, supported the labour campaign for an eight-hour working day, hoping to give it a more revolutionary character. Anarchists were involved in the famous Haymarket square incident of 1886 in Chicago (see CHICAGO: History).

In 1903 congress passed a law to bar foreign anarchists from the United States and to deport alien anarchists found within it. The movement survived, however, and in 1905 an anarchosyndicalist type of labour union was founded, the Industrial Workers of the World (q.v.), commonly known as the I.W.W. Despite strong opposition from employers and from the American Federation of Labor, the I.W.W. conducted many strikes, but after World War I it lost most of its importance. The conviction and execution of the I.W.W. organizer Joe Hill (Joseph Hillstrom) on a disputed murder charge at Salt Lake City, Utah, in 1915 is commemorated in a well-known labour song that bears his name.

More stringent legislation was enacted in 1918. During the antired excitement of 1919–20, some foreign-born anarchists were deported to the U.S.S.R., among them Alexander Berkman and Emma Goldman. They returned disappointed and published denunciations of the communist dictatorship. Since anarchists and syndicalists in the 1920s were popularly—and incorrectly—believed to be likely to commit any common crime, some of them were convicted on evidence that would not have been sufficient, in the opinion of many, to convict persons of less unpopular views. On Aug. 23, 1927, two anarchists, Nicola Sacco and Bartolomeo Vanzetti, were executed at Charlestown, Mass., after long delay and world-wide protests, for a murder with robbery that had occurred in April 1920 at South Braintree, Mass. World opinion, including considerable U.S. opinion, held that they had been convicted not so much on any evidence advanced as because of their extreme ideas (see SACCO-VANZETTI CASE). From 1952, when the earlier legislation was superseded, U.S. laws listed as deportable those "aliens who are anarchists" and "aliens who advocate or teach, or who are members of or are affiliated with any organization that advocates or teaches, opposition to all organized government." This language might be construed to enjoin aliens from advocating philosophical and nonviolent tenets of anarchism, which native-born U.S. citizens might lawfully do.

Continuing Interest in Anarchist Ideas.—Although anarchism by the mid-20th century had subsided as a political movement, its indirect intellectual influence continued. Anarchists in the late 1950s stressed particularly their belief in the necessity and desirability of decentralization in all areas of human activity. In this, they found some common ground with adherents of political pluralism (see POLITICAL PHILOSOPHY).

The development of modern science and technology convinced them more than ever of the necessity for decentralization into a stateless system of small communities. This view was strongly urged by Aldous Huxley in Science, Liberty and Peace (1946), which reaffirmed the view of Tolstoi that the application of science would make an unjust social system worse. A similar reaction was expressed by Sir Herbert Read (The Philosophy of Anarchism, 1940; Anarchy and Order, 1954) and George Orwell (Homage to Catalonia, 1938; Nineteen Eighty-Four, 1949). Anarchist ideas continued to appear in the English anarchist newspaper Freedom, and found new outlets in the Delphic Review (founded 1949) and the University Libertarian (founded 1955) in Britain and the Libertarian (founded 1958) of Sydney, Austr.

BIBLIOGRAPHY.—Max Nettlau, Bibliographie de l'anarchie (1897); V. Basch, L'individualisme anarchiste: Max Stirner (1904); K. A Mautz, Die Philosophie Max Stirners im Gegensatz zum Hegelschen Idealismus (1936); Karl Löwith, Von Hegel zu Nietzsche (1953); W. Bailie, Josiah Warren, the First American Anarchist (1900); E. H. Carr, Michael Bakunin (1937); Felix Frankfurter, The Case of Sacco and Vanzetti (1927); Rudolf Rocker, Anarcho-Syndicalism (1938); George Woodcock, Anarchy or Chaos (1944); Errico Malatesta, Anarchy, 8th rev. ed. (1949); G. D. H. Cole, Socialist Thought: Marxism and Anarchism, 1850–1890 (1954).   (K. W. D.)

ANASAZI, a term derived from the Navaho word meaning "ancient ones," is the archaeological name for the culture of the prehistoric inhabitants of the region around the Four Corners, the only point in the United States common to four states (Arizona, New Mexico, Colorado and Utah). The earliest Anasazi remains come from a Basket Maker village near Durango, Colo., with a tree-ring date of A.D. 46. Modern Pueblo Indians (q.v.) in Arizona and New Mexico, descendants of the Anasazi, preserve a way of life that began about 2,000 years ago. An unusually rich picture of Anasazi life has been reconstructed by analogy with the historic and modern Pueblo inheritors of the prehistoric tradition.

Anasazi characteristics include compact, cellular, masonry or adobe dwellings called pueblos; semisubterranean ceremonial structures called kivas; black-on-white painted pottery; corrugated, gray utility pottery; and a type of artificial head shaping which flattens the upper part of the back of the head. While these features are found from the upper Rio Grande river in New Mexico to the lower Virgin river in Nevada, and from the Dolores river in Colorado and the middle Colorado river in Utah to the Little Colorado river in Arizona, the Anasazi homeland was in the San Juan river basin. Anasazi farmers established their tenure of this semiarid plateau by developing special techniques for conserving and using the scarce water resources. The dry climate has preserved such perishable remains as cloth, basketry, wood, feather, fur and the so-called "mummies," which are only dessicated bodies.

The combination of remarkable preservation and standing masonry ruins in a colourful natural setting stimulated pioneer professional archaeologists and led to the early establishment of field schools where many U.S.-trained archaeologists received their field training digging in Anasazi ruins. The basic principles of stratigraphic analysis used by U.S. archaeologists were first demonstrated in the Anasazi area. Tree-ring dating, or dendrochronology (*q.v.*), made control of the time factor possible earlier than in other New World regions and fostered pioneer development of chronological concepts.

Early explorers and settlers of the Four Corners dug in the dry caves for specimens and noticed that deposits with pottery were superimposed over deposits without pottery but with many well-preserved baskets. They called the people who lived during the earlier period Basket Makers, and those who built masonry structures in caves and rock shelters in the canyon walls Cliff Dwellers. The early explorers and settlers thought the Cliff Dwellers were a race distinct from both the earlier Basket Makers and the historic Pueblos. This widespread popular belief persists despite archaeological demonstration that cliff dwellings are simply examples of pueblo architecture crammed into shallow caves.

Archaeologists referred to either Basket Maker or Pueblo remains until A. V. Kidder suggested "Anasazi" for the combined Basket Maker–Pueblo sequence. In 1927 Kidder sponsored an archaeological conference at Pecos, N.M., at which the long Anasazi sequence was subdivided into three Basket Maker and five Pueblo periods. Because of the complexity of the earliest Basket Maker culture then known, the first Basket Maker period was a hypothetical one reserved for the discovery of ancestral Basket Maker material, but nothing was found, and when Frank H. H. Roberts, Jr., revised the Pecos classification he eliminated this hypothetical stage.

About this same time physical anthropologists, especially C. C. Seltzer, showed by studying skeletons of Basket Makers and Pueblos that the physical differences recognized by earlier workers were not caused by the coming of a new race but by the introduction of the cultural practice of artificially shaping the heads of infants. Racial, as well as cultural, continuity was demonstrated for the Anasazi tradition.

Although Paleo-Indians were hunting now-extinct mammoth, horse, camel and bison 12,000 years ago in southern Arizona and on the High (Great) Plains, no evidence of such activity has been found in the Anasazi region. Basket Maker origins may ultimately be found in the Desert culture, a prehistoric way of life in arid North America similar to that of historic Indian groups in the Great Basin. Radiocarbon dates place the Desert culture as early as the Paleo-Indian hunters. The Cochise culture, the best-known Desert culture variant, was ancestral to the Hohokam (*q.v.*) and Mogollon (*q.v.*) cultures, southwestern groups contemporaneous with the Anasazi. The Hohokam (from a Pima Indian word meaning "those who have vanished") made red-on-buff pottery and lived in pole-and-mud houses in the southern Arizona desert, especially the Gila-Salt valley where they built an extensive network of irrigation canals. The Mogollon (named for the Mogollon mountains in southwestern New Mexico, which carry the surname of an early Spanish official) made polished red and brown pottery and lived in side-entered, semisubterranean pit houses in the mountainous regions of east-central Arizona and west-central New Mexico.

Whatever the exact local derivation of Anasazi culture may have been, Anasazi, Hohokam and Mogollon cultures emerged only after maize agriculture, pottery making and other sedentary arts were introduced from Mexico. The earliest Basket Makers raised maize and squash, although they depended as much on hunting and gathering of wild foods as on farming. They made baskets and twined bags, but no pottery; used the spearthrower instead of the bow; wore little except sandals, fur blankets, and ornaments;

and lived in "wood-and-mud masonry" houses. By A.D. 500 beans, new types of maize, pottery, the bow and arrow and possibly the domesticated turkey were added. Dwellings changed to roof-entered pit houses. The transition to Pueblo culture took place from A.D. 700 to 1100, pueblo-type dwellings replaced pit houses, and kivas were developed out of the pit-house idea. Head shaping, corrugated pottery, cotton, and loom weaving were introduced. The following period, A.D. 1100–1300, often called the Great or Classic Pueblo period, represents the peak of Anasazi achievements in their homeland area. During this time the cliff dwellings were built, but many villages were huge surface pueblos several stories high. The great kiva, a large and elaborate ceremonial structure, was added. The weaving of cotton was highly developed. Black-on-red and polychrome styles of painted pottery were introduced. Outstanding ruins of this period are preserved at Mesa Verde National park in Colorado and several national monuments in Arizona and New Mexico.

By A.D. 1300 the increasingly dry conditions of the 13th century became so severe that most of the Four Corners region was abandoned by Pueblo people who carried the Anasazi tradition into the Rio Grande valley, the Mogollon country in the White mountains of Arizona and even into Hohokam territory. The resulting contacts with other cultures added to the complexity and variety of Anasazi culture and changed the course of its development.

About A.D. 1450–1500 the Pueblo people withdrew from these southern regions into the area where the Spanish explorers first saw them. Navaho and Apache Indians arrived from the north about A.D. 1500. These Athapascan newcomers accelerated the withdrawal of the Pueblos from areas now largely occupied by Apache and Navaho. Although reduction in the area and the number of villages occupied by the Pueblos continued throughout the historic period, the Anasazi way of life was still preserved in the second half of the 20th century at the modern Hopi, Zuñi, Acoma and Rio Grande villages. *See also* NORTH AMERICA: *Prehistory and Archaeology.*

BIBLIOGRAPHY.—A. V. Kidder, *An Introduction to the Study of Southwestern Archaeology* (1924); A. E. Douglass, "The Secret of the Southwest Solved by Talkative Tree Rings," *National Geographic Magazine,* vol. 56, no. 6, pp. 737–770 (1929); Erik K. Reed, "The Distinctive Features and Distribution of the San Juan Anasazi Culture," *Southwestern Journal of Anthropology,* vol. 2, no. 3, pp. 295–305 (1946); H. M. Wormington, *Prehistoric Indians of the Southwest* (1947); J. D. Jennings (ed.), "The American Southwest: A Problem in Cultural Isolation," *Memoirs of the Society for American Archaeology,* no. 15, pp. 59–127 (1956); A. V. Kidder, *Pecos, New Mexico: Archaeological Notes* (Papers of the R. S. Peabody Foundation), vol. 5 (1958). (R. H. TH.)

ANASTASIUS, the name of four popes.

ANASTASIUS I, SAINT (d. 401), pope from 399 to 401, was elected on Nov. 27, 399, to succeed Siricius. He earned the praise of St. Jerome (*Epist.* 127) because of his censuring the works of the theologian Origen (d. *c.* 254), then but recently translated into Latin. In papal letters Anastasius condemned several Origenist writings, and disapproved the spread through translation of Origen's teaching. St. Anastasius died on Dec. 19, 401, and his feast is celebrated on the anniversary of his death.

ANASTASIUS II (d. 498), pope from 496 to 498, was consecrated on Nov. 24, 496. His first epistle to Emperor Anastasius displayed a conciliatory attitude toward Acacius, late patriarch of Constantinople, deposed in 484 by Pope Felix III. Anastasius' reception of the deacon Fotinus, probably occasioned by an anti-Acacian reaction at Salonika, was followed by schism at Rome and the charge of the *Liber pontificalis* that the pope desired to rehabilitate Acacius (*see* PAPACY: *The First Six Centuries: The Acacian Schism* and *Theodoric*). Because of Fotinus, Dante (*Inferno,* xi, 8) placed this pontiff in hell. Anastasius II died on Nov. 19, 498.

See P. Jaffé and W. Wattenbach, *Regesta pontificum Romanorum,* new ed., vol. 1 (1956). (H. G. J. B.)

ANASTASIUS III (d. 913), pope from 911 to 913, was a Roman, son of Lucian. He was consecrated about the middle of June 911. His pontificate falling during the period when Rome was under the control of the house of Theophylact, he had little freedom of action. Howel the Good, prince of Wales, consulted him in regard to a reformed law code. (A. G. Bɪ.)

ANASTASIUS IV (Conrad of Suburra) (d. 1154), pope from 1153 to 1154. This aged and amiable successor of Eugenius III, crowned on July 12, 1153, settled two long-standing problems: one with Frederick I over the see of Magdeburg, the other by restoring St. William of York to his see. As cardinal bishop of Sabina (1126) he had staunchly supported Innocent II, whom he served as vicar in Rome, during the schism of Anacletus II. Anastasius IV died on Dec. 3, 1154.

See H. K. Mann, *The Lives of the Popes in the Middle Ages,* 2nd ed., vol. ix, p. 221 ff. (1925). (J. J. Rɴ.)

ANASTASIUS I (*c.* 430–518), Byzantine emperor from 491 to 518, was born at Dyrrachium (Durazzo). An administrator of high character in the department of finance, he was chosen as emperor by Ariadne, the widow of his predecessor Zeno, who married him shortly after his accession. His reign began auspiciously. He gained popular favour in the towns by a judicious remission of taxation and displayed great vigour in administering the affairs of the empire. He succeeded in curbing Zeno's countrymen, the overpowerful Isaurians, driving them out of the capital and breaking their authority by a series of campaigns in Isauria itself which lasted until 498. Some of the Isaurians were transplanted and settled in Thrace. On the eastern frontier war was waged against Persia (502–505). Theodosiopolis (Erzurum) and Amida (Diyarbakir) were captured by the enemy, but the Persian provinces also suffered severely and the Byzantines recovered Amida. Peace was concluded in 506 by a treaty restoring the *status quo.* As Slavs and Bulgars were devastating the Balkan provinces of the empire, Anastasius in 512, in order to protect Constantinople and its vicinity, built the long wall stretching from the Black sea to the Sea of Marmara, about 30 mi. west of the capital.

In religious matters Anastasius began by maintaining the *Henoticon* (edict of union), Zeno's compromise, which satisfied neither Orthodox nor Monophysite. At his accession he had promised not to introduce any ecclesiastical innovations, but he gradually veered toward the Monophysite position. This won him the support of the Monophysites in Syria and Egypt, but antagonized the European provinces and the capital, particularly the city faction of the Blues, an important political party supporting Orthodoxy against the Greens who favoured Monophysitism. These differences caused many riots and revolts. The unpopularity of Anastasius' Monophysite policy gave an opportunity for a rebellion in 513 led by Vitalian, the commander in chief in Thrace, supported by Huns and Slavs. Vitalian attacked the capital by land and sea, and in 514 Anastasius came to terms and appointed him master of the soldiers in Thrace. Rebelling again, Vitalian was decisively defeated in 515. Seeing how any religious compromise with Syria and Egypt only caused trouble in Constantinople and the more central provinces, in his last years Anastasius attempted to treat with the papacy and with the Chalcedonian party, but was unsuccessful.

Anastasius' reign was marked by important financial reforms. He tried to stabilize the currency and reorganized the system of tax collection, both in urban and in rural districts. He tended to favour trade and industry at the expense of agriculture. His policy was not always popular and contributed to the unrest in the empire toward the end of his reign, but his careful and prudent administration filled the treasury and laid the foundation for the splendours of Justinian's reign. He died during the night of July 9, 518.

BIBLIOGRAPHY.—J. B. Bury, *History of the Later Roman Empire, 395–565,* vol. 1 (1923); E. Stein, *Histoire du Bas-Empire,* vol. 2 (1949); G. Ostrogorsky, *History of the Byzantine State* (1956); P. Charanis, *Church and State in the Later Roman Empire: the Religious Policy of Anastasius I, 491–518* (1939). (J. M. Hʏ.)

ANASTASIUS II (d. A.D. 721), Byzantine emperor from 713 to 715, was raised to the throne upon the deposition of Philippicus, whose chief secretary he had been. Formerly called Artemius, he took the name Anastasius in memory of one of his predecessors, another civilian whose reign was noted for its competent administration. Anastasius was a contrast to Philippicus. He immediately reversed the current ecclesiastical policy, rescinded the Monothelite decrees of Philippicus, and gave assurance of his orthodoxy to Pope Constantine. He was decisive in his military

action. He sent an army under the command of Leo the Isaurian (afterward emperor), who had distinguished himself in the army of Justinian II, to defend Syria against the Arabs. He took prudent and resolute measures to provision and defend Constantinople. He attempted to reorganize the army and sent a formidable naval force to Rhodes. In spite of the good intentions and ambitions of Anastasius, however, a stronger ruler was needed. The troops of the Opsician province mutinied, murdered the commander of the forces, and proclaimed a tax collector, Theodosius, emperor in 715. After a six-month siege, Theodosius took Constantinople. Anastasius, who had fled to Nicaea, submitted to the new emperor and became a monk in Thessalonica (716). In 720 he tried to regain his lost throne, heading a revolt against Theodosius' successor, Leo III; this failed, and Leo had him executed.

See G. Ostrogorsky, *History of the Byzantine State* (1956); J. B. Bury, *History of the Later Roman Empire,* vol. 2 (1889). (J. M. Hʏ.; X.)

ANASTIGMAT, or anastigmatic lens, a photographic lens free from astigmatism. *See* PHOTOGRAPHY: *Photographic Lenses.*

ANASTOMOSIS, in anatomy, the intercommunication between two vessels or nerves. In operative surgery the term means the formation of a passage joining two normally separated spaces or organs. *See* MEDICINE AND SURGERY, HISTORY OF.

ANATOLI, JACOB (fl. 13th century), physician, preacher and translator from the Arabic, was a member of the Jewish community of Narbonne in Languedoc. During a stay in Naples he enjoyed the friendship of the emperor Frederick II and of Michael Scot. Among his more important services were translations of works by Averroës. His philosophical homilies are collected in his book *Malmad ha-Talmidim* ("The Students' Instruction").

ANATOLIA (Gr. *anatolé,* "sunrise," *i.e.,* eastern land), in ancient geography, the country east of the Aegean, *i.e.,* Asia Minor (*q.v.*). It is now used by the Turks in the form *Anadolu* as the equivalent of Turkey in Asia.

See also references under "Anatolia" in the Index.

ANATOLIAN LANGUAGES are the indigenous languages (also called Asianic) spoken in ancient Asia Minor, or Anatolia, until the first centuries of the Christian era, when they were gradually supplanted by Greek. Archaeological exploration of this area lagged behind the 19th-century rediscoveries of more pivotal cultures of the ancient near east, notably Egypt and Mesopotamia. "Anatolian languages" has been a vague but comprehensive term, covering a general ignorance of the linguistic history of this exceptionally complex period and deriving from meagre, secondhand, Greek sources. Great progress, however, has been made, especially since 1900; there have been copious finds of inscriptional material. These epigraphs, together with archaeological and historical evidence, have led to important new conclusions.

History.—The history of Anatolia, like that of the Aegean world, begins about a millennium later than that of Mesopotamia. In Mesopotamia, the more fertile region, during the 3rd millennium B.C., the aboriginal Sumerian language (*q.v.*) was progressively absorbed by the expanding Semitic idiom of the Akkadian invaders; the presence of the likewise isolated Elamite language farther east is also recorded. Anatolia, however, exhibits only archaeological traces of a relatively primitive culture. Yet there is every indication of a basic stratum of autochthonous population from neolithic times, and of an irreducible substratum of indigenous languages, elements of which show an extraordinary persistence into historical times.

The early 2nd millennium B.C. was characterized by two important developments: the arrival of Indo-European-speaking conquerors (the Hittites and related tribes) from the north via the Bosporus or, more probably, the Caucasus; and the advent of literacy in the form of Mesopotamian cuneiform writing. The earliest recorded traces of Anatolian language are found in the records of Old Assyrian trading colonists at the ancient site of Kaneš (Kültepe) in central Asia Minor, where many proper names have a clearly indigenous character. The standard Anatolian cuneiform reached the Hittites via the Hurrians, who had invaded the eastern confines of Asia Minor and northern Mesopotamia from the northeast. Like the somewhat later Kassite conquerors of

Babylon, the Hurrians spoke a language of obscure affinities: it is related to the much later Haldian (9th–7th century B.C.), the immediate predecessor of the Indo-European Armenian in the general region of Lake Van. Ultimately it is perhaps connected with the Caucasian language group.

Subsequently, during most of the 2nd millennium B.C., the Hittites dominated in Asia Minor, and the official language was that of the capital city of Hattusas (now Boğazköy) in north-central Anatolia, an Indo-European speech which had been superimposed on Khattish (or Hattic), the native tongue of the aboriginal population. The central archives of the Hittite empire reflect a cosmopolitan culture and international intercourse in Hittite, Akkadian and Hurrian, which must have contrasted sharply with the dialectal multiplicity and localism of the hinterland. The ritual texts reveal the continued use of Khattish as a religious language in the worship of indigenous deities. Similar records show that in the province of Palâ, northwest of Hattusas, a different, though closely related, Indo-European language was in use. In the southern territories (Arzawa, Kizzuwatna) Lûish (also known as Luwian or Luvian) was spoken. Besides inherited distinctions, the influence of variant substrata differentiated Hittite, Palâ, and Lûish. In the centuries following the collapse of the Hittite empire (c. 1200 B.C.) political subdivision precipitated a decline in literacy. Cuneiform disappeared, but some literacy persisted in the form of hieroglyphic Hittite inscriptions in the so-called Late Hittite city-states. This peculiarly Anatolian word-syllabic writing system had also been in use during the empire for monumental purposes. The language seems to be a form of Lûish, and the same may be true of the still obscure stele of Ördek-burnu in the same region, written in an archaic West-Semitic consonantal alphabet.

Until the collapse of the empire, the central cultural orientation of Anatolia had been directed toward the southwest, and a corresponding preponderance of epigraphic material is found there. The connections of the Hittite empire with western Asia Minor are notoriously obscure, and there is little evidence of the language there in the 2nd millennium B.C. The centres of cultural diffusion in the west were Minoan Crete and Mycenaean Greece, which, however, exerted most of their influence on the maritime regions, especially Cyprus and the Syrian coast. The vast inland of Anatolia remained impervious to their penetration. Nevertheless, the ethnic and linguistic connections between the early inhabitants of the Aegean and those of western Asia Minor were considerable, as is shown clearly by the toponymy (place names) of both regions. The Greek mainland was settled by Indo-European-speaking Greeks in the early 2nd millennium B.C., and so at least was Cnossus in Crete in the late 15th century. Their variety of Minoan script represents the Greek language, but those attributed to the Minoan Eteo-Cretans and Cypro-Minoans remain undeciphered (*see* MINOAN LINEAR SCRIPTS).

Beginning about 750 B.C., after several centuries of illiteracy in the Aegean area and Anatolia, the advent of the Greek alphabet resulted in a profusion of written documents; most of Asia Minor was directed westward, especially after the ascendancy of the Ionian Greek colonies on the west coast. The exception was Cyprus, where the Cypriote syllabary, a late offshoot of the Cypro-Minoan script, was used not only for Greek inscriptions but also for the obscure Eteo-Cypriote texts from Amathus. The disunion of Asia Minor remained as pronounced as ever. Rarely did a strong political power emerge before the Persian conquest. Phrygia, which was founded by Indo-European invaders on the ruins of Hittite power in north-central Anatolia, held sway from the 9th to 7th century, and left a small number of Old Phrygian inscriptions, unquestionably Indo-European, written in a variety of early Greek alphabet. Many centuries later New Phrygian is attested in numerous inscriptions in the region.

Most sections of Asia Minor were reputed in Greek tradition to have distinct forms of indigenous speech. Many of these are known only by name or in scant and questionable traces, viz., Paphlagonian, Cappadocian, Cilician, Lycaonian, Isaurian and Pisidian. The Celtic Galatian, brought in by Indo-European invaders in the 3rd century B.C., was in a class by itself. Other languages are found in isolated inscriptions, as Sidetic in Pam-

phylia, Mysian and Tyrrhenian (stele of Lemnos, in the Aegean); the last is akin to Etruscan (*q.v.*) in Italy, being presumably a vestige of the ancient pre-Indo-European idioms of the Aegean region known in ancient tradition as Pelasgian, Tyrrhenian and Lelegian.

More important are the better attested languages of Caria, Lydia and Lycia. Carian is found in about 75 short inscriptions of Carian mercenaries in Egypt c. 600 B.C., and in a score of texts from Caria proper, notably the important Kaunos inscription. The writing system is a peculiar mixture of signs recalling either the Greek alphabet or the Cypriote syllabary. The language remains uninterpreted; it may be akin to the Eteo-Cretan of the 2nd millennium, traces of which are found in the later alphabetic Praesus inscriptions and in an Egyptian medical papyrus. Lydian appears in about 50 inscriptions, mostly from the old capital city of Sardis; these are generally monotonous epitaphs, some in verse, including a couple of short Lydian and Greek texts, and one longer Lydian-Aramaic bilingual, which is the chief clue to an understanding of Lydian so far available. Lycian is known from about 200 inscriptions and coin legends, including several short Lycian-Greek bilinguals and the long inscription of the stele of Xanthus, part of which is written in a divergent archaic type of Lycian known as Milyan.

Description.—Both Lydian and Lycian contain unmistakable Indo-European elements; the latter probably is merely a late vestige (5th–4th century B.C.) of the Lûish language in southern Anatolia. Their grammatical structure, though imperfectly known, has enough similarity with that of Hittite to enable us to speak of an Anatolian subdivision of Indo-European languages, comprising Hittite, Palâ, Lûish-Hieroglyphic-Lycian and Lydian. It belongs to the western (*centum*) branch of Indo-European, but has pronounced tendencies of its own. It includes the most anciently attested Indo-European speech material, but shows an advanced stage of formal evolution compared with both Greek and Sanskrit.

The influence of the native substrata appears in various ways. There is a tendency to lose the feminine gender (except perhaps in Lydian), or the gender altogether (Lycian). Most of the vocabulary is of uncertain or unknown, but presumably indigenous, origin, and differs from one language to another. It is to some extent possible to discern a northern substratum, actually attested in Khattish, and characterized by a suffix *-il* denoting appurtenance, which figures prominently in Hittite and Lydian as a grammatical element, largely as a substitute for the genitive case. The southern equivalent is also a native suffix (*-ass-*) of the pre-Lûish substratum, which expresses the genitive concept in Lûish and Lycian. This southern Anatolian stratum contains the toponymic suffixes *-nd-* and *-ss-* which loom large in the place names of southwestern Asia Minor and the whole Aegean world, and are seen in Greek *Korinthos* and *Halikarnassos, Labraunda* (Caria), Lûish *Purandas* and *Dattassas,* among many others. The pivotal point of the linguistic history of ancient Anatolia is the partial fusion of largely obscure and indirectly inferable native substrata with the languages of early Indo-European invaders. The influence of the indigenous element was strong in many fields, notably religion; it came to dominate the vocabulary of the intruding idioms, while the basic grammar remained Indo-European. *See also* HITTITES: *Language.*

BIBLIOGRAPHY.—J. Friedrich, *Kleinasiatische Sprachdenkmäler* ("Linguistic Monuments of Asia Minor") (1932), *Extinct Languages* (1957); E. Benveniste, in Meillet-Cohen, *Les Langues du monde,* 2nd ed. pp. 183–225 (1952). (J. Pl.)

ANATOMY (ARTICLES ON). The article ANATOMY, GROSS surveys the principles that govern this branch of biology, which deals with form and structure; describes the plan of construction that characterizes the higher vertebrates, including man; and summarizes the history and subdivisions of anatomical science. Botanical anatomy is outlined in PLANTS AND PLANT SCIENCE, and its major subdivisions are discussed in the articles listed under BOTANY (ARTICLES ON).

ANATOMY, COMPARATIVE discusses the branch of anatomical science which provided the source material for the concept of evolution, and which has since contributed an immense body of evidence to its validation. HOMOLOGY explains the distinction between homologues (similarities of animal structure that can be traced to an evolutionary relationship) and analogues (superficial similarities). Discussions of form and structure as the product of evolution will be found also in ANTHROPOLOGY, particularly the section *Old and New Concepts in Physical Anthropology;* BIOLOGY; EVOLUTION, ORGANIC; MAN, EVOLUTION OF; PALEONTOLOGY, particularly the section *Evolutionary Evidence;* TAXONOMY, which describes the methods used in classifying plant and animal forms; and ZOOLOGY. ANATOMY, MICROSCOPIC discusses the composition and architecture of organs, tissues, and cells, and the development of this science from the days of the first crude instruments to the era of the electron microscope.

The organization of protoplasm into the minuscule complications of cell structure is treated in CELL, and the types of tissue formed by groups of these cells are described in HISTOLOGY. Developmental anatomy (embryology), from fertilization of the egg until birth, is discussed in EMBRYOLOGY AND DEVELOPMENT, ANIMAL. Anatomical changes incident to old age, summarized in a section of ANATOMY, GROSS, are treated in detail in GERONTOLOGY AND GERIATRICS. Replacement of body parts by artificial devices is the subject of PROSTHETICS; of related interest are ARTIFICIAL ORGANS and TRANSPLANTS, TISSUE AND ORGAN.

The distinction between anatomy and physiology is largely a matter of emphasis; obviously, the form and structure of an arm, an eye, a hand, or an internal organ cannot be fully explained without reference to the functions with which these organs evolved. Therefore, PHYSIOLOGY and PHYSIOLOGY (ARTICLES ON) should be consulted. Human anatomy is discussed from the point of view of the artist in DRAWING (TECHNIQUES OF).

Many articles deal with the anatomy of components of the human body—for example: ARTERIES; BRAIN; CIRCULATORY SYSTEM; CONNECTIVE AND SUPPORTING TISSUES; EYE, HUMAN; HEART, ANATOMY OF; LIVER; LYMPH AND LYMPHATIC SYSTEM; NERVOUS SYSTEM; RESPIRATORY SYSTEM, ANATOMY OF; SKELETON, VERTEBRATE; URINARY SYSTEM; and VEINS. Ancillary material pertaining to the body components will be found in a variety of articles. For example, the article HAND is supplemented by portions of the articles BONE; DRAWING (TECHNIQUES OF); and JOINTS AND LIGAMENTS. Another example is PANCREAS: relevant material appears in GASTROINTESTINAL TRACT, DISEASES OF; DIABETES MELLITUS; DIGESTION; INSULIN; ENDOCRINOLOGY; HORMONES; and EMBRYOLOGY AND DEVELOPMENT, ANIMAL. For comprehensive information on any part of the body the Index is a guide not only to the survey article on the subject but also to specific sections of related articles.

The work of famous anatomists is discussed in their biographies. For additional articles of interest *see* MEDICINE AND SURGERY (ARTICLES ON).

ANATOMY, COMPARATIVE, is the branch of zoology that deals with the structure of related animals. It is largely confined to the study of vertebrates, since members of the major invertebrate groups do not show the evolutionary connections with which the science is now concerned.

Modern comparative anatomy may be dated from the work of Pierre Belon, who showed in 1555 that the skeletons of man and bird are constructed of similar elements arranged in the same way. Subsequent studies led to the realization that all animals are constructed according to a limited number of fundamental ground plans, each plan being subject to a great number of variations. This is particularly true among the vertebrates, in which a series of changes may be discerned from fishes through amphibians and reptiles to birds and mammals.

The likenesses discovered in the skeletal, digestive, circulatory and other systems of animals as diverse as the lizard, bird and dog did not at once lead to any inference about relationships. The resemblances were rather thought to reveal the basic ideas underlying the original creation. Not until the 19th century was it realized that different structures having some similarity may be developed through the alteration or loss of elements in a line of descent from a common ancestral structure. Darwin made extensive use of comparative anatomy in advancing the theory of evolution. Since Darwin the study of comparative anatomy has

largely centred on the theory of homology. Structures in two different animals are held to be homologous if they can be traced to a common structure in an animal ancestral to both. Thus the skeletons of the wing of a bat and the arm of a man are homologous because both are evolutionarily traceable to the fins of crossopterygian fishes, in which the arrangement of the skeletal elements was first established. In this case the homology is revealed by the obvious resemblance of the two skeletons, but in other cases study of fossil forms must be resorted to; *e.g.,* fossil ancestors of the horse reveal how loss and reduction of elements have made a one-toed hoof out of a five-toed paw (*see* EQUIDAE). Sometimes examination of developmental stages is essential, as in the establishment of homology between two tiny bones in the ears of mammals and the hinge bones in the jaws of reptiles. Embryology is also important in elucidating the relationships of the soft parts of the body, for which there is no fossil record.

See also references under "Anatomy, Comparative" in the Index.

See E. S. Goodrich, *Studies on the Structure and Development of Vertebrates* (1930); F. J. Cole, *A History of Comparative Anatomy* (1944). (F. MG.)

ANATOMY, GROSS. The science of anatomy is part of biology (*q.v.*), the comprehensive science which studies both plants and animals—those which are now living and those which have lived in the past. It seeks understanding of life—elucidation of the processes which constitute life and of the phenomena which those processes present. Anatomy is one of the morphological branches of biology. It is concerned with a critical analysis of structural detail of organisms, and is of general interest because all our activities are limited by our structure and because it tells us who our remote ancestors were and something of what they did. This article is restricted to gross anatomy as distinguished from microscopic anatomy (*see* ANATOMY, MICROSCOPIC).

The anatomy of plants, covered in the botanical articles, is excluded here, but it is in order to note that it has thrown much light on the anatomy of animals and that the word "anatomy" was introduced into scientific nomenclature by the botanist Theophrastus (d. 287 B.C.), who was Aristotle's pupil and successor.

Surface form may be studied from the outside, but the internal structure cannot. Some method of revealing internal structure must be used, and obviously the first method was dissection. The earliest record of its use was made by the Greeks, and Theophrastus called dissection "anatomy," from *ana temnein,* "to cut up." It is an unfortunate name, however, in two ways. First, dissection can be practised only on dead bodies, whereas the objective of anatomy is the understanding of living bodies—it is only a means to an end; second, it is only one of many techniques which anatomy uses to reveal structural detail. A better name for the science would be morphology. The term morphology (*q.v.*), however, has been used to indicate all the biologic disciplines concerned with the study of form and structure of organisms, without regard for the functions associated with structure. This definition establishes the morphological studies as antithetical to the physiological (*see* PHYSIOLOGY). Moreover, morphology has come to have another and a narrower meaning: it connotes a specific study of the general form and arrangement of parts of an organism and the relationships of parts to the whole.

Subdivisions.—Subdivisions of the science are made according to special interest: (1) in the part of the animal kingdom included—species anatomy (including human anatomy), comparative anatomy, paleontology (anatomy of extinct animals); (2) in the age of the animals studied—embryology, comparative embryology, gerontologic anatomy (old age) (*see* GERONTOLOGY AND GERIATRICS); (3) in the method of study—gross and microscopic anatomy, roentgenologic anatomy, anthropometry; (4) in parts of bodies to which the study is especially devoted—histology, histogenesis and tissue culture, organology (devoted to organs), systematic anatomy (devoted to systems of organs with associated functions), topographic anatomy (devoted to special regions); (5) in the special objective of study—descriptive anatomy, morphology (laws of structure), artistic anatomy, surgical anatomy, racial anatomy (physical anthropology) (*see* ANTHROPOL-

PRINCIPAL PARTS OF THE HUMAN BODY

This Plate on gross anatomy comprises 14 Views, 12 of which are transparent, showing all principal parts of the human anatomy. Below is a list in English (insofar as this is possible) of the names of the parts illustrated. The number immediately following the name is the code number for that part; the other number or numbers indicate the View or Views on which it is shown. A key to the Plate, with Latin names, is given on the last page.

Abdominal oblique muscle, external, 87: 1, 8
Abdominal oblique muscle, internal, 88: 1
Adductor longus muscle, 68: 6, 7, 14
Adductor brevis muscle, 67: 7
Adrenal gland: see Suprarenal gland
Aorta, 3: 5, 6, 10, 11, 14
Aponeurosis of external abdominal oblique muscle, 4: 1
Appendix, vermiform, 5: 4, 12, 13
Atrium, left, 19: 11
Axillary artery, 6: 5, 6, 14
Axillary vein, 178: 3, 10, 11
Biceps brachii muscle, 69: 5, 6, 10, 11
Bile duct, common, 35: 4, 5, 10, 11, 13
Brachial artery, 7: 5, 6, 14
Brachial muscle, 70: 14
Brachial plexus, 140: 5, 6, 7, 14
Brachial vein, 179: 3, 8, 10, 11
Brachiocephalic trunk, 164: 5, 14
Brachiocephalic vein, 180: 3, 4, 10, 11
Brachioradialis muscle, 71: 12, 13, 14
Breastbone, 160: 1, 2, 8, 9
Bronchus, left, 20: 5, 14
Buccinator muscle, 72: 1
Carotid artery, common, 8: 5, 14
Celiac trunk, 165: 5, 10, 12, 14
Cephalic vein, 183: 3, 4, 8, 9, 11, 12, 13, 14
Cerebellum, 22: 11, 14
Cerebrum, 23: 11, 14
Cheekbone, 134: 1
Collarbone, 24: 1, 2, 7, 8, 9, 14
Colon, ascending, 25: 3, 4, 12, 13
Colon, descending, 26: 3, 4, 12, 13
Colon, sigmoid, 27: 3, 4, 12, 13
Colon, transverse, 28: 3, 4, 11
Coracobrachialis muscle, 73: 5, 14
Corpus callosum, 32: 11, 14
Deltoid muscle, 74: 5, 6, 8, 9, 14
Depressor anguli oris muscle, 75: 1, 10
Diaphragm, 34: 2, 3, 4, 5, 6, 9, 10, 11, 14
Digastric muscle, 76: 3
Ductus deferens, 36: 5, 6
Duodenum, 37: 5, 12, 13
Epigastric vessels, deep, 169: 5, 8, 9
Esophagus, 122: 5, 6, 12, 13, 14
Extensor carpi radialis longus muscle, 77: 14
Falx cerebri, 38: 12, 13
Femoral artery, 9: 5, 6, 14
Femoral nerve, 114: 7, 14
Femoral vein, 184: 5, 6, 14
Femur, 39: 7
Flexor carpi radialis muscle, 78: 14
Fossa ovalis, 40: 8
Frontal bone, 126: 3, 7
Gall bladder, 200: 3, 4, 10, 11
Gastric vessels, 170: 11
Gastroepiploic vessels, 171: 10
Glans penis, 46: 1
Gluteus medius muscle, 79: 1, 5, 6, 7, 14
Gluteus minimus muscle, 80: 7
Gracilis muscle, 81: 6, 7, 14
Heart: see Atrium; Pericardium; Ventricle
Humerus, 48: 7
Ileum, 49: 12
Iliac artery, common, 10: 5, 6, 14
Iliac artery, external, 11: 5, 6, 14
Iliac artery, internal, 12: 5, 6, 14
Iliac spine, anterior superior, 159: 1, 2, 7, 8, 14
Iliacus muscle, 82: 7, 14

Iliac vein, common, 185: 5, 6, 14
Iliac vein, external, 186: 5, 6, 14
Iliac vein, internal, 187: 5, 6, 14
Iliohypogastric nerve, 115: 7
Ilioinguinal nerve, 116: 7
Inguinal ligament, 55: 1, 2, 3, 5, 6, 8, 13, 14
Inguinal ring, deep, 1: 1, 2
Inguinal ring, superficial, 2: 1
Innominate artery: see Brachiocephalic trunk
Innominate vein: see Brachiocephalic vein
Intercostal muscle, external, 83: 1
Intercostal muscle, internal, 84: 2, 9
Intestine, large: see Colon
Intestine, small, 50: 3, 4, 10, 11
Ischium, 127: 7
Jaw, lower, 61: 1, 2, 3, 4, 5, 6, 7, 11, 14
Jaw, upper, 62: 2, 3, 4, 5, 6, 7, 11, 12, 13, 14
Jugular vein, internal, 188: 3, 4, 5, 10
Kidney, 149: 5, 6, 14
Lacrimal gland, 41: 2
Larynx, 51: 4, 7, 11, 14
Ligament of the liver, falciform, 53: 3, 9
Ligament of the liver, round, 56: 2, 9
Ligament of the penis, fundiform, 54: 1
Line, arcuate, 58: 2
Line, semilunar, 59: 1, 2, 8, 9
Linea alba, 57: 1, 2, 8
Liver, 47: 3, 4, 9, 10, 11
Lumbosacral plexus, 141: 7
Lung, 146: 3, 4, 5, 6, 10, 11, 14
Mammary vessels, internal: see Thoracic vessels, internal
Masseter muscle, 85: 1
Median nerve, 117: 5, 6, 14
Medulla oblongata, 63: 11, 14
Mesenteric artery, inferior, 14: 5, 6, 14
Mesenteric artery, superior, 15: 14
Mesenteric vein, inferior, 189: 13
Mesenteric vein, superior, 190: 5
Mesenteric vessels, inferior, 173: 12, 13
Mesenteric vessels, superior, 174: 5, 12, 13
Mesentery, 65: 4, 11, 12
Mesocolon, transverse, 66: 11, 12
Mylohyoid muscle, 86: 2, 3
Nasal concha, inferior, 29: 4, 7, 11, 14
Nasal concha, middle, 30: 4, 7, 11, 14
Nasal concha, superior, 31: 4, 7, 11, 14
Nasal septum, 152: 5, 6, 12, 13
Obturator nerve, 118: 7
Occipital bone, 128: 4, 5, 7
Omentum, greater, 123: 10
Omentum, lesser, 124: 3, 4, 9, 10, 11
Omohyoid muscle, 89: 1, 2, 9
Orbicularis oris muscle, 90: 1
Ovarian vessels, 175: 14
Ovary, 135: 14
Pancreas, 136: 5, 12, 13
Parietal bone, 129: 3, 7
Parotid gland, 42: 1, 2
Pectoralis major muscle, 91: 1, 2, 5, 8, 9, 14
Pectoralis minor muscle, 92: 2, 5, 9, 10, 11
Penis, 137: 2, 3, 5
Pericardium, 138: 10
Phrenic nerve, 119: 10
Platysma muscle, 139: 8, 9
Pons, 144: 11, 14
Portal vein, 191: 5, 11, 12, 13
Pronator teres muscle, 93: 14
Prostate, 145: 6

Psoas major muscle, 94: 7, 14
Pterygoid muscle, internal, 95: 2
Pubis, 130: 3, 6, 7, 13, 14
Pulmonary artery, 16: 5, 10, 11, 14
Pulmonary vein, 192: 11, 14
Pylorus, 147: 12, 13
Quadratus lumborum muscle, 96: 14
Quadriceps femoris muscle, 97: 3, 4, 5, 6, 14
Rectum, 148: 7, 14
Rectus abdominis muscle, 98: 1, 2
Renal artery, 17: 6, 14
Renal vein, 193: 6, 14
Rib, 125: 1, 2, 7, 9
Sacrum, 131: 7
Saphenous vein, greater, 194: 8, 9
Sartorius muscle, 99: 1, 2, 9
Scalene muscle, anterior, 100: 14
Scrotum, 151: 1, 2, 5
Seminal duct: see Ductus deferens
Seminal vesicle, 202: 6
Serratus muscle, anterior, 101: 1
Shoulder blade, 150: 7
Sinus, frontal, 153: 2, 3, 4, 5, 6, 7, 11, 12, 13, 14
Sinus, inferior sagittal, 156: 12, 13
Sinus, maxillary, 154: 2, 3
Sinus, sphenoidal, 158: 4, 5, 6, 7, 11, 12, 13, 14
Sinus, straight, 155: 12, 13
Sinus, superior sagittal, 157: 12, 13
Skull, 33: 2
Sphenoid bone, 132: 7
Spinal cord, 64: 7, 14
Spleen, 52: 5, 12, 13
Splenic artery, 13: 5
Splenic vessels, 172: 12, 13
Sternohyoid muscle, 103: 1, 2, 9
Sternomastoid muscle, 102: 1, 2, 8, 9, 10
Sternothyroid muscle, 104: 2, 9
Stomach, 196: 3, 4, 10, 11
Styloglossus muscle, 105: 3
Subclavian artery, 18: 5, 6, 14
Subclavian vein, 195: 3, 4, 10, 11
Submandibular gland, 43: 1, 2
Suprarenal gland, 44: 5, 6, 14
Temporal bone, 133: 3, 7
Temporal muscle, 106: 1
Tensor fasciae latae muscle, 107: 1, 5, 6, 14
Tentorium cerebelli, 161: 11, 14
Testicle, 162: 5
Testicular vessels, 176: 5, 6
Thoracic vessels, internal, 177: 9, 10
Thyrohyoid muscle, 108: 2
Thyroid cartilage, 21: 3
Thyroid gland, 45: 3, 4, 10, 11
Tongue, 60: 3, 4, 5, 6, 7, 11, 14
Transversus abdominis muscle, 109: 1, 2
Transversus thoracis muscle, 110: 2, 9
Trapezius muscle, 111: 5, 6, 10, 14
Triceps brachii muscle, 112: 5, 6, 14
Turbinate bones: see Nasal concha
Ulnar nerve, 120: 5, 6, 14
Umbilical fold, medial, 142: 9
Umbilical fold, median, 143: 9
Ureter, 166: 5, 6, 13, 14
Urinary bladder, 201: 3, 4, 5, 6, 12, 13
Uterus, 167: 14
Vagina, 168: 14
Vagus nerve, 121: 14
Vena cava, inferior, 181: 5, 6, 11, 14
Vena cava, superior, 182: 4, 5, 10, 11
Ventricle, left, 198: 5, 10, 11
Ventricle, right, 197: 5, 10, 11
Vertebra, 199: 6, 7, 11, 14
Windpipe, 163: 5, 6, 14
Womb: see Uterus
Zygomaticus major muscle, 113: 1, 10

Abbreviations: A. (Arteria); L. (Ligamentum);
M. (Musculus); N. (Nervus); and V. (Vena).

KEY TO VIEW 14

3. Aorta
6. A. axillaris
7. A. brachialis
8. A. carotis communis
9. A. femoralis
10. A. iliaca communis
11. A. iliaca externa
12. A. iliaca interna
14. A. mesenterica inferior
15. A. mesenterica superior
16. A. pulmonalis
17. A. renalis
18. A. subclavia
20. Bronchus principalis
22. Cerebellum
23. Cerebrum
24. Clavicula
29. Concha nasalis inferior
30. Concha nasalis media
31. Concha nasalis superior
32. Corpus callosum
34. Diaphragma
44. Glandula suprarenalis
51. Larynx
55. L. inguinale
60. Lingua (tongue)
61. Mandibula
62. Maxilla
63. Medulla oblongata
64. Medulla spinalis
68. M. adductor longus
70. M. brachialis
71. M. brachioradialis
73. M. coracobrachialis
74. M. deltoideus
77. M. extensor carpi
    radialis longus
78. M. flexor carpi radialis
79. M. gluteus medius
81. M. gracilis
82. M. iliacus
91. M. pectoralis major
93. M. pronator teres
94. M. psoas major
96. M. quadratus lumborum
97. M. quadriceps femoris
    (rectus)
100. M. scalenus anterior
107. M. tensor fasciae latae
111. M. trapezius
112. M. triceps brachii
114. N. femoralis
117. N. medianus
120. N. ulnaris
121. N. vagus
122. Oesophagus (esophagus)
130. Os pubis
135. Ovarium (ovary)
140. Plexus brachialis
144. Pons
146. Pulmo (lung)
148. Rectum
149. Ren (kidney)
153. Sinus frontalis
158. Sinus sphenoidalis
159. Spina iliaca anterior superior
161. Tentorium cerebelli
163. Trachea
164. Truncus brachiocephalicus
165. Truncus coeliacus
166. Ureter
167. Uterus
168. Vagina
175. Vasa ovarica
181. V. cava inferior
183. V. cephalica
184. V. femoralis
185. V. iliaca communis
186. V. iliaca externa
187. V. iliaca interna   193. V. renalis
192. V. pulmonalis   199. Vertebra

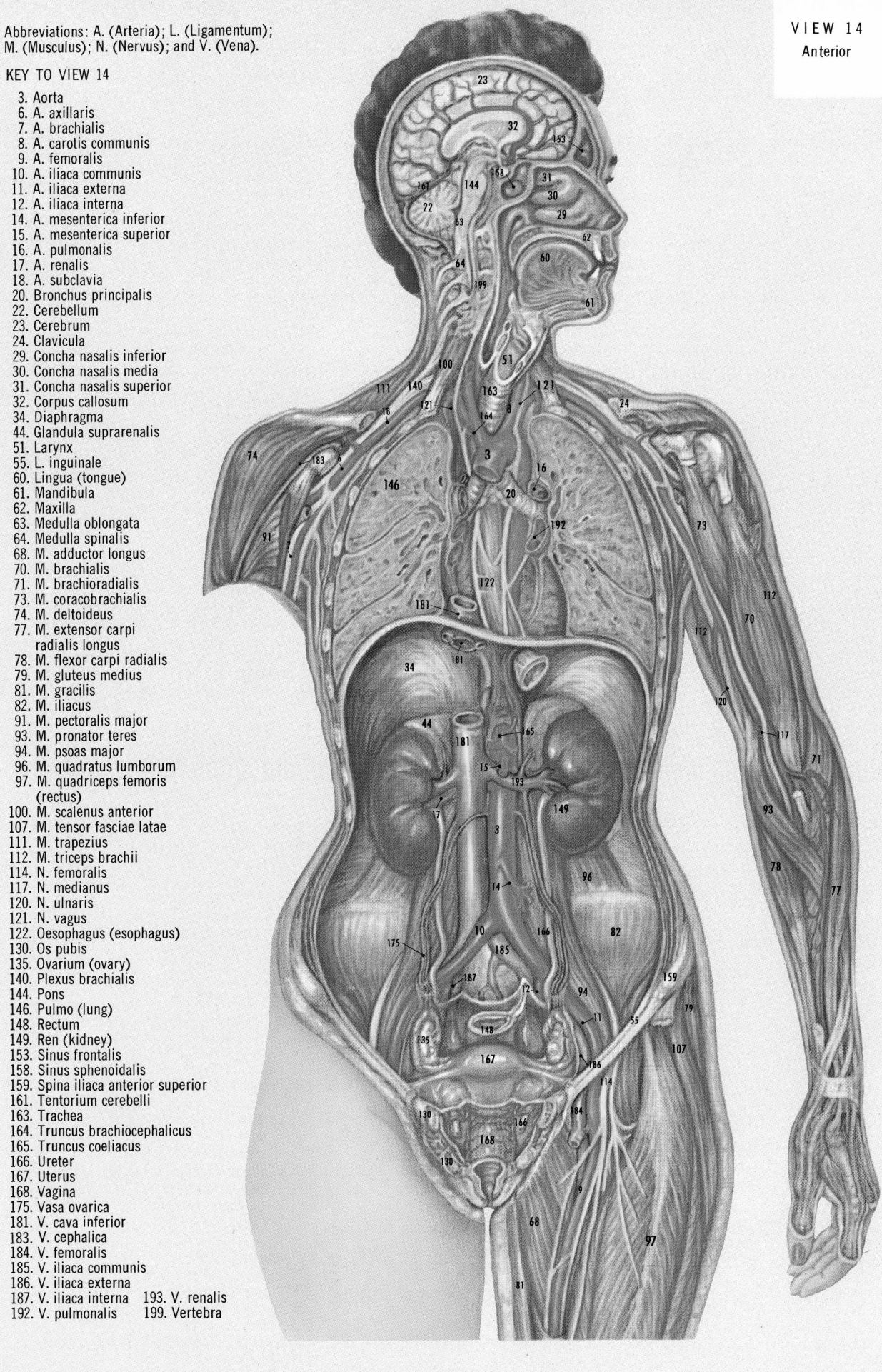

ANATOMY, GROSS

KEY TO PLATE, VIEWS 1-14

On the list below, the number at left is a code number for the part of the body named.
The number or numbers at right indicate the View or Views on which that part of the body is shown.

Abbreviations: A. (Arteria); L. (Ligamentum); M. (Musculus); N. (Nervus); and V. (Vena).

1. Anulus inguinalis profundus, 1,2
2. Anulus inguinalis superficialis, 1
3. Aorta, 5,6,10,11,14
4. Aponeurosis m. obliquus externus abdominis, 1
5. Appendix vermiformis, 4,12,13
6. A. axillaris, 5,6,14
7. A. brachialis, 5,6,14
8. A. carotis communis, 5,14
9. A. femoralis, 5,6,14
10. A. iliaca communis, 5,6,14
11. A. iliaca externa, 5,6,14
12. A. iliaca interna, 5,6,14
13. A. lienalis, 5
14. A. mesenterica inferior, 5,6,14
15. A. mesenterica superior, 14
16. A. pulmonalis, 5,10,11,14
17. A. renalis, 6,14
18. A. subclavia, 5,6,14
19. Atrium sinistrum, 11
20. Bronchus principalis, 5,14
21. Cartilago thyreoidea, 3
22. Cerebellum, 11,14
23. Cerebrum, 11,14
24. Clavicula, 1,2,7,8,9,14
25. Colon ascendens, 3,4,12,13
26. Colon descendens, 3,4,12,13
27. Colon sigmoideum, 3,4,12,13
28. Colon transversum, 3,4,11
29. Concha nasalis inferior, 4,7,11,14
30. Concha nasalis media, 4,7,11,14
31. Concha nasalis superior, 4,7,11,14
    Cor (heart): see 19,138,197,198
32. Corpus callosum, 11,14
33. Cranium, 2
34. Diaphragma, 2,3,4,5,6,9,10,11,14
35. Ductus choledochus, 4,5,10,11,13
36. Ductus deferens, 5,6
37. Duodenum, 5,12,13
    Esophagus: see 122
38. Falx cerebri, 12,13
39. Femur, 7
40. Fossa ovalis, 8
    Gall Bladder: see 200
41. Glandula lacrimalis, 2
42. Glandula parotis, 1,2
43. Glandula submandibularis, 1,2
44. Glandula suprarenalis, 5,6,14
45. Glandula thyreoidea, 3,4,10,11
46. Glans penis, 1
    Heart: see 19,138,197,198
47. Hepar (liver), 3,4,9,10,11
48. Humerus, 7
49. Ileum, 12
50. Intestinum tenue, 3,4,10,11
    Kidney: see 149
51. Larynx, 4,7,11,14
52. Lien (spleen), 5,12,13
53. L. falciforme hepatis, 3,9
54. L. fundiforme penis, 1
55. L. inguinale, 1,2,3,5,6,8,13,14
56. L. teres hepatis, 2,9
57. Linea alba, 1,2,8
58. Linea arcuata, 2
59. Linea semilunaris, 1,2,8,9
60. Lingua (tongue), 3,4,5,6,7,11,14
    Liver: see 47
    Lung: see 146
61. Mandibula, 1,2,3,4,5,6,7,11,14

62. Maxilla, 2,3,4,5,6,7,11,12,13,14
63. Medulla oblongata, 11,14
64. Medulla spinalis, 7,14
65. Mesenterium, 4, 11, 12
66. Mesocolon transversum, 11,12
67. M. adductor brevis, 7
68. M. adductor longus, 6,7,14
69. M. biceps brachii, 5,6,10,11
70. M. brachialis, 14
71. M. brachioradialis, 12,13,14
72. M. buccinator, 1
73. M. coracobrachialis, 5,14
74. M. deltoideus, 5,6,8,9,14
75. M. depressor anguli oris, 1,10
76. M. digastricus, 3
77. M. extensor carpi radialis longus, 14
78. M. flexor carpi radialis, 14
79. M. gluteus medius, 1,5,6,7,14
80. M. gluteus minimus, 7
81. M. gracilis, 6,7,14
82. M. iliacus, 7,14
83. M. intercostalis externus, 1
84. M. intercostalis internus, 2,9
85. M. masseter, 1
86. M. mylohyoideus, 2,3
87. M. obliquus externus abdominis, 1,8
88. M. obliquus internus abdominis, 1
89. M. omohyoideus, 1,2,9
90. M. orbicularis oris, 1
91. M. pectoralis major, 1,2,5,8,9,14
92. M. pectoralis minor, 2,5,9,10,11
93. M. pronator teres, 14
94. M. psoas major, 7,14
95. M. pterygoideus medialis, 2
96. M. quadratus lumborum, 14
97. M. quadriceps femoris, 3,4,5,6,14
98. M. rectus abdominis, 1,2
99. M. sartorius, 1,2,9
100. M. scalenus anterior, 14
101. M. serratus anterior, 1
102. M. sternocleidomastoideus, 1,2,8,9,10
103. M. sternohyoideus, 1,2,9
104. M. sternothyreoideus, 2,9
105. M. styloglossus, 3
106. M. temporalis, 1
107. M. tensor fasciae latae, 1,5,6,14
108. M. thyreohyoideus, 2
109. M. transversus abdominis, 1,2
110. M. transversus thoracis, 2,9
111. M. trapezius, 5,6,10,14
112. M. triceps brachii, 5,6,14
113. M. zygomaticus major, 1,10
114. N. femoralis, 7,14
115. N. iliohypogastricus, 7
116. N. ilioinguinalis, 7
117. N. medianus, 5,6,14
118. N. obturatorius, 7
119. N. phrenicus, 10
120. N. ulnaris, 5,6,14
121. N. vagus, 14
122. Oesophagus (esophagus), 5,6,12,13,14
123. Omentum majus, 10
124. Omentum minus, 3,4,9,10,11
125. Os costale, 1,2,7,9
126. Os frontale, 3,7
127. Os ischii, 7
128. Os occipitale, 4,5,7
129. Os parietale, 3,7
130. Os pubis, 3,6,7,13,14

131. Os sacrum, 7
132. Os sphenoidale, 7
133. Os temporale, 3,7
134. Os zygomaticum, 1
135. Ovarium (ovary), 14
136. Pancreas, 5,12,13
137. Penis, 2,3,5
138. Pericardium, 10
139. Platysma, 8,9
140. Plexus brachialis, 5,6,7,14
141. Plexus lumbosacralis, 7
142. Plica umbilicalis medialis, 9
143. Plica umbilicalis mediana, 9
144. Pons, 11,14
145. Prostata, 6
146. Pulmo (lung), 3,4,5,6,10,11,14
147. Pylorus, 12,13
148. Rectum, 7, 14
149. Ren (kidney), 5,6,14
150. Scapula, 7
151. Scrotum, 1,2,5
152. Septum nasi, 5,6,12,13
153. Sinus frontalis, 2,3,4,5,6,7,11,12,13,14
154. Sinus maxillaris, 2,3
155. Sinus rectus, 12,13
156. Sinus sagittalis inferior, 12,13
157. Sinus sagittalis superior, 12,13
158. Sinus sphenoidalis, 4,5,6,7,11,12,13,14
159. Spina iliaca anterior superior, 1,2,7,8,14
    Spleen: see 52
160. Sternum, 1,2,8,9
    Stomach: see 196
161. Tentorium cerebelli, 11,14
    Tongue: see 60
162. Testis, 5
163. Trachea, 5,6,14
164. Truncus brachiocephalicus, 5,14
165. Truncus coeliacus, 5,10,12,14
166. Ureter, 5,6,13,14
167. Uterus, 14
168. Vagina, 14
169. Vasa epigastrica inferior, 5,8,9
170. Vasa gastrica, 11
171. Vasa gastroepiploica, 10
172. Vasa lienalis, 12,13
173. Vasa mesenterica inferior, 12,13
174. Vasa mesenterica superior, 5,12,13
175. Vasa ovarica, 14
176. Vasa testicularis, 5,6
177. Vasa thoracicae internae, 9,10
178. V. axillaris, 3,10,11
179. V. comitans a. brachialis, 3,8,10,11
180. V. brachiocephalica, 3,4,10,11
181. V. cava inferior, 5,6,11,14
182. V. cava superior, 4,5,10,11
183. V. cephalica, 3,4,8,9,11,12,13,14
184. V. femoralis, 5,6,14
185. V. iliaca communis, 5,6,14
186. V. iliaca externa, 5,6,14
187. V. iliaca interna, 5,6,14
188. V. jugularis interna, 3,4,5,10
189. V. mesenterica inferior, 13
190. V. mesenterica superior, 5
191. V. portae, 5,11,12,13
192. V. pulmonalis, 11,14
193. V. renalis, 6,14
194. V. saphena magna, 8,9
195. V. subclavia, 3,4,10,11
196. Ventriculus (stomach), 3,4,10,11
197. Ventriculus dexter, 5,10,11
198. Ventriculus sinister, 5,10,11
199. Vertebra, 6,7,11,14
200. Vesica fellea (gall bladder), 3,4,10,11
201. Vesica urinaria, 3,4,5,6,12,13
202. Vesicula seminalis, 6

OGY). These subdivisions, which do not exist in nature, are all academic conveniences. All the laws of all nature co-operate harmoniously in everything we are and in everything we do. In addition to gross human anatomy, which is considered here, other subdivisions are treated in special articles. (*See* GASTROINTESTINAL TRACT; CIRCULATORY SYSTEM; MUSCLE AND MUSCULAR SYSTEM; NERVOUS SYSTEM; SKELETON, VERTEBRATE; *see also* BRAIN; EAR, ANATOMY OF; HEART, ANATOMY OF.)

GENERAL PLAN OF STRUCTURE

Comparative anatomists and comparative embryologists have shown that one common plan appears in the bodies of man and the higher vertebrates. In the adult it appears in the trunk region—the thorax and abdomen; in the embryos, with their less complex bodies, it is more evident.

The body wall is like a cylinder (*see* fig. 1), open at one end,

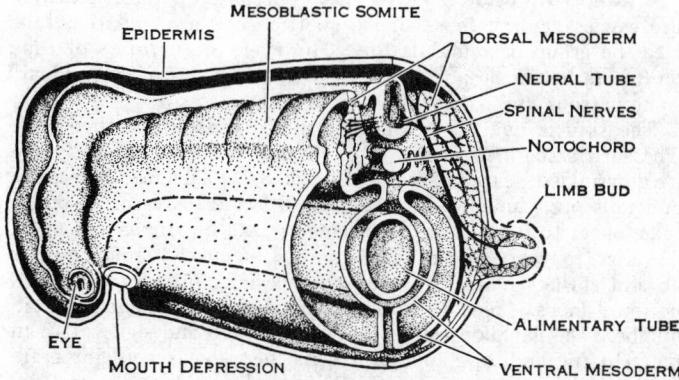

MODIFIED FROM J. S. KINGSLEY, "OUTLINE OF COMPARATIVE ANATOMY OF VERTEBRATES"; BY COURTESY OF MCGRAW-HILL BOOK COMPANY, INC.

FIG. 1.—GENERAL PLAN OF BODY STRUCTURE. DIAGRAM BASED ON EARLY EMBRYONIC STAGES. IN THE CROSS SECTION THE LEFT SIDE SHOWS A STAGE OF DEVELOPMENT EARLIER THAN THAT SHOWN ON THE RIGHT SIDE

tapering to a stem at the other. One rod and two tubes extend through the length of the cylinder. The tubes are on opposite sides of the rod, one, the neural tube, being dorsal and the other, the alimentary tube, being ventral. From the sides, somewhat ventral to the axial rod, four limbs grow out, two anterior and two posterior. The tubes extend above the open end of the cylinder, the neural tube to get information, the alimentary tube to get food. The whole is enclosed in a thin membrane, the epidermis, which covers it everywhere. The diagram represents simple embryonic stages of development, an earlier one on the left and a later one on the right. Both sides, of course, would actually be at the same stage of development at any one time.

The essential parts are: (1) the outer enclosing epidermal membrane (in the embryo called ectoderm); (2) the dorsal neural tube; (3) the supporting central rod around which the vertebral bodies grow (in the embryo called notochord); (4) the ventral alimentary tube which becomes the lining of the stomach and intestine (in the embryo called entoderm); (5) the intermediate mass (in the embryo called mesoderm); (6) a rather fluid tissue which fills the interspaces, derived from the mesoderm and in the embryo called mesenchyme.

The mesoderm constitutes a considerable pad of tissue on each side extending all the way from the most dorsal to the most ventral part of the body wall. It is hollow, for a cleftlike space appears in it on each side. These are the right and left body cavities. In the dorsal part of the body they are temporary; in the ventral part they are permanent, forming the two pleural cavities, the peritoneal cavity (originally double—most of the ventral mesentery is temporary) and the pericardial cavity. The dorsal mesoderm becomes separated from the ventral mesoderm and divides itself into serial parts like a row of blocks, 31 on each side (human); these are the mesodermal segments (mesoblastic somites). They grow dorsalward, ventralward, centralward (around the notochord) and outward toward the ectodermal membrane. They form bones, muscles and the deeper, leathery part of the skin. Dorsally they form bony arches protecting the

spinal cord, and ventrally the ribs protecting the alimentary canal and heart. Thus they form the body wall and the limbs—much the weightier part of the body. They give the segmental character to the body wall in neck and trunk and, following their lead, the spinal cord becomes correspondingly segmented. The ventral mesoderm is not so extensive; it remains near the alimentary tube, is never divided into segments and forms the continuous muscle layer of the stomach, intestine, etc., and the lining of the two body cavities; it becomes the smooth, shining, slippery pleura and peritoneum (fig. 3). The mesenchyme forms blood and lymph vessels, the heart and the loose cells of connective tissues. Everything in the body is formed from one or more of these six parts.

The neural tube itself is formed from the ectoderm at a very early stage. At first it dips in along the dorsal mid-line as a trough; fig. 2 shows it in cross section. Then the trough closes dorsally and it becomes a tube separate from the epidermis (fig. 3). Headward it extends above the open end of the cylinder and is enlarged to form the brain. It is not in immediate contact with the epidermis, for the dorsal mesoderm grows up around it and around the roots of the cranial nerves as a covering, separating the brain from the epidermis.

If the cylindrical body wall is followed headward it is found to terminate ventrally as the tongue, dorsally in the skull around the brain, ears and eyes. There is a considerable interval between eyes and tongue. This is occupied partly by a deep depression of the epidermis between them, which dips in to join the alimentary tube (lining of the mouth) (fig. 1).

Headward, the alimentary tube extends up in front of the notochord and projects above the upper part of the body wall (tongue) and in front of and below the brain to join the epidermal depression. From the epidermal depression are formed the teeth and most of the mouth lining; from the upper end of the alimentary canal is formed the pharynx with its gill slits and gill arches and the larynx, trachea and lungs.

The notochord terminates headward in a blunt mass under the middle of the brain.

Tailward, the neural tube terminates in the adult opposite the first lumbar vertebra (farther tailward in embryos). The notochord and mesoblastic somites extend to the tip of the tail (coccyx in man), the ventral body wall joins the dorsal at the coccyx, thus terminating the body cavities. The alimentary canal at its tail end splits longitudinally into two tubes—an anterior and a posterior—in all mammals except the lowest; the anterior tube becomes the bladder, urethra and lining of the vestibulum vaginae where it joins a depression of the ectoderm; the posterior (dorsal) tube becomes the rectum and ends just in front of the coccyx by joining another ectodermal depression (the anus).

The units of structure are the cells (*q.v.*). Each living cell comes from the division of a pre-existing cell and gets its life and its character from it. Living cells may be killed or die in the future; they have never died in the past. All cells now living in any living being have come in a continuous unbroken line from the first cells that lived on the earth.

Changes in Structure Appearing in Mammalia.—Among others, two new features introduced by the mammals were sucking and a long uterine gestation. The first required a small closable throat, which in turn required that food be masticated by

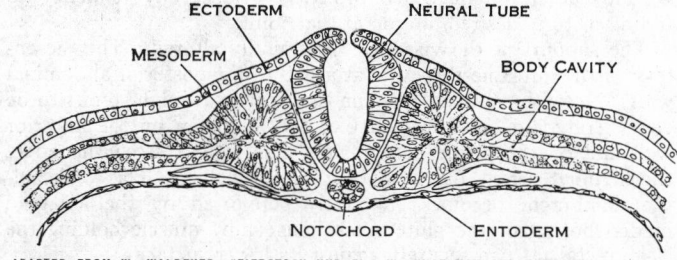

ADAPTED FROM W. WALDEYER, "EIERSTOCK UND EI," W. ENGELMAN AND COMPANY

FIG. 2.—FETAL MEMBRANE, SHOWING GERM LAYERS AND FORMATION OF THE NEURAL TUBE

molar teeth; it required also a firm imperforate hard palate. The second resulted in a fetus much larger at birth. But the parturient passages were smaller because the cloaca had been subdivided. This involved very high maternal intra-abdominal pressure at birth; it would have embarrassed the pumping apparatus—heart and mechanism of respiration. The diaphragm was interposed, increasing abdominal pressure by its action but not thoracic pressure. This interposition required the elongation of the esophagus to extend from the pharynx to the stomach which is caudad from the diaphragm.

Changes From Assumption of the Erect Position.—This posture, especially characteristic of the human animal, is not attained by simple rotation of the hind limbs through an angle of 90°, nor maintained without great modification of many parts of the body. The centre of gravity is shifted, involving changes in all the joints and especially in the vertebral column. The vertebrae are piled into a column of support, to which the thickened intervertebral discs give curvatures and elasticity. These discs reduce the impact of shocks, and the nucleus pulposus, like

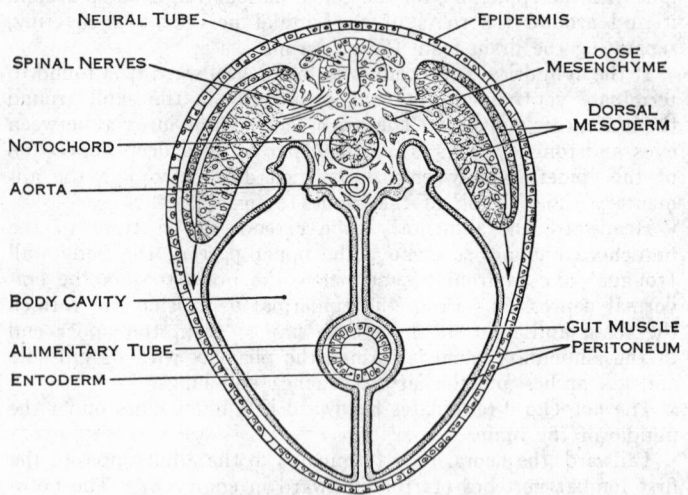

MODIFIED FROM J. S. KINGSLEY, "OUTLINE OF COMPARATIVE ANATOMY OF VERTEBRATES"; BY COURTESY OF McGRAW-HILL BOOK COMPANY, INC.

FIG. 3.—FORMATION OF THE BODY CAVITIES AND THEIR RELATION TO THE ALIMENTARY CANAL AND ITS MESENTERIES

a large marble in the centre of each, gives the whole column facility of movement. The cervical and lumbar curvatures appear and the lumbar segment is proportionally increased from 27% of total length in chimpanzees to 32% in adult men. It permits changing of the position of the relatively immobile thorax and its attached forelimbs.

The basis of bodily movement is reduced from the friction of four feet with the ground to that of two. This has important consequences for the feet, which develop heels and arches, a stronger bone structure and a very strong, half ligamentous bowstring muscle—the so-called abductor hallucis. The ankle joint becomes mortised and the work of knee and hip joints becomes greatly increased and complicated. The erect position requires the tonic contraction of muscles, especially of the extensors which prevent bending at the joints and the exquisitely delicate and automatic, unconscious action of the short (and other) muscles around the hip joint which promptly correct any tendency to falling or to undesired motion at that joint.

The support of the viscera is profoundly altered. The mesentery of the intestines becomes attached to the posterior abdominal wall. Notwithstanding this, almost the whole weight tends to be concentrated in the lower part of the abdomen on the anterior wall and on the pelvic diaphragm. The wall is strengthened in the inguinal region, but hernias occur through it. The weak pelvic diaphragm becomes effectively supported by the enlarged medial border of the gluteus maximus (hip) muscle holding the ischiorectal fat pad securely against its lower surface.

The mechanism of respiration is changed. The shoulder girdle is no longer supported from the ground and so cannot continue to be a base for muscular action producing inspiration. Instead it is a dead weight on inspiration. Some head muscles hold it up—trapezius and sternocleidomastoid. The thorax becomes flattened anteroposteriorly instead of laterally as in quadrupeds. Profound changes appear in the circulatory system. In fishes the heart is in the lowest part of the body. It pumps the blood up and gravity brings it back down. Land animals require limbs; they lift the heart to a height some distance above the lowest parts. Gravity can no longer effect all the return circulation. Assumption of erect posture in man lifts the heart higher above the ground than in any other animal now living except the giraffe and elephant. The return circulation is embarrassed. Valves are numerous in the veins of lower extremities but varicose veins are still common in later life. Changes throughout the body are required for the automatic adaptation through the sympathetic nerves of local blood supply during various activities.

Changes Incident to Old Age.—Because of the lengthening life expectancy, an increasing proportion of the population falls into the group past middle life. However, the imprints of time on human bodies do not come at the same age in each individual; some persons are as capable at 75 as others at 55.

The skin is one of the most accurate registers of the years. The soft, smooth, pink velvet of infancy becomes gradually the hard, wrinkled, seared parchment of old age. The head hair grays and falls out, though other hairs flourish and increase. Wounds take longer to heal; some replacements take five times as long at 60 as at 10 years of age. The brain is somewhat smaller after 40 and shrinks markedly after 75, especially in the frontal and occipital lobes. Sensory fibres in spinal nerves become fewer in number; the ganglion cells become pigmented and some of them die. In the auditory apparatus some nerve cells and fibres are lost and the ability to hear high notes diminishes. In the eye the lens loses its elasticity.

The bones become lighter and more brittle; they are friable and indentable; destruction overtakes new formation. They give up some of their calcium, which increases in arteries and cartilage, in ligaments and in the tendinous attachment of muscles. In joints the cartilage covering the ends of bone becomes thinner and sometimes disappears in spots, so bone meets bone directly and the old joints creak and burn. Muscular strength decreases but with marked individual variability.

Elastic tissue, like old rubber, loses its elasticity. This is the one tissue in the body which never rests. In the skin it makes cuts gape open, in the arteries it resists the ever-present blood pressure, in the connective tissues it restores the resting position after every movement. So it is apt to wear out early—in some families at 45; in others it may last until 90. In the lungs the air sacs (alveoli) get bigger because the elastic tissue in their walls degenerates and the lungs increase in size (emphysema of old age). Elastic tissue is at its best at 25 years. When lost in old age, it is not repaired.

The arteries become fibrous and sclerosed. Because of decreasing elasticity in their coats they tend to become rigid tubes. Yellow fatty spots, which appear in their lining even in youth, are always present in old age. Lymphoid tissue undergoes a general shrinkage after middle age. In glands the parenchyma shrinks and the protoplasm seems to become more sluggish.

Repairs of parts are made more slowly if at all and sometimes are made by tissue different from the original (metaplasia). Pigment appears in increasing amounts in the skin, the heart muscle, liver, kidney and nerve ganglia and in the cells of the central nervous system. Cells have less energy for division. Young tissues change and adapt themselves to changing conditions much more readily than do old fully differentiated tissues and thus the old lose a factor of safety.

These processes of aging are just as physiological as the processes of growing. Some of them appear in human embryos before birth. In evolution many structures which are functional in early forms undergo involution and are changed or replaced in later forms. The pronephros went; the mesonephros was changed. These involutions occur in human embryos. The ductus arteriosus goes at birth, the thymus during adolescence. Major involutions appear in increasing numbers as the higher decades pass.

Length of life differs greatly in different cells and body structures: nerve and muscle cells can live a lifetime and so never need replacement; head hairs live a few years. The longevity of the whole body differs for each species. The potential longevity of the human body has been estimated at 100 years; it appears to have been determined by man's gorillalike, anthropoid ancestors in the Pliocene period, perhaps 10,000,000 years ago.

Some scientific suggestions for the cause of old age, involution and death are failure of tissue nutrition through arterial degeneration, accumulation of waste products or of deleterious substances absorbed from the intestine or the atmosphere, failure of coordinated influence of hormones, the progressive diminution of oxygen consumption after 12 years of age or a combination of all of these. Doubtless all of these contribute.

FORM AND SIZE

Anatomists commonly recognize nine stages in a human life running its full course, and the body form changes from stage to stage. In none of these stages is the form static; it is reacting actively with the environment. Life before birth consists partly and after birth largely of such reaction, but though interaction with environment leads to local changes the body's deep fasciae preserve its general contours.

Form and size of the whole body and of its parts are inherited. The effects of present conditions modify the old adaptations. The resultant form is seldom perfect for life under present conditions but it is adapted to present needs well enough to maintain life with the least waste of energy.

Both form and size were determined in Pliocene times by a combination of internal and environmental forces. Among the internal forces were inheritance and growth. Among the external, gravity was one of the most important. In animals that moved on the surface of the earth, gravity confined life to one plane—the horizontal. Gravity dictated that one side should be up and one down and ventral and dorsal surfaces resulted. Limbs had to be on the underside. Since animals moved with one end first, head and tail evolved, and the head end, coming into contact with the environment first, developed sense organs. Animals that moved rapidly had to be bilaterally symmetrical.

Gravity was not only the chief agent in producing these qualities of form universal among the vertebrates, but also had a great influence on size. If a little animal with form perfectly adapted to its environment were to double its length while its form remained the same, it would have four times as much surface and eight times as much weight. Such a change of proportion might be serious in relation to gravity and water and air resistance.

Gravity has also an influence on the relative size of parts. The lancelet (amphioxus) has a straight and so a short intestine. As animals get longer the intestine becomes coiled. If the length of the animal were multiplied by ten and the form remained the same, the absorptive intestinal surface would be multiplied by only 100 but the weight by 1,000. To feed the greater bulk the intestine would have to be much longer than the body and so coiled. The human alimentary canal is 12 times as long as the straight line between its ends.

Gravity is thus an important determinant of form, but it works chiefly on large and heavy things. In early embryonic stages, when growth is most active, the body is too small for gravity to exert effective influence. In those tiny masses other intermolecular factors are more effective—capillarity, cohesion, surface tension, adsorption, electric charge, chemical action. These are the important internal and external forces operating at that stage of organization. They are co-operative with inheritance. Many antecedents and determinants of form in the early embryological stages have been revealed. The organizers of H. Spemann and the morphogenetic hormones of J. Needham are among them.

PHYSIOLOGICAL ANATOMY

For a long time physiology and anatomy were combined in universities; Johannes Müller was professor of both at the same time in Berlin. Later for academic convenience they were separated. In nature, however, all anatomy is physiological.

A new morphologic concept developed rapidly after 1940. Researches into the form and structure of small animal bodies and their parts (embryos and cells) showed them to be very sensitive to biochemical influences. Morphogenetic hormones are largely biochemical in nature and are the causes or determinants of many of the form changes in embryonic development.

The study of form in minute anatomy promised to be heuristically extended beyond the reach of visible light to include the structure of organic molecules, especially the giant protein molecules of which man's structure is composed.

HISTORY OF ANATOMY

The story of the development of the science of anatomy may properly be divided into four periods, during each of which the science had different orientations: (1) until thorough scientific dissection by Andreas Vesalius (A.D. 1543); (2) until the advent of scientific physiology with William Harvey (1628); (3) until the demonstration of the unity of all life by Charles Darwin (1859); and (4) after Darwin.

Until Thorough Scientific Dissection by Vesalius (A.D. 1543).—*The Period of Ignorance of Anatomy.*—None of the very early scientists dissected a human body. Men regarded the dead body with superstitious awe. Spirits were everywhere and surely the spirit of this body was hovering near its forsaken mansion. There was a belief in life after death and a disquieting uncertainty concerning the resurrection of the body. The disintegration of buried or drowned bodies was troubling. In the Talmudic writings is a theory of the "bone called Luz"—the resurrection bone (perhaps the sacrum). It was a nucleus around which the separated molecules were to be reassembled. The Mohammedan religion forbade dissection and the Christian church was not always mindful of St. Paul's statement, "It is sown a natural body, it is raised a spiritual body."

For surgeons, however, knowledge of the "natural body" was a vital necessity and for all men who could and dared to think it was of the greatest interest. Embalmers learned a little anatomy in preparing mummies, as did surgeons in treating wounds. The Edwin Smith surgical papyrus (3000–2500 B.C.) contains some anatomy of the head and brain. The Ebers papyrus (1600 B.C.) contains more. Early knowledge was pitifully vague.

Hippocrates and Aristotle.—More than a millennium later lived Hippocrates, the great physician (c. 460–c. 374 B.C.). Some writings on anatomy are dubiously ascribed to him, but there is no evidence that he dissected a human body. Nor did Aristotle (384–322 B.C.). Both thought the heart was the seat of the intellect.

Aristotle studied animals and was the founder of comparative anatomy. His comparisons of structure led him to construct a "ladder of nature" ascending from the lowest to the highest. He saw a unity in nature—the foundation of the concept of organic evolution. Aristotle did not see it, but Charles Darwin, standing on his shoulders, did. "Linnaeus and Cuvier were my Gods," said Darwin, "but they were mere schoolboys compared to old Aristotle."

Herophilus and Erasistratus.—About 40 years after the deaths of Aristotle and his patron, Alexander the Great, the Ptolemies ruled in Egypt and encouraged dissection. At Alexandria appeared Herophilus (fl. 300 B.C.), the greatest of the Greek anatomists. Before him, human anatomy was speculative rather than descriptive. But he dissected the human body, and for the first time anatomy was given a considerable factual basis. He dissected the brain and recognized it as the centre of the nervous system and the seat of intelligence. He distinguished motor and sensory nerves, showed that the aorta and arteries contained blood, not air, and described the lymphatic vessels of the intestine—the lacteals, which were "discovered" by Gasparo Aselli (1622), the contemporary of Harvey. He described and named the duodenum. If his book *On Anatomy* had not been lost, the world might not have had to wait 1,800 years for some account of structure of the human body resulting from thorough scientific dissection.

Erasistratus (fl. 300 B.C.) was a younger contemporary. He believed that arteries contained air or *spiritus vitalis*. Arteries, veins and nerves were in his view all tubes. He had a theory that the whole body was made of tubes, for the most part too fine to see. He might have arrived at an idea of the circulation of the blood, for he suspected that the ultimate branches of arteries and veins were connected by smaller branches beyond the limits of visibility. He first saw that the veins, like the arteries, centre in the heart, not the liver. He described the valves of the heart and named the tricuspid. Like Hippocrates, he called the trachea *arteria tracheia,* the rough air holder.

Marinus and Galen.—Three hundred years after Erasistratus, there lived in Alexandria the important teacher Marinus (*c.* A.D. 110), who wrote a book unfortunately lost. The influence of his personality and his teaching was so great that it reached down through four teachers who followed him and inspired Galen (*c.* A.D. 130–*c.* 200).

Galen was an Asiatic Greek who practised medicine in Rome from A.D. 164 to 199 (except when he fled from epidemics). He had ability, education, wealth, industry, self-assurance and a quarrelsome disposition. His patients (emperors and consuls) encouraged him to write and lecture. Some writings were lost in a fire; a vast number remain—59 books on anatomy. They abound in polemics and self-glorification. His nomenclature is inconsistent and indefinite. His science is vitiated by two a priori theories to which he adhered dogmatically. The first was the old one of the pneuma and spirits: the pneuma was cosmic life taken in with the breath; the spirits were three—natural in the liver, vital in the heart and animal (mental) in the brain; thence they traveled through veins, arteries and nerves respectively with an ebb and flow motion like the tides or the breath. The second was his self-made religion in which a creator had made every structure of the body perfect for its use. The first dogma precluded any thought of the blood circulation (he knew nothing of injections); its detail required the existence of canals through the interventricular septum of the heart. He could not find them in any animal but described them nevertheless. The religious dogma assumed that he knew everything of structure and function, and so could explain every phenomenon.

Much of what he knew of human anatomy, principally about bones and joints, he learned through Marinus. For other structures he offered the anatomy of the Barbary ape, the pig and the ox as human. But since his dogma suited the Stoics and also the new Christian religion, he was supported by the authority of state and church. His books were preserved while others were lost. Since Galen was perfect, no further study was needed or permitted. Galen's service consisted in assembling and arranging all the discoveries of Greek anatomy. His disservice consisted in the establishment of an authoritative fictitious anatomy.

Middle Ages.—Galen's period, which has been aptly called the Indian summer of Greek science, was followed by a long period during which anatomy as a science languished. For a dozen centuries the Arabs kept it barely alive. When they took Alexandria in A.D. 640, Paul of Aegina was there and he taught them Galen's anatomy. They also studied Greek science in commentaries translated into Arabic by Syrians, Nestorians, Christians and Jews. These were essentially Aristotle and Galen with an Arab colour. Rhazes, Ali Abbas and Avicenna made the most important ones and of these the last was the most famous. The *Canon of Medicine* of Avicenna, the "medical Bible," published in A.D. 1000, contained a considerable section of second- or third-hand anatomy, much of it from animals and scarcely ever tested by fresh observation. It spread throughout the Arab world, through Egypt and Africa to Spain.

Eventually the originals from which the Arab works had been abstracted were found, and through them men began to look at the wonders of nature. But at first, only through them. Men studied the books—not nature. Scholasticism made authorities of Galen and Aristotle. It did not attack problems by the study of nature but by metaphysical dialectic based on those books. Research was forbidden in some universities and physicians were punished if they dared to differ from Galen. But there was some interest in anatomy. The dissection of executed felons was authorized and public demonstrations, "anatomies," were held. An

"anatomie" was a reading from Galen (animal anatomy). Half of the names used were Arabic. The professor (of medicine) presided solemnly. Seated in his elevated chair, he read a translation of Galen. To a menial was given the task of verifying from the cadaver the text as read. He tried to do it though the text was wrong. The sessions were long and collations were served.

The law courts obtained permission to have autopsies made, being sometimes suspicious of the ostensible causes of death. Mondino de'Luzzi (Mondinus), professor of medicine at Bologna, performed some and published (1316) an autopsy manual of 40 small pages called *Anathomia.*

Leonardo.—Artists encouraged the study of anatomy, for they wanted accurate representations of the body. Dissections were performed by Leonardo da Vinci (1452–1519), Albrecht Dürer (1471–1528), Michelangelo (1475–1564) and Raphael (1483–1520). Leonardo began with surface measurements, proportions and anatomy of muscles, but it was not as an artist that he went on to study heart, brain, digestive system, fetus, etc. He became an anatomist and dissected 30 bodies (largely as autopsies) until stopped by Pope Leo X. He made more than 750 anatomical drawings and wrote 120 anatomical notebooks.

Altogether, his works on anatomy surpass in extent, accuracy and beauty the work of many centuries after his death. A long list of his discoveries has been made; all were rediscovered by later anatomists. Leonardo studied and trusted nature rather than books.

Leonardo's magnificent achievements in many fields brought him the admiration and reverence of his contemporaries. His spirit and influence prepared the way for the "restorer of anatomy," Vesalius, whose great book was published 24 years after Leonardo died.

Until the Advent of Scientific Physiology With Harvey (1628).—*Vesalius.*—Andreas Witing came of a distinguished medical family in Wesel on the Rhine; hence he was called Vesalius. In 1533 at the age of 19 he went to the University of Paris, where he studied medicine under the famous Sylvius (Jacques Dubois of Amiens), who was the most popular medical teacher of his time. In his lectures he presented Galen with so much eloquence and clearness that students flocked to Paris. Though he was professor of medicine, Sylvius lectured on anatomy. Sylvius knew Galen much better than he knew the body, however, and often the demonstrator could not find the structures Galen described. Neither could Sylvius. So Vesalius and his fellow student, Michael Servetus, would dissect bodies and confront the great professor with the evidence—an unforgivable offense.

At Paris Vesalius saw that he was an anatomist and that his teachers were not. He resolved that he would devote himself to the science of anatomy.

At the age of 22 he went to Venice. Within a year he took his doctor's degree in Padua where he became famous for his knowledge and skill in anatomy and surgery and accepted the chair of surgery and anatomy in the university (1537). He was the first to receive a salary as professor of anatomy in any university. Vesalius himself served as the dissector and his mechanical skill was marvelous, as was also his ability as a teacher. He covered the margins of Galen's book with notes of the author's mistakes.

Everyone came to his lectures—students, professors from all departments, artists, the élite of Padua and Venice, public officials and the clergy. In 1540 he demonstrated at Bologna the skeletons of a man and an ape, side by side. It became clear to Vesalius that where Galen was wrong for man he was right for the ape. Vesalius thus resolved to prepare a new account of human anatomy from his own dissections and illustrated with the best pictures that could be made. For three years he worked constantly; he dissected, wrote and made drawings. He engaged one of the best artists of Italy, said to be his friend and countryman, John de Calcar, Titian's pupil, to make drawings and woodcuts. The drawings of the skeleton reportedly were made by Calcar, those of the muscles probably by Vesalius himself. Many pictures are posed so as to show the entire body in the postures and environment of life. Vesalius was interested in the living man and the artists of Italy had much to do with securing the permission by which the few bodies were obtained on which Vesalius' work was done.

The book, *De humani corporis fabrica* (Basel, 1543), was a great success. For the first time men could see, in beautiful and accurate illustrations, the structure of their own bodies. There was fierce and bitter contemporary criticism, however. Many physicians and anatomists were opposed. Their reputations were at stake. They had taught Galen too long. Sylvius belittled the illustrations and wrote Vesalius asking why he had not published his little work as an appendix to Sylvius' edition of the complete works of Galen. Realdo Colombo, Vesalius' pupil at Padua, ridiculed him and said that he had overlooked important things like the duct between the stomach and the spleen. Vesalius challenged him to show it. He announced public dissections and invited all who knew him wrong to be present and show on the human body wherein he was mistaken. Crowds attended. Colombo could not find his gastrosplenic duct because it was not there. Vesalius says of others that, though urged to state his errors, they were silent as though their tongues had been cut out.

In a fit of despondency, Vesalius gave up anatomy. He burned everything he had on hand, the old Galen with the marginal notations and a great volume of anatomical notations. He became court physician to Charles V and afterward to Philip II of Spain.

But his work was well done, and his book triumphed by its own truth. It is the first real textbook of anatomy, but it is much more than that. With the publication of the *Fabrica*, medical science entered the modern period.

The Period of Discovery at Padua.—After Vesalius left Padua (about 1546) his chair was occupied by a series of five eminent anatomists following in succession until 1625. The first of these was his assistant Realdo Colombo (1516?–59), who, as mentioned previously, was critical of his former teacher. But he followed the methods of Vesalius and added to the knowledge of the serous membranes, the eye and the lung.

Gabriello Fallopius (1523–62), canon of Modena, succeeded. He also had been an assistant to Vesalius. He gave loyalty, admiration and affection to Vesalius and his students and colleagues gave them to him. Though he died at 39 he added much of permanent value to our knowledge of anatomy. Accuracy was his distinguishing characteristic. The uterine tubes and the canal carrying the facial nerve through the temporal bone are still known by his name. Two of his pupils became great anatomists—Volcher Coiter and Fabricius. The latter succeeded him.

Hieronymus Fabricius (Geronimo Fabrizio) (*c.* 1533–1619) came of a noble and wealthy family in Aquapendente near Orvieto. For nearly 50 years, from 1562 to 1613, he was professor of anatomy at Padua. His many publications cover anatomy, embryology and physiology. They contain excellent illustrations made from copper plates and justify his position among the greatest of anatomists. Bernard Albinus of Leyden republished his *Opera omnia* in 1738.

In his long life, he attained the greatest fame and it has not lessened. Galileo chose him as his physician. He was knighted in 1608. William Harvey lived in his house and began with him the study of blood circulation and of embryology.

Julius Casserio (Casserius) (1552–1616) was nominated by Fabricius as his successor. He had been a house servant, pupil and later assistant to Fabricius and was expert in all the techniques of anatomy of his time. Most of his plates were published after his death by his successor, Spigelius. There were 98, including 22 on the vocal organs and 17 on the ear.

The last of the six great Paduans was Adrian van der Spiegel (Spigelius) (1578–1625), who succeeded Casserius in 1618. Like Vesalius and Calcar, he was born in Belgium. His book, published in 1627, is illustrated by the magnificent plates of Casserius. His discoveries relate mainly to the muscles of the spinal column and to the viscera. The lobus caudatus of the liver is still commonly called the Spigelian lobe. He reformed the nomenclature, but died relatively young of blood poisoning from infections incurred in handling the poorly preserved material with which he worked; such infections were common among anatomists until after Pasteur's time. After Spigelius, Padua ceased to hold the

place so long maintained as leader in the work of gross anatomy. And as yet there was no other anatomy.

Other Italian and European Laboratories.—At Bologna, Jacopo Berengario da Carpi (d. 1530) had added knowledge of the vermiform appendix and the thymus gland. Giulio Aranzio (Arantius) (1530–89) studied the heart (corpora Arantii) and Costanzo Varoli (1543–75) described the brain (pons Varolii).

In Rome Bartolomeo Eustachio (Eustachius) (1524–74) made many discoveries. His great fame was posthumous, achieved through the drawings of his *Tabulae anatomicae.* He published only eight of these himself; 38 others did not appear until 1714, 140 years after his death, though completed much earlier (1552?). He made the drawings himself and was among the first to have them reproduced on copper plates instead of on wood. In accuracy of detail, they surpass the splendid illustrations of Vesalius. A list of the structures, of which he has given us the first accurate knowledge, is impressive. The tuba auditiva (Eustachian tube) is named for him. His drawings include a magnificent representation of the sympathetic nervous system far beyond any antecedent knowledge. He also introduced the study of variations.

Had his plates been published when they were made, the progress of anatomy would have been accelerated by a century and Eustachius would perhaps have taken his rightful place beside Vesalius as one of the two "fathers of anatomy."

In France Jacobus Sylvius (Jacques Dubois) (1478–1555), professor of medicine in Paris and sometime teacher of Vesalius, made some additions to knowledge of bones of the head and a real reform in anatomical nomenclature.

He unintentionally immortalized himself by his comments on the *Fabrica* of Vesalius when it was published in 1543. He said that anatomy had changed since Galen's time, that the femur was more curved then but had been straightened by the style of tight breeches; that the sternum did consist of eight bones when Galen described it—it needed more in the robust chests of ancient heroes than in men of the degenerate days of 1543. He made a pun on Vesalius' name and referred to him as Vesanus (madman).

In Switzerland Felix Platter (1536–1614) of Basel wrote an excellent account of the eye, the foundation of modern knowledge.

The learned, capable and religious Spaniard, Michael Servetus (1511–53) of Aragon, mentioned previously as the friend of Vesalius at Paris, described the pulmonary circulation accurately for the first time in his book *Christianismi restitutio* (1553). If he had lived longer it is probable that he would have discovered the general circulation 70 years before it was demonstrated by Harvey. An ardent Christian who made for himself a "Christocentric world," he did not agree with authorities in some doctrines concerning the Trinity, and Calvin and his associates condemned him to be burned alive.

In England Thomas Vicary published in 1548 a small book called the *Anatomie of the Bodie of Man,* probably the first book on anatomy in the English language. In 1651 the College of Physicians created a lectureship in anatomy and two years later built in Knight Rider street an anatomical theatre. In 1615 a lecturer in that foundation named William Harvey was appointed.

William Harvey.—Returning to England after four years with Fabricius, William Harvey (1578–1657) was already concerned with the problems of his life: circulation and generation.

Although he respected Galen and Aristotle, he had learned not to worship them. He learned all the facts anyone else had ever learned about the heart and added more which he perceived for the first time. Above all, he put all the facts together better than any other person and so saw the general principle underlying what formerly had been merely witnessed—the circulation of the blood. In anatomy and physiology this was a fundamental truth for all subsequent work and subsequent thought.

The physiologists hold that he was a physiologist; the anatomists that he was an anatomist. He was both; the separation is an artificial one. That he was an anatomist is attested by the fact that his work is based on structure and that he calls his book *Exercitatio anatomica de motu cordis.*

He had seen with everyone else the arterial tree and the venous tree (the metaphor comes from Hippocrates) with their great trunks and branches. He said the fluid blood passed somehow from the arterial twigs to the venous tree twigs. Many said that was like saying that the sap goes up this tree and then crosses over and goes down the tree over there. Harvey spent the rest of his life hunting the connecting capillaries. He never saw them, but he foresaw them. Actually, they are an enormous network connecting the terminal twigs of the arterial and venous trees. There are more than 60,000 mi. of them in the muscles alone. In 1628, when Harvey published his paper on circulation, a boy was born in Italy who did see them. Four years after Harvey died in 1657, Marcello Malpighi, then 32 years of age, stood on a hillside near Bologna looking toward the glow of the Italian sunset. He held up to the light a preparation—a spread-out piece of a frog's lung. He saw the terminal twigs of arteries and veins, and with a magnifying glass saw for the first time the tiny capillaries, with the blood in them, connecting the twigs.

Until the Demonstration of the Unity of Life by Darwin (1859).—*The Period of Consolidation, Illustration and Teaching.*—The century following Harvey became the heroic age of microscopic anatomy and embryology. Gross human anatomy was characterized in this period by the foundation of scientific and philosophic societies, the development of texts, atlases and museums, advances in knowledge made chiefly by surgeons and the establishment of special schools of anatomy, the beginning of anatomical work in the United States and the passing of anatomical acts.

Treatises.—The epoch-making *Fabrica* of Vesalius was followed by the text of another Paduan, Spigelius, in 1627. The intense interest aroused and nourished by the work of the Italians resulted in much anatomical investigation throughout western Europe, reported in many monographs on special topics. The scientific societies, founded about this time, were also receiving reports of similar work. It was desirable that all this should be brought together, and in several countries textbooks appeared in which all the knowledge available was assembled and arranged.

Investigations in Gross Human Anatomy.—This was left largely to surgeons. They were ardent anatomists. In preanesthetic days, speed in operation was of prime importance. This required exact detailed knowledge of structure and relations. They introduced the new overabundant detail of description and nomenclature in regions where operations were frequent—mouth, neck, inguinal region, perineum, etc.

Sometimes emulation had unhappy consequences. J. G. Wirsung and an associate "discovered" the pancreatic duct. Wirsung reported it (1642). He was later murdered. The associate was suspected, the motive being jealousy. O. Rudbeck of Sweden and T. Bartholinus of Denmark both "discovered," independently, 1651 and 1652 respectively, the lymphatic system and its termination in the neck veins. Their work was admirable, but their dispute over priority was bitter. All these jealousies were futile, for Eustachius' plates, so long unpublished, had shown the facts about a century before.

Schools of Anatomy.—On the continent, anatomy was taught throughout this period in the universities, usually in association with surgery or medicine. But in England, biology was an orphan child whom the dormant universities were slow to adopt. Anatomy was born and grew up outside them. The surgeons established extramural schools. It became clear to them that if the public were to have good medical service, medical students and physicians must know anatomy better than they did. William Hunter, at his own expense, established the famous school on Great Windmill street in 1770. It contained his collection of preparations, dissecting rooms, an amphitheatre and his dwelling house. He lived in the school and for it. When he died 13 years later, he had expended £100,000 on his museum. There he, his more famous brother, John Hunter, and William Hewson taught, superintended dissection and initiated many into investigation of special problems. The school, which continued 63 years, made a great contribution to the teaching and development of anatomy throughout the English-speaking world.

In the school's early days, Benjamin Franklin was a frequent

visitor and a great friend of Hewson. When the latter died from blood poisoning contracted in his work (one of nine who died of that cause in the school), Franklin induced his widow and children to move to Philadelphia, where some of their descendants became well-known physicians. Other similar schools were established. In 1828 there were in London seven private schools of anatomy plus four in the hospitals.

In Edinburgh anatomy was taught in the university. The Alexander Monros, father, son and grandson, held the chair for 126 continuous years—from 1720 to 1846. The two elders taught 12,800 students and made Edinburgh a great centre of medical teaching. There was also an extramural school in which the famous brothers John and Charles Bell taught. These schools gave to dissection the qualities of thoroughness and technical precision which have characterized it ever since.

William Hunter's museum was bequeathed to Glasgow, where it remained a centre of interest in modern times. John Hunter later parted from his brother and assembled his own famous anatomical collection, which became one of the most treasured and useful possessions of the Royal College of Surgeons in London.

Anatomy Acts.—The schools required human bodies to teach anatomy. Since there were no legal provisions for supplying them, they were obtained clandestinely. Resurrectionists dug them up and the schools bought them. Trouble came abundantly, culminating in the Burke and Hare atrocities in 1827 (*see* BURKE, WILLIAM). This led to the passing in 1832 of the British Anatomy act, long urged by leading medical men. It permitted use of unclaimed bodies by specially licensed teachers. A similar act had been passed in 1831 by the legislature of the state of Massachusetts, an example that was soon followed in other states.

Gross Anatomy in the United States.—In America anatomy followed the traditions of the old British schools, at first of the Monros of Edinburgh and later that of the Hunters of London. About 1730 Thomas Cadwalader opened a private school for anatomy in Philadelphia. He had been a pupil of Cheselden. New York had one in the 1750s. From 1752 to 1755, another William Hunter, of the same Scottish family as the famous brothers in London, gave a series of demonstrations in Newport, R.I.

In 1765 two young men, William Shippen and John Morgan, organized a school of medicine in connection with Pennsylvania college, afterward the University of Pennsylvania. They had been pupils of both the first Monro and of the Hunters. Shippen was professor of anatomy, surgery and obstetrics; Morgan wrote a monograph on the art of preserving material. Thus was founded the school of medicine of the University of Pennsylvania, which contributed much to making Philadelphia the medical capital of America throughout this period. Caspar Wistar, who was professor of anatomy there, 1808–18, wrote a textbook and founded a museum extended by William Horner (professor, 1831–53), who first described the tensor tarsi muscle and wrote a standard text.

This first American medical school was followed in 1768 by another at King's college (later Columbia university) in New York city. The departments of anatomy in both experienced difficulties in obtaining bodies for dissection similar to those experienced in Britain. Shippen's house in Philadelphia was mobbed and King's college was raided.

Afterward a department of anatomy was organized in Harvard college in Cambridge, Mass., in 1782, where John Warren, professor of anatomy and surgery, had 20 students in anatomy and had one cadaver dissected in each course. In that school, Oliver Wendell Holmes, Sr., the poet, the "autocrat of the breakfast table" and the apostle in America of I. P. Semmelweiss' demonstration of the cause of puerperal fever, became professor of anatomy in 1847, one of the ablest and most popular teachers of anatomy in U.S. schools. Departments of anatomy were founded at other U.S. colleges in rapid succession: Dartmouth, University of Maryland, Yale, Brown, Transylvania, Bowdoin and the University of Virginia. In 1825 Jefferson Medical college was organized in Philadelphia. G. S. Pattison of London was a professor there. In 1839 a third medical college was organized in Philadelphia with S. G. Morton as professor of anatomy. He published in 1839 an excellent monograph, *Crania Americana,* based on a thorough study of 600 skulls of various American stocks, and in 1849 an illustrated system of human anatomy.

Anatomy in the U.S. made some contributions to knowledge, but was active during this period mainly in teaching and encouraging dissection. It was a recognized laboratory discipline of medical students a century before such discipline was established in other subjects.

After Darwin.—*The Period of Biological Anatomy.*—The demonstration by Charles Darwin in 1859 of the origin of species from pre-existing species implies the unity of all life that has ever been on the earth—all came from the life that first existed. Each organism is just one manifestation of that life and all organisms are related. The form, structure, development and reactions of bodies other than ours could be experimentally studied with results of significance for our own.

This was the greatest generalization in the history of biology. It led to a radical revolution in biological sciences. It had been foreshadowed by Aristotle's ladder of life and by Harvey's *omne vivum ex ovo.* The comparative anatomists and paleontologists had gathered facts which indicated it, but it required the great synthetic mind of Darwin to see that living beings are hereditarily related. The conception and the demonstration were based on anatomical facts. The implication of the unity of all life was slowly appreciated and more slowly accepted. Even Darwin is said not to have used the word "evolution." But it was inescapable and before the end of the 19th century evolution had been generally accepted. This united human anatomy with animal anatomy and plant anatomy. All biological sciences entered an immeasurably wider field of research grounded in anatomy; human anatomy had a new orientation. Investigative work was no longer limited to dead human bodies. Most of it was not conducted on human material but on other animals with whom we share a common life. Even relatively simple organisms have told us much about ourselves. For example the study of chromosomes in fruit flies and J. G. Mendel's experiments on the hybrids of peas yielded results of great significance in heredity. Lower mammals became a field of study of most of man's life processes both in health and in disease.

Though research in anatomy of form, structure, growth and evolution was turning into the wider and more fertile fields of animal anatomy, where material is abundant and experiment on the living practicable, work in gross human anatomy continued in the medical schools and in laboratories of zoology, anthropology, biometry and other associated sciences.

In the medical schools, dissection is required. For centuries such dissection was dangerous; now it can be conducted in cleanliness and safety. Louis Pasteur's demonstration of the causes of infection and Joseph Lister's antiseptic campaign (begun in 1869) were followed by the injection of antiseptics, usually carbolic acid or formalin solutions, into the blood vessels of cadavers so that they became and long remained innocuous. Study by dissection was correlated with that of microscopic anatomy necessarily (but unfortunately) prosecuted in other laboratories, and correlated in study rooms with that of special preparations. Formalin hardening combined with freezing and cross sections preserved the form and relations of parts undisturbed by dissection. The relations of the brain and all other internal organs to one another and to the surface were seen as they appear in cadavers. But all this left the real objective unattained. The study of gross anatomy never was directed simply to mapping the topography of cadavers; that was only a step toward knowledge of the living. In the 20th century the main line of advance was emphasis on the study of the living rather than of cadavers. The latter continues, necessarily, with fossil discoveries, microscopic preparations, etc., but in the study of the living, action is added to structure. The time element is introduced; fluoroscopy permits observation of internal organs and motion pictures record what is seen; radiograms show changes in normal life and in disease.

The allotment of time to gross anatomy in the four-year medical curriculum was steadily (and rightly) reduced during the 20th century. Other essential sciences have been greatly and rapidly developed. This precipitated a problem in the medical teaching of anatomy. Attempts to solve it have been mainly along two lines: first, emphasis in the required courses on what appears now to be clinically essential; and, second, correlation with other parts of the curriculum. The textbooks have become ponderous reference tomes. A. B. Howell, J. C. B. Grant, D. Mainland and others published shorter ones for medical students.

While the curriculum of the medical schools must continue to put dissection of human bodies in a basic and important place, it constitutes, nevertheless, only a minor fraction of the work of anatomy. Structure, form and their response in living beings to the influences of environment are its real work. Those influences are demonstrated mainly by the physical sciences, which were developed so much by the middle of the 20th century that we seem only beginning to understand the nature of life and the relation of living beings to our universe.

All biology has a new outlook. Research in gross human anatomy seems almost completed. All the facts discovered from Hippocrates to D. J. Cunningham are in the reference textbooks. The idea that we know it all now or are on the road to complete understanding has been common but perilous in all ages of science, but work in anatomy has turned into new channels. Old methods and the old simple equipment are no longer adequate. To the dissecting rooms and lecture hall of the old period have been added many university laboratories where anatomy is studied on all kinds of animals and by many techniques. The larger university departments or institutes of anatomy provide space and equipment for investigation in many fields: microscopic anatomy (the new electron microscope); cytology (centrifuges, apparatus for sudden fixation in liquid air and for irradiation of tissues and even of individual constituents of cells); tissue culture; embryology (safes for storing precious human material and provision for experiments with hormones and other chemicals); fluoroscopy; neurology. Animal rooms provide for the maintenance of many kinds of animals, both terrestrial and aquatic, and operating rooms contain equipment for asepsis. Work in all these fields throws light on form and structure or on the processes of heredity and growth.

NOMENCLATURE

The study of anatomy has been carried on chiefly among Indo-European-speaking peoples, who are believed to have had a common ancestral language. Before writing was introduced, however, the race had separated into many branches. From the written records of these peoples, philologists have reconstructed what they believe were the words of that old, unwritten vanished speech.

The *Dictionary of Selected Synonyms in the Principal Indo-European Languages* by Carl D. Buck (1949) lists many such words. A few, selected because of their association with anatomy, are: blood-*esen* (Eng. sanguinous); bone-*ost* (osteo); eye-*ok* (ocular); brow-*bhru;* ear-*aus* (auditory); nose-*nas;* mouth-*os* (oral); tongue-*dnghwa;* tooth-*dont* (dental); throat-*gel* (gullet); chin (and knee)-*genu* (genuflection); shoulder-*omesos* (humerus, bone of the shoulder); arm-*armos;* elbow-*el;* finger-*deig* (digit); heart-*kerd* (cardiac); foot-*ped;* nail (finger or toe)-*onogh* (onychia). Such words constitute the beginning of anatomical nomenclature.

When physicians and surgeons appeared they were especially interested in anatomical names. The Greek physicians of the Coan (Hippocratic) school, 500–400 B.C., have given us a few names still in use: raphe, symphysis, arthron, diarthrosis, synarthrosis, brachium, olecranon, cubiton. Aristotle introduced the names colon and aorta (for the artery; Hippocrates used it for the trachea). The Alexandrian school, 300–250 B.C., gave us duodenum, choroid (plexus), calamus scriptorius. The Greeks adopted from their Cretan (Minoan) predecessors the shield idea in the name of the thyroid gland.

After 250 B.C. wars and politics greatly hampered the further development of anatomy in Greece and Egypt. After Rome had emerged as the dominant power, about A.D. 30, Aulus Cornelius Celsus compiled an encyclopaedic work. The anatomical section gathers up the results of the sporadic work of the three preceding centuries and presents it in beautiful literary Latin. From it have come our names abdomen, anus, cartilage, humerus, occiput, patella, radius, scrotum, tibia, uterus, vertebra and others.

The best Roman anatomist was the emperor's physician, Galen (*see* above). However, his nomenclature was unsystematic, indefinite and confused. Various phrases refer to single anatomic structures, and he used numbers instead of names to identify many of them. Despite his frequent carelessness, he passed on to us many of the names we use, among them anastomosis, carotid, epididymis, glottis, hyaloid, meconium, pancreas, peritoneum, psoas, ureter and zygoma. They are mostly of Greek origin.

Galen's contemporary, Julius Pollux (A.D. 139–192), wrote an *Onomasticon* (vocabulary) with definitions, explanations and quotations. To him we owe amnion, anthelix, antitragus, atlas (for the first vertebra), axis, canthus, clitoris, cricoid, epistropheus, gastrocnemius, tragus and trochanter.

After Galen there followed more than a millennium during which the old knowledge was maintained only in translations into Arabic and Hebrew. The Greek originals that were not lost were not rediscovered and reprinted until Renaissance times. During these dark ages, anatomic (and medical) names were Arab words except as Jewish translators used Hebrew names. Vesalius in his first publication (*Tabulae anatomicae sex*, 1538) used some Arabic and Hebrew names and many Hebrew characters. A few Arab words still appear in the nomenclature: nucha, basilic, cephalic, saphena (Arabic, "concealed"), dura and pia mater (translations from Arabic). Vesalius gave us the names atlas, alveolus, choana, mitral valve; Sylvius of Paris, corpus callosum and many names of muscles and blood vessels. From the strange and pathetic mind of Theophrastus Paracelsus comes the term synovia.

The introduction of printing did much to spread the use of anatomical names, but there was no uniformity in nomenclature. The enthusiastic activity in anatomical laboratories resulted in great increase in knowledge and still greater multiplication of names. Thousands were added, for each writer followed his own nomenclatorial fancy, usually expressing it in a Latin form. Some words were borrowed from botany—amygdala, arbor vitae. Some came from animals—tragus, hircus, hippocampus. Many words were used with a significance very different from the original one: *musculus* (originally "a little mouse"); *arteria* ("air holder"); *nervus* ("a bowstring"); *sacrum* ("sacred" or "big"); *glandula* ("a little acorn").

Association of muscles and mice suggests a probable origin of the name muscle. Some Stone Age hunter skinning an animal was startled when, in response to an accidental stimulus, he saw a contraction wave run along one of the long muscles. "Ah, a little mouse." Later another called it a little lizard. The little lizard which flashes along the sunny walls in Italy was called *lacertus*, which is an alternate name for muscle and is still used for part of the biceps. Sacrum is stated to be the neuter of sacer, the bone having been considered sacred. It probably meant big. The Greeks sometimes called big things "sacred"—"sacred Troy," "sacred bridge." It has been suggested that it may have been the resurrection bone, Luz, of rabbinical literature.

In the long list of names that have been used, mythology, religion, ribaldry and humour all played parts. Among the mythological are cornu ammonis (in the brain), tendo Achillis, iris, hymen, mons veneris. Among the religious are morsus diaboli (in the uterine tube), pomum Adami, musculus religiosus (inferior rectus of the eye), lyra Davidis and psalterium (in the brain). Among the ribald were musculus ani scalptor (latissimus dorsi) and many names for parts of the brain, mammae, nates, etc., introduced, says one Italian anatomist, to make neurology more interesting to the young. Among the humorous were musculus amatorius—the lateral rectus of the eye which makes the sidelong "come hither" glance; m. osculatorius—the orbicularis oris; m. humilis—the inferior rectus of the eye which makes the castdown eye of the humble; m. attentionis—the superior auricular, much used by horses; m. dormitator—the orbicularis oculi which helps to shut the eyes.

Origin of Curious Names.—*Bones.*—Astragalus and talus (originally taxillus) were bones used by Roman soldiers for dice—

"rolling the bones." Originally astragalus was a vertebra, talus was a horse's anklebone. Astragalus, because of its bad company, was degraded from the vertebral column to the ankle. Coccyx—cuckoo—was said to be so called because it is shaped like a cuckoo's bill. The coronoid processes were said to be so called because they are shaped like a crow's beak (*korone*, "a crow"). But *korone* was also a hook at the end of a bow to engage the bowstring which these processes resemble.

Muscles.—M. nauticus was one name for the tibialis posterior—it helped the sailor's foot in climbing the mast. M. cucullaris was the trapezius because the two trapezius muscles together are shaped like a monk's hood. M. sartorius is so called because it helps the tailor take the cross-legged position he assumes when sitting on the tailor's bench.

Viscera.—The origin of the word "stomach" is obvious if we leave off the final "ch." *Stoma* means "mouth." The stomach is part of the head gut and is innervated by the vagus. The old Greek name for intestine or gut was *chorde*. From the guts of animals the early Greeks made bowstrings, and just as we call some sutures "gut" they called these strings "gut" (*chorde*). Hence come the names spinal cord, notochord, spermatic cord, etc. The name ileum for intestine means twisted or folded.

The Bible talks of "bowels of mercies" (Col. iii, 12). Our emotions are expressed largely by our facial muscles; every one of them is a gut muscle derived from the first or second visceral arch and innervated by a gut nerve. The anatomical association is direct; the psychical association between our emotions and our viscera is closer perhaps than we realize or would like to admit.

The pancreas (*pan kreas*, "all flesh") is so called because it has so little connective tissue in it.

Vessels.—The word artery is Greek and means "air holder." After death the blood went to the veins, and the arteries when opened held air, hence the name. The big air holder (windpipe) was *arteria tracheia*—"the rough air holder." It is now called simply trachea. We have omitted "arteria" from the name of the only one that carries air and kept it for all those that do not. The "stupid" artery (carotid, from *karos*, "stupor") was so called by Galen because compressing it against the carotid tubercle of the sixth cervical vertebra caused stupor. Vesalius called that artery *somnifera*. The translation of venae cavae ("empty veins") is a mistake. The names are themselves a translation from Galen. Galen's name, *koilos*, meant "empty," but it also meant "cavity." The upper *koilos* was the thorax, the lower the abdomen. The superior vena cava is the upper cavity vein, the inferior the lower cavity vein.

Basilic and cephalic veins got their names from the Arabs. The Arab words *al-basilik* and *al-kifal* indicated medial and lateral veins. But when put in Latin form by the monk Gerard of Cremona, basilic was supposed to mean kingly or governing. The doctors of the middle ages said the left basilic vein governed the functions of the spleen and the right those of the liver, and the cephalic those of the head; they bled their patients accordingly from the proper side. The therapy was founded on a philological error, but was in any case futile. The word "anastomosis"—*ana stoma*, "mouth by mouth"—was sometimes thought to mean "kissing," but it did not. Erasistratus used it for bleeding—mouth forming—a hole in a blood vessel.

Nerves.—*Nervus* is the Latin form of the Greek *neuron*. Originally *neuron* meant "bowstring," and the name was given by Hippocrates and others indiscriminately to all strings—to nerves, tendons, ligaments and even to ducts (parotid). It is still used in the original sense in a hymn, "Awake my soul! stretch every nerve, and press with vigour on." The phrenic nerve was so named because it passed the heart, long regarded as the seat of the mind.

Use of the Vernacular.—Anatomical names are usually Latin. The names of diseases are usually Greek, for example, pulmo- and pneumonia, musculus and myositis. There is hardly an exception. It is amazing for how long a time Latin continued to be in all European countries the language of medical science. Harvey, Thomas Willis and Thomas Sydenham wrote in Latin. But in 1770 William Hunter published his atlas with a text in two parallel columns, one in Latin and one in English. About 1800 Latin began to yield to the vernacular on the continent, though it persisted in some medical lectures in Vienna until 1859.

Standardization of Anatomical Nomenclature.—By the end of the 19th century the confusion caused by the enormous number of names had become intolerable. Medical dictionaries sometimes listed as many as 20 synonyms for one name. More than 50,000 names were in use somewhere in the world and they differed in the various countries and schools. This placed a discouraging burden on students and hampered publication and diffusion of the results of investigation, not only in anatomy but in all medical sciences.

In 1887 the Deutsche Anatomische Gesellschaft undertook the task of standardization. A commission was appointed in 1889 and worked untiringly for six years. The co-operation of anatomists in other countries was sought. The Anatomical Society of Great Britain in 1893 appointed a special commission to adapt the proposed nomenclature to English needs. In 1890 a society of United States anatomists studied the question and submitted a list.

There was much divergence of opinion as to the inclusion of personal names. Against their use, it was urged that they often imply historical injustice. Thus the aqueduct of Sylvius was described long before either of the two Sylviuses lived; the circle of Willis was described by Casserius and dissected for Thomas Willis by Edmund King. It was decided to retain only those so firmly established in the language (and affection) of anatomists that they could not be left out—146 names of 103 men.

The attempt to include histological and comparative anatomical names was abandoned but some embryological names were given. There was much discussion of the "anatomical position." It was necessary to postulate a basic position for terms such as anterior and posterior, superior and inferior, etc. It was decided that this position should imagine the body standing erect, arms at the sides, palms forward. In the forearm and hand the terms volar and dorsal were used instead of anterior and posterior; in the foot, plantar and dorsal instead of superior and inferior.

The completed list was approved at the Basel meeting of the Gesellschaft in 1895 and published as the *Basle Nomina Anatomica* (B.N.A.). It reduced the 50,000 terms to 5,528, being the best of the terms already in use. It was immediately adopted in German-speaking countries, in Great Britain, Ireland, the U.S. and Japan. After World War I there was some tendency to regard it as a German nomenclature and to substitute nationalistic names. But the Deutsche Anatomische Gesellschaft was *anatomische* rather than *Deutsche*. Its membership in 1895 comprised 145 German and 129 non-German members from ten other nations.

But after 40 years, revision was needed on strictly scientific grounds. Parts of the science had grown and even metamorphosed. Neurology had developed so greatly that the B.N.A. nomenclature was inadequate and had many implied inaccuracies. In 1933 the Anatomical Society of Great Britain and Ireland made a British Revision (B.R.). In 1936 the International Anatomical congress meeting in Milan created an International Anatomical Nomenclature committee, which was to have reported at a meeting in London in 1939. The American Association of Anatomists appointed a committee to co-operate with the International commission. It sent to the International commission a 57-page report which was never published, apparently lost during the war. In 1936–37 the parent Gesellschaft adopted another nomenclature at its meeting in Jena, the *Jena Nomina Anatomica* (I.N.A.).

Because of wars, anatomists were unable to convene after 1936 for consideration of a report by the International Anatomical Nomenclature committee, looking toward a world-wide unity of names and co-operation in study and investigation.

In 1950 during the Fifth International Anatomical congress held at Oxford, the International Anatomical Nomenclature committee was appointed. This committee was composed of representatives from a large number of countries and adopted the following seven rules as principles upon which an international anatomical nomenclature should be based:

1. That, with a very limited number of exceptions, each structure shall be designated by one term only.
2. That every term in the official list shall be in Latin, each country to be at liberty to translate the official Latin terms into its own vernacular for teaching purposes.
3. That each term shall be, so far as possible, short and simple.
4. That the terms shall be primarily memory signs, but shall preferably have some informative or descriptive value.
5. That structures closely related topographically shall, as far as possible, have similar names—*e.g.*, Arteria femoralis, Vena femoralis, Nervus femoralis, etc., etc.
6. That differentiating adjectives shall be, in general, arranged as opposites—*e.g.*, major and minor, superficialis and profundus, etc., etc.
7. That eponyms shall not be used in the official nomenclature of gross or macroscopic anatomy.

In 1955 this committee submitted to the Sixth International Anatomical congress at Paris a revision of the B.N.A. which included many terms of the B.R. as well as of the I.N.A. This revision received approval by the congress and is now known as the Nomina Anatomica Parisiensa, or N.A.P.

BIBLIOGRAPHY.—*Textbooks:* Daniel J. Cunningham (ed.), *Textbook of Anatomy*, 9th ed., ed. by J. C. Brash (1951); Henry Gray, *Anatomy*, 27th ed., ed. by C. M. Goss (1959); Sir Henry Morris, *Human Anatomy*, ed. by J. P. Schaefer, 11th ed. (1953).

Atlases: J. C. B. Grant, *Atlas of Anatomy, by Regions*, 4th ed. (1956); J. Sobotta, *Atlas of Human Anatomy*, ed. from the 6th German edition by J. P. McMurrich (1927–28); W. Spalteholz, *Hand-Atlas of Human Anatomy*, trans. by L. F. Barker, 7th ed. (1943); C. Toldt and A. dalla Rosa, *Atlas of Human Anatomy for Students and Physicians*, adapted by M. E. Paul, 2nd ed. (1928); M. W. Woerdeman, *Atlas of Human Anatomy, Descriptive and Regional* (1948).

General: F. H. Garrison, *Introduction to the History of Medicine*, 4th ed. (1929); C. J. Singer, *Evolution of Anatomy* (1925).

(B. C. H. H.; X.)

USE OF X-RAYS IN ANATOMY

Although X-rays are widely used in clinical medicine, in anatomy dissection of the cadaver is, and presumably will continue to be, the basic approach. Fluoroscopy and radiography serve as secondary but valuable tools.

X-ray pictures or radiographs may be made of material from cadavers. Such radiographs supply information not easily obtained by other means. It is in the study of the anatomy of living subjects, however, that the X-rays are most useful.

When large, thick sections of the frozen cadaver are subjected to prolonged dehydration at low temperatures, individual muscle bundles become slightly separated from one another by layers of air so that they stand out in sharp contrast in radiographs. Radiographs of longitudinal sections of the long bones illustrate structural details not easily demonstrated by other means, and radiography is the method of choice for studying the development of bone in specimens too large to be made transparent.

One of the best means of demonstrating the size and distribution of the bursae about a joint such as the knee is to radiograph the joint after inflating the bursae with air. The study of stereoscopic radiographs of the vascular system (following the injection of a mixture of gelatin, glycerin and lead salts) is a helpful preliminary to the dissection of the part. By special techniques even the lymphatic vessels of the cadaver may be filled with a material such as mercury that casts a shadow when X-rayed, and then be demonstrated by radiographs.

One of the most important roles of X-rays in anatomy is the demonstration in the living subject of the variable size, shape and location of the organs. Even in the freshly dead body these features of the organs are altered, and by the time the cadaver has been made ready for dissection the deviation from the conditions existing during life may be very great.

Equally important is the use of X-rays in the study of function. In the past, functional anatomy was based largely on the study of structural relationships in the cadaver and examination of the surface of the living body; but as more and more of the functions of the body are submitted to direct study on the fluoroscopic screen or in X-ray motion pictures, more and more of the old deductions are found to be incomplete. The relative roles of the thoracic wall and of the diaphragm in breathing, the mechanism of swallowing and the change in the size and shape of the heart during the cardiac cycle are typical problems in which radiology provides the most direct avenue of approach. X-rays may also be used to advantage in analyzing the relationship of muscle function to changes in the joints in such structures as the shoulder and the spine.

X-rays serve also to increase the volume and selection of material available for study by the anatomist. Under the best of conditions, the available cadavers are scarce and constitute a distorted sample of the population with elderly, chronically ill males predominating. By the use of radiological procedures, however, certain anatomical studies may be made of healthy bodies throughout the entire prenatal and postnatal life span in both sexes.

Typical of the anatomical problems that have already yielded to the X-ray approach are: the cataloguing of abnormalities, individual variations, functional and age changes of the skeleton, organs and blood vessels; an understanding of the relationship of body build and changing posture to the position of the organs; and a clarification of the sexual differences in the pelvic bones and obstetrical significance of variation and size of the female pelvis.

See also Index references under "Anatomy, Gross" in the Index volume.   (S. H. By.)

ANATOMY, MICROSCOPIC. This division of the science of anatomy embraces all of the knowledge that can be gained only through the use of lens systems of some sort. Microscopic anatomy is usually considered as lying within the domain of biology; it involves the analysis and resynthesis of information concerning the finer structure of the organs and parts of living organisms. It might be possible to broaden the concept of microscopic anatomy by including also the intimate structure of organized inanimate matter. Indeed, the sciences of petrology and metallurgy have long used the microscope as a tool for obtaining data on the composition and arrangement of rocks and metals. But such types of endeavour are better assigned to the more general category of microscopy (*q.v.*). Certainly the examination of dust, single-celled animals, spores, pollen grains and the like clearly belongs in the province of microscopy, and this activity just as plainly lies outside the field of microscopic anatomy, which predicates a grosser sort of organization that permits the recognition of component systems. Actually the term microscopic anatomy has been used in two senses: probably the commoner usage is inclusive, embracing the subsciences of cytology (cell structure), histology (tissue structure) and organology (organ composition); but microscopic anatomy also has been used as a synonym for organology. In the latter usage the microscope is thought of as being employed to dissect the organs visually into component parts, somewhat as the scalpel and forceps reveal the grosser components of total organisms. The cytology of the animal and plant kingdoms is fundamentally the same; their histology and organology are parallel but unlike, and plant microstructure is much the simpler in both of these categories. When the term microscopic anatomy is employed, the connotation is always in contradistinction to gross anatomy and, usually, with regard to higher animals in general and mammals and man in particular. The development of form and structure is embryology; like anatomy of the adult, it is a category under the more inclusive science of morphology. A particular phase of microscopic anatomy is obviously contained in the development of tissues, organs and organ systems, but embryology is usually considered a coordinate discipline rather than an integral part of microscopic anatomy.

The Rise of Microscopy.—The discovery of the image-enhancing power of the simple lens is lost in antiquity. It seems reasonable that this property of water droplets and clear crystals of lenticular form must have been noted by primitive man. Seneca (4 B.C.–A.D. 65) was perhaps the first to record clearly the effect of a simple lens: "Letters though small and dim seem larger and more distinct through a glass-globe filled with water." But the use of such an optical aid in studying animalculae or other marvels of nature was never mentioned in any ancient writing. Not until the middle of the 17th century was the value of the simple microscope in discovering minute, previously unknown features coming to be understood and its application to the systematic pursuit of knowledge envisioned. Three pioneer microscopists, working in the last half of the 17th century with simple lenses, produced results that still stand as models of accurate, objective observation.

Foremost, in the sum of his contributions to anatomy and physiology, was Marcello Malpighi (*q.v.*). Among his achievements were the demonstration of the structure of the lungs (with the presence of air cells separated from the blood by a thin membrane) and the flow of blood through their capillaries, the germinative (Malpighian) layer of the epidermis, the renal (Malpighian) corpuscles, the splenic (Malpighian) nodules and the nature of the lingual papillae. Jan Swammerdam (*q.v.*) burned himself out in an intemperance of intense work and was the most critical and detailed observer of the three. His work dealt largely with minute anatomy in relation to the life history of insects; yet he was the first to observe and describe the blood corpuscles. Anton van Leeuwenhoek (*q.v.*) was a general microscopist who ground simple lenses capable of magnifying at least 270 diameters. Among his diverse microscopical observations was the important first demonstration of the capillary connection between arterioles and venules; he thus completed by ocular proof what William Harvey had left undone in his theory of the circulation of the blood, and he also extended the observations of Swammerdam on the red blood corpuscles to all vertebrate groups except reptiles. Among his other discoveries pertaining to anatomy were the cross striping of skeletal muscle, the branched character of cardiac muscle, the structure of the crystalline lens, the occurrence and action of cilia and the appearance of mammalian spermatozoa.

The compound microscope was invented about the end of the 16th century, but for a long time it was inferior to some of the simple instruments such as those used by Leeuwenhoek. A better compound microscope depended on improving the objective lens system, and two centuries passed before any notable advance was achieved. But from 1830 onward, one improvement followed another until, in 1886, the production of the apochromatic objective and compensating eyepiece brought the compound microscope to its highest peak of perfection (*see* MICROSCOPE). In general, the most exacting observation has been directed to the interpretation of cell structure.

The Discovery of Protoplasm.—The concept of protoplasm as the jellylike living substance that represents the physical basis of life was fundamental to any rational advances in the understanding of cells and tissues. Although protoplasm had been observed previously in the amoeba animalcule and in a few favourable plant cells, Félix Dujardin (*q.v.*) in 1835 was the earliest to study and describe this primitive slime of animal cells, which he named "sarcode," and to distinguish it from other viscid substances such as albumen. Several years later Hugo von Mohl (*q.v.*) distinguished the firmer, jellylike content of plant cells from the more internally located, watery cell sap and brought the word protoplasm, already suggested by Johannes Purkinje (1787–1869), into general use. Several workers began to realize that the sarcode of the zoologists and the protoplasm of the botanists were one and the same substance, but it was left to Max Johann Schultze (1825–74) to establish the identity of protoplasm in lower forms and higher forms, and in animals and plants alike, on an unassailable basis. Thus the two decades between 1840 and 1860 were extremely important for the future of biology, because an appreciation of the nature of protoplasm, both as to structure and function, is the foundation stone of biological understanding.

During this period the true import of such concepts was brought to a proper focus. Protoplasm can be defined as the essential substance of living organisms in which all the vital phenomena are manifested; as such, it represents the seat of chemical changes both constructive and destructive in nature. Physically this colloidal complex is colourless, translucent, viscous, ductile, hydrous, semifluid and jellylike.

Discovery of the Cell as a Biological Unit.—Yet another concept had to be established before the structural analysis of living organisms could be pursued intelligently and interpreted correctly. This was the concept of unit masses of protoplasm and the recognition of their role as the fundamental building stones out of which all tissues and organs are constructed. This idea of the cell, based on actual observations, had been vaguely foreshadowed for nearly two centuries before it became solidly established as a basic truth for both animals and plants. Various early observers saw and sketched cells without understanding their real significance. Even 2,000 years earlier, Aristotle had reached the theoretical conclusion, as the result of pure reasoning, "that animals and plants, complex as they may appear, are yet composed of comparatively few elementary parts, frequently repeated." In the 17th century Robert Hooke examined thin shavings of dead cork tissue, which he described as being composed of "little boxes or cells . . . in the manner of a honeycomb, but not so regular." His drawings are the earliest to depict cells, though it is more accurate to say that what he saw and emphasized were the prominent cellulose cell walls; indeed, it was the concept of a walled, empty compartment that suggested the term cell as an appropriate designation. Within a few years, several contemporaries published drawings showing the cellular construction of plants so plainly that it might seem that the foundation of the cell theory was then established, but actually these illustrations were little more than accurate records of plant fabric as seen. Malpighi came closest to the truth by understanding that the boxes he drew were separable "utricles," united to produce plant tissue, but he failed to generalize that these were uniform elements in the organized structure of living things. One century later C. F. Wolff (1733–94), as the result of his important studies in development and in support of his epoch-making opposition to the theory of preformation, concluded that every organ is composed at first of unorganized, viscous fluid in which cavities are developed that become the subsequent cells; and this process, he said, is identical in the early developing organs of an animal or a plant. Although he fell into the error of believing in a primitive semifluid mass which lacked organization of any kind, he nevertheless must be considered the chief forerunner of the more generally recognized co-founders of the cell theory.

For nearly a century after Wolff, the popular theory was that animals and plants are composed of "globules" and formless material; some of the globules that were described can now be identified with the nucleated cells depicted by later writers. The discovery of the nucleus in plant cells by Robert Brown (1773–1858) was an important preliminary to the enunciation of an ultimately satisfactory cell theory. In 1838 a collaborative conclusion by two friends, though separately presented and supported, produced what has been termed the "master stroke in generalization." M. J. Schleiden (1804–81) was a botanist and Theodor Schwann (q.v.) an anatomist; almost accidentally they came to realize the similarity of their independent observations, but the major role was played by Schwann, who formulated a comprehensive cell theory. Previously the prevailing view had been that cells existed as incidental components of plant and animal tissues, but at that time the character of the cell had not been determined clearly, and little importance was attached to it as a unit of organization. By contrast, Schwann maintained that "the elementary parts of all tissues are formed of cells in an analogous, though very diversified, manner; so that it may be asserted that there is one universal principle of development, and that this principle is the formation of cells." The original presentation of the cell theory, nevertheless, was imperfect and contained basic errors of fact. Other investigators showed later that the cell wall about a hollow cavity is not the important feature; that the essential part of the cell is an internal mass of protoplasm containing a nucleus; that the cell is not only the unit of structure but also the unit of function, since all vital activities take place within it; that parental sex cells, after merging, proliferate and lead to the production of a new organism; that the manner of propagation of cells by cell division is quite different from the method originally proposed; and that the nucleus plays a dominant role in hereditary transmissions. The corrected theory is now firmly established as a basic truth of biology, and its concept can better be designated as the cell doctrine. The cell can now be defined properly as a discrete, tiny mass of protoplasm, containing a nucleus and bounded by a limiting membrane; its cytoplasm contains living, self-perpetuating specializations called organoids, which serve as "cell organs," and also nonliving substances either synthesized by the cell or captured by ingestion; its nucleus contains threadlike chromosomes which, in turn, bear the definitely spaced genes that are concerned with the mechanism of hereditary transmissions.

The Rise of Histology.—When comparative anatomy, under the leadership of Georges Léopold Cuvier, was placing the organs of animals in comprehensive series, a contemporary scientist undertook a still deeper analysis into the kinds of structural materials out of which organs are fabricated. Marie F. X. Bichat (1771–1802) can be called the founder of the science dealing with the minute anatomy of the tissues, which he studied extensively even though, remarkably, he did not employ the microscope. He distinguished 21 kinds of tissues which enter into different combinations in producing the organs of the body; but of far greater importance was the method of inquiry he developed and the systematic treatment he gave to the study of histology in its relations to both physiology and pathology. This influence initiated a scientific epoch by providing the stimulus that set scientists to making new investigations of the minute structure of tissues and organs, investigations that presently placed the sciences of histology and organology on a sound basis.

Most notable as a successor to Bichat in the general field of histology was A. von Kölliker (1817–1905), equally famous in embryology. As a specialist in the field of the nervous system and sense organs, Santiago Ramón y Cajal (1852–1934) stands without peer. The extension of inquiry into all groups of multicellular animals (comparative histology) showed that common structural trends characterize the cells and tissues of all animal groups, and that comparable organs also have much in common architecturally.

Details of the minute anatomy of the cells and tissues can be found under the topics CYTOLOGY and HISTOLOGY, whereas the architecture of organs and organ systems is described under the individual entries for those parts. Similarly, the relations of microscopic structure to development, sex determination and heredity are included in the accounts of EMBRYOLOGY AND DEVELOPMENT, ANIMAL; and GENETICS, HUMAN. There remains, for a general account such as this, a review of the approaches, old and new, by which profitable information can be gained.

Microscopes and Techniques Used.—The ordinary brightfield microscope produces useful magnification to about 1,200 diameters and resolves point detail to 0.0002 mm. Phase contrast is a system by which objects, ordinarily transparent, become visible through the enhancement of contrast differences. Polarization refers to the use of Nicol prisms which detect double refraction in objects and demonstrate the orientation of particles too small to be seen. Fluorescence may occur under ultraviolet radiation, and objects then emit visible light of different colours and qualities. The dark-field microscope employs strong, oblique illumination; the only light that enters the objective comes by reflection, and the presence of particles far too small to be seen directly by bright light can be demonstrated. Invisible radiation is used successfully, images being recorded on suitably sensitized film. Thus ultraviolet rays and quartz lenses yield double the resolution (0.0001 mm.) possible with visible light. The electron microscope has beams of electron rays replacing light, and electromagnetic or electrostatic fields replacing lenses, the final image being visualized on a fluorescent screen and photographed; by these means a usable image of 50,000 diameters or more can be produced and the resolution pushed to 0.000001 mm. Electron microscopy is the favoured technique for revealing details hitherto deemed unapproachable.

The Observation of Living Tissue.—Direct observation can be done on some intact animals, such as the tail of a tadpole. Quartz-rod illumination can be used to transmit cold light into the interior of functioning organs. Glass windows can be inserted into a rabbit's ear and left indefinitely. Micromanipulation (q.v.) uses delicate needles to isolate, cut, tear or stretch cells, or capillary tubes to inject or suck the cell contents. Tissue cultures can be grown indefinitely in plasma. Motion pictures made with the microscope, in either slow motion or time lapse, can demonstrate motion otherwise not analyzable. Vital staining occurs when living cells store nontoxic dyes.

The Observation of Dead Tissue.—Fixation is the process of preserving protoplasm with the least amount of alteration, rendering it insoluble and increasing its affinity for future staining.

Chemical solutions are most commonly employed as fixing agents; the least alterations, however, are introduced by the freezing-drying technique, which freezes tissue in isopentane, chilled to −170° C. and dehydrated in a vacuum.

Embedding involves dehydrating and hardening the fixed tissue in alcohol, clearing it in a chemical that is soluble in both alcohol and the embedding medium and encasing the tissue in a solid block of paraffin or nitrocellulose. Sectioning produces thin slices (commonly 0.003–0.010 mm.) of the blocked tissue, which are affixed to a glass slide, whereupon the embedding medium is dissolved. By multiple staining the various cell constituents may be revealed.

Miscellaneous Techniques.—Teasing and spreading bits of tissue permit them to be examined fresh or after supravital staining. Maceration serves to soften binding material and hence to isolate cells, glandular units and the like. Microincineration of tissue slices leaves ash that retains the finest structural details, and so permits the localization of mineral content. Centrifuging gives information on the relative weights and sturdiness of displaced cell constituents.

By radioautography may be demonstrated the presence of tracer isotopes segregated in a tissue, and it also gives information as to their length of stay there; the radioactive elements will affect a photographic emulsion when brought into contact with it, thus recording their exact locations with respect to cells. Microchemical testing by qualitative analytical methods on local areas is possible, a large number of organic compounds, many more inorganic ones and numerous enzymes thereby becoming identified and localized by suitable tests; this field of vigorous current endeavour is consolidating into the new subscience of histochemistry.

BIBLIOGRAPHY.—A. B. Lee, *The Microtomists' Vade-Mecum*, 10th ed. (1937); E. B. Wilson, *The Cell in Development and Heredity*, 3rd ed. (1925); A. Oppel, *Lehrbuch der vergleichenden mikroskopischen Anatomie der Wirbeltiere* (1898–1914); K. C. Schneider, *Lehrbuch der vergleichenden Histologie der Tiere* (1902); W. A. Locy, *Biology and Its Makers* (1910); W. von Möllendorff, *Handbuch der mikroskopischen Anatomie des Menschen* (1927–56); E. R. Long, *A History of Pathology* (1928); A. Maximow and W. Bloom, *A Textbook of Histology*, 6th ed. (1952); A. W. Meyer, *The Rise of Embryology* (1939); E. De Robertis, W. W. Nowinsky and F. A. Saez, *General Cytology*, 2nd ed. (1954); A. W. Ham, *Histology*, 2nd ed. (1953); R. O. Greep, *Histology* (1954).
(L. B. Ay.)

ANATOMY OF PLANTS: *see* the section *Anatomy of Plants* under PLANTS AND PLANT SCIENCE. *See* further the separate articles on ROOT and SEED and various sections under the articles FLOWER; LEAF; STEM.

ANATTO: *see* ANNATTO.

ANAXAGORAS (*c.* 500–*c.* 428 B.C.), Greek philosopher, was born, probably about 500 B.C., at Clazomenae in Asia Minor. He went to Athens, which was rapidly becoming the headquarters of Greek culture (probably *c.* 480 B.C.), and it was he who brought philosophy and the spirit of scientific inquiry to Athens from Ionia. He had a great influence upon Pericles, and it was from him that the poet Euripides derived his great enthusiasm for science and humanity.

Anaxagoras was celebrated for his discovery of the true cause of eclipses and was known generally for the ascetic dignity of his nature and for his superiority to ordinary weaknesses. After 30 years' residence at Athens he was prosecuted on a charge of impiety (for holding the opinion that the sun was an incandescent stone somewhat larger than the Peloponnesus; *see* below). This prosecution was intended as an indirect political attack on Pericles; and although Pericles managed to save him, Anaxagoras was forced to leave Athens.

He retired to Lampsacus, the Milesian colony, where he died about 428 B.C.

Only a few fragments of Anaxagoras' writings have been preserved, and very divergent interpretations of his system have been given; it is unnecessary to describe them all here (*see* below, *Bibliography*). A careful examination of the existing fragments and of Aristotle's evidence makes it possible to arrive at an interpretation which yields a self-consistent and chronologically appropriate system and one by which Anaxagoras might reasonably have conceived himself to be solving the problems which in fact confronted him; no interpretation that fails in these respects can be satisfactory.

The Ionian predecessors of Anaxagoras had attempted to explain the physical universe on the assumption of a single ultimate stuff. Parmenides (*q.v.*) had shown that on this assumption it was impossible to explain the phenomena of movement and change. As a way out of the impasse, an obvious possible alternative assumption (which was in fact made by Empedocles and by Anaxagoras) is that of a plurality of ultimate stuffs. Empedocles posited four, Anaxagoras an infinite number. Anaxagoras says that at the beginning "all things were together" (fragment 1), that "all things are together now" (fr. 6) and that "there is a portion or 'share' of every thing in every thing" (fr. 6, fr. 12). What are these "things"? Earlier thinkers had selected their basic stuff or stuffs more or less directly from the traditional repertory—the cold stuff, the hot stuff, the solid, the fluid, the dark, etc. Anaxagoras, perhaps because he felt that these substances were not sufficiently relevant biologically, introduced for the first time in addition to them an entirely new set of ultimate stuffs; viz., those which are found in living bodies, substances such as flesh, bone, bark, leaf. (Aristotle when listing these substances applies to them his own generic term for them, "the uniform substances"; from this purely Aristotelian term some serious misunderstandings of Anaxagoras have arisen.) These substances, Anaxagoras held, as well as the hot stuff, the fluid stuff, etc., were ultimate, elementary; for, he asked, how can flesh come from what is not flesh? (fr. 10).

With these sets of elements Anaxagoras had a complete equipment for describing existing objects and for explaining change, especially biological change; and the latter problem accounts for the most striking feature in his system. The changes that we observe are manifold, varied and remarkable: we take food and drink, and our flesh, bone and hair grow. To meet the extraordinary range and multiplicity of change, Anaxagoras said that "there is a portion of every thing, *i.e.*, of every elementary stuff, in every thing"; but "each is and was most manifestly those things of which there is most in it" (fr. 12). For instance, in a pint of milk there is a portion of every thing; but it appears to us to be fluid and white and milk, because there is in it a larger portion of the fluid, of the white and of milk than of any other things, although there is a portion of each of them in it too, including flesh, hair and bone; and a pint of milk will differ from a lump of wood, because in the latter, although "all things" are present, wood, the hard and the dark will predominate. These elementary stuffs, then, are inseparable from each other; and their inseparability carries with it the further principle of infinite divisibility, as Anaxagoras himself points out (fr. 6), "because there cannot be a smallest, therefore all things are together." It is their ability to undergo unlimited division that enables them always to remain associated together. Thus there is an identical set of ingredients ("portions") in every lump of matter, though in one lump portions *a*, *b* and *c* will be the largest, in another lump portions *f*, *g* and *h*.

Hence there is in Anaxagoras no notion whatever of "atoms," indivisible particles of a fixed size and shape but possessing no other sensible characteristics. Anaxagoras carried to its utmost possible limit the old Ionian view, which assumed that the ultimate nature of physical reality consists in characteristics such as our senses perceive. The Ionian viewpoint was accepted by Aristotle; the other view, that sensible characteristics are not ultimate but are derived from shape, size, number and arrangement, originated with the Pythagoreans and was adopted in differing ways by the atomists and by Plato (in the *Timaeus*). But although there were no atoms in Anaxagoras' scheme, at the beginning the portions of all things were so minute that none of their characteristics would have been discernible, or only a few. The general appearance of the mixture was that of "air" and "aether" (fire), because the chief components of these were preponderant then, as they are now. (Note that for Anaxagoras earth, air, fire and water—and also minerals and metals—were not elements but conglomerations of portions of all the true elements.)

The stages in the formation of the cosmos were, broadly, two, and both were brought about by *nous* ("mind" or "reason"). At the first stage, *nous* caused the mixture to begin revolving (a process which is still extending), one result of which was that "like came to like" (the dark came together, the light came together, etc.), producing the large expanses of air, water, etc., which we see. Yet even so there was no complete separation; all things were still "together." The heavenly bodies were some of the stones which the eddy had carried to the circumference, where they became ignited as the aether swept them round. In the second stage, also controlled by *nous*, which is "in" living things especially, the process of "like to like" began to affect also the biological elements (flesh, etc.), and portions of these large enough to be significant were formed. This stage was effected not by a process of revolution but by means of the seeds of animals and plants, which had already existed in the original mixture. It is the power of *nous* in living organisms which enables them to extract from their foods those substances which their growth requires (though never so as to remove the whole of any one substance).

Anaxagoras uses physical language to describe his *nous:* it is the "thinnest" of all things, but it is not an ingredient of the mixture; it controls the mixture and determines what changes shall occur. It is incorrect to say that Anaxagoras uses *nous* as a *deus ex machina;* he states explicitly that it "knows" all things and has power over all things, and he clearly conceives it as controlling everything now.

The essence of the objection voiced by Socrates in the *Phaedo* (98 b) and repeated by Aristotle (*Metaphysics,* A 985 a) is that Anaxagoras did not show that *nous* acted and acts *for the best;* but Anaxagoras may have assumed that this was obvious. Aristotle commends Anaxagoras for his introduction of *nous* as the source of order in the universe: he was like a sober speaker coming after idle babblers (*Met.,* A 984 b, where Aristotle's words hint that this cosmic function of *nous* was suggested to Anaxagoras by its role in living organisms). It was for his introduction of *nous* that Anaxagoras was best known in succeeding ages.

See also Index references under "Anaxagoras" in the Index volume.

BIBLIOGRAPHY.—For the fragments *see* H. Diels and W. Kranz, *Die Fragmente der Vorsokratiker,* 6th ed. (1951–52). *See* also T. Gomperz, *Greek Thinkers,* Eng. trans. (1901); E. Zeller, *La Filosofia dei Greci,* Italian trans. ed. by R. Mondolfo (1932 *et seq.*); J. Beare, *Greek Theories of Elementary Cognition* (1906); L. Parmentier, *Euripide et Anaxagore* (1892); F. Lortzing, "Bericht über die griechischen Philosophen vor Sokrates" (1876–94) in *Bursians Jahresbericht,* vol. cxvi (1904); P. Tannery, *Pour l'histoire de la science hellène,* 2nd ed. (1930); J. Burnet, *Early Greek Philosophy,* 4th ed. (1930); C. Giussani, *Lucretius,* book i, exc. ii, pp. 147 ff. (1896); C. Bailey, *The Greek Atomists and Epicurus,* appendix i (1928); F. M. Cornford in *Classical Quarterly,* vol. xxiv, pp. 14 ff., 83 ff. (1930); A. L. Peck in *Classical Quarterly,* vol. xxv, pp. 27 ff., 112 ff. (1931) (giving the interpretation followed above); G. Vlastos in *Philosophical Review,* vol. lix, pp. 31 ff. (1950); J. E. Raven in *Classical Quarterly,* vol. iv, new series, pp. 123 ff. (1954) (for the influence of Zeno); J. Zafiropulo, *Anaxagore de Clazomène* (1948); F. M. Cleve, *The Philosophy of Anaxagoras* (1949).
On the date of the trial of Anaxagoras *see* Burnet, *Early Greek Philosophy,* ch. vi; A. E. Taylor in *Classical Quarterly,* vol. xi, p. 81 (1917).   (A. L. Pk.)

ANAXARETE, in Greek legend, was a beautiful young girl of Cyprus, loved by Iphis, who came incessantly to her home. But she, "like a rock," spurned him, so that he hanged himself at her door. Under her window passed his funeral procession, which she could not avoid seeing, and in seeing it she turned to stone. The story was told of a statue that stood in Salamis of Cyprus, inscribed "The Venus who looks from the window," in Ovid's *Metamorphoses.*   (T. V. B.)

ANAXIMANDER (fl. 6th century B.C.), Milesian natural philosopher, the first known to have developed anything like a cosmological system, was born, according to Apollodorus, in 610 B.C. and was alive in 546. He was an associate of Thales, and his interests were wide. Attributions of particular discoveries to early philosophers are usually dubious, but it seems certain that Anaximander left written treatises, which survived until late antiquity, covering geography, astronomy and cosmogony, and that he made a map of the known world.

Anaximander derived the world from a nonperceptible substance called the unlimited, a unity behind the multiplicity of phenomena, trying, it would seem, to describe a primitive condition before things were differentiated by the contrary characteristics (hot and cold, wet and dry, etc.) on which perceptibility depends. The only surviving sentence of his writings characterizes the emergence of individual substances such as water or fire in terms of human society as an "injustice" for which time makes them "give reparation," alluding to the fact that, for instance, neither hot nor cold ever prevails permanently, but a balance is kept in the whole (a clear reference to the cycle of the seasons).

The cosmos is generated by a process of "separating-out" of the opposites from the unlimited. As Aristotle saw, this implies that in some sense it contained them all the time and hence was not a genuine unity. Nevertheless it may be said that Anaximander's intention was monistic, to seek a unity behind multiplicity; the objection that, at least potentially, the opposites must always have been present belongs to a more advanced stage of thought. The "eternal motion" which brings about the separation is not itself explained, because, like all thinkers at that date, Anaximander regarded the primal being as animate. It was "the divine," which meant for a Greek everlasting, living (hence self-moving) and conscious. How far he had advanced from popular anthropomorphic ideas and what he retained from his religious heritage thus may be seen.

Cosmogony began when, somewhere in the unlimited, hot and cold began to separate, forming a nucleus in the shape of a sphere of fire enclosing a cold, moist mass with mist between. Thenceforth the process continued through the natural properties of the opposites. The centre dried and hardened into earth. The fiery envelope was parted and the dark mist closed around it forming separate rings of fire for the most part hidden from sight. Sun, moon and stars are really these rings of fire wheeling around the earth, but encased in tubes of mist with only a hole or holes through which the fire streams. The earth (which, by a remarkable advance in thought, remains unsupported at the centre "because of its equal distance from everything") is drum-shaped, its height one-third of its circumference. Relics of sacred numbers appear both here and when the sun's ring is said to be 27 times the earth's diameter away from it and the moon's ring 18. Further details are uncertain, but the process of "separation" still continues; *e.g.,* the sea, a relic of the primal moisture, is contracting and will one day dry up. As the cosmos had a beginning, Anaximander probably intended that it should end by reabsorption into the unlimited, but here the sources are obscure and the question is disputed.

Continuing "separation" accounts for the origin of life, which began in water through the action of heat. The first animals were a sort of sea urchin. Even human infants were produced first in a fishlike creature and protected by it until they could fend for themselves. (This, rather than an evolution of men from fish, seems to be the purport of some rather obscure passages.)

BIBLIOGRAPHY.—E. Zeller, *La Filosofia dei Greci,* Italian trans. ed. by R. Mondolfo, vol. i, ch. 2, pp. 135–205 (1938); J. Burnet, *Early Greek Philosophy,* 4th ed., pp. 50–71 (1930); F. M. Cornford, *Principium Sapientiae,* ch. x (1952); G. S. Kirk, "Some Problems in Anaximander," *Classical Quarterly,* vol. xlviii, pp. 21–38 (1955). For texts *see* H. Diels and W. Kranz, *Die Fragmente der Vorsokratiker,* vol. i, 7th ed. (1954).   (W. K. C. G.)

ANAXIMENES (fl. 6th century B.C.), of Miletus, Greek natural philosopher, was a younger contemporary of Anaximander (*q.v.*). His writings, which survived into the Hellenistic period, are now lost. For Anaximander's "unlimited" he substituted *aer* (meaning "mist" or "vapour" as well as "air") as the primary substance or matrix of everything. When "most evenly distributed" it is invisible atmospheric air, but by condensation it becomes visible first as mist or cloud, then as water and finally as solid matter such as earth or stones. When further rarefied it turns to fire; hotness and dryness go with rarity, cold and wetness with density.

Anaximenes' cosmology seems to have been more naïve than Anaximander's, but in the fragmentary sources not all details are clear. The earth (we are not told why) was formed first, by "felting" of the air. It is flat and buoyed up by the air beneath it. By thus returning to a material support, Anaximenes retreats from Anaximander's bold conception of an earth floating freely in space. The heavenly bodies arose from the earth, which gave off moisture that was finally rarefied into fire. However implausible, this account suggests remarkable emancipation from religious preconceptions, but it must be remembered that in the mythical cosmogony of Hesiod (*Theogony,* lines 126–127) "Earth first bore starry Heaven." Nearer to mythology also was Anaximenes' picture of the universe as effectively hemispherical, not a complete sphere like Anaximander's. The stars pass round, not under, the earth and disappear because hidden "by its higher parts." There are also earthy bodies in the sky, unseen because lacking fire to give light, which may have been intended to explain eclipses. The sun, being flat "like a leaf," "rides upon" the air like the earth; and so also do the stars. An isolated passage in Aëtius seems to say that the stars are "fixed like nails in the crystalline," but its accuracy is suspect. Some have supposed that Anaximenes distinguished fixed stars from planets. (It is just possible that the words translated "nails" and "crystalline" have another meaning. *See* W. K. C. Guthrie in *Classical Quarterly,* 1956.) He is reported to have said that the stars give no heat because of their great distance, thus contradicting Anaximander's strange view that they are nearer the earth than is the sun.

To account for the changes of density which produced the world, Anaximenes assumed (as Anaximander did) everlasting motion in the *aer.* For him too this implied that it possessed life; and that may be a clue to his choice of air as the origin of all things, since the primitive and universal identification of life with air or breath was certainly current among his contemporaries. Being everlastingly alive, *aer* was divine, and other gods, like everything else, were produced from it, though nothing further is said about these. There is evidence that, like his follower Diogenes of Apollonia, he emphasized the analogy between the divine air that sustains the universe and the air in us, that is, the human soul. This equation naturally played a great part in mystical religion as well as in philosophy, but Anaximenes can hardly be credited with mystical tendencies.

The evidence suggests that he was a practical man, with a taste for vivid imagery and a certain talent for observation. He notes an occasional moon rainbow and describes the phosphorescence from an oar blade breaking the water. His thought is typical of the transition from mythology to science, entirely rational in intent (the rainbow is no longer a goddess but the effect of the sun's rays on compacted air), yet only partly liberated from earlier mythological patterns. His permanent achievement is to have suggested a known natural process (condensation and rarefaction) as operative in the making of a world and to have reduced apparent qualitative differences to differences of quantity. This not only made Milesian monism consistent but had incalculable consequences for the future of scientific thought.

BIBLIOGRAPHY.—E. Zeller, *La Filosofia dei Greci,* Italian trans. ed. by R. Mondolfo, vol. i, ch. 2, pp. 206–238 (1938); J. Burnet, *Early Greek Philosophy,* 4th ed., pp. 72–79 (1930); G. B. Kerferd, "The Date of Anaximenes," *Museum Helveticum,* vol. xi, pp. 117–121 (1954). For texts *see* H. Diels and W. Kranz, *Die Fragmente der Vorsokratiker,* vol. i, 7th ed. (1954).   (W. K. C. G.)

ANAZARBUS, an ancient city in the eastern plain of Cilicia (*q.v.*), on the right bank of the Sumbas Chay, a tributary of the Ceyhan (Pyramus) in southern Turkey. The acropolis crag, which rises to more than 600 ft., dominates the lower walled city to the west of it. Under the Roman empire it was known as Caesarea by Anazarbus and reckoned as having been refounded in 19 B.C. In the 3rd century A.D. it rivaled Tarsus, the provincial capital, and later became the recognized metropolis of Cilicia Secunda. Under the Byzantine empire it was an archbishopric. Devastated by earthquakes in the 6th century, it was rebuilt, first as Justinopolis, later as Justinianopolis. Under Muslim occupation, Anazarbus (as Ayn Zarba) retained its strategic importance and so was refortified by the caliph Harun al-Rashid in 796 and probably also by al-Mutawakkil (847–861). Regained for Byzantium by Nicephorus Phocas about 962 and subsequently devastated during the crusades, it became, as Anavarza, the capital of Cilician Armenia early in the 12th century. Captured by the Egyptians in 1375, it was never again reoccupied.

The castle (Byzantine and Armenian) is the finest medieval monument in Cilicia. Inside the city are baths, a triumphal arch and two early Byzantine churches. Outside are two aqueducts, another church, the theatre, stadium and amphitheatre.

(M. R. E. G.)

ANBAR, a ruined town in Iraq, lies on the left bank of the Euphrates, downstream from the modern Ramadi and just south of the Sakhlawiye canal. Previously called Massice (Parthian *mshyk*), it was renamed Firuz-Shapur (Pirisabora) by King Shapur I after his victory there over the Roman emperor Gordian III (A.D. 244). Rebuilt after its destruction by the emperor Julian in 363, it became known from at least the 6th century as Anbar ("the Store"). Jews from the academy of Pumbeditha took refuge there from persecution in 588, and it became a Jewish centre. It was the capital of the Abbasid caliphs till the founding of Baghdad (A.D. 762), but thereafter slowly decayed.   (Ma. B.)

ANCAEUS, in Greek legend, son of Zeus or Poseidon, king of the Leleges of Samos. In the Argonautic expedition, after the death of Tiphys, helmsman of the "Argo," he took his place. It is said that, while planting a vineyard, he was told by a soothsayer that he would never drink of its wine. As soon as the grapes were ripe, he squeezed the juice into a cup, and raising it to his lips, mocked the seer, who retorted with the words, "there is many a slip between the cup and the lip." At that moment it was announced that a wild boar was ravaging the land. Ancaeus set down the cup, leaving the wine untasted, hurried out and was killed by the boar.

ANCASH, a department in Peru, lying between the Pacific ocean on the southwest and the Río Marañón on the northeast, with the department of La Libertad on the northwest, and that of Lima on the southeast. Area 14,019 sq.mi.; pop. (1961) 588,511. The capital is Huarás. The terrain of Ancash is extremely rugged, for the arid coast is separated from the deep Marañón valley by some of the highest mountains in Peru, the Cordillera Blanca. In the high country northwest of Cerro de Pasco, the Río Santa has its headwaters. This river, the largest on the Pacific coast of Peru, flows northwest between the Cordillera Blanca and the Cordillera Negra for about 100 mi., descending from nearly 14,000 ft. to about 7,000 ft. The zone in the midcourse of the Río Santa, where Huarás is located, is the most densely populated part of the department. At this point the Río Santa plunges into the Cañon del Pato, dropping 1,400 ft. in six miles. There it turns abruptly toward the ocean and empties into the sea a little north of Chimbote. The Río Santa has been harnessed with a series of hydroelectric plants.

Most of the people of Ancash support themselves by subsistence farming, growing potatoes and barley at the higher altitudes and maize, rice, alfalfa and sugar cane at the lower altitudes. The major economic production of Ancash comes from its mines and industries. The Ancos-Galgada coal field contains the largest reserve of good quality coal in all Latin America. Minerals include silver, lead, gold, copper and tungsten. At Chimbote there is a modern steel plant, supplied with coal from nearby mines and operated with electric power from the Río Santa development. The Pan-American highway runs along the coast, and a railroad climbs inland to the coal mines. But Huarás is reached only by a difficult mountain trail. Ancash was formed as a department in 1836 and was formerly called Ancachs.   (P. E. J.)

ANCESTOR WORSHIP. The worship, tendance and veneration of ancestors are manifestations of various attitudes toward the dead existent in diverse cultures and religions—primitive, middle and higher. The living and the dead are as much related as any other two classes of a given community, for death does not make a person cease to belong to his social unit (family, clan, tribe, village, nation). The dead may be regarded as friendly, as kindred beings with whom kindly relations are possible; they may be for a time displeased and angry with their people, but such displeasure may be dispelled when proper respect, reverence and worship are manifest. The dead, particularly the spirits of deceased strangers, also may be regarded as unfriendly to the living persons of a given community, as malevolent spirits capable of rendering harm to individuals or to the entire community. Attitudes toward the dead may be dominated by a continuation of the natural affections that preceded death in association with prospective beneficent efforts by the dead and living in behalf of each other; by fear, in light of the extensive powers the dead are thought to possess; or by respect, the ancestors being regarded as the repositories of the traditional wisdom of their people and, in certain societies, as influential elders and rulers of the people.

These attitudes toward the dead are further complicated by the following considerations: (1) All dead, as such, are terrible, because death is contagious, and where one person has died (especially if by violence), more deaths are likely to follow. (2) The dead are not able to provide for themselves and hence should be provided with necessities by the living, either because they are beloved and venerated members of the community or because in the absence of such provisions malevolent consequences might follow. (3) The dead, or those of the dead (such as chiefs, shamans, elders) who have been powerful in life, become even more powerful after death, for they are spirits relieved of bodily limitations and able to help or harm; propitiation of them hence is imperative. This often is reinforced by (1). (4) In some societies, the dead are thought of as capable of returning or of being reborn into the community. (5) Some older dead, if not quite forgotten, tend to become vague, idealized figures, often approaching the status of gods.

Indifference to or neglect of the dead is rare; awe or fear, with or without affection, as for kinsmen or fathers and mothers, is the prevailing attitude. Notions suggested in (2) lead to tendance of the dead (offerings of food, etc., at their graves, soul feasts, destruction of all or some of the dead man's property to be of use to him in the other world, proper funeral ceremonies) more than to actual worship. Attitudes toward the dead suggested in (1), (3) and (5) may and often do lead to worship of one sort or another, and this should be distinguished from mere tendance. With regard to (4), if it is possible for the dead to be reborn or to re-enter the community, it is imperative for such procedures to be followed as will assure the re-entry of only the "good" dead, the powerful, the wise, the efficient, the observers of community customs. Included in these procedures are proper funeral ceremonies, which vary for chiefs, for shamans, for ordinary custom-observing persons, for criminals, for men killed by wild beasts, for women who die in childbirth, etc. Worship is not necessarily implied by such procedures, but prayers are addressed to those of the dead who are expected to return.

A practice that appears, at first sight, to be like ancestor worship is the worship of what may be called the lifestream. The object of this cult is not any man, living or dead, but the power that enables the community to continue to exist by natural increase—a power that may be embodied for the time being in the head of the family or clan and worshiped by him and his dependents. An example of this is the Roman *genius,* in its earliest form.

Types of Ancestor Worship.—Worship directed toward ancestors, believed to possess such powers as those suggested above, is of several types.

Communal Worship.—The dead may be worshiped by an entire group—family, clan, tribe or nation—of which they were members while living. Such communal worship was manifest in the Roman cult of the *manes* or the cult of the *parentum,* which involved the tendance of all the dead of a particular line. The dead individual as such was not the object of worship, but the life-force or *genius.* The cultic practice involved the provision of food at the Lemuria or in the form of a communal banquet shared by the spirits of the dead.

Individual Worship.—More prevalent is the worship of individual ancestors, which may be combined in various ways with communal worship, as in the Roman emperor cult, Egyptian worship of ancestral rulers and Japanese worship of members of the imperial household.

Grades of Ancestors.—Not all ancestors are equally worthy of worship, for some are regarded as being more powerful than others. Ordinary members of a group, when dead, are tended only by their immediate relatives or perhaps not at all or not for very long, while the spirits of great personages become the focus for more elaborate cultic expression by an entire community. In the Greek

hero-cult, for example, prominent personages were singled out as those toward whom cultic expression was directed. Seniority as well as prominence may have brought about the emergence of a dead person to the rank of a worshipful ancestor. The founder of a family, for example, may be worshiped by that family for an indeterminate number of generations. The Aruntas of Australia direct reverence toward their mythical alcheringa, and the Greeks described themselves as "sons or descendants of such a One" (*e.g.,* Iamidae, descended from the legendary seer Iamus, son of Apollo) and worshiped their founder, honouring him above all intervening ancestors. Such a worshiped ancestor in time may fade vaguely away into the mass of the departed, for the number of generations that he can be remembered is not without limits.

Ancestors as Gods.—Some one ancestor may so combine in his image all the worshipful qualities desired in a worthy ancestor, or show such pre-eminence in some one quality, that he is no longer treated as a departed spirit but is given the status of a god. An apparent example is Asclepius, worshiped in many parts of Greece as a god but also spoken of as a hero, with a cultic clan (known as the Asclepiadae, a guild of physicians) committed to revere him (*see* ASCLEPIUS). The Fijian Ndengei, once representative of an ancestor and tutelary deity, became a symbol of creation and eternity, represented in serpent form.

Assistance Rendered.—Ancestral spirits may be called upon to assist the community of the living in many ways: to assure the continuation of the line, even if by intervening to beget a much desired child (the ancestors naturally would be interested in the continuance of the line that worships or tends them); to avert illness or plague; to assist in the obtaining of good crops (in many cultures ancestors are viewed as living in the ground); to intercede with gods, since they are associated with gods and often are viewed as living in the sky or in the abode of the deities. There is almost nothing that an ancestral spirit may not be called upon to grant or to avert. Generally, the relation of ancestral spirits to gods is that of inferior to superior, but they are commonly viewed as having a larger share of divine favour than the living.

Diffusion of Ancestor Worship.—Ancestor worship, though not so nearly universal as tendance and fear of spirits of the dead, occurs in widely distributed cultures. It is prevalent in primitive societies of Africa, Asia and the Pacific area; existed among the ancient Mediterranean peoples and the people of ancient Europe; and is manifest in Asian cultures, particularly in India, China and Japan.

Modern Primitive Society.—Among modern primitive societies ancestor worship has been observed in Melanesian cultures, where it provides a basis for the system of government. The Fijians direct worship to the ancestors of the chief, and this attitude forms a foundation for authority in a patriarchal society. Ancestors came to be regarded as *Kalou-vu* ("Root Gods"), with a temple and hereditary priesthood devoted to their worship. Among the Bantu peoples of South Africa, each family has its group of *chikwembo* (ancestral spirits) who are worshiped on occasions of family interest (marriage, death, etc.), while cultic prayers and sacrifices are directed to the ancestors of the reigning chief of a given tribe when the welfare of the community is concerned. The reverence the chief received during life is intensified after his death, when his powers are felt to be enhanced; a deceased chief hence becomes a focus of tribal worship until such time as his successor supplants him. In Polynesia, though ancestor worship is less pronounced than it is in Melanesia, attention is paid to *oramatuas* (ancestors) who dwell between the living and the *atuas* or gods; most often they are regarded as malevolent, though beneficence is not beyond their capacity.

Ancient Mediterranean World.—Among the ancient Mediterranean peoples, the Babylonians had a cult of the dead, which involved offerings necessary for their well-being in the life beyond, and ancestor worship, which applied only to families of rulers and chiefs and which included sacrifices, festivals in honour of the dead and the deification of certain ancestors. In Egypt, where the Pharaohs were regarded as representatives on earth of the sky-god Horus and as containing something of deity within them, ancestor worship was not highly developed except in the cases of Pharaohs (as Seti I and Ramses II) who made offerings to ancestors. Deceased royalty were venerated by Egyptians as symbolic of their loyalty to the ruling dynasty. Other dead were not worshiped as individuals but were thought to join Osiris, the god of the dead, who was worshiped.

Reference has been made above to the hero-cults of ancient Greece, in which it was thought that persons of exceptional merit or ability might be elevated after death to a status of immortality and hence be worthy of worship by members of the state, tribe or clan (*i.e.*, Asclepius). It is likely that heads of households, recent dead who had served their state and heads of colonies received honours and reverence tending toward worship (especially in the 5th and 6th centuries B.C.). A cult of the dead in the early Roman period (before the end of the republic) was associated with the notion that the dead, though not possessing individuality beyond death, joined collectively the *manes* (the "good gods"). On certain occasions the *manes* could return to earth, visit the living members of the families to which they had belonged and thus exercise an influence on the living. Offerings and sacrifices were included in the cultic worship of ancestors, especially during the Parentalia (a nine-day February festival including eight days of private worship of ancestors and a ninth day of public celebration) and the Lemuria, a May festival involving three days of family ceremony. Later, during the early centuries of the Christian era, as the *genius* came to be thought of in terms of individuality, the *manes* tended to become a group of individual deities, and the worship of the *genius* of the emperor (following his death, and even before his death in certain cases) became part of a state cult. (*See* GENIUS; MANES.)

Though the cult of the dead was not a part of the religion of Zoroaster and the early Avesta, it survived in popular belief in Iran and was reflected in later Zoroastrianism. The fravashi was regarded as a personification of the soul or *genius* of a person that looked after him during life and would receive him after death. The fravashis came to be regarded as the souls of the dead, and a cult of the fravashis developed. The fravashis were invoked, among other times, during the period of Hamaspathmaedaha, March 10–20, when they descended to the villages, capable of beneficent influence if the duties of the living in their behalf were fulfilled.

Europe.—Various European peoples looked to their ancestors in reverence and worship. Teutonic peoples regarded the spirits of the dead as proper recipients of worship. In Scandinavia deceased rulers and other prominent persons were the focus of cultic worship by families, friends and dependents. In Iceland the dead were thought to proceed to certain hills where sacrificial shrines were located. Banquets in commemoration of the dead were common among ancient Russians, and souls of dead relatives were worshiped in White Russia. Lithuanians worshiped deities of the dead and sacrificed to the dead on the anniversaries of their deaths. It is likely that the Celts and related peoples practised ancestor worship, though certain evidence to substantiate this is lacking.

Asia.—The sraddha (funeral) rites in India suggest the importance of ceremonies for the dead in Indian religious practice. These rites are intended to provide the departed spirit or subtle self with an "intermediate" body during that period between death and reincarnation. The sraddha rites performed by living relatives nourish, protect and support the spirit of the dead, aiding it in its pilgrimage from lower to higher realms before its reincarnation and reappearance on earth. In some villages in India there are annual rites during which those who have died during the preceding year are honoured, offerings of food are presented for them, and rites are conducted by the village priests.

In the traditional and complex culture and religion of China reverence for and worship of ancestors played a prominent part, apparently from the reign of Shun (perhaps 2255 B.C.) and certainly from the time of Wu Wang (early Chou dynasty, 1122 [or 1027] B.C. *et seq.*). Ancestral authority, so cardinal to the culture, was the dominant characteristic of the continuing relationship between the dead and the living. The family group—the dead, the living and coming generations—was regarded as a unit in which the strength and prestige of any member became the strength and prestige of the

group. The dead, who passed on to a "world of spirits," were not to be forgotten by the living. The dead generally were considered to have three residences: the graveyard; the family ancestral shrine of each household, in association with which the names of the most prominent and recent ancestors were kept on tablets; and clan temples in which resided all the spirits of the wider clan which were not in any family shrine. Ceremonies at death were intended to ease the spirit's entry into the "spirit world," to provide it with comfort and to make known the respect directed toward it by the living. Cultic and ritual commemoration of the ancestors through offerings of food and incense, pilgrimages to burial places and communal worship were intended to maintain the relationship between the living and the dead, to invoke the dead to pursue their duties to the living, to preserve remembrance of and knowledge about the dead, and to provide for the continuing life of the deceased.

In ancient Japan the cult of the dead was largely ambiguous, regard being directed to ancestors in proportion to their prominence during life. Under the influence of Chinese culture (6th century A.D. *et seq.*), Japanese tradition became more systematized, and the gods of nature were combined with the imperial ancestors in Japanese religion. The imperial household, its members descended from Amaterasu, came to be of central importance to the welfare of Japan and its people. In the *Nihongi* both prayer to and worship of the ancestors of the emperors were reflected. On a more popular level the dead spirits of the departed were thought to be present, especially on the anniversaries of their deaths, sharing in the efforts of the living.

See also Index references under "Ancestor Worship" in the Index volume.

BIBLIOGRAPHY.—There is no single work that treats this subject systematically. *See* J. T. Addison, *Chinese Ancestor Worship* (1925); C. N. E. Eliot, *Hinduism and Buddhism* (1921); *Encyclopaedia of Religion and Ethics,* "Ancestor Worship," vol. i, pp. 425–467, 2nd ed. (1951); J. G. Frazer, *The Belief in Immortality and Worship of the Dead* (1913–24) and *The Fear of the Dead in Primitive Religion* (1933–36); F. L. K. Hsu, *Under the Ancestors' Shadow* (1948); Morris Jastrow, *The Religion of Babylonia and Assyria* (1898); R. F. Johnston, *Confucianism and Modern China* (1935); G. W. Knox, *The Development of Religion in Japan* (1907); L. Lévy-Bruhl, *La Mentalité Primitive* (1922); E. B. Tylor, *Primitive Culture,* 7th ed. (1924); W. D. Wallis, *Religion in Primitive Society* (1939).   (F. S. L.)

ANCHIETA, JOSÉ DE (1534–1597), Jesuit missionary and educator, known as the "Apostle of Brazil," was born in the Canary Islands. He was educated in Portugal, and in 1551 joined the Society of Jesus at Coimbra. In 1553 Anchieta was sent by his superiors to Brazil, where he remained until his death. He was one of the founders of the Jesuit college of Piratininga (São Paulo) in 1554 and was also its most devoted teacher. He served as provincial of the Brazilian Jesuits from 1577 to 1587. In 1582 he founded, as some authorities believe, the Misericórdia hospital of Rio.

Anchieta was a man of many talents. He was a poet, a dramatist, epistler, nurse, teacher, philologist, shoemaker and historian. He wrote the first grammar of the Tupi Indian language and also the first dramatic pieces to be written in Brazil. His poem, *De Beata Virgine Dei Matre,* written in 1563 while he was a hostage of the Tamoio Indians, was the first composition of its kind in the new world. Anchieta's virtues were declared heroic on Aug. 10, 1736, by Pope Clement XII.   (M. CA.)

ANCHISES, in Greek legend, son of Capys and Themis, grandson (according to Hyginus, son) of Assaracus, of the junior branch of the royal family of Troy, king of Dardanus on Mt. Ida. There Aphrodite met him and, enamoured of his beauty, bore him Aeneas. For revealing the name of the child's mother, he was killed or struck blind by lightning. In later legend, adopted by Virgil in the *Aeneid,* he was conveyed out of Troy on the shoulders of his son Aeneas (*q.v.*) and died in Sicily.

ANCHOR. The most ancient anchors consisted of large stones, baskets full of stones, sacks filled with sand or logs of wood loaded with lead. Of this kind were the anchors of the ancient Greeks; they held the vessel merely by their weight and by the friction along the bottom. When iron was introduced for the construction of anchors, an improvement was made by forming them

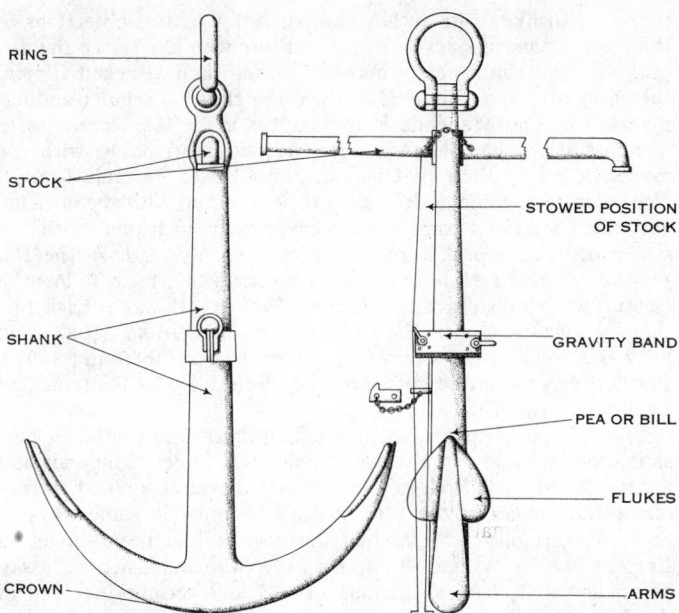

RING

STOCK

SHANK

CROWN

STOWED POSITION OF STOCK

GRAVITY BAND

PEA OR BILL

FLUKES

ARMS

FROM THE "MANUAL OF SEAMANSHIP," BY PERMISSION OF THE CONTROLLER OF H. M. STATIONERY OFFICE

FIG. 1.—FRONT AND SIDE VIEWS OF AN ADMIRALTY PATTERN ANCHOR

with teeth or flukes to fasten themselves to the bottom.

Until the beginning of the 19th century anchors were of imperfect manufacture, the means of effecting good and efficient welding being absent and the iron poor, while the arms, being straight, generally parted at the crown when weighing from good holding ground. However, curved arms were introduced in 1813, and after 1852 the admiralty anchor was supplied to ships of the British navy. The present form of admiralty pattern anchor, which is still used for light work and in boats, is shown in fig. 1. It will be noted that, by removing the keep pin, the anchor can be unstocked for stowing. The anchor must be stocked before letting go, to ensure that one of the flukes takes the ground.

The patent or stockless anchor, patented in England in 1821, became widely used principally because of the ease in handling and stowing in the hawsepipe. Its arms are in one plane and are pivoted so that they can turn through an angle from 35° to 45° on either side of the shank. One of the latest types is shown in fig. 2. Stockless anchors have replaced the old-fashioned stock anchor, fig. 1, almost entirely in ships of the U.S. navy and the merchant marine. However, the stock anchor is still widely used in fishing boats and small cargo vessels.

The principal advantage of the stockless anchor is that it can be hoisted into the hawsepipe, secured there and kept ready for letting go quickly. A disadvantage is that the anchor has a tendency to turn over with an upward pull on the ring or if the ship swings from side to side. Many attempts have been made to overcome this disadvantage while preserving the anchor's handiness; one of the best results is found in a lightweight anchor with extra-long, sharp flukes and an anti-rolling rod, called the stock, through the crown. Under a steady pull this anchor shows a tendency to bury itself deeper in the bottom and a disinclination to roll.

The mushroom anchor, fig. 3, so named because of its shape, has had wide use as a permanent mooring for lightships, dredges and lighters. Its excellent holding qualities result from its tendency to bury deeply and from the suction created by its shape.

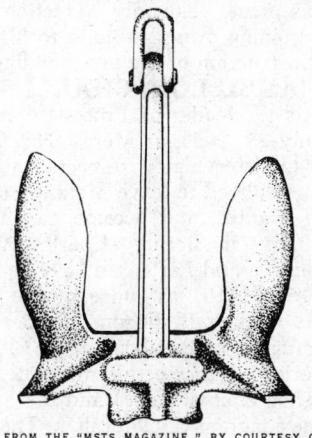

FROM THE "MSTS MAGAZINE," BY COURTESY OF U.S. NAVY

FIG. 2.—STOCKLESS ANCHOR

Types of Anchors.—Ships and boats may carry many kinds of anchors, among which are the following:

Bower anchors—starboard bower and port bower—are so named because they are carried in the bow; they are used for all anchoring except where a smaller anchor or a special type may be required.

The sea anchor is a floating device, usually made of spars and canvas, to keep the bow of a ship headed into the wind and sea; it also is used to reduce leeway and for riding heavy seas in greater safety.

The drogue is a sea anchor used by small boats when landing through a surf to prevent being thrown broadside (broaching).

The stream anchor is a medium-weight anchor, usually about one-fourth the weight of a bower, used to keep a ship from swinging.

FROM THE "MSTS MAGAZINE," BY COURTESY OF U.S. NAVY

FIG. 3.—MUSHROOM ANCHOR

The grapnel is a lightweight, stockless anchor with four or five curved, clawlike arms; it is used for dragging to recover objects on the bottom and for anchoring small boats such as skiffs and dories.

The kedge is a small anchor, of the stock or stockless type, used to move a ship short distances by carrying the anchor out in a boat, letting it go and then hauling the ship up to it; it also may be used to change the heading of a ship by moving the bow or stern around, a process called warping.

Windlasses.—A ship's windlass is used primarily for handling the anchor and chain, but it often is fitted with a concave metal drum, called a capstan, for handling mooring lines, lifting heavy loads, etc. Windlasses are generally classified according to the type of drive: hand, steam, electric or electric-hydraulic. The windlass consists of a vertical or horizontal shaft upon which is mounted a wildcat, a sprocket wheel, which engages the links of the anchor chain; the wildcat may be locked to the shaft for drawing in the anchor chain, or released to rotate independently

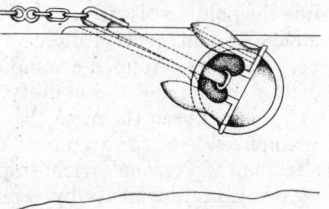

FROM THE "MANUAL OF SEAMANSHIP," BY PERMISSION OF THE CONTROLLER OF H. M. STATIONERY OFFICE

FIG. 4.—METHOD OF STOWING THE STOCKLESS ANCHOR ON SHIPBOARD

for dropping the anchor. The use of hand windlasses is limited to small vessels on which only light anchor gear is employed.

(M. O'N.)

ANCHORAGE, the largest city of Alaska, U.S., is a major air and railway transportation centre. Located at the head of Cook inlet, it was founded in 1915 as a construction port for the Alaska railroad, whose headquarters are there.

Construction of Elmendorf air force base and Ft. Richardson during World War II made Anchorage a key aviation and defense centre, and construction produced a boom as concrete and steel buildings crowded frontier shacks. Its achievement of third place among U.S. cities in volume of air traffic by the late 1950s was due to strategic location and favourable year-round flying weather. It became a regular stop on Seattle-Tokyo and transpolar Scandinavia-Japan air routes and air, rail and truck transportation provided a basic civilian industry.

Earth tremors are common in the area but on March 27, 1964, a severe earthquake, rated as more severe than the San Francisco earthquake of 1906, caused a number of deaths and extensive property damage. For comparative population figures see table in ALASKA: *Population.* (J. E. CL.)

ANCHOVY, common name for a family (Engraulidae) of small fishes related to the herring family and distinguished by the large mouth extending posterior to the eye. The pointed snout extends far in front of the mouth. Most of the species are less than five inches long. Members of the Indo-Pacific genus *Coilia* differ in having a longer posterior region, rounded caudal fin, and many more rays in the anal fin.

Most of the more than 100 species live in shallow tropical or warm temperate seas, where they often enter the brackish water around the river mouths. A few tropical anchovies are restricted to fresh water. Some occur in cold-temperate seas where their occurrence is associated with warm years or warm waters. Shallow waters such as the Zuider Zee have a higher summer temperature than the adjacent European seas and anchovies are able to spawn there. In the winter such fish migrate to other waters that have less seasonal change and therefore are relatively warmer.

Anchovies lay large numbers of elongate, transparent floating eggs. The eggs hatch in about two days and the larvae sink to the bottom. Young and adults feed on plankton, and growth is rapid. Adults congregate in small or large schools.

Anchovies grow to lengths of about four to ten inches. Temperate water types are important food fishes and tropical ones are important bait fishes, especially in the tuna fishery. Many species, however, are very susceptible to injury and are killed by contact with a net or other solid object.   (C. Hu.)

ANCIEN RÉGIME, a French expression meaning "old order," commonly used to denote the social and political system of the old kingdom of France (with particular reference to the form given to it under the Bourbon kings in the 17th and 18th centuries), overthrown by the Revolution of 1789. *See* FRANCE: *History.*

ANCIENS ET DES MODERNES, QUERELLE DES, a dispute in France in the 17th century between those who maintained that the classics were the only models for literary excellence and the "moderns," who challenged the supremacy of classical writers and recommended subjects from Romance legends and the Bible as proper for poetry. *See* also FRENCH LITERATURE: *The 17th Century.*

This is to state the case at its simplest. It is as difficult to define the points at issue in the dispute, as to trace its origins. It was an age of controversy: intellectual France was divided into a number of circles, grouped around outstanding thinkers and members of the church and the nobility, but with a constant ebb and flow of ideas between them, so that those apparently closely identified with one side of the argument may be found supporting the opposite view. Personal friendships and enmities became involved: extravagant judgments by reputable critics might depend on the vagaries of patronage. The violent feelings raised by the quarrel itself can only be understood against the background of Cartesianism (*see* CARTESIANS) with its emphasis on reason and distrust of historical tradition per se and Jansenism and Gallicanism (*qq.v.*) which, in their political aspects, affirmed the national principle against the claims of supranational authority. More purely aesthetic and literary problems with which the dispute became involved were the discussions of the idea of true beauty as the expression either of a perfected reality or a sublime ideal; and of the nature of poetry: whether it was best as it was most reasonable, pure and exact, or whether it should aim at representing what is most otherworldly in man and nature. A further confusion was introduced in that both sides made use of the same terms, and both might lay claim to Cartesian "good sense" (*le bon sens*), differing only in defining its meaning, and the best means to attain it.

The beginnings of the attack on the ancients (*c.* 1659) may be traced to circles influenced by Cartesian thought, especially those associated with Habert de Montmort and the abbé de Marolles. At first it was leveled at those who knew all languages but their own and all history but that of their own time, but it became concentrated on poetry with the publication of heroic poems based, not on classical mythology, but on Carolingian or biblical stories. Notable were *Clovis* (1657) by Desmarets de Saint-Sorlin (*q.v.*), one of the chief disputants, and *Charlemagne* (1664) by Louis le Laboureur, a friend of the abbé de Marolles. The dispute gained force in a number of treatises, and broke into storm on the publication of Boileau's *L'Art poétique* (1674) (*see* BOILEAU-DESPREAUX, NICOLAS). Boileau defined the case for the ancients. Essentially he upheld the great classical tradition in French poetry, established by the Pléiade (*q.v.*), and modified by Malherbe, Chapelain, Maynard and J. L. de Balzac (*qq.v.*). From then on the quarrel became personal, and more explicit. Desmarets' new edition of *Clovis* (1673) contained a "Traité pour juger poètes grecques, latines et françoises"; the abbé de Marolles, inspired

partly by dislike of its author and partly by critical objections to the poem, changed sides (a lesson to those who like to see the disputants ranged into neatly opposed camps) and attacked *Clovis;* the entry of Pierre Daniel Huet (*q.v.*), a classical scholar and humanist, into the Académie Française was made the occasion of a demonstration that the Académie was unquestionably with the moderns, led by Philippe Quinault and Charles Perrault (*qq.v.*). The salon of the duc de Richelieu took its stand with the ancients and the Cartesians were even more closely identified with the moderns. The appeal to patriotism was openly made in the *Défense de la poésie et de la langue française* (1675): to follow the classics was to disregard the glory of France. It was carried further by Perrault's poem *Le siècle de Louis le Grand* (1687) and his *Les Parallèles des anciens et des modernes* (1688 and 1697). Perrault was supported by Fontenelle, Boileau by La Fontaine and La Bruyère (*qq.v.*).

Like all such disputes, the affair died down and the bitter personalities exchanged in a series of polemical fables, lampoons and letters ended with Boileau's apology to Perrault (1700), recognizing the virtues of the 17th century as equal in some ways to those of antiquity. Meanwhile the dispute had been spread to England by Sir William Temple (*q.v.*), who published an essay on ancient and classical learning (1690) and became involved in the quarrels surrounding Richard Bentley. Its chief importance there, however, was to inspire Swift, then employed as Temple's secretary, to write his *Battle of the Books* (1704).

See studies by H. Rigault (1859) and H. Gillot (1914); R. F. Jones, *Ancients and Moderns: a Study of the Background of the Battle of the Books* (1936).

ANCIENT LIGHTS, a phrase in English law referring to windows and other openings in a building that have been used without interruption for at least 20 years, thus creating the right to prevent the owner of adjoining land from obstructing the light received through these openings. An owner of land can acquire an easement (*q.v.*) of light by express or implied grant. The doctrine of ancient lights permits acquisition of such an easement by prescription (*q.v.*). The fact that a window faces a boundary line does not bar the neighbour from building on his own land even though the effect of his action is to obstruct the flow of light to the first building. When, however, a window has been unobstructed for a long time (20 years under the Prescription act of 1832 in England), the light becomes an "ancient light," which English law protects from disturbance. An obstruction constitutes a disturbance if it shuts out enough light to render the occupation of the building uncomfortable according to "ordinary notions of mankind."

In the United States most courts rejected this doctrine at an early date. It was felt that there was sufficient land available so that the first to build did not have to locate his building on the boundary line; he could protect himself by setting his building back. It was also felt in the United States that it was improper to give an easement by prescription where the owner of the adjoining land had no judicial protection against acquisition of the easement. The only protection under the English rule was for the adjoining owner to build to his boundary line within 20 years of construction of the first building.   (A. DM.)

ANCILLON, CHARLES (1659–1715), French lawyer who was the leader of Protestant refugees in Germany, was born on July 28, 1659, at Metz. His father, David Ancillon (1617–92), a minister highly respected among the Huguenots of Lorraine, was obliged to leave Metz in 1685, on the revocation of the Edict of Nantes, and became pastor of the French Protestant community in Berlin. Charles Ancillon studied law at Marburg, Geneva and Paris. In 1699 he replaced his uncle Joseph Ancillon (1629–1719) as judge of the French refugees in Brandenburg. He died in Berlin on July 5, 1715. His history of the French refugees in Brandenburg (1690) is a valuable document of the period. Other of his works deal with the Edict of Nantes (published anonymously) and the habits of eunuchs (published under the anagram C. Ollincan). The biographical source on the family is C. Ancillon, *Mélange critique de littérature, recueilli des conversations de feu M. Ancillon*, 3 vol. (1698).

ANCILLON, JOHANN PETER FRIEDRICH (JEAN PIERRE FRÉDÉRIC (1767–1837), Prussian statesman and historian representative of the reaction against liberalism after 1814, was born in Berlin on April 30, 1767, of Huguenot descent. After studying theology at Geneva, he visited Paris in 1789 and was appointed pastor to the French Protestant community in Berlin in 1790. Through the favour of Prince Henry of Prussia, Ancillon became professor of history at the Berlin military academy in 1792 and official historiographer in 1803. His *Tableau des révolutions du système politique de l'Europe depuis le XVe siècle*, 4 vol. (1803–05), gained him admission to the Berlin Academy in 1805. He was appointed tutor to the royal princes in 1808, councilor of state in 1809 and private tutor to the future Frederick William IV in 1810. He powerfully influenced his pupil, instilling in him hatred and fear of revolution. Ancillon also strongly opposed K. A. von Hardenberg's constitutional projects, which he had at first favoured.

Ancillon entered the ministry of foreign affairs in 1814, becoming director of its political department in 1818 and head of the ministry in 1832. He aimed to preserve the Vienna settlement of 1815 in close association with Austria and believed the rigid Prussian class system to be the ideal basis for a state and representation by "estates" to be the essential constitutional principle. His ideas were rooted in Prussian nationalism, and he was close to the Romantic movement, which fertilized contemporary nationalism by its feeling for the past. Typical of his method of avoiding clear conclusions are his collected essays, *Zur Vermittlung der Extreme in den Meinungen* (1828). Ancillon died in Berlin on April 19, 1837.

His works include: *Mélanges de littérature et de philosophie*, 2 vol. (1809); *Über Souveränität und Staats-Verfassung* (1816); *Über die Staatswissenschaft* (1820); *Über Glauben und Wissen in der Philosophie* (1824); *Über den Geist der Staatsverfassungen* (1825); *Pensées sur l'homme*, 2 vol. (1829); and *Essais de philosophie, de politique et de littérature*, 4 vol. (1832).

See P. Haake, *J. P. F. Ancillon und Kronprinz Friedrich Wilhelm IV von Preussen* (1920) and *Der preussische Verfassungskampf vor 100 Jahren* (1921).

ANCONA, a city and Adriatic seaport on the east coast of central Italy, capital of Ancona province, lies 185 mi. N.E. of Rome by rail (132 mi. direct). Pop. (1961) 101,569 (commune). The town stands on the farthest branch of the promontory which descends among valleys and hills from the Conero massif. There the promontory divides into the two spurs of Monte Astagno and Monte Guasco, on which is the cathedral of S. Ciriaco. This is supposed to occupy the site of a temple of Venus, mentioned by Catullus and Juvenal as the tutelary deity, of which remains have been discovered. The present building, which has Romanesque-Gothic elements, is an enlargement (12th–13th century) and conversion into Greek cross shape of a basilica (5th–6th century). Two crypts have bishops' tombs and saints' relics. Pope Pius II died in the episcopal palace in 1464. Sta. Maria della Piazza has an elaborate arcaded façade (1210). The Palazzo del Comune (13th century, restored) has façade sculptures attributed to Marigaritone d'Arezzo. Fine late Gothic buildings include the churches of S. Francesco and S. Agostino, the Palazzo Benincasa and the Loggia dei Mercanti, all by Giorgio Orsini (da Sebenico), and the prefecture which has Renaissance additions. There is an archaeological museum in the Palazzo Ferretti, including material from the Picene Iron Age. To the west of the town is the harbour, originally protected only by the elbow-shaped promontory from which the town takes its name (Gr. *angkon*, "elbow"), now an oval basin.

Ancona is on the main east coast line of Italy from Milan and Bologna to Foggia and Brindisi; another main line runs to Rome. Ships ply to the Italian ports Rimini, Ravenna, Venice and Trieste, and Yugoslav ports. Industries include shipbuilding, and the production of machinery, metalwork, chemicals, medicines, foodstuffs, textiles, clothing, furniture, bricks and wood. Ancona is also an important market centre, trading in cloth, silk, stockings, skins, dried fish, coffee, drugs and colonial wares, cereals, chemical and pharmaceutical products, coal, timber, ironwork, building materials, liquid and compressed gas, rubber products, hygienic and sanitary materials, paper and pasteboard. Since World War II an oil refinery has much increased the port's activity.

Ancona was founded by Syracusan colonists in 390 B.C., Greek merchants establishing a purple dye factory there. The first Roman colony was in the time of the Gracchi (2nd century B.C.) and its own coinage was used for some time afterward. It was occupied as a naval station in the Illyrian War of 178 B.C. and taken by Caesar just after he had crossed the Rubicon. Trajan enlarged the harbour before starting on his second expedition to Moesia and Dacia in A.D. 105, the marble triumphal arch on the quay being set up in his honour in 115. Pope Clement II further enlarged the harbour. Attacked by Goths, Lombards and Saracens, Ancona recovered its importance in the middle ages, being one of the cities of the Pentapolis under the exarchate of Ravenna, the others being Fano, Pesaro, Senigallia and Rimini (*see* RAVENNA, EXARCHATE OF), and eventually became a semi-independent republic under papal control until Gonzaga took it for Clement VII in 1532. Captured by the French in 1797, it became a democratic state until absorbed into the Italian kingdom of 1808. It returned to papal control in 1816. Lamoricière capitulated there on Sept. 29, 1860, 11 days after his defeat at Castelfidardo, and Ancona became part of Italy. In World War I it was bombarded by the Austrian fleet on May 24, 1915, and thereafter. It was frequently bombed by Allied aircraft in 1943–44 during World War II. It fell to Polish forces under Gen. Wladyslaw Anders on July 18, 1944.

ANCRE, CONCINO CONCINI, MARQUIS D' (d. 1617), Italian adventurer whom the favour of Marie de Médicis made all-powerful in France during her regency. The errant son of a good family, Concini followed Marie de Médicis when she left Florence to marry Henry IV of France (1600). He married the queen's foster-sister, Leonora Galigai. The queen, already dominated by his wife, fell so completely under Concini's influence that Henry IV wanted more than once to banish him from the court. A Spanish agent, Concini was involved in the shady intrigues that led to the assassination of the king (1610). With Marie de Médicis as regent for the young Louis XIII, Concini, now marquis d'Ancre, and his wife enjoyed boundless influence, which they first used to enrich themselves. His ostentation and arrogance made him generally odious and particularly so to the young king, whom he constantly humiliated. He was made marshal of France in 1613. After two civil wars the prince de Condé (Henry II de Bourbon) seemed likely to seize power, whereupon the marshal intervened directly in politics by having Condé arrested and causing a strong government, including the future cardinal de Richelieu, to be formed (1616). His unpopularity, however, made failure inevitable. When another civil war was threatening, Louis on the advice of his own favourite Charles d'Albert de Luynes, decided to kill the marshal, who was shot by the royal guards on the drawbridge of the Louvre on April 24, 1617. The populace dismembered his corpse and sacked his house. His widow, condemned to death for sorcery, was beheaded and burned on July 8, 1617.

See F. Haylem, *Le Maréchal d'Ancre et Leonora Galigaï* (1910); H. d'Alméras, *Concini, maréchal d'Ancre* (1928). (P. ER.)

ANCUS MARCIUS (7th century B.C.), traditionally 4th king of ancient Rome 640–616 B.C. Although his name may be historically acceptable the details of his reign must be regarded as largely legendary. Among these are the settlement of the Aventine hill, the first extension of Rome beyond the Tiber to the Janiculum hill and the founding of the port of Ostia. (R. B. LD.)

ANCYLOPOD, a name applied to the chalicotheres, an extinct group of clawed ungulates, by those who believe these animals to be a separate order of mammals. However, despite their extraordinarily specialized feet, chalicotheres appear to form

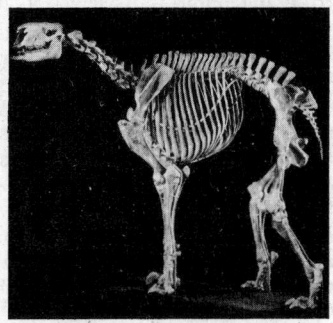

BY COURTESY OF AMERICAN MUSEUM OF NATURAL HISTORY

SKELETON OF LOWER MIOCENE MOROPUS

no more than a superfamily of the order Perissodactyla related to horses and titanotheres. *See also* PERISSODACTYL: *Chalicotheres.*

(B. PA.)

ANCYLOSTOMIASIS, or intestinal hookworm disease of man, is produced chiefly by *Ancylostoma duodenale* or *Necator americanus.* It is also called uncinariasis and miner's anemia. *See* HOOKWORM.

ANCYRA (mod. ANKARA in Turkey), an ancient city of Galatia in Asia Minor, on a tributary of the Sangarius (Sakarya). The date of its foundation is uncertain but it was a prosperous city under Phrygian rule. It was occupied by Alexander the Great in 333 B.C. and after his death fell to Antigonus I's share of his empire. In 281, however, it came under the rule of Seleucus Nicator. Later in the 3rd century B.C. it became the centre of the Tectosages, one of three Gaulish tribes that had settled in Galatia. In 189 B.C. it was occupied by the Roman general Gnaeus Manlius Vulso. In 63 B.C. Gnaeus Pompeius organized it and the surrounding territory under local Tectosagan rule, which continued until Ancyra was made the capital of the Roman province of Galatia in 25 B.C. Christianity was introduced perhaps as early as the 1st century A.D. The Ancyran Church is first mentioned in A.D. 192.

Later, as a city of the Byzantine empire, Ancyra occupied a position of considerable importance and was a target for attacks by several invading armies. A Persian army under the Sassanid king Khosrau II and an Arab army under the caliph Mu'awiya occupied it for short periods in the 7th century, and it was again occupied by Arab armies late in the 8th century during the reign of Harun al-Rashid. In 1073 it fell to the Seljuk Turks. (For the later history of the city *see* ANKARA.)

Of the many extant remains of the Roman and Byzantine periods the most important is the Augusteum, a temple of white marble erected to "Rome and Augustus" during Augustus' lifetime by the common council of the three Galatian tribes. On its walls is engraved the Monumentum Ancyranum (*see* ANCYRANUM, MONUMENTUM), a long inscription in Latin and Greek describing Augustus' achievements. *See also* GALATIA.

ANCYRANUM, MONUMENTUM, an inscription engraved soon after A.D. 14 on the walls of the temple of Rome and Augustus at Ancyra (*q.v.;* mod. Ankara) in the Roman province of Galatia, giving the Latin text and official Greek translation of the obituary of Augustus known as the *res gestae divi Augusti.* Fragments of the Latin version have also been discovered at Antioch in Pisidia and of the Greek version at Apollonia in Pisidia. The *res gestae* ("achievements") were composed by Augustus himself, who directed in his will that they should be engraved in bronze on two pillars in front of his mausoleum in Rome. The inscription recounts (1) his early career and the magistracies and other honours conferred upon him or offered to him by the senate and people; (2) the public benefactions which he had made from his private means, including games and buildings and distributions of money and land to citizens and veterans; (3) his warlike and diplomatic achievements. It ends with his claim to have restored the republic and with the honours that he received therefor. There follows a summary of his benefactions, added after his death. This inscription gives an invaluable picture of how Augustus wished to be remembered. It is factually accurate, but sometimes not entirely ingenuous in its selection and presentation of the facts.

See V. Ehrenberg and A. H. M. Jones, *Documents Illustrating the Reigns of Augustus and Tiberius,* 2nd ed. (1955); Jean Gagé, *Res Gestae Divi Augusti* (1935). (A. H. M. J.)

ANDALUSIA (Spanish ANDALUCÍA), a region including most of Spain south of the Sierra Morena, corresponding roughly to the Roman province of Baetica and divided after 1833 into the eight provinces of Almería, Cádiz, Córdoba, Huelva, Jaén, Málaga, Seville (*qq.v.*) and Granada. Area 33,964 sq.mi.; pop. (1960) 5,893,386. The origins of the name are uncertain; scholars have connected it with the occupation of the country by the Vandals in the 5th century A.D. The Arab form al-Andalus designated at various periods the whole peninsula, the area under Muslim rule, and the kingdoms of Seville, Córdoba, Jaén and Granada.

Andalusia consists mostly of high, heavily eroded mountain chains and their foothills, broken in the west by the Guadalquivir depression and in the east by the Almería and Almanzora rivers. Settlement has been heaviest in the valleys and coastal plains and in the folds of the south-facing mountain spurs. The climate and fauna and flora, often varying considerably within a few miles from subtropical coastal type to alpine, correspond to those of certain parts of the North African littoral. Other shared features are flat-roofed houses, cave-dwelling communities and the intensive cropping of irrigated hill terraces with the consequent proliferation of *minifundia* (small holdings), though stock-rearing *latifundia* are the rule in the plains. (For further description of physical features *see* SPAIN.)

History.—Andalusia's history was closely linked with that of the north African coast until the last decade of the 15th century, when the process of integration was partially suspended by the fall of Granada in 1492 to the monarchs of Castile and Aragon, who forbade their former Muslim subjects to communicate with Africa under pain of death, even after their conversion to Christianity. Both areas had been occupied successively by Punic, Roman and Visigothic settlers; after the invasion of southern Spain from Tangier by Tarik ibn Ziyad in 711, the strait of Gibraltar virtually ceased to exist as a human frontier for the next eight centuries, even though political strife between Spanish and African Muslim dynasties was often intense. In the 10th century the caliphate of Córdoba (*q.v.*) drew its military strength largely from Berber mercenaries, just as Algiers in the 17th was garrisoned largely by deported Spanish Moriscos (*q.v.*). Most of the distinguished figures of the Muslim period divided their lives between the two continents; for example, Averroës (*q.v.*), the greatest of Spanish Muslim philosophers, who was born at Córdoba in 1126, was qadi of Seville and later of his native city, and, except for a few years of banishment, served after 1182 until his death as court physician in Marrakesh, where he did most of his writing.

Whereas the Andalusian contribution to north Africa in the medieval period was mainly cultural and artistic, the African Muslims repaid their coreligionists in Spain by reinvigorating their fighting power and religious zeal at times when discord and tolerance were weakening their resistance to the Christians. The invasions of Spain by the Almoravids (*q.v.*) in the 11th century and by the Almohads (*q.v.*) in the 12th prolonged the life of the petty but highly cultured Muslim principalities which arose from the ruins of the caliphate. These invasions also played a part as important as, though less direct than, that of the rivalry between the Christian monarchs in the birth of the Nasrid sultanate of Granada in 1232. The defeat of the Marinids, one of the three great Berber groups, at the Salado (1340) and Palmones (1343) rivers, by Alfonso XI of Castile and León put an end to effective north African intervention in the peninsula; but the tide of the Christian reconquest of Spain was stemmed for a time by civil war in Castile, strife between crown and feudal nobility and mutual distrust among the Christian princes.

For more than a century the Muslims who had thronged to Granada for asylum were saved by the slowing of the Christian advance. While their frontiers were the scene of a fluctuating guerrilla warfare which inspired the most colourful and moving of the Spanish ballads, their cities saw the revival of a score of fine crafts; Almería and Málaga traded with Italy and north Africa; the *vegas* and terraced slopes were cultivated to yield a wealth of fruits; the mulberry-planted mountainsides produced the finest silks in Europe; and even the poorest hillsides bore fast-growing crops of panic grass and millets. Above the thickly populated city of Granada itself, on an outlying spur of the Sierra Nevada, rose the fortress and palace of the Alhambra (*q.v.*), flanked by the Generalife and other pleasure palaces which fell into ruins soon after the reconquest. (*See* SPAIN: *History.*)

Muslim Institutions.—The government of Muslim Spain, whether under the caliphs of Córdoba, the *taifa* kings or the sultans of Granada, was not radically different from that of the eastern caliphate. The office of ruler was nominally hereditary, though in practice he was frequently elected and deposed by military, aristocratic or merely local factions. A favourite of the ruler, or a military dictator who seized power, often took the title of hajib (chamberlain) and stood above the viziers (the ruler's delegates or ministers) who with the royal secretaries (kuttab) formed the diwan or council of state. Local authority was delegated to civil and military governors called walis, each of whom administered a province or chief city, while on every frontier there was a military chief who enjoyed a large measure of independence. Armies consisted of paid mercenaries or were recruited on a tribal or clan basis and rewarded with the spoils of a raid; frontiers, however, were garrisoned by ascetic warrior sects, the Sufis, who corresponded to the military orders of the Christians.

Muslim law, which is canonical insofar as it derives ultimately from the Koran, was administered by the qadis, who were chosen from scholars versed in the traditions of Islam (the fakihs). As the office of qadi became increasingly onerous in Spain, criminal offenses were relegated to a special judge, the *sahib-al-shurtah,* while under the caliphate a magistrate residing in Córdoba, the *sahib-al-mazalim,* reviewed complaints against all public officials. In addition, most cities had a municipal justice, the *muhtasib* (Sp. *almotacén*), who directed the police, judged offenses against public morality and retained after the reconquest his function of supervising markets, weights and measures.

The income of the state was derived from the *zakah,* a tithe imposed originally on the incomes of individual Muslims, but later on the products of agriculture, industry and commerce; from the capitation tax levied on non-Muslims, which declined after the expulsion of the Mozarabs (*q.v.*); from rents on the state lands recorded in the chancellery registers, which became increasingly important; and from import and export duties, supervised by the officials of the revenue minister. In Granada under the Nasrids the silk trade was an important source of revenue; silks could be bought and sold only in three marts, to which they were taken by elected deputies and stored until sold by the brokers. There was a variety of local taxes on consumer goods, public utilities and irrigation, mostly devoted to defraying the personal expenses of the ruler's household. In addition, the pious bequeathed property to a public welfare fund which supported mosques, schools, leper houses and lunatic asylums, provided maintenance for fakihs and students and ransoms for captives and even served to repair roads, bridges and defense works.

At the time of the reconquest, when Islamic law was completely replaced by Roman and canon law, many administrative and fiscal institutions of the Muslims were guaranteed to them in their capitulations; in this way they were retained or copied by the Christians and survived until the advent of the Bourbon dynasty in Spain. This was especially true of municipal and guild regulations, which were often translated from the Arabic and incorporated in local *ordenanzas.*

Survival of Islamic Influence.—While the most valuable contribution of Muslim Andalusia to the European heritage was in the realms of philosophy and literature (*see* ARABIC PHILOSOPHY; ARABIC LITERATURE), the most striking survivals of the Islamic occupation to be seen in modern Spain are agricultural and domestic. Many of the crops grown in Andalusia were introduced by the Arabs (for example, sugar cane, apricots and almonds—though two of the most characteristic features of the landscape, the maguey, or American aloe, and the prickly pear, come from the new world); and many of the elaborate irrigational constructions date from the Muslim period and have Arabic-derived names (*aljibe,* a well; *acequia,* a water channel; *noria,* a water wheel). The traditional Andalusian house, though Roman in origin, owes many of its refinements to the Muslims. A spacious porch gives access to the central patio, decorated with blue tiles and horseshoe arches with stuccowork arabesques, in the centre of which a fountain plays among citron trees, flowering shrubs and fragrant edgings of myrtle clipped in geometrical patterns. In summer life revolves around the patio and the cool rooms leading off it; in winter the family moves upstairs to heavily carpeted rooms heated by a large round copper brazier standing in a polygonal surround of marquetry and burning, by a process of downward combustion, powdered charcoal made from olive stones. The house is covered by a flat roof and from the outside presents an unrevealing white façade broken only by a few small openings with elaborate wrought-iron grilles. Behind these the family lives in greater seclusion than is usual elsewhere in Europe, and guests other than kinsfolk are rarely invited. Modern Andalusian cooking obtains many of its ingredients from the new world; but the use of olive oil is associated primarily with the Muslims, for the Christians proved their faith by using lard until a comparatively recent date.

Much of what is accepted as typically Andalusian derives from periods before the Muslim conquest (as castanets and some flamenco dancing) or from later periods, being attributable to the influence of the new world, the gypsies, the bandit and smuggler tradition of the 18th century, and the absentee landlords and political bosses of the 19th and 20th centuries. Perhaps the most lasting, though not the most immediately obvious, impress left by the Muslims on the Andalusian character is the gift for crystallizing the most fleeting emotion, aesthetic perception or witty thought in improvised music and verse. From the unknown poet who engraved on the tracery of the Alhambra

> This fountain is like a believer in ecstasy, rapt in prayer; and when the fountain shifts, it is the worshipper who stoops to genuflect and resumes his prayer

to the poetic vision of Luis de Góngora there is but a step; and the same tragic appreciation of the impermanence of material beauty unites both the Arab and the Góngoran tradition to Federico García Lorca.

BIBLIOGRAPHY.—For Andalusia in the Muslim period *see* R. P. A. Dozy, *Histoire des Musulmans d'Espagne,* 2nd ed. (1932), and E. Lévi-Provençal, *La Civilisation arabe en Espagne* (1948). As a general introduction, *see* J. B. Trend, *Spain From the South* (1928). The best travel books are Théophile Gautier, *Voyage en Espagne* (1870), Eng. trans. by Catherine Alison Phillips, *A Romantic in Spain* (1926); G. H. Borrow, *The Bible in Spain* (1843); Washington Irving, *The Alhambra* (1832); W. F. Starkie, *Don Gypsy* (1936); G. Brenan, *South From Granada* (1957); and J. Haycroft, *Babel in Spain* (1958). J. Pitt-Rivers, *The People of the Sierra* (1955), is a valuable sociological study. For a stimulating restatement of Muslim (and also Jewish) influence on Spanish literature, culture and life, *see* Américo Castro, *España en su historia* (1948), Eng. trans. by E. L. King, *The Structure of Spanish History* (1954). (K. GA.)

ANDALUSITE, an aluminum silicate mineral. The crystals usually are roughly developed and rude columnar masses, frequently partially altered to kaolinite or mica, are common. Such crystals, opaque and of a grayish or brownish colour, occur in a mica schist near Innsbruck, Tirol, Aus., and in Andalusia, Spain, from which the mineral derives its name. In addition to characteristic occurrences in small amounts in many contact metamorphic rocks (*see* METAMORPHISM), andalusite occurs in commercial quantities at White Mountain, Calif., Oreana, Nev., Kazakhstan, U.S.S.R., and the Transvaal, Africa. Such deposits are mined as a raw material for refractories and porcelain used in spark plugs and other products.

The unaltered mineral is found as transparent pebbles in the gem gravels of Minas Gerais, Braz., and in Ceylon. The pebbles are often dichroic, appearing greenish or reddish brown according to the direction of viewing, and are sufficiently hard (H. = 7.5) to make effective gem stones. A variety known as chiastolite, characteristic of clay slates near a granite contact, consists of elongated prismatic crystals enclosing symmetrically arranged wedges of carbonaceous material, and in cross section show a black cross on a grayish ground. Cross sections may be polished and worn as charms.

In addition to its natural occurrences, andalusite has been produced synthetically at moderate temperatures under moderate water-vapour pressures. It has the same chemical compositions as kyanite and sillimanite (*qq.v.*), Al_2SiO_5. As in sillimanite its crystalline form is orthorhombic, the latter having the form of almost square prisms. For discussion of its thermal behaviour, *see* MULLITE.

See *American Mineralogist,* vol. 39, 140 (1954). (DA. R.; RU. R.)

ANDAMAN AND NICOBAR ISLANDS, a centrally administered territory of the Republic of India. Formed in 1872 by uniting the Andaman Islands and the Nicobar Islands (*qq.v.*) under one administration, the territory was included under part D of the first schedule of the Indian constitution, 1950. It is administered by the president of the republic through a chief commissioner, who is advised by a local council of five members. The administrative headquarters are at Port Blair (pop. [1951] 8,014) on South Andaman; and an assistant commissioner is stationed on Car Nicobar in the Nicobar Islands. Port Blair is connected with India by a radio link, and a mail steamer running between Calcutta and Madras calls every three or four weeks. During the Japanese occupation of 1942–45 some roads were built, notably on Car Nicobar, and jetties were constructed at Malacca (Car Nicobar) and Nankauri (Nancowry) (central Nicobars). The total area of the territory is 3,215 sq.mi.; pop. (1961 census) 63,-438 excluding the aborigines of the Andamans, who try to avoid contacts with civilization.

See Andaman and Nicobar Islands *Administration Report* (annual).

ANDAMAN ISLANDS, a group of islands in the Bay of Bengal, administratively part of the Indian chief commissioner's territory of the Andaman and Nicobar Islands (*q.v.*). The total population of the Andaman Islands (see *The People,* below), was 48,985 in 1951. The seat of administration is Port Blair. The Andamans, area 2,461 sq.mi., include 204 islands and islets, which lie 650 mi. from the mouth of the Hooghly and 120 mi. from Cape Negrais in Burma, the nearest point on the mainland. The extreme length of the Andamans is about 310 mi.; the greatest width is under 30 mi. There are three chief islands in the main group— North, Middle and South Andaman—so closely adjoining each other that they have long been known collectively as Great Andaman. Grouped with the chief islands are, on the extreme north, Landfall Island; Interview Island, off the northwest coast of Middle Andaman; the Labyrinth Islands, off the southwest coast of South Andaman; Ritchie's archipelago (or the Archipelago Islands), off the east coast of South Andaman; Baratang, wedged in-between and on the east of Middle and South Andaman; and Rutland Island, at the southern end of South Andaman. Little Andaman, roughly 26 by 16 mi., forms the southern extremity of the whole Andaman group and lies 31 mi. S. of Rutland Island across Duncan passage, in which lie the Cinque and other islands. Besides these are a great number of islets lying off the shores of the main islands. The Andaman Islands are separated from the Nicobar Islands (*q.v.*) to the south by the 90 mi.-wide Ten Degree channel.

Topography.—The islands forming Great Andaman consist of a mass of hills enclosing very narrow valleys, the whole covered by dense tropical forest. The hills rise, especially on the east coast, to a considerable height; the highest is Saddle peak (2,402 ft.) on North Andaman. Little Andaman, with the exception of the extreme north, is practically flat. There are no rivers and few perennial streams in the islands. The scenery is everywhere strikingly beautiful and varied, and the coral beds of the more secluded bays in its harbours are conspicuous for their exquisite colouring. The coasts of the Andamans are deeply indented, forming a number of safe harbours and tidal creeks, often surrounded by mangrove swamps. The principal harbours are Port Blair in South Andaman, Port Cornwallis in North Andaman and Elphinstone and Mayabandar in Middle Andaman.

Geology.—The Andaman Islands form the higher parts of a lofty range of submarine mountains, 700 mi. long, stretching from Cape Negrais, the southernmost point of the Arakan Yoma range of Burma, through Sumatra and Java to the Lesser Sunda Islands and the Moluccas. This range separates the Bay of Bengal from the Andaman sea and contains much that is geologically characteristic of the Arakan Yoma (*see* BURMA: *Physical Geography*), and formations common also to the Nicobars and to Sumatra and the adjacent islands. The older rocks are probably early Tertiary or late Cretaceous, but there are no fossils to indicate age. Newer rocks, common also to the Nicobars and Sumatra, are chiefly in Ritchie's archipelago and contain radiolaria and foraminifera.

Climate.—Rarely affected by a cyclone, though within the influence of practically every one that blows in the Bay of Bengal, the Andamans are of the greatest importance because of the accurate information relating to the direction and intensity of storms which can be communicated from them, better than from any other point in the bay, to the vast amount of shipping in this part of the Indian ocean. A well-appointed meteorological station was established at Port Blair as early as 1868. Generally, the climate

of the Andamans may be described as normal for tropical islands of similar latitude. It is always warm, but tempered by pleasant sea breezes, and it is very hot when the sun is northing. The rainfall is irregular, but usually there is very little during the northeast and a great deal during the southwest monsoon.

Flora and Fauna.—A section of the forest department of India was established in the Andamans in 1883. In the neighbourhood of Port Blair 156 sq.mi. were set apart for regular forest operations, these being long conducted by convict labour. The chief timber of indigenous growth is Andaman redwood, or padauk (*Pterocarpus dalbergioides*), used for buildings, boats, furniture, fine joinery and all purposes to which teak, mahogany, hickory, oak and ash are applied. This tree is widely spread and forms a valuable export to European markets. Other first-class timbers are koko (*Albizzia lebbek*), white chuglam (*Terminalia bialata*), black chuglam (*Myristica irya*), marblewood or zebrawood (*Diospyros kurzii*) and satinwood (*Murraya paniculata*), which differs from the satinwood tree of Ceylon (*Chloroxylon swietenia*). Among the imported plants are tea, Siberian coffee, cocoa, Ceara rubber, abacá fibre (manila hemp), teak, coconut and a number of ornamental trees, fruit trees, vegetables and garden flowers. The general character of the forests is Burmese with an admixture of Malay types. Great mangrove swamps supply unlimited firewood.

Animal life is generally deficient throughout the Andamans, especially as regards mammalia, of which there are only 20 separate species in all, including the dugong of the surrounding seas. Some of these are peculiar to the islands and others, including a monkey (*Macaca leonina*), the house mouse and various rats, have been introduced. There is a small pig (*Sus scrofa andamanensis*), important to the food of the people, and a carnivore, a palm civet (*Paguma larvata tytleri*); but the bats and rats constitute four-fifths of the known mammals. Many of the Andaman species differ from those of the adjacent Nicobar Islands. Each island group has its distinct harrier eagle, red-cheeked parakeet, oriole, sunbird and bulbul. Fish are very numerous and many species are peculiar to the Andaman seas. Turtles are abundant and supply the Calcutta market. (X.)

The People.—The Andamanese belong to the negrito stock which is represented also by the Semang of Malaya and the pygmies of the Philippines. Their remoteness and their practice of killing all foreigners preserved them from any considerable physical or cultural modification. They live by hunting and collecting, cultivation being unknown. The dog, introduced in the 19th century, is the only domestic animal. The only indigenous weapon is the bow. Fish arrows have up to four points and pig arrows have detachable heads fastened by cord to the shafts, which catch in the undergrowth. They had no traps or fishhooks. Turtle, dugong and fish are caught with nets and harpoons; the latter are used from single-outrigger canoes. Pottery is made throughout the group, and fragments occur in ancient middens. Iron, obtained from wrecks, has been used for arrowheads, knives and adzes at least since the 18th century. It is shaped by breaking and grinding, a technique derived from the working of shell. The Andamanese were unique in knowing no method of making fire.

There were several tribes, each consisting of a number of small independent groups with a common language. Most Andamanese are now detribalized, but the old life survives among the Jarawa and Onge of the interior of South Andaman, Rutland Island and Little Andaman. (B. A. L. C.)

History.—Because of their position athwart the trade routes from India to Burma and the far east the existence of the islands has been known from earliest times. They are mentioned by the Chinese Buddhist monk I'Tsing (A.D. 672); the Arab travelers of the 9th century; Marco Polo (1286); Friar Odoric (1322); and Nicolo Conti (1430). The derivation of the name "Andaman" is uncertain. It seems possible that the Agathou Daimonos Nesos (Good Spirit Island) of Ptolemy was a misunderstanding of some form like Agdaman. It has been suggested that Angamanain (the name used by Marco Polo) is an Arabic dual indicating "the two Andamans." According to Conti the name means Island of Gold. The name is probably derived from the Malay Handuman, coming from the ancient Hanuman ("monkey"). Later travelers repeat the stories, too well founded, of the ferocious hostility of the people. In Sept. 1789 Capt. Archibald Blair, acting under instructions from the government of Bengal, established a penal colony on Chatham Island, in the southeast bay of the Great Andaman, now called Port Blair but then Port Cornwallis. Two years later, urged by Adm. Sir William Cornwallis, the government transferred the colony—together with its name of Port Cornwallis—to the northeastern part of Great Andaman, where a naval arsenal was to be established. But the scheme did poorly; and in 1796 the government put an end to it. In 1844 the troopships "Briton" and "Runnymede" were driven ashore there. The natives showed their usual hostility, killing all stragglers. Outrages on shipwrecked crews continued to be so frequent that the question of occupation was revived, and in 1855 a project was formed for a settlement and a convict establishment. This scheme was interrupted by the Indian Mutiny of 1857, but as soon as the revolt was broken it became more than ever urgent to provide such a resource on account of the great number of prisoners falling into British hands. A new settlement was established at the beginning of 1858 near the site of Blair's original Port Cornwallis and, to avoid confusion, was named Port Blair. For some time sickness and mortality were excessively high, but the reclamation of swamp and clearance of jungle on an extensive scale by Col. Henry Man was ultimately successful. The Andaman colony obtained a tragic notoriety from the murder, by a Muslim convict, of the viceroy, the earl of Mayo, when on a visit to the settlement on Feb. 8, 1872.

The islands were occupied by the Japanese on March 23, 1942, and reoccupied by the government of India on Oct. 8, 1945, when the abolition of the penal settlement, which had been going on gradually since 1926, was finally effected. As a result of the foundation of the penal settlement there is a considerable Indian population.

Development.—In the 1950s the islands were colonized with displaced persons from East Pakistan, evacuees from Burma and Indian emigrants from British Guiana. There were 20,000 ac. of forest land being cleared. Ten acres of land were given free to each family who also enjoyed exemption from land revenue for two years and received loans and facilities for cutting timber. Timber, especially Andaman redwood, gurjun for plywood and softwoods for match factories, coconuts and copra are exported to India. There is a high school and a well-equipped hospital.

BIBLIOGRAPHY.—M. V. Portman, *Notes on the Languages of the South Andaman Group of Tribes* (1898), *History of Our Relations with the Andamanese* (1899); Sir Richard C. Temple, *The Andaman and Nicobar Islands,* Indian Census (1901); G. S. Miller, "The Mammals of the Andaman and Nicobar Islands," *Proc. U.S. Nat. Mus.,* 24:751–795 (1902); C. B. Kloss, *In the Andamans and Nicobars* (1903); E. H. Man and A. J. Ellis, *On the Aboriginal Inhabitants of the Andaman Islands,* reprint from *J. R. Anthrop. Inst.* (1932); M. C. C. Bonington, *Census of India Report 1931,* vol. 2 (1932); A. R. Radcliffe-Brown, *The Andaman Islanders* (1933); "Andaman Islands," *Far East Review* (May 1940).

ANDEAN CIVILIZATION. The term Andean civilization refers to the aboriginal American Indian cultures that developed and flourished in the highlands of northwestern South America from several thousand years B.C. until their subjection by the Spanish in 1532. In its basic economic elements it persists today in the large Indian populations of Peru, Bolivia, Ecuador and Colombia. Though termed "Andean" it also includes, especially in its early phases, the peoples of the Peruvian coast.

The climatic range is even greater than the geographical one, extending from sea level to heights of over 13,000 ft. (4,000 m.) in the altiplano of Bolivia. The Peruvian coast is absolutely arid, with rain unknown in some parts, and vegetation only in the lush valleys of the many small rivers that descend from the Andes, while the highlands are verdant in the summer rainy season, October to May. On the coast, fish and seafoods are important staples, but in the highlands hunting is of slight importance. On the other hand, the highlands are characterized by the domestication of the American cameloids, the llama and alpaca.

Like all civilizations, the Andean was founded on agriculture, permitting a large and sedentary population with leisure time to devote to cultural improvement between harvest and sowing. This civilization naturally developed from an earlier and sparser hunting people.

PRE-INCA PEOPLES

The Inca were preceded during possibly 4,000 years by agricultural peoples who gradually developed high cultures; these are known only by archaeological excavations. The earliest known Andean people were a small group at Huaca Prieta at the mouth of the Chicama river. They lived in semisubterranean houses. Ignorant of maize and of pottery, they cultivated squash, gourds, chili pepper and cotton, fished and made coarse cloths and baskets. They are given a radiocarbon date of about 2500 B.C.

Chavín.—For 2,000 years, of which little is known, culture developed, maize was introduced, and the arts of pottery making, architecture and others were brought to a high state of development. One excavation at Guañape (Peru), dated at about 1250 B.C., affords data on the close of this period. The earliest-known culture of any sophistication was the Chavín with its apparent centre at Chavín de Huántar in the northern highlands of Peru, and a coastal phase at Cupisnique. Chavín, dated at about 700 B.C., was apparently the centre of a religious cult whose influence was felt over much of the Peruvian coast, especially in the art style in which the jaguar predominated. The main building at Chavín is immense, of excellent masonry, consisting of three stories, with stairs, ramps and even ventilating shafts. Maize was now the staple food, and all the arts including pottery, weaving and metallurgy had reached a high plane.

Experimental Period.—The cultures of the next period, sometimes called the Experimental, probably about 500–300 B.C., are not so well known, but include the Salinar, Gallinazo and several others. Several sites of this period have also been discovered in the highlands, Chanapata near Cuzco, and Chiripa on Lake Titicaca (Peru-Bolivia). The masonry architecture and the agricultural terraces show considerable skill, but apparently the highland cultures at this time lagged behind those on the coast. This cannot be stated with certainty, however, for in the highlands all objects made of perishable materials are gone while the cemeteries of the arid coast preserve all handicrafts in excellent condition. This was a dynamic period in which many new techniques appeared. The extent of agricultural lands was increased by irrigation canals, and agricultural terraces were built.

Florescent Period.—In the first few centuries of the Christian era—authorities differ by several centuries in their estimates, though allowing 600 to 800 years for the length of the period—high civilizations developed on the coast of Peru. In pottery making, weaving, metallurgy and other arts, as well as in engineering, this was the apogee of Peruvian culture; the period is known as the Florescent. The river valleys were densely populated, with intensive agriculture. The best-known civilization of that time is the Moche or Mochica of the region of Trujillo (Peru), where are found the enormous adobe mud pyramids of the Sun and the Moon. The former measures 750 by 450 ft. and, although much eroded, stands 60 ft. high; it has been estimated to contain 130,000,000 mud bricks. One of the great irrigation canals is said to have been 75 mi. long. Especially famous are the pottery vessels, modeled in naturalistic forms that reveal much of the native life. Apparently there were social classes, and, judging by figures of warriors, militarism had arisen.

On the southern coast, in the Pisco, Ica and Nazca valleys, other civilizations, the Paracas and Nazca, arose. The former are famous for their great exquisite embroidered mantles, the latter for their beautiful pottery vessels painted in polychrome colours. Other less-known peoples occupied the central coast. Less is known of the highland peoples of the period, but there must have been dozens of groups of slightly variant cultures and of a grade of civilization approaching that of the coastal peoples.

Tiahuanaco.—Probably early in the second half of the 1st millennium A.D. there arose the first of the great highland cultures. Its most important site, though probably not its actual centre, was at Tiahuanaco near Lake Titicaca in present Bolivia, an enormous, obviously ceremonial site with hundreds of great megalithic carved stones and monuments. The Tiahuanaco art style is very characteristic, and its influence spread all over Peru. It was probably the result of the spread of a religious cult, not a conquering megalithic empire as was once believed. This period throughout much of Peru seems to have been one of unrest, with increasing urbanization, social stratification and militarism.

Chimú.—In the last few centuries before the rise of Inca power one civilization is outstanding, that of the Chimú of the northern coast of Peru. It resembled the Inca on a smaller scale, with one great capital city, Chan Chan (*q.v.*), a large domain (probably achieved by conquest), a highly developed governmental system and social stratification from the humble farmer to the divine "king." The population was probably dense and largely urbanized, agriculture was carried to its ultimate limit, and craftsmanship was perfected. Handicrafts, however, were somewhat standardized, with quantity production. On a lesser scale, this was probably the pattern for most of Peru at this period, though the local cultures elsewhere are less well known. On the southern coast the successors of the Nazca people are known as the Ica.

The capital, Chan Chan, not far from Trujillo, now utterly deserted and uninhabitable for lack of water, is one of the world's most notable archaeological sites, with six to ten square miles of rectangular blocks and streets, great walls, reservoirs and pyramid temples, all built of adobe mud. The aboriginal population must have numbered many thousands.

PHILIP GENDREAU

RUINS OF MACHU PICCHU, 15TH-CENTURY INCA CITY IN CUZCO REGION OF PERU

INCA HISTORY

To most persons the term Andean civilization means the civilization of the Inca, and seldom is a popular concept more true. For practically our entire knowledge of Andean civilization is that of the Inca. In this it is not necessary to depend on archaeology, for the writings of many Spanish chroniclers of the time of the Conquest are extant. Unfortunately, however, there is considerable disagreement among them, especially regarding Inca history. As the Inca has no system of writing, the history was of course oral tradition. The following sketch seems to meet the known facts most logically, but in its earlier stages it differs greatly from other accounts preferred by some earlier historians.

Like the Aztec, the Inca came late upon the historical scene; even their legends do not predate A.D. 1200, with the first emperor. For, like old world peoples, and unlike other aboriginal Americans, the Inca recounted their history by kingly reigns. Most of the accounts agree on 13 emperors:

1. Manco Capac (*c.* A.D. 1200)
2. Sinchi Roca
3. Lloque Yupanqui
4. Mayta Capac
5. Capac Yupanqui
6. Inca Roca
7. Yahuar Huacac
8. Viracocha Inca
9. Pachacutec Inca Yupanqui (1438–71)
10. Tupac Inca Yupanqui (1471–93)
11. Huayna Capac (1493–1525)
12. Huascar (1525–32)
13. Atahualpa (1532–33)

The first seven emperors were legendary, local and of slight importance; their traditions are full of impossible or improbable events, especially those of the quasi-mythological founder Manco Capac. In this period the Inca were a small tribe, one of many, whose domain did not extend many miles around their capital, Cuzco (*q.v.*). They were almost constantly at war with neighbouring tribes of equal importance.

The incredibly rapid expansion of the Inca empire began with Viracocha's son Pachacutec (1438–71), one of the great conquerors, and one of the great men, of history. Also with his accession in 1438 reliable history began, almost all the chroniclers being in practical agreement. Pachacutec was called by Sir Clements Markham "the greatest man that the aboriginal race of America has produced." He and his son Tupac Inca may be aptly compared to Philip and Alexander of Macedon. Pachacutec was evidently a great civic planner as well; tradition ascribes to him the city plan of Cuzco as well as the erection of many of the massive masonry buildings that still awe the visitor to this ancient capital.

The sudden great expansion of the Inca empire was one of the most extraordinary events of history. It covered a little less than a century from the accession of Pachacutec in 1438 to the conquest by Francisco Pizarro (*q.v.*) in 1532, and most of it was apparently accomplished by Pachacutec and Tupac Inca in the 30 years between 1463 and 1493. At its maximum the empire extended from the present Colombia-Ecuador border to central Chile, a coastal distance of over 2,500 mi., encompassing approximately 380,000 sq.mi., about equal in area to France, Belgium, the Netherlands, Luxembourg, Switzerland and Italy combined. Inca expansion, like the other great conquests of history, was motivated by the thirst for power and aggrandizement.

First the Aymara-speaking rivals in the region of Lake Titicaca, the Colla and Lupaca, were defeated, and then the Chanca to the west; the latter attacked and nearly captured Cuzco. After that there was little effective resistance. First the peoples to the north were subjugated as far as Quito, Ecuador, including the powerful and cultured "kingdom" of Chimú on the northern coast of Peru. Tupac Inca then took over his father's role and turned southward, conquering all northern Chile as far as the Maule river, the southernmost limit of the empire. His son, Huayna Capac (1493–1525), continued conquests in Ecuador to the Ancasmayo river, the present border between Ecuador and Colombia. The difficulties of transport for such great distances being so great, it is doubtful that the empire could have been expanded farther.

The conquest of the great empire by Pizarro and 180 Spaniards is one of the most amazing events of history. Huayna Capac's two sons, Huascar and Atahualpa, had quarreled and fought over the throne, and Huascar was taken prisoner. Pizarro captured and executed Atahualpa, but not before the latter had ordered Huascar to be killed. So ended Inca rule. So well ordered was Inca authority that Pizarro stepped into Atahualpa's shoes, gave orders in his place, and the routine of government went on as before. The story has been well told by William H. Prescott and others.

INCA CULTURE

The basis of Inca culture was agriculture, including maize, white and sweet potatoes, squash, tomato, peanuts, chili peppers, coca, manioc and cotton; almost all of these were then unknown in Europe. Guinea pigs and ducks were raised and eaten; llamas and alpacas were used as beasts of burden and for their wool but rarely for food. Clothing was made of woven woolen and cotton cloth. Dwelling houses were of stone or adobe mud. Practically every man was a farmer, producing his own food and clothing.

The empire was a "welfare state" with complete regimentation. No one starved but there was little initiative; no one changed his location or work to improve his lot. The land was public and apportioned annually to families in relation to their size. It was divided into three classes, with the product for the state, for the church or for the people, though the latter were required to cultivate for all. The harvests of state lands went into storehouses for the use of the nobility, for the army and men engaged in other public service, and for the people in time of crop failure or other calamity. Llamas were also mainly the property of the state. In lieu of taxes every man was periodically called to service in the army or on public works such as building roads or temples, or mining; this service was known as *mita*.

Craftsmen were also government employees, their products going to the nobility and the priests. Others exempted from *mita* service were the *yanacuna,* superior boys selected to be permanent servants and aids to the emperor and the nobility. Beautiful girls were also chosen at a youthful age and taken to Cuzco for training as concubines of the emperor and nobles or as "Virgins of the Sun," living in a convent and weaving the clothing of the emperor, nobles and priests.

The emperor or "Inca" was divine, a descendant of the Sun, and enjoyed maximum privileges. He had a large seraglio and many descendants; most emperors married their sisters. The emperor's word was law, but, bound by custom, he was never a tyrant. His relatives formed a large body of nobility who were placed in positions of authority, especially over conquered lands. Beneath them were minor officers known as *curaca,* and so on down to foremen supervising ten households.

Religion was highly organized, with a numerous priesthood and many temples to the Sun. The priests conducted elaborate ceremonies, often lasting for many days, performed sacrifices, made divinations, consulted oracles and heard confessions. Sacrifices were usually of llamas; human sacrifice was rare, in contrast to the practice of the Aztec. The ceremonies were held at regular times, with one major one each month. There were hundreds of sacred places of various grades of sanctity, known as huacas. The great creator god, Viracocha, was little worshiped; the Inca adored primarily the Sun, with many subsidiary deities of various attributes.

Medicine and surgery were rather highly developed, and skulls were frequently trephined, whether to relieve fractures or to release demons is not clear. The Inca, like all American civilizations except the Maya, had no system of writing, and all knowledge and lore were orally transmitted. However, numerical records were kept on knotted cords called quipu, which were used primarily for such purposes as censuses but could be adapted by a trained *quipucamayoc* as mnemonic aids for almost anything.

Especially in later years, war was a state policy. All men were liable for service, and the Inca armies were large, well equipped and well trained. Like all ancient armies, they fought mainly hand to hand with clubs, axes and spears, plus the sling for short range. Their ability to conduct campaigns at great distances was due primarily to the system of roads with storehouses of food and equipment located at short intervals. As soon as the conflict ceased, conquered peoples were well treated, given Inca overlords, and most of them probably found their economic condition bettered. Intransigent groups were moved en masse to regions closer to Cuzco and replaced by more docile people; the latter were known as *mitimae.* Often some men from prominent families among conquered tribes were taken to Cuzco as hostages.

Works of engineering and architecture were outstanding. Roads were made from Cuzco to all parts of the empire, and on them relay runners (*chasqui*) were stationed at short distances to carry messages and packages quickly. Suspension bridges were built over small canyons, hillside terraces were constructed to increase agricultural production, long irrigation canals were built and immense fortresses were erected. Great edifices were built of massive and perfectly tooled masonry, many of which still remain in Cuzco. The stones brought to and erected in the fortress of Sacsahuaman at Cuzco are incredibly large.

Though the Inca did not excel some of their more ancient predecessors in handicraft, the Peruvians did admirable work in copper, silver, gold, pottery and especially textiles. Some of their weaving has never been surpassed for fineness and beauty, and they knew practically every technique known to the modern textile manufacturer. All textiles were woven by women on small backstrap looms.

See also SOUTH AMERICA: *Anthropology.*

BIBLIOGRAPHY.—J. Alden Mason, *The Ancient Civilizations of Peru* (1957); G. H. S. Bushnell, *Peru* (1957); J. H. Steward (ed.), *Handbook of South American Indians,* vol. ii, *The Andean Civilizations* (1946); Wendell C. Bennett and Junius B. Bird, *Andean Culture History* (1949); Philip A. Means, *Ancient Civilizations of the Andes* (1931). (J. A. Mn.)

ANDEIRO, JOÃO FERNANDES, COUNT OF OURÉM (d. 1383), a statesman in the service of Portugal, prominent in that country's negotiations with England. A Galician by birth, he supported the claim of Ferdinand I of Portugal to the throne of Castile after the murder of Pedro I of Castile by his bastard brother Henry (who then became king as Henry II) in 1369. Portuguese military reverses obliged Andeiro to seek refuge in England in 1371, whereupon he supported John of Gaunt, duke of Lancaster, as candidate to the throne of Castile. He acted as intermediary between the English and Portuguese courts during the treaty negotiations in 1372 and 1373, and when Anglo-Portuguese relations were resumed in 1380. He returned to Portugal in 1381 with the English naval squadron under Edmund of Langley (afterward duke of York) and was made count of Ourém. Hated for his part in arranging the marriage of Ferdinand's daughter Beatriz with John I of Castile, and for his own scandalous liaison with Ferdinand's wife, Leonor, Andeiro was murdered by the mestre de Aviz (later John I of Portugal) on Dec. 6, 1383. (V. R. R.)

ANDERMATT, a summer and winter resort in Uri canton, Switz., is situated 4,760 ft. high in the Alps below the Gurschenstock (9,401 ft.) and above the St. Gotthard tunnel, 111 km. (69 mi.) by road south of Zürich. Pop. (1960) 1,523. Wooden snow-deflectors protect the town from avalanches. The Schöllenen railway connects it with the St. Gotthard railway far below. The road from Lucerne and Zürich to Italy crosses the road from Lake Geneva to the Engadine there. Andermatt is also an important military station. St. Columban's church is mentioned in 712 and Ursern, or Andermatt, in 1309, but it remained unimportant until the opening of the St. Gotthard tunnel in 1882. (LE. M.)

ANDERS, WLADYSLAW (1892–   ), Polish army general, after 1945 a leader of the Poles in exile, was born on Aug. 11, 1892, at Blonie, near Warsaw, the son of a land agent. From 1911 he studied at the Technical college of Riga in Latvia (then part of Russia). In World War I he served in a Russian cavalry regiment, but after the Communist Revolution of Nov. 1917 he joined the Polish army corps in Belorussia. Appointed chief of staff of the Polish army in Poznania, he fought the Red army on the Polish eastern front (1919–20). In 1922–24 he studied at the Paris École Supérieure de Guerre. In World War II he fought the Germans and the Russians in Poland in Sept. 1939 and, severely wounded (for the eighth time), was captured by the Russians. He was confined at the Lubianka prison in Moscow. Released in Aug.

(LEFT) INCA SILVER ALPACA, CUZCO STYLE; (RIGHT) MOCHICA POTTERY WARRIOR

1941, under the Polish-Soviet agreement, he was appointed commander in chief of the Polish army to be formed of prisoners of war and deportees in the U.S.S.R. Finding that he could not organize an independent Polish army in the U.S.S.R., he suggested the transfer of his Polish soldiers to the middle east. As Winston Churchill was asking Stalin for the same, 115,000 Poles left the U.S.S.R. in the summer of 1942 for Iran and Iraq. In Italy in 1944–45 the 2nd Polish army corps, under Anders, fought alongside the British 8th army, captured Monte Cassino, took a major part in liberating the Adriatic coast and completed its campaign at Bologna. During the last months of World War II Anders was acting commander in chief of the Polish forces in the west. Being opposed to Communism, after the war he remained in Great Britain, where Polish forces were organized into the Polish Resettlement corps. On Sept. 26, 1946, the Warsaw Communist government deprived Anders and 75 senior officers of Polish citizenship. In 1954 the Polish national council in exile elected Anders a member of the Council of Three, a leading organ of Poles abroad. Anders received many Polish and foreign honours. His writings include *An Army in Exile* (1949) and *Hitler's Defeat in Russia* (1953).   (K. Sм.)

ANDERSEN, HANS CHRISTIAN (1805–1875), Danish writer of world-famous stories. He was born in the slums of Odense, on the island of Fyn (Fünen), on April 2, 1805, the son of a poor shoemaker and his superstitious and almost illiterate wife. His grandfather was insane, and his grandmother, a pathological liar, spoiled him. He was a sensitive child, and preferred daydreaming, playing with the puppet theatre made for him by his father and making up stories to playing with other children and learning a trade. His father volunteered for service in the Napoleonic Wars, and, returning broken in health and spirit, died in 1816. His mother married again, and Andersen, after apprenticeship to various trades, where he suffered from the crude jokes of his companions, determined to go to Copenhagen "in order to become famous." He set off in 1819, with very little money, centring all his ambitions on the Royal theatre, where he hoped to win fame as a singer, dancer, actor or even playwright. He succeeded in getting a job as a supernumerary there, but suffered great hardship and only survived because some of the best-known writers and composers of the period became his benefactors. When his voice broke, and he was dismissed from the Royal theatre, he tried writing tragedies, which were rejected as "completely unsuitable for performance." Jonas Collin, one of the directors of the theatre, then took an interest in him and raised money to send him, in 1822 at the age of 17, to the grammar school at Slagelse. The choice was unfortunate, for Simon Meisling, the headmaster, made Andersen the butt of his humour and reduced him to the brink of despair. In 1826 Meisling moved to Elsinore, taking Andersen with him, but he and his wife made his life so miserable that Collin arranged private tuition for him so that by 1828 he was able to enter Copenhagen university.

Andersen's first book, *Ungdoms-Forsøg* ("Youthful Attempts"), was published in 1822 under the pen name Villiam Christian Walter (his own name plus those of Shakespeare and Scott), and his first poem, "Det døende Barn" ("The Dying Child"), was printed in 1827. In 1829 came his first important work, *Fodreise fra Holmens Canal til Østpynten af Amager*, an imaginative arabesque in the style of E. T. A. Hoffman (*q.v.*), describing a journey on foot through the streets of Copenhagen. It brought him his first real fame, and in the same year his first play was performed at the Royal theatre. In 1831 he traveled in Germany and on return wrote the first of many travel sketches. For the next two years he tried writing poems, librettos, dramatic translations and original plays, but they were not well received and in 1833 he sought inspiration in Italy. The literary results were an unsuccessful dramatic poem, *Agnete og Havmanden* ("Agnete and the Merman"), and his first and most successful novel, *Improvisatoren* (1835), autobiographical in theme but in an Italian setting. The German and English translations (*The Improvisatore*, 1845) mark the beginning of his world fame. Other autobiographical novels followed: *O.T.* (1836; Eng. trans. 1845); *Kun en Spillemand* (1837; Eng. trans. *Only a Fiddler*, 1845); and, later, *De to Baronesser* (1848;

Eng. trans. *The Two Baronesses*, 1848); *At være eller ikker være* (1857; Eng. trans. *To Be, or Not to Be*, 1857); and *Lykke-Peer* (1870; Eng. trans. *Lucky Peer*, 1871).

While seeing *Improvisatoren* through the press, Andersen began to write his first four tales for children, *Eventyr, fortalte for Børn* ("The Tinderbox," "Little Claus and Big Claus," "The Princess and the Pea," "Little Ida's Flowers"), published in the spring of 1835.

THE BETTMANN ARCHIVE

HANS CHRISTIAN ANDERSEN

But neither he nor his Danish critics realized that he had entered the field in which he was to become the supreme master. Two further instalments of stories made up the first volume of *Eventyr* (1837); a second volume was completed in 1842: to these was added *Billedbog uden Billeder* (1840; Eng. trans. *A Picture-Book Without Pictures*, 1847). He continued to write fairy tales (*Eventyr*) and stories (*Historier*) (his own distinction between tales with and without supernatural elements) until 1872, writing 168 altogether. Many have become classics all over the world, being translated into more than 80 languages. Their perfection as works of art, their appeal to both children and grownups (for Andersen is never afraid of introducing feelings and ideas beyond a child's immediate comprehension, yet never loses touch with the child mind), their imaginative power and their roots in the folk legends he had heard in his own childhood and in the happenings he had himself known and observed have made them immortal.

In many of Andersen's tales inanimate things come alive, a darning needle or a shirt collar talk and behave like human beings, thus exposing and ridiculing some form of human weakness. In others, trees, plants and animals are endowed with human feelings; the fir tree, the daisy and the inhabitants of the farmyard are strange reflections of the human world. The fairy-tale world, too, acquires an oddly topical resemblance to our own world; thus both "The Swineherd and the Princess" and "The Nightingale" are aimed at those who prefer cheap imitation to genuine art, and "The Emperor's New Clothes" possesses a humour and satire that retains its topicality in every country. Many of Andersen's tales reveal an optimistic belief in the victory of goodness and beauty and harmony (*e.g.*, "The Snow Queen"), while others are deeply pessimistic, depicting the ultimate victory of the imitator and the parasite (*e.g.*, "The Shadow"). In the majority of his stories the autobiographical element is clearly distinguishable: Andersen himself is identified with the ugly duckling, the little mermaid, the fir tree, the soldier in "The Tinderbox" and the storyteller in "The Flying Trunk," etc., and yet his stories are all about universal human problems—that of being an outsider or outcast, that of lacking the capability to enjoy the moment of happiness, or of being predestined either to happiness or to a nostalgic longing for a lost happiness. As a stylist Andersen was an innovator who courageously used the idioms and constructions of the spoken language, thus deliberately breaking with the literary traditions of his time.

From 1840 to 1857 Andersen was constantly traveling, visiting the other Scandinavian countries, Italy, always the land of his dreams, and also Spain, Portugal, Greece, Asia Minor and Africa. His impressions are recorded in a number of travel books (*e.g.*, *En Digters Bazar*, 1842, Eng. trans. *A Poet's Bazaar*, 1846; *I Sverrig*, 1851, Eng. trans. *Pictures of Sweden*, 1852; and *I Spanien*, 1863, Eng. trans. *In Spain*, 1864), and in his diaries and pen drawings. In Germany and France he mixed with many leading writers and artists, and on his first visit to England (1847) he was lionized by society, and met many distinguished writers, among them Charles Dickens, with whom he stayed for five weeks at his home at Gad's Hill in 1857. In Denmark he was often the guest of members of the nobility, but he regarded the house of Jonas

Collin as his real home, though he suffered from never feeling entirely accepted by the family and his friendship with Edvard, the eldest son, was rent by violent storms. He remained a bachelor, though he fell deeply in love several times, notably with Jenny Lind, the Swedish singer, whom he met in 1843, and who became a close friend, inspiring some of his best stories. Much of his imaginative writing centres round himself, and he wrote three autobiographies: one private in 1832 (published in 1926), one for his German publisher (1847; Eng. trans. 1847) and one in Danish, *Mit Livs Eventyr* (1855; Eng. trans. 1871; a continuation was published posthumously in 1877). During his last years his closest friends were the families of M. R. Henriques and M. G. Melchior. He died at Melchior's house in Copenhagen on Aug. 4, 1875.

Few people are so intimately known to posterity as Andersen. He rarely destroyed anything connected with himself and his diaries (mainly unpublished) and thousands of letters reveal a man both vain and humble, sensitive to criticism, quick-witted, a keen observer and a true artist. The ingenious simplicity of his stories is appreciated all over the world, but his humour, vivid, racy style and mastery of form are often lost in translation.

BIBLIOGRAPHY.—The most important Danish editions are *Samlede Værker,* 15 vol. (1876–80); *Eventyr,* a critical ed., 5 vol. (1919); *Andersens Romaner og Rejseskildringer,* 7 vol. (1943–44); *Hundrede Digte* (1948); and *Mit Livs Eventyr. Revideret Tekstudgave,* 2 vol. (1951). Among the many editions of letters from and to Andersen the most important are those published by C. S. A. Bille and N. Bøgh (*Breve til Andersen,* 1877; *Breve fra Andersen,* 1878) and by H. Topsøe-Jensen (including Andersen's correspondence with Jonas Collin and others, 3 vol., 1945–48; with Edvard and Henriette Collin, 5 vol., 1933–37; and with Henriette Wulff, 3 vol., 1959–60). *Anderseniana* (1933 *et seq.*) contains many valuable essays and documents. For English editions, *see* E. Bredsdorff, *Danish Literature in English Translation,* with a supplement on Andersen (1950). The best translations are by R. P. Keigwin, *Fairy Tales,* world edition, 4 vol. (1950–60), Paul Leyssac, *Its Perfectly True, and Other Stories* (1938), R. Spink, *Fairy Tales and Stories* (1960), and Jean Hersholt, *The Complete Andersen,* 6 vol. (1952). For biography and criticism, *see* G. Brandes, *Kritiker og Portrætter* (1870); E. Collin, *Andersen og det Collinske Hus* (1882; new ed. 1929); H. Brix, *Andersen og hans Eventyr* (1907); H. Helweg, *H. C. Andersen: En psykiatrisk studie* (1927); P. V. Rubow, *H. C. Andersens Eventyr* (1927); H. Topsøe-Jensen, *Omkring Levnedsbogen* (1943); B. Grønbech, *Andersens Eventyrverden* (1945); H. G. Olrik, *Andersen. Undersøgelse og Kronikker* (1945); E. Bredsdorff, *Andersen og Charles Dickens* (1951; Eng. trans. 1955) and *Andersen og England* (1954); R. Nisbet Bain, *H. C. Andersen* (1895); E. Reumert, *Andersen som han var* (1925; Eng. trans. 1927); S. Toksvig, *The Life of Andersen* (1940); C. Burnett, *The Shoemaker's Son* (1943); Rumer Godden, *H. C. Andersen* (1955). (E. L. BF.)

ANDERSON, ALEXANDER (1775–1870), U.S. engraver, the first to make wood engravings in the United States, was born in New York city on April 21, 1775. At an early age he made his first attempts at metal engraving, fashioning his own tools and plates, but in 1789, in compliance with his father's wish, he began the study of medicine, graduating from Columbia in 1796. In 1793, having seen wood engravings by Thomas Bewick, he obtained boxwood blocks, made tools himself and began the practice of that technique. In 1798 his entire family died from yellow fever, and this caused him to abandon his career as a physician to devote himself entirely to engraving, finally working exclusively in wood engraving.

Anderson illustrated many books and produced an enormous volume of work, being active even during the last years of his long life. He was also skilled as a painter of miniatures and portraits. Best known of his book illustrations are those for Webster's *Elementary Spelling Book,* engravings for the plays of Shakespeare and about 300 cuts after the works of Thomas Bewick. He died in Jersey City, N.J., on Jan. 17, 1870.

See F. M. Burr, *Life and Works of Alexander Anderson* (1896); J. Lossing, "Memorial of Alexander Anderson" (1872) in *Bibliographical Society of America Papers 45,* no. 4 (1951). (H. Es.)

ANDERSON, CARL DAVID (1905–), U.S. physicist, received the 1936 Nobel prize in physics jointly for discovering the positron (1932). He participated in discovery of the meson (1937) and became a leading investigator of the properties of other new cosmic ray particles. He pioneered in magnetic cloud chamber studies of cosmic rays in 1930 with Robert A. Millikan (*q.v.*). Born in New York on Sept. 3, 1905, he received his Ph.D.

(1930) at the California Institute of Technology where he remained, becoming professor of physics in 1939. (L. A. D.)

ANDERSON, ELIZABETH GARRETT (1836–1917), English physician and pioneer in the professional education of Englishwomen, daughter of Newson Garrett, of Aldeburgh, Suffolk, was born in 1836. She was educated at home and at a private school. In 1860 she resolved to study medicine, an unheard-of procedure for a woman in those days. Miss Garrett managed to obtain some irregular instruction at the Middlesex hospital, London, but was refused admission as a full student there and at many other schools. She studied anatomy privately at the London hospital, as well as with some of the professors. She had difficulty in gaining a qualifying diploma to practise medicine; but in the end the Society of Apothecaries, London, allowed her to enter for the licence of Apothecaries' hall, which she obtained in 1865. In 1866 she was appointed general medical attendant to St. Mary's dispensary, a London institution started to enable poor women to obtain medical help from qualified practitioners of their own sex.

The dispensary soon developed into the New Hospital for Women. In 1870 she obtained the Paris degree of M.D. In 1871 she married, but did not give up practice. She worked steadily at the development of the New hospital, and also from 1874 at the creation of a school of medicine for women in London. Both the New hospital and London university have since been suitably housed and equipped; the New hospital is now the Elizabeth Garrett Anderson hospital. Dr. Anderson was elected president of the East Anglian branch of the British Medical association in 1897 and in 1908 mayor (the first woman) of Aldeburgh. She died at Aldeburgh on Dec. 17, 1917. Her daughter, Louisa Garrett Anderson (1873–1943), took an active part in the suffrage movement. During World War I she was joint organizer of the women's hospital corps and (1915–18) chief surgeon of the military hospital at Endell street.

BIBLIOGRAPHY.—O. M. Anderson, "Elizabeth Garrett Anderson and Her Contemporaries," *Ulster Med. J.,* 27:97 (Nov. 1, 1957); L. G. Anderson, *Elizabeth Garrett Anderson* (1939); E. H. C. M. Bell, *Storming the Citadel* (1953).

ANDERSON, MARIAN (1902–), U.S. singer, one of the foremost contraltos of her time, was born at Philadelphia, Pa., Feb. 17, 1902, of poor Negro parents. Her early musical training was in the choir of the Union Baptist church, which she joined when she was six, already having displayed a remarkable voice. Unable to afford private lessons, her church undertook to raise enough money for her to study privately with Giuseppe Boghetti. In 1925 Boghetti entered her for a contest for an appearance at Lewisohn stadium in New York city with the New York Philharmonic orchestra. She was placed first among 300 competitors. She had already undertaken several concert tours, and, despite struggles against poverty and racial discrimination, was beginning to make a name for herself. Real success came in 1933 when she went to Europe. She returned to New York in 1935, and succeeded in achieving at home the position due her voice. She was asked to sing at the White House, and also at the Metropolitan Opera. Her work for the people of her own race and her warmth of personality added to appreciation of her vocal and interpretative powers, and she was made a delegate to the United Nations. As a singer, her outstanding characteristics are wide range, richness and purity of tone and mastery of a variety of styles. For a portrait *see* NEGRO, AMERICAN.

See her autobiography *My Lord, What a Morning* (1957); K. Vehanen (her accompanist), *M. Anderson: a Portrait* (1941).

ANDERSON, MARY (1859–1940), U.S. actress, was born in Sacramento, Calif., on July 28, 1859. At the age of 15, with the advice of the actress Charlotte Cushman, she began to study for the stage, making her first appearance at the age of 16 in Louisville, Ky., as Juliet in 1875. Her remarkable beauty created an immediate success, and she played in all the large cities of the United States with increasing popularity. Between 1883 and 1889 she had several seasons in London, and was the Rosalind in the performance of *As You Like It* which opened the Shakespeare Memorial theatre at Stratford-on-Avon. Among her chief parts were Galatea (in W. S. Gilbert's *Pygmalion and Galatea*), Clarice (in his *Comedy and Tragedy*, written for her), Hermione and Perdita (in Shakespeare's *The Winter's Tale*), Lady Macbeth, and Ion (in Noon Talfourd's *Ion*). In 1889 she retired from the stage and in 1890 married a British subject, Antonio de Navarro, and settled in England. She died there on May 29, 1940.

See William Winter, *Stage Life of Mary Anderson* (1886), and her own *A Few Memories* (1896).

ANDERSON, MAXWELL (1888–1959), U.S. playwright who achieved success in many dramatic forms. Born in Atlantic, Pa., on Dec. 15, 1888, Anderson was educated at the University of North Dakota (Grand Forks) and Stanford university (California), taught English for a time and became a journalist. He first made his mark in the theatre with the pungent World War I comedy *What Price Glory?* (1924), a collaboration with Laurence Stallings. But Anderson was not content with realism and prose drama and became equally successful in the field of poetic drama, especially with his historical plays *Elizabeth the Queen* (1930), *Mary of Scotland* (1933) and *Anne of the Thousand Days* (1947). Even the success of his Pulitzer prize-winning satire *Both Your Houses* (1933) did not deflect him from his purpose, and he reached the peak of his career with two poetic plays set in his own times, *Winterset* (1935), a tragedy inspired by the Sacco and Vanzetti case of the 1920s, and *High Tor* (1936), a romantic comedy that expressed the author's displeasure with the materialism of the modern world. Collaborating with the composer Kurt Weill, Anderson also invaded the musical theatre with the political satire *Knickerbocker Holiday* (1938) and with *Lost in the Stars* (1949), a dramatization of Alan Paton's South African novel *Cry, the Beloved Country*. He died Feb. 28, 1959.   (J. W. G.)

ANDERSON, RICHARD HERON (1821–1879), Confederate general in the American Civil War, was born on Oct. 7, 1821, at Statesburg, S.C. After graduating from West Point in 1842 he saw routine cavalry duty for several years and served with distinction in the Mexican War. At the start of the Civil War he resigned from the U.S. army and entered the Confederate service. Anderson served in the army of northern Virginia from the Peninsula campaign through the battle of Gettysburg as an able and modest brigade and division commander, attaining the rank of major general on July 14, 1862. In the Wilderness campaign, in May 1864, he succeeded to the command of the 1st corps when Longstreet was wounded. After saving Spotsylvania by a brilliant night march, Anderson was given the rank of temporary lieutenant general. He later participated in the defense of Petersburg and Richmond. After the war Anderson became a railroad official in South Carolina and then state phosphate inspector. He died on June 26, 1879, at Beaufort, S.C.   (W. W. Ha.)

ANDERSON, ROBERT (1750–1830), Scottish author and critic, whose principal work was his edition of *The Works of the British Poets, With Prefaces Biographical and Critical* (1792–1807). He was born at Carnwath, Lanarkshire, Jan. 7, 1750, and died at Edinburgh, Feb. 20, 1830.

ANDERSON, SHERWOOD (1876–1941), U.S. author, whose *Winesburg, Ohio* strongly influenced the technique of the American short story, was born in Camden, O., Sept. 13, 1876. As a youth in Clyde, O., he attended school intermittently and worked as a newsboy, house painter, farm hand and race-track helper. At 22 he served in Cuba during the Spanish-American War. On his return, he studied for a year at Wittenberg academy, Springfield, O.; then he became a writer of advertising in Chicago and later a paint manufacturer in Ohio. In 1913, dissatisfied with the life of a businessman, he returned to Chicago to write fiction.

Encouraged by Floyd Dell, Theodore Dreiser, Carl Sandburg and Ben Hecht, leaders of a Chicago literary movement, Anderson began to contribute experimental verse and short fiction to the *Little Review*, the *Masses*, the *Seven Arts* and *Poetry*. Dell and Dreiser arranged the publication of his first two novels, *Windy McPherson's Son* (1916; rev., 1921) and *Marching Men* (1917), both written while he was still a manufacturer. His reputation as an author was made by *Winesburg, Ohio* (1919), his first mature book; this volume of interrelated short sketches and the short stories in *The Triumph of the Egg* (1921), *Horses*

and Men (1923) and *Death in the Woods* (1933) comprised his best work. Anderson's stories, simply told, presented sympathetically the lives of middle western townspeople who were warped into inarticulate grotesques by isolation and frustration of love and creativity. His novel *Poor White* (1920) studied one cause of these psychological ills—the industrialization of the small town.

In 1921 Anderson was awarded the first *Dial* prize of $2,000. His later books included *Many Marriages* (1923) and *Dark Laughter* (1925), highly subjective psychological novels; *A Story Teller's Story* (1924) and *Tar: a Midwest Childhood* (1926), autobiographical sketches; *Hello Towns* (1929); *Perhaps Women* (1931) and *Puzzled America* (1935), essays on American industrial conditions; and the posthumous *Memoirs* (1942) and *Letters* (1953).

In 1925 he moved to Marion, Va., where he published both of the town's newspapers, one Democratic, the other Republican. He died March 8, 1941, in Colón, Pan., while on a tour of South America.

See James Schevill, *Sherwood Anderson: His Life and Work* (1951); Irving Howe, *Sherwood Anderson* (1951).   (W. L. Ps.)

ANDERSON, a city of Indiana, U.S., 35 mi. N.E. of Indianapolis, in a rich corn- and wheat-producing region; seat of Madison county. Its importance as a manufacturing centre dates from the discovery of natural gas in 1887; the automobile parts industry aided later growth. Pop. (1960) 49,061. Madison county, designated in 1964 as the Anderson standard metropolitan statistical area, had a 1960 population of 125,819. (For comparative population figures *see* table in INDIANA: *Population*.)

Platted in 1823 by John Berry on the site of a Delaware Indian village, Anderson was named for a Delaware subchief, Kikthawenund, whose English name was Captain Anderson. First known as Anderson's Town, it was incorporated in 1838. Later it surrendered the incorporation and remained a village until 1853, when it was reincorporated as the town of Anderson; in 1865 it was incorporated as a city. The Anderson Bible Training school was founded there in 1917 by the Church of God. In 1929 it became a coeducational liberal arts college and was renamed Anderson College and Theological seminary. Mounds State park is 3 mi. E. of Anderson and contains the largest single known earthwork in Indiana as well as several other mounds erected by prehistoric inhabitants. *See* MOUND BUILDERS.   (E. R. Bo.)

ANDERSON, a city in northwestern South Carolina, U.S., in the foothills of the Blue Ridge mountains; the seat of Anderson county. The city and county were named for a local Revolutionary War hero, Gen. Robert Anderson. (For comparative population figures *see* table in SOUTH CAROLINA: *Population*.)

Anderson is one of the largest manufacturing areas in the state, with a large and long-established textile industry, as well as newer industries including fibre glass, metals, chemicals, plastics and sewing machines. After mid-20th century, cotton growing, once the county's chief agricultural occupation, was yielding to the cultivation of Turkish tobacco, grain, trees, legumes, vegetables and fruits and to livestock raising.

Although the area was settled by the end of the 18th century, on what had been Cherokee Indian land, the county was not created until 1826; the city was chartered the same year and was incorporated in 1882. The original settlers were, in large part, descendants of Scotch-Irish migrants from Virginia and Pennsylvania. Anderson has been called the "electric city" because of early (1898) long-distance transmission of power from the Seneca river.

The history of Anderson junior college began in 1848 when it was first opened as the Johnson Female seminary. Clemson university is located at Clemson, 17 mi. N.W. of Anderson. Near Anderson, on the Savannah river, is the $100,000,000 hydroelectric Hartwell dam.   (E. M. L.)

ANDERSONVILLE, a village of Sumter county, Ga., U.S., on the Central of Georgia railway, about 60 mi. S.W. of Macon, was the site of a Confederate military prison from Feb. 1864 to May 1865. In the summer of 1863 the federal authorities ended an agreement under which captives were exchanged; the increased number of prisoners of war confined in Richmond constituted a danger to the Confederacy and seriously pressed upon the food supply. In Nov. 1863, under orders of Gen. J. H. Winder, Capt. W. S. Winder selected the Andersonville site and began to construct a stockade of 16½ ac. (later enlarged to 26 ac.). Pressure in Richmond led to prisoners being sent to Andersonville before barracks and other facilities were constructed. Drainage was poor and the water supply was inadequate. Prisoners received poor and uncooked food. Many were diseased and fatigued before arrival and disease was rampant in the prison. In six months, 42,686 cases of diseased and wounded prisoners received treatment from the inadequate medical staff and hospital. Nearly 13,000 prisoners died. After Sept. 1864 the prison was largely a hospital. Conditions in Andersonville were utilized as propaganda material in the North, where Secretary of War Edwin M. Stanton ordered retaliation on Confederates held in Union prisons.

After the war, Capt. Henry Wirz, commander of the prison, was tried by a military commission and on Nov. 10, 1865, he was hanged. The site of the prison has been preserved as a federal park.

Partisan accounts of Andersonville abound. Hundreds of prisoners wrote their reminiscences. Conflicting views are to be found in J. McElroy, *Andersonville* (1879) and R. R. Stephenson, *The Southern Side* (1876). A later analysis is in W. B. Hesseltine, *Civil War Prisons* (1930). (W. B. HE.)

ANDES or LOS ANDES, the great mountain system which extends the full length of the western part of South America. It stretches from Tierra del Fuego at the southern tip of the continent to the Caribbean coast approximately 4,000 mi. to the north. Many of its peaks are more than 22,000 ft. high, and Aconcagua, north of Santiago (Chile), is the highest peak in the western hemisphere. The origin of the name is obscure. It has been suggested that it is derived from *anti*, the Quechua word for "east," a name applied by the Quechua Indians to the range east of Cuzco. Other suggested origins of the name are the Quechua words *antasuya*, "region of metal," or *anta*, "copper." The term "Cordillera of the Andes" is sometimes erroneously used as a name for the whole Andean system, and in South American nomenclature is often applied to the most important range of a given section of the system. From its original form, "Las Cordilleras de los Andes," a term applied by the Spanish conquerors to the series of parallel ranges of which the Andes appeared to be composed, is derived the present widespread use of the word "cordillera," meaning an extensive mountain range or system of ranges.

The Andes are narrowest at the southern end and broadest in the central or Bolivian section and at their northern end, where they divide into four distinct ranges. In Tierra del Fuego their trend is nearly east and west; on the mainland the trend is north and south as far north as latitude 18° S., where, in one of its two broadest sections, the system turns westward to form an almost semicircular curve convex to the west and follows the configuration of the west coast as far north as southern Colombia. There it spreads out into three distinct ranges, the easternmost of which again divides into two ranges, one of which forms the northern section of the Venezuela-Colombia boundary while the other crosses the boundary south of Lake Maracaibo and extends northeastward toward the Caribbean sea.

The following sections of this article describe the main ranges of the Andes—from the Patagonian Andes in the south to the Andes of Venezuela in the north—the geology of the region, climate, minerals, population, transportation and famous mountaineering expeditions.

The Patagonian Andes.—Until recently the Andean system was pictured as a great mountain barrier, with a well-defined crest line of lofty peaks which coincided with the water divide between the Pacific and Atlantic drainage systems and effectively separated them from each other. As late as 1881, when the governments of Chile and the Argentine republic signed a treaty in which their common boundary was defined, they described it as following the highest crest of the Andes, which formed the water divide between the Atlantic and Pacific oceans. When the demarcation of this boundary was undertaken it was found that throughout the greater part of the cordillera the topography did not correspond to the conception of it on which the treaty was based. South of

latitude 38° S. the Andes were found to be not a simple ridge but a broad zone, from 25 to 40 mi. wide, of mountain chains and narrow valleys. The higher summits shift back and forth from one chain to another and do not, except in a general way, mark the water divide. These summits rise above a broad base, represented by high valleys and broad passes, to an average elevation of about 6,500 ft. Few are lower than this average altitude, and some individual peaks exceed 7,500 ft. Those that have a fairly uniform altitude have been carved by erosion from the older Andean rocks of the plateaulike base. The higher peaks are volcanic cones built up on the plateau. The eastern side of this part of the Andes is divided into two sections—a northern from Lake Aluminé to Lake Nahuel Huapi, and a southern from Lake Nahuel Huapi southward, which includes the island of Tierra del Fuego. Both sections are characterized by a succession of glacier-fed lakes which stretch back like fiords into the heart of the cordillera, and by valleys cut from west to east across the Patagonian tableland through which, at one time, the lakes drained toward the Atlantic.

Settlement of the boundary came by arbitration in 1902 and was commemorated by erection of the famous statue known as "Christ of the Andes" near Uspallata Pass. (*See* ARGENTINA; CHILE.)

In the northern section high transverse ridges separate the lake basins and more or less effectively obstruct passage from one to another. These ridges connect the mountain zone with the Patagonian tableland, and all but one of the streams of this section rise in the westernmost range and flow eastward to the Collón Curá and Limay rivers. Lake Lacar now discharges across the western range to the Chilean lake region, but there is evidence that it, too, once drained to the Atlantic.

In the southern section the tableland is separated from the cordillera by a longitudinal depression which marks the line of contact between the folded cordillera and the flat tableland. It extends southward from the low pass between Lake Nahuel Huapi and Lake Bariloche and is continued beyond the mainland by the Canal Ancho of the Strait of Magellan, Useless bay, and Whiteside and Admiralty sounds. The continuity of this depression has, however, been frequently exaggerated. It is really divided into several compartments by masses of different kinds of rocks and by granite ridges. Between Lake Argentina and Lake Buenos Aires it is interrupted by the tableland which rises to a height of 5,000 ft. and butts against the cordillera. Similarly, between Lake Buenos Aires and Lake General Paz there is no great difference in level between the tableland and the depression.

Most of the lake basins there, as well as in the northern section, are continued eastward across the Patagonian tableland as distinct valleys. This is the case even in the submerged southern end of the depression, where the east end of the strait is a submerged valley on the axis of Otway bay and Useless bay and is continued eastward across northern Tierra del Fuego by the depression which ends in San Sebastián bay. The valleys are now, however, with few exceptions, dead valleys, for the drainage is mostly west to the Pacific by way of narrow canyons in the cordillera and the interoceanic water divide follows the terminal moraines of the old glaciers which confine the lakes on the east.

On the Pacific side of the cordillera a great longitudinal plain extends from the Chacabuco range, by which the basin of the Aconcagua river is enclosed on the south, southward to the Gulf of Ancud. The northern part of this region is narrow and irregular and is cut by ridges into small, almost completely separated valleys, and interrupted by isolated hills. At about latitude 36° S. it widens out to a width of 20 to 40 mi. A line of recent volcanoes begins a little south of Santiago and is aligned on the cordillera to about 35° S., where it gradually departs from the cordillera until in the south it stands well out in the central plain and forms a less continuous but higher chain west of the cordillera proper. The northern part of the plain is filled with recent geological deposits and forms the fertile Vale of Chile. South of latitude 39° S. it is sown with glacial lakes or depressions formerly occupied by lakes. Not only because of the greater precipitation on the west side of the cordillera in the belt of the westerly winds south of 39° S. but also because of the great condensation of moisture caused by the line of volcanoes in front of the cor-

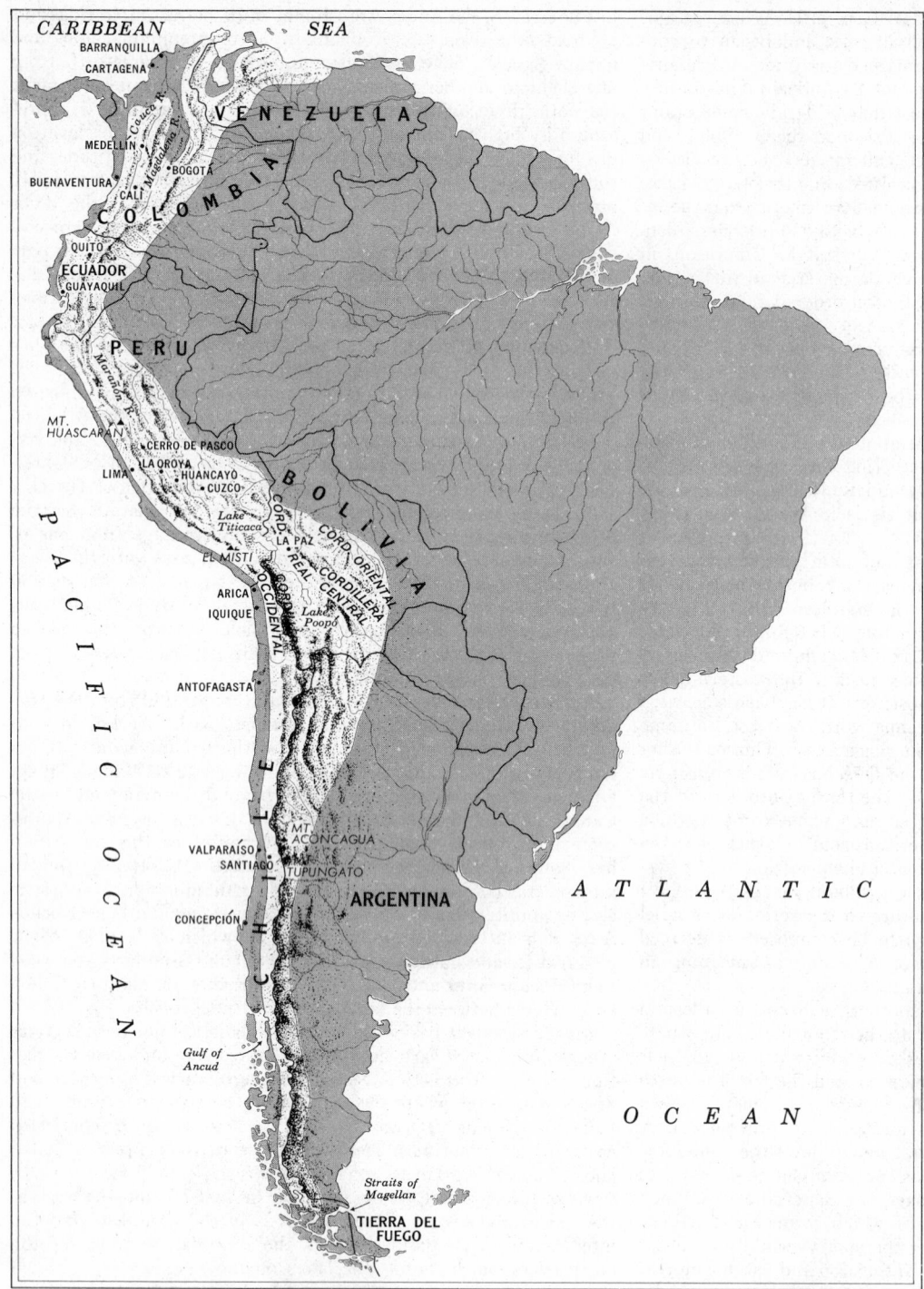

ANDES MOUNTAIN SYSTEM SHOWN IN RELATION TO THE CONTINENT OF SOUTH AMERICA

channel and the Strait of Magellan, but again rises to more than 6,500 ft. on Tierra del Fuego.

South Chilean Andes.— Northward from latitude 39° S. to 30° S. the character of the Andes is greatly simplified. It consists of a double line of crests, the westernmost of which carries the Argentina-Chile boundary. The high valleys between the crests are at an altitude of from 10,000 to 13,000 ft. The passes to the east and west in the northern part are between 13,000 and 15,000 ft. in altitude. South of 31° S. they are somewhat lower. Isolated summits rise from 5,000 to 7,000 ft. above the high valleys, and between 32° and 34° S. include three of the highest peaks of the Andes: Mercedario (22,-211 ft.), Aconcagua (22,831 ft.) and Tupungato (22,309 ft.). The interior valleys have a direction slightly oblique to the general trend of the cordillera and corresponding to the direction of the folds. The whole section has effective drainage of normal type. The water divide which the boundary follows shifts back and forth from one ridge to another, and the boundary pillars, which are located, in general, on high passes between head waters, follow a tortuous line. Eruptions from the chain of recent volcanoes which appears a little south of the latitude of Santiago and extends southward on the Pacific side of the main axis of the cordillera to the Gulf of Ancud have greatly complicated the topography of the cordillera by filling up high valleys or damming up lakes.

East of the cordillera in this section a continuous depression extends northward from the Mendoza river for more than 160 mi. between the cordillera and the precordillera (a series of short ranges reaching out into the Argentine plain). The precordillera continues south of the Mendoza river to about latitude 36° S.

dillera, the glaciers of the Glacial period advanced much farther from the water divide on the western slope than on the eastern, with the result that the glacial lakes on the Chilean side of the cordillera are at a much lower level than those on the Argentine side, and part of them, as, for instance, Ranco and Llanquihue, lie completely separated from the cordillera.

The cordillera of Patagonia is divided into a series of massifs separated by longitudinal and transverse depressions. Some of these depressions cut completely through the cordillera and are occupied by rivers which drain lakes on the Argentine side, or by fiords which extend through to the Argentine side. Between latitude 41° and 46° S. the altitude of these massifs is from 6,500 to 8,000 ft., only Tronador (11,660 ft.) attaining a higher altitude. Between 46° and 50° the cordillera reaches altitudes of from 10,000 to 13,000 ft. It is lower and broken up between Smith

It attains heights of 13,000 ft. in the latitude of San Juan and 11,000 ft. on the Paramillo plateau above Mendoza. In spite of their narrow width the Andes in this section offer serious obstacles to movement from one side to the other because of their elevation and covering of snow. They have no mineral wealth and the few routes across them, which include the Transandine railway between Santiago and Mendoza, are solely for the purpose of crossing the cordillera and not for exploiting its subsoil. The high valleys furnish some summer pasture and the rivers and lakes afford water for irrigation. Settlements lie not in the mountains but on their border, and the location of the more important of those on the Argentine side has been influenced by the position of the most practicable passes, since it is to cattle and goods trade with Chile that they owe their origin and growth.

The Puna de Atacama.—North of latitude 30° S. the Andes

again lose their simple character. The mountain belt widens and long extensions of it reach out southeastward to the Argentine plain, enclosing in the depressions between them long embayments of the plain. At about the 28th parallel the main range divides into a western and an eastern range, with a belt of very high and extremely cold and desolate country between them (called the Puna de Atacama), made up of mountain chains, isolated peaks, and basins of salt deposits known as salars, arranged along dominating north-south lines. The average height of the basin floors of the Puna is between 11,000 and 13,000 ft., with the interior peaks and ridges rising only from 1,000 to 5,000 ft. higher. The range which forms the western border of the Puna is known as the Cordillera de los Andes or Maritime cordillera and consists chiefly of a line of high volcanoes with lava flows between them. The passes in the Maritime cordillera average about 15,000 ft. while the peaks reach 20,000 to 23,000 ft. In the range that forms the eastern border of the Puna the passes are from 16,500 to 17,000 ft. high, but the peaks average only from 18,000 to 20,000 ft. In contrast with the western cordillera in which the volcanic cones are high and have been built up on a lower basement of lava, the cones of the eastern cordillera are low and have been built up on broad beds of lava. West of the western cordillera is a line of depressions between 3,000 and 4,000 ft. lower than the average level of the Puna and enclosed on the west by the Cordillera Domeyko, which contains a number of salars, among them the Salar de Atacama and the Salar de Punta Negra.

East of the eastern border of the Puna, the Andes of the Argentine provinces of Jujuy, Salta and Tucumán form a broad belt of ridges oriented from north to south and separated by deep depressions. Their altitudes diminish as they extend eastward into the Argentine plains, and their summits, as well as those of the secondary ranges along the main mountains, exhibit an older aspect than their ravined borders. The tops and high upper slopes are covered with grass. The steep headwater slopes and narrow declivities of the ravines, cut into them as the result of recent uplift, are youthful features in contrast to the lawnlike high-level slopes which they are gradually invading.

The Central Andes.—The northern limit of the Puna de Atacama is a transverse range of high snow-capped peaks and ridges at about the 23rd parallel, which separates it from the drainage basin of the Salar de Uyuni. The high plateau continues northward as the altiplano or *altiplanicie* of Bolivia. This altiplano has no outlet to the sea, and is therefore one of the world's great basins of interior drainage. It is about 500 mi. long by 80 mi. wide, and slopes gently from a little under 12,500 ft. at Lake Titicaca to slightly more than 12,100 ft. at Lake Poopó, and a little lower at the Salar de Uyuni. It differs from most interior drainage basins in that it contains a large body of fresh water (Lake Titicaca) and an important river drainage (the Desaguadero river). Lake Titicaca is the highest large body of navigable water in the world and has a length of about 110 mi. It owes its existence to a deep tectonic depression in close proximity to a high snow-capped mountain range (the Cordillera Real) that keeps it supplied with water. Farther south the altiplano becomes more and more like other interior semideserts, for the windward mountains become lower, so that they condense less moisture, and broader, so that the precipitation is more widely distributed. As it flows southward, the Desaguadero river, the outlet of Lake Titicaca, grows smaller and smaller until Lake Poopó, into which it empties, is a shallow pond with only a small overflow to the nearby salt lake or marsh called Coipasa. The altiplano lies between two great tablelands with superimposed peaks and ranges. Its eastern edge is particularly well defined by the sharp rise and straight form of the eastern cordillera. The western edge is less clearly defined because of the volcanic debris that has encroached upon it from the western or Maritime cordillera, forming hilly districts. Between the Salar de Coipasa and the Salar de Uyuni, the altiplano is divided into two interior drainage basins by a line of volcanoes and hills which extend from the western cordillera nearly across to the eastern. North of Lake Titicaca the bordering scarps converge in the Nudo de Vilcanota at about latitude 14° S., and enclose the altiplano on the north.

The western cordillera descends by relatively smooth slopes to the coastal deserts of Tarapacá and Atacama, famous for their nitrate deposits, and the desert region of southern Peru. In the rare cases in which its streams permanently reach the piedmont, they furnish water to small but important fields of vegetables and alfalfa. Viewed from the west, the cordillera presents, for long distances, a strikingly even skyline, generally the line along which the uplifted peneplain has been warped up to form the highlands, broken only by the summits of the highest volcanoes which stand back toward the altiplano, or, in places, by volcanoes like the Misti and Tacora, which rise on the western edge of the cordillera. The most recent of these volcanoes, such as Misti, Tacora and Sajama, are symmetrical cones surmounted by craters; but the greater number are much older than these and have more or less lost their original form by erosion.

The eastern cordillera, where it borders the altiplano, falls into two sections of quite different physiographic aspect. In the northern section the character of the uplifted peneplain has been almost completely destroyed because the concentration of the rainfall in a narrow belt in this region and the relatively steep gradient of the rivers have combined to enable the streams to cut the old surface to pieces, leaving only the lofty snow-clad Cordillera Real standing on a narrow base. The Cordillera Real is a central core of resistant rocks whose superior hardness and greater initial elevation have preserved it from the effects of great denudation recognizable all around it. The Cordillera Real is cut between the Nevado de Illimani and the Nevado de Quimsa-Cruz by the chasm of the La Paz river, a tributary of the Madeira river of the Amazon system, which, by virtue of the enormous condensation of moisture on the eastward slope of the eastern cordillera, has been able to break through this great barrier to the altiplano; but the axis of the Cordillera Real extends southward across the La Paz valley through the Nevados de Araca, Quimsa-Cruz and Vera Cruz, forming a line of heights as definite in trend and structure as the Cordillera Real and continuing its features southward nearly 50 mi.

Northward from Lake Titicaca the western range turns northwestward, while the eastern range, which has already in the Cordillera Real taken a northwesterly trend, turns still farther to the west and cuts off the altiplano by merging with the western range in a rough mountain mass known as the Nudo de Vilcanota. The eastern cordillera, there called the Cordillera de Carabaya, is a lofty snow-capped range separated from the Cordillera Real by a narrow and relatively low divide between the headwaters of the Mapiri river (a tributary of the Beni) and the Lake Titicaca drainage. On the west flank of the Cordillera de Carabaya is a group of glacial lakes in narrow depressions between the spurs of the range. There is no record of any soundings having been made in them, but from descriptions of their deep colouring and the character of the depressions in which they lie, they appear to be among the deepest of the high glacial-fed lakes of the Andes. The Cordillera of Carabaya lowers very rapidly to the northeast to the Amazon plain, and larger tributaries of the Beni cut directly across the lines of low ranges which front it on the east. Farther north, however, the valleys of the tributaries of the Madre de Dios have a longitudinal trend and have cut deep troughs oriented from southeast to northwest like the ridges which separate them.

The Peruvian Plateau.—The Andes of Peru, north from the Nudo de Vilcanota, are usually described as three distinct ranges which merge in the Nudo de Pasco and then continue north again as separate ranges. Recent studies show that they are a single broad plateau from 13,000 to 15,000 ft. high, on which narrow cordilleras rise to 18,000 and 21,000 ft.; and that the *nudos* or knots are only gigantic erosion remnants. The Amazon tributaries have cut deep gorges almost to the western edge of the plateau, while the numerous streams of the arid Pacific slope are short and, with the exception of the Rímac and Santa rivers, carry little water as far as the ocean.

The Andes are divided into three natural regions—the montaña, the eastern slopes of the Amazon forest; the sierra, the temperate regions of the slopes and secondary valleys of the

BERNARD G. SILBERSTEIN FROM EUROPEAN

URUBAMBA RIVER AND VALLEY IN THE ANDES, CUZCO DEPARTMENT, PERU

plateau; and the *puna*, cold, monotonous regions in the cordilleras, of vast extent at altitudes of from 10,000 to 15,000 ft. In isolated sections above the *puna* are areas known as *jalcas*, which resemble the paramos of Colombia and Ecuador. They are covered with a dense, steppelike vegetation that varies but little from season to season. Northwest of the Nudo de Vilcanota is a narrow trough sunk below the level of the plateau to an elevation of 11,000 ft., known as the Cuzco valley, from the city of Cuzco which lies at its upper end, on the site of the ancient Inca capital. The trough is 19 mi. long and is divided into three basins of flat-lying land arranged like the links of a chain. Its bordering rims have an average altitude of 13,500 ft., with peaks exceeding 14,500 ft., and are cut through in many places by streams leading to the Urubamba and Apurímac rivers. The valley itself is drained by the Huantaney river which flows through the chain of basins and joins the Urubamba through a broad pass in the mountain wall. The most broken section of the Peruvian Andes is between Abancay and Huancayo where the Apurímac, Pachachaca, Pampas and Mantaro rivers have cut deep gorges 6,000 ft. and more below the surface of the *puna*. The zone of the interoceanic water divide is there a gently undulating plateau, with lakes of glacial origin which the recently eroded valleys have not yet reached. The many secondary valleys, such as those of Ayacucho and Lircay, have long been centres of grain cultivation.

From the Huancayo to Cerro de Pasco the plateau is chiefly the basin of the upper Mantaro river. In the Cordillera de Huarochiri through which the Central railway from Lima to La Oroya cuts, at an altitude of nearly 16,000 ft., on red porphyritic sandstones between crests of dark andesites, the divide rises to elevations of over 17,000 ft. On the western slopes of the Cordillera de Huarochiri are many glacial cirques, and immediately north of the route of the Central railway as it enters the cordillera is a great cluster of lakes at different levels, still fed by glaciers, which drain into the Rímac river close to the edge of the plateau. East of the crest a network of glaciated valleys with many lakes descends in steps to the Mantaro river. East of the Mantaro a little-known range, whose snow-capped summits approach 16,500 ft., cuts off the horizon northeast of the plain of Jauja. Its altitude diminishes to the northwest, and north of Tarma no longer carries permanent snow.

The Mantaro river rises at an altitude of about 15,000 ft., near the mining town of Cerro de Pasco, in a marshy plain with many shallow lakes. Most of these are only small ponds, but Lake Junín, the largest of them, is about 20 mi. long. A group of partially glacier-fed lakes close to the main divide, of which Lake Punrún (7 mi. long) is the largest, also drains to the Mantaro river near the outlet of Lake Junín. The Mantaro flows southeastward in a long limestone gorge to the plains of Jauja and

Huancayo. These plains stand at 12,500 ft. and 11,600 ft. respectively, and together form a depression, 25 mi. long by 6 to 8 mi. wide, bordered on both sides by rows of bare hills behind which rise snow-capped ranges. The Mantaro leaves the depression in a deep gorge and swings round in a great bend to the Amazon plain about 80 mi. below Huancayo. The Cerro de Pasco region, north of the plain of Junín, has been given great importance in descriptions of the Peruvian Andes as a mountain knot in which are merged three distinct cordilleras. In reality it does not exceed the altitude of the *puna* and is only a fragment of the continuous plateau of sandstones and limestones, with occasional crests of andesite, which extends north of the plain of Junín and south between the plains of Junín and Jauja.

From Cerro de Pasco to the Pongo de Manseriche the plateau forms the drainage basin of the Huallaga and the upper Marañón rivers. Northwest of Cerro de Pasco the Cordillera de Huayhuash forms the interoceanic divide. The Marañón river flows from a chain of glacier-fed lakes on its northeast flank, while on the same slope, a short distance to the south, are the sources of the Huallaga river. The Huallaga valley is fairly wide as far as the gorge east of Huánuco in which it turns northward toward the Amazon and the valley floors of both the main streams and its tributaries in the plateau are well irrigated and have a considerable population. Below the Huánuco the Huallaga is a swift-flowing stream, with many rapids and gorges, and flows in a northerly direction through the foothills and low ranges for 180 mi. before it finally breaks through to the Amazon plain in the gorge or *pongo* of Aguirre, at latitude 6° 30′ S. The Marañón flows in a deep trench and has only a sparse population of Indian communities, which occupy the upper basins of its affluents, and occasional sugar plantations at the mouth of the larger tributaries or at rare points where the valley widens.

The Cordillera Blanca, north of the Cordillera de Huayhuash, has the same southeast to northwest trend as the latter but stands slightly to the west of its axis. These are both lofty snow-capped ranges with elevations that may be classed among the highest of the whole Andean highland, Cerro Carnicero in the Cordillera de Huayhuash being 21,688 ft. high and Cerro Huascarán in the Cordillera Blanca 22,198 ft. The valley of the Santa river (known as the Callejón de Huaylas), which separates the Cordillera Blanca from the Cordillera Negra (so called because its crests do not exceed 16,800 ft. and, therefore, bear no permanent snow), is the most densely populated district of this section of the Andes. The river has its source in Lake Conococha in the high *puna*; flows, with a descent of 6,500 ft. in 60 mi., through a string of lacustrine basins of rich alluvial soil; and carries a large permanent stream through a gorge across the Cordillera Negra to the Pacific ocean.

Ecuador.—North of the Peru-Ecuador boundary the plateau is higher, rising to altitudes of over 10,000 ft., but the interoceanic divide continues narrow as far north as latitude 3° S. From there northward to the Nudo de Pasto, in southern Colombia, the Andes appear to be a single broad plateau, the top of which is in places 40 mi. wide, surmounted by irregularly distributed volcanic masses which rise to elevations from 11,000 to 12,000 ft. above the plateau, and divide it into a number of separate basins (*hoyas*) at an average elevation of from 7,500 to 9,000 ft. It has been the custom to describe this section of the Andes as consisting of two parallel cordilleras (a western cordillera and an eastern cordillera, or Cordillera Real) with a high plateau between them which is divided into separate basins by cross ranges from the main cordilleras. Present knowledge does not support this description, and it seems to be only the rather general north and south alignment of some of the outstanding volcanoes on the east and west borders of the basins and, particularly, of the Quito and Latacunga-Riobamba basins themselves, that has given rise to such a characterization. In the interior basins is concentrated the population of the plateau. Their rich volcanic soil and temperate climate had permitted their Indian inhabitants to attain, long before the conquest, a state of civilization far above the savage. They are in the rain-shadow of the mountain masses which enclose them on the east and west, and have, at the most, only moderate rainfall and, in some cases, require irrigation. By contrast, both outer slopes have very heavy rainfall at about the level of the basins and are covered with luxuriant vegetation, while above 10,000 to 11,000 ft. they have very heavy rainfall on both sides. These high regions of heavy rainfall are the regions of the paramos, cold, desolate areas on both the slopes of the cordilleras and on the cross ranges, with a covering of moss and other bog growths and enshrouded in almost perpetual mist.

The Cuenca basin, in the south, and the Latacunga-Ambato and Riobamba basins, in the central plateau, drain to the Amazon; while the Alausí basin, north of the Cuenca basin, and the Quito and Ibarra basins in the north, drain to the Pacific. The Andes in this section slope steeply to both the Pacific and the Amazon plains. The streams from the basins have, therefore, steep gradients. Because of this and the steady supply of water from the adjoining mountaintop paramos, the streams have eroded deep beds and few lakes remain, of which San Pablo, in the Ibarra basin, is the only one of considerable area. Erosion is slight at the parts of the basins farthest from the outlet through the mountains, but deepens rapidly as the outlet is approached. In the case of the Guallabamba river, which drains the Quito basin, the total depth is over 3,000 ft., of which 1,200 is a steep-sided canyon.

An essential characteristic of the northern half of the Andes of Ecuador is the volcanoes which not only border the western side of the interior basins, from Chimborazo to the Nudo de Pasto in southern Colombia and the eastern side from nearly latitude 2° S. to the equator, but are grouped in many places between the basins and, in places, stand completely in them. They really owe more than half their height to the base of ancient rocks on which they stand, but so impressive are they that even conscientious observers have frequently exaggerated the steepness of their slopes. The principal volcanoes of the more westerly line of volcanoes are Chimborazo (20,702 ft.), Canhuairazo (16,784 ft.), Quilotoa (13,156 ft.), Illiniza (17,398 ft.), Pichincha (15,705 ft.), Cotacachi (16,292), Cimbal (15,715 ft.) and Chiles (15,682 ft.); of the eastern, Altar (17,729), Tungurahua (16,689 ft.), Cotopaxi (19,498 ft.), Antisana (18,228 ft.) and Cayambe (19,160 ft.). Sangay (17,464 ft.) lies still farther to the east, and Sumaco (12,559 ft.), which is believed to be a volcanic cone, lies far out on the eastern slope east of the Cordillera Guacamayo.

The eastern slopes of the Andes of Ecuador are little known. Recent explorers have described the Amazon lowland as joining the base of the plateau at elevations averaging between 3,600 and 4,000 ft., and sloping gently eastward with a descent of 1,000 ft. in the first 70 mi. There has been no exploration of the southern part of the lowland. North of the Napo river recent explorations have revealed a number of short ranges and mountain masses of moderate elevation rising above the general level. Among these are the Cordillera Guacamayo and the Cordillera Galeras, with elevations reaching 8,000 ft. and 6,000 ft., respectively, and the cone-shaped Sumaco. Still farther north a short range on the equator called the Cordillera Lumbaki and two high mountain masses northwest of Sumaco have been discovered.

The Cordilleras of Colombia.—In southern Colombia the Andes divide into three separate ranges: the western cordillera, or Cordillera de Chocó; the central cordillera, or Cordillera del Quindio; and the eastern cordillera, or Cordillera de Bogotá. The valley of the Magdalena river, which separates the eastern cordillera from the central, and part, at least, of the Patía and Cauca valley between the central and western cordilleras are not narrow, eroded trenches but broad tectonic depressions with a deep alluvial cover. The western cordillera forms the coast range of Colombia in the south and, to the north, extends on the east side of the valleys of the San Juan and Atrato rivers to the Caribbean coast. It is the lowest of the cordilleras, with elevations varying, in the southern section, from a little over 5,000 ft. on the Pacific railway between Buenaventura and Cali to 7,200 ft. west of Cartago and 10,000 ft. west of Popayán, and rising to elevations of 11,000 and 13,000 ft. in the west and northwest of the province of Antioquia. The southern 250 mi. of the depression between the western and central cordilleras is occupied by a series of three broad longitudinal plains. The southernmost is drained by the Patía river to the Pacific ocean, while the northernmost, with a length equal to the combined length of the other two, is the famous Cauca valley and drains to the Magdalena by the Cauca river. The central plain, in which is the city of Popayán, contains the low divide between these two drainage basins. Its elevation (6,000 ft.) is 3,000 ft. higher than those of the Cauca and Patía plains, and its northern and southern borders are, therefore, deeply trenched. The Cauca plain has many aspects of an old lake basin filled with detritus. The city of Cali stands slightly above the level of the plain on a gently sloping alluvial fan. North of the Cauca plain the Cauca river flows by a series of gorges through a region of hills and valleys between the western and central cordilleras. Its lower plain is bordered by gradually disappearing spurs until it finally merges in the plains of the lower Magdalena river.

The central cordillera is the highest of the cordilleras of Colombia and the shortest, its last spurs disappearing south of the junction of the Cauca river with the Magdalena, 170 mi. from the Caribbean. It contains the only recent volcanoes in the Colombian Andes. Of these, Tolima (18,425 ft.) and Ruiz (18,340 ft.) are the most important. At latitude 5° 30′ N. the cordillera widens to form the plateau of Antioquia, whose last spurs extend as far as 8° N., where they are lost in the plains of the Magdalena. This plateau appears to be a block of ancient crystalline rocks with intrusions of diorites and diabases divided into two parts by the deep trench of the Porce and Nechi rivers. The groups of highlands on both sides of the Porce river preserve, in their gently broken surfaces, traces of a very ancient cycle of erosion. The larger of these covers an area of about 1,200 sq.mi. N. of Medellín and has an average elevation of 8,500 ft., with diminishing heights toward the northeast. The other extends southeast of Medellín, and contains the upper valley of the Nare or Negro river. Medellín, the second city of Colombia, occupies an advantageous position in the Porce valley, where it widens out for a distance of about eight miles into a fertile alluvial plain.

The eastern cordillera is somewhat analogous to the Andes of Ecuador in that its most marked characteristic is a series of high intermontane plains or savannas, at a nearly uniform elevation of 8,000 to 9,000 ft., of which the most important are at the headwaters of the Bogotá, Suárez and Sogamoso rivers on the eastern border of the Magdalena basin. Their subsoil is formed of beds of fine gravels and clays, with some beds of peat, and the majority contain shallow lagoons and bogs which are partly submerged during the rainy season. Most of them have areas in their centres too wet for cultivation, so that the population is grouped about their edges. These high savannas were the centre of the precolonial Chibcha civilization and now contain a third of the entire population of Colombia. The Savanna de Bogotá is the largest and most densely populated of them, and has only a narrow strip of useless bog land in its centre. Bogotá is built on its eastern edge.

East of Girardot and Honda the cordillera is a series of parallel ranges, running from south-southwest to north-northeast, of which only the easternmost, the Sierra de Cocuy (18,044 ft.), reaches the level of permanent snow. North of the Sogamoso river the ranges have a north-south direction and in the latitude of Bucaramanga are united in a broad block. Farther north the central ranges stop and the western and eastern continue on, diverging toward the north and northeast as the Cordillera de Ocaña, of which the Sierra de Perijá forms the boundary between Colombia and Venezuela, west of Lake Maracaibo. Northeast of the delta of the Magdalena river, the Sierra Nevada de Santa Marta, a triangular massif with steep slopes to the north and west, rises abruptly from the Caribbean coast to snowy summits 17,000 ft. high. It is separated from the Sierra de Perijá by the valleys of the César and Ranchería rivers.

A great many lakes exist in the cordillera east of Bogotá and on both sides of the upper Sogamoso, but the paramos have usually gentle forms and show traces of a long erosion period. It is, however, only on the high plains and the paramos that the streams of the interior now meander. They are rapidly cutting the greater part of their courses and upon leaving the savannas they flow through deep canyons. The falls of Tequendama southwest of

Bogotá are the most striking example of the manner in which these streams have dissected the borders of the high plains, but the Suárez and Sogamoso rivers exhibit the same characteristics. Tributaries of the Orinoco river have cut through the eastern range to the neighbourhood of the savannas at points south of the Sogamoso and Tunja rivers. South of Bogotá the eastern cordillera is narrow. The Paramo de Sumapaz reaches elevations of 14,000 ft., and snow remains there throughout most of the year, but farther south the range is much lower. In the Sierra de Motilones, which forms its northern extremity, the cordillera narrows to about 16 mi., and its highest crests do exceed 12,000 ft.

Venezuela.—The Andes of Venezuela are separated from the eastern cordillera of Colombia by a depression of about 4,600 ft. altitude, between the Táchira and Torbes rivers, and extend northeast and east for about 500 mi., across the northern part of the country. Transverse valleys cut them into three sections, the area and altitude of which decrease from west to east. The westernmost section, from the sources of the Torbes river to the sources of the Tocuyo river, is known as the Sierra de Mérida. It is about 160 mi. long and 30 to 50 mi. wide. Its snow-capped summits are all above 10,000 ft., and in the Sierra de Santo Domingo and the Sierra de Mérida exceed 16,000 ft. In the Andes of Venezuela the coastal sierras have a west to east direction, and are separated from a second line of much lower mountains by a depression in which are the basins of Lake Valencia and the Tuy river. Eastward from Puerto Cabello the range rises steeply from the coast. Its western end is only a little over 5,000 ft. high near Nirgua, but it reaches 9,000 ft. on the Silla de Caracas northeast of Caracas, and falls to 7,500 ft. west of Cape Codera. The Caracas valley, in which is the city of Caracas at an altitude of 2,600 ft., is only six miles from the sea, and is not a part of the central depression. It appears to be, rather, a subsided local block covered with alluvial soil.

East of Cape Codera the Gulf of Barcelona interrupts the mountain zone for a distance of 80 mi. Only a narrow line of sandstones and limestones continues eastward from the interior range along the flat coast. Its altitude lowers rapidly from 4,000 to 1,600 ft., and it is completely interrupted by the Unari and Aragua rivers, which drain a part of the llanos to the Gulf of Barcelona. The Sierra de Cumaná extends for 80 mi. between the Aragua river and the Gulf of Paria. Its interior is a massif of sandstones and folded limestones which rises to 7,500 ft. in the Cerro Turumiquire. The double peninsula of Araya and Paria is a narrow belt of crystalline schists, with an altitude of 1,300 ft. west of the town of Carúpano and a little over 3,000 ft. at its eastern end near the Boca del Dragón, beyond which it is continued as the northern range of Trinidad Island.

Geology.—The beds of the Primary series are found in the Andes in a longitudinal zone on the eastern side of the cordillera. They form the eastern part of the plateaus of Bolivia and northern Argentina, where the high anticlinal ranges are of Cambrian quartzites, while Silurian schists, surrounding the recent granite crests of the Cordillera Real, cut by deep valleys and overlapped in the synclines by Devonian and Secondary red sandstones, form the base of the series. They are found, also as Silurian sandstones, schists and Devonian sandstones, on the eastern side of the Chile-Argentine cordillera as far south as latitude 35° S. and in the precordillera.

The zone of the Secondary beds is of much greater length. Breccias and porphyritic conglomerates are the most common formation, forming almost the whole of the western part of the Andean system. In Peru they are succeeded to the east by gray limestones, which cover the greater part of the plateau. Still farther east, on the Marañón and upper Huallaga rivers, the ridges are of Secondary sandstones above Silurian schists. In Ecuador the Secondary conglomerates of the western side of the plateau rest directly upon the Andean gneisses and mica schists, of which the eastern part is composed. In Colombia the central cordillera is formed of mica schists, with almost no trace of sedimentary covering; while, in the eastern cordillera, even on the border of the plains of the Orinoco, the conditions that prevail farther south are completely reversed and the Secondary beds have their greatest development. The importance of the Secondary marine deposits in the Andes, especially in the Jurassic and Cretaceous series, seems to indicate that, during the Secondary period the region of the Andes was a geosyncline inundated by the sea between two continental masses, one of which occupied the place of the present Pacific ocean. The relations between the Andes and the *vorland* to the east is obscured by an enormous development of alluvial forms which partly cover the zone of contact between the lowlands and the cordilleras. It has been suggested that it is a rigid zone against which were exerted the forces to which the folding of the geosynclinal Andes was due.

The beginning of the folding of the Andes dates from the upper Cretaceous and continued during a part, at least, of the Tertiary. Tertiary marine forms are, therefore, lacking in the interior of the cordillera and are known only in eastern Patagonia, on the extreme edge of the cordillera. The Tertiary is represented in the greater part of the Andes by continental deposits without fossils, which furnish no precise information on the age of the folding. North of the Patagonian Andes as far as latitude 4° S. the western ranges contain Jurassic rocks and porphyritic rocks of similar age folded together. Both are of interest, the Jurassic because they are the only marine sediments of that age south of the equator, the porphyritics because they are the most important evidence there is of volcanic activity in Mesozoic times. North of latitude 4° S. the Jurassic and porphyritic rocks are comparatively rare and the Primary rocks are absent. The majority of geological cross sections that have been made in the Andes indicates foldings of the simple Jura type rather than the complex type of the Alps. The cross sections are, however, still comparatively few, and greater complexity may be revealed by further studies.

Evidence of the uplift of the Andes is found not only in the existence of Tertiary and Quaternary marine deposits on the Pacific coast and many examples of uplifted shore-lines but also in the frequent occurrence throughout the cordillera of surfaces which could only have been formed at an altitude near sea level. These. areas are found even in the more humid parts, where the contrast between them and the deep ravines of the headwater streams which are now invading them is most striking. The peneplain has been most completely conserved, however, in the desertic Maritime cordillera of northern Chile and southern Bolivia. In the terracing of the valleys, particularly on the eastern side of the cordillera, there is evidence of a succession of vertical movements, interrupted by periods of rest; while in the coastal terraces all the way from Paita to Antofagasta there is evidence not only of periods of rest but also of at least one subsidence followed by an uplift, which is still in progress at the present time. In fact, along the entire western seaboard the region has suffered enormous disturbances in the past, while the frequent earthquakes that have occurred in recent years in many parts of the coastal region and the cordillera are evidence that these disturbances are still going on. The abrupt transition from high tableland to abysmal ocean depths that is characteristic of the entire coast indicates the remarkably unstable condition of the region. In addition to the general or regional movements of uplift and subsidence, the existence of drop faulting has been noted throughout the whole length of the cordillera. The upper Magdalena valley, the Cuzco basin, the Iglesia and Calingasta valleys between the cordillera and the precordilleras of Argentina, and the central valleys of Chile have all been thus explained.

The volcanoes of the Andes occur in three notable groups, southern Colombia and northern Ecuador, southern Peru and northern Chile, and the group of central Chile, Neuquén and Patagonia. All types are present, from ancient volcanoes almost completely destroyed by erosion and extinct volcanoes, with or without craters but still fresh in form, to active volcanoes. They have played an important part in the leveling of the interior basins. Fluid lavas exposed appear only on the Patagonian plateau. Elsewhere the lavas are chiefly of the viscous acidic type and, although accumulated to great depths in many places (as much as $1\frac{1}{2}$ mi. deep in the Cordillera de Vilca pampa in southern Peru), have not been removed far from the craters. The volcanic ash, however, has been carried away by erosion in such quantities that they have overcharged the streams and filled depressions and valleys to a great depth.

Climate.—It is not on the equator but between latitude 15° and 20° S. that the highest temperatures of the Andes are found, and it is necessary to go south of the tropics to find mean annual temperatures comparable to those on the equator. The abnormal depression of temperatures in the equatorial Andes is due to the heavy rainfall, and it is the lack of rainfall that raises the temperatures to the south. The effect of the higher temperatures of the drier Andes is to elevate the upper limit of agriculture and human occupation. In Colombia the highest agricultural zone is between 6,500 and 10,000 ft., while on the moister portions of the Bolivia altiplano agriculture is carried on over 3,000 ft. higher. The rich agricultural basins of Cuzco and Jauja, if they lay at the same elevation in the humid equatorial Andes, would not belong to the agricultural regions at all. The lower limit of the colder agricultural zone is not, however, parallel to the upper limit, and as one leaves the equator frosts occur at lower and lower levels. As a result, sugar cane, which grows at a level of 6,500 ft. and more in Ecuador and Colombia, does not reach above 3,000 ft. in northern Argentina.

The lower limit of perpetual snow in the tropical Andes is between 15,000 and 16,000 ft. Because of the increasing aridity, it rises rapidly south of the equatorial region to 17,000 ft. on the western ranges of the Peruvian Andes, above Lima, and to 18,000 and 20,000 ft. in the summits that border the Puna de Atacama, to the northeast. South of the Puna de Atacama it lowers again to 18,000 ft. in the Famatina ranges, and to between 14,500 and 16,500 ft. in the ranges of Juan and Mendoza. From these it falls rapidly to 6,500 ft. at latitude 37° S., 5,000 ft. at 40° S., and 2,300 ft. on Tierra del Fuego. In the tropical and subtropical sections of the Andes the present glaciers rarely extend beyond the snow line. South of 40° S., however, they have more extensive fields of supply, and come well down into the valleys. South of 46° S. the ice fields, though only a shrunken remnant of the ice fields of the Glacial period, still form a continuous cap over the entire central zone of the cordillera. Throughout the Andes there have been recognized, in front of the present glaciers and in regions today free of ice, glacial moraines, cirques, outwash plains and lakes confined behind glacial dams, which are proof of several periods of extensive Quaternary glaciation.

Minerals.—Mining is an important industry in all of the Andean countries. In Chile and Bolivia it far exceeds all other industries in the value of its products. The most important mineral deposits are those of the younger igneous rocks which include the gold quartz lodes of Colombia, the silver-bearing copper deposits of Peru and Chile, and the tin-silver-bismuth deposits of Bolivia. The copper deposits, which are found in many sections of the Andes but are particularly abundant in Chile and Peru and, to a lesser degree, in Bolivia, differ greatly in their geological occurrence and characteristics. They occur most frequently as replacements of rock near intrusions of igneous material. At Portrerillos, Chile, they have replaced the easily soluble limestone. At the Braden mines, near Rancagua, Chile, and the Cuquicamata mines, the copper minerals have filled cracks and openings in less soluble rocks with little or no replacement. In many places, as at Cerro de Pasco, Peru, rich silver ores at the surface give place to copper ores at lower levels. The tin deposits of Bolivia are true fissure veins or desseminations filled by products of igneous intrusives. The only gems occurring in the younger igneous rocks are the emeralds of Colombia. Of the ores that occur mainly in association with the ancient crystalline rocks, gold-bearing and silver-bearing veins in the Pre-Cambrian schists, gneisses and granites, in many places in the cordilleras, and iron ore, chiefly magnetite, in Chile, are the most important. Mineral deposits of economic value in the sedimentary rocks are not extensive. Chile, Peru and Colombia have extensive coal deposits, but they are of inferior quality as compared with foreign coals and, except in Chile, are so inaccessible that they have been worked but little, except for local use. Petroleum resources have been studied intensively, and indications of oil-bearing strata have been reported on the eastern border of the Andes all the way from Venezuela to Tierra

del Fuego. The areas that are at present yielding the most valuable flows are the Maracaibo basin in Venezuela, the basin of the Sogamoso river on the western border of the eastern cordillera of Colombia, and the coastal region of northern Peru at Talara. Of the placer minerals, gold is the most important, and the extensive placer operations have of recent years been mainly confined to Colombia, particularly in the Choco district, where they yield considerable platinum.

Population.—From the standpoint of human occupation, the Andes are divided into three sections—an unpopulated section extending north to the Puna de Atacama; an arid central section from the Puna de Atacama to northern Peru, where mining is the chief industry; and a humid northern section, of which the chief industry is agriculture. The southernmost section has little mineral or agricultural resources, and the population is, therefore, not in the mountain zone but on its borders, concentrated in irrigated districts on the eastern side and more uniformly distributed in the central valleys of Chile on the western side. In the Puna de Atacama there is a sparse population of shepherds, and a still smaller element engaged in collecting salt from the salars for sale in the settlements on the mountain border. From there north to the Caribbean sea, however, the greater part of the population of the west coast and Caribbean republics, and, with few exceptions, the chief cities, are on the plateau. This populated section of the Andes contains a third of the whole population of South America. It consists of two sections of distinctly different character. The southern and more arid section is a region in which mining is the dominant industry, and practically the only source of export. All other industries are maintained for the purpose of supplying it with food, clothing and means of transportation. Railways which penetrate into the cordillera from the Pacific coast were constructed solely to transport the products of the mines to the nearest ports. The influence of the mining industry, since the mining districts are mainly on the high paramos, combined with climatic conditions to raise human habitation to levels which are among the highest in the world. Since before the conquest the characteristic of this section of the Andes has been the establishment of small agricultural communities on the alluvial floors of high, sheltered valleys close to the mining centres which form the sole market for their produce. In the more humid Andes of Ecuador, Colombia and Venezuela mining is of secondary importance; the chief industries are agricultural and the chief exports the products of the tropical levels—cacao in Ecuador, coffee in Colombia and Venezuela. There the internal trade is not the supplying of agricultural products to a dominant industry but an exchange of products between zones at different levels and, therefore, of different climates.

Transportation.—Throughout the populated sections of the Andes, transportation between different parts of the plateau, between the plateau and the eastern lowlands and, to a considerable extent, between the plateau and the Pacific coast continued to be chiefly by pack trail. The mule came to be the principal pack animal, largely supplanting the llama of preconquest times, although the latter was still used locally in large numbers. In parts of Colombia the ox was still used for long trips with bulky commodities such as coffee and tobacco, while in the montañas of the eastern slopes and in the Chocó region of Colombia, transportation remained dependent upon Indian bearers. Everywhere the *arrieros,* or muleteers, became an important element of the population. Whereas the railway supplanted the pack train on most of the long routes from the plateau to the Pacific coast, the number of *arrieros* in the Andes as a whole probably was not decreased, since the penetration of the railways into the plateau increased the demand for foreign goods and, consequently, for means of distributing them from the railheads.

Except in the broad central plateau of Bolivia, the Andes offer such obstacles to road and railway construction that the west coast republics between Chile and Colombia are effectively divided into two lowland regions separated by the cordilleras. From the point of view of government administration and national solidarity, railways across the Andes to connect the two lowland regions are of much importance; but the great cost of construction and maintenance limited them. (Most rail connections in the mountain zone were built to connect important mining or agricultural districts with the nearest seaports.) The most famous of the routes crossing the Andes is the railway opened in 1911 between Los Andes, Chile, and Mendoza, Arg., which crosses the Chile-Argentine boundary by a tunnel 10,000 ft. long and 10,500 ft. above sea level, affording direct rail connection between Buenos Aires and Valparaíso. The transandine railway from the Bolivia-Argentine boundary to Uyuni was connected on the Bolivian altiplano with three railways to the Pacific coast, giving through routes from Buenos Aires to Antofagasta and Arica by rail, and by rail and steamer on Lake Titicaca, to Mollendo. In 1948 a railway between Antofagasta and Salta, Arg., was opened. Roads for motor transport have helped to improve communication in the Andes though the difficulties of construction have been great. Air travel, since the first flights over the Andes in 1918, has been of outstanding importance. (For railway lines eastward from the altiplano of Bolivia, *see* BOLIVIA. For railways, highways and air lines that penetrate the Andes in Peru, Ecuador, Colombia and Venezuela, *see* articles on these countries.)   (R. R. P.)

Mountaineering Expeditions.—Regions of the Andes offering the greatest challenge to mountaineers are found in Ecuador, Peru, Bolivia and the highest summits of the frontier between Argentina and Chile. Scientific exploration of the Andes began in the 18th century, but it was not until late in the 19th century that organized mountain climbing became established. The pioneer climbers concentrated upon the great volcanoes near the Pacific coast. Later they sought peaks farther inland, finally reaching the so-called "hidden ranges," mainly in Peru, the existence of which in many instances was unknown until the 20th century. The outstanding early climbers were Englishmen, Germans and Italians. More recently, climbers from the United States, France, the Netherlands, Belgium and Japan have appeared. After World War II, Europeans, North Americans and South Americans shared about equally in the activity.

The peaks of Ecuador were the first to be ascended and explored. Those best known among 30 important volcanoes located in the western cordillera are Cotacachi (16,292 ft.), Pichincha (15,705 ft.), Ihliniza (17,398 ft.), Canhuairazo (16,784 ft.), and Chimborazo (20,702 ft.); in the eastern cordillera, Cayambe (19,160 ft.), Antisana (18,228 ft.), Cotopaxi (19,498 ft.), Tungurahua (16,689 ft.), Altar (17,729 ft.) and Sangay (17,464 ft.). Chimborazo and Cotopaxi, whose summits are dominant in the group, were the objectives of the first climbing expeditions. Cotopaxi is usually regarded as the most active fire mountain in the world and one of the most beautiful.

The volcanic region of Ecuador was investigated between 1736 and 1744 by one of the first scientific expeditions to study a mountain range. This was led by Pierre Bouguer and C. M. de la Condamine of France and Antonio de Ulloa and Jorge Juan of Spain. From data gathered by this expedition it was concluded that Chimborazo was the highest mountain in the world, a misconception that persisted until the Himalayas and the southern Andes became known. In 1802 the German scientist Alexander von Humboldt and his companions, Aimé Bonpland and Carlos Montúfar, made attempts on the summits of Chimborazo and Cotopaxi, failing in each instance but reaching a height of 19,286 ft. on the former. Joseph Boussingault, in an attempt on Chimborazo in 1831, attained 19,698 ft. Chimborazo was finally ascended in 1880 by the great English alpinist Edward Whymper (*q.v.*), who had been first to climb the Matterhorn 15 years previously. In addition to Chimborazo, which he climbed twice, Whymper reached the summits of Cotopaxi, Sincholagua, Cayambe, Antisana, Saraurcu, Canhuairazo and Cotacachi. Hans Meyer and Rudolph Reschriter made two attempts upon Chimborazo in 1903, both unavailing, but ascended Cotopaxi and several other peaks.

Following the successes on the Ecuadorian volcanoes, mountaineers looked to the southern Andes for new peaks to conquer. One of the major triumphs there was the ascent of Aconcagua (22,831 ft.), the highest summit in the Americas. Lying on the boundary between Chile and Argentina, the peak itself is in Mendoza province of Argentina. The first attempt on Aconcagua was made in 1883 by Paul Güssfeldt, a noted German climber, who reached a point 1,300 ft. below the summit. Aconcagua fell to Stuart Vines and Matthias Zurbriggen of the Edward A. Fitzgerald expedition in 1896–97. Sir Martin Conway, another well known British climber, made the ascent soon thereafter.

The third great Andean region for mountaineering is in Peru and Bolivia. In Peru it was Huascarán (22,198 ft.), in the Cordillera Blanca, that first lured the mountaineers. In 1904 C. R. Enock, an Englishman, reached 17,000 ft. before being forced to retreat. In the same year, and again in 1906 and 1908, Miss Annie S. Peck of the United States made several attempts on Huascarán, finally reaching the north summit of the mountain's twin peaks. In the period 1932–39 members of the Austro-German Alpine club ascended the south summit of Huascarán and 14 other peaks exceeding 20,000 feet. In 1952 the summit of Huantsán (20,981 ft.) was reached by members of the Dutch party which included C. G. Egeler, T. de Booy and the French alpinist Lionel Terray. The Franco-Belgian expedition, with Georges Kogan, Raymond Leininger and their wives, climbed Alpamayo (20,080 ft.) in 1951. In the nearby Cordillera Huayhuash the summit of the formidable Yerupaja (21,765 ft.), also known as El Carnicero ("The Butcher"), was attained in 1950 by two members of the Harvard Andean expedition, David Harrah of Stanford university and James C. Maxwell of Harvard. Farther south in Peru rises Coropuna (21,079 ft.), a massive mountain of gently rounded form, first climbed in 1911 by members of the Yale Peruvian expedition led by Hiram Bingham.

Among the Andean ranges in Bolivia, the peaks bordering the plateau on the north, called the Cordillera Real, are better known to mountaineers than those to the south. Illimani (21,184 ft.), near La Paz, is the best known of this group. Conway ascended the most southerly of Illimani's twin peaks in 1898 in the belief that it was the higher of the two; it was not until 1950 that the north peak was discovered to be about 100 ft. higher. Sajama (21,555 ft.), the highest Bolivian mountain, was climbed in 1939 by Joseph Prem, a German, and Piero Ghiglioni, an Italian.

Peaks of lesser height, but in many instances of difficult character, are found in the far northern and southern limits of the Andes. Among them is the range called Sierra Nevada de Santa Marta, rising in Colombia near the Caribbean coast. Many of the peaks there were found to exceed 18,000 ft., which ranks them among the world's highest coastal mountains. Mountaineering has also been carried on in the ranges south of Santiago, Chile, and a large number of imposing peaks there remain unclimbed. The Fuegan archipelago, in the extreme south, was explored by the English expedition, which included Charles Darwin, during the period 1826–36. Mt. Sarmiento (7,333 ft.), the highest peak of the Darwin range, was explored by Conway in 1898.

See also Index references under "Andes" in the Index volume.

(J. L. TR.)

BIBLIOGRAPHY.—E. Whymper, *Travels Amongst the Great Andes of the Equator* (1892); E. A. Fitzgerald, *The Highest Andes* (1899); Sir Martin Conway, "Explorations in the Bolivian Andes," *Geographical Journal*, vol. xiv (1899), *The Bolivian Andes* (1901); L. R. Patrón, *Cordillera de los Andes*, Repúblic de Chile, Oficina de Límites (1903 *et seq.*); Sir Thomas Holdich, "The Patagonian Andes," *Geographical Journal*, vol. xxiii (1904); Isaiah Bowman, *The Andes of Southern Peru* (1916); B. Willis, *Northern Patagonia, Character and Resources* (1914); A. C. Veatch, *Quito to Bogotá* (1917); B. L. Miller and J. T. Singewald, *The Mineral Deposits of South America* (1919); J. H. Woods, *High Spots in the Peruvian Andes* (1935); A. M. Renwick, *Wanderings in the Peruvian Andes* (1939); J. L. Rich, *The Face of South America* (1942); F. A. Carlson, *Geography of Latin America* (1952); J. Sayle, *Along the Peruvian Andes* (1953); C. G. Egeler and T. de Booy, *Challenge of the Andes: the Conquest of Mount Huantsan* (1956); C. Arthaud and F. Hébert-Stevens, *Andes: Roof of America* (1956); Preston E. James, *Latin America* (1959).

ANDESINE: *see* FELDSPAR.

ANDESITE, a great family of rocks playing an important part in the geology of most of the volcanic areas of the globe. The name first was applied to a series of lavas from the Andes. Not only the Andes but most of the cordillera of Central and North America consist largely of andesites. The same rock type is found in abundance in volcanoes along practically the entire margin of the Pacific basin outside the andesite line. The volcanoes Montagne Pelée, the Soufrière of St. Vincent, Krakatoa, Bandaisan, Popocatepetl, Fuji, Ngauruhoe, Shasta, Hood and Adams have emitted great quantities of andesitic rock.

The term andesite has been used in many different definitions. Thus it has been used for rocks containing silica from an excess represented by 35% quartz to a deficiency represented by 15% olivine or 11% nepheline; rocks containing as much as 50% ferromagnesian minerals (pyroxene, biotite, etc.) have also been included. Most commonly the term andesite is used for fine-grained, usually porphyritic rocks, corresponding roughly to diorite in composition, and consisting essentially of a soda lime or plagioclase feldspar approximately andesine in composition (60 $Na_2O.Al_2O_3.6SiO_2 - 40\ CaO.Al_2O_3.2SiO_2$) and one or more ferromagnesian minerals. Smaller amounts of sanidine or potassium-rich feldspar may be present. The plagioclase feldspar of the phenocrysts is more calcic than that of the matrix, and is usually zoned, with still more calcic cores. The larger feldspars and ferromagnesian minerals are often visible to the naked eye, lying in a finer groundmass, usually crystalline, but sometimes to a large extent glassy or vitreous. When fresh they are dark-coloured if they contain much glass, but paler in colour and red, gray or pinkish when more thoroughly crystallized. Andesites occur mainly as surface deposits, and to a lesser extent as dikes and small plugs. Many of the deposits are not normal lava flows but rather flow breccias, mud flows, tuffs and other fragmental rocks; the peperino near Rome and the trass of the Eifel district in Germany are examples. There are three great subdivisions of this family of rocks, the quartz-bearing andesites or dacites (sometimes considered to be a separate family), the hornblende- and biotite-andesites and the pyroxene-andesites. The dacites, a term first applied to quartz-bearing andesites of Transylvania or Dacia, contain primary quartz and are the most siliceous members of the family; their quartz may appear in small blebs or phenocrysts, or may occur only as minute interstitial grains in the groundmass (see DACITE); other dacites are vitreous (dacite-pitchstones). The hornblende- and biotite-andesites, being comparatively rich in feldspar like the dacites, are usually pale pink, yellow or gray. They resemble the trachytes both in appearance and in structure, but their feldspar is mostly plagioclase, not sanidine. The biotite and hornblende are alike in both of these groups of rocks and are often surrounded by black borders, produced by corrosion and partial resorption by the magma. Augite is common in most andesites, and bronzite or hypersthene is common in many. Pyroxene-andesites are darker, more basic rocks, with a higher specific gravity, and approach basalts and dolerites, especially when they contain a small amount of olivine. They are the commonest type of andesite, both at the present and in former geological periods, and occur in amounts comparable to those of basalt.

In addition to the accessory minerals zircon, apatite and iron oxides, which are practically never absent, certain others occur which, because of their rarity and importance, are of special interest. Sharply formed little crystals of cordierite are occasionally found in andesites, presumably from the more or less complete digestion of fragments of aluminous rocks in the molten lava, although some of these crystals were later shown to be a new mineral, osumilite. A rose-red variety of epidote is a secondary product in certain altered andesitic rocks; the famous red porphyry (porfido rosso) is of this type (see PORPHYRY).

Many theories have been proposed for the origin of andesitic rocks. Andesitic magma is commonly thought to originate from basaltic magma, either by direct crystal fractionation or by reaction with siliceous rocks of the continents. Many ore deposits of gold, silver and other metals are associated with andesitic rocks. In most such cases, however, the minerals of the andesite have been altered to form an aggregate of chlorite, epidote, zeolites, carbonates and hematite termed propylite. The genetic relationships of this alteration to the ore are not certain.

(E. RR.)

ANDHRA PRADESH is one of the constituent states of the Republic of India, and was redefined by the States Reorganization act which came into force on Nov. 1, 1956. The realignment of the states of peninsular India was on a language basis and Andhra Pradesh is designed to include the bulk of the Telugu-speaking peoples. Prior to independence in 1947 the majority of Telugu speakers were in Madras presidency north of Madras city and in the eastern half of Hyderabad appropriately known as Telingana. In 1953 Andhra was first constituted a separate state by the partition of Madras; the big addition in 1956 was of half of Hyderabad when Hyderabad city became the capital. Hyderabad city had a population (1961) of 931,082. Other large towns are Vijayavada, Warangal, Guntur, Vishakhapatnam and Rajahmundry, all over 100,000. Andhra is bounded by Madras on the south; Mysore on the west; Maharashtra, Madhya Pradesh and Orissa on the north and by the Bay of Bengal on the east.

Physical Geography.—The state comprises two distinct parts: the western half which lies on the plateau of peninsular India and the eastern half which consists of coastal plains. The Andhra section of the plateau, in contrast with the lava-covered areas of the former Bombay state, consists of ancient metamorphic rocks. In places these are mineralized but the chief mineral product of the state is the mica of Nellore. The old rocks yield an indifferent soil and, as the state as a whole suffers from a low and somewhat precarious rainfall, cultivation is mainly in the shallow basins in the plateau surface where streams are dammed to form temporary lakes or tanks. These conserve the water beyond the rainy season but dry up later in the year. The plateau in the southern part of Andhra lies in the basin of the Penner river. Large-scale irrigation works were attempted many years ago but were only partly successful. The heart of the plateau lies in the basin of the great Krishna (q.v.) river. On its tributary, the Tungabhadra, a huge dam, inaugurated in 1953, irrigates nearly 1,000,000 ac. in Andhra and Mysore. The Nagarjunasagar irrigation and hydroelectric scheme on the main river was started in 1955. In the north of the state is the Godavari river; and on the Machkund river a joint scheme with the government of Orissa provides both hydroelectric power and irrigation water.

Although the eastern edge of the Deccan plateau is known as the Eastern Ghats it does not form a continuous range, being broken by the great river valleys. Spurs and isolated hills extend into parts of the coastal plain, but where the latter is broad it has been built up by the alluvial deltas of the great rivers, affording much fertile agricultural land.

Along this coastal belt is found an interesting range in climate. In the south, near Madras, October-November rains are added to the rains of the normal Indian wet season, June-September, but northward rainfall becomes inadequate. Irrigation is needed in the delta lands of Guntur, Krishna and Godavari districts, but northward again, along the Northern Circars (Sarkars) coast toward Orissa, the rainfall increases once more. (L. D. S.)

History.—The country of the Andhras is mentioned in Asokan inscriptions and appears in Sanskrit literature: it lay between Kalinga and Dravida; i.e., Orissa and Nellore. Jainism and Buddhism, once flourishing in Andhra, became extinct there by about the 9th century, except as philosophies. Well-known to the Puranas, the Satavahana, Satakarni or Andhra dynasty ruled the Deccan from the 1st century B.C. to the 3rd century A.D. except when expelled from its western side by Kshaharata satraps in the 1st century A.D. Simuka is said to have killed the last Brahman king of the Kanva dynasty in the Ganges valley about 28 B.C. Gautamiputra Yajna Sri was the most powerful Satavahana ruler. Successors of the dynasty were the Vakatakas (north central Deccan), Ikshvakus (east central), Pallavas (southeast) and Vishnukundins (east coast). Acquiring the greater part of the east coast the Pallavas from their capital at Kanchi or Kancheepuram (q.v.) fostered the arts and trade with the west and with Burma, and furthered the Hindu cultural colonization of southeast Asia. The Western Chalukyas (see CHALUKYA) gained a hold on Vengi (between the Godavari and the Krishna), and the Eastern Chalukyas ruled there as the Pallavas' rivals. In the 9th century the Cholas (q.v.) extinquished Pallava power, and the Eastern Chalukyas merged with the Cholas under Kulottunga in 1070. Thereafter the Western Chalukyas occupied Vengi fitfully until the Kakatiyas of Warangal subordinated it to an inland Andhra power. Ganapati Kakatiya, Rudramba (praised by Marco Polo) and Pratapa Rudra administered efficiently and founded Andhra nationality. Pressure from Delhi destroyed the dynasty in 1323. Muslims controlled as far south as the Krishna by 1354. After the disappearance of the Eastern Gangas of Orissa in the early 15th century, the Andhra coast was ruled by Reddis and Chodas, whose rivalries invited Muslim intervention and subsequently Vijayanagar conquest. The Gajapati dynasty of Orissa fought Vijayanagar (1428), annexing the Reddis' lands in 1446. Kapilesvara Gajapati reached the Tamil country by 1470, but a disputed succession gave Vijayanagar access to the southern and the Muslims to the northern districts of Andhra. Before 1510, however, Purushottama Gajapati took Warangal from the sultan of Golconda, and by 1515 he submitted to Krishnadevaraya of Vijayanagar and received back Andhra north of the Krishna. Yet by the middle of the century Muslims were in power over southern Andhra.

In the 17th century, the Mogul empire absorbed the Deccan sultanates. The viceroy of the Deccan gained the Northern Circars (see CIRCAR), and appointed the Nawab of the Carnatic to the remainder of Andhra. The British gained the Northern Circars from Hyderabad and administered them, somewhat inconveniently, from Madras. Masulipatam, which had been a British "factory" since 1611, did not grow into a centre of government. Bellary and other Telugu-speaking districts were added after the Mysore wars. The ryotwari system, in which the land revenue was periodically settled with the cultivators, was found more practical than the "permanent settlement" system imitated elsewhere from Bengal. For a fuller statement on the modern history of the states out of which Andhra Pradesh was created see HYDERABAD, former state; MADRAS, state; INDIA (Bharat).

(J. D. M. D.)

Population.—The area of the state is 106,052 sq.mi. and the population, adjusted on the basis of the 1961 census, 35,977,999. This figure includes a number of backward and tribal groups (such as the Chenchu) not fully integrated into the rural population. The state includes the following districts from the old Madras presidency, with district headquarters in parentheses and population figures from the 1961 census (many of the district boundaries were changed after 1951): Anantapur (Anantapur) 1,764,223; Chittoor (Chittoor) 1,913,169; Cuddapah (Cuddapah) 1,342,140; East Godavari (Kakinada) 2,609,311; Guntur (Guntur) 3,009,997; Krishna (Masulipatam) 2,076,103; Kurnool (Nandyal) 1,909,644; Nellore (Nellore) 2,033,963; Srikakulam (Srikakulam) 2,342,291; Vishakhapatnam (Vishakhapatnam) 2,288,976; West Godavari (Eluru) 1,978,434. The town of Kurnool, in Kurnool district, was for a time the capital of Andhra Pradesh, and consequently grew much larger than Nandyal. The districts of Telingana that were transferred from the former Hyderabad state to Andhra Pradesh are as follows: Mahbubnagar; Medak; Nizamabad; Karimnagar; Adilabad; Warangal; Nalgonda, Khamman and Hyderabad. A special feature of the governmental system is the regional committee for Telingana, whose duty is to see that the views of the people of Telingana are given proper consideration.

(S. CH.)

Social Conditions.—By the 1960s primary and secondary education was being imparted in over 33,500 recognized institutions to more than 3,000,000 pupils, two-thirds of whom belonged to rural areas. Compulsory education for children of the age group 6–12 had been introduced in over 300 towns and 1,600 villages and covered more than 400,000 children. The census for 1961 recorded 29.7% literacy for males and 11.8% for females. Filariasis is endemic in some parts of the state but government efforts in the field of preventive medicine produced remarkable results in reducing its incidence and that of malaria, cholera and other diseases. In 1958–59 there were 6 medical colleges, 376 hospitals and 921 dispensaries. Thirty-three welfare extension projects were functioning by 1959. These provided free educational facilities to children, crèches, maternity centres, social education, craft training and cultural activities for women. A separate social welfare department looks after the welfare of the scheduled castes and other backward classes by providing scholarships, free books and clothes to students, wells, free housing sites, cottage industries and agricul-

tural implements.

(S. B. L. N.)

Economy.—As elsewhere in India agriculture is the leading occupation and about 16,000,000 ac. are cultivated out of an estimated total of cultivable land of 24,000,000 ac. Where irrigation is not possible the chief "dry zone" crops are millets (jowar and bajra), peanuts and cotton; wherever irrigation is possible these give place to rice with some sugar cane and also, on the Orissa border, some jute. In the early 1960s it appeared certain that the extension of irrigation, then in hand, would add greatly to the area under rice and so to the ability of the state to support its population. A specialist crop is tobacco and Andhra produces about two-fifths of India's total. A fifth of the state is forested; especially on the hills of the Eastern Ghats there are valuable stands of sal (*Shorea*) and other timber trees.

Mineral deposits include manganese, mica and a little coal. The mica belt of Nellore also has uranium deposits.

As hydroelectric power becomes available industrial development is likely to increase. Especially in and near Hyderabad city there are textile mills; elsewhere sugar mills, paper mills, cement and glass factories have been developed and there remains a wide range of cottage industries.

The coast is a gently shelving one and breakers prevent the approach to the shore. For long the only harbour serving the whole coast was the artificial one of Madras; in the 1930s Vizagapatam (now Vishakhapatnam), partly sheltered by a rocky headland known as the Dolphin's nose, was provided with an artificial harbour and was at the same time linked by railway with the heart of the northern peninsula. This remains the state's chief port; it now has an oil refinery and the chief shipbuilding yards of India. The dangerous coastwise journey for shipping was early obviated by the salt water Buckingham canal running parallel to the coast, and leading from the Krishna river to Madras.

The railway system (Southern) affords broad-gauge lines along the coastal plain from Madras to Vishakhapatnam, where the Eastern line to Howrah (Calcutta) is joined. There is a broad gauge line inland from Vijayavada (formerly Bezwada), where the Krishna is bridged, to Nagpur in the heart of the plateau, but access to the capital Hyderabad is circuitous and a mixture of gauges is involved. Roads play an important role and the state of Andhra forms a relatively compact unit.

See also separate articles on the main towns and districts.

(L. D. S.)

BIBLIOGRAPHY.—*Geography:* O. H. K. Spate, *India and Pakistan*, ch. 23 and ch. 24, pp. 670–92 (1954).
History: K. Gopalachari, *Early History of the Andhra Country* (1941); D. C. Sarkar, *Successors of the Satavahanas* (1939); R. Gopalan, *Pallavas of Kanchi* (1928); N. Venkataramanayya, *Early Muslim Expansion in S. India* (1942), *Eastern Chalukyas* (1950); K. A. Nilakanta Sastri, *Cholas*, 2nd ed. (1955); M. Somasekhara Sarma, *Forgotten Chapter in Andhra History* (1945); M. Rama Rao, "Political History of the Kakatiyas," *J. Andhra Hist. Res. Soc.*, vol. v. (1930), vol. vi (1931); Y. Vitthal Rao, "The East India Company and Andhra," *J. Andhra Hist. Res. Soc.*, vol. xxiv (1956–58), vol. xxv (1958–60).
Economics: V. V. Ramanadham, *Economy of Andhra Pradesh* (1959); A. V. Raman Rau, *Economic Development of Andhra Pradesh* (1958).

ANDIZHAN, an *oblast* and town in the Uzbek Soviet Socialist Republic, U.S.S.R. The area is drained by the Syr-Darya and most of it is under cotton cultivation. Cattle are raised where water is available. The oil fields south of Andizhan town and east of Leninsk produce oil and natural gas, the latter being piped to these two cities. There is an oil refinery at Palvantash. The population—768,000 (173,000 urban) in 1959—is mostly Uzbek. There were 450 schools and 75 libraries in the *oblast* in 1956. Uzbek and Russian newspapers are published.

Andizhan town is the capital of the *oblast* (pop. [1959] 129,000) and is a railway centre. It has cotton-ginning and cottonseed oil extracting industries, food-processing plants and metal works. It lies in an earthquake area; the earthquake in 1902 destroyed the town.

(G. E. WR.)

ANDOCIDES (c. 440–after 391 B.C.), Athenian orator and politician, was born of one of the most prominent families in Athens. His career was interrupted when he was imprisoned on suspicion during the scandal of the mutilation of the Hermae in 415 (for the occasion, and the connected case of the profanation of the Eleusinian mysteries, see ALCIBIADES). He was then induced to turn informer to stop the general panic, and though the historian Thucydides is not sure that his information was genuine it was accepted, and those who were implicated were condemned. Andocides went into exile. After two unsuccessful attempts to return, he came back under the general amnesty of 403, when Thrasybulus restored the democracy. In 400 he was tried for impiety, but he had powerful support and was acquitted. In 392, during the Corinthian War (see GREECE: History), he went with three colleagues to negotiate peace with Sparta, but Athens rejected the terms and exiled the ambassadors.

Andocides is one of a canon of ten Attic orators who are the subject of Lives of the Ten Orators, a work wrongly attributed to Plutarch. An unconvincing politician, he was the least admired of these canonical orators, though he had a gift for vivid narrative. Three of his speeches survive: On His Return; On the Mysteries, his defense in 400; and On the Peace (392). A fourth, Against Alcibiades, has been attributed to him but is spurious.

See R. C. Jebb, Selections from the Attic Orators, 2nd ed. (1888).
(A. As.)

ANDORRA, a small, autonomous principality (officially PRINCIPALITY OF ANDORRA) in the Pyrenees between France and Spain, is bounded to the north and east by the French départements of Ariège and Pyrénées-Orientales and to the south and west by the Spanish province of Lérida. The population was 5,664 in 1954, about the same as it was in 1900, and in 1963 was given as 11,356. It has an area of 180 sq.mi. and the capital is Andorra la Vella (Andorra la Vieja).

Physical Geography.—Andorra is a cluster of mountain valleys whose waters unite to form the two-branched Valira, a tributary of the Segre, chief affluent of the Ebro. The frontier with France is determined largely by the watershed; that with Spain was finally delimited in 1863. The territory is ringed, save to the southwest, by towering peaks, the highest, the Pic d'Estats, being 10,295 ft. The main Pyrenean crestline exceeds 8,000 ft. Valleys, rarely below 3,000 ft., end in steep, impassable cirques. The ports (passes) of Siguer, Soldeu and Envalira may be blocked for months at a time, while the Valira defile below Sant Julià de Loria offers little easier, if more permanent, communication with Spain. The stratigraphy shows three main bands of Paleozoic crystalline formations running east-west: a southern granitic, a central of Silurian and Devonian slate and limestone, and a northern of metamorphic gneiss, the whole overlaid with Quaternary deposits and much influenced by glacier erosion.

The climate is severe, proportionately to altitude, for much of the year; extreme winter temperatures reach 5° F. at 3,800 ft. and —22° F. at 7,800 ft. Snow lies, on an average, from a month in Andorra la Vella to 7½ months in Portella Blanca. May, June and October are the rainiest months. Above 4,500 ft. drought becomes serious, making irrigation indispensable for the high meadows, which reach to the alpine zone; it is common in the lower valleys also, where torrents limit cultivable soil, the widest stretches being found about the capital. The best soil is provided by artificially terraced slopes. Forests have been largely destroyed. Trees include the evergreen oak, pine, spruce and poplar. Game abounds: there are hare, rabbit and partridge, with quail and chamois on the heights.

People and Population.—No prehistoric remains attest settlement earlier than that to be inferred from the Greek historian Polybius for the 3rd century B.C. Iberian and Roman coins have been found near Sant Julià. The territory was among the last occupied and first evacuated by the Muslims, who left no traces. The official language is Catalan (French and Spanish are widely understood), and the official religion Roman Catholic. The population of 5,664, according to the 1954 census, excluded about 1,400 foreigners, chiefly French and Spaniards; that of the parish comprising the capital was 1,382. Cluster-type settlements are both permanent and temporary. The former, found up to 6,000 ft., are generally on slopes facing south, the largest in the plains about Andorra la Vella and Encamp. Temporary (summer) habitations range from 5,200 to 6,500 ft., peasants spending up to nine months of the year in some districts at the high villages (cortals), where pastures are held in common.

History.—Andorran independence is traditionally associated with Charlemagne and his son Louis I, who recovered Barcelona from the Muslims in 801 and is reputed to have made over to the Spanish bishop of Urgel some part of his suzerainty. The bishop's mitre and crosier figure in the country's crest. Later bishops for long saw their overlordship contested by the French counts of Foix until, in 1278, arbitration confirmed the valleys in their independence under a popularly elected council with bishop and count as co-princes pro indiviso. The rights of the house of Foix passed by marriage to that of Béarn, thence, with the accession of Henri IV in 1589, to the French crown, and finally to the president of the French republic. In 1793 revolutionary France renounced, on grounds of principle, its feudal rights, which Napoleon reassumed in 1806, acceding to a petition from the Andorrans. The co-princes have mutually checked innovations, and on occasion each other, in a land where medieval usages persist. Differences of policy or interests between them, or between one and the council, have led periodically to the closing of one or another frontier. A feudal anachronism, it remains a suzerainty, paying nominal annual tribute of 960 fr. to the president of France and 460 pesetas to the bishop of Urgel.

Administration.—The Manual Digest of usages of Fiter Rosell (1748) enjoys semiofficial acceptance in lieu of a constitution; a "Reform" of 1866 introduced electoral modifications. Legislative power is vested in the co-princes. A council general of 24 elected by heads of families of the six parishes (Andorra la Vella, Encamp, La Massana, Ordino, Canillo, Sant Julià de Loria) chooses a syndic as chief executive (term unlimited). Representatives (veguers or viguiers) of the co-princes nominate two civil judges (bailles) of first instance. A judge of appeal is appointed alternately by the co-princes, with a supreme court at Perpignan and an ecclesiastical court at Urgel. Veguers and the appeal judge try criminal cases. Schools (primary only) are maintained by France and Spain, parish priests by the bishop of Urgel.

Economy.—With no ordinary taxes (until 1954 no budget), revenue comes chiefly from import duties. French and Spanish currencies are alike legal tender. Smuggling is rife, notably of tobacco and of consumer goods (especially automobiles) from France into Spain. Tobacco-growing and stock-raising are the major economic activities. In summer, with large-scale transhumance from the distant plains of the lower Segre and the Ariège, about 30,000 sheep graze on the high pastures. Lower slopes support horses, mules, cattle and goats. Difficulties of winter fodder mean large autumn fairs, held both in Andorra and across the Spanish border. Wheat, rye and potatoes are the chief crops. Mineral deposits include silver, lead and iron ores. A hydroelectric station at Les Escaldes (capacity 26,500 kw.) supplies Barcelona province. Industry is merely domestic; however, after World War II the tourist trade became important. A good road runs from L'Hospitalet, France, over the Port d'Envalira (8,022 ft.) to Andorra la Vella and on to Seo de Urgel, Spain. Another joins the capital to Ordino. Roads are maintained by Fuerzas Hidroeléctricas de Andorra, S.A., posts and telegraphs by France, telephones by Radio Andorra.

BIBLIOGRAPHY.—Violet Alford, Pyrenean Festivals (1937); W. Piesold, Andorra (1937); F. Weilenmann (ed.), Die Wahrheit über die Pyrenäenrepublik Andorra (1939); Santiago Alcobe, "Estudios antropológicos en tres altos valles de los Pirineos," Anales de la Universidad de Barcelona, pp. 239–305 (1941–42); J. Corts Peyret, Geografía e historia de Andorra (1945); Salvador Llobet, El medio y la vida en Andorra (1947); B. Riberaygua Argelich, Los valles de Andorra (1949); J. M. Vidal y Guitart, Instituciones políticas y sociales de Andorra (1949); Josef M. Guilera, Una història d'Andorra (1960).
(W. C. An.)

ANDOVER, a municipal borough and market town of Hampshire, Eng., lies among chalk hills on the Anton, a tributary of the Test, 14 mi. N.W. of Winchester by road and 17 mi. N.E. of Salisbury by rail. Pop. (1961) 16,985. The district is rich in prehistoric earthworks and tumuli. The witenagemot met there and it is the place where Aethelred II, "the Unready," met Olaf

Tryggvessön, afterward king of Norway, in 994. Andover is a borough by prescription, its earliest known charter having been granted in 1175. In the 14th century the town had a sheep fair, a woolen industry and an iron market and also manufactured parchments and silk fabrics. It is the centre of a large agricultural district; water cress is grown; there are flour mills, timber yards and printing works; and agricultural equipment and plastics are manufactured. Andover grammar school was founded in 1571. At Enham, in the northern part of the borough, is a village founded after World War I for disabled ex-servicemen. As the result of an Egyptian gift in Oct. 1945 of a substantial sum to commemorate the battle of El Alamein, the village was enlarged and officially renamed Enham-Alamein in Oct. 1947. There are many military and air force establishments in the locality, including the Royal Air Force staff college.

See O. G. S. Crawford, *The Andover District* (1922 and 1923).

ANDOVER, a township of Essex county, Mass., U.S., on the south rim of the Merrimack valley, 23 mi. N. of Boston. (For comparative population figures *see* table in MASSACHUSETTS: *Population.*) The original settlement was incorporated in 1646, and named after the English home of early colonists. North Andover was separated in 1855. A council-manager form of government became effective in 1959.

It is both an industrial and an educational centre. Textile mills began as early as 1813; woolen and worsted goods are still important products. Shawsheen village, once a "model" community, was created at Andover by the American Woolen company. Rubber goods have been produced for more than a century.

The first educational institution of note was Phillips academy, founded in 1778 "for the purpose of instructing youth, not only in English and Latin grammar, writing, arithmetic, and those sciences wherein they are commonly taught, but more especially to learn them the great end and real business of living," according to the constitution written by Samuel Phillips, Jr. (1752–1802). The extensive grounds include those occupied 1808–1908 by Andover Theological seminary, now Andover-Newton Theological school at Newton, Mass. The Addison Gallery of American Art and the archaeological museum house important collections.

The town is also the home of Abbot academy, founded in 1829 by Sarah Abbot. This was the earliest incorporated school exclusively for girls in New England. Merrimack college in North Andover opened in 1947.   (CA. M. C.)

ANDRADA E SILVA, JOSÉ BONIFÁCIO DE (*c.* 1763–1838), Brazilian scholar, statesman and father of Brazilian independence. Born at Santos, of a prominent colonial family, he went as a student to Portugal, where he remained until the age of 56. He was the outstanding Brazilian scholar of the time, a professor at the University of Coimbra (in Portugal), permanent secretary of the Lisbon Academy and internationally renowned as a naturalist and geologist. Returning to Brazil in 1819, he devoted himself to politics. As an adviser and later minister of Dom Pedro, he worked actively for independence under a monarchy, was instrumental in the establishment of the empire of Brazil on Sept. 7, 1822, and became prime minister.

In the constituent assembly of 1823, Andrada led the opposition to Pedro's Portuguese counselors and was exiled until 1829. However, Andrada returned to the emperor's cause and continued to support it even after Pedro's abdication in 1831, when he became the tutor of young Pedro II. He was arrested for political intrigue in 1833.

He retired to Niterói, where he died on April 6, 1838. *See also* BRAZIL: *History.*   (R. E. P.)

ANDRÁSSY, GYULA, COUNT (1823–1890), Hungarian statesman, the first premier of Hungary in the Austro-Hungarian dual monarchy and, as Austro-Hungarian foreign minister, a strong supporter of an alliance between Austria-Hungary and Germany, was born at Kassa (Kosice in Slovakia) on March 3, 1823, son of Count Károly Andrássy and Etelka Szapáry. He early joined the radical reformers in Hungary and entered the diet of 1847 pledged to their cause. In the subsequent hostilities (*see* HUNGARY: *History*) he saw some fighting in command of a battalion of volunteers against the Austrians, then was sent by Lajos Kossuth, in

May 1849, as diplomatic envoy to Turkey. After Hungary's surrender at Világos he spent some years in exile, chiefly in Paris; he was condemned to death *in absentia* by the Austrian government (Sept. 1851) and later hanged in effigy. In 1856 he married Countess Katinka Kendeffy. In 1857 he obtained an amnesty and returned to Hungary. When, in 1859, negotiations opened between the crown and the Hungarian leaders, Andrássy supported Ferencz Deák (*q.v.*), demanding the restoration of the 1848 legislation, and mediated between him and the court. When the Austrian emperor Francis Joseph agreed to appoint a responsible Hungarian ministry, Deák suggested that Andrássy should lead it. Appointed Hungarian premier and minister of defense on Feb. 17, 1867, Andrássy presided over the coronation of Francis Joseph as king of Hungary, the final codification of the Compromise (*Ausgleich*) and the settlement of certain questions left outstanding (over which he encountered stubborn resistance from Vienna).

Andrássy was always acutely aware of the Slav danger to Hungary, as represented by Russian ambitions and by the nationalist stirrings among the Slavs of the monarchy. For him safety against these two interlinked threats lay in the maintenance of the supremacy of the German element in Austria and of good relations between Austria and Germany. Consequently, already as Hungarian premier he intervened to quash both K. S. von Hohenwart's project for reorganizing Austria on a federal basis (as desired by the Czechs) and F. F. Beust's plan for taking revenge on Prussia for the Seven Weeks' War by means of alliance with France; it was because of his insistence that Austria declared itself neutral in the Franco-German War. When, thereafter, Francis Joseph abandoned the policy of revenge, he appointed Andrássy Austro-Hungarian foreign minister in place of Beust (Nov. 14, 1871). In this capacity Andrássy worked with much success to strengthen Austria's international position, always with an eye on the Russian danger. The outbreak of serious unrest in the Balkans in 1875 created a difficult situation for him (*see* EASTERN QUESTION). The *status quo* had vanished beyond recall; to let Russia alone profit by its disappearance was dangerous; but so was any increase of the number of Slav subjects of the monarchy, either in Hungary or in Austria. The occupation by the monarchy of Bosnia-Hercegovina, decided by the congress of Berlin in 1878, was Andrássy's solution as the least harmful course, but it was unpopular in both Hungary and Austria, and Andrássy resigned on Oct. 8, 1879. The previous day he had, however, secured the signature of the Austro-German alliance which until 1918 was to be the sheet anchor of the monarchy's foreign policy. Thereafter he still took part in the work of the upper house and the delegations. He died at Volosca in Istria on Feb. 18, 1890. He left a daughter and two sons, the younger of whom, Gyula, was also a distinguished statesman.

Andrássy was a man of great charm and natural ability. He was neither versed nor indeed interested in domestic politics, but in the field of foreign policy was undoubtedly a man of European outlook and format. There is an edition of his speeches, in Hungarian, by B. Lederer (1891).

See E. von Wertheimer, *Graf Julius Andrássy: sein Leben und seine Zeit*, 3 vol. (1910–13); G. Andrássy (the younger), *Bismarck, Andrássy and Their Successors*, Eng. trans. (1927).   (C. A. M.)

ANDRÁSSY, GYULA, COUNT (1860–1929), Hungarian statesman, the last foreign minister of Austria-Hungary, was born at Töketerebes (Trebisov in Slovakia) on June 30, 1860, the younger son of Count Gyula Andrássy (1823–90). After some diplomatic experience as attaché in the embassies in Berlin and Istanbul, he entered the Hungarian parliament in 1885. Dedicated to carrying on his father's work, especially in the foreign political field, he joined the Liberal party, the chief supporter of the Austro-Hungarian Compromise (*Ausgleich*) of 1867. His talents and his rectitude won for him great influence in the party, but he never got on well with its official leader, Count István Tisza, and was also not unsympathetic to some of the wishes of the opposition. In 1904 he left the Liberals in protest against Tisza's dictatorial methods and founded a Constitutional party. He was minister of the interior in the coalition government from April 6, 1906, to Jan. 17, 1910, when he resigned and dissolved his party. On

Oct. 25, 1918, in the last days of World War I, he became foreign minister of Austria-Hungary, in an attempt to save its integrity by a separate peace. Pres. Woodrow Wilson's unbending reply and revolution in the monarchy itself swept him from office. He re-entered the Hungarian parliament of 1920 as leader of the Christian National party. When, in Oct. 1921, King Charles (the ex-emperor of Austria) made his second attempt to recover his Hungarian throne, Andrássy joined him, was taken prisoner with him and was held in prison for several months. Released, he returned to parliament as a legitimist. He died in Budapest on June 11, 1929.

Andrássy wrote several works on Hungarian constitutional history, books of memoirs (including *Diplomacy and the War,* Eng. trans. 1927) and a study of his father's work, *Bismarck, Andrássy and Their Successors* (Eng. trans., 1927). (C. A. M.)

ANDRÉ, JOHN

ANDRÉ, JOHN (1750–1780), British soldier executed as a spy during the American Revolution, was born in London, May 2, 1750, of a Genevese father and Parisian mother. He was a younger friend of the poet Anna Seward and became engaged to her friend, the beautiful Honora Sneyd. When the engagement was terminated, without heartbreak on either side, André bought a commission in the army in Jan. 1771. He studied military engineering at the University of Göttingen, Ger., and traveled on the continent until 1774 when he joined his regiment in Quebec.

Taken prisoner in the surrender of Ft. St. John's on Nov. 3, 1775, André was interned in central Pennsylvania until exchanged at the end of 1776. He then went to New York, was promoted captain and became aide to the notorious Gen. Charles Grey. He was active in the successful Philadelphia campaign, 1777, and during the winter occupation of the city promoted various entertainments and wrote light verse. After the British forces evacuated Philadelphia and returned to New York, André became aide to Gen. Sir Henry Clinton, the new commander in chief.

In May 1779 the American general Benedict Arnold (*q.v.*) offered his services to the British in return for pay and equal rank. As André was in charge of intelligence and knew Mrs. Arnold, he carried on the secret correspondence. It was broken off in October because the British would not commit themselves on payments. André became deputy adjutant general with the rank of major. He sailed to Charleston, S.C., with General Clinton in December and took part in the siege of that city. Upon his return to New York in June 1780 he found a new note from Arnold stating that he expected to obtain the command of West Point.

André arranged to meet Arnold under a misuse of a flag of truce. They met up the Hudson river on the night of Sept. 21 and agreed on the sum of £20,000 for the surrender of West Point, including the garrison and supplies. Half that amount was to be paid if Arnold should fail and join the British empty-handed. As the British sloop "Vulture" which brought André to the rendezvous was fired upon and forced to drop downstream, André was compelled to pass the night within American lines. The next day he was persuaded to exchange his uniform for a civilian disguise and to set out overland for New York, carrying a pass provided by Arnold. Suspicious American militiamen stopped and searched him on the morning of Sept. 23 and found papers about West Point in his boot. They held him while word was innocently sent to Arnold, enabling him to escape down river to the British lines.

The stunning disclosure left André as scapegoat. Out of uniform and in disguise, he was clearly acting the role of spy and could be executed immediately, but General Washington moved cautiously. He convened a board of officers to examine the prisoner. The board concluded that André "ought to be considered a spy, and that, agreeable to the law and usage of nations, it is their opinion he ought to suffer death." During the few days' delay, word was carried to Clinton that André could be saved if Arnold were given up. Clinton refused the tempting proposition. André was hanged at Tappan, N.Y., on Oct. 2, 1780.

André had literary talent and personal charm, and his fate excited sympathy among several American officers who attended him. The British army went into mourning for him. A memorial to André was placed in Westminster abbey, and his brother was made a baronet. André's military journal of June 1777 to the close of 1778 was taken to England by General Grey and finally published in 1904.

BIBLIOGRAPHY.—James T. Flexner, *The Traitor and the Spy* (1953); the André-Arnold correspondence is found in Carl Van Doren, *Secret History of the American Revolution* (1941). (H. H. P.)

ANDREA DEL SARTO: *see* SARTO, ANDREA DEL.

ANDREANI, ANDREA

ANDREANI, ANDREA, Italian woodcut artist, is famous for his work in chiaroscuro printing. The dates of his birth and death are not known. He was active in Florence from 1584 until 1585, in Siena from 1586 to 1593 and in Mantua in 1599. Between 1607 and 1610 he appears as a publisher of prints, not his own. He is said to have died in Mantua in 1623 at an advanced age.

All of Andreani's woodcuts are from the works of others. His style possessed a fine vigour and simplicity, and he is best known for his use of the chiaroscuro, the method of technique of printing a subject from more than one block and with colour. His works are from the compositions of Giovanni da Bologna, Domenico Beccafumi, Jacopo Ligozzi, Alessandro Casolani and others. The most famous of all is the group of 12 large woodblocks representing the "Triumph of Julius Caesar," painted by Andrea Mantegna. Here each block has an individual character, yet fits into its place in the unified whole; the several sections were intended to be pasted together or mounted as a single frieze. The importance of this work is such that it is to be found in all large collections that attempt to give a survey of masterpieces of print making.

(H. Es.)

ANDREE, KARL THEODOR

ANDREE, KARL THEODOR (1808–1875), German geographer and writer, best known for his geography of world trade, which, though out of date, had not been replaced by the mid-20th century. Andree was born at Brunswick on Oct. 20, 1808. After studying history and political science at Jena, Berlin and Göttingen, he worked as a journalist until, influenced by Karl Ritter and Alexander von Humboldt, he turned entirely to geography and ethnography. In 1862 he founded the important periodical *Globus,* and with S. Ruge was the co-founder of the Dresden Geographical society. Andree's principal works include *Nordamerika in geographischen und geschichtlichen Umrissen* (1854), *Geographische Wanderungen* (1859) and *Geographie des Welthandels* (1862–77). He died suddenly at Bad Wildungen on Aug. 10, 1875.

RICHARD ANDREE (1835–1912), his son, edited *Globus* from 1891 to 1903 and in 1881 published *Allgemeiner Handatlas.*

(K. A. S.)

ANDREEV, LEONID NIKOLAEVICH

ANDREEV, LEONID NIKOLAEVICH (1871–1919), Russian novelist whose contemporary reputation has not lasted but whose best work has a place in Russian literature for its evocation of a mood of despair. Born at Orel, June 18, 1871, he went to St. Petersburg university in 1891, but attempted suicide and lived a restless life for some time. He subsequently studied law at Moscow and became a barrister and then a law and crime reporter, publishing his first stories in newspapers and periodicals. Encouraged by Gorki, who became a close friend, he was at first regarded as his successor as a realist. His "Zhili-byli" ("Once There Lived . . .") attracted attention, and was included in his first collection of short stories (1901). Two stories of 1902 caused a storm by their treatment of sex. Andreev's work became widely discussed and he acquired fame and wealth with a series of novels and short stories which at their best resemble Tolstoi, subdued in style but powerful in theme and showing an ironic sympathy for suffering humanity. They culminated in 1908 with *Rasskaz o semi poveshennykh (The Seven That Were Hanged,* 1909); among the best are *Gubernator* (1905; *His Excellency the Governor,* 1921) and *Krasny smekh* (1905; *The Red Laugh*). *T'ma* (1907; *The Dark,* 1922) shows his second style: its cloudy imagery reflects an increasingly nihilistic philosophy.

Andreev's fame as a novelist declined rapidly, however, and the ambitious *Sashka Zhegulev* (1912) attracted little attention. He began a career as a popular dramatist: his first play appeared in 1905. His most successful, *Zhizn' cheloveka* (1907; *The Life of Man,* 1915) and *Tot kts poluchayet poshchechiny* (1914; *He Who Gets Slapped,* 1921), were allegorical dramas, but he also attempted realistic comedy.

During World War I Andreev became editor of a government-inspired newspaper, and his writings were predominantly patriotic. A fervent antirevolutionary, he moved to Kuokkala, Fin., and his last work, *S.O.S.* (1919), was an appeal to the Allies to save imperial Russia. He died at Kuokkala, Sept. 12, 1919.

BIBLIOGRAPHY.— Andreev's collected works were published in 16 vol. (1910–15). Most have been translated into English. For full bibliography, *see* A. Kaun, *L. Andreyev: a critical study* (1924).

ANDREINI, FRANCESCO (1548–1624), Italian actor, was a distinguished exponent of the *commedia dell'arte* (q.v.) and a leader of its most famous company, the Gelosi, with which he visited Paris in 1600 at the invitation of Henry IV. His wife, ISABELLA ANDREINI (née Canali; 1562–1604), the company's brilliant and beautiful leading lady, whom he married in 1578, was also a minor poet, publishing a pastoral, *Mirtilla*, and a book of songs, sonnets and other poems. Of her seven children, the most famous was GIAMBATTISTA ANDREINI (*c.* 1578–1654), a distinguished actor who became well known in France under the name of Lelio. He was a leader, and probably founder, of the Fedeli company, which was popular with Louis XIII. He was also a prolific author, and it has been claimed that his play *L'Adamo* ("Adam"; 1613) suggested to Milton the idea of *Paradise Lost*.

ANDREIS, (ANDREW JAMES) FELIX (BARTHOLOMEW) DE (1778–1820), Vincentian priest and pioneer missionary to the American west, was born at Demonte, Piedmont, Italy, on Dec. 13, 1778. He pronounced his vows in the Congregation of the Mission of St. Vincent de Paul on Sept. 21, 1800, and was ordained at Piacenza, June 19, 1802. He performed numerous pastoral duties in that region until he was transferred in 1806 to Rome where he acquired a reputation as a preacher, professor of theology, retreat master and apostle to the poor. William DuBourg, bishop of Louisiana, visiting Rome in 1815, secured the services of Father Andreis for his diocese. Father Andreis was appointed temporary vicar-general and superior of a little band of missionaries that embarked for the American missions; among them was Joseph Rosati, first bishop of St. Louis. After a long delay at the Seminary of St. Thomas in Kentucky, where he spent several months teaching theology, Father Andreis arrived in St. Louis on Oct. 17, 1817. His first assignment was to the little village of St. Genevieve, but he was soon recalled to St. Louis and appointed vicar-general. He was professor and administrator of two colleges, one for clerical students and one for laymen, established by the bishop. He also supervised the erection of a novitiate for his congregation at the Barrens, 80 mi. S. of St. Louis. Although he appointed Rosati first superior of the novitiate, Andreis continued to train the novices in St. Louis while the new buildings were under construction. He died in St. Louis on Oct. 15, 1820. During his lifetime he gained a reputation for sanctity and several miracles were attributed to his intercession after his death.

See Joseph Rosati, *Life of the Very Reverend Felix De Andreis, C.M.* (1900).   (F. G. McM.)

ANDRÉ LE CHAPELAIN (ANDREAS CAPELLANUS), medieval French writer on the art of "courtly love," and chaplain at the French court (whence his surname), was born in the second half of the 12th century, and probably held his office under Philip Augustus (1180–1223). His famous treatise, *Liber de Arte honeste amandi et de Reprobatione inhonesti Amoris*, written at the beginning of the 13th century and translated twice into French during the century, is an interesting source of information concerning medieval manners and morals, and the "court of love" in particular. There are 12 manuscripts extant, of which the most important are the 13th-century manuscript in the Vatican, the 14th-century manuscript in the Bibliothèque Nationale and the 15th-century manuscript in the Ambrosian library, Milan. There is an English translation, *The Art of Courtly Love*, by J. J. Parry (1941).   (F. J. WE.)

ANDREW, SAINT, brother of Simon Peter, one of the 12 apostles, always mentioned in the first of the three groups of four names in the apostle lists (Matt. 10:2; Mark 3:18; Luke 6:14; Acts 1:13). The name is Greek, meaning "manly." In the Synoptic Gospels Andrew is a fisherman from Capernaum (Mark 1:16, 29); together with Peter, James, and John he asks Christ on the Mount of Olives about the signs of the end time, which is the occasion for the eschatological discourse in Mark 13:3. In John's Gospel he is the first disciple named; his home town is Bethsaida (1:44) and he was a disciple of John the Baptist before Christ's call. He plays a part in the multiplication of the barley loaves and fishes (6:8) and acts as a go-between for the Greeks who want to see Jesus (12:22).

Early Byzantine tradition (dependent on John 1:40) calls Andrew *protokletos*, "first called." Legends of the early church recount his missionary activity in the area about the Black Sea, in Scythia (according to Origen as quoted by Eusebius), in Epirus (Gregory of Nazianzus), and in Achaea (Jerome). Apocryphal writings about him include the Acts of Andrew, Acts of Andrew and Matthias, and Acts of Peter and Andrew. A 4th-century account reports his death by crucifixion at Patras in Greece in the year 60 under the governor Aegeates. From the 4th century on, his feast was celebrated on Nov. 30 (ancient Gothic calendar; Roman martyrology).

Jerome records that the relics of St. Andrew were taken from Patras to Constantinople by command of the emperor Constantius in 357. From there the body was taken to Amalfi, Italy (Church of S. Andrea) in 1208, and in the 15th century the head was taken to Rome (St. Peter's Basilica, Vatican). The relics and the legends about St. Andrew have always been closely associated with the claim of apostolic origin for the See of Byzantium. Thus when in September 1964 Pope Paul VI returned the head of St. Andrew to the Greek Orthodox Church in Patras—as Pius II, 500 years earlier, had promised would be done—it was a papal gesture of goodwill toward the separated Christians of Greece. St. Andrew is the patron saint of Scotland. *See also* APOSTLE.

See Peter M. Peterson, *Andrew, Brother of Simon Peter: His History and His Legends* (1958); F. Dvornik, *The Idea of Apostolicity in Byzantium and the Legend of the Apostle Andrew* (1958).   (J. A. FI.)

ANDREW, SAINT, OF CRETE (*c.* 660–740), who was born at Damascus *c.* 660 and died on the island of Hierissus in 740, is regarded by the Greek Church as one of its greatest hymn writers. From his monastery in Jerusalem he was sent to Constantinople where he stayed and became deacon of Hagia Sophia. During the reign of Philippicus Bardanes he was made archbishop of Gortyra in Crete, took part in the Monothelite synod in 712, but recanted his heretical views in 713. Andrew helped to introduce in Constantinople the liturgy of Jerusalem which was based upon the Rule of St. Sabas and favoured hymn singing. Byzantine hagiography ascribes to him the invention of the Kanon, the new genre of hymnography which consisted of nine odes in strophic form, each of them sung to a different melody, and replaced the Kontakion, a homiletic hymn of which all stanzas were sung to the same melody. Andrew was the author of many hymns and Kanons which still figure in Greek liturgical books. His most famous work is the "Great Kanon" for Thursday in the fifth week of Lent, consisting of 250 stanzas which are divided into four sections. The Greek Church keeps July 4 as his feast day.

See L. Petit, "André de Crète" in *Dict. d'archéol. chrétienne et de liturgie*, vol. i, 2034–41 (1903); R. Cantarella, *Poeti bizantini*, pp. 100–111 (1948).   (E. J. Wz.)

ANDREW II (1175–1235), king of Hungary, of the house of Árpád, was a son of Béla III and succeeded his nephew, the infant László III, in 1205. His reckless generosity, forced on him by the powerful magnates, impoverished the crown and made the monarchy dependent on the great feudatories, who reduced Hungary to a state bordering on anarchy. His first wife, Gertrude of Meran, was murdered in 1213 by rebellious nobles who objected to the prodigality of her German retinue. In 1217 Andrew set out on a crusade to the Holy Land with an army of 15,000 men, about 10,000 of whom sailed from Venice to Acre. The expedition failed, and on Andrew's return the barons extorted from him the Golden Bull (1222), which has been called the Hungarian Magna Carta. The Golden Bull, one of the most important sources of the Hungarian constitution, limited royal privileges and prerogatives, confirmed the basic rights of the nobles and smallholders, promised to improve the coinage of the realm and guaranteed justice for all. It also granted the nobles the right to resist by force any illegal royal decree (*jus resistendi*). Andrew came into conflict with the Teutonic Order (*q.v.*), which, after occupying parts of Transylvania for 14 years, challenged both royal and ecclesiastical authority. This controversy resulted in the Teutonic Order's expulsion from Hungary (1225). Andrew was married three times. St. Elizabeth of Hungary was his daughter by his first wife, Gertrude. (GE. GR.)

ANDREW (BOGOLYUBSKI) (ANDREI YURIEVICH) (1111?–1174), grand prince of Vladimir, the most powerful Russian prince of the 12th century. The son of the grand prince Yuri Dolgoruki, he ruled the "land of Rostov-Suzdal" in the upper Volga region from 1157. He moved his capital to the city of Vladimir on the Klyazma river and enlarged, fortified and beautified his new residence, as well as his summer residence, called Bogolyubovo (from which his surname is derived). He built many churches, among them a magnificent cathedral of Our Lady in Vladimir. He actively colonized the Rostov-Suzdal-Vladimir land, inviting servicemen, peasants and craftsmen from other regions into his realm. He strove to extend his authority over other Russian principalities. In 1169 his troops, with the troops of princes allied to him, stormed Kiev, the ancient Russian capital. Instead of coming himself to Kiev, however, Andrew put one of the allied princes on the throne there. In the following year his troops threatened the republic of Novgorod but were defeated by the Novgorodians. Soon after their victory, however, the Novgorodians saw themselves compelled to sue for peace and to accept a prince sent by Andrew. Andrew's policy aimed at establishing his sovereign power over other Russian princes, who regarded themselves as "younger brothers" of the grand prince but not as his vassals. Within his hereditary principality Andrew wished to be absolute master of all his subjects, including the boyars (*q.v.*), whom he treated as his common servitors and who were not accustomed to such full submission. When Andrew had inflicted the death penalty on one of his boyars, his embittered courtiers formed a conspiracy and in July 1174, at Bogolyubovo, killed their haughty prince.

See George Vernadsky, *Kievan Russia* (1948). (S. G. PU.)

ANDREW OF LONJUMEL (LONGJUMEAU, LONGUMEAU, etc.) (fl. 1238–1253), French Dominican, diplomat and traveler, noted for three diplomatic missions which he performed between 1238 and 1252. Nothing is known of Andrew's early life. In 1238 Louis IX (St. Louis) of France dispatched him to Constantinople to fetch the sacred Crown of Thorns which he had redeemed from the Latin emperor Baldwin II. Andrew carried the holy relic to Sens, where St. Louis met him, and thence to Paris where it was placed in the Sainte Chapelle. In 1247 he accompanied the mission under Friar Ascelin sent by Pope Innocent IV to the Mongols. At the Tatar camp near Kars, he met a certain David who appeared the following year at the court of Louis IX in Cyprus. Andrew, who was at that time with St. Louis, interpreted David's message, an offer of alliance from Elchigaday (Ilchikadi, Ilchikdai), the general in command of the Mongol hosts in Armenia and Persia, and a proposal for a joint attack upon Islam for the conquest of Syria. In reply St. Louis sent Andrew as ambassador to the great Khan Kuyuk.

Early in 1249 Andrew, accompanied by several ecclesiastics including John of Carcassonne, John Godericke and Gilbert of Sens, left Cyprus with letters from St. Louis and the papal legate, and rich presents including a chapel tent lined with scarlet cloth and embroidered with sacred pictures. From Cyprus the embassy went to Antioch and thence to the khan's court in central Asia; their route lay along the southern and eastern shores of the Caspian (its inland nature was demonstrated by their journey), and then through Talass, northeast of Tashkent; the journey took a year. On reaching the supreme Mongol court—located either on the Imyl river near Lake Ala-Kul or at or near Karakoram—Andrew found the great khan dead, poisoned as he concluded by agents of Batu Khan, who reigned supreme on the Volga.

The gifts which the embassy carried were regarded by the Mongols as evidence of submission to a dead khan. Andrew and his companions were received by the regent-mother, Ogul Gaimish (the "Camus" of Rubruquis), who dismissed them with presents and a letter for King Louis; the insolent language of the letter marked the mission a failure. It is generally held that Mangu Khan, Kuyuk's successor, was elected before the embassy left Tatary. The missionaries returned to the west to find St. Louis at Caesarea, sometime between March 1251 and May 1252.

Notwithstanding displeasure at the letter, St. Louis, on hearing shortly after that a son of Batu Khan was a "baptised Christian," sent William of Rubruquis (or Rubrouck) on an informal mission to the Mongols; it was William who recorded Andrew's account of his embassy. Andrew's narrative was a mixture of fact and fiction. His description of Tatar customs was fairly accurate, and his statements about the prosperity of Mongol Christianity, although exaggerated, were basically true. His route was marked by mounds of bones, witnesses to devastations recorded in detail by other historians. On the other hand his location of the Tatar homeland close to the prison of Gog and Magog and his account of the Mongols' rise to greatness and the struggles of their leader with Prester John rest upon fable. Nothing is heard of Andrew after 1253.

See especially William of Rubruquis in *Recueil de voyages*, Paris Geogr. Soc., iv, pp. 261, 265, 279, 296, 310, 353, 363, 370 (1839); Abel Rémusat, *Mémoires sur les relations politiques des princes chrétiens, et particulièrement des rois de France, avec les empereurs Mongols*, p. 52 ff. (1822 et seq.). (E. M. J. C.)

ANDREW, JOHN ALBION (1818–1867), U.S. political leader and Civil War governor of Massachusetts, was born at Windham, Me., on May 31, 1818. He graduated from Bowdoin college, Brunswick, Me., in 1837, studied law in Boston, was admitted to the bar in 1840 and practised his profession in Boston. He was a prominent member of the Unitarian Church and was assistant editor for some time of *The Christian World*. He entered political life as a "conscience Whig" in opposition to the Mexican War, joined the Free-Soil movement in 1848, and after the passage of the Kansas-Nebraska act in 1854 took part in the organization of the Republican party in Massachusetts. He served one term, 1858, in the state house of representatives. The following year he defended the abolitionist John Brown (*q.v.*) so vigorously that he was summoned to Washington to appear before a senatorial investigating committee. In 1860 he led the Massachusetts delegation at the Republican convention at Chicago, which nominated Lincoln for the presidency; and from 1861 to Jan. 1866 he was governor of Massachusetts, becoming known as one of the ablest and most energetic of the "war governors" of the North.

Governor Andrew anticipated military conflict with the South and had young men drilled and supplied so that Massachusetts troops began to muster in Boston on April 16, the day after Lincoln called for volunteers. At his own request, he was authorized by the secretary of war in 1863 to raise several Negro regiments with white commissioned officers. Although Governor Andrew criticized Lincoln for timidity during the war, he rejected in 1865 the more radical views of his party and supported most of Pres. Andrew Johnson's program. On retiring from the governor's office he resumed the practice of law with great success. In 1865 he presided at the first national convention of the Unitarian Church. He died suddenly of apoplexy, at Boston, on Oct. 30, 1867.

See Henry G. Pearson, *Life of John A. Andrew* (1904). (N. A. G.)

ANDREWES, LANCELOT (1555–1626), English bishop, was a key figure in the theological and liturgical development of the English Church from the uncertainties of the 16th century to the Restoration settlement. Descended from an ancient Suffolk family, he was born in London in 1555 and was educated at Cooper's Free school, Radcliffe, at Merchant Taylors' school and at Pembroke hall, Cambridge. Elected fellow of Pembroke in 1575, he was ordained deacon in 1580. He was master of Pembroke and vicar of St. Giles', Cripplegate, London (1589–1605), prebendary of St. Paul's and of Southwell minster (1589–1609), prebendary (1597–1601) and dean (1601–05) of Westminster. He refused the sees of Salisbury and Ely because Elizabeth I required his connivance in their spoliation by the crown. Consecrated bishop of Chichester in 1605, he was translated to Ely in 1609 and to Winchester in 1619. Andrewes was lord almoner to James I (1605–

19) and dean of the chapels royal (1619–26). He died at South-wark, Sept. 25, 1626.

The English Church's distinctive position in a divided Christendom was defined to the accompaniment of violent controversy, and Andrewes' own contribution to Anglican theology inevitably took a polemical form. His university career coincided with the great Puritan attempt to make Cambridge a stronghold of Calvinistic orthodoxy, while the years of his episcopate were marked by prolonged debates with Roman Catholics, precipitated by the Gunpowder plot and the resultant anti-Roman Catholic legislation. Despite his early exposure to Puritan influences, Andrewes was a cautious but consistent critic both of Calvinist dogmas and of Puritan reform platforms. His major writings, however, were devoted to anti-Roman Catholic apologetics, in which he combined a critique of distinctively Roman Catholic dogmas with a positive statement of Anglican teaching on such themes as patristic tradition, episcopacy and the sacraments.

The same Catholic-minded churchmanship was expressed both in Andrewes' learned, eloquent and influential preaching and in his dignified liturgical practice, and was further commended by his austere life and reputation for sanctity. His ardent devotion and private integrity were indisputable. However, his public failings, such as pluralism in his own career, nepotism in his exercise of patronage, an exaggerated deference to royal authority and a tendency to evade responsibility, both marred the image of sanctity and limited Andrewes' role in the rebuilding of the English Church.

BIBLIOGRAPHY.—P. A. Welsby, *Lancelot Andrewes, 1555–1626* (1958), is the only adequate biography; it contains full bibliographies. *See* also R. L. Ottley, *Lancelot Andrewes* (1894), a good sketch. The "Library of Anglo-Catholic Theology" includes Andrewes' *Collected Works*, 10 vol. (1841–54). Separate editions and translations of his *Preces privatae* are numerous. (E. R. F.)

ANDREWS, CHARLES McLEAN (1863–1943), U.S. educator and historian, was born in Wethersfield, Conn., on Feb. 22, 1863. He was educated at Trinity college, Hartford, Conn., graduating in 1884, and at Johns Hopkins university, where he received the degree of doctor of philosophy in 1889. He taught history at Bryn Mawr college from 1889 to 1907; was professor of history at Johns Hopkins university from 1907 to 1910; and served as professor of American history at Yale university from 1910 to 1931. For two years after his retirement as a professor he served as director of historical publications at Yale and continued to serve, as he had since 1912, as editor of the Yale Historical publications.

Though his graduate training and first teaching led him to work in European history, Andrews soon shifted to exclusive specialization in American colonial history. By the time he went to Yale in 1910 he was well started on his important guides to colonial materials in English archives. Emerging at once as a leader in the school of colonial historiography, since called "the imperial school," which insists that as the American colonies were dependent parts of the English system the centre of the colonial story belongs in the mother country, Andrews oriented all his work that way. Such an interpretation runs through his books, all of which received wide acceptance, and through the writings of historians trained in his seminar. He served as president of the American Historical association in 1924–25 and in 1935 the first volume of his four-volume work, *The Colonial Period of American History*, won a Pulitzer prize. He died in New Haven, Conn., Sept. 9, 1943.

Among his extensive historical writings are: *Colonial Self-Government, 1652–1689*, vol. v of *The American Nation, a History* (1904); (with F. G. Davenport) *Guide to the Manuscript Materials for the History of the United States to 1783 in the British Museum, in Minor London Archives and in the Libraries of Oxford and Cambridge* (1908); *The Colonial Period* (1912); *Guide to the Materials for American History, to 1783, in the Public Record Office of Great Britain*, 2 vol. (1912–14); *The British Merchants and the Non-Importation Movement* (1917); *Fathers of New England* and *Colonial Folkways* in "Chronicles of America Series" (1919); *The Colonial Background of the American Revolution* (1924); *The Colonial Period of American History*, 4 vol. (1934–37).

See A. S. Eisenstadt, *Charles McLean Andrews: a Study in American Historical Writing* (1956). (C. A. BA.)

ANDREWS, FRANK MAXWELL (1884–1943), U.S. soldier and air force officer, was born in Nashville, Tenn., on Feb. 3, 1884. Graduating from the U.S. Military academy at West Point in 1906, Andrews was commissioned in the cavalry, serving in the Philippines and Hawaii, but in 1917 he transferred into the new air service, rising to lieutenant colonel by the end of World War I.

After holding routine service assignments during the postwar period, in 1935 he was named commander of the new general headquarters air force, the first independent U.S. air striking force. A determined though moderate advocate of strategic air power, Andrews in his four years' command of G.H.Q. air force contributed signally to the evolution of American bombardment aviation; the development of the Boeing B-17 bomber during these years was in large measure attributable to his vision, and G.H.Q. air force became the model for the powerful army air forces of World War II. During the war, Andrews, as air commander in the Caribbean and later as head of the Caribbean defense command, was the first U.S. airman to hold theatre command. He was promoted to lieutenant general in 1941.

In Feb. 1943 he assumed command of all United States forces in Europe, succeeding Gen. Dwight D. Eisenhower. He was killed in an airplane accident in Iceland on May 3, 1943.

(W. R. E.)

ANDREWS, ROY CHAPMAN (1884–1960), U.S. naturalist and explorer, popularly known best for books on his central Asiatic field trips. Born at Beloit, Wis., on Jan. 26, 1884, he entered the American Museum of Natural History, New York, immediately after his graduation from Beloit college in 1906 and went to Alaska on his first exploring trip in 1908. In 1909–10 he accompanied, as a naturalist, the U.S.S. "Albatross" on its voyage to the Netherlands Indies, Borneo and Celebes; in 1911–12 he explored northern Korea; and in 1913 was with the Borden Alaska expedition.

Until 1914 he specialized in the study of whales and other water mammals. From that date he devoted himself, as chief of the division of Asiatic exploration of the American Museum of Natural History, to the exploration of the lesser known portions of central Asia, China and Borneo, also serving in the U.S. intelligence service in China in 1918.

The expeditions under his leadership explored successively Tibet, southwest China, Burma, north China, Mongolia and central Asia. In Mongolia they found some of the richest fossil fields known to the world. The fruits of the expeditions which he led in 1921–22 and 1925 into central Asia included the discovery of new geological formations, large fossil fields, dinosaur eggs and the skull and other parts of the *Baluchitherium*—the largest known land mammal.

The expeditions discovered some of the oldest known mammals and continued work in central Asia until 1932. He was director of the American Museum of Natural History from 1935 to 1942, when he retired. He died March 11, 1960, in Carmel, Calif.

He wrote *Whale Hunting With Gun and Camera* (1916), *Camps and Trails in China*, with Yvette Borup Andrews (1918), *Across Mongolian Plains* (1921), *On the Trail of Ancient Man* (1926–27), *Ends of the Earth* (1929), *The New Conquest of Central Asia* (1933), *This Business of Exploring* (1935), *This Amazing Planet* (1940), the autobiographical *Under a Lucky Star* (1943) and *An Explorer Comes Home* (1947), and *Beyond Adventure* (1954), as well as numerous monographs and scientific bulletins.

ANDREWS, THOMAS (1813–1885), Irish chemist and physicist, is best known for his experiments in the liquefaction of gases which displayed great skill and resourcefulness. He was born on Dec. 19, 1813, at Belfast. Following periods of study in Glasgow, Paris, Dublin and Belfast, he attended the University of Edinburgh, where he received a degree in medicine in 1835. In 1845 he was appointed vice-president of the newly established Queen's college, Belfast, and, in 1849, professor of chemistry, offices which he held until 1879, when failing health compelled his retirement. He died on Nov. 26, 1885.

Andrews carried out a very complete inquiry into the laws expressing the relations of pressure, temperature and volume in carbon dioxide, in particular establishing the conceptions of critical temperature and critical pressure, and showing that the gas passes from the gaseous to the liquid state without any breach of continuity.

ANDRIA, a city of southeastern Italy in the region of Puglia and province of Bari, is situated on the slopes of the Murge, 55 km. (34 mi.) W.N.W. of Bari by road. Pop. (1957 est.) 70,050 (commune). The city has several notable Roman remains and a restored 10th-century cathedral. The cloister of S. Domenico church is Gothic. There are several Renaissance palaces with decorated doorways and balconies; Casa Margiotti and Casa Toma are particularly good examples. The convent of Sta. Maria Vetere has pictures by Antonio Vivarini. Andria is on the railway from Bari to Foggia. Agriculture, especially the cultivation of vines, olives and almonds, is the chief industry; wine, oil and spun goods are also made. Andria may be the Netion of Strabo. Its recorded history began when the Normans came and Pietro I, count of Trani, enlarged and fortified the modest Locum Andrae. Subsequently it became the favourite home of Emperor Frederick II, who built in 1240 the Castel del Monte, 17 km. S., a massive octagonal Gothic structure, with plumbing installations exceptional for those days. Eventually the city passed to the Angevins, Otto of Brunswick, and the Orsini, Acquaviva and Carafa families. In World War II Andria was captured by the Allies in Sept. 1943.
(M. T. A. N.)

ANDRIC, IVO (1892–), Yugoslav novelist and author of short stories who was awarded the Nobel prize in literature in 1961. He was born at Travnik, Bosnia, and studied at Zagreb, Cracow, Vienna and Graz. His potentialities as a writer of both prose and verse were recognized early, and his reputation was established with *Ex Ponto* (1918), a contemplative lyrical prose work written during internment for political activities during World War I. Collections of his short stories were published at intervals from 1920 onward. Of his three novels, written during World War II, two—*Travnicka hronika* (1945; Eng. trans. *Bosnian Story,* 1959) and *Na Drini cuprija* (1945; Eng. trans. *The Bridge on the Drina,* 1959)—are concerned with the history of Bosnia. Although his career in the Yugoslav diplomatic service took him to Rome, Bucharest, Madrid, Geneva and Berlin, it is his native province that has provided the wealth of themes and psychological studies to be found in his works. These reveal his deterministic philosophy and his sense of compassion, and are written objectively and soberly, with economy and clarity, and in language of great beauty and purity. The Nobel prize committee commented particularly on the "epic force" with which he handled his material, especially in *The Bridge on the Drina.*
(V. J.)

ANDRIEUX, FRANÇOIS GUILLAUME JEAN STANISLAS (1759–1833), French lawyer hostile to Napoleon Bonaparte's civil code and dramatist who achieved contemporary fame as an ultraclassicist, was born at Strasbourg on May 6, 1759. Under the Convention (1792–95) he was a judge in the civil division of the court of cassation, which had power to annul the verdicts of lower tribunals. He became president of the Tribunat, the deliberative assembly opposed to the civil code, and was therefore displaced from the law in 1802. Andrieux then returned to dramatic writing, having achieved success with *Les Étourdis* (1787). His later plays include *Molière avec ses amis* (1804), *La Comédienne* (1816) and *Lucius Junius Brutus* (1830). As professor of literature at the Collège de France (1814) he maintained the classical tradition against the growing romantic school. His advice to the young Balzac (*q.v.*), to choose any profession rather than the writing of plays, is often remembered as a sign of his biased judgment. He became permanent secretary to the Académie Française in 1829, and the 1835 edition of the *Dictionnaire de l'Academie* was prepared partly under his direction.

Andrieux died in Paris on May 9, 1833.

ANDROCLES (ANDROCLUS) (fl. 1st century A.D.), a Roman slave, is the hero of a story by Aulus Gellius, taken originally from Apion's *Aiguptiaka* and also found in Aelian's *De natura animalium* (vii, 48), which tells that Androcles had taken refuge from the cruelties of his master in a cave in Africa, when a lion entered the cave and showed him his swollen paw, from which Androcles extracted a large thorn. The grateful animal subsequently recognized him when he had been captured and thrown to the wild beasts in the circus and, instead of attacking him, began to caress him; he was then set free. The story is the subject of the play *Androcles and the Lion* by G. Bernard Shaw.

ANDROMACHE, in Greek legend, the daughter of Eëtion, prince of Thebe in Mysia, and wife of Hector (*q.v.*). All her relations perished in or shortly after the taking of the town by Achilles. After the capture of Troy her son Astyanax (or Scamandrius) was hurled from the battlements. When the captives were allotted, Andromache fell to Neoptolemus (Pyrrhus), the son of Achilles, whom she accompanied to Epirus and to whom she bore three sons. When Neoptolemus was slain at Delphi, he left Andromache and the kingdom to Helenus, the brother of Hector. After his death Andromache returned to Asia Minor with her youngest son, Pergamus, who there founded a town named after himself.

ANDROMEDA, one of the constellations of the northern sky, near Perseus and Cassiopeia, named for the Andromeda of Greek legend, the daughter of Cepheus and Cassiopeia (*see* PERSEUS). The most famous feature of the constellation is the Great Andromeda Nebula, the brightest of the spiral nebulae. The distance of the nebula from the solar system was estimated by Walter Baade to be about 2,000,000 light-years, and it can be seen without much difficulty with the naked eye, being recognizable by its diffuse appearance. It is an "island universe" probably containing millions of stars and of the same general nature as our own stellar system, though apparently of somewhat smaller dimensions. (*See* NEBULA.) A number of outbursts of novae (temporary stars) have been observed in the nebula. Nearly all the spiral nebulae are receding from us with large velocities, but the Andromeda nebula is one of the exceptional approaching systems, its velocity in the line of sight being 300 km. per second. Photographs show in great detail its beautiful spiral structure; the plane of the spiral is tilted with respect to the Earth, giving the nebula an apparently elongated form.

The double star γ Andromedae is a favourite object for observation with a small telescope because of the striking contrast of colour of the two components.

The Andromedids are a swarm of meteors which made a notable display on Nov. 27, 1872, and provide some of the November meteors year by year; the swarm is believed to be the debris of Biela's comet which was last seen in 1852.

ANDRONICUS I (ANDRONICUS COMNENUS) (*c.* 1100–1185), Byzantine emperor from 1183 to 1185, was a son of Isaac and a grandson of Alexius I Comnenus. Captured by the Seljuk Turks in 1141 but ransomed a year later he went to Constantinople to the court of his cousin, the emperor Manuel I. Andronicus repeatedly fell into disgrace with the emperor because of his doubtful loyalty. Fascinating and well-educated, he was a born adventurer and most unscrupulous. He spent much of Manuel's reign in exile, wandering from court to court, living at Kiev or at Antioch or in Syria, Mesopotamia and the Caucasian districts. Finally he returned and submitted to Manuel and was then appointed governor of Pontus. The accession of a minor, Alexius II (*q.v.*), and the unpopular regency gave him his opportunity. He advanced through Asia Minor and reached Chalcedon. A revolt broke out in Constantinople, accompanied by a massacre of the Latins (May 1182), and Andronicus then entered the capital as the protector of Alexius II. He was crowned co-emperor in Sept. 1183, but soon killed Alexius and married Agnes, his child-widow.

The short reign of Andronicus was characterized by strong and wise measures. He attempted to suppress many administrative abuses, but, above all, to check the power of the great landed magnates and to reverse the pro-Latin policy of his predecessor. The people, who felt the severity of his laws, at the same time acknowledged their justice and found themselves protected from the rapacity of their superiors. The aristocrats, meanwhile, were infuriated against him and frequent conspiracies occurred, which he ruthlessly suppressed. He also faced external danger in the form of a Norman invasion. In 1185, William II of Sicily invaded Epirus and advanced as far as Thessalonica, which he took and sacked. At the news of the approaching Normans, a riot broke out in Constantinople. Isaac II Angelus was proclaimed emperor, and Andronicus was handed over to the mob, at whose hands he died on Sept. 12, 1185.

BIBLIOGRAPHY.—G. Ostrogorsky, *History of the Byzantine State* (1956); A. A. Vasiliev, *History of the Byzantine Empire* (1952); C. Diehl, *Figures byzantines,* vol. 2 (1906). (J. M. Hy.)

ANDRONICUS II (ANDRONICUS PALAEOLOGUS) (1258–1332), Byzantine emperor from 1282 to 1328, was the eldest son of Michael VIII, who proclaimed him heir-presumptive in 1261 and co-emperor in 1272 and whom he succeeded in Dec. 1282. An intellectual and a theologian rather than a statesman or soldier, he found it hard to deal with the new and urgent military problems of his reign. The danger from the west, which had determined his father's foreign policy, had collapsed with the Sicilian Vespers in 1282 (*see* SICILIAN VESPERS), but Andronicus was faced with the revived aspirations of the Serbs under Milutin (1282–1321) and with the fresh inroads of the Ottoman Turks. He held the Serbs off by giving his infant daughter in marriage to Milutin; but his attempt to stem the Turkish tide by accepting the help of Roger di Flor and his Catalan mercenaries, the Almogávares (*q.v.*), proved disastrous. The Catalans fell out of favour, their leader was murdered and they turned on their employers, while the Turks overran almost the whole of Asia Minor, leaving only a few isolated places (such as Nicaea and Nicomedia) in Byzantine control.

Internally Andronicus' reign was marked by a steady disintegration of centralized authority and by the concentration of power in the hands of the landed aristocracy. He tried to offset the depreciation of the currency by new measures of taxation and unwise economies. His reduction of the strength of the Byzantine army and navy led to an increasing reliance on foreign mercenaries; and by playing off the Genoese against the Venetians he involved the empire in their private disputes and made it almost entirely dependent on the Italian republics for its maritime trade and defense. In some respects, however, his reign was enlightened and progressive. Culture and the arts revived, and such men as the philosopher Theodore Metochites and the historian Nicephorus Gregoras were among his friends and counselors. He completely revised the diocesan lists of the empire and transferred Mount Athos from the jurisdiction of the emperor to that of the patriarch. He repudiated his father's attempt to save the empire by enforcing union with the Roman Church and deposed the unionist patriarch John Beccus. In 1320, however, Andronicus quarreled with his grandson Andronicus III and excluded him from the succession.

Civil war ensued and in May 1328 he was forced by his grandson to abdicate. He died on Feb. 13, 1332, as the monk Anthony.

See G. Ostrogorsky, *History of the Byzantine State* (1956). (D. M. N.)

ANDRONICUS III (ANDRONICUS PALAEOLOGUS) (1296–1341), Byzantine emperor from 1328 to 1341, was the son of Michael IX and the grandson of Andronicus II. His youthful extravagance lost him the favour of his grandfather, who deprived him of his right to the crown after one of his escapades had brought about the murder of his brother and the death of his father Michael (1320). The family quarrel then developed into civil war. Andronicus had many supporters among the younger Byzantine nobility, particularly the wealthy John Cantacuzenus. He obliged his grandfather to recognize him as ruler of Thrace and part of Macedonia in 1321, and to accept him as co-emperor in 1325. War broke out again in 1327, the Bulgars and the Serbs taking opposing sides, and the elder Andronicus was forced to abdicate in May 1328. Andronicus III, although a brave soldier, left the direction of imperial policy to his friend Cantacuzenus. His reign was one of constant warfare, principally with the Ottoman Turks and the Serbs. He encouraged the Seljuks against the Ottomans, and the Bulgars against the Serbs. But the Ottomans captured Nicaea and Nicomedia, and the Serbs defeated the

WÜRTTEMBERGISCHE LANDESBIBLIOTHEK

ANDRONICUS III. MINIATURE FROM A CONTEMPORARY MANUSCRIPT NOW IN THE LANDESBIBLIOTHEK, STUTTGART

Bulgars at Velbuzhd (Kyustendil) in July 1330. Andronicus' efforts to break the Genoese control of Byzantine waters and to reorganize an imperial fleet led to the recovery from Genoa of Lesbos, Chios and Phocaea. His greatest achievement, however, was to win back the districts of Epirus and Thessaly, which had been under separatist Greek rule since the fourth crusade (1204). He died on June 15, 1341.

See G. Ostrogorsky, *History of the Byzantine State* (1956). (D. M. N.)

ANDRONICUS OF CYRRHUS (*fl. c.* 100 B.C.), Greek astronomer, is best known as the builder of the horologium at Athens, the so-called "tower of the winds." A considerable portion of the tower still exists. It is octagonal, with sundials and figures carved on each side, these figures representing the eight principal winds. A brazen Triton on the summit, with a rod in his hand, turned round by the wind, pointed to the quarter from which it blew. From this model is derived the custom of placing weathercocks on steeples (*see* ATHENS: *Topography and Antiquities: Roman Period*). Andronicus also built a multiple-faced sundial in the sanctuary of Poseidon on the Island of Tenos.

ANDRONICUS OF RHODES (1st century B.C.), 11th head of the Peripatetic school and editor of the treatises of Aristotle and Theophrastus. The works Aristotle had published were mainly dialogues in a popular style; his mature thought had been expressed in lectures to his students, which had been transmitted through several generations in a state of confusion, the *disjecta membra* of important treatises being thrown together with trivial by-products of Peripatetic research. Andronicus disengaged the master's authentic works from this miscellaneous material and arranged them in a logical order, justifying his procedure in a long treatise (later lost) in which he gave a biography of Aristotle, treated of questions of authenticity and explained the structure of the Aristotelian system. He also collected Aristotle's letters and wrote commentaries on some of the treatises. He proceeded in the same way in his edition of Theophrastus.

A treatise *On the Emotions* and a paraphrase of Aristotle's *Ethics* which were printed under the name of Andronicus were not written by him.

See P. Moraux, *Les Listes anciennes des ouvrages d'Aristote* (1951). (D. J. A.)

ANDROS, SIR EDMUND (1637–1714), one of the ablest English colonial governors in 17th-century America. He was born in London on Dec. 6, 1637, the son of Amice Andros, royal bailiff of the Island of Guernsey. He was brought up as a page in the royal household and remained loyal during the Commonwealth exile. In 1674 his loyalty was rewarded by his appointment as governor of New York and the Jerseys. He was a military man of aristocratic background, able but tactless. His ability as an administrator and his conscientious devotion to the prerogatives of the crown made him unpopular and he was recalled in 1681.

The restoration policy of colonial consolidation returned Andros to America in 1686 as governor of the Dominion of New England, ultimately to include Massachusetts, Maine, Plymouth, Rhode Island, Connecticut and New Hampshire. Two years later his jurisdiction was extended to include New York and the Jerseys. His imposition of Episcopal worship in the Old South meetinghouse in Boston, his vigorous enforcement of the Navigation acts, his conservative financial policies, his demands that taxes and quit rents be paid, his requirement that landholders take out new land patents, and his limitations upon town meetings and right of local taxation antagonized the colonists. When the news of the overthrow of James II reached Boston, Andros was summarily deposed and arrested. In England he was tried and immediately released. In later years he served as governor of Virginia (1692–98) and Maryland (1693–94). Returning to England he served as governor of Guernsey (1704–06). In Virginia he encouraged cotton culture and promoted the establishment of William and Mary college. He died in London, Feb. 24, 1714.

(RA. MU.)

ANDROS, the most northerly island of the Cyclades (q.v.), Greece, lies 6 mi. S.E. of Euboea and about 2 mi. N. of Tenos. It is nearly 25 mi. long and its greatest breadth is 10 mi. The population was 12,928 (1961), among whom were many Albanians, especially in the north. It is mountainous, with many fruitful and well-watered valleys. Andros, the capital, on the east coast, has 2,032 inhabitants. The ruins of Palaeopolis, the ancient capital, are on the west coast; the town possessed a famous temple, dedicated to Dionysus. The ancient population was mainly Ionian, perhaps with a Thracian admixture. Originally dependent on Eretria, in the 7th century B.C. it sent colonies to Chalcidice (Acanthus, Stageirus, Argilus, Sane). In 480 it supplied ships to Xerxes and was subsequently harried by the Greek fleet. Though enrolled in the Delian league it remained disaffected toward Athens, and was obliged to admit Athenian settlers. It revolted in 411 and was attacked by Athens. In the 4th century it was again an uneasy member of the revived, anti-Spartan Delian league. In the Hellenistic period Andros was coveted as a frontier post by the naval powers of Macedonia and Egypt. In 200 it was captured by a combined Roman, Pergamene and Rhodian fleet, and remained a possession of Pergamum until the bequest of that kingdom to Rome in 133 B.C. Before falling under Turkish rule, Andros was from A.D. 1207 to 1566 governed by the Zeno and Sommariva families under Venetian protection. It became part of Greece in 1829 and is now an eparchy.

See T. Sauciuc, *Andros* (1914). (J. Bo.)

ANDROSCOGGIN, a river that serves as the outlet of Umbagog lake in Errol, N.H. It flows southerly 39 mi. to Gorham, N.H., thence easterly 65 mi. to Jay, Me., and southerly 67 mi. to the sea. The river drops a total of 1,245 ft. between Umbagog lake and tidewater with two steep drops at Berlin, N.H., and at Rumford, Me. Water power, process water and spruce fir forests of the drainage basin have combined to make it one of the leading pulp and paper manufacturing areas in New England. Similar resources account for textile manufacturing in Auburn and Lewiston, Me. Shoe manufacturing is most important in the diversified industry group. The excellent hunting, fishing and boating on the river and lakes attract thousands of sportsmen. (A. S. CN.)

ANEMIA is a condition of variable severity in which the concentration of hemoglobin in the circulating blood is reduced below normal. Hemoglobin, an iron-containing protein, gives the blood its red colour and is a direct measure of the capacity of blood to transport oxygen from the lungs to the tissues (*see* BLOOD). Consequently, the severity of anemia is best determined in practice by laboratory measurement with a photoelectric colorimeter of the intensity of the blood's hemoglobin colour. The reduced amount of oxygen in the blood of anemic patients is a major cause of their symptoms and of the concurrent dysfunction of organs such as the heart, skeletal muscle and brain. Anemia is always a sign, either predominant or incidental, of some underlying congenital condition or acquired disease.

Normally the blood consists of about five litres of a liquid containing a prodigious number of small hemoglobin-containing red corpuscles which are kept in suspension by the turbulence of the passage of the liquid through the blood vessels. When venous blood is centrifugated the slightly heavier red corpuscles pack to-

gether below the pale yellow plasma and occupy about 45% of the sample. Under the microscope the red cells appear as biconcave discs with an average diameter of about 0.0075 mm. (a common pin is about 1 mm. thick). Blood of normal human adult males contains on the average 5,400,000 red cells, that of normal adult females 4,800,000, per cubic millimetre, as enumerated after manifold dilution in a ruled counting chamber under the microscope. Each red cell holds about a third of its volume of hemoglobin. Collectively the red cells in 100 c.c. of adult male blood contain 16 g. of hemoglobin on the average, while the same quantity of adult female blood contains 14 g. Knowing the number of red cells, the amount of hemoglobin and the volume of the centrifugated red cells in a sample of blood permits easy calculation of the hemoglobin concentration and volume of the average red cell. These are often useful indexes of the nature of an anemia. Microscopic inspection of films of blood dried on glass slides and stained with aniline dyes allows observations of variations in the size and colour of individual red cells. It also permits identification of the two other cellular constituents of the blood, the so-called white corpuscles, which are nucleated and are larger than red cells, and the dustlike blood platelets.

SYMPTOMS AND SIGNS

In all types of anemia the decreased amount of oxygen carried by the blood requires compensatory adjustments by the body. These usually consist of (1) an increase in the amount of blood pumped through the tissues by the heart; and (2) an increase in the proportion of oxygen removed from the blood by the tissues. The effect of the first compensatory mechanism is perceived by the patient or his physician as more forceful or rapid heart action and pulse; the second is detectable only by laboratory analysis of the venous blood. The symptoms of tissue oxygen deficiency include pulsating noises in the ears, dizziness, fainting, poor appetite, shortness of breath and increased amounts of urine. In certain kinds of anemia the underlying condition itself may produce other symptoms in, for example, the nervous, digestive or genitourinary system. Abnormal physical signs include pallor, jaundice, skin hemorrhages, inflamed tongue or gums or enlargement of the heart, liver, spleen or lymph nodes. Aside from microscopic examination of the blood and bone marrow and chemical study of the blood plasma, X-ray examinations of the stomach, bowels, lungs or bones may be necessary for determination of the underlying cause of the anemia.

CAUSES AND TREATMENT

Red cells are formed within the marrow cavities of the central bones of the adult human skeleton (skull, spine, ribs, breastbone and pelvic bones), the marrow comprising altogether an organ larger than the liver. Samples of the active red bone marrow are easily obtained by needle or trephine puncture of the sternum or other accessible bones. Under the microscope the marrow shows hosts of nucleated red cells at all stages of development toward the mature, adult, nonnucleated, hemoglobin-containing cell that will be released into the circulation. When, as after a hemorrhage, more adult red cells are needed, the primitive cells develop rapidly, making possible a six- to eightfold increase in red cell production in certain types of anemia.

In the normal person sufficient red cells to contain about 7.5 g. of hemoglobin are released daily from the bone marrow into the blood stream. Those newly arrived in the circulation are recognizable for two or three days as reticulocytes when stained in a way to display their characteristic threadlike network. When the bone marrow is actively producing red cells, reticulocytes are numerous. Each day's crop of new red cells survives for about 100 days before succumbing to old age. The hemoglobin is then released and digested by specialized reticuloendothelial cells lining the capillary blood vessels, especially those of the spleen and liver, into its components: iron, a red pigment with a ring-shaped structural formula (porphyrin) and a protein (globin). The iron remains in the body to be used over and over again in the formation of new hemoglobin, but the porphyrin ring opens and changes chemically to become the yellow pigment of the blood plasma, bilirubin. This is then excreted by the liver, giving the bile its characteristic colour. In patients whose anemia is due to increased destruction of red cells, excess amounts of bilirubin in the yellow plasma cause the patient to appear to be slightly jaundiced, and the excess bile pigments darken the excreta.

In a healthy person, constant levels of red cells and hemoglobin exist in the circulating blood because the same enormous numbers of red cells are produced as are destroyed daily. Anemia results when either (1) the production of red cells and hemoglobin temporarily lags behind the normal rate of their destruction; or (2) an excessive rate of destruction temporarily exceeds the capacity of the bone marrow to produce red cells. Unless, at some reduced hemoglobin level consistent with life, these two opposed processes again become equivalent, the patient will die. This may happen quickly if too rapid destruction of red cells occurs. On the other hand, in chronic anemia in which only diminished red cell production is involved, this balance may result in a relatively constant but reduced level of circulating hemoglobin. The rate of production of red cells by the bone marrow is normally controlled by a physiological feedback mechanism analogous to the thermostatic control of temperature in a room. Thus, when the hemoglobin level in the circulating blood falls below normal, production of red cells in the bone marrow is accelerated, apparently as the result of a chemical signal carried to the marrow by the plasma.

REDUCED PRODUCTION OF RED CELLS

There are three principal causes of anemia of this type: (1) anatomical derangements of the bone marrow; (2) deficiency of essential chemical substances involved in the formation processes or required in the composition of the red cell; (3) "poisoning" or inhibition of the red cell forming processes. In general, in such anemias the reticulocytes in the peripheral blood are few and the bilirubin in the plasma is not increased.

Anatomical Derangements of Bone Marrow.—These may result from several causes, one of which is invasion by cancer cells carried by the blood stream from a tumour situated frequently in the breast, prostate gland or lung. The proliferating cells of leukemia (q.v.), a "cancer" of the white cell precursors in the bone marrow or lymph nodes, may also overgrow the bone marrow. Some forms of chronic marrow white cell leukemia (myeloid metaplasia) or chronic exposure to organic chemicals may stimulate replacement of the active red cellular bone marrow by fibrous tissue or bone. Only when very extensive, however, will any of these processes significantly reduce the production of red cells by the marrow. A characteristic sign in the peripheral blood of such mechanical interference is the appearance of many irregularities in the size and shape of the red cells and of nucleated red cells, which normally never leave the bone marrow. Unless the process invading the marrow can be suppressed (by use of X-rays, antileukemic or adrenocortical drugs), the patient's life can be prolonged only by frequent blood transfusions.

The so-called aplastic anemia (frequently of unknown cause) represents a challenging but fortunately comparatively rare form of anatomical bone marrow failure. In this condition the normally red bone marrow becomes fatty and yellow and fails to form enough of any of its three cellular products. Consequently, anemia with few reticulocytes, bone marrow white cells (granulocytes) and platelets in the peripheral blood is characteristic. The lack of granulocytes, which normally ingest bacteria when they invade the tissues, invites infections of the mouth or gums. The lack of platelets leads to bleeding, disfiguring and harmless in the skin but quickly fatal in the brain. In many patients it has been found that onset of aplastic anemia was preceded by extensive exposure to such organic chemicals as benzol or to hair dyes or insecticides containing benzollike chemicals. In some instances a peculiar sensitivity of the patient to a drug useful and harmless to hundreds of others has been responsible. Aplastic anemia also results from overexposure to various types of radiation, whether from external X-rays or internally absorbed radioactive substances, provided their destructive energy reaches the cells of the marrow. The only useful treatment is repeated blood transfusions and, when infection develops, administration of antibacterial drugs, in the hope of sus-

taining the patient until spontaneous recovery of bone marrow function occurs.

Deficiency of Essential Nutrients and Regulators of Bone Marrow Function.—Such deficiency causes several types of curable anemia and represents an area of great increase in knowledge that began in 1926. In that year, George R. Minot and William P. Murphy (qq.v.) of Harvard, reported that a large series of patients with pernicious anemia, previously an invariably fatal disease, showed prompt clinical improvement after being placed on a diet rich in liver, and that within a few weeks normal red cell and hemoglobin levels were attained. This work was suggested in part by experiments with chronically bled dogs, conducted by the pathologist George H. Whipple (q.v.), in which the efficacy of liver and meat in promoting formation of hemoglobin was demonstrated. It is now known that the activity of these foods in the dogs was due chiefly to their iron content, whereas the substance in liver active in pernicious anemia was principally vitamin B_{12}. The latter discovery was the result of scientific work of the pharmaceutical industry in the United States in 1948 and shortly afterward in England. Long before that time, liver extracts for oral use and later purified extracts for injection had been developed, providing one of the most dramatic of modern medical triumphs over death. The combined work of Whipple, Minot and Murphy, to whom the 1934 Nobel prize in medicine was awarded, converted the clinical study of anemia from a largely descriptive to a dynamic and actively pursued experimental subject.

Deficiency of Vitamin B_{12}.—This red, cobalt-containing vitamin is found in animal but not in vegetable foods. Unlike other vitamins, it is not formed by higher plants but only by certain bacteria and molds (as, for example, in its commercial production) and in the rumina of sheep and cattle, provided traces of cobalt are present in their fodder. In other species, including man, vitamin B_{12} must be obtained passively, by eating of animal foods. The vitamin, however, is successfully assimilated from the human intestinal tract only if a mucoprotein secretion of the stomach, the so-called intrinsic factor, is available to concentrate the vitamin on the intestinal wall.

In pernicious anemia, a condition first described by Thomas Addison of London in 1855 and usually affecting patients past middle life, all stomach secretion spontaneously fails and vitamin B_{12} ceases to be assimilated. However, if even as little as a millionth of a gram of vitamin B_{12} is injected daily, numerous reticulocytes begin to appear in the blood within a few days, and within six weeks the patient is well and no longer anemic. The half pound of liver a day originally prescribed by Minot and Murphy usually contained enough vitamin B_{12} to force the assimilation of the necessary daily millionth of a gram of vitamin B_{12} despite the absence of the stomach factor. Today it is possible but inefficient to treat the patient by a combination of hog stomach intrinsic factor and vitamin B_{12}. In practice the most reliable treatment is the injection of small amounts of vitamin B_{12} at monthly intervals.

Without vitamin B_{12} all bone marrow activity slows down and reticulocytes, granulocytes and platelets appear in reduced numbers in the circulation. In the marrow the nucleated red cells become abnormally large (megaloblastic) and show signs of delayed maturation of the nucleus. The adult red cells eventually formed are unusually large (macrocytic). Because they are well filled with hemoglobin, the bone marrow defect clearly lies in cell production rather than hemoglobin production. Deficiency of vitamin B_{12} also results in a red cell destroying process in the bone marrow, with elevated plasma bilirubin and clinical jaundice.

Lack of vitamin B_{12} also occasions defective formation of the papillae of the tongue, giving an appearance of abnormal smoothness. It often causes defective function of the intestine, resulting in "indigestion" and sometimes constipation and diarrhea. Most serious, because if it has been present for some time treatment with vitamin B_{12} may not correct it, is the degeneration of certain motor and sensory tracts of the spinal cord that vitamin B_{12} deficiency may cause. Initial complaints of numbness and tingling of fingers or toes may, without treatment, eventually progress to great instability of gait or virtual paralysis.

Vitamin B_{12} deficiency also may result from complete vegetarianism or from competition for vitamin B_{12} by the broad tapeworm or by intestinal bacteria growing in cul de sacs or above partial obstructions. In these, as in such primary intestinal diseases as chronic celiac disease, tropical sprue or regional ileitis that affect the absorptive capacity of the small bowel, additional nutritional deficiencies (as of folic acid or iron) are likely to develop.

Deficiency of Folic Acid.—Folic acid is found in leafy vegetables and is also synthesized by certain intestinal bacteria. In man, deficiency of this vitamin is sometimes the result of a highly defective diet, of chronic intestinal disease including celiac disease and tropical sprue, or of cirrhosis of the liver; and in some way pregnancy increases the requirement for the vitamin. The macrocytic anemia and megaloblastic bone marrow that folic acid deficiency causes are indistinguishable under the microscope from those of vitamin B_{12} deficiency, but the nervous system is never affected. In 1937 Lucy Wills of London found that some patients did not respond to the injection of purified liver extract, subsequently recognized to be virtually a pure solution of vitamin B_{12}. Eventually it was discovered that such patients have low levels of folic acid in the plasma and that they respond to the daily administration of as little as 250-millionths of a gram of pteroylglutamic acid, a synthetic folic acid. In 1946 it was found that 20 or more times that daily dosage also causes temporary blood response in pernicious anemia. However, anemia and nervous system damage may appear later. In rare instances additional dietary deficiency of vitamin C may produce clinical signs of scurvy and interfere with the conversion of dietary folic acid in the liver to its internally active form. Unless folic acid deficiency is complicated by the presence of intestinal or liver disease, its treatment rarely requires more than that a normal diet be instituted. Otherwise pteroylglutamic acid can be given daily by mouth.

Deficiency of Iron.—This is probably the commonest cause of anemia in all parts of the world. To it many different names have been applied: nutritional anemia in babies, chlorosis in adolescent girls, idiopathic hypochromic anemia in adult women, hookworm anemia, etc. To prevent such anemia, an adequate endowment of iron must be supplied by the mother to the unborn infant, and children of both sexes must obtain from food sufficient iron to maintain an ever-expanding pool of circulating hemoglobin until full growth is attained. At that time about 2.6 g. of iron, which constitutes 0.34% of the hemoglobin molecule, are present in the blood and 4.6 g. in the entire body. Thereafter, in the adult male, unless bleeding and consequent iron loss takes place (as from peptic ulceration, hookworm infestation, bowel cancer or hemorrhoids), there is virtually no more need for iron. In the adult female, however, recurrent menstruation or pregnancies make the demand for iron continuous. Milk is a poor source of iron; meat and green leafy vegetables are good sources, provided the normal stomach secretion of hydrochloric acid is present to render the iron soluble and provided there is no defect of assimilation due to intestinal disease.

Lack of iron quantitatively limits the hemoglobin available for red cell manufacture; hence the developing cells in the marrow have normal nuclei but small amounts of hemoglobin-containing cytoplasm. Red cell production is relatively less reduced than is that of hemoglobin, and the adult red cells released into the blood are small and pale. Granulocytes and platelets are produced in normal quantities. The plasma contains little bilirubin. The plasma iron is low and the granules of storage iron seen in the reticuloendothelial cells of the normal marrow are absent.

Victims of iron deficiency anemia are pale but not jaundiced. The deficiency of iron-containing enzymes in the tissues results in a smooth tongue, brittle, flattened fingernails and lustreless hair. The only treatment required is oral administration of iron salts in some palatable form. In instances of intestinal disease in which iron by mouth may be irritating or not well assimilated, organic iron compounds are available for injection. Within a few days the patient feels stronger, the reticulocytes increase temporarily and the hemoglobin level rapidly rises as new red cells, well filled with hemoglobin, pour into the blood stream.

Endocrine Deficiency.—Of more theoretical than practical interest are the mild anemias associated with deficiencies of the anterior pituitary, thyroid, adrenocortical or testicular hormones. The major symptoms of such patients are not due to the insignificant anemia; rather they are characteristic of the lack of a particular endocrine function as it affects general or specific metabolism. Unless complicated by deficiencies of vitamin B_{12} or iron, these anemias are never severe and are readily abolished by appropriate treatment with the lacking hormone.

Inhibition of Red Cell Forming Processes.—Such inhibition is due to the effect of various "poisonous" substances absorbed from outside or elaborated within the body by disease. In addition to anemia with few reticulocytes, reduction in the numbers of granulocytes and platelets may or may not occur. The so-called antifolic drugs, useful in the treatment of certain acute leukemias in children because they deprive the abnormal marrow white cells of an essential growth factor, may for the same reason also adversely affect red cell production. Chloramphenicol, a useful antibacterial drug, in rare patients has a toxic action upon the bone marrow. Far commoner are the anemias that result from the inhibitory effects of chronic infection, widespread cancer or uremia resulting from any kind of chronic kidney failure. The bone marrow looks surprisingly normal under the microscope, which suggests that it is powerless to increase its cellularity in response to the developing anemia. The removal of the offending drug may allow spontaneous recovery; but with toxins of internal origin only the elimination of the chronic infection, the temporary suppression of the cancerous growth or the relief of uremia will lessen the anemia.

Increased Destruction of Red Cells

There are two principal causes of anemia of this type: (1) inherently defective red cells; or (2) environment hostile to red cells. Both result in short red cell survival—sometimes of only a few days' duration in severe anemia. In general, the reticulocytes in the peripheral blood are numerous and the bilirubin in the plasma is increased as are the deposits of iron in the tissues. The patients look jaundiced, and the increased excretion of bile pigments may lead to the formation of gallstones.

Although profuse blood loss causes anemia, the immediate clinical symptoms and signs are due to the reduced blood volume, for which replacement by transfusion is urgently required. In fact, anemia develops only after the blood has become diluted with fluids derived from the tissues. Unless iron deficiency anemia results from continued bleeding, recovery is spontaneous over a few weeks and is initially associated with a transient rise of reticulocytes.

Defective Red Cells.—Of these, there are three principal hereditary types recognizable by the appearance under the microscope: spherocytic, target (target-oval) and sickle cell. One additional acquired type, an acid-sensitive red cell defect, causes chronic hemolytic anemia with paroxysmal hemoglobinuria.

Spherocytic Anemia.—In spherocytic anemia (hereditary hemolytic jaundice, spherocytosis) many of the red cells appear to be small, stain densely for hemoglobin and look nearly spherical. Such cells are mechanically fragile and readily swell up and burst osmotically in dilute salt solution. The chronic anemia is usually moderate or so slight that it may go unnoticed for years. However, anemia may become suddenly severe when an incidental respiratory infection briefly suppresses the increased production of red cells necessary to meet the constantly increased rate of red cell destruction (aplastic crisis). Congenital spherocytic anemia is transmitted by either parent as a Mendelian dominant. Studies with patients' red cells labeled with radioactive chromium, which emits gamma rays detectable at body surface, show that the radioactivity accumulates in the spleen. This occurs because the spheroidal shape of the red cells prevents them from readily passing through the spleen as normal discoidal cells do. Therefore, as might be expected, operative removal of the enlarged spleen permanently cures the anemia by eliminating this critical filter. Splenectomy is a harmless procedure except sometimes in infants. It does not, of course, prevent the future hereditary transmission of the disease.

Thalassemia.—In this disease (also called Cooley's anemia, Mediterranean anemia and target-cell anemia), which is genetically determined, the unusually flat red cells display central pale-staining areas (target cells) and irregular variations from the usual circular outline. The cells resist osmotic destruction in dilute salt solution. The mild form of the disease is associated with only slight anemia and a normal life expectancy. Development of the severely anemic form of the disease, which appears in infancy and is usually fatal before puberty, requires that both parents have the milder form. Although in the severe form the spleen and liver are usually enlarged, splenectomy is not usually beneficial, presumably because the short-lived red cells are destroyed elsewhere. Moreover, there is a diminished rate of hemoglobin production that is not corrected by iron therapy and that results in a blood level of hemoglobin constantly lower than that of red cells. Transfusions yield temporary benefit only.

Sickle-Cell Anemia.—In sickle-cell anemia (or sicklemia) most of the red cells of a sample of fresh blood look normally discoidal until deprived of oxygen, when the characteristic sickle- or crescent-shaped forms with threadlike extremities appear. Re-exposure to oxygen causes immediate reversion to the discoidal form. Only patients with the homozygous, *i.e.*, inherited from both parents, form of the disease are anemic. Their red cells begin to sickle when exposed to oxygen concentrations like those of the normal venous blood. Much lower oxygen concentrations are required to cause sickling of the cells of the nonanemic, heterozygous, *i.e.*, inherited from only one parent, form. In 1949 the sickling phenomenon was shown by Linus Pauling of the California Institute of Technology to be associated with the presence of hemoglobin with an abnormal electric charge on the molecule, accounting for most of the hemoglobin in the severely anemic form but for only about half that in the heterozygous patient's cells. In 1950 John W. Harris of Boston, Mass., demonstrated that cell-free solutions of sickle-cell hemoglobin when deoxygenated became viscous and under the microscope displayed parallel alignment of the hemoglobin molecules in elongated masses looking very like sickled cells. In the next few years, as a result of the wide clinical use of paper electrophoresis, several other hereditary varieties of abnormal hemoglobin were discovered in patients with mild forms of target-cell anemia alone or in genetically determined combinations with sickle-cell hemoglobin. Especially in these last, significant degrees of anemia may be present.

Sickle-cell anemia occurs almost exclusively in Negroes, of whom, in the United States, about 7% carry the sickle-cell trait. Only the homozygous form is clinically important because of the accompanying severe chronic anemia and painful crises. These last are apparently due to blockage of capillary beds in various organs by masses of sickled red cells, giving rise to fever and episodic pains in chest, abdomen or joints that are difficult to distinguish from other diseases. The homozygous anemic patients usually die in childhood after a period of some years of disability. At first the spleen is enlarged and congested with sickled red cells, but later it withers away. No treatment other than transfusion has been found useful. Oxygen inhalation suppresses red cell production more than it reduces sickling.

Environment Hostile to Red Cells.—This is invariably an acquired situation. It may be the result of (1) exposure to red cell destroying (hemolytic) chemicals; (2) development of antibodies (allergy) against red cells; or (3) increase of red cell trapping. The microscopic appearance of the red cells is not distinctive, and careful questioning and subtle tests for abnormalities of plasma or red cells are required for diagnosis.

Chemicals.—Chemicals that destroy red cells are usually themselves oxidants or are transformed into oxidizing substances in the body. Injury may be accidental, as with moth ball (naphthalene) ingestion in children or the undesirable effects of a drug such as sulfanilamide or primaquine. The anemia develops rapidly over a few days and without transfusions may be fatal. The oxidizing activity of the substance in the plasma may be sufficient to destroy any kind of red cell. In 1953 Alf S. Alving, of Chicago, Ill., discovered that the red cells of certain Negroes were abnormally susceptible. These particular red cells were lacking in a protective enzyme, and when exposed to oxidant chemicals in the patient or in the test tube readily developed oxidized hemoglobin (methemoglobin) and microscopic Heinz bodies. Treatment consists of transfusions for severe anemia and future avoidance of potentially toxic chemicals.

Allergy.—Antibodies against red cells are found in the plasma and clearly cause acute hemolytic anemias in paroxysmal hemoglobinuria due to cold, erythroblastosis fetalis of newborn infants, or after a drug such as stibophen has combined with and antigenically altered the red cells. Plasma antibodies are special proteins formed by the body against foreign protein (antigens), never against its own unaltered proteins. Syphilis occasionally causes a hemolytic plasma antibody to develop which quickly destroys red cells after exposure of the blood to cold in the test tube or in the patient. The hemoglobin released from the red cells pours out in the urine (hemoglobinuria). For such a patient, cold feet are indeed a hazard.

In erythroblastosis fetalis (hemolytic disease of fetus and newborn) no red cell destroying process can be demonstrated in the test tube. However, when the infant's plasma is slightly concentrated the red cells are clumped (agglutinated). When these "sensitized" or "coated" cells are labeled with radioactive chromium and are injected into a suitable normal person they are quickly removed by the spleen and destroyed by some unknown process. This is presumably also the case in the affected infant's own enlarged spleen. In 1940–42, chiefly through the researches of Philip Levine, Karl Landsteiner and Alexander Wiener of New York, the mechanism of sensitization was explained. It was found that 85% of normal persons had in their red cells, irrespective of Landsteiner's classical blood group ABO factors, a new factor, Rh (*Rhesus*). The other 15% did not, and hence were called Rh-negative. If an Rh-negative person was injected with Rh-positive red cells or if an Rh-negative mother received such cells from an Rh-positive fetus (father Rh-positive) through a break in the placental blood vessels during pregnancy, anti-Rh antibodies frequently developed in the mother, sometimes in high concentration in the plasma. When these antibodies passed into the fetus, as do other maternal plasma proteins, a red cell destroying process was set up with severe anemia and hemolytic jaundice. The jaundice may be so severe as to cause yellow staining and damage to the central nervous system (kernicterus). Fortunately the lives of most affected infants who survive to the end of pregnancy can be saved by prompt exchange transfusions, which remove Rh-antibodies and introduce Rh-negative, unagglutinable red cells into the infant's circulation. Although the mother develops no anemia she may again build up anti-Rh antibodies during any subsequent Rh-positive pregnancy. Rh-incompatibility between husband and wife is by no means necessarily followed by maternal sensitization, which in many past instances resulted from ill-considered transfusion or injection of Rh-positive blood into Rh-negative female children or young women. (*See also* FETAL DISORDERS: *Erythroblastosis Fetalis;* BLOOD: *Individuality of Human Blood.*)

Increase of Red Cell Trapping.—This occurs with true agglutinating antibodies, as noted above, and also in other acquired hemolytic anemias associated with obscure red cell agglutinating (but not hemolyzing) properties of the plasma. The circumstance that the red cells of these patients, like those in erythroblastosis fetalis, are apparently sensitized has understandably led to the assumption that they also are coated by antibodies. However, the antigens for the hypothetical "autoantibodies" are unknown. Moreover, in 1956, James H. Jandl of Boston, Mass., showed that exposure of normal red cells to certain heavy metal salts in plasma at once endowed them with the hallmarks of sensitized red cells. Conservatively it may be supposed therefore that the affinity of an abnormal plasma protein for the surface of the red cell is often merely fortuitous.

Whatever the initial coating mechanism, hemolytic anemias of this type are found in patients with leukemias and other tumours of the white cells, especially those arising from lymph node cells (Hodgkin's disease). Less commonly, patients with ovarian tumours, cancers and chronic infections resembling generalized tuberculosis (sarcoid) develop this kind of hemolytic anemia.

However, in half these patients no such association is found. The spleen is usually enlarged and in many patients can be shown to remove selectively and destroy the patient's red cells. Consequently, splenectomy is frequently useful in such patients. However, treatment by other means, including X-rays, antitumour chemotherapy or steroid drugs (cortisone), is effective only temporarily in those with underlying malignant disease.

Hemolytic anemia is also the result of an increase of the filtering capacity of the spleen for uncoated red cells (hypersplenism). Anemia in part due to this cause occurs acutely when the spleen enlarges in response to infections such as pneumonia, typhoid fever or endocarditis. When the spleen is enlarged as a result of chronic obstruction to its venous outflow, as in cirrhosis of the liver, or as a consequence of infiltration by certain types of leukemic cells, splenic sequestration of the patient's uncoated red cells is the dominant cause of the chronic hemolytic anemia.

See also Index references under "Anemia" in the Index volume.

BIBLIOGRAPHY.—G. A. Daland, *Color Atlas of Morphologic Hematology: With a Guide to Clinical Interpretation,* rev. ed. (1959); W. B. Castle, "Disorders of the Blood," in W. A. Sodeman, *Pathologic Physiology: Mechanisms of Disease,* 3rd ed., ch. 28, pp. 861–1012 (1961); M. M. Wintrobe, *Clinical Hematology,* 5th ed. (1961); L. Pauling *et al.,* "Sickle Cell Anemia, a Molecular Disease," *Science,* 110:543–548 (Nov. 25, 1949); V. M. Ingram, "How Do Genes Act?" *Scient. Am.,* 198:68–74 (Jan. 1958); V. Herbert, *The Megaloblastic Anemias* (1959); J. V. Dacie, *The Haemolytic Anaemias, Congenital and Acquired* (1954); V. C. Vaughan, III, "Current Status of Hemolytic Disease of the Newborn," *Postgrad. Med.,* 18:115–122 (Aug. 1955); P. E. Beutler *et al.,* "The Hemolytic Effect of Primaquine: VII. Biochemical Studies of Drug-Sensitive Erythrocytes," *J. Lab. & Clin. Med.,* 45:286–295 (Feb. 1955); J. H. Jandl *et al.,* "Clinical Determination of the Sites of Red Cell Sequestration in Hemolytic Anemias," *J. Clin. Invest.,* 35:842–867 (Aug. 1956); A. J. Erslev, "Hematology: Control of Red Cell Production," *Annu. Rev. Med.,* 11:315–332 (1960); "Haematology" ed. by D. A. G. Galton, *Brit. M. Bull.,* 15:1–40 and 54–67 (Jan. 1959). (W. B. C.)

ANEMOMETRY is the measurement of air speed. Because of the difficulty of visibly tagging a small volume of air, it is not practical to observe its motion directly for a known time interval and so compute its speed. Instead, it is necessary to observe some physical effect associated with air motion. Among such effects are: the drift of objects suspended in the moving air; the pressure developed by resisting the motion of the air; the cooling of heated objects by the air stream; and changes in the speed of sound waves resulting from their passage through moving air. Anemometers have been built utilizing each of these effects. The anemometers based on the drift of an object in air (rotating cup and fan types) are the most common means of obtaining wind-speed data for weather forecasting purposes. Pressure, heat-loss and acoustic types are special-purpose instruments used primarily for measurements taken under unusual conditions or for special speed ranges.

The rotating cup anemometer consists essentially of three or four cups, hemispherical or bluntly conical, placed at the ends of light arms arranged like spokes of a wheel around a vertical rotating shaft (*see* fig. 1). The wind force is greater on a cup that has its concave face to the wind than on a cup on the opposite side of the wheel that has its convex back to the wind. The net force on a pair of opposite cups is then such that the wheel will rotate in that direction which allows the concave faces to retreat before the wind. The useful range of a standard cup anemometer is about 5 to 100 m.p.h. In fluctuating winds, the cup anemometer does not slow down as rapidly as it speeds up. The resulting error, called overrunning, gives an indicated average wind always greater than the true wind.

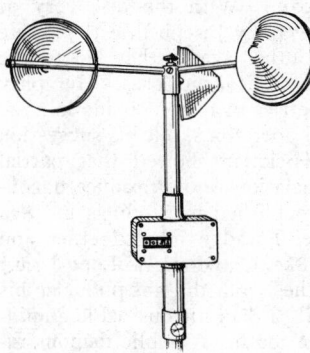

FRIEZ INSTRUMENT, BENDIX

FIG. 1.—A CUP ANEMOMETER
Standard anemometer used by the U.S. weather services. The rate of revolution of the cups is indicated or recorded at a distance by electrical means. The instrument body contains a transmitting mechanism and a counter dial

In very gusty wind, overrunning may produce an error as great as 30%. A contact mechanism within the box on the shaft housing allows a remote electrical indication to be made of each shaft revolution or mile of wind by means of a buzzer or flashing light. A simultaneous recording may be made by a magnetically operated pen bearing on a chart attached to a clock-driven drum.

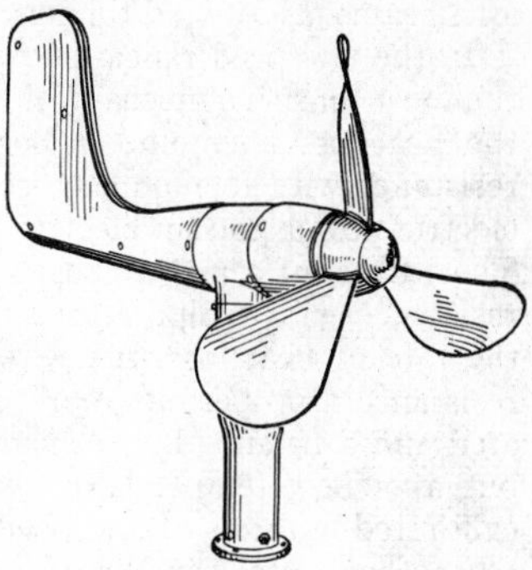

Another form of mechanical anemometer is the fan-type air meter. This consists of from 3 to 15 flat or curved blades mounted on a horizontal shaft which has a wind vane attached (*see* fig. 2) to keep the fan facing into the wind, in the manner of a windmill. When its rotating mechanism is very light and is mounted on jeweled bearings, the fan anemometer is especially adapted to measuring low air speeds in the range 1 to 25 m.p.h. (100–2,000 ft./sec., 1.5–35 ft./min.).

It is not feasible to compute the calibration factor of a mechanical anemometer from its dimensions. Its performance must be determined by observation in a wind tunnel whose air speed is known. This latter is best obtained by previous measurement with a pressure-type anemometer.

The common pressure anemometer consists of two thin-walled rigid tubes facing into the air stream. One is a Pitot tube (after Henri Pitot, French physicist [1695–1771]), its end cut off square and open to the air stream. The other is a static tube, closed and rounded at its upstream end, but having at some distance back a ring of small holes around the circumference of the tube. These permit an equalization of pressure within the tube and in the air streaming past just outside the holes. (*See* fig. 3; while the tubes are shown separated, it is common to surround the Pitot tube with the static tube.) A pressure gauge is connected to the tubes and indicates the differential pressure between them.

When a stream of air strikes the open mouth of the Pitot tube, it is brought to rest with a rise in pressure exactly equal to one-half the product of the air density and the square of its speed. When the static holes are located at least five tube diameters back on the cylindrical portion of the static tube, the air stream flowing smoothly over them will cause the pressure within the tube to be exactly equal to the static pressure outside. Since the static pressure also exists within the open Pitot tube, it will appear on both sides of the differential gauge with no effect. Only the dynamic pressure will be effective. The gauge may be calibrated either in pressure or air-speed units according to the rule given above. Pressure anemometers are best used in strong and steady

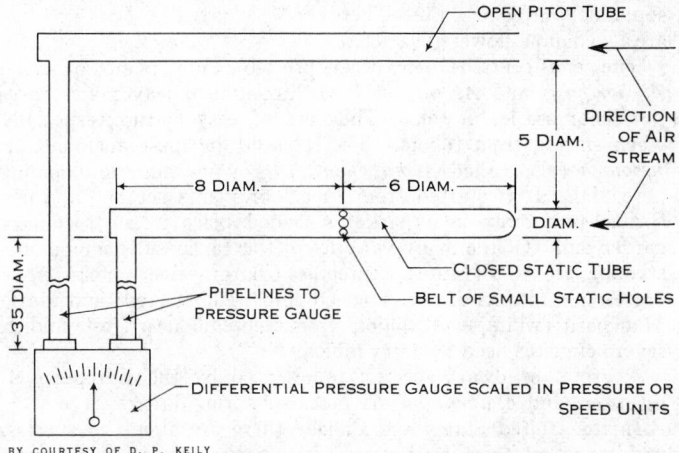

FRIEZ INSTRUMENT, BENDIX

FIG. 2.—PROPELLER ANEMOMETER. THE WIND VANE KEEPS IT FACING THE WIND

BY COURTESY OF D. P. KEILY

FIG. 3.—PITOT-STATIC PRESSURE TUBE ANEMOMETER
When proportioned as indicated, the instrument is a standard for the measurement of air speed

air streams, as in wind tunnels and on aircraft.

In the air-speed range below five miles per hour, where all but the most sensitive mechanical and pressure tube anemometers fail, the heat-loss anemometer becomes useful. One form, the hot resistance wire anemometer, consists of a heated wire, a source of electric power and an electric meter to show the heating current. The wire is of a metal chosen to give a large change in electrical resistance with temperature. When a rise in air speed increases the rate of heat loss, the wire temperature falls, the consequent resistance drop permits more current to flow, more heat is generated and a balance between heat gain and loss is again obtained, but at a new temperature. The electric-current meter may be calibrated in terms of air speed.

Another form, the heated thermocouple (*see* THERMOMETRY), employs an alternating current to heat the couple. The equilibrium temperature is measured as a direct current potential without interference by the heating current in the same circuit.

Heat-loss anemometers are especially valuable in observing air motion in very small spaces, where other types are too big to be inserted or would upset the flow they are intended to measure.

Acoustic anemometers measure the speed of sound in moving air. Since this speed is constant and known in still air, any deviation from it is a measure of the drift of the air in which the sound wave is traveling. The use of acoustic anemometers is limited to experimental researches in which small, rapid changes in very high air speed occur which cannot be detected by the more sluggish mechanical and pressure types.

See W. E. K. Middleton and A. F. Spilhaus, *Meteorological Instruments* (1953). (D. P. K.)

ANEMONE, or WINDFLOWER, a genus of the buttercup family (Ranunculaceae), containing about 100 species, mostly in the north temperate zone. *Anemone nemorosa,* wood anemone, occurs in Britain.

The plants are perennial herbs with an underground rootstock, or tuberous-rooted, and radical, deeply cut leaves. The elongated flower stem bears white, red, blue or, rarely, yellow flowers; there is an involucre of three bracts below each flower. The fruits comprise a cluster of short-beaked achenes, or long, plumose fruits in the pasqueflowers.

J. HORACE MCFARLAND CO.

MEADOW ANEMONE (ANEMONE CANADENSIS)

Many are favourite garden plants; among the best known is *Anemone coronaria,* the poppy anemone, a tuberous-rooted plant with divided leaves, and large, showy poppylike blossoms on stalks from six to nine inches high; the flowers are scarlet, crimson, blue, purple or white. There are also double-flowered varieties.

The genus contains many other spring-blooming plants, of which *A. hortensis* and *A. fulgens* have less-divided leaves and rosy-purple or scarlet flowers. They are of easy culture, especially when started from tubers. The splendid Japanese anemone, *A. japonica* (also called *A. hupehensis*), is a fine autumn-blooming perennial. It is started from tubers or plants set out in early spring, preferably in a partially shaded place in any ordinary garden soil. Of the many varieties of the Japanese anemone outstanding are Alba (white), September Charm (silvery pink), Alice (rose-pink), Prince Heinrich (deep pink), Rubra (red) and Marie Manchard (white). All bloom from September to frost, and in severe climates need a winter mulch.

A group of dwarf species, represented by the European *A. nemorosa* and *A. apennina,* are beautiful spring flowers.

In the United States and Canada there are about 20 species, with representatives in all regions from arctic America and Alaska south to Florida, Texas and California. Among these are some of the most attractive North American wild flowers. Noteworthy species are the American wood anemone (*A. quinquefolia*), very similar to the wood anemone of Europe; the tall windflower, or thimbleweed (*A. virginiana*), with greenish-white flowers, growing in woods from Nova Scotia to Alberta and south to Georgia and Arkansas; the mountain windflower (*A. lancifolia*), with large white flowers, often growing with the lily of the valley, native to the Appalachian region; and the red windflower (*A. multifida*), silky-hairy with red or greenish flowers, found throughout northern North America. The pasqueflower of Europe (*A. pulsatilla*) and its American representative (*A. patens*), both often called *Pulsatilla,* are showy examples of the genus.

The poppy anemone and its close relatives *A. hortensis* and *A. fulgens* are spring-flowering florist's plants.

The American species of *Anemone,* as well as the European wood anemone, are woodland plants that thrive in rich humus, in full or partial shade, and preferably out of the wind. The pasqueflowers do better in the gritty soil of the rock garden than in rich loam. Both species yield from their freshly crushed foliage an acrid volatile oil from which is extracted anemone camphor, somewhat used medicinally. *See* RANUNCULACEAE; PASQUEFLOWER.

(N. TR.)

ANESTHESIA AND ANESTHETICS. Anesthesia is loss of feeling or sensation, and anesthetics are agents capable of producing anesthesia. Anesthesia is induced to spare the patient the pain of surgical operations, but it also occurs as a symptom of certain diseases of the brain or spinal cord. Surgical anesthesia may be classified as general or local, general anesthesia being that in which total unconsciousness and muscular relaxation are produced and local anesthesia that in which only one area of the body is deprived of sensation.

The word analgesia (*q.v.*), which is sometimes erroneously used synonymously with anesthesia, describes a basically different phenomenon. "Analgesia" is used to indicate that either all or part of the patient's body has been so affected that the patient does not actually feel pain, but is conscious of touch and can sense pressure. Anesthesia, on the other hand, whether it affects part or all of the body, is brought about in such a manner that the patient is not conscious of any sensation in the anesthetized part of the body or in the whole body, whether the anesthesia is general or local.

History.—Oliver Wendell Holmes is credited with suggesting the words anesthesia and anesthetic, after William T. G. Morton (*q.v.*), on Oct. 16, 1846, first demonstrated publicly the use of ether to produce insensibility to pain during surgical operations. Before that time there had been, from the beginning of history, a search for means of relieving pain. With the discovery of nitrous oxide (1772) and oxygen (1774) by Joseph Priestley, there was continued study of these and other agents that led to the eventual discovery of anesthesia for surgical purposes. Humphry Davy described the anesthetic properties of nitrous oxide in 1799 and suggested its use during surgical operations, but his suggestion was not developed. Henry Hill Hickman showed that partial asphyxiation and carbon-dioxide inhalation would produce unconsciousness and relief of pain. He published his findings in 1824 without arousing interest. Michael Faraday inhaled ether and reported its effect. On March 30, 1842, Crawford W. Long (*q.v.*) used ether to produce surgical anesthesia but did not publicize his discovery. Horace Wells, in Dec. 1844, had nitrous oxide administered to himself for extraction of a tooth. A public demonstration by him of its use for a surgical operation ended in a fiasco. Later demonstrations proved successful. Local anesthesia dates from 1884, when Carl Koller, a Viennese physician, first used cocaine in surgery of the eye.

General Anesthesia.—*Inhalation.*—Inhalation anesthesia is produced by gaseous or volatile agents that are inhaled by the patient. The method of administering inhalation anesthetics by tube directly into the trachea, rather than through the mouth or nose, increased the safety and adaptability of these agents. Constant improvement and modifications of equipment contributed to the wider application of special anesthetic techniques. Soda lime is used to absorb the carbon dioxide from anesthetic mixtures, effecting a reduction in the amount of anesthetic agent necessary to maintain anesthesia. The explosion hazard in anesthesia has been studied, and safety measures have been recommended and used.

Nitrous oxide, which first was used for anesthetic purposes in 1844, has continued to be used extensively though with an increasing awareness by the anesthetist of the need for precaution against insufficient oxygenation and subsequent danger of cerebral damage. Because it is a weak anesthetic agent, its greatest usefulness is in combination with other agents.

Diethyl ether holds a dominant place among the inhalation anesthetics. Many ethers have been prepared and used experimentally, among these being cyclopropyl methyl, cyclopropyl ethyl, *n*-methyl propyl, ethyl-*n*-propyl, propenyl ethyl, Propethylene, cyprome, cypreth, cyprethylene and cyclopropyl vinyl ether. Some of these have been given clinical trial. Divinyl ether (vinethene, divinyl oxide) is more powerful than diethyl ether, but its usefulness is limited by the occasional ill effects that may result from prolonged administration.

Chloroform, which first was introduced by James Y. Simpson in 1847, is more potent and more toxic than ether. Its use as an anesthetic has decreased with increased knowledge of its dangers.

Trichloroethylene appears to be less toxic to the heart than chloroform, but it does not always produce complete muscular relaxation.

When trichloroethylene is administered in a closed circuit, toxic oxidation products caused by the interaction of trichloroethylene and soda lime may produce untoward results. The drug also may break down into toxic products under the influence of heat, such as heat from an electric cautery.

Ethylene, an explosive gas, was introduced in 1923. It is more potent than nitrous oxide and more oxygen may be used with it.

Ethyl chloride has a limited usefulness as an inhalation anesthetic, but it is similar to chloroform in its toxicity. Ethyl chloride is used for freezing of superficial tissues by applying it as a spray.

Cyclopropane, a potent, explosive gas, was first used clinically in 1934. It has the advantage that a large amount of oxygen may be used with it. The question of its action on the heart has been debated. The usefulness of this agent was enhanced by the introduction of curare (*see* below).

Halothane (Fluothane; 2-bromo-2-chloro-1,1,1-trifluoroethane) came into extensive use in the late 1950s. It is colourless, volatile, has a pleasant odour and is neither inflammable nor explosive when mixed with oxygen in any concentration. Halothane produces vasodilatation, hypotension and bradycardia, however, and a number of fatalities were reported from its use.

Rectal.—Rectal anesthesia is a method by which unconsciousness is produced by introducing the agent into the rectum. Ether, the barbiturates and tribromoethyl alcohol in amylene hydrate are the drugs that have been used most often in this method. Tribromoethyl alcohol in amylene hydrate has been used for release of a ureteral stricture around a kidney stone by direct injection of the agent into the ureter. It was used by the intravenous route to produce anesthesia in World War II.

Hypnotism.—Hypnotism has found a limited usefulness in obstetrics and in prisoner-of-war camps in the absence of adequate anesthetic agents, and in dentistry.

Intravenous.—Intravenous anesthesia, the method by which the anesthetic agent is introduced directly into the blood stream, has been used extensively and proved most valuable for anesthesia in warfare. The barbiturates have been employed satisfactorily. After a long search for a suitable agent, thiopental sodium (Pentothal Sodium) probably has gained more approval and use than any other barbiturate. Surital gives results comparable with those of thiopental sodium. Alcohol, injected intravenously, has been used for relief of postoperative pain. Procaine hydrochloride, administered intravenously, has been used to relieve many forms of pain and sometimes for operative anesthesia. Vascular spasm as well as itching has been relieved by this method of administering procaine hydrochloride.

Attempts to improve on thiopental sodium as an anesthetic agent for intravenous use have had little success. A widely favoured combination consists in premedication of the patient the night before and again on the morning of the operation, followed by intravenous administration of thiopental sodium and succinylcholine (a muscle relaxant), with nitrous oxide plus oxygen, just before the operation. This procedure also calls for the use of an intratracheal tube through which the gaseous anesthetic agent is given. Then, after the tube is in place and in use, curare is administered. By means of this combination, anesthesia and relaxation are produced without the hazard of fire and explosion attendant upon the use of open methods for giving gaseous agents.

Intraosseous.—It has been found that anesthetics such as thiopental sodium may be administered by injecting the solution into the bone marrow, called intraosseous anesthesia.

Local Anesthesia.—Local anesthesia is the method by which local insensibility is produced. Many agents have been used, the safest being procaine hydrochloride. Piperocaine hydrochloride, dibucaine hydrochloride and tetracaine hydrochloride also have been used.

Block.—When the local anesthetic agent is injected so that it blocks the nerve supply, the method is known as block or conduction anesthesia. Special types of blocks, such as caudal, sacral, brachial plexus and spinal, the name depending on what part of the spinal cord is injected, have been developed. A modification of caudal anesthesia is the continuous method, in which a needle or catheter is left within the caudal canal and repeated injections of the local anesthetic are made to produce continuous anesthesia. This method has been used chiefly in obstetrics.

Spinal anesthesia is a special form of block anesthesia in which the local anesthetic agent is deposited in the spinal fluid. The single-injection method has been modified by the continuous method, in which the needle or a catheter is left in position and intermittent injections are given to maintain continuing insensibility. By this method, smaller, safer doses of the drug may be given in each injection, and the value of the method is increased because the limited time element of the single-dose method is overcome.

Penicillin has been added to local anesthetic solutions in an attempt to increase the safety of the injection, especially in infected areas. Studies have shown that procaine hydrochloride did not interfere with penicillin activity.

One of the commonest applications of local anesthesia is in dentistry, where dental nerves are anesthetized with a local anesthetic agent to permit extraction of teeth and the use of many types of dental treatment that otherwise would be painful. General anesthesia has been employed in dentistry only for about 50 years. Usually, nitrous oxide and oxygen, with or without a local anesthetic agent, are used. However, there has been a tendency to employ intravenous anesthesia, even in the dental office, and sometimes trichloroethylene or vinethene is added in small doses to the nitrous oxide and oxygen to produce analgesia, rather than anesthesia. The current concept is that when teeth are extracted under local anesthesia, postoperative pain is greater than when a general anesthetic agent is employed for this purpose.

Refrigeration.—Refrigeration (crymo-anesthesia) also is a form of local anesthesia. By application of ice to an extremity or to a skin area, reducing the local temperature to near freezing, insensibility to pain of amputation has been produced. Skin grafts have been removed painlessly and amputation of an extremity, especially in cases of diabetes, has been done with greatly decreased operative risk.

Cold has been found to be valuable also in the treatment and prevention of shock and in the retardation of infection. It is also being used in cardiac surgery.

Dangers of Anesthesia.—Inhalation general anesthesia is brought about many times by the use of inflammable and explosive anesthetic agents, and therein lies a real danger, since an explosion may take place in the patient's lungs. This is especially true of ether, ethylene and cyclopropane. When gaseous anesthetic agents are used, a gas machine must be used to regulate the flow of gas from a cylinder to the breathing bag. There is always danger that the oxygen cylinder may become empty without being noticed immediately; if that occurs, the patient will experience asphyxia, which may be fatal. It has happened that the cylinders were not placed in the proper positions and that not enough oxygen was used for safety. The anesthetic gases and the oxygen are under considerable pressure in the cylinders, and occasionally difficulty has been experienced in the handling of the cylinders. Cylinder valves have been knocked off and when that happens the cylinder will speed about as if it were jet-propelled.

Certain anesthetic agents, such as trichloroethylene, can cause cardiac arrest when administered in full anesthetic dose. In the case of local anesthesia the danger is that the quantity of the local anesthetic introduced into the blood stream may be sufficient to cause convulsions or even cardiac arrest. Convulsions can be controlled by intravenous administration of a barbiturate such as thiopental sodium. Oxygen can be administered, the rationale for this being that death occurring during a convulsion is due essentially to inability to breathe. Blood pressure may fall to a dangerously low level. These catastrophes occur when anesthesia is administered by untrained and unskilful persons; they seldom take place when the anesthesiologist is experienced and skilful.

Even spraying the throat with a surface anesthetic may be dangerous if the patient swallows part of the local anesthetic, since the concentration of the solution used for spraying is fairly high, and therefore a small quantity of the solution contains a relatively large dose of the anesthetic agent.

A few persons are very sensitive to certain local anesthetics. Extreme care must be taken to keep them out of danger. Many times the addition of epinephrine to the anesthetic will detain the anesthetic in one spot longer than would be possible if epinephrine were not added, and it thus assures that the anesthetic effect at the desired site will not be dissipated. Epinephrine constricts blood vessels and reduces the blood flow to the area, so that the local anesthetic is carried away only slowly by the blood. At the same time, bleeding in the area is reduced, which is convenient for the surgeon. However, certain nervous persons in whom a considerable amount of epinephrine is produced by the body when the prospect of an operation is at hand will react unfavourably to the inclusion of epinephrine in the local anesthetic and sometimes will collapse.

Choice of Anesthetic Agent.—Many factors influence the choice of an anesthetic agent. If there is no one in the hospital who knows how to use a certain agent or method, that method or agent obviously is not the most desirable. The operation itself may be one that requires much relaxation of the patient. Such relaxation requires either a powerful anesthetic that can produce such an action or the addition of a muscle relaxant. Muscle relaxants have been great influencing factors in present-day anesthesia. Thiopental sodium does not produce muscular relaxation. Nitrous oxide and oxygen seldom do. The use of drugs such as succinylcholine or curare (*see* below) to produce relaxation is not a problem, and the development of these two agents greatly changed the use of anesthetics.

Intravenous anesthesia is very easy to produce. Once the vein has been punctured, no great skill is required to inject the solution, but it does require some judgment as to how fast the drug should be given or how much of it should be used. Rectal anesthesia is the method of choice for small children who are to undergo surgery. It is especially useful for tonsillectomy and adenoidectomy, since the child can go to sleep in his crib or his bed and then is taken to the operating room, where an inhalation anesthetic is administered. Usually an intratracheal tube is put in place to facilitate breathing. When the child returns to his room he has no knowledge that he left it, and he is not frightened by knowing that an operation has been performed.

There are times, however, when the anesthesiologist hesitates to administer a general anesthetic agent. For example, if a patient's heart is extremely irregular, cardiac arrest might develop if the patient became at all anoxic or did not have enough oxygen in his blood stream, whereas if he were under the influence of spinal anesthesia he probably would not experience much difficulty so long as the blood pressure did not become too low. However, the site of operation might not permit the use of spinal anesthesia at a high enough level.

Procedures.—Probably the most frequently used adjunct to anesthesia is medication the night before the operation to ensure the patient a good rest. The patient is asked not to smoke from the evening before operation until after operation the next day, so that coughing may be avoided. Then sufficient medication is used before operation so that the patient will be unexcited and may even be somewhat drowsy. Part of the burden of pain thus is relieved by the action of the preliminary medication. In the operating room thiopental sodium is administered by vein and succinylcholine is given. An intratracheal tube often is put in place; nitrous oxide and oxygen are administered through the tube, and thiopental sodium and curare are introduced intermittently into the vein. Patients are protected against too shallow breathing by the use of other drugs.

There are reasons why this combination, sometimes called "balanced anesthesia," is so useful, one of them being freedom from the danger of fire and explosion. Others are that the patient is better satisfied than when some other methods are used; relaxation can be produced to whatever degree is necessary; the patient remains quiet; relatively small doses of anesthetic agent can be used; and plenty of oxygen can be given.

Related Agents.—In 1954 F. H. Shaw called attention to the use of $\beta\beta$ methyl ethyl glutarimide as an antagonist for barbiturate poisoning; this substance later found application in anesthesia because of the fact that it will stimulate respiration when surgical anesthesia is to be terminated. The facility for terminating intravenous anesthesia by means of a barbiturate, added to the previously known fact that barbiturates will induce anesthesia, embodied a new concept. There are other antagonists, and by use of such drugs it was expected that many standard anesthetic drugs could be used in larger doses than previously, and with safety. Antagonists to standard drugs also can be very useful in the postoperative period for the control of pain. Amiphenazole, reported on by Shaw and G. Bentley in 1952, is a milder respiratory stimulant that permits the use of large doses of analgesic agents for the control of acute chronic pain.

Certain visual aids make it possible to teach technical steps quickly. One of these is a gauge for visualizing the position of the tip of the intratracheal tube when it is thrust the proper distance into the trachea. The tube is marked so that when it is inserted between the vocal cords the mark remains visible. This calibration prevents much of the difficulty that was encountered previously when the tube was thrust too far into the trachea.

The development of the esophageal stethoscope augmented the facilities for the immediate detection of difficulties of the heart and lungs, or all these structures.

Other related agents include the sulfonamide drugs, which have been studied in relation to anesthetics. Procaine hydrochloride was found to have an antisulfonamide action. Acetylation of the amino group of p-aminobenzoic acid leads to a 10,000-fold decrease in its antisulfonamide activity. Other studies of the sulfonamide drugs in relation to anesthetics showed that inhalation anesthetics were most controllable in patients who had sulfonamide therapy. Sulfonamide drugs in large doses were found to affect the toxicity of thiopental sodium in rats. In actual use, no ill effects were noted in patients heavily medicated with sulfonamides and anesthetized with thiopental sodium, and no synergism between the two drugs was seen. Sulfonamides were found not to increase the operative risk of animals in shock; indeed, in some instances, the sulfonamides seemed to be beneficial.

Curare (d-tubocurarine, intocostrin), which first was used in connection with anesthetics in 1942, is not an anesthetic but is used in conjunction with anesthetics to increase muscular relaxation. It may be administered intravenously or intramuscularly. Respiratory depression or arrest occurs from an overdose or from too rapid administration of curare. Artificial respiration and neostigmine and the quickly effective anticurare Tensilon are the antidotes for curare. Other drugs that have a curarelike action have been studied, including salts of erythroidine, quinine ethochloride, nicotine, thiamine, magnesium, quinine and quinine derivatives. (*See* CURARE.)

Vitamins in relation to anesthesia, as well as the vitamin state in the preanesthetic and postanesthetic periods, have been investigated. Vitamin C deficiency was found to increase the anesthetic induction time and recovery time. Vitamin B_2 has been found to be necessary for adequate functioning of the cell respiratory mechanism.

Shock existing before the administration of anesthetics as well as that which may develop during operation has been studied extensively, and supportive measures have been used successfully in its prevention and treatment. Blood transfusion, plasma transfusion and the so-called plasma substitutes, or plasma volume expanders, have decreased the incidence of operative shock.

Gas therapy is often given under the supervision of the anesthetist. Postanesthetic administration of oxygen, carbon dioxide and oxygen or helium has proved valuable in preventing complications. Helium, oxygen and carbon dioxide are used in conjunction with anesthetics as well as in gas therapy.

Diagnostic, preoperative, operative and postoperative tracheobronchial aspiration has reduced the incidence of serious pulmonary complications.

Postanesthesia observation rooms have been set aside in some institutions to facilitate the immediate postanesthetic care of the patient. Resuscitation is often done by the anesthetist because of his familiarity with the circulatory and respiratory physiology. Research in physiology as related to anesthesiology also added many factual data. *See* MEDICINE AND SURGERY, HISTORY OF and articles on the various anesthetic drugs. *See* also references under "Anesthesia and Anesthetics" in the Index.

BIBLIOGRAPHY.—R. C. Adams, *Intravenous Anesthesia* (1944); John Adriani, *The Chemistry of Anesthesia* (1945); *Anesthesia Abstracts*, compiled under direction of John S. Lundy and.Florence M. McQuillen (1937 *et seq.*); H. K. Beecher, *The Physiology of Anesthesia* (1938); *Current Researches in Anesthesia and Analgesia* (1922 et seq.); A. M. Dogliotti, *Anesthesia* (1939); N. A. Gillespie, *Endotracheal Anaesthesia* (1941); T. E. Keys, *The History of Surgical Anesthesia* (1945); C. B. Lull and R. A. Hingson, *Control of Pain in Childbirth* (1944); John S. Lundy, *Clinical Anesthesia* (1942); R. R. Macintosh and W. W. Mushin, *Local Anaesthesia, Brachial Plexus* (1946); F. H. Shaw, "Further Experiences With 'Megimide'—a Barbiturate Antagonist," *Med. J. Aust.*, 2:889–891 (1955); F. H. Shaw and G. Bentley, "Morphine Antagonism," *Nature*, 169:712–713 (1952); Code Smith, "An Endo-oesophageal Stethoscope," *Anesthesiology*, 15:566 (1954). (J. S. L.)

ANEURYSM (ANEURISM) is essentially an abnormal, localized dilatation of some artery that contains fluid or clotted blood. The causes are those that result in weakening of the arterial wall in a localized area, and they include a variety of injuries and diseases. Aneurysms are pulsating tumours that are progressive in character and may ultimately rupture, causing hemorrhages of varying degrees. They produce sounds called bruits. Aneurysms cause changes in the surrounding tissues mostly because of pressure and erosion from their enlargement and pulsation. They sometimes establish a communication with adjoining veins. Their names are derived from their shapes, characters and locations. Diagnosis is made by the clinical history, physical findings and X-ray examination. Treatment varies with the type and location, and its effectiveness depends upon early recognition, location and type. Surgical procedures may be valuable. *See also* BLOOD VESSELS, SURGERY OF. (F. L. A.)

ANGARA, a river in the U.S.S.R., the outlet for Lake Baikal (*q.v.*), is one of the major right bank tributaries of the Yenisei (*q.v.*). The river flows for 1,151 mi. across the southern part of the central Siberian plateau to join the Yenisei just above Yeniseisk and drains more than 400,000 sq.mi., which includes the drainage basin of Lake Baikal and its tributaries.

The upper Angara (Verkhnyaya Angara) rises in the Transbaikal mountains and flows west-southwest into the northern end of Lake Baikal, where it has formed a wide delta. It is 281 mi. long and its basin covers 8,436 sq.mi. The chief tributaries of the Angara proper are the Taseyeva (770 mi.), Oka (605 mi.) and Irkut (290 mi.) on the left bank and the Ilim (373 mi.) on the right. The Angara is navigable upstream as far as the village of Boguchany and again from Bratsk to Lake Baikal, but the middle reaches, where the river cuts across basalt flows, are broken by many rapids. Average annual discharge is 146,560 cu.ft. per second with maximum flow coming in autumn.

Flowing through the newly developing Angara industrial region,

the river has great value as a source of hydroelectric power. A barrage was completed at Irkutsk. (R. A. F.)

ANGARSK, a town of Irkutsk *oblast* of the Russian Soviet Federated Socialist Republic, U.S.S.R., lies southwest of the Angara river, about 30 mi. below Irkutsk on the Trans-Siberian railway. The town grew very rapidly in the 1950s, in connection with the development of a new major industrial region in the Angara basin. Machine-building (especially mining equipment for the nearby Cheremkhovo coal field) and timber-working are the major industries, power for which is supplied by a thermal power station in the town and from the Irkutsk hydroelectric plant. Pop. (1959) 134,390. (R. A. F.)

ANGARY, RIGHT OF. This term denotes the right of belligerents to requisition for their use neutral merchant vessels, aircraft and other means of transport that are within their territorial jurisdiction against payment of compensation. Although this right was received into international law only in the 17th century, the term "angary" itself is of great antiquity. It has been traced back to ancient Persia, where it applied to royal messengers or couriers, and to Greek usage. In Roman law it related to the compulsory service of means of transport, including ships for public purpose. The right was invoked frequently in the 18th century but rarely in the 19th. As originally practised, it included the right to requisition the crew along with the vessel. This is no longer regarded as justifiable.

It is generally agreed that the right of angary should be applied only in case of pressing need in time of war, and that compensation is due to the neutral owner. It was applied on several occasions during World Wars I and II. By proclamation of March 20, 1918, the president of the United States took over merchant vessels of Dutch registry lying in U.S. territorial waters. Similar action was taken by Great Britain, France and Italy. During World War I, neutral powers invoked the right of angary against ships of belligerents in their ports. Thus Italy in 1915 requisitioned 34 German vessels, Portugal in 1916 requisitioned 72, and Brazil in 1917 requisitioned 42. Germany declared war upon Portugal on the ground that, in requisitioning the ships, it had violated the treaty of 1908, which provided that agreement on compensation must precede requisition. Spain in 1918 took over about 90 German vessels but paid no compensation in view of the sinking of Spanish vessels by German submarines. In World War II some neutrals also requisitioned ships of belligerents but it is doubtful whether, juridically, their action was based on the right of angary or on other grounds. The United States in 1941, while formally still neutral, took over foreign vessels lying idle in waters within its jurisdiction. This, however, was not done pursuant to the right of angary but in virtue of the authority conferred on the president by the Idle Foreign Vessels act of June 6, 1941 (55 U.S. Stat. 242).

A specific recognition of the right of neutrals to apply the right of angary is seen in the Hague convention of 1907 respecting the rights and duties of neutral powers and persons in war on land. Article 19 of this convention confers upon neutral powers the right, in case of necessity and against compensation, to retain and utilize railway materials coming from the territory of a belligerent power which, under like conditions, requisitioned railway stock coming from the territory of that neutral. The difficulty in connection with the resort to the right of angary by neutrals against belligerents arises from the fact that the former cannot invoke its underlying reason, namely military necessity.

In World War I the question arose whether a belligerent may requisition neutral ships and cargoes seized on the high sea and brought in for, but prior to, adjudication by a prize court. The British judicial committee of the privy council (*The Zamora*, [1916], 2 A.C. 77) affirmed the right in principle, subject to the conditions that there must be urgent necessity, a real question to be tried and approval by a prize court. This is frequently regarded as an extension of the right of angary to things other than means of transport and other than those found within territorial jurisdiction. It is an open question whether the right of angary can be stretched so far or whether there is any need for this. Requisitions in such circumstances may well be explained on other grounds.

BIBLIOGRAPHY.—C. L. Bullock, "Angary," *British Year Book of International Law, 1922–23*, pp. 99–129; H. Lauterpacht, "Angary and Requisitions of Neutral Property," *British Year Book of International Law, 1950*, pp. 455–59; J. E. Harley, "The Law of Angary," *American Journal of International Law*, 13:267–301 (1919). (L. Gs.)

ANGEL, a term used in the Jewish and Christian religions and in others influenced by them (belief in the angels is an essential tenet of Islam) to designate a created spirit essentially inferior to God but superior to man in natural endowments of intellect and will. As St. Augustine notes (*Sermo* 7, 3), the name itself (from the Greek *angelos*, "messenger") indicates office or function rather than nature.

Belief in the existence of intermediary beings between God and the visible universe was common to most primitive religions, but the Judaeo-Christian doctrine of angels has its origins in the revealed word of God as contained in the Scriptures. Angels are mentioned repeatedly precisely in those parts of the Pentateuch and of other Old Testament books, *e.g.*, Job i, that, according to critics, derive from the most ancient documents or sources.

Old Testament.—In the pre-exilic period, the numerousness of the angels loomed large in the sacred writings, so that God himself was called the "Lord of hosts" (I Sam. i, 3, 11). Angels constitute God's heavenly court, and in his name fight Israel's battles. Most often, however, they are portrayed as God's servants charged with particular missions on earth, from guarding the entrance to the garden of Eden after man's fall (Gen. iii, 24) to protecting the faithful (Ps. xci, 11), punishing the remiss (Ps. xxxv, 5) and, above all, carrying God's important messages to man (Gen. xvi, 7 ff.; xxii, 11 ff.; Ex. iii, 2). Their appearances would seem to have been in human form (Gen. xviii, 2, 16).

In the Persian and Greco-Roman periods, after the exile, angels

FIG. 2.—"ST. MICHAEL TRIUMPHING OVER THE DEVIL" BY SIR JACOB EPSTEIN, 1959. COVENTRY CATHEDRAL, ENG.

play a still larger role (*cf.* the books of Job, Ezekiel, Daniel, Tobit). This was probably due to the growing emphasis on the transcendence of God as much as to the influence of neighbouring religious beliefs and folklore. A hierarchy among the angels is affirmed, and personal names occur: the archangel Michael is mentioned in Jude 9, and Gabriel and Raphael are traditionally identified as archangels.

Particularly prominent in Old Testament angelology are the cherubim and seraphim. Both are superior orders of angelic being, in close attendance on God's throne of majesty, guarding it from profanation (Ezek. i; Isa. vi, 2, 6). It is not surprising, therefore, that representations of the cherubim (and probably also of the seraphim) became accepted features of the Temple decorations. The figures of the two cherubim who with their wings overshadowed the mercy seat on the top of the ark in the Holy of Holies constituted nothing less than God's throne among his people (Ex. xxv, 18–21).

At the time of Christ, the inroads of hellenistic rationalism brought about a reaction: the Sadducees refused to acknowledge the very existence of angels (Acts xxiii, 8), though the Pharisees continued to believe in them, and among the Essenes and in contemporary apocalyptic writings angelology flourished as never before.

New Testament.—Very striking in the New Testament is the role which the evangelists assign to angels in the major events of Christ's life and work: his birth, the beginning of his public ministry, his agony, resurrection and ascension. In his teaching Jesus frequently refers to angels, suggests the idea of a guardian angel for children (Matt. xviii, 10) and stresses the presence of the angelic multitudes at his final coming in glory. But it is especially in St. Paul's letters and in Revelation that the doctrine concerning angels is presented with greatest amplitude. Christ is the head of the angels as well as of men. Seven group-names receive mention: angels, archangels, principalities, powers, virtues, dominions and thrones (I Thess. iv, 16; Rom. viii, 38; Eph. i; 21; Col. i, 16; ii, 15). Together with the cherubim and seraphim, named in the Old Testament, this listing gave rise in patristic times to the theory of the nine choirs of angels (*cf.* Dionysius the Areopagite, *The Celestial Hierarchy*). In the New Testament, too, is found clearer reference to the sin of the fallen angels (Jude 6; II Pet. ii, 4), and to the power of the Devil as "the ruler of this world" (John xiv, 30).

Doctrine.—Perhaps because of fear of syncretistic confusion with Gnostic and pagan doctrines of divine emanations and demigods, the early Fathers spoke of angels only incidentally. There was general agreement on their having been created by God, but not about the time of their creation: whether before or together with the visible world. Their role as messengers and agents of God was now extended to the performance of the Christian liturgy: Tertullian's famous "angel of baptism" has his counterpart in other sacraments, and especially in the Eucharist. In fact, the eucharistic celebration was widely viewed as an earthly participation as well as anticipation of the heavenly liturgy of the angels—a thought that has left its imprint on the Latin canon of the Mass to the present day (*cf.* the prayer "*Supplices*"). Very early, too, the doctrine of an angel assigned to each man as guardian gained currency.

Only very gradually, however, did Christian tradition arrive at the conviction of the nature of angels as pure spirits. Even Augus-

FIG. 1.—(LEFT) ST. MICHAEL, 6TH-CENTURY BYZANTINE MOSAIC FROM S. APOLLINARE NUOVO IN CLASSE, RAVENNA; (RIGHT) ANGEL FROM LINAIUOLI TRIPTYCH BY FRA ANGELICO, 1433; IN THE MUSEO DI SAN MARCO, FLORENCE

tine inclined to the view that angels possessed a body of some ethereal matter. The concept of pure spirit seemed too essentially a divine prerogative. Though Gregory of Nyssa, followed by Dionysius the Areopagite (*q.v.*) and Gregory the Great, taught clearly that angels were pure intelligences, it was not until the period of the scholastics that this teaching was fully accepted. Thomas Aquinas made it the basis of his extensive and pioneering speculation on angels: from it, for example, he concluded that angels were not composed of matter and form, that each of the myriads of individual angels consequently constitutes a distinct species, that their knowledge is intuitive and immediate rather than discursive like man's, that they are free from passions, etc.

Actual definitions of faith by the Catholic Church concerning angels are few. The fourth Council of the Lateran (1215), echoed by the first Vatican council (1870), teaches their creation by God "from the beginning of time"; but the exact meaning of the concluding phrase has not been clarified. Though not explicitly defined by any official solemn pronouncement, the nature of angels as pure spirits, their creation before man, the existence of different ranks or hierarchies (but not their number or nature) and the angels' guardianship over mankind (though not necessarily a special angel for each man) also are deemed to be sufficiently based on revelation to demand belief.

Veneration of angels in Christian tradition may appeal to certain Old Testament parallels (Gen. xviii, 2; Josh. v, 14), but a recognized and official cult of angels is a specifically Christian phenomenon. Initial hesitation generally disappeared about the time of Augustine, when there seemed to be no longer any danger of infiltration of pagan or idolatrous and superstitious misinterpretations. It was especially St. Michael, the powerful warrior, who attracted devotion. Shrines in his honour appear as early as the 4th century in both east and west, continued to be erected throughout the middle ages and play prominent roles in the devotional life of several countries. At present two feasts honouring St. Michael are celebrated annually according to the Roman calendar. Alcuin (d. 804) assigned a votive mass in honour of the angels to every Tuesday free of other feasts, a practice still retained in the Roman missal. In 1670 a feast of the guardian angels was promulgated for the universal church by Pope Clement X.

ALINARI

FIG. 3.—TWO PUTTI BY ANDREA DEL SARTO, 1528. IN THE UFFIZI, FLORENCE

Iconography.—The iconography of angels likewise has undergone development in the course of the centuries. It is generally agreed that Egyptian and Assyrian sculptures of winged beasts guarding the royal palaces were a major influence in determining the graphic representations of the cherubim of the Old Testament. Christian art in the catacombs offers no identifying traits for its angels; only toward the end of the 4th century do nimbus and wings begin to make their appearance. The figures themselves are those of men or youths, clad in white tunic and pallium. Under Byzantine influence, exemplified for instance in the magnificent mosaics of Ravenna, the angels are shown as noble winged attendants at Christ's or the Virgin's throne, vested in precious court apparel. At the height of the middle ages, when devotion to the humanity of Christ and his sufferings was predominant, artists pictured the angels carrying the instruments of the sacred passion and grieving over their Lord. Isolated instances of child-angels, or of winged child-heads, are found in the 12th century, and then became increasingly popular; in the time of the Renaissance, under the additional precedent of classic pagan representations of Eros

ALINARI

FIG. 4.—ASSYRIAN WINGED GENIUS FROM PALACE OF ASHURNASIRPAL II AT NIMRUD, 9TH CENTURY B.C. IN THE LOUVRE, PARIS

or Cupid, these find a joyous welcome among the sculptures and paintings of the baroque churches. The mighty cherubim at Yahweh's throne have become playful and all too obviously nonheavenly cherubs—not necessarily to the increase of sound Christian piety; Cupid refused to be baptized. The early Renaissance, finally, introduced the female angel, and before long, especially in Italy, she was decked in the current fashion, with occasionally a stole over it all to suggest sacred function. Angels in various stages of undress and without wings also appear, all for the laudable purpose of humanizing them and thus making them less forbidding to man's love and devotion. A return to a more worthy iconography of angels is making headway in the 20th century.

BIBLIOGRAPHY.—A. Vacant, "Ange," in *Dictionnaire de la Bible,* vol. i, col. 576–590 (1895); L. Blau and K. Kohler, "Angelology," in *The Jewish Encyclopedia,* vol. i, pp. 583–597 (1901); A. B. Davidson, "Angel," in *Dictionary of the Bible,* vol. i, pp. 93–97 (1902); H. Leclercq, "Anges," in *Dictionnaire d'archéologie chrétienne et de liturgie,* vol. i, col. 2080–2161 (1907); A. Lemonnyer, "Angélologie chrétienne," in *Dictionnaire de la Bible,* Supplément, vol. i, col. 255–262 (1928); J. Duhr, "Anges," in *Dictionnaire de spiritualité ascétique et mystique,* vol. i, col. 580–625 (1932); P. Auvray, A. Molien, J. de Mahuet, "Ange," in *Catholicisme,* vol. i, col. 538–547 (1948); W. Heidt, *Angelology of the Old Testament* (1949); Mortimer J. Adler (ed.), *The Great Ideas: A Syntopicon,* vol. i (1952), *cf.* "Angel," pp. 1–18; J. Daniélou, *Les Anges et leur mission d'après les Pères de l'Eglise* (1953); E. Peterson, *Das Buch von den Engeln,* 2nd ed. (1955); J. Michl, R. Haubst, E. Lucchesi-Palli, "Engel," in *Lexikon für Theologie und Kirche,* vol. iii, col. 863–874 (1959). (G. L. D.)

ANGELA MERICI, SAINT (1474–1540), Italian foundress of the Ursulines, the oldest and largest order of women in the Roman Catholic Church founded for teaching, was born on March 21, 1474 (or perhaps 1470), at Desenzano, a small town on Lake Garda in northern Italy. From a very early age she showed signs of a special religious vocation. Orphaned young, she went to Salò to live at the home of an uncle, and while there joined the Third Order of St. Francis in order to ensure the privilege of frequent communion. About the age of 20 she returned to Desenzano, where she gathered about her a group of girls who taught catechism to the children of the village. In 1506, while praying in the fields of Brudazzo, Angela Merici had a vision in which she was told that she would found at Brescia a society of virgins, and from that time her determination to fulfill this mission never wavered, although 40 years of waiting followed. During those years her motherly charity, deep prayer, humility, extraordinary penance and ability to help souls won her the love and esteem of all who knew her.

On Nov. 25, 1535, at Brescia, Angela Merici and 27 companions consecrated themselves to God by a vow of virginity, and the Company of St. Ursula was born. By the end of the year it numbered 60 members. The following year she drew up her Rule, which provided for the Christian education of girls in order to restore the family, and through the family all of Christian society. In 1537 she was unanimously elected superior-general of the company, which she ruled wisely and with great maternal affection. Before her death on Jan. 27, 1540, she dictated her *Testament and Souvenirs,* which contain her counsels to her daughters and are the embodiment of her spirit. They read like modern documents with their insistence on interest in the individual, gentleness and the efficacy of persuasion over force.

A cult to St. Angela grew up in and about Brescia almost immediately. She was not declared "blessed," however, until 1768. On May 24, 1807, Pius VII canonized her. Her feast day is celebrated on June 1.

St. Angela Merici is hailed not only as a foundress of a world-wide order of religious women famous for the education of girls, but also as a woman of extraordinary vision and courage who founded an entirely new form of religious life in the church and who enjoined her daughters to make changes according to the needs of the times.

BIBLIOGRAPHY.—Very Reverend Mother Marie de Saint Jean Martin, O.S.U., *The Spirit of Saint Angela* (1950); Sister Monica, O.S.U., *Angela Merici and Her Teaching Idea* (1927); Sigrid Undset, *Stages on the Road,* "Saint Angela Merici" (1934); Abbe V. Postel, *Histoire de Sainte Angèle Merici et tout l'ordre des Ursulines,* 2 vol. (1878); *Sainte Angèle Merici et l'ordre des Ursulines,* par une religieuse du même ordre (1922).   (M. E. McI.)

ANGELFISH, the popular name for several widely differing species of fishes.

Squatina squatina, also called the monkfish, is an elasmobranch skatelike shark found in tropical and subtropical seas, including the Mediterranean. It takes its name from the large winglike pectoral fins and reaches a length of four feet.

In Bermuda, fishes (family Chaetodontidae) of the genus *Holacanthus,* and especially *Angelichthys* are called angelfish. These fishes are laterally compressed and brilliantly coloured. They haunt coral reefs. *Angelichthys* may reach a weight of four pounds and are delicious eating. In this same family the genus *Pomacanthus,* also of warm seas, is known as angelfish.

BY COURTESY OF NEW YORK ZOOLOGICAL SOCIETY

BLUE ANGELFISH (ANGELICHTHYS ISABELITA)

Chaetodipterus faber, sometimes called spadefish, is also known as the angelfish. It occurs from Cape Cod to Rio de Janeiro. A very similar species occurs on the west coast of Mexico.

To the tropical fish hobbyist *Pterophyllum scalare* and two related species of South American origin are the popular angelfish of the aquarium. (*See* AQUARIUM: *Aquariums in the Home.*) They have silvery, black-barred, laterally compressed bodies, four to six inches long, with gracefully extended fins. Breeding has produced other form and colour variants of extraordinary beauty.

ANGELICA, a large genus of aromatic herbs of the family Umbelliferae. The most important species is the Eurasian *A. archangelica,* the roots and fruit of which yield angelica oil used to flavour liqueurs and in perfumery, while the tender shoots are used in making certain kinds of aromatic sweetmeats. In the Faeroe Islands and in Iceland, where the plant grows abundantly, it has been used as a vegetable. The genus is represented in Britain by one species, *A. sylvestris,* a tall perennial herb with large bipinnate leaves and large compound umbels of white or purple flowers. In the United States the common name alexanders (*q.v.*) is applied to *Angelica Atropurpurea.*

ANGELICO, FRA (GIOVANNI DA FIESOLE, originally GUIDO DI PIETRO) (*c.* 1400–1455), Italian painter, one of the greatest 15th-century religious artists, was born at Vicchio in the Mugello (Tuscany). If, as is likely, his reception into the Dominican order at S. Domenico at Fiesole took place about 1418–20, he would have been born about 1400. About 1423–25 he was ordained priest. At the Dominican house of Fiesole Angelico must have been deeply influenced by the teachings of Giovanni Dominici, the leader of the observant or reformed Dominicans and by the personalities of his disciples, St. Antoninus and the Blessed Lorenzo of Ripafratta. The writings of Dominici, in particular the *Lucula Noctis,* a defense of traditional spirituality against the onset of humanism, establish the intellectual and spiritual climate in which Angelico's style was formed.

His earliest surviving work, an altarpiece painted about 1425 for S. Domenico at Fiesole, where it is still preserved, was adapted about 1500 from a polyptych into a single panel altarpiece and has been stripped of its pilasters (two sections now in the Musée Condé, Chantilly) and its predella (now in the National gallery,

London). Other paintings executed at this time are a polyptych from S. Pietro Martire (now in the Museo di San Marco, Florence) and a "Virgin and Child Enthroned" in the same museum. More clearly indicative of the course Angelico was to pursue are three early frescoes painted for S. Domenico, in which an attempt was made to develop a style conducive to contemplation and capable of playing its own part in the community's spiritual life. One of these, a Crucifixion, is still in the convent of S. Domenico, and the others, a much damaged "Virgin and Child With SS. Dominic and Thomas Aquinas" and a second Crucifixion, are respectively in the Hermitage, Leningrad, and in the Louvre, Paris.

The earliest securely dated work by Angelico is a triptych (now in the Museo di San Marco) of the Virgin and Child, with the two SS. John on the interior of the mobile wings and SS. Peter and Mark on the exterior. Though this work owes its great popularity mainly to the small figures of music-making angels around the central figure, the Linaiuoli triptych is remarkable above all for the monumental treatment of the Virgin and the lateral saints, which reflect the influence of Masaccio. At a date not far removed from that of the Linaiuoli triptych, Angelico executed for S. Domenico at Cortona a great altarpiece of the Annunciation, now in the Museo del Gesù. This is one of the most inspired Florentine Renaissance paintings. Also for S. Domenico at Cortona, Angelico executed a fresco in a lunette over the west door of the church, and a polyptych with a predella containing scenes from the life of St. Dominic, which was probably painted about 1436. Closely related in style to the latter work is a polyptych in the Galleria Nazionale dell'Umbria, Perugia, painted for S. Domenico at Perugia in 1437. Thereafter Angelico abandoned the polyptych form and concentrated upon the production of altarpieces on single panels, boldly confronting the unfamiliar compositional demands presented by this new form. The most masterly of these altarpieces are a "Coronation of the Virgin" in the Louvre, painted for S. Domenico at Fiesole, and the high altarpiece of S. Marco in Florence.

The S. Marco altarpiece (now in the Museo di S. Marco) was probably completed in 1440. Its main panel is much abraded, but the eight panels of the predella, with scenes from the legend of SS. Cosmas and Damian, now distributed between the Museo di San Marco, the National Gallery of Art in Washington, the Alte Pinakothek at Munich, the Louvre and the National Gallery of Ireland, are in the main well preserved and exemplify the lucid command of narrative that is one of the glories of Angelico's work. On a larger scale these qualities are manifest again in two altarpieces, both in the Museo di San Marco, the first a "Lamentation Over the Dead Christ" executed for Sta. Maria della Croce al Tempio, and the second a moving "Deposition" painted about 1440 for S. Trinità. In the latter painting the Masacciesque idiom of the Linaiuoli triptych is developed into a soft and deeply individual style, in which a great wealth of emotion is expressed without disruption of the prevailing visual harmony. In the background is an extensive landscape; on the strength of this and of the landscapes in the predella panels at Cortona and in the Louvre, Angelico must be regarded as one of the greatest landscape painters of the 15th century.

The Dominican community had taken possession of the premises of S. Marco in Florence in 1436, and the rebuilding of the church and convent was begun in the following year. All of Fra Angelico's many frescoes in the convent appear to date from after 1443. These fulfilled the same function as the early frescoes in S. Domenico at Fiesole, and were intended for devotional and meditative purposes. They comprise, in the cloister, frescoes of "Christ on the Cross Adored by St. Dominic," and five lunettes; in the Sala del Capitolo on the ground floor a colossal fresco of the Crucifixion with attendant saints; and on the upper floor frescoes of "Christ on the Cross," the "Annunciation" and the "Virgin and Child With Saints" in the corridor, and 44 frescoes in the cells. The latter vary in quality, and many of them were executed by conventual pupils. The frescoes in the cloister and the Sala del Capitolo, however, are autograph paintings by Angelico, as are two of the three frescoes in the corridor. Outstanding among the cell frescoes are the "Noli Me Tangere," Annunciation, "Mocking of Christ," "Presentation in the Temple," "Coronation of the

ALINARI—ART REFERENCE BUREAU
"ST. THOMAS AQUINAS," BY FRA ANGELICO. IN THE MUSEO DI SAN MARCO, FLORENCE

Virgin" and "Transfiguration," in which each event is represented in its simplest terms with the minimum of visual distraction, and the monumental forms achieve the utmost eloquence. The bulk of these frescoes were probably completed by 1447, when Fra Angelico moved to Rome to undertake work in the Vatican.

Angelico's principal commissions in the Vatican at this time were for the decoration of the Chapel of Pope Nicholas V and of the pope's studio (destroyed). The chapel (which was probably completed by 1449) is frescoed on three walls with scenes from the lives of SS. Lawrence and Stephen. In the execution of these scenes some use was made of studio assistants, though Angelico was responsible for all of the designs. The style in which they are conceived is more closely related to that of the vivid panels of the S. Marco predella than to the austere scenes in the convent cells, but all of them are admirably organized, and the receding classical architecture of the "Ordination of St. Lawrence" and "St. Lawrence Distributing Alms" marks the farthest point of Angelico's development as a Renaissance artist.

In 1449 Angelico left Rome on his election as prior of S. Domenico at Fiesole. The most remarkable of the works executed at this time is a cycle of 35 panels of scenes from the life of Christ and other subjects, painted for the doors of a silver chest which stood in the church of SS. Annunziata. Though much damaged and extensively repainted, these scenes have become widely known. When Angelico's term of office as prior expired in 1452, he seems to have returned to Rome, where he decorated the Chapel of the Sacrament in the Vatican (destroyed). A triptych with the "Last Judgment" in the Galleria Nazionale in Rome and a "Christ on the Cross" in the Fogg museum at Cambridge, Mass., perhaps date from this time. Angelico died in Rome on March 18, 1455, and was buried in the north aisle of the church of Sta. Maria sopra Minerva, where his tomb slab is still preserved.

Fra Angelico occupies a unique position in the history of Italian painting. In G. Vasari's biography he is depicted as a naïve artist of great simplicity, whose appeal was due primarily to the sincerity of his convictions, and in the 19th century (when his work became more popular than that of any other religious artist except Raphael) this interpretation of his personality and work was widely propagated. Subsequent study has tended to lay stress on the artistic qualities which entitle him to rank with the greatest European painters.

BIBLIOGRAPHY.—J. Pope-Hennessy, *Fra Angelico* (1952); G. C. Argan, *Fra Angelico* (trans. by J. Emmons; 1955); S. Orlandi, *Beato Angelico; note cronologiche* (1955); M. Salmi, *Beato Angelico* (1958).

(J. W. P.-H.)

ANGELL, JAMES BURRILL (1829–1916), U.S. educator and diplomat, was born in Scituate, R.I., on Jan. 7, 1829. He was graduated in 1849 from Brown university, Providence, and was professor of modern languages and literature there from 1853 to 1860. He was president of the University of Vermont, Burlington, from 1866 to 1871 and of the University of Michigan, Ann Arbor, from 1871 to 1909. He was United States minister to China in 1880–81 and to Turkey in 1897–98. Angell's success in bringing the University of Michigan to a high standard of quality at a time when it was pioneering in many ways, his ability as an eloquent and persuasive orator, his achievements in active diplomacy and his scholarship in international law made him one of the most prominent and highly respected educators of his time. Besides contributions to periodicals, he published *Progress in International Law* (1875), *Reminiscences* (1912) and *Selected Addresses* (1912). He died at Ann Arbor, Mich., April 1, 1916.

(H. H. HR.)

ANGELL, JAMES ROWLAND (1869–1949), psychologist and university president, was born at Burlington, Vt., on May 8, 1869, the son of James Burrill Angell (q.v.). Graduating from the University of Michigan, he was drawn into philosophy and psychology under John Dewey and studied also at Harvard and Halle. While he was instructor in philosophy at Minnesota he was called by Dewey to be assistant professor of psychology at The University of Chicago (1894) where he rose to be professor and head of the department (1905), dean of the faculties (1911) and acting president (1918–19). In 1920 he accepted the presidency of the Carnegie corporation, whence he was called to be the 14th president of Yale, the first non-Yale president since the early Harvard-trained rectors. Under his administration (1921–37) Yale prospered materially, socially and intellectually. The spirit of inquiry replaced the spirit of discipline in Yale college, and the whole institution was infused with university standards. His works included *Psychology* (1904; rev. ed., 1908), *Chapters From Modern Psychology* (1911) and *American Education* (1937). Angell died at Hamden, Conn., on March 4, 1949.

See G. W. Pierson, *Yale: the University College, 1921–1937* (1955).

(G. W. P.)

ANGELL, SIR NORMAN (1874–), English economist and worker for international peace, awarded the Nobel peace prize in 1933 with Arthur Henderson, was born at Holbeach, Lincolnshire, on Dec. 26, 1874. He became a journalist on U.S., French and English newspapers successively, and was editor of *Foreign Affairs* from 1928 to 1931. In 1928 he invented "The Money Game," a card game teaching the elements of economics. Of his many publications the best known is *The Great Illusion* (1910; revised 1933), which has been translated into many languages. He was knighted in 1931 and published his autobiography, *After All*, in 1951.

ANGELUS, the name of a family that gave three emperors to the Byzantine throne. The Angelus family was famous neither for its breeding nor its wealth until the 12th century, when Theodora, youngest daughter of the emperor Alexius I Comnenus, married Constantine Angelus of Philadelphia (Asia Minor). Other members of the family held high positions under Manuel I Comnenus and were deeply involved in the aristocratic revolution that overthrew Andronicus I Comnenus (1185). Isaac II (q.v.), who was raised to the throne by that revolution, and his brother Alexius III (q.v.), who deposed and blinded him in 1195, were among the least competent of all the Byzantine emperors and contributed much by their intrigues and squabbles to the enfeeblement of the empire. Alexius IV (q.v.), by his appeal to the west to help him restore his father Isaac II to the throne, must bear part of the blame for the diversion of the fourth crusade to Constantinople. He and his father were set up as emperors for a few months by the crusaders in 1203. The despots of Epirus and Thessaly, who saved much of northern Greece from conquest by the Latins after 1204 and whose dynasty survived until 1318, were direct descendants of Constantine Angelus and Theodora. One of the last prominent members of the family was John Angelus, appointed governor of Thessaly by John VI Cantacuzenus in 1342.

See G. Ostrogorsky's article in the jubilee publication of the Russian Archaeological Society in the Kingdom of Yugoslavia, pp. 111–129 (1936).

(D. M. N.)

ANGELUS, a devotion in the Western Church in memory of the Incarnation. It consists of three Ave Marias with versicles and a collect. It is recited three times daily, about 6 A.M., noon and 6 P.M., when the Angelus bell is rung. In a simpler form the devotion can be traced back (as a night observance) to the 13th century, but it did not become widely used until the 17th.

See H. Thurston, S.J., "The Angelus," *The Month*, 98:483–499 and 607–616 (1901), and 99:61–73 and 518–532 (1902).

ANGELUS SILESIUS: see SCHEFFLER, JOHANNES.

ÅNGERMANÄLVEN (ANGERMAN RIVER), of Sweden, rises in Lapland and, joined near Näsåker by the Fjällsjöälven, flows for 279 mi. SE to the Gulf of Bothnia. In the plateau region crossed by this river and its tributaries are lakes such as the Vojmsjön (1,355 ft. above sea level, 31 sq.mi.) and Flåsjön (873 ft., 43 sq.mi.).

These long, narrow lakes have been formed by glacial dams and are valuable in regulating the river flow. There are a number of hydroelectric power stations. The estuary is navigable for large vessels for 20 mi. inland to Nyland. The river is much used for timber floating and alongside the estuary are extensive sawmills, but Solleteå and Kramfors, the largest towns, have less than 15,000 inhabitants. (A. C. O'D.)

ANGERONA, an early and obscure Roman goddess. According to ancient authorities, she relieved men from pain and sorrow, or delivered the Romans and their flocks from angina (quinsy); or she was the protecting goddess of Rome and the keeper of the sacred name of the city, which might not be pronounced lest it be revealed to Rome's enemies. The cult was older than the explanation of it, which tried to account for the goddess's name and her singular posture, with her mouth bound and sealed.

Modern scholars regard her as akin to Ops and Acca Larentia; or as the goddess of the new year and the returning sun. Her festival, called Divalia or Angeronalia, was celebrated Dec. 21, the winter solstice. The priests offered sacrifice in the temple of Volupia, the goddess of pleasure, in which stood a statue of Angerona. She was worshiped as Ancharia at Faesulae where an altar belonging to her was discovered.

See Georges Dumézil, *Déesses latines et mythes védiques* (1957). (T. V. B.)

ANGERS, a city and prefecture of the *département* of Maine-et-Loire in western France, and the former capital of Anjou, is situated on the Maine river 5 mi. above its junction with the Loire 55 mi. E.N.E. of Nantes. Pop. (1962) 109,614. Three bridges span the Maine at Angers, the old city being on the left bank and on the right the suburb of Doutre. The town is dominated by the cathedral of St. Maurice (12th- and 13th-century), which with its twin spires and magnificent portal possesses fine stained-glass windows and rich tapestries. The prominent castle (13th-century) is an irregular pentagon surrounded by a moat and bastioned by 17 large towers from 420 to 525 ft. high. Inside are the 16th-century chapel of Yolande of Aragon and the room containing the Apocalypse series of tapestries designed by Jean de Bandol and woven by Nicolas Bataille, unique in its size and artistic merit. The Logis Pincé, a Renaissance building, is now a museum. The Logis Barrault (15th-century) houses the public library, an art museum and the sculpture of Pierre Jean David d'Angers (q.v.), born in the city. Close by is the prefecture in the former St. Aubin's abbey (11th-century) with Roman arcades. The church of St. Serge was part of a former abbey and has a 13th-century chancel. The 12th-century Holy Trinity church is across the Maine in Doutre. Nearby is the hospital of St. Jean, a beautiful example of French Gothic style; part is an archaeological museum, but the main hall, chapel, cloisters, cellars and upper rooms are still to be seen. There are several fine 15th- and 16th-century houses. Angers is on the main line from Paris to Nantes, other lines run to Tours, Bordeaux and Brest. Cables, woolen goods, radio and television apparatus and umbrellas are manufactured. There is an important slate quarry. Angers is a market for the flowers, fruit and wines grown in the district.

Angers was first known as the capital of the Andegavi, the Celtic tribe of the state of Andes, and was called Juliomagus by the Romans. It had its hereditary counts from an early age, the best-known being Fulk Nerra, the "builder." The reign of the Plantagenets was marked by the construction of magnificent monuments of which the hospital of St. Jean is particularly well known. St. Louis (Louis IX) erected the castle. Philip Augustus in 1203 recaptured Anjou, which was attached to the crown of France by the treaty of Paris in 1259. The religious and revolutionary wars left their mark on the city. The medieval Universitas Andegavensis was refounded as the Facultés Catholiques de l'Ouest in 1875 by Bishop Charles Émile Freppel. In World War II Angers was occupied by the Germans from June 1940 to Aug. 1944; since then it has been almost entirely rebuilt. See also ANJOU.

(M. M.)

ANGILBERT (c. 740–814), Frankish poet and prelate at the court of Charlemagne. Of noble parentage, he was educated at the famous palace school at Aachen, under Alcuin. The known details of his life do little more than confirm his close connection with the court and the imperial family. In 800 he accompanied Charlemagne to Rome, and he was one of the witnesses to his will. He was made abbot of Centula (St. Riquier), Picardy, in 790 and died there in 814. He is said to have been the father of two children by Charlemagne's daughter Bertha, one of whom, Nithard, became a well-known chronicler.

Angilbert's Latin poems show the culture and tastes of a man of the world. A fragment of an epic, probably by him, describes life at the palace and the meeting between Charlemagne and Leo III, and earned him the nickname of "Homer" from Alcuin. Shorter poems show skill in versification and are interesting for their picture of the imperial circle. The passionate lover, the worldly cleric, the penitent abbot, depicted in contemporary references by other members of the court circle, is only glimpsed in Angilbert's own works.

BIBLIOGRAPHY.—Angilbert's poems were ed. by E. Dümmler in *Poetae latini Carolini Aevi*, vol. I (1881). See also D. Tardi, "Fortunat et Angilbert" in *Archivum Medii Aevi Latinitatis* (1925); F. J. E. Raby, *A History of Secular Latin Poetry in the Middle Ages* (1935).

ANGINA PECTORIS, a paroxysm of pain in the chest usually brought on by exertion in patients with diseased coronary arteries (see ARTERIES, DISEASES OF). An attack of angina pectoris begins suddenly as an agonizing pain, usually in the region of the heart but radiating through the chest in various directions and frequently extending down the left arm. A feeling of constriction and of suffocation accompanies the pain, although there is seldom actual difficulty in breathing. The sufferer becomes pale, his pulse feeble and he often feels that death is imminent. He is obliged to rest, and after two or three minutes the paroxysm subsides as quickly as it began. The attacks are apt to recur on less and less exertion as the coronary artery disease progresses. Attacks may be precipitated also by fits of anger. Angina pectoris is rare under middle life and is much commoner in males than in females.

(C. P. M.)

ANGIOLIERI, CECCO (c. 1260–1312), the best known of the Italian "comic" poets, was born at Siena. It is known that he married and had children, that he did military service, was exiled for a time and that he sometimes fell foul of the law. His sonnets should not be taken too seriously as revealing Cecco's own character and relationships, since their subjects and style belong to a European tradition which owes much to the "Goliard" poets (see GOLIARD). He expresses a love of women, wine, dice and money, and complains bitterly of his father's meanness and longevity. Many of the sonnets addressed to Becchina parody the *stil novo* writers, especially the Dante of the *Vita Nuova* and Guido Cavalcanti (q.v.).

Although Cecco is not original in his themes or in his deliberate use of colourful and unrefined language, he is a considerable artist whose lively verse expresses his sense of the comic and incongruous and reacts against the more exalted tone of love poetry in the "tragic" style.

BIBLIOGRAPHY.—M. Marti, *Poeti giocosi del tempo di Dante*, with texts (1956), *Cultura e stile nei poeti giocosi del tempo di Dante* (1953); S. Blancato, *Il Canzoniere* (1946). (S. Rs.)

ANGIOSPERMS (FLOWERING PLANTS), plants that bear flowers (not always conspicuous) and produce seeds enclosed within fruit (not always succulent); they include the majority of garden plants and most deciduous shrubs and trees.

All extant seed-bearing plants are divided into two groups, the

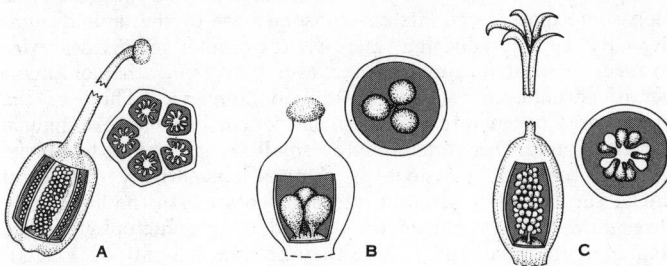

FIG. 1.—PLACENTAL AND CARPELLARY OVARIES

(A) with axile placentation; (B) with basal placentation; (C) with free-central placentation

angiosperms and gymnosperms. The gymnosperms—represented by conifers, cycads, and the ginkgo—have naked ovules and seeds (even though these may be hidden from view in cones), while the angiosperms have ovules enclosed within the ovary of a pistil, and the seeds are enclosed in the ripened ovary, the fruit. There are marked differences between these two groups in structure, life cycle, and development. After an introductory section, this article discusses the distinguishing characters of angiosperms, considers the descent of flowering plants, and gives a short survey of the subdivisions of the group.

GENERAL BACKGROUND

Concepts.—The botanical term Angiospermae (from the Greek *angeion*, "receptacle," and *sperma*, "seed") was coined by Paul Hermann in *Flore Lugduno-Batavae Flores* (1690) for one of his primary divisions of the plant kingdom that included flowering plants possessing seeds enclosed in capsules. (Hermann also coined the term Gymnospermae—from the Greek *gymnos*, "naked," and *sperma*, "seed"—defining that group as one in which the fruits either had only one seed or had divided into separate one-seeded portions, each piece being regarded as a naked seed.)

In 1827 Robert Brown established the existence of truly naked seeds in cycads and conifers, entitling them to be called correctly gymnosperms. Wilhelm Hofmeister demonstrated in 1851 the differences in embryology between the gymnosperms and angiosperms, a discovery showing the fallacy of acceptance to that time of the Gymnospermae as a subordinate group within the Angiospermae. August Wilhelm Eichler, in 1875, was the first to revise the classification of seed plants, treating the angiosperms and gymnosperms as the two primary and coordinate categories of the seed plants.

In earlier classifications Angiospermae was used as a class name in the phylum, or division, Spermatophyta (seed plants); in later schemes the angiosperms have been grouped as a subclass (Angiospermidae) of the class Pteropsida, which in turn is a unit of the division Tracheophyta (vascular plants), or, less commonly, as an entirely separate division, Anthophyta. Despite the confusion about the taxonomic rank and scientific terms used for these plants, the group is well defined and the common name of angiosperm serves to identify them.

Prevalence and Distribution.—The angiosperms are the dominant plants of the earth's vegetation and are the largest group of the plant kingdom, consisting of about 325 to 350 families, 12,500 genera, and somewhat more than 250,000 species. Economically they are the most important group of the plant kingdom, providing the majority of plants used for food, clothing, and shelter. Of even greater importance is their ecological significance as the dominant vegetation over the land surface of the earth. They preserve established watersheds and are essential to the maintenance of a balance in all of nature through their role in the nitrogen and carbon cycles.

The angiosperms occupy every land area of the earth. They are abundant in rivers and freshwater lakes; *e.g.*, members of Najadaceae and Potamogetonaceae. Some grow in shallow waters

of the oceans; *e.g.*, *Zostera*. Some persist in tropical desert areas with less than an inch of rainfall every few years; *e.g.*, certain cacti. Angiosperms are among the tallest of trees (*Eucalyptus*), the longest of rain-forest lianas (the rattan palm, *Calamus*), and the smallest of flowering plants, with tiny green thalloid bodies a fraction of an inch across (the duckweed *Wolffia*).

Between these extremes is every conceivable gradation, embracing aquatic and terrestrial herbs that develop a creeping, erect, or climbing habit; that grow as woody shrubs or trees; and that present great variety in size, shape, and colour of flower, fruit, and seed.

Derivation.—The origin of the angiosperms is unclear, but as a group they are of more recent evolvement than the gymnosperms or ferns. The most reliable evidence is that provided by the fossil record, but it is too fragmentary to be conclusive. Studies of this record, together with those of angiosperm analogies and homologies with other plant groups—living and extinct—have resulted in various theories and hypotheses in explanation of angiosperm origins.

Certainly these flowering plants are not derived from present-day gymnosperms or ferns. There is some suggestion of alliance with, or derivation from, extinct seed-bearing tree-fernlike plants called pteridosperms. It is believed that the angiosperms have been a dominant component of the earth's vegetation since the latter part of the Mesozoic Era (probably since the early Cretaceous Period) and that establishment of their dominance seemingly developed suddenly (in the sense of geologic time). There is also some evidence from the fossil record that there were plants clearly angiospermous in character existing back into the mid or early Jurassic Period.

FEATURES

Angiosperms are distinguished from gymnosperms by a number of vegetative and reproductive features. The articles FLOWER and PLANTS AND PLANT SCIENCE contain much information on terminology that will contribute greatly to a fuller understanding of the following discussion.

Vegetative Characters.—Distinctions are found in the roots, stem, and leaves. The roots of angiosperms and gymnosperms are similar except for the predominance in the former of fibrous

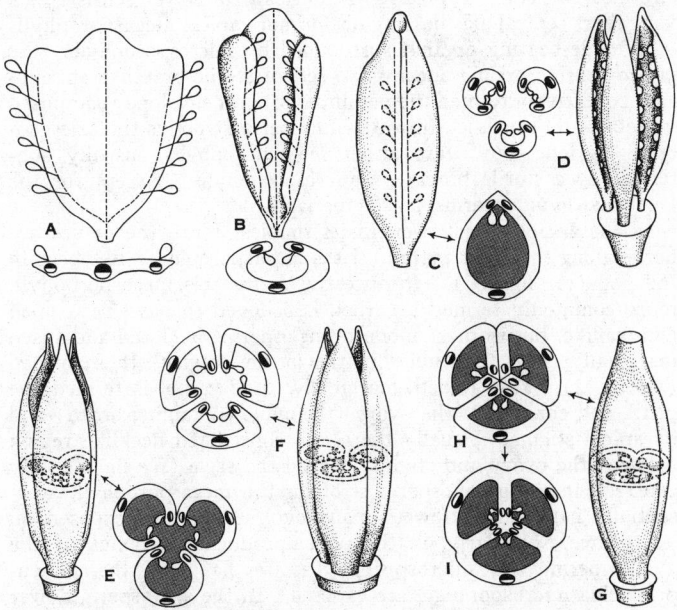

FIG. 2.—HYPOTHETICAL EVOLUTION OF SIMPLE AND COMPOUND OVARY

(A) three-lobed carpel with submarginal ovules (dotted lines indicate vascular strands); (B) the same, somewhat involute; (C) simple ovary derived from (B) by infolding of ovules and connation of ventral margins; (D) axis bearing three involute open carpels; (E) compound ovary derived from (D) by connation of edges of adjoining carpels; (F) axis with three open carpels with adjoining sides more or less parallel; (G) compound ovary derived from (F) by connation of adjoining sides and margins; (H) cross section of (G), hypothetical; (I) cross section of (G), actual, showing loss of carpellary demarcation in the three septa

roots and in the latter of taproots. The stem tissue of the typical angiosperm possesses a xylem element that includes vessels for water conduction (absent in a few primitive groups; *e.g.,* Winteraceae) and wood fibres for support, whereas the gymnosperm xylem consists primarily of tracheids that function both for conduction of liquids and for support.

The evolutionary advancement of the angiosperms over the gymnosperms is further evidenced by the appearance in the angiosperms of plants with soft herbaceous stem tissue (absent in gymnosperms) and by the usually diffuse mode of branching (deliquescent) as opposed to the single, primary axis, Christmas-tree type of branching (excurrent), characteristic of most gymnosperms. The leaves of angiosperms differ from those of most gymnosperms by the presence of extensive mesophytic tissue and of conspicuous pinnate or parallel venation.

Reproductive Characters.—The reproductive distinctions of the angiosperms, though more fundamental and significant than the vegetative, are often microscopic, and thus are not, for the

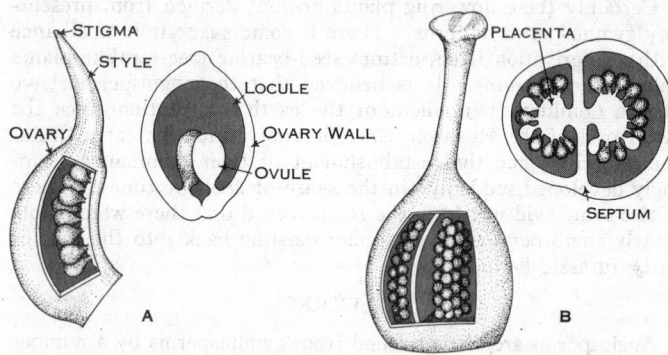

FIG. 3.—PLACENTAL AND CARPELLARY TYPES

(A) pistil with simple ovary and marginal placentation (unicarpellate); (B) compound ovary with parietal placentation, each placenta intruded and spreading (bicarpellate)

most part, so readily observable. The reproductive unit of the angiosperm is the flower, whereas in the gymnosperm it is the strobilus, or cone. Typically, the angiosperm flower consists of a very short central axis bearing one or more apical megasporophylls (the ovule-bearing organ), surrounded by microsporophylls (the pollen-bearing organ) and by two sets of sterile bractlike appendages collectively termed the perianth, or floral envelope (composed of petals and sepals). In the gymnosperm strobilus the axis generally is long and bears either megasporophylls (usually subtended by a sterile bract) or microsporophylls. Except for the Gnetales, gymnosperms lack a perianth.

In the angiosperm flower, in its simplest form, the ovules are borne along the inner margin of the megasporophyll—like peas in the pod (*see* fig. 2C). In ancestral forms this megasporophyll, more commonly termed a carpel, is believed to have been open and leaflike, but in most modern angiosperms is closed and fused marginally, with the ovules in the locule (cavity) thus formed (*see* fig. 2). This folded, marginally fused carpel is termed the pistil, and consists of the ovary (the ovule-containing organ) and its apical stigma. Usually there is a constricted necklike region between the ovary and stigma, termed the style (*see* fig. 3). By contrast, in the gymnosperm strobilus the megasporophyll is essentially flat, and its few to many ovules are borne exposed on its surface. Similarly, in the pollen-producing strobilus of the gymnosperm, the microsporophylls are flat and the pollen-producing microsporangia are exposed. In the angiosperm flower the microsporophylls are closed until maturity when they open and their pollen is released. They are termed stamens: the pollen-producing part is the anther and the supporting stalk the filament. The angiosperm gametes are microscopic and reduced to the simplest possible elements—an egg nucleus and a sperm nucleus.

The female gametophyte is enclosed within the ovule. The ovule consists typically of two outer, closely appressed, basally fused layers termed integuments. These open at the tip by a

pore known as the micropyle. The two integuments envelope a body of soft nutritive tissue, the nucellus. Borne within and near the micropylar end of the nucellus is a single multicellular megasporangium. One cell divides (mitotically) and produces the megaspore mother cell; its chromosomes are of the diploid number. By reduction division (meiosis) the mother cell divides twice to form a row of four megaspores, each possessing a haploid number of chromosomes (half the diploid number). Three of the megaspores degenerate and die; the fourth becomes the female gametophyte. This gametophyte (small sexual plant), by subsequent mitotic cell divisions, is composed eventually of several nuclei (up to eight) within a thin embryo sac. In the lily family three nuclei move to the micropylar end of the gametophyte, three remain at the other end (where they become the antipodal cells), and two remain together in the centre of the gametophyte. One of the three micropylar nuclei becomes the egg nucleus (the female gamete), the other two are the synergids, or "nurse" cells. There is no archegonium (flask-shaped organ containing an egg) in the angiosperm female gametophyte, as is present in vestigial form in gymnosperms.

The male gametophyte is simpler. Cells of meristematic tissue (tissues containing cells that retain the power of division) within the developing anther give rise to a microsporangium, or pollen sac. By mitotic division there is produced within the pollen sac a group of diploid pollen mother cells. Each divides twice by meiotic division to produce four microspores, which later become pollen grains, each containing the haploid number of chromosomes. The pollen grain divides once mitotically while yet in the anther, forming a generative nucleus and a tube nucleus. This is an immature stage of the male gametophyte. It is at this stage that the anther usually dehisces (splits open along definite lines) and pollination of the flower (transfer of pollen from anther to stigma) takes place.

Pollination in the angiosperms may be effected by wind, water, gravity, or insects and other animals. But unlike lower forms of plant life, angiosperms never produce free-swimming sperm. Fertilization in the angiosperms takes place entirely within the carpel of the flower.

Pollen grains have proved to be of considerable value in identification and classification studies. From these, the relatively new science of palynology (*q.v.*) has emerged, providing many data valuable as evidence of plant distributions and associations of earlier interglacial and preglacial periods. Studies of the morphology of the pollen grain have given new characters for classification purposes. These relate particularly to (1) the size, shape, and symmetry of the grain; (2) the position and number of its colpae (furrows) and germ pores (apertures); (3) the types of surface or adornment of the exine (outer spore wall, sporoderm); (4) the arrangement of the grains, whether they are borne singly, in tetrads (fours), or agglutinated in masses called pollinia; and (5) the number of nuclei present at the time the pollen grain (or microspore) is discharged from the anther.

Among these characters, that of furrow type is accepted to be of major phyletic significance. Monocolpate pollen grains (bearing a single furrow), characteristic of the extinct seed ferns, cycads, and ginkgo (all gymnosperms), and most monocotyledons, are considered primitive. A few dicot groups (all in the Ranales —*see* below) have monocolpate pollen. The order Ranales is also the only angiosperm group known to have both pollen types. In one angiosperm family, Casuarinaceae, the pollen grains lack furrows.

Fertilization follows pollination. The pollen grain (microgametophyte) reaches the receptive stigmatic surface of the pistil (megasporophyll) and develops a pollen tube into which moves the generative nucleus. This nucleus divides once and forms two male nuclei. Each of these male nuclei is a male gamete. Stimulated by the secretions on the stigma, the pollen tube grows through the wall of the pollen grain and into the tissue of the stigma. This tube continues down the style, penetrates the ovary and, when it reaches the ovule, enters the micropyle (or elsewhere through the integuments) and finally penetrates the female gametophyte.

As pollen-tube growth progresses from stigma to female gametophyte, it carries with it both male nuclei. Growth of the tube at the forward end is accompanied by degeneration at the other end. On approach to the egg nucleus, within the female gametophyte, the two haploid male nuclei are released. One unites with the haploid egg nucleus and forms the diploid zygote; the other unites with the polar nuclei to form an endosperm nucleus.

The zygote thus formed is a new generation. In contrast to the haploid gametophytes, it is a diploid sporophyte. It becomes the embryo within the seed. The endosperm nucleus, together with the embryo sac, multiplies to form the nutritive endosperm tissue of the seed. The angiosperm zygote (enclosed by a membrane) undergoes a series of divisions (not true at this stage in the gymnosperm embryo), each with its wall formation, the first of which separates the terminal cell from the basal cell. This wall may be transverse or longitudinal. The terminal cell continues to divide to produce the axis or hypocotyl of the embryo from which is later produced the cotyledons or seed leaves (one if a monocot). The basal cell divides to form a chain of cells that functions as a suspensor.

The endosperm tissue is the result of union of three nuclei ("double fertilization"): the two antipodal nuclei and the polar nucleus. In lilies the endosperm has a triploid (three times the haploid) number of chromosomes, unlike the embryo, which has a diploid number. The tissue multiplies as the embryo develops, but the bulk of it is digested by the embryo. In most angiosperms some of the endosperm remains in the seed (none is produced in orchids, where the initial cells of the tissue degenerate soon after formation). Endosperm character (amount, structure, etc.) and other seed features have been utilized in classifying flowering plants.

The seed consists typically of: (1) two seed coats—the outer is the testa, the inner the tegmen—developed from the ovule integuments; (2) the embryo with its radicle (root initial), hypocotyl, and cotyledon(s); and (3) the endosperm.

DIVISIONS

Since the last half of the 17th century the angiosperms have been divided into the Dicotyledonae (or dicotyledons) and Monocotyledonae (or monocotyledons). Nehemiah Grew, of England, was the first to propose this division (1672), but John Ray was the first to use it in a formal system of angiosperm classification (1686–88).

Main Identifying Characters.—The distinctions between the two groups are expressed by a combination of characters rather than by any single character. Characters identifying each group are:

Dicotyledons:
Embryo with two cotyledons (seed leaves)
Stems that acquire secondary growth do so by successive cylinders of xylem tissue
Veins of leaves typically arranged in a network
Leaves, generally petioled, margins often toothed
Flowers with petals and sepals mostly four or five, or in multiples of four or five
Pollen grains mostly tricolpate (with three furrows)
Monocotyledons:
Embryo with one cotyledon
Stems that acquire secondary thickening do so by vascular strands scattered through the stem, and no cylinders of secondary xylem tissue produced
Veins of leaves parallel, blades generally lacking a petiole, margins entire
Flower parts in multiples of three, sepals often petallike
Pollen grains always monocolpate (with one furrow)

The dicotyledons are the larger group, containing an estimated 260–270 families, 9,500 genera and in excess of 200,000 species. The monocotyledons comprise an estimated 65–70 families, 3,000 genera and 50,000 species.

Further Distinctions.—The dicotyledons were long considered to have been ancestral to the monocotyledons, but in recent decades evidence has been accumulating to indicate that either the reverse is true or that primitive forms of each group arose from a now extinct but common ancestor.

In mature dicot seeds that lack endosperm, *e.g.*, in beans, the embryo and its cotyledons are very large and possess abundant carbohydrate material. In those dicot seeds possessing endosperm tissue, *e.g.*, castor bean and buckwheat, the embryo is comparatively small. In all monocot seeds, except those of orchids, the embryo is small and the endosperm tissue abundant; *e.g.*, cereal grains, maize.

The structure and formation of the fruit varies markedly but is often constant for a particular genus or family. These variations provide many recognized types useful in angiosperm classification and identification. Many classifications have been made of fruit types but unfortunately most of them are so artificial as to have no direct correlation with the comparative morphology of the groups concerned; *e.g.*, most soft berrylike fruits are no different from that of a banana, or an orange, or a watermelon, yet each of these fruits is given a different name in most systems of fruit classification. There is much need for a thorough comparative study of all angiosperm fruits, correlating each with the floral morphology of the parent flower.

RELATIONSHIPS AND EVOLUTION

Darwin's and Alfred Russel Wallace's theories of descent and evolution, and information gained as the result of the development of the microscope, produced a more scientific system of plant classification. (*See* BOTANY: *Taxonomy*.)

Approach to Classification.—Modern scientific systems of flowering plant classification attempt to subdivide the dicotyledons and the monocotyledons into major groups called orders and families. The effort is made to arrange these in the sequence in which they are believed to have evolved. This is the phylogenetic approach. While it is comparatively easy to determine that two species are closely related, or belong in the same genus, it becomes increasingly difficult to postulate lines of evolution or degrees of relationship for larger groups. The problem is further complicated by the presumed extinction of entire groups that may have provided links to modern ones, or that may have been a common ancestor to two or more divergent lines of descent.

Phylogeny is the evolutionary history of a plant, or group of related plants—large or small. It attempts to account for the origin and development of the group. The goal of phylogenetic research within the angiosperms is to produce a system of classification that would place the oldest, most ancestral and most primitive units at the base, and the most recent and advanced units at the top. Although progress is being made, the absence of known origins for the angiosperms reduces most phylogenetic views close to the level of philosophical speculation.

There is abundant evidence that through evolutionary development, organs or floral parts common to their ancestors have been lost through reduction. This results in some seemingly "simple" flowers being evolutionarily and phylogenetically more advanced than a seemingly complex flower. Acceptance or rejection of this tenet of evolutionary theory, *i.e.*, a pattern of simple to complex and back to simple, has resulted in two groups of classification systems: those following the lines of Adolf Engler and Karl Prantl and those of Charles E. Bessey or John Hutchinson.

The German team of Engler and Prantl accepted Darwin's theories of evolution as fundamental to an understanding of plant relationships, but in their system of classification they rejected the view that simplicity of floral organization could be by reduction. They considered wind-pollinated flowers to be more primitive than insect-pollinated ones; the herbaceous habit to be ancestral to the woody; land plants to be derived from aquatic types; and monocotyledonous plants to be more primitive than the dicotyledons. This system became widely adopted because Engler and Prantl's great publication *Die natürlichen Pflanzenfamilien* (20 vol., 1887–1915, followed by the 2nd ed. in 1924) accounted for all the families and genera of the world's flora, complete with keys and descriptions. No other work was, or is, so comprehensive and detailed. A second and more ambitious publication, *Das Pflanzenreich* (107 vol., incomplete, 1900–), attempted to do the same for every species and variety of the higher plants. By these two publications Engler and Prantl provided botanists throughout the world with a common working tool. Because of this universality of application, their taxonomic system exerted a dominance for more than half a century.

The opposing concept, which holds that many apparently simple structures are derived by evolutionary reduction, has been advanced by the classification systems of Bessey of Nebraska (1897, 1915) and of Hutchinson of England (1926, 1935, 1948, 1959). These two systems were based on earlier ones dating back to Antoine Laurent de Jussieu of Paris (1789), and modified successively by Augustin Pyrame de Candolle (1813), John Lindley (1830), and George Bentham and Joseph D. Hooker (1862–83).

Primitive and Advanced Features.—Botanists from De Candolle to Hutchinson have listed criteria by which characters believed to indicate primitiveness are contrasted with those believed to represent evolutionary advancement. Those now most widely accepted postulate that: the woody habit is ancestral to the herbaceous in any one family or genus; herbaceous perennials are ancestral to annual or biennial plants; land plants are ancestral to aquatic plants; dicotyledons are ancestral to monocotyledons; spiral arrangement of parts preceded cyclic or whorled arrangement; numerous pistils or stamens in a flower is a more primitive condition than a solitary pistil or a few stamens in a flower; bisexual flowers preceded unisexual flowers; flowers with sepals and petals are ancestral to those without them; separate sepals and petals preceded conditions where fusion of parts occurs; flowers with superior (hypogynous) ovaries were ancestral to those with inferior (epigynous) ovaries; and radially symmetrical (actinomorphic) flowers were ancestral to bilaterally symmetrical (zygomorphic) ones.

Angiosperms having all of the primitive features, whether those listed above or others, would themselves be considered the most primitive, i.e., the least advanced, the lowest in terms of evolutionary development and the most simple; those with the most advanced features would be the most highly developed in the evolutionary scale, and likewise the most modern in terms of evolutionary development. These features only indicate probabilities; it is not possible to say that a particular genus or family is the most primitive or the most advanced.

Flowers with their parts (sepals, petals) distinct (not fused) and in spirals usually have numerous stamens and/or pistils that are also arranged in spirals and borne on a central axis; e.g., *Magnolia*. Flowers with their parts in whorls or cycles usually have a few or a definite number of stamens and pistils. There were believed to have been primitively two whorls of stamens and two whorls of perianth parts.

Flowers with a corolla of separate and distinct petals are more primitive than those with petals fused marginally into a tube- or saucer-shaped structure. Reduction of perianth parts to the point of extinction is considered to be an advanced condition. Similarly, reduction of stamens (in number of whorls or of individual stamens) is evidence of advancement, and a species bearing unisexual flowers (the extreme of sexual reduction) is considered to be more advanced than one producing bisexual flowers.

Flowers with the ovary borne above the point of origin of the perianth are hypogynous (the ovary superior). Those with the ovary borne seemingly below the point of origin of the perianth and stamens are epigynous (the ovary inferior). In those flowers where the perianth and stamens seemingly originate from the rim of a cuplike structure, within which "sits" the ovary, are perigynous. The hypogynous condition is accepted to be primitive. The epigynous condition is considered to be advanced, and in most instances is the result of fusion of the perianth and the filament bases to the sides of the ovary. The perigynous condition may be equally advanced and, with few exceptions, differs from epigyny only in that the fused parts are not adnate (fused to another structure from the beginning of development) to the ovary. The theory that the epigynous ovary is enveloped by the receptacle (stem tissue) is now generally rejected.

No one system of classification can be said to be more correct than another. There is increasing support for the view that the monocotyledons originated from primitive dicotyledons and that the Liliales (lily order) are among the most primitive of mono-

cotyledons and the Orchidales (orchid order) are the most advanced.

See FLOWER for more details on evolutionary relationships of flower types.

SURVEY OF FLOWERING PLANTS

The two groups, monocotyledons and dicotyledons are each further subdivided into orders. The Latin names of orders conventionally end in -ales, as Liliales, for the lily order. Exceptions of long standing are such ordinal names as Glumiflorae (the grass order), Centrospermae (the pink order), and Tubiflorae (the nightshade order). Each order, in turn, is composed of one or more families—whose Latin names conventionally end in -aceae, as Liliaceae for the lily family. For family names, also, exceptions exist to this identifying ending, notably Gramineae (the grass family), Cruciferae (the mustard family), Leguminosae (the pea family), Umbelliferae (the carrot family), Labiatae (the mint family), and Compositae (the aster or daisy family).

Each order has one or more, often minute and technical, characters that distinguish it from other orders. For this reason orders vary widely in the number of families they contain; sometimes only a single family constitutes an order, but more commonly many families are included. There is a growing belief that more natural plant relationships can be shown by grouping these families into a greater number of smaller and closer-knit orders than are given in the present article. Similarly, some of the large families are held to be unnatural assemblages as now constituted and are divided into still smaller units of the same rank (as in the Leguminosae and Saxifragaceae).

A growing body of opinion holds that monocotyledonous orders have been derived from some now extinct dicot, and that they represent a higher level of evolutionary advancement over the dicots. There is also a strong belief that the Heliobiae are not a natural group of interrelated families, and that the grasses and sedges (now comprising the Glumiflorae) are so unrelated as not to belong in the same order.

It is difficult to present these ideas diagramatically, for in the 20th century there exist angiosperm families of such great evolutionary advancement as to show no direct relationship with any other group, the linkages having been lost in the geologic past. These disjunctive dicotyledonous families include the Salicaceae (willows and poplars), Casuarinaceae (the Australian pine, *Casuarina*, and not a true pine), the Proteaceae of Australia and South Africa, and the Fagaceae (beeches and oaks). Rather than to think of these scores of families as analogous to the limbs of a much-branched tree, it is safer to view them as from above a cloud layer with their branches protruding through, sometimes as large clumps, sometimes as small ones, sometimes as solitary stalks, and each of varying degrees of remoteness, stature, and branching. "Islands in the sky" is an apt expression for this representation. Gradually some of the cloud formation clears and more islands are brought together. That is the state of knowledge of angiosperm interrelationship. It is a field rich in opportunities for further research along many lines.

MONOCOTYLEDONS

Pandanales (Pandanus Order).—A group of three families whose members have large grasslike or sword-shaped leaves and flowers usually with no perianth, or else reduced to bristles or scales. The order comprises cattails (Typhaceae), screw pines (Pandanaceae), and bur reeds (Sparganiaceae).

Heliobiae (Pondweed Order).—Similar to the above, but the plants mostly submerged aquatics, and the seed almost devoid of endosperm. Examples: pondweed (Potamogetonaceae), water plantain (Alismaceae), and elodea (Hydrocharitaceae).

Glumiflorae or Graminales (Grass and Sedge Order).—A group distinguished by minute flowers lacking perianth parts, situated in the axils of bracts or scales, and arranged in compact units called spikelets. The seed has abundant endosperm. The order consists of two families, the Gramineae (grasses) and Cyperaceae (sedges), and economically is perhaps the most important to man of all orders of plants. Examples: such important food plants as rice, wheat, corn, rye, oats, and barley; the bamboos, of many uses; turf and forage grasses; and scores of ornamental grasses.

Principes or Palmales (Palm Order).—A distinctive group composed only of the palm family (Palmae), typically woody plants with leaves generally deeply divided or compound and flowers minute but with a perianth. The ovary is composed of three carpels, basic units analogous to foliar leaves. The order, of pantropical distribution, is of economic importance ranking next to the grass order. It provides coconut products, oils, waxes, dates, fibres, ivory nuts; and locally palms yield abundant material for shelter, utensils, and food.

Cyclanthales (Panama-Hat-Palm Order).—A small order of tropical America, composed of one family of small palmlike plants (Cyclanthaceae), which differ from the true palms in that the flower has a two- to four- carpellate ovary, with many ovules. The importance of the order is as a source of material for Panama hats (from the leaves of *Carludovica*).

Spathiflorae or Arales (Aroid Order).—Mostly herbaceous plants or woody climbers, with very small flowers and pollen grains in groups of two or four. The order comprises two families: the Araceae (aroids), in which the flowers are aggregated on a single axis (termed a spadix), which is surrounded by an often large and showy bract (a spathe); and the Lemnaceae (aquatic duckweeds), in which the plant body is reduced to a tiny floating thallus and the flower to a single stamen and simple pistil. In the tropics a few aroids are important starch-producing food plants, notably taro from *Colocasia* and the large edible fruits of *Monstera*. Many ornamentals are members of the order including calla lily, anthurium, philodendron, pothos, and jack-in-the-pulpit.

Farinosae or Farinales (Pineapple Order).—A group of 13 small, mostly tropical families having neither habits nor floral characters in common, but united simply on the basis of the presence of a distinctive mealy endosperm in the seed (farinalike, hence the name Farinosae). Examples: bromeliads (Bromeliaceae), which include the pineapple; and the spiderworts (Commelinaceae).

Liliales (Lily Order).—A group of eight families, most characterized by showy flowers whose parts are in groups of three or multiples thereof. The sepals and petals generally look alike, and the seeds have a fleshy or bony endosperm. The three principal families are the Liliaceae (lilies; ovary usually superior, six stamens), the Amaryllidaceae (amaryllises; ovary usually inferior, six stamens, flowers in an umbel subtended by one or two bracts), and the Iridaceae (irises; ovary inferior, three stamens). Examples: such common ornamentals as the lily, tulip, hyacinth, amaryllis, narcissus, crocus, iris, gladiolus, agave, crinum, aloe, and day lily; and such plants as the onion and yam, and the fibreproducing (sisal) *Agave*.

Scitamineae or Scitaminales (Banana Order).—A natural group of four tropical families distinguished by each flower containing one functional stamen and the seeds usually bearing a fleshy or horny appendage termed an aril. The flowers are usually borne in dense spikelike clusters. Examples: banana and bird-of-paradise flower (Musaceae), ginger and torch flower (Zingiberaceae), canna (Cannaceae), and arrowroot (Marantaceae).

Microspermae or Orchidales (Orchid Order).—The most highly advanced group of monocots, having bilaterally symmetrical flowers with varying degrees of fusion of stamens to stamens and of stamens to pistil. The seeds are exceedingly minute and devoid of endosperm, or nearly so. The order is composed of two families, the Burmanniaceae and Orchidaceae. The orchid family is divided into two subfamilies, one with flowers having two stamens (*e.g.*, the lady's slippers, *Cypripedium*); the other, and much larger group, with flowers having one stamen (the *Cattleya* type). The Orchidales are a large and varied order, widely distributed but primarily tropical. They are important for the many showy ornamentals, and as the source of vanilla flavouring (from pods of certain *Vanilla* species).

DICOTYLEDONS

Verticillatae or Casuarinales (Casuarina Order).—A small, morphologically complex group from Australia, limited to the so-called Australian pines, constituting one genus (*Casuarina*) and one family (Casuarinaceae). They are distinguished anatomically by the ovule containing 20 or more embryo sacs (there is only one in all other dicots).

Piperales (Pepper Order).—Three families of predominately tropical plants, mostly herbaceous, the flowers minute and lacking a perianth, mostly bisexual and arranged in a spikelike cluster. Example: lizard's-tails (Saururaceae), black pepper (Piperaceae), and *Chloranthus* (Chloranthaceae).

Hydrostachyales (African Pondweed Order).—An order composed of a single genus of African aquatics (*Hydrostachys*), constituting the family Hydrostachyaceae. The plants are dioecious; *i.e.*, male and female flowers are borne on different plants. The flowers lack petals, the male flower being reduced to a single naked stamen.

Salicales (Willow Order).—One family, the Salicaceae, containing the willows and poplars. The plants are dioecious. The flowers of both sexes lack petals, and are borne in catkins; the tufted seeds are contained in capsules.

Garryales (Garrya Order).—An order composed of a single American dioecious genus, *Garrya*. The flowers, which lack petals, are on catkins; the ovary is unilocular (has one compartment), with several ovules; and the fruit is a globular berry.

Myricales (Sweet Gale Order).—One family, the Myricaceae, aromatic trees or shrubs. The flowers are unisexual; the ovary contains one ovule having one integument; the style is two-branched; and the fruit is a wax-coated drupe. Examples: bayberry, sweet fern, sweet gale.

Leitneriales (Corkwood Order).—An order composed of a single rare species, *Leitneria floridana*, of the southeastern U.S. It is distinguished from the Myricales by, among other features, the ovule having two integuments and the style being unbranched.

Balanopsidales (Balanops Order).—One family, the Balanopsidaceae, with two genera of Australia-Polynesian trees and shrubs. The order is distinguished from the Garryales by the ovary having two compartments, and from the Myricales in having several ovules in each ovary.

Juglandales (Walnut Order).—One family, the Juglandaceae, the walnuts and hickories. The order is distinguished by the plants being monoecious, *i.e.*, the male and female flowers are on the same plant. The leaves are pinnately compound. The male flowers are borne in catkins; the female ones are solitary or grouped a few in a cluster, each with a two-carpelled uniovulate ovary.

Julianiales (Juliania Order).—Tropical American woody dioecious plants superficially resembling the Juglandales but differing in having a three-carpelled ovary.

Batidales (Batis Order).—One species of maritime dioecious simple-leaved shrubs (*Batis maritima*), with unisexual flowers in small conelike inflorescences. The ovary has a single basal ovule in each of four locules, or compartments.

Fagales (Beech Order).—Trees and shrubs of temperate regions belonging to the beech (Fagaceae) and birch (Betulaceae) families, distinguished by having the male flowers in catkins and the inferior unilocular ovary with two or more ovules. Examples: beech, chestnut, oak, alder, birch, hornbeam.

Urticales (Nettle Order).—A group of four families of diverse habits, united by the unisexual flowers seldom borne in catkins. The female flower has a superior ovary, unilocular, two-carpellate, with a single ovule; the male flower has 4–12 stamens. Examples: elm, hackberry, mulberry, fig, hemp, breadfruit, nettle.

Podostemales (Riverweed Order).—One genus of American aquatic plants, *Podostemon*, differing technically from the Urticales in having bisexual flowers with numerous stamens.

Proteales (Protea Order).—Composed of more than 50 genera in the single family Proteaceae, of the Southern Hemisphere. It is distinguished by bisexual flowers with a perianth, and usually four stamens borne opposite the four perianth segments, with the filaments fused to the perianth. The seed lacks endosperm. Examples: Queensland, or macadamia, nut, showy species of *Banksia* and *Protea*, the she-oak (*Grevillea*).

Santalales (Sandalwood Order).—Three families of woody

plants, many semiparasites, with mostly unisexual flowers having small perianth parts opposite and fused to the stamens. The seed is endospermous. Examples: sandalwood (Santalaceae), *Olax* (Olacaceae), semiparasitic mistletoe (Loranthaceae).

Aristolochiales (Birthwort Order).—A small group of plants of diverse habits; among the many parasitic forms is the largest true plant parasite known, *Rafflesia arnoldii*. It is characterized by flowers usually with a single whorled petaloid perianth. The ovary is usually inferior with axile or free-central placentation (ovules attached to a central stalk). Stamens alternate with the perianth parts. The seed is endospermous. Examples: dutchman's-pipe (Aristolochiaceae); the parasitic monster flower, or rafflesia (Rafflesiaceae); and the Hydnoraceae.

Balanophorales (Balanophora Order).—One small family of fleshy parasitic herbs. The flowers are mostly unisexual, with the ovary superior and with free-central placentation.

Polygonales (Buckwheat Order).—One family, Polygonaceae, distinguished by the usually bisexual flowers, with a unilocular, uniovular, two- to four-carpelled ovary, and the perianth undifferentiated into sepals and petals. Examples: rhubarb, buckwheat, and knotweed.

Centrospermae or Centrospermales (Pink Order).—A large group of ten families, mostly of temperate herbs. The flowers usually have both sepals and petals. The order is distinguished from others by basal or free-central placentation. The seed has a coiled or S-shaped embryo. Examples: beets and spinach (Chenopodiaceae), amaranth (Amaranthaceae), four-o'clock and bougainvillea (Nyctaginaceae), pokeberry (Phytolaccaceae), carnation and baby's breath (Caryophyllaceae), and the large, primarily South African mesembryanthemum family (Aizoaceae).

Ranales (Buttercup Order).—A group of 19 families of woody and herbaceous plants, with showy bisexual flowers distinguished by the parts usually spirally arranged and numerous; there are many pistils in each flower and each pistil is unicarpellate. The woody members are separated as the Magnoliales by some authors. Examples: water lily and lotus (Nymphaeaceae); hornwort (Ceratophyllaceae); buttercup, delphinium, anemone, clematis, and columbine (Ranunculaceae); barberry (Berberidaceae); magnolia (Magnoliaceae); custard apple and pawpaw (Annonaceae); nutmeg (Myristicaceae); avocado, cinnamon, camphor, and sassafras (Lauraceae).

Rhoeadales or Papaverales (Poppy Order).—Seven families, mostly of herbs, characterized by bisexual hypogynous flowers usually with cyclic arrangement of sepals and petals. The ovary usually has parietal placentation. Examples: poppy (Papaveraceae), bleeding heart (Fumariaceae), caper (Capparidaceae), cabbage and mustard (Cruciferae), mignonette (Resedaceae).

Sarraceniales (Pitcher-Plant Order).—An order of three herbaceous families of carnivorous plants, whose leaves are often tubular and are provided with glandular hairs or other devices by which insects are entrapped. Examples: pitcher plant (Sarraceniaceae), *Nepenthes* (Nepenthaceae), sundew (Droseraceae).

Rosales (Rose Order).—One of the largest and most diverse of all orders of dicots, composed of 17 families. They are bonded into one order by a combination of technical characters: flowers with petals and sepals in whorls and typically bisexual; an hypanthium, or calyx-cup, often present; ovary unicarpellate with parietal placentation or multicarpellate with axile placentation; numerous stamens commonly in many whorls. Examples: sedum (Crassulaceae); currant, hydrangea, and mock orange (Saxifragaceae); sycamore, or plane tree (Platanaceae); apple, pear, cherry, peach, almond, strawberry, hawthorn, and rose (Rosaceae); pea, bean, peanut, clover, wisteria, sweet pea, mimosa, senna, and locust (Leguminosae).

Geraniales (Geranium Order).—A group of 21 families, distinguished by the stamens being usually twice the number of sepals, in two whorls (or those of the outer whorl missing). The ovules are pendulous, with a ventral raphe, or ridge, and the micropyle pointing upwards (or the ovule erect with the micropyle pointing downward). The styles of the compound ovary often persist in the fruit. The seeds generally lack endosperm. Examples: wood sorrel, or oxalis (Oxalidaceae); geranium and *Pelargonium* (Geraniaceae); nasturtium (Tropaeolaceae); flax (Linaceae); cocaine from leaves of coca (Erythroxylaceae); all citrus fruits (Rutaceae); tree of heaven (Simaroubaceae); mahogany (Meliaceae); poinsettia, Pará rubber tree, croton, castor bean (Euphorbiaceae).

Sapindales (Soapberry Order).—A group of 23 families, mostly tropical trees and shrubs, distinguished from the Geraniales by a pendulous ovule with a dorsal raphe and the micropyle directed upward (or erect ovules with a ventral raphe and the micropyle directed downward). Examples: boxwood and Japanese spurge (Buxaceae); cashew, pistachio, mango, poison ivy, and sumac (Anacardiaceae); leatherwood (Cyrillaceae); holly (Aquifoliaceae); bittersweet and euonymus (Celastraceae); maple (Aceraceae); horse chestnut (Hippocastanaceae); goldenrain tree and litchi (Sapindaceae); garden balsam (Balsaminaceae).

Rhamnales (Buckthorn Order).—Woody, temperate zone plants, mostly with unisexual and/or apetalous flowers with stamens in one whorl opposite the petals. The ovary is usually borne on, or within, a disc, and contains one or two ovules. Examples: buckthorn and jujube (Rhamnaceae); grape, Boston ivy, and Virginia creeper (Vitaceae).

Malvales (Mallow Order).—Eight families, mostly woody, predominately of tropical and subtropical distribution, often with stellate hairs and mucilage-producing tissues. The bisexual flowers have numerous stamens; the ovary is superior and syncarpous, with usually axile placentation; the sepals are mostly valvate. Examples: linden (Tiliaceae); cotton, okra, mallow, and hollyhock (Malvaceae); kapok, balsa wood, baobab tree, and cotton tree (Bombacaceae); cacao, source of cocoa, and cola (Sterculiaceae).

Parietales (Tea Order).—A group of 31 families, distinguished from the Malvales by the sepals usually overlapping and the placentation parietal. Current opinion considers this order an artificial assemblage whose families are still problematical. Examples: tara vine (Dilleniaceae), tea and camellia (Theaceae), St.-John's-wort (Hypericaceae), rockrose (Cistaceae), violet (Violaceae), passionflower (Passifloraceae), papaya (Caricaceae), begonia (Begoniaceae).

Opuntiales (Cactus Order).—Consisting of the single family Cactaceae, this order is distinguished by the plants being generally fleshy and spiny. The numerous sepals and petals are not clearly differentiated into calyx and corolla; the ovary is inferior, with parietal placentation. Examples: prickly pear and saguaro.

Myrtales (Myrtle Order).—A varied assemblage of 23 families. The flowers have a calyx-tube around a superior ovary (sometimes inferior by fusion to the calyx-tube); usually four or five sepals and petals; and several to many ovules in each locule. Examples: oleaster (Elaeagnaceae); loosestrife and crape myrtle (Lythraceae); pomegranate (Punicaceae); mangrove (Rhizophoraceae); sour gum tree (Nyssaceae); eucalyptus, guava, clove, allspice, and myrtle (Myrtaceae); water chestnut (Trapaceae); evening primrose, fuchsia, and fireweed (Onagraceae).

Umbellales (Carrot Order).—A small group of three families of temperate regions, characterized by the combination of flowers tending to be in clusters called umbels. The ovary is inferior, with each of two locules containing a single ovule. Examples: English ivy, ginseng, and rice-paper plant (Araliaceae); carrot, parsnip, celery, anise, caraway, and poison hemlock (Umbelliferae); dogwood (Cornaceae).

Diapensiales (Diapensia Order).—Composed of the one family, Diapensiaceae, of Nearctic regions, closely allied to the Ericales (*see* below) but differing in having the stamens inserted on the corolla or fused into a tube. The pollen is never in tetrads; the ovary is trilocular. Examples: *Galax, Pyxidanthera, Shortia.*

Ericales (Heather Order).—A small group of four families, mostly woody plants, characterized by flower parts usually in fives. The petals are fused basally. The stamens are separated from the corolla or joined only at extreme base and often at the edge of a nectar-bearing disc. The anthers often open by pores; the pollen is frequently in tetrads. Examples: sweet pepper bush (Clethraceae); heath, heather, rhododendron, mountain laurel, wintergreen, blueberry, and cranberry (Ericaceae).

Primulales (Primrose Order).—A conspicuous but small group of three families, characterized by the five-parted flowers, with petals fused partially. The ovary is superior; there is one style, one locule, and many carpels. Placentation is free-central and there are many ovules. Examples: *Ardisia* (Myrsinaceae); primrose, shooting star, and cyclamen (Primulaceae).

Plumbaginales (Plumbago Order).—Composed of the single family Plumbaginaceae, separated from the Primulales by the flowers having five styles or style-branches, and the ovary having a single basal or pendulous ovule. Examples: thrift, sea lavender, and leadwort.

Ebenales (Ebony Order).—A group of seven families of mostly tropical trees and shrubs, characterized by the stamens in two or three whorls. The ovary has two to five locules, with one to a few ovules in each on axile placentae. Examples: chicle, sapodilla, and star apple (Sapotaceae); ebony and persimmon (Ebenaceae); benzoin and silver bells (Styracaceae).

Gentianales or Contortae (Gentian Order).—A closely related group of six families, characterized by the petals fused at their bases, with the lobes usually twisted around each other. The stamens are inserted at or near the corolla base and alternate with the lobes. The ovary is superior, bicarpellate with the carpels fused; placentation is axile, free (at least basally) or parietal. Its most important families are the Oleaceae, Gentianaceae, Apocynaceae, and Asclepiadaceae. Examples: olive, ash, lilac, forsythia, and jasmine (Oleaceae); strychnine (Loganiaceae); gentian (Gentianaceae); milkweed and wax plant (Asclepiadaceae); periwinkle, oleander, and dogbane (Apocynaceae).

Tubiflorae (Nightshade Order).—A large group of 23 families, similar to the Gentianales but differing in the petal lobes overlapping. The stamens are usually attached to the corolla tube. The ovary is two- to five-carpelled with axile placentation. Examples: morning glory and sweet potato (Convolvulaceae); phlox and *Polemonium* (Polemoniaceae); heliotrope, borage, and forget-me-not (Boraginaceae); verbena and teak (Verbenaceae); mint, sage, and salvia (Labiatae); potato, tobacco, tomato, and petunia (Solanaceae); snapdragon, *Calceolaria,* and foxglove (Scrophulariaceae); catalpa and trumpet creeper (Bignoniaceae); broomrape (Orobanchaceae), parasites on roots; African violet and gloxinia (Gesneriaceae).

Plantaginales (Plantago Order).—An isolated group consisting only of the Plantaginaceae. It is characterized by the corolla being parchmentlike and the fruit, a capsule, opening by a lid. Psyllium seeds (from *Plantago psyllium*) are used to relieve constipation.

Rubiales (Madder Order).—A group of five families of pantropical distribution, characterized by having mostly opposite leaves, a cymose inflorescence, the petals partially fused, the stamens distinct and rarely joined, and the ovary inferior. Examples: coffee, quinine, and gardenia (Rubiaceae); honeysuckle and elderberry (Caprifoliaceae); valerian (Valerianaceae); teasel (Dipsacaceae).

Cucurbitales (Gourd Order).—Limited to the family Cucurbitaceae, a primarily pantropical group of herbaceous vines having commonly unisexual flowers, with a three-carpellate inferior ovary and parietal placentation; and the stamens more or less fused. Examples: squash, gourd, cucumber, citron, melon.

Campanulales (Bellflower Order).—Six families, but these contain collectively more than 1,000 genera and 22,000 species, with the bellflower (Campanulaceae) and the aster (Compositae) families being the dominant groups. The order is distinguished by the fused petals and inferior ovary of two to five carpels but a single locule and ovule. The stamens are often fused by their anthers. Examples: bellflower and *Lobelia;* and all members of the aster and daisy group, to which belong lettuce, artichoke, endive, safflower, ragweed, chicory, chrysanthemum, dahlia, pyrethrum, zinnia, marigold, sunflower, globe thistle, edelweiss.

See also references under "Angiosperms" in the Index.

BIBLIOGRAPHY.—Details of the subject and references to the literature will be found in the following works (the bibliographies in those by Constance and Lawrence are especially complete): C. E. Bessey, "The Phylogenetic Taxonomy of Flowering Plants," *Ann. Mo. Bot. Gdn.,* 2:109–164 (1915); J. Hutchinson, *The Families of Flowering Plants,* vol. i, *Dicotyledons,* vol. ii, *Monocotyledons,* 2nd ed. (1959); *British Flowering Plants* (worldwide in scope) (1948); A. Engler, *Syllabus der Pflanzenfamilien,* 12th ed., vol. i (1954) and vol. ii (1964); T. A. Just, "Gymnosperms and the Origin of the Angiosperm," *Bot. Gaz.,* 110:91–103, with bibliography (1948); I. W. Bailey, "Origin of the Angiosperms," *J. Arnold Arbor.,* 30:64–70 (1949); A. Gundersen, *Families of Dicotyledons* (1950); D. A. Johansen, *Plant Embryology: Embryogeny of the Spermatophyta* (1951); P. Maheshwari, *An Introduction to the Embryology of Angiosperms,* with bibliography (1950); C. R. Metcalfe and L. Chalk, *Anatomy of the Dicotyledons,* 2 vol. (1950); G. H. M. Lawrence, *Taxonomy of Vascular Plants,* with bibliography (1951); V. Puri, "The Role of Floral Anatomy in the Solution of Morphological Problems," *Bot. Rev.,* 17:471–553, with bibliography (1951); C. R. Metcalfe, "An Anatomist's Views on Angiosperm Classification," *Kew Bull.,* 3:427–440 (1954); A. L. Takhtajan, "Phylogenetic Principles of the System of Higher Plants," *Bot. Rev.,* 19:1–45, with bibliography (1953); L. Constance, "The Systematics of the Angiosperms," in *A Century of Progress in the Natural Sciences, 1853–1953,* pp. 405–483, with bibliography (1955); A. Cronquist, "Outline of a New System of Families and Orders of Dicotyledons," *Bull. Jard. Bot. État Brux.,* 27:13–40, with bibliography (1957); F. Němejc, "On the Problem of the Origin and Phylogenetic Development of the Angiosperms," *Acta Mus. Nat. Prag.,* 12–13:59–144, with bibliography (1956); R. F. Thorne, "Some Guiding Principles of Angiosperm Phylogeny," *Brittonia,* 10:72–77 (1958); A. Cronquist, "The Divisions and Classes of Plants," *Bot. Rev.,* 26:426–482, with bibliography (1960); H. Merxmüller, "Systematik der Spermatophyta," *Fortschr. Bot.,* 23:65–105, with bibliography (1961); P. H. Davis and V. H. Heywood, *Principles of Angiosperm Taxonomy,* with bibliography (1963). (G. H. M. L.)

ANGKOR, Cambodian word from Sanskrit *nagara,* city, state (cf. Malay *negeri, negara;* Thai *nakhon;* also Cambodian *nokor*). It is used loosely to refer to the region around Siemreap, the site of the ruins of the capital of the Khmer empire. The remains include those of Angkor Thom and Angkor Wat (*c.* 1140), and earlier remains. The capital city was founded in the 9th century A.D. and abandoned *c.* 1440.

See also CAMBODIA: *Archaeology;* INDONESIAN ARCHAEOLOGY AND ART. (A. H. CE.)

ANGLE, in plane geometry, a pair of half lines emanating from a point called the vertex of the angle. The half lines are called the arms, sides or legs of the angle. As shown in fig. 1, the angle consisting of the half lines (l_1, l_2) is distinct from the

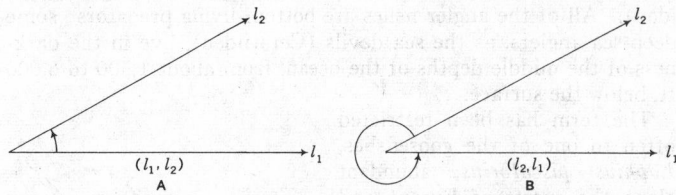

FIG. 1.—(A) ACUTE ANGLE; (B) REFLEX ANGLE

angle (l_2, l_1). If rotation is taken as a concept more primitive than angle, then the angle (l_1, l_2) can be defined as the (counterclockwise) rotation or amount of turning about the vertex required to make l_1 coincide with l_2. Two angles (l_1, l_2) and (m_1, m_2) with the same vertex are equal if the rotation sending l_1 into l_2 sends m_1 into m_2. A straight angle is an angle $(l, -l)$ made by the two half lines of any line through the vertex. (*See* fig. 2.) A right angle (l_1, l_2) is one for which $(l_1, l_2) = (l_2, -l_1)$.

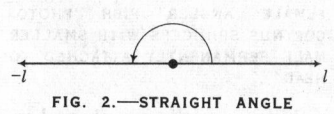

FIG. 2.—STRAIGHT ANGLE

Angles are measured either by radians or degrees. If a circle of radius 1 with centre at the vertex is drawn, an angle cuts out an arc of this circle. The radian measure of this angle is the length of this arc. Since the length of an arc is the same before and after a rotation, equal angles have equal radian measure. Also, if two angles have the same radian measure, they are equal. The radian measure of a straight angle is π while that of a right angle is $\frac{\pi}{2}$. If the radian measure of an angle is less than $\frac{\pi}{2}$ it is

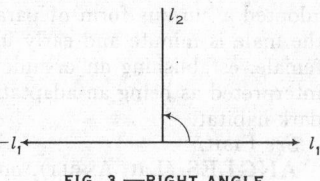

FIG. 3.—RIGHT ANGLE

called acute; if between $\frac{\pi}{2}$ and π, it is obtuse; if between π and 2π, it is a reflex angle. In rotary motion where rotations exceeding a complete revolution occur, it is useful to allow angles of radian measure greater than 2π. Nega-tive angles can be used to symbol-ize clockwise rotations, *i.e.*, $-(l_1, l_2) = (l_2, l_1)$. An angle of radian measure $-x$ also has radian measure $2\pi - x$. A straight angle is assigned a value of $180°$ so that an angle of x radians will be an angle of $\frac{180}{\pi} x$ degrees. The angle of $90 - a$ degrees is the complement of the angle with a degrees. The angle of $180 - a$ degrees is the supplement of the angle with a degrees.

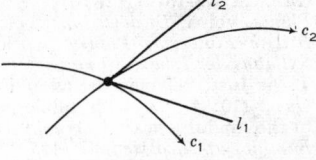

FIG. 4.—CURVILINEAR ANGLE

The curvilinear angle between a pair of intersecting smooth directed curves c_1 and c_2 in a plane is the angle of the pair of tangent half lines at their points of intersection (*see* fig. 4). If a pair of intersecting smooth directed curves lie on a surface, the angle between them is the angle of the pair of tangent half lines in the tangent plane of the surface. This angle is the spherical angle if the two curves are great circles on a sphere. Other ex-tensions of the original idea of angle include a dihedral angle (a pair of intersecting planes in space), a trihedral angle (three planes intersecting at a point in space) and a polyhedral angle (any number of planes intersecting at a point).

If two half lines l_1 and l_2 in three or higher dimensional space meet in a vertex, they lie in a plane and their angle is the angle in this plane. Since the plane is not oriented, that is, the counter-clockwise direction has not been specified, the convention is to use either (l_1, l_2) or (l_2, l_1) whichever is less than or equal to π.

BIBLIOGRAPHY.—Sir T. L. Heath (ed.), *The Thirteen Books of Euclid's Elements* (1956); D. Hilbert, *Grundlagen der Geometrie* (1956); H. Schotten, *Inhalt und Methode des planimetrischen Unter-richts* (1890). (I. M. S.)

ANGLER (ANGLER FISH), in a wide sense any fish of the order Lophiiformes (Pediculati), having the front dorsal spine modified to form a "fishing rod" whose "baited hook" projects over the mouth. The order includes the goosefishes (family Lophiidae), frogfishes (Antennariidae) and batfishes (Ogcocephal-idae). All of the angler fishes are bottom-living predators; some deep-sea anglers, as the sea devils (Ceratiidae), live in the dark-ness of the middle depths of the ocean, from about 1,500 to 6,000 ft. below the surface.

The term has been restricted often to one of the goosefishes, *Lophius piscatorius,* abundant along the coasts of Europe and eastern North America. It has an enormous mouth, with long, backwardly directed, depressible teeth and a large flattened head. The fish walks along the bottom by means of its paired fins, which are modified for this purpose. The first three rays of the ante-rior dorsal fin are long filaments placed on the head; the first, the longest, is freely movable and

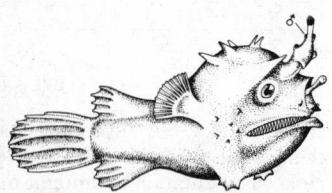

AFTER NORMAN IN W. C. ALLEE ET AL., "PRINCIPLES OF ANIMAL ECOLOGY" (1955); REPRODUCED BY PERMISSION OF W. B. SAUN-DERS CO.

FEMALE ANGLER FISH PHOTO-CORYNUS SPINICEPS WITH SMALLER MALE PERMANENTLY ATTACHED TO HEAD

acts as a lure to attract other fish. So large is the mouth and so extensible the stomach that the angler can engulf fish almost as big as itself. It may reach a length of five feet. The spawn consists of a transparent gelatinous sheet which may be 2 or 3 ft. broad and 25–30 ft. long; in this the eggs are embedded.

The small blackish sea devils, which have luminous lures, have adopted a curious form of parasitism between male and female: the male is minute and early in life attaches permanently to the female, establishing an organic union. This behaviour has been interpreted as being an adaptation to ensure mating in the fishes' dark habitat.

See FISH.

ANGLES (Lat. ANGLI), one of the Germanic tribes that in-vaded Britain in the 5th century A.D. Tacitus (1st century A.D.),

in his *Germania,* mentions them among the worshipers of Hertha (Nerthus), a divinity later revered mainly in Scandinavia. Bede in his account of the invaders of Britain places Angulus, the home of the Angles, on the European continent between the Jutes and the Saxons (*qq.v.*). It is natural to identify Angulus with Angel, a district in Schleswig between the Schlei and the fjord of Flensburg. This identification, made by King Alfred in his account of Ohthere's voyages and by Aethelweard (*c.* 990), is also supported by the legends of the early kings of the Angles, which are placed in Schleswig (*see* OFFA of Angel). Ptolemy's localization of the Angles on the middle Elbe (*Geographia,* ii, 11, 15) can therefore be regarded as wrong. Bede stresses that the continental home of the Angles was left deserted by them and there is no doubt that they practically all emigrated. Place names in Thuringia, such as Engelin and Englide, and a reference in the preface to one copy of the Thuringian laws show that they had had an earlier expansion in another direction. It has been objected that Angel was too small to have provided the invaders of so large a part of Britain, but it need only be regarded as their centre, and indeed Alfred assumes that they were widely dispersed in the area.

Bede's clear distinction of Angles and Saxons is not always observed by himself; *e.g.,* he writes *Anglorum sive Saxonum gens* (*Historia Ecclesiastica* i, 15). Both *Angli* and *Saxones* used of all the English are found elsewhere, and Gregory the Great ad-dresses Aethelberht of Kent as *rex Anglorum* (Bede, *Historia Ecclesiastica* i, 32). It may be said on the whole that *Angli* is in English and continental writings the commoner term, and in Old English *Engle* was the general term, *Seaxe* meaning specifically Saxons. But Celtic writers use *Saxones* of all the Germanic in-vaders, following the usage of their vernaculars. *See* also ANGLO-SAXONS.

See R. G. Collingwood and J. N. L. Myers, *Roman Britain and the English Settlements,* 2nd ed. (1937), and works there cited.

(AL. C.)

ANGLESEY, ARTHUR ANNESLEY, 1ST EARL OF (1614–1686), British statesman who exercised a moderating in-fluence in the religious controversies during the reign of Charles II, was born at Dublin, Ire., on July 10, 1614. His father was created Viscount Valentia in 1621. Annesley was educated at Magdalen college, Oxford, and admitted to Lincoln's Inn in 1634. He entered the house of commons as member for Radnorshire in 1647 and in June that year concluded a treaty with the duke of Ormonde, lord lieutenant of Ireland, on behalf of the parliamentary cause. He was hostile to Cromwell and by the end of 1659, as lord president of the council, was actively working for the Restoration. He was made a privy councilor in June 1660 and was created Baron Annesley and earl of Anglesey in 1661.

He was not a strong figure in the turbulent politics of the period; caught between the rivalry of the duke of Buckingham and the earl of Arlington he suffered from their alternating friendship and enmity. He was appointed treasurer of the navy in June 1667 but by Oct. 1668 Buckingham had secured his suspension. Arlington then helped him procure a pension in compensation. Yet in 1671 Buckingham promised to obtain high office for him and he became lord privy seal in April 1673. Although increasingly crippled by gout he was diligent in attending the house of lords and served on numerous committees of the privy council. In 1682 he published reflections on the duke of Ormonde's conduct of Irish affairs in the 1640s which angered Charles II, and Anglesey was dismissed from all his posts. Although critical of Charles II's later policy he maintained good relations with James, duke of York (afterward James II) up to and after his accession. Anglesey died on April 26, 1686, in Bletchingdon, Oxfordshire.

A devout Anglican, Anglesey showed moderation in the panic over the "popish plot," and between 1674 and 1680 he dissented from several bills penalizing Roman Catholics. He is credited with having interceded for the life of Lord Stafford although he voted him guilty of treason, and in 1683 he appeared as a witness in defense of Lord William Russell. His public career earned him charges of corruption but Samuel Pepys spoke highly of his admin-istrative ability. He was a learned and cultivated man, and after 1671 built up a fine library which, however, was dispersed at his death. (H. G. Ro.)

ANGLESEY, HENRY WILLIAM PAGET, 1ST MAR-
QUESS OF (1768–1854), British soldier who commanded the allied
cavalry during the Waterloo campaign, was born in London on May
17, 1768, the eldest son of Henry Paget, and took the title of Lord
Paget when his father was made earl of Uxbridge in 1784. After
being educated at Westminster school and Christ Church, Oxford,
he entered the army and rose rapidly. In the Corunna campaign
he commanded the cavalry with conspicuous success. In 1795
Paget married Lord Jersey's daughter Lady Caroline Villiers, who
bore him eight children, but he deserted her for Charlotte,
daughter of Lord Cadogan and wife of Henry Wellesley, later Lord
Cowley; in 1810, after two divorces and a duel, he married her,
and by her had six children. This connection with the duke of
Wellington's sister-in-law kept Paget from further service in Spain
and he saw no fighting, except in the disastrous affair of Walcheren,
until 1815. He succeeded his father as earl of Uxbridge in 1812.

In the Waterloo campaign (q.v.) Uxbridge skilfully covered the
retreat from Quatre Bras. At the battle of Waterloo he led in person the charge of the household cavalry that completed the rout
of Drouet d'Erlon's corps. One of the last shots of the day
wounded him badly; one leg was amputated. In 1815 he was created marquess of Anglesey for his services. He took George IV's
side in the quarrel with Queen Caroline; when a hostile mob forced
him to give her health he drank to "The Queen, and may all your
wives be like her." In 1827 he was a cabinet minister as master
general of the ordnance. Next year he became viceroy of Ireland
where his advocacy of Roman Catholic claims made him popular,
but disagreements with Wellington led to his recall. Changing
sides in politics he returned to Ireland as viceroy again (1830–33)
and established the Irish board of education. He was again
master general of the ordnance, but outside the cabinet, from 1846,
when he was made field marshal. He died on April 29, 1854.

One of his sons, LORD GEORGE PAGET (1818–80), was second-in-
command of the light brigade at Balaklava.

See 7th Marquess of Anglesey, *One-Leg: the Life and Letters of
Henry William Paget, 1st Marquess of Anglesey* (1961).

(M. R. D. F.)

ANGLESEY (ANGLESEA; Welsh MÔN [island], SIR FON
[administrative county]), the ancient Mona, is the largest island of England or Wales, but the second smallest county in Wales
(276.2 sq.mi.). It is a country of low relief, an old denuded
highland, whose highest points are Holyhead mountain in the
northwest (720 ft.) and Parys mountain in the northeast (418 ft.).
The island's main geological structure is Pre-Cambrian rock, highly
folded and metamorphized, known as the Mona Complex. Between Holyhead and Amlwch these rocks, a mixture of shales, grits,
jasper and lava flows, are forced up over the later and softer mud-
stones of the Lower Paleozoic systems, a distribution resulting
in a smooth and gently undulating landscape. To the south, in
the centre of the island, the Pre-Cambrian strata appears again
partly in the form of gneiss, giving rounded, knobbed hills and
outcrops. It is overlaid by the Carboniferous beds of the east
coast which stretch inland to Malltraeth marsh, with flat-topped
hills and bare platforms of rock along the shore, while the softer
Paleozoic shales recur along the southern coast and the great bays
of the west. A series of low ridges and little valleys runs from
northeast to southwest, the typical Caledonian trend. The Menai
strait (q.v.), which separates Anglesey from the mainland, is
merely another such cleft, made up of the sections of three river
beds whose old watershed is in the Swellies between the two
bridges. Along the west coast occur stretches of blown sand, penetrating two miles or more inland at Newborough and Aberffraw,
with great dunes 100 ft. in height.

The name Anglesey is usually accepted as meaning simply "the
island of the Angles." It lay on the prehistoric western sea route
linking the Mediterranean with the northern countries. Thus the
promontories and islands on both shores of the Irish sea were held
together in a network of coastal trading activities. The importance
of Anglesey in the Late Neolithic and Early Bronze Ages is attested
by the number of great megalithic burial chambers and the standing stones of Bronze Age religious significance. By 100 B.C. the

Celts had colonized the island and it became a famous centre of the
Druid religion. When the Romans finally occupied Britain it was
to this stronghold of resistance that Suetonius Paulinus swept in
his drive across the country in A.D. 61 to slay the Druid priests and
destroy the sacred groves. The conquest of the island was completed by Agricola in A.D. 78. The most noted hoard of Celtic objects of the Early Iron Age found in Anglesey was recovered in
1943 from the bog of Llyn Cerrig Bach near Valley and is associated
with this period and possibly with these events. Two well-
preserved Celtic villages, occupied throughout the Roman occupation, are Ty Mawr on the lower slopes of Holyhead mountain and
Din Lligwy on the hillside above Lligwy bay. The Romans left
their impress in the shape of two camps, a small rectangular enclosure near Brynsiencyn and the stone walls and bastions of a
4th-century fort at Holyhead (q.v.) built on the edge of low but
steep cliffs once washed by the sea and within whose shelter stands
the parish church of St. Gybi.

The foundation of a number of Anglesey churches in the dark
ages suggests that the "saints" of the early Celtic church followed
the old trade routes on their missionary enterprises traveling to
and fro between Anglesey, Ireland, Cornwall and south Wales.
The most noted of the Celtic monastic foundations were those of
St. Gybi on Holy (Holyhead) Island and St. Seiriol at Penmon.
Anglesey was constantly open to invasion from the sea; Irish pirates, Saxon, Viking and Norman venturers all laid temporary hold
upon it, but it was not finally subdued till the Edwardian conquest
of Wales in 1282–84. Edward I built the castle in Beaumaris
(q.v.), which was begun in 1295, and to make room for the English
colonists whom he settled beneath its walls he transferred the population of the neighbouring township of Llanfaes to the New
Borough which he created for them near the west coast, where a
village still bears this name.

The chief household and manor of the princes of Gwynedd, the
senior royal house of Wales, was at Aberffraw in the west of the
island. The farming of the land by clans of free tribesmen (as
distinct from the older villages of bond tenants) was developed in
the 12th century. Anglesey became the chief corn-growing district
of north Wales and so earned the name of *Môn Mam Cymru*
("Mona the mother of Wales"). After subjugation by the English
the chief developments were the slow transformation of the structure of Welsh society with its joint ownership and partitioning of
land and the replacement of the straggling Welsh holdings and
hamlets by consolidated farms in individual ownership. Two
hundred sites of medieval nuclei of settlement have been identified
in Anglesey and of these 153 are occupied by single modern farms
from 40 to 500 ac. or more in size.

Contact with Ireland has been maintained throughout the centuries and in 1801 Holyhead was established by the government as
a packet station for the Irish mail. Plans for an improved route
from London to Holyhead under the direction of Thomas Telford
as surveyor, began early in the 19th century. By 1823 Telford had
completed a road across the island (later part of the main London-
Holyhead road) and in 1826 his suspension bridge (reconstructed
1938–41) over the straits was opened, the first and longest in
Britain. The harbour at Holyhead was completed by 1824 and enlarged in 1880. Work on the railway from Chester to Holyhead
was begun in 1844 under Robert Stephenson (q.v.) and the foundations of the tubular bridge were laid in 1846. On June 18, 1849,
the Irish mails were carried to Holyhead by rail for the first time.

Though from its earliest settlement Anglesey has remained predominantly an agricultural and stock-raising county, with seafaring and fishing as secondary activities, industry has played a part
in its developments since about the middle of the 18th century.
Copper, with other minerals, is found in quantity in Parys mountain and in 1775 was first worked on a large scale. By 1800 half
the copper industry of Britain was in the hands of the Mona Mine
company, and for a time Anglesey with Cornwall dominated the
world market. But by 1844 the workings were largely abandoned
and the mine finally closed in 1871.

From the 15th century sporadic attempts were made to extract
coal from the seams underlying Malltraeth marsh but these always
ended in disappointment. Quarrying is carried on in various parts

of the island, principally at Penmon (whence came the stone for Caernarvon castle) and Holyhead. A few light industries have come to the island since World War II and are situated at Beaumaris, Amlwch and Holyhead and in the administrative centre of Llangefni.

The British railways (London Midland region, Chester to Holyhead branch) cross Anglesey from Menai Bridge to Holyhead (Caer Gybi) and a branch runs from Gaerwen to Amlwch. Beaumaris is the county town and the only municipal borough (pop. [1961] 1,962). There the assizes of the northwest circuit are held. Amlwch (pop. 2,902), Holyhead (10,412), Llangefni (3,206) and Menai Bridge (2,335) are urban districts. The population of the whole island was 51,705 in 1961.

Anglesey lies in the diocese of Bangor. The county returns one member to parliament.

BIBLIOGRAPHY.—A. H. Williams, *An Introduction to the History of Wales*, vol. i and pt. 1, vol. ii (1941, 1948); J. Hawkes, *Guide to the Prehistoric and Roman Monuments in England and Wales* (1951, 1952); T. G. Miller, *Geology and Scenery in Britain* (1953); E. Greenly, "A Short Summary of the Geological History of Anglesey," *Trans. Anglesea Antiq. Soc. Fld. Cl.* (1923); T. Jones-Pierce, "Medieval Settlement in Anglesey," *Trans. Anglesea Antiq. Soc. Fld. Cl.* (1951); G. R. J. Jones, "The Distribution of Medieval Settlement in Anglesey," *Trans. Anglesea Antiq. Soc. Fld. Cl.* (1951). (R. C. S.)

ANGLESITE, a mineral consisting of lead sulfate, is a minor ore of lead (*q.v.*). It was first recognized as a mineral species in 1783, by W. Withering, who discovered it in the Parys copper mine in Anglesey, Wales; the name anglesite, from this locality, was given by F. S. Beudant in 1832. Crystals from Anglesey are small in size and simple in form; they are brownish-yellow in colour, resulting from a stain of limonite or brown iron ore. Crystals from some other localities, notably from Monteponi in Sardinia, are transparent and colourless, possessed of a brilliant adamantine lustre and numerous faces. The mineral is of secondary origin, having been formed by the oxidation of the lead ore galena in the upper parts of mineral lodes, where these have been affected by weathering processes, and has been found in many localities in Europe, Africa and Australia and in the U.S.S.R., Mexico and the United States. Anglesite crystallizes in the orthorhombic system and there are distinct cleavages parallel to the faces of the prism and the basal plane, but these are not so well developed as in the isomorphous minerals barite and celestite. The formula is $PbSO_4$. The hardness is 3 and the specific gravity, 6.3.

ANGLICAN COMMUNION, a fellowship of independent churches in communion with the archbishop of Canterbury and acknowledging him as *primus inter pares*. They are the Church of England (*q.v.*), the Church in Wales, the Church of Ireland (*q.v.*), the Episcopal Church in Scotland (*q.v.*) and the following others, which originated directly or indirectly from the Church of England: Protestant Episcopal Church in the United States; Church of India, Pakistan, Burma and Ceylon; Church of the Province of South Africa; Anglican Church of Canada; Church of England in Australia and Tasmania; Church of the Province of New Zealand; Church of the Province of the West Indies; Chung Hua Sheng Kung Hui (Holy Catholic Church in China); Nippon Sei Ko Kai (Japan Holy Catholic Church); Church of the Province of West Africa; Church of the Province of Central Africa; Church of the Province of East Africa; Church of the Province of Uganda and Rwanda and Burundi. The Jerusalem archbishopric is semi-independent. There are two groups of missionary dioceses, some directly dependent on the archbishop of Canterbury and others, chiefly in Central and South America, under the jurisdiction of the Protestant Episcopal Church in the United States.

At intervals of about ten years the bishops of the Anglican communion meet in London for Lambeth conferences (*q.v.*).

The Old Catholic churches (*q.v.*) are not in the Anglican communion but are in communion with its member churches.

See *Official Year Book of the Church of England*. (H. M. W.)

ANGLICANISM, a general term for the ecclesiastical system, organization and doctrine of the Church of England and the churches throughout the world in communion with it. See ANGLICAN COMMUNION; ENGLAND, CHURCH OF.

ANGLIN, MARGARET MARY (1876–1958), U.S. actress who starred for 40 years in modern and classic roles, was born April 3, 1876, at Ottawa, Ont., daughter of T. W. Anglin, speaker of the Canadian house of commons, and Ellen (McTavish) Anglin. She was educated in Toronto and Montreal and was studying at the Empire Dramatic school, New York city, when Charles Frohman cast her as Madeline West in Bronson Howard's *Shenandoah* (1894). After touring with James O'Neill, E. H. Sothern and others, she scored as Roxane, to Richard Mansfield's Cyrano, in 1898. From 1900 to 1903 she was leading lady at the Empire theatre, where she made a great impression in *Mrs. Dane's Defence*. Frohman starred her first in his revival of *Camille* (1903). She was responsible for the production of William Vaughn Moody's *The Great Divide* (1907), in which she costarred with Henry Miller. She played Shakespearean repertory in Australia, 1908–09. In 1909 she produced and starred in *The Awakening of Helena Richie* from Margaret Deland's novel. Miss Anglin first tried Greek tragedy in 1910, playing *Antigone* in the Berkeley, Calif., open-air theatre, and she played *Electra* there in 1913. In 1916 she led 1,200 players in *As You Like It* for the Shakespeare tercentenary in Forest park, St. Louis, Mo. In New York she appeared in *Medea* in 1918 and in *Electra* in 1918 and 1927. Her last appearance was on tour as Sara Müller in *Watch on the Rhine* (1943). In 1911 she married Howard Hull, brother of the actor Henry Hull. She died at Toronto, Ont., on Jan. 7, 1958. (B. Ht.)

ANGLING: *see* FISHING.

ANGLO-JAPANESE ALLIANCE. On Jan. 30, 1902, because of the threat of Russian aggression in Manchuria and Korea, Great Britain and Japan concluded a defensive treaty of alliance. Pledging themselves to uphold the principles of the "open door" policy for commerce in the far east, the signatories also agreed upon mutual assistance in safeguarding their respective interests in China and Korea. Twice renewed during the next ten years the alliance was a cornerstone of British and Japanese policy in Asia until after World War I.

The agreement served Japanese purposes well in the Russo-Japanese War of 1904–05. Though Great Britain was not required to participate, the alliance was influential in deterring Russia's European ally, France, from entering the war. Even before the completion of a Russo-Japanese peace treaty the alliance was renewed on Aug. 12, 1905. Its scope was now, however, extended to include the far east and India, while Japan's paramount position in Korea was more explicitly recognized.

On July 23, 1911, after the Japanese annexation of Korea, the alliance was renewed for a period of ten years. An important addition to the new treaty was a specific provision exempting either contracting power from the obligation of assisting the other militarily in case of war against a state with whom either power had concluded a general arbitration treaty (art. iv). This provision was designed to allay British and U.S. fears that the alliance might necessitate British support of Japan in a war against the United States.

In keeping with the alliance Japan entered World War I on Aug. 23, 1914. At the end of the hostilities, however, the purposes of the treaty were strongly questioned. Not only did they seem to be inconsistent with the obligations imposed by the covenant of the new League of Nations but Great Britain especially was aware of the considerable uneasiness which the alliance was causing in the United States and China. Pressure for the ending of the Anglo-Japanese alliance finally came to a head at the Washington conference in December 1921. The aims of peace and security in the Pacific and the far east were met in the Four-Power Pacific treaty (United States, Great Britain, France and Japan), which called for the termination of the Anglo-Japanese alliance. With the exchange of ratifications of the Four-Power Pacific treaty on Aug. 17, 1923, the alliance between Great Britain and Japan was brought to an end. *See* JAPAN: *History*. (Hn. Kn.)

ANGLO-NORMAN LITERATURE, the literature in the French dialect of medieval England, also known as Norman-French or Anglo-French. The latter term is reserved by some for the period when central French influence was superseding Norman. The dialect was introduced into court circles in Edward the Confessor's time, but its history really begins with the Norman Conquest. It was the vernacular of the court, the law, the church, schools, universities, parliament and later of municipalities and of trade. Even for the aristocracy it became an acquired tongue and its use a test of gentility, but the more widely it was known the more it was corrupted. It was introduced into Wales and Ireland and used to a limited extent in Scotland before and during the wars of independence. The earliest extant literary texts belong to the reign of Henry I, the latest to that of Henry IV. Outside events, not so much the loss of Normandy as the unpopularity of foreigners in the reign of Henry III and the diminution of friendly relations with France during the Hundred Years' War, favoured an increasing use of English. The last strongholds of a French dialect were parliament, where it still survives in a few formulas, and the law. Reports and Readings continued to be in French until the beginning of the 18th century. Oliver Cromwell had abolished "Law French" but the judges revived it at the Restoration. As however there had just been time for a generation of lawyers unfamiliar with it to have grown up, it gradually disappeared.

Most types of literary works are represented in Anglo-Norman as in French, with a slight difference of emphasis. The *chanson de geste* is an exception. The type was not unknown in England, since the only surviving manuscript of the assonanced version of the *Chanson de Roland* is Anglo-Norman, as are the unique manuscripts of *Gormond et Isembard*, the *Chançun de Willame* and the *Pèlerinage de Charlemagne;* there is also an Anglo-Norman version of *Fierabras* but there seem to be no original works of the kind. Imitation was not all on one side. Many Anglo-Norman works were known, copied or imitated on the continent. Such were *St. Brendan*, the *Bestiaire*, the *Vie de Saint Édouard*, the *Vie de Sainte Catherine, Protesilaus, Amadas et Idoine*, the *Quatre Livre des Reis*, the *Apocalypse* and the debased Anglo-Norman Bible. Most of these occur either in manuscripts in the Picard dialect, probably because of the trade relations between England and the northeast of France, or in manuscripts made for the royal family. The clerkly and didactic nature of Anglo-Norman literature has been overstressed, but one important difference between continental and Anglo-Norman literature is that the fourth Lateran council of 1215 led to an outpouring of doctrinal and devotional works for the laity in England which is not paralleled in France. A curious and unexpected feature of Anglo-Norman is that in the early periods it is often in advance of the continent in the development of new literary kinds. History was popular both in Normandy and the continent and while it is true that after the Norman Conquest Latin took the place of English in documents and chronicles, examples of both in Anglo-Norman must not be overlooked. For political reasons the kings after Henry I were anxious to stress their connection with the old English line and particular attention was paid to Alfred and Edward the Confessor. Religious houses caused lives of native saints to be written and the nobility had a taste for romances about the deeds of imaginary English ancestors. Thus social and political differences between the two countries prevent Anglo-Norman literature from being a mere provincial imitation of French.

The Bible.—In the 12th century the oldest substantial prose work in French, *Li Quatre Livre des Reis*, ed. by E. R. Curtius (1911), was written in England, as also were many versions of the Psalter, including the Cambridge or rather Canterbury Psalter, published as *Le Livre des Psaumes*, ed. by F. Michel (1876)—the so-called Oxford Psalter is from Montebourg. Sanson de Nantuil translated into verse the proverbs of Solomon, with commentary, for Alice de Condet. In the 13th century Robert of Greatham wrote the *Miroir* or *Evangile des Domes*—the Sunday Gospels—for a noble lady. The same century saw the beginning of the magnificent series of Anglo-Norman Apocalypses (*see* the *Anglo-Norman Rhymed Apocalypse*, ed. by O. Rhys, Anglo-Norman Text society, no. 6, 1946), best known for their superb illustrations, which served as a model for the Angers tapestry. In the 14th century the Anglo-Norman Bible was begun, though never completed.

Saints' Lives.—The literature is rich in legends of the saints.

Benedeit's *Voyage of St. Brendan*, ed. by E. G. R. Waters (1928), which achieved popularity on the continent, was dedicated to one of the queens of Henry I and is perhaps the oldest purely narrative French poem in the octosyllabic couplet. The feminine lines are of the lyric type, the final -*e* counting as a syllable. Simund de Freine, a canon of Hereford and friend of Giraldus Cambrensis, wrote a Passion of St. George in heptasyllables which was published in *Oeuvres de Simund de Freine*, ed. by J. E. Matzke (Société des anciens textes français, 1909) and there is a *Passiun de seint Edmund* in stanzas. Wace (*q.v.*) was probably the first to write a saint's life in the standard form, but he was followed by Anglo-Norman writers in the 12th century—Denis Piramus, monk of Bury and former court poet, who refers to the *lais* of Marie de France (*q.v.*), wrote the life of *Seint Edmund le Rei*, ed. by H. Kjellman (1935), and Guillaume de Berneville that of *Saint Gilles*, ed. by G. Paris and A. Bos (Société des anciens textes français, 1881); the *Vie d'Édouard le Confesseur*, ed. by Ö. Södergård (1948), is by a nun of Barking, perhaps the Clemence of Barking who wrote the *Vie de S'einte Catherine*, ed. by J. U. Jarnik as *Dve verse starofrancouzské legendy o Sv. Kateriné* (1894). Adgar translated a collection of "Miracles of the Virgin" owned by St. Paul's, a revision of which is dedicated to the abbess of Barking, and these were issued as *Adgar's Marienlegenden*, ed. by C. Neuhaus (1886). In the 13th century Simon de Walsingham, monk of Bury, wrote *Seinte Foy (Saint Faith)*, ed. by A. T. Baker in *Romania*, vol. lxvi, pp. 49–84 (1940), and Angier, canon of St. Frideswide's, translated the dialogues and life of St. Gregory as the *Vie de Saint Grégoire le Grand*, ed. by P. Meyer in *Romania*, vol. xii, pp. 145–208 (1883). Matthew Paris (*q.v.*) translated four lives—*Vie de Seint Auban (Saint Alban)*, ed. by R. Atkinson (1876) in alexandrine *laisses*—probably holograph—and those of St. Edward, St. Edmund of Abingdon and Thomas Becket in octosyllables (*see* R. Vaughan, *Matthew Paris*, pp. 159–181, 1958). Benoit of St. Alban's wrote another life of Becket in tail rhyme, ed. by B. Schlyter (1941).

Lives connecting religious houses with their patron saints are: St. Modwenna (for the abbey at Burton Upon Trent), ed. by A. T. Baker and A. Bell (Anglo-Norman Text society, no. 7, 1947) and *St. Osyth* (for St. Osyth, Essex), ed. by A. T. Baker in *Modern Language Review*, vol. vi, no. 4, pp. 476–502 (1911), vol. vii, no. 1, pp. 74–93 and no. 2, pp. 157–92 (1912). Lives of St. Audrey, St. Richard of Chichester, St. Lawrence, St. Francis, St. Margaret, St. Eustace and many more too numerous to mention are also found. In the 14th century the Franciscan Nicole Bozon wrote seven short lives. For Temple Bruer, Lincolnshire, a version of the *Vitae Patrum* was written. Chardri's *Barlaam et Josaphat* and *Set Dormanz* are the only association of these stories in French, ed. by J. Koch (*Altfranzösische Bibliothek*, no. 1, 1879).

Drama.—The earliest play entirely in French, the semiliturgical *Mystère d'Adam*, ed. by P. Studer (1918, reissued 1949), unfortunately incomplete, is a continental copy of what was apparently an Anglo-Norman original. This is famous for its characterization and poetical quality, as well as for the minute stage directions in Latin. (*See also* DRAMA: *Medieval;* FRENCH LITERATURE.) The resurrection play, *La Seinte Resureccion*, ed. by T. A. Jenkins, J. M. Manly, M. K. Pope and J. G. Wright (Anglo-Norman Text society, no. 4, 1943) was probably 12th century, but was rewritten more than once in the 13th century. It is unique in having the stage setting and the action described in passages of verse which seem to have been designed to be read during the performance. Two later fragments of plays in alternative French and English versions have come to light.

Allegory.—There are a few religious allegories; the most important, the *Chasteau d'Amour*, ed. by J. Murray (1918), written by Robert Grosseteste (*q.v.*) in which he draws upon his work in optics, is the oldest in French. It was translated into Latin and English.

Moral, Mystical and Didactic Works.—The verse sermon was popular in Normandy and England in the 12th century. Among later sermons in prose is one by the Franciscan Thomas of Hales, who wrote the *Love Ron*. An Anglo-Norman version of the sermons of Maurice de Sully was frequently copied. The Franciscans John Pecham, archbishop of Canterbury, and Adam of Exeter wrote treatises and Nicole Bozon compiled a set of moral sayings illustrated by fables and tales, *Contes moralisés*, ed. by P. Meyer and L. T. Smith (Société des anciens textes français, 1889). The fourth Lateran council of 1215 led to the compilation of instructive works. The oldest and most attractive is the *Merure de seinte eglise*, by St. Edmund (*q.v.*) of Abingdon, ed. by H. W. Robbins (1925), translated into Latin and English. The *Manuel des Péchés* was translated into English by Robert Mannyng (*q.v.*) of Brunne as *Handlyng Synne*. Canon Peter of Peckham, Fetcham or Abernon's *Lumere as Lais* is cast in dialectic form. In the 13th–14th centuries countless treatises appeared on technical subjects—manuals for confession, agriculture, law, medicine, grammar, science, etc. There are also works dealing with manners, hunting, hawking, chess, etc. Two pioneer works on estate management are Walter of Henley's *Hosebanderie* and Grosseteste's *Reules Seynt Robert* written for the countess of Lincoln and translated into English. The legal literature includes the prose *Britton* and *Fet Asaver* and a poem *La Court de Baron*. The spelling treatises and "Manières de Langage" of the late 13th, 14th and 15th centuries are valuable for the light they shed on continental French as well as Anglo-Norman—*cf. La Manière de Langage*, ed. by J. Gessler (1934). They were compiled by grammar masters, scriveners or students returned from France for future lawyers, proctors of religious houses and merchants. A few are for children.

Romances.—Anglo-Norman literature is rich in romances. In the 12th century one Thomas wrote a courtly version of *Tristan*, ed. by J. Bédier (Société des anciens textes français, 1902–05; Eng. trans. 1960), which survives only in scattered fragments and was used by Gottfried von Strassburg (*q.v.*) in *Tristan und Isolde* as well as being the source of the Old Norse *Tristramssaga*, the Italian *Tavola Ritonda* and the Middle English *Sir Tristrem*. It is the ultimate source of the libretto of Wagner's opera. Béroul's *Tristan*, also 12th century, was probably written in England but by a Norman. (*See also* TRISTAN.) Hue de Rotelande (?Rhuddlan) of Credenhill wrote a lively romance of adventure, *Ipomedon*, ed. by E. Koelbing and E. Koschwitz (1889), with a setting in Calabria and Sicily probably provoked by the marriage of Henry II's daughter Joan to King William of Sicily. In this he refers to Walter Map as a notable inventor of lies. Less successful is the sequel *Protesilaus*, dedicated to Gilbert Fitz-Baderon, ed. by F. T. Kluckow (1924). In the next century *Gui de Warewic*, 2 vol., ed. by A. Ewert (1932), possibly by an Oseney canon, was popular and underwent revision. It was known on the continent. *Waldef*, a long confused story of an imaginary king of East Anglia and his sons, has passages of remarkable originality. In the 12th century some romances were composed in the form of the *chanson de geste*; for example, *Horn*, by Master Thomas, ed. by M. K. Pope (Anglo-Norman Text society, no. 9–10, 1955), which is connected with the Middle English *Horn Childe and Maiden Rimnild*, and which is claimed as a sequel of a lost *Aaluf*. Yet another Thomas wrote the *Roman de Toute Chevalerie*, an independent version of the Alexander romance, into which interpolations from the continental poems were afterward made. It is the source of the Middle English romance *Kyng Alisaunder*. Two versions of *Boeve de Haumtone* survive in overlapping fragments, ed. by A. Stimming (*Bibliotheca Normannica*, no. 7, 1899). This romance exists in English, French and other languages. In the 13th century the more courtly type of romance reappears in *Amadas et Idoine*, rewritten in Picard, ed. by J. R. Reinhard (1926), and in *Amis et Amiloun*, perhaps derived from the same source as the Middle English poem *Amis and Amiloun*, ed. by E. Koelbing (1884). (*See also* ALEXANDER ROMANCES.)

Lais and Fabliaux.—Marie de France wrote her *lais* for the English court and other *lais* were popular in England. Robert Biket's *Lai du Cor* is probably wrongly claimed for Anglo-Norman. The *Folie Tristan d'Oxford*, ed. by E. Hoepffner (1934; rev. ed. 1943), is a neat little work by an imitator of Thomas. Fabliaux are rare, but a few are found, probably for exemplary

purposes, copied in manuscripts from religious houses.

Lyrics and Political Songs.—There is no collection of Anglo-Norman lyrics, but a few occur on flyleaves or the blank pages of manuscripts. They are not of outstanding quality and do not differ in form from continental ones. Anglo-Norman is, however, rich in political satires and songs (see *Anglo-Norman Political Songs*, ed. by I. S. T. Aspin, Anglo-Norman Text society, no. 11, 1952).

Chronicles and History.—The earliest chronicle in French is the Anglo-Norman verse *Estoire des Engleis*, by Geffrei Gaimar, written *c.* 1140, ed. by A. Bell in 2 vol. (Anglo-Norman Text society, no. 14–15, 1960). About 1172 Jordan Fantosme wrote a chronicle of the war between the English and Scots, printed in *Chronicles of Stephen, Henry II and Richard I*, vol. iii, pp. 202–377, ed. by R. Howlett ("Rolls Series," no. 82, 1886), in the epic style later adopted by Peter Langtoft (*q.v.*), whose own *Chronicle*, ed. in 2 vol. by T. Wright ("Rolls Series," no. 47, 1866 and 1868), begins as a *Brut*—a complete chronicle of British history—but became a source for the times of Edward I. It contains fragments of political songs. The later part was translated by Robert Mannyng of Brunne. The Dominican Nicholas Trevet wrote a prose chronicle of European history for a nun at Amesbury, Mary, daughter of Edward I, from which Chaucer derived his *Man of Law's Tale*. Sir Thomas Gray of Heton began a huge prose *Brut* while a prisoner in Edinburgh castle from 1355 to 1357, the contemporary part of which is authoritative. A few monasteries which possessed a French *Brut* kept their annals in Anglo-Norman. Irish history produced some verse chronicles, the best of which is the *Song of Dermot and the Earl*, ed. by G. H. Orpen (1892). Two magnificent biographies of the first earl of Pembroke (William Marshal) and of Edward, the Black Prince, were written for English patrons by foreigners. Official documents, municipal records and letters were often in Anglo-Norman and the Yearbooks, unofficial reports of cases in the common pleas, run from the reign of Edward I to that of Henry VIII. English began to be used in parliament alongside French in the late 14th century.

Natural History and Science.—One of the earliest writers in Anglo-Norman, Philippe de Thaon or Thaün, wrote *Li Cumpoz* (the *Computus*), ed. by E. Mall (1873), the first French bestiary, *Le Bestiaire*, ed. by E. F. G. Walberg (1900), and a lapidary—a work on precious stones—included in *Anglo-Norman Lapidaries*, ed. by P. Studer and J. Evans (1924). Simund de Freine based his *Roman de Philosophie* on Boëthius, to whom the 13th-century *Petite Philosophie*, ed. by W. H. Trethewey (Anglo-Norman Text society, no. 1, 1939), also owes much. All these are allegorical or didactic.

BIBLIOGRAPHY.—J. Vising, *Anglo-Norman Language and Literature* (1923, under revision by R. J. Dean); E. Walberg, *Quelques Aspects de la littérature anglo-normande* (1936); P. Studer, *The Study of Anglo-Norman* (1920); M. D. Legge, *Anglo-Norman in the Cloisters* (1950).
(D. LE.)

ANGLO-SAXON CHRONICLE. This main source for Anglo-Saxon history was first compiled in the reign of Alfred (871–899), from materials which included some epitome of universal history: Bede's *Ecclesiastical History*, genealogies, regnal and episcopal lists, a few northern annals and probably some sets of earlier West Saxon annals. The compiler also had access to a set of Frankish annals for the late 9th century. Soon after 890 manuscripts were being circulated; one was available to Asser in 893, another, which appears to have gone no further than that year, to the late 10th-century chronicler Aethelweard, while one version, which eventually reached the north and which is best represented by the surviving E version, stopped in 892. Some of the manuscripts circulated at this time were continued in various religious houses, sometimes with annals which occur in more than one manuscript, sometimes with local material, confined to one version. The fullness and quality of the entries vary at different periods; thus the Chronicle is a rather barren document for the mid-10th century and for the reign of Canute, but an excellent authority for the reign of Aethelred the Unready and from the reign of Edward the Confessor until the version which was kept up longest ends with annal 1154.

The Chronicle is extant in seven manuscripts and a fragment. The seven manuscripts are generally known by the letters of the alphabet. The oldest, known as C. C. C. Cant. 173 from the fact that it is at Corpus Christi college, Cambridge, and generally referred to as A, is written in one hand up to 891, and then continued in various hands, approximately contemporary with the entries. It was at Winchester in the mid-10th century, and may have been written there. It is the only source for the account of the later campaigns of Edward the Elder. Little was added to this manuscript after 975, and in the 11th century it was removed to Christ church, Canterbury, where various interpolations and alterations were made, some by the scribe of the F version. The manuscript known as Cotton Otho B xi (from the fact that it forms part of the Cotton collection of manuscripts at the British museum), which was almost completely destroyed by fire in 1731, contained an 11th-century copy of A, before this was tampered with at Canterbury. Its text is known from a 16th-century transcript by L. Nowell and from Abraham Wheloc's edition (1644).

The B version (Cott. Tib. A vi) and the C version (Cott. Tib. B i) are copies made at Abingdon from a lost archetype. B ends at 977, whereas C, which is an 11th-century copy, ends, mutilated, in 1066. Their lost original incorporated into the text in a block after annal 915 a set of annals (902–924) known as the Mercian Register.

The D version (Cott. Tib. B iv) and the E version (kept at the Bodleian library, Oxford, Laud Misc. 636) share many features, including the interpolation of much material of northern interest taken from Bede and from annals also used by Simeon of Durham; hence they are known as the "northern recension." They contain also an entry in the style of Archbishop Wulfstan (q.v.). But D differs from E in including annals 893–915, the mid-10th century section with poems on Brunanburh and the recapture of the five boroughs, and some other entries, which are all missing from E but occur in A, B and C. D has also dovetailed into its text the Mercian Register, and contains a fair amount of northern material found in no other version. It is very much interested in the English descent of Queen Margaret of Scotland. C. Plummer accounted for the difference between D and E by postulating an early separation of their archetypes; but it is more likely that D (which is written in hands no earlier than the late 11th century) acquired its present form by a conflation of a version of the E type with a C version at some late period. After about 1031 the close connection between D and E ends; D, which is kept up until 1079, probably remained in the north (though Plummer thought it was moved into the Worcester diocese, to Evesham), whereas the archetype of E was taken south and continued at St. Augustine's, Canterbury, and was used by the scribe of manuscript F.

The extant manuscript E is a copy made at Peterborough, written in one stretch until 1121, and kept up there until the early part of 1155. It has several Peterborough interpolations in the earlier sections. It is the version that was continued longest, and it includes a famous account of the anarchy of Stephen's reign. Plummer believed that the additions to the "northern recension" were made at Ripon, but at least an equally good case can be made for York, and there is evidence pointing to York as the place where the D version was compiled.

The F version (Cott. Domit. A viii) is an abridgment, in both Old English and Latin, made in the late 11th or early 12th century, based on the archetype of E, but with some entries from A. It extends to 1058, and its scribe is responsible for some of the entries into A made at Canterbury. Finally, the fragment H (Cott. Domit. A ix) deals with 1113–14, and is independent of E, the only other version to continue so late.

Several Latin writers possessed versions of the Chronicle which have not survived. Those used by the writers of the Annals of St. Neots and by Aethelweard represented forms closer to the original than any surviving text. Various intermediate stages are seen in the versions available to Asser, William of Malmesbury, Henry of Huntingdon, the compiler of the Waverley Annals and the Anglo-Norman poet Gaimar, while Florence of Worcester seems to have possessed several versions.

BIBLIOGRAPHY.—The edition by B. Thorpe (1861) must be used to compare the various versions, since *Two of the Saxon Chronicles Parallel*, ed. by C. Plummer on the basis of an edition by J. Earle (i, 1892; ii, 1899), contains the full text of only A and E. Plummer's introduction remains a standard work on the subject, and the reprint of 1952 includes a new bibliography and note on the commencement of the year by D. Whitelock. The only edition of Cott. Otho B xi is that of A. Wheloc, *Venerabilis Bedae Historia Ecclesiastica* (1644). Facsimiles exist of A, *The Parker Chronicle and Laws*, by R. Flower and H. Smith (1941), and of E, *The Peterborough Chronicle*, by D. Whitelock (*Early English Manuscripts in Facsimile*, iv (1954). There is a separate edition of D, *An Anglo-Saxon Chronicle From British Museum Cotton MS., Tiberius B. iv*, by E. Classen and F. E. Harmer (1926); of C, *The C-Text of the Old English Chronicles*, by H. Rositzke (*Beiträge zur englische Philologie*, xxxiv [1940]), and of F, by F. P. Magoun, Jr., *Annales Domitiani Latini: an Edition* (*Mediaeval Studies of the Pontifical Institute of Mediaeval Studies*, ix, 1947). For translations *see* G. N. Garmonsway in Everyman's Library, rev. ed. (1955), and *English Historical Documents*, i, pp. 136–235 (60 B.C.–1042, by D. Whitelock); ii, pp. 107–203 (1042–1154, by S. I. Tucker) (1953–55).

For general description *see*, besides Plummer's introduction, F. M. Stenton, *Anglo-Saxon England*, 2nd ed., pp. 679–684 (1947); D. Whitelock, *English Historical Documents*, pp. 109–116. Some of Plummer's conclusions are challenged by F. M. Stenton, "The South-Western Element in the Old English Chronicle," *Essays in Medieval History presented to T. F. Tout* (1925); by Sir Ivor Atkins, "The Origin of the Later Part of the Saxon Chronicle known as D," *English Historical Review*, lv (1940); and by D. Whitelock, introduction to *The Peterborough Chronicle*, pp. 26–34. For further bibliography *see* the reprint of Plummer (1952), i, pp. 316a–316e; D. Whitelock, *English Historical Documents*, pp. 129–131; K. Sisam, "Anglo-Saxon Royal Genealogies," *Proceedings of the British Academy*, xxxix (1953); R. Vaughan, "The Chronology of the Parker Chronicle," *English Historical Review*, lxix (1954); Cecily Clark, "Notes on MS. Laud Misc. 636," *Medium Aevum*, xxiii (1954). (D. WK.)

ANGLO-SAXON LAW.

The body of legal rules and customs that prevailed in England before the Norman Conquest constitutes, with the Scandinavian laws, the most genuine expression of Teutonic legal thought. While the so-called "barbaric laws" (*leges barbarorum*) of continental Europe, including those compiled in the territory now called Germany, were largely the product of Roman influence, the continuity of Roman life was almost completely broken in the island, and even the church, the direct heir of Roman tradition, did not have a continuous existence: Canterbury was not a see formed in a Roman province in the same sense as Tours or Reims. One of the striking expressions of this Teutonism is presented by the language in which the Anglo-Saxon laws were written. They are uniformly worded in English, while continental laws, apart from the Scandinavian, are all in Latin. The English dialect in which the Anglo-Saxon laws have been handed down is in most cases a common speech derived from West Saxon—naturally enough since Wessex became the predominant English state. After the Conquest Latin or French took the place of English in the compilations made to meet the demand for Anglo-Saxon law texts still applicable in practice.

Classification.—The Anglo-Saxon laws may be divided into three groups: (1) laws and collections of laws promulgated by public authority; (2) authoritative statements of custom; (3) private compilations of legal rules and enactments. To the first division belong the laws of the Kentish kings, Aethelberht, Hlothhere, Eadric and Wihtred; those of Ine of Wessex, of Alfred, Edward the Elder, Aethelstan, Edmund, Edgar, Aethelred and Canute; the treaty between Alfred and Guthrum and the so-called treaty between Edward and Guthrum. The second division would include the law of the Northumbrian priests and fragments of local custumals entered in Domesday Book. The third division would consist of the post-Conquest collections of the so-called *Pseudo-leges Canuti*, the laws of Edward the Confessor (also spurious), of Henry I (a private venture which formed part of the great compilation of the *Quadripartitus*) and of a number of short notices on various matters, such as the formalities of betrothal (*Bewifmannes beweddung*), agricultural conditions (*Rectitudines singularum personarum*), the duties of a reeve (*Gerefa*) and of a judge (*Dema*), wergilds, oaths, ordeals, etc. A fourth group might be made of the charters since they are based on Old English private and public law and supply us with most important materials on the subject.

Direct statements of law would fall under the following heads from the point of view of their legal origins: (1) customary rules followed by divers communities capable of formulating law; (2) enactments of authorities, especially of kings; (3) private arrangements made under recognized legal rules. The first would comprise a great many of the rules entered in collections promulgated by kings; most of the paragraphs of Aethelberht's, Hlothhere's, Eadric's and Ine's laws are popular legal customs that have received the stamp of royal authority by their insertion in official codes. On the other hand, from Wihtred's and Alfred's laws downward, the element of enactment by central authority becomes increasingly prominent, though there are no outward signs enabling us to distinguish clearly between the various categories of laws in the codes nor can we draw a line between permanent laws and personal ordinances of single sovereigns, as has been attempted in the case of Frankish legislation.

Analysis of Content.—Even in the course of a general survey of the surviving legal lore, one cannot help being struck by peculiarities in the distribution of legal subjects. Matters which seem of primary importance and occupy a wide place in modern lawbooks are almost entirely absent in Anglo-Saxon laws or relegated to the background. While it is impossible to give here anything like a complete or exact survey of the field, a brief statistical analysis of the contents of the royal codes and laws may be made.

There are roughly 419 paragraphs devoted to criminal law and procedure as against 91 concerned with questions of private law and civil procedure. Of the criminal law clauses as many as 238 are taken up with lists of fines, while 80 deal with capital and corporal punishment, outlawry and confiscation, and 101 include rules of procedure. On the side of private law 18 clauses apply to rights of property and possession, 13 to succession and family law, 37 to contracts, including marriage when treated as an act of sale; 18 touch on civil procedure. A subject which attracted special attention was the law of status, and no less than 107 paragraphs contain dispositions dictated by the wish to discriminate between the classes of society. Questions of public law and administration are discussed in 217 clauses, while 197 concern the church in one way or another, apart from purely ecclesiastical collections.

In the public law division it is chiefly the power, interests and privileges of the king that are dealt with, in about 93 paragraphs, while local administration comes in for 39 and purely economic and fiscal matters for 13 clauses. Police regulations are very prominent and occupy no less than 72 clauses of the royal legislation. As to church matters the most prolific group is formed by general precepts based on religious and moral considerations, about 115, while secular privileges conferred on the church comprise approximately 62 and questions of organization about 20 clauses.

A consideration of chronological sequence in the elaboration of the laws reveals interesting results. The code of Aethelberht is almost entirely a list of "compositions" for various crimes, and similar lists figure largely in the laws of Hlothhere and Eadric, Ine and Alfred. In the codes of Edward the Elder and his successors, however, lists of fines for criminal offenses are much less prominent and gradually a new penal system is evolved, based on outlawry, confiscation, capital and corporal punishment.

Fines and compensations throughout the laws are graded carefully, in accordance with the social standing of the persons concerned. In early times it would appear that the different classes of society were more sharply distinguished than they were later. From the time of Aethelstan onward the distinction between the thegn or *twelfhynde* man (*i.e.,* the man with a wergild of 1,200 shillings) and the ceorl or *twihynde* man (*i.e.,* the man with a wergild of 200 shillings) is the chief dividing line between the classes of society. In the arrangements of the commonwealth the clauses dealing with royal privileges are more or less evenly distributed over all reigns, but the systematic development of police functions, especially in regard to responsibility for crimes, the catching of thieves and the suppression of lawlessness, is mainly the object of 10th- and 11th-century legislation.

Derivation.—The next question to be approached concerns the pedigree and natural affinities of Anglo-Saxon law. How far has it been influenced by non-Germanic elements, especially by Roman and canon law? The oldest Anglo-Saxon codes, especially the Kentish and the West Saxon ones, disclose a close relationship to the barbaric laws of Lower Germany—those of Saxons, Frisians, Thuringians. We find a division of social ranks which reminds us of the threefold gradation of Lower Germany (edelings, frilings, lazzen—Kentish eorls, ceorls, laets) and not of the twofold Frankish one (*ingenui Franci, Romani*), nor of the minute differentiation of the Upper Germans and Lombards. In subsequent history there is a good deal of resemblance between the legislation of the capitularies of Charlemagne and his successors on one hand and the acts of Alfred, Edward the Elder, Aethelstan and Edgar on the other, a resemblance called forth less by direct borrowing of Frankish institutions than by the similarity of political problems and conditions. Frankish law becomes a powerful modifying element in English legal history after the Conquest, when it was introduced wholesale in royal and in feudal courts. The Scandinavian invasions brought in many northern legal customs, especially in the districts thickly populated with Danes. The Domesday survey of Lincolnshire, Nottinghamshire, Yorkshire, Norfolk, etc., shows remarkable deviations in local organization and justice (lagmen, sokes), and great peculiarities as to status (socmen, freemen), while from laws and a few charters we can perceive some influence on criminal law (*nidingsvaerk*), special usages regarding fines (*lahslit*), the keeping of peace, attestation and sureties of acts (*festermen*), etc. But on the whole the importance of the introduction of Danish and Norse elements, apart from local cases, is due chiefly to the conflicts and compromises it called forth and to its social results; the Scandinavians coalesced easily with the natives.

The direct influence of Roman law was not great during the Saxon period: we notice neither the transmission of important doctrines nor the continuous stream of tradition in local usage. But indirectly Roman law did exert a by no means insignificant influence through the medium of the church, which, for all its insular character, was still permeated with Roman ideas and forms of culture. Thus Roman law had already turned its attention to the problem of intent and the church was much concerned with the problems of moral theology which the study of the Bible revealed: long before the matter was finally resolved by the scholastics, Archbishop Wulfstan secured the insertion, among the laws of Aethelred, of his moving appeal to distinguish between youth and age, wealth and poverty, accident and design when considering the moral nature of human acts.

The relations between church and state in Anglo-Saxon England were of capital importance and during the 19th century were variously estimated. It is now recognized that the Penitentials took an active part in supporting the efforts of the secular law to maintain law and order. Then, too, it was frequently suggested that Anglo-Saxon kings, for superstitious motives, allowed churches to exercise wide immunities and legal privileges, thus diminishing the powers of the crown. The more recent and probable view is that the crown was in fact casting upon wealthy churches (such as some of the greater abbeys) a large part of the duty of policing the countryside and that this policy was continued and developed under the Normans. Work of that sort was necessarily done by "the man on the spot"; it was expensive and a severe strain upon the resources of the Anglo-Saxon kings. The Old English "books" are derived in a roundabout way from Roman models, and the tribal law of real property was deeply modified by the introduction of individualistic notions concerning ownership, donations, wills, rights of women, etc. Yet here also the Norman Conquest increased the store of Roman conceptions by breaking the isolation of the English church and opening the way for closer intercourse with France and Italy.

Folkright and Privilege.—The Anglo-Saxon legal system cannot be understood unless one realizes the fundamental opposition between folkright and privilege. Folkright is the aggregate of rules, formulated or latent but susceptible of formulation, which can be appealed to as the expression of the juridical consciousness of the people at large or of the communities of which it is composed. It is tribal in its origin and differentiated not according to boundaries between states but on national and provincial lines. There may be the folkright of West and East Saxons, of East Angles, of Kentish men, Mercians, Northumbrians, Danes and Welshmen, and these main folkright divisions remain even when tribal kingdoms disappear. The centres for the formulation and application of folkright were, in the 10th and 11th centuries, the shire moots, while the councilors (witan) of the realm generally placed themselves on the higher ground of state expediency, although occasionally using folkright ideas. The older laws of real property, of succession, of contracts and the customary lists of fines were mainly regulated by folkright; the reeves employed by the king and great men were supposed to take care of local and rural affairs according to folkright. The law had to be declared and applied by the people themselves in their communities, while the spokesmen of the people were the leading men—the 12 eldest thanes or a similar quorum. Folkright could, however, be broken or modified by special law or special grant, and the fountain of such privileges was the royal power. Alterations and exceptions were, as a matter of fact, suggested by the interested parties themselves and chiefly by the church. Thus a privileged land tenure was created—bookland; the rules pertaining to the succession of kinsmen were replaced by concession of testamentary power and confirmations of grants and wills; special exemptions from the jurisdiction of the hundreds and special privileges as to levying fines were conferred. In time the rights originating in royal grants of privilege overbalanced folkright in many respects and became the starting point of a new legal system—the feudal one.

The King's Peace.—Another feature of vital importance in the history of Anglo-Saxon law is its tendency toward the preservation of peace. Already in Aethelberht's legislation we find characteristic fines inflicted for breach of the peace of householders of different ranks—the ceorl, the eorl and the king himself appearing as the most exalted among them. Peace is considered not so much a state of equilibrium or of friendly relations between parties but rather as the rule of a third within a certain region—a house, an estate, a kingdom. This leads on one side to the recognition of private authorities—the father's, the master's, the lord's—while on the other the tendency to maintain peace naturally takes its course toward the strongest ruler, the king, and we witness the gradual evolution of stringent rules in respect of the king's peace. A more metaphysical conception of "peace" was popularized by H. Brunner and adopted by F. W. Maitland. This concept regarded "peace" as proceeding from the folk and as being something like the theologian's "state of grace" which a criminal has forfeited by serious crime. J. Goebel cast serious doubts upon this interpretation, especially upon its alleged continental origins.

The more ancient documents of Anglo-Saxon law show us the individual not merely as the subject and citizen of a certain commonwealth but also as a member of some group, all the fellows of which are closely allied in claims and responsibilities. The most elementary of these groups is the *maegth*, the association of agnatic and cognatic relations. Personal protection and revenge, oaths, marriage, wardship, succession, supervision over settlement and good behaviour are regulated by the law of kinship. A man's actions are considered not as exertions of his individual will but as acts of the kindred, and all the fellows of the *maegth* are held responsible for them. What began as a natural alliance was used later as a means of enforcing responsibility and keeping lawless individuals in order. When the association of kinsmen failed (and it seems to have done so at an early period in England) the voluntary associations—guilds—appeared as substitutes. The guild brothers associated in mutual defense and support, and they had to share in the payment of fines. The township and the hundred were also involved in certain forms of collective responsibility.

In the course of time the natural associations get loosened and intermixed, and this calls forth the elaborate police legislation of the later Anglo-Saxon kings. Regulations are issued about the sale of cattle in the presence of witnesses. Enactments about the pursuit of thieves and the calling in of warrantors to justify sales of chattels are other expressions of the difficulties attending peaceful intercourse. Personal surety appears as a complement of and substitute for collective responsibility. The *hlaford* and his hiredmen are an institution not only of private patronage but also of police supervision for the sake of laying hands on malefactors and suspected persons. The *landrica* assumes the same part in a territorial district. Ultimately the laws of the 10th and 11th centuries show the beginnings of the frankpledge associations, which came to play so important a part in the feudal age.

See also ENGLISH LAW.

BIBLIOGRAPHY.—*Texts:*—*Domesday Book*, i, ii, Records Comm. (1833); J. M. Kemble (ed.), *Codex Diplomaticus Aevi Saxonici*, i-vi (1839–48); R. Schmid, *Gesetze der Angelsachsen*, 2nd ed. (1858); B. Thorpe, *Diplomatarium Anglicum: A Collection of English Charters . . . to . . . William the Conqueror*, with trans. (1865); A. W. Haddan and W. Stubbs, *Councils of Great Britain*, I–III (1869–78); W. de Gray Birch (ed.), *Cartularium Saxonicum*, 4 vol. (1885–99); J. Earle, *A Handbook to the Land-Charters* (1888); F. Liebermann, *Die Gesetze der Angelsachsen*, 3 vol. with trans. and notes (1898, 1906–16); F. E. Harmer, *Anglo-Saxon Writs* (1952); D. Whitelock (ed. and trans.), *Anglo-Saxon Wills* (1930); F. L. Attenborough (ed. and trans.), *The Laws of the Earliest English Kings* (1922); A. J. Robertson (ed. and trans.), *The Laws of the Kings of England from Edmund to Henry I* (1925).
Studies:—Sir F. Palgrave, *The Rise and Progress of the English Commonwealth*, 2 pt. (1832); W. Stubbs, *The Constitutional History of England . . .*, vol. i (1866); H. Adams *et al., Essays on Anglo-Saxon Law* (1876); J. M. Kemble (rev. by W. de Gray Birch), *The Saxons in England*, 2 vol. (1876); H. Brunner, *Zur Rechtsgeschichte der römischen und germanischen Urkunde . . .* (1880); J. C. H. R. Steenstrup, *Normannerne*, vol. iv (1882); Sir F. Pollock, "The King's Peace," *Oxford Lectures* (1890); P. Vinogradoff, "Folkland," *Eng. Hist. Rev.* (1893), "The Transfer of Land in Old English Law," *Harvard Law Review* (1907); Sir F. Pollock and F. W. Maitland, *The History of English Law before the Time of Edward I*, 2nd ed., 2 vol. (1898); F. Seebohm, *Tribal Custom in Anglo-Saxon Law* (1902), *The English Village Community . . .*, 2nd ed. (1926); H. M. Chadwick, *Studies on Anglo-Saxon Institutions* (1905); F. W. Maitland, *Domesday Book and Beyond . . .* (1907); J. Goebel, *Felony and Misdemeanor* (1937); T. P. Oakley, *English Penitential Discipline and Anglo-Saxon Law . . .* (1923); P. Fournier and G. Le Bras, *Histoire des Collections Canoniques en occident . . .*, 2 vol. (1931, 1932). (P. VI.; A. J. R.)

ANGLO-SAXONS. The title *rex Angulsaxonum*, with obvious variants like *rex Anglorum Saxonum*, was used sporadically by King Alfred (d. 899) and his successors down to King Edwy (d. 957) and was revived in the 11th century. The expression "Anglo-Saxons" probably arose to distinguish the Saxons of England from those of the continent, the *Antiqui Saxones* of Bede, translated *Ealdseaxe* in Old English. Hence the title "king of the Anglo-Saxons" would at first be merely a variant of "king of the Saxons" and "king of the West Saxons" also used by Alfred. Later the title would be interpreted as "king of the Angles and Saxons," and therefore equivalent to "king of the English."

Except in charters the term "Anglo-Saxons" is rare in English documents before 1066. In one 10th-century poem it occurs in the sense "people of England." It probably originated on the continent, where it was used from the time of Paulus Diaconus (*c.* 775) onward, and while at first it no doubt meant "Saxons of England," it can scarcely be said to mean more than "English" in surviving sources. Similarly writers in England after the Norman Conquest such as Florence of Worcester and Orderic Vitalis used it in the sense "English." It has been adopted since the 16th century to mean "English of the pre-Conquest period." From it were derived the adjective "Anglo-Saxon," used to describe the period of English history, language and literature which preceded the Norman Conquest, and the noun "Anglo-Saxon," meaning the Old English language. The latter term contrasts with the Old English usage in which the vernacular tongue was called *Englisc*, even by Saxon writers.

See also Index references under "Anglo-Saxons" in the Index volume.

See E. A. Freeman, *History of the Norman Conquest*, vol. i, appendix A, 3rd ed. (1887); K. Malone, "Anglo-Saxon: A Semantic Study," in *Review of English Studies*, vol. v (1929). (AL. C.)

ANGO, JEAN (*c.* 1480–1551), the most famous French shipowner of the Renaissance period, was born at Dieppe in Normandy. After taking over his father's import-export business early in the 16th century, he rose to control, by himself or in association with others, a fleet of 70 ships. With this he was able, in Francis I's reign, to ensure that France was represented wherever exploration had opened up new seas. It was Ango who in 1524 equipped the "Dauphine" in which Giovanni da Verrazano explored the east coast of North America, discovering the site of the future New York (which he named Angoulême), and in 1529 the brothers Jean and Raoul Parmentier reached the coast of Sumatra in Ango's ships the "Pensée" and the "Sacre." Ango also sponsored privateering. One of his captains, Jean Fleury, seized three ships on their way to Spain with Aztec treasures from Mexico (1523). When Francis I in 1530 authorized Ango to raid Portuguese shipping until he had compensated himself for losses sustained at Portuguese hands to the value of 250,000 ducats, the Portuguese were so much alarmed that their ambassador came to terms to have the authorization canceled. Francis I generally upheld Ango, as he both borrowed his ships for use against Spaniards and Englishmen and enjoyed the hospitality of his magnificent houses in Normandy. On Francis' death, however, Ango was exposed to his rivals' envy, was imprisoned for a time on a charge of malversation (1549) and died at Dieppe in 1551.

BIBLIOGRAPHY.—E. Guérin, *Ango et ses pilotes* (1901); M. Mollat, *Le Commerce maritime normand à la fin du moyen âge* (1952) and "Jean Ango," *Transmondia*, 69 (1960).   (MI. M.)

ANGOLA, a Portuguese overseas province on the west coast of Africa, south of the equator, is one of the eight Portuguese overseas provinces. The whole province, sometimes designated Portuguese West Africa, is situated south of the Republic of the Congo (former Belgian Congo), except the enclave of Cabinda (Kabinda), which is separated from the main territory by a strip of approximately 25 mi. belonging to the Republic of the Congo. The area of Angola is 481,351 sq.mi., and the population by the 1960 census was 4,830,449, including 172,529 Europeans. The capital is Luanda (São Paulo de Luanda); population (1960) 224,540. Nova Lisboa (formerly Huambo) was proposed as the capital in 1927 but this proposal was not made effective.

PHYSICAL GEOGRAPHY

Geology.—Angola is divided into two major zones: the first includes the continental plateau and the hills which separate it from the littoral, while the second is formed by the littoral itself. The most important geologic system is the Precambrian Oendolongo, corresponding to the Witwatersrand system in South Africa.

The central plateau consists of ancient crystalline rocks with granites overlain by unfossiliferous sandstones and conglomerates considered to be of the Paleozoic Age. The outcrops are largely hidden under laterite. The median hills parallel with the coast are composed largely of crystalline rocks with granites and some Paleozoic unfossiliferous rocks. The littoral zone contains the only fossiliferous strata; they are of Tertiary and Cretaceous Ages, the latter rocks resting on a reddish sandstone of an older date. The Cretaceous rocks of the Dombe Grande region (near Benguela) are of the Lower Cretaceous Albian Age and belong to the zone identified by the index fossil *Acanthoceras mamillari*, an ammonoid mollusk. The beds containing fossils of the ammonite *Schloenbachia inflata* are referable to the Gault. Tertiaries are at Dombe Grande, Moçâmedes and near Luanda. The sandstones with gypsum, copper and sulfur of Dombe may be Triassic. Recent eruptive rocks, mainly basalts, form a line of hills almost bare of vegetation between Benguela and Moçâmedes. Nepheline basalts and liparites occur at Dombe Grande. Copal, a fossil resin, occurs in quantity in some superficial rocks.

Physiography.—The northern boundary of Angola follows the Congo river, then goes east to the Kwango (Cuango) river. The eastern and southern boundaries, dividing Angola from the Republic of the Congo, Northern Rhodesia and South-West Africa, are highly irregular. They extend to 24° 05′ E. and 18° 03′ S. The enclave of Cabinda (*q.v.*) is separated from the neighbouring countries (Republic of Congo [former French Congo]) to the north and northeast and the Republic of the Congo to the south and southeast by land. This area near Matadi was ceded by Por-

tugal in 1927 for the laying of the Boma-Leopoldville railway; Belgium gave in exchange about 1,158 sq.mi. of the Bota de Dilolo, the frontier of the Republic of the Congo passing behind and almost parallel to the Luao river. South from the Congo river (6° S., 11° 41′ E.) the coast of Angola is about 1,000 mi. long and goes as far as the mouth of the Kunene (Cunene) river. The coast is divided into two different parts. North of the mouth of the Kwanza river it is hilly; south of that point it is for the most part flat, with occasional low cliffs of red sandstone. Great Fish bay (Baía dos Tigres), a little north of the Angola–South-West Africa frontier, is the one deep inlet. Farther north are Porto Alexandre, Little Fish bay (Baía de Moçâmedes) and Lobito bay, while shallower bays are numerous. The sparsely watered, sterile coastal plain extends 30 to 100 mi. inland. The great central plateau of Africa is approached by a series of irregular terraces covered with luxuriant vegetation. Water is fairly abundant although in the dry season obtainable only by digging in the sandy beds of the rivers. The plateau, altitude 4,000 to 6,000 ft., consists of well-watered, wide, rolling plains and low hills with scanty vegetation. In the east the tableland falls away to the basins of the Congo and Zambezi rivers, to the south it merges into barren sandy desert. The numerous westward rivers, except the Kwanza (Coanza) and Kunene (*qq.v.*), are unimportant. The mountain chains edging or dominating the plateau run generally parallel with the coast, as Tala Mugongo (3,937 ft.), Chela and Vissecua (7,611 to 5,751 ft.). In the district of Benguela are the highest points of the territory, Loviti (7,780 ft.) in 12° 5′ S. and Mt. Elonga (7,966 ft.). South of the Kwanza river is the volcanic mountain Caculo-Cabaza (3,592 ft.). From the tableland the Kwango and many other streams flow north to join the Kasai (*q.v.*), one of the largest affluents of the Congo. In its upper course the Kwango forms for fully 300 mi. the boundary between Angola and the Republic of the Congo. In the southeast the rivers flow to the Zambezi or, like the Cubango, drain to Lake Ngami.

Climate.—With the exception of the district of Moçâmedes, the coastal plains are unsuited to white people. In the interior, above 3,300 ft., temperature and rainfall, together with malaria, decrease. The plateau climate is healthful and invigorating. The mean annual temperature at São Salvador do Congo is 72.5° F.; at Luanda, 74.3°, and at Caconda, 67.2°. The prevailing winds are west, southwest and south-southwest. The cool season lasts from June to Sept.; and the rainy season from Oct. to May; the heaviest rainfall occurs with storms in April.

Vegetation.—As far south as Benguela the coast is rich in oil palms and mangroves. In the north are dense forests, some of which, especially in the enclave of Cabinda, contain valuable timber; in the south, toward the Kunene, are regions of dense thorn scrub. Rubber vines and trees are abundant but have been reduced by ruthless tapping; the commonest are various root rubbers, notably *Carpodinus chylorrhiza*; species of *Landolphia* are also found. Coffee, cotton and Guinea pepper are indigenous, and tobacco flourishes in several districts. Among timber trees are the tacula (*Pterocarpus tinctorius*), which grows to an immense size, its wood being blood red in colour, and the Angola mahogany. The bark of the musuemba (*Albizzia coriaria*) is used in tanning leather. The mulundo bears a hard green-shelled fruit, the size of a cricket ball (about 9 in. in circumference), with scarlet pips like a pomegranate.

Animal Life.—The fauna includes lion, leopard, cheetah, elephant, giraffe, rhinoceros, hippopotamus, buffalo, zebra, kudu and many other species of antelope, wild pig, ostrich and crocodile. Angola is one of the few territories where the great sable antelope (*Hippotragus niger variani*) still exists although it is very rare in spite of being protected. Only a few hundred individuals can be found on the banks of the Luando river. There are two major nature reserves; Quinçama (3,840 sq.mi.) and Moçâmedes (7,200 sq.mi.).

The maritime fauna is extremely rich. There are several kinds of whales, tortoises (*Chelonia imbricata*), lobsters, shell fish and a large variety of fish. Angola has the best fishing grounds of south and southwest Africa, where the Benguela cold current and the Agulhas warm current converge giving maritime temperatures and upsurges favourable to plankton. The sea is generally calm. Most of the fish common on the Atlantic coast of Europe are found off Angola, as well as African species. The most abundant are stickleback, mackerel, anchovy, tench, gilthead, sardine, whiting and tunny. The river fauna is also very rich, contributing an important part to the food supply of the native populations.

PEOPLE AND POPULATION

In 1960 the population of Angola was composed of 4,604,362 Natives, 172,529 Whites, 53,392 of mixed race, and 166 others. In 1960 the districts of greatest population density were those of Huambo (51 persons per sq.mi.), Benguela (32) and Luanda (26). The total urban population rose from 247,073 in 1950 to 512,543 in 1960, while the number of Negroes in urban centres rose from 94,818 in 1940 to 187,321 in 1950.

The great majority of the Negro population is of Bantu stock, though in the Congo district it is mixed with pure Negro. In the southeast there are various tribes of Bushmen. Bantu-Negroes include the Kongo and Ambundo in the north, and the Ambo in the south, etc., but the most important group is that of the Ovimbundo, whose language is spoken or understood by over 2,000,000 natives. Fetishism is the prevailing religion. (*See also* AFRICA: *Ethnography (Anthropology): West Central Africa.*)

Churches and Missions.—Angola forms a diocese of the Roman Catholic Church, in the province of Lisbon. This church began work at São Salvador do Congo in 1491 and controlled all educational activities until 1908. The Benidas, Cazombo, Cuando, Lilobo, Moxico and Vila Luso missions belong to the Benedictines, those of Andulo, Silva Porto, Cachingues, Chinguar, Entre Rios, Nova Sintra, Nhareia, Saurimo, Minungo, and Mussuco to the Order of the Holy Ghost; and those of Cuchi and Caiundo to the Redemptorists.

The Baptist Missionary society has headquarters at São Salvador do Congo. The American Methodist Episcopal Foreign Missionary society works in the Luanda district and the Canadian and American Congregational Churches and the Plymouth Brethren have missions in the highlands east of Lobito bay. In the Moçâmedes district are stations of the South African mission and the Swiss mission. There are in Angola about 50 non-Catholic missions, mostly British and American, which run schools, especially for agriculture; their welfare work has been outstanding.

Immigration and Settlement.—The Portuguese government has, since 1945, increased facilities for emigration; between 1950 and 1957 an average of 17,000 people a year left Portugal for Angola. The economic development of the territory is partly attributed to this immigration. In addition there have been some experimental settlements organized by the government. Those of Cela and the Kunene valley are of particular note. In Cela villages were prepared, fields cleared and bridges, roads, irrigation canals, etc., built before the settlers arrived. Each village has a community well, a public storehouse for crops, a combined church and schoolhouse and a first-aid station. Each family is provided with housing and a few livestock, and land for their support. There are tractor and machinery pools for the colony, though a few tractors are individually owned. Native labour cannot be hired, so that each European community has to be independent of the African. In this respect Cela is a positive experiment. The houses are similar to small farmhouses in Portugal and are well-built and attractive. Rice, wheat, maize (corn), potatoes, fruits and vegetables are the principal crops grown at Cela.

The Kunene valley settlement was created for natives and Europeans. Important crops grown there are sugar cane, tobacco and cotton. There are experimental colonies for natives only at Damba, Chimube, Toto, Loge, Culo and Caconda. (A. A. G. P.)

HISTORY

Very little is known about the early history of Angola. In the late Stone Age the northern part of the country was populated by groups of hunters and gatherers who left a variety of stone tools which the archaeologist can examine. Later, during the 1st millennium A.D., these early inhabitants were gradually absorbed by new, Bantu-speaking immigrants who introduced the revolutionary concepts of metalworking and agriculture. The Bantu communities in Angola remained for the most part small and isolated; the main exception to this was in the northwest where the Kongo people developed a large well-governed kingdom.

About 1483 Portuguese seafarers began to arrive on the coast. They came to trade but soon discovered that Angola had no gold or other precious metals with which to pay for the new luxuries they brought. The only salable commodity was labour and so within a few years an export trade in slaves developed. These slaves were mainly used to establish sugar plantations on the island of São Tomé and in Brazil.

The slave trade dominates the modern history of Angola. At first its effect was to increase the wealth and power of the rulers who controlled it; in particular the king of Ndongo (or Angola) greatly expanded his territory in the early 16th century. Later the trade caused internal divisions and rivalries which decayed the political fabric of the participating states and invited outside interference and conquest; it was in this manner that in 1568 Kongo fell prey to the depredations of a warrior nation from central Africa called the Jaga. Although the kingdom was later restored with the help of Portuguese troops it never recovered its former greatness and its position as the leading kingdom in Angola passed to Ndongo. Ndongo, however, soon clashed with the Portuguese.

For nearly a century the Portuguese who followed Diogo Cam (Cão) (*q.v.*) and other explorers down the African coast were mainly interested in commerce rather than in colonial dominion. They took with them missionaries, who taught European concepts and values to their trading partners, but not soldiers. When the Kongo kingdom began to crumble, however, the Portuguese changed their policy and decided to establish in Angola a conquest colony similar to those of the Spaniards in Mexico and Peru. Luanda became their military base and from 1576, under the leadership of Paulo Dias de Novais, they set out to subjugate the kingdom of Ndongo. In the ensuing wars the contestants proved fairly evenly matched and only after 100 years of intermittent fighting did the Portuguese prove successful. By 1680 their colony consisted of half a dozen forts in the lower Kwanza (Cuanza) valley and the small outlying territory of Benguela on the southern coast.

Throughout the Angolan wars the slave trade continued to flourish carrying off to the Americas more than 1,000,000 men, women, and children and killing countless others in the process. From the early 17th century Portuguese traders were joined by those of Holland, England and France and during the 18th century in particular these north Europeans heightened the devastation which the slave trade was causing in Angola. The only attempt to relieve the country's decay was made by Dom Francisco de Souza Coutinho who, while governor of Luanda, unsuccessfully tried to diversify the Angolan economy and establish sugar estates, iron mines and small factories.

The 19th century did not usher in a new era in Angola. The export of labour continued as before until British pressure forced the gradual suspension of the Brazilian slave trade in the 1850s. Thereafter the labourers, no longer called slaves but recruited in the same manner, were diverted to the cocoa estates of São Tomé, Portugal's original plantation island. By the end of the century Angola had suffered from four centuries of continuous slave trading and was as impoverished and underpopulated as any country in Africa.

When the colonial powers turned their attention to the partition of Africa in the 19th century the Portuguese were given a paper title to the vast area comprising Angola and at once set about gaining possession of it on the ground. Their endeavour was fiercely resisted by the Angolans and sporadic wars of conquest lasted for 30 years. The first campaign was fought in the south where the Cuanhama and other pastoralists fought a long but losing battle to resist the encroachments of both the Portuguese from the coast and the Boers from South Africa. The most decisive campaign was the Bailundo war of 1902 in which the Portuguese finally broke the power of the Ovimbundu kingdoms and captured the Bié plateau, thus enabling European entrepreneurs to build the

Benguela railway and establish white settlers on the highlands where Huambo became the Europeanized city of Nova Lisboa.

The first 30 years of colonial rule in Angola were a period of trial and experiment often hindered by political changes and unrest in Portugal; the main development projects such as the railways and diamond mines were launched with foreign capital and initiative. When in the 1930s Portugal began to settle down under a stable regime new emphasis was placed on colonial planning; progress, however, was long delayed first by the depression of the 1930s and then by World War II; only by the 1950s did new enterprise in education, harbour and airport construction, road building, and plantation work begin to show returns. By 1960 there were 6,000 children in high school. The annual value of exports had risen to over £40,000,000, the main exports being coffee, diamonds and sisal followed by fish products, maize, iron ore, cotton and sugar.

Throughout the colonial period the pressure to increase the development and exploitation of the country's resources led to a bitter conflict between colonial theory and practice. This was evident particularly in labour policy; various systems of forced and contract labour were used by private planters and companies as well as by the government. These abuses were undoubtedly one of the major factors causing the outbreak of civil war in 1961.

The Angolan civil war between the white settlers, backed by the Portuguese government, and the Angolan nationalists was far larger in scale than, for example, the Mau Mau war in Kenya; educated Africans and white planters were indiscriminately killed and about 250,000 people fled to the comparative haven of the Congo Republic. For five years Portugal strained every resource to build up and reequip its army to fight in Angola. Portugal was the first colonial power willing to use force on a large scale in an endeavour to retain its African possessions. In the short term the policy was successful and the opposition to its colonial policy muted; in the long run, however, the future of Portuguese control seemed to be linked with the survival of white minority rule in Rhodesia and South Africa.

While adopting a policy of the severest political repression Portugal launched an ambitious program of economic development after 1961. Faced with the danger of losing its African territories the Portuguese government began to encourage large-scale immigration of Portuguese peasants and to invite capital from Belgium, Germany, and elsewhere to partake in economic development and to expand such industries as oil and iron ore.   (D. B. B.)

ADMINISTRATION AND SOCIAL CONDITIONS

Government and Administration.—Angola is governed under the organic charter for overseas territories of June 1953 and the statute of July 1955. A governor general appointed by the Lisbon government and responsible to the minister for overseas territories has wide powers. He is advised by a legislative council of 26 persons, of whom 18 are elected and the other 8 appointed. The competence of the governor general to legislate normally requires the agreement of the legislative council.

The territory is divided into 15 districts: Cabinda, Zaire, Uíge, Luanda, Cuanza Norte, Cuanza Sul, Malanje, Lunda, Benguela, Huambo, Bié, Cuando Cubango, Moxico, Moçâmedes and Huíla. Each district is divided into *concelhos* (municipalities) and *circunscrições civis* (circumscriptions or subdistricts) each under an administrator who is the resident magistrate. Several minor local bodies with limited powers also exist, the most important of which are the *câmaras municipais*, which administer the *concelhos*. There are 64 *concelhos* and 21 subdistricts. The Portuguese overseas provinces situated on the west coast of Africa constitute a judicial district under an appeal court at Luanda.

Welfare Services.—Sleeping sickness appears but is rapidly decreasing because of the campaigns of mass vaccination. Common diseases are tuberculosis, malaria, hookworm, smallpox, leprosy, elephantiasis and goitre (among the women of the uplands). There are state and private hospitals, village infirmaries and leprosariums. In the Uíge district there is a special medical service for sleeping sickness and in the Baixo, Kunene and Gambos areas a special service for bubonic plague. There is a separate fund for medical assistance to natives.

Education.—By 1960 there were 5 state and 32 private secondary schools, 10 state and 5 private technical schools, and one teachers' training college. State primary education was provided by about 244 schools; primary and rudimentary education is also provided for native children in about 1,000 schools by the Portuguese Catholic and Evangelical missions. Schooling lasts for four years and all education is carried out in Portuguese. The teachers' training college, Teófilo Duarte, at Cuíma is subsidized by the state and entrusted to the Portuguese Catholic missions. Here educated natives of both sexes can graduate as primary school teachers. Two of the secondary schools are in Luanda and the other three in Benguela, Nova Lisboa and Sá da Bandeira.

Technical education covers commercial, industrial and agricultural fields. After 1949 it increased considerably to keep pace with the territory's economic development. The courses in highest demand are those in mechanics and bookkeeping. The Dr. Vieira Machado Agricultural and Husbandry college has accommodations for 100 resident pupils. The courses are of three or four years duration. The accommodations are modern and include stables, aviaries, laboratories and warehouses.

THE ECONOMY

Agriculture.—Angola is primarily an agricultural country that produces crops of both tropical and temperate zones. Coffee is the principal export crop and the chief market is the U.S. Maize is an important crop and is exported in large quantities. It is grown almost entirely by the Africans, mainly in the Benguela and Huambo districts. Sisal, also an export crop, is grown extensively in the Malanje and Benguela districts. Broad beans are a declining export from the same districts. Coconuts are grown in the north. Other oil-producing seeds are castor beans, grown almost exclusively by the Africans, chiefly in the Benguela, Bié, Malanje and Huíla districts; palm kernels, collected by the Africans in the coastal plain; peanuts, used mainly as a native food crop; and sesame, also used as a native food crop.

Cotton is grown chiefly in the Malanje district, and almost the entire crop is exported. Wheat does well on the Benguela plateau, in Bié and Huíla. Potatoes, rice, peas and other vegetables are commonly grown in the highlands. Cacao does well in Cabinda and in parts of the area around Amboim. Manioc is cultivated almost everywhere by the Africans. Tropical fruits, such as bananas, pineapples, guavas and pawpaws, grow almost everywhere, while Mediterranean fruits are successfully grown in the highlands. Tobacco is grown at middle altitudes as well as in the highlands, and its production in the 1960s was being developed, especially by the Europeans. Sugar cane, one of the most important products of Angola, contributes significantly to the territory's exports; and the extraction plants have modern machinery. Rubber is found in the interior districts and is the basis of trade with the Africans. Fine timber, principally hardwoods, is cut especially in the northern parts of the territory though it is still exported in only limited quantities. The chief woods are bulletwood, African mahogany and ebony. There are government agricultural stations at Luanda on the coast and in the interior.

Stock Raising.—There is excellent grazing land in many parts of Angola, especially in the Huíla, Huambo and Benguela districts. Forage is also available, but the tsetse fly has been prevalent in many districts. Cattle, goats, pigs, sheep, asses and horses are raised. Portuguese and French merino sheep have been imported to improve the quality of the wool, and Persian blackheads from South Africa have been introduced for mutton. Angola has an exceptional ability for Karacul raising. British firms have extensive cattle raising concessions in the vicinity of the Benguela railway. Honey and beeswax are produced almost entirely by the Africans. The export of beeswax has been on the decline.

Mining.—Thick beds of copper, probably outcrops of the Katanga mines of the Republic of the Congo, are found in the Bembe region in the north. Other deposits are found in the Quibala area and in the Moçâmedes district, also on the Cuvo. Iron is known in many parts: at Oeiras (on the Lucala affluent of the Kwanza river), near Andulo, around Bailundo and in other places in the south. It is believed that about 8,000,000 tons of ore are available and production is expanding. Petroleum was discovered in 1955 and proved to be of good quality. The Mulemba refinery was opened in 1958 with an initial capacity of 100,000 tons of refined oil per annum. Salt is worked by natives in several places along the coast. Gold occurs near the source of the Kunene and at Cassinga; lead on the Lucala east of Vila Salazar; lignite in the Kwanza valley; coal at Calucala, Quilungo, Dondo and on the Benguela plateau. The coal, of high volatile content, is exported while ordinary coal is imported. Diamonds are worked in the Lunda district under concession from the government which shares in the profits (see DIAMOND: *World Occurrence*). Other minerals are mica, manganese and sulfur.

Industries.—Much effort has been directed to the development of electric power resources. Angola had 450 thermal power stations by 1959. There were three dams supplying hydroelectric power: Mabubas on the Dande river, Biapio on the Catumbela river and Matala on the Kunene river. Others have been planned.

The most important manufacturing industries are those processing palm, whale and fish oil and resin and its derivatives; milling cereals; salting fish; preserving meat; and producing sugar, beer, cotton fabrics and cement. Fishing is an important occupation and includes a whaling station at Porto Amélia (near Moçâmedes).

Several factories produce vegetable fibres while other industries include ceramics, brick and tile making, carpentry and joinery, wagon building and sawmills. Tobacco is processed in modern factories in Luanda, local growths being mixed with imported ones. There are foundries and railway shops connected with the state railways. New factories include those for rubber tires, nitrogenous fertilizers, cellulose, cement and glass.

Trade.—The chief articles of import are textiles, foodstuffs, beverages, iron and steel goods, automobiles and industrial machinery. The chief exports are coffee, diamonds, fish meal, maize, cotton, sisal and sugar.

About one-third of the trade is with Portugal, which provides about half the imports and purchases one-fifth of the exports.

Finance.—The chief sources of revenue are customs, direct taxes (including native personal tax) and participation in private enterprises (mainly the diamond corporation). The chief expenditures are investments in the economic development of the territory, administration and defense.

Transport and Communications.—Benguela, Lobito, Luanda, Novo Redondo, Moçâmedes and Amboim are the principal ports along the coast, although there is some shipping from Ambriz, Great Fish bay and Ambrizete. There are regular steamship communications between Portugal, England, Germany and South Africa from Lobito. The Portuguese line which carries the bulk of the cargo is subsidized by the Portuguese government.

Railway mileage totals about 1,800 mi. Five lines run inland from the coast. The most important is the Benguela railway completed in 1927, 895 mi. from Lobito to its connection with the Katanga lines at the Republic of the Congo frontier. Of standard gauge (3′ 6″), it permits through shipment to the Republic of the Congo, Rhodesia, Mozambique and to South Africa by connecting lines. The service has been extended to Beira (Lobito to Beira, 2,920 mi.) and to Lourenço Marques (3,295 mi.). The Luanda-Malanje line, said to have been the most expensive railway to construct in tropical Africa, was bought by the government in 1918.

There are in Angola more than 4,900 mi. of primary roads and 17,000 of secondary roads. There are regular international air services from Lisbon, Kinshasa (formerly Léopoldville), Lourenço Marques, Pointe Noire, Brazzaville, etc., and internal lines connect Luanda (an international airport), Ambriz, Ambrizete, Cabinda, Lobito Sá da Bandeira, Moçâmedes, Nova Lisboa, Silva Porto, Porto Alexandre, etc. Land telegraph lines extend more than 8,000 mi. and telephone lines 3,500 mi. Cables connect Angola with Europe and South Africa. There are about 15 radio stations. *See* also references under "Angola" in the Index.   (A. A. G. P.)

BIBLIOGRAPHY.—R. Delgado, *Historia de Angola*, 4 vol. (1948-55); D. Birmingham, *Trade and Conflict in Angola* (1966); B. Davidson, *The African Awakening* (1955), *Black Mother* (1961); J. Duffy, *Portuguese Africa* (1959); T. Okuma, *Angola in Ferment* (1962); F. C. C. Egerton, *Angola in Perspective* (1957).   (D. B. B.; A. A. G. P.)

ANGORA GOAT: see GOAT; MOHAIR.

ANGOULÊME, CHARLES DE VALOIS, DUC D' (1573–1650), the natural son of Charles IX of France by Marie Touchet, chiefly remembered for the intrigues of his early life, was born at Fayet, near Montmélian, on April 28, 1573. Henriette d'Entragues, the future marquise de Verneuil and mistress of Henry IV of France, was his half sister. Favourably received at the French court because of his ready wit and good looks, he was granted the title of comte d'Auvergne and made colonel general of the cavalry. He served Henry IV in his campaigns against the Catholic league but became disaffected when Queen Margaret successfully contested his rights over Auvergne (though he retained his title).

Involved in the marshal de Biron's conspiracy in 1601, he was arrested with Biron but pardoned. He then engaged in more treasonable plots with Spain, in concert with his half sister (1604). When these were exposed he went into open rebellion. Captured in 1605 he was condemned to life imprisonment but was released from the Bastille in 1616 to serve against the enemies of the marshal d'Ancre. After the marshal's fall he was sent to campaign in Piedmont. Then in 1619 he was made duc d'Angoulême. The cardinal de Richelieu, whose favour he courted, gave him military commands at the sieges of Montáuban (1621), of La Rochelle (1627) and in Lorraine (1635), but was well aware of his proneness to peculation (Angoulême was accused even quite widely of coining). Cardinal Mazarin gave him a military command in the north in 1643. Old and wise enough to take no part in the Fronde, the duc died on Sept. 24, 1650. Angoulême had in 1644 married, as his second wife, the 20-year-old Françoise de Nargonne, who lived until 1713 and thus gave rise to the paradox whereby "Charles IX's daughter-in-law" is said to have been living 139 years after Charles's death (1574). The duc's *Mémoires*, first published in 1667, are reprinted in the Michaud-Poujoulat *Nouvelle collection des mémoires*, vol. 11 (1836).

ANGOULÊME, LOUIS ANTOINE DE BOURBON, DUC D' (1775–1844), the last dauphin of France, elder son of the comte d'Artois (afterward Charles X) and of Marie Thérèse of Savoy, was born in Versailles on Aug. 6, 1775. In 1789 he left France with his father. After residing in Poland and in England he returned to France in 1814 and with Wellington's help raised the royal standard again at Bordeaux. He did much for the restoration of the Bourbon rule after the overthrow of Napoleon and on Napoleon's return in 1815 made a valiant but futile attempt to raise a royalist army in the south. Unprepossessing and without personal ambitions he loyally supported the king's policies, being favourable to the Constitutionnels under Louis XVIII and to absolutism under Charles X. In 1823 he commanded the French expedition to Spain in support of Ferdinand VII. In 1830, when his father was compelled to abdicate, he renounced his claims to the throne and went into exile. He died at Gorizia, in Austrian Venetia, on June 3, 1844.

In 1799, at Mitau (Jelgava) in Courland, the duc d'Angoulême had married his cousin MARIE THÉRÈSE CHARLOTTE (1778–1851), daughter of Louis XVI and Marie Antoinette. Born at Versailles on Dec. 19, 1778, she was imprisoned during the French Revolution from Aug. 1792 until 1795, when she was released in exchange for members of the National Convention who had been handed over to the Austrians by Gen. Charles Dumouriez. In 1814 she returned to France with Louis XVIII. In March 1815, after Napoleon had re-entered Paris, she was able to maintain for ten days Bordeaux's loyalty to the royal family. She died at Frohsdorf, in Austria, on Oct. 19, 1851.

See Eugène de Guichen, *Le Duc d'Angoulême* (1909); Roger Langeron, *Madame Royale* (1958).   (G. DE B. DE S.)

ANGOULÊME, a city of southwestern France, capital of the *département* of Charente, is situated on a high plateau above the confluence of the Anguienne and the Charente rivers 72 mi. N.N.E. of Bordeaux by road. Pop. (1962) 46,924. Angoulême is surrounded by boulevards on the site of the fortifications. At the western end is the Jardin Vert, a park with extensive views. The centre of the town is the Place de l'Hôtel de Ville. The town hall (1868) is built on the site of the château of the counts of

Angoulême of which the tower of Valois (15th century) and the tower of Lusignan (13th century) remain. To the west is the cathedral of St. Pierre (1128, restored in the 19th century); its façade has 75 statues representing the last judgment and is flanked by two towers; the north transept is surmounted by a tower 194 ft. high. Inside, the roof of the nave is made into four cupolas, very typical of the region. Close by the cathedral is the former bishops' palace, now the museum. The shopping streets radiate from the Place Louvel, near which the church of St. André stands, with a 12th-century porch and 15th-century nave. On the neck of land joining the plateau with other high ground is the archaeological museum. Angoulême has cultural and economic links with Bury, in Lancashire, Eng. It also has U.S. connections, since the district on which New York is built was originally known as the Land of Angoulême. The city is on the main line from Paris to Bordeaux. There is an aerodrome at Ruelle (2 mi. N.E.). Papermaking is one of the chief industries and felt, wire gauze used in papermaking, iron, bricks, tiles, refrigerators and slippers are manufactured.

Angoulême was taken by Clovis from the Visigoths in 507 and attacked by the Normans in the 9th century. Ceded to England by the treaty of Brétigny in 1360, it was regained by the French under Charles V in 1373. Angoulême suffered in the religious wars when it was taken by the Protestants in 1569 under the orders of Admiral Coligny. The countship of Angoulême dates from the 9th century. (Fe. G.)

ANGOUMOIS, an old province of France, nearly corresponding to the modern *département* of Charente, represented the possessions of the counts of Angoulême (*q.v.*) in the feudal period. Having long shared the fortunes of Aquitaine (*q.v.*), it was recovered by France from the English in 1373. Henry IV subordinated it to the *gouvernement* of Orléanais. Under Louis XIV it was made part of a joint *gouvernement* of Saintonge and Angoumois.

ANGREN, a city on the Angren river in the Tashkent *oblast* of the Uzbek Soviet Socialist Republic, U.S.S.R. Pop. (1959) 55,789. Developed during World War II it is the newest and largest coal-mining centre in Soviet central Asia. It is linked by rail and a coal-gas pipeline with Tashkent, and furnishes coking coal to the Begovat steel mills. (G. E. Wr.)

ÅNGSTRÖM, ANDERS JONAS (1814–1874), Swedish physicist, was a pioneer in providing useful standards for spectroscopy (*q.v.*); the Ångström unit was named in his honour. Born on Aug. 13, 1814, at Lögdö, Medelpad, Sweden, he was educated at Uppsala university, where in 1839 he became *Privatdocent* in physics. In 1843 he became observer at Uppsala Observatory. In 1858 he succeeded Adolph Ferdinand Svanberg (1806–1857) in the chair of physics at Uppsala, and there he died on June 21, 1874.

His most important work was concerned with the conduction of heat and with spectroscopy. In his optical research *Optiska Undersökningar*, presented to the Stockholm academy in 1853, he not only pointed out that the electric spark yields two superposed spectra, one from the metal of the electrode and the other from the gas in which it passes, but deduced from Euler's theory of resonance that an incandescent gas emits luminous rays of the same refrangibility as those which it can absorb. This statement entitles him to rank as one of the founders of spectroscopy.

From 1861 onward he paid special attention to the solar spectrum. He announced in 1862 the existence of hydrogen, among other elements, in the sun's atmosphere, and in 1868 published his great map of the normal solar spectrum, which long remained authoritative in questions of wavelength although his measurements were inexact to the extent of one part in 7,000 or 8,000, the metre which he used as his standard having been slightly too short. He was the first, in 1867, to examine the spectrum of the aurora borealis and to detect and measure the characteristic bright line in its yellow green region; but he was mistaken in supposing that this same line, which is often called by his name, is also to be seen in the zodiacal light.

His son Knut Johan Ångström (1857–1910) became professor of physics at Uppsala in 1896. He investigated the radia-

tion of heat from the sun and its absorption by the earth's atmosphere and devised various delicate methods and instruments, including his electric compensation pyrheliometer, invented in 1893, and apparatus for obtaining a photographic representation of the infrared spectrum (1895).

ANGSTROM UNIT, that used for measuring wavelengths of light (also commonly applied to X rays), being equal to one ten-millionth of a millimetre; *i.e.*, 1×10^{-10} metre. The usual abbreviation for the angstrom is Å. *See* Light: *Introduction; see* also references under "Angstrom Unit" in the Index.

ANGTHONG, a province of central Thailand (Siam). It has an area of only 379 sq.mi. and, with a population (1960) of 197,865, has an average of 522 persons per sq.mi. The people live primarily in villages; the only city of any size is the provincial capital, Angthong, in which live about 6,454 (mun.). Angthong is about 55 mi. N. of Bangkok and occupies a bank site on the Chao Phraya river. It is linked by road to Ayutthaya. This province receives 50 in. of rainfall annually with 47 in. falling during the months of April through November. Its rich alluvial soils are irrigated by the Chao Phraya river. The province is noted for the production of rice, corn and oilseeds. (T. F. B.)

ANGUIER, FRANÇOIS (?1604–1669) and **MICHEL** (?1613–1686), French sculptors, were brothers, natives of Eu in Normandy. After some independent and local training, they traveled to Rome together in about 1641 and joined Alessandro Algardi's workshop. François stayed with him till 1643, Michel till 1651. The depth of feeling for contemporary Roman sculpture which they attained can be clearly measured in the tomb of the duc de Montmorency (Moulins) on which they worked between 1648 and 1652. This vast wall tomb, alike in design to Giacomo della Porta's Aldobrandini tomb in Sta. Maria sopra Minerva, is Italian in everything except the reticence and calm of the individual figures.

François' later works, almost all tombs, show no major change in style. His funerary statue of Gaspard de la Châtre (Louvre) is perhaps his most characteristic and distinguished work. He died in Paris, Aug. 9, 1669.

Michel, on the other hand, was a more restless and versatile artist. In 1655–58 he collaborated with G. F. Romanelli on the decoration of Anne of Austria's apartments in the Louvre, again with a Roman model in mind, this time Pietro da Cortona's scheme for the Pitti palace. He worked with Charles Le Brun and André Le Nôtre at Vaux. His most important commission was the decoration of the Val-de-Grâce in Paris, completed in 1667. He was responsible for the reliefs in the spandrels and vault of the nave and, in a totally different style, the dramatic marble "Nativity" group on the high altar (1665; moved to St. Roch). He returned to a rather severe classicism in his reliefs for the triumphal arch of the Porte Saint-Denis (1674). Michel died in Paris, July 11, 1686. The Anguiers' reputation was overshadowed by the importance of the following generation of sculptors.

(Aa. B.)

ANGUILLA: *see* Saint Kitts-Nevis.

ANGUISCIOLA (Angussola), **SOFONISBA** (*c.* 1528–*c.* 1625), Italian portrait painter of whom Van Dyck is said to have declared that he had derived much knowledge of the true principles of his art from her conversation. She was born at Cremona about 1528. In 1560, at the invitation of Philip II, she visited the court of Madrid, where her portraits elicited high praise. She painted several fine portraits of herself, one of which is at the Uffizi gallery in Florence. She had five sisters who were also celebrated artists. She died at Palermo.

ANGUS, EARLS OF. Angus was formerly one of the seven provinces of Pictish Scotland and was administered by a mormaor and later by an earl. The Celtic line of earls ended with Matilda (d. *c.* 1267), countess of Angus in her own right, but her marriage in 1243 to Gilbert de Umfraville (d. *c.* 1245) began the Norman line of four earls which lasted until 1381. They were in effect English barons, and their support of English against Scottish kings led to loss of their Scottish lands and to the creation, before 1329, of John Stewart (d. 1331) of Boncle in Berwickshire, as earl of Angus in a new line. This third creation ended with Margaret

STEWART (d. *c.* 1418), countess of Angus in her own right. By an irregular connection with William, 1st earl of Douglas, she became the mother of GEORGE DOUGLAS (*c.* 1378–1402 or 1403), who was created earl of Angus by Robert II in 1389. He died in England some time after being captured at the battle of Homildon hill (Sept. 1402).

George's great-grandson ARCHIBALD DOUGLAS (*c.* 1449–*c.* 1514), 5th earl in the Douglas line and known as the "Great Earl," was nicknamed "Bell the Cat" for his capture and execution (1482) of Robert Cochrane and the other favourites of James III. He engaged in frequent intrigues with English kings and in 1488 took part in the successful rebellion against James III. Ultimately he gained favour at the court of James IV and was chancellor from 1493 to 1498. He died at Whithorn in Galloway (mod. Wigtown) a few months after his two eldest sons were killed at the battle of Flodden (1513); a third son was Gavin Douglas (*q.v.*), bishop of Dunkeld.

ARCHIBALD DOUGLAS (*c.* 1489–1557), 6th earl, son of George, master of Angus, who was killed at Flodden, succeeded on his grandfather's death. By his second marriage in 1514 to the queen dowager Margaret (*q.v.*) Tudor, he aroused the jealousy of the nobles. Margaret was supplanted in 1515 as regent and guardian of the infant James V by the duke of Albany and fled to England. On her return she found that Angus had formed a liaison with a daughter of the laird of Traquair and she therefore allied with Albany against her husband. He was charged with high treason in 1522 and sent to France. But he returned two years later with the support of Henry VIII of England, entered Edinburgh in 1525 and called a parliament. He and the Douglases then wielded supreme power until Margaret obtained a divorce and James V escaped from his stepfather's tutelage (1528), issuing a decree of forfeiture against him. Angus took refuge in England, and James took vengeance on his relations, burning at the stake (July 17, 1537) Angus' sister Janet, Lady Glamis. After the death of James V in 1542, Angus returned to Scotland and the act of forfeiture was annulled. He was commissioned to arrange a marriage between Mary Stuart and Prince Edward (afterward Edward VI of England), but his English sympathies were mitigated by the earl of Hertford's marauding expedition of 1544. He was appointed lieutenant of southern Scotland, defeated the English at Ancrum moor on Feb. 27, 1545, and led the van when the Scots were defeated at Pinkie in 1547. He died at Tantallon castle in Jan. 1557, after a career in which national interests were completely subordinated to those of his family. His only surviving legitimate child, by Margaret Tudor, was Margaret who married Matthew, 4th earl of Lennox, and became the mother of Lord Darnley. He was succeeded by his nephew DAVID DOUGLAS (*c.* 1515–1557), 7th earl, son of Sir George Douglas of Pittendriech.

ARCHIBALD DOUGLAS (1555–1588), 8th earl and earl of Morton from 1586, was the son of the 7th earl. During the regency of his uncle, the earl of Morton, he rose rapidly to power. He became privy councilor and sheriff of Berwick (1573), lieutenant general of south Scotland (1574), warden of the west marches and steward of Fife (1577) and lieutenant general of the whole realm (1578). But when Morton fell in 1581 Angus was declared guilty of high treason for supporting him and fled to London. After a brief reconciliation with James VI he joined the rebellion of the earl of Mar and the master of Glamis, and sentence of attainder was pronounced against all three. The rebels fled to Newcastle, which became a centre of Presbyterianism and of projects against the Scottish government encouraged by Elizabeth I. They returned to Scotland in Oct. 1584 and secured from James the restoration of their estates and a share in the government. Angus was appointed warden of the marches and lieutenant general on the border, but his support of Presbyterianism prevented his gaining real favour with the king. He died at Smeaton near Dalkeith on Aug. 4, 1588.

His cousin, WILLIAM DOUGLAS (1533–1591), became the 9th earl. He was succeeded by his son WILLIAM (1554–1611), the 10th earl, who was converted to Roman Catholicism and became involved in various conspiracies against the government. He joined the rebellion of the earls of Huntly and Erroll in 1593, but the revolt failed and in 1597 all three renounced their religion, de-

clared themselves Presbyterians and were restored to the lands and honours they had forfeited. Angus recanted in 1608 and withdrew to France, dying at Paris on March 3, 1611. He was succeeded by his son WILLIAM (1589–1660), 11th earl, who became 1st marquess of Douglas in 1633. Thereafter the title earl of Angus was given by courtesy to the eldest son of the marquess or duke of Douglas. Since 1761 the title has been held by the dukes of Hamilton.

BIBLIOGRAPHY.—D. Hume of Godscroft, *History of the Houses of Douglas and Angus,* legendary in some respects, 4th ed. (1748); Sir W. Fraser, *The Douglas Book* (1885); Sir H. Maxwell, *History of the House of Douglas* (1902).　　　　　　　　　　(G. S. P.)

ANGUS (FORFARSHIRE), an eastern county of Scotland, is bounded on the north by the shires of Kincardine and Aberdeen, on the west by Perthshire, on the south by the Firth of Tay and on the east by the North sea. The Bell rock (*q.v.*) or Inchcape is also in the county. The ancient name of Angus was officially adopted in 1928 instead of Forfarshire. The land area is 874 sq.mi.

Physical Features.—The county is compact in shape, roughly bisected by the Highland boundary fault line running northeast-southwest from Edzell to Lintrathen. The Highland part contains dissected plateaus of 2,000–3,000 ft. rising to Glas Maol (3,502 ft.) to the south of the granite massif of Lochnagar and White Mounth. These high, rolling moorlands are cut by three broad glens trending northwest-southeast—Glen Isla, Glen Clova and Glen Esk—and by minor valleys. During the Quaternary glaciation the plateaus were protected by névé; the main glens carried weak glaciers; few ribbon lakes were excavated (*e.g.,* Loch Lee in Glen Esk now used as a reservoir), but there was considerable deposition of terminal moraine. The impressive Highland edge faces the softer, gentler Old Red Sandstone corridor of Strathmore strewn with ground moraine from great southwest Highland glaciers which came via the Tay (*e.g.,* the drumlins southwest of Kirriemuir). There are some fluvioglacial sands and gravels and a few lowland lakes in hollows in the glacial drift (*e.g.,* the Loch of Lintrathen supplying water to Dundee and parts of Angus). Then the Sidlaw hills, also with the northeast-southwest Caledonian trend, are a northwest-dipping hill range of andesite and basalt lavas of the Old Red Sandstone Age, scoured and molded by southwest Highland ice (*e.g.,* the three small lochs of Fithie, Rescobie and Balgavie near Forfar). The scarp face of the Sidlaws looks southeast across more till-covered Old Red Sandstone lowlands. Postglacial raised beaches, at about 25 ft., 50 ft. and 100 ft. above mean sea level, fringe the shore with its many sand dunes (as on the complex cuspate foreland at Buddon Ness at the mouth of the Firth of Tay).

The climate is generally the dry east coast type with many cool dry springs commonly accompanied by coastal sea mists (January mean coastal temperature about 37° F.; July about 59° F.; high inland areas a little colder in winter, especially in frost hollows). The late summer is fairly sunny (August mean approximately four and one-half hours per day) and it remains fairly sunny into the autumn enabling the generally late harvest to be gathered in.

In the uplands soils are thin and poor, an acid peaty layer overlying a whitish leached horizon, and there is much rock protruding, with peat on flat areas. A heather bilberry plant association predominates, with better grasses in the glens—a country of ptarmigan and red grouse, red deer and occasional golden eagles. In the lowlands soils are developed chiefly on the red boulder clays in which Old Red Sandstone is mixed with other glacial debris. Light, well-drained soils develop on the fluvioglacial and raised beach sands and gravels, while some fertile carse clays surround the Montrose basin. The lowlands are largely tilled except for the moorland crest of the Sidlaws and some wooded estates mainly on gravelly soils. Fulmar petrels breed in several coastal sites. Both the North Esk and South Esk rivers have heavy runs of salmon and sea trout.　　　　　　　　　　　　　　(A. T. A. L.)

History.—There are no authentic records of the struggles between the Picts and their predecessors the Scots, although at Forfar loch there are traces of crannogs, or lake dwellings, in which the early Caledonians must have defended themselves. By Roman times Angus was inhabited by the Picts. There are remains of weems or underground houses and there are vitrified forts at

Finavon, Drumsturdy Muir and the Laws near Monifieth, but the best examples of Pictish or pre-Pictish forts are found on the hills known as the White Caterthun and the Brown Caterthun near Menmuir. Traces of Roman camps and roads are common.

From A.D. 500 Teutons and Danes invaded Angus from the sea, and Angles from Northumbria invaded it by land. In 685 the Angles were defeated at the battle of Nechtansmere, near Dunnichen, and in the 11th century the Vikings were defeated at Barry and Aberlemno. In the next century the Flemings established linen and woolen industries and the county enjoyed a prosperity which was little affected by the War of Independence, although Brechin was one of the four places where John de Balliol resigned his kingdom to the English king Edward I in July 1296. However, during the English Civil War in the 17th century the marquis of Montrose and General Monk ravaged the countryside, both Dundee and Brechin being sacked.

Among interesting buildings are: Brechin cathedral with its 12th-century round tower; the ruins of Arbroath abbey and Edzell castle with a 17th-century walled garden; the remains of Forter castle, destroyed by the earl of Argyll in 1640; and 14th-century Glamis (q.v.) castle, the childhood home of Queen Elizabeth, consort of George VI, and the birthplace of Princess Margaret.

Population and Administration.—The population of Angus in 1961 was 278,399, including the county of the city of Dundee (182,978). Arbroath (19,537) is a large burgh, while Montrose (10,701), Forfar (10,294), Brechin (7,115), Carnoustie (5,511), Kirriemuir (3,486) and Monifieth (3,474) are small burghs. The county town is Forfar. Dundee returns two members to parliament, while Angus returns one member for South Angus and joins with Kincardineshire in returning another member who represents North Angus and Mearns. Sheriff courts are held at Arbroath, Dundee and Forfar and there are burgh courts in each of the other burghs.

Industries and Communications.—The higher parts of Angus are mainly in large sheep farms with only one sheep to several acres. There is also rearing of beef cattle in the glens. About two-fifths of the county is cultivated, mainly in the lowlands, where the large red sandstone farmsteads lie amid big, square, tidy fields showing red when ploughed. The rotation emphasizes the fodder crops—oats, particularly, and turnips—for this is an arable-and-stock economy, but potatoes are an important cash crop, high-grade seed potatoes being exported all over the world, while wheat, barley and sugar beet are also grown. Small holdings, in contrast, produce large quantities of raspberries and other soft fruit, partly for jam, especially on light, gravelly soils. Angus is the native county of the Aberdeen Angus black cattle, dating from 1808, and there are many well-known pedigree herds, as also of Shorthorns, while there are pedigree flocks of Border Leicesters and Black-face Highland sheep. (See CATTLE; SHEEP.) Fattening bullocks and sheep are brought in from the glens and elsewhere.

Although farming takes first place, Angus also has a well-balanced industrial economy. The staple industries in the towns are the manufacture of jute and linen products, carried on extensively at Dundee, Arbroath, Montrose, Brechin, Forfar and Kirriemuir. Other long-established industries are shipbuilding, particularly at Dundee, and engineering at Arbroath. There is however in Dundee a large, modern industrial estate providing employment in a considerable number of light industries, while in all the Angus towns alternative industries are being developed. In Carnoustie, for example, which is a holiday resort, there is a firm which specializes in stonecutting machinery, and in Brechin a precision-tool firm employs a considerable number of workers. In Arbroath there is a thriving whitefishing industry with ancillary fish-curing establishments, and the netting of salmon between Arbroath and Montrose is a profitable occupation. Throughout the county there has been a considerable increase in the facilities provided for the canning of fruit and vegetables.

Two main railway lines pass through Angus. The one from Glasgow to Aberdeen runs up Strathmore to Forfar, Guthrie, Dubton and Marykirk. That from Edinburgh to Aberdeen, which enters the county across the Firth of Tay by the Tay bridge (2 mi. long), follows the coast through Montrose and joins the other line

to the north of that town.   (I. A. M.)

BIBLIOGRAPHY.—A. J. Warden, *Angus or Forfarshire*, 5 vol. (1880–85); A. Jervoise, *Memorials of Angus and the Mearns* (1885); E. B. Dobson, *Angus* (pt. 27 of *The Land of Britain*, ed. by L. Dudley Stamp, 1946).

ANHALT, a former German state which was a duchy from 1863 to 1918 and a *Land* until 1945, when it was merged in Saxony-Anhalt. Saxony-Anhalt was a *Land* of the German Democratic Republic from 1949 to 1952, when it was broken up into *Bezirke* or districts, the former territories of Anhalt being divided between the *Bezirke* of Magdeburg and of Halle.

Territorially the duchy of Anhalt was divided into two major parts (the eastern one comprising Zerbst, Dessau, Cöthen and Bernburg, the western one being centred on Ballenstedt) and five smaller ones, all of them enclaves within the geographical boundaries of the Prussian province of Saxony.

The level country around the upper Elbe river from which Anhalt was constituted was in the 11th century still part of the duchy of Saxony. It was united in the 12th century in the possession of Albert (q.v.) the Bear, margrave of Brandenburg. With the death in 1212 of Albert's son Bernard, duke of Saxony, the countship of Anhalt was detached from the duchy and given to his son Henry, who in 1218 took the title of prince and was the real founder of the house of Anhalt. (*See* ASCANIAN DYNASTIES.)

On Henry's death (1252) his three sons partitioned Anhalt between the lines of Aschersleben (extinct in 1315 after which its lands passed to the bishops of Halberstadt, thus dividing the two major parts of the Anhalt possessions), of Bernburg (extinct in 1468) and of Zerbst. The Zerbst line inherited the Bernburg lands but was itself divided by the end of the 15th century into the lines of Anhalt-Dessau and Anhalt-Cöthen. All Anhalt, however, was reunited in 1570 under Joachim Ernest, but four of the latter's five sons partitioned the principality again in 1603, founding new lines of Dessau, Bernburg, Zerbst and Cöthen. The third son (who in 1611 was to receive Plötzkau, in appanage only, from Bernburg) reserved for himself and his descendants the right of succession to any princely line that should become extinct, with the result that in 1665 his line succeeded to Cöthen. In 1665 moreover the princes of the four lines agreed on an inheritance treaty intended to prevent further division of the territory. In 1793, on the extinction of the Zerbst line, its territory was divided among Dessau, Bernburg and Cöthen. The three princes each took the title of duke in 1806, on the dissolution of the Holy Roman empire. Cöthen passed to Anhalt-Dessau in 1847 and finally, with the extinction of the Bernburg line, all Anhalt was united under Leopold IV of Anhalt-Dessau in 1863.

In the 16th century Anhalt accepted the Reformation. Princes of Anhalt-Dessau served in the Prussian army in the 17th century and Anhalt came to be increasingly overshadowed by Prussia. The dukes joined the Confederation of the Rhine in 1807 and supported Napoleon till 1813. They joined the Germanic confederation in 1815 and the Prussian *Zollverein* in 1828. In 1859 a new constitution was established for Bernburg and Dessau jointly. Having been a state of the German empire from 1871, Anhalt in 1919 became a free state (*Land*) of the republican German Reich.

    (HE. K.)

ANHALT-DESSAU, LEOPOLD I, PRINCE OF (1676–1747), Prussian field marshal, the reorganizer of the Prussian army in the years immediately preceding the notable victories of Frederick the Great. The only surviving son of George II of Anhalt-Dessau, he was born at Dessau on July 3, 1676. His long career of active service began in the Netherlands in 1695–97, when he was present at the siege of Namur.

In 1698 he married Anna Luise Föse, the daughter of a chemist in Dessau. At the time this marriage was much resented by Leopold's family, especially by his mother, but in the event it proved a great success. Later his wife was accorded the title of princess. Anna Luise was a woman of ability and character. During her husband's absence on service she frequently acted as regent: at other times she accompanied him in the field. She died in 1745—the year of her husband's last battle. Leopold himself was a man of fiery temper, whose keen sense of duty and upbringing as a devout member of the Lutheran faith often led him to excessively hard measures against erring subordinates and delinquent subjects. It was said that his wife was very successful in mitigating the effect of some of his harsher judgments.

Leopold's career as a military commander of distinction began with the War of the Spanish Succession (q.v.), when he took the field as commander of a Prussian corps on the Rhine and participated in the sieges of Kaiserwerth and Venlo. He was also present at a number of other engagements, including Blenheim, Cassano, Turin, Tournai and Malplaquet, in most of which he played a distinguished part. In 1710 he became commander of all the Prussian forces at the front. In 1712 he was responsible for a particularly smart piece of work when the Dutch garrison at Mörs (near Düsseldorf) was surprised and the castle captured without a shot being fired or a single casualty occurring. In the same year he was made a field marshal. In 1715 he commanded a corps of about 40,000 men against Sweden. It was largely due to his skill that the campaign ended so favourably for Prussia, his most notable successes being on the island of Rügen (Nov. 16, 1715) and at the siege of Stralsund.

Up to this time Leopold had spent the greater part of his military career (1695–1715) on active service. There followed a long period of peace and it was probably during these years that he performed his greatest, although least spectacular, service to his country in the reorganization and training of the Prussian army. He was first and foremost an infantry soldier. It was said that he tolerated cavalry and artillery, but considered them entirely secondary to his own arm. Although Frederick the Great's victories were mostly won by cavalry action, infantry played a leading part in providing the firm base from which his mounted troops operated. Frederick's infantry was said to be superior to that of any other army in the proportion of five to three. This deservedly high reputation was due to the thorough training given to them by "Old Dessauer"—which was Leopold's popular name—in the years preceding Frederick's campaigns. This training was founded on the most rigid discipline: he also introduced the system of fire control for which Frederick's infantry became famous and which put them in a class by themselves in defense.

During the War of the Polish Succession (1733–35) Leopold served under Prince Eugène of Savoy. Although Frederick benefited from his prior preparation of the army and often sought his advice on matters of organization and training, the king did not often take Leopold on service. He found him a difficult and stubborn subordinate who, in his later years, regarded himself as the leading soldier in Europe—a not incorrect self-appraisement at a time when Frederick had yet to make his mark. In 1745 he was in command of an army on the Saxon frontier, in anticipation of trouble from that quarter, while Frederick was engaged elsewhere. His last battle was on Dec. 14, 1745, at Kesselsdorf, when he was in his 70th year. On this occasion Frederick was hastening toward Dresden to meet the Austrian-Saxon threat, but before he arrived the old marshal had engaged and defeated the enemy. A story is told of him on this day, the origin of which has since been attributed to others, who may perhaps have copied his example. As a devout churchman it was his custom to pray before battle, and at Kesselsdorf his prayer is said to have been as follows: "Oh God let me not be disgraced in my old days. Or if thou wilt not help me, do not help these scoundrels; but leave us to try it ourselves." After this campaign he retired to Dessau where he died on April 7, 1747.

Leopold of Anhalt-Dessau has hardly received the credit due to him as a soldier. In the field he was conspicuously successful and even more so as a trainer and organizer in peace. He introduced the iron ramrod—a big technical advance in musketry—and other improvements into the Prussian army. He was unfortunate in being an immediate predecessor of Frederick the Great, who captured most of the attention of military historians of that period; but much of Frederick's success was due to the spadework of Leopold. He was survived by three sons: Leopold II Maximilian who succeeded him as prince of Anhalt-Dessau; Dietrich; and Moritz. All had successful careers as generals in the Prussian army under Frederick the Great. Moritz was in Prussian service

from 1725 until two years before his death in 1760.

BIBLIOGRAPHY.—Anon., *Fürst Leopold I von Anhalt und seine Söhne* (1852); Curt Bökelmann, *Leopold I Fürst von Anhalt-Dessau* (1895); O. Krauske (ed.), *Die Briefe König Friedrich Wilhelms I an den Fürsten Leopold zu Anhalt-Dessau* (1905).   (C. N. B.)

ANHWEI (An-hui sheng), a province of China lying astride the Yangtze river on the western edge of its delta (area 54,015 sq.mi.; pop. [1957 est.] 33,560,000). Anhwei falls into two parts, divided almost equally north and south by the Ta-pieh range north of the Yangtze. Northern Anhwei is part of the north China or Yellow plain, a level depositional surface traditionally flooded by the Huai river and often the Yellow river. Wheat, millet, beans and cotton are grown there. Southern Anhwei is part of the green Yangtze hills country, with a more genial climate. Terraced hillsides produce the world-famous Ch'i-men tea, lumber and bamboo, while rice and tung oil grow on the valley floors. Huang shan rises there, 4,180 ft. high, a rugged granitic mass beloved by Chinese poets and artists for centuries for its strong shape and lush vegetation. Some 60 mi. W. at Ma-an-shan is a large high-grade iron ore deposit averaging 50% iron content, with 11 blast furnaces, the main supply centre for pig iron down the Yangtze to Shanghai. Near Huai-yuan in northern Anhwei is central China's largest coal-mining area, the Huai-nan mines, having a yearly output of over 1,000,000 tons. The government developed a great flood-control project for the Huai river after 1950. Nine concrete multiarch dams in the mountains of Anhwei, Hupeh and Honan have been erected to impound the tributaries of the Huai to irrigate farm land, to supply electric power and to improve navigation. Along with middle Huai in Anhwei, four sluice-gate dams with flood-detention basins have been built, with better drainage facilities downstream in Kiangsu also. Presumably the reconstruction of the Grand canal not only will open another flood outlet to the sea but will also permit Huai-nan coal to move south economically into the Yangtze delta cities. Formerly the largest cities, Wu-hu and Huai-ning, the one-time capital, were important as Yangtze trade and rice-shipping centres, but with the increase in mining and large water conservation projects along the Huai river, Peng-pu (pop. [1953] 253,000), where the Ch'ing-p'u railway spans the Huai, and Ho-fei (pop. [1953] 183,600), the provincial capital, are growing.   (Te. H.)

ANHYDRIDE, a compound which may be prepared by the removal of water or the elements of water from another compound. An oxide which combines with water to form an acid or which may be formed by the removal of water from an acid is called an acid anhydride; one which unites with water to form a base or which a base yields upon the loss of water is called a basic anhydride. *See also* Acids and Bases.

ANHYDRITE, an important calcium mineral, differing chemically from the more commonly occurring gypsum in containing no water of crystallization, being anhydrous calcium sulfate. Anhydrite is most frequently found with salt deposits in association with gypsum, as in the cap rock of the Texas-Louisiana salt domes. For discussion of its origins, occurrence and alterations, *see* Salt Dome; Gypsum. *See also* Calcium.

Anhydrite crystallizes in the orthorhombic system and has three directions of perfect cleavage parallel to the three planes of symmetry. Distinctly developed crystals are somewhat rare, the mineral usually presenting the form of cuboidal cleavage masses. The hardness is 3.5 and the specific gravity 2.9. The formula is $CaSO_4$. The colour is white, sometimes grayish, bluish or reddish. On the best developed of the three cleavages the lustre is pearly; on other surfaces it is of the ordinary glassy or vitreous type.

A peculiar variety of anhydrite occurring as contorted concretionary masses is known as tripestone, and a scaly granular variety, from Vulpino, near Bergamo, in Lombardy, as vulpinite; the latter is cut and polished for ornamental purposes.

ANICETUS, SAINT, pope from *c.* 155 to *c.* 166, called a martyr, worked to combat the errors of Valentine and Marcion and to prevent heresies. During his pontificate Polycarp (q.v.) visited Rome to confer with him about the controversy over the date of Easter. St. Anicetus' feast day is April 17.

ANIENE, a river of central Italy, is 67 mi. long, with a drainage basin of 569 sq.mi. The Aniene (anc. Anio), one of the main tributaries of the Tiber (*q.v.*), rises from two springs in the Simbruini mountains southeast of Rome, near the town of Subiaco, flows through a narrow valley to Tivoli (*q.v.*) where through a series of falls it descends to the level of the Roman Campagna and after numerous meanders joins the Tiber. Nero created a group of artificial lakes in the upper course of the river above Subiaco and built a villa there whose remains still can be seen. The falls at Tivoli were one of the main scenic attractions of the Roman countryside, but the heavy use made of the Aniene's waters by hydroelectric plants and by aqueducts reduced the once famous falls to a small trickle. The middle valley of the Aniene is followed by the Rome-Pescara railway and motor road.   (G. Kh.)

ANILINE, an organic base first obtained from the destructive distillation of indigo in 1826 by O. Unverdorben, who named it Crystallin. In 1834, F. Runge isolated from coal tar a substance which produced a beautiful blue colour on treatment with calcium chloride; this he named kyanol or cyanol. In 1841, C. J. Fritzsche showed that by treating indigo with potassium hydroxide it yielded an oil, which he named aniline, from the specific name of one of the indigo-yielding plants, *Indigofera anil*, *anil* being derived from the Sanskrit *nīla*, dark-blue, and *nīlā*, the indigo plant. About the same time N. N. Zinin found that on reducing nitrobenzene a base was formed, which he named benzidam. A. W. von Hofmann investigated these variously prepared substances and proved them to be identical, and thenceforth they took their place as one substance, under the name aniline or phenylamine having the composition $C_6H_5.NH_2$.

By the action of nitrous acid in acid solution, aniline is transformed into a diazonium salt. (*See* Diazo Compounds.) This reaction represents the first step in many important syntheses of dyes and other substances. The great commercial value of aniline is due to the readiness with which it yields, directly or indirectly, valuable dyestuffs. The discovery of mauve in 1856 by Sir W. H. Perkin was the first of a series of dyestuffs which are now to be numbered by hundreds. Reference should be made to the article Dyes and Dyeing for more details on this subject. It is a starting product for the manufacture not only of dyestuffs but of many drugs.

Aniline is manufactured by reducing nitrobenzene with iron borings and water slightly acidified with hydrochloric acid, the product being purified by steam distillation followed by distillation under reduced pressure. The action of ammonia on chlorobenzene at high pressure and temperature in the presence of a catalyst is also employed in the manufacture of aniline. Monomethyl- and dimethyl-aniline are colourless liquids prepared by heating in an autoclave at 220° aniline, aniline hydrochloride and methyl alcohol, or aniline, methyl alcohol and about 0.5% of iodine. They are of great importance in the dye industry. Monomethylaniline boils at 193–195°; dimethylaniline at 192°.

Properties.—Pure aniline is a basic substance of an oily consistence, colourless, melting at −8° and boiling at 184° C.; it dissolves in 31 parts of water. On exposure to air it absorbs oxygen and slowly resinifies, becoming deep brown in colour. It possesses a somewhat pleasant vinous odour and a burning aromatic taste; it is highly poisonous, having a destructive action on the red corpuscles of the blood.

Aniline is a weak base and forms salts with the mineral acids. Aniline hydrochloride is the "aniline salt" of commerce. Although aniline is but feebly basic, it precipitates zinc, aluminum and ferric hydroxides from their salts and expels ammonia from ammonium compounds when warmed with them. When aniline hydrogen sulfate is baked at 200° C. sulfanilic acid,

$$NH_2.C_6H_4.SO_3H,$$

is produced. Anilides, compounds in which the amino group is substituted by an acid radical, are prepared by heating aniline with certain acids; antifebrin or acetanilide (*q.v.*) is thus obtained from acetic acid and aniline. When aniline vapour and hydrogen are passed over finely divided nickel heated at 190° C., the reduction products, *cyclohexylamine*, *dicyclohexylamine* and *cyclohexylaniline* are produced. The oxidation of aniline has been carefully

investigated. Chromic acid converts it into quinone, while chlorates, in the presence of certain metallic salts (especially of vanadium), give aniline black. Hydrochloric acid and potassium chlorate give chloranil. Potassium permanganate oxidizes it in alkaline solution to azobenzene; Caro's acid, H_2SO_5, converts it into nitrosobenzene. Hypochlorous acid gives para-aminophenol and para-aminodiphenylamine (E. Bamberger). Bleaching powder gives a purple coloration.

See also Amines.

ANIMAL, in biology, any member of the kingdom Animalia, a group of living organisms distinguishable from plants (kingdom Plantae) on the basis of certain somewhat arbitrary differences, in morphology and physiology.

Until the discovery of the complexity of the cell and the series of investigations by which it was established that the cell was a fundamental structure essentially alike in both animals and plants (*see* Cell), there was a vague belief that plants, if they could really be regarded as animated creatures, exhibited at the most a lower grade of life. It is now known that insofar as life and living matter can be investigated by science, animals and plants cannot be described as being alive in different degrees. Animals and plants are extremely closely related, alike in their fundamental characters and each grading into organisms that possess some of the characters of both classes or kingdoms (*see* Protozoa).

The actual boundaries between animals and plants are artificial and are based solely on the ingenious analysis of the systematist. The most obvious distinction is that the animal cell wall is either absent or composed of a nitrogenous material, whereas the plant cell wall is composed of a carbohydrate material—cellulose.

The animal and the plant both require food to repair waste, to build up new tissue and to provide material which, by chemical change, may liberate the energy which appears in the processes of life. Both have the same general chemical composition, being made up of water, inorganic salts, carbohydrates, fats and proteins. Both animals and plants take their water and inorganic salts directly as such. The animal cell can absorb its carbohydrate and protein food only in the form of complex organic substances; it is dependent, in fact, on the pre-existence of these organic substances, themselves the products of living matter, and in this respect the animal is essentially a parasite on existing animal and plant life. The plant, on the other hand, if it is green (that is, containing chlorophyll) is capable, in the presence of light, of building up both carbohydrate material and protein material from inorganic salts; if it is a fungus (devoid of chlorophyll) it is dependent on pre-existing carbohydrate material and is also capable of absorbing, as an animal, protein material. (*See* Plants and Plant Science.)

On these basic differences are founded most of the characters which make the higher forms of animal and plant life so different. The animal body, if composed of many cells, follows a different architectural plan; the compact nature of its food and the relative elasticity of its cell walls, result in a structure, of more or less limited growth, consisting essentially of tubular or spherical masses of cells arranged concentrically round the food cavity. The relatively rigid nature of the plant cell wall and the attenuated inorganic food supply of plants make possible and necessary an unlimited form of growth in which the greatest surface is exposed to the exterior, and thus the plant body is composed of flattened blades and elongated branching growths.

The distinctions between animals and plants are in fact obviously secondary and adaptive and point clearly toward the conception of a common origin for the two forms of life, a conception which is made still more probable by the existence of many low forms, the protists—bacteria, protozoans, slime molds, etc.—in which the primary differences between animals and plants fade out.

An exact definition, delimiting all animals from all plants, is therefore impossible. In general, however, an animal is a living organism that is incapable of synthesizing carbohydrates and proteins from inorganic or simple organic substances, but must ingest them in complex form as food.

In general, also, animals are distinguished from plants by freedom of spatial movement.

For the classification of the animal kingdom, *see* Zoology.

See also references under "Animal" in the Index.

ANIMAL BEHAVIOUR, refers, generally speaking, to the action of an animal with reference to its entire repertory of behaviour and to its interaction with living and nonliving things. A given behaviour pattern may start in response to some external change or it may be initiated by internal stimuli, the nature of which escapes analysis. Behaviour is an aspect of response physiology, as contrasted with developmental, maintenance or toleration physiology. It is extremely hard to draw definite lines between these phases of physiology. The spinning of a cocoon by a moth involves complex behaviour patterns but is not greatly different in original stimulus or in end result from the hardening of the hypodermis to form the bare outer covering of the pupating butterfly.

It is difficult to observe animal behaviour without trying to understand its meaning and without trying to correlate the observed action with similar activities shown by other animals lower or higher in the evolutionary scale, particularly with the behaviour of man. Many students also attempt to puzzle out the complicated stimulus-response processes that are involved. Close study usually reveals a complex situation with many variables and leads directly to some of the most fundamental biological and philosophical problems. These include traditionally the problems associated with mechanism *versus* vitalism in biology; the extent to which nonhuman animals have what in man is called consciousness and mind; and much of the controversy about whether purpose exists in nature. (*See* also Mechanism; Teleology.)

Plants as well as animals show behaviour responses of many kinds. Some turn toward the sun; others give so-called sleep movements at night; and certain forms actively catch insect prey. Plant actions are usually so slow that they escape observation, yet viewed with the help of a motion-picture film made from time-lapse exposures, the self-propelled activity of plants rooted in the wind-free forest floor are quite evident. The leaflet-folding of sensitive mimosas is easily seen, and algal swarm spores swim across a microscope field as actively as do protozoans. The behaviour of plants is closely related to that of animals in many fundamentals, even though movements in higher plants are usually produced by changes in turgor or by growth responses. (*See* Tropism; Plants and Plant Science.)

Nonliving things also show varied behaviour patterns. The activity of electrons, ions, atoms, molecules, colloidal particles, the earth's crust, the planets and their satellites, the sun and other stars and galaxies of stars is as truly behaviour in the broad sense as is the flight of a bee or the tantrum of a child. One of the great problems is the extent to which the behaviour of living things is basically like that of nonliving nature. Those who believe that this unity will ultimately be demonstrated are called mechanists. This is the working hypothesis of students of experimental behaviour of lower organisms and other phases of experimental biology. In contrast, vitalists hold that a distinctively new vital principle or force is involved in the behaviour of living things. This fundamental problem is by no means solved.

Animal behaviour is not limited to that shown by the individual. Organisms are frequently integrated into more or less social communities that themselves behave as units of a higher order. Under such conditions animals give both individual and group responses. A further discussion of such matters will be found in the article Sociology, Animal.

Animal behaviour, as a part of biology, cuts across many boundaries. It is, of course, an integral part of psychology, of ecology and of the general and comparative phases of physiology, as well as of sociology. It draws from the lore and methods of all these fields and is used as a tool in the solution of problems in the four disciplines just mentioned.

Although it is difficult to give a definite outline of the subject matter usually treated under the heading of animal behaviour, there are at least four broad categories which will be discussed here.

1. The first of these deals with the sensory capacities of animals —the way in which organisms perceive the world around them. This has long been a fascinating subject for experimentalists in the various disciplines involved in animal behaviour. The sensory physiologist particularly has made many investigations of the colour vision of various animals, the limits of auditory behaviour, etc. (*See* also Hearing; Vision.)

2. A second area which has been explored is that of orientation, which deals not only with the primary orientation of animals—*i.e.*, the posture or attitude an organism takes in relation to its environment—but also with the way in which they find their way about. An example of the latter would of course be such behaviour as homing and migration (*see* Migration, Animal), which still remain one of the greatest riddles of animal behaviour.

3. A third category is that of innate behaviour patterns, which may be considered the heart of the study of animal behaviour. It was long a subject of controversy and reached a rather sterile plateau by the turn of the 20th century, when most of the work dealing with instinctive behaviour consisted largely of categorizing and pigeonholing various behaviour patterns. The trend, fortunately, has since changed and real attempts at analysis of instinctive behaviour have been made, particularly by the European ethologists.

4. The last of the general areas of investigation is that of learned behaviour. This has long been the province of the comparative or animal psychologist and in most instances has dealt with a determination of the learning ability of various species in the phylogenetic scale. The psychologist has sought, in particular, to rank animals in relation to their intelligence by attempting to use universal tests. The outstanding one of these tests has certainly been that utilizing the maze, an apparatus that has been responsible for thousands of papers. The animals that have been used for such experiments complete the entire phylogenetic range. Yet there is little that can be said about the intelligence of an animal on the basis of such maze-learning experiments, because the normal behaviour of the organism may lend itself very well to maze-learning behaviour and still give little index of the intelligence which the test was intended to measure. For example, a rat learns a maze very quickly, while an ape or a monkey may have considerably more difficulty with this problem because its normal behaviour does not involve traversing dark alleyways.

Below are discussed in more detail some representative examples of these broad categories of animal behaviour.

This article is divided into the following sections:

I. History
II. Problems of Animal Behaviour Study
   A. Methods
   B. Sensory Capacities of Animals
   C. Physicochemical Principles Applicable to Behaviour
III. Animal Behaviour Patterns
   A. Inherited Behaviour
   B. Instinctive and Learned Behaviour
   C. Conditioned or Learned Behaviour

I. HISTORY

Aristotle recorded a somewhat systematic account of the behaviour of many kinds of animals and exerted an influence on this phase of biology that was hardly equaled until the time of Charles Darwin. Well into the period after 1859, the men who contributed to knowledge concerning animal behaviour were, like Aristotle and Darwin, also prominent in other fields. The list includes Pliny the Elder and Plutarch, who, like other Romans, had a rather high opinion of animal intelligence. Thomas Aquinas and René Descartes separated man sharply from even the higher nonhuman animals. Konrad von Gesner (1516–65) helped in the revival of the spirit of inquiry of the classical Greeks. R. A. F. de Réaumur (1683–1757) worked actively with insects. Erasmus Darwin, Lamarck and Herbert Spencer were concerned, each in his own way, with the development of instinct and intelligence in animals.

In the Greek period students asked: (1) Do animals have souls? (2) If so, do their souls continue to live after their bodies die? (3) Do animals reason? By way of comparison, the queries of the early post-Darwinian students of behaviour were: (1) Have animals sensation? (2) Have animals memory? (3) How are these and other animal activities related to those of man? (4) Do animals reason? Darwin himself entered this field of study, and his followers have been concerned with the problem of the ancestry of the human mind. G. J. Romanes, W. Preyer, J. Fabre, K. Groos, C. O. Whitman and E. G. and G. W. Peckham were among the outstanding students of behaviour during the early Darwinian period.

Modern experimentation in behaviour dates from the 1880s. Of the four pioneers in the movement, Sir John Lubbock and later C. Lloyd Morgan stemmed from the post-Darwinian tradition. Max Verworn and Jacques Loeb developed their ideas in part from the studies of the plant physiologists, who, unaffected by the controversy over the ancestry of man, had been actively studying growth and movement in plants since T. A. Knight in 1805 demonstrated the effect of gravity on the direction of growth of seedlings.

These four early experimentalists were alike in discounting the use of anecdotes as a tool in analyzing animal activities. They all attempted to describe behaviour in objective terms and without anthropomorphisms. They studied animal behaviour for its own sake, without regard to the mental evolution of man. Loeb and later Lloyd Morgan applied what may be called the general scientific principle of parsimony. In the words of C. L. Morgan: "In no case may we interpret an action as the outcome of the exercise of a higher psychical faculty if it can be interpreted as the outcome of one which stands lower in the psychological scale" (*An Introduction to Comparative Psychology*). All four men adopted, to some extent, physicochemical explanations of behaviour, Loeb much more than others.

The next advance came with the work of H. S. Jennings (1897 and after), who, like Verworn and Loeb, concentrated upon the behaviour of the lower organisms. Although in the early years of the 20th century there was a sharp conflict between the supporters of the tropism theory of Loeb and those who accepted the more complex trial-and-error explanations of Jennings, the observations of the two groups were largely complementary.

By 1896 C. B. Davenport in his *Experimental Morphology*, which covered a much wider field, could give extensive historical treatment to such topics as the following reactions and the stimuli to which they are responses: chemotaxis (chemicals), hydrotaxis (water), tonotaxis (sound), thigmotaxis (touch), stereotaxis (space), rheotaxis (water currents), geotaxis (gravity), electrotaxis or galvanotaxis (electric current), phototaxis (light) and thermotaxis (heat).

The experimentalists did not always remember that they should master the normal responses of animals before introducing experimental complications. The implied naturalistic emphasis introduces the questions that ecologists began asking in the decades just before and after 1900: (1) Do animals have definite reactions that enable them to find habitat niches that match their ecological tolerances? (2) Are animal responses adaptive? (3) Is a given behaviour pattern innate or conditioned (learned)?

Outstanding advances during the 20th century include I. P. Pavlov's demonstration of conditioned reflexes. In a simple, direct experiment Pavlov showed that a dog on which the sound of a bell produces no observable effect can be trained to secrete saliva when the bell rings. This is done by ringing a bell when food is presented. A hungry dog salivates in the presence of food. After sufficient training, the sound of the bell stimulates the salivary glands to activity even in the absence of food.

A second major advance came from G. E. Coghill's proof that behaviour patterns in the developing vertebrate embryo depend on the growth of detailed nervous connections. Coghill also showed that the embryo first gives broadly generalized responses like the flexure of the trunk or generalized limb movements; finer, more individualized patterns develop later. Another set of recent advances came from the demonstration of the existence and effectiveness of neurohumoral substances and of the control of much of behaviour by hormones in general. Pituitary and sex hormones are especially potent in initiating and regulating behaviour.

The third major advance in the field of animal behaviour stems from the work of ethologists, a term that means, roughly, students of the objective behaviour of organisms. Konrad Lorenz, in 1935,

published a paper on social behaviour and early-experience effects in birds. This led to a development of behaviour study by workers such as N. Tinbergen, G. Baerends and others in which total life histories were observed and then behaviour was analyzed into component parts. The concepts of releaser (a simple stimulus which can result in a complex instinctive response) and "imprinting"—both discussed below—were developments of this group. Much of the modern work on animal behaviour comes from this group.

II. PROBLEMS OF ANIMAL BEHAVIOUR STUDY

There is a fundamental difficulty in the study of animal behaviour due to the inability of animals to convey to the student their perceptions or experiences. This is particularly true in the area of sensory processes, where it often is necessary to use devious means to determine what a particular animal can hear or see. Examples of methods in this area therefore may be discussed as representative for other types of behaviour.

A. Methods

There are four basic methods which can be used as testing procedures to determine given sensory capacities in organisms: (1) measurement of the electrical activity of the neurons involved in the sensory systems, called action potentials; (2) neural extirpation or interruption—the elimination of certain pathways leading from sense organ to central nervous system; (3) measurement of learned responses to certain stimuli; and (4) measurement of innate, or unlearned, responses.

Measurement of Action Potentials.—A major advantage of action-potential investigation is the fact that sensory processes can be measured directly. However, caution must certainly be used when evaluating experimental results obtained with this method. It is possible to record action potentials in neurons leading from sensory receptors that indicate a stimulus discrimination with the animal giving no behavioural evidence of such discrimination. Investigation by the microelectrode technique of colour receptors in the retinas of cats shows well-defined peaks of colour sensitivity, yet there is no evidence that colour vision plays a role in the behaviour of the cat. In other words, it appears that an animal may sometimes possess the requisite for discrimination of certain stimuli peripherally—that is, at the retinal level—without being able to make use of the information centrally, in the brain.

Neural Extirpation or Interruption.—In order to test a hypothesis of sensory physiology it is sometimes necessary to remove a part of the central nervous system or to sever a neural pathway. This method, obviously, seldom gives sufficient information by itself; it is usually supplemented by one of the two methods described below.

Measurement of Learned Responses.—This is the commonest method for determining sensory processes and capacities in organisms. The method may be adapted in a variety of ways. The classical conditioning procedure uses a natural (unconditioned) stimulus, such as food, to produce a natural (unconditioned) response, such as salivation. A neutral (conditionable) stimulus, such as a tone signal, is presented immediately prior to the natural stimulus. In this example, if the animal learns to salivate to the tone signal as it precedes the food, then it is possible to say that the particular tone used lies within the boundaries of the animal's discrimination. Many kinds of sensory discrimination have been tested in this manner.

Another variation on the same method is the one customarily called instrumental conditioning, where an animal has to act on the basis of a signal or cue to be rewarded or to escape punishment. The trend is away from the use of the discrimination apparatus in which the animal must move a certain distance to reach a goal; more popular is the Skinner-box type of discrimination apparatus, in which the animal may do nothing more than press an appropriate lever when the correct stimulus is presented. Failure to perform correctly in the learned-response method is sometimes taken as evidence that discrimination is lacking, but predictions based on such negative results are often unwarranted and sometimes incorrect. The animal may actually possess the discrimination ability but cannot show the ability by its behaviour because the experimenter has chosen to condition a response that may for some reason conflict with the animal's normal behaviour pattern.

Measurement of Innate or Unlearned Responses.—One of the advantages of this method is the ease with which experiments are usually performed, with respect to both experimental apparatus and time required. Another advantage is the greater probability of working within the actual response repertory of the animal. A common example of this method is the optokinetic response obtainable in most seeing animals when a field with some sort of articulation (*e.g.*, vertical stripes) is moved past the eyes of the animal. Usually if the animal can perceive the changes in the visual field, movements of the eye, the head or the whole body may be observed. With this technique, visual acuity, brightness discrimination, colour sensitivity and other visual phenomena have been explored.

B. Sensory Capacities of Animals

Man is the only animal whose behaviour can be described with even approximate completeness, since he is the only one for which objective behaviour observations may be supplemented by subjective knowledge gained personally or by communication with others. The experimenter or observer cannot learn by direct experience what animals of other species see, feel or otherwise sense; he can only find the stimuli to which they react and their methods of reacting. Using all available avenues of approach—observation, physical analysis of the environment, controlled experiments including discriminatory learning when possible—it has been found that many animals live in a sensory world different from that of human beings.

Much of the activity of ants indicates that within their dark nests, and outside for the blind species, ants live in a world of odour shapes somewhat as man lives primarily in a world of light and shade or of colour shapes. For many animals, smell is an important sense; it is blunted in man. Male moths of several species can find appropriate females though the latter may be over a mile away. The physics of the situation is little short of astounding, considering how scarce the minute odour-bearing particles must be, and yet the male is able not only to detect them but also to follow the very low intensity gradient that leads him to their source.

Dogs can be trained to react to a Galton whistle pitched so high that it is inaudible to man. Bats emit and react to supersonic vibrations of the order of 45,000–50,000 cycles per second. Man's hearing stops at about 20,000 cycles per second. Bats avoid obstacles in total darkness apparently by reacting to the radarlike reflections of the supersonic waves they have emitted.

As compared with man, the arthropods, as a rule, are relatively unresponsive to the red end of the spectrum. K. von Frisch failed in attempts to train honeybees to react to red paper when mixed with a series of grays and covered by clean glass; he could train them to find sugar water on the other spectral colours when similarly interspersed among shades of gray. The available experimental evidence indicates that the honeybee reacts to a spectrum of from 2,700–6,770 Å, extending from the ultraviolet region into the red, though hesitatingly at the red end. *Drosophila*, the common fruit fly, reacts to the range of wave lengths from 2,350 Å in the ultraviolet to about 5,780 Å in the yellow. The span to which some vertebrates respond, given in Angstrom units, is: *Phoxinus*, a fish, 3,400–8,000 (near ultraviolet to infrared); the common hen, 5,000–7,000 (green into red); adult man in daylight, 4,000–7,700 (violet through red).

A number of insects and other arthropods have been shown to be sensitive to ultraviolet radiation. Both *Drosophila* and the honeybee appear to find their highest luminosity values of light in short-wave lengths to which man is totally blind. *Trigona*, a stingless bee from the American tropics, has been trained to react to an ultraviolet pattern.

Enough has been said, perhaps, to document the general principle that it cannot be assumed that other animals, even other mammals, have the same sensory abilities and limitations found in man. One of the problems in comparative animal behaviour is to describe with all the accuracy possible the sensory field of representatives of all the major animal phyla and of the minor ones, too, when they are particularly interesting, either for functional or for evolutionary reasons.

C. Physicochemical Principles Applicable to Behaviour

The physiology of animal behaviour is very complex. Among the factors to be considered are: (1) the present external environment; (2) environments of the recent and sometimes of the more remote past; (3) the present physiological state; (4) recent physiological states and sometimes those of the more remote past; (5) the processes involved in the resolution of one physiological state into another; (6) the physiology and anatomy of the given animal, especially (7) of the sense organs (receptors), nerves or hormonal conductors (conductors), the central nervous system (adjustor) and the different kinds of effectors.

Considering its complexity, it is impressive to find the extent to which physicochemical principles (the "natural laws" of the older literature) apply in animal behaviour. The following incomplete list is long enough to make the point.

1. Most activities increase in speed with an increase in temperature between the threshold and the optimum points. The formula of Arrhenius and the Van't Hoff coefficient, devised from chemical considerations, holds in many instances.

2. With light, intensity varies inversely as the square of the distance. Animal reactions that are affected by light intensity clearly show the effect of this inverse-square relationship.

3. With light, the product of the strength of the stimulus and the length of time it operates, if constant, give constant results (Bunsen-Roscoe law).

4. The intensity of illumination of a surface element varies with the cosine of the angle of incidence (the cosine law of illumination).

5. Within the same modality and with constant experimental conditions, the ratio between two stimulus magnitudes that are correctly discriminated, in any intermediate proportion of the attempts, is a constant (Weber's law). As several others, this principle does not hold for relatively low or high magnitudes.

6. The stimulating effect of intermittent light equals that of a constant light if both emit the same amount of energy and if the interval between flashes is not too great (Talbot's law).

There is space to record only one illustration. *Limulus*, the horseshoe crab, is a photonegative animal. When it is exposed to light from two sources the animal swings to an orientation between the two beams. This orientation is independent of intensity (I) and of duration (D) of the light stimulus providing $I \times D$ of one equals $I \times D$ of the other. Under these conditions *Limulus* orients away from the lights and along a line equidistant from both. Given a situation in which $I \times D$ of one differs from $I \times D$ of the other light, the orientation shifts until $ID \times$ cosine-of-angle-of-incidence of one eye equals the product of similar values for the other eye. The reaction illustrates tropotactic behaviour.

In one of the original experiments, 38 individuals tested gave fairly diagrammatic responses; 10 did not. This serves to introduce a final principle of behaviour: At all levels of the animal kingdom, different individuals of the same kind show distinctly individualistic responses. Despite the remarkable extent to which many animals exhibit complex behaviour patterns that accord with physicochemical principles worked out for nonliving systems, the fact remains that under carefully controlled experimental conditions, animals often react in an unpredictable fashion. This means that even the best analyses of behaviour are incomplete. Such a situation is a cause for neither reproach nor defeatism, rather a stimulus to further study.

III. ANIMAL BEHAVIOUR PATTERNS

A. Inherited Behaviour

Inherited behaviour patterns may be divided into four classes: (1) unorganized or poorly organized responses; (2) reflexes proper; (3) reflexlike activities of entire organisms; (4) instincts.

Unorganized Responses.—Unorganized or poorly organized responses are those given by early embryos or by animals such as sponges that have no nervous systems.

Reflexes.—Reflexes proper, or reflex-arc movements, are those usually described, such as the immediate jerking away of the hand on touching a hot stove.

Reflexlike Activities of Entire Organisms.—These may be

unoriented or oriented.

Unoriented.—These include kineses—undirected speeding or slowing of the rate of locomotion or frequency of change from rest to movement (orthokinesis) or of frequency or amount of turning of the whole animal (klinokinesis; the avoiding or trial-and-error reaction of Jennings), the speed or frequency depending on the intensity of stimulation. Examples of orthokinesis are seen in lampreys, which are more active in high intensities of light, and cockroaches, which are more active in low intensities; flatworms and many fly larvae, among others, show orthokinesis. Klinokinesis is well demonstrated by *Paramecium.*

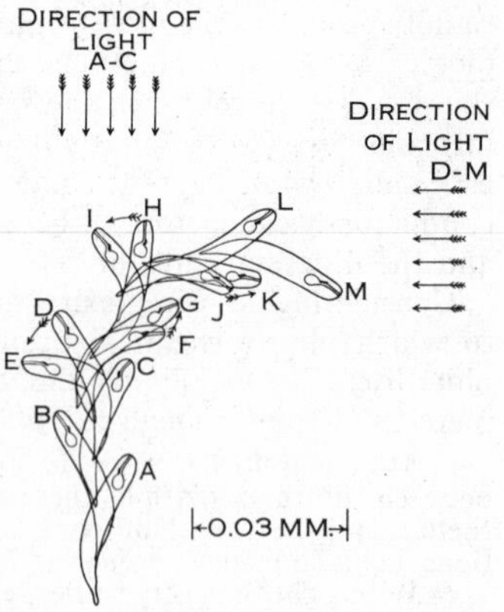

Oriented.—Among these activities may be included tropisms, taxes and orientations at an angle. Tropisms are those directed growth-curvature movements or other oriented reactions of sessile plants and sessile animals leading to equal intensities of stimulation of symmetrically placed parts of the body. They are shown by many plants and by hydroid animals such as *Eudendrium.*

Taxes may be described as oriented locomotory reactions of motile organisms. They exist in purest form as oriented, forced movements; that is, as reflex actions of entire organisms. When exposed to a single source of stimulation, the body is oriented in line with the source. Movement toward the source is said to be positive; that away from it is negative.

1. Klinotaxis is the achievement of orientation by interruption of regularly alternated lateral deviations of part or all of the body; there seems to be a comparison of intensities of stimulation that are successive in time. Klinotaxis is shown by animals with a single intensity receptor, such as fly larvae, *Euglena* and earthworms (*see* fig. 1).

2. In tropotaxis, attainment of orientation is direct, resulting from turning toward the less (negative) or more (positive) stimulated side as simultaneous, automatic comparisons of intensities on two sides of the body are made. No deviations (trial movements) are required. Tropotaxis is shown by animals with paired intensity receptors. If exposed to stimulation from two sources, orientation is to some intermediate point and is determined by the relative intensity of the sources. If one receptor is effectively covered, the animal goes around and around in spirals (circus movement). The locomotory reactions that Jacques Loeb called tropisms belong in this category. Tropotaxis is shown by many arthropods, especially insects. The reaction of *Notonecta,* the common back swimmer, to light is a good example.

3. In telotaxis, known only for responses to light, attainment of orientation is direct and again without apparent trial movements. When between lights from two sources, the animal orients to one

DIRECTION OF LIGHT
A-C

DIRECTION OF LIGHT
D-M

|-0.03 MM.-|

FROM S. O. MAST, "LIGHT AND BEHAVIOR OF ORGANISMS" (JOHN WILEY AND SONS, INC.)

FIG. 1.—EUGLENA, IN A CRAWLING STATE, SHOWING DETAILS IN THE PROCESS OF KLINOTACTIC ORIENTATION

light, not to some intermediate point. The animal switches orientation from one source to the other at unpredictable intervals and consequently follows a zigzag course. The response is given to the source as though it were a goal. Bilateral balance is not necessary, and circus movements, if given, demonstrate that the animal is reacting tropotactically rather than telotactically. Honeybees (*Apis*) and hermit crabs (*Eupagurus*), among others, show telotaxis.

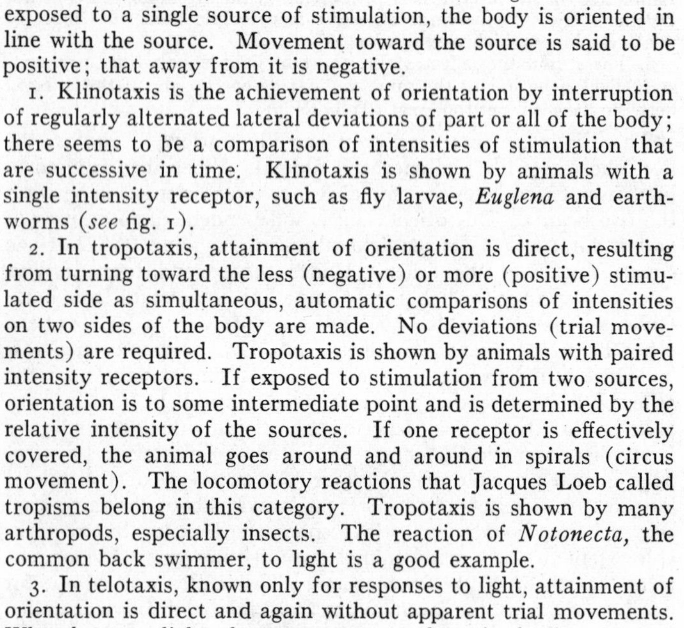

Orientations at an angle (transverse orientations) may or may not be accompanied by locomotion. They include:

1. The light-compass reaction, much given by foraging insects such as ants and bees that return to a fixed nest. The general principles involved are illustrated in fig. 2, in which an ant returning to nest at N, along a path approximately at right angles to the sun's rays, was covered over for 2.5 hours. On release the ant proceeded not toward the nest but at right angles to the rays of the late afternoon sun.

2. Dorsal (or ventral) transverse reaction is demonstrated when the impact of the stimulus is kept at right angles to both longitudinal and transverse axes of the body. Locomotion need not occur. This reaction is given to light by various aquatic crustaceans such as *Argulus,* the fish louse, and *Artemia,* the brine shrimp, and is given to gravity by crayfish.

Instincts.—Instinctive behaviour represents the most complicated of the inherited, unlearned behaviour patterns. Instincts are set off from kineses, tropisms and taxes by their greater intricacy. An instinct is a relatively complex activity of an animal that is acting (1) as a whole rather than by parts; (2) as the representative of a species rather than as an individual; (3) without previous experience or without modification caused by experience; and (4) with an end or purpose of which the reacting animal has no knowledge. Care must be taken to avoid confusion with early conditioned behaviour patterns. The difficulty is the greater since exhibition of instincts may be deferred pending the achievement of appropriate states of development. The lack of previous experience or of modification caused by experience before approximately perfect performance is crucial evidence of the action's being instinctive. Mating, nest building and rearing of new brood by a female ant are performed by instinct.

In view of the trend to dismiss instinctive or unlearned behaviour as an unknown and unlikely quantity, it is well to examine in some detail one example. Warblers, spring and summer residents of northern Europe, migrate during September and October to various parts of Africa, and in early spring fly back to their original points of departure. Some migrate over thousands of miles, from Scandinavia to southern Africa. This migration is accomplished by the birds individually; the warblers do not navigate in groups. Somehow the warblers know how to set their course, and this knowledge is not learned because young birds making their first migration reach their goal as surely as do experienced birds.

It has been proved that warblers can orient by the sun, but since these birds fly mainly at night, the question arises, do the warblers navigate by the stars? A systematic study of this question was made, over a period of several years, by means of specially designed cages in an aviary at Freiburg, Ger. It had already been observed that warblers hatched and raised in closed, soundproof chambers, under the illusion of constant summer, would nevertheless become restless during the nights of the year when they would normally be migrating.

To explore the question of orientation, warblers were placed in cages with glass tops so that they could see the sky but nothing else of their surroundings. At the seasons of migration the birds would begin to flutter about the cages and, like compass needles, take up positions pointing in particular directions. The direction in each case was characteristic of the particular species, depending on where the birds of each species migrated. When the stars were hidden by thick clouds, or when the skies were in diffuse light, the birds became disoriented. Birds were placed in a test cage in a planetarium. When the dome was illuminated with diffuse light, the birds would not choose any particular direction, but when the planetarium sky matched the night sky over Germany the

5ʰ 9′ P.M.
2ʰ 39′ P.M.
SUN
SUN
37½°
37°
N E W S
N

O 1 2 3 M.

ADAPTED FROM G. S. FRAENKEL AND D. L. GUNN, "THE ORIENTATION OF ANIMALS" (CLARENDON PRESS, OXFORD), AFTER BRUN, 1914

FIG. 2.—THE LIGHT-COMPASS REACTION GIVEN BY AN ANT

birds took up the proper direction as if seeing the natural sky.

By changing the positions of the planetarium stars, the birds could be made to change their positions and directions of flight. In one experiment with a lesser whitethroat warbler, which normally flies southeast across the Balkans and then turns due south, various positions of the planetarium sky were shown and the flight directions of the bird were observed. Under the approximate latitude of Germany, the warbler faced southeast. But as the sky was shifted, simulating more southerly latitudes, the bird turned more and more in a southern direction. When the longitude was changed to a position corresponding to a point near Lake Balkhash in Siberia, the bird hesitated for a minute and then changed its direction to the west; in natural circumstances, this would mean that the bird was returning to its take-off point in Germany. As the displacement was reduced, the bird shifted its direction gradually toward the south and when the sky again showed the placement of stars for Freiburg at that time of year, the warbler took up the normal southeasterly direction of flight.

This behaviour, confirmed by experiments with other birds, proves that the warblers have a hereditary mechanism for orienting themselves by the stars—an image of the star patterns in the sky coupled with a time sense relating the constellations to the geography of the earth at every time and season.

But what about getting at some of the real underlying mechanisms? Actually, most of the older investigators were willing to discover some such behaviour, call it instinct and then go on with something else. Modern psychology, however, cannot be satisfied by such a mere naming process. For this reason much work in this area of behaviour deals with attempts at finding physiological explanations for instinct. Migration, food hoarding, maternal and sexual behaviour have been studied with this end in view. The direction in which psychologists try to go is something like this: Birds brood their eggs not because of some mystical maternal instinct but because physiological changes occur during the nesting season which cause engorging of the blood capillaries in the breast of the bird. In order to keep this part of the body cool, the bird covers the eggs. Similarly, the eggs are turned because one part of the egg soon gets warm. This would be a fine way of accomplishing the necessary warming and turning of the eggs, but the answer is not always so simple. Nor is this one by any means complete. There are many unanswered parts—why the bird does not merely find some cool stones to brood, or why some birds sit only on their own eggs while others will accept the eggs of almost any bird, and so on.

Another group of students of behaviour believes that the problem of instinct can be approached by analysis of perception and behaviour. Although much more progress needs to be made, something can be said about what is known and what is suspected. A brief sketch of this work follows.

In the 1930s Lorenz suggested that instinctive behaviour is really a complex of several types of activity. Reflexes, taxes and instinctive movements make up the total pattern. The first two processes have been mentioned. The last-named Lorenz considers to be species-specific and always carried out in the same way. These movements are strictly inherited and characteristic of the species.

In most instances it is difficult to isolate and identify the individual behaviour components, but it has been done in certain cases. In these, instinctive movements and taxes were found to be the most important parts of the instinctive behaviour pattern. The instinctive movements themselves are relatively inaccurate and gross; taxes serve to refine them and make them more exact. For example, flies ordinarily clean their wings by passing their hind legs over and under the wings, meanwhile making small scrubbing movements. The gross movements of moving the legs back and forth in the area of the wings are instinctive. The finer scrubbing movements are taxes. To show this it is necessary only to remove the wings from the fly. It will then still attempt to clean its wings periodically and will move its legs in the direction where the wings were; the smaller taxic responses, however, will be missing. This is the key to the major differences between these two components of instinctive behaviour: Instinctive movements are

triggered off by some stimulus situation, but once started can continue to completion. Taxic responses, on the other hand, need continual stimulation and are therefore steered, rather than triggered, by some stimulus.

It is in the nature of this triggering of an instinctive response that the concept of the releaser has been developed. In the lives of most organisms there are types of unlearned behaviour that seem to be set off by extremely simple stimulus situations. In male sticklebacks, for example, the colour red is the releaser of an attack response. During the breeding season all male fish of this species develop bright red bellies. At that time they also drive away from the nesting area any intruding males. This simple stimulus of colour seems to be the key to the attack response. By making all kinds of models and presenting them to male sticklebacks, it can be shown that little else matters but the fact that the model has a red belly. This method of making models which serve as stimuli and then eliminating and adding certain characteristics is peculiar to those investigators who work with instinctive behaviour. In this way the perceptual aspect of behaviour can be analyzed in terms of the necessary stimulus components which result in a response. Most of the data collected by these investigators have been products of this method.

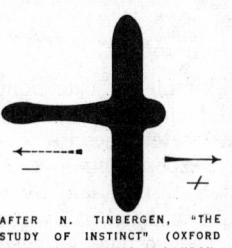

FIG. 3.—MODEL OF BIRD OF PREY, RELEASING NO ESCAPE REACTIONS WHEN SAILED TO THE LEFT, BUT RELEASING ESCAPE REACTIONS WHEN SAILED TO THE RIGHT

The releaser, however, may be somewhat more complex. It may involve relationships. Fig. 3 shows a bird silhouette. If it is moved overhead in the direction indicated by the arrow on the right, most young game birds will respond with fright reactions. Moved in the opposite direction it does not cause these responses. Apparently, when moved in the former direction it resembles a short-necked bird of prey (hawk) and is responded to in the appropriate manner. Moving in the opposite direction it appears to be merely a long-necked waterfowl and is ignored. The response in this case has been shown to be unlearned and may therefore be considered an instinctive movement.

One other aspect of instinctive movements, also differentiating these reactions from taxes and reflexes, is important. The longer the experimenter waits to elicit a particular instinctive response, the easier it is to set off. For example, in using models to set off the attack response in the stickleback, a model with only a suggestion of red colour will be enough to initiate the attack in a fish that has been undisturbed for some time. If, however, the response is elicited several times in succession then a more adequate colouring becomes necessary. This has been found in all cases where releasers and their appropriate reactions have been observed. In those cases where instinctive movements are involved, Lorenz thinks that this fluctuation of stimulus value is due to the essential accumulation of specific energy for an instinctive movement. When the level of energy is high because the response has not been made for some time, the stimulus need not be so accurately representative of the ideal one. The response, in fact, may go off without apparent stimulation, in a process called vacuum activity. If the energy level is low, because of repeated stimulation, then the releaser must resemble the normal one more accurately.

By using the method of isola-

FIG. 4.—HUMAN BABY AND THREE SUBSTITUTES (LEFT) PRESENTING SIGN STIMULI THAT RELEASE PARENTAL REACTIONS IN MAN, AS COMPARED WITH ADULT MAN AND THREE ADULT ANIMALS (RIGHT) WHICH DO NOT RELEASE PARENTAL REACTIONS

tion (*i.e.*, keeping an animal away from species members during its entire life), many of the data in this field have been collected. Because of its comparative newness much remains to be done, but the direction is clear. Problems in research methods make work on humans along this line difficult, but one example can be shown: the feeling for "babyishness" that most people have. If subjects are shown a number of pictures such as those in fig. 4 and asked which one of each pair they like better or think "cuter," most of them invariably choose the pictures in the column at the left. Lorenz thinks that this too is an example of a releaser, and, specifically, one working at the human level. Other examples of such releasers working in human behaviour are under investigation. (*See* also INSTINCT.)

B. INSTINCTIVE AND LEARNED BEHAVIOUR

The phenomenon of imprinting is an example of behaviour primarily learned, though formerly thought to be instinctive, by which an early experience of a young animal determines its consequent social behaviour. In one of the first experiments investigating this process, Lorenz divided a clutch of eggs laid by a graylag goose into two groups. One group was hatched by the goose, the other was incubator hatched. The goslings hatched by the goose followed it as soon as they could walk; the incubator-hatched offspring, however, were exposed not to the goose but to Lorenz, whom they then followed about as the other group followed the goose. This phenomenon has been observed in animals capable of locomotion shortly after birth.

In a series of experiments investigating this phenomenon, mallard ducklings were imprinted and tested in an apparatus consisting of a circular runway with walls of transparent plastic. The imprinting object was a male mallard decoy, suspended from a motor-driven arm pivoted at the centre of the apparatus. The imprinting was accomplished by placing a visually naïve duckling in the runway about a foot away from the decoy. A loudspeaker in the decoy emitted a recording of a human rendition of the sound "Gock, gock, gock, gock," and after a short interval was moved around the runway. The imprinting period usually lasted 10 minutes. Ducklings were tested for imprinting by placing each one in the apparatus between a male and female decoy and recording the choice of the animal.

To determine the age at which an imprinting exercise was most effective, ducklings were imprinted at various ages after hatching and tested for strength of imprinting. It was found that there is a critical age during which the animals are most strongly imprinted. Some imprinting can occur immediately after hatching, but the maximum score was made by those ducklings exposed to the decoy between 13 and 16 hours after hatching.

It was also found that the strength of imprinting (I) is dependent on the amount of effort (E) exerted by the young animal in following the imprinting object. Groups of ducklings were exposed to the model for the same length of time but were made to follow it for various distances. Up to distances of 50 ft., the strength of imprinting increases with the distance followed. There were no significant differences in the scores of ducklings which had followed the same distance but for different lengths of time. Ducklings were made to climb over four-inch hurdles and to follow the decoy up an inclined plane. The birds which had to climb hurdles or the inclined plane made higher imprinting scores than those which traveled the same distance without obstacles. It was found that the strength of imprinting equals the logarithm of the effort expended by the animal during the imprinting period; *i.e.*, $I = \log E$.

Thus, although learning seems to account almost entirely for imprinting, it is still necessary for some innate reaction to lead to the response of following in the first place, since if the animal does not follow it will not imprint.

The distinction between learned and unlearned behaviour is not so clear-cut as might appear. Instinctive elements enter into intelligent activities, and behaviour patterns that are primarily instinctive do not usually run their course automatically. Often they contain a variable element that is more or less adapted to the particular situation, in addition to the fixed, inherited aspects.

An act A is at one and the same time often a function of a constant C and a variable V; expressed as a formula it reads $A = f(C,V)$. In simplest cases the constant element is unlearned and the variable is either learned or is related to learned behaviour.

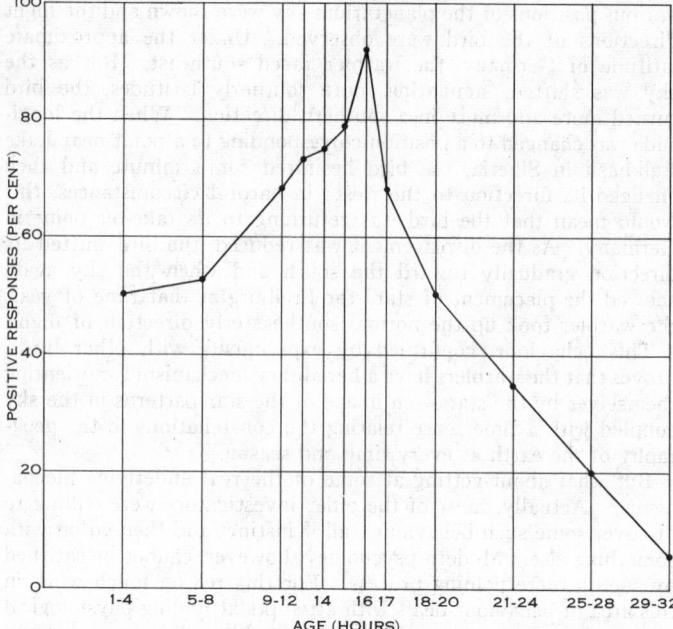

AFTER E. H. HESS, "IMPRINTING IN ANIMALS," IN "SCIENTIFIC AMERICAN" (MARCH 1958)

FIG. 5.—CRITICAL AGE AT WHICH DUCKLINGS ARE MOST STRONGLY IMPRINTED IS REFLECTED BY THIS CURVE
Each black dot on the curve is the average test score of the ducklings imprinted at that age

This analysis of action A into these two components is an abstract one. V and C do not represent more or less antagonistic agencies pushing the animal now in this direction, now in that, as they impinge on one another; they are rather two different phases of one whole. In instinctive reactions, C is greater than V, often very much greater; in intelligent behaviour, relations are reversed and V is greater than C.

The nest building of birds provides an interesting test case. The variable element appears in the way in which the individual bird sets about finding a suitable location and then by means of co-ordinated body movements collects available appropriate materials and weaves them into the structure of the nest. The general nest pattern is unlearned; it is representative of the genus or species rather than of the individual. On the other hand, older birds frequently weave more skillfully than do beginners. Nest building of birds thus is neither purely an automatic, inherited reaction nor purely learned behaviour. Both C and V are involved.

The complex activities of other animals, man included, similarly contain both of these elements. In this may be found an answer to one of the questions of the early Darwinians: The behaviour of man differs in degree rather than in kind from that of other animals; the differences, though often very great, are quantitative rather than qualitative.

The recording of total life histories of animals is not new. Indeed it represents many of the earlier attempts to study the behaviour of animals and was particularly carried on by the natural scientists who were called naturalists. Information recorded in such life histories is useful, but in most instances it is not specific enough for the purposes of an analytically oriented science. The ethologists take a new approach to life histories, in which very careful observations are supplemented by laboratory studies in such a way that the developmental schedule of abilities—sensory and motor capacities—is included in an "ethogram." Typical examples of such ethograms are those dealing with several species of birds as well as some rodents and other mammals. In these the kind of material useful to the student of animal behaviour in setting up problems that require prior knowledge of the capacities of the organism is available for the first time. Some of these ethograms provide insights into the innate behaviour patterns that determine social behaviour in an animal, and the various releasers and answering behaviours which make up such complex behaviour patterns.

C. CONDITIONED OR LEARNED BEHAVIOUR

In contrast with preceding categories, conditioned or learned behaviour is predominantly acquired or strongly modified as a result of individual experience. The following broad categories can be recognized: conditioned reflexes, trial-and-error learning and insight.

Conditioned reflexes or autonomisms represent simple associative learning. The unconditioned stimulus (presentation of food to dog) determines the response (secretion of saliva). The conditioned stimulus (ringing of bell), at first in contiguity with the unconditioned stimulus, at length elicits the response when acting alone. As soon as the conditioned stimulus begins to be effective, further improvement comes from trial-and-error learning. Conditioned reflexes are exemplified by the substitution of the sound of a bell for the sight of food to stimulate salivation. Conditioned autonomisms are more complex and involve reactions of the entire organism.

Trial-and-error learning, or selective learning, is independent of a specific unconditioned stimulus; it involves reward and punishment as well as contiguity. The animal does not learn something wholly new; rather a response, often a random response, is selected as a result of reward or punishment and becomes dominant. This kind of learning is shown under diverse problem situations in which the animal is not initially acquainted with all elements in the situation. In the 1960s interest was growing in the learning behaviour of animals in which the connections between the two brain hemispheres had been severed. Such split-brain animals learned as if they had two separate brains.

Insight is shown in those cases in which an animal that is accustomed to all elements in the situation taken separately finds them in new relations to each other. When typically exhibited, after the initial survey, the animal proceeds at once to make a smooth solution, or does so after a motionless pause. Reward speeds the performance (selective learning) and also repays the animal for displaying insight. An example is given with the aid

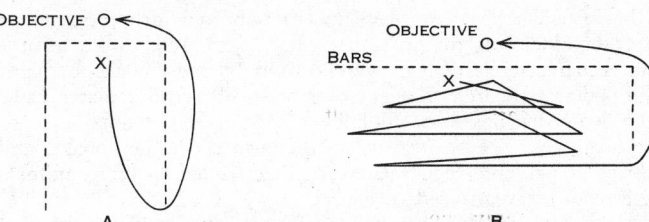

ADAPTED FROM WOLFGANG KÖHLER, "MENTALITY OF APES" (KEGAN PAUL, TRENCH, TRUBNER AND CO., LTD.)

FIG. 6.—(A) A SMOOTH SOLUTION AS GIVEN BY A DOG OR APE IN CONTRAST WITH (B) THE TRIAL-AND-ERROR BEHAVIOUR OF A HEN UNDER SIMILAR CONDITIONS

of fig. 6. A dog that has had the run of the surrounding yard is at X when he sees food being placed beyond the grill. His smooth solution of the situation is indicated by the curved line. A hen under similar conditions zigzags back and forth until she finds the solution by trial and error or until she ceases to react. These phases of learned behaviour and their general implications are discussed more fully in PSYCHOLOGY, COMPARATIVE.

See INSTINCT; PLAY, ANIMAL; SOCIOLOGY, ANIMAL; *see* also references under "Animal Behaviour" in the Index.

BIBLIOGRAPHY.—T. C. Barnes, *Textbook of General Physiology* (1937); C. M. Child, *Physiological Foundations of Behavior* (1924); G. S. Fraenkel and D. L. Gunn, *The Orientation of Animals* (1940); H. S. Jennings, *Behavior of the Lower Organisms* (1906); W. Köhler, *The Mentality of Apes* (1925); Jacques Loeb, *Forced Movements, Tropisms, and Animal Conduct* (1918); C. Lloyd Morgan, *Animal Behaviour* (1900); I. P. Pavlov, *Conditioned Reflexes* (1927); J. P. Scott, *Animal Behavior* (1958); W. H. Thorpe, *Learning and Instinct in Animals* (1956); N. Tinbergen, *The Study of Instinct* (1951); C. J. Warden, T. N. Jenkins and L. H. Warner, *Comparative Psychology*, 3 vol. (1935–40); R. M. Yerkes, *Chimpanzees* (1943).   (ED. H. H.)

ANIMAL BREEDING is based upon the mating of selected animals, usually livestock, for traits that man finds desirable aesthetically or economically. The science of genetics and knowledge of reproductive physiology are applied to improve animals by selecting the individuals that will produce the next generation and controlling how they will be mated. This article deals with the origin of breeds, the steps in selecting breeding stock, and the various methods of mating. The biologic factors involved in animal breeding are dealt with in GENETICS; HEREDITY; VARIATION; SELECTION; REPRODUCTION. The main breeds of various animals are described in the articles on the animals: CATTLE; HORSE; PIG; SHEEP; etc.

Improvement or favourable change in animals is brought about by changing the inheritance or the environment. Hereditary characteristics are those that arise from gene differences and account for common differences in animals as, for example, the white-face characteristic of Hereford cattle. Nonhereditary differences are mainly environmental; *e.g.*, animals poorly fed and managed will not develop to their maximum capacity. Environment, if markedly improved, can bring forth changes in animals with dramatic swiftness, but the changes continue only while the improved environment prevails. Changes in the hereditary make-up of a population are made slowly, but usually are fairly permanent. Some characteristics, however, revert to the original level when man withdraws his attention to selection.

Origin of Breeds.—Breeds were formed usually from small localized groups thought to be superior to the prevailing stock. Man began to isolate such groups to get a more desirable stock. Certain hereditary traits became characteristic of animals within an area, which tended to distinguish them from others of the same species. A type that met certain requirements in form or colour was accepted as a pattern and animals of that type were selected for breeding, with the result that animals exhibiting the desirable characteristics became more common.

As a breeder developed animals, he selected in his own herd what he thought was the best breeding stock for the next generation, supplementing it with stock from other sources. As the group improved, it became difficult to find stock outside for further improvement. It then became necessary to use more of the newly developed stock in the breeding program; consequently, inbreeding was not uncommon in the foundation of breeds.

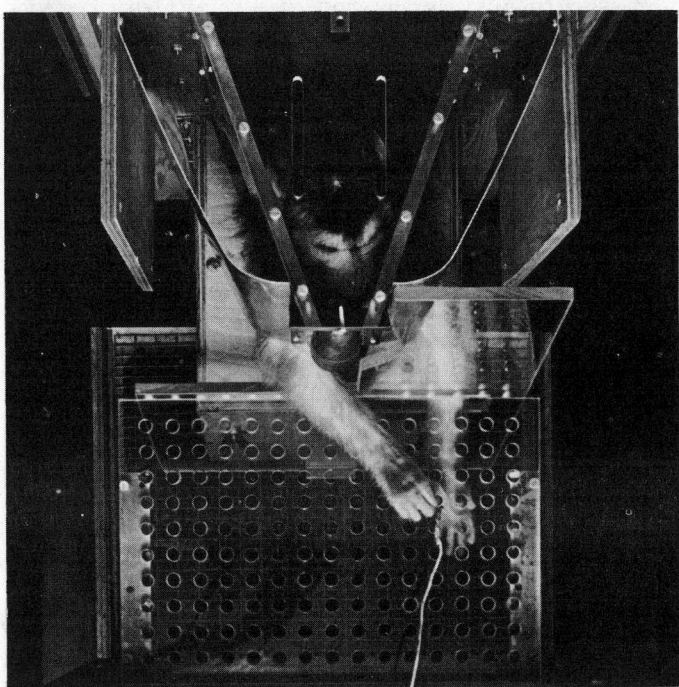

TODD WALKER

SPLIT-BRAIN MONKEY IN LEARNING APPARATUS (CONNECTIONS BETWEEN TWO HEMISPHERES OF THE BRAIN HAVE BEEN SEVERED); THE TWO HALVES OF THE BRAIN NOW LEARN INDEPENDENTLY OF EACH OTHER

The English began to develop the purebred idea for seed or breeding stock late in the 18th century. As breeds were formed and recognized, herdbooks were started by individuals to maintain pedigree records of selected animals. Breed organizations or record associations later took over control and maintenance of the pedigrees. These records were known as the herdbooks, and entries or pedigree registrations were restricted to those animals with record or registered ancestors.

As breeds were formed, standards were set mainly for the purpose of selling the breeding stock. The buyers of the stock demanded statements of breeding and also definite characteristics regarded as evidence of pure breeding. Thus, registration of pedigrees in herdbooks and description as to breed characteristics were stimulated. The term purebred, as used in the United States, refers to animals that are registered or are eligible for registry.

Defining the Ideal.—The animal breeder had in mind a type or ideal animal, representing particular desirable characteristics, these being determined by the purpose for which the animal was intended. Thus there are two common types of sheep—mutton and wool; two main types of cattle—dairy and beef; and analogous designations for other kinds of livestock. Starting with the animals available, which were quite variable, the early improver had to fashion his plans to include consideration of the feed supply and other environmental factors. The breeder of pet or fancy stock had mainly the human appeal to consider. With cattle, specialization moved mainly toward the two primary types of beef and dairy, although in some areas the draft type was developed. An animal type must be a compromise since it must suit the purpose or market requirement and also be adapted to the environment, including the feed supply.

Measuring Merit.—A breeding program, to be effective, must include measurements of the individual for comparison with the ideal. This is a more difficult task with some characteristics than with others, since certain features do not lend themselves to objective measurements. The measuring of milk production in terms of quantity and butterfat content was one of the first attempts at production evaluation (*see* DAIRY INDUSTRY). Evaluation of sheep in terms of the quantity and quality of their wool and of swine in terms of litter size are examples of fairly accurate assessments. The form and conformation of a meat animal can be appraised fairly accurately, but seldom can all of the features be measured objectively. While the external anatomical structure permits partial evaluation, the internal physiological functioning of the individual animal is difficult to appraise.

Many of the qualities that make for productivity cannot be determined from the live animal. Age is also a factor in production records. Information from slaughter records or lifetime records can be useful in evaluating an animal's descendants, or relatives.

Even with qualities subject to reasonably accurate measurement, such as yearly wool yields, variation occurs and the measured production for one period may not be typical of others. Further, over-all merit is not based on a few characteristics, but on several of them and on their interaction.

Selection.—With an ideal and methods of measurement established, the next step in animal breeding is to choose the breeding stock. The animal breeder bases his choice of breeding stock upon his estimate of the individual's genetic capability to produce the ideal. Merit of the individual, determined from the animal or its relatives, is used as a guide in estimating the breeding value.

It is common to distinguish the type of selection as follows:

Mass selection is the choosing of animals for producing the next generation wholly upon their own individual merit. It is sometimes referred to as phenotypic selection, as it is based on what an animal is and does.

Pedigree selection is based upon the merit of the individual's ancestors.

Family selection refers to selection based mainly upon collateral, or nonlineal, relatives or those descended from the same stock but from a different line.

Progeny testing is a means of estimating an animal's breeding worth and is based on the performance of offspring or lineal or direct descendants.

It is obvious that the various means of estimating breeding worth have advantages and disadvantages. The pedigree or record of ancestry is the first available information, while the progeny test can be made only after offspring have been born and tested. In unselected populations, individuality is generally the most accurate estimate of breeding ability and pedigree the least accurate. Progeny testing may be more accurate than individuality. Many characteristics affecting productivity are related to the reproductive process, and this complicates selection because such qualities (*e.g.*, milk production) may appear in only one sex.

As an animal grows older, progress in growth and development, adaptation to environment, resistance to parasites and disease and long-time productivity are recorded. Pedigree and family information is likewise accumulated. The average merit of the group can change as more individuals become available and their performance becomes known.

Complete certainty as to an animal's breeding ability is never attained except with regard to certain definite simple characteristics affected but little or not at all by environment. For example, the black of the Angus when pure (homozygous) is transmitted to the offspring. The mating of Angus that are not pure (heterozygous) for black may result in the production of both blacks and reds.

In practice, selection usually is based on several characteristics for which improvement is desired. Often an individual may be rated well above the average of the herd in all except one characteristic. Accordingly, selection on the basis of over-all merit has been sought. There is an interrelationship of body parts, a harmonious development essential for the proper functioning of any animal. Changing one particular part by selection may disturb the balance between the others. Selection indexes are calculated by evaluating the importance and heritability of each trait included in the index. The index, which considers many characteristics, is an attempt to guide the breeder in making the greatest possible improvement in performance.

Mass Selection.—Selection based wholly upon individual merit (phenotypic) involves choosing for breeding all or many of those animals exhibiting variation in the desired direction. Variations of some characteristics are low in heritability, whereas variations in other characteristics are high. With respect to characteristics of low heritability, the offspring will be only a little different from the population from which the parents were selected. Progress made by mass selection is also related to the intensity of selection.

Mass selection is generally most effective with characteristics that appear in varying degrees or quantities in different individuals; *e.g.*, the back fat of a pig. In the case of traits that appear in alternate forms, one form tends to become less prevalent, but progress is slow and the undesired form may still occur frequently. Characteristics sorted out and accumulated through mass selection have been the principal means of improving domesticated animals.

Pedigree Selection.—Individuals that may appear alike may differ vastly in their ability to transmit qualities to their offspring. Two offspring from the same parents (that is, with identical pedigrees) are not of the same genetic make-up unless they are identical or homozygous twins. If a pedigree is to be of value, the productive ability of the ancestors must be known, but even then pedigree selection is weak.

Family Selection.—In animal breeding the term family is used to describe a group in which there is high genetic relationship as compared with that of the breed of which it is a part. One family may be a group of close relatives that are not closely bred. Another kind of family is a linebred group which, with selection, has become quite distinctive.

Family selection is most effective when applied to inbred but unrelated lines. Since the family average is based upon the average merit of many individuals descended from some stock within a breed, the differences that are nonhereditary tend to be canceled out, and the individuals are closer genetically than is the case with individuals not belonging to the same family. This type of selection has its greatest value for characteristics that cannot be appraised accurately in the individual. It is also useful with characteristics that cannot be appraised in the young animal. To be fairly accurate with this type of selection, the family must be large enough to provide a representative average. For purposes of comparison, families should be exposed to a similar range of environmental conditions.

Family selection is not commonly used with animals in which there are relatively few full siblings (offspring of the same parents) and half siblings. It is most useful with animals having a high reproductive rate. A family of merit is made up of numerous animals with desirable qualities. Therefore, in either mass or family selection, many of the same animals would be chosen for breeding. However, an individual somewhat lacking in merit and due to be culled may be retained for breeding because of its family merit.

Progeny Selection.—This is the choosing of breeding stock on the basis of the performance or testing of their offspring. Individuals with desirable offspring are retained in the breeding herd while the ones with less desirable progeny are discarded. This system is especially valuable with features of low heritability that can be measured in young animals. For effective results, a representative sample of the progeny of different sets of parents must be tested under the same range of environment. Since the inheritance comes from both parents, the inheritance contribution from both should be considered. The progeny test results in choosing many of the same animals for the breeding group as would have been chosen under the other selection systems. These tests may take years to complete.

Systems of Mating.—After the breeding stock has been chosen, the next step is to decide how they should be mated. Systems of mating range all the way from the mating of closely related individuals, or inbreeding, to the mating of unrelated individuals, as in crossbreeding. Mating systems may also be assortative, that is, based upon similarity of characteristics. The mating system may change the various combinations of genes and thereby alter the range of variation within a group.

In practice, the term inbreeding is usually restricted to the mating of first cousins or closer relatives. Close inbreeding usually produces noticeable results in the first generation. Mild inbreeding may take several generations to produce distinguishable changes in the offspring. Individuals mated at random often bear some remote relationship, but this is not considered inbreeding.

Line breeding is a combination of inbreeding, usually in a fairly mild form, with selection. The purpose of the practice is to preserve and concentrate the good qualities of an ancestor by mating individuals related to that ancestor. By the natural halving process of Mendelian inheritance, characteristics of other ancestors are permitted to recede.

The main consequence of inbreeding and line breeding is to increase genetic purity or homozygosity (*see* INBREEDING). Therefore, it is necessary to form homogeneous families. When families or lines are formed by inbreeding, they become progressively more homozygous and distinct with each successive generation. Recessive characteristics may appear as a result of inbreeding. This may cause the merit of individuals to decline, because dominant characteristics are usually more desirable. However, some undesirable recessive traits may be uncovered by inbreeding, making it possible to use selection against these characteristics more effectively.

Selection and mating programs that involve inbred lines are designed to accumulate in the offspring genes that have a complementary effect.

Outbreeding is the mating of unrelated individuals. It is not uncommon for the progeny to surpass the parent stock in vigour and vitality. Hybrid vigour or heterosis (*see* HYBRIDISM) may be lost in mating the first offspring of the cross among themselves, but it can be maintained reasonably well by the alternate back crossing of two breeds or the rotation crossing of three breeds. Full advantage of crossbreeding is attained by retention of crossbred females for breeding. In meat animals, crossbreeding may result in faster and more economical gains.

The main use of crossbreeding has been in commercial livestock production. Breed crosses are very common throughout the United States in commercial hog production. Crosses between wool- and mutton-type sheep are common in the western range country. The crossbreeding of Brahman or zebu cattle with European breeds is quite common in the coastal plains of the south. The mule is an outstanding example of a hybrid resulting from a cross between species or an extremely wide outcross. In some such crosses fertility is impaired.

Artificial Insemination.—This is insemination of a breeding female by other than natural mating. The semen of the male is deposited in the reproductive tract of the female at the proper time in her reproductive cycle so as to effect fertilization. It was used long ago by the Arabs in horse breeding. Fowls, rabbits, dogs, and other animals have been bred by artificial insemination. Beginning about 1940 the practice became widespread in the United States, particularly with dairy cattle.

Artificial insemination permits extensive use of selected males, since more females can be bred to one male by this method than by natural service. It also permits the testing of more offspring of a sire in a shorter period of time and under a wider range of environment. Progeny tests can be more accurate if the offspring are reared in several different herds.

The semen may be collected in a number of ways. The first method used was that of obtaining the semen from a female that had just been served. Later the artificial vagina method was developed. The phallus is directed into a rubber artificial vagina when the male begins to mount a female or a dummy. Semen can also be secured from the male by electrical stimulation, massage of the male sex organs and other means. In most bull studs, the artificial vagina method of semen collection is preferred.

Since the semen of a bull can be extended or diluted, one ejaculation properly handled may be extended to 100 or more services. Some bulls in artificial breeding associations have served as many as 4,000 cows annually. Of the milk cows in this country, more than one-third are inseminated artificially.

Beef-cattle producers have made less use of artificial insemination than dairy farmers, as with the customary methods of beef-cattle management the sire usually runs with the herd. The practice of artificial insemination has been quite successful with horses. With the other common farm animals, the cost of keeping a sire is relatively low and there are technical difficulties that make artificial insemination rather impractical.

The careful collection and distribution of semen and proper handling of the material plus proper and timely insemination by trained personnel are essential for success. In cattle-producing areas organizations have been set up to provide the materials and personnel for the practice of artificial insemination. The semen is diluted and preserved by antibiotics and cooling. Freezing with dry ice has been used as a means of retaining the vitality of semen for over two years. Trained technicians make the actual inseminations and provide breeding supervision. Artificial insemination can be less costly than natural service as it saves the farmer the bother, expense, and danger of maintaining a herd sire. Further, properly handled, it may be a means of controlling infectious diseases and certain types of sterility.

Wider use of fewer sires of higher individual merit can make more selective breeding possible. The females, however, must also be carefully chosen for the greatest possible improvement of the herd.

The animal breeder can change the hereditary make-up and the merit of an animal population far beyond the limits of variation in the original population. Animal improvement is made by regrouping or forming new combinations of genes, resulting in animals with the collective desirable characteristics that formerly resided in separate individuals.

See also references under "Animal Breeding" in the Index.

BIBLIOGRAPHY.—J. L. Lush, *Animal Breeding Plans,* 3rd ed. (1945); Laurence M. Winters, *Animal Breeding,* 5th ed., with chapters on selection and the effectiveness of selection by William Rempel and chapters on fertility and artificial insemination by John N. Cummings (1954); J. E. Nichols, *Livestock Improvement,* 4th ed. (1957); Lester O. Gilmore, *Dairy Cattle Breeding,* ed. by R. W. Gregory (1952); Victor A. Rice *et al., Breeding and Improvement of Farm Animals,* 5th ed. (1957); Arthur L. Anderson and James J. Kiser, *Introductory Animal Science,* 4th ed. (1963).   (A. L. AN.)

ANIMAL EDUCATION. Animals are influenced to act in characteristic manners dependent upon learning achieved in various situations. Influences which guide or control learning may arise from experiences in the characteristic environment, from experiences with other animals or through human guidance.

Education through ordinary experience is typified by the manner in which many young vertebrate animals modify their inborn "snapping responses" to small moving objects. At first the young chick pecks at both edible and inedible objects in motion, but after certain kinds of objects (*e.g.*, hairy caterpillars) have been rejected repeatedly in response to their harsh effect in the mouth, these may be avoided while others of different visual appearance are snapped up.

Education through the activities of other animals may occur incidentally, or through individual relationships meriting the term "tuition." Often young mammals are weaned forcibly and thereby stimulated to acquire adult feeding habits, evidently more because physiological changes in the mother cause her to reject their advances than because she has a "teaching" attitude. In birds, parental behaviour frequently influences the appearance of adult behaviour in the young, as when fledgling birds of prey are at first given pieces of flesh and finally intact prey which they must handle independently, or when early flight is stimulated by pulling or forcing the young from the nest. In the higher mammals, situations in which one individual directly stimulates and guides learning in another are not uncommon. For example, a mother monkey may release herself and back away from her infant, thereby impelling it to follow independently. As another instance, in laboratory experiments one chimpanzee in a joint rope-pulling test stimulated its lagging partner by means of an identifiable gesture, a series of gentle taps with one hand. It must be remembered that an untrained animal profits only in a very general way from seeing another perform, unless the essential parts of the act have been learned previously.

An untrained dog which sees another open a door by twisting the knob with his paws is not thereby enabled to duplicate the act, although when tested alone he may be more persistent in his attacks on the door and perhaps work more around the knob than would otherwise be the case.

Education through human guidance in its simplest form, the "conditioned response," requires as basis a response which the animal makes at the outset to some definite excitatory stimulus. For example, to teach a dog to lie down on command, one begins by using the hands gently to force lying down, each time presenting the new stimulus ("lie down") until after many repetitions the words alone are sufficient. Similarly, in circus training the basic responses (*e.g.*, sitting still) essential for complicated training are fixed to particular stimulus cues through a conditioned-response procedure. However, for highly skilled acts a complex routine of special training is necessary, a process in which appropriate techniques are used to emphasize each step of the serial act and to exclude undesired acts. This holds both for the training of domestic animals and for less ordinary processes such as educating elephants to dance or dogs to lead the blind.

Obviously, the critical limits of animal educability vary in different animal forms, being particularly dependent upon the elaboration of the cerebral cortex in the brain. The cortex of a rat is inferior to that of a dog, for example, and the rat is found correspondingly inferior in learning complex tasks. Furthermore, brain operations reducing the amount of cerebral cortex lower the educability of given individuals. Once the potentialities and capacities of the given animal for new behaviour are known, established principles of learning may be utilized to devise a suitable training program. *See* PSYCHOLOGY, COMPARATIVE; CONDITIONING; ANIMAL BEHAVIOUR.

(T. C. S.)

ANIMAL EXPERIMENTATION. Animal experimentation is the use of animals to study living processes in health and disease. It includes their use for research in the panmedical sciences (including medicine, dentistry, pharmacology, veterinary medicine and the basic biological disciplines); for education and training in these sciences, including the development of surgical skill; for the manufacture of vaccines, toxoids, antiserums, anti-

toxins and antivenins; for the testing and standardization of drugs, biologicals and food additives; and for the diagnosis of disease.

The most fruitful approach to investigations in the panmedical sciences has been the comparative approach—the study of diverse forms of life to build up basic knowledge. Such investigations include the study of life forms ranging from the ultramicroscopic virus to the gorilla. The most frequently used laboratory animals are frogs, mice, rats, guinea pigs, hamsters, rabbits, chickens, pigeons, dogs, cats, sheep, goats, pigs and monkeys. The particular species used depends upon the nature of the project. The study of enzyme systems may well use one-celled organisms, and the fruit fly has been very helpful in genetic studies. The mouse is the mammal used in the greatest numbers.

The dog has been and continues to be particularly valuable in the development of new techniques in surgery. The basic techniques in chest and heart surgery were developed by use of the dog. Techniques for the prevention and control of shock and for the safe transfusion of blood and blood plasma substitutes were developed largely through experiments on dogs. The dog played a prominent role in the development of brain, bone and abdominal surgery. The dog has played a major role in the development of knowledge of many of the metabolic diseases of man, such as diabetes, pernicious anemia and adrenal cortical insufficiency (Addison's disease). There are more than 1,000,000 diabetics in the United States alone who are living useful and almost normal lives because of work done on the dog. Thousands of lives were saved during World War II as a result of research done on dogs after World War I, particularly beneficial being inquiries into shock and wound infections, each of which caused many deaths in World War I. The benefits of research were illustrated even more dramatically in the Korean war.

One of the less well-known uses of animals is for the routine testing of food additives, drugs and biologicals. Research into problems of food spoilage, processing and distribution, palatability and acceptability, and nutritive quality is a large industry in itself, requiring large numbers of animals. The animals used most commonly for such tests are mice, rats, dogs and monkeys.

The testing of potential new drugs requires large numbers of several species of animals. Every batch of many of these drugs, even after they are accepted for use, must be tested on animals before it is considered safe for man. For example, every batch of each antibiotic must be tested on rabbits to make sure there are no factors present that will produce fever and on mice to make sure that there are no toxic factors; and many antibiotics must be tested on dogs to make sure there are no factors present that will lower the blood pressure. Each batch of corticotrophin (ACTH) must be tested on rabbits, mice, dogs, cockerels, chickens, rats and cats. The 15th edition of the *United States Pharmacopoeia* (U.S.P. XV) lists 168 categories that require testing with one or more species of animals for safety, potency, antigenicity (the ability to stimulate the organism to produce antibodies) or some other important factor. Other drugs and biologicals not listed in the *Pharmacopoeia* but listed in the *National Formulary* or by the Food and Drug administration or the National Institutes of Health require animals for testing. The use of animals to test drugs and biologicals for safety and potency is widespread and necessary.

Antivivisection Activity.—An account of the prodigious advances in biological and medical knowledge that have followed the use of animal experimentation is convincing proof that it leads to profitable results and will continue to do so. There is not a single modern and substantial item of medical knowledge that does not owe something to animal experiment. Animal experimentation may cause pain to animals, and in any event is a form of using animals not for their own individual advantage but for the advantage of man in his pursuit of knowledge. The justification for using animals in this way depends on the individual's philosophical beliefs, as to man's obligation to animals and as to the rights that animals may be supposed to possess.

The origin of organized opposition to the use of animals in research, called antivivisectionism, came in the middle of the 19th century. At that time the panmedical sciences were benefited by the experimental work of the French genius Claude Bernard, the founder of physiology; his wife and daughter, however, became antivivisection leaders.

A militant organization was founded in England in 1875 under the name of the Society for the Protection of Animals Liable to Vivisection. In 1897 it adopted its present name, the National Antivivisection society. After the enactment of the Cruelty to Animals act of 1876, other antivivisection societies were founded in Great Britain, all of them pressing for the total abolition of animal experimentation. In Great Britain, money donated for the abolition of animal experimentation is not tax free.

The first antivivisection society in the United States, the American Antivivisection society, was founded in 1883. By 1955 there were over 200 antivivisection societies in the United States, including 5 national societies. Antivivisectionists join humane societies and in many cases, because of their zeal, dominate the societies and dictate their policies.

Laws Related to Experiments on Animals.—In most areas of the world, animal experimentation is accepted as approved practice by common law. In a number of countries it is legally defined.

United States.—In the United States, every large teaching hospital has a surgical research laboratory that uses dogs for both teaching and research. The federal congress can legislate in this matter only for the District of Columbia and for the territories. Bills against animal experimentation were introduced in congress each biennium after 1897, but none passed. Prior to 1945, six states (Illinois, Maine, Massachusetts, Oklahoma, South Dakota and Washington) had passed laws prohibiting animal experimentation in public schools.

Twelve cities had been supplying dogs to medical schools instead of killing them at local pounds. St. Louis, Mo., in 1922 and Chicago, Ill., in 1931 passed legislation defining these provisions. No states had passed legislation defining such provisions, although 11 states had legally endorsed animal experimentation.

In 1945 bills to prohibit the use of animals for teaching and research almost passed the legislatures of the states of New York and Massachusetts. In that year the National Society for Medical Research (N.S.M.R.) was founded. Supported chiefly by medical, dental and veterinary schools and research and philanthropic institutions, the N.S.M.R. became active in informing the public about animal experimentation. Subsequently, a number of states and cities passed laws making unclaimed stray animals from public pounds available to approved research institutions. In 1966, following reports of the laboratory use of stolen pets, congress empowered the secretary of agriculture to license dealers who buy and sell dogs and cats in interstate commerce, and to set standards of humane handling and transport. (NA. BR.)

Great Britain.—The law relating to animal experiments is the Cruelty to Animals act of 1876. It was drafted at a time when the majority of animal experiments were carried out by physiologists and were therefore more often than not of an acute surgical nature. Nevertheless, the wording of the act is so flexible, except for a system of certification that has proved cumbersome but by no means unworkable, that it has been possible to adapt it to the vastly changing conditions of animal experimentation.

The act covers experiments on mammals, birds, reptiles, amphibians and fish; invertebrates are not covered by it. All animal experiments under this act must be for the advancement of physiological knowledge, which includes the broad field of biological inquiry, or knowledge useful in saving or prolonging life or alleviating suffering, in man or in animals. It refers only to experiments on living animals of a kind that might cause pain, suffering or appreciable discomfort or departure from normal health. Such experiments must be carried out in places registered by the home office and regarded as suitable for the purpose, and these are regularly inspected by full-time qualified inspectors. Experimenters must hold licences granted by the home office, and they also require certificates controlling the use of anesthetics in any operative procedures from which the animal is allowed to recover, or to allow them to dispense with anesthetics altogether in the case of trivial procedures such as inoculations.

In operations followed by recovery, efficient anesthesia and full aseptic precautions must be observed. If in the course of an experiment the animal comes to suffer severe or enduring pain, and the main result of the experiment has been gained, the licensee must kill the animal forthwith; and he must also kill it regardless of the state of the experiment if severe and enduring pain develops. Today only a small proportion of experiments are performed under total anesthesia from which the animal does not recover. This includes a number used in illustration of lectures to medical and veterinary students.

Additional certificates are required for experiments on horses, asses and mules and, in most cases, on dogs and cats. These species thus have a special measure of protection. Licences and certificates are personal to the holder, who may not delegate his authority under them to another, not even a licence holder.

The act prohibits animal experiments whose object is the acquisition of manual skill, but this does not include research into surgical techniques, which is permissible. It also prohibits the exhibition of experiments to members of the public. A scientist working under home office licence cannot be prosecuted for any offense against the act without the written permission of the home secretary.

There have been no prosecutions under the act of 1876. This is partly due to the way in which British scientists have, by their co-operation, made a difficult law work as it was intended to work, and partly to the fact that the system of licensing places a very powerful sanction in the hands of the home secretary. The revocation of a professional physiologist's licence would be a more serious penalty than the penalties laid down in the act, because it would prevent his following his profession.

There have been two royal commissions on vivisection, one appointed in 1875, which was followed by the passing of the act of 1876, and one in 1906, which reported six years later. After exhaustive inquiries, both supported the need for animal experimentation and approved the ways in which British scientists carried it out. The act has been strictly but sensibly administered, so that it is possible to say that experimental animals enjoy a real and effective measure of protection against anything that could be described as cruelty, while at the same time science is not prevented from pursuing a profitable course. A similar act is in force in Northern Ireland and in the Isle of Man. (W. L.-PR.)

British Commonwealth.—There is no legal protection for laboratory animals in Canada, India, Pakistan, New Zealand or Tasmania. In Australia each state has legislation but none has inspection; experimenters are licensed in Queensland (1925) and Western Australia (1920 and regulation in 1944).

In Kenya only licensed persons may use experimental animals. Jamaica has an act passed in 1949 which provides for inspection, licensing of experimenters, registration of laboratories and obligatory keeping of records. Similar acts were passed, during 1957 and 1958, in the Bahamas, British Honduras, Montserrat, St. Vincent, Seychelles, Tanzania (Zanzibar), Fiji and Uganda. In Uganda the use of curare is restricted. By the 1960s legislation was being prepared in Barbados, Grenada, St. Kitts-Nevis-Anguilla, Guyana (British Guiana), Hong Kong and Sierra Leone.

Europe.—In Europe there is no legal control of the use of laboratory animals in France, the Netherlands, Spain, Portugal, Greece, Yugoslavia or the U.S.S.R. In the Republic of Ireland the British Cruelty to Animals act of 1876 still applies.

A comprehensive law was passed in Denmark in 1953 and a committee controls the use of vertebrate experimental animals. The duties of this committee include the granting of licences; supervision of experimenters' records (which must contain full details of anesthesia and euthanasia) and unannounced inspection of animals and experimental procedures. The Danish law also lays down that if animals have to recover from operation they are to be nursed carefully and their pain is to be relieved, and that students may not use, or have demonstrated to them, any procedure on a living animal unless that animal is anesthetized and never regains consciousness.

By the Swedish laws of 1944 and 1958 control of laboratory animals is vested in the Swedish Veterinary board, which licenses experimenters and has powers of inspection, which, however, it delegates to the director of each laboratory.

In the Swiss cantons of Basel and Berne laws passed in 1941 provide for unannounced inspection of laboratory animals by visiting committees of scientists and laymen. Both enactments provide for the licensing of experimenters and of laboratories and both contain a clause making good husbandry obligatory. In Vaud (1958) there is licensing of experimenters, and inspection by veterinary surgeons. In Zürich there is obligatory record keeping and licensing, but no inspection, and there, as in Austria, Czechoslovakia and Italy, an animal may not be used for more than one painful experiment.

In the German Federal Republic (law of 1933 and regulations in 1934 and 1951) invertebrates are protected as well as vertebrates, and there is inspection by state-employed doctors and veterinary surgeons. Italy (1941) made some provision for inspection.

In Austria, Norway and Poland experimenters are licensed. In Belgium, Czechoslovakia and Norway laboratories are registered. In Austria, Denmark and Czechoslovakia the law requires that the minimum number of animals must be used. Experimental animals may not be used at all in Liechtenstein.   (F. J. Vr.)

ANIMAL EXTRACTS. The animal kingdom provides a source for a large number of substances having nutritional and therapeutic value. Many of these active substances are complex proteins that have not been synthesized in the chemical laboratory. The structures of some of the hormones and other compounds isolated from animal extracts have been determined, and these compounds have been synthesized by the chemist at a cost much lower than the cost of extraction from the animal organ. The animal extracts are obtained by extraction of the active material from the animal organ with subsequent purification by chemical means; or the secretion, such as bile or pregnant mares' urine, of an organ is extracted and used as the source of the active compounds. Some of the potent adrenal hormones are produced by the perfusion in vitro of animal adrenal glands with blood and subsequent isolation of the crystalline hormones from the perfused blood. Many antibodies against diseases such as tetanus and diphtheria are obtained from the blood of animals inoculated with the organism producing the disease.

Substances such as honey and wax are obtained through the activity of members of the animal kingdom. Some of the common animal extracts are beeswax, cod-liver oil, gelatin, honey, insulin, lard, lanolin, suet, pancreatic solution, ox bile, and pituitary, testicular, liver, and ovarian extracts.

Pituitary Extracts.—The pituitary gland has anterior and posterior lobes. The posterior pituitary extract exhibits striking physiologic actions on the heart, circulatory system and the smooth muscle of the body.

Adrenal Extracts.—The adrenal gland produces at least two substances, epinephrine (adrenaline) and norepinephrine (noradrenaline or levarterenol), compounds with a profound stimulating action on the cardiovascular system. Epinephrine also is used in the treatment of certain allergic diseases.

Gonadal Extracts.—The testicular androgen, testosterone, is used in the treatment of hypogonadism and for the palliative treatment of certain breast cancers. The ovarian hormones, estrogens and progesterone, are used in certain menstrual disorders. Estrogens are helpful in relieving symptoms of the menopause and have been used in controlling certain types of cancer.

Parathyroid Extracts.—The parathyroid glands provide an extract used to treat hypoparathyroidism, characterized by muscle tetany associated with low blood calcium and high blood phosphorus.

Pancreatic Extracts.—The pancreas produces two types of secretions, exocrine and endocrine. The endocrine secretion, insulin, is of great importance in the treatment of diabetes mellitus. The exocrine secretion is made up of a number of enzymes activated in the intestine.

Thyroid Extract.—The thyroid gland produces a hormone, thyroxine, which is important in regulating the energy metabolism of the body. In certain deficiency states, such as myxedema in adults and cretinism in children, thyroid extract provides adequate re-

placement therapy.

Liver Extracts.—Liver extract was once widely used in the treatment of pernicious anemia, but it has been largely replaced by crystalline vitamin B_{12}, the active hematopoietic agent in liver extract. Animal bile provides bile acids that have been used in conditions of inadequate secretions of bile by the liver.

See also ENDOCRINOLOGY; HORMONES; and articles on the individual glands and their secretions. For synthetic analogues of animal extracts *see* NATURAL PRODUCTS, TOTAL SYNTHESIS OF.

ANIMAL FEEDS: *see* FEEDS, ANIMAL.

ANIMAL HEAT. This subject includes the physiology of the body temperature of animals, the paths of heat loss and the heat production that is necessary to maintain body temperature. The invention of the thermometer led to a marked increase in the knowledge of variations in body temperature of man and animals. The use of electrical resistance thermometers, thermocouples and radiometers also contributed measurably to the information concerning variations in different parts of the body, the paths of heat loss and the factors affecting them. The body temperature of man and animals is reliably obtained with a mercury thermometer placed in the rectum. With man the internal temperature is usually taken in the mouth.

Warm- and Cold-blooded Animals.—Animals in general are classified as homoiothermic (practically constant body temperature independent of environment) and poikilothermic (body temperatures varying with external temperature). The first class includes the so-called warm-blooded animals, all mammals and birds. The second class includes the so-called cold-blooded animals such as insects, snakes, lizards, tortoises, frogs and fishes. In a study of the rectal, mouth and skin temperatures of several varieties of snakes, turtles and tortoises, Francis G. Benedict found in 1932 that the body temperatures of these animals almost invariably were slightly lower than the temperature of the environment. These animals acted as a wet-bulb thermometer, because all of their heat elimination was by way of vaporization of water. When a snake was placed in a calorimeter to measure its heat elimination, no heat was given off; in fact, it absorbed heat from the surrounding air. Only in the case of a python incubating a group of eggs was the body temperature higher than that of the environment.

A few animals are warm-blooded at one season of the year and cold-blooded at another. The most noted example is the marmot or woodchuck. During the warm period of the year this animal is warm-blooded, but in the fall it goes into a state of hibernation and becomes cold-blooded. The state of hibernation is brought about by absence of food and cold external temperatures. The body temperature in hibernation has been observed to go down to 37° F. with recovery, being usually 2° to 5° F. above that of the environment. Warm-blooded animals can behave as cold-blooded under conditions of anesthesia. Sutherland Simpson demonstrated that when a monkey was kept deeply anesthetized with ether and placed in a cold chamber, its temperature gradually fell. When it had reached a sufficiently low point (87° F.), the use of an anesthetic was no longer necessary. The explanation was that the heat-regulating mechanism had been impaired. In studies on the marmot reported by Benedict in 1938, Nembutal was used to produce narcosis, and the marmots had body temperatures as low as 82° F. and were usually 2° to 4° F. above that of the environment. In man and animals, injuries to or severance of the spinal cord will bring about abolition of the heat-regulating mechanism and an approach to a condition like that of cold-blooded animals. These facts tend to show that the power of maintaining a constant temperature has been a gradual development and that anything that interferes with the working of the higher nerve centres puts the animal back again, for the time being, on to a lower plane of evolution.

Variations in Body Temperature.—The body temperature of animals ranges from 96° F. in the elephant to about 109° F. in small birds. Animals may be classified according to body temperature as follows: 96°–101° F., man, monkey, mule, ass, horse, rat, mouse and elephant; 100°–103° F., cattle, sheep, dog, cat, rabbit and pig; 104°–106° F., turkey, goose, duck, owl, pelican and vulture; 107°–109° F., chicken, pigeon and several small common birds. The body temperature of a healthy man may range from about 97° F. to 100° F. during the 24 hr.; the rectal temperature is between 1° and 2° F. higher than the mouth temperature. The temperature of infants and young children has a much greater range and changes readily from comparatively slight causes. The average temperature falls slightly from infancy to puberty, levels off and falls again from puberty to old age.

A diurnal variation of body temperature occurs in man and in most animals. In man the lowest body temperature is from 2 to 5 A.M. and the highest from 2 to 5 P.M. With this changing temperature throughout the day it is only coincidence that the temperature may be 98.6° F., which is considered to be normal. In the early morning the oral temperature may be as low as 97° F. and in the afternoon as high as 99° F. without being abnormal. Reversal of the activity from day to night, as in night workers, does not change this rhythm, but on a trip from New Haven, Conn., to Manila, Phil., R. B. Gibson found in 1905 that the rhythm changed with the progressive changes in the hours of night and day. Therefore, it would seem that the daily rhythm of man is affected by cosmic influences and not by cycles of activity. The daily rhythm of body temperature is surprisingly like the rhythm of the daily external temperature at certain times of the year on a different scale.

In women there is a monthly cycle of temperature in relation to menstruation and ovulation. T. T. Zuck in 1938 reported a study of rectal temperatures in women throughout the monthly cycle. Just before menstruation there was a slight fall in morning temperature to 98° F., which continued during menstruation. After menstruation there was usually an additional slight fall followed by a rise to 98° F., followed in turn by an abrupt fall to 97° F. or even lower at the midperiod. Thereafter it usually rose to normal and remained stationary until the next menstrual period. Records of the last menstrual cycles of 20 women identified ovulation with the approximate date of the midperiod low temperature. No pregnancy occurred before the 10th day or after the 20th day regardless of the length of the cycle.

The skin temperature of man is about 7° to 9° F. lower than the internal temperature, which is attained only at a depth of an inch or more (approximately 50% of the body is within one inch of the surface). In the basal state the rectal temperature may be 2° to 4° F. higher than the average body temperature. In fever the two may be practically alike. Men and women vary considerably in their reactions to environmental temperature.

Ingestion of food produces a rise in both skin and rectal temperatures for an hour to two hours, the skin temperature being elevated more than the rectal. Alcohol produces an elevation in skin temperature but a lowering of internal temperature, and therefore is to be avoided during exposure to cold environment. J. H. Weatherby in 1942 found that smoking decreased the skin temperature of the extremities 4° to 13° F., but removal of nicotine from cigarettes almost completely abolished this fall. Cold applications placed in various parts of the body cause a substantial lowering of the temperature of living tissues to a considerable depth from the contacting surfaces. Children about 13 years old had a temperature drop to 95° F. after swimming 45 min. in a pool at 73° F. Variations of external temperature within ordinary limits cause very slight changes although some individuals require a period of adaptation when they change from a temperate climate to a tropical one. Muscular work usually causes a temporary rise in temperature. This rise depends on the duration and severity of the work, the temperature and the per cent humidity of the environment.

Most animals (birds and mammals) have a daily rhythm in body temperature similar to that of man. The breadth of the rhythm varies with the type of animal. Pigs have a range of 2.5° F.; asses 2° F.; dogs and cattle 3.5° F.; and poultry 5° F. Hence man may represent the limit to which an evolutionary trend to homoiothermism has been attained.

Limits Compatible with Life.—There are limits both of heat and cold that a warm-blooded animal can bear. They depend on the classes of animals and upon whether or not they have sweat-ing mechanisms. The upper survival limit for fever in man is 107° F., but this may rise in premortal states to 110° F. The lower limit of human body temperature varies with the condition of the individual. In diabetic coma a temperature of 92° F. has been recorded with survival after recovery from the coma. Lawrence W. Smith and Temple Fay in 1940 subjected patients with incurable cancer to an artificial hibernation by means of ice packs that reduced their body temperatures to a range from 74° to 90° F. Their studies showed that patients may be kept at body temperatures in the 80s for from 5 to 8 days with recovery.

Cold-blooded animals will survive until the body temperature nearly reaches the freezing point. Small cold-blooded animals therefore descend below the frost line seasonally or like some insects migrate to warmer climates. Cold-blooded animals, on the other hand, have great difficulty surviving body temperatures above 98.6° F. Snakes and lizards in hot deserts will seek shade and if prevented from doing so will die.

Regulation of Body Temperature.—The body temperature of man and animals is maintained by the balance between heat production and heat loss. In cold-blooded animals the heat production varies with the external temperature and in general obeys the Q_{10} law of chemical processes, which is that for an increase of 10° C. (18° F.) the heat generated is about double that of the preceding rate. This law does not hold strictly throughout the range of possible body temperatures of cold-blooded animals. The lower the body temperature, the more rapid is the increase in heat production per degree rise in body temperature. However, even at body temperatures approaching those of the warm-blooded animals the heat production is much lower than that of the warm-blooded animals.

The larger the warm-blooded animal, the greater is the heat production, but the heat production decreases quite regularly per pound of additional body weight. Also, in general, the larger the animal, the lower the heat production per unit of body surface area. It was formerly considered that a general law governed the heat production at rest fasting per unit of body surface; *i.e.*, it was 1,000 cal. per square metre of body surface per 24 hr. in animals exposed to an environmental temperature of 16° C. (61° F.). However, Samuel Brody calculated that the average basal metabolism of the entire range of warm-blooded animals from the mouse to the elephant is equal to 70.5 cal. per 24 hr. per kilogram$^{0.73}$; *i.e.*, the body weight in kilograms raised to 0.73 power times 70.5 cal. Although man fits into this generalization, his basal heat production is usually referred to body surface. The body surface of man is calculated from the Eugene F. DuBois formula, $A = Wt.^{0.425} \times Ht.^{0.725} \times 71.84$ in which A equals area in square metres, Wt. equals weight in kilograms and Ht. equals height in centimetres. The normal basal heat production of men per 24 hr. varies from 46.0 cal. per square metre at 14–16 years of age to 35.5 at 70–80 years of age. Women have about 5% to 10% lower basal heat production.

The heat produced by various animals has to be eliminated in order to maintain a practically constant body temperature. The paths of heat loss are radiation, convection and vaporization of water. Radiation is actual heat rays, convection is carrying away of heat by air currents, and vaporization of water is heat used in evaporating water from the lungs and skin. In nonsweating animals there is little evaporation of water from the skin. Maintenance of constant body temperature in these animals is brought about in hot weather by increased panting and by increased exposure of the body surface so that radiation and convection are more effective. The cat licks itself in hot weather to increase evaporation, and the dog pants to accomplish the same end.

Domestic cattle do not stand hot weather well because they have few sweat glands, and the amount of panting they can do is sometimes insufficient to keep the body temperature within normal limits. Brody called attention to the ineffectiveness of electric fans in cooling cattle because they may actually increase the skin temperature by blowing hot air on the animals. He recommended use of wet blankets or wet spongy material on cattle in hot weather, together with electric fans. Milk production in cows is seriously affected by high body temperature, and the growth of chickens is markedly lowered in the hot months. On the contrary, cattle may be wintered at extremely low environmental temperatures in open range without serious injury. They develop highly insulating coats of fur and subcutaneous fat. Cattle native to hot countries withstand hot environments better than those native to temperate countries. The Brahman cattle, *Bos indicus*, are used in sections where high temperatures occur in summer. They probably have more sweat glands than European cattle, *Bos taurus*. Horses, mules and donkeys withstand hot weather much better than other farm animals because they have sweat glands. They, therefore, can be worked much more than cattle.

Poultry are likewise sensitive to hot weather. External temperatures above 80° F. produce disturbances, and temperatures of 100° F. or above cannot be withstood for more than seven hours. Good water supply in which fowls can dip their heads is required. The sheep is outstanding among domestic animals in tolerating hot atmospheres. Panting is not a marked feature since it occurs only at a rectal temperature of 106° F.

The greatest factor in heat regulation is the skin, which is regulated by the vasomotor system and by the nervous mechanism of perspiration. In hot weather the cutaneous blood vessels are dilated and there is increased blood flow so that more heat is eliminated. Contrariwise, in cold weather, the blood vessels of the skin contract, thus lowering the skin temperature and lowering heat loss. At rest in a comfortable environment, man's average loss by radiation is about 53%, by convection 19% and by vaporization 28%. The higher the external temperature the greater is the heat loss by vaporization of water, until at 97° F. external temperature all heat elimination is by vaporization. Above this temperature the body actually absorbs heat from the environment; this absorption is compensated for by increased vaporization.

Men and women behave differently on exposure to different environmental temperatures. J. D. Hardy and E. F. DuBois, in a study of the paths of heat elimination of nude men and women at external temperatures from 72° to 95° F., found that radiation decreased steadily in men until it disappeared at 95° F. In the cold zone, vaporization was about equal in the two sexes, but at 84° F. the men started to sweat whereas the women did not sweat until the external temperature reached 91° to 93° F. The heat loss for women in the cold zone was about 10% less than that of men because their skin temperature was lower than that of men, and in the warm zone the heat loss of most of the women was about 14% to 20% lower than that of men because they did not sweat so much. The comfort zone in which heat production and heat loss were equal had a range of 11° F. in women and only 4° to 5° F. in men. C. P. Yaglou and Anne Messer in 1941 pointed out that if women would dress in winter clothing comparable to that of men, they would be comfortable at 72° F. instead of 76° F. Conversely, if men would discard their coats, vests and collars in hot weather the temperature of buildings could be maintained at 83° F. for comfort instead of 76° to 80° F., and the problem of air conditioning for both sexes would be simplified.

In muscular work in hot, dry climates, enormous quantities of water are necessary to compensate for the loss of heat by vaporization. Losses of three quarts per hour have been recorded. A good acclimatization can be acquired rapidly during the first 7 days and then more gradually up to 23 days. Changes in heart rate are dramatic, as the principal reduction occurs in the first four to five days. The general course of the rectal temperature is downward as normal levels are attained in seven to ten days. Rates of sweating gradually increase. W. Machle and T. F. Hatch stated in 1947 that there was agreement among most observers that performance and appearance of men, degrees of vascular instability and cardiac rate and rectal temperature when evaluated together are so closely related to the state of acclimatization as to comprise the most reliable indexes of the state. Fever in men is caused in some diseases by interference with heat elimination and in others by both an increase in heat production and a lessening of heat elimination. In the human body the heat production follows the law of Q_{10} so that as the body temperature is raised the heat production is raised. T. M. Carpenter found that even in the range of normal body temperature the heat production varied directly with the body temperature.

All the arrangements in the animal economy for the production and loss of heat are themselves regulated by the central nervous system, and it is considered that the temperature centre is situated in the hypothalamus. *See also* references under "Animal Heat" in the Index.

BIBLIOGRAPHY.—Thomas Deighton, "Physical Factors in Body Temperature Maintenance and Heat Elimination," *Physiol. Rev.*, xiii (1933); Eugene F. DuBois, *Basal Metabolism in Health and Disease* (1936); Samuel Brody, *Bioenergetics and Growth* (1945).

(T. M. C.)

ANIMAL LOCOMOTION: *see* LOCOMOTION, ANIMAL.
ANIMAL MAGNETISM: *see* HYPNOSIS.
ANIMAL MIGRATION: *see* MIGRATION, ANIMAL.
ANIMAL PLAY: *see* PLAY, ANIMAL.
ANIMAL PSYCHOLOGY: *see* ANIMAL BEHAVIOUR; PSYCHOLOGY, COMPARATIVE.

ANIMALS, DISTRIBUTION OF. The subject of animal distribution can be approached from the viewpoint of (1) current spatial distribution; (2) life in past eras, along with the historical factors that molded present zoogeographic patterns; and (3) the environmental factors, both physical and biological (biotic), that channeled animal dispersions in the past and control present distribution. Primary attention is focused in this article on the role that physical environmental factors have played in determining the spread and limitations of animal life (fauna). Necessary data on the origin, rise and present diversity of different animal groups are included, but the history of animal evolution is surveyed primarily in the articles EVOLUTION, ORGANIC; ANIMALS, PHYLOGENY OF; PALEONTOLOGY; and under the names of major animal groups. The present distributions of nonmarine vertebrates are reviewed in ZOOGEOGRAPHY. Biotic factors associated with animal distribution are considered in the articles ECOLOGY; MARINE BIOLOGY; and PLANKTON; but a section on man as a factor in animal dispersal is included in this article.

This article is divided into the following sections:

I. Introduction
II. Animal Distribution in Time
    1. Life in the Early Seas
    2. Movement into Fresh Waters
    3. Movement onto Land
    4. Associated Evolutionary Changes
III. Geographical Distribution of Living Animals
    1. In the Sea
    2. In Fresh Water
    3. On Land
IV. Factors Affecting Ecological Distribution of Living Animals
    1. Water
    2. Temperature
    3. Light
    4. Food
    5. Oxygen and Carbon Dioxide
    6. Pressure
V. Animal Life in the Sea
    A. Conditions Influencing Sea Life
        1. Physical
        2. Chemical
    B. Zonation of Marine Animals
        1. Pelagic Division
        2. Benthic Division
VI. Animal Life in Fresh Waters
    A. Conditions Influencing Fresh-water Life
    B. Special Factors
        1. Low Salt Content
        2. Relative Impermanence of Fresh Waters
    C. Zonation of Fresh-water Animals
        1. Surface Film
        2. Standing Water
        3. Running Water
VII. Animal Life on Land
    A. Basic Adaptations to Terrestrial Life
        1. Air
        2. Water
        3. Other Environmental Factors
    B. Zonation of Land Animals
        1. Climatic Zonation
        2. Vegetative Zonation
        3. Topographic Zonation
    C. Dispersal of Animals on Land
VIII. Man as a Factor in Animal Distribution

I. INTRODUCTION

Information concerning the generalized adaptations and distribution patterns of different animal groups is basically dependent on the degree to which their systematics and ecology have been studied.

Zoological classification dates officially from 1758, when Linnaeus published his tenth edition of the *Systema naturae.* Prior to this time, there was a considerable body of general observations on animals, but no effective means of codifying these data so that scientists in all parts of the world would know to what species a particular observation referred. Linnaeus catalogued 4,236 animal species, of which 1,222 or nearly 29% were vertebrates. Insects accounted for 1,936 species or 46%, and the other phyla for the remaining 1,078 species.

In the more than 200 years since the *Systema naturae,* the number of known species has increased approximately as shown in fig. 1. Obviously, no catalogue of the more than 1,000,000 described species exists. New species are being named at the rate of more than 10,000 per year, and even estimates of the number of known species vary widely. Various authorities cite the number of known species of fish as low as 20,000 or as high as 40,000; of mollusks between 40,000 and 150,000; and of insects 650,000 to 1,000,000. Part of the problem lies in the fact that in many groups it is not yet known what is a species; many names listed as full species in old monographs actually refer to colour variants or to geographic races of species. Primarily the problem lies in the overwhelming diversity of animal life and in the comparatively small group of scholars attempting to systematize knowledge about animals.

Although the number of recognized vertebrate species increased more than 37 times since 1758, the vertebrates, with about 40,000 species, now comprise only about 4.4% of all the known animal species. The proportion of vertebrate species will further decrease in the future since there are probably close to another 1,000,000 species of invertebrates, mainly insects and other land arthropods, that have not yet been named. While 95% to 99% of the species of land vertebrates are described and classified, probably less than half of the insects and perhaps one tenth of the roundworms (nematodes) have been named.

Only very sketchy knowledge of the numbers and kinds of invertebrate life is available, and recent years have seen the discovery of the following groups: a new phylum (the Pogonophora—beard worms); a class of mollusks (Monoplacophora) thought to have been extinct for 350,000,000 years and found living in the ocean deeps; and a new subclass of phylum Crustacea (Cephalocarida) based on specimens of the genus *Hutchinsonella,* collected in waters off both coasts of North America.

The starting point for almost any biological study is a named and classified organism whose general geographic range has been established and for which some life history information is on record. Students of vertebrates have much of these basic data available and thus can work on ecological, physiological and behavioural problems. Students of the invertebrates, on the other hand, usually first become involved in the basic task of describing and classifying the organisms they wish to study; only with great difficulty can they attempt detailed distributional or ecological studies.

Data on distribution patterns of living organisms on earth are drawn almost entirely from nonmarine vertebrates (*see* ZOOGEOGRAPHY). The classification of most nonvertebral phyla is too poorly known to enable world-wide distributional studies. Fortunately, ecological information on the basic adaptations of organisms to their environment is more plentiful for the invertebrates than is information on spatial distribution.

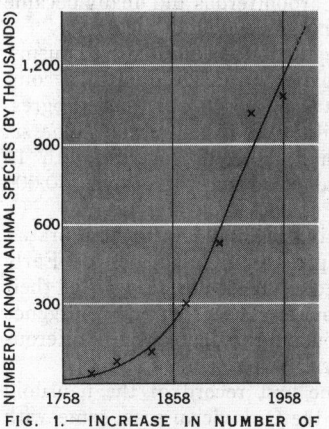

FIG. 1.—INCREASE IN NUMBER OF KNOWN ANIMAL SPECIES

II. ANIMAL DISTRIBUTION IN TIME

Life on earth probably originated between 1,500,000,000 and 2,000,000,000 years ago. Only a few scattered fossils provide information about early forms. It is not until comparatively recent times, geologically speaking, about 500,000,000 years ago, that a plentiful fossil record exists. Despite the abundance of fossils laid down since that time the inadequacy of the fossil record cannot be overemphasized. Fossilization is a rare accident, and it would be quite optimistic to say that one out of every 1,000,000 individual animals that ever lived had been preserved as a fossil (*see* FOSSIL).

Most fossils are of organisms that lived in comparatively shallow waters. Little knowledge is available of the deepwater creatures of the past: two zoological discoveries emphasize this fact. In 1938 a fish subsequently named *Latimeria* was caught off East London, U. of S. Af.; its relatives, the lobefins, or crossopterygian fishes, were known as fossils, and were presumed to have been extinct for 60,000,000 years (*see* COELACANTH). In the early 1950s a small mollusk, *Neopilina,* was dredged off the west coast of Costa Rica. Its relatives, the monoplacophorans, disappeared from the fossil record 350,000,000 years ago.

Organisms without skeletons, shells or at least some hard parts will leave few traces in the rocks. A group of soft, wormlike animals, the Onychophora (*Peripatus*), is known from Cambrian fossils and living species, but no fossils are evident in the 500,000,000-year gap between. Similarly, fossils of most worm phyla are very rare.

Despite obvious limitations and inadequacies, the fossil record does show that (1) there has been a definite history of rise, dominance, decline and extinction of animal groups; (2) many types of organisms abundant today were at one time absent or rare; and (3) some creatures that are rare today were formerly common. A brief discussion of a few major changes is given

Estimated Numbers of Known Species of Animals*

Phylum	Number of species
Protozoa (amoebas, parameciums, etc.)	20,000 (± 5,000)
Mesozoa (certain wormlike parasites)	50
Porifera (sponges)	5,000
Coelenterata (corals, jellyfish, etc.)	10,000
Ctenophora (comb jellies)	90 (± 10)
Platyhelminthes (flatworms)	10,000
Nemertina (ribbon worms)	650 (± 100)
Acanthocephala (spiny-headed worms)	300
Aschelminthes	
Class Rotifera (wheel animalcules)	1,500
Class Gastrotricha (microscopic aquatic forms)	180 (± 20)
Class Kinorhyncha (small marine forms)	100
Class Priapulida (aquatic wormlike forms)	6
Class Nematoda (roundworms)	10,000
Class Nematomorpha (hairworms)	75 (± 25)
Entoprocta (microscopic marine forms)	60
Phoronida (sedentary wormlike forms)	15
Ectoprocta (Bryozoa) (moss animals)	3,000
Brachiopoda (lamp shells)	245 (± 25)
Pogonophora (beard worms)	108
Sipunculida (peanut worms)	250
Annelida (segmented worms)	6,200
Mollusca (snails, clams, octopuses, etc.)	80,000 (± 25,000)
Arthropoda	
Class Onychophora ("walking worms")	80
Class Tardigrada (bear animalcules)	340
Class Crustacea (shrimps, crabs, etc.)	28,000 (± 2,000)
Class Arachnida (spiders, mites, etc.)	50,000
Class Pentastomida (Linguatulida) (wormlike parasites)	70
Class Pycnogonida ("sea spiders")	500
Class Pauropoda (small wormlike forms)	432
Class Diplopoda (millipedes)	6,300
Class Symphyla ("garden centipedes")	170
Class Chilopoda (centipedes)	1,700
Class Insecta (insects)	850,000 (± 100,000)
Echinodermata (starfish, sea urchins, etc.)	5,600
Chaetognatha (arrow worms)	30
Hemichordata (tongue worms)	80
Chordata	
Subphylum Urochordata (sea squirts)	1,500
Subphylum Cephalochordata (amphioxus)	28
Subphylum Vertebrata	
Classes Agnatha, Placodermi, Chondrichthyes and Osteichthyes (all the fish)	20,000 (± 5,000)
Class Amphibia (frogs, toads, etc.)	2,500
Class Reptilia (snakes, lizards, etc.)	6,000
Class Aves (birds)	8,600
Class Mammalia ("warm-blooded" animals with hair, mammary glands, etc.)	3,500

*The numbers of species given in this table are, as stated earlier, rough estimates that are continually being revised. Differences of opinion of course exist among students of taxonomy as to numbers of phyla and species, names of groups, etc.

below. A more complete account is in the article PALEONTOLOGY.

1. Life in the Early Seas.—By the Cambrian period, the first well-documented period, life was already varied. Radiolarian protozoans, many worms, a few echinoderms, many kinds of mollusks, primitive coelenterates, sponges, arthropods, brachiopods and several groups that subsequently became extinct, notably graptolites, trilobites and archaeocyathid sponges, were represented. Ocean reefs in the Early to Middle Cambrian were composed of archaeocyathid sponges; suddenly they died out, possibly having been replaced by calcareous algae.

The largest and perhaps dominant animals of Cambrian seas were the trilobites, primitive arthropods ranging from $\frac{1}{4}$ in. to 27 in. in size. Already diversified in the Early Cambrian, they rose to and maintained dominance until the Late Ordovician when they began to be replaced by the cephalopods; the trilobites then declined in numbers throughout the Carboniferous and finally became extinct in the Permian. (*See* TRILOBITE.)

Brachiopods, or lamp shells, were bottom-dwelling organisms, undergoing their greatest differentiation in the Ordovician, becoming most numerous in the Silurian and Devonian, then progressively declining from the Carboniferous to the present. The six superfamilies and perhaps 245 living species contrast with 19 Silurian superfamilies and a total fossil record of over 30,000 species. (*See* BRACHIOPODA.)

The graptolites, possible primitive relatives of the vertebrates, were tiny bottom-dwelling and planktonic organisms of Early Paleozoic seas. They differentiated in the Cambrian, reached their greatest development in the Ordovician, had a minor resurgence in the Silurian and finally died out in the Lower Carboniferous (Mississippian). (*See* GRAPTOLITE.)

Late in the Cambrian came the first record of the nautiloid cephalopods. These monsters of the Ordovician seas, some with shells 15 feet long, were the largest shelled invertebrates that ever lived. For a time they replaced the trilobites as the dominant animals, but declined in the Silurian and Devonian. Most forms were extinct by the end of the Paleozoic and only one genus, *Nautilus* (*q.v.*), exists today.

About the same time, the Bryozoa, or "moss animals" appear in the fossil strata. Two bryozoan groups, the Trepostomata and

Cryptostomata, were prominent during the Paleozoic, but died out in the Permian; another group, the Ctenostomata have never been important. The Cyclostomata (a bryozoan order, not to be confused with the class Cyclostomata that includes the lampreys, etc.) were moderately important during the Mesozoic, but have been overshadowed during the Tertiary by the Cheilostomata, which appeared in the Cretaceous and form the bulk of the present-day bryozoan fauna. Throughout their history, bryozoans have been important incrusting organisms. (*See* BRYOZOA.)

Of the coelenterates, primitive jellyfish forms have been reported from pre-Cambrian beds. The corals, reef-building coelenterates, are conspicuously absent from early rock strata, not appearing until the Lower Ordovician series of Vermont; by the Silurian and Devonian, however, the Tetracoralla and Tabulata were important organisms of the oceans and formed the major portion of extensive fossil reefs. At the close of the Paleozoic, these early coral organisms had declined in prominence and only a few stragglers persisted into the Mesozoic. Few corals are known between the Permian and Middle Triassic. By then the modern groups of corals had developed a calcareous skeleton and gradually begun to build the reefs so characteristic of modern tropical seas. (*See* COELENTERATA; CORAL; CORAL REEF.)

2. Movement into Fresh Waters.—It is uncertain when the first tentative movements into fresh waters were made by animals. Since animals depend upon plants for food, obviously plants migrated first, but the fossil record is inconclusive concerning the time of the emigration. Probably by the Silurian a good flora and a few animals (branchiopod, phyllocarid and possibly ostracod crustaceans, some mollusks and worms) were established in fresh waters.

The earliest remains of vertebrates are a few fragmentary toothlike structures in the Early Ordovician. More complete fossils occur in Late Ordovician and Early Silurian strata. There is considerable controversy concerning the original habitat of the first vertebrates (*see* A. S. Romer, 1955, and R. H. Denison, 1956). Probably both the earliest vertebrates and the eurypterids, large scorpionlike arthropods that reached their peak numbers in the Silurian and Devonian, with forms reaching 10 feet in length, were present first in brackish waters near the shore. The earliest vertebrates, the ostracoderms, were small, jawless, fishlike creatures with heavily armoured body covering. They fed by filtering food through their gills. The armour was probably a form of protection against predation by the much larger eurypterids.

Sometime during the latter part of the Silurian, both eurypterids and vertebrates colonized the fresh waters. The primitive, jawless ostracoderms were soon replaced by the jawed placoderms. During the Devonian, fish were common in fresh waters, and placoderms were superseded by the bony fishes (class Osteichthyes) still dominant today.

By the end of the Devonian many major fish groups had differentiated, though the modern bony fishes (teleosts) that now dominate the world of fish appeared only as recently as the Jurassic. Of the early fishes, a few fresh-water and marine relicts such as lampreys; lungfish; sharks and rays; sturgeons; and the coelacanth *Latimeria* still remain. From a stock of the crossopterygians, sometime near the end of the Devonian, came the amphibians, the first vertebrates to move from fresh water to the land. (*See* FISH.)

3. Movement onto Land.—The importance of this habitat shift is difficult to overemphasize. By then, plants were undoubtedly well established on land. Although the fossil record for Devonian land invertebrates is sparse and questionable, by the Upper Carboniferous and Permian there is evidence of a rich fauna of insects, land snails, scorpions, spiders, phalangids and mites. Not only were these groups established, but they had diversified considerably. Pennsylvanian strata contain at least three families of land snails, and the Permian beds yield 17 orders of insects, 10 of which still exist today. The origins of these invertebrate forms must have considerably predated the Permian and Carboniferous. Most probably the first invertebrates made the transition from fresh water to land in the Early or Middle Devonian.

All animals moving from water to land faced similar problems,

Geologic Column and Scale of Time
(Ages increase from top downward, as in a sequence of sedimentary rocks)

System and Period	Series and Epoch	Distinctive Records of Life	Began (Millions of Years Ago)
CENOZOIC ERA			
Quaternary	Recent (last 11,000 years)		
	Pleistocene	Early man	2+
	Pliocene	Large carnivores	10
	Miocene	Whales, apes, grazing forms	27
Tertiary	Oligocene	Large browsing mammals	38
	Eocene	Rise of flowering plants	55
	Paleocene	First placental mammals	65–70
MESOZOIC ERA			
Cretaceous		Extinction of dinosaurs; appearance of floras with modern aspects	130
Jurassic		Dinosaurs' zenith, primitive birds, first small mammals	180
Triassic		Appearance of dinosaurs	225
PALEOZOIC ERA			
Permian		Conifers abundant, reptiles developed	260
Carboniferous			
Upper (Pennsylvanian)		First reptiles, great coal forests	300
Lower (Mississippian)		Sharks abundant	340
Devonian		Amphibians appeared, fishes abundant	405
Silurian		Earliest land plants and animals	435
Ordovician		First primitive fishes	480
Cambrian		Large faunas of marine invertebrates	550–570
PRECAMBRIAN TIME			
No known basis for systematic division		Plants and animals with soft tissues, few fossils	Samples of isotopic dates 1,500* 1,900† 3,200‡ 3,490§

*Schist from Clark County, Nev. †Gunflint chert from Canada. ‡Basement rocks from Minnesota. §Basement rocks from the Congo region.

and a brief discussion of the necessary adaptations is included below under *Animal Life on Land*. The stimulus that produced the original invasion of the land is uncertain, but two major theories have been proposed to account for the vertebrate emergence. The most commonly accepted theory, put forward by Romer and summarized in 1958, is that the Devonian red rock beds, where the first amphibian fossils are found, were laid down during periods of increasing drought, and that the crossopterygian-amphibian moved from one drying pond to another in search of moisture and thus gradually became adapted to the rigours of dwelling on land. On the other hand, R. F. Inger in 1957 pointed out that the red beds probably were deposited under constant conditions of humidity; he suggested that the first movements were inspired by a search for food (insects, etc.) across land under conditions of high humidity. At the present time in the humid tropics of southeast Asia and Indonesia, there are several fish genera that venture across land.

The subsequent vertebrate story is well known: the rise of the huge amphibians in the Permian; the appearance of reptiles in the Late Carboniferous and their early radiation in the Permian; and the decline of the amphibians and the rise of the great dinosaurs in the Mesozoic. The end of the Permian saw not only the end of the amphibians as dominant animals but also major changes in the sea; with many bryozoans, trilobites, most nautiloids and corals becoming extinct. (*See* AMPHIBIA; REPTILE; DINOSAUR.)

The Mesozoic saw the dominance of dinosaurs; the evolution of small mammal forms from the therapsid reptiles in the Late Triassic; the appearance of birds in the Jurassic, opossumlike marsupials and primitive placental mammals in the Early Cretaceous; the great radiation of birds in the Cretaceous; and the sudden extinction of the dinosaurs. Finally, there was the tremendous radiation of mammals during the Tertiary and the appearance of man in very recent times. (*See* MAMMAL; BIRD; ANIMALS, PHYLOGENY OF.)

4. Associated Evolutionary Changes.—Compared with the major changes in dominant land species, comparatively minor changes occurred in the oceans from the Mesozoic to the present. The ammonite cephalopods were very important organisms in the Mesozoic, but died out with the dinosaurs at the end of the Cretaceous. Modern groups of corals appeared in the mid-Mesozoic, and modern families of marine snails were common in Cretaceous strata. Many families of marine clams originated in the Paleozoic, and the great majority of families go back well into the Mesozoic. Crustaceans are equally ancient.

Equally significant in any discussion of distribution is the history of land groups other than vertebrates. As mentioned earlier, insects are first known from the Upper Carboniferous and probably first appeared many millions of years before that.

By Late Permian times over one-third of the living orders of insects were established. By the Triassic all the ancient orders (except for the giant dragonflies—order Protodonata, which had wings up to 30 in. in spread) were extinct. The great majority of living orders were present sometime during the Mesozoic. The Tertiary fossil insects belong to modern families or, in many cases, even to modern genera. A few insects found in 50,000,000-year-old Baltic amber apparently belong to living species.

The nonmarine mollusks are equally conservative. A diversified fauna was already established in the Upper Carboniferous, and according to Cretaceous and Paleocene strata modern families and many modern genera were present. Some of these genera live apparently in the same area today that they did in the Paleocene. Species of the Recent epoch are common in Pliocene strata, and comparatively few of the Pleistocene species are extinct.

This conservative state of affairs contrasts greatly with the mammals. In this group orders arose in the Paleocene and modern genera in the very Late Tertiary. The reasons for this are exceedingly complex and a full discussion can be found in Simpson (1953) (*see also* EVOLUTION, ORGANIC). Basically, a type of organism such as a land snail, a reptile or a mammal will undergo an adaptive radiation, a rapid diversification, geologically speaking, by which it fulfills a role or series of roles in nature. After the rapid evolutionary change that produces a number of different

types, there is a stage, usually several times the length of the "explosive" diversification period, where the groups change only slightly. This stage can persist for long periods of time. Occasionally a group of organisms will have found a very suitable way of life under extremely constant environmental conditions, and under this regime the same genus can persist for millions of years. Opossums have changed but little since the Cretaceous; and virtually unchanged are "the horseshoe crab" (*Limulus*), dating from the Triassic, and *Lingula*, a brachiopod, from the Ordovician.

During rapid differentiation groups tend to spread rapidly as well as evolve quickly. When the initial major outburst is completed, diversification into the minor habitat niches occurs. A plateau of reasonable evolutionary stability is maintained until the opportunity for movement into a new region or a new ecological zone arises. Extinction of a group of animals can happen either through replacement by newly evolved, more efficient types (the Paleozoic cephalopods replaced the trilobites, and the mollusks possibly superceded the brachiopods), or through a change in environmental conditions so that the old group can no longer exist (possibly the great marine extinction at the close of the Permian and the dinosaur extinction at the end of the Cretaceous).

The stage of evolutionary activity that a group is in will have profound effects upon the meaning of current distributions. A group that appears to be in a relatively stable phase may represent a pattern of distribution much older than the pattern of a group that is rapidly evolving. Insects and land snails showed minor evolutionary changes in the Tertiary. They probably underwent their initial explosive evolution well back in the Paleozoic and Mesozoic. Mammals underwent their explosive evolution in the Paleocene and Early Tertiary and have continued to show rapid evolutionary change up to the present day.

III. GEOGRAPHICAL DISTRIBUTION OF LIVING ANIMALS

The distribution patterns of animals of the three main habitats—sea, fresh water and land—are usually discussed separately.

1. In the Sea.—It is significant that discussion of the marine distribution patterns is usually on a vertical, habitat or ecological rather than a geographic basis. The ocean presents a continuous medium only occasionally interrupted by major barriers (land masses). These barriers, in the course of geologic time, often have been lowered through encroachment of the sea across narrow necks of land (Bering strait, Isthmus of Panamá). Since most organisms have some form of floating or swimming larva the barriers in the ocean are more ecological than geographic. Also, the length of time that life has been present in the ocean has allowed the gradual movements of major types into essentially the entire geographic area with ecological conditions that would allow their successful reproduction and sustenance. The lower systematic categories, genera and species, and to a much lesser extent families do show at least partially geographically oriented distribution patterns. No faunal realms in the sea equivalent to Wallace's land divisions have been proposed, but some facets of marine animal geography have been presented by S. P. Ekman (1953).

2. In Fresh Water.—In contrast to the sea is the fresh-water habitat, which is, geologically speaking, extremely ephemeral. Fresh waters have existed for millions of years and have supported organisms since at least the Devonian, but individual lakes and river systems usually have a short life span. There has been a premium on organisms able to (1) pass through salt water barriers; (2) take advantage of passive dispersal by wind or other organisms (insects, birds, mammals, fish) from one body of water to another; (3) withstand a great variety of environmental conditions; and (4) start a permanent population from the introduction of one individual. The relative impermanence of fresh waters and the selection for organisms with at least some of the above attributes have resulted in few major groups of organisms colonizing fresh water. The successful invaders, however, tend to be very widely distributed, show an extreme amount of local variation in small bodies such as ponds and lakes and exhibit often very little specific level differentiation. Some species tend to be world-wide in distribution, such as the fresh-water sponge, *Ephydatia fluviatilis;* others widely spread over a major geographic area in many types of fresh-water habitats, as for example the finger-nail clams *Pisidium* and *Sphaerium;* still others are confined within major drainage basins, as are most unionid clams and prosobranch snails.

The only important exception to these generalizations concerns the fauna of ancient fresh-water lakes—Baikal in Siberia; Titicaca in Peru; Nyasa and Tanganyika in Africa; Ohrid in Yugoslavia; and Lakes Poso, Towoeti and Matana in the Celebes. These lakes have well differentiated faunas which, though derived from more generalized species found in external drainages, have undergone considerable divergence from both the ancestral form and habits during long isolation in these unusually permanent fresh waters (fig. 2). The major southern land masses, Australia, South America and Africa, have endemic (native and confined) fresh-water fish and mollusk faunas, whereas the North American and Eurasian land masses have a high percentage of groups, and even species, in common.

3. On Land.—The land habitat is much more permanent than the fresh water, but its own special features have drastically affected the evolution and dispersal of land organisms. Water gaps, which usually form almost impassable barriers for terrestrial organisms, divide the land masses into three great blocks, Australia;

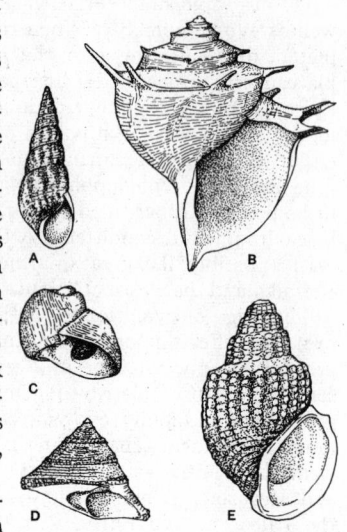

FIG. 2.—ANCIENT LAKE SPECIATION: (A) TYPICAL THIARID (MELANOIDES TUBERCULATA). (B–E) LAKE TANGANYIKA DERIVATIVES: (B) TIPHOBIA HOREI; (C) SPEKIA ZONATA; (D) LIMNOTROCHUS KIRKI; (E) PARAMELANIA DAMONI

the Americas; and Eurasia with Africa. It is now rather generally accepted that the rough outline of the present continental masses has persisted through most of geologic time (*see* ZOOGEOGRAPHY). There have been many minor alterations in contours and several major periods of mountain building. Both the Bering strait and Isthmus of Panamá, for example, have been alternately above and below water frequently during geological time. But at least portions of the main land masses have existed probably since the origin of the land animals and certainly during the major evolution and dispersal of the land vertebrates. These major land masses have at times been isolated from each other for considerable periods by more or less completely impassable water gaps. Notably Australia and, in the mid-Tertiary, South America formed "island continents." For millions of years at least, land mammals were not effectively introduced from other regions.

Evolution proceeded in the northern land masses with the replacement of the early mammals by newer types. The "theatres of evolution" in Australia and South America produced diversification within the primitive stocks. When South America and North America were rejoined in the Late Pliocene and Pleistocene, there was a sudden exchange of groups, with many of the more advanced North American types quickly replacing the more primitive South American forms. Australia has been effectively shielded from advanced organisms until the coming of man, and its fauna of primitive mammals, insects and other organisms is famous.

Less obviously spectacular than the water gaps but equally important in understanding the distribution and diversity of land animals is the extreme variability of environmental conditions on land. Life is based on chemical reactions in an aqueous medium. On land the availability and retention of water is a critical problem. Extremes in water availability range from scorching deserts with years between rainfalls to areas with over 300 inches of rain annually and a ground humidity at or near saturation. Temperature is relatively constant in the water, but on land it varies widely

from region to region and can fluctuate greatly within an area from season to season or even from day to night. Topographic features influence climate (rainfall, temperature and seasons) greatly and often a few miles is all that separates a near desert from a lush rain forest. These features at least temporarily tend to isolate animals into little groups and lead to extensive adaptations and diversifications in ways and areas of living.

Water gaps isolate geographic areas, and temperature and rainfall levels will generally fall into banded or otherwise zoned geographic patterns. The shifting gaps of water as well as climatic changes have channeled much of terrestrial evolution and dispersal along geographic lines, and the past history of animal dispersal can be glimpsed through a study of the geographic distribution of living organisms. This can be approached on the basis of distribution of animal groups (geographical zoology) or by the study of animal groups of a particular area (zoological geography). This sort of study has been done primarily for the land mammals and birds (*see* ZOOGEOGRAPHY) with occasional information on the cold-blooded vertebrates.

As mentioned earlier, the inventory of nonvertebral groups is very incomplete. Knowledge of their classification and distribution is so fragmentary that it is not yet possible to analyze fully their present or past distributions as has been done for the better known vertebrates. Evidence gradually accumulating about such diverse groups as termites, caddis flies and land snails suggests that the distribution patterns of the invertebrates show little conformity with the mammalian and bird patterns recognized by classic zoogeographic divisions. In particular, the invertebrate faunas of South America, south Africa and Australia-New Zealand often show striking similarities. Although very few vertebrates show discontinuous distribution in the southern hemisphere, interrupted distribution patterns are normal in many nonvertebral groups.

There is a very simple possible explanation for these differences in animal distribution patterns. The invertebrates and lower vertebrates had their adaptive radiations at a much earlier period than did the birds and mammals. During the Tertiary when sweeping changes in mammalian evolution and distribution were happening, the invertebrates were undergoing comparatively minor changes. They had probably reached more or less of a balance with their environment, and both Tertiary evolutionary changes and geographic dispersal, with obvious exceptions such as movement onto oceanic islands and into previously glaciated areas, were minimal. The present-day patterns of distribution shown by nonvertebral land-dwellers may represent much earlier adaptive radiations and dispersions than do the distribution patterns of mammals. Tertiary rates of evolution of invertebrates were much slower, and thus rates of dispersal may have been equally retarded.

IV. FACTORS AFFECTING ECOLOGICAL DISTRIBUTION OF LIVING ANIMALS

Each of the three major habitats presents its own set of problems for the successful dispersal and maintenance of life; but unless certain basic criteria are satisfied, no life can exist. Under conditions of extreme adversity life cannot survive: new lava flows; craters of active volcanoes; snows of the extreme polar regions or high mountains; springs rich in carbon dioxide; depths of the Black sea, abundant in hydrogen sulfide; and the Dead sea with its high concentrations of chlorides and bromides of magnesium are among the few areas where no animal life can be found.

These regions lack one or more of the following requisites for animal life: (1) an available set of chemicals to allow completion of metabolic activities and reproduction; (2) suitable temperatures for necessary activities; (3) proper density and pressure for chemical activities; (4) supplies of new materials and energy sources with controlled release of energy; and (5) shelter from lethal light rays. Life on earth evolved into the diverse forms seen today in accordance with the principles of the general environment outlined above.

Every species and individual has certain basic requirements, the fulfillment of which must be accomplished before its life cycle can be completed. Each of the many factors affecting the species varies at some time or other, and each species can tolerate a certain range of variation for each factor. Often the range of tolerated conditions can be greatly extended through avoidance, either a simple movement into a more favourable area or a complex physical adjustment involving a cessation or lowering of activity (dormancy) during the unfavourable period.

Each species has an innate capacity for reproduction far beyond the quantity needed to replace the living generation. Every organism, at some point in its life history, shows the tendency toward or has the capacity for dispersal, the spread by scattering of the original population from an occupied place into new areas. If the dispersed organisms settle in an area where the environment, the totality of factors affecting the organism, is favourable, the distribution, or area occupied by a species at any one moment, will be extended. Often there are barriers that prevent successful dispersal. Organisms are controlled in nature by limiting factors, materials for which there is an irreducible minimum needed or physical conditions that must be maintained within certain limits. The extremes of these factors which are acceptable to the organism represent that organism's limits of tolerance.

Every kind of animal in each of the three major habitats has its own particular limits of tolerance for different factors, its own distribution and pattern of dispersal and its own set of mechanisms for adjusting to or avoiding one or another factor of the environment. There are, however, certain basic adjustments and reactions common to all animals and certain limits of tolerance that cannot be exceeded by any animals. Also, each of the three major habitats presents certain major problems to which different groups of animals have had to adjust.

Basically, all animals must adjust to water, temperature, light, food, oxygen and carbon dioxide factors and to pressure problems in the environment. To indicate the relations of animals to particular factors, a convenient terminology has been established. For example, habitat preferences on land in relation to water supplies are called xerophilous, mesophilous or hygrophilous, going from the driest habitat to the wettest. The range of tolerance, or ecological valence, for any physical factor can be described by the prefixes steno-, meaning narrow, or eury-, meaning wide. Stenothermic, stenohygrous and stenoxybiont, for example, refer to narrow limits of toleration for variation in warmth, moisture and oxygen supply.

Environmental conditions change greatly not only from place to place but also in one area from season to season. In the temperate and arctic regions the obvious seasonal variation is from warm to cold; in the tropics the variation is often from dry to wet. To survive during seasons when conditions greatly exceed their normal limits of tolerance, animals have developed a remarkable group of responses known collectively as dormancy. These involve varying degrees of slowing or cessation of activity (quiescence), metabolic as well as locomotive. The most commonly known examples are hibernation and estivation.

Hibernation is a general term for winter dormancy and is associated with relatively low temperature and physiologically inaccessible water (snow and ice). Estivation is the term for summer dormancy in the temperate zones and dormancy during the dry season in the tropics; it is associated with relatively high temperature and physically inaccessible water (drought). A bear in its winter den; an earthworm in its mucous cocoon; a tree snail cemented to a limb with saliva; and pond protozoans in cysts are all examples of estivating or hibernating animals.

Two special cases deserve mention, not for being different in kind but because they carry dormancy to extreme lengths. The stage in an insect's (or other arthropod's) life cycle in which the animal is in a physiological state of arrested development is usually termed the diapause. Diapause can occur in the egg, larval, pupal or adult stages of insects. Sometimes it occurs in every generation and sometimes in only one of several generations each year. The line between diapause and quiescence is sometimes tenuous.

Even more striking is the anabiosis of certain protozoans, nematodes, rotifers and tardigrades. They normally live in water films on damp soil or vegetation. As dryness increases they encyst into a resting stage that has almost unbelievable powers of resistance

to freezing, having survived exposure to temperatures of −253° C. (near absolute zero), and to drying, having been revived from dried mud after 27 years. Whether all these processes are physiologically equivalent is still uncertain, but all perform the ecological function of enabling animals to survive unfavourable conditions.

1. Water.—Life began in water and the chemical activities of metabolism generally take place in a watery medium inside the animal. Each animal must maintain the internal watery environment at or near a certain level or die. Although the level of water can vary greatly from one stage in the life cycle to another, it always must be maintained within certain limits. Closely associated with the water supply is the question of proper concentration of salts and ions within the cell; the proportions of these substances in most marine animals are approximately the same as in sea water. In fresh water, the body fluids are hypertonic (more concentrated than the outside medium) and the animal has to prevent too much water from accumulating in the body. On land, animals must conserve water. Water relations are discussed in detail under the major habitats.

2. Temperature.—A distinction must be drawn between the temperature levels at which an organism can maintain normal activities and those which an animal can withstand. (All temperature measurements in this article are given in the Centigrade scale [0° C = 32° F. and 100° C. = 212° F.].)

Two blue-green algae, *Phormidium bijahense* and *Oscillatoria filiformis*, live in thermal springs at Yellowstone National park where the temperature is 85.2° C. (about 186° F.), and bacteria have been reported from waters reading 88° C. The upper limit for animals is probably somewhere near 55° C., at which point body chemicals may undergo destructive changes. In East Indian thermal springs, 57 species of animal were found in waters 36–40° C.; twelve in 41–45° C.; four in 46–50° C.; and only four in waters over 50° C. At the other extreme, a cave silphid beetle, *Astagobius angustatus*, carries out its life cycle in ice grottos where the temperature ranges from −1.7° to +1.0° C., and the marine clam, *Yoldia arctica*, is found only in waters 0° C. or colder.

Generally most animals are active somewhere between 6° and 35° C. Individual species will have a range of 16° to 20° in which they are active. Most of the known animal species are poikilothermous, that is, they cannot regulate their body temperature except by moving into warmer environments. Birds and mammals are homoiothermous, that is, they are able to regulate their body temperature by an internal physiological control.

Organisms vary greatly in their ability to withstand exposure to temperatures beyond their normal range of activity. Oceanic and tropical species will often die when a change of a few degrees occurs. Temperate and arctic species show a gradation in resistance to freezing. Some organisms (most mammals, some crustaceans) are killed by chilling to a point above actual freezing; others (many mollusks, insects, fish) can survive partial freezing of their tissues and can endure temperatures 20° or 30° below the freezing point of pure water. Finally, there are the anabiotic organisms mentioned above that can withstand temperatures near absolute zero.

3. Light.—Animals must receive their food at least indirectly from plants that depend on light for photosynthetic activity. Besides this secondary dependence on light, most animals have a daily rhythm of activity and recuperation, which is correlated with the alternation of day and night. Many animals orient themselves and move in relation to light. Quite often light seems to be the factor which triggers breeding behaviour and insures that all members of a species will breed at nearly the same time. Some animals need exposure to light in order for the young to develop. Corals with symbiotic algae need light for proper functioning, though this may reflect more directly the need of the algae than the coral.

4. Food.—A sufficient supply of organic food matter must be available before an area is inhabitable by animals. Usually the amount of available food is the deciding factor in controlling the density of life (number of individuals per unit area). Animals may feed on plants (herbivorous), animals (carnivorous) or both (omnivorous) with complete intergradation between categories.

The diet may be limited to one plant or animal (stenophagous) or a variety of prey (euryphagous). The former often have limited distributions, the latter, wide ones. Animals in caves, ground waters or oceanic deeps are far removed from the plant base of nutrition, but receive organic matter by seepage or gravity.

5. Oxygen and Carbon Dioxide.—Few animals, notably parasites and certain worms and larvae inhabiting waters polluted by garbage, can live without free oxygen. In other cases, however, oxygen is often a limiting factor in aquatic habitats. Polluted waters, sea areas with minimal circulation of water and many fresh-water lake bottoms have little free oxygen and therefore sparse animal populations. Excess carbon dioxide is equally harmful and land areas near fumaroles (holes where carbon dioxide escapes from the earth) form death traps. Carbon dioxide in water often limits the distribution of aquatic organisms. On land, oxygen is plentiful enough to seldom create a problem.

6. Pressure.—Animal life apparently can exist and function only in the range of temperature and pressure in which water is a relatively warm solid (ice) or a cool to warm liquid. On land, pressure is important only in high mountain areas, mainly because of decreased oxygen tension rather than a direct physical effect. Little is known of the effects of pressure on deep-sea organisms. It is known, however, that chemical reactions are speeded or hindered by pressure changes, but the metabolism of deep-sea creatures is essentially unstudied.

V. ANIMAL LIFE IN THE SEA

More than two-thirds of the earth is covered by ocean waters, which reach a greatest depth of 11,033 m. (almost six nautical miles) and an average depth of 3,975 m. (slightly more than two nautical miles). All oceans are connected, though land barriers, some of recent duration, form essentially two main divisions of the oceans—the Atlantic and Arctic with adjacent seas; and the Pacific and Indian oceans. These two divisions are joined in the north by the Bering strait, and in the south by broad bands of water. Smaller seas such as the Mediterranean and Baltic are connected to the major seas by narrow straits. Only a few isolated bodies, such as the Aral and Caspian seas, are separated from the major systems.

Except for those few regions mentioned earlier that are barren of life, animals are found, in widely differing degrees of abundance, throughout all levels and in all seas. The diversity of animal form in the sea is much greater than on the land. Ignoring purely parasitic types, of all the classes of free-living animals, only four—Onychophora, Chilopoda (centipedes), Diplopoda (millipedes) and Amphibia—are completely absent from the sea, while at least 27 seem to be confined to the oceans. Life originated in the ocean and probably was 500,000,000 years old before moving into fresh waters and onto land.

Despite the greater variety of types, the number of species of marine animals is only about one-fifth of the total number of animal species known to scientists. This is correlated with the relative uniformity of habitat conditions and the comparatively minor barriers to dispersal present in the oceans. Only in the transition zones (ecotones) between sea and land (shore areas) and between fresh water and sea (estuaries near river mouths) do conditions fluctuate widely, and here are found species with very limited geographic range because of their restricted dispersal capabilities.

A. Conditions Influencing Sea Life

Although living conditions in the sea are uniform compared with conditions on land and in fresh water habitats, there are distinct differences between areas and zones of the sea that profoundly affect the distribution and abundance of life. The basic chemistry and physics of the oceans are discussed in the article OCEAN AND OCEANOGRAPHY; here it is possible only to outline briefly some of the ways in which different chemical and physical factors govern the distribution of marine animals (see also MARINE BIOLOGY).

1. Physical.—*Light.*—The rate at which the different length rays of light are absorbed in the water depends upon several factors, including the angle at which they strike the water, the degree of surface disturbance (waves) and the amount of suspended particles in the water. Generally the ocean is divided into three strata of light: (1) The euphotic stratum, variously defined as running from the surface to 30 or 100 m. depth, has abundant light and supports most of the phytoplankton (see PLANKTON) that ultimately provides food for all marine animals—the herbivores and their predators; (2) The dysphotic or twilight stratum extends from 30 or 100 m. down to 200 or 500 m. and has very little light, consequently little phytoplankton, few herbivores and many predators. (3) The aphotic stratum lacks any light other than that provided by luminescent creatures, has no phytoplankton or herbivores, but only predators and scavengers. The euphotic zone is shallowest near the poles, and in polar waters life is densely concentrated in a rather narrow zone compared with tropical oceans.

Pressure and Density.—Most marine organisms are slightly denser than sea water. In order to keep from sinking to the bottom they must have special flotation mechanisms (see *Pelagic Division,* below). Also the density of sea water supports the bodies of marine animals and minimizes the need for supporting elements. Pressure increases tremendously from the surface to the depths, but seems to have relatively little influence on animal life. Many organisms will travel 400 m. vertically each day, while whales can move from the surface to below 1,600 m. Pressure affects the volume of gases and certain chemicals greatly. Most fish have a swim bladder, an air-filled sac that adjusts the density of the fish to that of sea water and enables it to stay at a given pressure level with a minimum of exertion. Vertical movements require changes in the amount of gas present and this is done by secretion or adsorption of gases through the membranes of the swim bladder. Many deep-sea fishes lack a swim bladder, and those that have one are often ruptured by the expanding gases when brought from the depths to the surface in a collecting net.

Waves, Tides and Currents.—Waves may reach to a depth of 500 m. and the adjustment that sea animals make to them takes several forms. In the areas of wave movement fixed animals such as Alcyonaria (*Spongodes*) and bryozoans are flexible, and bend with the water motion, as wheat in a wind; corals tend to have a rounded, flattened or thickened mass. In quieter waters the alcyonarians have stiff skeletons, and the corals have lightly calcified, finely branched stalks. In areas of wave pounding, where the force may reach 15 tons per square metre, the animals must protect themselves from injury and from being torn loose. Barnacles cement themselves to the rocks, mussels (*Mytilus*) attach themselves by byssus threads and snails anchor by a muscular foot, as in periwinkles, limpets and abalones.

Tides play an exceedingly important role in the life of shore zones (see *Benthic Zone,* below).

Ocean currents, continuous flows of water as opposed to the oscillations of tides and waves, mix the waters from different parts of the ocean. This maintains a more or less uniform chemical composition of the water, carries dissolved oxygen to all parts of the ocean and serves to spread the planktonic larvae of marine animals. For example, adult ghost crabs (*Ocypode albicans*) do not live north of New Jersey, but young, swimming stages have been collected off Rhode Island and Massachusetts, where they had been carried by currents from the southern breeding grounds. Currents are based on many factors: variations in temperature, salinity and turbidity; effects of the earth's rotation; and wind, to cite the major examples. The permanent currents (see OCEAN AND OCEANOGRAPHY) have particular impact on marine life, especially the areas of upwelling, where deep waters rich in nutriment are brought up to the surface. This upwelling results in regions that are rich in phytoplankton, herbivores and their predators. Areas off Peru, California and Portugal are good examples of such upwellings.

Heat and Temperature.—Most of the sun's radiated heat falls on the ocean and is used in evaporation of water that eventually drops back on the ocean or on land. While the sun's rays are fundamentally important in life processes, the related phenomenon of temperature is more directly responsible for limitations of animal distribution. Ocean temperatures range from about −3° to 42° C., although surface waters, except in lagoons and tide pools, seldom reach more than 30° C. Polar and tropical seas are relatively uniform in temperature, whereas temperate latitudes show greater fluctuations. The annual variation on almost ¾ of the ocean surface is less than 5°.

Temperature stratification is both horizontal and vertical. Generally, surface temperature decreases from the tropics to the poles, though this is greatly modified by currents that move warm waters toward the polar regions. Since cold water is denser than warm water, a constant flow of cold polar water is pushed down and under by the warmer tropical currents. Even near the surface in tropical waters the temperature drops rapidly. If it is 25° C. at the surface, at 200 m. it may be 20° C.; at 1,200 m. 5° C.; and in the abyssal regions, always 1° to 2° C. Seas, such as the Mediterranean, Gulf of Mexico, Red sea and Caribbean sea, that are connected to the larger masses by shallow straits have warmer bottom layers caused by (1) sinking of partially warmed surface water; (2) inflow of only slightly colder water from the major seas; and (3) exclusion of cold, deep waters by shallow entrances.

Many marine organisms are rigidly limited by water temperatures. The great colonies of reef-growing corals cannot tolerate water cooler than 20° C. and thus are restricted to tropical seas. Nearly all marine distributions can be correlated with temperature. Thus the European oyster (*Ostrea edulis*) breeds in water above 15° C., while the Portuguese oyster (*Ostrea angulata*) requires temperatures above 20° for breeding. Rates of metabolism are also greatly altered by temperature change. Often, size within a species increases from warm to cold waters. The snail *Nassarius clausus* is 12.7 mm. high in waters of the Skagerrak (an arm of the North sea south of Norway) and reaches 38 mm. at Spitsbergen, in the Arctic. The isopod *Serolis bromleyana* measures 16 mm. at 739 m. depth and 54 mm. at 3,600 m. The increase in number of vertebrae in related fishes from south to north waters (Jordan's rule) is well documented.

2. Chemical.—*Composition of Sea Water.*—Sea water is an assemblage of dissolved solids and gases, with a variable amount of suspended inorganic and organic matter. The continuous mixing of waters by currents results in a generally uniform composition. Salinity averages about 3.5%, with local variations caused by melting ice, river inflow or high evaporation. Thus polar surface waters may have a lower salinity because of ice melting, much of the Baltic sea has a lower salinity because of the many rivers it drains, while the Red sea and Mediterranean have slightly higher salinity because of rapid evaporation and little fresh water inflow. Estuaries have lower salinities, grading from that of open ocean water to that of the pure fresh water far upstream. The size and presence of species living in these areas can be closely correlated with the degree of salinity. Some animals, such as the mussel *Mytilus* and the lugworm *Arenicola*, are euryhaline; others, notably reef corals, are stenohaline and can tolerate almost no lowering of salinity.

Animals feed directly or indirectly on plants, and the abundance of plant life determines the numbers of animals. Plants need carbon dioxide, nitrogen compounds, phosphates and many trace chemicals; these elements must be present in the euphotic zone, not in the depths. Ocean areas supplied by river waters (Atlantic, Arctic) receive vast quantities of minerals from the fresh waters. All oceans receive animal waste products and decomposing animal bodies. Much of the latter sink to the ocean floor where the chemicals produced through decomposition are unavailable to plants unless carried up by a vertical current into an upwelling. In a shallow sea where waters are completely mixed decomposition substances are readily available. The great productivity of the North sea (especially along the Dogger bank) and of the waters of the Newfoundland banks are the result of vertical mixing and river inflow. The coasts of Portugal and Peru are rich in marine life because of deep upwellings. In contrast, the open eastern Pacific with few inflowing rivers and no major upwellings is poor in surface life.

Calcium is important to animals in building supporting structures. In sea water calcium sulfate is precipitated by ammonium carbonate into forms used to make spicules, skeletons, shells and armour. This reaction proceeds quickly at 26°–29° C., but very slowly at low temperatures. Thus the greatest use of calcium by animals occurs in tropical seas. In colder waters animals have soft bodies or skeletons composed primarily of silicon or protein. Calcareous sponges are restricted to shallow waters, and the siliceous hexactinellid sponges are found only in deep waters.

Oxygen is generally mixed in through surface disturbances and carried throughout the oceans by currents of polar surface water. Warm water carries less oxygen than cold water; therefore, warm areas that lack polar currents, such as the eastern Mediterranean, have little oxygen in their depths. If a rich surface fauna showers decomposing animal bodies on an oxygen-poor bottom, poisonous deposits of hydrogen sulfide can accumulate to the point of near exclusion of life (Black sea and some isolated lagoons).

Water Relations.—Exclusive of skeletal structures, the body of marine animals consists of 60% to 96% water. In this body water are suspended complex chemicals (protein, colloids, organic nonelectrolytes and electrolytes) necessary to life. In most marine animals the concentration of these chemicals is at approximately the same level as the salt concentration in sea water (isotonic). If exposed to sea water by a permeable or semipermeable membrane, these cells will neither give water to nor take water from the external environment. The body fluid of most invertebrates varies in concentration as the salinity of sea water changes (poikilosmotic). Many marine invertebrates can function in fluctuating salinities by salt loss or by swelling, but most species can stand only slight variations before death ensues. Species in estuarine situations generally can withstand a wide range of salinities, usually by regulating the water loss or intake. These homoiosmotic organisms accomplish this regulation by a variety of means fundamentally similar to those used by fresh-water organisms (*see* below). Generally the fresh-water forms must prevent or minimize water intake and salt loss, since the concentration in their body fluids is greater than the salinity of the surrounding medium.

Marine vertebrates have the opposite problem: the concentration of their body fluids is well below the salinity of sea water, and they must prevent or minimize water loss and salt intake. Elasmobranch fishes do this by having a relatively impervious body covering, by maintaining a high urea level in the blood and by secreting a dilute urine. Modern bony fishes (teleosts) actively secrete salt through the gills, drink large quantities of water and conserve water by passing little urine. Marine reptiles, birds and mammals have an impervious body covering; breathe air, thus respiratory surfaces are protected from salt water; and generally eat fish whose body fluids have low salt concentrations. Species feeding on invertebrates may satisfy their water needs through metabolizing the fat in their food. E. H. F. Baldwin (1948) gives an excellent summary of osmotic relations of animals.

B. ZONATION OF MARINE ANIMALS

The distributional division of marine animals into benthic (bottom dwellers) and pelagic organisms (ocean dwellers) parallels the strictly ecological distinction of benthos, nekton (swimmers) and plankton (floaters) (*see* ECOLOGY). All are terms of convenience, since most benthic species will have a brief floating or swimming larval stage, and some occasionally swim as adults (scallops, flounders). Generally, pelagic species are those permanently independent of any support other than water. Benthic forms are those that rest on the bottom, even if only occasionally.

The ocean habitat can be further divided in several ways. One scheme is presented in the article MARINE BIOLOGY. The area from the high tide mark to the limit of attached plants that carry on photosynthesis is called the littoral zone. The deep-sea province farther out is divided into the archibenthic (to 1,000 m.) and abyssal (below 1,000 m.) zones.

Generally, the limit of the littoral zone is at the edge of the continental shelf, or about 200 m. deep. The littoral zone can be divided into the (1) supratidal splash zone; (2) intertidal zone; (3) shallow-water zone, normally affected by waves; and (4) still water zone, extending to the beginning of the deep-sea province.

1. Pelagic Division.—Living matter is slightly heavier than sea water, and a flotation mechanism to prevent sinking is an essential adaptation for pelagic life. Floating is accomplished in

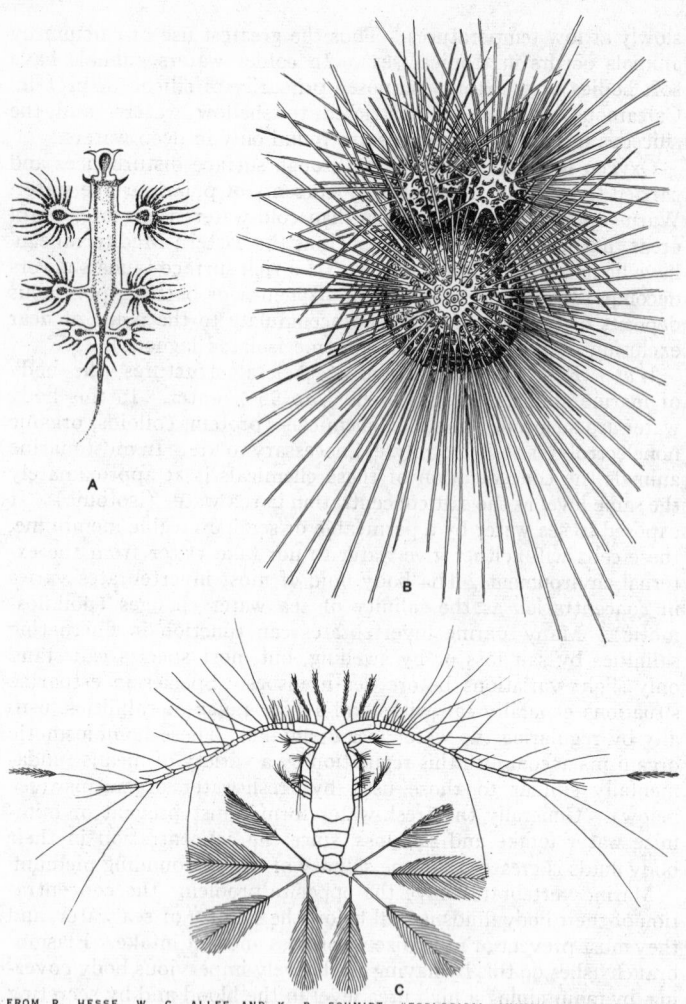

FROM R. HESSE, W. C. ALLEE AND K. P. SCHMIDT, "ECOLOGICAL ANIMAL GEOGRAPHY"; RE-
PRODUCED BY PERMISSION OF JOHN WILEY & SONS, INC.

FIG. 3.—PELAGIC LIFE FLOTATION MECHANISMS SHOWING USE OF BRISTLE-
LIKE EXTENSIONS TO RETARD SINKING: (A) MOLLUSK (GLAUCUS); (B)
FORAMINIFER (GLOBIGERINA); (C) CRUSTACEAN (CALOCALANUS)

ter motion. The larger forms are the nektonic animals, swimmers that are reasonably independent of currents; strictly speaking, they comprise only certain fishes and cephalopods, marine reptiles and mammals. The categories, however, are not sharply distinguished, such giants as the ocean sunfish being practically planktonic, and most small organisms being capable of some movement in still water. A good review of the plankton is given by A. C. Hardy (1956).

Oceanic pelagic animals spend their entire life in the plankton (holoplanktonic). These species can generally be found in all seas with suitable temperature conditions. Nearer to shore an additional element is present, animals which spend part of their life in the plankton and part on the bottom. They may be planktonic as adults, breeding on the bottom (meroplanktonic), or larval forms of benthic species that are dispersed in the larval stage.

No sponges, ascidians, brachiopods or bryozoans are pelagic as adults, and few actinians, echinoderms, worms (other than chaetognaths), clams, and snails (other than a few opisthobranchs and the heteropods and pteropods) are represented in the pelagic division. Radiolarians, jellyfishes (except *Lucernaria*), siphonophores, most ctenophores, chaetognaths, heteropods, pteropods, salpas and appendiculates are exclusively pelagic. Copepod crustaceans and cephalopods and fish are also important elements.

Below the level of the light penetration, there is still a considerable pelagic fauna consisting of fish, coelenterates, crustaceans, cephalopods and whales. No plant food is available, and the mid-zone pelagic fauna is one of predators. The water is still, except for slight currents, the temperature is uniformly low and the pressure per square inch is great. Luminescent organs are widely developed, and many deep-sea forms have huge eyes that enable them to spot the tiny glow from luminescent organs of other animals. Since sampling of the fauna has been very poor, little is known of deep-sea animals.

2. Benthic Division.—Conditions vary so widely in this division that it is difficult to make generalizations concerning its animal life. Even breaking it into its vertical strata does little to simplify the problem. A. Bruun (1956) provides excellent data on the deep-sea organisms, while C. M. Yonge (1949) treats the seashore and A. C. Hardy (1959) the bottom fauna. Remarks here are limited to a very few generalizations.

Both the number of marine species and the number of individuals are richest in the littoral benthos, especially in the subtidal areas. Problems of survival are the fewest, and both the pelagic and deep-sea faunas seem to be derived evolutionarily from littoral organisms. From the littoral zone, migrations, over geological time, have been made into the tidal zones, onto land, into brackish waters and finally into fresh waters.

The type of bottom has a profound influence on the habits and adaptations of life in the littoral zone. Sand and mud bottoms will have animals modified for burrowing or plowing through the substrate; clams having smooth flat shells, muscular feet for digging and long siphons projecting above the substrate for filtering food and breathing; echinoderms and worms eating their way through the sand and extracting nourishment from the debris; predatory snails, crustaceans and fish feeding on the other organisms.

Rocky shores are characterized by stationary (sessile) animals; attached worms, sponges and coelenterates; mussels anchored by byssal threads; snails secured by a muscular foot; and crabs, snails, fish and a myriad of other animals hiding in every conceivable rock crevice. Many of these organisms filter food from the water washed over them (barnacles, worms, bryozoans, clams); others graze on algae (snails); and many prey on other animals or scavenge (snails, echinoderms, crustaceans).

A coral reef, a special form of rocky shore formed by the calcareous skeletons of coelenterates, shelters an even more diverse fauna than a pure rock shore. Reef-building corals are limited to tropical seas and cannot grow in depths greater than 50 m. because the symbiotic algae associated with the coral-forming animals must have light to carry on photosynthesis. Coral reefs are zoned, with massive, blocklike colonies in the breaker zone and delicate, branched forms in calmer water. Associated animals are similarly

many ways. Reduction in weight through economy in skeletal material is shown by Foraminifera (*e.g., Globigerina*); snails (*e.g.,* heteropods and pteropods); squids (*e.g., Loliginidae*); and fish (*e.g., Crystallogobius*). Reduction in specific gravity through absorption of water is seen among all pelagic coelenterates, chaetognaths, tunicates and many mollusks and fish. Storage of materials lighter than sea water is demonstrated in the ctenophore *Beroë*, the protozoan *Noctiluca* and in the radiolarians; all these organisms contain a special fluid of low specific gravity. Oil droplets are stored by radiolarians and *Noctiluca*. Fat bodies are common in copepods and cladocerans, and enable the huge basking shark (*Cetorhinus maximus*) and ocean sunfish (*Mola mola*) to lie motionless at the ocean surface. Inclusion of air or other gases in part of the body is seen in the air sacs of siphonophores, the air chambers in the shells of the mollusks *Nautilus* and *Spirula* and the air bladder system of bony fishes. Tiny plankton organisms support themselves by increasing their body resistance to sinking through development of long bristles (fig. 3) and by enlarging the ventral surface through flattening of the body, as in jellyfish and many larvae. Support is also gained by muscular action: the oar-shaped limbs of crustaceans; the lashing cilia of larvae and ctenophores; the water-propelling devices of pulsating jellyfishes, tunicates and squids; the undulating fin motions of pelagic cephalopods, heteropods and rays; and the body undulations of fishes, whales and seals. Generally, several mechanisms are combined in one organism.

Herbivores and carnivores of all sizes are found in the pelagic division. The smallest forms are the planktonic animals, whose independent movements are insignificant when compared with wa-

oriented.

The littoral zone is greatly influenced by tidal rhythms and by the light alternations of day and night. Behaviour, breeding and colour are often correlated with light conditions. The tidal fluctuations expose to the air, for varying periods each day, the organisms of the intertidal zone. Many mechanisms for coping with water conservation, temperature variations, feeding problems, reproduction and salinity variations have developed in intertidal animals.

Estuaries, with fluctuating salinity levels, have a highly limited fauna and form a special ecotonal habitat between the sea and fresh water. In tropical and subtropical regions the mangrove with its associated brackish water fauna is a special type of estuarine habitat.

In contrast to the littoral zone the deep-sea area is without light, except for luminescence, and has no plant life. Only scavengers and predators exist in this domain. The recovery of more animals from great deeps, due to improved methods of collecting, has proved, contrary to former opinion, that the ocean deeps have a diverse fauna. Animals have been collected from 10,190 m. in the Philippine trench.

Abyssal creatures are relatively scarce compared with littoral forms, rather small in size and white or dark monochrome in colour. Many of these forms burrow in bottom ooze, but some, certain crustaceans, walk on stiltlike legs, and others creep over the surface. The topography of the bottom is as varied as that of littoral waters, and life is similarly specialized. The deep basins will often have endemic species, while shallow waters (above 1,000 m.) may have widely distributed forms around the fringes of the deeps. Stalked crinoids and many other ancient groups are confined to deep seas. The deep sea is not just a refuge for ancient types, for relatively modern mollusk groups (turrids) also live there.

Many deep-sea organisms were first recorded from shallow waters in the Arctic and Antarctic, only to be subsequently discovered in the deep seas between. Thus the old idea of bipolarity in distribution of marine animals had to be abandoned.

VI. ANIMAL LIFE IN FRESH WATERS

Probably less than 2% of the earth's surface is covered by inland bodies of water. These are generally small, only 18 lakes and inland seas having areas of more than 10,000 sq.km. An ecological division is made into salt and fresh waters, with the latter divided into lenitic, or standing waters (bog, marsh, swamp, puddle, pond, lake) and lotic or flowing waters (spring, stream, river). Many flowing waters drain great basins and eventually empty into lakes or the seas. Standing waters range from water films after rains, temporary ponds in small depressions that hold water a few weeks a year, permanent pools and small lakes to ancient deepwater lakes.

A. Conditions Influencing Fresh-water Life

The same factors that limit marine distributions act in fresh waters. Light penetrates very little into fresh water; temperatures fluctuate much more widely than in the ocean; calcium may be abundant (hard water) or absent (soft water); nitrate and phosphate supplies vary widely; some waters become clogged with organic debris; oxygen is abundant in streams but absent from many lake bottoms at least part of the year; currents may be swift or absent; and waters may be polluted by man. In addition, fresh-water life has to contend with the basic problems of osmotic regulation and effective dispersal. All these factors help determine the local distribution of organisms within an area since each species has its own limits of tolerance for variations in these conditions. Equally important in temperate areas is the fact that water is most dense at 4° C. at which temperature it sinks into the warmer water below. Below this temperature, however, water becomes less dense and at 0° C. freezes; therefore ice forms on the surface and, except in very shallow areas, does not reach the bottom. Because of this phenomenon some animals can winter over in the water beneath the ice. In some cases organisms can even withstand freezing in ice for relatively protracted periods.

The fragmentation of fresh waters into small bodies isolated from each other by ocean or land barriers, their very low salt content and their geologically brief life span have molded the habits of fresh-water organisms and restricted successful colonization to a comparatively few groups. Arthropods, mollusks and vertebrates are the dominant fresh-water organisms. Few sponges, hydrozoans, polychaetes, bryozoans, nemerteans, mysidaceans and amphipods reached fresh waters. Decapod crustaceans and fishes and clams are primarily marine but well represented in fresh water, while nematodes, turbellarians, oligochaetes, leeches, isopods and snails are found in all habitats. Rotifers, cladocerans, water mites and nematomorphs are predominantly fresh water; and tardigrades, gastrotrichs and ciliate and mastigophoran protozoans are more numerous in fresh water than in the sea. Only the branchiopods, except for a few forms, and the syncarid crustaceans are exclusively fresh-water dwellers. Amphibians, which generally must spend part of their life cycle in water, also wander widely on land, where they are most often found only under conditions of high humidity. Although insects are predominantly terrestrial, a few families live in fresh waters and many orders undergo their larval stages there.

B. Special Factors

1. Low Salt Content.—Since the salt content of fresh water is very low compared with both sea water and animal body fluids, there is a constant tendency for water to pass into the animal and dilute the body fluids. This can be combated and minimized by two general methods, a reduction in exposed permeable areas and excretion of copious quantities of very dilute urine. A hardened (chitinous or sclerotized) body covering in invertebrates (leeches, crustaceans, insects), the scales of fish and reptiles, the skin of mammals and the slime covering of eels and snails all represent means of reducing water intake. Gill breathers and forms such as amphibians with unprotected skin surfaces will absorb more water than air breathers or forms with protected body surfaces. Excretion of water is accomplished through the contractile vacuoles of protozoans, flame cells of flatworms (platyhelminthes) and various nephridial and glandular organs of higher animals.

Probably associated with the low salt level of fresh waters are the relatively few and large eggs laid by fresh-water animals as compared with marine relatives. Embryos of marine organisms apparently often absorb chemicals from the water, a feat which could not be accomplished by organisms working against the fresh-water osmotic gradient. Also, while marine organisms depend, to a large extent, on egg or larval dispersal by currents, fresh-water organisms in running waters would be swept away and could not move against the current. Most fresh-water organisms carry the eggs on or in the body or attach them to anchored structures. Compared with marine animals, free-swimming fresh-water larval forms are few; most of the young hatch as miniature replicas of the adult. Clam larvae (glochidia) are free for a while before parasitizing a fish; copepod, branchiopod and ostracod crustaceans, some insects and many amphibians have a free-swimming larval stage.

2. Relative Impermanence of Fresh Waters.—Many fresh-water habitats become dry during part of the year, and numerous adaptations exist for surviving the dry period. The encystment of rotifers, nematodes, tardigrades, protozoans and some copepods has been mentioned previously. Cladocerans, copepods, ostracods, caddis fly larvae, prosobranch snails, clams such as the sphaeriids and *Spatha* and some eels and lungfishes all bury themselves in mud during dry periods. Many water insects, salamanders, frogs and a few fishes (eels, callichthys, *Doras*) move across land areas to new water basins when their habitats dry out.

Marginal fresh-water habitats (ditches, grassy pools, desert lakes) may have water for only a few weeks a year or perhaps only once in several years. Only the most drought resistant organisms can survive. Certain branchiopods (fairy, tadpole and clam shrimps) exist today perhaps only because of their ability to adapt to this seemingly unfavourable niche. Some branchiopods can remain dormant for 15 years and then complete their life cycle in two weeks when water is available. Temporary ponds that have water for the same few weeks every year can support a diverse fauna consisting of microscopic encysting organisms, pulmonate snails, flatworms and small crustaceans besides providing breeding grounds for amphibians. Generally, the larger and more permanent bodies of water have more varied and larger faunas. Major river basins and larger lakes have endemic races or species, and very old basins and lakes may have endemic genera.

The encysted species found in water films and temporary pools tend to be world-wide in distribution; those of annual pools may range over one or two continents; those of permanent ponds and lakes may show numerous local varieties but a wide species range; and species found only in rivers may have a range limited to that basin. These distribution patterns are clearly correlated with dispersal capabilities. Encysted species may be blown about with dust particles by the wind or carried in dried mud on birds' feet. Severe storms have even produced showers of fish and frogs; and undoubtedly, many smaller animals are accidentally transported in this fashion. Insects and birds can carry organisms for short distances, and eggs occasionally fasten to their feet. Other species show little capacity for dispersal and are restricted in range.

Fresh-water mollusks show a series of distributional types correlated with dispersal mechanisms. Sphaeriid clams (*Pisidium* and *Sphaerium*) are hermaphroditic, and the young develop inside the adult's body. Ancylid, physid, lymnaeid and planorboid pulmonate snails are egg-laying hermaphrodites capable of self-fertilization. In the last two families of snails, if self-fertilization is followed by cross-fertilization, there is complete selection for the sperm from the cross-fertilization. This range of reproductive capacity allows not only for population of a new habitat by one individual but also for genetic variety through genetic recombination when more than one snail is present. The snail species named above are the only molluscan inhabitants of temporary ponds; they provide nearly all of the observed cases of accidental transport of mollusks by other organisms. All can burrow and encapsulate in mud and remain dormant for a long time. They are very widely distributed and often show bewildering local variations. In contrast, prosobranch snails have separate sexes and, except for tropical species, very seldom live in dried mud. Some small species can pass through fish or bird digestive tracts unharmed and in this way are distributed, but most species are restricted to definite areas, usually equivalent to drainage patterns. Finally, the larger fresh-water clams, Unionidae and related families, often have a

parasitic glochidial stage during which the larvae attach to fish. The fish can distribute the clams through a lake or river system, but intersystem transport is an extremely rare event. Unionids, because of their restricted distribution, are sometimes used to aid in the interpretation of past stream histories.

C. ZONATION OF FRESH-WATER ANIMALS

Lakes, ponds and oceans are zoned vertically; streams and rivers longitudinally. Lower reaches of streams with their muddy bottoms and much suspended organic material have many slow-moving detritus feeders. Upper parts of the rivers have clearer waters with rocky bottoms and crawling or swift-moving species. Some species may range from head waters to the entrance into a sea, many more are confined to the lower sections. Many fish spend part of their time in the sea and part in fresh water (*e.g.*, salmon). In the tropics many shallow-water marine organisms seem to have recently moved into fresh waters, notably thiarid snails and selachian fishes.

1. Surface Film.—The surface film of water has complex physical properties that enable a special fauna, the *neuston*, to develop. These are organisms adapted to gliding on top of or clinging to the bottom of the surface film. Gyrinid beetles, the hemipteran water striders, collembolans and even spiders may live on top, while cladocerans, protozoans and occasionally worms, snails, insect larvae and hydras may be attached to the underside.

2. Standing Water.—Standing bodies of water—ponds, swamps, bogs and lakes—have planktonic and bottom-dwellers just as the ocean, and with similar types of adaptations. In shallow areas of abundant plant growth, a rich fauna is present, with burrowing and creeping forms well represented. Normal variations in water levels, however, are such that only organisms capable of moving with the level or of encysting are present. Sessile and sedentary animals are found only in deeper waters. Cold-adapted organisms and detritus feeders (worms, snails, some clams, many protozoans) form the bulk of the deeper fresh-water lake fauna. In northern lakes these animals may live near the shore line, but in deep lakes with warmer surface waters they live only in the depths. Fishes range throughout lakes, often moving vertically with the seasons. Fishes feeding on bottom debris often have beardlike feelers.

Salty lakes can be isolated arms of the sea (Caspian sea) or the result of high evaporation (Great Salt lake). The former have marine animals, the latter a few highly salt-tolerant organisms (notably the brine shrimp *Artemia* and larvae of the dipteran *Ephydra*) derived from fresh-water species.

3. Running Water.—These can be divided into rapids and pools, with extensive transition zones between. Generally, running waters have more oxygen than still waters, a great runoff of chemicals from the land and an animal distribution primarily controlled by currents. Many lake animals exist in pool areas of running waters, but in the rapids of brooks and streams, special adaptations are needed for existence. A few sponges and bryozoans anchor by pedicels to rocks; some clams (*Byssanodonta*) and insects use attachment threads; snails and flatworms, a slimy undersurface; larval insects and mites, clawed legs; and such diverse animals as leeches, larval insects of many kinds, fishes and tadpoles, suction discs (fig. 4). Many of these animals have a flattened body enabling them to fit into narrow crevices; it is usually streamlined with a broadly rounded front and tapering posterior, offering minimum resistance to flowing water. Normally, these forms point upstream and move against the current, staying close to or in contact with a surface.

VII. ANIMAL LIFE ON LAND

Slightly more than one-quarter of the earth's surface is covered by land, which ranges from a few areas below sea level (Death valley) to 29,028 ft. above (Mt. Everest). Terrestrial animal life is most abundant in the tropical and temperate regions, becoming relatively scarce, both in species and individuals, in colder latitudes and at higher elevations. While many animals can fly or be carried to great heights by air currents, they are land-based for recuperation and breeding. Unlike in the sea and fresh water,

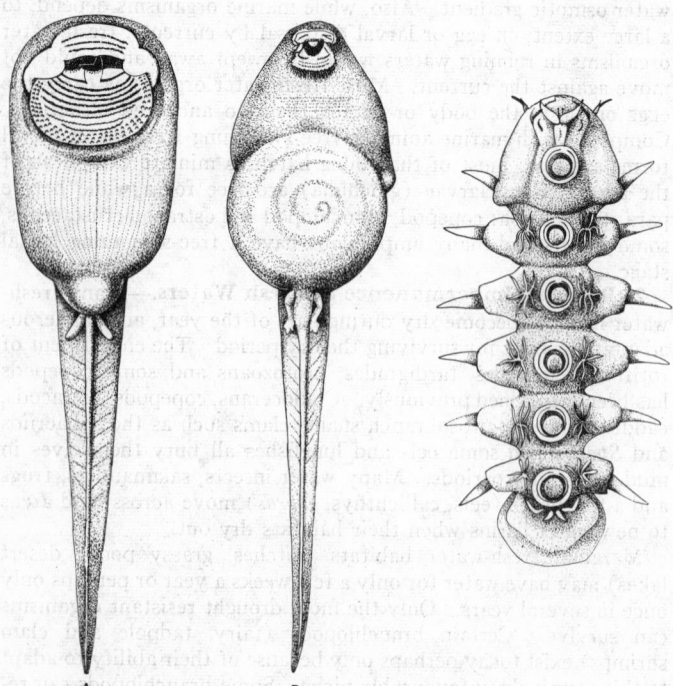

FIG. 4.—COMPARISON OF ADAPTATIONS TO STANDING AND RUNNING WATER: (A) POND TADPOLE (RANA PIPIENS); (B) SWIFT STREAM TADPOLE WITH SUCKER (ASCAPHUS TRUEI); (C) SWIFT STREAM DIPTERAN LARVA WITH SUCKERS (LIPONEURA)

animal life on land is confined to a narrow band extending at most from a few feet below the air-ground surface to the top of the highest vegetation (perhaps 250 ft. in tropical forests).

Vertebrates, arthropods and mollusks are the most successful land groups. Nematodes, oligochaete worms, a very few ostracods, leeches, onychophorans (*Peripatus*), a few nemerteans and flat-worms comprise the other terrestrial organisms. Protozoans, which live only in water films, are not truly terrestrial even though they are found in land habitats. Reptiles, birds and mammals are primarily terrestrial; amphibians usually spend part of their time in the water; and fish only rarely venture onto land. Snails are the only molluscan land dwellers, though a few finger-nail clams (*Sphaerium*) occasionally creep up into wet leaf litter. Most arachnids, millipedes and centipedes live on land, and insects are predominantly terrestrial with many fresh-water and a few marine species. Despite the paucity of major groups, it has been estimated that more than four-fifths of the known animal species are terrestrial. This is the result of the great diversity of land habitats, the many barriers to dispersal and the great variations in physical conditions.

A. Basic Adaptations to Terrestrial Life

1. Air.—In moving onto the land, animals gained an abundant oxygen supply, a diffuse medium (air) that allowed quick movements and offered less impediment to vision and a plentiful food supply (green plants). The decreased density of air, however, as contrasted with water created the need for support of the body by the animal itself instead of by the surrounding medium and presented the greatest problem of land animals—preserving an internal water balance. These two factors conditioned terrestrial animal form and adaptation.

Body Support.—Because air cannot support body tissues as does water, the very plastic, gelatinous animals are absent from the land. The tissues of flatworms, earthworms and snails are much firmer in terrestrial species than in water-dwellers. Soft-bodied organisms must rest their entire weight on the ground. Those with supporting structures, arthropods and vertebrates, reduce friction and ease movement by elevating the body on stiffened limbs. This, however, requires limitations of body size, since doubling body size requires a manifold increase in strength of the legs. Thus land animals generally are limited in size compared with oceanic relatives. The largest insect, the six-inch-long Hercules beetle (*Dynastes*) is tiny compared with even a small lobster, and an elephant about $11\frac{1}{2}$ ft. long, weighing almost four tons is a pigmy beside a 100-foot, 106-ton blue whale.

2. Water.—Terrestrial animals must maintain a narrow balance between water taken into the body (with food or by drinking or by absorption through the skin) and water lost to the environment (by excretion, ingestion, respiration or evaporation through the body covering). A few organisms (some snails, amphibians and insects) can survive large changes in the water content of their body, but most organisms must have a nearly constant level or they die.

In water sessile animals could filter prey out of passing currents; but the air has only a small temporary planktonic fauna, and no predatory sessile land animals evolved. A few spiders do strain animals into their webs from air currents, but that is more like a fisherman netting from the sea than a barnacle filtering from the water.

Most types of land-dwelling animals, nematodes, oligochaetes, amphibians, flatworms, leeches, ostracods, isopods (sow bugs), *Peripatus* and snails are marginally terrestrial. They can be active only during periods when the air in their micro-habitat is nearly saturated with water vapour, and they must encyst or estivate during dry periods. Arthropods and higher vertebrates alone have relatively impermeable cuticles and extensive water-conserving devices; these forms are the most successful land animals. Snails form the other major group, relying on lengthy estivation in their calcareous shell during dry periods. The opening can be sealed either by a disc on the snail's foot (the operculum) in prosobranchs, or by a calcified mucous sheet (the epiphragm) in pulmonates. Several species of snails have been

revived after six years of uninterrupted dormancy, and recorded cases of more than 20 years may be legitimate.

Water-conserving Mechanisms.—The water-conserving mechanisms enabling survival on land are quite varied. Impervious integuments or skins have been developed with great success by many insects, reptiles, birds and mammals. Some mammals and many insects, however, can lose large quantities of water through glandular structures in the integuments. Many land invertebrates and amphibians have a skin almost completely permeable to water and must stay in damp places.

Internal breathing systems are quite effective in reducing water loss. The high oxygen content of air (207 c.c. per litre) as compared with water (less than 7 c.c. per litre) allows terrestrial forms to have much smaller breathing area. Many stenohygric species breathe through their skin, but the most successful groups have the respiratory surface inside the body and connected to the outside by only a small opening. Snails and insects can even close the opening for brief periods to minimize water loss.

Dry body excretions, either in the form of crystalline or highly concentrated urine, help to save body water, as do the egestions of dry feces. Habitat conditions are an influencing factor: animals living in relatively dry situations (*e.g.*, antelopes) pass drier dung than do animals of moister habitats (*e.g.*, tapirs).

Various forms of dormancy, especially estivation or encystment, will allow species to survive when conditions are favourable for activity during only a few weeks each year.

The behaviour patterns of being active at the time of highest humidity (night or the early-morning dew period) or remaining in moist niches (damp pockets in woods or along the edges of ponds) are also common. Some social insects maintain "humidity control" by keeping the air in their enclosed nest and runways at a higher humidity than the outside.

Seasonal migration over a larger or smaller distance to a more favourable habitat is common among mammals and some birds and insects. Use of metabolic water is equally important: many desert animals derive all their water from their plant food, and many organisms use the water obtained from the breaking down of their own body sugars and carbohydrates to satisfy needs.

3. Other Environmental Factors.—Conditions of light, temperature, humidity and substrate vary widely on land and greatly influence the distribution of animals. Light, temperature and humidity change not only from place to place, but from time to time with definite rhythm. The numerous possible combinations of these variable factors have greatly increased the diversity of animal life, particularly when combined with the influence on land animals of barriers to dispersal.

Light.—Length of day quite often triggers mating behaviour and breeding, and exposure to light rays is a major limiting factor for many animals. Few organisms can withstand prolonged exposure to direct sunlight, for they may die either from heat or from actual lethal factors in light rays. Organisms normally exposed to light will have protective pigments not present in secretive organisms. Many animals hide during the day to avoid sunlight.

Temperature.—The extreme recorded temperatures on land surfaces are probably 71.5° C. near Tucson, Ariz., and −67.8° C. in eastern Siberia; the latter area also shows the greatest annual range in mean monthly maximum and minimum, 66.3°. Tropical forest floors may show an annual variation of only 3°, but temperate and cold regions have the seasonal periodicities of hot and cold, that is, summer and winter. In warmer areas temperature may allow activity throughout the year. In colder regions some form of dormancy between warm spells is frequently resorted to. The activity of poikilothermous (so-called cold-blooded) animals is usually governed by environmental temperature levels.

Poikilotherms can regulate their body temperature roughly through behaviour patterns such as moving from sun to shade to keep a constant temperature level. This is effective only part of the year. Generally poikilotherms are larger, more numerous and most varied in the tropics.

Homoiotherms, birds and mammals, control their body temperature through metabolism. In regions where the external temperature is below that inside their body, they must minimize heat loss. In regions where the external temperature is higher than their body level, they must minimize heat gain.

The line between poikilotherms and homoiotherms is indistinct. Young birds cannot regulate their temperature and many mammals and adult birds will vary within several degrees, yet the basic distinction between self-regulation and habitat-regulation is a useful one.

Heat conservation is accomplished in several ways. A shaggy coat of fur or heavy layer of feathers entraps an insulating layer of air next to the skin and thereby cuts loss of body heat. The dense fur of northern animals, wolves, yaks, reindeer and the Siberian tiger contrasts with the few hairs of many southern forms, monkeys, most hoofed mammals and the Bengal tiger.

Heat loss is greater from a body with a high surface-volume ratio than one with a low one. Thus, cold-adapted animals will be bulkier than warm-adapted relatives (Bergmann's rule). This holds true for the races of man, as well as for other animals. Following the same principle, cold-adapted animals have smaller appendages than warm-adapted species (Allen's rule). For example, the length of foxes' ears correlates with climate (fig. 5). Numerous exceptions to these two principles are known, but both Bergmann's and Allen's rules remain useful generalizations.

In tropical areas, species often will have long appendages and high surface-volume ratios. To avoid the sun's heat, many sleep during the day or are active only in shaded areas. Cooling by water evaporation is very effective since for each gram of water evaporated 500 cal. of heat are lost from the body. Sweating through the skin, increased water loss through rapid respiration and periodic immersion in cool water are commonly used cooling mechanisms.

FROM R. HESSE, W. C. ALLEE AND K. P. SCHMIDT, "ECOLOGICAL ANIMAL GEOGRAPHY"; REPRODUCED BY PERMISSION OF JOHN WILEY & SONS, INC.

FIG. 5.—ALLEN'S RULE ILLUSTRATED BY VARIATION IN LENGTH OF FOXES' EARS: (A) ARCTIC FOX; (B) COMMON FOX; (C) DESERT FOX

In cold regions many homoiotherms hibernate during the winter, partially to escape the severe cold but also because food supplies are limited during the winter period. This is only one example showing how both biotic and physical factors interact to limit a species distribution and behaviour.

Humidity.—Annual rainfall varies from a fraction of an inch to over 300 in. It can be evenly distributed throughout the year or concentrated within a few weeks or months. The latter situation is common in the tropics, with alternating dry and wet seasons providing an ecological equivalent of the hot and cold seasons of northern latitudes. Shaded areas, such as the ground stratum of tropical forests, have higher humidity for much longer periods than the forest canopy or grasslands. The distribution of animals that require a nearly saturated atmosphere will be limited by the time each year that suitable conditions prevail. Periods of dormancy afford survival of many animals over dry spells, but each species requires a certain minimum period suitable for activity in order to survive.

Substrate.—In the ocean and fresh waters most chemical and nutritive materials are suspended in the water. On land these must be obtained directly or indirectly from the substrate. Both physical state and chemical contents of the substrate greatly influence animal life. A barren rock bench or shifting sand dune will harbor little animal life, both for lack of shelter from weather or enemies and for paucity of food. On firm ground, running animals with tiny feet are present; in marshes and on snow or sand, animals with broad, often webbed feet are found. Loose-packed soils with high organic content (forest floor) have millions of burrowing organisms feeding on each other and on decaying matter.

The physical composition and structure of the soils, exceedingly important to animal distribution, is treated in the article SOIL.

Chemical composition is equally important. The availability of lime (calcium) for shells and skeletons limits snail and mam-

mal occurrence. Sodium chloride (common salt) is essential to animals that feed on plants, for it tends to counteract the high potassium content of the plant material. Many trace chemicals are essential to animal functions. The relative acidity or alkalinity of the soil also affects animal distribution. Alkaline and rocky soils hold heat for considerable periods.

Air Masses.—The movements of the great air masses above the earth affect the climate through determining rainfall. They also aid in the dispersal of organisms and are used by birds in flight. Pressure is important primarily in high mountain altitudes and has little direct effect on animal distribution.

B. ZONATION OF LAND ANIMALS

Similarity in (1) ecologic roles and adaptations or (2) systematic affinities and geographic distribution can be emphasized in discussing animal zonation. The former has grown out of ecological science; the latter is the methodology of classical systematics (*see* ZOOGEOGRAPHY).

The climatic elements of temperature, precipitation and wind are modified by latitude, distribution of the continental land masses, topography, barometric pressure and marine currents. It is possible to recognize areas that have basically similar cyclical variations in temperature, rainfall and light factors. A characteristic form of vegetation and associated animal communities has developed in every area of the world with similar sets of climatic conditions.

There are several ways of classifying these ecologic units, only a few of which are given below. None of these methods is fully satisfactory, primarily because these are not discrete units but patterns of operation that grade into one another. One division recognizes seven major biomes: tundra; taiga (coniferous forest); temperate deciduous forest; desert; tropical grasslands; temperate grasslands; and equatorial forest (fig. 6). These are characterized in the article, ECOLOGY. Another classification is the division into four biochores (forest, savanna, grassland, desert) with subdivisions into formation classes—geographic units of vegetation showing characteristic responses to a climatic trend of a particular intensity. In mountainous (montane) regions, the life-zone concept of C. H. Merriam, stripped of its theoretical temperature limits, accurately depicts the vertical zonation of plants and animals. It is less effective in dealing with nonmontane distributions.

All these systems are concerned with the idea of ecological equivalence—that grasslands will support grazing animals and

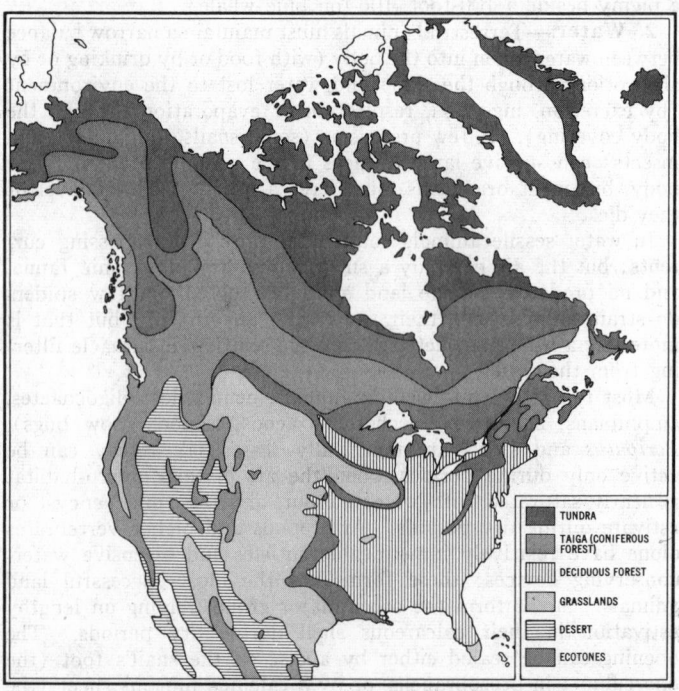

| TUNDRA |
| TAIGA (CONIFEROUS FOREST) |
| DECIDUOUS FOREST |
| GRASSLANDS |
| DESERT |
| ECOTONES |

FIG. 6.—PLANT AND ANIMAL COMMUNITIES (BIOMES) OF NORTH AMERICA

forests will have vertical stratification with arboreal and terrestrial forms. Grazing animals have similar teeth and digestive adaptations. Carnivores in all parts of the world, though they belong to very different taxonomic groups, have similar structures.

Equally important is the problem of ecological equivalents in the past. A considerable paleontological literature concerned with the ecological adaptations of past organisms was summarized by G. G. Simpson in 1953. (See *Bibliography,* below.)

Faunas can be ecologically zoned on the bases of climate, vegetation and topography. Extensive overlaps and intergradations occur, and these divisions present a gross oversimplification (*see* W. C. Allee and K. P. Schmidt, 1951).

1. Climatic Zonation.—*Tropical Faunas.*—Rain forests with nearly constant temperature and very high humidity at ground level have abundant rainfall throughout the year. These forests present the most favourable situation for terrestrial life. Dormancy is not needed, except in monsoon forests with dry seasons, and poikilothermic animals can be active during the entire year. Plant food production is continuous and life abounds.

Species are fantastically abundant—perhaps 2,000 species of moths alone having been caught on Barro Colorado Island in the Panama Canal Zone—but individuals are scattered; and it is far easier to collect 100 different species than 100 individuals of a single species. Most groups of poikilotherms reach their maximum size in the tropics.

Temperate Faunas.—The alternation of seasons and wide fluctuations in rainfall, light and temperature produce periods of plenty and of famine. The poikilotherms must have a period of dormancy, plant food production is suspended part of the year and homoiotherms must hibernate (mammals) or migrate (birds) during unfavourable conditions. Reproduction becomes restricted to seasonal periodicities. Species are much fewer in number, but, in contrast to the situation that pertains in the tropics, individuals of the same species are easier to find. Turnover of organic matter is much slower because of the dormant season, and climatic variations limit the groups that can inhabit temperate areas.

Polar Faunas.—The extreme changes in environmental conditions limit habitation of the polar areas to very few species. Homoiothermic animals are mainly marine or migratory, breeding during the warm summers. Large-bodied flies (Diptera) and butterflies and moths (Lepidoptera) are the dominant insects, but other poikilotherms are rare. Species are often present in huge numbers, though there is little variety, Greenland having only seven land mammals, for example. The snow-clouded air and lack of plant life in the Antarctic have practically eliminated terrestrial animals. Many arctic animals also live in the alpine zone of mountains.

2. Vegetative Zonation.—*Forest Faunas.*—Forests are found only where temperatures are above 10° C. during the vegetative season, annual rainfall above 50 cm. (about 20 in.) and humidity more than 50% saturation. In tropical forests arboreal animals are abundant, less so in temperate areas. Ground conditions are uniform, and the soil litter supports an abundant fauna. The animals have acute hearing and gregarious forms are noisy. Flying and running are hampered; gliding and climbing, well developed. In dense forests, conditions remain more uniform; in open forests they vary more widely. Generally, several distinct strata of life from ground to treetop can be recognized.

Open-country Faunas.—In open country, precipitation and/or temperature are lower than in forests, and the vegetation shades from savanna and steppe to desert, depending on rainfall. Protective foliage is absent in dry seasons, and vegetation gives minimum cover at most times. Dry-adapted animals can survive, and running forms are common among birds and mammals. Sight and scent are keenly developed, and gregarious animals are frequent. Burrowing species are common in all groups, and protective colorations are well developed.

3. Topographic Zonation.—*Mountain Faunas.*—In mountainous areas the abrupt rise in elevation results in lowered temperature and shortening of the warm season. Forest faunas ascend

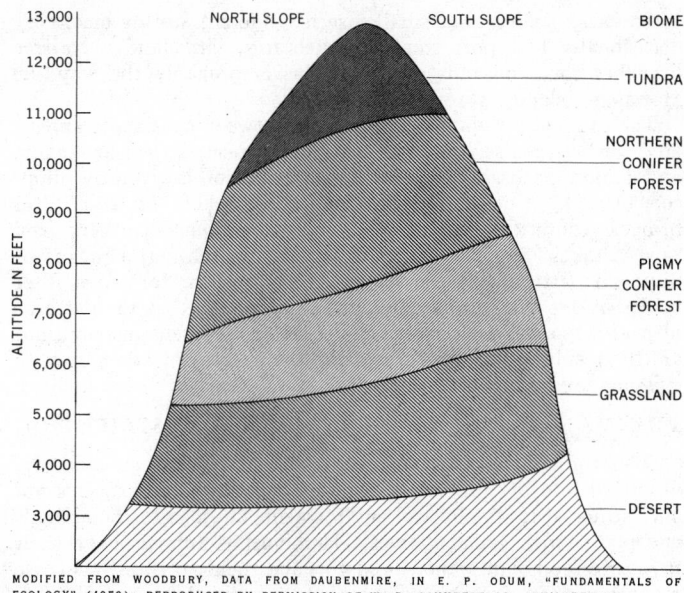

FIG. 7.—ZONATION IN MOUNTAINS OF WESTERN NORTH AMERICA

to the vegetational limit, and then a characteristic alpine fauna and flora appears. The number of species decreases rapidly, but some mammals (*e.g.,* the rabbitlike pika *Ochotona wollastoni*) live as high as about 20,000 ft. on Mt. Everest. During warm periods the strong light rays may heat the ground surface to 40°–50° C., and a considerable fauna of poikilotherms exists at moderate elevations. Mountain species generally bear live young and often seek shelter among rocks. High mountains show an especially clear pattern of zonation (fig. 7).

Island Faunas.—Some islands (Great Britain, Tasmania) formerly have been connected to continents; others (Hawaiian, Society) never have been connected to any land mass. The former group of islands have organisms very similar to those present on the mainland with which they were at one time connected. The latter group (oceanic islands) received its animal and plant life by chance dispersal over oceanic barriers. Few mammals, amphibians and reptiles; some birds and snails; and many insects live on oceanic islands.

Older oceanic islands have a great proliferation of species from a few chance introductions; the original stocks underwent minor adaptive radiations and filled habitat niches normally used by other organisms in balanced continental faunas. The flightless birds on oceanic islands probably could evolve because of the absence of mammalian competition.

C. DISPERSAL OF ANIMALS ON LAND

The division of land areas by oceans into three major blocks; the interruption of land masses by lakes, rivers, high mountain and desert regions; and the climatic zonations all tend to raise barriers to the spread of animals from one area to another. Oceanic barriers are particularly effective, but the fauna of the Hawaiian Islands is testimony to the occasional success of accidental dispersal by organisms across major barriers (*see* HAWAII: *Animal Life*).

On land most dispersal is the result of individual movement. Given enough time, any species could crawl from one land mass to another as long as conditions for survival were favourable. The world-wide distribution of ancient groups such as *Peripatus* may simply present a function of the time available for their dispersal. Similarly the wide range of amphibian and reptilian families and genera may be a function of the geological age of these groups, and the limited range of mammalian types a function of group youth. Paths for dispersal open to the older groups were closed to the younger ones by the time they evolved.

Floods are an effective means of dispersal for many organisms; the concept of natural rafts of trees carrying mammals or reptiles from a continent to an island has often been postulated. Winds often carry spiders and small insects. Violent storms may very occasionally transport small invertebrates, birds and even tree branches for thousands of miles; this is probably the way the Hawaiian Islands were populated.

The problems of faunal interchange between continents and islands or between separated or partially connected areas are many, and a good discussion of basic faunal evolution is given by Simpson (1953). Corridors (passageways for whole faunas), filter bridges (conditions that let some groups pass but not others) and "sweepstakes" routes (chance dispersal) are the major means of dispersal patterns. A particular area may have formed a filter bridge at one time and a corridor at another, so that the patterns of past dispersals are exceedingly complex. Present distributions are the result of past dispersals and the success of adaptation to existing environmental conditions.

VIII. MAN AS A FACTOR IN ANIMAL DISTRIBUTION

Over the course of geologic eras animal life has evolved and dispersed into the present distribution patterns; each species not only adjusted to its physical environment, but also to the animals and plants with which it lives. Herbivorous animals have their favourite food plants, their predators and their parasites. Disease organisms have a rough balance between their survival and the death of the species they attack.

Man has been able seriously to interrupt natural patterns by transporting an organism from an area in which it is in balance with physical and biotic factors to an area in which physical factors are favourable and food is available but the predators and parasites that keep it under control are lacking.

Major crop and forest pests—the Hessian fly, Japanese beetle, Colorado potato beetle, grape *Phylloxera*, spruce sawfly and gypsy moth; tree diseases—Dutch elm disease and chestnut blight; nuisance organisms—starlings and sparrows; and literally thousands of other examples testify to the ability of man to spread other organisms. Many serious epidemics of malaria and bubonic plague have been caused through man's accidental transport of infected animals.

Many well-intended transportations have not turned out satisfactorily. Thus, the rabbit in Australia, the giant African snail in the Pacific and the edible snail in California were purposely introduced to serve as food but multiplied beyond expectations to become pests.

The possibilities of further unwelcome introductions is con-

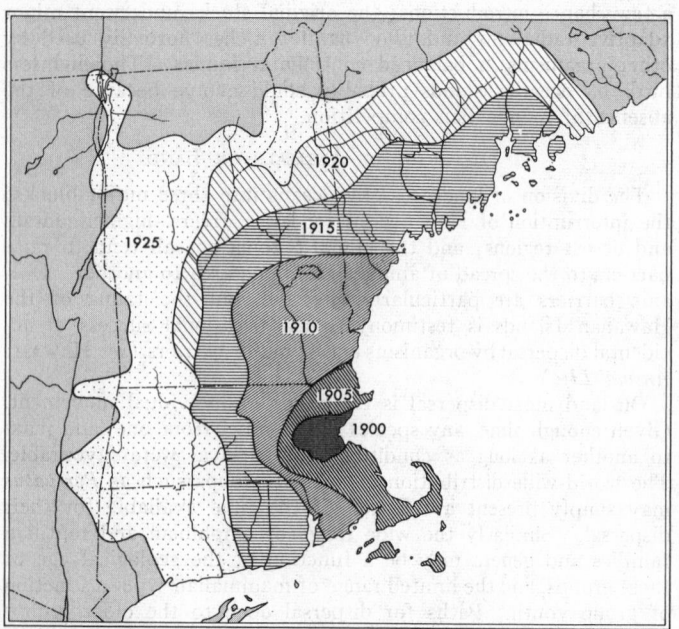

FROM R. C. BROWN AND R. A. SHEALS IN "JOURNAL OF FORESTRY"

FIG. 8.—SPREAD OF THE GYPSY MOTH, AN ECONOMIC PEST, AT FIVE YEAR INTERVALS, AFTER IT WAS INTRODUCED BY MAN INTO NORTH AMERICA LATE IN THE 19TH CENTURY

siderable, despite the rigid plant and animal quarantines maintained by almost every country. Man, through transplanting plants and animals, is now involved in one of the major distributional revolutions in the history of the earth. No one knows or can predict how it will end. A good review of some of the problems of man's disruption of natural distribution is given by C. S. Elton (1958).

See also references under "Animals, Distribution of" in the Index.

BIBLIOGRAPHY.—*General:* W. C. Allee and K. P. Schmidt, *Ecological Animal Geography,* 2nd ed. (1951); H. G. Andrewartha and L. C. Birch, *The Distribution and Abundance of Animals* (1954); W. C. Allee, et al., *Principles of Animal Ecology* (1949); E. P. Odum, *Fundamentals of Ecology,* 2nd ed. (1959).

Special: Historical: G. G. Simpson, *The Major Features of Evolution* (1953) and *Evolution and Geography* (1953); A. S. Romer, "Fish Origins—Fresh or Salt Water?" *Papers on Marine Biology and Oceanography, Deep-Sea Research,* Suppl. to vol. 3:261 (1955); R. H. Denison *A Review of the Habitat of the Earliest Vertebrates* (1956); R. F. Inger "Ecological Aspects of the Origins of the Tetrapods," *Evolution,* 11(3):373 (1957); A. S. Romer "Early Tetrapod Life," *Evolution,* 12:365 (1958).

Geographical: L. F. de Beaufort, *Zoogeography of the Land and Inland Waters* (1951); P. J. Darlington, *Zoogeography: The Geographical Distribution of Animals* (1957).

Marine Life: S. P. Ekman, *Zoogeography of the Sea* (1953); H. B. Moore, *Marine Ecology* (1958); J. A. C. Nicol, *The Biology of Marine Animals* (1960); C. M. Yonge, *The Sea Shore* (1949); A. C. Hardy, *The Open Sea, Its Natural History: The World of Plankton* (1956) and *The Open Sea, Its Natural History: Fish and Fisheries* (1959); N. B. Marshall, *Aspects of Deep Sea Biology* (1954). *Fresh-water Life:* T. T. Macan and E. B. Worthington, *Life in Lakes and Rivers* (1951).

Land Life: P. Dansereau, *Biogeography* (1957). *Man and Distribution:* C. S. Elton, *The Ecology of Invasions by Animals and Plants* (1958).   (G. A. S.)

ANIMALS, DOMESTICATION OF. Domestication implies: (1) tameness; (2) living in or near the dwelling places of man; (3) being kept by man to provide him with food, clothing, power or aesthetic satisfactions; (4) that the animal and its ancestors for many generations have had their movements and matings partially controlled by man; and (5) that the innate mental and physical qualities of the domesticated animal have been changed considerably from those of its wild ancestors.

Not all domesticated animals conform fully to all of this definition. Thus, man generally exercises little control over the movements and matings of the domestic cat. Although tameness is an important part of domestication, some domesticated animals, such as sows with very young pigs, cows with new calves or angry bulls, may be at times more dangerous to an incautious person than most wild animals are. Wild animals such as performing seals and bears sometimes become very tame, but they are not called domesticated. Yet wild elephants in India when caught and tamed are called domesticated.

Because domestication was accomplished in prehistoric times, the methods of doing it can only be surmised from such indirect evidence as the attitudes and habits of primitive peoples concerning the animals around them; paintings or carvings that archaeologists have found in ancient camp sites or tombs; and experiences of those who work in menageries. Presumably the initial steps toward domestication were taken largely through the widespread human practice of making pets of captured young or crippled wild animals. Religious customs, such as totemism, animal cults or the reverence accorded to cattle by the Hindus in India, may have been important. Many wild animals quickly lose much of their fear of man in game refuges. Some domestication deliberately may have been planned to serve definite needs. Prehistoric rock carvings in Egypt show hunters building a fence across the outlet of a steep-walled valley into which they had driven some wild game, presumably to keep a reserve food supply. Some wild species can be tamed easily, while others are extremely intractable. Some possibilities for domestication still may exist, although no important species has come completely from the wild to the domesticated condition within historic times. Perhaps fur-bearing animals, such as mink and foxes raised in captivity, are now being domesticated in the same slow way as cattle and sheep were many thousands of years ago.

The first date of domestication varied in different parts of the world and for different species. Peoples in a paleolithic (Old Stone Age) stage of culture generally had no truly domestic animal except, perhaps, the dog. This was true of the aborigines of Australia when white men first found them. Cattle and sheep were important domestic animals in Europe early in the neolithic (New Stone Age) culture. They may have been brought into Europe already domesticated by people who came from farther east. In Asia Minor they were domesticated by 7000 B.C. Horses first appeared as domesticated animals about 3000 B.C. but long had been hunted widely for food. Mounted invaders from the north brought them into the valleys of the Tigris and Euphrates as early as 2000 B.C. They had reached China well before 1500 B.C. Horses were kept at first for flesh as well as for riding; they were used for war chariots and other transport well before 1500 B.C. The ass was domesticated in southeastern Egypt before 3000 B.C. Cats were domesticated in or near Egypt long before 2000 B.C. Chickens were domesticated in southeastern Asia perhaps by 2500 B.C.

The only animals domesticated in the Americas were the llama, alpaca, guinea pig and turkey. American Indians north of Mexico had no domesticated animals except dogs. African tribes south of the Sahara probably acquired their domesticated animals from the northeast long after civilization had developed in Egypt.

The wild species that were originally tamed may have become extinct (*e.g.,* the *ur* or aurochs from which cattle are descended), or domestication may have changed the animal so that its ancestor cannot be identified with certainty (*e.g.,* the sheep comes from *Ovis ammon* but from which subspecies is uncertain). The dog is zoologically the same as the wolf of the northern hemisphere, although some investigators have argued that the jackal furnished part of the ancestry of some races of dogs in Africa and in southern Asia. The horse is descended from local races of Przhevalski's (Przewalski's) horse, which ranged from Poland to Mongolia. The chicken came from the wild jungle fowl still found in India. The local races of swine domesticated during the neolithic around the Baltic, on the northeast shores of the Mediterranean, in southeastern Asia and perhaps elsewhere are not considered to have belonged to one species, *Sus scrofa.*

Formerly it was widely believed that the diversity of form, size, colour and other characteristics within some domesticated species could be explained only by supposing that two or more wild species had been tamed and subsequently intercrossed. This view became less plausible as evidence accumulated to show that each wild species contains much genetic diversity and as it was demonstrated that isolation and continued selection can produce widely contrasting groups from the same initial population. Domestication did not change the laws of inheritance, but man's control over the movements and matings of the animals did increase the isolation of subgroups from each other. Also, domestication made possible wider outcrosses between local races because man in wars or commerce sometimes transports breeding animals over natural barriers that their wild contemporaries would not have crossed. From the very beginning of domestication man must have favoured for breeding purposes those animals that pleased him most. For aesthetic reasons he often desired variety, and for utilitarian reasons he often wanted several types of animals, each specialized for a purpose or set of conditions. This combination of continued artificial selection toward varied goals, inbreeding consequent upon isolation, and occasional wide outcrosses increased greatly the rate at which distinct local races were formed and changed.

BIBLIOGRAPHY.—J. H. Breasted, *Ancient Times,* 2nd ed., rev. (1935); W. Herre, *Abstammung und Domestikation der Haustiere,* pp. 1–58 in *Handbuch der Tierzüchtung,* vol. I (1958); Richard Lydekker, *The Horse and Its Relatives* (1912), *The Ox and Its Kindred* (1912), *The Sheep and Its Cousins* (1913); N. S. Shaler, *Domesticated Animals* (1895). (J. L. Lh.)

ANIMALS, LAWS CONCERNING. Legislation relating to animals is basically similar throughout the common-law countries, although with considerable regional variation. Historically two trends are recognizable: animals have been accorded increasing legal protection, and the principles of liability of those who control animals have been refined and extended. All creatures other than man are animals in the eyes of the law, but the law is concerned with those considered objects of property, usually excluding insects. They are classed as domestic (*domitae naturae*) and wild (*ferae naturae*); the former are objects of property by reason of ownership, and the latter may become property by reason of reduction to possession.

In determining what rules are applicable where the question is that of liability for injuries to persons or property by animals, the animals are classified by their natures: vicious wild animals; wild animals which have undergone some domestication; domestic animals known by their owners to be vicious; domestic animals not so known; and grazing domestic animals. A person keeps vicious wild animals at his peril and ordinarily is absolutely liable without regard to negligence for any injury done, but the rigour of this doctrine has been modified in some cases to require the existence of negligence. Keeping such animals may also constitute a public or private nuisance. In cases where the ordinarily wild animal has undergone some domestication, the owner is liable for injuries resulting from negligent keeping, unless a propensity of the animal to cause harm is known by the owner, in which case liability may be absolute. If a domestic animal with a known vicious or otherwise dangerous propensity is kept, some jurisdictions charge the keeper with absolute liability; others base liability on negligence. Knowledge of viciousness may be actual or based on the duty of the keeper to observe his animal. In the absence of a propensity toward viciousness, the owner is liable for injury following and foreseeably caused by a failure to exercise the care which a man of ordinary prudence would exercise.

The victim may be without recourse if he has acted negligently so as to contribute to his own injury. Where there are statutes forbidding letting animals run at large, criminal or civil liability may stem from a violation. The question of knowledge in the rules of liability has resulted in much litigation, particularly where dogs are concerned. The dog cases have given rise to the popular saying "Every dog is entitled to one bite"; that is a misconception, for the ordinary rules of liability apply to dogs. In many jurisdictions where the raising of animals is of economic importance, the common-law rule requiring knowledge of a dog's likelihood to do harm has been changed, either to impose absolute liability on the owner for injury to other domestic animals or to provide for judicial trials of dogs which have done certain acts, such as sheep-killing. Some statutes penalize the owner for keeping a vicious dog and may require the dog's destruction. Although liability for animals ordinarily depends upon ownership or control, a person may be liable for selling, without warning to the purchaser, an animal known to be dangerous.

The keeper of a wild animal must keep it penned up and is liable for trespasses (entries upon the land of another) and all resulting damages if he does not. The owner of land upon which wild animals live is not responsible for their natural wanderings unless he can be said to have actual control over them. Under common law the owner or possessors of domestic animals had an absolute duty to keep them off others' lands; this remains the modern rule in Great Britain, the United States and other common-law countries comprising heavily populated areas or agricultural areas where the protection of growing crops is important. Where raising livestock and the like is more important, the tendency has been to reject or modify the rule, and the modifications are extremely varied. Some jurisdictions have adopted the test of negligence, while others have schemes of negligence or absolute liability dependent upon the type of animal or land involved. Some jurisdictions permit recovery only where the injured party has attempted to fence animals out, while others require that animals be fenced in. Trespasses brought about wilfully are always wrongful. Owners of domestic animals may be liable by statute for letting them run at large or wander upon highways. In livestock-raising areas, statutes regulate grazing on open range land, and the government regulates and licenses the use of the public domain lands.

An estray at common law is an animal running at large whose owner is unknown, but not all modern definitions include the latter element. In the absence of a statute limiting the right, anyone may take up and impound estrays, but the taker does not become the owner simply by that act; public notice must be given about the taking. The taker has a right to compensation for his expenses and to possession until paid, but he may not use the animal for gain. He must take reasonable care of the estray, whose owner may recover it by paying the charges and proving ownership; otherwise, the taker after a time becomes the owner.

In English law the doctrine of distress damage feasant permits the distraint of animals for the payment of damages caused. A landowner may drive trespassing animals off his property, and municipal authorities may distrain and impound them. A pound is a place maintained by public authority for the keeping of animals picked up as estrays or for those running at large unlawfully. It is illegal to release an animal lawfully taken up. An animal may be killed where it is necessary to protect persons or property. For an unnecessary killing the owner may recover the value of the animal, and the killing may be criminal, particularly if malicious.

An agreement to take possession of another's animal is a bailment, which is regulated by contract between the parties, but the bailee is charged with exercising due care. An agreement to keep and care for an animal is a type of contract of bailment called agistment.

Ownership, possession and treatment of animals is the subject of extensive regulation. Commonly, zoning laws and deed restrictions limit the privilege of keeping animals to ordinary pets or nonoffensive agricultural types. In Great Britain and in most municipalities of the United States and Canada dogs are required to be licensed, for which a fee is paid. In the western United States, where livestock may run more or less at large, branding for identification is common, and statutes require registration of brands. Slaughtering animals for consumption is regulated by licensing, rules, reporting requirements and inspection by national and local governments. In the United States and Great Britain national legislation requires health inspection of live animals transported, imported or exported. Diseased animals may be quarantined or destroyed, and owners can be liable for spread of disease and the transportation or sale of diseased animals.

In ancient times animals had no rights under the law, though they could be charged with offenses and formally tried and convicted. Under common law, cruelty to animals was unlawful only when the act caused damage to the owner or constituted a nuisance to the public. Largely as a result of activities of the humane movement beginning in the early 19th century, infliction of unnecessary pain and suffering or wanton abuse of tame or wild animals, such as killing, shooting, starving, beating, overloading or overdriving, have been made criminal offenses (see HUMANE SOCIETIES). Hunting for sport is permitted, regulated and encouraged. The use of captive animals for games such as cockfighting, bearbaiting or bullfighting (which may be national sports in some countries) usually is prohibited. In the United States and Canada the use of animals in rodeos is not by itself cruelty, but such use is prohibited in Great Britain. Injury in the reasonable protection of property is not cruelty, nor in general is experimentation with live animals for scientific purposes (vivisection), but there are antivivisection laws in a few U.S. states. Vivisection is strictly regulated in Great Britain but not completely prohibited. (G. M. Jo.)

ANIMALS, PHYLOGENY OF, the branch of zoology concerned with tracing the lines of descent among animals. Its ideal is to do this at all evolutionary levels and so to give a complete exposition of the relatedness of all the members of the animal kingdom to each other. Phylogeny necessarily rests upon evolution as a fact of nature, but it is not concerned with theories about how evolution has been brought about; phylogenetic conclusions would not be altered by proof of the Darwinian, Lamarckian or any other explanation of evolution. For discussion of the theory of evolution in general, see EVOLUTION, ORGANIC.

Evidence: Paleontology.—The most direct evidence that can be used in phylogeny is that of paleontology, insofar as fossils show the actual changes that have taken place in animals with time. But this evidence is very incomplete. It is most complete

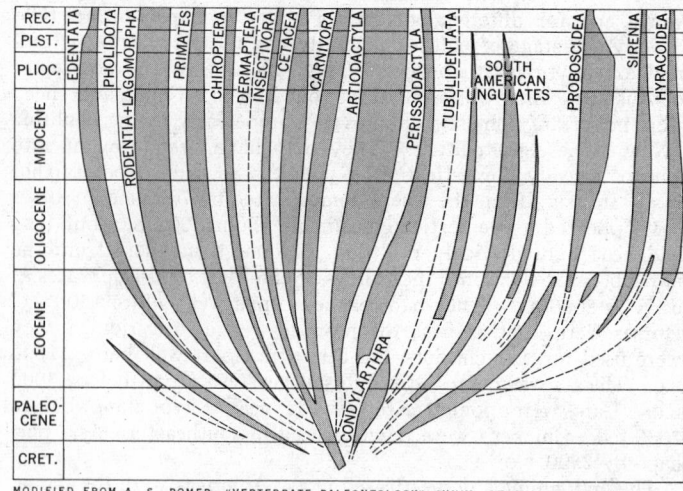

MODIFIED FROM A. S. ROMER, "VERTEBRATE PALEONTOLOGY" (UNIV. OF CHICAGO PRESS)

FIG. 1.—ADAPTIVE RADIATIONS OF THE ORDERS OF PLACENTAL MAMMALS. EACH LINE REPRESENTS AN ORDER, ALL OF WHICH CAN BE TRACED BACK INDEPENDENTLY TO NEAR THE BEGINNING OF THE RADIATION

where changes in species can be followed through long series of sedimentary layers evenly bedded upon each other and clearly laid down without large intermissions. Such complete geological records are rare. One example is in the Devonian rock strata of Iowa, where phylogenetic sequences of brachiopods (small marine animals with shells) have been worked out by Carroll Fenton; others occur in the Cretaceous and some Tertiary formations. Only the phylogeny of closely related species can be studied in these sequences; the periods of their formation are too short for larger results.

Elsewhere, the paleontological record gives occasional forms preserved at longer or shorter intervals, when the conditions for fossilization were favourable, and the paleontologist is forced to base his phylogenetic conclusions on study of their structure. The record is also very incomplete in its preservation of structure; in general, only the hard parts of animals are preserved, soft-bodied animals being rarely fossilized. With so incomplete a record, and since many of the animals of phylogenetic interest in the earlier stages of evolution had no hard skeleton, it is clear that a complete solution of the problems of phylogeny cannot be expected from paleontology alone.

Morphology and Embryology.—In general, related animals show their affinity by similarity of structure, the greater the similarity the closer the relationship. In using this evidence caution is necessary; similarity of structure may be due to causes other than evolutionary closeness. It may, for instance, arise in unrelated animals in response to similar environmental conditions; this is known as parallel evolution. Perhaps, in some cases, it may also arise as the result of inherent tendencies in animals to evolve in determined directions, and not at all in adaptation to the conditions of the environment. This possibility, which is the basis of the evolutionary theory of orthogenesis, is not generally accepted as a reality in evolution.

Special reasons may increase the phylogenetic significance of particular similarities of structure. The fundamental structure of an animal is laid down early in its development, and it is found that the earlier developmental stages of animals have altered less in evolution than have the later stages. Thus, resemblance in fundamental structure, and indeed in larval and embryonic structure in general, is often of special phylogenetic importance. Vestigial organs also provide good evidence. These are organs that are formed in development but later regress (or at least never become functional in the adult). Animals that have the same organ in a fully developed and functional condition are believed to be close to the ancestry of the animals having the vestigial organ. The presence of gill slits in the embryology of mammals and birds is strong evidence for the belief in the evolution of these groups from a fish ancestry. Again, where an organ is of a peculiar structure that has an easy explanation in view of the structure of some probably ancestral animal, but is otherwise inexplicable, it provides evidence for descent from these ancestors. Thus, the recurrent laryngeal nerve of terrestrial vertebrates passes from the neighbourhood of the brain to the thorax, where it loops round the systemic artery near the heart before returning up the neck to the larynx.

If the evolution of terrestrial vertebrates from fish ancestors is accepted, this extraordinary course is a natural result of the arrangement of the parts in the fishes. It has received no other explanation and must be accepted as evidence for this descent.

In reaching any conclusion in phylogeny other principles are looked to: the later structure always must be such that it can be derived by modification of the presumed earlier structure. And evolution has not always been in the direction of increasing complexity of structure; simplification has frequently occurred.

Conclusions.—In view of the uncertainty of the evidence phylogenetic conclusions always must be tentative; the larger the groups of animals they relate, and the earlier the evolutionary changes by which the groups were separated, the less certain these conclusions will be. It often is possible, however, to collect a body of evidence which, taken as a whole, bases the main conclusions on sure ground and makes it very unlikely that they will be upset or in many cases seriously modified by evidence added in the future. But it must be emphasized that such results can be reached only by a broad consideration of all the available morphological and paleontological evidence.

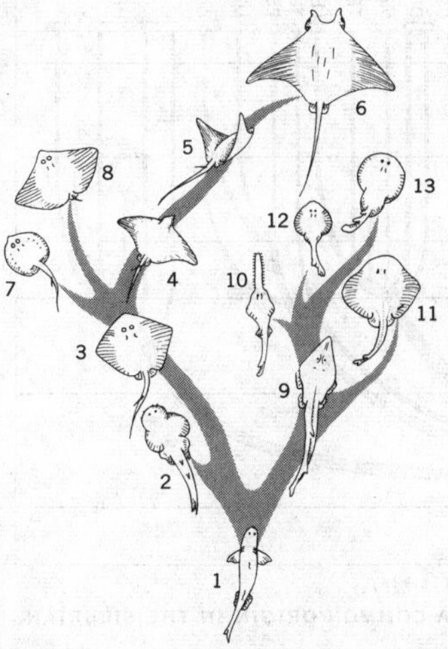

In one large group of animals, the backboned animals or vertebrates, knowledge of morphology and paleontology is much more detailed than in any other group of similar size.

VERTEBRATES

When vertebrate evolution is surveyed as a whole, several very distinct types of vertebrate organization stand out: the Agnatha (lampreys, hagfishes and related extinct forms); the various types of true fishes; the amphibians; reptiles; birds; and mammals. Each of these types has become successful in turn and has provided a dominant fauna in its own type of environment. In the Mesozoic era the reptiles were dominant in terrestrial environments; in Tertiary times, the mammals; and from the time of their origin in the Silurian period, fishes have dominated aquatic environments. Broadly, these conclusions are true in spite of frequent reversions of the later groups to earlier environments; many groups of mammals and reptiles have become secondarily aquatic.

Adaptive Radiation.—These main types of vertebrate organization were evolved from each other, but between any two of them the evolutionary changes were very great (*see* below). Within each of the large vertebrate groups the variation of structure is much less than that between groups, but almost as soon as a group became successful it differentiated into a large number of smaller groups adapted to different habits of life in parts of the wider environment of the dominant group as a whole. This differentiation of a successful group of animals is known as adaptive radiation, and it is to be noted that its changes are as much in adaptation to different habits of life as to environmental conditions.

For the placental mammals each of the smaller groups, the orders, can be traced almost to the beginning of mammalian dominance in the earliest Tertiary times (*see* fig. 1). The process is equally well displayed in the origin of birds or reptiles, and

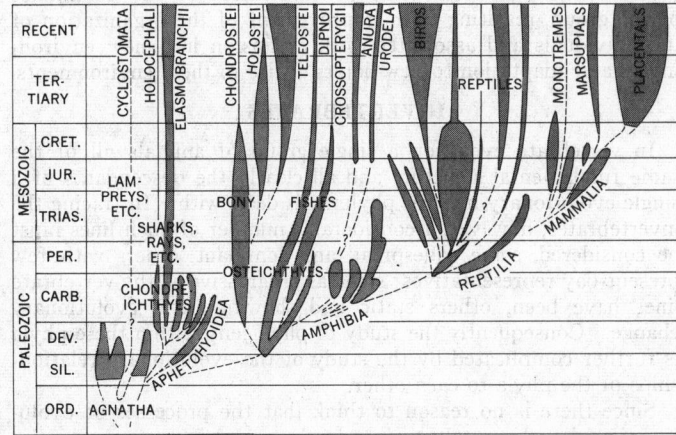

FROM W. K. GREGORY IN "BIOLOGICAL REVIEWS" (CAMBRIDGE PHILOSOPHICAL SOCIETY)

FIG. 2.—ADAPTIVE RADIATION OF SHARKS AND RAYS SHOWING COURSE THAT THEIR EVOLUTION IS BELIEVED TO HAVE FOLLOWED

similar phylogenetic "trees" can be drawn for these groups. For earlier radiations, however, there is less evidence.

It should be noted that these diagrams are unnaturally simplified. Radiation is a phenomenon that occurs not only at the beginning of the successful career of a group; it continues throughout the group's dominance, each of the adaptive lines frequently giving rise by further subdivision to groups adapted to more restricted environments and habits of life.

The structural changes of adaptive radiation are brought about mostly by alterations in the relative sizes of the parts of the body, alterations produced by changes in the relative growth rates of the parts during development. More fundamental changes, such as the formation of new organs, do not form any large part of the process, though physiological changes are associated with this as with other types of evolutionary change. The very large changes of form that may occur in adaptive radiation are exemplified in a phylogenetic tree of the sharks and rays (*see* fig. 2).

Evolution of the Main Vertebrate Types.—The process by which the main types of vertebrate organization are evolved appears, at first sight, to be very different from adaptive radiation (*see* fig. 3). It is so, both in the much greater extent of the structural changes involved and in the evolution of many new organs. In the example of which there is most detailed knowledge, the origin of the mammals from the reptiles, it is evident that early in the radiation of the reptiles one of the radiating lines, the Synapsida, began to show modification in the direction of what was to be mammalian structure. These tendencies are already to be found in some of the earliest members of the group in Permian times. Thereafter some synapsidans became more and more mammallike until toward the end of the Triassic period, when the first animals that can be classified as mammals appeared. Meanwhile the Synapsida as a whole was undergoing typical radiation, and many forms diverged from the line of mammalian descent to become specialized in various directions.

The origin of mammals from reptiles occupied a period of about 40,000,000 years. This is not a surprisingly long time when the great complexity of the changes involved is realized. Almost every organ in the body was altered in structure and there was much evolution of new organs. Nevertheless it may be that the evolutionary changes of this process are the same in nature as those of adaptive radiation, though greatly exaggerated. All changes of structure in organs already present may be produced by alterations in the growth rates of parts of the body, if these are on a sufficiently small and detailed scale; and new organs may be formed by differentiations in originally undifferentiated tissues. But at least these changes were extremely numerous and detailed, and they must have been correlated throughout the evolution so that the animal remained viable. It is not surprising that their evolution required a long time.

It is probable that the evolutionary process is of the same nature in the origin of all the main types of vertebrate organization.

MODIFIED FROM A. S. ROMER, "VERTEBRATE PALEONTOLOGY" (UNIV. OF CHICAGO PRESS)

FIG. 3.—PHYLOGENETIC TREE OF THE VERTEBRATES SHOWING SUCCESSIVE RADIATIONS OF EACH OF THE MAIN GROUPS

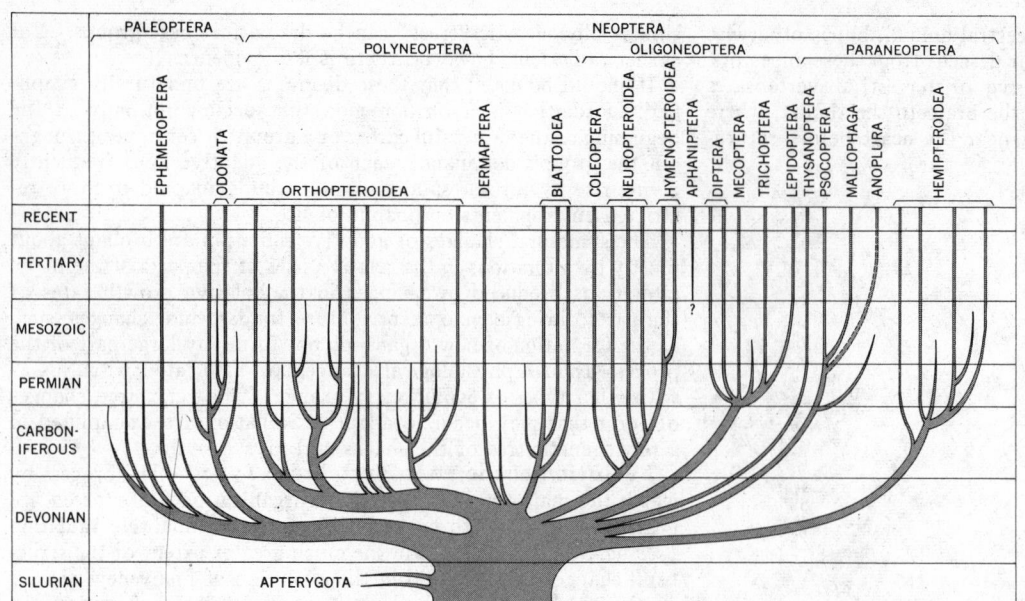

AFTER R. JEANNEL, IN "TRAITÉ DE ZOOLOGIE"; EDITED BY P. P. GRASSE, MASSON ET CIE, PARIS (1949)

FIG. 4.—ADAPTIVE RADIATION OF THE ORDERS OF PTERYGOTE INSECTS FROM A COMMON ORIGIN IN THE SILURIAN. *See* ALSO FIG. 3

Conclusions.—From this discussion it appears that vertebrate evolution has consisted of a succession of adaptive radiations as each new type became successful and that during each radiation another type was evolved. In the vertebrate phylogenetic tree the succession of radiations and types stands out clearly. It must be noted, however, that in the progress of this evolution the vertebrate has undergone other changes besides adaptation to its environment. It has for instance shown continuous improvement of its organization so that it has been able to live a more active life and one in greater isolation from and independence of its environment. Also, throughout their evolution, vertebrates have invaded and exploited new parts of the earth's surface. Starting as bottom-living and probably mud-eating fishes (Agnatha) that may have been either fresh-water, estuarine or marine, they first, as true fishes, took dominance over all aquatic environments, chiefly in the fresh waters (most early fishes) and later, on two occasions (Chondrichthyes and Teleostei), returning to the sea. The invasion of terrestrial habitats took place in two steps, to semiterrestrial life in the amphibians and to full terrestrial life in the reptiles.

Throughout evolution, passage from one environment to another has occurred more than once in smaller groups; pterodactyls (extinct reptiles) and bats (mammals) as well as birds became aerial. Phylogeny, then, in a successful group such as the vertebrates displays a course of evolution that is not merely a sequence of structural change but a continuous extension of the dominance of the group, resulting from improvement of the organization of its individuals and associated with expansion into new environments and adaptation to new habits of life in these environments.

INVERTEBRATES

In vertebrate evolution a single group of animals all of the same fundamental structure and all clearly the descendants of a single evolutionary line (or phylum) is dealt with. In tracing the invertebrates, however, a considerable number of such lines must be considered, some widespread and dominant, others with few present-day representatives; some as progressive as the vertebrate lines have been, others static and showing little evolutionary change. Consequently the study of phylogeny within these phyla is further complicated by the study of the evolutionary relationships of the phyla to each other.

Since there is no reason to think that the processes of evolution found to have taken place in the vertebrates were peculiar to that group and since knowledge of evolution is much more detailed for the vertebrates than for other animals, it is reason-

able to discuss invertebrate phylogeny in the light of conclusions derived from study of the vertebrates.

Phylogeny Within a Phylum.—It seems probable, then, that evolution within the invertebrate phyla will have proceeded, as in the vertebrate phyla, by a succession of adaptive radiations alternating with development of new types of organization. So far as the evidence goes, it supports this conception. The evolution in the insect orders gives a tree (fig. 4) that resembles that of the mammalian orders (fig. 1) in form. Many orders are traced back nearly to the beginning of insect dominance in the Devonian and Carboniferous, when extensive radiation occurred. There is also evidence of later radiations. For some other invertebrate groups, such as the gastropod mollusks (snails, slugs, etc.), similar trees could be drawn, but in very many groups the record is too incomplete. It may be assumed, until there is more evidence, that the evolution was of the same type in all.

Relations of Metazoan Phyla to Each Other.—The most difficult problems that phylogeny has to face are those of tracing the relationships of the animal phyla to each other. Here, paleontology is of little help, for the phyla were almost all separated before the period in which fossil-bearing strata were laid, and the animals were soft-bodied and unlikely to have been preserved.

Thus, in dealing with these questions, phylogeny is forced to rely entirely on the evidence of morphology and embryology, but in many phyla the adult structure has been altered so greatly in evolution that it is difficult to form any but the broadest conclusions by comparison of it between the phyla. It has been noted above that the early stages of the life history alter in general less than does the adult, and it has in fact been found that it is mainly on larval and embryonic structure that students must rely in discussing these basic problems of phylogeny.

The sponges (Parazoa or Porifera) must be set aside; they probably had an origin from unicellular organisms separate from that of all the other multicellular organisms (Metazoa). The sponges are certainly far from the main stock of the animal kingdom.

Adult Structure.—All the Metazoa are probably related. From their adult structure they may be classified on the general complexity of their bodies. Those with two cell layers (diploblastic), ectoderm and endoderm, are separated from those that also have an intermediate cell layer (triploblastic), mesoderm. On this evidence the diploblastic coelenterates are probably a very early offshoot of the metazoan stock, distantly related to the rest of the Metazoa, though it has been suggested that they evolved from an ancestor of the flatworms (Platyhelminthes) by reduction of the mesoderm. In turn, the triploblastic animals with a body cavity lined by epithelium (coelomate) may be separated from those in which such a body cavity is not present (acoelomate). But this distinction is probably not of phylogenetic value, for a coelom has been evolved more than once.

Only one other of these phylogenetic problems can be solved on the evidence of adult structure. This is the relationship of the arthropods to the annelids. Arthropod structure is in all its fundamentals so nearly identical with the simpler structure of the annelids that usually it is assumed that arthropods are descended from animals which, if they were present today, would be called annelids.

Larval Structure.—For further conclusions larval structure must be studied. Comparing development in the various triplo-

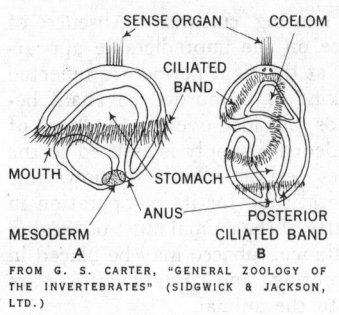

FROM G. S. CARTER, "GENERAL ZOOLOGY OF THE INVERTEBRATES" (SIDGWICK & JACKSON, LTD.)

FIG. 5.—(A) TROCHOPHORE LARVA;
(B) PLUTEUS LARVA

blastic phyla, it is found that the phyla fall into two large groups characterized by the presence of a larva of the "trochophore" type in the one, and by one of the "pluteus" type in the other. These two types of larva (fig. 5) are distinguished by the position of the ciliated band that forms the locomotory (and feeding) organ of the larva and by other fundamental characters such as the mode of origin of the coelom and the arrangement of the cells in the earliest divisions of the egg. The evidence of these characters does not correspond completely in all the phyla, but most of the phyla in which the larvae occur can be assigned to their groups.

The two groups, or superphyla, may be called the Trochophoralia (those having trochophore larvae) and the Plutealia (those having pluteus larvae) (*see* fig. 6). In some of the smaller phyla developmental as well as adult structure has been so altered in evolution that it is not possible to place them in the scheme with any certainty. This is true of such phyla as the Nematoda, Nematomorpha, Acanthocephala and Rotifera. These and some other small phyla are not included in fig. 6.

These larval resemblances imply descent in each of the two superphyla from an ancestral group that possessed these characters in its larvae. The form of the trees of fig. 6 suggests, when compared with the examples of adaptive radiation already considered, that the phyla diverged by very early radiations in these two groups of multicellular animals.

In each phylum the later development of the larva is characteristic of the phylum and different from that in other phyla. At this stage the organs typical of the phylum are formed; these organs are those required for the habit of life of the more primitive members of the phylum. If ancestral groups radiated to give rise to the early members of the phyla, it would be, on the analogy of vertebrate radiation, by each of the radiating lines becoming adapted to a distinct habit of life. It may be concluded, therefore, that the habits now found characteristic of the phyla were those adopted by their ancestors in this radiation and that the characteristic organs of the phyla were those evolved at that time in adaptation to these habits.

Larval Characteristics

On the basis of this larval kinship the major phyla may be characterized as follows (fig. 7):

1. Superphylum Trochophoralia
   a. Platyhelminthes, in which the trochophore (known as Müller's

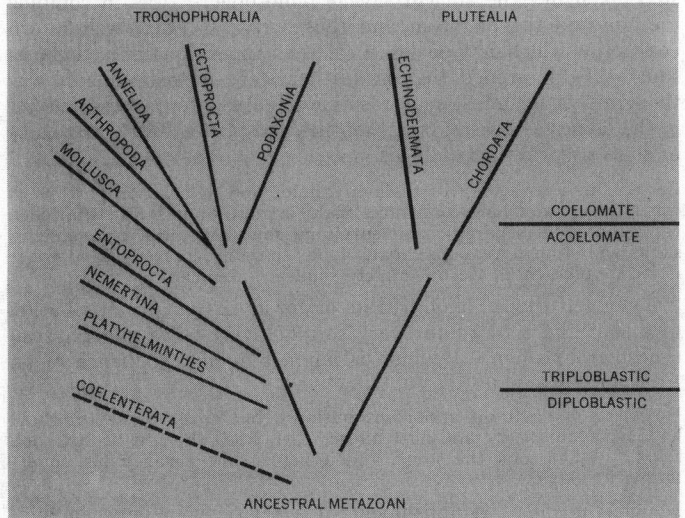

FIG. 6.—PHYLOGENY OF THE METAZOAN PHYLA

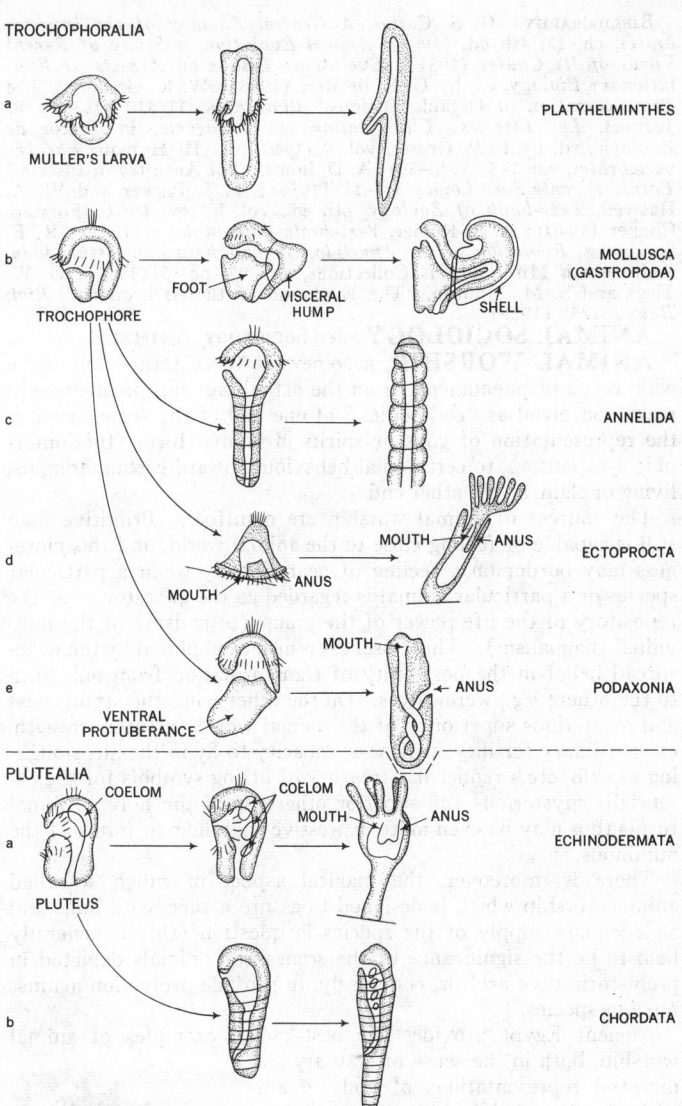

FROM G. S. CARTER, "GENERAL ZOOLOGY OF THE INVERTEBRATES" (SIDGWICK & JACKSON, LTD.)

FIG. 7.—LATER DEVELOPMENT IN THE METAZOAN PHYLA

larva) differs in some features from that in other phyla, were animals that took to gliding on their whole ventral surface, became elongate in an anteroposterior direction and flattened dorsoventrally. The Nemertina and Entoprocta were other acoelomate Trochophoralia that evolved in other ways.

b. Mollusca were also gliding animals but glided on the region between the mouth and anus and not on the whole ventral surface. A ventral protuberance, the foot, was formed and used as the gliding organ. On the dorsal side another protuberance, the visceral hump, developed and became covered by the shell.

c. Annelida took to a free life, moving by rhythmical contractions of the body, which was formed as an outgrowth in the anal region. Metameric segmentation arose in adaptation to this type of locomotion.

d. The Ectoprocta (Bryozoa) were a group that became sessile.

e. Podaxonia (sipunculids and perhaps *Phoronis,* though the latter is placed by some zoologists in the Plutealia) took to living in tubes. A protuberance was formed in the ventral region between the mouth and the anus, and this became covered by a tube.

2. Superphylum Plutealia
   a. Echinodermata became sessile by an attachment in front of the mouth and developed five-rayed radial symmetry around their free ends.
   b. Chordata were free-living with the same type of locomotion as the annelids. They developed metameric segmentation, as annelids did, in adaptation to their mode of locomotion.

The foregoing more or less general view of the probable phylogeny of the animal kingdom must be very tentative and liable to modification with the advance of knowledge in view of the incompleteness of the evidence on which many of the conclusions are based.

BIBLIOGRAPHY.—G. S. Carter, *A General Zoology of the Invertebrates,* ch. 23, 4th ed. (1961), *Animal Evolution, a Study of Recent Views of Its Causes* (1951); *Evolution: Essays on Aspects of Evolutionary Biology,* ed. by G. R. de Beer (1938); W. K. Gregory, "The Transformation of Organic Designs," *Biol. Rev.,* 11:310 (1936); R. Jeannel, *Les Insectes: Classification et Phylogenie,* in *Traite de Zoologie,* ed. by P. P. Grassé, vol. 9 (1940); L. H. Hyman, *The Invertebrates,* vol. 1–5 (1940–59): A. D. Imms, "The Ancestry of Insects," *Trans. R. ent. Soc. Lond.,* 3:1–32 (1936); T. J. Parker and W. A. Haswell, *Text-book of Zoology,* 6th ed., vol. ii, rev. by C. Forster-Cooper (1940); A. S. Romer, *Vertebrate Paleontology* (1945); R. E. Snodgrass, *Evolution of the Annelida, Onychophora and Arthropoda,* Smithsonian Miscellaneous Collections, vol. 97, no. 6 (1938); O. W. Tiegs and S. M. Manton, "The Evolution of the Arthropoda," *Biol. Rev.,* 33:258 (1958).   (G. S. Cr.)

ANIMAL SOCIOLOGY: see SOCIOLOGY, ANIMAL.

ANIMAL WORSHIP, a somewhat loose term, covering a wide range of phenomena, from the actual worship of divine animals, conceived as "god-bodies," at one end of the scale, through the representation of gods or spirits in animal form (theriomorphic symbolism), to ceremonial behaviour toward certain animals, living or slain, at the other end.

The sources of animal worship are manifold. Primitive man still is capable of feeling close to the animal world, and this closeness may border on a feeling of near-identity when a particular species or a particular animal is regarded as the ancestor or as the repository of the life power of the group (totemism) or the individual (nagualism). This closeness is also exemplified by the widespread belief in the possibility of transformation from one form to the other; *e.g.,* werewolves. On the other hand the strangeness and mysterious superiority of the animal world (greater strength, extraordinary fertility, swiftness, capacity to fly in the air, sloughing of skin, etc.) render it a treasury of fitting symbols for the essentially mysterious and superior otherness of the holy. Animal forms thus may be even more expressive than human forms of the numinous.

There is, moreover, the magical aspect of much so-called animal worship which is designed to assure a successful hunt and an adequate supply of the species in question (this is generally held to be the significance of the scenes and animals depicted in prehistoric cave art) or, conversely, to provide protection against noxious species.

Ancient Egypt provides the best-known examples of animal worship, both in the sense of statuary and pictorial representations of gods in animal or rather half-animal shape (human bodies with animal heads), and in the actual treatment of particular animals as divine (*e.g.,* the Apis bull). The animal ancestry, or at least animal aspects and symbolism, of many Greek gods is a well-established fact (*e.g.,* Poseidon Hippius, Dionysus as bull or kid, etc.).

Whenever a symbolic relationship between men (individuals or groups) and animals obtains, it may well be permissible to speak of "totemistic psychology," though the theory that totemism is a uniform phenomenon and at the origin of all religion has been rejected (*see* TOTEMISM). This relationship may be predominantly magical (*e.g.,* concerned with the increase of the species) as among the tribes of central Australia, or it may stress the taboo aspect as in Africa, or it may be focused on a

SEKHMET, EGYPTIAN GODDESS OF WAR, WITH HEAD OF LIONESS

personal guardian spirit or even animal alter ego, such as, for example, the nagual of Central American Indians or the *elanela,* usually a panther or serpent, among the African Fang. Military, medicine, dance and secret societies (*e.g.,* the leopard societies in west Africa or the medicine societies of the North American Pawnee) often have animal names or symbols; the same habit is still alive, though in an attenuated form, among various modern societies, clubs, military units, etc.

Ceremonial behaviour toward animals, as distinct both from worship and from the recognition of a bond of some kind, is a characteristic feature of many hunting cultures. Absence of animal husbandry and dependence on the unpredictable appearance of the necessary food supply at the right period are reflected in many myths which assume a kind of primordial covenant between the animal and human worlds, presided over by the "lord of life," or "lord of animals." An adequate supply is assured to the hunter, provided that he observes certain rules and shows due respect to the animal as well as gratitude for its co-operation in going for the kill. Thus certain parts of the animal must be treated or eaten in specified ways (for instance, tobacco may be placed in the mouth of a slain bear as an offering) and circumlocutions are respectfully used when referring to the animal.

Most mammals, birds and reptiles figure, in one way or another, in the religious and magical symbolism of mankind, some (*e.g.,* serpents) more frequently than others. But whereas animals play a large role in the ritual practice of many primitive religions and in the symbolism of some of the more highly developed (*e.g.,* Hinduism), actual worship of animals as incarnations or representations of the divine being or power are extremely rare.

BIBLIOGRAPHY.—G. van der Leeuw, *Religion in Essence and Manifestation,* pp. 75–82 (1938); F. G. Speck, *Naskapi, the Savage Hunters of the Labrador Peninsula,* pp. 76–126 (1935); J. G. Frazer, *The Golden Bough,* 12 vol., 3rd ed. (1907–12).   (R. J. Z. W.)

ANIMISM, derived from *anima,* "breath" or "soul," is the doctrine of the reality of souls. In biology and psychology it is the view that mind or soul is an immaterial element that co-operates with the body through the brain and nervous system. In philosophy it is the theory that all natural objects are animate, ensouled or spirit-directed from within, and that mental and physical life has as its source or ground soul or spirit. Animism, however, probably will always be known chiefly as the term used by Sir Edward Tylor in *Primitive Culture* (1871) to describe his theory of the origin of religion and the beliefs of primitive peoples.

Tylor's Theory.—Tylor wrote his great work, *Primitive Culture,* in order to prove that religion began in animism. Animism is the attribution of a soul or spirit to living things and inanimate objects. To a full-blown animism nothing is really inanimate; everything is alive with spirit, active or not. Tylor wrote:

It seems as though thinking men, as yet at a low level of culture, were deeply impressed by two groups of biological problems. In the first place, what is it that makes the difference between a living body and a dead one; what causes waking, sleep, trance, disease and death? In the second place, what are those human shapes which appear in dreams and visions? Looking at these two groups of phenomena, the ancient savage philosophers probably made their first step by the obvious inference that every man has two things belonging to him, namely a life and a phantom.

Both life and phantom are perceived to be separable from the body: the life as able to go away and leave it insensible or dead; and the phantom as appearing to people at a distance. The second step taken by "the ancient savage philosophers" was to combine the life and the phantom and thus arrive at "that well-known conception which may be described as an apparitional soul, a ghost-soul." Tylor argued that in further steps of reasoning it was thought that the ghost soul was able to enter into, possess and act in the bodies of beasts, birds, reptiles and plants. But the theory of souls stretches beyond this limit.

Certain high savage races distinctly hold, and a large proportion of other savage and barbarian races make a more or less close approach to, a theory of separable and surviving souls or spirits belonging to sticks and stones, weapons, boats, food, clothes, ornaments, and other objects which to us are not merely soulless but lifeless.

Tylor felt that religion had its origin in early man's attribution of a soul like his own to every sort of living being and physical object around him. Religion is implicit in the experience of an African Negro:

He was going out on important business, but crossing the threshold he trod on this stone and hurt himself. Ha! ha! thought he, art thou there? So he took the stone, and it helped him through his undertaking for days.

Religion is man's establishment of a relationship between himself and the spirits which he felt "possessed, pervaded, crowded" all nature.

Even though Tylor's theory has impressed anthropologists with its plausibility, it has been widely criticized as too intellectualistic. Was primitive man an "ancient savage philosopher" who felt a rational need to explain death and dreams and developed a theory? Hardly. Religion had a more intuitive, more emotional origin. Furthermore, was Tylor justified in imputing to primitive man a tendency to theorize that nature is universally animated, in all parts "possessed, pervaded, and crowded with spiritual beings"? It began to be felt that the facts are misinterpreted when it is said that the primitive man considers all objects to be alive. Two qualifications of Tylor's theory were seen to be necessary, and both were made by R. R. Marett in 1899 and later in his book *The Threshold of Religion* (1914).

Animatism.—Marett, in the first place, limited the primitive's conception of aliveness to objects that behave in an unusual way or queerly or that seem about to behave thus; such objects the primitive tends to regard as sacred, full of special potency. In the second place, the special potency or aliveness would not necessarily lead primitive man to attribute a soul or spirit to the object; for the notion of being alive is logically distinct from and historically and psychologically more rudimentary than the notion of possessing a soul or spirit. The object might be animated or alive without necessarily having a soul or spirit inside it; no sophisticated distinction between the body of the object and its soul was at first drawn. Marett called this animatism or preanimism. He was led to this view by the Melanesian conception of mana (*q.v.*), as it had been described by R. H. Codrington. Marett wrote:

Codrington defines mana as follows: "a force altogether distinct from physical power, which acts in all kinds of ways for good or evil, and which is of the greatest advantage to possess or control." ... He illustrates his point by examples: "If a man has been successful in fighting, it has not been his natural strength of arm, quickness of eye, or readiness of resource that has won success; he has certainly got the *mana* of a spirit or of some deceased warrior to empower him, conveyed in an amulet of stone round his neck or a tuft of leaves in his belt, in a tooth hung upon a finger of his bow hand, or in the form of words with which he brings supernatural assistance to his side. If a man's pigs multiply and his gardens are productive, it is not because he is industrious and looks after his property, but because of the stones full of *mana* for pigs and yams that he possesses. Of course a yam naturally grows when planted, that is well known, but it will not be very large unless *mana* comes into play." (R. R. Marett, *The Threshold of Religion,* London [1914]: Methuen & Co. Ltd., pp. 103–105.)

Mana is, then, "a kind of communicable energy," not a soul. Marett found in mana a confirmation of his theory that the primitive mind tends to treat the inanimate, insofar as it is regarded as unusual or sacred, "as if it were animated—that is, alive and endowed with feelings and a will of its own," without being possessed of a soul. He was sure that while animism is characteristic of primitive peoples, it is accompanied, and probably preceded, by animatism.

Prevalence of Animism.—Not only primitives but millions of people in the larger, more complex cultures are animists. They agree in attributing to all sorts of objects a soul or spirit separable from, and destined to survive the destruction or dissolution of, its physical shell or container. This belief is an essential part of their medicine, magic and religion. In general, the larger natural objects that make up the frame of the world are thought to be the abode of spirits; while animals, human beings and certain individual objects have souls, so long, that is, as they are "alive"; after death or departure from the body, souls become spirits or ghosts, until such time as they may gain another body.

In animistic medicine, illness, delirium and insanity are held to result from a mishap occurring to the soul, such as its being lured from its body and trapped or captured; or, again, these states may result from "possession," that is, from the fact that one or more additional souls or spirits have, perhaps with evil intent, entered the body and troubled the soul that belongs in it. In the latter case it becomes the function of the shaman or medicine man to exorcise the invading soul or spirit.

Ancestor worship (*q.v.*) and animism are interrelated phenomena; which is cause and which effect would be hard to determine. The souls of the dead are believed to survive the dissolution of their bodies, to linger near the scene of their former lives and to depend upon the living for food, remembrance and loyalty. This has been the basic factor in the popular religion of China for three millenniums.

Animism is also an aspect of nature worship. Not all nature worship is animistic. Sometimes the object is worshiped for the mana in it, its sacredness, its potencies; or, again, the object of worship may be far above the category of souls or spirits—some High God or Originator of all things. In between are all the spirits or souls found in stones, plants, trees, rivers, lakes, mountains, animals and men, and the gods and godlings of the polytheisms, as well as the evil spirits of demonology. *See* RELIGION, PRIMITIVE: *Manifestations of the Sacred; see* also references under "Animism" in the Index.

BIBLIOGRAPHY.—E. B. Tylor, *Primitive Culture* (1871); J. G. Frazer, *The Golden Bough* (1907–15), *The Fear of the Dead in Primitive Religion* (1933–36); R. R. Marett, *The Threshold of Religion* (1914); A. Lang, *The Making of Religion* (1898); B. Malinowski, *Magic, Science and Religion* (1925), especially "Baloma; the Spirits of the Dead in the Trobriand Islands"; R. F. Fortune, *The Sorcerers of Dobu* (1932); R. H. Lowie, *Primitive Religion* (1924); J. Murphy, *Primitive Man* (1927); W. C. Willoughby, *The Soul of the Bantu* (1928); W. W. Howells, *The Heathens: Primitive Man and His Religions* (1948); J. J. M. DeGroot, *The Religion of the Chinese* (1910).   (J. B. N.)

ANIMUCCIA, GIOVANNI (*c.* 1500–1571), Italian composer, chiefly remembered for his collaboration with St. Philip Neri (*q.v.*), for whose popular services in the Roman oratory of S. Girolamo he wrote a number of *Laudi spirituali*. These performances later gave rise to the oratorio (*q.v.*).

Animuccia was one of the first to simplify the structure of early 16th-century church music. Though he was a prolific master of the traditional Netherlandish style, handling canon and *cantus firmus* with great fluency, his later experiments in short, clear-cut forms, syllabic melody and homophonic declamation may well have influenced Palestrina.

Like his brother Paolo (d. 1563), also a composer, Animuccia was born in Florence. In 1555 he became choirmaster of the Julian chapel, St. Peter's, Rome, where he remained until his death in 1571. He published three books of madrigals (1547, 1551, 1554) and a mixed volume with some motets (1548), all in Venice; and in Rome books of *Masses* (1567), *Magnificat* (1568), madrigals, motets and *Madrigali spirituali* (1565) and two of *Laudi* (1563, 1570). Many sacred compositions remain unpublished.

(B. L. TR.)

ANION, a negatively charged particle or ion which moves toward the positive electrode or anode during an electrolysis or an electrical discharge. The anion is usually nonmetallic in character and consists of one or more atoms carrying a definite number of negative electric charges (*see* ELECTRON).

The chloride ion (Cl^-) and the nitrate ion (NO_3^-) are both univalent anions, while the sulfate ion ($SO_4^=$) is a bivalent anion. *See* also CATION.   (J. B. Ps.)

ANISE, an annual plant, *Pimpinella anisum* (Umbelliferae, or parsley family), native to the eastern Mediterranean region and extensively cultivated for its seedlike fruits, the anise seed of commerce. The anise plant, up to $2\frac{1}{2}$ ft. tall, has long-stalked basal leaves and shorter-stalked stem leaves. The small flowers, in loose umbels, are yellowish white. The fruits are about $\frac{1}{8}$ in. long, gray or greenish, ribbed, downy and aromatic. Principal anise-growing regions are southern Europe, southern U.S.S.R., the near east, north Africa, India, Pakistan, China, Chile, Mexico and the United States. Anise seed, or the essential oil therefrom, is used to flavour foods, beverages, medicines and dentifrices. The fruit of a tree (*Illicium verum*) of southeastern China and adjacent Vietnam, is the source of oil of star anise. The flavour and uses of star anise are similar to those of anise.   (J. W. TT.)

ANIUS, in Greek myth, was the son of Apollo and Rhoeo, a descendant of Dionysus. His mother, when pregnant, had been placed in a chest and cast into the sea by her father; floating to Delos she gave birth to Anius, who became a seer and a priest of Apollo. By his wife, Dorippe, Anius had three daughters, Oeno,

Spermo and Elais—that is, Wine, Grain Seed and Oil—who were granted by Dionysus the gift of bringing these three crops to fruition. They supplied both the Greek expedition on its way to Troy and Aeneas in his flight from Troy to Italy. (T. V. B.)

ANJOU, an ancient province of France, approximately corresponding to the modern *département* of Maine-et-Loire (*q.v.*) with the regions of La Flèche and Château-Gontier. The name is ultimately derived from that of the Andes, a Celtic tribe inhabiting the area before the Roman conquest of Gaul. Organized in the Gallo-Roman period as the Civitas Andegavensis and in the Frankish period first as the Pagus Andegavensis and then as the Comitatus Andegavensis, or countship of Anjou, the country was raised to the rank of duchy by King John II of France in 1360.

Anjou was bounded in the north by Maine, in the east by Touraine, in the south by Poitou and in the west by Brittany. Geographically it included the regions of Segré, Baugé, Saumur and the Mauges and the part of the valley of the Loire round Angers (*q.v.*), which was the capital of Anjou.

Earliest History.—Anjou was conquered for the Romans by one of Julius Caesar's lieutenants in 57 B.C. After the unsuccessful rising of the Gallic chieftain Dumnacus in 52 B.C., the country enjoyed peace and prosperity throughout the Gallo-Roman period. In the course of the 5th century, however, at the same time as it was being converted to Christianity, it suffered from barbarian invasions. Under the Merovingians, it formed part of Neustria (*q.v.*). Under the Carolingians, it was administered by a count representing the king.

In 845 Lambert, a former count of Nantes, aided by Nomenoë, the ruler of Brittany, invaded the whole of the western part of Anjou, certain areas of which he occupied. Shortly afterward the Northmen or Normans, moving up the Loire valley, laid waste the entire region. In order to keep the Normans in check, the Frankish king Charles II the Bald appealed for help to Robert (*q.v.*) the Strong, who engaged them in battle at Brissarthe (866). Robert was killed and his army defeated, and for some years the Normans were masters of Anjou. Angers was recaptured by Charles the Bald in 873, but until the end of the 9th century the Normans continued to make dangerous incursions into the territory of Anjou.

First Dynasty of Counts.—Under one of the sons of Robert the Strong, Anjou was entrusted to a certain Ingelger, who became the founder of the first Angevin dynasty. Ingelger's son Fulk I the Red rid the country of the Normans and enlarged his domains by taking part of Touraine. He died in 942, and under his successor, Fulk II the Good, the destruction caused by the preceding wars was repaired. Geoffrey I Grisegonelle, who succeeded Fulk II *c.* 960, began the policy of expansion which was to characterize this first feudal dynasty. He helped Hugh Capet to seize the French crown, but died some months after the new king's accession (987).

Geoffrey's successor Fulk III Nerra (*le Noir* or the Black; *see* FULK), one of the most remarkable figures of his period and the most powerful member of the dynasty, ruled from 987 to 1040. He finally drove back beyond the frontiers of Anjou the Bretons who were still harassing the country, defeating the count of Rennes, Conan I, at the battle of Conquereuil (992). Having made himself master in the west he turned his attention to the east and came into conflict with the count of Blois, Eudes II, over the territory of Saumur and a considerable part of Touraine. He defeated Eudes at Pontlevoy in 1016 and surprised and took Saumur ten years later. Fulk founded several abbeys and built strongly fortified castles of stone (instead of wood) along the border of his territory. He died on his return from a pilgrimage to the Holy Land, having reigned 53 years.

The victory won by Fulk's son Geoffrey II Martel (1040–60; *see* GEOFFREY) at Nouy (Aug. 21, 1044) assured to the Angevins the possession of the countship of Touraine. Pursuing the policy of expansion begun by his father, Geoffrey annexed the Vendômois and a part of Maine to Anjou. As he left no sons, his two nephews, Geoffrey III the Bearded and Fulk IV le Réchin, shared the succession. However, they soon came into armed conflict and Fulk defeated Geoffrey in 1068. Nevertheless he had to

give up most of the lands which Fulk Nerra had acquired and to defend his fief against the claims of the duke of Normandy. After the death of Fulk IV in 1109 his son Fulk V the Young (*see* FULK, king of Jerusalem) endeavoured to make good the losses caused by the various wars. He married his son Geoffrey Plantagenet to Matilda, the daughter of Henry I of England and widow of the emperor Henry V. In the crusade Fulk won such a reputation for valour that he was elected king of Jerusalem, where he died.

By his marriage to Matilda, Geoffrey Plantagenet acquired a claim to Normandy and England. Forced to spend his whole life fighting his rivals and the Angevin nobles, he nevertheless succeeded in pacifying Anjou, which in 1151 he left to his son Henry (later Henry II of England), count of Anjou and Maine and duke of Normandy, who married Eleanor (Aliénor) of Aquitaine after the annulment of her marriage to Louis VII of France. Thus the Anglo-Angevin empire of the Plantagenet dynasty was founded, extending from England to the Pyrenees. The existence of this empire was a threat to the Capetian monarchy in France, and the two dynasties entered into a struggle which lasted more than a century.

The Plantagenets never lost interest in the birthplace of their family, and Anjou was administered by a seneschal, who was not, however, always loyal. Henry II took steps to protect the valley of the Loire against flooding by building a dike along the banks of the river. He contributed to the foundation of the Hôtel Dieu (hospital) of Angers and bestowed many gifts upon the abbeys of Anjou, particularly Fontevrault, in which his remains lie next to those of Eleanor of Aquitaine.

Philip II Augustus of France conquered Anjou from John of England at the beginning of the 13th century. An attempt by the English to retake Anjou failed when they were defeated at La Roche-aux-Moines in 1214. Anjou was finally attached to the crown of France by the treaty of Paris (1259).

During the 12th and 13th centuries there was an economic expansion in Anjou; wines were already being exported to England and the working of the slate quarries in the region of Angers was begun.

Second Dynasty.—In 1246 Louis IX of France gave Anjou as an appanage to his brother Charles, the future king of Naples and Sicily. Charles was succeeded by his son Charles II and the latter by his son-in-law Charles of Valois, under whose rule the economic and social conditions of the people of Anjou improved.

The son of Charles of Valois became king of France, as Philip VI, in 1328. From that year until 1351 Anjou was once more united to the crown and benefited from royal attention. The Hundred Years' War, however, together with the war of succession in Brittany, brought a return of insecurity. In 1348 the black death inflicted widespread devastation.

Third Dynasty.—John II of France gave the countship of Anjou to his son Louis (*see* LOUIS, kings of Naples) in 1351. Thus began the third Angevin dynasty, which was raised to ducal rank in 1360. At this period bands of English soldiers under the command of Sir Robert Knollys were wandering through Anjou, causing great destruction. The later Angevin princes were more interested in the conquest of the kingdom of Naples than in the defense of their duchy, and Louis II, as his father, Louis I, spent most of his life away from Anjou. After his death his widow, Yolande of Aragon, strove to protect Anjou against attacks by the English. In 1421 Thomas duke of Clarence, brother of Henry V of England, was defeated by the Angevin nobles at Baugé. Despite several attempts the English never succeeded in taking possession of Anjou again.

The last of the rulers of Anjou was René I (*q.v.*), whose pleasant disposition, simplicity and taste for literature and the arts endeared him to his subjects. After his death (1480) Anjou was for the last time returned to the crown of France and its fate was thenceforth linked with that of the French kingdom.

Later History.—During the 16th century Anjou played a part in the literary and artistic developments of the Renaissance. Fine châteaux were built, and poets such as Joachim du Bellay took the Loire as a theme for their verses. However, in the second half of the 16th century the country experienced further troubles in the wars between Catholics and Huguenots. Members of the Holy league in Anjou refused for a long time to recognize Henry IV as king of France and abandoned their struggle only in 1598, shortly before the signing of the Edict of Nantes.

Anjou, then merely a province of France, was again during the 17th century the scene of disorders. In 1620 Marie de Médicis, the mother of Louis XIII, who had received the *gouvernement* of Anjou, rebelled against her son and took refuge in Anjou. After a brief struggle she submitted. More serious were the events which took place in the province during the Fronde. The people rose in revolt in protest against the severe taxes levied on them, and the royal army had to besiege Angers for three weeks before subduing it (1652).

In the 18th century, as a result of the efforts of the intendants of Tours, there was an upsurge of economic activity in Anjou. Roads and canals were built, and the textile industry (located in Cholet and in the district around Angers) and the slate quarries enjoyed great prosperity. On the eve of the Revolution Anjou was a rich province.

Administratively in 1789 Anjou formed two military *gouvernements* (Haut-Anjou and Bas-Anjou). It was part of the *généralité* (financial division) of Tours and comprised five *élections* (districts): Angers, Baugé, Saumur, Montreuil-Bellay, Château-Gontier and a part of the districts of La Flèche and Richelieu. One of the *pays de grande gabelle* (see GABELLE), it possessed 16 special tribunals or *greniers à sel* (salt warehouses). As regards judicial administration, Anjou was subject to the *parlement* of Paris. There was a presidial court at Angers, another at La Flèche and at Château-Gontier, seneschal's courts at Angers, Saumur, Baugé and Beaufort, and numerous seigniorial courts. Most of Anjou was included in the ecclesiastical diocese of Angers, although several parishes in the southern and western parts of the province belonged to the dioceses of Poitiers, Nantes and La Rochelle. When in 1790 France was divided into *départements*, Anjou, with the exception of La Flèche and Château-Gontier, formed the *département* of Maine-et-Loire.

BIBLIOGRAPHY.—*Principal Sources:* For the 10th, 11th and 12th centuries the most important text dealing with Anjou is the chronicle *Gesta consulum Andegavorum* or *Chroniques des comtes d'Anjou*, ed. by P. Marchegay and A. Salmon (1856–71) and by L. Halphen and R. Poupardin (1913). *See also* L. Halphen, *Étude sur les chroniques des comtes d'Anjou et des seigneurs d'Amboise* (1903).
Later works: The 11th century was treated in detail by L. Halphen in *Le Comté d'Anjou au XIe siècle* (1906), which has a preface with bibliography and an introduction dealing with the history of Anjou in the 10th century. The work of Célestin Port, *Dictionnaire historique, géographique et biographique de Maine-et-Loire*, 3 vol. (1874–78), and its volume of *Préliminaires* (including a summary of the history of Anjou) contain comprehensive information on Angevin history. *See also* J. Chartrou, *L'Anjou de 1109 à 1151* . . . (1928); J. Boussard, *Le Comté d'Anjou sous Henri Plantagenet et ses fils, 1151–1204* (1938) and "La Vie en Anjou aux XIe et XIIe siècles," *Le Moyen Age*, no. 1–2, 29–68 (1950); J. Levron, *Petite Histoire de l'Anjou* (1947); P. Wagret *et al.*, *Visages d'Anjou* (1951); J. Boussard, *Le Gouvernement d'Henri II Plantagenet* (1956). (J. Le.)

ANKARA, the second largest *il* (province) in Turkey, contains the capital city, Ankara (*q.v.*), situated, as other towns, on the green belt which encircles the steppe of central Anatolia and is linked by corridors with the other regions of Anatolia. Pop. (1960) 1,321,380. Area 11,850 sq.mi. (30,691 sq.km.). The province includes most of ancient Galatia (*q.v.*) and is surrounded by nine other provinces. It is famous for the Angora (Ankara) goat, bred for its long silky hair, which provides mohair, and for the Angora cat, which also has beautiful fur and often eyes of different colours: one blue, one amber. Outside the city there is a carpetmaking industry and local products include honey and a special variety of pear. (A. F. U.)

ANKARA (formerly transliterated ANGORA), the capital city of Turkey and of Ankara province, stands on a rocky hill 500 ft. above the plain and 3,400 ft. above sea level. Its position on the edge of a high inland plateau, with plains to the west and south and mountains to the north, gives it a dry continental climate. Chosen as the new capital by Mustafa Kemal Atatürk because its remoteness from the sea made it easy to defend and officially so designated in Oct. 1923, it reflects the character of modern

TEMPLE OF AUGUSTUS AND ROME, ANKARA, TURKEY. RESTORED BY AUGUSTUS. 1ST CENTURY B.C.

Turkey, with its emphasis on planning and westernization. Pop. (1960) 650,067; (1965) 902,000 (mun.).

The old town of Ankara is built on and around the hill on which stands the walled citadel with its inner fort and white tower still standing but its outer walls in ruins. The least densely populated part of the city is the old town which has mainly narrow, winding streets with houses mostly built of mud brick, brick and wood, with tile decorations, though the old houses are interspersed with modern buildings. It includes the commercial quarter and Ulus square, the scene of national celebrations. The most northerly area, untouched by the city's rapid development, contains most of the ancient remains: the temple of Augustus and Rome (possibly 2nd century B.C., later restored by Augustus); the 3rd-century Roman baths; and the Byzantine column of Julian (attributed to the 4th century). In the old town also are the mosques of Arslanhane (1290), Ahi Şeref et Tin (1330), Ahi Elvan (1331–61), and Haci Bayram (16th century). On the citadel hill is the archaeological museum (1951) containing outstanding Hittite remains. Near the inner citadel is the Alaeddin mosque (1178).

The main north-south artery is Atatürk boulevard, which runs from Ulus square to the presidential palace on Çankaya hill at the south, passing the National Opera house, the People's house, the ethnographical museum, in front of which is an equestrian statue of Atatürk by the Italian sculptor Canonica, and the faculty of letters. It then joins the new town (Yenisehir), passing Kizil Ay square, the centre of the most fashionable shopping and residential area. South of this is the Bakanliklar district, where the ministries are grouped, and the diplomatic quarter stretches to the south. The building of the grand national assembly is in the northwest of the city.

On the highest hill, to the west and visible from all parts of the city, is the impressive mausoleum of Atatürk, completed in 1953. Other modern memorials are the Victory monument, on Ulus square, which commemorates the annihilation of the Greek army in Aug. 1922, and the Confidence monument, at Kizil Ay, with its inscription *Ögün, Çaliş, Güven* ("Be Proud, Work, Be Confident"). Atatürk's house, in the grounds of the presidential palace, has become a museum.

Ankara has a university (founded 1946); a national library; a state-subsidized theatre; and a modern radio station. Ankara college, with over 4,000 pupils, boys and girls, is the largest school; the teaching of English is stressed and it has many British teachers. Gençlik parki (Youth park) lies between the railway station, to the west, and the old town. The racecourse is to the northwest and there are two sports stadiums. A favourite excursion is to Çubuk dam, with casino and restaurant, 8 mi. to the north.

The city is linked by rail with Istanbul, Izmir and Adana and has road connections to all parts. The airport at Esenboga, 16 mi. distant, is used by regular international services.

History.—The date of Ankara's foundation is uncertain. Archaeological evidence points to its foundation by people living in Anatolia before the Hittites. The name Ankara is derived from *Ank*, a gorge or ravine. It has been suggested that the citadel was built in the Phrygian period as a fortress at the junction of the east-west and north-south trade routes. The Galatians, who invaded the region in the 3rd century B.C., appear to have founded another city there on the same site. For its early history *see* ANCYRA, the form of the name known from the end of the 9th century B.C. until its fall to the Seljuk Turks in A.D. 1073.

Captured by the crusader Raymond, count of Toulouse, in 1101 it was reclaimed in 1127 and passed to the emir Gazi of the Danishmend dynasty but about 1150 fell again to the Seljuks. After a period of Mongol domination it was taken in 1356 by Orkhan, the second of the Ottoman sultans, and became part of the Ottoman empire in 1360. Invested again during Tamerlane's Anatolian campaign, and the scene of a Turkish defeat in 1402, it reverted to Ottoman rule in 1403 and became a trading centre on the caravan route to the eastern provinces.

Ankara achieved new importance in 1919 when Atatürk chose it as the seat of the representative body and his military headquarters. In April 1920 the grand national assembly met in Ankara for the first time. The city's progress thereafter was rapid; it was replanned in 1928 and had become by the early 1960s the most modern city in Turkey.   (A. F. U.)

ANKYLOSIS (ANCHYLOSIS), in medicine, stiffness of a joint, the result of injury or disease. The rigidity may be complete or partial and may be due to inflammation of the tendinous or muscular structures outside the joint or of the tissues of the joint itself. When the structures outside the joint are affected, the term false ankylosis has been used in contradistinction to true ankylosis, in which the disease is within the joint. When inflammation has caused the joint ends of the bones to be fused together the ankylosis is termed osseous or complete. Excision of a completely ankylosed shoulder or elbow may restore free mobility and usefulness to the limb. *See* JOINTS AND LIGAMENTS, DISEASES AND DISABILITIES OF.

ANNA (ANNA IVANOVNA) (1693–1740), empress of Russia from 1730 to 1740, was born in Moscow on Feb. 7 (new style; Jan. 28, old style), 1693, the second daughter of Peter the Great's feeble-minded half brother Ivan V (d. 1696). She spent her girlhood under the conflicting influences of her mother, Praskovia Fedorovna, née Saltykova, who was a bigoted woman of the old school, and of Peter, who wanted to endow his nieces with western accomplishments. On Nov. 11 (N.S., Oct. 31, O.S.), 1710, Peter married Anna to Frederick William, duke of Courland; but the young duke, whose health had been affected by the lavish wedding celebrations in St. Petersburg, died on the way home. In pursuance of his political aims Peter forced Anna to take up residence at Mitau (Jelgava). In spite of the efficiency of Peter's agent, P. M. Bestuzhev-Ryumin, who acted as her adviser, Anna's residence in Courland was embittered by the permanent inadequacy of her revenue and by political intrigues. After Catherine I (1725–27) had designated Peter's descendants as her successors, Anna's chances of ascending the Russian throne seemed remote. However, in 1730, at the death of Peter II, the supreme privy council, which was composed almost entirely of members of the old nobility, decided to offer the crown to Anna, as the council rightly calculated that she would agree to a drastic limitation of her powers in its favour.

On Feb. 26 (N.S., 15, O.S.), Anna made her public entry into Moscow. Meanwhile the oligarchic aims of the supreme privy council had been countered by claims put forward by the gentry; and on March 8 (N.S., Feb. 25, O.S.), encouraged by appeals in favour of autocracy, Anna tore up the "conditions" that she had signed a month earlier.

The privy council was abolished and the authority of the senate restored (1730). But since Anna was neither equipped nor disposed to deal with state business a cabinet of three ministers was formed (1731). Actually, however, all power was in the hands of Anna's German favourite Ernst Johann Biron (*q.v.*), who had supplanted Bestuzhev in Courland. Although Biron did not hold any responsible posts, his name became associated with all negative features of Anna's reign.

Prompted by dislike and fear, Biron instigated a continuous persecution of the Russian nobility, showing no mercy even to men not involved in the abortive attempt to impose the "conditions" and to keep him away from Russia. The support given by the gentry was rewarded by a gradual mitigation of the burdens imposed by Peter the Great. On the other hand, two new guards regiments with German officers (1730) provided a counterbalance to the old guards, who were the mainstay of the gentry. All external as well as important internal affairs and all military problems were in the care of two other foreigners, Andrei Ivanovich Osterman and Burkhard Christoph Münnich (*qq.v.*), who had entered Russian service under Peter. The empress herself was preoccupied with making up for lean years in Courland and had to be incessantly provided with sumptuous entertainments and crude amusements. The increased expenditure of the court, combined with war expenses, led to a relentless extortion of taxes from the peasants—whose social status steadily deteriorated in contrast with the advantages gained by the upper classes. Against the growing resentment among all groups of the population, the government applied the old remedies—spying, denunciations, torture, banishment and executions—so ruthlessly that posterity remembered them as the special hallmark of the Biron regime.

Even the brilliant military achievements in the War of the Polish Succession (1733–35) and in the Turkish War (1735–39) did not offset the gloomy picture, particularly since the outcome of the Turkish War scarcely justified the tremendous cost in life and money. Although Münnich had invaded the Crimea and inflicted several heavy defeats upon the Turks, the peace treaty of Belgrade (1739) gave Russia only an area of steppes with no immediate exit to the sea, since Azov (lost by Peter the Great and recaptured in this war) became no man's land. Another change of Russia's frontiers took place in the Caucasus, where Peter's acquisitions on the west coast of the Caspian sea were restored to Persia (1732). Russia's European policy was all the time based on a close alliance with Austria. A commercial treaty concluded by Osterman in 1734 improved Anglo-Russian relations.

The one problem that greatly worried the empress from the start was the succession, which she intended to reserve for a descendant of her father. In Aug. 1740, she made up her mind in favour of the newly born son of her young niece Anna Leopoldovna, whose marriage to Anton Ulrich of Brunswick she had arranged the previous year. On the eve of her death, which occurred in St. Petersburg on Oct. 28 (N.S., 17, O.S.), 1740 Anna appointed Biron to be regent during the infancy of the child, who succeeded her as Ivan VI.

See K. Waliszewski, *L'Héritage de Pierre le Grand* (1900); R. Nisbet Bain, *The Pupils of Peter the Great* (1897).   (Lo. L.)

ANNA (ANNA LEOPOLDOVNA) (1718–1746), regent of Russia for her son the emperor Ivan VI (*q.v.*) from Nov. 1740 to Dec. 1741, was the daughter of Catherine, sister of the empress Anna Ivanovna (*q.v.*), and Charles Leopold, duke of Mecklenburg-Schwerin. Born at Rostock, in Mecklenburg, on Dec. 18 (new style; Dec. 7, old style), 1718, she grew up in Russia and in 1739 reluctantly agreed to marry Prince Anton Ulrich of Brunswick (1714–74), a nephew of the Holy Roman emperor Charles VI who had been chosen for her by the empress Anna. On Aug. 13 (N.S.; Aug. 2, O.S.), 1740, Anna gave birth to her son Ivan, who on Oct. 27 (N.S.; Oct. 16, O.S.) was proclaimed heir to the Russian throne. The following day the empress Anna died, after having appointed her favourite, E. J. Biron (*q.v.*), as regent. The duchess Anna was soon forced to approach field marshal B. C. Münnich (*q.v.*) for help. Biron was deposed and Anna proclaimed regent (*pravitelnitsa*). Her ineptitude, however, together with the general dissatisfaction with the German domination in Russia, enabled Peter the Great's daughter Elizabeth (*q.v.*)—who was both popular with the guards and backed by France—to carry out her *coup d'état*, on Dec. 6 (N.S.; Nov. 25, O.S.), 1741. At first Elizabeth intended to send the Brunswick family to Germany, but on their arrival in Riga she became scared by plots, and the whole family was interned in the fortress of Dünamünde (Dec. 1742). In 1744 the prisoners were deported to Kholmogory in the far north, where Anna died in childbed, on March 18 (N.S.; 7, O.S.), 1746. Ivan, from 1756 on in solitary confinement in Schlüsselburg, was killed there in 1764. (Lo. L.)

ANNABA (formerly Bône), the capital of the *département* of Annaba, in Algeria, and a Mediterranean port on the Gulf of Bône near the mouth of the Seybouse River, lies 260 mi. (420 km.) E of Algiers near the Tunisian border. Pop. (1960) 164,844 (commune); 135,150 (city). The town rises from the shore up the cork-covered slopes of the Edough foothills. The old town with its narrow streets dominates the centre of the city and is grouped round the Place d'Armes where are the earliest French houses and the mosque of Salah Bey (1787). In the 11th-century mosque of Sidi-bou-Merouan the prayer room is divided into seven naves and seven bays, with columns taken from the ruined forum of the ancient city of Hippo. The synagogue, close by, was built in 1852.

West of the old town is the new town, built since 1870 along both sides of the Cours Jérôme Bertagna. Its straight roads cross at right angles, and the chief public buildings include the town hall (1888), the municipal theatre (1954), the prefecture (1958), the cathedral of St. Augustine (1850), the basilica of St. Augustine (1881), the Protestant church (1882), the hospital (1958), and schools, technical colleges, and the Hippo museum near the excavations of the Roman city. There are public gardens round the town hall; others are Randon Gardens and Jean Coggia Park.

Annaba, the chief exporter of minerals on the Mediterranean (iron ore and phosphates), is also a passenger, trading, and fishing port and a port of call. Main roads connect the city with Skikda, Constantine, Guelma, and Souk-Ahras. There are railways to Algiers and on to Morocco via Constantine, to Tunis via Souk-Ahras and to Biskra and Touggourt via Constantine. The airport, 6¾ mi. (11 km.) SE, serves France and North African towns.

In the surrounding countryside are farms (crops and livestock), forests, and mines. The important Karezas mine produces arsenic and tungsten. Major industries include automobile and railway workshops and aluminum and chemical works.

Annaba's exceptional situation on a coast poorly supplied with natural harbours, on a large bay between Cape Garde and Cape Rosa and protected from the west and northwest winds, attracted the earliest sailors. It seems certain that in the 12th century the Phoenicians founded a trading port there which later became Hippo Regius, the chosen residence of the kings of Numidia. At the end of the Punic Wars the inhabitants received their independence from Rome and Hippo became a flourishing town. St. Augustine (*q.v.*), bishop of Hippo from 396 to 430, made it the centre of Christian thought. Much of the town was destroyed by the Vandals in 431, but it was rescued by the emperor Justinian in 533. Two centuries later it was overcome by the Arabs, and the effects of Roman rule and Christianity soon disappeared. The remaining citizens, driven on to high ground nearby, built a new town, Bouna el Hadida, invisible from the sea. Surrounded by walls, it later became the headquarters of pirates and fugitives. For many centuries Annaba was one of the small cities of North Africa under the domination of successive rulers. In 1535 it was occupied by the soldiers of the emperor Charles V. In 1540, however, the Turks seized it, and it remained in their possession until 1832 when the French captured it with a small force. In 1848 Louis Philippe made it a commune administered from Paris, and by the end of the century Annaba had become the important Mediterranean port and city that it still remains. (P. A. Se.)

ANNA COMNENA (1083–after 1148), Byzantine historian whose *Alexiad* is an invaluable source for the period of the first crusade, was the elder daughter of the Emperor Alexius I Comnenus. She was born on Dec. 1, 1083, and received a good education, studying a wide range of subjects including literature and philosophy, history and geography. She also had a fairly ac-

curate knowledge of medicine and nursing. In 1097 she married Nicephorus Bryennius (*q.v.*), and she united with her mother the Empress Irene in a vain attempt to persuade her father, during his last illness, to disinherit his son in favour of her husband. She then conspired to depose her brother, John II Comnenus, after his accession in 1118, and on her failure she retired into a convent, where she wrote the *Alexiad*, the history of her father. This provides a continuation of her husband's work and deals with the period 1069–1118.

Anna had a keen sense of the Greek historical tradition, and the *Alexiad* gives a characteristically Byzantine point of view on the westerners. It also provides a picture of religious and intellectual activities within the empire and reflects the Byzantine conception of the imperial office.

BIBLIOGRAPHY.—For the *Alexiad* see editions by A. Reifferscheid in the Teubner series, 2 vol. (1884); by L. Schofen, vol. 1 (1839), and A. Reifferscheid, vol. 2 (1878), in the Bonn corpus with C. Du Cange's valuable commentary, and in J. P. Migne, *Patrologia Graeca*, vol. 131 (1864); by B. Leib, with French trans., in the Budé series, 3 vol. (1937–45). Eng. trans. by E. A. S. Dawes (1928). *See also* G. Moravcsik, *Byzantinoturcica*, vol. 1, pp. 219–223, 2nd ed. (1958); G. Ostrogorsky, *History of the Byzantine State*, pp. 311–312 and 333–334 (1956); and the detailed study by G. G. Buckler, *Anna Comnena* (1929).
(J. M. Hy.)

ANNALISTS, writers of annals (*annales*, "chronicles," properly "yearbooks"); a name commonly given to the Roman historians before Livy who drew up the conventional history of Rome from the foundation of the city. The form and content of the latest annalists may be judged from the books of Livy. Yet the term is too general, and it is necessary to distinguish various stages in the development of their work.

Although only scanty records survived from the period before 390 B.C.—and the Gallic sack of Rome in that year cannot be entirely to blame—there is evidence of more authentic tradition from the 4th century. Certainly after *c.* 300 B.C. the pontifical college kept regular records—the annual *tabulae pontificum*—containing the names of magistrates and notices of public events of religious significance. These tables provided the first *annales*, from which Quintus Ennius (239–169 B.C.) drew the title of his historical epic. That their character was still sacral in the time of Marcus Porcius Cato (*q.v.*) (called the Censor) (234–149 B.C.) is clear from his *Origines*, and there is little reason to suppose that they were yet published in the form of chronicles.

The first Roman historians were senators, who early in the 2nd century B.C., at the time of the Roman intervention in the east, wrote in Greek in order to interpret the traditions, institutions and policy of Rome to the Hellenistic world. They treated the origins of Rome fully, on the basis of Roman legends and Greek antiquarian studies; the early republic briefly, using such records as they could find, along with their family traditions; and recent and contemporary times again more fully, as they found more material, both in the public records and in personal memoirs that now began to be written (*see* the article COMMENTARII). Among these writers may be named Quintus Fabius Pictor, whose material can be identified in parts of the historian Polybius; L. Cincius Alimentus, who had been a prisoner of Hannibal; P. Cornelius Scipio, the son of Africanus; A. Postumius Albinus; and C. Acilius, whose work was used by Quintus Claudius Quadrigarius and so transmitted to Livy.

Cato brought this type of history to the Roman public by writing his *Origines* in Latin. He treated first the foundation stories of Rome and the Italian peoples—hence the title—and then the important episodes of recent history. This development led to more regular antiquarian research, notably by Lucius Cassius Hemina and L. Calpurnius Piso Frugi (*see* under Piso), who probably wrote in stricter annalistic style. About 123 B.C. the pontifex maximus, P. Mucius Scaevola, published a collection of records in his books, the *Annales Maximi*, covering from the earliest times (*ab initio rerum Romanarum*) to his own day. Although the first part may be open to suspicion, the work as a whole was systematic and authoritative, and it provided the conventional framework of annalistic history from then onward. The formal, even ritualistic, language of much of the later annalistic tradition may be attributed to the influence of the *Annales*

Maximi.

At this time, too, the Roman writers adopted the rhetorical technique of elaborating notices of public business, reports of debates and descriptions of battle scenes, so as to fill out the records, often in anachronistic terms derived from their own political situation. This development may have begun with the Gracchan annalist Gnaeus Gellius. Certainly it was carried on by the later annalists. Q. Claudius Quadrigarius was sufficiently critical of the early traditions to begin his history as late as the Gallic sack of Rome; he brought it down to Sullan times in at least 23 books, of which Livy made considerable use. A younger contemporary, Valerius Antias, who wrote the history of Rome from the foundation of the city down to his own day in at least 75 books, is notorious for willful exaggeration of casualty figures and distortion of historical material. Livy, however, though he continually cites him as untrustworthy, made extensive use of his narrative. The annalistic tradition was revised by Gaius Licinius Macer (d. 66 B.C.), who studied the evidence of magistrates' lists and wrote with a democratic and family bias; and by Q. Aelius Tubero, who fought on Pompey's side against Caesar. These historians brought the annalists' work down to a point at which Livy could pick it up and transform it from political writing into the national history of Rome. The literary form continued in the imperial historians to the *Annals* of Tacitus.

BIBLIOGRAPHY.—H. Peter, *Historicorum Romanorum Reliquiae*, vol. i, 2nd ed. (1914); A. Rosenberg, *Einleitung und Quellenkunde zur römischen Geschichte* (1921); M. Gelzer, "Der Anfang römischer Geschichtsschreibung," *Hermes* 69, p. 46 (1934); and *Hermes* 82, p. 342 (1954).   (A. H. McD.)

ANNALS (from Lat. *annus*, "year"), in a precise sense, are records of appointments and other noteworthy events, arranged in a chronological sequence, normally according to solar years. For the Roman compilers of such lists *see* ANNALISTS. In the Christian era (*see* CHRONOLOGY) "Paschal" or "Easter" annals developed in western Europe, mainly during the 8th century, from the practice of noting memoranda in the margins of tables of annual lunations governing the date of Easter. For more complex forms of strictly chronological historiography, *see* CHRONICLE.

ANNAM, the historic kingdom which extended along the coast of Indochina (*q.v.*) roughly between the Song Ma (river) to the north and Cap Bake to the south. Its territory is now divided so that the lesser part, north of latitude 17° N., is in the Communist state of North Vietnam, the rest in South Vietnam. Annam retained its integrity until 1954 after a history of over 21 centuries during which it repeatedly came under imperial Chinese suzerainty. It owed its creation in 207 B.C. to a Chinese general who established himself as a monarch during a period of imperial weakness. It was made a French protectorate in 1883 and its last emperor, Bao Dai, became emperor of all Vietnam before being deposed by popular vote in 1955. *See* VIETNAM.

(E. H. G. D.)

ANNAMESE LANGUAGE: *see* VIETNAMESE LANGUAGE.

ANNAN, a small and royal burgh of Dumfriesshire, Scot., lies on the river Annan, nearly 2 mi. from its mouth which opens into the Solway firth and 16 mi. E.S.E. of Dumfries by road or rail. Pop. (1961) 5,572. The Annan is crossed by a stone road bridge (1824); a railway bridge; and two foot bridges, one a suspension bridge. Shipping accommodation, improved in 1897, gives 15-ft. depth at high water spring tides. Industries include the making of boilers, machinery, cranes, chemicals and gloves. Flour milling and fishing, especially for salmon and shrimps, are important. In the 1950s four atomic reactors were built on the disused Creca airfield at Chapelcross, 3 mi. N.E. of Annan, a border town which was often raided and razed by the English between the 14th and 16th centuries. Gretna Green (*q.v.*) is 8 mi. E., while to the north is Ecclefechan, the birthplace of Thomas Carlyle.

ANNA PERENNA, an old Roman deity of the circle or ring of the year, as the name (per annum) clearly indicates. Her festival, characterized by popular merrymaking, fell on the full moon of the first month (March 15) and was held at the grove of the goddess at the first milestone on the Via Flaminia. Sac-

rifice was offered to her "that the circle of the year might be happily completed." This is all that is known for certain about the goddess and her cult, but the name naturally suggested myth-making, and Anna became a figure in stories in Ovid and in Silius Italicus. The myth related by Ovid in the *Fasti*, that Anna promised to procure Minerva for Mars but instead substituted herself in disguise, is probably an old Italian folk tale. She was occasionally confused with Anna, the sister of Dido.   (T. V. B.)

ANNAPOLIS, a city of Maryland, U.S., the capital of the state and seat of Anne Arundel county, is located on the Severn river about 2 mi. from its entrance into Chesapeake bay, 26 mi. S.E. of Baltimore and about the same distance northeast of Washington, D.C. It is a port of entry of the Maryland customs district, the seat of the U.S. Naval academy (*see* MILITARY, NAVAL AND AIR ACADEMIES) and the headquarters of the Severn river naval command. A council-manager form of government has been effective since 1949. The city's population more than doubled within a decade, in part because of the annexation of adjacent areas in May 1950. (For comparative population figures *see* table in MARYLAND: *Population*.) Since the late 19th century a large proportion of the Annapolis population has been associated with the national and state government activities located there.

Annapolis is one of the most picturesque and historically interesting cities of the United States. The grounds and buildings of the U.S. Naval academy (founded in 1845) occupy a beautiful 309-ac. site on the south bank of the Severn. On an elevation near the centre of the city stands the state house (1772), with its lofty white dome and pillared portico. Nearby are the old state treasury (1737) and St. Anne's Protestant Episcopal church, which was a state church in the later colonial days. More than 60 Annapolis residences were built before the American Revolution, including the homes of three of Maryland's signers of the Declaration of Independence. Outstanding as examples of Georgian architecture in America are the Brice house, Chase house and Hammond-Harwood house. Colonial associations are further preserved by the names of some of the principal streets, such as King George's, Prince George's, Hanover and Duke of Gloucester.

The city harbours several thousand pleasure craft during the season. The harbour is dredged but cannot accommodate deep-draft vessels. There are a number of boat yards, one of which produced several minesweepers during World War II. The seafood industry (crabs and oysters) offers seasonal employment, and there are a number of small manufacturing firms making plastics and instruments. Johns Hopkins university maintains an oceanographic laboratory near Annapolis.

History.—Annapolis was settled in 1649 by Puritan exiles from Virginia. First called Providence, later, Town of Proctor's, Town at the Severn and Anne Arundel Town, it was named Annapolis in 1694, in honour of Princess Anne, then heir to the throne of Great Britain. In the same year it was made the seat of the new (royal) government. It had considerable commerce until Baltimore, in 1780, became a port of entry. The U.S. congress was in session in the state house from Nov. 26, 1783, to June 3, 1784, and it was there that Washington, on Dec. 23, 1783, resigned his commission as commander in chief of the Continental army. The Annapolis convention (*q.v.*) of 1786 was a meeting to which all the states were invited to send delegates to consider measures for the better regulation of commerce; partly because only five states were represented (New York, Pennsylvania, Virginia, New Jersey and Delaware), however, the delegates merely passed a resolution calling for another convention to meet in Philadelphia the following year, to amend the Articles of Confederation. It was this convention that framed the constitution of the United States.

St. John's College.—Chartered in 1784 as a continuation of King William's school, founded by an act of the legislature in 1696, the college occupies a campus of 26 ac. adjoining the grounds of the Naval academy. One of the trees on the campus is believed to be more than 600 years old. The main building, McDowell hall, was built in the 18th century to be the governor's mansion and was the scene of many historic events. In 1937 a unique, unified, all-required curriculum was introduced, built around the reading and discussion of the great books of western civilization, supplemented by mathematics and language tutorials and by science laboratories. The college, which is private, is nonsectarian and coeducational. The state offers scholarships to students from each of the counties of Maryland and from the city of Baltimore.

(R. M. LA.)

ANNAPOLIS CONVENTION, in U.S. history, a gathering of delegates from five states in Sept., 1786, at Annapolis, Md., that was an important rallying point in the movement toward a federal convention to revise the Articles of Confederation (*q.v.*). It was a commercial convention which originated as one of a series of meetings held between Maryland and Virginia concerning the use of waterways lying between the two states. In 1784 George Washington had reaffirmed his long-established interest in improving communication with the west by taking a leading part in promoting plans for improving navigation of the Potomac and Chesapeake waterways. The conference held at Mount Vernon in March 1785 (but in which Washington did not participate), helped to smooth the way for a joint Virginia-Maryland project, but the co-operation of Pennsylvania was seen to be needed because western routes also involved that state. This factor gave James Madison and Washington the idea of using the regional meeting for national purposes. Madison arranged to have an invitation to the Annapolis meeting extended not only to Pennsylvania but to all of the states so that problems of commerce could be discussed on a national scale.

The need for such a meeting had become increasingly evident because of problems confronting foreign and domestic commerce. Since recognition of American independence in 1783, Britain had scorned the idea of a commercial treaty with the new nation, which she termed the "disunited states," by suggesting that not one treaty but 13 would be needed. The Barbary pirates were thwarting the efforts of U.S. citizens to trade with the Mediterranean area. Moreover, America's "perpetual ally," France, was too deeply involved in her own mercantilist policy to have room for commercial "friendship." These foreign factors, as well as the problems connected with interstate commerce, caused the belief to spread that the only solution lay in changing the Articles of Confederation to grant the central government power to regulate commerce.

In spite of the apparent need for concerted action, only Virginia, New Jersey, Delaware, New York and Pennsylvania were represented at Annapolis, Sept. 11–14. No delegates were named from Maryland (nominally the host state of the convention), Connecticut, Georgia or South Carolina. Delegates were chosen from New Hampshire, Massachusetts, Rhode Island and North Carolina but they did not attend. Of the 12 men who went to Annapolis, Alexander Hamilton and James Madison in particular hoped to broaden the agenda to include more than commercial matters and to use the convention as a sounding board for broad revision of the Articles of Confederation. The delegates realized, however, that with only 5 of the 13 states represented they could neither deal with national commercial problems nor recommend changes in the articles. They therefore drew up an address to the states citing the authority given to the New Jersey delegation as a useful example and urging that another meeting of commissioners from all the states be called to examine the defects of the system and design a plan to correct them. In agreeing to this address the delegates stretched their authority to the utmost, but in so doing they in effect issued the call which resulted in the meeting eight months later at Philadelphia where a new federal constitution was drafted. *See also* UNITED STATES (OF AMERICA): *History.*

BIBLIOGRAPHY.—George Bancroft, *History of the Formation of the Federal Constitution,* 2 vol. (1882); Irving Brant, *James Madison, the Nationalist* (1948); John C. Miller, *Alexander Hamilton: Portrait in Paradox* (1959); Edmund C. Burnett (ed.), *Letters of Members of the Continental Congress,* vol. viii (1936). (H. I. BE.)

ANNAPOLIS ROYAL, Nova Scotia, Can., capital of Annapolis county and till 1750 of Nova Scotia; on an arm of the Bay of Fundy, at the mouth of the Annapolis river, 95 mi. W. of Halifax; on the main Canadian Pacific railway, 63 mi. by steamer from Saint John, N.B. Pop. (1956) 765. It is one of the oldest settlements in North America, founded in 1605 by the French, who

called it Port Royal. It was captured by the British in 1710, ceded to them by the treaty of Utrecht in 1713, and renamed in honour of Queen Anne. Fort Anne, the oldest fortification in North America, is a historical museum. Once the centre of a shipbuilding and lumber industry, the town is now a market town and tourist resort. (C. T. BI.)

ANNAPURNA, a mountain massif, is part of the central section of the Nepal Himalayas. It forms a ridge about 30 mi. long between the basins of the Kali Gandaki and the Maryandi rivers and contains four main summits of which Annapurna I (26,391 ft. [8,044 m.]) and II (26,041 ft. [7,937 m.]) stand at the western and eastern ends of the range respectively; III (24,-858 ft. [7,577 m.]) and IV (24,688 ft. [7,525 m.]) stand between them. Annapurna I is the 11th highest peak in the world. Before 1950 it was almost unknown to the general public, but in that year it became famous as the first peak more than 8,000 m. high to be climbed. Though greater heights had been reached on mountains before (*e.g.,* by E. F. Norton and T. H. Somervell, who in 1924 reached 28,150 ft. on Mt. Everest), the climbing of the first 8,000-m. peak had long been an ambition of European mountaineers in the Himalayas.

The feat was achieved by a French expedition led by Maurice Herzog. Their original objective was Dhaulagiri which stands to the northwest across the Kali Gandaki, but having failed to find a practicable route up that mountain they turned their attention to Annapurna I. Neither mountain had previously been reconnoitred, and so much time had to be spent upon this task that when at length a route up the northern face of Annapurna was found, very little time was left before the onset of the monsoon. Five camps were established, the highest of which, at 24,600 ft. was occupied on June 2 by Herzog and Louis Lachenal, who reached the summit on the following day. During the course of their withdrawal to Camp IV, the party met with a series of misfortunes with the result that Herzog and Lachenal were severely frostbitten. Annapurna I was the first of the great peaks of the Himalayas to be climbed at the first attempt, a fact which greatly enhanced the quality of the French expedition's achievement.

Annapurna IV was climbed on May 30, 1955, by H. Biller, H. Steinmetz and J. Wellenkamp, and Annapurna II on May 17, 1960, by R. H. Grant and C. J. Bonnington in an expedition led by J. O. M. Roberts.

See M. Herzog, *Annapurna* (1952). (E. E. SH.)

ANN ARBOR, a city of Michigan, U.S., on the Huron river, 38 mi. W. of Detroit; seat of Washtenaw county. Pop. (1960) 67,340; standard metropolitan statistical area (Washtenaw county) 172,440. (For comparative population figures *see* table in MICHIGAN: *Population.*) John Allen and Elisha W. Rumsey founded Ann Arbor in 1824 and honoured their wives, both named Ann, in naming the town. It became the county seat in 1827; was incorporated as a village in 1833; and chartered as a city in 1851. The earliest settlers came from New York and Virginia; they were joined later by German and Irish immigrants. Favourably situated on the Huron river, the Territorial road, and the Michigan Central railroad, which brought the first train through from Detroit in 1839, the town became the trading centre of a rich farming area.

The opening of the University of Michigan in Ann Arbor in 1841 largely determined the future of the town. Feeding and housing students and providing for their other needs were important economically. On the other hand, the university made available to townspeople, as well as faculty and students, a great variety of cultural activities not usually enjoyed in a small city. The most noted of its annual programs, attended by persons from all parts of the state, are the drama season, the May music festival, the winter concert series and the lecture course.

Ann Arbor long ago crossed the Huron river and expanded far beyond the limits of the original village. Tree-lined streets, beautiful houses on gentle slopes and the university campus make it an attractive residential community.

About 80 industrial establishments produce tools, bearings, springs, photographic equipment, balers, gauges and instruments for automobiles. (F. CL. B.)

ANNATES, a term with varied meanings, refers in general to the whole or a part of the first year's fruits of a benefice (*q.v.*), to be surrendered by the new incumbent either to the bishop or to the pope (Lat. *annatae*, from *annus*, "year"; also primitiae, first fruits). The first mention of the practice appears in the time of Pope Honorius III (d. 1227). The earliest records show the *annatae* to have been sometimes a privilege conceded to the bishop for a term of years, sometimes a right based on immemorial precedent. In the course of time the popes claimed the privilege for themselves, at first only temporarily, in order to meet particular financial needs. Thus, in 1305, Clement V claimed the first fruits of all vacant benefices in England and in 1319 John XXII those of all Christendom vacated within the next two years. The more usual custom was for the pope to claim the first fruits only of those benefices the appointment of whose incumbents was reserved to himself. Thus arose the historically more significant papal annates.

The system never was applied with uniformity or effectiveness throughout the territories of the church; and the feeling that benefices were excessively reserved with a view to the unnecessary increase of the papal revenues led to such protests as that of the bishops and barons of England, headed by Robert Grosseteste of Lincoln, at the Council of Lyons in 1245. Later, under the Annates Statute of 1534, Henry VIII was to claim the English annates for the crown. With the gradual transformation of the system of benefices, papal annates fell into disuse.

From the time of Benedict XIV (1740–58) the term has referred to the half-portion (*media annata*) of the first year's income from parochial benefices, which, in Italy and the adjacent islands, was to be contributed toward the restoration of the cathedral and collegiate churches of the respective diocese. In the matter of annates the Code of Canon Law provided only that wherever the system still obtained in the form of particular statutes and customs, these should continue to be observed.

See W. E. Lunt (ed. and trans.), *Papal Revenues in the Middle Ages*, vol. i, pp. 93–99, and vol. ii, pp. 315–372 (1934).   (J. J. Re.)

ANNATTO (Anatto, Arnotto), a colouring matter that was much used by South American Indians for painting their bodies; among civilized communities its principal use is for colouring butter, cheese and varnishes. It is produced from the seeds of *Bixa orellana* (family Bixaceae), a small tree that grows in Central and South America. The seeds are surrounded with a thin coating of a waxy pulp, which is separated from them by washing in water, passing the liquid through a sieve and allowing the suspended pulp to deposit. The water is then drained away and the paste dried, till it is a thick, stiff unctuous mass. In this state it has a dark orange-red colour and is known as roll or flag annatto, according to the form in which it is put up; when further dried it is called cake annatto. It yields a fugitive bright orange colour and is used alone, or with other dyes, in the dyeing of silks and in calico printing. It contains a yellow colouring matter, bixin.

ANNE (1665–1714), queen of Great Britain and Ireland from 1702 to 1714, second daughter of James, duke of York, afterward James II, and of Anne Hyde, daughter of the 1st earl of Clarendon, was born on Feb. 6, 1665. She was brought up as a strict Protestant, and as a child formed a friendship with Sarah Jennings (afterward duchess of Marlborough). Later Sarah became Anne's lady of the bedchamber and intimate friend. All deference to the princess' rank was abandoned, and the two ladies called each other (nicknames) Mrs. Morley and Mrs. Freeman. On July 28, 1683, Anne married Prince George of Denmark (1653–1708), brother of King Christian V and second son of King Frederick III, an unpopular union politically, but one of great domestic happiness. Her husband was created earl of Kendal and duke of Cumberland in 1689.

On Feb. 6, 1685, James became king of England. In 1687 a project of settling the crown on the princess, to the exclusion of Mary, on the condition of Anne's embracing Roman Catholicism failed. But the birth of a son to James on June 10, 1688, made the religion of his daughters a matter of less importance. Anne was not present on the occasion, having gone to Bath, "I shall never now be satisfied," Anne wrote to Mary, "whether the child

be true or false. It may be it is our brother, but God only knows." In later years, however, she had no doubt that the Old Pretender was her half brother.

During the events immediately preceding the revolution Anne remained in seclusion. She refused to show any sympathy with the king after William had landed in November (1688) and wrote, with the advice of the Churchills (Marlboroughs), to the prince, declaring her approval of his action. Subsequently the Declaration of Right settled the succession of the crown upon her after William and Mary and their children.

Between 1684 and 1688 Anne had miscarried four times and given birth to two children who died infants. On July 24, 1689, the birth of a son, William, created duke of Gloucester, who survived his infancy, gave hopes that heirs to the throne under the Bill of Rights might be forthcoming. But Anne's happiness was soon troubled by quarrels with the king and queen. Money appears to have been the first cause of ill-feeling. The granting away by William of the private estate of James, amounting to £22,000 a year, to which Anne had some claim, was a grievance, and a motion brought forward in the house of commons to increase her civil list pension of £30,000, which she enjoyed in addition to £20,000 under her marriage settlement, greatly displeased William and Mary, who regarded it as a plot to make Anne the chief of a separate interest in the state. At the beginning of 1692 the breach between the royal sisters was made final by the dismissal of the duke of Marlborough, justly suspected of Jacobite intrigues, from all his appointments. Anne took the part of her favourites with great zeal against the court, but in all probability was unaware of Marlborough's treason; she retired with Lady Marlborough to the duke of Somerset's residence at Sion house. In Aug. 1693, however, the two sisters were temporarily reconciled, and on the occasion of Mary's last illness and death Anne showed an affectionate consideration.

The death of Mary weakened William's position and made it necessary to cultivate good relations with the princess. At the same time William kept her in the background and refrained from appointing her regent during his absence. In March 1695 after the reinstatement of Marlborough at court Anne gave her support to William's government. Meanwhile, since the birth of the duke of Gloucester, the princess had experienced six more miscarriages and had given birth to two children who survived only a few hours, and the last maternal hope flickered out on the death of the young prince on July 29, 1700. In default of her own issue, Anne acquiesced in the Act of Settlement in 1701 and the substitution of the Hanoverian branch.

On March 8, 1702, Anne became, by King William's death, queen of Great Britain, being crowned on April 23. In her first speech to parliament, as George III afterward, Anne declared her "heart to be entirely English," words which were resented by some as a reflection on the late king. A ministry, mostly Tory, with Lord Godolphin at its head, was established. She obtained a grant of £700,000 a year and hastened to bestow a pension of £100,000 on her husband, whom she created generalissimo of her forces and lord high admiral, while Marlborough obtained the Garter, with the captain-generalship and other prizes, including a dukedom, and the duchess was made mistress of the robes with the control of the privy purse.

The queen showed from the first a strong interest in church matters and declared her intention to keep church appointments in her own hands. She detested equally Roman Catholics and dissenters, showed a strong leaning toward the high-church party and gave zealous support to the bill forbidding occasional conformity. In 1704 she announced to the commons her intention of granting to the church the crown revenues, amounting to about £16,000 or £17,000 a year, from tenths and first fruits (paid originally by the clergy to the pope, but appropriated by the crown in 1534), for the increase of poor livings; her gift, under the name of Queen Anne's Bounty, still remaining as a testimony of her piety.

This devotion to the church, the strongest of all motives in Anne's conduct, dictated her hesitating attitude toward the two great parties in the state. In 1704 Anne acquiesced in the resignation of Lord Nottingham, the leader of the high Tory party. In the same year the great victory at Blenheim further consolidated the power of the Whigs and increased the influence of Marlborough, but she long resisted the influence and claims of the junto, as the Whig leaders Lord Somers, Lord Halifax, Robert Walpole, Lord Wharton and the earl of Sunderland were named. Marlborough's successive victories and the factious conduct of the Tories drove Anne farther to the side of the Whigs. But she opposed for some time the inclusion in the government of Sunderland. In 1708 she was forced to dismiss Robert Harley, who, with the aid of Mrs. Masham (*q.v.*), had been intriguing against the government. Abigail Hill, Mrs. (afterward Lady) Masham, a cousin of the duchess of Marlborough, had been introduced by the latter as a poor relation into Anne's service, while Anne was still princess of Denmark. In the summer of 1707 the duchess discovered to her indignation that her protégée had become the instrument of Harley's intrigue. Even after his retirement, Harley remained Anne's secret adviser, and the duchess never regained her former influence. The inclusion in the cabinet of Somers, whom she especially disliked as the hostile critic of Prince George's admiralty administration, was the subject of another prolonged struggle, ending again in the queen's submission, to avoid a motion from the Whigs for the removal of the prince, then actually on his deathbed. He died Oct. 28, 1708. But no reconciliation with the duchess of Marlborough took place. The queen showed her antagonism to the Whig administration on the occasion of the prosecution of Henry Sacheverell (*q.v.*), and the fall of the Whigs followed.

The queen rejoiced at being freed from what she called a long captivity, and the new parliament was returned with a Tory majority. On Jan. 17, 1711, in spite of Marlborough's efforts to ward off the blow, the duchess was compelled to give up her key of office. The queen was now able once more to indulge in her favourite patronage of the church, and by her influence an act was passed in 1712 for building 50 new churches in London. Later, in 1714, she approved the Schism bill. She gave strong support to Harley, now earl of Oxford and lord treasurer, in the intrigues and negotiations for peace. To break down the opposition to the terms of the peace of Utrecht, Marlborough was dismissed on Dec. 31, 1711, from all his employments, while the house of lords was "swamped" by Anne's creation of 12 peers, including Mrs. Masham's husband. The queen's conduct was generally approved, for the nation was now violently adverse to the Whigs, regarded as a war party. The peace of Utrecht was finally signed on March 31, 1713 (old style; April 11, new style).

As the queen's reign drew to its close, rumours were rife on the subject of the succession to the throne. Both Oxford and Viscount Bolingbroke were in communication with the Pretender's party, and on July 27, 1714, Oxford, who had gradually lost influence and quarreled with Bolingbroke was obliged to resign, leaving the supreme power in the hands of Bolingbroke. Anne herself had a natural feeling for her brother, but she had an intense dislike of any successor; and it is certain that religion and political wisdom kept Anne firm to the Protestant succession. Her sudden illness and death frustrated any schemes which Bolingbroke or others might have been contemplating. The final act of her life was to secure the Revolution settlement and the Protestant succession. During a last moment of returning consciousness, she placed the lord treasurer's staff in the hands of the duke of Shrewsbury, and the measures were immediately taken for assuring the succession of the elector. Her death took place on Aug. 1. The elector of Hanover, George Louis, son of the electress Sophia (daughter of Elizabeth, a daughter of James I), peacefully succeeded to the throne as George I.

By character and temperament unfitted to stand alone, Anne had led a life unhappy from its isolation. She had been separated in early years from her parents and sister, and her one great friendship had proved only baneful and ensnaring. Marriage had brought a mournful series of infant funerals. Constant ill-health and suffering had darkened her career. The claims of family attachment, of religion, of duty, of patriotism and of interest had dragged her in opposite directions, and her whole life had been a prey to jealousies and factions, which closed around her at her accession to the throne and surged to their height when she lay on her deathbed. The modern theory of the relations between the sovereign and the parties had not then been invented; and Anne, like her Hanoverian successors, maintained the struggle, though without success, to rule independently, finding support in Harley. Her motive for getting rid of the Whigs was the wish to escape from the domination of the party, and on the advent to power of the Tories she carefully left some Whigs in their employments, with the aim of breaking party alignments and acting upon what was called a moderate scheme.

Anne was a woman of small ability, of dull mind and of that kind of obstinacy which accompanies weakness of character. She took no interest in the art, the drama or the literature of her day. But she possessed the homely virtues; she was deeply religious, attached to the Church of England and concerned for the efficiency of the ministry; instances abound of her kindness and consideration for others. Her moderation toward the Jacobites in Scotland, after the Pretender's expedition in 1708, was much praised by the duc de Saint-Simon. She surrendered £10,000 a year for public purposes, and in 1706 she presented £30,000 to the officers and soldiers who had lost their horses. *See also* ENGLISH HISTORY: *The Restoration and the Revolution.*

BIBLIOGRAPHY.—H. Paul, *Queen Anne*, rev. ed. (1912); G. M. Trevelyan, *England Under Queen Anne*, 3 vol., with full bibliography (1930–34); R. Walcott, *English Politics in the Early Eighteenth Century* (1956). (P. C. Y.; D. Tn.)

ANNE (ANNE BOLEYN or BULLEN) (1507?–1536), second queen consort of Henry VIII of England, was the daughter of Sir Thomas Boleyn (later earl of Wiltshire and Ormonde) and of Elizabeth, daughter of Thomas Howard, earl of Surrey (later duke of Norfolk). According to William Camden she was born in 1507; the evidence adduced by some later writers for an earlier date (1501 or 1502) is not convincing. In 1519 she went with her father to France where she entered the royal service.

By 1522 she was back in England. Her father had long been rising steadily in the royal favour. Her grandfather was one of the king's leading ministers. Her elder sister Mary had been in the king's sister's service in France in 1514 and at a later date became the king's mistress. So Anne herself soon became fairly well known at the English court. The poet Sir Thomas Wyat was among her admirers and Henry Percy, heir to the earl of Northumberland, sought her in marriage. Cardinal Wolsey, however, broke that match, for the king was apparently planning then to marry Anne to the earl of Ormonde. It is impossible to say when Henry VIII himself began to be attracted by her, nor is it possible to tell whether this passion stimulated or followed upon his final decision to secure the annulment of his marriage to Catherine of Aragon, for his celebrated love letters to Anne are undated, and there is no positive evidence that his infatuation antedated the secret "divorce" proceedings of May 1527. It seems clear, however, that his determination to rid himself of the aging Catherine originated in his desire to beget a legitimate male heir to the throne and that the attractions of Anne strengthened rather than created this determination. After Henry's final separation from Catherine in July 1531, Anne accompanied him on a visit to Francis I in 1532 and about Jan. 25, 1533, Henry secretly married her, the union being made public the following Easter. On May 23 Archbishop Cranmer pronounced the marriage valid and that with Catherine null. In June Anne was crowned and in September she gave birth to a daughter, the future Elizabeth I.

This was a sharp disappointment to Henry and within a few years failure to bear him a son was to prove even more disastrous for Anne than it had proved for Catherine. Anne soon alienated her friends and made many enemies by her arrogance and lack of dignity. Her jealousy showed in spiteful malice toward Catherine and Catherine's daughter Mary and also in reproaches to the king. For Henry's passion soon cooled after marriage and his affections again began to wander. The birth of a son might have held them together but in 1534 Anne apparently had a miscarriage and on Jan. 29, 1536, the day of Catherine's funeral, she gave birth to a dead male child. Meanwhile she had, it seems, given Henry causes, or at least pretexts, for jealousy, and on May 2 she was committed to the Tower on a charge of adultery with various men, including her own brother, Lord Rochford. On May 12 Sir Francis Weston, Henry Norris, William Brereton and Mark Smeaton were tried and found guilty of high treason as her lovers.

Three days later Anne and her brother were condemned unanimously by a court of 26 peers presided over by her uncle, the duke of Norfolk, as lord steward. On May 17 her reputed lovers were executed and Cranmer pronounced her marriage with Henry invalid on grounds that were not disclosed. Anne was beheaded on the Tower green on May 19, meeting death with courage and even with jest. Next day Henry VIII was betrothed to Jane Seymour.

Anne's guilt remains unproved. She protested her innocence to her jailer and made no confession on the scaffold. Yet, despite her universal unpopularity and the king's weariness of her, it hardly seems likely that two grand juries, a petty jury and a tribunal of nearly all the lay peers of England should have passed sentence of guilt quite contrary to the evidence—which they had before them and which we do not possess—and that such a sentence should have been concurred in by her own uncle and father.

Anne was described as "not one of the handsomest women in the world; she is of middling stature, swarthy complexion, long neck, wide mouth, bosom not much raised, and in fact has nothing but the English king's great appetite and her eyes, which are black and beautiful and take great effect . . ."

BIBLIOGRAPHY.—H. W. Trovillion (ed.), *The Love Letters of Henry VIII to Anne Boleyn* (1945); P. Friedmann, *Anne Boleyn*, 2 vol. (1884); A. F. Pollard, *Henry VIII* (1902). (R. B. WM.)

ANNE OF AUSTRIA (1601–1666), queen consort and for a time regent of France, was born at Valladolid on Sept. 22, 1601, the eldest child of Philip III of Spain (of the house of Austria; *i.e.*, of the Habsburg dynasty). On Nov. 28, 1615, she was married, at Bordeaux, to Louis XIII of France. Her married life was unhappy: Louis was morbidly cold in his attitude to her (and to other women), yet expected an heir to be born from his infrequent and ceremonious approaches; Franco-Spanish hostilities in the Thirty Years' War cut her off from overt relations with her dearly loved family in Spain; and the omnipotent minister, the cardinal de Richelieu was concerned to prevent her exercising any rival influence over her husband. Frustrated in her sincere desire to serve France, she was open to the irresponsible advice of the intriguing Marie de Rohan, duchesse de Chevreuse (q.v.). Considerable scandal was made out of the duke of Buckingham's indiscreet advances to Anne during his embassy (1625). Further, Anne was suspected of being privy to a conspiracy against the king (1626) and of intending to marry the malcontent Gaston of Orléans, heir presumptive to the throne. She was deeply humiliated in the "affair of Val de Grâce" (1637) when she had to submit to interrogation by the king's ministers on the ground that she was frequenting the convent of Val de Grâce in order to conduct a treasonable correspondence with the Spaniards. Even after the birth of her sons (the future Louis XIV in 1638 and Philippe, later duc d'Orléans, in 1640), her husband remained unfriendly; and in his will he prescribed a council of regency for the child Louis XIV, so as to preclude Anne from being sole regent.

On Louis XIII's death (1643), this will was promptly annulled by the *parlement* of Paris; Anne was declared sole regent; and the ambitious princes, nobles and politicians who had been in disgrace under Richelieu began to demand rewards and favours from the queen in whose interests they claimed to have suffered. Anne disappointed them: able at last to play her due part in affairs of state, she was determined that her son should succeed to the absolute power that Richelieu had won for her husband; and for this she knew that she must rely on the heir to Richelieu's policy, Jules Mazarin (q.v.). The crisis came with the complex rebellion of the Fronde (q.v.); and Mazarin's eventual triumph would have been impossible without Anne's constant devotion to his guidance. The pamphleteers of the Fronde, of course, alleged that Mazarin was Anne's lover; and later writers, in view of her strong religious principles, have suggested that they were secretly married. There is no need to believe these tales any more than stories designed to show that Louis XIII was not the father of her children (an allegation often made either in spite against Louis XIV or in connection with the mystery of the Iron Mask, q.v.).

Anne's regency ended when Louis XIV was proclaimed of age to rule (1651). She lived to see not only the end of the Fronde but also peace between France and Spain (1659) and Louis XIV's marriage to her brother's daughter (1660). For the rest of Anne's life, moreover, Louis XIV refrained from publicly acknowledging his adulteries, out of respect for her sentiments; and her influence long withheld him from breaking the peace with Spain. She died of cancer of the breast on Jan. 20, 1666, in Paris.

BIBLIOGRAPHY.—Mme. de Motteville, *Mémoires pour servir à l'histoire d'Anne d'Autriche*, new ed., 4 vol. (1891), Eng. trans., 3 vol. (1906); M. W. Freer, *The Married Life . . .*, 2 vol., and *The Regency of Anne of Austria*, 2 vol. (1864–66); E. E. Herbillon, *Anne d'Autriche* (1939). (J. G. R.-S.)

ANNE OF BRITTANY (1477–1514), duchess of Brittany and queen consort of France, was born at Nantes on Jan. 25, 1477, the daughter of Francis II of Brittany and of Margaret of Foix. She succeeded to her father's duchy on Sept. 9, 1488. Brittany at that time enjoyed administrative independence, which the Bretons were anxious to protect against the French king even when this involved relying on foreign support. Anne, despite her youth, was firmly attached to these principles of independence, on which she was always to insist.

Clearly, the future of the duchy depended on her marriage. Alain d'Albret, the Great, with the support of her guardian Jean de Rieux, sought Anne for himself; the house of Rohan advanced rival claims; and in 1489 French troops invaded Brittany to assert King Charles VIII's authority, whereupon Jean de Rieux revolted. Against all these, Anne allied herself with Maximilian of Austria, who married her by proxy on Dec. 19, 1490. But Austrian affairs prevented Maximilian's defending his bride, and in 1491 she was besieged in Rennes and compelled to treat with Charles VIII, whose terms included the rupture of her Austrian marriage and her marriage (Dec. 6, 1491) with himself. The two sovereigns made a reciprocal arrangement as to Brittany, and Charles issued edicts whereby the duchy was recognized to be distinct from the kingdom of France and under a regime of personal union; but if Charles were to predecease her without issue, Anne was to marry the heir to his throne, and if Anne predeceased him, the duchy was to be his entirely.

Charles died without living issue in 1498; and on Jan. 8, 1499, Anne married Louis XII, who had just repudiated Joan of France. The marriage contract declared that Brittany should revert to the second son or to the eldest daughter of the marriage or, failing issue, to Anne's natural heirs. For the rest of her life Anne occupied herself personally with the administration of her duchy; and in 1504 she carried her jealousy of its autonomy to a point altogether prejudicial to the unity of the kingdom by concluding the treaties of Blois with Maximilian, whereby her daughter Claude of France was to marry his grandson Charles. This unpopular agreement, however, was broken, and Anne had to consent to Claude's betrothal (May 21, 1506) to Francis of Angoulême, the future Francis I of France. This led to the definitive union of Brittany and France. Anne died at Blois on Jan. 9, 1514. A devout Catholic and a patroness of the arts, Anne instituted the queen's maids of honour at the French court.

BIBLIOGRAPHY.—There is a life of Anne in Brantôme's *Vies des dames illustres*. See also A. Bailly, *Anne de Bretagne, reine de France* (1940); A. de La Borderie, *Choix de documents inédits sur le règne de la duchesse Anne de Bretagne* (1866 and 1902); A. J. V. Leroux de Lincy, *Vie de la reine Anne de Bretagne*, 4 vol. (1860–61); and A. Dupuy, *Histoire de la réunion de la Bretagne à la France* (1880). (R. DT.)

ANNE OF CLEVES (1515–1557), fourth queen consort of Henry VIII of England, was the second daughter of John, duke of Cleves, and of Mary, only child of William, duke of Jülich and Berg. Born on Sept. 22, 1515, Anne had a narrow upbringing. She learned no language but her own; was proficient in needlework, but had few other accomplishments; and had a meek, gentle temper but no great beauty. Her marriage to Henry VIII was a political arrangement, occasioned by Henry's momentary fear of a possible combination of the Catholic powers against him. Thomas Cromwell wished him to counter this by an alliance with the German Lutherans. Henry would not make the necessary doctrinal concessions, but did agree (Jan. 1539) to overtures for an alliance with Cleves. Duke John, although father-in-law to the Lutheran elector of Saxony, was not a Lutheran nor a member of the Protestant League of Schmalkalden. He, however, died in Feb. 1539 and was succeeded by his son William, who had also just inherited the duchy of Gelderland and its bitter quarrels with the emperor Charles V. The negotiations therefore proceeded very haltingly, as Henry did not wish to provoke the emperor unnecessarily. But news that Charles was to travel through France, to suppress a revolt at Ghent, suggested an alarmingly close understanding between the emperor and the French. So, on Oct. 6, 1539, the Cleves marriage treaty was signed. Anne landed at Deal on Dec. 27, Henry met her at Rochester on Jan. 1, 1540, and they were married on Jan. 6. The story that Henry found her immediately displeasing and "no better than a Flanders mare," although plausible, rests largely on evidence written by Cromwell from the Tower of London six months later in the faint hope of earning a pardon. By then the emperor had suppressed Ghent, was threatening Cleves and seemed also to be breaking with France. This revived Henry's hopes of finding safety in the mutual jealousies of the Catholic powers and made him increasingly reluctant to be dragged into needless quarrels with the emperor. The Cleves marriage had become a political embarrassment. Its validity was questioned in parliament on July 6, 1540, convocation annulled it on July 9, and parliament confirmed the annulment a few days later. Anne acquiesced and was rewarded with £4,000 a year in lands, on condition that she stayed in England. She was soon reported to be as joyous as ever and wearing new dresses every day. She lived at Richmond or Bletchingley, with occasional visits to court, until her death at Chelsea on July 16, 1557. (R. B. Wm.)

ANNE of Denmark (1574–1619), queen consort of James I of England and VI of Scotland, was the daughter of Frederick II of Denmark and Norway and of Sophia, daughter of Ulric III, duke of Mecklenburg. She was born on Dec. 12, 1574. She was married to James, by proxy, on Aug. 20, 1589, bringing him recognition of Scottish claims to the Orkney and Shetland islands, but no dowry. Storms, for which several supposed witches were burned in Denmark, delayed her voyage to Scotland and James sailed to Norway to meet her. Her Lutheran upbringing and innate frivolity did not endear her to the Calvinistic Scottish Kirk; and in 1595 James entrusted the upbringing of their first son, Henry (1594–1612), to the earl and countess of Mar, with instructions not to give him up to the queen or the estates until he was 18, if James himself should die. In 1603, after Elizabeth I's death, Anne followed James to England and was crowned with him on July 25. Her refusal of the Anglican sacrament on that occasion may have been due to her Lutheran scruples or to her flirtation with Roman Catholicism which was to continue for many years. Nevertheless, she lived in good harmony with the king, though in later years residing mostly apart from him. She favoured the ascendancy of the duke of Buckingham and Spanish marriages for her sons, Henry and Charles (afterward Charles I), and disapproved of her daughter Elizabeth's marriage to the Calvinist elector palatine. On the other hand, she appealed personally to Buckingham to save Sir Walter Raleigh from execution. But her interest in matters of state was spasmodic and her influence slight. Most of her time and energy were devoted to court entertainments, building, dress and jewels. Her patronage certainly contributed to the development of the arts, in particular of the masque; but her extravagant expenditure contributed also to the monarchy's growing financial difficulties and was contrasted unfavourably with the economy of Elizabeth I. She died, after a long illness, on March 2, 1619, and was buried in Westminster abbey. (R. B. Wm.)

ANNE of France (by marriage Dame de Beaujeu) (1461–1522), was the eldest daughter of Louis XI of France and Charlotte of Savoy. After several other plans for her marriage, Louis gave her, in 1474, to Pierre de Bourbon, seigneur de Beaujeu; and on his deathbed he entrusted to Pierre the charge of his 13-year-old son, Charles VIII. Thus from 1483 to the end of 1491 the Beaujeus were to exercise a virtual regency in France.

Anne's energy, strength of will, cunning and political sense en-

abled her to overcome the difficulties threatening the kingdom. Faced with the reaction of all who had suffered from Louis XI's callous oppressions, the Beaujeus managed to promote the king's authority by adroit concessions or, when these failed, by military action: for example, at the meeting of the states-general at Tours (1484) and in the "Mad War" and subsequent Breton campaigns (see France: History). Moreover, in 1491, despite Austrian and English opposition, they concluded the marriage of Charles VIII with Anne (q.v.) of Brittany. But when Charles freed himself from tutelage, his former guardians were exposed to the resentment of the new queen, whose duchy's independence had been compromised.

Pierre, who had become duc de Bourbon in 1488, died in Oct. 1503, leaving Anne to administer the Bourbonnais for their daughter Suzanne (1491–1521) and to protect Bourbon interests against royal encroachments. Suzanne was married to her second cousin Charles de Montpensier (see Bourbon, Charles, Duc de; also Bourbon: Table I) in 1505; and on Suzanne's death, when King Francis I's mother, Louise of Savoy, was trying to deprive Charles of his inheritance, Anne did not hesitate to encourage her son-in-law to seek support from the king's enemies in defense of his rights. She died at Chantelle on Nov. 14, 1522. There is an edition of the *Enseignements* (instructions) that she wrote for Suzanne by A. M. Chazaud (1878).

Bibliography.—P. Pelicier, *Essai sur le gouvernement de la dame de Beaujeu* (1882); J. S. C. Bridge, *History of France From the Death of Louis XI* (1921). (R. Dt.)

ANNEALING, the slow heating and cooling of a metal or alloy, usually to soften it and make it more workable (while cold) in presses, rolls or wire-drawing dies. The term has also been applied to a similar mild heat-treatment of age-hardenable alloys, for example, duralumin (q.v.), which results in hardening. The many varieties of conventional annealing are identified by the equipment used, the object to be attained or the final appearance of the metal.

Process Annealing.—Nearly all metallic alloys are more ductile (workable) when hot than cold; consequently most forging, pressing or rolling is done hot. Hot metal, however, reacts with the air and the resulting surface is unsightly and consumes metal, both effects becoming more objectionable as the part becomes thinner. Therefore much work is done on cold sheet, strip and wire. Here another problem arises: soft and ductile metal becomes harder and less workable as more and more cold work is done on it. Eventually a point is reached where the ductility is "exhausted"; cracking is imminent. If the piece is then heated to a moderate temperature and slowly cooled the original ductility is restored and further work can be safely performed. This is process annealing. Actual heat-treating schedules depend on the alloy, the degree of cold work it has endured and the mechanical and fabrication properties desired. Annealing temperature must be above recrystallization, where microscopic crystals form in the overstrained regions, yet not so high nor held so long that these new crystals can grow to objectionable size. In steels the annealing temperature is usually below the critical temperature required for quench hardening.

Bright Annealing.—Annealing in furnaces open to the air oxidizes the surface of the parts and this oxide has to be removed by cleaning and pickling. This expense can be avoided by annealing in controlled atmospheres where the metal remains bright or nearly so; in other words, the furnace atmosphere is a gas mixture substantially inert to the hot metal during the heating and cooling cycle. Steam is a common atmosphere for bright annealing of brass. Atmospheres for common carbon steels are made by partial combustion of natural gas, and the mixture of nitrogen, hydrogen, carbon oxides and moisture so adjusted that it will neither oxidize the iron nor add or subtract carbon at the surface. Traces of moisture will discolour hot stainless steel, so it is usually bright annealed in cracked ammonia, a mixture of hydrogen and nitrogen gases.

Full Annealing.—This term includes other designations such as malleableizing, isothermal annealing, spheroidizing and solution treatment. In general the heat-treating cycle is designed to make desirable changes in the microstructure and related properties of the metal, and consequently requires holding at temperatures where changes occur in the mutual solubilities of the microconstituents. A forged blank of tool steel, for example, high enough in carbon so there is excess iron carbide (cementite) in the microstructure, would probably have this constituent in rather massive plates. In such condition it is difficult to machine and responds poorly to hardening treatments; both circumstances can be corrected by changing the form of the excess cementite into a multitude of tiny globules. Such a spheroidizing anneal usually involves alternate slow heatings and coolings through the critical range during which the cementite is first dissolved and then precipitated. Another example of full annealing occurs in the manufacture of malleable iron castings. This high-carbon alloy is cast as brittle "white iron"—that is, all the carbon is held in unstable equilibrium in the microstructure as carbide. The castings, protected in iron boxes (box, or pack, annealing), are pushed slowly through a long furnace, eventually reaching 1,600° F. where all the iron carbide is in solution, and then cooled at a slow rate through the transformation range, whereupon practically all the carbon comes out of solution as elemental carbon. The cold casting contains tiny nodules of graphite in a matrix of soft iron, with a desirable combination of mechanical properties and machinability.

Stress Relief.—This is a type of anneal designed to prevent the bad effects of locked-up internal stresses. Complicated and thin-walled castings have regions which are highly stressed due to differential shrinkage on solidification in unyielding molds. Cold-headed bolts may spontaneously fracture at the ends due to exhaustion of ductility during fabrication. Metal alongside welded joints contains a complex system of thermal stresses. Temperature cycles for stress-relief annealing depend on the metal; it may be as low as 300° F. for copper and 900° F. for gray-iron castings. For steel pieces and weldments it varies from 900° to 1,300° F., depending on the mechanical properties desired in the base metal. Thus, if maximum strength and hardness is necessary, low stress-relieving temperatures would be used.

Furnaces.—Annealing furnaces vary with the product to be handled and the amount of work to be done and include small muffle furnaces for tool-steel blanks, long tunnel kilns through which carloads of castings are pushed, and long or high "continuous" furnaces, with prepared atmospheres contained behind entrance and exit locks. In mass production of sheet or wire the coils are stacked in large cylindrical boxes, the boxes sealed and filled with protective atmosphere; a cylindrical heating cover is then placed over the box. Wire is frequently bright annealed by being drawn, strand by strand, through a long bath of molten lead or salt. Stress-relieving furnaces for welded boilers or pressure vessels resemble big open rooms with barn-door ends. Pipe joints, welded in the field, are stress relieved by electrical heat from an induction coil wrapped around them. See METALLURGY: *Heat-Treatment*. See also CAST IRON; IRON AND STEEL INDUSTRY. See also references under "Annealing" in the Index.

BIBLIOGRAPHY.—American Society for Metals, *Metals Handbook* (1948); U.S. Steel Corporation, *The Making, Shaping and Treating of Steel* (1951); C. H. Samans, *Engineering Metals and Their Alloys* (1949); Lee Wilson Engineering Co., *Annealing of Low Carbon Steel* (1958). (E. E. T.)

ANNECY, the chief town of the *département* of Haute-Savoie, France, and the seat of a bishopric, is situated on the lake of Annecy 1,470 ft. above sea level and is 338 mi. from Paris by road. Pop. (1962), 42,304. The arcaded streets of the old town, lying below the castle (partly of the 12th and 14th centuries), now used as a refuge for homeless families, are intersected by canals, the chief of which, the Canal du Thiou, empties the waters of the lake into the river Fier. The climate is temperate, especially in the areas which lie below 1,500 ft., and the town is sheltered from violent winds by the mountains that surround it. Traces of the Gallo-Roman Boutae have been found nearby; but Annecy itself, after being the chief town of the counts of Genevois (10th century) and belonging after 1401 to the dukes of Savoy, became important only in 1535, when the bishop's see of Geneva was transferred there along with the monastic institutions expelled from Geneva at the Reformation. St. Francis of Sales was bishop

from 1602 to 1622 and founded with St. Jane Frances Chantal the first Congregation of the Visitation. In 1728 Jean Jacques Rousseau, then age 16, found a refuge there with Mme. de Warens. Annecy is joined by direct railway lines to Paris, Lyons, Marseilles and Nice. It is a holiday centre and the tourist trade is its biggest industry. Precision instrument industries also prevail.

ANNELIDA, the segmented worms, a major phylum of the animal kingdom. It numbers more than 8,000 species and includes three classes: the marine worms (Polychaeta), earthworms (Oligochaeta), and leeches (Hirudinea). Annelids, named for the transverse rings, or annulations, on the skin, are serially segmented metazoans having a body cavity (coelom) and movable bristles (setae). However, the coelom is reduced in the leeches, and setae are lacking in a few specialized forms, including leechs.

This article is divided into the following sections:

I. General Features
  A. Structure and Function
    1. Basic Body Plan
    2. Circulatory System
    3. Respiration
    4. Digestive System
    5. Excretory System
    6. Nervous System
    7. Neurosecretion
    8. Sense Organs
    9. Reproductive System
  B. Development
  C. Regeneration
  D. Biochemistry and Physiology
  E. Fossil Annelids
  F. Classification and Relationships
II. Polychaetes
  A. Structure and Function
    1. External Features
    2. Internal Structure
    3. Reproduction and Development
  B. Classification
III. Oligochaetes
  A. Structure and Function
    1. External Features
    2. Internal Structure
    3. Reproduction and Development
  B. Classification
IV. Leeches
  A. Structure and Function
    1. External Features
    2. Internal Features
    3. Reproduction and Development
  B. Classification

I. GENERAL FEATURES

Annelids range in size from minute water species to giant earthworms, known from the Southern Hemisphere, and a few large marine polychaetes, from the Pacific coast. The majority of polychaetes are oceanic; they float, burrow, or wander on the bottom, or inhabit tubes of their own construction. Earthworms and other oligochaetes burrow into soil; smaller relatives are found in fresh water, and a few are marine. Leeches, on land and in fresh water, are carnivorous or parasitic.

The estuarine mud flat area of the New England and Nova Scotia coasts are the principal source of the blood worm (*Glycera dibranchiata*), specimens of which are shipped to all coasts of the United States for use as bait for saltwater fishes. Polychaetes play the important role of turning over much of the bottom sediments, much as earthworms do on land. Certain species of polychaetes are abundant in the vicinity of domestic outfall sewers and are therefore useful as indicators of degrees of marine pollution. The swimming reproductive parts of the palolo worm (*q.v.*) are used as food during their annual fall swarming in the Samoa Islands.

Large earthworms, or nightcrawlers (*Lumbricus terrestris*), are cultivated on small farms for sale as bait for freshwater fishes and as humus-builders in gardens. Oligochaetes play an important role in burrowing into and turning over much of the surface soil. The importance of earthworms to the improvement of soil was first emphasized by Charles Darwin's *The Formation of Vegetable Mould Through the Action of Worms*. The sludge worm *Tubifex* is particularly abundant near domestic outfall sewers and is an indicator of pollution; this worm is also used as tropical fish food in aquariums.

The medicinal use of leeches dates from antiquity, having reached its peak in the first half of the 19th century. The European species *Hirudo medicinalis* was exported throughout the world for such purpose, but native species were also used. Use of leeches occasionally caused infections that sometimes resulted in death to the patient. Hirudin, an extract from the heads of leeches, is used as a blood anticoagulant.

See EARTHWORM and LEECH for further discussions of the distribution, ecology, and economics of these common annelids.

A. STRUCTURE AND FUNCTION

1. Basic Body Plan.—The body of an annelid is described as a tube within a tube (fig. 1). The inner tube, or digestive tract, is separated from the outer tube, or body wall, by the coelom. A pre-segmented head region (prostomium) is followed by a series of true segments, or metameres, more or less alike. The metameres do not always correspond in number or position with the superficial segmentation marked by the external rings. Body differentiation into two or three regions occurs in many forms, especially the sedentary polychaetes.

The epidermis is usually a simple columnar epithelium with a covering cuticle; parts of the body may be ciliated. The cuticle consists of thin layers of protein fibrils whose composition resembles that of collagen, found in some vertebrate tissue. An outer circular muscle layer and inner longitudinal muscle layer lie beneath the epithelium. Muscle fibres usually are smooth, rarely with cross striations.

The setae of polychaetes are borne upon projecting lobes (parapodia); in oligochaetes they are embedded in the body wall. Each seta, composed of a chitin-protein complex, is secreted by a single basal cell situated at the bottom of an epithelial invagination, the setal follicle. The form of the seta is determined by the changing activities of the basal cell, which dies when the function is completed. In certain polychaetes (and probably also in other annelids) the setae receive a superficial coating secreted by the follicle cells.

New setae are formed in reserve follicles and move forward to replace the old ones that are discarded. A typical seta has a basal portion sunken within the follicle and a projecting shaft. In many polychaetes the shaft has a blade that can be moved by protractor and retractor muscles inserted at the setae base.

The body cavity, or coelom, is of the schizocoelomic type, de-veloping in the embryonic worm as a split in the middle germ layer (mesoderm). In an idealized annelid the coelom is divided into compartments by transverse partitions, the septa, which correspond to the external segmentation. Septa may be reduced or lacking but typically they are strongly developed in the burrowing species. Within the coelom is a watery coelomic fluid, one of the functions of which is maintenance of turgor, which gives rigidity to the body and assists in locomotion. The coelomic fluid of marine polychaetes is of the same osmotic pressure as sea water and contains little or no protein; in earthworms it is more dilute, but proteins are present. Within the coelomic fluid are corpuscles of two types: leukocytes and chloragogue cells. Leukocytes collect wastes. Chloragogue tissue is the site of many phases of intermediary metabolism, temporary food storage, and nitrogenous excretion.

2. Circulatory System.—In annelids, except for some leeches, the circulatory system is closed, an improvement over the open-ended system of annelid precursors. The ventral blood vessel carries blood posteriorly and receives blood from the capillary network of the digestive tract. Lateral vessels arise segmentally and convey blood to the dorsal blood vessel, which is contractile and forces the blood anteriorly. Additional lateral contractile vessels, or "hearts," are present near the anterior end in oligochaetes. The circulatory system may be greatly modified by the presence of gills or tentacles in polychaetes. In certain leeches the circulatory system is rudimentary, with the coelom functioning as a secondary circulatory system.

The heartbeat of *Arenicola* (a polychaete) and *Lumbricus* (an oligochaete) appears to initiate in nerve cells, as in arthropods, rather than in muscle tissue, as in vertebrates. (*See* HEART, COMPARATIVE PHYSIOLOGY OF: *Pacemakers.*)

3. Respiration.—Gaseous exchange generally takes place through the skin; however, it may occur through gill filaments in some polychaetes or through the wall of the rectum in aquatic oligochaetes. Oxygen may be transported in solution, but more frequently it is carried by a respiratory pigment. Hemoglobin, of common occurrence, may be found either in coelomic corpuscles or in solution in the blood plasma. Chlorocruorin, peculiar to certain tube-dwelling polychaetes, is found in the blood plasma; it differs from hemoglobin in having a lower affinity for oxygen as a result of the nature of the iron-containing prosthetic group (hemin) and is green in dilute solutions, red in concentrated ones. The blood of the polychaete *Serpula vermicularis* contains both pigment types.

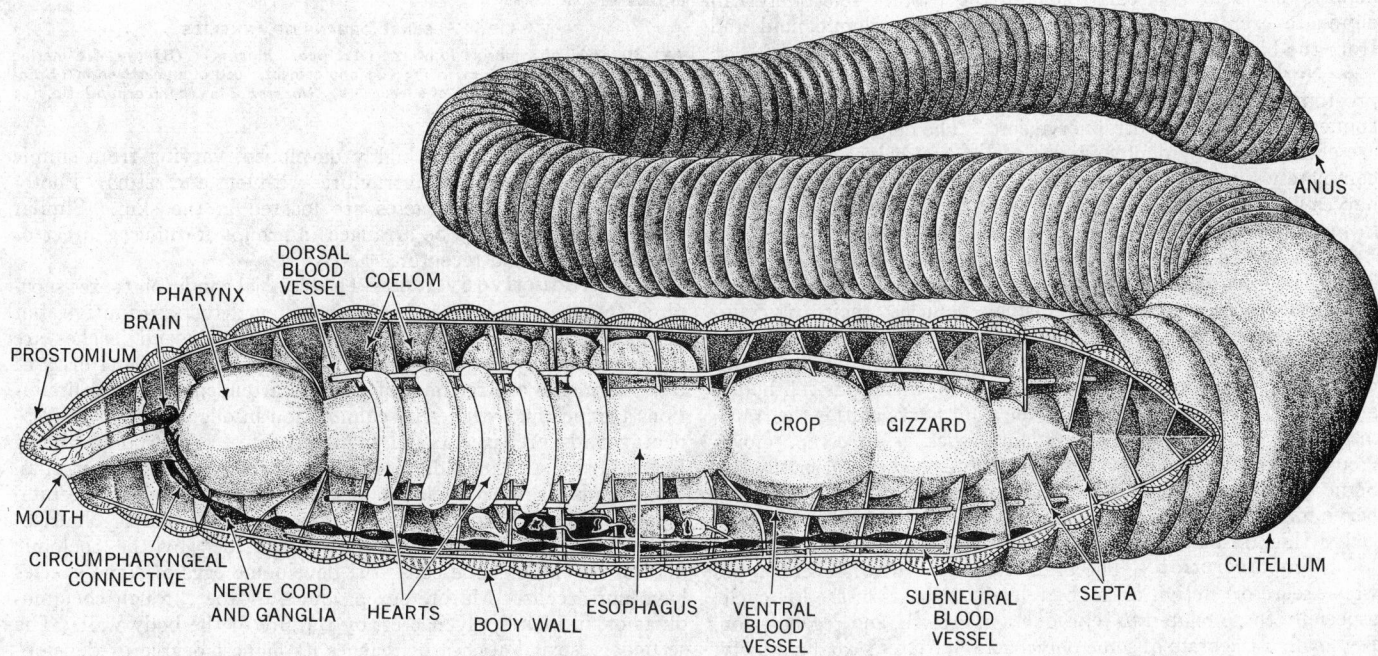

FIG. 1.—CUTAWAY VIEW OF AN EARTHWORM

The properties of annelid respiratory pigments are correlated with the mode of life of the worm. The hemoglobin of the lugworm *Arenicola*, which releases oxygen to the tissues only under conditions of extreme deficiency, may function either as a low tension transport system or serve as an emergency reserve. Hemoglobin of some earthworms, which takes up oxygen from a normal atmosphere but releases it only at low internal oxygen tensions, may protect the worm from oxygen poisoning.

4. Digestive System.—The structure of the digestive tract is diversified, according to the mode of life and the food habits of the worm. Except for the pharynx and rectal invaginations, which are ectodermal in origin, the digestive tract is derived from endoderm. Chitinous jaws are present in most free-living polychaetes and biting leeches but are absent in tube-dwelling polychaetes, most oligochaetes, and sucking leeches. The calciferous glands of earthworms are specialized esophageal pouches (diverticula). Diverticula of the mid-gut are rare in polychaetes and oligochaetes but common in leeches. Digestive enzymes are secreted in the digestive juices, but intracellular digestion, common in many invertebrates, has not been demonstrated.

5. Excretory System.—The excretory organs (nephridia) of annelids are straight, looped, or coiled tubes lying in the coelom and opening to the exterior or into the gut. The inner end may be closed by tufts of solenocytes (protonephridia), similar to the flame cells of flatworms, or there may be an open, ciliated funnel (metanephridium). A pair of protonephridia constitute the excretory system of the typical annelid larva, and there is reason to believe that this is the primitive condition. According to E. S. Goodrich, metanephridia are protonephridia that have acquired an internal opening, and both are of ectodermal origin, while coelomoducts are mesodermal funnels that function as reproductive ducts (gonoducts). A. Meyer advanced an alternate theory: open coelomic funnels are always coelomoducts, thus metanephridia are coelomic funnels attached to nephridia.

Ammonia is the chief nitrogenous excretory product of aquatic species; the urine of earthworms contains both ammonia and urea. As in the vertebrate kidney there are three aspects of nephridial function: filtration, resorption, and secretion. Coelomic fluid is filtered through closed solenocytes, but the ciliated funnels of open nephridia can retain only coelomic corpuscles and suspended particles of moderate size. In oligochaetes, whose coelomic fluid contains proteins, there is an active resorption of colloidal particles in the ciliated region of the tubule. In earthworms the tubules also must resorb inorganic ions, since the urine is more dilute than the body fluid. In addition to the activities of the end organ, the nephridium is well vascularized and the tubules selectively can eliminate excretory products both from the coelomic fluid and from the bloodstream.

6. Nervous System.—The brain is situated dorsally in the prostomium of the larva. It communicates by circumpharyngeal connectives with the ventral nerve cord. The nerve cord and brain are embryologically double in origin: the two halves may become completely fused or remain separate but united by transverse nerves like the rungs of a ladder. Ganglion cells are concentrated in segmental swellings of the nerve cord.

The nerve cord of many annelids is provided with giant nerve fibres (neurocords), which may be either simple or compound. Simple neurocords are very large single neurons; their axis cylinders arise from individual cells situated in either the brain or segmented ganglion. Compound neurocords are multiple structures with each axon receiving contributions from numerous cell bodies along its course. The function of the giant nerve cord is the transmission of rapid stereotyped responses such as an escape movement; in general, these systems are high-speed motor pathways. Some giant fibres conduct nerve impulses as fast as vertebrate nerve fibres (about 55 mph) but are of much larger diameter and lack a thick insulating myelin sheath.

7. Neurosecretion.—The brain contains cells of several types whose secretory activities can be related to phases of the life cycle, especially those related to reproduction, growth, and regeneration. Removal of the brain of some polychaetes initiates sexual maturity, and sexual maturation of a headless *Platynereis* can be inhibited by head implantation. The action of this inhibitory hormone is blocked by one given off by the gonads and sex cells. Conversely, in some oligochaetes removal of the brain *inhibits* maturation of the gonads and, independently, the development of the clitellum, a specialized part of the epithelium that gives rise to the cocoon. Posterior regeneration in nereids is under the influence of hormones produced by the brain.

8. Sense Organs.—Tactile endings and taste buds are especially numerous at the anterior end of the body. The so-called nuchal organs of sedentary polychaetes are probably chemoreceptors. Organs of equilibrium (statocysts) occur in many polychaetes, either as epidermal invaginations containing sand grains or as closed subepidermal pockets with calcareous granules (statoliths)

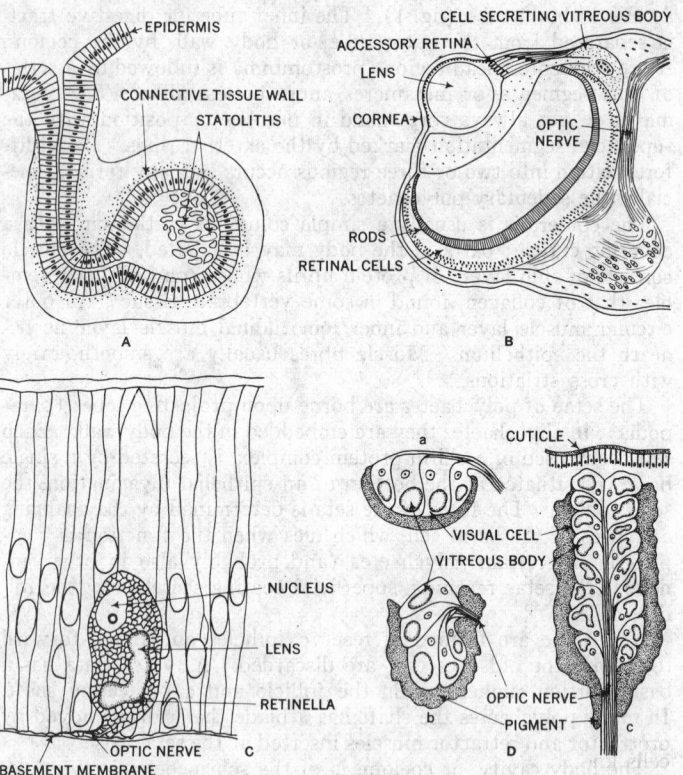

(A, B, D) FROM KÜKENTHAL'S "HANDBUCH D. ZOOLOGIE" (BERLIN); (C) FROM W. N. HESS IN "JOURNAL OF MORPHOLOGY," VOL. 41, NO. 1 (1925), PUBLISHED BY THE WISTAR INSTITUTE OF ANATOMY AND BIOLOGY

FIG. 2.—SENSE ORGANS OF ANNELIDS

(A) Statocyst of a marine lugworm (*Arenicola marina*); (B) eye of a marine polychaete (*Alciopa contarinii*); (C) photoreceptor cell of an earthworm (*Lumbricus terrestris*); (D) eye of a leech: (a) *Glossiphonia*, (b) *Herpobdella*, (c) *Hirudo medicinalis*

(fig. 2). Eyes are often highly developed, varying from simple pigment spots to elaborate structures with lens and retina. Photoreceptor cells of oligochaetes are located in the skin. Similar organs of leeches may be arranged in groups forming a direct or inverted compound receptor.

9. Reproductive System.—The bisexual condition (sexes separate) found in most polychaetes is believed to be primitive, but hermaphroditic forms are known. Oligochaetes and leeches are characteristically hermaphroditic. In polychaetes the majority of body segments are fertile, but there is a tendency toward limitation, a trend that reaches its culmination in oligochaetes. Permanent gonads are exceptional in polychaetes, sex products being formed from such mesodermal tissues as coelomic linings or septa. The gonads discharge their products into the coelom or into genital sacs of coelomic origin, where final maturation occurs. Nourishment for growth of the sex cells is provided by the coelomic fluid or by chloragogue cells; the developing eggs of some species have nurse cells. Mature sex products escape through coelomoducts or, in many polychaetes, by rupture of the body wall. The secondary sexual apparatus reaches its highest degree of development in the oligochaetes and leeches, the hermaphroditic condition of which is adapted to reciprocal copulation.

B. Development

Annelid eggs, like those of flatworms and mollusks, exhibit spiral cleavage (fig. 3A and B). The first four cells, called blastomeres, give rise by alternating clockwise and counterclockwise divisions to a cap of smaller cells, termed micromeres, at the animal pole. A ball of cells (solid gastrula) is formed by overgrowth of the micromeres, some of which are arranged in a characteristic pattern, the "annelid cross."

The typical marine larva is a pelagic trochophore (fig. 3C and D) named from the ciliated band (prototroch) that encircles the equator and divides the body. The upper portion consists of the apical plate and eyespots and will become the future prostomium containing the brain; the lower half of the trochophore contains the digestive tract, protonephridia, and other internal organs. Oligochaetes and leeches, which lay eggs enclosed in cocoons, as well as some polychaetes, bypass the trochophore larva; their development is, therefore, considerably modified.

Typically, the first three segments are formed practically simultaneously in the lower half of the trochophore. A resting stage follows in many species during which time many larvae begin to feed upon pelagic microscopic life. The body begins to grow in length by the addition of new segments from the preanal region, and pygidium. *See* also EMBRYOLOGY AND DEVELOPMENT, ANIMAL: *Invertebrate Development*.

C. Regeneration

L. H. Hyman pointed out that the Annelida contains the most highly organized animals that retain the power of complete regeneration. Regenerative abilities are lacking in leeches, however. Most polychaetes and oligochaetes can regenerate a new tail; ability to replace an amputated head is usually restricted to the anterior end and only the same number or fewer segments can be replaced. If a fewer number of segments is formed, then internal reorganization of organ systems follows. Regeneration from a single segment occurs naturally in the polychaetes *Ctenodrilus* and *Dodecaceria* and experimentally in *Chaetopterus* and *Myxicola*.

In regeneration, the wound first seals over; then the initial basis of the missing parts, a blastema, appears on the cut surface. In some species, growths appear from either side of the wound and later fuse together along the midline. New tissue probably arises from preexisting parent tissue, although mesodermal regenerative cells known as neoblasts, which migrate to the site of injury, are known in polychaetes and lower oligochaetes.

Reversal of anterio-posterior polarity was obtained in the Oriental earthworm *Perionyx excavatus*. In this species a piece cut out of the anterior end will regenerate a head at either cut end if the cuts are made simultaneously; then, if the newly formed anterior end is removed, the posterior head becomes dominant and evokes tail regeneration at the anterior cut surface. These phenomena of annelid regeneration reflect a physiological dominance of the anterior end, in accordance with C. M. Child's theory of axial metabolic gradient (*see* REGENERATION: *Polarity; Gradient Theory*).

D. Biochemistry and Physiology

Studies concerning the axial metabolic gradient have shown that enzyme systems that regulate intracellular tissue metabolism are more concentrated at the ends of the body. The role of chloragogue tissue in carbohydrate, nitrogen, and fat metabolism has been studied most thoroughly in earthworms. The chemical composition of representative annelids in different phases of their life cycle has been studied by M. Durchon and M. Lafon.

The contractile mechanism of annelid muscle depends on an actomyosin-myosin system similar to that found in other animals (*see* MUSCLE AND MUSCULAR SYSTEM: *Chemical Changes*). The acceptors of energy-rich phosphate present an interesting facet of comparative biochemistry: the muscle phosphagen of sedentary polychaetes contains an otherwise unknown monosubstituted guanidine, taurocyamine; errantiate polychaetes have glycocyamine; and earthworms have lumbricine. Some species utilize

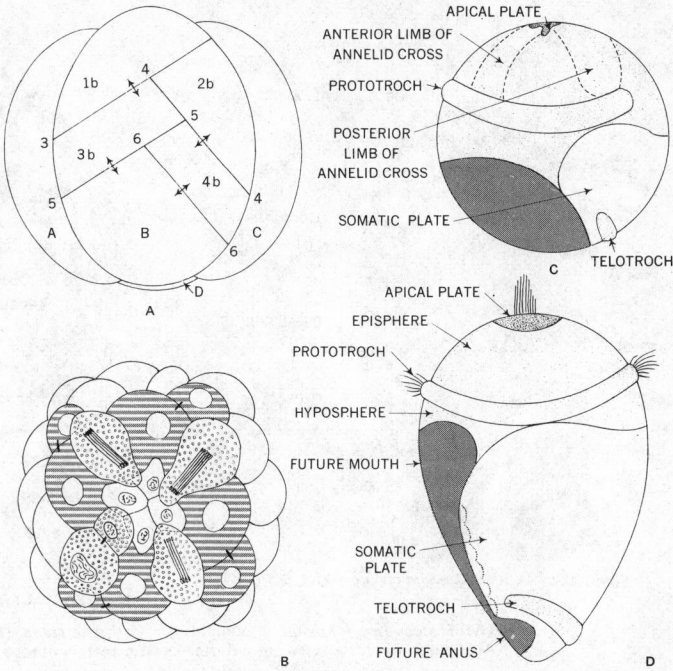

(A) FROM WILSON, "THE CELL"; (B) FROM MACBRIDE, "TEXTBOOK OF EMBRYOLOGY" BY PERMISSION OF THE MACMILLAN COMPANY, PUBLISHERS; (C, D) FROM KÜKENTHAL'S "HANDBUCH D. ZOOLOGIE" (BERLIN)

FIG. 3.—ANNELID DEVELOPMENT

(A) Diagram of spiral cleavage (numbers and letters used to indicate sequence of cleavage); (B) developing egg of *Polygordius* with micromeres arranged in "annelid cross" (stippled), anterior view; (C, D) development of a polychaete: larval ectoderm (stippled), blastopore (shaded)

creatine phosphate and/or arginine phosphate (*see* BIOCHEMISTRY).

The body fluids of marine polychaetes are isotonic with seawater and can withstand only moderate changes of external salinity. Certain polychaetes can survive in brackish or even in fresh water, and certain aquatic oligochaetes can live exclusively in fresh water, because of a physiological regulation of the internal medium.

A typical marine polychaete, such as *Perinereis cultrifera*, which cannot adapt to fluctuations of salinity, will burst when salinity is reduced to 20% seawater as the result of uncontrolled intake of water. On the other hand, races of *Nereis diversicolor* are capable of tolerating intertidal changes of salinity through an ability to excrete excess water; the nephridia of such species are enlarged. Differences in salinity tolerance are involved in long-term obligatory adaptation. Physiological races of *N. diversicolor* are adapted to about 60% seawater in the Black Sea and to about 100% seawater in a nearby saline lake. R. I. Smith found that fertilization and development of the same species occurred at lower salinities in Finland and at higher salinities in Sweden.

Adaptations of respiratory pigments to oxygen deficient environments have been treated under *Structure and Function: Respiration*, and the temperature-humidity relations of earthworms are discussed under *Class Oligochaeta: Ecology: Adaptation to Environment*.

E. Fossil Annelids

The fossil record of annelids is limited because of the near absence of hard body parts. The dwelling tubes and the jaws of polychaetes are the most commonly encountered fossil specimens; most records of fossil oligochaetes are doubtful, and fossil leeches are unknown. Burrows interpreted as those of wormlike creatures are known from Precambrian strata. C. D. Walcott described many forms from the rich invertebrate fossil bed of British Columbia. Some resembled the scale worm *Halosydna* and the sea mouse *Aphrodite*. From other areas a *Nereis*-like form, *Spriggina floundersi*, and calcareous tubes similar to those of present-day *Serpula* and *Spirorbis* species have been described. The shells of Paleozoic mollusks are occasionally marked by U-shaped mud-

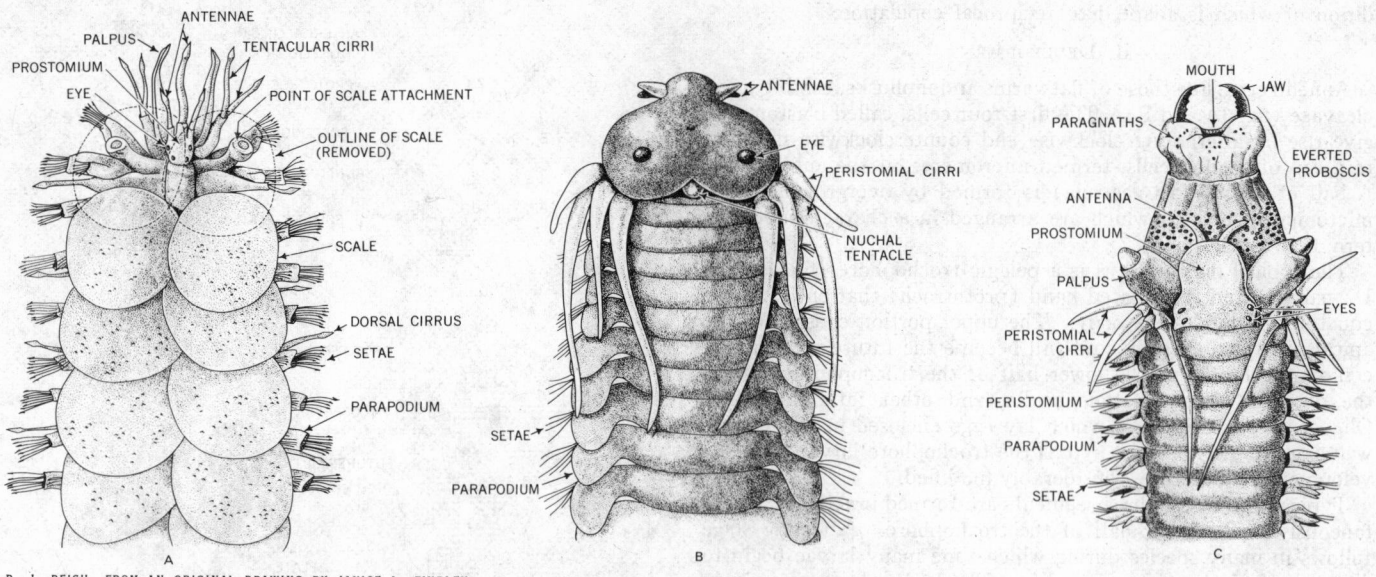

FIG. 4.—BODY FORM OF ERRANTIATE POLYCHAETES

(A) *Halosydna johnsoni* (Polynoidae); (B) *Anaitides* (Phyllodocidae); (C) *Neanthes arenaceodentata* (Nereidae).
All figures are dorsal views of anterior ends, greatly enlarged

blisters (*Caulostrepsis*) similar to those made by the polychaete *Polydora*, a modern-day pest of oysters.

The chitinous jaws of polychaetes, minute shiny black denticles known as scolecodonts, occur from the Cambrian period onward. Other toothlike objects called conodonts, once thought to be jaws of extinct annelids, differ in chemical composition and mode of formation from scolecodonts; they are now considered to be the remains of an extinct class, Conodontida, a jawless vertebrate group.

F. CLASSIFICATION AND RELATIONSHIPS

A current taxonomic system recognizes three classes: Polychaeta (including Archiannelida and Myzostomidae, aberrant groups), Oligochaeta, and Hirudinea. The Polychaeta are primarily marine; they are the most numerous (over 5,000 known species), the most diverse, and phylogenetically the oldest annelids. The Oligochaeta, numbering over 3,000 known species, are found on land, in fresh water, and rarely in salt water. The Hirudinea, constituting the smallest class (over 300 known species), are parasites found on land and in fresh and salt water. The Hirudinea are closely related to the Oligochaeta, so closely in fact that W. Michaelsen grouped them into one class, the Clitellata, named for the girdle, or clitellum, which in both groups secretes the egg cocoon. Most workers, however, now agree that leeches constitute a well-defined assemblage that is more conveniently treated as a separate class. The greatest gulf in intra-annelid phylogeny divides the polychaetes from the oligochaetes. At one time these two groups were united into the class Chaetopoda, on account of the presence of setae. The leeches were thus artificially separated from the oligochaetes, their closest relatives.

The annelids are considered to have evolved in the sea, perhaps from some ancestral flatworm through the trochophore larva, a characteristic early stage of polychaetes. The oligochaetes developed from polychaete stock perhaps by way of evasion through estuaries into freshwater streams. The leeches, with the clitellum in common with the oligochaetes, evolved from the latter.

The phylum Echiurida (*q.v.*), closely related to the Annelida, has members that possess setae but lack segmentation. The phylum Sipunculida (*q.v.*) comprises more highly modified species lacking both setae and segmentation; their annelidan affinities are obscured. Both the Echiurida and Sipunculida, along with the Mollusca (*see* MOLLUSK), display early developmental stages similar to the annelids. All their species possess the trochophore larval stage.

The nervous system of the annelid is especially significant in phylogeny. The nervous system in the trochophore resembles that of a platyhelminth, or flatworm, and in the adult resembles that of an arthropod. The gap between the annelids and arthropods is bridged by the intermediate features of the Onychophora (*q.v.*), a group that has become highly specialized at a low level of arthropodan evolution. Arthropods, which have jointed appendages that may be compared with annelidan parapodia, are regarded as the culmination of annelid evolution, a point of view that provides some justification for their union in a phylum Articulata, proposed long ago by Cuvier. *See also* ANIMALS, PHYLOGENY OF.

II. POLYCHAETES

Polychaeta, the largest class of the phylum Annelida, comprises 68 families and over 5,000 known species. The name refers to the numerous tufts of setae at the sides of the body. Polychaetes are distributed throughout the marine environment; a few live in brackish to fresh water and very few in moist earth. Commensal species number over 50 and are associated with sponges, echinoderms, or other polychaetes. More than 20 species are parasitic either on or within other animals.

A. STRUCTURE AND FUNCTION

1. External Features.—The body form (fig. 4 and 7) varies greatly, depending on whether the polychaete is errant, sedentary, or pelagic. Polychaetes vary in length from a fraction of an inch to over 20 ft. Colours range from brilliant to dull according to species; many forms are luminescent, especially during spawning. The body consists of a head, or prostomium, with associated parts; trunk (thorax and abdomen), which may be divisible; and a tail, or pygidium. The prostomium, anterior to the mouth, may be a simple lobe or a highly developed projection. The peristomium, the first body segment, surrounds the mouth; it is followed by a series of segments that may be similar or differentiated. The pygidium, the postsegmental region, may be surrounded by cirri, plaques, or other adornments. The number of segments may be few and limited or many and unlimited. Increase in number of segments occurs immediately in front of the pygidium.

Each body segment following the peristomium is usually provided with paired parapodia. These fleshy, lateral outgrowths (fig. 5) of the body may be prominent and ornate or reduced to rounded ridges. Bundles of extensile setae and embedded supporting acicula emerge from an upper notopodial and a lower neuropodial branch, or the upper branch may be lacking.

The setae differ in form and function and provide a remarkably accurate means of species identification. A simple seta originates as a secretion of an epidermal cell. The cell encloses a ciliary apparatus from which the seta arises and a lacuna in which the seta develops and through which it pushes to the outside (fig. 6). Composite or pointed setae are formed from two or more cells; ornamentations are the result of modifications of simple setae. Hairlike capillary setae are the most frequent type present.

Branchiae, or gills, are lacking in those species where respiration is accomplished through the body wall. They are simple filaments or divided tufts near the anterior end. The tentacular crown of sabellid and serpulid worms function both for food gathering and respiration.

Sense receptors include the eyes, lateral organs, dorsal ciliated ridges, statocysts, taste buds, papillae, stiff hairs, and others. The eyes range from simple pigment spots to complex eyes with lens. Eyes may be found on the prostomium (nereids), peristomium (terebellids), pygidium (sabellids), along the side of the body (opheliids), or on the tentacular crown (sabellids). Touch receptors, stiff hairs or modified cirri, may be diffuse. Statocysts function for maintaining equilibrium. Many other special sense organs are found among the errant polychaetes that evert the proboscis.

Luminescent structures are found in polynoids, pelagic polychaetes, chaetopterids, cirratulids, and terebellids. In polynoids the phenomenon is intracellular; the lower surface of some scales have photocells that luminesce when stimulated. In chaetopterids the process is extracellular, involving the discharge of a luminescent secretion from certain segments and antennae.

2. Internal Structure.—A mesodermal coelomic epithelium lines the body cavity. Successive body segments are separated from each other by transverse septa that correspond to the external rings. Circular, longitudinal, and transverse muscles are smooth or partially striated.

Digestive System.—The mouth is bounded by an upper and lower lip, and sometimes by an inner lip enclosing mucous glands. In some sedentary species, such as terebellids, much of the thoracic space is occupied by other systems, but in the errant polychaetes this space accommodates an eversible proboscis (fig. 4). The esophagus is followed by the stomach and the intestine.

Circulatory System.—The dorsal longitudinal blood vessel is the chief contractile one. Peristaltic contractile waves aided by cilia move the blood forward. The walls of the blood vessels consist

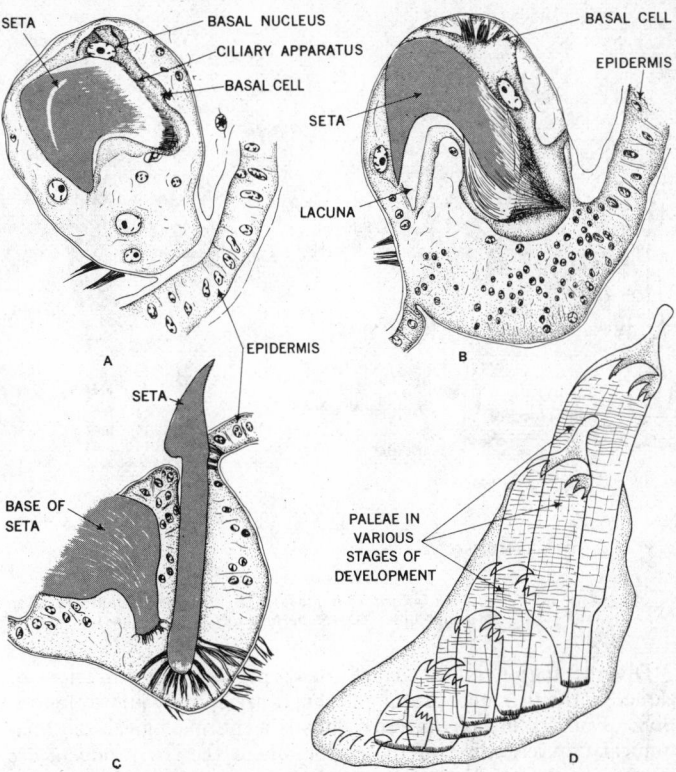

FROM BOBIN IN "ANNALES INSTITUT OCEANOGRAPHIQUE" (1944), MASSON & CIE, PARIS

FIG. 6.—DEVELOPMENT OF SETAE AMONG POLYCHAETES (SABELLIDAE AND SABELLARIDAE) (VIEWS MUCH ENLARGED)

(A) Early, (B) intermediate and (C) final stages in development of uncinus in *Sabella*; (D) series of developing paleae in *Sabellaria*

they are characteristic of nephthyids, glycerids, and phyllodocids. Metanephridia are coiled tubules that open internally as a funnel (nephrostome); they are characteristic of most sedentary and some errant polychaetes. Metanephridia collect and transport waste products from the coelom to the exterior through nephridiopores that are usually located near a part of the parapodium.

Nervous System.—A dorsal brain, or supra-esophageal ganglion, in the prostomium innervates the eyes, antennae, and other anterior sense receptors; it is connected to a ventral subesophageal ganglion and paired nerve cords. The ventral nerve cord has one ganglion per segment from which lateral nerves arise. Giant nerve fibres (axons) are widespread among polychaetes, but their occurrence presumably has no phylogenetic significance. Giant axons measure from a few microns to a millimeter across and attain their greatest size in *Myxicola*. They conduct impulses leading to rapid body contraction and thereby aid escape. Conduction rates vary from about 6.5 ft. per sec. to over 65 ft. per sec. in *Myxicola*.

Neurosecretory cells are found in the brain and are morphologically similar to neurons. They consist of fine projections (an axon and neurofibrillae) and a cell body whose cytoplasm contains Nissl bodies, small darkly stained granules. These cells do not innervate an end organ but terminate in the walls of a blood vessel, in other internal fluid systems, or in the epidermis; they secrete biologically active substances in microscopic droplets or granules. Evidence shows the neurosecretory cells may be derived from epidermal secretory cells that have been incorporated into the central nervous system. Their function has been discussed above in the introductory section.

3. Reproduction and Development.—Permanent gonads are exceptional in polychaetes. Prior to sexual maturity gonads appear on septa of certain segments. The underdeveloped eggs are shed into the coelom, where they are nourished by special nurse cells or other coelomic bodies. Ripe eggs and sperm may leave the body through special gonoducts or through nephridial pores, or they may be shed through ruptures of the body wall.

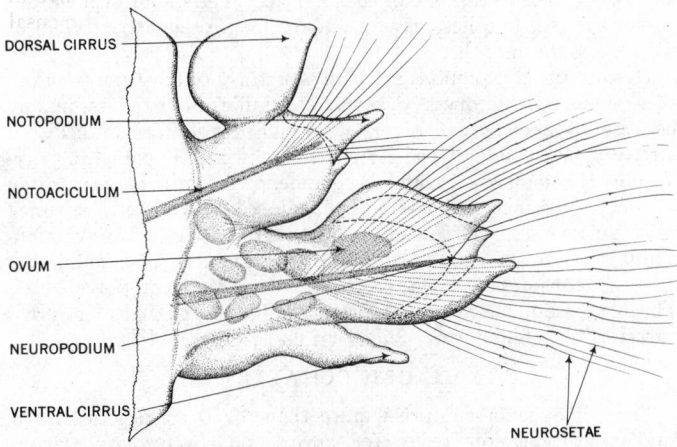

BY COURTESY OF OLGA HARTMAN

FIG. 5.—BIRAMOUS PARAPODIUM OF GONIADA (SEPARATED FROM THE BODY AND ENLARGED)

of an outer peritoneum layer with muscle fibres, a mid-skeletal coat of collagenous material, and an inner endothelium. The blood may be colourless or green (chlorocruorin) or red (hemoglobin). The respiratory pigments are either dissolved in the blood or in corpuscles.

Excretory System.—Nephridia (fig. 8) include protonephridia and metanephridia. Protonephridia originate blindly within the body and are each provided with a flagellated cell (solenocyte);

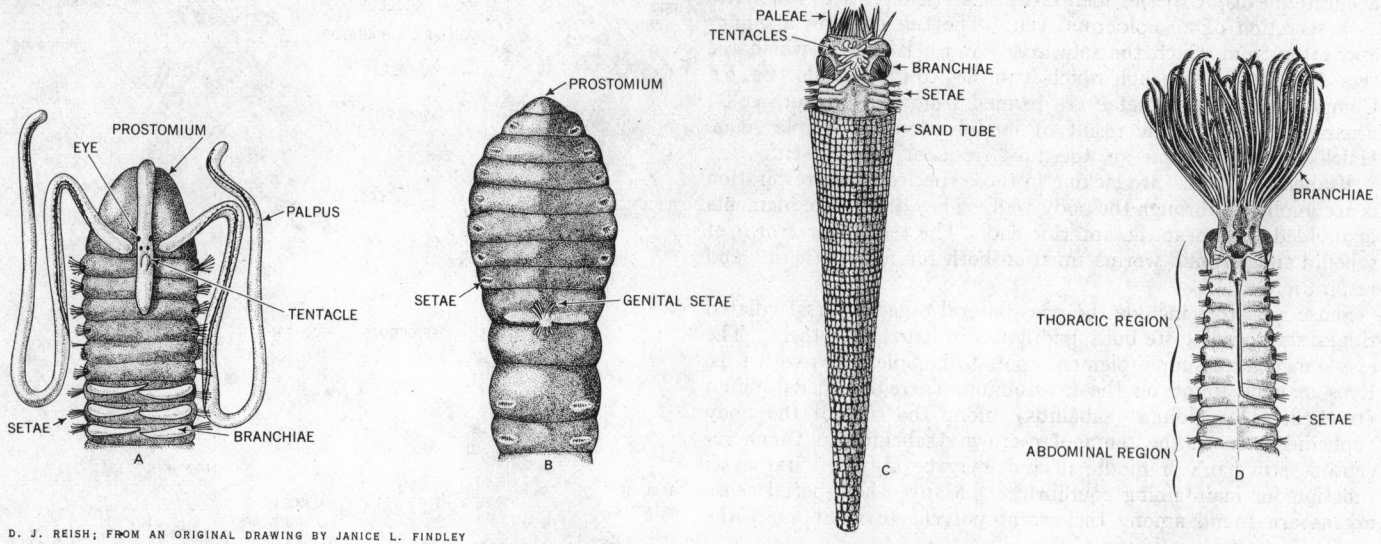

D. J. REISH; FROM AN ORIGINAL DRAWING BY JANICE L. FINDLEY

FIG. 7.—BODY FORM OF SEDENTARY POLYCHAETES

(A) *Polydora* (Spionidae); (B) *Capitella capitata* (Capitellidae); (C) *Pectinaria californiensis* (Pectinariidae) animal and tube; (D) *Sabella media* (Sabellidae). A, B, and D are dorsal views of anterior end

Diverse major body changes may precede the emission of gametes; the two most profound changes are epitoky and stolonization. Epitoky in nereids and syllids is a morphological and anatomical differentiation of the region where the sex products are concentrated. Stolonization in syllids is an isolation of the tail region, giving rise to new worms distinct from the stock. In some nereids surgical removal of a part of the brain effects precocious development of epitoky without influencing development of eggs or sperm. In some syllids removal of the proventriculus region of the digestive tract inhibits stolonization. Some hermaphroditic species (*e.g.*, *Ophryotrocha*) show marked sexual variability; male or female individuals may exist in association with hermaphroditic forms. Some hermaphroditic populations are limited as to numbers of various forms, others have varying numbers. Experiments on *Ophryotrocha* suggest that racial differences may exist regarding the age when passage from male to female phases can occur.

The fertilized egg, unless provided with much yolk, usually gives rise, through spiral cleavage, to a floating ciliated larva

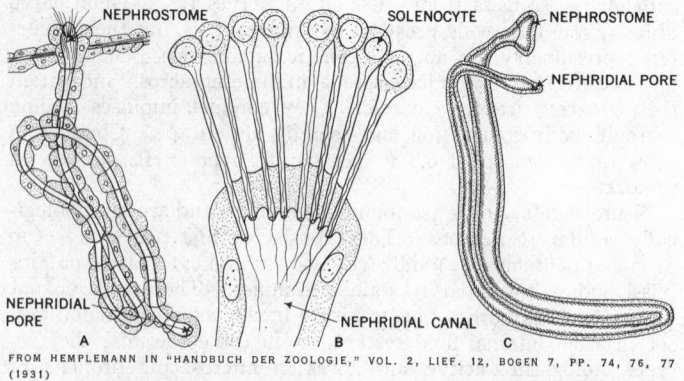

FROM HEMPLEMANN IN "HANDBUCH DER ZOOLOGIE," VOL. 2, LIEF. 12, BOGEN 7, PP. 74, 76, 77 (1931)

FIG. 8.—NEPHRIDIA OF POLYCHAETES (MUCH ENLARGED)

(A) Metanephridium of *Protodrilus*; (B) section of protonephridium with solenocytes of *Phyllodoce*; (C) nephridium of *Scalibregma*

called a trochophore. Both the mouth and anus may be derived from the blastopore, or the anus may arise secondarily. The trochophore stage is followed by a polytroch having a few segments, and this in turn by various larval, free-swimming stages. Metamorphosis in some polychaetes takes place in a capsule or cocoon, in others within the parent's body. Larvae of some polychaetes are cannibalistic.

B. CLASSIFICATION

The Polychaeta are most conveniently divided into the Errantia, or free-moving worms, having successive segments similar; and the Sedentaria, or tube-dwelling worms usually having the body divided into an anterior thoracic and a posterior abdominal region. This separation is only approximate since many species of Errantia occupy tubes, and some Sedentaria may be free-moving in habit; further, the division of the body into thorax and abdomen is sometimes obscure or altogether absent in the Sedentaria. The terms Phanerocephala ("head visible") and Cryptocephala ("head hidden") are also unreliable terms because the head structures are sometimes not distinguishable although they may be uncovered.

A more practical plan is to group families with obvious morphological affinities together into superfamilies insofar as is possible. For example, the scale worms, comprising five families, have the dorsal surface covered with segmentally arranged scales (modified dorsal cirri); the eunicids, comprising six families, have similar jaws at the anterior end of the pharynx. The spioniform worms, comprising six families, have a pair of long, prehensile feelers or palpi near the mouth.

Despite the conspicuous external structures of most polychaetes, there is no satisfactory key to the 68 families of the class, mainly because of their great diversity, which renders generalizations virtually impossible. The Errantia comprise 33, parasitic polychaetes 3, Sedentaria 29, and Archiannelida 3 families. Separation to genera and species is less difficult, especially when accompanied with illustrated keys and geographic lists of species. The Archiannelida were at one time treated as a separate class of annelids but now are considered as either primitive or aberrant polychaetes. The Myzostomidae are an aberrant family of external or internal parasites of echinoderms, chiefly crinoids.

III. OLIGOCHAETES

The Oligochaeta comprise more than 3,250 species of chiefly land, mud-living, or freshwater worms; only a few are marine. In a contracted state they vary in size from small aquatic species about $\frac{1}{25}$ in. long to earthworms several feet long and more than an inch in diameter.

A. STRUCTURE AND FUNCTION

1. External Features.—The prostomium is usually a simple lobe overhanging the mouth but sometimes is prolonged into a tentacle-like proboscis (fig. 9B); occasionally it is absent. The anus is terminal or, rarely, displaced dorsally. The body is usually cylindrical, sometimes flattened, rarely with projecting structures. The primary segmentation is usually conspicuous, but secondary

The sea mouse (*Aphrodite aculeata*), its underside showing bristle-bearing, segmented appendages, is found on north Atlantic shores; it reaches a length of 7 in. and width of almost 3 in.

A burrowing terebellid (*Amphitrite johnstoni*) and its commensal, a scale worm (*Gattyana cirrosa*)

MARINE POLYCHAETES

A paddle-footed worm (*Phyllodoce lamelligera*), with metallic iridescence, feeds at night on the sea bottom and lives by day under stones and shells

A large sabellid worm, the feather duster *Eudistylia*, from the California coast, reaches a length of 3 ft. and lives in a parchment-like tube. Its feathery tentacles are extended for food and respiration

Fan-shaped paddles propel water, which bears food and oxygen, through the tube (removed here) in which the parchment worm (*Chaetopterus*) lives

PHOTOGRAPHS, (BOTTOM LEFT) M. WOODBRIDGE WILLIAMS, (BOTTOM RIGHT) VISHNIAC—PUBLIX, (OTHERS) DOUGLAS P. WILSON

PLATE II   ANNELIDA

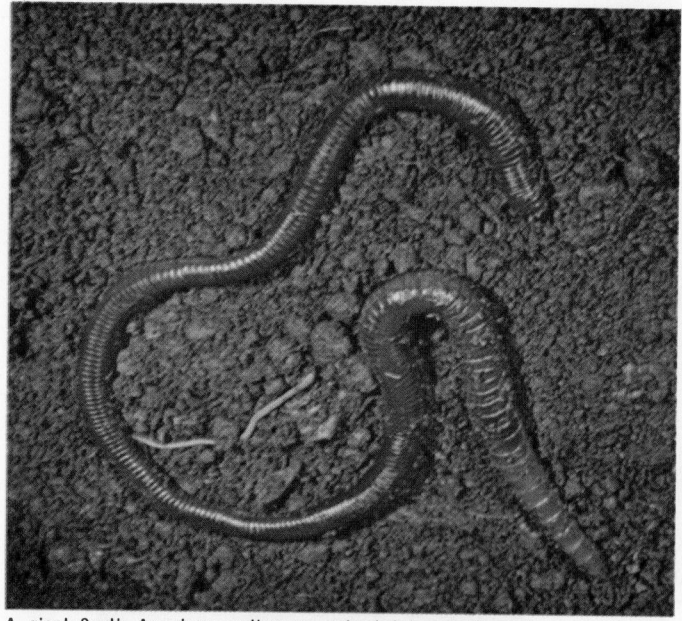

A giant South American earthworm, extended length five feet, encircling two *Lumbricus* earthworms, or night crawlers, a few inches long

Cocoons containing the eggs of a giant earthworm may be as large as two inches in size

EARTHWORMS AND LEECHES

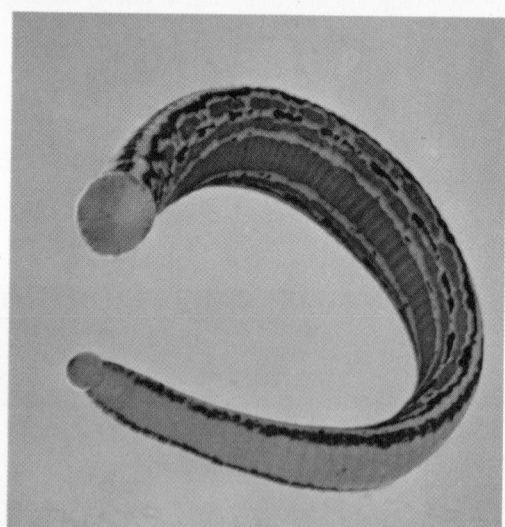

The medicinal leech (*Hirudo medicinalis*), showing both suckers, the larger sucker at the rear, thrives in ponds in America and Europe

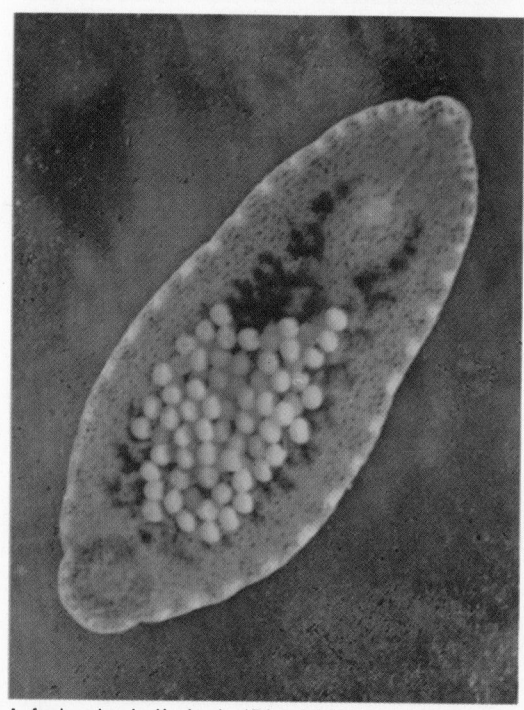

A fresh-water turtle leech (*Placobdella*) carrying its eggs beneath its body

The one-inch white worms (*Enchytraeus*), which tolerate salt water as well as fresh water, are sold in pet stores as food for aquarium animals

segmentation may occur in larger forms. The number of segments varies from seven in some aquatic species to 600 in the largest earthworms.

Setae, embedded in the body wall, are sometimes absent, as in the enchytraeid *Achaeta* and in Branchiobdellidae. They may be simple, S-shaped (sigmoid), forked, or hairlike. The lumbricine arrangement (fig. 10D), two pairs of sigmoid setae on every segment except the first, is possibly the primitive condition. The perichaetine arrangement (fig. 10E) appears in some terrestrial oligochaetes; a ring of small sigmoid setae encircle each segment. Many unrelated genera of the Megascolecidae possess this modification. There are many transitional conditions to these extremes in setae arrangement: The genus *Decachaetus* has five pairs of setae per segment. Other forms may have a greater number per segment in the middle and posterior parts of the body. Setae multiplication occurs in the ventral holdfast organ of the ectoparasitic enchytraeid *Aspidodrilus*. The so-called penial setae may be associated with the openings of the male ducts, and genital copulatory setae may occur on other segments. The replacement of sigmoid by modified setae during maturation takes place in periodic stages representing increasing degrees of transformation.

A simple columnar epithelium of interspersed glandular and sensory cells secretes a thin cuticle. In *Aeolosoma* the prostomium is ciliated below. The epidermis of earthworms assumes a pseudo-stratified appearance because of the presence of numerous small basal cells. Epidermal thickenings are found in species of the tubificid genus *Peloscolex*. The arrangement of circular and longitudinal muscles are as in other annelids.

All oligochaetes possess, at sexual maturity, a glandular de-

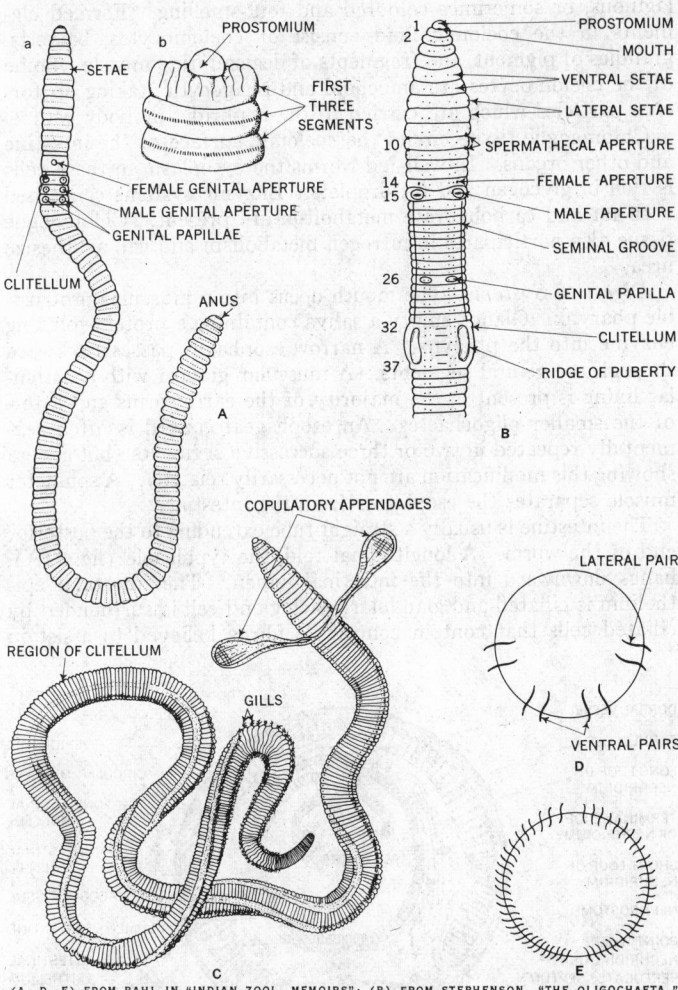

(A, D, E) FROM BAHL IN "INDIAN ZOOL. MEMOIRS"; (B) FROM STEPHENSON, "THE OLIGOCHAETA," BY PERMISSION OF THE CLARENDON PRESS, OXFORD; (C) FROM MICHAELSEN IN "HANDBUCH D. ZOOLOGIE"

FIG. 10.—BODY FORM IN HIGHER OLIGOCHAETES

(A) *Pheretima posthuma* (Megascolecidea): (a) ventral view, (b) dorsal view of anterior end; (B) *Lumbricus terrestris* (Lumbricidae), ventral view of anterior end; (C) *Alma eubranchiata* (Glossoscolecidae); diagrams of (D) Lumbricine arrangement of setae; (E) Perichaetine arrangement of setae

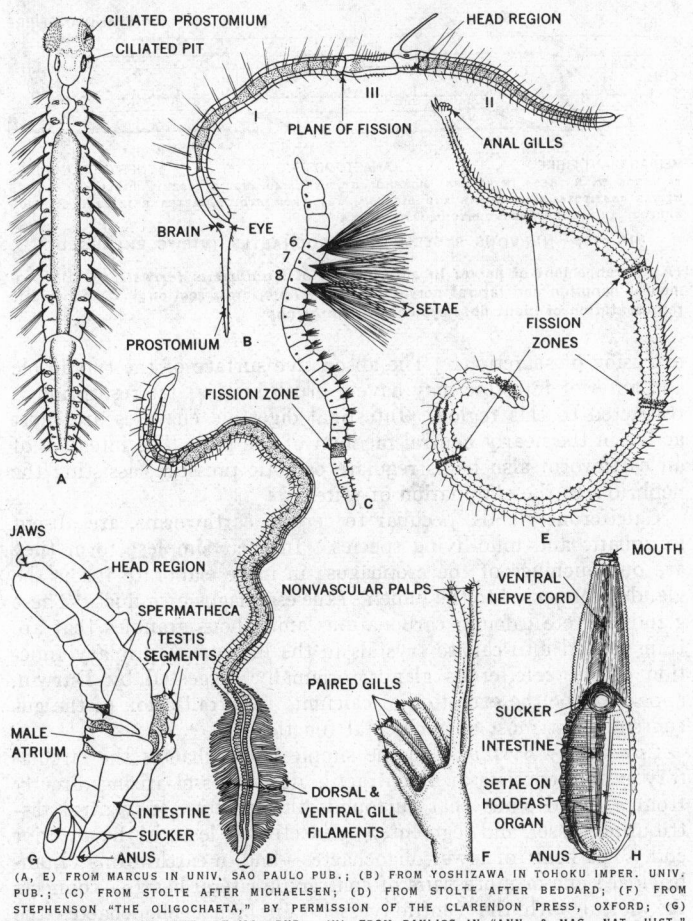

(A, E) FROM MARCUS IN UNIV. SÃO PAULO PUB.; (B) FROM YOSHIZAWA IN TOHOKU IMPER. UNIV. PUB.; (C) FROM STOLTE AFTER MICHAELSEN; (D) FROM STOLTE AFTER BEDDARD; (F) FROM STEPHENSON "THE OLIGOCHAETA," BY PERMISSION OF THE CLARENDON PRESS, OXFORD; (G) FROM GOODNIGHT IN UNIV. OF ILL. PUB.; (H) FROM BAYLISS IN "ANN. & MAG. NAT. HIST." (TAYLOR & FRANCIS, LTD.)

FIG. 9.—BODY FORM IN LOWER OLIGOCHAETES (VIEWS ENLARGED)

(A) *Aeolosoma headleyi* (Aeolosomatidae), chain of two zooids; (B) *Stylaria lacustris* (Naididae), chain of three zooids; (C) *Ripistes parasita* (Naididae); (D) *Branchiura sowerbyi* (Naididae); (E) *Aulophorus superterranus* (Naididae); (F) *Aulophorus furcatus* (Naididae), posterior end; (G) *Stephenodrilus obscurus* (Branchiobdellidae); (H) *Aspidodrilus kelsalli* (Enchytraeidae), ventral view

velopment of the epithelium, the clitellum or girdle, which secretes the egg capsule. It may be saddle-shaped or ring-shaped. The clitellum of earthworms occupies several segments and may be situated far behind the male pores. In lower oligochaetes it consists of a single layer of modified epithelial cells, but in the earthworms it has many layers.

The clitellum secretes the slime tube, the chitinous egg capsule, and the albumen of the cocoon. A clitellum may develop in animals in which the male reproductive system has been experimentally removed, but the coordinated maturation of the gonads and the clitellum is regulated by neurosecretion.

Free nerve endings, which probably respond to touch, heat, and pain, branch among the epidermal cells. Epithelial sense organs resembling taste buds stud the skin and mouth cavity; their appearance suggests that they are chemoreceptors. Photoreceptors (fig. 2C) contain a lenslike refractile body; in earthworms they are abundant at the anterior and posterior ends. Earthworms respond negatively to strong light but are attracted to weak illumination. All oligochaetes are strongly thigmotactic (attracted to surfaces). Some forms possess little studied receptors of pressure, sensory hairs, and pits.

2. Internal Structure.—*Coelom.*—The body cavity is well developed and segmentally partitioned by septa. The coelom often communicates with the exterior by pores, regulated by sphincter muscles. Dorsal pores are found in the intersegmental grooves of many terrestrial species through which coelomic fluid may be discharged. The fluid discharged may be milky, mucilaginous, or sometimes coloured and foul-smelling. Formed elements in the coelomic fluid consist of coelomocytes, bacteria, granules of pigment, and fragments of degenerating muscle. Some of the coelomocytes are amoeboid and phagocytic, taking up foreign particles which are carried to the nephridia or body wall.

Chloragogue tissue circles the coelomic surface of the intestine and other organs. In well-fed worms the cytoplasm in these cells is rich in glycogen and fat droplets. Enzyme systems concerned with fat and carbohydrate metabolism are present. Chloragogue tissue also participates in nitrogen metabolism and can synthesize urea.

Digestive System.—The mouth opens into a muscular protrusible pharynx. Glands empty a saliva containing a protein-splitting enzyme into the pharynx. A narrow esophagus passes backward through the genital segments. A muscular gizzard with a cuticular lining is present in the majority of the earthworms and a few of the smaller oligochaetes. An esophageal gizzard is often segmentally repeated in two or three successive segments (but genera showing this modification are not necessarily related). A sphincter muscle separates the esophagus from the intestine.

The intestine is usually a straight tube extending to the posterior end of the worm. A longitudinal fold, the typhlosole (fig. 11A), hangs downward into the intestinal lumen. The intestinal epithelium is ciliated and glandular; each gland cell is surrounded by ciliated cells that contain contractile fibrils believed to assist in

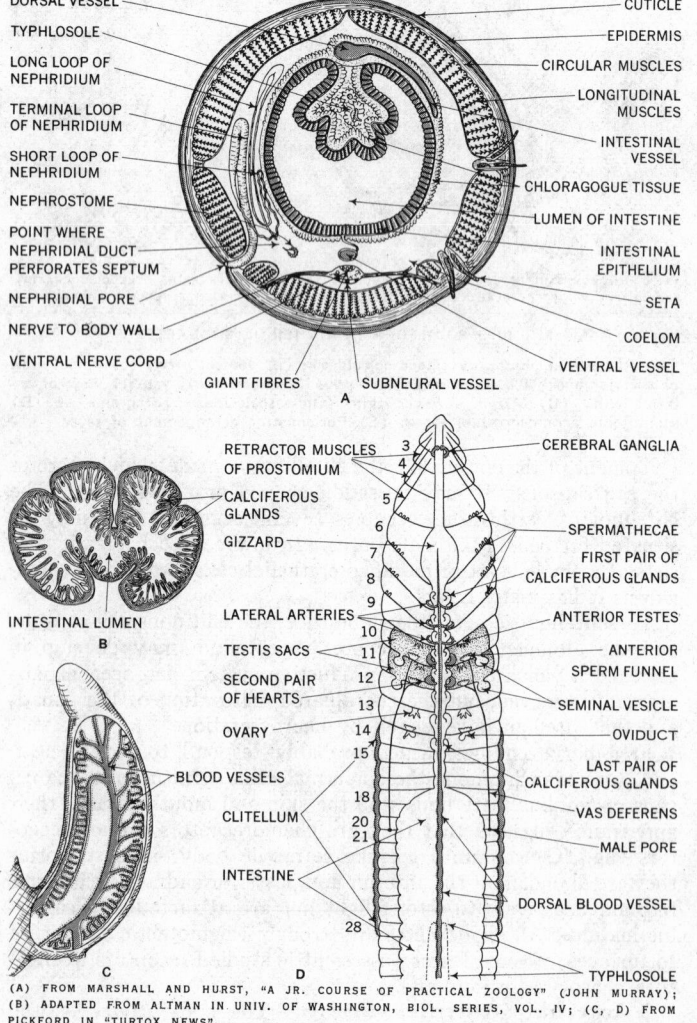

FIG. 11.—ANATOMY AND DIGESTIVE SYSTEM OF OLIGOCHAETES (VIEWS ENLARGED)

(A) FROM MARSHALL AND HURST, "A JR. COURSE OF PRACTICAL ZOOLOGY" (JOHN MURRAY); (B) ADAPTED FROM ALTMAN IN UNIV. OF WASHINGTON, BIOL. SERIES, VOL. IV; (C, D) FROM PICKFORD IN "TURTOX NEWS"

(A) Cross section through intestinal region of *Lumbricus terrestris*; (B) cross section of esophagus in *Plutellus kincaidi*; (C) calciferous gland of *Thamnodrilus crassus*; (D) diagram of anatomy of *Thamnodrilus crassus*

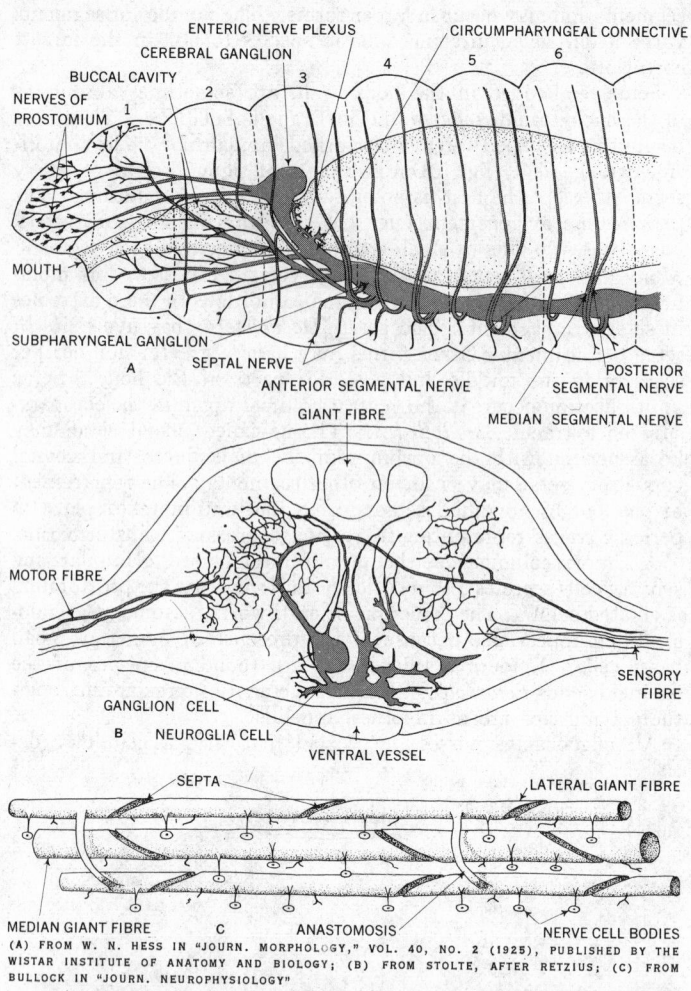

FIG. 12.—NERVOUS SYSTEM IN OLIGOCHAETES (VIEWS ENLARGED)

(A) FROM W. N. HESS IN "JOURN. MORPHOLOGY," VOL. 40, NO. 2 (1925), PUBLISHED BY THE WISTAR INSTITUTE OF ANATOMY AND BIOLOGY; (B) FROM STOLTE, AFTER RETZIUS; (C) FROM BULLOCK IN "JOURN. NEUROPHYSIOLOGY"

(A) Arrangement of nerves in anterior end of *Lumbricus terrestris*; (B) segmental ganglion and lateral nerves in *Lumbricus*, cross section; (C) schematic representation of giant fibre system in *Lumbricus*

extrusion of secretions. The absorptive surface of the typhlosole and anterior intestine may have a brush border; fat resorption is restricted to this region. Intestinal digestive enzymes are most active in the nearly neutral medium of the gut. The intestine of an earthworm also helps regulate osmotic pressure, assisting the nephridia in the elimination of water.

Calciferous glands, peculiar to certain earthworms, are absent in aquatic and mud-living species. In their simplest form they are outpouchings of the esophagus; in more elaborate forms the gland is connected to the lumen of the esophagus by a duct. These glands secrete calcium carbonate as amorphous granules that are transformed into calcite crystals in the lumen. A primary function of the calciferous glands, originally suggested by Darwin, appears to be the excretion of calcium. Neutralization of the gut contents is at most an incidental function.

Circulatory System.—In the simplest oligochaetes the circulatory system consists of a contractile dorsal vessel arising directly from a blood sinus that surrounds the intestine, a ventral distributing vessel, and segmented connective at least in the anterior end. The heart of lower oligochaetes—and in earthworms (Lumbricidae) one or more pairs of contractile lateral hearts—connects the dorsal with the ventral vessel. In higher oligochaetes the dorsal and ventral subneural vessel is generally present. The contractile lateral hearts are located in the esophageal region in the Megascolecidae and in the intestinal region in some Tubificidae. The dorsal vessel of the Lumbriculidae has peculiar blind contractile appendages.

The blood is colourless in some Microdrili; usually, however, it contains hemoglobin in solution in the plasma. According to some authors the blood carries nitrogenous excretory products to the nephridia. Only a small part of the osmotic pressure of the blood, which is much lower than that of marine polychaetes, is accounted for by chlorides. The only blood corpuscles are phagocytic amoebocytes.

Respiration.—Small aquatic species have anal respiration, in which water is pumped in and out of a rectal chamber. Some Naididae have anal gills (fig. 9F), and respiratory outgrowths of the body wall occur in a few aquatic genera (fig. 9D and 10C). In earthworms respiratory exchanges take place through well-vascularized moist skin. Earthworms can withstand considerable periods without oxygen, during which time they accumulate lactic acid and build up an oxygen debt, which is discharged as soon as oxygen again becomes readily available.

Excretory System.—The primitive (holonephric) condition is one pair of nephridia per segment, each nephridium consisting of a funnel (nephrostome), a duct that passes through the septum to the next segment posteriorly, and a coiled tube that frequently terminates in a bladderlike vesicle with an opening (nephridiopore). In earthworms the nephridium becomes more complex in structure, and in some forms there may be an increase in the number of nephriostomes for each nephridium (meronephric condition). The megascolecid genus *Perionyx* may have five pairs of nephridia per segment. The nephridiopore may open to the outside, into the esophagus or into the intestine. The highly evolved meronephore genus *Pheretima* has nephridia that open into the esophageal region, to the outside, and into the intestine.

Nervous System.—The central nervous system consists of a

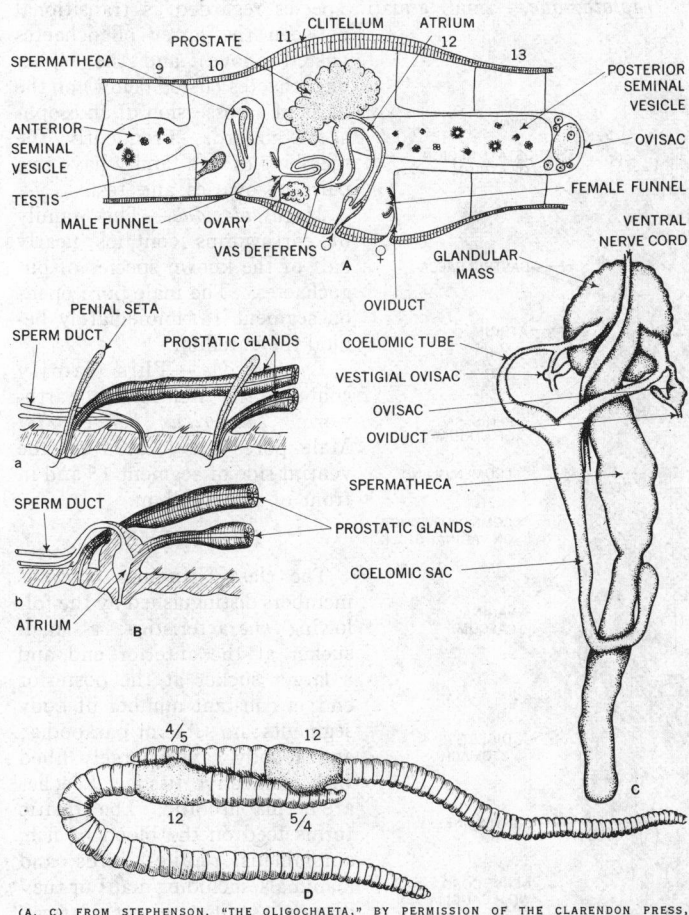

FIG. 13.—REPRODUCTIVE SYSTEM IN OLIGOCHAETES

(A) Genital organs (♂ male, ♀ female) of a tubificid, longitudinal section (enlarged, and segments numbered); (B) male terminal apparatus, longitudinal sections (much enlarged): (a) acanthodriline arrangement in *Eodrilus*, (b) transitional condition in *Gordiodrilus staudei;* (C) female reproductive organs in *Stuhlmannia stappersi* (enlarged); (D) two specimens of *Enchytraeus albidus* in copulation, the male pore, on segment 12, being directly opposed to the spermathecal pore of the other worm, between segments 4 and 5

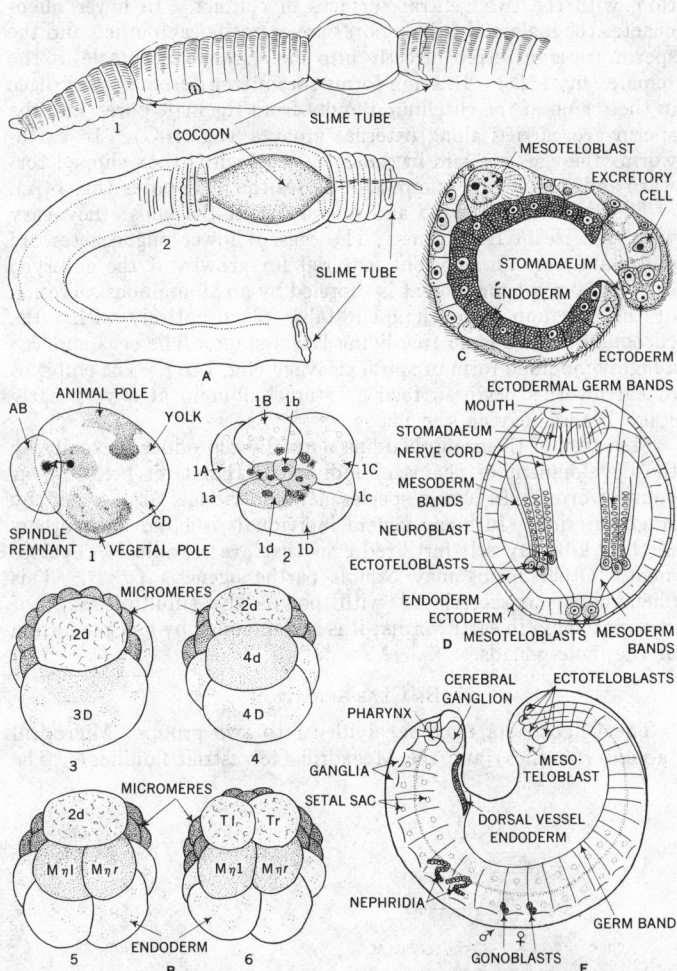

FIG. 14.—EMBRYOLOGY OF OLIGOCHAETES

(A) Formation of cocoon in *Eisenia foetida:* (1) cocoon forms on anterior end; (2) deposited cocoon hardens, slime tube dries and falls off. (B) Segmentation of ovum in *Tubifex tubifex:* (1) two-cell stage, (AB, CD) first blastomeres; (2) eight-cell stage, (1a-1d) first quartet of micromeres, (1A-1D) macromeres; (3-6) later stages showing formation of teloblasts, dorsal view; (2d) mother cell of ectoteloblasts, (4d) mother cell of mesoteloblasts (Tl, Tr) ectoteloblasts, (Mηl, Mηr) mesoteloblasts. (C) Advanced gastrula of *Dendrobaena rubida,* sagittal section. (D) Embryo of *Eisenia foetida,* ventral view. (E) Embryo of *Tubifex tubifex,* with 30 somites

bilobed brain, or supra-esophageal ganglion, circumpharyngeal connectives, and a ventral nerve cord. Each segmental ganglion gives off nerves (fig. 12B) that supply the epidermis and muscles. The visceral nerves are connected with the central nervous system anteriorly and segmentally. In *Lumbricus* the median giant fibre (fig. 12C) receives sensory messages from the anterior end and transmits them posteriorly. The two lateral fibres, connected with each other at intervals, transmit sensory impulses from the posterior end to the effector organs at the anterior part of the body.

3. Reproduction and Development.—Oligochaetes are primarily hermaphroditic, with the gonads normally restricted to a few segments. Lower oligochaetes have one pair of testes and one pair of ovaries in successive segments (fig. 13A). The Haplotaxidae have two pairs of testes in segments 10 and 11 and two pairs of ovaries in segments 12 and 13. Earthworms retain the two pairs of testes and the posterior pair of ovaries. Developing sperms are frequently stored in seminal vesicles before transfer to the female. The sperm ducts lead from the seminal vesicles to the male pores located one or more segments posterior to the testes. The ovaries are simple septal outpouchings (ovisacs) whose oviducts lead to the female pores located in the next posterior segment.

Copulation is reciprocal and takes place in a head-to-tail position, with the two ventral surfaces in contact. In lower oligo-chaetes the male and female pores are opposite each other, and the sperm are transferred directly into the seminal receptacle of the female (fig. 13D). In some forms sperm transference takes place in the region of the clitellum, remote from the male pores, and the sperm are carried along external grooves (fig. 10C). In earth-worms the eggs are laid in the cocoon, which is then slipped for-ward and receives the sperm as it passes the male pores (fig. 14A).

The cocoons are ovoid and drawn out at the ends; they vary with the size of the worms. The eggs of lower oligochaetes are yolky and contain sufficient material for growth of the embryo; in earthworms nourishment is supplied by an albuminous secretion of the clitellum. Development takes place entirely within the cocoon and there is no free-living larval stage. The eggs undergo a highly modified form of spiral cleavage (fig. 14B). The embryos of earthworms begin to feed on stored albumin at a very early stage before leaving the cocoon.

Members of the group Naidina normally reproduce asexually by the development of chains of individuals that later break off as young worms. In a few species new individuals are formed by fragmentation. In many genera individuals isolated from others of their kind lay self-fertilized eggs that are capable of develop-ment. Other forms may exhibit parthenogenesis (q.v.). This phenomenon is correlated with polyploidy (multiple sets of chromosomes) in earthworms; it is accompanied by a degeneration of the male gonads.

B. Classification

The Oligochaeta may be divided into two groups: Microdrili (aquatic families) and the Megadrili (terrestrial families). The distinction is merely one of convenience. Relationships of the families are based on the arrangement and number of gonads and the position of the gonaducts, particularly the male pores. In lower oligochaetes the male pores open on the segment following that containing the testes (Naididae, Tubificidae, and Enchytraei-dae). The Lumbriculidae are considered an offshoot from these lower oligochaetes since the male pores open on the same segment as that containing the testes. The Haplotaxidae are intermediate between the lower and higher oligochaetes. The higher oligo-chaetes have the male pore open several segments posterior to the segment that contains the testes (Megascolecidae and Lumbri-cidae).

The system of grouping the oligochaetes into 16 families by Michaelsen appears to reflect the natural relationship among them. A summary of the principal families follows:

Naididae.—Minute freshwater species reproducing mostly by asexual fission. Setae are usually in fanlike bundles. One pair of testes and one pair of ovaries are usually in segments 5 and 6.

Tubificidae.—Small species that frequently inhabit tubes in the bottom of lakes and streams; their projecting tails serve to permit anal respiration. The gonads are usually located in seg-ments 10 and 11.

Enchytraeidae.—Species may be terrestrial, freshwater, or marine. The testes and ovaries are usually in segments 11 and 12 but may be displaced forward.

Lumbriculidae.—Small or medium-sized worms found in mud. The number and arrangement of gonads vary; testes number from one to four pairs and are found in segments 7 to 11; ovaries num-ber from one to three pairs and are found from segments 9 to 12.

Haplotaxidae.—Small aquatic species regarded as transitional between the lower oligochaetes (listed above) and the higher oligochaetes (listed below) on the basis of a possession of an esoph-ageal gizzard. Frequently the members of this family have two pairs of ovaries and testes.

Megascolecidae.—This family of earthworms contains nearly half of the known species of oli-gochaetes. The male pore opens on segment 18, immediately be-hind the clitellum.

Lumbricidae.—This family contains the well-known earth-worm, *Lumbricus terrestris.* Male pores are located on the ventral side of segment 15 and in front of the clitellum.

IV. LEECHES

The class Hirudinea contains members distinguished by the fol-lowing characteristics: a small sucker at the anterior end and a larger sucker at the posterior end; a constant number of body segments; no setae or parapodia; and a body cavity largely filled with connective tissue. Leeches are hermaphroditic. The aquatic forms feed on the blood of fish, amphibians, reptiles, birds, and mammals, including man; or they devour snails, insect larvae, and worms. True land leeches feed exclusively on mammalian blood.

A. Structure and Function

1. External Features.—Leeches range in length from ⅜ to

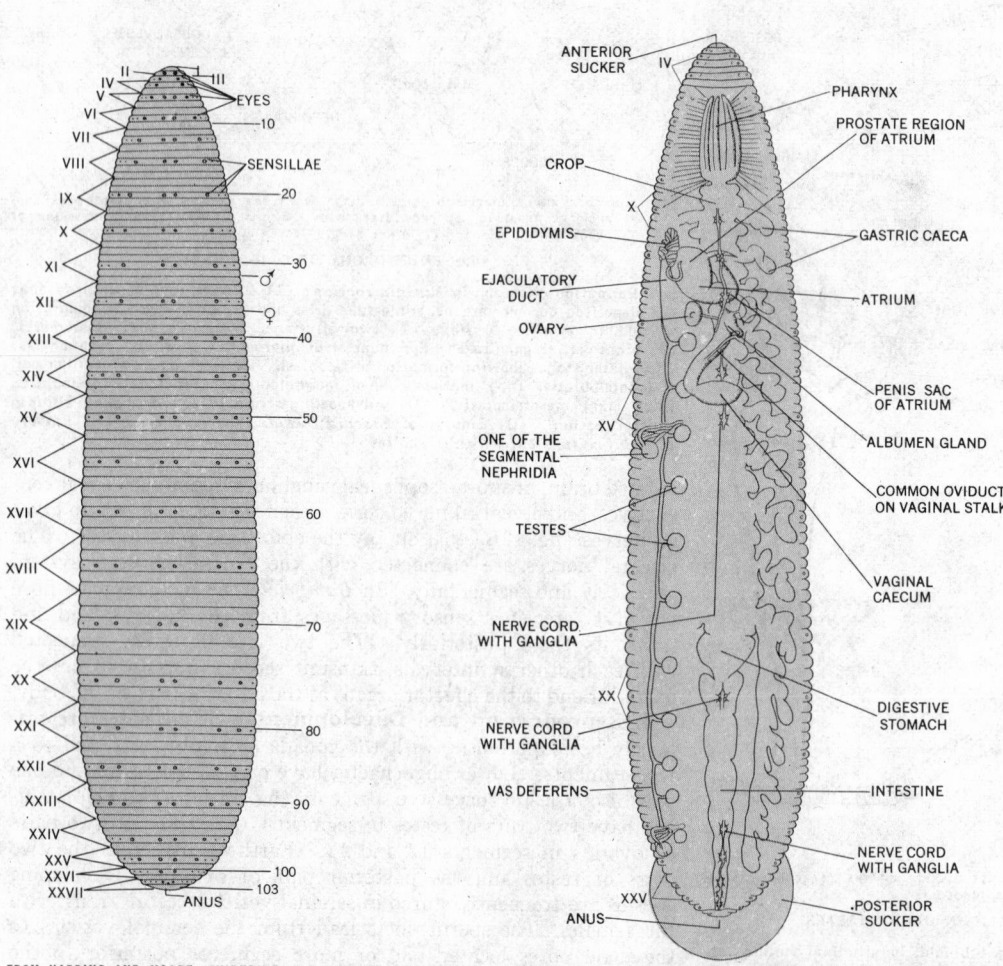

FROM HARDING AND MOORE, "HIRUDINEA," FAUNA OF BRITISH INDIA, BY COURTESY OF THE SECRETARY OF STATE FOR INDIA IN COUNCIL

FIG. 15.—HIRUDINEA: A TEN-EYED LEECH (HIRUDINARIA GRANULOSA). (LEFT) DORSAL VIEW; (RIGHT) INTERNAL ANATOMY. SOMITES INDICATED BY ROMAN NUMERALS; ANNULI BY ARABIC NUMERALS. GONOPORES OF MALE (♂) AND FEMALE (♀) INDICATED

about 17 in. and in form are elongate or elliptical, the length and shape of the body varying with the degree of muscular contraction. Since leeches have the number of segments fixed at 34, increase in length results from subdivision and elongation of the rings (annuli) into which the segments are divided. The number of annuli per segment in the mid-region is typical for a species, three to five being the commonest.

Eyes, placed anteriorly, usually vary from one to five pairs. The clitellar region, which secretes the cocoon, extends from segment X through XII and contains the male and female genital openings.

The skin of leeches consists of two cellular layers: the epidermis, consisting of a single layer of epithelium covered by a cuticle, and the dermis, consisting of fibrous connective tissue. The underlying musculature of the body wall consists of an outer circular layer, an intermediate crossed diagonal layer, and an inner, thicker, longitudinal layer.

Additional muscles are associated with the suckers and body systems.

2. Internal Features.—*Coelom.*—The coelom—characteristic of the other annelids—is largely replaced by the encroachment of connective tissue; it is reduced to a system of small spaces, constituting the lymphatic system, with various organs lying between the spaces. Five main longitudinal canals, or lacunae, with connecting branches and capillaries in the dermis, assist in respiration in the Glossiphoniidae. Contractile lateral lacunae and/or pulsating vesicles aid in circulation of coelomic fluid in many Piscicolidae.

The coelom is also invaded by the botryoidal tissue, believed to be excretory in function in the Arhynchobdellae.

Nervous System.—The nervous system consists of a chain of 34 paired ganglia connected by a double nerve cord. Six dorsal ganglia are aggregated to form the cephalic mass, followed by 21 spaced along the ventral nerve cord and 7 fused in the posterior sucker.

Digestive System.—The mouth, surrounded by the sucker, opens into the oral chamber, which is followed by the buccal sinus. The buccal sinus houses the jaws when they are present. Salivary glands, secreting anticoagulant substances, open either onto the jaws or proboscis of blood-sucking species.

The esophagus connects the pharynx with the stomach. The stomach is tubular with a few chambers in predaceous forms and diffuse with many paired pouches (caeca) in blood-sucking forms.

Circulatory System.—The blood is colourless in predaceous species and red (due to dissolved hemoglobin) in blood-sucking species.

In the Rhynchobdellae the circulatory system consists of a dorsal contractile vessel and a ventral vessel connected at the extremities by a system of loops. The coelomic cavity acts as a secondary circulatory system.

Excretory System.—The nephridia, numbering from 10 to 17 pairs, are convoluted tubules that may or may not open internally and exit individually on the ventrolateral surface.

3. Reproduction and Development.—In the male system the testes are segmentally arranged, with the organs on each side of the body, connected with tubules and leading to a muscular, often bulbous, ejaculatory duct. The female system consists of elongated ovisacs containing the ovaries. The ovisacs are connected to form an oviduct, which may serve as a vagina in those species that copulate.

Reproduction in leeches is exclusively sexual. Copulation occurs in Gnathobdellae with the sperms being transferred by the penis of one animal into the vagina of another. In the Rhynchobdellae and Erpobdellidae sperms are transferred by spermatophores onto the body of another. Sperms leave the spermatophore and enter the ovaries, resulting in fertilization. Eggs, numbering from one to more than 100, are usually deposited in cocoons. Development is direct, there being no larval stage.

B. CLASSIFICATION

The class Hirudinea is divided into four orders: (1) the Rhynchobdellae, characterized by a muscular protrusible proboscis, including the families Glossiphoniidae and Piscicolidae; (2) the Gnathobdellae, which have the mouth armed with toothed jaws, comprising the families Hirudidae, Haemadipsidae, and Semiscolecidae; (3) the Pharyngobdellae, with muscular ridges around the mouth but with no jaws, including families Erpobdellidae and Trematobdellidae; and (4) the Acanthobdellidae, known from a single species parasitic on salmon in the U.S.S.R. and Finland.

(D. J. R.)

BIBLIOGRAPHY.—R. P. Dales, *Annelids* (1963) (semi-popular); P. P. Grassé, *Traité de Zoologie*, vol. v, *Annélides, etc.*, fasc. i (1959; comprehensive; in French); O. Hartman, *Literature of the Polychaetous Annelids*, vol. 1, *Bibliography* (1951), and vol. 2, *Catalogue of the Polychaetous Annelids of the World* (1959); M. S. Laverack, *The Physiology of Earthworms* (1963); J. Stephenson, *The Oligochaeta* (1930); W. Michaelsen, "Oligochaeta," in W. Kükenthal and T. Krumbach, *Handbuch der Zoologie*, Bd. 2, Lief. 8 (1928) and "Nachtrag" (1930); K. H. Mann, *Leeches* (1962).

ANNEXATION, a formal act whereby a state proclaims its sovereignty over territory hitherto outside its domain. Unlike cession, where territory is given or sold by means of a treaty, annexation is a unilateral act made effective by actual possession and legitimized by general recognition.

Annexation is frequently preceded by conquest, a process by which a state ousts the existing government within a territory and places in authority its own military forces, thus setting up a condition of military occupation. Conceivably, as in the German conquest of Austria in 1938, this conquest may be accomplished by the threat of force without active hostilities. This military occupation does not *ipso facto* constitute annexation, nor will it necessarily lead to annexation. The military occupation of German territory by the United States, Great Britain, France and the Soviet Union after the cessation of hostilities in World War II was not in itself annexation, nor was it followed by annexation. To the contrary, the joint allied declaration of June 5, 1945, which announced the supreme authority of the occupying powers, expressly denied any intention to annex. For military occupation to eventuate in annexation an official announcement is necessary, to the effect that the sovereign authority of the annexing state has been established and will be maintained in the future.

Conquest and annexation may be limited to only a portion of the territory of a state but such acquisition is usually effected by cession by means of a treaty. An official announcement of annexation, before conquest has been completed, has long been deemed irregular and, according to the widely accepted Stimson doctrine of 1932, annexation following completed conquest should not be recognized if the conqueror has violated an antiwar obligation. The Italian annexation of Ethiopia in 1936, before conquest had been effected, was widely condemned and was not recognized by many states including the United States.

Conditions may exist which obviate the necessity for conquest prior to annexation. For instance, where a state already has a protectorate over a territory its authority there may be sufficient to sustain annexation. In 1910, as an example, Japan converted its protectorate of Korea into an annexed colony by means of proclamation. Preceding its annexation of the Svalbard Islands in 1925, Norway eliminated its competitors by means of a treaty in which they agreed to Norwegian possession. Annexation by the United States of Hawaii in 1898 was a peaceful act, based upon the willing acceptance by the Hawaiian government of U.S. authority.

The formalities of annexation are not defined by international law; whether it be done by one authority or another within a state is a matter of constitutional law. The annexation of Ethiopia was accomplished by a decree issued by the king of Italy on May 9, 1936. Joint resolutions of congress were the means by which the United States annexed Texas in 1845 and Hawaii in 1898. Subsequent recognition of annexation by other states may be explicit or implied. *See* CONQUEST.

BIBLIOGRAPHY.—M. F. Lindley, *The Acquisition and Government of Backward Territory in International Law* (1926); G. Hackworth, *Digest of International Law*, 8 vol. (1940-44). (N. L. HL.)

ANNICERIS (? fl. late 4th century B.C.), Greek philosopher, probably lived under Ptolemy I of Egypt. He gave his name to a sect of the Cyrenaics (*q.v.*), re-establishing the original doctrine in face of the innovations of Theodorus and of Hegesias. Against the former he emphasized that pleasure was to be found not only in sensual enjoyment but also in feelings of friendship, gratitude, patriotism, etc., apart from any benefits that they might secure. He also denied that to have understanding was adequate for a happy life, thinking that a habit must be formed before a man can feel no qualms in disregarding a false public opinion. Against the pessimist Hegesias he insisted on the value of positive pleasure as distinguished from the absence of pain.   (F. H. SH.)

ANNISTON, a city of Alabama, U.S., 61 mi. N.E. of Birmingham, on the slope of Blue mountain, seat of Calhoun county. (For comparative population figures *see* table in ALABAMA: *Population.*) Anniston makes nearly a third of the U.S. cast-iron soil pipe supply, and produces textiles, apparel and chemical products. Founded in 1872 as a company town by the Woodstock Iron company, it was chartered as a city in 1879 and opened to the public in 1882. The (Protestant Episcopal) Church of St. Michael and All Angels and the Regar Museum of Natural History with its famous habitat bird groups are points of interest. Nearby Fort McClellan, a permanent post of the U.S. army, is headquarters for the women's army corps and the chemical corps training command.   (J. A. TR.)

ANNO (HANNO), **SAINT** (*c.* 1010–1075), archbishop of Cologne, prominent in the political struggles of the Holy Roman empire, was born *c.* 1010 into a Swabian family and educated at Bamberg. He became confessor to the emperor Henry III, who appointed him archbishop of Cologne in 1056. Anno was the leader of the party that abducted the young king Henry IV from his mother Agnes. He then seized the regency, but was compelled to share it with Adalbert (*q.v.*), the powerful archbishop of Bremen. In 1064 he left the court but recovered some of his former influence on Henry when Adalbert fell in 1066. His most important service was his action at the Council of Mantua (May 1064), when he secured the recognition of Alexander II as pope against his rival Honorius, who was originally a nominee of the German court. He was killed at Cologne on Dec. 4, 1075, and canonized in 1183. His feast day is Dec. 4.

ANNOBÓN: *see* EQUATORIAL GUINEA.

ANNONA, Roman personification of the grain supply, originally associated with Ceres. Her attributes in works of art and on imperial coins were a grain bushel, a ship's prow pointing to the transport of the grain over the sea, ears of grain and a horn of plenty (*cornu copiae*).

The Latin word itself has various meanings: (1) the produce of the year's harvest; (2) all means of subsistence, especially grain stored in the public granaries for provisioning the city; (3) the market price of commodities, especially grain; (4) a direct tax in kind, levied in republican times in several provinces, chiefly employed in imperial times for distribution among officials and the support of the soldiery.

In order to insure a supply of grain sufficient to enable it to be sold at a very low price, it was procured in large quantities from Umbria, Etruria and Sicily. Almost down to the time of the empire, the care of the grain supply formed part of the duties of the aediles (*q.v.*), and possibly of certain special commissaries. As a consequence of the second Punic War, Roman agriculture was at a standstill; accordingly, recourse was had to Sicily and Sardinia (the first two Roman provinces) in order to keep up the supply of grain; a tax of one-tenth was imposed on it, and its export to any country except Italy forbidden. The price at which the grain was sold was always moderate; the grain law of Gracchus (123 B.C.) made it absurdly low, and Clodius (58 B.C.) bestowed it gratuitously. The number of the recipients of this gift grew so enormously that both Caesar and Augustus were obliged to reduce it. From the time of Augustus to the end of the empire the number of those who were entitled to receive a monthly allowance of grain on presenting a ticket was 200,000. A *praefectus annonae* was appointed by Augustus to superintend the grain supply. He was assisted by a large staff in Rome and the provinces. In the 3rd century bread formed the dole. The office lasted until the latest times of the empire.

ANNONACEAE, the custard apple family, an important group of dicotyledonous plants (those having two seed leaves) allied to the magnolias (*q.v.*). The Annonaceae are chiefly tropical shrubs and trees and comprise about 80 genera and 820 species. The leaves are simple, entire and alternate; the flowers are regular, usually with three sepals and six petals, the latter brown or tawny yellow, not showy; the stamens numerous; and the fruit an aggregation of berries (syncarp) in which the seeds are embedded or dry or capsular. Many species are grown for their edible fruits, for perfume and for ornament. A few extend into temperate regions, as the North American paw-paw (*Asimina triloba*), found northward to New York and Michigan. Many valuable fruits belong to the genus *Annona;* among these are the cherimoya (*A. cherimola*) of the American tropics, now cultivated in the southern United States; the custard apple or bullock's-heart (*A. reticulata*), of tropical America; the sugar apple, sweetsop or ate (*A. squamosa*), cultivated throughout the tropics; the soursop or *guanábana* (*A. muricata*), widely grown in tropical lands; the *ilama* (*A. diversifolia*) of Mexico and Guatemala; the alligator apple, or corkwood (*A. glabra*), of tropical America and the *posh-té* (*A. scleroderma*) of Guatemala and Mexico. The *biribá* (*Rollinsia deliciosa*) and related species are highly esteemed fruits from Brazil to Central America. A tree (*Porcelia saffordiana*) of Bolivia, named and described in 1927, bears immense fruits sometimes attaining 40 lb. weight. The ylang-ylang (*Canangium odoratum*), native to the East Indies, is the source of the famous perfume of Malaysia and the Philippines. The exceedingly fragrant climbing ylang-ylang (*Artabotrys uncinatus*), native to India and China, is sparingly planted in southern Florida. *See* CHERIMOYA; CUSTARD APPLE; SWEETSOP.

ANNUITY, in the simplest sense of the word, denotes a payment made yearly, as, for example, under a contract to provide retirement income. The term is also applied to any series of periodic payments made at regular, fixed intervals. Thus, an annuity may be payable every two years, every year, every half-year, quarterly, monthly or at other intervals. The length of the interval is called the annuity period. The size of an annuity may be described by referring either to the amount of each payment or to the amount payable in a year, the latter amount being called the annual rent. For example, a particular annuity may be described as an annuity calling for payments of $25 every quarter or a quarterly annuity with annual rent of $100.

In technical terminology an annuity is said to be payable during a given status, this being a word equally appropriate when the annuity is payable for a definite term of years and when payment is dependent upon some contingency. The most general definition of an annuity is, therefore, a series of payments made at regular intervals during the continuance of a given status.

There are two main classes of annuities: annuities certain and contingent annuities. Under an annuity certain the payments are to continue for a specified number of payments, and calculations are based on the assumption that each payment is certain to be made when due. With a contingent annuity each payment is contingent on the continuance of a given status. The most common form of contingent annuity is a life annuity, under which each payment is contingent on the survival of one or more specified persons. The person to whom an annuity is payable is the annuitant and the life involved is the nominee. A person who purchases an annuity on his own life is both annuitant and nominee.

Annuities certain issued in Great Britain are normally for terms of from 10 to 25 years, but shorter or longer contracts are available. The annuity payments continue for the whole of the term of years arranged at the outset whether or not the annuitant survives that period. Only the interest content of each annuity payment is assessable for income tax, and owing to this favourable taxation basis annuities certain were, until 1956 (when the Finance act extended this taxation basis to ordinary "purchased" life annuities), largely used in conjunction with a deferred annuity, the payments under which were arranged to commence at the expiration of the annuity certain period.

A perpetuity is a special case of an annuity certain and is defined as an annuity that is to continue forever. Perhaps the best-known example of a perpetuity would be the interest payments on British Consols (*q.v.*). Since these obligations of the government have no maturity date, it is intended that the interest payments will be continued indefinitely.

Definitions.—This section is devoted to definitions of some of the more common terms used to describe various types of annuities.

Under an annuity immediate the first payment is due one period after the date of the agreement.

Under an annuity due the first payment is due at the date of the agreement; *i.e.,* immediately.

Under a deferred annuity the first payment is due at some future time other than one period after the date of the agreement. If the first payment is due more than one period after the date of the agreement, the annuity can be described as either a deferred annuity due or a deferred annuity immediate. For example, an annuity with the first payment due in two years with payments due annually thereafter can be described as an annuity due deferred two years or as an annuity immediate deferred one year.

The words "immediate" and "due" may be unfortunate since an annuity due means an annuity under which the first payment is due immediately. There is, however, a reason for this seemingly odd choice of words. The reason is historical. A person was said to enter upon an annuity immediately if he received his first payment at the end of one year. The annuity was said to be deferred if the first payment was due later than at the end of one year. The concept of an annuity with the first payment due immediately was not important until the development of life insurance. Since life insurance premiums are paid in advance, the premium payments represent an annuity with the first payment due immediately. Thus the original terms were "annuity immediate" and "deferred annuity." When it became necessary to have a term to describe an annuity with the first payment due immediately, the word "immediate" was not available.

In Great Britain the first payment under a deferred annuity is made at the completion of the deferred term of years. For example, the first payment under an annuity deferred ten years would be made on the tenth anniversary of the inception of the annuity contract. A deferred annuity is usually purchased on an annual premium basis payable during the term of deferment, and a substantial volume of these contracts was effected after World War II in connection with occupational pension arrangements. An "approved" deferred annuity is one granted in accordance with provisions laid down in the Finance act of 1956, by which self-employed persons and others not entitled to benefit under schemes set up by their employers are enabled to obtain relief from income tax and surtax, on the whole of the premiums paid, so as to provide themselves with pensions on retirement. The annuity must be in "approved" form; it must, for instance, be noncommutable and nonassignable.

Unless otherwise stated, the first payment under an annuity in Great Britain is assumed to be made at the end of the first year in the case of yearly annuity and at the end of the first interval in the case of an annuity payable by half-yearly, quarterly or monthly installments.

Under a single life annuity each payment is contingent on the survival of a specified person.

Under a joint life annuity each payment is contingent on the survival of two or more specified persons.

Under a joint and survivor annuity payments are continued as long as any of the specified persons is alive. This type of annuity is a common option under pension plans, the specified lives usually being the pensioner and spouse.

Under a joint and two-thirds survivor annuity the full payment is made as long as both specified persons are alive with a two-thirds payment continued to the survivor after the first death. This type of annuity is a common option under pension plans, the theory being that living expenses for one person are about two-thirds as much as for two persons.

Under a whole life annuity (or straight life annuity) payments are made for the life of the specified person. The term "life annuity," without further qualification, almost always means a whole

life annuity on a single life. In addition, the absence of the word "joint" in any life annuity term almost always implies a single life.

Under a temporary life annuity each payment is contingent on the survival of a specified person and, in addition, the total payments are limited to some fixed number. Thus, in an annual 15-year temporary life annuity, no more than 15 payments will be made even if the person survives beyond the 15-year period.

Under an annuity for ten years certain and life thereafter payments for the first ten years are guaranteed and subsequent payments are contingent upon survival. The abbreviation "10cc" is frequently used in the United States for this annuity, the "cc" standing for certain and continuous. Although ten years is a common certain period, any other certain period is possible.

Under a refund annuity payments are continued for life with a guarantee that, in the event of death before total payments have amounted to the consideration paid for the annuity, payments will be continued until the total payments do amount to the consideration.

A cash-refund annuity in the United States is the same as a refund annuity except that any excess of consideration over total payments is paid in a lump sum at death rather than spread out over the regular payment intervals.

The general definition of a reversionary annuity is that payments depend on the existence of a particular status after the failure of another status. In the simple case of two persons, for example, there might be an agreement to make payments to B after the death of A. If B dies before A, no payments would be made. If a son is responsible for the support of a parent and wants to protect the parent against the son's early death, a reversionary annuity will provide this protection at comparatively small expense. Only a few life insurance companies, however, will issue this type of policy.

Although the original definition of a variable annuity was any annuity under which the payments varied in size, the term has come to have a more precise meaning: payments under a variable annuity vary as the market value of the fund varies. Since a variable annuity fund is invested in equities, the annuity payments vary with stock market quotations. The theory is that variations in the cost of living follow, in a general way, variations in the stock market, so that the variable annuity is a hedge against inflation.

The first large-scale use of variable annuities in the United States was made by the College Retirement Equities fund (C.R.E.F.), the companion organization to the Teachers Insurance and Annuity association (T.I.A.A.). Participation in T.I.A.A. and C.R.E.F. plans is limited to college and university staff members. C.R.E.F. commenced operations July 1, 1952.

Variable annuities were introduced into Great Britain in 1957. Only a few of the British life offices are interested in this type of annuity, for which there has been but little demand. Variable deferred annuities have inland revenue approval as a means of providing pensions "approved" under the Finance act of 1956. Under one such plan both the annuity and the premium that pays for it are expressed as a cash sum equal to the price of a stated number of trust units. According to another plan the benefits depend on the experience of a fund invested mainly in high-grade equities, created for the purpose and operated on a "mutual" basis, with the company taking such amounts as necessary to cover management expenses.

There has been considerable difference of opinion as to whether life insurance companies should issue variable annuities. The major argument in favour is, of course, that a retired person living on his annuity payments needs protection from inflation, that the variable annuity offers more protection than any other practical plan and that life insurance companies are the only organizations equipped, by knowledge and legal sanction, to issue annuities. Some of the arguments against life insurance companies issuing variable annuities to the general public are: (1) fear that the general public may not understand that payments can go down as well as up; (2) fear that increasing popularity of the variable annuity will result in pressures on the stock market and be self-defeating; and (3) reluctance to abandon the fixed-dollar philosophy under which the life insurance business has prospered.

Calculations of Present Values.—Over the years, techniques have been developed and tables prepared to simplify the necessary calculations in connection with annuities certain and life annuities. Although a full discussion is necessarily beyond the scope of this article, this section will be devoted to a brief discussion of the computation of the present value of (1) an *n*-year annuity certain immediate; and (2) a whole life annuity immediate to a life aged *x*, the annual payment being one in both cases.

The symbol $a_{\overline{n}|}$ represents the present value of the *n*-year annuity certain immediate. This present value must be the sum of the present values of each of the *n* payments; that is, $a_{\overline{n}|} = v + v^2 + v^3 + \ldots + v^n$ where v is the reciprocal of $1 + i$, i being the rate of interest. By using the formula for the sum of a geometric progression, we have $a_{\overline{n}|} = \dfrac{1 - v^n}{i}$.

The symbol a_x represents the present value of the life annuity immediate. This present value is the sum of the present values of all possible payments. By reasoning that the present value of a particular payment is the present value, discounted at interest only, multiplied by the probability that the payment will be made, we have $a_x = v \dfrac{l_{x+1}}{l_x} + v^2 \dfrac{l_{x+2}}{l_x} + \ldots$ where l_x is the number of persons alive at age *x* according to the mortality table used. By multiplying numerator and denominator of each term by v^x and defining the commutation symbols $D_x = v^x l_x$ and $N_x = D_x + D_{x+1} + \ldots$ (to the end of the mortality table), we have $a_x = \dfrac{N_{x+1}}{D_x}$.

Mortality Tables.—Scientific observation has shown that variations in rates of mortality are attributable to certain well-defined causes. The methods adopted in compiling the information so obtained into tables of mortality have progressed from crude beginnings to a state closely approaching perfection. In its simplest form a mortality table purports to show the life history, or a portion of the life history, of a body of lives unaffected by any influence other than death; because such tables are a record of life history they are sometimes termed life tables.

Work on reversionary payments carried out by Richard Price, published in Great Britain in 1771 (fourth and best-known edition, 1783), contained the Northampton table—the first mortality table recognized and adopted as a basis for the purpose of calculations of life assurance. In 1808, when British government annuities were first established, the annuity tables used were computed upon the Northampton table. However, a fallacy in their method of construction, together with the fact that the table was intended to be conservative for life insurance, resulted in annuities being granted at prices much below their value and the country sustained a loss of about £2,000,000 before the error was rectified. The reason the Northampton table was conservative for life insurance was that mortality according to the table was heavier than that actually experienced. Thus the death claims actually experienced were less than those contemplated in the premiums, the difference being a source of margin to the company. In the case of annuities the reverse is true. If the table shows mortality heavier than that experienced, the annuity payments will be greater than contemplated in the premiums and the issuing company (or government) will lose money. In short, a mortality table is conservative for insurance if the mortality rates are heavy but it is conservative for annuities if the rates are light.

There were four investigations into the mortality of persons who had purchased annuities from the British government. The period under observation extended from 1808 to 1875. The first investigation was made by John Finlaison and resulted in a new scheme being introduced in 1829. The mortality tables adopted were those constructed by Finlaison from an observation up to the end of 1822 of the duration of the lives of annuitants. Two main facts emerged from this investigation and have been confirmed

by subsequent experience: (1) annuitants as a class are remarkable for their longevity; and (2) the vitality of females is appreciably superior to that of males, so that separate mortality tables must be prepared for each sex. Further investigations were conducted by A. G. Finlaison and A. J. Finlaison, the son and the grandson of John Finlaison.

The effect of "selection" on annuitants' mortality was first taken into account by A. J. Finlaison when actuary to the National Debt office. He investigated the annuities granted by the national debt commissioners from 1808 to 1875. An annuity is not likely to be purchased on the life of a person thought to be in poor health and, as a result, the mortality experienced for several years after the date of purchase is likely to be lighter than that of the general body of annuitants of the same age. Finlaison found that the effects of selection were discernible for four years following the date of purchase and he recommended that revised tables based on the resulting select rates of mortality should be adopted. There followed many well-known mortality tables, the Carlisle table, the English Life tables, the Seventeen Offices' table, the Institute of Actuaries tables and the British Offices' tables.

Following an investigation of annuitant mortality experienced by British life offices during the years 1900–20, it was recommended that selection after the first year be ignored and that annuity values be based not on the rates of mortality derived directly from the observed experience but on these rates modified to allow for progressive future improvement in longevity. These recommendations were adopted and resulted in the publication in 1925 of the a(m) and a(f) tables. These tables gave only projected rates of mortality and annuity values derived from them. After the 1900–20 investigations, mortality experience was kept under continuous observation and, following a break during World War II, a further investigation was commenced in 1949 by the Institute and Faculty of Actuaries, which resulted in the a(55) tables for annuitants being published in 1953. These tables, which have been generally adopted, were compiled from data supplied by the life offices and make allowance for the future reduction in mortality.

A mortality table, partly based upon the experience of assured lives in the Mutual Life Insurance Company of New York and partly on previous tables, was compiled by a U.S. actuary, Sheppard Homans, and published in 1868. It was subsequently employed by all New York companies and, with the Seventeen Offices' table, became the standard adopted by a large number of U.S. companies. The experience upon which the elaborate Thirty American Offices' tables were constructed, under the superintendence of Levi W. Meech, was, up to the time of its publication in 1881, the largest ever published. It extended over a period of 30 years to the end of 1874.

Until 1899, when McClintock's Annuity table was published, annuity values in the United States were based largely on British experience. In 1920 Arthur Hunter prepared a table based on the experience of 20 of the principal U.S. companies under annuities issued in the United States. Called the American Annuitants' Mortality table, it was used with various modifications as a basis for premiums by U.S. companies until 1938. The Combined Annuity Mortality table published in 1928 and the 1937 Standard Annuity Mortality table published in 1938 were both based on the American Annuitants' Mortality table, with allowances for decreases in mortality.

In 1949 Wilmer A. Jenkins and Edward A. Lew, in a paper before the Society of Actuaries, made an important contribution to the study of mortality among annuitants. In addition to preparing the annuity table for 1949, which was designed to reflect mortality experience in that year, they also gave projection factors to provide for probable decreases in future mortality rates.

An outstanding feature of the annuity business in the United States has been the rapid development of group annuities since the early 1930s. A typical group annuity contract covers employees of a common employer under one master contract and provides annuity payments beginning at retirement. After 1938 most companies based their premiums for group annuities on the 1937 Standard Annuity Mortality table, or a modification; but by the middle 1950s many companies had shifted to the Group Annuity table for 1951, which was prepared by Ray M. Peterson and published in 1952. By the early 1960s various modifications of the 1951 table reflecting changes in mortality rates were in common use. *See* also DEATH RATE; LIFE EXPECTANCY; LIFE INSURANCE; PENSIONS; SOCIAL SECURITY.

BIBLIOGRAPHY.—R. E. Larson and E. A. Gaumnitz, *Life Insurance Mathematics* (1951); D. W. A. Donald, *Compound Interest and Annuities-Certain* (1953); C. W. Jordan, *Society of Actuaries' Textbook on Life Contingencies* (1952); P. F. Hooker and L. H. Longley-Cook, *Life and Other Contingencies*, vol. i (1953), vol. ii (1957); F. Baily, *The Doctrine of Life Annuities and Assurances* (1864); H. Boag, *Compound Interest, Annuities Certain and Logarithmic Calculations* (1948); R. E. Underwood, *The Elements of Actuarial Science* (1954); H. H. Edwards, *The Principles of Compound Interest, in Their Application to Annuities* (1934); Sir W. P. Elderton and R. C. Fippard, *The Construction of Mortality and Sickness Tables* (1959). Various papers in the volumes of the *Journal* of the Institute of Actuaries, *Transactions* of the Faculty of Actuaries and *Transactions* of the Society of Actuaries. (RT. E. L.; P. SS.)

ANNULMENT, in marriage law, signifies a judicial declaration that a marriage was null and void *ab initio* ("from the beginning"), as distinguished from divorce, the legal act by which a valid marriage is dissolved.

In the view of Christianity marriage is indissoluble, either completely, as under the doctrine of the Roman Catholic Church, or at least on principle, so that during the joint lifetime of both spouses it can be dissolved only, as in the Eastern Church, for adultery or, as in the Lutheran or Reformed view, only for adultery or other misconduct of the gravest kind. However, in order to be indissoluble the marriage must be valid. A situation may outwardly appear to be a marriage and yet not constitute a marriage within the meaning of the law of the church or the state. Rules meticulously indicating what does and what does not constitute a marriage were elaborated by the theological and legal scholars of the medieval church, in whose canon law they became crystallized. In postmedieval developments the rules were modified in many respects in the laws of the various churches and, even more, in the secular legislation of modern states. But in the ecclesiastical law of all Christian churches, as well as in all those secular laws in which marriage is treated as not freely dissolvable, the distinction between valid and invalid marriages is still of significance. In the Christian view the essential element of marriage is the free will of both parties to take each other as husband and wife; *i.e.,* to create a relationship of lasting and full community of life within which the procreation of children is permissible without sin and in which the parties have mutual and exclusive rights to their bodies. Where such mutual consent is absent, no marriage can exist. Since under the view developed by the church the procreation of children is an essential element of marriage, impotency to perform the marital act, but not impotency to procreate children, is also regarded as preventing the conclusion of a valid marriage. To these requirements the Roman Catholic Church, most Protestant churches and the secular laws of all western countries (with the sole exception of, as of 1958, 17 states of the United States) have added the further requirement of a ceremony to be conducted in accordance with the law of the church or state in question. Further requirements for the validity of a marriage have been added by the policies of churches and states to prohibit certain marriages as religiously or socially undesirable—for instance, marriages between a brother and his sister or between other persons closely related by blood.

However, not all prohibited marriages are necessarily invalid. In their rules about impediments to marriage the canonists developed a distinction between two groups of obstacles. Some impediments were regarded as so grave that their existence would not only subject the guilty parties to punishment but would also render the attempted marriage null and void. Other prohibitions were to be observed in the sense that no priest should officiate in their celebration and that the celebration knowingly concluded in spite of them would subject the guilty party to punishment. But the marriage, although it should not have been concluded, would be valid nevertheless. Impediments of the former, more serious character were called *impedimenta matrimonii dirimentia,* those of the latter *impedimenta matrimonii impedientia.* The distinction is still significant in modern canon law as well as in the secular laws, especially of England, Scotland, the commonwealth countries and the United States. Under all these laws a marriage between a brother and his sister is not only both prohibited and punishable if the parties knew of their blood relationship but is also null and void even if the parties were ignorant of their blood relationship. But a marriage concluded without the parties' first having obtained a medical certificate, though punishable in a considerable number of states of the United States, is nevertheless valid.

Positive law determines not only which violations shall render a marriage invalid, and whether a particular kind of a ceremony shall be necessary for the conclusion of a valid marriage, but also what exactly constitutes that free exchange of mutual consent without which the conclusion of a valid marriage is not possible. The religious and secular laws vary greatly in this respect. The fact, for instance, that the marital consent of one party was induced by his or her mistake about a personal characteristic of the other party does not render that consent invalid under the law of the Roman Catholic Church, as laid down in the *Codex juris canonici* of 1917, or of the secular laws of England or Illinois, while it is regarded as sufficient to allow an annulment under the laws of New York or of Germany if it is of so serious a nature that it would have prevented a reasonable person acting under the circumstances from entering upon the marriage in question. Ignorance of the other party's suffering from incurable cancer is thus irrelevant under the first-named laws, while it may be relevant under the latter.

Under the canon law a marriage is either valid or invalid. If it is valid, it has all its legal effects; if it is invalid, it has none at all. However, if there exists the outward appearance of a marriage the relation is presumed to be that of a valid marriage, and as long as both parties are alive neither of them nor any third person may deny its existence or derive any benefits from its invalidity. Neither party, *e.g.,* may remarry a third person. This presumption of validity is removed only when the invalidity of the marriage has been authoritatively declared by a court, and such a judgment of nullity is to be rendered only in proceedings specially instituted and conducted for the purpose of ascertaining the validity or invalidity of a marriage that has come to be questioned. Such a nullity suit may be instituted either by one of the parties or by a special official, the promoter of justice (*promotor iustitiae*), who is under a duty to do so where the continuance of an apparent marriage would amount to a scandal, for instance because of incest or bigamy.

In the secular laws of the Anglo-American countries these rules have been modified so that the validity of a relationship appearing to be a marriage may be attacked collaterally, a procedure allowed only under certain circumstances in the canon law after one of the parties to the relationship has died. Under these laws the question of the validity of a marriage may thus be raised and decided in any proceedings in which it appears to be relevant; *e.g.,* in those concerning the distribution of the estate of a decedent. If a relative of the decedent alleges that his marriage was invalid and that the person claiming to be his widow is therefore not entitled to a share in the estate, a decision may be rendered by the probate court in the course of the administration of the estate. Direct attack, *i.e.,* proceedings directly aimed at declaring the invalidity of a marriage, is also possible, but in Anglo-American law such an action, called a nullity suit, can be brought about only if one party to the marriage relationship is the petitioner and the other the respondent. If H, for instance, discovers that at the time of the celebration of his marriage to W there was still living a prior spouse of hers from whom no valid divorce had been obtained, H may simply leave W and enter upon a new marriage with another woman. However, he will do so at his risk. Some court may later hold a different opinion about W's freedom to marry H and, consequently, about the validity or invalidity of H's marriage to W and of his new marriage to his second wife. If a court should find that H's second marriage was bigamous, he may be punishable for bigamy, the children of his second marriage may be illegitimate, and upon his death his second wife may find herself to be without any rights to a pension or to survivor's benefits under social security. If H wishes to act safely he should bring, before remarrying, a nullity suit against W. If in that suit his marriage to W is declared null and void, he can remarry without running the risk of his new marriage being held bigamous and invalid.

Under canon law a marriage is either valid or void; *i.e.*, invalid. However, certain cases came to be treated in such a special way that they appeared to constitute a third category, viz., that of the voidable marriage. It was seen that under canon law the invalidity of a marriage could not be raised by anyone until it had been authoritatively declared in a judgment of nullity, and that the proceedings to obtain such a decree could be instituted only by one of the two parties to the marriage in question or by the promoter of justice. However, in certain situations the power to institute nullity proceedings is reserved to one of the two parties to the marriage, to the exclusion of the other and of the promoter of justice. These are the cases in which only one party's consent was not given freely, especially those in which the consent was brought about by coercion or by fraud of so serious a nature as to deprive the consent of its legal effectiveness. To let the party who has worked the coercion or fraud benefit from his own wrong and allow him to free himself of the marriage if it turns out to be disappointing would be unjust. Besides, the party coerced or defrauded may nevertheless desire to uphold the marriage. In such cases the power to initiate a suit for nullity is reserved to the party whose freedom the law seeks to protect. It is his decision whether or not he wishes the court to render that decree, without which no one may treat the marriage as invalid. In addition, if he desires such a decree he must act speedily upon the termination of the coercive situation or the discovery of the fraud. If he does not act at that time he is regarded as having ratified the marriage and neither he nor anyone else can at any time contest the validity of the marriage.

To these cases of coercion and fraud the secular laws have added that of nonage. Nobody but the party who was below the proper age at the time of the conclusion of the marriage can initiate the proceedings to have it declared void. Decrees rendered in proceedings initiated by the only party empowered to initiate them are frequently called decrees of annulment. In secular law, especially that of England but to some extent also in that of the United States, voidable marriages, being subject to annulment, have come to be clearly distinguished from void marriages, subject to be declared null and void by a decree of nullity or to be held void upon collateral attack. A decree of annulment is still similar to a decree of nullity in that it has retroactive effect. Once it is rendered or, more precisely, once it has become effective, the marriage is treated as if it had never existed. It also resembles, however, a decree of divorce in that the marriage must be treated as valid until it is annulled. In many respects annulment has thus been assimilated to divorce. Since annulment blots out the marriage retroactively, it seems that there is no place for any claims for maintenance or alimony. Worst of all, the children of the relationship are illegitimate. These harsh results have in most jurisdictions been removed by legislation or by judicial practice, and this tendency has come to make itself felt not only in cases of annulment but also of nullity.

In English law the Matrimonial Causes act, 1950, re-enacting the relevant provisions of the Matrimonial Causes act, 1938, sets out a number of additional grounds on which a marriage shall be voidable. These are: (1) that the marriage has not been consummated owing to the willful refusal of the respondent to consummate the marriage; (2) that either party to the marriage was at the time of the marriage of unsound mind or mentally defective, or subject to recurrent fits of insanity or epilepsy; (3) that the respondent was at the time of the marriage suffering from venereal disease in a communicable form; or (4) that the respondent was at the time of the marriage pregnant by some person other than the petitioner. These grounds are subject to certain provisos, namely: (*a*) that the petitioner was at the time of the marriage ignorant of the facts alleged; (*b*) that proceedings were instituted within a year from the date of the marriage; and (*c*) that

marital intercourse with the consent of the petitioner has not taken place since the discovery by the petitioner of the existence of the grounds for a decree. *See also* DIVORCE; MARRIAGE.

BIBLIOGRAPHY.—*England:* Matrimonial Causes Act, 1950, sec. 8; J. C. Arnold, *The Marriage Law of England* (1951); E. L. Johnson, *Family Law* (1958). *United States:* R. V. Mackay, *Law of Marriage and Divorce*, "Legal Almanac Series," 2nd ed., rev. by I. Mandell, no. 1, ch. 2 (1959); C. G. Vernier, *American Family Laws*, vol. 1 (1931) and, with R. A. Frank, supplement (1938); W. T. Nelson, *Divorce and Annulment*, 3 vol., 2nd ed. (1945–58). (M. RN.)

ANNUNCIATION, the announcement made by the angel Gabriel to the Virgin Mary of the incarnation of Christ (Luke i, 26–38). The feast of the Annunciation in the Christian church is celebrated on March 25 (Lady day). The first authentic allusions to the feast (apart from the Gelasian and Gregorian sacramentaries, in both of which it is mentioned) are in acts of the council of Toledo (656) and of the Trullan council (692).

ANNUNZIO, GABRIELE D': *see* D'ANNUNZIO, GABRIELE.

ANOA, a diminutive dark-brown buffalo confined to dense, mature forests of Celebes Island. It weighs about 600 lb. and measures about 40 in. at the shoulder. The straight, sharp-tipped horns are about 15 in. long. Its scientific name is *Anoa depressicornis*. Cultivation restricts the anoa to the island's protective interior. A mountain variety, measuring only 30 in. in height, is the smallest of all buffalo. Anoa are shy but vicious when harassed. A closely related species, *Anoa mindorensis*, occurs in the Philippine Islands. (H. K. B.)

ANODE, a positive electrode, the terminal from which electrons leave an electrolyte, electron tube, or any direct current load and return to the battery or other energy source. *See* BATTERY; ELECTROCHEMISTRY; *see* also Index references under "Anode" in the Index volume.

ANODYNE, anything that relieves pain. The term is commonly applied to medicines that lessen the sensibility of the brain or nervous system, such as morphia, etc.

ANOINTING, the ritual application of oil or fat. Like baptism (*q.v.*), the process of anointing is very nearly universal in the history of religion, although both the cultic practice followed and the sacred substance employed vary from one religion to another. It is possible to recognize three distinct, though not separate, meanings ascribed to ritual anointings by the devotees of various religions.

1. Anointing as healing. The medicine man of a tribe may be both its priest and its physician; "salvation" literally means "healing" or restoration to soundness. In the practice of ritual anointing this conjunction of religion and medicine is clear. Anointing seems intended to apply the power of natural and supernatural forces to the sick and thus to ward off the baneful influences of diseases and of demons.

2. Anointing as consecration. In preparation for battle, in danger from wild animals, in the hour of death (*see* EXTREME UNCTION) and at other special times anointing is used to endow an ordinary person with special holiness. He is "set aside" for a particular relation to that which is regarded as holy and good (*see* also CONFIRMATION). Anointing as consecration is frequently applied not only to persons but to objects as well. Altars, sacred vessels and temples, sometimes even weapons and items of clothing, are anointed to dedicate them to the service of the divine and to assure and symbolize the presence and pleasure of the divine in the holy place (*see* also CONSECRATION).

3. Anointing as ordination. Over and above the consecration applied to ordinary men, anointing has a place in the particular rituals by which certain men receive positions of eminence. In many religions priests are inducted into their sacred office with a holy chrism (*see* CHRISM). In ancient Israel and in various Christian cultures, the king was anointed in the rite of coronation (*q.v.*) as the one chosen of God to rule over the people.

See F. W. Puller, *The Anointing of the Sick in Scripture and Tradition* (1904). (J. J. PN.)

ANOMALY, a deviation from a regular, usual or expected pattern of action or result. As originally used in astronomy, anomaly described the nonuniform (anomalous) apparent motions of celestial bodies. In modern astronomical usage, the true anomaly is the angle between the radii drawn from the sun to a planet and to the perihelion point (the point in orbit closest to the sun). The mean anomaly is the angle between the radii drawn from the sun to the perihelion and to a point moving in the orbit at a uniform rate corresponding to the period of revolution of the planet. The eccentric anomaly is the eccentric angle defined in elementary conics. (R. L. DE.)

ANOMOEANS (from Gr. *anomoios*, "unlike"), a religious sect of the 4th century, representing an extreme form of Arianism (*q.v.*). Arianism held that the essential difference between God and Christ was that God had always existed while Christ was created by God. Aetius, the founder of the Anomoeans, reasoned that the doctrine carried to its logical conclusion must mean that God and Christ could not be alike. *Agennesia* ("innascibility," self-existence) being part of the essence of God, Christ could not be like God because he lacked this necessary quality. Aetius' chief convert and the second great leader of the Anomoeans was Eunomius, after whose death (*c.* 393) the sect soon became defunct.

ANONYMOUS AND PSEUDONYMOUS LITERATURE. Because much early literature was orally transmitted and was therefore remembered for its own sake, not the author's, the names of early poets and storytellers—if known at all—were often forgotten, so that traditional poetry (*e.g.*, *Beowulf*, the ballads [*qq.v.*], the Norse sagas) is usually anonymous. However, since classical times some authors have deliberately hidden their identity by withholding their names or using assumed names.

The reasons for this are various. In political and religious controversy it may be unsafe or unwise to publish the writer's name. The *Marprelate Tracts* (1588–89) by the pseudonymous Martin Marprelate (*see* MARPRELATE CONTROVERSY), attacking the episcopacy in somewhat ribald fashion, resulted in the rack for the printers and hanging for the supposed author. The letters of Junius (*q.v.*), published in the *London Public Advertiser* (1769–72), attacking the government of the day, have been attributed to or claimed by some 50 authors.

When it was not considered respectable for women to be writers, the author's identity was often hidden under the titlonym "A Lady." Other women writers adopted masculine names; *e.g.*, George Eliot (Mary Anne Evans) and George Sand (Amandine Lucile Aurore Dudevant). Some authors writing in more than one kind of literature prefer to keep their literary careers separate by using pseudonyms: the detective-story writer "Nicholas Blake" is the poet C. Day Lewis. Others prefer to adopt pseudonyms in deference to their professional standing; *e.g.*, James Bridie (the Scottish physician, O. H. Mavor).

In the 16th and 17th centuries, the golden age of pseudonyms, most writers used one at some stage in their careers—one of the more bizarre examples was "Aceeeffghhiillmmnnoorrssstuu," an alphabetical anagram of the name Christoffel von Grimmelshausen. A more predictable later derivation is Mark Twain (Samuel Langhorne Clemens) from the call meaning "two fathoms deep" used on Mississippi river boats. Initials are sometimes derived from the author's name, *e.g.*, "A.E.H.," Housman's initials, while others are quite unconnected, *e.g.*, "Y.Y.," used by Robert Lynd.

In the 19th and 20th centuries Scots authors were said to use pseudonyms most, with Poles coming next. Voltaire (François Marie Arouet) used at least 137 pseudonyms and Benjamin Franklin 57.

BIBLIOGRAPHY.—A. Taylor and F. J. Mosher, *The Bibliographical History of Anonyma and Pseudonyma* (1951). *International dictionaries:* Vincent Placcius, *Theatrum anonymorum et pseudonymorum,* 2 vol. (1708); J. C. Mylius, *Bibliotheca anonymorum et pseudonymorum* (1740), a supplement to Placcius' book; E. O. Weller, *Lexicon pseudonymorum* (1886). *English and American:* S. Halkett and J. Laing, *Dictionary of Anonymous and Pseudonymous English Literature,* new and enlarged ed. by J. Kennedy *et al.*, 8 vol. (1926–56); W. Cushing, *Anonyms* (1889), *Initials and Pseudonyms,* 2 series (1885, 1888). *French:* A. A. Barbier, *Dictionnaire des ouvrages anonymes,* 4 vol., 3rd ed. (1872–79). *Italian:* G. Melzi, *Dizionario di opere anonime e pseudonime di scrittori italiani,* 3 vol. (1848–59), with supplement by Passano (1887). *German:* M. Holzmann and H. Bohatta, *Deutsches Anonymen-Lexikon,* 7 vol. (1902–28), *Deutsches Pseudonymen Lexikon* (1906). *Spanish:* Maxiririarth, *Unos cuantos Seudónimos de Escritores españoles,* rev. ed. (1904); E. Ponce de León Freyre and F. Zamora Lucas, *1.500 Seudónimos Modernos de la Literatura Española, 1900–1942* (1942). (P. W. P.)

ANOPHELES, a genus of mosquitoes, species of which are the only known vectors of malaria. A few *Anopheles* also transmit filariasis and encephalitis. *See* MOSQUITO; MALARIA.

ANOPLURA, an order of small, wingless insects comprising the sucking lice, having mouth parts modified for puncturing skin and sucking blood. Anoplura are all ectoparasites (external parasites) on mammals, and some transmit diseases. *See* LOUSE.

ANORTHITE, a silicate of aluminum and calcium. Anorthite crystallizes in the triclinic system and has the chemical composition $CaAl_2Si_2O_8$. It is the calcium end member of the plagioclase series of feldspars (*see* FELDSPAR).

Pure anorthite is quite rare in nature, but is readily synthesized. The name is usually reserved for those solid solutions ranging in composition from pure anorthite to a mixture containing 10% of the albite (sodium) molecule. Such anorthite occurs in some gabbros and basalts, and also in contact metamorphosed limestones.

ANORTHOCLASE, the name given by the pioneer petrologist Karl (Harry) Rosenbusch in 1885 to include triclinic potashsoda feldspars that for reasons of symmetry should show cleavage angles different from 90° but which frequently do not show any measurable difference, although the deviation can be as high as about 4° (*see* FELDSPAR: *Unmixing at Low Temperature*).

The form development is variable, but the best-known crystals have a characteristic habit, giving rise to lozenge- or rhomb-shaped individuals. Anorthite is confined to alkaline igneous rocks; it appears in the larvikites and foyaitic rocks of Norway and Madagascar, as a prominent constituent of the rhomb-porphyry lavas of Norway and of the alkaline lavas of the island of Pantelleria (southwest of Sicily) and in the kenyte lavas of Mt. Kenya (Kenya) and of Mt. Erebus (Antarctica).

It is customary to call anorthoclase those feldspars which have a composition between Or_4Ab_6 and $Or_1Ab_9 \pm$, an An content that may reach 20% (Or = $KAlSi_3O_8$, Ab = $NaAlSi_3O_8$, An = $CaAl_2Si_2O_8$) and which show evidence of deviation from monoclinic to triclinic symmetry. Such evidence may be obtained by optical or X-ray methods. The optical evidence may be obscured by submicroscopical twinning produced by a displacive transformation whose temperature (lying between below 0° C. and approximately 1,000° C., *i.e.*, near the melting point) is a function of the potassium/sodium ratio and of the aluminum/silicon order-disorder distribution. The transformation temperature varies inversely as the potassium/sodium ratio and as the degree of aluminum/silicon disorder. In addition, anorthoclase is usually submicroscopically unmixed into potash-rich and sodium-rich domains and for this reason may exhibit a bluish schiller. According to the aluminum/silicon distribution within the structure and on the kind and coarseness of twinning and of unmixing, the optical properties vary considerably and cannot be considered to be significant for a definite phase. Usually, anorthoclase appears optically negative with $2V \approx 50°$. (F. H. L.)

ANOSMIA is lack of the sense of smell. This deficiency may be due to nasal obstruction or to disease of the nerves concerned in smelling. It is sometimes a manifestation of hysteria. In the first category, the common cold in the head is the most usual cause. Other frequent causes are adenoids, deviated septum and inflammation of the nasal passages.

Of nervous diseases causing anosmia, brain tumours are the commonest. Any brain lesion must be on both sides of the cortex in order to completely obliterate the sense of smell. *See also* OLFACTORY SYSTEM; SMELL AND TASTE.

ANOUILH, JEAN (1910–), French playwright who emerged as one of the foremost figures of the French theatre after World War II and whose work achieved great popularity also in other European countries and in the United States, was born on June 23, 1910, at Bordeaux. Anouilh came to the theatre by way of the post of secretary to the actor-producer Louis Jouvet. His first play to be staged was *L'Hermine* (1932; Eng. trans., *The Ermine*, 1958). This inaugurated a long series of dramatic works (published, according to his own classification, as *Pièces noires,*

1942; *Pièces roses*, 1942; *Nouvelles Pièces noires*, 1947; *Pièces brillantes*, 1951; and *Pièces grinçantes*, 1956), of which the dominant theme is a desperate and hopeless quest for an absolute purity and integrity. Little known before 1944, when his *Antigone* (Eng. trans., 1946; ed. by W. M. Landers, 1954), taken first for a Vichyite play and later for a Resistance play, brought him success, he rapidly won international fame. He has been considered both as the last of the *avant-garde* dramatists of the 1930s and as the first of the post-1945 generation.

Though Anouilh owes much as a dramatist to Jean Giraudoux and Luigi Pirandello, the intellectual content of his work links him to Albert Camus and Jean-Paul Sartre, particularly to the negative aspects of their thought. An anarchist, but not a revolutionary, he struck a resounding note in the 1930s with his passionate indictment of social evils. But the indictment became less convincing each time it was repeated and the message to which the *Pièces noires* and *Pièces roses* had seemed to point was never given. Instead, Anouilh whittled down his heroes' stature, and in the *Pièces brillantes* and the *Pièces grinçantes* mocked at the purity and integrity for which his earlier heroes and heroines had striven in vain. Bitter criticism of human nature (in *Ardèle*, 1948; *La Valse des Toréadors*, 1951, Eng. trans., *The Waltz of the Toreadors*, 1956; and *Ornifle*, 1955) replaced the social criticism of the *Pièces noires—L'Hermine, La Sauvage* (written, 1934), *Eurydice* (1941; Eng. trans., *Point of Departure*, 1951; U.S. title *Legend of Lovers*, 1952)—or the *Pièce rose, Le Rendez-vous de Senlis* (written 1937, performed 1941).

While his conception of the human predicament as pointless and absurd is made clear even in his first play, Anouilh did not formulate it explicitly until *Roméo et Jeannette* (1945; Eng. trans., 1958) in which he suggested that this life, pointless though it be, should nevertheless be accepted and lived, not renounced. He went further in *L'Alouette* (1953; Eng. trans., *The Lark*, 1955); here Jeanne d'Arc is proud of her achievements and loves mankind with all its failings. However, like his Antigone, his *sauvage* and other earlier heroes, she is not prepared to live a life of humiliating compromise. Fundamentally an escapist, Anouilh claimed the right to repudiate society (*Y'avait un prisonnier*, 1935), life itself (*Antigone*) or one's own past and personality (*Le Voyageur sans bagage*, 1937). A brilliant technician, Anouilh has successfully attempted a variety of types of plays: serious dramas constructed with classical simplicity of form, comedy ballet (*Le Bal des voleurs*, written in 1932, Eng. trans., *Thieves' Carnival*, 1952) and comedies of plot enlivened by the mistaken identities of traditional comedy (*L'Invitation au château*, 1947, Eng. trans., *Ring Round the Moon*, 1950).

See Hubert Gignoux, *Jean Anouilh* (1946).   (D. Ks.)

ANOXIA: *see* HYPOXIA.

ANSA, in astronomy, one of the apparent ends of the rings of Saturn as seen in perspective from the Earth; so-called because, viewed through the earlier telescopes, they looked like handles projecting from the planet (derived from the Latin *ansa* "a handle").

ANSBACH, a town of Germany which after partition of the nation following World War II was located in the *Land* of Bavaria of the Federal Republic of Germany. It lies 27 mi. S.W. of Nürnberg on the Rezat river, 1,509 ft. above sea level in beautiful forest land. Pop. (1961) 32,969. The 12th-century Romanesque Protestant church of St. Gumbertus was restored in the baroque style. Kaspar Hauser (*q.v.*) was killed in Ansbach and a museum dedicated to him is near the *Schloss* (castle). The latter, an 18th-century structure, was the palace of the margraves of Brandenburg-Ansbach and adjoining it is a public park with fine trees. Ansbach has metal, cardboard, leather and plastic industries. It was first mentioned about A.D. 750 and was a Hohenzollern residence from 1331 until 1791 when it became Prussian. In 1806 it passed to Bavaria. Queen Caroline, consort of George II of Great Britain, was born here in 1683. Today the town is the scene of the annual Bach music festival.   (H. J. DA.)

ANSELM, SAINT (1033–1109), archbishop of Canterbury, theologian and first of the scholastic philosophers, is one of the most important thinkers between Augustine and Thomas Aquinas.

In philosophy he is considered the author of the ontological argument for the existence of God (*see* THEISM). He was born in Piedmont, at Aosta, a town of strategic importance in Roman and medieval times because it stood at the juncture of the Great and Little St. Bernard routes. Ermenberga, his mother, belonged to a noble Burgundian family of Aosta and possessed considerable property. Gondolfo, his father, was a Lombard nobleman, who destined his son for a career in politics and opposed Anselm's choice of the monastic life. Anselm received an excellent classical training and was considered one of the best Latinists of his day. His writings excel in clarity and the precise use of words. As a result perhaps of his intense study as a young man, he was plagued with ill-health in his later years.

In 1056 Anselm left Aosta to enter the Norman Benedictine monastery of Bec (situated between Rouen and Lisieux), because of the reputation of its prior, Lanfranc (*q.v.*). En route he learned that Lanfranc was in Rome, so he tarried at Lyons, Cluny and Avranches, before entering Bec in 1060; he took his monastic vows in 1061. His intellectual ability and solid piety brought his election as prior, when Lanfranc became abbot of Caen (1066). He became abbot of Bec in 1078.

Under Anselm, Bec became a centre of monastic learning. Though Lanfranc had been a great theologian, Anselm far excelled his master. During his abbotship he composed his *Monologion* and *Proslogion*. Through benefactions of William I the Conqueror, Bec received lands in Normandy and England. Anselm made three visitations of the abbey's English lands, and when founding the priory at Chester he was named archbishop of Canterbury (March 1093) by the tyrannous William II (William Rufus), who had succeeded his father. The king had kept the see vacant since the death of Lanfranc, had stolen its revenues and pillaged its lands.

With reluctance and prompted by a desire to reform the English church, Anselm accepted the new post. He refused consecration until William restored the Canterbury lands and acknowledged Urban II, then opposed by the antipope Clement III. William, in fear of death from an illness, agreed and Anselm was consecrated Dec. 4, 1093. On his recovery, however, William showed his insincerity. He demanded an excessive sum of money from the new archbishop, who refused to pay it lest it look like simony. William blocked Anselm when he sought to go to Rome for the pallium, the symbol of papal approval of his archiepiscopal appointment. The Conqueror had often interfered in the English church, but his son sought its complete domination. William refused to accept Urban II, lest his control be weakened. He forbade Anselm to receive the pallium, for this implied royal recognition of Urban. Anselm insisted that such recognition was an ecclesiastical, not a secular matter. After two years of dispute the English bishops at the synod of Rockingham (March 11, 1095) sided with the king and abandoned Anselm. When the papal legate brought the pallium from Rome, Anselm refused to accept it from William lest it appear that he owed his spiritual authority to the king. He took it from the altar and placed it on his own shoulders (1095). William ultimately allowed Anselm to leave for Rome, but on his departure seized the lands of Canterbury.

Anselm attended the council of Bari (1098) and presented to the pope his grievances against the king. He also took an active part in the sessions and defended the traditional doctrine of the *Filioque* against the Greeks. The Bari council reapproved the decrees against lay investiture. At the end of the year, Anselm withdrew to the village of Liberi, near Capua, and completed his *Cur Deus Homo?* prior to attending a council at the Lateran at Easter 1099.

On the murder of William Rufus (1100), his brother Henry seized the throne, as Henry I. To win ecclesiastical support, Henry summoned Anselm to England, where the archbishop became for a time one of his most loyal supporters. Anselm broke with the king, however, when Henry insisted on his right to invest prelates with the spiritual insignia of their office. Three times the king sought an exemption, but Rome refused. During the controversy, Anselm was in exile from April 1103 to Aug. 1106. The dispute was settled at the synod of Westminster (1107). The king renounced investiture of bishops and abbots with the ring and crosier, but demanded that they do homage to him prior to consecration. The

Westminster agreement was a model for the Concordat of Worms (1122), which settled for a time the lay investiture controversy. (*See also* INVESTITURE CONTROVERSY.)

Anselm spent his last two years in peace and died on April 21, 1109. In 1163, with new canons requiring papal approval for canonizations, Archbishop Thomas Becket referred his cause to Rome. Anselm was probably canonized at this time, for the Canterbury records of 1170 make frequent mention of the pilgrimages to his new shrine in the cathedral. For several centuries he was venerated locally. Clement XI extended his mass and office to the whole church in 1720, when he declared him a doctor of the church. His feast day is April 21.

The singular position of Anselm in theology and philosophy is based not only on his confidence in human reason to investigate even the divine mysteries but, on his insight into the metaphysical and unitative character of being as a perfection. Though he often blends theology and philosophy, he is aware of the different principles underlying them. He betrays that hardy belief in the unity of truth which characterizes 12th- and 13th-century thought. He is a man of new ideas and new approaches.

Anselm's theory of knowledge is found in his *De Veritate* (1080), in which he shows that rectitude of thought and action arise from their agreement with the objective order of existence. Moral truth is the willing by the will of what-ought-to-be, but this is taught it by the mind. God is the supreme being and the supreme truth, and even reason puts man into contact with the whole order of being. Though Anselm holds that faith enlightens reason, the latter has its own principles of operation.

The *Monologion* (1077) was written at the request of certain monks of Bec; it is essentially a meditation by reason on the existence and the attributes of God. Nowhere in theology is there a more penetrating study of the divine attributes. Moving from an analysis of the inequalities of perfection, Anselm argues to the existence of an absolute norm by which the mind judges inequality. This norm is God, the absolute, ultimate, integrating standard of all perfection.

In the *Proslogion* or *Alloquium de Dei Existentia* (1078), Anselm attempts one all-inclusive proof for the existence of God. Chapters 2–3 give this ontological argument; the remaining 23 chapters treat the divine perfections. The essential significance of his proof lies in Anselm's discussion of being, which God possesses in its fullness. Even the fool has an idea of a being greater than which no other being can be conceived to exist. Such a being must really exist, for the very idea of such a being implies existence, otherwise it would not be an idea of a being greater than which no other being exists. The ontological argument is in the tradition of thinkers who hold that there must be some immediate idea of God in human experience.

Anselm was answered by Gaulino, a monk of Marmoutier, who denied in his *Liber pro Insipiente* that such an idea includes existence in the objective order. No direct intuition of God includes his existence. Anselm answered in his *Liber Apologeticus* that his argument is valid precisely because it deals with a necessary being. Bonaventura, John Duns Scotus, Descartes, Malbranche, Leibniz and Hegel have defended the Anselmian argument; Thomas Aquinas and Kant refute it.

The *Cur Deus Homo?* (1097–99) is the classic treatment of the Redemption. Sin was a formal affront to the divinity; man, as man, cannot make reparation. Nor is simple pardon adequate, for this does not change a man interiorly. The instrument of the Redemption must be the God-Man, by whose infinite merits man is purified in an act of co-operative re-creation. Anselm rejects the idea that man through sin owes a debt to the Devil, and puts the essence of the redemption for the individual in his union with Christ in the Eucharist, to which baptism opens the way. *See also* SCHOLASTICISM.

The best edition of Anselm's complete works is F. S. Schmitt's *Sancti Anselmi Opera Omnia* (1938–51), a definitive work with excellent notes. The best French translation is A. Rousseau, *Saint Anselme, Oeuvres philosophies* (1947). In English, S. N. Deane's *Saint Anselm* (1935) contains the *Proslogion, Monologion, Liber pro Insipiente* of Gaulino and the *Liber Apologeticus;* the *Proslogion* is also found in A. Pegis, *Wisdom of Catholicism* (1949). English selections are in R. McKeon, *Selections From Medieval Philosophers* (1929).

See also references under "Anselm, Saint" in the Index.

BIBLIOGRAPHY.—Major bibliographies are U. Chevalier, *Répertoire des sources historiques du moyen âge*, vol. i, pp. 256–259 (1905); for more recent periodical literature in English, French, German and Italian, see F. W. Bateson (ed.), *Cambridge Bibliography of English Literature*, vol. i, pp. 282–283 (1957); also F. van Steenberghen, *Philosophie des Mittelalters* (1950).

For Anselm's life and thought, *see* M. Rule, *Life and Times of St. Anselm* (1883), and Rule's edition of Eadmer's *Vita Anselmi*, "Rolls Series" (1884); R. W. Church, *St. Anselm* (1905); J. Clayton, *St. Anselm, a Critical Biography* (1933); J. McIntyre, *St. Anselm and His Critics, a Re-interpretation of the Cur Deus Homo* (1954); W. R. W. Stephens, "Saint Anselm," in *Dictionary of National Biography*, vol. i, pp. 482–503 (1908); E. Gilson, *History of Christian Philosophy in the Middle Ages* (1954); F. Copleston, *History of Philosophy* (1950); F. Cayré, *Manual of Patrology and History of Theology* (1940); Z. N. Brooke, *English Church and Papacy* (1952); E. Fairweather (ed.), *A Scholastic Miscellany: Anselm to Ockham* (1956).
(J. A. K.)

ANSELM OF LAON (ANSELME DE LAON) (d. 1117), French theologian, apparently studied at Bec under St. Anselm (*q.v.*) and like him became eminent in early scholasticism. In the final quarter of the 11th century Anselm of Laon taught with distinction at Paris, where with Guillaume de Champeaux he supported realism. Toward the close of the century, he returned to his native Laon, where his theological and exegetical school became famous. Peter Abelard came to Laon to continue his studies, and John of Salisbury referred to the late Anselm and his brother Rudolph as "those most brilliant lights of the Gauls." Anselm's *Interlinear Glosses*, a commentary on the entire Vulgate Bible, became a leading medieval authority. Some of his scriptural commentaries were ascribed to other writers, notably St. Anselm of Canterbury. His known works were published by J. P. Migne in *Patrologia Latina*, vol. clxii.
(D. D. McG.)

ANSELME (FATHER ANSELME OF THE VIRGIN MARY; originally PIERRE DE GUIBOURS) (1625–1694), French genealogist and friar, whose history of the French royal family and nobility is a valuable source of detailed and out-of-the-way information, was born in Paris in 1625. He entered the order of Barefooted Augustinians in 1644. His whole life was devoted to the study of genealogy. The first instalment of his most important work, *Histoire généalogique et chronologique de la maison royale de France, des pairs, grands officiers de la couronne et de la maison du roy: et des anciens barons du royaume*, appeared in 1674. After Père Anselme's death in Paris at the Couvent des Petits Pères, Jan. 17, 1694, the work was continued by Honoré Caille, seigneur du Fourny, who had encouraged its publication, and by two other Augustinian friars at the Couvent des Petits Pères, Père Ange de Sainte-Rosalie and Père Simplicien.

The third, and most complete edition (1726–33), consisted of nine folio volumes, and has remained a primary source, despite its inaccuracies, partly because its notes embody exact references to many original documents.

ANSERMET, ERNEST (1883–   ), Swiss conductor known for his authoritative interpretations of the works of Stravinsky and other 20th-century composers and for his keen intellectual approach to problems of contemporary musical aesthetics, was born at Vevey, Nov. 11, 1883. He studied at Lausanne and from 1906 to 1910 was professor of mathematics there. Later he studied music with A. Gédalge in Paris. He gained his experience as a conductor in Germany. About 1914 he met Stravinsky and in 1915 he became conductor of Diaghilev's Russian ballet. In 1918 he founded the Orchestre de la Suisse Romande in Geneva. He frequently toured Europe and the United States and introduced works by Stravinsky, Prokofiev, Hindemith and Bartók, as well as by the Swiss composers, Honegger and Frank Martin. He also recorded many orchestral works by French and Russian composers.

Ansermet's own works include a symphonic poem, settings of poems by Baudelaire and the orchestration of Debussy's *Épigraphes antiques*.

See E. Ansermet, *L'Expérience musicale et le monde d'aujourd'hui* (1948); *Hommage à Ernest Ansermet* (1943).   (E. LR.)

ANSGAR (ANSKAR or ANSCHAR), **SAINT** (801–865), Frankish missionary, the first archbishop of Hamburg and the apostle of Scandinavia, was born in 801. He received training at Corbie in Picardy and taught in the monastic school at Corvey ("New Corbie") in Westphalia as a young man. When Harald, an exiled Danish king, appealed to the emperor Louis I for support and accepted Christianity, Ansgar was attached to him to assist him in spreading the faith in his dominions. Harald seems never again to have had power beyond the Danish borders, but under his protection Ansgar began missionary work in Schleswig from 826. In 829–831, hearing that King Bjørn was not unfavourable to Christianity, he transferred his activities to Sweden. In 832 Ansgar was consecrated archbishop of Hamburg, but in 848 his see was transferred to Bremen. His suggested field of activity was all the peoples of the north, but political conditions enforced limitation. Denmark, however, was now united under King Haarik (Horec) I, who allowed Ansgar's work in Schleswig to be renewed and a church to be built in the town of Schleswig. His successor Haarik II also approved of Ansgar's work. The mission in Sweden had been extinguished by the expulsion of Bishop Gautbert in 845, but Ansgar sent a hermit to revive it in 851 and himself visited Sweden in 853–854. He died at Bremen on Feb. 3, 865.

The Swedish mission founded by Ansgar seems to have died out after the time of his successor Rimbert, who nourished it assiduously. Christianity probably then existed only sporadically in Sweden till the mission of Odinkar (c. 975). In Schleswig, similarly, there is no evidence that the early mission had permanent results.

A work by Ansgar on the miracles of St. Willehad is extant. His own life is known in considerable detail from the biography by Rimbert, his successor in the see of Bremen. The tone of Rimbert's last chapters suggests that veneration of Ansgar as a saint began soon after his death. His feast is celebrated at various places on Feb. 3, on Feb. 4 or on Sept. 9.

See É. de Moreau, *Saint Anschaire* (1930).   (AL. C.)

ANSHAN (ANZAN), an ancient city and country in southwestern Iran, closely associated with Elam (q.v.). Probably it was situated north of Elam, but its exact location is unknown. Anshan came into prominence about 2350 B.C. as an enemy of the Mesopotamian dynasty of Akkad. The third dynasty of Ur (c. 2130–2030 B.C.) sent merchants and expeditions to it. Its greatest days were in the 13th and 12th centuries when, as "kings of Anshan and Susa," Elamite rulers periodically raided Babylonian cities. A revived Elamite dynasty bore the same title in its contests with Assyria between 750 and 650, but about 675 B.C. the country appears to have come under the control of Achaemenid Persians, who bore the title "kings of Anshan" down to the accession of Darius I (522 B.C.). After this date, Anshan is virtually unknown to history.   (G. G. CA.)

AN-SHAN, the industrial centre of Liaoning province in south Manchuria, 60 mi. S. of Mukden on the east side of the Manchurian plain. Pop. (1953) 548,900; (1958 est.) 833,000. Iron ores have been worked at An-shan since the 10th century, but the modern discovery was by the Japanese in 1909. The South Manchurian Railway company began steel production there in 1919 and steadily expanded its capacity. An-shan contributed large quantities of iron and steel to the Japanese war effort between 1940 and 1945. Soviet Russia stripped the installations after World War II, but the Chinese Communists had restored them by 1952. Continuous expansion occurred after 1952 and by 1956 An-shan was China's primary iron and steel producer. Much of the iron ore is of low grade and requires enrichment to working quality. Cement and refractory plants, coke ovens, blast furnaces, steel converters and mills for the production of rails, bars, sheets and seamless tubing make up the heart of the complex.   (J. E. SR.)

ANSON, ADRIAN CONSTANTINE (1851–1922), U.S. baseball player and manager, known as "Cap" in his early days and "Pop" in his later ones, was an outstanding hitter in the 19th century with a lifetime batting average of .340. He was born in Marshalltown, Ia., on April 11, 1851. While playing with the Forest City team of Rockford, Ill., in the season of 1871, he came to the attention of the Philadelphia Athletics in the National

association, and from the 1872 through the 1875 season he caught, played first, second and third base, shortstop and in the outfield for that club. In 1876 when A. G. Spalding, star pitcher of the Boston team in the National association, was approached to become manager of the Chicago team, he in turn got Anson to join it as the team switched to the newly formed National league in the season of 1876. From 1876 through 1878 Anson was team captain, caught, played second and third base and in the outfield. In the 1879 season Anson became manager after Spalding's retirement and thereafter played only at first base, except that in both 1883 and 1884 he pitched but without record. He retired as a player after the 1897 season but was a nonplaying manager for the New York team in the National league in 1898. During his 27 seasons, the longest playing span of any major league baseball player, Anson won batting championships in 1879, 1881, 1887 and 1888; his 3,524 hits put him second only to Ty Cobb in number of hits made in a major league career. He threw and batted right handed. As a manager, Anson led the Chicago team to league pennants in 1880, 1881, 1882, 1885 and 1886. In 1888–89 he was part of the first baseball tour of the world, playing with his Chicago team against a team of other National league players. Anson was elected city clerk of Chicago in 1905 and served a two-year term. He died there on April 14, 1922. In 1939 he was elected to the Baseball Hall of Fame, the 17th player so honoured.

ANSON, GEORGE ANSON, BARON (1697–1762), British admiral, known from his reforms while a member of the board of admiralty as "father of the navy," was born on April 23, 1697. His mother was the sister-in-law of one lord chancellor (Lord Macclesfield) and his wife the daughter of another (Lord Hardwicke). He entered the navy in 1712 and became a captain at the age of 26. He is best known for his voyage around the world in the "Centurion" between 1740 and 1744. This voyage was inspired by the success of the privateer Woodes Rogers in 1704, but as a piece of naval strategy it was ill-conceived. The ships were badly equipped and manned, and out of the six that sailed, only the flagship returned. After a disastrous voyage around Cape Horn, Anson successfully raided the coast of Chile but nearly perished in crossing the Pacific, reaching Tinian Island just in time to save the health of his few remaining men. He then took the "Centurion" to Macao, whence he sailed to capture (1743) the Manila galleon "Nuestra Señora de Cobadonga," valued at £400,000. He sold the prize and cargo at Canton, the "Centurion" being the first British warship to enter Chinese waters. He returned to England with the specie payments on June 15, 1744. The voyage is a classical instance of the incidence of scurvy (q.v.): out of the 1,955 men who left England, 1,051 died, chiefly of scurvy. These losses inspired James Lind to discover the cure of lemon juice, which he published in *A Treatise on the Scurvy* (1753). The book was dedicated to Anson, who appointed Lind to the new naval hospital at Haslar in Hampshire.

In 1745 Anson was promoted to the board of admiralty, on which he sat, with only a brief interval, until his death in 1762. During this time he served twice at sea: in 1747, when by brilliant tactics he captured six out of the nine French warships escorting a convoy off Cape Finisterre, for which he was made Baron Anson, and again in 1758. His reforms at the admiralty included the classification of warships into six rates, distinguishing line-of-battle ships from the frigates of the fifth and sixth rates, which continued as long as the navy fought under sail, and the revision (1749) of the articles of war, which lasted with little change until the Naval Discipline act of 1865. Anson was instrumental in introducing a blue and white uniform for officers in 1748 and he created the permanent corps of marines under the direction of the admiralty in 1755. The increased efficiency of the navy in the Seven Years' War is mainly to be attributed to his administrative work, and, regarding strategy, he was largely responsible for the maintenance of a western squadron to blockade Brest, which was the key to British maritime success. He died during the war on June 6, 1762.

In society he was cold and reserved, so that he made as many enemies as he did friends. His character had little public appeal but his talents as an administrator and strategist were of the highest order, as Pitt recognized in a posthumous tribute: "To his wisdom, to his experience and care the nation owes the glorious successes of the last war."

BIBLIOGRAPHY.—There are contemporary narratives of the voyage around the world by Pascoe Thomas (1745) and by Anson's chaplain, Richard Walter (1748). *See* also H. B. T. Somerville, *Commodore Anson's Voyage* (1934); Sir J. Barrow, *Life of George Lord Anson* (1839); W. V. Anson, *Life of Admiral Lord Anson* (1912); S. W. C. Pack, *Admiral Lord Anson* (1960).   (C. C. L.)

ANSON, SIR WILLIAM REYNELL, BART. (1843–1914), English jurist and author of a noted study of the British constitution, was born in Walberton, Sussex, son of the second baronet. Educated at Eton and at Balliol College, Oxford, he became in 1874 Vinerian reader in English law at Oxford, a post which he held until he became in 1881 warden of All Souls College. He identified himself both with local and university interests, becoming an alderman of the city of Oxford (1892), chairman of quarter sessions for the county (1894), vice-chancellor of the university (1898–99), and chancellor of the diocese of Oxford (1899). In that year he was returned, without opposition, as member of Parliament for the university in the Liberal Unionist interests, and consequently resigned the vice-chancellorship.

In Parliament he preserved an active interest in education, being a member of the newly created consultative committee of the board of education in 1900, and in 1902 he became parliamentary secretary. He took an active part in the foundation of a school of law at Oxford, and his volumes on *The Principles of the English Law of Contract* (1884) and on *The Law and Custom of the Constitution,* in two parts, "The Parliament" and "The Crown" (1886–92), are standard works.

ANSONIA, an industrial city of New Haven County, Conn., U.S., is situated on the Naugatuck River about 10 mi. (16 km.) NW of New Haven.

Originally a part of the township of Derby, Ansonia was incorporated as a separate township in 1889 and chartered as a city in 1893. It was actually settled, however, in 1843 when Anson Greene Phelps (1781–1853) of New York City refused to pay an exorbitant price for land in Derby and established a factory at Ansonia in which he manufactured copper and brass goods. The settlement was named in Phelps's honour. Heavy machinery was manufactured there as early as 1848. These two industries remained dominant, though numerous other metal products were also produced. Ansonia and the neighbouring cities of Derby and Shelton form one of the important industrial communities of the state.

For comparative population figures *see* table in CONNECTICUT: *Population.*   (R. Lo.)

ANSTEY, CHRISTOPHER (1724–1805), English poet whose poem *The New Bath Guide* went through more than 30 editions between 1766 and 1830, was born on Oct. 31, 1724, at Brinkley, Cambridgeshire, and educated at Eton and King's College, Cambridge. In 1754 Anstey succeeded to an independent income, in 1756 he married, and in 1770 he settled permanently in Bath. *The New Bath Guide, or Memoirs of the B . . . r . . . d Family* (1766) is really a short epistolary novel in verse, the purpose of which is to satirize different aspects of Bath life. It is compounded from two sources: first, the type of versified caricature best known through poems like Swift's *The Lady's Dressing Room* (1732); and second, works like Goldsmith's *Citizen of the World* (1762) which use the ironic device of introducing an innocent countryman or foreigner to sophisticated pleasures. In the *Guide,* Simkin, a naïve countryman, is introduced to Bath and recounts his impressions in light anapaestic verse. Much of the poem's charm arises from Anstey's mastery of the difficult and somewhat repetitive anapaestic measure, but the element of parody, together with the simple caricature and occasional accurate delineation of scenes well known to 18th-century readers, helps to explain the poem's popularity. Anstey sustained his success with *An Election Ball in Poetical Letters from Mr. Inkle at Bath to His Wife at Glocester* (1776). He died in Bath in 1805.

See M. S. Day, "Anstey and Anapestic Satire in the Late Eighteenth Century" in *A Journal of English Literary History,* vol. xv (1948).
                                        (JN. C.)

END OF VOLUME ONE

PRINTED IN THE U. S. A. BY R. R. DONNELLEY & SONS CO.

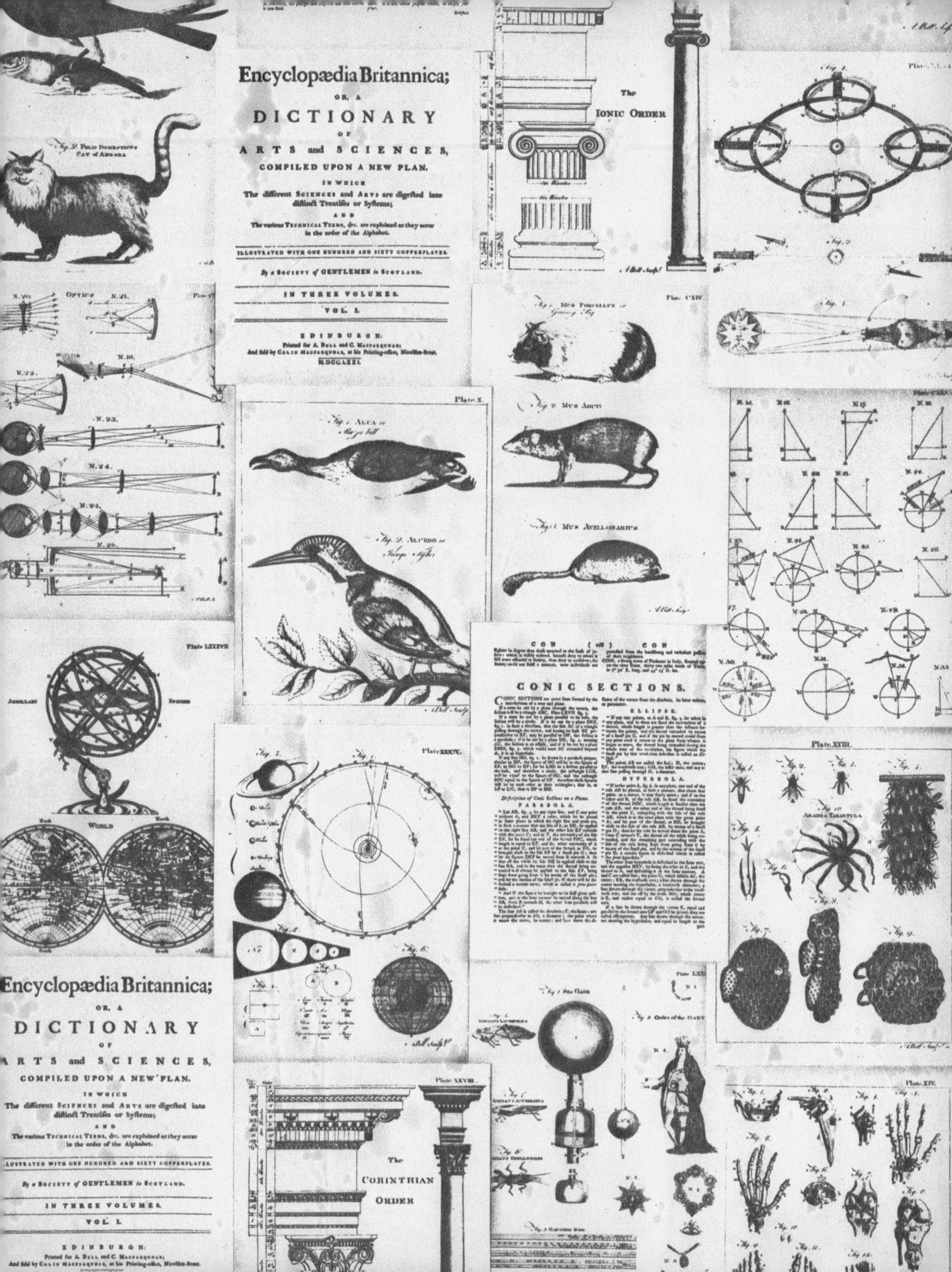